Reverse
Acronyms, Initialisms &
Abbreviations Dictionary

Gale's publications in the acronyms and abbreviations field consist of the following:

Acronyms, Initialisms & Abbreviations Dictionary series:

Volume 1 — *Acronyms, Initialisms & Abbreviations Dictionary*
(A guide to acronyms, initialisms, abbreviations, and similar contractions, arranged alphabetically by abbreviation)

Volume 2 — *New Acronyms, Initialisms & Abbreviations*
(Two interedition supplements, in which terms are arranged alphabetically both by abbreviation and by meaning)

Volume 3 — *Reverse Acronyms, Initialisms & Abbreviations Dictionary*
(A companion to Volume 1, in which terms are arranged alphabetically by meaning of the acronym, initialism, or abbreviation)

International Acronyms, Initialisms & Abbreviations Dictionary
(A guide to foreign and international acronyms, initialisms, abbreviations, and similar contractions, arranged alphabetically by abbreviation)

Periodical Title Abbreviations series:

Volume 1 — *Periodical Title Abbreviations: By Abbreviation*
(A guide to abbreviations commonly used for periodical titles, arranged alphabetically by abbreviation)

Volume 2 — *Periodical Title Abbreviations: By Title*
(A guide to abbreviations commonly used for periodical titles, arranged alphabetically by title)

Volume 3 — *New Periodical Title Abbreviations*
(Two interedition supplements, in which terms are arranged alphabetically both by abbreviation and by title)

ISSN 0270-4404

Reverse
Acronyms, Initialisms &
Abbreviations Dictionary

A Companion Volume to Acronyms, Initialisms & Abbreviations Dictionary,
with over 300,000 Terms Arranged Alphabetically by Meaning of Acronym, Initialism, or Abbreviation

*Covering: Aerospace, Associations, Biochemistry, Business and Trade,
Domestic and International Affairs, Education, Electronics, Genetics, Government,
Labor, Medicine, Military, Pharmacy, Physiology, Politics, Religion, Science, Societies,
Sports, Technical Drawings and Specifications, Transportation, and Other Fields*

Ninth Edition
1985-86

Volume 3

Part 1
A-K

Ellen T. Crowley
and
Helen E. Sheppard
Editors

Julie E. Towell
Associate Editor

OTHER VOLUMES
Volume 1—*Acronyms, Initialisms & Abbreviations Dictionary* (In two parts: A-K, L-Z)
Volume 2—*New Acronyms, Initialisms & Abbreviations* (Two interedition supplements to Volume 1)

GALE RESEARCH COMPANY • BOOK TOWER • DETROIT, MICHIGAN 48226

Editors: Ellen T. Crowley, Helen E. Sheppard

Associate Editor: Julie E. Towell
Assistant Editors: Pamela Dear, Prindle LaBarge
Editorial Assistants: Anthony J. Scolaro, Peter A. Smith

Contributing Editors: Leland G. Alkire, Jr., Mildred Hunt,
Edwin B. Steen, Miriam M. Steinert

Production Supervisor: Carol Blanchard
Production Associate: Mary Beth Trimper
Art Director: Arthur Chartow
Program Design: Donald G. Dillaman

Editorial Data Entry Supervisor: Doris Goulart
Senior Data Entry Assistant: Dorothy Cotter
Data Entry Assistants: Ann Blake, William P. Maher, Anna Marie Woolard

Publisher: Frederick G. Ruffner
Executive Vice President/Editorial: James M. Ethridge
Editorial Director: Dedria Bryfonski
Director, Indexes and Dictionaries Division: Ellen T. Crowley

Copyright © 1960, 1965, 1968, 1970, 1971, 1972, 1973, 1974,
1975, 1976, 1977, 1978, 1979, 1980, 1981, 1982, 1983, 1984
by Gale Research Company

ISBN 0-8103-0512-7
ISSN 0270-4404
Library of Congress Catalog Card Number 84-643188

Computerized photocomposition by
Computer Composition Corporation
Madison Heights, Michigan

Printed in the United States of America

Contents

Volume 3

Part 1 A-K

Volume 3

Part 2   L-Z

Acknowledgments

For suggestions, contributions of terms, permission to take material from personal or published sources, and for other courtesies during the preparation of previous editions and the present one, the editors are indebted to the following:

James Aguirre, former staff writer and editor, Quality Evaluation Laboratory, United States Naval Weapons Station, Concord, California

O.T. Albertini, Plans and Policy Directorate, Joint Chiefs of Staff, Department of Defense (retired)

Leland G. Alkire, Jr., humanities reference librarian, Eastern Washington University, editor of *Periodical Title Abbreviations,* 4th edition

Irving Allen, Professor of Sociology, University of Connecticut

Association of American Railroads

B-G-R Division, Associated Spring Corp. (publishers of *Civilian's Dictionary,* a dictionary of wartime abbreviations)

Burroughs Corp. (publishers of *Computer Acronyms and Abbreviations Handbook)*

Data Processing Division, International Business Machines Corp. (publishers of *IBM Glossary for Information Processing)*

Ethel M. Fair

David Glagovsky

Jack Gordon

Charles C. Hinckley, executive vice president, Union Central Life Insurance Co.

Roy Hubbard

Mildred Hunt, editorial consultant

Steven C. Krems, computer specialist, Internal Revenue Service

Robert E. Lacey, journalist

Mamie Meredith, late Professor of English, University of Nebraska

National Association of Securities Dealers (publishers of the *NASDAQ/CQS Symbol Directory)*

National Library of Medicine

Morgan Oates, late librarian, *Detroit Free Press*

Charles Parsons, formerly of Translation Research Institute

Eric Partridge, late author of *A Dictionary of Slang and Unconventional English; A Dictionary of Abbreviations, with Especial Attention to War-Time Abbreviations;* and other books

Harry Schecter, late chairman, Government Printing Office Style Board

Edward A. Schmerler

Edwin B. Steen, professor emeritus of biology, Western Michigan University, author of *Abbreviations in Medicine* and *Dictionary of Biology*

Miriam M. Steinert, editorial consultant

A. Marjorie Taylor, editor, *Language of World War II*

Edith Thompson

Translation Section, HQ US Air Force

Donald Weeks

Harvey J. Wolf

In addition, many suggestions concerning individual terms to be included or subjects to be covered have been received from individual users and have been most helpful. The editors invite all such comments and suggestions and will make every effort to incorporate them in future editions.

Preface to the Ninth Edition

Acronyms, initialisms, or other abbreviated letter symbols make up what is perhaps the fastest growing "language" in contemporary society. Whether one views the phenomenon with disdain or delight, it is apparent that the abbreviated form has established a lasting and ever-widening influence on both written and spoken communication.

For a number of years, Gale's *Acronyms, Initialisms, and Abbreviations Dictionary (AIAD)* has served as a reliable and up-to-date reference, guiding librarians, businessmen and businesswomen, technical writers, and other researchers through the alphabetical maze. Its scope has been broadened in recent years by publication of this companion volume, *Reverse Acronyms, Initialisms, and Abbreviations Dictionary (RAIAD)*, which is volume 3 of the *AIAD* series. *RAIAD* contains essentially the same entries as its *AIAD* companion (over 300,000 in this ninth edition), but in *RAIAD* the entries are arranged alphabetically by *meaning*, rather than by acronym or initialism.

Useful in Sorting Out Inconsistencies

If all abbreviated terms were as logically formed as Royal Artillery—RA, there would be little need for a tool such as *RAIAD*. The countless exceptions to this generalized formation, however, make a guide essential. Receipt Acknowledged, for instance, is not necessarily shortened to RA, but often to REACK; Sisters of the Most Holy Sacrament is abbreviated as MHS, not SMHS; and the military designation for First Available Air Transportation is not FAAT, but FAIRTRANS.

Another generality regarding the formation of acronyms and initialisms is that articles, prepositions, etc., are not usually represented in the shortened form: General Agreement on Tariffs and Trade—GATT. Yet it is becoming more common to find terms in which some or all of these minor words *are* abbreviated: Research in Laboratory Animal Medicine and Care—RILAMAC. Another popular practice is to tack on a stray letter that has no connection with the acronym's translation, but that renders it pronounceable or gives it an appropriate meaning: Greater Underwater Propulsive Power [*Type of submarine*]—GUPPY.

'Mistaken Identity' Avoided

An incorrect initialism can not only cause confusion, but may even change the meaning of a term. A Bachelor of Interior Architecture is designated BI Arch. Abbreviating it as BIA confers on the subject a Bachelor of Industrial Arts degree.

Some commercial firms and associations use their entire corporate name in their initials: Cancer Care, Inc.—CCI; while others use only the principal part of their name: American Airlines, Inc.—AA. If Cancer Care, Inc., is abbreviated to CC, it may indicate Chrysler Corporation; lengthening the initialism for American Airlines, Inc., to AAI may result in translation as Agricultural Ammonia Institute.

Even terms in the same subject field are not always shortened the same way. The abbreviation for Luggage and Leather Goods Manufacturers of America is formed as one might expect—LLGMA; however, the Luggage and Leather Goods Salesmen's Association of America is shortened simply to LLG.

A Valuable Key to Abbreviations and Symbols

Because simple abbreviations are also included in the *AIAD* series, a user will be able to find in *RAIAD* that the common abbreviated forms for Commission include CMSN, COM, COMM, COMMN, and COMSN. This type of information is often sought by users of data processing systems, where limited space makes the use of abbreviated terms necessary.

Both *AIAD* and *RAIAD* contain a number of letter symbols as well. These do not meet the criteria for being acronyms, initialisms, or abbreviations, but are included as an important part of an alphabetical reference. *Reverse Acronyms, Initialisms, and Abbreviations Dictionary* is especially valuable in assigning correct symbols to given terms, since the symbol often bears little or no resemblance to what it represents. For example, the meteorological symbol for Hail is A; the Navy symbol for a Heavy Cruiser is CA; the New York Stock Exchange symbol for Borden, Inc., is BN; the research code symbol for Travenol Laboratories is BAX.

Airport code names may also seem baffling. A few are apparent, such as the symbol for Denver—DEN. But in many cases the connection between subject and symbol seems remote at best: Michigan's Willow Run Airport is represented by YIP, illogical unless one realizes the airport's proximity to the city of Ypsilanti; the giant Chicago O'Hare Airport is represented by ORD—few remember that this is because its original name was Orchard Field.

Coverage Continues to Expand

The coverage of new fields and the updating of entries for *AIAD-9* are reflected in *RAIAD-9*.

Included for the first time in *RAIAD* are such diverse entries as over-the-counter stock symbols, antineoplastic drug regimens, geomagnetic observatory codes, and cable television networks.

The collection of MARC (Machine-Readable Cataloging) codes has been expanded by the addition of those used for geographic areas and languages. (It will be noticed that many of these codes consist of a combination of letters and hyphens, a feature familiar to librarians and others engaged in information retrieval.)

Coverage of accepted periodical title abbreviations, of particular interest to researchers and bibliographers, has increased by several thousand since the last edition.

Much *updating* in a wide variety of fields has taken place as well since the eighth edition. Included are changes in and additions of airport codes, government departments and agencies, New York and American Stock Exchange listings, and call letters for radio and television stations.

Because of these continual updating efforts and the ever-widening scope of coverage, *RAIAD* will increasingly eliminate guesswork and tiresome searches by providing acceptable alphabetical forms quickly and accurately.

Notes on Arrangement of Terms

Terms are arranged in alphabetical order, *according to the meaning* of the acronym, initialism, or abbreviation. If a particular translation has more than one initialism representing it, the various choices are then arranged alphabetically, as they were in volume 1 (*AIAD*). Thus:

Liquid Nitrogen .... LIN
Liquid Nitrogen .... LN

Treatment of Hyphens, Brackets, and Parentheses

Hyphenated terms are treated as separate words.

Material within brackets, such as categories or explanations, is not considered in alphabetizing. Material within parentheses *is* alphabetized, usually because it is considered to be an integral part of the term and is important to the logical placement of the term. Thus, the following entry is alphabetized using "(Destroyers)," which is represented in the initialism, but not "[*British*]," which is simply an explanatory addition:

Commodore, (Destroyers) Western Approaches
[*British*] .... COM(D)WA

Minor Parts of Speech

Articles, conjunctions, prepositions, etc., generally are not considered in the alphabetizing and appear entirely in lowercase:

Master Switch .... MS
Master *of* Textile Chemistry .... MTC
Not Less Than .... NLT
Not *in* Line *of* Duty .... NLD

Exceptions are those entries in which the preposition or other minor word is an *integral* part of the term or is part of a compound word:

***And/Or* Gate** [*Data processing*] .... AOG
Locked-*On* RADAR Bearing Indicator .... LORBI
Master *Under*-Panel Control .... MUC

Abbreviations and Initials

Certain words that are abbreviated within the translation of an acronym or initialism are alphabetized as though spelled out. Among these abbreviations are Co., Corp., Dr., Inc., Ltd., St., and Ste.

The translations of some entries contain other acronyms or initialisms within them. The acronyms or initialisms appearing in such entries are alphabetized as words themselves, although the less common ones may be followed by bracketed translations. Examples of such entries are:

EVA [*Extravehicular Activity*] **Life-Support**
System [*NASA*] .... ELSS
                [Alphabetized as "ev..."]

FMC Corp. [*NYSE symbol*] .... FMC
                [Alphabetized as "fm..."]

LASER Transceiver Device .... LXD
                [Alphabetized as "la..."]

When an entry begins with a single letter, that letter is treated as a word, and the entry will be found at the beginning of its particular letter section:

C & K Petroleum [*American Stock Exchange symbol*] . . . . CHK
[Precedes other C entries]

M-Day Mobilization Requirement . . . . MDMR
[Precedes other M entries]

Numerics

Entries containing *digits* precede all alphabetic forms:

Specialist 4 [*Army*] SP4
Specialist 5 [*Army*] SP5
Specialist, Archivist [*Navy rating*] . . . . SPXTS
Specialist, Mail Clerk [*Navy rating*] . . . . SPM
Specialist, V-Mail [*Navy rating*] . . . . SPPVM

Entries in which the number is spelled out are filed alphabetically:

Fountainwell Drama Series [*A publication*] . . . . FDS
Four-Bar Cutter Device . . . . FCD
Four Power Joint Military Commission . . . . FPJMC
Fourier Transform . . . . FT

Because of computer sorting limitations, Roman numerals are filed as letters:

World without War Council . . . . WWWC
World War I . . . . WWI
World War II Victory Medal . . . . WWIIVM
World War Tank Corps Association . . . . WWTCA

Reverse
Acronyms, Initialisms &
Abbreviations Dictionary

A-K

A

A-A-A Air Enterprises, Inc. [Omaha, NE] [FAA designator].......................TLA
A. A. Weinman [Designer's mark, when appearing on US coins].................AW
A/B Astra [Sweden] [Research code symbol]..A
A. Barton Hepburn Hospital, Ogdensburg, NY [Library symbol]............NOgH
A. C. Dougherty Memorial Township Library, Dupo, IL [Library
  symbol] ....IDup
A. Christiaens [Belgium] [Research code symbol]..AC
A & E Plastik Pak Co., Inc. [American Stock Exchange symbol]
  [Delisted]..AE
A Favor [In Favor] [Spanish]..AF
A. H. Brown Public Library, Mobridge, SD [Library symbol].................SdMo
A. H. Robins Co. [Research code symbol]...AHR
A. H. Robins Co., Richmond, VA [OCLC symbol] ....VIR
A. H. Robins Co., Richmond, VA [Library symbol]................................ViRRob
A. J. Hurley Ltd., London, United Kingdom [Library symbol] ....UkLHu
A. K. Smiley Public Library, Redlands, CA [Library symbol]..................CRedl
A & M Food Service, Inc. [NASDAQ symbol]...AMFD
A. Merritt's Fantasy Magazine [A publication]...AMF
A. N. Tupolev [Initialism used as designation for Russian aircraft
  designed by Tupolev]...ANT
A. Nattermann & Cie [Germany] [Research code symbol] ....CH
A. Philip Randolph Educational Fund ....APREF
A. Philip Randolph Institute ....APRI
A Protester [To Be Protested] [Business and trade]...................................AP
A and R (Analysis and Research) (Japan) [A publication] ....A and R (JP)
A Rat in the House May Eat the Ice Cream [Mnemonic guide for
  spelling "arithmetic"]...ARITHMETIC
A/S Norving [Norway] [ICAO designator]...WW
A-Strain Spontaneous Leukemia [Type of cell line]..................................ASL
A. Szekely Nemzeti Muzeum Ertesitoeje [A publication]
                                                  A Szekely Nemz Muz Ertes
A-T-O, Inc. [Later, FIG] [NYSE symbol]...ATO
A Tempo [In Strict Time] [Music]..AT
A Tempo [In Strict Time] [Music]...A TEMP
A. V. Roe & Co. Ltd. [Acronym used as designation for a British
  aircraft and is formed from the name of the aircraft's
  manufacturer]..AVRO
AA Importing Co. [NASDAQ symbol]...ANTQ
Aachen [Federal Republic of Germany] [Seismograph station
  code, US Geological Survey] [Closed] ....AAC
AADE [American Association of Dental Editors] Journal [A
  publication]...AADE J
AAEC [Australian Atomic Energy Commission] Nuclear News
  (Australia) [A publication]................................AAEC Nucl News (AU)
Aaland Islands ....AI
Aalborg [Denmark] [Airport symbol]..AAL
Aalesund [Norway] [Airport symbol]..AES
AANA [American Association of Nurse Anesthetists] Journal [A
  publication]...AANA J
AANNT [American Association of Nephrology Nurses and
  Technicians] Journal [A publication]...AANNT
AAPG [American Association of Petroleum Geologists] Bulletin [A
  publication]...AAPG Bull
AAPG [American Association of Petroleum Geologists] Studies in
  Geology [A publication]..AAPG Stud Geol
AAR Corp. [NYSE symbol]...AIR
Aarboeger foer Nordisk Oldkyndighed og Historie [A publication].......AaNo
Aarboeger foer Nordisk Oldkyndighed og Historie [A publication]......ANOH
Aarhus [Denmark] [Airport symbol]...AAR
Aarhus Universitet. Laboratoriet foer Fysisk Geografi Skrifter [A
  publication]..Aarhus Univ Lab Fys Geogr Skr
AARN [Alberta Association of Registered Nurses] News Letter [A
  publication]..AARN News Lett
AARN [Alberta Association of Registered Nurses] Newsletter [A
  publication]..AARN Newsl
Aaron Burr Association ....ABA
Aaron Rents, Inc. [NASDAQ symbol]...ARON
Aaronson, Huchra, and Moruld [Method of determining age of the
  universe] ....AHM

Aarsskrift den Kongelige Veterinaer og Landbohoejskole
  (Denmark) [A publication] ....Aarsskr K Vet Landbohoejsk (DK)
AAS [American Astronomical Society] Photo-Bulletin [A
  publication]...AAS Photo-Bull
AAS [American Astronautical Society] Science and Technology
  Series [A publication]...AAS Sci Technol Ser
AAT Airlines [Miami, FL] [FAA designator]...AAT
AAU [American Athletic Union of the United States] Junior
  Olympics ....AAU/USAJO
AAV Cos. [American Stock Exchange symbol] [Delisted].......................AAV
Aaxico Air Lines ....AXO
AB Bofors [Sweden] [Research code symbol] ....LAC
AB Bookman's Weekly [A publication] ....AB
AB Bookman's Weekly [A publication] ....AB Bkman's W
Ab Extra [From Without] [Latin]...ABEX
Ab Initio [From the Beginning] [Latin] ....AB INIT
Ab Urbe Condita [From the Founding of the City] [Refers
  especially to Rome] [Latin] ....AUC
ABA [American Bankers Association] Banking Journal [A
  publication] ....ABA Banking J
ABA Industries, Inc. [American Stock Exchange symbol] [Delisted] ....AB
Abaco [A publication] ....Aba
Abacus Fund [NYSE symbol] [Delisted]..ABJ
Abadan [Iran] [Airport symbol] ....ABD
Abaiang [Kiribati] [Airport symbol] ....ABF
Abal Air [Sweden] [ICAO designator]...KD
Abampere [Also, Bi] [Unit of electric current] ....aA
Abandon ....ABND
Abandon Call and Retry ....ACR
Abandon Ship ....ABDNSHP
Abandoned ....ABAND
Abandoned Lighthouse ....ABAND LT HO
Abandoned Police Post [Board on Geographic Names] ....PPQ
Abandoned Private Property ....APP
Abashiri [Japan] [Seismograph station code, US Geological Survey].......ABJ
Abastumani [USSR] [Seismograph station code, US Geological
  Survey] [Closed] ....ABS
Abatement of Nuisances Caused by Air Transport ....ANCAT
Abbaye de Saint-Benoit-du-Lac, Comte Brome, PQ, Canada
  [Library symbol]...CaQStBL
Abbe Sine Condition...ASC
Abbe's Sine Law...ASL
Abbess..ABS
Abbeville, AL [Radio station call letters]...WARI
Abbeville, AL [Radio station call letters]..WXLE
Abbeville, LA [Radio station call letters]..KASC-FM
Abbeville, LA [Radio station call letters]..KROF
Abbeville, SC [Radio station call letters]...WABV
Abbey [or Abbot]..AB
Abbey [or Abbot]..ABB
Abbey of Gethsemani, Trappist, KY [Library symbol] ....KyTrA
Abbotsford, BC [Radio station call letters] ....CFVR
Abbott Laboratories [Research code symbol]...A
Abbott Laboratories [NYSE symbol]..ABT
Abbott Laboratories [Research code symbol]...AG
Abbott Laboratories [Research code symbol]..MO
Abbott Laboratories [Research code symbol]..PR
Abbott Laboratories [Research code symbol]..PS
Abbott Laboratories Ltd. [Great Britain] [Research code symbol] ....ES
Abbott Laboratories Limited, Montreal, PQ, Canada [Library
  symbol]..CaQMALL
Abbott Laboratories, North Chicago, IL [Library symbol]..................INcA
Abbott Laboratories, North Chicago, IL [OCLC symbol].....................ITB
Abbott Memorial Library, Pomfret, VT [Library symbol].................. VtPom
Abbott-Northwestern Hospitals, Inc., Minneapolis, MN [Library
  symbol]..MnMAb
Abbreviated COBOL [Common Business-Oriented Language]
  Preprocessor [Data processing] ....ACOPP
Abbreviated Effectiveness Report [Air Force].......................................AER
Abbreviated Item Description ....AID

Abbreviated New Drug Application [*FDA*] ..... ANDA
Abbreviated Performance Characteristics [*Army*] ..... APC
Abbreviated Registered Address ..... ARA
Abbreviated Test Language for All Systems [*Data processing*] ..... ATLAS
Abbreviated Visual Approach Slope Indicator System [*Aviation*] ..... AVASIS
Abbreviation ..... ABBR
Abbreviation ..... ABBREV
Abbreviations and Related Acronyms Associated with Defense, Astronautics, Business, and Radio-Electronics [*Raytheon Co. publication*] ..... ABRACADABRA
Abbse [*Yemen Arab Republic*] [*Airport symbol*] ..... EAB
ABC Consolidated Corp. [*NYSE symbol*] [*Delisted*] ..... ABC
ABCA [*American Business Communication Association*] **Bulletin** [*A publication*] ..... ABCA Bul
Abcoulomb [*Unit of electric charge*] ..... aC
Abdomen ..... ABD
Abdomen ..... ABDOM
Abdominal Aortic Aneurysm [*Medicine*] ..... AAA
Abdominal Circumference ..... AC
Abdominal Hysterectomy [*Medicine*] ..... AH
Abdominal Surgery [*A publication*] ..... Abdom Surg
Abdominal Vena Cava [*Medicine*] ..... AVC
Abduction [*FBI standardized term*] ..... ABD
Abduction ..... ABDUC
Abeam ..... ABM
Abeche [*Chad*] [*Seismograph station code, US Geological Survey*] [*Closed*] ..... ABC
Abeille Medicale (Paris) [*A publication*] ..... Abeille Med (Paris)
Abelag Airways [*Belgium*] [*ICAO designator*] ..... VY
Abelson Leukemia Virus [*Medicine*] ..... ALV
Abelson-Murine Leukemia Virus ..... A-MuLV
Abemama [*Kiribati*] [*Airport symbol*] ..... AEA
Abengourou [*Ivory Coast*] [*Airport symbol*] ..... OGO
Aberbeeg [*Welsh depot code*] ..... ABEEG
Abercrombie & Fitch [*Retail stores*] ..... A & F
Abercynon [*Cardiff*] [*Welsh depot code*] ..... AYN
Aberdare [*Welsh depot code*] ..... ABDR
Aberdeen [*Scotland*] [*Seismograph station code, US Geological Survey*] ..... ABE
Aberdeen [*City and county in Scotland*] ..... ABERD
Aberdeen [*South Dakota*] [*Airport symbol*] ..... ABR
Aberdeen [*Scotland*] [*Airport symbol*] ..... ABZ
Aberdeen Airways Ltd. ..... AAW
Aberdeen/Amory, MS [*Location identifier*] [*FAA*] ..... HWF
Aberdeen Manufacturing Corporation [*American Stock Exchange symbol*] [*Delisted*] ..... AMC
Aberdeen Marine Laboratory ..... AML
Aberdeen, MD [*Location identifier*] [*FAA*] ..... APG
Aberdeen, MD [*Radio station call letters*] ..... WAMD
Aberdeen, MS [*Radio station call letters*] ..... WHAY
Aberdeen, MS [*Radio station call letters*] ..... WMPA
Aberdeen, NC [*Radio station call letters*] ..... WANC
Aberdeen Proving Ground [*Army*] ..... APG
Aberdeen Proving Ground/Ballistics Research Laboratory [*Army*] ..... APGBRL
Aberdeen Proving Ground/Human Engineering Laboratory [*Army*] ..... APG/HEL
Aberdeen Proving Ground/Materiel Testing Directorate [*Army*] ..... APG/MT
Aberdeen Proving Ground/Ordnance Bomb Disposal Center [*Army*] ..... APG/OBDC
Aberdeen Proving Ground/Ordnance Training Command [*Army*] ..... APG/OTC
Aberdeen Public Library, Aberdeen, WA [*Library symbol*] ..... WaA
Aberdeen Pulsed Reactor Facility ..... APRF
Aberdeen Research and Development Center ..... ARDC
Aberdeen & Rockfish Railroad Co. [*AAR code*] ..... AR
Aberdeen, SD [*Television station call letters*] ..... KABY-TV
Aberdeen, SD [*Television station call letters*] ..... KDSD-TV
Aberdeen, SD [*Radio station call letters*] ..... KGIM
Aberdeen, SD [*Radio station call letters*] ..... KKAA
Aberdeen, SD [*Radio station call letters*] ..... KQAA
Aberdeen, SD [*Radio station call letters*] ..... KSDN
Aberdeen, SD [*Radio station call letters*] ..... KSDN-FM
Aberdeen University Journal [*A publication*] ..... AUJ
Aberdeen University Review [*A publication*] ..... AUR
Aberdeen University Studies [*A publication*] ..... Aberdeen Univ Stu
Aberdeen, WA [*Radio station call letters*] ..... KJMD
Aberdeen, WA [*Radio station call letters*] ..... KXRO
Aberfoyle [*Scotland*] [*Seismograph station code, US Geological Survey*] ..... EAB
Aberration-Compensated Input Lens [*Optics*] ..... ACIL
Aberystwyth [*Borough in Wales*] ..... ABERY
Aberystwyth [*Welsh depot code*] ..... ABH
Aberystwyth Studies [*A publication*] ..... A St
Abfarad [*Unit of capacitance*] ..... aF
Abgekuerzt [*Abbreviated*] [*German*] ..... ABGK
Abha [*Saudi Arabia*] [*Airport symbol*] ..... AHB
Abhandlungen [*Transactions*] [*German*] ..... ABH
Abhandlungen der Akademie der Wissenschaften in Goettingen [*A publication*] ..... AAWG
Abhandlungen der Akademie der Wissenschaften in Goettingen. Mathematisch-Physikalische Klasse [*A publication*] ..... Abh Akad Wiss Goettingen Math-Phys Kl
Abhandlungen der Akademie der Wissenschaften in Goettingen. Philologisch-Historische Klasse [*A publication*] ..... AAWGPh
Abhandlungen der Akademie der Wissenschaften und der Literatur in Mainz. Geistes- und Sozialwissenschaftliche Klasse [*A publication*] ..... AAWL
Abhandlungen der Akademie der Wissenschaften in Mainz. Geistes- und Sozialwissenschaftliche Klasse [*A publication*] ..... AAWM
Abhandlungen der Bayerischen Akademie der Wissenschaften. Philosophisch-Historische Klasse [*A publication*] ..... ABAW
Abhandlungen und Berichte des Naturkundemuseums Goerlitz [*East Germany*] [*A publication*] ..... Abh Ber Naturkundemus Goerlitz
Abhandlungen und Berichte des Staatlichen Museums fuer Voelkerkunde Dresden [*Forschunsstelle*] [*A publication*] ..... Abh Ber Staat Mus Volk Dres
Abhandlungen der Braunschweigischen Wissenschaftlichen Gesellschaft [*A publication*] ..... Abh Braunschweig Wiss Gesellsch
Abhandlungen der Braunschweigischen Wissenschaftlichen Gesellschaft [*A publication*] ..... Abh Braunschw Wiss Ges
Abhandlungen der Deutschen Akademie der Wissenschaften zu Berlin. Klasse fuer Medizin [*A publication*] ..... Abh Dtsch Akad Wiss Berl Kl Med
Abhandlungen der Deutschen Akademie der Wissenschaften zu Berlin. Klasse fuer Sprachen, Literatur, und Kunst [*A publication*] ..... ADAW
Abhandlungen aus dem Gebiet der Hirnforschung und Verhaltenphysiologie [*A publication*] ..... Abh Geb Hirnforsch Verhaltenphysiol
Abhandlungen des Geologischen Dienstes (Berlin) [*A publication*] ..... Abh Geol Dienstes (Berl)
Abhandlungen der Gesellschaft der Wissenschaft zu Goettingen [*A publication*] ..... AGWG
Abhandlungen der Heidelberger Akademie der Wissenschaft [*A publication*] ..... AHAW
Abhandlungen der Heidelberger Akademie der Wissenschaften. Philosophisch-Historische Klasse [*A publication*] ..... AHAWPK
Abhandlungen fuer die Kunde des Morgenlandes [*A publication*] ..... AbhKM
Abhandlungen fuer die Kunde des Morgenlandes [*A publication*] ..... AKM
Abhandlungen der Kungliga. Gesselschaft der Wissenschaften zu Goettingen [*A publication*] ..... Gott Abh
Abhandlungen zur Kunst, Musik, und Literaturwissenschaft [*A publication*] ..... AKML
Abhandlungen aus dem Landesmuseum der Provinz Westfalen Museum fuer Naturkunde [*A publication*] ..... Abh Landes Prov Westfalen Mus Naturkd
Abhandlungen aus dem Mathematischen Seminar der Universitaet (Hamburg) [*A publication*] ..... Abh Math Sem Univ (Hamburg)
Abhandlungen des Meteorologischen Dienstes der Deutschen Demokratischen Republik [*A publication*] ..... Abh Meteorol Dienstes DDR
Abhandlungen Naturwissenschaftlichen Verein zu Bremen [*A publication*] ..... Abh Naturwiss Ver Bremen
Abhandlungen zur Philosophie, Psychologie, und Paedagogik [*A publication*] ..... APPP
Abhandlungen der Philosophisch-Historische. Klasse der Saechsischen Gesellschaft [*A publication*] ..... ASG
Abhandlungen der Preussischen Akademie der Wissenschaft [*A publication*] ..... APAW
Abhandlungen der Rheinisch-Westfaelischen Akademie der Wissenschaften [*A publication*] ..... Abh Rheinisch-Westfael Akad Wiss
Abhandlungen der Saechsischen Akademie der Wissenschaften zu Leipzig. Philosophisch-Historische [*A publication*] ..... ASAW
Abhandlungen der Saechsischen Akademie der Wissenschaften zu Leipzig. Philosophisch-Historische Klasse [*A publication*] ..... ASAWL PHK
Abhandlungen der Senckenbergischen Naturforschenden Gesellschaft [*A publication*] ..... Abh Senckenb Naturforsch Ges
Abhandlungen und Verhandlungen des Naturwissenschaftlichen Vereins in Hamburg [*A publication*] ..... Abh Verh Naturwiss Ver Hamb
Abhenry [*Unit of inductance*] ..... aH
ABIA [*Associacao Brasileira das Industrias de Alimentacao*] **SAPRO** [*Setor de Alimentos Calorico-Proteicos*] **Boletim Informativo** [*A publication*] ..... ABIA SAPRO Bol Inf
ABIA [*Associacao Brasileira das Industrias de Alimentacao*] **SAPRO** [*Setor de Alimentos Calorico-Proteicos*] **Revista** [*A publication*] ..... ABIA SAPRO Revista
Abidjan [*Ivory Coast*] [*Airport symbol*] ..... ABJ
Abigail Adams Historical Society, Weymouth, MA [*Library symbol*] ..... MWeyAA
Abilene [*Texas*] [*Airport symbol*] ..... ABI
Abilene Christian University, Abilene, TX [*Library symbol*] ..... TxAbC
Abilene Christian University, Abilene, TX [*OCLC symbol*] ..... TXC
Abilene Free Public Library, Abilene, KS [*Library symbol*] ..... KAb
Abilene, KS [*Radio station call letters*] ..... KABI
Abilene, KS [*Radio station call letters*] ..... KABI-FM

Abilene Public Library, Abilene, TX [*Library symbol*]	TxAb
Abilene Public Library, Abilene, TX [*OCLC symbol*]	TXB
Abilene & Southern Railway Co. [*AAR code*]	AS
Abilene, TX [*Location identifier*] [*FAA*]	DYS
Abilene, TX [*Radio station call letters*]	KEAN
Abilene, TX [*Radio station call letters*]	KEAN-FM
Abilene, TX [*Radio station call letters*]	KFMN
Abilene, TX [*Radio station call letters*]	KFMN-FM
Abilene, TX [*Radio station call letters*]	KORQ
Abilene, TX [*Radio station call letters*]	KRBC
Abilene, TX [*Television station call letters*]	KRBC-TV
Abilene, TX [*Television station call letters*]	KSUZ-TV
Abilene, TX [*Television station call letters*]	KTAB-TV
Abilene, TX [*Radio station call letters*]	KWKC
Abilene, TX [*Location identifier*] [*FAA*]	TYY
Abingdon [*Australia*] [*Airport symbol*]	ABG
Abingdon Mile [*Newmarket Racecourse*] [*Horseracing*] [*British*]	ABM
Abingdon, VA [*Location identifier*] [*FAA*]	ATX
Abingdon, VA [*Radio station call letters*]	WABN-FM
Abingdon, VA [*Radio station call letters*]	WBBI
Abinger [*United Kingdom*] [*Later, HAD*] [*Geomagnetic observatory code*]	ABN
Abington Free Library, Abington, PA [*Library symbol*]	PAb
Abington Library Society, Jenkintown, PA [*Library symbol*] [*Obsolete*]	PJA
Abington Township Public Library, Abington, PA [*OCLC symbol*]	ABG
Abisko [*Sweden*] [*Geomagnetic observatory code*]	ABK
Abisko [*Sweden*] [*Seismograph station code, US Geological Survey*] [*Closed*]	ABK
ABKCO Industries [*NASDAQ symbol*]	ABKC
Abkuerzungsfimmel [*Abbreviation Craze*]	ABKUFI
Ablating Blunt Body	ABB
Ablating Inner Surface	AIS
Ablative	ABL
Ablative	ABLAT
Ablative Heat Rate	AHR
Ablative Heat Shield	AHS
Ablative Insulative Plastic	AIP
Ablative Thrust Chamber [*NASA*]	ATC
Ablative Thrust Chamber Engine [*NASA*]	ATCE
Ablative Thrust Control	ATC
Ablator Insulated Ramjet Study [*NASA*]	AIRS
Ablauf- und Planungsforschung [*A publication*]	Ablauf-Planungsforsch
Able [*Phonetic alphabet*] [*World War II*]	A
[*To Be*] Able-Bodied, Bold, Courageous [*Promise made by members of the Junior Woodchucks, organization to which comic strip character Donald Duck's nephews belonged*]	ABC
Able-Bodied Seaman	AB
Able-Bodied Seaman	ABS
Able Chief	AC
ABM Computer Systems [*NASDAQ symbol*]	ABMC
Abnormal	ABNL
Abnormal	ABNML
Abnormal	ABNOR
Abnormal End [*Data processing*]	ABEND
Abnormal Fluctuation in the Economy	AFIE
Abnormal Frequency	AF
Abnormal Glucose Tolerance Test [*Medicine*]	AGTT
Abnormal Involuntary Movement Scale [*Medicine*]	AIMS
Abnormal Mission Routine	AMR
Abnormal Occurrence	AO
Abnormal Record Compatible with Myocardial Disease [*Lower-case c in acronym means "with"*] [*Cardiology*]	ARCcMD
Abnormal Record Compatible with Myocardial Drug Effect [*Lowercase c in acronym means "with"*] [*Cardiology*]	ARCcMDE
Abnormal [*or Anomalous*] Retinal Correspondence [*Ophthalmology*]	ARC
Abnormal Voltage	AV
Abo Akademi [*Swedish University of Abo*], Turku, Finland [*Library symbol*]	FiTA
Aboard	ABD
Aboard Sensing Control Unit	ASCO
Aboriginal Lands of Hawaiian Ancestry [*Hawaiian group seeking compensation for land*]	ALOHA
Aboriginal Research Club	ARC
Aborigine	ABOR
Aborigines Protection Society [*Later, Anti-Slavery Society for the Protection of Human Rights*]	APS
Abort	ABT
Abort Advisory Channel [*NASA*]	AAC
Abort Advisory Equipment [*NASA*]	AAE
Abort Advisory System [*NASA*]	AAS
Abort Electronics [*Apollo*] [*NASA*]	AE
Abort Electronics Assembly [*Apollo*] [*NASA*]	AEA
Abort Guidance Section [*NASA*]	AGS
Abort Guidance System [*or Subsystem*] [*Apollo*] [*NASA*]	AGS
Abort/Hold/Orbit [*NASA*]	A/H/O
Abort Inertial Digital System [*NASA*]	AIDS
Abort Interface Unit [*NASA*]	AIU
Abort Motor Facility [*NASA*]	AMF
Abort Once Around [*NASA*]	AOA
Abort Once around Cutoff	ACO
Abort-to-Orbit [*NASA*]	ATO
Abort Programer Assembly [*NASA*]	APA
Abort-Scan Table [*NASA*]	AST
Abort Sensing and Implementation System	ASIS
Abort Sensor Assembly [*Apollo*] [*NASA*]	ASA
Abort Solid Rocket Motor [*NASA*]	ASRM
Abort Time Assembly [*NASA*]	ATA
Abortion [*Medicine*]	ABOR
Abortion Fund	AF
Abortion Information Data Bank [*of Zero Population Growth, Inc.*] [*Defunct*]	AID
Abortion Patient [*Medicine*]	AB
Abortus Bang Ringprobe [*Test*] [*Medicine*]	ABR
Abortus, Militensis, Suis [*Microbiology*]	AMS
About	A
About	AB
About	ABT
About Buttonhooks, Spoons, and Patents [*An association*] [*Defunct*]	ABSP
About or On	A/O
Above	ABV
Above Aerodrome Level	AAL
Above Baseline	ABL
Above Clouds [*Aviation*]	ACLD
Above Core Load Pad [*Nuclear energy*]	ACLP
Above Field Level [*Aerospace*]	AFL
Above Ground Level	AGL
Above the Ground Review [*A publication*]	Ab G R
Above the Horizon	ATH
Above Knee [*Medicine*]	AK
Above Knee Amputation [*Medicine*]	AKA
Above Mean Sea Level [*Navigation*]	AMSL
Above Mountains [*Aviation*]	MON
Above-Named	AN
Above-Named Officer [*Army orders*]	ANO
Above Normal Loss [*Insurance*]	ANL
Above Proof	AP
Above Sea Level	ASL
Above Transmitted as Received	ATAR
Above Waist [*Medicine*]	AW
Above Water	AW
Above Water Torpedo Tube [*Navy*]	AWTT
Above Water Warfare [*Navy*]	AWW
Abra De Llog [*Philippines*] [*Seismograph station code, US Geological Survey*] [*Closed*]	ABP
Abraham Baldwin Agricultural College [*Georgia*]	ABAC
Abraham Baldwin Agricultural College, Tifton, GA [*Library symbol*]	GTiA
Abraham Baldwin Agricultural College, Tifton, GA [*OCLC symbol*]	GTM
Abraham Lincoln Association	ALA
Abraham Lincoln Birthplace National Monument	ABLI
Abraham Lincoln Quarterly [*A publication*]	ALQ
Abraham & Straus [*Retail store*]	A & S
Abrams Industries [*NASDAQ symbol*]	ABRI
Abrasive	ABRSV
Abrasive Engineering [*A publication*]	Abrasive Eng
Abrasive Engineering [*A publication*]	Abrasiv Eng
Abrasive Engineering Society [*Formerly, ASA, ASAM*]	AES
Abrasive Grain Association	AGA
ABRES [*Advanced Ballistic Reentry System*] Instrumentation Range Safety Systems [*Air Force*]	AIRSS
Abridged	ABR
Abridged Arrival Report [*Navy*]	HAVREP
Abridged Building Classification for Architects, Builders, and Civil Engineers	ABC
Abridged Index Medicus [*A publication*]	ABIM
Abridged Index Medicus [*A publication*]	AbrIMed
Abridged Index Medicus [*A publication*]	AIM
Abridged Index Medicus Accessed by Teletypewriter Exchange Service [*National Library of Medicine*]	AIM-TWX
Abridged Reader's Guide to Periodical Literature [*A publication*]	Abr RG
Abrupt Junction Varactor Doubler	AJVD
Abrupt Space Charge Edge [*Algorithm*]	ASCE
Abruzzo [*A publication*]	Ab
ABS Industries, Inc. [*NASDAQ symbol*]	ABSIC
Abschnittsbevollmaechtiger [*Section Deputy*] [*German*]	ABV
Abscisic Acid [*Biochemistry*]	ABA
Absent	A
Absent	ABS
Absent Bed Occupancy [*Medicine*]	ABO
Absent with Leave [*Military*]	AWL
Absent without Leave [*Military*] [*British*]	AWL
Absent-Minded Club	AMC
Absent without Official Leave [*Military*]	AWOL
Absent Over Leave [*Navy*]	AOL
Absent by Reason of Being Held by Civil Authorities [*Military*]	HCA
Absent on Temporary Additional Duty [*Navy*]	ATAD
Absent on Temporary Duty [*Navy*]	ATD
Absente Febre [*In the Absence of Fever*] [*Pharmacy*]	ABS FEB
Absente Reo [*The Defendant Being Absent*] [*Legal*] [*Latin*]	ABS RE
Absentee	ABSTEE
Abside [*A publication*]	ABs

Absiemens [*Unit of conductance*] ... aS
Absolute [*Temperature in Fahrenheit degrees*] ... A
Absolute ... ABS
Absolute ... ABSOL
Absolute Address ... AA
Absolute Altitude [*Navigation*] ... AA
Absolute Ampere ... ABAMP
Absolute Assembly Language [*Data processing*] ... AAL
Absolute Bed Rest [*Medicine*] ... ABR
Absolute Boiling Point ... ABP
Absolute Cardiac Dullness [*Medicine*] ... ACD
Absolute Ceiling [*Aviation*] ... ABS CLG
Absolute Ceiling [*Aviation*] ... AC
Absolute Coefficient of Yawing Moments ... CN
Absolute Electrical Unit Scale ... AEUS
Absolute Essential Equipment ... AEE
Absolute Filtration Rating ... AFR
Absolute Ground Level ... AGL
Absolute Iodine Uptake [*Medicine*] ... AIU
Absolute Limen [*Psychophysics*] ... AL
Absolute Magnitude [*Astronomy*] ... M
Absolute Memory Image ... AMI
Absolute Output [*Data processing*] ... AO
Absolute Rate Theory [*Statistics*] ... ART
Absolute Reaction of Degeneration ... ARD
Absolute Reaction Rate Theory [*Physical chemistry*] ... ARRT
Absolute Refractory Period ... ARP
Absolute Rod Position Indication [*Nuclear energy*] ... ARPI
Absolute Space-Time ... AST
Absolute Temperature [*Symbol*] [*IUPAC*] ... T
Absolute Temperature Scale ... ATS
Absolute Terminal Innervation Ratio [*Psychiatry*] ... ATIR
Absolute Threshold ... AT
Absolute Value ... ABV
Absolute Value BIT [*Binary Digit*] **Synchronizer** ... AVBS
Absolutely Bloody Final [*Especially with reference to a drink*] ... ABF
Absolutely to Die [*Slang*] ... ATD
Absolvo [*I Acquit*] [*Used by Romans in criminal trials*] [*Latin*] ... A
Absorb ... ABS
Absorbance [*Internal transmission density*] [*Symbol*] [*IUPAC*] ... A
Absorbent Paper Manufacturers Association [*Defunct*] ... APMA
Absorption ... ABSORB
Absorption Coefficient, Linear [*Symbol*] [*IUPAC*] ... a
Absorption Limiting Frequency ... ALF
Absorptivity ... A
Absorptivity-Emissivity [*Ratio*] ... A/E
Absque Ulla Nota [*Unmarked; literally, without any marking or note*] ... AUN
Abstaining Motorists' Association ... AMA
Abstract [*Data processing*] ... AB
Abstract ... ABS
Abstract ... ABST
Abstract ... ABSTR
Abstract Bulletin of the Institute of Paper Chemistry [*A publication*] ... ABIPC
Abstract Bulletin of the Institute of Paper Chemistry [*A publication*] ... Abstr Bull Inst Pap Chem
Abstract Family of Languages ... AFL
Abstract Information Digest Service [*Forest Products Research Society*] [*Information service*] ... AIDS
Abstract Journal in Earthquake Engineering [*A publication*] ... Abstr J Earthq Eng
Abstract Machine Description Language [*Data processing*] ... AMDL
Abstracted Business Information, Inc. ... ABI
Abstracting Board [*International Council of Scientific Unions*] [*Information service*] ... AB
Abstracting and Indexing ... A & I
Abstracting and Indexing Services Directory [*A publication*] ... AISD
Abstracts ... A
Abstracts of the Annual Meeting of the American Society for Microbiology [*A publication*] ... Abstr Annu Meet Am Soc Microbiol
Abstracts in Anthropology [*A publication*] ... AbAn
Abstracts in Anthropology [*A publication*] ... Abstr Anthropol
Abstracts in Biocommerce [*A publication*] ... ABC
Abstracts and Book Title Index Card Service [*Iron and Steel Institute*] [*A publication*] ... ABTICS
Abstracts of Bulgarian Scientific Literature [*A publication*] ... Abstr Bulg Scient Lit
Abstracts of Classified Reports [*A publication*] ... ACR
Abstracts of Computer Literature [*A publication*] ... Abstr Comput Lit
Abstracts of the Congress of Polish Phthisiopneumonological Society [*A publication*] ... Abstr Congr Pol Phthisiopneumonol Soc
Abstracts on Criminology and Penology [*A publication*] ... Abstr Crim & Pen
Abstracts on Criminology and Penology [*A publication*] ... CrimAb
Abstracts of Declassified Documents [*A publication*] ... ADD
Abstracts of English Studies [*A publication*] ... AbEnSt
Abstracts of English Studies [*A publication*] ... Abstr Engl Stud
Abstracts of Folklore Studies [*A publication*] ... AbFolkSt
Abstracts of Folklore Studies [*A publication*] ... AbFS
Abstracts of Folklore Studies [*A publication*] ... Abstr Folk Stud
Abstracts of Geochronology and Isotope Geology [*A publication*] ... Abstr Geochronology Isot Geol
Abstracts of Health Care Management Studies [*A publication*] ... Abstr Health Care Manage Stud
Abstracts of Hospital Management Studies [*A publication*] ... Abstr Hosp Manage Stud
Abstracts on Hygiene [*A publication*] ... Abstr Hyg
Abstracts of Instructional Materials/Abstracts of Research Materials ... AIM/ARM
Abstracts of Instructional Materials in Vocational and Technical Education [*ERIC*] ... AIM
Abstracts of Japanese Literature in Forest Genetics and Related Fields [*A publication*] ... Abstr Jap Lit Forest Genet
Abstracts. Meeting of the Weed Society of America [*A publication*] ... Abstr Meet Weed Soc Am
Abstracts. Meeting of the Weed Society of America [*A publication*] ... Abstr Mtg Weed Soc Amer
Abstracts of Military Bibliography [*A publication*] ... AbMilt
Abstracts of Military Bibliography [*A publication*] ... Abstr Mil Bibl
Abstracts of New World Archaeology [*A publication*] ... ANWA
Abstracts of North American Geology [*A publication*] ... Abstr N Amer Geol
Abstracts of North American Geology [*A publication*] ... ANAG
Abstracts of Papers. American Chemical Society [*A publication*] ... Abs Pap ACS
Abstracts of Papers. Journal of Japanese Society of Internal Medicine [*A publication*] ... Abstr Pap J Jpn Soc Intern Med
Abstracts of Papers. Meeting of American Chemical Society [*A publication*] ... Abstr Mtg ACS
Abstracts of Papers Presented at Annual Meeting of Korean Surgical Society [*A publication*] ... Abstr Pap Presented Annu Meet Korean Surg Soc
Abstracts of Papers. Society of American Foresters Meeting [*A publication*] ... Abstr Pap Soc Amer For
Abstracts of Photographic Science and Engineering Literature [*A publication*] ... AbPhoto
Abstracts of Photographic Science and Engineering Literature [*A publication*] ... APSE
Abstracts of Popular Culture [*A publication*] ... Abstr Pop Cult
Abstracts of Research and Related Materials in Vocational and Technical Education [*A publication*] ... AbVoc
Abstracts of Research and Related Materials in Vocational and Technical Education [*A publication*] ... ARM
Abstracts for Social Workers [*A publication*] ... AbSocWk
Abstracts for Social Workers [*A publication*] ... Absts Soc Workers
Abstracts of Technical Papers. Water Pollution Control Federation [*A publication*] ... Abstr Tech Pap Water Pollut Control Fed
Abstracts on Tropical Agriculture [*A publication*] ... Abstr Trop Agri
Abstracts of World Medicine [*A publication*] ... Abstr World Med
Abteilung [*Division*] [*German*] ... ABT
Abteilungsgewerkschaftaleitung ... AGL
Abteilungsparteiorganisation ... APO
Abtesla [*Unit of magnetic induction*] ... abT
Abu Dhabi [*United Arab Emirates*] [*Airport symbol*] ... AUH
Abu Simbel [*Egypt*] [*Airport symbol*] ... ABS
ABU [*Asian Broadcasting Union*] **Technical Review** [*A publication*] ... ABU Tech Rev
Abuja [*Nigeria*] [*Airport symbol*] ... ABV
Abundant [*With respect to occurrence of species*] ... A
Abundant ... ABNDT
Abundant Life Seed Foundation ... ALSF
Abused Women's Aid in Crisis ... AWAIC
Abuyama [*Japan*] [*Seismograph station code, US Geological Survey*] ... ABU
Abvolt [*Unit of electromotive force*] ... aV
Abweber [*Also, Mx*] [*Unit of magnetic flux*] ... abWb
Abwehrdienst [*Counterintelligence service*] [*German military - World War II*] ... AD
Abwehroffizier [*Counterintelligence officer*] [*German military - World War II*] ... AO
Abyssinia ... AB
Abyssinia ... ABYSS
AC [*Alternating Current*] **Control Unit** ... ACU
A.C. Owners Club - American Centre ... ACOC
AC Spark Plug Co., Electronics Division, Milwaukee, WI [*Library symbol*] ... WMACS
AC Spark Plug Co., General Motors Corp., Flint, MI [*Library symbol*] ... MiFliACS
Academia Brasileira de Ciencias [*Brazil*] ... ABC
Academia Brasileira de Ciencias. Anais [*A publication*] ... Acad Brasileira Cienc Anais
Academia de Ciencias de Cuba. Instituto de Geologia. Actas [*A publication*] ... Acad Cienc Cuba Inst Geol Actas
Academia de Ciencias de Cuba. Instituto de Geologia y Paleontologia. Publicacion Especial [*A publication*] ... Acad Cienc Cuba Inst Geol Paleontol Publ Espec
Academia de Ciencias de Cuba. Instituto de Geologia. Serie Geologica [*A publication*] ... Acad Cienc Cuba Inst Geol Ser Geol
Academia de Ciencias de Cuba. Serie Biologica [*A publication*] ... Acad Cienc Cuba Ser Biol
Academia de Ciencias Medicas, Fisicas, y Naturales de la Habana. Anales [*A publication*] ... Acad Cienc Med Fis y Naturales Habana Anales
Academia de Ciencias Medicas, Fisicas, y Naturales de la Habana. Annales [*A publication*] ... Ac Cienc Med Habana An

Academia Maria Reina, Rio Piedras, PR [*Library symbol*] ... PrRA
Academia Mexicana de Ciencias Exactas Fisicas y Naturales. Anuario [*A publication*] ... Ac Mex Cienc An
Academia Nacional de Ciencias Memorias y Revista [*A publication*] ... Acad Nac Cienc Mem Rev
Academia Republicii Populare Romine Filiala Cluj Studii Cercetari de Agronomie [*A publication*] ... Acad Repub Pop Rom Fil Cluj Stud Cercet Agron
Academia Republicii Populare Romine Studii si Cercetari de Biologie. Seria Biologie Vegetala [*A publication*] ... Acad Repub Pop Rom Stud Cercet Biol Ser Biol Veg
Academia Republicii Populare Romine Studii si Cercetari de Chimice [*A publication*] ... Acad Repub Pop Rom Stud Cercet Chim
Academia R.S. Romania [*Academy of Romania*]**, Bucharest, Romania** [*Library symbol*] ... RoBA
Academia Scientiarum Fennicae Annales. Series A-III. Geologica-Geographica [*A publication*] ... Acad Sci Fenn Ann Ser A-III Geol-Geogr
Academia Sinica Institute of Botany. Annual Report [*A publication*] ... Acad Sin Inst Bot Annu Rep
Academia Sinica Institute of Zoology. Monograph Series [*A publication*] ... Acad Sin Inst Zool Monogr Ser
Academiae Americanae Socius [*Fellow of the American Society*] ... AAS
Academic Administration Internship Program [*Later, AFP*] ... AAIP
Academic Clinical Laboratory Physicians and Scientists ... ACLPS
Academic Collective Bargaining Information Service ... ACBIS
Academic Committee on Soviet Jewry ... ACSJ
Academic Computing Group ... ACCOMP
Academic Instructor and Allied Officer School [*Military*] ... AIAOS
Academic Instructors School [*Air Force*] ... AIS
Academic Libraries of Brooklyn [*Library network*] ... ALB
Academic Press, Inc. [*Publishers*] ... AP
Academic Press, Incorporated [*Publishers*] ... API
Academic Remedial Training [*Navy*] ... ART
Academic and Social Anxiety Program [*Cornell University*] ... ASAP
Academic Therapy [*A publication*] ... Acad Ther
Academic Therapy [*A publication*] ... Acad Therapy
Academic Travel Abroad ... ATA
Academic Women Allied for Rights and Equality ... AWARE
Academic Women for Equality ... ACE
Academic Year Institute [*National Science Foundation*] ... AYI
Academical Rank of Civil Engineers ... ARCE
Academician [*or Academy*] ... A
Academician [*or Academy*] ... ACAD
Academie d'Agriculture de France. Comptes Rendus des Seances [*A publication*] ... Acad Ag France Comptes Rendus
Academie d'Agriculture de France. Comptes Rendus des Seances [*A publication*] ... Acad Ag France Compt Rend
Academie Imperiale des Sciences, Belles-Lettres, et Arts de Lyon. Classe des Sciences. Memoires [*A publication*] ... Ac Imp Lyon Cl Sc Mem
Academie des Inscriptions et Belles-Lettres. Comptes Rendus des Seances [*A publication*] ... AIBL
Academie des Inscriptions et Belles-Lettres. Comptes Rendus des Seances [*A publication*] ... AIBLCr
Academie des Inscriptions et Belles-Lettres [*Paris*]**. Fondation Eugene Piot. Monuments et Memoires** [*A publication*] ... Monuments Piot
Academie des Inscriptions et Belles-Lettres. Memoires [*Paris*] [*A publication*] ... Acad d Inscrip Memoires
Academie des Inscriptions et Belles-Lettres. Memoires (Paris) [*A publication*] ... Acad d Inscr (Paris) Mem
Academie des Inscriptions et Belles-Lettres. Monuments et Memoires [*Paris*] [*A publication*] ... Acad d Inscr Mon et Mem
Academie des Inscriptions et Belles-Lettres. Monuments et Memoires (Paris) [*A publication*] ... Acad d Inscr (Paris) Mon et Mem
Academie des Inscriptions et Belles-Lettres (Paris). Memoires Presentes par Divers Savants [*A publication*] ... Acad Inscr (Paris) Mem Div Savants
Academie Internationale de la Ceramique [*International Academy of Ceramics*] [*See also IAC*] ... AIC
Academie Internationale d'Heraldique [*International Academy of Heraldry*] ... AIH
Academie Polonaise des Sciences. Bulletin. Serie des Sciences de la Terre [*A publication*] ... Acad Pol Sci Bull Ser Sci Terre
Academie Roumaine. Bulletin de la Section Historique [*A publication*] ... Bull Roum
Academie Royale d'Archeologie de Belgique. Annales [*A publication*] ... ARABAn
Academie Royale d'Archeologie de Belgique. Bulletin [*A publication*] ... ARABBull
Academie Royale de Belgique [*A publication*] ... ABM
Academie Royale de Belgique. Annuaire [*A publication*] ... Acad R Belg Annu
Academie Royale de Belgique. Bulletin de la Classe des Beaux-Arts [*A publication*] ... BCBA
Academie Royale de Belgique. Bulletin de la Classe des Lettres et des Sciences Morales et Politiques et de la Classe des Beaux-Arts [*A publication*] ... ARBBull
Academie Royale de Belgique. Bulletin de la Classe des Lettres et des Sciences Morales et Politiques et de la Classe des Beaux-Arts [*A publication*] ... BARB
Academie Royale de Belgique. Bulletin de la Classe des Sciences [*A publication*] ... Acad Roy Belg Bull Cl Sci
Academie Royale de Belgique. Classe des Beaux-Arts. Bulletin [*A publication*] ... Acad Sci Belg Bul Cl Beaux-Arts
Academie Royale de Belgique. Classe des Lettres et des Sciences Morales et Politiques. Bulletin [*A publication*] ... Acad Sci Belg Bul Cl Lett
Academie Royale de Belgique. Classe des Lettres et des Sciences Morales et Politiques. Memoires. Collection in-8 [*A publication*] ... Acad Sci Belg Mem 8 Cl Lett
Academie Royale de Belgique. Classe des Sciences. Bulletin [*A publication*] ... Acad Sci Belg Bul Cl Sci
Academie Royale de Belgique. Classe des Sciences. Collection in Octavo. Memoires [*A publication*] ... Acad R Belg Cl Sci Collect Octavo Mem
Academie Royale de Belgique. Classe des Sciences. Collection in Quarto. Memoires [*A publication*] ... Acad R Belg Cl Sci Collect Quarto Mem
Academie Royale de Belgique. Classe des Sciences. Memoires [*A publication*] ... Acad R Belg Cl Sci Mem
Academie Royale de Belgique. Classe des Sciences. Memoires Collection in-8 [*A publication*] ... Acad Roy Belg Cl Sci Mem Coll in-8
Academie Royale de Belgique. Classe des Sciences. Memoires. Collection in-4 [*A publication*] ... Acad Sci Belg Mem 4 Cl Sci
Academie Royale de Belgique. Classe des Sciences. Memoires. Collection in-8 [*A publication*] ... Acad Sci Belg Mem 8 Cl Sci
Academie Royale de Belgique. Memoires de la Classe des Sciences. Collection in Octavo [*A publication*] ... Acad R Belg Mem Cl Sci Collect Octavo
Academie Royale de Belgique. Memoires de la Classe des Sciences. Collection in Quarto [*A publication*] ... Acad R Belg Mem Cl Sci Collect Quarto
Academie Royale de Langue et de Litterature Francaise de Belgique. Bulletin [*A publication*] ... AcLLB
Academie Royale des Sciences d'Outre-Mer. Bulletin des Seances [*A publication*] ... Acad Roy Sci O-Mer B
Academie des Sciences [*Academy of Science*] ... ADS
Academie des Sciences de Cracovie. Bulletin International [*A publication*] ... ASCBull
Academie des Sciences. Inscriptions et Belles-Lettres de Toulouse. Memoires [*A publication*] ... Acad Sci Toulouse Mem
Academie des Sciences Morales et Politiques (Paris). Memoires [*A publication*] ... Acad d Sci Mor et Pol (Paris) Mem
Academie des Sciences d'Outre Mer [*A publication*] ... ASOM
Academie des Sciences (Paris). Comptes Rendus [*A publication*] ... Ac Sc (Paris) C R
Academie des Sciences (Paris). Comptes Rendus Hebdomadaires des Seances. Serie B. Sciences Physiques [*A publication*] ... Acad Sci (Paris) CR Ser B
Academie des Sciences (Paris). Comptes Rendus Hebdomadaires des Seances. Serie C. Sciences Chimiques [*A publication*] ... Acad Sci (Paris) CR Ser C
Academie des Sciences (Paris). Comptes Rendus Hebdomadaires des Seances. Serie D. Sciences Naturelles [*A publication*] ... Acad Sci (Paris) CR Ser D
Academie des Sciences (Paris). Memoires [*A publication*] ... Acad d Sci (Paris) Mem
Academie des Sciences (Paris). Memoires [*A publication*] ... Acad Sci (Paris) Mem
Academie des Sciences (Paris). Memoires Presentes par Divers Savants [*A publication*] ... Acad d Sci (Paris) Mem Div Savants
Academie Serbe des Sciences et des Arts. Classe des Sciences Mathematiques et Naturelles. Glas [*A publication*] ... Acad Serb Sci Arts Classe Sci Math Nat Glas
Academie Serbe des Sciences et des Arts. Glas [*A publication*] ... Acad Serbe Sci Arts Glas
Academy of Air Traffic Control Medicine ... AATCM
Academy Airlines [*Griffin, GA*] [*FAA designator*] ... ACD
Academy of Ambulatory Foot Surgery ... AAFS
Academy of American Franciscan History ... AAFH
Academy of American Poets ... AAP
Academy of Aphasia ... AA
Academy of Applied Science ... AAS
Academy of Art and Literature [*British*] ... AAL
Academy of the Arts and Sciences of the Americas ... AASA
Academy Award [*Academy of Motion Picture Arts and Sciences film award*] ... AA
Academy of Certified Social Workers ... ACSW
Academy of Comic Book Artists ... ACBA
Academy of Comic-Book Fans and Collectors [*Defunct*] ... ACBFC
Academy of Country Music ... ACM
Academy of Criminal Justice Sciences [*Formerly, IAPP*] ... ACJS
Academy of Dentistry for the Handicapped ... ADH
Academy of Dentistry International ... ADI
Academy of Denture Prosthetics ... ADP
Academy for Educational Development ... AED
Academy of Electrical Contracting ... AEC
Academy of Family Films and Family Television ... AFFFT

Academy of General Dentistry ....AGD
Academy of Hazard Control Management ....AHCM
Academy of Health Care Consultants [Defunct]..............AHCC
Academy of Health Sciences [Health Services Command] [Army] ....AHS
Academy of Homiletics...AH
Academy of Hospital Counselors [Later, AHCC]...............AHC
Academy of Hospital Public Relations...........................AHPR
Academy of Human Rights...AHR
Academy on Human Rights and Peace...........................AHRP
Academy for Implants and Transplants.............................AIT
Academy of Independent Scholars......................................AIS
Academy Insurance Group [NASDAQ symbol].................ACIG
Academy of International Business......................................AIB
Academy of International Military History [Later, IMA].......AIMH
Academy for Interscience Methodology..............................AIM
Academy of Irish Art..AIA
Academy of Lighting Arts...ALA
Academy of Management..AM
Academy of Management. Journal [A publication] .... Acad Manage J
Academy of Management. Journal [A publication].............Acad Mgt J
Academy of Management. Review [A publication] .... Acad Manage Rev
Academy of Management. Review [A publication]............Acad Mgt R
Academy of Marketing Science..AMS
Academy of Master Wine Growers....................................AMWG
Academy of Medicine of New Jersey, Bloomfield, NJ [Library
   symbol]...NjBIM
Academy of Medicine of New Jersey. Bulletin [A publication]...............
                                                                          Acad Med NJ Bull
Academy of Medicine, Toronto, ON, Canada [Library symbol]............CaOTA
Academy of Model Aeronautics...AMA
Academy of Motion Picture Arts and Sciences................AMPAS
Academy of Motion Picture Arts and Sciences. Bulletin [A
   publication]..Acad Bul
Academy of Motion Picture Arts and Sciences, Los Angeles, CA
   [Library symbol]...CLAc
Academy of Natural Sciences. Journal [A publication] ......
                                                                          Acad of Nat Sci Jour
Academy of Natural Sciences of Philadelphia [Pennsylvania]...............ANSP
Academy of Natural Sciences of Philadelphia. Journal [A
   publication]...Ac N Sc Phila J
Academy of Natural Sciences of Philadelphia. Mineralogical and
   Geological Section. Proceedings [A publication]..................
                                                                          Ac N Sc Phila Min G Sec Pr
Academy of Natural Sciences of Philadelphia, Philadelphia, PA
   [OCLC symbol]...ANS
Academy of Natural Sciences of Philadelphia, Philadelphia, PA
   [Library symbol]..PPAN
Academy of Natural Sciences of Philadelphia. Proceedings [A
   publication]..Acad Natur Sci Phila Proc
Academy of Natural Sciences of Philadelphia. Proceedings [A
   publication]..Ac N Sc Phila Pr
Academy of Natural Sciences of Philadelphia. Special
   Publication [A publication]............... Acad Nat Sci Philadelphia Spec Pub
Academy of the New Church...ANC
Academy of the New Church, Bryn Athyn, PA [Library symbol] ....PBa
Academy of the New Church, Bryn Athyn, PA [OCLC symbol]................ PBA
Academy of Operative Dentistry...AOD
Academy of Oral Dynamics...AOD
Academy of Orthomolecular Psychiatry.............................AOP
Academy of Osteopathic Directors of Medical Education ....AODME
Academy of Parapsychology and Medicine........................APM
Academy of Parish Clergy...APC
Academy for Peace Research...APR
Academy of Pharmaceutical Sciences................................APS
Academy of Pharmacy Practice...APP
Academy of Political Science [A publication]........... Acad Pol Sci
Academy of Political Science...APS
Academy of Political Science. Proceedings [A publication] ....
                                                                          Acad Pol Sci Proc
Academy of Psychologists in Marital Counseling [Later, APMSFT] ....APMC
Academy of Psychologists in Marital Sex and Family Therapy ....APMSFT
Academy for the Psychology of Sports International ....APSI
Academy of Psychosomatic Medicine..................................APM
Academy of Rehabilitative Audiology..................................ARA
Academy of Religion and Mental Health [Later, Institutes of
   Religion and Health]..ARMH
Academy of Religion and Psychical Research ....ARPR
Academy Review [A publication]....................................Acad Rev
Academy of Richmond County, Augusta, GA [Library symbol] ....GAuAR
Academy of Science Fiction, Fantasy, and Horror Films..................ASFFHF
Academy of Science of Kansas City. Transactions [A
   publication]...Ac Sc Kansas City Tr
Academy of Science and Letters of Sioux City, Iowa.
   Proceedings [A publication].............................Ac Sc Sioux City Pr
Academy of Science of St. Louis. Transactions [A publication]............
                                                                          Acad of Sci of St Louis Trans
Academy of Science of St. Louis. Transactions [A publication] ....
                                                                          Acad Sci St Louis Trans
Academy of Science of St. Louis. Transactions [A publication] ....
                                                                          Ac Sc St L Tr
Academy of Science (Union of Soviet Socialist Republics)..............ASUSSR

Academy of Sciences..AS
Academy of Scientific Hypnotherapy...................................ASH
Academy of Screen Printing Technology............................ASPT
Academy of Security Educators and Trainees.....................ASET
Academy for Sports Dentistry...ASD
Academy for State and Local Government.........................ASLG
Academy of the Street of Puerto Rican Congress.............ASPRC
Academy (Syracuse) [A publication]..............................Acad (Syr)
Academy of Teachers of Occupations [Defunct]................ATO
Academy of Television Arts and Sciences.........................ATAS
Academy of Underwater Arts and Sciences.......................AUAS
Academy of Veterinary Allergy...AVA
Academy of Veterinary Cardiology......................................AVC
Academy of Wind and Percussion Arts.............................AWAPA
Academy of Zoology...AZ
Acadia National Park...ACAD
Acadia Parish Library, Crowley, LA [Library symbol]...............LCrA
Acadia University, Department of Geography, Wolfville, NS,
   Canada [Library symbol]...CaNSWAG
Acadia University, Wolfville, NS, Canada [Library symbol].............CaNSWA
Acadian Genealogical and Historical Association ....AGHA
Acandi [Colombia] [Airport symbol]..ACD
Acao Revolucionaria Armada [Portugal]..............................ARA
Acapulco [Mexico] [Airport symbol].....................................ACA
Acapulco y Los Arcos Restaurantes [NASDAQ symbol].................ALAR
Acarigua [Venezuela] [Airport symbol]................................AGV
Accademia..ACCAD
Accademia Gioenia de Scienze Naturali in Catania. Bollettino
   delle Sedute [A publication]................Ac Gioenia Sc Nat Catania B
Accademia di Mantova. Atti e Memorie [A publication] ....AMan
Accademia Nazionale dei Lincei. Atti. Classe di Scienze Fisiche,
   Matematiche, e Naturali. Rendiconti [A publication]......................
                                                                          Accad Naz Lincei Atti Cl Sci Fis Mat Nat Rend
Accademia Nazionale dei Lincei. Rendiconti della Classe di
   Scienze Morali, Storiche, e Filologiche [A publication]...........ANLMSF
Accademia Nazionale di Scienze, Lettere, e Arti (Modena). Atti
   e Memorie [A publication]..... Accad Naz Sci Lett Arti (Modena) Atti Mem
Accademia delle Scienze di Bologna. Memorie [A publication] ....ASB
Accademia delle Scienze Fisiche e Matematiche Rendiconto [A
   publication]................................... Accad Sci Fis e Mat Rend
Accademie e Biblioteche d'Italia [A publication]......................ABI
Accademie e Biblioteche d'Italia [A publication] ....Accad Bibliot d'Italia
Accademie e Biblioteche d'Italia [A publication]...............Accad e Bibl Italia
Accelerando [Quickening the Pace] [Music]..........................ACC
Accelerando [Quickening the Pace] [Music]......................ACCEL
Accelerate...ACCEL
Accelerate..ACLT
Accelerate/Stop Distance Available [Aviation]...................ASDA
Accelerated Assemblies...AA
Accelerated Business Collection and Delivery [Postal Service].............ABCD
Accelerated Christian Education [An association]...............ACE
Accelerated Construction Completion Date........................ACCD
Accelerated Cost Recovery System [Tax law]....................ACRS
Accelerated Declassification System..................................ADS
Accelerated Development Test...ADT
Accelerated Development Test Program.............................ADTP
Accelerated Evaluation Method...AEM
Accelerated Freeze-Drying [Food processing].....................AFD
Accelerated Growth Area [Embryology] ....AGA
Accelerated Intelligence Report...............................CELINTREP
Accelerated Inverse Voltage..AIV
Accelerated Item Reduction [Military]...................................AIR
Accelerated Learning of Logic...ALL
Accelerated Life Testing..ALT
Accelerated Pacification Campaign [South Vietnam]............APC
Accelerated Photosynthetic System [Sewage purification]...........APS
Accelerated Project to Automate Critical Hardware Hardcore
   Systems...APACHE
Accelerated Public Works [Program] [Department of the Interior] ....APW
Accelerated Public Works Program [Department of the Interior] ....APWP
Accelerated Readiness Analysis..ARA
Accelerated Reeducation of Emotions, Behavior, and Attitudes
   [Rehabilitation program]...AREBA
Accelerated Rural Development...ARD
Accelerated Service Test..AST
Accelerated Specialized Inspection Sites [Customs inspection at
   airports]...ASIST
Accelerated Strike Aircraft Program Requirement [DoD]...............ASAPR
Accelerated Test Technology..ATT
Accelerated Turn-Over to Vietnamese [Military]................ACTOV
Accelerating Rate Calorimeter [Instrumentation]...................ARC
Acceleration [or Accelerator]...A
Acceleration...ACC
Acceleration [Symbol]...f
Acceleration Compensation Unit..ACU
Acceleration Corp. [NASDAQ symbol].................................ACLE
Acceleration Correction...C
Acceleration-Deceleration Unit...ADU
Acceleration Monitoring Guidance System ....AMGS
Acceleration Switching Valve...ASV
Acceleration-Type Control Law..ATCL

Acceleration Vector Control	AVC
Accelerator	AC
Accelerator [Hematology]	Ac
Accelerator Globulin [Medicine]	AcG
Accelerator Information Center [ORNL]	AIC
Accelerator Mass Spectrometry	AMS
Accelerator for Physics and Chemistry of Heavy Metals	APACHE
Accelerator Pulsed Fast Assembly	APFA
Accelerometer	ACCEL
Accelerometer	ACCLRM
Accelerometer Calibration Vibration Exciter	ACVE
Accelerometer Monitoring Program [NASA]	AMP
Accelerometer Package	AP
Accelerometer Package	APK
Accelerometer Parameter Shift	APS
Accelerometer Pulse Converter	APC
Accelerometer Scale Factor Error	ASFE
Accelerometer Scale Factor Input Panel	ASFIP
Accelerometer Signal Conditioner	ASC
Accent [A publication]	Acc
Accent Before Cooking [Advertising slogan]	ABC
Accent on Developing Abstract Processes of Thought	ADAPT
Accent on Information [An association]	AI
Accent on Information [Data bank for the handicapped and rehabilitation professionals sponsored by association of the same name]	AOI
Accept [or Acceptance]	ACCPT
Accept	ACPT
Accept No Verbal Orders	ANVO
Accept-Reject Rule [Statistics]	AR
Acceptable Daily Intake [Toxicology]	ADI
Acceptable Defect Level	ADL
Acceptable Environmental Range Test	AERT
Acceptable Failure Rate	AFR
Acceptable Hazard Rate	AHR
Acceptable Limit for Dispersion	ALD
Acceptable Periodic Inspection	API
Acceptable Process Level	APL
Acceptable Quality Level [Quality control]	AQL
Acceptable Quality Rate [Quality control]	AQR
Acceptable Quality Test [Quality control]	AQT
Acceptable Reliability Level [Quality control]	ARL
Acceptable Supplier List	ASL
Acceptable Workload Factor [Management]	AWF
Acceptance	ACC
Acceptance	ACCEPTN
Acceptance Checkout [NASA]	ACO
Acceptance Checkout Equipment [NASA]	ACE
Acceptance Checkout Equipment - Space Craft [NASA]	ACE-S/C
Acceptance Checkout and Evaluation System [NASA]	ACES
Acceptance Checkout Procedure	ACP
Acceptance Control Equipment Section [NASA]	ACES
Acceptance Data Package	ADP
Acceptance and Ferry Flight [NASA]	AFF
Acceptance Functional Test Procedure [NASA]	A/FTP
Acceptance Inspection Equipment [Army]	AIE
Acceptance Inspection Instruction	AII
Acceptance Inspection Package	AIP
Acceptance Message [Aviation code]	ACP
Acceptance Number [Business and trade]	Ac
Acceptance and Operational Checkout Requirements Document [NASA]	AOCRD
Acceptance Readiness	AR
Acceptance Review	AR
Acceptance Summary Report	ASR
Acceptance Tag	AT
Acceptance Test Equipment	ATE
Acceptance Test Facility	ATF
Acceptance Test or Launch Language	ATOLL
Acceptance Test and Launch Operations	ATLO
Acceptance Test Plan [or Procedure]	ATP
Acceptance Test Specification	ATS
Acceptance Tests [NASA]	AT
Acceptance Thermal Testing	ATT
Acceptance and Transfer	A & T
Acceptance Trials [Shipbuilding]	AT
Acceptance Vibration Testing [NASA]	AVT
Accepte sous Protet [Accepted under Protest] [French]	ASP
Accepte sous Protet pour Compte [Accepted under Protest for Account] [French]	ASPC
Accepte sous Protet pour Compte [Accepted under Protest for Account] [French]	ASPPC
Accepted	A
Accepted Alternative Designation Of	AADO
Accepted Dental Remedies [A publication]	ADR
Accepted Dental Therapeutics	ADT
Accepted on Hire	AOH
Accepted Weight/Estimate [Ships]	AWE
Acceptor [Physiology]	A
Acceptor Energy Level	AEL
Accepts Transfer as Offered	ATRSO
Access [Credit card] [British]	A
Access	ACC
Access	ACES
Access	ACS
Access and Amendment Refusal Authority [Army]	AARA
Access Authorization	AA
Access Block Diagram	ABD
Access Door	AD
Access Floor Manufacturing Association	AFMA
Access Function Register	AFR
Access for the Handicapped [An association]	AH
Access Method	AM
Access Method Control Block [Data processing]	ACB
Access Method for Indexed Data Generalized for Operating System [Data processing]	AMIGOS
Access Method Service [Data processing]	AMS
Access Opening	ACS-O
Access Opening [Technical drawings]	AO
Access Panel [Technical drawings]	AP
Access Permit [or Permittee] [Nuclear energy]	AP
Access Permit Holder	APH
Access Point Pace	APP
Access Time	ACST
Access Time	AT
Accession Designation Number [Military]	ADN
Accession List	AL
Accessions Document [Air Force]	AD
Accessorial	ACCSL
Accessories Bulletin	AB
Accessory	ACC
Accessory	ACCES
Accessory	ACCESS
Accessory	ACCRY
Accessory	ACCY
Accessory Boring Organ [of a gastropod]	ABO
Accessory Bulletin	AYB
Accessory Change	AYC
Accessory Clinical Findings [Medicine]	ACF
Accessory Drive Gear Box	ADG
Accessory Drive Gear Box	ADGB
Accessory Drive System	ADS
Accessory and Equipment Technical Committee	AETC
Accessory Gear Box	AGB
Accessory Gland	AG
Accessory Pedal Ganglia	APG
Accessory Power Supply	APS
Accessory Power Unit	APU
Accessory Supply System	ASS
Acciaio Inossidabile [A publication]	Acciaio Inossid
Accident	ACC
Accident	ACCD
Accident	ACDNT
Accident	ACDT
Accident Analysis and Prevention [A publication]	Accid Anal Prev
Accident Analysis and Prevention [A publication]	Accident Anal Prev
Accident Benefits [Insurance]	AB
Accident and Emergency [Ward or Department] [Medicine]	A & E
Accident and Health Insurance	A & H
Accident, Incident, Deficiencies	AID
Accident and Indemnity [Insurance]	A & I
Accident Information Retrieval System	AIRS
Accident Injury	ACCI
Accident Intelligence [British police term]	AI
Accident Model Document [NASA]	AMD
Accident Notice [Aviation]	ACNOT
Accident Sequence Precursor Study [Nuclear Regulatory Commission]	ASP
Accidental Death Benefit [Insurance]	ADB
Accidental Death and Dismemberment [Insurance]	AD and D
Accidental Hypothermia [Medicine]	AH
Accidental Injury	AI
Accidental Loss [Nuclear energy]	AL
Accidentally Incurred	AI
Accidents Investigation Branch [Air Force] [British]	AIB
Accidents and Road Safety [British]	ARS
Accion Catolica Espanola	ACE
Accion Cultural Popular [Basic education organization] [Colombia]	ACPO
Accion Democratica [Democratic Action] [Venezuelan political party]	AD
Accion Democratica Popular [Popular Democratic Action] [Political party in Costa Rica]	ACP
ACCION International	AI
Accion Republicana Espanola	ARE
Accion Revolucionaria Nacional Ecuatoriana [National Revolutionary Action] [Political party in Ecuador]	ARNE
Acclimatization Experiences Institute	AEI
ACCO World [NYSE symbol]	ACO
Accokeek Foundation	AF
Accommodate	ACCOM
Accommodation	A
Accommodation	ACC
Accommodation	ACCN

Accommodation Convergence [*Ophthalmology*] ... AC
Accommodation Convergence/Accommodation [*A ratio*] [*Ophthalmology*] ... AC/A
Accommodation Sales Order ... ASO
Accommodation Sales Requisition ... ASR
Accommodation Weight Investigation ... AWI
Accompagnamento [*Accompaniment*] [*Music*] ... ACC
Accompanied ... ACC
Accompanied by Adult [*British Board of Film Censors*] ... AA
Accompaniment [*Music*] ... ACCOM
Accompaniment [*Music*] ... ACCOMP
Accompaniment [*Music*] ... ACCT
Accompany ... ACCOM
Accompany ... ACMP
Accompany ... ACPY
Accomplice [*FBI standardized term*] ... ACCPL
Accomplish ... ACCOMP
Accomplish ... ACCOMPL
Accomplishment of Assigned Mission Impeded by Deadline [*Army*] ... AAMID
Accomplishment/Cost Procedure ... ACP
Accomplishment Quotient ... AQ
Accord ... ACD
Accord Dangereuse Routier [*European agreement on the carriage of dangerous goods by road*] ... ADR
Accord Monetaire Europeen ... AME
Accord Transports Permissables [*European agreement on the transport of perishable foodstuffs*] ... ATP
Accordance With ... A/W
According ... ACCORD
According (To) ... ACC
Accordion Federation of North America ... AFNA
Accordion Teachers' Guild ... ATG
Account ... AC
Account ... ACC
Account [*or Accountant*] ... ACCT
Account Control ... AC
Account Current [*Business and trade*] ... A/C
Account Executive ... AE
Account Identification and Description Services [*Dun & Bradstreet*] ... AIDS
Account Identifier [*Data processing*] ... ACCTID
Account Mechanical ... AMECH
Account Number Change File [*IRS*] ... ANCF
Account Number File [*Integrated Data Retrieval System*] [*IRS*] ... ANF
Account Number Update File [*IRS*] ... ANUF
Account Of [*Business and trade*] ... AO
Account Paid ... AP
Account Sales ... AS
Account Traffic ... ATFC
Account Weather [*Aviation*] ... AWX
Accountability Data Package ... ADP
Accountable Property Officer [*Military*] ... ACTPO
Accountable Property Officer [*Military*] ... APO
Accountable Strength ... ACCTSTR
Accountancy ... ACCTCY
Accountancy ... ACCY
Accountant ... ACTNT
Accountant General ... AG
Accountant [*or Accounting*] **Officer** ... AO
Accountants Computer-Users Technical Exchange ... ACUTE
Accountants and Controllers ... AC
Accountants for the Public Interest ... API
Accounting ... ACCTG
Accounting ... ACCTNG
Accounting and Budget Distribution System [*Air Force*] ... ABDS
Accounting and Business Research [*A publication*] ... Acct & Bus Res
Accounting Careers Council [*Later, AICPA*] ... ACC
Accounting Classification Code ... ACC
Accounting Classification Reference Number ... ACRN
Accounting Control System ... ACS
Accounting and Data Processing Abstracts [*A publication*] ... ADPA
Accounting Data System ... ADS
Accounting Department Instructions ... ADI
Accounting and Disbursing ... A & D
Accounting and Disbursing Station Number [*Air Force*] ... ADSN
Accounting and Finance ... A & F
Accounting and Finance Office [*or Officer*] ... AFO
Accounting Information System ... AIS
Accounting Line Number ... ALN
Accounting Principles Board [*Later, Financial Accounting Standards Board*] [*American Institute of Certified Public Accountants*] ... APB
Accounting Processing Code ... APC
Accounting Program [*Association of Independent Colleges and Schools specialization code*] ... AC
Accounting and Reporting Management Improvement Program [*Army*] ... ARMIP
Accounting Requirements Code [*Military*] ... ARC
Accounting Researchers International Association ... ARIA
Accounting Review [*A publication*] ... Accounting R
Accounting Review [*A publication*] ... Account R
Accounting Review [*A publication*] ... Acc Review
Accounting Review [*A publication*] ... Acctg Rev
Accounting Review [*A publication*] ... Acct R
Accounting Review [*A publication*] ... AR
Accounting Tabulating [*Card*] ... AT
Accounting Tabulating Form ... ATF
Accounting Unit ... AU
Accounting Work Order ... AWO
Accounts ... A/C
Accounts of Chemical Research [*A publication*] ... Acc Chem Re
Accounts of Chemical Research [*A publication*] ... Acc Chem Res
Accounts of Chemical Research [*A publication*] ... Acct Chem Res
Accounts, Collection, and Taxpayer Service [*Internal Revenue Service*] ... ACTS
Accounts Control Area ... ACA
Accounts Maintenance [*IRS*] ... AM
Accounts Office [*Army*] ... AO
Accounts Payable ... AP
Accounts Receivable ... AR
Accounts Register [*Data processing*] ... AR
Accra [*Ghana*] [*Airport symbol*] ... ACC
Accreditation Association for Ambulatory Health Care ... AAAHC
Accreditation Board for Engineering and Technology [*Formerly, ECPD*] ... ABET
Accreditation Council for Accountancy ... ACA
Accreditation Council for Services for Mentally Retarded and Other Developmentally Disabled Persons ... AC/MRDD
Accreditation and Institutional Eligibility Staff [*Office of Education*] ... AIES
Accredited ... ACCRED
Accredited Appraiser, Canadian Institute ... AACI
Accredited Farm Manager [*Designation given by American Society of Farm Managers and Rural Appraisers*] ... AFM
Accredited Home Newspapers of America [*Later, SNA*] ... AHNA
Accredited Management Organization [*Designation given by Institute of Real Estate Management*] ... AMO
Accredited in Public Relations ... APR
Accredited Record Technician ... ART
Accredited Rural Appraiser [*Designation given by American Society of Farm Managers and Rural Appraisers*] ... ARA
Accrediting Association of Bible Colleges [*Later, American Association of Bible Colleges*] ... AABC
Accrediting Bureau of Health Education Schools ... ABHES
Accrediting Bureau of Medical Laboratory Schools [*Later, ABHES*] ... ABMLS
Accrediting Commission for Business Schools ... ACBS
Accrediting Commission on Education for Health Services Administration ... ACEHSA
Accrediting Commission for Specialized Colleges ... ACSC
Accrediting Council on Education in Journalism and Mass Communications [*Formerly, ACEJ*] ... ACEJMC
Accrington Public Library, Accrington, United Kingdom [*Library symbol*] ... UkAc
Accrual Accounting and Reporting System ... AARS
Accrued ... ACCR
Accrued Expenditure ... AE
Accrued Expenditure Paid ... AEP
Accrued Expenditure Unpaid ... AEU
Accrued Leave [*Military*] ... ACLV
Accrued Military Pay System ... AMPS
Accumulate ... ACCUM
Accumulation Area Ratio ... AAR
Accumulation Distribution Unit ... ADU
Accumulation Factor ... AF
Accumulation Time ... ACT
Accumulator ... A
Accumulator ... ACC
Accumulator High-Pressure Air ... AHPA
Accumulator Reservoir Manifold Assembly ... ARMA
Accumulator Switch ... ACS
Accumulators Shift Right [*Data processing*] ... ASR
Accuracy ... ACCRY
Accuracy Control Document ... ACD
Accuracy in Media [*An association*] ... AIM
Accurate ... ACCUR
Accurate and Reliable Prototype Earth Sensor Head [*NASA*] ... ARPESH
Accurate Tracking ... ACTRAC
Accurately Defined Systems [*Data processing*] ... ADS
Accuray Corp. [*NASDAQ symbol*] ... ACRA
Accusative ... ACC
Accusative ... ACCUS
Ace ... A
ACE [*Allied Command Europe*] **Communication Management Organization** [*NATO*] ... ACMO
ACE [*American Council on Education*] **Fellows Program in Academic Administration** [*Formerly, AAIP*] ... AFP
ACE [*Allied Command Europe*] **Mobile Force** [*NATO*] ... AMF
ACEC [*Ateliers de Constructions Electriques de Charleroi*] **Reviews** [*A publication*] ... ACEC Rev
(Acetamidol)Aminoethanesulfonic Acid [*A buffer*] ... ACES
(Acetamidol)Iminodiacetic Acid [*A buffer*] ... ADA
Acetate ... ACTT

Acetate Cloth Tape ... ACT
Acetate Film Tape ... AFT
Acetate Halftone Litho [*Du Pont*] ... AHL
Acetic Acid, Alcohol, Formalin [*Biology*] ... AAF
Aceto Chemical Co. [*NASDAQ symbol*] ... ACET
Acetone Cyanohydrin [*Organic chemistry*] ... ACN
Acetoxy [*Biochemistry*] ... AcO
Acetoxy-N-trimethylanilinium Iodide [*Organic chemistry*] ... ANTI
Acetoxycycloheximide [*Biochemistry*] ... AXM
Acetoxypregnenolone [*Pharmacology*] ... AOP
Acetyl [*As substituent on nucleoside*] [*Biochemistry*] ... ac
Acetyl [*Organic chemistry*] ... Ac
Acetyl Benzoyl Peroxide [*Organic chemistry*] ... ABP
Acetyl Coenzyme A [*Biochemistry*] ... AcCoA
Acetyl Ethyl Tetramethyl Tetralin [*Musk fragrance, neuro-toxic compound*] ... AETT
Acetyl-para-aminophenol [*Pharmacology*] ... APAP
Acetylacetonate [*Organic chemistry*] ... Acac
Acetylacetone [*Organic chemistry*] ... ACAC
Acetyl(alanyl)phenylalanylchloromethyl Ketone [*Biochemistry*] ... AAPCK
Acetylaminofluorene [*Also, AcAF, AcNHFln, FAA*] [*Organic chemistry*] ... AAF
Acetylaminofluorene [*Also, AAF, AcNHFln, FAA*] [*Organic chemistry*] ... AcAF
Acetylaminofluorene [*Also, AAF, AcAF, FAA*] [*Organic chemistry*] ... AcNHFln
Acetylcholine [*Biochemistry*] ... ACh
Acetylcholine Receptor [*Also, AChR*] [*Biochemistry*] ... AcChR
Acetylcholine Receptor [*Also, AcChR*] [*Biochemistry*] ... AChR
Acetylcholinesterase [*Also, AChe*] [*An enzyme*] ... AChE
Acetylene ... ACET
Acetylene Reduction Assay [*Botany*] ... ARA
(Acetylglycyl)lysine Methyl Ester Acetate [*Biochemistry*] ... AGLME
Acetylhomocysteinethiolactone [*Citiolone*] [*Organic chemistry*] ... AHCTL
Acetyllysine Methyl Ester [*Biochemistry*] ... ALME
Acetylneuraminic Acid [*Also, NAN, NANA*] [*Biochemistry*] ... AcNeu
Acetyl(p-nitrophenyl)sulfanilamide [*Pharmacology*] ... APNPS
Acetylpyridineadenine Dinucleotide [*Biochemistry*] ... APAD
Acetylsalicylic Acid [*Aspirin*] ... ASA
Acetylsalicylic Acid [*Aspirin*]**, Phenacetin, and Caffeine Compound** [*Slang translation is, "All Purpose Capsules"*] [*Pharmacy*] ... APC
Acetylstrophanthidin [*Organic chemistry*] ... ACS
Acetylsulfanilyl Chloride [*Organic chemistry*] ... ASC
Acetyltyrosine Ethyl Ester [*Biochemistry*] ... ATEE
ACF Industries, Inc. [*NYSE symbol*] ... ACF
ACF Industries, Inc., Albuquerque, NM [*Library symbol*] ... NmAACF
Achieve Successful Performance, Intensify Reliability Effort ... ASPIRE
Achieved Availability ... AA
Achievement ... ACHVIT
Achievement Age [*Psychology*] ... AA
Achievement Anxiety Scale [*Psychology*] ... AAS
Achievement through Counselling and Treatment [*Medicine*] ... ACT
Achievement Quotient ... AQ
Achievement Ratio ... AR
Achievement Rewards for College Scientists [*Foundation*] ... ARCS
Achievement Test ... AT
Achilles Tendon [*Anatomy*] ... AT
Achilles Tendon Lengthening [*Medicine*] ... ATL
Achilles Tendon Reflex [*Neurology*] ... ATR
Acholi [*MARC language code*] [*Library of Congress*] ... ach
Achutupo [*Panama*] [*Airport symbol*] ... ACU
Acid Cholesteryl Ester Hydrolase [*An enzyme*] ... ACEH
Acid-Citrate-Dextrose [*Hematology*] ... ACD
Acid-Detergent Fiber [*Food analysis*] ... ADF
Acid-Detergent Lignin [*Food analysis*] ... ADL
Acid-Detergent Residue [*Food analysis*] ... ADR
Acid-Fast [*Microbiology*] ... AF
Acid-Fast Bacillus [*Microbiology*] ... AFB
Acid Glycoprotein [*Biochemistry*] ... AGP
Acid Mucopolysaccharide [*Biochemistry*] ... AMP
Acid Mucopolysaccharide ... AMPS
Acid Number [*Chemistry*] ... AN
Acid Output [*Physiology*] ... AO
Acid Phosphatase [*Also, AP*] [*An enzyme*] ... ACP
Acid Phosphatase [*Also, ACP*] [*An enzyme*] ... AP
Acid-Precipitable Globulin [*Clinical chemistry*] ... APG
Acid-Precipitable Material [*Antiviral agent*] ... APM
Acid-Precipitated Protein [*Food analysis*] ... APP
Acid Precipitation Experiment ... APEX
Acid Rain Mitigation Strategies ... ARMS
Acid Resisting [*Technical drawings*] ... AR
Acid-Rinsing Solution [*Clinical chemistry*] ... ARS
Acid-Soluble-Collagen [*Biochemistry*] ... ASC
Acid Value [*Chemistry*] ... AV
Acid Waste ... AW
Acide Nucleique [*French*] [*Medicine*] ... AN
Acidic and Neutral [*Chemical analysis*] ... A/N
Acidproof ... AP
Acidproof Cement Manufacturers Association [*Defunct*] ... ACMA
Acidproof Floor [*Technical drawings*] ... APF
Acidulated Phosphofluoride ... APF
Aciers Speciaux [*A publication*] ... Aciers Spec
Acinic Cell Carcinoma [*Medicine*] ... ACC
Ackerman Institute for Family Therapy ... AIFT
Ackley Public Library, Ackley, IA [*Library symbol*] ... IaAc
Acknowledge ... ACK
Acknowledge ... ACKNE
Acknowledgment ... ACKGT
Acknowledgment Character [*Data processing*] ... ACK
Acknowledgment of Receipt [*Message handling*] ... AR
Acknowledgment of Receipt [*Message handling*] ... R
ACM [*Association for Computing Machinery*] **National Conference Proceedings** [*A publication*] ... ACM Proc
ACM [*Association for Computing Machinery*] **Transactions on Mathematical Software** [*A publication*] ... ACM Trans Math Softw
ACM [*Association for Computing Machinery*] **Transactions on Mathematical Software** [*A publication*] ... ACM Trans Math Software
ACMAT Corp. [*NASDAQ symbol*] ... ACMT
Acme-Cleveland Corp. [*NYSE symbol*] ... AMT
Acme Electric Corp. [*NYSE symbol*] ... ACE
Acme General Corp. [*NASDAQ symbol*] ... ACME
Acme-Hamilton Manufacturing Corp. [*American Stock Exchange symbol*] [*Delisted*] ... ACE
Acme Precision Products, Inc. [*American Stock Exchange symbol*] ... ACL
Acme Steel Company [*NYSE symbol*] [*Delisted*] ... ACO
Acme Steel Co., Chicago, IL [*Library symbol*] ... ICAS
Acme United Corp. [*American Stock Exchange symbol*] ... ACU
Acmite [*CIPW classification*] [*Geology*] ... ac
Acne Research Institute ... ARI
Aconite, Belladonna, and Chloroform [*Liniment compound*] ... ABC
Acoreana [*A publication*] ... Acor
Acorn Library District, Oak Forest, IL [*Library symbol*] ... IOf
Acoustic ... ACOUS
Acoustic ... ACST
Acoustic Add-On Unit ... AAU
Acoustic Comfort Index ... ACI
Acoustic Communication Program ... ACP
Acoustic Control ... ACCON
Acoustic Control and Telemetry System ... ACTS
Acoustic Correlation and Detection System ... ACCORDS
Acoustic Counter-Countermeasures [*Navy*] ... ACCM
Acoustic Countermeasures [*Navy*] ... ACM
Acoustic Data Analysis Center ... ADAC
Acoustic Data Processor ... ADP
Acoustic Delay Line ... ADL
Acoustic Depth Finder ... ADF
Acoustic Detection Device ... ADD
Acoustic Detection and Ranging [*Geophysics*] ... ACDAR
Acoustic Digital Memory ... ADM
Acoustic Discrimination of Decoys ... ADD
Acoustic Emission ... AE
Acoustic Environmental Support Detachment [*Office of Naval Research*] ... AESD
Acoustic Fatigue Test Article ... AFTA
Acoustic-Gravity Wave ... AGW
Acoustic Homing Torpedo ... AHT
Acoustic Intelligence [*Military*] ... ACINT
Acoustic Intelligence Data System [*Navy*] ... AIDS
Acoustic Intercept Receiver [*Navy*] ... AIR
Acoustic Intercept Receiver/Multimode Hydrophone System [*Navy*] ... AIR/MMH
Acoustic Isolation Chamber ... AIC
Acoustic-Magnetic ... AM
Acoustic Match Filter ... AMF
Acoustic Measurement System ... AMS
Acoustic, Meteorological, and Oceanographic Survey ... AMOS
Acoustic Minesweeping ... AMNSWP
Acoustic Model Test Facility ... AMTF
Acoustic Neuroma Association ... ANA
Acoustic Noise Environment ... ANE
Acoustic Noise Generator ... ANG
Acoustic Noise Test ... ANT
Acoustic Paramagnetic Resonance [*Physics*] ... APR
Acoustic-Pressure ... AP
Acoustic Radiation Element ... ARE
Acoustic Range-Finder ... ARF
Acoustic Reflex ... AR
Acoustic Reflex Ear Defender ... ARED
Acoustic Reflex Ear Defender System ... AREDS
Acoustic Reflex Test [*Audiology*] ... ART
Acoustic Research, Inc. [*Electronics firm*] ... AR
Acoustic Resistance Unit ... ARU
Acoustic-Seismic Intrusion Detector ... ACOUSID
Acoustic Sensor Operator ... ASO
Acoustic Sensor Range Prediction ... ASRAP
Acoustic Ship Positioning - Advanced ... ASPA
Acoustic Ship Positioning System ... ASPS
Acoustic Short-Pulse Echo Classification Technique ... ASPECT
Acoustic Signal Data Analysis and Conversion System [*Navy*] ... ASDACS
Acoustic Signal Generator System ... ASGE
Acoustic SONAR Range Prediction System ... ASRAPS

Acoustic Surface Wave ... ASW
Acoustic Target Sensor ... ATS
Acoustic Telemetry Bathythermometer ... ATBT
Acoustic Telemetry Subsystem ... ATS
Acoustic Test Laboratory ... ATL
Acoustic Transmission System ... ATS
Acoustic Trials ... ACTRL
Acoustic Underwater Range Determination Systems ... ACURAD
Acoustic Warfare ... AW
Acoustic Warfare Support Measures ... ACSM
Acoustic Warfare Support Measures ... AWSM
Acoustic Warfare System ... AWS
Acoustic Wave Analysis ... AWA
Acoustic Wave Analysis System ... AWAS
Acoustical Absorption Coefficient ... AAC
Acoustical Absorption Loss ... AAL
Acoustical Analysis Memo [*Navy*] ... AAM
Acoustical Attenuation Constant ... AAC
Acoustical and Board Products Association ... ABPA
Acoustical Door Institute ... ADI
Acoustical Emission Monitoring ... AEM
Acoustical Holography [*A publication*] ... Acoust Hologr
Acoustical and Insulating Materials Association [*Later, ABPA*] ... AIMA
Acoustical Intelligence [*Military*] ... ACOUSTINT
Acoustical Materials Association [*Later, ABPA*] ... AMA
Acoustical Phase Constant ... APC
Acoustical Plaster Ceiling [*Technical drawings*] ... APC
Acoustical Propagation Constant ... APC
Acoustical Society of America ... ACSA
Acoustical Society of America ... ACSOC
Acoustical Society of America ... ASA
Acoustical Society of America. Journal [*A publication*] ... Acoust Soc Am J
Acoustical Standards Board ... ASB
Acoustical Test Chamber ... ATC
Acoustical Tile Ceiling [*Technical drawings*] ... ATC
Acoustics Associates ... AA
Acoustics Laboratory ... AL
Acoustics Propellant Utilization ... APU
Acoustics, Speech, and Signal Processing ... ASSP
Acoustics of the Target ... ACTAR
Acousto-Optic ... A-O
Acousto-Optic Mode Locker and Frequency Doubler ... AMOL-FD
Acousto-Optical Imaging ... AOI
Acoyapa [*Nicaragua*] [*Seismograph station code, US Geological Survey*] ... ACY
Acquire on Jam ... AOJ
Acquired Immune Deficiency Syndrome [*Also, AID, GRID*] [*Medicine*] ... AIDS
Acquired Immunodeficiency [*Also, AIDS, GRID*] [*Medicine*] ... AID
Acquired Red Cell Aplasia [*Hematology*] ... ARCA
Acquisition ... ACQ
Acquisition ... ACQUIS
Acquisition ... AQUIS
Acquisition Advice Code [*NASA*] ... AAC
Acquisition Advisory Group [*Business and trade*] ... AAG
Acquisition Aid ... AQUAID
Acquisition Aid Vehicle [*Army*] ... AADV
Acquisition Based on Consideration of Logistic Effects [*Air Force*] ... ABLE
Acquisition Beacon ... AB
Acquisition Bus Monitor [*Data processing*] ... ABM
Acquisition and Command Support ... ACS
Acquisition and Control Module ... ACM
Acquisition and Control Query Executive [*A computer language*] ... ACQE
Acquisition, Control of Test [*Units*] ... ACT
Acquisition Costs ... AC
Acquisition Data Input Equipment ... ADIE
Acquisition Director ... AD
Acquisition and Distribution of Commercial Products [*Department of Defense program*] ... ADCOP
Acquisition and Distribution of Commercial Products ... ADCP
Acquisition Logistician ... AL
Acquisition Management Information System [*Air Force*] ... AMIS
Acquisition Management Plan ... AMP
Acquisition Management System List ... AMSL
Acquisition Manager ... AM
Acquisition Material List ... AML
Acquisition Message ... AQ
Acquisition Orbit Determination Program Assembly [*Space Flight Operations Facility, NASA*] ... AODP
Acquisition Plan ... AP
Acquisition Point ... AP
Acquisition Project Manager ... APM
Acquisition RADAR ... AR
Acquisition RADAR Jamming ... ARJ
Acquisition of Signal ... AOS
Acquisition Sun Sensor ... ASS
Acquisition on Target ... AOT
Acquisition Target and Search ... ATS
Acquisition Tracking and Recognition [*Aviation*] ... ATAR
Acquisition and Tracking Subsystem ... ATSS
Acquisition and Tracking System ... ATS
Acquisition Trigger at Zero Beat ... ATZ
Acquisitions, Cataloguing, Technical Systems [*Library service*] ... ACTS
Acquisitions Medicales Recentes [*A publication*] ... Acquis Med Recent
Acquisitions Section [*Resources and Technical Services Division of ALA*] ... AS
Acquittal ... ACQ
Acral Lentiginous Melanoma [*Medicine*] ... ALM
Acre ... A
Acre ... AC
Acre-Feet per Day ... ACRE-FT/D
Acre-Foot ... AF
Acreage Marketing Guide ... AMG
Acres American, Inc., Buffalo, NY [*Library symbol*] ... NBuAA
Acres Consulting Services Ltd., Niagara Falls, ON, Canada [*Library symbol*] ... CaONfA
Acridine Orange [*Dye*] ... AO
Acriflavine [*Anti-infective mixture*] ... Acr
Acro Energy Corp. [*NASDAQ symbol*] ... ACRO
Acro-Osteolysis [*Medicine*] ... AOL
Acrobatic ... ACRBT
Acrodermatitis Enteropathica [*Medicine*] ... AE
Acronym Data Base ... ACRODABA
[*The*] **Acronym Generator** [*An RCA computer program*] ... TAG
Acronym May Be Ignored Totally [*Data processing*] ... AMBIT/L
Acronym-Oriented Nut ... ACORN
Acronyms, Initialisms, and Abbreviations Dictionary [*Formerly, AID*] [*A publication*] ... AIAD
Acronyms and Initialisms Dictionary [*Later, AIAD*] [*A publication*] ... AID
Acropole. Revue du Monde Hellenique [*A publication*] ... Acr
Across ... ACR
Across ... ACRS
Across the Board [*A publication*] ... Across the Bd
Across the Board. Conference Board (New York) [*A publication*] ... Across Board (NY)
Across Flats ... ACRFLT
Across Tape [*Curve*] ... AT
Acrylic Acid [*Organic chemistry*] ... AA
Acrylic Eye Illustrator [*Medicine*] ... AEI
Acrylic Optics Corp. [*NASDAQ symbol*] ... AOPT
Acrylic Styrene [*Plastics technology*] ... AS
Acrylonitrile-Butadiene-Styrene [*Organic chemistry*] ... ABS
Acrylontrile [*Organic chemistry*] ... ACN
Acryloyloxyethyl N-Methylcarbamate [*Organic chemistry*] ... AEMC
ACS Enterprises, Inc. [*NASDAQ symbol*] ... ACSE
ACS Inustries, Inc. [*NASDAQ symbol*] ... ACSC
ACS [*American Chemical Society*] **Monograph** [*A publication*] ... ACS Monogr
ACS [*American Chemical Society*] **Symposium Series** [*A publication*] ... ACS Symp S
ACS [*American Chemical Society*] **Symposium Series** [*A publication*] ... ACS Symp Ser
Act ... A
Act in Crisis Today [*Fund sponsored by the Lutheran Church in America*] ... ACT
Act Inside the Army [*European antiwar group*] ... AITA
Act of the Parliaments of Scotland ... APS
Act Together ... AT
Acta Academiae Aboensis [*A publication*] ... AAA
Acta Academiae Aboensis [*A publication*] ... Acta Acad Aboensis
Acta Academiae Aboensis. Humaniora [*A publication*] ... AAAH
Acta Academiae Aboensis. Humaniora [*A publication*] ... AAA Hum
Acta Academiae Aboensis. Series B. Mathematica et Physica [*A publication*] ... Acta Acad Abo Ser B
Acta Academiae Internationalis Historiae Medicinae [*A publication*] ... Acta Acad Int Hist Med
Acta Academiae Paedagogicae Jyvaskylaensis [*A publication*] ... AAPJ
Acta Academiae Polytechnicae Pollack Mihaly Pecs [*A publication*] ... Acta Acad Polytech Pollack Mihaly Pecs
Acta Academiae Velehradensis [*A publication*] ... AAV
Acta Adriatica [*A publication*] ... Acta Adriat
Acta Agralia Fennica [*A publication*] ... Acta Agral Fenn
Acta Agraria et Silvestria. Series Agraria [*A publication*] ... Acta Agrar Silvestria Ser Agrar
Acta Agraria et Silvestria. Series Rolnictwo [*A publication*] ... Acta Agr Silv Ser Roln
Acta Agraria et Silvestria. Series Silvestris [*A publication*] ... Acta Agrar Silv Ser Silv
Acta Agraria et Silvestria. Series Zootechnia [*A publication*] ... Acta Agrar Silvestria Ser Zootech
Acta Agriculturae Scandinavica [*A publication*] ... Acta Agric Scand
Acta Agriculturae Scandinavica [*A publication*] ... Acta Agr Scand
Acta Agriculturae Scandinavica. Supplementum [*A publication*] ... Acta Agric Scand Suppl
Acta Agriculturae Scandinavica. Supplementum [*A publication*] ... Suppl Acta Agric Scand
Acta Agriculturae Sinica [*A publication*] ... Acta Agric Sin
Acta Agriculturae Sinica [*A publication*] ... Acta Agr Sinica
Acta Agriculturae Suecana [*A publication*] ... Acta Agric Suecana
Acta Agrobotanica [*A publication*] ... Acta Agrobot
Acta Agronomica. Academiae Scientiarum Hungaricae [*Budapest*] [*A publication*] ... Acta Agron Acad Sci Hung

Acta Agronomica. Academiae Scientiarum Hungaricae [*Budapest*] [*A publication*]....Acta Agron Hung
Acta Agronomica. Academiae Scientiarum Hungaricae [*Budapest*] [*A publication*]....Act Agron H
Acta Agronomica. Academiae Scientiarum Hungaricae (Budapest) [*A publication*]....Acta Agron (Budapest)
Acta Agronomica (Palmira) [*A publication*]....Acta Agron (Palmira)
Acta Alimentaria. Academiae Scientiarum Hungaricae [*A publication*]....Acta Aliment Acad Sci Hung
Acta Allergologica [*A publication*]....Acta Allergol
Acta Allergologica [*A publication*]....Act Allerg
Acta Allergologica. Supplementum [*A publication*]....Acta Allergol Suppl
Acta Americana [*A publication*]....Acta Am
Acta Anaesthesiologica [*A publication*]....ACAEA
Acta Anaesthesiologica Belgica [*A publication*]....Acta Anaesthesiol Belg
Acta Anaesthesiologica Italica [*A publication*]....Acta Anaesthesiol Ital
Acta Anaesthesiologica (Padova) [*A publication*]....Acta Anaesthesiol (Padova)
Acta Anaesthesiologica Scandinavica [*A publication*]....Acta Anaesthesiol Scand
Acta Anaesthesiologica Scandinavica [*A publication*]....Act Anae Sc
Acta Anaesthesiologica Scandinavica. Supplementum [*A publication*]....Acta Anaesthesiol Scand Suppl
Acta Anatomica [*A publication*]....Acta Anat
Acta Anatomica [*A publication*]....Act Anatom
Acta Anatomica (Basel) [*A publication*]....Acta Anat (Basel)
Acta Anatomica Nipponica [*A publication*]....Acta Anat Nippon
Acta Anatomica Sinica [*A publication*]....Acta Anat Sin
Acta Anatomica. Supplementum [*A publication*]....Acta Anat Suppl
Acta Anthropogenetica [*A publication*]....Acta Anthropogenet
Acta Antiqua. Academiae Scientiarum Hungaricae [*A publication*]....AAASH
Acta Antiqua. Academiae Scientiarum Hungaricae [*A publication*]....AAH
Acta Antiqua. Academiae Scientiarum Hungaricae [*A publication*]....AAnt
Acta Antiqua. Academiae Scientiarum Hungaricae [*A publication*]....AAntHung
Acta Antiqua. Academiae Scientiarum Hungaricae [*A publication*]....A Antiqua Acad Sci Hung
Acta Arachnologica [*A publication*]....Acta Arachnol
Acta ad Archaeologiam et Artium Historiam Pertinentia [*A publication*]....AAAH
Acta Archaeologica [*A publication*]....AArch
Acta Archaeologica [*A publication*]....Ac Ar
Acta Archaeologica [*A publication*]....Acta A
Acta Archaeologica [*A publication*]....Act Archaeo
Acta Archaeologica. Academiae Scientiarum Hungaricae [*A publication*]....A Arch Acad Sci Hung
Acta Archaeologica. Academiae Scientiarum Hungaricae [*A publication*]....AArchHung
Acta Archaeologica. Academiae Scientiarum Hungaricae [*A publication*]....Acta Archaeol Acad Sci Hung
Acta Archaeologica. Arheoloski Vestnik. Ljubljana, Academie Slovene [*A publication*]....AArchSlov
Acta Archaeologica (Budapest) [*A publication*]....Acta Archaeol (Budapest)
Acta Archaeologica Carpathica [*Crakow*] [*A publication*]....A Arch Carpathica
Acta Archaeologica (Kobenhavn) [*A publication*]....Acta Archaeol (Kobenhavn)
Acta Archaeologica Lodziensia [*A publication*]....A Arch Lodziensia
Acta Arctica [*A publication*]....Acta Arct
Acta Asiatica [*A publication*]....Ac As
Acta Asiatica [*A publication*]....ActaA
Acta Asiatica [*A publication*]....Acta Asiat
Acta Astronautica [*A publication*]....Acta Astronaut
Acta Astronautica [*A publication*]....Act Astron
Acta Astronomica [*A publication*]....Acta Astron
Acta Astronomica Sinica [*A publication*]....Acta Astron Sin
Acta Audiologica y Foniatrica Hispano-Americana [*A publication*]....Acta Audiol Foniat Hispano-Amer
Acta Baltica [*A publication*]....AB
Acta Baltico-Slavica [*A publication*]....ABalt-Slav
Acta Baltico-Slavica [*A publication*]....ABS
Acta Belgica de Arte Medicinali et Pharmaceutica Militari [*A publication*]....Acta Belg Arte Med Pharm Mil
Acta Biochimica [*A publication*]....Acta Biochim
Acta Biochimica et Biophysica. Academiae Scientiarum Hungaricae [*A publication*]....Acta Biochim Biophys Acad Sci Hung
Acta Biochimica et Biophysica. Academiae Scientiarum Hungaricae [*A publication*]....Act Bioch H
Acta Biochimica et Biophysica Sinica [*A publication*]....Acta Biochim Biophys Sin
Acta Biochimica et Biophysica Sinica [*A publication*]....Acta Biochim Biophys Sinica
Acta Biochimica Iranica [*A publication*]....Acta Biochim Iran
Acta Biochimica Iranica [*A publication*]....Act Bio Ira
Acta Biochimica Polonica [*A publication*]....Acta Biochim Pol
Acta Biochimica Polonica [*A publication*]....Acta Biochim Polon
Acta Biochimica Polonica [*A publication*]....Act Bioch P
Acta Biochimica Polonica (Translation) [*A publication*]....Acta Biochim Pol (Trans)
Acta Biochimica Sinica [*A publication*]....Acta Biochim Sin
Acta Biologiae Experimentalis. Polish Academy of Sciences [*A publication*]....Acta Biol Exp Pol Acad Sci
Acta Biologiae Experimentalis Sinica [*A publication*]....Acta Biol Exper Sinica
Acta Biologiae Experimentalis Sinica [*A publication*]....Acta Biol Exp Sin
Acta Biologiae Experimentalis (Warsaw) [*A publication*]....Acta Biol Exp (Warsaw)
Acta Biologica [*A publication*]....Acta Biol
Acta Biologica. Academiae Scientiarum Hungaricae [*A publication*]....Acta Biol Acad Sci Hung
Acta Biologica. Academiae Scientiarum Hungaricae [*A publication*]....Acta Biol Hung
Acta Biologica. Academiae Scientiarum Hungaricae [*A publication*]....Act Biol H
Acta Biologica. Academiae Scientiarum Hungaricae (Budapest) [*A publication*]....Acta Biol (Budapest)
Acta Biologica Cracoviensia. Series Botanica [*A publication*]....Acta Biol Cracov Ser Bot
Acta Biologica Cracoviensia. Series Botanica [*A publication*]....Act Bio C B
Acta Biologica Cracoviensia. Series Zoologia [*A publication*]....Acta Biol Cracov Ser Zool
Acta Biologica Cracoviensia. Series Zoologia [*A publication*]....Act Bio C Z
Acta Biologica Debrecina [*A publication*]....Acta Biol Debrecina
Acta Biologica Iugoslavica. Serija B. Mikrobiologija [*A publication*]....Acta Biol Iugosl Ser B Mikrobiol
Acta Biologica Iugoslavica. Serija E. Ichthyologia [*A publication*]....Acta Biol Iugosl Ser E Ichthyol
Acta Biologica Katowice [*A publication*]....Acta Biol Katowice
Acta Biologica et Medica (Gdansk) [*A publication*]....Acta Biol Med (Gdansk)
Acta Biologica et Medica Germanica [*A publication*]....ABMGA
Acta Biologica et Medica Germanica [*A publication*]....Acta Biol Med Ger
Acta Biologica et Medica Germanica [*A publication*]....Act Bio Med
Acta Biologica Paranaense [*A publication*]....Acta Biol Parana
Acta Biologica Venezuelica [*A publication*]....Acta Biol Venez
Acta Biotheoretica [*Leiden*] [*A publication*]....Acta Biotheor
Acta Biotheoretica (Leiden) [*A publication*]....Acta Biotheor (Leiden)
Acta Borealia a Scientia [*A publication*]....Acta Borealia a Sci
Acta Botanica. Academiae Scientiarum Hungaricae [*A publication*]....Acta Bot Acad Sci Hung
Acta Botanica. Academiae Scientiarum Hungaricae [*A publication*]....Acta Bot Hung
Acta Botanica. Academiae Scientiarum Hungaricae (Budapest) [*A publication*]....Acta Bot (Budapest)
Acta Botanica Croatica [*A publication*]....Acta Bot Croat
Acta Botanica Fennica [*A publication*]....Acta Bot Fenn
Acta Botanica Horti Bucurestiensis [*A publication*]....Acta Bot Horti Bucur
Acta Botanica Indica [*A publication*]....Acta Bot Indica
Acta Botanica Indica (India) [*A publication*]....Acta Bot Indica (IN)
Acta Botanica Instituti Botanici Universitatis Zagraebensis [*A publication*]....Acta Bot Inst Bot Univ Zagreb
Acta Botanica Islandica [*A publication*]....Acta Bot Isl
Acta Botanica Neerlandica [*A publication*]....Acta Bot Neerl
Acta Botanica Neerlandica [*A publication*]....Acta Bot Neerland
Acta Botanica Neerlandica [*A publication*]....Act Bot Nee
Acta Botanica Sinica [*A publication*]....Acta Bot Sin
Acta Botanica Sinica [*A publication*]....Acta Bot Sinica
Acta Botanica Venezuelica [*A publication*]....Acta Bot Venez
Acta Cancerologica [*A publication*]....Acta Cancerol
Acta Cardiologica [*Bruxelles*] [*A publication*]....ACCAA
Acta Cardiologica (Bruxelles) [*A publication*]....Acta Cardiol (Brux)
Acta Cardiologica. Supplementum [*Bruxelles*] [*A publication*]....Acta Cardiol Suppl
Acta Chemica Scandinavica [*A publication*]....Acta Chem Scand
Acta Chemica Scandinavica (Denmark) [*A publication*]....Acta Chem Scand (DK)
Acta Chemica Scandinavica. Series A. Physical and Inorganic Chemistry [*A publication*]....Acta Chem Scand Ser A
Acta Chemica Scandinavica. Series A. Physical and Inorganic Chemistry [*A publication*]....Act Chem A
Acta Chemica Scandinavica. Series B. Organic Chemistry and Biochemistry [*A publication*]....Acta Chem Scand (B)
Acta Chemica Scandinavica. Series B. Organic Chemistry and Biochemistry [*A publication*]....Acta Chem Scand Ser B
Acta Chemica Scandinavica. Series B. Organic Chemistry and Biochemistry [*A publication*]....Acta Chem Scand Ser B Org Chem Biochem
Acta Chemica Scandinavica. Series B. Organic Chemistry and Biochemistry [*A publication*]....Act Chem B
Acta Chimica. Academiae Scientiarum Hungaricae [*A publication*]....Acta Chim Acad Sci Hung
Acta Chimica. Academiae Scientiarum Hungaricae [*A publication*]....Act Chim H
Acta Chimica Sinica [*A publication*]....Acta Chim Sin
Acta Chimica Sinica [*A publication*]....Acta Chim Sinica
Acta Chimica. Societatis Scientiarum Lodziensis [*A publication*]....Acta Chim Soc Sci Lodz
Acta Chimica. Societatis Scientiarum Lodziensis (Poland) [*A publication*]....Acta Chim Soc Sci Lodz (PL)
Acta Chirurgiae Orthopaedicae et Traumatologiae Cechoslovaca [*A publication*]....Acta Chir Orthop Traumatol Cech

Acta Chirurgiae Plasticae [*A publication*] .... Acta Chir Plast
Acta Chirurgiae Plasticae (Prague) [*A publication*] .... Acta Chir Plast (Prague)
Acta Chirurgica. Academiae Scientiarum Hungaricae [*A publication*] .... ACAHA
Acta Chirurgica. Academiae Scientiarum Hungaricae [*A publication*] .... Acta Chir Acad Sci Hung
Acta Chirurgica. Academiae Scientiarum Hungaricae [*A publication*] .... Act Chir H
Acta Chirurgica Austriaca [*A publication*] .... Acta Chir Austriaca
Acta Chirurgica Austriaca. Supplement [*A publication*] .... Acta Chir Austriaca Suppl
Acta Chirurgica Belgica [*A publication*] .... Acta Chir Belg
Acta Chirurgica Belgica [*A publication*] .... Act Chir B
Acta Chirurgica Belgica. Supplement [*A publication*] .... Acta Chir Belg Suppl
Acta Chirurgica Italica [*A publication*] .... Acta Chir Ital
Acta Chirurgica Iugoslavica [*A publication*] .... Acta Chir Iugosl
Acta Chirurgica Scandinavica [*A publication*] .... Acta Chir Scand
Acta Chirurgica Scandinavica [*A publication*] .... Act Chir Sc
Acta Chirurgica Scandinavica. Supplementum [*A publication*] .... Acta Chir Scand Suppl
Acta Ciencia Indica [*A publication*] .... Acta Cienc Indica
Acta Ciencia Indica [*A publication*] .... Acta Ci Indica
Acta Ciencia Indica (India) [*A publication*] .... Acta Cienc Indica (IN)
Acta Ciencia Indica. Mathematics [*A publication*] .... Acta Cienc Indica Math
Acta Ciencia Indica. Physica [*A publication*] .... Acta Cienc Indica Physica
Acta Cientifica [*A publication*] .... Acta Cient
Acta Cientifica Compostelana [*A publication*] .... Acta Ci Compostelana
Acta Cientifica Compostelana [*A publication*] .... Acta Cient Compostelana
Acta Cientifica Potosina [*A publication*] .... Acta Cient Potosina
Acta Cientifica Venezolana [*A publication*] .... Acta Cient Venez
Acta Cientifica Venezolana [*A publication*] .... Act Cient V
Acta Classica. Universitates Scientiarum Debreceniensis [*A publication*] .... ACUSD
Acta Classica. Universitatis Scientiarum Debreceniensis [*A publication*] .... ACD
Acta Classica. Verhandelinge van die Klassieke Vereniging van Suid-Afrika [*A publication*] .... AClass
Acta Clinica Belgica [*A publication*] .... Acta Clin Belg
Acta Clinica Belgica [*A publication*] .... Act Clin B
Acta Clinica Belgica. Supplementum [*A publication*] .... Acta Clin Belg Suppl
Acta Comeniana [*A publication*] .... ACo
Acta Comeniana [*A publication*] .... ACom
Acta et Commentationes Universitatis Dorpatensis [*A publication*] .... AUD
Acta Criminologiae Medicinae Legalis Japonica [*A publication*] .... Acta Criminol Med Leg Jpn
Acta Crystallographica [*A publication*] .... Acta Cryst
Acta Crystallographica [*A publication*] .... Acta Crystallogr
Acta Crystallographica. Section A [*A publication*] .... Acta Crystallogr A
Acta Crystallographica. Section A [*A publication*] .... Act Cryst A
Acta Crystallographica. Section B [*A publication*] .... Acta Crystallogr B
Acta Crystallographica. Section B [*A publication*] .... Act Cryst B
Acta Cybernetica [*A publication*] .... Acta Cybernet
Acta Cytologica [*A publication*] .... Acta Cytol
Acta Cytologica [*A publication*] .... Act Cytol
Acta Cytologica [*A publication*] .... ACYTA
Acta Cytologica (Baltimore) [*A publication*] .... Acta Cytol (Baltimore)
Acta Dermato-Venereologica [*A publication*] .... Acta Derm-Venereol
Acta Dermato-Venereologica [*A publication*] .... Act Der-Ven
Acta Dermato-Venereologica (Stockholm) [*A publication*] .... Acta Derm-Venereol (Stockh)
Acta Dermato-Venereologica. Supplementum [*Stockholm*] [*A publication*] .... Acta Derm-Venereol Suppl
Acta Dermato-Venereologica. Supplementum (Stockholm) [*A publication*] .... Acta Derm-Venereol Suppl (Stockh)
Acta Dermatologica Kyoto (English Edition) [*A publication*] .... Acta Dermatol Kyoto (Engl Ed)
Acta Diabetologica Latina [*A publication*] .... Acta Diabetol Lat
Acta Diabetologica Latina [*A publication*] .... Act Diabet
Acta Electronica [*A publication*] .... Acta Electron
Acta Embryologiae Experimentalis [*Palermo*] [*A publication*] .... Acta Embryol Exp
Acta Embryologiae Experimentalis (Palermo) [*A publication*] .... Acta Embryol Exp (Palermo)
Acta Embryologiae et Morphologiae Experimentalis [*A publication*] .... Acta Embryol Morphol Exp
Acta Endocrinologica [*A publication*] .... Acta Endocrinol
Acta Endocrinologica [*A publication*] .... Act Endocr
Acta Endocrinologica (Copenhagen) [*A publication*] .... Acta Endocrinol (Copenh)
Acta Endocrinologica Panamericana [*A publication*] .... Acta Endocrinol Panam
Acta Endocrinologica. Supplementum [*Copenhagen*] [*A publication*] .... Acta Endocrinol Suppl
Acta Endocrinologica. Supplementum (Copenhagen) [*A publication*] .... Acta Endocrinol Suppl (Copenh)
Acta Entomologica Bohemoslovaca [*A publication*] .... Acta Entomol Bohemoslov
Acta Entomologica Bohemoslovaca [*A publication*] .... Act Ent Boh
Acta Entomologica Fennica [*A publication*] .... Acta Entomol Fenn
Acta Entomologica Jugoslavica [*A publication*] .... Acta Entomol Jugosl
Acta Entomologica Lituanica [*A publication*] .... Acta Entomol Litu
Acta Entomologica Sinica [*A publication*] .... Acta Entomol Sin
Acta Entomologica Sinica [*A publication*] .... Acta Entomol Sinica
Acta Ethnographica [*A publication*] .... Act Ethnogr
Acta Ethnographica [*A publication*] .... AE
Acta Ethnographica. Academiae Scientiarum Hungaricae [*A publication*] .... Acta Ethnog Hung
Acta Ethnographica. Academiae Scientiarum Hungaricae [*A publication*] .... Acta Ethnogr Acad Sci Hung
Acta Ethnographica. Academiae Scientiarum Hungaricae [*A publication*] .... AEASH
Acta Ethnographica. Academiae Scientiarum Hungaricae [*A publication*] .... AEH
Acta Ethnographica (Budapest) [*A publication*] .... Acta Ethnogr (Budapest)
Acta Europaea Fertilitatis [*A publication*] .... Acta Eur Fertil
Acta Facultatis Medicae Fluminensis [*A publication*] .... Acta Fac Med Fluminensis
Acta Facultatis Medicae Universitatis Brunensis [*A publication*] .... Acta Fac Med Univ Brun
Acta Facultatis Pharmaceuticae Bohemoslovenicae [*A publication*] .... Acta Fac Pharm Bohemoslov
Acta Facultatis Pharmaceuticae Universitatis Comenianae [*A publication*] .... Acta Fac Pharm Univ Comenianae
Acta Facultatis Rerum Naturalium Universitatis Comenianae. Botanica [*A publication*] .... Acta Fac Rerum Nat Univ Comenianae Bot
Acta Facultatis Rerum Naturalium Universitatis Comenianae. Chimia [*A publication*] .... Acta Fac Rerum Nat Univ Comenianae Chim
Acta Facultatis Rerum Naturalium Universitatis Comenianae. Formatio et Protectio Naturae (Czechoslovakia) [*A publication*] .... Acta Fac Rerum Nat Univ Comenianae Form Prot Nat (CS)
Acta Facultatis Rerum Naturalium Universitatis Comenianae. Genetica [*A publication*] .... Acta Fac Rerum Nat Univ Comenianae Genet
Acta Facultatis Rerum Naturalium Universitatis Comenianae. Microbiologia [*A publication*] .... Acta Fac Rerum Nat Univ Comenianae Microbiol
Acta Facultatis Rerum Naturalium Universitatis Comenianae. Mathematica [*A publication*] .... Acta Fac Rerum Natur Univ Comenian Math
Acta Facultatis Rerum Naturalium Universitatis Comenianae. Physica [*A publication*] .... Acta Fac Rerum Nat Univ Comenianae Phys
Acta Facultatis Rerum Naturalium Universitatis Comenianae. Zoologia [*A publication*] .... Acta Fac Rerum Nat Univ Comenianae Zool
Acta Faunistica Entomologica. Musei Nationalis Pragae [*A publication*] .... Acta Faun Entomol Mus Natl Pragae
Acta Forestalia Fennica [*A publication*] .... Acta For Fenn
Acta Gastro-Enterologica Belgica [*A publication*] .... Acta Gastro-Enterol Belg
Acta Gastro-Enterologica Belgica [*A publication*] .... Act Gastr B
Acta Gastroenterologica Latinoamericana [*A publication*] .... Acta Gastroenterol Latinoam
Acta Genetica Sinica [*A publication*] .... Acta Genet Sin
Acta Genetica et Statistica Medica [*A publication*] .... Acta Genet Stat Med
Acta Geneticae Medicae et Gemellologiae [*A publication*] .... Acta Genet Med Gemellol
Acta Geneticae Medicae et Gemellologiae [*A publication*] .... Act Genet M
Acta Geobotanica Barcinonensia [*A publication*] .... Acta Geobot Barc
Acta Geodaetica, Geophysica, et Montanistica [*A publication*] .... Acta Geod Geophys Montan
Acta Geographica [*A publication*] .... Acta Geogr
Acta Geographica [*France*] [*A publication*] .... Act Geogr
Acta Geographica Lodziensia [*A publication*] .... Acta Geogr Lodz
Acta Geographica Sinica [*A publication*] .... Acta Geogr Sinica
Acta Geologica. Academiae Scientiarum Hungaricae [*A publication*] .... Acta Geol Acad Sci Hung
Acta Geologica. Academiae Scientiarum Hungaricae [*A publication*] .... Acta Geol Hung
Acta Geologica et Geographica Universitatis Comenianae. Geologica [*A publication*] .... Acta Geol Geogr Univ Comenianae Geol
Acta Geologica Hispanica [*A publication*] .... Acta Geol Hisp
Acta Geologica Lilloana [*A publication*] .... Acta Geol Lilloana
Acta Geologica Polonica [*A publication*] .... Acta Geol Pol
Acta Geologica Sinica [*A publication*] .... Acta Geol Sin
Acta Geologica Sinica (English Translation) [*A publication*] .... Acta Geol Sin (Engl Transl)
Acta Geologica Taiwanica [*A publication*] .... Acta Geol Taiwan
Acta Geologica Taiwanica [*A publication*] .... Acta Geol Taiwanica
Acta Geophysica Polonica [*A publication*] .... Acta Geophys Pol
Acta Geophysica Polonica [*A publication*] .... Acta Geophys Polonica
Acta Geophysica Sinica [*A publication*] .... Acta Geophys Sin
Acta Germanica [*Capetown*] [*A publication*] .... ActaG
Acta Germanica zur Sprache und Dichtung Deutschlands [*A publication*] .... AGSD
Acta Gerontologica [*A publication*] .... Acta Gerontol
Acta Gerontologica et Geriatrica Belgica [*A publication*] .... Acta Gerontol Geriatr Belg
Acta Gerontologica Japonica [*A publication*] .... Acta Gerontol Jpn
Acta Haematologica [*A publication*] .... Acta Haematol
Acta Haematologica [*A publication*] .... Act Haemat
Acta Haematologica (Basel) [*A publication*] .... Acta Haematol (Basel)
Acta Haematologica Japonica [*A publication*] .... Acta Haematol Jpn
Acta Haematologica Polonica [*A publication*] .... Acta Haematol Pol

Acta Helvetica Physico Mathematico Botanico Medica [*A publication*]....Acta Helvet
Acta Hepato-Gastroenterologica [*Stuttgart/New York*] [*A publication*]....Acta Hepato-Gastroenterol
Acta Hepato-Gastroenterologica [*Stuttgart/New York*] [*A publication*]....Act Hep-Gas
Acta Hepato-Gastroenterologica (Stuttgart/New York) [*A publication*]....Acta Hepato-Gastroenterol (Stuttg)
Acta Herpetologica Japonica [*A publication*]....Acta Herpetol Jpn
Acta Histochemica [*A publication*]....Acta Histochem
Acta Histochemica [*A publication*]....Act Histoch
Acta Histochemica et Cytochemica [*A publication*]....Acta Histochem Cytochem
Acta Histochemica et Cytochemica [*A publication*]....Act Hist Cy
Acta Histochemica (Jena) [*A publication*]....Acta Histochem (Jena)
Acta Histochemica. Supplementband [*Jena*] [*A publication*]....Acta Histochem Supplementb
Acta Histochemica. Supplementband (Jena) [*A publication*]....Acta Histochem Suppl (Jena)
Acta Historiae Neerlandica [*A publication*]....AHN
Acta Historiae Rerum Naturalium Nec Non Technicarum [*A publication*]....Acta Hist Rerum Natur Nec Non Tech
Acta Historica. Academiae Scientiarum Hungaricae [*A publication*]....A HistHung
Acta Historica Leopoldina [*A publication*]....Acta Hist Leopold
Acta Historica Scientiarum Naturalium et Medicinalium [*Odense*] [*A publication*]....Acta Hist Sci Nat Med
Acta Historica Scientiarum Naturalium et Medicinalium (Odense) [*A publication*]....Acta Hist Sci Nat Med (Odense)
Acta Horti Gotoburgensis [*A publication*]....Acta Horti Gotob
Acta Horti Gotoburgensis [*A publication*]....Acta Horti Gotoburg
Acta Horticulturae (The Hague) [*A publication*]....Acta Hortic (The Hague)
Acta Horticulturalia [*Peking*] [*A publication*]....Acta Hort
Acta Horticulturalia (Peking) [*A publication*]....Acta Hortic (Peking)
Acta Hospitalia [*A publication*]....Acta Hosp
Acta Humboldtiana. Series Geographica et Ethnographica [*A publication*]....Acta Humboldtiana Ser Geog et Ethnograph
Acta Hydrobiologica [*A publication*]....Acta Hydrobiol
Acta Iberica Radiologia-Cancerologica [*A publication*]....Acta Iber Radiol-Cancerol
Acta Informatica [*A publication*]....Acta Inf
Acta de l'Institut d'Anesthesiologie [*A publication*]....Acta Inst Anesthesiol
Acta Instituti Forestalis Zvolenensis [*A publication*]....Acta Inst For Zvolenensis
Acta Instituti Psychologici Universitatis Zagrabiensis [*A publication*]....Acta Inst Psychol Univ Zagrabiensis
Acta Isotopica [*A publication*]....Acta Isot
Acta Juridica (Budapest) [*A publication*]....Acta Jur (Budapest)
Acta Juridica (Cape Town) [*A publication*]....Acta Jur (Cape Town)
Acta Latgalica [*A publication*]....ActaL
Acta Leidensia [*A publication*]....Acta Leiden
Acta Leprologica (Geneve) [*A publication*]....Acta Leprol (Geneve)
Acta Linguistica [*A publication*]....AcL
Acta Linguistica [*A publication*]....Acta Linguist
Acta Linguistica [*A publication*]....AL
Acta Linguistica. Academiae Scientiarum Hungaricae [*A publication*]....Acta Linguist Hung
Acta Linguistica. Academiae Scientiarum Hungaricae [*A publication*]....ActLingH
Acta Linguistica. Academiae Scientiarum Hungaricae [*A publication*]....ALASH
Acta Linguistica. Academiae Scientiarum Hungaricae [*A publication*]....ALH
Acta Linguistica. Academiae Scientiarum Hungaricae [*A publication*]....ALingHung
Acta Linguistica Hafniensia [*A publication*]....ALH
Acta Linguistica Hafniensia [*A publication*]....ALHa
Acta Litteraria. Academiae Scientiarum Hungaricae [*A publication*]....Acta Lit Hung
Acta Litteraria. Academiae Scientiarum Hungaricae [*A publication*]....ActLitH
Acta Litteraria. Academiae Scientiarum Hungaricae [*A publication*]....ALitASH
Acta Litteraria. Academiae Scientiarum Hungaricae [*A publication*]....ALitH
Acta Manilana. Series A. Natural and Applied Sciences [*A publication*]....Acta Manilana A
Acta Manilana. Series A. Natural and Applied Sciences [*A publication*]....Acta Manilana Ser A Nat Appl Sci
Acta Marxistica-Leninistica [*A publication*]....Acta Marx-Lenin
Acta Mathematica [*A publication*]....Acta Math
Acta Mathematica [*A publication*]....Act Math
Acta Mathematica. Academiae Scientiarum Hungaricae [*A publication*]....Acta Math Acad Sci Hungar
Acta Mathematica. Academiae Scientiarum Hungaricae [*A publication*]....Act Math H
Acta Mathematica Sinica [*A publication*]....Acta Math Sin
Acta Mathematica Sinica [*A publication*]....Acta Math Sinica
Acta Mathematica Vietnamica [*A publication*]....Acta Math Vietnam
Acta Mechanica [*A publication*]....Acta Mech
Acta Mechanica [*A publication*]....Act Mechan
Acta Mechanica Sinica [*A publication*]....Acta Mech Sinica
Acta Medica. Academiae Scientiarum Hungaricae [*A publication*]....Acta Med Acad Sci Hung
Acta Medica. Academiae Scientiarum Hungaricae [*A publication*]....Act Med H
Acta Medica Austriaca [*A publication*]....Acta Med Austriaca
Acta Medica Austriaca. Supplement [*A publication*]....Acta Med Austriaca Suppl
Acta Medica et Biologica [*A publication*]....Acta Med Biol
Acta Medica Bulgarica. Medicina i Fizkultura [*A publication*]....Acta Med Bulg
Acta Medica Costarricense [*A publication*]....Acta Med Costarric
Acta Medica (Fukuoka) [*A publication*]....Acta Med (Fukuoka)
Acta Medica Hidalguense [*A publication*]....Acta Med Hidalg
Acta Medica Hondurena [*A publication*]....Acta Med Hondur
Acta Medica Iranica [*A publication*]....Acta Med Iran
Acta Medica Iugoslavica [*A publication*]....Acta Med Iugosl
Acta Medica Iugoslavica (English Translation) [*A publication*]....Acta Med Iugosl (Eng Transl)
Acta Medica Medianae [*A publication*]....Acta Med Medianae
Acta Medica (Mexico) [*A publication*]....Acta Med (Mex)
Acta Medica Nagasakiensia [*A publication*]....Acta Med Nagasaki
Acta Medica Okayama [*A publication*]....Acta Med Okayama
Acta Medica Orientalia [*A publication*]....Acta Med Orient
Acta Medica Peruana [*A publication*]....Acta Med Peru
Acta Medica Philippina [*A publication*]....Acta Med Philipp
Acta Medica Polona [*A publication*]....Acta Med Pol
Acta Medica Romana [*A publication*]....Acta Med Roman
Acta Medica Romana [*A publication*]....Acta Med Romana
Acta Medica Scandinavica [*A publication*]....Acta Med Scand
Acta Medica Scandinavica [*A publication*]....Act Med Sc
Acta Medica Scandinavica. Supplementum [*A publication*]....Acta Med Scand Suppl
Acta Medica de Tenerife [*A publication*]....Acta Med Tenerife
Acta Medica Turcica [*A publication*]....Acta Med Turc
Acta Medica Turcica. Supplementum [*A publication*]....Acta Med Turc Suppl
Acta Medica Universitatis Kagoshimaensis [*A publication*]....Acta Med Univ Kagoshima
Acta Medica Venezolana [*A publication*]....Acta Med Venez
Acta Medica Veterinaria (Naples) [*A publication*]....Acta Med Vet (Naples)
Acta Medica Vietnamica [*A publication*]....Acta Med Vietnam
Acta Medicinae Legalis et Socialis [*Liege*] [*A publication*]....Acta Med Leg Soc
Acta Medicinae Legalis et Socialis (Liege) [*A publication*]....Acta Med Leg Soc (Liege)
Acta Medicinae Okayama [*A publication*]....Act Med Oka
Acta Metallurgica [*A publication*]....Acta Metall
Acta Metallurgica [*A publication*]....Act Metall
Acta Mexicana de Ciencia y Tecnologia [*A publication*]....Acta Mex Cienc y Tecnol
Acta Mexicana de Ciencia y Tecnologia [*A publication*]....Acta Mexicana Ci Tecn
Acta Microbiologica. Academiae Scientiarum Hungaricae [*A publication*]....Acta Microbiol Acad Sci Hung
Acta Microbiologica. Academiae Scientiarum Hungaricae [*A publication*]....Act Micro H
Acta Microbiologica Bulgarica [*A publication*]....Acta Microbiol Bulg
Acta Microbiologica Hellenica [*A publication*]....Acta Microbiol Hell
Acta Microbiologica Polonica [*A publication*]....Acta Microbiol Pol
Acta Microbiologica Polonica [*A publication*]....Acta Microbiol Polon
Acta Microbiologica Polonica. Series A. Microbiologia Generalis [*A publication*]....Acta Microbiol Pol Ser A
Acta Microbiologica Polonica. Series A. Microbiologia Generalis [*A publication*]....Acta Microbiol Pol Ser A Microbiol Gen
Acta Microbiologica Polonica. Series A. Microbiologia Generalis [*A publication*]....Act Mic P A
Acta Microbiologica Polonica. Series B. Microbiologia Applicata [*A publication*]....Acta Microbiol Pol Ser B
Acta Microbiologica Polonica. Series B. Microbiologia Applicata [*A publication*]....Acta Microbiol Pol Ser B Microbiol Appl
Acta Microbiologica Polonica. Series B. Microbiologia Applicata [*A publication*]....Act Mic P B
Acta Microbiologica Sinica [*A publication*]....Acta Microbiol Sinica
Acta Microbiologica, Virologica, et Immunologica (Sofiia) [*A publication*]....Acta Microbiol Virol Immunol (Sofiia)
Acta Mineralogica-Petrographica (Acta Universitatis Szegediensis) [*A publication*]....Acta Mineral-Petrogr (Szeged)
Acta Montana [*A publication*]....Acta Mont
Acta Morphologica. Academiae Scientiarum Hungaricae [*A publication*]....Acta Morphol Acad Sci Hung
Acta Morphologica. Academiae Scientiarum Hungaricae [*A publication*]....Act Morph H
Acta Morphologica. Academiae Scientiarum Hungaricae. Supplementum [*A publication*]....Acta Morphol Acad Sci Hung Suppl
Acta Morphologica Neerlando-Scandinavica [*A publication*]....Acta Morphol Neerl-Scand
Acta Morphologica Neerlando-Scandinavica [*A publication*]....Act Morph N
Acta Musei Macedonici. Scientiarum Naturalium [*A publication*]....Acta Mus Macedonici Sci Nat
Acta Musei Moraviae. Scientiae Naturales [*A publication*]....Acta Mus Morav Sci Natur

Acta Musei Moraviae. Scientiae Sociales [*A publication*] .... Acta Mus Morav Sci Soc
Acta Musei Napocensis [*A publication*]........A Mus Napocensis
Acta Musei Nationalis Pragae. Series B. Historia Naturalis [*A publication*]........Acta Mus Natl Pragae Ser B Hist Nat
Acta Musei Silesiae. Series A. Scientiae Naturales [*A publication*]........Acta Mus Silesiae Ser A Sci Nat
Acta Musicologica [*A publication*]........Ac M
Acta Musicologica [*A publication*]........Acta Mus
Acta Musicologica [*A publication*]........Acta Music
Acta Musicologica [*A publication*]........AM
Acta Mycologica [*A publication*]........Acta Mycol
Acta Naturalia Islandica [*A publication*]........Acta Nat Isl
Acta Neophilologica [*A publication*]........AN
Acta Neurobiologiae Experimentalis [*A publication*]........Acta Neurobiol Exp
Acta Neurobiologiae Experimentalis [*A publication*]........Act Neurob
Acta Neurobiologiae Experimentalis [*A publication*]........ANEXA
Acta Neurobiologiae Experimentalis. Supplementum [*A publication*]........Acta Neurobiol Exp Suppl
Acta Neurobiologiae Experimentalis (Warsaw) [*A publication*]........ Acta Neurobiol Exp (Warsaw)
Acta Neurobiologiae Experimentalis (Warszawa) [*A publication*]........ Acta Neurobiol Exp (Warsz)
Acta Neurochirurgica [*A publication*]........Acta Neurochir
Acta Neurochirurgica [*A publication*]........Act Neuroch
Acta Neurochirurgica. Supplementum [*Wien*] [*A publication*]........ Acta Neurochir Suppl
Acta Neurochirurgica. Supplementum (Wien) [*A publication*]........ Acta Neurochir Suppl (Wien)
Acta Neurochirurgica (Wien) [*A publication*]........Acta Neurochir (Wien)
Acta Neurologica Belgica [*A publication*]........Acta Neurol Belg
Acta Neurologica Latinoamericana [*A publication*]........Acta Neurol Latinoam
Acta Neurologica Latinoamericana [*A publication*]........ Acta Neurol Latinoamer
Acta Neurologica (Naples) [*A publication*]........Acta Neurol (Naples)
Acta Neurologica (Napoli) [*A publication*]........Acta Neurol (Napoli)
Acta Neurologica et Psychiatrica Belgica [*A publication*]........ Acta Neurol Psychiatr Belg
Acta Neurologica et Psychiatrica Belgica [*A publication*]........ANPBA
Acta Neurologica. Quaderni [*A publication*]........Acta Neurol Quad
Acta Neurologica Scandinavica [*A publication*]........Acta Neurol Scand
Acta Neurologica Scandinavica [*A publication*]........Act Neur Sc
Acta Neurologica Scandinavica. Supplementum [*A publication*]........ Acta Neurol Scand Suppl
Acta Neurologica Scandinavica. Supplementum [*A publication*]........ANSLA
Acta Neuropathologica [*A publication*]........Acta Neuropathol
Acta Neuropathologica [*A publication*]........Act Neurop
Acta Neuropathologica (Berlin) [*A publication*]........Acta Neuropathol (Berl)
Acta Neuropathologica. Supplement [*Berlin*] [*A publication*]........ Acta Neuropathol Suppl
Acta Neuropathologica. Supplement (Berlin) [*A publication*]........ Acta Neuropathol Suppl (Berl)
Acta Neurovegetativa [*A publication*]........Acta Neuroveg
Acta Numismatica [*A publication*]........Acta Num
Acta Numismatica [*A publication*]........ANum
Acta Obstetrica y Ginecologica Hispano-Lusitana [*A publication*]........ Acta Obstet Ginecol Hisp-Lusit
Acta Obstetrica y Ginecologica Hispano-Lusitana. Suplemento [*A publication*]........Acta Obstet Ginecol Hisp-Lusit Supl
Acta Obstetrica et Gynaecologica Japonica [*A publication*]........ Acta Obstet Gynaecol Jpn
Acta Obstetrica et Gynaecologica Japonica (English Edition) [*A publication*]........Acta Obstet Gynaecol Jpn (Engl Ed)
Acta Obstetricia et Gynecologica Scandinavica [*A publication*]........ Acta Obstet Gynecol Scand
Acta Obstetricia et Gynecologica Scandinavica [*A publication*]........ Act Obst Sc
Acta Obstetricia et Gynecologica Scandinavica. Supplement [*A publication*]........Acta Obstet Gynecol Scand Suppl
Acta Odontologica Scandinavica [*A publication*]........Acta Odontol Scand
Acta Odontologica Scandinavica [*A publication*]........Act Odon Sc
Acta Odontologica Scandinavica [*A publication*]........AOSCA
Acta Odontologica Scandinavica. Supplementum [*A publication*]........Acta Odontol Scand Suppl
Acta Odontologica Venezolana [*A publication*]........Acta Odontol Venez
Acta Oeconomica [*Budapest*] [*A publication*]........Acta Oecon
Acta Oeconomica [*Budapest*] [*A publication*]........Act Oecon
Acta Oncologica [*Madrid*] [*A publication*]........Acta Oncol
Acta Oncologica Brasileira [*A publication*]........Acta Oncol Bras
Acta Oncologica (Madrid) [*A publication*]........Acta Oncol (Madr)
Acta Ophthalmologica [*A publication*]........Acta Ophthalmol
Acta Ophthalmologica (Copenhagen) [*A publication*]........ Acta Ophthalmol (Copenh)
Acta Ophthalmologica Iugoslavica [*A publication*]........Acta Ophthalmol Iugosl
Acta Ophthalmologica (Kobenhavn) [*A publication*]........Act Ophth (K)
Acta Ophthalmologica. Supplementum [*Kobenhavn*] [*A publication*]........Acta Ophthalmol Suppl
Acta Ophthalmologica. Supplementum (Copenhagen) [*A publication*]........Acta Ophthalmol Suppl (Copenh)
Acta Orientalia [*A publication*]........AcOr
Acta Orientalia [*A publication*]........Acta O
Acta Orientalia [*A publication*]........Acta Or
Acta Orientalia [*A publication*]........Acta Orient
Acta Orientalia [*A publication*]........AO
Acta Orientalia [*A publication*]........AODNS
Acta Orientalia. Academiae Scientiarum Hungaricae [*A publication*]........AOASH
Acta Orientalia. Academiae Scientiarum Hungaricae [*A publication*]........AOH
Acta Orientalia. Academiae Scientiarum Hungaricae [*A publication*]........AOrientHung
Acta Orientalia. Academiae Scientiarum Hungaricae (Budapest) [*A publication*]........Acta Or (B)
Acta Ornithologica (English Translation) [*A publication*]........ Acta Ornithol (Engl Transl)
Acta Ornithologica (Warsaw) [*A publication*]........Acta Ornithol (Warsaw)
Acta Orthopaedica Belgica [*A publication*]........Acta Orthop Belg
Acta Orthopaedica Scandinavica [*A publication*]........Acta Orthop Scand
Acta Orthopaedica Scandinavica [*A publication*]........Act Orth Sc
Acta Orthopaedica Scandinavica. Supplementum [*A publication*]........Acta Orthop Scand Suppl
Acta Oto-Laryngologica [*A publication*]........Acta Oto-Laryngol
Acta Oto-Laryngologica [*A publication*]........Act Oto-Lar
Acta Oto-Laryngologica [*A publication*]........AOLAA
Acta Oto-Laryngologica. Supplementum [*A publication*]........ Acta Oto-Laryngol Suppl
Acta Oto-Rhino-Laryngologica Belgica [*A publication*]........Acta ORL Belg
Acta Oto-Rhino-Laryngologica Belgica [*A publication*]........ Acta Oto-Rhino-Laryngol Belg
Acta Oto-Rhino-Laryngologica Belgica [*A publication*]........AORLA
Acta Oto-Rino-Laringologica Espanola [*A publication*]........ Acta Oto-Rino-Laringol Esp
Acta Oto-Rino-Laringologica Ibero-Americana [*A publication*]........ Acta Oto-Rino-Laringol Ibero-Am
Acta Oto-Rino-Laringologica Ibero-Americana [*A publication*]........AORIA
Acta Otolaryngologica (Stockholm) [*A publication*]........ Acta Otolaryngol (Stockh)
Acta Otolaryngologica. Supplement (Stockholm) [*A publication*]........ Acta Otolaryngol Suppl (Stockh)
Acta Otorinolaringologica Espanola [*A publication*]........Acta Orl Espan
Acta Paediatrica [*A publication*]........Acta Paediatr
Acta Paediatrica. Academiae Scientiarum Hungaricae [*A publication*]........Acta Paediatr Acad Sci Hung
Acta Paediatrica. Academiae Scientiarum Hungaricae [*A publication*]........Act Paed H
Acta Paediatrica Belgica [*A publication*]........Acta Paediatr Belg
Acta Paediatrica Japonica (Overseas Edition) [*A publication*]........ Acta Paediatr Jpn (Overseas Ed)
Acta Paediatrica Scandinavica [*A publication*]........Acta Paediatr Scand
Acta Paediatrica Scandinavica [*A publication*]........Act Paed Sc
Acta Paediatrica Scandinavica. Supplementum [*A publication*]........ Acta Paediatr Scand Suppl
Acta Paediatrica Sinica [*A publication*]........Acta Paediatr Sin
Acta Paediatrica. Supplement [*A publication*]........Acta Paediatr Suppl
Acta Paediatrica (Uppsala) [*A publication*]........Acta Paediat (Uppsala)
Acta Paedopsychiatrica [*A publication*]........ACPDA
Acta Paedopsychiatrica [*A publication*]........Acta Paedopsychiat
Acta Paedopsychiatrica [*A publication*]........Acta Paedopsychiatr
Acta Paedopsychiatrica [*A publication*]........Act Paedops
Acta Paedopsychiatrica (Basel) [*A publication*]........ Acta Paedopsychiatr (Basel)
Acta Palaeobotanica [*A publication*]........Acta Palaeobot
Acta Palaeontologica Polonica [*A publication*]........Acta Palaeontol Pol
Acta Palaeontologica Sinica [*A publication*]........Acta Palaeontol Sin
Acta Parasitologica Lithuanica [*A publication*]........Acta Parasitol Lith
Acta Parasitologica Polonica [*A publication*]........Acta Parasitol Pol
Acta Pathologica Japonica [*A publication*]........Acta Pathol Jpn
Acta Pathologica Japonica [*A publication*]........Act Pat Jap
Acta Pathologica et Microbiologica Scandinavica [*A publication*]........ Acta Pathol Microbiol Scand
Acta Pathologica et Microbiologica Scandinavica. Section A [*A publication*]........Acta Pathol Microbiol Scand (A)
Acta Pathologica et Microbiologica Scandinavica. Section A [*A publication*]........Acta Pathol Microbiol Scand Sect A
Acta Pathologica et Microbiologica Scandinavica. Section A [*A publication*]........Act Pat S A
Acta Pathologica et Microbiologica Scandinavica. Section A. Pathology [*A publication*]........Acta Pathol Microbiol Scand Sect A Pathol
Acta Pathologica et Microbiologica Scandinavica. Section A. Pathology [*A publication*]........Acta Pathol Microbiol Sect A
Acta Pathologica et Microbiologica Scandinavica. Section A. Supplement [*A publication*]........Acta Pathol Microbiol Scand Sect A Suppl
Acta Pathologica et Microbiologica Scandinavica. Section B [*A publication*]........Acta Pathol Microbiol Scand (B)
Acta Pathologica et Microbiologica Scandinavica. Section B [*A publication*]........Acta Pathol Microbiol Scand Sect B
Acta Pathologica et Microbiologica Scandinavica. Section B [*A publication*]........Act Pat S B
Acta Pathologica et Microbiologica Scandinavica. Section B. Microbiology [*A publication*]........ Acta Pathol Microbiol Scand Sect B Microbiol

Acta Pathologica et Microbiologica Scandinavica. Section B. Microbiology and Immunology [*A publication*]...................... Acta Pathol Microbiol Scand Sect B Microbiol Immunol

Acta Pathologica et Microbiologica Scandinavica. Section C [*A publication*]...................Acta Pathol Microbiol Scand (C)

Acta Pathologica et Microbiologica Scandinavica. Section C [*A publication*]...................Acta Pathol Microbiol Scand Sect C

Acta Pathologica et Microbiologica Scandinavica. Section C [*A publication*]...................Act Pat S C

Acta Pathologica et Microbiologica Scandinavica. Section C. Immunology [*A publication*]...................Acta Pathol Microbiol Scand Sect C Immunol

Acta Pathologica et Microbiologica Scandinavica. Supplementum [*A publication*].......... Acta Pathol Microbiol Scand Suppl

Acta Pedologica Sinica [*A publication*]...................Acta Pedol Sin

Acta Pedologica Sinica [*A publication*]...................Acta Pedol Sinica

Acta Pharmaceutica Hungarica [*A publication*]...................Acta Pharm Hung

Acta Pharmaceutica Iugoslavica [*A publication*]...................Acta Pharm Iugosl

Acta Pharmaceutica Jugoslavica [*A publication*]...................Acta Pharmaceut Jugoslav

Acta Pharmaceutica Jugoslavica [*A publication*]...................Acta Pharm Jugosl

Acta Pharmaceutica Sinica [*A publication*]...................Acta Pharm Sin

Acta Pharmaceutica Suecica [*A publication*]...................Acta Pharm Suec

Acta Pharmaceutica Suecica [*A publication*]...................Act Pharm S

Acta Pharmacologica Sinica [*A publication*]...................Acta Pharmacol Sin

Acta Pharmacologica et Toxicologica [*A publication*]...................Acta Pharmacol Toxicol

Acta Pharmacologica et Toxicologica [*A publication*]...................Act Pharm T

Acta Pharmacologica et Toxicologica (Copenhagen) [*A publication*]...................Acta Pharmacol Toxicol (Copenh)

Acta Pharmacologica et Toxicologica. Supplementum [*A publication*]...................Acta Pharmacol Toxicol Suppl

Acta Philologica Scandinavica [*A publication*]...................Acta Philol Scand

Acta Philologica Scandinavica [*A publication*]...................APS

Acta Philologica Scandinavica. Tidsskrift foer Nordisk Sprogforskning [*A publication*]...................APhS

Acta Philologica. Societas Academica Dacoromana [*A publication*].......APh

Acta Philologica. Societas Academica Dacoromana [*A publication*]...................APhD

Acta Philosophica Fennica [*A publication*]...................Acta Philos Fenn

Acta Philosophica Fennica [*Elsevier Book Series*] [*A publication*]...........APF

Acta Physica. Academiae Scientiarum Hungaricae [*A publication*]...................Acta Phys Acad Sci Hung

Acta Physica. Academiae Scientiarum Hungaricae [*A publication*]...................Act Phys H

Acta Physica Austriaca [*A publication*]...................Acta Phys Austriaca

Acta Physica Austriaca [*A publication*]...................Act Phys Au

Acta Physica Austriaca. Supplementum [*A publication*]...................Acta Phys Austriaca Suppl

Acta Physica et Chemica [*A publication*]...................Acta Phys Chem

Acta Physica et Chemica [*A publication*]...................Act Phys Ch

Acta Physica et Chemica. Nova Series. Acta Universitatis Szegediensis [*A publication*]...................Acta Phys Chem Univ Szeged

Acta Physica Polonica [*A publication*]...................Acta Phys Pol

Acta Physica Polonica. Series A [*A publication*]...................Acta Phys Pol A

Acta Physica Polonica. Series A [*A publication*]...................Act Phy P A

Acta Physica Polonica. Series B [*A publication*]...................Acta Phys Pol B

Acta Physica Polonica. Series B [*A publication*]...................Act Phy P B

Acta Physica Sinica [*A publication*]...................Acta Phys Sin

Acta Physica Sinica [*A publication*]...................Acta Phys Sinica

Acta Physica Slovaca [*A publication*]...................Acta Phys Slov

Acta Physica Slovaca [*A publication*]...................APSVC

Acta Physiologica. Academiae Scientiarum Hungaricae [*A publication*]...................Acta Physiol Acad Sci Hung

Acta Physiologica. Academiae Scientiarum Hungaricae [*A publication*]...................Act Physl H

Acta Physiologica Latino Americana [*A publication*]...... Acta Physiol Lat Am

Acta Physiologica Latino Americana [*A publication*]...................Act Physl L

Acta Physiologica Latino Americana. Suplemento [*A publication*]...................Acta Physiol Lat Am (Supl)

Acta Physiologica Pharmacologica [*A publication*]...................APPBD

Acta Physiologica et Pharmacologica Bulgarica [*A publication*]...................Acta Physiol Pharmacol Bulg

Acta Physiologica et Pharmacologica Neerlandica [*A publication*]...................Acta Physiol Pharmacol Neerl

Acta Physiologica Polonica [*A publication*]...................Acta Physiol Pol

Acta Physiologica Polonica [*A publication*]...................Act Physl P

Acta Physiologica Polonica (English Translation) [*A publication*]...................Acta Physiol Pol (Engl Transl)

Acta Physiologica Polonica (Translation) [*A publication*]...................Acta Physiol Pol (Transl)

Acta Physiologica Scandinavica [*A publication*]............. Acta Physiol Scand

Acta Physiologica Scandinavica [*A publication*]...................Act Physl S

Acta Physiologica Scandinavica [*A publication*]...................APSCA

Acta Physiologica Scandinavica. Supplementum [*A publication*]...................Acta Physiol Scand Suppl

Acta Physiologica Sinica [*A publication*]...................Acta Physiol Sin

Acta Phytogeographica Suecica [*A publication*]......... Acta Phytogeogr Suec

Acta Phytomedica [*A publication*]...................Acta Phytomed

Acta Phytopathologica [*A publication*]...................Acta Phytopathol

Acta Phytopathologica. Academiae Scientiarum Hungaricae [*A publication*]...................Acta Phytopathol Acad Sci Hung

Acta Phytopathologica (Budapest) [*A publication*]...................Acta Phytopathol (Budapest)

Acta Phytopathologica Sinica [*A publication*]...........Acta Phytopathol Sinica

Acta Phytophylacica Sinica [*A publication*]............. Acta Phytophylacica Sin

Acta Phytophylacica Sinica [*A publication*].................Acta Phytophyl Sinica

Acta Phytophysiologica Sinica [*A publication*].........Acta Phytophysiol Sinica

Acta Phytotaxonomica Barcinonensia [*A publication*]...................Acta Phytotaxon Barc

Acta Phytotaxonomica et Geobotanica [*A publication*]...................Acta Phytotaxon Geobot

Acta Phytotaxonomica Sinica [*A publication*]................Acta Phytotaxon Sin

Acta Phytotherapeutica [*A publication*]...................Acta Phytother

Acta Politecnica Mexicana [*A publication*]...................Acta Politec Mex

Acta Politica [*A publication*]...................Acta Polit

Acta Poloniae Historica [*A publication*]...................APH

Acta Poloniae Pharmaceutica [*A publication*]...................Acta Pol Pharm

Acta Poloniae Pharmaceutica [*A publication*]...................Act Pol Ph

Acta Poloniae Pharmaceutica (English Translation) [*A publication*]...................Acta Pol Pharm (Engl Transl)

Acta Poloniae Pharmaceutica (English Translation) [*A publication*]...................Acta Pol Pharm (Transl)

Acta Polytechnica. Rada IV. Technicko-Teoreticka (Prague) [*A publication*]...................Acta Polytech IV (Prague)

Acta Polytechnica Scandinavica [*A publication*]............Acta Polytech Scand

Acta Polytechnica Scandinavica. Chemistry Including Metallurgy Series [*A publication*]...................Acta Polytech Scand Chem Incl Metall Ser

Acta Polytechnica Scandinavica. Chemistry Series [*A publication*]...................Act Poly Ch

Acta Polytechnica Scandinavica. Civil Engineering and Building Construction Series [*A publication*]...................Act Poly Ci

Acta Polytechnica Scandinavica. Electrical Engineering Series [*A publication*]................... Acta Polytech Scand Elec Eng Ser

Acta Polytechnica Scandinavica. Electrical Engineering Series [*A publication*]...................Act Poly El

Acta Polytechnica Scandinavica. Electrical Series [*A publication*]...................Acta Polytech Scand Electr Ser

Acta Polytechnica Scandinavica. Mathematics and Computing Machinery Series [*A publication*]...................Act Poly Ma

Acta Polytechnica Scandinavica. Mechanical Engineering Series [*A publication*]....................... Acta Polytech Scand Mech Eng Ser

Acta Polytechnica Scandinavica. Mechanical Engineering Series [*A publication*]...................Act Poly Me

Acta Polytechnica Scandinavica. Physics Including Nucleonics Series [*A publication*].....................Acta Polytech Scand Phys Nucl Ser

Acta Polytechnica Scandinavica. Physics Including Nucleonics Series [*A publication*]...................Act Poly Ph

Acta Polytechnica. Series III [*A publication*]...................Acta Polytech III

Acta Praehistorica et Archaeologica [*A publication*]...................Acta Praehist et Archaeol

Acta Praehistorica et Archaeologica [*A publication*]...................APA

Acta Protozoologica [*A publication*]...................Acta Protozool

Acta Psiquiatrica y Psicologica de America Latina [*A publication*]...................Acta Psiquiatr Psicol Am Lat

Acta Psiquiatrica y Psicologica de America Latina [*A publication*]...................Act Psiq Ps

Acta Psiquiatrica y Psicologica de America Latina [*A publication*]....APQPA

Acta Psychiatrica Belgica [*A publication*]................... Acta Psychiat Belg

Acta Psychiatrica Belgica [*A publication*].......................Acta Psychiatr Belg

Acta Psychiatrica et Neurologica Scandinavica [*A publication*]...................Acta Psychiatr Neurol Scand

Acta Psychiatrica et Neurologica Scandinavica [*A publication*]...................Acta Psychiat Scand

Acta Psychiatrica et Neurologica Scandinavica. Supplementum [*A publication*]...................Acta Psychiatr Neurol Scand Suppl

Acta Psychiatrica Scandinavica [*A publication*]...................Acta Psychiatr Scand

Acta Psychiatrica Scandinavica [*A publication*]...................Act Psyc Sc

Acta Psychiatrica Scandinavica. Supplementum [*A publication*]...................Acta Psychiatr Scand Suppl

Acta Psychologica [*Amsterdam*] [*A publication*]...................Acta Psychol

Acta Psychologica [*Amsterdam*] [*A publication*]...................Act Psychol

Acta Psychologica [*Amsterdam*] [*A publication*]...................APsych

Acta Psychologica (Amsterdam) [*A publication*]........... Acta Psychol (Amst)

Acta Psychologica (Amsterdam) [*A publication*]...................APSOA

Acta Psychologica Taiwanica [*A publication*]...............Acta Psychol Taiwan

Acta Psychologica Taiwanica [*A publication*]...................Act Psych T

Acta Psychologica Taiwanica [*A publication*]...................APT

Acta Psychotherapeutica et Psychosomatica [*A publication*]...................Acta Psychother Psychosom

Acta Psychotherapeutica et Psychosomatica [*A publication*]...........APYTA

Acta Radiologica [*A publication*]...................Acta Radiol

Acta Radiologica. Oncology Radiation Therapy, Physics, and Biology [*Stockholm*] [*A publication*]...................Acta Radiol Oncol Radiat Ther Phys Biol

Acta Radiologica. Series One. Diagnosis [*Stockholm*] [*A publication*]...................Acta Radiol Diagn

Acta Radiologica. Series One. Diagnosis [*Stockholm*] [*A publication*]...................Act Rad Dgn

Acta Radiologica. Series One. Diagnosis (Stockholm) [*A publication*]...................Acta Radiol Diagn (Stockh)

Acta Radiologica. Series Two. Oncology Radiation, Physics, and Biology [*Stockholm*] [*A publication*] .... Acta Radiol Oncol Radiat Phys Biol

Acta Radiologica (Stockholm) [*A publication*] .... Acta Radiol (Stockh)

Acta Radiologica. Supplementum [*Stockholm*] [*A publication*] .... Acta Radiol Suppl

Acta Radiologica. Supplementum (Stockholm) [*A publication*] .... Acta Radiol Suppl (Stockh)

Acta Radiologica. Therapy, Physics, Biology [*Stockholm*] [*Later, Acta Radiologica. Series Two. Oncology Radiation, Physics, and Biology*] [*A publication*] .... Acta Radiol Ther Phys Biol

Acta Radiologica. Therapy, Physics, Biology [*Stockholm*] [*Later, Acta Radiologica. Series Two. Oncology Radiation, Physics, and Biology*] [*A publication*] .... Act Rad TPB

Acta Radiologica. Therapy, Physics, Biology (Stockholm) [*Later, Acta Radiologica. Series Two. Oncology Radiation, Physics, and Biology (Stockholm)*] [*A publication*] .... Acta Radiol Ther (Stockh)

Acta Regiae Societatis Scientiarum et Litterarum Gothoburgensis Zoologica [*A publication*] .... Acta Regiae Soc Sci Litt Gothob Zool

Acta Rerum Naturalium Musei Nationalis Slovaci Bratislava [*A publication*] .... Acta Rerum Nat Mus Nat Slov Bratisl

Acta Rheumatologica Scandinavica [*A publication*] .... Acta Rheumatol Scand

Acta Rheumatologica Scandinavica. Supplementum [*A publication*] .... Acta Rheumatol Scand Suppl

Acta Rhumatologica [*A publication*] .... Acta Rhumatol

Acta Rhumatologica Belgica [*A publication*] .... Acta Rhumatol Belg

Acta Sagittariana [*A publication*] .... Acta Sag

Acta Salmanticensia [*A publication*] .... ASal

Acta Salmanticensia. Serie de Ciencias [*A publication*] .... Acta Salmanticensia Ser Cienc

Acta Salmanticensia. Serie de Medicina [*A publication*] .... Acta Salmanticensia Ser Med

Acta Sanctorum [*Acts of the Saints*] [*Latin*] .... ASS

Acta Scholae Medicinalis Universitatis in Gifu [*A publication*] .... Acta Sch Med Univ Gifu

Acta Scholae Medicinalis Universitatis in Kioto [*A publication*] .... Acta Sch Med Univ Kioto

Acta Scientiarum Mathematicarum [*A publication*] .... Act Sci Mat

Acta Scientiarum Mathematicarum (Szeged) [*A publication*] .... Acta Sci Math (Szeged)

Acta Scientiarum Naturalium. Academiae Scientiarum Bohemoslovacae Brno [*A publication*] .... Acta Sci Nat Acad Sci Bohemoslov Brno

Acta Scientiarum Naturalium. Universitatis Pekinensis [*A publication*] .... Acta Sci Natur Univ Pekinensis

Acta Scientiarum Vietnamicarum [*A publication*] .... Acta Sci Vietnam

Acta Semiotica et Linguistica [*A publication*] .... A S e L

Acta Societatis Botanicorum Poloniae [*A publication*] .... Acta Soc Bot Pol

Acta Societatis Botanicorum Poloniae [*A publication*] .... Acta Soc Bot Polon

Acta Societatis Entomologicae Cechosloveniae [*A publication*] .... Acta Soc Entomol Cech

Acta Societatis pro Fauna et Flora Fennica [*A publication*] .... Acta Soc Fauna Flora Fenn

Acta Societatis Humaniorum Litterarum Lundensis [*A publication*]......ASLL

Acta Societatis Linguisticae Upsaliensis [*A publication*]..................ASLU

Acta Societatis Medicorum Upsaliensis [*A publication*]....Acta Soc Med Ups

Acta Societatis Medicorum Upsaliensis [*A publication*] .... Acta Soc Med Upsal

Acta Societatis Ophthalmologicae Japonicae [*A publication*] .... Acta Soc Ophthalmol Jpn

Acta Societatis Scientiarum Fennicae. Series B [*A publication*] .... Acta Soc Sci Fenn Ser B

Acta Sociologica [*A publication*].......................... Acta Sociol

Acta Sociologica [*A publication*].......................... Act Sociol

Acta Stomatologica Belgica [*A publication*] .... Acta Stomatol Belg

Acta Stomatologica Belgica [*A publication*] ....ASBEB

Acta Stomatologica Croatica [*A publication*] .... Acta Stomatol Croat

Acta Technica. Academiae Scientiarum Hungaricae [*A publication*]..........................Acta Tech Acad Sci Hung

Acta Technica. Academiae Scientiarum Hungaricae [*A publication*]..........................Act Techn H

Acta Technica (Budapest) [*A publication*]..........Acta Tech (Budap)

Acta Technica. CSAV [*Ceskoslovenska Akademie Ved*] [*A publication*]..........................Acta Tech CSAV

Acta Technica Hungaricae [*A publication*]..........Acta Tech Hung

Acta Theologica Danica [*A publication*] .... ATD

Acta Theriologica [*A publication*] .... Acta Theriol

Acta Tropica [*A publication*] .... Acta Trop

Acta Tropica (Basel) [*A publication*] .... Acta Trop (Basel)

Acta Tuberculosea Japonica [*A publication*] .... Acta Tuberc Jpn

Acta Tuberculosea et Pneumologica Belgica [*A publication*]...................... Acta Tuberc Pneumol Belg

Acta Tuberculosea et Pneumologica Scandinavica [*A publication*].................. Acta Tuberc Pneumol Scand

Acta Tuberculosea et Pneumologica Scandinavica. Supplementum [*A publication*]....Acta Tuberc Pneumol Scand Suppl

Acta Tuberculosea Scandinavica [*A publication*] .... Acta Tuberc Scand

Acta Tuberculosea Scandinavica. Supplementum [*A publication*]...................... Acta Tuberc Scand Suppl

Acta Unio Internationalis Contra Cancrum [*A publication*] .... Acta Unio Int Contra Cancrum

Acta Universitatis Agriculturae (Brno). Section C. Facultas Silviculturae [*A publication*] .... Acta Univ Agr (Brno)

Acta Universitatis Agriculturae. Facultas Agronomica [*A publication*]..........................Acta Univ Agric Fac Agron

Acta Universitatis Agriculturae. Facultas Silviculturae [*A publication*]..........................Acta Univ Agric Fac Silvic

Acta Universitatis Agriculturae. Facultas Veterinaria [*A publication*]..........................Acta Univ Agric Fac Vet

Acta Universitatis Carolinae [*A publication*]..........................AUC

Acta Universitatis Carolinae. Biologica [*A publication*] .... Acta Univ Carol Biol

Acta Universitatis Carolinae. Geographica [*A publication*] .... Acta Univ Carol Geogr

Acta Universitatis Carolinae. Geographica [*A publication*] .... AUCG-B

Acta Universitatis Carolinae. Geologica [*A publication*] .... Acta Univ Carol Geol

Acta Universitatis Carolinae. Mathematica et Physica [*A publication*]..........................Acta Univ Carolinae Math et Phys

Acta Universitatis Carolinae. Mathematica et Physica [*A publication*]..........................Acta Univ Carol Math Phys

Acta Universitatis Carolinae. Medica [*A publication*]..... Acta Univ Carol Med

Acta Universitatis Carolinae. Medica Monographia [*A publication*]..........................Acta Univ Carol Med Monogr

Acta Universitatis Carolinae. Medica Monographia (Praha) [*A publication*] .... Acta Univ Carol Med Monogr (Praha)

Acta Universitatis Carolinae. Medica (Praha) [*A publication*] .... Acta Univ Carol Med (Praha)

Acta Universitatis Carolinae. Philologica [*A publication*] .... AUC-Ph

Acta Universitatis Carolinae. Pragensis [*A publication*] .... AUCP

Acta Universitatis Latviensis [*A publication*] .... AUL

Acta Universitatis Lodziensis [*A publication*].......................... Acta Univ Lodz

Acta Universitatis Lundensis [*A publication*]......................Acta Lund

Acta Universitatis Lundensis [*A publication*] .... AUL

Acta Universitatis Lundensis. Sectio II. Medica Mathematica Scientiae Rerum Naturalium [*A publication*] .... Acta Univ Lund Sect II Med Math Sci Rerum Nat

Acta Universitatis Nicolai Copernici. Biologia [*A publication*] .... Acta Univ Nicolai Copernici Biol

Acta Universitatis Nicolai Copernici. Geografia [*A publication*] .... Acta Univ Nicolai Copernici Geogr

Acta Universitatis Nicolai Copernici. Prace Limnologiczne [*A publication*].................. Acta Univ Nicolai Copernici Pr Limnol

Acta Universitatis Ouluensis. Series A. Scientiae Rerum Naturalium. Geologica [*A publication*] ..... Acta Univ Ouluensis Ser A

Acta Universitatis Ouluensis. Series A. Scientiae Rerum Naturalium. Mathematica [*A publication*] .... Acta Univ Oulu Ser A Sci Rerum Natur Math

Acta Universitatis Ouluensis. Series C. Technica [*A publication*] .... Acta Univ Ouluensis Ser C

Acta Universitatis Palackianae Olomucensis [*A publication*]............... AUPO

Acta Universitatis Palackianae Olomucensis. Facultas Philosophica, Philologica [*A publication*].......................AUO-Ph

Acta Universitatis Palackianae Olomucensis. Facultas Rerum Naturalium. Biologica [*A publication*] .... Acta Univ Palacki Olomuc Fac Rerum Nat Biol

Acta Universitatis Palackianae Olomucensis. Facultas Rerum Naturalium. Physica [*A publication*] .... Acta Univ Palacki Olomuc Fac Rerum Nat Phys

Acta Universitatis Palackianae Olomucensis. Facultatis Medicae [*A publication*] .... Acta Univ Palacki Olomuc Fac Med

Acta Universitatis Palackianae Olomucensis. Facultatis Medicae. Supplementum [*A publication*].................................. Acta Univ Palacki Olomuc Fac Med Suppl

Acta Universitatis Szegediensis. Acta Biologica [*A publication*] .... Acta Univ Szeged Acta Biol

Acta Universitatis Szegediensis. Acta Germanica et Romanica [*A publication*]..........................AUS AG & R

Acta Universitatis Szegediensis de Attila Jozsef Nominatae. Sectio: Acta Historiae Litterarum Hungaricarum [*A publication*]..........................AUS AHLH

Acta Universitatis Szegediensis de Attila Jozsef Nominatae. Sectio: Ethnographica et Linguistica [*A publication*].............AUS E & L

Acta Universitatis Tamperensis. Series A [*A publication*] .... Acta Univ Tamper Ser A

Acta Universitatis Upsaliensis. Abstracts of Uppsala Dissertations in Science [*A publication*] .... Acta Univ Ups Abstr Upps Diss Sci

Acta Universitatis Upsaliensis. Abstracts of Uppsala Dissertations from the Faculty of Science [*A publication*].................................. Acta Univ Upsal Abstr Upps Diss Fac Sci

Acta Universitatis Upsaliensis. Historia Litterarum [*A publication*] ... AUUHL

Acta Universitatis Upsaliensis. Studia Anglistica Upsaliensia [*A publication*]..........................AUUSAU

Acta Universitatis Upsaliensis. Studia Germanistica Upsaliensia [*A publication*] .... AUUSGU

Acta Universitatis Upsaliensis. Studia Romanica Upsaliensia [*A publication*].......................... AUUSRU

Acta Universitatis Wratislaviensis [*A publication*]............ Acta Univ Wratislav

Acta Universitatis Wratislaviensis [*A publication*]........................... AUW

Acta Universitatis Wratislaviensis. Matematyka, Fizyka, Astronomia [*A publication*] .... Acta Univ Wratislav Mat Fiz Astron
Acta Urologica Belgica [*A publication*] .... Acta Urol Belg
Acta Urologica Japonica [*A publication*] .... Acta Urol Jpn
Acta Vertebratica [*A publication*] .... Acta Vertebr
Acta Veterinaria. Academiae Scientiarum Hungaricae [*A publication*] .... Acta Vet Acad Sci Hung
Acta Veterinaria. Academiae Scientiarum Hungaricae [*A publication*] .... Act Vet H
Acta Veterinaria (Belgrade) [*A publication*] .... Acta Vet (Belgr)
Acta Veterinaria (Brno) [*A publication*] .... Acta Vet (Brno)
Acta Veterinaria Scandinavica [*A publication*] .... Acta Vet Scand
Acta Veterinaria Scandinavica [*A publication*] .... Act Vet Sc
Acta Veterinaria Scandinavica. Supplementum [*A publication*] .... Acta Vet Scand Suppl
Acta Veterinaria et Zootechnica Sinica [*A publication*] .... Acta Vet Zootech Sin
Acta Virologica [*English Edition*] [*A publication*] .... Act Virolog
Acta Virologica (Prague) [*A publication*] .... Acta Virol (Prague)
Acta Virologica (Prague) (English Edition) [*A publication*] .... Acta Virol (Prague) (Engl Ed)
Acta Virologica (Praha) [*A publication*] .... Acta Virol (Praha)
Acta Vitaminologica [*A publication*] .... Acta Vitaminol
Acta Vitaminologica et Enzymologica [*Milano*] [*A publication*] .... Acta Vitaminol Enzymol
Acta Vitaminologica et Enzymologica [*Milano*] [*A publication*] .... Act Vit Enz
Acta Vitaminologica et Enzymologica (Milano) [*A publication*] .... Acta Vitaminol Enzymol (Milano)
Acta Zoologica. Academiae Scientiarum Hungaricae [*A publication*] .... Acta Zool Acad Sci Hung
Acta Zoologica. Academiae Scientiarum Hungaricae [*A publication*] .... Act Zool H
Acta Zoologica Colombiana [*A publication*] .... Acta Zool Colomb
Acta Zoologica Cracoviensia [*A publication*] .... Acta Zool Cracov
Acta Zoologica Cracoviensia (English Translation) [*A publication*] .... Acta Zool Cracov (Engl Transl)
Acta Zoologica Fennica [*A publication*] .... Acta Zool Fenn
Acta Zoologica Lilloana [*A publication*] .... Acta Zool Lilloana
Acta Zoologica Mexicana [*A publication*] .... Acta Zool Mex
Acta Zoologica et Pathologica Antverpiensia [*A publication*] .... Acta Zool Pathol Antverp
Acta Zoologica et Pathologica Antverpiensia [*A publication*] .... Acta Zool Pathol Antverpiensia
Acta Zoologica Sinica [*A publication*] .... Acta Zool Sin
Acta Zoologica (Stockholm) [*A publication*] .... Acta Zool (Stockh)
Actas del Coloquio Internacional de Estudos Luso-Brasileiros [*A publication*] .... ACELB
Actas del Congresso Internacional de Americanistas [*A publication*] .... ACIAm
Actas do Congresso da Uniao Fitopatologica Mediterranea [*A publication*] .... Actas Congr Uniao Fitopatol Mediterr
Actas Dermosifiliograficas [*A publication*] .... Actas Dermosifiliogr
Actas Jornadas Forestales [*A publication*] .... Actas Jornadas For
Actas Luso-Espanolas de Neurologia, Psiquiatria, y Ciencias Afines [*A publication*] .... Actas Luso-Esp Neurol Psiquiatr
Actas Luso-Espanolas de Neurologia, Psiquiatria, y Ciencias Afines [*A publication*] .... Actas-Luso Esp Neurol Psiquiatr Cienc Afines
Actas y Memorias del Congreso International de Linguistica Romanica [*A publication*] .... AMCILR
Actas de la Primera Reunion de Toponimia Pirenaica [*A publication*] .... ATopPir
Actas Reunion Argentina de la Ciencia del Suelo [*A publication*] .... Actas Reun Argent Cienc Suelo
Actas Urologicas Espanolas [*A publication*] .... Actas Urol Esp
Actes du Colloque International [*A publication*] .... Actes Colloq Int
Actes du Congres de la Federation International des Association d'Etudes Classiques [*A publication*] .... ACEC
Actes Congres International d'Histoire des Sciences [*A publication*] .... Actes Congr Int Hist Sci
Actes du Congres International des Orientalistes [*A publication*] .... ACO
Actes du Congres International des Sciences Anthropologiques et Ethnologiques [*A publication*] .... ACAE
Actes. Congresso International de Linguistique Romanico [*A publication*] .... ACILR
Actes et Memoires du Congres International de Langue et Litterature du Midi de la France [*A publication*] .... AMCIM
Actes et Memoires du Congres International des Sciences Onomastiques [*A publication*] .... AMCISO
Actes et Memoires du Congres International de Toponymie [*A publication*] .... AMCIT
Actes de la Recherche en Sciences Sociales [*A publication*] .... Actes Rech Sci Soc
Actes de la Societe Helvetique des Sciences Naturelles. Parte Scientifique [*A publication*] .... Actes Soc Helv Sci Nat Parte Sci
Acting .... A
Acting .... ACT
Acting .... ACTG
Acting Air-Marshal [*British*] .... AAM
Acting Appointment .... AA
Acting Assistant Quartermaster [*Marine Corps*] .... AAQM
Acting Lieutenant [*Navy*] [*British*] .... A/L
Acting Pay Clerk [*Navy*] .... ACTPC
Acting Paymaster Sub-Lieutenant [*Navy*] [*British*] .... APSL
Acting Pilot Officer [*British*] .... APO
Acting Secretary of the Navy .... ACTSECNAV
Acting Sub-Lieutenant [*Navy*] [*British*] .... ASL
Acting Transportation Officer .... ATRO
Acting Wing-Commander [*British*] .... AWC
Actinides and Lanthanides. Reviews [*A publication*] .... Actinides Lanthanides Rev
Actinides Reviews [*A publication*] .... Actinides Rev
Actinium [*Chemical element*] .... Ac
Actinomycin [*Also, act*] [*Antibiotic compound*] .... A
Actinomycin [*Also, A*] [*Generic form*] [*Antibiotic compounds*] .... act
Actinomycin-C [*Antineoplastic drug*] .... act-C
Actinomycin-D [*Also, AMD, DACT*] [*Antineoplastic drug*] .... act-D
Actinomycin D [*Also, act-D, DACT*] [*Antineoplastic drug*] .... AMD
Actinomycin D, Dacarbazine, Vincristine [*Antineoplastic drug regimen*] .... ADV
Action .... A
Action .... ACTN
Action Against Burns [*Formerly, APBIC*] .... AAB
Action Air Carriers, Inc. [*Scottsdale, AZ*] [*FAA designator*] .... AAC
Action for Brain-Handicapped Children [*An association*] [*Defunct*] .... ABC
Action Change Card .... ACC
Action for Child Transportation Safety [*Defunct*] .... ACTS
Action for Children in Trouble .... ACT
Action for Children's Television .... ACT
Action Committee Against Narcotics .... ACAN
Action Committee on American-Arab Relations [*Later, AARC*] .... ACAAR
Action Committee for Higher Education .... ACHE
Action Committee for Narcotics Education and Enforcement .... ACNEE
Action Control Number [*Army*] .... ACN
ACTION Cooperative Volunteer Program .... ACV
Action Coordinating Committee to End Segregation in the Suburbs .... ACCESS
Action Coordinating Council for Comprehensive Child Care .... ACC-CCC
Action Council of Regional Dissemination Directors .... ACORDD
Action Cut-Out .... ACO
Action Data Automation .... ADA
Action Data Weapons System .... ADAWS
Action for Development [*FAO*] [*United Nations*] .... AD
Action for Former Military Wives [*An association*] .... AFMW
Action Group [*Nigeria*] .... AG
Action for Independent Maturity [*American Association of Retired Persons program*] .... AIM
Action for Industrial Recycling [*An association*] .... AIR
Action Industries, Inc. [*American Stock Exchange symbol*] .... ACX
Action Information Control Officer [*Navy*] .... AICO
Action Information Display System .... AIDS
Action Information Organization .... AIO
Action Information Training Center .... AITC
Action for Interracial Understanding [*Defunct*] .... AIU
Action Item .... AI
Action Item Directive .... AID
Action Item Report .... AIR
Action Item Tracking System [*Radiation measurement*] .... AITS
Action [*Indicator*] **Level** [*Radiation measurement*] .... AL
Action Library, Washington, DC [*OCLC symbol*] .... ACT
Action for Life .... AL
Action Nationale [*A publication*] .... ActN
Action Nationale [*A publication*] .... Act Nat
Action for Nuclear Disarmament Education Fund .... ANDEF
Action Officer [*Army*] .... ACTO
Action Officer [*Air Force*] .... AO
Action Potential [*of auditory nerve*] .... AP
Action Potential Duration [*Electrophysiology*] .... APD
Action for Prevention of Burn Injuries to Children [*Later, AAB*] .... APBIC
Action Program for Women .... APW
Action Register .... AR
Action pour la Renaissance de la Corse [*Corsica*] .... ARC
Action Research Model [*Program of Keep America Beautiful, Inc.*] .... ARM
Action on Smoking and Health [*Antismoking organization*] .... ASH
Action Sociale Tchadienne [*Chadian Social Action*] .... AST
Action Socialiste [*Socialist Action*] [*Congo*] .... AS
Action Socialiste Congolaise [*Congolese Socialist Action*] .... ASC
Action Speed Tactical .... AST
Action Sports Entertainment Cable [*Cable TV programing service*] .... ASEC
Action-Study Center for a Governed World [*Defunct*] .... ASCGW
Action Surveys, Incorporated [*Information service*] .... ASI
Action Taken .... AT
Action Technical Order .... ATO
Action Time [*Air Force*] .... A/T
Action Training Coalition [*Defunct*] .... ATC
Action Will Be Cancelled .... ACWCN
Actions per Time Interval .... APTI
Activate .... ACTV
Activate .... ACTVT
Activate IFR [*Instrument Flight Rules*] **Flight Plan** [*Aviation*] .... AIFP
Activate Test Article .... ACTA
Activate VFR [*Visual Flight Rules*] **Flight Plan** [*Aviation*] .... AVFP
Activated Partial Thromboplastin Time [*Hematology*] .... APTT

Activated Sludge Process ... ASP
Activated Thymus Cell [*s*] [*Immunochemistry*] ... ATC
Activating Factor [*Biochemistry*] ... AF
Activation ... ACT
Activation ... ACTIV
Activation Analysis ... AA
Activation Analysis Unit [*British*] ... AAU
Activation Coefficient ... AC
Activation Engineering Information Bulletin ... AEIB
Activation Project Control Plan ... APCP
Activation Test Program ... ATP
Activation Work Notice ... AWN
Activation Working Group ... AWG
Activator [*Genetics*] ... AC
Activator ... ACTVTR
Active ... A
Active ... ACT
Active Acoustic Device ... AAD
Active Air Defence [*British*] [*World War II*] ... AA
Active Air Target Fuse ... AATF
Active Arm External Load Stabilization System [*Army*] ... AAELSS
Active Army ... AA
Active Army Locator System ... AALS
Active Assistive Exercise [*Medicine*] ... AAE
Active Business Records [*Bell & Howell Co.*] ... ABR
Active Cavity Radiometer ... ACR
Active Cavity Radiometer Irradiance Monitor ... ACRIM
Active Certificate Information Program [*for stock certificates*] [*Data processing*] ... ACIP
Active Citizenship Campaign ... ACC
Active Cleaning Technique [*Optical surface*] ... ACT
Active Commission Base Date [*Military*] ... ACBD
Active Component ... AC
Active Contract File [*DoD*] ... ACF
Active Control Technique [*or Technology*] ... ACT
Active Corps of Executives [*Later, SCORE, ACE*] [*Small Business Administration*] ... ACE
Active Countermeasures ... ACM
Active Disk Table [*Data processing*] ... ADT
Active Dosimeter ... AD
Active Duty ... ACDU
Active Duty ... AD
Active Duty Agreement ... ADA
Active Duty Assistance Program Team ... ADAPT
Active Duty Base Date [*Later, PSD*] [*Navy*] ... ADBD
Active Duty Commitment ... ADC
Active Duty in a Flying Status, Operational and Training Flights [*Navy*] ... ACDIFOT
Active Duty in a Flying Status, Operational and Training Flights as Crewmember [*Navy*] ... ACDIFOTCREW
Active Duty in a Flying Status, Operational and Training Flights as Noncrewmember [*Navy*] ... ACDIFOTNONCREW
Active Duty under Instruction [*Navy*] ... ACDUINS
Active Duty under Instruction in a Flying Status, Operational and Training Flights [*Navy*] ... ACDIFOTINS
Active Duty under Instruction in a Flying Status, Operational and Training Flights as Crewmember [*Navy*] ... ACDIFOTINSCREW
Active Duty under Instruction in a Flying Status, Operational and Training Flights as Noncrewmember [*Navy*] ... ACDIFOTINSNONCREW
Active Duty Nondisability Retirement Branch [*BUPERS*] [*Navy*] ... ANDRB
Active Duty Obligation [*DoD*] ... ACDUOBLI
Active Duty Service Commitment [*Military*] ... ADSC
Active Duty for Training [*Army*] ... ADT
Active Electronic Gimballess Inertial System ... AEGIS
Active Element Array ... AEA
Active Element Group [*QCR*] ... AEG
Active Enlisted Plans Branch [*BUPERS*] ... AEPB
Active Federal Commissioned Service ... AFCS
Active File Table [*Data processing*] ... AFT
Active Filter Network ... AFN
Active Fuzing System ... AFS
Active Galactic Nucleus [*Astronomy*] ... AGN
Active Guard Reserve [*DoD*] ... AGR
Active High Resolution ... AHR
Active History File [*Army*] ... AHF
Active Hostility Index [*Psychology*] ... AHI
Active - In Commission [*Vessel status*] ... ACT/IC
Active - In Service [*Vessel status*] ... ACT/IS
Active Inert Missile ... AIM
Active Ingredient ... AI
Active Integral Defense ... AID
Active Integrated Module ... AIM
Active Isolation/Balance System [*for aircraft*] ... AIBS
Active LASER Seeker ... ALS
Active Lift Distribution Control System [*Aerospace*] ... ALDCS
Active Low-Light-Level Television [*Night vision device*] [*Air Force*] ... ALLTV
Active Magnetospheric Particle Tracer Explorer [*Project*] [*NASA/West Germany*] ... AMPTE
Active Maintenance Downtime ... AMDT
Active Maintenance Time ... AMT
Active Medium Propagation [*Amplifier*] ... AMP
Active Microwave Workshop ... AMW
Active Network Synthesis ... ANS
Active Night Covert Viewing System ... ANCOVS
Active Nutation Control ... ANC
Active Nutation Damper ... AND
Active Nutation Damper Electronics ... ANDE
Active Officer Promotion Branch [*BUPERS*] ... AOPB
Active Optical Fuze ... AOF
Active Optical Fuzing System ... AOFS
Active Optical Sensor ... AOS
Active Optical Target Detector ... AOTD
Active Optical Target Housing ... AOTH
Active Optics Simulation Program [*NASA*] ... AOSP
Active Optics Simulation System [*NASA*] ... AOSS
Active - Out of Commission [*Vessel status*] ... ACT/OC
Active - Out of Service [*Vessel status*] ... ACT/OS
Active Oxygen Method [*Food fat stability test*] ... AOM
Active Pulse Compression Network ... APCN
Active Purchase Request File [*DoD*] ... APRF
Active RADAR Seeker ... ARS
Active Range of Motion [*Medicine*] ... AROM
Active Reconnaissance Zone ... ARZ
Active Repeater Satellite [*Air Force*] ... ARS
Active Requisition Control and Status File [*DoD*] ... ARCSF
Active Resistance [*Occupational therapy*] ... AR
Active-Retired Lighthouse Service Employees' Association ... ARLSEA
Active Satellite Attitude Control ... ASAC
Active Scattering Aerosol Spectrometer [*Aerosol measurement device*] ... ASAS
Active Seismic Experiment [*NASA*] ... ASE
Active Service Career for Reserve Officers ... ASCRO
Active Singles Quest [*Technique*] [*In book title*] ... ASQ
Active Sleep [*Physiology*] ... AS
Active SONAR Frequency Analysis and Recording ... ASFAR
Active SONAR Processor ... ASP
Active Swept-Frequency Interferometer RADAR [*RADC*] ... ASFIR
Active Systems (Great Britain) [*A publication*] ... Act Syst (GB)
Active on Target ... AOT
Active Television System ... ATS
Active Thermal Control ... ATC
Active Thermal Control Subsystem ... ATCS
Active Thermal Control System ... ACTCS
Active Thermal Protection for Avionics Crew and Heat-Sensitive Equipment [*Air Force*] ... APACHE
Active Time List [*Data processing*] ... ATL
Active Token Collectors Organization ... ATCO
Active Transfer Command ... ATC
Active Vibration Isolation System ... AVIS
Active Zone ... AZ
Actively Shared Knowledge [*Data processing system*] ... ASK
Actividades Aereas Aragonesas [*ICAO designator*] ... AB
Activision, Inc. [*NASDAQ symbol*] ... AVSN
Activists for Protective Animal Legislation ... A-PAL
Activitas Nervosa Superior [*Praha*] [*A publication*] ... ACNSA
Activitas Nervosa Superior [*Praha*] [*A publication*] ... Activ Nerv
Activitas Nervosa Superior [*Praha*] [*A publication*] ... Act Nerv Super
Activitas Nervosa Superior (Praha) [*A publication*] ... Act Nerv Super (Praha)
Activities Committee on New Directions for ALA [*American Library Association*] ... ACONDA
Activities of Daily Living [*Medicine*] ... ADL
Activities Report [*Shipping*] ... ACTREP
Activity ... A
Activity ... ACT
Activity ... ACTV
Activity ... ACTVTY
Activity ... ACTY
Activity Account ... AA
Activity Address Code [*DoD*] ... AAC
Activity Balance Line Evaluation [*PERT*] ... ABLE
Activity Captain ... AC
Activity Characteristics Sheet [*Agency for International Development*] ... ACS
Activity Code [*DoD*] ... AC
Activity Control Number ... ACN
Activity Data Method ... ADM
Activity Data Sheet ... ADS
Activity Elements ... A/E
Activity Identification Code [*Navy*] ... AIC
Activity Index ... AI
Activity, Interest, and Opinion [*Factor scores*] [*Marketing*] ... AIO
Activity Level Dependent ... ALD
Activity Level Dependent Operations ... ALDO
Activity Level Independent ... ALI
Activity Level Independent Operations ... ALIO
Activity Median Aerodynamic Diameter ... AMAD
Activity Metabolic Rate ... AMR
Activity Operating Schedule ... AOS
Activity Processing Code ... APC
Activity Report ... AR
Activity Scheduling Processor [*NASA*] ... ASP

Activity Scheduling Program [*NASA*] ASP
Activity Time Status Report ATSR
Activity Vector Analysis [*Psychology*] AVA
ActMedia [*NASDAQ symbol*] ACTM
Actomyosin [*Biochemistry*] AM
Acton Corp. [*American Stock Exchange symbol*] ATN
Acton High School, Acton, ON, Canada [*Library symbol*] CaOAcH
Acton, MA [*Radio station call letters*] WHAB
Acton, TX [*Location identifier*] [*FAA*] AQN
Actors' Church Union [*Episcopalian*] ACU
Actor's Conservatory Theater ACT
Actors' Equity Association AEA
Actors' Fund of America AFA
Actors and Others for Animals [*An association*] A & O
Actors Studio AS
Actors Working for an Actors Guild AWAG
Actron Microprocessor Softwear Support System AMSSS
Actual ACT
Actual ACTL
Actual Block Processor [*Data processing*] ABP
Actual Cash Value ACV
Actual Completion Date of Activity [*Business and trade*] AA
Actual Cost [*Business and trade*] AC
Actual Cost Incurred ACI
Actual Cost Report ACR
Actual Cost of Work Flow ACWF
Actual Cost for Work Performed ACWP
Actual Departure Time ADT
Actual Development Cost Certification [*HUD*] ADCC
Actual Elapsed Time AET
Actual Evapotranspiration [*Biology*] AET
Actual Expenses Allowable [*Military*] AEA
Actual Exposure Time AET
Actual Gross Weight [*Railroads*] AGW
Actual Ground Zero [*Nuclear explosions*] AGZ
Actual Ground Zone AGZ
Actual Loss Ratio [*Insurance*] ALR
Actual Loss Sustained - No Specified Daily Indemnity [*Insurance*] ALS-NSDI
Actual Measurement Weight [*Railroads*] AMW
Actual Operating Time AOT
Actual Ship Position ASP
Actual Specifying Engineer [*A publication*] Actual Specif Eng
Actual Test Number [*NASA*] ATN
Actual Time of Arrival ATA
Actual Time of Departure ATD
Actual Time of Fall ATF
Actual Time of Interception ATI
Actual Time of Penetration [*Aviation*] ATP
Actual Time of Release [*Aviation*] ATRLS
Actual Time of Return to Operation ATRO
Actual Time over Target ATOT
Actual Total Loss ATL
Actual Unit Price AUP
Actual Value AV
Actual Weight [*Business and trade*] AW
Actual Weight Report AWR
Actual Wind Factor [*Meteorology*] ALWF
Actual Work Time [*Bell System*] AWT
Actualidades Biologicas [*A publication*] Actual Biol
Actualite Chimique [*A publication*] Actual Chim
Actualite en Chine Populaire [*A publication*] Actual Chine Popul
Actualite Economique [*A publication*] Act Ec
Actualite Economique [*A publication*] Actu Econ
Actualite de la Formation Permanente [*A publication*] Actual Formation Perm
Actualite Juridique [*A publication*] Actual Jur
Actualites Biochimiques [*A publication*] Actual Biochim
Actualites Endocrinologiques (Paris) [*A publication*] Actual Endocrinol (Paris)
Actualites de l'Hotel-Dieu [*A publication*] Actual Hotel-Dieu
Actualites Industrielles Lorraines [*A publication*] Actual Industr Lorraines
Actualites Marines [*A publication*] Actual Mar
Actualites Neurophysiologiques [*Paris*] [*A publication*] Actual Neurophysiol
Actualites Neurophysiologiques (Paris) [*A publication*] Actual Neurophysiol (Paris)
Actualites Odontostomatologiques [*Paris*] [*A publication*] Actual Odontostomatol
Actualites Odontostomatologiques (Paris) [*A publication*] Actual Odontostomatol (Paris)
Actualites Pharmacologiques [*A publication*] Actual Pharm
Actualites Pharmacologiques [*A publication*] Actual Pharmacol
Actualites Pharmacologiques (Paris) [*A publication*] Actual Pharmacol (Paris)
Actualites Scientifiques et Industrielles [*A publication*] Actualites Sci Indust
Actuarial Mail File [*IRS*] AMF
Actuarial Note [*A publication*] Actuar Note
Actuarial Society of America [*Later, SA*] ASA
Actuary ACT
Actuate ACT
Actuate ACTE
Actuating ACTG
Actuation Data Communication [*Naval Ordnance Laboratory*] ADC
Actuation Mechanism Subsystem AMS
Actuation Mine Simulator AMS
Actuator ACTR
Actuator/Indicator AI
Actuator Mechanism AM
Actuel Developpement [*A publication*] Actuel Develop
Actuelle Gerontologie [*A publication*] Actuelle Gerontol
Actum ut Supra [*Done as Above*] [*Latin*] AUS
Acupuncture Clinic [*British*] AC
Acupuncture and Electro-Therapeutics Research [*A publication*] Acupunct Electro-Ther Res
Acupuncture International Association AIA
Acupuncture Research Institute ARI
Acustica [*A publication*] ACUSA
Acute A
Acute [*Medicine*] AC
Acute Anxiety Attack [*Medicine*] AAA
Acute Bacterial Endocarditis [*Medicine*] ABE
Acute Bovine Pulmonary Emphysema [*Cattle disease*] ABPE
Acute Brain Syndrome [*Medicine*] ABS
Acute Care Bed Need Methodology [*Hospital management*] ACBNM
Acute Care Facility [*Medicine*] ACF
Acute Disseminated Encephalomyelitis [*Medicine*] ADE
Acute Encephalography and Fatty Degeneration of the Viscera [*Reye's syndrome*] [*Medicine*] AEFDV
Acute Erythroleukemia [*Oncology*] AEL
Acute Febrile Respiratory Illness [*Medicine*] AFRI
Acute Fibrinopurulent Pneumonia [*Medicine*] AFPP
Acute Fibrinoserous Pneumonia [*Medicine*] AFSP
Acute Glomerulonephritis [*Medicine*] AGN
Acute Heart Failure [*Medicine*] AHF
Acute Herpetic Gingival Stomatitis [*Dentistry*] AHGS
Acute Infectious Disease [*Medicine*] AID
Acute Intermittent Porphyria [*Medicine*] AIP
Acute Laryngotracheobronchitis [*Virus*] ALTB
Acute Launch Emergency Reliability Tip [*NASA*] ALERT
Acute Leukemia [*Medicine*] AL
Acute Lymphatic [*or Lymphoblastic or Lymphocytic*] **Leukemia** [*Medicine*] ALL
Acute Mesenteric Ischemia [*Medicine*] AMI
Acute Mesenteric Venous Thrombosis [*Medicine*] AMVT
Acute Monoblastic Leukemia [*Also, AMoL*] [*Medicine*] AMonoL
Acute Monocytic Leukemia [*Also, AMonoL*] [*Medicine*] AMoL
Acute Mountain Sickness AMS
Acute Myeloid [*or Myeloblastic or Myelocytic or Myelogenic*] **Leukemia** [*Medicine*] AML
Acute Myelomonoblastic Leukemia [*Medicine*] AMMOL
Acute Myelomonocytic Leukemia [*Medicine*] AMML
Acute Myocardial Infarction [*Medicine*] AMI
Acute Necrotizing Ulcerative Gingivitis [*Dentistry*] ANUG
Acute Nonlymphoblastic Leukemia [*Medicine*] ANL
Acute Nonlymphocytic Leukemia [*Medicine*] ANLL
Acute Pharyngo-Conjunctival Fever [*Medicine*] APCF
Acute Posterior Multifocal Placoid Pigment Epitheliopathy [*Ophthalmology*] APMPPE
Acute Progranulocytic [*or Promyelocytic*] **Leukemia** [*Hematology*] APL
Acute Respiratory Disease [*Medicine*] ARD
Acute Respiratory System Malfunction [*Medicine*] ARSM
Acute Respiratory Tract Illness ARTI
Acute Rheumatic Fever [*Medicine*] ARF
Acute Subdural Hematoma [*Medicine*] ASDH
Acute Transient Radiation Myelopathy [*Oncology*] ATRM
Acute Tubular Necrosis [*Nephrology*] ATN
Acute Undifferentiated Leukemia [*Hematology*] AUL
Acycloguanosine [*Also, ACV, Acyclovir*] [*Antiviral compound*] ACG
Acyclovir [*Also, ACG, Acycloguanosine*] [*Antiviral compound*] ACV
Acyl Carrier Protein [*Biochemistry*] ACP
Acyl Group Ac
Acylated Octapeptide [*Biochemistry*] A-OP
Acylcholine Acyl-Hydrolase [*Same as PCE*] [*An enzyme*] ACAH
Ad Defectionem Animi [*To the Point of Fainting*] [*Pharmacy*] AD DEF AN
Ad Effectum [*Until Effectual*] [*Pharmacy*] AD EFFECT
Ad Eundem Gradum [*To the Same Degree*] [*Of the admission of a graduate of one university to the same degree at another without examination*] AD EUND
Ad Eundem Gradum [*To the Same Degree*] [*Of the admission of a graduate of one university to the same degree at another without examination*] AEG
Ad Finem [*At or To the End*] [*Latin*] AD FIN
Ad Finem [*At or To the End*] [*Latin*] AF
Ad Gratum Aciditatem [*To an Agreeable Sourness*] [*Pharmacy*] AD GR ACID
Ad Gratum Gustum [*To an Agreeable Taste*] [*Pharmacy*] AD GR GUST
Ad Hanc Vocem [*At This Word*] [*Latin*] AHV
Ad Hoc Advisory Group on Science Programs [*Terminated, 1976*] [*National Science Foundation*] AGOSP
Ad Hoc Committee for American Silver AHCAS

Ad Hoc Committee on the Baltic States and the Ukraine ... AHCBSU
Ad Hoc Committee for Competitive Telecommunications ... ACCT
Ad Hoc Committee on Copyright Law ... AHCCL
Ad Hoc Committee on Equipment Interoperability [*NATO*] ... AHCEI
Ad Hoc Committee on Freedom of Scholarly Inquiry [*International Sociological Association*] ... AHCFSI
Ad Hoc Committee for Lebanese Freedom ... AHCLF
Ad Hoc Congressional Committee for Irish Affairs ... AHCCIA
Ad Hoc Crypto-Coordination Agency ... ACCA
Ad Hoc Group on US Policy toward the UN ... AHGUSPTUN
Ad Hoc Requirements Committee [*Later, COMOR*] ... ARC
Ad Hoc Working Group [*Army*] ... AHWG
Ad Hunc Locum [*To This Place*] [*Latin*] ... AD H L
Ad Hunc Locum [*At This Place*] [*Latin*] ... AHL
Ad Infinitum [*To Infinity*] [*Latin*] ... AD INF
Ad Initium [*At the Beginning*] [*Latin*] ... AD INIT
Ad Interim [*In the Meantime*] [*Latin*] ... AD INT
Ad Interim [*In the Meantime*] [*Latin*] ... AI
Ad Interim Specification [*Navy*] ... INT
Ad Jesum per Mariam [*To Jesus through Mary*] [*Latin*] ... AJPM
Ad Libitum [*At Pleasure, As Desired*] [*Latin*] ... AD LIB
Ad Locum [*To, or At, the Place*] [*Latin*] ... AD LOC
Ad Majorem Dei Gloriam [*To the Greater Glory of God*] [*Latin*] ... AMDG
Ad Manus Medici [*To Be Delivered into the Hands of the Physician*] [*Pharmacy*] ... AD MAN MED
Ad Nauseum [*To the Extent of Producing Nausea*] [*Latin*] ... AD NAUS
Ad Neutralizandum [*To Neutralization*] [*Pharmacy*] ... AD NEUT
Ad Pondus Omnium [*To the Weight of the Whole*] [*Pharmacy*] ... AD POND OM
Ad-Print, Belleville, NJ [*Library symbol*] ... NjBeA
Ad Saturandum [*To Saturation*] [*Pharmacy*] ... AD SAT
Ad Saturandum [*To Saturation*] [*Pharmacy*] ... AD SATUR
Ad Sectam [*At the Suit Of*] [*Latin*] ... ADS
Ad Tertiam Vicem [*Three Times*] [*Pharmacy*] ... AD TERT VIC
Ad Usum [*According to Custom*] [*Latin*] ... AD US
Ad Usum [*According to Custom*] [*Latin*] ... AU
Ad Usum Externum [*For External Use*] [*Pharmacy*] ... AD US EXTER
Ad Valorem [*According to the Value*] [*Latin*] ... AD VAL
Ad Valorem [*According to the Value*] [*Latin*] ... AV
Ad Valorem [*According to the Value*] **Equivalent** ... AVE
Ada Joint Program Office [*Data processing*] ... AJPO
Ada, OK [*Location identifier*] [*FAA*] ... ADH
Ada, OK [*Radio station call letters*] ... KADA
Ada, OK [*Radio station call letters*] ... KTEN
Ada, OK [*Television station call letters*] ... KTEN
Ada Programing Support Environments [*Data processing*] ... APSE
Ada Public Library, Ada, OK [*Library symbol*] ... OkAd
Adabietsunaslik va Tilsunaslik Masalalari/Voprosy Literaturovedenija i Jazykoznanija (Taskent) [*A publication*] ... ATMTas
ADAC Laboratories [*NASDAQ symbol*] ... ADAC
Adagdak [*Alaska*] [*Seismograph station code, US Geological Survey*] ... AD8
Adage Graphics Terminal ... AGT
Adage, Inc. [*NASDAQ symbol*] ... ADGE
Adagio [*Slow*] [*Music*] ... ADAG
Adagio [*Slow*] [*Music*] ... ADGO
Adagio [*Slow*] [*Music*] ... ADO
Adair-Koshland-Nemethy-Filmer [*Enzyme model*] ... AKNF
Adair News, Adair, IA [*Library symbol*] ... IaAdN
Adak [*Island*] [*Alaska*] [*Seismograph station code, US Geological Survey*] [*Closed*] ... ADA
Adak, AK [*Location identifier*] [*FAA*] ... NUD
Adak Island [*Alaska*] [*Airport symbol*] ... ADK
Adak Island [*Alaska*] [*Seismograph station code, US Geological Survey*] ... ADK
Adalbert Stifter Institut des Landes Oberoesterreich: Vierteljahresschrift [*A publication*] ... ASILO
ADAM [*Arts, Drama, Architecture, Music*] **International Review** [*A publication*] ... ADAM Int R
ADAM [*Arts, Drama, Architecture, Music*] **International Review** [*A publication*] ... AIR
Adam Walsh Child Resource Center ... AWCRC
Adams [*New York*] [*Seismograph station code, US Geological Survey*] [*Closed*] ... ADN
Adams County Juvenile Detention Center, Brighton, CO [*Library symbol*] ... CoBriJ
Adams County Public Library, Bennett, CO [*Library symbol*] ... CoBen
Adams County Public Library, Brighton, CO [*Library symbol*] ... CoBri
Adams County Public Library, Northglenn, CO [*Library symbol*] ... CoNgA
Adams County School District No. 12, Northglenn, CO [*OCLC symbol*]. DVA
Adams Drug Co. [*NYSE symbol*] ... ADG
Adams Express Co. [*NYSE symbol*] ... ADX
Adams Library (Chelmsford Public Library), Chelmsford, MA [*Library symbol*] ... MChelm
Adams, MA [*Television station call letters*] ... WCDC
Adams Mansion, Quincy, MA [*Library symbol*] ... MQA
Adams-Millis Corp. [*NYSE symbol*] ... ALL
Adams National Historic Site ... ADAM
Adams Resources & Energy, Inc. [*American Stock Exchange symbol*] ... AE
Adams-Russell Co., Inc. [*American Stock Exchange symbol*] ... AAR
Adams State College [*Colorado*] ... ASC
Adams State College, Alamosa, CO [*Library symbol*] ... CoAlC
Adamsville, TN [*Radio station call letters*] ... WPJM
Adana [*Turkey*] [*Airport symbol*] ... ADA
Adapt ... AD
Adaptable Data Base System ... ADABAS
Adaptable Surface Interface Terminal ... ASIT
Adaptable Terminal Interface Configuration [*Military*] ... ATIC
Adaptation ... ADAPT
Adaptation Level ... AL
Adaptation Mathematical Processor ... AMP
Adaptation Of [*Etymology*] ... AD
Adapted Identification Decision Equipment ... AIDE
Adapted Swimming-Pool Tank Reactor, Austria ... ASTRA
Adapter ... ADPT
Adapter ... ADPTR
Adapter, Binding Post ... ABP
Adapter Booster ... AB
Adapter, Bulkhead ... AB
Adapter Cable ... AC
Adapter Control Block [*Data processing*] ... ACB
Adapter Panel ... AP
Adapter, Right Angle ... ARA
Adapter Section [*NASA*] ... AS
Adapter, Straight ... AS
Adapter Subunit Tester ... ASUT
Adapter, Tee ... AT
Adapter Unit ... ADU
Adaption of Automatically Programed Tools [*Data processing*] ... ADAPT
Adaption Binary Load [*Program*] ... ABL
Adaption Error Note ... AEN
Adaption Kit ... AK
Adaptive Angle Bias ... AAB
Adaptive Arithmetical Method ... ADAM
Adaptive Beam Forming ... ABF
Adaptive Behavior [*Psychology*] ... AB
Adaptive Behavior Inventory for Children [*Psychology*] ... ABIC
Adaptive Behavior Scale [*Psychology*] ... ABS
Adaptive Control Process ... ACP
Adaptive Control System ... ACS
Adaptive Delta Modulation [*Electronics*] ... ADM
Adaptive Delta Voice Modulation [*Air Force*] ... ADVM
Adaptive Differential Pulse Code Modulation ... ADPCM
Adaptive Dynamic Decision-Aiding Method ... ADDAM
Adaptive Echo Cancellation [*Navy*] ... AEC
Adaptive Flight Control System ... AFCS
Adaptive Flight Training System ... AFTS
Adaptive Ground-Implemented Phased Array [*NASA*] ... AGIPA
Adaptive Injection Molding [*Engineering*] ... AIM
Adaptive Intercommunication Requirement ... AIR
Adaptive Iterated Extended Kalman Filtering ... AIEKF
Adaptive Learning Network [*Data processing*] ... ALN
Adaptive Linear Classifier ... ADALINE
Adaptive Linear Neuron [*Medicine*] ... ADALINE
Adaptive Long-Range Infrared Tracker ... ALIRT
Adaptive Man-Machine Nonarithmetic Information Processing [*Documentation*] ... AMNIP
Adaptive Mathematical Model ... AMM
Adaptive Microwave Proximity [*Military*] ... AMP
Adaptive Mission-Oriented Software System ... AMOSS
Adaptive Mobile Torpedo Decoy ... AMTD
Adaptive Mode Planning System [*Computer program*] ... AMPS
Adaptive Mode Planning System Input [*Computer program*] ... AMPSIN
Adaptive Multibeam Experiment for Aeronautical and Maritime Services ... AMEAMS
Adaptive Multibeam Phased Array [*RADAR*] ... AMPA
Adaptive Null Antenna ... ANA
Adaptive Pattern Perceiving Electronic Computer System ... APPECS
Adaptive Phase Array RADAR ... APAR
Adaptive Planning and Control Sequence [*Marketing*] ... APACS
Adaptive Side-Lobe Canceller [*RADAR*] ... ASLC
Adaptive Surface-Signal Recognition and Direction Indicator [*Navy*] ... ASRADI
Adaptive Video Processor ... AVP
Adaptive Wafer Scale Integration ... AWSI
Adaptive Waveform Recognition ... AWR
Adaptivnye Sistemy Avtomaticeskogo Upravlenija [*A publication*] ... Adapt Sistemy Avtomat Upravlenija
Adaptor ... ADAP
Adas Israel Congregation, Washington, DC [*Library symbol*] ... DAdI
ADAS [*Agricultural Development and Advisory Service*] **Quarterly Review** [*A publication*] ... ADAS Q Rev
Add with Carry ... ADC
Add, Initial, Multiprecision ... AIM
Add, Multiprecision ... AMP
Add-On Stabilization ... AOS
Add Packed [*Data processing*] ... AP
Add or Subtract ... AOS
Add-Subtract ... AS
Add-Subtract Time ... AST
Adde [*Add or Up To*] [*Pharmacy*] ... AD
Adde [*Add or Up To*] [*Pharmacy*] ... ADD
Adde cum Tritu [*Add Trituration*] [*Pharmacy*] ... ADD c TRIT

Added Entry .... AE
Addendum .... AD
Addendum .... ADD
Addendum to Monthly Collection [*IRS*] .... ADDM
Addendus [*To Be Added*] [*Pharmacy*] .... ADDEND
Adder .... ADDR
Adder .... ADR
Adder, Logical, and Transfer Unit [*Computer*] .... ALTU
Addict [*Drug*] [*Slang*] .... AD
Addict Rehabilitation Counselor .... ARC
Addiction Research Center [*National Institute of Mental Health*] .... ARC
Addiction Research Center Inventory [*Psychology*] .... ARCI
Addiction Research and Treatment Corporation .... ARTC
Addiction Workers Alerted to Rehabilitation and Education [*New York City*] .... AWARE
Addictive Behaviors [*A publication*] .... Addict Behav
Addictive Diseases [*A publication*] .... Addict Dis
Addicts Anonymous .... AA
Addis Ababa [*Ethiopia*] [*Airport symbol*] .... ADD
Addis Ababa [*Ethiopia*] [*Geomagnetic observatory code*] .... AAE
Addis Ababa [*Ethiopia*] [*Seismograph station code, US Geological Survey*] .... AAE
Addison, TX [*Location identifier*] [*FAA*] .... TBQ
Addison Wesley Publishers [*NASDAQ symbol*] .... ADSNB
Addition .... ADD
Addition .... ADDN
Addition Nucleophile Ring Opening Ring Closure [*Organic chemistry*] .... ANRORC
Addition, Subtraction, Timing, and Ratio .... ASTR
Additional .... ADDL
Additional .... ADDNL
Additional Air Force Specialty Code .... AAFSC
Additional Authorization List [*Army*] .... AAL
Additional Benefits [*Unemployment insurance*] .... AB
Additional Billet Requirements [*Military*] .... ABR
Additional Crew Member [*Military*] .... ACM
Additional Duty .... ADDU
Additional Duty .... ADY
Additional Expediting Expense [*Insurance*] .... AEE
Additional Extended Coverage [*Insurance*] .... AEC
Additional Fiscal Year Money Is Authorized by the Secretary of the Army .... AFYMOSAP
Additional Flight Training Period .... AFTP
Additional Living Expense [*Insurance*] .... ALE
Additional Military Production .... AMP
Additional Mobile SAM [*Surface-to-Air Missile*] **Site** .... AMOSS
Additional Personal Injury Protection [*Insurance*] .... APIP
Additional Places .... ADDPLA
Additional Premium [*Insurance*] .... AP
Additional Qualification Designator .... AQD
Additional Reference Number .... ARN
Additional Selection Factor .... ASF
Additional Skill Identifier [*Military*] .... ASI
Additional Sources .... AS
Additional Training Assemblies .... ATA
Additional Uniform Allowance [*Military*] .... ADDUNIFALW
Additional Voluntary Contribution [*Employee's wage contribution toward a company pension plan*] .... AVC
Additionally Awarded Military Occupational Specialty .... AMOS
Additive .... ADDT
Additive Color Process .... ACP
Additive Color Viewer Printer .... ACVP
Additive Gaussian Noise .... AGN
Additive Noise Linear Sequential Circuit .... ANLSC
Additives and Containments Committee [*British*] .... ACC
Addmaster Corporation [*NASDAQ symbol*] .... ADDC
Address .... A
Address .... ADD
Address .... ADDR
Address .... ADR
Address .... ADRS
Address .... ADS
Address [*Message handling*] .... ADS
Address Coding [*Business and trade*] .... AC
Address Coding Guide .... ACG
Address Constant [*Data processing*] .... ADCON
Address Control Unit [*Data processing*] .... ACU
Address Data Strobe [*Electronics*] .... ADS
Address to Index, True .... AXT
Address Indicating Group [*Data processing*] .... AIG
Address Latch Enable [*Data processing*] .... ALE
Address Locator Logic .... ALL
Address Plate Cabinet .... APC
Address Register .... ADR
Address-Selective [*British*] .... ADSEL
Address Space Identifier .... ASID
Address Verification Pulse .... AVP
Addressable Remote Multiplexer Unit .... ARMU
Addressee .... ADDEE
Addressee .... ADEE
Addresses .... ADSE
Addresses and Proceedings. Ontario Soil and Crop Improvement Association [*A publication*] .... Address Proc Ontario Soil Crop Impr Ass
Addresses and Proceedings. Saskatchewan University Farm and Home Week [*A publication*] .... Address Proc Saskatchewan Univ Farm Home Week
Addressograph-Multigraph Copier Duplicator .... AMCD
Adduction [*or Adductor*] [*Medicine*] .... ADD
Adductor Longus [*Anatomy*] .... AL
Adel, GA [*Radio station call letters*] .... WBIT
Adel, GA [*Radio station call letters*] .... WDDQ
Adelaide [*Mount Bonython*] [*Australia*] [*Seismograph station code, US Geological Survey*] .... ADE
Adelaide [*Australia*] [*Airport symbol*] .... ADL
Adelaide Airways Limited [*Australia*] .... AAL
Adelaide Law Review [*A publication*] .... Adelaide L Rev
Adelphi [*A publication*] .... Ad
Adelphi [*A publication*] .... Adel
Adelphi University, Garden City, NY [*Library symbol*] .... NGcA
Adelphi University, Garden City, NY [*OCLC symbol*] .... VJA
Aden [*People's Democratic Republic of Yemen*] [*Airport symbol*] .... ADE
Aden .... ADN
Aden Airways .... AD
Aden News Agency [*Yemen*] .... ANA
Aden Trade Union Congress .... ATUC
Adenine [*Also, Ade*] [*Biochemistry*] .... A
Adenine [*Also, A*] [*Biochemistry*] .... Ade
Adenine Arabinoside Monophosphate [*Biochemistry*] .... ara-AMP
Adenine Arabinoside Triphosphate [*Biochemistry*] .... ara-ATP
Adenine-D-ribose-phosphate-phosphate-D-ribose-nicotinamide [*Also, NAD, DPN*] [*Biochemistry*] .... ARPPRN
Adenine Phosphoribosyltransferase [*An enzyme*] .... APRT
Adenoid Cystic Carcinoma [*Medicine*] .... ACC
Adenoid Degenerative [*Viruses*] .... AD
Adenoidal-Pharyngeal-Conjunctival [*Virus*] [*Obsolete usage*] .... APC
Adenoma Malignum of the Cervix [*Oncology*] .... AMC
Adenomatosis of the Colon and Rectum [*Medicine*] .... ACR
Adenosine [*One-letter symbol; see Ado*] .... A
Adenosine [*Also, A*] [*A nucleoside*] .... Ado
Adenosine Deaminase [*An enzyme*] .... ADA
Adenosine Diphosphatase [*An enzyme*] .... ADPase
Adenosine Diphosphate [*Biochemistry*] .... ADP
Adenosine Diphosphate Ribosyltransferase [*An enzyme*] .... ADPRT
Adenosine Kinase [*An enzyme*] .... AK
Adenosine Monophosphate [*Biochemistry*] .... AMP
Adenosine Monophosphate Deaminase [*An enzyme*] .... AMPDA
Adenosine Monophosphate Succinate [*Biochemistry*] .... AMPS
Adenosine Phosphate Phosphosulfate [*Also, PAPS*] [*Biochemistry*] .... APPS
Adenosine Phosphoribosyltransferase [*An enzyme*] .... ADPT
Adenosine Phosphosulfate [*Biochemistry*] .... APS
Adenosine Tetraphosphate [*Biochemistry*] .... Atetra P
Adenosine Triphosphatase [*An enzyme*] .... ATPase
Adenosine Triphosphate [*Biochemistry*] .... ATP
Adenosinetriphosphatase (Na, K-Activated) [*An enzyme*] .... Na K-ATPase
Adenosylcobalamin [*Also, DBC*] [*A vitamin*] .... ADOCBL
Adenosylhomocysteine [*Biochemistry*] .... AdoHcy
Adenosylmethionine [*Also, SAM, SAMe*] [*Biochemistry*] .... AdoMet
Adenovirus .... AD
Adenylate Cyclase Inhibitor [*Biochemistry*] .... ACI
Adenylate Kinase [*An enzyme*] .... AK
Adenylic Acid [*Biochemistry*] .... AA
Adequate .... ADQT
Adhaesion [*A publication*] .... Adhaes
Adhere .... ADH
Adhesive .... ADH
Adhesive Bonding Repair .... ABR
Adhesive Film Mechanism .... AFM
Adhesive Insulation Material .... AIM
Adhesive and Sealant Council .... ASC
Adhesively Bonded Joint [*or Junction*] .... ABJ
Adhesives Age [*A publication*] .... Adhes Age
Adhesives Age [*A publication*] .... Adhesives
Adhesives Manufacturers Association [*Formerly, AMAA*] .... AMA
Adhesives Manufacturers Association of America [*Later, AMA*] .... AMAA
Adhibendus [*To Be Used*] [*Pharmacy*] .... ADHIBEND
Adi Dassler [*Founder of German sporting goods company; acronym used as brand name of shoes manufactured by the firm*] .... ADIDAS
ADI Electronics [*NASDAQ symbol*] .... XAID
Adiabatic Film Cooling .... ADFC
Adiabatic Low-Energy Injection and Capture Experiment .... ALICE
Adiabatic Storage Test [*For hazardous chemicals*] .... AST
Adiabatic Toroidal Compressor [*Nuclear energy*] .... ATC
Adipic, Glutaric, and Succinic [*Acids for flue-gas cleaning*] .... AGS
Adiponitrile [*Organic chemistry*] .... ADN
Adirondack [*National Weather Service*] .... ADRNDCK
Adirondack Community College, Glens Falls, NY [*Library symbol*] .... NGlfAC
Adirondack Forty-Sixers .... AFS
Adirondack Historical Association .... AHA

Adirondack Historical Association Museum Library, Blue Mountain Lake, NY [*Library symbol*] ... NBmIA
Adirondack Mountain Club ... ADK
Adirondack Trail Improvement Society ... ATIS
Adirondack World Affairs Resources for Education ... AWARE
ADIS [*Australasian Drug Information Services*] **Drug Information Retrieval System** ... ADIRS
Adjacent ... ADJ
Adjacent ... AJA
Adjacent Channel Attenuation ... ACA
Adjacent Channel Interference ... ACI
Adjacent Channel Rejection ... ACR
Adjective ... A
Adjective ... ADJ
Adjective Check List [*Psychology*] ... ACL
Adjoining ... ADJ
Adjoint Gamma-Ray Moments [*Computer code*] ... ADJMOM
Adjoint Wave Function ... AWF
Adjornator [*British*] ... ADJ
Adjourned ... ADJ
Adjournment in Contemplation of Dismissal [*Law*] ... ACD
Adjournment in Contemplation of Dismissal [*Law*] ... ACOD
Adjunct ... ADJ
Adjunct in Arts ... Adj A
Adjunctive Therapy [*Medicine*] ... AT
Adjustable Pawl Fastener ... APF
Adjustable Pitch Device ... APD
Adjustable Pressure Conveyor ... APC
Adjustable Ranging Telescope [*Army*] ... ART
Adjustable Rate Mortgage ... ARM
Adjustable Shock Absorber ... ASA
Adjustable Speed Drive ... ASD
Adjustable Stroke Kit ... ASK
Adjustable Thermal Wire Stripper ... ATWS
Adjustable Voltage Screwdown ... AVS
Adjustable Wire Stripper ... AWS
Adjustable Zero Adjustable Range ... AZAR
Adjusted Air Speed [*Navigation*] ... AAS
Adjusted Average per Capita Cost ... AAPCC
Adjusted on Basis of Photostat or Reviewed Copy of Temporary Pay Record from Finance Center, United States Army ... ADJFCUSA
Adjusted Gross Income ... AGI
Adjusted Megaton Equivalent ... AMTE
Adjusted Output [*Data processing*] ... AO
Adjusted Sequential Probability Ratio Test [*Statistics*] ... ASPRT
Adjusted Service Rating Score [*Military*] ... ASRS
Adjustment ... ADJ
Adjustment Assistance ... AA
Adjustment-Calibration ... AC
Adjustment File [*IRS*] ... ADJF
Adjustment Inventory [*Psychology*] ... AI
Adjustment Payment Level [*Social Security Administration*] ... APL
Adjutant ... A
Adjutant ... ADJ
Adjutant ... ADJT
Adjutant General ... AG
[*The*] **Adjutant General** [*Army*] ... TAG
[*The*] **Adjutant General Center** [*Army*] ... TAGCEN
Adjutant-General to the Forces [*British*] ... AGF
Adjutant General Management Information System ... AGMIS
Adjutant General Pool [*for Army officers*] ... AGP
Adjutant General Publications Center [*Army*] ... AGPC
Adjutant-General and Quartermaster-General [*British*] ... AG & QMG
Adjutant-General of the Royal Marines [*British*] ... AGRM
Adjutant General, War Department [*Obsolete*] ... AGWAR
[*The*] **Adjutant General's Board, United States Army** ... TAGBDUSA
Adjutant General's Corps ... AGC
Adjutant General's Department [*Army*] ... AGD
Adjutant General's Office [*Army*] ... AGO
[*The*] **Adjutant General's Office** [*Army*] ... TAGO
[*The*] **Adjutant General's Research and Development Command, United States Army** ... TAGRDCUSA
[*The*] **Adjutant General's School** [*United States*], **Army** ... TAGSUSA
Adjutant Inspector General [*Military*] ... AIG
Adjutants General Association of the United States [*Later, AGAUS*] ... AGA
Adjutants General Association of the United States [*Formerly, AGA*] ... AGAUS
Adjuvant Arthritis ... AA
ADL-Nachrichten [*A publication*] ... ADL-Nachr
Adler/Sochi [*USSR*] [*Airport symbol*] ... AER
ADM Industries, Inc. [*American Stock Exchange symbol*] [*Delisted*] ... ADI
ADM Industries, Inc. [*NASDAQ symbol*] ... ADND
ADM (Revista de la Asociacion Dental Mexicana) [*A publication*] ... ADM (Rev Asoc Dent Mex)
Administracion y Desarrollo [*A publication*] ... Adm y Desarr
Administration ... A
Administration ... ADM
Administration ... ADMN
Administration ... ADOM
Administration [*A publication*] ... Admin
Administration [*or Administrator*] ... ADMIN
Administration de Aeropuertos y Servicios Auxiliares a la Nauegacion Aerea [*Bolivian airline*] ... AASANA
Administration de Aeropuertos y Servicios Auxiliares a la Nauegacion Aerea [*AASANA*] [*Bolivia*] [*ICAO designator*] ... XV
Administration on Aging [*HEW*] ... AA
Administration on Aging [*HEW*] ... AOA
Administration de l'Assistance Technique des Nations Unies [*United Nations Technical Assistance Administration*] ... AATNU
Administration Center ... ADMCEN
Administration for Children, Youth, and Families [*Office of Human Development Services*] ... ACYF
Administration for Civil Affairs in Liberated Areas [*World War II*] ... ACALA
Administration by Competency [*Business and trade*] ... ABC
Administration on Developmental Disabilities [*Human Development Services*] ... ADD
Administration Duty Officer ... ADO
Administration Group Office ... AGO
Administration of Justice Branch [*US Military Government, Germany*] ... AJB
Administration and Management Operations [*Kennedy Space Center*] [*NASA*] ... AM
Administration in Mental Health [*A publication*] ... Admin Ment Hlth
Administration in Mental Health [*A publication*] ... Adm Ment He
Administration in Mental Health [*A publication*] ... Adm Ment Health
Administration for Native Americans [*Office of Human Development Services*] ... ANA
Administration by Objectives ... ABO
Administration Office ... AO
Administration du Petrole et du Gaz des Terres du Canada [*Canada Oil and Gas Lands Administration*] ... APGTC
Administration for Public Services [*Office of Human Development Services*] ... APS
Administration, Ryukyu Islands, Army ... ARIA
Administration in Social Work [*A publication*] ... Adm Soc Work
Administration and Society [*A publication*] ... Adm and Soc
Administration and Society [*A publication*] ... Adm Socie
Administration and Storage Building ... ASB
Administration of Territories Committee (Balkans) [*World War II*] ... AT(B)
Administration of Territories Committee (Europe) [*World War II*] ... AT(E)
Administration of Territories Committee (Europe), Shipping and Supply Subcommittee [*World War II*] ... AT(E)SSS
Administrativ Tidsskrift [*A publication*] ... Adm Tss
Administrative ... ADMINV
Administrative ... ADMIV
Administrative and Accounting Purposes ... ADANDAC
Administrative Aircraft [*When a suffix to Navy plane designation*] ... Z
Administrative Aircraft Standardization Office [*NASA*] ... AASO
Administrative Analysis, Information, and Statistics [*Red Cross*] ... AAIS
Administrative Area Control Centre [*Military*] [*British*] ... AACC
Administrative Area Unit [*Army*] ... AAU
Administrative Assistant ... AA
Administrative Assistant to the Secretary of the Army ... AASA
Administrative Board - Dress Industry ... ABDI
Administrative Change [*A publication*] ... Adm Change
Administrative Circular ... ADCIR
Administrative Clerical and Technical Programs [*Department of Labor*] ... ACT
Administrative Command ... ADCOM
Administrative Command, Amphibious Forces, Pacific Fleet ... ADCOMPHIBSPAC
Administrative Command, Amphibious Forces, Pacific Fleet, Subordinate Command ... ADCOMSUBORDCOMPHIBSPAC
Administrative Command, Minecraft, Pacific Fleet ... ADCOMINPAC
Administrative Commitment Document ... ACD
Administrative Committee on Administration [*UN*] ... ACA
Administrative Committee on Coordination [*of the United Nations*] [*Aviation*] ... ACC
Administrative Communications Distribution Center [*Air Force*] ... ACDC
Administrative Computing Service ... ACS
Administrative Conference of the United States [*A federal government body*] ... ACUS
Administrative Contract Document ... ACD
Administrative Contracting Officer [*Military*] ... ACO
Administrative Control ... ADCON
Administrative Data Processing ... ADP
Administrative Data Systems ... ADS
Administrative Data Systems - Teleprocessing ... ADS-TP
Administrative and Direct Support Logistics [*Company*] [*Army*] ... A & DSL
Administrative Directive ... AD
Administrative Division [*Municipality*] [*Board on Geographic Names*] ... ADMD
Administrative Engineering Information Management System ... AEIMS
Administrative Flagship [*Navy symbol*] ... APF
Administrative Information Data System ... AIDS
Administrative Inspection [*Military*] ... ADINSP
Administrative Inspection [*Military*] ... ADMININSP
Administrative Instructions ... ADMINI
Administrative Instructions ... ADMININST
Administrative Instructions ... AI
Administrative Law Judge [*Also, HE*] [*Federal trial examiner*] ... ALJ
Administrative Law Review [*A publication*] ... Ad Law Rev

Administrative Law Review [*A publication*] ... Adm Law R
Administrative Lead Time ... ALT
Administrative Liaison Officer ... ALO
Administrative Machine Branch [*Army*] ... AMB
Administrative Machine Division [*Army*] ... AMD
Administrative Management [*A publication*] ... Admin Mgmt
Administrative Management [*A publication*] ... Adm Manage
Administrative Management [*A publication*] ... Adm Mgt
Administrative Management Division [*Coast Guard*] ... CAM
Administrative Management Society ... AMS
Administrative Manual ... AM
Administrative-Material Inspection [*Military*] ... ADMAT
Administrative Medical Officer [*British*] ... AMO
Administrative Memo ... ADMM
Administrative and Miscellaneous Duties [*RAF*] [*British*] ... AMD
Administrative Motor Vehicle Management ... AMVM
Administrative Office [*or Officer*] ... ADMINO
Administrative Office Instruction ... AOINST
Administrative Office - Navy ... AO-N
Administrative Office, Navy Department ... AOND
Administrative Office of United States Courts ... AOUSC
Administrative Officer on Duty ... AOD
Administrative Operation and Support Services [*Kennedy Space Center*] [*NASA*] ... AD
Administrative Operations ... AO
Administrative Operations Branch [*NTIS*] ... AOB
Administrative Order ... ADMINO
Administrative Order ... ADMINORD
Administrative and Overhead ... AO
Administrative Plan ... ADMINPLAN
Administrative Procedures Act [*1946*] ... APA
Administrative Report ... ADMINREP
Administrative Research Bulletin ... ARB
Administrative Ruling [*US*] ... AR
Administrative Science Quarterly [*A publication*] ... Admin Sci Q
Administrative Science Quarterly [*A publication*] ... Adm Sci
Administrative Science Quarterly [*A publication*] ... Adm Sci Q
Administrative Science Quarterly [*A publication*] ... Adm Sci Qua
Administrative Science Quarterly [*A publication*] ... ASQ
Administrative Science Review [*A publication*] ... Admin Sci R
Administrative Section for Technical Cooperation [*United Nations*] ... ASTC
Administrative Service Centers ... ASC
Administrative Service Office ... ASO
Administrative Service Only ... ASO
Administrative Service Unit ... ASU
Administrative, Staff, and Technical [*Budget term*] ... AS & T
Administrative-Supply Technician [*Army*] ... AST
Administrative Support ... ADMINSUP
Administrative Support ... ADMSPT
Administrative Support ... AS
Administrative Support Group [*Army*] ... ASG
Administrative Support and Logistic Company [*Military*] ... AS & L
Administrative Support Operations Center [*Army*] ... ADSOC
[*The*] **Administrative Support Theaters Army** ... TASTA
Administrative Support Unit ... ASU
Administrative Terminal System [*IBM Corp.*] ... ATS
Administrative Trainee [*Civil Service*] [*British*] ... AT
Administrative Use Vehicle [*Military*] ... AUV
Administrative Use Vehicle Management Information System [*Military*] ... AUVMIS
Administrative Weight Limitation [*Military*] ... AWL
Administratively Uncontrollable Overtime ... AUO
Administrator ... ADMINR
Administrator ... ADMIR
Administrator ... ADMR
Administrator ... ADMTR
Administrator's Notebook [*A publication*] ... Adm Notebk
Administratrix ... ADMX
Admiral ... A
Admiral ... ADM
Admiral ... ADML
Admiral Commanding ... AC
Admiral Commanding Aircraft-Carriers [*British*] ... ACAC
Admiral Commanding Reserves [*Navy*] [*British*] ... ACR
Admiral Corp. [*NYSE symbol*] [*Delisted*] ... ADL
Admiral of the Fleet ... AF
Admiral of the Ocean Sea [*Annual award of US Merchant Marine; title originally bestowed on Christopher Columbus by the Spanish government*] ... AOTOS
Admiral's Club [*American Airlines' club for frequent flyers*] ... AC
Admiralty [*British*] ... ADM
Admiralty [*British*] ... ADMTY
Admiralty [*British*] ... ADMY
Admiralty Berthing Officer [*British*] ... ABQ
Admiralty Board [*British*] ... AB
Admiralty Centre for Scientific Information and Liaison [*British*] ... ACSIL
Admiralty Compass Observatory [*British*] ... ACO
Admiralty Corrosion Committee [*British*] ... ACC
Admiralty Engineering Laboratory [*British*] ... AEL
Admiralty Experiment Works [*British*] ... AEW
Admiralty Experimental Diving Unit [*British*] ... AEDU
Admiralty Fleet Order [*British*] ... AFO
Admiralty Fuel Experimental Station [*British*] ... AFES
Admiralty Gunnery Establishment [*British*] ... AGE
Admiralty Interview Board [*British*] ... AIB
Admiralty Islands ... AI
Admiralty Liaison Officer [*British*] ... ALO
Admiralty List of Lights [*British*] ... ALL
Admiralty List of Radio Signals [*British*] ... ALRS
Admiralty Marine Engineering Establishment [*British*] ... AMEE
Admiralty Materials Laboratory [*British*] ... AML
Admiralty Merchant Ship Defense Instructions [*British*] ... AMDI
Admiralty Merchant Shipping Instructions [*British*] ... AMSI
Admiralty Mining Establishment [*British*] ... AME
Admiralty Naval Staff [*British*] ... ANS
Admiralty Net Defence [*Antitorpedo nets*] [*British*] [*World War II*] ... AND
Admiralty Oil Laboratory [*British*] ... AOL
Admiralty Pattern [*The right procedure, the correct thing to do*] [*British*] ... AP
Admiralty Reactor Test Establishment ... ARTE
Admiralty Recruiting Service [*British*] ... ARS
Admiralty Research Laboratory [*British*] ... ARL
Admiralty Research Laboratory Extension [*British*] ... ARLE
Admiralty Signal Establishment [*British*] ... ASE
Admiralty Signal and RADAR Establishment [*British*] ... ASRE
Admiralty Supply Item ... ASI
Admiralty Surface Weapons Establishment [*British*] ... ASWE
Admiralty Underwater Weapons Establishment [*British*] ... AUWE
Admissible Linear Unbiased Estimator [*Statistics*] ... ALUE
Admissible Rank Test [*Statistics*] ... ART
Admission ... ADMSN
Admission and Disposition [*Military*] ... AAD
Admission Scheduling and Control System [*Hospital management*] ... ASCS
Admission Test for Graduate Study in Business ... ATGSB
Admissions ... ADM
Admissions ... ADMIS
Admissions Testing Program ... ATP
Admittance [*Symbol*] [*IUPAC*] ... Y
Admitting ... ADMG
Admove [*Apply*] [*Pharmacy*] ... ADM
Admove [*Apply*] [*Pharmacy*] ... ADMOV
Adobe Oil & Gas Corp. [*American Stock Exchange symbol*] ... AOI
Adolescence [*A publication*] ... ADOLA
Adolescence [*A publication*] ... Adoles
Adolescent ... ADOL
Adolescent Behavior Rating Scale [*Devereaux*] [*Also, DAB*] [*Psychology*] ... ABRS
Adolescent Psychiatry [*A publication*] ... Adolesc Psychiatry
Adolfo [*Couturier*] ... A
Adolph Meyer Mental Health Center, Decatur, IL [*Library symbol*] ... IDecM
Adopted Child ... AC
Adopted From [*or Adoption Of*] [*Etymology*] ... A
Adoptee/Natural Parent Locators ... ANPL
Adoptees Liberty Movement Association ... ALMA
Adoption Act [*British*] ... AA
Adoption Resource Exchange of North America [*Later, NAIES*] ... ARENA
Adoption Search Institute ... ASI
Adoption Triangle Ministry ... ATM
Adorers of the Blood of Christ [*Roman Catholic women's religious order*] ... ASC
ADP [*Adenosine Diphosphate*] **Ribosylated Enzyme** ... ADPR
ADP [*Automatic Data Processing*] **Systems Resources Analysis** ... ASRA
ADPE [*Automatic Data Processing Equipment*] **Resources Management System** ... ARMS
Adrar [*Algeria*] [*Airport symbol*] ... AZR
Adrenal [*Medicine*] ... Ad
Adrenal Androgen Stimulating Hormone [*Medicine*] ... AASH
Adrenal Cortex [*Medicine*] ... AC
Adrenal Cortex [*Medicine*] ... AdC
Adrenal Cortical Extract [*Endocrinology*] ... ACE
Adrenal Cortical Hormone [*Endocrinology*] ... ACH
Adrenal Medulla [*Medicine*] ... AdM
Adrenal Metabolic Research Society of the Hypoglycemia Foundation ... AMRSHF
Adrenal Weight Factor [*Endocrinology*] ... AWF
Adrenocortical Carcinoma [*Medicine*] ... ACC
Adrenocorticoid [*Medicine*] ... AC
Adrenocorticopolypeptide [*Endocrinology*] ... ACPP
Adrenocorticotrophic Hormone [*Endocrinology*] ... ACTH
Adrenocorticotrophic Polypeptide [*Endocrinology*] ... ACTP
Adrenocorticotrophin-Like Immunoreactivity [*Immunochemistry*] ... ACTH-LI
Adrenogenital Syndrome [*Medicine*] ... AGS
Adrenoglomerulotrophin [*Also, ASH*] [*Endocrinology*] ... AGTr
Adria Laboratories, Inc., Columbus, OH [*OCLC symbol*] ... OAD
Adriamycin [*See also ADR, Adriamycin*] [*Antineoplastic drug*] ... A
Adriamycin [*Hydroxydaunomycin*] [*Also, A, ADM, D, H*] [*Later, Doxorubicin*] [*Antineoplastic drug*] ... ADM
Adriamycin [*Hydroxydaunomycin*] [*Also, A, ADM, D, H*] [*Later, Doxorubicin*] [*Antineoplastic drug*] ... ADR
Adriamycin, Bleomycin, Prednisone [*Antineoplastic drug regimen*] ... ABP

Adriamycin [later, Doxorubicin], **Bleomycin, Vinblastine** [Oncovin], **Dacarbazine** [Antineoplastic drug regimen]..................ABVD
Adriamycin, CCNU [Lomustine] [Antineoplastic drug regimen]..............AC
Adriamycin, Cyclophosphamide [Antineoplastic drug regimen]..............AC
Adriamycin, Cyclophosphamide, Methotrexate [Antineoplastic drug regimen].................. ACM
Adriamycin, Dacarbazine, Bleomycin, CCNU [Lomustine] [Antineoplastic drug regimen].................ADBC
Adriamycin, DIC [Dacarbazine] [Antineoplastic drug regimen]...............ADIC
Adriamycin, Oncovin, ara-C, Prednisone [Antineoplastic drug regimen].....................ADOAP
Adriamycin, Vincristine, Cyclophosphamide [Antineoplastic drug regimen]......................AVC
Adrian C. and Leon Israel [in company name "ACLI International"] .... ACLI
Adrian College, Adrian, MI [OCLC symbol]...................EEA
Adrian College, Adrian, MI [Library symbol].................MiAdC
Adrian, MI [Location identifier] [FAA]..................ADG
Adrian, MI [Radio station call letters]..................WABJ
Adrian, MI [Radio station call letters]..................WLEN
Adrian, MI [Radio station call letters]..................WQTE
Adrian, MI [Radio station call letters]..................WVAC
Adrian Public Library, Adrian, MI [Library symbol]..................MiAd
Adrian Van Reypen Egerton [Near-acronym used as shortened first name of detective-story character Average Jones, in stories by Samuel Hopkins Adams].....................AVERAGE
Adriance Memorial Library, Poughkeepsie, NY [Library symbol]..............NP
Adriatic Base Command [Military].....................ABC
Adriatic Force [Military] .... ADFOR
Adriatic Sea Expanded Regional Oceanological Studies...................AS-EROS
Adsorbent......................ADSORB
Adstante Febre [When Fever Is Present] [Pharmacy] ....AD FEB
Adstante Febre [When Fever Is Present] [Pharmacy] ....ADST FEB
Adult......................A
Adult [Film certificate] [British]......................A
Adult Basic Education .... ABE
Adult Basic Learning Examination .... ABLE
Adult Basic Skill Training .... ABST
Adult-Child Interaction [Test]......................ACI
Adult Christian Education Foundation .... ACEF
Adult Community Movement for Equality [Civil rights]...................... ACME
Adult-Contemporary [Music]......................AC
Adult Education [A publication]......................Adult Ed
Adult Education [A publication].......................Adult Educ
Adult Education .... AE
Adult Education [A publication]...................... AE
Adult Education Association of the USA .... AEA
Adult Education Bulletin [A publication] .... Adult Ed Bul
Adult Education Centre [British] .... AEC
Adult Education Journal [A publication]...................Adult Ed J
Adult Education Journal [A publication] .... AEJ
Adult Education and the Library [A publication] ....Adult Ed and Lib
Adult Education and Lifelong Learning .... ADELL
Adult Education Program .... AEP
Adult Education-Washington [A publication] ....Adult Ed-W
Adult Film Association of America .... AFAA
Adult Heart .... AH
Adult Information on Drugs [Referral service] .... AID
Adult Jewish Education .... AJE
Adult Leadership [A publication]......................Adult Lead
Adult Leadership [A publication]......................A Lead
Adult Learning Association .... ALA
Adult Migrant Education [Department of Labor] .... AME
Adult Onset Diabetes Mellitus [Endocrinology]......................AODM
Adult-Onset Polycystic Kidney Disease [Medicine]......................APKD
Adult Operculum .... AO
Adult Opportunity Center [State employment service]......................AOC
Adult Performance Level [Education]......................APL
Adult Reading Improvement Association......................ARIA
Adult Respiratory Distress Syndrome [Medicine]......................ARDS
Adult Retraining Program......................ARP
Adult Services Division [American Library Association] [Later, RASD]......................ASD
Adult T-Cell Leukemia [Medicine]......................ATL
Adult Thymus-Cell Leukemia Antigen [Medicine]......................ATLA
Adult Thymus-Cell Leukemia-Lymphoma [Medicine]......................ATLL
Adult Thymus-Cell Leukemia Virus......................ATLV
Adult, Vocational, and Technical Education......................AVTE
Adult Vocational Training [HEW]......................AVT
Adult Vocational Training Program [HEW]......................AVTP
Adulteress [Letter embroidered on Hester Prynne's dress in Nathaniel Hawthorne's "The Scarlet Letter"] ....A
Adultery [FBI standardized term]......................ADLTY
Advance [or Advancement]......................ADV
Advance [or Advancement]......................ADVN
Advance Abstracts of Contributions on Fisheries and Aquatic Sciences in India [A publication] ....Adv Abstr Contrib Fish Aquat Sci India
Advance Base Section Dock [Floating drydock, first used in World War II]......................ABSD
Advance Bibliography of Contents: Political Science and Government [A publication]...................... ABC Pol Sci

Advance Book Information [Publishing]......................ABI
Advance Booking Charter [Airline fare] ....ABC
Advance Carrier Training Group [Navy] ....ACTG
Advance Cash Allowance Authorized ....ADCASHAL
Advance Change Notice ....ACN
Advance Circuits, Inc. [NASDAQ symbol]......................ADVC
Advance Command ....ADCOM
Advance Command Post ....ACP
Advance Concepts for Terrain Avoidance ....ADCON
Advance Contracting Officer ....ACO
Advance Corporate Contract Directive ....ACCD
Advance Corporation Tax [British] ....ACT
Advance Count Switch ....ACS
Advance Delivery of Correspondence [Military]......................ADC
Advance Development Group [Army] ....ADG
Advance Deviations Report ....ADR
Advance Discontinuance of Allotment ....ADVDISC
Advance Drawing Release Notice ....ADRN
Advance Engineering Material Order ....AEMO
Advance Engineering Memorandum ....AEM
Advance Engineering Order ....AEO
Advance Evaluation Note ....AEN
Advance Freight [Shipping] ....AF
Advance Guard [A publication]......................AG
Advance Information Letter [Military] ....AIL
Advance Information Memo ....AIM
Advance Investors Corp. [NYSE symbol]......................AIV
Advance Leave [Military] ....ADV/L
Advance List of Oversea-Returnees for Reassignment [Army]......................AOR
Advance Logistical Command [Army] ....ADLOG
Advance Manufacturing Directive ....AMD
Advance Material Order......................AMO
Advance Material Request ....AMR
Advance Missile Deviation Report ....AMDR
Advance Notice of Proposed Rulemaking [Also, ANPRM] [US Government agencies]......................ANPR
Advance Notice of Proposed Rulemaking [Also, ANPR] [US Government agencies]......................ANPRM
Advance Ordering Information ....AOI
Advance Pay......................AP
Advance of Pay and Allowances ....APA
Advance Payment......................ADVPMT
Advance Payment of Dislocation Allowance to Dependents [Air Force]......................ADVDLA-DEP
Advance Payment of Mileage Authorized [Army]......................APMA
Advance Payment of Monetary Allowance in Lieu of Transportation Is Authorized [Army]......................APMALTA
Advance Payment Plan [Airlines] ....APX
Advance Payment of Subsistence and Quarters ....APSQ
Advance Payment of Travel per Diem Authorized [Army]......................APTPDA
Advance Personnel Requirements Research Note ....APRRN
Advance Planning Procurement Information [Army]......................APPI
Advance Proceedings. Fluid Power Testing Symposium [A publication]......................Adv Proc Fluid Power Test Symp
Advance Process Engineering Order ....APEO
Advance Procurement List ....APL
Advance Procurement Plan [Navy] ....APP
Advance Production Release ....APR
Advance Programing and Proposal Operations......................AP & PO
Advance-Purchase Excursion [Airline fare] ....APEX
Advance Release [Military] ....ADVR
Advance Release Record ....ARR
Advance Ross Corp. [NASDAQ symbol]......................AROS
Advance in Schedule ....AIS
Advance in Schedule ....AVS
Advance Section [Military] ....AD SEC
Advance Sensor Development Program [Military] ....ASDP
Advance Services of Supply [Army]......................ADSOS
Advance Simulation Facility Interconnection and Setup System [Air Force]......................ASFISS
Advance STOL [Short Takeoff and Landing] **Transport (Medium)** [Aviation]......................ASTM
Advance Stoppage......................ADVST
Advance Surface-to-Air Weapons System......................ASAWS
Advance Surface Missile System......................ASMS
Advance Synthetic Aperture RADAR System ....ASARS
Advance Systems Engineering ....ASE
Advance Test Plant ....ATP
Advance Transportation Control and Movement Document ....ATCMD
Advance Weapon Ammunition Support Point ....AWASP
Advanced Academic Degree ....AAD
Advanced Academic Degree Management System ....AADMS
Advanced Accounting System ....AAS
Advanced Acoustic Search Sensors ....AASS
Advanced Action Manipulator System ....ADAMS
Advanced Administrative System [IBM Corp.]......................AAS
Advanced Aerial Fire Support System [Army]......................AAFSS
Advanced Aerial Fire Support System Office [Army] ....AAFSSO
Advanced Air Defense System......................AADS
Advanced Air Defense Weapon......................AADW
Advanced Air Depot Area [Air Force]......................AADA

Advanced Air Refueling Boom [*Air Force*] ... AARB
Advanced Air Striking Force [*British*] ... AASF
Advanced Air-to-Surface Missile Seeker [*Navy*] ... AASMS
Advanced Air Traffic Management System [*Department of Transportation*] ... AATMS
Advanced Air Training Command [*Military*] ... AATC
Advanced Airborne Command Post ... AABCP
Advanced Airborne Command Post ... AACP
Advanced Airborne Launch Center [*Air Force*] ... AALC
Advanced Airborne National Command Post ... AABNCP
Advanced Airborne Radio Position Location System [*Army*] ... AARPLS
Advanced Airborne Surveillance Sensor ... AASS
Advanced Aircraft Early Warning RADAR ... AAEWR
Advanced Aircraft Electrical System [*Navy*] ... AAES
Advanced Aircraft Programs Office ... AAPO
Advanced Allied Headquarters [*World War II*] ... AAHQ
Advanced Amphibious Training Base [*Navy*] ... AATB
Advanced Antenna System [*Air Force*] ... AAS
Advanced Antiarmor Vehicle Evaluation Test ... ARMVAL
Advanced Antiradiation Missile ... AARM
Advanced Antisubmarine Warfare Exercise ... ADEX
Advanced Antitank Weapon [*Army*] ... AATW
Advanced Applications Flight Equipment [*NASA*] ... AAFE
Advanced Applications Flight Experiments [*NASA*] ... AAFE
Advanced and Applied Concepts Office [*MERDC*] [*Army*] ... AACO
Advanced Army Aircraft Instrument System ... AAAIS
Advanced Army System Requirements ... AASR
Advanced Atmospheric Sounder and Imaging Radiometer [*NASA*] ... AAIR
Advanced Atmospheric Sounder and Imaging Radiometer [*NASA*] ... AASIR
Advanced Attack Helicopter [*Army*] ... AAH
Advanced Automatic Film Titles System ... AAFTS
Advanced Automatic Flight Control System ... AAFCS
Advanced Automation Research Laboratory [*Purdue University*] ... AARL
Advanced Automotive Power Systems ... AAPS
Advanced Aviation Base Ship [*Navy symbol*] ... AVB
Advanced Avionic Fault Isolation System [*Navy*] ... AAFIS
Advanced Avionics Data Handling System [*Air Force*] ... AADHS
Advanced Avionics Digital Computer [*Naval Air Systems Command*] ... AADC
Advanced Avionics Integration Program ... AAIP
Advanced Ballistic Missile Defense Agency [*Army*] ... ABMDA
Advanced Ballistic Missile Systems ... ABMS
Advanced Ballistic Reentry System ... ABRES
Advanced Ballistic Reentry Vehicle ... ABRV
Advanced Ballistic-Type Logistic Spacecraft System ... ABLSS
Advanced Ballistics Concepts [*Air Force*] ... ABC
Advanced Banking On-Line System ... ABOS
Advanced Base Aviation Training Unit [*Navy*] ... ABATU
Advanced Base Combat Communication Training Center [*Pearl Harbor*] ... ABCCTC
Advanced Base Components [*Military*] ... ABCO
Advanced Base Construction Depot ... ABCD
Advanced Base Depot [*or Dock*] [*Navy*] ... ABD
Advanced Base Depot Area Command ... ABDACOM
Advanced Base Functional Component [*Military*] ... ABFC
Advanced Base Functional Component System [*Military*] ... ABFCS
Advanced Base Hospital [*British*] ... ABH
Advanced Base Initial Outfitting List [*Military*] ... ABIOL
Advanced Base Personnel Administration ... ABPA
Advanced Base Personnel Officer ... ABPO
Advanced Base Personnel Unit ... ABPU
Advanced Base Proving Ground ... ABPG
Advanced Base Receiving Barracks ... ABRB
Advanced Base Receiving Depot ... ABRD
Advanced Base Repair Depot ... ABRD
Advanced Base Reshipment Depot ... ABRD
Advanced Base Supply Depot ... ABSD
Advanced Base Torpedo Unit [*Navy*] ... ABTU
Advanced Base Training Unit [*Navy*] ... ABTU
Advanced [*or Alternate*] **Battery Acquisition RADAR** ... ABAR
Advanced Beef Breeds Federation ... ABBF
Advanced Bill of Material ... ABM
Advanced Biomedical Capsule ... ABC
Advanced Bombardment System ... ABOSS
Advanced Cab and Visual System [*Army*] ... ACAVS
Advanced Capabilities RADAR ... ACR
Advanced Capability ... ADCAP
Advanced Capability Tanker ... ACT
Advanced Cardiac Life Support System ... ACLS
Advanced Cardiovascular Systems ... ACS
Advanced Career Training ... ACT
Advanced Ceramic System ... ACS
Advanced Certificate in Education ... Adv Cert in Ed
Advanced Certificate in Music Education ... Adv Cert in Mus Ed
Advanced Certification [*Canadian Society of Radiological Technicians*] ... AC
Advanced Chain Home [*RADAR*] ... ACH
Advanced Chemical Rocket Engine [*Air Force*] ... ACRE
Advanced Circuit Module ... ACM
Advanced Circular Scan Thermal Imaging System ... ACSTIS
Advanced Circular Scan Thermal Imaging System ... ACTIS
Advanced Combat Air Patrol ... ACAP
Advanced Combat Aircraft ... ACA
Advanced Combat Surveillance RADAR ... ACSR
Advanced Combat Training Academy [*Army*] ... ACTA
Advanced Command and Control Architectural Test Bed ... ACCAT
Advanced Command Data System ... ACDS
Advanced Communications-Electronics Requirements Plan [*Air Force*] ... ACERP
Advanced Communications Equipment Depot ... ACED
Advanced Communications Function [*Data processing*] ... ACF
Advanced Communications Service [*Later, AIS*] [*AT & T*] ... ACS
Advanced Compilation Equipment ... ACE
Advanced Composite Airframe Program [*Air Force*] ... ACAP
Advanced Compound Engine ... ACE
Advanced Computational Processor [*Data processing*] ... ACP
Advanced Computer for Array Processing ... ACAP
Advanced Computer for Medical Research [*Stanford University*] ... ACME
Advanced Computer Oriented System ... ACOS
Advanced Computer Services [*Honeywell Information Systems*] ... ACS
Advanced Computer System [*IBM Corp.*] ... ACS
Advanced Computer Techniques Corp. [*NASDAQ symbol*] ... ACTP
Advanced Computer Techniques Project ... ACTP
Advanced Concept Cost Model ... ACCM
Advanced Concept Ejection Seat [*Aviation*] ... ACES
Advanced Concept Escape System ... ACES
Advanced Concept Tire [*Firestone Tire & Rubber Co.*] ... ACT
Advanced Concepts Group ... ACG
Advanced Concepts Missile ... ACM
Advanced Concepts and Missions Division [*NASA*] ... ACMD
Advanced Concepts for Ordnance ... ACORD
Advanced Concepts Team [*Army*] ... ACT
Advanced Confidential Report ... ACR
Advanced Configuration Management System ... ACMS
Advanced Conformal Antenna Technique ... ACAT
Advanced Continuous Simulation Language [*Pronounced "axle"*] [*Data processing*] ... ACSL
Advanced Contract Administrator ... ACA
Advanced Control Experiments ... ACE
Advanced [*Flight*] **Control Programer** ... ADCP
Advanced Control Signal Processor [*For spacecraft*] ... ACSP
Advanced Conventional Standoff Missile ... ACSM
Advanced Converter Reactor [*Atomic energy*] ... ACR
Advanced Cooperative Countermeasure ... ADCOM
Advanced Cooperative Project [*NASA*] ... ACP
Advanced Copies Delivered ... ACD
Advanced Core Performance Reactor ... ACPR
Advanced Core Test [*Nuclear energy*] ... ACT
Advanced Coronary Treatment Foundation ... ACT
Advanced Cracking Reactor [*Fuel technology*] ... ACR
Advanced Credit Information System ... ACIS
Advanced Cruise Missile Program [*Navy*] ... ACMP
Advanced Cruise Missile Technology ... ACMT
Advanced Cryptographic System [*Air Force*] ... ACS
Advanced Data Communications Control Procedure ... ADCCP
Advanced Data Management ... ADAM
Advanced Data Scalar ... ADS
Advanced Data System [*DoD*] ... ADS
Advanced Dated Remittances [*IRS*] ... ADR
Advanced Deck-Launched Interceptor ... ADLI
Advanced Declassification Schedule ... ADS
Advanced Decoy Technology ... ADTECH
Advanced Deep-Dive System ... ADS
Advanced Deep-Running Acoustic Torpedo ... ADRAT
Advanced Defense Communications Satellite [*Air Force*] ... ADCS
Advanced Defense Communications Satellite Program [*Air Force*] ... ADCSP
Advanced Degree in Education ... Ed A2
Advanced Design ... AD
Advanced Design Aluminum Metal Shelter [*A prefabricated building known as an ADAMS hut*] ... ADAMS
Advanced Design Array RADAR ... ADAR
Advanced Design [*or Drawing*] **Change** ... ADC
Advanced Design [*or Drawing*] **Change Notice** ... ADCN
Advanced Design Team ... ADT
Advanced Destroyer/Aircraft Lightweight Torpedo ... AD/ALT
Advanced Developing Institutions Program ... ADIP
Advanced Development ... AD
Advanced Development [*Army*] ... ADDEV
Advanced Development Aims Processor Transponder [*Military*] ... ADAPT
Advanced Development Analysis ... ADA
Advanced Development Experimental [*Army*] ... ADX
Advanced Development Model ... ADM
Advanced Development Objective [*Military*] ... ADO
Advanced Development Plan (System) ... ADP(S)
Advanced Development Plans [*Air Force*] ... ADP
Advanced Development Report [*NASA*] ... ADR
Advanced Development Technology ... ADT
Advanced Development Vehicle ... ADV
Advanced Development Verification Tests ... ADVT
Advanced Diagnostic Engine Monitoring System [*Air Force*] ... ADEMS
Advanced Digital Ranging System [*NASA*] ... ADRAN

Advanced Digital Systems, Inc. [*NASDAQ symbol*] .... ADVA
Advanced Diploma in Art Education [*British*] .... ADAE
Advanced Direct-Landing Apollo Mission [*NASA*] .... ADAM
Advanced Direct Support Unit .... ADSU
Advanced Directional Warhead .... ADWAR
Advanced Display System .... ADS
Advanced Diving System .... ADS
Advanced Document Revision Notice [*NASA*] .... ADRN
Advanced Dressing Station [*British*] .... ADS
Advanced Dungeons and Dragons .... AD & D
Advanced Earned Income Credit [*IRS*] .... AEIC
Advanced Earth Satellite Weapon System [*Air Force*] .... AEWS
Advanced Echelon [*Marine Corps*] .... ADVON
Advanced Electric Distribution System .... AEDS
Advanced Electrical Development Package .... AEDP
Advanced Electrochemical Depolarized Concentrator Module [*NASA*] .... AEDCM
Advanced Electronic Design .... AED
Advanced Electronic Display System [*FAA*] .... ADEDS
Advanced Electronic Warfare System .... AEWS
Advanced Electronics Field .... AEF
Advanced Energy Projects [*Department of Energy*] .... AEP
Advanced Energy Technology .... AET
Advanced Engine Aerospike .... AEA
Advanced Engine Bell .... AEB
Advanced Engine Overhaul Base .... AEOB
Advanced Engineering Test Reactor .... AETR
Advanced Environmental Control System .... AECS
Advanced Environmental Research and Technology .... AERT
Advanced Epithermal Thorium Reactor .... AETR
Advanced [*or Aircrew*] **Escape/Rescue Capability** [*Navy - Air Force*] .... AERCAB
Advanced Extravehicular Protective System [*NASA*] .... AEPS
Advanced Extravehicular Suit [*NASA*] .... AES
Advanced - Far Infrared Search/Track .... A-FIRST
Advanced Field Array RADAR .... AFAR
Advanced Field Artillery Tactical Data System .... AFATDS
Advanced Field Operating System [*National Weather Service*] .... AFOS
Advanced Field Site Facility .... AFSF
Advanced Fighter Diagnostic System .... AFDS
Advanced Fighter RADAR System .... AFRS
Advanced Fighter Technology Integration [*Air Force*] .... AFTI
Advanced Figure Sensor .... AFS
Advanced Filament Wound Structure .... AFWS
Advanced Fire Support Avionics System .... AFSAS
Advanced Flash X-Ray Facility .... AFXF
Advanced Flexible Reusable Surface Insulation [*For space shuttles*] .... AFRSI
Advanced Flight Control Actuation System [*Navy*] .... AFCAS
Advanced Flight Control Programer .... AFCP
Advanced Flying Unit [*Air Force*] .... AFU
Advanced Foreign System Requirements .... AFSR
Advanced Forward Air Defense System [*Missiles*] .... AFADS
Advanced Forward Area Air Defense System .... AFAADS
Advanced Forward Area Air Defense Weapon .... AFAADW
Advanced Forward-Looking Infrared .... AFLIR
Advanced Gas-Cooled Reactor [*British*] .... AGR
Advanced Genetic Sciences [*NASDAQ symbol*] .... AGSI
Advanced Geosynchronous Observation Environment Satellite [*NASA*] .... AGOES
Advanced Ground Transport .... AGT
Advanced Guard .... AG
Advanced Guidance System .... AGS
Advanced Guidance Technology [*SAMSO*] [*Air Force*] .... AGT
Advanced Gun Weapon System .... AGWS
Advanced Gunnery Target Systems .... AGTS
Advanced Headquarters .... ADVHED
Advanced Heavy Antitank Missile System [*Army*] .... AHAMS
Advanced Helicopter Improvement Program [*Army*] .... AHIP
Advanced Helmet Sight Reticle Assembly [*Air Force*] .... AHRA
Advanced High-Performance Nuclear Attack Submarine .... AHPNAS
Advanced Hybrid Computer System .... AHCS
Advanced Hypersonic Manned Aircraft .... AHMA
Advanced Individual Training [*Army*] .... AIT
Advanced Individual Training Available [*Military*] .... AITA
Advanced Inertial Measurement System .... AIMS
Advanced Inertial Navigation System .... AINS
Advanced Inertial Reference Sphere [*ICBM technology*] .... AIRS
Advanced Information System/Net 1 Service [*Formerly, ACS*] [*American Bell, Inc.*] .... AIS
Advanced Institutional Development Program [*Under Title III of the Higher Education Act*] .... AIDP
Advanced Instruction Flying School .... AIFS
Advanced Instructional System .... AIS
Advanced Instrumentation and Data Analysis System .... AIDAS
Advanced Integrated Data System .... AIDS
Advanced Integrated Diagnostics .... AID
Advanced Integrated Landing System .... AILS
Advanced Integrated Life-Support System .... AILSS
Advanced Integrated Magnetic Anomaly Detection System .... AIMS
Advanced Integrated Modular Instrumentation System .... AIMIS
Advanced Integrated Safety and Optimizing Computer .... ADVISOR
Advanced Intelligence Center [*Navy*] .... ADINTELCEN
Advanced Intelligence Center [*Navy*] .... ADV INTEL CEN
Advanced Intelligence Center [*Navy*] .... AIC
Advanced Intelligence Center, Pacific Ocean Areas [*Navy*] .... AICPOA
Advanced Interactive Presentation System .... AIPS
Advanced Interceptor Air-to-Air Missile .... AIAAM
Advanced Intercontinental Missile System .... AIMS
Advanced Interior Communication System .... AICS
Advanced International Studies Institute .... AISI
Advanced Ion Exchange Cellulose [*Analytical biochemistry*] .... AIEC
Advanced Ionospheric Sounder [*A ground-based instrument*] .... AIS
Advanced Isotope Separation [*Process*] [*Nuclear energy*] .... AIS
Advanced Jet Trainer .... AJT
Advanced Kick Stage [*Missile launching*] .... AKS
Advanced Kinematic Bombing System .... AKBS
Advanced Landing Ground [*Air Force*] .... ALG
Advanced Language Program [*Institute for Defense Analysis*] .... ALP
Advanced LASER Spot Tracker .... ALAST
Advanced LASER System Study .... ALSS
Advanced Level [*School graduating grade*] [*British*] .... A
Advanced Library Systems, Inc. [*Information service*] .... ALS
Advanced Life Information System [*Data processing*] .... ALIS
Advanced Life Support [*System*] .... ALS
Advanced Light Antitank Weapon .... ALAW
Advanced Light Source [*For Synchrotron radiation*] [*High-energy physics*] .... ALS
Advanced Lightweight Torpedo [*Navy*] .... ALWT
Advanced Linear Programing System .... ALPS
Advanced Liquid Propulsion System [*NASA*] .... ALPS
Advanced List of Materials .... ALM
Advanced Location Strike System [*Formerly, Airborne Location and Strike System*] [*Air Force*] .... ALSS
Advanced Logistic System .... ALS
Advanced Logistics Development .... ALD
Advanced Logistics Information and Control System [*Air Force*] .... ALICS
Advanced Logistics Spacecraft .... ALS
Advanced Logistics System Project Advisory Committee [*Terminated, 1977*] [*DoD*] .... ALSPAC
Advanced Long-Range Interceptor .... ALRI
Advanced Low-Altitude Infrared Reconnaissance Sensor .... ALAIRS
Advanced Low-Altitude Technique .... ADLAT
Advanced Lunar Operation .... ALO
Advanced Lunar Orbital Rendezvous .... ALOR
Advanced Lunar Projects .... ALP
Advanced Lunar Projects Laboratory .... ALPL
Advanced Lunar Studies .... ALS
Advanced Lunar Transportation Systems .... ALTS
Advanced Magnetic Minesweeping .... AMMS
Advanced Mail Coding System .... AMCS
Advanced Management Information Service [*or System*] [*Air Force*] .... AMIS
Advanced Management Journal [*A publication*] .... Advanced Mgt
Advanced Management Journal [*A publication*] .... Advanced Mgt J
Advanced Management Journal [*A publication*] .... Advan Manage J
Advanced Management Journal [*A publication*] .... Adv Mgmt J
Advanced Management-Office Executive [*A publication*] .... Advanced Mgt-Office Exec
Advanced Management Program .... AMP
Advanced Maneuvering Orbit-to-Orbit Shuttle [*NASA*] .... AMOOS
Advanced Maneuvering Propulsion System .... AMPS
Advanced Maneuvering Propulsion Technology [*NASA*] .... AMPT
Advanced Maneuvering Reentry Vehicle .... AMARV
Advanced Manned Interceptor [*US Air Force Artillery Spotting Division interceptor*] .... AMI
Advanced Manned Missions Program [*NASA*] .... AMMP
Advanced Manned Penetrator .... AMP
Advanced Manned Penetrator System .... AMPS
Advanced Manned Precision Strike System [*Proposed Air Force plane*] .... AMPSS
Advanced Manned Space Simulator .... AMSS
Advanced Manned Spacecraft .... AMS
Advanced Manned Strategic Aircraft [*Air Force*] .... AMSA
Advanced Manufacturing Engineering Council .... AMEC
Advanced Manufacturing Technology .... AMT
Advanced Mapping System [*Geography*] .... AMS
Advanced Master of Education .... AME
Advanced Materials Fabrication Facility .... AMFF
Advanced Materiel Concepts Agency [*Army*] .... AMCA
Advanced Medical Imaging [*NASDAQ symbol*] .... ADIC
Advanced Medium-Caliber Aircraft Weapon System .... AMCAWS
Advanced Medium-Range Air-to-Air Missile .... AMRAAM
Advanced Medium STOL [*Short Takeoff and Landing*] **Transport** .... AMST
Advanced Memory Systems .... AMS
Advanced Metallic Air Vehicle Structure .... AMAVS
Advanced Metallic Structures [*Program*] [*Air Force*] .... AMS
Advanced Metals Research Corporation .... AMRC
Advanced Meteorological Sounding System .... AMSS
Advanced Meteorological System .... AMS
Advanced Micro Devices, Inc. [*NYSE symbol*] .... AMD
Advanced Microprogramable Processors .... AMPP
Advanced Midcourse Active System .... AMAS

Advanced Military Occupational Specialty [Army] .... ADVMOS
Advanced Millimeter Wave Device .... AMWD
Advanced Mine Countermeasures .... AMCM
Advanced Minuteman Accelerometer .... AMA
Advanced Minuteman Computer .... AMC
Advanced Minuteman Platform .... AMP
Advanced Minuteman System .... AMS
Advanced Missile Materials Research Technical Advisory
    Group [DoD] .... AMMRES
Advanced Missile Propulsion Definition Study [NASA] ..... AMPDS
Advanced Missile System .... AMS
Advanced Mission Studies [NASA] .... AMS
Advanced Missions Docking System [or Subsystem] [NASA] .. AMDS
Advanced Mobile Phone Service [Bell System] .... AMPS
Advanced Mobile Telephone System .... AMTS
Advanced Model Builder Shell [Data processing] .... AMBUSH
Advanced Modular RADAR .... AMR
Advanced Monitoring Systems Incorporated [NASDAQ symbol] ... AMSI
Advanced Moving Target Indicator, RADAR .... AMTIR
Advanced Multimission RADAR .... AMMR
Advanced Multimission Reconnaissance System [Military] .. AMMRS
Advanced Multimission Remotely Piloted Vehicle .... AMRPV
Advanced Multimission Torpedo .... AMMT
Advanced Multiplatform Navy Computer System .... AMNCS
Advanced Multipurpose Gas Turbine Program .... AMPGATT
Advanced Multipurpose Large Launch Vehicle .... AMLLV
Advanced Multipurpose Missile .... AMM
Advanced Multispectral Image Descriptor System [Photography] ... AMIDS
Advanced Mutual Security Act .... AMSA
Advanced Narrowband Digital Voice Terminal .... ANDVT
Advanced Naval Gun Weapon System .... ANGWS
Advanced Naval System Requirements .... ANSR
Advanced Naval Training School .... ANTS
Advanced Naval Vehicle Concepts Evaluation .... ANVCE
Advanced Navigator [Air Force] .... AN
Advanced Navy Display System .... ANDS
Advanced Navy Tactical Command and Control System ...... ANTACCS
Advanced Network System Architecture .... ANSA
Advanced NMR Systems [NASDAQ symbol] .... ANMR
Advanced Noncommissioned Officer Course [Army] .... ANCOC
Advanced Noncommissioned Officer Course .... ANOC
Advanced Nosetip [AEC] .... ANT
Advanced Nuclear Attack Submarine Program .... ANASP
Advanced Ocean Engineering Laboratory [Scripps Institution of
    Oceanography] .... AOEL
Advanced On-Board Processor [Computer] .... AOP
Advanced Operational Base [Navy] .... AOB
Advanced Operations Unit [Navy] .... ADVON
Advanced Optical Character Reader .... AOCR
Advanced Optical Countermeasures .... AOCM
Advanced Orbit/Ephemeris Subsystem .... AOES
Advanced Orbital Launch Operations .... AOLO
Advanced Orbiting Astronautical Observatory .... AOAO
Advanced Orbiting Geophysical Observatory .... AOGO
Advanced Orbiting Solar Observatory [NASA] .... AOSO
Advanced Ordnance Department [British] .... AOD
Advanced Parts Procurement .... APP
Advanced Parts Release .... APR
Advanced Passenger Train [British] .... ADP
Advanced Passenger Train [British] .... APT
Advanced Patent Technique .... APT
Advanced Patrol Sensor System .... ADPASS
Advanced Pay .... ADV/P
Advanced Penetration Model .... APM
Advanced Performance Computer .... APC
Advanced Performance Interceptor .... API
Advanced Personnel Data System .... APDS
Advanced Personnel System .... APS
Advanced Photosynthetic System .... APS
Advanced Physical Fitness Test [Army] .... APFT
Advanced Placement [Education] .... AP
Advanced Placement Program .... APP
Advanced Planetary Mission Technology [NASA] .... APMT
Advanced Planetary Probe .... APP
Advanced Planetary Spacecraft System .... APSS
Advanced Planning Briefing [Program] [DoD] .... APB
Advanced Planning Briefs for Industry .... APBI
Advanced Planning Data Sheet .... APDS
Advanced Planning and Design [NASA] .... AP & D
Advanced Planning Document .... APD
Advanced Planning Program Scheduling .... APPS
Advanced Point Defense Missile System [Navy] .... APDMS
Advanced Point Defense Surface Missile System [Navy] ... APDSMS
Advanced Pointing Tracking .... APT
Advanced Polar Orbiting Satellite .... APOS
Advanced Polaris Guidance Information .... APOGI
Advanced Post [Military] .... AP
Advanced Post Boost System [Military] .... APBS
Advanced Post Office [Military] .... APO
Advanced Power Conversion Experimental Facility .... APCEF
Advanced Power Management System [Jammer] .... APMS

Advanced Pressure Tube Reactor .... APTR
Advanced Procurement .... AP
Advanced Procurement Change [or Check] .... APC
Advanced Procurement Information .... API
Advanced Procurement Planning System for Security
    Assistance .... APPSSA
Advanced Product Planning Operation .... APPO
Advanced Production Engineering .... APE
Advanced Productivity Research and Technology .... APRT
Advanced Program Development .... APD
Advanced Programing Course [Data processing] .... APC
Advanced Programing Language [Data processing] .... APL
Advanced Programing Language Statistical Package .... APLSTATPACK
Advanced Programs Authorization .... APA
Advanced Progressive Matrices [Intelligence test] ...... APM
Advanced Project Planning .... APP
Advanced Propellant System .... APS
Advanced Propulsion Comparison Study [NASA] .... APC
Advanced Propulsion Cooling .... APC
Advanced Propulsion Payload Effects [NASA] .... APPLE
Advanced Propulsion Subsystem Integration [Air Force] .. APSI
Advanced PVO [Protivo-Voxdushnaia Oborona] Intercepter . APVOI
Advanced RADAR Experimental Systems Technology [Army] .. AREST
Advanced RADAR Information Evaluation System .... ARIES
Advanced RADAR Processing System .... ARPS
Advanced RADAR Terminal System .... ARTS
Advanced RADAR Traffic Control System [Air Force] ...... ARTCS
Advanced RADAR Traffic Control System [Air Force] ...... ARTS
Advanced RADAR Warning System .... ARWS
Advanced Radiation Effects Simulation .... ARES
Advanced Radiation Space Defense Application .... ARSDA
Advanced Range Instrumentation Aircraft .... ARIA
Advanced Range Instrumentation Ship .... ARIS
Advanced Range Instrumentation Systems .... ARIS
Advanced Range Testing, Reporting, and Control .... ARTRAC
Advanced Reactivity Measurement Facility [AEC] .... ARMF
Advanced Reactor .... AR
Advanced Reactor Development Associates .... ARDA
Advanced Reactor Technology .... ART
Advanced Real-Time Executive .... ARE
Advanced Real-Time Range Control .... ARTRAC
Advanced Receiver Model System .... ARMS
Advanced Recoilless Weapon .... ARW
Advanced Reconfigurable Computer System .... ARCS
Advanced Reconnaissance Helicopter .... ARH
Advanced Reconnaissance Satellite .... ARS
Advanced Reconnaissance System .... ARS
Advanced Reconnaissance and Target Acquisition Capabilities ... ARTAC
Advanced Record System [Air Force] .... ARS
Advanced Recovery System .... ADRECS
Advanced Reentry Concepts [Aerospace] .... ARC
Advanced Reentry Program [Aerospace] .... ARP
Advanced Reentry System [Aerospace] .... ARS
Advanced Registered Nurse Practitioner .... ARNP
Advanced Remotely Piloted Modular Aircraft .... ARPMA
Advanced Rescue and Recovery System [Proposed VTOL
    aircraft] [Also, ARS] .... ARRS
Advanced Rescue System [Proposed VTOL aircraft] [Also, ARRS] ... ARS
Advanced Research Consultants .... ARCON
Advanced Research Craft Hydrokeel .... ARCK
Advanced Research Division .... ARD
Advanced Research EMP [Electromagnetic Pulse] Simulator ... ARES
Advanced Research Instrument System, Inc. .... ARIS
Advanced Research Objective .... ARO
Advanced Research Program Directive .... ARPD
Advanced Research Projects .... ARP
Advanced Research Projects Agency [Later, DARPA] [DoD] .. ARPA
Advanced Research Projects Agency Network [DoD] .... ARPANET
Advanced Research Projects Agency Terminal [DoD] .... ARPAT
Advanced Research and Technology .... AR & T
Advanced Research and Technology .... ART
Advanced Research and Technology Development Program
    [Department of Energy] .... AR & TD
Advanced Research Workshop .... ARW
Advanced Resident Training Plan [Military] .... ARTP
Advanced Restricted Report .... ARR
Advanced Rocket Engine Storable .... ARES
Advanced Rocket Ramjet .... ARR
Advanced Rocket Ramjet .... ARRJ
Advanced Ruling Expiration Date [IRS] .... AD
Advanced Sales Index [LIMRA] .... ASI
Advanced Salvo Rifle .... ASR
Advanced Satellite Tracking Center .... ASTC
Advanced Scatterable Mine [Air Force] .... ASM
Advanced Schools .... ADVSCOL
Advanced Science Education Program [National Science
    Foundation] .... ASEP
Advanced Scientific Computer .... ASC
Advanced Scientific Instruments .... ASI
Advanced Scientific Instruments Symbolic Translator .... ASIST
Advanced Scout Helicopter [Military] .... ASH

Advanced Scout Helicopter Task Force [*Army*] ASH-TF
Advanced Sea-Based Deterrent [*Navy*] ASBD
Advanced Section Communication Zone [*World War II*] ADSC
Advanced Semiconductor Materials International [*NASDAQ symbol*] ASMIF
Advanced Sensor Analog Relay System [*Army*] ASARS
Advanced Sensor Evaluation and Test [*NASA*] ASET
Advanced Series in Agricultural Sciences [*A publication*] Adv Ser Agric Sci
Advanced Ship Concept Development ASCD
Advanced Ship Concepts ASC
Advanced Ship Development ASD
Advanced Ship Types and Combatant Craft ASTACC
Advanced Shipboard Communications ADSCOM
Advanced Short-to-Medium Range ASMR
Advanced Short-Range Air-to-Air Missile ASRAA
Advanced Short-Range Air-to-Air Missile ASRAAM
Advanced Signal Processor [*Data processing*] ASP
Advanced Simulation Center [*Army*] ASC
Advanced Simulation Facility [*Army*] ASF
Advanced Simulator for Undergraduate Pilot Training [*Air Force*] ASUPT
Advanced Skewed Sensory Electronic Triad [*Navy*] ASSET
Advanced Skills Education Program [*Army*] ASEP
Advanced Small Axial Turbine Technology ASATT
Advanced Small Launch Vehicle ASLV
Advanced Sodium-Cooled Reactor ASCR
Advanced Solar Observatory ASO
Advanced Solar Turbo-Electric Conversion ASTEC
Advanced Solid Logic Technology [*Data processing*] ASLT
Advanced Sonobuoy Communications Link [*Navy*] ASCL
Advanced Soviet [*Combined with GENS to form A Group*] [*Division of National Security Agency*] ADVA
Advanced Space Engine ASE
Advanced Space Ground Link Subsystem ASGLS
Advanced Space Station ASS
Advanced Spacecraft Subsystem Cost Analysis Structure ASSCAS
Advanced Special Projects in Radiation Effects ASPIRE
Advanced Static Test Recording Apparatus ASTRA
Advanced Statistical Analysis Program [*Data processing*] ASTAP
Advanced Strategic Air-Launched Missile ASALM
Advanced Strategic Missile System [*DoD*] ASM
Advanced Strategic Reconnaissance System [*Air Force*] ASRS
Advanced Studies Group [*Air Force*] ASG
Advanced Studies in Pure Mathematics [*Elsevier Book Series*] [*A publication*] ASPM
Advanced Study Institutes ASI
Advanced Study Program ASP
Advanced Submarine Control Program ASCOP
Advanced Submarine Detection ASD
Advanced Submarine Weapon Handling System ASWHS
Advanced Supersonic All-Purpose Dispenser ASAP
Advanced Supersonic Transport ASST
Advanced Supersonic Transport AST
Advanced Surface-to-Air Ramjet [*Navy*] ASAR
Advanced Surface-Air Rocket Ramjet ASARR
Advanced Surface Missile ASM
Advanced Surveillance Aircraft ASA
Advanced Surveillance RADAR ASR
Advanced Survival Avionics Program ASAP
Advanced Synchronous Meteorological Satellite ASMS
Advanced System for Communications and Education in National Development ASCEND
Advanced System Concept ASC
Advanced System Concepts Laboratory [*Army*] ASCL
Advanced System Data Processing Simulation ASDPSIM
Advanced System Planning [*Air Force*] ASP
Advanced System Synthesis and Evaluation Technique [*Lockheed Aircraft*] ASSET
Advanced System Technology AST
Advanced System Time Domain ASYSTD
Advanced Systems Buying ASB
Advanced Systems Division [*IBM Corp.*] ASD
Advanced Systems, Inc. [*NASDAQ symbol*] ADVS
Advanced Systems Laboratory ASL
Advanced Systems Requirements ASR
Advanced Systems Research Department ASRD
Advanced Systems and Technology AS & T
Advanced Systems Technology and Integration Office [*Army*] ASTIO
Advanced Tactical Air Command and Control System ATACCS
Advanced Tactical Assault Weapon ATAW
Advanced Tactical Avionics RADAR ATAR
Advanced Tactical Ballistic Missile [*AMC - Missile*] ATBM
Advanced Tactical Command and Control Capabilities ATCCC
Advanced Tactical Control System ATCS
Advanced Tactical Electronic Warfare System ATEWS
Advanced Tactical Fighter [*Air Force*] ATF
Advanced Tactical Inertial Guidance System [*Navy*] ATIGS
Advanced Tactical Jamming System [*Aircraft*] ATJS
Advanced Tactical Lightweight Air Superiority [*RADAR*] ATLAS
Advanced Tactical Lightweight Avionics System ATLAS
Advanced Tactical Stand-Off Missile ATSM
Advanced Tactical Support Base [*Navy*] ATSB
Advanced Tanker Cargo Aircraft ATCA
Advanced Technical Education Program ATEP
Advanced Technical Engagement Model ATEM
Advanced Technical Experimental Transportation ATET
Advanced Technical Objective Working Group ATOWG
Advanced Technical Training Center [*Military*] ATTC
Advanced Technical Training Facility [*Military*] ATTF
Advanced Techniques for Electrical Power Management, Control, and Distribution Systems [*Army*] ATEPS
Advanced Techniques for Imagery Interpretation ATII
Advanced Technology Bomber ATB
Advanced Technology Components [*Program*] [*Army, Navy*] ATC
Advanced Technology Cruise Missile ATCM
Advanced Technology Demonstration LASER Gyro ATDLG
Advanced Technology Demonstrator Engine ATDE
Advanced Technology Developments ATD
Advanced Technology Engine ATE
Advanced Technology Ground Attack Fighter [*Air Force*] ATGAF
Advanced Technology Group [*Navy*] ATG
Advanced Technology Laboratory [*NASA*] ATL
Advanced Technology Large Aircraft System [*Air Force*] ATLAS
Advanced Technology/Libraries [*Information service*] AT/L
Advanced Technology Light Twin Research Aircraft ATLIT
Advanced-Technology Medium-Range Transport ATMR
Advanced Technology Microelectronic Array Computer ATMAC
Advanced Technology Program [*Military*] ATP
Advanced Technology Satellite ATS
Advanced Telecommunications [*NASDAQ symbol*] ATEL
Advanced Telecommunications Sciences Office [*STRATCOM*] [*Army*] ATSO
Advanced Telescope Mission [*Skylab*] [*NASA*] ATM
Advanced Television Seeker ATVS
Advanced Terminal Aerial Weapon Delivery Simulation ATAWDS
Advanced Terminal Guidance System ATGS
Advanced Terminal Interceptor ATI
Advanced Test Accelerator [*Lawrence Livermore National Laboratory*] ATA
Advanced Test in Psychology ATP
Advanced Test Reactor ATR
Advanced Test Reactor Critical Experiment ATRCE
Advanced Test Reactor Critical Facility ATRC
Advanced Test Vehicle ATV
Advanced Text Management System [*IBM Corp.*] ATMS
Advanced Textbooks in Economics [*Elsevier Book Series*] [*A publication*] ATE
Advanced Thermal Flight Experiment ATFE
Advanced Thermal Imaging Scanner [*or System*] ATIS
Advanced Thermal Reactor ATR
Advanced Throttling Slurry Engine ATSE
Advanced Tracking Program ATP
Advanced Trainer [*Air Force*] AT
Advanced Training [*Military*] ADVTNG
Advanced Training Unit ATU
Advanced Transit Association ATRA
Advanced Transport Technology ATT
Advanced Transport Technology Program Office [*NASA*] ATTPO
Advanced Trauma Life Support System ATLS
Advanced Triga Prototype Reactor ATPR
Advanced Turbine Engine Gas Generator [*Air Force*] ATEGG
Advanced Turbofan Engine ATE
Advanced TV Systems Committee ATVSC
Advanced UHF Communication System AUCS
Advanced Underseas Weapons Circuitry AUWC
Advanced Underwater Missile AUM
Advanced Underwater Search System AUSS
Advanced Underwater Weapons AUW
Advanced Unit Training [*Army*] AUT
Advanced Universal Jamming System AUJS
Advanced User Terminal [*Navy*] AUT
Advanced Vehicle Design Department AVDD
Advanced Vehicle Simulation Technique AVST
Advanced Very-High-Resolution Radiometer [*NASA*] AVHRR
Advanced Very-Large-Scale Integration [*Electronics*] AVLSI
Advanced Vidicon Camera System AVCS
Advanced Visual Information Display AVID
Advanced Voyager AV
Advanced Warning and Control System AWACS
Advanced Warning System AWS
Advanced Waste Treatment [*of water*] AWT
Advanced Waste Treatment Laboratory [*National Environmental Research Center*] AWTL
Advanced Weapon/Aircraft Requirements Evaluation AWARE
Advanced Weapon Delivery RADAR AWDR
Advanced Weapons Support Command [*Army*] AWSCOM
Advanced Weather RADAR AWR
Advanced Wide-Area Antipersonnel Mine AWAAPM
Advanced Wild Weasel [*RADAR warning system*] AWW
Advanced X-Ray Astrophysics Facility AXAF
Advanced X-Ray Facility AXF
Advancement of Science [*A publication*] Advancement Sci

Advancement of Science [*A publication*] ..... Advmt Sci
Advancement of Science [*A publication*] ..... Adv Sci
Advancement of Science [*A publication*] ..... Adv of Science
Advancement, Strength, and Training Plan System ..... ADSTAP
Advances in Acarology [*A publication*] ..... Adv Acarol
Advances in Activation Analysis [*A publication*] ..... Adv Act Anal
Advances in Aerosol Physics [*A publication*] ..... Adv Aerosol Phys
Advances in Agronomy [*A publication*] ..... Adv Agron
Advances in Agronomy [*A publication*] ..... Advan Agron
Advances in Agronomy and Crop Science [*A publication*] ..... Adv Agron Crop Sci
Advances in Analytical Chemistry and Instrumentation [*A publication*] ..... Adv Anal Chem Instrum
Advances in Anatomy, Embryology, and Cell Biology [*A publication*] ..... Adv Anat Embryol Cell Biol
Advances in Animal Physiology and Animal Nutrition [*A publication*] ..... Adv Anim Physiol Anim Nutr
Advances in Antimicrobial and Antineoplastic Chemotherapy [*A publication*] ..... Adv Antimicrob Antineoplast Chemother
Advances in Applied Mechanics [*A publication*] ..... Advan Appl Mech
Advances in Applied Mechanics [*A publication*] ..... Adv Appl Mech
Advances in Applied Microbiology [*A publication*] ..... Adv Appl Microbiol
Advances in Applied Probability [*A publication*] ..... Advan Appl Probab
Advances in Applied Probability [*A publication*] ..... Adv Appl P
Advances in Applied Probability [*A publication*] ..... Adv Appl Probab
Advances in Applied Probability [*A publication*] ..... Adv Ap Pr
Advances in Aquatic Microbiology [*A publication*] ..... Adv Aquat Microbiol
Advances in the Astronautical Sciences [*A publication*] ..... Advan Astronaut Sci
Advances in the Astronautical Sciences [*A publication*] ..... Adv Astronaut Sci
Advances in Astronomy and Astrophysics [*A publication*] ..... Adv Astron Astrophys
Advances in Atomic and Molecular Physics [*A publication*] ..... Adv At Mol Phys
Advances in Behavioral Biology [*A publication*] ..... Adv Behav Biol
Advances in Biochemical Engineering [*A publication*] ..... Adv Biochem Eng
Advances in Biochemical Psychopharmacology [*A publication*] ..... Adv Biochem Psychopharmacol
Advances in Bioengineering [*A publication*] ..... Adv Bioeng
Advances in Bioengineering and Instrumentation [*A publication*] ..... Adv Bioeng Instrum
Advances in Biological and Medical Physics [*A publication*] ..... Adv Biol Med Phys
Advances in Biology of the Skin [*A publication*] ..... Adv Biol Skin
Advances in Biomedical Engineering [*A publication*] ..... Adv Biomed Eng
Advances in Biomedical Engineering and Medical Physics [*A publication*] ..... Adv Biomed Eng Med Phys
Advances in Biophysics [*Tokyo*] [*A publication*] ..... Adv Biophys
Advances in Biophysics (Tokyo) [*A publication*] ..... Adv Biophys (Tokyo)
Advances in the Biosciences [*A publication*] ..... Adv Biosci
Advances in Blood Grouping [*A publication*] ..... Adv Blood Grouping
Advances in Botanical Research [*A publication*] ..... Adv Bot Res
Advances in Cancer Research [*A publication*] ..... Adv Cancer Res
Advances in Carbohydrate Chemistry [*Later, Advances in Carbohydrate Chemistry and Biochemistry*] [*A publication*] ..... Adv Carbohydr Chem
Advances in Carbohydrate Chemistry and Biochemistry [*A publication*] ..... Adv Carbohyd Chem
Advances in Carbohydrate Chemistry and Biochemistry [*A publication*] ..... Adv Carbohydr Chem Biochem
Advances in Cardiology [*A publication*] ..... Adv Cardiol
Advances in Catalysis and Related Subjects [*A publication*] ..... Adv Catal
Advances in Cell and Molecular Biology [*A publication*] ..... Adv Cell Mol Biol
Advances in Cereal Science and Technology [*A publication*] ..... Adv Cereal Sci Technol
Advances in Chemical Engineering [*A publication*] ..... Advan Chem Eng
Advances in Chemical Physics [*A publication*] ..... Adv Chem Phys
Advances in Chemistry Series [*A publication*] ..... Advan Chem Ser
Advances in Chemistry Series [*A publication*] ..... Adv Chem Se
Advances in Chemotherapy [*A publication*] ..... Adv Chemother
Advances in Child Development and Behavior [*A publication*] ..... Adv Child Dev Behav
Advances in Chromatography [*A publication*] ..... Adv Chromatogr
Advances in Clinical Chemistry [*A publication*] ..... Advan Clin Chem
Advances in Clinical Chemistry [*A publication*] ..... Adv Clin Chem
Advances in Clinical Pharmacology [*A publication*] ..... Adv Clin Pharmacol
Advances in Colloid and Interface Science [*A publication*] ..... Adv Coll In
Advances in Colloid and Interface Science [*A publication*] ..... Adv Colloid Interface Sci
Advances in Comparative Physiology and Biochemistry [*A publication*] ..... Adv Comp Physiol Biochem
Advances in Cryogenic Engineering [*A publication*] ..... Advan Cryog Eng
Advances in Cryogenic Engineering [*A publication*] ..... Adv Cryog Eng
Advances in Cyclic Nucleotide Research [*A publication*] ..... Adv Cyclic Nucleotide Res
Advances in Cytopharmacology [*A publication*] ..... Adv Cytopharmacol
Advances in Drug Research [*A publication*] ..... Adv Drug Res
Advances in Ecological Research [*A publication*] ..... Adv Ecol Res
Advances in Electronics and Electron Physics [*A publication*] ..... Advan Electron and Electron Phys
Advances in Electronics and Electron Physics [*A publication*] ..... Adv Electron Electron Phys
Advances in Electronics and Electron Physics. Supplement [*A publication*] ..... Adv Electron Electron Phys Suppl
Advances in Environmental Sciences and Technology [*A publication*] ..... Adv Environ Sci Technol
Advances in Enzyme Regulation [*A publication*] ..... Adv Enzyme Regul
Advances in Enzymology [*A publication*] ..... Adv Enzym
Advances in Enzymology and Related Areas of Molecular Biology [*A publication*] ..... Adv Enzymol Relat Areas Mol Biol
Advances in Ethology [*A publication*] ..... Adv Ethol
Advances in Experimental Medicine and Biology [*A publication*] ..... Adv Exp Med Biol
Advances in Experimental Social Psychology [*A publication*] ..... Adv Exp Soc Psychol
Advances in Fluorine Chemistry [*A publication*] ..... Adv Fluorine Chem
Advances in Fluorine Research and Dental Caries Prevention [*A publication*] ..... Adv Fluorine Res Dent Caries Prev
Advances in Food Research [*A publication*] ..... Adv Food Res
Advances in Food Research. Supplement [*A publication*] ..... Adv Food Res Suppl
Advances in Genetics [*A publication*] ..... Advan Genet
Advances in Genetics [*A publication*] ..... Adv Genetic
Advances in Geophysics [*A publication*] ..... Advan Geophys
Advances in Geophysics [*A publication*] ..... Adv Geophys
Advances in Gerontological Research [*A publication*] ..... Adv Gerontol Res
Advances in Heat Transfer [*A publication*] ..... Adv Heat Transfer
Advances in Holography [*A publication*] ..... Adv Hologr
Advances in Human Genetics [*A publication*] ..... Adv Hum Gen
Advances in Hydroscience [*A publication*] ..... Adv Hydrosci
Advances in Image Pickup and Display [*A publication*] ..... Adv Image Pickup Disp
Advances in Immunology [*A publication*] ..... Adv Immunol
Advances in Information Systems Science [*A publication*] ..... Adv Inf Syst Sci
Advances in Infrared and Raman Spectroscopy [*A publication*] ..... Adv Infrared Raman Spectrosc
Advances in Inorganic Biochemistry [*Elsevier Book Series*] [*A publication*] ..... AIB
Advances in Inorganic Chemistry and Radiochemistry [*A publication*] ..... Adv Inorg Chem Radiochem
Advances in Insect Physiology [*A publication*] ..... Adv Insect Physiol
Advances in Instrumentation [*A publication*] ..... Adv Instrum
Advances in Internal Medicine [*A publication*] ..... Adv Intern Med
Advances in Lipid Research [*A publication*] ..... Adv Lipid Res
Advances in Liquid Crystals [*A publication*] ..... Adv Liq Cryst
Advances in Magnetic Resonance [*A publication*] ..... Adv Magn Reson
Advances in Marine Biology [*A publication*] ..... Adv Mar Bio
Advances in Mathematics [*A publication*] ..... Adv Math
Advances in Metabolic Disorders [*A publication*] ..... Adv Metab Disord
Advances in Metabolic Disorders. Supplement [*A publication*] ..... Adv Metab Disord Suppl
Advances in Microbial Physiology [*A publication*] ..... Adv Microb Physiol
Advances in Microcirculation [*A publication*] ..... Adv Microcirc
Advances in Modern Nutrition [*A publication*] ..... Adv Mod Nutr
Advances in Molecular Relaxation and Interaction Processes [*A publication*] ..... Adv Mol Relax Interact Processes
Advances in Molecular Relaxation Processes [*Later, Advances in Molecular Relaxation and Interaction Processes*] [*A publication*] ..... Advan Mol Relaxation Processes
Advances in Molecular Relaxation Processes [*Later, Advances in Molecular Relaxation and Interaction Processes*] [*A publication*] ..... Adv Mol Rel
Advances in Molecular Relaxation Processes [*Later, Advances in Molecular Relaxation and Interaction Processes*] [*A publication*] ..... Adv Mol Relaxation Processes
Advances in Molten Salt Chemistry [*Elsevier Book Series*] [*A publication*] ..... AMSC
Advances in Morphogenesis [*A publication*] ..... Adv Morphog
Advances for Mutual Defense Assistance ..... AMDA
Advances in Myocardiology [*A publication*] ..... Adv Myocardiol
Advances in Nephrology [*A publication*] ..... Adv Nephrol
Advances in Neurochemistry [*A publication*] ..... Adv Neurochem
Advances in Neurological Sciences [*A publication*] ..... Adv Neurol Sci
Advances in Neurology [*A publication*] ..... Adv Neurol
Advances in Neurosurgery [*A publication*] ..... Adv Neurosurg
Advances in Nuclear Physics [*A publication*] ..... Adv Nucl Phys
Advances in Nuclear Science and Technology [*A publication*] ..... Adv Nucl Sci Technol
Advances in Nursing Science [*A publication*] ..... ANS
Advances in Nutritional Research [*A publication*] ..... Adv Nutr Res
Advances in Obstetrics and Gynecology [*A publication*] ..... Adv Obstet
Advances in Obstetrics and Gynecology (Baltimore) [*A publication*] ..... Adv Obstet Gynecol (Baltimore)
Advances in Ophthalmology [*A publication*] ..... Adv Ophthal
Advances in Optical and Electron Microscopy [*A publication*] ..... Adv Opt Electron Microsc
Advances in Oral Biology [*A publication*] ..... Adv Oral Biol
Advances in Organic Chemistry. Methods and Results [*A publication*] ..... Adv Org Chem

Advances in Organic Chemistry. Methods and Results [*A publication*] ... Adv Org Chem Methods Results
Advances in Oto-Rhino-Laryngology [*A publication*] ... ADORB
Advances in Oto-Rhino-Laryngology [*A publication*] ... Adv Oto-Rhino-Laryngol
Advances in Pain Research and Therapy [*A publication*] ... Adv Pain Res Ther
Advances in Parasitology [*A publication*] ... Adv Parasitol
Advances in Pathobiology [*A publication*] ... Adv Pathobiol
Advances in Pediatrics [*A publication*] ... Adv Pediatr
Advances in Pest Control Research [*A publication*] ... Adv Pest Control Res
Advances in Pharmaceutical Sciences [*A publication*] ... Adv Pharm Sci
Advances in Pharmacology [*A publication*] ... Adv Pharmacol
Advances in Pharmacology and Chemotherapy [*A publication*] ... Adv Pharmacol Chemother
Advances in Photochemistry [*A publication*] ... Adv Photochem
Advances in Physical Organic Chemistry [*A publication*] ... Adv Phys Org Chem
Advances in Physics [*A publication*] ... Advan Phys
Advances in Physics [*A publication*] ... Adv in Phys
Advances in Physics [*A publication*] ... Adv Phys
Advances in Physics [*A publication*] ... Adv Physics
Advances in Planned Parenthood [*A publication*] ... Adv Planned Parent
Advances in Planned Parenthood [*A publication*] ... Adv Plann Parent
Advances in Plasma Physics [*A publication*] ... Adv Plasma Phys
Advances in Pollen-Spore Research [*A publication*] ... Adv Pollen-Spore Res
Advances in Polymer Science [*A publication*] ... Adv Polymer Sci
Advances in Polymer Science [*A publication*] ... Adv Polym Sci
Advances in Printing Science and Technology [*A publication*] ... Adv Printing Sci
Advances in Prostaglandin and Thromboxane Research [*A publication*] ... Adv Prostaglandin Thromboxane Res
Advances in Protein Chemistry [*A publication*] ... Adv Protein Chem
Advances in Psychobiology [*A publication*] ... Adv Psychobiol
Advances in Psychobiology [*A publication*] ... AVPBC
Advances in Psychosomatic Medicine [*A publication*] ... Adv Psychosom Med
Advances in Psychosomatic Medicine [*A publication*] ... Adv Psy Med
Advances in Quantum Chemistry [*A publication*] ... Adv Quantum Chem
Advances in Quantum Electronics [*A publication*] ... Adv Quantum Electron
Advances in Radiation Biology [*A publication*] ... Adv Radiat Biol
Advances in Radiation Chemistry [*A publication*] ... Adv Radiat Chem
Advances in Reproductive Physiology [*A publication*] ... Adv R Physl
Advances in Sex Hormone Research [*A publication*] ... Adv Sex Horm Res
Advances in Shock Research [*A publication*] ... Adv Shock Res
Advances in Sleep Research [*A publication*] ... Adv Sleep Res
Advances in Small Animal Practice [*A publication*] ... Adv Small Anim Pract
Advances in Space Science [*A publication*] ... Adv Space Sci
Advances in Space Science and Technology [*A publication*] ... Adv Space Sci Technol
Advances in Space Science and Technology [*A publication*] ... Adv Spa Sci
Advances in Stereoencephalotomy [*A publication*] ... Adv Stereoencephalotomy
Advances in Steroid Biochemistry and Pharmacology [*A publication*] ... Adv Steroid Biochem
Advances in Structure Research by Diffraction Methods [*A publication*] ... Adv Struct Res Diffr Methods
Advances in the Study of Behavior [*A publication*] ... Adv Study Behav
Advances in Surgery [*A publication*] ... Adv Surg
Advances in Teratology [*A publication*] ... Adv Teratol
Advances in Textile Processing [*A publication*] ... Adv Textile Process
Advances in Thanatology [*A publication*] ... Advan Thanatol
Advances in Theoretical Physics [*A publication*] ... Adv Theor Phys
Advances in Tracer Methodology [*A publication*] ... Adv Tracer Methodol
Advances in Tuberculosis Research [*A publication*] ... Adv Tuberc Res
Advances in Tumor Prevention, Detection, and Characterization [*Elsevier Book Series*] [*A publication*] ... ATPDC
Advances in Veterinary Medicine (Berlin) [*A publication*] ... Adv Vet Med (Berl)
Advances in Veterinary Science [*A publication*] ... Adv Vet Sci
Advances in Veterinary Science and Comparative Medicine [*A publication*] ... Adv Vet Sci Comp Med
Advances in Virus Research [*A publication*] ... Advan Virus Res
Advances in Virus Research [*A publication*] ... Adv Virus Res
Advances in X-Ray Analysis [*A publication*] ... Adv X-Ray Anal
Advancing Blade Concept [*Helicopter*] ... ABC
Advancing Developing Countries [*Economics*] ... ADC
Advancing Frontiers of Plant Sciences [*A publication*] ... Advan Front Plant Sci
Advancing Frontiers of Plant Sciences [*A publication*] ... Adv Frontiers Plant Sci
Advancing Frontiers of Plant Sciences [*A publication*] ... Advg Front Pl Sci
Advantage ... ADV
Advantage ... ADVTG
Advantage Companies [*NASDAQ symbol*] ... ADCO
Advection ... ADVCTN
Advent ... ADV
Adventist Health Network of North America ... AHN
Adventist Network of Georgia, Cumberland Elementary Library, Collegedale, TN [*OCLC symbol*] ... TCA
Adventitious Root Formation [*Botany*] ... ARF
Adventure Lands of America Corp. [*NASDAQ symbol*] ... ADLA
Adventurers Club of New York [*Defunct*] ... ACNY
Adventures in Experimental Physics [*A publication*] ... Adventures Exp Phys
Adventures in Movement for the Handicapped [*An association*] ... AIM
Adverb ... ADV
Adverbial ... ADVB
Adverse Drug Reaction [*Medicine*] ... ADR
Adverse Drug Reaction Bulletin [*A publication*] ... Adverse Drug React Bull
Adverse Weather [*or All-Weather*] **Aerial Delivery System** [*Ordnance delivery method*] ... AWADS
Adverse Weather Close Air Support [*Military*] ... AWCAS
Adversus [*Against*] [*Latin*] ... ADV
Advertise and Award ... A & A
Advertisement ... AD
Advertisement ... ADV
Advertisement ... ADVERT
Advertisement ... ADVT
Advertiser, Franklinville, NJ [*Library symbol*] ... NjFrvA
Advertisers Casting Service ... ACS
Advertising ... ADVTG
Advertising Age [*A publication*] ... AA
Advertising Age [*A publication*] ... Adv Age
Advertising Age Europe [*A publication*] ... Ad Age Eur
Advertising Agency Magazine [*A publication*] ... Adv Agency Mag
Advertising Agency Production Club of New York [*Later, APC*] ... AAPC
Advertising Agency Service Interchange [*Defunct*] ... AASI
Advertising Association of the West [*Later, AAF*] ... AAW
Advertising Checking Bureau ... ACB
Advertising Club of New York ... ACNY
Advertising Council ... AC
Advertising Dimensions Standards [*American Newspaper Publishers Association*] ... ADS
Advertising Educational Foundation ... AEF
Advertising Federation of America [*Later, AAF*] ... AFA
Advertising Information Services ... AIS
Advertising and Marketing Association ... A & MA
Advertising and Marketing Intelligence Service [*New York Times Information Service, Inc.*] ... AMI
Advertising and Marketing International Network ... AMIN
Advertising Matter [*Freight*] ... ADV MTR
Advertising Media Credit Executives Association ... AMCEA
Advertising News of New York [*Later, Adweek*] [*A publication*] ... Anny
Advertising Photographers of America ... APA
Advertising Production Club of New York [*Formerly, AAPC*] ... APC
Advertising Research Foundation ... ARF
Advertising and Sales Promotion [*A publication*] ... A & SP
Advertising and Sales Promotion [*A publication*] ... ASP
Advertising and Selling [*A publication*] ... Adv & Sell
Advertising Specialty Guild of America ... ASGA
Advertising Specialty National Association ... ASNA
Advertising Standards Authority [*British*] ... ASA
Advertising Standards Council [*Canada*] ... ASC
Advertising Training Center [*New York City*] ... ATC
Advertising Typographers Association of America ... ATA
Advertising Unlimited [*NASDAQ symbol*] ... AUNL
Advertising Women of New York ... AWNY
[*The*] **Advest Group, Inc.** [*NYSE symbol*] ... ADV
Advice ... AD
Advice ... ADVC
Advice of Allotment ... A/A
Advice of Allotment ... ADVALT
[*With the*] **Advice and Consent of the Senate** ... ADCONSEN
Advice of Payment ... AP
Advice of Receipt ... AR
Advise ... ADVS
Advise ... ADZ
Advise Acceptance ... ADVAC
Advise Action to Be Taken by This Office ... ADATT
Advise Action Taken ... ADACT
Advise by Airmail [*Army*] ... ADAML
Advise by Airmail as Soon as Practicable ... ADMAP
Advise All Concerned ... ADALCON
Advise [*or Issue Instructions to*] **All Concerned** ... ADCON
Advise Appropriate Command Having Cognizance of Transportation when Available for Transportation to Continental United States [*Military*] ... ADVAILTRANSCONUS
Advise Approximate Date ... ADADA
Advise Arrival ... ADZAR
Advise Availability [*Army*] ... ADAVAL
Advise Availability [*Army*] ... ADVAL
Advise Customs [*Aviation*] ... ADCUS
Advise [*Command Designated*] **Date Available for Transportation from Port of Embarkation** [*Military*] ... ADVAILTRANSPOE
Advise Date of Receipt ... ADARE
Advise Date of Reporting in Compliance with Orders [*Navy*] ... ADARCO
Advise Date of Shipment ... ADASH
Advise Disposition [*Aviation*] ... ADSPN
Advise Duration and Charge [*British telephone term*] ... AD and C
Advise Earliest Date ... ADSDA
Advise Effective Date ... ADEDA

Advise If Able [*Aviation*] ... AIA
Advise If Able to Proceed [*Aviation*] ... AAP
Advise Immediately by Dispatch ... ADIMD
Advise Individual Concerned of Change of Assignment [*Military*] ... CHASG
Advise Intentions ... ADZI
Advise Latest Address [*Military*] ... ADLATAD
Advise by [*Electronically Transmitted*] **Message** [*Army*] ... ADMSG
Advise by Message of Action the Following Individual Is Taking [*Military*] ... ADPERSACT
Advise by Message Reduction Current Period of Active Duty [*Military*] ... ADREDPRED
Advise by Message Why Individual Is Being Reduced [*Military*] ... ADPRORED
Advise Method, Bill of Lading, and Date Shipped ... AMBLADS
Advise Method and Date of Shipment ... ADMAD
Advise if Not Correct ... ADNOK
Advise Present Grade, Status, Physical Condition, and Mailing Address of Following Named [*Military*] ... STATREP
Advise Present Position and Altitude [*Aviation*] ... APPA
Advise Reason for Delay [*Aviation*] ... ADRDE
Advise [*names of*] **Representatives, Accommodations, and Transportation** [*desired*] [*Army*] ... ARAT
Advise Shipping Data ... ADSHIPDA
Advise Shipping Date ... ADSHPDAT
Advise Soldier Write Home ... ASWH
Advise as Soon as Possible ... ADSAP
Advise Status and/or Disposition [*Army*] ... ADSTADIS
Advise Stock on Hand [*Army*] ... ADSTKOH
Advise This Headquarters of Complete Action [*Army*] ... ADHCA
Advise This Office ... ADVOF
Advise This Office ... ADZOF
Advise What Action Has Been Taken [*Military*] ... ADTAKE
Advise When Able ... AWA
Advise When Established [*Aviation*] ... AWE
Advise Whether Individual May Be Properly Utilized in Your Installation [*Army*] ... ADIPU
Advised Not to Move Dependents until Suitable Quarters Located [*Military*] ... ADNOMOVPEN
Adviser on Combined Operations [*British*] ... ACO
Advisor ... ADVR
Advisor ... ADVSR
Advisor, Middletown, NJ [*Library symbol*] ... NjMiA
Advisory ... ADV
Advisory ... ADVRY
Advisory ... ADVSY
Advisory ... ADVY
Advisory ... ADZY
Advisory Area [*Aviation*] ... ADA
Advisory Board ... AB
Advisory Board on the Built Environment [*Formerly, BRAB*] ... ABBE
Advisory Board for Cooperative Systems [*of ICIREPAT*] ... ABCS
[*The*] **Advisory Board for the Research Councils** [*British*] ... ABRC
Advisory Centre for Education [*British*] ... ACE
Advisory Circular ... AC
Advisory Commission on Intergovernmental Relations ... ACIR
Advisory Commission on Parliamentary Accommodation [*Canada*] ... ACPA
Advisory Commission on Textbook Specifications ... ACTS
Advisory Committee ... AC
Advisory Committee on Administrative and Budgetary Questions [*United Nations*] ... ACABQ
Advisory Committee on the Application of Science and Technology to Development [*Also, ACASTD, ACST*] [*United Nations*] ... ACAST
Advisory Committee on the Application of Science and Technology to Development [*Also, ACAST, ACST*] [*United Nations*] ... ACASTD
Advisory Committee on the Application of Science and Technology to Development [*Also, ACAST, ACASTD*] [*United Nations*] ... ACST
Advisory Committee on the Arts [*Terminated, 1973*] ... ACA
Advisory Committee for Biology and Medicine [*AEC*] ... ACBM
Advisory Committee to the Board and to the Committee on Commodities [*UNCTAD*] ... ACBCC
Advisory Committee on Civilian Policy [*World War II*] ... ACCP
Advisory Committee to the Department of Housing and Urban Development ... ACHUD
Advisory Committee for the Education of Romany and Other Travellers ... ACERT
Advisory Committee on Energy Research and Development [*British government*] ... ACORD
Advisory Committee on Export Policy ... ACEP
Advisory Committee on Flight Information [*FAA*] ... ACFI
Advisory Committee on Immunization Practices [*Public Health Service*] ... ACIP
Advisory Committee on Marine Resources Research ... ACMRR
Advisory Committee on the NAIC [*National Astronomy and Ionosphere Center*] **Nation-Wide Marine Definition** ... COI
Advisory Committee on Nuclear Materials Safeguards ... ACNMS
Advisory Committee on Oceanic Meteorological Research [*United Nations*] ... ACOMR
Advisory Committee on Oil Pollution of the Sea [*British*] ... ACOPS
Advisory Committee for Operational Hydrology [*WMO*] ... ACOH
Advisory Committee on Personal Dosimetry Services [*National Science Foundation*] ... ACPDS
Advisory Committee on Reactor Safeguards [*Nuclear Regulatory Commission*] ... ACRS
Advisory Committee on Science and Technology and Foreign Affairs [*Terminated, 1975*] [*Department of State*] ... ACSTFA
Advisory Committee for Scientific and Technical Information [*British*] ... ACSTI
Advisory Committee, Statistics [*British*] ... AC(S)
Advisory Committee on Voluntary Foreign Aid [*Department of State*] ... ACVA
Advisory Committee on Voluntary Foreign Aid [*Department of State*] ... ACVFA
Advisory Committee on Weather Control [*Terminated, 1957*] ... ACWC
Advisory, Conciliation, and Arbitration Service [*British*] ... ACAS
Advisory Council, Allied Control Commission [*Italy*] [*World War II*] ... ACACC
Advisory Council for Applied Research and Development [*British government*] ... ACARD
Advisory Council on Camps ... ACC
Advisory Council on College Chemistry ... ACCC
Advisory Council on Federal Reports ... ACFR
Advisory Council on Historic Preservation ... ACHP
Advisory Council on Medical Education ... ACME
Advisory Council for Minority Enterprise [*White House*] ... ACME
Advisory Council on Naval Affairs ... ACNA
Advisory Council on Naval Affairs of the Navy League ... ACONA
Advisory Council for Orthopaedic Resident Education ... ACORE
Advisory Council on Scientific Policy ... ACSP
Advisory Council on Scientific Research and Technical Development [*British*] ... AC
Advisory Council on the Status of Women [*Canada*] ... ACSW
Advisory Council on Technology [*British*] ... ACT
Advisory Direction ... AD
Advisory Group [*Military*] ... ADGRU
Advisory Group for Aerospace Research and Development [*Formerly, Advisory Group for Aeronautical Research and Development*] [*NATO*] ... AGARD
Advisory Group on Electron Devices [*Army*] ... AGED
Advisory Group on Electronic Parts [*Military*] ... AGEP
Advisory Group on Energy [*Army*] ... AGE
Advisory Group on Management of Electronic Parts Specifications ... AGMEPS
Advisory Group on National Bibliographic Control ... AGNBC
Advisory Group on Reliability of Electronic Equipment [*Military*] ... AGREE
Advisory Leaflet. Ministry of Agriculture, Fisheries, and Food (Great Britain) [*A publication*] ... Adv Leafl Min Agr Fish Food (Gt Brit)
Advisory Leaflet. Queensland Department of Agriculture and Stock. Division of Plant Industry [*A publication*] ... Adv Leafl Queensland Dept Agr Stock Div Plant Ind
Advisory Leaflet. West of Scotland Agricultural College [*A publication*] ... Adv Leafl W Scot Agr Coll
Advisory Panel for Operations Research ... APOR
Advisory Panel on Safeguarding Special Nuclear Material ... APSSNM
Advisory Route [*Aviation*] ... ADR
Advisory Service Leaflet. Timber Research and Development Association [*A publication*] ... Ad Serv Leafl Timb Res Developm Ass
Advisory Support Force [*Military*] ... ASF
Advocate ... ADV
Advocate, East Orange, NJ [*Library symbol*] ... NjEoA
Advocates of International Trade and Comity [*Defunct*] ... AITC
Advocates to Save Legal Services ... ASLS
Advocates for Women [*An association*] ... AFW
Adyar Library Bulletin [*A publication*] ... AdLB
Adyar Library Bulletin [*A publication*] ... ALB
AE. Clemson Agricultural Experiment Station [*A publication*] ... AE Clemson Agr Exp Sta
AE. Delaware Agricultural Experiment Station. Department of Agricultural Economics [*A publication*] ... AE Del Agr Exp Stat Dept Agr Econ
AE Research. New York State College of Agriculture. Department of Agricultural Economics [*A publication*] ... AE Res NY State Coll Agr Dept Agr Econ
AE. University of Illinois. College of Agriculture. Experiment Station. Cooperative Extension Service [*A publication*] ... AE Univ Ill Coll Agr Exp Sta Coop Ext Serv
AEC Inc. [*NASDAQ symbol*] ... AECE
AECL [*Atomic Energy of Canada Ltd.*] **Research and Development in Engineering** [*A publication*] ... AECL Res & Dev Eng
AEDS [*Association for Educational Data Systems*] **Journal** [*A publication*] ... AEDS J
AEDS [*Association for Educational Data Systems*] **Journal** [*A publication*] ... AEDS Jrnl
AEDS [*Association for Educational Data Systems*] **Monitor** [*A publication*] ... AEDS Mon
AEDS [*Association for Educational Data Systems*] **Monitor** [*A publication*] ... AEDS Monit
AEG [*Allgemeine Elektrizitaets-Gesellschaft*] **Kernreaktoren** [*A publication*] ... AEG Kernreakt

AEG [*Allgemeine Elektrizitaets-Gesellschaft*] **- Telefunken Progress** [*A publication*] ... AEG-Telefunken Progr
Aegis Corp. [*American Stock Exchange symbol*] ... AO
Aegrus [*or Aegra*] [*The Patient*] [*Medicine*] ... AEG
Aegyptologische Abhandlungen [*A publication*] ... AA
Aegyptologische Forschungen [*A publication*] ... Aeg Forsch
Aegyptus: Rivista Italiana di Egittologia e di Papirologia [*A publication*] ... Aeg
Aehrodinamika Razrezhennykh Gazov [*A publication*] ... Aehrodin Razrezh Gazov
AEL Industries, Inc. Cl A [*NASDAQ symbol*] ... AELNA
Aeon [*10^9 years*] [*Geology*] ... AE
Aequales [*Equal*] [*Latin*] ... AEQ
Aequationes Mathematicae [*A publication*] ... Aequ Math
Aer Lingus Teoranta [*Ireland*] ... ALT
Aer Lingus Teoranta [*Ireland*] [*ICAO designator*] ... EI
Aer Turas Teoranta [*Ireland*] [*ICAO designator*] ... QT
Aerated Bread Company [*Chain of restaurants in London*] ... ABC
Aerated Stabilization Basin [*For water purification*] ... ASB
Aeration Test Burner [*Heating*] ... ATB
Aerial ... AERL
Aerial ... ARL
Aerial Ambulance Company [*Army*] ... AAC
Aerial Armored Reconnaissance Vehicle ... AARV
Aerial Biosensing Association ... ABA
Aerial Burst Bombs ... AB
Aerial Cartographic and Geodetic Squadron [*Air Force*] ... ACGSq
Aerial Combat Maneuvering Training ... ACMT
Aerial Combat Reconnaissance ... ACR
Aerial Delivered Land Mine ... ADLM
Aerial Delivery System ... ADS
Aerial Demonstration Squadron ... ADS
Aerial Demonstration Team ... ADT
Aerial Exposure Index ... AEI
Aerial Film Speed ... AFS
Aerial Fire Support ... AFS
Aerial Free Gunnery Instructions School [*Obsolete*] ... AFGIS
Aerial Free Gunnery Unit ... AFGU
Aerial Inspection Instrument ... AII
Aerial Intercept Missile ... AIM
Aerial Mail Terminal ... AMT
Aerial Nurse Corps of America ... ANCOA
Aerial Observer [*Military*] ... AO
Aerial Phenomena Research Organization ... APRO
Aerial Photographic Analysis Center ... APAC
Aerial Photographic Reconnaissance ... APR
Aerial Port ... AP
Aerial Port of Debarkation [*Military*] ... APOD
Aerial Port Detachment ... APD
Aerial Port Documentation and Management System ... ADAM II
Aerial Port of Embarkation [*Military*] ... APE
Aerial Port of Embarkation [*Military*] ... APOE
Aerial Port Group [*Air Force*] ... APG
Aerial Port Group [*Air Force*] ... APGp
Aerial Port Group [*Air Force*] ... APOG
Aerial Port Liaison Office [*or Officer*] [*Air Force*] ... APLO
Aerial Port Logistics Office [*Air Force*] ... APLO
Aerial Port Squadron [*Air Force*] ... APS
Aerial Port Squadron [*Air Force*] ... APSq
Aerial RADIAC Instrument ... ARI
Aerial RADIAC Instrument System ... ARIS
Aerial Radiological Measurements and Survey [*Program*] ... ARMS
Aerial Reconnaissance Laboratory ... ARL
Aerial Reconnaissance and Security ... ARS
Aerial Reconnaissance and Security Troop ... ARST
Aerial Reconnaissance and Surveillance Penetration Analysis [*Army*] ... ARSPA
Aerial Reconnaissance and Surveillance Survivability Analysis [*Army*] ... ARSSA
Aerial [*In-Flight*] **Refueling** ... AR
Aerial Refueling Operator ... ARO
Aerial Refueling Receptacle ... ARR
Aerial Rocket Antitank Program ... ARAT
Aerial Rocket Artillery ... ARA
Aerial Scout Helicopter ... ASH
Aerial Stores Lift Truck ... ASLT
Aerial Surveillance and Target Acquisition [*Military*] ... ASTA
Aerial Survey and Target Acquisition [*Military*] ... ASTA
Aerial Survey Team ... AST
Aerial Target Control Central ... ATCC
Aerial Torpedo ... AT
Aerial Tuning Condenser ... ATC
Aerial Tuning Inductance ... ATI
Aerie Airlines [*Nashville, TN*] [*FAA designator*] ... LTL
Aerlinte Eireann Teoranta [*Irish Air Lines*] ... AET
Aerlinte Eireann Teoranta [*Irish Air Lines*] [*ICAO designator*] ... IN
Aero/Acoustic Detection System [*Army*] ... AADS
Aero/Acoustic Rotor ... A/AR
Aero America, Inc. [*ICAO designator*] ... EO
Aero-Chem Research Laboratories, Inc. ... ACRL
Aero Club of America [*Later, National Aeronautic Association of the USA*] ... ACA
Aero-Elastic Research Laboratory [*MIT*] ... AERL
Aero-Electronic Technology Department [*Navy*] ... AETD
Aero Flotilla [*Soviet airline*] ... AEROFLOT
Aero-Flow Dynamics, Inc. [*American Stock Exchange symbol*] [*Delisted*] ... AER
Aero Geo Astro Corporation ... AGAC
Aero Gun Sights ... AGS
Aero Industries, Inc. [*Richmond, VA*] [*FAA designator*] ... WAB
Aero Industries Technical Institute ... AITI
Aero Lloyd [*West Germany*] [*ICAO designator*] ... LL
Aero Mech, Inc. [*Clarksburg, WV*] [*FAA designator*] ... AMH
Aero-Mechanical Engineering Laboratory [*Army*] ... AMEL
Aero-Mechanics Department [*Navy*] ... AMD
Aero O/Y [*Finnish airline*] ... FINNAIR
Aero-Propulsion Fuels Laboratory [*Air Force*] ... APFL
Aero-Propulsion Laboratory [*Air Force*] ... APL
Aero Rampart Corp. [*Colorado Springs, CO*] [*FAA designator*] ... RMP
Aero Repair ... AR
Aero Services, Inc. [*Wichita, KS*] [*FAA designator*] ... AOS
Aero Services International [*NASDAQ symbol*] ... AERO
Aero/Space Engineering [*A publication*] ... Aero/Space Eng
Aero Spacelines [*Air carrier designation symbol*] ... AERX
AERO Sun-Times [*A publication*] ... AERO Sun-T
Aero Surface Control ... ASC
Aero Systems [*NASDAQ symbol*] ... AESM
Aero Tour [*France*] [*ICAO designator*] ... FV
Aero Transportes, SA [*Mexican airline*] ... ATSA
Aero Transporti Italiani ... ATI
Aero Trends, Inc. [*San Jose, CA*] [*FAA designator*] ... CYR
Aeroamerica, Incorporated [*Air carrier designation symbol*] ... AAIX
Aeroballistic Reentry Vehicle ... ARV
Aerobic Plate Count [*Microbiology*] ... APC
Aerobics International Research Society ... AIRS
Aerobiology and Evaluation Laboratory [*Army*] ... AEL
Aerochemical Metal-Oxide Kinetics [*Program*] ... AMOK
Aerodespachos de El Salvador [*ICAO designator*] ... DN
Aerodex, Inc. [*American Stock Exchange symbol*] [*Delisted*] ... AOX
Aerodrome ... AD
Aerodrome ... ADRM
Aerodrome to Aerodrome ... A/A
Aerodrome Beacon ... ABN
Aerodrome Control [*British*] ... ADC
Aerodrome Defence Corps [*British*] ... ADC
Aerodrome [*or Airport*] **of Entry** ... AOE
Aerodrome Flight Information Service ... AFIS
Aerodrome Forecast [*Aviation*] ... TAF
Aerodrome Obstruction Chart ... AOC
Aerodrome RADAR/Radio Approach Aid ... ARAA
Aerodrome Reference Point ... ARP
Aerodrome Traffic Zone ... ATZ
Aerodromes, Air Routes, and Ground Aids [*Aviation*] ... AGA
Aerodynamic ... AERODYN
Aerodynamic Coefficients Identification Package ... ACIP
Aerodynamic Damping Moment in Pitch [*Helicopter rotor*] ... ADMP
Aerodynamic Data Analysis and Integration System [*Data processing*] ... ADAIS
Aerodynamic Data Book ... ADB
Aerodynamic Decelerator ... AD
Aerodynamic Deployable Decelerator Performance Evaluation Program ... ADDPEP
Aerodynamic Flight Control ... AFC
Aerodynamic Flight Test ... AFT
Aerodynamic Heat Test Plans ... AHTP
Aerodynamic Heating ... AEROHEAT
Aerodynamic Heating Indicator ... AHI
Aerodynamic-Influence Coefficient ... AIC
Aerodynamic Modeling [*Module*] ... AEROMOD
Aerodynamic Post-Processing [*Module*] ... AEROPOST
Aerodynamic Propulsive Interactive Force [*Air Force*] ... APIF
Aerodynamic Report ... AR
Aerodynamic Stability Augmentation System [*or Subsystem*] [*NASA*] ... ASAS
Aerodynamic Surface Assembly and Checkout ... ASAC
Aerodynamic Test Vehicle ... ATV
Aerodynamic Yaw Coupling ... AYC
Aerodynamic Yaw Coupling Parameters ... AYCP
Aerodynamically Neutral Spin-Stabilized Rocket ... ANSSR
Aerodynamically Neutral Spin-Stabilized Rocket Artillery System ... ANSSRAS
Aerodynamics ... ARODYN
Aerodynamics Advisory Panel [*AEC*] ... AAP
Aerodynamics Center ... AC
Aerodynamics Laboratory [*Naval Ship Research and Development Center*] ... AL
Aerodynamics Note ... AN
Aerodynamics Surface Control ... ASC
Aeroelastic and Structures Research Laboratory [*MIT*] ... ASRL
Aeroelastic Wind Tunnel ... AWT
Aeroelastically Conformable Rotor ... ACR

Aeroelectronic .... AE
Aeroflex Laboratories, Inc. [*NYSE symbol*] .... ARX
AEROFLOT [*Aero Flotilla*] [*USSR*] [*ICAO designator*] .... SU
Aerographer .... AERO
Aerographer's Mate .... AERM
Aerographer's Mate [*Navy rating*] .... AG
Aerographer's Mate, Chief [*Navy rating*] .... AGC
Aerographer's Mate, First Class [*Navy rating*] AG1
Aerographer's Mate, Master Chief [*Navy rating*] .... AGCM
Aerographer's Mate, Second Class [*Navy rating*] AG2
Aerographer's Mate, Senior Chief [*Navy rating*] .... AGCS
Aerographer's Mate, Third Class [*Navy rating*] AG3
Aerogulf Services Co. [*United Arab*] [*ICAO designator*] .... GZ
Aerojet/Bumblebee [*Navy missile*] .... AEROBEE
Aerojet Differential Analyzer .... ADA
Aerojet Electrosystems Co., Azusa, CA [*Library symbol*] .... CAzA
Aerojet-General Corp. .... AG
Aerojet-General Corporation .... AGC
Aerojet-General Nucleonics [*of Aerojet-General Corp.*] .... AGN
Aerojet Liquid Rocket Company .... ALRC
Aerojet Network Analyzer .... ANA
Aerojet Nuclear Co., Idaho Falls, ID [*Library symbol*] .... IdIfA
Aerojet Solid Propulsion Company .... ASPC
Aeroleasing [*Switzerland*] [*ICAO designator*] .... FP
Aerolineas Argentinas [*Argentine airline*] .... AA
Aerolineas Argentinas [*Argentine airline*] [*ICAO designator*] .... AR
Aerolineas Argentinas [*Argentine airline*] .... ARG
Aerolineas Colonia SA [*Uruguay*] [*ICAO designator*] .... KO
Aerolineas Dominicanas [*Dominican Republic*] [*ICAO designator*] .... SS
Aerolineas de El Salvador [*ICAO designator*] .... SZ
Aerolineas de Guatemala [*ICAO designator*] .... GU
Aerolineas Nacionales del Ecuador [*ICAO designator*] .... ED
Aerolinee Italiane Internazionali [*Italian International Airline*] .... ALITALIA
Aerological .... AEROL
Aerological Officer .... AER OF
Aerologist .... AEROG
Aeromarine, Inc. [*Honolulu, HI*] [*FAA designator*] .... AME
Aeromech Commuter Airlines [*Clarksburg, WV*] [*FAA designator*] .... KCI
Aeromechanics Laboratory [*Army*] .... AL
Aeromedica Acta [*A publication*] .... Aeromed Acta
Aeromedical .... AEROMED
Aeromedical Airlift Group [*Air Force*] .... AAGp
Aeromedical Airlift Squadron [*Air Force*] .... AASq
Aeromedical Airlift Wing [*Air Force*] .... AAW
Aeromedical Airlift Wing [*Air Force*] .... AAWg
Aeromedical Data .... AMD
Aeromedical Education Division [*FAA*] .... AED
Aeromedical Equipment Laboratory .... AMEL
Aeromedical Evacuation [*Later, AME*] .... AE
Aeromedical Evacuation [*Later, AME*] .... AMDLEVAC
Aeromedical Evacuation [*Formerly, AE, AMDLEVAC*] .... AME
Aeromedical Evacuation Control Center [*Military*] .... AECC
Aeromedical Evacuation Control Officer [*Military*] .... AECO
Aeromedical Evacuation Group [*Air Force*] .... AEGp
Aeromedical Evacuation Liaison Officer [*Air Force*] .... AELO
Aeromedical Evacuation Operations Office [*or Officer*] [*Military*] .... AEOO
Aeromedical Evacuation Squadron [*Air Force*] .... AESq
Aeromedical Evacuation Support Team .... AEST
Aeromedical Evacuation System [*Air Force*] .... AMES
Aeromedical Laboratory .... AML
Aeromedical Liaison Office [*or Officer*] [*Air Force*] .... AMLO
Aeromedical Library, 6571st Aeromedical Research Laboratory, Holloman AFB, NM [*Library symbol*] .... NmHARL
Aeromedical Monitor Console .... AMC
Aeromedical Research Laboratory [*NASA*] .... ARL
Aeromedical Research Unit [*Army*] .... ARU
Aeromedical Review [*A publication*] .... Aeromed Rev
Aeromedical Staging Facility .... ASF
Aeromedical Staging Unit .... ASU
Aerometric and Emissions Reporting System [*Environmental Protection Agency*] .... AEROS
Aeromexico [*Mexican airline*] [*ICAO designator*] .... AM
Aeronaut Society .... AS
Aeronautica and Air Label Collectors Club .... AALCC
Aeronautical .... AERON
Aeronautical Advisory Council .... AAC
Aeronautical Approach Chart [*Military*] .... AAC
Aeronautical Approach Chart [*Air Force*] .... AC
Aeronautical Army and Navy .... AAN
Aeronautical and Astronautical Engineering .... AAE
Aeronautical Board [*Air Force*] .... AB
Aeronautical Broadcast Station [*ITU designation*] .... FAB
Aeronautical Center [*FAA*] .... AC
Aeronautical Chamber of Commerce of America [*Later, AIA*] .... ACCA
Aeronautical Chart and Information Center [*Later, DMAAC*] [*Air Force*] .... ACIC
Aeronautical Chart and Information Center Technical Translation Section [*Air Force*] .... ACIC-TC
Aeronautical Chart and Information Squadron [*Air Force*] .... ACISQ
Aeronautical Communications Equipment Corp. .... AEROCOM
Aeronautical Communications Satellite System [*Proposed*] .... AEROSAT
Aeronautical Computers Laboratory [*Navy*] .... ACL
Aeronautical Data .... AD
Aeronautical Data Report [*Navy*] .... ADR
Aeronautical Design Standard [*Army*] .... ADS
Aeronautical Engine Laboratory [*Later, NAPTC*] [*Navy*] .... AEL
Aeronautical Engineer .... AE
Aeronautical Engineer .... AeEng
Aeronautical Engineering Department [*NASA*] .... AED
Aeronautical Engineering Duty [*Navy*] .... AED
Aeronautical Engineering and Electronic Laboratory [*Navy*] .... AEEL
Aeronautical Engineering Laboratory [*NASA*] .... AEL
Aeronautical Engineering Report .... AER
Aeronautical Engineering Review [*A publication*] .... Aero Eng R
Aeronautical Equipment Reference Number [*Military*] .... AERNO
Aeronautical Equipment Service Record .... AESR
Aeronautical Fixed Service .... AFS
Aeronautical Fixed Station [*ITU designation*] .... FAX
Aeronautical Fixed Telecommunications Network .... AFTN
Aeronautical Fixed Telecommunications Service .... AFTS
Aeronautical Icing Research Laboratory .... AIRL
Aeronautical Information Circular .... AIC
Aeronautical Information Publication [*FAA*] .... AIP
Aeronautical Information Regulation and Control .... AIRAC
Aeronautical [*or Aerospace*] **Information Report** .... AIR
Aeronautical Information Service .... AIS
Aeronautical Information Specialist .... AIS
Aeronautical Inspection Directorate [*British*] .... AID
Aeronautical Instruments Laboratory [*Military*] .... AIL
Aeronautical Journal [*A publication*] .... Aero J
Aeronautical Journal [*A publication*] .... Aeronaut J
Aeronautical Journal [*A publication*] .... Aeron J
Aeronautical Laboratory .... AL
Aeronautical Maintenance Duty Officer .... AMDO
Aeronautical Manufacturers' Planning Report .... AMPR
Aeronautical Marker Beacon [*ITU designation*] .... RLA
Aeronautical Material Specification .... AMS
Aeronautical Materials Laboratory .... AML
Aeronautical Medical Acceleration Laboratory [*Air Force*] .... AMAL
Aeronautical Militare [*Italy*] .... AM
Aeronautical Military Standards .... AMS
Aeronautical Mobile .... AEM
Aeronautical Mobile Service .... AMS
Aeronautical National Taper Pipe Threads .... ANPT
Aeronautical Operating Systems Division [*NASA*] .... AOSD
Aeronautical Order .... AO
Aeronautical Photographic Experimental Laboratory .... APEL
Aeronautical Planning Chart [*Military*] .... APC
Aeronautical Production Control System .... APCS
Aeronautical Propulsion Division [*NASA*] .... APD
Aeronautical Quality Assurance Directorate [*British*] .... AQD
Aeronautical Quality Assurance Field Office [*FAA*] .... AQAFO
Aeronautical Quarterly [*A publication*] .... Aeronaut Q
Aeronautical Quarterly [*A publication*] .... Aeron Q
Aeronautical RADAR Research Complex .... ARRC
Aeronautical Radio, Incorporated .... ARI
Aeronautical Radio, Incorporated .... ARINC
Aeronautical Radio, Incorporated .... ARINCO
Aeronautical Radio, Inc. [*ICAO designator*] .... XA
Aeronautical Radio and RADAR Laboratory [*Navy*] .... ARRL
Aeronautical Radio Range [*Nautical charts*] .... AERO R Rge
Aeronautical Radiobeacon [*Nautical charts*] .... AERO R Bn
Aeronautical Radionavigation Land Station [*ITU designation*] .... AL
Aeronautical Radionavigation Mobile Station [*ITU designation*] .... AM
Aeronautical Radionavigation RADAR .... ARR
Aeronautical [*or Aerospace*] **Recommended Practice** .... ARP
Aeronautical [*or Aircraft*] **Requirement** [*Military*] .... AR
Aeronautical Research Associates of Princeton .... ARAP
Aeronautical Research Council [*British*] .... ARC
Aeronautical Research Division [*NASA*] .... ARD
Aeronautical Research Foundation .... ARF
Aeronautical Research, Incorporated .... ARINC
Aeronautical Research Institute of Sweden .... ARIS
Aeronautical Research Laboratories. Department of Defence. Australia. Reports [*A publication*] .... Aeronaut Res Lab Dep Def Aust Rep
Aeronautical Research Laboratory [*OAR*] .... ARL
Aeronautical Research Scientist .... ARS
Aeronautical Services Communication Center [*Great Britain*] .... ASCC
Aeronautical Shipboard Installation Representative .... ASIR
Aeronautical Specifications .... AS
Aeronautical Standards .... AS
Aeronautical Standards Group [*Military*] .... AG
Aeronautical Standards Group [*Military*] .... ASG
Aeronautical Standards Group [*Military*] .... ASGp
Aeronautical Station [*ITU designation*] .... FA
Aeronautical Structures Laboratory [*Navy*] .... ASL
Aeronautical Support Equipment Type Designation System .... ASETDS
Aeronautical System Development .... ASD
Aeronautical Systems Center [*Air Force*] .... ASC
Aeronautical Systems Division [*AFSC*] .... ASD
Aeronautical Systems Division Form .... ASDF
Aeronautical Systems Division Manual .... ASDM

Aeronautical Systems Division Regulation .... ASDR
Aeronautical Technical Directive Requirement [*Obsolete*] .... ATDR
Aeronautical Telecommunications Operator .... ATO
Aeronautical Training Society .... ATS
Aeronautical Turbine Laboratory [*Navy*] .... ATL
Aeronautical Video Charts .... AVC
Aeronautical Video Plates .... AVP
Aeronautically Fixed .... AF
Aeronautics .... AER
Aeronautics .... AERO
Aeronautics and Astronautics Coordinating Board [*NASA*] .... AACB
Aeronautics and Space .... AEROSPACE
Aeronautics and Space Engineering Board [*National Academy of Engineering*] .... ASEB
Aeronautics Supply Officer .... ASO
Aeronautics Upper Atmosphere Impact Program [*NASA*] .... AUAIP
Aeronautique et l'Astronautique (Paris) [*A publication*] .... Aeronaut Astronaut (Paris)
Aeronaves de Mexico [*Mexican airline*] .... ADM
Aeronca, Inc. [*American Stock Exchange symbol*] .... ARN
Aeronomy Laboratory [*National Bureau of Standards*] .... AL
Aeronomy Satellite - Neutral Atmosphere Temperature Experiment .... AEROS-NATE
Aeronomy and Space Data Center [*Later, NGSDC*] [*National Oceanic and Atmospheric Administration*] .... ASDC
Aeronutronic Ford Corp., Newport Beach, CA [*Library symbol*] .... CNbAF
Aeronutronic General Perturbations Differential Correction Program .... AGPDC
Aeronutronics Division, Ford Motor Co. .... ADF
Aerophilatelic Federation of the Americas .... AFA
Aerophysics Development Corporation .... ADC
Aerophysics Laboratory .... AL
Aerophysics Laboratory Memorandum [*NASA*] .... ALM
Aeroplane and Armament Experimental Establishment [*British*] .... AAEE
Aeroplane Flag [*Navy*] [*British*] .... AP
Aeropropulsion Systems Test Facilities .... ASTF
Aeroquip Corp. [*NYSE symbol*] [*Delisted*] .... AQP
Aerosol Analyzer .... AA
Aerosol Climatic Effects [*NASA*] .... ACE
Aerosol Physical Properties of the Stratosphere [*NASA*] .... APPS
Aerosol Report [*A publication*] .... Aerosol Rep
Aerosol Sampling System .... ASS
Aerosol Techniques, Incorporated .... ATI
Aerosonic Corp. [*NASDAQ symbol*] .... ASON
Aerospace .... A
Aerospace .... AEROSP
Aerospace Audiovisual Service [*Air Force*] .... AAVS
Aerospace Auxiliary Equipment .... AAE
Aerospace Business Environment Simulator [*Computer-programed management game*] .... ABES
Aerospace Cartographic and Geodetic Service .... ACGS
Aerospace Catalog Automated Microfilm, Inc. .... ASCAM
Aerospace Center [*Defense Mapping Agency*] .... AC
Aerospace Communication and Controls Division [*NASA*] .... ACCD
Aerospace Communications .... AEROSPACECOM
Aerospace Communications Complex [*Air Force*] .... AIRCOM
Aerospace Computer Program [*Air Force*] .... ACP
Aerospace Contract Engineers .... ACE
Aerospace Control .... ASC
Aerospace Control Environment [*Air Force*] .... ACE
Aerospace Corporation .... AC
Aerospace Corp., El Segundo, CA [*Library symbol*] .... CEsA
Aerospace Crew Equipment Development .... ACED
Aerospace Crew Equipment Laboratory [*Philadelphia, PA*] .... ACEL
Aerospace Data Systems .... ADS
Aerospace Defense Command [*Formerly, Air Defense Command*] [*Air Force*] .... ADC
Aerospace Defense Command [*Formerly, Air Defense Command*] [*Air Force*] .... ADCOM
Aerospace Defense Division [*Air Force*] .... ADD
Aerospace Defense Systems Officer [*Air Force*] .... ADSO
Aerospace Department Chairmen's Association .... ADCA
Aerospace Digital Development .... ADD
Aerospace Draftsman's Education and Proficiency Training .... ADEPT
Aerospace Driver/Monitor .... ASDM
Aerospace Education .... AE
Aerospace Education Foundation .... AEF
Aerospace Education Instructor .... AEI
Aerospace Education Workshop Project .... AEWP
Aerospace Electrical Society .... AES
Aerospace and Electronic Systems .... AES
Aerospace Electronics Laboratories .... AEL
Aerospace Engineering Process Institute .... AEPI
Aerospace Engineering Test Establishment [*Canada*] .... AETE
Aerospace Environment .... AE
Aerospace Environment Simulation System .... ASESS
Aerospace and Environmental Medicine Information System .... AEMIS
Aerospace Environmental Support Unit [*Air Weather Service*] .... AESU
Aerospace Facilities Engineer .... AFE
Aerospace and Flight Test Radio Coordinating Council .... AFTRCC
Aerospace Flight Vehicle .... AFV
Aerospace Ground Equipment .... AGE
Aerospace Ground Equipment Department .... AGED
Aerospace Ground Equipment Installation .... AGEI
Aerospace Ground Equipment Out of Commission for Parts [*Air Force*] .... AGEOCP
Aerospace Ground Equipment Requirements Data .... AGERD
Aerospace Ground Equipment/Support Equipment .... AGE/SE
Aerospace Ground Unit .... AGU
Aerospace Group .... AG
Aerospace Guidance and Metrology Center [*Air Force*] .... AGE
Aerospace Guidance and Metrology Center [*Air Force*] .... AG & MC
Aerospace Guidance and Metrology Center [*Air Force*] .... AGMC
Aerospace Historian [*A publication*] .... Aerospace Hist
Aerospace Industrial Life Sciences Association [*of Aerospace Medical Association*] .... AILSA
Aerospace [*formerly, Aircraft*] **Industries Association of America** [*Formerly, ACCA*] .... AIA
Aerospace [*formerly, Aircraft*] **Industries Association of America** [*Formerly, ACCA*] .... AIAA
Aerospace Information Digest [*A publication*] .... AID
Aerospace Information Division [*Library of Congress*] .... AID
Aerospace Installation Diagnostic Equipment .... AIDE
Aerospace Instrumentation Laboratory [*Air Force*] .... AIL
Aerospace Instrumentation Range Station .... AESIR
Aerospace Intelligence Data System .... AIDS
Aerospace Intelligence File .... AIF
Aerospace Internal Data Report [*Air Force*] .... AIDR
Aerospace Maintenance and Operational Status .... AMOS
Aerospace Manufacturers Council [*Defunct*] .... AMC
Aerospace Material Specification .... AMS
Aerospace Materials Document .... AMD
Aerospace Materials Information .... AMI
Aerospace Materials Information Center [*Air Force*] .... AMIC
Aerospace Medical Association .... AMA
Aerospace Medical Association .... AsMA
Aerospace Medical Command [*Air Force*] .... AMC
Aerospace Medical Division [*Air Force*] .... AMD
Aerospace Medical Laboratory (Clinical) [*Air Force*] .... AMLC
Aerospace Medical Operations Office [*NASA*] .... AMOO
Aerospace Medical Research .... AMR
Aerospace Medical Research Laboratory [*Air Force*] .... AMRL
Aerospace Medicine [*A publication*] .... AEMEA
Aerospace Medicine [*A publication*] .... Aerospace Med
Aerospace Medicine [*A publication*] .... Aerosp Med
Aerospace Medicine .... AM
Aerospace Medicine and Biology .... AMB
Aerospace and Navigational Electronics .... ANE
Aerospace Nuclear Safety Information Center .... ANSIC
Aerospace Observation Platform .... AOP
Aerospace Photographic Reconnaissance Equipment .... APRE
Aerospace Plane .... ASP
Aerospace Planning Charts .... ASC
Aerospace Power Division [*Air Force*] .... APD
Aerospace Primus Club .... APC
Aerospace Radioisotope Power Information Center .... ARPIC
Aerospace Recovery Facility .... ARF
Aerospace Reference Project [*Formerly, ATP*] [*Library of Congress*] .... ARP
Aerospace Remote Calculator .... ARC
Aerospace Rescue and Recovery .... ARR
Aerospace Rescue and Recovery Center [*Air Force*] .... ARRC
Aerospace Rescue and Recovery Group [*Air Force*] .... ARRGp
Aerospace Rescue and Recovery Service [*Air Force*] .... ARRS
Aerospace Rescue and Recovery Squadron [*Air Force*] .... ARRSq
Aerospace Rescue and Recovery Training Center [*Air Force*] .... ARRTC
Aerospace Rescue and Recovery Wing [*Air Force*] .... ARRWg
Aerospace Research Applications Center [*Indiana University*] [*NASA*] .... ARAC
Aerospace Research Association .... ARA
Aerospace Research Chamber .... ARC
Aerospace Research Laboratory [*Air Force*] .... ARL
Aerospace Research Pilot School [*Air Force*] .... ARPS
Aerospace Research Pilot School - Edwards Air Force Base [*Air Force*] .... ARPSE
Aerospace Research Satellite .... ARS
Aerospace Research Support Program [*Air Force*] .... ARSP
Aerospace Research Vehicle .... ARV
Aerospace Safety [*A publication*] .... Aero Safe
Aerospace Safety Advisory Panel .... ASAP
Aerospace Safety Research and Data Institute [*Lewis Research Center*] [*NASA*] .... ASRDI
Aerospace Security Force .... ASF
Aerospace Services Division [*NASA*] .... ASD
Aerospace Spin-Off Laboratory .... AEROSOL
Aerospace Standards .... AS
Aerospace Static Converter .... ASC
Aerospace Static Inverter .... ASI
Aerospace Structural Material .... ASM
Aerospace Structures Information and Analysis Center [*Air Force*] .... ASIAC
Aerospace Structures Test Facility [*Air Force*] .... ASTF
Aerospace Studies [*AFROTC*] .... AS

Aerospace Studies Institute [*Air Force*] ... ASI
Aerospace Support Equipment ... ASE
Aerospace Support Systems ... ASS
Aerospace Surveillance and Control [*Air Force*] ... AS & C
Aerospace Surveillance and Control Squadron [*Air Force*] ... ASCS
Aerospace Surveillance System ... ASS
Aerospace Surveillance and Warning ... ASSAW
Aerospace System Test and Evaluation Complex ... ASTEC
Aerospace Systems Center [*Dayton, OH*] ... ASC
Aerospace Systems Safety Society ... ASSS
Aerospace Systems Security Program ... ASSP
Aerospace Systems Test Environment ... ASTE
Aerospace Systems Test Reactor [*Formerly, Aircraft Shield Test Reactor*] ... ASTR
Aerospace [*or Air*] **Technical Intelligence Center** ... ATIC
Aerospace Technologist [*or Technology*] [*NASA*] ... AST
Aerospace Technology [*A publication*] ... Aerospace Tech
Aerospace Technology Division [*Formerly, Aerospace Information Division; later, ARP*] [*Library of Congress*] ... ATD
Aerospace Technology Division [*Formerly, Aerospace Information Division; later, ARP*]**/Library of Congress** ... ATD/LC
Aerospace Test Equipment ... ATE
Aerospace Test Wing [*Air Force*] ... ASTWg
Aerospace Test Wing [*Air Force*] ... ATW
Aerospace Traffic Control Center ... ATCC
Aerospace Vehicle ... ASV
Aerospace Vehicle ... AV
Aerospace Vehicle Distribution Office [*or Officer*] [*Air Force*] ... AVDO
Aerospace Vehicle Electronics ... AVE
Aerospace [*or Airborne*] **Vehicle Equipment** ... AVE
Aerospace Vehicle Inventory, Status, and Utilization Reporting System ... AVISURS
Aerospace Vehicle System ... AVS
Aerosurface Driver Electronics ... ASDE
Aerosurface End-to-End Test ... AET
Aerosurface Position Indicator ... ASPI
Aerosurface Servo Amplifier ... ASA
Aerotechnica Missili e Spazio [*A publication*] ... Aerotec Missili & Spazio
Aerotherm Axisymmetric Transient Heating and Material Ablation [*Program*] ... ASTHMA
Aerothermodynamic Data Book ... ATDB
Aerothermodynamic Duct ... ATHODYD
Aerothermodynamic Elastic Vehicle ... AEV
Aerothermodynamic Integration Model ... AIM
Aerothermodynamic Structural Systems Environmental Test [*Military*] ... ASSET
Aerothermodynamic Structural Vehicle [*Air Force*] ... ASV
Aerotransporte de Espana SA [*Spain*] [*ICAO designator*] ... WK
Aerotransportes [*Argentina*] [*ICAO designator*] ... RS
Aerovia Sud Americana ... ASUD
Aerovias Ecuatoriana, SA ... AREA
Aerovias Interamericanas de Panama, SA ... AVISPA
Aerovias Nacionales de Colombia [*Avianca*] [*Colombia*] [*ICAO designator*] ... AV
Aerovias Nacionales de Colombia [*Colombian airline*] ... AVIANCO
Aerovias Panama Airways ... APA
Aerovias Quisqueyana [*Airlines*] [*Dominican Republic*] [*ICAO designator*] ... QQ
Aerovias Venezolanas, SA [*Venezuelan airline*] ... AVENSA
Aerovias Venezolanas, SA [*Venezuelan airline*] [*ICAO designator*] ... VE
Aerztliche Forschung [*A publication*] ... Aerztl Forsch
Aerztliche Jugendkunde [*A publication*] ... Aerztl Jugendkd
Aerztliche Laboratorium [*A publication*] ... Aerztl Lab
Aerztliche Monatshefte fuer Berufliche Fortbildung [*A publication*] ... Aerztl Monatsh Berufliche Fortbild
Aerztliche Praxis [*A publication*] ... Aerztl Praxis
Aerztliche Wochenschrift [*A publication*] ... Aerztl Wochenschr
Aes [*Obverse*] [*Numismatics*] ... AE
Aesculapian Club ... AC
Aesthetic Realism Foundation ... ARF
Aestheticians International Association ... AIA
Aesthetics [*A publication*] ... AE
Aesthetics ... AESTH
Aetatis [*Age*] [*Latin*] ... AE
Aetatis [*Age*] [*Latin*] ... Aet
Aetatis [*Age*] [*Latin*] ... AETAT
Aetherius Society ... AS
Aethylen-Rohrleitungs-Gesellschaft [*West Germany*] ... ARG
Aetna Life & Casualty Co. [*NYSE symbol*] ... AET
AEU-Archiv fuer Elektronik und Uebertragungstechnik [*A publication*] ... AEU-Arch El
AEU-Archiv fuer Elektronik und Uebertragungstechnik [*A publication*] ... AEU-Arch Elektron Uebertragungstech
Aevum [*A publication*] ... Ae
Aevum [*A publication*] ... Aev
Aevum Christianum. Salzburger Beitraege zur Religions- und Geistesgeschichte des Abandlandes [*A publication*] ... Ae Ch Salz
AFA Protective Systems [*NASDAQ symbol*] ... AFAP
Afar Locality [*Paleoanthropology*] ... AL
Afareaitu [*Society Islands*] [*Seismograph station code, US Geological Survey*] ... AFR
Affair ... AFFR
Affairs ... AFF
Affari Esteri [*A publication*] ... Aff Est
Affari Sociali Internazionali [*A publication*] ... Aff Soc Int
Affarsvarlden [*A publication*] ... Affarsvarld
Affect ... AFCT
Affect Adjective Check List [*Psychology*] ... AACL
Affect Elaboration [*Scale*] [*Psychology*] ... AE
Affected Areas ... AA
Affectionately ... AFF
Affective System ... AS
Affenpinscher Club of America [*Later, American Affenpinscher Association*] ... ACA
Afferent [*Medicine*] ... AFF
Affettuoso [*With Expression*] [*Music*] ... AFFET
Affettuoso [*With Expression*] [*Music*] ... AFFETTO
Affidavit ... AFDVT
Affidavit ... AFFT
Affiliate ... AFFL
Affiliate of the Royal Society of Health [*British*] ... Affil RSH
Affiliated ... AFFIL
Affiliated Advertising Agencies International ... AAAI
Affiliated Bank Corp. of Wyoming [*NASDAQ symbol*] ... ABWY
Affiliated Bankshares of Colorado [*NASDAQ symbol*] ... AFBK
Affiliated Capital Corp. [*American Stock Exchange symbol*] [*Delisted*] ... AFD
Affiliated Chiropodists-Podiatrists of America ... ACPA
Affiliated Dress Manufacturers ... ADM
Affiliated Drug Stores, Inc. [*An association*] ... ADS
Affiliated Government Employees' Distributing Co. [*California*] ... AGE
Affiliated Hospital Products, Inc. [*American Stock Exchange symbol*] ... AFH
Affiliated Leadership League of and for the Blind of America ... ALL
Affiliated Medical Research, Inc. [*Research code symbol*] ... AMR
Affiliated National Riding Commission [*Formerly, NRC*] ... ANRC
Affiliated Nutritional Retailers Association [*Commercial firm*] ... ANRA
Affiliated Publications, Inc. [*American Stock Exchange symbol*] ... AFP
Affiliated Warehouse Companies [*An association*] ... AWC
Affiliation ... AFFILTN
Affiliation Code [*IRS*] ... AFC
Affiliation Officer [*British*] ... AO
Affinely Connected Space ... ACS
Affirmative ... AFF
Affirmative ... AFIRM
Affirmative Action [*Employment policies for minorities*] ... AA
Affirmative Action Coordinating Center ... AACC
Affirmative Action Coordinating Center. Newsletter [*A publication*] ... AACC News
Affirmative Action Plan [*or Program*] [*Equal opportunity employment*] ... AAP
Affirmative Action Register [*A publication*] ... AAR
Affirmative Flag [*Navy*] [*British*] ... AF
Affirmative Replies Neither Required nor Desired ... NOAFIRM
Affirmed ... AFFD
Affirming ... AFFG
Affluent ... AFFL
Afford Service Member Opportunity to Apply for Ordinary Leave [*Army*] ... ASMOLV
Affray [*FBI standardized term*] ... AFFR
Affrettando [*Hurrying the Pace*] [*Music*] ... AFFRET
Affrettando [*Hurrying the Pace*] [*Music*] ... AFFRETTO
AFG Industries, Inc. [*NASDAQ symbol*] ... AFGN
Afghan Border Crusade ... ABC
Afghan Community in America ... ACA
Afghan Hound Club of America ... AHCA
Afghan Youth Council in America ... AYCA
Afghani [*Monetary unit in Afghanistan*] ... AF
Afghanistan [*MARC geographic area code*] [*Library of Congress*] ... a-af---
Afghanistan [*Three-letter standard code*] ... AFG
Afghanistan ... AFGH
Afghanistan [*Aircraft nationality and registration mark*] ... YA
Afghanistan [*MARC country of publication code*] [*Library of Congress*] ... af
Afghanistan [*Two-letter standard code*] ... AF
Afghanistan Information Center ... AIC
Afghanistan National Liberation Front ... ANLF
Afghanistan Relief Committee ... ARC
Afghanistan Studies Association ... ASA
Afiamalu [*Samoa Islands*] [*Seismograph station code, US Geological Survey*] ... AFI
AFL-CIO American Federationist [*A publication*] ... AFL-CIO Am Fed
Aflatoxicol [*Metabolite of AFB*] [*Biochemistry*] ... AFL
Aflatoxin [*A mycotoxin*] [*Generic form*] ... AFT
Aflatoxin [*s*] **B** [*Mycotoxins*] ... AFB
Aflatoxin [*s*] **G** [*Mycotoxins*] ... AFG
Aflatoxin [*s*] **M** [*Mycotoxins*] ... AFM
Aflatoxin [*s*] **P** [*Mycotoxins*] ... AFP
Aflatoxin [*s*] **Q** [*Mycotoxins*] ... AFQ
Afloat Communications Management Office [*Naval Ship Engineering Center*] ... ACMO
Afloat Consumption Cost and Effectiveness Surveillance System [*Navy*] ... ACCESS
Afore [*Papua New Guinea*] [*Airport symbol*] ... AFR
Aforesaid ... AFSD

AFP Imaging Corporation [*NASDAQ symbol*] ... AFPC
Africa ... AF
Africa ... AFR
Africa [*MARC geographic area code*] [*Library of Congress*] ... f------
Africa and Asia ... AFRASIA
Africa, Central [*MARC geographic area code*] [*Library of Congress*] ... fc-----
Africa Committee [*British*] [*World War II*] ... A
Africa Cooperative Savings and Credit Association ... ACOSCA
Africa Digest [*A publication*] ... Afr Dig
Africa, East [*MARC geographic area code*] [*Library of Congress*] ... fe-----
Africa, Equatorial [*MARC geographic area code*] [*Library of Congress*] ... fq-----
Africa (Ethiopia) Committee [*British*] [*World War II*] ... A(E)
[*The*] **Africa Fund** [*An association*] ... AF
Africa Guild ... AG
Africa Inland Mission ... AIM
Africa Inland Transport [*British*] [*World War II*] ... A(IT)
Africa Institute Bulletin [*A publication*] ... Afr Inst B
Africa Institute Bulletin [*A publication*] ... Afr Inst Bull
Africa. International African Institute [*A publication*] ... Africa IAI
Africa Italiana [*A publication*] ... AfrIt
Africa Italiana [*A publication*] ... AI
Africa (London) [*A publication*] ... AfricaL
Africa - Middle East Theater [*World War II*] ... AMET
Africa, North [*MARC geographic area code*] [*Library of Congress*] ... ff-----
Africa Quarterly [*A publication*] ... Afr Q
Africa Quarterly [*A publication*] ... AQ
Africa Report [*A publication*] ... Africa R
Africa Report [*A publication*] ... Africa Rep
Africa Report [*A publication*] ... Africa Rept
Africa Report [*A publication*] ... Afr Rep
Africa Report [*A publication*] ... Afr Report
Africa Research Bulletin Series [*A publication*] ... Afr Res Bull
Africa Research and Publications Project ... ARPP
Africa. Revista Espanola de Colonizacion [*A publication*] ... AFR
Africa Service Institute of New York [*Defunct*] ... ASI
Africa South of the Sahara [*Military*] ... ASOTS
Africa, Southern [*MARC geographic area code*] [*Library of Congress*] ... fs-----
Africa, Sub-Saharan [*MARC geographic area code*] [*Library of Congress*] ... fb-----
Africa-Tervuren [*A publication*] ... Afr-T
Africa Today [*A publication*] ... Africa T
Africa Today [*A publication*] ... Afr Today
Africa Today [*A publication*] ... AT
Africa, West [*MARC geographic area code*] [*Library of Congress*] ... fw-----
African [*Derogatory nickname for blacks in Zimbabwe and South Africa*] ... Af
African Abstracts [*A publication*] ... AfrAb
African Affairs [*A publication*] ... AfrAf
African Affairs [*A publication*] ... Afr Aff
African Affairs [*A publication*] ... Afr Affairs
African Affairs [*A publication*] ... Afric Affairs
African-American Institute ... AAI
African-American Labor Center [*AFL-CIO*] ... AALC
African American Museums Association ... AAMA
African-American Scholars Conference [*Defunct*] ... AASC
African Anti-Colonial Movement of Kenya ... AACM
African Arts [*Los Angeles*] [*A publication*] ... AfrA
African Arts [*Los Angeles*] [*A publication*] ... Afr Arts
African Bibliographic Center ... ABC
African Bibliographic Center, Washington, DC [*Library symbol*] ... DABC
African Book Publishing Record [*A publication*] ... ABPR
African, Caribbean, and Pacific [*Countries*] ... ACP
African Commune of Bad Relevant Artists [*Chicago*] ... AFRICOBRA
African Communications Liaison Service ... ACLS
African Communist [*A publication*] ... Afr Communist
African Development [*A publication*] ... Afr Develop
African Development Bank [*Also, AfDB*] ... ADB
African Development Bank [*Also, ADB*] ... AfDB
African Development Fund ... ADF
African Development Fund ... AFDF
African Ecclesial Review [*A publication*] ... AFER
African Economic Affairs Committee [*London*] [*World War II*] ... AEA
African Elected Members Organization ... AEMO
African Environment [*A publication*] ... AFRE
African Force Headquarters [*World War II*] ... AFHQ
African Forestry Commission [*UN Food and Agriculture Organization*] ... AFC
African Forum: A Quarterly Journal of Contemporary Affairs [*A publication*] ... AForum
African Green Monkey Kidney [*Type of cell line*] ... AGMK
African Groundnut Council ... AGC
African Heritage Center for African Dance and Music ... AHCADM
African Heritage Studies Association ... AHSA
African Historical Studies [*A publication*] ... Afr Hist Stud
African Imprint Library Services, Bedford, NY [*Library symbol*] ... AfrI
African/Indian Ocean [*Aviation*] ... AFI
African Jazz Art Society Studios ... AJASS
African Journal of Educational Research [*A publication*] ... African J Ednl Research
African Journal of Medical Sciences [*A publication*] ... Afr J Med Sci
African Journal of Medicine and Medical Sciences [*A publication*] ... Afr J Med Med Sci
African Journal of Psychiatry [*A publication*] ... Afr J Psychiatr
African Journal of Tropical Hydrobiology and Fisheries [*A publication*] ... Afr J Trop Hydrobiol Fish
African Journal of Tropical Hydrobiology and Fisheries. Special Issue [*A publication*] ... Afr J Trop Hydrobiol Fish Spec Issue
African Language Review [*A publication*] ... AfrLRev
African Language Studies [*A publication*] ... Afr Lang Stud
African Language Studies [*A publication*] ... AfrLS
African Language Studies [*A publication*] ... ALS
African Languages/Langues Africaines [*A publication*] ... AL/LA
African Law Association in America [*Superseded by INTWORLSA*] ... ALAA
African Law Studies [*A publication*] ... Afr Law Stud
African Literature Association ... ALA
African Literature Today [*A publication*] ... AFLT
African Literature Today [*A publication*] ... Afric Lit Today
African Literature Today [*A publication*] ... ALT
African Love Bird Society ... ALBS
African Medical and Research Foundation ... AMRF
African Methodist Episcopal [*Church*] ... AME
African Methodist Episcopal Mission ... AMEM
African Methodist Episcopal Zion [*Church*] ... AMEZ
African Music [*A publication*] ... Af Mus
African National Congress ... ANC
African National Congress of South Africa ... ANCSA
African National Congress Youth League ... ANCYL
African National Council [*Rhodesia*] ... ANC
African Nationalist Pioneer Movement [*Defunct*] ... ANPM
African Notes [*Ibadan*] [*A publication*] ... AfrN
African Peanut (Groundnut) Council ... APC
African Postal and Telecommunications Union ... APTU
African Postal Union ... AFPU
African Regional Organization ... AFRO
African Regional Standards Organization ... ARSO
African Religious Research [*A publication*] ... Afr Relig Res
African Research and Documentation [*A publication*] ... Afr Res Doc
African Research Foundation [*Later, IMRF, AMRF*] ... ARF
African Review [*A publication*] ... Afr R
African Rhino Group ... ARG
African Safari Airways [*ICAO designator*] ... QS
African Safari Club of Philadelphia ... ASCP
African Satellite ... AFROSAT
African Scholar [*A publication*] ... AfrSch
African Scholarship Program of American Universities [*Joint undertaking, headquartered in Cambridge, MA, to provide aid to African applicants for admission to American universities*] ... ASPAU
African Social Research [*A publication*] ... Afr Soc Res
African Social Security Series [*A publication*] ... Afr Soc Secur Ser
African Society for Human Rights ... ASHR
African Soils [*A publication*] ... Afr Soils
African Star [*Decoration*] [*British*] ... AS
African Studies [*A publication*] ... African Stud
African Studies [*A publication*] ... Afric Stud
African Studies [*Johannesburg*] [*A publication*] ... AfrS
African Studies [*A publication*] ... Afr Stud
African Studies Association ... ASA
African Studies Association, Brandeis University, Waltham, MA [*Library symbol*] ... MWalAF
African Studies Bulletin [*A publication*] ... African Stud Bul
African Studies Bulletin [*A publication*] ... ASB
African Studies Review [*A publication*] ... African Stud R
African Studies Review [*A publication*] ... Afric Stud R
African Studies Review [*A publication*] ... AfrSR
African Studies Review [*A publication*] ... Afr Stud R
African Succulent Plant Society [*Defunct*] ... ASPS
African Trade Union Confederation [*Confederation Syndicale Africaine*] [*Later, OATUU*] ... ATUC
African Trades Union Congress of Southern Rhodesia ... ATUC(SR)
African Violet Society of America ... AVSA
African Wildlife [*A publication*] ... Afr Wildl
African Wildlife Leadership Foundation ... AWLF
African Writers Series [*A publication*] ... Afr WS
Africana Bulletin [*Warsaw*] [*A publication*] ... AfB
Africana Journal [*A publication*] ... Africana J
Africana Library Journal [*A publication*] ... Africana Lib J
Africana Library Journal [*A publication*] ... AfrLJ
Africana Linguistica [*Tervuren*] [*A publication*] ... AfrL
Africana Marburgensia [*A publication*] ... Africana Marburg
Africana Marburgensia [*A publication*] ... AfrM
Africana Research Bulletin [*A publication*] ... Africana Res B
Africana Research Bulletin [*A publication*] ... ARB
Afrihili [*MARC language code*] [*Library of Congress*] ... afh
Afrika Heute [*A publication*] ... Afr Heute
Afrika Spectrum [*A publication*] ... Afr Spectrum
Afrika und Uebersee [*A publication*] ... AU
Afrika und Uebersee [*A publication*] ... AuU
Afrika-Wirtschaft [*A publication*] ... Afr-Wirtsch
Afrikaans [*MARC language code*] [*Library of Congress*] ... afr
Afrikaans ... AFRIK
Afrikaanse Christelike Vrouevereniging ... ACVV

Afrikan Airlines Ltd. [*Ghana*] [*ICAO designator*] ... KW
Afrique-Agriculture [*A publication*] ... Afr-Agric
Afrique et l'Asie [*Later, Afrique et l'Asie Modernes*] [*A publication*] ... Af A
Afrique-Asie [*A publication*] ... Afr-Asie
Afrique et l'Asie Modernes [*A publication*] ... Afr Asie
Afrique Contemporaine [*A publication*] ... Afr Contemp
Afrique Equatoriale Francaise [*French Equatorial Africa*] ... AEF
Afrique-Industrie-Infrastructure [*A publication*] ... Afr-Industr-Infrastruct
Afrique et l'Asie Modernes [*A publication*] ... Afr et Asie Mod
Afrique et l'Asie Modernes [*A publication*] ... Afr Asie Mod
Afrique Litteraire et Artistique [*A publication*] ... Afr Litter et Artist
Afrique Litteraire et Artistique [*A publication*] ... ALA
Afrique Medicale [*A publication*] ... Afr Med
Afrique Occidentale Francaise [*French West Africa*] ... AOF
Afro-American Art Institute ... AAAI
Afro-American Cultural Foundation ... AACF
Afro-American Cultural and Historical Society [*Later, AACHSM*] ... AACHS
Afro-American Cultural and Historical Society Museum [*Formerly, AACHS*] ... AACHSM
Afro-American Cultural Technological Scientific Olympics ... ACT-SO
Afro-American Historical and Genealogical Society ... AAHGS
Afro-American Museum of Detroit ... AAM
Afro-American Music Opportunities Association ... AAMOA
Afro-American Police League ... AAPL
Afro-American Society for International Relations ... AASIR
Afro-American Student Association ... AASA
Afro-American Studies [*A publication*] ... AfrAm S
Afro-American Studies [*A publication*] ... Afr-Am Stud
Afro-Asian Center ... AAC
Afro-Asian Journalists' Association ... AAJA
Afro-Asian Latin-American Students' Organization ... AALASO
Afro-Asian Lawyers' Conference ... AALC
Afro-Asian Organization for Economic Cooperation ... AFRASEC
Afro-Asian Peoples Solidarity Council ... AAPSC
Afro-Asian Peoples Solidarity Organization ... AAPSO
Afro-Asian Rural Reconstruction Organization ... AARRO
Afro-Asian Solidarity Organization ... AASO
Afro-Asian Solidarity Secretariat ... AASS
Afro-Asian Theatre Bulletin [*A publication*] ... AATB
Afro-Asian Workers' Organization ... AAWO
Afro-Asian and World Affairs [*A publication*] ... AAWA
Afro-Asian Writers' Permanent Bureau ... AAWPB
Afro-Asian Writings [*A publication*] ... AAW
Afro-Asian Youth Solidarity Organization ... AAYSO
Afro-Asiatic [*MARC language code*] [*Library of Congress*] ... afa
Afro-Hispanic Institute ... AHI
Afro-Mauritian Common Organization ... AMCO
Afro-Shirazi Party [*Zanzibar*] ... ASP
Afroasiatic Linguistics [*A publication*] ... Af L
Afroasiatic Linguistics [*A publication*] ... Afroasiatic Ling
AFS [*American Foundrymen's Society*] **Cast Metals Research Journal** [*A publication*] ... AFS Cast Met Res J
AFS [*American Field Service*] **International/Intercultural Programs** [*Formerly, AFS*] ... AFSIIP
AFSC Technical Information Center, Washington, DC [*OCLC symbol*] ... SCH
Aft ... A
Aft Crew Station ... ACS
Aft End Assembly ... AEA
Aft End Cone [*NASA*] ... AEC
Aft Equipment Bay [*NASA*] ... AEB
Aft Events Controller ... AEC
Aft Flight Deck ... AFD
Aft Flight Deck Control Panel ... AFDCP
Aft Flight Deck Power Distribution Box ... AFDPDB
Aft Fuselage ... AF
Aft Load Control Assembly ... ALCA
Aft Load Controller ... ALC
Aft Master Events Controller [*NASA*] ... AMEC
Aft Perpendicular [*Naval engineering*] ... AP
Aft Power Controller ... APC
Aft Power Controller Assembly ... APCA
Aft Propulsion System [*or Subsystem*] [*NASA*] ... APS
Aft Reaction Control Subsystem [*NASA*] ... ARCS
Aft Utility Bridge ... AUB
After ... A
After ... AFT
After Action Report [*Military*] ... AAR
After All [*Message handling*] ... AA
After Body ... AB
After Bottom Center [*Valve position*] ... ABC
After Bottom Dead Center [*Valve position*] ... ABDC
After Christ ... AC
After Cooler ... AFTCLR
After Dark ... AFDK
After Date [*Business and trade*] ... AD
After Deducting Freight ... ADF
After Delivery Economies ... ADE
After Engine Room ... AER
After England Failed [*Soldier slang for American Expeditionary Force in World War I*] ... AEF
After Ford [*Calendar used in Aldous Huxley's novel, "Brave New World;" refers to Henry Ford*] ... AF
After Hatch [*Shipping*] ... AH
After-Hyperpolarization [*Also, AHP*] [*Neurophysiology*] ... AH
After Image [*Psychology*] ... AI
After Initial Release ... AIR
After Japan [*Industry*] ... AJ
After Passage [*or Passing*] [*Aviation*] ... APSG
After Peak ... AP
After Peak Tank [*On ships*] ... APT
After Receipt of Order ... ARO
After Sight [*Business and trade*] ... AS
After Six, Inc. [*American Stock Exchange symbol*] ... TUX
After Top Center [*Valve position*] ... ATC
After Top Dead Center [*Valve position*] ... ATDC
After Torpedo Room ... ATRM
After Women or Liquor [*Slang*] ... AWOL
Afterburner [*on jet engines*] ... AB
Afterburner [*on jet engines*] ... AFTB
Afterdischarge [*Electrophysiology*] ... AD
Afterhyperpolarization [*Also, AH*] [*Neurophysiology*] ... AHP
Afterloaded Quick Release [*Physiology*] ... AQR
Aftermarket Body Parts Distributors Association ... ABPDA
Afternoon ... A
Afternoon ... AFT
Afternoon ... AFTN
AFTN [*Aeronautical Fixed Telecommunications Network*] **Communications Center** [*FAA*] ... AFCOM
Afton, OK [*Location identifier*] [*FAA*] ... AGB
Afton Star-Enterprise, Afton, IA [*Library symbol*] ... IaAfSE
Afton, WY [*Location identifier*] [*FAA*] ... AFO
AFWAL [*Air Force Wright Aeronautical Laboratories*] **Technical Information Center, Wright-Patterson AFB, OH** [*OCLC symbol*] ... SCW
AFWL [*Air Force Weapons Laboratory*] **LASER Engineering and Applications to Prototype Systems** ... AFWL/LEAPS
Agades [*Niger*] [*Airport symbol*] ... AJY
Agadir [*Morocco*] [*Airport symbol*] ... AGA
Again ... AGN
Against ... AGST
Against ... AGT
Against All Risks [*Business and trade*] ... AAR
Against Grain ... AG
Against Medical Advice ... AMA
Agana, GM [*Radio station call letters*] ... KGUM
Agana, GU [*Television station call letters*] ... KGTF
Agana, GU [*Radio station call letters*] ... KSTO
Agana, GU [*Radio station call letters*] ... KTWG
Agana, GU [*Radio station call letters*] ... KUAM
Agana, GU [*Radio station call letters*] ... KUAM-FM
Agana, GU [*Television station call letters*] ... KUAM-TV
Agar-Gel Diffusion [*Clinical chemistry*] ... AGD
AGARD [*Advisory Group for Aerospace Research and Development*] **Advisory Report** [*A publication*] ... AGARD Advis Rep
AGARD [*Advisory Group for Aerospace Research and Development*] **Advisory Report** [*A publication*] ... AGARD Adv Rep
AGARD [*Advisory Group for Aerospace Research and Development*] **Agardograph** [*A publication*] ... AGARD Agardogr
AGARD [*Advisory Group for Aerospace Research and Development*] **Conference Proceedings** [*A publication*] ... AGARD Conf Proc
AGARD [*Advisory Group for Aerospace Research and Development*] **Conference Proceedings** [*A publication*] ... AGARD CP
AGARD [*Advisory Group for Aerospace Research and Development*] **Lecture Series** [*A publication*] ... AGARD Lect Ser
AGARD [*Advisory Group for Aerospace Research and Development*] **(North Atlantic Treaty Organization)** [*A publication*] ... AGARD (NATO)
AGARD [*Advisory Group for Aerospace Research and Development*] **Report** [*A publication*] ... AGARD Rep
Agartala [*India*] [*Airport symbol*] ... IXA
Agathon Publication Services, Inc. [*Later, APS Publications*] ... APS
Age ... A
Age and Ageing Science. Annuals [*A publication*] ... Age & Ageing
Age and Ageing. Supplement [*A publication*] ... Age Ageing Suppl
Age Controlled Item ... ACI
Age Discrimination in Employment Act [*1967*] [*Department of Labor*] ... ADEA
Age Equivalent [*Development level*] [*Education*] ... AE
Age Module Test Set ... AMTS
Age Nouveau [*A publication*] ... AgN
Age Nouveau [*A publication*] ... AN
Age of Primary Taxpayer [*IRS*] ... AG
Age; Prior Service; Physical, Legal, Educational, and Marital Status; and Dependents [*Army recruiting questionnaire*] ... APPLE-MD
Age Replacement ... AR
Age Run Length ... ARL
Age Standardized Mortality Ratio ... ASMR
Age at Time of Bomb [*Of survivors at Hiroshima*] ... ATB
Aged, Blind, or Disabled [*HEW*] ... ABD
Aged Care and Services Review [*A publication*] ... Aged Care Serv Rev
Agen [*France*] [*Airport symbol*] ... AGF

Agena Class Lunar Orbiter [*NASA*] ... ACLO
Agena Control System [*NASA*] ... ACS
Agena Systems/Power-On Test [*NASA*] ... AS/POT
Agena Target Vehicle [*NASA*] ... ATV
Agenahambo [*Papua New Guinea*] [*Seismograph station code, US Geological Survey*] [*Closed*] ... AGE
Agence Camerounaise de Presse [*Cameroon Press Agency*] ... ACAP
Agence Centrafricaine de Voyages [*Airline*] ... ACAV
Agence Centrale des Approvisionnements [*Central Supplies Agency*] ... ACA
Agence Civile OTAN [*Organisation du Traite de l'Atlantique Nord*] **du Temps de Guerre** [*NATO Civil Wartime Agency*] ... ACOG
Agence Congolaise d'Information [*Press agency*] [*Congo*] ... ACI
Agence Congolaise de Presse [*Congolese Press Agency*] ... ACP
Agence Dahomeene de Presse [*Dahomean Press Agency*] ... ADP
Agence Europeenne d'Approvisionnement ... AEA
Agence Europeenne pour l'Energie Nucleaire ... AEEN
Agence Europeenne de Productivite ... AEP
Agence Francaise de Presse [*French Press Agency*] ... AFP
Agence Guineene de Presse [*Guinean Press Agency*] ... AGP
Agence Internationale de l'Energie Atomique ... AIEA
Agence Internationale d'Information du Mali [*Press agency*] [*Mali*] ... ANIM
Agence Ivoirienne de Presse [*Ivorian Press Agency*] ... AIP
Agence Khmere de Presse [*Press agency*] [*Cambodia*] ... AKP
Agence Lao Presse [*Laos Press Agency*] ... ALP
Agence Madagascar - Presse [*Press agency*] [*Malagasy Republic*] ... AMP
Agence Maritime Internationale [*International Maritime Agency*] ... AMI
Agence Nationale pour la Valorisation de la Recherche [*France*] ... ANVAR
Agence de Presse Libre du Quebec [*Free Press Agency of Quebec*] [*Canada*] ... APLQ
Agence de Presse Senegalaise [*Senegalese Press Agency*] ... APS
Agence Tchadienne de Presse [*Chad Press Agency*] ... ATP
Agence Telegraphique Suisse [*Press agency*] [*Switzerland*] ... ATS
Agence Transequatoriale des Communications [*Trans-Equatorial Communications Agency*] [*or CCEAE*] ... ATEC
Agence Zaire-Presse [*Zaire Press Agency*] ... AZAP
Agencia Centroamericana de Noticias, SA [*Press agency*] [*Panama*] ... ACAN
Agencia Ecuadoriana de Prensa [*Ecuador Press Agency*] ... AEP
Agencia Mexicana de Noticias, SA [*Press agency*] [*Mexico*] ... AMEX
Agencia Nacional [*Press agency*] [*Brazil*] ... AN
Agencia Nacionale de Informacoes [*National Information Agency*] [*Portugal*] ... ANI
Agencia Noticiosa Corporacion de Periodistas [*Press agency*] [*Chile*] ... COPER
Agencia Noticiosa Saporiti [*Press agency*] [*Argentina*] ... ANS
Agencies ... AGS
Agencja Robotricza [*Press agency*] [*Poland*] ... AR
Agency ... A
Agency ... AG
Agency ... AGCY
Agency ... AGNCY
Agency ... AY
Agency Activity Analysis [*LIMRA*] ... AAA
Agency Broadcast Producers Workshop [*Defunct*] ... ABPW
Agency for Business and Career Development ... ABCD
Agency for the Coordination of Transport in the Mediterranean [*NATO*] ... ACTIMED
Agency Danair [*Denmark*] [*ICAO designator*] ... DX
Agency of Industrial Science and Technology ... AIST
Agency for Instructional TV ... AIT
Agency for International Development [*State Department*] [*Also, USAID*] [*US International Development Cooperation Agency*] ... AID
Agency for International Development/Private Enterprise Promotion ... AID/PEP
Agency for International Development, Procurement Regulations ... AIDPR
Agency for International Development, Washington, DC [*OCLC symbol*] ... AID
Agency Management Conference [*LIMRA*] ... AMC
Agency Manager Survey [*LIMRA*] ... AMS
Agency for Navigation on the Rhine and the Moselle ... RHIMO
Agency Officers School [*Formerly, FOS*] [*LIMRA*] ... AOS
Agency to Prevent Evil [*Organization in TV series "Lancelot Link"*] ... APE
Agency Procedure ... AP
Agency Procurement Request ... APR
Agency Progress Report ... APR
Agency Rent-a-Car [*NASDAQ symbol*] ... AGNC
Agency for the Security of Air Navigation ... ASECNA
Agency for Toxic Substances and Disease Registry [*Department of Health and Human Services*] ... ATSDR
Agency-Wide Coding Structure ... AWCS
Agenda Item ... AI
Agent ... AGT
Agent Development Program [*LIMRA*] ... ADP
Agent Distributor Service [*Departments of State and Commerce*] ... ADS
Agent General ... AG
Agent to the Governor-General [*British*] ... AGG
Agent Job Review [*LIMRA*] ... AJR
Agent Orange Victims International ... AOVI
Agent Orange Working Group [*Cabinet Council on Human Resources*] ... AOWG
Agent Reference Material [*Used by airline agents*] ... ARM
Agent Report [*Army*] ... AREPT
Agent Selection Kit [*LIMRA*] ... ASK
Agents and Actions [*A publication*] ... Agent Actio
Agents and Actions. Supplement [*A publication*] ... Agents Actions Suppl
Agents Master File [*IRS*] ... AGMF
Agenzia Giornalistica Italia [*Press agency*] [*Italy*] ... AGI
Agenzia Nationale Stampa Associata [*Associated National Press Agency*] [*Italy*] ... ANSA
AGF [*Arbeitsgemeinschaft der Grossforschungseinrichtungen*] **Mitteilungen** [*A publication*] ... AGF Mitt
Aggeneys [*South Africa*] [*Airport symbol*] ... AGZ
Aggie Oil Co. [*NASDAQ symbol*] ... AGGY
Aggiornamenti Sociali [*A publication*] ... Aggiorn Soc
Agglutination ... AGG
Agglutination Activating Factor [*Medicine*] ... AAF
Aggrediente Febre [*When the Fever Increases*] [*Pharmacy*] ... AG FEB
Aggregate ... AGG
Aggregate ... AGGR
Aggregate [*Immunology*] ... agg
Aggregate Demand ... AD
Aggregate Expenditure [*Economics*] ... AE
Aggregate Expense Analysis [*LIMRA*] ... AEA
Aggregate Field Expense Study [*LIMRA*] ... AFES
Aggregate Supply ... AS
Aggregates of P-Protein [*Botany*] ... AgPp
Aggregation Factor [*Biochemistry*] ... AF
Aggressive Behavior [*A publication*] ... Aggressive Behav
Aggressive Growth [*Business and trade*] ... AG
Agile Combat Aircraft [*Proposed*] ... ACA
Agincourt [*Canada*] [*Later, OTT*] [*Geomagnetic observatory code*] ... AGN
Aging in America ... AIA
Aging and Human Development [*A publication*] ... Aging Hum Dev
Aging and Leisure Living [*A publication*] ... Aging Leis Living
Aging Research Institute [*Defunct*] ... ARI
Agita [*Shake*] [*Pharmacy*] ... AGIT
Agita Bene [*Shake Well*] [*Pharmacy*] ... AGIT BENE
Agita ante Usum [*Shake before Using*] [*Pharmacy*] ... AGIT A US
Agitate ... AG
Agitation and Propaganda [*Military*] ... AGIT-PROP
Agitato [*Agitatedly*] [*Music*] ... AGITO
Agitator [*FBI standardized term*] ... AGTR
Agkistrodon Contortrix Thrombin-Like Enzyme ... ACTE
Agmatine Iminohydrolase [*An enzyme*] ... AIH
Agnes Scott College [*Georgia*] ... ASC
Agnes Scott College, Decatur, GA [*OCLC symbol*] ... EGA
Agnes Scott College, Decatur, GA [*Library symbol*] ... GDS
Agnetha Faltskog, Bjorn Ulvaeus, Benny Andersson, Anni-Frid Lyngstad [*Swedish singing group; acronym formed from first letters of their first names*] ... ABBA
Agni Yoga Society ... AYS
Agnico-Eagle Mines [*NASDAQ symbol*] ... AEAGF
Agnogenic Myeloid Metaplasia [*Medicine*] ... AMM
Agnosia [*Medicine*] ... AGN
Agnostic ... AGNOS
Agnus Dei [*Lamb of God*] [*Latin*] ... AD
Agorot [*Monetary unit in Israel*] ... AG
Agra [*India*] [*Airport symbol*] ... AGR
Agra [*India*] [*Seismograph station code, US Geological Survey*] [*Closed*] ... AGR
Agra Europe [*A publication*] ... Ag Europe
Agra University Journal of Research Science [*A publication*] ... Agra Univ J Res Sci
Agrarische Rundschau [*A publication*] ... Agrar Rundsch
Agrarpolitische Revue [*A publication*] ... Agrarpolit Rev
Agrartorteneti Szemle [*A publication*] ... Agrartort Szemle
Agrartudomany [*A publication*] ... Agrartud
Agrartudomanyi Egyetem, Keszthely, Hungary [*Library symbol*] ... HuKeAgE
Agrartudomanyi Egyetem Mezoegazdasngtudomanyi Karanak Koezlemenyei (Goedoelloe) [*A publication*] ... Agrartud Egyet Mezoegtud Kar Koezl (Goedoelloe)
Agrartudomanyi Egyetem Tudomanyos Tajekoztatoja (Goedoelloe) [*A publication*] ... Agrartud Egyetem Tud Tajekoz (Goedoelloe)
Agrartudomanyi Foiskola Tudomanyos Koezlemenyei (Debrecen) [*A publication*] ... Agrartud Foisk Tud Koezlem (Debrecen)
Agrartudomanyi Kozlemenyek [*A publication*] ... Agrartud Kozl
Agrarwirtschaft [*A publication*] ... Agrarwirt
Agree ... AGR
Agreed ... AGD
Agreement ... AGRM
Agreement ... AGRMT
Agreement ... AGRT
Agreement to Extend Enlistment [*Military*] ... AEX
Agreement for Fighter Interceptor Operations ... AFIO
Agressologie [*A publication*] ... Agressolog
Agressologie [*A publication*] ... AGSOA
Agri-Energy Roundtable ... AER
Agri Hortique Genetica [*A publication*] ... Agr Hor Gen
Agri Hortique Genetica [*A publication*] ... Agri Hort Genet
Agri-Products Exporters Association ... APEA

Agri-Silviculture Institute ... ASI
Agribusiness Accountability Project [*Public interest research group*] [*Defunct*] ... AAP
Agribusiness Council ... AC
Agrichemical West [*A publication*] ... Agrichem W
Agrico Chemical Co., Memphis, TN [*Library symbol*] ... TMAC
Agricoltore Bresciano [*A publication*] ... Agr Bresciano
Agricoltore Ferrarese [*A publication*] ... Agr Ferrarese
Agricoltura d'Italia [*Rome*] [*A publication*] ... Agr Ital
Agricoltura Italiana (Pisa) [*A publication*] ... Agric Ital (Pisa)
Agricoltura Milanese [*A publication*] ... Agr Milanese
Agricoltura Napoletana [*A publication*] ... Agr Napoletana
Agricoltura della Spezia [*A publication*] ... Agr Spezia
Agricoltura della Venezie [*A publication*] ... Agr Venezie
Agricultor Mexicano y Hogar [*A publication*] ... Agric Mexicano
Agricultura [*A publication*] ... Agr
Agricultura de las Americas [*A publication*] ... Agr Amer
Agricultura en El Salvador [*A publication*] ... Agric El Salvador
Agricultura y Ganaderia [*A publication*] ... Agr Ganad
Agricultura y Ganaderia [*A publication*] ... Agric Ganad
Agricultura (Lisboa) [*A publication*] ... Agr (Lisboa)
Agricultura (Santo Domingo) [*A publication*] ... Agr (Santo Domingo)
Agricultura em Sao Paulo [*A publication*] ... Agr Sao Paulo
Agricultura Tecnica [*A publication*] ... Agricultura Tec
Agricultura Tecnica [*A publication*] ... Agr Tec
Agricultura Tecnica en Mexico [*A publication*] ... Agric Tec Mex
Agricultura Tecnica en Mexico [*A publication*] ... Agricultura Tec Mex
Agricultura Tecnica en Mexico [*A publication*] ... Agr Tec Mex
Agricultura Tecnica (Santiago) [*A publication*] ... Agric Tec (Santiago)
Agricultura Tropical [*A publication*] ... Agric Trop
Agricultura Tropical [*A publication*] ... Agricultura Trop
Agricultura Tropical [*A publication*] ... Agr Trop
Agricultura Venezolana [*A publication*] ... Agric Venez
Agricultural ... AGRL
Agricultural Adjustment Act [*1938, 1980*] ... AAA
Agricultural Adjustment Administration [*or Agency*] [*Production and Marketing Administration*] ... AAA
Agricultural Advisory Meteorologist ... AAM
Agricultural Aids Foundation ... AAF
Agricultural Aircraft Association [*Later, CAAA*] ... AAA
Agricultural Ammonia Institute [*Later, The Fertilizer Institute*] ... AAI
Agricultural Ammonia News [*A publication*] ... Agr Ammonia News
Agricultural Aviation [*A publication*] ... Agr Aviation
Agricultural Banking and Finance [*A publication*] ... Agr Banking Finan
Agricultural and Biological Chemistry [*Tokyo*] [*A publication*] ... Agr Biol Ch
Agricultural and Biological Chemistry [*Tokyo*] [*A publication*] ... Agr Biol Chem
Agricultural and Biological Chemistry [*Tokyo*] [*A publication*] ... Agric & Biol Chem
Agricultural and Biological Chemistry [*Tokyo*] [*A publication*] ... Agric Biol Chem
Agricultural and Biological Chemistry (Tokyo) [*A publication*] ... Agric Biol Chem (Tokyo)
Agricultural-Biological Literature Exploitation [*Systems study of National Agricultural Library*] ... ABLE
Agricultural Bulletin. Canterbury Chamber of Commerce [*A publication*] ... Agr Bull Canterbury Chamber Commer
Agricultural Bulletin. Oregon Department of Agriculture [*A publication*] ... Agr Bull Oreg Dept Agr
Agricultural Bulletin. Saga University [*A publication*] ... Agr Bull Saga Univ
Agricultural Bulletin. Saga University [*A publication*] ... Agric Bull Saga Univ
Agricultural Business and Commerce ... ABC
Agricultural Central Trading [*British*] ... ACT
Agricultural Chemicals [*A publication*] ... Ag Chem
Agricultural Chemicals [*A publication*] ... Ag Chemicals
Agricultural Chemicals [*A publication*] ... Agr Chem
Agricultural Chemicals [*A publication*] ... Agric Chem
Agricultural Climatological Office [*Department of Commerce*] ... ACO
Agricultural Communicators in Education [*Formerly, AAACE*] ... ACE
Agricultural Computer Association ... ACA
Agricultural Conservation Program [*Department of Agriculture*] ... ACP
Agricultural Cooperative Development International ... ACDI
Agricultural Credit Cooperative Farmers' Association [*Philippines*] ... ACCFA
Agricultural and Dairy Educational Political Trust ... ADEPT
Agricultural Decisions [*A publication*] ... AD
Agricultural Development and Advisory Service [*British*] ... ADAS
Agricultural Development Council ... ADC
Agricultural Digest [*A publication*] ... Ag Digest
Agricultural Economic Reports ... AER
Agricultural Economics Bulletin for Africa [*A publication*] ... Agric Econ B Afr
Agricultural Economics Division [*of AMS, Department of Agriculture*] ... AEC
Agricultural Economics Information Series. University of Maryland. Cooperative Extension Service [*A publication*] ... Agr Econ Inform Ser Univ MD Coop Ext Serv
Agricultural Economics Mimeo Report. Florida Agricultural Experiment Station [*A publication*] ... Agr Econ Mimeo Rep Fla Agr Exp Sta
Agricultural Economics Pamphlet. South Dakota Agricultural Experiment Station [*A publication*] ... Agr Econ Pam S Dak Agr Exp Sta
Agricultural Economics Report. Kansas Agricultural Experiment Station [*A publication*] ... Agr Econ Rep Kans Agr Exp Sta
Agricultural Economics Report. North Dakota Agricultural Experiment Station [*A publication*] ... Agr Econ Rep N Dak Agr Exp Sta
Agricultural Economics Research [*A publication*] ... Ag Econ Res
Agricultural Economics Research [*A publication*] ... AGER
Agricultural Economics Research [*A publication*] ... Agr Econ Re
Agricultural Economics Research [*A publication*] ... Agr Econ Res
Agricultural Economics Research [*A publication*] ... Agric Econ Res
Agricultural Economics Research Institution [*British*] ... AERI
Agricultural Education [*A publication*] ... Agric Educ
Agricultural Education Magazine [*A publication*] ... Ag Ed
Agricultural Education Magazine [*A publication*] ... Agr Educ Ma
Agricultural Education Magazine [*A publication*] ... Agric Educ Mag
Agricultural Electricity Institute Report [*A publication*] ... Agric Electr Inst Rep
Agricultural Engineer ... AE
Agricultural Engineering [*St. Joseph, Michigan*] [*A publication*] ... Ag Eng
Agricultural Engineering [*St. Joseph, Michigan*] [*A publication*] ... Agr Eng
Agricultural Engineering [*St. Joseph, Michigan*] [*A publication*] ... Agric Engin
Agricultural Engineering Extension Bulletin. New York State College of Agriculture. Department of Agricultural Engineering [*A publication*] ... Agr Eng Ext Bull NY State Coll Agr Dept Agr Eng
Agricultural Engineering Research Division [*of ARS, Department of Agriculture*] ... AE
Agricultural Engineering (St. Joseph, Michigan) [*A publication*] ... Agric Eng (St. Joseph Mich)
Agricultural Environmental Quality Institute [*Department of Agriculture*] ... AEQI
Agricultural Estimates Division [*of AMS, Department of Agriculture*] ... AES
Agricultural Executive Council [*British*] ... AEC
Agricultural Experiment Station. University of Vermont. Bulletin [*A publication*] ... Agric Exp Stn Univ VT Bull
Agricultural Finance Review [*A publication*] ... Agric Fin Rev
Agricultural Foreign Investment Disclosure Act ... AFIDA
Agricultural Gazette of Canada [*A publication*] ... Ag Gaz of Canada
Agricultural Gazette of New South Wales [*A publication*] ... Ag Gaz of New South Wales
Agricultural Gazette of New South Wales [*A publication*] ... Agr Gaz NSW
Agricultural Gazette of New South Wales [*A publication*] ... Agric Gaz NSW
Agricultural History [*A publication*] ... Ag Hist
Agricultural History [*A publication*] ... Agr Hist
Agricultural History [*A publication*] ... Agric Hist
Agricultural History [*A publication*] ... AH
Agricultural History Review [*A publication*] ... Ag Hist R
Agricultural History Review [*A publication*] ... Agr Hist Rev
Agricultural History Review [*A publication*] ... Agric Hist R
Agricultural History Society ... AHS
Agricultural and Horticultural Engineering Abstracts [*A publication*] ... Agric Hort Engng Abstr
Agricultural and Horticultural Engineering Abstracts [*A publication*] ... AHA
Agricultural Implements Hand [*Freight*] ... AG IMPS HND
Agricultural Implements Other Than Hand [*Freight*] ... AG IMPS O T HND
Agricultural Improvement Council [*British*] ... AIC
Agricultural Index ... AI
Agricultural and Industrial [*In a college name*] ... A & I
Agricultural and Industrial Manufacturers Representatives Association ... AIMRA
Agricultural Information Bank for Asia [*Information service*] [*SEARCA*] ... AIBA
Agricultural Information Bulletin ... AIB
Agricultural Information and Documentation Section [*Royal Tropical Institute*] [*Netherlands*] [*Information service*] ... AIDS
Agricultural Institute Review [*A publication*] ... Agric Inst Rev
Agricultural Institute Review [*A publication*] ... Agr Inst Rev
Agricultural Journal of British Columbia [*A publication*] ... Ag J of British Columbia
Agricultural Journal. Cape Town [*A publication*] ... Agric J Cape Town
Agricultural Journal. Department of Agriculture. Fiji Islands [*A publication*] ... Agric J Dep Agric Fiji Isl
Agricultural Journal. Department of Agriculture (Victoria, British Columbia) [*A publication*] ... Agric J Dept Agric (Victoria BC)
Agricultural Journal of Egypt [*A publication*] ... Ag J of Egypt
Agricultural Journal of Egypt [*A publication*] ... Agric J Egypt
Agricultural Journal of India [*A publication*] ... Ag J of India
Agricultural Journal and Mining Record. Maritzburg [*A publication*] ... Agric J & Mining Rec Maritzburg
Agricultural Laboratory Technology ... ALT
Agricultural Land Service [*Later, ADAS*] [*British*] ... ALS
Agricultural Leaders Digest [*A publication*] ... Agr Leaders Dig
Agricultural Libraries Information Network [*Department of Agriculture*] [*Library network*] ... AGLINET
Agricultural Libraries Information Network [*Department of Agriculture*] [*Library network*] ... ALIN
Agricultural Limestone Institute ... ALI
Agricultural Machinery Journal [*A publication*] ... Agric Mach J
Agricultural Marketing ... AM
Agricultural Marketing Administration [*World War II*] ... AMA
Agricultural Marketing (Nagpur) [*A publication*] ... Agr Market (Nagpur)

Agricultural Marketing Project..AMP
Agricultural Marketing Service [*Formerly, CMS*] [*Department of Agriculture*]..AMS
Agricultural Marketing (Washington, DC) [*A publication*]..
Agric Mark (Washington)
Agricultural Marketing (Washington, DC) [*A publication*]..
Agr Market (Washington DC)
Agricultural and Mechanical [*In a college name*]................................A & M
Agricultural Mechanization [*A publication*]................................Agr Mech
Agricultural Merchant [*A publication*]................................Agr Merchant
Agricultural Meteorology [*A publication*]................................Agric Met
Agricultural Meteorology [*A publication*]................................Agr Meteor
Agricultural Meteorology [*A publication*]................................Agr Meteorol
Agricultural Missions [*An association*]................................AM
Agricultural Network Serving Extension and Research [*University of Kentucky*] [*Information service*]................ANSER
Agricultural News (Barbados) [*A publication*]............Agric News (Barbados)
Agricultural Newsletter [*A publication*]................................Ag NL
Agricultural Newsletter [*A publication*]................................Agr Newslett
Agricultural On-Line Access [*Formerly, CAIN*] [*National Agricultural Library*] [*Information service*]................AGRICOLA
Agricultural Outlook [*A publication*]................................Agric Outl
Agricultural Pilots Association..APA
Agricultural Policy Review [*A publication*]................Agr Policy Rev
Agricultural Procurement Regulations................................AGPR
Agricultural Production and Management................................APM
Agricultural Progress [*A publication*]................................Agric Prog
Agricultural Progress [*A publication*]................................Agr Progr
Agricultural Property Management Regulations................AGPMR
Agricultural Publishers Association................................APA
Agricultural Record (South Australia) [*A publication*].......Agric Rec (S Aust)
Agricultural Relations Council..ARC
Agricultural Research [*A publication*]................................Ag Res
Agricultural Research [*A publication*]................................Agric Res
Agricultural Research [*A publication*]................................Agr Res
Agricultural Research..AR
Agricultural Research [*A publication*]................................ARES
Agricultural Research Administration [*Superseded by ARS, 1953*] [*Department of Agriculture*]................ARA
Agricultural Research Center [*of ARS, Department of Agriculture*]................ARC
Agricultural Research Center Operations [*of ARS, Department of Agriculture*]................ARCO
Agricultural Research Corporation (Gezira) Technical Bulletin [*A publication*]................Agric Res Corp (Gezira) Tech Bull
Agricultural Research Council [*British*]................................ARC
Agricultural Research Council. Food Research Institute (Norwich). Annual Report [*A publication*]................
Agric Res Counc Food Res Inst (Norwich) Annu Rep
Agricultural Research Council (Great Britain). Letcombe Laboratory Annual Report [*A publication*]................
Agric Res Counc (GB) Letcombe Lab Annu Rep
Agricultural Research Council (Great Britain). Radiobiological Laboratory [*A publication*]................Agric Res Counc (GB) Radiobiol Lab
Agricultural Research Council. Meat Research Institute (Bristol). Annual Report [*A publication*]................
Agric Res Counc Meat Res Inst (Bristol) Annu Rep
Agricultural Research Council. Meat Research Institute (Bristol). Memorandum [*A publication*]................
Agric Res Counc Meat Res Inst (Bristol) Memo
Agricultural Research Council Radiological Laboratory [*British*].......ARCRL
Agricultural Research Council. Report [*A publication*]................
Agric Res Counc Rep
Agricultural Research and Educational Center [*American University of Beirut*]................AREC
Agricultural Research (Guyana) [*A publication*]................Agric Res (Guyana)
Agricultural Research (India) [*A publication*]................Agr Res (India)
Agricultural Research Information Centre [*India*]................ARIC
Agricultural Research Information Index [*United Nations*]...........AGRINDEX
Agricultural Research Information System [*United Nations*]...........AGRIS
Agricultural Research Institute..ARI
Agricultural Research Institute. Ukiriguru Progress Report [*A publication*]................Agric Res Inst Ukiriguru Prog Rep
Agricultural Research Journal of Kerala [*A publication*]....Agric Res J Kerala
Agricultural Research Journal of Kerala [*A publication*].......Agr Res J Kerala
Agricultural Research (Kurashiki) [*A publication*].........Agric Res (Kurashiki)
Agricultural Research (New Delhi) [*A publication*]........Agric Res (New Delhi)
Agricultural Research News Notes (Lima) [*A publication*]................
Agric Res News Notes (Lima)
Agricultural Research Organization. Division of Forestry. Ilanot Leaflet [*A publication*]................Agric Res Organ Div For Ilanot Leafl
Agricultural Research Organization. Volcani Center. Special Publication [*A publication*]........Agric Res Organ Volcani Cent Spec Publ
Agricultural Research Policy Advisory Committee [*Terminated, 1977*] [*Department of Agriculture*]................ARPAC
Agricultural Research (Pretoria) [*A publication*]................Agr Res (Pretoria)
Agricultural Research Reports (Wageningen) [*A publication*]................
Agric Res Rep (Wageningen)
Agricultural Research Review [*Cairo*] [*A publication*]................Agr Res Rev
Agricultural Research Review (Cairo) [*A publication*]................
Agric Res Rev (Cairo)
Agricultural Research Service [*Department of Agriculture*]................ARS

Agricultural Research (Washington, DC) [*A publication*]................
Agric Res (Wash DC)
Agricultural Research (Washington, DC) [*A publication*]................
Agr Res (Washington DC)
Agricultural Review [*A publication*]................................Ag R
Agricultural and Rural Development Agreement................ARDA
Agricultural Science (Jogjakarta) [*A publication*].........Agric Sci (Jogjakarta)
Agricultural Science Journal [*A publication*]................Ag Sci J
Agricultural Science Review [*A publication*]................Agric Sci R
Agricultural Science Review [*A publication*]................Agr Sci Rev
Agricultural Science Review [*A publication*]................Ag Sci R
Agricultural Science Review [*A publication*]................ASR
Agricultural Science Review Cooperative. State Research Service. US Department of Agriculture [*A publication*]................
Agric Sci Rev Coop State Res Serv US Dep Agric
Agricultural Science (Sofia) [*A publication*]................Agric Sci (Sofia)
Agricultural Situation [*A publication*]................................Agric Situa
Agricultural Situation [*A publication*]................................Agr Situation
Agricultural Situation [*A publication*]................................Ag Situation
Agricultural Situation in India [*A publication*]................Agric Situation India
Agricultural Situation in India [*A publication*]................Agr Sit Ind
Agricultural Situation in India [*A publication*]................Agr Situation India
Agricultural Stabilization and Conservation................ASC
Agricultural Stabilization and Conservation Service [*Department of Agriculture*]................ASCS
Agricultural Statistics. North Dakota Crop and Livestock Reporting Service [*A publication*]................
Agr Statist N Dak Crop Livestock Rep Serv
Agricultural Supply Industry [*A publication*]................Ag Sply Ind
Agricultural System for Storage and Subsequent Selection of Information [*British*]................ASSASSIN
Agricultural and Technical [*In a college name*]................A & T
Agricultural Technical Assistance Foundation [*Defunct*]................ATAF
Agricultural Trade Council..ATC
Agricultural Trade Office [*Foreign Agricultural Service*]................ATO
Agricultural and Veterinary Chemicals [*A publication*].........Agric Vet Chem
Agricultural and Veterinary Chemicals [*A publication*]............Agr Vet Chem
Agricultural Wages Board [*British*]................................AWB
Agricultural Weather Service Center [*National Oceanic and Atmospheric Administration*]................AWSC
Agricultural Workers' Organization................................AWO
Agricultural Workers Organizing Committee [*Later, UFWA*] [*AFL-CIO*]................AWOC
Agriculture..AG
Agriculture..AGR
Agriculture..AGRIC
Agriculture Abroad [*A publication*]................................Agr Abroad
Agriculture Algerienne [*A publication*]................................Agr Alger
Agriculture in the Americas [*A publication*]................Ag Am
Agriculture and Animal Husbandry [*A publication*]................Agr Anim Husb
Agriculture Asia [*A publication*]................................Agr Asia
Agriculture Canada. Monograph [*A publication*]................Agric Can Monogr
Agriculture Canada. Research Branch Report [*A publication*]................
Agric Can Res Branch Rep
Agriculture Council of America..ACA
Agriculture Department [*US government*]................A
Agriculture Department's Automated Manpower................ADAM
Agriculture and Environment [*A publication*]................Agric Environ
Agriculture and Fishery Development Corporation [*South Korea*].......AFDC
Agriculture and Food Chemistry. Journal [*A publication*]............. Ag Food Jl
Agriculture, Food, and Nutrition Service. Publications [*A publication*]................FNS
Agriculture and Forestry Committee [*US Senate*]................A & F
Agriculture, Forestry, Fishing [*Department of Employment*] [*British*].......AFF
Agriculture (Great Britain). Ministry of Agriculture, Fisheries, and Food [*A publication*]................Agr (Gt Brit)
Agriculture Handbook..AH
Agriculture Handbook. United States Department of Agriculture [*A publication*]................Agric Handb US Dep Agric
Agriculture and Horticulture [*A publication*]................Agr Hort
Agriculture Index [*A publication*]................................Agri Ind
Agriculture Information Bulletin. United States Department of Agriculture [*A publication*]................Agric Inform Bull US Dep Agric
Agriculture Information Bulletin. United States Department of Agriculture [*A publication*]................Agr Inform Bull USDA
Agriculture Institute Review [*A publication*]................Ag Inst R
Agriculture in Israel [*A publication*]................................Agr Israel
Agriculture (Journal of the Ministry of Agriculture) [*A publication*]................J Ministry Ag
Agriculture and Livestock in India [*A publication*]..........Ag & Livestock India
Agriculture and Livestock in India [*A publication*]................Agr Livestock India
Agriculture and Livestock Professional Photographers Association................ALPPA
Agriculture (Montreal) [*A publication*]................Agr (Montreal)
Agriculture in Northern Ireland [*A publication*]................Agriculture in Ire
Agriculture in Northern Ireland [*A publication*]................Agr N Ireland
Agriculture Pakistan [*A publication*]................................Agric Pakistan
Agriculture Pakistan [*A publication*]................................Agr Pakistan
Agriculture (Paris) [*A publication*]................................Agr (Paris)
Agriculture Pratique [*A publication*]................................Agr Prat

Agriculture and Resources Inventory Survey through Aerospace Remote Sensing......AgRISTARS
Agriculture Romande [*A publication*]......Agr Romande
Agriservices Foundation......AF
Agro-Ecological Atlas of Cereal Growing in Europe [*Elsevier Book Series*] [*A publication*]...... AEA
Agro-Ecosystems [*A publication*]......Agro-Ecosyst
Agrobiologiya [*A publication*]......Agrobiol
Agrobotanika [*A publication*]......Agrobot
Agrochemia [*Bratislava*] [*A publication*]......Agrochem
Agrochemia (Bratislava) [*A publication*]......Agrochem (Bratislava)
Agrochimica [*A publication*]......Agrochim
Agrociencia. Serie A [*A publication*]...... Agrocienc Ser A
Agrociencia. Serie C [*A publication*]...... Agrocienc Ser C
Agrokemia es Talajtan [*A publication*]......Agrokem Talajtan
Agrokemia es Talajtan. Supplement [*A publication*]......Agrokem Talajtan Suppl
Agrokhimiya [*A publication*]......Agrokhim
Agronomia Angolana [*A publication*]...... Agron Angol
Agronomia Angolana [*A publication*]...... Agron Angolana
Agronomia Costarricense [*A publication*]......Agron Costarric
Agronomia (Lima) [*A publication*]......Agron (Lima)
Agronomia Lusitana [*A publication*]......Agron Lusit
Agronomia Lusitana [*A publication*]......Agronomia Lusit
Agronomia (Manizales) [*A publication*]......Agron (Manizales)
Agronomia Mocambicana [*A publication*]......Agron Mocambicana
Agronomia (Monterrey, Mexico) [*A publication*]......Agron (Mexico)
Agronomia Sulriograndense [*A publication*]......Agron Sulriogr
Agronomia Sulriograndense [*A publication*]...... Agron Sulriograndense
Agronomia Tropical [*Maracay, Venezuela*] [*A publication*]......Agron Trop
Agronomia Tropical (Maracay, Venezuela) [*A publication*]......Agron Trop (Maracay)
Agronomia Tropical. Revista del Instituto Nacional de Agricultura [*A publication*]......Agronomia Trop
Agronomia y Veterinaria [*A publication*]......Agron Vet
Agronomie Tropicale. Agronomie Generale. Etudes Scientifiques [*Paris*] [*A publication*]....... Agron Trop Agron Gen Etud Sci
Agronomie Tropicale. Agronomie Generale. Etudes Techniques [*Paris*] [*A publication*]...... Agron Trop Agron Gen Etude Tech
Agronomie Tropicale (Paris) [*A publication*]......Agron Trop (Paris)
Agronomie Tropicale. Riz et Riziculture et Cultures Vivrieres Tropicales [*A publication*]......Agron Trop Riz Rizic Cult Vivrieres Trop
Agronomski Glasnik [*A publication*]...... Agron Glas
Agronomy......AGRON
Agronomy [*A publication*]......Agron
Agronomy Abstracts [*A publication*]......Agron Abstr
Agronomy Department Series. Ohio Agricultural Experiment Station [*A publication*]......Agron Dept Ser Ohio Agr Exp Sta
Agronomy Journal [*A publication*]......Agron J
Agronomy. Mimeograph Circular. North Dakota Agricultural Experiment Station [*A publication*]......Agron Mimeogr Circ N Dak Agr Exp Sta
Agronomy Pamphlet. South Dakota Agricultural Experiment Station [*A publication*]......Agron Pam S Dak Agr Exp Sta
Agronomy and Soils Research Series. Clemson Agricultural Experiment Station [*A publication*]......Agron Soils Res Ser Clemson Agr Exp Sta
Agronomy Views. University of Nebraska. College of Agriculture and Home Economics. Extension Service [*A publication*]......Agron Views Univ Nebr Coll Agr Home Econ Ext Serv
Agrophysics Breeding Control Device [*Birth-control device for dogs*]......ABCD
Agrotecnia (Madrid) [*A publication*]...... Agrotec (Madrid)
Agrotekhnika Providnikh Kul'tur [*A publication*]....... Agrotekh Provid Kul'tur
AGS Computers, Inc. [*NASDAQ symbol*]......AGSC
Aguada, PR [*Radio station call letters*]......WRFE
Aguadilla [*Puerto Rico*] [*Airport symbol*]......BQN
Aguadilla, PR [*Location identifier*] [*FAA*]......JFF
Aguadilla, PR [*Radio station call letters*]......WABA
Aguadilla, PR [*Radio station call letters*]......WIVA-FM
Aguadilla, PR [*Television station call letters*]......WOLE-TV
Aguadilla, PR [*Radio station call letters*]......WTPM
Aguadilla, PR [*Radio station call letters*]......WUNA
Aguadilla, PR [*Television station call letters*]......WVEO
Aguan [*Papua New Guinea*] [*Airport symbol*]......AUP
Aguascalientes [*Mexico*] [*Airport symbol*]...... AGU
Agudas Harabonim [*Union of Orthodox Rabbis of the United States and Canada*]...... AH
Agudas Israel World Organization......AIWO
Agudath Israel [*Union of Israel*] [*World organization of Orthodox Jews*]...... AI
Agudath Israel of America......AIA
Aguilar Public Library, Aguilar, CO [*Library symbol*]......CoAg
Aguirre Co. [*NYSE symbol*] [*Delisted*]......AGG
Aguni [*Japan*] [*Airport symbol*]......AGJ
Agway Cooperator [*A publication*]......Agway Coop
Agway, Inc., Library, Syracuse, NY [*OCLC symbol*]......ZUL
Agway, Inc., Syracuse, NY [*Library symbol*]......NSyAg
Ah-Ah [*Lava-Flow*] [*Hawaiian*]......AA
Ahead......AHD
Ahead Flag [*Navy*] [*British*]......AD
Ahead-Throwing Weapon [*Antisubmarine*]......ATW

Ahmanson [*H. F.*] **& Co.** [*NYSE symbol*]......AHM
Ahmedabad [*India*] [*Airport symbol*]......AMD
[*The*] **Ahnapee & Western Railway Co.** [*Formerly, AW*] [*AAR code*]........ AHW
[*The*] **Ahnapee & Western Railway Co.** [*Later, AHW*] [*AAR code*].............AW
Ahoskie, NC [*Location identifier*] [*FAA*]......ASJ
Ahoskie, NC [*Radio station call letters*]......WQDK
Ahoskie, NC [*Radio station call letters*]......WRCS
Ahrens-Fox Fire Buffs Club......AFFBC
Ahrokhimia i Hruntoznavstvo Respublikanskii Mizhvidomchyi Tematichnyi Zbirnyk [*A publication*]......Ahrokhim Hruntozn Resp Mizhvid Temat Zb
Ahua [*Hawaii*] [*Seismograph station code, US Geological Survey*]...........AHA
Ahuachapan [*El Salvador*] [*Seismograph station code, US Geological Survey*]......AHU
Ahwaz [*Iran*] [*Airport symbol*] [*Obsolete*]......AWZ
AIA Industries, Inc. [*NASDAQ symbol*]......AIAI
AIA [*American Institute of Architects*] **Journal** [*A publication*]...... AIA J
AIAA [*American Institute of Aeronautics and Astronautics*] **Journal** [*A publication*]...... AIAA J
AIAA [*American Institute of Aeronautics and Astronautics*] **Student Journal** [*A publication*]......AIAA Stud J
AIBS [*American Institute of Biological Sciences*] **Bulletin** [*A publication*]......AIBS Bull
AIC Photo, Inc. [*American Stock Exchange symbol*]......APH
AIChE [*American Institute of Chemical Engineers*] **Annual Meeting. Preprints** [*A publication*]......AIChE Annu Meet Prepr
AIChE [*American Institute of Chemical Engineers*] **Annual Meeting. Program Abstracts** [*A publication*]......AIChE Annu Meet Program Abstr
AIChE [*American Institute of Chemical Engineers*] **Journal** [*A publication*]......AIChEJ
AIChE [*American Institute of Chemical Engineers*] **Monograph Series** [*A publication*]......AIChE Monogr Ser
AIChE [*American Institute of Chemical Engineers*] **Papers** [*A publication*]......AIChE Pap
AIChE [*American Institute of Chemical Engineers*] **Symposium Series** [*A publication*]......AIChE Symp Ser
Aichi Cancer Center Research Institute. Annual Report [*A publication*]......Aichi Cancer Cent Res Inst Annu Rep
Aichi Gakugei Daigaku Kenkyu Hokoku [*Bulletin of the Aichi Gakugei University: Cultural Sciences*] [*A publication*]......ACGKH
Aichi-Gakuin Journal of Dental Science [*A publication*]......Aichi-Gakuin J Dent Sci
Aid to Adoption of Special Kids [*An association*]......AASK
Aid for Afghan Refugees [*An association*]......AAR
Aid to the Aged, Blind, or Disabled......AABD
Aid Association for Lutherans......AAL
Aid Auto Stores, Inc. [*NASDAQ symbol*]......AASS
Aid to the Blind......AB
Aid to the Church in Need......ACN
Aid to Dependent Children......ADC
Aid to the Disabled......AD
Aid to Families with Dependent Children......AFDC
Aid to Families with Dependent Children of Unemployed Fathers...... AFDCUF
Aid to Families with Dependent Children - Unemployed Parents......AFDC-UP
Aid for International Medicine [*An association*]......AIM
Aid to the Permanently and Totally Disabled [*HEW*]......APTD
Aid Refugee Chinese Intellectuals [*Defunct*]......ARCI
AID [*Agency for International Development*] **Research and Development Abstracts** [*A publication*]......AID Res Dev Abstr
Aide-de-Camp [*Military*]......ADC
Aide-de-Camp General [*Appointment to the Queen*] [*British*]......ADCGEN
Aide-de-Camp Personal [*Appointment to the Queen*] [*British*]......ADC(P)
Aided Display Submarine Control System [*Navy*]......ADSCS
Aided LASER Tracking System......ALTS
Aided Tracking......ADT
Aided Visual Development Program......AVDP
Aided Visual Homing Missile......AVHOM
Aided Visual Sensor System......AVSS
Aided Visual System...... AVS
Aiding Leukemia Stricken American Children [*Later, ALSAC - St. Jude Children's Research Hospital*] [*Fund-raising organization*]......ALSAC
Aids to Navigation...... A to N
Aids to Navigation...... AN
Aids to Navigation......ATON
Aids to Navigation Boat......ANB
Aids to Navigation Radio Control [*Military*]......ANRAC
Aidu [*Inawashino*] [*Seismograph station code, US Geological Survey*] [*Closed*]......AID
Aiguebelle Resources [*NASDAQ symbol*]......AIRIF
AIIE [*American Institute of Industrial Engineers*] **Transactions** [*A publication*]......AIIE Trans
Aikawa [*Japan*] [*Seismograph station code, US Geological Survey*]..........AIK
Aiken-Bamberg-Barnwell-Edgefield Regional Library, Aiken, SC [*Library symbol*]......ScAi
Aiken Dahlgren Electronic Calculator......ADEC
Aiken Dynamic Algebra......ADA
Aiken Relay Calculator......ARC

Aiken, SC [*Radio station call letters*]....WAKN
Aiken, SC [*Radio station call letters*]....WNEZ
Aiken, SC [*Radio station call letters*]....WPBM
Aiken, SC [*Radio station call letters*]....WPBM-FM
Aikens, Macaulay, & Thorauldson Law Firm, Winnipeg, MB, Canada [*Library symbol*]....CaMWAMT
Aileen, Inc. [*NYSE symbol*]....AEE
Aileron....AIL
Aileron [*Martinique*] [*Seismograph station code, US Geological Survey*]....AIL
Aileron Rudder Interconnect....ARI
Aileron Station....AS
Ailing-In Difficulty....AID
Ailuk [*Marshall Islands*] [*Airport symbol*]....AIM
Aim-Point-Miss....APM
Aim Telephone, Inc. [*NASDAQ symbol*]....AIMT
Aimexico, Inc. [*NASDAQ symbol*]....AIMX
Aiming Point....AP
Aiming Point Determination....APD
Aimpoint Correlator [*Weaponry*]....APC
Aims College, Greeley, CO [*Library symbol*]....CoGrA
AIN Leasing Corp. [*NASDAQ symbol*]....AINS
Ainahou [*Hawaii*] [*Seismograph station code, US Geological Survey*]....AIN
Ainsworth, NE [*Radio station call letters*]....KBRB
Aiolika Grammata [*A publication*]....AiolikaG
Aiome [*Papua New Guinea*] [*Airport symbol*]....AIE
Aioun El Atrouss [*Mauritania*] [*Airport symbol*]....AEO
AIP [*American Institute of Physics*] **Conference Proceedings** [*A publication*]....AIP Conf Proc
AIP [*American Institute of Physics*] **Conference Proceedings. Particles and Fields Subseries** [*A publication*]....AIP Conf Proc Part Fields Subser
Air....A
Air Accounting and Finance Center [*Air Force*]....AAFC
Air Adjutant-General [*Military*]....AAG
Air Administrative Net [*Army*]....AIRAD
Air Afrique....AFQ
Air Aide-de-Camp [*RAF*] [*British*]....AADC
Air-to-Air....AA
Air-to-Air....ATA
Air-to-Air Armament Mission Analyses [*Air Force*]....AAAMA
Air-to-Air Guided Weapons....AAGW
Air-to-Air Gunnery Range....AAGR
Air-to-Air Identification [*Air Force*]....AAI
Air-to-Air Identification Control Panel [*Air Force*]....AAICP
Air-to-Air Identification Friend or Foe [*Air Force*]....AAIFF
Air-to-Air Intercept....AAI
Air-to-Air Interrogation....AAI
Air-to-Air Missile....AAM
Air-to-Air Missile Guidance Element....AAMGE
Air-to-Air Missile Weapons System Flight Report....AAMREP
Air-to-Air Recovery [*Air Force*]....ATAR
Air-to-Air Refueling....AAR
Air-to-Air Refueling Squadron....AARS
Air-to-Air Visual Recognition [*Aviation*]....ATAR
Air Algerie [*Algeria*] [*ICAO designator*]....AH
Air Alsace [*France*] [*ICAO designator*]....SY
Air America, Inc.....AA
Air America, Inc. [*Air carrier designation symbol*]....AAMX
Air America, Inc. [*ICAO designator*] [*Obsolete*]....FA
Air Anglia Ltd. [*Great Britain*] [*ICAO designator*]....AQ
Air Anjou Transports [*France*] [*ICAO designator*]....RZ
Air Antisubmarine Squadron....AIRANTISUBRON
Air Antisubmarine Squadron [*Navy*]....VS
Air Approach Control....AAC
Air Arc Heater....AAH
Air Arc Heater Housing....AAHH
Air Armament....AA
Air Assault [*Army*]....AASLT
Air Assault Division [*Army*]....AAD
Air Atlantic [*East Boston, MA*] [*FAA designator*]....ATL
Air Atlantic Airlines [*Centre Hall, PA*] [*FAA designator*]....NTY
Air Atlas/Air Maroc....ATM
Air Attache [*British*]....AA
Air Attache [*Air Force*]....AIRA
Air-Augmented Propulsion for Short-Range Air Defense....AAP/SHORAD
Air-Augmented Rocket....AAR
Air-Augmented Rocket Propulsion System....AARPS
Air Bag Impact Attentuation System....ABIAS
Air Bags....AB
Air Balear [*Spain*] [*ICAO designator*]....JI
Air Ballistics Missile Division [*Air Force*]....ABMD
Air Barrier Exercise [*Military*]....AIRBAREX
Air Base....AB
Air Base Advisory Team....ABAT
Air Base Augmentation Support Set [*Air Force*]....ABASS
Air Base Commander....AIRBASECOM
Air Base Damage Assessment Model....ADAM
Air Base Defense/Sensor Communications and Display System [*Air Force*]....ABD/SCADS
Air Base Group [*Obsolete*] [*Navy*]....ABG
Air Base Group [*Air Force*]....ABGP
Air Base Simulator [*Air Force*]....ABS
Air Base Squadron [*Air Force*]....ABS
Air Base Wing [*Air Force*]....ABW
Air Base Wing [*Air Force*]....ABWG
Air Bases Command, 1st Naval District....AB ONE
Air Bath Chamber....ABC
Air Battle Analysis Center Utility System [*Air Force*]....ABACUS
Air Battle Analysis Division [*Air Force*]....ABAD
[*Manual*] **Air Battle Management Operations Center** [*Army*]....ABMOC
Air Bearing....AB
Air Bearing Lift Pad....ABLP
Air Bearing Platform....ABP
Air Benin [*ICAO designator*]....BC
Air Blast....AB
Air Blast Circuit Breaker....ABCB
Air Blast Loading....ABL
Air Blast Transformer....ABT
Air Blast Valve....ABV
Air Board [*RAF*] [*British*]....AB
Air Bomber....AB
Air Bombers Training Unit [*Navy*]....ABTU
Air Botswana Pty. [*ICAO designator*]....BP
Air Brake Association....ABA
Air-Brake Switch....ABS
Air-Brake Switch....ABSW
Air-Breathing Electric LASER....ABEL
Air-Breathing Engine....ABE
Air-Breathing Engine System....ABES
Air-Breathing Propulsion System [*or Subsystem*] [*NASA*]....ABPS
Air-Breathing Propulsion System [*or Subsystem*] [*NASA*]....APS
Air-Breathing System....ABS
Air-Bridge Carriers Ltd. [*ICAO designator*]....AK
Air Bubble Craft....ABC
Air Bubble Vehicle....ABV
Air Burst Contact Maker....ABCM
Air Burst Effect....ABE
Air Burst Fuze....ABF
Air Burundi [*ICAO designator*]....PB
Air Caledonie [*France*] [*ICAO designator*]....TY
Air California [*Air carrier designation symbol*]....ACAX
Air California....ACF
Air California [*Newport Beach, CA*] [*FAA designator*]....ACL
Air Canada [*ICAO designator*]....AC
Air Canada....ACA
Air Canada, Montreal, PQ, Canada [*Library symbol*]....CaQMTC
Air Capable Ship....ACS
Air Cape [*South Africa*] [*ICAO designator*]....KP
Air Cargo Enterprises, Inc. [*Honolulu, HI*] [*FAA designator*]....ACE
Air Cargo Equipment [*NASDAQ symbol*]....ARCE
Air Cargo Express, Inc.....ACG
Air Cargo Glider....ACG
Air Carrier....ACR
Air Carrier Contract Personnel....AACP
Air Carrier District Office....ACDO
Air Carrier Engineering Service....ACES
Air Carrier Flight Engineers Association....ACFEA
Air Carrier Mechanic Association....ACMA
Air Carrier Safety District Office....ACSDO
Air Carrier Service Corporation....ACSC
Air Cavalry Combat Brigade [*Army*]....ACCB
Air Cavalry Combat Brigade/Triple Capability Division [*Army*]....ACCB/TRICAP
Air Cavalry Regiment....ACR
Air Center Commander....ACC
Air Center, Inc. [*El Dorado, AR*] [*FAA designator*]....ARK
Air Central, Inc. [*Enid, OK*] [*FAA designator*]....ACN
Air Central, Inc. [*Harlinger, TX*] [*FAA designator*]....ACS
Air Ceylon Ltd. [*ICAO designator*]....AE
Air Ceylon Ltd.....AIRCEY
Air Change per Hour [*Ventilation and infiltration rates*]....ACPH
Air Charter Austria [*ICAO designator*]....OE
Air Charter Services [*West Hartford, CT*] [*FAA designator*]....ASV
Air Charters [*ICAO designator*]....JV
Air Checkmate [*Tampa, FL*] [*FAA designator*]....CRW
Air Chief Commandant [*British*]....ACC
Air Chief Marshal [*RAF*] [*British*]....ACM
Air Circuit Breaker....ACB
Air Circulating....ACIRC
Air Cleaner....AIRCLNR
Air Coach Transport Association....ACTA
Air Collection Engine System....ACES
Air Collection and Enrichment....ACE
Air Collection and Enrichment System....ACES
Air Combat Analysis....ACA
Air Combat Engagement Experiment....ACEE
Air Combat Evaluation....ACEVAL
Air Combat Fighter....ACF
Air Combat Information....ACI
Air Combat Intelligence [*Navy*]....ACI
Air Combat Intelligence Office [*or Officer*] [*Navy*]....ACIO

Air Combat Maneuvering ... ACM
Air Combat Maneuvering Instrumentation System [*Air Force*] ... ACMI
Air Combat Maneuvering Range ... ACMR
Air Combat Maneuvering Simulator ... ACMS
Air Combat and Surveillance System ... ACSS
Air Combat Tactics ... ACT
Air Combat Training ... ACT
Air Command and Control Improvement System [*NATO*] ... ACCIS
Air Command and Control System ... ACCS
Air Command Net [*Army*] ... AIRCOMD
Air Command Operations Center [*NATO*] ... ACOC
Air Command, Southeast Asia ... ACSEA
Air Command and Staff College [*Air Force*] ... AC & SC
Air Command and Staff College [*Air Force*] ... ACSC
Air Command and Staff School [*Air Force*] ... AC & SS
Air Command and Staff School [*Air Force*] ... ACSS
Air Commandant [*British*] ... A CDT
Air Commander, Canadian Atlantic Subarea ... COMAIRCANLANT
Air Commander, Central Atlantic Subarea ... COMAIRCENTLANT
Air Commander-in-Chief, Eastern Atlantic Area ... CINCAIREASTLANT
Air Commander, North Norway [*NATO*] ... ACNN
Air Commander, Northeast Subarea Channel ... COMAIRNORECHAN
Air Commander, Northern Atlantic Subarea ... COMAIRNORLANT
Air Commander, Norway [*NATO*] ... ACN
Air Commander, Plymouth Subarea Channel ... COMAIRPLYMCHAN
Air Commando Squadron ... ACS
Air Commerce Bulletin [*A publication*] ... Air Commerce Bul
Air Commerce Manual ... ACM
Air Commodore [*RAF, RCAF*] ... A/C
Air Commodore [*RAF, RCAF*] ... A CDE
Air Communications Network ... AIRCOMNET
Air Communications and Weather [*Group*] [*Navy*] ... AC & W
Air Commuter, Incorporated ... ACI
Air Commuter Ltd. [*Great Britain*] [*ICAO designator*] ... CD
Air Comores [*France*] [*ICAO designator*] ... OR
Air Component Command [*Military*] ... ACC
Air Component Commander, Southeast Asia Treaty Organization ... ACCSEATO
Air Compressor ... AC
Air Compressor Research Council [*Defunct*] ... ACRC
Air Condensate Drain [*Aerospace*] ... ACD
Air Conditioned Microclimate System [*Army*] ... ACMS
Air Conditioning ... AC
Air-Conditioning Apparatus [*JETDS nomenclature*] [*Military*] ... HD
Air Conditioning Contractors of America ... ACCA
Air-Conditioning Equipment ... ACE
Air Conditioning, Heating, and Refrigeration News [*A publication*] ... Air Cond Heat & Refrig N
Air Conditioning, Heating, and Ventilating [*A publication*] ... Air Cond Heat & Ven
Air-Conditioning and Pneumatic System ... ACPS
Air-Conditioning and Refrigerating Machinery Association [*Later, ARI*] ... ACRMA
Air-Conditioning and Refrigeration Institute ... ACRI
Air-Conditioning and Refrigeration Institute ... ARI
Air Conditioning and Refrigeration News [*A publication*] ... Air Cond & Refrig N
Air Conditioning and Refrigeration Program [*Association of Independent Colleges and Schools specialization code*] ... AR
Air-Conditioning and Refrigeration Wholesalers ... ARW
Air-Conditioning Room ... AC/RM
Air Conduction ... AC
Air Containment Atmosphere Dilution [*Nuclear energy*] ... ACAD
Air Continental Ltd. [*Great Britain*] [*ICAO designator*] ... CW
Air Control Area Commander ... ACAC
Air Control Center [*Military*] ... ACC
Air Control Commission ... ACC
Air Control Intercept ... ACI
Air [*or Airborne*] **Control Officer** ... ACO
Air Control Point ... ACP
Air Control Products, Inc. [*NYSE symbol*] [*Delisted*] ... AIR
Air Control RADAR ... ACR
Air Control and Reporting ... ACR
Air Control Room ... ACR
Air Control Team [*Air Force*] ... ACT
Air Control Valve ... ACV
Air [*or Aircraft*] **Control and Warning** [*Military*] ... AC & W
Air [*or Aircraft*] **Control and Warning** [*Military*] ... ACW
Air Controller ... AC
Air Controlman [*Navy rating*] ... AC
Air Controlman, Chief [*Navy rating*] ... ACC
Air Controlman, First Class [*Navy rating*] ... AC1
Air Controlman, Master Chief [*Navy rating*] ... ACCM
Air Controlman, Second Class [*Navy rating*] ... AC2
Air Controlman, Senior Chief [*Navy rating*] ... ACCS
Air Controlman, Third Class [*Navy rating*] ... AC3
Air Cooperation Command [*RAF*] [*British*] ... AC/OC
Air Coordinating Committee [*Governmental policy body for civil aviation in US; terminated, 1960*] ... ACC
Air Coordinating Committee Airspace Subcommittee ... ACCASP
Air Coordinating Committee Communications Subcommittee ... ACC/COM
Air Coordinating Committee Meteorological Subcommittee ... ACC/MET
Air Coordinator [*Air Force*] ... AIRCO
Air-Core Gauge ... ACG
Air Corps [*Obsolete*] ... AC
Air Corps Board ... ACB
Air Corps Information Circular [*Obsolete*] ... ACIC
Air Corps Medical Forces [*Obsolete*] ... ACMF
Air Corps Reserve [*Obsolete*] ... ACR
Air Corps Tactical School [*Obsolete*] ... ACTS
Air Corps Technical Report [*Obsolete*] ... ACTR
Air Council Instruction [*World War II*] ... ACI
Air Court-Martial ... ACM
Air Crew Equipment Laboratory [*Navy*] ... ACEL
Air Crew Rescue ... ACR
Air Crew System Bulletin ... ACB
Air Crew System Change ... ACC
Air Crew Training System ... ACTS
Air-Cushion Landing Gear ... ACLG
Air-Cushion Landing System ... ACLS
Air-Cushion Logistic Vehicle [*Helicopter*] ... ACLV
Air-Cushion Restraint System [*General Motors*] ... ACRS
Air-Cushion Takeoff System ... ACTS
Air-Cushion Trailer [*or Transporter*] ... ACT
Air-Cushion Vehicle ... ACV
Air-Cushion Vehicle built by Air Bearings [*England*] [*Usually used in combination with numerals*] ... AB
Air-Cushion Vehicle built by Air Vehicles [*England*] [*Usually used in combination with numerals*] ... AV
Air-Cushion Vehicle built by Ajax Hovercraft [*England*] [*Usually used in combination with numerals*] ... AH
Air-Cushion Vehicle built by Canadian Cushion Craft [*Canada*] [*Usually used in combination with numerals*] ... CANAIR
Air-Cushion Vehicle built by Commercial Hovercraft Industries [*New Zealand*] [*Usually used in combination with numerals*] ... CH
Air-Cushion Vehicle built by Cushioncraft [*England*] [*Usually used in combination with numerals*] ... CC
Air-Cushion Vehicle built by De Haviland Canada [*Canada*] [*Usually used in combination with numerals*] ... DHC
Air-Cushion Vehicle built by Denny Brothers [*England*] [*Usually used in combination with numerals*] ... D
Air-Cushion Vehicle built by Flygtekniska Forsoksanstalen [*Sweden*] [*Usually used in combination with numerals*] ... FFA
Air-Cushion Vehicle built by Hover Vehicles [*New Zealand*] [*Usually used in combination with numerals*] ... HV
Air-Cushion Vehicle built by Hovercraft Development [*England*] [*Usually used in combination with numerals*] ... HD
Air-Cushion Vehicle built by Hoverjak [*England*] [*Usually used in combination with numerals*] ... HJ
Air-Cushion Vehicle built by Hoverjet [*Canada*] [*Usually used in combination with numerals*] ... HJ
Air-Cushion Vehicle built by Hovermarine (England) [*Usually used in combination with numerals*] ... HM
Air-Cushion Vehicle built by Hovermarine (US) [*Usually used in combination with numerals*] ... HM
Air-Cushion Vehicle built by Hoversport [*US*] [*Usually used in combination with numerals*] ... HS
Air-Cushion Vehicle built by Mitsubishi [*Japan*] [*Usually used in combination with numerals*] ... MH
Air-Cushion Vehicle built by Nakamura Seisakusho [*Japan*] [*Usually used in combination with numerals*] ... NAMCO
Air-Cushion Vehicle built by Neoteric Engineering Affiliates [*Australia*] [*Usually used in combination with numerals*] ... NEOVA
Air-Cushion Vehicle built by Research Vehicle Department [*Brazil*] [*Usually used in combination with numerals*] ... DEPV
Air-Cushion Vehicle built by Rhein Flugzeugbau [*West Germany*] [*Usually used in combination with numerals*] ... RFB
Air-Cushion Vehicle built by Saunders Roe [*England*] [*Usually used in combination with numerals*] ... SR
Air-Cushion Vehicle built by Sealan Air Cushion Vehicles [*US*] [*Usually used in combination with numerals*] ... SAVC
Air-Cushion Vehicle built by Sealand Hovercraft [*England*] [*Usually used in combination with numerals*] ... SH
Air-Cushion Vehicle built by Societe National Industrielle Aerospatiale [*France*] [*Usually used in combination with numerals*] ... SA
Air-Cushion Vehicle built by Universal Hovercraft [*US*] [*Usually used in combination with numerals*] ... UH
Air-Cushion Vehicle built by Vosper Thorneycroft [*England*] [*Usually used in combination with numerals*] ... VT
Air Cycle Air-Conditioning System ... ACACS
Air Cycle Air-Conditioning System ... ACAS
Air Data ... AD
Air Data Computer Static Pressure Compensator ... ADCSPC
Air Data Computers [*or Computing*] ... ADC
Air Data Computing System ... ADCS
Air Data Converter ... ADC
Air Data Measuring Unit ... ADMU
Air Data Probe ... ADP
Air Data Probe Assemblies ... ADPA
Air Data Sensor ... ADS
Air Data Subsystem ... ADS
Air Data Transducer ... ADT

Air Data Transducer Assembly ADTA
Air Decoy Missile ADM
Air Defence Cadet Corps [*Military*] [*British*] ADCC
Air Defence Experimental Establishment [*Later, ADRDE, RRE*] [*British*] ADEE
Air Defence Officer [*Navy*] [*British*] ADO
Air Defence Research and Development Establishment [*Later, RRE*] [*British*] ADRDE
Air Defense [*Air Force*] AD
Air Defense Annual Service Practice ADASP
Air Defense Antimissile ADAM
Air Defense Area [*Army*] ADA
Air Defense Area [*Army*] ADAR
Air Defense Area Monthly Report [*Army*] ADAM
Air Defense Artillery [*Military*] ADA
Air Defense Artillery Complex ADAC
Air Defense Artillery, Director [*Air Force*] ADAD
Air Defense Artillery Operations Detachment ADAOD
Air Defense Artillery Operations Officer ADAOO
Air Defense Board ADB
Air Defense Center ADC
Air Defense Command [*Air Force*] ADC
Air Defense Command Center ADCC
Air Defense Command Commendation Certificate ADCCC
Air Defense Command and Control [*MICOM*] ADCC
Air Defense Command, Control, and Coordination System ADCCCS
Air Defense Command and Control System ADCCS
Air Defense Command Headquarters, St. Hubert, Province of Quebec, Canada CANAIRDEF
Air Defense Command - Office of Operations Analysis ADC-OA
Air Defense Command Operation Control ADCOC
Air Defense Command Post ADCP
Air Defense Commander AIRDEFCOM
Air Defense Communications Office ADCO
Air Defense Computer ADC
Air Defense Control Center [*Air Force*] ADCC
Air Defense Control and Targets Office [*Army*] ADCAT
Air Defense Defended Area [*Army*] ADDA
Air Defense Defended Point [*Army*] ADDP
Air Defense Development ADD
Air Defense Direction Center [*Air Force*] ADDC
Air Defense District ADD
Air Defense Division [*NATO*] AIRDEF
Air Defense Early Warning ADEW
Air Defense Effectiveness Demonstration [*Army*] ADED
Air Defense Element ADE
Air Defense Emergency [*Military*] ADE
Air Defense Evaluation ADE
Air Defense Exercise ADEX
Air Defense Exercise ADX
Air Defense Filter Center [*Military*] ADFC
Air Defense Force ADF
Air Defense of Great Britain ADGB
Air Defense Ground Environment [*NATO*] ADGE
Air Defense Group [*Air Force*] ADG
Air Defense Group [*Air Force*] ADGp
Air Defense Hardware Committee [*NATO*] ADHC
Air Defense Identification Line [*Air Force*] ADIL
Air Defense Identification Zone [*Air Force, FAA*] ADIZ
Air Defense Institute ADI
Air Defense Integrated System [*Military*] ADIS
Air Defense Intercept [*Air Force*] ADI
Air Defense, Interdiction, and Photographic ADIP
Air Defense Liaison Officer ADLO
Air Defense Management Office ADMO
Air Defense Missile ADM
Air Defense Missile Battalion [*Army*] ADMSLBN
Air Defense Missile Command ADMC
Air Defense National Center ADNC
Air Defense of North American Continent [*Army*] ADNAC
Air Defense Notification Center ADNC
Air Defense Operations ADO
Air Defense Operations Center [*Air Force*] ADOC
Air Defense Planning Board ADPB
Air Defense Planning Group ADPG
Air Defense Position [*Military*] ADP
Air Defense Region ADR
Air Defense Sector [*Air Force*] ADS
Air Defense Ship ADS
Air Defense Software Committee ADSC
Air Defense Special Weapons Support Organization ADSWSO
Air Defense Squadron [*Air Force*] [*Vietnam*] ADSq
Air Defense Suppression Missile ADSM
Air Defense System ADS
Air Defense System Engineering Committee ADSEC
Air Defense System Management Office [*Air Force*] ADSMO
Air Defense Systems Command ADSC
Air Defense Systems Directorate ADSD
Air Defense Systems Integration Division [*Air Force*] ADSID
Air Defense Tactical Data Systems [*Missile minder*] ADTDS
Air Defense Technical Center ADTC
Air Defense Vulnerability Simulation [*Simulation game*] ADVUL
Air Defense Warning [*Air Force*] ADW
Air Defense Warning Key Point [*Air Force*] ADWKP
Air Defense Weapon ADW
Air Defense Weapons Center [*Air Force*] ADWC
Air Defense Weapons Cost Effectiveness Study ADWEPS
Air Defense Zone ADZ
Air Deflection and Modification [*NASA*] ADAM
Air Deflection and Modulation [*Air Force*] ADAM
Air-Deliverable Antipollution Transfer System ADAPTS
Air-Delivered Attack Marker [*Air Force*] ADAM
Air-Delivered Land Mine System [*Military*] ADLMS
Air-Delivered Seismic Intrusion Detectors ADSID
Air-Delivered Target-Activated Munitions ADTAM
Air Delivery Equipment Division [*Natick Laboratories*] [*Army*] ADED
Air Delivery Operations [*Aerial resupply*] [*Military*] AIRDELOPS
Air Delivery Platoon AIRDELPLT
Air Density [*Satellite*] [*NASA*] AD
Air Density A [*Explorer satellite*] [*NASA*] AD-A
Air Density Explorer [*Satellite*] [*NASA*] ADE
Air Density Gauge [*Aviation*] ADG
Air Density/Injun [*Explorer satellite*] AD/I
Air Department of the Admiralty [*British*] AD
Air-Deployed Towed-Array Surveillance System AIRTAS
Air Deployment Delivery System [*Military*] ADDS
Air Depot AD
Air Depot [*Army*] ADEP
Air Deputy [*NATO*] AIRDEP
Air Deputy [*NATO*] DEPAIR
Air-Derived Separation Assurance [*Aviation*] ADSA
Air-Derived Separation Assurance System [*Aviation*] ADSAS
Air Design Review ADR
Air Development Center [*Air Force*] ADC
Air Development Force ADF
Air Development Service ADS
Air Development Squadron AIRDEVRON
Air Development Squadron [*Navy*] VX
Air Development Station [*Navy*] ADS
Air Diffusion Council ADC
Air Direction Center ADC
Air Direction Finder ADF
Air Dispatch Letter Service [*Navy*] ADLS
Air Distribution Institute ADI
Air Division [*Air Force*] AD
Air Division [*Air Force*] A DIV
Air Division Defense [*Air Force*] AIRDIVDEF
Air Djibouti [*ICAO designator*] DJ
Air-Dried [*Lumber*] AD
Air-Driven Air Amplifier ADAA
Air-Driven Generator ADG
Air Drop Operator ADO
Air Droppable, Expendable Ocean Sensor ADEOS
Air Duct AD
Air and Earth Shock AES
Air East Airlines [*Westfield, MA*] [*FAA designator*] AEA
Air Ecosse (Charters) Ltd. [*Great Britain*] [*ICAO designator*] WG
Air Efficiency Award [*RAF*] [*British*] AEA
Air Efficiency Medal [*RAF*] [*British*] AEM
Air Ejector AE
Air Electrical [*NATO*] AE
Air Electrical Officer AIRELO
Air Electronics Officer [*British*] AEO
Air Encephalogram [*Medicine*] AEG
Air Engineer Officer AEO
Air Engineer Officer AIREO
Air Engineering Development Division [*Air Force*] AEDD
Air Entraining Agent [*Freight*] AEA
Air Equipment and Support AE & S
Air Equivalence Ratio [*For hydrocarbon combustion*] AER
Air Escape [*Technical drawings*] AE
Air-Espace Techniques [*A publication*] Air-Espace Tech
Air Europe Ltd. [*Great Britain*] [*ICAO designator*] KS
Air Evacuation AEVAC
Air Evacuation AIREVAC
Air Evacuation [*Military aircraft identification prefix*] E
Air Evacuation Wing AIREVACWING
Air Exchange, Inc. [*Dallas, TX*] [*FAA designator*] EXG
Air Executive, Inc. [*West Chicago, IL*] [*FAA designator*] EXC
Air Executive Norway A/S Busy Bee [*ICAO designator*] BS
Air Explorer Squadron AESQ
Air Express AXPS
Air Express International Corp. AEI
Air Express International Corp. [*American Stock Exchange symbol*] AEX
Air Faisal Ltd. [*Great Britain*] [*ICAO designator*] KV
Air Ferry Squadron [*Navy*] AIRFERRON
Air Field Attack Munition AFAM
Air Fighting Development Unit [*British*] AFDU
Air Filter AF
Air Filter [*Freight*] AIR FIL
Air Filter Institute [*Later, ARI*] AFI
Air Fleet Marine Force AFMF

Air Florida [*Air carrier designation symbol*] ... AFLX
Air Florida [*Miami, FL*] [*FAA designator*] ... FLA
Air Florida Systems [*NASDAQ symbol*] ... AIRLC
Air Flow Actuated Switch ... AFAS
Air Flow Indicator ... AFI
Air Flow Thermal Balance Calorimeter ... AFTBC
Air Force ... AF
Air Force Academy ... AFA
Air Force Academy and Aircrew Examining Center ... AFAAEC
Air Force Academy Board ... AFAB
Air Force Acceptance Team ... AFAT
Air Force Accountable Property Officer ... AFAPO
Air Force Accounting and Finance Center ... AFAFC
Air Force Acquisition Document ... AFAD
Air Force Acquisition Logistics Division ... AFALD
Air Force Administrative Order [*Canada, 1946-1964*] ... AFAO
Air Force Advanced Management Class ... AFADVMC
Air Force Advisory ... AFA
Air Force Advisory Group ... AFADGRU
Air Force Advisory Group ... AFAG
Air Force Advisory Group ... AFGP
Air Force Advisory Team ... AFAT
Air Force Aero-Propulsion Laboratory ... AFAPL
Air Force Aeronautical Chart and Information Center ... AFAC & IC
Air Force Aeronautical Systems Command ... AFASC
Air Force Aeronautical Systems Division ... AFASD
Air Force Aerospace Fuel Petroleum Supply Office ... AFAFPSO
Air Force Aerospace Fuels Field Office ... AFAFFO
Air Force Aerospace Medical Research Laboratory ... AFAMRL
Air Force Aerospace Rescue and Recovery Service ... AARS
Air Force Agent Installation ... AFAI
Air Force Aid Society ... AFAS
Air Force Air Base ... AAB
Air Force Air Materiel Area ... AFAMA
Air Force Alaskan Long Line System [*Communications*] ... AFALLS
Air Force Alternate Headquarters ... AFALT
Air Force Armament Center ... AFAC
Air Force Armament Development and Test Center ... AFADTC
Air Force Armament Technology Laboratory ... AFATL
Air Force/Armed Service Procurement Regulation ... AF/ASPR
Air Force with Army ... AFWA
Air Force Association ... AFA
Air Force Association - Space Education Foundation ... AFA-SEF
Air Force Audit Agency ... AFAA
Air Force Audit Branch ... AFAB
Air Force Auditor General ... AFAUD
Air Force Authorization Document ... AFAD
Air Force Auxiliary [*British*] ... AFA
Air Force Auxiliary Field ... AFAUX
Air Force Avionics Laboratory ... AFAL
Air Force Bailment Property ... AFBP
Air Force Ballistic Missile ... AFBM
Air Force Ballistic Missile Arsenal ... AFBMA
Air Force Ballistic Missile Center ... AFBMC
Air Force Ballistic Missile Committee ... AFBMC
Air Force Ballistic Missile Division ... AFBMD
Air Force Ballistic Missile Training Center ... AFBMTC
Air Force Ballistic Systems Division [*Later, Space and Missile Systems Operations*] ... AFBSD
Air Force Base ... AFB
Air Force Base Information Transfer System ... AFBITS
Air Force Base Unit ... AFBU
Air Force Board of Review ... AFBR
Air Force Bulletin ... AFB
Air Force Business Research Management Center ... AFBRMC
Air Force Cambridge Research Center [*Obsolete*] ... AFCRC
Air Force Cambridge Research Laboratories [*Later, AFGL*] ... AFCRL
Air Force Cambridge Research Library ... AFCRL
Air Force Central Review Board ... AFCRB
Air Force Chief of Operations Analysis ... AFCOA
Air Force Circulars ... AFC
Air Force Civil Engineer [*A publication*] ... AFCE
Air Force Civil Engineer [*A publication*] ... Air F Civ Eng
Air Force Civil Engineering Center ... AFCEC
Air Force Civilian Welfare Fund ... AFCWF
Air Force Combat Command ... AFCC
Air Force Combat Operations Staff ... AFCOS
Air Force Command and Control Development Center ... AFCCDC
Air Force Command and Control Development Division ... AFCCDD
Air Force Command and Control System ... AFCCS
Air Force Command Post ... AFCP
Air Force Command and Staff College ... AFCSC
Air Force Commendation Medal ... AFCM
Air Force Commendation Medal ... AFCOM
Air Force Communication Center ... AFCC
Air Force Communications [*Satellite*] ... AFCOM
Air Force Communications Program ... AIRCOM
Air Force Communications Security ... AFCOMSEC
Air Force Communications Security Center ... AFCOMSECCEN
Air Force Communications Security Letter ... AFCSL
Air Force Communications Security Manual ... AFCOMSECM
Air Force Communications Security Manual ... AFCSM
Air Force Communications Security Pamphlet ... AFCSP
Air Force Communications Service [*or System*] ... AFCS
Air Force Communications Service, Engineering and Installation ... AFCS E & I
Air Force Communications Service, Scott AFB, IL [*OCLC symbol*] ... ACS
Air Force Communications Station ... AFCOMMSTA
Air Force Communications Support System ... AFCSS
Air Force Component ... AFC
Air Force Component Command Post ... AFCCP
Air Force Component Commander ... AFCC
Air Force Component Headquarters ... AFCH
Air Force Comptroller ... AFC
Air Force Comptroller ... AFOC
Air Force Comptroller [*A publication*] ... Air F Comp
Air Force Computer Acquisition Office ... AFCAO
Air Force Configuration Control Board ... AFCCB
Air Force Contract Maintenance Center ... AFCMC
Air Force Contract Management Division ... AFCMD
Air Force Contract Management Office ... AFCMO
Air Force Contracting Office Approval ... AFCOA
Air Force Contracting Officer ... AFCO
Air Force Contractor Experience List ... AFCEL
Air Force Control Office ... AFCO
Air Force Controlled [*Units*] ... AFCON
Air Force Cost Reduction Program ... AFCRP
Air Force Council [*Advisory board to Air Force*] ... AFC
Air Force Cross [*British*] ... AFC
Air Force Cryptographic Aid, General ... AFKAG
Air Force Cryptographic Aid, Recognition and Identification Systems ... AFKAI
Air Force Cryptographic Code System ... AFKAC
Air Force Cryptographic Maintenance Manual ... AFKAM
Air Force Cryptographic One Time Pads ... AFKAP
Air Force Cryptologic Depot ... AFCD
Air Force Data Automation Agency ... AFDAA
Air Force Data Automation Planning Concepts [*Manual*] ... AFDAP
Air Force Data Communications System ... AFDATACOM
Air Force Data Station ... AFDASTA
Air Force Data Station ... AFDATASTA
Air Force Data Systems Design Center ... AFDSDC
Air Force Decorations Board ... AFDB
Air Force Departmental Catalog Coordinating Office ... AFDCCO
Air Force Departmental Industrial Equipment Reserve Storage Site ... AFDIERSS
Air Force Depot ... AFD
Air Force Depot Equipment Performance Tester ... ADEPT
Air Force Designated Acquisition Program ... AFDAP
Air Force Development Field Representative ... AFDFR
Air Force Directive ... AFD
Air Force Director of Accounting and Financing ... AFAF
Air Force Director of Data Automation ... AFDDA
Air Force Director of Inspection Services ... AFDIS
Air Force Director of Reconnaissance and Electronic Warfare ... AFRDR
Air Force Director of Requirements ... AFDRQ
Air Force Director [*or Directorate*] **of Research and Development** ... AFDRD
Air Force Directorate of Advanced Technology ... AFDAT
Air Force Directorate of Materials and Processes ... AFDMP
Air Force Directorate of Requirement ... AFDR
Air Force Directory of Resident Inspection Facilities ... AFDRIF
Air Force Disability Review Board ... AFDRB
Air Force Discharge Review Board ... AFDRB
Air Force Driver Magazine [*A publication*] ... AFDM
Air Force Duty Officer ... AFDO
Air Force Eastern Test Range ... AFETR
Air Force Educational Requirements Board ... AFERB
Air Force Edwards Research Center ... AFERC
Air Force Electro-Optical Site ... AFEOS
Air Force Electronic Data Processing Center ... AFEDPC
Air Force Electronic Security Command ... AFESC
Air Force Electronic Systems Division ... AFESD
Air Force Electronic Warfare Evaluation Simulator ... AFEWES
Air Force Emergency Operations Center ... AFEOC
Air Force Engineering and Logistics Information System ... AFELIS
Air Force Engineering Responsibility ... AFER
Air Force Engineering and Services Center ... AFESC
Air Force Engineering and Services Center/Engineering and Services Laboratory ... AFESC/ESL
Air Force Engineering and Services Quarterly [*A publication*] ... Air Force Eng Serv Q
Air Force Engineering and Technical Service ... AFETS
Air Force Engineering Technology Office ... AFETO
Air Force Environmental Rocket-Sounding System [*Meteorology*] ... AFERSS
Air Force Equipment Management Survey Team ... AFEMST
Air Force Equipment Management System ... AFEMS
Air Force Equipment Procurement Instruction ... AFEPI
Air Force in Europe ... AFE
Air Force European Office of Aerospace Research ... AFEOAR
Air Force Exchange Service ... AFES
Air Force Experiment ... AFE

Air Force Far East	AFFE
Air Force Field Office Manager	AFFOM
Air Force Field Technical Center [Edwards AFB]	AFFTC
Air Force Film Library Center	AFFLC
Air Force Finance Center	AFFC
Air Force Finance Center	AFN
Air Force Financial Postal Clerk	AFFPC
Air Force Flight Dynamics Laboratory	AFFDL
Air Force Flight Test Center [AFSC]	AFFTC
Air Force Flight Training Command	AFTC
Air Force Forces [Element of a joint task force]	AFFOR
Air Force Foreign Technology Division	AFFTD
Air Force General Order	AFGO
Air Force Geophysics Laboratory [Formerly, AFCRL]	AFGL
Air Force Geophysics Laboratory Research Library, Hanscom AFB, MA [OCLC symbol]	SCG
Air Force Global Weather Central	AFGWC
Air Force Global Weather Reconnaissance Program	AFGWRP
Air Force Good Conduct Medal	AFGCM
Air Force Guide for Writing	GW
Air Force Headquarters	AFHQ
Air Force Headquarters Command	AFHC
Air Force Headquarters, Ottawa, Ontario, Canada	CANAIRHED
Air Force Health Professions Scholarship Program	AFHPSP
Air Force Historical Foundation	AFHF
Air Force Hospital	AFH
Air Force Human Resources Laboratory	AFHRL
Air Force Human Resources Laboratory/Flying Training Division	AFHRL/FT
Air Force Human Resources Laboratory/Manpower Development Division	AFHRL/MD
Air Force Industrial Fund	AFIF
Air Force Industrial Security Regulations	AFISR
Air Force Inspection and Safety Center	AFISC
Air Force Installation Representative	AFIR
Air Force Installation Representative Officer	AFIRO
Air Force Institute of Technology	AFIT
Air Force Institute of Technology, Wright-Patterson AFB, OH [OCLC symbol]	SCT
Air Force Integrated Command and Control System	AFICCS
Air Force Intelligence Center	AFIC
Air Force Intelligence Data Handling System [ESD]	AIDS
Air Force Intelligence Service	AFIS
Air Force International Standard	AIR-STD
Air Force Inventory Manager	AFIM
Air Force JAG [Judge Advocate General] Law Review [A publication]	AF JAG L Rev
Air Force Jet	AFJ
Air Force Job Knowledge Test	AFJKT
Air Force Judge Advocate General	AFJAG
Air Force Junior Reserve Officers Training Corps	AFJROTC
Air Force Language Aptitude Test	AFLAT
Air Force Law Enforcement Terminal System	AFLETS
Air Force Law Review [A publication]	AF L R
Air Force Legislative Item	AFLI
Air Force Letter	AFL
Air Force Liaison	AFL
Air Force Logistics Center	AFLC
Air Force Logistics Command [Formerly, Air Materiel Command]	AFLC
Air Force Logistics Command Form	AFLCF
Air Force Logistics Command Letter	AFLCL
Air Force Logistics Command Manual	AFLCM
Air Force Logistics Command Operations Network	AFLCON
Air Force Logistics Command Pamphlets	AFLCP
Air Force Logistics Command Regulations	AFLCR
Air Force Logistics Communications Network	AFLCON
Air Force Logistics Control Group	AFLCG
Air Force Logistics Management Center	AFLMC
Air Force Longevity Service Award	AFLSA
Air Force - Los Alamos EMP [Electromagnetic Pulse] Calibration Simulator	ALECS
Air Force Machinability Data Center	AFMDC
Air Force Management Engineering Agency	AFMEA
Air Force Manpower Standards	AFMS
Air Force Manual	AFM
Air Force Material Review Board	AFMRB
Air Force Materials Information Center	AFMIC
Air Force Materials Laboratory	AFML
Air Force Medal [British]	AFM
Air Force Medical Materiel Field Office	AFMMFO
Air Force Medical Materiel Letter	AFMML
Air Force Medical Publications Agency	AFMPA
Air Force Medical Service	AFMS
Air Force Medical Specialist Corps	AFMSC
Air Force - Military Interdepartmental Purchase Requests	AF-MIPR
Air Force Military Personnel Center	AFMPC
Air Force Military Training Center	AFMTC
Air Force Missile Development Center [AFSC]	AFMDC
Air Force Missile Test Center [Later, AFETR]	AFMTC
Air Force Mission Element Need Statement	AFMENS
Air Force Museum	AFM

Air Force National Range Division	AFNRD
Air Force NATO Agreement	AFNAG
Air Force/Navy	AF/N
Air Force - Navy	AFNA
Air Force - Navy	AN
Air Force/Navy Aeronautical	AF/NA
Air Force - Navy Aeronautical	ANA
Air Force - Navy Aeronautical Bulletin	AFNAB
Air Force - Navy Aeronautical Standard	AFNAS
Air Force-Navy-Civil	ANC
Air Force-Navy Design	AND
Air Force Networks Station	AFNETSTA
Air Force News Service	AFNS
Air Force Noncommissioned Officer Academy [Graduate] Ribbon	AFNCOAR
Air Force NOTAM [Notice to Airmen] Exchange Area	AFNEA
Air Force NOTAM [Notice to Airmen] Exchange Office	AFNEO
Air Force Nuclear Engineering Test Facility [Reactor]	AF NETF
Air Force Nurse Corps	AFNC
Air Force Objective Series [Papers]	AFOS
Air Force Occupational Safety and Health [Standards]	AFOSH
Air Force Office of Aerospace Research [AFSC]	AFOAR
Air Force Office of Aerospace Sciences [AFOAR]	AFOAS
Air Force Office of Atomic Energy	AFOAT
Air Force Office of Manpower and Organization	AFOMO
Air Force Office of Research Analysis	AFORA
Air Force Office of Scientific Research	AFOSR
Air Force Office of Special Investigation	AFOSI
Air Force Officer in Charge	AFOIC
Air Force Officer Education Program	AFOEP
Air Force Officer Qualifying Test	AFOQT
Air Force On-Line Data System	AFOLDS
Air Force Operational Report	AFOREP
Air Force Operational Test Center	AFOTC
Air Force Operations Analysis Office	AFOAO
Air Force Operations Base	AFOB
Air Force Operations Center	AFOC
Air Force Organization Status Change Report	AFOSCR
Air Force Outstanding Unit Award	AFOUA
Air Force Outstanding Unit Award Ribbon	AFOUAR
Air Force Overseas Replacement Depot [World War II]	AFORD
Air Force Overseas Replacement Group [World War II]	AFORG
Air Force Packaging Evaluation Agency	AFPEA
Air Force Packaging Laboratory	AFPL
Air Force Pamphlet	AFP
Air Force Pamphlet	AFPAM
Air Force Personnel Board	AFPB
Air Force Personnel Council	AFPC
Air Force Personnel on Duty with Army	AFWAR
Air Force Personnel on Duty with Navy	AFWN
Air Force Personnel Processing Group	AFPG
Air Force Personnel Test	AFPT
Air Force Personnel and Training Research Center [Later, Air Force Personnel Research Laboratory]	AFPTRC
Air Force Petroleum Retail Distribution Station	AFPRDS
Air Force Physical Disability Appeal Board	AFPDAB
Air Force Planning Guide	AFPG
Air Force Plant	AFP
Air Force Plant Representative	AFPR
Air Force Plant Representative Office	AFPRO
Air Force Polaris Material Office	AFPMO
Air Force Police	AFP
Air Force Policy Council	AFPC
Air Force Post Office	APO
Air Force Postal Clerk	AFPC
Air Force Postal Unit	AFPU
Air Force Potential Contractor Program	AFPCP
Air Force Preliminary Evaluation	AFPE
Air Force Procurement Circulars	AFPC
Air Force Procurement Instructions	AFPI
Air Force Procurement Procedures	AFPP
Air Force Procurement Regulation	AFPR
Air Force Procurement Representative	AFPR
Air Force Production Reserve Policy	AFPRP
Air Force Professional Entertainment Branch	AFPEB
Air Force Project Representative	AFPR
Air Force Property Officer	AFPO
Air Force Purchase Item Description	AFPID
Air Force Purchasing Office	AFPO
Air Force Quality Assurance	AFQA
Air Force Quality Assurance Representative	AFQAR
Air Force Quality Control	AFQC
Air Force Quality Control Representative	AFQCR
Air Force Range Support Facility	AFRSF
Air Force Records Center	AFRC
Air Force Recoverable Assembly Management System	AFRAMS
Air Force Recruiter Assistance Program	AFRAP
Air Force Recurring Publication	AFRP
Air Force Regional Civil Engineers	AFRCE
Air Force Regulation	AFR
Air Force Representative [to the FAA]	AFREP

Air Force Rescue Coordination Center	AFRCC
Air Force Rescue Service	AFRS
Air Force Research and Development Branch	AFRDB
Air Force Research Directorate	AFRD
Air Force Research Division	AFRD
Air Force Research Objectives	AFRO
Air Force Research and Technology Division	AFRTD
Air Force Reserve	AFR
Air Force Reserve	AFRES
Air Force Reserve Base Support Group	AFRBSGP
Air Force Reserve Combat Support Training Center	AFRCSTC
Air Force Reserve Combat Training Center	AFRCTC
Air Force Reserve Coordination Center	AFRCC
Air Force Reserve Division	AFRD
Air Force Reserve Flying Training Center	AFRFTC
Air Force Reserve Navigation Squadron	AFRESNAVSQ
Air Force Reserve Officers Training Corps	AFROTC
Air Force Reserve Orders	AFRO
Air Force Reserve Policy Committee	AFRPC
Air Force Reserve Recovery Group	AFRRGp
Air Force Reserve Region	AFRR
Air Force Reserve Regions	AFRESR
Air Force Reserve Regions Base Support Group	AFRESBSGP
Air Force Reserve Regions Group	AFRESRGP
Air Force Reserve Sector	AFRS
Air Force Reserve Sectors	AFRESS
Air Force Reserve Specialist Training Center	AFRSTC
Air Force Reserve Training Center	AFRTC
Air Force Resident Officer in Charge	AFROIC
Air Force Resident Representative	AFRR
Air Force Retiring Board	AFRB
Air Force Rocket Propulsion Laboratory	AFRPL
Air Force Rome Air Development Center	AF/RADC
Air Force Routine Order [Canada, 1920-1945]	AFRO
Air Force Salary Impact Report	AFSIR
Air Force Satellite Communications System	AFSATCOM
Air Force Satellite Communications System	AFSCS
Air Force Satellite Control Center	AFSCC
Air Force Satellite Control Facility	AFSCF
Air Force Satellite Facility	AFSF
Air Force School of Aviation Medicine	AFSAM
Air Force Scientific Advisory Board	AFSAB
Air Force Screen Magazine [A publication]	AFSM
Air Force Section	AFSec
Air Force Section, Military Assistance Advisory Group	AFSMAAG
Air Force Security Service [Later, AFESC]	AFSS
Air Force Security Service Office of Production	AFSSOP
Air Force Senior Advisory	AFSA
Air Force Senior Advisory - Jefferson Barracks	AFSA-JB
Air Force Senior Noncommissioned Officers' Academy	AFSNCOA
Air Force Sergeants Association	AFSA
Air Force Serial Number	AFSN
Air Force Service Center [or Command]	AFSC
Air Force Service Information and News Center	AFSINC
Air Force Service Number	AFSN
Air Force Service Office	AFSO
Air Force Service Statement	AFSS
Air Force and Space Digest [A publication]	AF/SD
Air Force Space and Missile Systems Organization	AFSAMSO
Air Force Space Plane	AFSP
Air Force Space Program	AFSP
Air Force Space Systems Division	AFSSD
Air Force Space Test Center [Later, Western Test Range]	AFSTC
Air Force Special Activities Wing	AFSAW
Air Force Special Communications Center	AFSCC
Air Force Special Communications Center	AFSPCOMMCEN
Air Force Special Security Office [or Officer]	AFSSO
Air Force Special Weapons Center [AFSC]	AFSWC
Air Force Specialty	AFS
Air Force Specialty Code	AFSC
Air Force Specification Bulletin	AFSB
Air Force Standard	AFS
Air Force Standard Intelligence Publication	AFSIP
Air Force Standard Practice	AFSP
Air Force Station	AFS
Air Force Stock	AFS
Air Force Stock Fund	AFSF
Air Force Stock Number	AFSN
Air Force Stock Record Account Number	AFSRAN
Air Force Strike Command	AFSTRIKE
Air Force Supply	AFS
Air Force Supply Catalog	AFSC
Air Force Supply Code	AFSC
Air Force Supply Date	AFSD
Air Force Supply Depot	AFSD
Air Force Supply Directive	AFSD
Air Force Supply Force	AFSF
Air Force Supply Services System	AFSS
Air Force System Acquisition Review Council	AFSARC
Air Force Systems Command	AFSC
Air Force Systems Command Design Handbooks	AFSC-DH

Air Force Systems Command Form	AFSCF
Air Force Systems Command Letter	AFSCL
Air Force Systems Command Manual	AFSCM
Air Force Systems Command Pamphlet	AFSCP
Air Force Systems Command Procurement Production	AFSCPP
Air Force Systems Command Regulation	AFSCR
Air Force Systems Command, Scientific Technical Liaison Office	AFSC/STLO
Air Force Systems Command Space Systems Division	AFSC/SSD
Air Force Systems Project Division	AFSPD
Air Force Tactical Fighter Weapons Center	AFTFWC
Air Force Task Force	AFTF
Air Force Technical Applications Center	AFTAC
Air Force Technical Approval Team	AFTAT
Air Force Technical Intelligence Center	AFTIC
Air Force Technical Objectives Documents	AFTOD
Air Force Technical Order	AFTO
Air Force Technical Order Standardization Board	AFTOSB
Air Force Technical Report	AFTR
Air Force Technical Service Command	AFTSC
Air Force Technical Training Headquarters	AFTTH
Air Force Test Base	AFTB
Air Force Test and Evaluation Center	AFTEC
Air Force Test Unit	AFTU
Air Force Test Unit, Vietnam	AFTU-V
Air Force Training Auxiliary [British]	ATA
Air Force Training Category [48 inactive duty training periods and 15 days active duty training per year]	A
Air Force Training Category [24 inactive duty training periods and 15 days active duty training per year]	B
Air Force Training Category [Inactive duty training periods and 15 days active duty training per year]	D
Air Force Training Category [Inactive duty training periods and 30 days active duty training per year]	E
Air Force Training Category [No inactive duty periods and 4 months minimum initial active duty training per year]	F
Air Force Training Category [12 training periods and zero days active duty training per year]	G
Air Force Training Category	H
Air Force Training Category [No training]	I
Air Force Training Category [Officer training program]	J
Air Force Training Command	AFTRC
Air Force Unit Post Office	AFUPO
Air Force of the United States	AFUS
Air Force Visual Aid	AFVA
Air Force Weapon	AFW
Air Force Weapons Effectiveness Testing	AFWET
Air Force Weapons Effectiveness Testing System	AFWETS
Air Force Weapons Laboratory	AFWL
Air Force Weapons Laboratory, Kirtland AFB, NM [OCLC symbol]	SCK
Air Force Weather Observing and Forecasting System	AFWOFS
Air Force Welfare Board	AFWB
Air Force Western Test Range [Later, Space and Missile Test Center]	AFWTR
Air Force Western Test Range Manual	AFWTRM
Air Force World Wide Military Command and Control System	AFWWMCCS
Air Force Wright Aeronautical Laboratories	AFWAL
Air Forces, Atlantic	AFLANT
Air Forces, Atlantic Fleet [Navy]	AIRLANT
Air Forces Escape and Evasion Society	AFEES
Air Forces Europe Exchange	AFEX
Air Forces Ferry Command	AFFC
Air Forces, Iceland	AFI
Air Forces, Iceland	AFICE
Air Forces Pacific Advanced	AIRPAC(ADV)
Air Forces, Pacific Fleet	AIRPAC
Air Forces Pacific, Pearl Harbor	AIRPAC(PEARL)
Air Forces Subordinate Command, Forward Area	AIRPACSUBCOMFORD
Air Forces, Western Europe [NATO]	AFWE
Air Foundation	AF
Air Foyle Ltd. [Great Britain] [ICAO designator]	UP
Air France [ICAO designator]	AF
Air Freight [Air carrier designation symbol]	AFFX
Air Freight	AFRT
Air Freight Association of America [Formerly, AFFA]	AFA
Air Freight Forwarders Association of America [Later, AFA]	AFFA
Air Freight Motor Carriers Conference	AFMCC
Air Freight Motor Carriers Conference, Inc., Arlington VA [STAC]	AFM
Air Freight Terminal	AFT
Air Freighters [Air carrier designation symbol]	AFIX
Air Fret [ICAO designator]	FZ
Air/Fuel [Mixture ratio]	A/F
Air Gabon Cargo [ICAO designator]	PG
Air Gap Width	AGW
Air Gauge	AG
Air Gemini, Inc. [Tacoma, WA] [FAA designator]	GEM
Air Greater Than Bone [Conduction]	A > B
Air-to-Ground [Photos, missiles, etc.]	AG
Air-to-Ground [Photos, missiles, etc.]	ATG

Air-to-Ground Acquisition and Tracking Equipment ... AGATE
Air-to-Ground-to-Air ... AGA
Air-Ground-Air Communications System ... AGACS
Air-Ground Chart ... AGC
Air-Ground Communications ... AGC
Air-Ground Communications Channel ... AGCC
Air-Ground Cooperation Officer ... AGCO
Air-Ground Correlation Factor ... AGCF
Air-Ground Engagement Simulation ... AGES
Air Ground Equipment ... AGE
Air and Ground Forces Resources and Technical Staff [*Army*] ... AGFRTS
Air-to-Ground Gunnery Range ... AGGR
Air-Ground Information Center ... AGIC
Air-Ground Integration System ... AGIS
Air-to-Ground Liaison Code [*Air Force*] ... AGLC
Air-Ground Liaison Officer [*Marine Corps*] ... AGLO
Air-to-Ground Missile ... AGM
Air-to-Ground Moving Target Indicator ... AGMTI
Air-Ground Operations Section [*or School or System*] ... AGOS
Air-to-Ground Standoff Weapon ... AGSW
Air-Ground System ... AGS
Air Group ... AG
Air Group ... AIRGRP
Air Guinee [*Guinea*] [*ICAO designator*] ... GI
Air Gunner [*British*] ... AG
Air Gunnery Officer ... AGO
Air Haiti [*ICAO designator*] ... HJ
Air Hawaii [*Honolulu, HI*] [*FAA designator*] ... AHC
Air Header ... AHDR
Air Headquarters ... AHQ
Air to Heat Exchanger [*Aerospace*] ... AHE
Air Heater Blower ... AHB
Air Height Surveillance RADAR ... AHSR
Air Historical Branch [*Air Ministry*] [*British*] ... AHB
Air Horsepower [*Air Force*] ... AHP
Air Idaho, Inc. [*Twin Falls, ID*] [*FAA designator*] ... AID
Air Illinois, Inc. [*Air carrier designation symbol*] ... AILX
Air Illinois, Inc. [*Carbondale, IL*] [*FAA designator*] ... ILL
Air India [*ICAO designator*] ... AI
Air Indicator Not Operating [*Aviation*] ... ARNO
Air Induction ... AINDTN
Air Induction Control System [*Air Force*] ... AICS
Air Industries and Transports Association ... AITA
Air Inflatable Retarder [*for bombs*] ... AIR
Air Information Center ... AIC
Air Information Codification ... AIC
Air Information Division [*Library of Congress*] ... AID
Air Injection Reactor ... AIR
Air Inlet Controller ... AIC
Air Inspection Directorate [*British*] ... AID
Air Inspector ... AI
Air Inspector General ... AIG
Air Installation Compatible Use Zoning [*Air Force*] ... AICUZ
Air Installation Office ... AIO
Air Installations ... AI
Air Intake Panel ... AIP
Air Intelligence ... AI
Air Intelligence Force ... AIF
Air Intelligence Liaison [*British*] ... AIL
Air Intelligence Liaison Officer [*British*] ... AILO
Air Intelligence Officer [*Navy*] ... AIO
Air Intelligence Organization ... AIO
Air Intelligence Section [*Army*] ... AINTSEC
Air Intelligence Service ... AIS
Air Intelligence Training Center ... AITC
Air Intercept Battle Analysis ... AIBA
Air Intercept [*or Interception*] **Control** [*or Controller*] ... AIC
Air Intercept Control School ... AICS
Air Intercept Controller Supervisor ... AICS
Air Intercept Missile ... AIM
Air Intercept Missile Evaluation ... AIMVAL
Air Intercept Missile Package ... AIMP
Air Intercept Officer ... AIO
Air Intercept Rocket ... AIR
Air Interception Committee [*Air Ministry*] [*British*] ... AIC
Air Interceptor Fuze ... AIF
Air Interface Sub-Working Group [*NATO*] ... AISWG
Air Intergulf Ltd. [*United Arab*] [*ICAO designator*] ... II
Air Isolated Monolithic [*Circuit*] ... AIM
Air Jamaica Ltd. [*ICAO designator*] ... JM
Air Jet Control Unit ... AJCU
Air Jordan [*Airline*] ... AJ
Air Kentucky [*Owensboro, KY*] [*FAA designator*] ... AKY
Air-Land Assault ... ALA
Air-Land Forces Agency [*Air Force*] [*Army*] ... ALFA
Air-Land Operations Manual ... ALOM
Air-Land Resupply ... ALR
Air Landing Exercise [*Military*] ... AIRLEX
Air Lanka [*Sri Lanka*] [*ICAO designator*] ... UJ
Air Launch Sounding Rocket ... ALSOR
Air-Launched [*Missile launch environment symbol*] ... A
Air-Launched Advanced Ramjet Missile ... ALARM
Air-Launched, Air-Recoverable Rocket ... ALARR
Air-Launched Antiballistic Missile ... ALABM
Air-Launched AntiRADAR Missile ... ALARM
Air-Launched Ballistic Intercept ... ALBI
Air-Launched Ballistic Intercept System ... ALBIS
Air-Launched Ballistic Missile ... ALBM
Air-Launched Balloon System ... ALBS
Air-Launched Boost Intercept ... ALBI
Air-Launched Cruise Missile ... ALCM
Air-Launched Cruise Missile Guidance Set ... ALCMGS
Air-Launched Guided Missile [*Military*] ... ALGM
Air-Launched Intercept Missile ... ALIM
Air-Launched Intercept Missile Record System ... AIMS
Air-Launched Long-Range Air-to-Air Missile ... ALRAAM
Air-Launched Low-Altitude Cruise Missile ... ALLACM
Air-Launched Low-Volume Ramjet ... ALVRJ
Air-Launched Miniature Vehicle ... ALMV
Air-Launched Missile ... ALM
Air-Launched Missile Bulletin ... AMB
Air-Launched Missile Change ... AMC
Air-Launched Missile Intermediate Maintenance System Program [*Navy*] ... ALMIMSIP
Air-Launched Missile Inventory Objectives Study ... ALMIOS
Air-Launched Missile System ... ALMS
Air-Launched Nonnuclear Ordnance ... ALNNO
Air-Launched Platform ... ALP
Air-Launched Projected Sonobuoy ... ALPS
Air-Launched Report [*Navy*] ... ALREP
Air-Launched Ship-Attack Missile ... ALSAM
Air-Launched Trainer Rocket ... ATR
Air-Launched Vehicle ... ALV
Air-Launched Weapon ... ALW
Air Letter ... AL
Air Liaison ... AL
Air Liaison Officer ... AIRLO
Air Liaison Officer [*US Military, British Navy*] ... ALO
Air Liaison Officer Net ... ALON
Air Liaison Party ... ALP
Air Liberia [*ICAO designator*] ... NL
Air-Lift Associates, Inc. [*Morrisville, NC*] [*FAA designator*] ... WPK
Air Limousin T.A. [*France*] [*ICAO designator*] ... QY
Air Line of Communication [*Air Force*] ... ALOC
Air Line Communication Employees Association ... ACEA
Air Line Communication Employees Association ... ALCEA
Air Line Dispatchers Association [*Defunct*] ... ALDA
Air Line Employees Association, International ... ALEA
Air Line Pilots Association, International ... ALPA
Air Line Pilots Association, International ... ALPAI
Air Line Stewards and Stewardesses Association ... ALSSA
Air Lines of Communication ... AIRLOC
Air Liquide, Montreal, PQ, Canada [*Library symbol*] ... CaQMAL
Air Littoral [*France*] [*ICAO designator*] ... FU
Air Lock [*Technical drawings*] ... AL
Air Lock System ... ALS
Air Logistic Coordination Center ... ALCORCEN
Air Logistics [*Lafayette, LA*] [*FAA designator*] ... ALG
Air Logistics Center ... ALC
Air Logistics Service [*or System*] [*Military*] ... ALS
Air London [*Great Britain*] [*ICAO designator*] ... GG
Air Lowveld Pty. Ltd. [*South Africa*] [*ICAO designator*] ... LE
Air Lubricated Free Attitude [*NASA*] ... ALFA
Air Mail Center ... AMC
Air Mail Facility [*Post Office*] ... AMF
Air Mail Field ... AMF
Air Mail Pioneers ... AMP
Air Mail Transmission ... AMT
Air Malawi [*ICAO designator*] ... QM
Air Mali [*ICAO designator*] ... MY
Air Malta [*ICAO designator*] ... KM
Air Management Station ... AMS
Air Manila, Inc. [*Philippines*] [*ICAO designator*] ... UM
Air Marshal [*British*] ... AM
Air Mass [*Solar energy research*] ... AM
Air Mass ... AMS
Air Mass and Frontal Analysis [*Meteorology*] ... AMAFA
Air-Mass Transformation Experiment [*National Science Foundation/Japan*] ... AMTEX
Air Mass Zero ... AMO
Air Material Area Stock Control Point ... AMASCP
Air Material Armament Test Center ... AMATC
Air Material Command Headquarters, Ottawa, Ontario, Canada ... CANAIRMAT
Air Material Computer [*Air Force*] ... AIMACO
Air Material Proving Ground ... AMPG
Air Materiel Area [*Air Force*] ... AMA
Air Materiel Area System Management [*Air Force*] ... AMASM
Air Materiel Command [*Later, Air Force Logistics Command*] ... AMC
Air Materiel Command [*later, Air Force Logistics Command*] **- Air Force** ... AMC-AF

Air Materiel Command Ballistic Missile Center .... AMCBMC
Air Materiel Command [*later, Air Force Logistics Command*] **Command Forms** .... AMCF
Air Materiel Command [*later, Air Force Logistics Command*] **Compiling** [*System*] .... AIMACC
Air Materiel Command [*later, Air Force Logistics Command*] **Headquarters** .... AMCHQ
Air Materiel Command [*later, Air Force Logistics Command*] **Letter** .... AMCL
Air Materiel Command [*later, Air Force Logistics Command*] **Liaison Office** [*or Officer*] .... AMCLO
Air Materiel Command [*later, Air Force Logistics Command*] **Logistics Office** [*or Officer*] .... AMCLO
Air Materiel Command [*later, Air Force Logistics Command*] **Manual** .... AMCM
Air Materiel Command [*later, Air Force Logistics Command*] **Missile Field Office** .... AMCMFO
Air Materiel Command [*later, Air Force Logistics Command*] **Regulations** .... AMCR
Air Materiel Command [*later, Air Force Logistics Command*] **Test Site Office** .... AMCTSO
Air Materiel Force .... AMF
Air Materiel Force, European Area .... AMFEA
Air Materiel Force, Pacific Area .... AMFPA
Air Mattress [*Medicine*] .... AM
Air Mauritius [*ICAO designator*] .... MK
Air Medal [*Military*] .... AM
Air Member, Canadian Joint Staff, London, England .... CANAIRLON
Air Member, Canadian Joint Staff, Washington, DC .... CANAIRWASH
Air Member for Development and Production [*Air Ministry*] [*British*] .... AMDP
Air Member for Personnel [*Air Ministry*] [*British*] .... AMP
Air Member for Research and Development [*Later, TRE*] [*Air Ministry*] [*British*] .... AMRD
Air Member for Supply and Organisation [*Air Ministry*] [*British*] .... AMSO
Air Member for Supply and Research [*Air Ministry*] [*British*] .... AMSR
Air Midwest, Inc. [*Wichita, KS*] [*FAA designator*] .... AMW
Air Midwest, Incorporated [*NASDAQ symbol*] .... AMWI
Air Mileage Indicator [*Navigation*] .... AMI
Air Mileage Unit [*Navigation*] .... AMU
Air Mindanao Corp. [*Philippines*] [*ICAO designator*] .... MO
Air-Mining Mission [*Military*] .... AMM
Air Ministry [*British*] .... AM
Air Ministry Experimental Station [*British*] .... AMES
Air Ministry Local Staff Union [*Singapore*] .... AMLSU
Air Ministry Order [*British*] .... AMO
Air Ministry War Room [*British*] [*World War II*] .... AMWR
Air Ministry's Accident Branch [*British*] .... AMAB
Air Missile System .... AMS
Air Mission Unit [*Air Force*] .... AMU
Air Missouri [*Kirksville, MO*] [*FAA designator*] .... AMO
Air Mobile .... AM
Air Mobile Aircraft Refueling System .... AMARS
Air Mobile Task Force .... AMTF
Air-Mobile Van [*Trailer unit for use on ground or in air*] [*Military*] .... AIRVAN
Air Mobility Research and Development Laboratory [*Also, USAMR & DL*] [*Army*] .... AMR & DL
Air Monitoring Analysis and Prediction [*System*] .... AIRMAP
Air Monitoring Center [*Rockwell International Corp.*] .... AMC
Air Motor Servo Unit .... AMSU
Air Movement [*Message*] .... AIRMOVE
Air Movement and Control Association .... AM & CA
Air Movement and Control Association .... AMCA
Air Movement Data [*Air Force*] .... AMD
Air Movement Designator [*Army*] .... AMD
Air Movement Exercise [*Military*] .... AIRMOVEX
Air Movement Information Center [*NATO*] .... AMIC
Air Movement Recorder .... AMR
Air Movements Information Section .... AMIS
Air Munitions .... AMUN
Air Munitions Development Laboratory .... AMDL
Air Munitions Requirements and Development Committee [*Military*] .... AMRAD
Air National Guard .... ANG
Air [*or Army*] **National Guard** [*Military aircraft identification prefix*] .... G
Air National Guard Optometric Society .... ANGOS
Air National Guard Policy Council .... ANGPC
Air National Guard of the United States .... ANGUS
Air Nauru [*Republic of Nauru*] [*ICAO designator*] .... ON
Air and Naval Gunfire Liaison Company [*Military*] .... ANGLICO
Air Navigation .... AN
Air Navigation Act [*British*] .... ANA
Air Navigation Board .... ANB
Air Navigation Committee [*NATO*] .... ANC
Air Navigation Computer Unit .... ANCU
Air Navigation Development Board [*Functions absorbed by the FAA*] .... ANDB
Air Navigation Device .... AND
Air Navigation Directions .... AND
Air Navigation Facility .... ANF
Air Navigation Office [*Navy*] .... AIRNAVO
Air Navigation Office [*Navy*] .... ANO
Air Navigation Order .... ANO
Air Navigation Radio Aids .... ANRA
Air Navigation School [*British*] .... ANS
Air Navigation and Tactical Control .... ANTAC
Air Navigation and Traffic Control .... ANATC
Air Navigation Traffic Control .... ANTC
Air Navigation Training Unit .... ANTU
Air Navigational Aid [*Navy*] .... AIRNAVAID
Air Nebraska [*Kearny, NE*] [*FAA designator*] .... ANB
Air Nevada Airlines, Inc. [*Las Vegas, NV*] [*FAA designator*] .... ANV
Air New England, Inc. [*East Boston, MA*] [*FAA designator*] .... ANE
Air New York, Inc. [*Albany, NY*] [*FAA designator*] .... ABA
Air New Zealand Ltd. .... ANZ
Air New Zealand Ltd. [*ICAO designator*] .... TE
Air Niger [*ICAO designator*] .... AW
Air-Nitrogen Pressurization Control .... ANPC
Air Niugini [*New Guinea*] [*ICAO designator*] .... PX
Air North, Inc. [*Burlington, VT*] [*FAA designator*] .... ANO
Air Observer [*Military*] .... AOBSR
Air Observer School [*British*] .... AOS
Air Officer [*RAF*] [*British*] .... AO
Air Officer in Charge of Administration [*RAF*] [*British*] .... AOA
Air Officer Commander-in-Chief [*RAF*] [*British*] .... AOCINC
Air Officer Commanding [*RAF*] [*British*] .... AOC
Air Officer Commanding Base Air Forces [*RAF*] [*British*] .... AOCBAF
Air Officer Commanding-in-Chief [*RAF*] [*British*] .... AOC-in-C
Air Officer Commanding-in-Chief British Air Force Occupation [*RAF*] .... AOC in CBAFO
Air Officer of the Day [*Air Force*] .... AOD
Air O'Hare Ltd. [*Chicago, IL*] [*FAA designator*] .... LTD
Air Oil Cooler .... AOC
Air Oil Separator .... AOS
Air One [*NASDAQ symbol*] .... AONE
Air-Operated Plastic Valve .... AOPV
Air-Operated Unit .... AOU
Air Operational Network [*Air Force*] .... AIROPNET
Air Operational Training .... APTRA
Air Operations [*Military*] .... AIROPS
Air Operations [*Military*] .... AOPS
Air Operations Center [*Air Force*] .... AOC
Air Operations Room .... AOR
Air Operations Specialist .... AOS
Air Order of Battle .... AOB
Air Over .... AO
Air Over Hydraulic .... A/H
Air Pacific Airlines [*Eureka, CA*] [*FAA designator*] .... APA
Air Pacific Ltd. [*Fiji*] [*ICAO designator*] .... FJ
Air Panama International [*ICAO designator*] .... OP
Air Parcel Post .... APP
Air Passage .... AP
Air Patrol Area .... APA
Air Patrol Zone .... APZ
Air Permeability Meter .... APM
Air Photo Production Unit [*Canada*] .... APPU
Air Photographic and Charting Service .... APCS
Air Pictorial Service .... APS
Air Pilot .... AP
Air-Piloted Control Valve .... APCV
Air-Piloted Valve .... APV
Air to Pneumatic Distribution [*Aerospace*] .... APD
Air Police [*By extension, a person who is a member of the Air Police*] .... AP
Air Pollutant Emissions Report [*Environmental Protection Agency*] .... APER
Air Pollution [*A publication*] .... Air Pollut
Air Pollution .... AP
Air Pollution Abstracts [*A publication*] .... AirPolAb
Air Pollution Control .... APC
Air Pollution Control Association .... APCA
Air Pollution Control Association. Journal [*A publication*] .... Air Poll Cont Assn J
Air Pollution Control Association. Journal [*A publication*] .... Air Poll Control Assn J
Air Pollution Control District .... APCD
Air Pollution Control Office [*Obsolete*] [*Environmental Protection Agency*] .... APCO
Air Pollution Exercise .... APEX
Air Pollution Information and Computation System .... APICS
Air Pollution Meteorologist .... APM
Air Pollution Potential .... APP
Air Pollution Research Advisory Committee .... APRAC
Air Pollution Syndrome .... APS
Air Pollution Technical Data [*Series*] [*A publication*] .... APTD
Air Pollution Technical Information Center [*Also, NAPTIC*] [*Environmental Protection Agency*] .... APTIC
Air Polynesia, Inc. [*Honolulu, HI*] [*FAA designator*] .... BLA
Air Polynesie [*France*] [*ICAO designator*] .... VT
Air Position .... AP
Air Position Indicator [*Air Force*] .... API
Air Pressure .... AP
Air Pressure Analysis Program [*Bell System*] .... AIRPAP
Air Pressure Switch .... APS
Air Primary Training .... PRIMTRA

Air Priority	APRI
Air Priority Rating	APR
Air Prisoner of War Interrogation	APWI
Air Procurement District [Air Force]	APD
Air Procurement District Commander [Air Force]	APDC
Air Procurement Office	APO
Air Procurement Region, Europe	APRE
Air Procurement Region, Far East	APRFE
Air Products & Chemicals, Inc. [NYSE symbol]	APD
Air Products & Chemicals, Inc., Allentown, PA [OCLC symbol]	APA
Air Products & Chemicals, Inc., Allentown, PA [Library symbol]	PAtA
Air Programs Office [Environmental Protection Agency]	APO
Air Proving Ground	APG
Air Proving Ground Center [or Command]	APGC
Air Proving Ground Center - Eglin Air Force Base	APGCE
Air Provost Marshal	APM
Air Publication [Navy]	AP
Air Quality Act	AQA
Air Quality Advisory Board	AQAB
Air Quality Assessment Model [Air Force]	AQAM
Air Quality Control Region [Environmental Protection Agency]	AQCR
Air Quality Data Handling System [or Subsystem] [Environmental Protection Agency]	AQDHS
Air Quality Display Model	AQDM
Air Quality Forecast	AQF
Air Quality Index	AQI
Air Quality Management	AQM
Air Quality Region	AQR
Air Quality Related Values/Visibility Test [Environmental Protection Agency]	AQRV
Air Quality Simulation Model [Environmental Protection Agency]	AQSM
Air Quality Standard	AQS
Air Radio Officer	ARO
Air-Raid Defence [British] [World War II]	ARD
Air Raid Precautions [British] [World War II]	ARP
Air Raid Precautions Controller [British] [World War II]	ARPC
Air Raid Precautions Officer [British] [World War II]	ARPO
Air Raid Protection	ARP
Air Raid Reporting Control Ship [Navy]	ARRCS
Air Raid Warden	ARW
Air Raid Warning [Air Force]	ARW
Air Reactor Experiment	ARE
Air Receive	AR
Air Reconnaissance Detection Force	ARDF
Air Reconnaissance Liaison Officer	ARLO
Air Reconnaissance Support	ARSPT
Air Reconnaissance Support Battalion	ARSB
Air Reduction Center [NASA]	ARC
Air Reduction Company	AIRCO
Air Reduction Co., Inc., Central Research Department Library, Murray Hill, NJ [Library symbol]	NjMuA
Air Refueling	AIRFL
Air Refueling	AR
Air Refueling Boom	ARB
Air Refueling Control Point	ARCP
Air Refueling Control Time	ARCT
Air Refueling Egress Point [FAA]	AREP
Air Refueling Exit [Aviation]	AREX
Air Refueling Ingress Point [FAA]	ARIP
Air Refueling Initial Point [Air Force]	ARIP
Air Refueling Probe	ARP
Air Refueling Squadron	AREFS
Air Refueling Squadron	AREFSQ
Air Regenerative Exhaust	ARX
Air Regional Representative	ARR
Air Registration Board [British]	ARB
Air Regulating Squadron	ARS
Air Regulator	AR
Air Release Capacity [Aviation]	ARC
Air Report [Aviation]	AIREP
Air Report [Aviation]	ARP
Air Reporting Control	ARC
Air Reporting Net	ARN
Air Rescue	AIRRES
Air Rescue	AR
Air Rescue Operations Center [Air Force]	AROC
Air Rescue and Recovery Squadron	ARRS
Air Rescue Service [Air Force]	ARS
Air Rescue Ship	ARS
Air Research Bureau	ARB
Air Research and Development	AR & D
Air Research and Development Center [Later, Air Force Systems Command]	ARDC
Air Research and Development Command	ARDC
Air Research and Development Command - Andrews Air Force Base	ARDCA
Air Research and Development Command Forms	ARDCF
Air Research and Development Command Manual	ARDCM
Air Research and Development Command Regulations	ARDCR
Air Research and Development Council [NATO]	ARDC
Air Research and Testing Committee	ARTC

Air Reservations Interline Message Procedure	AIRIMP
Air Reserve	AR
Air Reserve Association [Later, Air Force Association]	ARA
Air Reserve Base	ARB
Air Reserve Center	ARC
Air Reserve District	ARD
Air Reserve Flying Center [Air Force]	ARFC
Air Reserve Forces	ARF
Air Reserve Forces Meritorious Service Ribbon	ARFMSR
Air Reserve Forces Personnel Data System	ARFPDS
Air Reserve Forces Policy Committee	ARFPC
Air Reserve Officers' Training Corps [Air Force]	AROTC
Air Reserve Pay and Allowance System	ARPAS
Air Reserve Pay System	ARPS
Air Reserve Personnel Center [Air Force]	ARPC
Air Reserve Records Center	ARRC
Air Reserve Specialist Training Squadron	ARSTS
Air Reserve Technician [Air Force]	ART
Air Reserve Technician Program [Air Force]	ARTP
Air Reserve Unit	ARU
Air Reserve Unit (General Training)	ARUG
Air Reserve Unit (General Training, Nonpay)	ARUSNP
Air Reserve Unit (General Training, Pay)	ARUSP
Air Reserve Volunteer Support Group	ARVSG
Air Reservist [A publication]	AIRR
Air Reservist [A publication]	Air Reserv
Air Resistance	AR
Air Resources Board [California]	ARB
Air Resources Laboratories [National Oceanic and Atmospheric Administration]	ARL
Air Resupply and Communication Service	ARCS
Air Revitalization System	ARS
Air Rhodesia [ICAO designator]	RH
Air Rouergue [ICAO designator]	UZ
Air Route Surveillance RADAR	ARSR
Air Route Traffic Control	ARTC
Air Route Traffic Control Center	ARTCC
Air Route Traffic Control Center Clearance Delivered [Symbol]	B
Air Routing International Corp. [ICAO designator]	XC
Air Safety Board	ASB
Air Safety Reporting System [NASA]	ASRS
Air Sampling System	ASS
Air Scatterable Antipersonnel Mine	ASPM
Air Screw	AS
Air-Sea-Rescue	ASR
Air-Sea Rescue Craft	ASRC
Air-Sea Service [Switzerland] [ICAO designator]	KF
Air Search Attack Team [Military]	ASAT
Air Search Attack Unit [Military]	ASAU
Air Search RADAR	ASR
Air Search RADAR Receiver [Shipborne]	SR
Air Section	AS
Air Self-Defense Force [Japan]	ASDF
Air Separation Unit [For oxygen production]	ASU
Air Service	AS
Air Service Area Command	ASAC
Air Service Command	ASC
Air Service Command Advisory Team	ASCAT
Air Service Group [Air Force]	ASG
Air Service Information Circular	ASIC
Air Service Signal Corps	ASSC
Air Service Support Squadron [Army]	ASSRON
Air Services [Military]	AIRSVC
Air Seychelles [ICAO designator]	CK
Air Shutoff	ASHOF
Air Shutoff Valve	ASV
Air Shutter	AIRSHTR
Air Siam Air Co. [Thailand] [ICAO designator]	VG
Air Signal Officer	ASO
Air Society, International	ASI
Air Solenoid Valve	ASV
Air Solomons Command [US]	AIRSOLS
Air South [Airline code]	KQ
Air Space	ASPA
Air Space Transportation	ASTRA
Air Space Travel Research Organization	ASTRO
Air Specification	AS
Air Speed & Executive Airline, Inc. [Cambridge, MA] [FAA designator]	ASE
Air Staff [Air Force]	AS
Air Staff Board	ASB
Air Staff Defense Force	ASDF
Air Staff Officer	ASO
Air Staff Orientation	ASO
Air Staff Training [Air Force]	ASTRA
Air Stagnation Advisories [National Weather Service]	ASA
Air Standard Efficiency	ASE
Air Standardization Coordinating Committee	ASCC
Air Standardization Coordination Program [NATO]	ASCP
Air Starting	ASTRG
Air Station	AS

Air Stations Weekly Orders [*Navy*] ASWO
Air Store Issuing Ship AIRIS
Air Stores Depot [*Navy*] AIRSTORDEP
Air Strike A/S
Air Superiority AS
Air Superiority Program ASP
Air Supply ASUP
Air Supply Board [*Ministry of Aircraft Production*] [*British*] ASB
Air Support Command ASC
Air Support Control ASC
Air Support Control Units ASCU
Air Support Director [*Military*] ASD
Air Support Operations Center [*Air Force*] ASOC
Air Support RADAR Team [*Marine Corps*] ASRT
Air Support Signal Unit ASSU
Air Support Test Unit ASTU
Air Support Training Units ASTU
Air-Supported Threat [*Army*] AST
Air-Supported Threat Defense [*Army*] ASTD
Air-Supported Threat Defense System [*Army*] ASTDS
Air-to-Surface [*Missiles*] AS
Air-to-Surface [*Missiles*] ATS
Air-to-Surface Ballistic Missile ASBM
Air, Surface, and Electronic Warfare Division [*Navy*] AS & EWD
Air-to-Surface Missile ASM
Air-to-Surface Vessel ASV
Air-to-Surface Weapon ASW
[*The*] **Air Surgeon** [*Army*] TAS
Air Surveillance [*Air Force*] AS
Air Surveillance Officer [*Air Force*] ASO
Air Surveillance RADAR ASR
Air Surveillance System ASS
Air Surveillance Technician [*Air Force*] AST
Air Survey Co. of India Ltd. [*ICAO designator*] [*Obsolete*] IS
Air Systems Command [*Navy*] AIRSYSCOM
Air Systems Command [*Navy*] ASC
Air Tactical Control Officer ATACO
Air Tactical Publication ATP
Air Tactical School [*Air Force*] ATS
Air Tactics Officer [*Air Force*] ATO
Air Tahiti [*ICAO designator*] QE
Air Tanzania [*ICAO designator*] TC
Air Target Chart ATC
Air Target Intelligence Liaison Program [*Air Force*] ATIL
Air Target Materials [*Military*] ATM
Air Target Materials Program ATMP
Air Targets Officer ATO
Air Task Force ATF
Air Task Force Commander ATFC
Air Taxi-Commercial Operator ATCO
Air Taxi and Commercial Pilots Association ATCPA
Air Technical Index ATI
Air Technical Information [*Used by Armed Services Technical Information Agency - later, Defense Documentation Center - to accession and identify documents*] ATI
Air Technical Intelligence [*Air Force*] ATI
Air Technical Intelligence Services Command [*Air Force*] ATISC
Air Technical Intelligence Study [*Air Force*] ATIS
Air Technical Service Command ATSC
Air Technical Training [*Navy*] TECHTRA
Air Technician [*Air National Guard*] AT
Air Temperature AT
Air Temperature Correction T
Air Terminal ATERM
Air Terminal Officer [*Air Force*] ATO
Air Terminal Team ATT
Air Test Vehicle ATV
Air Togo [*ICAO designator*] AX
Air Traffic (Area) Supervisor ATAS
Air Traffic Communication System [*NASA*] ATCS
Air Traffic Communications ATCOM
Air Traffic Communications Service ATCS
Air Traffic Communications Station ATCS
Air Traffic Conference of America ATC
Air Traffic Conference of America ATCA
Air Traffic Control ATC
Air Traffic Control Advisory Committee [*Department of Transportation*] ATCAC
Air Traffic Control Assigned Airspace ATCAA
Air Traffic Control Association ATCA
Air Traffic Control Automation Panel [*International Civil Aviation Organization*] ATCAP
Air Traffic Control Automation System ATCAS
Air Traffic Control Beacon Ground Station ATCBGS
Air Traffic Control Beacon Interrogator ATCBI
Air Traffic Control Center [*Air Force*] ATCC
Air Traffic Control Communication ATCC
Air Traffic Control Evaluation Unit ATCEU
Air Traffic Control Facility ATCF
Air Traffic Control Flight Advisory Service ATCFAS
Air Traffic Control Line ATCL
Air Traffic Control and Navigation Board ATCNB
Air Traffic Control Officer [*Air Force*] ATCO
Air Traffic Control Operations Representative ATCOR
Air Traffic Control Procedures ATCP
Air Traffic Control RADAR Beacon ATCRB
Air Traffic Control RADAR Beacon/Identification Friend or Foe/ Mark XII/System AIMS
Air Traffic Control RADAR Beacon System ATCRBS
Air Traffic Control RADAR System ATCRS
Air Traffic Control RADAR Unit ATCRU
Air Traffic Control Requests [*Aviation*] CR
Air Traffic Control Signaling System ATCSS
Air Traffic Control Specialist ATCS
Air Traffic Control Systems Command Center ATCSCC
Air [*or Airport*] **Traffic Control Tower** ATCT
Air Traffic Control Tower, Approach Control, and Departure Control Facility [*Aviation*] TAD
Air Traffic Control Transponder ATCT
Air Traffic Coordinating Officer ATCO
Air Traffic Coordinator ATCOR
Air Traffic Coordinator Europe ATCOREU
Air Traffic Data Processor ATDP
Air Traffic GmbH [*ICAO designator*] TJ
Air Traffic Management ATM
Air Traffic Management Automated Center ATMAC
Air Traffic Management System [*Army*] ATMS
Air Traffic Procedures ATP
Air Traffic Procedures Advisory Committee ATPAC
Air Traffic Regulation Center ATRC
Air Traffic Regulation Identification System [*Army*] ATRIS
Air Traffic Regulations ATR
Air Traffic Representative ATREP
Air Traffic Section ATS
Air Traffic Service [*of FAA*] [*Also known as AT, ATS*] AAT
Air Traffic Service [*of FAA*] [*Also known as AAT, ATS*] AT
Air Traffic Service [*of FAA*] [*Also known as AAT, AT*] ATS
Air Traffic Service Contingency Command Post [*of FAA*] ATSCCP
Air Traffic Service Flight Services Division [*of FAA*] ATSFSD
Air Traffic Services Reporting Office [*Aviation*] ARO
Air Traffic Transponder ATT
Air Training Advisor ATA
Air Training Advisory Group ATAG
Air Training Command [*Air Force*] ATC
Air Training Command [*Air Force*] ATRC
Air Training Command Manual [*Air Force*] ATCM
Air Training Command Pamphlet [*Air Force*] ATCP
Air Training Command Regulation [*Air Force*] ATCR
Air Training Corps [*RAF*] [*British*] ATC
Air Training Corps of America ATCA
Air Training Corps Cadet [*British*] ATCC
Air Training Squadron AIRTRAINRON
Air Training Squadron AIRTRARON
Air Training Team ATT
Air Trans Africa [*ICAO designator*] AG
Air Transcontinental Airlines Ltd. [*Great Britain*] [*ICAO designator*] WI
Air Transmit AT
Air Transport [*Military*] AT
Air Transport Advisory Council [*British*] ATAC
Air Transport Association of America ATA
Air Transport Association of America ATAA
Air Transport Association of Canada ATAC
Air Transport Auxiliary [*British*] [*World War II*] ATA
Air Transport Auxiliary Service [*British*] [*World War II*] ATAS
Air Transport Bureau [*ICAO*] ATB
Air Transport Command [*Military*] ATC
Air Transport Command Headquarters, Rockcliffe, Ontario, Canada CANAIRLIFT
Air Transport Committee [*ICAO*] ATC
Air Transport Coordinator for the United States ATCORUS
Air Transport Corp. [*Detroit, MI*] [*FAA designator*] TPT
Air Transport Development Unit [*British*] ATDU
Air Transport Licensing Authority [*British*] ATLA
Air Transport Licensing Board ATLB
Air Transport Movement Control Center ATMC
Air Transport Operation Centre [*Military*] [*British*] ATOC
Air Transport Pressurizing Unit ATPU
Air Transport of Radiation ATR
Air Transport Radio ATR
Air Transport Rating ATR
Air Transport Service [*Navy*] ATS
Air Transport Squadron AIRTRANSRON
Air Transport Squadron ATS
Air Transport Squadron, Atlantic AIRTRANSRONLANT
Air Transport Squadron, Pacific AIRTRANSRONPAC
Air Transport Squadron, West Coast AIRTRANSRONWESTCOAST
Air Transport Wing [*Air Force*] ATW
Air Transport Wing [*Air Force*] ATWg
Air Transport World [*A publication*] Air Transp World
Air Transportability Test Loading Agency ATTLA
Air-Transportable Clinic ATC
Air Transportable Communications Complex ATRAX

Air Transportable Communications Unit .... ATCU
Air Transportable Dispensary .... ATD
Air Transportable Hospital .... ATH
Air Transportable Loading Dock .... ATLD
Air Transportable Pantograph Fueling System .... ATPFS
Air Transportable Pulse RADAR Navigation Aid [*Aviation*] .... CPN
Air Transportable Pulse RADAR Search [*Aviation*] .... CPS
Air Transportable Radio Installations .... ATRI
Air Transportable SONAR .... ATS
Air Transportable SONAR Surveillance System .... ATSSS
Air Transportation Board .... ATB
Air Transportation Coordination Office .... ATCO
Air Transportation Exercise [*Military*] .... AIRTRANSEX
Air Transportation Rack .... ATR
Air Transportation Research Information Service .... ATRIS
Air Transportation Research International Forum .... ATRIF
Air Transportation Squadron (Medium) .... ATS(M)
Air Travel Card [*Airline notation*] .... ATC
Air Travel Card of High Credit [*Airline notation*] .... ATCQ
Air Travel Organisers Licence [*British*] .... ATOL
Air Travel Security Unit .... ATSU
Air Tungaru [*Gilbert Islands*] [*ICAO designator*] .... RT
Air Turbine Alternator .... ATA
Air Turbine Drive .... ATD
Air Turbine Generator .... ATG
Air Turbine Motor .... ATM
Air Turbine Starter .... ATS
Air Turbo Exchanger .... ATE
Air Turbo Rocket .... ATR
Air UK Ltd. [*Great Britain*] [*ICAO designator*] .... UK
Air-to-Umbilical Junction Box .... AUJ
Air-to-Underwater Missile [*Air Force*] .... AUM
Air University .... AU
Air University Board of Visitors .... AUBV
Air University Library .... AUL
Air University Library Index to Military Periodicals [*A publication*] .... AirUnLibI
Air University Press .... AUP
Air University Review [*A publication*] .... Air Univ Rev
Air US [*Denver, CO*] [*FAA designator*] .... AUS
Air Valve Silencer .... AVS
Air Vegas, Inc. [*Las Vegas, NV*] [*FAA designator*] .... AVG
Air Vehicle Detection .... AVD
Air Vehicle Synthesis [*Program*] .... AVSYN
Air Velocity Detector .... AVD
Air Velocity Index .... AVI
Air Velocity Meter .... AVM
Air Velocity Transducer .... AVT
Air Vendee [*France*] [*ICAO designator*] .... DV
Air Vent .... AV
Air Ventilation Garment [*NASA*] .... AVG
Air Ventures, Inc. [*Madison, CT*] [*FAA designator*] .... RCN
Air Vibrating Table .... AVT
Air Vice-Marshal [*British*] .... AVM
Air Viet-Nam [*ICAO designator*] .... VN
Air Viet-Nam .... VNA
Air Volta [*Upper Volta*] [*ICAO designator*] .... VH
Air Vosges [*France*] [*ICAO designator*] [*Obsolete*] .... GS
Air War College .... AWC
Air War College Associate Program .... AWCAP
Air Warfare Analysis Section [*British*] .... AWA
Air Warfare Analysis Section [*British*] .... AWAS
Air Warfare Control Officer .... AWCO
Air Warfare Division [*Navy*] .... AWD
Air Warfare Instructor [*Navy*] [*British*] .... AWI
Air Warfare Research Department [*Navy*] .... AWRD
Air Warfare Simulation Complex .... AWSC
Air Warfare Systems Analysis .... AWSA
Air Warfare Training Division [*Navy*] [*British*] .... AWTD
Air Warning .... AW
Air Warning Squadron [*Marine Corps*] .... AWS
Air Warning System .... AWS
Air-to-Water .... AW
Air and Water Pollution [*A publication*] .... Air Water Pollut
Air/Water Pollution Report [*A publication*] .... Air/Water Poll Rept
Air Weapon Systems [*Air Force*] .... AWS
Air Weapons Control System [*Air Force*] .... AWCS
Air Weapons Controller .... AWC
Air Weapons Systems Management .... AWSM
Air Weapons Systems Plan .... AWSP
Air Weapons Training Installation .... AWTI
Air Weather Service [*Air Force*] .... AWS
Air Weather Service Manual .... AWSM
Air Weather Service Office .... AWSWO
Air Weather Service, Technical Library, Scott AFB, IL [*OCLC symbol*] .... SCA
Air Weather Service Training Guide .... AWSTG
Air West Airlines Ltd. [*Richmond, BC*] [*FAA designator*] .... AWA
Air Wing Commander .... AWC
Air Wing Staffs .... AWS
Air Wisconsin [*Appleton, WI*] [*FAA designator*] .... AWI
Air Wisconsin [*Airline code*] .... ZW
Air Wisonsin [*NASDAQ symbol*] .... ARWS
Air Wonder Stories [*A publication*] .... AW
Air Wonder Stories [*A publication*] .... AWS
Air-World Co. .... AW
Air Xpress, Inc. [*Greensboro, NC*] [*FAA designator*] .... ARX
Air Yugoslavia [*ICAO designator*] .... JR
Airbama, Inc. [*Muscle Shoals, AL*] [*FAA designator*] .... ABM
Airblast Fuel Injection Tube [*Gas turbine engine*] .... AFIT
Airborne .... AB
Airborne .... ABN
Airborne Acoustic Information System (Intelligence) .... ACINF
Airborne Alert .... AA
Airborne Alert Indoctrination .... AAI
Airborne Alert Weapon System .... AAWS
Airborne Alternate Command Echelon [*NATO*] .... AACE
Airborne Angular Position Sensor .... AAPS
Airborne Antenna System .... AAS
Airborne Antiballistic Missiles .... AABM
Airborne Antisubmarine Warfare .... AASW
Airborne Argon Ion LASER .... AAIL
Airborne Armament Control [*Air Force*] .... AAC
Airborne Assault .... ABA
Airborne Assault Vehicle .... AAV
Airborne Associative Array Processor .... AAAP
Airborne Astrographic Camera System [*Air Force*] .... AACS
Airborne Audio Frequency Coder .... AAFC
Airborne Automatic Voice Communications System .... AAVCRS
Airborne Auxiliary Memory System .... AAMS
Airborne Backing Store .... ABS
Airborne Ballistic Missile Intercept System .... ABMIS
Airborne Ballistics Division [*NASA*] .... ABD
Airborne Battlefield Command and Control Center .... ABCCC
Airborne Battlefield Light Equipment System [*Army*] .... ABLES
Airborne Beacon Electronic Test Set .... ABETS
Airborne Beacon Processing System .... ABPS
Airborne Beacon Processor .... ABP
Airborne Bombing Evaluation .... ABE
Airborne Central Data Tape Recorder .... ACDTR
Airborne Collision-Avoidance System .... ACAS
Airborne Collision Warning .... ACW
Airborne Command Control Squadron [*Air Force*] .... ACCS
Airborne Command Control Squadron [*Air Force*] .... ACCSq
Airborne Command Post [*Air Force*] .... ABNCP
Airborne Command Post [*Air Force*] .... ACP
Airborne Communication Relay Station [*Air Force*] .... ACRES
Airborne Communications Center [*Military*] .... ABCC
Airborne and Communications-Electronics Board [*Army*] .... ACEBD
Airborne Communications Location Identification and Collection System .... ACLICS
Airborne Communications Reconnaissance Platform .... ACRP
Airborne Communications Reconnaissance Program .... ACRP
Airborne Control [*System*] .... ABC
Airborne Control Computer .... ACC
Airborne Controlled Intercept [*Air Force*] .... ACI
Airborne Cooperational Equipment .... ACE
Airborne Coordinating Group .... ACG
Airborne Corps Operation Plan [*Military*] .... ACOP
Airborne Countermeasures Environment and RADAR Target Simulation .... ACEARTS
Airborne Data Acquisition and Recording System .... ADARS
Airborne Data Acquisition System .... ADAS
Airborne Data Automation .... ADA
Airborne Data Link .... ADL
Airborne Data Link System .... ADLS
Airborne Data Processor [*Air Force*] .... ADP
Airborne Data Terminal .... ADT
Airborne Designation and Discrimination Study .... ADDS
Airborne Detection Discrimination Sensor .... ADDS
Airborne Digital Computer [*Air Force*] .... ADC
Airborne Digital Instrumentation System .... ADIS
Airborne Digital Processing Unit .... ADPU
Airborne Digital Recorder .... ADR
Airborne Digital Recording System .... ADRS
Airborne Digital Timer .... ADT
Airborne Digital Voltmeter .... ADV
Airborne Direct Air Support Center .... ABNDASC
Airborne Display Electrical Management System [*Aviation*] .... ADEMS
Airborne Doppler Velocity Altitude Navigation Compass Equipment .... ADVANCE
Airborne Dual-Channel Variable Input Severe Environmental Recorder/Reproducer [*Air Force*] .... ADVISER
Airborne Dual Detector Indicator .... ADDI
Airborne Dynamic Alignment System .... ADAS
Airborne [*or Aircraft*] **Early Warning** [*Station*] .... AEW
Airborne Early Warning Aircraft .... AEWA
Airborne Early Warning Combat Air Patrol .... AEWCAP
Airborne Early Warning and Control [*Army*] .... AEW & C
Airborne Early Warning and Control [*Army*] .... AEWC
Airborne Early Warning Fighter .... AEWF
Airborne Early Warning and Interceptor Control System .... AEWICS

Airborne Early Warning Squadron	AEWRON
Airborne Early Warning Training Unit	AEWTU
Airborne Early Warning Wing	AEWW
Airborne Electron Beam Recorder	AEBR
Airborne Electronic Equipment Modification	AEEM
Airborne Electronic LASER System	AELS
Airborne Electronic Ranging Instrumentation System	AERIS
Airborne Electronic Warfare	AEW
Airborne Electronics	AE
Airborne and Electronics Board [*Army*]	AEB
Airborne Emergency Actions Officer [*SAC*]	AEAO
Airborne Emergency Alternate Command Post	AEACP
Airborne Emergency Reaction Unit	ABERU
Airborne Environmental Reporting System	AERS
Airborne Equipment	A/BE
Airborne Equipment Division [*Bureau of Aeronautics; later, NASC*] [*Navy*]	AE
Airborne Equipment Failure [*Air Force*]	AEF
Airborne Equipment Repair Squadron	AERS
Airborne Evaluation Equipment	AEE
Airborne Expendable Bathythermograph	AXBT
Airborne Expendable Rocket System	AERS
Airborne Extended Range	AER
Airborne Fill-and-Drain	A/B F & D
Airborne Fire Control RADAR Set	AFCRS
Airborne Fire Fighting Equipment [*Air Force*]	AFFE
Airborne Fixed Array RADAR	AFAR
Airborne Flat Plate Array	AFPA
Airborne Flight Detection Measurement System	AFDMS
Airborne Formation Flight Simulator	AFFSIM
Airborne Forward Air Controller	AFAC
Airborne Forward Delivery Airfield Group	AFDAG
Airborne Fraunhofer Line Discriminator	AFLD
Airborne Freight Corp. [*NYSE symbol*]	ABF
Airborne Frequency Doubler	AFD
Airborne Frequency Multiplexing System	AFMS
Airborne General Illumination Light	AGIL
Airborne Ground Fire Locating System	AGFLS
Airborne Ground Fire Locator	AGFL
Airborne Gun-Laying	AGL
Airborne Gun-Laying RADAR	AGLR
Airborne Gun-Laying for Turrets	AGLT
Airborne Gunsight	AGS
Airborne Helmet Mounted Display	AHMD
Airborne Identification Kit	ABK
Airborne Identification Mobile System [*Military*]	AIMS
Airborne Infantry [*Military*]	ABNINF
Airborne Infrared Decoy Evaluation System	AIDES
Airborne Infrared Early Warning	AIREW
Airborne Infrared Equipment for Target Analysis	AIETA
Airborne Infrared Gunfire Locator	AIRGLO
Airborne Infrared Live Scanner	AILS
Airborne Infrared Mapper	AIM
Airborne Infrared Mapper	AIRM
Airborne Infrared Measurement Instrument	AIMI
Airborne Infrared Observatory [*NASA*]	AIO
Airborne Infrared Radiometer System	AIRS
Airborne Infrared Spectrometer	AIS
Airborne Infrared Surveillance Set	AISS
Airborne Insertion Display Equipment	AIDE
Airborne Institute Laboratories, Melville, NY [*Library symbol*]	NMelA
Airborne Instrumentation Platform	AIP
Airborne Instrumentation Subsystem	AIS
Airborne Instruments Laboratory [*Mineola, NY*]	AIL
Airborne Instruments Laboratory Approach	AILA
Airborne Integrated Flight Test Data System [*NASA*]	AIFTDS
Airborne Integrated Light Avionics System	AILAS
Airborne Integrated Maintenance System	AIMS
Airborne Integrated Reconnaissance System	AIRS
Airborne Intercept [*RADAR*] [*Air Force*]	AI
Airborne Interception Fire Control System [*Air Force*]	AIFCS
Airborne Interceptor Equipment	AIE
Airborne Interceptor Rocket	AIR
Airborne LASER	ABL
Airborne LASER Equipment Real-Time Surveillance	ALERTS
Airborne LASER Illuminator	ALI
Airborne LASER Illuminator Ranging and Tracking System	ALIRATS
Airborne LASER Laboratory [*Air Force*]	ALL
Airborne LASER Locator Designator	ALLD
Airborne LASER Range-Finder	ALR
Airborne LASER Receiver Module	ALARM
Airborne LASER System	ALS
Airborne LASER Tracker [*System*]	ALT
Airborne Launch Control Center	ALCC
Airborne Launch Control and Recovery System	ALCARS
Airborne Launch Control System [*Air Force*]	ALCS
Airborne Launching	ABLCHG
Airborne Law Enforcement Association	ALEA
Airborne LIDAR [*Light Detection and Ranging*] Oceanographic Probing Experiment [*NASA*]	ALOPE
Airborne Light Optical Fibre Technology	ALOFT

Airborne Lighting System [*Air Force*]	AIRLIGHT
Airborne Lightweight Optical Tracking [*Air Force*]	ALOT
Airborne Lightweight Optical Tracking System [*Air Force*]	ALOTS
Airborne Line Discriminator	ALD
Airborne Line Printer	ALP
Airborne Live Scanner	ALS
Airborne Long-Range Input	ALRI
Airborne Long-Range RADAR Input	ALRRI
Airborne Magnetic Recorder	AMR
Airborne Maintenance System	AMS
Airborne Microwave Scatterometer [*For measuring wind speed and direction*]	AMSCAT
Airborne Mine Countermeasure Equipment	AMCM
Airborne Mine Countermeasure System	AMCMS
Airborne Missile Control Subsystem	AMCSS
Airborne Missile Control System	AMCS
Airborne Mode Control	AMC
Airborne Modular Integrated System	AMIS
Airborne Moving Target Attack	AMTA
Airborne Moving Target Indicator [*Air Force*]	AMTI
Airborne Navigation Computer	ANC
Airborne Navigation Sensor	ANS
Airborne Navigational Multiple Indicators	ANMI
Airborne Night Classification System	ANCS
Airborne Night Observation Device	ANOD
Airborne Night Television System [*Obsolete*] [*Army*]	ANTS
Airborne Oil Surveillance System	AOSS
Airborne Operational Equipment	AOE
Airborne Operations Center [*NATO*]	ABNOC
Airborne Optical Beacon	AOB
Airborne Overland RADAR	AOR
Airborne Parabolic Arc Computer	APAC
Airborne Particle Monitoring System	APMS
Airborne Photography of the Eclipse of the Quiet Sun	APEQS
Airborne Power Supply	APS
Airborne Processing Unit	APU
Airborne Profile Recorder	APR
Airborne Propellant System	A/BPS
Airborne Provisioning Parts Breakdown	APPB
Airborne Pulse Search RADAR	APS
Airborne RADAR Approach	ARA
Airborne RADAR and Doppler	ARAD
Airborne RADAR Inflight Monitoring System	ARIMS
Airborne RADAR Navigational Aid	ARN
Airborne RADAR Orbital Determination System	ARODS
Airborne RADAR Platform [*Air Force*]	ARP
Airborne RADAR Target Simulator	ARTS
Airborne RADARscope Used in NAVAR [*Air Force*]	NAVASCOPE
Airborne Radiation Detection and Fixing [*Military*]	ARDF
Airborne Radiation Thermometer	ART
Airborne Radio Communicating	ARC
Airborne Radio Direction Finding	ARDF
Airborne Radio Installation [*RADAR*]	ARI
Airborne Radio Navigation	ARN
Airborne Radio Receiver	ARR
Airborne Range Instrumentation Station	ARIS
Airborne Range Only [*RADAR ranging set for use with various gun computers*]	ARO
Airborne Ranging and Orbit Determination System	AROD
Airborne Ranging System	ARS
Airborne Rapid-Scan Spectrometer	ARS
Airborne Real-Time Instrumentation System	ARTIS
Airborne Receiving Antenna	ARA
Airborne Reconnaissance Integrated Electronic System	ARIES
Airborne Refrigeration System	ARS
Airborne Relay Stations	ARS
Airborne Remote Sensing Oceanography Project	ARSOP
Airborne Remote Sensing System [*Coast Guard*]	ARSS
Airborne Research Capsule	ARC
Airborne Resupply	ABR
Airborne Satellite Receiving Station	ASRS
Airborne Scanning Radiometer	ASR
Airborne Science Program [*NASA*]	ASP
Airborne Science Spacelab Experiments System Simulation [*NASA*]	ASSESS
Airborne Search and Attack Plotter	ABSAP
Airborne Search Equipment	ASE
Airborne Self-Protection Jammer	ASPJ
Airborne Special Bombing	ASB
Airborne Special-Type Auxiliary Assembly	ASTAA
Airborne Special-Type Navigational Aid	ASN
Airborne Stabilized Viewing System	ASVS
Airborne Support Platform [*Army*]	ASP
Airborne and Surface Early Warning	ASEW
Airborne Surface Vessel Detection [*RADAR device*]	ASV
Airborne Surveillance and Control System [*ASD*]	ASACS
Airborne Surveillance and Intercept Defense System	ASIDS
Airborne Surveillance RADAR	ASR
Airborne Surveillance Set	ASS
Airborne Surveillance Warning and Control RADAR [*ASD/ADC*]	ASWCR
Airborne Systems Support Center	ASSC

Airborne Tactical Air Battle Control System .... ATABCS
Airborne Tactical Air Control Capability [*Air Force*] .... ATACC
Airborne Tactical Air Coordinator [*Navy*] .... ATAC
Airborne Tactical Command System [*Formerly, ATDS*] .... ATCS
Airborne Tactical Data Processing System .... ATDPS
Airborne Tactical Data System [*Later, ATCS*] .... ATDS
Airborne Tactical Jamming System [*Air Force*] .... ATJS
Airborne Tanker, Boom .... TAB
Airborne Tanker, Drogue .... TAD
Airborne Tanker, General .... TAG
Airborne Target Acquisition Control System .... ATACS
Airborne Target Acquisition and Fire Control System .... ATAFCS
Airborne Target Augmenter .... ATA
Airborne Task Force .... ABTF
Airborne Teletypewriter Equipment .... ATE
Airborne Test Bed .... ATB
Airborne Test Bed Mode Control .... ATBMC
Airborne Test Bed Turret .... ATBT
Airborne Test Conductor .... ATC
Airborne Test Instrumentation System [*Air Force*] .... ATIS
Airborne Test Safety Board .... ATSB
Airborne Time/Frequency Range/Altitude Monitor .... ATFRAM
Airborne Tracking .... ABT
Airborne Tracking, Acquisition, and Recognition .... ATAR
Airborne Traffic Situation Display [*FAA*] .... ATSD
Airborne Transponder Subsystem .... ABTSS
Airborne Two-Way Acoustic and Control System .... ATAC
Airborne Ultraviolet LASER .... AUVL
Airborne Vehicle Identification .... AVI
Airborne Vehicle Identification .... AVID
Airborne Very-Low-Frequency .... AVLF
Airborne Vibration Monitor .... AVM
Airborne Video Tape Recorder .... AVTR
Airborne Viewing System .... AVS
Airborne Visible-LASER Optical-Communications .... AVLOC
Airborne Warning and Control System [*Air Force*] .... AWACS
Airborne Warning and Recording Equipment .... AWARE
Airborne Waveguide Slotted Array .... AWSA
Airborne Waveguide Slotted Array Antenna .... AWSAA
Airborne Weapon and Control .... AWAC
Airborne Weapons Control .... AWC
Airborne Weapons Corrective Action Program .... AWCAP
Airborne Weather RADAR System .... AWRS
Airborne Weather and Reconnaissance System .... AWARS
Airborne Weather and Reconnaissance System .... AWRS
Aircal, Inc. [*NASDAQ symbol*] .... ACAL
Airco, Inc. [*Formerly, Air Reduction Co., Inc.*] [*NYSE symbol*] [*Delisted*] .... AN
Airco Speer Research & Development Laboratories, Niagara Falls, NY [*Library symbol*] .... NNiaA
Aircooled .... ACLD
Aircooled Beryllium Oxide with Integrated Gas Turbine .... ABORIGINE
Aircooled Motor .... AM
Aircraft [*or Airplane*] .... A
Aircraft .... AC
Aircraft .... ACFT
Aircraft .... ACRFT
Aircraft [*Wind triangle problems*] .... P
Aircraft [*Public-performance tariff class*] [*British*] .... AC
Aircraft Accident Board .... AAB
Aircraft Accident Investigation Board .... AAIB
Aircraft Accident Notification Procedures and Bureau Responsibilities [*Manual*] .... AANP
Aircraft Accident Record [*Obsolete*] [*Military*] .... AAR
Aircraft Accident Report [*Military*] .... AAR
Aircraft Acquisition and Support .... AIRACS
Aircraft Airworthiness Section .... AAS
Aircraft Anticollision Beacon System High-Intensity Light [*Army*] .... AABSHILL
Aircraft Antisubmarine Development Detachment, Atlantic Fleet .... AIRASDEVLANT
Aircraft Approach Light .... AAL
Aircraft Approach Limitation .... AAL
Aircraft Armament Bulletin [*Navy*] .... AAB
Aircraft Armament Change .... AAC
Aircraft and Armament Development .... AAD
Aircraft Armament Laboratory [*Naval Air Development Center*] .... AAL
Aircraft Armament Unit .... AIRARMUNIT
Aircraft Armaments, Incorporated .... AAI
Aircraft Arresting Gear .... A/G
Aircraft, Asiatic Fleet .... AIRAF
Aircraft Assembly Plant .... AAP
Aircraft Assignment Directive .... AAD
Aircraft Assignment Letter .... AAL
Aircraft-Based Infrared Detector .... ABIRD
Aircraft Battle Force [*Obsolete*] [*Navy*] .... ABF
Aircraft Battle Force, Pacific Fleet [*Navy*] .... AIRBATFORPAC
Aircraft Blast Interaction Tests .... ABIT
Aircraft of Bomber Command [*British*] .... ABC
Aircraft Bulletin .... A/B
Aircraft Capable of Satellite Operations .... ACSO
Aircraft Carrier .... A/CC
Aircraft Carrier [*Navy symbol*] CV
Aircraft Carrier Flag [*Navy*] [*British*] .... AC
Aircraft Carrier General Memorandum .... ACGM
Aircraft Carrier Intelligence Center CVIC
Aircraft Carrier, Medium Sized [*Navy symbol*] CVV
Aircraft Carrier, Nuclear Propulsion [*Navy symbol*] .... CVN
Aircraft Change Analysis .... ACA
Aircraft Change Application List .... ACAL
Aircraft Change Control Board [*DoD*] .... ACCB
Aircraft Checker's Report .... ACR
Aircraft Circular Letter .... ACL
Aircraft Coloring and Marking .... ACM
Aircraft Commander .... AC
Aircraft Commander Time .... ACT
Aircraft in Commission .... AIC
Aircraft Communication Control and Electronic Signaling System [*Air Force*] .... ACCESS
Aircraft Communication Procedures [*Navy*] .... ACP
Aircraft Communications System .... ACCS
Aircraft Communications System .... ACS
Aircraft Compatibility Control Drawing .... ACCD
Aircraft Component Intensive Management System [*Military*] .... ACIMS
Aircraft Component Mating Evaluation .... ACME
Aircraft Condition Evaluation [*Navy*] .... ACE
Aircraft Condition Inspection .... ACI
Aircraft Configuration Control Board [*DoD*] .... ACCB
Aircraft Control .... AC
Aircraft Control Link .... ACL
Aircraft Control Operator .... ACO
Aircraft Control Room .... ACR
Aircraft Control and Surveillance [*Air Force*] .... ACS
Aircraft Control System .... ACS
Aircraft Control Unit .... ACU
Aircraft Control and Warning .... ACAW
Aircraft Control and Warning Officer [*Military*] .... ACWO
Aircraft Control and Warning Squadron [*Military*] .... ACWRON
Aircraft Control and Warning Stations [*Military*] .... AC & WS
Aircraft Control and Warning System [*Military*] .... ACWS
Aircraft Crash Rescue Field Assistance and Evaluation Team [*Air Force*] .... ACRFAET
Aircraft Crew Interphone System .... ACIS
Aircraft Crewman Badge .... AcftCrmnBad
Aircraft Damage Sensing System .... ADSS
Aircraft Delivery Unit [*Air Force*] .... ADU
Aircraft Departing at [*number of minutes*] **Intervals** [*Aviation*] .... ADMIS
Aircraft Design-Induced Pilot Error [*National Transportation Safety Board*] .... ADIPE
Aircraft Design Research Division [*Navy*] .... ADR
Aircraft Destination Record .... ADR
Aircraft Development Service [*Air Force*] .... ADS
Aircraft Direction Room [*Navy*] .... ADR
Aircraft Directives Configuration [*Navy*] .... ADC
Aircraft Discrepancy Report .... ADR
Aircraft Dummy Deck Landing [*Navy*] .... ADDL
Aircraft Ejection Kit .... AEK
Aircraft Ejection Seat .... AES
Aircraft Ejection Seat System .... AESS
Aircraft Electrical Power System .... AEPS
Aircraft Electronic Warfare Self-Protection System [*Army*] .... AEWSPS
Aircraft Electronics Association .... AEA
Aircraft Emergency Procedures over Water .... AEPW
Aircraft Energy Efficiency .... ACEE
Aircraft Engine Laboratory .... AEL
Aircraft and Engine Mechanic .... AEM
Aircraft Engineering [*A publication*] .... Airc Engng
Aircraft Engineering [*A publication*] .... Aircr Eng
Aircraft Engineering District Office .... AEDO
Aircraft Engineering Foundation .... AEF
Aircraft Engineering Maintenance Company .... AEMCO
Aircraft and Engines .... A & E
Aircraft Environmental Support Office [*Naval Air Rework Facility*] .... AESO
Aircraft Equipment .... AE
Aircraft and Equipment Configuration List .... AECL
Aircraft Equipment List .... AEL
Aircraft Equipment Procedures .... AEP
Aircraft Equipment Requirement Schedule .... AERS
Aircraft Escort Vessel [*Navy symbol*] .... AVG
Aircraft and Facilities [*Navy appropriation*] .... A & F
Aircraft Familiarization .... AIRFAM
Aircraft Finance Association .... AFA
Aircraft, Fleet Marine Force, Atlantic [*Obsolete*] .... AIRFMFLANT
Aircraft, Fleet Marine Force, Pacific [*Obsolete*] .... AFMFP
Aircraft, Fleet Marine Force, Pacific [*Obsolete*] .... AIRFMFPAC
Aircraft Flight Report .... AFR
Aircraft Flying Training .... ACFT
Aircraft Force Projection Model [*Computer*] [*Navy*] .... AFPM
Aircraft Gas and Turbine .... AGT
Aircraft General Standards [*British*] .... AGS
Aircraft Generation Squadron .... AGS
Aircraft on Ground [*Navy*] .... ACOG
Aircraft on Ground [*Navy*] .... AOG

Aircraft Ground Fire Suppression and Rescue [*Air Force*] ... AGFSR
Aircraft Ground Fire Suppression and Rescue Systems [*Air Force*] ... AGFSRS
Aircraft Grounded for Lack of Parts ... AGP
Aircraft Gun Pod ... AGP
Aircraft Gunfire Detector ... AGD
Aircraft Handling Vehicle ... AHV
Aircraft Hangar ... ACH
Aircraft Identification ... ACID
Aircraft Identification ... AI
Aircraft IFF [*Identification, Friend or Foe*] **Mark XII System** ... AIMXS
Aircraft Incident Report [*Navy*] ... AIR
Aircraft Industries Center ... AIC
Aircraft Industry ... AI
Aircraft Industry Conference [*Navy*] ... AIC
Aircraft Inspection System ... AIS
Aircraft Inspections and Repair ... AIR
Aircraft Installation Diagnostic Equipment ... AIDE
Aircraft Instrument Bulletin [*Navy*] ... AIB
Aircraft Instrument Laboratory [*Navy*] ... AIL
Aircraft Instrument Repair Facility ... AIRF
Aircraft Instrument Subsystem [*Navy*] ... AIS
Aircraft Instruments and Aircrew Stations [*NATO*] ... AI
Aircraft Integrated Crew Station Concepts ... AICSC
Aircraft Integrated Data System ... AIDS
Aircraft Integrated Munition System ... AIMS
Aircraft Intermediate Maintenance Department [*Navy*] ... AIMD
Aircraft Intrusion Detection System [*RADAR*] ... AIDS
Aircraft Inventory Record ... AIR
Aircraft Inventory Reporting System ... AIRS
Aircraft Landing Gear ... ALG
Aircraft Landing Lamp ... ALL
Aircraft Landing Measurement System ... ALMS
Aircraft Landing System ... ALS
Aircraft Launch and Recovery Equipment Maintenance Program [*Navy*] ... ALREMP
Aircraft Launching Accessory Service Change ... ALASC
Aircraft Launching Bulletin ... ACLB
Aircraft Launching Bulletin ... ALB
Aircraft Limited Model ... ALM
Aircraft Load ... ACL
Aircraft Logistics Division [*Bureau of Aeronautics*] [*Later, NASC*] [*Navy*] ... AL
Aircraft Logistics Planning Board ... ALPB
Aircraft Machine Gunner ... AIRMG
Aircraft Machine Gunner ... AMG
Aircraft Maintenance Base ... AMB
Aircraft Maintenance Delayed for Parts [*Military*] ... AMDP
Aircraft Maintenance Manpower Information System ... AMMIS
Aircraft Maintenance Manpower Requirement [*Air Force*] ... AMMR
Aircraft Maintenance Manual ... AMM
Aircraft Maintenance Material Readiness List [*Navy*] ... AMMRL
Aircraft Maintenance Support Equipment ... AMSE
Aircraft Manufacturers Association [*Superseded by MAA*] ... AMA
Aircraft Manufacturing Company ... AMC
Aircraft Material Officer ... AMO
Aircraft Mechanics Fraternal Association ... AMFA
Aircraft Meteorological ... AC/M
Aircraft Military Mission ... AIRMILMIS
Aircraft/Missile Maintenance - Production Compression Report ... AMREP
Aircraft/Missile Project ... AMP
Aircraft Model Change ... AMC
Aircraft Monitor and Control ... AMAC
Aircraft Motion Compensation ... AMC
Aircraft Mounted Control System ... AMCS
Aircraft Movement Element ... AME
Aircraft Movement Information Service [*Air Force*] ... AMIS
Aircraft Multiplex Intercommunications ... AMI
Aircraft Multiplex Intercommunications System ... AMIS
Aircraft Multipurpose Test Inspection and Diagnostic Equipment ... AMTIDE
Aircraft Multispectral Photographic System [*NASA*] ... AMPS
Aircraft Noise Prediction Office [*NASA*] ... ANOPO
Aircraft Noise Prediction Program [*NASA*] ... ANOPP
Aircraft Nonflying-Electronics ... ANFE
Aircraft, Northern Solomons [*Military*] ... AIRNORSOLS
Aircraft Not Combat Ready ... ANCR
Aircraft Not Fully Equipped ... ANFE
Aircraft Nuclear Power [*or Propulsion*] ... ANP
Aircraft Nuclear Power Plant Facility ... ANPPF
Aircraft Nuclear Propulsion Department [*Navy*] ... ANPD
Aircraft Nuclear Propulsion Office [*of AEC*] [*Defunct*] ... ANPO
Aircraft Nuclear Propulsion Program ... ANPP
Aircraft Operating Cost Report ... AOCR
Aircraft Out of Commission for Maintenance [*Military*] ... AOCM
Aircraft Out of Commission for [*Lack of*] **Parts** [*Obsolete*] [*Military*] ... AOCP
Aircraft Out for Parts ... AOP
Aircraft Overhaul Work Stoppage ... AOWS
Aircraft Owners and Pilots Association ... AOPA
Aircraft Plume Analysis ... APA
Aircraft Position Information Converter [*Air Force*] ... APICON
Aircraft Procurement, Army ... APA
Aircraft Procurement, Navy ... APN
Aircraft Production Resources Agency ... APRA
Aircraft Program Data File ... APDF
Aircraft Proximity Warning Device ... APWD
Aircraft Proximity Warning System ... APWS
Aircraft Quality ... AQ
Aircraft Radio Laboratory ... ARL
Aircraft Reactor Equipment ... ARE
Aircraft Reactors Branch ... ARB
Aircraft Recording Instrumentation System [*British*] ... ARIS
Aircraft Recovery ... AIR
Aircraft Recovery Bulletin ... ARB
Aircraft Recovery Equipment ... ARE
Aircraft Reference Point ... ARP
Aircraft and Related Procurement, Navy ... ARPN
Aircraft Reliability and Maintainability Simulation ... ARMS
Aircraft Repair Division [*Military*] ... AIREPDIV
Aircraft Repair Division [*Military*] ... AIREPDN
Aircraft Repair Ship [*Navy*] ... ARS
Aircraft Repair Ship [*Navy symbol*] ... ARV
Aircraft Repair Ship (Aircraft) [*Navy symbol*] ... ARVA
Aircraft Repair Ship (Engine) [*Navy symbol*] ... ARVE
Aircraft Repair Ship (Helicopter) [*Navy symbol*] ... ARVH
Aircraft Repair and Supply Center ... ARSC
Aircraft Replaceable Assemblies ... ARA
Aircraft Report ... AIREP
Aircraft Requirements Computer System ... ARCS
Aircraft Rescue Boat [*Navy symbol*] ... AVH
Aircraft Rescue Vessel [*Navy*] ... ARV
Aircraft [*or Aviation*] **Rescue Vessel** [*Navy symbol*] ... AVR
Aircraft Research Instrumentation System ... ARIS
Aircraft Research and Testing Committee ... ARTC
Aircraft Resources Control Office ... ARCO
Aircraft Resources Management System [*Military*] ... ARMS
Aircraft Resources Management System, Pacific [*Military*] ... ARMSPAC
Aircraft Rocket ... AR
Aircraft and Rocket Design Engineers ... ARDE
Aircraft Rocket Subsystem ... ARS
Aircraft Safety Beacon ... ASB
Aircraft-to-Satellite Data Relay [*Meteorology*] ... ASDAR
Aircraft Schedule for Delivery to Fleet ... AIRSKEDELFLT
Aircraft Scheduling Unit ... ASU
Aircraft Scouting Force, Pacific Fleet ... AIRSCOFORPAC
Aircraft Security System ... ASS
Aircraft Security Vessel ... A/CS
[*The*] **Aircraft Service Association** ... TASA
Aircraft Service Change ... ASC
Aircraft Services Base ... ASB
Aircraft Services Facility ... ASF
Aircraft Shipment Readiness Date [*Army*] ... ASRD
Aircraft Sound Description System [*FAA*] ... ASDS
Aircraft, South Pacific Force [*Navy*] ... AIRSOPAC
Aircraft, Southwest Pacific Force [*Navy*] ... AIRSOWESPAC
Aircraft Specialties Lines ... ASL
Aircraft Specification Forum Committee ... ASFC
Aircraft Standard Parts ... ASP
Aircraft Standards ... AS
Aircraft Starting Unit ... ASU
Aircraft Station Keeper ... ASK
Aircraft Stations [*ITU designation*] ... MA
Aircraft Statistical Data ... ASD
Aircraft Storage and Disposition Group [*Air Force*] ... ASDG
Aircraft Storage Unit [*Military*] [*British*] ... ASU
Aircraft Stores Establishment [*Navy*] ... ASE
Aircraft Stores Interface Manual ... ASIM
Aircraft Structural Integrity Program ... ASIP
Aircraft Supply Council [*Ministry of Aircraft Production*] [*British*] ... ASC
Aircraft Supply Group ... ASG
Aircraft Survivability Equipment ... ASE
Aircraft Survivablility Equipment - Product Manager ... ASE-PM
Aircraft Survival Measures Programme [*NATO*] ... ASM
Aircraft Synthesis [*Data processing*] ... ACSYNT
Aircraft Synthesis Analysis Program ... ASAP
Aircraft Technical Bulletin ... ATB
Aircraft Technical Committee ... ATC
Aircraft Technical Order ... ATO
Aircraft Technical Publishers [*Information service*] ... ATP
Aircraft Test Equipment Modification ... ATEM
Aircraft Time Compliance Technical Manuals ... TCTM
Aircraft Torpedo Development Unit [*British*] ... ATDU
Aircraft Torpedo Maintenance Unit [*Navy*] ... ATMU
Aircraft Trailing Vortices ... ATV
Aircraft (Training) [*Navy symbol*] ... VTD
Aircraft Transfer Order ... ATO
Aircraft Transportation Lighter [*Non-self-propelled*] [*Navy symbol*] ... YCV
Aircraft Trouble Report ... ATR
Aircraft Trouble-Shooting System ... ATS
Aircraft Unitized Diagnostic Inspection and Test [*Boeing*] ... AUDIT
Aircraft Utilization Report ... AUR
Aircraft Warning Company [*Marine Corps*] ... AWRNCO

Aircraft Warning Service [*Military*] ... AWS
Aircraft and Weapons Control Interceptor ... AWCI
Aircraft and Weapons Control Interceptor System ... AWCIS
Aircraft Weapons Release Set ... AWRS
Aircraft Weapons Release Unit ... AWRU
Aircrafthand [*British*] ... ACH
Aircraftman [*British*] ... AC
Aircraftwoman [*British*] ... ACW
Aircrew ... ACRW
Aircrew Body Armor [*System*] [*Army*] ... ACBA
Aircrew Classification Test ... ACT
Aircrew Classification Test Battery ... ACTB
Aircrew Egress Trainer ... AET
Aircrew Electronic Warfare Tactics Facility ... AEWTF
Aircrew Escape Propulsion System [*Navy*] ... AEPS
Aircrew Flight Training Period ... AFTP
Aircrew Respiratory Protection ... ARP
Aircrew Station Standardization Panel ... ASSP
Aircrew Survival Equipmentman [*Navy rating*] ... PR
Aircrew Systems Change ... ASC
Aircrewman ... AC
Airdrome ... AD
Airdrome Battalion ... ADROBN
Airdrome Defense Corps [*Air Force*] ... ADC
Airdrome Officer ... AO
Airdrop [*Military*] ... ADRP
Airdrop by Parachute ... PARADROP
Airedale Terrier Club of America ... ATCA
AiResearch Manufacturing Company of Arizona ... AMCOA
Airfield ... A/F
Airfield ... AFLD
Airfield Control RADAR [*Air Force*] ... ACR
Airfield Heliport ... AH
Airfield Index ... AI
Airfield Marking and Lighting ... AML
Airfield Operations Designator ... AOD
Airfield Pavement [*Air Force*] ... AFPAV
Airfield and Seaplane Stations of the World ... ASSOTW
Airfield Surface Movement Indicator ... ASMI
Airfield Vehicle Obstacle Indication Device ... AVOID
Airfile ... A/F
Airflow Club of America ... ACA
Airfoil Design and Analysis Center [*Ohio State University*] ... ADAC
Airframe ... AF
Airframe ... AFME
Airframe ... AFR
Airframe ... AFRM
Airframe Bulletin ... AFB
Airframe Change ... AC
Airframe Change ... AFC
Airframe Design Division [*Bureau of Aeronautics; later, NASC*] [*Navy*] ... AD
Airframe and Engine ... A and E
Airframe Flight Qualification ... AFQ
Airframe Manufacturing Equipment Committee ... AMEC
Airframe Mounted Accessory Drive ... AMAD
Airframe and Powerplant [*Aviation*] ... A & P
Airframe Repair Technician-Repairman ... ART/R
Airframe and System Assembly/Test ... ASA/T
Airframe Unit Weight ... AUW
Airgo, Inc. [*Dallas, TX*] [*FAA designator*] ... ARD
Airhead [*Army*] ... AHD
Airhead Air Traffic Coordination Center [*Army*] ... AATOC
Airhead Maintenance Area [*Military*] [*British*] ... AMA
Airlantic Transport [*Air carrier designation symbol*] ... ATIX
Airletter Mail Express [*American Express Co.*] ... AMEX
Airlifeline [*An association*] ... ALL
Airlift ... AL
Airlift ... ALFT
Airlift ... ARLFT
Airlift Association ... AA
Airlift Clearance Authority ... ACA
Airlift Command Post ... ACP
Airlift Contingency Battalion Landing Team ... ACBLT
Airlift Control Center ... ALCC
Airlift Control Element ... ALCE
Airlift Field Maintenance Section ... AFMS
Airlift International, Inc. [*ICAO designator*] ... RD
Airlift International, Inc. [*Air carrier designation symbol*] ... RDLX
Airlift Launch Control Officer [*Air Force*] ... ALCO
Airlift Liaison Coordination Officer [*Air Force*] ... ALCO
Airlift Mission Planning and Scheduling System [*Air Force*] ... AMPSS
Airlift Operational Report ... ALOREP
Airlift Operations Directive ... AOD
Airlift Operations School Library, Scott AFB, IL [*OCLC symbol*] ... AOS
Airlift Service Industrial Fund [*Military*] ... ASIF
Airlift Simulation Model ... ASM
Airlift Summary Report [*Air Force*] ... LIFSUM
Airlift Task Force [*Air Force*] ... ALTF
Airlift and Training Division [*Air Force*] ... ATD
Airline Carriers of Goods ... ACG
Airline Carriers of Passengers ... ACP
Airline Charter Service ... ACS
Airline Credit Union Association ... ACUA
Airline Feed System ... AFS
Airline Ground Transportation Association [*Defunct*] ... AGTA
Airline Group, International Federation of Operational Research Societies ... AGIFORS
Airline Industrial Relations Conference ... AIR
Airline Interline Development ... AID
Airline Medical Directors Association ... AMDA
Airline Operational Control Society ... AOCS
Airline Operations Planning Model ... AOPM
Airline Operations Simulation Model ... AOSM
Airline Services Association ... ASA
Airline System Simulator ... ALSS
Airline Tariff Publishing Co. ... ATP
Airline Traffic Association ... ALTA
Airlines Communications Administrative Council ... ALCAC
Airlines Computer Tracing System [*Luggage retrieving system*] ... ACTS
Airlines Control Program [*IBM Corp.*] ... ACP
Airlines Electronic Engineering Committee ... AEEC
Airlines Load Optimization Recording and Display System [*Airport passenger-moving sidewalk*] ... AIRLORDS
Airlines Staff International Association ... ASIA
Airlock Adapter Plate ... AAP
Airlock Module [*NASA*] ... AM
Airlock Module Station [*NASA*] ... AMS
Airlock Multiple Docking Adapter [*NASA*] ... ALMDA
Airlock Stowage Bag ... ASB
Airlock Support Subsystem [*NASA*] ... ALSS
Airlock Support Subsystem [*NASA*] ... ASS
Airlock Systems Test [*NASA*] ... AST
Airlock Wall ... AW
Airmail ... AM
Airmail ... ARML
Airmailgram ... AMGM
Airman ... A
Airman ... AMN
Airman [*Nonrated enlisted man*] [*Navy*] ... AN
Airman, Aerographer's Mate, Striker [*Navy rating*] ... AGAN
Airman, Air Controlman, Striker [*Navy rating*] ... ACAN
Airman Apprentice [*Navy rating*] ... AA
Airman Apprentice, Aerographer's Mate, Striker [*Navy rating*] ... AGAA
Airman Apprentice, Air Controlman, Striker [*Navy rating*] ... ACAA
Airman Apprentice, Aviation ASW [*Antisubmarine Warfare*] **Operator, Striker** [*Navy rating*] ... AWAA
Airman Apprentice, Aviation ASW [*Antisubmarine Warfare*] **Technician, Striker** [*Navy rating*] ... AXAA
Airman Apprentice, Aviation Boatswain's Mate, Striker [*Navy rating*] ... ABAA
Airman Apprentice, Aviation Electrician, Striker [*Navy rating*] ... AEAA
Airman Apprentice, Aviation Fire Control Technician, Striker [*Navy rating*] ... AQAA
Airman Apprentice, Aviation Machinist's Mate, Reciprocating Engine Mechanic, Striker [*Navy rating*] ... ADRAA
Airman Apprentice, Aviation Maintenance Administrationman, Striker [*Navy rating*] ... AZAA
Airman Apprentice, Aviation Storekeeper [*Navy rating*] ... AKAA
Airman Apprentice, Aviation Structural Mechanic, Striker [*Navy rating*] ... AMAA
Airman Apprentice, Aviation Support Equipment Technician, Striker [*Navy rating*] ... ASAA
Airman Apprentice (High School) ... AA(HS)
Airman Apprentice, Jet Striker [*Navy rating*] ... ADJAA
Airman Apprentice, Parachute Rigger, Striker [*Navy rating*] ... PRAA
Airman Apprentice, Photographer's Mate, Striker [*Navy rating*] ... PHAA
Airman Apprentice, Photographic Intelligenceman, Striker [*Navy rating*] ... PTAA
Airman Apprentice, TRADEVMAN [*Training Devices Man*], **Striker** [*Navy rating*] ... TDAA
Airman, Aviation ASW [*Antisubmarine Warfare*] **Operator, Striker** [*Navy rating*] ... AWAN
Airman, Aviation ASW [*Antisubmarine Warfare*] **Technician, Striker** [*Navy rating*] ... AXAN
Airman, Aviation Boatswain's Mate, Striker [*Navy rating*] ... ABAN
Airman, Aviation Electrician, Striker [*Navy rating*] ... AEAN
Airman, Aviation Electronics Technician [*Navy rating*] ... ATAN
Airman, Aviation Fire Control Technician, Striker [*Navy rating*] ... AQAN
Airman, Aviation Machinist's Mate, Reciprocating Engine Mechanic, Striker [*Navy rating*] ... ADRAN
Airman, Aviation Maintenance Administrationman, Striker [*Navy rating*] ... AZAN
Airman, Aviation Storekeeper [*Navy rating*] ... AKAN
Airman, Aviation Structural Mechanic, Striker [*Navy rating*] ... AMAN
Airman, Aviation Support Equipment Technician, Striker [*Navy rating*] ... ASAN
Airman Basic ... AB
Airman Commissioning Program [*Air Force*] ... ACP
Airman Education and Commissioning Program ... AECP
Airman Effectiveness Report [*Air Force*] ... AER
Airman, First Class ... A/1C
Airman, Jet Striker [*Navy rating*] ... ADJAN

Airman Military Record [*Air Force*] AMR
Airman, Parachute Rigger, Striker [*Navy*] PRAN
Airman Performance Report APR
Airman Performance Report Review Board APRRB
Airman, Photographer's Mate, Striker [*Navy rating*] PHAN
Airman, Photographic Intelligenceman, Striker [*Navy rating*] PTAN
Airman Qualifying Examination AQE
Airman Records [*Air Force*] AR
Airman Recruit AR
Airman, Second Class A/2C
Airman, Third Class A/3C
Airman, TRADEVMAN [*Training Devices Man*], **Striker** [*Navy rating*] TDAN
Airman's Guide [*A publication*] AIRGI
Airman's Information Manual [*FAA*] AIM
Airman's Medal AmnM
Airmen Classification Battery [*Military tests*] ACB
Airmen Proficiency Test APT
Airmen's Advisory [*A notice to airmen*] AIRAD
Airmen's Meteorological Information AIRMET
Airmobile AMBL
AIRPAC [*Seattle, WA*] [*FAA designator*] APC
Airplane [*Freight*] AIRPL
Airplane AP
Airplane APL
Airplane Avionics AA
Airplane Avionics/AUTOLAND AA/AL
[*The*] **Airplane Co.** [*Pensacola, FL*] [*FAA designator*] HRN
Airplane Economic Design Evaluator [*Boeing Co.*] AEDE
Airplane Engine, Propeller, and Accessory Overhaul [*Navy*] AIRENGPROPACCOVERHAUL
Airplane Model List of America AMLA
Airplane Nose Down AND
Airplane Nose Up ANU
Airplane Pilot AP
Airplane Sizing and Mission Performance [*Computer program*] ASAMP
Airplane Summary List ASL
Airplane Test Equipment ATE
Airport AP
Airport APRT
Airport ARPRT
Airport ARPT
Airport Advisory Service AAS
Airport and Airway Development Act of 1970 AADA
Airport and Airways Surveillance RADAR [*Air Force*] AASR
Airport Associations Coordinating Council AACC
Airport Bird Detection Equipment ABDE
Airport Control Station [*ITU designation*] FAC
Airport Control Tower ACT
Airport Data System [*FAA*] ADS
Airport Development Aid Program [*FAA*] ADAP
Airport Development Program ADP
Airport Directory [*FAA*] APD
Airport District Office [*FAA*] ADO
Airport District Office APDO
Airport Engineering Data Sheet [*FAA*] AEDS
Airport/Facility Directory AFD
Airport Ground Traffic Control [*Department of Transportation*] AGTC
Airport Hangar [*New York*] [*Seismograph station code, US Geological Survey*] APH
Airport Information Desk AID
Airport Information Retrieval System [*FAA*] AIRS
Airport Layout Plan ALP
Airport Lighting Equipment ALE
Airport Lights APL
Airport Location Point ALP
Airport Mail Facility AMF
Airport Manager AMGR
Airport Master Plan AMP
Airport Operating Certificate AOC
Airport Operators Council [*Later, AOCI*] AOC
Airport Operators Council International AOCI
Airport Reference Point ARP
Airport Reservation Office ARO
Airport Reservation Position ARP
Airport Security Council ASC
Airport Surface Detection [*RADAR*] ASDR
Airport Surface Detection Equipment [*RADAR*] ASDE
Airport Surface Traffic RADAR Equipment ASTRE
Airport Surface Traffic Simulator ASTS
Airport Surveillance RADAR ASR
Airport System Plan ASP
Airport Traffic Area ATA
Airport [*or Airway*] **Traffic Control** ATC
Airport Trailing Vortex Warning System ATVWS
Airport Transportation AIRTRANS
Airport Vicinity Air Pollution AVAP
Airports [*Public-performance tariff class*] [*British*] ARP
Airports Field Office AFO
Airports Program Report APR
Airports Service [*of FAA*] AS
Airscoop AS
Airsearch Manufacturing Co., Los Angeles, CA [*Library symbol*] CLAi
Airship ASHP
Airship, Air-Sea Rescue [*Navy symbol*] ZNH
Airship Experimental Center [*Navy*] AEC
Airship Group AIRSHIPGR
Airship Group [*Navy symbol*] ZPG
Airship (Nonrigid) [*Navy symbol*] ZN
Airship Rigger AR
Airship Squadron AIRSHIPRON
Airship Tender [*Navy symbol*] AZ
Airship, Utility [*Navy symbol*] ZNJ
Airship Utility Squadron [*Navy symbol*] ZUTRON
Airspace ASP
Airspace Control [*or Coordination*] **Element** [*Army*] ACE
Airspace Docket ASD
Airspace Flight Inspection Pilot ASIP
Airspace Reservation Coordination Office [*Canada*] ARCO
Airspace Subcommittee [*ACC*] ASP
Airspace Surveillance Station ASS
Airspeed AS
Airspeed ASP
Airspeed Indicator AI
Airspeed Indicator ASI
Airspeed Mach Indicator AMI
Airstream Direction Sensing Unit ADSU
Airtight [*Technical drawings*] AT
Airtight Containers [*Freight*] AT C
Airtouring Charter Ltd. [*ICAO designator*] HG
Airway AWY
Airway, Breathing, and Circulation [*Cardiopulmonary resuscitation*] [*Medicine*] ABC
Airway Express, Inc. [*Mesa, AZ*] [*FAA designator*] AEX
Airway Facilities Service [*FAA*] AAF
Airway Opened, Breathing Restored, Circulation Restored, and Definitive Therapy [*Cardiopulmonary resuscitation*] [*Medicine*] ABCD
Airway Operations Specialist [*Airport*] AOSAP
Airway Pressure [*Pulmonary ventilation*] AWP
Airway Reactivity Index [*Physiology*] ARI
Airway Resistance [*Medicine*] RAW
Airways and Air Communications Service AACS
Airways and Air Communications Service Manual AACSM
Airways Communication Station ACS
Airways Communications System AIRCOM
Airways Data Collection and Distribution [*Data processing*] ADCAD
Airways Engineer AENG
Airways Engineering Society [*Defunct*] AES
Airways Facilities Sector AFS
Airways Facilities Sector Field Office AFSFO
Airways Facilities Sector Field Office Plus Unit AFSFOU
Airways Facilities Sector Office AFSO
Airways Flight Inspector AFINS
Airways Inspector AI
Airways Integrating and Monitoring System AIMS
Airways Modernization Board [*Functions transferred to FAA*] AMB
Airways of New Mexico [*Alamogordo, NM*] [*FAA designator*] ANM
Airways Operations Evaluation Center AOEC
Airways Operations Specialist AOSS
Airways Operations Specialist (General) AOSG
Airways Operations Supervisor AOSPV
Airways Technical District Office [*FAA*] ATDO
Airways Technical District Supervisor [*FAA*] ATDS
Airways Technical Field Office [*FAA*] ATFO
Airwork Ltd. AW
Airworthiness Directive AD
Airworthiness Qualification Program AQL
Airworthiness Qualification Specification AQS
Airworthiness Requirements Committee ARC
Airworthiness Standards Evaluation Committee [*FAA*] ASEC
Aishalton [*Guyana*] [*Airport symbol*] [*Obsolete*] AHL
Aitape [*Papua New Guinea*] [*Airport symbol*] ATP
Aitkin, MN [*Radio station call letters*] KEZZ
Aitkin, MN [*Radio station call letters*] KKIN
Aitutaki [*Cook Islands*] [*Airport symbol*] AIT
Aiyura [*Papua New Guinea*] [*Airport symbol*] [*Obsolete*] AYU
AJ Industries, Inc. [*NYSE symbol*] [*Delisted*] AJ
Ajaccio [*Corsica*] [*Airport symbol*] AJA
Ajax, ON [*Radio station call letters*] CHOO
Ajax Public Library, Ajax, ON, Canada [*Library symbol*] CaOAj
Ajia Bunka [*Asian Culture*] [*A publication*] ABK
Ajia Keizai. Journal of the Institute of Developing Economics [*A publication*] Ajia Keizai
Ajiro [*Japan*] [*Seismograph station code, US Geological Survey*] AJI
AJNR. American Journal of Neuroradiology [*A publication*] AJNR
Ajoutez [*Add*] [*Music*] AJ
AJR. American Journal of Roentgenology [*A publication*] AJR
Akademi Militer Nasional [*Indonesia*] AKMIL
Akademi Seni Rupa Indonesia ASRI
Akademi Tehnik Angkatan Darat [*Indonesia*] ATEKAD
Akademia Sztuk Pieknych [*Poland*] ASP

Akademie der Wissenschaften der DDR. Zentralinstitut fuer Physik der Erde. Veroeffentlichungen [*A publication*] .... Akad Wiss DDR Zentralinst Phys Erde Veroeff
Akademie der Wissenschaften in Goettingen. Mathematisch-Physikalische Klasse. Abhandlungen. Folge 3 [*A publication*] .... Akad Wiss Goettingen Math Phys Kl Abh Folge 3
Akademie der Wissenschaften in Goettingen. Nachrichten. Mathematisch-Physikalische Klasse [*A publication*] .... Akad Wiss Gottingen Nachr Math-Physikal Kl
Akademie der Wissenschaften in Goettingen. Philologisch-Historische Klasse [*A publication*] .... AWG Phk
Akademie der Wissenschaften und der Literatur. Abhandlungen der Mathematisch-Naturwissenschaftlichen Klasse (Mainz) [*A publication*] .... Akad Wiss Lit Abh Math-Naturwiss Kl (Mainz)
Akademie der Wissenschaften und der Literatur in Mainz. Abhandlungen der Geistes- und Sozialwissenschaftlichen Klasse [*A publication*] .... AWLM AGSK
Akademie der Wissenschaften und der Literatur in Mainz. Abhandlungen der Geistes- und Sozialwissenschaftlichen Klasse [*A publication*] .... AWLMGS
Akademie der Wissenschaften und der Literatur in Mainz. Abhandlungen der Mathematisch-Naturwissenschaftlichen Klasse [*A publication*] .... Akad Wiss Lit Mainz Abh Math-Natur Kl
Akademie der Wissenschaften und der Literatur in Mainz. Klasse der Literatur [*A publication*] .... AWLML
Akademie der Wissenschaften. Muenchen. Abhandlungen [*A publication*] .... AWMAbh
Akademie der Wissenschaften. Muenchen. Philosophische-Historische Klasse. Sitzungsberichte [*A publication*] .... AWMSb
Akademie der Wissenschaften in Wien. Philosophisch-Historische Klasse. Denkschriften [*A publication*] .... Akad d Wiss Denksch Philos-Hist KL
Akademie der Wissenschaften (Wien). Sitzungsberichte [*A publication*] .... AWWSb
Akademiet for de Tekniska Videnskaber [*Academy of Technical Sciences*] [*Denmark*] .... ATV
Akademiia Nauk Belorusskaia SSR, Fundamemtalnaia Biblioteka Imeni Ia. Kolasa [*Academy of Sciences of the Belorussian SSR, J. Kolasa Fundamental Library*]**, Minsk, Belorussian SSR, Soviet Union** [*Library symbol*] .... RuBeMiA
Akademiia Nauk Kirgizskoi SSR, Tsentralnaia Nauchaia Biblioteka [*Academy of Sciences of the Kirghiz SSR, Central Scientific Library*]**, Frunze, Kirghiz SSR, Soviet Union** [*Library symbol*] .... RuKiFrA
Akademiia Nauk Moldavskoi SSR, Tsentralnaia Nauchnaia Biblioteka [*Academy of Sciences of the Moldavian SSR, Central Scientific Library*]**, Kishivev, Moldavian SSR, Soviet Union** [*Library symbol*] .... RuMoKisA
Akademiia Nauk SSSR. Doklady. Izvestiia. Seriia Geologicheskaia [*A publication*] .... Akad Nauk SSSR Doklady Izvestiia Ser Geol
Akademiia Nauk SSSR. Institut Narodov Azii. Kratkie Soobshcheniia [*Moscow*] [*A publication*] .... KS
Akademiia Nauk SSSR [*Academy of Sciences of the USSR*]**, Leningrad, Soviet Union** [*Library symbol*] .... RuLA
Akademiia Nauk Tarkmenskoi SSR, Tsentralnaia Nauchnaia Biblioteka [*Academy of Sciences of Turkmen SSR, Central Scientific Library*]**, Ashkhabad, Turkmen, SSR, Soviet Union** [*Library symbol*] .... RuTuAsA
Akademija Nauk Armjanskoi SSR. Doklady [*A publication*] .... Akad Nauk Armjan SSR Dokl
Akademija Nauk Azerbaidzanskoi SSR. Doklady [*A publication*] .... Akad Nauk Azerbaidzan SSR Dokl
Akademija Nauk Kazahskoi SSR. Trudy Astrofiziceskogo Instituta [*A publication*] .... Akad Nauk Kazah SSR Trudy Astrofiz Inst
Akademija Nauk Kazahskoi SSR. Trudy Instituta Matematiki i Mehaniki [*A publication*] .... Akad Nauk Kazah SSR Trudy Inst Mat i Meh
Akademija Nauk SSSR [*A publication*] .... ANSSSR
Akademija Nauk SSSR. Radiotehnika i Elektronika [*A publication*] .... Radiotehn i Elektron
Akademija Nauk UzSSR. Karakalpakskii Filial. Vestnik [*A publication*] .... Vestnik Karakalpak Fil Akad Nauk UzSSR
Akademiska Dzive [*A publication*] .... ADz
Akademiya Nauk Armyanskoy SSR. Doklady [*A publication*] .... Akad Nauk Arm SSR Dokl
Akademiya Nauk Azerbaydzhanskoy SSR. Doklady [*A publication*] .... Akad Nauk Azerb SSR Dokl
Akademiya Nauk BSSR. Doklady [*A publication*] .... Akad Nauk BSSR Dokl
Akademiya Nauk Gruzinskoy SSR. Geologicheskiy Institut. Trudy [*A publication*] .... Akad Nauk Gruz SSR Geol Inst Tr
Akademiya Nauk Gruzinskoy SSR. Soobshcheniya [*A publication*] .... Akad Nauk Gruz SSR Soobshch
Akademiya Nauk Kazakhskoy SSR. Institut Geologicheskikh Nauk. Trudy [*A publication*] .... Akad Nauk Kaz SSR Inst Geol Nauk Tr
Akademiya Nauk Kazakhskoy SSR. Izvestiya. Seriya Geologicheskaya [*A publication*] .... Akad Nauk Kaz SSR Izv Ser Geol
Akademiya Nauk SSSR. Doklady [*A publication*] .... Akad Nauk SSSR Dokl
Akademiya Nauk SSSR. Geologicheskiy Institut. Trudy [*A publication*] .... Akad Nauk SSSR Geol Inst Tr
Akademiya Nauk SSSR. Geologicheskiy Institut. Trudy [*A publication*] .... Akad Nauk SSSR Geol Inst Trudy
Akademiya Nauk SSSR. Izvestiya. Seriya Fizicheskaya [*A publication*] .... Akad Nauk SSSR Izv Ser Fiz
Akademiya Nauk SSSR. Izvestiya. Seriya Geograficheskaya [*A publication*] .... Akad Nauk SSSR Izv Ser Geogr
Akademiya Nauk SSSR. Izvestiya. Seriya Geologicheskaya [*A publication*] .... Akad Nauk SSSR Izv Ser Geol
Akademiya Nauk SSSR. Komi Filial. Institut Geologii. Trudy [*A publication*] .... Akad Nauk SSSR Komi Fil Inst Geol Tr
Akademiya Nauk SSSR. Paleontologicheskiy Institut Trudy [*A publication*] .... Akad Nauk SSSR Paleontol Inst Tr
Akademiya Nauk SSSR. Sibirskoye Otdeleniye. Institut Geologii i Geofiziki. Trudy [*A publication*] .... Akad Nauk SSSR Sib Otd Inst Geol Geofiz Tr
Akademiya Nauk SSSR. Ural'skii Filiak. Trudy Instituta Khimii [*A publication*] .... Akad Nauk SSSR Ural Fil Tr Inst Khim
Akademiya Nauk SSSR. Vestnik [*A publication*] .... Akad Nauk SSSR Vestn
Akademiya Nauk Tadzhikskoy SSR. Doklady [*A publication*] .... Akad Nauk Tadzh SSR Dokl
Akademiya Nauk Ukrainskoi SSR. Metallofizika [*A publication*] .... Akad Nauk Ukr SSR Metallofiz
Akademiya Nauk Ukrainskoy RSR. Dopovidi. Seriya B. Geologiya, Geofizika, Khimiya, ta Biologiya [*A publication*] .... Akad Nauk Ukr RSR Dopov Ser B
Akhalkalaki [*USSR*] [*Seismograph station code, US Geological Survey*] [*Closed*] .... AKH
Akhiok [*Alaska*] [*Airport symbol*] .... AKK
Akiachak [*Alaska*] [*Airport symbol*] .... KKI
Akiak [*Alaska*] [*Airport symbol*] .... AKI
Akieni [*Gabon*] [*Airport symbol*] .... AKE
Akinetic .... A
Akita [*Japan*] [*Seismograph station code, US Geological Survey*] .... AKI
Akita [*Japan*] [*Airport symbol*] .... AXT
Akita Central Hospital Medical Journal [*A publication*] .... Akita Cent Hosp Med J
Akita Club of America .... ACA
Akkadian [*MARC language code*] [*Library of Congress*] .... akk
Aklavik [*Canada*] [*Airport symbol*] .... LAK
Akro Agate Art Association .... AAAA
[*The*] **Akron & Barberton Belt Railroad Co.** [*AAR code*] .... ABB
Akron/Canton [*Ohio*] [*Airport symbol*] .... CAK
Akron-Canton, OH [*Location identifier*] [*FAA*] .... HJM
[*The*] **Akron, Canton, & Youngstown Railroad Co.** [*AAR code*] .... ACY
Akron Child Guidance Center, Akron, OH [*Library symbol*] .... OAkCh
Akron Law Review [*A publication*] .... Akron L Rev
Akron, OH [*Location identifier*] [*FAA*] .... ACO
Akron, OH [*Location identifier*] [*FAA*] .... GGZ
Akron, OH [*Location identifier*] [*FAA*] .... RGO
Akron, OH [*Radio station call letters*] .... WAEZ
Akron, OH [*Radio station call letters*] .... WAKR
Akron, OH [*Television station call letters*] .... WAKR-TV
Akron, OH [*Radio station call letters*] .... WAPS
Akron, OH [*Radio station call letters*] .... WAUP
Akron, OH [*Television station call letters*] .... WEAO
Akron, OH [*Radio station call letters*] .... WHLO
Akron, OH [*Radio station call letters*] .... WKDD
Akron, OH [*Radio station call letters*] .... WSLR
Akron Public Library, Akron, CO [*Library symbol*] .... CoAk
Akron Public Library, Akron, OH [*Library symbol*] .... OAk
Akron Register-Tribune, Akron, IA [*Library symbol*] .... IaAkRT
Akron-Summit County Public Library, Akron, OH [*OCLC symbol*] .... APL
Aksu [*China*] [*Airport symbol*] .... AKU
Akten des Internationalen Amerikanisten Kongresses [*A publication*] .... AIAK
Aktiebolaget [*Company*] [*Swedish*] .... AB
Aktiebolaget Aero Transport [*Swedish airline*] .... ABA
Aktiebolaget Atomenergi [*Swedish nuclear development company*] .... ABA
Aktiebolaget Atomenergi Computer-Based User-Oriented Service .... ABACUS
Aktiebolaget Svenska Metallverken .... ABSM
Aktiengesellschaft [*Joint Stock Company*] [*German*] .... AG
Aktiengesellschaft fuer Anilinfabrikaten [*German photographic manufacturer*] .... AGFA
Aktieselskapet- [*Joint Stock Company*] [*Norwegian*] .... A/S
Aktualne Problemy Informacji i Dokumentacji [*A publication*] .... Akt Probl Inf Dokum
Aktualne Problemy Informacji i Dokumentacji [*A publication*] .... Aktual Probl Inf & Dok
Aktuelle Fragen der Psychiatrie und Neurologie [*A publication*] .... Aktuel Fragen Psychiatr Neurol
Aktuelle Fragen der Psychotherapie [*A publication*] .... Aktuel Fragen Psychother
Aktuelle Gerontologie [*A publication*] .... Aktuel Gerontol
Aktuelle Neurologie [*A publication*] .... Aktuel Neurol
Aktuelle Otorhinolaryngologie [*A publication*] .... Aktuel Otorhinolaryngol
Aktuelle Probleme in der Chirurgie [*A publication*] .... Aktuel Probl Chir
Aktuelle Probleme in Chirurgie Orthopaedie [*A publication*] .... Aktuel Probl Chir Orthop
Aktuelle Probleme der Phoniatrie und Logopaedie [*A publication*] .... Aktuel Probl Phoniatr Logop
Aktuelle Probleme der Polymer-Physik [*A publication*] .... Aktuel Probl Polym-Phys

Aktuelle Traumatologie [*A publication*]....Aktuel Traumatol
Aktuelle Urologie [*A publication*]....Aktuel Urol
Aktuellt fran Lantbrukshogskolan [*A publication*]....Aktuellt Lantbrukshogs
Akulivik [*Canada*] [*Airport symbol*]....AKV
Akureyri [*Iceland*] [*Airport symbol*]....AEY
Akureyri [*Iceland*] [*Seismograph station code, US Geological Survey*]....AKU
Akusherstvo i Ginekologiya (Moscow) [*A publication*]....Akush Ginekol (Mosc)
Akusherstvo i Ginekologiya (Sofia) [*A publication*]....Akush Ginekol (Sofia)
Akusticheskii Zhurnal [*A publication*]....Akust Zh
Akustika i Ul'trazvukovaya Tekhnika [*A publication*]....Akust Ul'trazvuk Tekh
Akutan [*Alaska*] [*Airport symbol*]....KQA
Akwesasne Notes [*A publication*]....Akw Notes
Akyab [*Burma*] [*Airport symbol*]....AKY
Akzente [*A publication*]....Akz
Akzona, Inc. [*NYSE symbol*] [*Delisted*]....AXO
Al-Andalus [*A publication*]....Al-An
Al-Anon Family Group Headquarters....AAFGH
Al Arish [*Egypt*] [*Airport symbol*]....AAC
Al-Baha [*Saudi Arabia*] [*Airport symbol*]....BBH
Al Bahrain Arab African Bank....AL-BAAB
Al Fine [*To the End*] [*Music*]....AF
Al Hoceima [*Morocco*] [*Airport symbol*]....AHU
Al-Mustansiriya University. Review [*Baghdad*] [*A publication*]....MUR
Al Segno [*At the Sign*] [*Music*]....AL SEG
Al Sigl Center Library, Rochester, NY [*OCLC symbol*]....VQA
Ala Moana Hawaii Properties [*NYSE symbol*]....ALA
ALA Zurnals [*A publication*]....ALAZ
Alabama [*Postal code*]....AL
Alabama....ALA
Alabama [*MARC country of publication code*] [*Library of Congress*]....alu
Alabama [*MARC geographic area code*] [*Library of Congress*]....n-us-al
Alabama Academy of Science Journal [*A publication*]....Ala Acad Sci Jour
Alabama Agricultural Experiment Station. Auburn University. Agronomy and Soils Departmental Series [*A publication*]....Ala Agric Exp Stn Auburn Univ Agron Soils Dep Ser
Alabama Agricultural Experiment Station. Auburn University. Forestry Departmental Series [*A publication*]....Ala Agric Exp Stn Auburn Univ For Dep Ser
Alabama Agricultural Experiment Station. Bulletin (Auburn University) [*A publication*]....Ala Agric Exp Stn Bull (Auburn Univ)
Alabama Agricultural Experiment Station. Leaflet (Auburn University) [*A publication*]....Ala Agric Exp Stn Leafl (Auburn Univ)
Alabama Agricultural Experiment Station. Progress Report Series (Auburn University) [*A publication*]....Ala Agric Exp Stn Prog Rep Ser (Auburn Univ)
Alabama Agricultural Experiment Station. Publications [*A publication*]....Ala Ag Exp
Alabama Agricultural and Mechanical University, Normal, AL [*Library symbol*]....ANA
Alabama Army Ammunition Plant....ALAAP
Alabama Central R. R. [*AAR code*]....ALC
Alabama Conservation [*A publication*]....Ala Conserv
Alabama Corn Variety Report [*A publication*]....Ala Corn Variety Rep
Alabama Department of Archives and History, Library, Montgomery, AL [*OCLC symbol*]....AAR
Alabama Department of Archives and History, Montgomery, AL [*Library symbol*]....A-Ar
Alabama Department of Archives and History, State Documents, Montgomery, AL [*OCLC symbol*]....AAS
Alabama. Geological Society. Bulletin [*A publication*]....Alabama Geol Soc Bull
Alabama. Geological Survey [*A publication*]....Ala G S
Alabama. Geological Survey. Atlas Series [*A publication*]....Ala Geol Surv Atlas Ser
Alabama. Geological Survey. Bulletin [*A publication*]....Ala Geol Surv Bull
Alabama. Geological Survey. Circular [*A publication*]....Ala Geol Surv Circ
Alabama. Geological Survey. Geo-Petro Notes [*A publication*]....Ala Geol Surv Geo-Petro Notes
Alabama. Geological Survey. Information Series [*A publication*]....Alabama Geol Survey Inf Ser
Alabama. Geological Survey. Information Series [*A publication*]....Ala Geol Surv Inf Ser
Alabama. Geological Survey. Map [*A publication*]....Alabama Geol Survey Map
Alabama. Geological Survey. Map [*A publication*]....Ala Geol Surv Map
Alabama. Geological Survey and State Oil and Gas Board. Annual Reports [*A publication*]....Ala Geol Survey and State Oil and Gas Board Ann Repts
[*The*] **Alabama Great Southern Railroad Co.** [*AAR code*]....AGS
[*The*] **Alabama Great Southern Railroad Co.** [*NYSE symbol*]....AGT
Alabama Historical Quarterly [*A publication*]....AlaHQ
Alabama Historical Society. Transactions [*A publication*]....Ala His S
Alabama Industrial and Scientific Society. Proceedings [*A publication*]....Ala Ind Sc Soc Pr
Alabama Journal of Medical Sciences [*A publication*]....Ala J Med Sci
Alabama Law Review [*A publication*]....Ala L Rev
Alabama Lawyer [*A publication*]....Ala Law
Alabama Librarian [*A publication*]....Ala Libn
Alabama Linguistic and Philological Series [*A publication*]....ALPS
Alabama Lutheran College, Selma, AL [*Library symbol*]....ASeLC
Alabama Marine Resources Bulletin [*A publication*]....Ala Mar Resour Bull
Alabama Nurse [*A publication*]....Ala Nurse
Alabama Polytechnic Institute....API
Alabama Power Co. [*NYSE symbol*]....ALP
Alabama Power Co., Birmingham, AL [*Library symbol*]....ABAP
Alabama Public Library Service, Montgomery, AL [*Library symbol*]....A
Alabama Public Library Service, Montgomery, AL [*OCLC symbol*]....ASL
Alabama Review [*A publication*]....Ala R
Alabama Review [*A publication*]....Ala Rev
Alabama Review [*A publication*]....AR
Alabama State Normal School, Daphne, AL [*Library symbol*] [*Obsolete*]....ADaN
Alabama State Supreme Court Library, Montgomery, AL [*Library symbol*]....A-SC
Alabama State University, Montgomery, AL [*Library symbol*]....AMS
Alabama State University, Montgomery, AL [*OCLC symbol*]....AMU
Alabama Supreme Court and State Law Library, Montgomery, AL [*OCLC symbol*]....ALS
Alabama, Tennessee, & Northern R. R. [*AAR code*]....ATN
Alabama Trucking Association, Montgomery AL [*STAC*]....ALT
Alabamine [*Superseded by astatine*] [*Chemical element*]....Ab
Alabaster, AL [*Location identifier*] [*FAA*]....AOA
Alabaster, AL [*Radio station call letters*]....WQMS
Alabaster Cavern State Park [*Oklahoma*] [*Seismograph station code, US Geological Survey*]....ACO
Aladdin Knights of the Mystic Light....AKML
Alagasco, Inc. [*NYSE symbol*]....AGA
Alah [*Philippines*] [*Airport symbol*]....AAV
ALAIR, Inc. [*Anniston, AL*] [*FAA designator*]....ALA
Alakanuk [*Alaska*] [*Airport symbol*]....AUK
Alamagordo, NM [*Radio station call letters*]....KPSA-FM
Alamco, Inc. [*American Stock Exchange symbol*]....AXO
Alameda Belt Line [*AAR code*]....ABL
Alameda, CA [*Radio station call letters*]....KJAZ
Alameda County Health Department, Oakland, CA [*Library symbol*]....COH
Alameda County Law Library, Oakland, CA [*Library symbol*]....COAL
Alameda County Library, Fremont, CA [*Library symbol*]....CFrA
Alameda County Public Library, Hayward, CA [*Library symbol*]....CHA
Alameda Free Library, Alameda, CA [*Library symbol*]....CAla
Alamethicin [*An antibiotic*]....ALA
Alamo [*Nevada*] [*Seismograph station code, US Geological Survey*]....ALA
Alamo Community, NM [*Radio station call letters*]....KABR
Alamo Commuter Airlines [*San Antonio, TX*] [*FAA designator*]....ALO
Alamo Heights, TX [*Radio station call letters*]....KDRY
Alamo Savings Association of Texas [*NASDAQ symbol*]....ALMO
Alamo, TN [*Radio station call letters*]....WCTA
Alamo, TX [*Radio station call letters*]....KJAV
Alamogordo [*New Mexico*] [*Airport symbol*]....ALM
Alamogordo, NM [*Radio station call letters*]....KINN
Alamogordo, NM [*Radio station call letters*]....KINN-FM
Alamogordo, NM [*Radio station call letters*]....KKEE
Alamogordo, NM [*Radio station call letters*]....KPSA
Alamogordo, NM [*Location identifier*] [*FAA*]....MUK
Alamogordo Public Library, Alamogordo, NM [*OCLC symbol*]....AMO
Alamogordo Public Library, Alamogordo, NM [*Library symbol*]....NmAl
Alamosa [*Colorado*] [*Airport symbol*]....ALS
Alamosa, CO [*Radio station call letters*]....KALQ
Alamosa, CO [*Radio station call letters*]....KALQ-FM
Alamosa, CO [*Radio station call letters*]....KASF
Alamosa, CO [*Radio station call letters*]....KGIW
Alamosa, CO [*Radio station call letters*]....KRZA
Alan Guttmacher Institute [*Planned Parenthood Federation of America*]....AGI
Alanco Ltd. [*NASDAQ symbol*]....ALAN
Alandsk Odling: Arsbok [*A publication*]....AO
Alanine [*One-letter symbol; see Ala*]....A
Alanine [*Also, A*] [*An amino acid*]....Ala
Alanine Aminotransferase [*Also, ALT, GPT*] [*An enzyme*]....AAT
Alanine Aminotransferase [*Also, AAG, GPT*] [*An enzyme*]....ALT
Alanine Nitroanilide [*Biochemistry*]....ANA
Alanine Nitrogen Mustard [*L-PAM*] [*Antineoplastic drug*]....A
Alanson Public Library, Alanson, MI [*Library symbol*]....MiAln
Alarm....ALM
Alarm Check Valve....ACV
Alarm Communications and Display Segment....ACADS
Alarm Communications and Display System....ACAD
Alarm Control Center....ACC
Alarm Control Panel....ACP
Alarm Control Unit [*Bell System*]....ACU
Alarm Indicating Monitor....AIM
Alarm Industry Committee for Combating Crime [*Defunct*]....AICCC
Alarm and Jettison Panel....AJP
Alarm Monitor Computer....AMC
Alarm Monitoring System....AMS
Alarm Network Group....ANG
Alarm Panel Monitor....APM
Alarm Products International [*NASDAQ symbol*]....ALPI
Alarm Reaction [*Physiology*]....AR
Alarm Reporting Telephone....ART
Alarm and Status Module....ASM

Alarm System Control Unit .... ASCU
Alarm System Operation .... ASO
Alaska .... AAA
Alaska [*Postal code*] .... AK
Alaska [*MARC country of publication code*] [*Library of Congress*] .... aku
Alaska .... ALAS
Alaska [*MARC geographic area code*] [*Library of Congress*] .... n-us-ak
Alaska Aeronautical Industries [*Anchorage, AK*] [*FAA designator*] .... ALR
Alaska Agricultural Experiment Station. Publications [*A publication*] .... Alaska Ag Exp
Alaska Air Command [*Air Force*] .... ALAC
Alaska Airlines, Inc. [*NYSE symbol*] .... ALK
Alaska Airlines, Inc. [*ICAO designator*] .... AS
Alaska Airlines, Inc. [*Air carrier designation symbol*] .... ASA
Alaska Apollo Gold [*NASDAQ symbol*] .... APLOF
Alaska Bancorp [*NASDAQ symbol*] .... ASKA
Alaska British Columbia Transportation Co. [*AAR code*] .... ABCK
Alaska-Canada [*Highway*] .... ALCAN
Alaska, Canada, United States .... ALCANUS
Alaska Carriers Association, Inc., Anchorage AK [*STAC*] .... ACA
Alaska Central Air [*Fairbanks, AK*] [*FAA designator*] .... ACC
Alaska Coalition .... AC
Alaska Coastal Airlines .... ACA
Alaska Coastal Management Office .... ACMO
Alaska Communication System Industrial Fund .... ACSIF
Alaska Conservation Society .... ACS
Alaska Defense Command [*Known to many of the soldiers who served in it as "All Damn Confusion"*] [*World War II*] .... ADC
Alaska Defense Frontier [*Military*] .... ADF
Alaska Department of Fisheries Research Report [*A publication*] .... Alaska Dep Fish Res Rep
Alaska Department of Mines. Report of the Commissioner of Mines. Biennium [*A publication*] .... Alaska Dept Mines Rept Commissioner Mines Bienn
Alaska Department of Natural Resources. Division of Mines and Geology. Geochemical Report [*A publication*] .... Alaska Div Mines and Geology Geochem Rept
Alaska Department of Natural Resources. Division of Mines and Geology. Geologic Report [*A publication*] .... Alaska Div Mines and Geology Geol Rept
Alaska Division of Geological and Geophysical Surveys. Geologic Report [*A publication*] .... Alaska Div Geol Geophys Surv Geol Rep
Alaska Division of Mines and Minerals. Information Circular. Report [*A publication*] .... Alaska Div Mines and Minerals Inf Circ Rept
Alaska Engineering Commission [*Later, the Alaska Railroad*] .... AEC
Alaska Federation of Natives .... AFN
Alaska Forest Fire Council .... AFFCO
Alaska Game Commission [*Terminated, 1959*] .... AGC
Alaska Historical Library and Museum, Juneau, AK [*Library symbol*] .... AkHi
Alaska Hydro-Train [*AAR code*] .... AHT
Alaska Institute for Fisheries Development .... AIFD
Alaska International Air [*Air carrier designation symbol*] .... AIAX
Alaska International Industries, Inc. [*ICAO designator*] .... KA
Alaska International Rail and Highway Commission [*Terminated, 1961*] .... AIRHC
Alaska Interstate Co. [*NYSE symbol*] [*Delisted*] .... AKI
Alaska Medicine [*A publication*] .... Alaska Med
Alaska Methodist University .... AMU
Alaska Methodist University, Anchorage, AK [*Library symbol*] .... AkAM
Alaska Military Highway .... AMH
Alaska Mineral Resource Assessment Program [*Department of the Interior*] .... AMRAP
Alaska Mutual Bancorp [*NASDAQ symbol*] .... AMAB
Alaska National Interest Land Conservation Act [*1980*] .... ANILCA
Alaska Native Arts and Crafts Cooperative Association .... ANAC
Alaska Native Claims Settlement Act .... ANCSA
Alaska Natural Gas Transportation System .... ANGTS
Alaska Northwest Properties [*NASDAQ symbol*] .... ANPI
Alaska Pacific Bancorp [*NASDAQ symbol*] .... ABPC
Alaska Power Administration [*Department of Energy*] .... APA
[*The*] **Alaska Railroad** [*Department of Transportation*] .... AAR
[*The*] **Alaska Railroad** [*AAR code*] .... ARR
Alaska Science Conference. Proceedings [*A publication*] .... Alaska Sci Conf Proc
Alaska Standard Time .... ALST
Alaska State Court System, Law Library, Anchorage, AK [*Library symbol*] .... Ak-L
Alaska State Library, Juneau, AK [*Library symbol*] .... Ak
Alaska University. Anthropological Papers [*A publication*] .... Alaska Univ Anthrop Pa
Alaska University. Geophysical Institute. Report [*A publication*] .... Alaska Univ Geophys Inst Rep
Alaska University. School of Mines Publication. Bulletin [*A publication*] .... Alaska Univ School Mines Pub Bull
Alaska Village Demonstration Project [*Environmental Protection Agency*] .... AVDP
Alaska Yukon Pioneers .... AYP
Alaskan Air Command [*Air Force*] .... AAC
Alaskan Air Command [*Air Force*] .... ALAIRC
Alaskan Collectors Club .... ACC
Alaskan Command [*Discontinued, 1975*] [*Military*] .... AC
Alaskan Command [*Discontinued, 1975*] [*Military*] .... ALCOM
Alaskan Communications Region [*Air Force*] .... ACR
Alaskan Communications System [*Air Force*] .... ACS
Alaskan Daylight Time .... ADT
Alaskan Integrated Air Defense System .... ALIADS
Alaskan Integrated Communications Exchange .... ALICE
Alaskan Long-Period Array .... ALPA
Alaskan Malamute Club of America .... AMCA
Alaskan Region [*FAA*] .... AAL
Alaskan Sea Frontier [*Navy*] .... AL SEA FRON
Alaskan Sea Frontier [*Navy*] .... ASF
Alaskan Sector .... AL SEC
Alaskan Standard Time [*Aviation*] .... A
Alaskan Territorial Guard .... ATG
Alatenn Resources, Inc. [*NASDAQ symbol*] .... ATNG
Alba-Waldensian, Inc. [*American Stock Exchange symbol*] .... AWS
Alban Institute .... AI
Albania [*MARC country of publication code*] [*Library of Congress*] .... aa
Albania [*Two-letter standard code*] .... AL
Albania [*A publication*] .... Alb
Albania [*MARC geographic area code*] [*Library of Congress*] .... e-aa---
Albania [*Three-letter standard code*] .... ALB
Albanian [*MARC language code*] [*Library of Congress*] .... alb
Albanian-American National Organization .... AANO
Albanian Telegraph Agency .... ATA
Albany [*Georgia*] [*Airport symbol*] .... ABY
Albany [*New York*] .... ALB
Albany [*Australia*] [*Airport symbol*] .... ALH
Albany [*New York*] [*Airport symbol*] .... ALB
Albany College of Pharmacy, Albany, NY [*Library symbol*] .... NAIP
Albany County Public Library, Laramie, WY [*Library symbol*] .... WyLar
Albany Felt Guidelines [*A publication*] .... Albany Felt Guide
Albany Free Public Library, Albany, CA [*Library symbol*] .... CAlb
Albany, GA [*Television station call letters*] .... WALB-TV
Albany, GA [*Radio station call letters*] .... WALG
Albany, GA [*Radio station call letters*] .... WGPC
Albany, GA [*Radio station call letters*] .... WGPC-FM
Albany, GA [*Radio station call letters*] .... WJAZ
Albany, GA [*Television station call letters*] .... WJFT-TV
Albany, GA [*Radio station call letters*] .... WJIZ
Albany, GA [*Radio station call letters*] .... WKAK
Albany, GA [*Radio station call letters*] .... WQDE
Albany, GA [*Television station call letters*] .... WTSG-TV
Albany General Hospital, Albany, OR [*Library symbol*] .... OrAlH
Albany Institute of History of Art, Albany, NY [*Library symbol*] .... NAII
Albany Institute. Proceedings [*A publication*] .... Albany Inst Pr
Albany Institute. Transactions [*A publication*] .... Albany Inst Tr
Albany International Corp. [*NYSE symbol*] .... ABY
Albany International Weekly News Digest [*A publication*] .... Albany News Dig
Albany Junior College, Albany, GA [*Library symbol*] .... GAlJC
Albany, KY [*Radio station call letters*] .... WANY
Albany, KY [*Radio station call letters*] .... WANY-FM
Albany Law Review [*A publication*] .... Albany L R
Albany Law School, Albany, NY [*Library symbol*] .... NAILS
Albany Law School, Albany, NY [*OCLC symbol*] .... YZA
Albany Medical College, Albany, NY [*Library symbol*] .... NAIA
Albany Medical College, Schaffer Library of Health Sciences, Albany, NY [*OCLC symbol*] VXL
Albany, MN [*Radio station call letters*] .... KASM
Albany & Northern Railway Co. [*AAR code*] .... ALN
Albany, NY [*Radio station call letters*] .... WABY
Albany, NY [*Radio station call letters*] .... WAMC
Albany, NY [*Radio station call letters*] .... WCDB
Albany, NY [*Radio station call letters*] .... WGNA
Albany, NY [*Radio station call letters*] .... WHRL
Albany, NY [*Television station call letters*] .... WNYT
Albany, NY [*Radio station call letters*] .... WPTR
Albany, NY [*Radio station call letters*] .... WPYX
Albany, NY [*Radio station call letters*] .... WROW
Albany, NY [*Radio station call letters*] .... WROW-FM
Albany, NY [*Television station call letters*] .... WTEN
Albany, NY [*Radio station call letters*] .... WWCN
Albany, NY [*Radio station call letters*] .... WWOM
Albany, NY [*Television station call letters*] .... WXXA-TV
Albany, OR [*Radio station call letters*] .... KHPE
Albany, OR [*Radio station call letters*] .... KRKT
Albany, OR [*Radio station call letters*] .... KRKT-FM
Albany, OR [*Radio station call letters*] .... KWIL
Albany Port District [*AAR code*] .... APD
Albany Public Library, Albany, GA [*Library symbol*] .... GAI
Albany Public Library, Albany, NY [*Library symbol*] .... NAI
Albany Public Library, Albany, OR [*Library symbol*] .... OrAI
Albany State College [*Georgia*] .... ASC
Albany State College, Albany, GA [*Library symbol*] .... GAISC
Albemarle, NC [*Location identifier*] [*FAA*] .... SWY
Albemarle, NC [*Radio station call letters*] .... WABZ-FM
Albemarle, NC [*Radio station call letters*] .... WWWX
Albemarle, NC [*Radio station call letters*] .... WZKY

Albemarle-Stanly County Public Library, Albemarle, NC [*Library symbol*]...NcAlb

Albermarle Regional Library, Winton, NC [*Library symbol*]..............NcWintA

Alberni [*British Columbia*] [*Seismograph station code, US Geological Survey*]..ALB

Alberni Valley Museum, Port Alberni, BC, Canada [*Library symbol*]...CaBPaM

Albert Einstein Medical Center..............................AEMC

Albert Einstein Medical Center, Northern Division, Philadelphia, PA [*Library symbol*].........................PPAEM

Albert Einstein Peace Prize Foundation.....................AEPPF

Albert F. Simpson Historical Research Center...............AFSHRC

Albert Lea, MN [*Location identifier*] [*FAA*]................AEL

Albert Lea, MN [*Radio station call letters*]................KATE

Albert Lea, MN [*Radio station call letters*]................KCPI

Albert Lea Public Library, Albert Lea, MN [*Library symbol*]..........MnAlb

Albert Medal [*British*]......................................AM

Albert Rolland [*France*] [*Research code symbol*]............ANP

Albert Rolland [*France*] [*Research code symbol*].............Rd

Albert Schweitzer Fellowship................................ASF

Albert W. Thompson Memorial Library, Clayton, NM [*Library symbol*]....................................NmCla

Albert-Westmoreland-Kent Regional Library, Moncton, NB, Canada [*Library symbol*]...................CaNBMoW

Alberta [*Canadian province*] [*Postal code*]................AB

Alberta [*MARC country of publication code*] [*Library of Congress*]...........abc

Alberta [*Canadian province*]..............................ALB

Alberta [*Canadian province*].............................ALBA

Alberta [*Canadian province*].............................ALTA

Alberta [*MARC geographic area code*] [*Library of Congress*]..............n-cn-ab

Alberta Alcoholism and Drug Abuse Commission Library, Edmonton, AB, Canada [*OCLC symbol*]...........AAD

Alberta Cancer Clinic, Edmonton, AB, Canada [*Library symbol*].....CaAECC

Alberta College of Art, Calgary, AB, Canada [*Library symbol*].......CaACSAA

Alberta Culture, Edmonton, AB, Canada [*Library symbol*]..............CaAECYR

Alberta Culture, Heritage Resources Development, Edmonton, AB, Canada [*Library symbol*]..........CaAECYRH

Alberta Department of Advanced Education and Manpower, Edmonton, AB, Canada [*Library symbol*]...........CaAEAE

Alberta Department of Agriculture, Edmonton, AB, Canada [*Library symbol*]..........................CaAEAg

Alberta Department of Agriculture, Laboratory, Edmonton, Canada [*Library symbol*]....................CaAEAgL

Alberta Department of Agriculture, O. S. Longman Building, Edmonton, AB, Canada [*Library symbol*]........CaAEAO

Alberta Department of the Attorney General, Edmonton, AB, Canada [*Library symbol*]....................CaAEAtG

Alberta Department of the Attorney General, Planning, Research, and Development Division, Edmonton, AB, Canada [*Library symbol*]......................CaAEPRD

Alberta Department of Business Development and Tourism, Edmonton, AB, Canada [*Library symbol*]..........CaAEIC

Alberta Department of Consumer and Corporate Affairs, Edmonton, AB, Canada [*Library symbol*].........CaAECA

Alberta Department of Education, Audio Visual Services Branch, Edmonton, AB, Canada [*Library symbol*]...........CaAEEAV

Alberta Department of Education, Edmonton, AB, Canada [*Library symbol*]...........................CaAEE

Alberta Department of Education, Special Education, Materials Resource Centre, Edmonton, AB, Canada [*Library symbol*]....CaAEESE

Alberta Department of Energy and Natural Resources, Edmonton, AB, Canada [*Library symbol*] [*Obsolete*]................CaAEMM

Alberta Department of Energy and Natural Resources, Edmonton, AB, Canada [*Library symbol*].........CaAENR

Alberta Department of Energy and Natural Resources, Renewable Resources Division, Edmonton, AB, Canada [*Library symbol*] [*Obsolete*]....................CaAELF

Alberta Department of the Environment, Edmonton, AB, Canada [*Library symbol*]......................CaAEEN

Alberta Department of Federal and Intergovernmental Affairs, Edmonton, AB, Canada [*Library symbol*]...........CaAEFIA

Alberta Department of Government Services, Computing and Systems Division, Edmonton, AB, Canada [*Library symbol*].....CaAEDC

Alberta Department of Government Services, Edmonton, AB, Canada [*Library symbol*]....................CaAEGS

Alberta Department of Housing and Public Works, Edmonton, AB, Canada [*Library symbol*]..................CaAEPW

Alberta Department of Labour, Edmonton, AB, Canada [*Library symbol*]............................CaAEML

Alberta Department of Labour, Occupational Health and Safety Division, Edmonton, AB, Canada [*Library symbol*]...............CaAEMLOH

Alberta Department of Municipal Affairs, Edmonton, AB, Canada [*Library symbol*].......................CaAEMA

Alberta Department of Recreation, Parks, and Wildlife, Edmonton, AB, Canada [*Library symbol*]........CaAERPW

Alberta Department of Social Services and Community Health, Edmonton, AB, Canada [*Library symbol*].........CaAEHSD

Alberta Department of Transportation, Edmonton, AB, Canada [*Library symbol*]..........................CaAEHT

Alberta Department of Transportation, Highways Testing Laboratory, Edmonton, AB, Canada [*Library symbol*]..............CaAEHTT

Alberta Energy Co., Calgary, AB, Canada [*Library symbol*]..............CaACAE

Alberta Energy Resources Conservation Board, Calgary, AB, Canada [*Library symbol*]....................CaACER

Alberta Environmental Centre, Vegreville, AB, Canada [*Library symbol*]...........................CaAVeE

Alberta Folklore Quarterly [*A publication*]....................AFQ

Alberta Gas Ethylene Co., Calgary, AB, Canada [*Library symbol*]....CaACAG

Alberta Government Telephones Commission, Edmonton, AB, Canada [*Library symbol*].....................CaAEGT

Alberta Government Union Catalogue, Edmonton Concordia College, Edmonton, AB, Canada [*Library symbol*].................CaAEAUC

Alberta Historical Resources, Edmonton, AB, Canada [*Library symbol*]...............................CaAEA

Alberta Historical Review [*A publication*]..............Alta Hist R

Alberta Horticultural Research Centre, Brooks, AB, Canada [*Library symbol*]...........................CaABAH

Alberta Hospital, Oliver, AB, Canada [*Library symbol*]........CaAEHO

Alberta Hospital, Staff Library, Ponoka, AB, Canada [*Library symbol*].............................CaAPH

Alberta Housing Corporation, Edmonton, AB, Canada [*Library symbol*]..............................CaAEHC

Alberta Human Rights Commission, Edmonton, AB, Canada [*Library symbol*].........................CaAEHR

Alberta Journal of Educational Research [*A publication*]...................AJER

Alberta Journal of Educational Research [*A publication*].........Alber J Edu

Alberta Journal of Educational Research [*A publication*]..................
Alberta J Educ Res

Alberta Labour-Building Standards Library, Edmonton, AB, Canada [*Library symbol*]......................CaAELBS

Alberta Lands and Forests Annual Report [*A publication*]..................
Alberta Lands For Annu Rep

Alberta Law Review [*A publication*]....................Alberta L R

Alberta Legislature Library, Edmonton, AB, Canada [*Library symbol*]..............................CaAEP

Alberta Modern Language Journal [*A publication*].............Alberta M L J

Alberta Oil Sands Index [*Canada*] [*Information service*]............AOSI

Alberta Oil Sands Information Centre, Edmonton, AB, Canada [*Library symbol*]............................CaAEAOS

Alberta Ombudsman, Edmonton, AB, Canada [*Library symbol*].....CaAEOM

Alberta Petroleum Marketing Commission, Calgary, AB, Canada [*Library symbol*]..........................CaACPMC

Alberta Provincial Courts, Edmonton, AB, Canada [*Library symbol*].............................CaAEPC

Alberta Public Utilities Board, Edmonton, AB, Canada [*Library symbol*]............................CaAEPU

Alberta Research. Annual Report [*A publication*]..........Alberta Res Annu Rep

Alberta Research Council. Bulletin [*A publication*]....Alberta Res Counc Bull

Alberta Research Council. Bulletin [*A publication*]..................
Alberta Research Council Bull

Alberta Research Council. Information Series [*A publication*]..................
Alberta Res Counc Inf Ser

Alberta Research Council. Information Series [*A publication*]..................
Alberta Research Council Inf Ser

Alberta Research Council. Memoir [*A publication*]..................
Alberta Research Council Mem

Alberta Research Council. Mimeographed Circular [*A publication*]....................Alberta Research Council Mimeo Circ

Alberta Research Council. Preliminary Soil Survey Report [*A publication*]................Alberta Research Council Prelim Soil Survey Rept

Alberta Research Council. Report [*A publication*]......Alberta Res Counc Rep

Alberta Research Council. Report [*A publication*]..................
Alberta Research Council Rept

Alberta Research. Economic Geology Report [*A publication*]..................
Alberta Res Econ Geol Rep

Alberta Research, Edmonton, AB, Canada [*Library symbol*]..............CaAER

Alberta Research. Report [*A publication*]............................Alberta Res Rep

Alberta School for the Deaf, Edmonton, AB, Canada [*Library symbol*]...........................CaAESD

Alberta Society of Petroleum Geologists. Journal. News Bulletin [*A publication*]..............Alberta Soc Petroleum Geologists Jour News Bull

Alberta Solicitor General's Department, Edmonton, AB, Canada [*Library symbol*]............................CaAESG

Alberta Treasury Department, Bureau of Statistics, Edmonton, AB, Canada [*Library symbol*]....................CaAETBS

Alberta Treasury Department, Edmonton, AB, Canada [*Library symbol*].............................CaAET

Alberta Union of Civil Service Employees, Edmonton, AB, Canada [*Library symbol*].......................CaAECS

Alberta Vocational Centre, Calgary, AB, Canada [*Library symbol*]..............................CaACVC

Alberta Vocational Centre, Edmonton, AB, Canada [*Library symbol*].............................CaAEVC

Alberta Vocational Centre, Grouard, AB, Canada [*Library symbol*].............................CaAGVC

Alberta Vocational Centre, Lac La Biche, AB, Canada [*Library symbol*].............................CaALLbVC

Albertina Studien [*A publication*]........................Alb Stud

Alberto-Culver Co. [*NYSE symbol*]...........................ACV

Alberto-Culver Co., Melrose Park, IL [*Library symbol*]..............IMelpA

Albertsons, Inc. [*NYSE symbol*]..............................ABS

Albertus Electus Imperator Optimus Vivat [*Inscription used by Albert II, 15th-century German king*] ... AEIOU
Albertus Magnus College [*Connecticut*] ... AMC
Albertus Magnus College, New Haven, CT [*Library symbol*] ... CtNhA
Albertus Magnus Guild ... AMG
Albertville, AL [*Location identifier*] [*FAA*] ... ARF
Albertville, AL [*Radio station call letters*] ... WAVU
Albertville, AL [*Radio station call letters*] ... WQSB
Albertville, AL [*Radio station call letters*] ... WXBK
Albi [*France*] [*Airport symbol*] ... LBI
Albia Christiana [*A publication*] ... AC
Albia, IA [*Radio station call letters*] ... KLBA
Albia Public Library, Albia, IA [*Library symbol*] ... IaAlb
Albia Union-Republican, Albia, IA [*Library symbol*] ... IaAlbUR
Albion College, Albion, MI [*OCLC symbol*] ... EXA
Albion College, Albion, MI [*Library symbol*] ... MiAlbC
Albion, MI [*Radio station call letters*] ... WELL
Albion, MI [*Radio station call letters*] ... WUFN
Albion, NE [*Television station call letters*] ... KBGT-TV
Albion Public Library, Albion, IL [*Library symbol*] ... IAlb
Albion Public Library, Albion, MI [*Library symbol*] ... MiAlb
Albion State Normal School, Albion, ID [*Library symbol*] ... IdAlN
Albite [*CIPW classification*] [*Geology*] ... ab
Albrecht Duerer [*German artist, 1471-1528*] ... AD
Albrecht Duerer Study Unit [*American Topical Association*] ... ADSU
Albrecht Von Graefe's Archiv fuer Klinische und Experimentelle Ophthalmologie [*A publication*] ... A Graefe's A
Albrecht Von Graefe's Archiv fuer Ophthalmologie [*A publication*] ... Albrecht V Graefe's Arch Ophthal
Albrecht Von Graefe's Archiv fuer Ophthalmologie [*A publication*] ... Albrecht Von Graefe's Arch Ophthalmol
Albrecht Von Graefe's Archive for Clinical and Experimental Ophthalmology [*A publication*] ... Albrecht Von Graefe's Arch Clin Exp Ophthalmol
Albright College, Reading, PA [*Library symbol*] ... PRA
Albright-Knox Art Gallery Library, Buffalo Fine Arts Academy, Buffalo, NY [*Library symbol*] ... NBuAK
Album-Oriented Rock [*Music*] ... AOR
Albumin ... ALB
Albumin/Globulin [*Medicine*] ... A/G
Albuq [*Yemen*] [*Airport symbol*] ... BUK
Albuquerque [*New Mexico*] [*Seismograph station code, US Geological Survey*] ... ALQ
Albuquerque [*New Mexico*] [*Seismograph station code, US Geological Survey*] ... ANMO
Albuquerque [*New Mexico*] [*Airport symbol*] ... ABQ
Albuquerque [*New Mexico*] [*Seismograph station code, US Geological Survey*] ... ABQ
Albuquerque, NM [*Radio station call letters*] ... KABQ
Albuquerque, NM [*Radio station call letters*] ... KAMX
Albuquerque, NM [*Radio station call letters*] ... KANW
Albuquerque, NM [*Radio station call letters*] ... KDAZ
Albuquerque, NM [*Radio station call letters*] ... KDEF
Albuquerque, NM [*Radio station call letters*] ... KFLQ
Albuquerque, NM [*Radio station call letters*] ... KFMG
Albuquerque, NM [*Television station call letters*] ... KGGM-TV
Albuquerque, NM [*Television station call letters*] ... KGSW-TV
Albuquerque, NM [*Radio station call letters*] ... KHFM
Albuquerque, NM [*Radio station call letters*] ... KKIM
Albuquerque, NM [*Radio station call letters*] ... KKJY-FM
Albuquerque, NM [*Radio station call letters*] ... KLTN
Albuquerque, NM [*Radio station call letters*] ... KLYT-FM
Albuquerque, NM [*Television station call letters*] ... KNAT-TV
Albuquerque, NM [*Television station call letters*] ... KNME-TV
Albuquerque, NM [*Television station call letters*] ... KOAT-TV
Albuquerque, NM [*Radio station call letters*] ... KOB
Albuquerque, NM [*Radio station call letters*] ... KOB-FM
Albuquerque, NM [*Television station call letters*] ... KOB-TV
Albuquerque, NM [*Radio station call letters*] ... KQEO
Albuquerque, NM [*Radio station call letters*] ... KRKE
Albuquerque, NM [*Radio station call letters*] ... KRST
Albuquerque, NM [*Radio station call letters*] ... KRZY
Albuquerque, NM [*Radio station call letters*] ... KUNM
Albuquerque, NM [*Radio station call letters*] ... KWXL
Albuquerque, NM [*Radio station call letters*] ... KXKS
Albuquerque, NM [*Radio station call letters*] ... KZIA
Albuquerque, NM [*Radio station call letters*] ... KZZX
Albuquerque Operations Office [*Department of Energy*] ... ALO
Albuquerque Operations Office [*Department of Energy*] ... ALOO
Albuquerque Public Library, Albuquerque, NM [*Library symbol*] ... NmA
Albuquerque Public Library, Albuquerque, NM [*OCLC symbol*] ... QUE
Albuquerque Public Library, Ernie Pyle Memorial Branch, Albuquerque, NM [*Library symbol*] ... NmA-EP
Albuquerque Public Library, Los Griegos Branch, Albuquerque, NM [*Library symbol*] ... NmA-LG
Albuquerque Public Library, Prospect Park Branch, Albuquerque, NM [*Library symbol*] ... NmA-PP
Albury [*Australia*] [*Airport symbol*] ... ABX
Albus [*White*] [*Pharmacy*] ... ALB
Alcadd Test [*Psychology*] ... AT
Alcan Aluminium Limited [*Formerly, Aluminium Limited*] [*NYSE symbol*] ... AL
Alcan Aluminum Co., Cleveland, OH [*Library symbol*] ... OClA
Alcan Research & Development Ltd., Kingston, ON, Canada [*Library symbol*] ... CaOKA
Alcantara [*A publication*] ... Alc
Alcester Public Library, Alcester, SD [*Library symbol*] ... SdAl
Alchemy ... ALCH
Alcheringa (Association of Australasian Palaeontologists) [*A publication*] ... Alcheringa (Assoc Australas Palaeontol)
Alcide Corp. [*NASDAQ symbol*] ... ALCD
Alclad [*Metallurgy*] ... ALCD
Alco Products, Inc. [*Later, ASN*] [*NYSE symbol*] ... AP
Alco Standard Corp. [*NYSE symbol*] ... ASN
ALCOA Smelting Process ... ASP
Alcoa, TN [*Radio station call letters*] ... WEAG
Alcobaca [*Brazil*] [*Airport symbol*] ... ABC
Alcohol ... ALC
Alcohol ... ALCH
Alcohol ... ALCOL
Alcohol on Breath [*Police term*] ... AOB
Alcohol, Chloroform, Ether [*An early anesthetic mixture*] ... ACE
Alcohol Dehydrogenase [*An enzyme*] ... ADH
Alcohol and Dependency Intervention Council [*Military*] ... ADDIC
Alcohol, Drug Abuse, and Mental Health [*Block grant*] ... ADA/MH
Alcohol, Drug Abuse, and Mental Health Administration [*Formerly, HSMHA*] [*Department of Health and Human Services*] ... ADAMHA
Alcohol and Drug Abuse Prevention and Control Program [*Military*] ... ADAPCP
Alcohol and Drug Abuse Prevention Treatment ... ADAPT
Alcohol and Drug Control Office [*Military*] ... ADCO
Alcohol and Drug Problems Association of North America [*Formerly, NAAAP*] ... ADPA
Alcohol Education for Youth [*An association*] ... AYE
Alcohol, Ether, Acetone [*Solvent mixture*] ... AEA
Alcohol Health and Research World [*A publication*] ... Alcoh Health & Res W
Alcohol Health and Research World [*A publication*] ... Alcohol Health Res World
Alcohol Insoluble Solids [*Food analysis*] ... AIS
Alcohol Level Evaluation Road Tester ... ALERT
Alcohol Quotient ... AQ
Alcohol Rehabilitation Center ... ARC
Alcohol Rub [*Medicine*] ... AlcR
Alcohol Safety Action Project [*Department of Transportation*] ... ASAP
Alcohol Safety Interlock System ... ASIS
Alcohol Tax Unit [*Department of the Treasury*] ... ATU
Alcohol, Tobacco, and Firearms [*Bureau*] [*Department of the Treasury*] ... ATF
Alcohol and Tobacco Tax Division [*Internal Revenue Service*] ... ATTD
Alcoholic [*Freight*] ... ALCOLIC
Alcoholic Beverage Control [*Board*] ... ABC
Alcoholics Anonymous World Services [*An association*] ... AA
Alcoholism Center for Women ... ACW
Alcoholism Commission of Saskatchewan, Regina, SK, Canada [*Library symbol*] ... CaSRAC
Alcoholism and Drug Abuse Commission, Calgary, AB, Canada [*Library symbol*] ... CaACAD
Alcoholism and Drug Abuse Commission, Edmonton, AB, Canada [*Library symbol*] ... CaAEAD
Alcolac, Inc. [*American Stock Exchange symbol*] [*Delisted*] ... ALC
Alcon Laboratories, Inc. [*NYSE symbol*] [*Delisted*] ... ALB
Alcon Laboratories, Inc., Fort Worth, TX [*Library symbol*] ... TxFAl
Alcona County Library, Harrisville, MI [*Library symbol*] ... MiHarv
Alcor Life Extension Foundation ... ALEF
Alcorn Agricultural and Mechanical College, Lorman, MS [*Library symbol*] ... MsAM
Alcuin Society ... AS
Aldebaran Drilling Co. [*NASDAQ symbol*] ... ALDB
Aldehyde Fuchsin [*A dye*] ... AF
Aldehyde Oxidase [*An enzyme*] ... AO
Alden Ocean Shell Association ... AOSA
Alden Public Library, Alden, IA [*Library symbol*] ... IaAld
Aldens, Inc. [*NYSE symbol*] [*Delisted*] ... AUD
Alderman ... ALD
Aldermaston Mechanised Cataloging and Ordering System [*British*] ... AMCOS
Alderney [*Channel Islands*] [*Airport symbol*] ... ACI
Alderson-Broaddus College, Philippi, WV [*OCLC symbol*] ... WVA
Alderson-Broaddus College, Philippi, WV [*Library symbol*] ... WvPhA
Aldolase [*An enzyme*] ... ALD
Aldosterone [*Endocrinology*] ... ALDO
Aldosterone-Binding Protein [*Endocrinology*] ... ABP
Aldosterone Excretion Rate [*Endocrinology*] ... AER
Aldosterone-Induced Protein [*Biochemistry*] ... AIP
Aldosterone-Producing Adenoma [*Clinical chemistry*] ... APA
Aldosterone Secretion Rate [*Endocrinology*] ... ASR
Aldosterone-Stimulating Hormone [*Also, AGTr*] [*Endocrinology*] ... ASH
Ale, Bread, and Cheese ... ABC
Alector Airways Corp. [*Newburg, NY*] [*FAA designator*] ... WYA
Aledo, IL [*Radio station call letters*] ... WRMJ

Alegrete [Brazil] [Airport symbol] [Obsolete].................ALQ
Aleknagik [Alaska] [Airport symbol].........................WKK
Aleknagik, AK [Location identifier] [FAA]...................WKK
Aleksandr Solzhenitsyn Society for Freedom and Justice...........ASSFJ
Alemannisches Jahrbuch [A publication].....................ALJ
Aleph Zadik Aleph [Society]................................AZA
Aleppo [Syria] [Airport symbol]............................ALP
Alert [Northwest Territories] [Seismograph station code, US Geological Survey].................................ALE
Alert Area [Military]..A
Alert Area Supervisor [Military]...........................AAS
Alert Availability...AA
Alert Bay Air Service Ltd. [Canada] [ICAO designator]........BF
Alert Building..AB
Alert Condition [Military]...............................LERTCON
Alert Crew Billet Security.................................ACBS
Alert Exercise...ALEX
Alert Force Capability Test................................AFCT
Alert Implementation Reports...........................ALIMPREPS
Alert Message...AM
Alert Notice..ALNOT
Alert, NT [Radio station call letters]....................CHAR-FM
Alert Phase [Aviation code].............................ALERFA
Alert Reaction Time...ART
Alerting Long-Range Airborne RADAR for MTI [Moving Target Indicator]..ALARM
Alerting Message [Aviation code]...........................ALR
Alerting Search Service from Kinokuniya [Kinokuniya Book Store Co. Ltd.] [Information service]....................ASK
Aleut [MARC language code] [Library of Congress]...........ale
Aleutian [FAA]...ALUTN
Aleutian Islands...ALUTS
Alex [Aarons] and Vinton [Freedley] [Theatrical producers of the 1920's and 1930's, after whom the Alvin Theatre in New York City was named]................................ALVIN
Alexander & Alexander Services, Inc. [NYSE symbol]..........AAL
Alexander & Baldwin [NASDAQ symbol]......................ALEX
Alexander Bay [South Africa] [Airport symbol]..............ALJ
Alexander Bay [New York] [Seismograph station code, US Geological Survey].................................ALX
Alexander City, AL [Radio station call letters]...........WACD
Alexander City, AL [Radio station call letters]...........WRFS
Alexander City, AL [Radio station call letters].........WRFS-FM
Alexander City State Junior College, Alexander City, AL [Library symbol]......................................AAcC
Alexander County Public Library, Taylorsville, NC [Library symbol]....................................NcTayA
Alexander Energy Corp. [NASDAQ symbol]....................AEOK
Alexander Graham Bell Association for the Deaf.............AGBA
Alexander Graham Bell Association for the Deaf............AGBAD
Alexander M. Poniatoff, Excellence [Acronym is name of electronics company and brand name of its products; formed from name of firm's founder, plus "excellence"]........AMPEX
Alexander Mitchell Library, Aberdeen, SD [Library symbol]...SdAbA
Alexander Railroad Company [AAR code]......................ARC
Alexander's, Inc. [NYSE symbol]............................ALX
Alexandra [New Zealand] [Airport symbol]...................ALR
Alexandra [Newport and South Wales] Docks & Railway [Wales].....AD
Alexandria [Egypt] [Airport symbol]........................ALY
Alexandria [Minnesota] [Airport symbol] [Obsolete].........AXN
Alexandria [Louisiana] [Airport symbol]....................ESF
Alexandria Dental Journal [A publication].............Alex Dent J
Alexandria, IN [Radio station call letters]...............WAXT
Alexandria Journal of Agricultural Research [A publication]......................................Alexandria J Agric Res
Alexandria Journal of Agricultural Research [A publication]......................................Alexandria J Agr Res
Alexandria, LA [Location identifier] [FAA].................AEX
Alexandria, LA [Location identifier] [FAA].................ERJ
Alexandria, LA [Location identifier] [FAA].................ESF
Alexandria, LA [Radio station call letters]...............KALB
Alexandria, LA [Television station call letters].........KALB-TV
Alexandria, LA [Radio station call letters]...............KDBS
Alexandria, LA [Radio station call letters]...............KDEI
Alexandria, LA [Television station call letters].........KLAX-TV
Alexandria, LA [Television station call letters].........KLPA-TV
Alexandria, LA [Radio station call letters]...............KQID
Alexandria, LA [Radio station call letters]...............KRRV
Alexandria, LA [Radio station call letters]...............KSYL
Alexandria, LA [Radio station call letters]...............KTIZ
Alexandria Library, Alexandria, VA [Library symbol].........ViAl
Alexandria Medical Journal [A publication].........Alexandria Med J
Alexandria, MN [Radio station call letters]...............KCMT
Alexandria, MN [Radio station call letters]...............KXRA
Alexandria, MN [Radio station call letters].............KXRA-FM
Alexandria, MN [Television station call letters]..........KCMT
Alexandria Public Library, Alexandria, SD [Library symbol]...SdAle
Alexandria Public Library, Alexandria, VA [OCLC symbol].....VAX
Alexandria, VA [Radio station call letters]...............WRMR
Alexandroupolis [Greece] [Airport symbol]..................AXD
Alexis De Tocqueville Society...............................ATS

Alfa [Phonetic alphabet].....................................A
Alfa Romeo Nissan Autoveicoli [Italian-Japanese alliance for the joint manufacture of automobiles with Alfa engines and Nissan bodies]......................................ARNA
Alfacell Corp. [NASDAQ symbol].............................ACEL
Alfalfa Club...AC
Alfalfa Mosaic Virus.......................................AMV
Alfalfa Pest Management.....................................APM
Alfin Fragrances, Inc. [NASDAQ symbol]....................ALFN
Alfoeld: Irodalmi es Muvelodesi Folyoirat [A publication].......Alfold
Alfred [New York] [Seismograph station code, US Geological Survey]...ALF
Alfred Adler Institute.....................................AAI
Alfred Dickey Free Library, Jamestown, ND [Library symbol]......NdJ
Alfred Holbrook College, Manchester, OH [Library symbol] [Obsolete]....................................OMancAH
Alfred, NY [Radio station call letters]...................WALF
Alfred, NY [Radio station call letters]...................WETD
Alfred P. Sloan Foundation Report [A publication]......................................Alfred P Sloan Found Rep
Alfred University, Alfred, NY [Library symbol]............NAlf
Alfred University, Alfred, NY [OCLC symbol]................YAH
Alfred University, School of Theology, Alfred, NY [Library symbol] [Obsolete]............................NAlf-ST
Alfven Number [IUPAC].......................................Al
Alfven Propulsion Engine [Aerospace].......................APE
Algebra..ALG
Algebra and Logic [A publication]......................Alg Log
Algebra Package...ALPAK
Algebraic Compiler [Data processing]....................ALCOM
Algebraic Compiler and Translator [Data processing]........ACT
Algebraic Interpretive Dialogue [Data processing]..........AID
Algebraic Logic Investigation of Apollo Systems..........ALIAS
Algebraic Manipulation by Identity Translation...........AMBIT
Algebraic Operating System.................................AOS
Algebraic Reconstruction Technique.........................ART
Algebraic Technological Function...........................ATF
Algebraic Transistorized Automatic Computer Translator....ALTAC
Algebraic Translator [Data processing]..................ALTRAN
Algemeen Nederlandisch Persbureau [Press agency] [Netherlands]......ANP
Algemeen Nederlands Tijdschrift voor Wijsbegeerte [A publication].....................................ANTW
Algemeen Nederlands Tijdschrift voor Wijsbegeerte en Psychologie [A publication].........................ANTsW
Algemeen Rijksarchief te s'Gravenhage (Central State Archives), The Hague, Netherlands [Library symbol].........Ne
Algemeen Vrijzinnig Vakverbond in Nederland [General Liberal Labor Federation] [Netherlands]....................AVV
Algemene Bedrijfsgroepen Centrale [General Union of Workers in Miscellaneous Industries] [Netherlands]............ABC
Algemene Kunstzijde Unie [Later, AKZO] [Commercial firm] [Netherlands].......................................AKU
Algemene Kunstzijde Unie [AKU] - Koninklijke Zout-Organon [KZO] [Two companies whose merger formed AKZO].........AKZO
Alger-Bouzareah [Algeria] [Seismograph station code, US Geological Survey].................................ABA
Algeran, Inc. [NASDAQ symbol]............................ALGR
Algeria [MARC country of publication code] [Library of Congress]...ae
Algeria..ALG
Algeria [Two-letter standard code]..........................DZ
Algeria [Three-letter standard code].......................DZA
Algeria [MARC geographic area code] [Library of Congress]......f-ae---
Algeria [Aircraft nationality and registration mark]........7T
Algeria. Service Geologique. Bulletin [A publication]......Alger Serv Geol Bull
Algerie Medicale [A publication]......................Alger Med
Algerie Presse Service [Press agency] [Algeria]............APS
Algers, Winslow, & Western Railway Co. [AAR code]..........AWW
Alghero [Italy] [Airport symbol]...........................AHO
Algiers [Algeria] [Airport symbol].........................ALG
Algiers [Algeria] [Seismograph station code, US Geological Survey]...ALG
Algodon Boletin de la Camara Algodonera del Peru [A publication].....................Algodon Bol Cam Algodonera Peru
ALGOL [A publication]......................................ALG
ALGOL [Algorithmic Language] Compiler [Data processing]....ALCOM
ALGOL [Algorithmic Language] Extended for Design [Data processing].....................................AED
ALGOL [Algorithmic Language]-to-FORTRAN [Formula Translation] Translator [Data processing]............ALFTRAN
Algological Studies [A publication]....................Algol Stud
Algoma Central Railway [AAR code]...........................AC
Algoma College, Sault Ste. Marie, ON, Canada [Library symbol]......................................CaOStMA
Algoma Steel Corp., Quality Control and Research Department, Sault Ste. Marie, ON, Canada [Library symbol].......CaOStMAS
Algona, IA [Radio station call letters]..................KLGA
Algona, IA [Radio station call letters]................KLGA-FM
Algona Public Library, Algona, IA [Library symbol].........IaAlg
Algonquian [MARC language code] [Library of Congress]......alg
Algonquin College, Ottawa, ON, Canada [Library symbol]....CaOOAC
Algonquin Regional Library, Parry Sound, ON, Canada [Library symbol]......................................CaOPsA

Algonquin Regional Library System, Sturgeon Falls Branch, Sturgeon Falls, ON, Canada [*Library symbol*] ... CaOSfAR
Algood, TN [*Radio station call letters*] ... WWRT
Algorex Corp. [*NASDAQ symbol*] ... ALGO
Algorithm ... ALGO
Algorithm Development Facility [*for spacecraft data*] [*Jet Propulsion Laboratory*] ... ADF
Algorithm Simulation Test and Evaluation Program [*NASA*] ... ASTEP
Algorithmic and Business Oriented Language [*Data processing*] ... ALABOL
Algorithmic Language [*Data processing*] ... ALGOL
Algorithmic Language for Economic Calculations [*Data processing*] ... ALGEC
Algorithmic Remote Manipulation [*Data processing language*] ... ARM
Algoritmy i Algoritmiceskie Jazyki [*A publication*] ... Algoritmy i Algoritm Jazyki
Algot Holmbergs Arsbok [*A publication*] ... Algot Holmbergs Arsb
Alhambra Public Library, Alhambra, CA [*Library symbol*] ... CAlh
ALI-ABA [*American Law Institute - American Bar Association*] **Committee on Continuing Professional Education** ... ALI-ABA
Alia [*Others*] [*Latin*] ... AL
Alianca Renovadora Macional [*National Renewal Alliance*] [*Brazil*] ... ARENA
Alianza Anticomunista Argentina ... AAA
Alianza Democratica Revolucionaria [*Democratic Revolutionary Alliance*] [*Bolivia*] ... ADR
Alianza Interamericana ... AI
Alianza Nacional Popular [*Colombian political party*] ... ANAPO
Alianza Popular Revolucionaria Americana [*Peruvian political party*] ... APRA
Alias [*Otherwise*] [*Latin*] ... AL
Alias ... ALS
Alibag [*India*] [*Geomagnetic observatory code*] ... ABG
Alicahue [*Chile*] [*Seismograph station code, US Geological Survey*] ... ALH
Alicante [*Spain*] [*Airport symbol*] ... ALC
Alicante [*Spain*] [*Seismograph station code, US Geological Survey*] ... ALI
Alice Arm/Kitsault [*Canada*] [*Airport symbol*] ... ZAA
Alice Meynell [*British poet, 1847-1922*] ... AM
Alice Springs [*Australia*] [*Airport symbol*] ... ASP
Alice Springs [*Australia*] [*Seismograph station code, US Geological Survey*] ... ASP
Alice, TX [*Radio station call letters*] ... KBIC
Alice, TX [*Radio station call letters*] ... KDSI
Alice, TX [*Radio station call letters*] ... KOPY
Alico, Inc. [*NASDAQ symbol*] ... ALCO
Alicudi [*Lipari Islands*] [*Seismograph station code, US Geological Survey*] ... ACL
Alicyclic [*Chemistry*] ... ac
Alidade [*Engineering*] ... ALDD
Alien Cell ... AC
Alien Declared Intention ... ADI
Alien Documentation, Identification, and Telecommunications [*Immigration and Naturalization Service*] ... ADIT
Alien Firearms Act ... AFA
Alien Grange ... AGR
Alien, Penumbral, Umbral, Penumbral, Alien ... APUPA
Alien Priory ... APR
Alien Property Custodian [*World War II*] ... APC
Aligarh Bulletin of Mathematics [*A publication*] ... Aligarh Bull Math
Aligarh Journal of English Studies [*A publication*] ... AJES
Aligarh Muslim University Publications. Zoological Series [*A publication*] ... Aligarh Muslim Univ Publ Zool Ser
Alighieri [*A publication*] ... AL
Alighting [*Aviation*] ... ALGTG
Alighting Area [*Aviation*] ... ALA
Align ... ALN
Alignment ... ALGN
Alignment ... ALIGN
Alignment ... ALNMT
Alignment Control Panel ... ACP
Alignment Countdown Set [*Aerospace*] ... A-CS
Alignment Countdown Set Inertial Guidance [*Aerospace*] ... ACSIG
Alignment and Diagnostic Display Console ... ADDC
Alignment Group ... AG
Alignment Group Sensing Platform ... AGSP
Alignment Lab ... AL
Alignment Optical Telescope ... AOT
Alignment Periscope ... AP
Alignment Procedures ... AP
Alignment Progress Indicator ... API
Alignment and Test Facility for Optical Systems [*Navy*] ... ATFOS
Alignment Unit ... AU
Alignment Window ... AW
Alii Air Hawaii [*Honolulu, HI*] [*FAA designator*] ... ALL
Alimentary System [*Medicine*] ... AS
Alimentary Toxic Aleukia ... ATA
Alimentation et la Vie [*A publication*] ... Aliment Vie
Alimentazione Animale [*A publication*] ... Aliment Anim
Alimentos para Animales, SA [*Feed plant*] [*Guatemala*] ... ALIANSA
Aliquippa & Southern Railroad Co. [*AAR code*] ... ALQS
Alishan [*Republic of China*] [*Seismograph station code, US Geological Survey*] ... ALS
Alison Mortgage Investment Trust [*NYSE symbol*] ... AMV
Alitak [*Alaska*] [*Airport symbol*] ... ALZ
Alitalia [*Aerolinee Italiane Internazionali*] [*Italian airline*] ... ALI
Alitalia [*Aerolinee Italiane Internazionali*] [*Italian airline*] [*ICAO designator*] ... AZ
Alitalia, Lufthansa, Air France, Sabena [*Consortium of airlines*] ... ATLAS
Alive and Well ... A & W
Alizarin Red S [*An indicator*] [*Chemistry*] ... ARS
Aljamia [*MARC language code*] [*Library of Congress*] ... ajm
Alkali-Extractable Light Chain [*Biochemistry*] ... ALC
Alkali Flame Ionization Detector [*Instrumentation*] ... AFID
Alkali Metal Cleaning Facility [*Nuclear energy*] ... AMCF
Alkali Metal Thermoelectric Converter [*Power source*] ... AMTEC
Alkali-Metal Turbine ... AMT
Alkali Plasma Hall Accelerator ... ALPHA
Alkaline ... ALK
Alkaline Calcium Petroleum Sulfonate ... ACPS
Alkaline Electrolyte Fuel Cell ... AEFC
Alkaline Phosphatase [*Also, AP*] [*An enzyme*] ... ALP
Alkaline Phosphatase [*Also, ALP*] [*An enzyme*] ... AP
Alkaline Phosphatase:Antialkaline Phosphatase [*Immunochemistry*] ... APAAP
Alkalinity ... ALKY
Alkalmazott Matematikai Lapok [*A publication*] ... Alkalmaz Mat Lapok
Alkyl [*Chemistry*] ... Alk
Alkyl Benzenesulfonate [*Organic chemistry*] ... ABS
Alkyl Sulfate [*Surfactant*] [*Organic chemistry*] ... AS
Alkyldimethylamine [*Acronym is a trademark of Erhyl Corp. for its brand of alkyldimethylamine products*] ... ADMA
Alkylethoxylated Sulfate [*Surfactant*] [*Organic chemistry*] ... AES
All [*When used as prefix*] [*FAA*] ... AL
All Accident Notice Offices [*FAA*] ... ALANO
All-African Farmers' Union ... AAFU
All African Peoples' Conference ... AAPC
All-African Trade Union Federation [*Later, OATUU*] ... AATUF
All-African Women's Conference ... AAWC
All [*text*] **After** [*specified point*] [*Message handling*] ... AA
All Air Carrier Field Offices [*FAA*] ... ALACFO
All Air Defense Liaison Officers in Region [*FAA*] ... ALADLO
All Air Route Traffic Control Centers in Region [*FAA*] ... ALARTC
All Air Traffic Control Towers in Region [*FAA*] ... ALTWR
All Air Traffic Field Facilities [*FAA*] ... ALATF
All Air Traffic Field Offices [*FAA*] ... ALATFO
All Air Traffic Service Personnel in Region [*FAA*] ... ALAT
All Air Traffic [*Area*] **Supervisors in Region** [*FAA*] ... ALATAS
All Airway Facilities Sector and Field Offices [*FAA*] ... ALAFFO
All-Altitude Air-Bearing Research and Training Simulator ... ARTS
All-Altitude Spin Projected [*Munition*] ... ASP
All Aluminum Conductor ... AAC
All-America Football Conference [*Major league 1946-49, merged with NFL 1950*] ... AAFC
All-America Gladiolus Selections [*An association*] ... AAGS
All-America Rose Selections [*An association*] ... AARS
All-America Selections [*An association*] ... AAS
All-American Amateur Baseball Association ... AAABA
All American Association of Contest Judges ... AAACJ
All-American Bronze Club ... AABC
All American Cables & Radio, Inc. ... AAC & R
All-American Conference to Combat Communism ... AACCC
All American Life & Financial Corp. [*NYSE symbol*] [*Delisted*] ... AAL
All Applications Digital Computer [*Navy*] ... AADC
All Army Activities ... ALARACT
All-Articles Configuration Inspection Log [*Aerospace*] ... AACIL
All AT [*Air Traffic Service*] **Combined Station/Centers in Region** [*FAA*] ... ALCS/C
All AT [*Air Traffic Service*] **Combined Station/Towers in Region** [*FAA*] ... ALCS/T
All-Attitude Control Capability [*Aerospace*] ... AACC
All-Attitude Indicator ... AAI
All-Attitude Indicator Bombing System ... AABS
All-Band Intercept Receiver ... ABIR
All [*text*] **Before** [*specified point*] [*Message handling*] ... AB
All Between_____ and_____ [*Message handling*] ... BN
All Body Type [*Army*] ... ABT
All Bureaus [*Navy*] ... ALBUS
All Busy Low [*AT & T*] ... ABL
All But the Dissertation [*PhD candidates*] ... ABD
All Cargo Airlines Ltd. [*Great Britain*] [*ICAO designator*] ... UF
All Ceylon Federation of Free Trade Unions ... ACFFTU
All-Ceylon Harbor and Dock Workers' Union ... ACHDWU
All Chiefs, No Indians ... ACNI
All-China Federation of Trade Unions [*Communist China*] ... ACFTU
All Commands [*A dispatch to all commands in an area*] [*Navy*] ... ALCOM
All Commands, [*US*] **Atlantic Fleet** [*Navy*] ... ALCOMLANT
All Commands, [*US*] **Pacific Fleet** [*Navy*] ... ALCOMPAC
All Commands Process as Attached [*Army*] ... ACPATT
All Composite Aircraft ... ACA
All Concerned [*Army*] ... ALCON
All Concerned Notified ... ACN
All Courses and Quadrants [*Aviation*] ... ACQ
All-Craft Foundation ... ACF
All Damn Confusion ... ADC

All Dielectric Filter ADF
All-Digital Attack Center ADAC
All-Digital Data Tape ADDT
All-Digital Phase-Locked Loop ADPLL
All-Digital Simulator ADS
All Engines Operating [*Aviation*] AEO
All England AE
All England Law Reports AER
All England Lawn Tennis Club AELTC
All Equipment OK [*Expression meaning "in perfect working order." Popularized during early development of NASA's space program*] A-OK
All FAA [*Federal Aviation Administration*] **Field Offices** ALFOF
All FAA [*Federal Aviation Administration*] **Field Offices and Personnel** ALFAA
All FAA [*Federal Aviation Administration*] **Offices on Service B** ALFAB
All in the Family [*TV program*] AITF
All Flight Service Stations in Region [*FAA*] ALFSS
All Flight Standards Field Offices [*FAA*] ALFSFO
All Food Activities [*DoD*] ALFOODACT
All Fouled-Up [*Bowdlerized version*] AFU
All-India Bank Employees' Association AIBEA
All-India Bank Employees' Federation AIBEF
All-India Congress Committee AICC
All India Congress Committee. Economic Review [*A publication*] AICCER
All-India Coordinated Millet Improvement Programme AICMIP
All-India Coordinated Rice Improvement Program AICRIP
All-India Federation of Electricity Employees AIFEE
All-India Insurance Employees' Association AIIEA
All-India Jute Textile Workers' Federation AIJWF
All-India Port and Dock Workers' Federation AIPDWF
All-India Radio AIR
All-India Railwaymen's Federation AIRF
All-India Trade Union Congress AITUC
All-Industry Electronics Conference AIEC
All-Industry Research Advisory Council AIRAC
All Inertial Guidance [*Aerospace*] AIG
All Inertial Guidance System [*Aerospace*] AIGS
All International Aeronautical Telecommunications Switching Centers [*FAA*] ALIATSC
All International Air Traffic Communications Stations [*FAA*] ALIATCS
All International Air Traffic Switching Centers [*FAA*] AIATSC
All International Field Offices [*FAA*] ALIFO
All International Flight Service Stations in Region [*FAA*] ALIFSS
All Iron AI
All Is Well [*Search and rescue symbol that can be stamped in sand or snow*] LL
All-Language Services, Inc. ALS
All Lengths [*Lumber*] AL
All Major Commands ALMAJCOM
All Major Commands AMC
All Marine Corps Activities ALMAR
All Military Activities ALMILACT
All Nations Women's League ANWL
All Naval Stations [*A dispatch to all Naval stations in an area*] ALLNAVSTAS
All Naval Stations [*A dispatch to all Naval stations in an area*] ALNAVSTA
All Navy Activities [*A dispatch to all activities in an area*] ALNAV
All Navy Activities [*A dispatch to all activities in an area*] NAVACT
All-Nigeria Trade Union Federation ANTUF
All Nippon Airways ANA
All Nippon Airways Co. Ltd. [*Japan*] [*ICAO designator*] NH
All Numbers Calling [*Telephone*] ANC
All-Ordnance Destruct System AODS
All-Ordnance Thrust Termination AOTT
All Other Perils [*Insurance*] AOP
All Others [*Later, G Group*] [*Division of National Security Agency*] ALLO
All' Ottava [*At the Octave*] [*Music*] ALL' OTT
All Out-of-Kilter [*Slang*] AOK
All-Pakistan Confederation of Labor APCOL
All-Pakistan Post and Telegraph Union APPTU
All-Pakistan Railwaymen's Federation APRF
All Party Alliance [*British*] APA
All Pass Network APN
All-Peoples Congress APC
All Personnel Communication [*Military*] ALPERSCOM
All Points Bulletin [*Police call*] APB
All Present or Accounted For APOAF
All-Purpose AP
All-Purpose Communications System ALPURCOMS
All-Purpose Electronic Computer APEC
All-Purpose Rocket for Collecting Atmospheric Soundings [*Navy*] ARCAS
All-Purpose Room APR
All Quadrants [*Aviation*] ALQDS
All RADAR Air Traffic Control Facilities in Region [*FAA*] ALRAFAC
All Rail [*Railroad*] AR
All Regional Offices [*FAA*] ALRGN
All Right [*From Oll Korrect; or from Old Kinderhook, a Democratic party organization that supported Martin Van Buren in 1840; or from Aux Cayes, Caribbean Keys on which was produced a rum of superior quality*] OK
All Risk Management [*Insurance*] ARM
All Risks [*Business and trade*] AR
All-Russian Monarchist Front ARMF
All Safety Commands [*Air Force*] ALSAFECOM
All Saints' Day ASD
All Savers Certificate [*Banking*] ASC
All Seasons Aviation Ltd. [*ICAO designator*] JC
All Sectors [*FAA*] ALSEC
All-Service Close Air Support [*Military*] ASCAS
All-Services Evaluation Group [*Military*] ASEG
All Ships and Stations Letters AS & SL
All-Sky Camera ASC
All-Sky Monitor [*Optics*] ASM
All Source Analysis System [*DoD*] ASAS
All States Hobby Club [*Later, NASHC*] ASHC
All Stations ALSTA
All Stations, Continental United States ALSTACON
All-Steel Equipment, Inc. ASE
All Systems Test AST
All Systems Test Equipment Group ASTEG
All Systems Vehicle ASV
All Tariffs Computerized [*Project*] ATAC
All-Terrain Cycle ATC
All-Terrain Remote Control Vehicle ATRCV
All-Terrain Vehicle ATV
All Things Considered [*Radio program*] ATC
All Thrust Terminate Relay ATTR
All Thrust Termination ATT
All Together [*An association*] AT
All Trunks Busy [*Communications*] ATB
All-Ukrainian Evangelical Baptist Fellowship AUEBF
All Union Central Council of Trade Unions [*USSR*] AUCCTU
All Up Around AUR
All Up Weight [*Aviation*] AUW
All Volatile Treatment [*Nuclear energy*] AVT
All-Volunteer Force [*Army*] AVF
All Water AW
All Wave Antenna AWA
All-Weather A/W
All-Weather [*As applied to fighter aircraft, etc.*] AW
All-Weather Aircraft AWX
All-Weather Attack AWA
All-Weather Carrier Landing System [*Navy*] ACLS
All-Weather Carrier Landing System [*Navy*] AWCLS
All-Weather Electronics AWE
All-Weather Flare AWF
All-Weather Ground Surveillance RADAR AGSR
All-Weather Interceptor AWI
All-Weather Landing AWL
All-Weather Landing System [*Also, AWLS*] ALS
All-Weather Landing System [*Also, ALS*] AWLS
All-Weather Low-Altitude Route [*Aviation*] AWLAR
All-Weather Operations Committee [*ATA*] AWOC
All-Weather Operations Panel [*International Civil Aviation Organization*] AWOP
All-Weather Reconnaissance System AWRS
All-Weather Sea Target Acquisition System [*Navy*] AWSTAS
All-Weather Short-Range Air Defense Missile System AW-SHORADS
All-Weather Station AWSTA
All-Weather System AWS
All-Weather Tactical Bombing System AWTBS
All-Weather Tactical Strike System [*Air Force*] AWTSS
All-Weather Test Bed AWTB
All-Weather Topographic Mapping System [*Army*] AWTMS
All-Weather Yaw Damper Computer AWYDC
All Widths [*Lumber*] AW
All the Year Round [*A publication*] All the Year
Alla Bottega [*A publication*] AllaB
Allagash [*Maine*] [*Seismograph station code, US Geological Survey*] AGM
Allahabad [*India*] [*Airport symbol*] IXD
Allahabad Farmer [*A publication*] Allahabad Fmr
Allahabad University Studies [*A publication*] Allahabad Univ Studies
Allakaket [*Alaska*] [*Airport symbol*] AET
Allam- es Jogtudomany [*A publication*] Allam- es Jogtud
Allamin Gorkij Konyvtar, Budapest, Hungary [*Library symbol*] HuBG
Allamvedelmi Hivatal [*Hungarian secret police*] AVH
Allamvedelmi Osztaly [*Hungarian secret police*] AVO
Allan Hancock College [*California*] AHC
Allan Hancock College, Santa Maria, CA [*Library symbol*] CStmaAH
Allan Hancock Foundation Publications. Occasional Paper [*A publication*] Allan Hancock Found Publ Occas Pap
Allan Hancock Monographs in Marine Biology [*A publication*] Allan Hancock Monogr Mar Biol
Allan Hills [*Antarctic meteorology*] ALH
[*Sir*] **Allan Patrick Herbert** [*British humorist*] APH
Allard Owners Club USA AOC-USA
Allard Register AR

Allatorvosi Lapok [*A publication*] ..... Allat Lapok
Allattani Kozlemenyek [*A publication*] ..... Allattani Kozl
Allattenyesztestani Tanszek [*A publication*] ..... Allatteny
Allegan Public Library, Allegan, MI [*Library symbol*] ..... MiAlle
Allegany Community College, Cumberland, MD [*Library symbol*] ..... MdCuAC
Allegany County Library, Cumberland, MD [*Library symbol*] ..... MdCu
Alleghany Corp. [*NYSE symbol*] ..... Y
Allegheny [*National Weather Service*] ..... ALGHNY
Allegheny Airlines [*Air carrier designation symbol*] ..... AAA
Allegheny Airlines [*American Stock Exchange symbol*] [*Delisted*] ..... ALA
Allegheny Airlines ..... ALL
Allegheny Ballistics Laboratory ..... ABL
Allegheny Beverage [*NASDAQ symbol*] ..... ABEV
Allegheny College, Meadville, PA [*OCLC symbol*] ..... AVL
Allegheny College, Meadville, PA [*Library symbol*] ..... PMA
Allegheny County Law Library, Pittsburgh, PA [*OCLC symbol*] ..... PAL
Allegheny County Law Library, Pittsburgh, PA [*Library symbol*] ..... PPiAL
Allegheny International, Inc. [*NYSE symbol*] ..... AG
Allegheny International, Inc. [*Formerly, Allegheny Ludlum Industries, Inc.*], **Brackenridge, PA** [*Library symbol*] ..... PBracAL
Allegheny Ludlum Horizons [*A publication*] ..... Allegheny Ludlum Horiz
Allegheny Ludlum Steel Corp. [*Later, Allegheny International, Inc.*] ..... ALS
Allegheny Portage Railroad National Historic Site ..... ALPO
Allegheny Power System, Inc. ..... APS
Allegheny Power System, Inc. [*NYSE symbol*] ..... AYP
Allegheny & South Side [*AAR code*] ..... AYSS
Allegheny/Western Energy [*NASDAQ symbol*] ..... ALGH
Allegheny & Western Railway Co. [*NYSE symbol*] [*Delisted*] ..... AY
Allegiance ..... ALLEG
Allegro [*Quick*] [*Music*] ..... ALLO
Alleluia [*An old abbreviation, formed from the vowels of the word*] ..... AEUIA
Allemagnes d'Aujourd'hui [*A publication*] ..... Allem Aujourd
Allen Academy, Bryan, TX [*Library symbol*] ..... TxBryA
Allen-Bradley Co. ..... A-B
Allen County Law Library, Lima, OH [*Library symbol*] ..... OLimaAL
Allen County Public Library, Fort Wayne, IN [*OCLC symbol*] ..... IMF
Allen Group, Inc. [*NYSE symbol*] ..... ALN
Allen & Hanburys [*Great Britain*] [*Research code symbol*] ..... AH
Allen & Hanburys [*Great Britain*] [*Research code symbol*] ..... CB
Allen Industries, Inc. [*NYSE symbol*] [*Delisted*] ..... ANL
Allen Organ Co. Cl B [*NASDAQ symbol*] ..... AORGB
Allen Parish Library, Oberlin, LA [*Library symbol*] ..... LObA
Allen Park Public Library, Allen Park, MI [*Library symbol*] ..... MiAp
Allen Township Consolidated Community School District 65, Ransom, IL [*Library symbol*] ..... IRanASD
Allen Video-Enhanced Contrast [*Microscopy*] ..... AVEC
Allen and Wright [*Root beer*] [*Initialism also used as name of franchised drive-in restaurants*] ..... A & W
Allendale, MI [*Radio station call letters*] ..... WGVC-FM
Allendale, SC [*Radio station call letters*] ..... WDOG
Allendale, SC [*Television station call letters*] ..... WEBA-TV
Allendale, SC [*Radio station call letters*] ..... WYXZ
Allendale Township Library, Allendale, MI [*Library symbol*] ..... MiAll
Allentown/Bethlehem/Easton [*Pennsylvania*] [*Airport symbol*] ..... ABE
Allentown Borough Hall, Allentown, NJ [*Library symbol*] ..... NjAlB
Allentown College of Saint Francis de Sales, Center Valley, PA [*OCLC symbol*] ..... ALL
Allentown College of Saint Francis de Sales, Center Valley, PA [*Library symbol*] ..... PCvA
Allentown Historical Society, Allentown, NJ [*Library symbol*] ..... NjAlHi
Allentown, PA [*Location identifier*] [*FAA*] ..... BXY
Allentown, PA [*Radio station call letters*] ..... WAEB
Allentown, PA [*Radio station call letters*] ..... WFMZ
Allentown, PA [*Television station call letters*] ..... WFMZ-TV
Allentown, PA [*Radio station call letters*] ..... WHOL
Allentown, PA [*Radio station call letters*] ..... WKAP
Allentown, PA [*Television station call letters*] ..... WLVT-TV
Allentown, PA [*Radio station call letters*] ..... WMUH
Allentown, PA [*Radio station call letters*] ..... WSAN
Allentown, PA [*Radio station call letters*] ..... WXKW
Allentown Printing Service, Allentown, NJ [*Library symbol*] ..... NjAlA
Allentown Public Library, Allentown, NJ [*Library symbol*] ..... NjAl
Allentown Public Library, Allentown, PA [*OCLC symbol*] ..... AYP
Allentown Public Library, Allentown, PA [*Library symbol*] ..... PAt
Allentown State Hospital, Allentown, PA [*OCLC symbol*] ..... PHL
Aller Ehren Ist Oesterreich Voll [*Austria Is Crowned with All Honor*] [*Variation of 15th-century inscription*] ..... AEIOU
Aller Erst Ist Oesterreich Verdorben [*Variation of 15th-century inscription*] ..... AEIOU
Allergan Pharmaceuticals, Inc. [*NYSE symbol*] [*Delisted*] ..... AGN
Allergic Bronchopulmonary Aspergillosis [*Medicine*] ..... ABPA
Allergic Bronchopulmonary Aspergillosus [*Medicine*] ..... ABA
Allergic to Combat [*A play on the initialism for the Air Transport Command*] ..... ATC
Allergic Rhinitis [*Medicine*] ..... AR
Allergie und Asthma [*A publication*] ..... Allerg Asthma
Allergie und Asthmaforschung [*A publication*] ..... Allerg Asthmaforsch
Allergie und Immunologie [*A publication*] ..... Allerg Immunol
Allergie und Immunologie (Leipzig) [*A publication*] ..... Allerg Immunol (Leipz)
Allergologia et Immunopathologia [*Madrid*] [*A publication*] ..... Allergol Immunopathol
Allergologia et Immunopathologia (Madrid) [*A publication*] ..... Allergol Immunopathol (Madr)
Allergy Foundation of America [*Later, A & AFA*] ..... AFA
Allergy Relief Medicine [*Trademark*] ..... ARM
Allerton Public Library, Allerton, IA [*Library symbol*] ..... IaAll
Alles Erdreich Ist Oesterreich Unterthan [*Variation of 15th-century inscription*] ..... AEIOU
Alley ..... ALL
Alley ..... ALY
Alley Music [*A publication*] ..... Alley Mus
Allgemeine Berg- und Huettenmaennische Zeitung [*A publication*] ..... Allgem Berg- u Huettenm Ztg
Allgemeine Deutsche Naturhistorische Zeitung [*A publication*] ..... Allg Deutsche Naturh Ztg
Allgemeine Elektrizitaets-Gesellschaft [*West Germany*] ..... AEG
Allgemeine Fischerei-Zeitung [*A publication*] ..... Allg Fisch-Ztg
Allgemeine Forst- und Holzwirtschafte Zeitung [*A publication*] ..... Allg Forst Holzwirtsch Zeit
Allgemeine Forst- und Jagdzeitung [*A publication*] ..... Allg Forst Jagdztg
Allgemeine Forst- und Jagdzeitung [*A publication*] ..... Allg Forst- u Jagdztg
Allgemeine Forstzeitschrift [*A publication*] ..... Allg Forstzeitschr
Allgemeine Forstzeitung [*A publication*] ..... Allg Forstztg
Allgemeine Musikalische Zeitung [*A publication*] ..... AMZ
Allgemeine Nahrungs und Genussmittel Ausstellung [*General Food and Delicacies Fair*] [*West Germany*] ..... ANUGA
Allgemeine Papier-Rundschau [*A publication*] ..... Allg Papier-Rundschau
Allgemeine und Praktische Chemie [*A publication*] ..... Allg Prakt Chem
Allgemeine Wiener Medizinische Zeitung [*A publication*] ..... Allg Wien Med Ztg
Allgemeine Zeitschrift fuer Psychiatrie und Psychisch-Gerichtliche Medicin [*A publication*] ..... Allg Ztschr Psychiat
Allgemeiner Deutscher Automobil Club [*Pre-World War II*] [*Germany*] ..... ADAC
Allgemeiner Deutscher Nachrichtendienst [*General German Press Agency*] [*East Germany*] ..... ADN
Allgemeines Bucher-Lexikon [*A publication*] ..... ABl
Allgemeines Krankenhaus [*Austria*] [*Largest hospital in Europe*] ..... AKH
Allgemeines Literaturblatt [*A publication*] ..... ALB
Allgemeines Statistisches Archiv [*A publication*] ..... Allgemein Statist Arch
Alliance [*Nebraska*] [*Airport symbol*] ..... AIA
Alliance Against Sexual Coercion ..... AASC
Alliance of American Insurers [*Formerly, AMIA*] ..... AAI
Alliance for Arts Education ..... AAE
Alliance of Associations for the Advancement of Education ..... AAAE
Alliance de Baboma-Bateke du Kwamouth [*Alliance of Baboma-Bateke People of Kwamouth*] ..... ABAKWA
Alliance des Bakongo [*Alliance of the Bakongo People*] ..... ABAKO
Alliance Balkanique [*Balkan Alliance*] ..... AB
Alliance des Bateke [*Alliance of Bateke*] ..... ABATE
Alliance des Bayanzi [*Alliance of Bayanzis*] ..... ABAZI
Alliance Biblique Universelle ..... ABU
Alliance for Cannabis Therapeutics ..... ACT
Alliance for Coal and Competitive Transportation ..... ACCT
Alliance College, Cambridge Springs, PA [*Library symbol*] ..... PCamA
Alliance Cooperative Internationale [*International Cooperative Alliance*] ..... ACI
Alliance Defense Industry and Technology ..... ADIT
Alliance for Democracy in Korea ..... ADK
Alliance to End Repression ..... AER
Alliance for Engineering in Medicine and Biology ..... AEMB
Alliance for Environmental Education ..... AEE
Alliance Europeenne des Agences de Presse ..... AEAP
Alliance Francaise de New York [*Later, FIAF*] ..... AFNY
Alliance of Gay Artists ..... AGA
Alliance Graphique Internationale [*International Graphical Alliance*] ..... AGI
Alliance of Independent Telephone Unions [*Later, TIU*] ..... AITU
Alliance of Independent Telephone Unions [*Later, TIU*] ..... ATU
Alliance Industrielle [*A publication*] ..... Alliance Ind
Alliance of Information and Referral Systems ..... AIRS
Alliance Internationale de la Distribution par Fil [*International Alliance for Distribution by Wire*] ..... AID
Alliance Internationale des Femmes [*International Alliance of Women*] [*See also IAW*] ..... AIF
Alliance Internationale pour le Merite ..... AIM
Alliance Internationale de Tourisme [*International Touring Alliance*] ..... AIT
Alliance Israelite Universelle [*Universal Israelite Alliance*] ..... AIU
Alliance de Jeunesse Angolaise pour la Liberte [*Alliance of Angolan Youth for Freedom*] ..... AJEUNAL
Alliance Journal [*A publication*] ..... AJ
Alliance for Justice ..... AJ
Alliance for Labor Action [*Defunct*] ..... ALA
Alliance of Latin Artistes Society ..... ALAS
Alliance of Metalworking Industries ..... AMI
Alliance of Natives of Zombo [*Angola*] ..... ALIAZO
Alliance, NE [*Location identifier*] [*FAA*] ..... AOQ
Alliance, NE [*Radio station call letters*] ..... KCOW
Alliance, NE [*Radio station call letters*] ..... KPNY
Alliance, NE [*Television station call letters*] ..... KTNE-TV
Alliance for Neighborhood Government [*Later, NAN*] ..... ANG

Alliance of NGOs on Crime Prevention and Criminal Justice ANCPCJ
Alliance, OH [*Radio station call letters*] WDJQ
Alliance, OH [*Radio station call letters*] WFAH
Alliance, OH [*Television station call letters*] WNEO-TV
Alliance, OH [*Radio station call letters*] WRMU
Alliance of Pan American Round Tables APART
Alliance des Patriotes Independents du Congo [*Alliance of Independent Patriots of the Congo*] APIC
Alliance for Perinatal Research and Services APRS
Alliance for Philippine Concerns APC
Alliance of Poles of America APA
Alliance for Progress [*OAS*] AP
Alliance des Proletaires Independents du Congo [*Alliance of Independent Proletarians of the Congo*] APIC
Alliance of Rail Citizens for Progress [*Formerly, ARC*] ARCP
Alliance for Rail Commuter Progress [*Later, ARCP*] ARC
Alliance Record [*A publication*] Alliance Recd
Alliance Reformee Mondiale [*World Alliance of Reformed Churches*] [*See also WARC*] ARM
Alliance of Resident Theatres/New York [*Formerly, OOBA*] ART/NY
Alliance for Responsible CFC [*Chlorofluorocarbon*] **Policy** ARCFCP
Alliance to Save Energy ASE
Alliance for Social Security Disability Recipients ASSDR
Alliance of Television Film Producers [*Later, Association of Motion Picture and Television Producers*] ATFP
Alliance Tire & Rubber Co. Ltd. [*American Stock Exchange symbol*] ATR
Alliance for Traffic Safety ATS
Alliance of Transylvanian Saxons ATS
Alliance for Undesirable but Necessary Tasks [*From book title, "The Woman from AUNT"*] AUNT
Alliance Universelle des Ouvriers Diamantaires [*Universal Alliance of Diamond Workers*] [*See also UADW*] AUOD
Alliance Universelle des Unions Chretiennes de Jeunes Gens [*World Alliance of Young Men's Christian Associations*] UCJG
Alliance for Volunteerism [*Defunct*] AFV
Alliance Witness [*A publication*] AW
Alliance of Women in Architecture AWA
Alliance of Women for Equality AWE
Allianz Berichte fuer Betriebstechnik und Schadenverhuetung [*A publication*] Allianz Ber Betriebstech Schadenverhuetung
Allied ALLD
Allied Administrative Publication AAP
Allied Aerial Photographic Interpretation Unit [*Obsolete*] AAPIU
Allied African Economic Affairs Committee [*World War II*] AAEA
Allied Agencies Center, Peoria, IL [*Library symbol*] IPA
Allied Air Forces AAF
Allied Air Forces, Baltic Approaches [*NATO*] AIRBALTAP
Allied Air Forces, Central Europe [*Later, AIRCENT*] [*NATO*] AAFCE
Allied Air Forces, Central Europe [*Formerly, AAFCE*] [*NATO*] AIRCENT
Allied Air Forces in Italy [*World War II*] AAFI
Allied Air Forces, North Norway [*NATO*] AIRNON
Allied Air Forces, Northern Europe [*Later, AIRNORTH*] [*NATO*] AAFNE
Allied Air Forces, Northern Europe [*Formerly, AAFNE*] [*NATO*] AIRNORTH
Allied Air Forces, South Norway [*NATO*] AIRSONOR
Allied Air Forces, Southern Europe [*Later, AIRSOUTH*] [*NATO*] AAFSE
Allied Air Forces, Southern Europe [*Formerly, AAFSE*] [*NATO*] AIRSOUTH
Allied Air Headquarters [*Obsolete*] AAHQ
Allied Air Intelligence Center AAIC
Allied Air Support Command [*Mediterranean*] AASC
Allied Armies in Italy [*Obsolete*] AAI
Allied Army Procedures AAP
Allied Army Publications AAP
Allied Artists of America AAA
Allied Artists Industries, Inc. [*American Stock Exchange symbol*] [*Delisted*] AAX
Allied Bancshares [*NASDAQ symbol*] ALBN
Allied Board of Trade ABT
Allied Camouflage and Concealment Publication [*NATO*] ACAMP
Allied Capital [*NASDAQ symbol*] ALLC
Allied Captured Intelligence Center [*US and Britain*] ACIC
Allied Central Air Bureau [*World War II*] ACAB
Allied Central Interpretation Unit [*World War II*] ACIU
Allied Central Mediterranean Force [*Later, AAI*] [*World War II*] ACMF
Allied Chemical Corporation [*Later, Allied Corp.*] ACC
Allied Chemical Corp. [*Later, ALD*] [*NYSE symbol*] ACD
Allied Chemical Corp., Fibers Division, Technical Center Library, Petersburg, VA [*Library symbol*] ViPetA
Allied Chemical Corp., Library, Solvay, NY [*OCLC symbol*] ZUB
Allied Chemical Technology [*Trademark*] ACT
Allied Chief Commissioner [*World War II*] ACC
Allied Chiefs of Staff [*World War II*] ACS
Allied Civil Affairs Office [*World War II*] ACAO
Allied Civil Defense [*World War II*] ACD
Allied Command Atlantic [*NATO*] ACLANT
Allied Command Atlantic Frequency Allocation Panel [*Obsolete*] [*NATO*] LANTFAP
Allied Command Baltic Approaches [*NATO*] COMBALTAP
Allied Command Channel [*NATO*] ACCHAN
Allied Command Channel Intelligence Plan [*NATO*] CHIP
Allied Command Europe [*NATO*] ACE
Allied Command Europe ACEUR
Allied Command Europe Communications Network [*NATO*] ACENET
Allied Command Europe Report ACEREP
Allied Command Southeast Asia [*World War II*] ACSEA
Allied Commander-in-Chief [*World War II*] ACC
Allied Commission [*World War II*] AC
Allied Commission, Agriculture Subcommission [*World War II*] ACAGR
Allied Commission, Austria [*World War II*] ACA
Allied Commission, Austria, British Element [*World War II*] ACABRIT
Allied Commission, Commerce Subcommission, Exports [*World War II*] ACCCE
Allied Commission, Economic Section [*World War II*] ACECO
Allied Commission, Industry Subcommission [*World War II*] ACIDY
Allied Commission, Military Government Subcommission [*World War II*] ACMG
Allied Commission, Mining Subcommission [*World War II*] ACMNG
Allied Commission on Reparations ACR
Allied Commission, Requisitions Subcommittee [*World War II*] ACREQ
Allied Communications Publications [*Military*] ACP
Allied Communications Security Agency [*NATO*] ACSA
Allied Container Advisory Committee [*Obsolete*] ACAC
Allied Control Authority [*Allied German Occupation Forces*] ACA
Allied Control Center [*NATO*] ACC
Allied Control Commission [*World War II*] ACC
Allied Control Commission for Austria [*World War II*] AACA
Allied Control Commission for Bulgaria [*World War II*] AACB
Allied Control Commission for Hungary [*World War II*] AACH
Allied Control Commission for Italy [*World War II*] AACI
Allied Control Commission for Rumania [*World War II*] AACR
Allied Control Council [*World War II*] ACC
Allied Control Council for Germany [*World War II*] AACG
Allied Control Council for Japan [*World War II*] AACJ
Allied Corp. [*Initialism is trademark*] A-C
Allied Corp. [*Formerly, ACO*] [*NYSE symbol*] ALD
Allied Corp., Hopewell, VA [*Library symbol*] ViHopA
Allied Corp., Solvay Process Division, Syracuse, NY [*Library symbol*] NSyA
Allied Corp., Specialty Chemicals Division, Buffalo, NY [*Library symbol*] NBuA
Allied Data Publications ADatP
Allied Data System Interoperability Agency [*NATO*] ADSIA
Allied Defense Publications ADP
Allied Demands, Supplies [*World War II*] AD(S)
Allied Distribution [*An association*] AD
Allied Electrical Publications AEIP
Allied Electronics Publications AEtP
Allied Engineering Publications AEP
Allied Equipment Publications AEP
Allied Equipment Publications AEqP
Allied Exercise Publications AXP
Allied Expeditionary Air Force AEAF
Allied Expeditionary Force AEF
Allied Explosive Ordnance Disposal Publications AEoP
Allied Finance Adjusters Conference AFAC
Allied Financial Agency [*World War II*] AFA
Allied Fiscal Administration [*World War II*] AFA
Allied Forces ALFOR
Allied Forces Baltic Approaches [*NATO*] AFBALTAP
Allied Forces Baltic Approaches [*NATO*] BALTAP
Allied Forces Central Europe [*NATO*] AFCE
Allied Forces Central Europe [*NATO*] AFCENT
Allied Forces Headquarters [*Might refer to any theater of war*] [*World War II*] AFHQ
Allied Forces Headquarters (Counter Intelligence Corps) [*World War II*] AFHQ (CIC)
Allied Forces Headquarters Petroleum Section [*World War II*] AFHQPS
Allied Forces Local Resources Section [*World War II*] AFLRS
Allied Forces Mediterranean [*NATO*] AFMED
Allied Forces North Norway AFNON
Allied Forces Northern Europe [*NATO*] AFNE
Allied Forces Northern Europe [*NATO*] AFNORTH
Allied Forces South Norway AFSONOR
Allied Forces Southern Europe [*NATO*] AFSE
Allied Forces Southern Europe [*NATO*] AFSOUTH
Allied Freighter Guard AFG
Allied Geographic Section [*Southwest Pacific*] [*Obsolete*] AGS
Allied Hat Manufacturers Association AHMA
Allied Headquarters AHQ
Allied Health and Behavioral Sciences [*A publication*] Allied Health & Behav Sci
Allied Health Program [*Association of Independent Colleges and Schools specialization code*] AH
Allied High Commission [*Germany*] AHC
Allied Hydrographic Publication AHP
Allied Independent Unions [*Lebanon*] AIU
Allied Intelligence Committee [*London*] AIC
Allied Intelligence Publications AIP
Allied Interrogating Organization AIO
Allied Invasion Forces [*World War II*] AIF
Allied Irish Investment Bank AIIB

Allied Kid Co. [*NYSE symbol*] [*Delisted*]......................AKD
Allied Kommandatura......................AK
Allied Land Forces......................ALF
Allied Land Forces Central Europe [*NATO*]......................ALFCE
Allied Land Forces Central Europe [*NATO*]......................LANDCENT
Allied Land Forces Denmark [*NATO*]......................LANDENMARK
Allied Land Forces North Norway [*NATO*]......................LANDNON
Allied Land Forces Northern Europe [*NATO*]......................LANDNORTH
Allied Land Forces Norway [*NATO*]......................LANDNORWAY
Allied Land Forces Schleswig-Holstein [*NATO*]......................ALFSH
Allied Land Forces Schleswig-Holstein and Jutland [*NATO*]........LANDJUT
Allied Land Forces South Norway [*NATO*]......................LANDSONOR
Allied Land Forces Southeast Asia [*NATO*]......................ALFSEA
Allied Land Forces Southeastern Europe [*NATO*]......................ALFSEE
Allied Land Forces Southeastern Europe [*NATO*]..........LANDSOUTHEAST
Allied Land Forces Southern Europe [*NATO*]......................ALFSE
Allied Land Forces Southern Europe [*NATO*]......................LANDSOUTH
Allied Land Forces Zealand [*NATO*]......................LANDZEALAND
Allied Land Headquarters [*World War II*]......................LHQ
Allied Liaison Office [*Military*]......................ALO
Allied Liaison and Protocol [*Military*]......................ALP
Allied Linens and Domestics Association [*Defunct*]......................ALDA
Allied Logistics Publication [*Military*]......................ALP
Allied Longline Agency [*NATO*]......................ALLA
Allied Longline Agency Annual Conference [*NATO*]......................AAC
Allied Maintenance Corp. [*NYSE symbol*] [*Delisted*]......................ALM
Allied Maritime Air Commander-in-Chief, Channel ..........CINCMAIRCHAN
Allied Medical Publications......................AMed P
Allied Mediterranean Commission [*World War II*]......................AMC
Allied Meteorological Office......................AMO
Allied Military Administration Civil Affairs Branch [*World War II*]......................
AMACAB
Allied Military Communications-Electronics Committee ....AMCEC
Allied Military Financial Agency [*World War II*]......................AMFA
Allied Military Government [*of occupied territory*] [*Formerly,*
AMGOT] [*Post-World War II*]......................AMG
Allied Military Government of Occupied Territory [*Later, AMG*]
[*Post-World War II*]......................AMGOT
Allied Military Liaison [*Balkans*] [*World War II*]......................AML
Allied Military Liaison, Greece [*World War II*]......................AMLG
Allied Military Mission [*World War II*]......................AMM
Allied Military Publication [*NATO*]......................AMP
Allied Military Security Publication ....AMSP
Allied Military Staff Conference [*Quebec, Yalta, etc.*] [*World War II*]....AMSC
Allied Mills, Inc. [*NYSE symbol*] [*Delisted*]......................ADS
Allied Minimum Imports Program [*World War II*]......................AMIP
Allied Mining and Mine Countermeasures Publications ....AMP
Allied Mobile Force [*NATO*]......................AMF
Allied Mobile Force (Air) [*NATO*]......................AMF(A)
Allied Mobile Force (Land) [*NATO*]......................AMF(L)
Allied Naval Commander-in-Chief [*World War II*]......................ANC-in-C
Allied Naval Commander Expeditionary Forces......................ANCXF
Allied Naval Communications Agency [*NATO*]......................ANCA
Allied Naval Forces......................ANF
Allied Naval Forces, Baltic Approaches [*NATO*]......................NAVBALTAP
Allied Naval Forces, Central Europe......................NAVCENT
Allied Naval Forces, North Norway [*NATO*]......................NAVNON
Allied Naval Forces, Northern Europe......................NAVNORTH
Allied Naval Forces, Scandinavian Approaches [*NATO*]......................NAVSCAP
Allied Naval Forces, Southern Europe......................NAVSOUTH
Allied Naval Maneuvering Instructions [*NATO*]......................ANMI
Allied Navigation Publications......................ANP
Allied/Neutral [*Military*]......................A/N
Allied Ordnance Publications......................AOP
Allied Papers......................A/P
Allied Petroleum Service Organization ....APSO
Allied Pilots Association......................APA
Allied Political and Military Commission [*World War II*]......................APMC
Allied Press Information Center [*NATO*]......................APIC
Allied Procedures Publications......................APP
Allied Products Corp. [*NYSE symbol*]......................ADP
Allied Publication......................AP
Allied Publications Board [*World War II*]......................APB
Allied Quality Assurance Provision [*NATO*]......................AQAP
Allied Quality Assurance Publication [*NATO*]......................AQAP
Allied Radio Frequency Agency [*Formerly, ERFA*] [*NATO*]......................ARFA
Allied Railway Supply Association [*Later, RSA*]......................ARSA
Allied Research Associates, Inc.......................ARA
Allied Research Institute [*Later, Aluminum Recycling Association*]..........ARI
Allied Secretariat [*Allied German Occupation Forces*]......................ASEC
Allied Security, Inc. [*NASDAQ symbol*]......................ASCY
Allied Social Science Associations......................ASSA
Allied Staff, Berlin [*Post-World War II*]......................ASB
Allied Staff Chiefs [*World War II*]......................ASC
Allied Standing Procedure [*NATO*]......................ASP
Allied States Association of Motion Picture Exhibitors [*Later,*
NATO]......................ASAMPE
Allied Stores Corp. [*NYSE symbol*]......................ALS
Allied Supply Executive [*World War II*]......................ASE
Allied Supply Executive, China [*World War II*]......................ASE(C)
Allied Supply Executive, Chinese Oil Supplies [*World War II*] ....ASE(OC)

Allied Supply Executive, Middle East [*World War II*]......................ASE(ME)
Allied Supply Executive, Other Allies [*World War II*]......................ASE(OA)
Allied Supply Executive, Persian Gulf [*World War II*]......................ASE(PG)
Allied Supply Executive, Russia and Persian Gulf [*World War II*]........ASE(R)
Allied Supply Executive, Transportation [*World War II*] ....ASE(T)
Allied Supreme Council [*World War II*]......................ASC
Allied Tactical Air Force [*NATO*]......................ATAF
Allied Tactical Air Force, Northern Norway [*NATO*]......................TAFNORNOR
Allied Tactical Air Force, South Norway [*NATO*]......................TAFSONOR
Allied Tactical Communications Agency [*NATO*]......................ATCA
Allied Tactical Data Systems Interoperability Agency [*NATO*]........ATADSIA
Allied Tactical Publication......................ATP
Allied Tanker Coordinating Committee in London......................ATCC (L)
Allied Tanker Coordinating Committee in Washington ....ATCC (W)
Allied Task Force Commander, North Norway [*NATO*]......................ATFCNN
Allied Task Force, North Norway [*NATO*]......................TASKFORNON
Allied Technical Publication [*Navy*]......................ATP
Allied Telecommunications Committee [*Allied Control*
Commission for Italy]......................ATC
Allied Thermal Corp. [*American Stock Exchange symbol*] [*Delisted*]..........AT
Allied Trades of the Baking Industry ....ATBI
Allied Training Publications......................ATrP
Allied Translator and Interpreter Service......................ATIS
Allied Travel Office......................ATO
Allied Underwear Association......................AUA
Allied Weather Publications......................AWP
Allied Workers International Union (Independent)......................AWIU(I)
Allied Works Council [*World War II*]......................AWC
Allied Youth......................AY
Allis-Chalmers Corp.......................AC
Allis-Chalmers Corp. [*NYSE symbol*] [*Wall Street slang name: "Alice"*]....AH
Allis-Chalmers Critical Experimental Facility......................AC-CEF
Allis-Chalmers Engineering Review [*A publication*]......................
Allis-Chalmers Eng Rev
Allmaenna Svenska Laekartidningen [*A publication*] ....
Allm Sven Laekartidn
Allmaenna Svenska Utsaedesaktiebolaget Svaloef [*A*
publication]......................Allmaenna Svenska Utsaedesaktiebol Svaloef
Allmanna Svenska Electriska Aktiebolaget [*Sweden*]......................ASEA
Allnet Commercial Services [*NASDAQ symbol*]......................ALNT
Allocate [*or Allocation*]......................ALLOC
Allocate [*or Allocation*]......................ALOC
Allocated Configuration Identification [*NASA*]......................ACI
Allocated Configuration Item [*Navy*]......................ACI
Allocated Reserve......................AR
Allocations for Budgetary Control ....ABC
Allocator......................A
Allogeneic Effect Factor [*Immunochemistry*]......................AEF
Allopurinol Phosphate [*Biochemistry*]......................APP
Allopurinol Phosphate Ribonucleotide [*Biochemistry*]......................APPR
Allotment......................ALOT
Allotment......................ALOTM
Allotment Division [*Navy*]......................NAVALOT
Allotment Serial Number......................ASN
Allowable Cabin Load [*in an aircraft*] ....ACL
Allowable Container Load......................ACL
Allowable Daily Intake [*Toxicology*]......................ADI
Allowable Deficiency......................AD
Allowable [*Takeoff*] Gross Weight [*for an aircraft*]......................AGW
Allowable Ship Turn......................AST
Allowable Steering Error......................ASE
Allowable Takeoff Gross [*Weight*] [*for an aircraft*]......................ATOG
Allowance......................ALLOW
Allowance......................ALW
Allowance Appendix Package......................AAPG
Allowance Appendix Page......................AAP
Allowance Change Request......................ACR
Allowance Equipage List......................AEL
Allowance for Funds Used during Construction ....AFUDC
Allowance List......................AL
Allowance Parts List......................APL
Allowance Parts List/Component Identification Number ....APL/CID
Allowance Parts List Master Index......................APLMI
Allowance Prescribed in Joint Travel Regulations [*Military*]................AJTR
Allowance for Project Adjustment......................APA
Allowance Race [*Horse racing*]......................ALW
Allowance Source Code [*Military*]......................ASC
Alloway Air [*Oak Harbor, WA*] [*FAA designator*]......................AAY
Allowed......................ALLD
Allowed Failure Effect......................AFE
Allowed-Off Aircraft Time......................AOAT
Alloxazine Adenine Dinucleotide [*Biochemistry*] ....AAD
Alloxazine Mononucleotide [*Pharmacology*]......................AMN
Alloy......................ALY
Alloy Casting Institute [*Later, SFSA*]......................ACI
Alloy-Coated Aluminum......................ALCAL
Alloy Data Center [*National Bureau of Standards*]......................ADC
Alloy Digest [*A publication*]......................Alloy Dig
Alloy Junction......................AJ
Alloy-Steel Protective Plating......................ASPP
Alloyed Zinc Sheet......................AZS

Allport-Vernon-Lindzey [*Study of values*] ... AVL
Allright Auto Parks, Inc. [*NYSE symbol*] [*Delisted*] ... ALR
All's Well That Ends Well [*Shakespearean work*] ... AWW
Allstates-Programming & Systems, Incorporated ... APSI
ALLTEL Corp. [*Formerly, Allied Telephone Co.*] [*NYSE symbol*] ... AT
Alltransport International Group ... AIG
Alluminio e Nuova Metallurgia [*A publication*] ... Allum Nuova Met
Allusion ... ALLUS
Ally & Gargano, Incorporated [*NASDAQ symbol*] ... AGAI
Allyl Chloride [*Organic chemistry*] ... AC
Allylisopropylacetamide [*Biochemistry*] ... AIA
Alma-Ata [*USSR*] [*Airport symbol*] ... ALA
Alma-Ata [*USSR*] [*Geomagnetic observatory code*] ... AAA
Alma-Ata [*USSR*] [*Seismograph station code, US Geological Survey*] ... AAA
Alma-Atinskii Gosudarstvennyi Pedagogiceskii Institut Imeni Abaja. Ucenye Zapiski [*A publication*] ... Alma-Atin Gos Ped Inst Ucen Zap
Alma College, Alma, MI [*OCLC symbol*] ... EZA
Alma College, Alma, MI [*Library symbol*] ... MiAC
Alma, GA [*Radio station call letters*] ... WULF
[*The*] **Alma & Jonquieres Railway Co.** [*AAR code*] ... AJ
Alma Mater [*A publication*] ... AM
Alma, MI [*Radio station call letters*] ... WFYC
Alma, MI [*Radio station call letters*] ... WFYC-FM
Alma, PQ [*Radio station call letters*] ... CFGT
Alma Public Library, Alma, MI [*Library symbol*] ... MiA
Alma Urbis [*Beloved City*] [*Rome*] ... AU
Alma White College [*New Jersey*] ... AWC
Alma White College, Zarephath, NJ [*Library symbol*] ... NjZaA
Almaden [*California*] [*Seismograph station code, US Geological Survey*] ... AMC
Almaden Air Charter [*San Jose, CA*] [*FAA designator*] ... ALM
Almanacco Letterario Bompiani [*A publication*] ... ALB
Almanach des Lettres [*A publication*] ... AIL
Almanach der Oesterreichischen Akademie der Wissenschaften [*A publication*] ... AlmOAW
Almanak Agricola Brasileiro [*A publication*] ... Almanak Agric Brasil
Almanor Railroad Co. [*AAR code*] ... AL
Almenara [*Brazil*] [*Airport symbol*] [*Obsolete*] ... AMJ
Almeria [*Spain*] [*Geomagnetic observatory code*] ... ALM
Almeria [*Spain*] [*Airport symbol*] ... LEI
Almeria [*Spain*] [*Seismograph station code, US Geological Survey*] ... ALM
Almirall [*Spain*] [*Research code symbol*] ... LAS
Almond Leaf Scorch [*Plant pathology*] ... ALS
Almost-Developed Country ... ADC
Almost Everywhere ... AE
Almost Uncirculated [*Condition of coins*] [*Numismatics*] ... AU
Almy Stores, Inc. [*American Stock Exchange symbol*] ... ALY
Alo-Scherer Healthcare [*NASDAQ symbol*] ... ALOE
Aloft ... ALF
Aloha Airlines [*American Stock Exchange symbol*] ... ALO
Aloha Airlines [*ICAO designator*] ... TS
Aloha Airlines [*Air carrier designation symbol*] ... TSA
Aloin, Strychnine, and Belladonna [*Pills*] ... AS & B
Aloin, Strychnine, Belladonna, and Ipecac [*Pills*] ... ASB & I
Alon Hahevra Hanumismatit le'Israel [*A publication*] ... AHHI
Along ... ALG
Alongside ... AS
Alor [*Indonesia*] [*Airport symbol*] ... ARD
Alor Setar [*Malaysia*] [*Airport symbol*] ... AOR
Alotau [*Papua New Guinea*] [*Airport symbol*] ... GUR
Alouette Topside Sounder Synoptic [*NASA*] ... ALOSYN
Alpena [*Michigan*] [*Airport symbol*] ... APN
Alpena Community College [*Michigan*] ... ACC
Alpena Community College, Alpena, MI [*Library symbol*] ... MiAlpC
Alpena County Library, Alpena, MI [*Library symbol*] ... MiAlp
Alpena, MI [*Location identifier*] [*FAA*] ... CLO
Alpena, MI [*Radio station call letters*] ... WATZ
Alpena, MI [*Radio station call letters*] ... WATZ-FM
Alpena, MI [*Radio station call letters*] ... WCML-FM
Alpena, MI [*Television station call letters*] ... WCML-TV
Alpena, MI [*Radio station call letters*] ... WHSB
[*Herb*] **Alpert and** [*Jerry*] **Moss** [*Initialism, from surnames of founders, is used as name of record company*] ... A & M
Alpes Maritimes ... AM
Alpha ... A
Alpha [*Australia*] [*Airport symbol*] ... ABH
Alpha-1-Antitrypsin [*Protease inhibitor*] [*Serology*] ... A_1AT
Alpha Airlines, Inc. [*Jamaica, NY*] [*FAA designator*] ... NGS
Alpha-(Alkyl)olefinsulfonate [*Surfactant*] [*Organic chemistry*] ... AOS
Alpha-Aminoisobutyric Acid [*Organic chemistry*] ... AIBA
Alpha-Antitrypsin [*Biochemistry*] ... AAT
Alpha Block Control Number [*Data processing*] ... ABC
Alpha Control Guidance ... ACG
Alpha Counter Tube ... ACT
Alpha Cutoff ... ACO
Alpha Delta [*Society*] ... AD
Alpha Delta Phi [*Fraternity*] ... ADP
Alpha Delta Pi [*Sorority*] ... ADP
Alpha Disintegration Energy ... ADE
Alpha-Fetoprotein [*Clinical chemistry*] ... AFP
Alpha Hand and Shoe Monitor [*Radiation detection*] ... AHSM
Alpha-Hydroxybutyric Dehydrogenase [*An enzyme*] ... AHBD
Alpha Industries, Inc. [*American Stock Exchange symbol*] ... AHA
Alpha Kappa Kappa [*Fraternity*] ... AKK
Alpha Kappa Psi [*Fraternity*] ... AKP
Alpha Mach Indicator ... AMI
Alpha Meter ... AM
Alpha-Methyl-m-tyrosine [*Pharmacology*] ... MMT
Alpha-Methyl-p-tyrosine [*Also, MPT*] [*Pharmacology*] ... AMPT
Alpha-Methyl-p-tyrosine [*Also, AMPT*] [*Pharmacology*] ... MPT
Alpha-Methyldopa [*Also, MD*] [*Antihypertensive compound*] ... AMD
Alpha-Methylphenethylamine [*CNS stimulant*] ... AMPHETAMINE
Alpha Microsystems [*NASDAQ symbol*] ... ALMI
Alpha-Naphthoflavone [*Biochemistry*] ... ANF
Alpha-Naphthyl Butyrate Esterase [*An enzyme*] ... ANBE
Alpha-Naphthylisothiocyanate [*Organic chemistry*] ... ANIT
Alpha-Naphthylthiourea [*Organic chemistry*] ... ANTU
Alpha Omega Computer System ... AOCS
Alpha Park Public Library District, Pekin, IL [*OCLC symbol*] ... ISF
Alpha Particle Spectrometer ... AP
Alpha Petrol Explorations [*NASDAQ symbol*] ... APET
Alpha Portland Cement Co. [*Later, APC*] [*NYSE symbol*] ... AHP
Alpha Portland Industries [*NYSE symbol*] ... APC
Alpha Ray Spectrometer ... ARS
Alpha Ray Spectrometric Equipment ... ARSE
ALPHA [*AMC Logistics Program - Hardcore Automated*] **Remote Terminal Interactive System** ... ARTIS
Alpha Repertory Television Service [*Cable-television service*] ... ARTS
Alpha Research and Development ... ARAD
Alpha Tau Alpha ... ATA
Alpha Tau Omega [*Fraternity*] ... ATO
Alpha Temperature Probe Assembly ... ATPA
Alpha Waste Storage Facility [*Nuclear energy*] ... AWSF
Alpha Xi Delta [*Sorority*] ... AXD
Alpha Zeta ... AZ
Alpha Zeta Omega [*Fraternity*] ... AZO
Alphabetic ... A
Alphabetic Subject Index [*A publication*] ... ASI
Alphabetical ... ALPHA
Alphabetical Index of Names ... AION
Alphanumeric ... AN
Alphanumeric Display ... AND
Alphanumeric Display Equipment ... ADE
Alphanumeric Display Equipment ... ANDE
Alphanumeric Keyboard ... ANK
Alphanumeric Keyboard ... ANKB
Alphanumeric Language for Music Analysis ... ALMA
Alphanumeric Output ... ANO
Alphanumeric Photocomposer System ... APS
Alphanumeric System for Classification of Recordings ... ANSCR
Alpharetta, GA [*Radio station call letters*] ... WMOE
Alphonsus College, Woodcliff Lake, NJ [*Library symbol*] ... NjWolA
Alpine Air Charter, Inc. [*Englewood, CO*] [*FAA designator*] ... ALP
Alpine Club [*British*] ... AC
Alpine Club, Banff, AB, Canada [*Library symbol*] ... CaABAC
Alpine Club of Canada ... ACC
Alpine Garden Society ... AGS
Alpine Geophysical [*NASDAQ symbol*] ... ALGAC
Alpine International Corp. [*NASDAQ symbol*] ... APIN
Alpine Journal [*A publication*] ... Alpine J
Alpine Luft-Transport AG [*ICAO designator*] ... NO
Alpine Luft-Transport Aktiengesellschaft [*Airline*] ... ALAG
Alpine Tourist Commission ... ATC
Alpine, TX [*Location identifier*] [*FAA*] ... BWR
Alpine, TX [*Radio station call letters*] ... KVLF
Alps Region [*MARC geographic area code*] [*Library of Congress*] ... ea-----
Already Had ... A/H
Alside, Inc. [*NYSE symbol*] [*Delisted*] ... ASD
Alsip-Merrionette Park Library District, Alsip, IL [*Library symbol*] ... IAlsA
Also Known As ... AKA
Alston Wilkes Society ... AWS
Alta [*Utah*] [*Seismograph station code, US Geological Survey*] [*Closed*] ... AAU
Alta [*Norway*] [*Airport symbol*] ... ALF
Alta Advertiser, Alta, IA [*Library symbol*] ... IaAltaA
Alta Energy Corp. [*NASDAQ symbol*] ... ALTE
Alta Frequenza [*A publication*] ... Alta Freq
Alta Frequenza. Supplemento [*A publication*] ... Alta Freq Suppl
Alta Public Library, Alta, IA [*Library symbol*] ... IaAlta
Altadena Library District, Altadena, CA [*OCLC symbol*] ... ALD
Altadena Library District, Altadena, CA [*Library symbol*] ... CAlt
Altair Airlines, Inc. [*Philadelphia, PA*] [*FAA designator*] ... AAR
Altair Corp. [*NASDAQ symbol*] ... ALTA
Altalanos Nyelveszeti Tanulmanyok [*A publication*] ... ANT
Altamil Corp. [*American Stock Exchange symbol*] [*Delisted*] ... ALW
Altamira [*Brazil*] [*Airport symbol*] ... ATM
Altamont Aviation, Inc. [*Livermore, CA*] [*FAA designator*] ... ALT
Altavista, VA [*Radio station call letters*] ... WKDE
Altavista, VA [*Radio station call letters*] ... WKDE-FM
Altay [*China*] [*Airport symbol*] ... AAT
Altdeutsche Textbibliothek [*A publication*] ... AdTb

Altdeutsche Textbibliothek [*A publication*] ATB
Alte Kaempfer [*Old Fighters*] [*German*] AK
Alte und Moderne Kunst. Oesterreichische Fachzeitschrift des Marktes fuer Antiquitaeten, Bilder, Kunstgegenstaende Alter, und Moderner Kunst [*A publication*] Alte Mod Kunst
Altec Corp. [*American Stock Exchange symbol*] [*Delisted*] ALE
Alten Sprachen [*A publication*] AS
Alter Course [*Navigation*] A/C
Alter Heading [*Navigation*] AH
Alter Ridge [*Washington*] [*Seismograph station code, US Geological Survey*] ALD
Alterable Read-Only Memory [*Data processing*] AROM
Alteration ALT
Alteration ALTERON
Alteration ALTR
Alteration ALTRN
Alteration Equivalent to a Repair AER
Alteration Identification ALTID
Alteration and Improvement Program [*Navy*] A & I
Alteration and Inspection A & I
Alteration Management System AMS
Alteration Request Number ARN
Altered ALTRD
Altered State of Consciousness ASC
Altered State of Consciousness Induction Device ASCID
Altering [*FBI standardized term*] ALT
Alterman Foods, Inc. [*American Stock Exchange symbol*] [*Delisted*] ALF
Alternate [*Approach and landing charts*] [*Aviation*] A
Alternate ALT
Alternate ALTER
Alternate ALTN
Alternate ALTR
Alternate Acquisition RADAR AAR
Alternate Airport ALTPT
Alternate Alerting Network [*Air Force*] ALTAN
Alternate Antiair Warfare Commander AAAWC
Alternate Binaural Loudness Balancing [*Audiometry*] ABLB
Alternate Captain [*Sports*] A
Alternate Care Plan [*Health Care Financing Administration*] ACP
Alternate Command [*or Commander*] [*Navy*] ALTCOM
Alternate Command Center [*Navy*] ACC
Alternate Command Center [*Navy*] ALTCOMCEN
Alternate Command and Control Center [*Air Force*] ACCC
Alternate Command Elements [*Navy*] ACE
Alternate Command Facility [*Navy*] ACF
Alternate Command Post [*Military*] ACP
Alternate Command Post [*Military*] ALCOP
Alternate Commander, Atlantic [*Navy*] ALTCOMLANT
Alternate Commander, Pacific [*Navy*] ALTCOMPAC
Alternate Communications Facility [*Military*] ACF
Alternate CPU [*Central Processing Unit*] **Recovery** [*Data processing*] ACR
Alternate-Day Treatment [*Medicine*] ADT
Alternate Days AD
Alternate Definition of Accident [*Insurance*] A/D
Alternate Detection and Control Unit ADCU
Alternate Device Support [*NASA*] ADS
Alternate Drop [*Electroanalysis*] AD
Alternate Emergency Action Center AEAC
Alternate Energy Institute AEI
Alternate Flight Plan AFP
Alternate Headquarters [*Military*] AH
Alternate Headquarters [*Military*] ALTHQ
Alternate Health Services AHS
Alternate Inspection Policy AIP
Alternate Interim Successor [*Military*] AIS
Alternate Joint Communications Center AJCC
Alternate Joint War Room [*Later, ANMCC*] AJWR
Alternate Landing Site [*NASA*] ALS
Alternate Launch Officer [*Air Force*] ALO
Alternate Launch Officer Console [*Air Force*] ALOC
Alternate Library [*Computer program*] [*NASA*] ALTLIB
Alternate Life Style ALS
Alternate Management Summary Report AMSR
Alternate Media Center AMC
Alternate Military Occupational Specialty AMOS
Alternate Mission Equipment AME
Alternate Molecular Orbital AMO
Alternate National Military Command Center [*Formerly, AJWR*] ANMCC
Alternate Net Control Officer [*Navy*] ANCO
Alternate Net Control Station ANCS
Alternate Path Retry [*Data processing*] APR
Alternate Record-Voice ARV
Alternate Source Council ASC
Alternate Source Development ASD
Alternate Squadron Commander [*Air Force*] ASC
Alternate Target Docking Adapter [*NASA*] ATDA
Alternate Target Point ATP
Alternate Voice Data AVD
Alternate Weapon AW
Alternating [*Polymer*] [*Organic chemistry*] alt
Alternating Continuous Waves [*Radio*] ACW
Alternating Current A
Alternating Current AC
Alternating Current Circuit ACC
Alternating Current Continuous Wave ACCW
Alternating Current/Direct Current A-C/D-C
Alternating Current Dump ACD
Alternating Current Generator ACG
Alternating Current Signal Generator AC-SG
Alternating Current Synchronous ACS
Alternating Current Synthesizer [*Exxon Corp.*] ACS
Alternating Current Test Volts VACT
Alternating Current Volts ACV
Alternating Current Volts VAC
Alternating Current Working Volts VACW
Alternating Direction Implicit [*Algorithm*] ADI
Alternating Exotropia [*Ophthalmology*] AXT
Alternating Field AF
Alternating Field Demagnetization AFD
Alternating Fixed and Flashing [*Lights*] ALTFFL
Alternating Fixed and Group Flashing [*Lights*] ALTFGPGL
Alternating Flashing [*Lights*] ALTFL
Alternating Flow AF
Alternating Gradient Focusing AGF
Alternating Gradient Synchrotron AGS
Alternating Group Occulting [*Lights*] ALTGPOCC
Alternating Guidance Section AGS
Alternating Light [*Navigation signal*] AI
Alternating Light [*Navigation signal*] Alt
Alternating Monocular Deprivation [*Optics*] AMD
Alternating Motion Rate AMR
Alternating Occulting [*Lights*] ALTOCC
Alternative Automotive Power Systems [*Environmental Protection Agency*] AAPS
Alternative Birth Crisis Coalition ABCC
Alternative Broadcasting [*An association*] AB
Alternative Center for International Arts ACIA
Alternative Complement Pathway [*Hematology*] ACP
Alternative Dispute Resolution ADR
Alternative Energy AE
Alternative Energy Resources Organization AERO
Alternative Environmental Futures [*An association*] AEF
Alternative Fertility [*Demography*] AF
Alternative Fertility Proportion [*Demography*] AFP
Alternative Information Network AIN
Alternative Intermediate Services for the Mentally Retarded AIS/MR
Alternative Launch-Point System ALPS
Alternative Lifestyle Checklist ALC
Alternative Marriage and Relationship Council of the United States AMRCUS
Alternative Minimum Tax AMT
Alternative Mortgage Instrument AMI
Alternative to the New York Times Committee ANYTC
Alternative Operational Concepts in Europe [*Military*] AOCEUR
Alternative Press Center APC
Alternative Press Centre, Toronto, ON, Canada [*Library symbol*] CaOTAP
Alternative Press Index [*A publication*] Alt Press Ind
Alternative Press Index [*A publication*] API
Alternative Press Syndicate [*Formerly, UPS*] APS
Alternative Release Procedures ARP
Alternative Resource Allocation Priorities [*Military*] ARAP
Alternative Sources of Energy [*A publication*] Alt Energy
Alternative Sources of Energy [*An association*] ASE
Alternative Technology AT
Alternative Vote AV
Alternatives [*A publication*] Alternatv
Alternatives to Abortion International AAI
Alternatives in Higher Education [*Program*] [*National Science Foundation*] AHE
Alternatives to Laboratory Animals [*A publication*] ATLA
Alternatives Non-Violentes [*A publication*] Alternat Non-Violentes
Alternator ALT
Alternator ALTNR
Alternator ALTNTR
Alternator Research Package ARP
Alternis Diebus [*Every Other Day*] [*Pharmacy*] ALT DIEB
Alternis Horis [*Every Other Hour*] [*Pharmacy*] ALTERN HOR
Alternis Horis [*Every Other Hour*] [*Pharmacy*] ALT HOR
Alternis Nocte [*Every Other Night*] [*Pharmacy*] ALT NOCT
Altertuemer von Pergamon [*A publication*] AvP
Altes Testament [*Old Testament*] [*German*] AT
Altesse [*Highness*] [*French*] ALT
Altesse Imperiale [*Imperial Highness*] [*French*] AI
Altesse Royale [*Royal Highness*] [*French*] AR
Altesses [*Highnesses*] [*French*] AA
Altex Oil Corporation [*American Stock Exchange symbol*] [*Delisted*] AOC
Altex Oil Corp. Wts [*NASDAQ symbol*] ALTXL
Althydusamband Islands [*Icelandic Federation of Labor*] ASI
Altimeter A
Altimeter ALT
Altimeter ALTM
Altimeter Check Location [*Aviation*] ACL

Altimeter Checkpoint [*Aviation*] .... ACP
Altimeter Indicator .... AI
Altimeter Setting [*Aviation*] .... ALSTG
Altimeter Setting Indicator [*Aviation*] .... ASI
Altimeter Setting Region [*Aviation*] .... ASRGN
Altimeter Station [*ITU designation*] .... ROA
Altimeter Subscale Setting to Obtain Elevation When on the
   Ground [*Aviation code*] .... QNH
Altimeter/Velocity Sensor Antenna .... A/VSA
Altintas [*Turkey*] [*Seismograph station code, US Geological Survey*] .... ALT
Altitude .... ALT
Altitude .... H
Altitude Command Indicator .... ACI
Altitude Control Electronics .... ACE
Altitude Control System .... ACS
Altitude Controller Assembly .... ACA
Altitude Conversion Kit .... ACK
Altitude Deviation .... AD
Altitude Difference [*Navigation*] .... A
Altitude Direction Indicator .... ADI
Altitude Encoder Unit .... AEU
Altitude Engine Control .... AEC
Altitude Engine Control Panel .... AECP
Altitude Error .... ALTE
Altitude Identification Military System .... AIMS
Altitude Indicator .... AI
Altitude Indoctrination .... AI
Altitude Layer Surveillance Terminal Area RADAR .... ALSTAR
Altitude Manned Penetrator .... AMP
Altitude Marking Range .... AMR
Altitude Measurement System .... AMS
Altitude Proximity Sensor .... APS
Altitude Radial [*Aviation*] .... ARAD
Altitude Rate Command .... ARC
Altitude Rate Command System .... ARCS
Altitude Reconnaissance Probe .... ARP
Altitude Referenced Radiometer .... ARR
Altitude Reservation [*Air Force*] .... ALTRV
Altitude Reservation Void for Aircraft Not Airborne by_____
   [*Aviation*] .... AVANA
Altitude Sensing System .... ASS
Altitude Sensor Bypass .... ASB
Altitude Sounding Projectile .... ASP
Altitude Transmitting Equipment [*FAA*] .... ATE
Altitude Variation Rate and Displacement .... AVRAD
Altitude Velocity Chart .... AVC
Altitude-Vertical Scale .... AVS
Altitude-Vertical Velocity Indicator .... AVVI
Altitude Warning System .... AWS
Alto .... A
Alto .... ALT
Alto Rio Senguerr [*Argentina*] [*Airport symbol*] .... ARR
Altocumulus [*Also, ACU, ALCU*] [*Meteorology*] .... AC
Altocumulus [*Also, AC, ALCU*] [*Meteorology*] .... ACU
Altocumulus [*Also, AC, ACU*] [*Meteorology*] .... ALCU
Altocumulus Castellanus [*Also, ACCAS*] [*Meteorology*] .... ACC
Altocumulus Castellanus [*Also, ACC*] [*Meteorology*] .... ACCAS
Altoff High School, Belleville, IL [*Library symbol*] .... IBelHS
Alton Community Unit 11, Alton, IL [*Library symbol*] .... IAICU
Alton Downs [*Australia*] [*Airport symbol*] [*Obsolete*] .... AWN
Alton, IL [*Location identifier*] [*FAA*] .... CVM
Alton, IL [*Radio station call letters*] .... WOKZ
Alton, IL [*Radio station call letters*] .... WZEN
Alton Memorial Hospital, Alton, IL [*Library symbol*] .... IAIH
Alton Mental Health Center, Development and Training Center,
   Staff Library, Alton, IL [*Library symbol*] .... IAIMH
Alton Public Library, Alton, IA [*Library symbol*] .... IaAltn
[*The*] Alton & Southern Railway Co. [*AAR code*] .... ALS
[*The*] Alton & Southern Railway Co. .... ALT & S
Altona, MB [*Radio station call letters*] .... CFAM
Altona Medical Centre, Altona, MB, Canada [*Library symbol*] .... CaMAMC
Altoona [*Pennsylvania*] [*Airport symbol*] .... AOO
Altoona Area Public Library, Altoona, PA [*OCLC symbol*] .... AOP
Altoona Area Public Library, Altoona, PA [*Library symbol*] .... PAlt
Altoona, PA [*Radio station call letters*] .... WFBG
Altoona, PA [*Radio station call letters*] .... WFBG-FM
Altoona, PA [*Television station call letters*] .... WOPC
Altoona, PA [*Radio station call letters*] .... WPRR
Altoona, PA [*Radio station call letters*] .... WRTA
Altoona, PA [*Television station call letters*] .... WTAJ-TV
Altoona, PA [*Radio station call letters*] .... WVAM
Altoona Public Library, Altoona, IA [*Library symbol*] .... IaAlto
Altos Computer Systems [*NASDAQ symbol*] .... ALTO
Altostratus [*Also, AS*] [*Meteorology*] .... ALST
Altostratus [*Also, ALST*] [*Meteorology*] .... AS
Altostratus and Altocumulus [*Meteorology*] .... ASAC
Altpreussische Forschungen [*A publication*] .... APrF
Altpreussische Monatschrift [*A publication*] .... APMS
Altrusa International .... AI
Alturas, CA [*Location identifier*] [*FAA*] .... ARU
Alturas, CA [*Radio station call letters*] .... KCNO

Altus [*Oklahoma*] [*Airport symbol*] .... AXS
Altus Flying Service [*Altus, OK*] [*FAA designator*] .... ATU
Altus Library, Altus, OK [*Library symbol*] .... OkAl
Altus, OK [*Location identifier*] [*FAA*] .... HVU
Altus, OK [*Radio station call letters*] .... KWHW
Altus, OK [*Radio station call letters*] .... KWHW-FM
Altus, OK [*Location identifier*] [*FAA*] .... LTS
Alula [*Somalia*] [*Airport symbol*] .... ALU
Alum, Blood, and Charcoal [*A method of deodorizing by addition
   of a compound of these*] [*Medicine*] .... ABC
Alum Precipitated [*Medicine*] .... AP
Alum Precipitated Toxoid [*Medicine*] .... APT
Alumina Ceramic Manufacturers Association [*Defunct*] .... ACMA
Alumina Ceramic Test .... ACT
Alumina Trihydrate [*Inorganic chemistry*] .... ALTH
Alumina Trihydrate [*Inorganic chemistry*] .... ATH
Aluminium Courier [*A publication*] .... Alumin Cour
Aluminium Federation .... AF
Aluminium Suisse, SA [*Commercial firm*] .... AS
Aluminium-Zentrale eV .... AZ
Aluminosilicate Polyacrylate [*Type of dental cement*] .... ASPA
Aluminum [*Chemical element*] .... AI
Aluminum [*Chemical symbol is Al*] .... ALUM
Aluminum [*Chemical symbol is Al*] .... ALUMN
Aluminum Alloy .... ALALY
Aluminum Association .... AA
Aluminum, Brick, and Clay Workers International Union .... ABCWIU
Aluminum, Brick, and Glass Workers International Union .... ABGW
Aluminum Building Products Credit Association [*Defunct*] .... ABPCA
Aluminum Cable Steel Reinforced .... ACSR
Aluminum Chlorohydrate [*Inorganic chemistry*] .... ACH
Aluminum Chlorohydroxyallantoinate [*Organic chemistry*] .... ALCA
Aluminum Co. of America [*NYSE symbol*] [*Wall Street slang
   names: "Ack Ack" and "All American"*] .... AA
Aluminum Company of America .... ALCOA
Aluminum Co. of America, Alcoa Research Laboratories Library,
   New Kensington, PA [*Library symbol*] .... PNkA
Aluminum Co. of Canada Ltd. .... ALCAN
Aluminum Co. of Canada Ltd., Arvida, PQ, Canada [*Library
   symbol*] .... CaQAA
Aluminum Conductor Steel Reinforced .... ACSR
Aluminum Crown [*Dentistry*] .... AL CR
Aluminum Dihydroxyaminoacetate [*Also, ALGLYN*] [*Pharmacology*] ..... ADA
Aluminum Electrical Lead .... AEL
Aluminum Extension Jacket .... AEJ
Aluminum Extruders Council .... AEC
Aluminum Field Coil .... AFC
Aluminum Foil Container Manufacturers Association .... AFCMA
Aluminum Foil Field Coil .... AFFC
Aluminum-Free Inorganic Suspended Material .... AFISM
Aluminum Glycinate [*Also, ADA*] [*Pharmacology*] .... ALGLYN
Aluminum Isopropoxide [*or Isopropylate*] [*Organic chemistry*] .... AIP
Aluminum Manufacturers Credit Bureau [*Defunct*] .... AMCB
Aluminum Matting [*Military*] .... AM
Aluminum, Nickel, Cobalt [*Alloy*] .... ALNICO
Aluminum-Oxide Electrolytic Capacitor .... ALOXCON
Aluminum Perchlorate .... AP
Aluminum and Polyethylene [*Components of a type of
   telecommunications cable*] .... ALPETH
Aluminum Powder Metallurgy .... APM
Aluminum Recycling Association .... ARA
Aluminum Research Institute .... ARI
Aluminum Review [*A publication*] .... Alum Rev
Aluminum Secretariat Ltd., Montreal, PQ, Canada [*Library
   symbol*] .... CaQMA
Aluminum Siding Association [*Later, AAMA*] .... ASA
Aluminum Silicate Pigment .... ASP
Aluminum Silicon [*An alloy*] .... ALSI
Aluminum Smelters Research Institute [*Later, ARA*] .... ASRI
Aluminum and Steel [*Freight*] .... AS
Aluminum Wares Association [*Later, CMA*] .... AWA
Aluminum Window Manufacturers Association [*Later,
   Architectural Aluminum Manufacturers Association*] .... AWMA
Aluminum Workers International Union [*Later, ABCWIU*] .... AWIU
Aluminum Workers International Union [*Later, ABCWIU*] .... AWU
Aluminum(dihydroxy)allantoinate [*Organic chemistry*] .... ALDA
Alumnae Advisory Center [*Later, CCP*] .... AAC
Alumni Bulletin. School of Dentistry. Indiana University [*A
   publication*] .... Alumni Bull Sch Dent Indiana Univ
Alumni Bulletin. University of Michigan. School of Dentistry [*A
   publication*] .... Alumni Bull Univ Mich Sch Dent
Alumni Memorial Library, Orchard Lake, MI [*Library symbol*] .... MiOIA
Alumni Presidents' Council of Independent Secondary Schools ..... APCISS
Alushta [*USSR*] [*Seismograph station code, US Geological
   Survey*] [*Closed*] .... ALU
Alva, OK [*Radio station call letters*] .... KALV
Alva, OK [*Radio station call letters*] .... KRKA
Alveolar [*Gas*] [*Medicine*] .... A
Alveolar Macrophage [*s*] [*Hematology*] .... AM
Alverno College, Milwaukee, WI [*OCLC symbol*] .... GZA
Alverno College, Milwaukee, WI [*Library symbol*] .... WMA

Alverthorpe Gallery, Rosenwald Collection, Jenkintown, PA [*Library symbol*] ... PJAIG
Alvi Dejectiones [*Discharge from the Bowels*] [*Pharmacy*] ... ALV DEJECT
Alvin Junior College [*Texas*] ... AJC
Alvin Junior College, Alvin, TX [*Library symbol*] ... TxAlvC
Alvin, Mid-Atlantic Ridge [*Oceanography*] ... AMAR
Alvin, TX [*Radio station call letters*] ... KACC
Alvin, TX [*Radio station call letters*] ... KTEK
Alvo Adstricta [*When the Bowels Are Constipated*] [*Pharmacy*] ... ALV ADST
Always Afloat ... AA
Alyeska Air Service [*Anchorage, AK*] [*FAA designator*] ... ALY
Alyuminievye Splavy Sbornik Statej [*A publication*] ... Alyum Splavy Sb Statej
Alza Conference Series [*A publication*] ... Alza Conf Ser
ALZA Corp. Cl A [*American Stock Exchange symbol*] ... AZAA
Alzheimer Type Dementia [*Medicine*] ... ATD
Alzheimer's Disease [*Medicine*] ... AD
Alzheimer's Disease and Related Conditions [*Medicine*] ... ADRC
Alzheimer's Disease and Related Disorders Association ... ADRDA
Am Angefuehrten Orte [*At the Place Quoted*] [*German*] ... AAO
AM Cable TV Industries, Inc. [*NASDAQ symbol*] ... AMTV
AM International, Inc. [*NYSE symbol*] ... AIN
AM International, Inc. [*Formerly, Addressograph-Multigraph Corp.*] ... AM
Ama [*Papua New Guinea*] [*Airport symbol*] ... AMF
AMA [*American Management Associations*]**/International** [*Formerly, IMA*] ... AMA/I
Amacan Resources Corp. [*NASDAQ symbol*] ... AMCN
Amadac Industries [*NASDAQ symbol*] ... AMDA
Amador Central Railroad Co. [*AAR code*] ... AMC
Amador County Free Library, Jackson, CA [*Library symbol*] ... CJ
Amagansett Free Library, Amagansett, NY [*Library symbol*] ... NAma
Amagansett Historical Association, Amagansett, NY [*Library symbol*] ... NAmaHi
Amagat-Leduc Rule [*Physics*] ... ALR
Amahai [*Indonesia*] [*Airport symbol*] ... AHI
Amalgam [*Metallurgy*] ... AMLG
Amalgamated ... AMALG
Amalgamated Association of Street, Electric Railway, and Motor Coach Employees of America [*Later, ATU*] ... SERMCE
Amalgamated Association of Wistful War Wives [*World War II*] ... AAWWW
Amalgamated Clothing and Textile Workers Union [*Formerly, ACWA, TWUA*] ... ACTWU
Amalgamated Clothing Workers of America [*Later, ACTWU*] ... ACWA
Amalgamated Engineering Union [*United Kingdom*] ... AEU
Amalgamated Flying Saucer Clubs of America ... AFSCA
Amalgamated Lace Operatives of America ... ALO
Amalgamated Lace Operatives of America ... ALOA
Amalgamated Lithographers of America [*Later, GAIU*] ... ALA
Amalgamated Meat Cutters and Butcher Workmen of North America [*Later, UFCWIU*] ... AMCBW
Amalgamated Meat Cutters and Butcher Workmen of North America [*Later, UFCWIU*] ... MCBW
Amalgamated National Union of Local Authorities Employees' Federation of Malaya ... ANULAE
Amalgamated Printers' Association ... APA
Amalgamated Publishers, Incorporated ... API
Amalgamated Society of Railway Servants [*New Zealand*] ... ASRS
Amalgamated Sugar Co. [*NYSE symbol*] ... AGM
Amalgamated Tin Mines of Nigeria ... ATMN
Amalgamated Transit Union ... ATU
Amalgamated Union of Public Employees [*Singapore*] ... AUPE
Amami O Shima [*Japan*] [*Airport symbol*] ... ASJ
Amanab [*Papua New Guinea*] [*Airport symbol*] ... AMU
(Amanitinylazobenzoyl)glycylglycine ... ABGG
Amanu [*Tuamotu Archipelago*] [*Seismograph station code, US Geological Survey*] ... AMN
Amarco Resources Corp. [*NASDAQ symbol*] ... AMAR
Amarex, Inc. [*NASDAQ symbol*] ... AMRQC
Amarillo [*Texas*] [*Airport symbol*] ... AMA
Amarillo College, Amarillo, TX [*OCLC symbol*] ... ACC
Amarillo College, Amarillo, TX [*Library symbol*] ... TxAmC
Amarillo Grain Exchange ... AGE
Amarillo Public Library, Amarillo, TX [*OCLC symbol*] ... TAP
Amarillo Public Library, Amarillo, TX [*Library symbol*] ... TxAm
Amarillo, TX [*Radio station call letters*] ... KACV-FM
Amarillo, TX [*Television station call letters*] ... KAMR-TV
Amarillo, TX [*Radio station call letters*] ... KBUY
Amarillo, TX [*Radio station call letters*] ... KDJW
Amarillo, TX [*Television station call letters*] ... KFDA-TV
Amarillo, TX [*Radio station call letters*] ... KGNC
Amarillo, TX [*Radio station call letters*] ... KGNC-FM
Amarillo, TX [*Radio station call letters*] ... KIXZ
Amarillo, TX [*Television station call letters*] ... KJTV
Amarillo, TX [*Radio station call letters*] ... KMML-FM
Amarillo, TX [*Radio station call letters*] ... KPUR
Amarillo, TX [*Radio station call letters*] ... KQIZ
Amarillo, TX [*Radio station call letters*] ... KQIZ-FM
Amarillo, TX [*Television station call letters*] ... KVII-TV
Amarillo, TX [*Radio station call letters*] ... KWAS
Amarillo, TX [*Radio station call letters*] ... KZIP
Amark Explorations Ltd. [*NASDAQ symbol*] ... AMAEF
Amaryllis Research Institute ... ARI
Amateur ... A
Amateur Astronomers [*An association*] ... AA
Amateur Astronomers Association [*Later, AAANY*] ... AAA
Amateur Astronomers Association, Brooklyn, NY [*Library symbol*] ... NBA
Amateur Astronomers Association of New York [*Formerly, AAA*] ... AAANY
Amateur Athletic Association ... AAA
Amateur Athletic Club ... AAC
Amateur Athletic Union of the United States ... AAU
Amateur Basketball Association of the United States of America ... ABAUSA
Amateur Bicycle League of America [*Later, United States Cycling Federation*] ... ABLA
Amateur Cartoonist Extraordinary [*National Cartoonists' Society award*] ... ACE
Amateur Chamber Music Players ... ACMP
Amateur Dramatic Club [*British*] ... ADC
Amateur Entomologists' Society ... AES
Amateur Fencers League of America [*Later, USFA*] ... AFLA
Amateur Field Trial Clubs of America ... AFTCA
Amateur Golfers' Association of America ... AGA
Amateur Hockey Association of the United States ... AHAUS
Amateur Organist Association International ... AOAI
Amateur Press Alliance [*Defunct*] ... APA
Amateur Press Association [*Generic term*] ... APA
Amateur Publishers' Association ... APA
Amateur Publishers' Association Magazine [*Generic term for one-person science-fiction fan magazine*] ... APAZINE
Amateur Radio Emergency Corps [*of ARPSC*] ... AREC
Amateur Radio Emergency Service ... ARES
Amateur Radio Monitor ... ARM
Amateur Radio Public Service Corps ... ARPSC
Amateur (Radio) Station [*ITU designation*] ... AR
Amateur Rocketeers of America ... ARA
Amateur Scientist Research Organization ... ASRO
Amateur Skating Union of the United States ... ASU-USA
Amateur Softball Association of America ... ASA
Amateur Station [*ITU designation*] ... AT
Amateur Swimming Association ... ASA
Amateur Television Association ... ATA
Amateur Trapshooting Association ... ATA
Amateur Yacht Research Society ... AYRS
Amatex Export Trade Association ... AETA
Amatignak Island [*Alaska*] [*Seismograph station code, US Geological Survey*] [*Closed*] ... AMA
Amatol [*Materials*] ... AM
Amatsia [*Israel*] [*Geomagnetic observatory code*] ... AMT
Amaurotic Familial Idiocy ... AFI
AMAX, Inc. [*Formerly, Alumax, Inc., American Metal Climax, Inc.*] [*NYSE symbol*] ... AMX
AMAX, Inc., Golden, CO [*Library symbol*] ... CoGA
Amazing Detective Tales [*A publication*] ... AD
Amazing Detective Tales [*A publication*] ... ADT
Amazing Magic Pivot Swing [*Training device for baseball batter's rear foot*] ... AMPS
Amazing Science Stories [*A publication*] ... ASS
Amazing Stories [*A publication*] ... AMZ
Amazing Stories Annual [*A publication*] ... AA
Amazing Stories Annual [*A publication*] ... AMA
Amazing Stories Quarterly [*A publication*] ... AMQ
Amazing Stories Quarterly [*A publication*] ... AQ
Amazing Stories Quarterly Reissue [*A publication*] ... AMR
Amazing Stories Science Fiction Novels [*A publication*] ... AMN
Amazon Bay [*Papua New Guinea*] [*Airport symbol*] ... AZB
Amazon River and Basin [*MARC geographic area code*] [*Library of Congress*] ... sa-----
AMB. Revista da Associacao Medica Brasileira [*A publication*] ... AMB
Ambac Industries, Inc. [*NYSE symbol*] [*Delisted*] ... AB
Ambanja [*Madagascar*] [*Airport symbol*] ... IVA
Ambar [*Pakistan*] [*Seismograph station code, US Geological Survey*] ... AMP
Ambassador ... AMB
Ambassador College, Pasadena, CA [*OCLC symbol*] ... ACL
Ambassador College, Pasadena, CA [*Library symbol*] ... CPA
Ambassador Extraordinary and Plenipotentiary [*Diplomacy*] ... AE & P
Ambassador Group, Inc. [*NASDAQ symbol*] ... AMBA
Ambassador of the United States ... AUS
Ambassador's Club [*TWA's club for frequent flyers*] ... AC
Ambassadors for Friendship ... AF
Ambassadors of Mary ... AM
Ambatomainty [*Madagascar*] [*Airport symbol*] ... AMY
Ambatondrazaka [*Madagascar*] [*Airport symbol*] ... WAM
Amber ... A
Amber ... AM
Amber ... AMB
Amber Light ... AL
Amber Resources Co. [*NASDAQ symbol*] ... AMBR
Amberley [*New Zealand*] [*Later, EYR*] [*Geomagnetic observatory code*] ... AML
Ambient [*Electronics*] ... A
Ambient ... AM
Ambient ... AMB

Ambient Air Ventilation Microclimate System [*Army*] ... AVMCS
Ambient Multimedia Environmental Goals [*Environmental Protection Agency*] ... AMEG
Ambient Noise [*Composite of sounds present at a given spot in the ocean*] ... AN
Ambient Noise Background ... ANB
Ambient Noise and Data System [*Pacific Missile Range*] ... ANADS
Ambient Temperature ... AT
Ambient Temperature and Pressure, Dry [*Medicine*] ... ATPD
Ambient Temperature and Pressure, Saturated [*Medicine*] ... ATPS
Ambient Temperature Range ... ATR
Ambiguity Eliminator [*Electronics*] ... AMBEL
Ambiguous [*Used in correcting manuscripts, etc.*] ... AMB
Ambilobe [*Madagascar*] [*Airport symbol*] ... AMB
Ambio Special Report [*A publication*] ... Ambio Spec Rep
Ambler [*Alaska*] [*Airport symbol*] ... ABL
Amboin [*Papua New Guinea*] [*Airport symbol*] ... AMG
Amboina [*Indonesia*] [*Seismograph station code, US Geological Survey*] ... AMO
Ambon [*Indonesia*] [*Seismograph station code, US Geological Survey*] ... AAI
Ambon [*Indonesia*] [*Airport symbol*] ... AMQ
Ambra Oil & Gas Company [*NASDAQ symbol*] ... AOGC
Ambridge, PA [*Radio station call letters*] ... WMBA
Ambulance ... AMB
Ambulance Association of America ... AA of A
Ambulance Association of America ... AAOA
Ambulance Design Criteria [*National Highway Transportation Safety Administration*] ... ADC
Ambulance Driver ... AD
Ambulance Journal [*A publication*] ... Ambulance J
Ambulance Loading Post [*Military*] ... ALP
Ambulance Manufacturers Association [*Later, TBEA*] ... AMA
Ambulance and Medical Service Association of America [*Later, AAA*] ... AMSAA
Ambulance Plane [*Navy symbol*] ... VH
Ambulate with Assistance [*Medicine*] ... AWA
Ambulatory [*Also, AMBUL*] [*Medicine*] ... AMB
Ambulatory ... AMBT
Ambulatory [*Also, AMB*] [*Medicine*] ... AMBUL
Ambulatory Medical Care [*NASDAQ symbol*] ... AMCR
Ambulatory Pediatric Association ... APA
Ambulong [*Philippines*] [*Seismograph station code, US Geological Survey*] [*Closed*] ... AMB
Ambunti [*Papua New Guinea*] [*Airport symbol*] ... AUJ
Ambush ... AB
Ambush ... AMB
Ambush Communication Equipment [*Military*] ... ACE
Ambush Patrol ... AP
AMC Entertainment [*NASDAQ symbol*] ... AMCE
AMC [*Army Materiel Command*] **Logistics Program - Hardcore Automated** ... ALPHA
AMC [*American Motors Corporation*] **Rambler Club** ... AMCRC
AMCA International Corp. [*NYSE symbol*] ... AIL
AMCA Resources Ltd. [*NASDAQ symbol*] ... AMCIF
Amcast Industrial Corp. [*NASDAQ symbol*] ... ACST
Amcel Propulsion Company ... APC
Amcel Propulsion Co., Asheville, NC [*Library symbol*] ... NcAAP
Amchitka [*Alaska*] [*Seismograph station code, US Geological Survey*] [*Closed*] ... AEB
Amchitka [*Alaska*] [*Seismograph station code, US Geological Survey*] [*Closed*] ... ANA
Amchitka [*Alaska*] [*Seismograph station code, US Geological Survey*] [*Closed*] ... ANB
Amchitka [*Alaska*] [*Seismograph station code, US Geological Survey*] [*Closed*] ... AND
Amchitka [*Alaska*] [*Seismograph station code, US Geological Survey*] [*Closed*] ... ASB
Amchitka [*Alaska*] [*Seismograph station code, US Geological Survey*] [*Closed*] ... ASC
Amchitka [*Alaska*] [*Seismograph station code, US Geological Survey*] [*Closed*] ... ASD
Amchitka [*Alaska*] [*Seismograph station code, US Geological Survey*] [*Closed*] ... AWA
Amchitka Central A [*Alaska*] [*Seismograph station code, US Geological Survey*] [*Closed*] ... ACA
Amchitka Central B [*Alaska*] [*Seismograph station code, US Geological Survey*] [*Closed*] ... ACB
Amchitka Central C [*Alaska*] [*Seismograph station code, US Geological Survey*] [*Closed*] ... ACC
Amchitka Central D [*Alaska*] [*Seismograph station code, US Geological Survey*] [*Closed*] ... ACD
Amchitka Central E [*Alaska*] [*Seismograph station code, US Geological Survey*] [*Closed*] ... ACE
Amchitka Central F [*Alaska*] [*Seismograph station code, US Geological Survey*] [*Closed*] ... ACF
Amchitka East [*Alaska*] [*Seismograph station code, US Geological Survey*] [*Closed*] ... AME
Amcord, Inc. [*Formerly, American Cement Corp.*] [*NYSE symbol*] [*Delisted*] ... AAC
Amdahl Corp. [*American Stock Exchange symbol*] ... AMH
Amdahl Users Group ... AUG
AMDEL [*Australian Mineral Development Laboratories*] **Bulletin** [*A publication*] ... AMDEL Bul
AMDEL [*Australian Mineral Development Laboratories*] **Bulletin** [*A publication*] ... AMDEL Bull
Amderma [*USSR*] [*Seismograph station code, US Geological Survey*] [*Closed*] ... AMD
AMDF [*Army Master Data File*] **Reader Microfilm System** [*Formerly, AMDFRMS*] ... ARMS
Amedco, Inc. [*American Stock Exchange symbol*] ... AMY
Amelia Earhart Collectors Club ... AECC
Amenagement et Nature [*A publication*] ... Amenag et Nature
Amenagement du Territoire et Developpement Regional [*A publication*] ... Amenag Territ Develop Region
Amenagement du Territoire et Droit Foncier [*A publication*] ... Amenage Territ Droit Foncier
Amend ... AMD
Amend [*or Amendment*] ... AMND
Amend Existing Orders Pertaining To ... AEOP
Amended Clearance [*Aviation*] ... AMCL
Amended Program Decision Memorandum [*Navy*] ... APDM
Amended Route of Flight [*Aviation*] ... AMRF
Amended Shipping Instruction ... ASI
Amendment ... AM
Amendment ... AMDT
Amendment ... AMEND
Amendment ... AMENDT
Amendment Request [*Navy*] ... AR
Amerace Corp. [*Formerly, Amerace Esna Corp.*] [*NYSE symbol*] ... AAE
Amerada Hess Corporation [*NYSE symbol*] ... AHC
Amerada Petroleum Corporation [*Later, AHC*] [*NYSE symbol*] ... ARC
Amerasia Journal [*A publication*] ... Amerasia J
Amercian Association of Applied Psychology [*Division of American Psychological Association*] ... AAAP
Amerford International Corp. [*NASDAQ symbol*] ... AMRF
Ameribanc, Inc. [*NASDAQ symbol*] ... ABNK
America [*A publication*] ... A
America [*A publication*] ... AM
America the Beautiful Fund [*An association*] ... ABF
America, Britain, China, and Dutch East Indies [*The ABCD Powers*] [*World War II*] ... ABCD
America: History and Life [*A publication*] ... AmerH
America Indigena. Organo Oficial del Instituto Indigenista Interamericano [*A publication*] ... AI
America-Israel Cultural Foundation ... AICF
America Israel Friendship League ... AIFL
America-Italy Society ... AIS
America Kenkyu [*A publication*] ... Amer Kenkyu
America Latina [*A publication*] ... Amer Lat
America-Mideast Educational and Training Services ... AMIDEAST
America. Revista de la Asociacion de Escritores y Artistas Americanos [*A publication*] ... AEA
American ... A
American ... AM
American ... AMER
American [*A publication*] ... Amer
American Abolitionist Movement ... AAM
American Abstract Artists ... AAA
American Academic Environments, Inc. ... AAE
American Academy of Actuaries ... AAA
American Academy of Advertising ... AAA
American Academy of Allergy ... AAA
American Academy of Ambulatory Nursing Administration ... AAANA
American Academy of Applied Nutrition [*Later, ICAN*] ... AAAN
American Academy of Art ... AAA
American Academy of Arts and Letters [*Later, AAIAL*] ... AAAL
American Academy of Arts and Letters [*Later, AAIAL*] ... AAA & L
American Academy of Arts and Letters [*Later, AAIAL*], **New York, NY** [*Library symbol*] ... NNAL
American Academy of Arts and Sciences ... AAAS
American Academy of Arts and Sciences ... AAA & S
American Academy of Arts and Sciences, Boston, MA [*Library symbol*] ... MBA
American Academy of Arts and Sciences. Memoirs [*A publication*] ... Am Acad Arts & Sci Mem
American Academy of Arts and Sciences. Memoirs [*A publication*] ... Amer Acad Arts & Sci Mem
American Academy of Arts and Sciences. Proceedings [*A publication*] ... Am Acad Arts & Sci Proc
American Academy of Asian Studies ... AAAS
American Academy of Behavioral Medicine ... AABM
American Academy for Cerebral Palsy [*Later, AACPDM*] ... AACP
American Academy for Cerebral Palsy and Developmental Medicine ... AACPDM
American Academy of Child Psychiatry ... AACP
American Academy of Clinical Psychiatrists ... AACP
American Academy of Clinical Toxicology ... AACT
American Academy of Compensation Medicine ... AACM
American Academy of Craniomandibular Disorders ... AACD
American Academy of Criminalistics ... AAC
American Academy of Crisis Interveners ... AACI
American Academy of Crown and Bridge Prosthodontics ... AACBP

American Academy of Dental Electrosurgery .... AADE
American Academy of Dental Group Practice .... AADGP
American Academy of Dental Medicine [*Later, AAOM*] .... AADM
American Academy of Dental Practice Administration .... AADPA
American Academy of Dental Radiology .... AADR
American Academy of Dentists [*Defunct*] .... AAD
American Academy of Dermatology .... AAD
American Academy of Diplomacy .... AAD
American Academy of Environmental Engineers .... AAEE
American Academy of Esthetic Dentistry .... AAED
American Academy of Facial Plastic and Reconstructive Surgery .... AAFPRS
American Academy of Family Physicians [*Formerly, AAGP*] .... AAFP
American Academy of Forensic Sciences .... AAFS
American Academy of General Practice [*Later, AAFP*] .... AAGP
American Academy of Gnathologic Orthopedics .... AAGO
American Academy of Gold Foil Operators .... AAGFO
American Academy of Health Administration .... AAHA
American Academy of the History of Dentistry .... AAHD
American Academy of Homiletics [*Later, AH*] .... AAH
American Academy of Husband-Coached Childbirth .... AAHCC
American Academy of Implant Dentistry .... AAID
American Academy and Institute of Arts and Letters [*Formerly, AAAL, AAA & L, NIAL*] .... AAIAL
American Academy for Jewish Research .... AAJR
American Academy of Matrimonial Lawyers .... AAML
American Academy of Maxillofacial Prosthetics .... AAMP
American Academy of Mechanics .... AAM
American Academy of Medical Administrators .... AAMA
American Academy of Medical Administrators Research and Educational Foundation [*Formerly, HCREF*] .... AAMAREF
American Academy of Medical Directors .... AAMD
American Academy of Medical Preventics .... AAMP
American Academy on Mental Retardation .... AAMR
American Academy of Microbiology .... AAM
American Academy of Neurological Surgery .... AANS
American Academy of Neurology .... AAN
American Academy of Nursing .... AAN
American Academy of Nutrition .... AAN
American Academy of Occupational Medicine .... AAOM
American Academy of Ophthalmology .... AAO
American Academy of Ophthalmology and Otolaryngology .... AAOO
American Academy of Optometry .... AAO
American Academy of Optometry Series [*A publication*] .... Am Acad Optom Ser
American Academy of Oral Medicine .... AAOM
American Academy of Oral Pathology .... AAOP
American Academy of Oral Roentgenology [*Later, AADR*] .... AAOR
American Academy of Organ .... AAO
American Academy of Orthodontics for the General Practitioner .... AAOGP
American Academy of Orthopaedic Surgeons .... AAOS
American Academy of Orthotists and Prosthetists .... AAOP
American Academy of Osteopathic Surgeons .... AAOS
American Academy of Osteopathy [*Formerly, Academy of Applied Osteopathy*] .... AAO
American Academy of Otolaryngologic Allergy [*Formerly, ASOOA*] ... AAOA
American Academy of Otolaryngology - Head and Neck Surgery .... AAO-HNS
American Academy of Pediatrics .... AAP
American Academy of Pedodontics .... AAP
American Academy of Periodontology .... AAP
American Academy of Philately [*Later, APC*] .... AAP
American Academy of Physical Education .... AAPE
American Academy of Physical Medicine and Rehabilitation .... AAPMR
American Academy of Physicians' Assistants. Journal [*A publication*] .... PA J
American Academy of Physiologic Dentistry .... AAPD
American Academy for Plastics Research in Dentistry .... AAPRD
American Academy of Podiatric Sports Medicine .... AAPSM
American Academy of Podiatry Administration .... AAPO
American Academy of Political and Social Science .... AAPSS
American Academy of Political and Social Science. Annals [*A publication*] .... AAPSSA
American Academy of Political and Social Science. Annals [*A publication*] .... Am Acad Pol & Soc Sci Ann
American Academy of Political and Social Science. Annals [*A publication*] .... APSS
American Academy of Political and Social Science. Monographs [*A publication*] .... AAPSS Mg
American Academy of Pro-Life Physicians .... AAPLP
American Academy for Professional Law Enforcement .... AAPLE
American Academy of Psychiatry and the Law .... AAPL
American Academy of Psychoanalysis .... AAP
American Academy of Psychotherapists .... AAP
American Academy of Religion .... AAR
American Academy of Religion. Journal [*A publication*] .... Am Acad Relig J
American Academy of Restorative Dentistry .... AARD
American Academy in Rome .... AAR
American Academy in Rome. Memoirs [*A publication*] .... Am Acad Rome Mem
American Academy in Rome. Papers and Monographs [*A publication*] .... PAAR
American Academy of Safety Education .... AASE
American Academy of Sanitarians .... AAS
American Academy of Sports Physicians .... AASP
American Academy of Stress Disorders .... AASD
American Academy of Teachers of Singing .... AATS
American Academy of Transportation .... AAT
American Academy of Tuberculosis Physicians .... AATP
American Academy of Veterinary Dermatology .... AAVD
American Academy of Veterinary Pharmacology and Therapeutics .... AAVPT
American Accordion Musicological Society .... AAMS
American Accordionists' Association .... AAA
American Accounting Association .... AAA
American Adoption Congress .... AAC
American Advertising Federation [*Formerly, AFA*] .... AAF
American Affenpinscher Association [*Formerly, ACA*] .... AAA
American Afghan Action .... AAA
American-African Affairs Association .... AAAA
American Afro-Asian Educational Exchange [*Later, AAEE*] .... AAAEE
American Aggregates Corp. [*NASDAQ symbol*] .... AMAG
American Aging Association .... AGE
American Agri-Women [*An association*] .... AAW
American Agricultural Chemical Co. [*NYSE symbol*] [*Delisted*] .... AHD
American Agricultural Economics Association .... AAEA
American Agricultural Economics Documentation Center [*Department of Agriculture*] .... AAEDC
American Agricultural Economics Documentation Center, Washington, DC [*OCLC symbol*] .... AGU
American Agricultural Editors' Association .... AAEA
American Agricultural Law Association .... AALA
American Agricultural Marketing Association .... AAMA
American Agriculture Movement .... AAM
American Agronomics Corp. [*NYSE symbol*] .... AGR
American Aid for Afghans .... AAF
American Aid Society of Paris .... AASP
American Aid Society for the West Indies .... AASWI
American Aid to Ulster .... AAU
American Air Export & Import Company .... AAXICO
American Air Filter Co., Inc. [*NYSE symbol*] .... AAF
American Air Mail Society .... AAMS
American Airlines, Inc. [*ICAO designator*] .... AA
American Airlines, Inc. [*Air carrier designation symbol*] .... AAL
American Airship Association .... AAA
American Albino Association [*Later, WWWCRW*] .... AAA
American Albino Horse Club [*Later, WWWCRW*] .... AAHC
American All-Hobbies Association .... AAHA
American Allergy Association .... AAA
American Alliance for Health, Physical Education, and Recreation [*Later, AAHPERD*] .... AAHPER
American Alliance for Health, Physical Education, Recreation, and Dance [*Formerly, AAHPER*] .... AAHPERD
American Alligator Council [*Defunct*] .... AAC
American Almanac [*A publication*] .... Am Alma
American Alpine Club .... AAC
American Alpine Club, New York, NY [*Library symbol*] .... NNAAI
American Alpine Journal [*A publication*] .... Am Alpine Jour
American Alumni Council [*Later, Council for the Advancement and Support of Education*] .... AAC
American Amaryllis Society .... AAS
American Amateur Baseball Congress .... AABC
American Amateur Inventors Club .... AAIC
American Amateur Karate Federation .... AAKF
American Amateur Press Association .... AAPA
American Amateur Racquetball Association [*Formerly, IPRA, IPA, IRA*] .... AARA
American Ambulance Association [*Formerly, AMSAA*] .... AAA
American Ambulance and Rescue Association [*Defunct*] .... AARA
American Angora Goat Breeders' Association .... AAGBA
American Angus Association .... AAA
American Animal Health Pharmaceutical Association [*Defunct*] ..... AAHPhA
American Animal Hospital Association .... AAHA
American Annals of the Deaf [*A publication*] .... Am Ann Deaf
American Annals of the Deaf [*A publication*] .... ANDFA
American Annual [*A publication*] .... AmA
American Annual Register [*A publication*] .... Ann Reg
American Anorexia Nervosa Association .... AANA
American Antarctic Association .... AAA
American Antarctic Mountaineering Expedition .... AAME
American Anthropological Association .... AAA
American Anthropologist [*A publication*] .... AA
American Anthropologist [*A publication*] .... AAn
American Anthropologist [*A publication*] .... A ANTH
American Anthropologist [*A publication*] .... AAnthr
American Anthropologist [*A publication*] .... AAR
American Anthropologist [*A publication*] .... AmA
American Anthropologist [*A publication*] .... Am Anthrop
American Anthropologist [*A publication*] .... Am Anthropol
American Anthropologist [*A publication*] .... Amer Anthropol
American Anti-Vivisection Society .... AAVS

American Antiquarian [*A publication*]................ Am Antiq
American Antiquarian Society............................. AAS
American Antiquarian Society. Proceedings [*A publication*]............... AAS
American Antiquarian Society. Proceedings [*A publication*]...............
Am Antiq Soc Proc
American Antiquarian Society. Proceedings [*A publication*]...............
Amer Antiq Soc Proc
American Antiquarian Society, Worcester, MA [*OCLC symbol*]............. AQM
American Antiquarian Society, Worcester, MA [*Library symbol*]...........MWA
American Antiques & Crafts Society [*Commercial firm*].......AACS
American Antiquity [*A publication*] .... Am Ant
American Antiquity [*A publication*] .... Am Antiq
American Antiquity [*A publication*] .... Am Antiquit
American Antiquity [*A publication*] .... Amer Antiq
American Apparel Manufacturers Association ....AAMA
American Appraisal Association [*NASDAQ symbol*]..............AMCA
American-Arab Affairs Council............................AAAC
American-Arab Anti-Discrimination Committee ....ADC
American-Arab Association for Commerce and Industry ....AAACI
American-Arab Relations Committee ....AARC
American Arab Relief Agency [*Defunct*] ....AARA
American Arabic Association.............................AMERA
American Arbitration Association .... AAA
American Arbitration Association, New York, NY [*Library symbol*] .... NNAAr
American Archaeological Expedition to Syria. Publication [*A publication*]...............AAES
American Archery Council ....AAC
American Architect [*A publication*] .... Am Arch
American Architectural Foundation [*Later, AIAF*]...............AAF
American Archives of Rehabilitation Therapy [*A publication*]...............
Am Arch Rehabil Ther
American Archives of Rehabilitation Therapy [*A publication*]...............
Amer Arch Rehab Ther
American Archivist [*A publication*] ....AA
American Archivist [*A publication*] ....A Arch
American Archivist [*A publication*] ....Am Archiv
American Archivist [*A publication*] ....Am Archivis
American Archivist [*A publication*] ....Am Archivist
American Art Association [*Predecessor of Parke-Bernet, New York*]...... AAA
American Art Journal [*A publication*]................ Am Art J
American Art Therapy Association ....AATA
American Artist [*A publication*] ....AArt
American Artist [*A publication*] ....Am Artist
American Artists Professional League ....AAPL
American Artists Series................................AAS
American Arts Alliance................................AAA
American Arts Documentation Centre ....AMARTS
American-ASEAN [*Association of South East Asian Nations*] Trade Council...............AATC
American-Asian Educational Exchange [*Formerly, AAAEE*] ....AAEE
American Assembly [*An association*]....................AA
American Assembly of Collegiate Schools of Business ....AACSB
American Associates, Ben-Gurion University of the Negev ....AABGU
American Association [*Baseball league*].................AA
American Association of Aardvark Aficionados ....AAAA
American Association for the Abolition of Involuntary Mental Hospitalization [*Defunct*]...............AAAIMH
American Association of Academic Editors...............AAAE
American Association for Accreditation of Ambulatory Plastic Surgery Facilities...............AAAPSF
American Association for Accreditation of Laboratory Animal Care...............AAALAC
American Association for the Advancement of Atheism [*Later, AA*]....AAAA
American Association for the Advancement of the Humanities ....AAAH
American Association for the Advancement of Science...............AAAS
American Association for the Advancement of Science. Proceedings. Memoirs [*A publication*]............... Am As Pr Mem
American Association for the Advancement of Science. Publication [*A publication*]...............Am Assoc Adv Sci Publ
American Association for the Advancement of Science. Symposium [*A publication*]...............Am Assoc Adv Sci Symp
American Association for the Advancement of Slavic Studies .... AAASS
American Association for the Advancement of Tension Control [*Later, ISTC*]...............AAATC
American Association of Advertising Agencies...............AAAA
American Association of Advertising Agencies, New York, NY [*Library symbol*]...............NNAdv
American Association for Aerosol Research...............AAAR
American Association for Affirmative Action...............AAAA
American Association Against Addiction...............AAAA
American Association of Agricultural College Editors [*Later, Agricultural Communicators in Education*]...............AAACE
American Association of Agricultural Communicators of Tomorrow .... ACT
American Association of Airport Executives...............AAAE
American Association of Aluminum Importers and Warehouse Distributors [*Later, American Metal Importers Association*].......AAAIWD
American Association of Anatomists...............AAA
American Association for Applied Linguistics...............AAAL
American Association of Architectural Bibliographers...............AAAB
American Association of Architectural Bibliographers. Papers [*A publication*]...............American Assoc Arch Bib

American Association for Artificial Intelligence ....AAAI
American Association of Attorney-Certified Public Accountants ....
AAA-CPA
American Association of Audio Analgesia [*Defunct*] ....AAAA
American Association for Automotive Medicine ....AAAM
American Association of Avian Pathologists ....AAAP
American Association of Backgammon Clubs...............AABC
American Association of Baggage Traffic Managers [*Defunct*]...........AABTM
American Association of Bible Colleges ....AABC
American Association of Bicycle Importers ....AABI
American Association of Bioanalysts ....AAB
American Association of Biofeedback Clinicians...............AABC
American Association of Black Women Entrepreneurs ....AABWE
American Association of Blacks in Energy...............AABE
American Association of Blood Banks ....AABB
American Association of Book Wholesalers ....AABW
American Association of Botanical Gardens and Arboreta...............AABGA
American Association of Bovine Practitioners ....AABP
American Association of Cable TV Owners ....AACTVO
American Association for Cancer Education ....AACE
American Association for Cancer Research ....AACR
American Association for Career Education ....AACE
American Association of Cereal Chemists...............AACC
American Association of Certified Allergists...............AACA
American Association of Certified Allied Health Personnel in Ophthalmology...............AACAHPO
American Association of Certified Appraisers ....AACA
American Association of Certified Orthoptists ....AACO
American Association of Chairmen of Departments of Psychiatry ... AACDP
American Association of Children's Residential Centers ....AACRC
American Association for Chinese Studies...............AACS
American Association of Christian Schools...............AACS
American Association of Classified School Employees ....AACSE
American Association for Cleft Palate Rehabilitation [*Later, ACPA*]...............AACPR
American Association of Clinic Physicians and Surgeons [*Defunct*]...............AACPS
American Association of Clinical Chemistry ....AACC
American Association for Clinical Histocompatibility Testing ....AACHT
American Association for Clinical Immunology and Allergy...............AACIA
American Association of Clinical Urologists...............AACU
American Association of College Baseball Coaches...............AACBC
American Association of College and University Business Officers [*Defunct*]...............AACUBO
American Association of Colleges of Chiropody-Podiatry ....AACCP
American Association of Colleges of Nursing...............AACN
American Association of Colleges of Osteopathic Medicine [*Formerly, AAOC*]...............AACOM
American Association of Colleges of Pharmacy ....AACP
American Association of Colleges of Podiatric Medicine ....AACPM
American Association of Colleges of Podiatry [*Later, AACPM*]...........AACP
American Association of Colleges for Teacher Education...............AACTE
American Association of Colleges for Teacher Education. Yearbook [*A publication*]...............Am Assn Col Teach Educ Yrbk
American Association of Collegiate Registrars and Admissions Officers...............AACRAO
American Association of Collegiate Registrars. Journal [*A publication*]...............Am Assn Coll Reg J
American Association of Commerce Publications [*Later, American Chamber of Commerce Executives Communications Council*]...............AACP
American Association of Commodity Traders...............AACT
American Association of Community and Junior Colleges...............AACJ
American Association of Community and Junior Colleges...............AACJC
American Association for the Comparative Study of Law...............AACSL
American Association for Comprehensive Health Planning [*Later, AHPA*]...............AACHP
American Association for Conservation Information [*Later, ACI*]..........AACI
American Association of Conservators and Restorers...............AACR
American Association for Contamination Control [*Later, IES*]...............AACC
American Association for Continuity of Care...............AACC
American Association of Convention Planners [*Defunct*]...............AACP
American Association of Correctional Facility Officers [*Later, AACO*]...............AACFO
American Association of Correctional Officers [*Formerly, AACFO*] .... AACO
American Association of Correctional Psychologists...............AACP
American Association of Correctional Training Personnel...............AACTP
American Association of Cosmetic Surgeons ....AACS
American Association of Cost Engineers ....AACE
American Association of Cost Engineers. Bulletin [*A publication*]...............
AACE Bull
American Association of Councils of Medical Staffs [*Later, PDA*].........CMS
American Association of Creative Artists ....AACA
American Association of Credit Counselors ....AACC
American Association of Crimean Turks...............AACT
American Association of Critical-Care Nurses...............AACCN
American Association of Critical-Care Nurses...............AACN
American Association for Crystal Growth...............AACG
American Association of Dental Consultants ....AADC
American Association of Dental Editors...............AADE
American Association of Dental Examiners...............AADE

American Association for Dental Research................................AADR
American Association of Dental Schools..................................AADS
American Association of Dental Victims...................................AADV
American Association of Diabetes Educators.........................AADE
American Association of Doctors' Nurses...............................AADN
American Association of Electromyography and Electrodiagnosis .... AAEE
American Association of Elementary/Kindergarten/Nursery
   Educators [Defunct] ....AAE/K/N/E
American Association on Emeriti [Later, NCE] ....AAE
American Association of Endodontists......................................AAE
American Association of Engineering Societies.......................AAES
American Association of Engineers [Later, NSPE] ....AAE
American Association of Equine Practitioners.........................AAEP
American Association of Equipment Lessors [Formerly, AEL]............AAEL
American Association of Esthetics...AAE
American Association for Ethiopian Jews..............................AAEJ
American Association of Evangelical Students......................AAES
American Association of Exporters and Importers [Formerly,
   NCAI, AIA]..AAEI
American Association of Feed Exporters [Defunct]................AAFE
American Association of Feed Microscopists.........................AAFM
American Association of Feline Practitioners.........................AAFP
American Association of Fitness Directors in Business and
   Industry ....AAFDBI
American Association of Food Stamp Directors.....................AAFSD
American Association of Foot Specialists...............................AAFS
American Association of Foreign Medical Graduates [Defunct]........AAFMG
American Association of Forms Executives............................AAFE
American Association of Foundations for Medical Care.........AAFMC
American Association of Fund-Raising Counsel ....AAFRC
American Association of Genito-Urinary Surgeons................AAGUS
American Association for Geodetic Surveying........................AAGS
American Association for Geriatric Psychiatry.......................AAGP
American Association for Gifted Children ....AAGC
American Association of Gynecological Laparoscopists.......AAGL
American Association for Hand Surgery.................................AAHS
American Association of Handwriting Analysts......................AAHA
American Association of Health Data Systems......................AAHDS
American Association of Hides, Skins, and Leather Merchants..... AAHSLM
American Association for Higher Education............................AAHE
American Association for the History of Medicine ....AAHM
American Association of Homeopathic Pharmacists..............AAHP
American Association of Homes for the Aging.......................AAHA
American Association of Hospital Accountants [Later, HFMA]............AAHA
American Association of Hospital Consultants.......................AAHC
American Association of Hospital Dental Chiefs [Later, AAHD] ....AAHDC
American Association of Hospital Dentists [Formerly, AAHDC]...........AAHD
American Association for Hospital Planning...........................AAHP
American Association of Hospital Podiatrists.........................AAHP
American Association of Hospital Purchasing Agents ....AAHPA
American Association of Housing Educators..........................AAHE
American Association for Humanistic Psychology [Later, AHP]...........AAHP
American Association of Immunologists..................................AAI
American Association of Imported Car Dealers [Defunct].....................AAICD
American Association of Independent News Distributors......AAIND
American Association of Individual Investors..........................AAII
American Association of Industrial Dentists [Defunct].....................AAID
American Association of Industrial Editors [Later, IABC] ......AAIE
American Association of Industrial Engineers........................AAIE
American Association of Industrial Management [Later, AME] ....AAIM
American Association of Industrial Nurses [Later, AAOHN] ....AAIN
American Association of Industrial Social Workers ....AAISW
American Association of Industrial Veterinarians [Formerly, IVA]........AAIV
American Association of Inhalation Therapists [Later, AART]..............AAIT
American Association of Instructors of the Blind [Later, AEVH]..........AAIB
American Association of Insurance Services [Formerly, TIRB].............AAIS
American Association for International Aging.........................AAIA
American Association for the International Commission of Jurists .... AAICJ
American Association of IV Therapy ....AAIVT
American Association of Jesuit Scientists [Defunct]..............AAJS
American Association for Jewish Education [Later, JESNA] ..AAJE
American Association of Journalism School Administrators ....AAJSA
American Association of Junior Colleges [Later, AACJC]......AAJC
American Association of Laban Movement Analysts.............AALMA
American Association for Laboratory Accreditation ....AALA
American Association for Laboratory Animal Science...........AALAS
[The] American Association of Language Specialists ....TAALS
American Association of Law Libraries...................................AALL
American Association for Legal and Political Philosophy......AALPP
American Association for Leisure and Recreation................AALR
American Association of Library Trustees [Later, ALTA].......AALT
American Association of Limited Partners..............................AALP
American Association of Machinery Importers [Defunct]........................AAMI
American Association of Managing General Agents..............AAMGA
American Association of Marriage Counselors [Later, AAMFT].........AAMC
American Association of Marriage and Family Counselors
   [Later, AAMFT]...AAMFC
American Association for Marriage and Family Therapy
   [Formerly, AAMFC]...AAMFT
American Association for Maternal and Child Health [Formerly,
   AAMIH]...AAMCH

American Association for Maternal and Infant Health [Later,
   AAMCH]...AAMIH
American Association of Meat Processors.............................AAMP
American Association of Medical Assistants..........................AAMA
American Association of Medical Clinics [Later, AGPA]........AAMC
American Association of Medical Milk Commissions.............AAMMC
American Association of Medical Record Librarians [Later,
   AMRA]...AAMRL
American Association of Medical Society Executives............AAMSE
American Association for Medical Systems and Informatics
   [Formerly, SAMS, SCM]...AAMSI
American Association of Medico-Legal Consultants ....AAMC
American Association on Mental Deficiency...........................AAMD
American Association of Mental Health Professionals in
   Corrections ....AAMHPC
American Association of Meta-Science...................................AAMS
American Association for Middle East Studies [Defunct].................AAMES
American Association of Minority Enterprise Small Business
   Investment Companies ....AAMESBIC
American Association of Motor Vehicle Administrators ....AAMVA
American Association of Museums...AAM
American Association of Museums. Proceedings [A publication]...............
                                        Am As Museums Pr
American Association of Music Festivals [Defunct]...............AAMF
American Association for Music Therapy [Formerly, UFMT]...............AAMT
American Association of Nephrology Nurses and Technicians ....AANNT
American Association of Neurological Surgeons [Formerly, HCS].......AANS
American Association of Neuropathologists...........................AANP
American Association of Neurosurgical Nurses.....................AANN
American Association of Newspaper Representatives [Later,
   NASA]..AANR
American Association of Nurse Anesthetists..........................AANA
American Association of Nurse Attorneys...............................AANA
American Association of Nurse-Midwives [Later, ACNM].....AANM
American Association of Nurserymen.....................................AAN
American Association of Nursing Assistants..........................AANA
American Association of Obstetricians and Gynecologists
   [Later, AGOS]..AAOG
American Association of Occupational Health Nurses [Formerly,
   AAIN]...AAOHN
American Association of Oilwell Drilling Contractors [Later,
   IADC]...AAODC
American Association of Ophthalmology.................................AAO
American Association of Oral and Maxillofacial Surgeons ... AAOMS
American Association of Orthodontists....................................AAO
American Association of Orthopaedic Medicine ....AAOM
American Association of Orthoptic Technicians [Later, AACO]..........AAOT
American Association of Osteopathic Colleges [Later, AACOM].......AAOC
American Association of Osteopathic Examiners....................AAOE
American Association of Osteopathic Medical Examiners.............. AAOME
American Association of Owners and Breeders of Peruvian Paso
   Horses...AAOBPPH
American Association of Passenger Rate Men [Defunct] ....AAPRM
American Association of Passenger Traffic Officers [Defunct].........AAPTO
American Association of Pastoral Counselors.......................AAPC
American Association of Pathologists [Formerly, AAPB, ASEP]...........AAP
American Association of Pathologists' Assistants..................AAPA
American Association of Pathologists and Bacteriologists
   [Later, AAP]...AAPB
American Association for Pediatric Ophthalmology and
   Strabismus..AAPO & S
American Association of Petroleum Geologists ....AAPG
American Association of Petroleum Geologists. Bulletin [A
   publication]...Am As Petroleum G B
American Association of Petroleum Geologists. Bulletin [A
   publication]...Am Assn Pet Geol Bul
American Association of Petroleum Geologists. Bulletin [A
   publication]...Am Assn Pet Geologists Bull
American Association of Petroleum Geologists. Bulletin [A
   publication]..Am Assoc Pet Geol Bull
American Association of Petroleum Geologists. Bulletin [A
   publication]..Amer Assoc Pet Geol Bull
American Association of Petroleum Geologists. Memoir [A
   publication]..Am Assoc Pet Geol Mem
American Association of Petroleum Geologists. Memoir [A
   publication]...Am Assoc Petroleum Geologists Mem
American Association of Petroleum Geologists. Reprint Series
   [A publication]...Am Assoc Pet Geol Repr Ser
American Association of Petroleum Landmen.........................AAPL
American Association of Phonetic Sciences...........................AAPS
American Association of Physical Anthropologists................AAPA
American Association of Physicians' Assistants [Defunct]................AAPA
American Association of Physicists in Medicine ....AAPM
American Association of Physics Teachers.............................AAPT
American Association of Planned Parenthood Physicians [Later,
   APPP]...AAPPP
American Association of Plastic Surgeons..............................AAPS
American Association of Poison Control Centers....................AAPCC
American Association of Police Polygraphists........................AAPP
American Association of Political Consultants........................AAPC
American Association of Port Authorities................................AAPA

American Association of Presidents of Independent Colleges and Universities ... AAPICU
American Association of Private Railroad Car Owners ... AAPRCO
American Association of Pro Life Obstetricians and Gynecologists ... AAPLOG
American Association of Professional Bridal Consultants ... AAPBC
American Association of Professional Hypnologists ... AAPH
American Association of Professional Hypnotherapists ... AAPH
American Association of Professional Standards Review Organizations ... AAPSRO
American Association of the Professions ... AAP
American Association of Professors in Sanitary Engineering [*Later, AEEP*] ... AAPSE
American Association of Professors of Yiddish ... AAPY
American Association for the Promotion of Science ... AAPS
American Association of Psychiatric Administrators [*Formerly, AMSMH*] ... AAPA
American Association of Psychiatric Clinics for Children [*Later, AAPSC*] ... AAPCC
American Association of Psychiatric Services for Children ... AAPSC
American Association of Public Health Dentists ... AAPHD
American Association of Public Health Physicians ... AAPHP
American Association for Public Opinion Research ... AAPOR
American Association of Public Welfare Attorneys ... AAPWA
American Association of Public Welfare Information Systems Management ... AAPWISM
American Association of Railroad Superintendents ... AARS
American Association of Railroad Ticket Agents [*Defunct*] ... AARTA
American Association of Railway Surgeons ... AARS
American Association of Registered Patent Attorneys and Agents ... AARPAA
American Association for Rehabilitation Therapy ... AART
American Association of Religious Therapists ... AART
American Association for Respiratory Therapy ... AART
American Association of Retired Persons ... AARP
American Association of School Administrators ... AASA
American Association of School Administrators. Official Report [*A publication*] ... Am Assn Sch Adm Off Rep
American Association of School Librarians ... AASL
American Association of School Personnel Administrators ... AASPA
American Association of Schools and Departments of Journalism ... AASDJ
American Association of Schools of Religious Education [*Later, ATS*] ... AASRE
American Association of Scientific Workers ... AASW
American Association of Securities Representatives ... AASR
American Association of Senior Physicians ... AASP
American Association of Sex Educators and Counselors [*Later, AASECT*] ... AASEC
American Association of Sex Educators, Counselors, and Therapists [*Formerly, AASEC*] ... AASECT
American Association of Sheep and Goat Practitioners ... AASP
American Association of Sheriff Posses and Riding Clubs ... AASPRC
American Association of Small Business [*Later, NSB*] ... AASB
American Association of Small Cities ... AASC
American Association of Small Research Companies ... AASRC
American Association of Soap and Glycerin Producers [*Later, SDA*] ... AAS & GP
American Association for Social Psychiatry ... AASP
American Association for Social Security ... AASS
American Association of Special Educators ... AASE
American Association of Specialized Colleges ... AASC
American Association of State Climatologists ... AASC
American Association of State Colleges and Universities ... AASCU
American Association of State Highway Officials [*Later, AASHTO*] ... AASHO
American Association of State Highway and Transportation Officials [*Formerly, AASHO*] ... AASHTO
American Association of State Libraries [*Later, ASCLA*] ... AASL
American Association of State Libraries [*Later, ASCLA*] ... ASL
American Association for State and Local History ... AASLH
American Association for State and Local History. Bulletin [*A publication*] ... Am Assoc State Local Hist Bull
American Association of Stratigraphic Palynologists ... AASP
American Association for the Study of Headache ... AASH
American Association for the Study of Liver Diseases ... AASLD
American Association for Study of Neoplastic Diseases ... AASND
American Association for the Study of the United States in World Affairs ... USWA
American Association of Suicidology ... AAS
American Association of Sunday and Feature Editors ... AASFE
American Association for the Surgery of Trauma ... AAST
American Association of Swine Practitioners ... AASP
American Association of Swiss Alpine Club Members [*Defunct*] ... AASACM
American Association of Teacher Educators in Agriculture ... AATEA
American Association of Teachers of Arabic ... AATA
American Association of Teachers of Chinese Language and Culture [*Later, AACS*] ... AATCLC
American Association of Teachers of English as a Second Language ... AATESL
American Association of Teachers of Esperanto ... AATE
American Association of Teachers of French ... AATF
American Association of Teachers of French. National Bulletin [*A publication*] ... AATFNB
American Association of Teachers of German ... AATG
American Association of Teachers of Italian ... AATI
American Association of Teachers of Slavic and East European Languages ... AATSEEL
American Association of Teachers of Slavic and East European Languages. Bulletin [*A publication*] ... AATSEEL
American Association of Teachers of Slavic and East European Languages. Bulletin [*A publication*] ... AATSEEL Bull
American Association of Teachers of Slavic and East European Languages. Journal [*A publication*] ... AATSEEL Jour
American Association of Teachers of Spanish and Portuguese ... AATSP
American Association of Textile Chemists and Colorists ... AATCC
American Association for Textile Technology ... AATT
American Association of Theological Schools [*Later, ATS*] ... AATS
American Association for Thoracic Surgery ... AATS
American Association for Tissue Banks ... AATB
American Association of Trauma Specialists [*Defunct*] ... AATS
American Association of Traveling Passenger Agents [*Defunct*] ... AATPA
American Association for the United Nations [*Later, United Nations Association of the United States*] ... AAUN
American Association of University Administrators ... AAUA
American Association of University Affiliated Programs for the Developmentally Disabled ... AAUAP
American Association of University Professors ... AAUP
American Association of University Professors. Bulletin [*A publication*] ... AAUPB
American Association of University Professors. Bulletin [*A publication*] ... AAUP Bul
American Association of University Professors. Bulletin [*A publication*] ... AAUP Bull
American Association of University Professors. Bulletin [*A publication*] ... Am Assn Univ Prof B
American Association of University Professors of Urban Affairs and Environmental Sciences ... AAUP-UAES
American Association of University Students ... AAUS
American Association of University Teachers of Insurance [*Later, ARIA*] ... AAUTI
American Association of University Women ... AAUW
American Association of University Women Educational Foundation ... AAUWEF
American Association of University Women Educational Foundation, Washington, DC [*Library symbol*] ... DAAUW
American Association of University Women. Journal [*A publication*] ... Am Assn Univ Women J
American Association of Variable Star Observers ... AAVSO
American Association of Veterinary Anatomists ... AAVA
American Association of Veterinary Bacteriologists [*Defunct*] ... AAVB
American Association of Veterinary Laboratory Diagnosticians ... AAVLD
American Association of Veterinary Nutrition ... AAVN
American Association of Veterinary Parasitologists ... AAVP
American Association of Veterinary State Boards ... AAVSB
American Association for Vital Records and Public Health Statistics [*Later, AVRHS*] ... AAVRPHS
American Association of Volunteer Services Coordinators [*Later, AVA*] ... AAVSC
American Association of Waterbed Manufacturers [*Later, WMA*] ... AAWM
American Association of Wildlife Veterinarians ... AAWV
American Association of Women in Community and Junior Colleges ... AAWCJC
American Association of Women Dentists ... AAWD
American Association of Women Ministers [*Later, IAWM*] ... AAWM
American Association for Women Podiatrists ... AAWP
American Association of Workers for the Blind ... AAWB
American Association of Workers for Children ... AAWC
American Association for World Health [*Formerly, NCCWHO*] ... AAWH
American Association of Youth Museums ... AAYM
American Association of Zoo Keepers ... AAZK
American Association of Zoo Veterinarians ... AAZV
American Association of Zoo Veterinarians. Annual Proceedings [*A publication*] ... Am Assoc Zoo Vet Annu Proc
American Association for Zoological Nomenclature ... AAZN
American Association of Zoological Parks and Aquariums ... AAZPA
American Associations of Spanish Speaking CPA's ... AASSCPA
American Associations for Vocational Instructional Materials ... AAVIM
American Astronautical Federation [*Defunct*] ... AAF
American Astronautical Society ... AAS
American Astronautical Society. Publications. Science and Technology [*A publication*] ... Am Astronaut Soc Publ Sci Technol
American Astronomers Association ... AAA
American Astronomical Society ... AAS
American Astronomical Society. Bulletin [*A publication*] ... Am Astron Soc Bull
American Astronomical Society, Tarzana, CA [*Library symbol*] ... CTarA
American Atheist Addiction Recovery Groups ... AAARG
American Atheist Women [*An association*] ... AAW
American Athletic Association for the Deaf ... AAAD
American Athletic Trainers Association and Certification Board ... AATACB
American Audio Institute ... AAI

American Austin-Bantam Club ... AABC
American Australian Association ... AAA
American Austrian Society ... AAS
American Auto Laundry Association [*Later, International Carwash Association/National Carwash Council*] ... AALA
American Auto Racing Writers and Broadcasters Association ... AARWBA
American Automatic Control Council ... AACC
American Automobile Association ... AAA
American Automobile Touring Alliance ... AATA
American Automotive Leasing Association ... AALA
American Aviation [*A publication*] ... Am Aviation
American Aviation Historical Society ... AAHS
American Award Manufacturers Association [*Defunct*] ... AAMA
American Baby [*A publication*] ... Am Baby
American Bach Foundation ... ABF
American Backgammon Players Association ... ABPA
American Backgammon Society ... ABS
American Badminton Association [*Later, United States Badminton Association*] ... ABA
American Bail Bondsman Association ... ABBA
American Baker [*A publication*] ... Amer Baker
American Bakeries Co. [*NYSE symbol*] ... ABA
American Bakers Association ... ABA
American Bakery and Confectionery Workers' International Union [*Later, BCTWIU*] ... ABCW
American Ballet Competition [*An association*] ... ABC
American Ballet Theater ... ABT
American Bamboo Society ... ABS
American Bancorp [*NASDAQ symbol*] ... AMBC
American Bandmasters Association ... ABA
American Banjo Fraternity ... ABF
American Bank of Connecticut [*NASDAQ symbol*] ... AMSA
American Bank Note Co. [*NYSE symbol*] [*Delisted*] ... ABN
American Banker [*A publication*] ... Am Bank
American Bankers Association ... ABA
American Bankers Association, New York, NY [*Library symbol*] ... NNABA
American Bankers Insurance Group [*NASDAQ symbol*] ... ABIG
American Bankruptcy Law Journal [*A publication*] ... Am Bankr L J
American Bankruptcy Law Journal [*A publication*] ... Am Bankrupt
American Bankruptcy Reports ... AMBANKRREP
American Bantam Association ... ABA
American Baptist Black Caucus ... ABBC
American Baptist Churches ... ABC
American Baptist Education Association [*Defunct*] ... ABEA
American Baptist Extension Corporation ... ABEC
American Baptist Foreign Mission Society [*Congo - Leopoldville*] ... ABFMS
American Baptist Historical Society ... ABHS
American Baptist Historical Society Library, Rochester, NY [*OCLC symbol*] ... RXP
American Baptist Historical Society, Rochester, NY [*Library symbol*] ... NRAB
American Baptist Home Mission Society [*Later, Board of National Ministries*] ... ABHMS
American Baptist Missionary Union [*Later, Board of International Ministries*] ... ABMU
American Baptist Publication Society, Philadelphia, PA [*Library symbol*] [*Obsolete*] ... PPABP
American Baptist Theological Seminary, Nashville, TN [*Library symbol*] ... TNBT
American Baptist Women ... ABW
American Bar Association ... ABA
American Bar Association. Antitrust Law Journal [*A publication*] ... ABA Antitrust L J
American Bar Association. Journal [*A publication*] ... ABA J
American Bar Association. Journal [*A publication*] ... Am Bar A J
American Bar Association. Journal [*A publication*] ... Am Bar Assn J
American Bar Association. Section of Antitrust Law [*A publication*] ... ABA Sect Antitrust L
American Bar Association. Section of Criminal Law [*A publication*] ... ABA Sect Crim L
American Bar Association. Section of Insurance, Negligence, and Compensation Law [*A publication*] ... ABA Sect Ins N & CL
American Bar Association. Section of International and Comparative Law [*A publication*] ... ABA Sect Int & Comp L
American Bar Association. Section of International and Comparative Law. Bulletin [*A publication*] ... ABA Sect Int & Comp L Bull
American Bar Association. Section of Labor Relations Law [*A publication*] ... ABA Sect Lab Rel L
American Bar Association. Section of Mineral and Natural Resources Law [*A publication*] ... ABA Sect M & NRL
American Bar Association. Section of Real Property, Probate, and Trust Law. Proceedings [*A publication*] ... ABA Sect Real Prop L
American Bar Association Traffic Court Program ... ABA/TCP
American Bar Foundation ... ABF
American Bar Foundation, Chicago, IL [*Library symbol*] ... ICABF
American Barred Plymouth Rock Bantam Club [*Defunct*] ... ABPRBC
American Barred Plymouth Rock Club [*Later, Plymouth Rock Fanciers Club*] ... ABPRC
American Bashkir Curly Registry ... ABCR
American Basketball Association [*Later, NBA*] [*League of professional basketball players*] ... ABA
American Battle Monuments Commission [*Independent government agency*] ... ABMC
American Battleship Association ... ABA
American Bay Horse Registry ... ABHR
American Beagle Club ... ABC
American Bee Breeders Association ... ABBA
American Bee Journal [*A publication*] ... Am Bee J
American Bee Journal [*A publication*] ... Amer Bee J
American Beefalo Association ... ABA
American Beekeeping Federation ... ABF
American Begonia Society ... ABS
American Behavioral Scientist [*A publication*] ... ABHSA
American Behavioral Scientist [*A publication*] ... ABS
American Behavioral Scientist [*A publication*] ... Am Behavioral Sci
American Behavioral Scientist [*A publication*] ... Am Behav Sci
American Behavioral Scientist [*A publication*] ... Amer Behav Scientist
American Behcet's Foundation ... ABF
American Belgian Hare Club ... ABHC
American Belgian Tervuren Club ... ABTC
American Bell Association ... ABA
American Bell, Incorporated ... ABI
American Belted Galloway Cattle Breeders' Association [*Later, BGS*] ... BGA
American Benedictine Academy ... ABA
American Benedictine Review [*A publication*] ... A Ben R
American Benedictine Review [*A publication*] ... ABR
American Berkshire Association ... ABA
American Beveren Club ... ABC
American Bible Society ... ABS
American Bible Society, New York, NY [*Library symbol*] ... NNAB
American Biblical Encyclopedia Society ... ABES
American Biblical Repository [*A publication*] ... Am Bib Repos
American Bibliographical Center ... ABC
American Bibliopolist [*A publication*] ... Am Bibliop
American Bicentennial Commemorative Society ... ABCS
American Bicycle Association ... ABA
American Bike Month Committee ... ABMC
American Bikeways Foundation [*Defunct*] ... ABF
American Bill of Rights Day Association [*Defunct*] ... ABRDA
American Billiard Association ... ABA
American Biltrite, Inc. [*American Stock Exchange symbol*] ... ABL
American Biological Society ... ABS
American Biology Teacher [*A publication*] ... Am Biol Tea
American Biology Teacher [*A publication*] ... Am Biol Teach
American Birding Association ... ABA
American Birds [*A publication*] ... Am Birds
American Black Chiropractors Association ... ABCA
American Black Maine-Anjou Association ... ABMMA
American Black and Tan Coonhound Association ... ABTCA
American Blade Collectors ... ABC
American Bladesmith Society ... ABS
American Blake Foundation ... ABF
American Bleached Shellac Manufacturers Association ... ABSMA
American Blind Bowling Association ... ABBA
American Blind Lawyers Association ... ABLA
American Blind Skiing Foundation ... ABSF
American Blood Commission ... ABC
American Blood Resources Association ... ABRA
American Bloodhound Club ... ABC
American Bloodpressure Center [*NASDAQ symbol*] ... BPRC
American Blue Cheese Association ... ABCA
American Blue and White Rabbit Club ... ABWRC
American Board of Abdominal Surgery ... ABAS
American Board of Allergy and Immunology ... ABAI
American Board of Anesthesiology ... ABA
American Board Association ... ABA
American Board of Bio-Analysis [*Defunct*] [*No connection with ABB*] ... ABB-A
American Board of Bioanalysis [*Defunct*] [*No connection with ABB-A*] ... ABB
American Board for Certification in Orthotics and Prosthetics ... ABC
American Board of Clinical Biofeedback ... ABCB
American Board of Clinical Chemistry ... ABCC
American Board of Clinical Hypnosis ... ABCH
American Board of Clinical Immunology and Allergy ... ABCIA
American Board of Colon and Rectal Surgery ... ABCRS
American Board of Commissioners for Foreign Missions [*Later, UCBWM*] ... ABCFM
American Board of Commissioners for Foreign Missions [*Later, UCBWM*], **Boston, MA** [*Library symbol*] ... MBACFM
American Board on Counseling Services [*Later, IACS*] ... ABCS
American Board of Dental Public Health ... ABDPH
American Board of Dermatology ... ABD
American Board of Emergency Medicine ... ABEM
American Board of Endodontics ... ABE
American Board of Examiners in Professional Psychology [*Later, ABPP*] ... ABEPP
American Board of Examiners in Psychological Hypnosis [*Later, ABPH*] ... ABEPH
American Board of Examiners in Psychotherapy ... ABEP
American Board of Foreign Missions ... ABFM

American Board of Forensic Psychology ... ABFP
American Board of Funeral Service Education ... ABFSE
American Board of Health Physics ... ABHP
American Board of Internal Medicine ... ABIM
American Board of International Missions ... ABIM
American Board of Medical Microbiology ... ABMM
American Board of Medical Specialties ... ABMS
American Board of Medical Toxicology ... ABMT
American Board of Missions to the Jews ... ABMJ
American Board of National Missions ... ABNM
American Board of Neurological and Orthopaedic Medicine and Surgery ... ABNOMS
American Board of Neurological Surgery ... ABNS
American Board of Nutrition ... ABN
American Board of Obstetrics and Gynecology ... ABOG
American Board of Ophthalmology ... ABO
American Board of Opticianry ... ABO
American Board of Oral and Maxillofacial Surgery [*Formerly, ABOS*] ... ABOMS
American Board of Oral Pathology ... AMBOP
American Board of Oral Surgery [*Later, ABOMS*] ... ABOS
American Board of Orthodontics ... ABO
American Board of Orthopaedic Surgery ... ABOS
American Board of Otolaryngology ... ABO
American Board of Pathology ... ABP
American Board of Pediatrics ... ABP
American Board of Pedodontics ... ABP
American Board of Periodontology ... ABP
American Board of Physical Medicine and Rehabilitation ... ABPMR
American Board of Plastic Surgery ... ABPS
American Board of Podiatric Dermatology ... ABPD
American Board of Podiatric Orthopedics ... ABPO
American Board of Podiatric Surgery ... ABPS
American Board of Preventive Medicine ... ABPM
American Board Products Association [*Later, AHA*] ... ABPA
American Board of Professional Liability Attorneys ... ABPLA
American Board of Professional Psychology ... ABPP
American Board of Prosthodontics ... ABP
American Board of Psychiatry and Neurology ... ABPN
American Board of Psychological Hypnosis ... ABPH
American Board of Quality Assurance and Utilization Review Physicians ... ABQAURP
American Board of Radiology ... ABR
American Board of Surgery ... ABS
American Board of Thoracic Surgery ... ABTS
American Board of Trade ... ABT
American Board of Trial Advocates ... ABOTA
American Board of Trial Advocates ... ABTA
American Board of Tropical Medicine ... ABTM
American Board of Urology ... ABU
American Board of Veterinary Toxicology ... ABVT
American Boarding Kennels Association ... ABKA
American Boards of Examiners in Speech Pathology and Audiology [*Later, COPS*] ... ABESPA
American Boat Builders and Repairers Association ... ABBRA
American Boat and Yacht Council ... ABYC
American Boccaccio Association ... ABA
American Boiler Manufacturers Association ... ABMA
American Bonanza Society ... ABS
American Bonsai Society ... ABS
[*The*] American Book Award [*Later, ABA*] ... TABA
American Book Awards [*Formerly, TABA*] ... ABA
American Book Collector [*A publication*] ... ABC
American Book Collector [*A publication*] ... Am Bk Collec
American Book Producers Association ... ABPA
American Book Publishers Council [*Later, AAP*] ... ABPC
American Book Publishers Political Action Committee ... ABPPAC
American Book Publishing Record [*A publication*] ... ABPR
American Book Publishing Record [*A publication*] ... Am Book Publ Recd
American Book Review [*A publication*] ... AMR
American Book Trade Directory [*A publication*] ... ABTD
(American) Bookman [*A publication*] ... AB
American Booksellers Association ... ABA
American Border Fancy Canary Club ... ABFCC
American-Born Chinese ... ABC
American Bosch Arma Corp. [*NYSE symbol*] [*Delisted*] ... AB
American Bosch Arma Corporation ... ABAC
American Bosch Arma Corporation ... AMBAC
American Bosch Arma Corp. ... ARMA
American Bottled Water Association ... ABWA
American Bottlers of Carbonated Beverages [*Later, NSDA*] ... ABCB
American Bouvier des Flandres Club ... ABDFC
American Bowhunters Association [*Defunct*] ... ABA
American Bowling Congress ... ABC
American Boxer Club ... ABC
American Boxwood Society ... ABS
American Boys Club in Defense of Errol Flynn [*Facetious organization*] ... ABCDEF
American Brahma Club ... ABC
American Brahman Breeders Association ... ABBA
American Brake Shoe Co. [*NYSE symbol*] [*Delisted*] ... ABK
American Brands, Inc. [*NYSE symbol*] ... AMB
American Brazilian Association [*Later, Brazilian American Chamber of Commerce*] ... ABA
American Breed Association ... ABA
American Breeder Service ... ABS
American Brewer [*A publication*] ... Am Brew
American Brewer [*A publication*] ... Amer Brewer
American Bridge Association ... ABA
American Bridge Teachers' Association ... ABTA
American Bridge, Tunnel, and Turnpike Association [*Later, IBTTA*] ... ABTTA
American, British, Australian [*Military*] ... ABA
American British Cab Society ... ABCS
American, British, and Canadian ... ABC
American-British-Canadian Air Standardization Agreement ... ABCAIRSTD
American-British-Canadian Army Standardization Program ... ABC-ASP
American, British, Canadian, and Australian [*Armies*] ... ABCA
American-British-Canadian Standardization Program ... ABCSP
American-British-Canadian Stores Catalogue ... ABCSC
American and British Commonwealth Association ... ABC
American-British Conversation [*as ABC-1, a 1941 report that set forth Allied worldwide strategy*] [*World War II*] ... ABC
American-British-Dutch-Australian Air Operational Command [*1942*] ... ABDAIR
American-British-Dutch-Australian Army Operational Command [*1942*] ... ABDARM
American-British-Dutch-Australian Naval Operational Command [*1942*] ... ABDAFLOAT
American-British-Dutch-Australian Supreme Command [*1942*] ... ABDA
American-British-Dutch-Australian Supreme Command [*1942*] ... ABDACOM
American-British Forces [*World War II*] ... ABFOR
American-British Intelligence [*NATO*] ... ABI
American-British Laboratory [*Harvard University*] ... ABL
American British Numismatic Society ... ABNS
American Brittany Club ... ABC
American Brittle Bone Society ... ABBS
American Broadcasting Companies, Inc. [*NYSE symbol*] ... ABC
American Broadcasting-Paramount Theatres [*Later, ABC*] [*NYSE symbol*] ... ABP
American Broadcasting Station in Europe [*OWI*] ... ABSIE
American Broncho-Esophagological Association ... ABEA
American Brown Leghorn Club ... ABLC
American Brush Manufacturers Association ... ABMA
American Brussels Griffon Association ... ABGA
American Bryological and Lichenological Society ... ABLS
American Bryological Society [*Later, ABLS*] ... ABS
American Buckskin Registry Association ... ABRA
American Buddhist Academy ... ABA
American Buddhist Association ... ABA
American Budgerigar Society ... ABS
American Buff Plymouth Rock Club ... ABPRC
American Buff Wyandotte Club [*Defunct*] ... ABWC
American Buffalo Association ... ABA
American Builder [*A publication*] ... Am Bld
American Building Contractors Association ... ABCA
American Building Maintenance Industries [*NYSE symbol*] ... ABM
American Bulgarian League [*Defunct*] ... ABL
American Bullmastiff Association ... ABA
American Bureau of Geography. Bulletin [*A publication*] ... Am Bur Geog B
American Bureau for Medical Advancement in China ... ABMAC
American Bureau of Metal Statistics ... ABMS
American Bureau of Shipping ... AB
American Bureau of Shipping ... ABS
American Burn Association ... ABA
American Bus Association ... ABA
American Business [*A publication*] ... Am Bsns
American Business [*A publication*] ... Am Business
American Business Cancer [*in name "ABC Research Foundation"*] ... ABC
American Business Cancer Research Foundation ... ABCRF
American Business Communication Association [*Formerly, ABWA*] ... ABCA
American Business Conference ... ABC
American Business Council, Malaysia ... ABC
American Business Council of Singapore ... ABCS
American Business Education [*A publication*] ... Am Bsns Ed
American Business Education Yearbook [*A publication*] ... Am Bsns Ed Yrbk
American Business Law Association ... ABLA
American Business Law Journal [*A publication*] ... Am Bus Law
American Business Law Journal [*A publication*] ... Am Bus L J
American Business Media Council ... ABMC
American Business Men's Research Foundation ... ABMRF
American Business Press [*Formerly, Associated Business Publications*] [*An association*] ... ABP
American Business Products, Inc. [*NYSE symbol*] ... ABP
American Business Women's Association ... ABWA
American Business Writing Association [*Later, ABCA*] ... ABWA
American Butter and Cheese Review [*A publication*] ... Am Butter R
American Butter Institute ... ABI
American Buyers Federation ... ABF
American-Byelorussian Cultural Relief Association ... ABCRA

American Cable & Radio Corp. ... AC & R
American Cadet Alliance ... ACA
American Camellia Society ... ACS
American Camp and Hospital Service ... ACHS
American Campaign Medal ... ACM
American Camping Association ... ACA
American Can Co. [*NYSE symbol*] ... AC
American Can Co., Barrington, IL [*Library symbol*] ... IBarA
American, Canadian, Australian, British Urban Game [*Computer-assisted simulation wargame*] [*Army*] ... ACABUG
American-Canadian Genealogical Society ... ACGS
American Canal Society ... ACS
American Cancer Society ... ACS
American Cancer Society, New York, NY [*Library symbol*] ... NNACS
American Canoe Association ... ACA
American Canvas Institute ... ACI
American Capital Bond Fund, Inc. [*NYSE symbol*] ... ACB
American Capital Convertible Securities, Inc. [*NYSE symbol*] ... ACS
American Capital Corporation [*American Stock Exchange symbol*] ... ACC
American Capitol Insurance Company [*NASDAQ symbol*] ... ACIC
American Capon Producers Association ... ACPA
American Car and Foundry ... ACF
American Car Rental Association ... ACRA
American Carbon Society ... ACS
American Cardiology Technologists Association ... ACTA
American Cargo War Risk Reinsurance Exchange ... ACWRRE
American Carnation Society [*Defunct*] ... ACS
American Carnival Glass Association ... ACGA
American Carnivals Association ... ACA
American Carousel Society ... ACS
American Carpet Institute [*Later, CRI*] ... ACI
American Carriers, Incorporated [*NASDAQ symbol*] ... ACIX
American Cartographic Association ... ACA
American Casino Enterprises [*NASDAQ symbol*] ... ACES
American Casting Association ... ACA
American Cat Association ... ACA
American Cat Fanciers Association ... ACFA
American Catalogue [*A bibliographic publication*] ... AmC
American Catfish Marketing Association ... ACMA
American Catholic Committee ... ACC
American Catholic Conference ... ACC
American Catholic Correctional Chaplains Association ... ACCCA
American Catholic Esperanto Society ... ACES
American Catholic Historical Association ... ACHA
American Catholic Historical Researches [*A publication*] ... ACHR
American Catholic Historical Society ... ACHS
American Catholic Historical Society, Philadelphia, PA [*Library symbol*] ... PPACHi
American Catholic Historical Society. Records [*A publication*] ... ACHS
American Catholic Historical Society. Records [*A publication*] ... Am Cath His Rec
American Catholic Historical Society. Records [*A publication*] ... AmCathHS
American Catholic Philosophical Association ... ACPA
American Catholic Psychological Association [*Later, PIRI*] ... ACPA
American Catholic Quarterly Review [*A publication*] ... ACQR
American Catholic Quarterly Review [*A publication*] ... Am Cath Q
American Catholic Sociological Review [*A publication*] ... ACSR
American Catholic Sociological Society [*Later, ASR*] ... ACSS
American Catholic Truth Society ... ACTS
American Cattle Producer [*A publication*] ... Am Cattle Prod
American Cattle Producer [*A publication*] ... Amer Cattle Prod
American Cause [*An association*] ... AC
American Cavy Breeders Association ... ACBA
American Celiac Society ... ACS
American Cellular Network [*NASDAQ symbol*] ... AMLL
American Cemetery Association ... ACA
American Center for the Alexander Technique ... ACAT
American Center for Chinese Medical Sciences ... ACCMS
American Center for Homeopathy ... ACH
American Center for Quality of Work Life ... ACQWL
American Center for Stanislavski Theatre Art ... ACSTA
American Center for Students and Artists ... ACSA
American Center of the Union Internationale de la Marionnette [*International Puppeteers Union*] ... UNIMA-USA
American Central NOTAM [*Notice to Airmen*] **Facility** [*Military*] ... ACNF
American Century Corp. [*Formerly, American Century Trust SBI*] [*NYSE symbol*] ... ACT
American Ceramic Society ... ACerS
American Ceramic Society ... ACS
American Ceramic Society. Bulletin [*A publication*] ... Am Ceram S
American Ceramic Society. Bulletin [*A publication*] ... Am Ceram Soc Bull
American Ceramic Society. Bulletin [*A publication*] ... Am Cer Soc Bul
American Ceramic Society. Bulletin [*A publication*] ... Amer Ceram Soc Bull
American Ceramic Society. Bulletin [*A publication*] ... Ceramic S B
American Ceramic Society, Columbus, OH [*Library symbol*] ... OCoAC
American Ceramic Society. Journal [*A publication*] ... Am Ceramic Soc Jour
American Ceramic Society. Journal [*A publication*] ... Am Cer Soc J
American Certified Morticians Association [*Defunct*] ... ACMA
American Cetacean Society ... ACS
American Chain Association ... ACA
American Chain of Warehouses ... ACW
American Chamber of Commerce in Austria ... ACCA
American Chamber of Commerce of Bolivia ... ACCB
American Chamber of Commerce of El Salvador ... ACCES
American Chamber of Commerce Executives ... ACCE
American Chamber of Commerce in Japan ... ACCJ
American Chamber of Commerce of the Philippines ... ACCP
American Chamber of Commerce in Republic of China ... ACC-ROC
American Chamber of Commerce Researchers Association ... ACCRA
American Chapter, International Real Estate Federation ... AC/IREF
American Charbray Breeders Association [*Later, AICA*] ... ACBA
American Checker Federation [*Governing body for sport in US*] ... ACF
American Checkered Giant Club [*Later, ACGRC*] ... ACGC
American Checkered Giant Rabbit Club [*Formerly, ACGC*] ... ACGRC
American Cheerleader Association ... ACA
American Cheese Society ... ACS
American Chemical Exchange ... ACE
American Chemical Society ... ACS
American Chemical Society. Division of Environmental Chemistry. Preprints [*A publication*] ... Am Chem Soc Div Environ Chem Prepr
American Chemical Society. Division of Fuel Chemistry. Preprints [*A publication*] ... Am Chem Soc Div Fuel Chem Prepr
American Chemical Society. Division of Fuel Chemistry. Preprints [*A publication*] ... Am Chem Soc Div Fuel Prepr
American Chemical Society. Division of Fuel Chemistry. Preprints [*A publication*] ... Amer Chem Soc Div Fuel Chem Prepr
American Chemical Society. Division of Polymer Chemistry. Preprints [*A publication*] ... Am Chem Soc Div Polym Chem Prepr
American Chemical Society. Journal [*A publication*] ... Am Chem Soc J
American Chemical Society. Monograph [*A publication*] ... Am Chem Soc Mon
American Chemical Society, Washington, DC [*Library symbol*] ... DACS
American Chesapeake Club ... ACC
American Chess Academy [*Commercial firm*] ... ACA
American Chess Foundation ... ACF
American Chestnut Foundation ... ACF
American Cheviot Sheep Society ... ACSS
American Chianina Association ... ACA
American Child [*A publication*] ... Am Child
American Child Guidance Foundation [*Defunct*] ... ACGF
American Childhood [*A publication*] ... Am Childh
American Chinchilla Rabbit Breeders Association ... ACRBA
American Chinese Medical Society ... ACMS
American Chiropractic Association ... ACA
American Choral Directors Association ... ACDA
American Choral Foundation ... ACF
American Choral Review [*A publication*] ... Am Choral R
American Christian Action Council ... ACAC
American Christian Association for Israel [*Later, American-Israel Cultural Foundation*] ... ACAI
American Christian Committee for Refugees [*Post-World War II, Europe*] ... ACCR
American Christian Palestine Committee [*Defunct*] ... ACPC
American Christian Television Service [*Network*] ... ACTS
American Christians for the Abolition of Torture ... ACAT
American Christmas Crib Society [*Defunct*] ... ACCS
American Church Building Fund Commission [*Later, Episcopal Church Building Fund*] ... ACBFC
American Church Monthly [*A publication*] ... Am Church Mo
American Church Review [*A publication*] ... Am Church R
American Church Review [*A publication*] ... American Church R
American Church Union ... ACU
American Cinema Editors ... ACE
American Cinematographer [*A publication*] ... Am Cin
American Cinematographer [*A publication*] ... Am Cinematog
American Circus Memorial Association ... ACMA
American Citizens Band Operators Association ... ACBOA
American Citizens Concerned for Life ... ACCL
American Citizens for Honesty in Government [*Defunct*] ... ACHG
American Citizenship Center ... ACC
American City [*A publication*] ... AC
American City [*A publication*] ... Am City
American City [*A publication*] ... Amer City
American City (City Edition) [*A publication*] ... Am City (C ed)
American City and County [*A publication*] ... Am City Cty
American City Planning Institute ... ACPI
American City (Town and Country Edition) [*A publication*] ... Am City (T & C ed)
American Civic Association ... ACA
[*The*] **American Civil Defense Association** ... TACDA
American Civil Liberties Union ... ACLU
American Civilian Internee Information Bureau ... ACIIB
American Classical League ... ACL
American Classical Review [*A publication*] ... ACR
American Clean Water Association ... ACWA
American Cleft Palate Association ... ACPA
American Clinical and Climatological Association ... ACCA
American Clinical Laboratory Association ... ACLA
American Clinical Products Review [*A publication*] ... ACPR
American Clipper Owners Club ... ACOC
American Cloak and Suit Manufacturers Association ... ACSMA

American Club of Paris...ACP
American Co-Operative Journal [A publication]..........Am Co-Op J
American Coalition of Citizens with Disabilities................ACCD
American Coalition of Patriotic Societies ....ACPS
American Coaster Enthusiasts ....ACE
American Cockatiel Society ....ACS
American Cocoa Research Institute ....ACRI
American Coke and Coal Chemicals Institute ....ACCCI
American Collection Association ....ACA
American Collector [A publication].............................Am Coll
American Collectors Association ....ACA
American Collectors of Infant Feeders .... ACIF
American College Admissions Advisory Center [Formerly,
   ACAC]..ACAAC
American College Admissions Center [Later, American College
   Admissions Advisory Center] ....ACAC
American College of Allergists ....ACA
American College of Anesthesiologists ....ACA
American College of Angiology......................................ACA
American College of Animal Laboratory Medicine ....ACALM
American College of Apothecaries ....ACA
American College, Bryn Mawr, PA [OCLC symbol] ....AMC
American College of Cardiology......................................ACC
American College of Cardiology. Extended Learning [A
   publication]...ACCEL
American College of Cardiology Extended Study Services...........ACCESS
American College of Chemosurgery................................ACC
American College of Chest Physicians............................ACCP
American College of Chiropractic Orthopedists ....ACCO
American College of Clinic Administrators [Defunct].........ACCA
American College of Clinic Managers [Later, American College
   of Medical Group Administrators].................................ACCM
American College of Clinical Hypnosis ....ACCH
American College of Clinical Pharmacology ....ACCP
American College of Clinical Pharmacy ....ACCP
American College of Cryosurgery....................................ACC
American College Dance Festival Association ....ACDFA
American College of Dentists ....ACD
American College of Ecology..ACE
American College of Emergency Physicians ....ACEP
American College of Foot Orthopedists ....ACFO
American College of Foot Roentgenologists [Later, American
   College of Podiatric Radiologists] ....ACFR
American College of Foot Specialists ....ACFS
American College of Foot Surgeons ....ACFS
American College of Gastroenterology ....ACG
American College of General Practice ....ACGP
American College of General Practitioners in Osteopathic
   Medicine and Surgery ....ACGPOMS
American College Health Association ....ACHA
American College of Heraldry ....ACH
American College of Home Obstetrics ....ACHO
American College of Hospital Administrators ....ACHA
American College of International Physicians [Formerly, NAFMG] ....ACIP
American College of Laboratory Animal Medicine ....ACLAM
American College of Legal Medicine ....ACLM
American College of Life Underwriters [Later, The American
   College]..ACLU
American College of Life Underwriters, Bryn Mawr, PA [Library
   symbol]..PBmA
American College of Medical Group Administrators [Formerly,
   ACCM] ....ACMGA
American College of Medical Technologists.....................ACMT
American College of Musicians ....ACM
American College of Neuropsychiatrists ....ACN
American College of Neuropsychopharmacology ....ACNP
American College of Nuclear Medicine ....ACNM
American College of Nuclear Physicians ....ACNP
American College of Nurse-Midwives ....ACNM
American College of Nursing Home Administrators ....ACNHA
American College of Nutrition ....ACN
American College of Obstetricians and Gynecologists.........ACOG
American College of Oral and Maxillofacial Surgeons ....ACOMS
American College of Orgonomy.......................................ACO
American College of Osteopathic Emergency Physicians ....ACOEP
American College of Osteopathic Hospital Administrators ....ACOHA
American College of Osteopathic Internists ....ACOI
American College of Osteopathic Obstetricians and
   Gynecologists ....ACOOG
American College of Osteopathic Pediatricians ....ACOP
American College of Osteopathic Surgeons ....ACOS
American College of Otorhinolaryngologists ....ACO
American College Personnel Association ....ACPA
American College of Pharmacists ....ACP
American College of Physician Executives ....ACPE
American College of Physicians ....ACP
American College of Physicians Assistants......................ACPA
American College of Podiatric Radiologists......................ACPR
American College of Podopediatrics ....ACP
American College of Preventive Medicine ....ACPM
American College of Probate Counsel.............................ACPC

American College of Prosthodontists...............................ACP
American College of Psychiatrists....................................ACP
American College of Psychoanalysts ....ACPn
American College Public Relations Association [Later, Council
   for the Advancement and Support of Education].............ACPRA
American College of Radiology.......................................ACR
American College of Real Estate Consultants [Later, RECP]...........ACREC
American College of Sports Medicine ....ACSM
American College of Surgeons ....ACS
American College of Surgeons, Chicago, IL [Library symbol] ....ICAC
American College Test [or Testing] [Program] ....ACT
American College Testing. Research Reports [A publication]...........
                                             ACT Res Rep
American College of Theriogenologists ....ACT
American College of Trial Lawyers..................................ACTL
American College of Utilization Review Physicians ....ACURP
American College of Veterinary Dermatology ....ACVD
American College of Veterinary Internal Medicine............ACVIM
American College of Veterinary Microbiologists ....ACVM
American College of Veterinary Ophthalmologists ....ACVO
American College of Veterinary Pathologists ....ACVP
American College of Veterinary Radiology ....ACVR
American College of Veterinary Surgeons ....ACVS
American College of Veterinary Toxicologists...................ACVT
American Collegiate Retailing Association ....ACRA
American Colonization Society..ACS
American Color Print Society...ACPS
American Comedy Museum Association [Defunct].............ACMA
American Commercial Barge Lines, Inc. [AAR code] ....ACBL
American Commercial Collectors Association ....ACCA
American Commercial Lines, Inc. [NYSE symbol] [Delisted] ....ABR
American Commercial Lines, Inc.......................................ACL
American Commission on Ministerial Training...................ACMT
American Commission for Protection and Salvage of Artistic
   and Historical Monuments in War Areas [World War II]
   [Defunct]...ACPSAHMWA
American Committee to Advance the Study of Petroglyphs and
   Pictographs..ACASPP
American Committee on Africa ....ACOA
American Committee for Democracy and Freedom in Greece.........ACDFG
American Committee on East-West Accord ....ACEWA
American Committee for Flags of Necessity [Later, FACS].........ACFN
American Committee on the History of the Second World War.....ACHSWW
American Committee for International Conservation [Formerly,
   ACIWLP] [Later, ACI]...ACIC
American Committee for International Wild Life Protection
   [Later, ACIC]...ACIWLP
American Committee for Irish Studies ....ACIS
American Committee for Irish Studies. Newsletter [A
   publication]...ACIS Newsletter
American Committee on Italian Migration ....ACIM
American Committee on Japan...ACJ
American Committee for Liberation [Later, RFE/RL] ....ACL
American Committee for the National Sick Fund of Israel.........ACNSFI
American Committee of OSE [Defunct].............................AMEROSE
American Committee for Rescue and Resettlement of Iraqi
   Jews...AMCORR
American Committee of Slavists ....ACS
American Committee for South Asian Art.........................ACSAA
American Committee for Ulster Justice ....ACUJ
American Committee of United Europe ....ACUE
American Committee for the Weizmann Institute of Science...........ACWIS
American Communications Association ....ACA
American Communications & TV [NASDAQ symbol]............ASTV
American Community Cultural Center Association ....ACCCA
American Community Schools [In foreign countries]............ACS
American Community Services [NASDAQ symbol] ....ACSI
American Community Theatre Association ....ACTA
American Commuters Association ....ACA
American Comparative Literature Association ....ACLA
American Comparative Literature Association. Newsletter [A
   publication]...ACLAN
American Compensation Association ....ACA
American Component Dealers Association ....ACDA
American Composers Alliance ....ACA
American Composers Alliance. Bulletin [A publication].........ACA
American Composers Orchestra ....ACO
American Concert Choir [Defunct]....................................ACC
American Concert Choir and Choral Foundation [Later, ACF] ....ACCCF
American Concrete Agricultural Pipe Association [Defunct]............ACAPA
American Concrete Institute..ACI
American Concrete Institute, Detroit, MI [Library symbol].........MiDACI
American Concrete Institute. Journal [A publication].......Am Concrete Inst J
American Concrete Institute. Monograph [A publication]...........
                                           Am Concr Inst Monogr
American Concrete Institute. Monograph [A publication]...........
                                           Amer Concr Inst Monogr
American Concrete Institute. Standards [A publication]...........
                                           Amer Concr Inst Stand
American Concrete Pavement Association ....ACPA
American Concrete Pipe Association.................................ACPA

American Concrete Pressure Pipe Association ... ACPP
American Concrete Pumping Association ... ACPA
American Conference of Academic Deans ... ACAD
American Conference of Cantors ... ACC
American Conference of Governmental Industrial Hygienists ... ACGIH
American Conference of Real Estate Investment Trusts ... ACREIT
American Conference of Therapeutic Selfhelp/Selfhealth Social Action Clubs ... ACT
American Congregation of Jews from Austria ... ACJA
American Congregational Association ... ACA
American Congregational Association, Boston, MA [*Library symbol*] ... MBC
American Congregational Union ... ACU
American Congress of Physical Medicine and Rehabilitation [*Later, ACRM*] ... ACPMR
American Congress of Rehabilitation Medicine ... ACRM
American Congress on Surveying and Mapping ... ACSM
American Connemara Pony Society ... ACPS
American Conservative Union ... ACU
American Conservative Union Education and Research Institute ... ACU-ERI
American Conservatory of Music ... ACM
American Conservatory of Music, Chicago, IL [*OCLC symbol*] ... IVI
American Conservatory Theatre ... ACT
American Constitutional Rights Association ... ACRA
American Consul ... AMCON
American Consular Reporting Officer ... AMCONREPO
American Consulate General ... AMCONGEN
American Consulting Engineers Council ... ACEC
American Consumer Industries, Inc. [*NYSE symbol*] [*Delisted*] ... ACA
American Continental Corporation [*NASDAQ symbol*] ... AMCC
American Contract Bridge League ... ACBL
American Controlled Industries, Inc. [*American Stock Exchange symbol*] ... ACI
American Coon Hunters Association ... ACHA
American Coordinated Medical Society ... ACMS
American Coordinating Committee for Equality in Sport and Society ... ACCESS
American Copper Council ... ACC
American Coptic Association ... ACA
American Cormo Sheep Association ... ACSA
American Corn Millers' Federation ... ACMF
American Corporate Counsel Association ... ACCA
American Corporation [*A publication*] ... Amer Corp
American Correctional Association ... ACA
American Correctional Chaplains Association ... ACCA
American Correctional Food Service Association ... ACFSA
American Correctional Health Services Association ... ACHSA
American Corrective Therapy Association ... ACTA
American Corrective Therapy Journal [*A publication*] ... Am Correct Ther J
American Corrective Therapy Journal [*A publication*] ... Amer Correct Ther J
American Corriedale Association ... ACA
American Cotswold Record Association ... ACRA
American Cottage Cheese Institute [*Later, ACDPI*] ... ACCI
American Cotton Cooperative Association ... ACCA
American Cotton Exporters' Association ... ACEA
American Cotton Linter Association [*Defunct*] ... ACLA
American Cotton Manufacturers Institute [*Later, ATMI*] ... ACMI
American Cotton Shippers Association ... ACSA
American Cotton Waste Exchange ... ACWE
American Council for the Advancement of Human Rights ... ACAHR
American Council on Alcohol Problems ... ACAP
American Council on Alcoholism ... ACA
American Council of Applied Clinical Nutrition ... ACACN
American Council for the Arts ... ACA
American Council for the Arts in Education [*Defunct*] ... ACAE
American Council for Better Broadcasts ... ACBB
American Council of the Blind ... ACB
American Council of the Blind Enterprises and Services ... ACBES
American Council of the Blind Federal Employees ... ACBFE
American Council of the Blind Parents ... ACBP
American Council for Capital Formation ... ACCF
American Council on Capital Gains and Estate Taxation [*Later, ACCF*] [*Tax lobbying organization*] ... ACCGET
American Council for Career Women ... ACCW
American Council on Chiropractic Physiotherapy ... ACCP
American Council on Chiropractic Roentgenology [*Later, Council on Roentgenology of the American Chiropractic Association*] ... ACCR
American Council of Christian Churches ... ACCC
American Council of Christian Laymen [*Later, Laymen's Commission of the American Council of Christian Churches*] ... ACCL
American Council of Commercial Laboratories [*Later, ACIL*] ... ACCL
American Council for Construction Education ... ACCE
American Council on Consumer Interests ... ACCI
American Council for Coordinated Action [*Absorbed by Enterprise America*] ... ACCA
American Council on Cosmetology Education ... ACCE
American Council on Education ... ACE
American Council on Education for Journalism [*Later, ACEJMC*] ... ACEJ
American Council on Educational Simulation and Gaming ... ACESG
American Council for Elementary School Industrial Arts ... ACESIA
American Council for Emigres in the Professions [*Defunct*] ... ACEP
American Council on the Environment ... ACE
American Council of Executives in Religion ... ACER
American Council on German Studies ... ACGS
American Council on Germany ... ACG
American Council of Human Rights ... ACHR
American Council to Improve Our Neighborhoods [*Later, NUC*] ... ACTION
American Council of Independent Laboratories [*Formerly, ACCL*] ... ACIL
American Council of Industrial Arts State Association Officers ... ACIASAO
American Council of Industrial Arts Supervisors ... ACIAS
American Council of Industrial Arts Teacher Education ... ACIATE
American Council of the International Institute of Welding ... ACIIW
American Council on International Sports ... ACIS
American Council for Judaism ... ACJ
American Council of Learned Societies ... ACLS
American Council of Learned Societies. Newsletter [*A publication*] ... ACLSN
American Council of Life Insurance ... ACLI
American Council on Marijuana and Other Psychoactive Drugs ... ACM
American Council on the Middle East ... ACME
American Council for Nationalities Service ... ACNS
American Council on NATO [*Later, Atlantic Council of the United States*] ... ACN
American Council of Otolaryngology [*Later, ACO-HNS*] ... ACO
American Council of Otolaryngology - Head and Neck Surgery [*Formerly, ACO*] ... ACO-HNS
American Council of Parent Cooperatives [*Later, PCPI*] ... ACPC
American Council on Pharmaceutical Education ... ACPE
American Council of Polish Cultural Clubs ... ACPCC
American Council for Private International Communications, Inc. [*Proposed corporation to replace Radio Free Europe*] ... ACPIC
American Council on Race Relations ... ACRR
American Council of Railroad Women ... ACRW
American Council for Romanians ... ACR
American Council on Rural Special Education ... ACRSE
American Council on Schools and Colleges ... ACSC
American Council on Science and Health ... ACSH
American Council of Spotted Asses ... ACSA
American Council of Taxpayers [*Formerly, COST*] ... ACT
American Council of Teachers of Russian ... ACTR
American Council of Teachers of Uncommonly Taught Asian Languages ... ACTUAL
American Council on the Teaching of Foreign Languages ... ACTFL
American Council for Turfgrass ... ACT
American Council for University Planning and Academic Excellence ... ACUPAE
American Council of Venture Clubs ... ACVC
American Council of Voluntary Agencies for Foreign Service ... ACVAFS
American Council of Women Chiropractors [*Formerly, NCWC, CWC*] ... ACWC
American Council for World Freedom ... ACWF
American Council of Young Political Leaders ... ACYPL
American Counseling Association ... ACA
American Country Life Association ... ACLA
American Court and Commercial Newspapers ... ACCN
American Craft [*A publication*] ... Am Craft
American Craft [*formerly, Craftsmen's*] **Council** ... ACC
American Cranberry Growers' Association [*Defunct*] ... ACGA
American Cream Draft Horse Association ... ACDHA
American Creamery and Poultry Produce Review [*A publication*] ... Am Creamery
American Credit Corp. [*NYSE symbol*] ... ACR
American Cricket Growers Association ... ACGA
American Criminal Justice Association - Lambda Alpha Epsilon ... ACJA-LAE
American Criminal Law Quarterly [*A publication*] ... Am Crim L Q
American Criminal Law Review [*A publication*] ... Am Crim Law
American Criminal Law Review [*A publication*] ... Am Crim L Rev
American Croatian Academic Club [*Later, ACAS*] ... ACAC
American Croatian Academic Society [*Formerly, ACAC*] ... ACAS
American Crossbow Association ... ACA
American Crossbred Pony Registry ... ACPR
American Cryptogram Association ... ACA
American Crystal Sugar Co. [*NYSE symbol*] [*Delisted*] ... ACS
American Crystallographic Association ... ACA
American Crystallographic Association Polycrystal Book Service. Transactions [*A publication*] ... Am Cryst Assoc Trans
American Crystallographic Community ... ACC
American Culinary Federation ... ACF
American Cultural Society [*Defunct*] ... ACS
American Cultured Dairy Products Institute ... ACDPI
American Custard Glass Collectors ... ACGC
American Cut Glass Association ... ACGA
American Cutlery Manufacturers Association ... ACMA
American Cyanamid Company ... ACC
American Cyanamid Company ... ACCO
American Cyanamid Co. [*NYSE symbol*] ... ACY
American Cyanamid Co., Agricultural Division, Princeton, NJ [*Library symbol*] ... NjPA

American Cyanamid Co., Lederle Laboratories, Pearl River, NY [*Library symbol*] ... NPrA
American Cyanamid Co., Organic Chemicals Division, Bound Brook, NJ [*Library symbol*] ... NjBbA
American Cyanamid Co., Pigments Division, Piney River, VA [*Library symbol*] ... ViPrA
American Cyanamid Co., Princeton, NJ [*OCLC symbol*] ... ACA
American Cyanamid Co., Stamford, CT [*Library symbol*] ... CtSA
American Cycling Union ... ACU
American Cytogenetics, Inc. [*NASDAQ symbol*] ... ACYT
American Daffodil Society ... ADS
American Dahlia Society ... ADS
American Dairy Association ... ADA
American Dairy Goat Association ... ADGA
American Dairy Products Review [*A publication*] ... Am Dairy Prod R
American Dairy Review [*A publication*] ... Am Dairy R
American Dairy Review [*A publication*] ... Amer Dairy Rev
American Dairy Science Association ... ADSA
American Dance Festival ... ADF
American Dance Guild ... ADG
American Dance Therapy Association ... ADTA
American Dart Association ... ADA
American Darts Organization ... ADO
American/Davey Corp. [*NASDAQ symbol*] ... ADAX
American Deafness and Rehabilitation Association [*Formerly, PRWAD*] ... ADARA
American Decartelization Agency [*Post-World War II*] ... AMDAG
American Defenders ... AD
American Defenders Against Animal Mistreatment ... ADAM
American Defenders of Bataan and Corregidor ... ADBC
American Defense Preparedness Association ... ADPA
American Defense Service Medal ... ADSM
American Dehydrated Onion and Garlic Association ... ADOGA
American Dehydrators Association ... ADA
American and Delaine-Merino Record Association ... ADMRA
American Democratic Political Action ... ADPAC
American Dental Assistants Association ... ADAA
American Dental Assistant's Program ... ADAP
American Dental Association ... ADA
American Dental Association, Chicago, IL [*Library symbol*] ... ICADA
American Dental Association, Chicago, IL [*OCLC symbol*] ... JAA
American Dental Hygienists' Association ... ADHA
American Dental Interfraternity Council ... ADIC
American Dental Society of Anesthesiology ... ADSA
American Dental Society of Europe ... ADSE
American Dental Trade Association ... ADTA
American Dentists for Foreign Service ... ADFS
American Denture Society ... ADS
American Depositary Receipt ... ADR
American Dermatologic Society of Allergy and Immunology ... ADSAI
American Dermatological Association ... ADA
American Deserters Committee, France ... ADC
American Design Bicentennial [*An association*] [*Defunct*] ... ADB
American Devon Cattle Club [*Later, Devon Cattle Association*] ... ADCC
American Dexter Cattle Association ... ADCA
American Diabetes Association ... ADA
American Diagnostics Corp. [*NASDAQ symbol*] ... ADGN
American Dialect Dictionary [*A publication*] ... ADD
American Dialect Society ... ADS
American Dialog [*A publication*] ... AmD
American Diamond Industry Association ... ADIA
American Die Casting Institute ... ADCI
American Dietetic Association ... ADA
American Dietetic Association. Journal [*A publication*] ... Am Dietet Assn J
American Digestive Disease Society ... ADDS
American Dinner Theatre Institute ... ADTI
American Diopter and Decibel Society ... ADDS
American Distilling Company [*NYSE symbol*] [*Delisted*] ... ADC
American District Telegraph Co. [*NYSE symbol*] ... ADT
American Divorce Association for Men ... ADAM
American Doctoral Dissertations [*A publication*] ... ADD
American Doctors [*Later, AMDOC/Option Agency*] ... AMDOC
American Documentation [*A publication*] ... AD
American Documentation [*A publication*] ... Am Doc
American Documentation [*A publication*] ... Amer Doc
American Documentation Institute [*Later, American Society for Information Science*] ... ADI
American Dog Breeders Association [*Defunct*] ... ADBA
American Dog Feed Institute [*Defunct*] ... ADFI
American Donkey and Mule Society ... ADMS
American Double Dutch League ... ADDL
American Dove Association ... ADA
American Down Association ... ADA
American Dressage Institute ... ADI
American Driver Education Association [*Later, ADTSEA*] ... ADEA
American Driver and Traffic Safety Education Association ... ADTSEA
American Driving Society ... ADS
American Drug Manufacturers' Association [*Later, PMA*] ... ADMA
American Druggist [*A publication*] ... Am Druggist
American Druggist [*A publication*] ... Amer Drug
American Druggist Merchandising [*A publication*] ... Am Druggist Merch
American Druze Public Affairs Committee ... AD-PAC
American Dry Milk Institute ... ADMI
American Dutch Rabbit Club ... ADRC
American Duty Free ... ADF
American Dyestuff Reporter [*A publication*] ... Am Dye Rep
American Dyestuff Reporter [*A publication*] ... Am Dyest Rep
American Dyestuff Reporter [*A publication*] ... Am Dyestuff Reptr
American Dyestuff Reporter [*A publication*] ... Amer Dyestuff Rep
American Eagle Airlines, Inc. [*ICAO designator*] ... WX
American Ecclesiastical Review [*A publication*] ... AER
American Ecclesiastical Review [*A publication*] ... Am Eccles Rev
American Eclectic [*A publication*] ... Am Ecl
American Ecology Services ... AES
American Economic Association ... AEA
American Economic Association. Bulletin [*A publication*] ... Am Econ Assn Bul
American Economic Association. Publications [*A publication*] ... Am Econ Assoc Publ
American Economic Council ... AEC
American Economic Development Council [*Formerly, AIDC*] ... AEDC
American Economic Foundation ... AEF
American Economic Review [*A publication*] ... AER
American Economic Review [*A publication*] ... Am Econ R
American Economic Review [*A publication*] ... Am Econ Rev
American Economic Review [*A publication*] ... Am Ec Rev
American Economic Review [*A publication*] ... Amer Econ R
American Economic Review [*A publication*] ... Amer Econ Rev
American Economic Review. Papers and Proceedings [*A publication*] ... Am Econ R Pa & Proc
American Economist [*A publication*] ... Am Econ
American Economist [*A publication*] ... Am Economist
American Economist [*A publication*] ... Amer Economist
American Edge Collectors Association ... AECA
American Education [*A publication*] ... A Ed
American Education [*A publication*] ... AMED
American Education [*A publication*] ... Am Educ
American Education Association ... AEA
American Education Finance Association ... AEFA
American Education Week ... AEW
American Educational Computers [*NASDAQ symbol*] ... AEDC
American Educational Publishers Institute [*Later, AAP*] ... AEPI
American Educational Research Association ... AERA
American Educational Research Journal [*A publication*] ... Am Ed Res J
American Educational Research Journal [*A publication*] ... Am Educ Res
American Educational Studies Association ... AESA
American Educational Television Network [*Cable-television system*] ... AETN
American Educational Theatre Association [*Later, ATA*] ... AETA
American Egg Board ... AEB
American Egg and Poultry Review [*A publication*] ... Am Egg & Poultry R
American Electric Power Co., Inc. [*Group of investor-owned public utility companies*] [*NYSE symbol*] ... AEP
American Electro Metal Corporation ... AEMC
American Electrochemical Society [*Later, ECS*] ... AES
American Electrochemical Society. Transactions [*A publication*] ... Am Electrochem Soc Trans
American Electroencephalographic Society ... AEEGS
American Electroencephalographic Society ... AES
American Electrolysis Association ... AEA
American Electromechanical Society ... AES
American Electromedics [*NASDAQ symbol*] ... AECO
American Electronical Society ... AES
American Electronics Association [*Formerly, WEMA*] ... AEA
American Electroplaters' Society ... AES
American Embassy ... AE
American Embassy ... AMEMB
American Emergency Committee for Tibetan Refugees [*Defunct*] ... AECTR
American Emigrants' League ... AEL
American Endodontic Society ... AES
American Endurance Ride Conference ... AERC
American Energy Corp. [*NASDAQ symbol*] ... ACEVF
American Energy Week [*An association*] ... AEW
American Engineer [*A publication*] ... Amer Eng
American Engineering Association [*Defunct*] ... AEA
American Engineering Council ... AEC
American Engineering Model Society ... AEMS
American Engineering Standards Committee [*Later, ANSI*] ... AESC
American English Spot Rabbit Club ... AESRC
American Enka Corp. [*NYSE symbol*] [*Delisted*] ... ANK
American Enka Corp., Enka, NC [*Library symbol*] ... NcEnk
American Ensemble [*A publication*] ... Am Ens
American Enterprise Association [*Later, AEI*] ... AEA
American Enterprise Institute for Public Policy Research [*Formerly, AEA*] ... AEI
American Enterprise Institute for Public Policy Research ... AEIPPR
American Entomological Society ... AES
American Entrepreneurs Association [*Formerly, IEA*] ... AEA
American Epidemiological Society ... AES
American Epilepsy Society ... AES
American Equilibration Society ... AES
American Equity Investment Trust [*NASDAQ symbol*] ... AEQTS

American Ethical Union ... AEU
American Ethnological Society ... AES
American Ethnologist [*A publication*] ... Amer Ethnol
American Ethnologist [*A publication*] ... Am Ethnol
American Eugenics Society [*Later, Society for the Study of Social Biology*] ... AES
American European Foundation ... AEF
American Euthanasia Foundation ... AEF
American Ex-Prisoners of War ... XPW
American Examiner [*A publication*] ... Am Ex
American Exiles ... AMEX
American Expeditionary Force [*World War I*] ... AEF
American Exploration Company [*NASDAQ symbol*] ... AXCO
American Export Airlines ... AEA
American Export Industries Co. [*NYSE symbol*] [*Delisted*] ... AEX
American Export Isbrandtsen Lines [*Later, American Export Industries Co.*] ... AEIL
American Exporter [*A publication*] ... Am Exporter
American Express Card [*Credit card*] ... AEC
American Express Co. ... AMEX
American Express Company ... AMEXCO
American Express Co. [*NYSE symbol*] ... AXP
American Express International Banking Corporation ... AEIBC
American Fabricating Institute of Technology ... AFIT
American Fabrics [*A publication*] ... AF
American Fabrics [*A publication*] ... Am Fabrics
American Fair Trade Council [*Defunct*] ... AFTC
American Family Communiversity [*An association*] ... AFCO
American Family Corp. [*NYSE symbol*] ... AFL
American Family Farm and Ranch Association ... AFFRA
American Family Foundation ... AFF
American Family Heritage Society [*Defunct*] ... AFHS
American Family Physician [*A publication*] ... AFPYB
American Family Physician [*A publication*] ... Am Fam Phys
American Family Physician [*A publication*] ... Am Fam Physician
American Family Pizza Uts [*NASDAQ symbol*] ... AFPZU
American Family Therapy Association ... AFTA
American Fan Association ... AFA
American Far Eastern Society ... AFES
American Farm Bureau ... AFB
American Farm Bureau Federation ... AFBF
American Farm Bureau Federation. Weekly News Letter [*A publication*] ... Am Farm Bur N L
American Farm Bureau Research Foundation ... AFBRF
American Farm Economic Association [*Later, AAEA*] ... AFEA
American Farm Research Association [*Superseded by AFBRF*] ... AFRA
American Farriers Association ... AFA
American Fashion Homesewing Council ... AFHSC
American Federal Savings & Loan Association of Colorado [*NASDAQ symbol*] ... AFSL
American Federation of Arts ... AFA
American Federation of Astrologers ... AFA
American Federation of Aviculture ... AFA
American Federation of Catholic Workers for the Blind [*Later, AFCWBVH*] ... AFCWB
American Federation of Catholic Workers for the Blind and Visually Handicapped [*Formerly, AFCWB*] ... AFCWBVH
American Federation for Clinical Research ... AFCR
American Federation of Film Societies ... AFFS
American Federation of Government Employees ... AFGE
American Federation of Grain Millers ... AFGM
American Federation of Guards ... AFG
American Federation of Home Health Agencies ... AFHHA
American Federation of Hosiery Workers [*Later, ACTWU*] ... AFHW
American Federation of Information Processing Societies ... AFIPS
American Federation of International Institutes [*Later, ACNS*] ... AFII
American Federation of Italian Evangelicals [*Later, Association of Evangelicals for Italian Missions*] ... AFIE
American Federation of Jewish Fighters, Camp Inmates, and Nazi Victims ... AFJFCINV
American Federation of Jews from Central Europe ... AFJCE
American Federation of Labor [*Later, AFL-CIO*] ... AFL
American Federation of Labor [*Later, AFL-CIO*] ... AF of L
American Federation of Labor and Congress of Industrial Organizations ... AFL-CIO
American Federation of Labor and Congress of Industrial Organizations Library, Washington, DC [*Library symbol*] ... DAFL
American Federation of Medical Accreditation ... AFMA
American Federation of Mineralogical Societies ... AFMS
American Federation of Musicians of the United States and Canada ... AFM
American Federation of New Zealand Rabbit Breeders ... AFNZRB
American Federation of the Physically Handicapped ... AFPH
American Federation of Police ... AFP
American Federation of Polish Jews ... AFPJ
American Federation of Poultry Producers Associations [*Defunct*] ... AFPPA
American Federation of Priests ... AFP
American Federation of Radio Artists ... AFRA
American Federation of Retail Kosher Butchers ... AFRKB
American Federation of School Administrators ... AFSA
American Federation of School Administrators and Supervisors [*AFL-CIO*] ... AFSAS
American Federation of Small Business ... AFSB
American Federation of Soroptimist Clubs [*Later, Soroptimist International of the Americas*] ... AFSC
American Federation of State, County, and Municipal Employees ... AFSCME
American Federation of State, County, and Municipal Employees ... SCME
American Federation of Teachers ... AFT
American Federation of Technical Engineers [*Later, International Federation of Professional and Technical Engineers*] ... AFTE
American Federation of Television and Radio Artists ... AFTRA
American Federation of World Citizens [*Later, Fellowship of World Citizens*] ... AFWC
American Federationist [*A publication*] ... Amer Feder
American Federationist [*A publication*] ... Am Fed
American Feed Manufacturers Association ... AFMA
American Feed Manufacturers Association Proceedings. Meeting of the Nutrition Council [*A publication*] ... Am Feed Manuf Assoc Proc Meet Nutr Counc
American Feline Society ... AFS
American Fern Journal [*A publication*] ... Am Fern J
American Fern Society ... AFS
American Fertility Society ... AFS
American Fertilizer and Allied Chemicals [*A publication*] ... Am Fert
American Fiber Institute ... AFI
American Fiber Optics [*NASDAQ symbol*] ... FIBR
American Fiber, Textile, Apparel Coalition ... AFTAC
American Field Service [*Later, AFSIIP*] ... AFS
American Fighter Aces Association ... AFAA
American Film [*A publication*] ... Amer F
American Film [*A publication*] ... Am Film
American Film Export Association ... AFEA
American Film Institute ... AFI
American Film Marketing Association ... AFMA
American Film Theater ... AFT
American Filtrona Corp. [*NASDAQ symbol*] ... AFIL
American Finance Association ... AFA
American Finance Conference [*Later, NCFA*] ... AFC
American Finance System [*NYSE symbol*] [*Delisted*] ... AFS
American Financial Corp. H Pfd [*NASDAQ symbol*] ... AFINM
American Fine Arts Society ... AFAS
American Fine China Guild ... AFCG
American Fire Sprinkler Association ... AFSA
American Firearm Association ... AFA
American First Corporation [*NASDAQ symbol*] ... AFCO
American First Day Cover Foundation [*Affiliated with AFDCS*] ... AFDCF
American First Day Cover Society [*Affiliated with AFDCF*] ... AFDCS
American Fish Farmers Federation ... AFFF
American Fisheries Advisory Committee ... AFAC
American Fisheries Protection Act ... AFPA
American Fisheries Society ... AFS
American Fisheries Society. Monograph [*A publication*] ... Am Fish Soc Monogr
American Fisheries Society. Special Publication [*A publication*] ... Am Fish Soc Spec Publ
American Fishing Tackle Manufacturers Association ... AFTMA
American Flag Association [*Defunct*] ... AFA
American Flag Committee ... AFC
American Flag Flying, Inc. [*Ft. Lauderdale, FL*] [*FAA designator*] ... FLG
American Flag Institute ... AFI
American Flagship Available ... AFSA
American Fletcher Corp. [*NASDAQ symbol*] ... AFLT
American Fletcher Mortgage Investors [*American Stock Exchange symbol*] [*Delisted*] ... AFM
American Flight Strips Association ... AFSA
American Flint Glass Workers Union ... AFGWU
American Flint Glass Workers' Union of North America ... AFGW
American Florist [*A publication*] ... Am Flor
American Flyers Airline ... AFA
American Folklife Center [*Library of Congress*] ... AFC
American Folklore Society ... AFS
American Food for Peace Council [*Defunct*] ... AFPC
American Foot Care Institute [*Defunct*] ... AFCI
American Foot Health Foundation ... AFHF
American Football Coaches Association ... AFCA
American Football Conference [*of NFL*] ... AFC
American Football League [*Reorganized as part of AFC and NFC*] ... AFL
American Footwear Industries Association [*Later, FIA*] ... AFIA
American Footwear Manufacturers' Association [*Later, FIA*] ... AFMA
American Forage and Grassland Council ... AFGC
American Forces in Action [*Military*] ... AFA
American Forces Information Service [*DoD*] ... AFIS
American Forces Information Service [*Military*] ... AMFINFOS
American Forces Network ... AFN
American Forces Network, Europe ... AFNE
American Forces Press Service [*Formerly, AFNB*] ... AFPS
American [*formerly, Armed*] **Forces Radio and Television Service** [*or System*] ... AFRTS
American [*formerly, Armed*] **Forces Vietnam Network** ... AFVN

American and Foreign Bible Society ... AFBS
American and Foreign Christian Union ... AFCU
American Foreign Insurance Association ... AFIA
American Foreign Law Association ... AFLA
American Foreign Policy Institute [*Formerly, AIPEU*] ... AFPI
American & Foreign Power Co., Inc. [*NYSE symbol*] [*Delisted*] [*Wall Street slang name: "Airforce"*] ... AF
American & Foreign Power Co., Inc. ... A & FP
American Foreign Service Association ... AFSA
American Foreign Service Journal [*A publication*] ... Am For Serv Jour
American Foreign Service Protective Association ... AFSPA
American Forensic Association ... AFA
American Forest Institute ... AFI
American Forest Products Industries [*Later, AFI*] ... AFPI
American Forestry Association ... AFA
American Forestry Association, Washington, DC [*Library symbol*] ... DAFA
American Forests [*A publication*] ... AF
American Forests [*A publication*] ... Am For
American Forests [*A publication*] ... Am Forests
American Forged Fitting and Flange Association [*Defunct*] ... AFFFA
American Formalwear Association ... AFA
American Foundation for Aging Research ... AFAR
American Foundation for Alternative Health Care ... AFAHC
American Foundation on Automation and Employment [*Later, CNB-TV*] ... AFAE
American Foundation for the Blind ... AFB
American Foundation for the Blind, New York, NY [*Library symbol*] ... NNAF
American Foundation for the Blind. Research Bulletin [*A publication*] ... AFBRB
American Foundation for the Blind. Research Bulletin [*A publication*] ... Am Found Blind Res Bull
American Foundation for Continuing Education ... AFCE
American Foundation for Homoeopathy ... AFH
American Foundation for Learning Disabilities ... AFLD
American Foundation for Management Research [*Later, AMA*] ... AFMR
American Foundation for Management Research, Hamilton, NY [*Library symbol*] ... NHA
American Foundation for Management Research, Library, Hamilton, NY [*OCLC symbol*] ... ZUC
American Foundation for Maternal and Child Health ... AFMCH
American Foundation for Mental Hygiene ... AFMH
American Foundation for Negro Affairs ... AFNA
American Foundation for Overseas Blind [*Later, HKI*] ... AFOB
American Foundation for Pharmaceutical Education ... AFPE
American Foundation for Political Education ... AFPE
American Foundation for Psychoanalysis and Psychoanalysis in Groups ... AFPPG
American Foundation of Religion and Psychiatry [*Later, Institutes of Religion and Health*] ... AFRAP
American Foundation of Religion and Psychiatry [*Later, Institutes of Religion and Health*] ... AFRP
American Foundation for the Science of Creative Intelligence ... AFSCI
American Foundation for Tropical Medicine ... AFTM
American Foundation for World Youth Understanding ... AFWYU
American Foundrymen's Association [*Later, AFS*] ... AFA
American Foundrymen's Society [*Formerly, AFA*] ... AFS
American Foundrymen's Society, Des Plaines, IL [*Library symbol*] ... IDesA
American Fox and Fur Farmer [*A publication*] ... Am Fox and Fur Farmer
American Fox Terrier Club ... AFTC
American Fox Trotting Horse Breed Association ... AFTHBA
American Foxhound Club ... AFC
American Fracture Association ... AFA
American Franciscan Society for Vocations [*Later, FVC*] ... AFSV
American Fraternal Union ... AFU
American Freedom Association ... AFA
American Freedom Center ... AFC
American Freedom from Hunger Foundation [*Later, MFM/FFH*] ... AFFHF
American Freedom of Residence Fund [*Defunct*] ... AFRF
American-French Genealogical Society ... AFGS
American Friends of Afghan Refugees ... AFAR
American Friends of the Alliance Israelite Universelle ... AFAIU
American Friends of Anne Frank Center ... AFAFC
American Friends of the Anti-Bolshevik Bloc of Nations ... AFABBN
American Friends of the Association for Welfare of Soldiers in Israel ... AWSI
American Friends of Boys Town of Jerusalem ... BTJ
American Friends of Cambridge University ... AFCU
American Friends of the Captive Nations [*Defunct*] ... AFCN
American Friends of Chung-Ang University ... AFC-AU
American Friends of Greece ... AFG
American Friends of the Gutenberg Museum ... AFGM
American Friends of the Hebrew University ... AFHU
American Friends of Israel ... AFI
American Friends of the Israel Museum ... AFIM
American Friends of the Jerusalem Society for World Fellowship ... AFJSWF
American Friends of Lafayette ... AFL
American Friends of the Middle East [*Later, AMIDEAST*] ... AFME
American Friends of Refugees [*Defunct*] ... AFR
American Friends of Religious Freedom in Israel ... AFRFI
American Friends of Russian Freedom [*Later, AFR*] ... AFRF
American Friends of Scottish Opera ... AFSO
American Friends of Scottish War Blinded ... AFSWB
American Friends Service Committee ... AFSC
American Friends of the Vatican Library ... AFVL
American Friends of Vietnam ... AFV
American Frontier Explorations [*NASDAQ symbol*] ... AFEX
American Frozen Food Institute [*Formerly, NAFFP*] ... AFFI
American Fruit Grower [*A publication*] ... Am Fruit Grower
American Fuchsia Society ... AFS
American Fuel Technology [*NASDAQ symbol*] ... AFTI
American Fund for Alternatives to Animal Research ... AFAAR
American Fund for Czechoslovak Refugees ... AFCR
American Fund for Dental Education [*Later, AFDH*] ... AFDE
American Fund for Dental Health [*Formerly, AFDE*] ... AFDH
American Fund for Free Jurists ... AFFJ
American Fund for Slovak Refugees ... AFSR
American Funeral Directors and Embalmers Association ... AFDEA
American Fur Liner Contractors Association ... AFLCA
American Fur Merchants' Association ... AFMA
American Furniture Co. [*NASDAQ symbol*] ... AFUR
American Galloway Breeders' Association ... AGBA
American Game. Bulletin. American Game Protective Association [*A publication*] ... Am Game Bull Am Game Protect Ass
American Garden Products, Inc. [*American Stock Exchange symbol*] [*Delisted*] ... AGP
American Gas Association ... AGA
American Gas Association Laboratories ... AGAL
American Gas Association. Monthly [*A publication*] ... AGA
American Gas Association. Monthly [*A publication*] ... Amer Gas Ass Mon
American Gas Association. Monthly [*A publication*] ... Am Gas As M
American Gas Association, New York, NY [*Library symbol*] ... NNAG
American Gas Association. Operating Section. Proceedings [*A publication*] ... Amer Gas Ass Oper Sect Proc
American Gas Association. Operating Section. Proceedings [*A publication*] ... Am Gas Assoc Oper Sect Proc
American Gas Association. Preprints [*A publication*] ... Am Gas Assoc Prepr
American Gas Association. Proceedings [*A publication*] ... Am Gas Assoc Proc
American Gas and Electric Services ... AGES
American Gas Journal [*A publication*] ... Amer Gas J
American Gas Journal [*A publication*] ... Am Gas J
American Gasoline Dealers Association ... AGDA
American Gastroenterological Association [*Later, ASGE*] ... AGA
American Gathering of Jewish Holocaust Survivors ... AGJHS
American Gauge Design Committee ... AGD
American Gauge Design Committee ... AGDC
American Gauge Design Standard ... AGDS
American Gear Manufacturers Association ... AGMA
American Gear Manufacturers Association. Standards [*A publication*] ... Amer Gear Mfr Ass Stand
American Gelbvieh Association ... AGA
American Gem and Mineral Suppliers Association ... AGMSA
American Gem Society ... AGS
American Genealogical Research Institute ... AGRI
American Genealogist [*A publication*] ... Am Geneal
American General Bond Fund, Inc. [*NYSE symbol*] [*Delisted*] ... AGB
American General Convertible Securities, Inc. [*NYSE symbol*] [*Delisted*] ... AGS
American General Insurance Company [*NYSE symbol*] ... AGC
American Genetic Association ... AGA
American Genetics International [*NASDAQ symbol*] ... AMGI
American Geographical Institute ... AGI
American Geographical Society ... AGS
American Geographical Society [*A publication*] ... Am Geog Soc
American Geographical Society. Bulletin [*A publication*] ... Am Geog Soc Bul
American Geographical Society. Bulletin. Journal [*A publication*] ... Am Geog Soc B J
American Geographical Society. Journal [*A publication*] ... Am Geog Soc Jour
American Geographical Society, New York, NY [*Library symbol*] ... NNA
American Geographical Society. Special Publication [*A publication*] ... Am Geog Soc Special Pub
American Geographical and Statistical Society ... AGSS
American Geographical and Statistical Society. Journal [*A publication*] ... Am Geog Stat Soc J
American Geological Association. Bulletin [*A publication*] ... Am G As B
American Geological Institute ... AGI
American Geological Institute. Report [*A publication*] ... Am Geol Inst Rept
American Geological Institute. Reprint Series [*A publication*] ... Am Geol Inst Repr Ser
American Geologist [*A publication*] ... Am G
American Geophysical Union ... AGU
American Geophysical Union. Transactions [*A publication*] ... Am Geophys Union Trans
American Geriatric Research Foundation [*Later, ARI*] ... AGRF
American Geriatrics Society ... AGS
American-German Review [*A publication*] ... AGR
American Gesneria Society [*Later, GSI*] ... AGS
American Glassware Association [*Defunct*] ... AGA
American Gloxinia and Gesneriad Society ... AGGS

American Gloxinia Society [*Later, AGGS*] .... AGS
American Go Association .... AGA
American Goat Society .... AGS
American Goiter Association [*Later, American Thyroid Association*] .... AGA
American Gold Association [*Defunct*] .... AGA
American Gold Minerals [*NASDAQ symbol*] .... AGMC
American Gold Star Mothers .... AGSM
American Golf Sponsors [*Formerly, IGSA*] .... AGS
American Good Government Society .... AGGS
American Gotland Horse Association .... AGHA
American Gourd Society .... AGS
American Graduate School of International Management [*Formerly, Thunderbird Graduate School of International Management*] .... AGSIM
American Grand Prix Association .... AGA
American Graniteware Association .... AGA
American Graphological Society .... AGS
American Grassland Council [*Later, AFGC*] .... AGC
American Graves Registration Command [*Military*] .... AGRC
American Graves Registration Command [*Military*] .... AGRCO
American Graves Registration Service [*Military*] .... AGRS
American Greek Exchange Society .... AGES
American Greenhouse Vegetable Growers Association .... AGVGA
American Greetings Cl A [*NASDAQ symbol*] .... AGREA
American Greyhound Track Operators Association .... AGTOA
American Groomer's Guild .... AGG
American Ground Flat Stock Association .... AGFSA
American Group of CPA Firms .... TAG
American Group Practice Association .... AGPA
American Group Psychotherapy Association .... AGPA
American Guaranty Financial [*NASDAQ symbol*] .... AMGR
American Guernsey Cattle Club .... AGCC
American Guides Association .... AGA
American Guild of Animal Artists .... AGAA
American Guild of Authors and Composers .... AGAC
American Guild of English Handbell Ringers .... AGEHR
American Guild of Hypnotherapists .... AGH
American Guild of Luthiers .... AGL
American Guild of Music .... AGM
American Guild of Musical Artists .... AGMA
American Guild of Organists .... AGO
American Guild of Organists. Quarterly [*A publication*] .... AGO
American Guild of Patient Account Management .... AGPAM
American Guild of Variety Artists .... AGVA
American Gulf West Indies Co. .... AGWI
American Gun Dealers Association .... AGDA
American Guppy Association [*Superseded by IFGA*] .... AGA
American Gynecological and Obstetrical Society [*Formerly, AGS, AAOG*] .... AGOS
American Gynecological Society [*Later, AGOS*] .... AGS
American Habonim Association [*Later, Labor Zionist Alliance*] .... AHA
American Hackney Horse Society .... AHHS
American Hair Replacement Association .... AHRA
American Half-Paso Association [*Defunct*] .... AHPA
American Hampshire Sheep Association .... AHSA
American Handwriting Analysis Foundation .... AHAF
American Hanoverian Society .... AHS
American Hardboard Association .... AHA
American Hardware Corporation [*NYSE symbol*] [*Delisted*] .... AHC
American Hardware Manufacturers Association .... AHMA
American Harlequin Rabbit Club .... AHRC
American Harp Journal [*A publication*] .... Am Harp J
American Harp Society .... AHS
American Healing Association .... AHA
American Health Assistance Foundation .... AHAF
American Health and Beauty Aid Institute .... AHBAI
American Health Care Association [*Formerly, ANHA*] .... AHCA
American Health Care Association. Journal [*A publication*] .... Am Health Care Assoc J
American Health Foundation .... AHF
American Health Industries Institute .... AHII
American Health Planning Association .... AHPA
American Health Professionals .... AHP
American Hearing Research Foundation .... AHRF
American Hearing Society [*Later, NAHSA*] .... AHS
American Heart Association .... AHA
American Heart Association. Monograph [*A publication*] .... Am Heart Assoc Monogr
American Heart Journal [*A publication*] .... Am Heart J
American Helicopter Company [*Air Force*] .... AHC
American Helicopter Society .... AHS
American-Hellenic Chamber of Commerce .... AHCC
American Hellenic Congress .... AHC
American Hellenic Educational Progressive Association .... AHEPA
American Helvetia Philatelic Society .... AHPS
American Hemerocallis Society .... AHS
American Hepatic Foundation .... AHF
American Herb Association .... AHA
American Herbal Products Association .... AHPA
American Hereford Association .... AHA
American Heritage [*A publication*] .... AH
American Heritage [*A publication*] .... Am Her
American Heritage [*A publication*] .... Am Heritage
American Heritage Dictionary [*A publication*] .... AHD
American Heritage Foundation .... AHF
American Heritage Life Investment Corp. [*NYSE symbol*] .... AHL
American Hibiscus Society .... AHS
American High-Density Gradient .... AHG
American Highways [*A publication*] .... Amer Highways
American Highways [*A publication*] .... Am Highw
American Hiking Society [*Formerly, IBA*] .... AHS
[*The*] **American Hispanist** [*A publication*] .... TAH
American Histadrut Cultural Exchange Institute .... AHCEI
American Historic and Cultural Society .... AHCS
American Historical Association .... AHA
American Historical Association. Newsletter [*A publication*] .... AHA Newsletter
American Historical Association. Reports [*A publication*] .... Am Hist Assn Rept
American Historical Philatelic Society [*Formerly, AHPS-CWPS*] .... AHPS
American Historical Philatelic Society - Civil War Philatelic Society [*Later, AHPS*] .... AHPS-CWPS
American Historical Print Collectors Society .... AHPCS
American Historical Record [*A publication*] .... Am Hist Rec
American Historical Register [*A publication*] .... Am Hist Reg
American Historical Review [*A publication*] .... AHR
American Historical Review [*A publication*] .... Am His R
American Historical Review [*A publication*] .... Am Hist R
American Historical Review [*A publication*] .... Am Hist Rev
American Historical Society of Germans from Russia .... AHSGR
American History Illustrated [*A publication*] .... Am Hist Illus
American Hitchhiker Association .... AHA
American Hobbit Association .... AHA
American Hobby Federation [*Defunct*] .... AHF
American Hockey Coaches Association .... AHCA
American Hockey League .... AHL
American Hoist & Derrick Co. [*NYSE symbol*] .... AHO
American Holistic Health Sciences Association .... AHHSA
American Holistic Medical Association .... AHMA
American Holistic Medical Institute [*of the American Holistic Medical Association*] [*Formerly, BIA*] .... AHMI
American Holistic Nurses Association .... AHNA
American Holstein Horse Association .... AHHA
American Home [*A publication*] .... Am Home
American Home Economics Association .... AHEA
American Home Industries [*NASDAQ symbol*] .... AHIC
American Home Laundry Manufacturers Association [*Later, AHAM*] .... AHLMA
American Home Lighting Institute .... AHLI
American Home Mission Society .... AHMS
American Home Patient Center [*NASDAQ symbol*] .... AHOM
American Home Products Corp. [*Formerly, HPT*] [*NYSE symbol*] .... AHP
American Home Products Corp. [*Later, AHP*] [*NYSE symbol*] .... HPT
American Home Products Corp., Ayerst Medical Library, New York, NY [*Library symbol*] .... NNAy
American Home Sewing Association [*Formerly, NNA, AHSC*] .... AHSA
American Home Sewing Council [*Later, AHSA*] .... AHSC
American Home Shield [*NASDAQ symbol*] .... AHSCD
American Homebrewers Association .... AHA
American Homeowners Association [*Commercial firm*] [*Defunct*] .... AHA
American Homes and Gardens [*A publication*] .... Am Homes
American Hominological Association .... AHA
American Honey Institute [*Later, HICA*] .... AHI
American Honey Producers Association .... AHPA
American Horse Council .... AHC
American Horse Protection Association .... AHPA
American Horse Publications [*An association*] .... AHP
American Horse Shows Association .... AHSA
American Horticultural Council [*Later, AHS*] .... AHC
American Horticultural Magazine [*A publication*] .... Am Hort Mag
American Horticultural Society .... AHS
American Horticulturist [*A publication*] .... Am Hort
American Hospital Association .... AHA
American Hospital Association, Chicago, IL [*Library symbol*] .... ICAH
American Hospital Association Library, Chicago, IL [*OCLC symbol*] .... IHD
American Hospital Corps .... AHC
American Hospital Formulary [*A publication*] .... AHF
American Hospital Formulary Service .... AHFS
American Hospital Radiology Administrators .... AHRA
American Hospital Society .... AHS
American Hospital Supply Corp. [*NYSE symbol*] .... AHS
American Hospital Supply Corp., Evanston, IL [*OCLC symbol*] .... JAU
American Hospital Video Network [*Satellite television system*] .... AHVN
American Host Foundation .... AHF
American Hosta Society .... AHS
American Hot Dip Galvanizers Association .... AHDGA
American Hot Rod Association .... AHRA
American Hotel Association [*Later, AH & MA*] .... AHA
American Hotel and Motel Association [*Formerly, AHA*] .... AH & MA
American Hotel Trade Association Executives .... AHTAE
American Hound Association .... AHA
American Hovercraft Association [*Superseded by HA*] .... AHA

American Hull Insurance Syndicate ... AHIS
American Humane Association ... AHA
American Humane Association, Denver, CO [*Library symbol*] ... CoDAH
American Humane Education Society ... AHES
American Humane Society ... AHS
American Humanics [*Formerly, AHF*] [*An association*] ... AH
American Humanics Foundation [*Later, AH*] ... AHF
American Humanist Association ... AHA
American Humor [*A publication*] ... A Humor
American Humor Studies Association ... AHSA
American Hungarian Catholic Society [*Later, William Penn Association*] ... AHCS
American Hungarian Educators' Association ... AHEA
American Hungarian Folklore Centrum ... AHFC
American Hungarian Foundation ... AHF
American Hungarian Library and Historical Society ... AHLHS
American Hungarian Studies Foundation [*Later, AHF*] ... AHSF
American Hypnodontic Society ... AHS
American Hypnotists' Association ... AHA
American Imago [*A publication*] ... AI
American Imago [*A publication*] ... Amer Imago
American Imago [*A publication*] ... AMIAA
American Imago [*A publication*] ... Am Im
American Imago [*A publication*] ... Am Imago
American Immigration and Citizenship Conference ... AICC
American Immigration Lawyers Association [*Formerly, AINL*] ... AILA
American Import/Export Bulletin [*A publication*] ... Am Import/Export Bull
American Import/Export Management [*A publication*] ... Am Import/Export Mgt
American Importers Association [*Later, AAEI*] ... AIA
American Incense Manufacturers Association ... AIMA
American Income Life Insurance [*NASDAQ symbol*] ... AINC
American Indemnity Financial [*NASDAQ symbol*] ... AIFC
American Independent Designers and Engineers Society ... AIDES
American Independent Oil Co. ... AMINOIL
American Independent Party ... AIP
American Indian ... AMERIND
American Indian ... AMIND
American Indian/Alaska Native Nurses Association ... AIANNA
American Indian Archaeological Institute ... AIAI
American Indian Culture Research Center ... AICRC
American Indian Development Association ... AIDA
American Indian Environmental Council ... AIEC
American Indian and Eskimo Cultural Foundation [*Defunct*] ... AIECF
American Indian Ethnohistorical Conference [*Later, American Society for Ethnohistory*] ... AIEC
American Indian Historical Association ... AIHA
American Indian Historical Society ... AIHS
American Indian Horse Registry ... AIHR
American Indian Law Center ... AILC
American Indian Law Students Association ... AILSA
American Indian Liberation Crusade ... AILC
American Indian Lore Association ... AILA
American Indian Movement ... AIM
American Indian Press Association [*Defunct*] ... AIPA
American Indian Projects Foundation [*Defunct*] ... AIPF
American Indian Quarterly [*A publication*] ... AIQ
American Indian Refugees [*An association*] ... AIR
American Indian Scholarships [*An association*] ... AIS
American Indian Travel Commission [*Defunct*] ... AITC
American Indicator Digest Average [*American Stock Exchange*] ... AIDA
American Indigena [*A publication*] ... Amer Indig
American Industrial Arts Association ... AIAA
American Industrial Arts Student Association ... AIASA
American Industrial Bankers Association [*Later, NCFA*] ... AIBA
American Industrial Development Council [*Later, AEDC*] ... AIDC
American Industrial Health Council ... AIHC
American Industrial Hygiene Association ... AIHA
American Industrial Hygiene Association. Journal [*A publication*] ... AIHAA
American Industrial Hygiene Association. Journal [*A publication*] ... Amer Industr Hyg Assoc J
American Industrial Hygiene Association. Journal [*A publication*] ... Am Ind Hyg
American Industrial Hygiene Association. Journal [*A publication*] ... Am Ind Hyg Assoc J
American Industrial Hygiene Association. Journal [*A publication*] ... Am Ind Hygiene Assn J
American Industrial Music Association ... AIMA
American Industrial Radium and X-Ray Society [*Later, ASNT*] ... AIRXRS
American Industrial Real Estate Association ... AIR
American Industrial Transport, Inc. ... AIT
American Industrial Writing Institute ... AIWI
American Industries [*A publication*] ... Am Ind
American Inkmaker [*A publication*] ... Am Ink
American Innerspring Manufacturers ... AIM
American Institute ... AI
American Institute of Aerological Research ... AIAR
American Institute of Aeronautics and Astronautics ... AIAA
American Institute of Aeronautics and Astronautics, New York, NY [*Library symbol*] ... NNIA
American Institute of Aeronautics and Astronautics, Pacific Aerospace Library, Los Angeles, CA [*Library symbol*] ... CLIA
American Institute of Aeronautics and Astronautics - Technical Information Service ... AIAA-TIS
American Institute of Architects ... AIA
American Institute of Architects Foundation ... AIAF
American Institute of Architects. Journal [*A publication*] ... Am Inst Arch J
American Institute of Architects, Washington, DC [*Library symbol*] ... DAIA
American Institute of Baking ... AIB
American Institute of Baking, Chicago, IL [*Library symbol*] ... ICAI
American Institute of Banking ... AIB
American Institute of Banking. Bulletin [*A publication*] ... Am Inst Bank Bul
American Institute of Biological Sciences ... AIBS
American Institute of Bolt, Nut, and Rivet Manufacturers [*Later, Industrial Fasteners Institute*] ... AIBNRM
American Institute of Building Design ... AIBD
American Institute of Certified Planners ... AICP
American Institute of Certified Public Accountants ... AICPA
American Institute of Certified Public Accountants, New York, NY [*Library symbol*] ... NNAIA
American Institute of Ceylonese Studies ... AICS
American Institute for Character Education ... AICE
American Institute of Chefs [*Later, ACF*] ... AIC
American Institute of Chemical Engineers ... AICE
American Institute of Chemical Engineers ... AIChE
American Institute of Chemists ... AIC
American Institute of Child Care Centers [*Defunct*] ... AICCC
American Institute of Commemorative Art ... AICA
American Institute for Conservation of Historic and Artistic Works ... AIC
American Institute of Constructors ... AIC
American Institute of Consulting Engineers [*Later, ACEC*] ... AICE
American Institute for Contemporary German Studies ... AICGS
American Institute of Cooperation ... AIC
American Institute of Crop Ecology ... AICE
American Institute for Decision Sciences ... AIDS
American Institute for Design and Drafting ... AIDD
American Institute for Economic Research ... AIER
American Institute of Electrical Engineers [*Later, IEEE*] ... AIEE
American Institute of Electrical Engineers [*Later, IEEE*] ... AmInstEE
American Institute for Exploration ... AIFE
American Institute of Family Relations ... AIFR
American Institute of Financial Brokers ... AIFB
American Institute of Fishery Research Biologists ... AIFRB
American Institute of Floral Designers ... AIFD
American Institute of Food Distribution ... AIFD
American Institute for Foreign Study ... AIFS
American Institute for Foreign Trade ... AIFT
American Institute of France [*Defunct*] ... AIF
American Institute for Free Labor Development ... AIFLD
American Institute of Graphic Arts ... AIGA
American Institute of Group Counseling [*Defunct*] ... AIGC
American Institute of the History of Pharmacy ... AIHP
American Institute of Homeopathy ... AIH
American Institute for Human Engineering and Development ... AIHED
American Institute of Hydrology ... AIH
American Institute for Imported Steel ... AIIS
American Institute of Indian Studies ... AIIS
American Institute of Industrial Engineers [*Later, IIE*] ... AIIE
American Institute of Instruction [*A publication*] ... Am Inst of Instruc
American Institute of Interior Designers [*Later, ASID*] ... AID
American Institute of Iranian Studies ... AIIS
American Institute for Islamic Affairs ... AIIA
American Institute of Islamic Studies ... AIIS
American Institute of Islamic Studies, Denver, CO [*Library symbol*] ... CoDAmI
American Institute of Kitchen Dealers ... AIKD
American Institute of Landscape Architects [*Later, ASLA*] ... AILA
American Institute of Laundering [*Later, IFI*] ... AIL
American Institute of Maintenance ... AIM
American Institute of Management ... AIM
American Institute of Marine Underwriters ... AIMU
American Institute of Maritime Services ... AIMS
American Institute for Marxist Studies ... AIMS
American Institute of Medical Climatology ... AIMC
American Institute for the Medical Research of Trauma ... AIMRT
American Institute of Men's and Boys' Wear [*Later, MFA*] ... AIMBW
American Institute for Mental Studies ... AIMS
American Institute of Merchant Shipping ... AIMS
American Institute of Mining Engineers. Transactions. Bulletin [*A publication*] ... Am I M Eng Tr B
American Institute of Mining, Metallurgical, and Petroleum Engineers ... AIME
American Institute of Mining, Metallurgical, and Petroleum Engineers. Transactions [*A publication*] ... AIME Trans
American Institute of Musical Studies ... AIMS
American Institute of Musicology ... AIM
American Institute of Nautical Archaeology [*Later, INA*] ... AINA
American Institute of Nutrition ... AIN
American Institute of Oral Biology ... AIOB
American Institute of Oral Biology. Annual Meeting [*A publication*] ... Am Inst Oral Biol Annu Meet

American Institute of Pacific Relations [*Defunct*] ... AIPR
American Institute of Park Executives [*Later, APRS*] ... AIPE
American Institute of Parliamentarians ... AIP
American Institute of Pathologic Science ... AIPS
American Institute of Physics ... AIP
American Institute of Physics. Conference Proceedings [*A publication*] ... Am Inst Phys Conf Proc
American Institute of Physics, New York, NY [*Library symbol*] ... NNAIP
American Institute of Planners [*Later, American Planning Association*] ... AIP
American Institute of Planners. Journal [*A publication*] ... Am Inst Plan
American Institute of Planners. Journal [*A publication*] ... Am Inst Plan J
American Institute of Plant Engineers ... AIPE
American Institute for Polish Culture ... AIPC
American Institute for Political Communication ... AIPC
American Institute for the Prevention and Eradication of Dental Disease ... AIPEDD
American Institute on Problems of European Unity [*Later, AFPI*] ... AIPEU
American Institute for Professional Education ... AIPE
American Institute of Professional Geologists ... AIPG
American Institute of Professional Geologists. California Section. Annual Meeting. Proceedings [*A publication*] ... Am Inst Prof Geol Calif Sect Annu Meet Proc
American Institute for Property and Liability Underwriters ... AIPLU
American Institute of Real Estate Appraisers ... AIREA
American Institute of Reciprocators ... AIR
American Institute of Refrigeration [*Defunct*] ... AIR
American Institute for Research in the Behavioral Sciences ... AIRBS
American Institute for Research and Education in Naturopathy ... AIREN
American Institute for Shippers' Associations ... AISA
American Institute of Steel Construction ... AISC
American Institute of Stress ... AIS
American Institute of Supply Associations [*Formerly, AIWPHSA; later, ASA*] ... AISA
American Institute in Taiwan ... AIT
American Institute of Tax Practice ... AITP
American Institute of Technical Illustrators Association ... AITIA
American Institute of Technology ... AIT
American Institute of Timber Construction ... AITC
American Institute of Ultrasound in Medicine ... AIUM
American Institute of Urban and Regional Affairs ... AIURA
American Institute for Verdi Studies ... AIVS
American Institute of Vocal Pedagogy ... AIVP
American Institute of Weights and Measures ... AIWM
American Institute of Wholesale Plumbing and Heating Supply Associations [*Later, AISA*] ... AIWPHSA
American Institutes for Research in the Behavioral Sciences ... AIR
American Institutions Food Service Association ... AIFSA
American Instructors of the Deaf ... AID
American Instrument Company ... AMINCO
American Insulator Corporation ... AICO
American Insurance Association ... AIA
American Insurance Group [*Commercial firm*] ... AIG
American Insurers Highway Safety Alliance ... AIHSA
American Inter-Island, Inc. [*Virgin Islands*] [*FAA designator*] ... ITL
American International Academy [*Defunct*] ... AIA
American International Association for Economic and Social Development [*Defunct*] ... AIA
American International Automobile Dealers Association ... AIADA
American-International Charolais Association ... AICA
American International Checkers Society ... AICS
American International College [*Massachusetts*] ... AIC
American International College, Springfield, MA [*Library symbol*] ... MSAI
American International Corporation [*NYSE symbol*] [*Delisted*] ... AMC
American International Dragon Association ... AIDA
American International Group ... AIG
American International Group, Inc. [*NASDAQ symbol*] ... AIGR
American International Managers Society ... AIMS
American International Marchigiana Society ... AIMS
American International Music Fund ... AIMF
American International Pictures, Inc. ... AIP
American International Pictures, Inc. [*American Stock Exchange symbol*] [*Delisted*] ... ANP
American International Underwriters ... AIU
American Interprofessional Institute ... AII
American Intra-Ocular Implant Society ... AIOIS
American Inventors Association ... AIA
American Investment Company [*NYSE symbol*] [*Delisted*] ... AIC
American Investors Life [*NASDAQ symbol*] ... AILI
American Ionospheric Propagation Association ... AIPA
American Iris Society ... AIS
American Irish Bicentennial Committee ... AIBC
American Irish Historical Society ... AIHS
American Irish Historical Society. Journal [*A publication*] ... Am Irish His S J
American Irish Historical Society, New York, NY [*Library symbol*] ... NNAI
American Irish Unity Committee ... AIUC
American Iron Ore Association ... AIOA
American Iron and Steel Institute ... AISI
American Iron and Steel Institute. Steel Products Manual [*A publication*] ... AISI Steel Prod Man
American Israel Numismatic Association ... AINA
American Israel Public Affairs Committee ... AIPAC
American Israeli Civil Liberties Coalition ... AICLC
American Israeli Lighthouse ... AIL
American Israeli Paper Mills Ltd. [*American Stock Exchange symbol*] ... AIP
American Issues Forum [*American bicentennial project*] ... AIF
American Italian Congress ... AIC
American Italian Historical Association ... AIHA
American-Italian Women of Achievement ... AMITA
American-Italy Society, Incorporated ... AISI
American Ivy Society ... AIS
American Jail Association [*Formerly, NJA, NJMA*] ... AJA
American Japanese Trade Committee ... AJTC
American Jazz Alliance [*Formerly, CJOA*] ... AJA
American Jersey Cattle Club ... AJCC
American Jesuit Missionary Association [*Later, JM*] ... AJMA
American Jewish Alternatives to Zionism ... AJAZ
American Jewish Archives [*A publication*] ... AJA
American Jewish Archives [*A publication*] ... Am Jew Arch
American Jewish Archives [*An association*] ... AJA
American Jewish Archives, Cincinnati, OH [*Library symbol*] ... OCAJA
American Jewish Commission on the Holocaust ... AJCH
American Jewish Committee ... AJC
American Jewish Committee, New York, NY [*Library symbol*] ... NNAJ
American Jewish Conference ... AJC
American Jewish Congress ... AJC
American Jewish Correctional Chaplains Association ... AJCCA
American Jewish Historical Quarterly [*A publication*] ... AJHQ
American Jewish Historical Quarterly [*A publication*] ... Am Jew Hist Q
American Jewish Historical Quarterly [*A publication*] ... Am Jewish H
American Jewish Historical Society ... AJHS
American Jewish Historical Society. Publications [*A publication*] ... AJHS
American Jewish Historical Society. Publications [*A publication*] ... Am Jew His
American Jewish Historical Society. Publications [*A publication*] ... Am Jew Hist Soc Publ
American Jewish Historical Society, Waltham, MA [*Library symbol*] ... MWalA
American Jewish History Center of the Jewish Theological Seminary [*Defunct*] ... AJHC
American Jewish Institute [*Later, JIB*] ... AJI
American Jewish Joint Distribution Committee ... JDC
American Jewish League Against Communism ... AJLAC
American Jewish League for Israel ... AJLI
American Jewish Periodical Center ... AJPC
American Jewish Periodical Center, Cincinnati, OH [*Library symbol*] ... OCAJ
American Jewish Physicians' Committee [*Later, AFHU*] ... AJPC
American Jewish Press Association ... AJPA
American Jewish Public Relations Society ... AJPRS
American Jewish Society for Service ... AJSS
American Jewish Year Book [*A publication*] ... AJYB
American Jewish Year Book [*A publication*] ... Am Jew Yr Bk
American Jewish Yearbook [*A publication*] ... AJY
American Jews Opposed to Israeli Aggression ... AJOIA
American Joint Committee on Cancer [*Formerly, AJC*] ... AJCC
American Joint Committee for Cancer Staging and End Results Reporting [*Later, AJCC*] ... AJC
American Joint Committee on Cancer Staging and End Stage Reporting ... AJCCS
American Joint Distribution Committee ... AJDC
American Journal of Acupuncture [*A publication*] ... Am J Acupunct
American Journal of Agricultural Economics [*A publication*] ... AJAE
American Journal of Agricultural Economics [*A publication*] ... Amer J Agr Econ
American Journal of Agricultural Economics [*A publication*] ... Amer J Agric Econ
American Journal of Agricultural Economics [*A publication*] ... Am J Ag Econ
American Journal of Agricultural Economics [*A publication*] ... Am J Agr Ec
American Journal of Agricultural Economics [*A publication*] ... Am J Agr Econ
American Journal of Agricultural Economics [*A publication*] ... Am J Agric Econ
American Journal of Agriculture and Science [*A publication*] ... Am J Agr
American Journal of Anatomy [*A publication*] ... Am J Anat
American Journal of Archaeology [*A publication*] ... AJA
American Journal of Archaeology [*A publication*] ... AJAr
American Journal of Archaeology [*A publication*] ... Amer J Archaeol
American Journal of Archaeology [*A publication*] ... Am J Archae
American Journal of Archaeology [*A publication*] ... Am J Archaeol
American Journal of Archaeology [*A publication*] ... Am Jnl Archae
American Journal of Art Therapy [*A publication*] ... AJATA
American Journal of Art Therapy [*A publication*] ... Amer J Art Ther
American Journal of Art Therapy [*A publication*] ... Am J Art Th
American Journal of Art Therapy [*A publication*] ... Am J Art Ther
American Journal of Botany [*A publication*] ... Amer J Bot
American Journal of Botany [*A publication*] ... Am J Bot
American Journal of Cardiology [*A publication*] ... Am J Card
American Journal of Cardiology [*A publication*] ... Am J Cardiol
American Journal of Chinese Medicine [*A publication*] ... Amer J Chinese Medicine

American Journal of Chinese Medicine [*A publication*]..........Am J Chin Med
American Journal of Clinical Hypnosis [*A publication*]..........Amer J Clin Hypnosis
American Journal of Clinical Hypnosis [*A publication*]..........Am J Clin Hypn
American Journal of Clinical Hypnosis [*A publication*].... Am J Clin Hypnosis
American Journal of Clinical Nutrition [*A publication*]..........Amer J Clin Nutr
American Journal of Clinical Nutrition [*A publication*]..........Am J Clin N
American Journal of Clinical Nutrition [*A publication*]..........Am J Clin Nutr
American Journal of Clinical Nutrition [*A publication*]...... Am J Clin Nutrition
American Journal of Clinical Pathology [*A publication*].....Amer J Clin Pathol
American Journal of Clinical Pathology [*A publication*]..........Am J Clin P
American Journal of Clinical Pathology [*A publication*]........Am J Clin Pathol
American Journal of Community Psychology [*A publication*]..........Am J Community Psychol
American Journal of Comparative Law [*A publication*]..........AJCL
American Journal of Comparative Law [*A publication*]......Amer J Comp Law
American Journal of Comparative Law [*A publication*]......Am J Compar Law
American Journal of Comparative Law [*A publication*]..........Am J Comp L
American Journal of Comparative Law [*A publication*]......... Am J Comp Law
American Journal of Conchology [*A publication*]..........Am J Conch
American Journal of Correction [*A publication*]..........Am J Correction
American Journal of Criminal Law [*A publication*]..........Am J Crim L
American Journal of Dermatopathology [*A publication*]..........Am J Dermatopathol
American Journal of Digestive Diseases [*A publication*]..........AJDDA
American Journal of Digestive Diseases [*A publication*] ....Amer J Digest Dis
American Journal of Digestive Diseases [*A publication*]..........Am J Dig Di
American Journal of Digestive Diseases [*A publication*]........... Am J Dig Dis
American Journal of Diseases of Children [*A publication*]..........Amer J Dis Child
American Journal of Diseases of Children [*A publication*]..........Am J Dis Ch
American Journal of Diseases of Children [*A publication*]....... Am J Dis Child
American Journal of Drug and Alcohol Abuse [*A publication*]..........Am J Drug Alcohol Abuse
American Journal of Economics and Sociology [*New York*] [*A publication*]..........AJES
American Journal of Economics and Sociology [*New York*] [*A publication*]..........Amer J Econ Sociol
American Journal of Economics and Sociology [*New York*] [*A publication*]..........Am J Econ
American Journal of Economics and Sociology [*New York*] [*A publication*]..........Am J Econ S
American Journal of Economics and Sociology [*New York*] [*A publication*]..........Am J Econ & Sociol
American Journal of Economics and Sociology [*New York*] [*A publication*]..........Am Jnl Econ & Soc
American Journal of Economics and Sociology [*New York*] [*A publication*]..........Am Jour Econ Sociol
American Journal of Economics and Sociology (New York) [*A publication*]..........Am J Econ Sociol (New York)
American Journal of Education [*A publication*]..........Am J Educ
American Journal of EEG Technology [*A publication*]...... Am J EEG Technol
American Journal of Enology and Viticulture [*A publication*]......Am J Enol V
American Journal of Epidemiology [*A publication*]..........Am J Epidem
American Journal of Epidemiology [*A publication*]..........Am J Epidemiol
American Journal of Forensic Medicine and Pathology [*A publication*]..........Am J Forensic Med Pathol
American Journal of Gastroenterology [*A publication*]..........Am J Gastro
American Journal of Gastroenterology [*A publication*].... Am J Gastroenterol
American Journal of Health Planning [*A publication*].........Am J Health Plann
American Journal of Hematology [*A publication*]..........Am J Hematol
American Journal of Hospital Pharmacy [*A publication*]..........Am J Hosp P
American Journal of Hospital Pharmacy [*A publication*].... Am J Hosp Pharm
American Journal of Human Genetics [*A publication*]..........Amer J Hum Genetics
American Journal of Human Genetics [*A publication*]..........Am J Hu Gen
American Journal of Human Genetics [*A publication*] ..... Am J Human Genet
American Journal of Human Genetics [*A publication*]......... Am J Hum Genet
American Journal of Hygiene [*A publication*]..........Amer J Hyg
American Journal of Hygiene [*A publication*]..........Am J Hyg
American Journal of Hygiene. Monographic Series [*A publication*]..........Am J Hyg Monogr Ser
American Journal of Infection Control [*A publication*]..... Am J Infect Control
American Journal of International Law [*A publication*]..........AJIL
American Journal of International Law [*A publication*]..........A J I Law
American Journal of International Law [*A publication*].......... Amer J Int Law
American Journal of International Law [*A publication*]..........Am J Int L
American Journal of International Law [*A publication*]..........Am J Int Law
American Journal of International Law [*A publication*]..........Am Jour Internatl Law
American Journal of International Law. Proceedings [*A publication*]..........Am J Int Law Proc
American Journal of International Law. Supplement [*A publication*]..........Am J Int L Supp
American Journal of Intravenous Therapy and Clinical Nutrition [*A publication*]..........Am J IV Clin Nutr
American Journal of Intravenous Therapy and Clinical Nutrition [*A publication*]..........Am J IV Ther Clin Nutr
American Journal of I.V. Therapy [*A publication*]..........Am J IV Ther
American Journal of I.V. Therapy [*A publication*]..........Am J IV Therapy
American Journal of Jurisprudence [*A publication*]..........Amer J Juris
American Journal of Jurisprudence [*A publication*]..........Am J Juris
American Journal of Law and Medicine [*A publication*]..........Am J Law Med
American Journal of Legal History [*A publication*]..........Am J Legal Hist
American Journal of Legal History [*A publication*]..........Am Jour Legal Hist
American Journal of Maternal Child Nursing [*A publication*]..........MCN
American Journal of Mathematics [*A publication*]..........Am J Math
American Journal of Medical Electronics [*A publication*]..........Am J Med Electron
American Journal of Medical Genetics [*A publication*]........ Am J Med Genet
American Journal of the Medical Sciences [*A publication*] .... Am J Med Sc
American Journal of the Medical Sciences [*A publication*] ...... Am J Med Sci
American Journal of Medical Technology [*A publication*] .... Am J Med Te
American Journal of Medical Technology [*A publication*]..........Am J Med Technol
American Journal of Medicine [*A publication*]..........Am J Med
American Journal of Mental Deficiency [*A publication*]..........AJMD
American Journal of Mental Deficiency [*A publication*]..........AJMDA
American Journal of Mental Deficiency [*A publication*].....Amer J Ment Defic
American Journal of Mental Deficiency [*A publication*]..........Am J Men Deficiency
American Journal of Mental Deficiency [*A publication*]..........Am J Mental Deficiency
American Journal of Mental Deficiency [*A publication*]..........Am J Ment D
American Journal of Mental Deficiency [*A publication*]........ Am J Ment Defic
American Journal of Microscopy and Popular Science (New York) [*A publication*]..........Am J Micr (NY)
American Journal of Numismatics [*A publication*]..........AJN
American Journal of Numismatics [*A publication*]..........AJNum
American Journal of Nursing [*A publication*]..........AJNUA
American Journal of Nursing [*A publication*]..........Am J Nurs
American Journal of Nursing [*A publication*]..........Am J Nursing
American Journal of Nursing Co., New York, NY [*Library symbol*].... NNAJN
American Journal of Obstetrics and Gynecology [*A publication*]....... AJOGA
American Journal of Obstetrics and Gynecology [*A publication*]..........Am J Obstet Gynecol
American Journal of Obstetrics and Gynecology [*A publication*]..........Am J Obst G
American Journal of Occupational Therapy [*A publication*].......... AJOT
American Journal of Occupational Therapy [*A publication*]..........Am J Occup Ther
American Journal of Occupational Therapy [*A publication*].......Am J Occu T
American Journal of Ophthalmology [*A publication*].......... Am J Ophth
American Journal of Ophthalmology [*A publication*] ....Am J Ophthalmol
American Journal of Optometry [*A publication*]..........AJOYA
American Journal of Optometry and Archives of American Academy of Optometry [*Later, American Journal of Optometry and Physiological Optics*] [*A publication*]..........Am J Optom Arch Am Acad Optom
American Journal of Optometry and Physiological Optics [*A publication*]..........Am J Optom
American Journal of Optometry and Physiological Optics [*A publication*]..........Am J Optom & Physiol Opt
American Journal of Optometry and Physiological Optics [*A publication*]..........Am J Optom Physiol Opt
American Journal of Orthodontics [*A publication*]..........AJOHA
American Journal of Orthodontics [*A publication*]..........Am J Orthod
American Journal of Orthodontics and Oral Surgery [*Later, American Journal of Orthodontics*] [*A publication*]..........Am J Orthod Oral Surg
American Journal of Orthopsychiatry [*A publication*]..........AJOPs
American Journal of Orthopsychiatry [*A publication*]..........AJORA
American Journal of Orthopsychiatry [*A publication*]..........Amer J Orthopsychiat
American Journal of Orthopsychiatry [*A publication*]..........Am J Orthop
American Journal of Orthopsychiatry [*A publication*]..........Am J Orthopsych
American Journal of Orthopsychiatry [*A publication*]......Am J Orthopsychiat
American Journal of Orthopsychiatry [*A publication*].... Am J Orthopsychiatr
American Journal of Otolaryngology [*A publication*] .... Am J Otolaryngol
American Journal of Otology [*A publication*]..........Am J Otol
American Journal of Pathology [*A publication*]..........Amer J Pathol
American Journal of Pathology [*A publication*]..........Am J Path
American Journal of Pathology [*A publication*]..........Am J Pathol
American Journal of Pediatric Hematology/Oncology [*A publication*]..........Am J Pediatr Hematol Oncol
American Journal of Pharmaceutical Education [*A publication*]..........Am J Phar E
American Journal of Pharmaceutical Education [*A publication*]..........Am J Pharm Educ
American Journal of Pharmacy and the Sciences Supporting Public Health [*A publication*]..........Am J Pharm
American Journal of Pharmacy and the Sciences Supporting Public Health [*A publication*]..........Am J Pharm Sci Supporting Public Health
American Journal of Philology [*A publication*]..........AJP
American Journal of Philology [*A publication*]..........AJPh
American Journal of Philology [*A publication*]..........AJPhil
American Journal of Philology [*A publication*]..........Amer J Philo
American Journal of Philology [*A publication*]..........Am Jnl Philol
American Journal of Philology [*A publication*]..........Am J Phil
American Journal of Philology [*A publication*]..........Am J Philol

American Journal of Physical Anthropology [*A publication*] ... Amer J Phys Anthropol
American Journal of Physical Anthropology [*A publication*] ... Am Jour Phys Anthropol
American Journal of Physical Anthropology [*A publication*] ... Am J P Anth
American Journal of Physical Anthropology [*A publication*] ... Am J Phys Anthro
American Journal of Physical Anthropology [*A publication*] ... Am J Phys Anthrop
American Journal of Physical Anthropology [*A publication*] ... Am J Phys Anthropol
American Journal of Physical Anthropology. New Series [*A publication*] ... Am J Phys Anthrop ns
American Journal of Physical Medicine [*A publication*] ... Amer J Phys Med
American Journal of Physical Medicine [*A publication*] ... Am J Phys M
American Journal of Physical Medicine [*A publication*] ... Am J Phys Med
American Journal of Physics [*A publication*] ... AJPIA
American Journal of Physics [*A publication*] ... Amer J of Phys
American Journal of Physics [*A publication*] ... Amer J Phys
American Journal of Physics [*A publication*] ... Am J Phys
American Journal of Physics [*A publication*] ... Am J Physics
American Journal of Physiology [*A publication*] ... Amer J Physiol
American Journal of Physiology [*A publication*] ... Am J Physiol
American Journal of Physiology [*A publication*] ... Am J Physl
American Journal of Physiology. Renal, Fluid Electrolyte Physiology [*A publication*] ... Am J Physiol Renal Fluid Electrolyte Physiol
American Journal of Political Science [*A publication*] ... Amer J Polit Sci
American Journal of Political Science [*A publication*] ... Am J Pol Sc
American Journal of Political Science [*A publication*] ... Am J Pol Sci
American Journal of Politics [*A publication*] ... Am J Pol
American Journal of Proctology [*Later, American Journal of Proctology, Gastroenterology, and Colon and Rectal Surgery*] [*A publication*] ... Am J Proctol
American Journal of Proctology, Gastroenterology, and Colon and Rectal Surgery [*A publication*] ... Am J Proctol Gastroenterol Colon Rectal Surg
American Journal of Proctology, Gastroenterology, and Colon and Rectal Surgery (Georgetown) [*A publication*] ... Am J Proctol Gastroenterol Colon Rectal Surg (Georgetown)
American Journal of Psychiatry [*A publication*] ... AJP
American Journal of Psychiatry [*A publication*] ... AJPSA
American Journal of Psychiatry [*A publication*] ... AJPsy
American Journal of Psychiatry [*A publication*] ... Amer J Psychiatry
American Journal of Psychiatry [*A publication*] ... Am Jour Psychiatry
American Journal of Psychiatry [*A publication*] ... Am J Psych
American Journal of Psychiatry [*A publication*] ... Am J Psychi
American Journal of Psychiatry [*A publication*] ... Am J Psychiatry
American Journal of Psychoanalysis [*A publication*] ... AJP
American Journal of Psychoanalysis [*A publication*] ... Amer J Psychoanal
American Journal of Psychoanalysis [*A publication*] ... Am J Psycha
American Journal of Psychoanalysis [*A publication*] ... Am J Psychoanal
American Journal of Psychology [*A publication*] ... AJPCA
American Journal of Psychology [*A publication*] ... AJPs
American Journal of Psychology [*A publication*] ... A J Psy
American Journal of Psychology [*A publication*] ... AJPsych
American Journal of Psychology [*A publication*] ... Amer Jour Psych
American Journal of Psychology [*A publication*] ... Amer J Psychol
American Journal of Psychology [*A publication*] ... Am J Psycho
American Journal of Psychology [*A publication*] ... Am J Psychol
American Journal of Psychotherapy [*A publication*] ... AJPst
American Journal of Psychotherapy [*A publication*] ... Amer J Psychother
American Journal of Psychotherapy [*A publication*] ... Am J Psychother
American Journal of Psychotherapy [*A publication*] ... Am J Psycht
American Journal of Public Health [*A publication*] ... AJHEA
American Journal of Public Health [*A publication*] ... Am J Pub He
American Journal of Public Health [*A publication*] ... Am J Pub Health
American Journal of Public Health [*A publication*] ... Am J Public Health
American Journal of Reproductive Immunology [*A publication*] ... AJRI
American Journal of Roentgenology [*A publication*] ... Am J Roentg
American Journal of Roentgenology [*A publication*] ... Am J Roentgenol
American Journal of School Hygiene [*A publication*] ... Am J School Hygiene
American Journal of Science [*A publication*] ... AJS
American Journal of Science [*A publication*] ... Amer J Sci
American Journal of Science [*A publication*] ... Am J Sci
American Journal of Science and Arts [*A publication*] ... Am J Sc and Arts
American Journal of Science. Radiocarbon Supplement [*A publication*] ... Amer J Sci Radiocarbon Suppl
American Journal of Semitic Languages and Literatures [*A publication*] ... AJSemL
American Journal of Semitic Languages and Literatures [*A publication*] ... AJSL
American Journal of Semitic Languages and Literatures [*A publication*] ... Am J Sem Lang
American Journal of Small Business [*A publication*] ... Jl Small Bus
American Journal of Social Science [*A publication*] ... Am J Soc Sci
American Journal of Social Science [*A publication*] ... Am Soc Sci J
American Journal of Sociology [*A publication*] ... AJS
American Journal of Sociology [*A publication*] ... AJSOA
American Journal of Sociology [*A publication*] ... Amer J Sociol
American Journal of Sociology [*A publication*] ... Am Jnl Soc
American Journal of Sociology [*A publication*] ... Am Jour Sociol
American Journal of Sociology [*A publication*] ... Am J Soc
American Journal of Sociology [*A publication*] ... Am J Sociol
American Journal of Sports Medicine [*A publication*] ... Am J Sports Med
American Journal of Surgery [*A publication*] ... Am J Surg
American Journal of Surgical Pathology [*A publication*] ... Am J Surg Pathol
American Journal of Theology [*A publication*] ... AJT
American Journal of Theology [*A publication*] ... AJTh
American Journal of Theology [*A publication*] ... Am J Theol
American Journal of Therapeutics and Clinical Reports [*A publication*] ... Am J Ther Clin Rep
American Journal of Tropical Diseases and Preventive Medicine (New Orleans) [*A publication*] ... Am J Trop Dis (New Orleans)
American Journal of Tropical Medicine and Hygiene [*A publication*] ... Am J Trop M
American Journal of Tropical Medicine and Hygiene [*A publication*] ... Am J Trop Med Hyg
American Journal of Veterinary Medicine [*A publication*] ... Am J Vet Med
American Journal of Veterinary Research [*A publication*] ... Amer J Vet Res
American Journal of Veterinary Research [*A publication*] ... Am J Vet Re
American Journal of Veterinary Research [*A publication*] ... Am J Vet Res
American Judges Association ... AJA
American Judicature Society ... AJS
American Judo Association ... AJA
American Junior Academy of Sciences ... AJAS
American Junior Bowling Congress ... AJBC
American Junior College of Puerto Rico, Bayamon, PR [*Library symbol*] ... PrBayA
American Junior College of Puerto Rico, Bayamon, PR [*OCLC symbol*] ... PRJ
American Junior Golf Association ... AJGA
American Junior Hereford Association ... AJHA
American Junior Red Cross ... AJRC
American Junior Shorthorn Association ... AJSA
American Junior Simmental Association [*Later, ASA*] ... AJSA
American Justice Institute ... AJI
American Karakul Fur Sheep Registry ... AKFSR
American Kennel Club ... AKC
American Kennel Club, New York, NY [*Library symbol*] ... NNAKC
American Kidney Fund ... AKF
American Killifish Association ... AKA
American Kitefliers Association ... AKA
American Knit Glove Association ... AKGA
American-Korean Foundation [*Later, IHAP*] ... AKF
American Labor Education Service [*Defunct*] ... ALES
American Labor Health Association [*Later, GHAA*] ... ALHA
American Labor Legislation Review [*A publication*] ... Am Labor Leg R
American Labor Party ... ALP
American Laboratory [*A publication*] ... Am Lab
American Laboratory (Fairfield, Connecticut) [*A publication*] ... Am Lab (Fairfield Conn)
American Lace Manufacturers Association ... ALMA
American Ladder Institute ... ALI
American Lamancha Club ... ALC
American Lancia Club ... ALC
American Land Alliance ... ALA
American Land Development Association ... ALDA
American Land Forum ... ALF
American Land Title Association ... ALTA
American Landrace Association ... ALA
American Langshan Club ... ALC
American Laryngological Association ... ALA
American Laryngological, Rhinological, and Otological Society ... ALROS
American Latvian Association in the United States ... ALA
American Laundry Digest [*A publication*] ... Am Laund Dig
American Law Enforcement Officers Association ... ALEOA
American Law Institute ... ALI
American Law Reports ... ALR
American Law Review [*A publication*] ... Am Law R
American Law Student Association [*Later, Law Student Division - American Bar Association*] ... ALSA
American Lawn Bowls Association ... ALBA
American Lawyers Association [*Later, TAG*] ... ALA
American League [*Baseball*] ... A
American League [*Baseball*] ... AL
American League to Abolish Capital Punishment [*Defunct*] ... ALACP
American League of Anglers ... ALA
American League for Exports and Security Assistance ... ALESA
American League of Lobbyists ... ALL
American League of Professional Baseball Clubs ... ALPBC
American Leather Belting Association [*Later, NIBA*] ... ALBA
American Leather Chemists Association ... ALCA
American Lebanese League ... ALL
American Lebanese Syrian Association Charities ... ALSAC
American Lecture Series [*A publication*] ... Am Lect Ser
American Legal Foundation ... ALF
American Legal Studies Association ... ALSA
American Legation, United States Naval Attache ... ALUSNA
American Legation, United States Naval Liaison Officer ... ALUSLO
American Legation, United States Naval Observer ... ALUSNOB
American Legion ... AL
American Legion Auxiliary ... ALA

American Legion Auxiliary Library, Cheyenne Wells, CO [*Library symbol*] ... CoChey
American Legion Baseball [*An association*] ... ALB
American Legion of Honor ... AL of H
American Legion, National Headquarters Library, Indianapolis, IN [*Library symbol*] ... InIAL
American Legion Press Association [*Later, NALPA*] ... ALPA
American Legion Transportation Post ... ALTP
American Legislative Exchange Council ... ALEC
American Leisure Corporation [*NASDAQ symbol*] ... AMCO
American Leprosy Missions [*An association*] ... ALM
American Lessing Society [*Later, LS*] ... ALS
American Lhasa Apso Club ... ALAC
American Liaison Office ... ALO
American Liberal Association ... ALA
American Liberation League ... ALL
American Libraries [*Chicago*] [*A publication*] ... A Lib
American Libraries [*Chicago*] [*A publication*] ... Am Lib
American Libraries [*Chicago*] [*A publication*] ... Am Libr
American Libraries [*Chicago*] [*A publication*] ... Am Libs
American Libraries (Chicago) [*A publication*] ... Am Libr (Chicago)
American Library Association ... ALA
American Library Association. Adult Services Division. Joint Committee on Library Service to Labor Groups. Library Service to Labor Newsletter [*A publication*] ... ALA Lib Serv to Labor News
American Library Association. Association of Hospital and Institution Libraries. Book Guide. [*A publication*] ... ALA Hosp Bk Guide
American Library Association. Booklist [*A publication*] ... Booklist
American Library Association, Booklist, Chicago, IL [*OCLC symbol*] ... JAB
American Library Association. Bulletin [*A publication*] ... ALA Bul
American Library Association. Bulletin [*A publication*] ... Am Lib Assn Bul
American Library Association, Chicago, IL [*Library symbol*] ... ICALA
American Library Association, Chicago, IL [*OCLC symbol*] ... IEH
American Library Association. Intellectual Freedom Committee Newsletter [*A publication*] ... ALA Intellectual Freedom Newsl
American Library Association. Library Periodicals Round Table. Newsletter [*A publication*] ... ALA Lib Period Round Table Newsl
American Library Association. Reference Services Division. RQ [*A publication*] ... ALA Ref Serv Div
American Library Association. Washington Newsletter [*A publication*] ... ALA Wash Newsl
American Library Directory [*A publication*] ... ALD
American Library for Education, Research, and Training ... ALERT
American Library and Educational Services Company ... ALESCO
American Library History Round Table ... ALHRT
American Library Scholarship [*A publication*] ... Am L S
American Library Society [*Defunct*] ... ALS
American Library Trustee Association ... ALTA
American Life Convention [*Later, ACLI*] ... ALC
American Life Foundation [*Press*] ... ALF
American Life Insurance Association [*Later, ACLI*] ... ALIA
American Life Lobby [*An association*] ... ALL
American Lifesaving Emergency Response Team ... ALERT
American List Corp. [*NASDAQ symbol*] ... ALST
American Liszt Society ... ALS
American Literary Anthology ... ALA
American Literary Magazine [*A publication*] ... Am Lit M
American Literary Realism, 1870-1910 [*A publication*] ... ALR
American Literary Realism, 1870-1910 [*A publication*] ... Am Lit Realism
American Literary Translators Association ... ALTA
American Literature [*A publication*] ... AL
American Literature [*A publication*] ... AmLit
American Literature Abstracts [*A publication*] ... AmerLitAb
American Literature, English Literature, and World Literature in English [*A publication*] ... ALELWLE
American Lithuanian Catholic Federation Ateitis [*Later, LCFA*] ... ALCFA
American Lithuanian Engineers' and Architects' Association ... ALEAA
American Lithuanian Organist - Musicians Alliance [*Formerly, ALRCOA*] ... ALOMA
American Lithuanian Press and Radio Association ... ALPRA
American Lithuanian Press and Radio Association - Viltis ... ALPRA-V
American Lithuanian Roman Catholic Organist Alliance [*Later, ALOMA*] ... ALRCOA
American Lithuanian Roman Catholic Women's Alliance ... ALRCWA
American Lithuanian Workers Literary Association ... ALWLA
American Littoral Society [*For underwater study of shore life*] ... ALS
American Littoral Society. Special Publication [*A publication*] ... Am Littoral Soc Spec Publ
American Liver Foundation ... ALF
American Lives Endowment ... ALE
American Livestock Journal [*A publication*] ... Amer Livestock J
American Livestock Journal [*A publication*] ... Am Livestock J
American Loan Fund ... ALF
American Lock Collectors Association ... ALCA
American Locomotive Company ... ALCO
American Logistics Association ... ALA
American Longevity Association ... ALA
American Loudspeaker Manufacturers Association ... ALMA
American Lumber Standards ... ALS
American Lumber Standards Committee ... ALSC
American Lung Association ... ALA
American Lung Association. Bulletin [*A publication*] ... Am Lung Assoc Bull
[*The*] **American Lupus Society** ... TALS
American Lutheran Church ... ALC
American Lutheran Church Men ... ALCM
American Lutheran Church Women ... ALCW
American Lutheran Education Association ... ALEA
American Lutheran Publicity Bureau ... ALPB
American Luxembourg Society ... ALS
American Machine Tool Distributors Association ... AMTDA
American Machine Tool Export Associates ... AMTEA
American Machinery Association ... AMA
American Machinist [*A publication*] ... AM
American Machinist [*A publication*] ... Amer Mach
American Machinist [*A publication*] ... Am Mach
American Machinist/Metalworking Manufacturing [*A publication*] ... Am Mach/Metalwork Manuf
American Magazine [*A publication*] ... Am M
American Magazine [*A publication*] ... Am Mag
American Magazine of Art [*A publication*] ... Am Mag Art
American Magazine of Art [*A publication*] ... Am M Art
American Magazine of Civics [*A publication*] ... Am M Civics
American Magnetics Corp. [*NASDAQ symbol*] ... AMMG
American Magnolia Society ... AMS
American Mail Line ... AML
American Mail-Order Merchants Association ... AMMA
American Mailorder Association ... AMOA
American Maine-Anjou Association ... AMAA
American Maize-Products Co. [*American Stock Exchange symbol*] ... AZE
American Majority Party ... AMP
American Malacological Union ... AMU
American Malacological Union. Annual Report [*A publication*] ... Am Malacolog Union Ann Rept
American Malacological Union. Bulletin [*A publication*] ... Am Malacol Union Bull
American Malacological Union, Incorporated. Annual Report [*A publication*] ... Am Malacol Union Inc Annu Rep
American Malacological Union, Incorporated. Bulletin [*A publication*] ... Am Malacol Union Inc Bull
American Maltese Association ... AMA
American Management Associations ... AMA
American Management Associations, New York, NY [*Library symbol*] ... NNAMA
American Management Associations. Research Study [*A publication*] ... Amer Manage Ass Res Stud
American Management Review [*A publication*] ... Am Management R
American Management Systems [*Information service*] ... AMS
American Management Systems [*NASDAQ symbol*] ... AMSY
American Manchester Terrier Club ... AMTC
American Manganese Producers Association [*Defunct*] ... AMPA
American Manufacturing Co., Inc. [*American Stock Exchange symbol*] [*Delisted*] ... AFT
American Marine Insurance Clearinghouse ... AMIC
American Marine Insurance Forum ... AMIF
American Marine Insurance Syndicate for Insurance of Builder's Risks [*Defunct*] ... AMISIBR
American Maritime Association ... AMA
American Maritime Cases ... AMC
American Market Selection [*Cigars*] ... AMS
American Marketing Association ... AMA
American Massage and Therapy Association ... AMTA
American Material Handling Society [*Later, IMMS*] ... AMHS
American Mathematical Association of Two Year Colleges ... AMATYC
American Mathematical Monthly [*A publication*] ... Am Math M
American Mathematical Monthly [*A publication*] ... Am Math Mo
American Mathematical Monthly [*A publication*] ... Am Math Mon
American Mathematical Society ... AMS
American Mathematical Society. Bulletin [*A publication*] ... Am Math Soc Bul
American Mathematical Society. Memoirs [*A publication*] ... Am Math Soc Mem
American Mathematical Society. Memoirs [*A publication*] ... Am Math Soc Memoirs
American Mathematical Society, Providence, RI [*Library symbol*] ... RPAM
American Mathematical Society. Translations [*A publication*] ... Amer Math Soc Transl
American Matthay Association ... AMA
American McAll Association ... AMA
American Measuring Tool Manufacturers Association [*Defunct*] ... AMTMA
American Meat Institute ... AMI
American Meat Institute Foundation ... AMIF
American Meat Science Association ... AMSA
American Medallic Sculpture Association ... AMSA
American Medcare Corp. [*NASDAQ symbol*] ... AMMC
American Medi-Dent, Inc. [*NASDAQ symbol*] ... AMED
American Medical Alert Corporation [*NASDAQ symbol*] ... AMAC
American Medical Association ... AMA
American Medical Association Auxiliary [*Formerly, WAAMA*] ... AMAA
American Medical Association, Chicago, IL [*Library symbol*] ... ICAM
American Medical Association Committee on Insurance and Prepayment Plans ... AMA-CIPP

American Medical Association, Division of Library and Archival Services, Chicago, IL [OCLC symbol] .... AMA
American Medical Association Drug Evaluation .... AMA-DE
American Medical Association Education and Research Foundation .... AMA-ERF
American Medical Association. Journal [A publication] .... Am Med Assn J
American Medical Association, Washington Office, Washington, DC [Library symbol] .... DAMA
American Medical Buildings, Inc. [American Stock Exchange symbol] .... A
American Medical Center for Burma [Defunct] .... AMCB
American Medical Center, Medical Library, Denver, CO [Library symbol] .... CoDAMC-M
American Medical College Application Service .... AMCAS
American Medical Curling Association .... AMCA
American Medical Electroencephalographic Association .... AMEEGA
American Medical Fly Fishing Association .... AMFFA
American Medical Golf Association .... AMGA
American Medical International, Inc. [NYSE symbol] .... AMI
American Medical Joggers Association .... AMJA
American Medical News [A publication] .... Am Med News
American Medical Political Action Committee .... AMPAC
American Medical Publishers' Association .... AMPA
American Medical Qualification [British] .... AMQ
American Medical Record Association .... AMRA
American Medical Services [NASDAQ symbol] .... AMSR
American Medical Society on Alcoholism .... AMSA
American Medical Students Association [Formerly, SAMA] .... AMSA
American Medical Systems, Inc., Minneapolis, MN [Library symbol] .... MnMAM
American Medical Technologists .... AMT
American Medical Tennis Association .... AMTA
American Medical Women's Association .... AMWA
American Medical Writers' Association .... AMWA
American Medicine [A publication] .... Am Med
American Medicorp, Inc. [NYSE symbol] [Delisted] .... AAM
American Melting Point .... AMP
American Men and Women of Science [A publication] .... AMWS
American Mental Health Counselors Association .... AMHCA
American Mental Health Foundation .... AMHF
American Mental Health Fund .... AMHF
American Merchant Marine Institute [Later, AIMS] .... AMMI
American Merchant Marine Library Association .... AMMLA
American Merchant Marine Library Association, New York, NY [Library symbol] .... NNAMM
American Mercury [A publication] .... AM
American Mercury [A publication] .... AmM
American Mercury [A publication] .... AmMerc
American Mercury [A publication] .... Am Mercury
American Messianic Fellowship .... AMF
American Metal Climax, Inc. [Later, AMAX, Inc.] .... AMAX
American Metal Climax, Inc. [Later, AMX] [NYSE symbol] .... AMM
American Metal Detector Manufacturers Association .... AMDMA
American Metal Importers Association .... AMIA
American Metal Market [A publication] .... Am Met Mark
American Metal Market [A publication] .... Am Mtl Mkt
American Metal Products Co. [NYSE symbol] [Delisted] .... APS
American Metal Repair Association [Defunct] .... AMRA
American Metal Stamping Association .... AMSA
American Metals Service [NASDAQ symbol] .... AMTS
American Meteor Society .... AMS
American Meteorite Laboratory .... AML
American Meteorological Journal [A publication] .... Am Meteorological J
American Meteorological Society .... AMS
American Meteorological Society. Bulletin [A publication] .... Am Meteorol Soc Bull
American Meter Co. [NYSE symbol] [Delisted] .... AEM
American Metered Postage Society [Defunct] .... AMPS
American Methodist Magazine [A publication] .... Am Meth M
American Mexican Claims Commission [Terminated, 1947] .... AMCC
American MGB Association .... AMGBA
American MGC Register .... AMGCR
American Micro Company, Kansas City, MO [Library symbol] .... AmCo
American Microchemical Society .... AMS
American Microscopical Society .... AMS
American Microscopical Society. Proceedings [A publication] .... Am Micro Soc Pr
American Microscopical Society. Transactions [A publication] .... Am Micros Soc Trans
American Microsystems, Incorporated .... AMI
American Middle East Rehabilitation .... AMER
American Midland Naturalist [A publication] .... Amer Midl Nat
American Midland Naturalist [A publication] .... Am Midland Natural
American Midland Naturalist [A publication] .... Am Midl Nat
American Military Assistance Staff .... AMAS
American Military Government .... AMG
American Military Industrial Complex .... AMERIMIC
American Military Institute .... AMI
American Military Mission to China [World War II] .... AMMISCA
American Military Mission, Delhi [World War II] .... AMMDEL
American Military Precision Flying Teams Association .... AMPFTA
American Military Retirees Association .... AMRA

American Milk Goat Record Association [Later, ADGA] .... AMGRA
American Milk Review [A publication] .... Am Milk R
American Milking Shorthorn Society .... AMSS
American Miller and Processor [A publication] .... Amer Miller Process
American Miller and Processor [A publication] .... Am Miller Process
American Millinery Manufacturers Association [Defunct] .... AMMA
American Mime Theatre .... AMT
[The] American Mime Theatre .... TAMT
American Mineral Spirits Company .... AMSCO
American Mineralogical Journal [A publication] .... Am Miner J
American Mineralogist [A publication] .... Amer Mineral
American Mineralogist [A publication] .... Am Min
American Mineralogist [A publication] .... Am Mineral
American Miniature Horse Registry .... AMHR
American Miniature Racing Car Association .... AMRCA
American Miniature Schnauzer Club .... AMSC
American Mining Congress .... AMC
American Mining Congress [A publication] .... Am M Cong
American Ministerial Association .... AMA
American Minor Breeds Conservancy .... AMBC
American Miscellaneous Society .... AMSOC
American Mission for Aid to Greece .... AMAG
American Mission for Aid to Turkey .... AMAT
American Mission to the Chinese [Later, American Mission to the Chinese and Asian] .... AMC
American Mission to the Chinese and Asian .... AMCA
American Mission to Greeks [Later, AMG International] .... AMG
American Mission in Korea .... AMIK
American Mission for Opening Churches [Formerly, AMOCC] .... AMOC
American Mission for Opening Closed Churches [Later, AMOC] ..... AMOCC
American Missionary Association .... AMA
American Missionary Fellowship [Formerly, ASSU] .... AMF
American Mizrachi Women [Formerly, MWOA] .... AMW
American Mobilehome Association .... AMA
American Modern Dance Caucus .... AMDC
American Mohammedan Society [Later, Moslem Mosque] .... AMS
American Monitor Corp. [NASDAQ symbol] .... AMON
American Montessori Society .... AMS
American Monthly Magazine [A publication] .... Am Mo M
American Monthly Review [A publication] .... Am Mo R
American Monument Association .... AMA
American Morab Horse Association .... AMHA
American Morgan Horse Association .... AMHA
American Mosquito Control Association .... AMCA
American Motel Association .... AMA
American Mothers Committee [Later, American Mothers, Inc.] .... AMC
American Mothers of Korean Orphans .... AMKO
American Motion Picture Export Company/Africa [An association] .... AMPECA
American Motor Hotel Association .... AMHA
American Motor Inns, Inc. [American Stock Exchange symbol] .... INN
American Motor Owners Association .... AMO
American Motorcycle Drag Racing Association [of the National Hot Rod Association] [Later, NMRA] .... AMDRA
American Motorcyclist Association .... AMA
American Motors Corporation .... AMC
American Motors Corp. [NYSE symbol] [Wall Street slang name: "Ammo"] .... AMO
American Movement for World Government .... AMWG
American Movers Conference .... AMC
American Mule Association .... AMA
American Municipal Association [Later, National League of Cities] .... AMA
American Murray Grey Association .... AMGA
American Museum of Immigration .... AMI
American Museum Journal [A publication] .... Am Mus J
American Museum of Marine Archaeology .... AMMA
American Museum of Natural History .... AMNH
American Museum of Natural History. Bulletin [A publication] .... Am Mus Nat History Bull
American Museum of Natural History. Bulletin. Memoirs [A publication] .... Am Mus N H B Mem
American Museum of Natural History, New York, NY [Library symbol] .... NNM
American Museum of Natural History, New York, NY [OCLC symbol] .... YAM
American Museum Novitates [A publication] .... Am Mus Novit
American Museum Novitates [A publication] .... Am Mus Novitates
American Museum of Safety .... AMS
American Mushroom Institute .... AMI
American Music Center .... AMC
American Music Conference .... AMC
American Music Teacher [A publication] .... Am Mus Tcr
American Music Teacher [A publication] .... Am Mus Teach
American Music Teacher [A publication] .... AMUTA
American Musical Digest [A publication] .... Am Mus Dgt
American Musical Instrument Society .... AMIS
American Musical Instrument Society. Journal [A publication] .... AMIS J
American Musical Instrument Society. Newsletter [A publication] .... AMIS N
American Musicians Union .... AMU
American Musicological Society .... AMS
American Musicological Society. Journal [A publication] .... Am Musicol Soc J

American Musicological Society. Journal [*A publication*]....AMS
American Musicological Society. Journal [*A publication*]....AMS Jl
American Mustang Association....AMA
American Mutual Alliance [*Insurance association*] [*Later, Alliance of American Insurers*]....AMA
American Mutual Insurance Alliance [*Later, Alliance of American Insurers*]....AMIA
American Mutual Life Association....AMLA
American Nail Producers Council....ANPC
American Name Society....ANS
American Naprapathic Association....ANA
American Narcolepsy Association....ANA
American National Archives....ANA
American National Cattlemen's Association [*Later, NCA*]....ANCA
American National Commission for the Accreditation of Colleges and Universities....ANCACU
American National Committee to Aid Homeless Armenians....ANCHA
American National Council for Health Education of the Public....ANCHEP
American National Cowbelles....ANC
American National Cowbelles....ANCB
American National Enterprises [*NASDAQ symbol*]....AMNT
American National Heritage Association....ANHA
American National Holding Company [*NASDAQ symbol*]....ANHC
American National Insurance Co. [*NASDAQ symbol*]....ANAT
American National Insurance Co.....ANI
American National Insurance Company....ANICO
American National Metric Council....ANMC
American National Petrol [*NASDAQ symbol*]....ANPC
American National Postal Employees Retirees Association....ANPERA
American National Red Cross [*Later, ARC*]....ANRC
American National Red Cross, Washington, DC [*Library symbol*]....DARC
American National Standard....ANS
American National Standard Character Set for Optical Character Recognition....ANSCS OCR
American National Standard Code for Information Interchange....ANSCII
American National Standard Labels....ANL
American National Standards Institute [*Formerly, AESC, ASA, USASI*]....ANSI
American National Standards (Institute) Committee....ANSC
American National Standards Institute, New York, NY [*Library symbol*]....NNASA
American National Theatre and Academy [*Liquidated, 1969*]....ANTA
American Natural Gas Co. [*Later, ANR*] [*NYSE symbol*]....ANG
American Natural Hygiene Society....ANHS
American Natural Resources Co. [*Formerly, ANG*] [*NYSE symbol*]....ANR
American Naturalist [*A publication*]....Amer Nat
American Naturalist [*A publication*]....Am Nat
American Naturalist [*A publication*]....Am Natural
American Naturalized Citizen Welfare Association [*Later, US Naturalized Citizen Association*]....ANCWA
American Nature Association....ANA
American Nature Study Society....ANSS
American Naturopathic Medical Association....ANMA
American Navion Society....ANS
American Near East Refugee Aid [*An association*]....ANERA
American-Nepal Education Foundation....ANEF
American Neptune [*A publication*]....Am Neptune
American Neurological Association....ANA
American Newcomen Society....ANS
American News Company [*NYSE symbol*] [*Delisted*]....ANC
American News Women's Club....ANWC
American Newspaper Association....ANA
American Newspaper Guild [*Later, TNG*]....ANG
American Newspaper Publishers Abstracting Technique....ANPAT
American Newspaper Publishers Association....ANPA
American Newspaper Publishers Association. Newsprint Statistics [*A publication*]....ANPA Stat
American Newspapers, 1821-1936 [*A bibliographic publication*]....AN
American Normande Association....ANA
American North Country Cheviot Sheep Association....ANCCSA
American Norwich Society....ANS
American Notes and Queries [*A publication*]....Am Notes & Queries
American Notes and Queries [*A publication*]....Am N & Q
American Notes and Queries [*A publication*]....AN & Q
American Notes and Queries [*A publication*]....ANQ
American Nuclear Corp. [*NASDAQ symbol*]....ANUC
American Nuclear Energy Council....ANEC
American Nuclear Insurers....ANI
American Nuclear Science Corporation....ANSC
American Nuclear Society....ANS
American Nucleonics Corp. [*NASDAQ symbol*]....AMNU
American Numismatic Association....ANA
American Numismatic Association Certification Service....ANACS
American Numismatic Association, Colorado Springs, CO [*Library symbol*]....CoCAN
American Numismatic Society....ANS
American Numismatic Society. Museum Notes [*A publication*]....Am Num Soc Mus Notes
American Numismatic Society. Museum Notes [*A publication*]....ANSMN
American Numismatic Society. Museum Notes [*A publication*]....ANSMusN
American Numismatic Society. Museum Notes [*A publication*]....ANSN
American Numismatic Society, New York, NY [*Library symbol*]....NNAN
American Numismatic Society. Numismatic Notes and Monographs [*A publication*]....ANSNNM
American Numismatic Society. Numismatic Studies [*A publication*]....ANSNS
American Nurse [*A publication*]....Am Nurse
American Nurseryman [*A publication*]....Amer Nurserym
American Nurses' Association....ANA
American Nurses' Association, Kansas City, MO [*Library symbol*]....MoKA
American Nurses' Association. Nursing Research Conferences [*A publication*]....ANA Nurs Res Conf
American Nurses' Association. Publications [*A publication*]....ANA Publ
American Nurses' Foundation....ANF
American Nursing Assistants' Association....ANAA
American Nursing Home Association [*Later, AHCA*]....ANHA
American Nut Journal [*A publication*]....Am Nut J
American Nutrition Society....ANS
American Occupational Medical Association....AOMA
American Occupational Therapy Association....AOTA
American Oceanic Organization....AOO
American Office Supply Exporters Association [*Defunct*]....AOSEA
American Oil Chemists' Society....AOCS
American Oil Chemists' Society. Journal [*A publication*]....Am Oil Chem Soc J
American Oil Company [*Later, Amoco Oil Co.*]....AMOCO
American Oil Co. [*Later, Amoco Oil Co.*], **Texas City, TX** [*Library symbol*]....TxTA
American Old Time Fiddlers Association....AOTFA
American Ontoanalytic Association....AOA
American Ophthalmological Color [*Chart*]....AOC
American Ophthalmological Society....AOS
American Opinion [*A publication*]....Amer O
American Opinion [*A publication*]....Am Opinion
American Optical Co.....AO
American Optical Company [*NYSE symbol*] [*Delisted*]....AOC
American Optical Corp., Southbridge, MA [*Library symbol*]....MSbrA
American Optometric Association....AOA
American Optometric Foundation....AOF
American Optometric Student Association....AOSA
American Orchid Society....AOS
American Orchid Society. Bulletin [*A publication*]....Am Orchid Soc Bull
American Order of the French Croix de Guerre....AOFCG
American Order of Stationary Engineers....AOSE
American [*or Army*] **Ordnance Association** [*Later, ADPA*]....AOA
American Orff-Schulwerk Association....AOSA
American Organist [*A publication*]....Am Org
American Organization for the Education of the Hearing Impaired....AOEHI
American Organization of Tour Operators to Israel [*Defunct*]....AOTOI
American Oriental Series [*A publication*]....AOS
American Oriental Society....AOS
American Oriental Society. Journal [*A publication*]....Amer Oriental Soc Jour
American Oriental Society. Journal [*A publication*]....Am Orient Soc J
American Ornithologists' Union....AOU
American Orthodontic Society....AOS
American Orthopaedic Association....AOA
American Orthopaedic Foot Society....AOFS
American Orthopaedic Society for Sports Medicine....AOSSM
American Orthopsychiatric Association....AOA
American Orthopsychiatric Association....ORTHO
American Orthoptic Council....AOC
American Orthoptic Journal [*A publication*]....Am Orthopt J
American Orthotic and Prosthetic Association....AOPA
American Osler Society....AOS
American Osteopathic Academy of Orthopedics....AOAO
American Osteopathic Academy of Sclerotherapy....AOAS
American Osteopathic Academy of Sports Medicine....AOASM
American Osteopathic Association....AOA
American Osteopathic Association, Chicago, IL [*Library symbol*]....ICAO
American Osteopathic Board of General Practice....AOBGP
American Osteopathic Board of Pediatrics....AOBP
American Osteopathic College of Allergy and Immunology....AOCAI
American Osteopathic College of Anesthesiologists....AOCA
American Osteopathic College of Dermatology....AOCD
American Osteopathic College of Nuclear Medicine....AOCNM
American Osteopathic College of Pathologists....AOCP
American Osteopathic College of Pathologists....AOCPA
American Osteopathic College of Physical Medicine and Rehabilitation [*Later, AOCRM*]....AOCPMR
American Osteopathic College of Proctology....AOCP
American Osteopathic College of Proctology....AOCPR
American Osteopathic College of Radiology....AOCR
American Osteopathic College of Rehabilitation Medicine....AOCRM
American Osteopathic College of Rheumatology....AOCR
American Osteopathic Historical Society [*Defunct*]....AOHS
American Osteopathic Hospital Association....AOHA
American Osteopathic Hospital Research and Education Foundation....AOHREF
American Otological Society....AOS

American Otorhinologic Society for Plastic Surgery [*Later, American Academy of Facial Plastic and Reconstructive Surgery*] ... AOSPS
American Overseas Airlines ... AOA
American Overseas Association ... AOA
American Oxford Down Record Association [*Later, AOSA*] ... AODRA
American Oxford Sheep Association [*Formerly, AODRA*] ... AOSA
American Oxonian [*A publication*] ... AmOx
American Oxonian [*A publication*] ... AO
American Pacific Corp. [*NASDAQ symbol*] ... APFC
American Pacific International [*NASDAQ symbol*] ... APIC
American Package Express Carriers Association ... APECA
American Pain Society ... APS
American Paint Horse Association ... APHA
American Paint Journal [*A publication*] ... Am Paint
American Palestine Committee [*Defunct*] ... APC
American Pancreatic Association ... APA
American Paper Co. ... AP
American Paper Exchange Club ... APEC
American Paper Industry [*A publication*] ... Amer Pap Ind
American Paper Industry [*A publication*] ... Am Paper Ind
American Paper Industry [*A publication*] ... Am Pap Ind
American Paper Institute [*A publication*] ... Am Paper Inst
American Paper Institute ... API
American Paper Institute. Food Additives Reference Manual [*A publication*] ... API Food Add Ref
American Paper Institute. Monthly Statistical Summary [*A publication*] ... API Statist Sum
American Paper Institute. Newsprint Division. Bulletin [*A publication*] ... API Newsprint Bull
American Paper Institute. Wood Pulp Statistics [*A publication*] ... API Wood Pulp Statist
American Paper Merchant [*A publication*] ... Am Paper Merch
American Paper and Pulp Association [*Later, API*] ... APPA
American Paralysis Association ... APA
American Paramedical Institute [*Hawaii*] ... API
American Parapsychological Research Foundation ... APRF
American Parents Committee ... APC
American Park and Recreation Society ... APRS
American Parkinson Disease Association ... APDA
American Parquet Association ... APA
American Part-Blooded Horse Registry ... APB
American Partridge Plymouth Rock Club ... APPRC
American Paso Fino Horse Association ... APFHA
American Patent Law Association ... APLA
American Pathology Foundation ... APF
American Patients Association ... APA
American Pawnbrokers Association ... APA
American Pax Association [*Later, PC-USA*] ... APA
American Peace Society ... APS
American Peanut Product Manufacturers, Incorporated ... APPMI
American Peanut Research and Education Association [*Later, APRES*] ... APREA
American Peanut Research and Education Society [*Formerly, APREA*] ... APRES
American Pedestrian Association ... APA
American Pediatric Gross Assessment Record ... APGAR
American Pediatric Society ... APS
American Pencil Collectors Society ... APCS
American Penstemon Society ... APS
American Peony Society ... APS
American People for American Prisoners ... APAP
American People's Mobilization [*Formerly, American Peace Mobilization*] [*World War II*] ... APM
American Performing-Rights Society ... APRS
American Perfumer and Aromatics [*A publication*] ... Am Perfumer & Aromatics
American Perfumer and Cosmetics [*A publication*] ... Am Perfumer
American Personnel and Guidance Association ... APGA
American Peruvian Paso Horse Registry ... APPHR
American Pet Products Manufacturers Association ... APPMA
American Petanque Association ... APA
American Petrofina, Incorporated [*American Stock Exchange symbol*] ... API
American Petroleum Credit Association ... APCA
American Petroleum Institute ... API
American Petroleum Institute. Bulletin [*A publication*] ... Am Pet Inst Bul
American Petroleum Institute. Medical Research Publications [*A publication*] ... API Med Res Publ
American Petroleum Institute. Proceedings [*A publication*] ... Am Pet Inst Proc
American Petroleum Institute. Publications [*A publication*] ... API Publ
American Petroleum Institute. Refining Department. Midyear Meeting. Preprints [*A publication*] ... API Refining Dep Midyear Meet Prepr
American Petroleum Institute Research ... APIR
American Petroleum Institute Research Project ... APIRP
American Petroleum Institute. Standards [*A publication*] ... Amer Petrol Inst Stand
American Petroleum Institute, Washington, DC [*Library symbol*] ... DAPI
American Petroleum Refiners Association ... APRA
American Pewter Guild ... APG
American Pharmaceutical Association ... APA
American Pharmaceutical Association ... APhA
American Pharmaceutical Association, Washington, DC [*Library symbol*] ... DAPh
American Pharmacopeia ... AP
American Pharmacy [*A publication*] ... Am Pharm
American Pheasant Society [*Later, AP & WS*] ... APS
American Pheasant and Waterfowl Society ... AP & WS
American Phenolic Corp. ... AMPHENOL
American Philatelic Congress ... APC
American Philatelic Research Library ... APRL
American Philatelic Research Library, State College, PA [*Library symbol*] ... PStcA
American Philatelic Society ... APS
American Philatelic Society Writers Unit [*American Philatelic Society*] ... APSWU
American Philological Association ... APA
American Philosophical Association ... APA
American Philosophical Quarterly [*A publication*] ... Amer Phil Quart
American Philosophical Quarterly [*A publication*] ... Am Philos Q
American Philosophical Quarterly [*A publication*] ... APQ
American Philosophical Society ... APS
American Philosophical Society. Library Bulletin [*A publication*] ... Am Philos Soc Lib Bull
American Philosophical Society, Philadelphia, PA [*Library symbol*] ... PPAmP
American Philosophical Society. Proceedings [*A publication*] ... Amer Philos Soc Proc
American Philosophical Society. Proceedings [*A publication*] ... Am Philos Soc Proc
American Philosophical Society. Proceedings [*A publication*] ... APS
American Philosophical Society. Transactions [*A publication*] ... Amer Philos Soc Trans
American Philosophical Society. Transactions [*A publication*] ... Am Philos Soc Trans
American Philosophical Society. Yearbook [*A publication*] ... Am Philos Soc Yearbook
American Phonemeter Cl A [*NASDAQ symbol*] ... APMCA
American Photograph Equipment Company ... APECO
American Photographic Artisans Guild ... APAG
American Photographic Book Publishing Co. ... AMPHOTO
American Photography [*A publication*] ... Am Phot
American Photography [*A publication*] ... Am Photog
American Photoplatemakers Association [*Later, IAP*] ... APA
American Physical Education Association. Research Quarterly [*A publication*] ... Am Phys Ed Assn Res Q
American Physical Education Review [*A publication*] ... Am Phys Educ R
American Physical Fitness Research Institute ... APFRI
American Physical Society ... APS
American Physical Therapy Association ... APTA
American Physicians Art Association ... APAA
American Physicians Fellowship for the Israel Medical Association ... APF
American Physicians Poetry Association ... APPA
American Physicians Service [*NASDAQ symbol*] ... AMPH
American Physiological Society ... APS
American Physiotherapy Association [*Later, APTA*] ... APA
American Phytopathological Society ... APS
American Phytopathological Society. Monograph [*A publication*] ... Am Phytopathol Soc Monogr
American Piedmontese Association ... APA
American Pilots' Association ... APA
American Pinto Horse Association ... APHA
American Pinzgauer Association ... APA
American Pioneer Trails Association ... APTA
American Pipe Fittings Association ... APFA
American Pistol Institute ... API
American Pistol and Revolver Association [*Defunct*] ... APRA
American Place Theatre ... APT
American Plan Corp. [*American Stock Exchange symbol*] ... APN
American Planning Association ... APA
American Planning Association. Journal [*A publication*] ... Am Plan Assn J
American Planning Civic Association [*Later, NUC*] ... APCA
American Planning and Civic Planning [*A publication*] ... Am Planning
American Plant Life Society ... APLS
American Plant Selections [*An association*] [*Defunct*] ... APS
American Plate Number Single Society ... APNSS
American Platform Tennis Association ... APTA
American Playwrights Theatre [*Defunct*] ... APT
American Plywood Association ... APA
American Podiatry Association ... APA
American Podiatry Association Auxiliary ... APAA
American Poetry League ... APL
American Poetry Review [*A publication*] ... Amer Po R
American Poetry Review [*A publication*] ... Am Poetry
American Poetry Review [*A publication*] ... APR
American Poinsettia Society ... APS
American Pointer Club ... APC
American Polar Society ... APS
American-Polish National Relief for Poland ... APNRP
American Polish War Relief [*Post-World War II*] ... APWR
American Political Item Collectors ... APIC

American Political Science Association......APSA
American Political Science Association. Quarterly [*A publication*]......PS
American Political Science Review [*A publication*]......Amer Polit Sci R
American Political Science Review [*A publication*]......Am Poli Sci
American Political Science Review [*A publication*]......Am Pol Sci R
American Political Science Review [*A publication*]......APSR
American Politics Quarterly [*A publication*]......Amer Polit Quart
American Politics Quarterly [*A publication*]......Am Polit Q
American Politics Quarterly [*A publication*]......Am Pol Q
American Polled Hereford Association......APHA
American Polled Shorthorn Society......APSS
American Polygraph Association......APA
American Polypay Sheep Association......APSA
American Pomeranian Club......APC
American Pomological Society......APS
American Pomological Society. Proceedings [*A publication*]......Am Pom Soc Pro
American Portuguese Cultural Society [*Later, APS*]......APCS
American Portuguese Society [*Formerly, APCS*]......APS
American Postal Chess League [*Defunct*]......APCL
American Postal Chess Tournaments......APCT
American Postal Workers Union......APWU
American Potash & Chemical Corp. [*NYSE symbol*] [*Delisted*]......APO
American Potash & Chemical Corp., Whittier, CA [*Library symbol*]......CWhA
American Potash Institute [*Later, PPI*]......API
American Potato Journal [*A publication*]......Am Potato J
American Poultry Advocate [*A publication*]......Am P Advocate
American Poultry Association......APA
American Poultry and Hatchery Federation [*Later, PEIA*]......APHF
American Poultry Historical Society......APHS
American Poultry International......API
American Poultry Journal [*A publication*]......Am P J
American Poultry Journal [*A publication*]......Am Poultry J
American Powder Metallurgy Institute......APMI
American Power Boat Association......APBA
American Power Committee......APC
American Power Drinkers Association......APDA
American Power Jet Co.......APJ
American Power Net Association [*Later, EFMCNTA*]......APNA
American Practitioner and Digest of Treatment [*A publication*]......Am Pract Dig Treat
American Precision Industries, Inc. [*American Stock Exchange symbol*]......APR
American Prefaces [*A publication*]......Am Prefs
American Prepaid Legal Services Institute......API
American Presbyterian Congo Mission......APCM
American Presbyterian Review [*A publication*]......Am Presb R
American President Lines......APL
American President Lines, Ltd. [*NYSE symbol*]......APS
American Press Institute [*Columbia University*]......API
American Pressman Reports [*A publication*]......Am Pressman Rept
American Primrose Society......APS
American Printed Fabrics Council......APFC
American Printer and Lithographer [*A publication*]......Am Ptr & Lith
American Printing History Association......APHA
American Printing House for the Blind, Inc.......APH
American Printing House for the Blind, Inc.......APHB
American Prison Ministry [*An association*]......APM
American Prisoner of War......APW
American Prisoner of War Information Bureau......APWIB
American Pro Life Council......APLC
American Probation and Parole Association......APPA
American Proctologic Society [*Later, ASCRS*]......APS
American Produce Review [*A publication*]......Am Prod R
American Producers of Italian Type Cheese Association......APITCA
American Production and Inventory Control Society......APICS
American Productivity Center......APC
American Professional Basketball Association [*Game*] [*Pronounced "ap-bah"*]......APBA
American Professional Needlework Retailers Association [*Formerly, MPNA*]......APNRA
American Professional Practice Association......APPA
American Professional Racquetball Organization......APRO
American Professional Surfing Association......APSA
American Professors for Peace in the Middle East......APPME
American Program Bureau [*Lectures*]......APB
American Progress Foundation......APF
American Prosthodontic Society......APS
American Protective Association [*Late-19th-century organization opposed to so-called encroachments of the Catholic Church in the US; initialism was also used by Catholics as an epithet for Protestants*]......APA
American Protestant Association......APA
American Protestant Correctional Chaplains Association......APCCA
American Protestant Hospital Association......APHA
American Protestant Society......APS
American Psychiatric Association......APA
American Psychical Institute......API
American Psychoanalytic Association......APA
American Psychoanalytic Association......APsaA
American Psychoanalytic Association. Journal [*A publication*]......Am Psychoana Assn J
American Psychoanalytic Association. Journal [*A publication*]......Am Psychoanal Assn J
American Psychoanalytic Association. Journal. Monograph Series [*A publication*]......Am Psychoanal Assoc J Monogr Ser
American Psychological Association......APA
American Psychological Association. Proceedings of the Annual Convention [*A publication*]......AMPCB
American Psychological Foundation......APF
American Psychologist [*A publication*]......Amer Psychol
American Psychologist [*A publication*]......Am P
American Psychologist [*A publication*]......AMPSA
American Psychologist [*A publication*]......Am Psychol
American Psychologist [*A publication*]......AP
American Psychologist [*A publication*]......APs
American Psychologist [*A publication*]......A Psy
American Psychologists for Social Action [*Later, PSA*]......APSA
American Psychology-Law Society......AP-LS
American Psychopathological Association......APA
American Psychopathological Association......APPA
American Psychosomatic Society......APS
American Psychotherapy Association......APA
American Public Energy Co. [*American Stock Exchange symbol*] [*Delisted*]......AEN
American Public Gas Association......APGA
American Public Health Association......APHA
American Public Health Association. Reports [*A publication*]......Am Pub Health Ass Rep
American Public Power Association......APPA
American Public Radio......APR
American Public Relations Association [*Later, PRSA*]......APRA
American Public Transit Association [*Formerly, ATA, IRT*]......APTA
American Public Welfare Association......APWA
American Public Works Association......APWA
American Publicists Guild......APG
American Puerto-Rican Action League......APAL
American Pulpwood Association......APA
American Pulpwood Association. Legislative Bulletin [*A publication*]......APA Legisl Bull
American Pulpwood Association. Monthly Pulpwood Summary [*A publication*]......APA Pulpwood Sum
American Pulpwood Association. Pulpwood Highlights [*A publication*]......APA Pulpwood Highl
American Pulpwood Association. Pulpwood Statistics [*A publication*]......APA Pulpwood Statist
American Pulpwood Association. Safety Alert [*A publication*]......APA Safety Alert
American Pulpwood Association. Technical Papers [*A publication*]......APA Tech Papers
American Pulpwood Association. Technical Release [*A publication*]......APA Tech Release
American Puppet Arts Council [*Defunct*]......APAC
American Purchasing Society......APS
American Puritan Ethic......APE
American Pyramid Resources, Inc. [*NASDAQ symbol*]......AMPYF
American Pyrotechnics Association......APA
American Quarter Horse Association......AQHA
American Quarterly [*A publication*]......Am Q
American Quarterly [*A publication*]......Am Quar
American Quarterly [*A publication*]......AQ
American Quarterly Journal of Agriculture and Science [*A publication*]......Am Q J Agr
American Quarterly Microscopical Journal [*A publication*]......Am Q Micro J
American Quarterly Observer [*A publication*]......Am Q Obs
American Quarterly Register [*A publication*]......Am Q Reg
American Quarterly Review [*1827-1837*] [*A publication*]......Am Q
American Quasar Petroleum Co. [*NASDAQ symbol*]......AQAS
American Quaternary Association......AMQUA
American Quick Printing Association......AQPA
American Quilt Study Group......AQSG
American Rabbit Breeders Association......ARBA
American Rabbit Journal [*A publication*]......Am Rabbit J
American Racing Driver's Club......ARDC
American Racing Pigeon Union......ARPU
American Radiator & Standard Sanitary Corp. [*Later, American Standard, Inc.*]......AMSTAN
American Radiator & Standard Sanitary Corp. [*Later, American Standard, Inc.*]......ARSS
American Radio Association......ARA
American Radio Council [*Later, PRO-IF*]......ARC
American Radio Importers Association......ARIA
American Radio Relay League......ARRL
American Radiography Technologists......ART
American Radium Society......ARS
American Rafting Association......ARA
American Railroad Foundation......ARF
American Railway Association [*Later, AAR*]......ARA
American Railway Bridge and Building Association......ARBBA
American Railway Car Export Association......ARCEA
American Railway Car Institute......ARCI

American Railway Cases [*Legal*] ... ARC
American Railway Development Association ... ARDA
American Railway Engineering Association ... AREA
American Railway Engineering Association. Bulletin [*A publication*] ... Am Railw Eng Assoc Bull
American Railway Magazine Editors Association [*Later, Association of Railroad Editors*] ... ARMEA
American Railway Master Mechanics' Association ... ARMMA
American Railway Supervisors Association [*Later, American Railway and Airline Supervisors Association*] ... RSA
American Railway Union ... ARU
American Rambouillet Sheep Breeders Association ... ARSBA
American Rationalist Federation ... ARF
American Rayon Institute [*Defunct*] ... ARI
American Reading Council ... ARC
American Real Estate Exchange ... AMREX
American Real Estate and Urban Economic Association. Journal [*A publication*] ... Am Real Estate & Urb Econ Assn J
American Real Estate and Urban Economics Association ... AREUEA
American Realty Trust SBI [*American Stock Exchange symbol*] ... ARB
American Record Guide [*A publication*] ... Am Rec G
American Record Guide [*A publication*] ... Am Rec Guide
American Record Guide [*A publication*] ... Am Record Gd
American Record Guide [*A publication*] ... AR
American Record Guide [*A publication*] ... ARG
American Record Merchandisers and Distributors Association [*Defunct*] ... ARMADA
American Recorder [*A publication*] ... Am Recorder
American Recorder Society ... ARS
American Recovery Association ... ARA
American Recreation Centers [*NASDAQ symbol*] ... AMRC
American Recreation Coalition ... ARC
American Recreation Society [*Later, APRS*] ... ARS
American Recreational Activities ... ARA
American Recreational Equipment Association ... AREA
American Recreational Vehicle Living Association [*Defunct*] ... ARVLA
American Red Brangus Association ... ARBA
American Red Cross ... AMCROSS
American Red Cross ... ARC
American Red Cross Children's Fund ... ARCCF
American Red Magen David for Israel [*An association*] ... ARMD
American Red Magen David for Israel [*An association*] ... ARMDI
American Red Poll Association ... ARPA
American Reference Books Annual [*A publication*] ... ARBA
American Refrigeration Transit Co. [*AAR code*] ... ART
American Refugee Committee ... ARC
American Registered Inhalation Therapist [*Academic degree*] ... ARIT
American Registered Respiratory Therapist ... ARRT
American Registry of Architectural Antiquities ... ARAA
American Registry of Clinical Radiography Technologists ... ARCRT
American Registry of Diagnostic Medical Sonographers ... ARDMS
American Registry of Inhalation Therapists [*Later, NBRT*] ... ARIT
American Registry of Medical Assistants [*Later, RMA*] ... ARMA
American Registry of Pathologists ... ARP
American Registry of Physical Therapists [*Defunct*] ... ARPT
American Registry of Professional Entomologists ... ARPE
American Registry of Radiologic Technologists ... ARRT
American Rehabilitation [*A publication*] ... Amer Rehab
American Rehabilitation Committee [*Later, FEGS*] ... ARC
American Rehabilitation Counseling Association ... ARCA
American Rehabilitation Foundation [*Later, SKI*] ... ARF
American Rehabilitation Foundation [*Later, SKI*], **Minneapolis, MN** [*Library symbol*] ... MnMAR
American Relief Administration Association ... ARA
American Relief for Poland [*Defunct*] ... ARP
American Reloaders Association ... ARA
American Remount Association ... ARA
American Rental Association ... ARA
American Repair Service ... ARS
American Repertory Theatre ... ART
American Republics Area [*Department of State*] ... ARA
American Rescue Dog Association ... ARDA
American Rescue Workers ... ARW
American Research Bureau ... ARB
American Research & Development Corp. [*NYSE symbol*] [*Delisted*] ... ARD
American Research Institute for Community Development ... ARICD
American Research Institute in Turkey ... ARIT
American Research Merchandising Institute [*Later, NASM*] ... ARMI
American Resources Management [*NASDAQ symbol*] ... ARMC
American Restaurant China Council ... ARCC
American Retail Association Executives ... ARAE
American Retail Coal Association ... ARCA
American Retail Federation ... ARF
American Retreaders Association ... ARA
American Reuseable Textile Association ... ARTA
American Revenue Association ... ARA
American Review [*Formerly, New American Review*] [*A publication*] ... Am R
American Review [*Formerly, New American Review*] [*A publication*] ... Am Rev
American Review [*Formerly, New American Review*] [*A publication*] ... AR
American Review of Respiratory Disease [*A publication*] ... Am Rev Resp Dis
American Review of Respiratory Disease [*A publication*] ... Am Rev Respir Dis
American Review of Respiratory Disease [*A publication*] ... Am R Resp D
American Review of Respiratory Disease [*A publication*] ... ARRDA
American Review of Tuberculosis and Pulmonary Diseases [*A publication*] ... Am Rev Tuberc Pulm Dis
American Revised Version [*of the Bible*] ... ARV
American Revolution Bicentennial Administration [*Formerly, ARBC*] [*Disbanded, 1977*] ... ARBA
American Revolution Bicentennial Advisory Council [*American Revolution Bicentennial Administration*] ... ARBAC
American Revolution Bicentennial Board [*American Revolution Bicentennial Administration*] ... ARBB
American Revolution Bicentennial Commission [*Later, ARBA*] ... ARBC
American Revolution II Committee ... AR II
American Revolution Round Table ... ARRT
American Reye's Syndrome Association ... ARSA
American Rheumatism Association ... ARA
American Rheumatism Association Medical Information System ... ARAMIS
American Rhinologic Society ... ARS
American Rhododendron Society ... ARS
American Rice Growers Cooperative Association [*Defunct*] ... ARGCA
American Riding Association of Berlin [*Post-World War II*] ... ARAB
American Right to Read ... ARR
American Right of Way Association [*Later, IRWA*] ... ARWA
American Risk and Insurance Association ... ARIA
American River College, Sacramento, CA [*OCLC symbol*] ... ASR
American River College, Sacramento, CA [*Library symbol*] ... CSAR
American River Touring Association ... ARTA
American Rivers Conservation Council ... ARCC
American Road Builders' Association [*Later, ARTBA*] ... ARBA
American Road Race of Champions ... ARRC
American Road Racing Association ... ARRA
American Road and Transportation Builders Association ... ARTBA
American Rock Garden Society ... ARGS
American Rocket Society [*Later, AIAA*] ... ARS
American Roentgen Ray Society ... ARRS
American Romagnola Association ... ARA
American Romanian Orthodox Youth [*An association*] ... AROY
American Romney Breeders' Association ... ARBA
American Roque League ... ARL
American Rose Foundation ... ARF
American Rose Society ... ARS
American Rottweiler Club ... ARC
American Rowing Association ... ARA
American Royal Association ... ARA
American RSROA [*Roller Skating Rink Operators Association of America*] **Roller Hockey Association** ... ARRHA
American Rubberband Duckpin Bowling Congress ... ARDBC
American Running and Fitness Association [*Formerly, NJA*] ... ARFA
American Rural Health Association ... ARHA
American Russian Aid Association ... ARAA
American Russian Institute, San Francisco, CA [*Library symbol*] ... CSfAR
American Sabbath Tract Society ... ASTS
American Saddle Horse Breeders Association [*Later, ASHA*] ... ASHBA
American Saddle Horse Youth Club ... ASHYC
American Saddlebred Horse Association [*Formerly, ASHBA*] ... ASHA
American Saddlebred Pleasure Horse Association ... ASPHA
[*The*] **American Safe Deposit Association** ... TASDA
American Safety Council ... ASC
American Safety Equipment Corp. [*American Stock Exchange symbol*] [*Delisted*] ... ASQ
American Sail Training Association ... ASTA
American Sailing Council ... ASC
American Saluki Association ... ASA
American Samoa [*MARC country of publication code*] [*Library of Congress*] ... as
American Samoa [*Three-letter standard code*] ... ASM
American Samoa [*MARC geographic area code*] [*Library of Congress*] ... poas---
American Samoa [*Two-letter standard code*] [*Postal code*] ... AS
American Sanitary Engineering Intersociety Board [*Later, AAEE*] ... ASEIB
American Satin Rabbit Breeders' Association ... ASRBA
American Savings & Loan Association of Florida [*NYSE symbol*] ... AAA
American Savings and Loan Institute [*Later, Institute of Financial Education*] ... ASLI
American Savings and Loan League ... ASLL
American-Scandinavian Foundation ... ASF
American-Scandinavian Foundation, New York, NY [*Library symbol*] ... NNASF
American-Scandinavian Review [*A publication*] ... Am Scand R
American-Scandinavian Review [*A publication*] ... ASR
American Scenic and Historic Preservation Society ... ASHPS
American Scenic and Historic Preservation Society. Annual Report [*A publication*] ... Am Scenic and Historic Preservation Soc An Rp
American Schizophrenia Association ... ASA
American Scholar [*A publication*] ... Amer Scholar
American Scholar [*A publication*] ... Am Sch
American Scholar [*A publication*] ... Am Schol
American Scholar [*A publication*] ... Am Scholar

American Scholar [*A publication*]....AS
American Scholar [*A publication*]....ASc
American Scholar [*A publication*]....ASch
American School Band Directors' Association....ASBDA
American School Board Journal [*A publication*]....Am Sch Bd J
American School Board Journal [*A publication*]....Am Sch Board J
American School and Community Safety Association....ASCSA
American School Counselor Association....ASCA
American School Food Service Association....ASFSA
American School Health Association....ASHA
American School in London....ASL
[*The*] **American School in Switzerland**....TASIS
American School and University [*A publication*]....Am Sch & Univ
American School and University [*A publication*]....ASU
American Schools Association....ASA
American Schools and Hospitals Abroad [*Program*] [*Agency for International Development*]....ASHA
American Schools of Oriental Research [*Later, W. F. Albright Institute*]....ASOR
American Schools of Oriental Research. Bulletin [*A publication*]....Am Sch Orient Res Bul
American Schools of Oriental Research. Newsletter....ASOR
American Schools of Oriental Research. Publications of the Jerusalem School. Archaeology [*A publication*]....ASOR PJSA
American Schooner Association....ASA
American Science & Engineering, Inc.....AS & E
American Science & Engineering, Inc. [*American Stock Exchange symbol*]....ASE
American Science Fiction Association....ASFA
American Science Film Association....ASFA
American Science Information Institute....ASII
American Scientific Affiliation....ASA
American Scientific Engineering....ASE
American Scientific Glassblowers Society....ASGS
American Scientist [*A publication*]....Amer Sci
American Scientist [*A publication*]....Am Sci
American Scientist [*A publication*]....Am Scient
American Scientist [*A publication*]....ASci
American Scotch Highland Breeders' Association....ASHBA
American Scottish Foundation....ASF
American Scripture Gift Mission....ASGM
American Seafood Distributors Association....ASDA
American Seafood Retailers Association....ASRA
American Sealyham Terrier Club....ASTC
American Seamen's Friend Society [*Defunct*]....ASFS
American Seat Belt Council....ASBC
American Seating Co. [*American Stock Exchange symbol*] [*Delisted*]....AMZ
American Secondary Education [*A publication*]....Am Sec Educ
American Section of the International Association for Philosophy of Law and Social Philosophy....AMINTAPHIL
American Section of the International Solar Energy Society....AS of ISES
American Section of the Societe de Chimie Industrielle....ASSCI
American Security Corp. [*NASDAQ symbol*]....ASEC
American Security Council....ASC
American Security Council Foundation....ASCF
American Seed Research Foundation....ASRF
American Seed Trade Association....ASTA
American Self-Protection Association....ASP
American Self-Protection Association....ASPA
American Selling Price....ASP
American Selling Price System....ASPS
American Sentic Association....ASA
American Sephardi [*A publication*]....Am Seph
American Sephardi Federation....ASF
American-Serbian Cultural Association....ASCA
American Servicemen's Union....ASU
American Sewing Guild....ASG
American Shark Association....ASA
American Sheep Breeder and Wool Grower [*A publication*]....Am Sheep B & W
American Sheep Producers Council....ASPC
American Shellfisheries Association....ASA
American Shetland Pony Club....ASPC
American Shetland Sheepdog Association....ASSA
American Shih Tzu Club....ASTC
American Ship Building Co. [*NYSE symbol*]....ABG
American Shire Horse Association....ASHA
American Shore and Beach Preservation Association....ASBPA
American Short Line Railroad Association....ASLRA
American Short Line Railroads....ASLR
American Shorthorn Association....ASA
American Shorthorn Breeders Association [*Later, ASA*]....ASBA
American Shortwave Listeners Club....ASWLC
American Shrimp Canners Association [*Later, ASCPA*]....ASCA
American Shrimp Canners and Processors Association [*Formerly, ASCA*]....ASCPA
American Shrimpboat Association....ASA
American Shropshire Registry Association....ASRA
American Shuffleboard Company [*An association, not a commercial firm*]....ASC
American Shuffleboard Leagues....ASL
American Sightseeing Association [*Later, ASI*]....ASA
American Sightseeing International [*Formerly, ASA*]....ASI
American Sign Language [*for the deaf*]....AMESLAN
American Sign Language [*for the deaf*]....ASL
American Silk Council [*Defunct*]....ASC
American Simmental Association....ASA
American Simplified Keyboard [*Typewriter*]....ASK
American Singers Club....ASC
American Single Shot Rifle Association....ASSRA
American Ski Association....ASA
American Ski Federation....ASF
American Ski Manufacturers' Association....ASMA
American Ski Teachers Association of Natur Teknik....ASTAN
American Skibob Association [*Later, USSBF*]....ASBA
American Slavic and East European Review [*A publication*]....Am Slavic R
American Slavic and East European Review [*A publication*]....ASEER
American Slavic Review [*A publication*]....ASR
American Slovenian Catholic Union of the USA....KSKJ
American Small and Rural Hospital Association....ASRHA
American Smelting & Refining Co., Research Department Library, South Plainfield, NJ [*Library symbol*]....NjSopA
American Smoking Pipe Manufacturers Association [*Defunct*]....ASPMA
American Snowmobile Association [*Defunct*]....ASA
American Snowshoers Union....ASU
American Snuff Co. [*NYSE symbol*] [*Delisted*]....SNU
American Soccer League....ASL
American Social Communications Conference....ASCC
American Social Health [*formerly, Hygiene*] **Association**....ASHA
American Society of Abdominal Surgery....ASAS
American Society for Abrasive Methods [*Later, AES*]....ASAM
American Society for Abrasives [*Superseded by AES*]....ASA
American Society of Access Professionals....ASAP
American Society for Adolescent Psychiatry....ASAP
American Society for Advancement of Anesthesia in Dentistry [*Formerly, ASAGAD*]....ASAAD
American Society for Advancement of General Anesthesia in Dentistry [*Later, ASAAD*]....ASAGAD
American Society of Aeronautical Engineers [*Later, SAE*]....ASAE
American Society for Aerospace Education....ASAE
American Society of Aerospace Pilots....ASAP
American Society for Aesthetic Plastic Surgery....ASAPS
American Society for Aesthetics....ASA
American Society of African Culture [*Defunct*]....AMSAC
American Society of Agricultural Consultants....ASAC
American Society of Agricultural Engineers....ASAE
American Society of Agricultural Engineers. Transactions [*A publication*]....Am Soc Ag Eng
American Society of Agronomy....ASA
American Society of Agronomy. Journal [*A publication*]....Am Soc Agron J
American Society of Allied Health Professions....ASAHP
American Society of Ancient Instruments....ASAI
American Society of Anesthesiologists....ASA
American Society of Anesthesiologists, Park Ridge, IL [*Library symbol*]....IParkA
American Society of Animal Production [*Later, ASAS*]....ASAP
American Society of Animal Science [*Formerly, ASAP*]....ASAS
American Society of Anthropometric Medicine and Nutrition [*Defunct*]....ASAMN
American Society of Appraisers....ASA
American Society of Architectural Hardware Consultants [*Later, DHI*]....ASAHC
American Society of Arms Collectors....AS of AC
American Society of Arms Collectors....ASAC
American Society for Artificial Internal Organs....ASAIO
American Society of Artists....ASA
American Society of Association Executives....ASAE
American Society of Auctioneers [*Defunct*]....ASA
American Society of Aviation Writers....ASAW
American Society of Bakery Engineers....ASBE
American Society of Bariatric Physicians [*Formerly, ASB*]....ASBP
American Society of Bariatrics [*Later, ASBP*]....ASB
American Society of Biological Chemists....ASBC
American Society of Body Engineers....ASBE
American Society for Bone and Mineral Research....ASBMR
American Society of Bookplate Collectors and Designers....ASBC & D
American Society of Brewing Chemists....ASBC
American Society of Business Press Editors....ASBPE
American Society of Cartographers....ASC
American Society for Cell Biology....ASCB
American Society of Certified Engineering Technicians....ASCET
American Society of Chartered Life Underwriters....ASCLU
American Society of Childbirth Educators....ASCE
American Society of Chinese Medicine [*Inactive*]....ASCM
American Society of Chiropodical Roentgenology....ASCR
American Society of Christian Ethics [*Later, SCE*]....ASCE
American Society for Church Architecture [*Later, IFRAA*]....ASCA
American Society of Church History....ASCH
American Society of Church History. Papers [*A publication*]....Am Soc Church Hist Papers
American Society of Cinematographers....ASC
American Society of Civil Engineers....ASCE

American Society of Civil Engineers. Proceedings [*A publication*].................................Am Soc C E Proc
American Society of Civil Engineers. Proceedings [*A publication*]......................... Am Soc Civil Eng Proc
American Society of Civil Engineers. Proceedings. Journal. Geotechnical Engineering Division [*A publication*]........... Am Soc Civil Eng Proc J Geotech Eng Div
American Society of Civil Engineers. Proceedings. Journal. Hydraulics Division [*A publication*] .... Am Soc Civ Eng Proc J Hydraul Div
American Society of Civil Engineers. Proceedings. Journal. Hydraulics Division [*A publication*] .... Am Soc Civil Engineers Proc Jour Hydraulics Div
American Society of Civil Engineers. Proceedings. Journal. Irrigation and Drainage Division [*A publication*]........... Am Soc Civ Eng Proc J Irrig Drain Div
American Society of Civil Engineers. Proceedings. Journal. Sanitary Engineering Division [*A publication*]......... Am Soc Civil Engineers Proc Jour Sanitary Eng Div
American Society of Civil Engineers. Proceedings. Journal. Structural Division [*A publication*] .... Am Soc Civil Engineers Proc Jour Structural Div
American Society of Civil Engineers. Proceedings. Journal. Surveying and Mapping Division [*A publication*]........... Am Soc Civil Engineers Proc Jour Surveying and Mapping Div
American Society of Civil Engineers. Proceedings. Transportation Engineering Journal [*A publication*]........... Am Soc Civ Eng Proc Transp Eng J
American Society of Civil Engineers. Transactions [*A publication*].........................Am Soc Civ Eng Trans
American Society of Civil Engineers. Transactions [*A publication*]...........Am Soc Civil Engineers Trans
American Society of Clincial Oncology .... ASCO
American Society of Clinical Hypnosis.........................ASCH
American Society of Clinical Hypnosis - Education and Research Foundation .... ASCH-ERF
American Society for Clinical Investigation......................... ASCI
American Society of Clinical Laboratory Technicians [*Later, ASMT*].........................ASCLT
American Society for Clinical Nutrition.........................ASCN
American Society of Clinical Pathologists.........................ASCP
American Society of Colon and Rectal Surgeons [*Formerly, APS*] .... ASCRS
American Society for Colposcopy and Cervical Pathology .... ASCCP
American Society of Composers, Authors, and Publishers .... ASCAP
American Society of Computer Dealers.........................ASCD
American Society for Concrete Construction.........................ASCC
American Society for Conservation Archaeology.........................ASCA
American Society of Construction Inspectors.........................ASCI
American Society of Consultant Pharmacists .... ASCP
American Society of Consulting Arborists.........................ASCA
American Society of Consulting Planners.........................ASCP
American Society of Contemporary Artists .... ASCA
American Society of Contemporary Medicine and Surgery.............ASCMS
American Society on Contemporary Ophthalmology....................... ASCO
American Society of Corporate Secretaries.........................ASCS
American Society of Criminology .... ASC
American Society for Cybernetics .... ASC
American Society of Cytology .... ASC
American Society for Cytotechnology.........................ASCT
American Society of Danish Engineers .... ASDE
American Society for Dental Aesthetics.........................ASDA
American Society of Dental Radiographers .... ASDR
American Society of Dentistry for Children .... ASDC
American Society for Dermatologic Surgery .... ASDS
American Society of Directors of Volunteer Services.........................ASDVS
American Society of Disk Jockeys [*Defunct*].........................ASDJ
American Society of Dowsers .... ASD
American Society for Eastern Arts .... ASEA
American Society of Echocardiography .... ASE
American Society of Educators .... ASE
American Society for Eighteenth-Century Studies .... ASECS
American Society of Electroencephalographic Technologists............. ASET
American Society of Electroplated Plastics .... ASEP
American Society for Engineering Education .... ASEE
American Society for Engineering Education. Computers in Education Division. Transactions [*A publication*]........... Am Soc Eng Educ COED Trans
American Society for Engineering Management.........................ASEM
American Society of Engineers.........................ASE
American Society of Engineers and Architects .... ASEA
American Society of Enologists .... ASE
American Society for Environmental Education .... ASEE
American Society for Environmental History.........................ASEH
American Society for Ethnohistory.........................ASE
American Society for Experimental Pathology [*Later, AAP*]................ ASEP
American Society of Extracorporeal Technology .... AmSECT
American Society of Farm Managers and Rural Appraisers ....ASFMRA
American Society for Head and Neck Surgery.........................ASHNS
American Society of Forensic Odontology.........................ASFO
American Society of the French Legion of Honor .... ASFLH
American Society for Friendship with Switzerland [*Later, ASA*] .... ASFS

American Society of Furniture Designers .... ASFD
American Society of Gas Engineers [*Formerly, GAES*].........ASGE
American Society for Gastrointestinal Endoscopy.........................ASGE
American Society of Genealogists.........................ASG
American Society of Geolinguistics.........................ASG
American Society for Geriatric Dentistry .... ASGD
American Society for German Literature of the 16th and 17th Centuries.........................ASGLSSC
American Society of Golf Course Architects .... ASGCA
American Society of Group Psychotherapy and Psychodrama ..... ASGP & P
American Society of Hand Therapists.........................ASHT
American Society of Handicapped Physicians .... ASHP
American Society for Health Manpower Education and Training.......ASHET
American Society of Heating and Air-Conditioning Engineers [*Later, ASHRAE*].........................ASHACE
American Society of Heating and Air-Conditioning Engineers [*Later, ASHRAE*].........................ASHAE
American Society of Heating, Refrigerating, and Air-Conditioning Engineers [*Formerly, ASHACE, ASHAE*].............ASHRAE
American Society of Heating, Refrigerating, and Air-Conditioning Engineers. Bulletin [*A publication*] ....ASHRAE B
American Society of Heating, Refrigerating, and Air-Conditioning Engineers. Handbook of Fundamentals [*A publication*]...........ASHRAE Handb Fundam
American Society of Heating, Refrigerating, and Air-Conditioning Engineers. Journal [*A publication*]................... ASHRAE J
American Society of Heating, Refrigerating, and Air-Conditioning Engineers. Transactions [*A publication*] ....ASHRAE Trans
American Society of Heating and Ventilating Engineers ....ASHVE
American Society of Hematology.........................ASH
American Society of Home Inspectors .... ASHI
American Society for Horticultural Science.........................ASHS
American Society for Horticultural Science. Journal [*A publication*].........................Am Soc Hort Sci J
American Society of Hospital Attorneys.........................ASHA
American Society of Hospital-Based Emergency Air Medical Services.........................ASHBEAMS
American Society for Hospital Central Service Personnel..............ASHCSP
American Society for Hospital Engineers [*of American Hospital Association*].........................ASHE
American Society for Hospital Food Service Administrators [*of American Hospital Association*].........................ASHFSA
American Society for Hospital Personnel Administration..............ASHPA
American Society of Hospital Pharmacists .... ASHP
American Society of Hospital Pharmacists Research and Education Foundation .... ASHPREF
American Society for Hospital Planning.........................ASHP
American Society for Hospital Purchasing and Materials Management .... ASHPMM
American Society for Hospital Risk Management .... ASHRM
American Society of Human Genetics .... ASHG
American Society of Ichthyologists and Herpetologists .... ASIH
American Society of Indexers .... ASI
American Society of Industrial Auctioneers .... ASIA
American Society of Industrial Designers [*Later, IDSA*].........................ASID
American Society for Industrial Security .... ASIS
American Society for Information Science [*Formerly, American Documentation Institute*].........................ASIS
American Society for Information Science. Journal [*A publication*].........................Am Soc Inf Sci J
American Society for Information Science, Washington, DC [*Library symbol*].........................ASIS
American Society of Insurance Management [*Later, RIMS*]..............ASIM
American Society of Interior Designers .... ASID
American Society of Internal Medicine .... ASIM
American Society of International Executives .... ASIE
American Society of International Law.........................ASIL
American Society of International Law. Proceedings [*A publication*].........................Am Soc Int Law Proc
American Society of International Law. Proceedings [*A publication*].........................Am Soc Int L Proc
American Society of Interpreters.........................ASI
American Society of Inventors .... ASI
American Society of Irrigation Consultants .... ASIC
American Society for Jewish Music.........................ASJM
American Society of Journalism School Administrators .... ASJSA
American Society of Journalists and Authors.........................ASJA
American Society of Knitting Technologists .... ASKT
American Society of Laboratory Animal Practitioners ....ASLAP
American Society of Landscape Architects .... ASLA
American Society for Laser Medicine and Surgery .... ASLMS
American Society of Law and Medicine .... ASLM
American Society of Learned Societies on the Protection of Cultural Treasures in War Areas [*World War II*] ....ASLSPCTWA
American Society for Legal History.........................ASLH
American Society of the Legion of Honor Magazine [*A publication*] ..... ASLH
American Society of the Legion of Honor Magazine [*A publication*].........................ASLHM
American Society of Limnology and Oceanography ....ASLO
American Society of Lubrication Engineers.........................ASLE
American Society of Magazine Editors.........................ASME

American Society of Magazine Photographers ... ASMP
American Society of Mammalogists ... ASM
American Society for Mass Spectrometry ... ASMS
American Society of Master Dental Technologists ... ASMDT
American Society of Mature Catholics ... ASMC
American Society of Maxillofacial Surgeons ... ASMS
American Society of Mechanical Engineers ... ASME
American Society of Mechanical Engineers Auxiliary ... ASMEA
American Society of Mechanical Engineers. Boiler and Pressure Vessel Code [*A publication*] ... ASME Boiler Pressure Vessel Code
American Society of Mechanical Engineers. Papers [*A publication*] ... Am Soc Mech Eng Pap
American Society of Mechanical Engineers. Papers [*A publication*] ... ASME Pap
American Society of Mechanical Engineers. Transactions [*A publication*] ... Am Soc Mechanical Engineers Trans
American Society of Mechanical Engineers. Transactions [*A publication*] ... ASME Trans
American Society of Mechanical Engineers. Transactions. Series F. [*A publication*] ... ASME Trans Ser F
American Society of Mechanical Engineers. Transactions. Series I. [*A publication*] ... ASME Trans Ser I
American Society for Medical Technology ... ASMT
American Society of Mental Hospital Business Administrators [*Later, AMHA*] ... ASMHBA
American Society for Metals ... ASM
American Society for Metals Monographs ... ASMM
American Society for Microbiology ... ASM
American Society of Military Comptrollers ... ASMC
American Society of Military Insignia Collectors ... ASMIC
American Society of Missiology ... ASM
American Society of Motion Picture Engineers [*Later, ASMPTE*] ... ASMPE
American Society of Motion Picture and Television Engineers [*Formerly, ASMPE*] ... ASMPTE
American Society for Municipal Improvements. Proceedings [*A publication*] ... Am Soc Munic Imp
American Society of Music Arrangers ... ASMA
American Society of Music Copyists ... ASMC
American Society of Naturalists ... ASN
American Society of Naval Engineers ... ASNE
American Society of Naval Engineers. Journal [*A publication*] ... Am Soc Naval Eng J
American Society for Neo-Hellenic Studies ... ASNHS
American Society of Nephrology ... ASN
American Society for Netherlands Philately ... ASNP
American Society for Neurochemistry ... ASN
American Society of Neuroimaging ... ASN
American Society of Neuroradiology ... ASNR
American Society of Newspaper Editors ... ASNE
American Society for Nondestructive Testing [*Nuclear energy*] ... ASNT
American Society of Notaries ... ASN
American Society for Nursing Service Administrators ... ASNSA
American Society for Oceanography [*Later, MTS*] ... ASO
American Society of Veterinary Ethology ... ASVE
American Society of Onomatologists [*Defunct*] ... ASO
American Society of Ophthalmologic and Otolaryngologic Allergy [*Later, AAOA*] ... ASOOA
American Society of Oral Surgeons [*Later, AAOMS*] ... ASOS
American Society of Orthodontists [*Later, AAO*] ... ASO
American Society of Papyrologists ... ASP
American Society of Paramedics ... ASPM
American Society of Parasitologists ... ASP
American Society for Parenteral and Enteral Nutrition ... ASPEN
American Society for Pediatric Neurosurgery ... ASPN
American Society of Pension Actuaries ... ASPA
American Society for Performance Improvement ... ASPI
American Society of Perfumers [*Defunct*] ... ASP
American Society of Periodontists [*Later, AAP*] ... ASP
American Society for Personnel Administration ... ASPA
American Society of Pharmacognosy ... ASP
American Society for Pharmacology and Experimental Therapeutics ... ASPET
American Society for Pharmacy Law ... ASPL
American Society for Photobiology ... ASP
American Society of Photogrammetry ... ASP
American Society of Photogrammetry. Annual Meeting. Proceedings [*A publication*] ... Am Soc Photogramm Annu Meet Proc
American Society of Photogrammetry. Fall Convention. Proceedings [*A publication*] ... Am Soc Photogramm Fall Conv Proc
American Society of Photographers ... ASP
American Society of Physician Analysts ... ASPA
American Society of Picture Professionals ... ASPP
American Society of Planning Officials [*Later, American Planning Association*] ... ASPO
American Society of Plant Physiologists ... ASPP
American Society of Plant Taxonomists ... ASPT
American Society of Plastic and Reconstructive Surgeons ... ASPRS
American Society of Plastic and Reconstructive Surgical Nurses ... ASPRSN
American Society of Plumbing Engineers ... ASPE
American Society of Podiatric Assistants ... ASPA
American Society of Podiatric Dermatology ... ASPD
American Society of Podiatric Medicine ... ASPM
American Society of Polar Philatelists ... ASPP
American Society for Political and Legal Philosophy ... ASPLP
American Society of Post-Anesthesia Nurses ... ASPAN
American Society of Practicing Architects ... ASPA
American Society of Pre-Dental Students ... ASPS
American Society of Precision Nailmakers [*Defunct*] ... ASPN
American Society for the Preservation of Sacred, Patriotic, and Operatic Music ... ASPSPOM
American Society for the Prevention of Crime [*Defunct*] ... ASPC
American Society for the Prevention of Cruelty to Animals ... ASPCA
American Society for Preventive Dentistry [*Defunct*] ... ASPD
American Society of Primatologists ... ASP
American Society of Professional Biologists [*Later, AIBS*] ... ASPB
American Society of Professional Draftsmen and Artists ... ASPDA
American Society of Professional Ecologists ... ASPE
American Society of Professional Estimators ... ASPE
American Society of Professional and Executive Women ... ASPEW
American Society of Professional Salesmen ... ASPS
American Society for Psychical Research ... ASPR
American Society for Psychical Research. Journal [*A publication*] ... Am Soc Psychical Res J
American Society for Psychical Research, New York, NY [*Library symbol*] ... NNASP
American Society of Psychopathology of Expression ... ASPE
American Society for Psychoprophylaxis in Obstetrics ... ASPO
American Society of Psychosomatic Dentistry and Medicine ... ASPDM
American Society for Public Administration ... ASPA
American Society for Quality Control ... ASQC
American Society of Questioned Document Examiners ... ASQDE
American Society of Radiologic Technologists ... ASRT
American Society of Range Management [*Later, SRM*] ... ASRM
American Society of Real Estate Counselors ... ASREC
American Society for Reformation Research ... ASRR
American Society of Refrigerating Engineers [*Later, ASHRAE*] ... ASRE
American Society of Regional Anesthesia ... ASRA
American Society of Rocketry ... ASR
American Society of Roommate Services [*Formerly, NRA*] ... ASRS
American Society for Russian Naval History ... ASRNH
American Society of Safety Engineers ... ASSE
American Society of Safety Engineers. Journal [*A publication*] ... Am Soc Safety Eng J
American Society of Sanitary Engineering ... ASSE
American Society to Save Biharis and Other Minorities ... ASSB & OM
American Society of Scientific and Engineering Translators ... ASSET
American Society of Senior Wire Rope Engineers ... AS²WRE
American Society of Sephardic Studies ... ASOSS
American Society for Steel Treaters [*Later, ASM*] ... ASST
American Society for Stereotactic and Functional Neurosurgery ... ASSFN
American Society for the Study of Arteriosclerosis [*Later, Council on Arteriosclerosis of the American Heart Association*] ... ASSA
American Society for the Study of Orthodontics ... ASSO
American Society for the Study of Religion ... ASSR
American Society for the Study of Sterility [*Later, AFS*] ... ASSS
American Society of Sugar Beet Technologists ... ASSBT
American Society for Surgery of the Hand ... ASSH
American Society of Swedish Engineers ... ASSE
American Society of Teachers of Dancing ... ASTD
American Society of Test Engineers ... ASTE
American Society for Testing and Materials ... ASTM
American Society for Testing and Materials. Book of ASTM Standards [*A publication*] ... ASTM Book ASTM Stand
American Society for Testing and Materials. Bulletin [*A publication*] ... ASTM Bul
American Society for Testing and Materials. Meeting. Preprints [*A publication*] ... ASTM Meet Prepr
American Society for Testing and Materials. Special Technical Publication [*A publication*] ... Am Soc Testing Materials Special Tech Pub
American Society for Testing and Materials. Special Technical Publication [*A publication*] ... Am Soc Testing and Materials Spec Tech Pub
American Society for Testing and Materials. Special Technical Publication [*A publication*] ... Am Soc Test Mater Spec Tech Publ
American Society for Theatre Research ... ASTR
American Society of Therapeutic Radiologists ... ASTR
American Society of Tool Engineers [*Later, SME*] ... ASTE
American Society of Tool and Manufacturing Engineers [*Later, SME*] ... ASTME
American Society of Tool and Manufacturing Engineers. ASTME/ASM Western Metal and Tool Conference [*A publication*] ... ASTME/ASM West Metal Tool Conf
American Society of Tool and Manufacturing Engineers. ASTME Collected Papers [*A publication*] ... ASTME Collect Papers
American Society of Traffic and Transportation ... ASTT
American Society for Training and Development ... ASTD
American Society of Transplant Surgeons ... ASTS
American Society of Travel Agents ... ASTA
American Society of Tropical Medicine and Hygiene ... ASTMH

American Society of Tropical Medicine. Papers [*A publication*] .... Am Soc Trop Med Papers
American Society of TV Cameramen .... ASTVC
American Society of Ultrasound Technical Specialists [*Later, SDMS*] .... ASUTS
American Society of University Composers .... ASUC
American Society of University Composers. Proceedings [*A publication*] .... ASUC
American Society of Utility Investors .... ASUI
American Society for Value Inquiry .... ASVI
American Society of Veterinary Ophthalmology .... ASVO
American Society of Veterinary Physiologists and Pharmacologists .... ASVPP
American Society of Women Accountants .... ASWA
American Society of X-Ray Technicians [*Later, ASRT*] .... ASXT
American Society for Zero Defects [*Later, American Society for Performance Improvement*] .... ASZD
American Society of Zoologists .... ASZ
American Sociological Association .... ASA
American Sociological Review [*A publication*] .... Amer Sociol R
American Sociological Review [*A publication*] .... Am Sociol R
American Sociological Review [*A publication*] .... Am Sociol Rev
American Sociological Review [*A publication*] .... Am Soc R
American Sociological Review [*A publication*] .... A Soc R
American Sociological Review [*A publication*] .... ASR
American Sociological Society. Publications [*A publication*] .... Am Sociol S
American Sociologist [*A publication*] .... Amer Sociologist
American Sociologist [*A publication*] .... Am Sociol
American Sociometric Association [*Defunct*] .... ASA
American Sod Producers' Association .... ASPA
American Software Cl A [*NASDAQ symbol*] .... AMSWA
American Software Technology [*NASDAQ symbol*] .... ASTK
American Sokol Educational and Physical Culture Organization .... ASO
American Sokol Educational and Physical Culture Organization .... SOK
American Solar Energy Association .... ASEA
American Solar King [*NASDAQ symbol*] .... AMSK
American Soldier .... AMSOL
American-South African Study and Educational Trust .... ASSET
American Southdown Breeders' Association .... ASBA
American-Southern Africa Chamber of Trade and Industry .... ASACOT
American-Southern Africa Council [*Defunct*] .... ASAC
American-Soviet Medical Society, New York, NY [*Library symbol*] [*Obsolete*] .... NNASovM
American Soybean Association .... ASA
American Soybean Institute [*Defunct*] .... ASI
American Spaniel Club .... ASC
American Spanish Committee .... ASC
[*The*] **American Specialty Surety Council** .... TASSC
American Specification Institute [*Defunct*] .... ASI
American Spectator [*A publication*] .... Am Spect
American Speech [*A publication*] .... Amer Sp
American Speech [*A publication*] .... AmS
American Speech [*A publication*] .... Am Sp
American Speech [*A publication*] .... Am Speech
American Speech [*A publication*] .... AS
American Speech-Language-Hearing Association .... ASHA
American Spelean Historical Association .... ASHA
American Spice Trade Association .... ASTA
American Spinal Injury Association .... ASIA
American Spoon Collectors .... ASC
American Sports Advisors [*NASDAQ symbol*] .... PIKS
American Sports Education Institute .... ASEI
American Sportscasters Association .... ASA
American Sportsman's Club [*Commercial firm*] .... ASC
American Sprocket Chain Manufacturers Association [*Later, American Chain Association*] .... ASCMA
American Squadron of Aviation Historians .... ASAH
American Stamp Club of Great Britain .... ASCGB
American Stamp Dealers Association .... ASDA
American Standard .... AS
American Standard Building Code .... ASBC
American Standard Chinchilla Association [*Later, ASCRA*] .... ASCA
American Standard Chinchilla Rabbit Association .... ASCRA
American Standard Code for Information Interchange [*Acronym pronounced "ask-ee"*] [*Data processing*] .... ASCII
American Standard Elevator Codes .... ASEC
American Standard, Inc. [*NYSE symbol*] .... AST
American Standard Version [*of the Bible, 1901*] .... ASV
American Standard Vocabulary for Information Processing .... ASVIP
American Standardbred Breeders Association .... ASBA
American Standards Association [*Later, USASI, ANSI*] .... ASA
American States Leasing [*NASDAQ symbol*] .... AMST
American Statistical Association .... ASA
American Statistical Association. Journal [*A publication*] .... Am Stat Assn J
American Statistical Association. Proceedings of Business and Economic Statistics Section [*A publication*] .... ASA Pro Bu Ec
American Statistical Association. Proceedings of Social Statistics Section [*A publication*] .... ASA Pro So St
American Statistical Association. Proceedings of Statistical Computing Section [*A publication*] .... ASA Pro St Cp
American Statistical Association. Quarterly Publications [*A publication*] .... Am Stat Assoc Quar Publ
American Statistical Association. Quarterly Publications [*A publication*] .... Am Statis Assn
American Statistician [*A publication*] .... Amer Stat
American Statistician [*A publication*] .... Am Stat
American Statistician [*A publication*] .... Am Statistician
American Statistician [*A publication*] .... Am Statistn
American Statistics Index [*A publication*] .... Amer Stat Ind
American Statistics Index [*A publication*] .... ASI
American Steamship Traffic Executives Committee .... ASTEC
American Steel Foundrymen's Association .... ASFA
American Steel Warehouse Association [*Later, SSCI*] .... ASWA
American Steel & Wire Gauge .... AS & W
American Steel & Wire Gauge .... ASWG
American Sterilizer Company .... AMSCO
American Sterilizer Co. [*NYSE symbol*] .... ASZ
American Stock Exchange .... A
American Stock Exchange .... AMEX
American Stock Exchange .... ASE
American Stock Yards Association .... ASYA
American Stockman [*A publication*] .... Am Stockman
American Stone Importers Association .... ASIA
American Stores Company [*NYSE symbol*] .... ASC
American Street Machines .... ASM
American String Teacher [*A publication*] .... AST
American String Teachers Association .... ASTA
American Striped Bass Society .... ASBS
American Student Association .... ASA
American Student Dental Association .... ASDA
American Student Information Service .... ASIS
American Student Media Association .... ASMA
American Student Union .... ASU
American Studies [*A publication*] .... AmerS
American Studies [*A publication*] .... AmS
American Studies [*A publication*] .... Am Stud
American Studies Association .... ASA
American Studies in Papyrology [*A publication*] .... ASPap
American Subcontractors Association .... ASA
American Suffolk Horse Association .... ASHA
American Suffolk Sheep Society .... ASSS
American Sugar Beet Industry Policy Committee [*Defunct*] .... ASBIPC
American Sugar Cane League of the USA .... ASCL
American Sugar Refining Co., Philadelphia, PA [*Library symbol*] [*Obsolete*] .... PPAmSR
American Sugarbeet Growers Association .... ASGA
American Sunbathing Association .... ASA
American Sunday School Union [*Later, AMF*] .... ASSU
American Sunday School Union, Philadelphia, PA [*Library symbol*] [*Obsolete*] .... PPAmS
American Supply Association .... ASA
American Supply and Machinery Manufacturers Association .... ASMMA
American Surfing Association .... ASA
American Surgeon [*A publication*] .... Am Surg
American Surgery Centers Corp. [*NASDAQ symbol*] .... SRGY
American Surgical Association .... ASA
American Surgical Trade Association .... ASTA
American Survival Association [*Defunct*] .... ASA
American Swedish Historical Foundation .... ASHF
American Swedish Historical Foundation, Philadelphia, PA [*Library symbol*] .... PPAmSwM
American Swedish Historical Foundation. Yearbook [*A publication*] .... ASHFY
American Swedish Historical Foundation. Yearbook [*A publication*] .... ASHY
American Swedish Institute .... ASI
American Swedish Monthly [*A publication*] .... ASM
American Swimming Coaches Association .... ASCA
American-Swiss Association .... ASA
American Swiss Foundation for Scientific Exchange .... ASFSE
American Symphony Orchestra .... ASO
American Symphony Orchestra League .... ASOL
American Symphony Orchestra League. Newsletter [*A publication*] .... ASOL
American Synthetic Rubber Corporation .... ASRC
American Tan Rabbit Specialty Club .... ATRSC
American Tarantula Society [*Defunct*] .... ATS
American Tarentaise Association .... ATA
American Tariff League [*Later, TRC*] .... ATL
American Tarpan Studbook Association .... ATSA
American Tax Reduction Movement .... ATRM
American Tax Reform Project .... ATRP
American Tax Token Society .... ATTS
American Taxation Association .... ATA
American Taxicab Association [*Later, ITA*] .... ATA
American Taxpayers Association .... ATA
American Teacher [*A publication*] .... Am Teach
American Teachers Association [*Later, NEA*] .... ATA
American Technical Education Association .... ATEA
American Technical Industries, Inc. [*American Stock Exchange symbol*] [*Delisted*] .... ATM
American Technical Society .... ATS

American Technological University .... ATU
American Teilhard Association for the Future of Man [*Formerly, ATCA*] .... ATAFM
American Teilhard de Chardin Association [*Later, ATAFM*] .... ATCA
American Telemarketing Association .... ATA
American Telephone & Telegraph Co. .... AT & T
American Telephone & Telegraph Co. .... ATT
American Telephone & Telegraph Co. [*NYSE symbol*] [*Wall Street slang name: "Telephone"*] .... T
American Telephone & Telegraph Co., Corporate Research Library, New York, NY [*Library symbol*] .... NNAT
American Telephone & Telegraph Co., Long Lines, Bedminister, NJ [*OCLC symbol*] .... ATT
American Telephone & Telegraph Co., Technical Process, Piscataway, NJ [*OCLC symbol*] .... ATP
American Telephone & Telegraph, Resource Center, Piscataway, NJ [*Library symbol*] .... NjPwAT
American Television and Communications [*Cable TV operator*] .... ATC
American Telnet Corp. [*NASDAQ symbol*] .... TNET
American Temperance Society .... ATS
American Tennis Association .... ATA
American Tentative Society .... ATS
American Terms [*Business and trade*] .... AT
American Textbook Publishers Institute [*Later, AAP*] .... ATPI
American Textile Machinery Association .... ATMA
American Textile Manufacturers Institute .... ATMI
American Theater Critics Association .... ATCA
American Theater Productions, Inc. .... ATP
American Theatre Arts for Youth .... TAFY
American Theatre Association [*Formerly, AETA*] .... ATA
American Theatre Organ Enthusiasts [*Later, ATOS*] .... ATOE
American Theatre Organ Society [*Formerly, ATOE*] .... ATOS
American Theatre Society [*Commercial firm*] .... ATS
American Theatre Wing .... ATW
American Theological Library Association .... ATLA
American Theological Library Association Indexes .... ATLAI
American Theological Library Association. Newsletter [*A publication*] .... Am Theol Lib Assn Newsl
American Theological Library Association, Princeton, NJ [*OCLC symbol*] .... ATL
American Theological Library Association. Proceedings [*A publication*] .... ALTAPro
American Theological Library Association, Yale University Divinity School, New Haven, CT [*Library symbol*] .... ATLA
American Theological Society - Midwest Division .... ATS
American Therapeutic Society [*Later, American Society for Clinical Pharmacology and Therapeutics*] .... ATS
American Thermographic Society .... ATS
American Thesaurus of Slang .... ATS
American Thoracic Society .... ATS
American Thresherman [*A publication*] .... Am Thresherman
American Thyroid Association .... ATA
American Time Travel Society [*Defunct*] .... ATTS
American Tin Trade Association .... ATTA
American Tinnitus Association .... ATA
American Title Association [*Later, ALTA*] .... ATA
American Tobacco Co. [*Later, AMB*] [*NYSE symbol*] .... AT
American Tobacco Co., Department of Research and Development, Hopewell, VA [*Library symbol*] .... ViHopAT
American Tolkien Society .... ATS
American Topical Association .... ATA
American Torah Shelemah Committee .... ATSC
American Toy Export Association .... ATEA
American Toy Retailers Association .... ATRA
American Track [*National Railroad Passenger Corp.; formerly, Railpax*] .... AMTRAK
American Tract Society .... ATS
American Trade Association for British Woolens .... ATABW
American Trade Association Executives [*Later, ASAE*] .... ATAE
American Trade and Industrial Development .... ATID
American Trade Union Council for Histadrut .... ATUCH
American Traffic Association .... ATA
American Traffic Services Association .... ATSA
American Train Dispatchers Association .... ATDA
American Train Dispatchers Association .... TDA
American Trainers Association .... ATA
American Training Services, Inc. [*American Stock Exchange symbol*] [*Delisted*] .... ATZ
American Trakehner Association .... ATA
American Tramp Shipowners Association .... ATSA
American Transcendental Quarterly [*A publication*] .... ATQ
American Transfer Printing Institute [*Later, ITPI*] .... ATPI
American Transit Association [*Later, APTA*] .... ATA
American Transit Collectors' Association .... ATCA
American Translators Association .... ATA
American Transportation Advisory Council .... ATAC
American Transportation Bowling Association .... ATBA
American Trauma Society .... ATS
American Travel Association [*Later, ATI*] .... ATA
American Travel Inns [*Formerly, ATA*] [*An association*] .... ATI
American Tree Association .... ATA
American Trial Lawyers Journal [*A publication*] .... ATI L J
American Truck Historical Society .... ATHS
American Truck Stop Operators Association .... ATSOA
American Truckers Benevolent Association .... ATBA
American Trucking Associations .... ATA
American Trudeau Society [*Later, American Thoracic Society*] .... ATS
American Trust Review of the Pacific [*A publication*] .... Am Trust Rev Pacific
American Trustee, Incorporated [*NASDAQ symbol*] .... AMTI
American Tunaboat Association .... ATA
American Tung Oil Association [*Defunct*] .... ATOA
American-Turkish Society .... ATS
American Turners [*An association*] .... AT
American Turners [*An association*] .... TUR
American Turpentine Farmers Association Cooperative .... ATFAC
American Type Culture Collection .... ATCC
American Typecasting Fellowship .... ATF
American Underground-Space Association .... AUA
American Underground-Space Association .... AUSA
American Underwriters Group [*NASDAQ symbol*] .... AUND
American Union of Students .... AUS
American Union of Swedish Singers .... AUSS
American Unitarian Association .... AUA
American Unitarian Christian Association .... AUCA
American Universities Field Staff [*Later, UFSI-IWA*] .... AUFS
American Universities Field Staff - Institute of World Affairs [*Later, UFSI-IWA*] .... AUFS-IWA
American Universities Field Staff. Reports. East Asia Series [*A publication*] .... AUFS EA
American Universities Field Staff. Reports Series [*A publication*] .... AUFSRS
American Universities Field Staff. Reports. South Asia Series [*A publication*] .... AUFS SA
American Universities Field Staff. Reports. Southeast Asia Series [*A publication*] .... AUFS SEA
American University .... AU
American University of Beirut [*Lebanon*] .... AUB
American University of Beirut, Beirut, Lebanon [*Library symbol*] .... LeBAU
American University of the Caribbean .... AUC
American University Law Review [*A publication*] .... Am U L Rev
American University Publishers Group Ltd. .... AUPG
American University, Washington College of Law, Washington, DC [*Library symbol*] .... DAU-L
American University, Washington, DC [*Library symbol*] .... DAU
American University, Washington, DC [*OCLC symbol*] .... EAU
American Urological Association .... AUA
American Utility Shares, Inc. [*American Stock Exchange symbol*] [*Delisted*] .... AU
American Vacuum Society .... AVS
American Vaulting Association .... AVA
American Vecturist Association .... AVA
American Vegan Society .... AVS
American Vegetable Grower [*A publication*] .... Amer Veg Grower
American Vegetable Grower [*A publication*] .... Am Veg Grower
American Vegetarian, Inc. .... AV
American Vegetarian Union [*Defunct*] .... AVU
American Veneer Package Association .... AVPA
American Venereal Disease Association .... AVDA
American Ventilation Association .... AVA
American Veterans Committee .... AVC
American Veterans of Israel .... AVI
American Veterans of World War II, Korea, and Vietnam .... AMVETS
American Veterinary Dental Society .... AVDS
American Veterinary Exhibitors' Association .... AVEA
American Veterinary Holistic Medical Association .... AVHMA
American Veterinary Medical Association .... AVMA
American Veterinary Medical Association, Chicago, IL [*Library symbol*] .... ICAV
American Veterinary Medical Association. Journal [*A publication*] .... Am Vet Med Assn J
American Veterinary Medical Association. Proceedings [*A publication*] .... Am Vet Med Assn Proc
American Veterinary Medical Association. Scientific Proceedings of the Annual Meeting [*A publication*] .... Am Vet Med Assoc Sci Proc Annu Meet
American Veterinary Neurology Association .... AVNA
American Veterinary Radiology Society [*Defunct*] .... AVRS
American Veterinary Review [*A publication*] .... Am Vet Rev
American Video Association .... AVA
American Viewcard Club .... AVC
American Viewpoint [*Later, ERC*] .... AV
American Vineyard Foundation .... AVF
American Viola Society .... AVS
American Viscose Co. [*NYSE symbol*] [*Delisted*] .... VIS
American Viscose Co., Front Royal, VA [*Library symbol*] .... ViFroA
American Viscose Co., Roanoke, VA [*Library symbol*] .... ViRoA
American Viticultural Area Association .... AVAA
American Vocational Association .... AVA
American Vocational Education Personnel Development Association .... AVEPDA
American Vocational Education Research Association .... AVERA
American Vocational Journal [*A publication*] .... Am Voc J

American Volkssport Association ... AVA
American Volunteer Group [*Flying Tigers*] [*World War II*] ... AVG
American Waldensian Aid Society ... AWAS
American Walking Horse Association ... AWHA
American Walnut Manufacturers Association [*Later, FHAWA*] ... AWMA
American War Dads ... AWD
American War Mothers ... AWM
American War Standards ... AWS
American Warehousemen's Association ... AWA
American Warmblood Registry ... AWR
American Wash and Wear Institute ... AWWI
American Watch Association ... AWA
American Watch Workers Union ... AWWU
American Watchmakers Institute ... AWI
American Water Resources Association ... AWRA
American Water Resources Association. (Symposium) Proceedings [*A publication*] ... Am Water Resour Assoc (Symp) Proc
American Water Ski Association ... AWSA
American Water Works Association ... AWWA
American Water Works Association, Denver, CO [*Library symbol*] ... CoDAW
American Water Works Association. Journal [*A publication*] ... Am Water Works Assn J
American Water Works Association. Journal. Southeastern Section [*A publication*] ... Am Water Works Assoc Jour Southeastern Sec
American Water Works Co., Inc. [*NYSE symbol*] ... AWK
American Watercolor Society ... AWS
American Waterfowl Association ... AWA
American Watershed Council ... AWC
American Waterways Operators ... AWO
American Waterways Shipyard Conference ... AWSC
American Wax Importers and Refiners Association ... AMERWAX
American Wax Importers and Refiners Association ... AWIRA
American Weight Lifting Association ... AWLA
American Welders Association ... AWA
American Welding Society ... AWS
American Welding Society. Standards [*A publication*] ... Amer Welding Soc Stand
American Well Servicing Corporation [*American Stock Exchange symbol*] ... AWC
American West [*A publication*] ... Am West
American West [*A publication*] ... AW
American West African Freight Conference ... AWAFC
American West Airlines [*NASDAQ symbol*] ... AWAL
American West Overseas Association ... AWOA
American Western Corp. [*NASDAQ symbol*] ... AWST
American Wheelchair Bowling Association ... AWBA
American Whig Review [*A publication*] ... Am Whig R
American Whippet Club ... AWC
American Whitewater Affiliation [*An association*] ... AWA
American Wholesale Horticultural Dealers Association [*Later, HDA*] ... AWHDA
American Wilderness Alliance ... AWA
American Wind Energy Association ... AWEA
American Wine Association ... AWA
American Wine Society ... AWS
American Wire Cloth Institute [*Formerly, IWCI*] ... AWCI
American Wire Gauge [*Standard*] ... AWG
American Wire Producers Association ... AWPA
American Wire Weavers Protective Association ... AWWPA
American Wit and Gags [*Book title*] ... AWAG
American Woman's Association [*Defunct*] ... AWA
American Woman's Economic Development Corp. ... AWED
American Woman's Society of Certified Public Accountants ... AWSCPA
American Women Buyers Club ... AWBC
American Women Composers ... AWC
American Women Playwrights Association ... AWPA
American Women in Radio and Television ... AWRT
American Women's Clergy Association ... AWCA
American Women's Himalayan Expeditions ... AWHE
American Women's Hospitals [*Later, AWHS*] ... AWH
American Women's Hospitals Service [*Formerly, AWH*] ... AWHS
American Women's Voluntary Services [*World War II*] ... AWVS
American Wood Chip Export Association ... AWCEA
American Wood Council ... AWC
American Wood Fabric Institute ... AWFI
American Wood Inspection Agency ... AWIA
American Wood-Preservers' Association ... AWPA
American Wood-Preservers Bureau ... AWPB
American Wood Preservers Institute ... AWPI
American Wooden Money Guild ... AWMG
American Woods. US Forest Service [*A publication*] ... Amer Woods US For Serv
American Wool Council [*Later, ASPC*] ... AWC
American Word Processing Association ... AWPA
American Working Terrier Association ... AWTA
American Wrestling Coaches and Officials Association [*Later, NWCA*] ... AWCOA
American Writers Theatre Foundation ... AWTF
American Y-Flyer Yacht Racing Association ... AYFYRA
American Yachtsmen's Association [*Later, BOAT/US*] ... AYA
American Yarn Spinners Association ... AYSA
American Year Review [*A publication*] ... AYR
American Yorkshire Club ... AYC
American Youth Congress ... AYC
American Youth for Democracy ... AYD
American Youth Foundation ... AYF
American Youth Hostels ... AYH
American Youth Soccer Organization ... AYSO
American Yugoslav Claims Committee ... AYCC
American Zellter, Incorporated ... AZI
American Zinc Institute [*Later, ZI*] ... AZI
American Zinc Institute, Incorporated [*Later, ZI*] ... AZII
American Zinc, Lead, & Smelting Co. [*NYSE symbol*] [*Delisted*] ... ZA
American Zionist Council [*Later, AZF*] ... AZC
American Zionist Federation [*Formerly, AZC*] ... AZF
American Zionist Youth Council ... AZYC
American Zionist Youth Foundation ... AZYF
American Zoologist [*A publication*] ... Amer Zool
American Zoologist [*A publication*] ... Am Zool
American Zoologist [*A publication*] ... Am Zoolog
Americana Annual [*A publication*] ... Am Ann
Americana Hotels & Realty Corp. [*NYSE symbol*] ... AHR
Americana Illustrated [*A publication*] ... Am Ill
Americana Norvegica [*A publication*] ... AN
Americana Unit [*American Topical Association*] ... AU
Americanae Antiquarianae Societatis Socius [*Fellow of the American Antiquarian Society*] ... AASS
Americanae Orientalis Societatis Socius [*Fellow of the American Oriental Society*] ... AOSS
Americanism Educational League ... AEL
Americans Against Abortion ... AAA
Americans Against Union Control of Government ... AAUCG
Americans for Better Care ... ABC
Americans for Children's Relief [*Defunct*] ... ACR
Americans for Common Sense ... ACS
Americans for the Competitive Enterprise System [*Later, ACEE*] ... ACES
Americans Concerned about Corporate Power ... ACACP
Americans Concerned about Southern Africa ... ACSA
Americans for Constitutional Action ... ACA
Americans for Customary Weight and Measure ... ACWM
Americans for Democratic Action ... ADA
Americans for Economic Freedom ... AEF
Americans for Effective Law Enforcement ... AELE
Americans for Energy Independence ... AFEI
Americans of European Ancestry [*Psychometrics*] ... AEA
Americans for God ... AFG
Americans for God ... AG
Americans for Human Rights and Social Justice ... AHRSJ
Americans for Indian Opportunity ... AIO
Americans of Italian Descent ... AID
Americans of Japanese Ancestry [*Psychometrics*] ... AJA
Americans for Justice on the Job ... AJJ
Americans for Justice in the Middle East ... AJME
Americans (of Lebanese-Syrian Ancestry) for America ... ALSAA
Americans for Medical Freedom ... AMF
Americans for Middle East Understanding ... AMEU
Americans for More Power Sources ... AMPS
Americans for a Music Library in Israel [*Defunct*] ... AMLI
Americans Mutually Interested in Giving Others a Start [*Defunct*] ... AMIGOS
Americans in New Caledonia [*Army's 23rd infantry; acronym used as name of division. Active in World War II, disbanded 1945; reactivated 1967-71*] ... AMERICAL
Americans for Nuclear Energy ... AFNE
Americans for Nuclear Energy ... ANE
Americans for Peace [*Defunct*] ... AFP
Americans for Peace and Democracy in the Middle East ... APDME
Americans for Progressive Israel ... API
Americans for Progressive Israel - Hashomer Hatzair ... API-HH
Americans for a Safe Israel ... AFSI
Americans for Undivided Israel USA ... AUIUSA
Americans United for God and Country ... AUGC
Americans United for Life ... AUL
Americans United Research Foundation ... AURF
Americans United for Separation of Church and State ... AUSCS
Americans Want to Know [*Defunct*] ... AWK
Americares Foundation ... AF
[*The*] **Americas** [*Academy of American Franciscan History*] [*A publication*] ... AmF
Americas [*A publication*] ... Ams
[*The*] **Americas** [*Academy of American Franciscan History*] [*A publication*] ... TAm
Americas Boychoir Federation ... ABF
America's Foundation ... AF
America's Future [*An association*] ... AF
America's Manifest Destiny [*An association*] ... AMD
[*The*] **Americas: A Quarterly Review of Inter-American Cultural History** [*A publication*] ... AM
[*The*] **Americas: a Quarterly Review of Inter-American Cultural History** [*A publication*] ... AMS

Americas Society ... AS
America's Society of Divorced Men [*Later, ASSDM*] ... ASDM
America's Society of Separated and Divorced Men [*Formerly, ASDM*] ... ASSDM
America's Sound Transportation Review Organization [*AAR*] [*Defunct*] ... ASTRO
America's Textiles Reporter Bulletin [*A publication*] ... Textil Rep
Americas UNIVAC [*Universal Automatic Computer*] **Users Association** [*Formerly, UUA*] ... AUUA
America's Victory Force [*An association*] ... AVF
Americium [*Chemical element*] ... Am
Americus [*Georgia*] [*Seismograph station code, US Geological Survey*] ... AMG
Americus, GA [*Location identifier*] [*FAA*] ... ACJ
Americus, GA [*Radio station call letters*] ... WADZ
Americus, GA [*Radio station call letters*] ... WDEC
Americus, GA [*Radio station call letters*] ... WISK
Americus, GA [*Radio station call letters*] ... WPUR
Amerifax Cattle Association ... ACA
Amerifin Corp. [*NYSE symbol*] ... AFN
Amerihealth, Inc. [*NASDAQ symbol*] ... AHTH
Amerikastudien/American Studies [*A publication*] ... Amst
Amerikos Lietuviu Tautine Sajunga [*National Lithuanian Society of America*] ... ALTS
Amerind Foundation ... AF
Amerique Francaise [*A publication*] ... AF
Ameritech Corp. [*NYSE symbol*] ... AIT
Ameritrust Corp. [*NASDAQ symbol*] ... AMTR
Ameriwest Financial [*NASDAQ symbol*] ... AMWS
Ameron, Corrosion Control Division, Brea, CA [*Library symbol*] ... CBreA
Ameron, Inc. [*NYSE symbol*] ... AMN
Amertool Services ... AS
Amery, WI [*Radio station call letters*] ... WXCE
Ames Aeronautical Laboratory [*Air Force*] ... AAL
Ames Cubic Precision Ranging System [*NASA*] ... ACPRS
Ames Daily Tribune, Ames, IA [*Library symbol*] ... IaAT
Ames Department Stores, Inc. [*NYSE symbol*] ... ADD
Ames, IA [*Radio station call letters*] ... KASI
Ames, IA [*Radio station call letters*] ... KCCQ
Ames, IA [*Radio station call letters*] ... KEZT
Ames, IA [*Radio station call letters*] ... KUSR
Ames, IA [*Radio station call letters*] ... WOI
Ames, IA [*Radio station call letters*] ... WOI-FM
Ames, IA [*Television station call letters*] ... WOI-TV
Ames Laboratory Research Reactor ... ALRR
Ames Prototype Hypersonic Free Flight Facility ... APHFFF
Ames Public Library, Ames IA [*Library symbol*] ... IaA
Ames Research Center [*NASA*] ... ARC
Amesbury Historical Society, Amesbury, MA [*Library symbol*] ... MAmHi
Amesbury Public Library, Amesbury, MA [*Library symbol*] ... MAm
Ametek, Inc. [*NYSE symbol*] ... AME
Amethopterin [*Methotrexate*] [*Also, M, MTX*] [*Antineoplastic drug*] ... A
AMEX-Canada [*A publication*] ... AMEX
AMEX [*American Stock Exchange*] **Communications** [*Network*] ... AMCOM
AMEX [*American Stock Exchange*] **Computerized Order Display and Execution System** ... AMCODE
AMF Apollo Sailing Class Association ... ASCA
AMF, Inc. [*Formerly, American Machine & Foundry Co.*] [*NYSE symbol*] ... AMF
AMF Sunfish Racing Class Association ... SRC
AMF Windflite Sailboard Class Association ... AMFWSCA
Amfac, Inc. [*NYSE symbol*] ... AMA
Amfesco Industries [*NYSE symbol*] ... AFS
Amfonelic Acid [*Biochemistry*] ... AFA
Amgen [*NASDAQ symbol*] ... AMGN
Amharic [*MARC language code*] [*Library of Congress*] ... amh
Amherst Associates [*NASDAQ symbol*] ... AASI
Amherst College, Amherst, MA [*OCLC symbol*] ... AMH
Amherst College, Amherst, MA [*Library symbol*] ... MA
Amherst Historical Society, Amherst, MA [*Library symbol*] ... MAHi
Amherst, MA [*Radio station call letters*] ... WAMH
Amherst, MA [*Radio station call letters*] ... WFCR
Amherst, MA [*Radio station call letters*] ... WMUA
Amherst, MA [*Radio station call letters*] ... WTTT
Amherst, NS [*Radio station call letters*] ... CKDH
Amherst, NY [*Radio station call letters*] ... WUFO
Amherst, VA [*Radio station call letters*] ... WAMV
Amherst, VA [*Radio station call letters*] ... WCNV
AMI Systems, Inc. [*NASDAQ symbol*] ... AMIS
AMIC Corp. [*NYSE symbol*] [*American Stock Exchange symbol*] [*Delisted*] ... AMM
Amicor, Inc. [*NASDAQ symbol*] ... AMIR
AMIGOS [*Access Method for Indexed Data Generalized for Operating System*] **Bibliographic Council, Dallas, TX** [*OCLC symbol*] ... IIC
AMIGOS Bibliographic Council, Dallas, TX [*OCLC symbol*] ... TPQ
AMIGOS Bibliographic Council, Dallas, TX [*OCLC symbol*] ... TPR
Amilcar Register ... AR
AMINCO Laboratory News [*A publication*] ... AMINCO Lab News
Amine Precursor Uptake and Decarboxylation [*Cytology*] ... APUD
Amino [*As substituent on nucleoside*] [*Biochemistry*] ... n
Amino Acid [*As substituent on nucleoside*] [*Biochemistry*] ... aa
Amino Acid [*Biochemistry*] ... AA
Amino Acid Formula [*Biochemistry*] ... AAF
Amino Acid Formula with Glutamate [*Biochemistry*] ... AAFG
Amino Acid and Nucleic Acid [*A publication*] ... Amino Acid Nucleic Acid
Amino Acid Oxidase [*An enzyme*] ... AAO
Amino Acid Racemization [*Dating process*] ... AAR
Amino-Acid Residue [*Biochemistry*] ... AA
Amino Acid, Unknown or Other [*Symbol*] [*Biochemistry*] ... X
Amino Acids, Peptide, and Protein. Abstracts [*A publication*] ... AAPP Abstr
Amino-Form Bind Medium [*Analytical biochemistry*] ... ABM
Amino-(nitro)cyclopentanecarboxylic Acid [*Organic chemistry*] ... ANCPA
Aminoacetone [*Organic chemistry*] ... AA
Aminoacetonitrile [*Organic chemistry*] ... AAN
Aminoacetylcatechol [*or Acetamidocatechol*] [*Biochemistry*] ... AAC
Aminoadipic Acid [*Biochemistry*] ... Aad
AminoAzobenzene [*Organic chemistry*] ... AB
Aminobenzamidine [*Biochemistry*] ... ABD
Aminobenzophenone [*Organic chemistry*] ... AB
Amino(bromo)(phenyl)pyrimidinone [*Antiherpes compound*] ... ABPP
(Aminobutyl)ethylisoluminol [*Biochemistry*] ... ABEI
Aminobutyric Acid [*Also, Abu*] [*Organic chemistry*] ... ABA
Aminobutyric Acid [*Also, ABA*] [*Biochemistry*] ... Abu
Aminocaproic Acid [*Biochemistry*] ... Acp
Aminocaprolactam [*Organic chemistry*] ... ACL
Aminocephalosporanic Acid [*Pharmacology*] ... ACA
Aminochlorobenzophenone [*Organic chemistry*] ... ACB
Aminocyclopropane-Carboxylic Acid [*Organic chemistry*] ... ACC
Aminodecephalosporanic Acid [*Biochemistry*] ... ADCA
Aminodihydroxytetrahydronaphthalene [*Organic chemistry*] ... ADTN
Aminodiphenyl [*Organic chemistry*] ... ADP
Aminoethoxyvinylglycine [*Organic chemistry*] ... AVG
Aminoethyl [*Biochemistry*] ... Aet
Aminoethylethanolamine [*Organic chemistry*] ... AEEA
Aminoethylisothiuronium [*Radiology*] ... AET
Aminoethylphosphonic Acid [*Organic chemistry*] ... AEP
Aminoethylpiperazine [*Organic chemistry*] ... AEP
Amino(ethyl)propanediol [*Organic chemistry*] ... AEPD
Aminofluorene [*Also, FA*] [*Carcinogen*] ... AF
Aminohexanoic Acid [*Biochemistry*] ... Ahx
Aminohydroxynaphthalenesulfonic Acid [*Organic chemistry*] ... ANSA
Aminohydroxypropane Diphosphonate ... APDP
Aminoimidazole Ribonucleotide [*Biochemistry*] ... AIR
Aminoimidazolecarboxamide [*Also, AICA*] [*Organic chemistry*] ... AIC
Aminoimidazolecarboxamide [*Also, AIC*] [*Organic chemistry*] ... AICA
Aminoimidazolecarboxamide Ribonucleotide [*Biochemistry*] ... AICAR
Aminoimidazolecarboxylic Acid [*Organic chemistry*] ... AICA
Aminoisobutyric Acid [*Biochemistry*] ... AIB
Aminolaevulinate [*or Aminolaevulinic*] **Acid** [*Biochemistry*] ... ALA
Aminolaevulinate Dehydratase [*Also, ALD*] [*An enzyme*] ... ALAD
Aminolaevulinate Dehydratase [*Also, ALAD*] [*An enzyme*] ... ALD
Aminolaevulinate Synthase [*An enzyme*] ... ALAS
Aminolevulinic Acid [*Biochemistry*] ... AmLev
Aminomethylalizarindiacetic [*Organic chemistry*] ... AMADAC
Aminomethylcyclohexanecarboxylic Acid [*Pharmacology*] ... AMCHA
Amino(methyl)propanediol [*Organic chemistry*] ... AMPD
Amino(methyl)propanol [*Organic chemistry*] ... AMP
Aminomethyltrimethylpsoralen [*Cytology*] ... AMT
Aminonaphtholsulfonic Acid [*Organic chemistry*] ... ANSA
Aminooxyacetic Acid [*Biochemistry*] ... AOAA
Aminopenicillanic Acid [*Biochemistry*] ... APA
Amino(phenyl)butanoic Acid [*Organic chemistry*] ... APBA
Aminophosphonobutyric Acid [*Organic chemistry*] ... APB
Aminopropylmorpholine [*Organic chemistry*] ... APM
Aminopteroylglutamic Acid [*Organic chemistry*] ... APGA
Aminopurine [*Biochemistry*] ... AP
Aminopyrazolopyrimidine [*Biochemistry*] ... APP
Aminopyrazolopyrimidine Ribonucleoside [*Biochemistry*] ... APPR
Aminosalicyclic Acid [*Biochemistry*] ... ASA
Aminotransferase [*An enzyme*] ... AT
Aminotriazole [*Herbicide*] ... ATA
Amiprophos Methyl [*Organic chemistry*] ... APM
Amiral Commandant l'Escadre [*Admiral, French Fleet*] ... ALESC
Amiral Commandant l'Escadre Legere [*Admiral, Light Squadron*] [*France*] ... ALLEG
Amiral Commandant le Groupe Anti-Sous-Marin [*Commander, Antisubmarine Force*] [*France*] ... ALGASM
Amiral Commandant les Porte-Avions [*Admiral, Aircraft Carriers*] [*France*] ... ALPA
Amis du Film et de la Television [*A publication*] ... AMIS
Amistad Airlines [*Del Rio, TX*] [*FAA designator*] ... ASD
Amistad Recreation Area [*National Park Service designation*] ... AMIS
Amite, LA [*Radio station call letters*] ... WABL
Amitie Charles Peguy [*A publication*] ... ACP
Amitie Charles Peguy. Feuillets Mensuels [*A publication*] ... ACPFM
Amities Belgo-Congolaises [*Belgian-Congolese Friendship Association*] ... ABC
Amitriptyline [*Also, AT*] [*Antidepressant compound*] ... AMI
Amitriptyline [*Also, AMI*] [*Antidepressant compound*] ... AT
Amity Public Library, Amity, OR [*Library symbol*] ... OrAm
Amityville Public Library, Amityville, NY [*Library symbol*] ... NAmi

Amman [*Jordan*] [*Airport symbol*] ... AMM
Ammanford [*District in Wales*] ... AMMAN
Ammeter ... A
Ammeter ... AM
Ammeter ... AMM
Ammeter ... AMTR
Ammeter Switch ... AS
Ammo War Reserve Level ... AWRL
AMMOHOUSE [*Ammunition House*] **Bulletin** [*A publication*] ... AMMOHOUSE Bull
Ammonia ... AMNA
Ammoniaque Synthetique et Derives [*Belgium*] ... ASED
Ammonium Dihydrogen Arsenate [*Inorganic chemistry*] ... ADA
Ammonium Dihydrogen Phosphate [*Inorganic chemistry*] ... ADP
Ammonium Dimolybdate [*Inorganic chemistry*] ... ADM
Ammonium Diuranate [*Inorganic chemistry*] ... ADU
Ammonium Heptamolybdate [*Inorganic chemistry*] ... AHM
Ammonium Metatungstate [*Inorganic chemistry*] ... AMT
Ammonium Molybdophosphate [*Inorganic chemistry*] ... AMP
Ammonium Nitrate [*Inorganic chemistry*] ... AN
Ammonium Nitrate, Copper, Aluminum, and Plywood [*Proposed currency*] ... ANCAP
Ammonium Nitrate and Fuel Oil [*Explosive*] ... ANFO
Ammonium Paratungstate [*Metallurgy*] ... APT
Ammonium Perchlorate [*Inorganic chemistry*] ... AP
Ammonium Perchlorate [*Inorganic chemistry*] ... APC
Ammonium Persulfate [*Inorganic chemistry*] ... APS
Ammonium Polyphosphate [*Fertilizer*] ... APP
Ammonium Pyrrolidinedithiocarbamate [*Also, APDTC*] [*Organic chemistry*] ... APDC
Ammonium Pyrrolidinedithiocarbamate [*Also, APDC*] [*Organic chemistry*] ... APDTC
Ammonium Sulfamate [*Inorganic chemistry*] ... AMS
Ammonium Thioglycolate ... ATG
Ammunition ... AMM
Ammunition ... AMMO
Ammunition ... AMN
Ammunition Bearer [*Military*] ... AMMOBR
Ammunition Condition Report ... ACR
Ammunition Consolidated Stock Status Report ... ACSSR
Ammunition Control Point ... ACP
Ammunition Distribution and Control [*Military*] ... AD & C
Ammunition Engineering Directorate [*Army*] ... AED
Ammunition, Explosives, and Other Dangerous Articles ... AEDA
Ammunition Group - Picatinny Arsenal ... AGPA
Ammunition Hoist ... AMOHST
Ammunition Hoist Drive ... AMOHSTDR
Ammunition Identification Code ... AIC
Ammunition Loading Production Engineering Center [*Army*] ... ALPEC
Ammunition Lot Number ... ALN
Ammunition Peculiar Equipment ... APE
Ammunition Performance Report [*Military*] ... APR
Ammunition Point ... AP
Ammunition Procurement and Supply Agency [*Army*] ... APSA
Ammunition Rack ... AMMORK
Ammunition Railhead ... ARH
Ammunition Refilling Point ... ARP
Ammunition Reliability Division [*Military*] ... ARD
Ammunition Repair Workshop ... ARW
Ammunition Reporting Management System [*Air Force*] ... ARMS
Ammunition Ship [*Navy symbol*] ... AE
Ammunition Ship ... AFD
Ammunition Shipment Order [*Army*] ... AMSO
Ammunition Stock Recording System ... ASRS
Ammunition Storage Facility [*Military*] ... ASF
Ammunition Stores Issue Ship ... ASIS
Ammunition Subdepot [*United Kingdom*] ... ASD
Ammunition Supply Depot ... ASD
Ammunition Supply Dump [*British*] [*World War II*] ... ASD
Ammunition Supply Officer ... ASO
Ammunition Supply Point ... ASP
Ammunition Systems Reliability and Safety Division [*Picatinny Arsenal*] [*Army*] ... ASRSD
Ammunition Technical Officer [*Ireland*] ... ATO
Ammunition Transport ... AKE
Ammunition War Reserve ... AWR
Amnesty International [*An association*] ... AI
Amnesty International, USA Affiliate ... AIUSA
Amnesty Review Board [*Terminated, 1976*] ... ARB
Amniotic Fluid [*Obstetrics*] ... AF
Amniotic Fluid Glucose [*Obstetrics*] ... AFG
Amoco Canada Petroleum Co. Ltd., Calgary, AB, Canada [*Library symbol*] ... CaACAC
AMOCO Chemicals Customer Service System ... ACCESS
AMOCO Production Co., Library, Tulsa, OK [*OCLC symbol*] ... OUD
Amoco Production Co., Research Center Geology Library, Tulsa, OK [*Library symbol*] ... OkTAm
Amon Carter Museum of Western Art, Fort Worth, TX [*Library symbol*] ... TxFACM
Among ... AMG
Among Others ... AO
Amook [*Alaska*] [*Airport symbol*] ... AOS
Amor de Libro [*A publication*] ... ALi
Amor de Libro [*A publication*] ... AmL
Amore Resources, Inc. [*NASDAQ symbol*] ... AMORF
Amorphous Hydrous Calcium Phosphate [*Inorganic chemistry*] ... ACP
Amortization and Partial Prepayment ... APP
Amory, MS [*Radio station call letters*] ... WAFM
Amory, MS [*Radio station call letters*] ... WAMY
Amory, MS [*Radio station call letters*] ... WZBR
Amos [*Old Testament book*] ... Am
Amos [*California*] [*Seismograph station code, US Geological Survey*] ... AMS
Amos, PQ [*Radio station call letters*] ... CHAD
Amoskeag Bank Shares [*NASDAQ symbol*] ... AMOS
Amoskeag Co. [*NASDAQ symbol*] ... AMKG
Amount ... AMT
Amount of Critical View ... ACV
Amount of Substance [*Molecular quantity*] [*Symbol*] [*IUPAC*] ... n
Amount Tendered ... AT
AMP, Inc. [*NYSE symbol*] ... AMP
AMP, Inc., Harrisburg, PA [*Library symbol*] ... PHarA
Ampad Corp. [*NASDAQ symbol*] ... AMPD
Ampal-American Israel Corp. Cl A [*American Stock Exchange symbol*] ... AISA
Ampal-American Israel Corp. Pfd [*NASDAQ symbol*] ... AMPLP
Ampanihy [*Madagascar*] [*Airport symbol*] ... AMP
Ampco-Pittsburgh Corp. [*NYSE symbol*] ... AP
Ampere [*Unit of electric current*] [*SI symbol*] ... A
Ampere [*Unit of electric current*] ... AMP
Ampere Demand Meter ... AD
Ampere Direct Current ... ADC
Ampere Hour ... A h
Ampere/Hour ... A/HR
Ampere-Hour ... AMP-HR
Ampere-Hour Capacity ... AHC
Ampere-Hour Meter ... AHM
Ampere per Meter [*Unit of magnetic field strength*] ... A/M
Ampere Second ... As
Ampere-Turn [*Technical drawings*] ... A-T
Ampere-Turn per Meter ... AT/M
Amperes ... AMPS
Amperes per Meter ... A/M
Amperes per Square Foot ... ASF
Amperes per Square Inch ... APSI
Amperes per Square Meter ... A/M^2
Amperes per Terminal ... A/T
Ampex Corp. [*NYSE symbol*] [*Delisted*] ... APX
Ampex Corp., Redwood City, CA [*Library symbol*] ... CRcAm
Amphenol-Borg Electronics Corporation ... ABEC
Amphenol Corp. [*NYSE symbol*] [*Delisted*] ... ABE
Amphetamine [*Also, AMT*] [*CNS stimulant*] ... A
Amphetamine [*Also, A*] [*CNS stimulant*] ... AMT
Amphibian [*or Amphibious*] ... A
Amphibian [*Russian aircraft symbol*] ... E
Amphibian Boat Reconnaissance Aircraft ... ABR
Amphibian Imperial Forces ... AIF
Amphibian Reconnaissance [*Military*] ... AR
Amphibian [*or Amphibious*] **Tractor** [*or Truck*] ... AMTRAC
Amphibian [*or Amphibious*] **Tractor** [*or Truck*] **Battalion** ... AMTRACBN
Amphibians and Watercraft ... AWC
Amphibious ... AMPH
Amphibious ... AMPHIB
Amphibious ... PHIB
Amphibious Assault Bulk Fuel System [*Navy*] ... AABFS
Amphibious Assault Fuel System [*Navy*] ... AAFS
Amphibious Assault Landing Craft [*Navy symbol*] ... AALC
Amphibious Assault Ship [*Landing Helicopter Assault Ship*] [*Navy symbol*] ... LHA
Amphibious Assault Ship [*Landing Platform, Helicopter*] [*Navy symbol*] ... LPH
Amphibious Auto Club of America ... AACA
Amphibious Bases, United Kingdom ... PHIBSUKAY
Amphibious Car [*British*] ... AC
Amphibious Cargo Ship [*Navy symbol*] ... LKA
Amphibious Coastal Reconnaissance Ship [*Navy symbol*] ... LSSR
Amphibious Command Car ... ACC
Amphibious Command Ship [*Formerly, AGC*] [*Navy symbol*] ... LCC
Amphibious Construction Battalion [*Also, PHIBCB*] ... ACB
Amphibious Construction Battalion [*Also, ACB*] ... PHIBCB
Amphibious Corps [*Marine Corps*] ... AC
Amphibious Corps [*Marine Corps*] ... PHIBCORPS
Amphibious Corps, Atlantic Fleet [*Marine Corps*] ... ACAF
Amphibious Corps, Pacific Fleet [*Marine Corps*] ... ACPF
Amphibious Corps, Pacific Fleet [*Marine Corps*] ... PHIBCORPAC
Amphibious Detachment ... PHIBDET
Amphibious Detachment, India ... PHIBDETIND
Amphibious Exercise [*Navy, Marine Corps*] ... AMPHIBEX
Amphibious Fire Support Ship [*Navy symbol*] ... LFS
Amphibious Flagship Data System [*Military*] ... AFDS
Amphibious Force Flagship [*Later, LCC*] [*Navy symbol*] ... AGC
Amphibious Forces ... AMPHIBFOR
Amphibious Forces ... PHIBFOR

Amphibious Forces, Atlantic.................................. AMPHFORLANT
Amphibious Forces, Atlantic.................................. AMPHIBFORLANT
Amphibious Forces, Atlantic Fleet .... PHIBLANT
Amphibious Forces, Atlantic Fleet .... PHIBSLANT
Amphibious Forces, Central Pacific ..................AMPHIBFORCENPAC
Amphibious Forces, Europe .... PHIBEU
Amphibious Forces, Europe .... PHIBSEU
Amphibious Forces, Mediterranean .... AMPHFORMED
Amphibious Forces, Mediterranean .... AMPHIBFORMED
Amphibious Forces, Northwest African Waters............. PHIBNAW
Amphibious Forces Ordnance Material Mobile Instruction Unit
　[Obsolete] [Navy].. AF(F)MMIU
Amphibious Forces, Pacific .... AMPHFORPAC
Amphibious Forces, Pacific .... AMPHIBFORPAC
Amphibious Forces, Pacific Fleet .... PHIBPAC
Amphibious Forces, Pacific Fleet .... PHIBSFORPAC
Amphibious Forces, Pacific Fleet .... PHIBSPAC
Amphibious Group .... PHIBGROUP
Amphibious Group .... PHIBGRU
Amphibious Group Command .... AGC
Amphibious Infantry Support Vehicle .... AISV
Amphibious Landing Exercise [Navy]........................ PHIBLEX
Amphibious Logistics Systems [Navy] .... ALS
Amphibious Objective Area [Navy] .... AOA
Amphibious Objective Study [Navy] .... AOS
Amphibious Operational Training Element................... AOTE
Amphibious Operations [Navy] .... PHIBOPS
Amphibious Raid Exercise [Navy] .... PHIBRAIDEX
Amphibious Ready Group .... ARG
Amphibious Reconnaissance Exercise [Navy] .... PHIBRECONEX
Amphibious Refresher Training [Navy] .... PHIBRFT
Amphibious Research Craft .... ARC
Amphibious River Crossing Equipment [Military]............. ARCE
Amphibious Schoolship [Navy] .... PHIBSS
Amphibious Ship, Dock .... LSD
Amphibious Ship Shakedown Cruise [Navy]................. PHIBSKDN
Amphibious Ship, Tank .... LST
Amphibious Squadron .... PHIBRON
Amphibious Supply Platform [Army] .... ASP
Amphibious Support Battalion [Military] .... ASB
Amphibious Support Information System.................... ASIS
Amphibious Tank [Military]................................... AMTANK
Amphibious Tank [Military].................................. AMTK
Amphibious Tanker Terminal Facility [Navy] .... ATTF
Amphibious Task Force [Navy] .... ATF
Amphibious Task Force [Navy] .... PHIBTF
Amphibious Tractor Exercise [Navy] .... TRACEX
Amphibious Training Base [Navy]............................. ATB
Amphibious Training Base [Navy]............................. PHIBTRABASE
Amphibious Training Base [Navy]............................. PHIBTRBASE
Amphibious Training Command Liaison Officer [Navy]....... ATCLO
Amphibious Training Demonstrator .... ADT
Amphibious Training Exercise [Navy] .... AMTREX
Amphibious Training Exercise [Navy] .... PHIBTRAEX
Amphibious Training Unit, Royal Marines [British] .... ATURM
Amphibious Transport [Navy ship symbol].................... LPA
Amphibious Transport [Navy] .... PHIBTRANS
Amphibious Transport Dock [Landing Platform, Dock] [Navy ship
　symbol]... LPD
Amphibious Transport (Small) [Navy ship symbol]............ LPR
Amphibious Transport Submarine [Landing Platform,
　Submarine] [Navy ship symbol]............................. LPSS
Amphibious Truck, 2 1/2-ton Cargo.......................... DUKW
Amphibious Warfare [Navy].................................. AMW
Amphibious Warfare Communications [Navy]................ AWC
Amphibious Warfare Lift Capability [Navy] .... AMWL
Amphibious Warfare Training Center [Navy] ... PHIBWARTRACEN
Amphibious Warfare Working Party .... AWWP
Amphibious Warping Tug [Navy symbol]...................... LWT
Amphicar Owners Club .... AOC
Amphotericin B [Antifungal agent] .... AMB
Amphotericin B Methyl Ester [A drug]....................... AME
AMPI (Association of Medical Physicists of India) Medical
　Physics Bulletin [A publication].............................
　　　　　　AMPI (Assoc Med Phys India) Med Phys Bull
Ampicillin [Also, AM] [Antibacterial compound] .... A
Ampicillin [Also, A] [Antibacterial compound] .... AM
Amplidyne [Electricity]...................................... ADYN
Amplidyne [Electricity]...................................... AMPLDN
Amplidyne Generator [Electricity] .... AMPLG
Amplidyne Motor Generator [Electricity] .... AMPLMG
Amplification Factor .... AF
Amplification by Stimulated Emission of Radiation .... ASER
Amplified .... AMPLFD
Amplified Automatic Level Control [Air Force] .... AALC
Amplified Failure or Unsatisfactory Report.................. AFUR
Amplified Failure or Unsatisfactory Report [Obsolete]....... AMFUR
Amplified Spontaneous Emission .... ASE
Amplifier ....
Amplifier [JETDS nomenclature] [Military] .... AM
Amplifier .... AMP

Amplifier .... AMPL
Amplifier Buffer Attenuator .... ABA
Amplifier-Control Intercommunications ....ACI
Amplifier Detector ....AD
Amplifier Detector Assembly .... ADA
Amplifier Input .... AI
Amplifier Open Loop Response .... AOLR
Amplifier Oscillator, Radiofrequency .... AORF
Amplifier Output .... AO
Amplifier Output Stage...................................... AOS
Amplifier Power Supply .... APS
Amplifier Subsystem .... AMS
Amplifier and Switch Assembly .... ASA
Amplifying Failure, Unsatisfactory, or Removal Report.......... AMPFUR
Amplitude [Physics]... A
Amplitude .... AMP
Amplitude .... AMPL
Amplitude .... AMPTD
Amplitude Absorption Coefficient .... AAC
Amplitude-Frequency Distortion .... AFD
Amplitude Gain Control ....AGC
Amplitude Keyed ....AK
Amplitude and Latency Measuring Instrument with Digital
　Output... ALMIDO
Amplitude Miss Distance Acoustical Scoring System .... AMASS
Amplitude Modulated Link .... AML
Amplitude-Modulated Transmitter .... AMT
Amplitude Modulation [Electronics] .... AM
Amplitude Modulation, Double Sideband [Electronics].......... AMDSB
Amplitude Modulation, Double-Sideband, Suppressed Carrier
　[Electronics].. AMDSB/SC
Amplitude Modulation Generator .... AMG
Amplitude Modulation Link Program .... AMLP
Amplitude Modulation, Single Sideband [Electronics] .... AMSSB
Amplitude Modulation, Single Sideband, Suppressed Carrier
　[Electronics].. AMSSB/SC
Amplitude Noise Limiting .... ANL
Amplitude Phase Shift Keying .... APK
Amplitude Probability Distribution [Communications] .... APD
Amplitude Shift Keying .... ASK
Amplus [Large] [Pharmacy] .... AMPL
Ampoule .... AM
Ampower Instrument [NASDAQ symbol]......................APOW
Ampule .... AMP
Ampulla [Ampule] [Pharmacy] .... AMPUL
Ampullary-Isthmic Junction [Anatomy] .... AIJ
Ampurias [A publication]..................................... Amp
Amputation [Medicine]...................................... AMP
Amputee Shoe and Glove Exchange .... ASGE
Amputees in Motion .... AIM
AmQuest Corp. [American Stock Exchange symbol] .... AMQ
AMR Corp. [NYSE symbol] .... AMR
AMREP Corp. [NYSE symbol] .... AXR
Amritsar [India] [Airport symbol] .... ATQ
Amron Information Services .... AIS
AMS Press, Inc., New York, NY [Library symbol] .... AmS
AMSAC [American Society of African Culture] Newsletter [A
　publication]...AMSAC
AmSouth Bancorporation [NYSE symbol] .... ASO
Amstar Corp. [Formerly, American Sugar Co.] [NYSE symbol]........ ASR
Amsted Industries, Inc. [NYSE symbol] .... AD
Amstelodamum [A publication] .... Amstel
Amsterdam [Netherlands] [Airport symbol] .... AMS
Amsterdam Free Library, Amsterdam, NY [Library symbol]........ NAms
Amsterdam, NY [Radio station call letters]................... WCSS
Amsterdam, NY [Radio station call letters]................... WKOL
Amsterdam, NY [Radio station call letters]................... WMVQ
Amsterdam, Rotterdam, Antwerp .... ARA
Amsterdam-Rotterdam Bank .... AMRO
Amsterdamer Beitraege zur Aelteren Germanistik [A publication]...... ABAG
Amsterdamer Beitraege zur Neueren Germanistik [A publication]...... ABNG
Amsterdamer Publikationen zur Sprache und Literatur [A
　publication].. APSL
Amsterdams Sociologisch Tijdschrift [A publication] ....
　　　　　　　　　　　　　　　　　Amsterdams Sociol Tijds
Amtel, Inc. [NYSE symbol] [Delisted].......................... ATI
Amtliche Berichte aus den Koeniglichen Kunstsammlungen [A
　publication].. Amtl Ber
Amtliche Zeitung des Deutsche Fleischer-Verbandes [A
　publication].................... Amtl Ztg Deutsch Fleischer-Verbandes
AMTRAK Commuter Services Corporation [Later, CSC] ....ACSC
AMTRAK [American Track] Library, Washington, DC [OCLC symbol]...... ATK
Amts- und Mitteilungsblatt der Bundesanstalt fuer
　Materialpruefung [A publication]............................
　　　　　　　Amts- Mitteilungsbl Bundesanst Materialpruef
Amtsblatt des Bayerischen Staatsministeriums fuer
　Landesentwicklung und Umweltfragen [A publication]............
　　　Amtsbl Bayer Staatsminist Landesentwickl Umweltfragen
Amur River and Basin [MARC geographic area code] [Library of
　Congress] .... aa-----
Amusement Game Manufacturers Association .... AGMA

Amusement and Music Operators Association [*Formerly, MOA*]......... AMOA
Amusement Parks and Arcades [*Public-performance tariff class*] [*British*]......... AP
Amusement with Prizes [*Pinball machines*] [*British*]......... AWP
Amusement and Vending Machine Distributors Association......... AVMDA
Amvets Auxiliary......... AA
Amyl [*Organic chemistry*]......... Am
Amylase Inhibitor Activity [*Food technology*]......... AIA
Amyloglucosidase [*An enzyme*]......... AMG
Amyloid-A [*Protein*] [*Medicine*]......... AA
Amyloid-A-Degrading Protease [*An enzyme*]......... AADP
Amyloid of Immunoglobulin Origin [*Medicine*]......... AIO
Amyloid Substance [*Medicine*]......... AS
Amyloid of Unknown Origin [*Medicine*]......... AUO
Amyotrophic Lateral Sclerosis [*Medicine*]......... ALS
Amyotrophic Lateral Sclerosis Society of America......... ALSSOA
An Comunn Gaidhealach [*The Highland Association*]......... ACG
An-Con Genetics, Inc. [*NASDAQ symbol*]......... ANCN
AN [*Army-Navy*] **and MS** [*Manufacturing Status*] **Manual**......... AAMM
An Party Kenethlegek Kernow [*An organization supporting Cornish ethnic solidarity*]......... APKK
Ana [*Of Each*] [*Pharmacy*]......... A
Ana [*Of Each*] [*Pharmacy*]......... AA
ANA [*American Nurses' Association*] **Clinical Conferences** [*A publication*]......... ANA Clin Conf
ANA [*American Nurses' Association*] **Clinical Session** [*A publication*]......... ANA Clin Sess
Anacapa Island [*California*] [*Seismograph station code, US Geological Survey*]......... AIC
Anachronism......... ANAC
Anaco [*Venezuela*] [*Airport symbol*]......... AAO
Anacomp, Inc. [*NYSE symbol*]......... AAC
Anaconda American Brass Co., Waterbury, CT [*Library symbol*]......... CtWAB
Anaconda Co. [*NYSE symbol*] [*Delisted*]......... A
Anaconda, MT [*Radio station call letters*]......... KANA
Anaconda, MT [*Radio station call letters*]......... KGLM
Anaconda Wire & Cable Co. [*NYSE symbol*] [*Later, A*]......... AWC
Anacortes, WA [*Radio station call letters*]......... KAGT
Anadarko, OK [*Radio station call letters*]......... KRPT
Anadite, Inc. [*NASDAQ symbol*]......... ADIT
Anadolu Arastirmalari [*A publication*]......... AnAr
Anaelectrodiabatic [*Nuclear wave*]......... AED
Anaerobic Attached-Film Expanded-Bed [*For treating wastewater*]......... AAFEB
Anaerobic Bacterial Flora [*Microbiology*]......... ABF
Anaerobic Upflow Fixed-Film Process [*For treating wastewater*]......... ANFLOW
Anaesthesia [*A publication*]......... ANASA
Anaesthesia and Intensive Care [*A publication*]......... Anesth Intensive Care
Anaesthesiologie und Wiederbelebung [*A publication*]......... Anaesthesiol Wiederbelebung
Anaesthesiologische und Intensivmedizinische Praxis [*A publication*]......... Anaesthesiol Intensivmed Prax
Anaesthesiology and Resuscitation [*A publication*]......... Anaesthesiol Resuscitation
Anaesthetics [*Medical Officer designation*] [*British*]......... A
Anaheim, CA [*Television station call letters*]......... KDOC-TV
Anaheim, CA [*Radio station call letters*]......... KEZY-FM
Anaheim, CA [*Radio station call letters*]......... KNWZ
Anaheim Public Library, Anaheim, CA [*Library symbol*]......... CAna
Anahuac, TX [*Location identifier*] [*FAA*]......... CBC
Anais. Academia Brasileira de Ciencias [*A publication*]......... An Acad Bras Cienc
Anais. Academia Brasileira de Ciencias [*A publication*]......... An Ac Brasi
Anais. Academia Brasileira de Ciencias. Suplemento [*A publication*]......... An Acad Bras Cienc Supl
Anais Azevedos [*A publication*]......... An Azevedos
Anais. Biblioteca Nacional [*Rio De Janeiro*] [*A publication*]......... ABN
Anais. Bibliotecas e Arquivos de Portugal [*A publication*]......... ABAP
Anais Botanicos. Herbario "Barbosa Rodrigues" [*A publication*]......... An Bot Herb "Barbosa Rodrigues"
Anais Brasileiros de Dermatologia [*A publication*]......... An Bras Dermatol
Anais Brasileiros de Dermatologia e Sifilografia [*A publication*]......... An Bras Dermatol Sifilogr
Anais. Congresso Latino-Americano de Zoologia [*A publication*]......... An Cong Lat-Am Zool
Anais. Congresso Nacional. Sociedade Botanica do Brasil [*A publication*]......... An Cong Nac Soc Bot Bras
Anais. Escola Nacional de Saude Publica e de Medicina Tropical [*A publication*]......... An Esc Nac Saude Publica Med Trop
Anais. Escola Superior de Agricultura "Luiz De Queiroz" [*A publication*]......... Anais Esc Sup Agric "Luiz Queiroz"
Anais. Escola Superior de Agricultura "Luiz De Queiroz" [*A publication*]......... An Esc Super Agr "Luiz De Queiroz"
Anais. Escola Superior de Agricultura "Luiz De Queiroz." Universidade de Sao Paulo [*A publication*]......... An Esc Super Agric "Luiz De Queiroz" Univ Sao Paulo
Anais. Escola Superior de Medicina Veterinaria (Lisbon) [*A publication*]......... An Esc Super Med Vet (Lisb)
Anais. Faculdade de Ciencia. Universidade do Porto [*A publication*]......... An Fac Cienc Univ Porto
Anais. Faculdade de Ciencia. Universidade do Porto [*A publication*]......... An Fac Ci Univ Porto
Anais. Faculdade de Farmacia e Odontologia. Universidade de Sao Paulo [*A publication*]......... An Fac Farm Odontol Univ Sao Paulo
Anais. Faculdade de Farmacia do Porto [*A publication*]......... An Fac Farm Porto
Anais. Faculdade de Medicina de Porto Alegre [*A publication*]......... An Fac Med Porto Alegre
Anais. Faculdade de Medicina. Universidade Federal de Minas Gerais (Belo Horizonte) [*A publication*]......... An Fac Med Univ Fed Minas Gerais (Belo Horizonte)
Anais. Faculdade de Medicina. Universidade Federal de Pernambuco [*A publication*]......... An Fac Med Univ Fed Pernambuco
Anais. Faculdade de Medicina. Universidade do Parana (Curitiba) [*A publication*]......... An Fac Med Univ Parana (Curitiba)
Anais. Faculdade de Medicina. Universidade do Recife [*A publication*]......... An Fac Med Univ Recife
Anais. Faculdade de Medicina. Universidade de Sao Paulo [*A publication*]......... An Fac Med Univ Sao Paulo
Anais. Faculdade de Odontologia. Universidade Federal do Rio De Janeiro [*A publication*]......... An Fac Odontol Univ Fed Rio De J
Anais da Farmacia e Quimica de Sao Paulo [*A publication*]......... An Farm Quim Sao Paulo
Anais de Historia [*A publication*]......... An Hist
Anais. Instituto de Higiene e Medicina Tropical [*Lisbon*] [*A publication*]......... An Inst Hig Med Trop
Anais. Instituto de Higiene e Medicina Tropical (Lisbon) [*A publication*]......... An Inst Hig Med Trop (Lisb)
Anais. Instituto de Medicina Tropical [*Lisbon*] [*A publication*]......... An Inst Med Trop
Anais. Instituto de Medicina Tropical (Lisbon) [*A publication*]......... An Inst Med Trop (Lisb)
Anais. Instituto Superior de Agronomia (Lisboa) [*A publication*]......... An Inst Agron (Lisboa)
Anais. Instituto Superior de Agronomia (Lisboa) [*A publication*]......... An Inst Super Agron (Lisboa)
Anais. Instituto Superior de Agronomia. Universidade Tecnica de Lisboa [*A publication*]......... Anais Inst Sup Agron Univ Tec Lisb
Anais. Instituto Superior de Agronomia. Universidade Tecnica de Lisboa [*A publication*]......... An Inst Super Agron Univ Tec Lisb
Anais. Instituto do Vinho do Porto [*A publication*]......... An Inst Vinho Porto
Anais. Junta de Investigacoes do Ultramar [*A publication*]......... An Junta Invest Ultramar
Anais de Microbiologia (Rio De Janeiro) [*A publication*]......... An Microbiol (Rio De J)
Anais Paulistas de Medicina e Cirurgia [*A publication*]......... An Paul Med Cir
Anais. Reuniao de Fitossanitarisatas do Brasil [*A publication*]......... An Reuniao Fitossanit Brasil
Anais de Santa Casa de Santos [*A publication*]......... An St Casa Santos
Anais. Seminario Brasileiro de Herbicidas e Ervas Daninhas [*A publication*]......... An Seminar Brasil Herbic Ervas Danin
Anais. Sociedade de Biologia de Pernambuco [*A publication*]......... An Soc Biol Pernambuco
Anais. Sociedade Botanica do Brasil [*A publication*]......... An Soc Bot Bras
Anais. Sociedade Entomologica do Brasil [*A publication*]......... An Soc Entomol Bras
Anais. Sociedade de Medicina de Pernambuco [*A publication*]......... An Soc Med Pernambuco
Anaktuvuk Pass [*Alaska*] [*Airport symbol*]......... AKP
Anal Pore......... AP
Analalava [*Madagascar*] [*Airport symbol*]......... HVA
Anale. Institutul Central de Cercetari Agricole. Sectiei de Economice Agricole (Bucharest) [*A publication*]......... An Inst Cent Cercet Agr Sect Econ Agr (Bucharest)
Anale. Institutul Central de Cercetari Agricole. Sectiei de Pedologie [*A publication*]......... Anal Inst Cent Cerc Agric Sect Pedol
Anale. Institutul Central de Cercetari Agricole. Series A (Bucharest) [*A publication*]......... An Inst Cent Cercet Agr Ser A (Bucharest)
Anale. Institutul Central de Cercetari Agricole. Series B (Bucharest) [*A publication*]......... An Inst Cent Cercet Agr Ser B (Bucharest)
Anale. Institutul Central de Cercetari Agricole. Series C (Bucharest) [*A publication*]......... An Inst Cent Cercet Agr Ser C (Bucharest)
Analecta Augustiniana [*A publication*]......... AAug
Analecta Biblica [*A publication*]......... An Bi
Analecta Bollandiana [*A publication*]......... AB
Analecta Bollandiana [*A publication*]......... Anal Boll
Analecta Bollandiana [*A publication*]......... AnBol
Analecta Cartusiana [*A publication*]......... A Car
Analecta Cisterciensia [*A publication*]......... AC
Analecta Cisterciensia [*A publication*]......... ACist
Analecta Franciscana [*A publication*]......... Anal Fran
Analecta Linguistica [*A publication*]......... Anal Ling
Analecta Mediaevalia Namurcensia [*A publication*]......... AMN
Analecta Monastica [*A publication*]......... AMon
Analecta Montserratensia [*A publication*]......... AMontserr
Analecta Montserratensia [*A publication*]......... AMt
Analecta Orientalia [*A publication*]......... Anal O
Analecta Praemonstratensia [*A publication*]......... AnPraem
Analecta Praemonstratensia [*A publication*]......... APr
Analecta Praemonstratensia [*A publication*]......... APraem
Analecta Romana Instituti Danici [*A publication*]......... ARID

Analecta Sacra Tarraconensia [*A publication*] ... AnST
Analecta Sacra Tarraconensia [*A publication*] ... AST
Analecta Sacri Ordinis Cisterciensis [*Roma*] [*A publication*] ... ASOC
Analecta Sacri Ordinis Fratrum Praedicatorum [*A publication*] ... AnFP
Analecta Tarraconensia [*A publication*] ... AT
Analecta Veterinaria [*A publication*] ... Analecta Vet
Analectes. Ordre de Premontre [*A publication*] ... AOP
Analectes pour Servir a l'Histoire Ecclesiastique de la Belgique [*A publication*] ... AHEB
Analectic Magazine [*A publication*] ... Anal M
Analele. Institutul Central de Cercetari Agricole. Sectiei de Pedologie [*A publication*] ... An Inst Cent Cercet Agric Sect Pedol
Analele. Institutului de Cercetari Agronomice. Academia Republicii Populare Romine [*A publication*] ... Anal Inst Cerc Agron
Analele. Institutului de Cercetari pentru Pedologie si Agrochimie [*A publication*] ... An Inst Cercet Pedol Agrochim
Analele. Institutului de Cercetari pentru Protectia Plantelor [*A publication*] ... An Inst Cercet Prot Plant
Analele. Institutului de Studii si Cercetari Pedologice [*A publication*] ... An Inst Stud Cercet Pedol
Analele Stiintifice. Universitatii Al. I. Cuza din Iasi. Sectiunea I-C. Chimie [*A publication*] ... Anal Stiint Univ Cuza Iasi Chim
Analele Stiintifice. Universitatii Al. I. Cuza din Iasi (Serie Noua) Sectiunea III (Stiinte Sociale) E. Lingvistica [*A publication*] ... AnUILingv
Analele Stiintifice. Universitatii (Iasi) [*A publication*] ... ASUI
Analele. Universitatii Al. I. Cuza (Iasi) [*A publication*] ... AUI
Analele. Universitatii Bucuresti [*A publication*] ... AUB
Analele. Universitatii Bucuresti. Biologie Animala [*A publication*] ... An Univ Bucur Biol Anim
Analele. Universitatii Bucuresti. Biologie Vegetala [*A publication*] ... An Univ Bucur Biol Veg
Analele. Universitatii Bucuresti. Chimie [*A publication*] ... An Univ Bucur Chim
Analele. Universitatii Bucuresti. Fizica [*A publication*] ... An Univ Bucuresti Fiz
Analele. Universitatii Bucuresti. Fizica [*A publication*] ... An Univ Bucur Fiz
Analele. Universitatii Bucuresti. Geologie [*A publication*] ... An Univ Bucur Geol
Analele. Universitatii Bucuresti. Limba Literara [*A publication*] ... AUB-LLR
Analele. Universitatii Bucuresti. Limba si Literatura Romana [*A publication*] ... AUBLL
Analele. Universitatii Bucuresti. Limbi Clasice si Orientale [*A publication*] ... AUB-LCO
Analele. Universitatii Bucuresti. Limbi Germanice [*A publication*] ... AnUBLG
Analele. Universitatii Bucuresti. Limbi Germanice [*A publication*] ... AUB-LG
Analele. Universitatii Bucuresti. Limbi Romanice [*A publication*] ... AUBLR
Analele. Universitatii Bucuresti. Literatura Universala Comparata [*A publication*] ... AnUBLUC
Analele. Universitatii Bucuresti. Literatura Universala Comparata [*A publication*] ... AUB-LUC
Analele. Universitatii Bucuresti. Matematica [*A publication*] ... An Univ Bucuresti Mat
Analele. Universitatii Bucuresti. Matematica-Mecanica [*A publication*] ... An Univ Bucur Mat Mec
Analele. Universitatii Bucuresti. Seria Stiintele Naturii. Biologie [*A publication*] ... Anal Univ Buc Ser Stiint Nat Biol
Analele. Universitatii Bucuresti. Seria Stiintele Naturii. Chimie [*A publication*] ... An Univ Bucur Ser Stiint Nat Chim
Analele. Universitatii Bucuresti. Stiinte Sociale, Seria Istorie [*A publication*] ... Anal Univ Bucuresti
Analele. Universitatii Bucuresti. Stiintele Naturii [*A publication*] ... An Univ Bucuresti Sti Natur
Analele. Universitatii Bucuresti. Stiintele Naturii [*A publication*] ... An Univ Bucur Stiint Nat
Analele. Universitatii C. I. Parhoun. Seria Stiintele Naturii [*A publication*] ... An Univ C I Parhon Ser Stiint Nat
Analele. Universitatii din Craiova. Biologie Stiinte Agricole. Seria A III-A [*A publication*] ... An Univ Craiova Biol Stiinte Agric Ser A III-A
Analele. Universitatii. Limbi Slave [*A publication*] ... AUB-LS
Analele. Universitatii din Timisoara. Seria Stiinte Filologice [*A publication*] ... AnUTFil
Analele. Universitatii din Timisoara. Seria Stiinte Filologice [*A publication*] ... AUT
Analele. Universitatii din Timisoara. Seria Stiinte Fizice-Chimice [*A publication*] ... An Univ Timisoara Ser Sti Fiz-Chim
Analele. Universitatii din Timisoara. Seria Stiinte Matematice [*A publication*] ... An Univ Timisoara Ser Sti Mat
Anales. Academia Chilena de Ciencias Naturales [*A publication*] ... An Acad Chil Cienc Nat
Anales. Academia de Ciencias Morales y Politicas [*A publication*] ... AACMP
Anales de Anatomia [*A publication*] ... An Anat
Anales de Arqueologia y Etnologia [*A publication*] ... An Arqueol Etnol
Anales. Asociacion Espanola para el Progreso de las Ciencias [*A publication*] ... AAEPC
Anales. Asociacion Quimica [*Argentina*] [*A publication*] ... An As Quim
Anales. Asociacion Quimica (Argentina) [*A publication*] ... An Asoc Quim (Argent)
Anales de Bromatologia [*A publication*] ... An Bromatol
Anales. Casa de Salud Valdecilla Santander [*A publication*] ... An Casa Salud Valdecilla Santander
Anales. Catedra Francisco Suarez [*A publication*] ... A Catedra F Suarez
Anales. Catedra Francisco Suarez [*A publication*] ... An Cated Suarez
Anales. Centro de Cultura Valenciana [*A publication*] ... ACCV
Anales Cervantinos [*A publication*] ... AC
Anales Cervantinos [*A publication*] ... ACer
Anales Cientificos (La Molina) [*A publication*] ... An Cient (La Molina)
Anales Cientificos (Lima) [*A publication*] ... An Cient (Lima)
Anales. Circa Medico Argentino [*A publication*] ... An Circ Med Argent
Anales de Cirugia (Rosario) [*A publication*] ... An Cir (Rosario)
Anales. Congreso Nacional de Medicina Veterinaria y Zootecnia [*A publication*] ... An Congr Nac Med Vet Zootec
Anales del Desarrollo [*A publication*] ... An Desarrollo
Anales de Edafologia y Agrobiologia [*A publication*] ... An Edafol Agrobiol
Anales de Edafologia y Fisiologia Vegetal [*A publication*] ... An Edafol Fisiol Veg
Anales. Escuela Nacional de Ciencias Biologicas (Mexico) [*A publication*] ... An Esc Nac Cienc Biol (Mex)
Anales. Escuela de Quimica y Farmacia y Bioquimica. Universidad de Concepcion [*A publication*] ... An Esc Quim Farm Bioquim Univ Concepcion
Anales Espanoles de Odontoestomatologia [*A publication*] ... An Esp Odontoestomatol
Anales Espanoles de Pediatria [*A publication*] ... An Esp Pediatr
Anales. Estacion Experimental de Aula Dei. Consejo Superior de Investigaciones Cientificas [*A publication*] ... An Estac Exp Aula Dei Cons Super Invest Cient
Anales. Estacion Experimental de Aula Dei (Zaragoza) [*A publication*] ... An Estac Exp Aula Dei (Zaragoza)
Anales. Facultad de Medicina de Lima [*A publication*] ... An Fac Med Lima
Anales. Facultad de Medicina. Universidad de la Republica (Montevideo) [*A publication*] ... An Fac Med (Montevideo)
Anales. Facultad de Medicina. Universidad de la Republica (Montevideo) [*A publication*] ... An Fac Med Univ Repub (Montev)
Anales. Facultad de Odontologia (Universidad de la Republica, Uruguay) [*A publication*] ... An Fac Odontol (Univ Repub Urug)
Anales. Facultad de Quimica y Farmacia. Universidad de Chile [*Santiago*] [*A publication*] ... An Fac Quim Farm Univ Chile
Anales. Facultad de Quimica y Farmacia. Universidad de Chile (Santiago) [*A publication*] ... An Fac Quim Farm (Santiago)
Anales. Facultad de Quimica y Farmacia. Universidad de Concepcion [*A publication*] ... An Fac Quim Farm Univ Concepcion
Anales. Facultad de Veterinaria de Leon [*A publication*] ... An Fac Vet Leon
Anales. Facultad de Veterinaria del Uruguay [*A publication*] ... An Fac Vet Urug
Anales de Farmacia Hospitalaria [*A publication*] ... An Farm Hosp
Anales de Filologia Clasica [*A publication*] ... AFC
Anales de Fisica [*A publication*] ... An Fis
Anales de Fisica [*A publication*] ... An Fisica
Anales Galdosianos [*A publication*] ... AG
Anales de Historea Antigua y Medieval [*A publication*] ... AHAM
Anales. Hospital de la Santa Cruz y San Pablo [*A publication*] ... An Hosp St Cruz San Pablo
Anales. Instituto de Biologia. Universidad Nacional Autonoma de Mexico [*A publication*] ... An Inst Biol (Mexico)
Anales. Instituto de Biologia. Universidad Nacional Autonoma de Mexico [*A publication*] ... An Inst Biol Univ Mex
Anales. Instituto de Biologia. Universidad Nacional Autonoma de Mexico [*A publication*] ... An Inst Biol Univ Nac Auton Mex
Anales. Instituto de Biologia. Universidad Nacional Autonoma de Mexico. Serie Biologia Experimental [*A publication*] ... An Inst Biol Univ Nac Auton Mex Ser Biol Exp
Anales. Instituto de Biologia. Universidad Nacional Autonoma de Mexico. Serie Botanica [*A publication*] ... An Inst Biol Univ Nac Auton Mex Ser Bot
Anales. Instituto de Biologia. Universidad Nacional Autonoma de Mexico. Serie Zoologia [*A publication*] ... An Inst Biol Univ Nac Auton Mex Ser Zool
Anales. Instituto Botanico A. J. Cavanilles [*A publication*] ... An Inst Bot A J Cavanilles
Anales. Instituto Botanico A. J. Cavanilles (Madrid) [*A publication*] ... An Inst Bot A J Cavanilles (Madrid)
Anales. Instituto de Estudios Gerundenses [*A publication*] ... AIEG
Anales. Instituto de Estudios Madrilenos [*A publication*] ... AIEM
Anales. Instituto Etnico Nacional. Argentina [*A publication*] ... AIEN
Anales. Instituto de Etnografia Americana. Universidad Nacional de Cuyo [*A publication*] ... AIEC
Anales. Instituto de Farmacologia Espanola [*A publication*] ... An Inst Farmacol Esp
Anales. Instituto Forestal de Investigaciones y Experiencias (Madrid) [*A publication*] ... An Inst For Invest Exper (Madr)
Anales. Instituto de Investigaciones Esteticas [*A publication*] ... AIIE
Anales. Instituto de Investigaciones Veterinarias [*A publication*] ... An Inst Invest Vet
Anales. Instituto de Investigaciones Veterinarias (Madrid) [*A publication*] ... An Inst Invest Vet (Madrid)

Anales. Instituto de Linguistica. Universidad Nacional de Cuyo [*A publication*]....AIL
Anales. Instituto de Linguistica. Universidad Nacional de Cuyo [*A publication*]....AILC
Anales. Instituto de Literaturas Clasicas [*A publication*]....AILC
Anales. Instituto de Matematicas. Universidad Nacional Autonoma de Mexico [*A publication*]....An Inst Mat Univ Nac Autonoma Mexico
Anales. Instituto de Medicina Regional [*A publication*]....An Inst Med Reg
Anales. Instituto Medico Nacional (Mexico) [*A publication*]....An Inst Med Nac (Mexico)
Anales. Instituto Nacional de Antropologia e Historia [*A publication*]....AINAH
Anales. Instituto Nacional de Antropologia e Historia [*A publication*]....AnINA
Anales. Instituto Nacional de Antropologia e Historia [*A publication*]....An Inst Nac Antropol Hist
Anales. Instituto Nacional de Investigaciones Agrarias. Serie General [*A publication*]....An Inst Nac Invest Agrar Ser Gen
Anales. Instituto Nacional de Investigaciones Agrarias. Serie Produccion Animal [*A publication*]....An Inst Nac Invest Agrar Ser Prod Anim
Anales. Instituto Nacional de Investigaciones Agrarias. Serie Produccion Vegetal [*A publication*]....An Inst Nac Invest Agrar Ser Prod Veg
Anales. Instituto Nacional de Investigaciones Agrarias. Serie Proteccion Vegetal [*A publication*]....An Inst Nac Invest Agrar Ser Prot Veg
Anales. Instituto Nacional de Investigaciones Agrarias. Serie Recursos Naturales [*A publication*]....An Inst Nac Invest Agrar Ser Recur Nat
Anales. Instituto Nacional de Investigaciones Agronomicas (Madrid) [*A publication*]....An Inst Nac Invest Agron (Madr)
Anales. Instituto Nacional de Microbiologia (Buenos Aires) [*A publication*]....An Inst Nac Microbiol (B Aires)
Anales. Instituto de Oncologia "Angel H. Roffo" (Buenos Aires) [*A publication*]....An Inst Oncol "Angel H Roffo" (B Aires)
Anales. Instituto de la Patagonia [*A publication*]....An Inst Patagonia
Anales. Istituto di Linguistica di Mendoza [*A publication*]....AILM
Anales de Lactologia y Quimica Agricola (Zaragoza) [*A publication*]....An Lactol Quim Agric (Zaragoza)
Anales de Mecanica y Electricidad [*A publication*]....An Mec Elect
Anales de Mecanica y Electricidad [*A publication*]....An Mec & Electr
Anales de Medicina [*A publication*]....An Med
Anales de Medicina. Academia de Ciencias Medicas de Cataluna y Baleares [*A publication*]....An Med Acad Cienc Med Cataluna Baleares
Anales de Medicina Cirugia [*A publication*]....An Med Cir
Anales de Medicina Especialidades [*A publication*]....An Med Espec
Anales de Medicina (Lima) [*A publication*]....An Med (Lima)
Anales Medicos. Asociacion Medica. Hospital Americano Britanico Cowdray [*A publication*]....An Med Assoc Med Hosp Am Br Cowdray
Anales Mexicanos de Ciencias [*A publication*]....An Mex Cienc
Anales. Museo Nacional David J. Guzman [*A publication*]....An Mus Nac David J Guzman
Anales. Museo Nacional de Historia Natural de Montevideo [*A publication*]....An Mus Nac Hist Nat Montev
Anales. Oto-Rhino-Laryngologicos Ibero-Americanos [*A publication*]....An ORL Ibero-Amer
Anales Otorrinolaringologicos Ibero-Americanos [*A publication*]....An Otorrinolaringol Iber-Am
Anales de Parques Nacionales (Buenos Aires) [*A publication*]....An Parques Nac (B Aires)
Anales de Quimica [*A publication*]....An Quim
Anales de Quimica [*A publication*]....An Quimica
Anales de Quimica. Serie A. Quimica Fisica y Quimica Tecnica [*A publication*]....An Quim A-Fis Tec
Anales de Quimica. Serie B. Quimica Inorganica y Quimica Analytica [*A publication*]....An Quim B Inorg Anal
Anales de Quimica. Serie C. Quimica Organica y Bioquimica [*A publication*]....An Quim C Org Bioquim
Anales. Real Academia de Farmacia [*A publication*]....An R Acad Farm
Anales. Real Academia Nacional de Medicina (Madrid) [*A publication*]....An R Acad Nacl Med (Madr)
Anales. Real Academia Nacional de Medicina (Madrid) [*A publication*]....An R Acad Nac Med (Madr)
Anales. Real Sociedad Espanola de Fisica y Quimica [*A publication*]....An R Soc Esp Fis Quim
Anales. Real Sociedad Espanola de Fisica y Quimica. Serie B. Quimica [*A publication*]....An R Soc Esp Fis Quim Ser B Quim
Anales. Sociedad Cientifica (Argentina) [*A publication*]....An Soc Cient (Argent)
Anales. Sociedad de Geografia e Historia [*A publication*]....An Soc Geogr Hist
Anales. Sociedad de Geografia e Historia [*A publication*]....ASGH
Anales. Sociedad Medico-Quirurgica del Guayas [*A publication*]....An Soc Med-Quir Guayas
Anales. Sociedad Mexicana de Oftalmologia [*A publication*]....An Soc Mex Oftalmol
Anales. Sociedad Mexicana de Otorinolaringologia [*A publication*]....An Soc Mex Otorinolaringol
Anales. Sociedad Rural Argentina [*A publication*]....An Soc Rural Argent
Anales. Sociedad Rural Argentina [*A publication*]....An Soc Rur Argent
Anales. Sociedad Veterinaria de Zootecnia [*A publication*]....An Soc Vet Zootec
Anales de la Universidad [*A publication*]....AnU
Anales. Universidad Central del Ecuador [*A publication*]....An Univ Cent Ecuador
Anales. Universidad Central del Ecuador [*A publication*]....AUCE
Anales. Universidad de Chile [*A publication*]....AUC
Anales. Universidad de Cuenca [*A publication*]....An Univ Cuenca
Anales. Universidad de Guayaquil [*A publication*]....AUG
Anales. Universidad Hispalense [*A publication*]....An Univ Hispalense
Anales. Universidad Hispalense [*A publication*]....AUH
Anales. Universidad Hispalense [*A publication*]....AUHisp
Anales. Universidad Hispalense. Serie de Ciencias [*A publication*]....An Univ Hispalense Ser Cienc
Anales. Universidad Hispalense. Serie Veterinaria [*A publication*]....An Univ Hisp Ser Vet
Anales. Universidad de Murcia [*A publication*]....AUM
Anales. Universidad de Valencia [*A publication*]....AUV
Analgesic [*Medicine*]....ANAL
Analgesic-Associated Nephropathy [*Medicine*]....AAN
Analgesic Dose....AD
Anali Filoloskog Fakulteta [*Belgrade*] [*A publication*]....AFF
Anali Filoloskog Fakulteta Beogradskog Univerziteta [*A publication*]....AnaliFF
Anali Klinicke Bolnice Dr. M. Stojanovic [*A publication*]....An Klin Boln Dr M Stojanovic
Anali Klinicke Bolnice Dr. M. Stojanovic. Suplement [*A publication*]....An Klin Boln Dr M Stojanovic Supl
Anali za Sumarstvo (Zagreb) [*A publication*]....An Sumar (Zagreb)
Analise Social [*A publication*]....Anal Soc
Analiticheskaya Khimiya Neorganicheskikh Soedinenij [*A publication*]....Anal Khim Neorg Soedin
Analog....ANL
Analog....ANLG
Analog Alarm Section....AAS
Analog Antenna Positioner....AAP
Analog Autopilot....AAP
Analog Computer....AC
Analog Computer....ANACOM
Analog Computer Facility....ACF
Analog Computer Subsystem....ACSS
Analog Computer System....ACS
Analog Conditioning and Test System....ACTS
Analog Data Acquisition Module....ADAM
Analog Data Digitizer....ADD
Analog Data Distributor and Control....ADDAC
Analog Data Handling System....ADHS
Analog Data Recorder Transcriber....ADRT
Analog Delay Unit....ADU
Analog Devices, Incorporated [*NYSE symbol*]....ADI
Analog-to-Digital [*Converter*] [*Data processing*]....A-to-D
Analog-to-Digital [*Converter*] [*Data processing*]....AD
Analog-Digital Automatic Program Tester [*Data processing*]....ADAPT
Analog-to-Digital Conversion System [*Data processing*]....ADIC
Analog-to-Digital Converter [*Data processing*]....ADC
Analog-to-Digital Converter [*Data processing*]....ADCON
Analog-to-Digital Data Recording System....ADRS
Analog-to-Digital Data Reduction System for Oceanographic Research....ADDRESOR
Analog-Digital-Designer [*Trademark*]....ADD
Analog-Digital Integrating Translator [*Data processing*]....ADIT
Analog and Digital Monitoring System [*Data processing*]....ADMS
Analog-Digital Recorder [*Data processing*]....ADR
Analog Display Unit....ADU
Analog Electronic Computer....AEC
Analog Event Distribution System [*Data processing*]....AEDS
Analog Event System [*Data processing*]....AES
Analog Factor Calibration Network....AFCAN
Analog Filter Assembly....AFA
Analog Fly by Wire [*Aviation*]....AFBW
Analog to Frequency Converter....AFC
Analog Function Generator....AFG
Analog Ground Bus....AGBUS
Analog Input Module [*Data processing*]....AIM
Analog Input/Output Package [*Data processing*]....AIOP
Analog Instrumentation Subsystem....AIS
Analog Line Driver [*Data processing*]....ALD
Analog Major Alarm....AMA
Analog Matched Filter....AMF
Analog Multiplexer Quantitizer....AMQ
Analog Output....AO
Analog Output Differential [*Data processing*]....AOD
Analog Panel Meter....APM
Analog to Pressure Converter....APC
Analog Program Tape....APT
Analog Programing and Checking [*Data processing*]....APACHE
Analog-to-Pulse Duration....APD

Analog-to-Pulse Width Converter A/PW
Analog RADAR Absorber ARA
Analog RADAR Signal Processor ARSP
Analog Recording Dynamic Analyzers [*Data processing*] ARDA
Analog Recording System ARS
Analog Remote Unit ARU
Analog Response Conditioner ARC
Analog Response Unit ARU
Analog Rotation Speed Control ARSC
Analog Schematic Translator to Algebraic Language [*Data processing*] ASTRAL
Analog Science Fiction [*A publication*] ASF
Analog Select Keyboard ASK
Analog Self-Checking Automatic Tester ASCAT
Analog Shift Register ASR
Analog Signal Converter ASC
Analog Signal Correlator ASC
Analog Signal to Discrete Time Interval Converter [*NASA*] ASDTIC
Analog Simulation System ASS
Analog Stimulus Unit ASU
Analog Strip Chart ASC
Analog Strip Chart Recorder ASCR
Analog System Assembly Pack ASAP
Analog Tape Recorder ATR
Analog Technology Company ATC
Analog Threshold Logic ATL
Analog Translator [*Data processing*] ANATRAN
Analog Tree-Organized Multiplexer ATOM
Analog Video Bandwidth AVB
Analogic Corp. [*NASDAQ symbol*] ALOG
Analogue Simulation of Competitive Operational Tactics [*Game*] ASCOT
Analogy ANAL
Anals de Antropologia [*A publication*] A Antropol
Analyse Financiere [*A publication*] Anal Financ
Analyse et Prevision [*A publication*] Anal et Previs
Analyse et Prevision [*A publication*] Anal Previs
Analysen und Prognosen ueber die Welt von Morgen [*A publication*] Anal Progn
Analyser og Problemer [*A publication*] AOP
Analyses. Revue Technique Merlin Gerin [*A publication*] Anal Rev Tech Merlin Gerin
Analysis ANAL
Analysis ANALYS
Analysis ANLYS
Analysis of Accounts A/A
Analysis of Automatic Line Insulation Test [*Bell System*] ANALIT
Analysis and Characterization of Oils, Fats, and Fat Products [*A publication*] Anal Charact Oils Fats Fat Prod
Analysis Computer System ACS
Analysis of Covariance ANCOVA
Analysis of Digitized Seismic Signals [*Data processing*] ADSS
Analysis and Evaluation A & E
Analysis Instrumentation [*A publication*] Anal Instrum
Analysis of Internal Management Systems AIMS
Analysis Mathematica [*A publication*] Anal Math
Analysis Production Persistency [*LIMRA*] APP
Analysis and Program for Calculation of Optimum Propellant Performance for Liquid and Solid Rocket Fuels APCOPPLSRF
Analysis Program Linear Active Circuits APLAC
Analysis of Random Data [*System documentation*] [*Oregon State University*] ARAND
Analysis, Refinement, and Extension of Nuclear Methodology [*Military*] ARENUM
Analysis and Research of Methods for Management ARMM
Analysis of Spare Parts Change ASPC
Analysis Time AT
Analysis of Variance [*Also, ANOVA*] ANOV
Analysis of Variance [*Also, ANOV*] ANOVA
Analyst [*A publication*] Anal
Analysts International Corp. [*NASDAQ symbol*] ANLY
Analysts Journal [*A publication*] Analysts J
Analytic [*or Analytical*] **Chemist** AC
Analytic Ephemeris Generator AEG
Analytic Intelligence Test [*Psychology*] AIT
Analytic Language Manipulation System ALMS
Analytic Methodology for System Evaluation and Control [*Army*] AMSEC
Analytic Plotter Coordinagraph [*Geoscience*] APC
[*The*] **Analytic Sciences Corporation** TASC
Analytic Services, Inc. ANSER
Analytica Chimica Acta [*A publication*] Anal Chim Acta
Analytica Chimica Acta [*A publication*] Anal Chimica Acta
Analytica Chimica Acta [*A publication*] Analyt Chim
Analytical Abstracts AA
Analytical Abstracts [*A publication*] Anal Abstr
Analytical Abstracts [*A publication*] Analyt Abstr
Analytical Advances [*A publication*] Anal Adv
Analytical Biochemistry [*A publication*] Anal Biochem
Analytical Biochemistry [*A publication*] Analyt Bioc
Analytical Biochemistry [*A publication*] Analyt Biochem
Analytical Chemistry [*A publication*] Anal Chem
Analytical Chemistry [*A publication*] Analyt Chem
Analytical Chemistry [*A publication*] An Chem
Analytical Chemistry and Applied Spectroscopy ACAS
Analytical Chemistry Laboratory ACL
Analytical Chemistry Symposia Series [*Elsevier Book Series*] [*A publication*] ACSS
Analytical and Computer Laboratory ACL
Analytical Computer Program ACP
Analytical Condition Inspection ACI
Analytical Condition Inspection Program ACIP
Analytical Electron Microscopy AEM
Analytical and Enumerative Bibliography [*A publication*] AEB
Analytical Grade [*Organic chemistry*] AG
Analytical Instrument Development, Inc. AID
Analytical Isoelectrofocusing Scanning Apparatus [*Analytical chemistry*] AISA
Analytical Laboratory Managers Association [*Formerly, ULMA*] ALMA
Analytical Letters [*A publication*] Anal Lett
Analytical Letters [*A publication*] Anal Letter
Analytical Letters [*A publication*] Anal Letters
Analytical Limits AL
Analytical Liquid Chromatograph ALC
Analytical Maintenance Program [*Navy*] AMP
Analytical Methodology Information Center [*Environmental Protection Agency*] AMIC
Analytical Photogrammetric Positioning System APPS
Analytical Proceedings [*A publication*] Anal Proc
Analytical Profile Index [*Microbiology*] API
Analytical Psychology AP
Analytical Psychology Club of New York APCNY
Analytical Quality Control Laboratory AQCL
Analytical and Quantitative Cytology [*A publication*] Anal Quant Cytol
Analytical Reagent [*Chemistry*] AR
Analytical Reports Gathering and Updating System [*Navy*] ARGUS
Analytical Research and Development Unit [*British*] ARDU
Analytical Rework Program [*Navy*] ARP
Analytical Studies of Surface Effects of Submerged Submarines [*Navy*] ASSESS
Analytical Transmission Electron Microscope ATEM
Analyze ANALY
Analyzer ANLYZ
Analyzer-Recorder-Controller ARC
Anamilo Club of Detroit ACD
Anamosa Eureka, Anamosa, IA [*Library symbol*] IaAnaE
Anamosa, IA [*Radio station call letters*] KLEH
Anamosa Journal, Anamosa, IA [*Library symbol*] IaAnaJ
Anamosa Public Library, Anamosa, IA [*Library symbol*] IaAna
Ananda Airways, Inc. [*Lahaina, Maui, HI*] [*FAA designator*] ANA
Ananda Marga [*An association*] AM
Ananda Marga Universal Relief Team [*India*] AMURT
Anaphylatoxin [*Immunology*] AT
Anaphylaxis [*Medicine*] A
Anarchism [*A publication*] Anarch
Anarchist Association of the Americas AAA
Anarchist Red Cross ARC
ANARE [*Australian National Antarctic Research Expeditions*] **Interim Reports. Series A** [*A publication*] ANARE Interim Rep Ser A
ANARE [*Australian National Antarctic Research Expeditions*] **Scientific Reports. Series B-I. Zoology** [*A publication*] ANARE Sci Rep Ser B I Zool
ANARE [*Australian National Antarctic Research Expeditions*] **Scientific Reports. Series B-IV. Medical Science** [*A publication*] ANARE Sci Rep Ser B IV Med Sci
Anaren Microwave, Inc. [*NASDAQ symbol*] ANEN
Anasco, PR [*Radio station call letters*] WVID
Anasthesie, Intensivtherapie, Notfallmedizin [*A publication*] Anasth Intensivther Notfallmed
Anatolian Studies [*A publication*] AnatS
Anatolian Studies [*A publication*] Anat Stud
Anatolian Studies [*A publication*] An St
Anatolian Studies [*A publication*] AS
Anatomia, Histologia, Embryologia [*A publication*] Anat Histol Embryol
Anatomia, Histologia, Embryologia/Zentralblatt fuer Veterinaermedizin, Reihe C [*A publication*] Anat His Em
Anatomical Record [*A publication*] Anat Rec
Anatomischer Anzeiger; Zentralblatt fuer die Gesamte Wissenschaftliche Anatomie [*A publication*] Anat Anz
Anatomy [*or Anatomical*] ANAT
Anatomy and Embryology [*A publication*] Anat Embryo
Anatuberculina Diagnostica Petragnani [*Petragnani Diagnostic Anatuberculin*] [*Medicine*] ADP
Anches [*Reeds*] [*Music*] ANCH
Anchor AHR
Anchor Bolt [*Technical drawings*] AB
Anchor Hocking Corp. [*NYSE symbol*] ARH
Anchor Order AOR
Anchor Placement Equipment APE
Anchor Review [*A publication*] Anchor Rev
Anchor Windlass AWNDLS
Anchorage [*Alaska Methodist University*] [*Alaska*] [*Seismograph station code, US Geological Survey*] [*Closed*] AMU
Anchorage [*Alaska*] [*Airport symbol*] ANC

Anchorage [*Maps and charts*] ... ANCH
Anchorage, AK [*Location identifier*] [*FAA*] ... CMQ
Anchorage, AK [*Television station call letters*] ... KAKM
Anchorage, AK [*Radio station call letters*] ... KBYR
Anchorage, AK [*Radio station call letters*] ... KCMG
Anchorage, AK [*Radio station call letters*] ... KENI
Anchorage, AK [*Radio station call letters*] ... KFQD
Anchorage, AK [*Radio station call letters*] ... KGOT
Anchorage, AK [*Radio station call letters*] ... KHAR
Anchorage, AK [*Television station call letters*] ... KIMO-TV
Anchorage, AK [*Radio station call letters*] ... KKLV
Anchorage, AK [*Radio station call letters*] ... KNIK
Anchorage, AK [*Radio station call letters*] ... KRKN
Anchorage, AK [*Radio station call letters*] ... KSKA
Anchorage, AK [*Television station call letters*] ... KTBY
Anchorage, AK [*Radio station call letters*] ... KTNX
Anchorage, AK [*Television station call letters*] ... KTUU-TV
Anchorage, AK [*Television station call letters*] ... KTVA
Anchorage, AK [*Radio station call letters*] ... KWHL
Anchorage, AK [*Radio station call letters*] ... KYAK
Anchorage, AK [*Location identifier*] [*FAA*] ... LHD
Anchorage Community College, Anchorage, AK [*Library symbol*] ... AkAC
Anchorage Higher Education Consortium Library, Anchorage, AK [*Library symbol*] ... AkACon
Anchorage Prohibited [*Nautical charts*] ... Anch prohib
Anchored ... ANCH
Anchored Filament ... ANCFIL
Anchored Filament ... ANF
Anchored Interplanetary Monitoring Platform ... AIMP
Anchorite ... A
Anchors and Chains Proved [*Shipping*] ... A & CP
Ancien Pays de Looz [*A publication*] ... APL
Ancien Testament [*Old Testament*] [*French*] ... AT
Ancient ... ANC
Ancient ... ANCT
Ancient Accepted Scottish Rite [*Masonic*] ... AASR
Ancient Astronaut Society ... AAS
Ancient Egypt [*A publication*] ... AncEg
Ancient Egyptian Arabic Order Nobles of the Mystic Shrine ... AEAONMS
Ancient Egyptian Arabic Order Nobles of the Mystic Shrine ... NMS
Ancient Egyptian Order of Sciots ... AEOS
Ancient Free and Accepted Masons ... AF & AM
Ancient Free and Accepted Masons ... AFAM
Ancient Gneiss Complex [*Geology*] ... AGC
Ancient and Illustrious Order Knights of Malta ... AIOK of M
Ancient India [*A publication*] ... AI
Ancient Mediterranean Research Association ... AMRA
Ancient and Modern [*Hymns*] ... A and M
Ancient Mystic Order of Bagmen of Bagdad Imperial Guild ... AMOB
Ancient Mystic Order of Samaritans ... AMOS
Ancient Mystical Order Rosae Crucis [*Rosicrucian Order*] ... AMORC
Ancient Order of Druids ... AOD
Ancient Order of Foresters ... AOF
Ancient Order of Foresters of California ... AOFC
Ancient Order of Frothblowers [*British*] ... AOFB
Ancient Order of Hibernians in America ... AOH
Ancient Order of Shepherds ... AOS
Ancient Order United Workmen ... AOUW
Ancient Petition ... AP
Ancient Society [*A publication*] ... Anc Soc
Ancient York Mason ... AYM
Ancilla College [*Formerly, Ancilla Domini College*] [*Indiana*] ... AC
Ancona [*Italy*] [*Airport symbol*] ... AOI
Ancorp National Services, Inc. [*NYSE symbol*] [*Delisted*] ... ANC
And Elsewhere [*Mathematics*] ... ae
And Gate [*Data processing*] ... AG
And/Or ... A/OR
And-Or Invert ... AOI
And Others ... AO
Andahuaylas [*Peru*] [*Airport symbol*] [*Obsolete*] ... ANS
Andal Corp. [*American Stock Exchange symbol*] ... ADL
Andalgala [*Argentina*] [*Seismograph station code, US Geological Survey*] [*Closed*] ... ANL
Andalusia, AL [*Radio station call letters*] ... WAAO
Andalusia, AL [*Radio station call letters*] ... WKYD
Andalusia, AL [*Radio station call letters*] ... WKYD-FM
Andalusia, AL [*Radio station call letters*] ... WTCG
Andalusian Horse Registry ... AHR
Andamooka [*Australia*] [*Airport symbol*] ... ADO
Andante [*Slow*] [*Music*] ... AND
Andante [*Slow*] [*Music*] ... ANDTE
Andantino [*Slow*] [*Music*] ... ANDNO
Andantino [*Slow*] [*Music*] ... ANDO
Andapa [*Madagascar*] [*Airport symbol*] ... ZWA
Andco, Inc., Buffalo, NY [*Library symbol*] ... NBuAn
Andean Area [*MARC geographic area code*] [*Library of Congress*] ... sn-----
Andean Common Market ... ANCOM
Andean Pact Organization [*Chile, Peru, Bolivia, Ecuador, Colombia*] ... APO
Andelin Foundation for Education in Family Living ... AFEFL
Andenes [*Norway*] [*Airport symbol*] ... ANX
Andersen 2000, Inc. [*NASDAQ symbol*] ... ANDN
Andersen Group, Inc. [*NASDAQ symbol*] ... ANDR
Anderseniana [*A publication*] ... And
Anderson [*South Carolina*] [*Airport symbol*] ... AND
Anderson, CA [*Radio station call letters*] ... KEWB
Anderson Carnegie Public Library, Anderson, IN [*Library symbol*] ... InAnd
Anderson, Clayton, & Co. [*NYSE symbol*] ... AYL
Anderson, Clayton, & Co., Foods Division Technical Library, Dallas, TX [*Library symbol*] ... TxDaAC
Anderson Clayton Foods [*of Anderson, Clayton, & Co.*], **Richardson, TX** [*Library symbol*] ... TxRiA
Anderson College, Anderson, IN [*OCLC symbol*] ... INA
Anderson College, Anderson, IN [*Library symbol*] ... InAndC
Anderson College, Graduate School of Theology, Anderson, IN [*Library symbol*] ... InAcdC-T
Anderson County Library, Anderson, SC [*OCLC symbol*] ... SAL
Anderson County Library, Anderson, SC [*Library symbol*] ... ScAn
Anderson - Darling Test [*Statistics*] ... AD
Anderson Galleries ... AG
Anderson, Greenwood, & Co. [*NYSE symbol*] ... AGV
Anderson, IN [*Radio station call letters*] ... WHBU
Anderson, IN [*Radio station call letters*] ... WHUT
Anderson, IN [*Radio station call letters*] ... WLHN
Anderson Industries, Inc. [*NASDAQ symbol*] ... ANDS
Anderson Jacobson, Inc. [*American Stock Exchange symbol*] ... AJ
Anderson Model [*Physics*] ... AM
Anderson Public Library, Anderson, IN [*OCLC symbol*] ... IAM
Anderson Reservoir [*California*] [*Seismograph station code, US Geological Survey*] ... ADR
Anderson, SC [*Radio station call letters*] ... WAIM
Anderson, SC [*Radio station call letters*] ... WAIM-FM
Anderson, SC [*Radio station call letters*] ... WANS
Anderson, SC [*Radio station call letters*] ... WANS-FM
Anderson, SC [*Television station call letters*] ... WAXA
Andhra Agricultural Journal [*A publication*] ... Andhra Agric J
Andhra Agricultural Journal [*A publication*] ... Andhra Agr J
Andhra Pradesh ... AP
Andhra Pradesh Ground Water Department. District Series [*A publication*] ... Andhra Pradesh Ground Water Dep Dist Ser
Andizhan [*USSR*] [*Seismograph station code, US Geological Survey*] ... ANR
Andorra [*Two-letter standard code*] ... AD
Andorra [*MARC country of publication code*] [*Library of Congress*] ... an
Andorra [*Three-letter standard code*] ... AND
Andorra [*MARC geographic area code*] [*Library of Congress*] ... e-an---
Andorran Philately Study Circle ... APSC
Andover Controls [*NASDAQ symbol*] ... ANDO
Andover Historical Society, Andover, MA [*Library symbol*] ... MAnHi
Andover, MA [*Radio station call letters*] ... WPAA
Andover Newton Quarterly [*A publication*] ... AndNewQ
Andover Newton Quarterly [*A publication*] ... ANQ
Andover Newton Theological School ... ANTS
Andover Newton Theological School, Newton Center, MA [*OCLC symbol*] ... BAN
Andover Newton Theological School, Newton Center, MA [*Library symbol*] ... MNtcA
Andover Review [*A publication*] ... And R
Andover Service Center [*IRS*] ... ANSC
Andre and Coquelin [*Often used as a pattern on clothes designed by Courreges, the initials represent the first names of the couturier and his wife*] ... AC
Andre Marsan & Associes, Inc., Montreal, PQ, Canada [*Library symbol*] ... CaQMAMA
Andrea Radio Corp. [*American Stock Exchange symbol*] ... AND
Andreafsky/St. Marys, AK [*Location identifier*] [*FAA*] ... SMA
Andrew Bayne Memorial Library, Bellevue, PA [*Library symbol*] ... PBvu
Andrew College, Cuthbert, GA [*Library symbol*] ... GCuA
Andrew Corp. [*NASDAQ symbol*] ... ANDW
Andrew County Historical Society, Savannah, MO [*Library symbol*] ... MoSavHi
Andrew W. Mellon Foundation, New York, NY [*Library symbol*] ... NNMel
Andrews Air Force Base [*Washington, DC*] ... AAFB
Andrews, TX [*Radio station call letters*] ... KACT
Andrews, TX [*Radio station call letters*] ... KACT-FM
Andrews University, Berrien Springs, MI [*OCLC symbol*] ... EXN
Andrews University, Berrien Springs, MI [*Library symbol*] ... MiBsA
Andrews University Seminary Studies [*A publication*] ... An U S S
Andrews University Seminary Studies [*A publication*] ... AUSem St
Andrews University Seminary Studies [*A publication*] ... AUSS
Andriamena [*Madagascar*] [*Airport symbol*] ... WAD
Androecium [*Botany*] ... A
Androgen Binding Protein [*Endocrinology*] ... ABP
Androgen Insensitivity Syndrome [*Endocrinology*] ... AIS
Androgen Receptors [*Endocrinology*] ... AR
Andrologie [*A publication*] ... ANDLA
Andromeda [*Constellation*] ... And
Andromeda [*Constellation*] ... Andr
Andronicus Publishing Company, Inc., New York, NY [*Library symbol*] ... ApC
Andros Analyzers [*NASDAQ symbol*] ... ANDY
Andros Town [*Bahamas*] [*Airport symbol*] ... ASD
Androstatrienedione [*Organic chemistry*] ... ATD
Androstenedione [*Endocrinology*] ... AD

Andrus Gerontological Information Center [*University of Southern California*] ... AGIC
Anechoic Water Tank ... AWT
Aneco Reinsurance Co. [*NASDAQ symbol*] ... ANECF
Anegada [*Virgin Islands*] [*Seismograph station code, US Geological Survey*] ... ABV
Aneityum [*Vanuata*] [*Airport symbol*] ... AUY
Anejos de Estudios Filologicos [*A publication*] ... AEF
Anesteziologiya i Reanimatologiya [*A publication*] ... Anesteziol Reanimatol
Anesthesia [*or Anesthetic*] [*Medicine*] ... ANESTH
Anesthesia and Analgesia [*Cleveland*] [*A publication*] ... Anesth Anal
Anesthesia and Analgesia (Cleveland) [*A publication*] ... Anesth Analg (Cleve)
Anesthesia Progress [*A publication*] ... Anesth Prog
Anesthesie, Analgesie, Reanimation [*Paris*] [*A publication*] ... AAREA
Anesthesie, Analgesie, Reanimation [*Paris*] [*A publication*] ... Anesth Analg Reanim
Anesthesie, Analgesie, Reanimation [*Paris*] [*A publication*] ... Anesth An R
Anesthesie, Analgesie, Reanimation (Paris) [*A publication*] ... Anesth Analg (Paris)
Anesthesiologie et Reanimation [*A publication*] ... Anesthesiol Reanim
Anesthesiology ... ANES
Anesthesiology [*A publication*] ... ANESA
Anesthesiology [*A publication*] ... Anesthesiol
Anesthesiology ... ANESTHLGY
Anesthetic [*Medicine*] ... A
Aneurysm ... AN
Angavokely [*Madagascar*] [*Seismograph station code, US Geological Survey*] ... AVY
Angeborener Ausolsender Mechanismus [*Innate Release Mechanism*] [*Psychology*] ... AAM
Angel Collectors Club of America ... ACCA
Angel Island [*California*] [*Seismograph station code, US Geological Survey*] ... AGC
Angel, Jerald J., Los Angeles CA [*STAC*] ... AJJ
Angel, Second Class [*Classification of angel Clarence Oddbody in 1947 film, "It's a Wonderful Life"*] ... AS2
Angeles Corp. [*American Stock Exchange symbol*] ... ANG
Angeles Corp. [*NASDAQ symbol*] ... ANGS
Angelholm/Helsingbord [*Sweden*] [*Airport symbol*] ... AGH
Angelic Warfare Confraternity [*Defunct*] ... AWC
Angelica Corp. [*NYSE symbol*] ... AGL
Angelina College, Lufkin, TX [*Library symbol*] ... TxLufA
Angelina & Neches River Railroad Co. [*AAR code*] ... ANR
Angelini Francesco [*Italy*] [*Research code symbol*] ... AF
Angelo State University, San Angelo, TX [*Library symbol*] ... TxSaIA
Angel's Peak [*Nevada*] [*Seismograph station code, US Geological Survey*] ... APK
Angewandte Botanik [*A publication*] ... Angew Bot
Angewandte Chemie [*A publication*] ... Angew Chem
Angewandte Chemie. International Edition in English [*A publication*] ... Angew Chem Int Ed Engl
Angewandte Chemie. International Edition in English [*A publication*] ... Angew Chem Intern Ed
Angewandte Elektronik [*A publication*] ... Angew Elektron
Angewandte Elektronik. Mess und Regeltechnik [*A publication*] ... Angew Elektron Mess & Regeltech
Angewandte Informatik/Applied Informatics [*A publication*] ... Angew Inf
Angewandte Informatik/Applied Informatics [*A publication*] ... Angew Inf Appl Inf
Angewandte Informatik/Applied Informatics [*A publication*] ... Angew Infor
Angewandte Makromolekulare Chemie [*A publication*] ... Angew Makro
Angewandte Makromolekulare Chemie [*A publication*] ... Angew Makromol Chem
Angewandte Meteorologie [*A publication*] ... Angew Met
Angewandte Ornithologie [*A publication*] ... Angew Ornithol
Angewandte Parasitologie [*A publication*] ... Angew Parasitol
Angewandte Pflanzensoziologie [*A publication*] ... Angew Pflanzensoziol
Angina Pectoris [*Medicine*] ... AP
Angiocardiography [*Medicine*] ... ACG
Angiogenesis Factor [*Biochemistry*] ... AF
Angiogenesis Inhibitor [*Physiology*] ... AI
Angiogram [*Medicine*] ... ANG
Angioimmunoblastic Lymphadenopathy [*Medicine*] ... AIL
Angioimmunoblastic Lymphadenopathy with Dysproteinemia [*Medicine*] ... AILD
Angiotensin [*Biochemistry*] ... ANG
Angiotensin Converting Enzyme ... ACE
Angiotensin II [*Biochemistry*] ... AII
Angiotensin Pressor Dose [*Medicine*] ... APD
Angiotensin Sensitivity Test [*Medicine*] ... AST
Angle ... ANG
Angle-of-Approach Indicator [*Aviation*] ... AAI
Angle of Attack [*Military*] ... A/A
Angle of Attack [*Military*] ... AOA
Angle-of-Attack Indicator [*Military*] ... AAI
Angle-of-Attack Indicator [*Military*] ... AOAI
Angle-of-Attack Sensor [*Military*] ... AOAS
Angle of Bank ... AOB
Angle of Beam ... AOB
Angle on the Bow [*Navy*] ... AOB
Angle Bulkhead Jack ... ABHJ
Angle Bulkhead Jack ... ABJ
Angle Data Assembly ... ADA
Angle Data Recorder ... ADR
Angle Data Subsystem ... ADS
Angle Deception Jamming ... ADJ
Angle Deception Jamming System ... ADJS
Angle of Descent ... AOD
Angle of Greatest Extension ... AGE
Angle of Greatest Flexion ... AGF
Angle of Incidence ... I
Angle of Inner Gimbal ... AIG
Angle Iron [*Freight*] ... AI
Angle on Jam ... AOJ
Angle Jamming System ... AJS
Angle Lock ... AL
Angle Measuring Equipment ... AME
Angle Measuring Equipment, Correlation Tracking and Ranging ... AME/COTAR
Angle of Middle Gimbal ... AMG
Angle Order ... ANLOR
Angle Orthodontist [*A publication*] ... Angl Orthod
Angle Panel Jack ... APJ
Angle Point ... AP
Angle Position Indicator ... API
Angle Rate Bombing System ... ARBS
Angle of Reflection ... AOR
Angle-Resolved Photoelectron Spectroscopy ... ARPES
Angle-Resolved Ultraviolet Photoelectron Spectroscopy ... ARUPS
Angle of Site ... AOS
Angle Stop Valve [*Technical drawings*] ... ASV
Angle on Target ... AOT
Angle Template ... AT
Angle, Time, Range [*Data processing*] ... ATR
Angle Track on Target [*Military*] ... ATOT
Angle Tracker ... A/T
Angle Tracking System [*NASA*] ... ATS
Angle Versus Length [*Data processing*] ... AVL
Angle of Yaw Indicator ... AYI
Angleplied Laminate ... APL
Anglesey [*Island and county in Wales*] ... ANG
Anglia [*A publication*] ... Ang
Anglia Beiblatt [*A publication*] ... Ang Bbl
Anglia Beiblatt [*A publication*] ... AnglB
Anglia Beiblatt [*A publication*] ... Angl Bei
Anglica Germanica [*A publication*] ... AG
Anglican ... A
Anglican ... ANG
Anglican ... ANGL
Anglican Association of Musicians ... AAM
Anglican Church of Canada ... ACC
Anglican Church of Canada, Archives, Toronto, ON, Canada [*Library symbol*] ... CaOTCHAr
Anglican Church House, Toronto, ON, Canada [*Library symbol*] ... CaOTCH
Anglican Communion ... AC
Anglican and Eastern Churches Association ... A & ECA
Anglican Roman Catholic International Commission ... ARCIC
Anglican Theological Review [*A publication*] ... Angl Th R
Anglican Theological Review [*A publication*] ... AThR
Anglican Theological Review [*A publication*] ... ATR
Anglican Young People's Association ... AYPA
Anglice [*In English*] [*Latin*] ... ANGL
Anglistik und Amerikanistik [*A publication*] ... AuA
Anglistische Forschungen [*A publication*] ... AF
Anglistisches Seminar [*A publication*] ... AS
Anglo-American ... AA
Anglo-American Associates [*An association*] ... AAA
Anglo-American Catalog Code Revision Committee [*American Library Association*] ... AACR
Anglo-American Cataloging Rules [*Library science*] ... AACR
Anglo-American Code [*Cataloging*] ... AAC
Anglo-American Committee [*World War II*] ... AAC
Anglo American Corp. of South Africa ADR [*NASDAQ symbol*] ... ANGLY
Anglo-American Food Committee [*World War II*] ... AAFC
Anglo American Gold ADR [*NASDAQ symbol*] ... AAGIY
Anglo-American-Hellenic Bureau of Education [*Defunct*] ... AAHBE
Anglo-American Joint Chiefs of Staff ... AAJCS
Anglo-American Press Association of Paris ... AAPAP
Anglo-American Sporting Club ... AASC
Anglo-Bomarc Mines [*NASDAQ symbol*] ... ANGBF
Anglo Co. Ltd. [*American Stock Exchange symbol*] [*Delisted*] ... AGO
Anglo-Dutch-United States ... ANDUS
Anglo Energy Limited [*American Stock Exchange symbol*] ... AEL
Anglo-French [*Language, etc.*] ... AF
Anglo-French [*Language, etc.*] ... AFR
Anglo-French Review [*A publication*] ... AFR
Anglo-French Supply and Purchases [*World War II*] ... AFSP
Anglo-French Variable-Geometry [*Combat aircraft*] ... AFVG
Anglo-Frisian [*Language, etc.*] ... AF
Anglo-German Medical Review [*A publication*] ... Anglo-Ger Med Rev
Anglo-German Review [*A publication*] ... AglGr

Anglo-Indian [Language, etc.] .... AI
Anglo-Irish [Language, etc.] .... AI
Anglo-Irish Free Trade Area [British] .... AIFTA
Anglo-Israelism [or Anglo-Israelite] .... AI
Anglo-Jewish Association [British] .... AJA
Anglo-Latin [Language, etc.] .... AL
Anglo-Malaysian Defence Agreement .... AMDA
Anglo-Norman [Language, etc.] .... AN
Anglo-Norman Text Society [A publication] .... ANTS
Anglo-Rhodesian Society .... ARS
Anglo-Saxon [MARC language code] [Library of Congress] .... ang
Anglo-Saxon [Language, etc.] .... A-S
Anglo-Saxon Chronicle .... ASC
Anglo-Saxon England [A publication] .... ASE
Anglo-Saxon Protestant .... ASP
Anglo-Soviet Recognition Signals .... ASRS
Anglo-Vernacular .... AV
Anglo-Welsh Review [A publication] .... AWR
Angola [Three-letter standard code] .... AGO
Angola [MARC country of publication code] [Library of Congress] .... ao
Angola [MARC geographic area code] [Library of Congress] .... f-ao---
Angola [Two-letter standard code] .... AO
Angola, IN [Location identifier] [FAA] .... SJZ
Angola, IN [Radio station call letters] .... WEAX
Angola, IN [Radio station call letters] .... WLKI
Angola, IN [Television station call letters] .... WXJC-TV
Angoon [Alaska] [Airport symbol] .... AGN
Angoram [Papua New Guinea] [Airport symbol] .... AGG
Angra Do Heroismo [Azores] [Seismograph station code, US
    Geological Survey] .... ADH
Angstrom [Also, AU] .... A
Angstrom Pyrheliometric Scale .... APS
Angstrom Unit [Also, A] .... AU
Angstromeinheit [Angstrom Unit] [German] .... AE
Anguganak [Papua New Guinea] [Airport symbol] .... AKG
Anguilla [West Indies] [Airport symbol] .... AXA
Anguilla, MS [Location identifier] [FAA] .... RFK
Anguilla Tourist Information Office .... ATIO
Angular .... ANLR
Angular Acceleration Susceptibility [Orientation] .... AAS
Angular Accelerometer .... AA
Angular Accelerometer Unit .... AAU
Angular Aperture .... AA
Angular Differentiating-Integrating Accelerometer ..... ADA
Angular Distribution Data Tape .... ADDT
Angular Magnetic-Hydrodynamic Integrating Accelerometer .... AMIA
Angular Mapping Transformation [Data processing] ..... AMT
Angular Momentum .... AM
Angular Momentum [Symbol] [IUPAC] L
Angular Momentum [Symbol] [Physics] .... M
Angular Momentum Wheel .... AMW
Angular Motion Compensator .... AMC
Angular Position Digitizer .... APD
Angular Position Sensor .... APS
Angular Rate Sensor .... ARS
Angular Second Moment .... ASM
Angular Yaw Velocity .... r
Angwin, CA [Radio station call letters] .... KCDS-FM
Angwin, CA [Radio station call letters] .... KPRN
Anhaltische Geschichtsblaetter [A publication] .... AGB
Anheuser-Busch Companies [NYSE symbol] .... BUD
Anheuser-Busch, Inc. .... AB
Anheuser-Busch, Inc., Corporation Library, St. Louis, MO [OCLC
    symbol] .... ABS
Anheuser-Busch, Inc., St. Louis, MO [Library symbol] ...... MoSAB
Anhwei Province [China, Mainland] [MARC geographic area
    code] [Library of Congress] .... a-cc-an
Anhydride .... ANHYD
Anhydrobis(beta-hydroxyethyl)biguanide [Antiviral agent] .... ABOB
Anhydroenneahepitol [Organic chemistry] .... AEH
Anhydrous .... AN
Anhydrous .... ANH
Anhydrous .... ANHY
Anhydrous Monocalcium Phosphate [Inorganic chemistry] ...... AMCP
Anhysteretic Remanent Magnetization .... ARM
Aniak [Alaska] [Airport symbol] .... ANI
Aniline Gentian Violet .... AGV
(Anilino)naphthalenesulfonic Acid [Also, ANSA] [Organic chemistry] .... ANS
(Anilino)naphthalenesulfonic Acid [Also, ANS] [Organic chemistry] .... ANSA
Anima Dulcis [Sweet Soul] [Latin] .... AD
Anima e Pensiero [A publication] .... AeP
Anima e Pensiero [A publication] .... APen
Anima Quiescat in Christo [May His, or Her, Soul Repose in
    Christ] [Latin] .... AQIC
Animal [Psychology] .... A
Animal. .... AN
Animal. .... ANI
Animal Air Transportation Association .... AATA
Animal Behavior Society .... ABS
Animal Behaviour [A publication] .... AnB
Animal Behaviour [A publication] .... Animal Behav

Animal Behaviour [A publication] .... Anim Behav
Animal Behaviour. Monographs [A publication] ..... Anim Behav Monogr
Animal Blood Groups and Biochemical Genetics [A publication] ....
    Anim Blood Groups Biochem Genet
Animal Breeding [A publication] .... Anim Breed
Animal Breeding Abstracts [A publication] ...... Anim Breed Abstr
Animal Care Panel [Later, AALAS] .... ACP
Animal Detail [Rorschach] [Psychology] .... Ad
Animal Disease Eradication Division [of ARS, Department of
    Agriculture] .... ADE
Animal Disease and Parasite Research Division [of ARS,
    Department of Agriculture] .... ADP
Animal Educational League [Defunct] .... AEL
Animal Feed and Tissue Residue Research Center [Department
    of Health and Human Services] .... AFTRRC
Animal Guild of America .... AGA
Animal Health [A publication] .... Anim Health
Animal Health Institute .... AHI
Animal Husbandry [A publication] .... Anim Husb
Animal Husbandry and Agricultural Journal [A publication] ....
    Anim Husb Agric J
Animal Husbandry Mimeograph Series. Florida Agricultural
    Experiment Station [A publication] ....
    Anim Husb Mimeogr Ser Fla Agr Exp Sta
Animal Husbandry Research Division [of ARS, Department of
    Agriculture] .... AH
Animal Improvement Programs Laboratory [Formerly, DHIA] ...... AIPL
Animal Inspection and Quarantine Division [of ARS, Department
    of Agriculture] .... AIQ
Animal Kingdom [A publication] .... Anim Kingdom
Animal Learning and Behavior [A publication] .... ALBVA
Animal Learning and Behavior [A publication] ..... Anim Lear B
Animal Learning and Behavior [A publication] ... Anim Learn Behav
Animal Liberation [An association] .... AL
Animal Liberation Front .... ALF
Animal Medical Center .... AMC
Animal Models of Protecting Ischemic Myocardium [Cardiology
    project] .... AMPIM
Animal Nutrition and Health [A publication] ...... Anim Nutr Health
Animal Nutrition Research Council .... ANRC
Animal and Plant Health Inspection Service [Department of
    Agriculture] .... APHIS
Animal Political Action Committee .... ANPAC
Animal Procurement Office [Military] .... APO
Animal Production [A publication] .... Animal Prod
Animal Production [A publication] .... Anim Prod
Animal Production [A publication] .... Anim Produc
Animal Protection Institute of America .... API
Animal Protein Factor .... APF
Animal Psi [Parapsychology] .... ANPSI
Animal Research Facilities .... ARF
Animal Rights Mobilization .... ARM
Animal Rights Network .... ARN
Animal Science Mimeograph Circular. Louisiana State
    University. Agricultural Experiment Station [A publication] ....
    AS Mimeogr Circ LA State Univ Agr Exp Sta
Animal Science Mimeograph Report. Florida Agricultural
    Experiment Station [A publication] ....
    Anim Sci Mimeogr Rep Fla Agr Exp Sta
Animal Science Mimeograph Series. Ohio State Agricultural
    Experiment Station [A publication] ....
    Anim Sci Mimeogr Ser Ohio State Agr Exp Sta
Animal Science (Sofia) [A publication] .... Anim Sci (Sofia)
Animal Transport [Navy ship symbol] [Obsolete] .... APA
Animal-Tub-Sized [Paper] .... ATS
Animal-Unit Month .... AUM
Animal Welfare Institute .... AWI
Animated Backlighted Burtek Trainer .... ABBT
Animated Burtek Trainer .... ABT
Animated Computer Education .... ACE
Animated Film Language .... AFL
Animated Movie Language .... AML
Animated Reconstruction of Telemetry .... ART
Animation [Films, television, etc.] .... ANIM
Animation Producers' Association [Defunct] .... APA
Animato [Lively, Animated] [Music] .... ANIMO
Anion-Responsive Electrode .... ARE
Anisometropia [Ophthalmology] .... AN
Anisotropy of Magnetic Susceptibility [Geophysics] ..... AMS
Anisoyl [As substituent on nucleoside] [Biochemistry] ...... an
Anita Tribune, Anita, IA [Library symbol] .... IaAniT
Anixter Brothers, Inc. [NYSE symbol] .... ANX
Anjou Historique [A publication] .... AH
Anjouan [Comoro Islands] [Airport symbol] .... AJN
Ankang [China] [Airport symbol] .... AKA
Ankara [Turkey] [Airport symbol] .... ANK
Ankara [Turkey] [Seismograph station code, US Geological Survey] .... ANK
Ankara-Esenboga [Turkey] [Airport symbol] .... ESB
Ankara Universitesi. Dil ve Tarih Cografya Fakultesi Dergisi [A
    publication] .... AnkUDerg

Ankara Universitesi Tip Fakultesi Mecmuasi [*A publication*] .... Ankara Univ Tip Fak Mecm
Ankara Universitesi Tip Fakultesi Mecmuasi. Supplementum [*A publication*] .... Ankara Univ Tip Fak Mecm Suppl
Ankara Universitesi Veteriner Fakultesi Dergisi [*A publication*] .... Ankara Univ Vet Fak Derg
Ankavandra [*Madagascar*] [*Airport symbol*] .... JVA
Ankazoabo [*Madagascar*] [*Airport symbol*] .... WAK
Anken Chemical & Film Corp. [*NYSE symbol*] [*Delisted*] .... AKF
Anken Industries [*American Stock Exchange symbol*] [*Delisted*] .... ANK
Ankeny, IA [*Radio station call letters*] .... KJJY
Ankeny Press-Citizen, Ankeny, IA [*Library symbol*] .... IaAnkP
Ankina Breeders [*An association*] .... AB
Ankle-Foot Arthrosis [*Medicine*] .... AFO
Ankle Jerk [*Neurology*] .... AJ
Ankole Watusi International Registry .... AWIR
Ankylosing Spondylitis [*Medicine*] .... AS
Anleitungen Bienenzuechter [*A publication*] .... Anleit Bienenzuechter
Anmerkung [*Note*] [*German*] .... ANM
Ann Arbor [*Michigan*] .... A²
Ann Arbor [*Michigan*] [*Seismograph station code, US Geological Survey*] .... AAM
Ann Arbor, MI [*Location identifier*] [*FAA*] .... ARB
Ann Arbor, MI [*Radio station call letters*] .... WAAM
Ann Arbor, MI [*Radio station call letters*] .... WCBN-FM
Ann Arbor, MI [*Television station call letters*] .... WIHT-TV
Ann Arbor, MI [*Radio station call letters*] .... WIQB
Ann Arbor, MI [*Radio station call letters*] .... WPAG
Ann Arbor, MI [*Radio station call letters*] .... WPAG-FM
Ann Arbor, MI [*Radio station call letters*] .... WUOM
Ann Arbor Public Library, Ann Arbor, MI [*Library symbol*] .... MiAa
Ann Arbor Railroad Co. [*AAR code*] .... AA
Ann Arbor Review [*A publication*] .... AAR
Ann Arbor Sun [*A publication*] .... Arbor Sun
Anna [*Monetary unit in India*] .... A
Anna [*Ohio*] [*Seismograph station code, US Geological Survey*] AN1
Anna [*Ohio*] [*Seismograph station code, US Geological Survey*] AN3
Anna, IL [*Radio station call letters*] .... WRAJ
Anna, IL [*Radio station call letters*] .... WRAJ-FM
Anna Regina [*Queen Anne*] .... AR
Annaba [*Algeria*] [*Airport symbol*] .... AAE
Annai [*Guyana*] [*Airport symbol*] .... NAI
Annale. Natalse Museum [*A publication*] .... Ann Natal Mus
Annale. Universita di Padova. Facolta di Economia e Commercio in Verona [*A publication*] .... Ann Univ Padova
Annale. Universiteit van Stellenbosch. Serie A [*A publication*] .... Ann Univ Stellenbosch Ser A
Annalen der Chemie [*Justus Liebigs*] [*A publication*] .... Ann Chem
Annalen der Chemie (Justus Liebigs) [*A publication*] .... Ann Chem (Justus Liebigs)
Annalen des Historischen Vereins fuer den Niederrhein [*A publication*] .... AHNRH
Annalen des Historischen Vereins fuer den Niederrhein [*A publication*] .... AHVNR
Annalen des Historischen Vereins fuer den Niederrhein [*A publication*] .... AHVNRh
Annalen. Naturhistorischen Museums in Wien [*A publication*] .... Ann Naturhist Mus Wien
Annalen van de Oudheidkundige Kring van het Land van Waas [*A publication*] .... AOKW
Annalen der Philosophie und Philosophischen Kritik [*A publication*] .... AP
Annalen der Physik [*A publication*] .... Ann Physik
Annalen der Physik und Chemie [*A publication*] .... An Physik
Annalen der Physik (Germany) [*A publication*] .... Ann Phys (Germ)
Annalen der Physik (Leipzig) [*A publication*] .... Ann Phys (Leipzig)
Annalen van het Thijmgenootschap [*A publication*] .... AnnThijm
Annalen van het Thijmgenootschap [*A publication*] .... AThijmG
Annalen der Vereeniging tot het Hevorderen van de Beoefening der Wetenschap Onder de Katholieken in Nederland [*A publication*] .... AVBWKN
Annalen des Vereins fuer Nassauische Altertumskunde und Geschichtsforschung [*A publication*] .... AVNAG
Annalen des Vereins fuer Nassauische Altertumskunde und Geschichtsforschung [*A publication*] .... AVNAKGF
Annales de l'Abeille (Paris) [*A publication*] .... Ann Abeille (Paris)
Annales. Academiae Medicae Gedanensis [*A publication*] .... Ann Acad Med Gedanensis
Annales. Academiae Medicae Lodzensis [*A publication*] .... Ann Acad Med Lodz
Annales. Academiae Medicae Lodzensis. Suplement [*A publication*] .... Ann Acad Med Lodz Supl
Annales. Academiae Medicae Stetinensis [*A publication*] .... Ann Acad Med Stetin
Annales. Academiae Medicae Stetinensis. Suplement [*A publication*] .... Ann Acad Med Stetin Supl
Annales. Academiae Regiae Scientiarum Upsaliensis [*A publication*] .... Ann Acad Regiae Sci Ups
Annales. Academiae Scientiarum Fennicae [*A publication*] .... AASF
Annales. Academiae Scientiarum Fennicae [*A publication*] .... Ann Ac Fenn
Annales. Academiae Scientiarum Fennicae. Series A-I (Mathematica) [*A publication*] .... Ann Acad Sci Fenn A I
Annales. Academiae Scientiarum Fennicae. Series A-I (Mathematica) [*A publication*] .... Ann Acad Sci Fenn Ser A I
Annales. Academiae Scientiarum Fennicae. Series A-II (Chemica) [*A publication*] .... Ann Acad Sci Fenn A II
Annales. Academiae Scientiarum Fennicae. Series A-II (Chemica) [*A publication*] .... Ann Acad Sci Fenn Ser A II
Annales. Academiae Scientiarum Fennicae. Series A-II (Chemica) [*A publication*] .... Ann Acad Sci Fenn Ser A II Chem
Annales. Academiae Scientiarum Fennicae. Series A-III (Geologica-Geographica) [*A publication*] .... Ann Acad Sci Fenn Ser A III
Annales. Academiae Scientiarum Fennicae. Series A-IV (Biologia) [*A publication*] .... Ann Acad Sci Fenn (Biol)
Annales. Academiae Scientiarum Fennicae. Series A-IV (Biologia) [*A publication*] .... Ann Acad Sci Fenn Ser A IV
Annales. Academiae Scientiarum Fennicae. Series A-IV (Biologia) [*A publication*] .... Ann Acad Sci Fenn Ser A IV Biol
Annales. Academiae Scientiarum Fennicae. Series A-V (Medica) [*A publication*] .... Ann Acad Sci Fenn (Med)
Annales. Academiae Scientiarum Fennicae. Series A-V (Medica) [*A publication*] .... Ann Acad Sci Fenn Ser A V
Annales. Academiae Scientiarum Fennicae. Series A-V (Medica) [*A publication*] .... Ann Acad Sci Fenn Ser A V Med
Annales. Academiae Scientiarum Fennicae. Series A-V (Medica-Anthropologica) [*A publication*] .... Ann Acad Sci Fenn Ser A-V Med-Anthropol
Annales. Academiae Scientiarum Fennicae. Series A-VI (Physica) [*A publication*] .... Ann Acad Sci Fenn A VI
Annales. Academiae Scientiarum Fennicae. Series A-VI (Physica) [*A publication*] .... Ann Acad Sci Fenn Ser A VI
Annales. Academie Royale d'Archeologie de Belgique [*A publication*] .... AAAB
Annales. Academie Royale d'Archeologie de Belgique [*A publication*] .... AABAn
Annales. Academie Royale d'Archeologie de Belgique [*A publication*] .... AARAB
Annales. Academie des Sciences de Russie [*A publication*] .... AAR
Annales. ACFAS [*Association Canadienne Francaise pour l'Avancement des Sciences*] [*A publication*] .... Ann ACFAS
Annales Africaines [*A publication*] .... A Afr
Annales Agriculturae Fenniae [*A publication*] .... Ann Agr Fenn
Annales Agriculturae Fenniae [*A publication*] .... Ann Agric Fenn
Annales Agriculturae Fenniae [*A publication*] .... Annls Agric Fenn
Annales Agriculturae Fenniae. Supplementum [*A publication*] .... Suppl Annls Agric Fenn
Annales Agronomiques [*A publication*] .... Ann Agron
Annales Agronomiques [*A publication*] .... Annls Agron
Annales Agronomiques (Paris) [*A publication*] .... Ann Agron (Paris)
Annales Algeriennes de Chirurgie [*A publication*] .... Ann Alger Chir
Annales de l'Amelioration des Plantes [*Paris*] [*A publication*] .... Ann Amelior Plantes
Annales de l'Amelioration des Plantes [*Paris*] [*A publication*] .... Ann A Plant
Annales de l'Amelioration des Plantes (Paris) [*A publication*] .... Ann Amelior Plant (Paris)
Annales d'Anatomie Pathologique [*Paris*] [*A publication*] .... Ann Anat Pathol
Annales d'Anatomie Pathologique (Paris) [*A publication*] .... Ann Anat Pathol (Paris)
Annales de l'Anesthesiologie Francaise [*A publication*] .... Ann Anesthesiol Fr
Annales Archeologiques [*A publication*] .... Ann Arch
Annales Archeologiques de Syrie [*A publication*] .... AArchSyr
Annales. Association Internationale pour le Calcul Analogique [*A publication*] .... Ann Ass Int Calcul Analogique
Annales. Association Internationale pour le Calcul Analogique [*A publication*] .... Ann Assoc Int Calcul Analogique
Annales. Belgische Vereniging voor Tropische Geneeskunde [*A publication*] .... Ann Belg Ver Trop Geneeskd
Annales de Biologie Animale, Biochimie, et Biophysique [*A publication*] .... Ann Biol An
Annales de Biologie Animale, Biochimie, et Biophysique [*A publication*] .... Ann Biol Anim Biochim Biophys
Annales de Biologie Clinique [*Paris*] [*A publication*] .... Ann Biol Cl
Annales de Biologie Clinique (Paris) [*A publication*] .... Ann Biol Clin (Paris)
Annales Biologiques [*A publication*] .... Ann Biol
Annales Bogoriensis [*A publication*] .... Ann Bogor
Annales Botanici Fennici [*A publication*] .... Ann Bot Fenn
Annales Botanici Societatis Zoologicae Botanicae Fennicae "Vanamo" [*A publication*] .... Ann Bot Soc Zool Bot Fenn "Vanamo"
Annales de Bourgogne [*A publication*] .... ABourg
Annales de Bourgogne [*A publication*] .... AnB
Annales de Bourgogne [*A publication*] .... AnnBourg
Annales de Bourgogne [*A publication*] .... Ann Bourgogne
Annales de Bretagne [*Later, Annales de Bretagne et des Pays de l'Ouest*] [*A publication*] .... ABret
Annales de Bretagne [*Later, Annales de Bretagne et des Pays de l'Ouest*] [*A publication*] .... AnBr
Annales de Bretagne [*Later, Annales de Bretagne et des Pays de l'Ouest*] [*A publication*] .... AnBret
Annales de Bretagne [*Later, Annales de Bretagne et des Pays de l'Ouest*] [*A publication*] .... Ann de Bret
Annales de Bretagne [*Later, Annales de Bretagne et des Pays de l'Ouest*] [*A publication*] .... AnnBret

Annales de Bretagne et des Pays de l'Ouest [*A publication*] ... ABr
Annales de Cardiologie et d'Angeiologie [*A publication*] ... Ann Card An
Annales de Cardiologie et d'Angeiologie [*A publication*] ... Ann Cardiol Angeiol
Annales. Centre d'Etude des Religions [*A publication*] ... ACER
Annales. Centre de Recherches Agronomiques de Bambey au Senegal [*A publication*] ... Annls Cent Rech Agron Bambey
Annales. Centre Universitaire Mediterraneen de Nice [*A publication*] ... ACUM
Annales. Centre Universitaire de Nice [*A publication*] ... ACUN
Annales. Cercle Archeologique du Canton de Soignies [*A publication*] ... ACACS
Annales. Cercle Archeologique d'Enghien [*A publication*] ... ACAE
Annales. Cercle Archeologique de Mons [*A publication*] ... ACAM
Annales. Cercle Archeologique du Pays de Waes [*A publication*] ... AAW
Annales. Cercle Archeologique du Pays de Waes [*A publication*] ... ACAPW
Annales. Cercle Hutois des Sciences et Beaux-Arts [*A publication*] ... ACHSB
Annales de Chimie (Paris, France) [*A publication*] ... Ann Chim Fr
Annales de Chimie (Paris, France) [*A publication*] ... Ann Chim (Paris)
Annales Chirurgiae et Gynaecologiae Fenniae [*Helsinki*] [*A publication*] ... Ann Chir Gy
Annales Chirurgiae et Gynaecologiae Fenniae [*Helsinki*] [*A publication*] ... Ann Chir Gynaecol
Annales Chirurgiae et Gynaecologiae Fenniae [*Helsinki*] [*A publication*] ... Ann Chir Gynaecol Fenn
Annales Chirurgiae et Gynaecologiae Fenniae. Supplementum [*Helsinki*] [*A publication*] ... Ann Chir Gynaecol Fenn Suppl
Annales Chirurgiae et Gynaecologiae Fenniae. Supplementum [*Helsinki*] [*A publication*] ... Ann Chir Gynaecol Suppl
Annales de Chirurgie [*A publication*] ... Ann Chir
Annales de Chirurgie Infantile [*A publication*] ... Ann Chir In
Annales de Chirurgie Infantile [*A publication*] ... Ann Chir Infant
Annales de Chirurgie (Paris) [*A publication*] ... Ann Chir (Paris)
Annales de Chirurgie Plastique [*A publication*] ... Ann Chir Pl
Annales de Chirurgie Plastique [*A publication*] ... Ann Chir Plast
Annales de Chirurgie Thoracique et Cardio-Vasculaire [*A publication*] ... Ann Chir Thorac Cardio-Vasc
Annales. College Royal des Medecins et Chirurgiens du Canada [*A publication*] ... Ann Coll R Med Chir Can
Annales. Comite Flamand de France [*A publication*] ... ACFF
Annales-Conferencia [*A publication*] ... AC
Annales Cryptogamici et Phytopathologici [*A publication*] ... Ann Cryptogam Phytopathol
Annales de Demographie Historique [*A publication*] ... Ann Dem Hist
Annales de Dermatologie et de Syphiligraphie [*Later, Annales de Dermatologie et de Venereologie*] [*A publication*] ... Ann Dermatol Syphiligr
Annales de Dermatologie et de Syphiligraphie [*Later, Annales de Dermatologie et de Venereologie*] [*A publication*] ... Ann Der Syp
Annales de Dermatologie et de Venereologie [*A publication*] ... Ann Dermatol Venereol
Annales de la Direction des Etudes et de l'Equipement. Service d'Exploitation Industrielle des Tabacs et des Allumettes [*A publication*] ... Annls SEITA
Annales de Droit [*A publication*] ... A Dr
Annales de Droit International Medical [*A publication*] ... Ann Droit Int Med
Annales. Ecole des Hautes-Etudes de Gand [*A publication*] ... AEHEG
Annales. Ecole Nationale d'Agriculture d'Alger [*A publication*] ... Ann Ecole Nat Agr Alger
Annales. Ecole Nationale Superieure Agronomique [*A publication*] ... Ann Ecole Nat Super Agron
Annales. Ecole Nationale Superieure de Mecanique (Nantes) [*A publication*] ... Ann Ecole Nat Sup Mec (Nantes)
Annales d'Economie Politique [*A publication*] ... A Econ Polit
Annales de l'Economie Publique, Sociale, et Cooperative [*A publication*] ... A Econ Publ Soc Coop
Annales d'Economie et de Sociologie Rurales [*A publication*] ... Ann Econ So
Annales: Economies, Societes, Civilisations [*A publication*] ... AESC
Annales: Economies, Societes, Civilisations [*A publication*] ... Annales-ESC
Annales Economiques (Clermont) [*A publication*] ... A Econ (Clermont)
Annales d'Embryologie et de Morphogenese [*A publication*] ... Ann Embryol Morphog
Annales d'Endocrinologie [*Paris*] [*A publication*] ... Ann Endocr
Annales d'Endocrinologie [*Paris*] [*A publication*] ... Ann Endocrinol
Annales d'Endocrinologie (Paris) [*A publication*] ... Ann Endocrinol (Paris)
Annales Entomologici Fennici [*A publication*] ... Ann Ent Fenn
Annales Entomologici Fennici [*A publication*] ... Ann Entomol Fenn
Annales des Epiphyties [*Paris*] [*A publication*] ... Ann Epiphyt
Annales des Epiphyties (Paris) [*A publication*] ... Ann Epiphyt (Paris)
Annales des Epiphyties et de Phytogenetique [*Paris*] [*A publication*] ... Ann Epiphyt Phytogenet
Annales des Epiphyties et de Phytogenetique [*Paris*] [*A publication*] ... Annls Epiphyt
Annales de l'Est [*A publication*] ... AE
Annales de l'Est [*A publication*] ... Ann Est
Annales de l'Est et du Nord [*A publication*] ... AEN
Annales de l'Est et du Nord [*A publication*] ... AnE
Annales de l'Est et du Nord [*A publication*] ... AnEN
Annales d'Esthetique [*A publication*] ... Ann Esth
Annales d'Ethiopie [*A publication*] ... AnnEth
Annales d'Etudes Internationales [*A publication*] ... A Et Int
Annales pro Experimentis Foresticis [*A publication*] ... Ann Exp For
Annales. Faculdade de Medicina de Sao Paulo [*A publication*] ... Ann Fac Med S Paulo
Annales. Faculte de Droit de Liege [*A publication*] ... A Fac Dr Liege
Annales. Faculte de Droit de Lyon [*A publication*] ... A Fac Dr Lyon
Annales. Faculte de Droit et de Science Politique (Clermont) [*A publication*] ... A Fac Dr Sci Polit (Clermont)
Annales. Faculte des Lettres d'Aix [*A publication*] ... AFLA
Annales. Faculte des Lettres d'Aix-en-Provence [*A publication*] ... ALA
Annales. Faculte des Lettres de Besancon [*A publication*] ... ALB
Annales. Faculte des Lettres et Sciences Humaines de Nice [*A publication*] ... AFLNice
Annales. Faculte des Lettres et Sciences Humaines de l'Universite de Dakar [*A publication*] ... AFLD
Annales. Faculte des Lettres et Sciences Humaines de Yaounde [*A publication*] ... AFLSHY
Annales. Faculte des Lettres de Toulouse [*A publication*] ... ALT
Annales. Faculte des Sciences du Cameroun [*A publication*] ... Ann Fac Sci Cameroun
Annales. Faculte des Sciences de Marseille [*A publication*] ... Ann Fac Sci Mars
Annales. Faculte des Sciences. Section Biologie, Chimie, et Sciences de la Terre (Universite Nationale du Zaire) [*A publication*] ... Ann Fac Sci Sect Biol Chim Sci Terre (Univ Natl Zaire)
Annales. Faculte des Sciences. Universite de Dakar [*A publication*] ... Ann Fac Sci Univ Dakar
Annales. Faculte des Sciences. Universite de Toulouse [*A publication*] ... Ann Fac Sci Univ Toulouse
Annales. Faculte des Sciences de Yaounde [*A publication*] ... Ann Fac Sci Yaounde
Annales des Falsifications et de l'Expertise Chimique [*A publication*] ... Ann Falsif Expert Chim
Annales des Falsifications et de l'Expertise Chimique [*A publication*] ... Ann Falsif Expertise Chim
Annales des Falsifications et des Fraudes [*Later, Annales des Falsifications et de l'Expertise Chimique*] [*A publication*] ... Ann Falsif Fraudes
Annales. Fondation Louis de Broglie [*A publication*] ... Ann Fond Louis de Broglie
Annales Fonds Maeterlinck [*A publication*] ... AFM
Annales Forestales (Zagreb) [*A publication*] ... Ann For (Zagreb)
Annales Francaises de Chronometrie et de Micromecanique [*A publication*] ... Ann Fr Chronom Micromec
Annales de Gastroenterologie et d'Hepatologie [*A publication*] ... Ann Gastro
Annales de Gastroenterologie et d'Hepatologie [*A publication*] ... Ann Gastroenterol Hepatol
Annales de Gembloux [*A publication*] ... Ann Gembloux
Annales de Gembloux [*A publication*] ... Annls Gembloux
Annales de Genetique [*A publication*] ... Ann Genet
Annales de Genetique et de Selection Animale [*A publication*] ... Ann Genet Sel Anim
Annales de Geographie [*A publication*] ... A Geogr
Annales de Geographie [*A publication*] ... An Geog
Annales de Geographie [*A publication*] ... Ann Geog
Annales de Geographie [*A publication*] ... Ann Geogr
Annales de Geologie et de Paleontologie [*A publication*] ... An G Paleont
Annales Geologiques de Madagascar [*A publication*] ... Ann Geol Madagascar
Annales Geologiques de la Peninsule Balkanique [*A publication*] ... Ann Geol Peninsule Balk
Annales Geologiques. Service des Mines (Madagascar) [*A publication*] ... Ann Geol Serv Mines (Madagascar)
Annales de Geophysique [*A publication*] ... Ann Geophys
Annales Guebhard [*A publication*] ... Ann Guebhard
Annales d'Histochimie [*A publication*] ... Ann Histoch
Annales d'Histochimie [*A publication*] ... Ann Histochim
Annales d'Histoire Economique [*A publication*] ... AHE
Annales d'Histoire Economique et Sociale [*A publication*] ... AHES
Annales d'Histoire Sociale [*A publication*] ... AHS
Annales d'Histoire Sociale [*A publication*] ... AHSoc
Annales Historico-Naturales. Musei Nationalis Hungarici [*A publication*] ... Ann Hist-Nat Mus Natl Hung
Annales Historiques de la Revolution Francaise [*A publication*] ... AHRF
Annales Homeopathiques Francaises [*A publication*] ... Ann Homeopath Fr
Annales d'Hydrobiologie [*A publication*] ... Ann Hydrob
Annales d'Hydrobiologie [*A publication*] ... Ann Hydrobiol
Annales d'Hygiene de Langue Francaise. Medecine et Nutrition [*A publication*] ... Ann Hyg Lang Fr Med Nutr
Annales d'Hygiene et de Medecine Coloniales [*A publication*] ... Ann Hyg et Med Colon
Annales d'Hygiene Publique et de Medecine Legale [*A publication*] ... Ann Hyg Pub et Med Legale
Annales Immunologiae Hungaricae [*A publication*] ... Ann Immunol Hung
Annales d'Immunologie [*A publication*] ... Ann Immunol
Annales. INSEE [*Institut National de la Statistique et des Etudes Economiques*] [*A publication*] ... Ann INSEE
Annales. Institut Archeologique du Luxembourg [*A publication*] ... AIAL
Annales. Institut d'Etudes Occidentes [*A publication*] ... AnnIEOc

Annales. Institut d'Etudes Occitanes [*A publication*]....AIEO
Annales. Institut d'Etudes Orientales. Faculte des Lettres d'Alger [*A publication*]....AnnIEO
Annales. Institut d'Etudes du Travail et de la Securite Sociale [*A publication*]....A Inst Et Trav Secur Soc
Annales. Institut Experimental du Tabac de Bergerac [*A publication*]....Ann Inst Exp Tabac Bergerac
Annales. Institut Fourier [*A publication*]....Ann I Four
Annales. Institut Francais de Zagreb [*A publication*]....AIF
Annales. Institut Henri Poincare. Section A (Physique Theorique) [*A publication*]....Ann I Hen A
Annales. Institut Henri Poincare. Section A (Physique Theorique) [*A publication*]....Ann Inst Henri Poincare A
Annales. Institut Henri Poincare. Section A (Physique Theorique) [*A publication*]....Ann Inst Henri Poincare Sect A
Annales. Institut Henri Poincare. Section A (Physique Theorique) [*A publication*]....Ann Inst Poincare Sect A
Annales. Institut Henri Poincare. Section B (Calcul des Probabilites et Statistique) [*A publication*]....Ann I Hen B
Annales. Institut Henri Poincare. Section B (Calcul des Probabilites et Statistique) [*A publication*]....Ann Inst Henri Poincare B
Annales. Institut Henri Poincare. Section B (Calcul des Probabilites et Statistique) [*A publication*]....Ann Inst Poincare Sect B
Annales. Institut Michel Pacha [*A publication*]....Ann Inst Michel Pacha
Annales. Institut National Agronomique [*Paris*] [*A publication*]....Ann Inst Nat Agron
Annales. Institut National Agronomique [*Paris*] [*A publication*]....Ann Inst Natl Agron
Annales. Institut National Agronomique (Paris) [*A publication*]....Annls Inst Natn Agron (Paris)
Annales. Institut National de la Recherche Agronomique de Tunisie [*A publication*]....Ann Inst Natl Rech A
Annales. Institut National de la Recherche Agronomique de Tunisie [*A publication*]....Ann Inst Natl Rech Agron Tunis
Annales. Institut National de la Recherche Agronomique de Tunisie [*A publication*]....Annls Inst Natn Rech Agron Tunisie
Annales. Institut National de Recherches Forestieres de Tunisie [*A publication*]....Ann Inst Nat Rech For Tunis
Annales. Institut Oceanographique [*A publication*]....Ann Inst Oceanogr
Annales. Institut Oceanographique [*A publication*]....Ann I Ocean
Annales. Institut Pasteur [*A publication*]....Ann Inst Pasteur
Annales. Institut Pasteur de Lille [*A publication*]....Ann Inst Pasteur Lille
Annales. Institut Pasteur (Paris) [*A publication*]....Ann Inst Pasteur (Paris)
Annales. Institut Pasteur (Paris) [*A publication*]....Annls Inst Pasteur (Paris)
Annales. Institut Phytopathologique. Benaki [*A publication*]....Ann Inst Phytopathol Benaki
Annales. Institut Phytopathologique. Benaki [*A publication*]....Annls Inst Phytopath Benaki
Annales. Institut Superieur de Philosophie [*A publication*]....AISP
Annales. Institut Technique du Batiment et des Travaux Publics [*A publication*]....Ann Inst Tech Batim Trav Publics
Annales. Instituti Biologici (Tihany). Hungaricae Academiae Scientiarum [*A publication*]....Ann Inst Biol (Tihany) Hung Acad Sci
Annales. Instituti Geologici Publici Hungarici [*A publication*]....Ann Inst Geol Publ Hung
Annales Institutorum [*A publication*]....Ann Inst
Annales Institutorum Quae in Urbe Erecta Sunt [*A publication*]....AInst
Annales Internationales de Criminologie [*A publication*]....A Int Criminol
Annales de Kinesitherapie [*A publication*]....Ann Kinesither
Annales Latini Montium Arvernorum. Bulletin du Groupe d'Etudes Latines. Universite de Clermont [*A publication*]....ALMArv
Annales de Limnologie [*A publication*]....Ann Limnol
Annales de Medecine Belge et Etrangere [*A publication*]....Ann de Med Belge
Annales de Medecine et Chirurgie Infantiles [*A publication*]....Ann Med et Chir Inf
Annales de Medecine Interne [*A publication*]....Ann Med In
Annales de Medecine Interne [*A publication*]....Ann Med Intern
Annales de Medecine Legale [*A publication*]....Ann Med Leg
Annales de Medecine et de Pharmacie Coloniales [*A publication*]....Ann Med et Pharm Colon
Annales de Medecine et de Pharmacie de Reims [*A publication*]....Ann Med Pharm Reims
Annales de Medecine de Reims [*A publication*]....Ann Med Reims
Annales de Medecine Veterinaire [*A publication*]....Ann Med Vet
Annales Medicales Belges [*A publication*]....Ann Med Belges
Annales Medicales de Nancy [*A publication*]....Ann Med Nancy
Annales Medicinae Experimentalis et Biologiae Fenniae [*A publication*]....AMEBA
Annales Medicinae Experimentalis et Biologiae Fenniae [*A publication*]....Ann Med Exp Biol Fenn
Annales Medicinae Internae Fenniae [*A publication*]....Ann Med Intern Fenn
Annales Medicinae Militaris Fenniae [*A publication*]....Ann Med Mil Fenn
Annales Medico-Psychologiques [*A publication*]....AM-Ps
Annales Medico-Psychologiques [*A publication*]....AMPYA
Annales Medico-Psychologiques [*A publication*]....Ann Med-Psy
Annales Medico-Psychologiques [*A publication*]....Ann Med-Psychol
Annales de Microbiologie [*Institut Pasteur*] [*Paris*] [*A publication*]....Ann Microb
Annales de Microbiologie (Paris) [*A publication*]....Ann Microbiol (Paris)
Annales du Midi [*Toulouse*] [*A publication*]....AM
Annales du Midi [*Toulouse*] [*A publication*]....AMid
Annales du Midi [*Toulouse*] [*A publication*]....AnM
Annales du Midi [*Toulouse*] [*A publication*]....Ann Midi
Annales du Midi. Revue de la France Meridionale [*A publication*]....A d M
Annales des Mines [*Paris*] [*A publication*]....An Mines
Annales des Mines [*Paris*] [*A publication*]....Ann Mines
Annales des Mines de Belgique [*A publication*]....An M Belgique
Annales des Mines de Belgique [*A publication*]....Annls Mines Belg
Annales des Mines de Belgique [*A publication*]....Ann Mines Belg
Annales des Mines (Paris) [*A publication*]....Annls Mines (Paris)
Annales. Musee Colonial de Marseille [*A publication*]....Ann Mus Colon Mars
Annales. Musee Royal de l'Afrique Centrale [*A publication*]....AMRAC
Annales. Musee Royal de l'Afrique Centrale [*A publication*]....AnnMAfrC
Annales. Musee Royal de l'Afrique Centrale. Serie in Quarto. Zoologie [*A publication*]....Ann Mus R Afr Cent Ser Quarto Zool
Annales. Musee Royal du Congo Belge. Linguistique [*A publication*]....AnnMCB-L
Annales Musei Goulandris [*A publication*]....Ann Mus Goulandris
Annales Musicologiques [*A publication*]....AMu
Annales Musicologiques [*A publication*]....Ann M
Annales de Normandie [*A publication*]....AnN
Annales de Normandie [*A publication*]....AnnNorm
Annales de Normandie [*A publication*]....Ann Normandie
Annales de Normandie; Revue Trimestrielle d'Etudes Regionales [*A publication*]....A Normandie
Annales de la Nutrition et de l'Alimentation [*A publication*]....Ann Nutr Al
Annales de la Nutrition et de l'Alimentation [*A publication*]....Ann Nutr Aliment
Annales de l'Observatoire de Besancon [*A publication*]....Ann Obs Besancon
Annales d'Oculistique [*Paris*] [*A publication*]....Ann Ocul
Annales d'Oculistique [*Paris*] [*A publication*]....Ann Oculist
Annales d'Oculistique (Paris) [*A publication*]....Ann Ocul (Paris)
Annales d'Oto-Laryngologie [*Later, Annales d'Oto-Laryngologie et de Chirurgie Cervico-Faciale*] [*A publication*]....Ann Oto-Laryngol
Annales d'Oto-Laryngologie et de Chirurgie Cervico-Faciale [*A publication*]....Ann Oto-Lar
Annales d'Oto-Laryngologie et de Chirurgie Cervico-Faciale [*A publication*]....Ann Oto-Laryngol Chir Cervico-Fac
Annales d'Oto-Laryngologie et de Chirurgie Cervico-Faciale [*A publication*]....AOCCA
Annales Paediatriae Fenniae [*A publication*]....Ann Paediatr Fenn
Annales Paediatrici [*A publication*]....Ann Paediatr
Annales Paediatrici Japonici. Kioto Universitatis [*A publication*]....Ann Pediatr Jpn Kioto Univ
Annales de Paleontologie [*A publication*]....Ann Paleontol
Annales de Paleontologie [*A publication*]....An Paleont
Annales de Paleontologie Invertebre [*A publication*]....Ann Paleontol Invertebr
Annales de Paleontologie Vertebre [*A publication*]....Ann Paleontol Vertebr
Annales de Parasitologie Humaine et Comparee [*A publication*]....Ann Parasitol
Annales de Parasitologie Humaine et Comparee [*A publication*]....Ann Parasitol Hum Comp
Annales de Pathologie [*A publication*]....Ann Pathol
Annales Paulistas de Medicina e Cirurgia [*A publication*]....Ann Paulist Med e Cirurg
Annales de Pediatrie [*Paris*] [*A publication*]....Ann Pediatr
Annales de Pediatrie (Paris) [*A publication*]....Ann Pediatr (Paris)
Annales Pharmaceutici (Poznan) [*A publication*]....Ann Pharm (Poznan)
Annales Pharmaceutiques Francaises [*A publication*]....Ann Pharm F
Annales Pharmaceutiques Francaises [*A publication*]....Ann Pharm Fr
Annales de la Philosophie Chretienne [*A publication*]....AnPC
Annales de la Philosophie Chretienne [*A publication*]....APC
Annales de Physiologie Vegetale [*Bruxelles*] [*A publication*]....Ann Physiol Veg
Annales de Physiologie Vegetale (Bruxelles) [*A publication*]....Annls Physiol Veg (Brux)
Annales de Physiologie Vegetale (Paris) [*A publication*]....Annls Physiol Veg (Paris)
Annales de Physiologie Vegetale (Paris) [*A publication*]....Ann Physiol Veg (Paris)
Annales de Physiologie Vegetale de l'Universite de Bruxelles [*A publication*]....Ann Physiol Veg Univ Brux
Annales de Physique [*Paris*] [*A publication*]....Ann Physiq
Annales de Physique Biologique et Medicale [*A publication*]....Ann Phys Bi
Annales de Physique Biologique et Medicale [*A publication*]....Ann Phys Biol Med
Annales de Physique (Paris) [*A publication*]....Ann Phys (Paris)
Annales de Phytopathologie [*A publication*]....Ann Phytopath
Annales de Phytopathologie [*A publication*]....Ann Phytopathol
Annales Politiques et Litteraires [*A publication*]....Ann Pol et Litt
Annales Politiques et Litteraires [*A publication*]....APL
Annales Polonici Mathematici [*A publication*]....Ann Polon Math
Annales des Ponts et Chaussees [*A publication*]....Ann Ponts Chaussees
Annales. Prince de Ligne [*A publication*]....APL
Annales Publiees par la Faculte des Lettres et Sciences Humaines de Toulouse [*Via Domitia*] [*A publication*]....AFLToul
Annales Publiees par la Faculte des Lettres de Toulouse [*A publication*]....AFLT

Annales de Radioelectricite [*A publication*]........................... Ann Radioelectr
Annales de Radiologie [*A publication*] ....Ann Radiol
Annales de Radiologie; Medecine Nucleaire [*A publication*] ....
Ann Radiol Med Nucl
Annales de la Recherche Forestiere au Maroc [*A publication*] ....
Ann Rech For Maroc
Annales de Recherches Veterinaires [*A publication*].................Ann Rech Vet
Annales de Saint-Louis des Francais [*A publication*]........................ASLF
Annales de la Science Agronomique [*A publication*] .... Ann Sci Agron
Annales des Sciences Economiques Appliquees [*A publication*] ....
Ann Sci Econ Appl
Annales des Sciences Economiques Appliquees [*A publication*] ....
A Sci Econ Appl
Annales des Sciences Forestieres (Paris) [*A publication*]........................
Ann Sci For (Paris)
Annales des Sciences Geologiques [*A publication*] .... An Sc Geol
Annales des Sciences Naturelles [*A publication*] .... Ann Sc Nat
Annales des Sciences Naturelles (A) Botanique [*A publication*] ....
Ann Sci Nat Bot
Annales des Sciences Naturelles (B) Zoologie [*A publication*] ....
Ann Sci Nat Zool
Annales des Sciences Naturelles. Botanique et Biologie
Vegetale [*A publication*]....................................Ann Sci Nat Bot Biol Veg
Annales des Sciences Naturelles. Botanique et Biologie
Vegetale [*A publication*]................................ Ann Sci Natur Bot Biol Veg
Annales des Sciences Naturelles. Zoologie [*A publication*] ....
Ann Sc Nat Zool
Annales des Sciences Naturelles. Zoologie [*A publication*].... An Sc Nat Zool
Annales des Sciences Naturelles. Zoologie et Biologie Animale
[*A publication*]................................... Ann Sci Nat Zool Biol Anim
Annales Scientifiques. Ecole Normale Superieure [*A
publication*] .... Ann Sci Ec
Annales Scientifiques. Ecole Normale Superieure [*A
publication*]................................... Ann Sci Ecole Norm Sup
Annales Scientifiques. Universite de Besancon. Botanique [*A
publication*] .... Ann Sci Univ Besancon Bot
Annales Scientifiques. Universite de Besancon. Geologie [*A
publication*]................................Ann Sci Univ Besancon Geol
Annales Scientifiques. Universite de Besancon. Mathematiques
[*A publication*]............................Ann Sci Univ Besancon Math
Annales Scientifiques. Universite de Besancon. Mecanique et
Physique Theorique [*A publication*] ....
Ann Sci Univ Besancon Mec Phys Theor
Annales Scientifiques. Universite de Besancon. Medecine [*A
publication*] ....Ann Sci Univ Besancon Med
Annales Scientifiques. Universite de Besancon. Physiologie et
Biologie Animale [*A publication*] ....
Ann Sci Univ Besancon Physiol Biol Anim
Annales Scientifiques. Universite de Besancon. Zoologie [*A
publication*]....................................Ann Sci Univ Besancon Zool
Annales Scientifiques. Universite de Besancon. Zoologie et
Physiologie [*A publication*] ....Ann Sci Univ Besancon Zool Physiol
Annales Scientifiques. Universite de Besancon. Zoologie,
Physiologie, et Biologie Animale [*A publication*]......................
Ann Sci Univ Besancon Zool Physiol Biol Anim
Annales Scientifiques. Universite de Clermont. Serie
Mathematique [*A publication*]............Ann Sci Univ Clermont Math
Annales Scientifiques. Universite de Reims et de l'ARERS
[*Association Regionale pour l'Etude et la Recherche
Scientifiques*] [*A publication*] .... Ann Sci Univ Reims ARERS
Annales. Section Dendrologique. Societe Botanique de Pologne
[*A publication*] .... Ann Sect Dendrol Soc Bot Pol
Annales. Seminario de Metafisica [*A publication*]............ Ann Seminar Metaf
Annales. Service des Antiquites de l'Egypte [*A publication*]...........Ann Serv
Annales. Service des Antiquites de l'Egypte [*A publication*].................. ASAE
Annales. Service Archeologique de l'Iran [*A publication*]..................... ASAI
Annales. Service Botanique et Agronomique de Tunisie [*A
publication*]....................Ann Serv Bot Agron Tunis
Annales Silesiae [*A publication*] ....AnnS
Annales. Societa Retorumantscha [*A publication*]....................AnnSR
Annales. Societa Retorumantscha [*A publication*]....................ASR
Annales. Societe d'Archeologie de Bruxelles [*A publication*]...............AnAB
Annales. Societe d'Archeologie de Bruxelles [*A publication*]...............ASAB
Annales. Societe Archeologique de l'Arrondissement de
Nivelles [*A publication*] .... ASAAN
Annales. Societe Archeologique de Namur [*A publication*]..................ASAN
Annales. Societe Archeologique de Namur [*A publication*]..................
A Soc Arch Namur
Annales. Societe Belge de Medecine Tropicale [*A publication*].....................
Ann Soc Belge Med Trop
Annales. Societe d'Emulation de Bruges [*A publication*].....................ASEB
Annales. Societe d'Emulation pour l'Etude de l'Histoire et des
Antiquites de Flandre [*A publication*]....................................... ASEF
Annales. Societe Entomologique de France [*A publication*]....... Ann Soc Ent
Annales. Societe Entomologique de France [*A publication*].....................
Ann Soc Entomol Fr
Annales. Societe Entomologique du Quebec [*A publication*]....................
Ann Soc Entomol Que
Annales. Societe Geologique de Belgique [*A publication*].....................
Ann Soc Geol Belg

Annales. Societe Geologique de Belgique. Memoires [*A
publication*]........................... Ann Soc Geol Belg Mem
Annales. Societe Geologique du Nord [*A publication*] ..... Ann Soc Geol Nord
Annales. Societe d'Histoire et d'Archeologie de Gand [*A
publication*]... AHAG
Annales. Societe d'Histoire et d'Archeologie de Gand [*A
publication*].. ASHAG
Annales. Societe Historique et Archeologique de Tournai [*A
publication*]..ASHAT
Annales. Societe Jean-Jacques Rousseau [*A publication*] ....AJJR
Annales. Societe Linneenne de Lyon [*A publication*]........ Ann Soc Linn Lyon
Annales. Societe Medico-Chirurgicale de Bruges [*A publication*] ....
Ann Soc Med-Chir Bruges
Annales. Societe Royale d'Archeologie de Bruxelles [*A
publication*]... ASRAB
Annales. Societe Royale d'Histoire et d'Archeologie de Tournai
[*A publication*]..................................... ASRHAT
Annales. Societe Royale Zoologique de Belgique [*A publication*]..................
Ann Soc R Zool Belg
Annales. Societe des Sciences Naturelles de la Charente-
Maritime [*A publication*]..........................Ann Soc Sci Nat Charente-Marit
Annales. Societe Scientifique de Bruxelles [*A publication*]......................
Ann Soc Sci Bruxelles
Annales. Societe Scientifique de Bruxelles. Serie B. Sciences
Physiques et Naturelles [*A publication*] ....
Ann Soc Scient Bruxelles S B Sc Phys Nat
Annales. Societe Scientifique de Bruxelles. Serie C. Sciences
Medicales [*A publication*].............. Ann Soc Scient Bruxelles S C Sci Med
Annales. Societe Scientifique de Bruxelles. Serie I [*A
publication*]...Ann Brux I
Annales. Societe Scientifique de Bruxelles. Serie I [*A
publication*]................................... Ann Soc Sci Brux Ser I
Annales. Societe Scientifique Litteraire de Cannes et de
l'Arrondissement de Grasse [*A publication*]...........A Soc Sci Litt Cannes
Annales. Societes Belges de Medecine Tropicale, de
Parasitologie, et de Mycologie [*A publication*] ....
Ann Soc Belg Med Trop Parasitol Mycol
Annales Sociologiques [*A publication*] ....ASoc
Annales de Speleologie [*A publication*] .... Ann Speleol
Annales. Station Biologique de Besse-En-Chandesse [*A
publication*]....................Ann Stn Biol Besse-En-Chandesse
Annales. Station Centrale d'Hydrobiologie Appliquee [*A
publication*]....................Ann Stn Cent Hydrobiol Appl
Annales du Tabac. Section 2 [*A publication*] ....Ann Tab Sect 2
Annales de Technologie Agricole [*Paris*] [*A publication*]........... Ann Tec Agr
Annales de Technologie Agricole [*Paris*] [*A publication*]......Ann Technol Agr
Annales de Technologie Agricole (Paris) [*A publication*] ....
Ann Technol Agric (Paris)
Annales des Telecommunications [*A publication*] .... Ann Telecom
Annales des Telecommunications [*A publication*] .... Ann Telecommun
Annales des Travaux Publics de Belgique [*A publication*].....................
Ann Trav Publics Belg
Annales des Travaux Publics de Belgique [*A publication*].....................
An Trav Pub Belgique
Annales. Universitatis Mariae Curie-Sklodowska [*A publication*]..................
Annls Univ Mariae Curie-Sklodowska
Annales. Universitatis Mariae Curie-Sklodowska [*A publication*]..................
A Univ M Curie-Sklodowska
Annales. Universitatis Mariae Curie-Sklodowska. Sectio A.
Mathematica [*A publication*]...
Ann Univ Mariae Curie-Sklodowska Sect A
Annales. Universitatis Mariae Curie-Sklodowska. Sectio C.
Biologia [*A publication*] ....Ann Univ Mariae Curie-Sklodowska Sect C
Annales. Universitatis Mariae Curie-Sklodowska. Sectio C.
Biologia [*A publication*]
Ann Univ Mariae Curie-Sklodowska Sect C Biol
Annales. Universitatis Mariae Curie-Sklodowska. Sectio D.
Medicina [*A publication*] .... Ann Univ Mariae Curie-Sklodowska Med
Annales. Universitatis Mariae Curie-Sklodowska. Sectio DD.
Medicina Veterinaria [*A publication*].....................................
Ann Univ Mariae Curie-Sklodowska Sect DD
Annales. Universitatis Mariae Curie-Sklodowska. Sectio EE.
Agraria [*A publication*] ....Ann Univ Mariae Curie-Sklodowska Sect EE
Annales. Universitatis Mariae Curie-Sklodowska. Section AA.
Physics and Chemistry [*A publication*] ....
Ann Univ M Curie-Sklodowska Sect AA
Annales. Universitatis Mariae Curie-Sklodowska. Section AAA
(Physica) [*A publication*]...
Ann Univ M Curie-Sklodowska Sect AAA (Phys)
Annales. Universitatis Mariae Curie-Sklodowska. Section C.
Biology [*A publication*].............Ann Univ M Curie-Sklodowska Sect C
Annales. Universitatis Mariae Curie-Sklodowska. Section D.
Medicine [*A publication*] ....Ann Univ M Curie-Sklodowska Sect D
Annales. Universitatis Mariae Curie-Sklodowska. Section F.
Nauki Filozoficzne i Humanistyczne [*A publication*] .... AUMCS
Annales. Universitatis Saraviensis [*A publication*]................................ AUS
Annales. Universitatis Saraviensis. Mathematisch-
Naturwissenschaftliche Fakultaet [*A publication*]..........................
Ann Univ Sarav Math-Natur Fak
Annales. Universitatis Saraviensis. Medizin [*A publication*]......................
Ann Univ Saraviensis Med

Annales. Universitatis Saraviensis. Medizin [*A publication*].........................
Ann Univ Sarav Med

Annales. Universitatis Saraviensis. Philosophie- Lettres [*A publication*]..AnnUS

Annales. Universitatis Saraviensis. Reihe. Mathematisch-Naturwissenschaftliche Fakultaet [*A publication*]..................
Ann Univ Sarav Reihe Math-Naturwiss Fak

Annales. Universitatis Scientiarum Budapestensis de Rolando Eoetvoes Nominatae [*A publication*]........................ AUB

Annales. Universitatis Scientiarum Budapestensis de Rolando Eoetvoes Nominatae. Sectio Philologica [*A publication*]..............AUBud

Annales. Universitatis Turkuensis [*A publication*]................ AUT

Annales. Universitatis Turkuensis. Series A-I. Astronomica-Chemica-Physica-Mathematica [*A publication*]........................
Ann Univ Turku Ser A I

Annales. Universitatis Turkuensis. Series A-II. Biologica-Geographica [*A publication*]................ Ann Univ Turk Ser A II Biol-Geogr

Annales. Universitatis Turkuensis. Series A-II. Biologica-Geographica [*A publication*]................ Ann Univ Turku Ser A II

Annales. Universite d'Abidjan [*A publication*] ....As U A

Annales. Universite d'Abidjan. Ethnosociologie [*A publication*] ....
A Univ Abidjan Ethnosociologie

Annales. Universite d'Abidjan. Histoire [*A publication*] ....
A Univ Abidjan Histoire

Annales. Universite d'Abidjan. Lettres [*A publication*] ....
A Univ Abidjan Lettres

Annales. Universite d'Abidjan. Linguistique [*A publication*] ....
A Univ Abidjan Linguist

Annales. Universite d'Abidjan. Medecine [*A publication*]......................
Ann Univ Abidjan Med

Annales. Universite d'Abidjan. Serie A. Droit [*A publication*] ....
A Univ Abidjan Ser A Dr

Annales. Universite d'Abidjan. Serie B. Medecine [*A publication*]....................
Ann Univ Abidjan Ser B Med

Annales. Universite d'Abidjan. Serie C. Sciences [*A publication*].....................
Ann Univ Abidjan Ser C Sci

Annales. Universite d'Abidjan. Serie E. Ecologie [*A publication*]....................
Ann Univ Abidjan Ser E Ecol

Annales. Universite et de l'ARERS [*Association Regionale pour l'Etude et la Recherche Scientifiques*] [*A publication*] .... Ann Univ ARERS

Annales. Universite de Besancon [*A publication*]................ AUB

Annales. Universite de Brazzaville [*A publication*]............................ A d U B

Annales. Universite de Brazzaville. Serie C. Sciences [*A publication*]................Ann Univ Brazzaville Ser C Sci

Annales. Universite de Grenoble [*A publication*]....................AnUG

Annales. Universite de Grenoble [*A publication*].....................AUG

Annales. Universite de Lyons [*A publication*] ....AnUL

Annales. Universite de Lyons [*A publication*] ....AUL

Annales. Universite de Madagascar. Serie de Droit et des Sciences Economiques [*A publication*]....................
A Univ Madagascar Ser Dr Sci Econ

Annales. Universite de Madagascar. Serie Sciences de la Nature et Mathematiques [*A publication*] ....
Ann Univ Madagascar Ser Sci Nature Math

Annales. Universite de Madagascar. Series Science de la Nature et Mathematiques [*A publication*] ....
Ann Univ Madagascar Ser Sci Nat Math

Annales. Universite de Montpellier. Supplement Scientifique. Serie Botanique [*A publication*] .... Ann Univ Montp Suppl Sci Ser Bot

Annales. Universite de Paris [*A publication*]....................Ann Paris

Annales. Universite de Paris [*A publication*]....................AnnUP

Annales. Universite de Paris [*A publication*]....................AUP

Annales. Universite des Sciences Sociales de Toulouse [*A publication*]....................A Univ Sci Soc Toulouse

Annales d'Urologie [*A publication*]....................Ann Urol

Annales Valaisannes [*A publication*] ....AV

Annales Zoologici Fennici [*A publication*]....................Ann Zool Fenn

Annales Zoologici. Societatis Zoologicae-Botanicae Fennicae "Vanamo" [*A publication*] ....Ann Zool Soc Zool-Bot Fenn "Vanamo"

Annales Zoologici (Warsaw) [*A publication*]....................Ann Zool (Warsaw)

Annales de Zoologie - Ecologie Animale [*A publication*]....................
Ann Zool Ecol Anim

Annales de Zootechnie [*A publication*] ....Ann Zootech

Annales de Zootechnie. Institut National de la Recherche Agronomique [*A publication*].............. Ann Zootech Inst Nat Rech Agron

Annali. Accademia Italiana de Scienze Forestali [*A publication*] ....
Ann Accad Ital Sci For

Annali di Botanica (Rome) [*A publication*]....................Ann Bot (Rome)

Annali di Ca' Foscari [*A publication*] ....ACF

Annali di Chimica [*A publication*] ....Ann Chim

Annali di Chimica (Rome) [*A publication*]....................Ann Chim (Rome)

Annali. Facolta di Agraria (Bari) [*A publication*]....................A Fac Agrar (Bari)

Annali. Facolta di Agraria (Milano) [*A publication*]........ A Fac Agrar (Milano)

Annali. Facolta di Agraria (Perugia) [*A publication*].....Ann Fac Agr (Perugia)

Annali. Facolta di Agraria di Portici della Reale Universita di Napoli [*A publication*] ....Annali Fac Agr Portici

Annali. Facolta di Agraria. Universita di Bari [*A publication*]....................
Annali Fac Agr Univ Bari

Annali. Facolta di Agraria. Universita di Bari [*A publication*]....................
Ann Fac Agrar Univ Bari

Annali. Facolta di Agraria. Universita Cattolica del Sacro Cuore [*A publication*]...............................Ann Fac Agrar Univ Catt Sacro Cuore

Annali. Facolta di Agraria. Universita Cattolica del Sacro Cuore (Milan) [*A publication*].........Ann Fac Agr Univ Cattol Sacro Cuore (Milan)

Annali. Facolta di Agraria. Universita di Pisa [*A publication*]....................
Ann Fac Agrar Univ Pisa

Annali. Facolta di Agraria. Universita di Pisa [*A publication*]....................
Ann Fac Agr Univ Pisa

Annali. Facolta di Agraria. Universita degli Studi Milano [*A publication*]....................Ann Fac Agrar Univ Studi Milano

Annali. Facolta di Agraria. Universita degli Studi di Perugia [*A publication*]....................Annali Fac Agr Univ Perugia

Annali. Facolta di Agraria. Universita degli Studi di Perugia [*A publication*]....................Ann Fac Agrar Univ Stud Perugia

Annali. Facolta di Agraria. Universita degli Studi di Perugia [*A publication*]....................Ann Fac Agr Univ Studii Perugia

Annali. Facolta di Economia e Commercio (Palermo) [*A publication*]....................A Fac Econ Com (Palermo)

Annali. Facolta di Lettere e Filosofia [*A publication*]....... Ann Fac Lett Filosof

Annali. Facolta di Lettere e Filosofia. Bari Universita [*A publication*] ... AFLB

Annali. Facolta di Lettere, Filosofia, e Magistero. Universita di Cagliari [*A publication*]....................AFLC

Annali. Facolta di Lettere, Filosofia, e Magistero. Universita di Cagliari [*A publication*]....................AUCal

Annali. Facolta di Lettere e Filosofia (Perugia) [*A publication*] .... AFLPer

Annali. Facolta di Lettere e Filosofia. Universita di Bari [*A publication*]....................AFLFB

Annali. Facolta di Lettere e Filosofia. Universita di Macerata [*A publication*]....................AFLFUM

Annali. Facolta di Lettere e Filosofia. Universita di Napoli [*A publication*]....................AFLN

Annali. Facolta di Lettere e Filosofia. Universita di Napoli [*A publication*]....................AUN

Annali. Facolta di Lettere e Filosofia. Universita di Perugia [*A publication*]....................AFLFP

Annali. Facolta di Lettere di Lecce [*A publication*]....................AFLL

Annali. Facolta di Magistero [*University of Palermo*] [*A publication*]....................AFMag

Annali. Facolta di Magistero (Universita di Bari) [*A publication*]........ AFMUB

Annali. Facolta di Magistero (Universita di Lecce) [*A publication*] ....AFML

Annali. Facolta di Medicina e Chirurgia [*A publication*]....................
Ann Fac Med Chirurg

Annali. Facolta di Medicina Veterinaria. Universita degli Studi di Pisa [*A publication*]....................Ann Fac Med Vet Univ Studi Pisa

Annali. Facolta di Medicina Veterinaria. Universita di Torino [*A publication*]....................Ann Fac Med Vet Univ Torino

Annali. Facolta di Science Agrarie. Universita di Napoli. Ser 3 [*A publication*]....................Ann Fac Sci Agr Univ Napoli Ser 3

Annali. Facolta di Science Agrarie. Universita degli Torino [*A publication*]....................Ann Fac Sci Agr Univ Torino

Annali. Facolta di Scienza Politica (Genova) [*A publication*]....................
A Fac Sci Polit (Genova)

Annali. Facolta di Scienze Agrarie. Universita degli Studi di Napoli Portici [*A publication*]....................
Ann Fac Sci Agrar Univ Studi Napoli Portici

Annali. Facolta di Scienze Agrarie. Universita degli Studi di Napoli Portici [*A publication*].... Ann Fac Sci Agr Univ Stud Napoli Portici

Annali di Fitopatologia [*A publication*]....................Ann Fitopatol

Annali. Fondazione Giangiacomo Feltrinelli [*A publication*]....................
A Fond G Feltrinelli

Annali. Fondazione Luigi Einaudi [*A publication*]................A Fond L Einaudi

Annali di Geofisica [*A publication*] ....Annali Geofisica

Annali di Geofisica [*A publication*] ....Ann Geofis

Annali Idrologici [*A publication*] ....Annali Idrol

Annali Idrologici [*A publication*] ....Ann Idrol

Annali d'Igiene [*A publication*] ....Ann Ig

Annali d'Igiene. Sperimentali [*A publication*] ....Ann Ig Sper

Annali. Istituto di Corrispondenza Archeologica [*A publication*] ....AdI

Annali. Istituto Italiano di Numismatica [*A publication*]....................AIIN

Annali. Istituto Sperimentale per l'Assestamento Forestale e per l'Alpicoltura [*A publication*]....................Ann Ist Sper Asses For Alpic

Annali. Istituto Sperimentale per la Cerealicoltura [*A publication*]....................Ann Ist Sper Cerealic

Annali. Istituto Sperimentale per le Colture Foraggere [*A publication*]....................Ann Ist Sper Colt Foraggere

Annali. Istituto Sperimentale per l'Enologia (Asti) [*A publication*]....................
Ann Inst Sper Enol (Asti)

Annali. Istituto Sperimentale per la Floricoltura [*A publication*]....................
Ann Ist Sper Floricolt

Annali. Istituto Sperimentale per la Frutticoltura [*A publication*]....................
Ann Ist Sper Frutticolt

Annali. Istituto Sperimentale per la Selvicoltura [*A publication*]....................
Ann Ist Sper Selvic

Annali. Istituto Sperimentale per lo Studio e la Difesa del Suolo [*A publication*]....................Ann Ist Sper Stud Dif Suolo

Annali. Istituto Sperimentale per il Tabacco [*A publication*]....................
Ann Ist Sper Tab

Annali. Istituto Sperimentale per la Zoologia Agraria [*A publication*]....................Ann Ist Sper Zool Agrar

Annali. Istituto Sperimentale per la Zootecnia [*A publication*]....................
Ann Ist Sper Zootec

Annali. Istituto Sperimentale Zootecnico di Roma [*A publication*] ... Ann Ist Sper Zootec Roma
Annali. Istituto di Studi Danteschi [*A publication*] ... AISD
Annali. Istituto Superiore di Sanita [*A publication*] ... Ann Ist Super Sanita
Annali. Istituto Universitario Orientale (Napoli) [*A publication*] ... AION
Annali. Istituto Universitario Orientale (Napoli) [*A publication*] ... AnnION
Annali. Istituto Universitario Orientale (Napoli) [*A publication*] ... Ann Or (Napoli)
Annali. Istituto Universitario Orientale. Sezione Germanica [*Napoli*] [*A publication*] ... AIUO
Annali. Istituto Universitario Orientale. Sezione Germanica (Napoli) [*A publication*] ... AION-G
Annali. Istituto Universitario Orientale. Sezione Germanica (Napoli) [*A publication*] ... AION-SG
Annali. Istituto Universitario Orientale. Sezione Linguistica (Napoli) [*A publication*] ... AION-L
Annali. Istituto Universitario Orientale. Sezione Linguistica (Napoli) [*A publication*] ... AION-SL
Annali. Istituto Universitario Orientale. Sezione Orientale (Napoli) [*A publication*] ... AION-O
Annali. Istituto Universitario Orientale. Sezione Orientale (Napoli) [*A publication*] ... AION-SO
Annali. Istituto Universitario Orientale. Sezione Romanza (Napoli) [*A publication*] ... AION-R
Annali. Istituto Universitario Orientale. Sezione Romanza (Napoli) [*A publication*] ... AION-SR
Annali. Istituto Universitario Orientale. Sezione Slava (Napoli) [*A publication*] ... AION-S
Annali. Istituto Universitario Orientale. Sezione Slava (Napoli) [*A publication*] ... AION-SS
Annali dell'Isturzione Media [*A publication*] ... AIM
Annali Italiani di Chirurgia [*A publication*] ... Ann Ital Chir
Annali di Laringologia, Otologia, Rinologia, Faringologia [*A publication*] ... Ann Laringol
Annali di Laringologia, Otologia, Rinologia, Faringologia [*A publication*] ... Ann Laringol Otol Rinol Faringol
Annali Lateranensi [*A publication*] ... AL
Annali Lateranensi [*A publication*] ... AnnLat
Annali del Liceo Classico Garibaldi di Palermo [*A publication*] ... ALCGP
Annali Manzoniani [*A publication*] ... AM
Annali di Matematica Pura ed Applicata [*A publication*] ... Ann Mat Pura Appl
Annali di Medicina Navale [*A publication*] ... Ann Med Nav
Annali di Medicina Navale e Coloniale [*A publication*] ... Ann Med Nav e Colon
Annali del Mezzogiorno [*A publication*] ... A Mezzogiorno
Annali di Microbiologia [*A publication*] ... Ann Microbiol
Annali di Microbiologia. Ed. Enzimologia [*A publication*] ... Annali Microbiol
Annali di Microbiologia. Ed. Enzimologia [*A publication*] ... Ann Microbiol Enzimol
Annali. Museo Civico di Storia Naturale "Giacomo Doria" [*A publication*] ... Ann Mus Civ Stor Nat "Giacomo Doria"
Annali di Oftalmologia e Clinica Oculistica [*A publication*] ... Ann Oftalmol Clin Ocul
Annali. Ospedale Maria Vittoria di Torino [*A publication*] ... Ann Osp Maria Vittoria Torino
Annali di Ostetricia, Ginecologia, Medicina Perinatale [*A publication*] ... Ann Ostet Ginecol Med Perinat
Annali. Pontificio Museo Missionario Etnologico (Vatican) [*A publication*] ... Ann Pontif Mus Miss Etnol (Vatican)
Annali della Pubblica Istruzione [*A publication*] ... API
Annali della Pubblica Istruzione [*A publication*] ... A Pubbl Istr
Annali di Radiologia Diagnostica [*A publication*] ... Ann Radiol Diagn
Annali. Reale Scuola Normale Superiore di Pisa. Sezione di Lettere [*A publication*] ... Ann Pisa
Annali. Reale Stazione Chimico-Agraria Sperimentale di Roma [*A publication*] ... Annali Staz Chim-Agr Sper Roma
Annali della Sanita Pubblica [*A publication*] ... Ann Sanita Pubblica
Annali Sclavo [*A publication*] ... Ann Sclavo
Annali. Scuola Normale Superiore di Pisa [*A publication*] ... ASN
Annali. Scuola Normale Superiore di Pisa [*A publication*] ... ASNP
Annali. Scuola Normale Superiore di Pisa [*A publication*] ... ASNSP
Annali. Scuola Normale Superiore di Pisa. Classe di Scienze [*A publication*] ... Ann Scuola Norm Sup Pisa Cl Sci
Annali. Seminario Giuridico di Palermo [*A publication*] ... ASGP
Annali di Sociologia (Milano) [*A publication*] ... A Sociol (Milano)
Annali della Sperimentazione Agraria [*A publication*] ... Annali Sper Agr
Annali della Sperimentazione Agraria [*A publication*] ... Ann Sper Agr
Annali della Sperimentazione Agraria [*A publication*] ... Ann Sper Agrar
Annali. Stazione Chimico-Agraria Sperimentale di Roma. Ser 3 [*A publication*] ... Ann Sta Chim-Agr Sper Roma Ser 3
Annali. Stazione Sperimentale di Risicoltura e delle Colture Irrigue. Vercelli [*A publication*] ... Annali Staz Sper Risicolt Vercelli
Annali di Stomatologia [*Roma*] [*A publication*] ... Ann Stomatol
Annali di Stomatologia (Roma) [*A publication*] ... Ann Stomatol (Roma)
Annali di Storia del Diritto [*A publication*] ... ASD
Annali di Storia Naturale [*A publication*] ... Ann Storia Nat
Annali Triestini [*A publication*] ... AnnTriest
Annali. Universita di Ferrara. Nuovo Serie. Sezione VII. Scienze Matematiche [*A publication*] ... Ann Univ Ferrara Sez VII
Annali. Universita di Ferrara. Sezione I. Ecologia [*A publication*] ... Ann Univ Ferrara Sez I Ecol
Annali. Universita di Ferrara. Sezione III. Biologia Animale [*A publication*] ... Ann Univ Ferrara Sez III Biol Anim
Annali. Universita di Ferrara. Sezione IV. Botanica [*A publication*] ... Ann Univ Ferrara Sez IV Bot
Annali. Universita di Ferrara. Sezione IX. Scienze Geologiche e Paleontologiche [*A publication*] ... Ann Univ Ferrara Sez IX Sci Geol Paleontol
Annali. Universita di Ferrara. Sezione VI. Fisiologia e Chimica Biologica [*A publication*] ... Ann Univ Ferrara Sez VI Fisiol Chim Biol
Annali. Universita di Ferrara. Sezione XI. Farmacologia e Terapia [*A publication*] ... Ann Univ Ferrara Sez XI Farmacol Ter
Annali. Universita di Ferrara. Sezione XIII. Anatomia Comparata [*A publication*] ... Ann Univ Ferrara Sez XIII Anat Comp
Annali. Universita di Lecce [*A publication*] ... AUL
Annali. Universita Toscane [*A publication*] ... AUT
Annals ... ANN
Annals. Academy of Medicine (Singapore) [*A publication*] ... Ann Acad Med (Singapore)
Annals of Agricultural Science (Cairo) [*A publication*] ... Ann Agric Sci (Cairo)
Annals of Agricultural Science. University of A'in Shams [*A publication*] ... Ann Agric Sci Univ A'in Shams
Annals of Agriculture Science [*A publication*] ... Ann Agri Sci
Annals of Allergy [*A publication*] ... Ann Allergy
Annals. American Academy of Political and Social Science [*A publication*] ... AAA
Annals. American Academy of Political and Social Science [*A publication*] ... AAAPSS
Annals. American Academy of Political and Social Science [*A publication*] ... A Amer Acad Polit Soc Sci
Annals. American Academy of Political and Social Science [*A publication*] ... AAPS
Annals. American Academy of Political and Social Science [*A publication*] ... An Am Acad Pol Soc Sci
Annals. American Academy of Political and Social Science [*A publication*] ... Annals Am Acad
Annals. American Academy of Political and Social Science [*A publication*] ... Ann Am Acad
Annals. American Academy of Political and Social Science [*A publication*] ... Ann Amer Acad Polit Soc Sci
Annals. American Academy of Political and Social Science [*A publication*] ... Ann Am Poli
Annals of American Geographers [*A publication*] ... AAG
Annals of Applied Biology [*A publication*] ... Ann Ap Biol
Annals of Applied Biology [*A publication*] ... Ann App Biol
Annals of Applied Biology [*A publication*] ... Ann Appl Biol
Annals of Archaeology and Anthropology (Liverpool) [*A publication*] ... Ann Liv
Annals of Archaeology. University of Liverpool [*A publication*] ... AAL
Annals of Arid Zone [*A publication*] ... Ann Arid Zone
Annals. Association of American Geographers [*A publication*] ... AAAG
Annals. Association of American Geographers [*A publication*] ... A Assoc Amer Geogr
Annals. Association of American Geographers [*A publication*] ... Ann As Am G
Annals. Association of American Geographers [*A publication*] ... Ann Ass Amer Geogr
Annals. Bhandarkar Oriental Research Institute [*A publication*] ... A Bhandarkar Or Res Inst
Annals. Bhandarkar Oriental Research Institute [*A publication*] ... ABORI
Annals. Bhandarkar Oriental Research Institute [*A publication*] ... An Bhand Or Res Inst
Annals. Bhandarkar Oriental Research Institute [*A publication*] ... AnnBhI
Annals of Biochemistry and Experimental Medicine [*Calcutta and New Delhi*] [*A publication*] ... Ann Biochem Exp Med
Annals of Biochemistry and Experimental Medicine (Calcutta and New Delhi) [*A publication*] ... Ann Biochem Exp Med (Calcutta)
Annals of Biomedical Engineering [*A publication*] ... Ann Biomed
Annals of Biomedical Engineering [*A publication*] ... Ann Biomed Eng
Annals of Botany [*A publication*] ... Ann Bot
Annals. Cape Provincial Museums. Natural History [*A publication*] ... Ann Cape Prov Mus Nat Hist
Annals. Carnegie Museum [*A publication*] ... Ann Carnegie Mus
Annals of the CIRP [*A publication*] ... Ann CIRP
Annals of Clinical Biochemistry [*A publication*] ... Ann Clin Biochem
Annals of Clinical and Laboratory Science [*A publication*] ... Ann Clin Lab Sci
Annals of Clinical Research [*A publication*] ... Ann Clin R
Annals of Clinical Research [*A publication*] ... Ann Clin Res
Annals of Clinical Research. Supplement [*A publication*] ... Ann Clin Res Suppl
Annals of Collective Economy [*Later, Annals of Public and Co-Operative Economy*] [*A publication*] ... ACE
Annals. College of Medicine (Mosul) [*A publication*] ... Ann Coll Med (Mosul)
Annals of Dentistry [*A publication*] ... Ann Dent
Annals of Development [*A publication*] ... Ann Dev
Annals of Discrete Mathematics [*Elsevier Book Series*] [*A publication*] ... ADM

Annals of Economic and Social Measurement [*A publication*].......................
A Econ Soc Measurement
Annals of Economic and Social Measurement [*A publication*].......................
Ann Econ Sm
Annals of Emergency Medicine [*A publication*].................... Ann Emerg Med
Annals. Entomological Society of America [*A publication*]....................
Ann Entomol Soc Am
Annals. Entomological Society of America [*A publication*]....................
Ann Entom Soc Am
Annals. Entomological Society of America [*A publication*].......... Ann Ent S A
Annals. Entomological Society of America [*A publication*]....................
Ann Ent Soc Am
Annals. Entomological Society of Quebec [*A publication*]....................
Ann Entomol Soc Que
Annals of Eugenics [*A publication*]..Ann Eugen
Annals of Family Studies [*A publication*] ....A Family Stud
Annals of Human Biology [*A publication*]...............................Ann Hum Bio
Annals of Human Genetics [*A publication*] ....Ann Hum Gen
Annals of Human Genetics [*A publication*] ....Ann Hum Genet
Annals. ICRP [*International Commission on Radiological
Protection*] [*A publication*] ....Ann ICRP
Annals. Indian Academy of Medical Sciences [*A publication*]....................
Ann Indian Acad Med Sci
Annals. Institute of Comparative Studies of Culture [*A
publication*]....................................A Inst Comp Stud Cult
Annals. Institute of Statistical Mathematics [*A publication*].........An In St Ma
Annals. Institute of Statistical Mathematics [*A publication*]...........Ann I Stat
Annals of Internal Medicine [*A publication*]...................................... AIMEA
Annals of Internal Medicine [*A publication*]............................Ann Intern Med
Annals of Internal Medicine [*A publication*]............................Ann Int Med
Annals of Iowa [*A publication*] .... AI
Annals of Iowa [*A publication*] ....Ala
Annals of Iowa [*A publication*] ....AnIowa
Annals of Iowa [*A publication*] ....Ann IA
Annals of Iowa [*A publication*] ....Ann Iowa
Annals. Japan Association for Philosophy of Science [*A
publication*]....................................Ann Japan Assoc Philos Sci
Annals. Japan Association for Philosophy of Science [*A
publication*]....................................Ann Jpn Assoc Philos Sci
Annals of Kentucky Natural History [*A publication*] .....Annals KY Nat History
Annals of Kentucky Natural History [*A publication*] ....Ann KY Nat Hist
Annals of Library Science [*A publication*]...................................Annals Lib Sci
Annals of Library Science and Documentation [*A publication*]....................
Ann Libr Sci
Annals of Library Science and Documentation [*A publication*]....................
Ann Libr Sci Docum
Annals. Lyceum of Natural History (New York) [*A publication*]....................
Ann Lyceum Nat Hist (NY)
Annals and Magazine of Natural History [*A publication*]..............An Mag N H
Annals and Magazine of Natural History [*A publication*]....................
Annals and Mag Nat History
Annals and Magazine of Natural History [*A publication*]....................
Ann and Mag Nat Hist
Annals and Magazine of Natural History [*A publication*].... Ann Mag Nat Hist
Annals and Magazine of Natural History [*A publication*]....................
Ann Mag Natur Hist
Annals of Mathematical Logic [*A publication*] ....Annals Math Log
Annals of Mathematical Logic [*A publication*] ....Ann Math Logic
Annals of Mathematical Statistics [*A publication*].....................Ann Math Stat
Annals of Mathematics [*A publication*] ....Ann Math
Annals of Medical History [*A publication*]..................................Ann Med Hist
Annals. Medical Section. Polish Academy of Sciences [*A
publication*]....................... Ann Med Sect Pol Acad Sci
Annals. Medicina Academia de Ciencias Mediques de
Catalunya i de Balears [*A publication*]....................
Ann Med Acad Cienc Med Catalunya Balears
Annals. Missouri Botanical Garden [*A publication*].......................Ann MO Bot
Annals. Missouri Botanical Garden [*A publication*]............Ann MO Bot Gard
Annals. Missouri Botanical Garden [*A publication*]..............Ann MO Bot Gdn
Annals of Neurology [*A publication*] .... Ann Neurol
Annals. New York Academy of Sciences [*A publication*] .... Ann NY Acad
Annals. New York Academy of Sciences [*A publication*] ..... Ann NY Acad Sci
Annals. New York Academy of Sciences [*A publication*] ....ANYAA
Annals of Nuclear Energy [*A publication*]..............................Ann Nuc Eng
Annals of Nuclear Energy [*A publication*] ....Ann Nucl Energy
Annals of Nuclear Science and Engineering [*A publication*]....................
Ann Nucl Sci & Eng
Annals of Nuclear Science and Engineering [*A publication*]....................
Ann Nucl Sci Eng
Annals of Nuclear Science and Engineering [*A publication*]....................
Ann Nucl Sci Engng
Annals of Nutrition and Metabolism [*A publication*]..............Ann Nutr Metab
Annals of Occupational Hygiene [*A publication*] ....Ann Occup Hyg
Annals of Occupational Hygiene [*A publication*] ....AOHYA
Annals. Oklahoma Academy of Science [*A publication*] ... Ann Okla Acad Sci
Annals of Ophthalmology [*A publication*] .... Ann Ophthalmol
Annals of Oriental Research [*A publication*] ....An Or Res
Annals of Oriental Research [*A publication*] ....AOR
Annals of Oto-Rino-Laryngologica Ibero-Americana [*A
publication*]... AOIAA

Annals of Otology, Rhinology, and Laryngology [*A publication*]....................
Ann Otol Rh
Annals of Otology, Rhinology, and Laryngology [*A publication*]....................
Ann Oto Rhinol Laryngol
Annals of Otology, Rhinology, and Laryngology [*A publication*].........AORHA
Annals of Otology, Rhinology, and Laryngology. Supplement [*A
publication*]....................Ann Otol Rhinol Laryngol Suppl
Annals. Philippine Chinese Historical Association [*A
publication*]....................................An Phil Chin Hist Asso
Annals of Physical Medicine [*A publication*]............................. Ann Phys Med
Annals of Physics [*New York*] [*A publication*] .... Ann Phys
Annals of Physics [*New York*] [*A publication*] ....Ann Physics
Annals of Physics (New York) [*A publication*] ....Ann Phys (New York)
Annals. Phytopathological Society of Japan [*A publication*]....................
Ann Phytopathol Soc Jap
Annals. Phytopathological Society of Japan [*A publication*] ....
Ann Phytopathol Soc Jpn
Annals of Plastic Surgery [*A publication*] .... Ann Plast Surg
Annals of Probability [*A publication*]...Anls Prob
Annals of Probability [*A publication*]... Ann Probab
Annals of Public and Co-Operative Economy [*Formerly, Annals
of Collective Economy*] [*A publication*] .... ACE
Annals of Public and Co-Operative Economy [*Formerly, Annals
of Collective Economy*] [*A publication*] ....APCE
Annals of Regional Science [*A publication*] ....AARS
Annals. Research Institute of Epidemiology and Microbiology [*A
publication*] .... Ann Res Inst Epidemiol Microbiol
Annals of the Rheumatic Diseases [*A publication*].................... Ann Rheum D
Annals of the Rheumatic Diseases [*A publication*]....................Ann Rheum Dis
Annals. Royal College of Physicians and Surgeons of Canada [*A
publication*] .... Ann R Coll Physicians Surg Can
Annals. Royal College of Surgeons of England [*A publication*] ....
Ann R Coll Surg Eng
Annals. Royal College of Surgeons of England [*A publication*] ....
Ann R Coll Surg Engl
Annals. Royal College of Surgeons of England [*A publication*] ....
Ann RC Surg
Annals of Science [*London*] [*A publication*] .... Ann Sci
Annals of Science [*London*] [*A publication*] ....ASc
Annals of Science (Cleveland) [*A publication*] ....An Sc (Cleveland)
Annals of Science. Kanazawa University [*A publication*]....................
Ann Sci Kanazawa Univ
Annals of Science. Kanazawa University. Part 2. Biology-
Geology [*A publication*].............. Ann Sci Kanazawa Univ Part 2 Biol-Geol
Annals. South Africa Museum [*A publication*] .... Ann S Afr Mus
Annals of Statistics [*A publication*] ....Anls Stat
Annals of Statistics [*A publication*] ....Ann Statist
Annals of Surgery [*A publication*].. Ann Surg
Annals of Systems Research [*A publication*] .... Ann Syst Res
Annals of Thoracic Surgery [*A publication*].................................Ann Thorac
Annals of Thoracic Surgery [*A publication*] .... Ann Thorac Surg
Annals. Tokyo Astronomical Observatory [*A publication*]....................
Ann Tokyo Astron Obs
Annals. Transvaal Museum [*A publication*].......................Ann Transvaal Mus
Annals of Tropical Medicine and Parasitology [*A publication*].... Ann Trop M
Annals of Tropical Medicine and Parasitology [*A publication*]....................
Ann Trop Med Parasitol
Annals. Ukrainian Academy of Arts and Sciences in the US [*A
publication*].. AnnUA
Annals. Ukrainian Academy of Arts and Sciences in the US [*A
publication*]....................Ann Ukr Acad Arts Sci US
Annals. Ukrainian Academy of Arts and Sciences in the US [*A
publication*].. AUA
Annals of the University [*Grenoble*] [*A publication*]................................AU
Annals of Veterinary Research [*A publication*] ....Ann Vet Res
Annals of Wyoming [*A publication*] ....Ann Wyo
Annals of Wyoming [*A publication*] ....AW
Annals of Zoology [*A publication*] .... Ann Zool
Annals of Zoology (Agra) [*A publication*] .... Ann Zool (Agra)
Annamalainagar [*India*] [*Geomagnetic observatory code*]..................ANN
Annandale Corp. [*NASDAQ symbol*] .... ANNA
Annapolis, MD [*Radio station call letters*]....................................WANN
Annapolis, MD [*Television station call letters*] ....WAPB
Annapolis, MD [*Radio station call letters*] ....WFSI
Annapolis, MD [*Radio station call letters*] ....WHFS
Annapolis, MD [*Radio station call letters*] ....WNAV
Annapolis, MD [*Radio station call letters*] ....WYRE
Annapolis Science Center..ASC
Annapolis Valley Regional Library, Annapolis Royal, NS, Canada
[*Library symbol*]..CaNSAR
Anneal..ANL
Annealed...ANN
Annealed Copper-Covered Steel..ACS
Annecy [*France*] [*Airport symbol*] ....NCY
Annee Africaine [*A publication*] ....Annee Afr
Annee Agricole [*A publication*] .... Annee Agr
Annee Balzacienne [*A publication*]..ABa
Annee Balzacienne [*A publication*] ....A Balzac
Annee Biologique [*A publication*] .... Annee Biol
Annee Courante [*Current Year*] [*French*]...AC
Annee Endocrinologique [*A publication*] ....Annee Endocrinol

Annee Epigraphique [*A publication*] .... AEpigr
Annee Geophysique Internationale [*International Geophysical Year*] [*French*] .... AGI
Annee de Lumiere [*Light Year*] [*French*] .... AL
Annee Mondiale du Refugie .... AMR
Annee Philologique [*A publication*] .... APh
Annee Politique et Economique [*A publication*] .... Annee Polit Econ
Annee Propedeutique [*A publication*] .... AnP
Annee Psychologique [*A publication*] .... Annee Psychol
Annee Psychologique [*A publication*] .... AnnPsych
Annee Psychologique [*A publication*] .... Ann Psychol
Annee Psychologique [*A publication*] .... ANPQA
Annee Sociologique [*A publication*] .... Annee Sociol
Annee Sociologique [*A publication*] .... ASoc
Annee Theologique Augustinienne [*A publication*] .... ATA
Annee Theologique Augustinienne [*A publication*] .... AThAug
Annee Therapeutique et Clinique en Ophtalmologie [*A publication*] .... Annee Ther Clin Ophtalmol
Annette Island [*Alaska*] [*Airport symbol*] [*Obsolete*] .... ANN
Annex .... AN
Annex .... ANN
Annex .... ANX
Anniston [*Alabama*] [*Airport symbol*] .... ANB
Anniston, AL [*Radio station call letters*] .... WANA
Anniston, AL [*Radio station call letters*] .... WDNG
Anniston, AL [*Radio station call letters*] .... WHMA
Anniston, AL [*Radio station call letters*] .... WHMA-FM
Anniston, AL [*Television station call letters*] .... WHMA-TV
Anniston Army Depot [*Alabama*] .... ANAD
Anniston Museum of Natural History, Anniston, AL [*Library symbol*] .... AAnnM
Anniston Public Library, Anniston, AL [*Library symbol*] .... AAnn
Anniversary .... ANNIV
Anniversary Bulletin of Chuo University [*A publication*] .... Anniv Bull Chuo Univ
Anno [*or Annus*] [*Year*] [*Latin*] .... A
Anno [*or Annus*] [*Year*] [*Latin*] .... AN
Anno [*or Annus*] [*Year*] [*Latin*] .... ANN
Anno Ante Christum [*In the Year before Christ*] [*Latin*] .... AAC
Anno Christi [*In the Year of Christ*] [*Latin*] .... AC
Anno Christianis Aerae [*In the Year of the Christian Era*] [*Latin*] .... ACE
Anno Domini [*In the Year of Our Lord*] [*Latin*] .... AD
Anno Domini [*In the Year of Our Lord*] [*Latin*] .... AN DO
Anno Hebraico [*In the Hebrew Year*] [*Latin*] .... AH
Anno Hegirae [*In the Year of the Hegira*] [*The flight of Mohammed from Mecca*] [*Latin*] .... AH
Anno Humanae Salutis [*In the Year of Human Salvation*] [*Latin*] .... AHS
Anno Inventionis [*In the Year of the Discovery*] [*Latin*] .... AI
Anno Lucis [*In the Year of Light*] [*Latin*] .... AL
Anno Mundi [*In the Year of the World*] [*Latin*] .... AM
Anno Orbis Conditi [*In the Year of the Creation*] [*Latin*] .... AOC
Anno Post Christum Natum [*In the Year after Christ Was Born*] [*Latin*] .... APCN
Anno Post Romam Conditam [*In the Year after the Building of Rome*] [*Latin*] .... APRC
Anno Regni [*In the Year of the Reign of*] [*Latin*] .... AR
Anno Regni Regis [*or Reginae*] [*In the Year of the King's - or Queen's - Reign*] [*Latin*] .... ARR
Anno Reparatae Salutis [*In the Year of Our Redemption*] [*Latin*] .... ARS
Anno Salvatoris [*or Salutis*] [*In the Year of Salvation*] [*Latin*] .... AS
Anno Urbis [*In the Year of the City of Rome*] [*Latin*] .... AU
Anno Urbis Conditae [*In the Year from the Building of the City (Rome)*] [*753 BC*] [*Latin*] .... AUC
Anno Vixit [*He Lived (a given number of) Years*] [*Latin*] .... AV
Annotate .... ANOT
Annotated .... ANNOT
Annotated Bibliography. Commonwealth Forestry Bureau (Oxford) [*A publication*] .... Bibliogr For Bur (Oxf)
Annotated Bibliography of Economic Geology [*A publication*] .... Annot Bibliography of Econ Geology
Annotated Manual of Statutes and Regulations [*of the Federal Home Loan Bank Board*] .... AMSR
Annotated Tax Cases .... ATC
Annotationes Zoologicae et Botanicae [*A publication*] .... Annot Zool Bot
Annotationes Zoologicae Japonenses [*A publication*] .... Annot Zool Japon
Annotationes Zoologicae Japonenses [*A publication*] .... Annot Zool Jpn
Annotatsii Dokladov. Seminar Instituta Prikladnoj Matematiki. Tbilisskij Universitet [*A publication*] .... Annot Dokl Semin Inst Prikl Mat Tbilis Univ
Announce .... ANN
Announce .... ANNC
Announcement of Flight Opportunity [*NASA*] .... AFO
Announcement of Opportunities [*NASA*] .... AO
Announcing .... ANCG
Annoyance Call Bureau [*Telephone-pest control*] .... ACB
Annoyance Level [*Aircraft noise*] .... ANL
Annuaire. Academie Royale de Belgique [*A publication*] .... AARB
Annuaire. Academie Royale de Belgique [*A publication*] .... AnnAB
Annuaire. Afrique du Nord [*A publication*] .... Annu Afr Nord
Annuaire Agricole de la Suisse [*A publication*] .... Annu Agric Suisse
Annuaire des Auditeurs et Anciens Auditeurs. Academie de Droit International de la Haye [*A publication*] .... Annu A A A
Annuaire-Bulletin. Societe de l'Histoire de France [*A publication*] .... ABSHF
Annuaire. College de France [*A publication*] .... ACF
Annuaire de Droit Maritime et Aerien [*A publication*] .... A Dr Marit Aer
Annuaire de Droit Maritime et Aerien [*A publication*] .... Annu Dr Marit Aer
Annuaire. Ecole Pratique des Hautes Etudes, IVeme Section [*A publication*] .... Ann Ec Prat HEt
Annuaire Europeen [*A publication*] .... Annu Europ
Annuaire. Faculte d'Agriculture et de Sylviculture. Universite de Skopie [*A publication*] .... Annu Fac Agric Univ Skopie
Annuaire. Federation Historique de Lorraine [*A publication*] .... AFHL
Annuaire Francais de Droit International [*A publication*] .... Annuaire Francais Droit Int
Annuaire Francais de Droit International [*A publication*] .... Annu Franc Dr Int
Annuaire Francais des Droits de l'Homme [*A publication*] .... Annu Franc Dr Homme
Annuaire d'Histoire Liegeoise [*A publication*] .... AHL
Annuaire d'Histoire Liegeoise [*A publication*] .... AnnHL
Annuaire. Institut Europeen de Securite Sociale [*A publication*] .... Annu Inst Europ Secur Soc
Annuaire. Institut de Philologie et d'Histoire Orientales [*Bruxelles*] [*A publication*] .... AIPhO
Annuaire. Institut de Philologie et d'Histoire Orientales et Slaves [*Bruxelles*] [*A publication*] .... AIPhOS
Annuaire. Institut de Philologie et d'Histoire Orientales et Slaves [*Bruxelles*] [*A publication*] .... AIPS
Annuaire International de la Fonction Publique [*A publication*] .... Annu Int Fonction Publ
Annuaire. Musee d'Histoire de la Religion et de l'Atheisme [*A publication*] .... AMHR
Annuaire. Musee National Archeologique (Plovdiv) [*A publication*] .... AMNP
Annuaire. Musee National Archeologique (Plovdiv) [*A publication*] .... Ann Mus Nat Arch (Plovdiv)
Annuaire. Museum National d'Histoire Naturelle [*A publication*] .... Annu Mus Natl Hist Nat
Annuaire Roumain d'Anthropologie [*A publication*] .... Annu Roum Anthropol
Annuaire. Societe d'Histoire et d'Archeologie de la Lorraine [*A publication*] .... ASAL
Annuaire. Societe d'Histoire et d'Archeologie de la Lorraine [*A publication*] .... ASHAL
Annuaire. Societe Suisse de Philosophie [*A publication*] .... ASSPh
Annuaire Suisse de Science Politique [*A publication*] .... Annu Suisse Sci Polit
Annuaire du Tiers-Monde [*A publication*] .... Annu Tiers-Monde
Annuaire. Universite de Sofia. Faculte de Biologie [*A publication*] .... Annu Univ Sofia Fac Biol
Annuaire. Universite de Sofia. Faculte des Lettres [*A publication*] .... AUS
Annuaire. Universite de Sofia. Faculte de Mathematiques et Mecanique [*A publication*] .... Annuaire Univ Sofia Fac Math Mec
Annuaire. Universite de Sofia. Faculte de Physique [*A publication*] .... Annuaire Univ Sofia Fac Phys
Annuaire. Universite de Sofia. Faculte de Physique [*A publication*] .... Annu Univ Sofia Fac Phys
Annuaire de l'URSS et des Pays Socialistes Europeens [*A publication*] .... Annu URSS
Annual .... A
Annual .... ANL
Annual .... ANN
Annual Active Duty for Training [*Army*] .... ANACDUTRA
Annual Advance Retainer Pay .... AARP
Annual. American Schools of Oriental Research [*A publication*] .... AASOR
Annual of Animal Psychology [*A publication*] .... Ann Anim Ps
Annual of Animal Psychology [*A publication*] .... Annu Anim Psychol
Annual Average Daily Traffic [*on highways*] .... AADT
Annual Average Score .... AAS
Annual Biology Colloquium [*A publication*] .... Annu Biol Colloq
Annual Book of ASTM [*American Society for Testing and Materials*] **Standards** [*A publication*] .... Annu Book ASTM Stand
Annual. British School of Archaeology at Athens [*A publication*] .... Ann B S Arch Ath
Annual. British School at Athens [*A publication*] .... ABSA
Annual Budget Authorization .... ABA
Annual Capital Charge .... ACC
Annual Conference on Research in Medical Education [*A publication*] .... Annu Conf Res Med Educ
Annual Conference. Soil Mechanics and Foundation Engineering [*A publication*] .... Annu Conf Soil Mech Found Eng
Annual Confidential Report .... ACR
Annual Contributions Contract [*Public housing development*] .... ACC
Annual Convention Proceedings. Washington Association of Wheat Growers [*A publication*] .... Annu Conv Proc Wash Ass Wheat Growers
Annual Cycle Energy System [*Energy Research and Development Admininistration*] .... ACES
Annual. Department of Antiquities of Jordan [*A publication*] .... ADAJ
Annual Digest of International Law [*A publication*] .... ADIL
Annual Efficiency Index [*Army*] .... AEI
Annual Execution Plan .... AEP
Annual Field Training [*Army*] .... AFT
Annual Financial Plan .... AFP

Annual Fuel Utilization Efficiency [*Department of Energy*] .... AFUE
Annual Funding Program [*Army*] .... AFP
Annual General Inspection [*Army*] .... AGI
Annual General Meeting .... AGM
Annual Goal [*Education*] .... AG
Annual Highway Geology Symposium. Proceedings [*A publication*] .... Annu Highway Geol Symp Proc
Annual Hospital Report [*Program of the Department of Health and Human Services*] .... AHR
Annual Implementation Plan [*Health Planning and Resource Development Act of 1974*] .... AIP
Annual Journal. Institution of Engineers [*A publication*] .... Annu J Inst Eng
Annual Leave [*US Civil Service*] .... AL
Annual. Leeds University Oriental Society [*A publication*] .... ALOS
Annual Logistic Estimate .... LOGEST
Annual Maintenance Manhours [*Military*] .... AMMH
Annual Material Forecast [*Military*] .... AMF
Annual Meeting-Proceedings. American Society of Photogrammetry [*A publication*] .... Annu Meet Proc Am Soc Photogramm
Annual Military Inspection .... AMI
Annual Military Personnel Inspection .... AMPI
Annual Minerals Symposium [*American Institute of Mining, Metallurgical, and Petroleum Engineers*] **Proceedings** [*A publication*] .... Annu Miner Symp Proc
Annual National Information Retrieval Colloquium .... ANIRC
Annual National Information Retrieval Colloquium [*A publication*] .... Annu Natl Inf Retr Colloq
Annual Northeast Regional Antipollution Conference .... ANERAC
Annual Operating Budget [*Army*] .... AOB
Annual Operating Program [*Army*] .... AOP
Annual Percentage Rate .... APR
Annual Plan .... AP
Annual Planning Estimate [*Navy*] .... APE
Annual Planning Report .... APR
Annual Proceedings. Associated Scientific and Technical Societies of South Africa [*A publication*] .... Annu Proc Assoc Sci & Tech Soc S Afr
Annual Proceedings. Gifu College of Pharmacy [*A publication*] .... Annu Proc Gifu Coll Pharm
Annual Proceedings. Phytochemical Society [*A publication*] .... Annu Proc Phytochem Soc
Annual Proceedings. Reliability Physics (Symposium) [*A publication*] .... Annu Proc Reliab Phys (Symp)
Annual Procurement Agreement .... APA
Annual Program Objectives [*Navy*] .... APO
Annual Progress in Child Psychiatry and Child Development [*A publication*] .... Annu Prog Child Psychiatry Chil Dev
Annual Progress Report .... APR
Annual Progress Report. SEATO [*Southeast Asia Treaty Organization*] **Medical Research Laboratories** [*A publication*] .... Annu Prog Rep SEATO Med Res Lab
Annual of Psychoanalysis [*A publication*] .... Annu Psychoanal
Annual Qualifications Questionnaire [*Navy*] .... AQQ
Annual Renewable Term [*Insurance*] .... ART
Annual Report .... ANREP
Annual Report .... AR
Annual Report. Alabama Agricultural Experiment Station [*A publication*] .... Annu Rep Ala Agr Exp Sta
Annual Report. American Institute of Physics [*A publication*] .... Annu Rep Am Inst Phys
Annual Report of Biological Works. Faculty of Science. Osaka University [*A publication*] .... Annu Rep Biol Works Fac Sci Osaka Univ
Annual Report. Board of Regents of the Smithsonian Institution [*A publication*] .... ARBRSI
Annual Report on Cacao Research. University of the West Indies [*A publication*] .... Annu Rep Cacao Res Univ West Indies
Annual Report. Canadian Seed Growers Association [*A publication*] .... Annu Rep Can Seed Growers Ass
Annual Report. Cancer Research Institute. Kanazawa University [*A publication*] .... Annu Rep Cancer Res Inst Kanazawa Univ
Annual Report. Center for Adult Diseases (Osaka) [*A publication*] .... Ann Rep Cent Adult Dis (Osaka)
Annual Report. Central and Regional Arecanut Research Stations [*A publication*] .... Annu Rep Cent Reg Arecanut Res Stn
Annual Report. Clemson Agricultural Experiment Station [*A publication*] .... Annu Rep Clemson Agr Exp Sta
Annual Report Council .... ARC
Annual Report. CSIR [*Council for Scientific and Industrial Research*] [*A publication*] .... Annu Rep CSIR
Annual Report. Dante Society [*A publication*] .... ARDS
Annual Report of the Director. Department of Terrestrial Magnetism. Carnegie Institution [*A publication*] .... Annu Rep Dir Dep Terr Magn Carnegie Inst
Annual Report. East African Agriculture and Forestry Research Organization [*A publication*] .... Annu Rep E Afr Agr Forest Res Organ
Annual Report. East Malling Research Station [*A publication*] .... Rep E Malling Res Stn
Annual Report. Engineering Research Institute. Faculty of Engineering. University of Tokyo [*A publication*] .... Annu Rep Eng Res Inst Fac Eng Univ Tokyo
Annual Report. Faculty of Education. Gunma University Art and Technology Series [*A publication*] .... Annu Fac Educ Gunma Univ Art Technol Ser
Annual Report. Faculty of Education. University of Iwate [*A publication*] .... Annu Rep Fac Educ Univ Iwate
Annual Report. Faculty of Pharmaceutical Sciences. Nagoya City University [*A publication*] .... Annu Rep Fac Pharm Sci Nagoya City Univ
Annual Report. Farmers Union Grain Terminal Association [*A publication*] .... Annu Rep Farmers Union Grain Terminal Ass
Annual Report. Florida University. Agricultural Experiment Station [*A publication*] .... Annu Rep Fla Univ Agr Exp Sta
Annual Report to the Governor. Kansas Wheat Commission [*A publication*] .... Annu Rep Governor Kans Wheat Comm
Annual Report. Hokkaido Branch. Government Forest Experiment Station [*A publication*] .... Annu Rep Hokkaido Branch Gov For Exp Stn
Annual Report. Hokkaido Branch. Government Forest Experiment Station [*A publication*] .... Rep Forest Exp Stn Hokkaido
Annual Report. Hokusei Gakuin Junior College [*A publication*] .... Annu Rep Hokusei Gakuin Jr Coll
Annual Report. Institute for Fermentation. Osaka [*A publication*] .... Annu Rep Inst Ferment Osaka
Annual Report. Institute of Food Microbiology. Chiba University [*A publication*] .... Annu Rep Inst Food Microbiol Chiba Univ
Annual Report. Institute for Nuclear Study. University of Tokyo [*A publication*] .... Annu Rep Inst Nucl Stud Univ Tokyo
Annual Report. Institute of Phonetics. University of Copenhagen [*A publication*] .... ARIPUC
Annual Report. Institute of Sociology [*A publication*] .... Annu Rep Inst Sociol
Annual Report. Institute for Virus Research. Kyoto University [*A publication*] .... Annu Rep Inst Virus Res Kyoto Univ
Annual Report. International Crop Improvement Association [*A publication*] .... Annu Rep Int Crop Impr Ass
Annual Report. Kyoritsu College of Pharmacy [*A publication*] .... Annu Rep Kyoritsu Coll Pharm
Annual Report. Laboratory of Algology. Trebon [*A publication*] .... Annu Rep Lab Algol Trebon
Annual Report. Mississippi State University. Agricultural Experiment Station [*A publication*] .... Annu Rep Miss State Univ Agr Exp Sta
Annual Report. National Institute of Genetics [*A publication*] .... Annu Rep Natl Inst Genet
Annual Report. National Institute of Genetics (Japan) [*A publication*] .... Annu Rep Nat Inst Genet (Jap)
Annual Report. National Institute of Nutrition [*A publication*] .... Annu Rep Natl Inst Nutr
Annual Report. National Veterinary Assay Laboratory [*A publication*] .... Annu Rep Natl Vet Assay Lab
Annual Report of Natural Science and Home Economics. Kinjo Gakuin College [*A publication*] .... Annu Rep Natur Sci Home Econ Kinjo Gakuin Coll
Annual Report. Nebraska Grain Improvement Association [*A publication*] .... Annu Rep Nebr Grain Impr Ass
Annual Report. Nebraska Wheat Commission [*A publication*] .... Annu Rep Nebr Wheat Comm
Annual Report. New Mexico Agricultural Experiment Station [*A publication*] .... Annu Rep N Mex Agr Exp Sta
Annual Report. Noto Marine Laboratory [*A publication*] .... Annu Rep Noto Mar Lab
Annual Report. Oregon State Horticultural Society [*A publication*] .... Annu Rep Oreg State Hort Soc
Annual Report Producers Council .... ARPC
Annual Report. Radiation Center of Osaka Prefecture [*A publication*] .... Annu Rep Radiat Cent Osaka Prefect
Annual Report. Record Research. East African Agriculture and Forestry Research Organisation [*A publication*] .... A Rep Rec Res
Annual Report. Research Institute for Chemobiodynamics. Chiba University [*A publication*] .... Annu Rep Res Inst Chemobiodyn Chiba Univ
Annual Report. Research Institute of Environmental Medicine. Nagoya University [*A publication*] .... Annu Rep Res Inst Environ Med Nagoya Univ
Annual Report on Research and Technical Work. Department of Agriculture. Northern Ireland [*A publication*] .... Annu Rep Res Tech Work Dep Agric North Irel
Annual Report. Sado Marine Biological Station. Niigata University [*A publication*] .... Annu Rep Sado Mar Biol Stn Niigata Univ
Annual Report. Sankyo Research Laboratories [*A publication*] .... Annu Rep Sankyo Res Lab
Annual Report to Shareholders [*Securities and Exchange Commission*] .... ARS
Annual Report. Shionogi Research Laboratory [*A publication*] .... Annu Rep Shionogi Res Lab
Annual Report. Smithsonian Institution [*A publication*] .... Annu Rep Smiths Inst
Annual Report. Society for Libyan Studies [*A publication*] .... Ann Rep Soc Libyan Stud
Annual Report. Society of Plant Protection of North Japan [*A publication*] .... Annu Rep Soc Plant Prot N Jap

Annual Report of Studies. Doshisha Women's College of Liberal
Arts [*A publication*]........ Annu Rep Stud Doshisha Women's Coll Lib Arts
Annual Report. Takeda Research Laboratories [*A publication*]
Annu Rep Takeda Res Lab
Annual Report. Tobacco Research Institute [*A publication*]
Annu Rep Tob Res Inst
Annual Report. Tobacco Research Institute (Taiwan) [*A
publication*]................................Rep Tob Res Inst (Taiwan)
Annual Report. Tohoku College of Pharmacy [*A publication*]
Annu Rep Tohoku Coll Pharm
Annual Report. Tokyo College of Pharmacy [*A publication*]
Annu Rep Tokyo Coll Pharm
Annual Report. Tokyo University of Agriculture and Technology
[*A publication*]................ Ann Rept Tokyo Univ Agr Technol
Annual Report. Tokyo University of Agriculture and Technology
[*A publication*]................Annu Rep Tokyo Univ Agric Technol
Annual Report on Transport Statistics .... ARTS
Annual Report. United Fruit Company. Medical Department [*A
publication*]................Ann Rep United Fruit Co Med Dept
Annual Report. University of Georgia. College of Agriculture.
Experiment Stations [*A publication*]
Annu Rep Univ GA Coll Agr Exp Sta
Annual Report. Vegetable Growers Association of America [*A
publication*]................ Annu Rep Veg Growers Ass Amer
Annual Reports. Faculty of Pharmaceutical Sciences.
Tokushima University [*A publication*]
Annu Rep Fac Pharm Sci Tokushima Univ
Annual Reports. Institute of Population Problems [*A publication*]
Annu Rep Inst Popul Probl
Annual Reports. Kinki University Atomic Energy Research
Institute [*A publication*]............... Annu Rep Kinki Univ At Energy Res Inst
Annual Reports in Medicinal Chemistry [*A publication*]
Annu Rep Med Chem
Annual Reports on the Progress of Chemistry [*A publication*]
Ann Rept Progr Chem
Annual Reports on the Progress of Chemistry. Section A.
General, Physical, and Inorganic Chemistry [*A publication*]
Ann Rp Ch A
Annual Reports on the Progress of Chemistry. Section A.
General, Physical, and Inorganic Chemistry [*A publication*]
Annu Rep Prog Chem Sect A
Annual Reports on the Progress of Chemistry. Section A.
General, Physical, and Inorganic Chemistry [*A publication*]
Annu Rep Prog Chem Sect A Gen Phys Inorg Chem
Annual Reports on the Progress of Chemistry. Section B.
Organic Chemistry [*A publication*]................Ann Rp Ch B
Annual Reports on the Progress of Chemistry. Section B.
Organic Chemistry [*A publication*]............... Annu Rep Prog Chem Sect B
Annual Reports. Research Reactor Institute. Kyoto University [*A
publication*]................Annu Rep Res Reactor Inst Kyoto Univ
Annual Research Task Summary .... ARTS
Annual Return ....AR
Annual Review ....AR
Annual Review of Anthropology [*A publication*]................Ann R Anthr
Annual Review of Anthropology [*A publication*]................ Annu Rev Anthropol
Annual Review of Astronomy and Astrophysics [*A publication*]
Ann R Astro
Annual Review of Astronomy and Astrophysics [*A publication*]
Annu Rev Astron Astrophys
Annual Review of Astronomy and Astrophysics [*A publication*]............ARAA
Annual Review in Automatic Programming [*A publication*]
Annu Rev Autom Program
Annual Review of Behavior Therapy Theory and Practice [*A
publication*]................ Annu Rev Behav Ther Theory Pract
Annual Review of Biochemical and Allied Research in India [*A
publication*]................ Annu Rev Biochem Allied Res India
Annual Review of Biochemistry [*A publication*]................Ann R Bioch
Annual Review of Biochemistry [*A publication*]................ Ann Rev Biochem
Annual Review of Biochemistry [*A publication*]................ Annu Rev Biochem
Annual Review of Biophysics and Bioengineering [*A publication*]
Ann R Bioph
Annual Review of Biophysics and Bioengineering [*A publication*]
Annu Rev Biophys Bioeng
Annual Review Committee [*NATO*]................ARC
Annual Review of Earth and Planetary Sciences [*A publication*]
Ann R Earth
Annual Review of Earth and Planetary Sciences [*A publication*]
Annu Rev Earth Planet Sci
Annual Review of Ecology and Systematics [*A publication*].......... Ann R Ecol
Annual Review of Ecology and Systematics [*A publication*]...... Ann Rev Ecol
Annual Review of Ecology and Systematics [*A publication*]
Annu Rev Ecol Syst
Annual Review of Energy [*A publication*] ....Annu Rev Energy
Annual Review of Entomology [*A publication*]................Ann R Entom
Annual Review of Entomology [*A publication*]................Ann Rev Entomol
Annual Review of Entomology [*A publication*]................Annu Rev Entomol
Annual Review of Entomology [*A publication*]................A Rev Ent
Annual Review of Fluid Mechanics [*A publication*]................Ann R Fluid
Annual Review of Fluid Mechanics [*A publication*]........ Annu Rev Fluid Mech
Annual Review of Food Technology (Mysore) [*A publication*]
Annu Rev Food Technol (Mysore)

Annual Review of Genetics [*A publication*]................Ann R Genet
Annual Review of Genetics [*A publication*]................ Annu Rev Genet
Annual Review of Information Science and Technology [*A
publication*]................Ann R Infor
Annual Review of Information Science and Technology [*A
publication*]................ Annu Rev Inf Sci Technol
Annual Review of Information Science and Technology [*A
publication*]................ ARIST
Annual Review and Information Symposium on the Technology
of Training, Learning, and Education [*DoD*]................ARISTOTLE
Annual Review. Institute of Plasma Physics. Nagoya University
[*A publication*]................ Annu Rev Inst Plasma Phys Nagoya Univ
Annual Review of Materials Science [*A publication*]................ Ann R Mater
Annual Review of Materials Science [*A publication*]........Annu Rev Mater Sci
Annual Review of Medicine [*A publication*]................Ann R Med
Annual Review of Medicine [*A publication*]................ Annu Rev Med
Annual Review of Microbiology [*A publication*]................Ann Rev Microbiol
Annual Review of Microbiology [*A publication*]................Ann R Micro
Annual Review of Microbiology [*A publication*]................Annu Rev Microbiol
Annual Review of Microbiology [*A publication*]................A Rev Microbiol
Annual Review of Neuroscience [*A publication*]................Annu Rev Neurosci
Annual Review of Nuclear Science [*A publication*]................Ann Rev Nuclear Sci
Annual Review of Nuclear Science [*A publication*]................Ann R Nucl
Annual Review of Nuclear Science [*A publication*]................Annu Rev Nucl Sci
Annual Review of Pharmacology [*A publication*]................ Ann R Pharm
Annual Review of Pharmacology [*A publication*]................Annu Rev Pharmacol
Annual Review of Pharmacology and Toxicology [*A publication*]................
Annu Rev Pharmacol Toxicol
Annual Review of Physical Chemistry [*A publication*].....Ann Rev Phys Chem
Annual Review of Physical Chemistry [*A publication*]................ Ann R Ph Ch
Annual Review of Physical Chemistry [*A publication*]................
Annu Rev Phys Chem
Annual Review of Physiology [*A publication*]................Ann R Physl
Annual Review of Physiology [*A publication*]................ Annu Rev Physiol
Annual Review of Phytopathology [*A publication*]................ Ann R Phyto
Annual Review of Phytopathology [*A publication*]....... Annu Rev Phytopathol
Annual Review of Phytopathology [*A publication*]................ A Rev Phytopath
Annual Review of Plant Physiology [*A publication*] ...... Ann R Plant Physiol
Annual Review of Plant Physiology [*A publication*]................ Ann R Plant
Annual Review of Plant Physiology [*A publication*] .... Annu Rev Plant Physiol
Annual Review of Plant Physiology [*A publication*]................ A Rev Pl Physiol
Annual Review of Psychology [*A publication*]................ Ann R Psych
Annual Review of Psychology [*A publication*]................ Annu Rev Psychol
Annual Review of Psychology [*A publication*]................ ARPSA
Annual Review Questionnaire [*Military*]................ARQ
Annual Review of the Schizophrenic Syndrome [*A publication*]................
Annu Rev Schizophr Syndr
Annual Review of Sociology [*A publication*] .... Ann R Sociol
Annual Review Traveling Team [*NATO*] .... ARTT
Annual Reviews [*An association*]................AR
Annual Sanitary Report of the Province of Assam [*A publication*]................
Ann San Rep Prov Assam
Annual Service Practice [*Firings*] [*Military*]................ ASP
Annual Simulation Symposium (Record of Proceedings) [*A
publication*]................ Annu Simul Symp (Rec Proc)
Annual Summary Report .... ASR
Annual Supply Inspection [*Military*]................ASI
Annual Survey of Manufacturers [*Census Bureau*]................ASM
Annual. Swedish Theological Institute [*A publication*] ....ASTI
Annual Symposium on Biomathematics and Computer Science
in the Life Sciences. Abstracts [*A publication*]................
Annu Symp Biomath Comput Sci Life Sci Abstr
Annual Symposium on Foundations of Computer Science
(Proceedings) [*A publication*]........ Annu Symp Found Comput Sci (Proc)
Annual Technical Conference [*Society of Plastics Engineers*]............ANTEC
Annual Technical Progress Report ....ATPR
Annual Training [*Military*] ....AT
Annual Training Deployment .... ATD
Annual Training Duty [*Marine Corps*] ....ATD
Annual Training Equipment Pools ....ATEP
Annual Work Plan................ AWP
Annuale Mediaevale [*A publication*]................AnM
Annuale Mediaevale [*A publication*]................ Ann Med
Annuario. Accademia Etrusca di Cortona [*A publication*] ....AAEC
Annuario. Istituto Giapponese di Cultura in Roma [*A publication*]........AIGC
Annuario. Liceo Ginnasio G. Mameli [*A publication*]................ALGGM
Annuario. Liceo Ginnasio Statale G. Palmieri [*A publication*]................ALGP
Annuario di Politica Internazionale [*A publication*]................Annu Polit Int
Annuario. Reale Accademia d'Italia [*A publication*] .... ARAI
Annuario. Reale Scuola Archeologica di Atene [*A publication*]............ASAA
Annuario. Scuola Archeologica di Atene e delle Missioni Italiane
in Oriente [*A publication*] .... Ann Scu Archeol Atene
Annuario. Stazione Chimico-Agraria Sperimentale di Torino [*A
publication*]................ Annu Sta Chim-Agr Sper Torino
Annuario. Universita Cattolica del Sacro Cuore [*A publication*]......... AUCC
Annuarium van de Apologetische Vereeniging (Petrus
Canisius) [*A publication*]................AAVPC
Annuarium Historiae Conciliorum [*A publication*]................ AHC
Annuarium des Roomsch-Katholieke Studenten in Nederland [*A
publication*]................ ARKSN
Annuity ....ANNY

Annular ... A
Annular ... ANLR
Annular Base Drag ... ABD
Annular Bearing Engineering Committee ... ABEC
Annular Core Pulsed Reactor ... ACPR
Annular Fire Missile ... AFM
Annular Linear Induction Pump [*Nuclear energy*] ... ALIP
Annular Momentum Control Device [*NASA*] ... AMCD
Annular Primary Combustor ... APC
Annular Turbojet Combustor ... ATC
Annular Turbojet Combustor ... ATJC
Annulus Gas System [*Nuclear energy*] ... AGS
Annulus Vacuum Maintenance System [*Nuclear energy*] ... AVMS
Annunciation ... ANNUN
Annunciator [*Electronically controlled signal board*] ... ANN
Annunciator Control Assembly ... ACA
Annunciator Control Unit ... ACU
Annunciator Display Unit ... ADU
Annus [*Year*] [*Latin*] ... ANN
Annus [*Year*] [*Latin*] ... ANO
Annus Mirabilis [*The Wonderful Year*] [*1666*] [*Latin*] ... AM
Annville-Cleona, PA [*Radio station call letters*] ... WAHT
Anodal Closing Odor ... ACO
Anodal Closing Picture ... ACP
Anodal Closing Sound ... ACS
Anodal Closure ... AC
Anodal Closure Contraction [*Also, AnCC*] [*Physiology*] ... ACC
Anodal Closure Contraction [*Also, ACC*] [*Physiology*] ... AnCC
Anodal Closure Tetanus [*Physiology*] ... ACTe
Anodal Contraction ... AC
Anodal Deviation ... AD
Anodal Duration Contraction ... ADC
Anodal Duration Tetanus ... AnDTe
Anodal Opening ... AO
Anodal Opening Clonus [*Physiology*] ... AOCL
Anodal Opening Contraction [*Also, AOC*] [*Physiology*] ... AnOC
Anodal Opening Contraction [*Also, AnOC*] [*Physiology*] ... AOC
Anodal Opening Odor ... AOO
Anodal Opening Picture [*Physiology*] ... AOP
Anodal Opening Sound ... AOS
Anode [*Technical drawings*] ... A
Anode ... AD
Anode Circuit ... AC
Anode Reaction ... AR
Anode Supply Voltage ... ASV
Anode Voltage Drop ... AVD
Anodic Behavior of Metals and Semiconductors Series [*A publication*] ... Anodic Behav Met Semicond Ser
Anodic Stripping Voltammetry [*Chemical analysis*] ... ASV
Anodize ... ANDZ
Anodize ... ANOD
Anoka County Genealogical Society, Anoka, MN [*Library symbol*] ... MnAnGS
Anoka County Historical Society, Anoka, MN [*Library symbol*] ... MnAnHi
Anoka County Library, Minneapolis, MN [*Library symbol*] ... MnMAC
Anoka, MN [*Radio station call letters*] ... KKKC
Anoka, MN [*Radio station call letters*] ... KTWN-FM
Anoka-Ramsey Community College, Anoka, MN [*Library symbol*] ... MnAnA
Anomalous Atrioventricular Conduction [*Cardiology*] ... AAVC
Anomalous Dispersion Spherical Array Target [*for increasing radio reflectivity*] ... ADSAT
Anomalous Magnetic Moment ... AMM
Anomalous Propagation ... ANAPROP
Anomalous Propagation [*Electronics*] ... AP
Anomalous Retinal Correspondence [*Ophthalmology*] ... ARC
Anomaly Dynamics Study [*NORPAX*] ... ADS
Anomaly Report ... AR
Anonima Lombarda Fabbrica Automobili ... ALFA
Anonymous ... A
Anonymous ... ANON
Anonymous Arts Recovery Society ... AARS
Anonymous Families History Project ... AFHP
Anordnung [*Order or Directive*] [*German*] ... AO
Anorexia Nervosa [*Medicine*] ... AN
Anorexia Nervosa and Associated Disorders [*Later, ANAD-National Association of Anorexia Nervosa and Associated Disorders*] ... ANAD
Anorthite [*CIPW classification*] [*Geology*] ... an
Anorthotion Komma Ergazomanou Laou [*Reform Party of the Working People*] [*Cyprus*] ... AKEL
Anotati Diokisis Enosios Demosion Ypallilon [*Supreme Council of Civil Servants*] [*Greece*] ... ADEDY
Another ... ANO
Another Mother for Peace [*An association*] ... AMP
Anovular Menstruation ... AM
Anoxic Encephalopathy [*Medicine*] ... AE
ANPA/RI [*American Newspaper Publishers Association. Research Institute*] **Bulletin** [*A publication*] ... ANPA/RI Bull
ANPHI [*Academy of Nursing of the Philippines*] **Papers** [*A publication*] ... ANPHI Pap
Anpu [*Republic of China*] [*Seismograph station code, US Geological Survey*] ... ANP
Anritsu Technical Bulletin [*A publication*] ... Anritsu Tech Bull
Ansett Airlines of Australia [*ICAO designator*] ... AN
Ansett Airlines of Australia ... ANSETT
ANSI [*American National Standards Institute*] **Reporter** [*A publication*] ... ANSI Reptr
ANSI [*American National Standards Institute*] **Standards** [*A publication*] ... ANSI Stand
ANSI [*American National Standards Institute*] **Standards Action** [*A publication*] ... ANSI Std Action
Anson Technical Institute, Ansonville, NC [*Library symbol*] ... NcAnA
Ansonia, CT [*Radio station call letters*] ... WADS
Ansul Co. [*NYSE symbol*] ... AFX
Answer [*In transcripts*] ... A
Answer ... AN
Answer ... ANS
Answer Construct ... AC
Answering Flag [*Navy*] [*British*] ... AN
Answering Machine Owner ... AMO
Anta [*Peru*] [*Airport symbol*] ... ATA
Anta Corp. [*NYSE symbol*] ... ANA
Antagonist Cimetidine [*Ulcer medicine manufactured by SmithKline Beckman Corp.*] ... TAGAMET
Antaios [*A publication*] ... Ant
Antalaha [*Madagascar*] [*Airport symbol*] ... ANM
Antalya [*Turkey*] [*Airport symbol*] ... AYT
Antananarivo [*Madagascar*] [*Airport symbol*] ... TNR
Antarctic ... A
Antarctic [*Marguerite Bay*] [*Antarctica*] [*Seismograph station code, US Geological Survey*] [*Closed*] ... ANC
Antarctic ... ANT
Antarctic [*MARC geographic area code*] [*Library of Congress*] ... t-------
Antarctic Bottom Water [*Oceanography*] ... AABW
Antarctic Journal of the United States [*A publication*] ... AJUS
Antarctic Journal of the United States [*A publication*] ... Antarctic J
Antarctic Journal of the United States [*A publication*] ... Antarct J US
Antarctic Journal of the United States [*A publication*] ... Antar Jour US
Antarctic Observation Team ... AOT
Antarctic Operations [*Military*] ... ANTOPS
Antarctic Record [*A publication*] ... Antarct Rec
Antarctic Research Programs ... ARP
Antarctic Research Series [*A publication*] ... Antarct Res Ser
Antarctic Support Activities ... ANTARCTICSUPPORT
Antarctic Task Force ... ATF
Antarctica [*Two-letter standard code*] ... AQ
Antarctica [*Three-letter standard code*] ... ATA
Antarctica [*MARC country of publication code*] [*Library of Congress*] ... ay
Antarctica [*MARC geographic area code*] [*Library of Congress*] ... t-ay---
Antarctica Service Medal [*US*] ... ASM
Antarctican Society ... AS
Antares Oil Corp. [*NASDAQ symbol*] ... ANTS
Antares SpA [*ICAO designator*] ... SL
Antarktika Doklady Komissii [*A publication*] ... Antarktika Doklady Kom
Ante [*Before*] [*Latin*] ... A
Ante [*Before*] [*Latin*] ... an
Ante Christum [*Before Christ*] [*Latin*] ... AC
Ante Christum Natum [*Before the Birth of Christ*] [*Latin*] ... ACN
Ante Cibum [*Before Meals*] [*Pharmacy*] ... AC
Ante-Communion ... AC
Ante Diem [*Before the Day*] [*Latin*] ... AD
Ante Jentaculum [*Before Breakfast*] [*Pharmacy*] ... ANT JENTAC
Ante Meridiem [*Forenoon*] [*Latin*] ... AM
Ante Prandium [*Before Dinner*] [*Pharmacy*] ... ANT PRAND
Ante Prandium [*Before Dinner*] [*Pharmacy*] ... AP
Antecedent Precipitation Index ... API
Antediluvian Order of Buffaloes [*British*] ... AOB
Antelope Island [*Utah*] [*Seismograph station code, US Geological Survey*] ... ANU
Antelope Valley Junior College [*California*] ... AVJC
Antelope Valley Junior College, Lancaster, CA [*Library symbol*] ... CLAV
Antenatal [*Medicine*] ... AN
Antenna ... ANT
Antenna Aspect Processor ... AAP
Antenna Base Spring ... ABS
Antenna Contour Measuring Equipment ... ACME
Antenna Control Console ... ACC
Antenna Control Display ... ACD
Antenna Control and Display Panel ... ACDP
Antenna Control Unit ... ACU
Antenna Counterbalance Cylinder Assembly ... ACCA
Antenna Coupler Receiver ... ACR
Antenna Coupling Regulator ... ACR
Antenna Cross Talk ... ACT
Antenna Directive Gain ... ADG
Antenna Dish Control ... ADC
Antenna Dummy Load ... ADL
Antenna Effective Height ... AEH
Antenna Effective Length for Electric-Field Antennas ... LE
Antenna Effective Length for Magnetic-Field Antennas ... LEM
Antenna Effective Resistance ... AER

Antenna Elevation Angle .... AEA
Antenna Feed Horn .... AFH
Antenna Feed System .... AFS
Antenna Field Charge Kit .... AFCK
Antenna Field Gain .... AFG
Antenna Homing System .... AHS
Antenna Impedance .... AI
Antenna Input Resistance .... AIR
Antenna Laboratory .... AL
Antenna Lightning Arrester .... ALA
Antenna Loading Coil .... ALC
Antenna Lobe for Variable Ionospheric Nimbus .... ALVIN
Antenna Mast Group [*PATRIOT*] [*Army*] .... AMG
Antenna Measurement Techniques Association .... AMTA
Antenna Noise Temperature .... ANT
Antenna Ohmic Resistance .... AOR
Antenna Pattern Analyzer .... APA
Antenna Pattern Correction [*for spacecraft data*] .... APC
Antenna Pattern Error Analysis .... APEA
Antenna Pattern Measurement Test [*Army*] .... APMT
Antenna Pattern Test System [*Army*] .... APATS
Antenna Pointing Angle Change .... APAC
Antenna Pointing Subsystem .... APS
Antenna Position Indicator .... API
Antenna Position Programer [*Manned Space Flight Network*] .... APP
Antenna Position Recorder .... APR
Antenna Positioning Device .... ANPOD
Antenna Positioning Mechanism .... APM
Antenna Power Gain .... APG
Antenna Radiation Pattern .... ARP
Antenna Radiation Resistance .... ARR
Antenna RADOME [*RADAR Dome*] **Heater** .... ARH
Antenna Range Equipment .... ARE
Antenna with Reflector .... R
Antenna Rotation Rate .... ARR
Antenna Select Logic Unit .... ASLU
Antenna Solar Panel Positioner .... ASPP
Antenna Steering Group .... ASG
Antenna Supports [*JETDS nomenclature*] [*Military*] .... AB
Antenna Switching Matrix .... ASM
Antenna System Readiness Monitor .... ASRM
Antenna Test Facility .... ATF
Antenna Test Group [*Army*] .... ATG
Antenna Test Model .... ATM
Antenna and Transmitter Improvement Study .... ATIS
Antennas, Complex [*JETDS nomenclature*] [*Military*] .... AS
Antennas and Propagation .... A/P
Antennas, Simple [*JETDS nomenclature*] [*Military*] .... AT
Antepartum Hemorrhage [*Medicine*] .... APH
Anterior .... A
Anterior .... ANT
Anterior Aorta .... AA
Anterior Axillary Line .... AAL
Anterior Bulbar Cell [*Neurobiology*] .... ABC
Anterior Burster [*Neuron*] .... AB
Anterior Chest Diameter .... ACD
Anterior Convex Side .... ACS
Anterior Cruciate Ligament [*Anatomy*] .... ACL
Anterior Facial Height .... AFH
Anterior Fold from Typhlosole .... AFT
Anterior [*Part of*] **Foot** .... AF
Anterior Hypothalamic Area .... AHA
Anterior Hypothalamic Nucleus [*Brain anatomy*] .... AH
Anterior Hypothalamus, Preoptic Area [*Brain anatomy*] .... AHPOA
Anterior [*Wall of*] **Kidney** .... AK
Anterior Lateral Myocardial Infarct [*Cardiology*] .... ALMI
Anterior Lateral Nerve .... ALN
Anterior Latissimus Dorsi [*Anatomy*] .... ALD
Anterior Lobe of Pituitary [*Gland*] .... ALP
Anterior Middle Suprasylvian Association [*Area of cat cortex*] .... AMSA
Anterior Mitral Leaflet [*Cardiology*] .... AML
Anterior Pituitary [*Endocrinology*] .... ANT PIT
Anterior Pituitary .... AP
Anterior Pituitary Extract [*Endocrinology*] .... APE
Anterior Pituitary Hormone [*Endocrinology*] .... APH
Anterior Pituitary-Like [*Endocrinology*] .... APL
Anterior Sorting Area .... ASA
Anterior Superior Iliac Spine .... ASIS
Anterior Superior Spine .... ASS
Anterior Tibialis [*Anatomy*] .... ATB
Anterior Trabeculae Carneae [*Heart anatomy*] .... ATC
Anterior Ventral Microtubule [*Anatomy*] .... AVM
Anterior Ventral Neuron [*Neurophysiology*] .... AV
Anterograde Amnesia [*Medicine*] .... AA
Anteroposterior .... AP
Anteroposterior Diameter .... A-PD
Anteroventral Cochlear Nucleus .... AVCN
Anteversion [*Medicine*] .... AV
Anthem Electronics [*American Stock Exchange symbol*] .... ATM
Anther [*Botany*] .... AN
Anthocyanin [*Fruit pigment*] .... ACN
Anthology .... ANTH
Anthology .... ANTHOL
Anthology Film Archives [*An association*] .... AFA
Anthon Herald, Anthon, IA [*Library symbol*] .... IaAntH
Anthon Public Library, Anthon, IA [*Library symbol*] .... IaAnt
Anthony Industries, Inc. [*NYSE symbol*] .... ANT
Anthony, KS [*Location identifier*] [*FAA*] .... ANY
Anthracite Information Bureau [*Defunct*] .... AIB
Anthracite Institute .... AI
Anthranilic Acid [*Organic chemistry*] .... AA
Anthrax Antiserum [*Medicine*] .... AAS
Anthropologiai Koezlemenyek [*A publication*] .... Anthr Kozl
Anthropologiai Koezlemenyek [*A publication*] .... Anthropol Koezlem
Anthropologiai Koezlemenyek [*A publication*] .... Anthropol Kozl
Anthropologica [*A publication*] .... Anthrplgica
Anthropological .... ANTHROPOL
Anthropological Forum [*A publication*] .... Ant F
Anthropological Forum [*A publication*] .... Anthro Forum
Anthropological Forum [*A publication*] .... Anthropol Forum
Anthropological Index [*A publication*] .... Antrol
Anthropological Index to Current Periodicals in the Library of the Royal Anthropological Institute [*A publication*] .... AICP
Anthropological Institute. Journal [*A publication*] .... Anthrop J
Anthropological Journal of Canada [*A publication*] .... Anthr J Can
Anthropological Linguistics [*A publication*] .... AnL
Anthropological Linguistics [*A publication*] .... AnthL
Anthropological Linguistics [*A publication*] .... Anthr Ling
Anthropological Linguistics [*A publication*] .... Anthro Ling
Anthropological Linguistics [*A publication*] .... Anthropol Ling
Anthropological Papers [*Smithsonian Institution*] [*A publication*] .... AP
Anthropological Papers. American Museum of Natural History [*A publication*] .... Anthropol Pap Am Mus Nat Hist
Anthropological Papers. American Museum of Natural History [*A publication*] .... Anthr Pap
Anthropological Papers. Museum of Anthropology. University of Michigan [*A publication*] .... Anthropol Pap Mus Anthropol Univ Mich
Anthropological Papers. Museum of Anthropology. University of Michigan [*A publication*] .... Anthr P Mic
Anthropological Quarterly [*A publication*] .... ANQU-A
Anthropological Quarterly [*A publication*] .... AnthQ
Anthropological Quarterly [*A publication*] .... Anth Quart
Anthropological Quarterly [*A publication*] .... Anthropol Quart
Anthropological Quarterly [*A publication*] .... Anthrop Q
Anthropological Quarterly [*A publication*] .... Anthr Q
Anthropological Records. University of California [*A publication*] .... Anthropol Rec Univ Calif
Anthropological Research Council [*British*] .... ARC
Anthropological Review [*A publication*] .... Anthrop R
Anthropologische Gesellschaft in Wien. Mitteilungen [*A publication*] .... Anthrop Gesell Wien Mitt
Anthropologischer Anzeiger [*A publication*] .... Anthro Anz
Anthropologischer Anzeiger [*A publication*] .... Anthropol Anz
Anthropology .... ANTHRO
Anthropology .... ANTHROP
Anthropology Case Materials Project [*National Science Foundation*] .... ACMP
Anthropology Film Center Foundation [*Formerly, AFI*] .... AFCF
Anthropology Film Institute [*Later, AFCF*] .... AFI
Anthropology Resource Center .... ARC
Anthropology-UCLA [*A publication*] .... Anthr-UCLA
Anthropomorphic Test Dummy .... ATD
Anthroponymica Suecana [*A publication*] .... ASu
Anthropos [*A publication*] .... Anthr
Anthroposophical Society in America .... ASA
Anti-alpha-staphylolysin [*Immunology*] .... ASTA
Anti-Antimissile Missile .... AAM
Anti-Apartheid Movement .... AAM
Anti-Beevers-Ross [*Beta-alumina crystallography*] .... aBR
Anti-Bureaucracy Special Interest Group [*Mensa*] .... ABSIG
Anti-Comintern Pact .... ACP
Anti-Communist Advisory Committee .... ACAC
Anti-Communist Committee .... ACC
Anti-Communist Confederation of Polish Freedom Fighters in USA .... ACCPFF
Anti-Communist League of America .... ACLA
Anti-Concorde Project .... A-CP
Anti-Corrosion Methods and Materials [*A publication*] .... Anti-Corros
Anti-Corrosion Methods and Materials [*A publication*] .... Anti-Corros Methods Mater
Anti-Defamation League of B'nai B'rith .... ADL
Anti-Defamation League of B'nai B'rith, New York, NY [*Library symbol*] .... NNAD
Anti-Digit Dialing League .... ADDL
Anti-Drug Coalition [*Later, NADC*] .... ADC
Anti-ETA [*Euzkadi ta Azkatasuna*] **Terrorism** [*Spain*] .... ATE
Anti-Fascist Organization [*Later, AFPFL*] [*Burma*] [*World War II*] .... AFO
Anti-Fascist People's Freedom League [*Formerly, AFO*] [*Burma*] [*World War II*] .... AFPFL
Anti-Friction Bearing Distributors Association [*Later, BSA*] .... AFBDA
Anti-Friction Bearing Manufacturers Association .... AFBMA
Anti-G-Suit .... AGS

Anti-Helicopter Device ... AHD
Anti-Icing [*Technical drawings*] ... AI
Anti-Icing Additive ... AIA
Anti-Icing System [*Aircraft*] ... AIS
Anti-Inflammatory Corticoid [*Endocrinology*] ... AC
Anti-Inflation Act [*Canada*] ... AIA
Anti-Inflation Appeal Tribunal [*Canada*] ... AIAT
Anti-Inflation Board ... AIB
Anti-Intercontinental Ballistic Missile ... AICBM
Anti-Intermediate Range Ballistic Missile ... AIRBM
Anti-Intrusion Alarm ... AIA
Anti-Intrusion Alarm Set ... AIAS
Anti-Invasion Factor [*In bone resorption*] ... AIF
Anti-Knock Index [*Automotive industry*] ... AKI
Anti-Locust Bulletin [*A publication*] ... Anti-Locust Bull
Anti-Locust Memoir [*A publication*] ... Anti-Locust Mem
Anti-Locust Research Centre [*Later, Centre for Overseas Pest Research*] [*British*] ... ALRC
Anti-Locust Research Centre [*Later, Centre for Overseas Pest Research*] **Report** [*A publication*] ... Anti-Locust Res Cent Rep
Anti-Missile Research Advisory Council ... AMRAC
Anti Nuclear [*A publication*] ... Anti Nk
Anti-Ovotransferrin [*Biochemistry*] ... AOT
Anti-Repression Resource Team ... ARRT
Anti-Revolutionaire Partij ... ARP
Anti-Slavery Society for the Protection of Human Rights ... ASSPHR
Anti-Tetany Substance 10 [*Same as DHT, Dihydrotachysterol*] [*Pharmacology*] ... AT-10
Anti-Torture Research [*An association*] ... ATR
Anti-Transmit-Receive ... ATR
Anti-Transmit-Receive Tube ... ATRT
Anti-U-Boat Warfare [*British*] [*World War II*] ... AU
Anti-Vivisection Party [*British*] ... AV
Anti-Vivisection Society [*Later, VIL*] ... AVS
Anti-Whole Rabbit Serum [*Immunology*] ... AWRS
Antiair Output ... AAO
Antiair Warfare ... AAW
Antiair Warfare Center ... AAWC
Antiair Warfare Commander [*or Coordinator*] ... AAWC
Antiair Warfare Exercise [*Navy*] ... AAWEX
Antiair Warfare Exercises in Port [*Navy*] ... AAWEXINPT
Antiair Warfare Reporting [*Navy*] ... AAW(R)
Antiair Warfare Support ... AAWSUP
Antiair Warfare Systems [*Navy*] ... AAWS
Antiair Warfare Training in Port [*Navy*] ... AAWIPT
Antiaircraft ... AA
Antiaircraft Armament ... AAA
Antiaircraft Artillery ... AAA
Antiaircraft Artillery Command ... AAAC
Antiaircraft Artillery and Guided Missile Center ... AAGMC
Antiaircraft Artillery Information [*or Intelligence*] **Service** ... AAAIS
Antiaircraft Artillery Information [*or Intelligence*] **Service** ... AAIS
Antiaircraft Artillery Operation Center ... AAAOC
Antiaircraft Artillery Reception Center ... AAARC
Antiaircraft Balloon [*Obsolete*] ... AA/B
Antiaircraft Cannon ... AAC
Antiaircraft Command ... AAC
Antiaircraft Common [*Projectile*] ... AAC
Antiaircraft Defences [*British*] ... AAD
Antiaircraft Defended Point ... AADP
Antiaircraft Defense Area ... AADA
Antiaircraft Defense System ... AADS
Antiaircraft Director Center ... AADC
Antiaircraft Fire Control ... AAFC
Antiaircraft Guided Missile ... AAGM
Antiaircraft Guided Missile System ... AAGMS
Antiaircraft Gun-Laying ... AAGL
Antiaircraft Light Cruiser [*Navy symbol*] ... CLAA
Antiaircraft Light Machine Gun ... AALMG
Antiaircraft Machine Gun ... AAMG
Antiaircraft Missile ... AAM
Antiaircraft Missile Battalion [*Marine Corps*] ... AAMSBN
Antiaircraft Observation Post ... AAOP
Antiaircraft Operations Center [*Air Force*] ... AAOC
Antiaircraft Searchlight ... AASL
Antiaircraft Self-Destroying ... AASD
Antiaircraft Station ... AASTA
Antiaircraft Technician ... AAT
Antiaircraft Training Center [*Navy*] ... AATC
Antiaircraft Training Center [*Navy*] ... AATRACEN
Antiaircraft Training and Test Center [*Navy*] ... AAT & TC
Antiaircraft Volunteer ... AAV
Antiarmor Cluster Munition ... ACM
Antiarmor Fuze ... AAF
Antibacklash Gear ... ABG
Antibacklash Gear ... ABLG
Antiballistic Missile [*Air Force*] ... ABM
Antiballistic Missile Early Warning System [*Air Force*] ... ABMEWS
Antiballistic-Missile Missile [*Air Force*] ... ABMM
Antibiotic-Associated Pseudomembranous Colitis [*Medicine*] ... AAPMC
Antibiotic Medicine and Clinical Therapy [*A publication*] ... Antibio Med Clin Ther
Antibiotica et Chemotherapia [*A publication*] ... Antibiot Chemother
Antibiotics Annual [*A publication*] ... Antibiot Annu
Antibiotics and Chemotherapy [*A publication*] ... Antibiot and Chemother
Antibiotics and Chemotherapy (Basel) [*A publication*] ... Antibiot Chemother (Basel)
Antibiotics and Chemotherapy (Washington, DC) [*A publication*] ... Antibiot Chemother (Wash DC)
Antibiotiki [*A publication*] ... Antibiot
Antibiotiki Respublikanskii Mezhvedomstvennyi Sbornik [*A publication*] ... Antibiot Resp Mezhved Sb
Antibodies to Nuclear Antigen [*Immunology*] ... ANA
Antibody [*Also, ABY*] [*Immunology*] ... Ab
Antibody Activity [*Immunology*] ... AA
Antibody-Coated Bacteria [*Immunology*] ... ACB
Antibody-Dependent Cell-Mediated Cytotoxicity [*Immunology*] ... ADCC
Antibody-Dependent Cell-Mediated Cytotoxicity [*Immunology*] ... ADCMC
Antibody-Forming Cell [*Immunology*] ... AFC
Antibody Mediated Cell Dependent Immune Lympholysis [*Immunology*] ... ABCIL
Antibody-Negative Mice with Latent Infection [*Immunology*] ... ANLI
Antibolshevic Bloc of Nations ... ABN
Anticar Theft [*Campaign or Committee*] ... ACT
Anticenter ... AC
Antichaff Circuit ... ANTC
Antichita Altoadriatiche [*A publication*] ... AAAd
Anticipate ... ANCPT
Anticipate ... ANTCP
Anticipated Level of Business ... ALB
Anticipated Life Span ... ALS
Anticipated Not Mission Capable, Supply [*Military*] ... ANMCS
Anticipated Not Operationally Ready, Maintenance ... ANORM
Anticipated Not Operationally Ready, Supply ... ANORS
Anticipated Transient without Scram [*Physics*] ... ATWS
Anticipated Vacancy [*Civil Service*] ... AV
Anticipatory Avoidance [*Medicine*] ... AA
Anticipatory Goal Response [*Medicine*] ... AGR
Anticircling Run [*Navy*] ... ACR
Anticlutter ... AC
Anticoagulant Citrate Dextrose [*Hematology*] ... ACD
Anticoagulant Therapy [*Medicine*] ... ACT
Anticoagulation ... AC
Anticoincidence Detection System ... ADS
Anticomplement Immunofluorescence Test [*Immunochemistry*] ... ACIF
Anticomplementary [*Immunology*] ... AC
Anticompromise Emergency Destruction ... ACED
Anticompromise Technique ... ACT
Anticonstipation Regimen [*Medicine*] ... ACR
Anticorrosive ... AC
Anticountermeasures Trainer ... ACTER
Anticrime Unit ... ACU
Anticyclonic [*Meteorology*] ... ACYC
Antidetonation Injection ... ADI
Antidiuretic Hormone [*Vasopressin*] [*Endocrinology*] ... ADH
Antidiuretic Substance ... ADS
Antiepileptic Drug ... AED
Antietam National Battlefield Site ... ANTI
Antiexposure Flight Suit ... AEFS
Antiferromagnetic Resonance ... AFMR
Antifriction Bearing ... AFB
Antifriction Metal ... AFM
Antigas [*Military*] ... AG
Antigen [*Also, a, Ag*] [*Immunology*] ... A
Antigen [*Also, A, a*] [*Immunology*] ... Ag
Antigen-Antibody [*Immunology*] ... Ag-AB
Antigen-Binding [*Immunology*] ... AB
Antigen-Binding Capacity [*Immunology*] ... ABC
Antigen-binding fragment [*Immunology*] ... Fab
Antigen-Carrier Lipid [*Immunology*] ... ACL
Antigen Presenting Cell [*Immunology*] ... APC
Antigen-Reactive Cell [*Immunology*] ... ARC
Antigenic Determinant [*Medicine*] ... AD
Antiglobulin Test [*Hematology*] ... AGT
Antigo Public Library, Antigo, WI [*Library symbol*] ... WAn
Antigo, WI [*Radio station call letters*] ... WATK
Antigo, WI [*Radio station call letters*] ... WRLO
Antigonish, NS [*Television station call letters*] ... CJCB-TV-2
Antigonish, NS [*Radio station call letters*] ... CJFX
Antigonish Review [*A publication*] ... AntigR
Antigravity ... AG
Antigravity Suit [*Air Force clothing for supersonic flight*] ... G (Suit)
Antigua [*Two-letter standard code*] ... AG
Antigua [*Antigua*] [*Seismograph station code, US Geological Survey*] ... ANG
Antigua [*Antigua*] [*Airport symbol*] ... ANU
Antigua [*MARC country of publication code*] [*Library of Congress*] ... aq
Antigua [*Three-letter standard code*] ... ATG
Antigua [*Antigua*] [*Seismograph station code, US Geological Survey*] [*Closed*] ... AWI
Antigua [*MARC geographic area code*] [*Library of Congress*] ... nwaq---

Antihemophilic Factor [*Factor VIII*] [*Also, AHG, PTF, TPC*] [*Hematology*] ... AHF
Antihemophilic Globulin [*Factor VIII*] [*Also, AHF, PTF, TPC*] [*Hematology*] ... AHG
Antihuman Globulin [*Consumption test*] [*Medicine*] ... AHG
Antihunt [*Circuit*] [*Electronics*] ... AH
Antihyaluronidase [*Clinical chemistry*] ... AH
Antijam Display ... AJD
Antijam Equipment ... AJE
Antijam Frequency ... AJF
Antijam Frequency Hopper ... AJFH
Antijam Hopper ... AJH
Antijam Operator ... AJO
Antijam Synthesizer ... AJS
Antijam Technique ... AJT
Antijamming [*RADAR*] ... AJ
Antijamming/Anti-Interference ... AJ/AI
Antijamming Improvements ... AJI
Antik Tanulmanyok [*A publication*] ... AT
Antike [*A publication*] ... Ant
Antike und Abendland [*A publication*] ... A & A
Antike, Alte Sprachen und Deutsche Bildung [*A publication*] ... AntAS
Antike und Christentum [*A publication*] ... AuChr
Antike Denkmaeler [*A publication*] ... Ant Denk
Antike Kunst [*A publication*] ... AK
Antike Kunst [*A publication*] ... AntK
Antike Plastik [*A publication*] ... AntP
Antike Welt [*A publication*] ... AW
AntiLASER Beam Coating ... ALBC
Antilles Air Boats, Inc. [*ICAO designator*] ... AD
Antilles Command, United States Army Caribbean ... ANTCOMDUSARCARIB
Antilles Research Program [*Yale University*] ... ARP
Antilliaanse Luchtvaart Maatschappi [*Netherlands*] [*ICAO designator*] ... LM
Antilogarithm ... ANTILOG
Antilymphocyte Globulin [*Immunology*] ... ALG
Antilymphocyte [*or Antilympholytic*] **Serum** [*Immunology*] ... ALS
Antimalaria Campaign ... AMC
Antimalarial Agent ... AMA
Antimassed Armor Strike Weapon System ... AASWS
Antimateriel [*Munitions*] ... AM
Antimateriel Warhead ... AMW
Antimateriel Warhead ... AMWH
Antimechanized [*Army*] ... AMECZ
Antimicrobial Agents and Chemotherapy ... AAC
Antimicrobial Agents and Chemotherapy [*A publication*] ... Antim Ag Ch
Antimicrobial Agents and Chemotherapy [*A publication*] ... Antimicrob Agents Chemother
Antiminesweeping Explosive Float ... AMSEF
Antimissile Array RADAR ... AMAR
Antimissile Missile [*Air Force*] ... AMM
Antimissile Missile and Space Defense Office ... AMMSDO
Antimissile Missile Test Range [*Military*] ... AMMTR
Antimissile Surface-to-Air Missile ... AMSAM
Antimissile Warfare ... AMW
Antimisting Kerosene [*Aviation*] ... AMK
Antimitochondral Antibodies [*Immunology*] ... AMA
Antimony Trisulfide Oxysulfide ... ASOS
Antimotor Torpedo Boat ... AMTB
Antimotorboat ... AMB
Antimultipath Equipment ... AME
Antimuscle Factor [*Immunology*] ... AMF
Antinuclear Antibody [*Immunology*] ... ANA
Antinuclear Factor [*Immunology*] ... ANF
Antinuclear Submarine Warfare [*Navy*] ... ANSW
Antioch College, Yellow Springs, OH [*OCLC symbol*] ... ANC
Antioch College, Yellow Springs, OH [*Library symbol*] ... OYesA
Antioch Program for Interracial Education [*Antioch College*] ... APIE
Antioch Review [*A publication*] ... Antioch R
Antioch Review [*A publication*] ... Ant R
Antioch Review [*A publication*] ... AR
Antioxidant Activity [*Food technology*] ... AA
Antipernicious Anemia Factor [*Also, EF, LLD*] [*Hematology*] ... APAF
Antipersonnel [*Projectile*] ... AP
Antipersonnel [*Projectile*] ... APER
Antipersonnel [*Projectile*] ... APERS
Antipersonnel Antimaterial [*Weaponry*] ... APAM
Antipersonnel Bomb ... APB
Antipersonnel Missile ... APM
Antipersonnel Projectile ... APP
Antiphase Boundaries [*Mineralogy*] ... APB
Antiphase Domains [*Mineralogy*] ... APD
Antiphlogistic-Corticoid Conditioning Effect [*Medicine*] ... A-CC
Antiplugging Relay ... APR
Antipodal Propagation Phenomena ... APP
Antipolo [*Philippines*] [*Later, MUT*] [*Geomagnetic observatory code*] ... ANO
Antiprostaglandin Antiserum [*Immunology*] ... APS
Antipsychotic Drug ... APD
Antiquarian [*or Antiquities*] ... ANTIQ
Antiquarian Book Monthly Review [*A publication*] ... ABMR
Antiquarian Bookman [*A publication*] ... AB
Antiquarian Bookman [*A publication*] ... Ant Bk
Antiquarian Bookman [*A publication*] ... Antiq Bkman
Antiquarian Booksellers Association [*International*] ... ABA
Antiquarian Booksellers Association of America ... ABAA
Antiquarian Booksellers' Center ... ABC
Antiquarian Horological Society ... AHS
Antiquarian Horological Society Monograph [*A publication*] ... AHSM
Antiquarian House, Plymouth, MA [*Library symbol*] ... MPIA
Antiquarian Trade List Annual [*A publication*] ... ATLA
Antiquaries Journal [*A publication*] ... Antiq J
Antiquaries Journal [*A publication*] ... Antiq Jnl
Antiquaries Journal [*A publication*] ... Antiquar J
Antiquaries Journal [*A publication*] ... AntJ
Antiquariorum Regiae Societatis Socius [*Fellow of the Royal Society of Antiquaries*] [*British*] ... ARSS
Antiquarische Gesellschaft in Zuerich. Mitteilungen [*A publication*] ... Antiq Gesell in Zuerich Mitt
Antiquary, Jewitt's [*A publication*] ... Antiquary
Antiquary (New Series) [*A publication*] ... Antiq n s
Antique Airplane Association ... AAA
Antique Appraisal Association of America ... AAAA
Antique Auto Racing Association ... AARA
Antique Automobile Club of America ... AACA
Antique Bicycle Club of America ... ABCA
Antique Boat and Yacht Club ... ABYC
Antique Bottle Collectors Association [*Defunct*] ... ABCA
Antique and Classic Boat Society ... ACBS
Antique Engine and Thresher Association ... AETA
Antique and Historical Glass Foundation ... AHGF
Antique Motorcycle Club of America ... AMCA
Antique Phonograph Collectors Club ... APCC
Antique Radio Club of America ... ARCA
Antique Radio Guild of America ... ARGA
Antique Snowmobile Club of America ... ASCOA
Antique Studebaker Club ... ASC
Antique Telephone Collectors Association ... ATCA
Antique Toy Collectors of America ... ATCA
Antique Wireless Association ... AWA
Antiques [*A publication*] ... Antiq
Antiques Journal [*A publication*] ... Antiques J
Antiquitaeten-Rundschau [*A publication*] ... AR
Antiquitas Hungarica [*A publication*] ... AntHung
Antiquite Classique [*A publication*] ... AC
Antiquite Classique [*A publication*] ... An Cl
Antiquite Classique [*A publication*] ... AntC
Antiquite Classique [*A publication*] ... Ant Cl
Antiquites Africaines [*A publication*] ... Ant Afr
Antiquites Africaines [*A publication*] ... Antiq Afr
Antiquities ... ANT
Antiquity [*A publication*] ... Antiq
Antiquo [*I Oppose*] [*Latin*] [*Used by Romans to signify a negative vote*] ... A
Antirabies Serum [*Medicine*] ... ARS
Antiracketeering ... AR
AntiRADAR ... AR
AntiRADAR Missile ... ARM
AntiRADAR Surveillance and Target Acquisition System ... ASTAS
Antiradiation Guidance Sensor ... ARGS
Antiradiation Homer ... ARH
Antiradiation Missile ... ARM
Antiradiation Projectile ... ARP
Antiradiation Weapon System ... ARWS
Antireceptor Antibody [*Immunology*] ... ARA
Antirecession Fiscal Assistance ... ARFA
Antireflection ... AR
Antireflection Coated Metal-Oxide Semiconductor ... AMOS
Antirepeat Relay ... ARR
Antireticular Cytotoxic Serum ... ACS
Antiriot Laws ... ARL
Antisatellite ... ASAT
Antisaturation Inverter ... ASI
Antiself Homing [*System*] [*Torpedo safety device*] [*Navy*] ... ASH
Antiserum [*Immunology*] ... AS
Antiship Capable Missile ... ASCM
Antiship Cruise Missiles ... ASCM
Antiship Missile ... ASM
Antiship Missile Defense ... ASMD
Antiship Missile Target ... ASMT
Antiship Phoenix ... ASP
Antiship Surveillance and Targeting [*Navy*] ... ASST
Antiship Torpedo ... ASTOR
Antiship Torpedo Defense ... ASTD
Antiship Underwater Warfare ... ASUW
Antishock Body ... ASB
Antislack Device ... ASD
Antisolar ... A-SOL
Antistatic Additive ... ASA
Antistatic Compound ... ASC
Antistreptolysin [*Immunology*] ... ASL
Antistreptolysin-O [*Also, ASO*] [*Clinical chemistry*] ... ASLO
Antistreptolysin-O [*Also, ASLO*] [*Clinical chemistry*] ... ASO
Antisubmarine ... AS

Antisubmarine [*Designation for all US military aircraft*] ... S
Antisubmarine Air Control [*Navy*] ... ASAC
Antisubmarine Attack Plotter [*Navy*] ... ASAP
Antisubmarine Attack Teacher ... ASAT
Antisubmarine Attack Teacher Training Unit ... ASATTU
Antisubmarine Classification and Analysis Center [*Navy*] ... ASCAC
Antisubmarine Classification Analysis Test ... ASCAT
Antisubmarine Composite Engineering Squadron ... ACES
Antisubmarine Contact Evaluation System [*Navy*] ... ASCES
Antisubmarine Defense Forces, Atlantic [*Obsolete*] [*Navy*] ... ASDEFORLANT
Antisubmarine Defense Forces, Pacific [*Obsolete*] [*Navy*] ... ASDEFORPAC
Antisubmarine Defense Group ... ASDG
Antisubmarine Detection Investigation Committee [*A group in World War I that gave rise to the device that bore its name in World War II*] ... ASDIC
Antisubmarine Development Detachment [*Navy*] ... ASDD
Antisubmarine Development Detachment, Atlantic Fleet [*Navy*] ... ASDEVLANT
Antisubmarine Establishment [*Navy*] [*British*] ... ASE
Antisubmarine Experimental Establishment ... A/SEE
Antisubmarine Fighter Squadron [*Navy*] ... ANTISUBFITRON
Antisubmarine Fighter Squadron [*Navy*] ... VSF
Antisubmarine Fixed Defenses Officer ... A/SFDO
Antisubmarine Helicopter ... HPS
Antisubmarine Launched Ballistic Missile ... ASLBM
Antisubmarine Patrol ... ASP
Antisubmarine Rocket [*Navy*] ... ASROC
Antisubmarine Submarine [*Navy symbol*] ... SSK
Antisubmarine Systems Project Office [*Navy*] ... ASPO
Antisubmarine Technical Evaluation Center [*Military*] ... ASTEC
Antisubmarine Terrier ... ASTER
Antisubmarine Test Requirement Outline ... ASTRO
Antisubmarine War Division [*British*] ... A/SWD
Antisubmarine Warfare ... ASW
Antisubmarine Warfare Advisory Committee ... ASWAC
Antisubmarine Warfare Air Control Ship ... ASWACS
Antisubmarine Warfare and Antiair Warfare ... ASW/AAW
Antisubmarine Warfare Barrier Submarine Patrol Area [*Navy*] ... SUBPA
Antisubmarine Warfare Barrier Submarine Patrol Zone [*Navy*] ... SUBPZ
Antisubmarine Warfare Barrier Surface Patrol Area [*Navy*] ... SURFPA
Antisubmarine Warfare Barrier Surface Patrol Ship [*Navy*] ... SURF
Antisubmarine Warfare Barrier Surface Patrol Zone [*Navy*] ... SURFPZ
Antisubmarine Warfare Barriers [*Military*] ... ASWB
Antisubmarine Warfare Center [*NATO*] ... ASWC
Antisubmarine Warfare Commander [*Navy*] ... ASWC
Antisubmarine Warfare Electronic Countermeasures System ... ASWEC
Antisubmarine Warfare Environmental Prediction Service [*Navy*] ... ASWEPS
Antisubmarine Warfare Exercise ... ASWEX
Antisubmarine Warfare Force, Sixth Fleet [*Navy*] ... ASWFORSIXTHF
Antisubmarine Warfare Group ... ASWGRU
Antisubmarine Warfare Improved Localization System ... ASWILS
Antisubmarine Warfare Information Exchange System [*Navy*] ... ASWIXS
Antisubmarine Warfare Installations [*NATO*] ... ASWI
Antisubmarine Warfare Integrated Combat System ... ASWICS
Antisubmarine Warfare Laboratory [*Military*] ... ASWL
Antisubmarine Warfare Operational Research Group [*World War II*] ... ASWORG
Antisubmarine Warfare Operations Centers [*Navy*] ... ASWOC
Antisubmarine Warfare Operations Patrol ... ASWPTL
Antisubmarine Warfare Programs [*Navy*] ... AWP
Antisubmarine Warfare Project Office [*Navy*] ... ASWPO
Antisubmarine Warfare Research Center [*NATO*] ... ASWRC
Antisubmarine Warfare Research Center [*NATO*] ... ASWRECEN
Antisubmarine Warfare Schoolship [*Navy*] ... ASWSS
Antisubmarine Warfare Ship Command and Control System ... ASWSCCS
Antisubmarine Warfare Standoff Weapon ... ASW/SOW
Antisubmarine Warfare Systems [*Navy*] ... ASWS
Antisubmarine Warfare Systems Analysis Group [*Navy*] ... ASWSAG
Antisubmarine Warfare Systems Project Office [*Navy*] ... ASWR
Antisubmarine Warfare Systems Project Office [*Navy*] ... ASWSPO
Antisubmarine Warfare Tactical Data System [*Navy*] ... ASWTDS
Antisubmarine Warfare Tactical Navigation System [*Navy*] ... ASWTNS
Antisubmarine Warfare Tactical School ... ASWTACSCOL
Antisubmarine Warfare Target Vehicle ... ASWTV
Antisubmarine Warfare Test Requirement Outline ... ASWTRO
Antisubmarine Warfare Training Center [*Navy*] ... ASWTC
Antisubmarine Warfare Training Center [*Navy*] ... ASWTRACEN
Antisubmarine Warfare Training in Port [*Navy*] ... ASWIPT
Antisubmarine Warfare Training Unit ... ASWTU
Antisubmarine Warfare/Underwater Warfare ... ASW/UW
Antisubmarine Warfare Unit [*Navy*] ... ASWU
Antisubmarine Warning - Long Range ... ASW-LR
Antisubmarine Warning - Short Range ... ASW-SR
Antisubmarine Weapon ... ASW
Antisurface [*Military*] ... A/S
Antisurface Raiders Exercise ... RAIDEX
Antisurface Ship Missile [*NATO*] ... ASSM
Antisurface Warfare [*Navy*] ... ASUW
Antisurface Warfare Commander [*Navy*] ... ASUWC
Antisyphilitic Treatment [*Medicine*] ... AST
Antitactical Ballistic Missile ... ATB
Antitactical Ballistic Missile ... ATBM
Antitank [*Also, ATk*] ... AT
Antitank [*Also, AT*] ... ATk
Antitank Aircraft Rocket ... ATAR
Antitank Assault Air Defense ... ATAAD
Antitank Battalion [*Marine Corps*] ... ATBN
Antitank Battery [*Military*] ... ATB
Antitank Grenade Launcher ... ATGL
Antitank Guided Air Rocket ... ATGAR
Antitank Guided Missile ... ATGM
Antitank Guided Weapon ... ATGW
Antitank Gun [*Military*] ... ATG
Antitank Mine Dispensing System ... ATMDS
Antitank Missile [*Air Force*] ... ATM
Antitank, Nonmetallic ... ATNM
Antitank Regiment [*Military*] ... ATR
Antitank Rocket Launcher Imagery Interpretation ... ATRL
Antitank Weapon ... ATW
Antitank Weapons Effect Signature Simulator [*Army*] ... ATWESS
Antiterrain Avoidance RADAR System ... ATARS
Antitetanus Serum [*Medicine*] ... ATS
Antithrombin [*Hematology*] ... AT
Antithymocyte Gamma-Globulin [*Immunology*] ... ATGAM
Antithymocyte Globulin [*Immunochemistry*] ... ATG
Antithymocyte Serum [*Immunochemistry*] ... ATS
Antithyroglobulin Antibody [*Immunochemistry*] ... ATA
Antitorpedo [*Nets*] ... AT
Antitorpedo ... ATORP
Antitorque Pedal ... ATP
Antitoxin Unit [*Immunology*] ... AU
Antitracking Control ... ATRC
Antitrust Bulletin [*A publication*] ... Antitrust B
Antitrust Bulletin [*A publication*] ... Antitrust Bull
Antitrust Law ... ATL
Antitrust Law and Economics Review [*A publication*] ... Antitrust L & Econ Rev
Antitrust Law Symposium [*A publication*] ... Antitrust L Sym
Antitrust and Monopoly Subcommittee [*US Senate*] ... A & M
Antitrust and Trade Regulation Report [*of Bureau of National Affairs*] ... ATRR
Antiunderwater Warfare ... AUW
Antivehicle [*Munitions*] ... AV
Antivehicle Device [*Air Force*] ... AVD
Antivehicle Land Mine ... AVLM
Antivehicle Mine ... AVM
Antivibration Joint ... AVJ
Antiviral Factor ... AVF
Antiviral Protein [*Immunology*] ... AVP
Antiviral Research [*A publication*] ... AR
Antivoice-Operated Transmission ... ANTIVOX
Antiwear ... AW
Antiyeast Factor [*Medicine*] ... AYF
Antlers, OK [*Location identifier*] [*FAA*] ... AEE
Antlia [*Constellation*] ... Ant
Antlia [*Constellation*] ... Antl
Antofagasta [*Chile*] [*Airport symbol*] ... ANF
Antofagasta [*Chile*] [*Seismograph station code, US Geological Survey*] ... ANT
Antokon'ny Kongresin'ny Fahaleovantenan' i Madagasikara [*Party for the Congress for the Independence of Madagascar*] ... AKFM
Anton Chico, NM [*Location identifier*] [*FAA*] ... ACH
Antoniani Benedictini Armeni [*Mechitarists*] ... ABA
Antonianum [*A publication*] ... An
Antonianum [*A publication*] ... Anton
Antonie Van Leeuwenhoek Journal of Microbiology and Serology [*A publication*] ... Antonie Van Leewenhoek J Microbiol Serol
Antonie Van Leeuwenhoek Journal of Microbiology and Serology [*A publication*] ... A Van Leeuw
Antony and Cleopatra [*Shakespearean work*] ... Ant
Antonym ... ANT
Antropologica [*A publication*] ... Antropologi
Antropologicky Archiv [*A publication*] ... Antropol Arch
Ants, Mice, and Gophers [*Electromagnetic antipest device*] ... AMIGO
Antsalova [*Madagascar*] [*Airport symbol*] ... WAQ
Antsohihy [*Madagascar*] [*Airport symbol*] ... WAI
Antwerp [*Belgium*] [*Airport symbol*] ... ANR
Antwerpiensia [*A publication*] ... Antw
Antwerpsch Archievenblad [*A publication*] ... AA
Anuar de Lingvistica si Istorie Literara [*A publication*] ... ALIL
Anuari. Oficina Romanica [*A publication*] ... AOR
Anuario. Asociacion Francisco de Vitoria [*A publication*] ... AAFV
Anuario Brasileiro de Economia Florestal. Instituto Nacional de Pinho [*A publication*] ... Anu Bras Econ Flor Inst Nac Pinho
Anuario Brasileiro de Odontologia [*A publication*] ... Anu Bras Odontol
Anuario de Derecho de la Universidad de Panama [*A publication*] ... Anu Der Univ Panama
Anuario Ecuatoriano de Derecho Internacional [*A publication*] ... Anu Ecuator Der Int
Anuario Espanol e Hispano-Americano [*A publication*] ... AEHA

Anuario Estadistico de la Mineria Mexicana [*A publication*]........ Anu Estad Min Mex
Anuario de Estudios Atlanticos [*A publication*]........ AEA
Anuario de Estudios Medievales [*A publication*]........ AEM
Anuario. Facultad de Derecho [*A publication*]........ Anu Fac Der
Anuario de Filologia [*A publication*]........ AnuarioF
Anuario Filosofico [*A publication*]........ Anu Filosof
Anuario de la Historia del Derecho Espanol [*A publication*]........ AHDE
Anuario Indigenista [*A publication*]........ Anu Indig
Anuario. Institut de'Estudios Catalans [*A publication*]........ AIEC
Anuario. Instituto de Ciencias Penales y Criminologicas [*A publication*]........ Anu Inst Cienc Pen Criminol
Anuario de Letras [*A publication*]........ AdL
Anuario da Literatura Brasileira [*A publication*]........ ALBr
Anuario Mineral Brasileiro [*A publication*]........ Anu Miner Brasil
Anuario Musical [*A publication*]........ An M
Anuario Musical [*A publication*]........ Anu Mus
Anuario de Prehistoria Madrilena [*A publication*]........ APM
Anuario. Sociedad Folklorico de Mexico [*A publication*]........ ASFM
Anuario. Sociedade Broteriana [*A publication*]........ Anu Soc Broteriana
Anuario Tecnico. Instituto de Pesquisas Zootecnicas "Francisco Osorio" [*A publication*]........ Anu Tec Inst Pesqui Zootec "Francisco Osorio"
Anuarul Comisiunii Monumentelor Istorice. Sectia pentru Transilvania [*A publication*]........ ACM
Anuarul. Institutul de Studii Clasice [*A publication*]........ AICS
Anuarul. Institutului de Patologie si Igiena Animala Bucuresti [*A publication*]........ Anu Inst Patol Ig Anim Bucur
Anuarul. Universitatea Cluj [*A publication*]........ AUC
Anus........ A
Anvik [*Alaska*] [*Airport symbol*]........ ANV
Anvil Mountain [*Alaska*] [*Seismograph station code, US Geological Survey*]........ ANV
Anxiety Index [*Psychology*]........ AI
Anxiety Scale for the Blind [*Psychology*]........ ASB
Anxiety Scale Questionnaire [*Psychology*]........ ASQ
Anxiety Score [*Psychology*]........ AS
Anxiety Sign [*Psychology*]........ AxS
Anxiety State [*Psychology*]........ AS
Anxiety Tension State [*Psychology*]........ ATS
Any Acceptable........ A/A
Any Boy Can [*Program*] [*Defunct*]........ ABC
Any-to-Come [*Type of wager where any cash forthcoming from earlier bets finances further bets*] [*British*]........ ATC
Any Good Brand........ AGB
Any Quantity........ AQ
Any Tape Search [*Computer program*]........ ANTS
Anybody But Carter [*Movement within Democratic Party to deny Jimmy Carter the 1976 Presidential nomination*]........ ABC
Anybody But Wallace [*Political slogan concerning Alabama governor George Wallace*]........ ABW
Anybody but McGovern [*Democratic movement during 1972 presidential campaign*]........ ABM
Anything That You Desire [*Notation in a placebo prescription*] [*Medicine*]........ ADT
Anzar Road [*California*] [*Seismograph station code, US Geological Survey*]........ ANZ
Anzeiger. Akademie der Wissenschaften (Wien) [*A publication*]........ AAWW
Anzeiger. Akademie der Wissenschaften (Wien) [*A publication*]........ Anz (Wien)
Anzeiger fuer die Altertumswissenschaft [*A publication*]........ Anz Alt
Anzeiger fuer die Altertumswissenschaft [*A publication*]........ Anz Altertumsw
Anzeiger fuer die Altertumswissenschaft [*A publication*]........ Anz Altertumswiss
Anzeiger fuer die Altertumswissenschaft. Herausgegeben von der Oesterreichischen Humanistischen Gesellschaft [*A publication*]........ AAHG
Anzeiger fuer Deutsches Altertum [*A publication*]........ Anz f D Altert
Anzeiger fuer Deutsches Altertum und Deutsche Literatur [*A publication*]........ ADA
Anzeiger des Germanischen Nationalmuseums [*A publication*]........ AGN
Anzeiger des Germanischen Nationalmuseums [*A publication*]........ AGNM
Anzeiger fuer Indogermanische [*A publication*]........ Idg Anz
Anzeiger fuer Indogermanische Sprach- und Altertumskunde [*A publication*]........ AIF
Anzeiger der Kaiserlich Akademie der Wissenschaften [*Wien*] [*A publication*]........ AKAW
Anzeiger. Oesterreichischen Akademie der Wissenschaften [*Wien*]. **Mathematisch-Naturwissenschaftliche Klasse** [*A publication*]........ Anz Oesterr Akad Wiss Math Naturwiss Kl
Anzeiger. Oesterreichischen Akademie der Wissenschaften [*Wien*]. **Philosophisch-Historische Klasse** [*A publication*]........ AOAW
Anzeiger. Oesterreichischen Akademie der Wissenschaften (Wien). Philosophisch-Historische Klasse [*A publication*]........ AAWW
Anzeiger der Ornithologischen Gesellschaft in Bayern [*A publication*]........ Anz Ornithol Ges Bayern
Anzeiger fuer Schaedlingskunde [*A publication*]........ Anz Schaedlingskd
Anzeiger fuer Schaedlingskunde und Pflanzenschutz [*Later, Anzeiger fuer Schaedlingskunde, Pflanzenschutz, Umweltschutz*] [*A publication*]........ Anz Schaedlingskd Pflanzenschutz
Anzeiger fuer Schaedlingskunde, Pflanzenschutz, Umweltschutz [*A publication*]........ Anz Schaedlingskd Pflanzenschutz Umweltschutz
Anzeiger fuer Schaedlingskunde, Pflanzenschutz, Umweltschutz [*A publication*]........ Anz Schaedlingskd Pflanzen- und Umweltschutz
Anzeiger fuer Schweizerische Altertumskunde [*A publication*]........ Anz Schweiz
Anzeiger fuer Schweizerische Altertumskunde [*A publication*]........ ASA
Anzeiger fuer Schweizerische Altertumskunde [*A publication*]........ ASAK
Aomori [*Japan*] [*Airport symbol*]........ AOJ
Aomori [*Japan*] [*Seismograph station code, US Geological Survey*]........ AOM
Aomori Outpost [*Japan*] [*Seismograph station code, US Geological Survey*]........ AOMJ
Aortacoronary Bypass Graft [*Cardiology*]........ ACBG
Aortic Arch Syndrome [*Medicine*]........ AAS
Aortic Incompetence [*or Insufficiency*] [*Medicine*]........ AI
Aortic Pressure [*Medicine*]........ AP
Aortic Regurgitation [*Medicine*]........ AR
Aortic Root [*Cardiology*]........ AR
Aortic Second Sound [*Medicine*]........ A_2
Aortic Stenosis [*Medicine*]........ AS
Aortic Valve [*Cardiology*]........ AV
Aortic Valve Echophonocardiogram [*Cardiology*]........ AVE
Aortic Valve Replacement [*Cardiology*]........ AVR
Aorto-Femoral Bypass [*Medicine*]........ AFB
Aorto-Iliac Occlusive Disease [*Medicine*]........ AIOD
Aortopulmonary [*Cardiology*]........ AP
Aoyama Journal of General Education [*A publication*]........ Aoyama J Gen Educ
APA-PSIEP [*American Psychological Association-Project on Scientific Information Exchange in Psychology*] **Report** [*A publication*]........ APA-PSIEP Rep
Apache [*MARC language code*] [*Library of Congress*]........ apa
Apache, Black Hawk, and Chinook Self-Deployments [*Military*]........ ABCD
Apache Corp. [*NYSE symbol*]........ APA
Apache Energy & Mining Co. [*NASDAQ symbol*]........ APCH
Apache Junction, AZ [*Radio station call letters*]........ KSTM
Apache Petroleum [*NYSE symbol*]........ APP
[*The*] **Apache Railway Co.** [*AAR code*]........ APA
Apalachee Community Mental Health Services, Inc., Tallahassee, FL [*Library symbol*]........ FTaA
Apalachicola, FL [*Location identifier*] [*FAA*]........ AAF
Apalachicola, FL [*Location identifier*] [*FAA*]........ AQQ
Apalachicola Northern Railroad Co. [*AAR code*]........ AN
Aparatura Naukowa i Dydaktyczna [*A publication*]........ Apar Nauk Dydakt
Apartado [*Colombia*] [*Airport symbol*]........ APO
Apartment........ APT
Apartment Owners and Managers Association of America........ AOMA
Apartments........ APTS
Apataki [*French Polynesia*] [*Airport symbol*]........ APK
Apatite [*CIPW classification*] [*Geology*]........ ap
Apatite Subgroup [*Apatite, fluorite, calcite, pyrite, iron*] [*CIPW classification*] [*Geology*]........ A
Apatity [*USSR*] [*Seismograph station code, US Geological Survey*]........ APA
APAVE, Revue Technique du Groupement des Associations de Proprietaires d'Appareils a Vapeur et Electriques [*A publication*]........ APAVE
APCHE [*Automatic Program Checkout Equipment*] **Relay Box**........ ARB
APCO Argentina, Inc. [*NASDAQ symbol*]........ APAGF
Apco Oil Corp. [*NYSE symbol*] [*Delisted*]........ AOL
APE [*Amalgamated Power Engineering Ltd.*] **Engineering** [*A publication*]........ APE Eng
APEA [*Australian Petroleum Exploration Association*] **Journal** [*A publication*]........ APEA J
Apeco Corp. [*Formerly, American Photocopy Equipment Co.*] [*NYSE symbol*] [*Delisted*]........ APY
Apeiranthos Of Naxos [*Greece*] [*Seismograph station code, US Geological Survey*]........ APE
Apercus sur l'Economie Tchecoslovaque [*A publication*]........ Apercus Econ Tchecosl
Aperture........ AP
Aperture........ APER
Aperture........ APERT
Aperture Current Setting [*In Coulter counter*] [*Microbiology*]........ ACS
Aperture Distribution and Maintenance [*System*]........ ADAM
Aperture Lip........ APL
Aperture Plate Character Generator........ APCG
Aperture Relay Experiment Definition........ ARED
Apex Beat [*Medicine*]........ AB
Apex Cardiogram [*Medicine*]........ ACG
Apex Cardiogram [*Medicine*]........ APCG
Aphorism........ APH
Aphoxide [*Also, TEPA*] [*Mutagen*]........ APO
Apia [*Samoa Islands*] [*Geomagnetic observatory code*]........ API
Apia [*Samoa Islands*] [*Airport symbol*]........ APW
Apia [*Samoa Islands*] [*Seismograph station code, US Geological Survey*]........ API
Apiary Inspectors of America........ AIA
Apical Cell [*Botany*]........ AC
Apical/Radial [*Pulse*] [*Medicine*]........ A/R
Apical Rate [*Medicine*]........ AR

Apicoltore d'Italia [*A publication*]....Apicolt Ital
Apicultura in Romania [*A publication*]....Apic Rom
Apicultural Abstracts [*A publication*]....AA
Apicultural Abstracts [*A publication*]....Apic Abstr
APL Corp. [*Formerly, Admiral Plastics Corp.*] [*NYSE symbol*]....APL
APL Management Planning and Engineering Resources Evaluation [*Navy*]....AMPERE
APL [*Applied Physics Laboratory*] **Technical Digest** [*A publication*]....APL Tech Dig
Aplikace Matematiky [*A publication*]....Apl Mat
Aplington Legion Memorial Library, Aplington, IA [*Library symbol*]....IaAp
Apneustic Center [*Brain anatomy*]....APC
Apocalypse [*Writings from about 200 BC to 150 AD which principally deal with a cataclysmic end to the world followed by resurrection and judgment*]....Apoc
Apocrypha....APOCR
Apogee....APG
Apogee....APO
Apogee....APOG
Apogee Boost Motor [*Aerospace*]....ABM
Apogee Enterprises, Inc. [*NASDAQ symbol*]....APOG
Apogee Injection Module [*NASA*]....AIM
Apogee Kick [*NASA*]....AK
Apogee Kick Motor [*NASA*]....AKM
Apogee Motor Assembly with Paired Satellites [*NASA*]....AMAPS
Apogee Motor Fire [*Aerospace*]....AMF
Apogee Motor Igniter [*NASA*]....AMI
Apogee Motor Timer [*NASA*]....AMT
Apollo [*A publication*]....Apo
Apollo Access Arm [*NASA*]....AAA
Apollo Airways [*Detroit, MI*] [*FAA designator*]....BKS
Apollo Airways, Inc. [*Goleta, CA*] [*FAA designator*]....SNC
Apollo Applications [*NASA*]....AA
Apollo Applications Program [*NASA*]....AAP
Apollo Applications Program Office [*NASA*]....AAPO
Apollo Applications Test Requirements [*NASA*]....AATR
Apollo Command [*or Communications*] **System** [*NASA*]....ACS
Apollo Computer Address Matrix [*NASA*]....ACAM
Apollo Computer, Incorporated [*NASDAQ symbol*]....APCI
Apollo Contractor Information Center [*NASA*]....ACIC
Apollo Crew Systems Branch [*NASA*]....ACSB
Apollo Data Bank [*NASA*]....ADB
Apollo Data [*or Document*] **Descriptions Standards** [*NASA*]....ADDS
Apollo Data Manager [*NASA*]....ADM
Apollo Development [*NASA*]....AD
Apollo Display Console [*NASA*]....ADC
Apollo Docking Test Device [*NASA*]....ADTD
Apollo Document Distribution Requirements Index [*NASA*]....ADDRI
Apollo Document Index [*NASA*]....ADI
Apollo Document Preparation Standards [*Handbook*] [*NASA*]....ADPS
Apollo Documentation Administration Instruction [*NASA*]....ADAI
Apollo Documentation List [*NASA*]....ADL
Apollo Dynamic Programs [*NASA*]....ADP
Apollo Earth-Orbiting Station [*NASA*]....AES
Apollo Engineering Documentation Board [*NASA*]....AEDB
Apollo Engineering and Technology Index [*NASA*]....AETI
Apollo Experiment Pallet [*NASA*]....AEP
Apollo Experiment Support [*NASA*]....AES
Apollo Extension Program [*NASA*]....AEP
Apollo Extension System [*NASA*]....AES
Apollo Flight Control [*NASA*]....AFC
Apollo/GOSS [*Ground Operations Support System*] **Navigation Qualifications** [*NASA*]....AGNQ
Apollo Guidance Computer [*NASA*]....AGC
Apollo Guidance Equipment [*NASA*]....AGE
Apollo Guidance Ground Display [*NASA*]....AGGD
Apollo Guidance and Navigation Industrial Support [*NASA*]....AGNIS
Apollo Guidance and Navigation Information [*NASA*]....AGANI
Apollo Implementing Instructions [*NASA*]....AII
Apollo Industries, Inc. [*NASDAQ symbol*]....APOL
Apollo Initiator Resistance Measuring Equipment [*NASA*]....AIRME
Apollo Instrumentation Ships [*NASA*]....AIS
Apollo Intermediate Chart [*NASA*]....AIC
Apollo Launch Data System [*NASA*]....ALDS
Apollo Launch Operation Panel [*NASA*]....ALOP
Apollo Launch Operations Committee [*NASA*]....ALOC
Apollo Launch Trajectory Data System [*NASA*]....ALTDS
Apollo Light-Flash Moving-Emulsion Detector [*NASA*]....ALFMED
Apollo Logistic Support System [*NASA*]....ALSS
Apollo Lunar Excursion Module Sensors [*NASA*]....ALEMS
Apollo Lunar Exploration Mission [*NASA*]....ALEM
Apollo Lunar Hand Tool [*NASA*]....ALHT
Apollo Lunar Hand Tool Carrier [*NASA*]....ALHTC
Apollo Lunar Logistic Support [*NASA*]....ALLS
Apollo Lunar Module [*NASA*]....ALM
Apollo Lunar Orbit [*NASA*]....ALO
Apollo Lunar Orbital Science [*NASA*]....ALOS
Apollo Lunar Polar Orbiter [*NASA*]....ALPO
Apollo Lunar Radioisotopic Heater [*NASA*]....ALRH
Apollo Lunar Sample Return Container [*NASA*]....ALSRC
Apollo Lunar Sounder Experiment [*NASA*]....ALSE
Apollo Lunar Surface Closeup Camera [*Apollo 11*] [*NASA*]....ALSCC
Apollo Lunar Surface Drill [*NASA*]....ALSD
Apollo Lunar Surface Experiments Package [*NASA*]....ALSEP
Apollo Master Measurements Program [*NASA*]....AMMP
Apollo Mission Planning Task Force [*NASA*]....AMPTF
Apollo Mission Programs [*NASA*]....AMP
Apollo Mission Simulator [*NASA*]....AMS
Apollo Navigation Working Group [*NASA*]....ANWG
Apollo Network [*NASA*]....ANW
Apollo Network Simulations [*NASA*]....ANS
Apollo Operations Handbook [*NASA*]....AOH
Apollo Orbital Research Laboratory [*NASA*]....AORL
Apollo Orbiting Laboratory Module [*NASA*]....AOLM
Apollo Owners Register....AOR
Apollo, PA [*Radio station call letters*]....WAVL
Apollo Pad Test [*NASA*]....APT
Apollo Part Task Trainer [*NASA*]....APTT
Apollo Parts Information Center [*NASA*]....APIC
Apollo Payload Exploration [*NASA*]....APPLE
Apollo Personnel Identification Program [*NASA*]....APIP
Apollo Personnel Investigation Program [*NASA*]....APIP
Apollo Preflight Operations Procedures [*NASA*]....APOP
Apollo Problem Bulletin [*NASA*]....APB
Apollo Program [*NASA*]....AP
Apollo Program Control Center [*NASA*]....APCC
Apollo Program Control Room [*NASA*]....APCR
Apollo Program Definition Phase [*NASA*]....APDP
Apollo Program Directive [*NASA*]....APD
Apollo Program Logic Network [*NASA*]....APLN
Apollo Program Office [*NASA*]....APO
Apollo Program Requirements [*NASA*]....APR
Apollo Program Specifications [*NASA*]....APS
Apollo Propellant Gauging System [*NASA*]....APGS
Apollo Propulsion Analysis Program [*NASA*]....APAP
Apollo Qualification [*NASA*]....AQ
Apollo Range Instrumentation Aircraft [*NASA*]....ARIA
Apollo Reentry Communications Blackout Working Group [*NASA*]....ACBWG
Apollo Reentry Ship [*NASA*]....ARS
Apollo Reliability Engineering [*NASA*]....ARE
Apollo Reliability Engineering Electronics [*NASA*]....AREE
Apollo Requirements Manual [*NASA*]....ARM
Apollo Saturn [*NASA*]....AS
Apollo Ship's Operational Readiness Force [*NASA*]....ASORF
Apollo Signal Definition Document [*NASA*]....ASDD
Apollo Simple Penetrometer [*NASA*]....ASP
Apollo Simulated Remote Site [*NASA*]....ASRS
Apollo Simulation Checkout and Training System [*NASA*]....ASCATS
Apollo Site Selection Board [*NASA*]....ASSB
Apollo-Soyuz Docking Module [*NASA*]....ASDM
Apollo-Soyuz Test Project [*NASA*]....ASTP
Apollo Spacecraft Development Test Plan [*NASA*]....ASDTP
Apollo Spacecraft Hardware Utilization Request [*NASA*]....ASHUR
Apollo Spacecraft Parts and Materials Information Services [*NASA*]....ASPMIS
Apollo Spacecraft Project Office [*NASA*]....ASPO
Apollo Special Task Team [*NASA*]....ASTT
Apollo Standard Detonator [*NASA*]....ASD
Apollo Standard Initiator [*NASA*]....ASI
Apollo Supplemental Procedural Information [*NASA*]....ASPI
Apollo Support Department [*NASA*]....ASD
Apollo Technical Documentation Distribution List [*NASA*]....ATDDL
Apollo Telemetry Aircraft Project [*NASA*]....ATAP
Apollo Telescope Mount [*NASA*]....ATM
Apollo Telescope Mount Console [*NASA*]....ATMC(O)
Apollo Telescope Mount - Deployed [*NASA*]....ATM-D
Apollo Telescope Mount Deployment Assembly [*NASA*]....ATMDA
Apollo Telescope Mount Digital Computer [*NASA*]....ATMDC
Apollo Telescope Mount - Stowed [*NASA*]....ATM-S
Apollo Test Integration Working Groups [*NASA*]....ATIWG
Apollo Test Operations [*NASA*]....ATO
Apollo Test Requirements [*NASA*]....ATR
Apollo Time Conditioner [*NASA*]....ATC
Apollo Trajectory Decision Logic Prototype [*NASA*]....ATDLP
Apollo Unified S-Band Circuit Margin [*Program*] [*NASA*]....AUSBCM
Apollo Validation Test [*NASA*]....AVT
Apollo Vehicle Systems Section [*NASA*]....AVSS
Apollo Wind-Tunnel Testing Program [*NASA*]....AWTTP
Apollo XI Collector Society [*Defunct*]....AXICS
Apomorphine [*Neurochemistry, pharmacology*]....APO
Apopka, FL [*Radio station call letters*]....WTLN
Apopka, FL [*Radio station call letters*]....WTLN-FM
Apostilb [*Unit of luminance*]....Asb
Apostle [*Church calendars*]....A
Apostle....AP
Apostle and Evangelist [*Church calendars*]....AE
Apostles....APP
Apostles of the Sacred Heart of Jesus [*Roman Catholic women's religious order*]....ASCJ
Apostleship of Prayer....AP
Apostleship of the Sea [*See also AM*]....AOS

Apostleship of the Sea in the United States ... ASUS
Apostolado del Mar [*Apostleship of the Sea - AOS*] ... AM
Apostolado Sacerdotal [*A publication*] ... AS
Apostolate of Christ the Worker ... ACW
Apostolate for Family Consecration ... AFC
Apostolic Anti-Communist Alliance [*Spain*] ... AAA
Apostolic Church ... AC
Apostrophe ... APOS
Apothecary ... APOTH
Apoyeque [*Nicaragua*] [*Seismograph station code, US Geological Survey*] ... APY
Appalachia Education Laboratory ... AEL
Appalachia Magazine [*A publication*] ... Appalachia Mag
Appalachian [*FAA*] ... APLCN
Appalachian Airport Safety Improvement Program ... AASIP
Appalachian Area [*MARC geographic area code*] [*Library of Congress*] ... n-usa--
Appalachian Bible Institute, Bradley, WV [*Library symbol*] ... WvBrA
Appalachian Community Service Network [*Cable-television system*] ... ACSN
Appalachian Consortium ... AC
Appalachian Educational Laboratory, Inc., Charleston, WV [*Library symbol*] ... WvCAE
Appalachian Finance Association ... APFA
Appalachian Flying Service, Inc. [*Blountville, TN*] [*FAA designator*] ... APL
Appalachian Hardwood Manufacturers, Incorporated ... AHMI
Appalachian Journal [*A publication*] ... Appal J
Appalachian Laboratory for Occupational Respiratory Diseases ... ALFORD
Appalachian Land Stabilization and Conservation Program ... ALSCP
Appalachian Mountain Club ... AMC
Appalachian News Service [*A publication*] ... Appl News
Appalachian Power Co. [*NYSE symbol*] ... AEW
Appalachian Power Company ... APC
Appalachian Regional Commission ... ARC
Appalachian State Teachers College [*Later, ASU*] [*North Carolina*] ... ASTC
Appalachian State University [*Formerly, ASTC*] [*North Carolina*] ... ASU
Appalachian State University, Boone, NC [*Library symbol*] ... NcBoA
Appalachian State University, Boone, NC [*OCLC symbol*] ... NJB
Appalachian Trail ... AT
Appalachian Trail Conference ... ATC
Appalachian Volunteers, Incorporated ... AVI
Appaloosa Horse Club ... AHC
Appaloosa Horse Club ... ApHC
Apparatura i Metody Rentgenovskogo Analiza [*A publication*] ... Appar Metody Rentgenovskogo Anal
Apparatus ... APAR
Apparatus ... APP
Apparatus ... APPAR
Apparatus ... APTUS
Apparatus Mounted in Plastic ... AMPLAS
Apparel Business Control [*System*] [*Data processing*] ... ABC
Apparel Guild ... AG
Apparel Industries Inter-Association Committee ... AIIC
Apparel Industry Committee on Imports ... AICI
Apparel Manufacturing Executives Association ... AMEA
Apparel Performance Level Standards [*Pronounced "apples"*] ... APLS
Apparel Research Foundation [*Defunct*] ... ARF
Apparent ... APPAR
Apparent ... APRNT
Apparent Activation Energy ... AAE
Apparent Candle Power ... ACP
Apparent Digestible Energy [*Nutrition*] ... ADE
Apparent Free Testosterone Concentration [*Clinical chemistry*] ... AFTC
Apparent Molar Quantity ... AMQ
Apparent Oxygen Utilization ... AOU
Apparent Polar Wander [*Paleomagnetism*] ... APW
Apparent Polar Wander Path [*Paleomagnetism*] ... APWP
Apparent Power [*Symbol*] ... S
Apparently ... APP
Appeal ... APPL
Appeal Cases [*Legal*] [*British*] ... AC
Appeal of Conscience Foundation ... ACF
Appeal and Marathon Republic, Albert City, IA [*Library symbol*] ... IaAlcAM
Appeal, Plain Facts, Personalities, Local Angle, Action, Uniqueness [*or Universality*], **Significance, Energy** ... APPLAUSE
Appeals Examining Office [*CSC*] ... AEO
Appeals Review Board [*Formerly, BAR*] [*Civil Service Commission*] ... ARB
Appear ... APPR
Appearance ... APP
Appearance Potential Spectroscopy [*Physics*] ... APS
Appelbo [*Sweden*] [*Seismograph station code, US Geological Survey*] ... APP
Appellate Division [*Legal*] ... AD
Appellation d'Origine Controlle [*Official place name for wine*] ... AOC
Appendage ... APPEN
Appendix ... APP
Appendix ... APPX
Applanation [*Ophthalmology*] ... APPLAN
Apple Computer, Inc. [*NASDAQ symbol*] ... AAPL
Apple Valley [*California*] [*Airport symbol*] [*Obsolete*] ... APV
Apple Valley, CA [*Radio station call letters*] ... KAPV
Apple Valley, CA [*Radio station call letters*] ... KAVR
Appleby College, Oakville, ON, Canada [*Library symbol*] ... CaOOakA
Applejack ... AJ
Appleton [*Wisconsin*] [*Airport symbol*] ... ATW
Appleton-Century-Crofts [*Publisher*] ... ACC
Appleton Memorial Hospital, Appleton, WI [*Library symbol*] ... WAM
Appleton, MN [*Television station call letters*] ... KWCM-TV
Appleton, OH [*Location identifier*] [*FAA*] ... APE
Appleton Public Library, Appleton, WI [*Library symbol*] ... WA
Appleton Public Library, Appleton, WI [*OCLC symbol*] ... WIQ
Appleton, WI [*Radio station call letters*] ... WAPL-FM
Appleton, WI [*Television station call letters*] ... WBUD
Appleton, WI [*Radio station call letters*] ... WHBY
Appleton, WI [*Radio station call letters*] ... WLFM
Appleton, WI [*Radio station call letters*] ... WVMS
Appleton's Journal [*A publication*] ... Appleton
Appliance ... APPL
Appliance Manufacturer [*A publication*] ... Appl Mfr
Appliance Parts Distributors Association ... APDA
Appliance Parts Jobbers Association [*Later, APDA*] ... APJA
Appliance, Range, Adjust [*Data processing*] ... ARGA
Applicability Code ... APCOD
Applicable ... APPL
Applicable Analysis [*A publication*] ... App Anal
Applicable Analysis [*A publication*] ... Appl Anal
Applicable Analysis [*A publication*] ... Applicable Anal
Applicandus [*To Be Applied*] [*Pharmacy*] ... APPLICAND
Applicant Data System [*Department of Labor*] ... ADS
Applicant File Search [*US Employment Service*] [*Department of Labor*] ... AFS
Applicant Holding Office [*Employment*] ... AHO
Applicant Outreach Program [*Department of Labor*] ... AOP
Applicant Qualification Test [*Navy*] ... AQT
Application ... APP
Application ... APPLN
Application ... APPLON
Application of the 1973 Middle East War to CAA [*Concepts Analysis Agency*] **War Games, Models, and Simulations** ... AMWAR
Application of Autonomous Passive Classification ... AAPC
Application Data Material Readiness List [*DoD*] ... ADMRL
Application Design Service [*IBM Corp.*] ... ADS
Application Development Facility [*Data processing*] ... ADF
Application Development Systems [*Data processing*] ... ADS
Application Development Task Group [*Navy*] ... ADTG
Application Engineering ... AE
Application Explorer Mission [*NASA*] ... AEM
Application Functions Module [*Data processing*] ... AFM
Application Module Library [*IBM Corp.*] ... AML
Application Oriented Language [*Data processing*] ... AOL
Application Package for Chemical Engineers ... APACHE
Application for Passport for Self and/or Dependents Accordance BUPERS Manual [*Navy*] ... PLYPASSPORT
Application Program [*Data processing*] ... AP
Application Program Generator [*Data processing*] ... APG
Application Program Interface [*Data processing*] ... API
Application of RADAR Ballistic Acceptance Testing ... ARBAT
Application of Remote Manipulators in Space [*Robot*] [*NASA*] ... ARMS
Application Replacement Factor ... ARF
Application and Resource Control ... A & RC
Application of Science and Technology to Rural Areas [*An association*] ... ASTRA
Application of Space Techniques Relating to Aviation [*International Civil Aviation Organization*] ... ASTRA
Application Systems Developer [*Army*] ... ASD
Application Transfer Teams [*IBM Corp.*] ... ATT
Applications Control Language [*Data processing*] ... ACL
Applications Explorer [*NASA*] ... AE
Applications and Industry ... AI
Applications of Mathematics [*A publication*] ... Appl Math
Applications of Moessbauer Spectroscopy [*A publication*] ... Appl Moessbauer Spectrosc
Applications Processor ... AP
Applications Program Integration Board [*NASA*] ... APIB
Applications of Surface Science [*A publication*] ... Appl Surf Sci
Applications Systems Verification Test [*NASA*] ... ASVT
Applications Technology Satellite [*NASA*] ... ATS
Applications Technology Satellite Operations Control Center [*NASA*] ... ATSOCC
Applications Vertical Test Program [*Communication Satellite program*] ... AVT
Applicative Language Idealized Computing Engine ... ALICE
Applicatur [*Let It Be Applied*] [*Pharmacy*] ... APPLICAT
Applied ... APP
Applied ... APPL
Applied ... APPLD
Applied Acoustics [*A publication*] ... AACOB
Applied Acoustics [*A publication*] ... Appl Acoust
Applied Behavior Analysis [*Psychology*] ... ABA
Applied Biochemistry and Bioengineering [*A publication*] ... Appl Biochem Bioeng
Applied Biochemistry and Biotechnology [*A publication*] ... ABB

Applied Biochemistry and Microbiology [*A publication*] ... Appl Biochem Microbiol
Applied Biosystems [*NASDAQ symbol*] ... ABIO
Applied Circuit Technology [*NASDAQ symbol*] ... ACRT
Applied Communication Research, Inc. [*Information service*] ... ACR
Applied Communications [*NASDAQ symbol*] ... ACIS
Applied Communications Systems Center [*AT & T*] ... ACSC
Applied Computer Research [*Information service*] ... ACR
Applied Data Communications [*NASDAQ symbol*] ... ADCC
Applied Data Research, Inc. [*American Stock Exchange symbol*] ... ADR
Applied Decision Analysis ... ADA
Applied Decision Systems [*Temple, Barker, & Sloane, Inc.*] [*Information service*] ... ADS
Applied Devices Corp. [*American Stock Exchange symbol*] [*Delisted*] ... ADE
Applied Digital Data Systems, Inc. [*NASDAQ symbol*] ... ADDS
Applied Digital Data Systems, Inc. [*NYSE symbol*] [*Delisted*] ... ADS
Applied DNA Systems [*NASDAQ symbol*] ... ADNA
Applied Economics [*A publication*] ... Appl Econ
Applied Electrical Phenomena [*A publication*] ... Appl Electr Phenom
Applied Energy [*A publication*] ... Appl Energy
Applied Entomology ... AE
Applied Entomology and Zoology [*A publication*] ... Appl Entomol Zool
Applied and Environmental Microbiology [*A publication*] ... Appl Environ Microbiol
Applied Ergonomics [*A publication*] ... AERGB
Applied Ergonomics [*A publication*] ... Appl Ergon
Applied Forest Research Institute [*Syracuse University*] ... AFRI
Applied Information and Data Management Systems Section [*Battelle Memorial Institute*] [*Information service*] ... AIDMS
Applied Information Management System [*Data processing*] ... AIMS
Applied Journalism ... AJ
Applied LASER Projects Staff ... ALPS
Applied Magnetics Corp. [*NYSE symbol*] ... APM
Applied Manufacturing Research and Process Development ... AMRPD
Applied Materials [*NASDAQ symbol*] ... AMAT
Applied Mathematical Modelling [*A publication*] ... Appl Math Model
Applied Mathematical Sciences [*A publication*] ... Appl Math Sci
Applied Mathematics and Computation [*A publication*] ... Appl Math Comput
Applied Mathematics and Computation (New York) [*A publication*] ... Appl Math Comput (New York)
Applied Mathematics Group ... AMG
Applied Mathematics Laboratory ... AML
Applied Mathematics and Mechanics [*A publication*] ... Appl Math Mech
Applied Mathematics and Mechanics [*A publication*] ... App Math & Mech
Applied Mathematics Notes [*A publication*] ... Appl Math Notes
Applied Mathematics and Optimization [*A publication*] ... Appl Math O
Applied Mathematics and Optimization [*A publication*] ... Appl Math Optim
Applied Mathematics Panel [*of NDRC*] [*World War II*] ... AMP
Applied Mathematics Series ... AMS
Applied Mathematics and Statistics Laboratory [*Stanford University*] ... AMSL
Applied Mechanics Division [*American Society of Mechanical Engineers*] ... AMD
Applied Mechanics Engineer [*Academic degree*] ... App ME
Applied Mechanics Reviews [*A publication*] ... AMR
Applied Mechanics Reviews [*A publication*] ... ApMec
Applied Mechanics Reviews [*A publication*] ... Appl Mech Rev
Applied Medical Devices [*NASDAQ symbol*] ... AMDI
Applied Microbiology [*A publication*] ... ApMicrobiol
Applied Microbiology [*A publication*] ... Appl Microb
Applied Microbiology [*A publication*] ... Appl Microbiol
Applied Microbiology [*A publication*] ... App Microbiol
Applied Microbiology Group [*Natick Laboratories*] [*Army*] ... AMG
Applied Mineralogy. Technische Mineralogie [*A publication*] ... Appl Mineral
Applied Naturalist Guild [*Defunct*] ... ANG
Applied Neurophysiology [*A publication*] ... Appl Neurop
Applied Neurophysiology [*A publication*] ... Appl Neurophysiol
Applied Optics [*A publication*] ... Ap Optics
Applied Optics [*A publication*] ... Appl Opt
Applied Optics [*A publication*] ... App Op
Applied Optics [*A publication*] ... App Optics
Applied Ornithology [*A publication*] ... Appl Ornithol
Applied Parallel Programing Language Experiment [*Data processing*] ... APPLE
Applied Physics ... AP
Applied Physics [*A publication*] ... Appl Phys
Applied Physics [*A publication*] ... App Phys
Applied Physics Branch [*Air Proving Ground Center*] ... APB
Applied Physics and Engineering [*A publication*] ... Appl Phys Eng
Applied Physics Laboratory [*Johns Hopkins University*] ... APL
Applied Physics Laboratory, Johns Hopkins University ... APL/JHU
Applied Physics Laboratory (University of Washington) ... APL(UW)
Applied Physics Letters [*A publication*] ... Appl Phys L
Applied Physics Letters [*A publication*] ... Appl Phys Lett
Applied Physics Research Section ... APRS
Applied Plastics [*A publication*] ... Appl Plast
Applied Polymer Symposia [*A publication*] ... Appl Polym Symp
Applied Power B Pfd [*NASDAQ symbol*] ... APWRP
Applied Psychological Measurement [*A publication*] ... Appl Psychol Meas
Applied Psychological Services ... APS
Applied Psychology Corporation ... APC
Applied Psychology Panel [*of NDRC*] [*World War II*] ... APP
Applied Psychology Unit ... APU
Applied Radiology [*A publication*] ... Applied Radiol
Applied Radiology [*A publication*] ... Appl Radiol
Applied Radiology and Nuclear Medicine [*A publication*] ... Appl Radiol Nucl Med
Applied Research ... APPRES
Applied Research ... AR
Applied Research [*of ASRA*] [*National Science Foundation*] ... AR
Applied Research Corporation ... ARC
Applied Research Laboratories [*Commercial firm*] ... ARL
Applied Research Laboratory [*Johns Hopkins University*] ... ARL
Applied Research Management ... ARM
Applied Research in Mental Retardation [*A publication*] ... Appl Res Ment Retard
Applied Research Objective ... ARO
Applied Research: Operation Weather Analysis [*Navy*] ... AROWA
Applied Research Program ... ARPO
Applied Science [*A publication*] ... Applied Sc
Applied Science ... AS
Applied Science Corporation ... ASC
Applied Science Corporation of Princeton ... ASCOP
Applied Science Laboratory ... ASL
Applied Science and Research Applications [*Program*] [*Supersedes RANN*] [*National Science Foundation*] ... ASRA
Applied Science through Research and Engineering ... ASTRE
Applied Science and Technology Index [*A publication*] ... Appl Sci Technol Index
Applied Science and Technology Index [*A publication*] ... AST
Applied Science and Technology Index [*A publication*] ... ASTI
Applied Science and Technology Index [*A publication*] ... A S & T Ind
Applied Scientific Research [*A publication*] ... Appl Sci Re
Applied Scientific Research Corporation of Thailand. Annual Report [*A publication*] ... Appl Sci Res Corp Thail Annu Rep
Applied Scientific Research (The Hague) [*A publication*] ... Appl Sci Res (The Hague)
Applied Solar Energy [*A publication*] ... Appl Sol Energy
Applied Solar Energy [*NASDAQ symbol*] ... SOLR
Applied Solid State Science [*A publication*] ... Appl Solid State Sci
Applied Space Technology Regional Advancement ... ASTRA
Applied Spectroscopy [*A publication*] ... Appl Spectr
Applied Spectroscopy [*A publication*] ... Appl Spectrosc
Applied Spectroscopy [*A publication*] ... Appl Spectry
Applied Spectroscopy Reviews [*A publication*] ... Appl Spectrosc Rev
Applied Spectroscopy Reviews [*A publication*] ... Appl Sp Rev
Applied Statistics [*A publication*] ... Appl Stat
Applied Statistics [*A publication*] ... AS
Applied Statistics. Proceedings of Conference at Dalhousie University [*A publication*] ... P Ap St Dalho
Applied Statistics Training Institute ... ASTI
Applied Systems Development Evaluation Center ... ASDEC
Applied Systems and Personnel ... ASAP
Applied Technology Advanced Computer ... ATAC
Applied Technology Council ... ATC
Applied Technology Laboratory [*Army*] ... ATL
Applied Therapeutics [*A publication*] ... Appl Ther
Applied Urbanetics, Incorporated [*Information service*] ... AUI
Applique ... APLQ
Apply Fixture ... APFX
Apply Template ... AT
Appoint ... APNT
Appoint ... APT
Appointed ... APP
Appointed ... APPTD
Appointing Order ... AO
Appointment ... APPMT
Appointment ... APPT
Appointment and Promotion Advisory Committee [*UN Food and Agriculture Organization*] ... APAC
Appointment Recommended ... APRMD
Appointment Will Be Regarded as Having Terminated upon This Date ... POINTERM
Appointments Register ... AR
Appomattox Court House National Historic Park ... APCO
Appomattox Regional Library, Hopewell, VA [*Library symbol*] ... ViHop
Appomattox, VA [*Radio station call letters*] ... WTTX
Appomattox, VA [*Radio station call letters*] ... WTTX-FM
Apportioned Effort ... AE
Appraisal. Children's Science Books [*A publication*] ... ACSB
Appraisal Journal [*A publication*] ... Appraisal J
Appraisal of Language Disturbance [*Test*] ... ALD
Appraisal of the Navy RDT & E [*Research, Development, Test, and Evaluation*] **Program** ... ANREP
Appraisers Association of America ... AAA
Appreciation of Capital, Protection, Income [*Finance*] ... API
Appreciation Index [*Television ratings*] [*British*] ... AI
Apprehend ... APP
Apprehend ... APPR
Apprentice ... APP
Apprentice ... APR

Apprentice Seaman ... AS
Apprentices' Free Library, Philadelphia, PA [*Library symbol*] [*Obsolete*] ... PPAp
Apprentices National Insurance [*British*] ... ANI
Apprenticeship ... APPR
Apprenticeship Committee [*Department of Labor*] ... AC
Apprenticeship Information Center [*Department of Labor*] ... AIC
Apprenticeship, Referral, and Outreach for Women [*An association*] [*Defunct*] ... AROW
Apprenticeship and Training Conference [*Bureau of Apprenticeship and Training*] [*Department of Labor*] ... ATC
Apprenticeship and Training Representative [*Bureau of Apprenticeship and Training*] [*Department of Labor*] ... ATR
Approach ... APCH
Approach ... APP
Approach ... APRCH
Approach [*A publication*] ... APP
Approach Astrophysics Payload ... APP
Approach Chart ... AC
Approach by Concept [*Information retrieval*] ... ABC
Approach Control [*Aviation*] ... A/C
Approach Control [*Aviation*] ... APC
Approach Control [*FAA*] ... APCON
Approach Control [*Air Force*] ... APPCON
Approach Control Center ... ACC
Approach Control Office [*Aviation code*] ... APP
Approach Control RADAR ... ACR
Approach and Departure Control [*Aviation*] ... AADC
Approach End Barrier Engagement ... AEBE
Approach End Runway [*Aviation*] ... AER
Approach Indexer ... APEXER
Approach and Landing [*Aviation*] ... A & L
Approach Landing Autopilot System ... ALAS
Approach and Landing Flight Test ... ALFT
Approach and Landing Procedures Simulator ... ALPS
Approach and Landing Simulator ... ALS
Approach Landing System ... ALS
Approach and Landing Test ... ALT
Approach and Landing Test Requirement ... ALTR
Approach Light Contact Height ... ALCH
Approach Light Lane [*Aviation*] ... YL
Approach Light System [*Aviation*] ... ALS
Approach Lighting System with Sequenced Flashers [*Aviation*] ... ALSF
Approach, Naval Aviation Safety Review [*A publication*] ... ANAR
Approach Path Control System [*Navy*] ... APCS
Approach Power Compensator [*or Control*] ... APC
Approach Power Compensator System [*Navy*] ... APCS
Approach Power Control Set ... APCS
Approaches ... AP
Approaches [*Maps and charts*] ... Apprs
Approaching ... APCHG
Approbation ... APPRO
Approdo Letterario [*A publication*] ... ApL
Appropriate ... APROP
Appropriate Authority [*Office of Censorship*] [*World War II*] ... AA
Appropriate Duty [*Air Force*] ... APDY
Appropriate for Gestational Age [*Medicine*] ... AGA
Appropriate Health Resources and Technology Action Group [*ITDG*] [*British*] ... AHRTAG
Appropriate National Authorities ... ANA
Appropriate Technology ... AT
Appropriate Technology International ... ATI
Appropriate Technology - United Kingdom Unit [*ITDG*] [*British*] ... AT-UK
Appropriated Funds ... APF
Appropriating Property in Possession of Common Carrier [*FBI standardized term*] ... APIPOCC
Appropriation ... APPN
Appropriation ... APPROP
Appropriation Account Data [*Business and trade*] ... AAD
Appropriation Accounts and Data Processing Division [*Ministry of Agriculture, Fisheries, and Food*] [*British*] ... AA & DPD
Appropriation and Budget Activity [*Army*] ... ABA
Appropriation and Expense ... A & E
Appropriation Purchases Account ... APA
Appropriation Transfer Account ... ATA
Approval ... APPR
Approval ... APPRO
Approval ... APPVL
Approval ... APRVL
Approval ... APVL
Approval in Principle ... AIP
Approval Requests [*Military*] ... APREQS
Approval for Service Use [*Military*] ... ASU
Approve ... APPV
Approve ... APRV
Approve ... APV
Approved ... A
Approved ... APPD
Approved ... APVD
Approved as Amended ... AAA
Approved to British Standard [*British Standards Institution*] ... ABS
Approved Conference Rate and Interconference Agreement [*of Steamship Lines in the Foreign Commerce of the United States*] ... ACRA
Approved Cult ... AC
Approved Data Element ... ADE
Approved Departure Time ... ADT
Approved Equivalent Parts List ... AEPL
Approved Fastener Substitution List ... AFSL
Approved Force Acquisition Objective [*Army*] ... AFAO
Approved Force Budget Objective [*Army*] ... AFBO
Approved Force Gross Requirement [*Army*] ... AFGR
Approved Force Inventory Objective [*Army*] ... AFIO
Approved Force War Reserves ... AFWR
Approved Item Name ... AIN
Approved Marine Devices Co. ... AMD
Approved Material Substitution List ... AMSL
Approved Materials List [*NASA*] ... AML
Approved Modernization Maintenance Program ... AMMP
Approved Operating Budget [*Army*] ... AOB
Approved Parts List ... APL
Approved Production Inspection System ... APIS
Approved for Release ... AR
Approved and Removed ... A & R
Approved Spare Parts List ... ASPL
Approved Supplier Tab List ... ASTL
Approved System Requirement ... ASR
Approved Tank Wagon ... ATW
Approved Type Certificate [*Governmental airworthiness certification for planes*] ... ATC
Approved Vendors List ... AVL
Approving Authority ... AA
Approximate [*Rate*] [*Value of the English pound*] ... A
Approximate ... APPRX
Approximate ... APRX
Approximate Absolute ... AA
Approximate Cubic Search [*Mathematics*] ... ACS
Approximate Degrees of Freedom [*Statistics*] ... ADF
Approximate Exposure Time ... AET
Approximate Lethal Dose ... ALD
Approximate Quadratic Search [*Mathematics*] ... AQS
Approximately ... APP
Approximately ... APPROX
Approximately ... APRXLY
APRA [*Australasian Performing Right Association*] **Journal** [*A publication*] ... APRA J
Apres Jesus-Christ [*After Christ*] [*French*] ... AP JC
Apres Livraison [*After Delivery*] [*French*] ... AL
Apricot Producers of California ... APC
April ... A
April ... AP
April ... APL
April ... APR
April Fools' Day ... AFD
Apron [*Aviation*] ... APN
APS, Inc. [*American Stock Exchange symbol*] [*Delisted*] ... APS
Aptechnoe Delo [*A publication*] ... Aptechn Delo
Aptitude ... APT
Aptitude Area ... APTA
Aptitude Assessment Battery Programing [*Data processing*] ... AABP
Aptitude Index ... AI
Aptitude Index Battery [*LIMRA*] ... AIB
Aptitude-Treatment Interactions [*Education*] ... ATI
Aptos-Capitola, CA [*Radio station call letters*] ... KMFO
Apud [*At, In the Works Of*] [*Latin*] ... AP
Apus [*Constellation*] ... Aps
Aqaba [*Jordan*] [*Airport symbol*] ... AQJ
Aqua [*Water*] [*Latin*] ... A
Aqua [*Water*] [*Latin*] ... AQ
Aqua Bulliens [*Boiling Water*] [*Pharmacy*] ... AQ BULL
Aqua Calida [*Hot Water*] [*Pharmacy*] ... AQ CAL
Aqua-Cat Catamaran Sailing Association ... ACSA
Aqua Communis [*Tap Water*] [*Pharmacy*] ... AQ COM
Aqua Destillata [*Distilled Water*] [*Pharmacy*] ... AQ DEST
Aqua Fervens [*Warm Water*] [*Pharmacy*] ... AQ FERV
Aqua Frigida [*Cold Water*] [*Pharmacy*] ... AQ FRIG
Aqua Gelida [*Cold Water*] [*Pharmacy*] ... AQ GEL
Aqua Lung Dealers Association ... ALDA
Aqua-Sol, Inc. Uts [*NASDAQ symbol*] ... AQSLU
Aqua Tepida [*Lukewarm Water*] [*Pharmacy*] ... AQ TEP
Aquaculture Products Technology [*NASDAQ symbol*] ... AQUA
Aquanautics Corp. [*NASDAQ symbol*] ... AQNT
Aquaplaning Risk Indicator for Landings ... APRIL
Aquarian Research Foundation ... ARF
Aquarien Magazin [*A publication*] ... Aquarien Mag
Aquarium Journal [*A publication*] ... Aquarium J
Aquarius [*Constellation*] ... Aqar
Aquarius [*Constellation*] ... Aqr
Aquarius Resources Ltd. [*NASDAQ symbol*] ... AQRLF
Aquatic Biology Abstracts [*A publication*] ... Aqua Biol Ab
Aquatic Botany [*A publication*] ... Aquat Bot
Aquatic Plant ... AP
Aquatic Plant Management Society ... APMS

Aquatic Research Institute ... ARI
Aquatic Sciences and Fisheries Abstracts [*A publication*] ... Aqua Sci & Fish Abstr
Aquatic Sciences and Fisheries Abstracts [*A publication*] ... ASFA
Aquatic Sciences and Fisheries Information System [*United Nations*] ... ASFIS
Aquatic Sciences Information Retrieval Center [*University of Rhode Island*] ... ASIRC
Aqueous ... AQ
Aqueous Extraction Process ... AEP
Aqueous Film-Forming Foam [*Firefighting chemical for ships*] ... AFFF
Aqueous Flare Response [*Physiology*] ... AFR
Aqueous Homogeneous Reactor ... AHR
Aqueous Powder Suspension [*For coating plastics*] ... APS
Aqueous Procaine Penicillin G [*Antibiotic*] ... APPG
Aqueous Solution ... AS
Aqueous Suspension ... AS
Aquila [*Constellation*] ... Aqil
Aquila [*Constellation*] ... Aql
Aquila [*Italy*] [*Geomagnetic observatory code*] ... AQU
Aquila [*Italy*] [*Seismograph station code, US Geological Survey*] ... AQU
Aquila Airways Ltd. ... AQU
Aquileia Nostra [*A publication*] ... AN
Aquilo Serie Botanica [*A publication*] ... Aquilo Ser Bot
Aquilo Serie Zoologica [*A publication*] ... Aquilo Ser Zool
Aquinas College, Grand Rapids, MI [*OCLC symbol*] ... EXQ
Aquinas College, Grand Rapids, MI [*Library symbol*] ... MiGrA
Aquinas High School, Augusta, GA [*Library symbol*] ... GAuAH
Aquinas Institute, Dubuque, IA [*Library symbol*] ... IaDuA
Aquinas Institute Library, Rochester, NY [*OCLC symbol*] ... RVO
Aquitaine Co. of Canada Ltd. [*American Stock Exchange symbol*] [*Delisted*] ... AQC
ARA Services, Inc. [*Formerly, Automatic Retailers of America, Inc.*] [*NYSE symbol*] ... ARA
Arab Airways (Jerusalem) Ltd. ... AAJ
Arab, AL [*Radio station call letters*] ... WCRQ-FM
Arab, AL [*Radio station call letters*] ... WRAB
Arab Bankers' Association ... ABA
Arab Common Market [*United Arab Republic, Iraq, Jordan, Kuwalt, and Syria*] ... ACM
Arab Energy Institute ... AEI
Arab Film and Television Center News [*A publication*] ... Arab F & TV
Arab International Aviation Co. [*Egypt*] [*ICAO designator*] ... KK
Arab Journal of Nuclear Science and Applications [*A publication*] ... Arab J Nucl Sci Appl
Arab Latin American Bank ... ARLABANK
Arab League ... AL
Arab League Educational, Cultural, and Scientific Organization ... ALECSO
Arab Liberation Army ... ALA
Arab Liberation Front ... ALF
Arab Marketing & Finance, Incorporated ... AMFI
Arab Monetary Fund ... AMF
Arab Organization of Petroleum Exporting Countries ... AOPEC
Arab Petroleum Investments Corporation [*Owned by the member countries of OPEC*] ... APICORP
Arab Postal Union ... APU
Arab Relief Agency ... ARA
Arab Report & Record [*A publication*] ... ARR
Arab Republic of Egypt ... ARE
Arab Revolution News Agency ... ARNA
Arab Socialist Renaissance Party [*Syria*] ... ASRP
Arab Socialist Union ... ASU
Arab States [*MARC geographic area code*] [*Library of Congress*] ... ma-----
Arab States Broadcasting Union ... ASBU
Arab States Fundamental Education Centre ... ASFEC
Arab Wings Co. [*ICAO designator*] ... SI
Arab Women's Council ... AWC
Arab World [*A publication*] ... ArabW
Arabian-American Oil Company ... ARAMCO
Arabian Communication Satellite ... ARCOMSAT
Arabian Horse Club Registry of America [*Later, AHR*] ... AHCRA
Arabian Horse Owners Foundation ... AHOF
Arabian Horse Registry of America ... AHR
Arabian Journal for Science and Engineering [*A publication*] ... Arabian J Sci Engrg
Arabian Peninsula [*MARC geographic area code*] [*Library of Congress*] ... ar-----
Arabian Sea and Area [*MARC geographic area code*] [*Library of Congress*] ... au-----
Arabian Shield Development [*NASDAQ symbol*] ... ARSD
Arabic ... AR
Arabic ... ARA
Arabic [*MARC language code*] [*Library of Congress*] ... ara
Arabidopsis Information Service ... AIS
Arabidopsis Information Service [*A publication*] ... Arabidopsis Inf Serv
Arabinofuranosyladenine [*or Adenine Arabinoside*] [*Also, Vira-A*] [*Antiviral compound*] ... ara-A
Arabinofuranosylfluorocytosine [*Also, FCA*] [*Antineoplastic drug*] ... ara-FC
Arabinofuranosylthymine [*Biochemistry*] ... ara-T
Arabinose [*One-letter symbol; see Ara*] ... a
Arabinose [*Also, a*] [*A sugar*] ... Ara
Arabinosylhypoxanthine [*Biochemistry*] ... ara-H
Arabinosylmercaptopurine [*Antineoplastic drug*] ... ara-MP
Aracaju [*Brazil*] [*Airport symbol*] ... AJU
Aracatuba [*Brazil*] [*Airport symbol*] ... ARU
Aracca Petroleum Corp. [*NASDAQ symbol*] ... ARAC
Arachidonic Acid [*Biochemistry*] ... AA
Arachnology ... ARACH
Aracytidine [*Cytarabine*] [*Also, CA, CAR*] [*Antineoplastic drug*] ... ara-C
Arad [*Romania*] [*Airport symbol*] ... ARW
Aragarcas [*Brazil*] [*Airport symbol*] ... ARS
Aragip [*Papua New Guinea*] [*Airport symbol*] ... ARP
Araguaina [*Brazil*] [*Airport symbol*] ... AUX
Aram Public Library, Delavan, WI [*Library symbol*] ... WDA
Aramac [*Australia*] [*Airport symbol*] ... AXC
Aramaic ... ARAM
Aramaic [*MARC language code*] [*Library of Congress*] ... arc
Aramco World Magazine [*A publication*] ... Aramco W
Araneta Journal of Agriculture [*A publication*] ... Araneta J Agric
Araneta Research Journal [*A publication*] ... Araneta Res J
Aranuka [*Kiribati*] [*Airport symbol*] ... AAK
Arapaho [*MARC language code*] [*Library of Congress*] ... arp
Arapaho Petroleum, Inc. [*NASDAQ symbol*] ... ARHO
Arapahoe Community College, Littleton, CO [*Library symbol*] ... CoLiAJ
Arapahoe Community College, Littleton, CO [*OCLC symbol*] ... DVZ
Arapahoe County Evaluation Center, Englewood, CO [*Library symbol*] ... CoEnE
Arapahoe County School District 6, Littleton, CO [*Library symbol*] ... CoLiSD
Arapahoe Regional Library District, Littleton, CO [*Library symbol*] ... CoLiA
Arapuni [*New Zealand*] [*Seismograph station code, US Geological Survey*] [*Closed*] ... ARA
Arar [*Saudi Arabia*] [*Airport symbol*] ... RAE
Araracuara [*Colombia*] [*Airport symbol*] ... ACR
Araraquara [*Brazil*] [*Airport symbol*] [*Obsolete*] ... AQA
Ararat [*Australia*] [*Airport symbol*] [*Obsolete*] ... ARY
Arauca [*Colombia*] [*Airport symbol*] ... AUC
Araucanian [*MARC language code*] [*Library of Congress*] ... arn
Araucariana. Serie Botanica [*A publication*] ... Araucariana Ser Bot
Araucariana. Serie Geociencias [*A publication*] ... Araucariana Ser Geocienc
Arawa [*Papua New Guinea*] [*Airport symbol*] ... RAW
Arawak [*MARC language code*] [*Library of Congress*] ... arw
Arawak Airlines ... LK
Araxa [*Brazil*] [*Airport symbol*] ... AAX
Arba Sicula [*Sicilian Dawn*] [*An association*] ... AS
Arbeiten aus Anglistik und Amerikanistik [*A publication*] ... Ar A A
Arbeiten zur Bayerisch-Oesterreichischen Dialektgeografie [*A publication*] ... ABOD
Arbeiten. Biologischen Reichanstalt fuer Land- und Forstwirtschaft. Berlin [*A publication*] ... Arb Biol Reichanst Land Forstw Berlin
Arbeiten. Botanischen Instituts in Wurzburg [*A publication*] ... Arb Bot Inst Wurz
Arbeiten. Deutsche Landwirtschafts-Gesellschaft [*A publication*] ... Arb Deut Landwirt Ges
Arbeiten zur Deutschen Philologie [*A publication*] ... ADPh
Arbeiten aus dem Gebiete des Futterbaues [*A publication*] ... Arb Gebiete Futterbaues
Arbeiten zur Geschichte des Spaetjudentums und Urchristentums [*A publication*] ... AGSU
Arbeiten. Paul-Ehrlich-Institut [*A publication*] ... Arb Paul-Ehrlich-Inst
Arbeiten. Paul-Ehrlich-Institut, Georg-Speyer-Haus, und Ferdinand-Blum-Institut [*A publication*] ... Arb Paul Ehrlich Inst Georg Speyer Haus Ferdinand Blum Inst
Arbeiten und Texte zur Slavistik [*A publication*] ... ATS
Arbeiten. Universitaet Hohenheim (Landwirtschaftliche Hochschule) [*A publication*] ... Arb Univ Hohenheim (Landwirtsch Hochsch)
Arbeiter-und-Bauern-Fakultaet ... ABF
Arbeiter-und-Bauern-Inspektion ... ABI
Arbeits Gemeinschaft der Offentlichrechtlichen Rundfunk Anstalten der Bundesrepublik Deutschland [*Broadcasting organization*] ... ARD
Arbeitseinheit ... AE
Arbeitsgemeinschaft fuer Forschung des Landes Nordrhein-Westfalen [*A publication*] ... Arbeitsgem Forsch Landes Nordrh-Westfalen
Arbeitsgemeinschaft fuer Forschung des Landes Nordrhein-Westfalen Geisteswissenschaften [*A publication*] ... AFNG
Arbeitsgemeinschaft fuer Industrielle Forschung [*Cooperative Group for Industrial Research*] [*Germany*] ... AIF
Arbeitsgemeinschaft Satellitentragersystem [*Germany*] ... ASAT
Arbeitsgemeinschaft der Waehlerinnen [*Association of Women Voters*] [*Germany*] ... ADW
Arbeitskraft ... AK
Arbeitsmedizin, Sozialmedizin, Arbeitshygiene [*Later, Arbeitsmedizin, Sozialmedizin, Praeventivmedizin*] [*A publication*] ... Arbeitsmed Sozialmed Arbeitshyg
Arbeitsmedizin, Sozialmedizin, Praeventivmedizin [*A publication*] ... Arbeitsmed Sozialmed Praeventivmed
Arbeitsschutzinformationssystem [*Information System for Occupational Safety and Health*] [*West Germany*] ... ASIS

Arbeitsverwendungsfaehig [*Fit for labor duty only*] [*German military - World War II*] ... AV
Arbetsmarknadsstyrelsen [*Labor-Market Agency*] [*Sweden*] ... AMS
Arbetsstudietekniska Institutet [*Stockholm*] ... ASTI
Arbitrary ... ARB
Arbitrary Correction to Hit [*Gunnery term*] [*Navy*] ... ACTH
Arbitrary Function Generator ... AFG
Arbitrary Unit ... AU
Arbitration Journal [*A publication*] ... Arbitrat J
Arbitration Journal [*A publication*] ... Arbitr J
Arbitration Journal [*A publication*] ... Arb J
Arbok Det Norske Videnskapsakademi [*A publication*] ... ArNVA
Arbok fuer Universitetet i Bergen. Matematisk-Naturvitenskapelig Serie [*A publication*] ... Arbok Univ Bergen Mat-Naturvitensk Ser
Arbok fuer Universitetet i Bergen. Matematisk-Naturvitenskapelig Serie [*A publication*] ... Arb U B Mat
Arbok fuer Universitetet i Bergen. Medisinsk Serie [*A publication*] ... Arbok Univ Bergen Med Ser
Arboletas [*Colombia*] [*Airport symbol*] ... ARO
Arbor [*A publication*] ... Arb
Arboretum Kornickie [*A publication*] ... Arbor Kornickie
Arboricultural Association ... AA
Arboricultural Association Journal [*A publication*] ... Arbor Ass J
Arboriculture ... ARBOR
Arboriculture Fruitiere [*A publication*] ... Arboricult Fruit
Arc Current Time Simulator ... ACTS
Arc Detector Unit ... ADU
Arc Drop Voltage ... ADV
Arc Gas Heater ... AGH
Arc-Heated Materials Jet [*Langley Research Center*] ... AHMJ
Arc Heater Housing ... AHH
Arc Heating Device ... AHD
ARC International [*NASDAQ symbol*] ... ASSRF
Arc Jet ... AJ
Arc-Jet Wind Tunnel ... AWT
Arc Lamp Assembly ... ALA
Arc Lamp Igniter ... ALI
Arc LASER Light ... ALL
Arc LASER Light Pump ... ALLP
Arc Melting Furnace ... AMF
Arc-Plasma Spraying [*Magnetic film*] ... APS
Arc Resistance Tester ... ART
Arc Tangent Mechanism ... ATM
Arc Vacuum Cast ... AVC
Arc Weld ... ARC/W
Arc Welding Machine ... AWM
Arc Xenon Lamp ... AXL
Arcade ... ARC
Arcade & Attica Railroad Corp. [*AAR code*] ... ARA
Arcadia [*Berlin*] [*A publication*] ... Arc
Arcadia, Accademia Letteraria Italiana. Atti e Memorie [*A publication*] ... AALIAM
Arcadia, CA [*Radio station call letters*] ... KMAX
Arcadia, FL [*Radio station call letters*] ... WAPG
Arcadia, FL [*Radio station call letters*] ... WOKD
Arcadia Public Library, Arcadia, CA [*Library symbol*] ... CAr
Arcana Workshops [*Teaches philosophy of Alice A. Bailey toward human relations*] ... AW
Arcane Order [*An association*] ... AO
ARCAS [*Atlantic Research Corporation Atmospheric Sounding Missile*] **Piggyback Emulsion Experiment** ... APEX
Arcata [*California*] [*Seismograph station code, US Geological Survey*] ... ARC
Arcata, CA [*Radio station call letters*] ... KAHN
Arcata, CA [*Radio station call letters*] ... KATA
Arcata, CA [*Radio station call letters*] ... KHSU-FM
Arcata, CA [*Radio station call letters*] ... KXGO
Arcata Corp. [*NYSE symbol*] [*Delisted*] ... ACA
[*The*] **Arcata & Mad River Rail Road Co.** [*AAR code*] ... AMR
Arcata Microfilm Corporation, Winston-Salem, NC [*Library symbol*] ... AmC
Arcata Public Library, Arcata, CA [*Library symbol*] ... CArc
Arcato [*With the Bow*] [*Music*] ... ARC
Arcavacata [*Italy*] [*Seismograph station code, US Geological Survey*] ... ACI
Arch-Chancellor ... AC
Arch-Loop-Whorl [*Basis of Galton's System of Fingerprint Classifications*] ... ALW
Arch-Treasurer ... AT
Archaeologia [*A publication*] ... ARCH
Archaeologia [*A publication*] ... Archaeol
Archaeologia Austriaca [*A publication*] ... Archaeol Austr
Archaeologia Austriaca [*A publication*] ... Arch Austr
Archaeologia Cambrensis [*A publication*] ... AC
Archaeologia Cambrensis [*A publication*] ... Arch Camb
Archaeologia Cambrensis [*A publication*] ... Arch Cambrensis
Archaeologia Cantiana [*A publication*] ... Arch Cant
Archaeologia Classica [*A publication*] ... AC
Archaeologia Geographica [*A publication*] ... Arch Geogr
Archaeologia Homerica [*A publication*] ... Arch Hom
Archaeologia Iugoslavica [*A publication*] ... ArchIug
Archaeologia Polona [*A publication*] ... Archaeol Polona
Archaeologia Polona [*A publication*] ... Arch Polon
Archaeologiae Christianae Doctor [*Doctor of Christian Archeology*] ... ACD
Archaeologiai Ertesito [*A publication*] ... AErt
Archaeologiai Ertesito [*A publication*] ... Arch Ert
Archaeologica Aeliana [*A publication*] ... Arch Aeliana
Archaeological Conservancy ... AC
Archaeological Institute of America ... AIA
Archaeological Journal [*A publication*] ... AJ
Archaeological Journal [*A publication*] ... Archaeol J
Archaeological Journal [*A publication*] ... Arch J
Archaeological Journal (London) [*A publication*] ... Archaeol J (London)
Archaeological News [*A publication*] ... Arch N
Archaeological Reports [*A publication*] ... AR
Archaeological Reports [*A publication*] ... Archaeol Rep
Archaeological Survey Association of Southern California, La Verne, CA [*Library symbol*] ... CLavA
Archaeological Survey of Egypt [*A publication*] ... ASE
Archaeologisch-Epigraphische Mitteilungen aus Oesterreich [*Ungarn*] [*A publication*] ... AEM
Archaeologische Bibliographie [*A publication*] ... Archaeol Biblio
Archaeologische Mitteilungen aus Iran [*A publication*] ... AMIran
Archaeologische Nachrichten aus Baden [*A publication*] ... Arch Nachr Baden
Archaeologische Zeitung [*A publication*] ... AZ
Archaeologischer Anzeiger [*A publication*] ... AA
Archaeology [*A publication*] ... Arch
Archaeology ... ARCHAEOL
Archaeology and Physical Anthropology in Oceania [*A publication*] ... Archaeol Phy Anthrop Oceania
Archaeology and Physical Anthropology in Oceania [*A publication*] ... Archaeol & Phys Anthropol Oceania
Archaeometry [*A publication*] ... Archaeometr
Archaic ... ARCH
Archaiologika Analekta ex Athenon [*A publication*] ... Arch An Ath
Archaiologike Ephemeris [*A publication*] ... Arch Eph
Archaiologike Ephemeris [*A publication*] ... Arch Ephemeris
Archaiologikon Deltion [*A publication*] ... A Delt
Archaiologikon Deltion [*A publication*] ... Deltion
Archangelos [*Greece*] [*Seismograph station code, US Geological Survey*] ... ARG
Archangelos [*Greece*] [*Seismograph station code, US Geological Survey*] ... RHD
Archbishop ... ABP
Archbishop ... ABSHP
Archbishop ... ARCHBP
Archbishop of Canterbury's Diploma in Church Music [*British*] ... ADCM
Archbishop Oscar Arnulfo Romero Relief Fund ... AOARRF
Archbold, OH [*Radio station call letters*] ... WHFD
Archconfraternity of Christian Mothers ... ACM
Archconfraternity of Perpetual Adoration [*Defunct*] ... APA
Archconfraternity of Prayer for Israel ... API
Archdeacon ... ADCON
Archdeacon ... ADN
Archdeacon [*or Archdeaconry*] ... ARCHD
Archdeaconry ... AD
Archdiocesan Development Fund [*Catholic*] ... ADF
Archduke ... AD
Archduke ... ARCHD
Arche [*A publication*] ... Ar
Archeia tes Pharmakeutikes (Athens) [*A publication*] ... Arch Pharm (Athens)
Archeion ton Byzantinon Mnemeion tes Hellados [*A publication*] ... Arch Byz Mnem
Archeion Euboikon Meleton [*A publication*] ... AEM
Archeion Pontou [*A publication*] ... ArcP
Archeion Thrakes [*A publication*] ... ArchT
Archeion tou Thrakikou Laographikou kai Glossikou Thesaurou [*A publication*] ... ATLGT
Archeolgrafo Triestino [*A publication*] ... Arch Triest
Archeolgrafo Triestino [*A publication*] ... AT
Archeolgrafo Triestino [*A publication*] ... ATriest
Archeologia Classica [*A publication*] ... Arch Cl
Archeologia Classica [*A publication*] ... ArchClass
Archeologia Polski [*A publication*] ... Arch Pol
Archeological ... ARCHEOL
Archeological Resources Protection Act [*1979*] ... ARPA
Archeologicke Rozhledy [*A publication*] ... Archeol Rozhl
Archeologicke Rozhledy [*A publication*] ... Arch Rozhledy
Archeologie Armoricaine [*A publication*] ... ArchArm
Archeologie (Sofia) [*A publication*] ... Arch (Sofia)
Archeology and Ecology [*Coined by Paolo Soleri, Italian-born architect*] ... ARCHOLOGY
Archer-Daniels-Midland Co. [*NYSE symbol*] ... ADM
Archery ... ARCH
Archery Manufacturers Association [*Later, AMO*] ... AMA
Archery Manufacturers and Dealers Association [*Later, AMO*] ... AMADA
Archery Manufacturers Organization ... AMO
Archery Range and Retailers Organization ... ARRO
Arches National Monument ... ARCH
Archeveche de Sherbrooke, Sherbrooke, PQ, Canada [*Library symbol*] ... CaQSherA
Archibald Library, Caronport, SK, Canada [*Library symbol*] ... CaSCA

Archidux Electus Imperator Optime Vivat [*Inscription used by Frederick III, 15th-century German king*] .... AEIOU
Archief voor de Geschiedenis van het Aartsbisdom Utrecht [*A publication*] .... AGAU
Archief voor de Geschiedenis van de Katholieke Kerk in Nederland [*A publication*] .... AGKKN
Archiginnasio [*A publication*] .... Archig
Archignac [*France*] [*Seismograph station code, US Geological Survey*] .... ARH
Archipelago [*Maps and charts*] .... ARCH
Architect [*or Architecture*] .... ARCH
Architect .... ARCHT
Architect of the Capitol [*US*] .... AC
Architect of the Capitol [*US*] .... AOC
Architect-Engineer .... A-E
Architect and Engineer [*A publication*] .... Arch & Eng
Architect-Engineer-Manager [*Plan*] .... AEM
Architect-Engineers Liaison Commission .... AELC
Architect-Engineers - Spanish Bases .... AESB
Architect and Surveyor [*A publication*] .... Archit Surv
[*The*] **Architects Collaborative** [*Design firm*] .... TAC
Architects and Designers [*Building*] [*New York City*] .... A & D
Architects' Emergency Committee .... AEC
Architects' Journal [*A publication*] .... AJ
Architects' Journal [*A publication*] .... Architects J
Architects' Journal [*A publication*] .... Archit J
Architects Law Reports [*British*] .... ARCHLR
Architects, Professional Engineers, Land Surveyors Council on Registration .... APELSCOR
Architects' Registration Council [*British*] .... ARC
Architects Renewal Committee in Harlem [*Defunct*] .... ARCH
Architects for Social Responsibility .... ASR
Architect's Yearbook [*A publication*] .... Arch Yr
Architect's Yearbook [*A publication*] .... Arch Yrbk
Architectural Acoustics Society .... AAS
Architectural Aluminum Manufacturers Association .... AAMA
Architectural Association .... AA
Architectural Association Quarterly [*A publication*] .... AAQ
Architectural Barriers .... A/B
Architectural Barriers Committee .... ABC
Architectural Design [*A publication*] .... AD
Architectural Design [*A publication*] .... Arch Des
Architectural Design [*A publication*] .... Archit Des
Architectural Digest [*A publication*] .... AD
Architectural Engineer .... Arch E
Architectural Engineer .... Ar E
Architectural and Engineering [*Also, A-E*] .... A & E
Architectural and Engineering [*Also, A & E*] .... A-E
Architectural Fabric Structures Institute .... AFSI
Architectural Forum [*A publication*] .... AF
Architectural Forum [*A publication*] .... Arch Forum
Architectural Forum [*A publication*] .... Archit Forum
Architectural Heritage Foundation .... AHF
Architectural History Foundation .... AHF
Architectural Interaction Design System .... AIDS
Architectural League of New York .... ALNY
Architectural Periodicals Index [*Royal Institute of British Architects*] [*Information service*] .... API
Architectural Periodicals Index [*A publication*] .... Archit Per Ind
Architectural Photographers Association .... APA
Architectural Precast Association .... APA
Architectural Projected Window [*Technical drawings*] .... APW
Architectural Psychology Newsletter [*British*] .... AP
Architectural Record [*A publication*] .... ACUR-A
Architectural Record [*A publication*] .... Archit Rec
Architectural Record [*A publication*] .... Arch Rec
Architectural Record [*A publication*] .... ARD
Architectural Review [*A publication*] .... AARV-A
Architectural Review [*A publication*] .... AR
Architectural Review [*A publication*] .... Archit R
Architectural Review [*A publication*] .... Arch R
Architectural Review [*A publication*] .... Arch Rev
Architectural Science Review [*A publication*] .... Archit Sci Rev
Architectural Secretaries Association .... ASA
Architectural and Transportation Barriers Compliance Board [*Office of Human Development Services*] .... A & TBCB
Architectural and Transportation Barriers Compliance Board [*Office of Human Development Services*] .... ATBCB
Architectural Woodwork Institute [*Formerly, MCB*] .... AWI
Architecture .... AR
Architecture .... ARCHIT
Architecture d'Aujourd'hui [*A publication*] .... Arch Aujourd'hui
Architecture d'Aujourd'hui [*A publication*] .... Arch d'Aujourd'hui
Architecture d'Aujourd'hui [*A publication*] .... Archit Aujourd
Architecture d'Aujourd'hui [*A publication*] .... ARDH-A
Architecture-Batiment-Construction [*A publication*] .... Arch-Bat-Constr
Architecture and Building [*A publication*] .... Arch & B
Architecture and Building [*A publication*] .... Arch & Bldg
Architecture Canada [*A publication*] .... Arch Can
Architecture Concept [*A publication*] .... Arch Concept
Architecture Description Language [*Data processing*] .... ADL
Architecture Mouvement Continuite [*A publication*] .... ARMC
Architektura [*A publication*] .... ARKT-B
Architektura a Urbanizmus [*A publication*] .... ARCU
Archiv fuer Acker- und Pflanzenbau und Bodenkunde [*A publication*] .... Arch Acker-Pflanzenbau Bodenkd
Archiv fuer Anatomie, Physiologie, und Wissenschaftliche Medicin [*A publication*] .... Arch Anat Phys Wiss Med
Archiv fuer Anthropologie [*A publication*] .... AAn
Archiv fuer Anthropologie [*A publication*] .... Arch Anthrop
Archiv fuer Anthropologie und Voelkerforschung [*A publication*] .... Archiv Anthrop
Archiv und Atlas der Normalen und Pathologischen Anatomie in Typischen Roentgenbildern [*A publication*] .... Arch Atlas Norm Pathol Anat Roentgenbild
Archiv fuer Begriffsgeschichte [*A publication*] .... ABG
Archiv fuer Begriffsgeschichte [*A publication*] .... Arch Begriff
Archiv fuer Bergbau und Huettenwesen [*A publication*] .... Arch Bergbau
Archiv fuer Bienenkunde [*A publication*] .... Arch Bienenkd
Archiv fuer Dermatologie und Syphilis [*A publication*] .... Arch Dermat u Syph
Archiv fuer Dermatologische Forschung [*A publication*] .... Arch Dermatol Forsch
Archiv fuer Dermatologische Forschung [*A publication*] .... Arch Derm F
Archiv fuer Diplomatik [*A publication*] .... AD
Archiv fuer Diplomatik [*A publication*] .... AfD
Archiv fuer Eisenbahntechnik [*A publication*] .... Arch Eisenbahntech
Archiv fuer das Eisenhuettenwesen [*A publication*] .... Arch Eisenh
Archiv fuer das Eisenhuettenwesen [*A publication*] .... Arch Eisenhuettenwes
Archiv der Elektrischen Uebertragung [*A publication*] .... Arch Elektr Uebertrag
Archiv der Elektrischen Uebertragung [*A publication*] .... Arch Elek Uebertragung
Archiv fuer Elektronik und Uebertragungstechnik [*A publication*] .... Arch Elektron Uebertragungstech
Archiv fuer Elektrotechnik [*Berlin*] [*A publication*] .... Arch Elektr
Archiv fuer Elektrotechnik (Berlin) [*A publication*] .... Arch Elektrotech (Berlin)
Archiv fuer Elsaessische Kirchengeschichte [*A publication*] .... AEKG
Archiv fuer Energiewirtschaft [*A publication*] .... Arch Energiewirtsch
Archiv fuer Entwicklungsmechanik der Organismen [*A publication*] .... Arch Entwicklungsmech Org
Archiv fuer Entwicklungsmechanik der Organismen (Wilhelm Roux) [*A publication*] .... Arch Entwicklungsmech Org (Wilhelm Roux)
Archiv fuer Experimentelle Pathologie und Pharmakologie [*A publication*] .... Arch Exp Pathol Pharmakol
Archiv fuer Experimentelle Veterinaermedizin [*A publication*] .... Arch Exp Veterinaermed
Archiv fuer Experimentelle Veterinaermedizin [*A publication*] .... AXVMA
Archiv fuer Fischereiwissenschaft [*A publication*] .... Arch Fisch
Archiv fuer Fischereiwissenschaft [*A publication*] .... Arch Fischereiwiss
Archiv fuer Forstwesen [*A publication*] .... Arch Forstw
Archiv fuer Frankfurts Geschichte und Kunst [*A publication*] .... AFGK
Archiv fuer Gartenbau [*A publication*] .... Arch Gartenb
Archiv fuer Gartenbau [*A publication*] .... Arch Gartenbau
Archiv fuer Gefluegelkunde [*A publication*] .... Arch Gefluegelk
Archiv fuer Gefluegelkunde [*A publication*] .... Arch Gefluegelkd
Archiv fuer Gefluegelzucht und Kleintierkunde [*A publication*] .... Arch Gefluegelzucht Kleintierk
Archiv fuer Genetik [*Zurich*] [*A publication*] .... Arch Genet
Archiv fuer Genetik (Zurich) [*A publication*] .... Arch Genet (Zur)
Archiv fuer die Gesamte Physiologie des Menschen und der Tiere (Pfluegers) [*A publication*] .... Arch Gesamte Physiol Mens Tiere (Pfluegers)
Archiv fuer die Gesamte Psychologie [*A publication*] .... AGEPB
Archiv fuer die Gesamte Psychologie [*A publication*] .... APsyc
Archiv fuer die Gesamte Virusforschung [*A publication*] .... Arch Gesamte Virusforsch
Archiv fuer Geschichte des Buchwesens [*A publication*] .... ADGB
Archiv fuer Geschichte des Buchwesens [*A publication*] .... AGB
Archiv fuer Geschichte des Buchwesens [*A publication*] .... Archiv Gesch Buchw
Archiv fuer Geschichte des Buchwesens [*A publication*] .... Archiv Gesch Buchwes
Archiv fuer Geschichte des Hochstifts Augsburg [*A publication*] .... AGHA
Archiv fuer Geschichte der Philosophie [*A publication*] .... AGP
Archiv fuer Geschichte der Philosophie [*A publication*] .... AGPh
Archiv fuer Geschichte der Philosophie [*A publication*] .... Arch Gesch Phil
Archiv fuer Geschwulstforschung [*A publication*] .... Arch Geschw
Archiv fuer Geschwulstforschung [*A publication*] .... Arch Geschwulstforsch
Archiv fuer Gewerbepathologie und Gewerbehygiene [*A publication*] .... Arch Gewerbepathol Gewerbehyg
Archiv fuer Gynaekologie [*A publication*] .... Arch Gynaekol
Archiv fuer Hessische Geschichte und Altertumskunde [*A publication*] .... AHGAK
Archiv des Historischen Vereins von Mainfranken [*A publication*] .... AHVMF
Archiv des Historischen Vereins von Unterfranken und Aschaffenburg [*A publication*] .... AHVUA
Archiv fuer Hydrobiologie [*A publication*] .... Arch Hydrob
Archiv fuer Hydrobiologie [*A publication*] .... Arch Hydrobiol
Archiv fuer Hydrobiologie [*A publication*] .... Archiv Hydrobiologie

Archiv fuer Hydrobiologie und Planktonkunde [*A publication*] ... Arch Hydrobiol u Planktonkunde
Archiv fuer Hydrobiologie. Supplementband [*A publication*] ... Arch Hydrobiol Supplementb
Archiv fuer Hygiene [*A publication*] ... Arch Hyg
Archiv fuer Hygiene und Bakteriologie [*A publication*] ... Arch Hyg Bakteriol
Archiv fuer Japanische Chirurgie [*A publication*] ... Arch Jpn Chir
Archiv fuer Katholisches Kirchenrecht [*A publication*] ... AKK
Archiv fuer Katholisches Kirchenrecht [*A publication*] ... AKKR
Archiv fuer Keilschriftforschung [*A publication*] ... ArKF
Archiv fuer Kinderheilkunde [*A publication*] ... Arch Kinderh
Archiv fuer Kinderheilkunde [*A publication*] ... Arch Kinderheilkd
Archiv fuer Klinische Chirurgie [*A publication*] ... Arch Klin Chir
Archiv fuer Klinische und Experimentelle Dermatologie [*A publication*] ... Arch Klin Exp Dermatol
Archiv fuer Klinische und Experimentelle Ohren-, Nasen-, und Kehlkopfheilkunde [*A publication*] ... AKONA
Archiv fuer Klinische und Experimentelle Ohren-, Nasen-, und Kehlkopfheilkunde [*A publication*] ... Arch Klin Exp Ohren- Nasen- Kehlkopfheilkd
Archiv fuer Klinische und Experimentelle Ophtalmologie [*A publication*] ... Arch Klin Exp Ophtalmol
Archiv fuer Klinische Medizin [*A publication*] ... Arch Klin Med
Archiv fuer Kommunalwissenschaften [*A publication*] ... Archiv Kommunalwiss
Archiv des Kreises Asch, Fernleihe, Bayern, Federal Republic of Germany [*Library symbol*] ... GyBaA
Archiv fuer Kreislaufforschung [*A publication*] ... Arch Kreislaufforsch
Archiv fuer Kriminologie [*A publication*] ... Arch Kriminol
Archiv fuer Kulturgeschichte [*A publication*] ... AKG
Archiv fuer Kulturgeschichte [*A publication*] ... ArchK
Archiv fuer Lagerstaettenforschung in den Ostalpen [*A publication*] ... Arch Lagerstaettenforsch Ostalpen
Archiv fuer Landtechnik [*A publication*] ... Arch Landtech
Archiv fuer Lateinische Lexikographie und Grammatik [*A publication*] ... ALLG
Archiv fuer Lebensmittelhygiene [*A publication*] ... Arch Lebensmittelhyg
Archiv fuer Literatur und Kirchengeschichte des Mittelalters [*A publication*] ... ALKM
Archiv fuer Literatur und Volksdichtung [*A publication*] ... ALV
Archiv fuer Literatur und Volksdichtung [*A publication*] ... ArchLit
Archiv fuer Liturgiewissenschaft [*A publication*] ... ALW
Archiv fuer Liturgiewissenschaft [*A publication*] ... Ar Lw
Archiv der Mathematik [*A publication*] ... Arch Math
Archiv fuer Mathematische Logik und Grundlagen Forschung [*A publication*] ... Arch Math Log
Archiv fuer Meteorologie, Geophysik, und Bioklimatolgie. Serie A. Meteorologie und Geophysik [*A publication*] ... Archiv Meteorologie Geophysik u Bioklimatolgie Ser A
Archiv fuer Meteorologie, Geophysik, und Bioklimatologie. Serie A [*A publication*] ... Arch Meteorol Geophys Bioklimatol Ser A
Archiv fuer Meteorologie, Geophysik, und Bioklimatologie. Serie A [*A publication*] ... Arch MGB A
Archiv fuer Meteorologie, Geophysik, und Bioklimatologie. Serie B [*A publication*] ... Arch Meteorol Geophys Bioklimatol Ser B
Archiv fuer Meteorologie, Geophysik, und Bioklimatologie. Serie B [*A publication*] ... Arch MGB B
Archiv fuer Mikrobiologie [*A publication*] ... Arch Mikrobiol
Archiv fuer Mikroskopische Anatomie [*A publication*] ... Arch Mikr Anat
Archiv fuer Mineralogie Geognosie, Bergbau und Huettenkunde [*A publication*] ... Arch Miner
Archiv fuer Mittelrheinische Kirchengeschichte [*A publication*] ... AMrhKG
Archiv fuer Molluskenkunde [*A publication*] ... Arch Molluskenkd
Archiv fuer Musikforschung [*A publication*] ... A Mf
Archiv fuer Musikwissenschaft [*A publication*] ... AfM
Archiv fuer Musikwissenschaft [*A publication*] ... AMW
Archiv fuer Musikwissenschaft [*A publication*] ... Archiv fuer Mus
Archiv fuer Musikwissenschaft [*A publication*] ... Arch Mus
Archiv fuer Naturgeschichte [*A publication*] ... Arch Naturg
Archiv fuer Naturgeschichte (Berlin) [*A publication*] ... Arch Naturg (Berlin)
Archiv fuer Naturschutz und Landschaftsforschung [*A publication*] ... Arch Naturschutz Landschaftsforsch
Archiv des Oeffentlichen Rechts [*A publication*] ... Archiv Off Rechts
Archiv fuer Oesterreichische Geschichte [*A publication*] ... AOG
Archiv fuer Oesterreichische Geschichte [*A publication*] ... Archiv Oesterr Gesch
Archiv fuer Oesterreichische Geschichte [*A publication*] ... Archiv f Oesterr Geschichte
Archiv fuer Ohren-, Nasen-, und Kehlkopfheilkunde [*A publication*] ... Arch Ohren- Nasen- Kehlkopfheilkd
Archiv fuer Ohren-, Nasen-, und Kehlkopfheilkunde [*A publication*] ... Arch Ohr-Nas Kehlkopfheilk
Archiv fuer Ohrenheilkunde [*A publication*] ... Arch Ohrenh
Archiv Orientalni [*A publication*] ... AO
Archiv Orientalni [*A publication*] ... Archiv Or
Archiv Orientalni [*A publication*] ... ArchOrient
Archiv Orientalni [*A publication*] ... ArO
Archiv Orientalni [*A publication*] ... Ar Or
Archiv fuer Orientforschung [*A publication*] ... AFO
Archiv fuer Orientforschung [*A publication*] ... AOF
Archiv fuer Orientforschung [*A publication*] ... Archiv Orientforsch
Archiv fuer Orthopaedische und Unfall-Chirurgie [*A publication*] ... Arch Orthop
Archiv fuer Orthopaedische und Unfall-Chirurgie [*A publication*] ... Arch Orthop Unfall-Chir
Archiv fuer Papyrus Forschung und Verwandte Gebiete [*A publication*] ... APF
Archiv fuer Papyrusforschung [*A publication*] ... Arch P
Archiv fuer Papyrusforschung [*A publication*] ... Ar Pf
Archiv fuer Pathologische, Anatomie, und Physiologie und fuer Klinische Medicin [*A publication*] ... Arch Path Anat
Archiv fuer Pflanzenschutz [*A publication*] ... Arch Pflanzenschutz
Archiv fuer Pflanzenschutz [*A publication*] ... Arch Pflsch
Archiv for Pharmaci og Chemi [*A publication*] ... Arch Pharm Chem
Archiv for Pharmaci og Chemi. Scientific Edition [*A publication*] ... Arch Pharm Chem Sci Ed
Archiv der Pharmazie [*A publication*] ... Arch Pharm
Archiv der Pharmazie und Berichte der Deutschen Pharmazeutischen Gesellschaft [*A publication*] ... Arch Pharm Ber Dtsch Pharm Ges
Archiv fuer Philosophie [*A publication*] ... ArchivPhilos
Archiv fuer Physikalische Therapie [*A publication*] ... Arch Phys Ther
Archiv fuer Phytopathologie und Pflanzenschutz [*A publication*] ... Arch Phytopathol Pflanzenschutz
Archiv fuer Politik und Geschichte [*A publication*] ... APG
Archiv fuer Protistenkunde. Protozoen-Algen-Pilze [*A publication*] ... Arch Protistenkd
Archiv fuer Psychiatrie und Nervenkrankheiten [*A publication*] ... Arch Psychi
Archiv fuer Psychiatrie und Nervenkrankheiten [*A publication*] ... Arch Psychiat Nervenkr
Archiv fuer Psychiatrie und Nervenkrankheiten [*A publication*] ... Arch Psychiatr Nervenkr
Archiv fuer Psychologie [*A publication*] ... Arch Psych
Archiv fuer Psychologie (Frankfurt Am Main) [*A publication*] ... Arch Psychol (Frankf)
Archiv fuer Rechts- und Sozialphilosophie [*A publication*] ... Archiv Rechts u Soz-Philos
Archiv fuer Rechts- und Sozialphilosophie [*A publication*] ... Arch Rechts Soz
Archiv fuer Rechts- und Sozialphilosophie [*A publication*] ... ARSP
Archiv fuer Rechts- und Wirtschaftsphilosophie [*A publication*] ... ARPh
Archiv fuer Rechts- und Wirtschaftsphilosophie [*A publication*] ... ARWP
Archiv fuer Reformationsgeschichte [*A publication*] ... AR
Archiv fuer Reformationsgeschichte [*A publication*] ... Archiv
Archiv fuer Reformationsgeschichte [*A publication*] ... ARG
Archiv fuer Reformationsgeschichte. Texte und Untersuchungen [*A publication*] ... AFR
Archiv fuer Reformationsgeschichte. Texte und Untersuchungen [*A publication*] ... AFTU
Archiv fuer Reformationsgeschichte. Texte und Untersuchungen [*A publication*] ... ARGTU
Archiv fuer Reformationsgeschichte. Texte und Untersuchungen [*A publication*] ... ARTU
Archiv fuer Religionspsychologie [*A publication*] ... ARPs
Archiv fuer Religionswissenschaft [*A publication*] ... ArchRW
Archiv fuer Religionswissenschaft [*A publication*] ... ARW
Archiv fuer Schiffs-und Tropen-Hygiene [*A publication*] ... Arch Schiffs-u Tropen-Hyg
Archiv fuer Schlesische Kirchengeschichte [*A publication*] ... Arch Schlesische Kirchengesch
Archiv fuer Schlesische Kirchengeschichte [*A publication*] ... ASKG
Archiv fuer Slavische Philologie [*A publication*] ... ASP
Archiv fuer das Studium der Neueren Sprachen [*A publication*] ... A
Archiv fuer das Studium der Neueren Sprachen [*A publication*] ... ANS
Archiv fuer das Studium der Neueren Sprachen und Literaturen [*A publication*] ... Archiv
Archiv fuer das Studium der Neueren Sprachen und Literaturen [*A publication*] ... Archiv f Stud
Archiv fuer das Studium der Neueren Sprachen und Literaturen [*A publication*] ... ASNS
Archiv fuer das Studium der Neueren Sprachen und Literaturen [*A publication*] ... ASNSL
Archiv fuer Systematische Philosophie [*A publication*] ... ASPh
Archiv fuer Technisches Messen und Industrielle Messtechnik [*A publication*] ... Arch Tech Mess Ind Messtech
Archiv fuer Technisches Messen und Messtechnische Praxis [*A publication*] ... Arch Tech Mess Messtech Prax
Archiv fuer Tierernaehrung [*A publication*] ... Arch Tierernaehr
Archiv fuer Toxikologie [*Later, Archives of Toxicology*] [*A publication*] ... Arch Toxikol
Archiv fuer Urkundenforschung [*A publication*] ... Archiv Urk
Archiv fuer Urkundenforschung [*A publication*] ... AUF
Archiv fuer Verdauungs-Krankheiten mit Einschluss der Stoffwechselpathologie und der Diaetetik [*A publication*] ... Arch Verdauungskr
Archiv des Vereins fuer Siebenbuergische Landeskunde [*A publication*] ... AVSLK
Archiv fuer Voelkerkunde [*A publication*] ... Archiv Voelkerk
Archiv fuer Voelkerkunde [*A publication*] ... ArchV
Archiv fuer Voelkerkunde [*A publication*] ... Ar Vk
Archiv des Voelkerrechts [*A publication*] ... Archiv Volkerrechts

Archiv fuer Wissenschaftliche und Praktische Tierheilkunde [*A publication*]....Arch Wissensch u Prakt Tierh
Archiva Veterinaria (Bucharest) [*A publication*]....Arch Vet (Buchar)
Archival Micrographics, Midland Park, NJ [*Library symbol*]....ArcM
Archival Security Program [*An association*] [*Defunct*]....ASP
Archivalische Zeitschrift [*A publication*]....AZ
Archive [*Quezon City*] [*A publication*]....Ar
Archive....ARCH
Archive Corp. [*NASDAQ symbol*]....ACHV
Archive for History of Exact Sciences [*A publication*]....Arch Hist E
Archive for History of Exact Sciences [*A publication*]....Arch Hist Exact Sci
[*The*] **Archive (Philippines)** [*A publication*]....ArchiveP
Archive for Rational Mechanics and Analysis [*A publication*]....Arch Ration Mech Anal
Archive for Rational Mechanics and Analysis [*A publication*]....Arch R Mech
Archives of Acoustics [*A publication*]....ARACC
Archives of Acoustics [*A publication*]....Arch Acoust
Archives of American Art....AAA
Archives d'Anatomie et de Cytologie Pathologiques [*A publication*]....Arch Anat Cytol Pathol
Archives d'Anatomie, d'Histologie, et d'Embryologie [*A publication*]....Arch Anat Histol Embryol
Archives d'Anatomie, d'Histologie, et d'Embryologie; Normales et Experimentales [*A publication*]....Arch Anat Histol Embryol Norm Exp
Archives d'Anatomie, d'Histologie, et d'Embryologie (Strasbourg) [*A publication*]....Arch Anat Histol Embryol (Strasb)
Archives d'Anatomie Microscopique et de Morphologie Experimentale [*A publication*]....Arch Anat M
Archives d'Anatomie Microscopique et de Morphologie Experimentale [*A publication*]....Arch Anat Microsc Morphol Exp
Archives d'Anatomie Pathologique (Paris) [*A publication*]....Arch Anat Pathol (Paris)
Archives of Andrology (New York) [*A publication*]....Arch Androl (New York)
Archives de l'Archeveche de Quebec, Quebec, PQ, Canada [*Library symbol*]....CaQQAA
Archives of Asian Art [*A publication*]....Archiv As Art
Archives Belges [*A publication*]....ABelges
Archives Belges de Dermatologie [*A publication*]....Arch Belg Dermatol
Archives Belges de Dermatologie et de Syphiligraphie [*A publication*]....Arch Belg Dermatol Syphiligr
Archives Belges de Medecine Sociale, Hygiene, Medecine du Travail, et Medecine Legale (Belgium) [*A publication*]....Arch Belges Med Soc Hyg Med Trav Med Leg (Belgium)
Archives Belges de Medecine Sociale, Hygiene, Medecine du Travail, et Medecine Legale [*A publication*]....Arch Belg Med Soc
Archives Belges de Medecine Sociale, Hygiene, Medecine du Travail, et Medecine Legale [*A publication*]....Arch Belg Med Soc Hyg Med Trav Med Leg
Archives et Bibliotheques [*A publication*]....Aeb
Archives et Bibliotheques de Belgique [*A publication*]....ABB
Archives et Bibliotheques de Belgique [*A publication*]....Arch Bibl
Archives et Bibliotheques de Belgique [*A publication*]....Archives & Bibl
Archives, Bibliotheques, Collections, Documentation [*A publication*]....ABCD
Archives, Bibliotheques, et Musees de Belgique [*Later, Archives et Bibliotheques de Belgique*] [*A publication*]....ABMB
Archives, Bibliotheques, et Musees de Belgique [*Later, Archives et Bibliotheques de Belgique*] [*A publication*]....Arch Bibl et Mus
Archives of Biochemistry and Biophysics [*A publication*]....Arch Bioch
Archives of Biochemistry and Biophysics [*A publication*]....Arch Biochem Biophys
Archives of Biological Sciences [*A publication*]....Arch Biol Sci
Archives de Biologie [*Liege*] [*A publication*]....Arch Biol
Archives de Biologie (Liege) [*A publication*]....Arch Biol (Liege)
Archives of the Canadian Rockies, Banff, AB, Canada [*Library symbol*]....CaABA
Archives de la Chancellerie, Montreal, PQ, Canada [*Library symbol*]....CaQMAA
Archives of Child Health [*A publication*]....Arch Child Health
Archives for Dermatological Research [*A publication*]....Arch Dermatol Res
Archives for Dermatological Research [*A publication*]....Arch Derm R
Archives of Dermatology [*A publication*]....Arch Dermat
Archives of Dermatology [*A publication*]....Arch Dermatol
Archives of Dermatology and Syphilology [*Chicago*] [*A publication*]....Arch Dermatol Syphilol
Archives of Dermatology and Syphilology (Chicago) [*A publication*]....Arch Dermat and Syph (Chicago)
Archives of Diagnosis [*A publication*]....Arch Diagn
Archives Diplomatiques et Consulaires [*A publication*]....Archiv Diplom Consul
Archives of Disease in Childhood [*A publication*]....Arch Dis Ch
Archives of Disease in Childhood [*A publication*]....Arch Dis Child
Archives of Disease in Childhood [*A publication*]....Arch Dis Childhood
Archives of the Ecclesiastical Province of British Columbia, Vancouver, BC, Canada [*Library symbol*]....CaBVaRE
Archives de l'Eglise d'Alsace [*A publication*]....AEAls
Archives of Environmental Contamination and Toxicology [*A publication*]....Arch Environ Contam Toxicol
Archives of Environmental Health [*A publication*]....AEHLA
Archives of Environmental Health [*A publication*]....Arch Env He
Archives of Environmental Health [*A publication*]....Arch Environ Health
Archives of Environmental Health [*A publication*]....Arch Environ Hlth
Archives of Environmental Health [*A publication*]....Archives Environ Health
Archives Europeenes de Sociologie [*A publication*]....Archiv Eur Sociol
Archives Europeennes de Sociologie [*A publication*]....AES
Archives Europeennes de Sociologie [*A publication*]....Arch Eur So
Archives Europeennes de Sociologie [*A publication*]....Archives Eur Sociol
Archives Europeennes de Sociologie [*A publication*]....Archiv Europ Sociol
Archives de Folklore [*A publication*]....A Folk
Archives de Folklore [*A publication*]....Arch Folk
Archives de Folklore. Universite Laval (Quebec) [*A publication*]....AFLQ
Archives Francaises des Maladies de l'Appareil Digestif [*A publication*]....Arch Fr Mal
Archives Francaises des Maladies de l'Appareil Digestif [*A publication*]....Arch Fr Mal App Dig
Archives Francaises de Pediatrie [*A publication*]....Arch Fr Ped
Archives Francaises de Pediatrie [*A publication*]....Arch Fr Pediatr
Archives of General Psychiatry [*A publication*]....Arch Gen Psychiatr
Archives of General Psychiatry [*A publication*]....Arch G Psyc
Archives of General Psychiatry [*A publication*]....Archives Gen Psychiat
Archives of General Psychiatry [*A publication*]....ARGPA
Archives Generales de Medecine [*A publication*]....Arch Gen Med
Archives Geologiques du Vietnam [*A publication*]....Arch Geol Vietnam
Archives of Gynecology [*A publication*]....Arch Gynecol
Archives Heraldiques Suisses [*A publication*]....AHS
Archives Heraldiques Suisses. Annuaire [*A publication*]....Arch Herald Suisses
Archives d'Histoire Doctrinale et Litteraire du Moyen-Age [*A publication*]....AHDLMA
Archives d'Histoire Doctrinale et Litteraire du Moyen-Age [*A publication*]....AHMA
Archives d'Histoire Dominicaine [*A publication*]....AHD
Archives d'Histoire du Droit Oriental [*A publication*]....AHDO
Archives Historique de la Gironde [*A publication*]....AHG
Archives of Hygiene (Athens) [*A publication*]....Arch Hyg (Athens)
Archives of Industrial Health [*A publication*]....Arch Industr Hlth
Archives of Industrial Hygiene and Occupational Medicine [*A publication*]....Arch Ind Hyg Occup Med
Archives of Industrial Hygiene and Occupational Medicine [*A publication*]....Archives Ind Hyg & Occup Med
Archives. Institut de Botanique. Universite de Liege [*A publication*]....Arch Inst Bot Univ Liege
Archives. Institut d'Hessarek (Institut Razi) [*A publication*]....Arch Inst Hessarek (Inst Razi)
Archives. Institut Pasteur d'Algerie [*A publication*]....Arch Inst Pasteur Alger
Archives. Institut Pasteur d'Algerie [*A publication*]....Arch Inst Pasteur Algerie
Archives. Institut Pasteur Hellenique [*A publication*]....Arch Inst Pasteur Hell
Archives. Institut Pasteur de Madagascar [*A publication*]....Arch Inst Pasteur Madagascar
Archives. Institut Pasteur de Tunis [*A publication*]....Arch Inst Pasteur Tunis
Archives. Institut Razi [*A publication*]....Arch Inst Razi
Archives. Instituts Pasteur de l'Afrique du Nord [*A publication*]....Arch Inst Pasteur Afrique Nord
Archives of Internal Medicine [*A publication*]....Arch In Med
Archives of Internal Medicine [*A publication*]....Arch Intern Med
Archives Internationales d'Histoire des Idees [*A publication*]....AIHI
Archives Internationales d'Histoire des Sciences [*A publication*]....AIHS
Archives Internationales d'Histoire des Sciences [*A publication*]....Arch Int Hist Sci
Archives Internationales de Pharmacodynamie et de Therapie [*A publication*]....Arch Int Pharmacodyn Ther
Archives Internationales de Pharmacodynamie et de Therapie [*A publication*]....Arch I Phar
Archives Internationales de Physiologie et de Biochimie [*A publication*]....Arch Int Physiol Biochim
Archives Internationales de Physiologie et de Biochimie [*A publication*]....Arch I Phys
Archives Internationales de Sociologie de la Cooperation et du Developpement [*A publication*]....Archiv Int Sociol Coop Develop
Archives Italiennes de Biologie [*A publication*]....AIBLA
Archives Italiennes de Biologie [*A publication*]....Arch Ital Biol
Archives Italiennes de Biologie [*A publication*]....Arch It Bio
Archives Jean Piaget, Geneve, Switzerland [*Library symbol*]....SzGPAr
Archives Juives. Cahiers de la Commission des Archives Juives [*A publication*]....Arch Juives
Archives des Lettres Modernes [*A publication*]....ALM
Archives des Maladies de l'Appareil Digestif et des Maladies de la Nutrition [*A publication*]....Arch Mal Appar Dig Mal Nutr
Archives des Maladies du Coeur et des Vaisseaux [*A publication*]....Arch Mal C
Archives des Maladies du Coeur et des Vaisseaux [*A publication*]....Arch Mal Coeur Vaiss
Archives des Maladies Professionelles de Medecine du Travail et de Securite Sociale [*A publication*]....AMPMA
Archives des Maladies Professionelles de Medecine du Travail et de Securite Sociale [*A publication*]....Arch Mal Pr
Archives des Maladies Professionelles de Medecine du Travail et de Securite Sociale [*A publication*]....Arch Mal Prof Med Trav Secur Soc
Archives and Manuscripts [*A publication*]....A & M

Archives of Meat, Fish, and Dairy Science [*A publication*]....Arch Meat Fish Dairy Sci
Archives of Mechanics [*Archiwum Mechaniki Stosowanej*] [*A publication*]....Arch Mech
Archives of Mechanics (Archiwum Mechaniki Stosowanej) [*A publication*]....Arch Mech (Arch Mech Stosow)
Archives de Medecine des Enfants [*A publication*]....Arch Med Enf
Archives de Medecine Experimentale et d'Anatomie Pathologique [*A publication*]....Arch Med Exper et Anat Path
Archives de Medecine Navale [*A publication*]....Arch Med Nav
Archives Medicales [*A publication*]....Arch Med
Archives of Microbiology [*A publication*]....Arch Microb
Archives of Microbiology [*A publication*]....Arch Microbiol
Archives des Missions Scientifiques et Litteraires [*A publication*]....Arch Miss
Archives du Monastere Notre Dame des Anges, Quebec, PQ, Canada [*Library symbol*]....CaQQAND
Archives of the Moravian Church, Bethlehem, PA [*Library symbol*]....PBMCA
Archives. Musee Teyler [*A publication*]....Arch Mus Teyler
Archives. Museum d'Histoire Naturelle de Lyon [*A publication*]....Arch Mus Hist Nat Lyon
Archives. Museum National d'Histoire Naturelle (Paris) [*A publication*]....Arch Mus Natl Hist Nat (Paris)
Archives Nationales du Quebec, Trois-Rivieres, PQ, Canada [*Library symbol*]....CaQTA
Archives Neerlandaises de Phonetique Experimentale [*A publication*]....Arch Neerl Phon Exp
Archives Neerlandaises de Phonetique Experimentale [*A publication*]....ArchNPhonExp
Archives Neerlandaises de Zoologie [*A publication*]....Arch Neerl Zool
Archives of Neurology [*A publication*]....Archives Neurol
Archives of Neurology [*A publication*]....Arch Neurol
Archives of Neurology [*A publication*]....ARNEA
Archives of Neurology and Psychiatry [*A publication*]....Arch Neurol Psychiatry
Archives. Office du Niger [*A publication*]....Arch Off Niger
Archives d'Ophtalmologie [*A publication*]....Arch Ophtal
Archives d'Ophtalmologie [*A publication*]....Arch Ophtalmol
Archives d'Ophtalmologie (Paris)....Arch Opht (Paris)
Archives d'Ophtalmologie et Revue Generale d'Ophtalmologie [*A publication*]....Arch Ophtalmol Rev Gen Ophtalmol
Archives d'Ophtalmologie et Revue Generale d'Ophtalmologie (Paris) [*A publication*]....Arch Ophtalmol (Paris)
Archives of Ophthalmology [*Chicago*] [*A publication*]....Arch Ophth
Archives of Ophthalmology [*Chicago*] [*A publication*]....Arch Ophthalmol
Archives of Ophthalmology (Chicago) [*A publication*]....Arch Ophthalmol (Chicago)
Archives of Oral Biology [*A publication*]....Arch Oral B
Archives of Oral Biology [*A publication*]....Arch Oral Biol
Archives of Orthopaedic and Traumatic Surgery [*A publication*]....Arch Orthop Trauma Surg
Archives of Oto-Rhino-Laryngology [*A publication*]....Arch Oto-R
Archives of Oto-Rhino-Laryngology [*A publication*]....Arch Oto-Rhino-Laryngol
Archives of Otolaryngology [*A publication*]....Arch Otolar
Archives of Otolaryngology [*A publication*]....Arch Otolaryngol
Archives of Otolaryngology [*A publication*]....AROTA
Archives de Parasitologie (Paris) [*A publication*]....Arch Parasitol (Paris)
Archives of Pathology [*Later, Archives of Pathology and Laboratory Medicine*] [*A publication*]....Arch Path
Archives of Pathology [*Later, Archives of Pathology and Laboratory Medicine*] [*A publication*]....Arch Pathol
Archives of Pathology and Laboratory Medicine [*A publication*]....Arch Path and Lab Med
Archives of Pathology and Laboratory Medicine [*A publication*]....Arch Pathol Lab Med
Archives of Pediatrics [*A publication*]....Arch Pediat
Archives of Pediatrics [*A publication*]....Arch Pediatr
Archives de Philologie. Academie Polonaise des Sciences et des Lettres [*A publication*]....APhAP
Archives de Philosophie [*A publication*]....APhilos
Archives de Philosophie [*A publication*]....Archives Philos
Archives de Philosophie [*A publication*]....Arch Phil
Archives de Philosophie [*A publication*]....Arch Philos
Archives de Philosophie [*A publication*]....Ar Ph
Archives de Philosophie du Droit [*A publication*]....Archiv Philos Dr
Archives of Physical Medicine and Rehabilitation [*A publication*]....Arch Phys M
Archives of Physical Medicine and Rehabilitation [*A publication*]....Arch Phys Med Rehabil
Archives of Podiatric Medicine and Foot Surgery [*A publication*]....Arch Podiatr Med Foot Surg
Archives Portugaises des Sciences Biologiques [*A publication*]....Arch Port Sci Biol
Archives of Poultry Science [*A publication*]....Arch Poult Sci
Archives Provinciales de Capucins, Montreal, PQ, Canada [*Library symbol*]....CaQMArC
Archives of Psychiatry and Neurological Sciences [*A publication*]....Arch Psychiatry Neurol Sci
Archives des Recherches Agronomiques et Pastorales au Vietnam [*A publication*]....Arch Rech Agron Pastorales Vietnam
Archives Roumaines de Pathologie Experimentale et de Microbiologie [*A publication*]....Arch Roum Pathol Exp Microbiol
Archives of Rubber Cultivation (Bogor) [*A publication*]....Arch Rubber Cultiv (Bogor)
Archives de Science Avicole [*A publication*]....Arch Sci Avicole
Archives des Sciences [*A publication*]....Archives Sci
Archives des Sciences [*A publication*]....Arch Sci
Archives des Sciences Biologiques (Belgrade) [*A publication*]....Arch Sci Biol (Belgrade)
Archives des Sciences Physiologiques [*A publication*]....Arch Sci Ph
Archives des Sciences Physiologiques [*A publication*]....Arch Sci Physiol
Archives des Sciences Physiques et Naturelles [*A publication*]....Arch Sc Phys Nat
Archives des Sciences Physiques et Naturelles. Supplement a la Bibliotheque Universelle [*A publication*]....Arch Sci Phys Nat
Archives de Sciences Sociales des Religions [*A publication*]....Archives Sci Sociales Relig
Archives de Sciences Sociales des Religions [*A publication*]....Archiv Sci Soc Rel
Archives de Sciences Sociales des Religions [*A publication*]....Archiv Sci Soc Relig
Archives de Sciences Sociales des Religions [*A publication*]....Arch SS Rel
Archives du Seminaire de Quebec, Quebec, PQ, Canada [*Library symbol*]....CaQQAS
Archives du Seminaire de Saint-Sulpice, Montreal, PQ, Canada [*Library symbol*]....CaQMAS
Archives of Sexual Behavior [*A publication*]....Archiv Sex Behav
Archives of Sexual Behavior [*A publication*]....Arch Sex Be
Archives of Sexual Behavior [*A publication*]....Arch Sex Behav
Archives de Sociologie des Religions [*A publication*]....Archives Sociol Relig
Archives de Sociologie des Religions [*A publication*]....Archiv Soc Rel
Archives de Sociologie des Religions [*A publication*]....ASR
Archives Suisses d'Anthropologie Generale [*A publication*]....Archives Suisses Anthrop Gen
Archives Suisses d'Anthropologie Generale [*A publication*]....Archiv Suisses Anthropol Gen
Archives Suisses d'Anthropologie Generale [*A publication*]....Arch Suisses Anthropol Gen
Archives Suisses de Neurologie, Neurochirurgie, et de Psychiatrie [*A publication*]....Arch Suisses Neurol Neurochir Psychiatr
Archives Suisses des Traditions Populaires [*A publication*]....ASTP
Archives of Surgery [*A publication*]....Arch Surg
Archives of Toxicology [*Berlin*] [*A publication*]....Arch Toxic
Archives of Toxicology [*Berlin*] [*A publication*]....Arch Toxicol
Archives of Toxicology (Berlin) [*A publication*]....Arch Toxicol (Berl)
Archives of Toxicology. Supplement (Berlin) [*A publication*]....Arch Toxicol (Suppl)
Archives de l'Union Medicale Balkanique [*A publication*]....Arch Union Med Balk
Archives des Ursulines, Trois-Rivieres, PQ, Canada [*Library symbol*]....CaQTUrA
Archives of Virology [*A publication*]....Arch Virol
Archives de Zoologie Experimentale et Generale [*A publication*]....Arch Zool Exper et Gen
Archives de Zoologie Experimentale et Generale [*A publication*]....Arch Zool Exp Gen
Archives de Zoologie Experimentale et Generale. Notes et Revue [*A publication*]....Arch Zool Exp Gen Notes Rev
Archivi (Rome) [*A publication*]....ArR
Archivio [*A publication*]....Ar
Archivio [*A publication*]....Arch
Archivio. Alto Adige [*A publication*]....AAA
Archivio. Alto Adige [*A publication*]....AAAd
Archivio per l'Antropologia e la Etnologia [*A publication*]....Arch Antropol Etnol
Archivio per l'Antropologia e la Etnologia [*A publication*]....Archiv Antropol Etnol
Archivio ed Atti. Societa Italiana di Chirurgia [*A publication*]....Arch ed Atti Soc Ital Chir
Archivio Bibliographico. Bibliotheca da Universidade de Coimbra [*A publication*]....ABUC
Archivio Botanico [*A publication*]....Arch Bot
Archivio Botanico e Biogeografico Italiano [*A publication*]....Arch Bot Biogeogr Ital
Archivio di Chirurgia del Torace [*A publication*]....Arch Chir Torace
Archivio di Chirurgia Toracica e Cardiovascolare [*A publication*]....Arch Chir Torac Cardiovasc
Archivio Dati e Programmi per le Scienze Sociali [*Data and Program Archive for the Social Sciences*] [*Italy*] [*Information service*]....ADPSS
Archivio "De Vechi" per l'Anatomia Patologica e la Medicina Clinica [*A publication*]....Arch "De Vechi" Anat Patol Med Clin
Archivio di Diritto Ecclesiastico [*A publication*]....ADE
Archivio "E Maragliano" di Patologie e Clinica [*A publication*]....Arch "E Maragliano" Patol Clin
Archivio di Filosofia [*A publication*]....AF
Archivio di Filosofia [*A publication*]....AFilos
Archivio di Filosofia [*A publication*]....Arch Filosof
Archivio di Filosofia [*A publication*]....Ar Fi

Archivio di Filosofia [*A publication*] ... Ar Fil
Archivio di Fisiologia [*A publication*] ... Arch Fisiol
Archivio Glottologico Italiano [*Torino*] [*A publication*] ... AGI
Archivio Italiano di Anatomia e di Embriologia [*A publication*] ... Arch Ital Anat Embriol
Archivio Italiano di Chirurgia [*A publication*] ... Arch Ital Chir
Archivio Italiano di Clinica Medica [*A publication*] ... Arch Ital Clin Med
Archivio Italiano di Istologia Patologica [*A publication*] ... Arch Ital Anat Istol Patol
Archivio Italiano di Otologia, Rinologia, e Laringologia [*A publication*] ... Arch Ital Otol Rinol Laringol
Archivio Italiano di Patologia e Clinica dei Tumori [*A publication*] ... Arch Ital Patol Clin Tumori
Archivio Italiano di Scienze Farmacologiche [*A publication*] ... Arch Ital Sci Farmacol
Archivio Italiano di Scienze Mediche Coloniali [*A publication*] ... Arch Ital Sc Med Colon
Archivio Italiano di Scienze Mediche Tropicali e di Parassitologia [*A publication*] ... Arch Ital Sci Med Trop Parassitol
Archivio Italiano di Urologia e Nefrologia [*A publication*] ... Arch Ital Urol Nefrol
Archivio Monaldi [*A publication*] ... Arch Monaldi
Archivio Muratoriano [*A publication*] ... AM
Archivio Muratoriano [*A publication*] ... AMur
Archivio di Oceanografia e Limnologia [*A publication*] ... Arch Oceanogr Limnol
Archivio di Ortopedia e Reumatologia [*A publication*] ... Arch Ortop Reumatol
Archivio Ospedale al Mare [*A publication*] ... Arch Osp Mare
Archivio di Ostetricia e Ginecologia [*A publication*] ... Arch Ostet Ginecol
Archivio di Patologia e Clinica Medica [*A publication*] ... Arch Patol e Clin Med
Archivio di Patologia e Clinica Medica [*A publication*] ... Arch Patol Clin Med
Archivio di Psicologia, Neurologia, e Psichiatria [*A publication*] ... APNPA
Archivio di Psicologia, Neurologia, e Psichiatria [*A publication*] ... Arch Psicol Neurol Psichiatr
Archivio Putti di Chirurgia degli Organi di Movimento [*A publication*] ... Arch Putti Chir Organi Mov
Archivio. R. Deputazione Romana di Storia Patria [*A publication*] ... ADRS
Archivio. R. Deputazione Romana di Storia Patria [*A publication*] ... ADRSP
Archivio. R. Deputazione Romana di Storia Patria [*A publication*] ... ARDRSP
Archivio di Radiologia (Napoli) [*A publication*] ... Arch Radiol (Napoli)
Archivio di Scienze Biologiche [*Bologna*] [*A publication*] ... Arch Sci Biol
Archivio di Scienze Biologiche (Bologna) [*A publication*] ... Arch Sci Biol (Bologna)
Archivio per le Scienze Mediche [*Torino*] [*A publication*] ... Arch Sci Med
Archivio per le Scienze Mediche (Torino) [*A publication*] ... Arch Sc Med (Torino)
Archivio. Societa Romana di Storia Patria [*A publication*] ... ASRS
Archivio. Societa Romana di Storia Patria [*A publication*] ... ASRSP
Archivio Stomatologico [*A publication*] ... Arch Stomatol
Archivio de Storia della Filosofia [*A publication*] ... ASF
Archivio di Storia della Scienza [*A publication*] ... ASSc
Archivio Storico [*A publication*] ... Archiv Stor
Archivio Storico per Belluno, Feltre, e Cadore [*A publication*] ... ASBFC
Archivio Storico per la Calabria e la Lucania [*A publication*] ... ASCL
Archivio Storico di Corsica [*A publication*] ... ASC
Archivio Storico per la Dalmazia [*A publication*] ... ASD
Archivio Storico Italiano [*A publication*] ... Arch Stor
Archivio Storico Italiano [*A publication*] ... ASI
Archivio Storico Lodigiano [*A publication*] ... ASLod
Archivio Storico Lombardo [*A publication*] ... ASL
Archivio Storico Messinese [*A publication*] ... ASM
Archivio Storico Pratese [*A publication*] ... ASP
Archivio Storico per le Provincie Napolitane [*A publication*] ... ASPN
Archivio Storico per le Provincie Parmensi [*A publication*] ... ASPP
Archivio Storico Pugliese [*A publication*] ... ASP
Archivio Storico del Risorgimento Umbrio [*A publication*] ... ASRU
Archivio Storico Sardo [*A publication*] ... ASSar
Archivio Storico per la Sicilia Orientale [*A publication*] ... Arch Stor Sicilia Orient
Archivio Storico per la Sicilia Orientale [*A publication*] ... ASSO
Archivio Storico Siciliano [*A publication*] ... ArchSS
Archivio Storico Siciliano [*A publication*] ... ASS
Archivio Storico Ticinese [*A publication*] ... ASTic
Archivio per lo Studio delle Tradizioni Populari [*A publication*] ... ATP
Archivio Trentino [*A publication*] ... ATren
Archivio de Vecchi per l'Anatomia Patologica e la Medicina Clinica [*A publication*] ... Arch de Vecchi Anat Patol
Archivio Veneto [*A publication*] ... AV
Archivio Veneto [*A publication*] ... AVen
Archivio Veneto-Tridentino [*A publication*] ... AVT
Archivio Veterinario Italiano [*A publication*] ... Arch Vet Ital
Archivio Zoologico Italiano [*A publication*] ... Arch Zool Ital
Archivium Hibernicum [*A publication*] ... AH
Archivo Agustiniano [*A publication*] ... AAg
Archivo de Derecho Publico [*A publication*] ... ADP
Archivo Espanol de Arqueologia [*A publication*] ... AEA
Archivo Espanol de Arqueologia [*A publication*] ... AEArq
Archivo Espanol de Arqueologia [*A publication*] ... Archivo Esp Arq
Archivo Espanol de Arte [*A publication*] ... AEA
Archivo Espanol de Arte [*A publication*] ... Arch Esp Art
Archivo Espanol de Arte [*A publication*] ... Archivo Esp Arte
Archivo Espanol de Arte y Arqueologia [*A publication*] ... AEAA
Archivo Espanol de Arte y Arqueologia [*A publication*] ... Arch Esp
Archivo Espanol de Morfologia [*A publication*] ... Arch Esp Morfol
Archivo de Filologia Aragonesa [*A publication*] ... AFA
Archivo de Filologia Aragonesa [*A publication*] ... ArchFAr
Archivo General de Indias [*Archives of the Indies*], **Seville, Spain** [*Library symbol*] ... SpSAG
Archivo Giuridico [*A publication*] ... AG
Archivo Hispalense [*A publication*] ... AH
Archivo Hispalense [*A publication*] ... ArH
Archivo Ibero-Americano [*Madrid*] [*A publication*] ... AIA
Archivo Ibero-Americano [*Madrid*] [*A publication*] ... ArchIA
Archivo Ibero-Americano [*Madrid*] [*A publication*] ... ArI
Archivo Jose Marti [*Cuba*] [*A publication*] ... AJM
Archivo del Libertador, Caracas, Venezuela [*Library symbol*] ... VeCAL
Archivo Nacional de Historia [*Ecuador*] ... ARNAHIS
Archivo de Prehistoria Levantina [*A publication*] ... APL
Archivo per la Storia Ecclesiastica dell'Umbria [*A publication*] ... ASEU
Archivo Teologico Granadino [*A publication*] ... ATG
Archivos Argentinos de Neurologia [*A publication*] ... Arch Argent Neurol
Archivos Argentinos de Pediatria [*A publication*] ... Arch Argent Pediatr
Archivos Argentinos de Tisiologia y Neumonologia [*A publication*] ... Arch Argent Tisiol Neumonol
Archivos de Biologia Andina [*A publication*] ... Arch Biol Andina
Archivos de Biologia y Medicina Experimentales [*A publication*] ... Arch Biol M
Archivos de Biologia y Medicina Experimentales [*A publication*] ... Arch Biol Med Exp
Archivos de Bioquimica, Quimica, y Farmacia (Tucuman) [*A publication*] ... Arch Bioquim Quim Farm (Tucuman)
Archivos Brasileiros de Medicina [*A publication*] ... Arch Brasil Med
Archivos de Cardiologia y Hematologia [*A publication*] ... Arch Cardio y Hematol
Archivos del Colegio Medico de El Salvador [*A publication*] ... Arch Col Med El Salv
Archivos de Criminologia Neuro-Psiquiatria y Disciplinas Conexas [*A publication*] ... Arch Criminol Neuro Psiquiatr Discip Conexas
Archivos Espanoles de Urologia [*A publication*] ... Arch Esp Urol
Archivos. Facultad de Medicina de Madrid [*A publication*] ... Arch Fac Med Madrid
Archivos de Farmacia y Bioquimica del Tucuman [*A publication*] ... Arch Farm Bioquim Tucuman
Archivos de Farmacologia y Toxicologia [*A publication*] ... Arch Farmacol Toxicol
Archivos del Folklore Chileno [*A publication*] ... AC
Archivos del Folklore. Chileno Universidad de Chile [*A publication*] ... AFCU
Archivos. Fundacion Roux-Ocefa [*A publication*] ... Arch Fund Roux-Ocefa
Archivos de Histologia Normal y Patologica [*A publication*] ... Arch Histol Norm Patol
Archivos del Hospital Vargas [*A publication*] ... Arch Hosp Vargas
Archivos Iberoamericanos de Historia de la Medicina [*A publication*] ... AIHM
Archivos. Instituto de Aclimatacion Almeria Espana [*A publication*] ... Arch Inst Aclim Almeria Esp
Archivos. Instituto de Biologia Andina (Lima) [*A publication*] ... Arch Inst Biol Andina (Lima)
Archivos. Instituto de Cardiologia de Mexico [*A publication*] ... Arch I Card
Archivos. Instituto de Cardiologia de Mexico [*A publication*] ... Arch Inst Cardiol Mex
Archivos. Instituto de Estudios Africanos [*A publication*] ... AIEA
Archivos. Instituto de Farmacologia Experimental (Medicina) [*A publication*] ... Arch Inst Farmacol Exp (Med)
Archivos Internacionales de la Hidatidosis [*A publication*] ... Arch Int Hidatidosis
Archivos de Investigacion Medica [*A publication*] ... AIVMB
Archivos de Investigacion Medica [*A publication*] ... Arch Invest Med
Archivos de Investigacion Medica [*A publication*] ... Arch Inv M
Archivos Latinoamericanos de Nutricion [*A publication*] ... Arch Latinoamer Nutr
Archivos Latinoamericanos de Nutricion [*A publication*] ... Arch Latinoam Nutr
Archivos de Medicina (Lisbon) [*A publication*] ... Arch Med (Lisbon)
Archivos de Medicina Veterinaria (Valdivia) [*A publication*] ... Arch Med Vet (Valdivia)
Archivos Mexicanos de Anatomia [*A publication*] ... Arch Mex Anat
Archivos de Neurobiologia [*Madrid*] [*A publication*] ... Arch Neurobiol
Archivos de Neurobiologia (Madrid) [*A publication*] ... Arch Neurobiol (Madr)
Archivos de Oftalmologia de Buenos Aires [*A publication*] ... Arch Oftalmol B Aires
Archivos de Oftalmologia Hispano-Americanos [*A publication*] ... Arch Oftal Hispano-Am
Archivos de Pediatria del Uruguay [*A publication*] ... Arch Pediatr Urug
Archivos. Real Instituto Bacteriologico Camara Pestana [*A publication*] ... Arch R Inst Bacteriol Camara Pestana
Archivos. Sociedad Americana Oftalmologia y Optometria [*A publication*] ... Arch S A Of

Archivos. Sociedad Americana de Oftalmologia y Optometria [A publication].................... Arch Soc Am Oftalmol Optom
Archivos. Sociedad de Biologia de Montevideo [A publication]................... Arch Soc Biol Montev
Archivos. Sociedad Espanola de Oftalmologia [A publication] .... Arch Soc Esp Oftalmol
Archivos. Sociedad de Estudios Clinicos de la Habana [A publication].................Arch Soc Estud Clin Habana
Archivos. Sociedad Oftalmologica Hispano-Americana [A publication].................. Arch Soc Oftalmol Hisp-Am
Archivos Uruguayos de Medicina Cirujia y Especialidades [A publication]................Arch Urug Med Cir Espec
Archivos Venezolanos de Folklore [A publication]................AVF
Archivos Venezolanos de Medicina Tropical y Parasitologia Medica [A publication] .... Arch Venez Med Trop Parasitol Med
Archivos Venezolanos de Nutricion [A publication] .... Archos Venez Nutr
Archivos Venezolanos de Nutricion [A publication] .... Arch Venez Nutr
Archivos Venezolanos de Patologia Tropical y Parasitologia Medica [A publication].................Arch Venez Patol Trop Parasitol Med
Archivos Venezolanos de Puericultura y Pediatria [A publication].................. Arch Venez Pueric Pediatr
Archivos de Zootecnia [A publication] ....Arch Zootec
Archivum [Oviedo] [A publication]...Arch
Archivum Balatonicum [A publication] ....Arch Balatonicum
Archivum Chirurgicum Neerlandicum [A publication].........Arch Chir Neerl
Archivum Europae Centro-Orientalis [A publication] ....AECO
Archivum Europae Centro-Orientalis [A publication] ....ArchEurCO
Archivum Franciscanum Historicum [Firenze] [A publication] .... AFH
Archivum Fratrum Praedicatorum [Roma] [A publication] ....AFP
Archivum Histologicum Japonicum [A publication].............Arch Hist J
Archivum Histologicum Japonicum [A publication].............Arch Histol Jpn
Archivum Historiae Pontificiae [A publication] ....AHP
Archivum Historicum Societatis Iesu [A publication]..................AHSI
Archivum Historicum Societatis Iesu [A publication]..................Archivum Hist Soc Iesu
Archivum Historii Filozofii i Mysli Spolecznej [A publication] .... AHF
Archivum Hydrobiologii i Rybactwa [A publication]..................Arch Hydrobiol Rybactwa
Archivum Immunologiae et Therapiae Experimentalis [A publication].........................Arch Immunol Ther Exp
Archivum Immunologiae et Therapiae Experimentalis (Warszawa) [A publication].................Arch Immunol Ther Exp (Warsz)
Archivum Latinitatis Medii Aevi [A publication] .... ALMA
Archivum Linguisticum [A publication]..................................ALing
Archivum Linguisticum [A publication]...............................Archiv Ling
Archivum Linguisticum [A publication].....................................ArchL
Archivum Linguisticum [A publication]...................................Arch Ling
Archivum Linguisticum [A publication]...ArL
Archivum Mathematicum (Brno) [A publication]..................Arch Math (Brno)
Archivum Orientale Pragense [A publication] ....AOP
Archivum Romanicum [A publication]...AR
Archivum Romanicum [A publication]....................................Archiv Rom
Archivum Romanicum [A publication]..................................Arch Rom
Archivum Romanicum [A publication]......................................ARom
Archivum. Societatis Zoologicae-Botanicae Fennicae "Vanamo" [A publication] .... Arch Soc Zool-Bot Fenn "Vanamo"
Archivus Historii Medycyny [A publication]..................ARHMB
Archiwa, Biblioteki, i Muzea Koscielne [A publication]......................ABMK
Archiwum Akustyki [A publication]..................................Arch Akust
Archiwum Automatyki i Telemechaniki [A publication]..................Arch Automat Telemech
Archiwum Automatyki i Telemechaniki [A publication]..................Arch Autom Telemech
Archiwum Budowy Maszyn [A publication].......................Arch Budowy Masz
Archiwum Elektrotechniki [Warsaw] [A publication] .... Arch Elektrotech
Archiwum Elektrotechniki (Warsaw) [A publication]..................Arch Elektrotech (Warsaw)
Archiwum Energetyki [A publication].....................................Arch Energ
Archiwum Gornictwa [A publication] ....Arch Gorn
Archiwum Gornictwa [A publication] ....Archwm Gorn
Archiwum Historii Medycyny [A publication]...........................Arch Hist Med
Archiwum Historii Medycyny (Warszawa) [A publication].................. Arch Hist Med (Warsz)
Archiwum Hutnictwa [A publication] .... Arch Hutn
Archiwum Hutnictwa [A publication] ....Archwm Hutn
Archiwum Hydrotechniki [A publication].........................Arch Hydrotech
Archiwum Inzynierii Ladowej [A publication]....................Arch Inz Ladowej
Archiwum Mechaniki Stosowanej [A publication]............. Arch Mech Stosow
Archiwum Mechaniki Stosowanej [Archives of Mechanics] [A publication]......................Arch Mech Stosowanej
Archiwum Termodynamiki [A publication] ....Arch Termodyn
Archiwum Thermodynamiki i Spalania [A publication]..................Arch Thermodyn Spal
Archonist Club ....AC
Archons of Colophon ....AC
Archuleta County Public Library, Pagosa Springs, CO [Library symbol] ....CoPs
Arcing ....ARNG
Arcispedale S. Anna di Ferrara [A publication]..................AAFRA
ARCO Chemical Co., Channelview, TX [Library symbol] ....TxCvS
Arcola, TX [Location identifier] [FAA]..................................SYG

Arctic [Air mass] [Meteorological symbol]...............................A
Arctic ....ART
Arctic Aeromedical Laboratory [Later, AMRL] [Air Force].....................AAL
Arctic Aeromedical Laboratory [Later, AMRL] [Air Force]...................AAML
Arctic and Alpine Research [A publication].................... Arct Alp Res
Arctic and Alpine Research (Boulder, Colorado) [A publication]................... Arct Alp Res (Boulder Colo)
Arctic and Antarctic Scientific Research Institute ....AASRI
Arctic Anthropology [A publication]...............................Arct Anthropol
Arctic Anthropology [A publication]...............................Arctic Anthropol
Arctic Anthropology [A publication]...............................Artic Anth
Arctic Approach Limitation..AAL
Arctic Bibliography [A publication] ....AB
Arctic Bibliography [A publication]...............................Arct Bibl
Arctic Bulletin [A publication] ....Arct Bull
Arctic Bulletin [A publication] ....Arctic Bul
Arctic Circle ....AC
Arctic Construction and Frost Effects Laboratory [Army].....................ACFEL
Arctic-Desert-Tropic Information Center [Air Force] ....ADTIC
Arctic Drift Barge ....ADB
Arctic Drift Station ....ADS
Arctic Drilling System ....ADS
Arctic Enterprises, Incorporated [NYSE symbol] [Delisted] ....AEI
Arctic Environmental Engineering Laboratory [University of Alaska]... AEEL
Arctic Environmental Information and Data Center [University of Alaska]..................AEIDC
Arctic Health Research Laboratory [HEW].........................AHRL
Arctic Health Services Research Center [HEW].........................AHSRC
Arctic Ice Dynamics Joint Experiment [National Science Foundation - Canada]..................AIDJEX
Arctic Institute ....AI
Arctic Institute of North America......................................ACNA
Arctic Institute of North America.....................................AINA
Arctic Institute of North America. Annual Report [A publication] .... Arct Inst N Am Annu Rep
Arctic Institute of North America. Annual Report [A publication] .... Arct Inst North Am Annu Rep
Arctic Institute of North America, Calgary, AB, Canada [Library symbol].....................CaACAI
Arctic Institute of North America, Montreal, PQ, Canada [Library symbol] [Obsolete].....................CaQMAI
Arctic Institute of North America. Research Paper [A publication]............... Arctic Inst North America Research Paper
Arctic Institute of North America. Special Publication [A publication]...................Arct Inst N Am Spec Publ
Arctic Institute of North America. Technical Papers [A publication]...................Arct Inst N Am Tech Pap
Arctic International Wildlife Range Society ....AIWRS
Arctic Marine Locomotive [An icebreaker used in oil exploration in the Arctic]..................AML
Arctic Marine Pipelaying System ....AMPS
Arctic Meteorology Photographic Probe............................AMPP
Arctic Ocean Environment Simulator..................................AOES
Arctic Ocean and Region [MARC geographic area code] [Library of Congress] ....r------
Arctic Operations [Military] ....ARCOPS
Arctic Research Laboratory [Army].....................................ARL
Arctic Research Laboratory Island [A floating ice island in the Arctic Ocean] [Navy].....................ARLIS
Arctic Science and Technology Information System [Arctic Institute of North America]..................ASTIS
Arctic Slope Native Association ....ASNA
Arctic Surface Effects Vehicle [Navy]...............................ASEV
Arctic Tent Stake Driver...ATSD
Arctic Test Branch [Army]...ATB
Arctic Test Center [Army]...ATC
Arctic Village [Alaska] [Airport symbol] ....ARC
Arctos: Acta Philologica Fennica [A publication] ....AAPF
Arcuate [Brain anatomy]...AR
Arcuate-Median Eminence [Anatomy]...................................A-ME
Ardeer Double Cartridge Test [Sensitivity to propagation test of an explosive]..................ADC
Arden Group, Inc. [NASDAQ symbol] ....ARDN
Arden Hill Hospital Medical Library, Goshen, NY [Library symbol] .....NGosA
Ardmore [Oklahoma] [Airport symbol] [Obsolete] ....ADM
Ardmore [Oklahoma] [Airport symbol] [Obsolete] ....AHD
Ardmore [New Zealand] [Airport symbol].............................AMZ
Ardmore, OK [Location identifier] [FAA].............................AUV
Ardmore, OK [Radio station call letters] ....KELS
Ardmore, OK [Radio station call letters] ....KKAJ
Ardmore, OK [Radio station call letters] ....KVSO
Ardmore, OK [Television station call letters].........................KXII
Ardmore, TN [Radio station call letters]..............................WSLV
Ardsley Public Library, Ardsley, NY [Library symbol] ....NArd
Are [Also, a] [A unit of area in the metric system] ....A
Are You? [Communication]...RU
Area ....A
Area ....AR
Area Air Defense System...AADS
Area Airports Checked...ARAC
Area Chart ....A

Area Clearance Officer	ACO
Area Combined Headquarters [World War II]	ACHQ
Area Combined Movements Center	ACMC
Area Command Post	ACP
Area Commanders' Meeting [NATO]	ARCOMET
Area Communications Operations Center	ACOC
Area Communications Terminal Subsystem [Ground Communications Facility, NASA]	ACTS
Area Computing Facilities	ACF
Area Concept Papers [Military]	ACP
Area Confinement Facility [Military]	ACF
Area Control Center [Aviation]	ACC
Area Cooperative Educational Services [Information service]	ACES
Area Coordinating Paper	ACP
Area Coordination Group [Air Force]	ACG
Area Coordination Group [Air Force]	ACGp
Area Coordination Review	ACR
Area Coordination Subgroup [Air Force]	ACSG
Area Coordination Subgroup [Air Force]	ACSGp
Area Coordination Subgroup [Air Force]	ACSGRP
Area Correlation Tracker [Air Force]	ACT
Area Council for Economic Education	ACEE
Area of Critical Environmental Concern [Bureau of Land Management designation]	ACEC
Area and Culture Studies [Tokyo] [A publication]	A & CS
Area Damage Control Center [Army]	ADCC
Area Damage Control Center [Army]	ADCOC
Area Damage Control Party [Army]	ADCOP
Area Data Center	ADC
Area Defense Homing Interceptor	ADHI
Area Defense Missile	ADM
Area Denial Artillery Munition	ADAM
Area Denial Munition	ADM
Area Denial Visual Indication Security Equipment	ADVISE
Area Director	AD
Area Discriminator [SAGE]	AD
Area Distribution Officers [Military] [British] [World War II]	ADOS
Area Distribution Panel	ADP
Area of Dominant Influence [Television ratings term used by American Research Bureau]	ADI
Area Drain [Technical drawings]	AD
Area Education Officer [Military] [British]	AEO
Area Electronic Supervisor	AES
Area Engineering Officer [Army Corps of Engineers]	AEO
Area Equipment Compounds [Military]	AEC
Area Forecast [Aviation]	ARFOR
Area Forecast [Aviation code]	FA
Area Forecast Center	AFC
Area Forecast of Upper Winds and Temperatures [Aviation code]	ARMET
Area Frequency Coordinator	AFC
Area Headquarters	AHQ
Area Health Authority	AHA
Area Health Authority Full Time [Chiropody] [British]	AHF
Area Health Authority (Teaching) [British]	AHA(T)
Area Health Education Center [Library network]	AHEC
Area II Library Services Authority [Library network]	ALSA 2
Area Imaging Device	AID
Area Inspector [British railroad term]	AI
Area Interdiction Mine [Air Force]	AIM
Area of Interest	AOI
Area Learning Resource Center	ALRC
Area Library Services Authority [Indiana]	ALSA
Area Local Control Panel	ALCP
Area Logistics Command	ALC
Area Mail Processing [US Postal Service]	AMP
Area Mail Processing Center [US Postal Service]	AMPC
Area Maintenance Facility	AMF
Area Maintenance Supply Facility [Army]	AMSF
Area Maintenance Support Activity	AMSA
Area Manpower Instructional Development Systems	AMIDS
Area Manpower Review [Department of Labor]	AMR
Area Medical Laboratory [Military]	AML
Area Microwave Assembly [Ground Communications Facility, NASA]	AMWA
Area Moving Target Indicator [NASA]	AMTI
Area Naval Commander [NATO]	ANC
Area Navigation	ANAV
Area Office	AO
Area Office Notice [FAA]	ARNOT
Area of Operations [Military]	AO
Area-Oriented Depots [Military]	AOD
Area of Outstanding Natural Beauty [Great Britain]	AONB
Area Passive Dosimeter	APD
Area Petroleum Office [or Officer]	APO
Area Planning	AP
Area Planning-Action Councils	APAC
Area Planning Report	APR
Area under Plasma Concentration Curve [Hematology]	AUC
Area of Positive Control [FAA]	APC
Area Postal Directory	APD
Area Precipitation Measurement Equipment	APME

Area Precipitation Measurement Indicator	APMI
Area of Probability	AOP
Area Production Urgency Committee	APUC
Area Radiation Monitor	ARM
Area Real Estate Office	AREO
Area Recruiting Concept Special Test Army Reserve	ARCSTAR
Area Redevelopment Act	ARA
Area Redevelopment Administration [Terminated, 1965; functions transferred to Economic Development Administration] [Department of Commerce]	ARA
Area Redevelopment Program	ARP
Area Reference Resource Center [Library network]	ARRC
Area of Resolution	AR
Area Resource Center [Library network]	ARC
Area Resource File [Public Health Service] [Information service]	ARF
Area of Responsibility	AOR
Area of Responsibility Centre [Aviation]	ARC
Area Resupply	ARS
Area Safety Officer	ASO
Area Scale Temperature Display	ASTD
Area Scanning Alarm	ASA
Area Security Coordination Center	ASCC
Area Security Information Center	ASIC
Area Service Unit	ASU
Area Signal Center [Army]	ASIGCEN
Area Specialist Program [Air Force training program]	ASP
Area Specialist Team [Army]	AST
Area of Substantial Unemployment [CETA] [Department of Labor]	ASU
Area Supervisor [FAA]	ARSUP
Area Supervisor [Bureau of Apprenticeship and Training] [Department of Labor]	AS
Area Supply Officer [Army]	ASO
Area Supply Support Activity	ASSA
Area Support Group [Military]	ASG
Area Surveillance	AS
Area Surveillance Control System	ASCS
Area Surveillance RADAR	ASR
Area Test Equipment	ATE
Area Traffic Officer	ATO
Area Training Director [Red Cross]	TD
Area Utilization Office [GSA]	AUO
Area VI Library Services Authority [Library network]	ALSA 6
Area Wage and Classification Office	AWCO
Area Weighted Average Resolution [Photography]	AWAR
Area Weighted Average T-Number	AWAT
Area Working Standards	AWS
Areal Hypolimnetic Oxygen Deficit [Hydrobiology]	AHOD
Arecibo [Puerto Rico] [Seismograph station code, US Geological Survey]	APR
Arecibo Ionospheric Observatory [Later, National Astronomy and Ionospheric Observatory] [Puerto Rico]	AIO
Arecibo, PR [Location identifier] [FAA]	ABO
Arecibo, PR [Television station call letters]	WATX-TV
Arecibo, PR [Radio station call letters]	WCMN
Arecibo, PR [Radio station call letters]	WCMN-FM
Arecibo, PR [Radio station call letters]	WMIA
Arecibo, PR [Radio station call letters]	WNIK
Arecibo, PR [Radio station call letters]	WNIK-FM
Arena [A publication]	Ar
Arena Managers Association [Defunct]	AMA
Arena Managers Association, Incorporated [Defunct]	AMAI
Arequipa [Peru] [Airport symbol]	AQP
Arequipa [Peru] [Seismograph station code, US Geological Survey]	ARE
Arethuse [A publication]	Areth
Arfendazam [Biochemistry]	ARF
Argensola [A publication]	Arg
Argent [Heraldry]	A
Argent [Heraldry]	ARG
Argenteuil Symposia Series [Elsevier Book Series] [A publication]	ASS
Argentia, NF [Radio station call letters]	CFOZ-FM
Argentia, NF [Television station call letters]	CJAP-TV
Argentina [MARC country of publication code] [Library of Congress]	ag
Argentina [Two-letter standard code]	AR
Argentina [Three-letter standard code]	ARG
Argentina [Aircraft nationality and registration mark]	LQ
Argentina [Aircraft nationality and registration mark]	LV
Argentina [MARC geographic area code] [Library of Congress]	s-ag---
Argentina, Brazil, Chile	ABC
Argentina Electroenergetica [A publication]	Argent Electroenerg
Argentine Commission for Human Rights	ACHR
Argentine Information Service Center [An association]	AISC
Argentine Interplanetary Association	AIA
Argentine Island [Antarctica] [Geomagnetic observatory code]	AIA
Argentine Island [Antarctica] [Seismograph station code, US Geological Survey]	AIA
Argentum [Silver] [Chemical element]	Ag
Argentum [Silver] [Numismatics]	AR
Argentum [Silver]	ARG
Arges [Romania] [Seismograph station code, US Geological Survey]	ARR
Arginase [An enzyme]	AS
Arginine [Also, R] [An amino acid]	Arg

Arginine [*One-letter symbol; see Arg*] ... R
Arginine Decarboxylase [*An enzyme*] ... ADC
Arginine, Glutamate, alpha-Ketoglutarate Oxalacetate ... AGKO
Arginine Maturity Index [*For prediction of peanut harvest date*] ... AMI
Arginine Vasopressin [*Antidiuretic hormone*] ... AVP
Arginine Vasotocin [*Endocrinology*] ... AVT
Argininosuccinate Lyase [*Also, ASL*] [*An enzyme*] ... AL
Argininosuccinate Synthetase [*An enzyme*] ... AS
Argininosuccinate Synthetase [*An enzyme*] ... ASS
Argo Petroleum Corp. [*American Stock Exchange symbol*] ... ARG
ARGO Systems, Incorporated [*NASDAQ symbol*] ... ARGI
ARGO Systems, Inc., Sunnyvale, CA [*OCLC symbol*] ... ASI
Argon [*Chemical symbol is Ar*] [*Chemical element*] ... A
Argon [*Preferred form, but also see A*] [*Chemical element*] ... Ar
Argon Gas LASER ... AGL
Argon Glow Lamp ... AGL
Argon Ion LASER ... AIL
Argon LASER Discharge Tube ... ALDT
Argon LASER Lining ... ALL
Argon-Oxygen Decarburization [*Steelmaking*] ... AOD
Argon Purge Cart [*Nuclear energy*] ... APC
Argonaut Energy Corp. [*NASDAQ symbol*] ... ARGN
Argonne Advanced Research Reactor ... AARR
Argonne Advanced Research Reactor ... A^2R^2
Argonne Boiling Water Reactor ... ARBOR
Argonne Cancer Research Hospital [*Illinois*] ... ACRH
Argonne Code Center [*Department of Energy*] ... ACC
Argonne Fast Source Reactor ... AFSR
Argonne High-Flux Reactor ... AHFR
Argonne Institute of Nuclear Science and Engineering [*AEC*] ... AINSE
Argonne Low-Power Reactor [*Obsolete*] ... ALPR
Argonne National Laboratory [*Department of Energy*] ... ANL
Argonne National Laboratory, Argonne, IL [*OCLC symbol*] ... ANL
Argonne National Laboratory, Argonne, IL [*Library symbol*] ... IArg
Argonne National Laboratory Engineering and Technology Division ... ANL/ETD
Argonne National Laboratory, Idaho Division ... ANL ID
Argonne National Laboratory. Water Resources Research Program (Report) ANL/WR [*A publication*] ... Argonne Natl Lab Water Resour Res Program (Rep) ANL/WR
Argonne Nuclear Assembly for University Training ... ARGONAUT
Argonne Reactor Computation ... ARC
Argonne Reviews [*A publication*] ... Argonne Rev
Argonne Tandem/LINAC Accelerator System [*Department of Energy*] ... ATLAS
Argonne Thermal Source Reactor ... ATSR
Argonne Universities Association ... AUA
Argostolion [*Greece*] [*Airport symbol*] ... EFL
Argosy Air Lines, Inc. [*Ft. Lauderdale, FL*] [*FAA designator*] ... ARG
Argument Programing ... AP
Argumento [*By an argument drawn from such a law*] [*Latin*] ... ARG
Argus Printing & Publishing Co., Butler, NJ [*Library symbol*] ... NjButA
Argyll [*County in Scotland*] ... ARG
Argyll Light Infantry [*Military unit*] [*British*] ... ALI
Argyll and Sutherland Highlanders [*Military unit*] [*British*] ... A & SH
Argyllshire [*County in Scotland*] ... ARGYL
Argyrophil, Fluorescent, Granulated [*Cells*] [*Anatomy*] ... AFG
Arheologia Moldovei [*A publication*] ... Arh Moldovei
Arheologija un Etnografija [*A publication*] ... AE
Arheologija un Etnografija [*A publication*] ... AuE
Arheoloski Vestnik [*A publication*] ... ArhV
Arhitektura SSSR [*A publication*] ... Arhitekt SSSR
Arhiv Bioloskih Nauka [*A publication*] ... Arh Biol Nauka
Arhiv za Farmaciju (Belgrade) [*A publication*] ... Arh Farm (Belgr)
Arhiv za Higijenu Rada i Toksikologiju [*A publication*] ... Arh Hig Rada Toksikol
Arhiv za Higijenu Rada i Toksikologiju [*A publication*] ... Arh Hig Rad Toksikol
Arhiv za Poljoprivredne Nauke [*A publication*] ... Arh Poljopriv Nauke
Arhiv za Poljoprivredne Nauke [*A publication*] ... Arh Poljopr Nauke
Arhiv za Poljoprivredne Nauke i Tehniku [*A publication*] ... Arh Poljopr Nauke Teh
ARIA [*Apollo Range Instrumentation Aircraft*] **Operations Control Center** [*NASA*] ... AOCC
Ariana Afghan Airline Co. Ltd. [*Afghanistan*] [*ICAO designator*] ... FG
Arica [*Chile*] [*Airport symbol*] ... ARI
Arica [*Chile*] [*Seismograph station code, US Geological Survey*] ... ARI
Arica Institute ... AI
Arid Land Ecology [*AEC project*] ... ALE
Arid Lands Agricultural Development [*Program*] [*Middle East*] ... ALAD
Arid Lands Information Center [*University of Arizona*] ... ALIC
Arid Lands Information System [*University of Arizona*] ... ALIS
Arid Lands Resource Information Paper [*A publication*] ... Arid Lands Resour Inf Pap
Arid Zone Research. United Nations Educational, Scientific, and Cultural Organization [*A publication*] ... Arid Zone Res UNESCO
Arida [*Japan*] [*Seismograph station code, US Geological Survey*] ... ARD
Ariel Owners' Motorcycle Club ... AOMC
Ariel: a Review of International English Literature [*A publication*] ... Ariel E
Aries [*Constellation*] ... Ari
Aries [*Constellation*] ... Arie
Aries Air Cargo International [*Air carrier designation symbol*] ... AACX
Aril Society International ... ASI
Arion's Dolphin [*A publication*] ... Ari D
Aristar, Inc. [*NYSE symbol*] [*Delisted*] ... ARR
Aristek Communities [*NASDAQ symbol*] ... ARIS
Aristotelian Society: Supplementary Volume [*A publication*] ... Aris Soc
Arithmetic ... ARITH
Arithmetic Array Identification ... AAID
Arithmetic Assignment Statement ... AAS
Arithmetic Average ... AA
Arithmetic Computation Test [*Military*] ... AC
Arithmetic Computer ... ACU
Arithmetic and Control Unit ... ACU
Arithmetic Device ... AD
Arithmetic Element ... AE
Arithmetic Element Program ... ARELEM
Arithmetic Expression ... AE
Arithmetic Function Designator ... AFD
Arithmetic Function Identifier ... AFID
Arithmetic and Logic Unit [*Data processing*] ... A & LU
Arithmetic and Logic Unit [*Data processing*] ... ALU
Arithmetic mean ... X
Arithmetic Processing Unit [*Data processing*] ... APU
Arithmetic Proficiency Training Program [*Computer-assisted training program*] ... APTP
Arithmetic Progression ... AP
Arithmetic Project [*National Science Foundation*] ... AP
Arithmetic Reading Test [*Military*] ... ART
Arithmetic Reasoning Test ... ART
Arithmetic Shift Left ... ASL
Arithmetic Shift Right ... ASR
Arithmetic Simple Variable ... ASV
Arithmetic Statement Function ... ASF
Arithmetic Teacher [*A publication*] ... Arith Teach
Arithmetic Underachievers [*Education*] ... AUA
Arithmetic Unit ... ARITHU
Arithmetic Unit ... AU
Arivaca Silver Mines [*NASDAQ symbol*] ... AVCMF
Arizona ... ARI
Arizona ... ARIZ
Arizona [*Postal code*] ... AZ
Arizona [*MARC country of publication code*] [*Library of Congress*] ... azu
Arizona [*MARC geographic area code*] [*Library of Congress*] ... n-us-az
Arizona Academy of Science. Journal [*A publication*] ... Arizona Acad Sci Jour
Arizona Agricultural Experiment Station. Publications [*A publication*] ... Ariz Ag Exp
Arizona Agricultural Experiment Station. Research Report [*A publication*] ... Ariz Agric Exp Stn Res Rep
Arizona Agricultural Experiment Station. Technical Bulletin [*A publication*] ... Ariz Agric Exp Stn Tech Bull
Arizona Bancwest Corp. [*NASDAQ symbol*] ... AZBW
Arizona Bureau of Mines. Bulletin [*A publication*] ... Ariz Bur Mines Bull
Arizona Bureau of Mines. Bulletin [*A publication*] ... Arizona Bur Mines Bull
Arizona Bureau of Mines. Bulletin. Geological Series [*A publication*] ... Ariz Bur Mines Bull Geol Ser
Arizona Bureau of Mines. Bulletin. Mineral Technology Series [*A publication*] ... Ariz Bur Mines Bull Mineral Technology Ser
Arizona Bureau of Mines. Circular [*A publication*] ... Ariz Bur Mines Circ
Arizona Bureau of Mines. Field Notes [*A publication*] ... Ariz Bur Mines Field Notes
Arizona City, AZ [*Radio station call letters*] ... KKAF
Arizona Commission of Agriculture and Horticulture. Annual Report [*A publication*] ... Ariz Comm Agric Hortic Annu Rep
Arizona Department of Library Archives, Tempe, AZ [*OCLC symbol*] ... AZP
Arizona Department of Mineral Resources. Annual Report [*A publication*] ... Ariz Dept Mineral Res Ann Rept
Arizona Foreign Language Teachers Forum [*A publication*] ... AFLT Forum
Arizona Forestry Notes [*A publication*] ... Ariz For Notes
Arizona Game and Fish Department. Wildlife Bulletin [*A publication*] ... Ariz Game Fish Dep Wildl Bull
Arizona Geological Society Digest. Annual [*A publication*] ... Ariz Geol Soc Digest Ann
Arizona Highways [*A publication*] ... Ariz H
Arizona Historical Foundation, Arizona State University, Tempe, AZ [*Library symbol*] ... AzTeS-Hi
Arizona Historical Review [*A publication*] ... Ariz His R
Arizona Historical Review [*A publication*] ... Ariz Hist Rev
Arizona Historical Society, Tucson, AZ [*Library symbol*] ... AzTP
Arizona Job Colleges [*An association*] [*Defunct*] ... AJC
Arizona Jojoba Growers Association ... AJGA
Arizona Law Review [*A publication*] ... Ariz Law R
Arizona Law Review [*A publication*] ... Ariz L Rev
Arizona Librarian [*A publication*] ... Ariz Libn
Arizona Librarian [*A publication*] ... Ariz Librn
Arizona Medical Center, University of Arizona, Tucson, AZ [*Library symbol*] ... AzTAM
Arizona Medicine [*A publication*] ... Ariz Med
Arizona Motor Tariff Bureau, Inc., Phoenix AZ [*STAC*] ... AZB
Arizona Nurse [*A publication*] ... Ariz Nurse
Arizona Photopolarimeter Telescope ... APT

Arizona Public Service Co. [*NYSE symbol*] ... AZP
Arizona Quarterly [*A publication*] ... AQ
Arizona Quarterly [*A publication*] ... Ariz Q
Arizona Quarterly [*A publication*] ... ArQ
Arizona Regional Ecological Test Site [*Department of the Interior*] ... ARETS
Arizona Regional Library for the Blind and Physically Handicapped, Phoenix, AZ [*Library symbol*] ... Az-BPH
Arizona Review [*A publication*] ... AR
Arizona Review [*A publication*] ... Arizona R
Arizona Silver Corp. [*NASDAQ symbol*] ... ARZNF
Arizona Sports Network [*Cable TV programing service*] ... ASN
Arizona State Bureau of Mines. Bulletin [*A publication*] ... Ariz St Bur Mines B
Arizona State College ... ASC
Arizona State Department of Library and Archives, Phoenix, AZ [*Library symbol*] ... Az
Arizona State Land Department. Water Resources Report [*A publication*] ... Ariz State Land Dept Water Res Rept
Arizona State Law Journal [*A publication*] ... Ariz State Law J
Arizona State Law Journal [*A publication*] ... Ariz St L J
Arizona State Prison Library, Florence, AZ [*Library symbol*] ... AzFlP
Arizona State University [*Arizona*] [*Seismograph station code, US Geological Survey*] ... ASU
Arizona State University, College of Educational Technology and Library Science, Tempe, AZ [*OCLC symbol*] ... ASE
Arizona State University, College of Law Library, Tempe, AZ [*OCLC symbol*] ... AZC
Arizona State University, Tempe, AZ [*OCLC symbol*] ... AZS
Arizona State University, Tempe, AZ [*Library symbol*] ... AzTeS
Arizona Statistical Repetitive Analog Computer ... ASTRAC
Arizona Teacher [*A publication*] ... Ariz Teach
Arizona Trade-Off Model [*State of Arizona and Department of Commerce project to resolve conflicts between economic and environmental goals*] ... ATOM
Arizona University. Agricultural Experiment Station. Bulletin [*A publication*] ... Ariz Univ Agr Expt Bull
Arizona University. Agricultural Experiment Station. Bulletin. Physical Science Bulletin [*A publication*] ... Ariz Univ Agr Expt Bull Phys Sci Bull
Arizona University. Laboratory of Tree-Ring Research. Papers [*A publication*] ... Ariz Univ Lab Tree-Ring Res Pap
Arizona University. Lunar and Planetary Laboratory. Communications [*A publication*] ... Ariz Univ Lunar Planet Lab Commun
Arizona Water Commission. Bulletin [*A publication*] ... Ariz Water Comm Bull
Arizona and the West [*A publication*] ... ArizW
Arizona and the West [*A publication*] ... Ariz and West
Arizona Western College, Yuma, AZ [*OCLC symbol*] ... AZY
Arizona Western College, Yuma, AZ [*Library symbol*] ... AzYAW
Ark-La-Tex Genealogical Association ... ALTGA
Ark River Review [*A publication*] ... Ark Riv
Ark Valley Airways [*Arkansas City, KS*] [*FAA designator*] ... SMY
Arkadelphia, AR [*Location identifier*] [*FAA*] ... ADF
Arkadelphia, AR [*Radio station call letters*] ... KDEL
Arkadelphia, AR [*Television station call letters*] ... KETG
Arkadelphia, AR [*Radio station call letters*] ... KSWH
Arkadelphia, AR [*Radio station call letters*] ... KVRC
Arkansas [*Postal code*] ... AR
Arkansas ... ARK
Arkansas [*MARC country of publication code*] [*Library of Congress*] ... aru
Arkansas [*MARC geographic area code*] [*Library of Congress*] ... n-us-ar
Arkansas Academy of Science. Proceedings [*A publication*] ... Ark Acad Sci Proc
Arkansas Academy of Science. Proceedings [*A publication*] ... Arkansas Acad Sci Proc
Arkansas Agricultural Experiment Station. Bulletin [*A publication*] ... Arkansas Agric Exp Stn Bull
Arkansas Agricultural Experiment Station. Mimeograph Series [*A publication*] ... Arkansas Agric Exp Stn Mimeogr Ser
Arkansas Agricultural Experiment Station. Publications [*A publication*] ... Ark Ag Exp
Arkansas Agricultural Experiment Station. Report Series [*A publication*] ... Arkansas Agric Exp Stn Rep Ser
Arkansas Agricultural Experiment Station. Special Report [*A publication*] ... Arkansas Agric Exp Stn Spec Rep
Arkansas Arts Center, Little Rock, AR [*OCLC symbol*] ... AKA
Arkansas Arts Center, Little Rock, AR [*Library symbol*] ... ArLA
Arkansas Best Corp. [*NYSE symbol*] ... ABZ
Arkansas City, KS [*Radio station call letters*] ... KSOK
Arkansas College ... AC
Arkansas College, Batesville, AR [*Library symbol*] ... ArBaA
Arkansas Democrat, Little Rock, AR [*Library symbol*] ... ArLAD
Arkansas Dental Journal [*A publication*] ... Arkansas Dent J
Arkansas Farm Research [*A publication*] ... Arkans Fm Res
Arkansas Farm Research [*A publication*] ... Ark Farm Res
Arkansas Geological and Conservation Commission. Information Circular [*A publication*] ... Arkansas Geol Comm Inform Circ
Arkansas Geological Survey [*A publication*] ... Ark G S
Arkansas Historical Association. Publications [*A publication*] ... Ark His As
Arkansas Historical Association. Publications [*A publication*] ... Ark Hist Assoc Publ
Arkansas Historical Quarterly [*A publication*] ... AHQ
Arkansas Historical Quarterly [*A publication*] ... ArHQ
Arkansas Historical Quarterly [*A publication*] ... Ark Hist Q
Arkansas Historical Quarterly [*A publication*] ... Ark Hist Quar
Arkansas Historical Quarterly [*A publication*] ... ArkHQ
Arkansas History Commission, Department of Archives and History, Little Rock, AR [*Library symbol*] ... Ar-Hi
Arkansas Law Review [*A publication*] ... Ark Law R
Arkansas Law Review [*A publication*] ... Ark L Rev
Arkansas Libraries [*A publication*] ... Arkansas Lib
Arkansas Libraries [*A publication*] ... Ark Lib
Arkansas Library Commission, Little Rock, AR [*OCLC symbol*] ... AKF
Arkansas Library Commission, Little Rock, AR [*Library symbol*] ... Ar
Arkansas Louisiana Gas Co. ... ARKLA
Arkansas & Louisiana Missouri Railway Co. [*AAR code*] ... ALM
Arkansas Nurse [*A publication*] ... Ark Nurse
Arkansas & Ozarks Railway [*AAR code*] ... AO
Arkansas Polytechnic College [*Later, Arkansas Technical University*] ... APC
Arkansas Polytechnic College [*Later, Arkansas Technical University*], **Russellville, AR** [*Library symbol*] ... ArRuA
Arkansas Post National Monument ... ARPO
Arkansas Research Test Station ... ARTS
Arkansas Resources and Development Commission. Division of Geology Bulletin. Information Circular [*A publication*] ... Ark Res Devel Comm Div Geology Bull Inf Circ
Arkansas River Valley Regional Library, Dardanelle, AR [*Library symbol*] ... ArDar
Arkansas River Valley Regional Library, Dardanelle, AR [*OCLC symbol*] ... AVR
Arkansas State College [*Later, ASU*] ... ASC
Arkansas State Library, Little Rock, AR [*OCLC symbol*] ... AST
Arkansas State Nurses' Association. Newsletter [*A publication*] ... Ark State Nurses Assoc Newsl
Arkansas State Teachers College [*Later, University of Central Arkansas*] ... ASTC
Arkansas State University ... ASU
Arkansas State University Library, State University, AR [*OCLC symbol*] ... ASU
Arkansas State University, State University, AR [*Library symbol*] ... ArStC
Arkansas Supreme Court Library, Little Rock, AR [*Library symbol*] ... Ar-SC
Arkansas Technical University, Russellville, AR [*OCLC symbol*] ... AKP
Arkansas University. Institute of Science and Technology. Research Series [*A publication*] ... Ark Univ Inst Sci and Technology Research Ser
Arkansas University. Seismological Bulletin [*A publication*] ... Arkansas Univ Seismol Bull
Arkansas Valley Regional Library Service System [*Library network*] ... AVRLSS
[*The*] **Arkansas Western Railway Co.** [*AAR code*] ... ARW
Arkhangelsk [*USSR*] [*Geomagnetic observatory code*] ... ARK
Arkheograficheskii Ezhegodnik [*A publication*] ... AE
Arkheologicheskie Otkrytiia [*A publication*] ... Ark Otkr
Arkheologichi Pamiatniki URSR [*A publication*] ... Ark Pam URSR
Arkheologiia i Istoriia Bospora. Sbornik Statei [*A publication*] ... AIB
Arkheologiia (Kiev) [*A publication*] ... Ark (Kiev)
Arkheologija. Publies par l'Academie des Sciences d'Ukraine [*A publication*] ... ArkUkr
Arkhiv Anatomii Gistologii i Embriologii [*A publication*] ... Arkh Anat Gistol Embriol
Arkhiv Biologicheskikh Nauk [*A publication*] ... Arkh Biol Nauk
Arkhiv Klinicheskoi i Eksperimental'noi Meditsiny (Moskva) [*A publication*] ... Arkh Klin i Eksper Med (Moskva)
Arkhiv Meditsinskikh Nauk [*A publication*] ... Arkh Med Nauk
Arkhiv Patologii [*A publication*] ... Arkh Patol
Arkhiv Russkogo Protistologicheskogo Obshchestva [*A publication*] ... Arkh Russk Protist Obsh
Arkhivi Ukraini. Naukovo Informatsiinii Biuleten' Arkhivnogo Upravliniia pri Radi Ministriv URSR [*A publication*] ... Arkhivi Ukr
Arkia Israel Inland Airlines [*ICAO designator*] ... IZ
Arkib Negara [*National Archives of Malaysia*], **Federal Government Building, Kuala Lumpur, Malaysia** [*Library symbol*] ... MlyKA
Arkiv foer Astronomi [*A publication*] ... Ark Astron
Arkiv foer Botanik [*A publication*] ... Ark Bot
Arkiv foer Fysik [*A publication*] ... Ark Fys
Arkiv foer det Fysiske Seminar i Trondheim [*A publication*] ... Ark Fys Semin Trondheim
Arkiv foer Geofysik [*A publication*] ... Ark Geofys
Arkiv fuer Kemi [*A publication*] ... Ark Kemi
Arkiv foer Matematik [*A publication*] ... Ark Mat
Arkiv foer Matematik [*A publication*] ... Ark Matemat
Arkiv foer Mineralogi och Geologi [*A publication*] ... Ark Mineral Geol
Arkiv foer Nordisk Filologi [*A publication*] ... ANF
Arkiv foer Nordisk Filologi [*A publication*] ... Arkiv
Arkiv foer Nordisk Filologi [*A publication*] ... Arkiv f Nord Filologi
Arkiv foer Zoologi [*A publication*] ... Ark Zool
Arkiv foer Zoologi (Stockholm) [*A publication*] ... Ark Zool (Stockholm)
Arkkitehti [*A publication*] ... ARKK-A
Arkla Industries, Inc. [*Formerly, Arkansas Louisiana Gas Co.*] [*NYSE symbol*] ... ALG
Arlans Department Stores, Inc. [*NYSE symbol*] [*Delisted*] ... AAD

Arlen Realty & Development Corp. [*NYSE symbol*] ARE
Arlington Annex [*Navy*] AA
Arlington Baptist Junior College, Arlington, TX [*Library symbol*] TxArB
Arlington College, Arlington, CA [*Library symbol*] CArlA
Arlington County Department of Libraries, Arlington, VA [*OCLC symbol*] VIA
Arlington County Department of Libraries, Arlington, VA [*Library symbol*] ViAr
Arlington County Department of Libraries, Aurora Hills Branch, Arlington, VA [*Library symbol*] ViAr-A
Arlington County Department of Libraries, Cherrydale Branch, Arlington, VA [*Library symbol*] ViAr-Ch
Arlington County Department of Libraries, Clarendon Branch, Arlington, VA [*Library symbol*] ViAr-Cl
Arlington County Department of Libraries, Fairlington Branch, Arlington, VA [*Library symbol*] ViAr-F
Arlington County Department of Libraries, Glencarlyn Branch, Arlington, VA [*Library symbol*] ViAr-G
Arlington County Department of Libraries, Westover Branch, Arlington, VA [*Library symbol*] ViAr-W
Arlington Hall Station [*Virginia*] [*Army*] AHS
Arlington Heights, IL [*Location identifier*] [*FAA*] JLH
Arlington Heights, IL [*Radio station call letters*] WSEX
Arlington Memorial Amphitheater Commission [*Abolished 1960, functions transferred to Department of Defense*] AMAC
Arlington National Cemetery ANC
Arlington Public Library, Arlington, IA [*Library symbol*] IaArl
Arlington Public Library, Arlington, SD [*Library symbol*] SdAr
Arlington Public Library, Genealogy Department, Arlington, TX [*Library symbol*] TxAr-G
Arlington Quarterly [*A publication*] ArlQ
Arlington State College [*Texas*] ASC
Arlington, TN [*Location identifier*] [*FAA*] LHC
Arlington, TN [*Radio station call letters*] WGSF
Arlington, TX [*Radio station call letters*] KWJS
Arlington, VA [*Radio station call letters*] WABS
Arlington, VA [*Radio station call letters*] WAVA
Arlington, VA [*Radio station call letters*] WEAM
ARLIS [*Art Libraries Society/North America*] **Newsletter** [*A publication*] ARLIS Newsl
Arlit [*Niger*] [*Airport symbol*] RLT
Arm/Destruct A/D
Arm/Firing Mechanism A/FM
Arm Girth, Chest Depth, and Hip Width [*Anatomical index*] ACH
Arm and Hammer [*Brand of soda*] A & H
Arm Length AL
Arm Length Index ALI
Arm Length Order ALO
Arm Retracting Strut [*Nuclear energy*] AR-RET-ST
Arm Width AW
Arm Width Index AWI
Armac Enterprises, Incorporated [*American Stock Exchange symbol*] [*Delisted*] ARI
Armada Corp. [*NYSE symbol*] ABW
Armada Free Public Library, Armada, MI [*Library symbol*] MiArm
Armadillo Breeders Association [*Defunct*] ABA
Armak Co., McCook, IL [*Library symbol*] IMccA
Armament A
Armament ARM
Armament ARMT
Armament Boresight Line ABL
Armament Command [*Army*] ARMCOM
Armament Concepts Office [*Army*] ACO
Armament Control Computer ACC
Armament Control and Delivery System ARCADS
Armament Control Panel ACP
Armament Control Relay Panel ACRP
Armament Control System [*Air Force*] ACS
Armament Data Line [*Military*] ADL
Armament Depot [*Military*] [*British*] AD
Armament Design Establishment [*British*] ADE
Armament Development Center [*Army*] ADC
Armament Development Enfield/Direction Etude Fabrication [*Military*] ADEN/DEFA
Armament Development Laboratory [*Air Force*] ADL
Armament Development and Test Center [*Air Force*] ADTC
Armament Division [*Air Force Systems Command*] AD
Armament and Electronics [*Air Force*] A & E
Armament and Electronics Laboratory AEL
Armament and Electronics Test Laboratory [*NATO*] AETL
Armament Maintenance Management Information Center [*Navy*] AMMIC
Armament Material Bulletin AMB
Armament Material Change AMC
Armament Research Development [*British*] ARD
Armament Station Control Unit ASCU
Armament Supply Department [*Navy*] [*British*] ASD
Armament System Test Set ASTS
Armament Systems Personnel Research Laboratory [*Air Force*] ASPRL
Armament Technology Division [*Air Force*] ATL
Armament Test AT
Armament Test Center [*Military*] ATC
Armament Test Preparation Facility ATPF
Armaments Command [*Formerly, Munitions Command*] [*Army*] AC
Armaments Control Agency [*Western European Union*] ACA
Armaments Design Department [*Ministry of Supply*] [*British*] [*World War II*] ADD
Armaments Research Department [*Ministry of Supply*] [*British*] ARD
Armaments Research and Development Establishment [*British*] ARDE
Armaments Standardization and Interoperability [*NATO*] ASI
Armas y Letras [*A publication*] ALet
Armatron International [*American Stock Exchange symbol*] ART
Armature ARM
Armature ARMA
Armature Accelerator AA
Armature Shunt [*Electromagnetism*] ARMSHT
Armature Shunt [*Electromagnetism*] ASH
[*The*] **Armchair Detective** [*A publication*] Armchair Det
[*The*] **Armchair Detective** [*A publication*] Arm D
[*The*] **Armchair Detective** [*A publication*] TAD
Armco, Inc. [*Formerly, Armco Steel Corp.*] [*NYSE symbol*] AS
Armco, Inc., Advanced Materials Division, Research Library, Baltimore, MD [*Library symbol*] MdBAS
Armco, Inc., Research Center, Technical Library, Middletown, OH [*Library symbol*] OMidAR
Arme Blindee-Cavalerie [*Armored Forces Cavalry*] [*France*] ABC
Armed ARMD
Armed Advanced Scout Helicopter ARMEDASH
Armed Aircraft Qualification AAQ
Armed Boarding Vessel ABV
Armed Forces AF
Armed Forces Acquisition Document AFAD
Armed Forces Act AFA
Armed Forces Air Intelligence Training Center AFAITC
Armed Forces Assistance to Korea [*Military*] AFAK
Armed Forces Benefit and Aid Association AFBAA
Armed Forces Broadcasters Association AFBA
Armed Forces Chemical Association [*Later, ADPA*] AFCA
Armed Forces Combat Bulletin AFCB
Armed Forces Communications Association [*Later, AFCEA*] AFCA
Armed Forces Communications and Electronics Association AFCEA
Armed Forces Council AFC
Armed Forces Courier Service AFCOS
Armed Forces Courier Service ARFCOS
Armed Forces Courier Station ARFCOSTA
Armed Forces Day AFD
Armed Forces Dental Officers Association AFDOA
Armed Forces Development Board AFDB
Armed Forces Disciplinary Control Board AFDCB
Armed Forces Enlisted Personnel Benefit Association [*Later, MBA*] AFEPBA
Armed Forces Epidemiological Board AFEB
Armed Forces Examining and Entrance Stations AFEES
Armed Forces Examining and Induction Stations AFEIS
Armed Forces Examining Station AFES
Armed Forces Expeditionary Medal AFEM
Armed Forces Hostess Association AFHA
Armed Forces Induction Station AFIS
Armed Forces Information and Education AFIE
Armed Forces Information and Education Division AFIED
Armed Forces Information Film AFIF
Armed Forces Information Program AFIP
Armed Forces Information School AFIS
Armed Forces Information Service [*DoD*] AFIS
Armed Forces Institute AFI
Armed Forces Institute of Pathology AFIP
Armed Forces Institute of Technology AFIT
Armed Forces Intelligence Training Center AFITC
Armed Forces Journal [*A publication*] AFJ
Armed Forces Language Program AFLP
Armed Forces Liaison Representative [*Red Cross*] AFLR
Armed Forces Mail Call AFMC
Armed Forces Management AFM
Armed Forces Management Association [*Later, ADPA*] AFMA
Armed Forces Marketing Council [*DoD*] AFMC
Armed Forces Master Records [*Solicited phonograph records, and money to buy records, for the armed forces*] [*See also RFOFM*] [*World War II*] AFMR
Armed Forces Medical Journal. India [*A publication*] Armed Forces Med J India
Armed Forces Medical Library [*Later, National Library of Medicine, 1956*] AFML
Armed Forces Medical Procurement Agency AFMPA
Armed Forces Menu Service Committee AFMSC
Armed Forces Military Report [*DoD*] AFMR
Armed Forces Movement [*Portugal*] AFM
Armed Forces National Research Council [*National Academy of Sciences*] AFNRC
Armed Forces Network [*Military*] AFN
Armed Forces News Bureau [*Later, AFPS*] AFNB
Armed Forces Optometric Society AFOS
Armed Forces Pest Control Board AFPCB
Armed Forces of the Philippines AFP

Armed Forces Philippines Supply Center	AFPSC
Armed Forces Police	AFP
Armed Forces Police Department [or Detachment]	AFPD
Armed Forces Policy Council	AFPC
Armed Forces Procurement Regulation	AFPR
Armed Forces Product Evaluation Committee	AFPEC
Armed Forces Production Resources Agency	APRA
Armed Forces Professional Entertainment Office	AFPEO
Armed Forces Qualification Test	AFQT
Armed Forces Qualification Test, Verbal Arithmetic Subtest	AFQTVA
Armed Forces Radio Service [Military]	AFRS
Armed Forces Radiobiology Research Institute	AFRADBIORSCHINST
Armed Forces Radiobiology Research Institute	AFRRI
Armed Forces Radiobiology Research Institute, Bethesda, MD [OCLC symbol]	AFR
Armed Forces Recipe Service Committee	AFRSC
Armed Forces Recruiting Stations [DoD]	AFRS
Armed Forces Relief and Benefit Association	AFRBA
Armed Forces Reporting Unit [Red Cross]	AFRU
Armed Forces of the Republic of Korea	AFK
Armed Forces Reserve Act of 1952, as Amended	AFRA
Armed Forces Reserve Center	AFRC
Armed Forces Reserve Medal [US]	AFRESM
Armed Forces Reserve Medal [US]	AFRM
Armed Forces Revolutionary Council [Ghana]	AFRC
Armed Forces Screen Reports	AFSR
Armed Forces Security Agency [Obsolete]	AFSA
Armed Forces Security Agency [Obsolete]	AFSAG
Armed Forces Security Agency Council [Obsolete]	AFSAC
Armed Forces Security Agency Council Intelligence Requirements Committee [Obsolete]	AFSAC/IRC
Armed Forces and Society [A publication]	Armed Forces Soc
Armed Forces Special Weapons Agency	AFSWA
Armed Forces Special Weapons Project [Later, DASA]	AFSWP
Armed Forces Special Weapons Project [Later, DASA], Technical Publications [A publication]	AFSWP-TP
Armed Forces Staff College	AFSC
Armed Forces Stamp Exchange Club	AFSEC
Armed Forces Supply Control Center [DoD]	AFSCC
Armed Forces Supply Support Center [Merged with Defense Logistics Services Center]	AFSSC
Armed Forces Surplus Property Bidders Registration and Sales Information Office [Later, Defense Surplus Bidders Control Office]	AFSPBRSIO
Armed Forces Technical Information Agency	AFTIA
Armed Forces of the United States	AFUS
Armed Forces Vocational Testing Group	AFVTG
Armed Forces Women's Selection Test	AFWST
Armed Forces Writers League [Later, NAGC]	AFWL
Armed Guard	AG
Armed Guard	ARMGRD
Armed Guard Center	AGC
Armed Guard Center Training School [Obsolete]	AGCTS
Armed Guard Inspection Officer	AGIO
Armed Guard Inspection Service	AGIS
Armed Guard School	AGS
Armed Merchant Cruiser [Navy] [British]	AMC
Armed Merchant Cruiser [Navy symbol]	XCL
Armed Nuclear Bombardment Satellite	ANBS
Armed Proletarian Nuclei [Italy]	NAP
Armed Propaganda Team [Military]	APT
Armed Public Security Force	APSF
Armed Reconnaissance	A/R
Armed Resistance Movement	ARM
Armed Revolutionary Movement [Puerto Rico]	ARM
Armed Services Board of Contract Appeals	ASBCA
Armed Services Bulletin	ASB
Armed Services Committee [US Senate]	AS
Armed Services Committee [US Senate]	ASC
Armed Services Documents Intelligence Center	ASDIC
Armed Services Edition [Publishing] [World War II]	ASE
Armed Services Electro-Standards Agency [Later, DESC]	ASESA
Armed Services Electron Tube Committee	ASETC
Armed Services Exchange Regulation [DoD]	ASER
Armed Services Explosive Ordnance Disposal Coordinating Group	ASEODCG
Armed Services Explosives Safety Board [Army]	ASESB
Armed Services Explosives Safety Board [Army]	ASESBD
Armed Services Graves Registration Office	ASGRO
Armed Services Industrial Readiness Council	ASIRC
Armed Services Medical Material Coordination Committee	ASMMCC
Armed Services Medical Procurement Agency [Later, Medical Material Directorate]	ASMPA
Armed Services Medical Regulating Office	ASMRO
Armed Services Papers	ASP
Armed Services Patent Advisory Board [DoD]	ASPAB
Armed Services Personnel Interrogation Center	ASPIC
Armed Services Petroleum Agency	ASPA
Armed Services Petroleum Board	ASPB
Armed Services Petroleum Purchasing Agency	ASPPA
Armed Services Procurement Act	ASPA
Armed Services Procurement Medal	ASPM
Armed Services Procurement Planning Officer	ASPPO
Armed Services Procurement Regulation	ASPR
Armed Services Procurement Regulation Manual	ASPRM
Armed Services Procurement Regulation Supplement	ASPRS
Armed Services Procurement Regulation Supplement	ASPS
Armed Services Procurement Regulations	ASPERS
Armed Services Renegotiation Board [Later, RB]	ASRB
Armed Services Research Specialists Committee	ASRSC
Armed Services Technical Information Agency [Later, Defense Documentation Center]	ASTIA
Armed Services Vocational Aptitude Battery [Tests]	ASVAB
Armed Services Whole Blood Processing Laboratory	ASWBPL
Armed Strike Reconnaissance	ASR
Armee Korps [Army Corps] [German]	AK
Armee de Liberation Nationale [National Liberation Army] [Algeria]	ALN
Armee de Liberation Nationale de l'Angola [Angolan Army of National Liberation]	ALNA
Armee de Liberation Nationale Kamerounaise [Cameroonese National Liberation Army]	ALNK
Armee-Munitionslager [Army ammunition depot] [German military - World War II]	AML
Armee Nationale Congolaise [Congolese National Army]	ANC
Armees d'Aujourd'hui [A publication]	Armees Aujourd
Armel, Inc. [NASDAQ symbol]	AMLT
Armement. Bulletin d'Information et de Liaison [A publication]	Armement Bull Inf Liaison
Armenia	ARM
Armenia [Colombia] [Airport symbol]	AXM
Armenian [MARC language code] [Library of Congress]	arm
Armenian Assembly Charitable Trust	AACT
Armenian Church Youth Organization of America	ACYOA
Armenian Educational Foundation	AEF
Armenian Film Foundation	AFF
Armenian General Benevolent Union of America	AGBU
Armenian General Benevolent Union of America	AGBUA
Armenian Literary Society	ALS
Armenian Missionary Association of America	AMAA
Armenian National Committee	ANC
Armenian National Council of America	ANCA
Armenian Numismatic Journal [A publication]	Armenian N J
Armenian Progressive League of America	APLA
Armenian Relief Society [Later, ARSNA]	ARS
Armenian Relief Society of North America [Formerly, ARS]	ARSNA
Armenian Revolutionary Federation of America	ARFA
Armenian Secret Army for the Liberation of Armenia	ASALA
Armenian Soviet Socialist Republic [MARC country of publication code] [Library of Congress]	air
Armenian Soviet Socialist Republic	ArmSSR
Armenian Soviet Socialist Republic [MARC geographic area code] [Library of Congress]	e-ur-ai
Armenian Students Association of America	ASA
Armenian Students Association of America	ASAA
Armenian Women's Welfare Association	AWWA
Armenian Youth Federation of America - Youth Organization of the ARF [Armenian Revolutionary Federation of America]	AYF
Armidale [Australia] [Airport symbol]	ARM
Armidale City and Dumarasq Shire War Memorial Library, Armidale, NSW, Australia [Library symbol]	AuAr
Armidale Newspaper Co. Ltd., Armidale, NSW, Australia [Library symbol]	AuArA
Armin Corp. [American Stock Exchange symbol] [Delisted]	ARP
Arming	ARM
Arming Decision Device	ADD
Arming Device	ARMDEV
Arming Device Assemblies [Army]	ADA
Arming and Fusing	A & F
Arming and Fusing Device	AFD
Arming and Fusing System	AFS
Arming System Tester	AST
Arming Unit Distribution Box	AUDB
Arming Wire [Bombs]	AW
Armistice and Post-War Committee [British] [World War II]	APW
Armistice Terms and Civil Administration [British] [World War II]	ACA
Armitage Academy Library, Kenosha, WI [Library symbol]	WKenA
ARMMS [Automated Reliability and Maintenance Management System] Control Executive System [NASA]	ACES
Armor, Armament, and Ammunition	AA & A
Armor and Arms Club	AAC
Armor, Artillery, and Engineers Aptitude Area [Army]	AE
Armor Board	AB
Armor Combat Operations Model Support [TCATA]	ARCOMS
Armor Grating [Technical drawings]	AG
Armor di Libro [A publication]	AdL
Armor-Piercing [Army]	AP
Armor-Piercing Capped [Ammunition]	APC
Armor-Piercing-Capped Incendiary [Ammunition]	APCI
Armor-Piercing-Capped Incendiary with Tracer [Ammunition]	APCIT
Armor-Piercing-Capped with Tracer [Ammunition]	APCT
Armor-Piercing, Carbide, Ballistic Cap [Ammunition]	APCBC
Armor-Piercing Discarding Sabot [Ammunition]	APDS

Armor-Piercing Discarding Sabot with Tracer [*Ammunition*] .... APDS-T
Armor-Piercing Fin Stabilized Discarding Sabot [*Ammunition*] ...... APFSDS
Armor-Piercing High Explosive [*Ammunition*] .... APHE
Armor-Piercing Incendiary [*Ammunition*] .... API
Armor-Piercing Incendiary Tracer [*Ammunition*] .... APIT
Armor-Piercing Infantry Light-Arm System [*Ammunition*] .... APILAS
Armor-Piercing Reduced (Caliber) [*Ammunition*] .... APCR
Armor-Piercing with Tracer [*Ammunition*] .... APT
Armor Plate .... A/PL
Armor Plate .... ARM-PL
Armor Remoted Target System .... ARETS
Armor School [*Army*] .... AS
Armor Training Devices .... ATD
Armored .... ARM
Armored .... ARMD
Armored Antiaircraft System .... AAAS
Armored Assault Vehicle .... AAV
Armored Box Launcher [*Shipboard launching system*] .... ABL
Armored Cable .... AC
Armored Cavalry Assault Vehicle .... ACAV
Armored Cavalry Regiment .... ACR
Armored Cavalry Trainer [*Army*] .... ACT
Armored Combat Earthmover [*Army*] .... ACE
Armored Combat Vehicle .... ACV
Armored Combat Vehicle Technology .... ACVT
Armored Command and Reconnaissance Vehicle .... ACRV
Armored Crew Seat .... ACS
Armored Cruiser [*Navy symbol*] .... ACR
Armored Division [*Military*] .... ARMD
Armored Division Equivalent [*Military*] .... ADE
Armored Fighting Vehicle [*Marine Corps*] .... AFV
Armored Force Vehicle .... AFV
Armored Infantry Battalion .... AIB
Armored Infantry Combat Vehicle .... AICV
Armored Infantry Fighting Vehicle .... AIFV
Armored-Infantry-Mechanized .... AIM
Armored Infantry Vehicle .... AIV
Armored Personnel Carrier [*Military*] .... APC
Armored Personnel Carrier/Qualification Course [*Army*] .... APC/QC
Armored Reconnaissance .... AR
Armored Reconnaissance Airborne Assault Vehicle .... ARAAV
Armored Reconnaissance Scout Vehicle [*Army*] .... ARSV
Armored Reconnaissance Scout Vehicle [*Army*] .... RSV
Armored Recovery Vehicle .... ARV
Armored Rifle Battalion .... ARB
Armored Support Patrol Boat [*Military*] .... ASPB
Armored Training Devices [*Army*] .... ARD
Armored Transport Vehicle .... ATV
Armored Transportation Institute .... ATI
Armored, Universal Engineer Tractor .... AUET
Armored Utility Vehicle .... AUV
Armored Vehicle General Purpose [*General Motors armored car*] [*Canada*] .... AVGP
Armored Vehicle Launched .... AVL
Armored Vehicle Launched Bridge [*Military*] .... AVLB
Armorer .... ARMR
Armour & Co. [*NYSE symbol*] .... AM
Armour & Co., Chicago, IL [*Library symbol*] [*Obsolete*] .... ICArmour
Armour Pharmaceutical Co. [*Research code symbol*] .... AB
Armour Pharmaceutical Co. [*Research code symbol*] .... P
Armour Public Library, Armour, SD [*Library symbol*] .... SdArm
Armour Research Center Library, Scottsdale, AZ [*Library symbol*] .... AzSArm
Armour Research Center, Scottsdale, AZ [*OCLC symbol*] .... AZR
Armour Research Foundation .... ARF
Armour Research Foundation Reactor .... ARR
Armoured Tractor [*British*] .... AT
Armoured Train [*British*] .... AT
Arms and Ammunition Division [*Army*] .... AAD
Arms and Armour Society .... AAS
Arms Control Association .... ACA
Arms Control Computer Network .... ACCN
Arms Control and Disarmament [*A publication*] .... ACD
Arms Control and Disarmament [*A publication*] .... ArmC
Arms Control and Disarmament Agency .... ACDA
Arms Control and Disarmament Agency Military and Economic Affairs Bureau .... ACDA/MEA
Arms Control and Disarmament Agency Weapons Evaluation and Control Bureau .... ACDA/WEC
Arms Control and Disarmament Agency Weapons Evaluation and Control Bureau Field Operations Division .... ACDA/WEC/FO
Arms Control Observation Satellite .... ACOS
Arms Control Technical Information and Analysis Center [*Department of State*] .... ACTIAC
Arms Export Control Act .... AECA
Arms Export Control Board .... AECB
ARMS/FIRMS Users Association .... AFUA
Arms Material .... AM
Arms Memorandum .... AM
Arms and Services with the Army Air Forces .... ASWAAF
Arms and Services on Duty with Air Force .... ASWAF
Arms Transfer Management Group .... ATMG
Armstrong Association of Philadelphia, Philadelphia, PA [*Library symbol*] [*Obsolete*] .... PPArmA
Armstrong Journal, Armstrong, IA [*Library symbol*] .... IaArmJ
Armstrong Rubber Co. [*NYSE symbol*] .... ARM
Armstrong Siddeley Owners Club .... ASOC
Armstrong State College, Savannah, GA [*OCLC symbol*] .... GAC
Armstrong State College, Savannah, GA [*Library symbol*] .... GSA
Armstrong World Industries, Inc. [*Formerly, Armstrong Cork Co.*] [*NYSE symbol*] .... ACK
Army .... A
Army [*Military aircraft identification prefix*] .... R
Army Acquisition Objective .... AAO
Army Adaptation Inventory .... AAI
Army Administration Center, Fort Benjamin Harrison .... ADMINCEN
Army Advanced Marksmanship Unit .... AAMU
Army Advisory Group, China .... AGC
Army Aerial Reconnaissance System .... AARS
Army Aeromedical Research Laboratory .... AARL
Army Aeronautical Depot Maintenance Center [*AMC-ASMC*] .... ARADMAC
Army Aeronautical Research Center [*Ames Research Center*] .... AARL
Army Air Base .... AAB
Army Air Corps .... AAC
Army Air Defense .... AAD
Army Air Defense Area .... AADA
Army Air Defense Board .... AADB
Army Air Defense Command [*or Commander*] [*Later, AADCOM*] .... AADC
Army Air Defense Command [*or Commander*] [*Formerly, AADC, ARADCOM*] .... AADCOM
Army Air Defense Command [*or Commander*] [*Later, AADCOM*] .... ARADCOM
Army Air Defense Command Post .... AADCP
Army Air Defense Control and Coordination System .... AADCCS
Army Air Defense Information Service .... AADIS
Army Air Defense Operations Office [*or Officer*] .... AADOO
Army Air Defense School .... AADS
Army Air Defense School .... ARADSCH
Army Air Defense Site .... AADS
Army Air Defense System [*Formerly, FABMDS*] .... AADS
Army and Air Force Air Intelligence School [*British*] .... AAFAIS
Army and Air Force Base .... AAFB
Army Air Force Board .... AAFB
Army Air Force Central Flying Training Command .... AAFCFTC
Army Air Force Central Technical Training Command .... AAFCTTC
Army and Air Force Civilian Welfare Fund .... AAFCWF
Army Air Force Classification Center .... AAFCC
Army Air Force Clemency and Parole Board .... AAFCPB
Army Air Force Eastern Flying Training Command .... AAFEFTC
Army Air Force Eastern Technical Training Command .... AAFETTC
Army and Air Force Exchange and Motion Picture Service .... AAFEMPS
Army and Air Force Exchange and Motion Picture Services Board of Directors [*DoD*] .... AAFBD
Army and Air Force Exchange Service .... A & AFES
Army and Air Force Exchange Service .... AAFES
Army Air Force Flying Training Detachment .... AAFFTD
Army Air Force Headquarters, Mediterranean Theater of Operations .... AAFMTO
Army and Air Force Intelligence Staff [*British*] .... AAFIS
Army/Air Force Motion Picture Service .... AAFM
Army and Air Force Motion Picture Service .... AAFMPS
Army Air Force Officer-in-Charge .... AAFOIC
Army and Air Force Postal Service .... AAFPS
Army and Air Force Wage Board .... AAFWB
Army Air Forces .... AAF
Army Air Forces Aid Society [*World War II*] .... AAFAS
Army Air Forces Air Adjutant General [*World War II*] .... AFMAG
Army Air Forces Antisubmarine Command .... AFSUB
Army Air Forces Assistant Secretary of War for Air [*World War II*] .... AFSWA
Army Air Forces Base Unit .... AAFBU
Army Air Forces Basic Training Center .... AAFBTC
Army Air Forces Bombardier School .... AAFBS
Army Air Forces Center .... AAFC
Army Air Forces Chief of the Air Staff [*World War II*] .... AFCAS
Army Air Forces Commanding General [*World War II*] .... AFACG
Army Air Forces Deputy Chiefs of Air Staff [*World War II*] .... AFIAS
Army Air Forces Engineer Command .... AAFEC
Army Air Forces Gunnery School .... AAFGS
Army Air Forces Intelligence School .... AAFIS
Army Air Forces Materiel Center .... AAFMC
Army Air Forces Military Personnel [*World War II*] .... AFPMP
Army Air Forces Navigation School .... AAFNS
Army Air Forces, Pacific Ocean Areas .... AAFPOA
Army Air Forces, Pacific Ocean Areas (Administrative) ... AAFPOA (ADMIN)
Army Air Forces Pilot School .... AAFPS
Army Air Forces Pre-Flight School (Pilot) .... AAFPFS(P)
Army Air Forces Requirements Division [*World War II*] .... AFREQ
Army Air Forces School of Applied Tactics [*World War II*] .... AAFSAT
Army Air Forces Service Command .... AAFSC
Army Air Forces Southeast Training Command [*World War II*] ...... AAFSETC
Army Air Forces Tactical Center [*World War II*] .... AAFTAC
Army Air Forces Technical School [*World War II*] .... AAFTS

Army Air Forces Technical Training Command [*World War II*] ... AAFTTC
Army Air Forces Training Aids Division [*World War II*] ... AAFTAD
Army Air Forces Training Command [*World War II*] ... AAFTC
Army Air Forces Western Flying Training Command [*World War II*] ... AAFWFTC
Army Air Forces Western Technical Training Command [*World War II*] ... AAFWTTC
Army Air-Ground System ... AAGS
Army Air Mobility Research and Development Laboratories [*Army*] ... AAMRDL
Army Air Operations ... AA
Army Air Reconnaissance for Damage Assessment in the Continental United States ... AARDAC
Army Air Service ... AAS
Army Air Traffic Control and Navigation System ... AATCAN
Army Air Traffic Coordinating Office ... AATCO
Army Air Traffic Regulation and Identification ... AATRI
Army Air Traffic Regulation and Identification System ... AATRIS
Army Air Transport Training and Development Centre [*England*] ... AATDC
Army Airborne Electronics and Special Warfare Board [*Army*] ... AAESWB
Army Aircraft ... AACFT
Army Aircraft Maintenance ... AAM
Army Aircraft Maintenance Shop ... AAMS
Army Aircraft Mobile Technical Assistance Program ... AAMTAP
Army Aircraft Repair Ship ... AARS
Army Aircraft Requirements Review Committee ... AARRC
Army Airfield ... AAF
Army Airways Communications System ... AACS
Army Alaska Communication System [*Air Force*] ... AACS
Army Amateur Radio System ... AARS
Army Ammunition Plant ... AAP
[*The*] Army Ammunition Reporting System ... TAARS
Army Analysis of Intelligence ... AAI
Army Apprenticeship Program ... AAP
Army Area Communications System ... AACOMS
Army Area Representative ... AAR
Army Area Signal Center ... AASC
Army Armament Materiel Readiness Command ... ARRCOM
Army Armament Research Ballistic Research Laboratory ... ARBRL
Army Armament, Research and Development Command [*Dover, NJ*] ... ARRADCOM
Army Armament Research and Development Command Chemical Systems Laboratory ... ARCSL
Army Armament Research and Development Command Product Assurance Directorate ... ARPAD
Army Armament Research and Development Command Technical Support Directorate ... ARTSD
Army Armor School ... AAMS
Army Artillery Board ... AAB
Army Artillery Group ... AAG
Army Artillery and Missile Center ... AAMC
Army Artillery and Missile School ... AAMS
Army Atomic Weapons Systems Safety Committee [*Later, DNA*] ... AAWSSC
Army Attache [*Military*] ... ARMA
Army Attache System ... AAS
Army Attrition Rates Committee ... AARC
Army Audiovisual Center ... AAC
Army Audit Agency ... AAA
Army Authority for Major Commands to Disseminate Information and Take Appropriate Action ... ACTCOM
[*The*] Army Authorization Document System ... TAADS
[*The*] Army Automated Budget System ... TAABS
[*The*] Army Automated Logistic Data System ... TAALODS
Army Aviation ... AAVN
Army Aviation Association of America ... AAAA
Army Aviation Board ... AAB
Army Aviation Control Center ... AACC
Army Aviation Digest [*A publication*] ... AAD
Army Aviation Element ... AAE
Army Aviation Engineering Flight Activity ... AAEFA
Army Aviation Engineers ... AAE
Army Aviation Maintenance Support Activity ... AAMSA
Army Aviation Materiel Command ... AAMC
Army Aviation Materiel Laboratory ... AAML
Army Aviation Medical Officer's Badge ... AR Av MO Bad
Army Aviation Operating Detachment ... AAOD
Army Aviation Planning Manual ... AAPM
Army Aviation Research and Development Command ... AVRADCOM
Army Aviation Support Element ... AASE
Army Aviation Systems Test Activity [*Also, USAASTA*] ... AASTA
Army Aviation Test Board ... AATB
Army Aviation Test Command [*ATEC*] ... AATC
Army Aviation Unit Training Command ... AAUTC
Army Aviator ... ARAV
Army Aviator Badge ... AR Av Bad
Army Aviator Badge ... AVBAD
Army Avionics Program ... AAP
Army Ballistic Missile Agency ... ABMA
Army Base Information Transfer System ... ARBITS
Army Benevolent Fund [*British*] ... ABF
Army Biological Laboratory ... ABL
Army Biological Warfare Research Center ... ABWRC
Army Board for Correction of Military Records ... ABCMR
Army Board of Review for Eliminations ... ABRE
Army Bureau of Current Affairs [*To encourage British soldiers to think and talk about what they were fighting for*] [*World War II*] ... ABCA
Army Cadet Force [*Military unit*] [*British*] ... ACF
Army Calibration System ... ACS
Army Career Group ... ACGP
Army Catering Corps [*British*] ... ACC
Army Central Logistics Data Bank ... ACLDB
Army Central Welfare Fund ... ACWF
Army Chemical Center ... ACC
Army Chemical Center ... ACMLC
Army Chemical Center Procurement Agency ... ACCPA
Army Chemical Corps Medical Laboratories ... ACCML
Army Chemical Typewriter [*Data processing*] ... ACT
Army Chemical Warfare Laboratory ... ACWL
Army Chief of Support Services ... ACSS
Army Civil Services' Union [*Singapore*] ... ACSU
Army Class Manager Activity ... ACMA
Army Classification Battery [*Military tests*] ... ACB
Army Clerical Speed Test ... ACST
Army Clothing, Textile, and Materiel Center ... ACTMC
Army Coastal Engineering Research Center ... ACERC
Army Coating and Chemical Laboratory ... ACCL
Army Cohesion and Stability Program ... ARCOST
Army Combat Artist Program ... ACAP
Army Combat Development Committee [*British*] ... ACDC
Army Combat Development Experimental Center ... ACDEC
Army Combat Developments Command ... ACDC
Army Combat Engineers ... ACE
Army Combat Operations Vietnam ... ARCOV
Army Command and Administration Communication Agency ... ACACA
Army Command and Administrative Network [*Domestic and overseas integrated system of fixed radio, wire, cable, and associated communications facilities*] ... ACAN
Army Command and Control Network ... ACCNET
Army Command and Control System ... ACCS
Army Command and General Staff School ... ACGSC
Army Command Management System ... ACMS
Army [*Forces*] Command Post ... ARCP
Army Commanding Service ... ACS
Army Commendation Medal [*US*] ... ARCOM
Army Commercial Vehicle Code ... ACVC
Army Commissary Computer Entry Store System ... ACCESS
Army Communication Operations Center Agency ... ACOCA
Army Communications Board ... ACB
Army Communications Command ... ACC
Army Communications Command Advanced Concepts Office ... ACC-ACO
Army Communications Division ... ACD
Army Communications and Electronic Command ... ACEC
Army Communications and Electronics Management Information System ... ACEMIS
Army Communications and Equipment Coordination ... AC & EC
Army Communications Equipment Support ... ACES
Army Communications - Service Division ... ACSD
Army Communicative Technology ... ACT
Army Communicative Technology Office ... ACTO
Army Community Service ... ACS
Army Component Command ... ACC
Army Computer Systems Command [*Also, CSC*] ... ACSC
Army COMSEC [*Communications Security*] Central Office of Record ... ACCOR
Army COMSEC [*Communications Security*] Commodity, Logistical, and Accounting Information Management System ... ACCLAIMS
Army Concept Team in Vietnam ... ACTIV
Army Consideration of Tactical Air Support ... ACTAS
Army Container-Oriented Distribution Systems ... ACODS
Army Continuing Education System ... ACES
Army Contract Adjustment Board ... ACAB
Army Contract Appeals Panel ... ACAP
Army Control Program Directive ... ACPD
Army Cooperation Command [*British*] ... ACC
Army Corps ... AC
Army Corps of Engineers ... ACE
Army Corps of Engineers/Naval Facilities Engineering Command ... CE/NAVFAC
Army Correspondence Course Program ... ACCP
Army Cost Analysis Information and Data System ... ARCAIDS
Army Cost Analysis Paper ... ACAP
Army Cost Reduction Program ... ACRP
Army Council Instruction [*World War II*] ... ACI
Army Council of Review Boards ... ACRB
Army Countermine Mobility Equipment System ... ACMES
Army Damage Assessment System ... ARMDAS
Army Data Retrieval Engineering System ... ADRES
Army Defense Acquisition Regulation Supplement ... ADARS
Army Dental Corps [*British*] ... AD
Army Dental Corps [*British*] ... ADC

Army Dental Service	ADS
Army Department [British]	AD
Army Department Establishments [British]	ADE
Army Deployment Reporting System	ADEPREP
Army Depot	AD
Army Depot Automatic Diagnostic System	ADADS
Army Development and Employment Agency	ADEA
Army Digest [A publication]	AD
Army Disability Rating Review Board	ADRRB
Army Disability Review Board	ADRB
Army Discharge Review Board	ADRB
Army Distaff Foundation	ADF
Army Dollar Resource Allocation	ADRA
Army Education	AE
Army Education Center	AEC
Army Educational Corps [Later, RAEC] [British]	AEC
Army Educational Requirements Board	AERB
Army Electronic Proving Ground	AEPG
Army Electronic Warfare Information System	AEWIS
Army Electronics Command	AEC
Army Electronics Command	AECOM
Army Electronics Laboratories	AEL
Army Electronics Logistics Research Office	AELRO
Army Electronics Material Support Agency	AEMSA
Army Electronics Research and Development Activity	AERDA
Army Electronics Research and Development Laboratory	AERDL
Army Emergency Relief	AER
Army Emergency Reserve [British]	AER
Army Engineer District, Far East	FED
Army Engineer Reactors Group	AERG
Army Engineer Topographic Laboratories	AETL
Army Engineer Waterways Experiment Station	AEWES
[US] Army Enlisted Personnel Support Center	AGPERSCEN
Army Entertainment Scholarships and Awards Program	AESAP
Army Environmental Health Laboratory	AEHL
Army Environmental Hygiene Agency	AEHA
Army Equipment Authorizations Review Center	AEARC
Army Equipment Engineering Establishment	AEEE
Army Equipment Policy Committee	AEPC
[The] Army Equipment Record System [Later, TAMMS]	TAERS
Army Equipment Status Reporting System	AESRS
Army in Europe	AE
Army Excess Property	AES
Army Exchange Service [Centralized the control of PX's in US] [World War II]	AES
Army Exhibit Unit	AEU
Army Extension Course Program	AECP
Army Extension Training System	AETS
Army Facilities Components System	AFCS
Army Field Commands	AFC
Army Field Forces	AFF
Army Field Forces Board	AFFB
Army Field Stock Control System	AFSCS
Army Field Workshop	AFW
Army Finance Association [Defunct]	AFA
Army Finance Center	AFC
Army Fixed Wing Aptitude Battery	AFWAB
Army Flight Activity	AFA
Army Food Service Energy Management	AFSEM
Army Force	AF
Army Force Development Plan	AFDP
Army Force/Materiel Cost Methodology Improvement Project	ACMIP
Army Force Planning Cost Handbook	AFPCH
Army Force Planning Data and Assumptions	AFPDA
Army Force Status Reporting System	ARFORSTAT
Army Forces [Element of a joint task force]	ARFOR
Army Forces Far East	AFFE
[US] Army Forces, Middle Pacific [Official name for the theater of war more commonly called MIDPAC] [World War II]	AFMIDPAC
[US] Army Forces in the Pacific [World War II]	AFPAC
[US] Army Forces, Western Pacific	AFWESPAC
Army Foreign Science and Technology Center	AFSTC
Army Form	AF
Army Forwarding Officer [British]	AFO
Army Fuels and Lubricants Laboratory	AFLL
Army Fuels and Lubricants Research Laboratory	AFLRL
[The] Army Functional Files System	TAFFS
Army Gas-Cooled Reactor Systems Program	AGCRSP
Army General Classification Test [Measurement of intelligence]	AGCT
Army General Equipment Command	AGEC
Army General Staff	AGS
Army General Staff Civilian Personnel Office, Office of the Chief of Staff	AGSCPO
Army General Supplies Commodity Center	AGSCC
Army Good Conduct Medal	AGCMDL
Army Ground Forces	AGF
Army Ground Pool [for officers]	AGP
Army Group	AG
Army Group	AGP
Army Group Effects Department	AGED
Army Group Headquarters	AGH

Army Group Royal Artillery [British]	AGRA
Army Gun Air Defense Systems	ARGADS
Army Handicapped Employe of the Year	AHEY
Army Headquarters	AHQ
Army Health Nurse	AHN
Army Helicopter Improvement Program	AHIP
Army Heliport	AHP
Army Help for Education and Development	AHEAD
Army Hospital	AH
Army Hospital Corps	AHC
Army Housing Committee	ARHOC
Army Human Engineering Laboratory	AHEL
Army Human Factors Research Advisory Committee	AHFRAC
Army Human Factors Research and Development Committee	AHFRDC
Army Imagery Intelligence Corps	AIIC
Army In-Flight Data Transmission System	AIDATS
Army Industrial College	AIC
Army Industrial Fund	AIF
Army Industrial Preparedness Program	AIPP
Army/Industry Materiel Information Liaison Office	AIMILO
Army Infantry Board	AIB
Army Infantry School	AIS
Army Information and Data Systems Command	AIDSCOM
Army Information Digest	AID
Army Information Management System	AIMS
Army Information Program	AIP
Army Installation Management	AIM
Army Installation Management Course	AIMC
Army Installations Planning Committee	AIPC
Army Institute of Advanced Studies	AIAS
Army Institute of Dental Research	AIDR
Army Institute of Surgical Research	AISR
Army Integrated Decision Equipment	AIMS
Army Integrated Meteorological Systems	AIMS
Army Integrated Microfilm System	AIMS
Army Intelligence	AI
Army Intelligence Center	AIC
Army Intelligence Department [British]	AID
Army Intelligence Interpreter	AII
Army Intelligence Reserve	AIR
Army Intelligence School	AIS
Army Intelligence and Security	AIS
Army Intelligence Translator	AIT
Army Inventory Control Point	AICP
Army Inventory of Data Systems	AIDS
Army Inventory Objective	AIO
Army Investigational Drug Review Board	AIDRB
Army Job Activities Questionnaire	AJAQ
Army Job Questionnaire	AJQ
Army Laboratory of the Year Award	ALYA
Army Land Forces	ALANF
Army Language Aptitude Test [Later, DLAT]	ALAT
[The] Army Language School	TALS
Army LASER Target Designator System	ALTDS
Army Launch Area	ALA
Army Lawyer [A publication]	Army Law
Army Liaison Officer	ALO
Army Liaison Officer	ARLO
Army Library	ALIB
Army Library Automated Systems	ALAS
Army Life Cycle Cost Analysis Model	ALCCAM
Army Life-Support Power Source System	ALPSS
Army Limited War Laboratory	ALWL
Army Logistic Development Committee [British]	ALDC
Army Logistician [A publication]	ALOG
Army Logistician [A publication]	Army Logis
Army Logistics Assessment	ALA
Army Logistics Center	ALC
Army Logistics Command Japan	ALCJ
Army Logistics Data Center	ALDC
Army Logistics Management Center [Fort Lee, VA]	ALMC
Army Logistics Management Integrated Data Systems	ALMIDS
Army Logistics Manpower Office [Merged with Operations Personnel Office]	ALMO
Army Logistics Objectives Program	ALOP
Army Logistics Policy Council	ALPC
Army Logistics Research and Development	ALRD
Army Logistics Study Program	ALSP
Army Long-Range Appraisal	ALRA
Army Long-Range Capabilities Plan	ALRCP
Army Long-Range Technological Forecast	ALRTF
Army Low-Speed Air Research Tasks	ALART
Army Maintenance Board	AMB
[The] Army Maintenance Management System [Formerly, TAERS]	TAMMS
Army Maintenance and Supply Procedures [or Publications]	AMSP
Army Management Engineering Training Activity	AMETA
Army Management Fund	AMF
Army Management Information Program	AMIP
Army Management Information System	AMIS
Army Management Information Systems Course	AMISC

Army Management Intern Program ... AMIP
Army Management School ... AMS
Army Management Structure ... AMS
Army Manual ... AM
Army Map Service [*Later, Defense Mapping Agency Topographic Center*] ... AMS
Army Marksmanship Training Unit [*CONARC*] ... AMKTU
Army Marksmanship Unit ... AMU
Army Master Data File ... AMDF
Army Master Data File Reader Microfilm System [*Later, ARMS*] ... AMDFRMS
Army Master Study Program ... AMSP
Army Material Supply Command ... AMSC
Army Materials and Mechanics Research Center ... AMMRC
Army Materials Research Agency [*Later, AMMRC*] ... AMRA
Army Materials Research Reactor ... AMRR
Army Materiel Acquisition Review Committee ... AMARC
Army Materiel Command [*Later, MDRC, DARCOM*] ... AMC
Army Materiel Command Administrative Data Center ... AMCADC
Army Materiel Command Automated Logistics Management Systems Agency ... AMCALMSA
Army Materiel Command Board ... AMCB
Army Materiel Command Catalog Data Office ... AMCCDO
Army Materiel Command Data Center ... AMCDC
Army Materiel Command Depot Data Center ... AMCDDC
Army Materiel Command Facilities and Services Center ... AMCFASC
Army Materiel Command Field Office ... AMCFO
Army Materiel Command Field Safety Agency ... AMCFSA
Army Materiel Command General Order ... AMCGO
Army Materiel Command Information Center ... AMCIC
Army Materiel Command Inspector General, Western Inspection Activity ... AMCIGW
Army Materiel Command Installation Division ... AMCID
Army Materiel Command Installations and Service Agency ... AMCI & SA
Army Materiel Command International Logistics Directorate ... AMCIL
Army Materiel Command Logistic Data Center ... AMCLDC
Army Materiel Command Logistics Systems Support Agency ... AMCLSSA
Army Materiel Command Materiel Requirements Directorate ... AMCMR
Army Materiel Command Memorandum ... AMCM
Army Materiel Command Pamphlet ... AMCP
Army Materiel Command Procurement Instructions ... AMCPI
Army Materiel Command Procurement and Production Directorate ... AMCPP
Army Materiel Command Regulations ... AMCR
Army Materiel Command Research and Development ... AMCRD
Army Materiel Command Support Activity ... AMCSA
Army Materiel Command Technical Committee ... AMCTC
Army Materiel Plan ... AMP
Army Materiel Status Committees ... ARMATSC
Army Materiel Systems Analysis Activity [*or Agency*] ... AMSAA
Army Materiel Test and Evaluation Directorate ... ARMTE
Army Mathematics Research Center [*Madison, Wisconsin*] ... AMRC
Army Mathematics Steering Committee ... AMSC
Army Medical Bioengineering Research and Development Laboratory ... AMBRDL
Army Medical Center ... AMC
Army Medical Corps ... AMC
Army Medical Department ... AMD
Army Medical Department ... AMEDD
Army Medical Department Property Accounting System ... AMEDDPAS
Army Medical Department. Reports (London) [*A publication*] ... Army Med Dept Rep (London)
Army Medical Intelligence and Information Agency ... AMIIA
Army Medical Library [*Became Armed Forces Medical Library, 1952; later, NLM*] ... AML
Army Medical Nutrition Laboratory ... AMNL
Army Medical Research and Development Command ... AMRDC
Army Medical Research Institute of Chemical Defense ... AMRICD
Army Medical Research Institute of Infectious Diseases ... AMRIID
Army Medical Research Laboratory ... AMRL
Army Medical Research Laboratory, Alaska ... AMRLA
Army Medical Research and Nutrition Laboratory ... AMRNL
Army Medical Service ... AMEDS
Army Medical Service [*British*] ... AMS
Army Medical Service Graduate School ... AMSGS
Army Medical Service Research and Development Command ... AMSRDC
Army Medical Service School [*Later, Medical Field Service School*] ... AMSS
Army Medical Specialist Corps ... AMSC
Army Medical Staff ... AMS
Army Medical Supply Control Officer ... AMSCO
Army Medical Supply Support Activity ... AMSSA
Army Medical Unit ... AMU
Army Member, Inter-American Defense Board ... AMIADB
Army Metrology and Calibration Center ... AMCC
Army Metrology and Calibration Center Metrology Development and Engineering Division ... AMCC-MM
Army Mine Planter ... AMP
Army Mine Planter Service ... AMPS
Army Missile Command ... AMC
Army Missile Command ... AMICOM
Army Missile Command ... ARMSLC
Army Missile Defense Command ... AMDC
Army Missile Development Center ... AMDC
Army Missile Laboratory ... AML
Army Missile Research and Development Command ... AMRDC
Army Missile and Rockets Directorate ... AMRD
Army Missile and Rockets Division - NATO Supply Center ... AMRD-NASC
Army Missile Test Center ... AMTC
Army Missile Test and Evaluation ... ARMTE
Army Missile Transport Systems ... AMTRANS
Army Mobile Missile Operation ... AMMO
Army Mobility Command ... AMC
Army Mobility Command ... AMOCOM
Army Mobility Equipment Research and Development Center ... AMERADC
Army Mobility Model ... AMM
Army Mobility Research Center ... AMRC
Army Mobility Research and Development Center ... AMRDC
Army Mobility Support Center ... AMSC
Army Mobilization Capabilities Study ... AMCS
Army Mobilization and Operations Planning System ... AMOPS
Army Mobilization Planning and Programing Directive ... AMPPD
Army Mobilization Planning and Programing Guidance Document ... AMPPGD
Army Mobilization Program Directive ... AMPD
Army Model Improvement Program ... AMIP
Army Modernization Information Memorandum ... AMIM
Army Molecular Sieve Oxygen Generator ... AMSOG
Army Morale Support Fund ... AMSF
Army Mortar Program ... ARMOP
Army Motion Picture Service ... AMPS
Army Munitions Command [*Later merged with Army Weapons Command*] ... AMC
Army Munitions Command [*Later merged with Army Weapons Command*] ... AMUCOM
Army Munitions Command [*Later merged with Army Weapons Command*] ... AMUNC
Army Mutual Aid Association ... AMAA
Army Natick Laboratory ... ANL
Army National Guard ... ANG
Army National Guard ... ARNG
Army National Guard ... RNG
Army National Guard of the United States ... ARNGUS
Army and Navy ... A & N
Army and Navy ... AN
Army with Navy [*Personnel*] ... ARNA
Army-Navy Aeronautical ... ANA
Army-Navy-Air Force ... ANAF
Army-Navy-Air Force Journal [*A publication*] ... ANAFJ
Army-Navy Anticorrosion Compound ... ANC
Army-Navy-British ... ANB
Army-Navy-Civil ... ANC
Army and Navy Club, Washington, DC [*Library symbol*] ... DAN
Army-Navy-Commerce ... ANC
Army-Navy Communications Intelligence Board [*Later, STANCIB*] ... ANCIB
Army-Navy Communications Intelligence Coordinating Committee [*Later, ANCIB*] ... ANCICC
Army-Navy Communications Production Expediting Agency ... ANCPEA
Army-Navy Country Club ... ANCC
Army-Navy Design ... AND
Army, Navy Electronics Evaluation Group ... ANEEG
Army-Navy Electronics Production Agency ... ANEPA
Army-Navy-Industry ... ANI
Army-Navy Instrumentation Program ... ANIP
Army-Navy Joint Specifications Board ... ANJSB
Army-Navy Joint Type Ordnance ... AN
Army-Navy Liquidation Commission [*World War II*] ... ANLC
Army-Navy Munitions Board [*Later, Munitions Board*] ... ANMB
Army, Navy, NASA, Air Force Geodetic Satellite ... ANNA
Army/Navy Number ... A/N
Army-Navy Petroleum Board ... ANPB
Army-Navy Petroleum Pool, Pacific Coast ... ANPPPC
Army-Navy Shipping Information Agency ... ANSIA
Army and Navy Staff College [*Redesignated National War College, 1946*] ... ANSC
Army and Navy Staff College [*See ANSC*] ... ANSCOL
Army and Navy Union, USA ... ANU
Army Net Assessment, Central Europe ... ANACE
Army News Features ... ANF
Army News Service ... ANS
Army Newspaper Service ... ANS
Army of Northern Virginia [*Civil War*] ... ANV
Army Nuclear Data System [*Study*] ... ANUDS
Army Nuclear Defense Laboratory ... ANDL
Army Nuclear Power Program ... ANPP
Army Nuclear Weapon Coordination Group ... ANWCG
Army Nurse Corps ... ANC
Army Nursing Service [*British*] ... ANS
Army of Occupation of Germany Medal ... AOGM
Army of Occupation of Germany Medal ... OCCGERMDL
Army of Occupation Medal [*Germany-Japan*] [*US*] ... AOM
Army of Occupation Medal [*Germany-Japan*] [*US*] ... OCCMDL
Army Occupational Survey Program [*Formerly, MODB*] ... AOSP

Army Officers' Emergency Reserve [*British*]	AOER
Army Oil Analysis Program	AOAP
Army Operating Availability Data	AOAD
Army Operational Research	AOR
Army Operational Research Establishment	AORE
Army Operational Research Group [*British*]	AORG
Army Operations Center	AOC
[*The*] Army Operations Center	TAOC
[*The*] Army Operations Center System	TARMOCS
Army Operations Research Symposia	AORS
Army Order [*British*]	AO
Army Ordnance Ammunition Command [*Merged with Munitions Command*]	AOAC
Army Ordnance Ballistic Missile Office	AOBMO
Army Ordnance Combat Equipment Office	AOCEO
Army Ordnance Corps [*Later, RAOC*] [*British*]	AOC
Army Ordnance Corps [*US*]	AOC
Army Ordnance Department [*British*]	AOD
Army Ordnance Guided Missile School	AOGMS
Army Ordnance Missile Center	AOMC
Army Ordnance Missile Command [*Later, Missile Command*]	AOMC
Army Ordnance Missile Support Agency	AOMSA
Army Ordnance Missile Support Center	AOMSC
Army Ordnance Stores [*British*]	AOS
Army Ordnance Submarine Mine Laboratory	AOSML
Army Ordnance Weapons Command	AOWC
Army Pacific	ARPAC
Army Package Power Reactor	APPR
Army Packaging Board	APB
Army Parachute Team	APT
Army Pay Corps [*Later, RAPC*] [*British*]	APC
Army Pay Department [*British*]	APD
Army Pearl Harbor Board [*World War II*]	APHB
Army Pensions	AP
Army Personnel Attached to the Air Force for Duty	ARWAF
Army Personnel Letter	APL
Army Personnel Newsletter	APNL
Army Personnel Research Committee	APRC
Army Personnel Research Establishment [*British*]	APRE
Army Personnel Research Office	APRO
Army Personnel Research Service	APRS
Army Petroleum Center	APC
Army Photo Interpretation Center	APIC
Army Photo Interpretation Detachment	APID
Army Photo Interpretation Unit	APIU
Army Photographic Interpretation Section [*British*]	APIS
Army Physical Disability Activity	APDA
Army Physical Disability Appeal Board	APDAB
Army Physical Evaluation Board	APEB
Army Physical Readiness Test	APRT
Army Physical Review Council	APRC
Army Physical Training Corps [*British*]	APTC
Army Pictorial Center	APC
Army Pictorial Division	APD
Army Pictorial Service	APS
Army Pilot School	APS
[*The*] Army Plan for Equipment Records	TAPER
Army Planning Group	APG
Army Point of Contact	APOC
Army Policy Council	APC
Army Port and Service Command	AP & SC
[*The*] Army Portion of Force Status and Identify Report [*Force Status Report*]	TAPFOR
Army Post Office	APO
Army Postal Clerk	APC
Army Postal Service	APS
Army Postal Service Agency	ARPSA
Army Postal Unit	APU
Army Precommission Extension Course	APCEC
Army Preliminary Evaluation	APE
Army Printing and Stationery Services [*British*]	APSS
Army Procurement Appropriation Reporting System	APARS
Army Procurement District	APD
Army Procurement Procedure	APP
Army Procurement - Sharpe General Depot	APSGD
Army Program for Individual Training	ARPRINT
Army Program Memorandum	APM
Army Promotion List	APL
Army Propulsion Laboratory and Center	APLC
Army Prosthetics Research Laboratory	APRL
Army Proving Grounds	APG
Army Pulse Radiation Facility	APRF
Army Pulsed Experimental Research Assembly	APRA
Army Qualification Battery [*of tests*]	AQB
Army Quartermaster Corps [*Merged with Supply and Maintenance Command*]	AQMC
Army Quartermaster Research and Engineering Command	AQREC
Army RADAR Approach Control Facility	ARAC
Army Radiation Laboratory	ARL
Army Radio Code	ARC
Army Radio Code Aptitude Test	ARCT
Army Ration Credit System	ARCS
Army Reactor Experimental Area [*Army*]	AREA
Army Reactor Systems Health and Safety Review Committee	ARCHS
Army Readiness Measurement System	ARMS
Army Readiness Regions	ARR
Army Ready Materiel	ARM
Army Rearming Base	ARB
Army Registry of Physical Therapists	ARPT
Army Registry of Special Educational Materials	ARSEM
Army Regulation	AR
Army Relief Society [*Later, AER*]	ARS
Army Renegotiation Division [*of ASRB*]	ARD
Army of the Republic of Vietnam [*Also, ARVN*] [*South Vietnam*]	ARVIN
Army of the Republic of Vietnam [*Also, ARVIN*] [*South Vietnam*]	ARVN
Army Requirements Control Office	ARCO
Army Requirements Development Plan	ARDP
Army Requirements for Tactical Communications	ARTACOM
[*The*] Army Research Council	TARC
Army Research and Development [*A publication*]	Army Res & Devel
Army Research, Development, and Acquisition	ARDAC
Army Research and Development Group	ARDG
Army Research and Development Group (Europe)	ARDG(E)
Army Research and Development Group (Far East)	ARDG(FE)
Army Research and Development Information Systems	ARDIS
Army Research and Development Information Systems Office	ARDISO
Army Research Institute for the Behavioral and Social Sciences	ARI
Army Research Institute of Environment Medicine	ARIEM
Army Research Office	ARO
Army Research Office - Durham	ARO-D
Army Research Office - Europe	ARO-E
Army Research Office - Far East	ARO-FE
Army Research Office - Japan	ARO-J
Army Research Plan	ARP
Army Research Task Summary	ARTS
Army Reserve [*Formerly, ERC, ORC*]	AR
Army Reserve Command	ARCOM
Army Reserve Components Achievement Medal	ARCAM
Army Reserve Magazine [*A publication*]	Army Reserv
Army Reserve Personnel Center [*St. Louis, MO*]	ARPERCEN
Army Reserve Readiness Training Center [*Fort McCoy, WI*]	ARRTC
Army Reserve and Reserve Officers Training Corps Affairs	ARROTCA
Army Retail Requirements	ARR
Army Retiring Board	ARB
Army Rocket and Guided Missile Agency	ARGMA
Army Rocket Transportation System	ARTP
Army Rotary Wing Aptitude Battery	ARWAB
Army Routine Order [*Military*]	ARO
Army Satellite Tracking Center	AST
Army School of Education [*British*]	ASE
Army School of Physical Training [*British*]	ASPT
Army Science Board [*Formerly, ASAP*]	ASB
Army Scientific Advisory Panel [*Later, ASB*]	ASAP
[*The*] Army Scientific Advisory Panel	TASAP
Army Scientific and Technical Information Program	ASTIP
Army Scientific and Technical Intelligence Bulletin [*A publication*]	ASTIB
Army Seal of Approval	ASA
Army Security	AS
Army Security Agency [*Later, INSCOM*]	ASA
Army Security Agency, Pacific	ASAPAC
Army Security Agency School [*Merged with Defense Security Agency School*]	ASAS
Army Security Review Board	ASRB
Army Selection Centre [*British*]	ASC
Army Selective Aerial Rocket	ASAR
Army Serial Number	ASN
Army Service Command	ASCOM
Army Service Corps [*Initialism also facetiously translated during World War I as "Ally Sloper's Cavalry," Ally Sloper being a comic-paper buffoon*] [*Later, RASC*] [*British*]	ASC
Army Service Forces [*Formerly, SOS*]	ASF
Army Service Forces Training Center	ASFTC
Army Service Forces Training Center Unit	ASFTCU
Army Service Number	ASN
Army Service Squadron [*Corresponds to Navy's CASU*]	ASSERON
Army Shipping Document	ASD
Army Signal Corps [*Later, CEC*]	ASC
Army Signal Corps, Communications Security Service	ASCCSS
Army Signal Intelligence Agency	ASIA
Army Signal Material [*or Missile*] Support Agency	ASMSA
Army Signal Radio Propagation Agency	ASRPA
Army Signal Research and Development Laboratory	ASRDL
Army Signal School [*British*]	ASS
Army Signal Supply Agency	ASSA
[*The*] Army Signal Supply Agency	TASSA
Army Small Arms Program	ASARP
Army Small Arms Requirements Studies	ASARS
Army Snow, Ice, and Permafrost Research Establishment	ASIPRE
Army Special Award for Accomplishment	ASAA
Army Special Operations Pictorial Detachment	ASOPD
Army Special Staff	ASS
Army Special Warfare Center	ASWC

Army Special Weapons Depot ASWD
Army Specialist Corps [*Functions transferred to Officer Procurement Service*] ASC
Army Specialized Training AST
Army Specialized Training Division ASTD
Army Specialized Training Program [*World War II*] ASTP
Army Specialized Training Reserve Program ASTRP
Army Specialized Training Unit ASTU
Army Spectrometric Oil Analysis Program ASOAP
Army Sports Control Board [*British*] ASCB
Army Staff ARSTAF
Army Staff AS
[*The*] **Army Staff** TAS
Army Standard Program Languages ASPL
Army Standards Laboratory ASL
Army Stationing and Installation Plan ASIP
Army Status Report ASR
Army Stock Fund ASF
Army Stock Fund/Non-Stock Fund ASF/NSF
Army Strategic Capabilities Plan ASCP
Army Strategic Communications Command ASCC
Army Strategic Objectives Plan ASOP
Army Strategic Plan [*A document*] ASP
Army Strategic and Tactical Reorganization Objective ASTRO
[*US*] **Army Strike** [*STRICOM*] ARSTRIKE
Army Student Nurse Program ASNP
Army Student Nurse Program Identification Badge [*Military decoration*] ASNPIdentBad
[*The*] **Army Studies Program** TASP
Army Study Advisory Committee ASAC
Army Study Documentation and Information Retrieval System [*Later, ALAS*] ASDIRS
[*The*] **Army Study System** TASS
Army Subject Schedule ASUBJSCD
Army Subordinate Command Management Information System [*Formerly, CARMOCS*] ASMIS
Army Subsistence Center ASC
Army Subsistence Supply Center [*Merged with Defense Subsistence Supply Center*] ASSC
Army Supply and Maintenance Command ASMC
Army Supply and Maintenance Command ASMCOM
[*The*] **Army Supply and Maintenance System** TASAMS
Army Supply Program ASP
Army Support Center ASPTC
Army Surgeon General ASG
Army Survival Measures Plan ASMP
Army Switched Data and Secure Voice Network ASDSVN
Army System Management ASM
Army System for Standardized Intelligence Support Terminals ASSIST
Army Systems Acquisitions Review Council ASARC
Army Systems Coordinating Documents ASCOD
Army Tactical Airspace Regulation System ATARS
Army Tactical Command ATC
Army Tactical Communication System Simulator ATCSS
Army Tactical Communications System ATACS
Army Tactical Data Systems ARTADS
Army Tactical Operations Central ARTOC
Army Tank-Automotive Center [*or Command*] ATAC
Army Tank Office ATO
Army Technical Library Improvement Studies ATLIS
Army Technical Service Corps ATSC
Army Telecommunications Center Automatic Programing ATCAP
Army of Tennessee, CSA [*An association*] AT
Army Terminal Command ATC
Army Terrain Information System ARTINS
Army Test and Evaluation Command [*AMC*] ATEC
Army Test and Evaluation Command [*AMC*] ATECOM
Army Test and Evaluation Seminar ATES
Army Theatre Arts Association ATTA
Army TMDE Modernization ATM
Army Topographic Command [*Formerly, Army Map Service*] ATC
Army Topographic Station ATS
Army Training Board ATB
Army Training Center ATC
Army Training Device Agency ATDA
Army Training and Evaluation Program ARTEP
Army Training Extension Course Program ATECP
Army Training Film ATF
Army Training Memorandum [*British*] ATM
Army Training Program ATP
[*The*] **Army Training Requirements and Resource System** ATARRS
Army Training Study ARTS
Army Training Support Center ATSC
Army Training Test ATT
Army Transport Service [*Obsolete*] [*Became Military Sea Transportation Service, then Military Sealift Command*] ATS
Army Transport Service Quartermaster Corps [*Obsolete*] ATSQMC
Army Transportation Association ATA
Army Transportation Board ATB
Army Transportation Corps ATC
Army Transportation Plan in Support of the Army Strategic Capabilities Plan ATP-ASCP
Army Transportation Research Command ATRC
Army Uniform Data Inquiry System AUDIT
Army Unit AU
Army Unit Resiliancy Analysis [*Data processing*] AURA
Army of the United States AUS
Army Validation Program AVP
Army Veterinary Corps [*Initialism also facetiously translated during World War I as "All Very Cushy"*] [*Later, RAVC*] [*British*] AVC
Army Veterinary Department [*British*] AVD
Army Victualling Department [*British*] AVD
Army Vietnam ARV
Army Volunteer Reserve [*British*] AVR
Army Volunteers Corps [*British*] AVC
Army War College ARWC
Army War College AWC
Army War Room AWR
Army War Room Information System AWRIS
Army Wartime Asset Distribution Study AWADS
Army Weapons Command [*AMC*] AWC
Army Weapons Command [*AMC*] AWECOM
Army Weapons and Mobility Command AWMC
Army Weather Service AWS
Army Welfare Officer [*British*] AWO
Army Welfare Services [*British*] AWS
Army Wholesale Logistic System AWLOG
Army-Wide AW
Army-Wide Library Council ALC
Army-Wide Training Literature Program ATLP
Army-Wide Training Support AWTS
Army Work Study Group AWSG
Army Youth Team [*British*] AYT
Armyanskii Khimicheskii Zhurnal [*A publication*] Arm Khim Zh
Army's Incentive Awards Program AIAP
ARN [*Association of Rehabilitation Nurses*] **Journal** [*A publication*] ARN J
Arnold Air Development Center [*Air Force*] AADC
Arnold Air Society AAS
Arnold Bax Society. Bulletin [*A publication*] Bax S
Arnold Bennett Newsletter [*A publication*] ABN
Arnold Constable Corp. [*NYSE symbol*] [*Delisted*] ACT
Arnold Engineering Development Center [*Air Force*] AEDC
Arnold Engineering Development Center, Arnold Air Force Station, TN [*OCLC symbol*] TAF
Arnold Gregory Memorial Hospital, Albion, NY [*Library symbol*] NAlbiH
Arnold Industries [*NASDAQ symbol*] AIND
Arnold, MD [*Radio station call letters*] WACC
Arnold Ranch [*California*] [*Seismograph station code, US Geological Survey*] ARN
Arnold Schoenberg Institute. Journal [*A publication*] Schoenberg Inst
Arnold Transit Company [*Later, ATCO*] [*AAR code*] ATC
Arnold Transit Company [*Formerly, ATC*] [*AAR code*] ATCO
Arnold, White, & Durkee, Houston, TX [*Library symbol*] TxHAWD
Arnolt-Bristol Owners Club ABOC
Arnolt-Bristol Registry ABR
Aro Corp. [*NYSE symbol*] ARO
ARO, Inc., AEDC Library, Arnold Air Force Station, TN [*Library symbol*] TArnA
Aromatic [*Chemistry*] ar
Aromatic AROM
Aromatic Amino Acid Decarboxylase [*Also, AADC*] [*An enzyme*] AAAD
Aromatic Amino Acid Decarboxylase [*Also, AAAD*] [*An enzyme*] AADC
Aromatic Amino Acids [*Biochemistry*] AAA
Aromatic Hydrocarbon Hydroxylase [*An enzyme*] AHH
Aromatic Red Cedar Closet Lining Manufacturers Association ARCCLMA
Aroostook Airways, Inc. [*Presque Isle, ME*] [*FAA designator*] ATK
Aroostook State Teachers College [*Merged with University of Maine*] ASTC
Aroostook Valley Railroad Co. [*AAR code*] AVL
Arorae [*Kiribati*] [*Airport symbol*] AIS
Around ARND
Around the Clock [*Medicine*] ATC
Arousal A
Arousal Mechanism [*Medicine*] AM
ARPA [*Advanced Research Projects Agency*] **Environmental Test Satellites** ARENTS
ARPA [*Advanced Research Projects Agency*]**/Lincoln C-Band Observable RADAR** [*Army*] ALCOR
ARPA [*Advanced Research Projects Agency*] **Long-Range Tracking and Instrument RADAR** ALTAIR
ARPA [*Advanced Research Projects Agency*] **Maui Optical Station** AMOS
ARPA [*Advanced Research Projects Agency*] **Measurements RADAR** [*Raytheon*] AMRAD
Arpeggio [*Music*] ARP
Arpeggio [*Music*] ARPO
Arqueologo Portugues [*A publication*] Arq Port
Arquitectura [*A publication*] ARQT
Arquivo de Anatomia e Antropologia [*A publication*] Arq Anat Antropol
Arquivo de Bibliografia Portuguesa [*A publication*] ABP
Arquivo do Distrito de Aveiro [*A publication*] ADA

Arquivo. Instituto Gulbenkian de Ciencia. A. Estudos Matematicos e Fisico-Matematicos [*A publication*] ... Arquivo Inst Gulbenkian Ci A Estud Mat Fis-Mat
Arquivo de Patologia [*A publication*] ... Arq Patol
Arquivos de Biologia (Sao Paulo) [*A publication*] ... Arq Biol (Sao Paulo)
Arquivos de Biologia e Tecnologia [*A publication*] ... Arq Biol Tecnol
Arquivos de Biologia e Tecnologia (Curitiba) [*A publication*] ... Arq Biol Tecnol (Curitiba)
Arquivos de Botanica do Estado de Sao Paulo [*A publication*] ... Arq Bot Estado Sao Paulo
Arquivos Brasileiros de Cardiologia [*A publication*] ... Arq Bras Cardiol
Arquivos Brasileiros de Cardiologia [*A publication*] ... Arq Brasil Cardiol
Arquivos Brasileiros de Endocrinologia e Metabologia [*A publication*] ... Arq Bras Endocrinol Metabol
Arquivos Brasileiros de Medicina [*A publication*] ... Arq Bras Med
Arquivos Brasileiros de Nutricao [*A publication*] ... Arq Bras Nutr
Arquivos Brasileiros de Oftalmologia [*A publication*] ... Arq Bras Oftalmol
Arquivos Brasileiros de Psicologia Aplicada [*A publication*] ... Arq Bras Ps
Arquivos Brasileiros de Psicologia Aplicada [*A publication*] ... Arquivos Brasil Psicol Ap
Arquivos Brasileiros de Psicotecnica [*A publication*] ... AQBPA
Arquivos Brasileiros de Tuberculose e Doencas do Torax [*A publication*] ... Arq Bras Tuberc Doencas Torax
Arquivos Catarinenses de Medicina [*A publication*] ... Arq Catarinenses Med
Arquivos. Centro Cultural Portugues [*A publication*] ... ACCP
Arquivos. Centro Cultural Portugues [*Paris*] [*A publication*] ... ArCCP
Arquivos de Ciencias do Mar [*A publication*] ... Arq Cienc Mar
Arquivos de Cirurgia Clinica e Experimental (Sao Paulo) [*A publication*] ... Arq Cir Clin Exp (Sao Paulo)
Arquivos de Dermatologia e Sifiligrafia de Sao Paulo [*A publication*] ... Arq Dermatol Sifiligr Sao Paulo
Arquivos de Entomologia. Serie A [*A publication*] ... Arq Entomol Ser A
Arquivos de Entomologia. Serie B [*A publication*] ... Arq Entomol Ser B
Arquivos. Escola de Veterinaria. Universidade Federal de Minas Gerais [*A publication*] ... Arq Esc Vet Univ Fed Minas Gerais
Arquivos. Escola de Veterinaria. Universidade Federal de Minas Gerais [*A publication*] ... Arq Esc Vet Univ Minas Gerais
Arquivos. Estacao de Biologia Marinha da Universidade Federal do Ceara [*A publication*] ... Arq Estac Biol Mar Univ Ceara
Arquivos. Estacao de Biologia Marinha da Universidade Federal do Ceara [*A publication*] ... Arq Estac Biol Mar Univ Fed Ceara
Arquivos. Faculdade de Higiene e Saude Publica da Universidade de Sao Paulo [*A publication*] ... Arq Fac Hig Saude Publica Univ Sao Paulo
Arquivos de Gastroenterologia [*A publication*] ... Arq Gastroenterol
Arquivos de Higiene (Rio De Janeiro) [*A publication*] ... Arq Hig (Rio De J)
Arquivos de Higiene e Saude Publica (Sao Paulo) [*A publication*] ... Arq Hig Saude Publica (Sao Paulo)
Arquivos de Historia de Cultura Portuguesa [*A publication*] ... AHCP
Arquivos. Instituto de Anatomia Universidade do Rio Grande Do Sul [*A publication*] ... Arq Inst Anat Univ Rio Grande Do Sul
Arquivos. Instituto Bacteriologico Camara Pestana [*A publication*] ... Arq Inst Bacteriol Camara Pestana
Arquivos. Instituto Bacteriologico Camara Pestana [*A publication*] ... Arq Inst Bacteriol Cam Pestana
Arquivos. Instituto de Biologia Animal (Rio De Janeiro) [*A publication*] ... Arq Inst Biol Anim (Rio De J)
Arquivos. Instituto de Biologia do Exercito [*A publication*] ... Arq Inst Biol Exerc
Arquivos. Instituto de Biologia Vegetal (Rio De Janeiro) [*A publication*] ... Arq Inst Biol Veg (Rio De J)
Arquivos. Instituto Biologico [*A publication*] ... Arq Inst Biol
Arquivos. Instituto Biologico (Sao Paulo) [*A publication*] ... Arq Inst Biol (Sao Paulo)
Arquivos. Instituto de Pesquisas Agronomicas [*A publication*] ... Arq Inst Pesqui Agron
Arquivos. Instituto de Pesquisas Veterinarias Desiderio Finamor [*A publication*] ... Arq Inst Pesqui Vet Desiderio Finamor
Arquivos. Jardim Botanico do Rio De Janeiro [*A publication*] ... Arq Jard Bot Rio De J
Arquivos Mineiros de Leprologia [*A publication*] ... Arq Min Leprol
Arquivos. Museu Bocage [*A publication*] ... Arq Mus Bocage
Arquivos. Museu de Historia Natural. Universidade Federal de Minas Gerais [*A publication*] ... Arq Mus Hist Nat Univ Fed Minas Gerais
Arquivos. Museu Nacional do Rio De Janeiro [*A publication*] ... Arq Mus Nac Rio De J
Arquivos. Museu Paranaense [*A publication*] ... Arq Mus Parana
Arquivos de Neuro-Psiquiatria [*A publication*] ... Arq Neuro-Psiquiatr
Arquivos de Oncologia [*A publication*] ... Arq Oncol
Arquivos de Patologia Geral e Anatomia Patologica de Universidade de Coimbra [*A publication*] ... Arq Patol Geral Anat Patol Univ Coimbra
Arquivos de Patologia (Lisbon) [*A publication*] ... Arq Patol (Lisbon)
Arquivos Portugueses de Bioquimica [*A publication*] ... Arq Port Bioquim
Arquivos. Seminario de Estudos Galegos [*A publication*] ... ASEG
Arquivos. Servico Florestal (Rio De Janeiro) [*A publication*] ... Arq Serv Florestal (Rio De J)
Arquivos de Tisiologia [*A publication*] ... Arq Tisiol
Arquivos da Universidade de Baia. Faculdade de Filosofia [*A publication*] ... AUBFF
Arquivos de Zoologia do Estado de Sao Paulo [*A publication*] ... Arq Zool Estado Sao Paulo
Arquivos de Zoologia (Sao Paulo) [*A publication*] ... Arq Zool (Sao Paulo)
Arrange ... ARNG
Arranged ... ARR
Arranged ... ARRD
Arrangement [*Music*] ... ARR
Arrangement ... ARRANGT
Array Element Study ... AES
Array Processor [*Data processing*] ... AP
Array Processor Access Method [*Data processing*] ... APAM
Array Processor Subroutine Package [*Data processing*] ... APSP
Array Transform Processor ... ATP
Arrears in Pay [*Military*] ... ARSIP
Arrecife [*Canary Islands*] [*Airport symbol*] ... ACE
Arrester [*Electricity*] ... ARR
Arrester [*Electricity*] ... ARSR
Arresting ... ARG
Arresting Gear [*Aviation*] ... A-G
Arresting Gear Officer [*Military*] ... AGO
Arresting Gear Tester ... AGT
Arrick, Douglas B., Denver CO [*STAC*] ... ARK
Arriflex [*Camera*] [*Named for manufacturers Arnold and Richter*] ... ARRI
Arrival ... AR
Arrival [*or Arrive*] ... ARR
Arrival Airfield Control Group [*Military*] ... AACG
Arrival Angle ... AA
Arrival Approved [*Aviation*] ... AA
Arrival Approved Request for IFR [*Instrument Flight Rules*] **Flight** [*Aviation*] ... AI
Arrival Further Proceed Immediately and Report [*Navy*] ... ARPROIMREP
Arrival Further Proceed Port in which Activity Designated May Be [*Navy*] ... ARPROPORICH
Arrival Locator ... AL
Arrival Message [*Aviation code*] ... ARR
Arrival Notice [*Shipping*] ... AN
Arrival Report [*Navy*] ... ARREP
Arrival Report [*Military*] ... ARRIVEDREP
Arrival Report Commanding Officer that Vessel Duty [*Navy*] ... ARREPCOVES
Arrival Report Immediate Superior in Command [*Navy*] ... ARREPISIC
Arrival Report Will Be Filed with____ [*Aviation*] ... FIRIV
Arrival Report Will Be Filed With [*Aviation*] ... FIRAV
Arrival and Return [*Shipping*] ... AR
Arrival Time ... AT
Arrival Time [*Aviation*] ... PX In
Arrival Unknown [*Aviation*] ... ARUNK
Arrived ... ARRD
Arrived Within Continental Limits of US [*Navy*] ... ARRUS
Arrow Automotive Industries, Inc. [*American Stock Exchange symbol*] ... AI
Arrow Aviation Ltd. [*Abbotsford, BC*] [*FAA designator*] ... ARO
Arrow Bank Corp. [*NASDAQ symbol*] ... AROW
Arrow Electronics, Inc. [*NYSE symbol*] ... ARW
Arrowhead [*Military decoration*] ... Ahd
Arrowhead Energy Corporation [*NASDAQ symbol*] ... AHEC
Arrowhead Library System [*Library network*] ... ALS
Arrowhead Library System, Janesville Public Library, Janesville, WI [*OCLC symbol*] ... WIJ
Arrowhead Professional Libraries Association [*Library network*] ... APLA
Arroyo Grande, CA [*Radio station call letters*] ... KKAL
Ars Curandi em Odontologia [*A publication*] ... Ars Curandi Odontol
Ars Islamica [*A publication*] ... AI
Ars Islamica [*A publication*] ... Ars Islam
Ars Journal [*A publication*] ... Ars J
Ars Medici (Edition Francaise) [*A publication*] ... Ars Med (Ed Fr)
Ars Orientalis [*A publication*] ... Ars Orient
Ars Pharmaceutica [*A publication*] ... Ars Pharm
Ars Poetica [*A publication*] ... AP
Ars Semiotica [*A publication*] ... Ars S
ARS [*American Rocket Society*] **Structures and Materials Committee** ... ASTMC
Arsanilic Acid [*Organic chemistry*] ... ARS
Arsberetning Norges Fiskerier [*A publication*] ... Arsberet Nor Fisk
Arsbok. Finska Vetenskaps Societeten [*A publication*] ... Arsb Finska Vetensk Soc
Arsbok. Sodermanlands Lans Hushallningssallskaps [*A publication*] ... Arsb Sodermanlands Lans Hushallningssallsk
Arsbok Utgiven av Seminarierna i Slaviska Sprak, Jamforande Sprakforskning, Finsk-Ugriska Sprak och Ostasiatiska Sprak Vid Lunds Universitet [*A publication*] ... ASLund
Arsenal ... ARS
Arsenal ... ARSL
Arsenal Management Information System ... ARMIS
Arsenal Operations Directorate [*Rock Island Arsenal*] [*Army*] ... AOD
Arsenic [*Chemical element*] ... As
Arshan [*USSR*] [*Seismograph station code, US Geological Survey*] ... ARS
Arsine [*Inorganic chemistry*] ... ARS
Arson Task Force Assistance Program ... ATFAP
Arsphenamine [*Antisyphilitic compound*] ... ARS
Arsskrift. Bohuslaens Hembygdsfoerbund [*A publication*] ... A Bohuslaens Hembygds

Arsskrift foer Modersmalslararnas Forening [*A publication*] .... Arsskr f Modersmalslararnas Foren
Art in America [*A publication*]................................ Art in Am
Art in America [*A publication*]................................ Art Am
Art in America [*A publication*]................................ Art in Amer
Art and Antique Dealers League of America ....AADLA
Art and Archaeology [*A publication*]........................A & A
Art and Archaeology [*A publication*]................ Art & Arch
Art and Archaeology. Research Papers [*A publication*] .... Art Archaeol Res Papers
Art and Archaeology. Technical Abstracts [*A publication*]...ArtArch
Art and Archaeology. Technical Abstracts [*A publication*]............................. Art Archaeol Tech Abstr
Art and Architecture [*A publication*] ....AA
Art and Architecture [*A publication*] ....ARAC
Art Bulletin [*A publication*]..AB
Art Bulletin [*A publication*]....................................ABul
Art Bulletin [*A publication*]....................................ABull
Art Bulletin [*A publication*]....................................ArtB
Art Bulletin [*A publication*].................................. Art Bul
Art Bulletin [*A publication*].................................. Art Bull
Art Center College of Design, Los Angeles, CA [*Library symbol*].........CLArt
Art Center School ....ACS
Art Circle Public Library, Crossville, TN [*Library symbol*] ....TCrA
Art Class Teacher's Certificate [*British*]....................ACTC
Art Collectors Club of America ....ACCA
Art Complete ....AC
Art Dealers Association of America ....ADAA
Art Deco Societies of America ....ADSA
Art and Decoration [*A publication*]..................... Art & Dec
Art Digest [*A publication*]..AD
Art Direction [*A publication*]............................... Art Dir
Art Director [*Films, television, etc.*]............................AD
Art Directors Annual [*A publication*].........................ADA
Art Directors Club ....ADC
Art Dreco Institute ....ADI
Art Education [*A publication*]............................ Art Educ
Art Exhibitions Bureau... AEB
Art Explosion, Inc. [*NASDAQ symbol*].......................ARTX
Art/Film/Criticism [*A publication*] ....Art
Art Gallery ....AG
Art Gallery of Cobourg, Cobourg, ON, Canada [*Library symbol*] ...... CaOCoA
Art Gallery of Hamilton, Hamilton, ON, Canada [*Library symbol*] .... CaOHAG
Art Gallery of Nova Scotia, Halifax, NS, Canada [*Library symbol*] .... CaNSHAG
Art Gallery of Ontario, Audiovisual Library, Toronto, ON, Canada [*Library symbol*] ....CaOTAGAV
Art Gallery of Ontario, Toronto, ON, Canada [*Library symbol*]..........CaOTAG
Art Gallery of Windsor, Windsor, ON, Canada [*Library symbol*].......CaOWAG
Art Hazards Information Center [*of the Center for Occupational Hazards*]................ AHIC
Art Index [*A publication*] ....AInd
Art Index [*A publication*] ....ArtI
Art Index [*A publication*] .... Art Ind
Art and Industry [*A publication*]........................ Art & Ind
Art Information Center [*Information service*].................AIC
Art Institute of Chicago, Chicago, IL [*Library symbol*] .....ICA
Art Institute of Light ....AIL
Art International [*A publication*] ....AI
Art International [*A publication*] .... Art Int
Art Journal [*A publication*] ....AJ
Art Journal [*A publication*] .... Art J
Art Journal [*A publication*] .... Art Jnl
Art Journal [*A publication*] .... Art Jour
Art Libraries Journal [*A publication*].....................Art Lib J
Art Libraries Society/North America ....ARLIS/NA
Art Master's Certificate ....AMC
Art Master's Teaching Certificate [*British*]...............AMTC
Art Material Board of Trade ....AMBOT
Art Material Club [*Later, AMMA*]..............................AMC
Art Material Manufacturers Association [*Formerly, AMC*]................. AMMA
Art Museum of South Texas, Corpus Christi, TX [*Library symbol*]................. TxCcMST
Art News [*A publication*]... AN
Art News [*A publication*]......................................Art N
Art Patrons Association of America..........................APAA
Art Psychotherapy [*A publication*].....................Art Psychot
Art Quarterly [*A publication*] ....AQ
Art Quarterly [*A publication*] ....ArtQ
Art Research Libraries of Ohio [*Library network*]..........ARLO
Art Scholar [*A publication*] ....AS
Art Services Grants [*British*].................................ASG
Art Students' League of New York ....ASLNY
Art Teacher [*A publication*]..............................Art Teach
Art Teacher's Certificate [*British*]...........................ATC
Art Teacher's Diploma [*British*]..............................ATD
Art Therapist, Registered ....ATR
Art for World Friendship [*Defunct*]...........................AWF
Arta [*Djibouti*] [*Seismograph station code, US Geological Survey*] [*Closed*]....................................ART
Arta si Arheologia [*A publication*]..........................A & A

Arta Observatory [*Djibouti*]....................................ARO
Arte Antica e Moderna [*A publication*] ....AAM
Arte Figurativa [*A publication*]...................................AF
Arte (Milan) [*A publication*].....................................ArM
Arte Musical [*A publication*]................................Arte Mus
Arte e Poesia [*A publication*].................................ArteP
Arte Stampa [*A publication*]...................................ArtSt
Arte y Variedades [*A publication*] ....Arte y Var
Artel Communications [*NASDAQ symbol*]................... AXXX
Arterial Blood Gases ....ABG
Arterial Blood Pressure [*Medicine*] ....ABP
Arterial Hypertension [*Medicine*] .... AH
Arterial Occlusive Disease [*Medicine*] ....AOD
Arterial Pulse Wave Transducer...............................APWT
Arteriosclerosis [*Medicine*] ....AS
Arteriosclerosis [*Medicine*] ....ASC
Arteriosclerosis Obliterans [*Medicine*] ....ASO
Arteriosclerotic Cardiovascular Disease [*Cardiology*].......ASCVD
Arteriosclerotic Heart Disease [*Cardiology*]................AHD
Arteriosclerotic Heart Disease [*Cardiology*]................ASHD
Arteriovenous [*Medicine*]..AV
Arteriovenous Anastomosis [*Medicine*] ....AVA
Arteriovenous Malformation [*Medicine*] ....AVM
Artery .... A
Artesia, NM [*Location identifier*] [*FAA*].....................ATS
Artesia, NM [*Radio station call letters*].....................KSVP
Artesia, NM [*Radio station call letters*].....................KTZA
Artesia Public Library, Artesia, NM [*OCLC symbol*] ...... ANM
Artesia Public Library, Artesia, NM [*Library symbol*] ......NmAr
Artesian Petroleum [*NASDAQ symbol*]....................APCOF
Artforum [*A publication*] .... Artf
Artha Vijnana [*A publication*] ....Artha Vij
Artha Vijnana [*A publication*] ....AV
Artha Vikas [*A publication*] ....Artha Vik
Arthaniti [*A publication*] ....Arth
Arthritis Foundation ....AF
Arthritis Health Professions Association.....................AHPA
Arthritis Information Clearinghouse ....AIC
Arthritis Rehabilitation Center..................................ARC
Arthritis and Rheumatic Diseases Abstracts [*A publication*]...... ARD
Arthritis and Rheumatism [*A publication*].............Arth Rheum
Arthritis and Rheumatism [*A publication*].........Arthritis Rheum
Arthritis and Rheumatism Foundation [*Later, Arthritis Foundation*]........ARF
Arthrogryposis Association......................................AA
Arthrogryposis Multiplex Congenita [*Medicine*] ....AMC
Arthropod-Borne [*Also, ARBOR*] [*Virology*] .... ARBO
Arthropod-Borne [*Also, ARBO*] [*Virology*].................ARBOR
Arthropod-Borne Animal Diseases Research Laboratory [*Department of Agriculture*]................ABADRL
Arthropods of Florida and Neighboring Land Areas [*A publication*]................ Arthropods Fla Neighboring Land Areas
Arthroscopy Association of North America ....AANA
Arthur Adaptation of the Leiter International Performance Scale [*Psychology*]................AALIPS
Arthur Andersen Chronicle [*A publication*] ....A A Chron
Arthur D. Little, Inc. [*Research code symbol*] ....ADL
Arthur D. Little, Incorporated ....ALI
Arthur D. Little, Inc. [*Research code symbol*] ....NSC
Arthur D. Little, Inc., Cambridge, MA [*OCLC symbol*] .....ADL
Arthur D. Little, Inc., Cambridge, MA [*Library symbol*] ....MCA
Arthur G. McKee & Co., Cleveland, OH [*Library symbol*].......OCIAM
Arthur Johnson Memorial Library, Raton, NM [*OCLC symbol*] ....AJM
Arthur Johnson Memorial Library, Raton, NM [*Library symbol*] ....NmRa
Arthur Machen Society [*Defunct*].............................AMS
Arthur Vining Davis Corp..................................... ARVIDA
Arthuriana [*A publication*] .... A
Arthur's Town [*Bahamas*] [*Airport symbol*].................ATC
Arti [*USSR*] [*Seismograph station code, US Geological Survey*]...............ARU
Arti Figurative. Rivista d'Arte Antica e Moderna [*A publication*]............AFig
Arti Musices [*A publication*] ....Arti Mus
Artibus Asiae [*A publication*] ....AA
Artichoke Advisory Board ....AAB
Article .... A
Article ....ART
Articles Contributed for Intelligence and Dollars [*Education program*]................AID
Articles for the Government of the Navy [*Obsolete*] ....AGN
Articles of War ....AOW
Articles of War .... AW
Articulare [*Craniometric point*].................................AR
Articulated.. ARTCLD
Articulated Computing Hierarchy [*British*]................ ARCH
Articulated Mirror System [*Astronomy*]......................AMS
Articulation .... ARTIC
Articulation Control Subsystem [*NASA*]....................ARTC
Articulation Index ....AI
Articulation Score [*Percentage of words correctly understood over a radio channel perturbed by interference*]................AS
Artificer..ART
Artificial ....ART
Artificial ....ARTF

Artificial .... ARTIF
Artificial .... ARTIFCL
Artificial Aerial .... AA
Artificial Breeding Box .... ABB
Artificial Cerebrospinal Fluid .... ACSF
Artificial Cloud Nucleation [*Rainmaking*] .... ACN
Artificial Compression Method .... ACM
Artificial Earth Research and Orbiting Satellite .... AEROS
Artificial Earth Satellite [*NASA*] .... AES
Artificial Earth Satellite Observation Program [*Navy*] .... AESOP
Artificial Endocrine Pancreas .... AEP
Artificial Flower Manufacturers Board of Trade .... AFMBT
Artificial Gravity .... AG
Artificial Gravity Structure .... AGS
Artificial Heart [*Medicine*] .... AH
Artificial Heart Energy System .... AHES
Artificial Horizon .... AH
Artificial Horizon Indicator .... AHI
Artificial Insemination [*Medicine*] .... AI
Artificial Insemination by Donor [*Medicine*] .... AID
Artificial Insemination by Husband [*Medicine*] .... AIH
Artificial Intelligence .... AI
Artificial Intelligence [*A publication*] .... Artif Intel
Artificial Intelligence [*A publication*] .... Artif Intell
Artificial Intelligence [*Elsevier Book Series*] [*A publication*] .... AI
Artificial Intelligence Group [*MIT*] .... AIG
Artificial Intelligence in Medicine .... AIM
Artificial Interference to Transmission or Reception [*Broadcasting*] .... QRM
Artificial Luminous Cloud .... ALC
Artificial Methods Analyst .... ARMAN
Artificial Neuron .... ARTRON
Artificial Organs [*A publication*] .... Artif Organs
Artificial Pneumothorax [*Medicine*] .... AP
Artificial Pneumothorax [*Medicine*] .... APN
Artificial Respiration [*Medicine*] .... AR
Artificial Rupture of Membranes [*Medicine*] .... ARM
Artificial Satellite .... AS
Artificial Satellite Time and Radio Orbit .... ASTRO
Artificial Seawater .... ASW
Artificial Site Tuff [*Geology*] .... AST
Artificial Sweetener .... AS
Artificial Top Component [*Virology*] .... ATC
Artificial Transmission Line .... ATL
Artificially Induced Aurora .... AIA
Artigas [*Uruguay*] [*Airport symbol*] .... ATI
Artilleriefuehrer [*Division artillery commander*] [*German military - World War II*] .... AF
Artillery .... A
Artillery .... ART
Artillery .... ARTIL
Artillery .... ARTILL
Artillery .... ARTLY
Artillery .... ARTY
Artillery .... AT
Artillery Ammunition and Rocket Development Laboratory [*Army*] .... AARDL
Artillery Barge [*Navy symbol*] [*Obsolete*] .... APB
Artillery Computer System .... ACS
Artillery Control Console [*British*] .... ACC
Artillery Controller .... AC
Artillery-Delivered Antipersonnel Mine .... ADAM
Artillery-Delivered Multipurpose Submunition .... ARDEMS
Artillery Destruction Program .... ADP
Artillery Direct Fire Trainer .... ADFT
Artillery-Fired Atomic Projectiles .... AFAP
Artillery Flash Ranging [*Army*] .... AFR
Artillery Forward Observer .... AFO
Artillery Intelligence Officer [*Army*] .... AIO
Artillery-Locating RADAR .... ALR
Artillery Location Acoustic System .... ALAS
Artillery Meteorological System .... AMETS
Artillery and Missile School [*Army*] .... AMS
Artillery Repair Truck [*British*] .... ART
Artillery Siege Train Traction Engine [*British*] .... ASTTE
Artillery Spotting Division [*Air Force*] .... ASD
Artillery Supply Truck [*British*] .... AST
Artillery Tactical Terminal .... ATT
Artillery Test Board [*Army*] .... ATB
Artillery Towing Light Auxiliary System .... ATLAS
Artillery Tractor [*British*] .... AT
Artillery Volunteer Corps [*British*] .... AVC
Artillery Volunteers .... AV
Artillery Weapons Data Transmission System .... AWDATS
ARTINS [*Army Terrain Information System*] **Requirements Coordination Committee** .... ARCC
Artisans Order of Mutual Protection .... AOMP
Artist .... ART
Artist Blacksmith Association of North America .... ABANA
Artist in Residence [*Signs used in NoHo district of New York City - often followed by floor number and meant to advise night-duty firemen that someone may be sleeping on that floor*] .... AIR
Artistic Roller Skating Federation .... ARSF
Artists and Athletes Against Apartheid .... AAAA
Artists Civil Rights Assistance Fund [*Defunct*] .... ACRAF
Artists Equity Association .... AEA
Artists Equity Fund .... AEF
Artists' Fellowship .... AF
Artists' General Benevolent Institution [*British*] .... AGBI
Artists Guild .... AG
Artists Guild of Chicago .... AGC
Artists Guild of New York .... AGNY
Artists for Nuclear Disarmament .... AND
Artists and Repertory .... A and R
Artists' Representatives Association .... ARA
Artists Rights Association .... ARA
Artists Technical Research Institute .... ATRI
Artium Baccalaureus [*Bachelor of Arts*] .... AB
Artium Elegantium Doctor [*Doctor of Fine Arts*] .... AED
Artium Liberalium Magister [*Master of the Liberal Arts*] .... ALM
Artium Magister [*Master of Arts*] .... AM
Artra Group, Inc. [*NYSE symbol*] .... ATA
Arts d'Afrique Noire [*A publication*] .... Arts Afr Noire
Arts and Architecture [*A publication*] .... A & A
Arts and Architecture [*A publication*] .... Arts & Arch
Arts of Asia [*A publication*] .... Arts As
Arts Asiatique [*A publication*] .... Arts Asiat
Arts Asiatiques [*A publication*] .... Ar As
Arts and Business Council .... ABC
Arts Council of Great Britain .... ACGB
Arts Councils of America [*Later, American Council for the Arts*] .... ACA
Arts and Decoration [*A publication*] .... Arts & D
Arts and Decoration [*A publication*] .... Arts and Dec
[*The*] **Arts, Education, and Americans** .... AEA
Arts and Humanities .... AH
Arts and Humanities Citation Index [*A publication*] .... AHCI
Arts and Humanities Citation Index [*A publication*] .... Arts & Hum Cit Ind
Arts International .... AI
Arts and Letters Club, Toronto, ON, Canada [*Library symbol*] .... CaOTAL
Arts, Letters, Printers and Publishers, and Systems [*A publication*] .... ALPS
Arts Magazine [*A publication*] .... Arts
Arts Magazine [*A publication*] .... Arts Mag
Arts et Manufactures [*A publication*] .... Arts Manuf
Arts et Metiers [*Arts and Crafts*] [*French*] .... A et M
Arts et Metiers [*A publication*] .... Arts Metiers
Arts Recognition and Talent Search [*National Foundation for Advancement in the Arts*] .... ARTS
Arts Reporting Service [*A publication*] .... Arts Reptg Ser
Arts and Sciences .... A & S
Arts and Sciences [*A publication*] .... A & S
Arts and Sciences Basic to Human Biology and Medicine [*Program in medical education*] .... ASHUM
Arts in Society [*A publication*] .... ARSOB
Arts in Society [*A publication*] .... Arts in Soc
Arts in Society [*A publication*] .... AS
Arts in Society [*A publication*] .... ASoc
Arts et Traditions Populaires [*A publication*] .... ATP
Art's Way Manufacturing Co., Inc. [*NASDAQ symbol*] .... ARTW
Artscanada [*A publication*] .... Artscan
Arturo Toscanini Society .... ATS
Arua [*Uganda*] [*Airport symbol*] .... RUA
Aruba [*Netherlands Antilles*] [*Airport symbol*] .... AUA
Aruba, Bonaire, and Curacao [*Islands*] .... ABC
Arundel Corp. [*American Stock Exchange symbol*] .... ARL
Arvada, CO [*Radio station call letters*] .... KQXI
Arvada Public Library, Arvada, CO [*Library symbol*] .... CoAr
Arvin Industries, Inc. [*NYSE symbol*] .... ARV
Aryan Path [*A publication*] .... AP
Aryl [*Chemistry*] .... Ar
Aryl Hydrocarbon Hydroxylase [*An enzyme*] .... AHH
Arylene Isopropylidene Polymers [*Organic chemistry*] .... AIP
Arzneimittel-Forschung [*A publication*] .... ARZNA
Arzneimittel-Forschung [*A publication*] .... Arznei-For
Arzneimittel-Forschung [*A publication*] .... Arzneim-Forsch
Arzneimittel-Forschung/Drug Research [*A publication*] .... Arzneim Forsch Drug Res
As Amended By [*Army*] .... AABY
As Before .... AB
As-Built Configuration Lists .... ABCL
As-Built Configuration Record .... ABCR
As Design Changes Occur .... ADCO
As Drawn .... AD
As Generated .... ASGEN
As Good As .... AGA
As Interest May Appear [*Insurance*] .... AIMA
As Low as Practical .... ALAP
As Low as Reasonably Achievable [*Radiation exposure*] [*Nuclear Regulatory Commission*] .... ALARA
As Needed .... A/N
As-Of Date .... AOD
As Planned Parts List .... APPL
As Prescribed .... AP
As Purchased .... AP

As Required...AR
As Soon as Possible...ASAP
As Soon as Possible...ASP
As Stated...AS
As You Like It [*Shakespearean work*]...AYL
ASA Ltd. [*Formerly, American-South African Investment Co. Ltd.*] [*NYSE symbol*]...ASA
ASA [*American Society of Agronomy*] **Newsletter** [*A publication*]...ASA Newsl
ASA [*American Society of Agronomy*] **Special Publication** [*A publication*]...ASA Spec Publ
Asahikawa [*Japan*] [*Airport symbol*]...AKJ
Asahikawa [*Japan*] [*Seismograph station code, US Geological Survey*]...ASA
Asama [*Japan*] [*Seismograph station code, US Geological Survey*]...ASM
Asamera, Inc. [*American Stock Exchange symbol*]...ASM
ASAP Air, Inc. [*Fort Worth, TX*] [*FAA designator*]...SAP
ASARCO, Inc. [*Formerly, American Smelting & Refining Company*] [*NYSE symbol*]...AR
Asatru Free Assembly...AFA
ASB [*Association of Southeastern Biologists*] **Bulletin** [*A publication*]...ASB Bull
Asbestos...A
Asbestos...ASB
Asbestos...ASBSTS
Asbestos Cement...A/C
Asbestos Cement [*Technical drawings*]...AC
Asbestos-Cement Board [*Technical drawings*]...ACB
Asbestos-Cement Products Association [*Defunct*]...A-CPA
Asbestos Claims Council...ACC
Asbestos Compensation Coalition...ACC
Asbestos-Covered Metal [*Technical drawings*]...ACM
Asbestos & Danville [*AAR code*]...ASDA
Asbestos Hill [*Canada*] [*Airport symbol*] [*Obsolete*]...YAF
Asbestos Information Association/North America...AIA/NA
Asbestos Insulated Wire...AIW
Asbestos International Association...AIA
Asbestos Mill Board [*Technical drawings*]...AMB
Asbestos, PQ [*Radio station call letters*]...CJAN
Asbestos Roof Shingles [*Technical drawings*]...ARS
Asbestos Textile Institute...ATI
Asbestos Victims of America...AVA
Asbury College, Wilmore, KY [*OCLC symbol*]...KWW
Asbury College, Wilmore, KY [*Library symbol*]...KyWA
Asbury Park Free Public Library, Asbury Park, NJ [*Library symbol*]...NjAs
Asbury Park/Monmouth County [*New Jersey*] [*Airport symbol*]...ARX
Asbury Park, NJ [*Radio station call letters*]...WJLK
Asbury Park, NJ [*Radio station call letters*]...WJLK-FM
Asbury Park Press, Asbury Park, NJ [*Library symbol*]...NjAsP
Asbury Seminarian [*A publication*]...AS
Asbury Theological Seminary, Wilmore, KY [*OCLC symbol*]...KAT
Asbury Theological Seminary, Wilmore, KY [*Library symbol*]...KyWAT
ASC [*American Society for Cybernetics*] **Communications** [*A publication*]...ASC Commun
ASCAP [*American Society of Composers, Authors, and Publishers*] **in Action** [*A publication*]...ASCAP
ASCAP [*American Society of Composers, Authors, and Publishers*] **Today** [*A publication*]...ASCAP
ASCE [*American Society of Civil Engineers*] **Engineering Issues. Journal of Professional Activities** [*A publication*]...ASCE Eng Issues J Prof Activ
ASCE [*American Society of Civil Engineers*] **Journal of the Construction Division** [*A publication*]...ASCE J Constr Div
ASCE [*American Society of Civil Engineers*] **Journal of the Engineering Mechanics Division** [*A publication*]...ASCE J Eng Mech Div
ASCE [*American Society of Civil Engineers*] **Journal of Professional Activities** [*A publication*]...ASCE J Prof Activ
ASCE [*American Society of Civil Engineers*] **Journal of the Sanitary Engineering Division** [*A publication*]...ASCE J Sanit Eng Div
ASCE [*American Society of Civil Engineers*] **Journal of the Soil Mechanics and Foundations Division** [*A publication*]...ASCE J Soil Mech Found Div
ASCE [*American Society of Civil Engineers*] **Journal of the Structural Division** [*A publication*]...ASCE J Struct Div
ASCE [*American Society of Civil Engineers*] **Journal of the Surveying and Mapping Division** [*A publication*]...ASCE J Surv Mapp Div
ASCE [*American Society of Civil Engineers*] **Manuals and Reports on Engineering Practice** [*A publication*]...ASCE Man Rep Eng Pract
Ascend...ASND
Ascend To [*or Ascending To*] [*Aviation*]...ASC
Ascendance-Submission [*Psychology*]...AS
Ascending...ASC
Ascending Reticular Activating [*or Activation*] **System**...ARAS
Ascension [*Bolivia*] [*Airport symbol*] [*Obsolete*]...ASC
Ascension Island [*MARC geographic area code*] [*Library of Congress*]...lsai---
Ascension Island Tracking Station [*NASA*]...ACN
Ascension Parish Library, Donaldsonville, LA [*Library symbol*]...LDA
Ascent Air Data System...AADS
Ascent Engine Arming Assembly [*NASA*]...AEAA
Ascent Engine Latching Device [*NASA*]...AELD
Ascent Flight Systems Integration Group [*NASA*]...AFSIG
Ascent Guidance and Control System [*NASA*]...AGS
Ascent Phase...AP
Ascent Propulsion System [*NASA*]...APS
Ascent Stage [*NASA*]...AS
Ascent Thrust Vector Control Driver...ATVCD
Ascheim-Zondek Test [*Medicine*]...AZT
ASCII [*American Standard Code for Information Interchange*] **COBOL** [*Data processing*]...ACOB
ASCII [*American Standard Code for Information Interchange*] **COBOL** [*Common Business-Oriented Language*] **Data Manipulation Language-Preprocessor** [*Data processing*]...ADMLP
Ascites Hepatoma [*Medicine*]...AH
Ascorbic Acid [*Vitamin C*] [*Biochemistry*]...AA
Ascorbic Acid Factor [*Biochemistry*]...AAF
Ascorbic Free Radical [*Biochemistry*]...AFR
ASEA AB ADR [*NASDAQ symbol*]...ASEAY
ASEA [*Allmaenna Svenska Elektriska Aktiebolaget*] **Journal** [*A publication*]...ASEA J
ASEA [*Allmaenna Svenska Elektriska Aktiebolaget*] **Research** [*A publication*]...ASEA Res
ASEA [*Allmaenna Svenska Elektriska Aktiebolaget*] **Tidning** [*A publication*]...ASEA Tidn
ASEA [*Allmaenna Svenska Elektriska Aktiebolaget*] **Zeitschrift** [*A publication*]...ASEA Z
ASEAN [*Association of South East Asian Nations*] **Council on Petroleum**...ASCOPE
Aseki [*Papua New Guinea*] [*Airport symbol*] [*Obsolete*]...AEK
Aseptic Bone Necrosis [*Medicine*]...ABN
Aseptic Fluid Transfer System [*NASA*]...AFTS
Aseptic Maintenance by Pressurization [*NASA*]...AMP
Aseptic Necrosis [*Medicine*]...AN
Aserradero [*Nicaragua*] [*Seismograph station code, US Geological Survey*]...ASE
ASG Industries, Inc. [*Formerly, American St. Gobain*]...ASG
Ash-Free Dry Mass [*Analytical chemistry*]...AFDM
Ash Lighter [*Navy symbol*]...YA
ASHA. Journal of the American Speech and Hearing Association [*A publication*]...ASHA J Am Speech Hear Assoc
ASHA [*American Speech and Hearing Association*] **Monographs** [*A publication*]...ASHA Monogr
ASHA [*American Speech and Hearing Association*] **Reports** [*A publication*]...ASHA Rep
Ashbrooke-Pembleton-Ffrench [*Mythical British family appearing in "Announcements" column of Times of London*]...A-P-F
Ashburn, GA [*Radio station call letters*]...WMES
Ashdown, AR [*Radio station call letters*]...KMLA
Asheboro, NC [*Radio station call letters*]...WCSE
Asheboro, NC [*Radio station call letters*]...WGWR
Asheboro, NC [*Radio station call letters*]...WZOO
Asher's Guide to Botanical Periodicals [*A publication*]...Ash G Bot Per
Asheville [*North Carolina*] [*Airport symbol*]...AVL
Asheville-Buncombe Technical Institute, Asheville, NC [*Library symbol*]...NcAAB
Asheville, NC [*Radio station call letters*]...WBMU-FM
Asheville, NC [*Television station call letters*]...WHNS
Asheville, NC [*Radio station call letters*]...WISE
Asheville, NC [*Radio station call letters*]...WLOS
Asheville, NC [*Television station call letters*]...WLOS-TV
Asheville, NC [*Radio station call letters*]...WRAQ
Asheville, NC [*Radio station call letters*]...WSKY
Asheville, NC [*Radio station call letters*]...WUNF-FM
Asheville, NC [*Television station call letters*]...WUNF-TV
Asheville, NC [*Radio station call letters*]...WWNC
Ashizuri [*Japan*] [*Seismograph station code, US Geological Survey*]...ASZ
Ashkhabad [*USSR*] [*Airport symbol*]...ASB
Ashkhabad [*USSR*] [*Geomagnetic observatory code*]...ASH
Ashkhabad [*USSR*] [*Seismograph station code, US Geological Survey*]...ASH
Ashland [*Wisconsin*] [*Airport symbol*] [*Obsolete*]...ASX
Ashland, AL [*Radio station call letters*]...WASZ
Ashland Chemical Co., Research Library, Columbus, OH [*OCLC symbol*]...ASO
Ashland City, TN [*Radio station call letters*]...WAJN
Ashland College, Ashland, OH [*OCLC symbol*]...ASC
Ashland College, Ashland, OH [*Library symbol*]...OAsC
Ashland, KY [*Radio station call letters*]...WAMX
Ashland, KY [*Radio station call letters*]...WCMI
Ashland, KY [*Television station call letters*]...WKAS
Ashland, KY [*Television station call letters*]...WTSF
Ashland, OH [*Location identifier*] [*FAA*]...AAU
Ashland, OH [*Radio station call letters*]...WNCO
Ashland, OH [*Radio station call letters*]...WNCO-FM
Ashland, OH [*Radio station call letters*]...WRDL
Ashland Oil Canada Ltd. [*American Stock Exchange symbol*] [*Delisted*]...AHX
Ashland Oil Canada Ltd., Calgary, AB, Canada [*Library symbol*]...CaACAO
Ashland Oil, Inc. [*NYSE symbol*]...ASH
Ashland, OR [*Radio station call letters*]...KCMX

Ashland, OR [*Radio station call letters*]....KCMX-FM
Ashland, OR [*Radio station call letters*]....KDOV
Ashland, OR [*Radio station call letters*]....KSOR
Ashland Public Library, Ashland, KY [*Library symbol*]....KyA
Ashland Public Library, Ashland, MA [*Library symbol*]....MAsl
Ashland State General Hospital, Ashland, PA [*OCLC symbol*]....PHZ
Ashland Theological Seminary, Ashland, OH [*Library symbol*]....OAsT
Ashland, VA [*Radio station call letters*]....WIVE
Ashland, VA [*Radio station call letters*]....WYFJ
Ashland, WI [*Location identifier*] [*FAA*]....ENY
Ashland, WI [*Radio station call letters*]....WATW
Ashland, WI [*Radio station call letters*]....WATW-FM
Ashley Community Consolidated District 15, Ashley, IL [*Library symbol*]....IAsyCD
Ashley, Drew, & Northern Railway Co. [*AAR code*]....ADN
Ashley, ND [*Location identifier*] [*FAA*]....ASY
Ashley Public Library, Ashley, IL [*Library symbol*]....IAsy
Ashmolean Museum [*A publication*]....Ash M
Ashmont, AB [*Television station call letters*]....CFRN-TV-4
Ashmore and Cartier Islands [*at (Australia) used in records cataloged after January 1978*] [*MARC country of publication code*] [*Library of Congress*]....ac
Ashmore and Cartier Islands [*MARC geographic area code*] [*Library of Congress*]....u-ac---
Ashtabula County District Library, Ashtabula, OH [*Library symbol*]....OAsht
Ashtabula, OH [*Radio station call letters*]....WAQI
Ashtabula, OH [*Radio station call letters*]....WFUN
Ashtabula, OH [*Radio station call letters*]....WREO-FM
Ashton-Tate [*NASDAQ symbol*]....TATE
Ashton-Under-Lyne Public Library, Ashton-Under-Lyne, United Kingdom [*Library symbol*]....UkAul
Asia [*MARC geographic area code*] [*Library of Congress*]....a------
Asia....AS
Asia and Africa Review [*A publication*]....Asia Afr R
Asia and the Americas [*A publication*]....Asia
Asia, Central [*MARC geographic area code*] [*Library of Congress*]....ac-----
Asia, East [*MARC geographic area code*] [*Library of Congress*]....ae-----
Asia Electronics Union. Journal [*A publication*]....AEU
[*The*] **Asia Foundation**....TAF
Asia House [*An association*]....AH
Asia Library Services, Auburn, NY [*Library symbol*]....AIS
Asia Major [*A publication*]....AM
Asia Major [*A publication*]....AsM
Asia Major [*A publication*]....As Ma
Asia Oceania Journal of Obstetrics and Gynaecology [*A publication*]....Asia Oceania J Obstet Gynaecol
Asia-Pacific Council of American Chambers of Commerce....APCAC
Asia-Pacific Forestry Commission [*UN Food and Agriculture Organization*]....APFC
Asia-Pacific News Network....ANN
Asia-Philippines Leader [*A publication*]....Le
Asia Quarterly [*A publication*]....Asia Quart
Asia Quarterly [*A publication*]....As Q
Asia Research Centre....ARC
Asia Society [*Formerly, CAA, CASA*]....AS
Asia, Southeastern [*MARC geographic area code*] [*Library of Congress*]....as-----
Asia, Southwestern [*MARC geographic area code*] [*Library of Congress*]....aw-----
Asian Affairs [*A publication*]....AA
Asian Affairs [*A publication*]....Asian Aff
Asian Affairs. Journal of the Royal Central Asian Society (London) [*A publication*]....Asian Aff (London)
Asian Affairs (New York) [*A publication*]....Asian Aff (New York)
Asian African Legal Consultative Committee....AALCC
Asian and African Studies [*A publication*]....AAS
Asian and African Studies (Bratislava) [*A publication*]....Asian & African Stud (Bratislava)
Asian American Caucus for Disarmament....AACD
Asian American Free Labor Institute....AAFLI
Asian American Legal Defense and Education Fund....AALDEF
Asian American Librarians Association [*Defunct*]....AALA
Asian American Librarians Caucus....AALC
Asian American Psychological Association....AAPA
Asian-American Women's Political Caucus....AAWPC
Asian Archives of Anaesthesiology and Resuscitation [*A publication*]....Asian Arch Anaesthesiol Resusc
Asian Association of Agricultural Colleges and Universities [*Philippines*]....AAACU
Asian Benevolent Corps....ABC
Asian Broadcasting Union....ABU
Asian Bureau Australia Newsletter [*A publication*]....ABAN
Asian Business and Industry [*A publication*]....Asian Bus
Asian Clearing Union....ACU
Asian Coconut Community....ACC
Asian Communist [*Later, B Group*] [*Division of National Security Agency*]....ACOM
Asian Cultural Centre for UNESCO....ACCU
Asian Cultural Council....ACC
Asian Cultural Exchange Foundation....ACEF
Asian Cultural Forum on Development....ACFOD-USA
Asian Defence Journal [*A publication*]....As Def J
Asian Development Bank [*Philippines*]....ADB
Asian Development Bank....AsDB
Asian Development Center....ADC
Asian Development Fund....ADF
Asian Economic Review [*A publication*]....Asian Econ R
Asian Economics [*A publication*]....Asian Econ
Asian Economies [*A publication*]....As Econ
Asian Federation of Library Associations....AFLA
Asian Folklore Studies [*A publication*]....AFS
Asian Folklore Studies [*A publication*]....As Folk Stud
Asian Folklore Studies [*A publication*]....Asian Folkl Stud
Asian Folklore Studies Group....AFSG
Asian Information Center for Geotechnical Engineering [*Asian Institute of Technology*]....AGE
Asian Institute for Economic Development and Planning....AIEDP
Asian Institute of Management [*Philippines*]....AIM
Asian Institute of Technology [*Thailand*]....AIT
Asian Journal of Infectious Diseases [*A publication*]....Asian J Infect Dis
Asian Literature Division [*of MLA*] [*Formerly, COWLR*]....ALD
Asian Manpower Skill Development Program [*United Nations*]....AMSDEP
Asian Medical Journal [*Tokyo*] [*A publication*]....Asian Med J
Asian Medical Journal (Tokyo) [*A publication*]....Asian Med J (Tokyo)
Asian Monetary Unit....AMU
Asian Music [*A publication*]....AMus
Asian Music [*A publication*]....Asian Mus
Asian Music [*A publication*]....As Music
Asian Oceanic Postal Union [*China, Korea, Philippines, Thailand*]....AOPU
Asian Outlook [*A publication*]....As Outlook
Asian/Pacific American....APA
Asian Pacific American Heritage Council....APAHC
Asian/Pacific American Librarians Association....APALA
Asian and Pacific Coconut Community [*Indonesia*]....APCC
Asian and Pacific Council....ASPAC
Asian and Pacific Population Programme News [*A publication*]....Asian Pac Popul Programme News
Asian and Pacific Professional Language and Education Services....APPLES
Asian Pacific Quarterly of Cultural and Social Affairs [*A publication*]....Asian Pacif Quart Cult Soc Aff
Asian Parliamentarians' Union....APU
Asian Peoples' Anti-Communist League....APACL
Asian Perspectives [*A publication*]....AP
Asian Perspectives [*A publication*]....Asian Persp
Asian Perspectives [*A publication*]....Asian Perspect
Asian Perspectives (Honolulu) [*A publication*]....As Perspect (H)
Asian Perspectives (Seoul) [*A publication*]....As Perspect (S)
Asian Political Scientists Group in USA....APSGUSA
Asian Productivity Organization [*Japan*]....APO
Asian Profile [*A publication*]....As Profile
Asian Program for Education Innovation for Development....APEID
Asian Racing Conference....ARC
Asian Regional Organization....ARO
Asian Regional Organization - International Confederation of Free Trade Unions....ARO-ICFTU
Asian Regional Training and Development Organization....ARTDO
Asian Religio-Cultural Forum on Development....ARCFOD
Asian Review [*A publication*]....AR
Asian Review [*A publication*]....Asian R
Asian Socialist Conference....ASC
Asian Statistical Institute....ASI
Asian Student [*A publication*]....AsSt
Asian Studies [*A publication*]....Asian Stud
Asian Studies [*A publication*]....ASt
Asian Studies. Professional Review [*A publication*]....Asian Stud Prof R
Asian Survey [*A publication*]....AS
Asian Survey [*A publication*]....Asian S
Asian Survey [*A publication*]....Asian Surv
Asian Survey [*A publication*]....As Surv
Asian Thought and Society [*A publication*]....As Thought Soc
Asian Vegetable Research and Development Center [*Taiwan*]....AVRDC
Asiatic Fleet [*Obsolete*] [*Navy*]....AF
Asiatic-Pacific Campaign Medal....APCM
Asiatic-Pacific Theater of War....APTW
Asiatic Review [*A publication*]....Asiatic R
Asiatic Review. New Series [*A publication*]....Asiatic R ns
Asiatic Society of Japan. Transactions [*A publication*]....Asiatic Soc Japan Trans
Asiatic Society of Pakistan. Publication [*A publication*]....ASPP
Asiatische Forschungen [*A publication*]....AF
Asiatische Forschungen [*A publication*]....As For
Asiatische Studien [*A publication*]....AS
Asiatische Studien [*A publication*]....Asiat Stud
Asiatische Studien [*A publication*]....AsS
Asiatische Studien [*A publication*]....ASt
Asiatische Studien/Etudes Asiatiques [*A publication*]....ASEA
Asiatische Studien/Etudes Asiatiques [*A publication*]....Asi St/Et As
Asie et l'Afrique [*A publication*]....As A
Asie du Sud-Est et Monde Insulindien [*A publication*]....Asie Sud-Est Monde Insulind
Ask Computer Systems [*NASDAQ symbol*]....ASKI

Ask a Friend to Explain Reconstruction [*An association*] ... AFTER
Askania Cine-Theodolite Optical-Tracking Range ... ACTOR
Askania Optical Tracker ... AOT
Askania Theodolite Camera ... ASK
Asked ... A
Askin Service Corp. [*American Stock Exchange symbol*] [*Delisted*] ... ASK
Asking Price ... AP
ASL [*American Scientific Laboratories*] **Research Report** [*A publication*] ... ASL Res Rep
ASLE [*American Society of Lubrication Engineers*] **Preprints** [*A publication*] ... ASLE Prepr
ASLE [*American Society of Lubrication Engineers*] **Transactions** [*A publication*] ... ASLE Trans
Aslib Proceedings [*A publication*] ... Aslib Proc
ASM [*American Society for Metals*] **Transactions Quarterly** [*A publication*] ... ASM Trans Q
ASM [*American Society for Metals*] **Transactions Quarterly** [*A publication*] ... ASM Trans Quart
Asmara [*Ethiopia*] [*Airport symbol*] ... ASM
Asmat Sketch Book [*A publication*] ... Asmat Sketch Bk
ASNA [*Alabama State Nurses' Association*] **Reporter** [*A publication*] ... ASNA Reporter
Asnuntuck Community College, Learning Resources Center, Enfield, CT [*Library symbol*] ... CtEnA
Aso [*Japan*] [*Seismograph station code, US Geological Survey*] [*Closed*] ... ASO
Asociacion [*Association*] [*Spanish*] ... ASOC
Asociacion Colombiana de Bibliotecarios. Boletin [*A publication*] ... Asoc Colombiana Bibl Bol
Asociacion del Congreso Panamericano de Ferrocarriles [*Pan-American Railway Congress Association*] ... ACPF
Asociacion Cubana de Bibliotecarios. Boletin [*A publication*] ... Asoc Cuba Bibl Bol
Asociacion Filatelica de Filipinas [*Philatelic Association of the Philippines*] ... AFF
Asociacion Folklorica Argentina. Anales [*A publication*] ... AFA
Asociacion Geologica Argentina. Monografia [*A publication*] ... Asoc Geol Argent Monogr
Asociacion Hispano-Islamica ... AHI
Asociacion para la Historia de la Ciencia Espanola [*A publication*] ... AHCE
Asociacion Iberoamericana de Camaras de Comercio [*Ibero-American Association of Chambers of Commerce - IAACC*] ... AICO
Asociacion de Industriales Latino-Americanos ... AILA
Asociacion de Ingenieros y Arquitectos de Mexico ... AIAM
Asociacion de Ingenieros del Uruguay. Revista de Ingenieria [*A publication*] ... Asoc Ing Uruguay Rev Ingenieria
Asociacion Interamericana de Bibliotecarios y Documentalistas Agricolas [*Interamerican Association of Agricultural Librarians and Documentalists*] ... AIBDA
Asociacion Interamericana pro Democracia y Libertad [*Interamerican Association for Democracy and Freedom*] ... AIDL
Asociacion Interamericana de Gastroenterologia [*Interamerican Association of Gastroenterology*] ... AIGE
Asociacion Interamericana de Ingeniera Sanitaria [*Inter-American Association of Sanitary Engineering*] ... AIDIS
Asociacion Interamericana de la Propiedad Industrial [*Interamerican Association of Industrial Property*] ... ASIPI
Asociacion Interamericana de Radiodifusion [*Interamerican Association of Broadcasters*] ... AIR
Asociacion Internacional de Beisbol Amateur [*International Association of Amateur Baseball*] ... AINBA
Asociacion Internacional de Derecho de Aguas [*International Association for Water Law - IAWL*] ... AIDA
Asociacion Internacional de Estructuras Laminares y Espaciales [*International Association for Shell and Spatial Structures*] ... AIEL
Asociacion Internacional de Estudio Integral del Deporte [*International Association of Sport Research*] ... AIEID
Asociacion Internacional de Fomento [*International Development Association*] ... AIF
Asociacion Internacional de Hispanistas ... AIH
Asociacion Internacional de los Profesores de Italiano [*International Association of Teachers of Italian*] ... AIPI
Asociacion Latinoamericana de Administracion Publica ... ALAP
Asociacion Latinoamericana de Derecho Aeronautico y Espacial ... ALADA
Asociacion Latinoamericana de Editores en Geociencias ... ALEGEO
Asociacion Latinoamericana de Educacion Agricola Superior ... ALEAS
Asociacion Latinoamericana de Entomologia. Publicacion [*A publication*] ... Asoc Latinoam Entomol Publ
Asociacion Latinoamericana de Escuelas de Bibliotecologia y Ciencias de la Informacion ... ALEBCI
Asociacion Latinoamericana de Ferrocarriles [*Latin American Railways Association*] ... ALAF
Asociacion Latinoamericana de Instituciones Financieras de Desarrollo ... ALIDE
Asociacion Latinoamericana de Libre Comercio [*Also, LAFTA*] [*Latin American Free Trade Association*] ... ALALC
Asociacion Latinoamericana de Produccion Animal ... ALPA
Asociacion Latinoamericana de Produccion Animal. Memoria [*A publication*] ... Asoc Latinoam Prod Anim Mem
Asociacion de Linguistica y Filologia de America Latina ... ALFAL
Asociacion Mexicana de Geofisicos de Exploracion. Boletin [*A publication*] ... Asoc Mexicana Geofisicos Explor Bol
Asociacion Mexicana de Geologos Petroleros. Boletin [*A publication*] ... Asoc Mex Geol Pet Bol
Asociacion Mexicana de Ingenieros Industriales [*Mexico*] ... AMII
Asociacion Mexicana de Investigacion de Operaciones y Administracion Cientifica [*Mexico*] ... AMIOAC
Asociacion Mundial Veterinaria de Avicola [*World Veterinary Poultry Association - WVPA*] ... AMVA
Asociacion Mundial Veterinaria de Pequenos Animales [*World Small Animal Veterinary Association - WSAVA*] ... AMVPA
Asociacion Mundial de Veterinarios Higienistas de los Alimentos [*World Association of Veterinary Food-Hygienists - WAVFH*] ... AMVHA
Asociacion Nacional de Bibliotecarios, Arquiveros, y Arqueologos [*Madrid*] [*A publication*] ... ANABA
Asociacion Nacional de Comerciantes y Industriales ... ANCI
Asociacion Nacional de Fomento Economico [*National Economic Development Association*] [*Costa Rica*] ... ANFE
Asociacion Nacional de Industriales [*National Association of Industrialists*] [*Colombia*] ... ANDI
Asociacion Nacional pro Personas Mayores [*National Association for Hispanic Elderly*] ... ANPPM
Asociacion de Tecnicos Azucareros de Cuba [*Cuban Association of Sugar Experts*] ... ATAC
Asociacion Universal de Federalistas Mundiales [*World Association of World Federalists*] ... AUFM
Asociacion pro Zarzuela en America ... APZA
Asociatiunea Reuniunilor Femeilor Ortodoxe Romane-Americane [*Association of Romanian-American Orthodox Ladies Auxiliaries*] ... ARFORA
Asomante [*A publication*] ... As
Asomante [*A publication*] ... Aso
Asosa [*Ethiopia*] [*Airport symbol*] ... ASO
Asosan [*Japan*] [*Seismograph station code, US Geological Survey*] ... ASJ
Asosiasi Perpustakaan, Arsip dan Dokumentasi Indonesia ... APADI
Asotin County Library, Clarkston, WA [*Library symbol*] ... WaCl
Asparagine [*One-letter symbol; see Asn*] ... A
Asparagine [*or Asp(NH_2)*] [*Also, N*] [*An amino acid*] ... Asn
Asparagine [*or Asn*] [*Also, N*] [*An amino acid*] ... Asp(NH_2)
Aspartame [*Sweetening agent*] ... APM
Aspartate Aminotransferase [*Also, AST, GOT*] [*An enzyme*] ... AAT
Aspartate Aminotransferase [*Also, AAT, GOT*] [*An enzyme*] ... AST
Aspartate Transcarbamylase [*Also, ATCase*] [*An enzyme*] ... ATC
Aspartate Transcarbamylase [*Also, ATC*] [*An enzyme*] ... ATCase
Aspartic Acid [*Also, D*] [*An amino acid*] ... Asp
Aspartic Acid [*or Asparagine*] [*Also, B*] [*An amino acid*] ... Asx
Aspartic Acid [*or Asparagine*] [*Also, Asx*] [*An amino acid*] [*Symbol*] ... B
Aspartic Acid [*One-letter symbol; see Asp*] ... D
Aspect Ratio ... AR
Aspects of Allergy and Applied Immunology [*A publication*] ... Aspects Allergy Appl Immunol
Aspects of Education [*A publication*] ... Aspects of Ed
Aspects of Education [*A publication*] ... Aspects Ed
Aspects of Plant Sciences [*A publication*] ... Aspects Plant Sci
Aspects Statistiques de la Region Parisienne [*A publication*] ... Aspects Statist Region Paris
Aspen [*Colorado*] [*Airport symbol*] ... ASE
Aspen Airways [*Air carrier designation symbol*] ... APN
Aspen Airways [*Denver, CO*] [*FAA designator*] ... ASP
Aspen Anthology [*A publication*] ... Aspen
Aspen Anthology [*A publication*] ... Aspen A
Aspen, CO [*Location identifier*] [*FAA*] ... BUK
Aspen, CO [*Radio station call letters*] ... KSNO
Aspen, CO [*Radio station call letters*] ... KSPN
Aspen, CO [*Location identifier*] [*FAA*] ... PKN
Aspen, CO [*Location identifier*] [*FAA*] ... RDY
Aspen Explorations Corp. [*NASDAQ symbol*] ... ASPN
Aspen Institute for Humanistic Studies ... AIHS
Aspen Law Center, Aspen, CO [*Library symbol*] ... CoAsL
Aspergillus niger [*Factor*] ... AN
Aspetti Letterari [*A publication*] ... ALet
Asphalt ... ASP
Asphalt ... ASPH
Asphalt Composition ... AC
Asphalt Emulsion Manufacturers Association ... AEMA
Asphalt Institute ... AI
Asphalt-Plank Floor ... ASPHPF
Asphalt Recycling and Reclaiming Association ... ARRA
Asphalt Roof Shingles [*Technical drawings*] ... ASPHRS
Asphalt Roofing Industry Bureau [*Later, ARMA*] ... ARIB
Asphalt Roofing Manufacturers' Association [*Formerly, ARIB*] ... ARMA
Asphalt-Tile Base [*Technical drawings*] ... ATB
Asphalt-Tile Floor [*Technical drawings*] ... ATF
Asphalt and Vinyl Asbestos Tile Institute [*Later, RFCI*] ... AVATI
Asphaltenic Bottom Cracking [*Hydrocarbon processing*] ... ABC
Asphaltic Concrete ... AC
Asphaltic Concrete Pavement ... ACP
Aspira of America ... AOA
Aspirator ... ASPRTR
Aspirin Foundation of America ... AFA

Aspirin Myocardial Infarction Study [*Medicine*] .... AMIS
Aspro, Inc. [*American Stock Exchange symbol*] [*Delisted*] .... ASP
ASR [*Automatizovane Systemy Rizeni*] **Bulletin INORGA** [*A publication*] .... ASR Bull INORGA
ASROC [*Antisubmarine Rocket*] **Missile Assembly** .... AMA
Assab [*Ethiopia*] [*Airport symbol*] .... ASA
Assamese [*MARC language code*] [*Library of Congress*] .... asm
Assassination Information Bureau [*An association*] .... AIB
Assateague Island National Seashore [*National Park Service designation*] .... ASIS
Assault [*FBI standardized term*] .... A
Assault .... ASLT
Assault Airlift Control Officer .... AACO
Assault and Battery .... A & B
Assault and Battery with Intent to Kill .... ABWIK
Assault Breaker .... AB
Assault Craft Unit .... ACU
Assault Crisis Center .... ACC
Assault with Deadly Weapon .... ADW
Assault Echelon .... AE
Assault Fire Command Console [*Army*] .... AFCC
Assault Fire Unit [*Army*] .... AFU
Assault Follow-On Echelon .... AFOE
Assault Gun .... ASLTG
Assault Gun Battalion .... AGB
Assault Helicopter Aircraft Carrier [*Navy symbol*] .... CVHA
Assault Helicopter Battalion [*Military*] .... AHB
Assault Helicopter Company [*Army*] .... AHC
Assault Helicopter Company [*Air Force*] .... AHCo
Assault Helicopter Support Company [*Air Force*] .... AHSCo
Assault to Kill [*FBI standardized term*] .... A to K
Assault Landing Zone .... ALZ
Assault Support Helicopter [*Military*] .... ASH
Assault Support Patrol Boat [*Navy symbol*] .... ASPB
Assault Vehicle, Royal Engineers [*British*] .... AVRE
Assaulting Federal Officer [*FBI standardized term*] .... AFO
Assay Ton .... AT
ASSE Journal [*A publication*] .... ASSE J
Asselin, Benoit, Boucher, Ducharme, & Lapointe, Inc., Montreal, PQ, Canada [*Library symbol*] .... CaQMABB
Assemble .... ASBL
Assemble .... ASSEM
Assemble and Checkout .... A/C
Assemble/Load .... A/L
Assemble and Test .... A & T
Assembled .... ASMBD
Assembled Air-Launched Weapon .... AALW
Assembled Electronic Component .... AEC
Assemblee de l'Atlantique Nord [*North Atlantic Assembly*] .... AAN
Assemblee des Franco-Americains/Association of Franco-Americans .... AFA
Assemblee Generale des Federations Internationales Sportives [*General Assembly of International Sports Federations*] .... AGFIS
Assemblee Generale Permanente des Comites Nationaux Olympiques [*Permanent General Assembly of National Olympic Committees*] .... AGP-CNO
Assemblee Mondiale de la Jeunesse [*World Assembly of Youth*] .... AMJ
Assemblee des Nations Captives d'Europe [*Assembly of Captive European Nations*] .... ANCE
Assemblee Parlementaire Europeenne .... APE
Assemblee Permanente des Chambres de Commerce et d'Industrie .... APCCI
Assembler [*Data processing*] .... ASM
Assemblies, Components, Spare Parts, and Materials .... ACSM
Assemblies of God Graduate School, Springfield, MO [*OCLC symbol*] .... MOG
Assemblies of God Graduate School, Springfield, MO [*Library symbol*] .... MoSpA
Assembling [*FBI standardized term*] .... ASMB
Assembly .... ASBLY
Assembly .... ASS
Assembly .... ASSY
Assembly Aid [*Tool*] .... ASAD
Assembly Area Command .... AAC
Assembly for Behavioral and Social Sciences [*National Research Council*] .... ABASS
Assembly Bill [*in state legislatures*] .... AB
Assembly Breakdown List .... ABL
Assembly of Captive European Nations .... ACEN
Assembly Control System [*IBM Corp.*] .... ACS
Assembly Coordination Advice .... ACA
Assembly Department Shortage List .... ADSL
Assembly Detail Purchased Parts .... ADPP
Assembly/Disassembly Facility .... A/D
Assembly District .... AD
Assembly Drawing .... AD
Assembly Engineering [*A publication*] .... Assem Eng
Assembly of Episcopal Hospitals and Chaplains .... AEHC
Assembly Facility Tool .... AFT
Assembly Fixture .... AF
Assembly Fixture [*Tool*] .... ASFX
Assembly Fixture Accessory .... AFA
Assembly of Governmental Employees .... AGE
Assembly, Handling, and Shipping Equipment .... AHSE
Assembly History Tag .... AHT
Assembly of Hospital Schools of Nursing .... AHSN
Assembly Identification Number .... AIN
Assembly Instruction Mnemonics [*Data processing*] .... AIM
Assembly Jig .... AJ
Assembly Language [*Data processing*] .... AL
Assembly Language Coding [*Data processing*] .... ALC
Assembly Language Program [*Data processing*] .... ALP
Assembly of Librarians of the Americas [*Defunct*] .... ALA
Assembly of Librarians of the Americas [*Defunct*] .... ALOA
Assembly List Shortage Log .... ALSL
Assembly Machine Fixture .... AMF
Assembly and Maintenance .... A & M
Assembly Management Operating System .... AMOS
Assembly of Mathematical and Physical Sciences [*National Research Council*] .... AMPS
Assembly of National Tourist Office Representatives in New York .... ANTOR
Assembly and Operations Plan .... AOP
Assembly Operations Record .... AOR
Assembly Order .... AO
Assembly Outline .... AO
Assembly Part List .... APL
Assembly of Parties [*INTELSAT*] .... AP
Assembly Production Order .... APO
Assembly Programing Language [*Data processing*] .... APL
Assembly Programing System [*Data processing*] .... APS
Assembly Quality Record .... AQR
Assembly and Repair .... A & R
Assembly Sequence Record Sheet - Work Sheet .... ASRSWS
Assembly Shortage Control .... ASC
Assembly and Structure Test .... AST
Assembly System for Central Processor [*Data processing*] .... ASCENT
Assembly System for the Peripheral Processors [*Data processing*] .... ASPER
Assembly and Test [*Aerospace*] .... A/T
Assembly and Test Area [*NASA*] .... ATA
Assembly and Test Pit [*Nuclear energy*] .... A & TP
Assembly Test Recording System .... ATRS
Assembly Tool .... ASTO
Assembly of Turkish American Associations .... ATAA
Assembly Work Schedule Order .... AWSO
Assembly Workstand [*NASA*] .... AW
Assented .... ASST
Assented .... AST
Assessment .... ASMT
Assessment .... ASSESMT
Assessment .... ASST
Assessment .... AST
Assessment Biological and Chemical [*Warfare*] .... ABC
Assessment Center [*Business and trade*] .... AC
Assessment of Children's Language Comprehension [*Education*] .... ACLC
Assessment of Combat Effectiveness [*Army*] .... ACE
Assessment for Community Care Services [*Health Care Financing Administration*] .... ACCESS
Assessment, Improvement, and Monitoring System [*School milk programs*] .... AIMS
Assessment Paid .... AP
Assessment of Performance Unit [*Education*] [*British*] .... APU
Assessment Statute Expiration Date [*IRS*] .... ASED
Assessment Subgroup [*NATO*] .... ASG
Asset [*or Availability*] **Balance File** [*Military*] .... ABF
Asset Control System [*or Subsystem*] [*Army*] .... ACS
Asset Depreciation Range [*IRS*] .... ADR
Asset Master Balance File [*Military*] .... AMBF
Asset Status Cards .... ASC
Assets Accounting [*Business and trade*] .... AA
Assets Management System .... AMS
Assiduously Capable Crossworder .... ACC
Assign .... ASG
Assign .... ASGN
Assign .... ASSN
Assignable Square Feet .... ASF
Assigned .... ASGD
Assigned Procurement Responsibility .... APR
Assigned Responsible Agency [*DoD*] .... ARA
Assigned Service Contractor .... ASC
Assignment .... ASGMT
Assignment Action Number .... AAN
Assignment Children [*A publication*] .... Assignment Chil
Assignment Control Authority [*Military*] .... ACA
Assignment Control Number [*Army*] .... ACN
Assignment Eligibility and Availability [*Military*] .... AEA
Assignment Instructions Remain Firm [*Army*] .... AIRF
Assignment Instructions Were Furnished Your Command .... AIFURC
Assignment Instructions Will Include MOS [*Military Occupational Specialty*] **within Army Career Group** .... AIMOSACGP
Assignment Memorandum [*Army*] .... AM

Assignment Oriented Training ... AOT
Assignment Selection Date [*Military*] ... ASD
Assimilated ... ASSIM
Assimilations per Second ... APS
Assimulatory Quotient ... AQ
Assist [*Sports*] ... A
Assist Card International [*An association*] ... ACI
Assist Order ... AO
Assist Ship's Force Funds [*Navy*] ... ASF
Assist Work Authorization ... AWA
Assistance for the Blind ... AB
Assistance Dogs International [*Defunct*] ... ADI
Assistance Information and Data Acquisition Center [*Navy*] ... AIDAC
Assistance-in-Kind [*Funds*] ... AIK
Assistance Payments [*Social Security Administration*] ... AP
Assistance Payments Administration [*Later, Office of Family Assistance*] [*Social Security Administration*] ... APA
Assistance Technique de l'Organisation des Nations Unies ... ATONU
Assistant ... ASS
Assistant ... ASSIST
Assistant ... ASST
Assistant Adjutant-General [*Military*] ... AAG
Assistant Adjutant and Quartermaster-General [*British*] ... AA & QMG
Assistant Air Attache [*British*] ... AAA
Assistant Air Force Postal Clerk ... AAFPC
Assistant [*US*] **Army Military Attache** ... AARMA
Assistant Base Operations Manager [*NASA*] ... ABOM
Assistant Beach Master [*British*] ... ABM
Assistant Camp Commandant [*British*] ... ACC
Assistant Captain [*Worn on assistant captains' uniforms*] [*Hockey*] ... A
Assistant Casework Supervisor [*Red Cross*] ... ACWS
Assistant Cashier [*Banking*] ... AC
Assistant Chaplain-General [*British*] ... ACG
Assistant Chief ... AC
Assistant Chief of Air Staff [*Army*] [*British*] ... AC of AS
Assistant Chief of Air Staff [*Army*] [*British*] ... ACAS
Assistant Chief of Air Staff (Intelligence) [*Army*] [*British*] ... ACAS(I)
Assistant Chief of Air Staff (Operations) [*Army*] [*British*] ... ACAS(O)
Assistant Chief of Air Staff (Policy) [*Army*] [*British*] ... ACAS(P)
Assistant Chief of Air Staff (Technical) [*Army*] [*British*] ... ACAS(T)
Assistant Chief of Air Staff (Technical Requirements) [*Army*] [*British*] ... ACAS(TR)
Assistant Chief, Chemical Warfare Service ... ACCWS
Assistant Chief of Defence Staff [*British*] ... ACDS
Assistant Chief of Fleet Support [*Navy*] [*British*] ... ACFS
Assistant Chief of the General Staff (Operational Requirements) [*British*] ... ACGS(OR)
Assistant Chief of the Imperial General Staff [*British*] ... ACIGS
Assistant Chief of Mission [*Foreign Service*] ... ACM
Assistant Chief of Mission Operations [*NASA*] ... ACMO
Assistant Chief of Naval Operations ... ACNO
Assistant Chief of Naval Operations (Transportation) ... ACNOT
Assistant Chief of the Naval Staff [*British*] ... ACNS
Assistant Chief of the Naval Staff (Air) [*British*] ... ACNS(A)
Assistant Chief Observer [*Navy*] ... ACHOBS
Assistant Chief Patrol Inspector [*Immigration and Naturalization Service*] ... ACPI
Assistant Chief for Research ... ACR
Assistant Chief of Staff ... ACOFS
Assistant Chief of Staff ... ACOS
Assistant Chief of Staff ... AC of S
Assistant Chief of Staff ... ACS
Assistant Chief of Staff, Air Force ... AC/SAF
Assistant Chief of Staff for Automation and Communications [*Military*] ... ACSAC
Assistant Chief of Staff for Communications - Electronics [*Army*] ... ACSC-E
Assistant Chief of Staff for Force Development [*Army*] ... ACSFOR
Assistant Chief of Staff, Intelligence ... ACINTEL
Assistant Chief of Staff for Intelligence [*Army*] ... ACSI
Assistant Chief of Staff, Logistics ... ACLOG
Assistant Chief of Staff, Organization and Training Division ... ACOT
Assistant Chief of Staff, Plans and Policy Division ... ACPANDP
Assistant Chief of Staff, Programs Division ... ACPROG
Assistant Chief of Staff for Reserve Components [*Army*] ... ACSRC
Assistant Chief of Staff, Studies and Analysis [*Air Force*] ... ACS/S & A
Assistant Chief of Staff for Studies and Analysis [*Air Force*] ... CSA
Assistant Chief of Transportation [*Army*] ... AC of T
Assistant Civil Engineer Adviser [*Military*] [*British*] ... ACEA
Assistant Combat Information Center Officer ... ACICO
Assistant Commandant [*Coast Guard*] ... CA
Assistant Commissary General ... ACG
Assistant-Commissary-General [*British*] ... Ass Com Gen
Assistant Commissioner ... AC
Assistant Controller of the Navy [*British*] ... AC of N
Assistant Controller, Personnel and Logistics [*Navy*] [*British*] ... ACPL
Assistant Controller, Research and Development [*Admiralty*] [*British*] ... AC(R & D)
Assistant County Architect [*British*] ... ACA
Assistant Data Recording System Analyst ... ADRSA
Assistant Defense Counsel ... ADC
Assistant Deputy Chief of Staff for Logistics [*Army*] ... ADCSLOG
Assistant and Deputy Director of Naval Recruiting [*British*] ... ADDNR
Assistant Deputy Judge Advocate General [*Military*] [*British*] ... ADJAG
Assistant Deputy Military Governor [*US Military Government, Germany*] ... ADMG
Assistant for Development Planning [*Air Force*] ... AFDAP
Assistant Director ... AD
Assistant Director of Administrative Planning [*Military*] [*British*] ... ADAP
Assistant Director of Army Psychiatry [*British*] ... ADAP
Assistant Director of Army Welfare Services [*British*] ... ADAWS
Assistant Director of Artillery [*British*] ... ADA
Assistant Director of Contracts [*Military*] [*British*] ... ADC
Assistant Director of Dental Services ... ADDS
Assistant Director for Education [*Vietnam*] ... ADEDU
Assistant Director of Expense Accounts [*Navy*] [*British*] ... ADEA
Assistant Director, Flight Operations [*NASA*] ... ADFO
Assistant Director of Fortifications and Works [*Military*] [*British*] ... ADFW
Assistant Director-General [*British*] ... ADG
Assistant Director-General of Medical Services [*Military*] [*British*] ... ADGMS
Assistant Director of Hygiene [*Military*] [*British*] ... ADH
Assistant Director of Intelligence, Department K [*Air Ministry*] [*British*] ... ADI(K)
Assistant Director for Legal and Legislative Affairs [*Obsolete*] [*National Security Agency*] ... ADLA
Assistant Director of Medical Services ... ADMS
Assistant Director of Naval Accounts [*British*] ... ADNA
Assistant Director of Naval Construction [*British*] ... ADNC
Assistant Director of Naval Intelligence [*British*] ... ADNI
Assistant Director of Ordnance Factories [*Ministry of Supply*] [*British*] [*World War II*] ... ADOF
Assistant Director of Ordnance Services [*British*] ... ADOS
Assistant Director of Pathology [*Military*] [*British*] ... ADP
Assistant Director for Plans and Resources [*Obsolete*] [*National Security Agency*] ... ADPR
Assistant Director for Policy and Liaison [*Obsolete*] [*National Security Agency*] ... ADPL
Assistant Director of Public Relations [*Military*] [*British*] ... ADPR
Assistant Director of Supplies and Transport [*Military*] [*British*] ... ADS & T
Assistant Director for Training [*National Security Agency*] ... ADT
Assistant Director of Veterinary Services [*Military*] [*British*] ... ADVS
Assistant Director of Works, Electrical and Mechanical [*Military*] [*British*] ... ADWE & M
Assistant District Attorney ... ADA
Assistant Division Commander [*Military*] ... ADC
Assistant Division Communications Electronics Officer [*Military*] ... ADCEO
Assistant Division Engineer [*Army*] ... ADE
Assistant Division Supply Officer [*Army*] ... ADSO
Assistant Engineer ... AE
Assistant Experimental Officer [*Ministry of Agriculture, Fisheries, and Food*] [*Also, AExO, AXO*] [*British*] ... AEO
Assistant Experimental Officer [*Ministry of Agriculture, Fisheries, and Food*] [*Also, AEO, AXO*] [*British*] ... AExO
Assistant Experimental Officer [*Ministry of Agriculture, Fisheries, and Food*] [*Also, AEO, AExO*] [*British*] ... AXO
Assistant Field Director [*Red Cross*] ... AFD
Assistant Fighter Director Office [*Navy*] ... AFDO
Assistant Fire Support Coordinator [*Military*] ... AFSCOORD
Assistant Flight Director [*NASA*] ... AFD
Assistant Flight Dynamics Officer [*NASA*] ... AFDO
Assistant Freight Traffic Manager ... AFTM
Assistant General Freight Agent ... AGFA
Assistant General Manager [*AEC*] ... AGM
Assistant General Manager for Administration [*AEC*] ... AGMA
Assistant General Manager for International Activities [*AEC*] ... AGMIA
Assistant General Manager for Operations [*AEC*] ... AGMO
Assistant General Manager for Plans and Production [*AEC*] ... AGMPP
Assistant General Manager for Research and Development [*AEC*] ... AGMRD
Assistant Grand Director of Ceremonies [*Masonry*] ... AGDC
Assistant Grand Sojourner [*Masonry*] ... AGS
Assistant House Physician ... AHP
Assistant House Surgeon ... AHS
Assistant Industrial Manager [*of Naval District*] ... AIM
Assistant Industrial Manager [*of Naval District*] ... ASTINDMAN
Assistant Inspector General [*Military*] ... AIG
Assistant Inspector of Naval Materiel ... AINM
Assistant Inspector of Naval Materiel ... AINSMAT
Assistant Inspector of Naval Ordnance ... AINO
Assistant Inspector of Physical Training [*Military*] [*British*] ... AIPT
Assistant Instrumentation Operations Coordination ... AIOC
Assistant Judge Advocate General [*Army*] ... AJAG
[*The*] **Assistant Judge Advocate General** [*Army*] ... TAJAG
Assistant Judge Advocate General for Civil Law [*Army*] ... AJAG/CIV
Assistant Judge Advocate General for Military Law [*Army*] ... AJAG/MIL
Assistant Laboratory Director ... ALD
Assistant Librarian [*A publication*] ... Assist Libn
Assistant Librarian [*A publication*] ... Asst Libn
Assistant Manager ... AM
Assistant Marshal of the Diplomatic Corps [*British*] ... AMDC
Assistant Master-General of Ordnance [*British*] ... AMGO

Assistant for Materiel Program Control [*Air Force*] .... AFMPC
Assistant Medical Officer .... AMO
Assistant Military Secretary [*British*] .... AMS
Assistant Missile Flight Safety Officer .... AMFSO
Assistant Naval Stores Officer .... ANSO
Assistant Navy Mail Clerk .... ANMC
Assistant Network Controller [*NASA*] .... ANC
Assistant Network Operations Manager [*NASA*] .... ANOM
Assistant Officer in Charge [*DoD*] .... AOIC
Assistant Operations Director .... AOD
Assistant Paymaster .... AP
Assistant Paymaster [*Marine Corps*] .... APM
Assistant Postmaster-General [*British*] .... APMG
Assistant in Private Practice [*Chiropody*] [*British*] .... P
Assistant Private Secretary to the First Sea Lord [*Navy*] [*British*] .... APSFSL
Assistant Project Engineer .... APE
Assistant Project Manager [*NASA*] .... APM
Assistant Project Manager for Business Administration .... APMBA
Assistant Project Officer .... APO
Assistant Provost Marshal [*Initialism also facetiously translated as "A Permanent Malingerer"*] .... APM
Assistant Public Works Officer .... APWO
Assistant Quartermaster .... AQM
Assistant Quartermaster-General [*Military*] .... AQMG
Assistant Regional Commissioner [*IRS*] .... ARC
Assistant Regional Manager .... ARM
Assistant Research Officer [*Ministry of Agriculture, Fisheries, and Food*] [*British*] .... ARO
Assistant Secretary .... AS
Assistant Secretary for Administration and Management [*Department of Labor*] .... ASAM
Assistant Secretary of the Air Force .... AS of AF
Assistant Secretary of the Air Force .... ASOFAF
Assistant Secretary of the Air Force .... ASTSECAF
Assistant Secretary of the Air Force (Manpower and Personnel) .... SAFMP
Assistant Secretary of the Air Force (Materiel) .... ASAFMA
Assistant Secretary of the Air Force (Research and Development) .... SAFRD
Assistant Secretary of the Army .... AS of A
Assistant Secretary of the Army .... ASA
[*The*] **Assistant Secretary of the Army** .... TASA
Assistant Secretary of the Army (Civil Works) .... ASA(CW)
Assistant Secretary of the Army (Financial Management) .... ASA (FM)
Assistant Secretary of the Army (Financial Management) .... OASA (FM)
Assistant Secretary of the Army (Installations and Logistics) .... ASA (I & L)
Assistant Secretary of the Army (Installations and Logistics) .... OASA (I & L)
Assistant Secretary of the Army (Installations, Logistics, and Financial Management) .... ASA(IL & FM)
Assistant Secretary of the Army (Manpower and Reserve Affairs) .... ASA (M & RA)
Assistant Secretary of the Army (Research and Development) .... ASA (R & D)
Assistant Secretary of the Army (Research and Development) .... OASA (R & D)
Assistant Secretary, Controller [*Admiralty*] [*British*] .... AS(C)
Assistant Secretary of Defense .... ASD
Assistant Secretary of Defense (Administration) .... ASD (A)
Assistant to the Secretary of Defense (Atomic Energy) .... ATSD (AE)
Assistant Secretary of Defense (Civil Defense) .... ASD (CD)
Assistant Secretary of Defense (Communications, Command-Control, and Intelligence) .... ASD(C3I)
Assistant Secretary of Defense (Comptroller) .... ASD (C)
Assistant Secretary of Defense (Health Affairs) .... ASD(HA)
Assistant Secretary of Defense (Health and Environment) .... ASD (H & E)
Assistant Secretary of Defense (Health and Medical) .... ASD/H & M
Assistant Secretary of Defense (Installations and Logistics) .... ASD (I & L)
Assistant Secretary of Defense (Intelligence) .... ASD (I)
Assistant Secretary of Defense (International Security Affairs) .... ASD/ISA
Assistant Secretary of Defense (Manpower) .... ASD (M)
Assistant Secretary of Defense (Manpower, Personnel, and Reserves) .... ASD/MP & R
Assistant Secretary of Defense (Manpower and Reserve Affairs) [*Later, ASD (MRA & L)*] .... ASD (M & RA)
Assistant Secretary of Defense (Manpower, Reserve Affairs, and Logistics) [*Formerly, ASD(M & RA)*] .... ASD(MRA & L)
Assistant Secretary of Defense (Program Analysis and Evaluation) .... ASD (PA & E)
Assistant Secretary of Defense (Properties and Installations) .... ASD/P & I
Assistant Secretary of Defense (Public Affairs) .... ASD (PA)
Assistant Secretary of Defense (Research and Development) .... ASD/R & D
Assistant Secretary of Defense (Research and Engineering) .... ASD/R & E
Assistant to the Secretary of Defense (Review and Oversight) .... ATSD(R & O)
Assistant Secretary of Defense (Supply and Logistics) .... ASD/S & L
Assistant Secretary of Defense (Systems Analysis) .... ASD (SA)
Assistant Secretary of Defense (Telecommunications) .... ASD (T)
Assistant Secretary for Employment Standards [*Department of Labor*] .... ASES
Assistant Secretary for Employment and Training [*Department of Labor*] .... ASET
Assistant Secretary General .... ASG
Assistant Secretary General .... ASYG
Assistant Secretary General for Air Navigation [*ICAO*] .... ASGAN
Assistant Secretary of the General Staff .... ASGS
Assistant Secretary for Health [*HEW*] .... ASH
Assistant Secretary for Labor-Management Relations [*Department of Labor*] .... ASLMR
Assistant Secretary of the Navy .... ASN
Assistant Secretary of the Navy .... ASTSECNAV
Assistant Secretary of the Navy for Air .... ASTSECNAVAIR
Assistant Secretary of the Navy (Financial Management) .... ASN (FM)
Assistant Secretary of the Navy (Financial Management) .... ASTSECNAVFIN
Assistant Secretary of the Navy (Installation and Logistics) .... ASN(I & L)
Assistant Secretary of the Navy (Installation and Logistics) .... ASTSECNAVINSLOG
Assistant Secretary of the Navy (Research and Development) .... ASN(R & D)
Assistant Secretary of the Navy (Research and Development) .... ASTSECNAVRESDEV
Assistant Secretary for Occupational Safety and Health [*Department of Labor*] .... ASOSH
Assistant Secretary for Policy Evaluation and Research [*Department of Labor*] .... ASPER
Assistant Secretary of War .... ASW
Assistant Secretary of War for Air [*World War II*] .... ASWA
Assistant Secretary's Office [*Navy*] .... ASO
Assistant Section Officer [*Air Force*] [*British*] .... ASO
Assistant Special Agent in Charge .... ASAIC
Assistant Staff Duty Officer .... ASDO
Assistant Staff Judge Advocate [*Air Force*] .... ASJA
Assistant Staff Meteorologist [*NASA*] .... ASM
Assistant Stage Manager .... ASM
Assistant State Director .... ASD
Assistant Superintendent, Range Operations [*NASA*] .... ASRO
Assistant Supervisor of Shipbuilding [*Navy*] .... ASOS
Assistant Test Chief .... ATC
Assistant Test Conductor .... ATC
Assistant Test Director .... ATD
Assistant Town Clerk [*British*] .... ATC
Assistant Traffic Manager .... ATM
Assistant Transmission Controller .... ATC
Assistant Trial Counsel .... ATC
Assistant Under-Secretary, General [*Air Ministry*] [*British*] .... AUS(G)
Assistant Veterans Employment Representative [*Department of Labor*] .... AVER
Assistant Vice Chief of Staff .... AVCS
Assistant Vice Chief of Staff, Army [*Formerly, AVC of SA*] .... AVCSA
Assistant Vice Chief of Staff, Army [*Later, AVCSA*] .... AVC of SA
Assistant Weapons Control Officer .... AWCO
Assistant Yard Master [*British railroad term*] .... AYM
Assisted Health Insurance Plan .... AHIP
Assisted Takeoff [*British aviation and rocket term*] .... ATO
Assisted Takeoff System .... ATOS
Assistenza Sociale [*A publication*] .... Assist Soc
Assisting .... ASSTG
Assisting Work Center .... AWC
Assiut University. Faculty of Science. Bulletin [*A publication*] .... Assiut Univ Fac Sci Bull
Assize Rolls [*British*] .... ASS
Associacao de Assistencia a Crianca Defeituosa .... AACD
Associacao Brasileira de Credito e Assistencia Rural [*Brazilian Association of Credit and Rural Assistance*] .... ABCAR
Associacao Brasileira de Imprensa [*Brazilian press association*] .... ABI
Associacao Brasileira de Normas Technicas [*Brazilian national standards organization*] .... ABNT
Associacao Brasileira de Refrigeracao, Ar Condicionado, Ventilacao, e Aquecimento [*Brazil*] .... ABRAVA
Associacao de Credito e Assistencia Rural [*Association of Credit and Rural Assistance*] [*Brazil*] .... ACAR
Associacao de Educacao Catolica do Brasil .... AEC
Associacao dos Geografos Brasileiros .... AGB
Associacao Latino-Americana de Direito Agrario .... ALADA
Associate [*In an academic degree*] .... A
Associate .... ASSO
Associate [*or Association*] .... ASSOC
Associate in Accountancy, University of Queensland [*Australia*] .... AAUQ
Associate of Accountants' and Executives' Corporation of Canada .... AAE
Associate in Accounting .... AA
Associate in Administration .... A Adm
Associate Administrator [*NASA*] .... AA
Associate Administrator for Administration [*FAA*] .... AAD
Associate Administrator for Air Traffic and Airway Facilities [*FAA*] .... ATF
Associate Administrator for Airports [*FAA*] .... AAP
Associate Administrator for Aviation Safety [*FAA*] .... ASA
Associate Administrator for Engineering and Development [*FAA*] .... AED
Associate Administrator for Information Systems [*Social and Rehabilitation Service, HEW*] .... AAIS
Associate Administrator for Management [*Social and Rehabilitation Service, HEW*] .... AA/M
Associate Administrator for Manned Space Flight [*NASA*] .... AA/MSF

Associate Administrator for Policy Development and Review [*FAA*] ..... APD
Associate in Aeronautical Engineering .... A Ae E
Associate in Agriculture .... A Agri
Associate in Air-Conditioning and Refrigeration Technology ....
AA-C & Ref Tech
Associate of American Guild of Organists .... AAGO
Associate of the American Institute of Electrical Engineers .... AAIEE
Associate of the American Institute of Mining and Metallurgical
Engineers .... AAIMME
Associate of the American Institute of Physics........................ AAIP
Associate of the American Society of Mechanical Engineers........... AASME
Associate in Applied Arts .... AAA
Associate in Applied Science .... AAS
Associate in Architecture ....A Arch
Associate in Arts .... AA
Associate in Arts in Agriculture .... AA Ag
Associate in Arts in Arts and Science .... AAA & S
Associate in Arts in Business .... AAB
Associate in Arts in Business .... AA Bus
Associate in Arts in Fine Arts....................................AAFA
Associate in Arts in Home Economics............................AAHE
Associate in Arts in Law Enforcement .... AALE
Associate in Arts in Liberal Arts .... AALA
Associate in Arts in Music...................................... AAMus
Associate in Arts in Nursing....................................AAN
Associate in Arts in Terminal Education .... AA Ter Ed
Associate of Association of Certified and Corporate
Accountants [*British*] .... AACCA
Associate of the Association of International Accountants [*British*] ..... AAIA
Associate of the Australian Society of Accountants.................... AASA
Associate in Automotive Technology .... AA Tech
Associate in Aviation Technology................................ A Av Tech
Associate of the Birmingham and Midland Institute School of
Music [*British*]....................................... ABSM
Associate of the British Ballet Organisation .... ABBO
Associate of the British Institution of Radio Engineers .... Assoc Brit IRE
Associate of the British Psychological Society .... AB Ps S
Associate of the British Society of Commerce .... ABSC
Associate in Business .... AB
Associate in Business Administration................................ ABA
Associate in Business Administration.............................. ABus
Associate in Business Management .... ABM
Associate in Business Management .... ASBM
Associate in Business Science .... ABS
Associate in Business Technology .... ABT
Associate of the Camborne School of Mines [*British*]............ ACSM
Associate of the Canadian College of Organists .... ACCO
Associate of Canadian Institute of Chemistry.................... ACIC
Associate of the Casualty Actuarial Society .... ACAS
Associate of the Chartered Auctioneers' and Estate Agents'
Institute [*British*]..................................... AAI
Associate of the Chartered Institute of Secretaries [*British*]
[*Later, Institute of Chartered Secretaries and Administrators*].......... ACIS
Associate of the Chartered Insurance Institute [*British*] .... ACII
Associate of the Chartered Land Agents' Society [*British*] .... ALAS
Associate in Chemistry....................................... A Chem
Associate Citizens for Responsible Education [*Group opposing
sex education in schools*] .... ACRE
Associate of the City and Guilds of London Institute [*British*]................. ACGI
Associate Client Program [*Business International Corp.*]
[*Information service*].................................. ACP
Associate of the College of Preceptors [*British*]..................... ACP
Associate of the College of Technology [*British*] .... ACT
Associate, College of Violinists................................ ACV
Associate Collegiate Players .... ACP
Associate in Commerce .... AC
Associate in Commerce ....A Com
Associate in Commercial Arts .... ACA
Associate in Commercial Education .... AC Ed
Associate in Commercial Science .... ACS
Associate Committee on Aviation Medical Research [*Canada*]........ ACAMR
Associate Committee of Geodesy and Geophysics [*Canada*].............. ACGG
Associate Contractor... AC
Associate Contractor [*NASA*]................................ A/C
Associate Contractor Agreements .... ACA
Associate Contractor Program Manager [*NASA*]................. ACPM
Associate Contractor Projects Office [*NASA*].................. ACPO
Associate of the Corporation of Insurance Brokers [*British*]................ ACIB
Associate in Criminal Justice................................... ACJ
Associate Degree.. AD
Associate Degree Completion Program [*Navy*]................. ADCOP
Associate in Diesel Technology .... A Dies Tech
Associate Director .... AD
Associate Directorate for Design [*Kennedy Space Center*] [*NASA*] .... DD
Associate Directorate for Facilities and Systems Management
[*Kennedy Space Center*] [*NASA*].......................... DF
Associate Directorate for LPS [*Launch Processing System*]
Development [*Kennedy Space Center*] [*NASA*] .... DL
Associate in Drafting and Design............................ A Dr & Dgn
Associate in Education... AE
Associate in Education.......................................A Ed

Associate of the Educational Institute of Scotland................................ AEIS
Associate in Electrical Technology................................ AET
Associate in Elementary Education .... A El Ed
Associate in Engineering..................................... AE
Associate in Engineering....................................... AEE
Associate in Engineering....................................A Eng
Associate in Engineering................................... A Engr
Associate in Engineering..................................... ASE
Associate in Engineering Administration.......................... AEA
Associate in Engineering Electronics.......................... A Eng Elect
Associate in Engineering Technology .... AET
Associate in English .... A En
Associate Engraver, Royal Academy [*British*] .... AERA
Associate of the Faculty of Actuaries [*British*] .... AFA
Associate of the Faculty of Architects and Surveyors [*British*]........... AFAS
Associate of the Faculty of Astrological Studies [*British*]............. AFAS
Associate of the Faculty of Physiatrics [*British*]................ AFPhys
Associate of the Federal Institute of Accountants [*Australia*]............... AFIA
Associate Fellow of the American Institute of Aeronautics and
Astronautics [*Formerly, AFIAS*]........................... AFAIAA
Associate Fellow of the Canadian Aeronautical Institute.................. AFCAI
Associate Fellow of the Institute of Aeronautical Sciences
[*Later, AFAIAA*] .... AFIAS
Associate Fellow of the Institute of Civil Defence [*British*]................. AFICD
Associate Fellow of the Institute of Petroleum [*British*]............... AF Inst Pet
Associate Fellow of the Royal Aeronautical Society [*British*]........... AFR Ae S
Associate Fellow of the Royal Aeronautical Society [*British*].............. AFRAS
Associate in Fine Arts... AFA
Associate in Fine Arts in Art................................ AFA Art
Associate in Fine Arts in Dance .... AFA Dance
Associate in Fine Arts in Drama .... AFA Drama
Associate in Fine Arts in Music.............................. AFA Mus
Associate in General Education .... AGE
Associate in General Education .... A in G Ed
Associate in General Education .... AGEd
Associate in General Studies .... AGS
Associate of the Guildhall School of Music [*British*] .... AGSM
Associate of Heriot-Watt College, Edinburgh .... AH-WC
Associate in Home Economics................................ AHE
Associate in Home Economics................................AH Ec
Associate of the Imperial College of Tropical Agriculture [*British*]...... AICTA
Associate of Incorporated Secretaries Association .... AISA
Associate in Industrial Education .... AI Ed
Associate in Industrial Management .... AIM
Associate in Industrial Management .... ASIM
Associate Infantry Officer Career Course [*Army*] .... AIOCC
Associate of the Institute of Actuaries [*British*]................. AIA
Associate of the Institute of Arbitrators [*British*] .... AI Arb
Associate of the Institute of Automobile Engineers [*British*]............ AIAE
Associate of the Institute of Bankers [*British*]................. AIB
Associate of the Institute of British Decorators .... AIBD
Associate of the Institute of British Photographers................. AIBP
Associate of the Institute of Builders [*British*]................. AIOB
Associate of the Institute of Ceramics [*British*] .... AI Ceram
Associate of the Institute of Certificated Grocers [*British*]................. AGI
Associate of the Institute of Chartered Accountants [*British*]............. ACA
Associate of the Institute of Chartered Shipbrokers [*British*]............ AICS
Associate of the Institute of Chemistry [*Later, ARIC*] [*British*] .... AIC
Associate of the Institute of Civil Engineers [*British*]................. AICE
Associate of the Institute of Cost and Management Accountants
[*British*] .... ACMA
Associate of the Institute of Cost and Works Accountants [*British*] ....ACWA
Associate of the Institute of Electrical Engineers [*British*] .... AIEE
Associate of the Institute of Hospital Almoners [*British*]................. AIHA
Associate of the Institute of Information Scientists [*British*]............ AI Inf Sc
Associate of the Institute of Landscape Architects [*British*]............. AILA
Associate of the Institute of Linguists [*British*] .... AIL
Associate of the Institute of Marine Engineers [*British*] ....AI Mar E
Associate of the Institute of Marine Engineers [*British*] .... AIME
Associate of the Institute of Marketing and Sales Management
[*British*] .... A Inst MSM
Associate of the Institute of Mechanical Engineers.................... AIME
Associate of the Institute of Mining Engineers .... AIME
Associate of the Institute of Mining and Metallurgy [*British*]..............
Assoc Inst MM
Associate of the Institute of Municipal Treasurers and
Accountants [*British*] .... AIMTA
Associate of the Institute of Naval Architects.................... AINA
Associate of the Institute of Patentees and Inventors [*British*] .... AInstPI
Associate of the Institute of Physics and the Physical Society
[*British*].. AInstP
Associate of the Institute of the Rubber Industry [*British*]....................... AIRI
Associate of the Institute of Statisticians [*Later, MIS*] [*British*]............ AIS
Associate of the Institute of Structural Engineers [*British*]........... AI Struct E
Associate of the Institution of Certified Public Accountants
[*British*] .... ACPA
Associate of the Institution of Electrical Engineers [*British*]......... Assoc IEE
Associate of the Institution of Electronic and Radio Engineers
[*British*] .... AIERE
Associate of the Institution of Fire Engineers [*British*] .... AIFireE
Associate of the Institution of Locomotive Engineers [*British*]........ AI Loco E

Associate of the Institution of Mechanical Engineers [*British*]....... AI Mech E
Associate of the Institution of Mechanical Engineers [*British*]........... AIMEE
Associate of the Institution of Mechanical Engineers [*British*]...................
Assoc I Min E
Associate of the Institution of Metallurgists [*British*].....................AIM
Associate of the Institution of Mining and Metallurgy [*British*].............AIMM
Associate of the Institution of Naval Architects [*British*]..............Assoc INA
Associate of the Institution of Production Engineers [*British*] ....AIPE
Associate of the Insurance Institute of America ....AIIA
Associate of the Insurance Institute of Canada ....AIIC
Associate of Iron and Steel Institute...............................AISI
Associate of the Iron and Steel Institute [*British*]...................AssocISI
Associate Jewelers [*Defunct*].......................................AJ
Associate in Journalism ....AJ
Associate Justice [*US Supreme Court*]..............................AJ
Associate of King's College [*London*].............................AKC
Associate of King's College London................................AKCL
Associate in Letters ....A Litt
Associate in Letters, Arts, and Sciences ....ALAS
Associate in Liberal Arts ....ALA
Associate of the Library Association [*British*] ....ALA
Associate of the Library Association of Australia.....................ALAA
Associate of the Linnaean Society [*British*].........................ALS
Associate in Literature ....A Lit
Associate Logistics Executive Development Course ....ALEDC
Associate of the London Association of Certified and Corporate
  Accountants [*British*] ....ALAA
Associate of the London College of Divinity [*British*]...............ALCD
Associate of the London College of Music [*British*] ....ALCM
Associate of Manchester College of Technology [*British*]...........AMCT
Associate in Mechanical Technology ....AMT
Associate in Medical Technology ....AMT
Associate Member...AM
Associate Member of the American Society of Civil Engineers................
AM Am Soc CE
Associate Member of the American Society of Mechanical
  Engineers ....AMASME
Associate Member of the Australian Institute of Mining and
  Metallurgy ....AM Aus IMM
Associate Member of the British Institute of Management...............AMBIM
Associate Member of the British Institution of Radio Engineers
  [*Later, AMIERE*]...AM Brit IRE
Associate Member of the Commonwealth Institute of
  Accountants [*British*] ....AICA
Associate Member of Engineering Institute of Canada..................AMEIC
Associate Member of Institute of Accredited Public Accountants.........APA
Associate Member of the Institute of Electronics [*British*].............AM Inst E
Associate Member of the Institute of Export [*British*]................AMIEx
Associate Member of the Institute of Fuel [*British*]...............AM Inst F
Associate Member of the Institute of Marine Engineers [*British*]................
AMI Mar E
Associate Member of the Institute of the Motor Industry [*British*].......AMIMI
Associate Member of the Institute of Plant Engineers [*British*].................
AMI Plant E
Associate Member of the Institute of Radio and Electronic
  Engineers (Australia) ....AMIREE (Aust)
Associate Member of the Institute of Refrigeration [*British*]............ AMInstR
Associate Member of the Institute of Structural Engineers
  [*British*] ....AMIStruct E
Associate Member of the Institute of Transport [*British*] ....AMInstT
Associate Member of the Institute of Water Engineers [*British*] ....
AMI Water E
Associate Member of the Institute of Welding [*British*] ....AM Inst W
Associate Member of the Institute of Welding [*British*] ....AMIW
Associate Member of the Institute of Work Study Practitioners
  [*British*] ....AIWSP
Associate Member of Institution of Aeronautical Engineers
  [*British*] ....AMI Ae E
Associate Member of the Institution of Aeronautical Engineers
  [*British*] ....AssocMIAeE
Associate Member of the Institution of Agricultural Engineers
  [*British*] ....AMIAgrE
Associate Member of the Institution of British Engineers.............AMInstBE
Associate Member of the Institution of Chemical Engineers
  [*British*] ....AMI Chem E
Associate Member of the Institution of Civil Engineers [*Later,
  MICE*] [*British*]..AMICE
Associate Member of the Institution of Civil Engineers [*British*] ... AMInstCE
Associate (Member) of the Institution of Civil Engineers [*British*]................
Assoc (M) Inst CE
Associate Member of the Institution of Electrical Engineers
  [*Later, MIEE*] [*British*] .... AMIEE
Associate Member of the Institution of Electronic and Radio
  Engineers [*Formerly, AM Brit IRE*] [*British*] ....AMIERE
Associate Member of the Institution of Engineering Designers
  [*British*] ....AMIED
Associate Member of the Institution of Engineers of Australia..... AMIE Aust
Associate Member of the Institution of Fire Engineers [*British*] ..... AMIFireE
Associate Member of the Institution of Gas Engineers [*British*] ..... AMIGasE
Associate Member of the Institution of Locomotive Engineers
  [*British*] ....AMILocoE

Associate Member of the Institution of Mechanical Engineers
  [*Later, MIMechE*] [*British*]................................AMIMechE
Associate Member of the Institution of Mining Engineers [*British*] ....AMIME
Associate Member of the Institution of Mining Engineers
  [*British*] ....AMIMinE
Associate Member of the Institution of Mining and Metallurgy
  [*British*] ....AMIMM
Associate Member of the Institution of Naval Architects [*British*] ......AMINA
Associate Member of the Institution of Production Engineers
  [*British*] ....AMIPE
Associate Member of the Institution of Works Managers [*British*].... AMIWM
Associate Member of the International Institute of Arts and Letters .....AIAL
Associate Member of the Nautical Institute [*British*] ....AMNI
Associate Member of the Royal Institution of Naval Architects
  [*British*] ....AMRINA
Associate Member of the Royal School of Church Music [*British*].....ARSCM
Associate Member of the Royal Society of Health [*Formerly,
  ARSH*] [*British*]...AMRSH
Associate Member of the Town Planning Institute [*British*] ....AMTPI
Associate in Metallurgy [*British*]..................................A Met
Associate of the Museums Association [*British*]......................AMA
Associate in Music ....AMus
Associate, National Academician ....ANA
Associate of the National Academy of Design ....ANA
Associate of the New Zealand Institute of Chemistry.................ANZIC
Associate of the Non-Destructive Testing Society [*British*] ....ANDTS
Associate of the Normal School of Science ....ANSS
Associate of the Northeast Coast Institution of Engineers and
  Shipbuilders [*British*]...................................ANECInst
Associate in Nursing.. AN
Associate in Nursing..ASN
Associate in Nursing Science..ASN
Associate in Philosophy ....A Ph
Associate in Physical Education ....AP Ed
Associate of the Plastics Institute [*British*]..........................API
Associate in Practical Arts ....APA
Associate of the Psychological Society of Ireland....................APsSI
Associate in Public Administration ....APA
Associate in Public Service Technology ....APST
Associate Pulmonary Technologist [*Academic degree*]................A-Put
Associate of Queen's College [*London*]..............................AQC
Associate in Recreation Leadership ....ARL
Associate Regional Administrator ....ARA
Associate in Religion ....A Rel
Associate in Religious Arts..ARA
Associate in Religious Education ....ARE
Associate in Retailing ....AR
Associate of the Royal Academy [*British*]............................ARA
Associate of the Royal Academy of Dancing [*British*]................ARAD
Associate of the Royal Academy of Music [*British*]..................ARAM
Associate of the Royal Aeronautical Society [*British*]...............ARAeS
Associate of the Royal Astronomical Society [*British*]................ARAS
Associate of the Royal Australian Chemical Institute.................ARACI
Associate of the Royal British Colonial Society of Artists..............ARBC
Associate of the Royal Cambrian Academy [*British*] ....ARCamA
Associate of the Royal Canadian Academy ....ARCA
Associate of the Royal College of Advanced Technology [*British*] ....
Assoc RCATS
Associate of the Royal College of Art [*British*]......................ARCA
Associate of the Royal College of Dancing [*British*].................ARCD
Associate of the Royal College of Music [*British*]..................ARCM
Associate of the Royal College of Organists [*British*]...............ARCO
Associate of the Royal College of Organists (Choir-Training
  Diploma) [*British*].....................................ARCO(CHM)
Associate of the Royal College of Science [*British*] ....ARCS
Associate of the Royal College of Science [*British*].................ARCSc
Associate of the Royal College of Science and Technology,
  Glasgow [*Later, ARTC*] [*Scotland*]........................ARCST
Associate of the Royal College of Veterinary Surgeons [*British*] .... ARCVS
Associate of the Royal Colonial Institute [*British*]...................ARCI
Associate of the Royal Conservatory of Music of Toronto...............ARCT
Associate of the Royal Drawing Society [*British*]...................ARDS
Associate of the Royal Hibernian Academy [*British*].................ARHA
Associate of the Royal Incorporation of Architects in Scotland ....ARIAS
Associate of the Royal Institute of British Architects ....ARIBA
Associate of the Royal Institute of Chemistry [*Formerly, AIC*]
  [*British*] ....ARIC
Associate of the Royal Institute of Public Health and Hygiene
  [*British*] ....ARIPHH
Associate of the Royal Institution of Chartered Surveyors
  [*Formerly, PASI*] [*British*].................................ARICS
Associate of the Royal Institution of Naval Architects [*British*]....AssocRINA
Associate of the Royal Photographic Society [*British*]...............ARPS
Associate of the Royal Red Cross [*British*] ....ARRC
Associate of the Royal Sanitary Institute [*British*]..................ARSI
Associate of the Royal School of Mines [*British*]....................ARSM
Associate of the Royal Scottish Academy............................ARSA
Associate of the Royal Society of Antiquaries [*British*]...............ARSA
Associate of the Royal Society of Arts [*British*] ....ARSA
Associate of the Royal Society of British Artists......................ARBA
Associate of the Royal Society of British Sculptors....................ARBS

Associate of the Royal Society of Health [Later, AMRSH] [British].......ARSH
Associate of the Royal Society of Literature [British].............ARSL
Associate of the Royal Society of Miniature Painters [British] ....ARMS
Associate of the Royal Society of Musicians [British] ....ARSM
Associate of the Royal Society of Painter-Etchers and
　Engravers [British]..................................ARE
Associate of the Royal Society of Painters in Water Colours
　[British]..................................ARWS
Associate of the Royal Technical College, Glasgow [Formerly,
　ARCST]..................................ARTC
Associate of the Royal Technical College (Salford) [British].............ARTC(S)
Associate of the Royal Victoria Institute of Architects [British] ....ARVIA
Associate of the Royal West of England Academy ....ARWA
Associate in Science..................................AS
Associate in Science..................................ASc
Associate in Science..................................Assoc Sc
Associate in Science in Basic Engineering ....ASBE
Associate in Science in Business ....ASB
Associate in Science in Commerce ....ASC
Associate in Science Education ....ASEd
Associate in Science in Electronic Engineering Technology............ASEET
Associate in Science in Engineering ....ASE
Associate in Science in Medical Secretarial ....ASMS
Associate in Science in Recreation Leadership..................ASRL
Associate in Science in Secretarial Studies ....ASSS
Associate in Science in Teacher Training ....ASTT
Associate in Secretarial Administration..................ASA
Associate in Secretarial Science ....A Se S
Associate in Secretarial Science ....A Se Sc
Associate in Secretarial Science ....ASS
Associate in Secretarial Science ....SSA
Associate in Secretarial Studies ....ASS
Associate of the Society of Actuaries [British] ....ASA
Associate of the Society of Art Masters [British] ....ASAM
Associate of the Society of Incorporated Accountants and
　Auditors [British]..................................ASAA
Associate of the Society of Industrial Artists (Education)
　[British]..................................ASIA(Ed)
Associate of the South African Institute of Mechanical
　Engineers ....ASAI Mech E
Associate in Specialized Business ....ASB
Associate Surveyor Member of the Incorporated Association of
　Architects and Surveyors [British]..................AIAS
Associate of the Sydney Technical College [Australia] ....ASTC
Associate Technical Aide ....ATA
Associate in Technical Arts..................ATA
Associate in Technical Education ....ATE
Associate in Technology..................AT
Associate of the Textile Institute [British]..................ATI
Associate of Theological Study [British]..................ATS
Associate in Theology ....A Th
Associate in Therapy ....ATh
Associate of the Toronto Conservatory of Music..................ATCM
Associate of Trinity College of Music, London [British]..................ATCL
Associate in Wildlife Technology..................AWT
Associated..................................ASSOCD
Associated Accounting Firms International..................AAFI
Associated Actors and Artistes of America ....AAA
Associated Actors and Artistes of America ....AAAA
Associated Agents of America..................AAA
Associated Air Balance Council ....AABC
Associated Antique Dealers of America ....AADA
Associated Baby Carriage Dealers ....ABCD
Associated Bancorp [NASDAQ symbol]..................ASBC
Associated Biomedic Systems, Inc. ....ABS
Associated Booksellers of Great Britain and Ireland ....ABGBI
Associated Brewing Co. [NYSE symbol] [Delisted]..................ABW
Associated British Cinemas ....ABC
Associated with Brokers [London Stock Exchange]..................AB
Associated Builders and Contractors..................ABC
Associated Building Materials, Inc. [An association] ....ABM
Associated Business Publications [Later, American Business
　Press] [An association]..................ABP
Associated Business Writers of America ....ABWA
Associated Chain Drug Stores ....ACDS
Associated Chiropodists of America..................ACA
[The] Associated Christian Colleges of Oregon [Library network].......ACCO
Associated Church Press ....ACP
[The] Associated Clubs..................AC
Associated Collectors of El Salvador [Philately] ....ACES
Associated College Libraries of Central Pennsylvania [Library
　network]..................ACLCP
Associated Colleges of the Chicago Area..................ACCA
Associated Colleges of the Midwest..................ACM
Associated Colleges of the Midwest, Periodical Bank, Chicago,
　IL [Library symbol]..................ICACM
Associated Colleges of Upper New York..................ACUNY
Associated Collegiate Press ....ACP
Associated Committee of Friends on Indian Affairs ....ACFIA
Associated Communications CI A [NASDAQ symbol] ....ACCMA
Associated Companies [NASDAQ symbol]..................ASCI

Associated Construction Distributors..................ACD
Associated Construction Publications..................ACP
Associated Container Transportation..................ACT
Associated Contractor Originated Change..................ACOC
Associated Cooperage Industries of America ....ACIA
Associated Corpuscular Emission..................ACE
Associated Correspondents News Service..................ACNS
Associated Corset and Brassiere Manufacturers..................ACBM
Associated Councils of the Arts [Later, American Council for the
　Arts]..................ACA
Associated Country Women of the World ....ACWW
Associated Credit Bureaus..................ACB
Associated Day Care Centers ....ADCC
Associated Drug and Chemical Industries of Missouri ....ADACIOM
Associated Dry Goods Corp. [NYSE symbol] ....DG
Associated with Dual Capacity Firms [London Stock Exchange]..................AD
Associated Electrical Industries [British]..................AEI
Associated Engineering Services Ltd., Vancouver, BC, Canada
　[Library symbol]..................CaBVaAE
Associated Equipment Distributors ....AED
Associated Factory Mutual Fire Insurance Companies [Later,
　FMS]..................AFMFIC
Associated Fantasy Publishers..................AFP
Associated Funeral Directors Service ....AFDS
Associated Fur Manufacturers..................AFM
Associated Gas Distributors ....AGD
Associated General Contractors of America ....AGC
Associated General Contractors of America ....AGCA
Associated Geographers of America..................AGA
Associated Glass and Pottery Manufacturers..................AGPM
Associated Granite Craftsmens Guild ....AGCG
Associated Ground Equipment ....AGE
Associated Health Foundation ....AHF
Associated Hosts, Inc. [NASDAQ symbol] ....AHST
Associated In-Group Donors ....AID
Associated Independent Dairies of America ....AIDA
Associated Independent Distributors..................AID
Associated Independent Electrical Contractors of America
　[Later, IEC]..................AIECA
Associated Industrial Photographic Dealers [Defunct] ....AIPD
Associated Industries of Massachusetts..................AIM
Associated Information Managers ....AIM
Associated Japan-America Societies of the United States..................AJAS
Associated Japanese Bank (International) Ltd...................AJB
Associated with Jobbers [London Stock Exchange] ....AJ
Associated Koi Clubs of America ....AKCA
Associated Laboratories [An association] ....AL
Associated Landscape Contractors of America ....ALCA
Associated Legislative Rabbinate of America ....ALRA
Associated Locksmiths of America ....ALA
Associated Locksmiths of America ....ALOA
Associated Logic Parallel System..................ALPS
Associated Lutheran Charities [Later, Lutheran Social Welfare
　Conference of America]..................ALC
Associated Madison Companies, Inc. [NYSE symbol] [Delisted]............AMC
Associated Male Choruses of America ....AMC of A
Associated Marine Officers Association of the Philippines ....AMOAP
Associated Master Barbers and Beauticians of America ....AMBBA
Associated Medical Devices [NASDAQ symbol] ....ASMD
Associated Memory Equipment ....AME
Associated Merchandising Corporation ....AMC
Associated Microfilming Service, Inc., Mountain Lakes, NJ
　[Library symbol]..................AssM
Associated Midwestern Universities, Inc. ....AMU
Associated Migrant Opportunity Services ....AMOS
Associated Milk Producers, Incorporated..................AMPI
Associated Millinery Men ....AMM
Associated Minority Contractors of America ....AMC
Associated Missile Products Corporation ....AMPCO
Associated Motion Picture Advertisers ....AMPA
Associated Motor Carriers Tariff Bureau..................AMCTB
Associated Motor Carriers Tariff Bureau, Saint Paul MN [STAC] ....AMC
Associated Music Publishers [Musical slang]..................AMPS
Associated Newspapers Ltd., London, United Kingdom [Library
　symbol]..................UkLA
Associated Nursery Guides Emphatically Lacking in Leisure ....ANGELL
Associated Organizations for Professionals in Education
　[Formerly, AOTE]..................AOPE
Associated Organizations for Teacher Education [Later, AOPE]..........AOTE
Associated Parishes ....AP
Associated Person [Commodities trading term] ....AP
Associated Photographers International ....API
Associated Pimiento Canners ....APC
Associated Pot and Kettle Clubs of America [Later, IPKC] ....APKCA
Associated Poultry and Egg Industries [Defunct] ....APEI
Associated Press ....AP
Associated Press Broadcasters [Formerly, APBA, APRTA]..................APB
Associated Press Broadcasters Association [Later, APB]..................APBA
Associated Press Managing Editors ....APME
Associated Press of Pakistan ....APP
Associated Press Radio ....APR

Associated Press Radio-Television Association [*Later, APB*] .... APRTA
Associated Press Service .... APS
Associated Press Sports Editors Association .... APSEA
Associated Public-Safety [*formerly, Police*] **Communications Officers** .... APCO
Associated Public School Systems .... APSS
Associated Publishers .... AP
Associated Purchasing Publications .... APP
Associated Rare Breeds of New England [*Defunct*] .... ARBNE
Associated Rediffusion [*Television*] .... AR
Associated Reformed Presbyterian .... ARP
Associated Regional Accounting Firms .... ARAF
Associated Reinforcing Bar Producers .... ARBP
Associated Retail Bakers of America [*Later, Retail Bakers of America*] .... ARBA
Associated Retail Confectioners of North America [*Later, RCI*] .... ARC
Associated Retail Confectioners of the United States [*Later, RCI*] .... ARCUS
Associated Rocky Mountain Universities [*AEC*] .... ARMU
Associated Sandblasting Contractors .... ASC
Associated Schools of Construction .... ASC
Associated Scientific and Technical Societies of South Africa. Annual Proceedings [*A publication*] .... Assoc Sci Tech Soc S Afr Annu Proc
Associated Seattle Prostitutes .... ASP
Associated Specialty Contractors .... ASC
Associated Spring Corp. [*NYSE symbol*] [*Delisted*] .... AAS
Associated Spring Corporation .... ASCO
Associated States of Indochina .... ASIC
Associated Stenotypists of America [*Later, NSRA*] .... ASA
Associated Students Promoting Individual Rights for Everyone .... ASPIRE
Associated Students of the University of California .... ASUC
Associated Surplus Dealers .... ASD
Associated Technical Services, Inc. [*Information service*] .... ATS
Associated Technical Services, Inc., Glen Ridge, NJ [*Library symbol*] .... NjGlriA
Associated Technical Services, Inc., List of Translations [*A publication*] .... ATS List Transl
Associated Telephone Answering Exchanges [*Formerly, ATE*] .... ATAE
Associated Telephone Exchanges [*Later, ATAE*] .... ATE
Associated Television Ltd. [*British independent, commercial television company*] .... ATV
Associated Third Class Mail Users [*Later, TCMA*] .... ATCMU
Associated Tobacco Manufacturers [*Defunct*] .... ATM
Associated Traffic Clubs of America [*Later, TCI*] .... ATC
Associated Transport, Inc. [*NYSE symbol*] [*Delisted*] .... ATP
[*The*] **Associated Turtles** .... TAT
Associated Unions of America [*Later, OPEIU*] .... AUA
Associated Universities .... AU
Associated Universities, Incorporated .... AUI
Associated University Bureaus of Business and Economic Research [*Later, AUBER*] .... AUBBER
Associated Veterinary Laboratories [*Defunct*] .... AVL
Associated Video Dealers of America [*Defunct*] .... AVDA
Associated Western Universities .... AWU
Associated Wire Rope Fabricators .... AWRF
Associated With [*Aviation*] .... ASSW
Associated Workers' Union [*Philippines*] .... AWU
Associated Writing Programs [*An association*] .... AWP
Associates of the Graymoor Ecumenical Institute [*Formerly, ECA*] .... AGEI
Associates Investment Co. [*NYSE symbol*] [*Delisted*] .... ATS
Associates for Radio Astronomy .... ARA
Associates for Religion and Intellectual Life .... ARIL
Associateship of the Manchester College of Technology [*British*] .... AssocMCT
Association .... A
Association .... ASS
Association .... ASSCN
Association .... ASSN
Association .... ASSOCN
Association of Academic Health Centers .... AAHC
Association of Academic Health Sciences Library Directors .... AAHSLD
Association of Academic Physiatrists .... AAP
Association for Academic Surgery .... AAS
Association for Academic Travel Abroad .... ATA
Association of Academies of Science [*Later, NAAS*] .... AAS
Association of Accounting Administrators [*Commercial firm*] .... AAA
Association of Accredited Medical Laboratory Schools [*Later, NAHCS*] .... AAMLS
Association of Acrobats .... AA
Association Adjustment Inventory [*Psychology*] .... AAI
Association for Administration of Volunteer Services [*Formerly, AAVSC*] [*Later, AVA*] .... AAVS
Association of Administrative Assistants and Secretaries to United States Senators .... AAASUSS
Association to Advance Ethical Hypnosis .... AAEH
Association for Advanced Life Underwriting .... AALU
Association of Advanced Rabbinical and Talmudic Schools [*Formerly, Council of Roshay Hayeshivoth*] .... AARTS
Association for the Advancement of Aeronautical Research [*France*] .... AAAR
Association for the Advancement of Aging Research [*Defunct*] .... AAAR
Association for the Advancement of Agricultural Sciences in Africa .... AAASA
Association for the Advancement of Baltic Studies .... AABS
Association for Advancement of Behavior Therapy .... AABT
Association for Advancement of Blind Children [*Later, AABR*] .... AABC
Association for Advancement of Blind and Retarded [*Formerly, AABC*] .... AABR
Association for Advancement of Creative Musicians .... AACM
Association for the Advancement of Family Stability [*Later, AFCO*] .... AAFS
Association of the Advancement of Health Education .... AAHE
Association for the Advancement of Instruction about Alcohol and Narcotics [*Defunct*] .... AAIAN
Association for the Advancement of Invention and Innovation [*Patent lobby*] [*Defunct*] .... AAII
Association for the Advancement of Medical Education [*Defunct*] .... AAME
Association for the Advancement of Medical Instrumentation .... AAMI
Association for the Advancement of Ophthalmology .... AAO
Association for the Advancement of Policy, Research, and Development in the Third World .... AAPRDTW
Association for the Advancement of Psychoanalysis .... AAP
Association for Advancement of Psychology .... AAP
Association for the Advancement of Psychotherapy .... AAP
Association for the Advancement of Sports Potential .... AASP
Association of Advertising Film Companies .... AAFC
Association of Advertising Lawyers .... AAL
Association of Advertising Men and Women [*Later, Advertising and Marketing Association*] .... AAMW
Association for African American Education .... AAAE
Association of African Industrial Technology Organizations .... AAITO
Association of African Physicians in North America .... AAPNA
Association for the Aid of Crippled Children [*Later, Foundation for Child Development*] .... AACC
Association of Air Transport Unions [*Defunct*] .... AATU
Association of Allergists for Mycological Investigations .... AAMI
Association for the Alleviation of Asinine Abbreviations and Absurd Acronyms [*Satirical nonassociation*] .... AAAAAA
Association for Ambulatory Pediatric Services [*Later, APA*] .... AAPS
Association of American Agricultural Colleges and Experiment Stations. Proceedings [*A publication*] .... Assn Am Ag Coll & Exp Pro
Association of American Air Travel Clubs .... AAATC
Association of American Battery Manufacturers [*Later, BCI*] .... AABM
Association of American Boards of Examiners in Veterinary Medicine [*Later, AAVSB*] .... AABEVM
Association of American and Canadian Importers of Green Olives [*Later, Green Olive Trade Association*] .... AACIGO
Association of American Chambers of Commerce in Latin America .... AACCLA
Association of American Choruses [*Later, Drinker Library of Choral Music*] .... AAC
Association of American CIRP [*College Internationale pour l'Etude Scientifique des Techniques de Production Mechanique*] **Industrial Sponsors** .... AACIS
Association of American Colleges .... AAC
Association of American Colleges. Bulletin [*A publication*] .... Assn Am Col Bul
Association of American Collegiate Literary Societies .... AACLS
Association of American Correspondents in London .... AACL
Association of American Dance Companies [*Defunct*] .... AADC
Association of American Dentists .... AAD
Association of American Editorial Cartoonists .... AAEC
Association of American Feed Control Officials .... AAFCO
Association of American Fertilizer Control Officials [*Later, AAPFCO*] .... AAFCO
Association of American Foreign Service Women .... AAFSW
Association of American Geographers .... AAG
Association of American Geographers. Annals [*A publication*] .... As Am Geog
Association of American Geographers. Annals [*A publication*] .... Assn Am Geog Ann
Association of American Geographers. Annals [*A publication*] .... Assoc Am Geographers Annals
Association of American Geologists and Naturalists. Reports [*A publication*] .... As Am G Rp
Association of American Indian Affairs .... AAIA
Association of American Indian and Alaska Native Social Workers [*Formerly, AAISW*] .... AAIANSW
Association of American Indian Physicians .... AAIP
Association of American Indian Social Workers [*Later, AAIANSW*] .... AAISW
Association of American Jurists .... AAJ
Association of American Law Schools .... AALS
Association of American Law Schools. Proceedings [*A publication*] .... AALS Proc
Association of American Library Schools .... AALS
Association of American Library Schools. Newsletter [*A publication*] .... AALS News
Association of American Medical Book Publishers [*Later, AMPA*] .... AAMBP
Association of American Medical Colleges .... AAMC
Association of American Military Uniform Collectors .... AAMUC
Association of American Motorcycle Road Racers .... AAMRR
Association of American Pesticide Control Officials .... AAPCO

Association of American Physicians .... AAP
Association of American Physicians and Surgeons .... AAPS
Association of American Plant Food Control Officials .... AAPFCO
Association of American Playing Card Manufacturers [*Defunct*] .... AAPCM
Association of American Publishers [*Formerly, ABPC, AEPI*] .... AAP
Association of American Railroad Dining Car Officers .... AARDCO
Association of American Railroads .... AAR
Association of American Railroads, Economics and Finance Department Library, Washington, DC [*Library symbol*] .... DBRE
Association of American Rhodes Scholars .... AAR
Association of American Rod and Gun Clubs in Europe .... AARGCE
Association of American Seed Control Officials .... AASCO
Association of American Ship Owners .... AASO
Association of American State Boards of Examiners in Veterinary Medicine [*Later, AAVSB*] .... AASBEVM
Association of American State Geologists .... AASG
Association of American Steel Manufacturers .... AASM
[*The*] **Association of American Sword Collectors** .... TAASC
Association of American Universities .... AAU
Association of American University Presses .... AAUP
Association of American Veterinary Medical Colleges .... AAVMC
Association of American Vintners .... AAV
Association of American Volunteer Physicians .... AAVP
Association of American Wives of Europeans .... AAWE
Association of American Wood Pulp Importers .... AAWPI
Association of Americans and Canadians for Aliyah [*Later, North American Aliyah Movement*] .... AACA
Association of Americans and Canadians in Israel .... AACI
Association of Americans Resident Overseas .... AARO
Association des Amidonneries de Mais de la CEE [*Association of the Maize Starch Industries of the European Economic Community*] .... AAM
Association des Amis d'Andre Rey .... AAAR
Association of Analytical Chemists, Inc. .... AAC
Association of Analytical Chemists, Inc. .... ANACHEM
Association des Anciens Eleves des Ecoles des Freres Chretiennes [*Association of Former Students of Catholic Schools*] .... ASSANEF
Association des Anciens Fonctionnaires Internationaux [*Association of Former International Civil Servants*] .... AAFI
Association of Ancient Historians .... AAH
[*The*] **Association for the Anthropological Study of Play** .... TAASP
Association of Apollo-Soyuz Test Project Philatelists .... A-ASTP-P
Association of Appliance and Home Entertainment Distributors .... AAHED
Association of Applied Insect Ecologists .... AAIE
Association for Applied Psychoanalysis .... AAP
Association for Applied Solar Energy [*Later, International Solar Energy Society*] .... AASE
Association for Applied Solar Energy [*Later, International Solar Energy Society*] .... AFASE
Association of Arab-American University Graduates .... AAUG
Association of Architectural Hardware Manufacturers .... AAHM
Association of Architectural Librarians .... AAL
Association of Area Business Publications .... AABP
Association for Arid Lands Studies .... AALS
Association of Art Museum Directors .... AAMD
Association des Artisans Glaciers et des Fabricants de Mix pour Glace des Pays de la CEE [*Association of Home-Made Ice-Cream and Ice-Mix Manufacturers in the European Economic Community*] .... ASSOGLACE
Association of Artist-Run Galleries .... AARG
Association of Arts Administration Educators .... AAAE
Association of Asbestos Cement Pipe Producers .... AACPP
Association of Asian-American Chambers of Commerce .... AAACC
Association of Asian/Pacific American Artists .... AAPAA
Association for Asian Studies .... AAS
Association for Asian Studies, Committee on American Library Resources on the Far East, Center for Research Libraries, Chicago, IL [*Library symbol*] .... CALRFE
Association for Asian Studies. Newsletter [*A publication*] .... Assn Asian Stud Newsletter
Association of Asphalt Paving Technologists .... AAPT
Association of Assistant Librarians .... AAL
Association of Atlantic Universities/Blackwell North America [*Project*] [*Information service*] .... AAU/BNA
Association of Attenders and Alumni of The Hague Academy of International Law .... AAA
Association of Audio-Visual Technicians .... AAVT
Association of Auto and Truck Recyclers [*Later, ADRA*] .... AATR
Association pour l'Avancement des Sciences et des Techniques de la Documentation [*Formerly, ACBLF. Acronym alone now used as organization's name*] .... ASTED
Association of Average Adjusters of the United States .... AAA
Association of Average Adjusters of the United States .... AAAUS
Association of Aviation Psychologists .... AAP
Association of Aviation and Space Museologists .... AASM
Association for Balance of Political Power .... BOP
Association of Balloon and Airship Constructors .... ABAC
Association des Baluba du Katanga [*Association of the Baluba of Katanga*] .... BALUBAKAT
Association of Bank Holding Companies [*Formerly, ARBHC*] .... ABHC
Association of Bank Travel Bureaus [*Defunct*] .... ABTB
Association of Baptist Homes and Hospitals .... ABHH
Association of Baptist Professors of Religion .... ABPR
Association of Baptists for World Evangelism .... ABWE
Association of the Bar of the City of New York, New York, NY [*Library symbol*] .... NNB
Association of the Bar of the City of New York. Record [*A publication*] .... Assn Bar City NY Rec
Association des Batetela de Lodja [*Association of Batetelas of Lodja*] .... ASSOBELA
Association of Bay Area Governments [*Northern California*] .... ABAG
Association of Bedding and Furniture Law Officials .... ABFLO
Association for Behavior Analysis .... ABA
Association Belge pour le Developpement Pacifique de l'Energie Atomique [*Belgian Association for the Peaceful Development of Atomic Energy*] .... ADEA
Association Belgo-Americaine [*Belgian-American Association*] .... ABA
Association of Bendectin Children .... ABC
Association of Better Business Bureaus [*Later, CBBB*] .... ABBB
Association of Better Computer Dealers .... ABCD
Association of Beverage Container Recyclers .... ABCR
Association for the Bibliography of History .... ABH
Association des Bibliothecaires Francais. Bulletin d'Informations [*A publication*] .... Ass Bibliot Fr Bull Inf
Association des Bibliothecaires Francais. Bulletin d'Informations [*A publication*] .... Assn Bibl Francais Bull Inf
Association des Bibliothecaires Francais. Bulletin d'Informations [*A publication*] .... Assoc Bibl Francais Bul
Association of Biological Collections Appraisers .... ABCA
Association of Biomedical Communication .... ABCD
Association for Biomedical Research .... ABR
Association of Biotechnology Companies .... ABC
Association for Birth Psychology .... ABP
Association of Bituminous Contractors .... ABC
Association of Black Motion Picture and Television Producers .... ABMPTP
Association of Black Psychologists .... ABP
Association of Black Psychologists .... ABPsi
Association of Black Sociologists .... ABS
Association of Black Women in Higher Education .... ABWHE
Association of Black Women Historians .... ABWH
Association of Blind Chartered Physiotherapists .... ABCP
Association of Bone and Joint Surgeons .... ABJS
Association of Book Travelers .... ABT
Association of Boys and Students Clothing Manufacturers .... ABSCM
Association for Brain Tumor Research .... ABTR
Association of Brass and Bronze Ingot Manufacturers .... ABBIM
Association of Bridal Consultants .... ABC
Association for Bridge Construction and Design .... ABCD
Association of British Chambers of Commerce .... ABCC
Association of British Library and Information Science Schools .... ABLISS
Association of British Library Schools .... ABLS
Association of British Orientalists .... ABO
Association of British Picture Restorers .... ABPR
Association of British Secretaries in America .... ABSA
Association of British Theological and Philosophical Libraries .... ABTAPL
Association of British Travel Agents .... ABTA
Association for Broadcast Engineering Standards .... ABES
Association on Broadcasting Standards [*Later, Association for Broadcast Engineering Standards*] .... ABS
Association of Business Forms Manufacturers [*Defunct*] .... ABFM
Association of Business Officers of Preparatory Schools .... ABOPS
Association of Business and Professional Women in Construction .... ABPWC
Association for Business Simulation and Experiential Learning .... ABSEL
Association of Buying Offices .... ABO
Association of Byelorussian American Veterans in America .... ZBAV
Association of Cable Television Suppliers .... ACTS
Association de Cadres Dirigeants de l'Industrie pour le Progres Social et Economique. Bulletin [*A publication*] .... Assoc Cadres Dir Industr B
Association of Cambodian Survivors of America .... ACSA
Association of Canadian Archivists .... ACA
Association for Canadian Studies in the United States .... ACSUS
Association of Canadian Television and Radio Artists .... ACTRA
Association Canadienne des Bibliothecaires de Langue Francaise [*Later, ASTED*] .... ACBLF
Association Canadienne des Bibliothecaires de Langue Francaise. Bulletin [*A publication*] .... ACBLF Bul
Association Canadienne des Bibliotheques [*Canadian Library Association*] [*Also known as CLA*] .... ACB
Association Canadienne des Bibliotheques Musicales [*Canadian Association of Music Libraries*] .... ACBM
Association Canadienne des Ecoles de Bibliothecaires [*Canadian Association of Library Schools*] .... ACEB
Association Canadienne-Francaise pour l'Avancement des Sciences .... ACFAS
Association Canadienne-Francaise pour l'Avancement des Sciences. Annales [*A publication*] .... Assoc Canadienne-Francaise Av Sci Annales
Association Canadienne des Sciences de l'Information [*Canadian Association for Information Science*] .... ACSI

Association Canado-Americaine ... ACA
Association for the Care of Asthma ... ACA
Association for the Care of Children's Health ... ACCH
Association of Career Training Schools [*Defunct*] ... ACTS
Association of Caribbean Historians ... ACH
Association of Caribbean Studies ... ACS
Association of Caribbean University and Research Institute Libraries ... ACURIL
Association Cartographique Internationale [*International Cartographic Association*] ... ACI
Association of Casualty Accountants and Statisticians [*Later, SIA*] ... ACAS
Association of Casualty and Surety Companies [*Later, AIA*] ... ACSC
Association of Catholic Colleges and Universities ... ACCU
Association of Catholic Teachers [*Defunct*] ... ACT
Association of Catholic Trade Unionists ... ACTU
Association of Catholic TV and Radio Syndicators ... ACTRS
Association Catholique Internationale des Oeuvres de Protection de la Jeune Fille [*Later, ACISJF*] ... ACIOPJF
Association Catholique Internationale des Services de la Jeunesse Feminine [*International Catholic Girls Society*] [*Formerly, ACIOPJF*] ... ACISJF
Association of Centers of Medieval and Renaissance Studies [*Later, CARA*] ... ACOMARS
Association of Certified Public Accountant Examiners [*Later, NASBA*] ... ACPAE
Association of Chairmen of Departments of Mechanics ... ACDM
Association of Chief State School Audio-Visual Officers [*Defunct*] ... ACSSAVO
Association for Child Psychoanalysis ... ACP
Association for Childbirth at Home, International ... ACHI
Association for Childhood Education International ... ACE
Association for Childhood Education International ... ACEI
Association for Children and Adults with Learning Disabilities ... ACALD
Association for Children and Adults with Learning Disabilities ... ACLD
Association for Children with Retarded Mental Development ... A/CRMD
Association of Chinese and American Engineers ... ACAE
Association of Chinese from Indochina ... ACI
Association of Choral Conductors ... ACC
Association of Christian Church Educators ... ACCE
Association of Christian Librarians ... ACL
Association for Christian Schools ... ACS
Association of Christian Schools International ... ACSI
Association for Christian Training and Service ... ACTS
Association of Church Missions Committees ... ACMC
Association of Cinema Laboratories [*Later, ACVL*] ... ACL
Association of Cinema and Video Laboratories [*Formerly, ACL*] ... ACVL
Association of Civilian Technicians ... ACT
Association of Civilian Technicians ... CTA
Association des Classes Moyennes Africaines [*African Middle Classes Association*] ... ACMAF
Association for Classical Music ... ACM
Association of Classroom Teachers [*Defunct*] ... ACT
Association for Clinical Pastoral Education ... ACPE
Association of Clinical Pathologists ... ACP
Association of Clinical Scientists ... ACS
Association of College Admissions Counselors [*Later, NACAC*] ... ACAC
Association of College Auxiliary Services [*Later, NACAS*] ... ACAS
Association of College Honor Societies ... ACHS
Association of College and Research Libraries ... ACRL
Association of College Unions [*Later, ACU-I*] ... ACU
Association of College Unions - International [*Formerly, ACU*] ... ACU-I
Association of College and University Auditors ... ACUA
Association of College, University, and Community Arts Administrators [*Formerly, ACUCM*] ... ACUCAA
Association of College and University Concert Managers [*Later, ACUCAA*] ... ACUCM
Association of College and University Housing Officers [*Later, ACUHO-I*] ... ACUHO
Association of College and University Housing Officers - International [*Formerly, ACUHO*] ... ACUHO-I
Association of College and University Printers ... ACUP
Association of College and University Telecommunications Administrators ... ACUTA
Association of Colleges and Secondary Schools [*Later, SACS*] ... ACSS
Association of Colleges and Secondary Schools for Negroes [*Later, ACSS*] ... ACSSN
Association of Colleges and Universities for International-Intercultural Studies [*Defunct*] ... ACUIIS
Association of Collegiate Entrepreneurs ... ACE
Association of Collegiate Schools of Architecture ... ACSA
Association of Collegiate Schools of Nursing [*Later, NLN*] ... ACSN
Association of Collegiate Schools of Planning ... ACSP
[*The*] **Association of Comedy Artists** ... TACA
Association des Commercants Indigenes du Burundi [*Association of Indigenous Merchants of Burundi*] ... ACIBU
Association du Commerce et de l'Industrie du Cafe dans la CEE [*Association for the Coffee Trade and Industry in the EEC*] ... ACICAFE
Association of Commercial Finance Attorneys [*Defunct*] ... ACFA
Association of Commercial Finance Companies of New York ... ACFC
Association of Commercial Mail Receiving Agencies ... ACMRA
Association of Commercial Records Centers ... ACRC
Association of Commodity Exchange Firms [*Later, Futures Industry Association*] ... ACEF
Association for Commonwealth Literature and Language Studies ... ACLALS
Association of Commonwealth Universities ... ACU
Association for Communication Administration ... ACA
Association for Community Based Educational Institutions ... ACBEI
Association of Community Cancer Centers ... ACCC
Association of Community College Trustees ... ACCT
Association of Community Colleges for Excellence in Systems and Services [*Consortium*] ... ACCESS
Association of Community Organizations for Reform Now ... ACORN
Association of Community Travel Clubs ... ACTC
Association of Commuter Airlines [*Later, NATA*] ... ACA
Association for Comparative Economic Studies ... ACES
Association for Comparative Economics [*Later, ACES*] ... ACE
Association for Computational Linguistics ... ACL
Association of Computer Programmers and Analysts ... ACPA
Association of Computer Users [*Formerly, ATSU, ASCU*] ... ACU
Association for Computers and the Humanities ... ACH
Association for Computing Machinery ... ACM
Association for Computing Machinery. Journal [*A publication*] ... Assn Comp Mach J
Association of Concern for Ultimate Reality and Meaning ... ACURM
Association of Concerned African Scholars ... ACAS
Association of Concert Bands [*Formerly, ACBA*] ... ACB
Association of Concert Bands of America [*Later, ACB*] ... ACBA
Association for Conflict Resolution ... ACR
Association of Conservation Engineers ... ACE
Association for Conservation Information [*Formerly, AACI*] ... ACI
Association pour la Conservation et la Reproduction Photographique de la Presse, Paris, France [*Library symbol*] ... ACRPP
Association des Constructeurs de Machines a Coudre de la CEE [*Association of Sewing Machine Manufacturers of the EEC*] ... ASCOMACE
Association of Consulting Chemists and Chemical Engineers ... ACC & CE
Association of Consulting Engineers of Canada ... ACEC
Association of Consulting Engineers of Great Britain ... ACEGB
Association of Consulting Foresters ... ACF
Association of Consulting Management Engineers ... ACME
Association for Consumer Research ... ACR
Association of Contemplative Sisters ... ACS
Association of Contemporary Historians ... ACH
Association for Continuing Higher Education [*Formerly, AUEC*] ... ACHE
Association of Continuing Legal Education Administrators ... ACLEA
Association for Continuing Professional Education [*Formerly, AFSTE*] ... ACPE
Association for Cooperation in Engineering [*Defunct*] ... ACE
Association of Cooperative Educators ... ACE
Association of Cooperative Library Organizations [*Later, ASCLA*] ... ACLO
Association for the Coordination of University Religious Affairs ... ACURA
Association for Corporate Growth ... ACG
Association for Corporate Growth and Diversification [*Later, PCG*] ... ACGD
Association of Correctional Administrators ... ACA
Association of Correctional Psychologists ... ACP
Association for Correctional Research and Information Management ... ACRIM
Association of Cotton Textile Merchants of New York [*Later, ATMI*] ... ACTM
Association of Cotton Yarn Distributors [*Later, AYD*] ... ACYD
Association of Council Secretaries [*Later, NAES*] ... ACS
Association for Counselor Education and Supervision ... ACES
Association of Country Entertainers ... ACE
Association of County Councils [*British*] ... ACC
Association of Couples for Marriage Enrichment ... ACME
Association for Creative Change within Religious and Other Social Systems ... ACC
Association of Credit Union League Executives ... ACULE
Association of Cuban Architects in Exile ... ACAE
Association for Cultural Exchange ... CULTUREX
Association for Cultural Interchange ... ACI
Association of Customers' Brokers [*Later, AIB*] ... ACB
Association of the Customs Bar [*Later, CITBA*] ... ACB
Association of Cycle Exhibitors ... ACE
Association of Cytogenetics Technologists ... ACT
Association of Dark Leaf Tobacco Dealers and Exporters ... ADLTDE
Association of Data Communications Users ... ADCU
Association of Data Processing Service Organizations [*Includes American and Canadian companies*] ... ADAPSO
Association of Data Processing Service Organizations [*Includes American and Canadian companies*] ... ADPSO
Association of Database Producers ... ADP
Association pour Defendre la Memoire de Petain ... ADMP
Association of Departments of English ... ADE
Association of Departments of English. Bulletin [*A publication*] ... ADEB
Association of Departments of Foreign Languages ... ADFL
Association of Departments of Foreign Languages. Bulletin [*A publication*] ... ADFLB
Association of Desk and Derrick Clubs ... ADDC

Association for Development of Computer-Based Instructional Systems [Formerly, ADIS]............ADCIS
Association for the Development of Human Potential......................ADHP
Association of Development Institutes for the Pacific and Asia..........ADIPA
Association for Development of Instructional Systems [Later, ADCIS]............ADIS
Association for the Development of Religious Information Systems............ADRIS
Association pour le Developpement des Bibliotheques Publiques en Afrique [Association for the Development of Public Libraries in Africa]............ADBPA
Association pour le Developpement de l'Exportation des Vins de Bordeaux............ADEP
Association of Diesel Specialists............ADS
Association of Direct Marketing Agencies............ADMA
Association of Disciples for Theological Discussion............ADTD
Association of District Councils [British]............ADC
Association of Diving Contractors............ADC
Association for Dressings and Sauces............ADS
Association of Drilled Shaft Contractors............ADSC
Association of Drinkwatchers International [Defunct]............DW
Association of Earth Science Editors............AESE
Association des Ecoles Internationales............AEI
Association des Ecrivains de Langue Francaise [Association of French-Language Writers]............ADELF
Association of Edison Illuminating Companies............AEIC
Association of Editorial Businesses............AEB
Association of Education Committees [British]............AEC
Association for Education and Cultural Advancement [South Africa]............ASECA
Association for Education in International Business [Later, AIB]..........AEIB
Association for Education in Journalism............AEJ
Association for Education by Radio. Journal [A publication]............ Assn Ed Radio J
Association of Education by Radio-Television. Journal [A publication]............AERTJ
Association for the Education of Teachers in Science............AETS
Association for Education of the Visually Handicapped............AEVH
Association for Educational Communications and Technology [Formerly, DAVI]............AECT
Association for Educational Data Systems............AEDS
Association of Educational Negotiators [Later, NAEN]............AEN
Association of Educators of Homebound and Hospitalized Children [Later, DPH]............AEHHC
Association of Electronic Distributors............AED
Association of Electronic Manufacturers [Later, EIA]............AEM
Association of Electronic Manufacturers, Eastern Division............AEM-ED
Association of Electronic Parts and Equipment Manufacturers [Later, EIA]............AEPEM
Association pour l'Emancipation de la Femme Camerounaise [Association for the Emancipation of Cameroonian Women]............ ASSOFECAM
Association of Energy Engineers............AEE
Association of Engineering Geologists............AEG
Association of Engineering Geologists. Bulletin [A publication]............ Assoc Eng Geol Bull
Association of Engineering Societies. Journal [A publication]............ As Eng Soc J
Association of Engineers and Scientists of the Bureau of Naval Weapons [Later, ASE]............AESBNW
Association of Engineers and Scientists (Independent)............AES(I)
Association of Enrolled Agents [Later, NAEA]............AEA
Association of Environmental Engineering Professors............AEEP
Association for Environmental and Outdoor Education............AEOE
Association of Environmental Scientists and Administrators............AESA
Association of Episcopal Colleges............AEC
Association of Equipment Lessors [Later, AAEL]............AEL
Association des Etablissements Multiplicateurs de Semences Fourrageres de CE [Association of Forage Seed Breeders of the European Community]............AMUFOC
Association pour l'Etude et le Developpement de la Traduction Automatique et de la Linguistique Appliquee............ATALA
Association pour l'Etude des Problemes de l'Europe [Association for the Study of European Problems]............AEPE
Association pour l'Etude Taxonomique de la Flore d'Afrique Tropicale [Association for the Taxonomic Study of Tropical African Flora]............AETFAT
Association des Etudiants Guineens de France [Association of Guinean Students in France]............AEGF
Association des Etudiants Malgaches [Association of Malagasy Students]............AEM
Association des Etudiants Nigeriens en France [Association of Niger Students in France]............AENF
Association des Etudiants d'Origine Malgache [Association of Students of Malagasy Origins Studying in France]............AEOM
Association of European Conjuncture Institutes............AECI
Association of European Jute Industries............AEJI
Association Europeenne de Ceramique [European Ceramic Association]............AEC
Association Europeenne pour la Cooperation [European Association for Cooperation]............AEC

Association Europeenne des Enseignants [European Association of Teachers]............AEDE
Association Europeenne pour l'Etude du Probleme des Refugies..........AER
Association Europeenne des Exploitations Frigorifiques [European Association of Refrigeration Enterprises] [Common Market]............AEEF
Association Europeenne de Libre-Echange [European Free Trade Association]............AELE
Association Europeenne des Organisations Nationales des Commercants Detaillants en Textiles [European Association of National Organizations of Textile Manufacturers]............AEDT
Association Europeenne des Photographes Professionnels [European Association of Professional Photographers]..........EUROPHOT
Association Europeenne Rubans, Tresses, Tissus Elastiques [European Ribbon, Braid, and Elastic Material Association]........AERTEL
Association of Evangelical Lutheran Churches............AELC
Association of Evangelical Professors of Missions............AEPM
Association of Evangelicals for Italian Missions [Formerly, AFIE, IBAA]............AEIM
Association for Evolutionary Economics............AFEE
Association of Executive Recruiting Consultants............AERC
Association Executives Human Rights Caucus............AEHRC
Association of Existential Psychology and Psychiatry............AEPP
Association for Experiential Education............AEE
Association des Fabricants de Cafe Soluble des Pays de la CEE [Association of Soluble Coffee Manufacturers of the Countries of the European Economic Community]............AFCASOLE
Association des Fabricants de Glucose de la CEE [Association of the Glucose Producers in the European Economic Community]........AFG
Association des Fabricants de Laits de Conserve des Pays de la CEE [Association of Powdered Milk Manufacturers of the EEC]............ASFALEC
Association of Fair Housing Committees [Defunct]............AFHC
Association of Family Conciliation Courts............AFCC
Association of Family Farmers............AFF
Association for Family Living [Defunct]............AFL
Association of Federal Appraisers [Later, Association of Governmental Appraisers]............AFA
Association of Federal Architects............AFA
Association of Federal Communications Consulting Engineers........AFCCE
Association of Federal Fiscal Technicians............AFFT
Association for Federal Information Resources Management............AFFIRM
Association of Federal Investigators............AFI
Association of Federal Photographers............AFP
Association of Federal Women's Award Recipients............AFWAR
Association Feeling Truth and Living It............AFTLI
Association for Field Archaeology............AFFA
Association of Field Service Managers............AFSM
Association for Field Services in Teacher Education [Later, ACPE]............AFSTE
Association of Film Commissioners............AFC
Association for Finishing Processes............AFP
Association of Finnish Electric Industries............AFEI
Association of Firearm and Tool Mark Examiners............AFTE
Association of First Class Mailers............AFCM
Association of Flight Attendants............AFA
Association of Flock Processors [Defunct]............AFP
Association des Fonctionnaires et Agents de la Colonie [Association of Civil Servants and Agents of the Colony] [European Civil servants] [East Congo]............AFAC
Association of Food Distributors [Later, AFI]............AFD
Association of Food and Drug Officials [Formerly, AFDOUS]............AFDO
Association of Food and Drug Officials of the United States [Later, AFDO]............AFDOUS
Association of Food Industries [Formerly, AFD]............AFI
Association for Food Service Management [Later, SFM]............AFSM
Association of Footwear Distributors............AFD
Association Foret-Cellulose [A publication]............AFOCEL
Association of Former Agents of the United States Secret Service............AFAUSSS
Association of Former Intelligence Officers............AFIO
Association of Former International Civil Servants............AFICS
Association of Former Members of Congress [Formerly, FMC]..........AFMC
Association of Former Secretaries of [the Department of] Health, Education, and Welfare [Mythical group]............AFSHEW
Association of Former Senate Aides............AFSA
Association Francaise pour l'Augmentation de la Productivite [France]............AFAP
Association Francaise pour l'Avancement des Sciences [France]........AFAS
Association Francaise pour l'Avancement des Sciences. Comptes-Rendus [A publication]............ As Franc C R
Association Francaise pour l'Avancement des Sciences. Comptes-Rendus [A publication]............Ass Franc Avance Sc C R
Association Francaise de Calcul............AFCAL
Association Francaise pour la Communaute Atlantique [French Association for the Atlantic Community]............AFCA
Association Francaise pour la Cybernetique Economique et Technique [France]............AFCET
Association Francaise pour l'Etude du Quaternaire. Bulletin [A publication]............ Assoc Fr Etude Quat Bull

Association Francaise de Gemmologie. Bulletin [*A publication*] .... Assoc Fr Gemmol Bull
Association Francaise des Ingenieurs et Techniciens de l'Aeronautique et de l'Espace [*France*] .... AFITAE
Association Francaise des Journalistes Agricoles [*France*] .... AFJA
Association Francaise de Normalisation [*France*] [*National standards organization*] .... AFNOR
Association Francaise des Techniciens du Petrole .... AFTP
Association Francaise des Techniciens du Petrole. Revue [*A publication*] .... Assoc Fr Tech Pet Rev
Association France-Etats-Unis [*France-United States Association*] .... AFEU
Association Francophone de Spectrometrie de Masse de Solides [*French-Speaking Association of Solids Mass Spectrometry*] .... AFSMAS
Association of Fraternity Advisors .... AFA
Association of the Free French in the United States .... AFFUS
Association of Free Lutheran Congregation and Seminary Headquarters, Minneapolis, MN [*Library symbol*] .... MnMFL
Association of Free Lutheran Congregations .... AFLC
Association of Free Methodist Educational Institutions .... AFMEI
Association of Free Trade Unions [*USSR*] .... AFTU
Association of Fund-Raising Directors .... AFRD
Association of Fundamental Institutions of Religious Education .... AFIRE
Association of Fundraising List Professionals .... AFLP
Association of Gay Psychologists .... AGP
Association of General and Liberal Studies .... AGLS
Association of General Merchandise Chains .... AGMC
Association Generale des Etudiants de France en Afrique Noire [*General Association of French Students in Black Africa*] .... AGEFAN
Association Generale des Hygienistes et Techniciens Municipaux .... AGHTM
Association de Geographes Francais. Bulletin [*A publication*] .... Assoc Geographes Francais Bull
Association de Geographes Francais. Bulletin [*A publication*] .... Assoc Geogr Fr Bull
Association des Geologues du Bassin de Paris. Bulletin [*A publication*] .... Assoc Geol Bassin Paris Bull
Association des Geologues du Bassin de Paris. Bulletin d'Information [*A publication*] .... Assoc Geol Bassin Paris Bull Inf
Association of Geoscientists for International Development .... AGID
Association of German Broadcasters .... AGB
Association of German Language Authors in America [*Defunct*] .... AGLAA
Association for Gerontology in Higher Education .... AGHE
[*The*] **Association for the Gifted** .... TAG
Association of Girl Scout Executive Staff [*Formerly, AGSPW*] .... AGSES
Association of Girl Scout Professional Workers [*Later, AGSES*] .... AGSPW
Association for Gnotobiotics .... AG
Association of Governing Boards of Universities and Colleges .... AGB
Association of Government Accountants .... AGA
Association for Government Assisted Housing .... AGAH
Association of Governmental Appraisers .... AGA
[*The*] **Association for Graduate Education and Research** .... TAGER
Association of Graduate Liberal Studies Programs .... AGLSP
Association of Graduate Schools [*in Association of American Universities*] .... AGS
Association of Graphic Arts Consultants .... AGAC
Association for Gravestone Studies .... AGS
Association for Group Psychoanalysis and Process .... AGPP
Association of Group Travel Executives .... AGTE
Association des Groupements de Negoce Interieur du Bois et des Produits Derives dans les Pays de la CEE [*Association of National Trade Groups for Wood and Derived Products in Countries of the European Economic Community*] .... AGNIB
Association Guillaume Bude. Bulletin [*A publication*] .... AGB
Association of Halfway House Alcoholism Programs of North America .... AHHAP
Association of Handicapped Artists .... AHA
Association on Handicapped Student Services Programs in Postsecondary Education .... AHSSPPE
Association of Health Occupations Teacher Educators .... AHOTE
Association for Health Records [*Later, AHQ*] .... AHR
Association for Health Services Research .... AHSR
Association for Healthcare Quality [*Formerly, AHR*] .... AHQ
Association Henri Capitant .... AHC
Association for Higher Education [*of the NEA*] [*Later, AAHE*] .... AHE
Association for Higher Education, Dallas, TX [*OCLC symbol*] .... IUC
Association of Highway Steel Transporters .... AHST
Association of Hispanic Arts .... AHA
Association for the History of Chiropractic .... AHC
Association for Holistic Health .... AHH
Association of Home Appliance Manufacturers .... AHAM
Association of Home Study Schools [*Later, ACTS*] .... AHSS
Association of Hospital Directors of Medical Education [*Later, AHME*] .... AHDME
Association of Hospital and Institution Libraries [*of ALA*] [*Later, ASCLA*] .... AHIL
Association of Hospital and Institution Libraries Quarterly [*A publication*] .... AHIL Q
Association of Hospital Management Committees .... AHMC
Association for Hospital Medical Education .... AHME
Association of Hospital Security Administrators .... AHSA
Association of House Democratic Press Assistants .... AHDPA
Association for Human Emergence [*Defunct*] .... AHE
Association for Humanist Sociology .... AHS
Association for Humanistic Education .... AHE
Association for Humanistic Education and Development .... AHEAD
Association for Humanistic Psychology .... AHP
Association of Humanistic Rabbis .... AHR
Association of Hungarian Students in North America [*Defunct*] .... AHS
Association of the Hungarian Telecommunication Industry [*A publication*] .... Assoc Hung Telecommun Ind
Association of Hydraulic Equipment Manufacturers .... AHEM
Association of Immigration and Nationality Lawyers [*Later, AILA*] .... AINL
Association of Importers-Manufacturers for Muzzle Loading .... AIMM
Association for the Improvement of Community College Teaching .... AICCT
Association for the Improvement of the Mississippi River .... AIMR
Association of Independent Camps [*Formerly, APC*] .... AIC
Association of Independent Colleges of Music .... AICM
Association of Independent Colleges and Schools .... AICS
Association of Independent Commercial Producers .... AICP
Association of Independent Composers and Performers .... AICP
Association of Independent Copy Machine Dealers and Manufacturers .... AICMDM
Association of Independent Corrugated Converters .... AICC
Association of Independent Medical Equipment Suppliers .... AIMES
Association of Independent Optical Wholesalers [*Later, OLA*] .... AIOW
Association of Independent Software Companies [*Later, ADAPSO*] .... AISC
Association of Independent Television Stations .... INTV
Association of Independent Video and Filmmakers .... AIVF
Association of Indians in America .... AIA
Association for Individually Guided Education .... AIGE
Association of Industrial Advertisers [*Later, B/PAA*] .... AIA
Association of Industrial Manufacturers' Representatives .... AIMR
Association of Industrial Metallizers, Coaters, and Laminators .... AIMCAL
Association of Industrial Scientists [*affiliated with*] **Marine Engineers Beneficial Association** [*A union*] .... AIS-MEBA
Association de l'Industrie de la Fonte de Fromage de la CEE [*Association of the Processed Cheese Industry of the European Economic Community*] .... ASSIFONTE
Association de l'Industrie Laitiere de la CEE [*Milk Industry Association of the EEC*] .... ASSILEC
Association des Industries des Aliments Dietetiques de la CEE [*Association of Dietetic Foods Industries of the European Economic Community*] .... IDACE
Association des Industries de Glaces Alimentaires de la CEE [*Association of the Ice Cream Industries of the European Economic Community*] .... EUROGLACES
Association des Industries du Jute Europeennes [*Association of European Jute Industries*] .... AIJE
Association des Industries Margarinieres des Pays de la CEE [*Association of Margarine Industries of the EEC Countries*] .... IMACE
Association for Infant Massage .... AIM
Association for Informal Logic and Critical Thinking .... AILACT
Association of Information and Dissemination Centers .... ASIDIC
Association of Information Managers for Savings Institutions .... AIM
Association des Ingenieurs, Liege [*Association of Engineers, Liege*] [*Belgium*] .... AILg
Association for Innovation in Higher Education .... AIHE
Association Institute .... AI
Association of Institutional Distributors [*Later, FOOD*] .... AID
Association for Institutional Research .... AIR
Association des Instituts d'Etudes Europeennes [*Association of Institutes for European Studies*] .... AIEE
Association of Insulin-Dependent Diabetics .... AIDD
Association of Insurance Advertisers [*Defunct*] .... AIA
Association of Insurance Attorneys .... AIA
Association for the Integration of Management .... AIM
Association for Intercollegiate Athletics for Women .... AIAW
Association Intercontinentale du Mais Hybride .... INTERHYBRID
Association des Interets Coloniaux Belges [*Merged with AIIB into FEC*] .... AICB
Association des Interets Industriels au Congo [*Merged with AICB into FEC*] .... AIIB
Association des Interets Portuaires .... ASSIPORT
Association of Interior Decor Specialists .... AIDS
Association Internacional de Asmologia [*International Association of Asthmology*] .... INTERASMA
Association of Internal Management Consultants .... AIMC
Association of International Accountants .... AIA
Association of International Advertising Agencies .... AIAA
Association of International Bond Dealers .... AIBD
Association of International Border Agencies .... AIBA
Association of International Colleges and Universities .... AICU
Association for International Cotton Emblem .... AFICE
Association for International Development [*Defunct*] .... AID
Association of International Health Researchers .... AIHR
Association of International Institute of Arts and Letters .... AIAL
Association of International Insurance Agents [*Later, Intersure*] .... AIIA
Association of International Libraries .... AIL
Association of International Libraries/North America .... AIL/NA
Association for International Medical Study .... AIMS
Association of International Photography Art Dealers .... AIPAD

Association for International Practical Training .... AIPT
Association of International Relations Clubs .... AIRC
Association for International Technical Promotion .... AITEP
Association Internationale d'Allergologie [*International Association of Allergology*] .... AIA
Association Internationale des Arts Plastiques [*International Association of Art - Painting, Sculpture, Graphic Art*] [*See also IAA*] .... AIAP
Association Internationale des Assureurs Contre la Grele [*International Association of Hail Insurers*] .... AIAG
Association Internationale de Bibliophile [*International Association of Bibliophiles - IAB*] .... AIB
Association Internationale des Bibliotheques, Archives, et Centres de Documentation Musicaux [*International Association of Music Libraries, Archives, and Documentation Centers*] [*See also IAML*] .... AIBM
Association Internationale de la Boulangerie Industrielle [*International Association of the Bread Industry*] .... AIBI
Association Internationale de Boxe Amateur [*International Amateur Boxing Association*] .... AIBA
Association Internationale pour le Calcul Analogique [*International Association for Analogue Computation*] [*Later, IMACS*] .... AICA
Association Internationale pour le Calcul Analogique [*International Association for Analogue Computation*] .... ASICA
Association Internationale de Chimie Cerealiere [*International Association for Cereal Chemistry*] [*Also, ICC*] .... AICC
Association Internationale de Chimie Cerealiere [*International Association for Cereal Chemistry*] [*Also, AICC*] ICC
Association Internationale du Cinema Scientifique [*International Scientific Film Association*] .... AICS
Association Internationale des Circuits Permanents .... AICP
Association Internationale du Congres des Chemins de Fer [*International Railway Congress Association*] .... AICCF
Association Internationale des Constructeurs de Materiel Aerospatial [*International Association of Aerospace Equipment Manufacturers*] .... AICMA
Association Internationale des Constructeurs de Materiel Roulant [*International Association of Rolling Stock Builders*] [*See also IARSB*] .... AICMR
Association Internationale Contre le Bruit [*International Association Against Noise*] .... AICB
Association Internationale Contre la Torture [*International Association Against Torture*] .... AICT
Association Internationale de la Couleur [*International Colour Association*] .... AIC
Association Internationale des Critiques d'Art [*International Association of Art Critics*] .... AICA
Association Internationale des Critiques Litteraires [*International Association of Literary Critics*] .... AICL
Association Internationale des Critiques de Theatre [*International Association of Theatre Critics*] .... AICT
Association Internationale de Cybernetique [*International Association for Cybernetics - IAC*] .... AIC
Association Internationale de Defense des Artistes [*International Association for the Defense of Artists*] .... AIDA
Association Internationale de Developpement et d'Action Communautaires [*International Association for Community Development*] .... AIDAC
Association Internationale pour le Developpement des Bibliotheques en Afrique [*International Association for the Development of Libraries in Africa*] .... AIDBA
Association Internationale pour le Developpement des Universites Internationales et Mondiales [*International Association for the Development of International and World Universities*] .... AIDUM
Association Internationale de la Distribution des Produits Alimentaires et des Produits de Grande Consommation [*International Association for the Distribution of Food Products*] ...... AIDA
Association Internationale des Distributions d'Eau .... AIDE
Association Internationale des Documentalists et Techniciens de l'Information [*International Association of Documentalists and Information Officers*] .... AID
Association Internationale des Documentaristes [*International Association of Documentary Filmmakers*] .... AID
Association Internationale du Droit de l'Assurance [*International Association for Insurance Law*] .... AIDA
Association Internationale de Droit Penal [*International Association of Penal Law*] .... AIDP
Association Internationale des Ecoles Privees Europeennes .... AIEPE
Association Internationale des Ecoles des Sciences de l'Information [*International Association of Information Sciences Schools*] .... AIESI
Association Internationale des Ecoles de Service Social [*International Association of Schools of Social Work*] .... AIESS
Association Internationale des Ecoles Superieures d'Education Physique [*International Association of Schools or Higher Institutes of Physical and Sportive Education*] .... AIESEP
Association Internationale des Educateurs de Jeunes Inadaptes [*International Association of Workers for Maladjusted Children*] [*See also IAWMC*] .... AIEJI

Association Internationale des Entreprises d'Equipment Electrique [*International Association of Electrical Contractors - IAEC*] .... AIE
Association Internationale d'Epigraphie Latine [*International Association for Latin Epigraphy*] .... AIEL
Association Internationale pour l'Etude des Argiles [*International Association for the Study of Clays*] .... AIPEA
Association Internationale d'Etude des Civilisations Mediterraneennes [*International Association of Studies on Mediterranean Civilizations*] .... AIECM
Association Internationale pour l'Etude de la Mosaique Antique [*International Association for the Study of Ancient Mosaics*] .... AIEMA
Association Internationale des Etudes Francaises .... AIEF
Association Internationale des Etudes de l'Asie du Sud-Est .... AIEAS
Association Internationale d'Etudes pour la Protection des Investissements .... ADPI
Association Internationale des Etudes et Recherches sur l'Information [*International Association of Mass Communications Research*] .... AIERI
Association Internationale d'Etudes du Sud-Est Europeen [*International Association of South-East European Studies*] .... AIESEE
Association Internationale des Etudiants en Agriculture [*International Association of Agricultural Students*] [*See also IAAS*] .... AIEA
Association Internationale des Etudiants Dentaires [*International Association of Dental Students*] .... AIED
Association Internationale des Etudiants en Sciences Economiques et Commerciales [*International Association of Students in Business and Economics*] .... AIESEC
Association Internationale d'Experts Scientifiques du Tourisme [*International Association of Scientific Experts in Tourism*] .... AIEST
Association Internationale des Femmes Medecins [*Medical Women's International Association*] .... AIFM
Association Internationale du Film d'Animation [*International Animated Film Association*] .... ASIFA
Association Internationale Futuribles [*Futuribles International*] .... AIF
Association Internationale de Geodesie [*International Association of Geodosy*] .... AIG
Association Internationale de Geologie de l'Ingenieur [*International Association of Engineering Geology*] .... AIGI
Association Internationale de Geomagnetisme et d'Aeronomie [*International Association of Geomagnetism and Aeronomy*] .... AIGA
Association Internationale de Grands Magasins [*International Association of Department Stores*] .... AIGM
Association Internationale de l'Hotellerie [*International Hotel Association*] .... AIH
Association Internationale d'Hydrologie Scientifique .... AIH
Association Internationale d'Hydrologie Scientifique .... AIHS
Association Internationale d'Information Scolaire Universitaire et Professionnelle [*International Association for Educational and Vocational Information*] .... AIISUP
Association Internationale des Interets Radio-Maritimes .... AIIRM
Association Internationale des Interpretes de Conference [*International Association of Conference Interpreters*] .... AIIC
Association Internationale des Jeunes Avocats [*Young Lawyers' International Association*] .... AIJA
Association Internationale des Journalistes Philateliques [*International Association of Philatelic Journalists*] .... AIJP
Association Internationale des Journalistes de la Presse Feminine et Familiale [*International Association of Women and Home Page Journalists*] .... AIJPF
Association Internationale des Juges des Enfants .... AIJE
Association Internationale de Juristes Democrates [*International Association of Democratic Lawyers*] .... AIJD
Association Internationale de Limnologie Theoretique et Appliquee. Travaux [*A publication*] ...... Assoc Int Limnol Theor Appl Trav
Association Internationale de Limnologie Theorique et Appliquee [*International Association of Theoretical and Applied Limnology*] .... AIL
Association Internationale de Linguistique Applique [*International Association of Applied Linguistics*] .... AILA
Association Internationale de Litterature Comparee [*International Comparative Literature Association*] .... AILC
Association Internationale des Lotteries d'Etat [*International Association of State Lotteries*] .... AILE
Association Internationale des Magistrats de la Jeunesse [*International Association of Youth Magistrates*] .... AIJE
Association Internationale de Medecine et de Biologie de l'Environnement [*International Association of Medicine and Biology of Environment - IAMBE*] .... AIMBE
Association Internationale de Meteorologie et de Physique de l'Atmosphere [*International Association of Meteorology and Atmospheric Physics*] .... AIMPA
Association Internationale des Metiers et Enseignements d'Art [*International Association for Crafts and the Teaching of Art*] .... AIMEA
Association Internationale de la Meunerie [*International Milling Association - IMA*] .... AIM
Association Internationale de Musees de Transports [*International Association of Transport Museums - IATM*] .... AIMT
Association Internationale de la Mutualite [*International Association for Mutual Assistance*] .... AIM

Association Internationale des Numismates Professionnels [*International Association of Professional Numismatists*] [*See also IAPN*] ... AINP
Association Internationale d'Oceanographie Biologie [*International Association of Biological Oceanography*] ... AIOB
Association Internationale d'Oceanographie Physique ... AIOP
Association Internationale d'Organisateurs de Courses Cyclistes [*International Association of Organizers of Cycle Competitions*] ... AIOCC
Association Internationale d'Orientation Professionnelle ... AIOP
Association Internationale d'Orientation Scolaire et Professionnelle [*International Association for Educational and Vocational Guidance*] [*See also IAEVG*] ... AIOSP
Association Internationale des Palais des Congres [*International Association of Congress Centers*] ... AIPC
Association Internationale de Papyrologues [*International Association of Papyrologists*] ... AIP
Association Internationale de Pediatrie [*International Pediatric Association*] [*See also IPA*] ... AIP
Association Internationale Permanente des Congres de Navigation [*Permanent International Association of Navigation Congresses*] ... AIPCN
Association Internationale Permanente des Congres de la Route [*Permanent International Association of Road Congresses*] [*See also PIARC*] ... AIPCR
Association Internationale des Ponts et Charpentes [*International Association for Bridge and Structural Engineering*] ... AIPC
Association Internationale de la Presse Echiqueenne [*International Association of Chess Press*] ... AIPE
Association Internationale de Presse pour l'Etude des Problemes d'Outre-Mer [*International Press Association for Studying Overseas Problems*] ... AIPEPO
Association Internationale de la Presse Sportive [*International Sporting Press Association*] ... AIPS
Association Internationale pour la Prevention du Suicide [*International Association for Suicide Prevention*] ... AIPS
Association Internationale des Producteurs de l'Horticulture [*International Association of Horticultural Producers*] ... AIPH
Association Internationale des Professeurs de Philosophie [*International Association of Teachers of Philosophy*] ... AIPPh
Association Internationale pour le Progres Social ... AIPS
Association Internationale de Prophylaxie de la Cecite [*International Association for the Prevention of Blindness*] ... AIPC
Association Internationale pour la Protection de la Propriete Industrielle [*International Association for the Protection of Industrial Property*] ... AIPPI
Association Internationale de la Psychologie Adlerienne [*International Association of Adlerian Psychology*] ... AIPA
Association Internationale de Psychologie Appliquee [*International Association of Applied Psychology*] ... AIPA
Association Internationale pour la Recherche et la Diffusion des Methodes Audio-Visuelles et Structuroglobales [*International Association for the Study and Promotion of Audio-Visual and Structuro-Global Methods*] ... AIMAV
Association Internationale pour la Recherche Medicale et les Echanges Culturels [*International Association for Medical Research and Cultural Exchange*] ... AIRMEC
Association Internationale pour les Recherches au Bas Fourneau d'Ougree ... AIRBO
Association Internationale de Recherches Hydrauliques [*International Association of Hydraulic Research*] ... AIRH
Association Internationale du Registre des Bateaux du Rhin [*International Association of the Rhine Ships Register*] ... AIRBR
Association Internationale de la Savonnerie et de la Detergence [*International Association of the Soap and Detergent Industry*] ... AIS
Association Internationale de Science Politique [*International Political Science Association*] ... AISP
Association Internationale de la Science du Sol [*International Society of Soil Science*] [*See also ISSS*] ... AISS
Association Internationale des Sciences Economiques [*International Economic Association*] ... AISE
Association Internationale des Sciences de l'Education [*International Association for the Advancement of Educational Research*] ... AISE
Association Internationale des Sciences Hydrologiques [*International Association of Hydrological Sciences*] ... AISH
Association Internationale des Sciences Hydrologiques. Publication [*A publication*] ... Assoc Int Sci Hydrol Publ
Association Internationale des Sciences Juridiques [*International Association of Legal Science*] ... AISJ
Association Internationale des Sciences Physique de l'Ocean [*International Association for the Physical Sciences of the Ocean*] ... AISPO
Association Internationale pour la Securite Aerienne [*International Air Safety Association*] ... AISA
Association Internationale de la Securite Sociale [*International Social Security Association*] ... AISS
Association Internationale de Seismologie et de Physique de l'Interieur de la Terre ... AISPIT
Association Internationale des Selectionneurs pour la Protection des Obtentions Vegetales [*International Association of Plant Breeders for the Protection of Plant Varieties*] ... ASSINSEL
Association Internationale de Signalisation Maritime [*International Association of Lighthouse Authorities*] ... AISM
Association Internationale des Skal Clubs [*International Association of Skal Clubs*] ... AISC
Association Internationale des Societes d'Assurance Mutuelle [*International Association of Mutual Insurance Companies - IAMIC*] ... AISAM
Association Internationale des Societes de Microbiologie [*International Association of Microbiology Societies*] ... AISM
Association Internationale de Sociologie [*International Sociological Association*] ... AIS
Association Internationale de la Soie [*International Silk Association*] ... AIS
Association Internationale pour le Sport des Aveugles [*International Blind Sports Association - IBSA*] ... AISA
Association Internationale de Standardisation Biologique [*International Association of Biological Standardization - IABS*] ... AISB
Association Internationale de la Teinture et de l'Impression Textiles [*International Association of Textile Dyers and Printers - IATDP*] ... AITIT
Association Internationale du Theatre d'Amateurs [*International Amateur Theatre Association*] ... AITA
Association Internationale du Theatre pour l'Enfance et la Jeunesse [*International Association of Theater for Children and Youth*] ... ASSITEJ
Association Internationale des Traducteurs de Conference [*International Association of Conference Translators*] ... AITC
Association Internationale des Travailleurs [*International Association of Workers*] [*France*] ... AIT
Association Internationale des Universites [*International Association of Universities*] ... AIU
Association Internationale Urbanisme et Commerce [*International Association for Town Planning and Distribution*] ... URBANICOM
Association Internationale des Urbanistes [*International Society of City and Regional Planners*] [*See also ISoCaRP*] ... AIU
Association Internationale des Usagers d'Embranchements Particuliers [*International Association of Users of Private Sidings*] ... AIEP
Association Internationale des Utilisateurs de Files de Fibres Artificielles et Synthetiques [*International Association of Users of Yarn of Man-Made Fibers*] ... AIUFFAS
Association Internationale Veterinaire de Production Animale [*International Veterinary Association for Animal Production*] [*See also IVAAP*] ... AIVPA
Association Internationale pour les Voiles Minces [*en Beton*] [*International Association for Shell Structures*] ... AIVM
Association Internationale de Volcanologie [*International Association of Volcanology*] ... AIV
Association Internationale de Volcanologie et de Chimie de l'Interieur de la Terre [*International Association of Volcanology and Chemistry of the Earth's Interior*] ... AIVCIT
Association Interparlementaire du Tourisme [*Interparliamentary Association for Tourism*] ... AIDT
Association of Interpretive Naturalists ... AIN
Association of Interracial Marriages ... AIM
Association of Interstate Commerce Commission Practitioners ... AICCP
Association of Interstate Motor Carriers ... AIMC
Association of Interstate Motor Carriers, Newark NJ [*STAC*] ... AIC
Association for the Introduction of New Biological Nomenclature ... AINBN
Association of Investment Brokers ... AIB
Association of Iron Ore Exporting Countries ... AIOEC
Association of Iron and Steel Engineers ... AISE
Association of Island Marine Laboratories of the Caribbean ... AIMLC
Association on Japanese Textile Imports [*Defunct*] ... AJTI
Association of Jensen Owners ... AJO
Association of Jesuit Colleges and Universities [*Later, JSEA*] ... AJCU
Association de la Jeunesse Bakoko [*Association of Bakoko Youth*] ... AJBA
Association de la Jeunesse Camerounaise [*Cameroonian Youth Association*] ... AJC
Association de la Jeunesse Mauritanienne [*Mauritanian Youth Association*] ... AJM
Association des Jeunesse Nationalistes du Kongo [*Association of Nationalist Youth of the Congo*] [*Leopoldville*] ... AJENAKO
Association of Jewish Anti-Poverty Workers [*Superseded by ECJF*] ... AJAPW
Association of Jewish Book Publishers ... AJBP
Association of Jewish Center Workers ... AJCW
Association of Jewish Chaplains of the Armed Forces ... AJCAF
Association of Jewish Community Relations Workers ... AJCRW
Association of Jewish Family and Children's Agencies ... AJFCA
Association of Jewish Libraries ... AJL
Association of Jewish Refugees in Great Britain ... AJR
Association of Jewish Sponsored Camps ... AJSC
Association for Jewish Studies ... AJS
Association for Jewish Youth [*British*] ... AJY
Association des Juifs Anciens Resistants [*Association of Jews in the Resistance*] [*Acronym is pseudonym of writer Romain Gary*] ... AJAR

Association of Junior Leagues .... AJL
Association of the Junior Leagues of America [*Later, AJL*] .... AJLA
Association of Kew Gardeners in America .... AKGA
Association of Kinsmen Clubs .... KIN
Association of Knitted Fabrics Manufacturers .... AKFM
Association for Korean Studies .... AKS
Association of Korean University Presses .... AKUP
Association of Labor-Management Administrators and Consultants on Alcoholism .... ALMACA
Association of Labor Mediation Agencies [*Later, ALRA*] .... ALMA
Association of Labor Relations Agencies [*Formerly, ASMA, ALMA*] .... ALRA
Association of Ladies of Charity of the United States .... ALCUS
Association of Land Grant Colleges and Universities [*Later, NASULGC*] .... ALGCU
Association of Land and Property Owners .... ALPO
Association for Latin American Studies [*Defunct*] .... ALAS
Association for Latin Liturgy .... ALL
Association of Latvian Academic Societies .... ALAS
Association of Learned and Professional Society Publishers [*British*] .... ALPSP
Association of Learning Disabled Adults .... ALDA
Association of Legal Administrators .... ALA
Association of Legal Aid Attorneys of the City of New York .... ALAA
Association for the Liberation of Ukraine .... ALU
Association of Libertarian Feminists .... ALF
Association of Libraries of Judaica and Hebraica in Europe .... ALJH
Association for Library Automation Research Communications .... LARC
Association for Library Information, Pittsburgh, PA [*OCLC symbol*] .... AFL
Association for Library Service to Children [*Formerly, CSD*] [*American Library Association*] .... ALSC
Association of Life Agency Officers [*Later, LIMRA*] .... ALAO
Association of Life Insurance Counsel .... ALIC
Association of Life Insurance Medical Directors of America .... ALIMDA
Association for Literary and Linguistic Computing .... ALLC
Association for Literary and Linguistic Computing. Bulletin [*A publication*] .... ALLCB
Association of Literary Magazines of America [*Later, CCLM*] .... ALMA
Association of Lithuanian Foresters in Exile .... LMSI
Association of Lithuanian Workers .... ALW
Association Litteraire et Artistique Internationale [*International Literary and Artistic Association*] .... ALAI
Association for Living Historical Farms and Agricultural Museums .... ALHFAM
Association of Local Air Pollution Control Officials .... ALAPCO
Association of Local Housing Finance Agencies .... ALHFA
Association of Local Transport Airlines .... ALTA
Association of Long Distance Telephone Companies .... ALTEL
Association for Loss Prevention and Security .... ALPS
Association of Lunar and Planetary Observers .... ALPO
Association of Lutheran College Faculties .... ALCF
Association of Lutheran Secondary Schools .... ALSS
Association for Machine Translation and Computational Linguistics [*Later, Association for Computational Linguistics*] .... AMTCL
Association of Machinery and Equipment Appraisers .... AMEA
Association for Macular Diseases .... AMD
Association for Major Symphony Orchestras [*Formerly, WASO*] .... AMSO
Association Management [*A publication*] .... Assoc Manage
Association of Management Analysts in State and Local Government .... AMASLG
Association of Management Analysts in State and Local Government .... MASLIG
Association of Management Consultants .... AMC
Association for Management Excellence [*Formerly, NMTA, AAIM*] .... AME
Association of Management in Public Health [*Later, AAHA*] .... AMPH
Association of Manufacturers of Confectionery and Chocolate .... AMCC
Association of Marian Helpers .... AMH
Association of Marine Engineering Schools [*British*] .... AMES
Association of Marine Underwriters of the United States .... AMUUS
Association Marketing Roundtable .... AMR
Association of Married Women .... AMW
Association of Master of Business Administration Executives .... AMBAE
Association of Maximum Service Telecasters .... AMST
Association of Maximum Service Telecasters .... MST
Association for Measurement and Evaluation in Guidance .... AMEG
Association for Media-Based Continuing Education for Engineers .... AMCEE
Association of Media Producers .... AMP
Association for Media Psychology .... AMP
Association of Medical Advertising Agencies .... AMAA
Association of Medical Group Psychoanalysts .... AMGP
Association of Medical Illustrators .... AMI
Association of Medical Record Consultants [*Defunct*] .... AMRC
Association of Medical Rehabilitation Directors and Coordinators .... AMRDC
Association of Medical School Pediatric Department Chairmen .... AMSPDC
Association of Medical Superintendents of Mental Hospitals [*Later, American Association of Psychiatric Administrators*] .... AMSMH
Association Medicale Franco-Americaine .... AMFA
Association Medicale Internationale pour l'Etudes des Conditions de Vie et de Sante [*International Medical Association for the Study of Living Conditions and Health*] .... AMIEV
Association Medicale Mondiale [*World Medical Association*] .... AMM
Association of Members and Friends of the Historic Southern Tenant Farmers Union .... AMFHSTFU
Association for Men in Psychology .... AMP
Association Men (Rural Manhood) [*A publication*] .... Assn Men
Association of Men's Belt Manufacturers .... AMBM
Association of Mental Health Administrators .... AMHA
Association for Mental Health Affiliation with Israel .... AMHAI
Association of Mental Health Practitioners with Disabilities .... AMHPD
Association of Mental Hospital Clergy .... AMHC
Association of Mercy Colleges .... AMC
Association of Messenger Services .... AMS
Association of Methodist Historical Societies [*Later, General Commission on Archives and History of the United Methodist Church*] .... AMHS
Association of Metropolitan Authorities [*British*] .... AMA
Association of Metropolitan Chief Librarians [*London*] .... AMCL
Association of Metropolitan Sewerage Agencies .... AMSA
Association for Mexican Cave Studies .... AMCS
Association for Middle-Income Housing [*Later, MMHA*] .... AMIH
Association of Midwest Fish and Game Commissioners [*Later, AMFWA*] .... AMFGC
Association of Midwest Fish and Wildlife Agencies [*Formerly, AMFGC, AMFWC*] .... AMFWA
Association of Midwest Fish and Wildlife Commissioners [*Formerly, AMFGC*] [*Later, AMFWA*] .... AMFWC
Association of Military Colleges and Schools .... AMCS
Association of Military Dental Surgeons .... AMDS
Association of Military Surgeons of the United States .... AMS
Association of Military Surgeons of the United States .... AMSUS
Association of Mill and Elevator Mutual Insurance Companies .... AMEMIC
Association of Minicomputer Users .... AMU
Association of Missile and Rocket Industries .... AMRI
Association Mondiale des Amis de l'Enfance [*World Association of Young People's Friends*] .... AMADE
Association Mondiale pour l'Ecole Instrument de Paix [*World Association for the School as an Instrument of Peace*] .... EIP
Association Mondiale des Femmes Chefs d'Enterprises [*World Association of Women Business Leaders*] [*Formerly, Les Femmes Chefs d'Enterprises Mondiales*] [*Association retains the earlier acronym*] .... FCEM
Association Mondiale des Guides et des Eclaireuses [*World Association of Girl Guides and Girl Scouts - WAGGGS*] .... AMGE
Association Mondiale des Inventeurs [*World Association of Inventors and Researchers*] .... AMINA
Association Mondiale de Lutte Contre la Faim [*World Association for the Struggle Against Hunger*] .... ASCOFAM
Association Mondiale des Medecins Francophones .... AMMF
Association Mondiale de Prospective Sociale [*World Social Prospects Study Association*] .... AMPS
Association Mondiale des Sciences de l'Education [*World Association for Educational Research - WAER*] .... AMSE
Association Mondiale des Travailleurs Scientifiques [*Scientific Workers World Association*] .... AMTS
Association Mondiale Veterinaire [*World Veterinary Association*] [*See also WVA*] .... AMV
Association Mondiale des Veterinaires Microbiologistes, Immunologistes, et Specialistes des Maladies Infectieuses [*World Association of Veterinary Microbiologists, Immunologists, and Specialists in Infectious Diseases*] [*See also WAVMI*] .... AMVMI
Association Mondiale de Zootechnie [*World Association for Animal Production*] .... AMZ
Association Montessori Internationale [*International Montessori Association*] .... AMI
Association of Motion Picture Producers [*Later, AMPTP*] .... AMPP
Association of Motion Picture and Television Producers [*Formerly, AMPP*] .... AMPTP
Association for Multi-Image .... AMI
Association of Multiracial Playgroups .... AMP
Association of Municipal Corporations [*British*] .... AMC
Association of Museum Stores .... AMS
Association of Muslim Scientists and Engineers .... AMSE
Association of Muslim Social Scientists .... AMSS
Association of Mutual Fire Insurance Engineers [*Later, ILCA*] .... AMFIE
Association of Mutual Fund Plan Sponsors [*Later, ICI*] .... AMFPS
Association of Mutual Insurance Engineers [*Later, ILCA*] .... AMIE
Association of National Advertisers .... ANA
Association of National Grasslands .... ANG
Association for a National Recycling Policy .... ANRP
Association Nationale de la Recherche Technique [*France*] .... ANRT
Association of Natural Rubber Producing Countries .... ANRPC
Association of Naval Aviation .... ANA
Association of Naval Weapons, Engineers, and Scientists [*Later, ASE*] .... ANWES
Association du Negoce des Grains Oleagineuses, Huiles, et Graisses Animales et Vegetales et Leurs Derives de la CEE [*Trade Association for Oilseeds, Oil, Vegetable and Animal Fats and Their Derivatives of the European Economic Community*] .... ANGO
Association of Negro Press Photographers .... ANPP

Association of Newspaper Classified Advertising Managers .... ANCAM
Association for Non-White Concerns in Personnel and Guidance ...... ANWC
Association of North American Directory Publishers .... ANADP
Association of North American Missions .... ANAM
Association of North American Radio Clubs .... ANARC
Association for Nuclear Development and Research in Electrical Engineering .... ANDREE
Association of Nuclear Instrument Manufacturers [*Later, SAMA*]........ ANIM
Association of Obedience Clubs and Judges .... AOCJ
Association des Obtenteurs de Pommes de Terre du Marche Commun [*Association of Certified Seed Potato Suppliers of the Common Market*].. ASSOPOMAC
Association of Official Agricultural Chemists. Journal [*A publication*]... Assn Offic Ag Chem J
Association of Official Agricultural Chemists. Journal [*A publication*]... Assoc Official Agr Chemists Jour
Association of Official Analytical [*formerly, Agricultural*] **Chemists**..... AOAC
Association of Official Racing Chemists .... AORC
Association of Official Seed Analysts .... AOSA
Association of Official Seed Certifying Agencies .... AOSCA
Association of Oil Pipe Lines .... AOPL
Association of Oilwell Servicing Contractors .... AOSC
Association of Old Crows .... AOC
Association of Operating Room Nurses .... AORN
Association of Operating Room Nurses. Journal [*A publication*]........ AORN J
Association of Operating Room Technicians [*Later, AST*] .... AORT
Association of Operative Millers .... AOM
Association of Optometric Educators .... AOE
Association des Organisations Nationales d'Entreprises de Peche de la CEE [*Association of National Organizations of Fishing Enterprises in the European Economic Community*] .... EUROPECHE
Association des Organisations Professionnelles du Commerce des Sucres pour les Pays de la CEE [*Association of Sugar Trade Organizations for the EEC Countries*] .... ASSUC
Association des Originaires de Bandounga [*Association of Natives of Bandounga*] .... AOB
Association of Orthodox Jewish Scientists .... AOJS
Association of Orthodox Jewish Teachers .... AOJT
Association of Orthopaedic Chairmen .... AOC
Association of Osteopathic Publications [*Defunct*] .... AOP
Association of Osteopathic State Executive Directors .... AOSED
Association of Our Lady of Salvation [*Defunct*]................................. AOLS
Association of Outplacement Consulting Firms .... AOCF
Association of Overseas Educators .... AOE
Association of Pacific Fisheries [*Later, PSPA*]...................................... APF
Association Package Sequence Number .... APSN
Association Parlementaire Europe-Afrique [*Eur-African Parliamentary Association*]... APEA
Association of Parliamentary Librarians in Canada .... APLIC
Association of Paroling Authorities .... APA
Association of Part-Time Professionals .... AP-TP
Association of Pathology Chairmen .... APC
Association des Pays Exportateurs de Mineral de Fer [*Association of Iron Ore Exporting Countries*]................................. APEF
Association of Pediatric Oncology Nurses .... APON
Association of Personnel Agencies of New York .... APANY
Association of Petroleum Re-Refiners .... APR
Association of Petroleum Writers .... APW
Association of Philippine-American Women .... APAW
Association of Philippine Coconut Desiccators .... APCD
Association of Philippine Practicing Physicians in America .... APPPA
Association of Philosophy Journals Editors .... APJE
Association for Philosophy of the Unconscious .... APU
Association Phonetique Internationale [*International Phonetic Association*] .... API
Association of Photo Sensitizers .... APS
Association of Photographic Importers and Distributors .... APID
Association of Physical Fitness Centers .... APFC
Association for Physical and Mental Rehabilitation [*Later, ACTA*] ...... APMR
Association of Physical Plant Administrators of Universities and Colleges .... APPA
Association of Physical Plant Administrators of Universities and Colleges .... APPAUC
Association for Physical and System Mathematics .... APSM
Association of Physician Assistant Programs .... APAP
Association of Planned Parenthood Physicians .... APPP
Association of Podiatrists in Federal Service [*Formerly, MAP*]............ APFS
Association for Poetry Therapy [*Later, NAPT*] .... APT
Association of Polish Women of the United States .... APWUS
Association of Political Risk Analysts .... APRA
Association for Politics and the Life Sciences .... APLS
Association for Population/Family Planning Libraries and Information Centers, International .... APLICI
Association of Port Authorities .... APA
Association of Poultry Slaughterhouse Operators .... APSO
Association for Practitioners in Infection Control .... APIC
Association for Precision Graphics [*Defunct*] .... APG
Association of Presbyterian Colleges and Universities .... APCU
Association for the Preservation of Anti-Psychiatric Artifacts .... APAPA
Association for the Preservation of the Auction Markets .... APAM
Association for the Preservation of Political Americana .... APPA
Association for the Preservation and Presentation of the Arts .... APPA
Association for Preservation Technology .... APT
Association for the Preservation of Virginia Antiquities .... APVA
Association of Private Camps [*Later, AIC*] .... APC
Association of Private Enterprise Education .... APEE
Association of Private Hospitals .... APH
Association of Private Libraries .... APL
Association of Private Office Personnel Agencies .... APOPA
Association of Private Pension and Welfare Plans .... APPWP
Association of Private Postal Systems .... APPS
Association of Producing Artists .... APA
Association des Producteurs d'Isoglucose de la CE [*Association of the Producers of Isoglucose of the European Community*] [*Common Market*].. API
Association des Producteurs de Sorbitol de la CEE [*Association of Sorbitol Producers within the European Economic Community*] .... ASPEC
Association of Productivity Specialists .... APS
Association des Professeurs Franco-Americains [*Defunct*]................... APFA
Association of Professional Ball Players of America .... APBPA
Association of Professional Baseball Physicians .... APBP
Association for Professional Broadcasting Education [*Later, Broadcast Education Association*] .... APBE
Association of Professional Color Laboratories .... APCL
Association for Professional Education for Ministry .... APEM
Association of Professional Genealogists .... APG
Association of Professional Geological Scientists [*Later, AIPG*] .... APGS
Association of Professional Insurance Women [*Acronym now used as name of association*] .... APIW
Association of Professional Material Handling Consultants .... APMHC
Association of Professional Photogrammetrists .... APP
Association of Professional Vocal Ensembles .... APVE
Association Professionnelle Apolitique du Katanga [*Non-Political Professional Association of Katanga*]................................. APAK
Association Professionnelle de Colons Individuels [*Professional Association of Colonials*] .... APROCOLIN
Association Professionnelle International des Medicins [*International Professional Association of Physicians*]...................... APIM
Association of Professors of Gynecology and Obstetrics .... APGO
Association of Professors of Medicine .... APM
Association of Professors of Missions .... APM
Association of Professors and Researchers in Religious Education .... APRRE
Association of Program Directors in Internal Medicine .... APDIM
Association of Programmed Learning .... APL
Association for Programmed Learning and Educational Technology .... APLET
Association on Programs for Female Offenders .... APFO
Association of Progressive Rental Organizations .... APRO
Association for Promoting Christian Knowledge [*Church of Ireland*] .... APCK
Association for Promoting the Reform of Convocation [*British*] .... APRC
Association for Promoting Unity of Christendom .... APUC
Association for the Promotion of Humor in International Affairs .... APHIA
Association for the Promotion of the International Circulation of the Press [*Distipress*] .... APICP
Association pour la Promotion Sociale de la Masse [*Association for the Social Betterment of the People*] [*Rwanda and Burundi*] .... APROSOMA
Association for the Protection of the Adirondacks .... APA
Association of Psychiatric Outpatient Centers of America .... POCA
Association for Psychiatric Treatment of Offenders .... APTO
Association for Psychoanalytic Medicine .... APM
Association de Psychologie Scientifique de Langue Francaise [*French-Language Association of Scientific Psychology*] .... APSLF
Association for the Psychophysiological Study of Sleep .... APSS
Association for Psychotheatrics [*Defunct*] .... AP
Association of Public Data Users .... APDU
Association for Public Justice .... APJ
Association of Public and Private Labor Employees .... APPLE
Association of Public Radio Stations [*Later, NPR*]................................ APRS
Association of Publication Production Managers .... APPM
Association of Publicly Traded Investment Funds .... APTIF
Association of Publishers Representatives [*Later, NAPR*] .... APR
Association for Puerto Rican-Hispanic Culture .... APRHC
Association of Pulp Consumers, Inc. [*Later, American Paper Institute*] .... APC
Association of Pulp Consumers, Incorporated .... APCI
Association of Racquetsports Manufacturers and Suppliers .... ARMS
Association of Radio News Analysts [*Later, ARTNA*]............................ ARNA
Association of Radio-Television News Analysts .... ARTNA
Association of Railroad Advertising Managers .... ARAM
Association of Railroad Editors [*Formerly, ARMEA*] .... ARE
Association of Railway Museums .... ARM
Association of Railway Trainmen and Locomotive Firemen .... ARTLF
Association of Railway Trainmen and Locomotive Firemen .... RTLF
Association of Rain Apparel Contractors .... ARAC
Association for Rational Environmental Alternatives .... AREA
Association of Real Estate Syndicators .... ARES
Association for Realistic Philosophy .... ARP

Association pour les Recherches sur les Parodontopathies [*International Association for Research in Paradentosis*] ... ARPA
Association for Recorded Sound Collections ... ARSC
Association for Recorded Sound Collections. Journal [*A publication*] ... ARSC
Association for Recorded Sound Collections. Journal [*A publication*] ... ARSCJ
Association of Records Executives and Administrators [*Later, ARMA*] ... AREA
Association of Records Managers and Administrators [*Formerly, AREA*] ... ARMA
Association for the Reduction of Aircraft Noise ... ARAN
Association Referral Information Service ... ARIS
Association of Reform Zionists of America ... ARZA
Association of Regional Religious Communicators ... ARRC
Association of Registered Bank Holding Companies [*Later, Association of Bank Holding Companies*] ... ARBHC
Association of Regular Army Sergeants ... ARAS
Association of Rehabilitation Centers [*Later, NARF*] ... ARC
Association of Rehabilitation Nurses ... ARN
Association of Rehabilitation Programs in Data Processing ... ARPDP
Association of Religion and Applied Behavioral Science [*Later, ACC*] ... ARABS
Association for Religious Education ... ARE
Association for Religious Education Aspects of Education. Bulletin [*A publication*] ... AREA
Association for Religious and Value Issues in Counseling ... ARVIC
Association to Remind Husbands to Remember Birthdays and Anniversaries [*Probably mythical*] ... ATRHTRBAA
Association to Repeal Abortion Laws ... ARAL
Association of Representatives of Professional Athletes ... ARPA
Association of Reproduction Materials Manufacturers ... ARMM
Association for Research, Administration, Professional Councils and Societies ... ARAPCS
Association for Research of Childhood Cancer ... AROCC
Association for Research in Cosmecology ... ARC
Association of Research Directors ... ARD
Association for Research and Enlightenment ... ARE
Association for Research and Enlightenment, Virginia Beach, VA [*Library symbol*] ... ViVbRE
Association for Research in Growth Relationships ... ARGR
Association of Research Libraries ... ARL
Association of Research Libraries Collection Analysis Project ... ARLCAP
Association of Research Libraries. Minutes [*A publication*] ... ARL Mins
Association for Research in Nervous and Mental Disease ... ARNMD
Association for Research in Ophthalmology [*Later, ARVO*] ... ARO
Association for Research in Vision and Ophthalmology [*Formerly, ARO*] ... ARVO
Association of Reserve City Bankers ... ARCB
Association of Reserve Officers of the US Public Health Service ... AROUSPHS
Association des Ressortissants du Haut et du Moyen Congo [*Association of Natives of the Upper and Middle Congo*] ... ASSORECO
Association des Restauratrices-Cuisinieres ... ARC
Association for Restriction of TV Commercials ... ARTVC
Association pour le Retablissement des Institutions et Oeuvres Israelites en France ... ARIF
Association of Retail Candy Shops ... ARCS
Association of Retail Travel Agents ... ARTA
Association of Retailer-Owned Wholesalers in Foodstuffs [*See also UGAL*] ... AROWF
Association for Retarded Citizens [*Formerly, NARC*] ... ARC
Association of Retired Persons International [*Later, IARP*] ... ARP
Association of Rhode Island Health Sciences Librarians [*Library network*] ... ARIHSL
Association of Rhodesian and Nyasaland Industries ... ARNI
Association of Road Racing Athletes ... ARRA
Association of Romanian-American Orthodox Ladies Auxiliaries ... ARAOLA
Association of Romanian Catholics of America ... ARCA
Association of Rotational Molders ... ARM
Association of Round Tables in Central Africa ... ARTCA
Association Royale Sportive Congolaise [*Congolese Royal Sporting Association*] ... ARSC
Association for Rural Mental Health [*Later, NARMH*] ... ARMH
Association of Russian-American Scholars in the USA ... ARASUSA
Association of Russian Imperial Medical Officers [*Defunct*] ... ARIMO
Association of Russian Imperial Naval Officers in America ... ARINOA
Association of Russian War Invalids of World War II ... ARWI
Association of Safety Council Executives ... ASCE
Association of Sales Administration Managers ... ASAM
Association for Sane Psychiatric Practices ... ASPP
Association of School Business Officials of the United States and Canada ... ASBO
Association for School, College, and University Staffing ... ASCUS
Association of Schools and Colleges of Optometry ... ASCO
Association of Schools of Public Health ... ASPH
Association for Science Education [*British*] ... ASE
Association of Science Museum Directors ... ASMD
Association of Science-Technology Centers ... ASTC
Association of Science-Technology Centers ... ASTEC
Association for Science, Technology, and Innovation ... ASTI
[*The*] **Association of the Scientific, Engineering, and Technological Community of Canada** ... SCITEC
Association for Scientific Journals ... ASJ
Association of Scientific, Technical, and Managerial Staffs [*British*] ... ASTMS
Association of Scientific Workers [*British*] ... AScW
Association Scientifique Europeenne pour la Prevision Economique a Moyen et Long Terme [*European Scientific Association for Medium and Long-Term Economic Forecasts*] ... ASEPELT
Association Scientifique Internationale du Cafe [*International Scientific Association of Coffee*] ... ASIC
Association Scientifique et Technique pour la Recherche en Informatique Documentaire [*Scientific and Technical Association for Research in Documentary Information*] [*Information service*] [*Belgium*] ... ASTRID
Association of Scientists and Engineers of the Naval Sea Systems Command [*Formerly, ASEBS*] ... ASE
Association of Scientists and Professional Engineering Personnel ... ASPEP
Association of Screen Magazine Publishers [*Defunct*] ... ASMP
Association of Seafood Importers ... ASI
Association of Second Class Mail Publishers ... ASCMP
Association of Secretaries General of Parliaments ... ASGP
Association of Secretaries Young Men's Christian Associations [*Later, YMCA*] ... ASYMCA
Association of Seminary Professors in the Practical Fields [*Later, APEM*] ... ASPPF
Association Senegalaise pour l'Etude du Quaternaire de l'Ouest Africain ... ASEQUA
Association of Senior Engineers [*NAVSHIPS*] ... ASE
Association of Senior Engineers of the Bureau of Ships [*Later, ASE*] ... ASEBS
Association of Seventh-Day Adventist Educators ... ASDAE
Association of Seventh Day Pentecostal Assemblies ... ASDPA
[*The*] **Association for the Severely Handicapped** ... TASH
Association of Ship Brokers and Agents (USA) ... ASBA
Association of Short-Circuit Testing Authorities. Publication [*A publication*] ... ASS Short-Circuit Test Auth Publ
Association for Short Term Psychotherapy ... ASTP
Association for Sickle Cell Anemia [*Defunct*] ... ASCA
Association for Singles ... AS
Association des Sinistres et Repatries de Cote d'Ivoire [*Association of the Wounded and Repatriates of the Ivory Coast*] ... ASSOSIRACI
Association of Sleep Disorders Centers ... ASDC
Association for Small Business Advancement ... ASBA
Association of Small Computer Users [*Later, ACU*] ... ASCU
Association of Smoked Fish Processors ... ASFP
Association of Social Anthropologists of the Commonwealth ... ASA
Association for Social Anthropology in Oceania ... ASAO
Association of Social and Behavioral Scientists ... ASBS
Association for Social Design [*Later, BRI*] ... ASD
Association for Social Economics [*Formerly, CEA*] ... ASE
Association of Social Science Teachers [*Later, ASBS*] ... ASST
Association for Social Work Education in Africa ... ASWEA
Association and Society Manager [*A publication*] ... Assoc Soc Manager
Association for the Sociological Study of Jewry ... ASSJ
Association for the Sociology of Religion ... ASR
Association of Software Brokers ... ASB
Association for Software Protection ... ASP
Association of Soil Conservation Officer Trainees ... ASCOT
Association of Soil and Foundation Engineers ... ASFE
Association in Solidarity with Guatemala ... ASOGUA
Association of the Sons of Poland ... SSP
Association of South East Asia [*Later, ASEAN*] ... ASA
Association of South East Asian Nations [*Indonesia, Malaysia, the Philippines, Singapore, and Thailand*] [*Formerly, Association of South East Asia*] ... ASEAN
Association of South-East Asian States ... ASAS
Association of Southeast Asian Institutions of Higher Learning ... ASAIHL
Association of Southeast Asian University Students ... ASEAUS
Association of Southeastern Research Libraries [*Library network*] ... ASERL
Association of Southern Agricultural Workers [*Later, SAAS*] ... ASAW
Association of Southern Baptist Campus Ministers ... ASBCM
Association of Southern Baptist Colleges and Schools ... ASBCS
Association of Special Libraries of the Philippines ... ASLP
Association of Special Libraries of the Philippines. Bulletin [*A publication*] ... ASLP Bul
Association of Special Libraries of the Philippines. Bulletin [*A publication*] ... ASLP Bull
Association for Specialists in Group Work ... ASGW
Association of Specialized and Cooperative Library Agencies [*American Library Association*] ... ASCLA
Association of Specialized Film Exhibitors ... ASFE
Association of Sports Information Directors ... ASID
Association of Sports Museums and Halls of Fame ... ASMHF
Association of Sprocket Chain Manufacturers [*Defunct*] ... ASCM
Association of Sri-Lankans in America ... ASIA

Association pour les Stages et l'Accueil des Techniciens d'Outre-Mer [*Association for the Reception and Instruction of Overseas Technicians*] ASATOM
Association for Stamp Exhibitions [*Defunct*] ASE
Association of Standards Laboratories ASL
Association of State Colleges and Universities [*Later, AASCU*] ASCU
Association of State Colleges and Universities Forestry Research Organizations ASCUFRO
Association of State Correctional Administrators [*Formerly, CAA*] ASCA
Association of State Democratic Chairs ASDC
Association of State Foresters [*Later, NASF*] ASF
Association of State and Interstate Water Pollution Control Administrators ASIWPCA
Association of State Juvenile Justice Administrators ASJJA
Association of State Labor Relations Agencies ASLRA
Association of State Library Agencies [*Formerly, Association of State Libraries*] [*Later, ASCLA*] ASLA
Association of State Library Agencies. President's Newsletter [*A publication*] ASLA Pres Newsl
Association of State Maternal and Child Health and Crippled Children's Directors ASMCHCCD
Association of State Mediation Agencies [*Later, ALRA*] ASMA
Association of State Planning and Development Agencies [*Later, NASDA*] ASPDA
Association of State and Provincial Safety Coordinators [*Later, ASPSO*] ASPSC
Association of State and Provincial Safety Officials [*Formerly, ASPSC*] ASPSO
Association of State Public Health Veterinarians [*Later, NASTPHV*] ASPHV
Association of State and Territorial Chronic Disease Program Directors ASTCDPD
Association of State and Territorial Dental Directors ASTDD
Association of State and Territorial Directors of Local Health Services [*Defunct*] ASTDLHS
Association of State and Territorial Directors of Nursing [*Formerly, ASTDPHN*] ASTDN
Association of State and Territorial Directors of Public Health Nursing [*Later, ASTDN*] ASTDPHN
Association of State and Territorial Health Officers ASTHO
Association of State and Territorial Nutrition Directors ASTND
Association of State and Territorial Public Health Laboratory Directors ASTPHLD
Association of State and Territorial Public Health Nutrition Directors ASTPHND
Association of State and Territorial Solid Waste Management Officials ASTSWMO
Association of State Universities and Land-Grant Colleges ASULGC
Association of Statisticians of American Religious Bodies ASARB
Association of Steel Distributors ASD
Association of Stock Exchange Firms [*Later, Securities Industry Association*] ASEF
Association Stomatologique Internationale [*International Stomatological Association*] ASI
Association-Storing Processor [*Data processing*] ASP
Association of Strategic Planning Consultants ASPC
Association of Structural Draftsmen of America ASDA
Association of Student Chapters, American Institute of Architects ASC/AIA
Association of Student Governments ASG
Association of Student International Law Societies ASILS
Association of Student and Professional Italian-Americans ASPI
Association for Student Teaching [*Later, ATE*] AST
Association for Student Teaching. Yearbook [*A publication*] Assn Stud Teach Yrbk
Association for the Study of Abortion [*Later, NAF*] ASA
Association for the Study of Afro-American Life and History ASALH
Association for the Study of Animal Behavior ASAB
Association for the Study of Dada and Surrealism ASDS
Association for the Study of the Grants Economy ASGE
Association for the Study of Higher Education ASHE
Association for the Study of Man-Environment Relations ASMER
Association for the Study of Medical Education ASME
Association for the Study of the Nationalities [*USSR and East Europe*] ASN
Association for the Study of Negro Life and History [*Later, Association for the Study of Afro-American Life and History*] ASNLH
Association for the Study of Soviet-Type Economies [*Later, ACES*] ASTE
Association for the Study of the World Refugee Problem AWR
Association of Sugar Producers of Puerto Rico [*Defunct*] ASPPR
Association Suisse des Syndicats Evangeliques [*Swiss Federation of Protestant Trade Unions*] ASSE
Association of Summer Session Deans and Directors [*Later, AUSS*] ASSDD
Association for Supervision and Curriculum Development ASCD
Association for Supervision and Curriculum Development. Yearbook [*A publication*] Assn Sup & Curric Devel Yrbk
Association of Supervisory Staff and Technicians [*British*] ASST
Association of Supervisory Staffs, Executives, and Technicians ASSET
Association of Surf Angling Clubs ASAC
Association of Surgical Technologists AST
Association for Symbolic Logic ASL
Association of Synthetic Yarn Manufacturers ASYM
Association of System 2000 Users for Technical Exchange ASTUTE
Association of Systematics Collections ASC
Association for Systems Management [*Formerly, SPA*] ASM
Association of Talent Agents ATA
Association of Tax Consultants ATC
Association of Teacher Educators ATE
Association of Teachers of English to Pupils from Overseas ATEPO
Association of Teachers of English as a Second Language ATESL
Association of Teachers in Independent Schools of New York City and Vicinity ATISNYCV
Association of Teachers of Japanese ATJ
Association of Teachers of Latin American Studies ATLAS
Association of Teachers of Maternal and Child Health ATMCH
Association of Teachers of Preventive Medicine ATPM
Association of Teachers of Russian. Journal [*A publication*] ATRJ
Association of Teachers of Technical Writing ATTW
Association of Technical Artists [*Later, IG*] ATA
Association of Technical Institutions ATI
Association of Technical Professionals ATP
Association Technique Internationale des Bois Tropicaux [*International Technical Association of Tropical Timber*] ATIBT
Association Technique Maritime et Aeronautique [*France*] ATMA
Association of Telephone Answering Services ATAS
Association of Temporary Office Services ATOS
Association of Temporary Personnel Contractors ATPC
Association of Tennis Professionals ATP
Association of Tequila Producers ATP
Association of Thalidomide-Damaged Children ATDC
Association of Theaters of Emilia and Romagna [*Ballet company*] ATER
Association of Theatre Benefit Agents [*Defunct*] ATBA
Association of Theatre Screen Advertising Companies [*Defunct*] ATSAC
Association of Theatrical Press Agents and Managers ATPAM
Association for Theological Education in the Near East ATENE
Association of Theological Schools ATS
Association of Third World Affairs ATWA
Association of Time-Sharing Users [*Later, ACU*] ATSU
Association of Tongue Depressors ATD
Association of Track and Field Statisticians ATFS
Association of Track and Structure Suppliers [*Later, REMSA*] ATSS
Association de Traducteurs et Reviseurs des Organisations et Conferences Intergouvernementales ATOCI
Association of Training and Employment Professionals ATEP
Association for Transarmament Studies ATS
Association for Transpersonal Psychology ATP
Association of Travel Marketing Executives ATME
Association of Trial Behavior Consultants ATBC
Association of Trial Lawyers of America [*Formerly, NACCA*] ATLA
Association for Tropical Biology ATB
Association des Tshokwe de Congo Belge, de l'Angola, et de la Rhodesie [*Association of Belgian Congolese, Angolan, and Rhodesian Tshokwe*] ATCAR
Association Typographique Internationale [*International Typographic Association*] ATYPI
Association of Ukrainian Sports Clubs in North America AUSC-NA
Association of Umbrella Manufacturers and Suppliers [*Defunct*] AUM
Association of Unclaimed Property Administrators [*Later, NAUPA*] AUPA
Association for the Understanding of Man AUM
Association for Union Democracy AUD
Association of United Contractors of America [*Defunct*] AUCOA
Association of the United States Army AUSA
Association of United States Members of International Institute of Space Law [*of International Astronautical Federation*] AUSMIISL
Association of United States Night Vision Manufacturers AUSNVM
Association of United States University Directors of International Agricultural Programs AUSUDIAP
Association Universelle d'Aviculture Scientifique [*World's Poultry Science Association*] [*See also WPSA*] AVI
Association Universitaire pour le Developpement de l'Enseignement et de la Culture en Afrique et a Madagascar AUDECAM
Association des Universitaires d'Europe AUE
Association d'Universites Partiellement ou Entierement de Langue Francaise [*Association of Partially or Wholly French-Language Universities*] AUPELF
Association of Universities of the British Commonwealth AUBC
Association of Universities and Colleges of Canada AUCC
Association of Universities and Colleges of Canada, Ottawa, ON, Canada [*Library symbol*] CaOOCU
Association of Universities for Research in Astronomy [*National Science Foundation*] AURA
Association of University Affiliated Facilities [*Later, AAUAP*] AUAF
Association of University Anesthetists AUA
Association of University Architects AUA
Association for University Business and Economic Research AUBER
Association of University Evening Colleges [*Later, Association for Continuing Higher Education*] AUEC
Association of University Professors of Ophthalmology AUPO
Association of University Programs in Health Administration AUPHA
Association of University Radiologists AUR

Association of University Summer Sessions .... AUSS
Association for Unmanned Vehicle Systems .... AUVS
Association of Uptown Converters .... AUC
Association of Urban Universities [*Defunct*] .... AUU
Association of US Chess Journalists [*Later, CJA*] .... AUSCJ
Association of Vacuum Equipment Manufacturers .... AVEM
Association Value [*Psychometrics*] .... AV
Association of Veterinary Inspectors .... AVI
Association of Viewdata Information Providers .... AVIP
Association of Visual Merchandise Representatives .... AVMR
Association of Visual Science Librarians .... AVSL
Association for Vital Records and Health Statistics .... AVRHS
Association of Vitamin Chemists .... AVC
Association of Voluntary Action Scholars .... AVAS
Association of Voluntary Agencies on Narcotics Treatment .... AVANT
Association for Voluntary Sterilization .... AVS
Association for Voluntary Sterilization, Inc., International Project, New York, NY [*Library symbol*] .... NNAVS
Association for Volunteer Administration [*Formerly, AAVSC, AAVS*] .... AVA
Association of Volunteer Bureaus .... AVB
Association of the Wall and Ceiling Industries-International .... AWCI
Association of Water Transportation Accounting Officers .... AWTAO
Association of Western Hospitals .... AWH
Association of Western Pulp and Paper Workers .... AWPPW
Association of Western Pulp and Paper Workers .... WPPW
Association of Western Railways [*Later, WRA*] .... AWR
Association of Woman Mathematicians [*Later, Association for Women in Mathematics*] .... AWM
Association of Women in Architecture .... AWA
Association of Women Broadcasters .... AWB
Association for Women in Computing .... AWC
Association for Women in Development .... AWD
Association for Women Geoscientists .... AWG
Association of Women Highway Safety Leaders .... AWHSL
Association for Women in Psychology .... AWP
Association for Women in Science .... AWIS
Association of Women Soil Scientists .... AWSS
Association for Women Veterinarians .... AWV
Association for Women's Active Return to Education [*Defunct*] .... AWARE
Association for Workplace Democracy .... AWD
Association of World Colleges and Universities [*Later, AWE*] .... AWCU
Association for World Education [*Formerly, AWCU*] .... AWE
Association for World Evangelism .... AWE
Association for a World Language .... AWL
Association of World Trade Chamber Executives .... AWTCE
Association for World Travel Exchange .... AWTE
Association for the World University .... AWU
Association of Yarn Distributors .... AYD
Association of Yugoslav Jews in the USA .... AYJUSA
Associations des Industries du Poisson de la CEE [*Association of the Fish Industries of the European Economic Community*] .... AIPCEE
Associative Array Processor .... AAP
Associative Computer Device .... ACD
Associative Interactive Dictionary [*for data bases*] [*National Library of Medicine*] .... AID
Associative Learning from Relative Environmental Data .... ALFRED
Associative List Selection .... ALS
Associative Memory Computer .... AMC
Associative Memory Device .... AMD
Associative Memory Organizing System .... AMOS
Associative Memory Processor [*Data processing*] .... AMP
Associative Memory System .... AMS
Associative Parallel Processor [*Data processing*] .... APP
Associative Principle for Addition [*New math*] .... APA
Associative Principle for Multiplication [*New math*] .... APM
Associative Processor [*Data processing*] .... AP
Associative Processor Microelectronic Element .... APME
Associative Programing Language [*Data processing*] .... APL
Associative Registers for Generalized User Switching [*Computer typesetting system*] .... ARGUS
Associative Structure Computer .... ASC
Associative Structures Package .... ASP
Associative Visual Cortex [*Anatomy*] .... AVC
Associazione Cristiana Artigiani Italiani .... ACAI
Associazione Elettrotecnica Italiana .... AEI
Associazione Generale tra i Magistrati Italiani .... AGMI
Associazione Internazionale di Archeologia Classica [*International Association for Classical Archeology*] [*See also IACA*] .... AIAC
Associazione Internazionale per gli Studi di Lingua e Letteratura Italiane [*International Association for the Study of the Italian Language and Literature - IASILL*] .... AISLLI
Associazione Internazionale Uomo nello Spazis .... AIUS
Associazione Italiana de Aeronautica e Astronautica .... AIDAA
Associazione Italiana di Aerotecnica .... AIDA
Associazione Italiana Biblioteche .... AIB
Associazione Italiana Biblioteche. Bollettino d'Informazioni [*A publication*] .... AIB Boll
Associazione Italiana Biblioteche. Bollettino d'Informazioni [*A publication*] .... Assn Italiana Bibl Boll Inf
Associazione Italiana per il Calcolo Automatico .... AICA
Associazione Italiana di Metallurgia .... AIM
Associazione Italiana Relazioni Pubbliche [*Italian public relations organization*] .... AIRP
Associazione Nazionale degli Ingegneri ed Architetti Italiani. Quaderni [*A publication*] .... Ass Naz Ing Architetti Ital Quad
Associazione Sindacati Lavoratore della Somalia [*Workers' Trade Union Association of Somalia*] .... ASLS
Associazione Studentesca Universitaria della Somalia [*University Students' Association of Somalia*] .... ASUS
Associazioni Cristiane Lavoratori Italiani .... ACLI
Associometrics Data Management System .... ADAM
Associometrics Remote Terminal Inquiry Control System .... ARTIC
Assort .... ASRT
Assort .... ASST
Assorted .... ASSTD
Assortment .... ASMT
Assortment .... AT
Assumed .... ASMD
Assumed Latitude [*Navigation*] .... AL
Assumed Mean .... AM
Assumed Position [*Navigation*] .... AP
Assumption College, Worcester, MA [*OCLC symbol*] .... AZM
Assumption College, Worcester, MA [*Library symbol*] .... MWAC
Assumption of Control Message [*Aviation*] .... AOC
Assumption Guild .... AG
Assumption High School, East St. Louis, IL [*Library symbol*] .... IEsAHS
Assumption Parish Library, Napoleonville, LA [*Library symbol*] .... LNapA
Assurance .... ASSCE
Assurance .... ASSNCE
Assurance Control Economics System .... ACES
Assurance Mutuelle [*Mutual Assurance*] [*French*] .... AM
Assurance sur la Vie [*Life Insurance*] [*French*] .... ASLV
Assure Competitive Transportation [*Truckers' lobby*] .... ACT
Assure Contre l'Incendie [*Assured Against Fire*] [*French*] .... ACI
Assured Depot Task .... ADT
Assured Destruction [*Capability*] [*of missiles*] .... AD
Assured Destruction Force [*Military*] .... ADF
Assured Field Shop Task .... AFST
Assurex International [*Formerly, ISAA, ISA*] .... AI
Assyria .... ASS
Assyria .... ASSYR
Assyriological Studies [*A publication*] .... Assyr S
Asta Werke AG [*Germany*] [*Research code symbol*] .... A
Asta Werke AG [*Germany*] [*Research code symbol*] .... P
Astable Blocking Oscillator .... ABO
Astable Multivibrator .... AMV
Astatine [*Chemical element*] .... At
Astern .... ASTN
Astern Flag [*Navy*] [*British*] .... AT
Asteroid Belt Probe .... ABP
Asteroid Meteoroid Detector .... AMD
Asterriquinone [*Antineoplastic drug*] .... ARQ
Asthma and Allergy Foundation of America .... A & AFA
Asthma Care Association of America .... ACAA
Asthma Research Council [*British*] .... ARC
Asthmatic Children's Foundation of New York .... ACFNY
ASTIA [*Armed Services Technical Information Agency*] **Document** .... AD
ASTIA [*Armed Services Technical Information Agency*] **Report Bibliography** .... ARB
Astigmatic Spectral Line .... ASL
Astigmatism [*Also, Ast*] [*Ophthalmology*] .... As
Astigmatism [*Also, As*] [*Ophthalmology*] .... Ast
Astigmatism [*Electronics*] .... ASTIG
Astigmatism, Hypermetropic [*Also, AsH*] [*Ophthalmology*] .... AH
Astigmatism, Hypermetropic [*Also, AH*] [*Ophthalmology*] .... AsH
Astigmatism, Myopic [*Also, AsM*] [*Ophthalmology*] .... AM
Astigmatism, Myopic [*Also, AM*] [*Ophthalmology*] .... AsM
ASTM [*American Society for Testing and Materials*] **Journal of Testing and Evaluation** [*A publication*] .... ASTM J Testing Evaln
ASTM [*American Society for Testing and Materials*] **Proceedings** [*A publication*] .... ASTM Proc
ASTM [*American Society for Testing and Materials*] **Special Technical Publications** [*A publication*] .... ASTM Spec Tech Publ
ASTM [*American Society for Testing and Materials*] **Standardization News** [*A publication*] .... ASTM Stand N
ASTM [*American Society for Testing and Materials*] **Standardization News** [*A publication*] .... ASTM Stand News
ASTM [*American Society for Testing and Materials*] **Standardization News** [*A publication*] .... ASTM Stdn News
ASTM [*American Society for Testing and Materials*] **Standards** [*A publication*] .... ASTM Std
Aston Dark Space [*Physics*] .... ADS
Aston Martin Owners Club .... AMOC
Aston Whole Number [*Chemistry*] .... AWN
Astonishing Stories [*A publication*] .... Ash
Astonishing Stories [*A publication*] .... AST
Astor Home for Children, Rhinebeck, NY [*Library symbol*] .... NRhbA
Astor Library, Astoria, OR [*Library symbol*] .... OrAst
Astoria [*Oregon*] [*Airport symbol*] [*Obsolete*] .... AST
Astoria, OR [*Radio station call letters*] .... KAST
Astoria, OR [*Radio station call letters*] .... KMUN

Astoria, OR [*Radio station call letters*] ..... KVAS
Astounding Science Fiction [*A publication*] ..... ASF
Astounding Stories Yearbook [*A publication*] ..... ASY
Astradyne Computer [*NASDAQ symbol*] ..... ACII
Astragal ..... A
Astrex, Incorporated [*American Stock Exchange symbol*] ..... ASI
Astrida [*Rwanda*] [*Seismograph station code, US Geological Survey*] [*Closed*] ..... AST
Astro Airways Corp. [*Pine Bluff, AR*] [*FAA designator*] ..... AST
Astro Communications System [*NASA*] ..... ACS
Astro Drilling Company [*American Stock Exchange symbol*] ..... ADC
Astro-Electronics Division [*RCA*] ..... AED
Astro Guidance Digital Computer ..... AGDIC
Astro Launch Circuit [*NASA*] ..... ALC
Astro-Med, Incorporated [*NASDAQ symbol*] ..... ASDI
Astro Research Corporation ..... ARC
Astro-Space Lab, Inc. ..... ASL
Astro-Wing Airlines [*Dallas, TX*] [*FAA designator*] ..... AWG
Astrocom Corp. [*NASDAQ symbol*] ..... ACOM
Astrodigital Doppler Speedometer [*Electronics*] ..... ADDS
Astrofizicheskie Issledovaniya [*A publication*] ..... Astrofiz Issled
Astrofizika [*A publication*] ..... Astrofiz
Astrogeodetic World Datum ..... AWD
Astrogeophysical Transmission Network [*Air Force's Air Weather Service Teletypewriter circuit*] ..... ATN
Astrograph Mean Time [*Navigation*] ..... AMT
Astroinertial Guidance Equipment ..... AIGE
Astrologers' Guild of America ..... AGA
Astrologers International [*Defunct*] ..... AI
Astrology ..... AST
Astrology ..... ASTROL
Astrology '77 [*A publication*] ..... Astrol 77
Astrology '78 [*A publication*] ..... Astrol 78
Astrology Now [*A publication*] ..... Astrol Now
Astrometriya i Astrofizika [*A publication*] ..... Astrom Astrofiz
Astrometriya i Astrofizika [*A publication*] ..... Astrometriya & Astrofiz
Astronaut Activities Office [*NASA*] ..... AAO
Astronaut-Actuated Abort ..... AAA
Astronaut Control Console [*NASA*] ..... ACC
Astronaut Control Panel [*NASA*] ..... ACP
Astronaut Life Support Assembly [*NASA*] ..... ALSA
Astronaut Maneuvering Equipment [*NASA*] ..... AME
Astronaut Maneuvering Research Vehicle [*NASA*] ..... AMRV
Astronaut Maneuvering Unit [*Gemini*] [*NASA*] ..... AMU
Astronaut Operations Requirement Document [*NASA*] ..... AORD
Astronaut Preference Kit [*NASA*] ..... APK
Astronaut Preference Test [*NASA*] ..... APT
Astronaut Rescue Air Pack [*NASA*] ..... ARAP
Astronaut Survival Kit [*NASA*] ..... ASK
Astronaut Work Station [*NASA*] ..... AWS
Astronautica Acta [*A publication*] ..... Astronaut Acta
Astronautical ..... ASTRO
Astronautical Defensive-Offensive System ..... ADOS
Astronautical Society of Canada ..... ASC
Astronautics and Aeronautics [*A publication*] ..... A & A
Astronautics and Aeronautics [*A publication*] ..... Astro Aeron
Astronautics and Aeronautics [*A publication*] ..... Astronaut Aeronaut
Astronautics Notice ..... AN
Astronautics and Space ..... ASTROSPACE
Astronautics Standard Practice ..... ASP
Astronautics Support Center ..... ASC
Astronautics Test Procedures ..... ATP
Astronavigation ..... AN
Astronics Corp. [*NASDAQ symbol*] ..... ATRO
Astronomia-Optika Institucio. Universitato de Turku. Informo [*A publication*] ..... Astron-Opt Inst Univ Turku Inf
Astronomiae Professor Greshamii [*Professor of Astronomy at Gresham College, London*] ..... APG
Astronomic ..... ASTN
Astronomical ..... Astro
Astronomical Constant ..... AC
Astronomical Explorer Satellite ..... AES
Astronomical Great Circle Course ..... ACC
Astronomical Herald [*A publication*] ..... Astron Her
Astronomical Journal [*A publication*] ..... Astron J
Astronomical Journal [*A publication*] ..... Astronom J
Astronomical League ..... AL
Astronomical Netherlands Satellite ..... ANS
Astronomical Observatory ..... AO
Astronomical Observatory Satellite ..... AOS
Astronomical Radio Interferometric Earth Survey [*or Surveying*] [*NASA*] ..... ARIES
Astronomical Society of Australia. Proceedings [*A publication*] ..... Astron Soc Aust Proc
Astronomical Society of the Pacific ..... ASP
Astronomical Society of the Pacific. Publications [*A publication*] ..... Astron Soc Pacific Pubs
Astronomical and Space Techniques for Research on the Atmosphere [*National Science Foundation project*] ..... ASTRA
Astronomical Space Telescope Research Assembly ..... ASTRA
Astronomical Telescope Orientation Mount [*NASA*] ..... ATOM
Astronomical Time ..... AT
Astronomical Time Switch ..... ATS
Astronomical Unit [*Equal to average distance from earth to sun*] ..... AU
Astronomicheskii Vestnik [*A publication*] ..... Astron Vestn
Astronomicheskii Zhurnal [*A publication*] ..... Astronom Zh
Astronomicheskii Zhurnal [*A publication*] ..... Astron Zh
Astronomie (Paris) [*A publication*] ..... Astron (Paris)
Astronomie (Paris). Supplement [*A publication*] ..... Astron (Paris) Suppl
Astronomie und Raumfahrt [*A publication*] ..... Astron Raumfahrt
Astronomische Einheit [*Astronomical Unit*] [*German*] ..... AE
Astronomische Nachrichten [*A publication*] ..... Astronom Nachr
Astronomischer Jahresbericht [*A publication*] ..... Astron Jahresber
Astronomisk Tidsskrift [*A publication*] ..... Astron Tidsskr
Astronomy ..... AST
Astronomy ..... ASTR
Astronomy ..... ASTRON
Astronomy and Astrophysics [*A publication*] ..... Astron
Astronomy and Astrophysics [*A publication*] ..... Astron Astr
Astronomy and Astrophysics [*A publication*] ..... Astron & Astrophys
Astronomy and Astrophysics [*A publication*] ..... Astron Astrophys
Astronomy and Astrophysics. Abstracts [*A publication*] ..... Ast & AstroAb
Astronomy and Astrophysics. Supplement Series [*A publication*] ..... Astron Astrophys Suppl Ser
Astronomy and Astrophysics. Supplement Series [*A publication*] ..... Astron & Astrophys Suppl Ser
Astronomy (Milwaukee) [*A publication*] ..... Astron (Milwaukee)
Astronomy Missions Board [*NASA*] ..... AMB
Astronomy and Space [*A publication*] ..... Astron & Space
Astronomy Spacelab Payloads [*NASA*] ..... ASP
Astronomy Study Unit [*Formerly, AU*] [*American Topical Association*] ..... ASU
Astronomy Unit [*Later, ASU*] [*American Topical Association*] ..... AU
Astronuclear Laboratory [*Westinghouse Electric Corp.*] ..... AL
Astrophysical Journal [*A publication*] ..... Astrophys J
Astrophysical Journal. Letters to the Editor [*A publication*] ..... Astrophys J Lett Ed
Astrophysical Journal. Supplement [*A publication*] ..... Astrophys J Suppl
Astrophysical Journal. Supplement Series [*A publication*] ..... Astroph J S
Astrophysical Journal. Supplement Series [*A publication*] ..... Astrophys J Suppl Ser
Astrophysical Letters [*A publication*] ..... Astrophys L
Astrophysical Letters [*A publication*] ..... Astrophys Lett
Astrophysical Observatory [*Smithsonian Museum*] ..... APO
Astrophysics [*A publication*] ..... Astrophys
Astrophysics and Space Science [*A publication*] ..... Astrophys & Space Sci
Astrophysics and Space Science [*A publication*] ..... Astrophys Space Sci
Astrophysics and Space Science [*A publication*] ..... Astro Sp Sc
Astrophysics and Space Science Library [*A publication*] ..... Astrophys Space Sci Libr
Astrophysics Transient Explorer ..... ATREX
Astropower Laboratory [*Douglas Aircraft Corp.*] ..... AL
Astrosurveillance Science Laboratory ..... ASL
Astrosystems, Inc. [*NASDAQ symbol*] ..... ASTR
Asuncion [*Paraguay*] [*Airport symbol*] ..... ASU
ASW [*Antisubmarine Warfare*] **Acoustic Deception Device** ..... ADDS
ASW [*Antisubmarine Warfare*]**, Gun, and Missile Escort Ship** [*Navy symbol*] ..... DX/DXG
ASW [*Antisubmarine Warfare*] **Module** [*Navy*] ..... ASWM
ASW [*Antisubmarine Warfare*] **Submarine System Evaluation Technique** ..... ASSET
ASW [*Antisubmarine Warfare*] **Support Aircraft Carrier** [*Navy symbol*] ..... CVS
Aswan [*Egypt*] [*Airport symbol*] ..... ASW
ASWEPS [*Antisubmarine Warfare Environmental Prediction Service*] **Submarine Oceanographic Digital Data System** ..... ASODDS
Asylum ..... ASY
Asylum ..... ASYL
Asymmetric ..... A
Asymmetric [*Chemistry*] ..... as
Asymmetric ..... ASYM
Asymmetric Epoxidation [*Organic chemistry*] ..... AE
Asymmetric Septal Hypertrophy [*Medicine*] ..... ASH
Asymmetric Stress Analysis of Axisymmetric Solids [*Computer program*] ..... ASAAS
Asymmetrical Sideband ..... ASB
Asymptote [*Mathematics*] ..... ASYMP
Asymptotic Relative Efficiency [*Statistics*] ..... ARE
Asymptotic Standard Error [*Statistics*] ..... ASE
Asymptotic Threshold Shift [*Hearing*] ..... ATS
Asymptotically Admissible Linear Unbiased Estimator [*Statistics*] ..... AALUE
Asymptotically Best Linear Unbiased Estimator [*Statistics*] ..... ABLUE
Asymptotically Most Powerful Rank Test [*Statistics*] ..... AMPRT
Asynchronous ..... ASYNC
Asynchronous Communication Procedure ..... ASC
Asynchronous Communications Interface Adapter [*Data processing*] ..... ACIA
Asynchronous Data Multiplexer Synchronizer ..... ADMS
Asynchronous Look-Ahead Simulator ..... ALAS
Asynchronous State Machine ..... ASM
Asynchronous Task Storage ..... ATS
Asynchronous Time Diversity Device ..... ATDD

At ... A
At or Above [*Aviation*] ... AOA
At All Times ... AATM
At Bat [*Baseball*] ... AB
At or Below [*Aviation*] ... AOB
At the Coast [*Aviation code*] ... COT
AT & E Corporation [*NASDAQ symbol*] ... ATEC
At a Later Date ... ALD
At Least [*Followed by altitude*] [*Aviation*] ... AL/
At No Expense to the Government ... ANEXGOVT
At the Rate Of ... A/R
At Same Time ... AST
At Sea [*Aviation code*] ... MAR
At-Sea Calibration Procedure ... ASCAP
At Sight ... AS
At the Suit Of ... ATS
At This Time ... ATTM
At (Time or Place) [*Aviation*] ... ATP
Ata Reumatologica Brasileira [*A publication*] ... Ata Reumatol Bras
Atalanta Corp. [*American Stock Exchange symbol*] [*Delisted*] ... ALT
Atalanta Norvegica [*A publication*] ... Atalanta Norv
Atanasoff-Berry Computer [*Early computer*] ... ABC
Atar [*Djibouti*] [*Seismograph station code, US Geological Survey*] ... ATA
Atar [*Mauritania*] [*Airport symbol*] ... ATR
Atari Message and Information System ... AMIS
Atas. Instituto de Micologia da Universidade Federal de Pernambuco [*A publication*] ... Atas Inst Micol Univ Fed Pernambuco
Atas. Simposio Sobre a Biota Amazonica [*A publication*] ... ASBA
Atas. Sociedade de Biologia do Rio De Janeiro [*A publication*] ... Atas Soc Biol Rio De J
Atascadero, CA [*Radio station call letters*] ... KIQO
Atascadero State Hospital, Atascadero, CA [*Library symbol*] ... CAtaH
Ataxia Telangiectasia [*Genetic disease*] ... AT
Atbara [*Sudan*] [*Airport symbol*] ... ATB
Atchison, KS [*Location identifier*] [*FAA*] ... JNL
Atchison, KS [*Radio station call letters*] ... KARE
[*The*] **Atchison, Topeka & Santa Fe Railway Co.** ... AT & SF
[*The*] **Atchison, Topeka & Santa Fe Railway Co.** ... AT & SFR
[*The*] **Atchison, Topeka & Santa Fe Railway Co.** [*Later, SFF*] [*NYSE symbol*] ... SF
[*The*] **Atchison, Topeka & Santa Fe Railway Co.** [*AAR code*] ... ATSF
[*The*] **Atchison, Topeka & Santa Fe Railway Co. - DF Loaders** [*AAR code*] ... SFRB
[*The*] **Atchison, Topeka & Santa Fe Railway Co. - Refrigerator Cars** [*AAR code*] ... SFRD
Atco Industries, Inc. [*American Stock Exchange symbol*] [*Delisted*] ... ATL
Atcor, Inc. [*NASDAQ symbol*] ... ATCO
ATE Enterprises, Inc. [*NASDAQ symbol*] ... ATEE
ATE Management Service Co., Inc., Cincinnati, OH [*OCLC symbol*] ... ATE
Ateitis Association of Lithuanian Catholic Intellectuals ... AALCI
Ateliers de Construction Electriques de Charleroi [*Atomic power plant*] [*Belgium*] ... ACEC
Atemswegs- und Lungenkrankheiten [*A publication*] ... Atemswegs- Lungenkr
Atene e Roma [*A publication*] ... AeR
Atene e Roma [*A publication*] ... A & R
Atenea [*A publication*] ... At
Atenea [*Formerly, Nueva Atenea*] [*A publication*] ... Ate
Ateneo de Manila University, Manila, Philippines [*Library symbol*] ... PiMA
Ateneo Parmense. Acta Bio-Medica [*A publication*] ... Ateneo Parmense Acta Bio-Med
Ateneo Parmense. Acta Naturalia [*A publication*] ... Ateneo Parmense Acta Nat
Ateneo Parmense. Sezione 1. Acta Bio-Medica [*A publication*] ... Ateneo Parmense Sez 1
Ateneo Veneto [*A publication*] ... AtV
Ateneo Veneto [*A publication*] ... AV
Ateneum Kaplanskie [*A publication*] ... AK
Athabasca, AB [*Television station call letters*] ... CBXT-1
Athapascan [*MARC language code*] [*Library of Congress*] ... ath
Atheists Association [*Formerly, AAAA*] ... AA
Athenaeum [*A publication*] ... Ath
Athenaeum of Ohio, Norwood, OH [*OCLC symbol*] ... ATO
Athenaeum of Ohio, Norwood, OH [*Library symbol*] ... ONowdM
Athenaeum of Philadelphia, Philadelphia, PA [*OCLC symbol*] ... PAT
Athenaeum of Philadelphia, Philadelphia, PA [*Library symbol*] ... PPA
Athenische Mitteilungen. Beiheft [*A publication*] ... Ath Mitt-BH
Athens [*Georgia*] [*Airport symbol*] ... AHN
Athens [*Greece*] ... ATH
Athens [*Greece*] [*Airport symbol*] ... ATH
Athens [*Greece*] [*Later, PEN*] [*Geomagnetic observatory code*] ... ATH
Athens, AL [*Radio station call letters*] ... WJMW
Athens, AL [*Radio station call letters*] ... WKAC
Athens, AL [*Radio station call letters*] ... WZYP
Athens Annals of Archaeology [*A publication*] ... AAA
Athens Center for Ekistics ... ACE
Athens College, Athens, GA [*Library symbol*] ... AAthC
Athens, GA [*Radio station call letters*] ... WAGQ
Athens, GA [*Radio station call letters*] ... WCCD
Athens, GA [*Radio station call letters*] ... WGAU
Athens, GA [*Television station call letters*] ... WGTV
Athens, GA [*Radio station call letters*] ... WNGC
Athens, GA [*Radio station call letters*] ... WRFC
Athens, GA [*Radio station call letters*] ... WUOG
Athens, GA [*Radio station call letters*] ... WXAG
Athens News Agency [*Greece*] ... ANA
Athens Observatory [*Greece*] [*Seismograph station code, US Geological Survey*] ... ATH
Athens, OH [*Radio station call letters*] ... WATH
Athens, OH [*Radio station call letters*] ... WOUB
Athens, OH [*Radio station call letters*] ... WOUB-FM
Athens, OH [*Television station call letters*] ... WOUB-TV
Athens, OH [*Radio station call letters*] ... WXTQ
Athens Regional Library, Athens, GA [*Library symbol*] ... GAt
Athens, TN [*Location identifier*] [*FAA*] ... MMI
Athens, TN [*Radio station call letters*] ... WJSQ-FM
Athens, TN [*Radio station call letters*] ... WLAR
Athens, TN [*Radio station call letters*] ... WYXI
Athens, TX [*Radio station call letters*] ... KBUD
Athens, TX [*Location identifier*] [*FAA*] ... LIQ
Athens University [*Greece*] [*Seismograph station code, US Geological Survey*] ... ATU
Atherogenic Index [*Medicine*] ... AI
Atherosclerosis [*A publication*] ... Atheroscler
Atherosclerosis [*Medicine*] ... ATHSC
Atherosclerosis Reviews [*A publication*] ... Atheroscler Rev
Atherton, CA [*Radio station call letters*] ... KWAP
Athinaikon Praktoreion Eidiseon [*Athens News Agency*] [*Greece*] ... APE
Athletes in Action ... AIA
Athletes for a Better Education ... AthBE
Athletes United for Peace ... AUP
Athletic ... ATH
Athletic ... ATHL
Athletic Association ... AA
Athletic Club [*Usually in combination with proper noun, as, DAC, Detroit Athletic Club*] ... AC
Athletic Conference of American College Women [*Later, ARFCW*] ... ACACW
Athletic Director ... AD
Athletic Equipment Managers Association ... AEMA
Athletic Goods Manufacturers Association [*Later, SGMA*] ... AGMA
Athletic Goods Team Distributors [*National Sporting Goods Association*] ... AGTD
Athletic Journal [*A publication*] ... Ath J
Athletic and Recreation Federation of College Women ... ARFCW
Athletic Training Council ... ATC
[*The*] **Athletics Congress** [*Track*] [*An association*] ... TAC
[*The*] **Athletics Congress/USA** ... TAC/USA
[*The*] **Athletics Congress/USA Trust Fund** ... TACTRUST
Athlone French Poets [*A publication*] ... AFrP
Athlone Industries, Inc. [*NYSE symbol*] ... ATH
Athwartships ... ATH
Athwartships Reference Axis ... ASRA
ATI, Inc. [*American Stock Exchange symbol*] ... ATQ
Atico [*Peru*] [*Seismograph station code, US Geological Survey*] ... ATI
Atico Financial Corporation [*NASDAQ symbol*] ... ATFC
Atico Mortgage Investors [*NYSE symbol*] [*Delisted*] ... ACO
Atigaru Point, AK [*Location identifier*] [*FAA*] ... AUJ
Atikokan [*Canada*] [*Airport symbol*] ... YIB
Atikokan High School, Atikokan, ON, Canada [*Library symbol*] ... CaOAtH
Atikokan, ON [*Radio station call letters*] ... CFAK
Atiu [*Cook Islands*] [*Airport symbol*] ... AIU
Atkasuk Village, AK [*Location identifier*] [*FAA*] ... ATK
Atlan-Tol Industries, Inc. [*NASDAQ symbol*] ... ALOT
Atlanta [*Georgia*] [*Airport symbol*] ... ATL
Atlanta [*Georgia*] [*Seismograph station code, US Geological Survey*] ... ATL
Atlanta Army Depot [*Georgia*] ... ATAD
Atlanta, Birmingham, & Coast Railroad Co. ... AB & C
[*USS*] **Atlanta,** [*USS*] **Boston,** [*USS*] **Chicago,** [*USS*] **Dolphin** [*The ABCD ships, so called because their construction began in the same year, 1883*] ... ABCD
Atlanta Chamber of Commerce, Atlanta, GA [*Library symbol*] ... GACC
Atlanta College of Art Library, Atlanta, GA [*OCLC symbol*] ... GAA
Atlanta [*Georgia*] **De Kalb/Peachtree Airport** [*Airport symbol*] [*Obsolete*] ... PDK
Atlanta Economic Review [*A publication*] ... Atl Econ R
Atlanta, GA [*Location identifier*] [*FAA*] ... AFA
Atlanta, GA [*Location identifier*] [*FAA*] ... FSQ
Atlanta, GA [*Location identifier*] [*FAA*] ... FTY
Atlanta, GA [*Location identifier*] [*FAA*] ... FUN
Atlanta, GA [*Location identifier*] [*FAA*] ... HZK
Atlanta, GA [*Location identifier*] [*FAA*] ... LYN
Atlanta, GA [*Location identifier*] [*FAA*] ... RHX
Atlanta, GA [*Location identifier*] [*FAA*] ... SZJ
Atlanta, GA [*Radio station call letters*] ... WABE
Atlanta, GA [*Radio station call letters*] ... WAEC
Atlanta, GA [*Television station call letters*] ... WAGA-TV
Atlanta, GA [*Television station call letters*] ... WANX-TV
Atlanta, GA [*Radio station call letters*] ... WAOK
Atlanta, GA [*Television station call letters*] ... WATL-TV
Atlanta, GA [*Radio station call letters*] ... WCLK
Atlanta, GA [*Television station call letters*] ... WETV

Atlanta, GA [*Radio station call letters*] ... WGKA
Atlanta, GA [*Radio station call letters*] ... WGST
Atlanta, GA [*Radio station call letters*] ... WGUN
Atlanta, GA [*Radio station call letters*] ... WIGO
Atlanta, GA [*Radio station call letters*] ... WKLS
Atlanta, GA [*Radio station call letters*] ... WKLS-FM
Atlanta, GA [*Radio station call letters*] ... WPCH
Atlanta, GA [*Radio station call letters*] ... WQXI
Atlanta, GA [*Radio station call letters*] ... WRAS
Atlanta, GA [*Radio station call letters*] ... WREK
Atlanta, GA [*Radio station call letters*] ... WRFG
Atlanta, GA [*Radio station call letters*] ... WSB
Atlanta, GA [*Radio station call letters*] ... WSB-FM
Atlanta, GA [*Television station call letters*] ... WSB-TV
Atlanta, GA [*Television station call letters*] ... WTBS
Atlanta, GA [*Radio station call letters*] ... WVEE
Atlanta, GA [*Television station call letters*] ... WVEU
Atlanta, GA [*Television station call letters*] ... WXIA-TV
Atlanta, GA [*Radio station call letters*] ... WYZE
Atlanta, GA [*Radio station call letters*] ... WZGC
Atlanta Gas Light Co. [*NASDAQ symbol*] ... AGLT
Atlanta Historical Society, Atlanta, GA [*Library symbol*] ... GAHi
Atlanta Junior College, Atlanta, GA [*Library symbol*] ... GAJ
Atlanta Public Library, Atlanta, GA [*Library symbol*] ... GA
Atlanta Public Library, Atlanta, GA [*OCLC symbol*] ... GAP
Atlanta Public Schools, Professional Library, Atlanta, GA [*Library symbol*] ... GAP
Atlanta & Saint Andrews Bay Railway Co. [*AAR code*] ... ASAB
Atlanta School of Art, Atlanta, GA [*Library symbol*] ... GAA
Atlanta Service Center [*IRS*] ... ATSC
Atlanta Skylark Club, Inc. [*Atlanta, GA*] [*FAA designator*] ... SLK
[*The*] **Atlanta, Stone Mountain, & Lithonia Railway Co.** [*AAR code*] ... ASML
Atlanta, TX [*Location identifier*] [*FAA*] ... ATA
Atlanta, TX [*Radio station call letters*] ... KALT
Atlanta, TX [*Radio station call letters*] ... KPYN
Atlanta University, Atlanta, GA [*Library symbol*] ... GAU
Atlanta University Center, Atlanta, GA [*OCLC symbol*] ... AUU
Atlanta & West Point Rail Road Co. ... A & WP
Atlanta & West Point Rail Road Co. [*AAR code*] ... AWP
Atlantic ... ATL
Atlantic ... ATLC
Atlantic ... LANT
Atlantic Advocate [*A publication*] ... Atl Adv
Atlantic Advocate [*A publication*] ... Atlan Adv
Atlantic Air Charter [*Baltimore, MD*] [*FAA designator*] ... ATN
Atlantic Airborne Early Warning [*Military*] ... AAEW
Atlantic American Corp. [*NASDAQ symbol*] ... AAME
Atlantic Amphibious Force [*Navy*] ... AAF
Atlantic Antisubmarine Warfare Communication Net ... AMANET
Atlantic Area [*Services to the Armed Forces*] [*Red Cross*] ... AA
Atlantic Art Institute ... AAI
Atlantic Association of Young Political Leaders ... AAYPL
Atlantic Ballistic Missile Range ... ABMR
Atlantic Bancorp [*NASDAQ symbol*] ... ABAN
Atlantic Barrier Patrol [*Eastern seaward extension of the DEW Line*] [*Obsolete*] ... BARLANT
Atlantic Base Section ... ABS
Atlantic Beach, FL [*Radio station call letters*] ... WFYV
Atlantic Beach, FL [*Radio station call letters*] ... WJNJ
Atlantic Booster Test ... ABT
Atlantic Central Airlines Ltd. [*Canada*] [*ICAO designator*] ... CN
Atlantic Central Airlines Ltd. [*St. John, NB*] [*FAA designator*] ... CNA
Atlantic Charter ... AC
Atlantic Christian College [*North Carolina*] ... ACC
Atlantic Christian College, Wilson, NC [*Library symbol*] ... NcWilA
Atlantic City [*New Jersey*] [*Airport symbol*] ... ACY
Atlantic City [*New Jersey*] [*Airport symbol*] ... AIY
Atlantic City Electric Co. [*NYSE symbol*] [*Delisted*] ... ATE
Atlantic City Free Public Library, Atlantic City, NJ [*OCLC symbol*] ... ACP
Atlantic City Free Public Library, Atlantic City, NJ [*Library symbol*] ... NjAc
Atlantic City, NJ [*Radio station call letters*] ... WAYV
Atlantic City, NJ [*Radio station call letters*] ... WFPG
Atlantic City, NJ [*Radio station call letters*] ... WIIN
Atlantic City, NJ [*Radio station call letters*] ... WMGM
Atlantic City, NJ [*Radio station call letters*] ... WMID
Atlantic City, NJ [*Radio station call letters*] ... WUSS
Atlantic City, NJ [*Television station call letters*] ... WWAC-TV
Atlantic City Reporter, Atlantic City, NJ [*Library symbol*] ... NjAcR
Atlantic Coast Air Service ... ACAS
Atlantic Coast Conference [*College sports*] ... ACC
Atlantic Coast Football League ... ACFL
Atlantic Coast Line R. R. [*AAR code*] ... ACL
Atlantic Coast Line R. R. ... ACLRR
Atlantic Coast Line R. R. [*NYSE symbol*] [*Delisted*] ... AX
Atlantic Command ... LANTCOM
Atlantic Command Operational Control Center ... LANTCOMOPCONCEN
Atlantic Command Operational Control Center ... LCOCC
Atlantic [*Fleet*] **Commander Operational Control Center** [*Navy*] ... ACOCC
Atlantic Community College, Mays Landing, NJ [*OCLC symbol*] ... ANJ
Atlantic Community College, Mays Landing, NJ [*Library symbol*] ... NjMlAC
Atlantic Community Development Group for Latin America [*Joint US-European private investment company*] ... ADELA
Atlantic Community Quarterly [*A publication*] ... Atlan Com Q
Atlantic Community Quarterly [*A publication*] ... Atl Community Quar
Atlantic Congress ... AC
Atlantic Council [*Later, ACUS*] [*NATO*] ... AC
Atlantic Council of the United States ... ACUS
Atlantic County Advertiser, Northfield, NJ [*Library symbol*] ... NjNoA
Atlantic County Clerk, Atlantic City, NJ [*Library symbol*] ... NjAcCoC
Atlantic County Clerk, Mays Landing, NJ [*Library symbol*] ... NjMlCoC
Atlantic County Historical Society, Somers Point, NJ [*Library symbol*] ... NjSomHi
Atlantic County Library, Mays Landing, NJ [*Library symbol*] ... NjMlA
Atlantic County Record, Mays Landing, NJ [*Library symbol*] ... NjMlR
Atlantic Daylight Time ... ADT
Atlantic Deeper Waterways Association ... ADWA
Atlantic Deutsche Luftverkehrs AG [*West Germany*] [*ICAO designator*] ... ID
Atlantic Division Naval Facilities Engineering Command ... LANTNAVFACENGCOM
Atlantic Division Transport Control Center [*Military*] ... ATCC
Atlantic & East Carolina Railway Co. [*AAR code*] ... AEC
Atlantic Economic Society ... AES
Atlantic Environmental Group [*National Marine Fisheries Service*] ... AEG
Atlantic Estuarine Research Society ... AERS
Atlantic Estuarine Society ... AES
Atlantic Federal Savings & Loan [*NASDAQ symbol*] ... ASAL
Atlantic Ferry Organization [*Based in Canada under Ministry of Aircraft Production*] [*British*] [*World War II*] ... ATFERO
Atlantic Ferry Service [*World War II*] ... AFS
Atlantic Financial Federal [*NASDAQ symbol*] ... ATLF
Atlantic Fleet ... LANTFLT
Atlantic Fleet Amphibious Force [*Navy*] ... AFAF
Atlantic Fleet Antisubmarine Warfare Tactical School [*Navy*] ... LANTFLEASWTACSCOL
Atlantic Fleet Combat Camera Group [*Obsolete*] ... AFCCG
Atlantic Fleet Organization ... AFO
Atlantic Fleet Training Support Facilities ... LANTFLTRANSUPPFAC
Atlantic Fleet Weapons Range [*Later, AFRSF*] [*Navy*] ... AFWR
Atlantic Fleet Weapons Range [*Later, AFRSF*] [*Navy*] ... LANTFLTWPNRAN
Atlantic Fleet Weapons Training Facility [*Navy*] ... AFWTF
Atlantic Free Trade Area ... AFTA
Atlantic and Gulf American Flag Berth Operators ... AGAFBO
Atlantic-Gulf Coastwise Steamship Freight Bureau ... AGCSB
Atlantic-Gulf Coastwise Steamship Freight Bureau, Elizabeth NJ [*STAC*] ... AGC
Atlantic Highlands Public Library Association, Atlantic Highlands, NJ [*Library symbol*] ... NjAt
Atlantic, IA [*Radio station call letters*] ... KJAN
Atlantic, IA [*Radio station call letters*] ... KJAN-FM
Atlantic Independent Union ... AIU
Atlantic Information Centre for Teachers [*Defunct*] ... AICT
Atlantic Institute of Education, Halifax, NS, Canada [*Library symbol*] ... CaNSHAI
Atlantic Institute for International Affairs ... AIIA
Atlantic Intelligence Center [*Navy*] ... AIC
Atlantic Intelligence Center [*Navy*] ... LANTINTCEN
Atlantic International Marketing Committee [*Maryland, Virginia, North Carolina, and South Carolina*] ... AIM
Atlantic Margin Coring Project ... AMCOR
Atlantic Marine Center [*National Oceanic and Atmospheric Administration*] ... AMC
Atlantic Merchant Shipping Instructions ... AMSI
Atlantic Metropolitan [*NYSE symbol*] ... ATC
Atlantic Missile Range [*Later, Eastern Test Range*] ... AMR
Atlantic Missile Range [*later, Eastern Test Range*] **Operations** ... AMRO
Atlantic Missile Range [*later, Eastern Test Range*] **Operations Office** ... AMROO
Atlantic Missile Test Range ... AMTR
Atlantic Monthly [*A publication*] ... AM
Atlantic Monthly [*A publication*] ... AMo
Atlantic Monthly [*A publication*] ... Atl
Atlantic Monthly [*A publication*] ... Atlan
Atlantic Monthly [*A publication*] ... Atlan Mo
Atlantic Monthly [*A publication*] ... Atlantic
Atlantic Monthly [*A publication*] ... Atl M
Atlantic Monthly [*A publication*] ... Atl Mo
Atlantic Monthly [*A publication*] ... AtM
Atlantic Naturalist [*A publication*] ... Atl Nat
Atlantic News-Telegraph, Atlantic, IA [*Library symbol*] ... IaAtNT
Atlantic Nuclear Force [*NATO*] ... ANF
Atlantic Ocean [*MARC geographic area code*] [*Library of Congress*] ... l------
Atlantic Ocean Air Traffic Control ... AOATC
Atlantic Ocean Area ... AOA
Atlantic Ocean Recovery Area [*NASA*] ... AORA
Atlantic Ocean Region [*INTELSAT*] ... AOR
Atlantic Ocean Ship [*INTELSAT*] ... AOS
Atlantic Oceanographic Laboratories [*of Environmental Science Services Administration*] ... AOL
Atlantic Oceanographic and Meteorological Laboratories [*NOAA*] ... AOML
Atlantic Offshore Fishermen's Association ... AOFA
Atlantic Outer Continental Shelf ... AOCS

Atlantic Papers [*A publication*] .... Atlantic Pap
Atlantic Pilotage Authority .... APA
Atlantic Political Advisory Group [*NATO*] .... APAG
Atlantic Provinces Economic Council .... APEC
Atlantic Provinces Library Association. Bulletin [*A publication*] .... APLA Bull
Atlantic Public Library, Atlantic, IA [*Library symbol*] .... IaAt
Atlantic Quarterly [*A publication*] .... AQ
Atlantic Range Instrumentation Ship .... ARIS
Atlantic Refining Co. [*Later, Atlantic Richfield Co.*] [*NYSE symbol*] .... AFI
Atlantic Refining Co., Philadelphia, PA [*Library symbol*] .... PPAtR
Atlantic Research Center .... ARC
Atlantic Research Corporation .... ARC
Atlantic Research Corporation [*NASDAQ symbol*] .... ATRC
Atlantic Research Corporation Atmospheric Sounding [*Missile*] .... ARCAS
Atlantic Research Laboratories .... ARL
Atlantic Reserve Fleet .... LANTRESFLT
Atlantic Richfield Canada Ltd. .... ARCAN
Atlantic Richfield Company [*NYSE symbol*] .... ARC
Atlantic Richfield Company .... ARCO
Atlantic Richfield Co., Geoscience Library, Dallas, TX [*OCLC symbol*] .... ATR
Atlantic Richfield Co., Geoscience Library, Dallas, TX [*Library symbol*] .... TxDaAR-G
Atlantic Richfield Co., R and D Library, Dallas, TX [*OCLC symbol*] .... ATC
Atlantic Richfield Co., R and D Library, Dallas, TX [*Library symbol*] .... TxDaAR-R
Atlantic Richfield Co., Technical Library, Dallas, TX [*Library symbol*] .... TxDaAR-T
Atlantic Richfield Hanford Co. .... ARH
Atlantic Richfield Hanford Company .... ARHCO
Atlantic Richfield Hanford Co., Richland, WA [*Library symbol*] .... WaRiAR
Atlantic Salmon Association .... ASA
Atlantic Salmon Journal [*A publication*] .... Atl Salmon J
Atlantic Salmon Research Trust .... ASRT
Atlantic School of Theology, Halifax, NS, Canada [*Library symbol*] .... CaNSHPH
Atlantic Sea Run Salmon Commission .... ASRSC
Atlantic Seaboard Circuit [*Horse racing*] .... ASC
Atlantic Southeast Airlines, Incorporated [*NASDAQ symbol*] .... ASAI
Atlantic Southeast Airlines, Inc. [*Air carrier designation symbol*] .... ASEX
Atlantic Southeast Airlines, Inc. [*Hapeville, GA*] [*FAA designator*] .... ASO
Atlantic Squadron .... ATRON
Atlantic Standard Time .... AST
Atlantic Standard Time .... AT
Atlantic Standard Time .... ATST
Atlantic States Marine Fisheries Commission .... ASMFC
Atlantic Systems Conference .... ASC
Atlantic Tracking Range [*NASA*] .... ATR
Atlantic Tracking Ship [*NASA*] .... ATS
Atlantic Trade Study .... ATS
Atlantic Tradewind [*or Tropical*] **Experiment** [*National Science Foundation*] .... ATEX
Atlantic Transportation Terminal Command [*Army*] .... ATTC
Atlantic Treaty Association .... ATA
Atlantic Treaty Education Committee [*NATO*] .... ATEC
Atlantic Undersea Test and Evaluation Center [*Navy*] [*Acronym also used to refer to device for detection, amplification, and transmission of undersea noise*] .... AUTEC
Atlantic Union College [*Massachusetts*] .... AUC
Atlantic Union College, South Lancaster, MA [*Library symbol*] .... MSIA
Atlantic Varnish & Paint Co., Richmond, VA [*Library symbol*] .... ViRAV
Atlantic Waterfowl Council .... AWC
Atlantic and West Indies .... A & WI
Atlantic & Western Railway Co. [*AAR code*] .... ATW
Atlantico [*A publication*] .... Atl
Atlantida [*A publication*] .... At
Atlantide Report [*A publication*] .... Atl Rep
Atlantis [*A publication*] .... Atla
Atlantis Airlines [*Myrtle Beach, SC*] [*FAA designator*] .... AAO
Atlantis Commodities Purchasing Service .... ATCOPS
Atlantis Research Centre .... ARC
Atlantische Passatwind Experiment [*Atlantic Tradewind Experiment*] [*US, England, Germany*] .... APEX
Atlas Agena [*NASA*] .... AA
Atlas Airlines [*Muncie, IN*] [*FAA designator*] .... ATR
Atlas Basic Language [*Data processing*] .... ABL
Atlas Biomedical Literature System .... ABLS
Atlas-Centaur [*Missile*] .... A-C
Atlas Chemical Industries, Inc. [*NYSE symbol*] [*Delisted*] .... ACI
Atlas Chemical Industries, Inc. [*Research code symbol*] .... AT
Atlas Chemical Industries, Inc., Wilmington, DE [*Library symbol*] .... DeWAt
Atlas Commercial Language [*Data processing*] .... ACL
Atlas Configuration Control Board [*Aerospace*] .... ACCB
Atlas Consolidated Mining & Development Corp. [*American Stock Exchange symbol*] .... ACM
Atlas Corp. [*NYSE symbol*] .... AZ
Atlas Crew Procedures Laboratory .... ACPL
Atlas Educational Center .... AEC
Atlas Gemini [*NASA*] .... AG
Atlas General Survey Program .... AGSP
Atlas of Japanese Fossils [*A publication*] .... Atlas Jap Fossils
Atlas Mountain Region [*MARC geographic area code*] [*Library of Congress*] .... fa-----
Atlas [*Missile*] **Operational Data Summary** .... AODS
Atlas Reliability Group .... ARG
Atlas Van Lines [*American Stock Exchange symbol*] .... AVL
ATM [*Apollo Telescope Mount*] **Electrical Power System** [*NASA*] .... AEPS
ATM [*Apollo Telescope Mount*] **Experiments Officer** [*NASA*] .... AEO
ATM [*Archiv fuer Technisches Messen*] **Messtechnische Praxis** [*A publication*] .... ATM Mess Pr
ATM [*Apollo Telescope Mount*] **Navigation and Timing Summary** [*NASA*] .... ANTS
Atmautluak [*Alaska*] [*Airport symbol*] .... ATT
ATMDC [*Apollo Telescope Mount Digital Computer*] **Software Control Officer** [*NASA*] .... ASCO
Atmore, AL [*Radio station call letters*] .... WASG
Atmore, AL [*Radio station call letters*] .... WATM
Atmore, AL [*Radio station call letters*] .... WSKR
Atmosphere .... ATM
Atmosphere .... ATMOS
Atmosphere Control System [*NASA*] .... ACS
Atmosphere Explorer B [*Satellite*] [*NASA*] .... AE-B
Atmosphere, Magnetosphere, and Plasmas in Space [*Space shuttle payload*] [*NASA*] .... AMPS
Atmosphere Normale Internationale [*International Normal Atmosphere*] .... ANI
Atmosphere Reactants Supply Subsystem .... ARSS
Atmosphere Reactants Supply Subsystem Group .... ARSSG
Atmosphere Revitalization Section [*or System*] [*NASA*] .... ARS
Atmosphere Sensing and Maintenance System [*NASA*] .... ASMS
Atmosphere Sounding Projectile .... ASP
Atmosphere and Space .... AS
Atmosphere, Standard [*Unit of pressure*] .... atm
Atmosphere, Technical [*Unit of pressure*] .... at
Atmospheric .... ATMO
Atmospheric Analysis and Prediction [*National Center for Atmospheric Research*] .... AAP
Atmospheric Applications .... AA
Atmospheric Cloud Physics Laboratory [*Spacelab*] [*NASA*] .... ACPL
Atmospheric Composition Satellite [*NASA*] .... ATCOS
Atmospheric Contamination Potential .... ACP
Atmospheric Control Experimentation .... ACE
Atmospheric Devices Laboratory [*Cambridge, MA*] .... ADL
Atmospheric Diffusion of Beryllium Program [*NASA*] .... ADOBE
Atmospheric Diffusion Measuring System .... ADMS
Atmospheric Electric Detection System .... AEDS
Atmospheric Entry .... AE
Atmospheric Environment [*A publication*] .... Atmos Envir
Atmospheric Environment [*A publication*] .... Atmos Environ
Atmospheric Explorer [*Satellite*] [*NASA*] .... AE
Atmospheric Flight .... AF
Atmospheric Flight Test .... AFT
Atmospheric Fluidized Bed [*Chemical engineering*] .... AFB
Atmospheric Fluidized-Bed Combustion [*Fuel technology*] .... AFBC
Atmospheric Gas Oil [*Petroleum technology*] .... AGO
Atmospheric Head .... H
Atmospheric Infrared Attenuation Coefficient .... AIRAC
Atmospheric Layer and Density Distribution of Ions and Neutrals [*Rocket*] [*NASA*] .... ALADDIN
Atmospheric and Oceanic Physics [*A publication*] .... Atmos Oceanic Phys
Atmospheric and Oceanic Physics (English Edition) [*A publication*] .... Atmos Oceanic Phys (Engl Ed)
Atmospheric and Oceanographic Information Processing System .... AOIPS
Atmospheric Pollution Sensor .... APS
Atmospheric Pressure .... AP
Atmospheric Pressure at Aerodrome Elevation [*or Runway Threshold*] [*Aviation code*] .... QFE
Atmospheric Pressure and Ambient Temperature .... APAT
Atmospheric Pressure Chemical Ionization .... APCI
Atmospheric Pressure Supply Subsystem [*NASA*] .... APSS
Atmospheric Quality and Modification [*National Center for Atmospheric Research*] .... AQM
Atmospheric Radio Noise .... ARN
Atmospheric Radio Wave .... ARW
Atmospheric Release Advisory Capability [*Energy Research and Development Administration*] .... ARAC
Atmospheric Rendezvous Space Logistics [*NASA*] .... ARSL
Atmospheric Research Information Exchange Study .... ARIES
Atmospheric Research Program .... ARP
Atmospheric Revitalization .... AR
Atmospheric Revitalization Pressure Control System .... ARPCS
Atmospheric Science Facility .... ASF
Atmospheric Sciences Laboratory [*Army*] .... ASL
Atmospheric Sciences Research Center [*State University of New York*] .... ASRC
Atmospheric Sound-Focusing Gain .... ASFG
Atmospheric Sound Refraction .... ASR
Atmospheric and Space Plasma Physics .... ASPP
Atmospheric Storage and Control Section [*Spacelab*] [*NASA*] .... ASCS
Atmospheric Transmission Measurement Equipment .... ATME
Atmospheric Turbulence and Diffusion Laboratory [*Oak Ridge, Tennessee*] .... ATDL

Atmospheric Turbulence Measuring Set .... ATMS
Atmospheric Variability Experiment [*NASA*] .... AVE
Atmospheric Wind Velocity .... AWV
Atmospheric Winds Aloft .... AWA
Atmospherics .... SFERICS
Atmospherics .... XS
Atoka, OK [*Radio station call letters*] .... KEOR
Atoka, OK [*Radio station call letters*] .... KEOR-FM
Atoll Commander [*In Pacific operations*] [*World War II*] .... ATCOM
Atoll Research Bulletin [*A publication*] .... Atoll Res Bull
Atom [*or Atomic*] .... A
Atom Bomb .... A (Bomb)
Atom Indonesia [*A publication*] .... At Indones
Atom-Informationen [*A publication*] .... At-Inf
Atom und Strom [*A publication*] .... At & Strom
Atom und Strom [*A publication*] .... At Strom
Atomedic Research Center .... ARC
Atomes et Molecules par Etudes Radio-Electriques [*Switzerland*] .... AMPERE
Atomgewicht [*Atomic Weight*] [*German*] .... AG
Atomic .... AT
Atomic Absorption .... AA
Atomic Absorption Coefficient .... AAC
Atomic Absorption Flame Spectrometer .... AAFS
Atomic Absorption Newsletter [*A publication*] .... At Absorpt Newsl
Atomic Absorption Spectrometer [*or Spectroscopy*] .... AAS
Atomic Bargain Analysis Report .... ATBAN
Atomic Beam Method .... ABM
Atomic, Biological, and Chemical [*as, ABC Officer, ABC Warfare*] .... ABC
Atomic, Biological, Chemical, and Damage Control .... ABCD
Atomic, Biological, Chemical, and Radiological [*Warfare*] .... ABCR
Atomic, Biological, Chemical Warfare .... ABCW
Atomic Bomb Casualty Commission [*Later, RERF*] .... ABCC
Atomic Bomb Casualty Commission, Seattle, WA [*Library symbol*] .... WaSAB
Atomic Cesium Beam MASER .... ACBM
Atomic Collision Cross Sections Information Center [*ORNL*] .... ACCSIC
Atomic Coordinating Office (Washington, DC) [*British Defense Staff*] .... ACO(W)
Atomic Coordination Office [*British*] .... ACO
Atomic Damage Template [*Military drafting*] .... ADT
Atomic Data [*A publication*] .... At Data
Atomic Data and Nuclear Data Tables [*A publication*] .... At Data Nucl Data Tables
Atomic Data and Nuclear Data Tables [*A publication*] .... Atomic Data
Atomic Defense .... ATOMDEF
Atomic Defense Engineering .... ADE
Atomic Defense and Space Group [*Westinghouse Electric Corp.*] .... ADSG
Atomic Defense Support Agency .... ADSA
Atomic Demolition Munition .... ADM
Atomic Development Authority [*Proposed by Bernard Baruch to exercise control over those aspects of atomic energy inimical to global security, never organized*] .... ADA
Atomic Device [*Military*] .... ATOMDEV
Atomic Drive .... AD
Atomic Drive .... A-DRV
Atomic Emission .... AE
Atomic Emission Spectroscopy .... AES
Atomic Energy Act [*1954*] .... AEA
Atomic Energy in Australia [*A publication*] .... At Energy Aust
Atomic Energy in Australia [*A publication*] .... Atom Ener A
Atomic Energy Authority [*British*] .... AEA
Atomic Energy Bureau of Science and Technics Agency [*Japan*] .... AEBSTA
Atomic Energy of Canada, Chalk River, ON, Canada [*Library symbol*] .... CaOCkA
Atomic Energy of Canada Limited .... AECL
Atomic Energy of Canada Limited. AECL (Report) [*A publication*] .... At Energy Can Ltd AECL (Rep)
Atomic Energy of Canada, Ottawa, ON, Canada [*Library symbol*] .... CaOOAE
Atomic Energy of Canada, Toronto, ON, Canada [*Library symbol*] .... CaOTAE
Atomic Energy of Canada, Whiteshell Nuclear Research Establishment, Pinawa, MB, Canada [*Library symbol*] .... CaMPW
Atomic Energy Centre - Lahore .... AECL
Atomic Energy Commission [*Functions divided, 1975, between Nuclear Regulatory Commission and Energy Research and Development Administration*] .... AEC
Atomic Energy Commission Manual .... AECM
Atomic Energy Commission Procurement Regulations [*Obsolete*] .... AECPR
Atomic Energy Control Board [*Canada*] .... AECB
Atomic Energy Control Board, Ottawa, ON, Canada [*Library symbol*] .... CaOOAECB
Atomic Energy Detection System [*Nuclear energy*] .... AEDS
Atomic Energy Establishment [*British*] .... AEE
Atomic Energy Establishment, Winfrith [*England*] .... AEEW
Atomic Energy Labor Management Relations Panel .... AELMRP
Atomic Energy Law Journal [*A publication*] .... At Energy Law J
Atomic Energy Law Journal [*A publication*] .... Atomic Energy L J
Atomic Energy Level .... AEL
Atomic Energy Levels Data Center .... AELDC
Atomic Energy Levels and Grotrian Diagrams [*Elsevier Book Series*] [*A publication*] .... AEL
Atomic Energy Research Department [*NASA*] .... AERD
Atomic Energy Research Establishment [*of United Kingdom Atomic Energy Authority*] [*Harwell, England*] .... AERE
Atomic Energy Research Establishment, Didcot, Oxfordshire, United Kingdom [*Library symbol*] .... UkHA
Atomic Energy Review [*A publication*] .... At Energy Rev
Atomic Energy Review [*A publication*] .... Atom Ener R
Atomic Energy Review. Special Issue [*A publication*] .... At Energy Rev Spec Issue
Atomic Explosion .... ATXPL
Atomic Fluorescence Spectroscopy .... AFS
Atomic Frequency Standard .... AFS
Atomic Fuel Corporation [*Japan*] .... AFC
Atomic Hydrogen Weld .... AT/W
Atomic Incident Control Plan .... AICP
Atomic Industrial Forum [*Information service*] .... AIF
Atomic International - Combustion Engineering .... AI-CE
Atomic Mass Number .... AMN
Atomic Mass Unit .... AMU
Atomic Masses and Fundamental Constants [*A publication*] .... At Masses Fundam Constants
Atomic Migration .... AM
Atomic and Molecular Physical Data Program [*American Society for Testing and Materials*] .... AMD
Atomic and Molecular Processes Information Center [*ORNL*] .... AMPIC
Atomic/Nuclear Energy Study Group [*Philately*] .... ANESG
Atomic Number .... AN
Atomic Number .... ATNO
Atomic Number [*Symbol*] .... Z
Atomic Orbital .... AO
Atomic Ordnance Cataloging Office .... AOCO
Atomic Ordnance Platoon .... AOP
Atomic Packing Factor .... APF
Atomic Photoelectric Effect .... APE
Atomic Physics [*A publication*] .... At Phys
Atomic Physics Consortium at Oak Ridge .... APCOR
Atomic Post-Strike Analysis Report .... ATPOS
Atomic Power Construction Ltd. .... APC
Atomic Power Construction Limited .... APCL
Atomic Power Development Associates, Inc. .... APDA
Atomic Powered .... AP
Atomic Reactors in Space .... ARIS
Atomic Resolution Microscope .... ARM
Atomic Safety and Licensing Appeal Board .... ASLAB
Atomic Safety and Licensing Appeal Panel [*Nuclear Regulatory Commission*] .... ASLAP
Atomic Safety and Licensing Board [*Nuclear Regulatory Commission*] .... ASLB
Atomic Safety and Licensing Board Panel [*Nuclear Regulatory Commission*] .... ASLBP
Atomic Scattering Factor .... ASF
Atomic Scientists' Association [*Great Britain*] .... ASA
Atomic Security Agency [*Army*] .... ASA
Atomic Solution Diffusion .... ASD
Atomic and Space Development Authority .... ASDA
Atomic Standing Operating Procedures .... ASOP
Atomic Status Report .... ATOMSTATSREP
Atomic Strike Evaluation Center .... ASTREC
Atomic Strike Net .... ASN
Atomic Strike Plan .... ASP
Atomic Strike Plan Control Group Alternate .... ASPCGA
Atomic Strike Recording [*Air Force*] .... ASR
Atomic Strike Recording System [*Air Force*] .... ASTREC
Atomic Time .... AT
Atomic Torpedo [*Military*] .... ATORP
Atomic Transition Probabilities Data Center .... ATPDC
Atomic Units .... AU
Atomic Vapor LASER Isotope Separation .... AVLIS
Atomic Warfare .... AW
Atomic Weapon Retrofit Order .... AWRO
Atomic Weapons Research Establishment [*British*] .... AWRE
Atomic Weapons Training Group [*DASA*] .... AWTG
Atomic Weight .... A
Atomic Weight .... ATWT
Atomic Weight .... AW
Atomic Weight Unit .... AWU
Atomics International, Canoga Park, CA [*Library symbol*] .... CCpA
Atomics International Evaluated Nuclear Data Files .... AIENDF
Atomized Suspension Technique .... AST
Atomizing .... ATMG
Atomkernenergie [*A publication*] .... Atomkernene
Atomkernenergie-Dokumentation .... AED
Atomkernenergie Kerntechnik [*A publication*] .... Atomkernenerg Kerntech
ATOMKI [*Atommag Kutato Intezet*] **Kozlemenyek** [*A publication*] .... ATOMKI Kozl
Atomnaya Energiya [*USSR*] [*A publication*] .... At Energ
Atomnaya Energiya [*USSR*] [*A publication*] .... Atomnaya En
Atomnaya Energiya [*USSR*] [*A publication*] .... Atomn Energ

Atomnaya Energiya (USSR) [*A publication*]....At Energiya (USSR)
Atomnaya Tekhnika za Rubezhom [*A publication*]....At Tekh Rubezhom
Atompraxis [*A publication*]....Atomprax
Atoms in Japan [*A publication*]....At Jpn
Atomtechnikai Tajekoztato [*A publication*]....Atomtech Tajek
Atomwirtschaft Atomtechnik [*A publication*]....Atomwirtsch
Atomwirtschaft Atomtechnik [*A publication*]....Atomwirtsch Atomtech
Atonement Seminary of the Holy Ghost, Washington, DC [*Library symbol*]....DAtS
Atoomenergie en Haar Toepassingen [*A publication*]....Atoomenerg Haar Toepass
Atqasuk [*Alaska*] [*Airport symbol*]....ATK
ATR, Australian Telecommunication Research [*A publication*]....ATR Aust Telecommun Res
Atrial Ectopic Tachycardia [*Medicine*]....AET
Atrial Fibrillation [*Cardiology*]....AF
Atrial Fibrillation [*Cardiology*]....AFIB
Atrial Fibrillation [*Cardiology*]....AT FIB
Atrial Natriuretic Factor [*Biochemistry*]....ANF
Atrial Premature Beats [*Cardiology*]....APB
Atrial Premature Contractions [*Cardiology*]....APC
Atrial Premature Depolarization [*Cardiology*]....APD
Atrial Septal Defect [*Cardiology*]....ASD
Atrial Synchronous Ventricular Inhibited Pacemaker [*Cardiology*]....ASVIP
Atrial Vascular Relaxant Substance [*Biochemistry*]....AVRS
Atrioventricular [*Cardiology*]....AV
Atrioventricular Canal [*Cardiology*]....AVC
Atrioventricular Conduction System [*Cardiology*]....AVCS
Atrioventricular Nodal Reentry [*Cardiology*]....AVNR
Atrioventricular Node [*Cardiology*]....AVN
Atrium Pace [*Cardiology*]....AP
Attach [*or Attachment*]....ATCH
Attach....ATT
Attach-Detach Kit....ADK
Attach on Morning Report the Following Named EM [*Enlisted Man*] **Who Has Been Authorized to Report to Your Station upon Expiration of Leave. Retain Him/Her Pending Further Instructions and Advise This Office by Message the Date(s), the Report(s), PMOS, and AMOS**....ATCHEMPI
Attach Points Only....APO
Attache....ATT
Attached....ATCHD
Attached FORTRAN Processor [*Data processing*]....AFP
Attached Inflatable Decelerator [*Aerodynamics*]....AID
Attached to Other Correspondence....AOC
Attached Processor [*Data processing*]....AP
Attached Support Processor [*Data processing*]....ASP
Attachie [*British Columbia*] [*Seismograph station code, US Geological Survey*] [*Closed*]....ATC
Attachment....ATCHMT
Attachment....ATTACHT
Attack....ATCK
Attack....ATK
Attack....ATTK
Attack [*Designation for all US military aircraft*]....A
Attack [*Men's lacrosse position*]....A
Attack Aircraft Carrier [*Navy symbol*]....CVA
Attack Aircraft Carrier (Nuclear Propulsion) [*Navy symbol*]....CVAN
Attack Assessment [*Military*]....AA
Attack Cargo Ship [*Navy symbol*]....AKA
Attack Carrier Air Wing....ATKCARAIRWING
Attack Carrier Air Wing [*Navy symbol*]....CVW
Attack Carrier Striking Force....ACSF
Attack Center....AC
Attack Center Display....ACD
Attack Center Indicator Panel....ACIP
Attack Center Panel....ACP
Attack Center Switchboard....ACS
Attack Console....AC
Attack Control Console....ACC
Attack Cut Out [*Military*]....ACO
Attack Director [*Military*]....AD
Attack Display Group....ADG
Attack Experimental....AX
Attack Helicopter....AH
Attack Helicopter Company [*Military*]....ATKHC
Attack Helicopter Organization [*Military*]....ATHELO
Attack Helicopter Team....AHT
Attack Information Center....AIC
Attack Jet....AJ
Attack Plotter....AP
Attack Squadron [*Navy*]....ATKRON
Attack Squadron [*Symbol*]....VA
Attack Surveillance Committee [*Army*]....ATKSC
Attack Surveillance Coverage [*Army*]....ATKSC
Attack Teacher....A/T
Attack Transport [*Later, LPA*] [*Navy symbol*]....APA
Attack Warning System [*Civil Defense*]....AWS
Attainment Quotient....AQ
Attawapiskat [*Canada*] [*Airport symbol*]....YAT
Attempt....ATMT
Attempt to Contact....ATMTC
Attempt to Locate....ALCT
Attempted [*FBI standardized term*]....ATT
Attempted Corporate Integration of Dividends [*Economics*]....ACID
Attempts....ATT
Attend....ATND
Attendance [*Sports*]....A
Attendant....ATDNT
Attendant....ATTND
Attendant Control of Facilities [*Western Electric*]....ACOF
Attending....ATT
Attending....ATTG
Attending....ATTNG
Attending Physician's Statement....APS
Attention....ATT
Attention....ATTEN
Attention....ATTN
Attention Deficient Disorder [*Psychology*]....ADD
Attention Display [*Military communications device*]....AD
Attention-Interest-Desire-Action [*Formula*] [*Marketing*]....AIDA
Attention Operating Characteristic [*Psychometrics*]....AOC
Attenuated Total Reflectance [*Used in field of analytical instruments*]....ATR
Attenuation....AT
Attenuation Reaction....AR
Attenuator....ATTEN
Attenuator....ATTN
Attenuator-Thermoelement Voltmeter....ATVM
Attestation....ATTESTN
Atti. Accademia di Agricoltura, Scienze, e Lettere di Verona [*A publication*]....AAV
Atti. Accademia degli Arcadi [*A publication*]....AAAr
Atti. Accademia Fiorentina [*A publication*]....AAF
Atti. Accademia Fisio-Medico-Statistica di Milano [*A publication*]....Atti Accad Fis-Med-Statist Milano
Atti. Accademia dei Fisiocritici in Siena. Sezione Agraria [*A publication*]....Atti Accad Fisiocrit Siena Sez Agrar
Atti. Accademia dei Fisiocritici in Siena. Sezione Medico-Fisica [*A publication*]....AAMFA
Atti. Accademia dei Fisiocritici in Siena. Sezione Medico-Fisica [*A publication*]....Atti Accad Fisiocrit Siena Sez Med-Fis
Atti. Accademia Gioenia di Scienze Naturali in Catania [*A publication*]....Atti Accad Gioenia Sci Nat Catania
Atti. Accademia Ligure di Scienze e Lettere [*A publication*]....Atti Accad Ligure Sci & Lett
Atti. Accademia Ligure di Scienze e Lettere [*A publication*]....Atti Accad Ligure Sci Lett
Atti. Accademia dei Lincei [*A publication*]....AAL
Atti. Accademia Medica Lombarda [*A publication*]....Atti Accad Med Lomb
Atti. Accademia Medica Lombarda [*A publication*]....Atti Accad Med Lombarda
Atti. Accademia Nazionale dei Lincei [*A publication*]....AANL
Atti. Accademia Nazionale dei Lincei. Memorie. Classe di Scienze [*A publication*]....Atti Accad Naz Lincei Mem Cl Sci Fis Mat Nat
Atti. Accademia Nazionale dei Lincei. Memorie. Classe di Scienze Morali, Storiche, e Filologiche [*A publication*]....MAL
Atti. Accademia Nazionale dei Lincei. Memorie. Classe di Scienze Morali, Storiche, e Filologiche [*A publication*]....MALinc
Atti. Accademia Nazionale dei Lincei. Memorie. Classe di Scienze Morali, Storiche, e Filologiche [*A publication*]....MALincei
Atti. Accademia Nazionale dei Lincei. Rendiconti. Classe di Scienze Fisiche, Matematiche, e Naturali [*A publication*]....Att ANL R F
Atti. Accademia Nazionale dei Lincei. Rendiconti. Classe di Scienze Morali, Storiche, e Filologiche [*A publication*]....AANLR
Atti. Accademia Nazionale dei Lincei (Series Ottava) [*A publication*]....Atti Accad Naz Lincei (Series Ottava)
Atti. Accademia di Palermo [*A publication*]....AAP
Atti. Accademia di Palermo [*A publication*]....AAPal
Atti. Accademia Pontaniana [*Naples*] [*A publication*]....AAP
Atti. Accademia Pontaniana [*Naples*] [*A publication*]....AAPont
Atti. Accademia Pontaniana (Naples) [*A publication*]....AAPN
Atti. Accademia Roveretana degli Agiati [*A publication*]....AARA
Atti. Accademia delle Scienze di Ferrara [*A publication*]....Atti Accad Sci Ferrara
Atti. Accademia delle Scienze Fisiche e Matematiche di Napoli [*A publication*]....Atti Accad Sci Fis Mat Napoli
Atti. Accademia delle Scienze dell'Istituto di Bologna [*A publication*]....AASB
Atti. Accademia delle Scienze dell'Istituto di Bologna. Classe di Scienze Fisiche. Rendiconti [*A publication*]....Atti Accad Sci Ist Bologna Cl Sci Fis Rend
Atti. Accademia di Scienze, Lettere, e Arti di Palermo [*A publication*]....AAPal
Atti. Accademia di Scienze, Lettere, e Arti di Palermo. Parte Prima. Scienze [*A publication*]....Atti Accad Sci Lett Arti di Palermo Parte I
Atti. Accademia di Scienze, Lettere, e Arti di Udine [*A publication*]....AAU
Atti. Accademia di Scienze Morali e Politiche di Napoli [*A publication*]....AASN
Atti. Accademia di Scienze Morali e Politiche della Societa Nazionale di Scienze, Lettere, ed Arti di Napoli [*A publication*]....AAN

Atti. Accademia delle Scienze di Siena Detta de Fisiocritici [*A publication*]....Atti Accad Sci Siena Fisiocrit
Atti. Accademia delle Scienze di Torino [*A publication*]....AAT
Atti. Accademia delle Scienze di Torino [*A publication*]....Atti Accad Sci Torino
Atti. Accademia delle Scienze di Torino. Classe di Scienze Fisiche, Matematiche, e Naturali [*A publication*]....Atti Accad Sci Torino Cl Sci Fis Mat Nat
Atti. Associazione Genetica Italiana [*A publication*]....Att Ass Gen
Atti. Associazione Genetica Italiana [*A publication*]....Atti Ass Genet Ital
Atti. Associazione Genetica Italiana [*A publication*]....Atti Assoc Genet Ital
Atti. Centro Nazionale Meccanico Agricolo [*A publication*]....Atti Cent Naz Mecc Agr
Atti. Colloquio Slavistico di Uppsala [*A publication*]....ACSU
Atti. Congresso Internazionale per l'Elettronica [*A publication*]....Atti Congr Int Elettron
Atti. Congresso Internazionale di Estetica [*A publication*]....Atti
Atti. Congresso Internazionale di Studi Romanzi [*A publication*]....ACISR
Atti. Congresso del Naturalis i Italiani [*A publication*]....Atti Cong Nat Ital
Atti. Congresso Nazionale di Studi Romani [*A publication*]....Atti C St R
Atti del Congresso. Societa Italiana di Ortodonzia [*A publication*]....Atti Congr Soc Ital Ortod
Atti. Convegno Internazionale del Grano Duro [*A publication*]....Atti Conv Int Grano Duro
Atti. Convegno Internazionale di Studie Etiopici [*A publication*]....ACISE
Atti. Fondazione Giorgio Ronchi [*A publication*]....Atti Fond Ronchi
Atti. Fondazione Giorgio Ronchi e Contributi dell'Istituto Nazionale di Ottica [*A publication*]....Atti Fond Giorgio Ronchi & Contrib Ist Naz Ottica
Atti della Giornate Fitopatologiche [*A publication*]....Atti Giornate Fitopatol
Atti. Istituto Botanico e Laboratorio Crittogamico dell'Universita di Pavia [*A publication*]....Atti Ist Bot Labor Crittog Univ Pavia
Atti. Istituto Geologico della Universita di Pavia [*A publication*]....Atti Ist Geol Univ Pavia
Atti. Istituto Veneto di Scienze, Lettere, ed Arti [*A publication*]....Atti Ist Veneto
Atti. Istituto Veneto di Scienze, Lettere, ed Arti [*A publication*]....Atti Ven
Atti. Istituto Veneto di Scienze, Lettere, ed Arti. Classe di Scienze Matematiche e Naturali [*A publication*]....Atti Ist Veneto Sci Lett Arti Cl Sci Mat Nat
Atti e Memorie. Accademia di Padova [*A publication*]....AAP
Atti e Memorie. Accademia di Padova [*A publication*]....AAPad
Atti e Memorie. Accademia Patavina [*A publication*]....AAPat
Atti e Memorie. Accademia Patavina di Scienze, Lettere, ed Arti [*A publication*]....AMAP
Atti e Memorie. Accademia Petrarca [*A publication*]....AMAPe
Atti e Memorie. Accademia di Scienze, Lettere, ed Arti di Modena [*A publication*]....AAM
Atti e Memorie. Accademia di Scienze, Lettere, ed Arti di Modena [*A publication*]....AAMod
Atti e Memorie. Accademia di Scienze, Lettere, ed Arti di Modena [*A publication*]....AMAM
Atti e Memorie. Accademia di Storia dell'Arte Sanitaria [*A publication*]....AMAAA
Atti e Memorie. Accademia Toscana la Colombaria [*A publication*]....AATC
Atti e Memorie. Accademia Toscana la Colombaria [*A publication*]....AMAT
Atti e Memorie dell'Arcadia [*A publication*]....AMA
Atti e Memorie. Deputazione di Storia Patria per le Antiche Provincie Modenesi [*A publication*]....ADSPM
Atti e Memorie. Deputazione di Storia Patria per le Antiche Provincie Modenesi [*A publication*]....AMDM
Atti e Memorie. Deputazione di Storia Patria per le Antiche Provincie Modenesi [*A publication*]....AMDSPAM
Atti e Memorie. Deputazione di Storia Patria per le Antiche Provincie Modenesi [*A publication*]....AMSAPM
Atti e Memorie. Deputazione di Storia Patria per le Provincie delle Marche [*A publication*]....AMDSPPM
Atti e Memorie. Deputazione di Storia Patria per le Provincie di Romagna [*A publication*]....ADSPR
Atti e Memorie. Deputazione di Storia Patria per le Provincie di Romagna [*A publication*]....AMSPR
Atti e Memorie. Istituto Italiano di Numismatica [*A publication*]....AIIN
Atti e Memorie. Istituto Italiano di Numismatica [*A publication*]....AIN
Atti e Memorie. Reale Accademia di Modena [*A publication*]....Atti Mod
Atti e Memorie. Reale Accademia di Scienze, Lettere, ed Arti in Padova [*A publication*]....AAP
Atti e Memorie. Reale Accademia Virgiliana di Scienze, Lettere, ed Arti di Montova [*A publication*]....AAM
Atti e Memorie. Reale Deputazione di Storia Patria per l'Emilia et la Romagna [*A publication*]....AMSER
Atti e Memorie. Reale Deputazione di Storia Patria per le Marche [*A publication*]....AMSM
Atti e Memorie. Societa Dalmata di Storia [*A publication*]....AMSDSP
Atti e Memorie. Societa Istriana di Archeologia e Storia Patria [*A publication*]....AMSI
Atti e Memorie. Societa Istriana di Archeologia e Storia Patria [*A publication*]....AMSIstriana
Atti e Memorie. Societa Istriana di Archeologia e Storia Patria [*A publication*]....Atti Istr
Atti e Memorie. Societa Magna Grecia [*A publication*]....ASMG
Atti e Memorie. Societa Magna Grecia [*A publication*]....Atti Mem Soc Magna Grecia
Atti e Memorie. Societa Magna Grecia [*A publication*]....Atti M Grecia
Atti e Memorie. Societa Tiburtina di Storia e d'Arte [*A publication*]....AST
Atti e Memorie. Societa Tiburtina di Storia e d'Arte [*A publication*]....Atti Mem Soc Tiburtina
Atti. Museo Civico di Storia Naturale di Triesti [*A publication*]....Atti Mus Civ Stor Nat Triesti
Atti Notizie. Associazione Italiana di Metallurgia [*A publication*]....Atti Not Assoc Ital Metall
Atti della Pontificia. Accademia Romana di Archeologia [*A publication*]....APAA
Atti della Pontificia. Accademia Romana di Archeologia [*A publication*]....Atti Pont Acc
Atti della Pontificia. Accademia Romana di Archeologia. Memorie [*A publication*]....Mem Pont Acc
Atti della Pontificia. Accademia Romana di Archeologia. Rendiconti [*A publication*]....APARAR
Atti. Reale Accademia di Archeologia, Lettere, e Belle Arti di Napoli [*A publication*]....AAN
Atti. Reale Accademia d'Italia. Rendiconti. Classe di Scienze Morali [*A publication*]....Rend Acc It
Atti. Reale Accademia d'Italia (Roma). Memorie. Classe di Scienze Morali e Storiche [*A publication*]....AAR
Atti. Reale Accademia dei Lincei. Notizie degli Scavi [*Rome*] [*A publication*]....ARALNS
Atti. Reale Accademia Nazional dei Lincei (Roma) [*A publication*]....Atti R Accad Naz Lincei (Roma)
Atti. Reale Accademia delle Scienze di Torino [*A publication*]....ARAST
Atti. Reale Accademia della Scienze di Torino [*A publication*]....Atti Tor
Atti. Reale Accademia delle Scienze di Torino. Classe di Scienze Morali, Storiche, e Filologiche [*A publication*]....AAST
Atti. Reale Istituto Veneto di Scienze, Lettere, ed Arti. Classe di Scienze Morali e Lettere [*A publication*]....AIV
Atti. Reale Istituto Veneto di Scienze, Lettere, ed Arti. Classe di Scienze Morali e Lettere [*A publication*]....AIVSML
Atti. Reale Scuola Normale Superiore di Pisa [*A publication*]....ARSNSP
Atti. Reale Universita di Genova [*A publication*]....Atti R Univ Genova
Atti. Regia Accademia dei Fisiocritici in Siena [*A publication*]....Atti R Accad Fisiocrit Siena
Atti Scientifici. Societa Elvetica di Scienze Naturali [*A publication*]....Atti Sci Soc Elv Sci Nat
Atti. Seminario Matematico e Fisico dell'Universita di Modena [*A publication*]....Atti Semin Mat & Fis Univ Modena
Atti. Seminario Matematico e Fisico dell'Universita di Modena [*A publication*]....Atti Sem Mat Fis Univ Modena
Atti. Simposio Internazionale di Zootecnia [*A publication*]....Atti Simp Int Zootec
Atti. Societa Astronomica Italiana [*A publication*]....Atti Soc Astron Ital
Atti. Societa fra i Cultori delle Scienze Mediche e Naturali in Cagliari [*A publication*]....Atti Soc Cultori Sc Med e Nat Cagliari
Atti. Societa Elvetica di Scienze Naturali. Parte Scientifica [*A publication*]....Atti Soc Elv Sci Nat Parte Sci
Atti. Societa Italiana di Cardiologia [*A publication*]....Atti Soc Ital Cardiol
Atti. Societa Italiana per il Progresso delle Scienze [*A publication*]....ASPS
Atti. Societa Italiana di Scienze Naturali Milano [*A publication*]....Atti Soc Ital Sc Nat Milano
Atti. Societa Italiana delle Scienze Veterinarie [*A publication*]....Atti Soc Ital Sci Vet
Atti. Societa Italiana di Statistica [*A publication*]....ASIS
Atti. Societa Ligure di Storia Patria [*A publication*]....ASLSP
Atti. Societa Ligure di Storia Patria [*A publication*]....Atti Soc Lig Stor Patria
Atti. Societa Ligustica di Scienze Naturali e Geografiche [*A publication*]....Atti Soc Ligust Sc Nat e Geogr
Atti. Societa Linguistica di Scienze e Lettere di Genova [*A publication*]....ASLG
Atti. Societa dei Naturalisti e Matematici di Modena [*A publication*]....Atti Soc Nat Mat Modena
Atti. Societa Peloritana di Scienze Fisiche, Matematiche, e Naturali [*A publication*]....Atti Soc Peloritana Sci Fis Mat Nat
Atti. Societa Piemontese di Archeologia e Belle Arti [*A publication*]....ASPA
Atti. Societa Piemontese di Archeologia e Belle Arti [*A publication*]....ASPABA
Atti. Societa Toscana di Scienze Naturali. Processi Verbali e Memorie. Serie B [*A publication*]....Atti Soc Toscana Sci Nat P-V Mem Ser B
Atti. Societa Toscana di Scienze Naturali Residente in Pisa. Memorie. Serie A [*A publication*]....Atti Soc Toscana Sci Nat Resid Pisa Mem Ser A
Atti. Societa Toscana di Scienze Naturali Residente in Pisa. Processi Verbali e Memorie. Serie A [*A publication*]....Atti Soc Toscana Sci Nat Pisa P V Mem Ser A
Atti. Sodalizio Glottologico Milanese [*A publication*]....ASGLM
Atti. Sodalizio Glottologico Milanese [*A publication*]....ASGM
Atti del V Simposio Internazionale di Agrochimica su "Lo Zolfo in Agricoltura" [*A publication*]....Atti V Simp Int Agrochim "Zolfo in Agricoltura"
Attic Black-Figure Vase-Painters [*A publication*]....ABV
Attic Red-Figure Vase-Painters [*A publication*]....ARV
Attica [*New York*] [*Seismograph station code, US Geological Survey*] [*Closed*]....ATT

Attica, NY [*Radio station call letters*] .... WBTF
Attitude .... ATT
Attitude .... ATTD
Attitude Acquisition Technique .... AAT
Attitude Angle Transducer .... AAT
Attitude and Antenna Control System .... AACS
Attitude and Articulation Control Subsystem [*NASA*] .... AACS
Attitude Axis Emergency Control [*Aerospace*] .... AAEC
Attitude Command System .... ACS
Attitude Control [*System*] [*Aerospace*] .... AC
Attitude Control Electronics .... ACE
Attitude Control Jet .... ACJ
Attitude Control and Maneuver Rate .... ACMR
Attitude Control and Maneuvering Electronics .... ACME
Attitude Control and Maneuvering Electronics System .... ACMES
Attitude Control Propulsion Motors .... ACPM
Attitude Control Propulsion System [*or Subsystem*] [*NASA*] .... ACPS
Attitude Control and Stabilization [*NASA*] .... ACS
Attitude Control System [*or Subsystem*] [*Aerospace*] .... ACS
Attitude Control Torquing Device .... ACTD
Attitude Control and Translation System .... ACTS
Attitude Control and Translation System/Propulsion .... ACTS/PROP
Attitude Control and Translation System/Stabilization and Control Electronics .... ACTS/SCE
Attitude Controller Assembly [*NASA*] .... ACA
Attitude Coordinate Converter System .... ACCS
Attitude Direction Indicator .... ADI
Attitude Display Indicator .... ADI
Attitude Display System .... ADS
Attitude Gyro .... AG
Attitude Gyro Accelerometer Assembly .... AGAA
Attitude Gyro Accelerometer Package .... AGAP
Attitude Gyro Assembly .... AGA
Attitude Gyro Coupling Unit .... AGCU
Attitude Heading Reference System .... AHRS
Attitude Hold .... AH
Attitude Indicating System .... AIS
Attitude Indicator [*NASA*] .... AI
Attitude-Interest Analysis Test [*Psychology*] .... AIAT
Attitude and Orbit Control System .... AOCS
Attitude and Pointing .... AP
Attitude and Pointing Control System [*NASA*] .... APCS
Attitude and Pointing Control System [*NASA*] .... APS
Attitude Propulsion Subsystem .... APS
Attitude and Rate Indicating System .... ARIS
Attitude Reaction Wheel .... ARW
Attitude Reference Assembly .... ARA
Attitude Reference Bombing Computer .... ARBC
Attitude Reference Bombing Computer Set [*or System*] .... ARBCS
Attitude Reference Program [*NASA*] .... ATTREF
Attitude Reference System .... ARS
Attitude Reference Unit .... ARU
Attitude-Referenced Radiometer Study [*NASA*] .... ARRS
Attitude Set .... AS
Attitude Set Control Panel .... ASCP
Attitude Set and Gimbal Position Display [*NASA*] .... AS/GPD
Attitude Set and Gimbal Position Indicator [*NASA*] .... AS/GPI
Attitude and Spin Control Subsystem [*NASA*] .... ASCS
Attitude Thrustor System .... ATS
Attitude and Translation Control Assembly .... ATCA
Attitude and Translation Control Electronics .... ATCE
Attitude and Translation Control Unit .... ATCU
Attitudes Toward Disabled Persons [*Psychology*] .... ATDP
Attitudes Toward Industrialization [*Psychology*] .... ATI
Attitudes Toward Parental Control of Children [*Psychology*] .... ATPCC
Attitudinal Information Data System .... AIDS
Attleboro, MA [*Radio station call letters*] .... WARA
Attleboro Public Library, Attleboro, MA [*Library symbol*] .... MAtt
Atto [*A prefix meaning divided by 10 to the 18th power*] [*SI symbol*] .... a
Attock Oil Company [*Pakistan*] .... AOC
Attorney .... ATT
Attorney .... ATTY
Attorney General .... AG
Attorney General of Ontario, Crown Law Office, Toronto, ON, Canada [*Library symbol*] .... CaOTAGC
Attorney General's Opinion .... AGO
Attorneys for Animal Rights .... AFAR
Attorneys, Certified Public Accountants, and Enrolled Agents [*In "Operation ACE," IRS investigation of these occupations as sources of income tax evasion*] .... ACE
[*The*] **Attorneys Group** .... TAG
Attraktiv und Preiswert [*Attractive and Priced Right*] [*West German grocery products brand*] .... A & P
Attributed .... ATTRIB
Attrition and Pregnancy [*Refers to reasons for high turnover rate among women employees*] .... A and P
Attrition, Utilization, and Loss Rate .... AULR
Attu, AK [*Location identifier*] [*FAA*] .... ATU
Attualita di Ostetricia e Ginecologia [*A publication*] .... Attual Ostet Ginecol
Attualita Zoologiche [*A publication*] .... Attual Zool
Atualidades Agronomicas [*A publication*] .... Atual Agron
Atualidades Agronomicas (Sao Paulo) [*A publication*] .... Atual Agron (Sao Paulo)
Atualidades Agroveterinarias [*A publication*] .... Atual Agrovet
Atualidades Medico Sanitarias [*A publication*] .... Atual Med Sanit
Atualidades Veterinarias [*A publication*] .... Atual Vet
Atualidades Veterinarias (Sao Paulo) [*A publication*] .... Atual Vet (Sao Paulo)
Atuona [*Marquesas Islands*] [*Airport symbol*] .... AUQ
ATV Systems [*NASDAQ symbol*] .... ATVS
Atwater Kent Museum, Philadelphia, PA [*Library symbol*] .... PPAK
Atwater Library, Montreal, PQ, Canada [*Library symbol*] .... CaQMMI
Atwood, KS [*Location identifier*] [*FAA*] .... ADT
Atwood Oceanics, Inc. [*NASDAQ symbol*] .... ATWD
Atypical Legionella-Like Organism .... ALLO
Atypical Lymphoepitheloid Cell Proliferation [*Medicine*] .... ALEP
Atypical Measles Syndrome [*Medicine*] .... AMS
Au Tau [*Hong Kong*] [*Later, HKO*] [*Geomagnetic observatory code*] .... AUT
Aua [*Papua New Guinea*] [*Airport symbol*] .... AUI
AUAA [*American Urological Association Allied*] **Journal** [*A publication*] .... AUAA J
Aubenas [*France*] [*Airport symbol*] .... OBS
Auberger [*Blood group*] .... Au
Auburn [*Nebraska*] [*Seismograph station code, US Geological Survey*] .... ABN
Auburn, AL [*Radio station call letters*] .... WAUD
Auburn, AL [*Radio station call letters*] .... WEGL
Auburn, AL [*Radio station call letters*] .... WFRI
Auburn, CA [*Location identifier*] [*FAA*] .... AUN
Auburn, CA [*Radio station call letters*] .... KAHI
Auburn Community College [*New York*] .... ACC
Auburn-Cord-Duesenberg Club .... ACDC
Auburn Dam [*California*] [*Seismograph station code, US Geological Survey*] .... ADC
Auburn Enterprise, Auburn, IA [*Library symbol*] .... IaAubE
Auburn Heights, MI [*Radio station call letters*] .... WAHS
Auburn, IN [*Radio station call letters*] .... WIFF
Auburn, IN [*Radio station call letters*] .... WIFF-FM
Auburn/Lewiston, ME [*Location identifier*] [*FAA*] .... LEW
Auburn, ME [*Radio station call letters*] .... WKZS
Auburn, ME [*Radio station call letters*] .... WRXV
Auburn Memorial Hospital, Learning Resources Center, Auburn, NY [*Library symbol*] .... NAuMH
Auburn, NY [*Radio station call letters*] .... WAUB
Auburn, NY [*Radio station call letters*] .... WDWN
Auburn, NY [*Radio station call letters*] .... WMBO
Auburn, NY [*Radio station call letters*] .... WPCX
Auburn/Opelika [*Alabama*] [*Airport symbol*] .... AUO
Auburn-Placer County Library, Auburn, CA [*OCLC symbol*] .... APR
Auburn-Placer County Library, Auburn, CA [*Library symbol*] .... CAuP
Auburn Public Library, Auburn, IA [*Library symbol*] .... IaAub
Auburn Public Library, Auburn, IL [*Library symbol*] .... IAub
Auburn Public Library, Auburn, ME [*Library symbol*] .... MeAu
Auburn Public Library, Auburn, WA [*Library symbol*] .... WaAu
Auburn Research Foundation .... ARF
Auburn Theological Seminary, Auburn, NY [*Library symbol*] [*Obsolete*] .... NAuT
Auburn University [*Alabama*] .... AU
Auburn University, Auburn, AL [*OCLC symbol*] .... AAA
Auburn University, Auburn, AL [*Library symbol*] .... AAP
Auburn University at Montgomery, Montgomery, AL [*OCLC symbol*] .... AAM
Auburn University at Montgomery, Montgomery, AL [*Library symbol*] .... AMU
Auburn, WA [*Radio station call letters*] .... KASY
Auburn, WA [*Radio station call letters*] .... KGRG
Auburndale, FL [*Radio station call letters*] .... WTWB
Auburndale, WI [*Radio station call letters*] .... WLBL
Auchinoon [*Scotland*] [*Seismograph station code, US Geological Survey*] .... EAU
Auckland [*New Zealand*] [*Airport symbol*] .... AKL
Auckland [*New Zealand*] [*Seismograph station code, US Geological Survey*] .... AUC
Auckland University, Auckland, New Zealand [*Library symbol*] .... NzAU
Auckland University Law Review [*A publication*] .... Auckland U L Rev
Auctorum [*Of Authors*] [*Biology, taxonomy*] .... auct
Audible Rumble Loudness Level [*Stereo*] .... ARLL
Audible Signal Devices [*JETDS nomenclature*] [*Military*] .... BZ
Audibly Instructed Manufacturing Operations [*Military*] .... AIMO
Audience [*A publication*] .... Aud
Audience [*A publication*] .... Audn
Audience Development Committee [*Theatre*] .... AUDELCO
Audience Interest Factor .... AIF
Audience Reaction Assessment [*Television ratings*] [*British*] .... AURA
Audience Studies, Incorporated [*Television program testing system*] .... ASI
Audio [*A publication*] .... Au
Audio [*or Audible or Audiology*] .... AUD
Audio [*A publication*] .... AUDUA
Audio Bandpass Filter .... ABF
Audio Bandpass Filter .... ABPF
Audio Bandwidth .... AB
Audio Center [*Command and Service Module*] [*NASA*] .... AC
Audio Center - Receiver .... ACRC

Audio Center - Receiver ... ACRV
Audio Center - Transmitter ... ACTM
Audio Central Control Unit ... ACCU
Audio Commercial Message Repeating Unit [*Device delivering a recorded commercial from cigarette vending machines*] ... ACMRU
Audio Communications System ... ACS
Audio Control Center ... ACC
Audio Control Panel ... ACP
Audio Decode Oscillator ... ADO
Audio Distribution Amplifier ... ADA
Audio Distribution System ... ADS
Audio Engineering [*A publication*] ... Audio Engg
Audio Engineering Society ... AES
Audio Engineering Society. Journal [*A publication*] ... Audio Eng Soc J
Audio Engineering Society. Preprint [*A publication*] ... Audio Eng Soc Prepr
Audio Frequency [*Electronics*] ... AF
Audio Frequency Amplifier ... AFA
Audio Frequency Coder ... AFC
Audio Frequency Magnetotelluric ... AMT
Audio Frequency Shift ... AFS
Audio Function Generator ... AFG
Audio High Density ... AHD
Audio Input Frequency Tolerance ... AIFT
Audio Input Level ... AIL
Audio Level Meter ... ALM
Audio Lingual Education Press ... ALEP
Audio Load Compensator ... ALC
Audio-Only ... AO
Audio Oscillator ... AO
Audio Peak Clipping Amplifier ... APCA
Audio Playback Unit ... APU
Audio and Power Connectors [*JETDS nomenclature*] [*Military*] ... U
Audio Recording Rights Coalition ... ARRC
Audio Reply ... AUDREY
Audio Response ... AR
Audio Response [*International Harvester Co. computer*] ... AUDRE
Audio Response Control ... ARC
Audio Response Unit ... ARU
Audio Scene Canada [*A publication*] ... Audio Scene Can
Audio Sensitivity ... AS
Audio Support Equipment ... ASE
Audio Switch Assembly [*Ground Communications Facility, NASA*] ... ASWA
Audio Tape Cassette Player Set ... ATCPS
Audio Tape Recording ... ATR
Audio Techniques and Evaluation Laboratory [*NASA*] ... ATEL
Audio Terminal Unit ... ATU
Audio Thermal Unit ... ATU
Audio Tone Decoder ... ATD
Audio-Video Recording System [*Air Force*] ... AVRS
Audio Visual [*A publication*] ... AV
Audio-Visual Credit Interchange ... AVCI
Audio Visual Guide [*A publication*] ... Audio Visual G
Audio-Visual Index [*A publication*] ... A-V Ind
Audio, Visual, Kinesthetic, and Oral [*Teaching techniques*] ... AVKO
Audio-Visual Language Journal [*A publication*] ... Audio-Visual Language J
Audio-Visual Language Journal [*A publication*] ... A-V L J
Audio-Visual Management Association [*Formerly, IAVA*] ... AVMA
Audio-Visual Media [*A publication*] ... A-V Media
Audio Warning Amplifier ... AWA
Audio Wave Analyzer ... AWA
Audiofrequency Magnetic Fields [*Prospecting technique*] ... AFMAG
Audiogenic Seizure [*Neurophysiology*] ... AS
Audiolingual Language Programing [*Data processing*] ... ALLP
Audiology [*A publication*] ... Audiol
Audiology [*A publication*] ... AUDLA
Audiology (Japan) [*A publication*] ... Audiol (Jap)
Audiology Society of Japan [*A publication*] ... AUDIB
Audiometry Sweep Test ... AST
Audiotronics Corp. [*American Stock Exchange symbol*] ... ADO
Audiovisual ... AV
Audiovisual Annunciator ... AVA
Audiovisual, Computer, and Communication Office Automation ... AVCCOA
Audiovisual Conference of Medical and Allied Sciences ... ACMAS
Audiovisual Display Unit ... AVDU
Audiovisual Education in Neurosurgery ... AVENS
Audiovisual Information System ... AVIS
Audiovisual Instruction [*A publication*] ... Audiovis Instr
Audiovisual Instruction [*A publication*] ... Av I
Audiovisual Instruction [*A publication*] ... AV Inst
Audiovisual Instruction [*A publication*] ... Av Instr
Audiovisual Instructional Technology [*Military*] ... AVIT
Audiovisual Kit [*Army*] ... AVK
Audiovisual Liaison Officer [*Army*] ... AVLO
Audiovisual Market Place [*A publication*] ... AMP
Audiovisual Modulator ... AVM
Audiovisual Superimposed Electrocardiogram Presentation ... AVSEP
Audiovisual Support Center [*Army*] ... AVSC
Audiovisual-Tutorial [*Instruction*] ... AVT
Audiovisuals On-Line [*Data base*] [*National Library of Medicine*] ... AVLINE
Audit [*or Audited*] ... A
Audit [*or Auditor*] ... AUD
Audit Base Inventory System [*IRS*] ... ABIS
Audit Bureau of Circulations ... ABC
Audit Discrepancy Report ... ADR
Audit Entry ... AE
Audit Error List ... AEL
Audit Information Management System [*Department of the Treasury*] ... AIMS
Audit Information Management-Systems File [*IRS*] ... AIMF
Audit Integrated Reporting System [*IRS*] ... AIRS
Audit Reports Handbook [*IRS*] ... ARH
Audit Technical Time Report [*IRS*] ... ATTR
Auditing Order Error ... AOE
Auditor Camerae [*Auditor of the Papal Treasury*] ... AC
Auditor Freight Accounts ... AFA
Auditor Freight Claims ... AFC
Auditor Freight Receipts ... AFR
Auditor Freight Traffic ... AFT
Auditor General [*Military*] ... AG
Auditor General of the Navy ... AUDGENAV
Auditor General's Department [*Air Force*] ... AGD
Auditor General's Office ... AGO
Auditor Overcharge Claims ... AOC
Auditorium and Training Facility [*NASA*] ... ATF
Auditory Apperception Test [*Psychology*] ... AAT
Auditory Brainstem Response [*Neurophysiology*] ... ABR
Auditory Discrimination in Depth [*Program*] [*Education*] ... ADD
Auditory Discrimination Test [*"Wepman"*] [*Education*] ... ADT
Auditory Evoked Potential [*Neurophysiology*] ... AEP
Auditory Evoked Response [*Neurophysiology*] ... AER
Auditory Gross Error ... AGE
Auditory Induction ... AI
Auditory Information Display ... AID
Auditory Input Task [*Data processing*] ... AUDIT
Auditory, Kinesthetic, Tactile Approach [*Teaching method*] ... AKT
Auditory Memory Span [*Psychometrics*] ... AMS
Auditory Nerve Activating Substance [*Physiology*] ... ANAS
Auditory Sensation Area ... ASA
Audubon [*A publication*] ... Aud
Audubon Artists ... AA
Audubon County Courthouse, Audubon, IA [*Library symbol*] ... IaAuCoC
Audubon, IA [*Location identifier*] [*FAA*] ... ADU
Audubon Magazine [*A publication*] ... Audubon Mag
Audubon News-Advocate, Audubon, IA [*Library symbol*] ... IaAuNA
Audubon Public Library, Audubon, IA [*Library symbol*] ... IaAu
Audubon Regional Library, Clinton, LA [*Library symbol*] ... LCli
Audubon Society of Rhode Island. Bulletin [*A publication*] ... Audubon Soc RI Bull
Audubon Society of Rhode Island, Providence, RI [*Library symbol*] ... RPAS
Auerbach Reporter [*A publication*] ... Auerbach Rep
Auf Zeit [*On Credit*] [*German*] ... AZ
Aufbau [*A publication*] ... A
Aufbau [*A publication*] ... AUFB-A
Aufbereitungs-Technik [*A publication*] ... Aufbereit-Tech
Aufbereitungs-Technik [*A publication*] ... Aufbereitungs-Tech
Aufklaerungsgruppe [*Air forces reconnaissance unit*] [*German military - World War II*] ... AG
Auflage [*Edition*] [*German*] ... AUFL
Aufsaetze zur Portugiesischen Kulturgeschichte [*A publication*] ... APK
Aufschlagzuender ohne Verzoegerung [*Nondelay fuze*] [*German military - World War II*] ... AZOV
Aufstieg und Niedergang der Roemischen Welt [*A publication*] ... Au N
Augat, Inc. [*NYSE symbol*] ... AUG
Auger Electron Analysis ... AEA
Auger Electron Spectrometry [*or Spectroscopy*] ... AES
Auger and Elevator Manufacturers Council ... AEMC
Augere [*Increase*] [*Pharmacy*] ... AUG
Aughey Spark Chamber ... ASC
Augment ... AGMT
Augment ... AUG
Augmentation [*Music*] ... A
Augmentation ... AGN
Augmentation Concentration [*Biochemistry*] ... AC
Augmentation Research Center [*Stanford Research Institute*] ... ARC
Augmentation System ... AS
Augmentative ... AUGM
Augmented Air Jet ... AAJ
Augmented Assault Fire Units ... AAFU
Augmented Built-In Test ... AMBIT
Augmented Colombian El Nino Tuna Oceanography [*Project of IATTC*] ... ACENTO
Augmented Deflector Exhaust Nozzle [*Aviation*] ... ADEN
Augmented Human Intellect ... AHI
Augmented Logistics Support ... ALS
Augmented Lunar Module ... ALM
Augmented Off-Gas System [*Nuclear energy*] ... AOG
Augmented Phase Wave [*Thermodynamics*] ... APW
Augmented Plane Wave ... APW
Augmented Predictive Analyzer [*Data processing*] ... APA
Augmented Programing Training [*Data processing*] ... APT
Augmented Spark Igniter ... ASI

Augmented Support Period [*or Plan*] ... ASP
Augmented Surveyor ... AS
Augmented System Igniter [*NASA*] ... ASI
Augmented Target Docking Adapter [*Gemini*] [*NASA*] ... ATDA
Augmented Target Screening Subsystem ... ATSS
Augmented Thermally Electric Propulsion ... ATEP
Augmented Thrust Propulsion ... ATP
Augmented Transmission Network ... ATN
Augmenter Wing Jet STOL [*Short Takeoff and Landing*] **Research Aircraft** ... AWJSRA
Augmenting Unit [*Navy*] ... AUGU
Augmentor-Wing [*Aviation*] ... AW
Augsburg College, Minneapolis, MN [*OCLC symbol*] ... MNA
Augsburg College and Seminary, Minneapolis, MN [*Library symbol*] ... MnMA
Augsburg Transmission Upgrade ... ATU
August ... AG
August ... AUG
August Derleth Society ... ADS
August Thyssen Huette [*German steel producer*] ... ATH
Augusta [*Georgia*] [*Airport symbol*] ... AGS
Augusta [*Maine*] [*Airport symbol*] ... AUG
Augusta, AR [*Radio station call letters*] ... KABK
Augusta, AR [*Radio station call letters*] ... KABK-FM
Augusta, AR [*Radio station call letters*] ... KMCW
Augusta Area Committee for Health Information Resources [*Library network*] ... AACHIR
Augusta Chronicle-Herald, Augusta, GA [*Library symbol*] ... GAuACH
Augusta College, Augusta, GA [*Library symbol*] ... GAuA
Augusta College, Augusta, GA [*OCLC symbol*] ... GJG
Augusta, GA [*Location identifier*] [*FAA*] ... EMR
Augusta, GA [*Location identifier*] [*FAA*] ... MZX
Augusta, GA [*Radio station call letters*] ... WACG-FM
Augusta, GA [*Television station call letters*] ... WAGT
Augusta, GA [*Radio station call letters*] ... WBBQ
Augusta, GA [*Radio station call letters*] ... WBBQ-FM
Augusta, GA [*Radio station call letters*] ... WCKJ
Augusta, GA [*Radio station call letters*] ... WGAC
Augusta, GA [*Radio station call letters*] ... WHGI
Augusta, GA [*Television station call letters*] ... WJBF
Augusta, GA [*Television station call letters*] ... WRDW-TV
Augusta, GA [*Radio station call letters*] ... WTHB
Augusta, GA [*Radio station call letters*] ... WYMX
Augusta, GA [*Radio station call letters*] ... WZZW
Augusta, ME [*Television station call letters*] ... WCBB
Augusta, ME [*Radio station call letters*] ... WFAU
Augusta, ME [*Radio station call letters*] ... WKCG
Augusta, ME [*Radio station call letters*] ... WRDO
Augusta, ME [*Radio station call letters*] ... WSCL
Augusta Mental Health Institute, Augusta, ME [*Library symbol*] ... MeAM
Augusta Mental Health Institute, Augusta, ME [*OCLC symbol*] ... MEZ
Augusta Railroad Co. [*AAR code*] ... AUG
Augusta-Richmond County Library, Augusta, GA [*Library symbol*] ... GAu
Augusta-Ross Township District Library (McKay Library), Augusta, MI [*Library symbol*] ... MiAu
Augusta & Summerville Railroad Co. [*AAR code*] ... AUS
Augusta Warshaw Advertising Library, New York, NY [*Library symbol*] ... NNAA
Augustan Reprint Society ... ARS
Augustan Society ... AS
Augustana Bulletin [*A publication*] ... AB
Augustana College, Rock Island, IL [*OCLC symbol*] ... ICY
Augustana College, Rock Island, IL [*Library symbol*] ... IRA
Augustana College, Sioux Falls, SD [*OCLC symbol*] ... SDA
Augustana College, Sioux Falls, SD [*Library symbol*] ... SdSifA
Augustana Historical Society [*Formerly, ASI*] ... AHS
Augustana Hochschule Bibliothek, Neuendettelsau, Federal Republic of Germany [*Library symbol*] ... GyNeA
Augustana Institute Bulletin [*A publication*] ... AIB
Augustana Library Publications [*A publication*] ... Augustana Libr Pub
Augustana Luther League [*Later, ILLL*] ... ALL
Augustana Swedish Institute [*Later, AHS*] ... ASI
Augustine Island [*Alaska*] [*Seismograph station code, US Geological Survey*] ... AGI
Augustine Island [*Alaska*] [*Seismograph station code, US Geological Survey*] ... AUF
Augustine Island [*Alaska*] [*Seismograph station code, US Geological Survey*] ... AUI
Augustine Island [*Alaska*] [*Seismograph station code, US Geological Survey*] ... AUM
Augustinian Educational Association ... AEA
Augustinian Historical Institute, Villanova University, Villanova, PA [*Library symbol*] ... PVAHI
Augustinian Studies [*A publication*] ... Augustin Stud
Augustiniana [*A publication*] ... Aug
Augustiniani Assumptionis [*Assumptionists*] [*Roman Catholic men's religious order*] ... AA
Augustus Downs [*Australia*] [*Airport symbol*] [*Obsolete*] ... AUD
Aujourd'hui [*Today*] [*French*] ... AUJ
Aujourd'hui: Art et Architecture [*A publication*] ... Aujourd'hui
Auki [*Solomon Islands*] [*Airport symbol*] ... AKS
Auki [*Solomon Islands*] [*Seismograph station code, US Geological Survey*] ... AUK
Ault, Inc. [*NASDAQ symbol*] ... AULT
Ault Public Library, Ault, CO [*Library symbol*] ... CoAul
Aur [*Marshall Islands*] [*Airport symbol*] ... AUL
Aurakhmat [*USSR*] [*Seismograph station code, US Geological Survey*] [*Closed*] ... AUR
Aural Bearing Generator ... ABG
Aural Perception Heterodyne Exciter [*Inter-Technology Exchange Ltd.*] [*Psychoacoustics*] ... APHEX
Aurangabad [*India*] [*Airport symbol*] ... IXU
Aurea Parma [*A publication*] ... AP
Aurea Parma [*A publication*] ... APar
Aurelia Public Library, Aurelia, IA [*Library symbol*] ... IaAur
Aurelia Sentinel, Aurelia, IA [*Library symbol*] ... IaAurS
Aures Unitas [*Both Ears*] [*Latin*] ... AU
Auricular [*or Auricle*] [*Also, AUR*] [*Medicine*] ... A
Auricular [*or Auricle*] [*Also, A*] [*Medicine*] ... AUR
Auricular Fibrillation [*Medicine*] ... AF
Auriculo-Osteodysplasia [*Medicine*] ... AOD
Auriculoventricular [*Medicine*] ... AV
Auriga [*Constellation*] ... Aur
Auriga [*Constellation*] ... Auri
Aurigny Air Services Ltd. [*Great Britain*] [*ICAO designator*] ... GR
Aurillac [*France*] [*Airport symbol*] [*Obsolete*] ... AUR
Aurinarium [*Ear Cone*] [*Pharmacy*] ... AURIN
Auris [*Ear*] [*Latin*] ... A
Auris [*Ear*] [*Latin*] ... AUR
Auris Dextra [*Right Ear*] [*Latin*] ... AD
Auris Sinistra [*Left Ear*] [*Latin*] ... AS
Auris Uterque [*Each Ear*] [*Latin*] ... AU
Auristillae [*Ear Drops*] [*Pharmacy*] ... AURIST
Auristillae [*Ear Drops*] [*Pharmacy*] ... AURISTILL
Auropalpebral Reflex [*Response to sound*] ... APR
Aurora [*A publication*] ... Aur
Aurora Air Service, Inc. [*Fairbanks, AK*] [*FAA designator*] ... ARA
Aurora Borealis ... AURBO
Aurora College, Aurora, IL [*Library symbol*] ... IAurC
Aurora College, Aurora, IL [*OCLC symbol*] ... ICA
Aurora, Elgin, & Fox River Electric R. R. [*AAR code*] ... AEFR
Aurora, IL [*Location identifier*] [*FAA*] ... ARR
Aurora, IL [*Radio station call letters*] ... WAUR
Aurora, IL [*Radio station call letters*] ... WFVR
Aurora, IL [*Radio station call letters*] ... WKKD-FM
Aurora, IL [*Radio station call letters*] ... WMRO
Aurora, IL [*Television station call letters*] ... WPWR-TV
Aurora, IN [*Radio station call letters*] ... WSCH
Aurora, MO [*Radio station call letters*] ... KELE
Aurora, MO [*Radio station call letters*] ... KSWM
Aurora, NC [*Location identifier*] [*FAA*] ... AUR
Aurora, NE [*Location identifier*] [*FAA*] ... AUH
Aurora, NE [*Radio station call letters*] ... KIAE
Aurora, OR [*Location identifier*] [*FAA*] ... HBU
Aurora Public Library, Aurora, CO [*Library symbol*] ... CoAur
Aurora Public Library, Aurora, CO [*OCLC symbol*] ... COB
Aurora Public Library, Aurora, IL [*Library symbol*] ... IAur
Aurora Public Library, Aurora, ON, Canada [*Library symbol*] ... CaOAu
Auroral Absorption Index ... Ka
Auroral Electrojet [*Index*] ... AE
Auroral Hydrogen Line ... AHL
Auroral Hydrogen Line Emission ... AHLE
Auroral Infrasonic Wave [*Substorm*] ... AIW
Auroral Time [*Geophysics*] ... AT
Aurukun Mission [*Australia*] [*Airport symbol*] ... AUU
Aurum [*Gold*] [*Chemical element*] ... Au
Aurum [*Gold*] [*Latin*] ... AUR
Aurum [*Gold*] [*Numismatics*] ... AV
Aus Aachens Vorzeit [*A publication*] ... AAV
Aus Aachens Vorzeit [*A publication*] ... AV
Auscultation and Percussion [*Medicine*] ... A & P
Ausgabe [*Edition*] [*German*] ... AUSG
Ausgabestelle [*Distribution point*] [*German military - World War II*] ... A
Ausgrabungen und Funde [*A publication*] ... Au Fu
Ausgrabungen und Funde [*A publication*] ... Ausgrab Fun
Ausgrabungen und Funde. Nachrichtenblatt fuer Vor- und Fruehgeschichte [*A publication*] ... AF
Ausonia [*A publication*] ... Au
Ausonia [*A publication*] ... Aus
Aussen Politik [*A publication*] ... Aussen Poli
Aussenhandelsunternehmen [*Foreign Trade Enterprise*] [*German*] ... AHU
Ausser Dienst [*Retired*] [*German*] ... AD
Austell, GA [*Radio station call letters*] ... WCKZ
Austen Riggs Center, Inc., Stockbridge, MA [*Library symbol*] ... MStocA
Austere Airborne Ranging and Sighting System ... AARSS
Austere Heads-Up Display [*Aviation*] ... AHUD
Austere Surface-to-Air Missile System ... ASAMS
Austin [*Nevada*] [*Airport symbol*] [*Obsolete*] ... ASQ
Austin [*Texas*] [*Airport symbol*] ... AUS
Austin [*Texas*] [*Seismograph station code, US Geological Survey*] [*Closed*] ... AUS

Austin Area Vocational-Technology Institute, Austin, MN [OCLC symbol]..AVT
Austin College, Sherman, TX [OCLC symbol]...............................IAU
Austin College, Sherman, TX [Library symbol].....................TxShA
Austin Community College, Austin, MN [OCLC symbol].........ACO
Austin Community College, Austin, TX [OCLC symbol] ....TAC
Austin Community College, Austin, TX [Library symbol]..................TxAuCC
Austin-Healey Club of America...AHCA
Austin-Healey Sports Touring Club..AHSTC
Austin Junior College [Later, Austin Community College] [Minnesota].....AJC
Austin, MN [Location identifier] [FAA]..AUM
Austin, MN [Television station call letters]...............................KAAL
Austin, MN [Radio station call letters]......................................KAUS
Austin, MN [Radio station call letters]...............................KAUS-FM
Austin, MN [Radio station call letters]...............................KAVT-FM
Austin, MN [Television station call letters]........................KAVT-TV
Austin, MN [Radio station call letters].....................................KQAQ
Austin, Nichols, & Co., Inc. [NYSE symbol] [Delisted].............ANO
Austin Peay State College [Later, APSU] [Tennessee]............APSC
Austin Peay State University [Formerly, APSC] [Tennessee].................APSU
Austin Peay State University, Clarksville, TN [Library symbol]...............TCIA
Austin Peay State University, Clarksville, TN [OCLC symbol]..............TPA
Austin Presbyterian Theological Seminary, Austin, TX [Library symbol]...............TxAuP
Austin Public Library, Austin, MN [Library symbol].................MnAu
Austin Public Library, Austin, TX [Library symbol]..................TxAu
Austin Public Library, Austin, TX [OCLC symbol] ....TXG
Austin Public School Media, Austin, MN [Library symbol]................MnAuPS
Austin Public Schools Media, Austin, MN [OCLC symbol].......APS
Austin Service Center [IRS]..AUSC
Austin State Hospital, Austin, TX [Library symbol].............TxAuSHos
Austin State Junior College, Austin, MN [Library symbol].....MnAuS
Austin Ten Drivers Club..ATDC
Austin, TX [Location identifier] [FAA]..EBL
Austin, TX [Radio station call letters]......................................KASE
Austin, TX [Radio station call letters]....................................... KAZI
Austin, TX [Television station call letters]...............................KBVO
Austin, TX [Radio station call letters].......................................KHFI
Austin, TX [Radio station call letters]..KIXL
Austin, TX [Radio station call letters].......................................KLBJ
Austin, TX [Radio station call letters]..................................KLBJ-FM
Austin, TX [Television station call letters]................................KLRU
Austin, TX [Radio station call letters]......................................KMFA
Austin, TX [Radio station call letters].....................................KMMM
Austin, TX [Radio station call letters]..................................KMMM-FM
Austin, TX [Radio station call letters]....................................KNOW
Austin, TX [Radio station call letters]......................................KPEZ
Austin, TX [Television station call letters]............................KTBC-TV
Austin, TX [Television station call letters]............................KTVV-TV
Austin, TX [Radio station call letters]..................................KUT-FM
Austin, TX [Radio station call letters]......................................KVET
Austin, TX [Television station call letters]...........................KVUE-TV
Austin, TX [Location identifier] [FAA].......................................MMR
Austin Vocational Technical Institue, Austin, MN [Library symbol] ....MnAuV
Austral [or Australian] English...AE
Austral Lineas Aereas [Argentina] [ICAO designator] ....AU
Austral Oil Company, Inc. [American Stock Exchange symbol] [Delisted]..AOC
Australasia [MARC geographic area code] [Library of Congress] ....u------
Australasian Annals of Medicine [A publication]............Australas Ann Med
Australasian Association for the Advancement of Science. Reports [A publication]...............................Australasian As Rp
Australasian Baker and Millers' Journal [A publication] ....Australas Baker Millers J
Australasian Bulletin of Medical Physics and Biophysics [A publication]...........................Australas Bull Med Phys Biophys
Australasian Corrosion Engineering [A publication]..... Australas Corros Eng
Australasian Drug Information Services ....ADIS
Australasian Engineer [A publication]..................... Australas Eng
Australasian Institute of Mining and Metallurgy. Conference Series [A publication]...............Australas Inst Min Metall Conf Ser
Australasian Institute of Mining and Metallurgy. Monograph Series [A publication]...............Australas Inst Min Metall Monogr Ser
Australasian Institute of Mining and Metallurgy. Proceedings [A publication]................................Australas Inst Mining Met Proc
Australasian Institute of Mining and Metallurgy. Proceedings [A publication]............................. Australas Inst Min Metall Proc
Australasian Journal of Dermatology [A publication]...................Aust J Derm
Australasian Journal of Dermatology [A publication].....Australas J Dermatol
Australasian Journal of Pharmacy [A publication]..............Australas J Pharm
Australasian Journal of Pharmacy. Science Supplement [A publication]..Australas J Pharm Sci Suppl
Australasian Journal of Philosophy [A publication].......................Austl J Phil
Australasian Manufacturing Engineer [A publication] ....Australas Manuf Eng
Australasian Nurses Journal [A publication]...................... Australas Nurses J
Australasian Nursing Journal (Port Adelaide) [A publication]..Australas Nurs J (Port Adelaide)
Australasian Oil and Gas Review [A publication]..........Australas Oil Gas Rev
Australasian Physical and Engineering Sciences in Medicine [A publication]................................ Australas Phys Eng Sci Med

Australasian Physical Sciences in Medicine [A publication] ....
Australas Phys Sci Med
Australasian Radiology [A publication] ....Aust Radiol
Australasian Radiology [A publication] ....Australas Radiol
Australasian Society of Engineers... ASE
Australasian Universities Modern Language Association. Journal [A publication] ....AUMLA
Australia ....AS
Australia [MARC country of publication code] [Library of Congress] .... at
Australia [Two-letter standard code]...AU
Australia [Three-letter standard code]...AUS
Australia ....AUSTL
Australia ....AUSTR
Australia ....AUSTRAL
Australia [MARC geographic area code] [Library of Congress] ....u-at---
Australia [Aircraft nationality and registration mark].....................VH
Australia Antigen [Also, AA, HB_S, HBSAg] [Immunology].........................Au
Australia Building Forum [A publication]................ Aust Bldg Forum
Australia Bureau of Mineral Resources, Geology, and Geophysics. Bulletin [A publication] ....
Aust Bur Miner Resour Geol Geophys Bull
Australia Bureau of Mineral Resources, Geology, and Geophysics. Report [A publication]..
Aust Bur Miner Resour Geol Geophys Rep
Australia Commonwealth Scientific and Industrial Research Organisation. Animal Research Laboratories. Technical Papers [A publication]......................Aust CSIRO Anim Res Lab Tech Pap
Australia Commonwealth Scientific and Industrial Research Organisation. Annual Report [A publication] .... Aust CSIRO Annu Rep
Australia Commonwealth Scientific and Industrial Research Organisation. Bulletin [A publication] .... Aust CSIRO Bull
Australia Commonwealth Scientific and Industrial Research Organisation. Division of Animal Genetics. Research Report [A publication]...............Aust CSIRO Div Anim Genet Res Rep
Australia Commonwealth Scientific and Industrial Research Organisation. Division of Applied Chemistry. Annual Report [A publication]..................Aust CSIRO Div Appl Chem Annu Rep
Australia Commonwealth Scientific and Industrial Research Organisation. Division of Atmospheric Physics. Technical Paper [A publication]......................Aust CSIRO Div Atmos Phys Tech Pap
Australia Commonwealth Scientific and Industrial Research Organisation. Division of Building Research. Annual Report [A publication] .... Aust CSIRO Div Build Res Annu Rep
Australia Commonwealth Scientific and Industrial Research Organisation. Division of Dairy Research. Annual Report [A publication] .... Aust CSIRO Div Dairy Res Annu Rep
Australia Commonwealth Scientific and Industrial Research Organisation. Division of Entomology. Technical Paper [A publication].....................Aust CSIRO Div Entomol Tech Pap
Australia Commonwealth Scientific and Industrial Research Organisation. Division of Fisheries and Oceanography. Circular [A publication] .... Aust CSIRO Div Fish Oceanogr Circ
Australia Commonwealth Scientific and Industrial Research Organisation. Division of Food Research. Report of Research [A publication]................Aust CSIRO Div Food Res Rep Res
Australia Commonwealth Scientific and Industrial Research Organisation. Division of Food Research. Technical Paper [A publication]................Aust CSIRO Div Food Res Tech Pap
Australia Commonwealth Scientific and Industrial Research Organisation, Division of Horticulture. Research Report [A publication]......................Aust CSIRO Div Hortic Res Rep
Australia Commonwealth Scientific and Industrial Research Organisation. Division of Irrigation Research. Annual Report [A publication]...............Aust CSIRO Div Irrig Res Annu Rep
Australia Commonwealth Scientific and Industrial Research Organisation. Division of Mathematical Statistics. Technical Paper [A publication]........................ Aust CSIRO Div Math Stat Tech Pap
Australia Commonwealth Scientific and Industrial Research Organisation. Division of Mechanical Engineering. Annual Report [A publication] .... Aust CSIRO Div Mech Eng Annu Rep
Australia Commonwealth Scientific and Industrial Research Organisation. Division of Plant Industry. Annual Report [A publication]...............Aust CSIRO Div Plant Ind Annu Rep
Australia Commonwealth Scientific and Industrial Research Organisation. Division of Plant Industry. Technical Paper [A publication]...............Aust CSIRO Div Plant Ind Tech Pap
Australia Commonwealth Scientific and Industrial Research Organisation. Division of Soil Mechanics. Technical Paper [A publication]............... Aust CSIRO Div Soil Mech Tech Pap
Australia Commonwealth Scientific and Industrial Research Organisation. Division of Soils. Report on Progress [A publication]...................... Aust CSIRO Div Soils Rep Prog
Australia Commonwealth Scientific and Industrial Research Organisation. Division of Soils. Technical Paper [A publication]............................... Aust CSIRO Div Soils Tech Pap
Australia Commonwealth Scientific and Industrial Research Organisation. Division of Tropical Agronomy. Technical Paper [A publication]...............Aust CSIRO Div Trop Agron Tech Pap
Australia Commonwealth Scientific and Industrial Research Organisation. Division of Wildlife. Research Report [A publication]......................Aust CSIRO Div Wildl Res Rep

Australia Commonwealth Scientific and Industrial Research Organisation. Irrigation Research Stations. Technical Paper [*A publication*].....................................Aust CSIRO Irrig Res Stn Tech Pap

Australia Commonwealth Scientific and Industrial Research Organisation. Land Research Series [*A publication*]..................... Aust CSIRO Land Res Ser

Australia Commonwealth Scientific and Industrial Research Organisation. National Measurement Laboratory. Technical Paper [*A publication*].....................Aust CSIRO Natl Meas Lab Tech Pap

Australia Commonwealth Scientific and Industrial Research Organisation. National Standards Laboratory. Technical Paper [*A publication*].....................Aust CSIRO Natl Stand Lab Tech Pap

Australia Commonwealth Scientific and Industrial Research Organisation. Soil Mechanics Section. Technical Paper [*A publication*].....................Aust CSIRO Soil Mech Sect Tech Pap

Australia Commonwealth Scientific and Industrial Research Organisation. Soil Publication [*A publication*]........Aust CSIRO Soil Publ

Australia Commonwealth Scientific and Industrial Research Organisation. Soils and Land Use Series [*A publication*]..................... Aust CSIRO Soils Land Use Ser

Australia Day.....................AD

Australia Defence Standards Laboratories. Technical Note [*A publication*].....................Aust Def Stand Lab Tech Note

Australia Department of Agriculture. Biology Branch. Technical Paper [*A publication*].....................Aust Dep Agric Biol Branch Tech Pap

Australia-New Guinea Administrative Unit [*World War II*].................ANGAU

Australia-New Zealand Army Corps ....ANZAC

Australia New Zealand Closer Economic Relationship ....ANZCER

Australia, New Zealand, and Malaysia ....ANZAM

Australia, New Zealand, and United Kingdom ....ANZUK

Australia, New Zealand, and the United States [*The ANZUS Pact nations*] .... ANZUS

Australian ....A

Australian ....AUST

Australian Academic and Research Libraries [*A publication*]..................... Aust Acad and Res Lib

Australian Advertising Rate and Data Service ....AARDS

Australian Advisory War Council ....AAWC

Australian Air Mission.....................AAM

Australian Antarctic Territory ....AAT

Australian Armed Forces, Vietnam.....................AAFV

Australian Army Medical Corps ....AAMC

Australian Army Training Team ....AATT

Australian Army Training Team, Vietnam ....AATTV

Australian Associated Press Party Ltd. ....AAP

Australian Association of British Manufacturers ....AABM

Australian Atomic Energy Commission ....AAEC

Australian Biblical Review [*A publication*] ....ABR

Australian Bibliographic Network [*National Library of Australia*] [*Information service*] ....ABN

Australian Broadcasting Commission.....................ABC

Australian Broadcasting Corporation.....................ABC

Australian Capital Territory [*Formerly, FCT*] ....ACT

Australian Chemical Engineering [*A publication*] ....Aust Chem Eng

Australian Chemical Processing and Engineering [*A publication*]..................... Aust Chem Process Eng

Australian Civil Engineering [*A publication*]...................Aust Civ Eng

Australian Coin Review [*A publication*].....................ACR

Australian College of Theology.....................ACT

Australian Commonwealth Military Forces ....ACMF

Australian Commonwealth Naval Board [*Obsolete*] [*Navy*]...................ACNB

Australian Computer Journal [*A publication*] ....Aus Comp J

Australian Computer Journal [*A publication*] ....Aust Comput J

Australian Computer Journal [*A publication*] ....Austral Comput J

Australian Council for Aeronautics.....................ACA

Australian Council for Educational Research, Hawthorn, V, Australia [*Library symbol*].....................AuHaA

Australian Council of Salaried and Professional Associations ....ACSPA

Australian Council of Trade Unions.....................ACTU

Australian Dental Journal [*A publication*] ....Aust Dent J

Australian Dictionary of Biography [*A publication*] ....ADB

Australian Economic History Review [*A publication*] ....AEHR

Australian Economic History Review [*A publication*]...................Aust Econ H

Australian Economic Papers [*A publication*] ....AEP

Australian Economic Papers [*A publication*] ....Aust Econ

Australian Economic Papers [*A publication*] ....Aust Econ Pap

Australian Economic Review [*A publication*] ....AER

Australian Education Index [*Australian Council for Educational Research*] [*Information service*] ....AEI

Australian Education Index [*A publication*] ....Aus Educ Ind

Australian Electrical World [*A publication*]...................Aust Electr World

Australian Electronics Engineering [*A publication*] ....Aust Electron Eng

Australian Embassy, Washington, DC [*Library symbol*].....................DAusE

Australian Entomological Magazine [*A publication*]...................Aust Entomol Mag

Australian Entomological Society. Miscellaneous Publication [*A publication*].....................Aust Entomol Soc Misc Publ

Australian Family Physician [*A publication*] ....Aust Fam Physician

Australian Financial Review [*A publication*] ....Aust Financ Rev

Australian Financial Review [*A publication*] ....Austrl Fin

Australian Fisheries [*A publication*] ....Aust Fish

Australian Fisheries Newsletter [*A publication*] ....Aust Fish Newsl

Australian Force, Vietnam [*Military*].....................AFV

Australian Foreign Affairs Record [*A publication*]..........Aust Foreign Aff Rec

Australian Foreign Affairs Record [*A publication*]...........Austral For Aff Rec

Australian Forest Research [*A publication*] ....Aust For Res

Australian Forestry [*A publication*].....................Aust For

Australian Forestry Journal [*A publication*].....................Australian For J

Australian Gas Journal [*A publication*].....................Aust Gas J

Australian Gemmologist [*A publication*] ....Aust Gemmol

Australian General Hospital ....AGH

Australian Geographer [*A publication*].....................Aust Geogr

Australian Geographical Studies [*A publication*] ....Aust Geog S

Australian Geomechanics Journal [*A publication*] ....Aust Geomech J

Australian Hospital [*A publication*].....................Aust Hosp

Australian Imperial Forces ....AIF

Australian Information Network ....AUSINET

Australian Inland Mission ....AIM

Australian Institute of Aboriginal Studies. Newsletter [*A publication*].....................Austr Inst Aborig Stud Newsletter

Australian Institute of Nuclear Science and Engineering ....AINSE

Australian Institute of Park Administration.....................AIPA

Australian Institute of Refrigeration, Air Conditioning, and Heating.....................AIRAH

Australian Joint Staff Service.....................AJSS

Australian Journal of Agricultural Economics [*A publication*]......Aust J Ag E

Australian Journal of Agricultural Economics [*A publication*].....................Aust J Agr Econ

Australian Journal of Agricultural Economics [*A publication*].....................Austral J Agric Econ

Australian Journal of Agricultural Research [*A publication*]..........Aust J Agr

Australian Journal of Agricultural Research [*A publication*].....................Aust J Agric Res

Australian Journal of Agricultural Research [*A publication*].....................Aust J Agr Res

Australian Journal of Applied Science [*A publication*]...................Aust J Appl Sci

Australian Journal of Biblical Archaeology [*A publication*]...................AJBA

Australian Journal of Biological Sciences [*A publication*] ....Aust J Biol

Australian Journal of Biological Sciences [*A publication*] ....Aust J Biol Sci

Australian Journal of Biological Sciences [*A publication*] ... Austral J Biol Sci

Australian Journal of Botany [*A publication*] ....Aust J Bot

Australian Journal of Botany [*A publication*] ....Austral J Bot

Australian Journal of Botany. Supplementary Series [*A publication*].....................Aust J Bot Suppl Ser

Australian Journal of Chemistry [*A publication*].....................Aust J Chem

Australian Journal of Chemistry [*A publication*].....................Austral J Chem

Australian Journal of Dairy Technology [*A publication*].................Aust J Dair

Australian Journal of Dairy Technology [*A publication*].....................Aust J Dairy Technol

Australian [*later, Australasian*] Journal of Dermatology [*A publication*].....................Aust J Dermatol

Australian Journal of Ecology [*A publication*].....................Aust J Ecol

Australian Journal of Education [*A publication*] ....Aust J Educ

Australian Journal of Experimental Agriculture [*A publication*].....................Aust J Exper Agric

Australian Journal of Experimental Agriculture and Animal Husbandry [*A publication*] ....Aust J Exp Agr Anim Husb

Australian Journal of Experimental Agriculture and Animal Husbandry [*A publication*] ....Aust J Exp Agric Anim Husb

Australian Journal of Experimental Biology and Medical Science [*A publication*].....................Aust J Ex B

Australian Journal of Experimental Biology and Medical Science [*A publication*] ....Aust J Exp Biol Med Sci

Australian Journal of Forensic Sciences [*A publication*].....................Aust J Forensic Sci

Australian Journal of French Studies [*A publication*].....................AJFS

Australian Journal of Human Communication Disorders [*A publication*].....................Austral J Hum Commun Dis

Australian Journal of Instrument Technology [*A publication*].....................Aust J Instrum Technol

Australian Journal of Instrumentation and Control [*A publication*].....................Aust J Inst

Australian Journal of Instrumentation and Control [*A publication*].....................Aust J Instrum & Control

Australian Journal of Marine and Freshwater Research [*A publication*].....................Aust J Mar

Australian Journal of Marine and Freshwater Research [*A publication*].....................Aust J Mar Freshwater Res

Australian Journal of Marine and Freshwater Research [*A publication*].....................Aust J Mar Freshw Res

Australian Journal of Medical Technology [*A publication*].....................Aust J Med Technol

Australian Journal of Mental Retardation [*A publication*]...................AJMNA

Australian Journal of Music Education [*A publication*].....................AJMEA

Australian Journal of Music Education [*A publication*] ... Australian J Mus Ed

Australian Journal of Ophthalmology [*A publication*].........Aust J Ophthalmol

Australian Journal of Pharmaceutical Sciences [*A publication*].....................Aust J Pharm Sci

Australian Journal of Physics [*A publication*].....................Aust J Phys

Australian Journal of Physics [*A publication*].....................Austral J Phys

Australian Journal of Physics. Astrophysical Supplement [*A publication*].....................Aust J Phys Astrophys Suppl

Australian Journal of Plant Physiology [*A publication*] ....Aust J Plant Physiol

Australian Journal of Politics and History [*A publication*]........Aust J Pol Hist
Australian Journal of Politics and History [*A publication*]........Aust J Poli
Australian Journal of Politics and History [*A publication*]........Austral J Polit Hist
Australian Journal of Psychology [*A publication*]........ASJPA
Australian Journal of Psychology [*A publication*]........Aust J Psyc
Australian Journal of Psychology [*A publication*]........Aust J Psychol
Australian Journal of Psychology [*A publication*]........Australian J Psychol
Australian Journal of Science [*A publication*]........Aust J Sci
Australian Journal of Scientific Research. Series B. Biological Sciences [*A publication*]........Aust J Sci Res B
Australian Journal of Social Issues [*A publication*]........Aust J Soc
Australian Journal of Soil Research [*A publication*]........Aust J Soil
Australian Journal of Soil Research [*A publication*]........Aust J Soil Res
Australian Journal of Statistics [*A publication*]........Aust J Stat
Australian Journal of Statistics [*A publication*]........Austr J St
Australian Journal of Zoology [*A publication*]........Aust J Zool
Australian Journal of Zoology. Supplementary Series [*A publication*]........Aust J Zool Suppl Ser
Australian Labor Party........ALP
Australian Law Journal [*A publication*]........Aust Law J
Australian Law Journal [*A publication*]........Aust L J
Australian Lawyer [*A publication*]........Aust Law
Australian Legal Monthly Digest [*A publication*]........Aus Leg Mon Dig
Australian Letters [*A publication*]........AusL
Australian Library Journal [*A publication*]........ALJ
Australian Library Journal [*A publication*]........Aust Lib J
Australian Library Journal [*A publication*]........Aust Libr J
Australian Library Journal [*A publication*]........Australian Lib J
Australian Literary Studies [*A publication*]........ALS
Australian Machinery and Production Engineering [*A publication*]........Aust Mach Prod Eng
Australian Mammalogy [*A publication*]........Aust Mammal
Australian Marine Science Bulletin [*A publication*]........Aust Mar Sci Bull
Australian Marine Sciences Association........AMSA
Australian Mathematical Society. Gazette [*A publication*]........Austral Math Soc Gaz
Australian Medical Association........AMA
Australian Medical Journal [*A publication*]........Austral Med J
Australian Military Forces........AMF
Australian Mineral Development Laboratory........AMDEL
Australian Mineral Industries Research Association........AMIRA
Australian Mineral Industry [*A publication*]........Aust Miner Ind
Australian Mineral Industry [*A publication*]........Aust Min Ind
Australian Mining [*A publication*]........Aust Min
Australian Mining and Petroleum Law Journal [*A publication*]........Aust Min Pet Law J
Australian Museum. Magazine [*A publication*]........Aust Mus Mag
Australian Museum. Records [*A publication*]........Aust Mus Rec
Australian Museum (Sydney). Memoirs [*A publication*]........Aust Mus (Sydney) Mem
Australian Mutual Provident Society [*Insurance*]........AMP
Australian National Airways........ANA
Australian National Antarctic Research Expeditions........ANARE
Australian National Bibliography........ANB
Australian National University........ANU
Australian National University, Canberra, ACT, Australia [*Library symbol*]........AuU
Australian Natural History [*A publication*]........Aust Nat Hist
Australian Natural History [*A publication*]........Aust Natur Hist
Australian and New Zealand Association for the Advancement of Science........ANZAAS
Australian and New Zealand Association for the Advancement of Science. Report [*A publication*]........Australian and New Zealand Assoc Adv Sci Rept
Australian-New Zealand Conference on Geomechanics. Proceedings [*A publication*]........Aust NZ Conf Geomech Proc
Australian and New Zealand Journal of Criminology [*A publication*]........Aust NZ J C
Australian and New Zealand Journal of Medicine [*A publication*]........Aust NZ J M
Australian and New Zealand Journal of Medicine [*A publication*]........Aust NZ J Med
Australian and New Zealand Journal of Obstetrics and Gynaecology [*A publication*]........Aust NZ J O
Australian and New Zealand Journal of Obstetrics and Gynaecology [*A publication*]........Aust NZ J Obstet Gynaecol
Australian and New Zealand Journal of Obstetrics and Gynaecology [*A publication*]........AZOGB
Australian and New Zealand Journal of Obstetrics and Gynaecology (Supplement) [*A publication*]........Aust NZ J Obstet Gynaecol (Suppl)
Australian and New Zealand Journal of Psychiatry [*A publication*]........Aust NZ J P
Australian and New Zealand Journal of Psychiatry [*A publication*]........Aust NZ J Psychiat
Australian and New Zealand Journal of Psychiatry [*A publication*]........Aust NZ J Psychiatry
Australian and New Zealand Journal of Sociology [*A publication*]........Aust NZ J Sociol
Australian and New Zealand Journal of Sociology [*A publication*]........Aust NZ Soc
Australian and New Zealand Journal of Sociology [*A publication*]........Australian and NZ J Sociol
Australian and New Zealand Journal of Surgery [*A publication*]........Aust NZ J S
Australian and New Zealand Journal of Surgery [*A publication*]........Aust NZ J Surg
Australian and New Zealand Scientific Research Liaison........ANZSRL
Australian-New Zealand Society of New York........ANZSNY
Australian Numismatic Journal [*A publication*]........ANJ
Australian Nurses' Journal (Melbourne) [*A publication*]........Aust Nurses J (Melbourne)
Australian Orthodontic Journal [*A publication*]........Aust Orthod J
Australian Outlook [*A publication*]........Aust Outloo
Australian Outlook [*A publication*]........Aust Outlook
Australian Outlook [*A publication*]........Austral Outlook
Australian Packaging [*A publication*]........Austral Pkg
Australian Paediatric Journal [*A publication*]........Aust Paedia
Australian Paediatric Journal [*A publication*]........Aust Paediatr J
Australian Paint Journal [*A publication*]........Austral Paint J
Australian Pharmaceutical Manufacturers Association........APMA
Australian Physicist [*A publication*]........Aust Phys
Australian Plants [*A publication*]........Aust Plants
Australian Plastics and Rubber Journal [*A publication*]........Aust Plast Rubber J
Australian Process Engineering [*A publication*]........Aust Process Eng
Australian Psychologist [*A publication*]........Aust Psychl
Australian Psychologist [*A publication*]........Aust Psychol
Australian Public Affairs Information Service [*A publication*]........Aus PAIS
Australian Quarterly [*A publication*]........AQ
Australian Quarterly [*A publication*]........AusQ
Australian Quarterly [*A publication*]........Aust Q
Australian Quarterly [*A publication*]........Aust Quart
Australian Quarterly [*A publication*]........Austral Quart
Australian Railway Historical Society........ARHS
Australian Road Research [*A publication*]........Aust Road Res
Australian Road Research Board. Bulletin [*A publication*]........Aust Road Res Board Bull
Australian Safety News [*A publication*]........Aust Saf News
Australian School Librarian [*A publication*]........Aust Sch Librn
Australian Science Index [*A publication*]........Aus Sci Ind
Australian Science Index [*A publication*]........Austral Sci Index
Australian Science Teachers Journal [*A publication*]........Aust Sci Teach J
Australian Scientific Liaison Office [*US*]........ASLO
Australian Scientific Research Liaison [*British*]........ASRL
Australian Scientist [*A publication*]........Aust Sci
Australian Security Intelligence Organization........ASIO
Australian Society of Dairy Technology. Technical Publication [*A publication*]........Aust Soc Dairy Technol Tech Publ
Australian Society of Exploration Geophysicists. Bulletin [*A publication*]........Aust Soc Explor Geophys Bull
Australian Society of New York [*Later, Australia-New Zealand Society of New York*]........AS of NY
Australian Special Libraries News [*A publication*]........Aust Spec Libr News
Australian Speleo Abstracts [*A publication*]........Aus Speleo Abstr
Australian Stock Exchange Journal [*A publication*]........Aust Stock Exch J
Australian Surveyor [*A publication*]........Aust Surv
Australian Task Force........ATF
Australian Teacher of the Deaf [*A publication*]........Austral Teacher Deaf
Australian Telecommunications Research [*A publication*]........ATR
Australian Telecommunications Research [*A publication*]........Aust Telecommun Res
Australian Terrier Club of America........ATCA
Australian Timber Journal [*A publication*]........Aust Timb J
Australian Tobacco Grower's Bulletin [*A publication*]........Aust Tob Grow Bull
Australian Trade Commission........ATC
Australian Transport [*A publication*]........Aust Transp
Australian Veterinary Journal [*A publication*]........Aust Vet J
Australian Water Resources Council. Stream Gauging Information [*A publication*]........Aust Water Resour Counc Stream Gauging Inf
Australian Water Resources Council. Technical Paper [*A publication*]........Aust Water Resour Counc Tech Pap
Australian Water and Wastewater Association........AuWWA
Australian Welding Journal [*A publication*]........Aust Weld J
Australian Welding Research [*A publication*]........Aust Weld Res
Australian Welding Research Association. Bulletin [*A publication*]........Aust Weld Res Ass Bull
Australian Wildlife Research [*A publication*]........Aust Wildl Res
Australian Women's Home Army........AWHA
Australian Wool Commission........AWC
Australian Workers' Union........AWU
Australian Yearbook of International Law [*A publication*]........Aust Yearbook Int L
Australian Zoologist [*A publication*]........Aust Zool
Australia's Neighbours [*A publication*]........Aust Neighbours
Australisch-Neuseelaendische Studien zur Deutschen Sprache und Literatur [*A publication*]........ANSDSL
Austria........A
Austria [*Two-letter standard code*]........AT

Austria ... AU
Austria ... AUS
Austria ... AUST
Austria [*Three-letter standard code*] ... AUT
Austria [*MARC geographic area code*] [*Library of Congress*] ... e-au---
Austria [*Aircraft nationality and registration mark*] ... OE
Austria [*MARC country of publication code*] [*Library of Congress*] ... au
Austria Erit In Orbe Ultima [*Austria Will Be The Last in the World*] [*Variation of 15th-century inscription*] ... AEIOU
Austria Philatelic Society of New York ... APSNY
Austria Presse Agentur [*Press agency*] [*Austria*] ... APA
Austriae Est Imperare Orbi Universo [*It Is Given to Austria to Rule the Whole World*] [*Variation of 15th-century inscription*] ... AEIOU
Austrian Airlines ... AUA
Austrian Airlines [*ICAO designator*] ... OS
Austrian Airtransport [*ICAO designator*] ... OB
Austrian Forum ... AF
Austrian Institute ... AI
Austrian Journal of Oncology [*A publication*] ... Austrian J Oncol
Austrian RADAR Site Analysis ... ARSA
Austrian Trade News [*A publication*] ... Aus Trade
Austrian Trade Union Federation ... ATUF
Austria's Empire Is Obviously Upset [*Variation of 15th century inscription*] ... AEIOU
Austria's Empire Is Overall Universal [*Variation of 15th-century inscription*] ... AEIOU
Austron, Inc. [*NASDAQ symbol*] ... ATRN
Auswaertiges Amt [*Foreign Office*] [*German*] ... AA
Aut Aut [*A publication*] ... AA
Authentic ... AUTH
Authentic ... AUTHEN
Authentic Reproduction of an Independent Earth Satellite ... ARIES
Authentic Science Fiction [*A publication*] ... Aut
Authentication ... AUTHN
Authentication Maneuver [*Aviation*] ... ATM
Authenticolor, Inc. [*NASDAQ symbol*] ... ATCR
Author ... A
Author [*Data processing*] ... AU
Author ... AUTH
Author Biographies Master Index [*A publication*] ... ABMI
Author Earn-Out [*Publishing*] ... AEO
Author Index ... AUTDEX
Authority ... AUT
Authority ... AUTH
Authority ... AUTHY
Authority for the Coordination of Inland Transport in Central Europe [*NATO*] ... ACTICE
Authority for the Coordination of Inland Transport in Southern Europe [*NATO*] ... ACTISUD
Authority Directing Arrest or Confinement [*Military*] ... ADA
Authority for Expenditure ... AFE
Authority Granted ... AUGRA
Authority Granted [*Military*] ... AUTHGR
Authority Granted [*Military*] ... AUTHGRA
Authority Granted to Execute Acceptance and Oath of Office for____ ... AUTHEXANDO
Authority Is Requested ... AUREQ
Authority Is Requested to Inter [*the remains of*] [*Army*] ... ARI
Authority for Material Substitution ... AMS
Authority to Pay [*or Purchase*] ... A/P
Authority to Proceed ... ATP
Authority for Purchase ... AFP
Authority for Removal of Accepted Spacecraft Installations ... AFROASI
Authorization [*or Authorized*] ... AUTH
Authorization for Program Development [*NASA*] ... AFPD
Authorization to Purchase [*Food stamp card*] [*Department of Agriculture*] ... ATP
Authorization for Sale of Salvage Material ... ASSM
Authorization for Temporary Admission [*Customs*] ... ATA
Authorization to Transfer Material ... ATTM
Authorize ... AUZ
Authorized About ... AUTHAB
Authorized in Accordance with Bureau of Naval Personnel Manual ... ABPM
Authorized Accounting Activity [*DoD*] ... AAA
Authorized Acquisition Objective [*Army*] ... AAO
Authorized Allowance ... AA
Authorized in Bureau of Naval Personnel Manual ... AUTHBUPERSMAN
Authorized Code Number ... ACN
Authorized Commanders Atomic Air Defense ... ACAAD
Authorized Consumption List [*Military*] ... ACL
Authorized Controller Material ... ACM
Authorized Data Chain ... ADC
Authorized Data Element ... ADE
Authorized Data List [*DoD*] ... ADL
Authorized to Delay [*Number of Days*], **Any Portion of Which May Be Taken in CONUS** [*Navy*] ... DELINUS
Authorized to Delay [*Number of Days*], **Any Portion of Which May Be Taken Prior to or after Arrival in United States** [*Navy*] ... DELREPARUS
Authorized to Delay [*Number of Days*], **Any Portion of Which May Be Taken Prior to or after Departure** [*Navy*] ... DELPARTURE
Authorized to Delay [*Number of Days*], **in Reporting** [*Navy*] ... DELREP
Authorized to Delay [*Number of Days*], **in Reporting, Any Portion of Which May Be Taken Prior to or after Reporting at Temporary Duty Station** [*s*] [*Navy*] ... DELREPANY
Authorized to Delay [*Number of Days*], **in Reporting, to Count as Graduation Leave** [*Navy*] ... DELREPGRAD
Authorized to Delay [*Number of Days*], **in Reporting, Keep New Station Advised Address** [*Navy*] ... DELREPVAN
Authorized Depot Stockage List [*Army*] ... ADSL
Authorized Equipment Listing ... AEL
Authorized "In Excess" ... AIE
Authorized Inspector ... AI
Authorized Item Identification Data Collaborator Code ... AIIDC
Authorized Item Identification Data Receiver Code ... AIIDR
Authorized Item Identification Data Submitter Code ... AIIDS
Authorized Level of Organization ... ALO
Authorized Military Occupational Specialty Code ... AMOSC
Authorized Notice of Change ... ANOC
Authorized Order ... AO
Authorized Organizational Storage List [*Army*] ... AOSL
Authorized Part Number ... APN
Authorized Possession Limits [*Nuclear energy*] ... APL
Authorized Price List ... APL
Authorized to Proceed On or About [*Date*] [*Military*] ... AUTHPROBOUT
Authorized Procurement Information Requirements Description [*NASA*] ... APIRD
Authorized Procurement Information Requirements List [*NASA*] ... APIRL
Authorized Program Analysis Report [*Data processing*] ... APAR
Authorized Program Facility [*Data processing*] ... APF
Authorized Retention Level [*Military*] ... ARL
Authorized Revisit Above-Mentioned Places and Vary Itinerary as Necessary ... REVAR
Authorized Rotational Retention [*Navy*] ... RORET
Authorized Shortages and Discrepancies ... ASAD
Authorized Stock Level ... ASL
Authorized Stockage List [*Army*] ... ASL
Authorized Version [*or King James Version of the Bible, 1611*] ... AV
Author's Alteration [*Publishing*] ... AA
Authors at Auction [*A publication*] ... AAA
Author's Correction [*Publishing*] ... AC
Authors Guild ... AG
Authors Guild of the Authors League of America ... AGALA
Authors League of America ... ALA
Author's Proof [*Publishing*] ... AP
Authors' and Publishers' Lending Right Association Committee ... APLA
Author's Time [*Publishing*] ... AT
Autism Services Center ... ASC
Auto Acquisition [*RADAR*] ... AA
Auto Beacon ... AB
Auto Car Guard ... ACG
Auto Dealers Traffic Safety Council [*Later, HUF*] ... ADTSC
Auto Defense Ordinance ... ADO
Auto-Diesel Technician Program [*Association of Independent Colleges and Schools specialization code*] ... AD
Auto Enthusiasts International [*Defunct*] ... AEI
Auto-Fiche ... AF
Auto Glass Industry Committee for Highway Safety ... AGICHS
Auto Hold Fire ... AHF
Auto Industries Highway Safety Committee [*Later, HUF*] ... AIHSC
Auto Insurance Plans Services Office [*A rule and rate-making association*] ... AIPSO
Auto Internacional Association ... AIA
Auto-Lock Channel Tuning [*TV*] ... ACT
Auto/Manual ... A/M
Auto Merchandising News [*A publication*] ... Auto Merch
Auto-Mitrailleuse Legere [*French armored car*] ... AML
Auto-Resonant Accelerator [*For atomic particles*] ... ARA
Auto-Train Corporation [*American Stock Exchange symbol*] [*Delisted*] ... ATC
Auto-Trol Technology [*NASDAQ symbol*] ... ATTC
Auto Workers Action Caucus ... AWAC
Autoanalyzer ... AA
Autobody Filler Manufacturers Association ... AFMA
Autobody Supply and Equipment Manufacturers Council ... ASEMC
Autobond Welder ... ABW
Autoclave Engineers [*NASDAQ symbol*] ... ACLV
Autocoder to COBOL Conversion Aid Program [*Data processing*] ... ACCAP
Autocoder-to-COBOL [*Common Business-Oriented Language*] **Translating Service** [*Data processing*] ... ACTRAN
Autocollimator ... AC
Autocorrelation Function [*Aviation*] ... ACF
Autocovariance Generating Function [*Statistics*] ... ACGF
Autocycle Union [*British*] ... ACU
AUTODIN/AUTOVON [*Automatic Digital Network/Automatic Voice Network*] **Interface** ... AAI
AUTODIN [*Automatic Digital Network*] **Coordination Station** ... ADCS
AUTODIN [*Automatic Digital Network*] **Digital Subscriber Terminal** ... ADST
AUTODIN [*Automatic Digital Network*] **Multimedia Terminal** ... AMT
AUTODIN [*Automatic Digital Network*] **Station Maintenance Console** ... ASMC
AUTODIN [*Automatic Digital Network*] **Switch Upgrade Project** ... ASUP

AUTODIN [*Automatic Digital Network*] **Switching Center** ... ASC
Autodynamics Cl A [*NASDAQ symbol*] ... AUDYA
Autodyne Detection and Ranging ... AUDAR
Autogenic Training [*Influencing the body through autosuggestion*] ... AT
Autogestion et Socialisme [*A publication*] ... Autogestion et Social
Autograph ... AUT
Autograph ... AUTOG
Autograph Card Signed [*Manuscript descriptions*] ... ACS
Autograph Chapter of the American First Day Cover Society ... ACAFDCS
Autograph Document [*Manuscript descriptions*] ... AD
Autograph Document Signed [*Manuscript descriptions*] ... ADS
Autograph Letter [*Manuscript descriptions*] ... AL
Autograph Letter Signed [*Manuscript descriptions*] ... ALS
Autograph Manuscript Signed [*Manuscript descriptions*] ... AMSS
Autograph Note Signed [*Manuscript descriptions*] ... ANS
Autograph Postcard Signed [*Manuscript descriptions*] ... APS
Autographa Californica Nuclear Polyhedrosis Virus ... AcNPV
Autographed Presentation Copy ... APC
Autographic Theme Extraction [*System*] ... ATE
Autographics International ... AI
Autoignition Temperature ... AIT
Autoimmune Complement Fixation [*Immunochemistry*] ... AICF
Autoimmune Deficiency [*or Disease*] [*Immunology*] ... AID
Autoimmune Encephalomyelitis [*Hematology*] ... AE
Autoimmune Hemolytic Anemia [*Hematology*] ... AHA
Autoimmune Hemolytic Anemia [*Hematology*] ... AIHA
Autoland Flight Tests ... AFL
Autoland Rollout ... A/R
Autoleather Guild [*Formerly, ULG*] ... AG
Autologous Mixed Lymphocyte Reaction [*Immunochemistry*] ... AMLR
Autologous Rosette-Forming Cell [*s*] [*Immunology*] ... ARFC
Automatech Graphics Corporation [*Information service*] ... AGC
Automated Accounting System ... AAS
Automated Agency Accounting ... AAA
Automated Air Facilities Intelligence File [*Naval Oceanographic Office*] ... AAFIF
Automated Air Facility Information File [*Defense Mapping Agency*] ... AAFIF
Automated Amino Acid Analysis [*Food technology*] ... AAA
Automated Analytical Electrophoresis Facility [*NASA*] ... AAEF
Automated Armed Forces Examining and Entrance Station System ... AAFEESS
Automated Astronomic Positioning Device [*Defense Mapping Agency*] ... AAPD
Automated Astronomic Positioning System [*Defense Mapping Agency*] ... AAPS
Automated Attendance Accounting System [*Jet Propulsion Laboratory, NASA*] ... AAAS
Automated Attendance Reporting System ... AARS
Automated Auger Microprobe ... A²M
Automated Batch Mixing [*Data processing*] ... ABM
Automated Batch Weighing ... ABW
Automated Biological and Chemical Data [*System*] ... ABCD
Automated Biological Laboratory [*NASA*] ... ABL
Automated Budget System ... AUTOBUS
Automated Building Components, Inc. [*American Stock Exchange symbol*] [*Delisted*] ... ATD
Automated Camera Effects System ... ACES
Automated Carrier Landing System [*Military*] ... ACLS
Automated Carrier Landing Systems Project [*Military*] ... ACLSP
Automated Chemistry Program [*Data processing*] ... ACP
Automated Circuit Card Etching Layout [*Data processing*] ... ACCEL
Automated Circulation System [*Data processing*] ... ACS
Automated Clearinghouse [*Banking*] ... ACH
Automated Coder of Report Narrative [*Data processing*] ... ACORN
Automated Combustor [*Computer code*] ... AUTOCOM
Automated Communications and Control System [*Navy*] ... ACCS
Automated Communications and Message Processing System [*Army*] ... ACAMPS
Automated Communications and Message Processing System [*Army*] ... ACMPS
Automated Communications Set ... ACS
Automated Computer Controlled Editing Sound System ... ACCESS
Automated Computer Science Education ... ACSED
Automated CONARC Command Echelon Standard Systems ... ACCESS
Automated Contingency Support Capability ... ACSC
Automated Contingency Translator [*Data processing*] ... ACT
Automated Control and Checking of Electrical Systems Support ... ACCESS
Automated Control and Distribution of Trainees [*Army*] ... ACT
Automated Control of a Document Management System [*Data processing*] ... ACDMS
Automated Control and Landing System [*Navy*] ... ACLS
Automated Conversion Routine ... ACORN
Automated Cost Estimates ... ACE
Automated Cross-Section Analysis Program [*Data processing*] ... ACSAP
Automated Custom Terminal System ... ACTS
Automated Data Acquisition System [*GCA Corp.*] ... ADAS
Automated Data Analysis and Presentation Techniques ... ADAPT
Automated Data on Instructional Technology ... ADIT
Automated Data Interchange Systems [*International Civil Aviation Organization*] ... ADIS
Automated Data Management Information System ... ADMIS
Automated Data Preparation by Electronic Photocomposition ... ADPEP
Automated Data Preparation Evaluation Program ... ADPEP
Automated Data Reports Submission System ... ADRSS
Automated Data Subsystem ... ADSS
Automated Data System ... ADS
Automated Data System Analysis Technique ... AUTOSATE
Automated Data and Telecommunications Service [*Later, Office of Information and Resources Management*] ... ADTS
Automated Data Unit Movement ... ADUM
Automated Data Wiring ... ADW
Automated Depot Maintenance ... ADM
Automated Depot Maintenance Study ... ADMS
Automated Design Engineering ... ADE
Automated Design System ... ADS
Automated Digital Design System [*Raytheon Co.*] ... ADDS
Automated Digital Weather Communications Program [*Air Force*] ... ADWCP
Automated Direct Labor Reporting ... ADLR
Automated Document Control System ... ADCS
Automated Documentation Systems [*Data processing*] ... ADS
Automated Drafting and Digitizing Machine [*Data processing*] ... ADDM
Automated Drafting Machine ... ADM
Automated Drafting System ... ADS
Automated Drawing Parts List System ... ADPLS
Automated Drug Identification ... AUDRI
Automated Educational Services On-Line Processing ... AESOP
Automated Electrocardiograph Interpretive System [*Veterans Administration*] ... AECGIS
Automated En-Route Air Traffic Control [*Proposed*] [*FAA*] ... AERA
Automated Engineering Design [*Data processing*] ... AED
Automated Engineering Design Circuit Analysis Program ... AEDCAP
Automated Engineering Document Preparation System ... AEDPS
Automated Engineering and Scientific Optimization Program [*NASA*] ... AESOP
Automated Environmental Prediction System ... AEPS
Automated Fare Collections ... AFC
Automated Field Interview System ... AFIS
Automated Flaw Detector ... AFD
Automated Flight Service Station ... AFSS
Automated Frequency Assignment System [*Communications*] ... AFAS
Automated General Experimental Device [*Animal performance testing*] ... AGED
Automated Gyro Test Set ... AGTS
Automated Hospital Information System [*Veterans Administration*] ... AHIS
Automated Identification Division System [*FBI*] ... AIDS
Automated Image Data Extraction System ... AIDES
Automated Image Device Evaluator [*Electronics*] ... AIDE
Automated Immunoprecipitin [*System*] [*Clinical chemistry*] ... AIP
Automated Industrial Management System ... AIMS
Automated Information Data System ... AIDS
Automated Information Management ... AIM
Automated Information and Management Systems ... AIMES
Automated Information and Management Systems ... AIMS
Automated Information and Reservation Computer Operated Network ... AIRCON
Automated Information System ... AIS
Automated Information Systems ... AIS
Automated Input and Document Update Service [*International Data Corp.*] ... AIDUS
Automated Inspection of Data ... AIDA
Automated Instructional Management System [*Army*] ... AIMS
Automated Instructional Materials Services [*Developed by the System Development Corp.*] ... AIMS
Automated Instrumentation System ... AIS
Automated Insurance Service ... AIS
Automated Integrated Design Engineering ... AIDE
Automated Intelligence Data System [*Air Force*] ... AIDS
Automated Intelligence File [*Military*] ... AIF
Automated Intelligence Processing System ... AIPS
Automated Intelligent Microscope ... AIM
Automated Inventory Distribution System ... AIDS
Automated Inventory Management Evaluation System ... AIMES
Automated Jail Information System ... AJIS
Automated Large Experiment [*NASA*] ... ALE
Automated Layout Design Program [*IBM Corp.*] ... ALDEP
Automated Learning Process ... ALP
Automated Library Information System [*Dataphase Systems, Inc.*] ... ALIS
Automated Library Issue Document ... ALID
Automated Library Processing Services [*System Development Corp.*] ... ALPS
Automated Library Program ... ALP
Automated Library Technical Services [*Program*] ... ALTS
Automated Linguistic Extraction and Retrieval Technique ... ALERT
Automated Linguistic Fieldworker [*Data processing*] ... AUTOLING
Automated Liquid Sampler [*Instrumentation*] ... ALS
Automated Literature Alerting System [*Data processing*] ... ALAS
Automated Location of Isolation and Continuity Error [*Module*] [*Raytheon Co.*] ... ALICE
Automated Logic Diagram [*Data processing*] ... ALD
Automated Logic Implementation ... ALI

Automated Logistics Data Processing System ... ALDPS
Automated Logistics Management Systems Agency [*DoD*] ... ALMSA
Automated Maintenance Depot ... AMD
Automated Management Information System ... AMIS
Automated Management Reports ... AMR
Automated Manpower Management Information System ... AMMIS
Automated Material Parts Request System ... AMPRS
Automated Material Processing System [*Data processing*] ... AMPS
Automated Materials Handling System ... AMHS
Automated Medical History ... AMH
Automated Medical Laboratories [*NASDAQ symbol*] ... AUML
Automated Merchandise Processing System [*US Customs Service*] ... AMPS
Automated [*formerly, Atlantic*] **Merchant Vessel Report** [*Coast Guard*] ... AMVER
Automated [*formerly, Atlantic*] **Merchant Vessel Report System** [*Coast Guard*] ... AMVERS
Automated Message Handling System ... AMHS
Automated Meteorological and Terminal Information Service ... AMATIS
Automated Microbial Metabolism Laboratory [*NASA*] ... AMML
Automated Microfilm Aperture Card Updating System [*Army*] ... AMACUS
Automated Microfilm Storage and Retrieval [*Army*] ... AMSR
Automated Microhemagglutination Assay for Antibodies to Treponema pallidum [*Serology*] ... AMHA-TP
Automated Military Justice Analysis and Management System ... AMJAMS
Automated Military Outpatient System ... AMOS
Automated Minefield System ... AMS
Automated Multimedia Exchange [*Communications*] [*Army*] ... AMME
Automated Multiparameter Analyzer for Cells ... AMAC
Automated Multiphasic Health Testing ... AMHT
Automated Multiphasic Health Testing and Services ... AMHTS
Automated Multitest Laboratory ... AML
Automated Nautical Chart Index File [*System*] [*DoD*] ... ANCIF
Automated Near-Term Improvement ... ANTI
Automated Network Schedule with Evaluation of Resources ... ANSWER
Automated Offset Unit [*Air Force*] ... AOU
Automated Orbit Control System ... AOCS
Automated Overseas Employment Referral Program ... AOERP
Automated Packaging Code ... APC
Automated Packaging Planning System ... APPS
Automated Parking Lot Control ... APLC
Automated Payload Processing Facility [*NASA*] ... APPF
Automated Payroll, Cost, and Personnel System [*Defense Supply Agency*] ... APCAPS
Automated PEMA [*Procurement of Equipment and Munition Appropriations*] **Budget System** [*Military*] ... APBS
Automated Pilot Aptitude Measurement System ... APAMS
Automated Powder Diffractometer ... APD
Automated Procedures for Engineering Consultants ... APEC
Automated Process Information File [*Library of Congress*] ... APIF
Automated Procurement Planning, Execution, and Control ... APEX
[*The*] **Automated Procurement Planning System** ... TAPPS
Automated Procurement and Production Scheduling and Management System [*Army*] ... APPSMS
Automated Production System ... APS
Automated Professional Systems [*NASDAQ symbol*] ... APSI
Automated Program for Aerospace-Vehicle Synthesis ... APAS
Automated Program Support System [*Data processing*] ... APSS
Automated Programable Assembly System [*Data processing*] ... APAS
Automated Programing, Budgeting, and Operational Evaluation [*Army*] ... AUTOPROBE
Automated Project Management Information System [*Data processing*] ... APMIS
Automated Pronunciation Instructor ... API
Automated RADAR Terminal System ... ARTS
Automated Radioimmunoassay ... AR
Automated Readability Index ... ARI
Automated Reagin [*Serology*] ... AR
Automated Reagin Test [*Serology*] ... ART
Automated Record Management Study ... ARMS
Automated Reliability Assessment Program [*FAA*] ... ARAP
Automated Reliability and Maintenance Management System [*Navy*] ... ARMMS
Automated Rent Collections ... ARC
Automated Reports Control Handling ... ARCH
Automated Requirement Computation System Initial Provisioning [*Army*] ... ARCSIP
Automated Requirements Allocation Data ... ARAD
Automated Resource Planning and Analysis System ... ARPAS
Automated Responsive Environment ... ARE
Automated Ring Code Search ... ARCS
Automated Route Management ... ARM
Automated Runbook/Library System ... ARLS
Automated Schedule Procedures ... ASP
Automated Seat Reservation System [*Aviation*] ... ASRS
Automated Service Center ... AUTOSERVCEN
Automated Shell Theory for Rotating Structures [*NASA*] ... ASTROS
Automated Ship Data Library ... ASDL
Automated Ship Location and Attitude Measuring System ... ASLAMS
Automated Shipboard Forecasting System ... ASFS
Automated Signal Excess Prediction ... ASEP
Automated Small Purchase System [*DoD*] ... ASPS
Automated Sneak Program ... ASP
Automated Soft Lander [*Aerospace*] ... ASL
Automated Spares Simulation Estimating Technique [*Boeing*] ... ASSET
Automated Specifications [*Data processing*] ... AUTOSPEC
Automated Speed Enforcement Device ... ASED
Automated Spooling Priority [*Data processing*] ... ASP
Automated Statistical Analysis Program ... ASAP
Automated Status Board ... ASB
Automated Storage Control System ... ASCS
Automated Storage/Retrieval Systems ... AS/RS
Automated Structural Design [*NASA*] ... ASD
Automated Structural Optimization Program [*Air Force*] ... ASOP
Automated Switched Communications Network ... ASCON
Automated System for Composing, Revising, Illustrating, and Phototypesetting ... AUTOSCRIPT
Automated System for Sequential Extraction and Tabulation ... ASSET
Automated System for Transportation Data [*Military*] ... AUTOSTRAD
Automated System for Transportation Intelligence [*Army*] ... ASTI
Automated Systems Army Commissaries ... ASAC
Automated Systems Management System ... ASMS
Automated Systems and Services Branch [*NTIS*] ... AS & SB
Automated Tactical Environmental System ... ATESS
Automated Tactical Fusion Division ... ATFD
Automated Tactical Target Graphic ... ATTG
Automated Tape Label Assignment System ... ATLAS
Automated Tape Library ... ATL
Automated Technical Control [*System*] [*Army*] ... ATC
Automated Technical Control [*System*] [*Honeywell*] ... ATEC
Automated Technical Order Maintenance Sequences [*or Systems*] [*Boeing*] ... ATOMS
Automated Technique for Spacecraft Monitoring [*NASA*] ... ATSM
Automated [*or Automatic*] **Teller Machine** [*Banking*] ... ATM
Automated Terminal Weather Dissemination Display System ... ATWDDS
Automated Test Plan ... ATP
Automated Time Standards ... ATS
Automated Trading System [*NYSE computer*] ... ATS
Automated Traffic Advisory and Resolution Service [*Collision-avoidance system*] [*Aviation*] ... ATARS
Automated Travel Agents Reservation ... ATAR
Automated Ultrasonic Scanner ... AUS
Automated Urease-Chromous Method [*Analytical chemistry*] ... AUCM
Automated Vacuum ... AVAC
Automated Verification System [*Data processing*] ... AVS
Automated Video Target Scoring System ... AVTSS
Automated Visual Sensitivity Tester ... AVST
Automated Vocabulary Control [*Subsystem of PLIS*] [*Data processing*] ... AVOCON
Automated Want and Warrant System [*Data processing system used in police work*] ... AWWS
Automated Weapons Test Analysis System ... AWTAS
Automated Weather Distribution System ... AWDS
Automated Weather Network [*Air Force*] ... AWN
Automated Weather Network Coordinating Station [*Air Force*] ... AWNCS
Automated Wire Data System ... AWDS
Automated Wire List ... AWL
Automated Work Authorization System ... AWAS
Automated Work Request ... AWR
Automated Worthless Document Index ... AWDI
Automatic ... AUTM
Automatic ... AUTO
Automatic Abort-Sensing System [*NASA*] ... AASS
Automatic Addressing System ... AAS
Automatic Air Traffic Control [*System*] ... AATC
Automatic Air-Valving Surface Effects Device [*Army*] ... AAVSED
Automatic Aircraft Diagnostic System ... AADS
Automatic Aircraft Intercept Control System ... AAICS
Automatic Aircraft Vectoring Control System [*Air Force*] ... AAVCS
Automatic Aircraft Vectoring System [*Air Force*] ... AAVS
Automatic Alternate Voice/Data [*Data processing*] ... AAVD
Automatic Altitude Trim System [*for helicopters*] ... AATS
Automatic Amplitude Control ... AAC
Automatic Anechoic Chamber Test System [*Navy*] ... AACTS
Automatic Antenna Timer ... AAT
Automatic Antijam Circuit ... AAJAC
Automatic Antitheft System [*Electronic lock*] ... AATS
Automatic Aperture Control ... AAC
Automatic Approach/AUTOLAND ... AA/AL
Automatic Approach Control [*Aviation*] ... AAC
Automatic Approach Control Coupler [*Aviation*] ... AACC
Automatic Attack Warning System ... AAWS
Automatic Autocollimator ... AAC
Automatic Aviation Weather Service ... AAWS
Automatic Azimuth Laying Theodolite ... AALT
Automatic Back Bias [*RADAR*] ... ABB
Automatic Bandwidth Control ... ABC
Automatic Bar Checker ... ABC
Automatic Bass Compensation [*Radio*] ... ABC
Automatic Bass Control ... ABC
Automatic Battery Test ... ABT
Automatic Bias Compensation [*Air Force*] ... ABC

Automatic Bias Control ... ABC
Automatic Bill Calling [*Later, MCCS*] [*Telecommunications*] ... ABC
Automatic Binary Data Link ... ABDL
Automatic BIT [*Binary Digit*] **Error Rate Test** [*Data processing*] ... ABERT
Automatic Blip Counter ... ABC
Automatic Blip Counter System ... ABCS
Automatic Blip-Scan Counter ... ABSC
Automatic Blip-Scan Counter System ... ABSCS
Automatic Boiling-Column Reactor ... ABC
Automatic Bridge Control [*Navy*] ... ABC
Automatic Brightness Control ... ABC
Automatic Broadcast ... ABCST
Automatic Broadcasting Control System [*Japan*] ... ABCS
Automatic Bulk Tape Degausser ... ABTD
Automatic Bus Transfer ... ABT
Automatic Cable Tester ... ACT
Automatic Call Distribution [*Telecommunications*] ... ACD
Automatic Calling Equipment ... ACE
Automatic Calling Unit ... ACU
Automatic Cancellation of Extended Targets ... ACET
Automatic Canteen Co. of America [*NYSE symbol*] [*Delisted*] ... AUM
Automatic Capacitor Tester ... ACT
Automatic Car Identification [*Railroads*] ... ACI
Automatic Car Wash Association International [*Later, International Carwash Association/National Carwash Council*] ... ACWA
Automatic Card Control Entrance Security System [*Data processing*] ... ACCESS
Automatic Card Reader ... ACR
Automatic Carriage Return ... ACR
Automatic Carrier Landing System [*Military*] ... ACL
Automatic Cartographic System ... ACS
Automatic Celestial Navigation [*Air Force*] ... ACN
Automatic Centrifugal Tinning Apparatus ... ACTA
Automatic Channel and Time [*Programable television set*] [*Toshiba America Inc.*] ... ACT
Automatic Checkout ... AC
Automatic Checkout and Control System ... ACCS
Automatic Checkout Equipment ... ACE
Automatic Checkout Equipment ... ACOE
Automatic Checkout Equipment Sequencer ... ACES
Automatic Checkout and Evaluation System [*Air Force*] ... ACES
Automatic Checkout and Readiness Equipment ... ACRE
Automatic Checkout and Recording Equipment ... ACORN
Automatic Checkout Set ... ACOS
Automatic Checkout System ... ACHS
Automatic Checkout System [*NASA*] ... ACS
Automatic Checkout Technician [*or Technique*] ... ACT
Automatic Checkout Test Equipment ... ACTE
Automatic Chemical Agent Alarm [*Army*] ... ACAA
Automatic Chemical Biological Warning System ... ACBWS
Automatic Chemical Reaction System ... ACRS
Automatic Chrominance Control ... ACC
Automatic Circuit Analysis Program ... ACAP
Automatic Circuit Analyzer ... ACA
Automatic Circuit Assurance Feature ... ACAF
Automatic Circuit Board Card Tester ... ACBCT
Automatic Circuit Board Tester ... ACBT
Automatic Circuit Exchange ... ACE
Automatic Circuit Tester ... ACT
Automatic Classification and Interpretation of Data ... ACID
Automatic Clutter Eliminator [*FAA*] ... ACE
Automatic Clutter Mapping ... ACM
Automatic Coating Machine ... ACM
Automatic Code Translation [*Data processing*] ... ACT
Automatic Coding Machine ... ACOM
Automatic Coin Telephone Service ... ACTS
Automatic Collision Avoidance System [*Aviation*] ... ACAS
Automatic Color Control ... ACC
Automatic Color-Scanned Device ... ACSD
Automatic Combustion Control ... ACC
Automatic Command to Line of Sight [*Military*] [*British*] ... ACLOS
Automatic Communication Relay ... AUTOCAT
Automatic Component Tester ... ACT
Automatic Comprehensive Display System ... ACDS
Automatic Compression Regulator ... ACR
Automatic Compression - Release ... ACR
Automatic Compression - Release Device ... ACRD
Automatic Computer ... AC
Automatic Computer-Controlled Electronic Scanning System [*National Bureau of Standards*] ... ACCESS
Automatic Computer Evaluation ... ACE
Automatic Computer, Ministry of Supply [*British*] ... AMOS
Automatic Computer Telex Services ... ACTS
Automatic Computerized Transverse Axial [*Computer X-ray system*] ... ACTA
Automatic Computing Engine ... ACE
Automatic Computing Transfer Oscillator ... ACTO
Automatic Conference Arranger ... ACA
Automatic Continuity Equipment ... ACE
Automatic Continuous Evaporation ... ACE
Automatic Continuous Function Generation [*Data processing*] ... ACFG
Automatic Contour Digitizer ... ACD
Automatic Contrast Control ... ACC
Automatic Control ... AC
Automatic Control of Air Transmissions ... AUTOCAT
Automatic Control and Computer Sciences [*A publication*] ... Automat Control and Computer Sci
Automatic Control and Computer Sciences [*A publication*] ... Autom Control Comput Sci
Automatic Control Console ... ACC
Automatic Control Equipment ... ACE
Automatic Control Evaluation Simulator [*Spaceflight training machine*] ... ACES
Automatic Control Instrumentation ... ACI
Automatic Control System ... ACS
Automatic Control Theory and Applications [*A publication*] ... Automatic Control Theory Appl
Automatic Control Theory and Applications [*A publication*] ... Autom Control Theory & Appl
Automatic Controlled Exposure ... ACE
Automatic Controlled Instrument Landing ... ACIL
Automatic Correlation Guidance ... ACG
Automatic Counter System ... ACS
Automatic Crane Control Storage System ... ACCESS
Automatic Daily System Operability Test ... ADSOT
Automatic Damper Arm ... ADA
Automatic Damper Manufacturers Association ... ADMA
Automatic Data Accumulation and Transfer ... ADAT
Automatic Data Acquisition ... ADA
Automatic Data Acquisition and Computer Complex [*Air Force*] ... ADACC
Automatic Data Acquisition and Processing Techniques [*Army*] ... ADAPT
Automatic Data Collection System ... ADCS
Automatic Data Collector [*National Weather Service*] ... ADC
Automatic Data Descriptor ... ADD
Automatic Data Digitizing System [*Air Force*] ... ADDS
Automatic Data Distribution System [*Army*] ... ADDS
Automatic Data Entry [*Air Force*] ... ADE
Automatic Data Equalized Modern ... ADEM
Automatic Data Evaluation ... ADE
Automatic Data Exchange ... ADX
Automatic Data Extractor and Plotting Table ... ADEPT
Automatic Data Field Systems Command [*Army*] ... ADFSC
Automatic Data Handling [*Data processing*] ... ADH
Automatic Data Interchange System ... ADIS
Automatic Data Link [*Data processing*] ... ADL
Automatic Data Plotter ... ADP
Automatic Data Processing ... ADP
Automatic Data Processing Budget Control Totals ... ADPBCT
Automatic Data Processing Center ... ADPC
Automatic Data Processing Engineering ... ADPE
Automatic Data Processing Equipment ... ADPE
Automatic Data Processing Equipment Selection Office [*Navy*] ... ADPESO
Automatic Data Processing by Equipment Systems ... ADPES
Automatic Data Processing Field Branch [*BUPERS*] ... ADPFB
Automatic Data Processing, Inc. [*Trademark for data processing services*] ... ADP
Automatic Data Processing, Inc. [*NYSE symbol*] ... AUD
Automatic Data Processing Information Bulletin [*A publication*] ... Automat Data Process Inform B
Automatic Data Processing Machine ... ADPM
Automatic Data Processing Management Information System ... ADPMIS
Automatic Data Processing Modification Order ... ADPMO
Automatic Data Processing Planning and Development Branch [*BUPERS*] ... ADPP & DB
Automatic Data Processing Production Branch [*BUPERS*] ... ADPPB
Automatic Data Processing Programing and Processing Branch [*BUPERS*] ... ADPP & PB
Automatic Data Processing Programs ... ADPP
Automatic Data Processing Requirements Office [*Jet Propulsion Laboratory, NASA*] ... ADPRO
Automatic Data Processing Resource Estimating Procedures ... ADPREP
Automatic Data Processing Resource Estimating Procedures ... ADREP
Automatic Data Processing Service Center ... ADPSC
Automatic Data Processing Systems [*or Subsystems*] ... ADPS
Automatic Data Rate Changer ... ADRC
Automatic Data Reporting System ... ADRS
Automatic Data Routing Group ... ADRG
Automatic Data and Select Program ... ADASP
Automatic Data Service Center ... ADSC
Automatic Data Set Editing Program [*NASA*] ... ADSEP
Automatic Data Switching System [*Deep Space Network*] ... ADSS
Automatic Data System [*Data processing*] ... ADS
Automatic Data System within the Army in the Field ... ADSAF
Automatic Data Systems Uniform Practices ... ADSUP
Automatic Data Test System [*Bell System*] ... ADTS
Automatic Data Translator [*or Transmitter*] ... ADT
Automatic Dead Reckoning Instrument Systems [*Navigation*] [*Canada*] ... ADRIS
Automatic Debit Transfer [*Banking*] ... ADT
Automatic Decisions Optimizing Predicted Estimates ... ADOPE
Automatic Degreasing Machine ... ADM
Automatic Depositor ... AD

Automatic Depressurization System [*Nuclear energy*] ... ADS
Automatic Depth/Deployed Moored Sweep ... ADDMS
Automatic Derivation of Invariants ... ADI
Automatic Destruct Program ... ADP
Automatic Detection [*Air Force*] ... AD
Automatic Detection/Automatic Classification [*Antisubmarine warfare*] ... AD/AC
Automatic Detection and Integrated Tracking ... ADIT
Automatic Detection Mark ... ADM
Automatic Detection and Tracking ... ADT
Automatic Development System ... ADS
Automatic Device for Mechanical Order Selection ... ADMOS
Automatic Diagnostic Maintenance Information Retrieval [*Data processing*] ... ADMIRE
Automatic Dial Order Wire [*Military*] ... ADOW
Automatic Dialing Unit ... ADU
Automatic Diffemic Identification of Speakers [*University of Bonn*] ... ADIS
Automatic Digit Recognition ... AUDREY
Automatic Digital Assembly Test Equipment ... ADATE
Automatic Digital Data Acquisition and Recording ... ADDAR
Automatic Digital Data Assembly System ... ADDAS
Automatic Digital-Data-Error Recorder ... ADDER
Automatic Digital Encoding System [*Data processing*] ... ADES
Automatic Digital Input-Output System [*Data processing*] ... ADIOS
Automatic Digital Message Switching ... ADMS
Automatic Digital Message Switching Center [*AUTODIN*] ... ADMSC
Automatic Digital Network ... AUTODIN
Automatic Digital On-Line Instrumentation System ... ADONIS
Automatic Digital Optical Tracker [*Army*] ... ADOT
Automatic Digital Recording and Control ... ADRAC
Automatic Digital Switch ... ADS
Automatic Digital Switching Center ... ADSC
Automatic Digital Test Unit ... ADTU
Automatic Digital Tracking Analyzer Computer [*Data processing*] ... ADTAC
Automatic Digital Weather Switch [*Air Force*] ... ADWS
Automatic Direct Access to Information with the On-Line UDC [*Universal Decimal Classification*] **System** ... AUDACIOUS
Automatic Direct Analog Computer ... ADAC
Automatic Direct-Distance Dialing System ... ADDDS
Automatic Direction Finder [*Military*] ... ADF
Automatic Direction Finder, Remote Control ... ADFR
Automatic Direction Finding Approach ... ADFAP
Automatic Direction Finding System ... ADFS
Automatic Direction Indicator ... ADI
Automatic Dispatching Stick Repeater ... ADSP
Automatic Display ... AD
Automatic Display Finder ... ADF
Automatic Display Mode [*Data processing*] ... ADM
Automatic Display and Plotting System ... ADAPS
Automatic Display Plotting System ... ADPS
Automatic Display Switching Oscilloscope ... ADSO
Automatic Distance and Angle Measurement ... ADAM
Automatic Distribution of Documents [*DoD*] ... ADD
Automatic Distribution of Microfiche ... ADM
Automatic Document Analysis ... ADA
Automatic Document Storage and Retrieval [*Data processing*] ... ADSTAR
Automatic Documentation and Mathematical Linguistics [*A publication*] ... ADML
Automatic Documentation and Mathematical Linguistics [*A publication*] ... Autom Doc Math Linguist
Automatic Door Isolating Cock [*British railroad term*] ... DIC
Automatic Door Seal [*Technical drawings*] ... ADS
Automatic Drafting Equipment ... ADE
Automatic Drafting Machine ... ADMA
Automatic Drawing Device ... ADD
Automatic Drift Control ... ADC
Automatic Drip Coffee [*Brand name*] ... ADC
Automatic Dynamic Evaluation by Programed Organizations ... ADEPO
Automatic Dynamic Evaluation by Programed Test ... ADEPT
Automatic and Dynamic Monitor with Immediate Relocation, Allocation, and Loading ... ADMIRAL
Automatic Earnings Recomputation Operation [*Social Security*] ... AERO
Automatic Electric Technical Journal [*A publication*] ... Automat Elec Tech J
Automatic Electronic Switching Center ... AESC
Automatic Electronic Voice Switch ... AEVS
Automatic End Point ... AEP
Automatic Environment Monitoring ... AEM
Automatic Equalization/Analyzation System ... AEAS
Automatic Error Analysis ... AEA
Automatic Error Correction [*Aviation*] ... ARQ
Automatic Error Correction Equipment [*Aviation*] ... ARQ
Automatic Exciter Control ... AEC
Automatic Exposure Control ... AEC
Automatic Exposure Control Technique ... AECT
Automatic External Standard [*or Standardization*] [*Radioactivity measurement*] ... AES
Automatic Extracting Program ... AEP
Automatic False Alarm Rate ... AFAR
Automatic Fare Collection System ... AFCS
Automatic Fast Demagnetization ... AFD
Automatic Fault Isolation ... AFI
Automatic Fault Isolation Test ... AFIT
Automatic Fault Location ... AFL
Automatic Field Analog Computer ... AFAC
Automatic Field Assistant ... AFA
Automatic Film Data Collection System ... AFDCS
Automatic Fine Tuning ... AFT
Automatic Fire Alarm Association ... AFAA
Automatic Fire Control ... AFC
Automatic Fire Control System ... AFCS
Automatic Firearms Identification System [*Jet Propulsion Laboratory, NASA*] ... AFIDS
Automatic Firing Sequencer ... AFS
Automatic Flexible Test Station ... AFTS
Automatic Flight Control ... AFC
Automatic Flight Control Equipment ... AFCE
Automatic Flight Control System [*Air Force*] ... AFCS
Automatic Flight Management ... AFM
Automatic Flight Operation Center [*Army*] ... AFOC
Automatic Flight Termination ... AFT
Automatic Flow Control ... AFC
Automatic Flow Process Analysis ... AFPA
Automatic Focusing Random Scene Tracker ... AFRST
Automatic Following [*RADAR*] ... AF
Automatic Frequency Assignment Model [*Communications*] ... AFAM
Automatic Frequency Control [*Electronics*] ... AFC
Automatic Frequency Follower ... AFF
Automatic Frequency/Phase-Controlled [*Loop*] ... AF/PC
Automatic Frequency Stabilization ... AFS
Automatic Frequency Tone Shift ... AFTS
Automatic Fuel Cutoff [*NASA*] ... AFCO
Automatic Functional Test and Evaluation Routine [*Raytheon Co.*] ... AFTER
Automatic Funds Transfer ... AFT
Automatic Gain Adjusting Amplifier ... AGAA
Automatic Gain Calibration Program ... AGCP
Automatic Gain Control [*Electronics*] ... AGC
Automatic Gain Stabilization ... AGS
Automatic Generation of Requests [*Data processing*] ... AUTOQEST
Automatic Gimbaled-Antenna Vectoring Equipment [*Air Force*] ... AGAVE
Automatic Government Source Inspection ... AGSI
Automatic Gravity Gradient ... AGGD
Automatic Ground-to-Air Communications System ... AGACS
Automatic Ground Checkout System ... AGCS
Automatic Ground Computer System ... AGCS
Automatic Ground Control Station ... AGCS
Automatic Ground Control System Computer ... AGCSC
Automatic Ground-Controlled Approach [*RADAR*] ... AGCA
Automatic Ground-Controlled Intercept ... AGCI
Automatic Ground-Controlled Landing ... AGCL
Automatic Ground Equipment ... AGE
Automatic Ground Position Indicator [*Military*] ... AGPI
Automatic Ground Transportable Emitter Location and Identification System [*Army*] ... AGTELIS
Automatic Ground Unit ... AGU
Automatic Guard Receiver Terminals [*Navy*] ... AGRT
Automatic Guidance Electronics ... AGE
Automatic Guidance Programing ... AGP
Automatic Guided Flight ... AGF
Automatic Guided Vehicle Systems ... AGVS
Automatic Gun-Laying ... AGL
Automatic Heading Reference System ... AHRS
Automatic Headway Control ... AHC
Automatic Helicopter Approach System [*Army*] ... AHAS
Automatic Hydrologic Observing System [*National Weather Service*] ... AHOS
Automatic Identification Manufacturers ... AIM
Automatic Identified Outward Dialing ... AIOD
Automatic Illustrated Documentation System [*Information International, Inc.*] ... AIDS
Automatic Image Retrieval System ... AIRS
Automatic Imagery Interpretation ... AII
Automatic Implantable Defibrillator [*Medicine*] ... AID
Automatic In-Flight Insertion ... AIFI
Automatic Indexing and Proofreading System ... AIPS
Automatic Information Retrieval System ... AIRS
Automatic Information Station ... AIST
Automatic Information Test [*Military*] ... AIT
Automatic Inlet Control System ... AICS
Automatic Input [*Data processing*] ... AI
Automatic Inspection Device for Explosive Charge Shell ... AIDECS
Automatic Inspection, Diagnostic, and Prognostic [*System*] [*Army*] ... AIDAP
Automatic Inspection, Diagnostic, and Prognostic System [*Army*] ... AIDAPS
Automatic Instrument Landing Approach System ... AILAS
Automatic Instrument Landing System [*Aviation*] ... AILS
Automatic Instrumented Diving Assembly ... AIDA
Automatic Integrated Circuit Tester ... AICT
Automatic Integrated Debugging System [*Data processing*] ... AIDS
Automatic Integrated Director Equipment ... AIDE
Automatic Integrated Dynamic Avionics Tester ... AIDAT

Automatic Integrating Fluctuation Meter .... AIFM
Automatic Interaction Detection [*or Detector*] [*Data processing*] .... AID
Automatic Intercept Center [*Bell System*] .... AIC
Automatic Intercept System [*Bell System*] .... AIS
Automatic Intercom Switching System .... AISS
Automatic Intermediate Station .... AIS
Automatic Interplanetary Station [*USSR*] .... AIS
Automatic Intruder Detector Alarm [*Military*] [*British*] .... AIDA
Automatic Jamming Avoidance Circuitry .... AJAC
Automatic Landing .... AUTOLAND
Automatic Landing Autopilot Subsystem [*NASA*] .... ALAS
Automatic Landing Positioning System .... ALPS
Automatic Landing System .... ALS
Automatic Language Data Processing .... ALDP
Automatic Language Processing Advisory Committee [*National Research Council*] .... ALPAC
Automatic LASER Encoder .... ALE
Automatic Lead Former .... ALF
Automatic Letter Facer .... ALF
Automatic Level Control .... ALC
Automatic Level Control Assembly .... ALCA
Automatic Level Recorder .... ALR
Automatic Level Setting .... ALS
Automatic License Plate Scanning .... ALPS
Automatic Light Aircraft Readiness Monitor .... ALARM
Automatic Light Control .... ALC
Automatic Lightning Detection System [*To aid in the prevention of forest fires*] .... ALDS
Automatic Line Buildout [*Bell Laboratories*] .... ALBO
Automatic Line Insulation Test [*or Tester*] [*Bell System*] .... ALIT
Automatic Line Integration .... ALI
Automatic Line Tracer and Programing Equipment .... ALTAPE
Automatic Linear Positioning System .... ALPS
Automatic Linear Temperature Programer .... ALTP
Automatic Liquid Agent Detector .... ALAD
Automatic Liquid Nitrogen Transfer System .... ALNTS
Automatic List Classification and Profile Production .... ALCAPP
Automatic Literature Processing, Handling, and Analysis .... ALPHA
Automatic Load Alleviation System .... ALAS
Automatic Load Control .... ALC
Automatic Location Identification [*Street crime locator*] .... ALI
Automatic Lock-On .... ALO
Automatic Logging Electronic Reporting and Telemetering System [*Maintains surveillance over petroleum wells and pipelines*] .... ALERT
Automatic Logic Testing and Recording Equipment .... ALTARE
Automatic Logical Equipment Readiness Tester .... ALERT
Automatic Logical Translation and Information Retrieval [*Data processing*] .... ALTAIR
Automatic Low-Altitude Bombing System .... AUTOLABS
Automatic Low Date Rate Input .... ALDRI
Automatic Low-Frequency Gain-Limiting Circuit .... ALFGL
Automatic Machine Loading .... AML
Automatic Machining [*A publication*] .... Autom Mach
Automatic Machining Program .... AUTOMAP
Automatic Magazine Loading .... AML
Automatic Magnetic Guidance .... AMG
Automatic Magnetic Tape Dissemination .... AMTD
Automatic Maintenance Monitor .... AMM
Automatic Malfunction Analysis .... AMA
Automatic Manifold Pressure Regulator [*Aviation*] .... AMPR
Automatic Map Display .... AMD
Automatic Master Sequence Selector .... AMSS
Automatic Mathematic Analysis and Symbolic Translation [*Data processing*] .... AUTOMAST
Automatic Mathematical Translator [*Data processing*] .... AMTRAN
Automatic Measuring Computing and Sorting .... AMECOS
Automatic Memory Allocation [*Data processing*] .... AMA
Automatic Message Accounting [*Telecommunications*] .... AMA
Automatic Message Accounting Recording System [*Bell System*] .... AMARS
Automatic Message Accounting System .... ALMAS
Automatic Message Accounting System .... AMAS
Automatic Message Address Routing System .... AMARS
Automatic Message Counting .... AMC
Automatic Message Distribution System .... AMDS
Automatic Message Entry System [*Data processing*] .... AMES
Automatic Message Exchange .... AMX
Automatic Message Processing Center .... AMPC
Automatic Message Processing System [*USAERDL*] .... AMPS
Automatic Message Recording .... AMR
Automatic Message Registering .... AMR
Automatic Message Routing .... AMR
Automatic Meteorological Correction [*A missile guidance technique*] .... AUTOMET
Automatic Meteorological Data Acquisition and Processing System .... AMDAPS
Automatic Meteorological Observation [*or Observing*] **Station** [*or System*] .... AMOS
Automatic Meteorological Oceanographic Buoy .... AMOB
Automatic Meteorological, Oceanographic, (and Radiation) Station .... AMO(R)S
Automatic Meteorological System .... AMS
Automatic Meter Reading .... AMR
Automatic Microfilm Information System .... AMFIS
Automatic Miss Distance Indicator .... AMDI
Automatic Mission Control .... AMC
Automatic Mixture Control .... AMC
Automatic Modal Tuning and Analysis System .... AMTAS
Automatic Modulation Control .... AMC
Automatic Module for Industrial Control Analysis .... AMICA
Automatic Monitoring .... AM
Automatic Monitoring and Measuring [*A publication*] .... Automat Monit Mea
Automatic Monitoring System [*Aviation*] .... AMS
Automatic Moon Tracking .... AMT
Automatic Motor Tester .... AMT
Automatic Moving Target Indicator .... AMTI
Automatic Multiloop Optimal Approach Controller [*Navy*] .... AMOAC
Automatic Multimode Mass Spectrometry .... AMMS
Automatic Multiparameter Semiconductor Test Set .... AMSTS
Automatic Multiple-Parameter Collection Processing System [*Air Force*] .... AMCAPS
Automatic Musical Instrument Collectors Association .... AMICA
Automatic Navigation Computer for Land and Amphibious Vehicles .... ANCLAV
Automatic Navigation System .... ANS
Automatic Network Analyzer .... ANA
Automatic Network Display .... AUTONET
Automatic New Structure Alert [*A publication*] .... ANSA
Automatic Nitrogen Transfer System .... ANTS
Automatic Noise Figure Indicator .... ANFI
Automatic Noise Limiter [*Electronics*] .... ANL
Automatic Number Identification [*Telecommunications*] .... ANI
Automatic Observer .... AO
Automatic Operating and Scheduling Program [*Data processing*] .... AOSP
Automatic Operating System [*IBM Corp.*] .... AUTOPSY
Automatic Operation Control .... AOC
Automatic Operations Panel .... AOP
Automatic Outgoing Message Processor System .... AOMPS
Automatic Outgoing Trunk Test [*Bell System*] .... AOTT
Automatic Output Control .... AOC
Automatic Overdrive .... AOD
Automatic Overload Circuit .... AOC
Automatic Overload Control .... AOC
Automatic Paralleling Relay .... APR
Automatic Parts Handler .... APH
Automatic Passbook Reader .... APR
Automatic Patching System .... APS
Automatic Pattern Recognition .... APR
Automatic Performance Analysis System .... APAS
Automatic Performance Control .... APC
Automatic Personal Identification Code .... AUTOPIC
Automatic Phase and Amplitude Data System .... APADAS
Automatic Phase Control .... APC
Automatic Phase Lock .... APL
Automatic Phonograph Manufacturers Association .... APMA
Automatic Photographic Analysis .... APA
Automatic Picture Taking .... APT
Automatic Picture Transmission [*NASA*] .... APT
Automatic Picture Transmission System [*or Subsystem*] [*NASA*] .... APTS
Automatic Pilot .... A/P
Automatic Pilot System .... APS
Automatic Pistol .... AUTOP
Automatic Pitch Control .... APC
Automatic Plate Processor .... APP
Automatic Point Marking, Measuring, and Recording Instrument .... APMMRI
Automatic Position Planning .... APP
Automatic Position Reference System .... APRS
Automatic Position Telemetering .... APT
Automatic Positioning Equipment .... APE
Automatic Positioning Telemetering Antenna .... APOTA
Automatic Power-Factor-Control Systems .... APFCS
Automatic Power Input Controller .... APIC
Automatic Power Plant Checker .... APPC
Automatic Premium Loan .... APL
Automatic Press Feed .... APF
Automatic Pressure Conveyor .... APC
Automatic Pressure Relief [*Nuclear energy*] .... APR
Automatic Priority Group .... APG
Automatic Priority Interrupt [*Data processing*] .... API
Automatic Processing of Jezebel [*Sonobuoy System*] **Information** .... APOJI
Automatic Production Line .... APL
Automatic Production Recording .... APR
Automatic Program Analysis Report [*Data processing*] .... APAR
Automatic Program Finding [*Electronics*] .... APF
Automatic Program Loading Unit .... APLU
Automatic Program System .... APS
Automatic Program Unit High Speed [*Component of ADIS*] .... APUHS
Automatic Program Unit Low Speed [*Component of ADIS*] .... APULS
Automatic Programed Checkout Equipment .... APCHE
Automatic Programer and Data System [*Air Force*] .... APADS
Automatic Programer and Test System [*Army*] .... APATS

Automatic Programer and Test System [*Army*] ... APTS
Automatic Programing [*Data processing*] ... AP
Automatic Programing Information Centre [*British*] ... APIC
Automatic Programing of Machine Tools ... AUTOPROMT
Automatic Programing and Recording [*Data processing*] ... APAR
Automatic Programing and Recording [*Data processing*] ... APR
Automatic Programming [*A publication*] ... Automat Programming
Automatic Proof of Delivery ... AUTOPOD
Automatic Quench Calibration [*or Correction*] ... AQC
Automatic Quench Compensation [*Beckman Instruments, Inc.*] [*Instrumentation*] ... AQC
Automatic RADAR Beacon ... ARB
Automatic RADAR Beacon Sequencer ... ARBS
Automatic RADAR Chain Acquisition System [*Air Force*] ... ARCAS
Automatic RADAR Control and Data Equipment ... ARCADE
Automatic RADAR Data Measuring Equipment ... ARDME
Automatic RADAR Pattern Recognition ... ARPR
Automatic RADAR Plotting Aids ... ARPA
Automatic RADAR Reconnaissance Exploitation System ... ARRES
Automatic Radiating Tester ... ART
Automatic Radiation Monitoring System ... ARMS
Automatic Radio Manufacturing Co., Inc. ... AR
Automatic Radio Manufacturing Co., Inc. [*American Stock Exchange symbol*] [*Delisted*] ... ART
Automatic Radiotheodolite [*Meteorology*] ... ART
Automatic Random Access Transport ... ARAT
Automatic Range Control ... ARC
Automatic Range Only ... ARO
Automatic Range Tracker [*or Tracking*] ... ART
Automatic Range Tracking Unit [*Military*] ... ARTU
Automatic Ranging Telescope [*Weaponry*] ... ART
Automatic Rate Changer ... ARC
Automatic Rate Control ... ARC
Automatic Ratio Control ... ARC
Automatic Reaction of Mobile Electronic Defenses [*Auto theft alarm*] [*Digequip Security Industries, Inc.*] ... ARMED
Automatic Receiving and Measuring System ... ARMS
Automatic Record Analysis Language ... ARAL
Automatic Record Evaluation ... ARE
Automatic Record Evaluation System ... ARES
Automatic Recording Infrared Spectrometer ... ARIS
Automatic Recording and Reduction Facility ... ARRF
Automatic Recording Spectrometer ... ARS
Automatic Reel Mounting ... ARM
Automatic Reentry Flight Dynamics Simulator [*NASA*] ... ARFDS
Automatic Reference System/Sequential Launch ... AR/SLA
Automatic Relay Calculator ... ARC
Automatic Release Date [*Military*] ... ARD
Automatic Remote Control ... ARC
Automatic Remote Manned System ... ARMS
Automatic Repeat Request [*Data processing*] ... ARQ
Automatic Reporting Feature ... ARF
Automatic Reporting Post [*Air defense*] [*NATO*] ... ARP
Automatic Reporting Telephone ... ART
Automatic Request ... ARQ
Automatic Reset Counter ... ARC
Automatic Resistance Test Set ... ARTS
Automatic Resupply ... AR
Automatic Resupply Logistics System ... ARLS
Automatic Retailers of America ... ARA
Automatic Retrieval of Text from Europe's Multinational Information Service ... ARTEMIS
Automatic Return Fire [*ARPA*] ... ARF
Automatic Return Items ... ARI
Automatic Rifle [*or Rifleman*] [*DoD*] ... AR
Automatic Rocket Impact Predictor ... ARIP
Automatic Route Control System [*Truck-delivery computer system*] ... ARCS
Automatic Route Selection [*Also known as MERS*] [*Bell System*] ... ARS
Automatic Routine Generating and Updating System [*Data processing*] ... ARGUS
Automatic Rudder Control ... ARCON
Automatic Sample Processor ... ASP
Automatic Scan Counter ... ASC
Automatic Scan Counter System ... ASCS
Automatic Scanning Control Unit ... ASCU
Automatic Scanning Correlator ... AUSCOR
Automatic Scanning Unit Inoperative [*Aviation*] ... SCANO
Automatic Scanning Unit Operative [*Aviation*] ... SCAOK
Automatic Schedule Procedures ... ASP
Automatic Scheduling and Operating Program ... ASOP
Automatic Scheduling with Time-Integrated Resource Allocation ... ASTRA
Automatic Science Citation Alerting ... ASCA
Automatic Secure Voice Communications ... AUTOSEVOCOM
Automatic Selection of Digital Electronic Computers ... ASDEC
Automatic Selective Dissemination of Information ... ASDI
Automatic Selectivity Control ... ASC
Automatic Self-Verification ... ASV
Automatic Send/Receive [*Communications equipment*] ... AS/R
Automatic Sensitivity Control ... ASC
Automatic Sequence Controlled Calculator [*First all-automatic calculating machine*] ... ASCC
Automatic Sequence Execution and Processor ... ASEP
Automatic Services and Products ... ASP
Automatic Servo Plotter ... ASP
Automatic Shaft-Position Data Encoder ... ASPDE
Automatic Shipboard Checkout and Readiness Equipment ... ASCORE
Automatic Shipboard Launch Aircraft Data System ... ASLADS
Automatic Shot Dispensing Pump ... ASDP
Automatic Shuttle Valve ... ASV
Automatic Skin [*NASA*] ... AS
Automatic SONAR Readout ... ASR
Automatic Sorting, Testing, Recording Analysis ... ASTRA
Automatic Spares Analysis Technique ... ASAT
Automatic Specimen Positioning ... ASP
Automatic Specimen Positioning System ... ASPS
Automatic Spectrum Display and Signal Recognition System ... ASDSRS
Automatic Speech Recognition ... ASR
Automatic Spray Gun ... ASG
Automatic Sprinkler [*Technical drawings*] ... AS
Automatic Sprinkler Riser [*Technical drawings*] ... ASR
Automatic Stabilization and Control System ... ASCS
Automatic Stabilization Equipment ... ASE
Automatic Stabilization System ... ASS
Automatic Start-Up System [*Reactor*] ... ASS
Automatic Starter ... AUTOSTRT
Automatic Starting ... AUTOSTRTG
Automatic Statewide Theft Inquiry System [*California Highway Patrol*] ... AUTO-STATIS
Automatic Station Identification Device ... ASID
Automatic Station Keeping System ... ASKS
Automatic Steerable Null Antenna Processor ... ASNAP
Automatic Steering Antenna ... ASA
Automatic Step Regulator ... ASR
Automatic Stereo Recording Amplifier ... ASRA
Automatic Stop and Check Valve ... AUTO S & CV
Automatic Store and Forward ... ASF
Automatic Storm Observation Service [*AFCRL*] ... ASOS
Automatic Strobe Tracking ... ASTRA
Automatic Structure Analysis of Mass Spectra ... ASAMS
Automatic Subject Citation Alert [*A publication*] ... ASCA
Automatic Submarine Control [*Navy*] ... ASC
Automatic Support Equipment ... ASE
Automatic Support Systems for Advanced Maintainability ... ASSC
Automatic Surveillance Receiver ... ASR
Automatic Sustainer Cutoff ... ASCO
Automatic Switch Co. [*American Stock Exchange symbol*] ... ASV
Automatic Switching Center ... ASC
Automatic Switching Panel ... ASP
Automatic Synchronized Control ... ASC
Automatic Synchronized Discriminator ... ASD
Automatic Synthesis Program ... ASP
Automatic System Control ... ASC
Automatic System for Positioning Tools ... AUTOSPOT
Automatic System Self-Test [*Aviation*] ... ASST
Automatic Systems Analysis ... ASA
Automatic Systems for Kinematic Analysis ... ASKA
Automatic Systems Test Unit ... ASTU
Automatic Tap Changing ... ATC
Automatic Tape Degausser ... ATD
Automatic Tape Load Audit System ... ATLAS
Automatic Target and Battery Evaluation [*Military*] ... ATABE
Automatic Target Counting ... ATC
Automatic Target Designation ... ATAD
Automatic Target Designation ... ATD
Automatic Target Detection ... ATD
Automatic Target Evaluator and Weapon Assignor ... ATEWA
Automatic Target Follow ... ATF
Automatic Target Identification ... ATI
Automatic Target Recognition ... ATR
Automatic Target Recognition Analysis ... AUTRAN
Automatic Target Recognition Device ... ATRD
Automatic Target Recognition, Identification, and Detection ... ATRID
Automatic Target Scoring Systems ... ATSS
Automatic Target Selection File ... ATSF
Automatic Target Tracking ... ATT
Automatic Teaching Device ... ATD
Automatic Techniques for Selection and Identification of Targets ... ATSIT
Automatic Telegraph Subsystem [*Navy*] [*British*] ... ATSS
Automatic Telemetry Decommutation System ... ATDS
Automatic Telemetry System ... ATS
Automatic Telemetry Tracking Antenna System ... ATTRAS
Automatic Telemetry Tracking System ... ATTS
Automatic Teleprinter Exchange Service [*of Western Union*] ... TEX
Automatic Teletypewriter Exchange Service [*of Western Union*] ... TELEX
Automatic Temperature Compensation ... ATC
Automatic Temperature Control ... ATC
Automatic Temporary Roof Support [*Mining industry*] ... ATRS
Automatic Terminal Information Service [*Aviation*] ... ATIS
Automatic Terminal System ... ATS
Automatic Terrain Avoidance [*Military*] ... ATA
Automatic Terrain Following [*Military*] ... ATF

Automatic Terrain Following/Automatic Terrain Avoidance [*Military*] ... ATF/ATA
Automatic Terrain-Following RADAR [*Military*] ... ATFR
Automatic Terrain Recognition and Navigation Guidance System ... ATRAN
Automatic Test ... AT
Automatic Test Analysis System ... ATAS
Automatic Test and Checkout Equipment ... ATCE
Automatic Test Equipment ... ATE
Automatic Test Equipment for Internal Combustion Engines ... ATE/ICE
Automatic Test Grading ... ATG
Automatic Test Line ... ATL
Automatic Test Program Generation ... ATPG
Automatic Test Scoring ... ATS
Automatic Test Support Systems ... ATSS
Automatic Test System ... ATS
Automatic Test System Jet Engine Accessories ... ATSJEA
Automatic Testing, Evaluation, and Reporting ... ATER
Automatic Testing Multiple Operating System ... ATMOS
Automatic Thin-Layer Analytical System ... ATLAS
Automatic Three-Axis Stabilization ... ATAS
Automatic Three-Dimensional Electronics Scanning Array ... ATHESA
Automatic Threshold Circuit ... ATC
Automatic Threshold Variation ... ATV
Automatic Throttle/Speed Control System ... ATS
Automatic Thrust Vector Control [*NASA*] ... ATVC
Automatic Ticketing ... AT
Automatic Time Interval Measurement System [*Air Force*] ... ATIMS
Automatic Track Acquisition ... ATA
Automatic Track-while-Scan [*Radar*] ... ATWS
Automatic Tracking Antenna ... ATA
Automatic Tracking Antenna System ... ATAS
Automatic Tracking Control ... ATC
Automatic Tracking Feature ... ATF
Automatic Tracking LASER Illumination System ... ATLIS
Automatic Tracking Razor Action [*The Gillette Co.*] ... ATRA
Automatic Tracking Unit ... ATU
Automatic Train Control ... ATC
Automatic Transformer ... AXFMR
Automatic Transient Detection System ... ATDS
Automatic Transistor Test Equipment ... ATTE
Automatic Translation ... AT
Automatic Translation ... AUTOTRAN
Automatic Transmission Fluid ... ATF
Automatic Transmission Measuring System ... ATMS
Automatic Transmission Rebuilders Association ... ATRA
Automatic Transmitter Identification System [*Citizens band radio*] ... ATIS
Automatic Trunk Measuring System [*Bell System*] ... ATMS
Automatic Trunk Routiner ... ATR
Automatic Tuning Control ... ATC
Automatic Turret Lathe ... ATL
Automatic Type Placement System ... ATPS
Automatic Unattended Detection Inspection Transmitter [*Raytheon*] ... AUDIT
Automatic Universal Translator ... AUNT
Automatic Unmanned Weather Station ... AUWS
Automatic Utility Translator ... AUTRAN
Automatic Variable Perforating ... AVP
Automatic Vehicle Location ... AVL
Automatic Vehicle Monitoring [*Antihijack device*] ... AVM
Automatic Vehicle Monitoring System [*Antihijack device*] ... AVMS
Automatic Verification, Evaluation, and Readiness Tester ... AVERT
Automatic Vertical Electrophoresis System [*Instrumentation*] ... AVES
Automatic Vibration Control ... AVC
Automatic Vibration Exciter Control ... AVEC
Automatic Video Noise Limiter ... AVNL
Automatic Visual Inspection System [*NASA*] ... AVIS
Automatic Voice Data ... AVD
Automatic Voice Link Observation ... AVOLO
Automatic Voice Network [*DoD*] ... AUTOVON
Automatic Voice Relay ... AVR
Automatic Voltage Control ... AVC
Automatic Voltage Digitizer ... AVD
Automatic Voltage Regulator ... AVR
Automatic Volume Control [*Radio*] ... AVC
Automatic Volume Expansion ... AVE
Automatic Volume Recognition ... AVR
Automatic Voting Machine ... AVM
Automatic Warning and Control System ... AWCS
Automatic Water Check [*Freight*] ... AUTM WTR CK
Automatic Waveform Digitizing System ... AWDS
Automatic Weapons ... AW
Automatic Weapons Control System ... AWCS
Automatic Weapons (Self-Propelled) [*Military*] ... AWSP
Automatic Weather Broadcast Equipment ... AWBE
Automatic Weather Station ... AWS
Automatic Welding [*USSR*] [*A publication*] ... Autom Weld
Automatic Welding Machinery Association [*Defunct*] ... AWMA
Automatic Welding System ... AWS
Automatic Welding (USSR) [*A publication*] ... Aut Weld R
Automatic Wire Wrap Machine ... AWWM
Automatic Writing Machine ... AWM
Automatic X-Ray Radiograph ... AXR
Automatic Zero Set ... AZS
Automatica si Electronica [*A publication*] ... Autom & Electron
Automatica: the Journal of IFAC [*International Federation of Automatic Control*] [*A publication*] ... Automatica-J IFAC
Automatically Controlled Electrical System [*NASA*] ... ACES
Automatically Controlled Transportation [*Airport passenger shuttle*] [*Ford Motor Co.*] ... ACT
Automatically Controlled Turbine Run-Up System [*Navigation*] ... ACTRUS
Automatically Cued Target Detecting System ... ACTDS
Automatically Directed Outgoing Intertoll Trunk [*Bell System*] ... ADOIT
Automatically Directed Outgoing Trunk [*Bell System*] ... ADOT
Automatically Erectable Modular Torus ... AEMT
Automatically Operated Inlet Valve ... AOIV
Automatically Processed Wire List ... APWL
Automatically Programed Remote Indication Logged ... APRIL
Automatically Programed Tools [*Data processing*] ... APT
Automatically Reconfigurable Modular Multiprocessor [*or Multiprocessing*] **System** [*Data processing*] ... ARMMS
Automatically Stabilized Maneuvering Unit [*NASA*] ... ASMU
Automatically Synchronous [*Remote-indicating system*] [*Trade name*] ... AUTOSYN
Automation ... AUTOMN
Automation ... AUTON
Automation of Bibliography through Computerization [*ABC-Clio Press*] ... ABC
Automation (Cleveland) [*A publication*] ... Automation (Cleve)
Automation Engineering Laboratory ... AEL
Automation Foundation ... AF
Automation in Housing and Systems Building News [*A publication*] ... Auto Housg
Automation Industries, Incorporated [*NYSE symbol*] [*Delisted*] ... AII
Automation Industries Research Laboratory ... AIRL
Automation Institute ... AI
Automation Instrument Data Service [*Computer-based industrial information system*] [*British*] ... AIDS
Automation Management Office [*Military*] ... AMO
Automation Planning and Technology ... APT
Automation and Remote Control [*USSR*] [*A publication*] ... Automat Remote Contr
Automation and Remote Control [*USSR*] [*A publication*] ... Autom & Remote Control
Automation and Remote Control [*USSR*] [*A publication*] ... Autom Remote Control
Automation and Remote Control (USSR) [*A publication*] ... Aut Remot R
Automation Services - System Improvement - Solution and Tracking ... ASSIST
Automation System for Scientific Experiments ... ASSE
Automation Techniques, Incorporated ... ATI
Automation Training Center ... ATC
Automatique, Inc. [*NASDAQ symbol*] ... ATOM
Automatique et Informatique Industrielles [*A publication*] ... Autom & Inf Ind
Automatisierungspraxis fuer Grundlagen Geratebau und Betriebserfahrungen [*A publication*] ... Automatisierungspraxis
Automatix, Inc. [*NASDAQ symbol*] ... AITX
Automazione e Strumentazione [*A publication*] ... Autom Strum
Automazione e Strumentazione [*A publication*] ... Autom & Strum
Automedica Corp. [*An association*] [*Defunct*] ... AM
Automicrobic System ... AMS
Automix Keyboards, Incorporated ... AKI
Automized Medical Anamnesis Dialog Assistant [*Computer*] ... AMANDA
Automobil Versuchs- und Untersuchungs Strecke [*Automobile Test Track*] ... AVUS
Automobile ... A
Automobile ... AUTO
Automobile Association [*British*] ... AA
Automobile Builders' Combination Designed Especially for Getting Hitler including Japan [*Suggested name for Automotive Council for War Production*] [*World War II*] ... ABCDEFGHIJ
Automobile Club ... AC
Automobile Club of Great Britain and Ireland [*Later, Royal Automobile Club*] ... ACGBI
Automobile Club of Philadelphia, Philadelphia, PA [*Library symbol*] [*Obsolete*] ... PPAuC
Automobile Competition Committee for the United States ... ACCUS
Automobile Dealers Association ... ADA
Automobile Engineer [*A publication*] ... Auto Eng
Automobile Importers of America ... AIA
Automobile Information Disclosure Act ... AIDA
Automobile Labor Board ... ALB
Automobile Legal Association ... ALA
Automobile Liability [*Insurance*] ... AL
Automobile License Plate Collectors Association ... ALPCA
Automobile Manufacturers Association [*Later, MVMA*] ... AMA
Automobile Manufacturers' Association, Inc., Detroit, MI [*Library symbol*] ... MiDAMA
Automobile Mutual Insurance Company of America ... AMICA
Automobile Owners Action Council ... AOAC
Automobile Parts [*Freight*] ... AUTO PTS
Automobile Physical Damage [*Insurance*] ... APD
Automobile Quarterly [*A publication*] ... Automob Q

Automobile Racing Club of America ARCA
Automobile Seat Cover Association of America ASCAA
Automobile Transporters Tariff Bureau, Inc., Southfield MI [*STAC*] ATB
Automobile Utility Trailer Rental Association AUTRA
Automobiltechnische Zeitschrift [*A publication*] Automobiltech Z
Automotive AUTMV
Automotive AUTOM
Automotive AUTOMV
Automotive Advertisers Council AAC
Automotive Affiliated Representatives AAR
Automotive Air Conditioning Association [*Later, IMACA*] AACA
Automotive and Aviation Industries [*A publication*] Automotive & Aviation Ind
Automotive Battery Charger Manufacturers Council ABCMC
Automotive Booster Clubs International ABC
Automotive Booster Clubs International ABCI
Automotive Committee for Air Defense [*World War II*] ACAD
Automotive and Construction Equipment Overhaul and Repair Plant [*Navy*] ACEORP
Automotive and Construction Equipment Parts Depot [*Navy*] ACEPD
Automotive Consumer Action Program AUTOCAP
Automotive Cooling Systems Institute ACSI
Automotive Crash Injury Research ACIR
Automotive Design Engineering [*A publication*] Automot Des Eng
Automotive Dismantlers and Recyclers of America ADRA
Automotive Electric Association AEA
Automotive Energy Efficiency Program [*Department of Transportation*] AEEP
Automotive Engine Rebuilders Association AERA
Automotive Engineer [*A publication*] AE
Automotive Engineer (London) [*A publication*] Automot Eng (Lond)
Automotive Engineering [*A publication*] Aut Eng
Automotive Engineering [*A publication*] Automot Eng
Automotive Engineering (Pittsburgh) [*A publication*] Automot Eng (Pittsb)
Automotive Exhaust Research Institute [*Defunct*] AERI
Automotive Exhaust Systems Manufacturers Committee AESMC
Automotive Filter Manufacturers Council AFMC
Automotive Fleet and Leasing Association AFLA
Automotive Industrial Motor AIM
Automotive Industries [*A publication*] Auto Ind
Automotive Industries [*A publication*] Automot Ind
Automotive Industries. Truck and Off Highway [*A publication*] Auto Highwy
Automotive Information Council AIC
Automotive Information Test AIT
Automotive Legislative Council of America ALCA
Automotive Lift Institute ALI
Automotive Manufacturers EDP [*Electronic Data Processing*] **Council** AMEDPC
Automotive Market Research Council AMRC
Automotive Mechanical and Electrical [*Test*] AME
Automotive News [*A publication*] Automot N
Automotive Occupant Protection Association AOPA
Automotive Organization Team AOT
Automotive Original Equipment Manufacturers AOEM
Automotive Parts and Accessories Association APAA
Automotive Parts Rebuilders Association APRA
Automotive Pigeon Loft APL
Automotive Presidents Council APC
Automotive Products Emissions Committee APEC
Automotive Products Export Council APEC
Automotive Public Relations Council APRC
Automotive Refrigeration Products Institute ARPI
Automotive Safety Foundation [*Later, HUF*] ASF
Automotive Sales Council ASC
Automotive Service Councils ASC
Automotive Service Industry Association ASIA
Automotive Study Unit [*American Topical Association*] ASU
Automotive Trade Association Managers ATAM
Automotive Warehouse Distributors Association AWDA
Autonetics AN
Autonetics Base-Line Equipment ABLE
Autonetics Business & Control United Systems, Inc. ABACUS
Autonetics General Information Learning Equipment AGILE
Autonetics Generalized Reset AGR
Autonetics Kalman Utilization of Reference for Optimal Navigation AKURON
Autonetics Modular Airborne RADAR System AMARS
Autonome Transfer Unit [*Data processing*] ATU
Autonomic Hyperreflexia [*Medicine*] AH
Autonomic Lability Score [*In ion detection*] ALS
Autonomic Nervous System [*Medicine*] ANS
Autonomous Line Scanning Unit ALSU
Autonomous Listening Stations [*Instrumentation*] ALS
Autonomous Missile Site RADAR AMSR
Autonomous Navigation System ANS
Autonomous Navigation System Concept ANSC
Autonomous Navigation Technology ANT
Autonomous Oblast AO
Autonomous Republic AR
Autonomous Soviet Socialist Republic ASSR
Autonomous Tactical All-Weather Strike ATAWS
Autonomously Functioning Thyroid Nodule [*Endocrinology*] AFTN
Autopilot AP
Autopilot Capsule A/PC
Autopilot Control Unit A/P CTL
Autopilot Disengage Switch ADS
Autopilot Flight Director APFD
Autopilot Ground Control Unit AGCU
Autopilot Ground Control Unit APGCU
Autopilot Mode Selector AMS
Autopilot Monitor and Control Unit A/P MCU
Autopilot Monitor Unit A/P MON
Autopilot Positioning Indicator A/P POI
Autopilot Rate Control ARC
Autopilot Surface Servo ASS
Autopilot Test Monitor A/P TSTMN
Autopilot Test Programer A/P TSTPG
Autoplot Controller APC
Autopsy [*Also, AUT*] [*Medicine*] AU
Autopsy [*Also, AU*] AUT
Autoradiographic AR
Autoradiography ARG
Autoregressive [*Mathematical bioscience*] AR
Autoregressive-Integrated-Moving-Average [*Statistics*] ARIMA
Autoregressive Moving Average [*Statistics*] ARMA
Autorite pour l'Amenagement de la Region du Sud-Ouest [*Ivory Coast*] ARSO
AUTOSEVOCOM Life Cycle Extension Program ALCEP
Autosomal Dominant [*Genetics*] AD
Autosomal Recessive [*Genetics*] AR
Autotrack Vulcan Air Defense System AVADS
Autotransaction Industry Report [*A publication*] Auto Ind Rep
Autotransformer AUTOTR
Autotrol Corp. [*NASDAQ symbol*] AUTR
AUTOVON [*Automatic Voice Network*] **Centralized Alarm System** ACAS
Autumn [*A publication*] AT
Autumnal Equinox AE
Aux Bons Soins De [*Care Of, c/o*] [*French*] ABS
Aux Soins De [*Care Of, c/o*] [*French*] A/S
Aux Soins De [*Care Of, c/o*] [*French*] A/S DE
Auxi-Atome [*French association*] AA
Auxiair [*France*] [*ICAO designator*] AJ
Auxiliary AUX
Auxiliary AUXIL
Auxiliary Air Force [*Later, R Aux AF*] [*British*] AAF
Auxiliary Air Force Base AAFB
Auxiliary Air Force Reserve [*British*] AAFR
Auxiliary Air Units [*Naval Reserve*] AAU
Auxiliary Airborne Command Post AUXCP
Auxiliary Aircraft Carrier [*Navy symbol*] ACV
Auxiliary Aircraft Transport [*Navy symbol*] AVT
Auxiliary to the American Optometric Association AAOA
Auxiliary to the American Osteopathic Association AAOA
Auxiliary Amplifier XA
Auxiliary Attitude Control System [*Aviation*] AACS
Auxiliary Aviation Weather Facility [*FAA*] AAWF
Auxiliary Ballast Tank ABT
Auxiliary Building Filter System [*Nuclear energy*] ABFS
Auxiliary Checkpoint ACP
Auxiliary Coastguard [*British*] ACG
Auxiliary Combat Information Center ACIC
Auxiliary Command AC
Auxiliary Computer Input Multiplexer ACIM
Auxiliary Computer Power Unit ACPU
Auxiliary Computer Room [*Apollo*] [*NASA*] ACR
Auxiliary Conditioning Unit ACU
Auxiliary Control Panel [*Aerospace*] ACP
Auxiliary Conversion Equipment ACE
Auxiliary Cooling System [*Nuclear energy*] ACS
Auxiliary Core Memory [*Data processing*] ACM
Auxiliary Core Storage [*Data processing*] ACS
Auxiliary Crew Compartment ACC
Auxiliary Data Annotation Set [*or System*] ADAS
Auxiliary Data Processing Equipment ADPE
Auxiliary Data Translator Unit ADTU
Auxiliary of the Decalogue Society of Lawyers ADSL
Auxiliary Deep Submergence Support Ship [*Navy symbol*] AGDS
Auxiliary Detonation Fuze ADF
Auxiliary Display Equipment Group ADEG
Auxiliary Display Request Keyboard ADRK
Auxiliary Drum AXD
Auxiliary Encoder System AES
Auxiliary Engineering Signal Processor AESP
Auxiliary Equipment AE
Auxiliary Equipment Building [*Nuclear energy*] AEB
Auxiliary Ferry Service Unit AFSU
Auxiliary Field AF
Auxiliary Fighter Director Ship [*Navy*] AFDS
Auxiliary Fire Service [*British*] AFS
Auxiliary Floating Dry Dock [*Navy symbol*] AFD

Auxiliary Floating Dry Dock, Concrete [*Navy symbol*] .... AFDC
Auxiliary Functional Unit [*Data link*] .... AFU
Auxiliary General Electronics Research Ship [*Navy*] .... AGERS
Auxiliary General Missile .... AGM
Auxiliary General Oceanographic Research .... AGOR
Auxiliary General Survey .... AGS
Auxiliary Ground Control Station [*NASA*] .... AUXGCS
Auxiliary Ground Equipment .... AGE
Auxiliary Hydraulic Power Supply .... AHPS
Auxiliary Inerting Gas Subsystem [*Nuclear energy*] .... AIGS
Auxiliary Interface Unit [*NASA*] .... AIU
Auxiliary Intermediate Heat Exchanger [*Nuclear energy*] .... AIHX
Auxiliary Landing Field .... ALF
Auxiliary Library Service Collections .... ALSC
Auxiliary Library Service Organization .... ALSO
Auxiliary Light [*Navigation signal*] .... Aux
Auxiliary Liquid Metal System [*Nuclear energy*] .... ALMS
Auxiliary Loans to Assist Students .... ALAS
Auxiliary Memory .... AM
Auxiliary Memory Drum .... AMD
Auxiliary Memory Set .... AMS
Auxiliary Memory Unit .... AMU
Auxiliary Mexican Border Veterans .... AMBV
Auxiliary Military Pioneer Corps [*British*] .... AMPC
Auxiliary Minelayer [*Navy symbol*] .... ACM
Auxiliary Minelayer .... AML
Auxiliary Motor Launches .... MLA
Auxiliary Motor Minesweeper [*Navy symbol*] .... YMS
Auxiliary to the National Dental Association [*Formerly, LANDA*] .... ANDA
Auxiliary to the National Medical Association .... ANMA
Auxiliary Ocean Tug [*Navy symbol*] .... ATA
Auxiliary Operational Members [*Coast Guard*] .... AUXOPS
Auxiliary Oscillator .... AO
Auxiliary Oscillator .... AUXOSC
Auxiliary Output Tester .... AOT
Auxiliary Pastoral Ministry [*Church of England*] .... APM
Auxiliary Payload Power System .... APPS
Auxiliary Personnel, Attack [*Navy designation for combat landing craft*] [*World War II*] .... APA
Auxiliary Pneumatic .... APNEU
Auxiliary Pneumatics Panel .... APP
Auxiliary Power Distribution .... APD
Auxiliary Power Package .... APP
Auxiliary Power Plant .... APP
Auxiliary Power Supply .... APS
Auxiliary Power [*or Propulsion*] **Unit** [*Military*] .... APU
Auxiliary Power Unit Subsystem .... APUS
Auxiliary Power Unit Test .... APUT
Auxiliary Processing Unit .... APU
Auxiliary Program Storage [*Data processing*] .... APS
Auxiliary Propulsion System [*or Subsystem*] [*Apollo*] [*NASA*] .... APS
Auxiliary Pump-Drive Assembly .... APDA
Auxiliary Recording Control [*Circuit*] [*Bell System*] .... AUXRC
Auxiliary Recovery Antenna [*NASA*] .... ARA
Auxiliary Register .... AUXR
Auxiliary Repair Dry Dock [*Non-self-propelled*] [*Navy ship symbol*] .... ARD
Auxiliary Repair Dry Dock, Concrete [*Later, AFDL*] [*Navy symbol*] .... ARDC
Auxiliary Report .... XREP
Auxiliary Rescue Team Chief [*Air Force*] .... ARTC
Auxiliary Resources Control Office .... ARCO
Auxiliary Rocket Engine .... ARE
Auxiliary Roll Control .... ARC
Auxiliary Seaplane Tender [*Ship symbol*] .... XAV
Auxiliary Service Force, Transition Training Squadron, Pacific .... ASFTRNTRARONPAC
Auxiliary to Sons of Union Veterans of the Civil War .... ASUVCW
Auxiliary Spacecraft Power .... ASP
Auxiliary Stabilizing Support - "A" Frame .... ASF
Auxiliary Stage [*NASA*] .... A/S
Auxiliary Storage Manager [*Data processing*] .... ASM
Auxiliary Storage and Playback [*Assembly*] [*Apollo Telescope Mount*] [*NASA*] .... ASAP
Auxiliary Storage and Playback Assembly [*Apollo Telescope Mount*] [*NASA*] .... ASPA
Auxiliary Submarine [*Navy symbol*] .... AGSS
Auxiliary Submarine Rescue Ship [*Navy symbol*] .... ASR
Auxiliary Support Reaction System .... ASRS
Auxiliary Switch [*Electricity*] .... ASW
Auxiliary Switch [*Breaker*] **Normally Closed** [*Electricity*] .... ASC
Auxiliary Switch [*Breaker*] **Normally Open** [*Electricity*] .... ASO
Auxiliary System for Interactive Statistics [*Sweden*] [*Information service*] .... AXIS
Auxiliary Systems Function Test Stand [*NASA*] .... ASFTS
Auxiliary Tape Memory [*Spacecraft guidance*] .... ATM
Auxiliary Territorial Service [*Later, WRAC*] [*British women's service*] [*World War II*] .... ATS
Auxiliary Test Unit .... ATU
Auxiliary Timer .... AT
Auxiliary Timer Assembly .... ATA
Auxiliary Track .... AUXTRAC
Auxiliary Training Submarine [*Navy symbol*] .... ATSS
Auxiliary Turbopump Assembly .... ATPA
Auxiliary Unit .... AU
Auxiliary Vessels [*Navy symbol*] .... AA
Auxiliary Video Switching Matrix .... AVSM
Auxton Computer Enterprises [*NASDAQ symbol*] .... AUXT
AV Communication Review [*A publication*] .... AV
AV Communication Review [*A publication*] .... AV Comm R
AV Communication Review [*A publication*] .... AV Commun Rev
AV Communication Review [*A publication*] .... AVCR
Ava, IL [*Radio station call letters*] .... WXAN
Ava, MO [*Location identifier*] [*FAA*] .... AOV
Ava, MO [*Radio station call letters*] .... KSOA
Avacare [*NASDAQ symbol*] .... AVAC
Availability .... AVBLTY
Availability Balance File [*Military*] .... ABF
Availability Code .... AC
Availability Factor .... AVF
Available [*or Availability*] .... A
Available [*or Availability*] .... AVAIL
Available [*or Availability*] .... AVAL
Available [*or Availability*] .... AVBL
Available [*or Availability*] .... AVLBL
Available-to-Load Date .... ALD
Available Machine Time .... AMT
Available Manhours .... AVMH
Available but Not Installed .... ABNI
Available Phosphoric Acid .... APA
Available Potential Energy [*Geophysics*] .... APE
Available Power Efficiency .... APE
Available Power Response .... APR
Available for Reassignment .... AVFR
Available for Release .... AFR
Available Seat Miles [*Airlines term*] .... ASM
Available Supply Rate .... ASR
Available Time .... AVT
Available Water-Holding Capacity [*Soil science*] .... AWC
Avair Ltd. [*Ireland*] [*ICAO designator*] .... WV
Avalanche Diode .... AD
Avalanche Diode Oscillator .... ADO
Avalanche-Induced Migration .... AIM
Avalanche Injection Diode .... AID
Avalanche Mode Photodiode .... AMP
Avalanche Photodiode Detector .... APD
Avalanche Punch-Through Erase .... APTE
Avalanche Transit Time .... ATT
Avalanche Transit Time Diode .... ATTD
Avalanching Junction Light Output .... AJLO
Avalon, CA [*Radio station call letters*] .... KBRT
Avalon, NJ [*Radio station call letters*] .... WWOC
Avancer [*Fast, as clocks*] .... A
Avances en Alimentacion y Mejora Animal [*A publication*] .... Av Aliment Mejora Anim
Avances en Alimentacion y Mejora Animal. Suplemento [*A publication*] .... Av Aliment Mejora Anim Supl
Avances en Produccion Animal [*A publication*] .... Av Prod Anim
Avant-Garde Computing [*NASDAQ symbol*] .... AVGA
Avant Jesus-Christ [*Before Christ*] [*French*] .... AV J-C
Avant Scene du Cinema [*A publication*] .... Avant Scene
Avantek, Inc. [*NASDAQ symbol*] .... AVAK
Avanti Owners Association International .... AOAI
Avaric [*MARC language code*] [*Library of Congress*] .... ava
Avatar Holdings, Inc. [*NASDAQ symbol*] .... AVTR
AVC Corp. [*Formerly, American Viscose Corporation*] [*American Stock Exchange symbol*] .... AVC
Avco Corp. [*NYSE symbol*] .... AV
Avco Corporation. Research Reports [*A publication*] .... Avco Corp Res Rep
Avco Data Analysis and Prediction Technique [*for sunspot prediction*] .... ADAPT
Avco-Everett Research Laboratory .... AERL
Avco-Everett Research Laboratory, Everett, MA [*OCLC symbol*] .... AVC
Avco-Everett Research Laboratory, Everett, MA [*Library symbol*] .... MEvA
Avco Systems Development .... AVSD
Ave Maria .... AM
Ave Maria .... AVM
AVEMCO Corp. [*NYSE symbol*] .... AVE
Avenida [*Avenue*] .... AVDA
Avenir Agriculture [*A publication*] .... Avenir Agr
Avenue .... AV
Avenue .... AVE
Avenue of Approach .... AA
Average .... AV
Average .... AVE
Average .... AVER
Average .... AVG
Average Alarm .... AVA
Average Aptitude Requirement per Unit Time .... AARPUT
Average Audience [*Television ratings*] .... AA
Average Australian Voters .... AVOZVOTS
Average Blank Data [*Data processing*] .... AVEBD
Average Business Day [*Bell System*] .... ABD
Average Cost per Patient Day [*Medicine*] .... ACPPD

Average Daily Attendance .... ADA
Average Daily Gain [of weight] [Cattle] .... ADG
Average Daily Member Load .... ADML
Average Daily Membership .... ADM
Average Daily Patient Load [Medicine] .... ADPL
Average Daily Service Charge [Hospitals] .... ADSC
Average Daily Traffic .... ADT
Average Decreasing Line .... ADL
Average Depth .... AVDTH
Average Deviation [Statistics] .... AD
Average Efficiency Index .... AEI
Average Electrode Current .... AEC
Average Evoked Potential [Neurophysiology] .... AEP
Average Evoked Response [Neurophysiology] .... AER
Average Extent of Burning .... AEB
Average Failure Number .... AFN
Average Fixed Cost .... AFC
Average Freight Rate Assessment [Shipping] .... AFRA
Average Global Automobile [Emissions to atmosphere] .... AGA
Average Goals Against per Period [Hockey] .... AGP
Average Heading .... AVH
Average Hearing Level .... AHL
Average Indexed Monthly Earnings [Social Security Administration] ..... AIME
Average Instructions per Second [Data processing] .... AIP
Average Inventory Level .... AIL
Average Length of Stay [of patients in a health care institution] ..... ALOS
Average Linear Planar Heat Generation Rate [Nuclear energy] ..... ALPHGR
Average Mean Pressure .... AMP
Average Monthly Consumption .... AMC
Average Monthly Earnings .... AME
Average Monthly Sales .... AMS
Average Monthly Usage .... AMU
Average Monthly Weather Outlook [A publication] .... AWO
Average Operating Cost .... AOC
Average Operation Time .... AOT
Average Outgoing Quality [Quality control term] .... AOQ
Average Outgoing Quality Level [or Limit] [Quality control term] ..... AOQL
Average Particle Diameter .... APD
Average Percentage Damage [Meteorology] .... APD
Average Picture Level .... APL
Average Pore Diameter [Filtration] .... APD
Average Power Dissipation .... APD
Average Power Range Monitor [Nuclear energy] .... APRM
Average Price .... AP
Average Propensity to Consume [Economics] .... APC
Average Propensity to Save [Economics] .... APS
Average Quality Limit .... AQL
Average Quarterly Demand .... AQD
Average Rating .... AR
Average Response Amplitude .... ARA
Average Response Amplitude Data .... ARAD
Average Response Computer .... ARC
Average Response Data .... ARD
Average Revenue .... AR
Average Revenue per Message .... ARPM
Average Run Length [Statistics] .... ARL
Average Sample Number [Quality control] .... ASN
Average Sampling Time [Statistics] .... AST
Average Service Life .... ASL
Average Speech Power .... ASP
Average Straight Time Hourly Earnings .... ASTHE
Average Task Time .... ATT
Average Temperature .... AVTMP
Average Time of Burning .... ATB
Average Time between Maintenance .... ATBM
Average Time to Repair .... ATTR
Average Total Cost .... ATC
Average Total Inspection [QCR] .... ATI
Average Total Operating Cost .... ATOC
Average Total Unit Cost .... ATUC
Average Turnaround [Data processing] .... ATA
Average Useful Life .... AUL
Average Value .... AV
Average Variability .... AV
Average Variable Costs .... AVC
Average Visual Evoked Potential [Neurophysiology] ...... AVEP
Average Weekly Earnings .... AWE
[The] Average White Band [Rock music group] .... AWB
Average Width .... AVW
Average Work Load .... AWL
Average Work Time .... AWT
Average Working Depth .... AWD
Averette College, Danville, VA [Library symbol] .... ViDA
Averroes [Morocco] [Geomagnetic observatory code] ..... AVE
Averroes [Morocco] [Seismograph station code, US Geological Survey] ..... AVE
Avert Disruption of Operation .... AVERDISROP
Avery Index to Architectural Periodicals of Columbia University [A publication] ..... Avery Ind Archit Per
Avery International Corp. [NYSE symbol] .... AVY

Avery-Mitchell-Yancey Regional Library, Spruce Pine, NC [Library symbol] ..... NcSppA
Avery Point [Connecticut] [Seismograph station code, US Geological Survey] [Closed] ..... APT
Avesta [MARC language code] [Library of Congress] .... ave
Avesta Stainless Bulletin [A publication] ...... Avesta Stainless Bull
Avhandlingar Utgitt av Norsk Videnskaps-Akademi I Oslo. I. Mathematisk-Naturvidenskaplige Klasse [A publication] ..... Avh Nor Vidensk-Akad Oslo I
Avhandlinger Utgitt av Norsk Videnskaps-Akademi I Oslo [A publication] ..... ANVA
Avhandlinger Utgitt av Norsk Videnskaps-Akademi I Oslo. II [A publication] ..... ANVAO
Avia Transport [France] [ICAO designator] .... JA
Aviacion y Comercio SA [AVIACO] [Spanish airline] [ICAO designator] ..... AO
Aviacion y Comercio SA [Spanish airline] .... AVIACO
Aviaeskadra [Russian term for an air squadron] .... AS
Avian Diseases [A publication] .... Avian Dis
Avian Leukosis Virus .... ALV
Avian Myeloblastosis Virus .... AMV
Avian Pancreatic Polypeptide .... APP
Avian Philately Unit [American Topical Association] .... APU
Avian Sarcoma Virus [Same as RSV] .... ASV
AVIANCA [Aerovias Nacionales de Colombia, SA; Colombian airline] ..... AVN
Aviapolk [Russian term for an air regiment] .... AP
Aviation .... AV
Aviation .... AVN
Aviation Advisory Commission [Report presented to Congress in 1972] ..... AAC
Aviation Annex [Air Force] .... AA
Aviation Armament Bulletin .... AAB
Aviation Armament Change .... AAC
Aviation Armament Laboratory [Later, Naval Air Development Center] [Navy] ..... AAL
Aviation ASW [Antisubmarine Warfare] Operator [Navy rating] ..... AW
Aviation ASW [Antisubmarine Warfare] Operator, First Class [Navy rating] AW1
Aviation ASW [Antisubmarine Warfare] Operator, Master Chief [Navy rating] ..... AWCM
Aviation ASW [Antisubmarine Warfare] Operator, Second Class [Navy rating] AW2
Aviation ASW [Antisubmarine Warfare] Operator, Senior Chief [Navy rating] ..... AWCS
Aviation ASW [Antisubmarine Warfare] Operator, Third Class [Navy rating] AW3
Aviation ASW [Antisubmarine Warfare] Technician [Navy rating] ..... AX
Aviation ASW [Antisubmarine Warfare] Technician, Chief [Navy rating] ..... AXC
Aviation ASW [Antisubmarine Warfare] Technician, First Class [Navy rating] AX1
Aviation ASW [Antisubmarine Warfare] Technician, Master Chief [Navy rating] ..... AXCM
Aviation ASW [Antisubmarine Warfare] Technician, Second Class [Navy rating] AX2
Aviation ASW [Antisubmarine Warfare] Technician, Senior Chief [Navy rating] ..... AXCS
Aviation ASW [Antisubmarine Warfare] Technician, Third Class [Navy rating] AX3
Aviation Baseship .... AVB
Aviation Battalion [Army] .... AB
Aviation Battalion [Army] .... AVBAT
Aviation Boatswain [Navy rating] .... AB
Aviation Boatswain's Mate [Navy rating] .... ABM
Aviation Boatswain's Mate, Arresting Gear and Barriers [Navy rating] ..... ABMAG
Aviation Boatswain's Mate, Catapult [Navy rating] ..... ABMCP
Aviation Boatswain's Mate, Chief [Navy rating] .... ABC
Aviation Boatswain's Mate, First Class [Navy rating] AB1
Aviation Boatswain's Mate, Fuel [Navy rating] .... ABF
Aviation Boatswain's Mate, Fuel, Airman [Navy rating] ..... ABFAN
Aviation Boatswain's Mate, Fuel, Airman Apprentice [Navy rating] ..... ABFAA
Aviation Boatswain's Mate, Gasoline System [Navy rating] ..... ABMGA
Aviation Boatswain's Mate, Handler [Navy rating] .... ABH
Aviation Boatswain's Mate, Handler, Airman [Navy rating] ..... ABHAN
Aviation Boatswain's Mate, Handler, Airman Apprentice [Navy rating] ..... ABHAA
Aviation Boatswain's Mate, Launch and Recovery Equipment [Navy rating] ..... ABE
Aviation Boatswain's Mate, Launch and Recovery Equipment, Airman [Navy rating] ..... ABEAN
Aviation Boatswain's Mate, Launch and Recovery Equipment, Airman Apprentice [Navy rating] ..... ABEAA
Aviation Boatswain's Mate, Plane Handler [Navy rating] ..... ABMPH
Aviation Boatswain's Mate, Second Class [Navy rating] AB2
Aviation Boatswain's Mate, Senior Chief [Navy rating] ..... ABCS
Aviation Boatswain's Mate, Third Class [Navy rating] AB3
Aviation Cadet [Air Force] .... AC
Aviation Cadet [Navy] .... AVCAD
Aviation Cadet Qualifying Test [Military] .... ACQT
Aviation Career Incentive Act [1974] .... ACIA

Aviation Career Incentive Pay [*Air Force*] ACIP
Aviation Centers of America [*Jackson, TN*] [*FAA designator*] CNN
Aviation Chief Boatswain's Mate, Arresting Gear and Barriers [*Navy rating*] ACBMAG
Aviation Chief Boatswain's Mate, Catapult [*Navy rating*] ACBMCP
Aviation Chief Boatswain's Mate, Gasoline System [*Navy rating*] ACBMGA
Aviation Chief Boatswain's Mate, Plane Handler [*Navy rating*] ACBMPH
Aviation Chief Electrician's Mate [*Navy*] ACEM
Aviation Chief Fire Controlman [*Navy*] ACFC
Aviation Chief Machinist's Mate [*Navy*] ACMM
Aviation Chief Machinist's Mate, Carburetor Mechanic [*Navy*] ACMMC
Aviation Chief Machinist's Mate, Flight Engineer [*Navy*] ACMMF
Aviation Chief Machinist's Mate, Gas Turbine Mechanic [*Navy*] ACMMT
Aviation Chief Machinist's Mate, Hydraulic Mechanic [*Navy*] ACMMH
Aviation Chief Machinist's Mate, Instrument Mechanic [*Navy*] ACMMI
Aviation Chief Machinist's Mate, Propeller Mechanic [*Navy*] ACMMP
Aviation Chief Metalsmith [*Navy*] ACM
Aviation Chief Ordnanceman [*Navy*] ACOM
Aviation Chief Ordnanceman, Turret Mechanic [*Navy*] ACOMT
Aviation Chief Radio Technician [*Navy*] ACRT
Aviation Chief Radioman [*Navy*] ACRM
Aviation Circular Letter ACL
Aviation Classification Repair Activity Depot [*Army*] AVCRAD
Aviation Classification Test ACT
Aviation Clothing and Survival Equipment Bulletin ACSEB
Aviation Combat Development Agency [*CDC*] ACDA
Aviation Command [*Army*] AVCOM
Aviation Consolidated Allowance List [*Military*] AVCAL
Aviation Construction Engineers [*Military*] ACE
Aviation Consumer Action Project ACAP
Aviation Control Center ACC
Aviation Crash Injury Research ACIR
Aviation Credit Corps ACC
Aviation Daily AD
Aviation Data Service, Inc. [*Information service*] ADS
Aviation Depot Group ADG
Aviation Depot Squadron ADS
Aviation Design Research [*Navy*] ADR
Aviation Development Advisory Committee ADAC
Aviation Development Council ADC
Aviation Development Test Activity [*Test and Evaluation Command*] ADTA
Aviation Development Test Activity [*Army*] AVNDTA
Aviation Distributors and Manufacturers Association ADMA
Aviation Electric Ltd., Montreal, PQ, Canada [*Library symbol*] CaQMAE
Aviation Electrician's Mate [*Navy rating*] AE
Aviation Electrician's Mate [*Navy*] AEM
Aviation Electrician's Mate, Chief [*Navy rating*] AEC
Aviation Electrician's Mate, First Class [*Navy rating*] AE1
Aviation Electrician's Mate, Master Chief [*Navy rating*] AECM
Aviation Electrician's Mate, Second Class [*Navy rating*] AE2
Aviation Electrician's Mate, Senior Chief [*Navy rating*] AECS
Aviation Electrician's Mate, Third Class [*Navy rating*] AE3
Aviation Electronic Equipment Information Exchange System AVEXS
Aviation Electronic Technician's Mate [*Navy*] AETM
Aviation Electronic Technician's Mate, Combat Aircrewman [*Navy*] AETAC
Aviation Electronics AVIONICS
Aviation Electronics Technician [*Navy rating*] AT
Aviation Electronics Technician Airborne CIC [*Combat Information Center*] **Equipment** ATW
Aviation Electronics Technician, Chief [*Navy rating*] ATC
Aviation Electronics Technician, First Class [*Navy rating*] AT1
Aviation Electronics Technician, Master Chief [*Navy rating*] ATCM
Aviation Electronics Technician, Second Class [*Navy rating*] AT2
Aviation Electronics Technician, Senior Chief [*Navy rating*] ATCS
Aviation Electronics Technician, Third Class [*Navy rating*] AT3
Aviation Electronicsman [*Military*] AL
Aviation Engineer Battalion [*Marine Corps*] AVNENGRBN
Aviation Engineer Force AEF
Aviation Engineering Corp. AVIEN
Aviation Engineering Flight Activity [*Formerly, ASTA*] AEFA
Aviation Evaluation Group AEG
Aviation Facilities AF
Aviation Facilities Service [*of FAA*] AFS
Aviation Financial Services, Incorporated AFSI
Aviation Fire Control Technician [*Navy rating*] AQ
Aviation Fire Control Technician, Bomb Direction [*Navy rating*] AQB
Aviation Fire Control Technician, Chief [*Navy rating*] AQC
Aviation Fire Control Technician, Fire Control [*Navy rating*] AQF
Aviation Fire Control Technician, First Class [*Navy rating*] AQ1
Aviation Fire Control Technician, Master Chief [*Navy rating*] AQCM
Aviation Fire Control Technician, Second Class [*Navy rating*] AQ2
Aviation Fire Control Technician, Senior Chief [*Navy rating*] AQCS
Aviation Fire Control Technician, Third Class [*Navy rating*] AQ3
Aviation Fire Controlman [*Navy*] AFC
Aviation Fleet Maintenance AFM
Aviation Forum [*British*] AF
Aviation Fuel AVFUEL
Aviation Fuels, Lubricants, and Associated Products [*NATO*] F & L
Aviation Gas Turbine AGT
Aviation Gasoline [*Navy*] AGAS
Aviation Gasoline AVGAS
Aviation Ground Unit [*Naval Reserve*] AGU
[*The*] **Aviation Group** [*NASDAQ symbol*] LIFT
Aviation Guided Flight AGF
Aviation Gunnery Officers School AGOS
Aviation Historical Society AHS
Aviation Human Research Unit [*Army*] AHRU
Aviation Information Services Limited AISL
Aviation Instrument Laboratory [*Navy*] AIL
Aviation Insurance Rating Bureau AIRB
Aviation Intensive Management Items AIMI
Aviation Intermediate Maintenance [*Army*] AVIM
Aviation Item Reports AIR
Aviation Laboratories [*Army*] AVLABS
Aviation Life Support Equipment ALSE
Aviation Lubricant AVLUB
Aviation Machinist Mate Jet, Chief [*Navy rating*] ADJC
Aviation Machinist Mate Jet, Master Chief [*Navy rating*] ADJM
Aviation Machinist Mate Jet, Senior Chief [*Navy rating*] ADJS
Aviation Machinist's Mate [*Navy rating*] AD
Aviation Machinist's Mate, Carburetor Mechanic [*Navy rating*] AMMC
Aviation Machinist's Mate, Combat Aircrewman [*Navy rating*] AMMAC
Aviation Machinist's Mate, Flight Engineer [*Navy rating*] AMMF
Aviation Machinist's Mate, Hydraulic Mechanic [*Navy rating*] AMMH
Aviation Machinist's Mate, Instrument Mechanic [*Navy rating*] AMMI
Aviation Machinist's Mate, Jet Engine Mechanic [*Navy rating*] ADJ
Aviation Machinist's Mate, Propeller Mechanic [*Navy rating*] AMMP
Aviation Machinist's Mate, Reciprocating Engine Mechanic [*Navy rating*] ADR
Aviation Machinist's Mate, Reciprocating Engine Mechanic, Chief [*Navy rating*] ADRC
Aviation Machinist's Mate, Reciprocating Engine Mechanic, First Class [*Navy rating*] ADR1
Aviation Machinist's Mate, Reciprocating Engine Mechanic, Master Chief [*Navy rating*] ADRCM
Aviation Machinist's Mate, Reciprocating Engine Mechanic, Second Class [*Navy rating*] ADR2
Aviation Machinist's Mate, Reciprocating Engine Mechanic, Senior Chief [*Navy rating*] ADRCS
Aviation Machinist's Mate, Reciprocating Engine Mechanic, Third Class [*Navy rating*] ADR3
Aviation Machinist's Mate, Turret Mechanic [*Navy rating*] AMMT
Aviation Maintenance Administrationman [*Navy rating*] AZ
Aviation Maintenance Administrationman, Chief [*Navy rating*] AZC
Aviation Maintenance Administrationman, First Class [*Navy rating*] AZ1
Aviation Maintenance Administrationman, Master Chief [*Navy rating*] AZCM
Aviation Maintenance Administrationman, Second Class [*Navy rating*] AZ2
Aviation Maintenance Administrationman, Senior Chief [*Navy rating*] AZCS
Aviation Maintenance Administrationman, Third Class [*Navy rating*] AZ3
Aviation Maintenance Costs AMC
Aviation Maintenance Foundation, Incorporated AMFI
Aviation Maintenance Officer [*Military*] AMO
Aviation Materiel Laboratories [*Army*] AML
Aviation Materiel Management Center AMMC
Aviation Materiel Management Improvement Program [*Military*] AMMIP
Aviation Medical AVM
Aviation Medical Examiner AME
Aviation Medical Officer [*Military*] AMO
Aviation Medical Reports AMR
Aviation Medicine AM
Aviation Medicine [*A publication*] Aviat Med
Aviation Medicine [*Military*] AVNMED
Aviation Medicine [*Medical officer designation*] [*British*] A/M
Aviation Medicine Technician [*Navy*] AVT
Aviation Metalsmith AM
Aviation Meteorological Facsimile [*National Weather Service*] AMFAX
Aviation Modernization Program AMP
Aviation News [*A publication*] Aviation N
Aviation News [*A publication*] AVN
Aviation News Features ANF
Aviation Observation AVIOB
Aviation Officer Candidate [*Navy*] AOC
Aviation Officer Continuation Pay [*Navy*] AOCP
Aviation Officers' Quarters AOQ
Aviation Officers Training Corps AOTC
Aviation Oil [*Military*] A OIL
Aviation Oil [*Military*] AVOIL
Aviation Operating Detachment AOD
Aviation Ordnance Officer AOO
Aviation Ordnanceman [*Navy rating*] AO
Aviation Ordnanceman [*Navy rating*] [*Obsolete*] AOM
Aviation Ordnanceman, Airman Apprentice, Striker [*Navy rating*] AOAA
Aviation Ordnanceman, Airman, Striker [*Navy rating*] AOAN
Aviation Ordnanceman, Bombsight Mechanic [*Navy rating*] [*Obsolete*] AOMB
Aviation Ordnanceman, Chief [*Navy rating*] AOC

Aviation Ordnanceman, Combat Aircrewman [*Navy rating*] [*Obsolete*] .... AOMAC
Aviation Ordnanceman, Combat Aircrewman, Air Bomber [*Navy rating*] [*Obsolete*] .... AOACB
Aviation Ordnanceman, First Class [*Navy rating*] AO1
Aviation Ordnanceman, Master Chief [*Navy rating*] .... AOCM
Aviation Ordnanceman, Second Class [*Navy rating*] AO2
Aviation Ordnanceman, Senior Chief [*Navy rating*] .... AOCS
Aviation Ordnanceman, Third Class [*Navy rating*] AO3
Aviation Ordnanceman, Turret Mechanic [*Navy rating*] .... AOMT
Aviation Pay [*Navy*] .... AVIA
Aviation Pay (Crewmember) [*Navy*] .... AVN(CM)
Aviation Pay (Non-Crewmember) [*Navy*] .... AVN(NCM)
Aviation Personnel Planning Data [*Navy*] .... APPD
Aviation Personnel and Survival Equipment Team [*Navy*] .... APSET
Aviation Petroleum Coordinating Committee, Latin American .... APCCLA
Aviation Petroleum Products Allocation Committee .... APPAC
Aviation Petroleum Products Allocation Committee, London .... APPAC-L
Aviation Pilot [*Navy*] .... AP
Aviation Pilot, Airship [*Navy*] .... APLA
Aviation POL [*Petroleum, Oil, and Lubrication*] **Handling Equipment** .... PHE
Aviation Qualification Test .... AQT
Aviation Radio and RADAR Countermeasures Technician [*Navy*] .... RCM
Aviation Radio Technician .... ART
Aviation Radioman [*Navy*] .... ARM
Aviation Radioman, Combat Aircrewman [*Navy*] .... ARMAC
Aviation Radionavigation, Land [*FCC*] .... AR
Aviation Readiness Evaluation .... ARE
Aviation Repair and Overhaul Unit .... AROU
Aviation Repair Supply Depot .... ARSD
Aviation Requirements for the Combat Structure of the Army .... ARCSA
Aviation Research and Development Service [*of FAA*] .... ARDS
Aviation Research Monographs [*A publication*] .... Aviat Res Monogr
Aviation Reserve Officers Candidate Program .... AVROC
Aviation Resources Management and Control System .... ARMACS
Aviation Review [*A publication*] .... Aviat Rev
Aviation Routine Weather Report .... AERO
Aviation Routine Weather Report [*Aviation code*] .... METAR
Aviation Safety District Office .... ASDO
Aviation Safety Engineering and Research .... AVSER
Aviation Safety Institute .... ASI
Aviation Safety Officer .... ASO
Aviation Safety Regulation .... ASR
Aviation Safety Reporting System .... ASRS
Aviation School of Medicine .... ASM
Aviation Section Signal Reserve Corps .... ASSRC
Aviation Security Association of America - International .... ASAA-I
Aviation Security Command [*Philippines*] .... AVSECOM
Aviation Selected Reserve Programs Branch [*BUPERS*] .... ASRPB
Aviation Service Code .... ASC
Aviation Service Date .... ASD
Aviation Service Entry Data .... ASED
Aviation Services, Incorporated .... ASI
Aviation Services, Inc. [*Reno, NV*] [*FAA designator*] .... GEN
Aviation, Space, and Environmental Medicine [*A publication*] .... ASEMC
Aviation, Space, and Environmental Medicine [*A publication*] .... Aviat Space Environ Med
Aviation, Space, and Environmental Medicine [*A publication*] .... Aviat Sp En
Aviation/Space Writers Association .... A/SWA
Aviation/Space Writers Association .... AWA
Aviation Storekeeper [*Navy rating*] .... AK
Aviation Storekeeper, Chief [*Navy rating*] .... AKC
Aviation Storekeeper, First Class [*Navy rating*] AK1
Aviation Storekeeper, Master Chief [*Navy rating*] .... AKCM
Aviation Storekeeper, Second Class [*Navy rating*] AK2
Aviation Storekeeper, Senior Chief [*Navy rating*] .... AKCS
Aviation Storekeeper, Third Class [*Navy rating*] AK3
Aviation Structural Mechanic [*Navy rating*] .... AM
Aviation Structural Mechanic, Chief [*Navy rating*] .... AMC
Aviation Structural Mechanic, First Class [*Navy rating*] AM1
Aviation Structural Mechanic, Hydraulic Mechanic [*Navy rating*] .... AMH
Aviation Structural Mechanic, Hydraulics, Airman [*Navy rating*] .... AMHAN
Aviation Structural Mechanic, Hydraulics, Airman Apprentice [*Navy rating*] .... AMHAA
Aviation Structural Mechanic, Master Chief [*Navy rating*] .... AMCM
Aviation Structural Mechanic, Safety Equipment [*Navy rating*] .... AME
Aviation Structural Mechanic, Safety Equipment, Airman [*Navy rating*] .... AMEAN
Aviation Structural Mechanic, Safety Equipment, Airman Apprentice [*Navy rating*] .... AMEAA
Aviation Structural Mechanic, Second Class [*Navy rating*] AM2
Aviation Structural Mechanic, Senior Chief [*Navy rating*] .... AMCS
Aviation Structural Mechanic, Structures [*Navy rating*] .... AMS
Aviation Structural Mechanic, Structures, Airman [*Navy rating*] .... AMSAN
Aviation Structural Mechanic, Structures, Airman Apprentice [*Navy rating*] .... AMSAA
Aviation Structural Mechanic, Third Class [*Navy rating*] AM3
Aviation Supply Annex .... ASA
Aviation Supply Control Center .... ASCC
Aviation Supply Depot .... ASD
Aviation Supply Depot - Naval Supply Center .... ASD-NSC
Aviation Supply Office [*Air Force*] .... ASO
Aviation Supply Office/Inventory Control Point .... ASO/ICP
Aviation Supply Office Philadelphia [*Navy*] .... ASOP
Aviation Supply Ship [*Navy symbol*] .... AVS
Aviation Support, Electrical [*Navy rating*] .... ASE
Aviation Support Equipment Technician [*Navy rating*] .... AS
Aviation Support Equipment Technician, Chief [*Navy rating*] .... ASC
Aviation Support Equipment Technician, First Class [*Navy rating*] AS1
Aviation Support Equipment Technician, Master Chief [*Navy rating*] .... ASCM
Aviation Support Equipment Technician, Second Class [*Navy rating*] AS2
Aviation Support Equipment Technician, Senior Chief [*Navy rating*] .... ASCS
Aviation Support Equipment Technician, Third Class [*Navy rating*] AS3
Aviation Support, Hydraulic [*Navy rating*] .... ASH
Aviation Support Material and Equipment .... ASME
Aviation Support, Mechanical [*Navy rating*] .... ASM
Aviation and Surface Effects Department [*David W. Taylor Naval Ship Research and Development Center*] .... ASED
Aviation and Surface Material Command [*Air Force*] .... AVSCOM
Aviation Systems Command [*Army*] .... ASC
Aviation Systems Command [*Army*] .... AVSCOM
Aviation Systems Command [*Army*] .... AVSYCOM
Aviation Systems Laboratory .... ASL
Aviation Systems Test Activity [*Later, AEFA*] .... ASTA
Aviation Tactical Coordinator [*Navy*] .... ATACCO
Aviation Tactical Data System .... ATDS
Aviation Technical Training Center .... ATTC
Aviation Technician Education Council .... ATEC
Aviation Technician, Navigation .... ATN
Aviation Technician, RADAR .... ATR
Aviation Test Office [*Army*] .... ATO
Aviation Training Aids .... ATA
Aviation Training Record .... ATR
Aviation Turbine Fuel .... ATF
Aviation Unit [*Marine Corps*] .... AVNU
Aviation Unit Maintenance [*Army*] .... AVUM
Aviation Warrant Officer Career Course [*Army*] .... WOCAR
Aviation Weapons Movement Control System .... AWMCS
Aviation Weather Facility .... AWF
Aviation Weather and Notice to Airmen System .... AWANS
Aviation Weather Reporting Station .... AWRS
Aviation Weather Service [*of National Weather Service*] .... AWS
Aviation Week [*A publication*] .... Aviation W
Aviation Week [*A publication*] .... AW
Aviation Week and Space Technology [*A publication*] .... Aviat Week Space Technol
Aviation Week and Space Technology [*A publication*] .... Avia Week
Aviation Wide-Angle Visual System .... AWAVS
Aviator .... AVR
Aviator's Breathing Oxygen [*Air Force*] .... ABO
Aviator's Night Vision Imaging System .... ANVIS
Aviator's Oxygen Helmet .... AOH
Aviator's Protective Helmet .... APH
Aviatsiia Dalnego Deistviia [*Long-Range Aviation*] [*Strategic bombing force of USSR*] .... ADD
Aviatsionnaya Armiya [*Air Army*] [*USSR*] .... AA
Aviatsionnaya Diviziya [*Air Division*] [*USSR*] .... AD
Aviatsiya Voenno Morskogo Flota [*Aviation - Naval Fleet*] [*USSR*] .... AVMF
Avicultura Tecnica [*A publication*] .... Avicult Tec
Avicultural Magazine [*A publication*] .... Avic Mag
Avicultural Society of America .... ASA
Avicultural Society of America .... ASOA
Avidin-Biotin-Peroxidase [*Immunochemistry*] .... ABC
Avignon [*France*] [*Airport symbol*] .... AVN
Avila College, Kansas City, MO [*OCLC symbol*] .... HOO
Avila College, Kansas City, MO [*Library symbol*] .... MoKAv
Avino Mines & Resources [*NASDAQ symbol*] .... AVMRF
Avio Linee Italiane .... ALI
Aviogenex [*Yugoslavia*] [*ICAO designator*] .... JJ
Avioligure [*Italy*] [*ICAO designator*] .... ML
Avionic Integration Support Facility .... AISF
Avionic Observation of Intruder Danger Systems [*Army*] .... AVOIDS
Avionic System Integration Plan .... ASIP
Avionics .... AV
Avionics Automatic Transmission Line .... AATE
Avionics Bay .... AB
Avionics Bulletin .... AVB
Avionics Change .... AVC
Avionics, Control, and Information Systems .... ACIS
Avionics Cooling Loop .... ACL
Avionics Cooling Unit .... ACU
Avionics Depot Test Station .... ADTS
Avionics Development Lab [*Downey, CA*] [*NASA*] .... ADL
Avionics Engineering Center, Ohio University [*Athens, OH*] [*FAA designator*] .... FDT
Avionics Equipment Design Review .... AEDR
Avionics Integration Laboratories [*NASA*] .... AIL
Avionics Integration Plan [*NASA*] .... AIP
Avionics Interface Unit .... AIU

Avionics Intermediate Shop ... AIS
Avionics Laboratory [*Air Force*] ... AL
Avionics Laboratory Technical Information Handling Profile ... ALTIHP
Avionics Maintenance Conference ... AMC
Avionics Maintenance Shop ... AMS
Avionics Maintenance Squadron [*Air Force*] ... AMSq
Avionics Module Repair Improvement Program [*Navy*] ... AMRIP
Avionics Multiplex ... AMUX
Avionics Overall Test ... AOT
Avionics Requirements ... AR
Avionics Research and Development Activity [*Army*] ... AVRADA
Avionics Shop Maintenance ... ASM
Avionics Status Panel ... ASP
Avionics Subsystem Group [*NASA*] ... ASG
Avionics Subsystem Interface Unit ... ASSIU
Avionics Subsystem for Strategic Bombers ... ASSB
Avionics Subsystems Interface Contractor [*Air Force*] ... ASIC
Avionics System Project Officer ... ASPO
Avionics System Review ... ASR
Avionics Test Article ... ATA
Avis de Reception [*Return receipt*] ... AR
AVKO Educational Research Foundation ... AVKOERF
AVM Corporation [*NASDAQ symbol*] ... AVMC
Avnet, Inc. [*NYSE symbol*] ... AVT
Avoca Journal-Herald, Avoca, IA [*Library symbol*] ... IaAvJH
Avoca Public Library, Avoca, IA [*Library symbol*] ... IaAv
Avocado Growers Bargaining Council [*Formerly, AGC*] ... AGBC
Avocado Growers Council [*Later, AGBC*] ... AGC
Avogadro Constant [*Symbol*] [*IUPAC*] ... L
Avogadro Number [*Number of molecules in one gram-molecular weight of a substance*] ... N
Avoid Verbal Instructions ... AVI
Avoid Verbal Orders ... AVO
Avoidable Delay ... AD
Avoir [*Credit*] [*French*] ... AV
Avoirdupois ... AV
Avoirdupois ... AVDP
Avoirdupois ... AVDPS
Avoirdupois ... AVOIR
Avon [*Australia*] [*Seismograph station code, US Geological Survey*] ... AVO
Avon, CO [*Location identifier*] [*FAA*] ... VON
Avon Fantasy Reader [*A publication*] ... AFR
Avon Junior/Senior High School Library, Avon, NY [*OCLC symbol*] ... RVP
Avon Park, FL [*Location identifier*] [*FAA*] ... AGR
Avon Park, FL [*Radio station call letters*] ... WAPR
Avon Park, FL [*Radio station call letters*] ... WWOJ-FM
Avon Products, Inc. [*NYSE symbol*] ... AVP
Avon Products, Inc., Suffern, NY [*Library symbol*] ... NSufA
Avon Science Fiction Reader [*A publication*] ... ASFR
Avon Science Fiction Reader [*A publication*] ... ASR
Avondale Mills [*American Stock Exchange symbol*] ... AVD
Avoyelles Parish Library, Marksville, LA [*Library symbol*] ... LMarA
Avril Sur Loire [*France*] [*Seismograph station code, US Geological Survey*] ... AVF
AVSCOM [*Aviation Systems Command*] **Integrated Microfilm Systems** [*Army*] ... AIMS
Avtomat Kalashnikov [*Submachine Gun*] [*USSR*] ... AK
Avtomaticheskaya Svarka [*A publication*] ... Avtom Svarka
Avtomatika i Izcislitelna Tehnika [*A publication*] ... Avtomat i Izcisl Tehn
Avtomatika i Telemekhanika [*A publication*] ... Avtomat i Telemekh
Avtomatika i Telemekhanika [*A publication*] ... Avtom & Telemekh
Avtomatika i Telemekhanika [*A publication*] ... Avtom Telemekh
Avtomatika Telemekhanika Svyaz [*A publication*] ... Avtom Telemekh Svyaz
Avtomatika i Vychislitel'naya Tekhnika [*A publication*] ... Avtom & Vychisl Tekh
Avtomatika i Vycislitel'naja Tehnika (Riga) [*A publication*] ... Avtomat i Vycisl Tehn (Riga)
Avtomatizirovannye Sistemy Upravlenija i Pribory Avtomatiki [*A publication*] ... Avtomat Sistemy Upravlenija i Pribory Avtomat
Avu Avu [*Solomon Islands*] [*Airport symbol*] ... AVU
Avvenire Agricolo [*A publication*] ... Avven Agr
Avvocato ... AVV
AVX Corp. [*NYSE symbol*] ... AVX
AW Computer Systems Cl A [*NASDAQ symbol*] ... AWCSA
AWA [*Amalgamated Wireless Australasia*] **Technical Review** [*A publication*] ... AWA Tech Rev
Awadhi [*MARC language code*] [*Library of Congress*] ... awa
Await ... AWT
Awaiting Action Deck Court-Martial ... AADCM
Awaiting Action General Court-Martial ... AAGCM
Awaiting Action [*of*] **Higher Authority** [*Army*] ... AAHA
Awaiting Action Summary Court-Martial ... AASCM
Awaiting Aircraft Availability ... AAA
Awaiting Bad Conduct Discharge [*Military*] ... ABCD
Awaiting Combat Assignment ... ACA
Awaiting Delivery ... A/D
Awaiting Disciplinary Action This Command [*Army*] ... AWDISCOM
Awaiting Maintenance ... AM
Awaiting Maintenance ... AWM
Awaiting Office Hours ... AOH
Awaiting Overhaul ... AOH
Awaiting Parts ... AP
Awaiting Parts ... AWP
Awaiting Results of Trial [*Military*] ... ARTL
Awaiting Sentence [*of court-martial*] ... AWS
Awaiting Transportation ... AT
Awaiting Trial ... ATL
Awaiting Trial [*by court-martial*] ... AWT
Awamia Revue de la Recherche Agronomique Marocaine [*A publication*] ... Awamia Rev Rech Agron Maroc
Awana Youth Association ... AYA
Award ... AWD
Award of Contract ... AOC
Award Fee ... AF
Award Fee Evaluation Board [*NASA*] ... AFEB
Award Fee Evaluation Committee [*NASA*] ... AFEC
Awards for Cablecasting Excellence ... ACE
Awards, Honors, and Prizes [*A publication*] ... AHP
Awards in Nuclear Medicine and Radiopharmacology [*A publication*] ... Awards Nucl Med Radiopharmacol
Awareness ... AWRN
Awareness Center [*Defunct*] ... AC
Away without Authorization ... AWA
Away from Reactor [*Storage facilities*] ... AFR
Awkward Expression or Construction [*Used in correcting manuscripts, etc.*] ... AWK
Awning ... AWN
AXIA, Inc. [*NYSE symbol*] ... AX
Axial Centrifugal ... AC
Axial Flow ... AF
Axial Flow ... AXFL
Axial Flow Compressor ... AFC
Axial Flow Wheel ... AFW
Axial Pitch ... AXP
Axial Power Distribution Monitoring Systems [*Nuclear energy*] ... APDMS
Axial Power Shaping Rods [*Nuclear energy*] ... APSR
Axial Pressure Angle [*Gears*] ... APA
Axial Turbo Machine ... ATM
Axial Vector Dominance Model ... AVDM
Axial Velocity Ratio ... AVR
Axial Width ... AW
Axially Magnetized Plasma ... AMP
Axially Symmetric Nozzle ... ASN
Axilla, Shoulder, Elbow [*Bandage*] ... ASE
Axillary [*Medicine*] ... AX
Axio-Occlusal [*Dentistry*] ... AO
Axiobuccocervical [*Dentistry*] ... ABC
Axiobuccogingival [*Dentistry*] ... ABG
Axiobuccolingual [*Dentistry*] ... ABL
Axiocervical [*Dentistry*] ... AC
Axiodistal [*Dentistry*] ... AD
Axiodisto-Occlusal [*Dentistry*] ... ADO
Axiodistocervical [*Dentistry*] ... ADC
Axiodistogingival [*Dentistry*] ... ADG
Axiodistoincisal [*Dentistry*] ... ADI
Axiogingival [*Dentistry*] ... AG
Axioincisal [*Dentistry*] ... AI
Axiolabial [*Dentistry*] ... ALa
Axiolabiogingival [*Dentistry*] ... ALaG
Axiolabiolingual [*Dentistry*] ... ALaL
Axiolingual [*Dentistry*] ... AL
Axiolinguo-Occlusal [*Dentistry*] ... ALO
Axiolinguocervical [*Dentistry*] ... ALC
Axiolinguogingival [*Dentistry*] ... ALG
Axiom ... AX
Axiom of Choice [*Logic*] ... AC
Axiomesial [*Dentistry*] ... AM
Axiomesio-Occlusal [*Dentistry*] ... AMO
Axiomesiocervical [*Dentistry*] ... AMC
Axiomesiodistal [*Dentistry*] ... AMD
Axiomesiogingival [*Dentistry*] ... AMG
Axiomesioincisal [*Dentistry*] ... AMI
Axiopulpal [*Dentistry*] ... AP
Axis ... AX
Axis Crossing Interval Meter [*SONAR*] ... ACIM
Axis [*or Axes*] **of Signal Communication** ... AXSIGCOMM
Axisymmetric Blunt Body ... ABB
Axisymmetric Jet Stretcher ... AJS
Axisymmetrical Conical Flow ... ACF
Axisymmetrical Flow Field ... AFF
Axon Cylinder Membrane ... ACM
Axum [*Ethiopia*] [*Airport symbol*] ... AXU
Ayacucho [*Peru*] [*Airport symbol*] ... AYP
Ayagualo [*El Salvador*] [*Seismograph station code, US Geological Survey*] [*Closed*] ... AYA
Aydin Corp. [*NYSE symbol*] ... AYD
Ayenquera [*Peru*] [*Seismograph station code, US Geological Survey*] ... AYE
Ayer Information Center [*N. W. Ayer, Inc.*] [*Information service*] ... AIC
Ayer Public Library, Delavan, IL [*OCLC symbol*] ... ISG
Ayers Rock [*Australia*] [*Airport symbol*] ... AYQ
Ayerst Laboratories [*Research code symbol*] ... AY

Ayerst, McKenna, & Harrison Ltd., Montreal, PQ, Canada [*Library symbol*]...CaQMAy
Ayerst Science Laboratory, Rouses Point, NY [*Library symbol*]...........NRpA
Aylesford Review [*A publication*]...AYLR
Aymara [*MARC language code*] [*Library of Congress*].............................aym
Ayn Rand Memorial Library Association ....ARMLA
Ayres Space Test [*Psychology*]...AST
Ayrshire [*County in Scotland*]...AYRS
Ayrshire Breeders' Association ....ABA
Az Egri Muzeum Evkoenyve [*A publication*] ....Egri Muz Ev
Aza [*As substituent on nucleoside*] [*Biochemistry*]....................................z
Azacycloheptane Diphosphonate [*Organic chemistry*]....................AHDP
Azacytidine [*or Azacitidine*] [*Also, Aza-C*] [*Antineoplastic drug*]..............AZA
Azacytidine [*or Azacitidine*] [*Also, AZA*] [*Antineoplastic drug*]............Aza-C
Azad Hind Fauj [*Indian National Army*]..AHF
Azalea Society of America..ASA
Aza(methyl)pregnanedione [*Biochemistry*]....................................AMPD
Azania Liberation Front ....ALF
Azathioprine [*Immunosuppressive drug*]...AZ
Azerbaidzhanskii Meditsinskii Zhurnal [*A publication*] ....
                                         Azerbaidzhan Med Zhurnal
Azerbaidzhanskii Meditsinskii Zhurnal [*A publication*] ....Azerb Med Zh
Azerbaijan Soviet Socialist Republic [*MARC country of publication code*] [*Library of Congress*].....................................ajr
Azerbaijan Soviet Socialist Republic [*MARC geographic area code*] [*Library of Congress*].......................................e-ur-aj
Azerbaijani [*MARC language code*] [*Library of Congress*].........................aze
Azerbajdzhanskij Khimicheskij Zhurnal [*A publication*]..........Azerb Khim Zh
Azerbajdzhanskoe Neftyanoe Khozyajstvo [*A publication*]......................
                                          Azerb Neft Khoz
Azerbaydzhani Soviet Socialist Republic..............................AzerSSR
Azia Keizai Kenkyujo [*Institute for Developing Economies*], Tokyo, Japan [*Library symbol*]..JTA
Azienda Generale Italiana Petroli [*Italian petroleum enterprise*]..............AGIP
Azienda de Stato per i Servizi Telefonici [*Italy*] ....ASST
Azimuth..AZ
Azimuth ....AZM
Azimuth Alignment System [*Aerospace*]..AAS
Azimuth Versus Amplitude..AVA
Azimuth Angle..Z
Azimuth Angle Increment..AAI
Azimuth Change Pulse...ACP
Azimuth Comparator ....AC
Azimuth Control Amplifier ....ACA
Azimuth Control System ....ACS
Azimuth Control Torquer ....ACT
Azimuth and Elevation...A & E
Azimuth-Elevation...AZEL
Azimuth Elevation Range ....AER
Azimuth Error Indicator..AEI
Azimuth Error Test Feature ....AETF
Azimuth Follow-Up Amplifier...AFA

Azimuth Follow-Up System...AFS
Azimuth Guidance Nose in Stands ....AGNIS
Azimuth Indicator ....AI
Azimuth Laying Set...ALS
Azimuth Mark Pulse Amplifier ....AMPA
Azimuth Only...AZON
Azimuth Orientation System [*Military*]...AOS
Azimuth Orientation Unit [*Military*]...AOU
Azimuth Pulse Generator ....APG
Azimuth Quantized Gated Video [*Air Force*]...................................AQGV
Azimuth/Range...A/R
Azimuth and Range...AZRAN
Azimuth Range and Timing Group...ARTG
Azimuth Reference Pulse [*Aviation*]..ARP
Azimuth Servo Assembly ....ASA
Azimuth, Speed, Altitude ....AZUSA
Azimuth Speed Indicator...ASI
Azimuth-Stabilized Plan Position Indicator ....ASPPI
Azimuth Steering Line...ASL
Azimuth Torquer Amplifier..ATA
Azimuthal Quantum Number...AQN
Azimuthal Quantum Number [*or Orbital Angular Momentum Quantum Number*] [*Symbol*]...I
Azimuthal Quantum Number [*or Orbital Angular Momentum Quantum Number*] - **Total** [*Symbol*]....................................L
Azimuthally Varying Field..AVF
Azione Cattolica Italiana...ACI
Azione Dynamico-Specifico [*Dynamic-Specific Action*] [*Medicine*].........ADS
AZL Resources, Inc. [*Formerly, Arizona-Colorado Land & Cattle Co.*] [*American Stock Exchange symbol*] [*Delisted*]...........................AZL
Azobenzenearsonate [*Organic chemistry*] ....ARS
Azobisformamide [*Organic chemistry*]..ABFA
Azobisisobutyronitrile [*Organic chemistry*] ....AIBN
Azores Fixed Acoustic Range [*NATO*]..AFAR
Azores Islands [*MARC geographic area code*] [*Library of Congress*]....lnaz---
Azote [*Nitrogen*] [*French*]...AZ
Aztec Manufacturing [*NASDAQ symbol*] ....AZTC
Aztec, NM [*Radio station call letters*]..KKBK
Aztec, NM [*Radio station call letters*]...KWYK
Aztec Oil & Gas Co. [*NYSE symbol*] [*Delisted*] ....AOG
Aztec Resources Corporation [*NASDAQ symbol*]...........................AZCO
Aztec Ruins National Monument ....AZRU
Aztech International Ltd. [*NASDAQ symbol*] ....AZIN
Azure [*Heraldry*] ....AZ
Azusa Ground Station ....AZGS
Azusa Pacific College, Azusa, CA [*OCLC symbol*] ....CAP
Azusa Pacific College, Azusa, CA [*Library symbol*].......................CAzPC
Azusa Public Library, Azusa, CA [*Library symbol*] ....CAz
Azusa Transponder...AZT
Azusa Transponder B-1 ....AZTB1
Azusa Transponder B-2 ....AZTB2
Azusa Transponder Coherent ....AZTC

B

B and Better [Lumber] .... BB
B-Cell Chronic Lymphocytic Leukemia [Medicine] .... B-CLL
B-Cell Growth Factor [Immunochemistry] .... BCGF
B-Cell Leukemia [Medicine] .... B-ALL
B. F. Goodrich Chemical Co. [of B. F. Goodrich Co.],
   Development Center Library, Avon Lake, OH [Library symbol] ...... OAvG
B. F. Goodrich Co. .... BFG
B. F. Goodrich Co., Akron, OH [Library symbol] .... OAkGr
B. F. Goodrich Co., Information Center, Brecksville, OH [OCLC
   symbol] .... OGR
B. F. Goodrich Co., Technical Library, Brecksville, OH [Library
   symbol] .... OBrG
B. F. Goodrich Institute for Personnel Development .... GIPD
B. F. Jones Memorial Library, Aliquippa, PA [OCLC symbol] .... BFJ
B. F. Jones Memorial Library, Aliquippa, PA [Library symbol] .... PA
Ba [Fiji] [Airport symbol] .... BFJ
BA [Bansilal Amritlal] College of Agriculture Magazine [India] [A
   publication] .... BA Coll Agric Mag
Baader-Meinhof Group [Revolutionary group] [West Germany] .... BMG
[The] Babbage Society .... BABS
Babbing [Fishing for eels] .... BAB
Babbitt [Metallurgy] .... BAB
Babbitt [B. T.], Inc. [NYSE symbol] [Delisted] .... BAB
Babbitt Metal [Freight] .... BAB MTL
Babcock Test of Mental Efficiency [Psychology] .... BTME
Babcock & Wilcox Co. [NYSE symbol] .... BAW
Babcock & Wilcox Co. .... B & W
Babcock & Wilcox Co., Alliance, OH [Library symbol] .... OAIB
Babcock & Wilcox Co., Lynchburg, VA [Library symbol] .... ViLBW
Babcock and Wilcox Test Reactor .... BAWTR
Babcock and Wilcox Test Reactor .... BWTR
Babe Ruth Baseball [An association] .... BRB
Babe Ruth League .... BRL
Babel. International Journal of Translation [Budapest] [A publication] ...... Ba
Babel. Journal of the Australian Federation of Modern Language
   Teachers Association [Darlinghurst, New South Wales] [A
   publication] .... Bab J A
Babinet Absorption Rule .... BAR
Babinet Jamin Compensator .... BJC
Babinski [Reflex] [Medicine] .... BAB
Babo [Indonesia] [Airport symbol] .... BXB
Baboon Endogenous Virus .... BEV
Babson College, Babson Park, MA [OCLC symbol] .... BAB
Babson College, Babson Park, MA [Library symbol] .... MBBI
Babson Institute of Business Administration [Massachusetts] .... BIBA
Baby Born Dead [Medicine] .... BBD
Baby Brother Tender Love [Doll manufactured by Mattel, Inc.] .... BBTL
Baby or Doll [Freight] .... BB DL
Baby Hamster Kidney .... BHK
Baby Incendiary Bomb .... B/B
Baby Incendiary Bomb .... BIB
Baby "N" Connector .... BNC
Babylon, NY [Radio station call letters] .... WBAB-FM
Babylon, NY [Radio station call letters] .... WGLI
Babylon, NY [Radio station call letters] .... WNYG
Babylon Public Library, Babylon, NY [Library symbol] .... NBab
Bac-Giang [Vietnam] [Seismograph station code, US Geological
   Survey] .... BGV
Baca County Public Library, Springfield, CO [Library symbol] .... CoSp
Bacardi Corp. CI A [NASDAQ symbol] .... BACAA
Bacau [Romania] [Seismograph station code, US Geological Survey] ...... BAC
Bacau [Romania] [Airport symbol] .... BCM
Baccalaureate .... B
Baccalaureate .... BACC
Baccalaureate Exam [France] .... BAC
Baccalaureus .... BAC
Baccalaureus in Arte Ingeniaria [Bachelor of Engineering] .... BAI
Baccalaureus Artium [Bachelor of Arts] [Latin] .... BA
Baccalaureus Chirurgiae [Bachelor of Surgery] .... BC
Baccalaureus Chirurgiae [Bachelor of Surgery] .... B Ch

Baccalaureus Chirurgiae [Bachelor of Surgery] .... B Chir
Baccalaureus Chirurgiae Dentium [Bachelor of Dental Surgery] .... B Ch D
Baccalaureus Literarum [Bachelor of Literature] .... LB
Baccalaureus Medicinae, Chirurgiae Magister [Bachelor of
   Medicine, Master of Surgery] .... MBCM
Baccalaureus Scientiae [Bachelor of Science] [Latin] .... B Sc
Baccalaureus Scientiae Didacticae [Bachelor of Didactic Science] .... BSD
Baccalaureus Utriusque Juris [Bachelor of Both Laws; i.e., Canon
   and Civil Laws] .... BUJ
[Johann Sebastian] Bach, [Ludwig van] Beethoven, and
   [Johannes] Brahms [Classical composers] .... 3B's
[Johann Sebastian] Bach, [Ludwig van] Beethoven, and
   [Johannes] Brahms [Classical composers] .... BBB
Bach Jahrbuch [A publication] .... B JB
Bachad Organization of North America .... BONA
Bache Group, Inc. [Formerly, Bache & Co.] [NYSE symbol] [Delisted] ..... BAC
Bachelier des Arts [Bachelor of Arts] .... B des A
Bachelier en Arts Visuels [Bachelor of Visual Arts] .... BAV
Bachelier en Droit [Bachelor of Laws] .... B en Dr
Bachelier en Droit Canonique [Bachelor of Canon Law] .... BDC
Bachelier des Lettres [Bachelor of Letters] .... B des L
Bachelier des Sciences [Bachelor of Science] .... B des S
Bachelier en Sciences Administratives [Bachelor in
   Administrative Sciences] .... BSA
Bachelier es Sciences Appliquees [Bachelor of Applied Science] .... BScA
Bachelier en Service Social [Bachelor of Social Work] .... BSerSoc
Bachelor .... B
Bachelor .... BACH
Bachelor .... BACHR
Bachelor of Accountancy .... B Acc
Bachelor of Accounts .... B Ac
Bachelor of Accounts .... B Acc's
Bachelor of Administration .... B Adm
Bachelor of Administration .... BAdmin
Bachelor of Administrative Engineering .... B Adm Eng
Bachelor of Advertising Arts and Design ....B of Adv Art & Des
Bachelor of Aeronautical Administration .... B of AA
Bachelor of Aeronautical Engineering .... B of AE
Bachelor of Aeronautical Engineering .... BAE
Bachelor of Aeronautical Engineering .... B Ae E
Bachelor of Aeronautical Engineering .... B Ae Eng
Bachelor of Aeronautical Engineering .... B Aero E
Bachelor of Aeronautical Science .... B Ae S
Bachelor of Aeronautical Science .... B Ae Sc
Bachelor of Aeronautics .... B Ae
Bachelor of Agricultural Engineering .... BAE
Bachelor of Agricultural Engineering .... B Ag E
Bachelor of Agricultural Engineering .... B Agr E
Bachelor of Agricultural Engineering .... B Eng A
Bachelor of Agricultural Science .... B Agr S
Bachelor of Agricultural Science .... B Agr Sc
Bachelor of Agricultural Science .... BAS
Bachelor of Agricultural Science .... BA Sc
Bachelor of Agriculture .... BA
Bachelor of Agriculture .... B Ag
Bachelor of Agriculture .... B Agr
Bachelor of Agriculture .... BAgri
Bachelor of Air Conditioning Engineering .... BACE
Bachelor of Air Conditioning Engineering .... BAC Eng
Bachelor Airmen's Quarters [Air Force] .... BAQ
Bachelor of Applied Arts .... BAA
Bachelor of Applied Chemistry .... BA Chem
Bachelor of Applied Mathematics .... BAM
Bachelor of Applied Music .... BMusA
Bachelor of Applied Science .... B Applied Sc
Bachelor of Applied Science .... BAS
Bachelor of Applied Science .... BA Sc
Bachelor of Architectural Design .... B Arch Des
Bachelor of Architectural Engineering .... BAE
Bachelor of Architectural Engineering .... B Arc E

Bachelor of Architectural Engineering	B Arch Eng
Bachelor of Architectural Engineering	B Ar E
Bachelor of Architectural History	BArchHist
Bachelor of Architectural Science	BAS
Bachelor of Architectural Technology	BArchTech
Bachelor of Architecture	B Ar
Bachelor of Architecture	B Arch
Bachelor of Architecture in Architectural Engineering	B Arch (ArchE)
Bachelor of Architecture in Architecture	B Arch (Arch)
Bachelor of Architecture in City Planning	B Arch in City Pl
Bachelor of Art Education	BAE
Bachelor of Art Education	BA Ed
Bachelor of the Art of Obstetrics	BAO
Bachelor of Art of Oratory	BAO
Bachelor of Arts	BA
Bachelor of Arts [A publication]	Bach of Arts
Bachelor of Arts in Arts and Sciences	BA in A & Sci
Bachelor of Arts in Bible	AB (Bible)
Bachelor of Arts in Business Administration	BA in BA
Bachelor of Arts in Business and Economics	BA in B & E
Bachelor of Arts in Ceramic Art	BA in Cer A
Bachelor of Arts in Chemical Engineering	AB in Ch E
Bachelor of Arts in Civil Engineering	AB in CE
Bachelor of Arts - Classical	BA Class
Bachelor of Arts (Economics)	BA (Econ)
Bachelor of Arts in Economics and Business	BA in E & B
Bachelor of Arts in Education	AB Ed
Bachelor of Arts in Education	BAE
Bachelor of Arts in Education	BA Ed
Bachelor of Arts (Education)	BA(Educ)
Bachelor of Arts in Electrical Engineering	AB in EE
Bachelor of Arts in Elementary Education	BA in E Ed
Bachelor of Arts in General Studies	BAGS
Bachelor of Arts in Home Economics	AB in H Ec
Bachelor of Arts in Human Relations	BAH Re
Bachelor of Arts in Journalism	AB in J
Bachelor of Arts in Journalism	BA in J
Bachelor of Arts in Journalism	BAJ
Bachelor of Arts in Law	BA(Law)
Bachelor of Arts in Library Science	ABLS
Bachelor of Arts, Master of Science	BASM
Bachelor of Arts in Mechanical Engineering	AB in ME
Bachelor of Arts in Mechanical Engineering	ABME
Bachelor of Arts in Music	BAM
Bachelor of Arts (Music)	BA (Mus)
Bachelor of Arts in Music Education	BA in M Ed
Bachelor of Arts - Non-Classical	BA Non-Class
Bachelor of Arts in Practical Christian Training	BAPCT
Bachelor of Arts in Religious Education	BA in Rel Ed
Bachelor of Arts with Religious Major	AB (Rel)
Bachelor of Arts and Sciences	B Ar Sc
Bachelor of Arts and Sciences	BAS
Bachelor of Arts in Secondary Education	AB in Sec Ed
Bachelor of Arts in Speech	BAS
Bachelor of Arts in Speech	BA in Sp
Bachelor of Arts in Teaching	BAT
Bachelor of Arts in Theology	AB in TH
Bachelor of Arts in Theology	BA Theo
Bachelor of Association Science	B As S
Bachelor of Association Science	B As Sc
Bachelor of Automobile Engineering	B Au E
Bachelor of Automobile Engineering	B Au Eng
Bachelor of Ayurvedic Medicine	BAM
Bachelor of Bacteriology	BB
Bachelor of Bacteriology	B Bac
Bachelor of Beauty Culture	BBC
Bachelor of Biblical Arts	B Bib Arts
Bachelor of Biological Chemistry	B Bi Ch
Bachelor of Biological Chemistry	B Bi Chem
Bachelor of Biological Engineering	B Bi E
Bachelor of Biological Engineering	B Bi Eng
Bachelor of Biological Physics	B Bi Phy
Bachelor of Biological Sciences	B Bi S
Bachelor of Biological Sciences	B Bi Sc
Bachelor of Building Construction	B of BC
Bachelor of Building Construction	BBC
Bachelor of Business Administration	BBA
Bachelor of Business Administration	BB Ad
Bachelor of Business Administration	BB Adm
Bachelor of Business Education	BB Ed
Bachelor of Business Management	BBM
Bachelor of Business Science	BBS
Bachelor of Business Science	BB Sc
Bachelor of Business Studies	BBS
Bachelor of Canon Law	B Can L
Bachelor of Canon Law	BCL
Bachelor of Cement Engineering	B Ce Eng
Bachelor of Ceramic Engineering	B Cer E
Bachelor of Ceramic Engineering	B Cer Eng
Bachelor of Chemical Engineering	BCE
Bachelor of Chemical Engineering	B Ch E
Bachelor of Chemical Engineering	B Chem E
Bachelor of Chemical Engineering	B Ch Eng
Bachelor of Chemical Science	BCS
Bachelor of Chemistry	BC
Bachelor of Chemistry	B Ch
Bachelor of Chemistry	B Chem
Bachelor of Chemistry	Ch B
Bachelor of Christian Education	BCE
Bachelor of Christian Education	B Chr Ed
Bachelor of Christian Science	BSC
Bachelor of Christian Science	CSB
Bachelor of Christian Training	BCT
Bachelor of Chromatics	BChrom
Bachelor of Church Music	BCM
Bachelor of City Forestry	BCF
Bachelor of City Planning	BCP
Bachelor of Civil Engineering	BCE
Bachelor of Civil Law	BCL
Bachelor of Civil Law	CLB
Bachelor of Classics	BC
Bachelor of College Studies	BCS
Bachelor of Commerce	BC
Bachelor of Commerce	B Com
Bachelor of Commerce	B Comm
Bachelor of Commercial Administration	B Com Adm
Bachelor of Commercial Arts	BCA
Bachelor of Commercial Education	BC Ed
Bachelor of Commercial Law	BCL
Bachelor of Commercial Science	BComSc
Bachelor of Commercial Science	BCS
Bachelor of Commercial Science	BC Sc
Bachelor of Commercial Science	BScCom
Bachelor of Commercial Service	BC Se
Bachelor of Computer Science	BCS
Bachelor of Creative Arts	BCA
Bachelor of Criminology	B Cr
Bachelor in Dental Science [British]	BDentSc
Bachelor of Dental Science	BD Sc
Bachelor of Dental Surgery	BDS
Bachelor of Design	B Des
Bachelor of Design in Art Education	B Des A Ed
Bachelor of Didactics	BDi
Bachelor of Didactics	B Did
Bachelor of Diesel Engineering	B Di E
Bachelor of Diesel Engineering	B Di Eng
Bachelor of Diplomacy	B Dipl
Bachelor of Divine Literature	BDL
Bachelor of Divinity	BD
Bachelor of Divinity	DB
Bachelor of Divinity in Education	BD in E
Bachelor of Domestic Arts	ADB
Bachelor of Domestic Arts	BDA
Bachelor of Dramatic Art	BDA
Bachelor of Dramatic Art	B Dr Art
Bachelor of Economics	B Ec
Bachelor of Economics	BEcon
Bachelor of Education	BE
Bachelor of Education	B Ed
Bachelor of Education	Ed B
Bachelor of Educational Studies	BEdStud
Bachelor of Electrical Engineering	BEE
Bachelor of Electrical Engineering	BEngE
Bachelor of Electrical Engineering, Communication Option	B of EE (Com Opt)
Bachelor of Electrical Engineering, Power Option	B of EE (Power Opt)
Bachelor of Electro-Chemical Engineering	BECE
Bachelor of Elements	B Ele
Bachelor of Elocution	BE
Bachelor of Elocution	B El
Bachelor of Engineering	BE
Bachelor of Engineering	BEn
Bachelor of Engineering	B Eng
Bachelor of Engineering (Agriculture)	BE(Ag)
Bachelor of Engineering Construction	BEC
Bachelor of Engineering in Mechanical Engineering	BE-ME
Bachelor of Engineering of Mines	BEM
Bachelor of Engineering Physics	B of EP
Bachelor of Engineering Physics	BEP
Bachelor of Engineering Physics	BE Phy
Bachelor of Engineering Science	BESc
Bachelor of Engineering Sciences	BES
Bachelor of Engineering (Technology)	B Eng (Tech)
Bachelor of Engineering Technology	BET
Bachelor of English	BE
Bachelor of English	B En
Bachelor of English Divinity	BED
Bachelor of English Literature	BEL
Bachelor of English Literature	ELB
Bachelor Enlisted Quarters	BEQ
Bachelor of Entomology	B Ent
Bachelor of Environmental Studies	BES

Bachelor of Expression	BE
Bachelor of Expression	B Ex
Bachelor of Family Life	BFL
Bachelor of Finance	BF
Bachelor of Fine Arts	BFA
Bachelor of Fine Arts in Dramatic Art	BFA in DA
Bachelor of Fine Arts in Education	BFA in Ed
Bachelor of Fine Arts in Landscape Architecture	BFALA
Bachelor of Fine Arts in Music	BFA in Mus
Bachelor of Fine Arts in Painting and Sculpture	BFA in PS
Bachelor of Fine Arts in Speech	BFA in Sp
Bachelor of Fisheries Science	BFSc
Bachelor of Foreign Service	BFS
Bachelor of Foreign Trade	BFT
Bachelor of Forest Engineering	BFE
Bachelor of Forest Engineering	BF Eng
Bachelor of Forestry	BF
Bachelor of General Education	B Gen Ed
Bachelor of General Studies	BGS
Bachelor of Geological Engineering	BGE
Bachelor of Geological Engineering	B Ge E
Bachelor of Geological Engineering	B Ge Eng
Bachelor of Hamburgerology [McDonald's Corp. Hamburger University]	BH
Bachelor of Health Science	BHS
Bachelor of Hebrew	BH
Bachelor of Hebrew Letters	BHL
Bachelor of Hebrew Literature	BHL
Bachelor of Home Economics	BH Ec
Bachelor of Home Science	BHS
Bachelor of Horticultural Science	BHortSc
Bachelor of Horticulture	B Hor
Bachelor of Horticulture	BHort
Bachelor of Hospital Administration	BHA
Bachelor of Hospital Administration	BH Adm
Bachelor of Household Economics	BHE
Bachelor of Household Economy	B Ho Ec
Bachelor of Household Science	B Ho Sc
Bachelor of Household Science	BHSc
Bachelor of Humane Letters	BHL
Bachelor of Humane Letters [or Bachelor of Literature or Bachelor of the More Humane Letters]	LHB
Bachelor of Humanics	BH
Bachelor of Humanities	B Hu
Bachelor of Hygiene	B Hy
Bachelor of Hygiene	B HYG
Bachelor of Industrial Arts	BIA
Bachelor of Industrial Design	BID
Bachelor of Industrial Education	B Ind Ed
Bachelor of Industrial Engineering	BIE
Bachelor of Industrial Engineering	BI Eng
Bachelor of Industrial Engineering	B Ind E
Bachelor of Industrial Management	B of IM
Bachelor of Industrial Management	BIM
Bachelor of Industrial Management	B Ind Mgt
Bachelor of Industrial Technology	BIndTech
Bachelor of Industrial Technology	BIT
Bachelor of Industry	B Ind
Bachelor of Interdisciplinary Studies	BIS
Bachelor of Interior Architectural Engineering	BI Arch E
Bachelor of Interior Architectural Engineering	BI Arch Eng
Bachelor of Interior Architecture	BI Arch
Bachelor in Interior Architecture	BIntArch
Bachelor of Interior Design	B of ID
Bachelor in Interior Design	BIntDesign
Bachelor of International Law	B Int L
Bachelor of Irrigation Engineering	B Ir E
Bachelor of Irrigation Engineering	B Ir Eng
Bachelor of Jewish Education	BJ Ed
Bachelor of Jewish Pedagogy	BJP
Bachelor of Journalism	BJ
Bachelor of Judicial Science	JSB
Bachelor of Jurisprudence	B Jur
Bachelor of Jurisprudence	BJuris
Bachelor of Landscape Architecture	BLA
Bachelor in Landscape Architecture	BLandArch
Bachelor of Landscape Architecture	BL Arch
Bachelor of Landscape Design	BL Des
Bachelor of Landscape Engineering	BL Eng
Bachelor of Landscape Management	BLM
Bachelor of Latin Letters	B La L
Bachelor of Latin Letters	BLL
Bachelor of Law	LLB
Bachelor of Laws	BL
Bachelor of Laws	BLL
Bachelor of Letters	BL
Bachelor of Letters	B Lit
Bachelor of Letters	B Litt
Bachelor of Letters in Journalism	BLJ
Bachelor of Liberal Arts	BLA
Bachelor of Liberal Studies	BLS

Bachelor of Library Economics	BLE
Bachelor of Library Economics	BL Ec
Bachelor of Library and Information Studies	BLS
Bachelor of Library Science	BLS
Bachelor of Library Science	BL Sc
Bachelor of Life Science	LSB
Bachelor of Literary Interpretation	BLI
Bachelor of Literature	BL
Bachelor of Literature	B Lit
Bachelor of Literature	B Litt
Bachelor of Literature	B Lt
Bachelor of Literature	Lt B
Bachelor of Management Engineering	B Mgt E
Bachelor of Marine Engineering	B Ma E
Bachelor of Marine Engineering	B Ma Eng
Bachelor of Marine Engineering	B Mar E
Bachelor of Marine Science	BMS
Bachelor of Mathematics	BM
Bachelor of Mathematics	BMath
Bachelor of Mechanic Arts	AMB
Bachelor of Mechanical Engineering	BME
Bachelor of Mechanical Engineering	B Mech E
Bachelor of Mechanical Engineering	BM Eng
Bachelor of Mechanical Engineering (Aeronautical Option)	BME (Aero Option)
Bachelor of Mechanical Science	BMS
Bachelor of Mechanical Science	BM Sc
Bachelor of Mechanical Sciences	B Ms Sc
Bachelor of Medical Biology	B Med Biol
Bachelor of Medical Laboratory Science	BMedLabSc
Bachelor of Medical Science	BMS
Bachelor of Medical Sciences	B Med Sc
Bachelor of Medical Sciences	B Med Sci
Bachelor of Medical Technology	BMT
Bachelor of Medicine	BM
Bachelor of Medicine	B Med
Bachelor of Metallurgical Engineering	B Metal E
Bachelor of Metallurgical Engineering	B Met E
Bachelor of Metallurgical Engineering	B Met Eng
Bachelor of Metallurgy	B Met
Bachelor of Metaphysics	Me B
Bachelor of Microbiology	B Mic
Bachelor of Mining Engineering	BEM
Bachelor of Mining Engineering	BME
Bachelor of Mining Engineering	B Mi E
Bachelor of Mining Engineering	B Mi Eng
Bachelor of Mining and Metallurgy	BMM
Bachelor of Ministry	BMin
Bachelor of Modern Languages	BML
Bachelor of Municipal Administration	BMA
Bachelor of Music	BM
Bachelor of Music	B Mu
Bachelor of Music	B Mus
Bachelor of Music Education	BME
Bachelor of Music in Education	BME
Bachelor of Music Education	BM Ed
Bachelor of Music Education	B Mus E
Bachelor of Music in Education	B Mus Ed
Bachelor of Music Education	Mus Ed B
Bachelor of Music in Public School Music	B Mus (PSM)
Bachelor of Naval Architecture	BN Arch
Bachelor of Naval Engineering	BNE
Bachelor of Naval Engineering	BN Eng
Bachelor of Naval Science	BNS
Bachelor of Navigation	B Na
Bachelor Noncommissioned Officers' Quarters [Air Force]	BNCOQ
Bachelor of Nursing	BN
Bachelor of Nursing Education	BN Ed
Bachelor of Nursing Science	BNS
Bachelor of Nursing Science	BN Sc
Bachelor of Occupational Therapy	BOT
Bachelor Officers' Quarters [Army]	BOQ
Bachelor of Optometry	B Opt
Bachelor of Oral English	BOE
Bachelor of Oratory	BO
Bachelor of Oratory	B Or
Bachelor of Oriental Language	BOL
Bachelor of Oriental Studies	B Orient
Bachelor of Osteopathy	BO
Bachelor of Painting	BP
Bachelor of Painting	B Pa
Bachelor of Patent Law	BPL
Bachelor of Pedagogy	BP
Bachelor of Pedagogy	BPaed
Bachelor of Pedagogy [or Pedagogics]	B Pd
Bachelor of Pedagogy	B Pe
Bachelor of Pedagogy [or Pedagogics]	B Ped
Bachelor of Pedagogy	B Py
Bachelor of Pedagogy	Pd B
Bachelor of Pedagogy	Ped B
Bachelor of Pedagogy	Pg B

Bachelor of Pedagogy ... Py B
Bachelor of Pediatrics ... Pe B
Bachelor of Performing Arts ... BPerfArts
Bachelor of Petroleum Engineering ... B Pe E
Bachelor of Petroleum Engineering ... B Pe Eng
Bachelor of Petroleum Engineering ... B Pet E
Bachelor of Pharmaceutical Chemistry ... B Ph C
Bachelor of Pharmacy ... BP
Bachelor of Pharmacy ... B Pharm
Bachelor of Pharmacy ... Phar B
Bachelor of Pharmacy ... Ph B
Bachelor of Pharmacy ... Phm B
Bachelor of Philosophy ... BP
Bachelor of Philosophy ... B Ph
Bachelor of Philosophy ... B Phil
Bachelor of Philosophy ... PB
Bachelor of Philosophy ... Ph B
Bachelor of Philosophy in Architecture ... Ph B in Arch
Bachelor of Philosophy in Commerce ... Ph B in Com
Bachelor of Philosophy in Education ... Ph B in Ed
Bachelor of Photography ... B Pho
Bachelor of Physic ... BM
Bachelor of Physical Biology ... BPB
Bachelor of Physical Culture ... Ph B
Bachelor of Physical Education ... BPE
Bachelor of Physical Education ... BP Ed
Bachelor of Physical and Health Education ... BPHE
Bachelor of Physical Health Education ... BPhysHlthEd
Bachelor of Physical Science ... B Ph S
Bachelor of Physical Therapy ... BPT
Bachelor of Physics ... B Phy
Bachelor of Political Science ... B Pol Sc
Bachelor of Practical Theology ... P Th B
Bachelor of Professional Arts ... BPA
Bachelor of Professional Studies ... BPS
Bachelor of Psychic Sciences ... B Ps Sc
Bachelor of Psychology ... B Ps
Bachelor of Psychology ... BPsych
Bachelor of Psychotherapy ... B Ps Th
Bachelor of Public Administration ... BPA
Bachelor of Public Administration ... BP Adm
Bachelor of Public Health ... BPH
Bachelor of Public Health Education ... BPH Ed
Bachelor of Public Health Engineering ... BPHE
Bachelor of Public Health Engineering ... BPH Eng
Bachelor of Public Health Nursing ... BPHN
Bachelor of Public School Art ... BPSA
Bachelor of Public School Music ... BPSM
Bachelor of Radio Engineering ... B Ra E
Bachelor of Radio Engineering ... B Ra Eng
Bachelor of Radio and Television Engineering ... BRTE
Bachelor of Radio and Television Engineering ... BRT Eng
Bachelor of Refrigeration Engineering ... B Re E
Bachelor of Refrigeration Engineering ... B Re Eng
Bachelor of Religion ... B Re
Bachelor of Religious Education ... BRE
Bachelor of Religious Education ... BR Ed
Bachelor of Rural Engineering ... BRuE
Bachelor of Rural Engineering ... B Ru Eng
Bachelor of Sacred Literature ... BSL
Bachelor of Sacred Music ... BSM
Bachelor of Sacred Music ... BS Mu
Bachelor of Sacred Music ... BS Mus
Bachelor of Sacred Music ... SMB
Bachelor of Sacred Sciences ... B Sa Sc
Bachelor of Sacred Theology ... BST
Bachelor of Sanitary Engineering ... BSE
Bachelor of Sanitary Engineering ... BS Eng
Bachelor of Sanitary Science ... BSS
Bachelor of Sanitary Science ... BS Sc
Bachelor of School Music ... B Sch Mus
Bachelor of School Music ... BSM
Bachelor of School Music ... BS Mus
Bachelor of School Music ... Sch Mus B
Bachelor of Science ... BS
Bachelor of Science ... B Sc
Bachelor of Science ... SB
Bachelor of Science ... Sc B
Bachelor of Science in Accounting ... BS (Acc)
Bachelor of Science in Accounting ... BS in Acc
Bachelor of Science in Administrative Engineering ... BS in AE
Bachelor of Science in Advertising ... BS Adv
Bachelor of Science in Aeronautical Administration ... BS in Aero Adm
Bachelor of Science in Aeronautical Engineering ... BS in AE
Bachelor of Science in Aeronautical Engineering ... BSAE
Bachelor of Science in Aeronautical Engineering ... BS in Ae E
Bachelor of Science in Aeronautical Engineering ... BS Ae E
Bachelor of Science in Aeronautical Engineering ... BS (Aero E)
Bachelor of Science in Aeronautical Engineering ... BS in Aero E
Bachelor of Science with Aeronautical Engineering Electives ... BS (Ae Elec)

Bachelor of Science in Aeronautical Engineering - Electronics Major ... BSAE-E
Bachelor of Science in Agricultural Administration ... BSA Adm
Bachelor of Science in Agricultural Administration ... BS in AM
Bachelor of Science in Agricultural Education ... BS in AD
Bachelor of Science in Agricultural Education ... BS in Agr Ed
Bachelor of Science in Agricultural Engineering ... BS in Ag E
Bachelor of Science in Agricultural Engineering ... BS Ag E
Bachelor of Science in Agricultural Engineering ... BS in Agr E
Bachelor of Science in Agricultural Engineering ... BS in Agr Eng
Bachelor of Science in Agricultural Engineering ... BS in AN
Bachelor of Science in Agricultural Engineering ... B Sc in Agr Engr
Bachelor of Science in Agricultural Engineering ... BSc(AgricEng)
Bachelor of Science in Agriculture ... BSA
Bachelor of Science in Agriculture ... BS in Ag
Bachelor of Science in Agriculture ... BS Ag
Bachelor of Science in Agriculture ... BS Agr
Bachelor of Science in Agriculture ... BScA
Bachelor of Science in Agriculture ... BScAg
Bachelor of Science in Agriculture ... B Sc Agr
Bachelor of Science in Agriculture ... BScAgri
Bachelor of Science in Agriculture ... BScAgric
Bachelor of Science in Agriculture and Chemistry ... BS in Agr & Chem
Bachelor of Science in Agriculture in Dairy Manufacturing ... BS in Ag (DM)
Bachelor of Science in Agriculture and Education ... BS in Ag & Ed
Bachelor of Science in Air Transportation ... BSAT
Bachelor of Science in Aircraft Maintenance Engineering ... BSAME
Bachelor of Science in Applied Mathematics ... BS (A Math)
Bachelor of Science in Applied Mathematics ... BS in Math
Bachelor of Science in Applied Mathematics ... Sc BAM
Bachelor of Science in Architectural Engineering ... BS in AE
Bachelor of Science in Architectural Engineering ... BSAE
Bachelor of Science in Architectural Engineering ... BS Arch E
Bachelor of Science in Architecture ... BS in Arch
Bachelor of Science in Architecture ... BS Arch
Bachelor of Science (Architecture) ... BSc(Arch)
Bachelor of Science in Architecture in Architectural Engineering ... BS Arch (Arch E)
Bachelor of Science in Architecture in Architecture ... BS Arch (Arch)
Bachelor of Science in Art Education ... BS Art Ed
Bachelor of Science in Bacteriology ... B Sc in Bact
Bachelor of Science in Basic Medical Science ... BS in Med S
Bachelor of Science in Basic Medical Sciences ... BS in BMS
Bachelor of Science in Biology ... BS Biol
Bachelor of Science in Biomedical Engineering ... BS in Biomed Eng
Bachelor of Science in Business ... BSB
Bachelor of Science in Business ... BS Bus
Bachelor of Science in Business ... BS in Bus
Bachelor of Science in Business Administration ... BS in BA
Bachelor of Science in Business Administration ... BSBA
Bachelor of Science in Business Administration ... BS in B Ad
Bachelor of Science in Business Administration ... BSB Ad
Bachelor of Science in Business Administration ... BS in Bus Ad
Bachelor of Science in Business Administration ... BS Bus Ad
Bachelor of Science in Business Education ... BSB Ed
Bachelor of Science in Business Education ... BS in B Ed
Bachelor of Science in Business Education ... BS in Bus Ed
Bachelor of Science in Business Education ... BSBusEd
Bachelor of Science in Business - Medical Records ... BS (Bus-MR)
Bachelor of Science in Cartography ... BS in Cart
Bachelor of Science in Ceramic Engineering ... BS in Cer E
Bachelor of Science in Ceramic Engineering ... BS (Cer E)
Bachelor of Science in Ceramic Engineering ... BS Cr E
Bachelor of Science in Ceramic Technology ... BS in Cer Tech
Bachelor of Science in Ceramics ... BS in Cer
Bachelor of Science in Chemical Engineering ... BS in CE
Bachelor of Science in Chemical Engineering ... BS in Ch E
Bachelor of Science in Chemical Engineering ... BS Ch E
Bachelor of Science in Chemical Engineering ... BS in Chem E
Bachelor of Science in Chemical Engineering ... BS Chem E
Bachelor of Science in Chemical Engineering ... BS in Ch Eng
Bachelor of Science in Chemical Engineering ... BS Ch Eng
Bachelor of Science in Chemical Engineering ... BS in Chm E
Bachelor of Science in Chemical Engineering ... BS in CN
Bachelor of Science with Chemical Engineering Electives ... BS (Ch E Elect)
Bachelor of Science in Chemical Technology ... BS in Chem Tech
Bachelor of Science in Chemistry ... BS in C
Bachelor of Science in Chemistry ... BS in Ch
Bachelor of Science in Chemistry ... BSCh
Bachelor of Science in Chemistry ... BS in Chm
Bachelor of Science in Chemistry ... Sc BC
Bachelor of Science in Christian Education - Music ... BS in CE - Music
Bachelor of Science in Civil Engineering ... B Sc in CE
Bachelor of Science in Civil Engineering ... BS in CE
Bachelor of Science in Civil Engineering ... BSCE
Bachelor of Science in Civil Engineering ... SBCE
Bachelor of Science in Commerce ... BS in C
Bachelor of Science in Commerce ... BSC
Bachelor of Science in Commerce ... BS in Comm
Bachelor of Science in Commerce and Business ... BS in Com & Bus

Bachelor of Science in Commerce and Economics	BS in C & Ec
Bachelor of Science in Commercial and Business Administration	BS in C & BA
Bachelor of Science in Commercial Education	BS in Com Ed
Bachelor of Science in Communications	BS Com
Bachelor of Science in Community Recreation	BS in Comm Rec
Bachelor of Science in Computer Science	BSCompSci
Bachelor of Science in Criminal Justice	BSCJ
Bachelor of Science in Dental Hygiene	BS in DH
Bachelor of Science in Dental Hygiene	BSD Hyg
Bachelor of Science in Dentistry	BSc (Dent)
Bachelor of Science in Dentistry	BS in Dent
Bachelor of Science in Design	BSD
Bachelor of Science in Design	BS Des
Bachelor of Science in Design in Decorative Design	BS Des (Dec Des)
Bachelor of Science in Dianoetics	B Sc (Dn)
Bachelor of Science (Domestic Science)	B Sc (Dom Sc)
Bachelor of Science in Economics	B Sc Econ
Bachelor of Science in Economics	BS in Ec
Bachelor of Science in Economics	BS Ec
Bachelor of Science in Education	BScEd
Bachelor of Science (Education)	BSc(Educ)
Bachelor of Science in Education	BS in E
Bachelor of Science in Education	BSE
Bachelor of Science in Education	BS in Ed
Bachelor of Science in Education	BS Ed
Bachelor of Science in Electrical Engineering	B Sc in EE
Bachelor of Science in Electrical Engineering	BS in EE
Bachelor of Science in Electrical Engineering	BSEE
Bachelor of Science in Electrical Engineering	SBEE
Bachelor of Science in Electrical and Mechanical Engineering	BSEE-ME
Bachelor of Science in Electronic Engineering	BS El E
Bachelor of Science in Electronic Engineering	BS in Elect Eng
Bachelor of Science in Elementary Education	BSEE
Bachelor of Science in Elementary Education	BS El Ed
Bachelor of Science in Elementary Education	BS Elem
Bachelor of Science in Elementary Education	BS in Elem Ed
Bachelor of Science in Engineering	BES
Bachelor of Science (Engineering)	BSc(Eng)
Bachelor of Science (Engineering)	BSc(Engg)
Bachelor of Science (Engineering)	BSc(Engin)
Bachelor of Science in Engineering	BS in E
Bachelor of Science in Engineering	BSE
Bachelor of Science in Engineering	BS in Eng
Bachelor of Science in Engineering	Sc BE
Bachelor of Science in Engineering Administration	BS Engr Ad
Bachelor of Science in Engineering in Aeronautical Engineering	BSE (Ae E)
Bachelor of Science in Engineering in Chemical Engineering	BSE (Ch E)
Bachelor of Science in Engineering and Civil Engineering	BSE (CE)
Bachelor of Science in Engineering and Economics	BSE & E
Bachelor of Science in Engineering in Electrical Engineering	BSE (EE)
Bachelor of Science in Engineering in Engineering Mechanics	BSE (EM)
Bachelor of Science in Engineering in Geodesy and Surveying	BSE (Geod & Surv)
Bachelor of Science in Engineering in Industrial Engineering	BSE (Ind E)
Bachelor of Science in Engineering in Materials Engineering	BSE (Mat E)
Bachelor of Science in Engineering Mathematics	BS in E Math
Bachelor of Science in Engineering in Mechanical Engineering	BSE (ME)
Bachelor of Science in Engineering in Mechanical and Industrial Engineering	BSE (M & Ind E)
Bachelor of Science in Engineering Mechanics	BS in Mech
Bachelor of Science in Engineering in Metallurgical Engineering	BSE (Met E)
Bachelor of Science in Engineering of Mines	BS in EM
Bachelor of Science in Engineering of Mines	BSEM
Bachelor of Science in Engineering in Naval Architecture and Marine Engineering	BSE (Nav Arch & Mar E)
Bachelor of Science in Engineering Physics	BS Engr Phys
Bachelor of Science in Engineering Physics	BS in EP
Bachelor of Science in Engineering Physics	BSEP
Bachelor of Science in Engineering Physics	BS in E Phys
Bachelor of Science in Engineering Physics	BSE Phys
Bachelor of Science in Engineering Science	BS Engr Sci
Bachelor of Science in Engineering Sciences	BS Eng Sci
Bachelor of Science in Engineering Sciences	BS in ES
Bachelor of Science in Engineering Sciences	BSES
Bachelor of Science in Engineering Sciences	BSE Sc
Bachelor of Science and English Literature	BSEL
Bachelor of Science (Estate Management)	B Sc (Est Man)
Bachelor of Science in Finance	BS (Fin)
Bachelor of Science in Finance	BS in Fin
Bachelor of Science in Fisheries Management	BSF Mgt
Bachelor of Science in Foreign Service	BS in FS
Bachelor of Science in Foreign Service	BSFS
Bachelor of Science in Forest Management	BSFM
Bachelor of Science in Forestry	B Sc F
Bachelor of Science in Forestry	B Sc For
Bachelor of Science (Forestry)	BSc(Forestry)
Bachelor of Science in Forestry	BSF
Bachelor of Science in Forestry	BS in For

Bachelor of Science in Forestry	BS For
Bachelor of Science in Forestry	BS Fsty
Bachelor of Science in Forestry	BS in Fy
Bachelor of Science in Fuel Technology	BSFT
Bachelor of Science in Game Management	BSG Mgt
Bachelor of Science in General Business	BS in Gen Bus
Bachelor of Science in General Education	BS Gen Ed
Bachelor of Science in General Engineering	BS in GE
Bachelor of Science in General Engineering	BSGE
Bachelor of Science in General Engineering	BS in Gen Eng
Bachelor of Science in General Nursing	BS in Gen Nurs
Bachelor of Science in General Science	BS in Gen Sci
Bachelor of Science in General Science and Mathematics	BS in GSM
Bachelor of Science in General Studies	BS in Gen Std
Bachelor of Science in General Studies	BS in GS
Bachelor of Science in Geodesy and Surveying	BS in Geod & Surv
Bachelor of Science in Geography	BS (Geog)
Bachelor of Science in Geography	BS Ggr
Bachelor of Science in Geological Engineering	BS in Ge E
Bachelor of Science in Geological Engineering	BS in Geol E
Bachelor of Science in Geological Engineering	BS Geol E
Bachelor of Science in Geological Engineering	BS Gl E
Bachelor of Science in Geology	BS (Geol)
Bachelor of Science in Geology	BS Gl
Bachelor of Science in Geology and Physics	BSGP
Bachelor of Science in Geophysical Engineering	BS in Gph E
Bachelor of Science in Geophysics	BS Gph
Bachelor of Science in Group Work Education	BS in GWE
Bachelor of Science in Health Education	BSHE
Bachelor of Science in Health Education	BS in H Ed
Bachelor of Science in Health and Physical Education	BS in H & PE
Bachelor of Science in Health and Physical Education	BS in HPE
Bachelor of Science in Home Economics	B Sc in HE
Bachelor of Science in Home Economics	BSc(HEc)
Bachelor of Science in Home Economics	BS (HE)
Bachelor of Science in Home Economics	BS in HE
Bachelor of Science in Home Economics	BSHE
Bachelor of Science in Home Economics	BS in H Ec
Bachelor of Science in Home Economics	BS H Ec
Bachelor of Science in Home Economics	BS in H Econ
Bachelor of Science in Home Economics Education	BS in HD
Bachelor of Science (Home Science)	BSc(HomeSc)
Bachelor of Science (Home Science)	BSc(HomeSci)
Bachelor of Science in Home Science	BSc(HomeScience)
Bachelor of Science in Horticulture	BSc(Hort)
Bachelor of Science in Hospital Administration	BSHA
Bachelor of Science in Hotel and Restaurant Administration	BS in H & RA
Bachelor of Science in Industrial Art	BS in Ind Art
Bachelor of Science in Industrial Arts	BS in IA
Bachelor of Science in Industrial Chemistry	BS in Ind Ch
Bachelor of Science in Industrial Education	BSIE
Bachelor of Science in Industrial Education	BS in Ind Ed
Bachelor of Science in Industrial Education	BSIndEd
Bachelor of Science in Industrial Engineering	BS in IE
Bachelor of Science in Industrial Engineering	BSIE
Bachelor of Science in Industrial Engineering	BS in Ind E
Bachelor of Science in Industrial Engineering	BS Ind Eng
Bachelor of Science in Industrial Engineering and Management	BS in IE & M
Bachelor of Science in Industrial Management	BS in IM
Bachelor of Science in Industrial Management	BSIM
Bachelor of Science in Industrial Management	BS Ind Mgt
Bachelor of Science in Industrial Relations	BSIR
Bachelor of Science in Industrial Technology	BSIndTech
Bachelor of Science in Industrial Technology	BSIT
Bachelor of Science in Journalism	BS in J
Bachelor of Science in Journalism	BSJ
Bachelor of Science in Journalism	BS Jr
Bachelor of Science in Labor Relations	BS Lab Rel
Bachelor of Science in Laboratory Technology	BS in LT
Bachelor of Science in Land Planning	BS in LP
Bachelor of Science in Landscape Architecture	BSLA
Bachelor of Science in Landscape Architecture	BSL Arch
Bachelor of Science in Landscape Management	BSLM
Bachelor of Science in Languages	BSL
Bachelor of Science in Latin	BS in Lat
Bachelor of the Science of Law	B Sc L
Bachelor of Science in Law	BSL
Bachelor of Science in Letters and Science	BS in L & S
Bachelor of Science in Library Science	BSLS
Bachelor of Science in Library Service	BS in LS
Bachelor of Science in Linguistics	BSL
Bachelor of Science in Management Engineering	BS in Mgt Engr
Bachelor of Science in Management Science	BS in Mgt Sc
Bachelor of Science in Mathematical Statistics	BS in Math Stat
Bachelor of Science in Mathematics and Chemistry	BSMC
Bachelor of Science in Mechanical Arts	BS in MA
Bachelor of Science in Mechanical Engineering	B Sc in ME
Bachelor of Science in Mechanical Engineering	BS (ME)
Bachelor of Science in Mechanical Engineering	BS in ME

Bachelor of Science in Mechanical Engineering	BSME
Bachelor of Science in Mechanical Engineering	BS in Mech Eng
Bachelor of Science in Mechanical Engineering	BS in M Engr
Bachelor of Science with Mechanical Engineering Electives	BS (ME Elect)
Bachelor of Science in Mechanical Industries	BS in Mech Ind
Bachelor of Science in Mechanics	BS in Mech
Bachelor of Science (Medical)	BSc(Med)
Bachelor of Science in Medical Record Library Science	BS in MRL
Bachelor of Science in Medical Records	BS in Med Rec
Bachelor of Science in Medical Records Librarianship	BS in Med Rec Lib
Bachelor of Science (Medical Science)	B Sc (Med Sci)
Bachelor of Science in Medical Secretarial Science	BS in Med Sc
Bachelor of Science in Medical Technology	B Sc in Med Tech
Bachelor of Science in Medical Technology	BS in Md
Bachelor of Science in Medical Technology	BS Med T
Bachelor of Science in Medical Technology	BS in Med Tech
Bachelor of Science in Medical Technology	BS Med Tech
Bachelor of Science in Medical Technology	BS (MT)
Bachelor of Science in Medical Technology	BS in MT
Bachelor of Science in Medical Technology	BSMT
Bachelor of Science in Medicine	B Sc in Med
Bachelor of Science in Medicine	BSM
Bachelor of Science in Medicine	BS in Med
Bachelor of Science in Metallurgical Engineering	BS in Met E
Bachelor of Science in Metallurgical Engineering	BS Met E
Bachelor of Science in Metallurgical Engineering	BS Met Eng
Bachelor of Science in Metallurgical Engineering	BS in Met Engin
Bachelor of Science in Metallurgical Engineering	BS Mt E
Bachelor of Science in Metallurgy	B Sc Met
Bachelor of Science in Metallurgy	BS in Met
Bachelor of Science in Meteorology	BS in Met
Bachelor of Science in Meteorology	BS Met
Bachelor of Science in Military Science	BS in MS
Bachelor of Science in Mineralogy	BS Min
Bachelor of Science in Mining	BS in Min
Bachelor of Science in Mining Engineering	BSME
Bachelor of Science in Mining Engineering	BS Mg E
Bachelor of Science in Mining Engineering	BS in Min E
Bachelor of Science in Mining Engineering	BS Min E
Bachelor of Science in Mining Engineering	BS in Min Eng
Bachelor of Science in Mining Engineering	BS Mng E
Bachelor of Science in Music	BSM
Bachelor of Science in Music	BS Mus
Bachelor of Science in Music Education	BSME
Bachelor of Science in Music Education	BSM Ed
Bachelor of Science in Music Education	BS in M Educ
Bachelor of Science in Music Education	BS in Mu Ed
Bachelor of Science in Music Education	BS Mus Ed
Bachelor of Science in Musical Education	BS in Mus Ed
Bachelor of Science in Natural-Gas Engineering	BS in Nat G Engin
Bachelor of Science in Natural History	BS in Nat Hist
Bachelor of Science in Natural Science	BS in NS
Bachelor of Science in Natural Science	BS in N Sc
Bachelor of Science in Nursing	BScN
Bachelor of Science in Nursing	B Sc in Nurs
Bachelor of Science (Nursing)	BSc(Nursing)
Bachelor of Science in Nursing	BS in N
Bachelor of Science in Nursing	BSN
Bachelor of Science in Nursing	BS in Nr
Bachelor of Science in Nursing	BS Nurs
Bachelor of Science in Nursing	BS in Nurs
Bachelor of Science in Nursing Administration	BSNA
Bachelor of Science in Nursing Education	BS in NE
Bachelor of Science in Nursing Education	BSNE
Bachelor of Science in Nursing Education	BS in N Ed
Bachelor of Science in Nursing Education	BSN Ed
Bachelor of Science in Nursing Education	BS in Nurs Ed
Bachelor of Science in Nursing Education	BS Nurs Ed
Bachelor of Science (Nutrition)	BSc(Nutr)
Bachelor of Science in Occupational Therapy	B Sc in Occ Ther
Bachelor of Science (Occupational Therapy)	BSc(OT)
Bachelor of Science in Occupational Therapy	BS in Occ Ther
Bachelor of Science in Occupational Therapy	BS in OT
Bachelor of Science in Occupational Therapy	BSOT
Bachelor of Science in Oceanography	BS in Ocean
Bachelor of Science in Optics	BS in Opt
Bachelor of Science in Optometry	B Sc in Opt
Bachelor of Science in Optometry	BS (Opt)
Bachelor of Science in Optometry	BS in Opt
Bachelor of the Science of Oratory	B Or Sc
Bachelor of the Science of Oratory	B Sc O
Bachelor of the Science of Oratory	BSO
Bachelor of Science in Ornamental Horticulture	BS in OH
Bachelor of Science in Ornamental Horticulture	BS Orn Hort
Bachelor of Science in Orthoptics	BS in Ortho
Bachelor of Science in Personnel and Industrial Relations	BS (Per & Ind Rel)
Bachelor of Science in Petroleum	BS in Pet
Bachelor of Science in Petroleum Engineering	BS in PE
Bachelor of Science in Petroleum Engineering	BS in Pet Engin

Bachelor of Science in Petroleum Engineering	BS in Petr E
Bachelor of Science in Pharmacy	B Sc in Phar
Bachelor of Science in Pharmacy	BSc(Pharm)
Bachelor of Science in Pharmacy	BSP
Bachelor of Science in Pharmacy	BS in Ph
Bachelor of Science in Pharmacy	BS Ph
Bachelor of Science in Pharmacy	BS in Phar
Bachelor of Science in Pharmacy	BS Phar
Bachelor of Science in Pharmacy	BSPharm
Bachelor of Science in Physical Education	BS (PE)
Bachelor of Science in Physical Education	BS in PE
Bachelor of Science in Physical Education	BSPE
Bachelor of Science in Physical Education	BS in P Ed
Bachelor of Science in Physical Education	BS in Phy Ed
Bachelor of Science in Physical Education	BS in Phys Ed
Bachelor of Science in Physical and Occupational Therapy	BSc (P & OT)
Bachelor of Science in Physical and Occupational Therapy	BS in Th
Bachelor of Science in Physical Therapy	B Sc in Phys Ther
Bachelor of Science (Physical Therapy)	BSc(PT)
Bachelor of Science in Physical Therapy	BS Ph Th
Bachelor of Science in Physical Therapy	BS in Phys Th
Bachelor of Science in Physical Therapy	BS in Phys Ther
Bachelor of Science in Physical Therapy	BS (PT)
Bachelor of Science in Physical Therapy	BS in PT
Bachelor of Science in Physical Therapy	BSPT
Bachelor of Science in Physics	B Sc in Phys
Bachelor of Science in Physics	BS Phys
Bachelor of Science in Physics	Sc BP
Bachelor of Science in Practical Arts	BS in PA
Bachelor of Science in Practical Arts	BS in Prac Arts
Bachelor of Science in Practical Arts and Letters	BS in PAL
Bachelor of Science in Professional Geology	BS in Pr Ge
Bachelor of Science in Professional Meteorology	BS in Pr Met
Bachelor of Science in Public Administration	BS in PA
Bachelor of Science in Public Administration	BSPA
Bachelor of Science in Public Health	BSPH
Bachelor of Science in Public Health Nursing	BS in PHN
Bachelor of Science in Public Health Nursing	BSPHN
Bachelor of Science in Public Health and Preventative Medicine	BS in PHPM
Bachelor of Science in Public School Music	BS in PSM
Bachelor of Science in Pure Science	BS
Bachelor of Science in Radiological Technology	BS in RT
Bachelor of Science in Radiological Technology	BSRT
Bachelor of Science in Railway and Mechanical Engineering	BS in Ry ME
Bachelor of Science in Range Animal Husbandry	BS in RAH
Bachelor of Science in Recreation	BSR
Bachelor of Science in Recreation	BS in Rec
Bachelor of Science in Recreation	BS Rec
Bachelor of Science in Recreation Leadership	BS in Rec Lead
Bachelor of Science in Religious Education	BA in RE
Bachelor of Science in Restaurant Management	B Sc in Rest Mgt
Bachelor of Science in Retailing	BS Ret
Bachelor of Science in Sanitary Engineering	BS in San E
Bachelor of Science in Sanitary Engineering	BSSanE
Bachelor of Science in Sanitary Engineering	SBSanE
Bachelor of Science in Sanitary Science	BS in San Sci
Bachelor of Science in Science	BSS
Bachelor of Science in Science Engineering	BS Sc E
Bachelor of Science in Secondary Education	BSSE
Bachelor of Science in Secondary Education	BS Sec
Bachelor of Science in Secondary Education	BS (Sec Ed)
Bachelor of Science in Secondary Education	BS in Sec Ed
Bachelor of Science in Secondary Education	BS Sec Ed
Bachelor of Science in Secretarial Administration	BSSA
Bachelor of Science in Secretarial Administration	BS (Sec Adm)
Bachelor of Science in Secretarial Science	BS in Sec Sc
Bachelor of Science in Secretarial Science	BS in Sec Sci
Bachelor of Science in Secretarial Science	BSS Sci
Bachelor of Science in Secretarial Studies	BSSS
Bachelor of Science in Social Administration	B Sc in Soc Adm
Bachelor of Science in Social Science	BS in SS
Bachelor of Science in Social Science	BSSS
Bachelor of Science in Social Science	BS (SS)
Bachelor of Science in Social Science	BS in S Sc
Bachelor of Science (Social Sciences)	BSc(SocSc)
Bachelor of Science in Social Service	BS in Soc Serv
Bachelor of Science in Social Studies	BS in Soc St
Bachelor of Science in Social Work	BS (Soc Wk)
Bachelor of Science (Sociology)	B Sc (Soc)
Bachelor of Science in Special Fields	BS in Spec Flds
Bachelor of Science in Speech	BS Sp
Bachelor of Science in Statistics	BS in Stat
Bachelor of Science in Structural Engineering	BS in Struc E
Bachelor of Science in Teaching	BST
Bachelor of Science (Technology)	B Sc (Tech)
Bachelor of Science in Technology	BSTech
Bachelor of Science in Textile Engineering	BS in TE
Bachelor of Science in Textiles	BA in Text
Bachelor of the Science of Theology	STB
Bachelor of Science in Trade and Industrial Engineering	BST & IE

Bachelor of Science in Transportation	BS Trans
Bachelor of Science (Veterinary)	BSc(Vet)
Bachelor of Science in Vocational Agriculture	BS in Voc Ag
Bachelor of Science in Vocational Education	BS in Voc Ed
Bachelor of Science in Zoological Sciences	BS in ZS
Bachelor of Scientific Agriculture	BSA
Bachelor of Scientific Didactics	BS Di
Bachelor of Scientology	B Scn
Bachelor of Secretarial Arts	B Se A
Bachelor of Secretarial Science	B Sec Sc
Bachelor of Secretarial Science	BSS
Bachelor of Secretarial Studies	B Se St
Bachelor Sergeant Quarters [Air Force]	BSQ
Bachelor of Social Science	BScSoc
Bachelor of Social Science	B Soc Sc
Bachelor of Social Science	B So Sc
Bachelor of Social Science	BSS
Bachelor of Social Science	BS Sc
Bachelor of Social Sciences	BSocSc
Bachelor of Social Service	B So Se
Bachelor of Social Work	BSocWk
Bachelor of Social Work	B So W
Bachelor of Social Work	BSW
Bachelor of Sociology	B So
Bachelor of Special Education	BSpEd
Bachelor of Special Studies	BSS
Bachelor of Speech	B Sp
Bachelor of Statistics	B St
Bachelor of Structural Engineering	B St E
Bachelor of Structural Engineering	B St Eng
Bachelor of Surgery	BS
Bachelor of Surgery	B Sur
Bachelor of Surgery	Ch B
Bachelor of Surveying	BSurv
Bachelor of Systematic Theology	B Sy Th
Bachelor of Teaching	BT
Bachelor of Technical Science	B Sc Tech
Bachelor of Technological Science	BTS
Bachelor of Technology	BT
Bachelor of Technology	B Tech
Bachelor in Technology	BTech
Bachelor of Textile Chemistry	B of TC
Bachelor of Textile Chemistry	BTC
Bachelor of Textile Chemistry	BT Ch
Bachelor of Textile Design	BT Des
Bachelor of Textile Dyeing	BTD
Bachelor of Textile Engineering	B of TE
Bachelor of Textile Engineering	BTE
Bachelor of Textile Engineering	BT Eng
Bachelor of Textile Management	B of TM
Bachelor of Textile Technology	BTT
Bachelor of Textiles	BText
Bachelor of Theology	BT
Bachelor of Theology	B Th
Bachelor of Theology	Th B
Bachelor of Town Planning	BTP
Bachelor of Unani Medicine and Surgery	BUMS
Bachelor of Urban Planning	B Urb Pl
Bachelor of Urban Studies	BUS
Bachelor of Veterinary Medicine	B Vet Med
Bachelor of Veterinary Medicine	BVM
Bachelor of Veterinary Medicine	Vet MB
Bachelor of Veterinary Medicine and Surgery	BVM & S
Bachelor of Veterinary Medicine and Surgery	BVMS
Bachelor of Veterinary Science	BVS
Bachelor of Veterinary Science	BV Sc
Bachelor of Veterinary Science and Animal Husbandry	BVSc & AH
Bachelor of Veterinary Surgery	BVS
Bachelor of Vocational Agriculture	BVA
Bachelor of Vocational Arts	BVocArts
Bachelor of Vocational Education	BVE
Bachelor of Vocational Education	BVocEd
Bachelor of Welding Engineering	BWE
Bachelor of Zoological Science	BZ Sc
Bachman-Turner Overdrive [Rock music group]	BTO
Bacillary White Diarrhea [Veterinary medicine]	BWD
Bacille Acido-Resistant [Acid-Fast Bacillus] [Medicine]	BAR
Bacillus [Bacteriology]	B
Bacillus Calmette-Guerin [TB vaccine]	BCG
Bacillus globigii [Biological warfare with bacteria]	BG
Bacillus thuringiensis [Also, Bt] [Bacteriology]	BT
Bacillus thuringiensis israelensis [Bacteriology]	BTI
Bacitracin V [Antibacterial compound]	BV
Bacitracin V and X [Antibacterial compound]	BVX
Bacitracin X [Antibacterial compound]	BX
Back	B
Back	BCK
Back Again to Hoover [Slogan during 1974 economic downturn]	BATH
Back to Back [Technical drawings]	B to B
Back of Board	B of B
Back to the City, Incorporated [An association]	BCI

Back-Connected [Technical drawings]	BC
Back Course [Aviation]	BC
Back Course Marker [Aviation]	BCM
Back Dividends	BD
Back Door Trot [i.e., a call of nature] [Obsolete slang]	BDT
Back Electromotive Force	BEMF
Back End	BE
Back-Feed	BF
Back Focal	BF
Back Focal Distance	BFD
Back Focal Length	BFL
Back Folded [Freight]	BF
Back Gear [Technical drawings]	BG
Back Judge [Football]	BJ
Back Marker [Aviation]	BM
Back Order	BO
Back Pain Association	BPA
Back Porch Effect	BPE
Back Pressure	BP
Back-Pressure Control	BPC
Back Projection	BP
Back Shelf	BKSLF
Back Shunt Keying	BSK
Back Stage Left [A stage direction]	BSL
Back Stage Right [A stage direction]	BSR
Back, Training [Parachute]	BT
Back-Up Quantity	BQ
Back View	BV
Back-Water Valve	BWV
Backache [Medicine]	BA
Backbord [Portside] [German military]	BB
Backface	BF
Background	BG
Background	BKGD
Background Heat Flux	BHF
Background Illumination Intensity	BII
Background Information Document [Environmental Protection Agency]	BID
Background Information and User Guide [Helicopter]	BIUG
Background Investigation	BI
Background-Limited Infrared Photoconductor	BLIP
Background-Limited Infrared Photography	BLIP
Background Listening [Music]	BL
Background Mapping Sensor	BMS
Background Measurement Satellite	BMS
Background Noise Power	BNP
Background Notes [A publication]	Backgr Notes
Background Notes on the Countries of the World. US Department of State [A publication]	Back Notes
Background Operating System	BOS
Background Storage and Control Unit	BSCU
Backing [Aviation]	BCKG
Backlash Allowance	BA
Backlight Burtek Trainer	BBT
Backlog of Essential Maintenance and Repair	BEMAR
Backorder Problem Working Group [DoD]	BOPWG
Backpack	BP
Backscatter Electron	BSE
Backscatter Ultraviolet [Spectrometry]	BUV
Backscatter Ultraviolet Spectrometer	BUS
Backscatter Ultraviolet Spectrometer	BUVS
Backscattered LASER Energy Digitizing Equipment	BLEDE
Backspace	BKSP
Backspace	BS
Backspace Contact	BSC
Backspace File	BSF
Backspace Recorder	BSR
Backstairs [Gossip]	BS
Backstamp	BKST
Backup	BKUP
Backup	BU
Backup Acquisition System	BACS
Backup Air Data Sensor Assembly	BADSA
Backup Attitude Reference System	BARS
Backup Avionics Subsystem Software	BASS
Backup Block	BUB
Backup Computer	BUC
Backup Control System	BCS
Backup Digital Computer	BDC
Backup Digital Computer	BUDC
Backup Digital System	BUDS
Backup Drive Amplifier	BDA
Backup Emergency Communications	BUEC
Backup Flight Control	BFC
Backup Flight Control System [NASA]	BFCS
Backup Flight System	BFS
Backup Gimbal Servo	BGS
Backup Guidance System [NASA]	BGS
Backup Guidance System [NASA]	BUGS
Backup Interceptor Control [System] [Air Force]	BUIC
Backup Interceptor Control System [Air Force]	BUICS

Backup Optical Unit ... BUOU
Backup Plate ... BUP
Backup Plate, Perforated ... BUPP
Backup Rate ... BUR
Backup Rate of Pitch ... BURP
Backup Rate of Roll ... BURR
Backup Rate of Yaw ... BURY
Backus Naur [*or Normal*] **Form** [*Data processing*] ... BNF
Backward ... BKWD
Backward Edge [*Skating*] ... B
Backward Limit Photocell ... BLPC
Backward Traveling Wave ... BTW
Backward Wave Amplifier ... BWA
Backward Wave Converter ... BWC
Backward Wave Magnetron ... BWM
Backward Wave Oscillator ... BWO
Backward Wave Oscillator Synchronizer ... BWOS
Backward Wave Oscillator Tube ... BWOT
Backward Wave Power Amplifier ... BWPA
Backward Wave Sweep Oscillator ... BWSO
Backward Wave Tube [*Physics*] ... BWT
Backwardation [*Business and trade*] ... BK
BACM Industries Ltd. [*Formerly, British-American Construction & Materials Ltd.*] ... BACM
Bacolod [*Philippines*] [*Airport symbol*] ... BCD
Bacon, Lettuce, and Tomato [*Sandwich*] [*Waitress's call to a short order cook*] ... BLT
Bacon Memorial Public Library, Wyandotte, MI [*Library symbol*] ... MiWy
Baconiana [*A publication*] ... Ba
Bacteria ... BACT
Bacterial Adherent Colonies ... BAC
Bacterial Alkaline Phosphatase [*or Bacterial Alkaline Phosphomonoesterase*] [*An enzyme*] ... BAP
Bacterial Antigen Complex [*Immunochemistry*] ... BAC
Bacterial Automated Identification Technique ... BAIT
Bacterial Phosphatidylethanolamine [*Physiological chemistry*] ... BPE
Bacteriochlorophyll [*Biochemistry*] ... BChl
Bacteriologia, Virusologia, Parazitologia, Epidemiologia (Bucharest) [*A publication*] ... Bacteriol Virusol Parazitol Epidemiol (Buchar)
Bacteriological Analytical Manual [*A publication*] ... BAM
Bacteriological Oxygen Demand [*Water pollution*] ... BOD
Bacteriological Proceedings [*A publication*] ... Bacteriol Proc
Bacteriological Proceedings [*A publication*] ... Bact Proc
Bacteriological Reviews [*A publication*] ... Bacteriol Rev
Bacteriological Reviews [*A publication*] ... Bact R
Bacteriological Reviews [*A publication*] ... Bact Rev
Bacteriological Reviews [*A publication*] ... Bact Rs
Bacteriological Warfare ... BW
Bacteriological Warfare, Defence [*British*] [*World War II*] ... BW(D)
Bacteriological Warfare, Operational Panel [*British*] [*World War II*] ... BW(O)
Bacteriological Warfare, Policy Panel [*British*] [*World War II*] ... BW(P)
Bacteriological Warhead ... BW
Bacteriology ... BACTER
Bacteriology ... BACTLGY
Bacteriopheophytin [*Biochemistry*] ... BPheo
Bacteriorhodopsin [*Biochemistry*] ... bR
Bacteroids Bile Esculin [*Agar*] [*Microbiology*] ... BBE
Bad Axe, MI [*Radio station call letters*] ... WLEW
Bad Axe, MI [*Radio station call letters*] ... WLEW-FM
Bad Axe Public Library, Bad Axe, MI [*Library symbol*] ... MiBa
Bad Breath ... BB
Bad Character ... BC
Bad Check ... BC
Bad Conduct Discharge [*Military*] ... BCD
Bad Conduct Discharge, General Court-Martial, after Confinement in Prison [*Navy*] ... BDGC
Bad Conduct Discharge, General Court-Martial, after Violation of Probation [*Navy*] ... BDGP
Bad Conduct Discharge, General Court-Martial, Immediate [*Navy*] ... BDGI
Bad Conduct Discharge, Sentence of Summary Court-Martial, Immediate [*Navy*] ... BDSI
Bad Conduct Discharge, Summary Court-Martial, after Violation of Probation [*Navy*] ... BDSP
Bad Data Lister ... BDL
Bad Demographic Risk [*Television*] ... BDR
Bad Hersfelder Jahresheft [*A publication*] ... Bad Hersfelder Jh
Bad Order [*i.e., requiring repair*] ... BO
Bad Reichenhall [*Federal Republic of Germany*] [*Seismograph station code, US Geological Survey*] ... BHG
Badajoz [*Spain*] [*Airport symbol*] ... BJZ
Badan Kongress Kebathinan Indonesia ... BKKI
Badan Perdjoangan Buruh [*Board for the Defense of Labor Interest*] [*Indonesia*] ... BPB
Badana [*Saudi Arabia*] [*Airport symbol*] [*Obsolete*] ... BDN
Bade [*Indonesia*] [*Airport symbol*] ... BXD
Badger Army Ammunition Plant ... BAAP
Badger Meter, Incorporated [*American Stock Exchange symbol*] ... BMI
Badger Mountain [*Washington*] [*Seismograph station code, US Geological Survey*] ... BDG
Badger Union High School District, Lake Geneva, WI [*Library symbol*] ... WLagB
Badische Anilin-und Soda-Fabrik [*Chemical company*] [*West Germany*] ... BASF
Badische Historische Kommission Neujahrsblaetter [*A publication*] ... Badische Hist Komm Neujahrsbl
Badlands National Monument ... BADL
Bado Lite [*Zaire*] [*Airport symbol*] ... BDT
Baende [*Volumes*] [*German*] ... BDE
Baessler-Archiv. Beitraege zur Voelkerkunde [*A publication*] ... Baessler-Arch
Baffle [*Regulating device*] ... BAF
Baffle/Liner Interface Seal [*Nuclear energy*] ... BLIS
Bafoussam [*Cameroon*] [*Airport symbol*] ... BFX
Bag ... B
Bag ... BG
Bag All Garbage ... BAG
Bag of Waters [*Medicine*] ... BOW
Bagdogra [*India*] [*Airport symbol*] ... IXB
Bage [*Brazil*] [*Airport symbol*] ... BGX
Baggage ... BAG
[*Number of Pounds Indicated*] **- Baggage to Accompany Authorized for Air Travel Outside Continental US** ... BAGAIR
Baggage for Air Cargo ... CARBAGAIR
Baghdad [*Iraq*] [*Airport symbol*] ... BGW
Baghdad Pact ... BP
Baghdad-Saddam [*Iraq*] [*Airport symbol*] ... SDA
Baghdad University. College of Science. Bulletin [*A publication*] ... Baghdad Univ Coll Sci Bull
Baghdader Mitteilungen [*A publication*] ... BM
Bagley Gazette, Bagley, IA [*Library symbol*] ... IaBagG
Bagley Public Library, Bagley, IA [*Library symbol*] ... IaBag
Baglung [*Nepal*] [*Airport symbol*] ... BGL
Bagneres De Bigorre [*France*] [*Seismograph station code, US Geological Survey*] ... BDB
Bagra [*Pakistan*] [*Seismograph station code, US Geological Survey*] ... BGP
Bags ... BGS
Bags, Barrels, or Boxes [*Freight*] ... BBB
Baguio [*Philippines*] [*Airport symbol*] ... BAG
Baguio [*Philippines*] [*Geomagnetic observatory code*] ... BAG
Baguio [*Philippines*] [*Seismograph station code, US Geological Survey*] ... BAG
Bahaa Esperanto-Ligo ... BEL
Baha'i International Community ... BIC
Bahamas [*MARC country of publication code*] [*Library of Congress*] ... bf
Bahamas [*Three-letter standard code*] ... BHS
Bahamas [*Two-letter standard code*] ... BS
Bahamas [*MARC geographic area code*] [*Library of Congress*] ... nwbf---
Bahamas World Airlines Ltd. [*ICAO designator*] ... WQ
Bahamasair Holding Ltd. [*Bahamas*] [*ICAO designator*] ... BH
Bahar Dar [*Ethiopia*] [*Airport symbol*] ... BJR
Bahia Blanca [*Argentina*] [*Airport symbol*] ... BHI
Bahia De Los Angeles [*Mexico*] [*Seismograph station code, US Geological Survey*] ... LAX
Bahia Solano [*Colombia*] [*Airport symbol*] ... BSC
Bahn Post Amt [*Railway Post Office*] [*German*] ... BPA
Bahrain [*MARC geographic area code*] [*Library of Congress*] ... a-ba---
Bahrain [*MARC country of publication code*] [*Library of Congress*] ... ba
Bahrain [*Two-letter standard code*] ... BH
Bahrain [*Three-letter standard code*] ... BHR
Bahrain Islands [*Airport symbol*] ... BAH
Bahrain Monetary Agency ... BMA
Baht [*Monetary unit in Thailand*] ... B
Baht [*Tical*] [*Monetary unit in Thailand*] ... BHT
Baia Mare [*Romania*] [*Airport symbol*] ... BAY
Baibara [*Papua New Guinea*] [*Airport symbol*] ... BAP
Baie Comeau [*Canada*] [*Airport symbol*] ... YBC
Baie Comeau, PQ [*Radio station call letters*] ... CBMI-FM
Baie Johan Beetz [*Canada*] [*Airport symbol*] ... YBJ
Baie-Trinite, PQ [*Television station call letters*] ... CIVF-TV
Baie Verte, NF [*Television station call letters*] ... CBNAT-1
Baie Verte, NF [*Radio station call letters*] ... CKIM
Baikal-Amur Mainline [*USSR railroad in Siberia*] ... BAM
Baikonur [*Satellite launch complex*] [*USSR*] ... BAI
Bail Bond ... BB
Bail Court Cases [*Legal*] [*British*] ... BCC
Bail Court Reports [*Legal*] [*British*] ... BCR
Bail Out ... BO
Bailadores [*Venezuela*] [*Seismograph station code, US Geological Survey*] ... BLV
Bailett Weighting Function ... BWF
Bailey, G. R., Escanaba MI [*STAC*] ... BGR
Bailey Oil Content Monitor [*Ship ballast discharge*] ... BOCM
Bailiff Grand Cross ... BGC
Bailment Flight Test Program ... BFTP
Baimuru [*Papua New Guinea*] [*Airport symbol*] ... VMU
Bainbridge, GA [*Location identifier*] [*FAA*] ... BGE
Bainbridge, GA [*Radio station call letters*] ... WAZA
Bainbridge, GA [*Radio station call letters*] ... WJAD
Bainbridge, GA [*Radio station call letters*] ... WMGR
Bainbridge Junior College, Bainbridge, GA [*Library symbol*] ... GBaB

Bainbridge, OH [Radio station call letters]..................WKHR
Baird-Associates, Incorporated ....BAI
Baird Corp. [NASDAQ symbol] ....BATM
Bairnco Corp. [NYSE symbol] ....BZ
Bairnsdale [Australia] [Airport symbol] [Obsolete]..................BSJ
Baitadi [Nepal] [Airport symbol]..................BIT
Baiting Hollow Free Library, Calverton, NY [Library symbol]..................NCalv
Baja California - Territorio Norte..................BCTN
Baja California - Territorio Sur..................BCTS
Baja Cortez Airlines [Los Angeles, CA] [FAA designator]..................BJA
Bajawa [Indonesia] [Airport symbol]..................BJW
Bajhang [Nepal] [Airport symbol]..................BJH
Bakalalan [Malaysia] [Airport symbol]..................BKM
Bakel [Senegal] [Seismograph station code, US Geological Survey]..................BKL
Bakel [Senegal] [Airport symbol]..................BXE
Bakelite Review [A publication] ....Bakelite Rev
Baker [Phonetic alphabet] [World War II]..................B
Baker Analyzed Reagent [Chemistry] ....BAR
Baker, Botts, Shepherd, & Coates, Houston, TX [Library symbol]..................TxHBB
Baker Communications [NASDAQ symbol]..................BAKR
Baker [Michael] Corp. [American Stock Exchange symbol] ....BKR
Baker, Fentress & Co. [NASDAQ symbol] ....BKFR
Baker Gold Ltd. [NASDAQ symbol] ....BKGDF
Baker Industries, Inc. [American Stock Exchange symbol] ....BAK
Baker International Corp. [Formerly, Baker Oil Tools, Inc.] [NYSE symbol]..................BKO
Baker Lake [Northwest Territories] [Geomagnetic observatory code]..................BLC
Baker Lake [Canada] [Airport symbol]..................YBK
Baker Lake [Northwest Territories] [Seismograph station code, US Geological Survey]..................BLC
Baker Lake, NT [Radio station call letters]..................CKQN-FM
Baker, MT [Location identifier] [FAA]..................BKU
Baker, MT [Radio station call letters] ....KFLN
Baker, MT [Radio station call letters]..................KFLN-FM
Baker, OR [Location identifier] [FAA]..................BKE
Baker, OR [Radio station call letters] ....KBKR
Baker, OR [Radio station call letters]..................KBKR-FM
Baker River Audiovisual Center [Library network]..................BRAVC
Baker-Schulberg Community Mental Health Ideology Scale [Psychology]..................CMHI
Baker Street Irregulars [An association]..................BSI
Baker Street Journal [A publication]..................BSJ
Baker and Taylor's Automated Buying System [Baker & Taylor Cos.] [Information service]..................BATAB
Baker University, Baldwin City, KS [Library symbol]..................KBB
Baker University, Baldwin City, KS [OCLC symbol]..................KKB
Baker's Digest [A publication]..................Baker's
Baker's Digest [A publication]..................Baker's Dig
Baker's Review [A publication]..................Baker's Rev
Bakersfield [California] [Airport symbol]..................BFL
Bakersfield Aviation Services [Bakersfield, CA] [FAA designator]..................RWG
Bakersfield, CA [Radio station call letters]..................KAFY
Bakersfield, CA [Television station call letters]..................KBAK-TV
Bakersfield, CA [Television station call letters]..................KERO-TV
Bakersfield, CA [Radio station call letters]..................KGEO
Bakersfield, CA [Radio station call letters]..................KGFM
Bakersfield, CA [Radio station call letters]..................KHIS
Bakersfield, CA [Radio station call letters]..................KHIS-FM
Bakersfield, CA [Radio station call letters]..................KKXX
Bakersfield, CA [Radio station call letters]..................KLYD
Bakersfield, CA [Radio station call letters]..................KPMC
Bakersfield, CA [Television station call letters]..................KPWR-TV
Bakersfield, CA [Radio station call letters]..................KQXR
Bakersfield, CA [Radio station call letters]..................KUZZ
Bakersfield, CA [Radio station call letters]..................KWAC
Bakery..................BAK
Bakery..................BKRY
Bakery, Confectionery, and Tobacco Workers' International Union [Formerly, TWIU, BCW, BCWIU of A, ABCW]..................BCTWIU
Bakery and Confectionery Workers' International Union of America [Later, BCTWIU]..................BCW
Bakery and Confectionery Workers' International Union of America [Later, BCTWIU]..................BCWIU of A
Bakery Equipment Manufacturers Association ....BEMA
Bakery Production and Marketing [A publication]..................Baker Prod
Bakhtar Afghan Airlines [Afghanistan] [ICAO designator]..................BJ
Baking Industry [A publication]..................Baking Ind
Baking Industry Sanitation Standards Committee..................BISSC
Bakkafjordur [Iceland] [Airport symbol]..................BJD
Baku [USSR] [Airport symbol]..................BAK
Baku [USSR] [Seismograph station code, US Geological Survey]..................BAK
Bakuriani [USSR] [Seismograph station code, US Geological Survey]..................BKR
Balair SA [Switzerland] [ICAO designator]..................BB
Balalae [Solomon Islands] [Airport symbol]..................BAS
Balance..................BAL
Balance Agriculture with Industry Program..................BAWI
Balance Calibration Machine..................BCM
Balance Fixture..................BAF
Balance Forward Master..................BFC
Balance General Mobilization Reserve Acquisition Objective [DoD]..................BGMRAO

Balance Mobilization Reserve Materiel Objective [Army]..................BMRMO
Balance of Need Campaign [Red Cross fund-raising]..................BON
Balance of Payments..................BALPA
Balance of Payments..................BOP
Balance of Payments..................B-of-P
Balance of Payments..................BP
Balance of Payments Act..................BOPA
Balance of Payments Programed..................BOPP
Balance of Plant [Nuclear energy]..................BOP
Balance Sheet [A publication]..................Bal Sheet
Balance Sheet..................BS
Balance of Space to Space Control Agencies..................BALSPACON
Balance of State [Department of Labor]..................BOS
Balance of Trade..................BOT
Balance of Trade..................B-of-T
Balance-to-Unbalance Network..................BALUN
Balanced Colorimeter Chamber..................BCC
Balanced Diet Certificates [Economics simulation game]..................BALDICER
Balanced Digital Transmission Device [Army]..................BDTD
Balanced Electrolyte Solution [Physiology]..................BES
Balanced Force Requirements Analysis..................BALFRAM
Balanced Forearm Orthosis [Medicine]..................BFO
Balanced Fund [Business and trade]..................B
Balanced Half-Sample Replication [Statistics]..................BHSR
Balanced Incomplete Block [Statistical design]..................BIB
Balanced Incomplete Block Design [Mathematics]..................BIBD
Balanced Indigenous Population..................BIP
Balanced Inductor Logical Element..................BILE
Balanced Line Logical Element..................BLLE
Balanced Line System..................BLS
Balanced Magnetic Amplifier..................BMA
Balanced Parametric Amplifier..................BPA
Balanced in Plane..................BIP
Balanced Pressure Joint..................BPJ
Balanced Pressure Plane Swivel Joint..................BPPSJ
Balanced Pressure Swivel Joint..................BPSJ
Balanced Repeated Replication [Statistics]..................BRR
Balanced Salt Solution [Cell incubation medium]..................BSS
Balanced Swivel Joint..................BSJ
Balanced Tape Drive..................BTD
Balanced Valve Regulator..................BVR
Balanced Voltage..................BV
Balancing Rheostat..................BALRHEO
Balancing Set..................BALS
Balancing Unit [Radio]..................BALUN
Balasovkii Gosudarstvennyi Pedagogiceskii Institut. Ucenye Zapiski [A publication]..................Balasov Gos Ped Inst Ucen Zap
Balboa [Monetary unit in Panama]..................B
Balboa Heights [Canal Zone] [Seismograph station code, US Geological Survey]..................BHP
Balch Institute [Philadelphia, PA]..................BI
Balch Institute Library, Philadelphia, PA [OCLC symbol]..................BAI
Balch Institute, Philadelphia, PA [Library symbol]..................PPBI
Bald with Bridgework, Bifocals, Baywindow, and Bunions [A humorous unofficial Selective Service Class]..................5B
Bald Eagle [District of Columbia] [Seismograph station code, US Geological Survey] [Closed]..................BED
Bald-Headed Men of America..................BHMA
Bald Knob, AR [Radio station call letters]..................KAPZ
Baldor Electric Co. [NYSE symbol]..................BEZ
Baldwin City, KS [Radio station call letters]..................KNBU
Baldwin-Lima-Hamilton Corp. [NYSE symbol] [Delisted]..................B
Baldwin Locomotive Works, Eddystone, PA [Library symbol] [Obsolete]..................PEddyB
Baldwin & Lyons, Inc. [NASDAQ symbol]..................BWIN
Baldwin Public Library, Baldwin, NY [Library symbol]..................NBald
Baldwin Public Library, Birmingham, MI [Library symbol]..................MiBir
Baldwin Securities Corp. [American Stock Exchange symbol]..................BAL
Baldwin-United Corp. [NYSE symbol]..................BDW
Baldwin-Wallace College [Ohio]..................BWC
Baldwin-Wallace College, Berea, OH [Library symbol]..................OBerB
Baldwin-Wallace College, Berea, OH [OCLC symbol]..................OXB
Baldwinsville, NY [Radio station call letters]..................WBXL
Baldwinsville, NY [Radio station call letters]..................WSEN
Baldwinsville, NY [Radio station call letters]..................WSEN-FM
Baldwyn, MS [Radio station call letters]..................WESE
Bale..................B
Bale..................BE
Bale..................BL
Balearic Islands..................BI
Bales..................BLS
Bales of Cotton [Shipping]..................B/C
Bales or Rolls [Freight]..................B or R
Balgarska Dialektologija [A publication]..................BDial
Balgarski Ezik [A publication]..................BE
Balgarski Ezik i Literatura [A publication]..................BEL
Bali [Papua New Guinea] [Airport symbol]..................BAJ
Bali [Cameroon] [Airport symbol]..................BLC
Balikpapan [Indonesia] [Airport symbol]..................BPN
Balimo [Papua New Guinea] [Airport symbol]..................OPU
Balkan Archiv [A publication]..................BA

Balkan-Bulgarian Airlines [*ICAO designator*] ... LZ
Balkan Intelligence Centre [*British*] [*World War II*] ... BIC
Balkan Studies [*A publication*] ... Balkan Stud
Balkan Studies [*A publication*] ... Bal St
Balkan Studies [*A publication*] ... BASU
Balkan Supply Center [*Navy*] ... BSC
Balkansko Ezikoznanije [*A publication*] ... BalkE
Balkansko Ezikoznanije [*A publication*] ... B Ez
Balks [*Baseball*] ... BK
Ball ... B
Ball ... BA
Ball Bearing [*Technical drawings*] ... BB
Ball Bearing ... BBRG
Ball Bearing Joint ... BBJ
Ball Bearing Journal [*A publication*] ... Ball Bear J
Ball Bearing Swivel Joint ... BBSJ
Ball Bearing Torque ... BBT
Ball Brothers Research Corporation ... BBRC
Ball Brothers Research Corporation, Boulder, CO [*Library symbol*] ... CoBBRC
Ball-Burton-Hill-Hatch Plan [*Senate resolution calling for international cooperation in waging war, planning postwar rehabilitation, etc. Introduced after World War II by Senators Joseph Ball, Harold Burton, Lister Hill, and Carl Hatch*] ... B2H2
Ball and Chain [*Slang for a wife*] ... B & C
Ball Check Valve ... BCV
Ball Corp. [*NYSE symbol*] ... BLL
Ball Joint Actuator ... BJA
Ball Joint Fitting ... BJF
Ball Lock Pin ... BLP
Ball-Lock Separation Bolt ... BLSB
Ball Manufacturers Engineers Committee ... BMEC
Ball Reduction Drive ... BRD
Ball and Roller Bearing Engineering [*A publication*] ... Ball Roller Bear Eng
Ball and Socket Joint ... BSJ
Ball and Socket Upper Bearing ... BSUB
Ball Spinning Friction ... BSF
Ball State Journal for Business Educators [*A publication*] ... Ball State J
Ball State Teachers College [*Later, Ball State University*] [*Indiana*] ... BSTC
Ball State Teachers College Forum [*Later, BSUF*] [*A publication*] ... BSTCF
Ball State University Forum [*A publication*] ... BSUF
Ball State University, Muncie, IN [*OCLC symbol*] ... IBS
Ball State University, Muncie, IN [*Library symbol*] ... InMuB
Ball Tooth Gear ... BTG
Ball Tooth Gear Joint ... BTGJ
Ball Tooth Joint ... BTJ
Ball and Tube [*Photography*] ... B & T
Ballade Tidsskrift for Ny Musikk [*A publication*] ... Ballade
Ballard Medical Products [*NASDAQ symbol*] ... BMED
Ballast ... BALL
Ballast ... BLST
Ballast Control Panel ... BCP
Ballast Flood Valve ... BFV
Ballast Rack ... BR
Ballast Tank Meter ... BTM
Ballast Tube Resistor ... BTR
Ballastable Earthmoving Sectionalized Tractor [*Formerly, UET*] [*Army*] ... BEST
Ballastable Tractor ... BALTRAC
Balled [*Freight*] ... BLD
Ballet News [*A publication*] ... Ballet N
Ballet Theatre Foundation ... BTF
Ballinger, TX [*Radio station call letters*] ... KRUN
Ballinger, TX [*Radio station call letters*] ... KRUN-FM
Ballistic ... B
Ballistic ... BAL
Ballistic ... BALL
Ballistic Advanced Missile ... BAM
Ballistic Aerial Target System ... BATS
Ballistic Analysis Research System ... BARS
Ballistic Attack Game ... BAG
Ballistic Camera ... BC
Ballistic Camera Control ... BCC
Ballistic Compressor Computer Code ... BCCC
Ballistic Data Acquisition System ... BALDAS
Ballistic Density ... BALDNY
Ballistic Environmental Characteristics and Measurement Program [*Army*] ... BECAMP
Ballistic LASER Holographic System ... BLHS
Ballistic LORAN Assist Device ... BALLAD
Ballistic Missile ... BALMI
Ballistic Missile ... BM
Ballistic Missile Acquisition RADAR ... BMAR
Ballistic Missile Analyst Technician-Specialist ... BMAT/S
Ballistic Missile Bombardment [*or Boost*] **Interceptor** [*Military*] ... BAMBI
Ballistic Missile Center [*Air Materiel Command*] [*Obsolete*] ... BMC
Ballistic Missile Center, Air Materiel Command [*Obsolete*] ... BMC/AMC
Ballistic Missile Checkout Equipment Technician-Specialist ... BMCET/S
Ballistic Missile Construction Office ... BMCO
Ballistic Missile Cost Study ... BMCS
Ballistic Missile Defense ... BMD
Ballistic Missile Defense Advanced Technology Center ... BMDATC
Ballistic Missile Defense Center ... BMDC
Ballistic Missile Defense Command Post ... BMDCP
Ballistic Missile Defense Committee ... BMDC
Ballistic Missile Defense Emergency Action Report ... BMDEAR
Ballistic Missile Defense Integrated Training Plan ... BMDITP
Ballistic Missile Defense Master Plan ... BMDMP
Ballistic Missile Defense Missile Battalion ... BMDMB
Ballistic Missile Defense - Nuclear Effects and Threat Committee ... BMD-NEAT
Ballistic Missile Defense Operations ... BMDO
Ballistic Missile Defense Operations Activity ... BMDOA
Ballistic Missile Defense Program Manager ... BMDPM
Ballistic Missile Defense Program Office ... BMDPO
Ballistic Missile Defense Surveillance Battalion ... BMDSB
Ballistic Missile Defense System ... BMDS
Ballistic Missile Defense Systems Command ... BMDSCOM
Ballistic Missile Defense Test Program ... BMDTP
Ballistic Missile Division [*Ballistic Research Laboratory*] ... BMD
Ballistic Missile Early Warning [*System*] ... BMEW
Ballistic Missile Early Warning System ... BMEWS
Ballistic Missile Inertial Guidance Technician-Mechanic ... BMIGT/M
Ballistic Missile Interceptor ... BMI
Ballistic Missile Launch Equipment Technician-Repairman ... BMLET/R
Ballistic Missile Logistics Office ... BMLO
Ballistic Missile Manager ... BMM
Ballistic Missile Office [*or Officer*] [*Air Force*] ... BMO
Ballistic Missile Operational Training Readiness ... BMOTR
Ballistic Missile Orientation Course ... BMOC
Ballistic Missile Radiation Analysis Center ... BAMIRAC
Ballistic Missile Reentry System ... BMRS
Ballistic Missile Reentry System ... BMRSYS
Ballistic Missile Ship [*Navy*] ... BMS
Ballistic Missile Surface Force ... BMSF
Ballistic Missile Systems Command [*Army*] ... BMSC
Ballistic Missile Target System ... BMTS
Ballistic Missile Terminal Defense ... BMTD
Ballistic Missile Test System ... BMTS
Ballistic Missile Test Vessel ... BMTV
Ballistic Missiles European Task Organization [*Military*] ... BMETO
Ballistic Missiles Management Group ... BMMG
Ballistic Missiles Weapon System ... BMWS
Ballistic Offense Suppressive System [*Military*] ... BOSS
Ballistic Range Experimental Program ... BREP
Ballistic Recording System ... BRS
Ballistic Recoverable Booster ... BRB
Ballistic Recovery of Orbiting Man ... BROOM
Ballistic Reentry Body ... BRB
Ballistic Reentry Vehicle ... BRV
Ballistic Research Laboratories Electronic Scientific Computer ... BRLESC
Ballistic Research Laboratory [*Military*] ... BRL
Ballistic Rocket Air Suppression ... BRAS
Ballistic Shell ... BS
Ballistic Simulated Round ... BSR
Ballistic Systems Education Division [*Air University*] [*Air Force*] ... BSED
Ballistic Systems Zeus [*Aerospace*] ... BSZ
Ballistic Test and Evaluation Systems ... BATES
Ballistic Test Facility [*Air Research and Development Command*] ... BTF
Ballistic Test Submodule ... BTSM
Ballistic Track Assignor ... BTA
Ballistic Wind ... BALLWIN
Ballistic Wind ... BALWND
Ballistic Wind Plotter ... BWP
Ballistically Launched Aerodynamic Missile ... BLAM
Ballistics ... BAL
Ballistics Dispensing System ... BDS
Ballistocardiogram [*Medicine*] ... BCG
Ballon De Servance [*France*] [*Seismograph station code, US Geological Survey*] ... BSF
Balloon ... BLN
Balloon Altitude Mosaic Measurements ... BAMM
Balloon-Assisted Takeoff [*Air Force*] ... BATO
Balloon Astronomy ... BALAST
Balloon Atmospheric Propagation Experiment [*NASA*] ... BAPE
Balloon Barrage ... BB
Balloon-Borne Astronomical Studies ... BBAS
Balloon-Borne Filter ... BBF
Balloon-Borne Filter Radiometer ... BBFR
Balloon-Borne Microwave Limb Sounder [*Atmospheric research*] ... BMLS
Balloon-Borne Nephelometer ... BBN
Balloon-Borne Polar Nephelometer ... BBPN
Balloon-Borne Polar Nephelometer ... BPN
Balloon-Borne Radio ... BBR
Balloon-Borne Radio System ... BBRS
Balloon-Borne Solar Pointer ... BBSP
Balloon-Borne Ultraviolet Stellar Spectrometer ... BUSS
Balloon Ceiling [*Meteorology*] ... B
Balloon Destroyer [*British*] ... BD
Balloon Federation of America ... BFA
Balloon Infrared Astronomy Platform ... BIRAP
Balloon Interrogation Package ... BIP

Balloon-Launched Decelerator Test [*Air Force*] ... BLDT
Balloon Launching Station ... BLS
Balloon and Nike Scaled High Explosive Experiment ... BANSHEE
Balloon Parachute ... BALLUTE
Balloon Platoon of America [*Later, HBC*] ... BPA
Balloon Post Collectors Club ... BPCC
Balloon Radio System ... BRS
Balloon Supported Rocket ... BSR
Balloon Temperature and Humidity [*Sonde*] [*Meteorology*] ... BALTHUM
Balloon Transport System ... BTS
Ballstop ... BSP
Ballwin, MO [*Radio station call letters*] ... KYMC
Bally Manufacturing Corp. [*NYSE symbol*] ... BLY
Bally's Park Place [*NYSE symbol*] ... BPP
Balmaceda [*Chile*] [*Airport symbol*] ... BBA
Balmoral Shoe [*Orthosis*] ... Bal
Balneologia Polska [*A publication*] ... Balneol Pol
Balneological Society of Japan. Journal [*A publication*] ... Balneol Soc Japan Jour
Balneum [*Bath*] [*Medicine*] ... B
Balneum Arenae [*Sand Bath*] [*Medicine*] ... BA
Balneum Arenae [*Sand Bath*] [*Medicine*] ... BAL ARENAE
Balneum Mariae [*Salt-Water Bath*] [*Medicine*] ... BAL MAR
Balneum Marinum [*Sea-Water Bath*] [*Medicine*] ... BM
Balneum Maris [*Sea Bath*] [*Medicine*] ... BAL MAR
Balneum Vapor [*Vapor Bath*] [*Medicine*] ... BAL VAP
Balneum Vapor [*Vapor Bath*] [*Medicine*] ... BV
Balsamum [*Balsam*] [*Pharmacy*] ... BALS
Baltek Corp. [*NASDAQ symbol*] ... BTEK
Balthazar Scales of Adaptive Behavior [*Psychology*] ... BSAB
Baltic [*MARC language code*] [*Library of Congress*] ... bat
Baltic-American Freedom League ... BAFL
Baltic Aviation, Inc. [*Denver, CO*] [*FAA designator*] ... BLT
Baltic and International Maritime Conference ... BIMCO
Baltic Review [*A publication*] ... Bal R
Baltic Review [*New York*] [*A publication*] ... BR
Baltic States [*MARC geographic area code*] [*Library of Congress*] ... eb-----
Baltic Student Federation ... BSF
Baltic Women's Council ... BWC
Baltic World Conference ... BWC
Baltimore [*Maryland*] ... BALT
Baltimore [*Maryland*] ... BALTO
Baltimore [*Maryland*] [*Airport symbol*] [*Name derived from Baltimore-Washington International Airport*] ... BWI
[*The*] **Baltimore & Annapolis Railroad Co.** [*AAR code*] ... BLA
Baltimore Bar Library, Baltimore, MD [*Library symbol*] ... MdBB
Baltimore Biological Laboratory ... BBL
Baltimore Bulletin of Education [*A publication*] ... Baltimore B of Ed
Baltimore City Court House, Baltimore, MD [*Library symbol*] ... MdBCH
Baltimore City Hospitals, Doctors' Library, Baltimore, MD [*Library symbol*] ... MdBH
Baltimore College of Commerce [*Maryland*] ... BCC
Baltimore Conference, Inc., United Methodist Historical Society, Baltimore, MD [*Library symbol*] ... MdBBC
Baltimore County Public Library, Towson, MD [*Library symbol*] ... MdBCP
Baltimore & Eastern Railroad Co. [*Absorbed into Consolidated Rail Corp.*] [*AAR code*] ... BE
Baltimore Gas & Electric Co. [*NYSE symbol*] ... BGE
Baltimore Hebrew College, Baltimore, MD [*Library symbol*] ... MdBHC
Baltimore Junior College [*Maryland*] ... BJC
Baltimore, MD [*Location identifier*] [*FAA*] ... FND
Baltimore, MD [*Location identifier*] [*FAA*] ... MTN
Baltimore, MD [*Location identifier*] [*FAA*] ... RUX
Baltimore, MD [*Radio station call letters*] ... WAYE
Baltimore, MD [*Radio station call letters*] ... WBAL
Baltimore, MD [*Television station call letters*] ... WBAL-TV
Baltimore, MD [*Television station call letters*] ... WBFF-TV
Baltimore, MD [*Radio station call letters*] ... WBJC
Baltimore, MD [*Radio station call letters*] ... WBMD
Baltimore, MD [*Radio station call letters*] ... WBSB
Baltimore, MD [*Radio station call letters*] ... WBYQ
Baltimore, MD [*Radio station call letters*] ... WCAO
Baltimore, MD [*Radio station call letters*] ... WCBM
Baltimore, MD [*Radio station call letters*] ... WEAA
Baltimore, MD [*Radio station call letters*] ... WEBB
Baltimore, MD [*Radio station call letters*] ... WFBR
Baltimore, MD [*Radio station call letters*] ... WITH
Baltimore, MD [*Radio station call letters*] ... WITH-FM
Baltimore, MD [*Radio station call letters*] ... WIYY
Baltimore, MD [*Radio station call letters*] ... WJHU-FM
Baltimore, MD [*Television station call letters*] ... WJZ-TV
Baltimore, MD [*Television station call letters*] ... WKJL-TV
Baltimore, MD [*Radio station call letters*] ... WLIF
Baltimore, MD [*Television station call letters*] ... WMAR-TV
Baltimore, MD [*Television station call letters*] ... WMPB
Baltimore, MD [*Television station call letters*] ... WNUV-TV
Baltimore, MD [*Radio station call letters*] ... WPOC
Baltimore, MD [*Radio station call letters*] ... WRBS
Baltimore, MD [*Radio station call letters*] ... WWIN
Baltimore, MD [*Radio station call letters*] ... WXVY
Baltimore, MD [*Radio station call letters*] ... WYST
Baltimore, MD [*Radio station call letters*] ... WYST-FM
Baltimore Museum of Art, Baltimore, MD [*Library symbol*] ... MdBMA
Baltimore Museum of Art. News [*A publication*] ... Baltimore Mus Art N
Baltimore Museum of Art. News [*A publication*] ... Baltimore Mus N
[*The*] **Baltimore & Ohio Chicago Terminal Railroad Co.** ... B & OCT
[*The*] **Baltimore & Ohio Chicago Terminal Railroad Co.** [*AAR code*] ... BOCT
[*The*] **Baltimore & Ohio Railroad Co.** [*Chessie System, Inc.*] ... B & O
[*The*] **Baltimore & Ohio Railroad Co.** [*Chessie System, Inc.*] ... B & O RR
[*The*] **Baltimore & Ohio Railroad Co.** [*Chessie System, Inc.*] [*AAR code*] ... BO
[*The*] **Baltimore & Ohio Railroad Co., Employees' Library, Baltimore, MD** [*Library symbol*] [*Obsolete*] ... MdBBO
Baltimore Photo & Blue Print Co., Baltimore, MD [*Library symbol*] ... BPB
Baltimore Regional Planning Commission [*Library network*] ... RPC
Baltimore Steam Packet Co. [*AAR code*] ... BSP
Baltische Hefte [*A publication*] ... B He
Baluchi [*MARC language code*] [*Library of Congress*] ... bal
Balwant Vidyapeeth Journal of Agricultural and Scientific Research [*A publication*] ... Balwant Vidyapeeth J Agric Sci Res
Balwant Vidyapeeth Journal of Agricultural and Scientific Research [*A publication*] ... Balwant Vidyapeeth J Agr Sci Res
Balzac Deflection Door ... BDD
BAM-Berichte. Forschung und Entwicklung in der Bundesanstalt fuer Materialpruefung [*A publication*] ... BAM-Ber
BAM Berlin Amtsblatt und Mitteilungsblatt der Bundesanstalt fuer Materialpruefung [*A publication*] ... BAM Amtsbl Mitteilungsbl
Bamaga [*Australia*] [*Airport symbol*] ... ABM
Bamako [*Mali*] [*Airport symbol*] ... BKO
Bambara [*MARC language code*] [*Library of Congress*] ... bam
Bamberg, SC [*Radio station call letters*] ... WWBD
Bamberg, SC [*Radio station call letters*] ... WWBD-FM
Bamberger Abhandlungen und Forschungen [*A publication*] ... BAF
Bamburi [*Kenya*] [*Airport symbol*] [*Obsolete*] ... BMQ
Bamian [*Afghanistan*] [*Airport symbol*] [*Obsolete*] ... BIN
Bamu [*Papua New Guinea*] [*Airport symbol*] ... BMZ
Ban Unsafe Schoolbuses Which Regularly Endanger Children [*Student legal action organization*] ... BUSWREC
Banana Plug Resistor ... BPR
Banana River Repeater Station [*NASA*] ... BRRS
Banasthali Patrika [*A publication*] ... BP
Banber Erevani Hamalsarani-Vestnik Erevanskogo Universiteta [*A publication*] ... Banb Erev Hamal
Banber Matenadarani [*A publication*] ... BM
Banbury [*British depot code*] ... BAN
Banc One Corp. [*NYSE symbol*] ... ONE
Banc One Corp. A Pfd [*NASDAQ symbol*] ... BONEP
Banca Commerciale Italiana [*Italy*] ... BCI
Banca Nazionale del Lavoro [*Italy*] ... BNL
Banca Nazionale del Lavoro. Quarterly Review [*A publication*] ... Banca Naz Lav Quart R
Banca Nazionale del Lavoro. Quarterly Review [*A publication*] ... BNL
BanCal Tri-State Corporation [*NYSE symbol*] ... BNC
Banco Central SA ADS [*NYSE symbol*] ... BCM
Banco De Ponce [*NASDAQ symbol*] ... BDEP
Banco Industrial del Mediterraneo [*Industrial Bank of the Mediterranean*] [*Spain*] ... BIM
Banco Industrial del Peru [*Industrial Bank of Peru*] ... BIP
Banco Industrial de Venezuela [*Industrial Bank of Venezuela*] ... BIV
Banco Interamericano de Desarrollo [*Interamerican Development Bank*] ... BID
Banco de Intercambio Regional [*Argentina*] ... BIR
Banco Internacional de Reconstruccion y Fomento [*International Bank for Reconstruction and Development*] ... BIRF
Banco Nacional do Desanvolvimento Economico [*National Economic Development Bank*] [*Brazil*] ... BNDE
Banco Nacional de Mexico [*National Bank of Mexico*] ... BANAMEX
Banco Popular de Puerto Rico [*NASDAQ symbol*] ... BPOP
Banco Regis [*or Reginae*] [*The King's (or Queen's) Bench*] [*Latin*] ... BR
Bancohio Corp. [*NASDAQ symbol*] ... BOHI
Bancoklahoma Corporation [*NASDAQ symbol*] ... BOKC
Bancorp Hawaii, Incorporated [*NASDAQ symbol*] ... BNHI
Bancroft Convertible Fund, Inc. [*American Stock Exchange symbol*] ... BCV
Bancroft, ON [*Television station call letters*] ... CIII-TV-2
Bancroft, ON [*Radio station call letters*] ... CJNH
Bancroft Public Library, Salem, NY [*Library symbol*] ... NSa
Bancroft Register, Bancroft, IA [*Library symbol*] ... IaBanR
Banctec, Inc. [*NASDAQ symbol*] ... BTEC
BancTEXAS Group [*NYSE symbol*] ... BTX
BancTexas Group Pfd [*NASDAQ symbol*] ... BTXGO
Bancus [*Bench*] ... B
Band ... B
Band ... BD
Band ... BND
Band [*Volume*] [*German*] ... BD
Band Amplitude Product ... BAP
Band Display ... BNDDIS
Band Edge Energy ... BEE
Band Elimination ... BE
Band Elimination Filter ... BEF
Band Filter Cutoff ... BFCO
Band Filter Set ... BFS

Band Ignitor Tube ... BIT
Band-Limited Hiss [*NASA*] ... BLH
Band-Limited Signal ... BLS
Band and Orchestra [*Musical slang*] ... B & O
Band Pressure Level ... BPL
Banda Aceh [*Indonesia*] [*Airport symbol*] ... BTJ
Bandag, Inc. [*NYSE symbol*] ... BDG
Bandanaira [*Indonesia*] [*Airport symbol*] ... NDA
Bandar Abbas [*Iran*] [*Airport symbol*] ... BND
Bandar Lampung [*Indonesia*] [*Airport symbol*] ... TKG
Bandar Lengeh [*Iran*] [*Airport symbol*] ... BDH
Bandar Seri Begawan [*Brunei*] [*Airport symbol*] ... BWN
Bande Dessinee [*Comic strip*] [*French*] ... BD
Bandelier National Monument ... BAND
Bandera, TX [*Radio station call letters*] ... KQRK
Bandmaster ... BMSTR
Bandoleer ... BAND
Bandon Public Library, Bandon, OR [*Library symbol*] ... OrBan
Bandpass ... BP
Bandpass Crystal ... BPC
Bandpass Crystal Filter ... BCF
Bandpass Crystal Filter ... BPCF
Bandpass Filter ... BPF
Bandpass Network ... BPN
Bandpass Transformer ... BPT
Bands (Civilian and Military) [*Public-performance tariff class*] [*British*] ... B
Bandsman [*Military*] [*British*] ... BDSMN
Bandundu [*Zaire*] [*Airport symbol*] ... FDU
Bandung [*Indonesia*] [*Airport symbol*] ... BDO
Bandung [*Indonesia*] [*Seismograph station code, US Geological Survey*] [*Closed*] ... BND
Bandwidth ... B
Bandwidth ... BW
Bandwidth Compression Technique ... BCT
Bandwidth Ratio ... BWR
Bandwidth Shape Factor ... BSF
Banff [*Alberta*] [*Seismograph station code, US Geological Survey*] [*Closed*] ... BAN
Banff School of Fine Arts, Banff, AB, Canada [*Library symbol*] ... CaABSFA
Bangalore [*India*] [*Airport symbol*] ... BLR
Bangkok [*Thailand*] [*Airport symbol*] ... BKK
Bangladesh [*MARC geographic area code*] [*Library of Congress*] ... a-bg---
Bangladesh [*Two-letter standard code*] ... BD
Bangladesh [*MARC country of publication code*] [*Library of Congress*] ... bg
Bangladesh [*Three-letter standard code*] ... BGD
Bangladesh Agricultural Sciences Abstracts [*A publication*] ... Bangladesh Agr Sci Abstr
Bangladesh Biman [*ICAO designator*] ... BG
Bangladesh Cultural Association ... BCA
Bangladesh Development Studies [*A publication*] ... Bangladesh Devel Stud
Bangladesh Development Studies [*A publication*] ... Bangla Dev Stud
Bangladesh Development Studies [*A publication*] ... BGLE
Bangladesh Geological Survey. Records [*A publication*] ... Bangladesh Geol Surv Rec
Bangladesh Historical Studies [*A publication*] ... Bangla Hist Stud
Bangladesh Horticulture [*A publication*] ... Bangladesh Hortic
Bangladesh Journal of Agricultural Sciences [*A publication*] ... Bangladesh J Agric Sci
Bangladesh Journal of Biological and Agricultural Sciences [*A publication*] ... Bangladesh J Biol Agric Sci
Bangladesh Journal of Botany [*A publication*] ... Bangladesh J Bot
Bangladesh Journal of Scientific and Industrial Research [*A publication*] ... Bangladesh J Sci & Ind Res
Bangladesh Journal of Scientific and Industrial Research [*A publication*] ... Bangladesh J Sci Ind Res
Bangladesh Journal of Zoology [*A publication*] ... Bangladesh J Zool
Bangladesh Medical Research Council Bulletin [*A publication*] ... Bangladesh Med Res Counc Bull
Bangladesh National Scientific and Technical Documentation Centre [*Information service*] ... BANSDOC
Bangladesh News Agency ... BNA
Bangladesh Press International ... BPI
Bangladesh Sanwad Sanstha [*News agency*] ... BSS
Bangladesh Veterinary Journal ... Bangladesh Vet J
Bango Whiplash [*Military*] ... BW
Bangor [*Maine*] [*Airport symbol*] ... BGR
Bangor [*New York*] [*Seismograph station code, US Geological Survey*] ... BGR
Bangor & Aroostook Railroad Co. ... B & AR
Bangor & Aroostook Railroad Co. [*AAR code*] ... BAR
Bangor Historical Society, Bangor, ME [*Library symbol*] ... MeBaHi
Bangor Hydro-Electric Co. [*NASDAQ symbol*] ... BANG
Bangor International Airport ... BIA
Bangor, ME [*Radio station call letters*] ... WABI
Bangor, ME [*Television station call letters*] ... WABI-TV
Bangor, ME [*Radio station call letters*] ... WACZ
Bangor, ME [*Radio station call letters*] ... WBGW
Bangor, ME [*Radio station call letters*] ... WHCF
Bangor, ME [*Radio station call letters*] ... WHSN
Bangor, ME [*Television station call letters*] ... WLBZ-TV
Bangor, ME [*Radio station call letters*] ... WMEH
Bangor, ME [*Radio station call letters*] ... WMLI
Bangor, ME [*Radio station call letters*] ... WPBC
Bangor, ME [*Television station call letters*] ... WVII
Bangor Mental Health Institute, Bangor, ME [*OCLC symbol*] ... MEB
Bangor [*Wales*] **Orange Position Estimating Equipment for Pastures** [*Electronic beeper to be attached to sheep*] ... BO PEEP
Bangor Public Library, Bangor, ME [*OCLC symbol*] ... BYN
Bangor Public Library, Bangor, ME [*Library symbol*] ... MeBa
Bangor Punta Corp. [*NYSE symbol*] ... BNK
Bangor Theological Seminary, Bangor, ME [*Library symbol*] ... MeBaT
Bangui [*Central African Republic*] [*Airport symbol*] ... BGF
Bangui [*Central African Republic*] [*Geomagnetic observatory code*] ... BNG
Bangui [*Central African Republic*] [*Seismograph station code, US Geological Survey*] ... BNG
Bani [*Monetary unit in Romania*] ... B
Bani Yas Airlines [*United Arab Emirates*] [*ICAO designator*] ... DC
Banister Continental Ltd. [*American Stock Exchange symbol*] ... BAN
Banja Luka [*Yugoslavia*] [*Seismograph station code, US Geological Survey*] ... BLY
Banjarmasin [*Indonesia*] [*Airport symbol*] ... BDJ
Banjo ... BJO
Banjul [*Gambia*] [*Airport symbol*] ... BJL
Bank ... BK
Bank Administration Institute [*Formerly, National Association for Bank Audit, Control, and Operation*] ... BAI
Bank of America ... BA
Bank Angle ... BA
Bank Automated Service Information System ... BASIS
Bank Book ... BB
Bank Book ... BK
Bank of Boston [*NYSE symbol*] ... BKB
Bank Building & Equipment Corp. of America [*American Stock Exchange symbol*] ... BB
Bank Burglary ... BB
Bank of Canada, Ottawa, ON, Canada [*Library symbol*] ... CaOOB
Bank of China Economic Review [*A publication*] ... BCER
Bank for Cooperatives ... BC
Bank of Delaware Corp. [*NASDAQ symbol*] ... BDEL
Bank Descriptor Index [*Data processing*] ... BDI
Bank Descriptor Registers [*Data processing*] ... BDR
Bank Descriptor Word [*Data processing*] ... BDW
Bank Draft ... BD
Bank of England ... B of E
Bank of England ... BE
Bank Error ... BE
Bank of Finland. Monthly Bulletin [*A publication*] ... Bank Finland Mthly B
Bank fuer Gemeinwirtschaft [*Frankfurt, Germany*] ... BfG
Bank of Hawaii. Monthly Review [*A publication*] ... Bk Hawaii
Bank Holding Company ... BHC
Bank Holiday ... BH
Bank for International Settlements ... BIS
Bank of Kuwait and the Middle East ... BKME
Bank Larceny ... BL
Bank Leumi ADR [*NASDAQ symbol*] ... BKLMY
Bank of London & South America Ltd. ... BOLSA
Bank of London & South America Ltd. Review [*A publication*] ... Bank London South Amer R
Bank of Los Angeles [*NASDAQ symbol*] ... BKLA
Bank Marketing Association ... BMA
Bank Marketing Association, Chicago, IL [*Library symbol*] ... ICBM
Bank Marketing Association, Chicago, IL [*OCLC symbol*] ... IDZ
Bank of Montana Systems [*NASDAQ symbol*] ... BMON
Bank of Montreal, Canadian Imperial Bank of Commerce, Bank of Nova Scotia, and Toronto-Dominion Bank ... MINT
Bank of Montreal, Montreal, PQ, Canada [*Library symbol*] ... CaQMBMo
Bank Negara Malaysia. Bulletin [*A publication*] ... BNMB
Bank of New England Corp. [*NASDAQ symbol*] ... BKNE
Bank of New York Co., Inc. [*NYSE symbol*] ... BK
Bank Note Reporter [*A publication*] ... BNR
Bank of Nova Scotia, Toronto, ON, Canada [*Library symbol*] ... CaOTNS
Bank Officers Guild [*Later, Banking, Insurance, and Finance Union*] ... BOG
Bank Post Bill [*Business and trade*] ... BPB
Bank Public Relations and Marketing Association [*Later, BMA*] ... BPRMA
Bank Rate ... BR
Bank Robbery ... BR
Bank Securities, Inc. [*NASDAQ symbol*] ... BNKS
Bank-Share Owners Advisory League ... BSOAL
Bank South Corp. [*NASDAQ symbol*] ... BKSO
Bank Stationers Association ... BSA
Bank Street College of Education, New York, NY [*Library symbol*] ... NNBSC
Bank Street Writer [*A computer program manufactured by Bank Street and Intentional Educations, Inc.*] ... BSW
Bank of Sudan Economic and Financial Bulletin [*A publication*] ... Bank Sudan Ec Fin Bull
Bank Systems and Equipment [*A publication*] ... Bank Sys
Bank and Trust ... B & T
Bank to Turn [*Aviation*] ... BTT
Bank and Turn Indicator [*Aviation*] ... BTI
Bank of the United States ... BUS
Bank of Virginia Co. [*NYSE symbol*] ... BKV
Bank Wire Transfer of Funds ... BWTF

Bankair, Inc. [*West Columbia, SC*] [*FAA designator*] ... BKA
BankAmerica Corporation [*NYSE symbol*] ... BAC
BankAmerica Realty Investors SBI [*NYSE symbol*] ... BRE
BankAmericard [*Later, Visa*] [*Credit card*] ... BA
BankAmericard [*Later, Visa*] [*Credit card*] ... BAC
BankAmericard Service Exchange ... BASE
Bankcard Holders of America ... BHA
Bankeast Corp. [*NASDAQ symbol*] ... BENH
Banker-Farmer [*A publication*] ... Banker-F
Bankers' [*Rate*] [*Value of the English pound*] ... BK
Bankers Association for Foreign Trade ... BAFT
Bankers' Blanket Bond ... BBB
Bankers Committee to Eliminate Favoritism to Credit Unions ... BCEFCU
Bankers Committee for Tax Equality ... BCTE
Bankers' Magazine [*A publication*] ... Bankers' M
Bankers' Magazine [*A publication*] ... Bankers' Mag
Bankers' Magazine (London) [*A publication*] ... Bank M (L)
Bankers' Magazine (London) [*A publication*] ... Bank M (Lond)
Bankers' Magazine (New York) [*A publication*] ... Bank M (NY)
Bankers' Monthly [*A publication*] ... Bankers' Mo
Bankers' Monthly [*A publication*] ... Bankers' Mon
Banker's Note, Inc. [*NASDAQ symbol*] ... BKNT
Banker's Order [*British*] ... BO
Bankers Trust New York Corp. [*NYSE symbol*] ... BT
Bankers Trust of South Carolina [*NASDAQ symbol*] ... BTSC
Banking ... BKG
Banking and Currency Committee [*US Senate*] ... B & C
Banking Information Processing System ... BIPS
Banking Law Journal [*A publication*] ... Bank Law J
Banking On-Line Package System ... BOPS
Banking Profession Political Action Committee [*Acronym now used as official name of organization*] ... BANKPAC
Banking Research and Economic Analysis [*Unit*] [*Department of the Treasury*] ... BR & EA
Banking and Securities Industry Committee ... BASIC
Banknote ... BN
Banknote Quarterly [*A publication*] ... BQ
Bankroll [*Slang*] ... BR
Bankrupt ... BKRPT
Bankruptcy ... BANKCY
Bankruptcy ... BKCY
Bankruptcy ... BKRPTCY
Bankruptcy ... BKTCY
Bankruptcy ... BKY
Bankruptcy and Insolvancy Cases [*Legal*] [*British*] ... B & I
Banks of Iowa, Inc. [*NASDAQ symbol*] ... BIOW
BankVermont Corp. [*NASDAQ symbol*] ... BKVT
Banner Industries, Inc. [*NYSE symbol*] ... BNR
Banning, CA [*Radio station call letters*] ... KGUD
Banning Union Public Library, Banning, CA [*Library symbol*] ... CBan
Bannon, E. J., Buffalo NY [*STAC*] ... BEJ
Bannu [*Pakistan*] [*Airport symbol*] ... BNP
Banque Afrique Occidentale [*Bank of French West Africa*] ... BAO
Banque Arabe et Internationale d'Investissement [*France*] ... BAII
Banque Belge d'Afrique [*Belgian African Bank*] ... BBA
Banque Canadienne Nationale ... BCN
Banque des Etats de l'Afrique Centrale ... BEAC
Banque Europeenne pour l'Amerique Latine SA ... BEAL
Banque Europeenne de Credit [*Brussels*] ... BEC
Banque Europeenne d'Investissement [*European Investment Bank*] ... BEI
Banque Francaise du Commerce Exterieur [*French state-owned bank*] ... BFCE
Banque de France [*Bank of France*] ... BF
Banque Franco-Arabe d'Investissements Internationaux ... FRAB
Banque d'Informations Politiques et d'Actualites [*Political and Current Events Information Bank*] [*France*] [*Information service*] ... BIPA
Banque Internationale pour la Reconstruction et le Developpement [*International Bank for Reconstruction and Development; also known as the World Bank*] ... BIRD
Banque Marocaine du Commerce Exterieur [*Morocco*] ... BMCE
Banque Nationale de Belgique [*National Bank of Belgium*] ... BNB
Banque Nationale pour le Commerce et l'Industrie [*National Bank for Commerce and Industry*] ... BNCI
Banque Nationale de Paris [*National Bank of Paris*] ... BNP
Banque des Reglements Internationaux [*Bank for International Settlements*] ... BRI
Banque de Terminologie du Quebec [*Terminology Bank of Quebec*] [*French Language Board*] [*Information service*] ... BTQ
Banqueting/Catered Functions [*Public-performance tariff class*] [*British*] ... BF
Banta [*George*] **Co.** [*NASDAQ symbol*] ... BNTA
[*The*] **Bantock Society** ... BS
Banyaszati es Kohaszati Lapok. Banyaszat [*A publication*] ... Banyasz Kohasz Lap Banyasz
Banyaszati es Kohaszati Lapok. Banyaszat [*A publication*] ... Banyasz Kohasz Lapok Banyasz
Banyaszati es Kohaszati Lapok. Koeolaj es Foeldgaz [*A publication*] ... Banyasz Kohasz Lapok Koeolaj Foeldgaz
Banyaszati es Kohaszati Lapok. Kohaszat [*A publication*] ... Banyasz Kohasz Lapok Kohasz
Banz [*Papua New Guinea*] [*Airport symbol*] [*Obsolete*] ... BNZ
Baoshan [*China*] [*Airport symbol*] ... BSD
Baotou [*China*] [*Airport symbol*] ... BAV
BAPTA [*Bearing and Power Transfer Assembly*] **Accelerometer and Conditioner** [*Aerospace*] ... BAC
Baptist ... B
Baptist ... BAP
Baptist ... BAPT
Baptist Association of Hospital Chaplains ... BAHC
Baptist Bible College, Denver, CO [*Library symbol*] ... CoDBB
Baptist Bible College of Pennsylvania, Clarks Summit, PA [*Library symbol*] ... PCsB
Baptist Bible Fellowship International ... BBFI
Baptist Bulletin [*A publication*] ... Bapt B
Baptist College at Charleston, Charleston, SC [*OCLC symbol*] ... SBC
Baptist History and Heritage [*A publication*] ... Bapt Hist and Heritage
Baptist History and Heritage [*A publication*] ... BHH
Baptist Hospital Association ... BHA
Baptist Information Retrieval System [*Library network*] ... BIRS
Baptist Joint Committee on Public Affairs ... BJCPA
Baptist Life Association ... BLA
Baptist Medical Center (Montclair), Medical Library, Birmingham, AL [*Library symbol*] ... ABBM-M
Baptist Medical Center (Princeton), Medical Library, Birmingham, AL [*Library symbol*] ... ABBM-P
Baptist Medical Center, School of Nursing, Birmingham, AL [*Library symbol*] ... ABBM
Baptist Memorial Hospital, Kansas City, MO [*Library symbol*] ... MoKBH
Baptist Mid-Missions ... BMM
Baptist Mission Society ... BMS
Baptist Missionary Association Theological Seminary, Jacksonville, TX [*Library symbol*] ... TxJaB
Baptist Peace Fellowship ... BPF
Baptist Public Relations Association ... BPRA
Baptist Quarterly [*London*] [*A publication*] ... Bapt Q
Baptist Quarterly [*A publication*] ... BQ
Baptist Quarterly Review [*London*] [*A publication*] ... Bapt Q
Baptist Students Concerned [*Defunct*] ... BSC
Baptist Union ... BU
Baptist World Aid ... BWA
Baptist World Alliance ... BWA
Baptist World Relief [*Later, Baptist World Aid*] ... BWARF
Baptist Young People's Union ... BYPU
Baptists for Life ... BFL
Baptized ... BA
Baptized ... BAP
Baptized ... BAPT
Baptized ... BP
Bar ... B
Bar [*s*] [*Freight*] ... BA
Bar ... BR
Bar Association of the District of Columbia, Washington, DC [*Library symbol*] ... DBA
Bar Bulletin of the Boston Bar Association [*A publication*] ... Bar Bull (Boston)
Bar Draft [*Depth of water over a bar*] ... BD
Bar Examiner [*A publication*] ... Bar Exam
Bar Harbor [*Maine*] [*Airport symbol*] ... BHB
Bar Library Association of Kansas City, Kansas City, MO [*Library symbol*] ... MoKB
Baraboo, WI [*Radio station call letters*] ... WLVE
Baraboo, WI [*Radio station call letters*] ... WRPQ
Baracoa [*Cuba*] [*Airport symbol*] ... BCA
Barahona [*Dominican Republic*] [*Airport symbol*] ... BRX
Barakoma [*Solomon Islands*] [*Airport symbol*] ... VEV
Baramita [*Guyana*] [*Airport symbol*] ... BMJ
Barat College of the Sacred Heart [*Illinois*] ... BCSH
Barat College of the Sacred Heart, Lake Forest, IL [*OCLC symbol*] ... ICB
Barat College of the Sacred Heart, Lake Forest, IL [*Library symbol*] ... ILfB
Barat Review [*A publication*] ... Barat R
Baratropic ... BATROP
Barbados [*MARC country of publication code*] [*Library of Congress*] ... bb
Barbados [*Seismograph station code, US Geological Survey*] ... BDS
Barbados [*Airport symbol*] ... BGI
Barbados [*Seismograph station code, US Geological Survey*] [*Closed*] ... BRB
Barbados [*MARC geographic area code*] [*Library of Congress*] ... nwbb---
Barbados [*Aircraft nationality and registration mark*] ... 8P
Barbados [*Three-letter standard code*] ... BRB
Barbados [*Two-letter standard code*] ... BB
Barbados Board of Tourism ... BBT
Barbados Nursing Journal [*A publication*] ... Barbados Nurs J
Barbados Oceanographic and Meteorological Analysis Project ... BOMAP
Barbados Oceanographic and Meteorological Experiment [*National Oceanic and Atmospheric Administration*] ... BOMEX
Barbecue Briquet Institute [*Later, BIA*] ... BBI
Barbecue Industry Association ... BIA
Barber [*Charles E.*] [*Designer's mark, when appearing on US coins*] ... B
Barber, Albert P., Kenosha WI [*STAC*] ... BAA
Barber Greene Co. [*NASDAQ symbol*] ... BARB
Barber Oil Corp. [*NYSE symbol*] [*Delisted*] ... BBO
Barber Pole ... BP
Barber-Scotia College [*North Carolina*] ... BSC

Barber-Scotia College, Concord, NC [*OCLC symbol*] ... NCB
Barber-Scotia College, Concord, NC [*Library symbol*] ... NcCoB
Barber Suggestibility Scale [*Psychology*] ... BBS
Barberton Public Library, Barberton, OH [*Library symbol*] ... OBarb
Barbette [*Military*] ... BARB
Barbourville, KY [*Radio station call letters*] ... WYWY
Barbourville, KY [*Radio station call letters*] ... WYWY-FM
Barbuda [*West Indies*] [*Airport symbol*] ... BBQ
Barbuda [*MARC geographic area code*] [*Library of Congress*] ... nwbc---
Barcaldine [*Australia*] [*Airport symbol*] ... BCI
Barcelona [*A publication*] ... B
Barcelona [*Spain*] [*Airport symbol*] ... BCN
Barcelona [*Venezuela*] [*Airport symbol*] ... BLA
Barcelona. Instituto de Investigaciones Geologicas. Publicaciones [*A publication*] ... Barc Inst Invest Geol Publ
Barcelona. Instituto Provincial de Paleontologia. Actividades [*A publication*] ... Barc Inst Prov Paleontol Actividades
Barcelona. Instituto Provincial de Paleontologia. Paleontologia y Evolucion [*A publication*] ... Barc Inst Prov Paleontol Paleontol Evol
Barcelona Universidad. Facultad de Ciencias. Miscellanea Alcobe [*A publication*] ... Barc Univ Fac Cienc Misc Alcobe
Barcelona Universidad. Instituto Geologia. Memorias y Communicaciones [*A publication*] ... Barc Univ Inst Geol Mem Commun
Barch, John R., New York NY [*STAC*] ... BJR
Barcklay Flying Service [*Spokane, WA*] [*FAA designator*] ... ACH
Barclay Industries, Inc. [*American Stock Exchange symbol*] [*Delisted*] ... BLA
Barco of California [*American Stock Exchange symbol*] ... BRC
Barco Rotary Joint ... BRJ
Bard College, Annandale-On-Hudson, NY [*Library symbol*] ... NAnB
Bard College, Annandale-On-Hudson, NY [*OCLC symbol*] ... VVP
Bard [*C. R.*], **Inc.** [*NYSE symbol*] ... BCR
Bardeen-Cooper-Schrieffer [*Theory of superconductivity*] ... BCS
Barden Corp. [*NASDAQ symbol*] ... BARD
Bardstown, KY [*Radio station call letters*] ... WBRT
Bardstown, KY [*Radio station call letters*] ... WOKH
Bardufoss [*Norway*] [*Airport symbol*] ... BDU
Bare Aluminum Wire ... BAW
Bare Base [*Air Force*] ... BB
Bare Base Set [*Air Force*] ... BBS
Bare Base Support Package ... BBSP
Bare Beryllium Copper Wire ... BBCW
Bare Brass Wire ... BBW
Bare Copper ... BC
Bare Copper-Clad Wire ... BCCW
Bare Copper Wire ... BCW
Bare Gold-Plated Wire ... BGPW
Bare Molybdenum Wire ... BMW
Bare Nickel Chrome Wire ... BNCW
Bare Phosphor Bronze Wire ... BPBW
Bare Platinum Wire ... BPW
Bare Reactor Experiment at Nevada ... BREN
Bare Refractory, Double Containment [*Boiler*] [*NASA*] ... BRDC
Bare Silver-Plated Wire ... BSPW
Bare Stainless-Steel Wire ... BSSW
Bare Steel Wire ... BSW
Bare Tungsten Wire ... BTW
Bare Zirconium Wire ... BZW
Baretti [*A publication*] ... Bar
Barge ... B
Barge ... BG
Barge Aboard Catamaran ... BACAT
Barge, Amphibious, Resupply, Cargo ... BARC
Barge Cargo ... BC
Barge Cargo Ship ... TALS
Barge Carrying Vessel ... BCV
Barge, Knockdown ... BK
Barge Off Loading Facility ... BOLF
Barge, Training ... BT
Barge Transportation Appraisal Program [*Military*] ... BARTAP
Barges on Board [*Shipping*] ... BOB
Bari [*Italy*] [*Seismograph station code, US Geological Survey*] [*Closed*] ... BAI
Bari [*Italy*] [*Airport symbol*] ... BRI
Barile-Yaguchi-Eveland [*Growth medium*] [*Microbiology*] ... BYE
Barinas [*Venezuela*] [*Airport symbol*] ... BNS
Bario [*Malaysia*] [*Airport symbol*] ... BBN
Barisan Socialist Party [*Malaysia*] ... BSP
Baritone ... BAR
Barium [*Chemical element*] ... Ba
Barium Cloud Experiment [*NASA*] ... BCE
Barium Crown ... BC
Barium Enema [*Medicine*] ... BaE
Barium Enema [*Medicine*] ... BE
Barium Ferrite Magnet ... BFM
Barium Ion Cloud [*NASA*] ... BIC
Barium Meal [*Medicine*] ... BaM
Barium Oxide Ferrite ... BOF
Barium Sodium Niobate [*Crystal*] ... BSN
Bark ... BK
Barker Free Library, Barker, NY [*Library symbol*] ... NBar
Barker-Henderson [*Theory*] [*Chemical physics*] ... BH
Barkhausen-Kurz Oscillator ... BKO
Barking Sands Tactical Underwater Range [*Naval Oceanographic Office*] ... BARSTUR
Barking Sands Underwater Range Expansion [*Naval Oceanographic Office*] ... BSURE
Barksdale, LA [*Location identifier*] [*FAA*] ... BYU
Barley Canyon [*New Mexico*] [*Seismograph station code, US Geological Survey*] ... BRC
Barley and Malt Institute ... BMI
Barley Stripe Mosaic Virus ... BSMV
Barley Yellow Dwarf Virus ... BYDV
Barlow Sanatorium, Elks Tuberculosis Library, Los Angeles, CA [*Library symbol*] ... CLE
Barn [*Area of nuclear cross-section*] ... b
Barn Cleaner, Cattle Feeder, and Silo Unloader Association [*Later, FEA*] ... BCCFSUA
Barn Equipment Association [*Later, FEA*] ... BEA
Barnabites [*Also, CRSP*] [*Roman Catholic men's religious order*] ... Barn
Barnard College, Columbia University, New York, NY [*Library symbol*] ... NNBa
Barnaul'skii Gosudarstvennyi Pedagogiceskii Institut. Ucenye Zapiski [*A publication*] ... Barnaul Gos Ped Inst Ucen Zap
Barnes Engineering Company ... BEC
Barnes Engineering Co. [*American Stock Exchange symbol*] ... BIR
Barnes Group, Inc. [*NYSE symbol*] ... B
Barnes, Hickam, Pantzer, & Boyd, Indianapolis, IN [*OCLC symbol*] ... IHB
Barnes, Hickam, Pantzer, & Boyd, Law Library, Indianapolis, IN [*Library symbol*] ... InIBHP
Barnesboro, PA [*Radio station call letters*] ... WNCC
Barnesville, GA [*Radio station call letters*] ... WBAF
Barnesville Public Library, Barnesville, OH [*Library symbol*] ... OBarn
Barnett Banks of Florida, Inc. [*NYSE symbol*] ... BBF
Barnett Mortgage Trust [*NYSE symbol*] ... BMT
Barney Children's Medical Center, Dayton, OH [*Library symbol*] ... ODaMC
Barnstable, MA [*Radio station call letters*] ... WQRC
Barnwell Industries, Inc. [*American Stock Exchange symbol*] ... BRN
Barnwell, SC [*Radio station call letters*] ... WBAW
Barnwell, SC [*Radio station call letters*] ... WBAW-FM
Baroclinic ... BACLIN
Baroda Journal of Nutrition [*A publication*] ... Baroda J Nutr
Baroda. Museum and Picture Gallery. Bulletin [*A publication*] ... BBMPG
Barograph Display Unit ... BDU
Barometer ... BAR
Barometer ... BARO
Barometer ... BRM
Barometric Altimeter ... BA
Barometric Altitude Control ... BAC
Barometric Altitude Indicator ... BAI
Barometric Pressure ... BP
Barometric Pressure Correction [*Symbol*] ... B
Baron ... B
Baron ... BN
Baron Data Systems [*NASDAQ symbol*] ... BDSY
Baronet ... BART
Baronet ... BT
Baronial Order of Magna Charta ... BOMC
Baroque All Style High [*Acronym is title of silk screen by sculptor Eduardo Paolozzi*] ... BASH
Barora [*Solomon Islands*] [*Airport symbol*] ... RRI
Barostat ... BARO
Baroswitch ... BS
Barque ... BQ
Barque ... BQUE
Barquentine [*Ship*] ... BKN
Barquisimeto [*Venezuela*] [*Airport symbol*] ... BRM
Barra [*Brazil*] [*Airport symbol*] ... BQQ
Barra [*Hebrides Islands*] [*Airport symbol*] ... BRR
Barra Colorado [*Costa Rica*] [*Airport symbol*] ... BCL
Barracks ... BAKS
Barracks ... BKS
Barracks Craft [*Non-self-propelled*] [*Navy symbol*] ... APL
Barracks Master-at-Arms ... BMAA
Barracks and Quarters [*Army*] ... B & Q
Barrage Balloon ... BRGBLN
Barrage Balloon [*Navy symbol*] ... ZK
Barrage Jammers [*RADAR*] ... BJ
Barrage Mansour Eddahbi [*Morocco*] [*Seismograph station code, US Geological Survey*] ... BME
Barrage Rocket ... BR
Barrancabermeja [*Colombia*] [*Airport symbol*] ... EJA
Barranquilla [*Colombia*] [*Airport symbol*] ... BAQ
Barranquitas, PR [*Radio station call letters*] ... WOLA
Barrasiha-Ye Tarikhi [*A publication*] ... ByT
Barratry [*FBI standardized term*] ... BARR
Barre Granite Association ... BGA
Barre du Jour [*A publication*] ... BdJ
Barre-Montpelier, VT [*Radio station call letters*] ... WNCS
Barre-Montpelier, VT [*Radio station call letters*] ... WSKI
Barre, VT [*Radio station call letters*] ... WORK
Barre, VT [*Radio station call letters*] ... WSNO
Barreau de Montreal, Bibliotheque des Avocats, Montreal, PQ, Canada [*Library symbol*] ... CaQMAv

Barred	BRRD
Barreiras [Brazil] [Airport symbol]	BRA
Barrel	BAR
Barrel	BBL
Barrel	BL
Barrel	BRL
Barrel Coating	BC
Barrel Roll	BR
Barrel-Tile Roof [Technical drawings]	BTR
Barrels [or Boxes] [Freight]	BB
Barrels	BBLS
Barrels	BLS
Barrels or Bags [Freight]	B BGS
Barrels, Boxes, or Crates [Freight]	BBC
Barrels per Calendar Day	BPCD
Barrels per Day	BD
Barrels per Day	BPD
Barrels per Day Oil Equivalent	B/DOE
Barrels per Hour	BPH
Barrels of Oil Equivalent	BOE
Barrels of Oil Equivalent per Day	BOED
Barrels per Stream Day	BPSD
Barren Foundation	BF
Barrett [California] [Seismograph station code, US Geological Survey]	BAR
Barrett Memorial Library, Williams Bay, WI [Library symbol]	WWil
Barrette [Hawaii] [Seismograph station code, US Geological Survey] [Closed]	BAH
[The] Barretts of Wimpole Street [A play by Rudolf Besier]	BOWS
Barrie, ON [Radio station call letters]	CHAY-FM
Barrie, ON [Radio station call letters]	CKBB
Barrie, ON [Television station call letters]	CKVR-TV
Barrie Public Library, Barrie, ON, Canada [Library symbol]	CaOBa
Barrier	BAR
Barrier	BARR
Barrier Combat Air Patrol [Navy]	BARCAP
Barrier and Countersurveillance Division [Army]	B & CD
Barrier Doctrine [Military]	BARDOC
Barrier Film Rectifier	BFR
Barrier, Grease Proof	BGP
Barrier Injection Transit Time [Physics]	BARITT
Barrier Layer Cell	BLC
Barrier Layer Rectifier	BLR
Barrier, Moisture Vapor Proof	BMVP
Barrier Operations [Military]	BAROPS
Barrier Paper Manufacturers Association [Defunct]	BPMA
Barrier Ready Light System	BRLS
Barrier Terminal Strip	BTS
Barrier Up Indicator System	BUIS
Barrier Up Indicator System	BUISYS
Barrier, Waterproof	BWP
Barring	BRRG
Barringer Research Ltd., Rexdale, ON, Canada [Library symbol]	CaOTBR
Barringer Resources, Inc. [NASDAQ symbol]	BARR
Barrington College, Barrington, RI [Library symbol]	RBaB
Barrington Historical Society, Barrington, NJ [Library symbol]	NjBarHi
Barrington, IL [Radio station call letters]	WPBR-FM
Barrio Florida [Puerto Rico] [Seismograph station code, US Geological Survey]	PWP
Barris Industries [NASDAQ symbol]	BRRS
Barrister	BARR
Barrister-at-Law	BL
Barro Colorado Island [Canal Zone] [Site of Smithsonian Tropical Research Institute]	BCI
Barron-Welsh Art Scale [Psychology]	BWAS
Barrow [Alaska] [Airport symbol]	BRW
Barrow [Alaska] [Geomagnetic observatory code]	BRW
Barrow [Alaska] [Seismograph station code, US Geological Survey] [Closed]	BRW
Barrow, AK [Radio station call letters]	KBRW
Barry [Cardiff] [Welsh depot code]	BRY
Barry College, North Miami, FL [OCLC symbol]	FBC
Barry College, North Miami, FL [Library symbol]	FNmB
Barry [R. G.] Corp. [American Stock Exchange symbol]	RGB
Barry Melton Band [Pop music group]	BMB
Barry Railway [Wales]	BR
Barry Wright Corp. [NYSE symbol]	BAR
Barryton Public Library, Barryton, MI [Library symbol]	MiBar
Barstow, CA [Location identifier] [FAA]	BYS
Barstow, CA [Radio station call letters]	KIOT
Barstow, CA [Radio station call letters]	KPRD
Barstow, CA [Radio station call letters]	KZNS
Barter Clubs	BC
Barter Island [Alaska] [Seismograph station code, US Geological Survey]	BI1
Barter Island [Alaska] [Seismograph station code, US Geological Survey]	BI2
Barter Island [Alaska] [Seismograph station code, US Geological Survey]	BI3
Barter Island [Alaska] [Seismograph station code, US Geological Survey]	BI4
Barter Island [Alaska] [Airport symbol]	BTI

Barth-Spencer Corp. [American Stock Exchange symbol] [Delisted]	BTH
Bartholin and Skene [Glands] [Medicine]	B & S
Bartholomew County Library, Columbus, IN [OCLC symbol]	INB
Bartholomew County Library, Columbus, IN [Library symbol]	InColo
Bartica [Guyana] [Airport symbol]	GFO
Bartlesville Energy Research Center [Department of Energy]	BERC
Bartlesville Energy Technology Center [Department of Energy]	BETC
Bartlesville, OK [Location identifier] [FAA]	BVO
Bartlesville, OK [Television station call letters]	KDOR
Bartlesville, OK [Radio station call letters]	KWON
Bartlesville, OK [Radio station call letters]	KYFM
Bartlesville Public Library, Bartlesville, OK [Library symbol]	OkB
Bartok Archives Z-Symbol Rhythm Extraction [Data processing]	BARZREX
Barton County Community College, Great Bend, KS [Library symbol]	KGbB
Barton & Guestier [Wine]	B & G
Barton Valve Co., Inc. [NASDAQ symbol]	BART
Bartonian Metaphysical Society, Ottawa, ON, Canada [Library symbol]	CaOOBM
Barton's Candy Corp. [American Stock Exchange symbol] [Delisted]	BBB
Bartow, FL [Radio station call letters]	WBAR
Bartow, FL [Radio station call letters]	WPUL
Bartow Public Library, Bartow, FL [Library symbol]	FB
Bartram Trail Regional Library, Washington, GA [Library symbol]	GWasB
Baruch [Old Testament book] [Roman Catholic canon]	Bar
Baruch College, New York, NY [OCLC symbol]	VVB
Baruch-Foster Corp. [American Stock Exchange symbol]	BFO
Baruch Retrieval of Automated Information for Negotiations [City University of New York] [Information service]	BRAIN
Barwick [E. T.] Industries, Inc. [American Stock Exchange symbol] [Delisted]	ETB
Baryon-Isobar Rest System	BARS
Baryta Light Fling	BLF
Barzone Breeders Association of America	BBAA
Basal Acid Output [Medicine]	BAO
Basal Body Temperature [Medicine]	BBT
Basal Cell Carcinoma [Medicine]	BCC
Basal Cell Epithelioma [Obsolete] [Medicine]	BCE
Basal Cell Hyperplasia [Medicine]	BCH
Basal Cerebral Vigilance [Sleep]	BCV
Basal Fold	BF
Basal Granule	BGR
Basal Groove	BG
Basal Heart Rate [Medicine]	BHR
Basal Medium [Microbiology]	BM
Basal Metabolic Rate [Medicine]	BMR
Basal Metabolism [Medicine]	BM
Basal [or Baseline] Skin Resistance [Medicine]	BSR
Basal Web	BW
Basalt Public Library, Basalt, CO [Library symbol]	CoBa
Basalt Waste Isolation Project [Department of Energy]	BWIP
Basaltic Achondrite Parent [Planetary body]	BAP
Basankusu [Zaire] [Airport symbol]	BSU
Basco [Philippines] [Airport symbol]	BSO
Base	B
Base Accountable Supply Officer [Air Force]	BASO
Base Accounting and Finance Office [Air Force]	BAFO
Base Activation	BA
Base Activation Central Control Committee	BACCC
Base Activation Change Order	BACO
Base Activation Instruction	BAI
Base Activation Notice	BAN
Base Activation Statistical Control	BASC
Base Activation Test Equipment	BATE
Base Address Register [Data processing]	BAR
Base Air Depot Area [Air Force]	BADA
Base of Air Operations	BAO
Base Allowance List	BAL
Base Ammunition Depot	BAD
Base Assembly	BA
Base Augmentation Support Set	BASS
Base Authorization List	BAL
Base Automated Mobility System	BAMS
Base Automotive Maintenance	BAM
Base Auxiliary Power	BAP
Base Civil Engineer [Military]	BCE
Base Closing Economic Injury [Loan]	BCEI
Base Collector	BC
Base Command	BC
Base Condemnation Percent	BCP
Base Consolidation Control Office	BCCO
Base Construction Depot Detachment [Navy]	BCDD
Base Data Processing Installation	BDPI
Base Data System	BDS
Base Defense Force [Military]	BDF
Base Deficit	BD
Base Detonating	BD
Base Detonating Fuse	BDEF
Base Detonating Fuze	BDF
Base Detonating, Self-Destroying	BDSD

Base Development Board [Military]	BDB
Base Development Feasibility Study [Navy]	BDFS
Base Development Plan	BDP
Base Diameter	BD
Base Diameter	BDIA
Base Distribution System [Air Force]	BDS
Base Divider Strip	BDS
Base of Dorsal Lip	BDL
Base Ejection	BE
Base Electronics System Engineering Plan	BESEP
Base Engineer Emergency Force [Air Force]	BEEF
Base Engineering Automated Management System	BEAMS
Base Equipment Container	BEC
Base Equipment Management Office [Air Force]	BEMO
Base Excess	BE
Base Excess [Medicine]	BXS
Base Exchange	BX
Base Extension Course	BEC
Base Facilities for SACLANT [NATO]	BFS
Base Flight Management Data System	BFMDS
Base Force	BASEFOR
Base Fuels Management Officer [Air Force]	BFMO
Base Fuels Supply Officer [Air Force]	BFSO
Base Funded	BF
Base Fuze	BF
Base Fuze Hole Plug	BFHP
Base Heat Shield	BHS
Base-Height Ratio	B/H
Base Helix Angle [NASA]	BHA
Base Hospital [Military]	BH
Base Ignition	BI
Base and Increment [Technical drawings]	B & I
Base Industrial Relations Office [or Officer] [Military]	BIRO
Base Inspection Questionnaire [Air Force]	BIQ
Base Installation Action Requirements	BIAR
Base Installation Officer	BIO
Base and Installation Security System [Military]	BISS
Base Intrusion Detection System	BIDS
Base Intrusion Surveillance System	BISS
Base of Lateral Lip	BLL
Base Level Military Personnel System	BLMPS
Base Level Self-Sufficiency [Air Force]	BLSS
Base Loaded Antenna	BLA
Base Logistical Command	BALOG
Base Mail Distribution Scheme [Air Force]	BMDS
Base Maintenance [Air Force]	BM
Base Maintenance Division [Navy]	BMD
Base Maintenance and Operations Model	BMOM
Base Maintenance and Repair	BMAR
Base Management Engineering Data System	BMEDS
Base Manager's Notice	BMN
Base Manpower Data System [Air Force]	BMDS
Base Medical Supply Office [or Officer] [Air Force]	BMSO
Base Mount Valve	BMV
Base Operating Information System [Formerly, COCOAS]	BASOPS
Base Operating Information System (Supply Management System)	BASOPS (SMS)
Base Operating Service [Contract] [DoD]	BOS
Base Operating Supplies	BOS
Base Operating Supply System	BOSS
Base Operating Support	BOS
Base Operation Manager	BOM
Base Operations	BAOPS
Base Operations	BASEOPS
Base Operations Division [NASA]	BOD
Base Operations Office	BASOPS
Base Order	BO
Base of Overcast [Meteorology]	BOVC
Base Pairs in DNA [Genetics]	BP
Base Percussion	BP
Base Perimeter Security System	BPSS
Base Personnel Staff Officer [Air Force] [British]	BPSO
Base Pitch	BP
Base Planning Board	BPB
Base Plate	BP
Base Point	BP
Base Point	BPT
Base Point Configuration	BPC
Base Post Office	BPO
Base Postal Section [Air Force]	BPS
Base Precision Measurement Equipment Laboratories	BPMEL
Base of Preference Program [for reenlisting airmen]	BOP
Base Procured	BP
Base Procured/Central Procured	BP/CP
Base Procurement Office [Air Force]	BPO
Base Procurement Service Stores [Air Force]	BPSS
Base Production Unit [Army]	BPU
Base Quartermaster [Marine Corps]	BQM
Base Quota [Red Cross fund-raising]	BQ
Base Reclamation [of critical materials]	BR
Base Recovery Course [Military]	BRC

Base Repair Cycle	BRC
Base Requirements Overseas	BRO
Base Residence Course	BRC
Base Resistance Transistor	BRT
Base [or Basic] Retirement Date [Air Force]	BRD
Base Salvage	BS
Base Section [Military]	BASEC
Base Section [Military]	BS
Base Security Council [Air Force]	BSC
Base Service Battalion [Marine Corps]	BSERBN
Base Service Unit [Navy]	BASESERVUNIT
Base Service Unit [Navy]	BSU
Base Shell	BS
Base Shop Tester	BST
Base Skirt	BS
Base Spares Allowance List	BSAL
Base Spares Group	BSG
Base Station [ITU designation]	FB
Base Statistical Control	BSC
Base Supply	BS
Base Supply Management Office [Air Force]	BSMO
Base Supply Officer [Navy]	BSO
Base Support Equipment [Military]	BSE
Base Support Group [Air Force]	BSGP
Base Support Group System [Air Force]	BSGS
Base Target	BT
Base Ten Systems Cl A [NASDAQ symbol]	BASEA
Base of Terminal Service [for airmen]	BTS
Base for Uniform Language Definition [Data processing]	BUILD
Base Unit	BU
Base Vehicle Reporting Officer	BVRO
Base Weather Station	BWS
Base Wire Communications Program [Air Force]	BWCP
Base Wire Communications System [Air Force]	BWCS
Base Wire and Telephone System [Air Force]	BWTS
Base Wire and Telephone System Development Schedule [Air Force]	BWTSDS
Base Work Order	BWO
Baseball Writers Association of America	BBWAA
Baseball Writers Association of America	BWAA
Baseband	BB
Baseband	BSB
Baseband Assembly Unit	BAU
Baseband Breadboard	BBB
Baseband Distribution Unit	BDU
Baseboard Hot Water [Heating system] [Classified advertising]	BBHW
Basegram [Navy]	BGM
Basel [Bale] [Switzerland] [Seismograph station code, US Geological Survey]	BAS
Basel Club	BC
Basel/Mulhouse [Switzerland] [Airport symbol]	BSL
Baseline	BL
Baseline Accounting and Reporting System	BARS
Baseline Armor Reliability Test [Army]	BART
Baseline Calibration Equipment	BLCE
Baseline Configuration	BLC
Baseline Cost Estimate	BCE
Baseline Definition Document	BDD
Baseline Demonstration LASER	BDL
Baseline Electronic Warfare System	BLEWS
Baseline Flight Vehicle Mission Time Line	BFVMTL
Baseline Operations Plan	BOP
Baseline Program Document	BPD
Baseline Reference Flight Plan	BRFP
Baseline Reference Mission	BRM
Basement	BSMT
Basement Membrane [Medicine]	BM
Basenji Club of America	BCA
Basenji Club of America	BCOA
Baseplate	BAPE
Baseplate [Technical drawings]	BP
Bases on Balls [Baseball]	BB
BASF [Badische Anilin- und Sodafabrik] Information [A publication]	BASF Inf
BASF [Badische Anilin- und Sodafabrik] Review [A publication]	BASF Rev
Bashkimet Profesionale te Shqiperise [Union of Albanian Trade Unions]	BPSH
Bashkir [MARC language code] [Library of Congress]	bak
Bashkir Soviet Socialist Republic	BashSSR
Basic [Rate] [Value of the English pound]	BAS
Basic	BSC
Basic Access Method [Data processing]	BAM
Basic Acoustic Warfare System	BAWS
Basic Active Service Date	BASD
Basic Adaptive Hardware	BAH
Basic Additional Teleprocessing Support	BATS
Basic Administration and Management	BAAM
Basic Advance Training	Bas Adv Tra
Basic Advanced Integrated Navigation System	BAINS
Basic Agreement	BA
Basic Air Defense Ground Environment [Air Force]	BADGE

Basic Air Temperature .... BAT
Basic Airspeed [*Aviation*] .... BAS
Basic Algebraic Symbolic Interpretive Compiler .... BASIC
Basic Allowance for Quarters [*Military*] .... BAQ
Basic Allowance for Quarters for Adopted Child [*Military*] .... BAQ(AC)
Basic Allowance for Quarters for Father [*Military*] .... BAQ(F)
Basic Allowance for Quarters for Husband [*Military*] .... BAQ(H)
Basic Allowance for Quarters for Legitimate Children [*Military*] .... BAQ(LC)
Basic Allowance for Quarters for Mother [*Military*] .... BAQ(M)
Basic Allowance for Quarters Pending Disability Retirement [*Military*] .... BAQ(DIS RET)
Basic Allowance for Quarters for Stepchildren [*Military*] .... BAQ(SC)
Basic Allowance for Quarters for Wife [*Military*] .... BAQ(W)
Basic Allowance for Subsistence [*Military*] .... BAS
Basic American Medical [*NASDAQ symbol*] .... BAMI
Basic Angle System .... BAS
Basic and Applied Histochemistry [*A publication*] .... Basic Appl Histochem
Basic Appraisal System for Incoming Components .... BASIC
Basic Armed Forces Communication Plan .... BAFCOM
Basic Army Administrative Course .... BAAC
Basic Army Strategic Estimate [*A document*] .... BASE
Basic Assembler Program [*Data processing*] .... BAP
Basic Assembly Language [*Data processing*] .... BAL
Basic Attack Helicopter Team [*Army*] .... BAHT
Basic Authorization .... BA
Basic Automatic Checkout Equipment .... BACE
Basic Automatic Stored Instruction Computer .... BASIC
Basic Biology in Color Series [*A publication*] .... Basic Biol Color Ser
Basic Boxed Base .... BBB
Basic Business Language [*Data processing*] .... BBL
Basic Cardiac Life Support [*System*] [*Medicine*] .... BCLS
Basic Combat Maneuver .... BCM
Basic Combat Training [*Later, BT*] .... BCT
Basic Computer Unit .... BCU
Basic Concepts Inventory [*Psychology*] .... BCI
Basic Consolidated Requirements Document .... BCRD
Basic Contour Line .... BCL
Basic Contract Specification .... BCS
Basic Control [*Mode*] [*Data processing*] .... BC
Basic Control Frequency .... BCF
Basic Control Monitor .... BCM
Basic Control System [*For satellites*] .... BCS
Basic Copy [*Genetics*] .... BC
Basic Cryptanalysis Course .... BCC
Basic Daily Food Allowance .... BDFA
Basic Data Set Project [*National Science Foundation*] .... BDSP
Basic Democrats [*Pakistan*] .... BD
Basic Device Unit [*Data processing*] .... BDU
Basic Direct Access Method [*Data processing*] .... BDAM
Basic Direct Shipping Instructions .... BDSI
Basic Disk Operating System .... BDOS
Basic Display Unit [*Data processing*] .... BDU
Basic Earth Science Systems [*NASDAQ symbol*] .... BSIC
Basic Education [*A publication*] .... BE
Basic Education Assistance Material Service [*National Multimedia Center for Adult Basic Education*] .... BEAMS
Basic Educational Opportunity Grants [*Office of Education*] .... BEOG
Basic Educational Skills Test .... BEST
Basic Electrical Rhythm [*Neurophysiology*] .... BER
Basic Electricity and Electronics .... BE & E
Basic Encyclopedia [*Army*] .... BE
Basic Energy Reduction Technology .... BERT
Basic Energy Sciences Program [*Department of Energy*] .... BES
Basic Engineering Casualty Control Exercise [*Military*] .... BECCE
Basic Engineering Damage Control Exercise [*Military*] .... BEDCE
Basic Engineering Development .... BED
Basic English .... BE
Basic Enlisted Service Date .... BESD
Basic Entry Pay Date .... BEPD
Basic Equipment List .... BEL
Basic Essential Skills Testing .... BEST
Basic Exercises .... BX
Basic Facility Requirements List [*Navy*] .... BFRL
Basic Field Manual [*Military*] .... BFM
Basic Flight Maneuver [*Aviation*] .... BFM
Basic in Flow .... BIF
Basic Health Profile .... BHP
Basic Hole System .... BHS
Basic Human Needs .... BHN
Basic Impulse Insulation Level [*Electronics*] .... BIL
Basic Incidence Rate [*Medicine*] .... BIR
Basic, Incorporated [*NYSE symbol*] [*Delisted*] .... BAI
Basic Indexed Sequential Access Method [*Data processing*] .... BISAM
Basic Indexing and Retrieval System [*Data processing*] .... BIRS
Basic Industrial Materials [*Program*] [*Navy*] .... BIM
Basic Infantry .... BI
Basic Information Unit .... BIU
Basic Input-Output System .... BIOS
Basic Institutional Development Program [*Under Title III of the Higher Education Act*] .... BIDP
Basic Insulation Level .... BIL
Basic Integrated Aircraft Command and Control [*Navy*] .... BIACC
Basic Intrinsic Noise Ratio .... BINR
Basic Inventory of Natural Language [*Test*] .... BINL
Basic Iron Aluminum Silicate [*Du Pont trademark*] .... BIASILL
Basic Issue Items [*Army*] .... BII
Basic Issue Items List [*Army*] .... BIIL
Basic Issue List Items [*Army*] .... BILI
Basic Journal Abstracts [*A publication*] .... BJA
Basic Language for the Implementation of System Software [*Data processing*] .... BLISS
Basic Language Machine [*Data processing*] .... BLM
BASIC Language Translator [*Data processing*] .... BLT
Basic Launch Plan [*NASA*] .... BLP
Basic Learning Institute .... BLI
Basic Level Automation of Data through Electronics .... BLADE
Basic Liberation of Smokers and Sympathizers of Marijuana .... BLOSSOM
Basic Library Inquiry Subsystem [*Data processing*] .... BLISS
Basic Life Sciences [*A publication*] .... Basic Life Sci
Basic Life Support [*System*] .... BLS
Basic Link Unit [*Data processing*] .... BLU
Basic Literal Automatic Coding .... BALITAC
Basic Load [*Ammunition*] .... BL
Basic Logic Unit .... BLU
Basic and Logically Applied Norms - Civil Engineering .... BALANCE
Basic Magnesium, Inc., Las Vegas, NV [*Library symbol*] [*Obsolete*] .... NvLBM
Basic Main Frame .... BMF
Basic Maintenance Allowance .... BMA
Basic Mapping Support [*Data processing*] .... BMS
Basic Medical Insurance Plan [*UN Food and Agriculture Organization*] .... BMIP
Basic Message Switching Center [*Data processing*] .... BSC
Basic Metabolism Rate and Electrocardiogram [*Medicine*] .... BMR & ECG
Basic Meteorological Services .... BMS
Basic Military Requirement .... BMR
Basic Military Training .... BMT
Basic Military Training School .... BMTS
Basic Missile Checker .... BMC
Basic Mission, Design Number, and Series [*Aircraft*] .... BMDNS
Basic Motion-Time Study .... BMT
Basic Motor Ability Test [*Education*] .... BMAT
Basic National Security Police .... BNSP
Basic Naval Establishment Plan .... BNEP
Basic Noncommissioned Officer Course [*Army*] .... BNCOC
Basic Noncommissioned Officer Course .... BNOC
Basic Notch Unit .... BNU
Basic Oblate Spheroid .... BOS
Basic Occupational Language Training .... BOLT
Basic Occupational Literacy Test .... BOLT
Basic Occupational Preparation .... BOP
Basic Officers Training Battalion [*Army*] .... BOTB
Basic Operating Consumer-Oriented Language [*Data processing*] .... BOCOL
Basic Operating Monitor .... BOM
Basic Operating System .... BOS
Basic Operation Plan [*Army*] .... BOP
Basic Operational Data .... BOD
Basic Operational Training Unit (Fixed Wing) .... BOTU(FW)
Basic Operational Training Unit (Rotary Wing) .... BOTU(RW)
Basic Ordering Agreement .... BOA
Basic Oxygen Furnace [*Steelmaking*] .... BOF
Basic Oxygen Process [*Steelmaking*] .... BOP
Basic Oxygen Steel [*Steelmaking*] .... BOS
Basic Partitioned Access Method [*Data processing*] .... BPAM
Basic Pay .... BP
Basic Pay Entry Date .... BPED
Basic Planning Document [*Military*] .... BPD
Basic Planning Memorandum .... BASPM
Basic Point Defense [*Military*] .... BPD
Basic Point Defense Missile System .... BPDMS
Basic Point Defense Surface Missile System .... BPDSMS
Basic Pole Unit .... BPU
Basic Pressure Altitude .... BPA
Basic Processing Unit .... BPU
Basic Products Corp. [*NYSE symbol*] [*Delisted*] .... BPD
Basic Programing Knowledge Test .... BPKT
Basic Programing Support .... BPS
Basic Programing System .... BPS
Basic Protein [*Immunology*] .... BP
Basic Query Language [*Data processing*] .... BQL
Basic Radiation Effects Reactor .... BRER
Basic Reference Coordinate System .... BRCS
Basic Research .... BR
Basic Research in Cardiology [*A publication*] .... Basic Res Cardiol
Basic Research in Cardiology [*A publication*] .... Bas R Card
Basic Research, Incorporated [*Formerly, PRI*] [*An association*] .... BRINC
Basic Resources International Bahamas [*NASDAQ symbol*] .... BBAHF
Basic School Skills Inventory [*Education*] .... BSSI
Basic School Skills Inventory - Diagnostic .... BSSI-D
Basic School Skills Inventory - Screen .... BSSI-S
Basic Sediment [*Petroleum*] .... BS
Basic Sediment and Water [*In crude oil*] .... BS & W

Basic Semantic Element [*Data processing*] ... BASE
Basic Sequential Access Method [*Data processing*] ... BSAM
Basic Shaft System ... BSS
Basic Shipping Instructions ... BSI
Basic Skills Education Program [*Army*] ... BSEP
Basic Standardization Agreement [*Military*] ... BSA
Basic Stock Allowance [*Military*] ... BSA
Basic Stock Allowance List [*Military*] ... BSAL
Basic Storage Module ... BSM
Basic Subsystem Module ... BSM
Basic System ... BASYS
Basic System Memory [*Data processing*] ... BSM
Basic Systems, Inc., Huntington, WV [*Library symbol*] ... WvHuB
Basic Tables of Commissioning Allowances [*Navy*] ... BTCA
Basic Takeoff Gross Weight [*Aviation*] ... BTOGW
Basic Technical Course [*Military*] ... BTC
Basic Technique [*Parapsychology*] ... BT
Basic Telecommunication ... BTMA
Basic Telecommunications Access Method [*Data processing*] ... BTAM
Basic Test Battery [*Navy*] ... BTB
Basic Time-Sharing System ... BTSS
Basic and Traditional Food Association ... BTFA
Basic Trainer [*Air Force*] ... BT
Basic Training [*Military*] ... BASICTNG
Basic Training [*Military*] ... BT
Basic Training Center [*Military*] ... BTC
Basic Training School ... BTS
Basic Transient Diode Logic [*Data processing*] ... BTDL
Basic Transmission Header [*Data processing*] ... BTH
Basic Transmission Unit [*Data processing*] ... BTU
Basic Transportation Vehicle ... BTV
Basic Underwater Demolition/SEAL [*Sea, Air, and Land Capability*] **Training Department** [*Navy*] ... BUD/S
Basic Underwater Demolition Team [*Marine Corps*] ... BUD
Basic Unit Training ... BUT
Basic War Plan [*Navy*] ... BWP
Basic Weight Controller ... BWC
Basics of Language [*Method*] ... BOL
Basilar Membrane [*Ear anatomy*] ... BM
Basilian Salvatorian Fathers [*Roman Catholic religious order*] ... BS
Basin [*Board on Geographic Names*] ... BSN
Basion [*Craniometric point*] ... BA
[*Classified on the*] **Basis of Information Revealed** ... BIR
Basis of Issue [*Army*] ... BOI
Basis of Issue Monitoring and Recording System [*Army*] ... BOIMARS
Basis of Issue Plan [*Army*] ... BOIP
Basis of Issue Plan - Complete [*Army*] ... BOIP-C
Basis of Issue Plan II [*Army*] ... BOIP II
Basis of Issue Plan - Tentative [*Army*] ... BOIP-T
Basis of Issue System [*Army*] ... BOIS
BASIX Corp. [*NYSE symbol*] ... BAS
Basket ... BKT
Basket ... BSK
Basket ... BSKT
Basketball Federation of the United States of America [*Defunct*] ... BFUSA
Baskets or Hampers [*Freight*] ... BH
Baskirskii Gosudarstvennyi Universitet. Ucenye Zapiski [*A publication*] ... Baskir Gos Univ Ucen Zap
Basle Nomina Anatomica [*Basel Anatomical Nomenclature*] [*Medicine*] ... BNA
Basler Airlines, Inc. [*Air carrier designation symbol*] ... BASX
Basler Beitraege zur Deutschen Literatur-und Geistesgeschichte [*A publication*] ... BBLG
Basler Beitraege zur Ethnologie [*A publication*] ... Basler Beitr Ethnol
Basler Beitraege zur Geographie [*A publication*] ... Basler Beitr Geogr
Basler Beitraege zur Geschichtswissenschaft [*A publication*] ... BBG
Basler Flight Service, Inc. [*Oshkosh, WI*] [*FAA designator*] ... BAS
Basler Studien zur Deutschen Sprache und Literatur [*A publication*] ... BSDSL
Basler Zeitschrift fuer Geschichte und Altertumskunde [*A publication*] ... Basler Z Gesch & Altertumsk
Basler Zeitschrift fuer Geschichte und Altertumskunde [*A publication*] ... BZG
Basler Zeitschrift fuer Geschichte und Altertumskunde [*A publication*] ... BZGA
Basler Zeitschrift fuer Geschichte und Altertumskunde [*A publication*] ... BZGAK
Basophil Chemotactic Factor [*Hematology*] ... BCF
Basophils [*Hematology*] ... Bas
Basque [*MARC language code*] [*Library of Congress*] ... bag
Bass [*or Basso*] [*Music*] ... B
Bass Air Corp. [*Pine Bluff, AR*] [*FAA designator*] ... BCC
Bass Anglers Sportsman Society ... BASS
Bass Clarinet ... BC
Bass Research Foundation ... BRF
Bass Sound Post [*A publication*] ... Bass Sound
Basse Pression [*Low Pressure*] [*French*] ... BP
Basse-Terre [*Guadeloupe*] [*Airport symbol*] ... BBR
Bassein [*Burma*] [*Airport symbol*] ... BSX
Bassett Furniture [*NASDAQ symbol*] ... BSET
Bassett Hound Club of America ... BHCA
Bassett, NE [*Television station call letters*] ... KMNE-TV
Bassett, NE [*Location identifier*] [*FAA*] ... RBE
Bassett, VA [*Radio station call letters*] ... WODY
Bassett-Walker, Inc. [*NASDAQ symbol*] ... BWKR
Basso [*Music*] ... BAS
Basso Continuo [*Continued Bass*] [*Music*] ... BASS CONT
Basso Continuo [*Continued Bass*] [*Music*] ... BC
Bassoon ... BN
Bastard [*Size or material*] ... BSTD
Bastardy [*FBI standardized term*] ... BAST
Bastia [*Corsica*] [*Airport symbol*] ... BIA
Bastian Industries [*NASDAQ symbol*] ... BSIN
Bastrop, LA [*Radio station call letters*] ... KJBS
Bastrop, LA [*Radio station call letters*] ... KTRY
Bastrop, LA [*Radio station call letters*] ... KTRY-FM
Bastrop, LA [*Radio station call letters*] ... KVOB
Basutoland ... BL
Basutoland Congress Party [*Lesotho*] ... BCP
Basutoland Congress of Trade Unions ... BCTU
Basutoland Congress of Trade Unions ... BTU
Basutoland National Party [*Lesotho*] ... BNP
Bat ... B
BAT Industries Ltd. [*American Stock Exchange symbol*] ... BTI
Bat Research News [*A publication*] ... Bat Res News
Bataan Ocean Petroleum Depot ... BOPD
Bataille [*A publication*] ... BAT
Batavia [*Indonesia*] [*Later, TNG*] [*Geomagnetic observatory code*] ... BTV
Batavia Area Office [*Energy Research and Development Administration*] ... BAO
Batavia Beacon, Batavia, IA [*Library symbol*] ... IaBatB
Batavia, NY [*Radio station call letters*] ... WBTA
Batavia, OH [*Radio station call letters*] ... WCNE
Batch Fabrication ... BF
Batch Fabrication Technique ... BFT
Batch Mixer ... BMXR
Batch Processing Monitor [*Data processing*] ... BPM
Batch Terminal Simulator [*Data processing*] ... BTS
Batch Time-Sharing Monitor [*Data processing*] ... BTM
Batch Weighing Kit ... BWK
Batch Weighing System ... BWS
Bateau Torpilleur [*Torpedo Boat*] [*French*] ... BT
Bateman Eichler and Hill Richards. Research Report [*A publication*] ... Bateman E
Bateria de Examenes de Aptitud General [*General Aptitude Test Battery*] ... BEAG
Bateria General de Preubas de Aptitud [*General Aptitude Test Battery*] ... BGPA
Bates College, Lewiston, ME [*OCLC symbol*] ... BTS
Bates College, Lewiston, ME [*Library symbol*] ... MeLB
Batesburg, SC [*Radio station call letters*] ... WBLR
Batesburg, SC [*Radio station call letters*] ... WKWQ-FM
Batesville [*Arkansas*] [*Airport symbol*] ... BVX
Batesville, AR [*Location identifier*] [*FAA*] ... BVX
Batesville, AR [*Radio station call letters*] ... KAAB
Batesville, AR [*Radio station call letters*] ... KBTA
Batesville, AR [*Radio station call letters*] ... KGED
Batesville, AR [*Radio station call letters*] ... KZLE
Batesville, AR [*Location identifier*] [*FAA*] ... LYY
Batesville, IN [*Location identifier*] [*FAA*] ... HLB
Batesville, IN [*Radio station call letters*] ... WRBI
Batesville, MS [*Radio station call letters*] ... WBLE
Batesville, MS [*Radio station call letters*] ... WWUN
Bath ... B
Bath & Hammondsport Railroad Co. [*AAR code*] ... BH
Bath Industries, Inc. [*Formerly, Bath Iron Works Corp.*] [*Later, COG*] [*NYSE symbol*] ... BIW
Bath, ME [*Radio station call letters*] ... WIGY
Bath, ME [*Radio station call letters*] ... WJTO
Bath, ME [*Radio station call letters*] ... WMOS
Bath, NY [*Radio station call letters*] ... WCIK
Bath, NY [*Radio station call letters*] ... WVIN
Bath Road [*Bristol*] [*British depot code*] ... BL
Bathophenanthroline [*Analytical chemistry*] ... BP
Bathroom ... BR
Bathroom Privileges [*Medicine*] ... BP
Bathroom Privileges [*Medicine*] ... BRP
Bathurst [*Australia*] [*Airport symbol*] ... BHS
Bathurst College, Bathurst, NB, Canada [*Library symbol*] ... CaNBBB
Bathurst Island [*Australia*] [*Airport symbol*] ... BRT
Bathurst, NB [*Radio station call letters*] ... CKBC
Bathyconductograph ... BC
Bathymetric Navigation Equipment ... BNE
Bathyscaphe Oceanographic Program ... BOP
Bathythermal Traces ... BT
Bathythermograph ... BATHY
Bathythermograph ... BT
Bathythermographic Data Collection and Processing Facility ... BTDCPF
Bathythermographic Data Processing and Analysis Facility ... BTDPAF
Bati Edebiyatlari Arastirma Dergisi (Ankara, Turkey) [*A publication*] ... BEAD (Ankara Turkey)

Batiment International/Building Research and Practice [*A publication*] ... Batim Int Build Res Pract
Baton Rouge [*Louisiana*] [*Airport symbol*] ... BTR
Baton Rouge, LA [*Location identifier*] [*FAA*] ... CLZ
Baton Rouge, LA [*Radio station call letters*] ... KLSU
Baton Rouge, LA [*Radio station call letters*] ... WAFB
Baton Rouge, LA [*Television station call letters*] ... WAFB-TV
Baton Rouge, LA [*Radio station call letters*] ... WBRH
Baton Rouge, LA [*Television station call letters*] ... WBRZ
Baton Rouge, LA [*Radio station call letters*] ... WFMF
Baton Rouge, LA [*Radio station call letters*] ... WIBR
Baton Rouge, LA [*Radio station call letters*] ... WJBO
Baton Rouge, LA [*Radio station call letters*] ... WLCS
Baton Rouge, LA [*Television station call letters*] ... WLPB
Baton Rouge, LA [*Radio station call letters*] ... WLUX
Baton Rouge, LA [*Radio station call letters*] ... WQXY
Baton Rouge, LA [*Television station call letters*] ... WRBT
Baton Rouge, LA [*Radio station call letters*] ... WRKF
Baton Rouge, LA [*Radio station call letters*] ... WTKL
Baton Rouge, LA [*Radio station call letters*] ... WXOK
Baton Rouge, LA [*Radio station call letters*] ... WYNK
Baton Rouge, LA [*Radio station call letters*] ... WYNK-FM
Batouri [*Cameroon*] [*Airport symbol*] ... OUR
Batrachotoxin [*Biochemistry*] ... BTX
Bats Both Right-Handed and Left-Handed [*Baseball*] ... BB
Bats Left-Handed [*Baseball*] ... BL
Bats Right-Handed [*Baseball*] ... BR
Batsfjord [*Norway*] [*Airport symbol*] ... BJF
Battalion ... BAT
Battalion ... BATT
Battalion ... BN
Battalion ... BTN
Battalion Antitank Recoilless Rifle ... BAT
Battalion Automated Personnel System ... BAPERS
Battalion Beachhead [*Army*] ... BBH
Battalion Close Support Weapon System ... BCSWS
Battalion Combat Team ... BCT
Battalion Control Group [*Army*] ... BCG
Battalion Equipment Evaluation Program [*DoD*] ... BEEP
Battalion Expeditionary Force ... BEF
Battalion Field Exercise [*Military*] ... BNFEX
Battalion Fire Distribution Center ... BFDC
Battalion Ground Surveillance Section [*Army*] ... BGSS
Battalion Headquarters [*Marine Corps*] ... BNHQ
Battalion Infantry ... BI
Battalion Landing Exercise [*Military*] ... BLTLEX
Battalion Landing Team [*Military*] ... BLT
Battalion Landing Team Landing Exercise [*Military*] ... BTLEX
Battalion Mortar and Davy Crockett Platoon [*Army*] ... BMDCP
Battalion Operations Center ... BOC
Battalion Orderly Room [*British*] ... BOR
Battalion Shore Fire Control Party ... BNSFCP
Battalion Training Management System [*Army*] ... BTMS
Battalion Training Model [*Military*] ... BTM
Batted In [*Short form for RBI, Runs Batted In*] [*Baseball*] ... BI
Battelle Automated Search Information System [*Battelle Memorial Institute*] [*Information service*] ... BASIS
Battelle-Columbus Laboratories ... BCL
Battelle-Columbus Laboratories, Columbus, OH [*Library symbol*] ... OCoB
Battelle - Defense Information Analysis Center [*Battelle Memorial Institute*] ... BDIAC
Battelle - Defense Information Center [*Battelle Memorial Institute*] ... BDIC
Battelle Information (Frankfurt) [*A publication*] ... Battelle Inf (Frankfurt)
Battelle Institute Learning Automation [*Battelle Memorial Institute*] ... BILA
Battelle Memorial Institute ... BMI
Battelle Memorial Institute, Columbus, OH [*OCLC symbol*] ... BKM
Battelle Memorial Institute. Defense Ceramic Information Center. DCIC Report [*A publication*] ... Battelle Mem Inst DCIC Rep
Battelle Memorial Institute. Defense Metals Information Center. DMIC Memorandum [*A publication*] ... Battelle Mem Inst DMIC Memo
Battelle Memorial Institute. Defense Metals Information Center. DMIC Report [*A publication*] ... Battelle Mem Inst DMIC Rep
Battelle Memorial Institute, Pacific Northwest Laboratory, Richland, WA [*Library symbol*] ... WaRiB
Battelle Memorial Institute. Probable Levels of R and D Expenditures [*A publication*] ... Battel R & D
Battelle Monographs [*A publication*] ... Battelle Mg
Battelle Monte Carlo [*Data processing*] ... BMC
Battelle Northwest Laboratories ... BNL
Battelle Northwest Laboratories ... BNWL
Battelle Research Outlook [*A publication*] ... Battelle Res Outlook
Battelle Research Reactor ... BRR
Battelle Technical Review [*A publication*] ... Battelle Tech R
Battelle Today [*A publication*] ... Battelle T
Battelle's Educational Computer User's Network [*Battelle Memorial Institute*] [*Information service*] ... BECUN
Batten ... BATT
Batten, Barton, Durstine, & Osborn [*Advertising agency*] ... BBD & O
Batten-Turner Muscular Dystrophy [*Syndrome*] [*Medicine*] ... BTMD
Batten's Disease [*Medicine*] ... BD
Batter ... BAT
Battered Child Syndrome ... BCS
Batterers Anonymous ... BA
Batters Faced by Pitcher [*Baseball*] ... BFP
Battery ... B
Battery ... BAT
Battery ... BATRY
Battery ... BATT
Battery ... BATTY
Battery ... BTRY
Battery ... BTY
Battery [*FBI standardized term*] ... BATT
Battery Acquisition RADAR ... BAR
Battery Adjust ... BA
Battery Booster Cable ... BBC
Battery Charge Regulator ... BCR
Battery Chargers [*Military*] ... BC
Battery Command Post ... BCP
Battery Commander [*Army*] ... BC
Battery Computer System ... BCS
Battery Condition Indicator ... BCI
Battery Control Area [*Army*] ... BCA
Battery Control Building [*Army*] ... BCB
Battery Control Central [*Army*] ... BCC
Battery Control Data Processor [*Army*] ... BCDP
Battery Control and Monitor [*Army*] ... BCM
Battery Control Officer [*Army*] ... BCO
Battery Control RADAR [*Army*] ... BCR
Battery Control Trailer ... BCT
Battery Control Van ... BCV
Battery/Coolant Unit ... BCU
Battery Council International [*Formerly, AABM*] ... BCI
Battery Data Link [*Air Force*] ... BDL
Battery Data Link System [*Air Force*] ... BDLS
Battery Display Unit [*Army*] ... BDU
Battery Echelon Operating Control ... BEOC
Battery Energy Storage Test ... BEST
Battery Firing Device ... BFD
Battery Guidance Command Group ... BGCG
Battery Information Index [*Battelle Memorial Institute*] ... BII
Battery Integration and RADAR Display Equipment [*Air defense system*] ... BIRDIE
Battery Interconnecting Cables ... BIC
Battery Inverter ... BI
Battery Inverter Accessory Power Supply ... BIAPS
Battery Operations Center [*Air Force*] ... BOC
Battery Package ... BP
Battery Park City [*New York City*] ... BPC
Battery Powered Recorder ... BPR
Battery Quartermaster-Sergeant [*British*] ... BQMS
Battery Sergeant-Major ... BSM
Battery Shop Maintenance [*NASA*] ... BSM
Battery Simulator ... BS
Battery Status Indicator ... BSI
Battery Terminal Equipment ... BTE
Battery Test Set ... BTS
Battery Timing Equipment ... BTE
Battery Timing Group ... BTG
Battery Training Corps [*British*] ... BTC
Battery-Voltage Limit System ... BVLS
Batting Average [*Baseball*] ... BA
Batting Practice [*Baseball*] ... BP
Battle ... B
Battle ... BAT
Battle Area Control Unit [*Military*] ... BACU
Battle Area Surveillance and Integrated Communication System ... BASICS
Battle Area Surveillance and Integrated Communications System [*Marine Corps*] ... BASIC
Battle Area Surveillance and Integrated Communications System Processor and Computer [*Marine Corps*] ... BASICPAC
Battle of Atlantic [*World War II*] ... BA
Battle Correlator Display ... BCD
Battle Creek [*Michigan*] [*Airport symbol*] ... BTL
Battle Creek College, Battle Creek, MI [*Library symbol*] [*Obsolete*] ... MiBatC
Battle Creek, MI [*Radio station call letters*] ... WBCK
Battle Creek, MI [*Radio station call letters*] ... WDFP
Battle Creek, MI [*Radio station call letters*] ... WKFR-FM
Battle Creek, MI [*Radio station call letters*] ... WKNR
Battle Creek, MI [*Television station call letters*] ... WUHQ-TV
Battle Creek, MI [*Radio station call letters*] ... WWKQ
Battle Creek Public School, Battle Creek, MI [*Library symbol*] ... MiBat
Battle Creek Times, Battle Creek, IA [*Library symbol*] ... IaBcT
Battle Cruiser ... BC
Battle Cruiser [*Navy symbol*] ... CB
Battle Cruiser Flag [*Navy*] [*British*] ... BC
Battle Cruiser Squadron ... BCS
Battle Damage Assessment ... BDA
Battle Damage Assessment and Reporting Team ... BDART
Battle Damage Repair [*Army*] ... BDR
Battle Damage Repair Ship [*Navy symbol*] ... ARB
Battle Dress ... BD

Battle Dress Uniform [*Military*] .... BDU
Battle Dressing Station [*Military*] .... BDS
Battle Force .... BATFOR
Battle Group .... BG
Battle Group Landing Team .... BGLT
Battle Injury or Wound .... BIW
Battle Mountain [*Nevada*] [*Airport symbol*] [*Obsolete*] .... BAM
Battle Mountain [*Nevada*] [*Seismograph station code, US Geological Survey*] .... BMN
Battle Mountain, NV [*Radio station call letters*] .... KLME
Battle Position .... BP
Battle Practice Target [*Navy*] [*British*] .... BPT
Battle Readiness and Competition Instructions .... BATREADCOM
Battle Readiness and Competition Instructions .... BATREADCOMP
Battle Short Relay .... BSR
Battle Staff Teams .... BSTS
Battle Star .... BS
Battle-Unit Short-Range Antitank Weapon System .... BUSRAT
Battle Wound Injury .... BWI
Battlefield Air Interdiction .... BAI
Battlefield Airborne Illumination System .... BAIS
Battlefield Area Reconnaissance System [*RADAR*] [*Army*] .... BARCS
Battlefield Area Surveillance System .... BASS
Battlefield Artillery Target Engagement System .... BATES
Battlefield Automated Systems [*Data processing*] [*Military*] .... BAS
Battlefield Damage Assessment and Repair [*Technical manual*] [*Army*] .... BDAR
Battlefield Data System .... BDS
Battlefield Day .... BFD
Battlefield Environment System Simulation .... BELDWSS
Battlefield Estimate .... BFE
Battlefield Exploitation and Target Acquisition .... BETA
Battlefield Identification Friend or Foe .... BIFF
Battlefield Identification System Study [*NATO*] .... BISS
Battlefield Illumination .... BI
Battlefield Illumination Airborne System .... BIAS
Battlefield Illumination System .... BIS
Battlefield Information Center [*Army*] .... BIC
Battlefield Information Control Center [*Army*] .... BICC
Battlefield Information Control Center/Battlefield Information Center [*Army*] .... BICC/BIC
Battlefield Information Distribution System .... BIDS
Battlefield Integration Management System [*Army*] .... BIMS
Battlefield Interdiction .... BFI
Battlefield Interdiction .... BI
Battlefield Surveillance Devices .... BSD
Battlefield Systems Project Management .... BSPM
Battlefield Visualization Graphics .... BVG
Battlefield Weapons System .... BWS
Battlefield Weapons System Laboratory .... BWSL
Battleship .... BAT
Battleship .... BATSHIP
Battleship [*Navy symbol*] .... BB
Battleship .... BS
Battleship Division .... BATDIV
Battleship Flag [*Navy*] [*British*] .... BS
Battleship Observation Squadron [*Navy symbol*] .... VO
Battleship Squadron .... BATRON
Battleship Squadron .... BS
Battleships, Atlantic Fleet .... BATLANT
Battleships, Atlantic Fleet .... BATSHIPSLANT
Battleships, Battle Force, Pacific Fleet .... BATSHIPSBATFORPAC
Battleships and Cruisers, Atlantic Fleet .... BATCRULANT
Battleships and Cruisers, Pacific Fleet .... BATCRUPAC
Battleships, Pacific Fleet .... BATPAC
Battleships, Pacific Fleet .... BATSHIPSPAC
Batu Besar [*Indonesia*] [*Airport symbol*] .... BTH
Batumi [*USSR*] [*Airport symbol*] .... BUS
Baubau [*Indonesia*] [*Airport symbol*] .... BUW
Baud [*Unit of data transmission speed*] .... B
Baud .... Bd
Bauelemente der Elektrotechnik [*A publication*] .... Bauelem Elektrotech
Bauer Hospital-Saint Mary Medical Center, Long Beach, CA [*Library symbol*] .... CLobB
Bauer Publishing & Printing Ltd., Rahway, NJ [*Library symbol*] .... NjRahB
Baughan, E. F., Baltimore MD [*STAC*] .... BEF
Baukunst und Werkform [*A publication*] .... Bau & Werk
Baumaschine und Bautechnik [*A publication*] .... Baumasch Bautech
Baume .... B
Baume .... BA
Baume .... Be
Bauplanung Bautechnik [*A publication*] .... Bauplanung Bautech
Bauru [*Brazil*] [*Airport symbol*] .... BAU
Bausch & Lomb, Inc. [*NYSE symbol*] .... BOL
Bausch & Lomb, Inc., Library, Rochester, NY [*OCLC symbol*] .... VQB
Bausch & Lomb, Inc., Rochester, NY [*Library symbol*] .... NRBL
Bausch & Lomb, Inc., SOFLENS Division, Technical Information Center, Rochester, NY [*Library symbol*] .... NRBL-S
Bausteine zum Deutschen Nationaltheater [*A publication*] .... BDN
Bausteine zur Geschichte der Literatur bei den Slaven [*A publication*] .... BGLS
Baustoffindustrie. Ausgabe B. Bauelemente [*A publication*] .... Baustoffind Ausg B
Bautechnik-Archiv [*A publication*] .... Bautech-Arch
Bauteile Report [*A publication*] .... Bauteile Rep
Bauteile Report. Siemens [*A publication*] .... Bauteile Rep
Bauwelt [*A publication*] .... BAWT-A
Bauxite & Northern Railway Co. [*Later, BXN*] [*AAR code*] .... BN
Bauxite & Northern Railway Co. [*AAR code*] .... BXN
BAV Liquidating [*Formerly, Bates Manufacturing Co., Inc.*] [*NYSE symbol*] [*Delisted*] .... BAT
Bavarian Border Police [*Germany*] .... BBP
Bavarian Dance Group of North America .... BDGNA
Baw Faw Mountain [*Washington*] [*Seismograph station code, US Geological Survey*] .... BFW
Baxley, GA [*Radio station call letters*] .... WBYZ
Baxley, GA [*Radio station call letters*] .... WUFE
Baxter Laboratories, Inc. [*of Baxter Travenol Laboratories, Inc.*] [*Research code symbol*] .... BAX
Baxter New Era, Baxter, IA [*Library symbol*] .... IaBaxNE
Baxter Springs, KS [*Radio station call letters*] .... KBLT
Baxter Travenol Laboratories, Inc. [*NYSE symbol*] .... BAX
Baxter Women's Club, Baxter, IA [*Library symbol*] .... IaBaxWC
Bay .... B
Bay [*Maps and charts*] .... B
Bay [*Thoroughbred racing*] .... B
Bay Area Army Terminal Center .... BAATC
Bay Area Cryonics Society .... BACS
Bay Area Leg Lovers [*San Francisco group opposing below-the-knee fashions introduced in 1970*] .... BALL
Bay Area Library and Information System [*Library network*] .... EBC
Bay Area Library and Information System, Hayward, CA [*OCLC symbol*] .... BAS
Bay Area Physicians for Human Rights .... BAPHR
Bay Area Rapid Transit [*San Francisco area, California*] .... BART
Bay Area Rapid Transit District [*San Francisco area, California*] .... BARTD
Bay Area Reference Center [*Library network*] .... BARC
Bay Area Religious Channel [*Cable TV programing service*] .... BARC
Bay Area Worker [*A publication*] .... Bay Workr
Bay Cabinet Unit .... BCU
Bay City Junior College [*Michigan*] .... BCJC
Bay City, MI [*Radio station call letters*] .... WBCM
Bay City, MI [*Radio station call letters*] .... WCHW-FM
Bay City, MI [*Radio station call letters*] .... WGER
Bay City, MI [*Radio station call letters*] .... WHNN
Bay City, MI [*Television station call letters*] .... WNEM-TV
Bay City, MI [*Television station call letters*] .... WVCI
Bay City, MI [*Radio station call letters*] .... WXOX
Bay City Public Library, Bay City, MI [*Library symbol*] .... MiBay
Bay City, TX [*Location identifier*] [*FAA*] .... BYY
Bay City, TX [*Radio station call letters*] .... KIOX
Bay County Library System, Auburn Branch Library, Auburn, MI [*Library symbol*] .... MiBayS-A
Bay County Library System, Bay City, MI [*Library symbol*] .... MiBayS
Bay County Library System, Broadway Branch Library, Bay City, MI [*Library symbol*] .... MiBayS-B
Bay County Library System, Linwood Branch Library, Linwood, MI [*Library symbol*] .... MiBayS-L
Bay County Library System, Pinconning Branch Library, Pinconning, MI [*Library symbol*] .... MiBayS-P
Bay County Library System, Sage Branch Library, Bay City, MI [*Library symbol*] .... MiBayS-S
Bay County Public Library, Panama City, FL [*Library symbol*] .... FPc
Bay De Noc Community College, Escanaba, MI [*Library symbol*] .... MiEscB
Bay Financial Corp. [*NYSE symbol*] .... BAY
Bay Gelding [*Horse*] .... BG
Bay Microfilm, Incorporated, Palo Alto, CA [*Library symbol*] .... BMI
Bay Minette, AL [*Radio station call letters*] .... WBCA
Bay Minette, AL [*Radio station call letters*] .... WWSM
Bay Path Junior College [*Massachusetts*] .... BPJC
Bay of Pigs Veterans Association .... BPVA
Bay St. Louis, MS [*Radio station call letters*] .... WXGR
Bay Shore-Brightwaters Public Library, Brightwaters, NY [*Library symbol*] .... NBri
Bay Springs, MS [*Radio station call letters*] .... WHII
Bay Springs, MS [*Radio station call letters*] .... WXIY
Bay State Gas Company [*NYSE symbol*] .... BGC
Bay State Librarian [*A publication*] .... Bay State Libn
Bay State Librarian [*A publication*] .... Bay St Librn
Bay State Monthly [*A publication*] .... Bay State Mo
Bayamo [*Cuba*] [*Airport symbol*] .... BYM
Bayamon Central University, Bayamon, PR [*OCLC symbol*] .... BCU
Bayamon, PR [*Radio station call letters*] .... WGSX
Bayamon, PR [*Radio station call letters*] .... WLUZ
Bayamon, PR [*Radio station call letters*] .... WRSJ
Bayamon, PR [*Radio station call letters*] .... WXYX
Bayandai [*USSR*] [*Seismograph station code, US Geological Survey*] [*Closed*] .... BAY
Bayard News, Bayard, IA [*Library symbol*] .... IaBayN
Bayard, NM [*Radio station call letters*] .... KLCJ
Bayard, NM [*Radio station call letters*] .... KNFT
Bayard Public Library, Bayard, IA [*Library symbol*] .... IaBay

BayBanks, Inc. [*NASDAQ symbol*] .... BBNK
Bayer-Symposium [*A publication*] .... Bayer-Symp
Bayerische Akademie der Wissenschaften. Jahrbuch [*A publication*] .... Bayerische Akad Wiss Jahrbuch
Bayerische Akademie der Wissenschaften. Mathematisch-Naturwissenschaftliche Klasse. Abhandlungen [*A publication*] .... Bayer Akad Wiss Math-Natur Kl Abh
Bayerische Akademie der Wissenschaften. Mathematisch-Naturwissenschaftliche Klasse. Sitzungsberichte [*A publication*] .... Bayer Akad Wiss Math-Natur Kl S-B
Bayerische Akademie der Wissenschaften. Mathematisch-Naturwissenschaftliche Klasse. Abhandlungen [*A publication*] .... Bayer Akad Wiss Math-Naturwiss Kl Abh
Bayerische Akademie der Wissenschaften. Mathematisch-Naturwissenschaftliche Klasse. Sitzungsberichte [*A publication*] .... Bayer Akad Wiss Math-Naturwiss Kl Sitzungsber
Bayerische Akademie der Wissenschaften. Philosophisch Historische Klasse. Sitzungsberichte [*A publication*] .... BADWS
Bayerische Akademie der Wissenschaften. Philosophisch Historische Klasse. Sitzungsberichte [*A publication*] .... BAW PHK
Bayerische Akademie der Wissenschaften. Philosophisch Historische Klasse. Sitzungsberichte [*A publication*] .... BAWS
Bayerische Akademie der Wissenschaften. Sitzungsberichte [*A publication*] .... Bayer Sitzb
Bayerische Koenigpartei [*Bavarian Royalist Party*] [*Pre-World War II*] .... BKP
Bayerische Motoren Werke [*Bavarian Motor Works*] [*German automobile manufacturer; initialism used as name of its cars*] .... BMW
Bayerische Rundfunk [*Radio network*] [*West Germany*] .... BR
Bayerische Staatssammlung fuer Palaeontologie und Historische Geologie. Mitteilungen [*A publication*] .... Bayer Staatssamml Palaeontol Hist Geol Mitt
Bayerische Vereinsbank [*Union Bank of Bavaria*] .... BV
Bayerische Volkspartei [*Bavarian People's Party*] [*Pre-World War II*] .... BVP
Bayerische Vorgeschichtsblaetter [*A publication*] .... Bayer Vorgeschbl
Bayerisches Landwirtschaftliches Informationssystem [*Bavarian Agricultural Information System*] [*West Germany*] .... BALIS
Bayerisches Landwirtschaftliches Jahrbuch [*A publication*] .... Bayer Landwirt Jahrb
Bayerisches Landwirtschaftliches Jahrbuch [*A publication*] .... Bayer Landwirtsch Jahrb
Bayerisches Zahnaerzteblatt [*A publication*] .... B Zb
Bayes Fixed Sample-Size Procedure [*Statistics*] .... BFP
Bayes Operating Characteristic .... BOC
Bayes Sequential Procedure [*Statistics*] .... BSP
Bayesian Analysis Modified by Inspection [*Data processing*] .... BAMBI
Bayesian Reliability Demonstration Test [*Data processing*] .... BRDT
Bayfield Public Library, Bayfield, CO [*Library symbol*] .... CoBay
Bayless [*A. J.*] **Markets, Inc.** [*NASDAQ symbol*] .... BAYM
Baylis Public Library, Sault Ste. Marie, MI [*Library symbol*] .... MiSsB
Baylor College of Dentistry, Dallas, TX [*OCLC symbol*] .... IBD
Baylor Geological Studies. Bulletin [*A publication*] .... Baylor Geol Stud Bull
Baylor Law Review [*A publication*] .... Baylor Law
Baylor Law Review [*A publication*] .... Baylor L Rev
Baylor Nursing Educator [*A publication*] .... Baylor Nurs Educ
Baylor University, Armstrong Browning Library, Waco, TX [*Library symbol*] .... TxWB-B
Baylor University in Dallas, Dallas, TX [*Library symbol*] .... TxDaBU
Baylor University, Law School Library, Waco, TX [*Library symbol*] .... TxWB-L
Baylor University, Museum Collection, Waco, TX [*Library symbol*] .... TxWB-Mus
Baylor University, Waco, TX [*OCLC symbol*] .... IYU
Baylor University, Waco, TX [*Library symbol*] .... TxWB
Bayly Corp. [*NASDAQ symbol*] .... BAYL
Bayonet .... BAY
Bayonet Candelabra .... BAYC
Bayonet Candelabra Double Contact .... BAYCANDDC
Bayonet Candelabra Single Contact .... BAYCANDSC
Bayonet Cap .... BC
Bayonet Skirted .... BAYSK
Bayonne Free Public Library, Bayonne, NJ [*Library symbol*] .... NjBa
Bayou [*Maps and charts*] .... B
Bayou .... BYU
Bayou Resources, Inc. [*NASDAQ symbol*] .... BYOU
Bayou Vista, LA [*Radio station call letters*] .... KQKI
Bayou Vista, LA [*Radio station call letters*] .... KQKI-FM
Bayport-Blue Point Public Library, Blue Point, NY [*Library symbol*] .... NBp
Bayram-Ali [*USSR*] [*Seismograph station code, US Geological Survey*] [*Closed*] .... BAT
Bayreuth [*West Germany*] [*Airport symbol*] .... BYU
Bayreuther Blaetter [*A publication*] .... BB
Bayrock Utility Securities, Inc. [*American Stock Exchange symbol*] [*Delisted*] .... BAY
Bayshore Independent, Matawan, NJ [*Library symbol*] .... NjMatB
Bayswater Realty & Capital [*NASDAQ symbol*] .... BAYS
Bayu Indonesia Air Pt. [*Indonesia*] [*ICAO designator*] .... DD
Bayuk Cigars, Inc. [*NYSE symbol*] [*Delisted*] .... BYK
Bayview Community Hospital, Mastic Beach, NY [*Library symbol*] .... NMbCH
Bayville Free Library, Bayville, NY [*Library symbol*] .... NBayv
Bazillenemulsion [*Bacillary emulsion*] [*Immunology*] .... BE
BBA [*Biochimica et Biophysica Acta*] **Library** [*A publication*] .... BBA Libr
BBC [*British Broadcasting Corporation*] **Engineering** [*A publication*] .... BBC Eng
BBC [*British Broadcasting Corporation*] **Engineering Division Monograph** [*A publication*] .... BBC Eng Div Monogr
BBC [*Brown, Boveri, und Cie*] **Nachrichten** [*A publication*] .... BBC Nachr
BBDO International, Inc. [*NASDAQ symbol*] .... BBDO
BC Central Credit Union, Vancouver, BC, Canada [*Library symbol*] .... CaBVaCCU
BCA Credit Information [*Formerly, Broadcast Credit Association*] .... BCA
BCA [*Business Committee for the Arts*] **News** [*A publication*] .... BCA News
BCIRA [*British Cast Iron Research Association*] **Journal** [*A publication*] .... BCIRA J
BCLA [*British Columbia Library Association*] **Reporter** [*A publication*] .... BCLA Rept
BCNU [*Carmustine*], **ara-C, Cyclophosphamide, Thioguanine** [*Antineoplastic drug regimen*] .... BACT
BCNU [*Carmustine*], **Cyclophosphamide, Oncovin** [*Vincristine*], **Prednisone** [*Antineoplastic drug regimen*] .... BCOP
BCNU [*Carmustine*], **Cyclophosphamide, Vinblastine, Procarbazine, Prednisone** [*Antineoplastic drug regimen*] .... BCVPP
BCNU [*Carmustine*], **Oncovin** [*Vincristine*], **Prednisone** [*Antineoplastic drug regimen*] .... BOP
BCNU [*Carmustine*], **Oncovin** [*Vincristine*], **Procarbazine, Prednisone** [*Antineoplastic drug regimen*] .... BOPP
BCNU [*Carmustine*], **Prednisone** [*Antineoplastic drug regimen*] .... BP
BCNU [*Carmustine*], **Vincristine, Procarbazine, Prednisone** [*Antineoplastic drug regimen*] .... BVPP
BCS [*Boeing Computer Services*] **Interactive Graphics** .... BIG
BCURA [*British Coal Utilization Research Association*] **Gazette** [*A publication*] .... BCURA Gaz
BDM International, Inc. [*American Stock Exchange symbol*] .... BDM
Be Ever Alert, Vigilant/Error Removal [*United States Air Force Security System's acronym for the Zero Defects Program*] .... BEAVER
Be On the Lookout [*Police term*] .... BOL
Be On the Lookout [*Police term*] .... BOLO
Be Specific .... BS
Beach .... BCH
Beach Abort .... BA
Beach Armored Recovery Vehicle .... BARV
Beach, Dewey W., Denver CO [*STAC*] .... BDW
Beach Discharge Lighter .... BDL
Beach Erosion Board [*Army*] .... BEB
Beach Group .... BG
Beach Jump Unit .... BJU
Beach Master Unit [*Navy*] .... BMU
Beach Modulator Oscillator .... BMO
Beach Party .... BP
Beach Party Division [*Navy*] .... BPD
Beach Party Group [*Navy*] .... BPG
Beach Party Guard [*Navy*] .... BPG
Beach Party Team [*Navy*] .... BPT
Beach Support Area .... BSA
Beachcomber, Ship Bottom, NJ [*Library symbol*] .... NjSbB
Beachhead .... BHD
Beachhead Air Defense .... BHAD
Beachmaster .... BM
Beachmaster .... BMR
Beacon [*Aviation*] .... B
Beacon .... BCN
Beacon .... BN
Beacon Aircraft Position .... BAP
Beacon Antenna Equipment .... BAE
Beacon Collision Avoidance System [*Aviation*] .... BCAS
Beacon Explorer [*Satellite*] [*NASA*] .... BE
Beacon Explorer A [*Satellite*] [*NASA*] .... BE-A
Beacon Explorer B [*Satellite*] [*NASA*] .... BE-B
Beacon Instrumented Guided Ordnance .... BINGO
Beacon, NY [*Radio station call letters*] .... WBNR
Beacon Only Bombing System .... BOBS
Beacon, Pequannock, NJ [*Library symbol*] .... NjPeqB
Beacon Processing System .... BPS
Beacon Ranging Pulse .... BRP
Beacon Tracking Level .... BTL
Beacon Tracking System .... BTS
Beacon Trigger Generator .... BTG
Beacon, Ultra Portable "S" Band [*Navy*] .... BUPS
Beacon Video Digitizer .... BVD
Beacon Video Processing System .... BVPS
Beacon Video Processor .... BVP
Beaconsfield Public Library, Beaconsfield, PQ, Canada [*Library symbol*] .... CaQBE
Bead Journal [*A publication*] .... Bead J
Bead Society .... BS
Bead and Stone Importers Association .... BSIA
Beaded One Side [*Lumber*] B1S
Beaded Two Sides [*Lumber*] B2S
Beading Device [*Tool*] .... BDDV
Beading Die .... BDDI
Beak .... B
Beak Line .... BL

Bealanana [*Madagascar*] [*Airport symbol*] ... WBE
Beale Cypher Association ... BCA
Bealoideas [*A publication*] ... Be
Beam [*or Breadth*] [*of a ship*] ... B
Beam ... BM
Beam Approach ... B/A
Beam Approach Beacon System [*Aviation*] ... BABS
Beam Approach Seeker Evaluation System [*Air Force*] ... BASES
Beam Approach Training [*Military*] ... BAT
Beam-to-Beam Correlation ... BBC
Beam Candlepower ... BCP
Beam Candlepower Seconds ... BCPS
Beam Collimation Error ... BCE
Beam Collimator ... BC
Beam Communications Set ... BCS
Beam Control Subsystem ... BCS
Beam Correction Factor ... BCF
Beam Coupling Coefficient ... BCC
Beam Coupling Tube ... BEACOTRON
Beam Deflection Tube ... BDT
Beam Degrader ... BD
Beam [*James B.*] **Distilling Co.** [*NYSE symbol*] [*Delisted*] ... BJD
Beam-Foil Spectroscopy ... BFS
Beam Forming ... BF
Beam-Forming Electrode ... BFE
Beam-Heated Cathode ... BHC
Beam-Lead Device ... BLD
Beam Lead Sealed Junction Integrated Circuit Package ... BLSJICP
Beam of Light Transistor ... BOLT
Beam Monitor ... BM
Beam Plasma Amplification ... BPA
Beam Positioning Magnet ... BPM
Beam Ride ... BR
Beam Ride Actuator ... BRA
Beam Ride Error ... BRE
Beam-Rider Tail Control ... BT
Beam Rider - Terrier ... BT
Beam-Riding Tail-Controlled Nuclear Missile ... BTN
Beam Steering ... BS
Beam Steering Device ... BSD
Beam Steering Group ... BSG
Beam Steering System ... BSS
Beam Steering Transducer ... BST
Beam Steering Ultrasonic Transducer ... BSUT
Beam Stop ... BS
Beam-Switching Tube ... BST
Beam Transport System ... BTS
Beam Width ... BW
Beaman Corporation [*NASDAQ symbol*] ... BECO
Beams and Stringers [*Technical drawings*] ... B & S
Beamsville District Secondary School, Beamsville, ON, Canada [*Library symbol*] ... CaOBeD
Beamwidth ... BMW
Bean Golden Mosaic Virus ... BGMV
Bear Canyon [*Utah*] [*Seismograph station code, US Geological Survey*] [*Closed*] ... BCU
Bear Creek Corp. [*NASDAQ symbol*] ... BCRK
Bear Gulch [*California*] [*Seismograph station code, US Geological Survey*] ... BGH
Bear Island [*Formerly, Bjornoya*] [*Norway*] [*Geomagnetic observatory code*] ... BJN
Bear River Range [*Idaho*] [*Seismograph station code, US Geological Survey*] ... BEI
Bear Valley [*California*] [*Seismograph station code, US Geological Survey*] ... BVL
Bear Valley Observatory [*California*] [*Seismograph station code, US Geological Survey*] [*Closed*] ... BVC
Bearcat Explorations Ltd. [*NASDAQ symbol*] ... BCATF
Beard Oil Company [*American Stock Exchange symbol*] ... BOC
Beardstown, IL [*Radio station call letters*] ... WRMS
Beardstown, IL [*Radio station call letters*] ... WRMS-FM
Bearing [*Angle*] ... B
Bearing ... BRG
Bearing Altitude Indicator [*Aerospace*] ... BAI
Bearing Deviation Indicator [*Aerospace*] ... BDI
Bearing, Distance, and Heading ... BDH
Bearing, Distance, and Heading Indicator ... BDHI
Bearing Doubtful [*Aviation code*] ... DO
Bearing Frequency Indicator ... BFI
Bearing per Gyro Compass [*Navigation*] ... BPGC
Bearing Indicator and Navigator to Grounded Operator ... BINGO
Bearing Mounted Clutch ... BMC
Bearing Pennant [*Navy*] [*British*] ... BG
Bearing and Power Transfer Assembly [*Aerospace*] ... BAPTA
Bearing and Range Indicator ... BRI
Bearing Specialists Association ... BSA
Bearing per Standard Compass [*Navigation*] ... BPSC
Bearing per Steering Gyro Compass [*Navigation*] ... BPSTGC
Bearing Technology ... BT
Bearing Time Recorder ... BTR
Bearingless Main Rotor ... BMR
Bearings, Inc. [*NYSE symbol*] ... BER
Bearn-Fabre, PQ [*Television station call letters*] ... CKRN-TV-3
Bears Bluff Laboratories. Progress Report [*A publication*] ... Bears Bluff Lab Prog Rep
Bears, Lions, Eagles, Steelers, Vikings, Colts, Dolphins, and Bills [*Computerized scouting combine for professional football teams; name comprises membership teams*] ... BLESTO-VIII
Beat ... BT
Beat-Frequency ... BF
Beat-Frequency Oscillator ... BFO
Beat Oscillator ... BO
Beata Maria [*The Blessed Virgin*] [*Latin*] ... BM
Beata Maria Virgo [*Blessed Mary the Virgin*] [*Latin*] ... BMV
Beata Virgo [*Blessed Virgin*] [*Latin*] ... BV
Beata Virgo Maria [*Blessed Virgin Mary*] [*Latin*] ... BVM
Beatae Memoriae [*Of Blessed Memory*] [*Latin*] ... BM
Beaten Favourite [*Horse racing*] [*British*] ... BF
Beating [*FBI standardized term*] ... BTG
Beatissime Pater [*Most Holy Father*] [*Latin*] ... BP
Beatitudo Vestra [*Your Holiness*] [*Latin*] ... BV
Beatrice Foods Co. [*NYSE symbol*] ... BRY
Beatrice M. Murphy Foundation ... BMMF
Beatrice, NE [*Location identifier*] [*FAA*] ... BIE
Beatrice, NE [*Location identifier*] [*FAA*] ... BJU
Beatrice, NE [*Radio station call letters*] ... KMAZ
Beatrice, NE [*Radio station call letters*] ... KWBE
Beatrice Public Library, Beatrice, NE [*Library symbol*] ... NbB
Beats per Minute [*Cardiology*] ... BPM
Beats per Second ... BPS
Beatty [*Nevada*] [*Seismograph station code, US Geological Survey*] [*Closed*] ... BEA
Beatty [*Nevada*] [*Seismograph station code, US Geological Survey*] [*Closed*] ... BTY
Beatty, NV [*Location identifier*] [*FAA*] ... BTY
Beattyville, KY [*Radio station call letters*] ... WLJC
Beattyville, KY [*Television station call letters*] ... WLJC-TV
Beauchemin, Beaton, LaPointe, Inc., Montreal, PQ, Canada [*Library symbol*] ... CaQMBBL
Beaufort [*South Carolina*] [*Airport symbol*] ... BFT
Beaufort County Library, Beaufort, SC [*Library symbol*] ... ScB
Beaufort County Technical Institute, Washington, NC [*Library symbol*] ... NcWaB
Beaufort & Morehead Railroad Co. [*AAR code*] ... BMH
Beaufort, NC [*Radio station call letters*] ... WBTB
Beaufort, SC [*Location identifier*] [*FAA*] ... NBC
Beaufort, SC [*Radio station call letters*] ... WBEU
Beaufort, SC [*Radio station call letters*] ... WJWJ-FM
Beaufort, SC [*Television station call letters*] ... WJWJ-TV
Beaufort, SC [*Radio station call letters*] ... WQLO-FM
Beaufort, SC [*Radio station call letters*] ... WVBG
Beaufort Wind Scale ... BWS
Beaumont Art Museum, Beaumont, TX [*Library symbol*] ... TxBeaAM
Beaumont, CA [*Location identifier*] [*FAA*] ... BUO
Beaumont Enterprise & Journal, Beaumont, TX [*Library symbol*] ... TxBeaE
Beaumont Library District Library, Beaumont, CA [*Library symbol*] ... CBea
Beaumont/Port Arthur [*Texas*] [*Airport symbol*] ... BPT
Beaumont, Sour Lake, & Western Railway Co. ... BSL & W
Beaumont, TX [*Radio station call letters*] ... KAYC
Beaumont, TX [*Radio station call letters*] ... KAYD
Beaumont, TX [*Television station call letters*] ... KBMT-TV
Beaumont, TX [*Television station call letters*] ... KFDM-TV
Beaumont, TX [*Radio station call letters*] ... KIEZ
Beaumont, TX [*Radio station call letters*] ... KLVI
Beaumont, TX [*Radio station call letters*] ... KQXY
Beaumont, TX [*Radio station call letters*] ... KTRM
Beaumont, TX [*Radio station call letters*] ... KVLU
Beaumont, TX [*Radio station call letters*] ... KWIC
Beaumont, TX [*Radio station call letters*] ... KZZB
Beaunit Corp. [*NYSE symbol*] [*Delisted*] ... BEM
Beauregard Parish Library, DeRidder, LA [*Library symbol*] ... LDeB
Beautiful Old House ... BOH
Beautiful People [*Slang for the wealthy, world-traveling, partying set*] ... BP
Beauty and Barber Supply Institute ... BBSI
Beauty Counselors International [*NASDAQ symbol*] ... BTYCF
Beauty Without Cruelty ... BWC
Beauvoir, the Jefferson Davis Shrine, Biloxi, MS [*Library symbol*] ... MsBB
Beaux-Arts Institute of Design Bulletin [*A publication*] ... Beaux-Arts Inst Des Bul
Beaver [*Alaska*] [*Airport symbol*] ... WBQ
Beaver, AK [*Location identifier*] [*FAA*] ... WBQ
Beaver Army Terminal [*Oregon*] ... BEART
Beaver College, Glenside, PA [*OCLC symbol*] ... BEA
Beaver College, Glenside, PA [*Library symbol*] ... PGIB
Beaver County Court House, Beaver, PA [*Library symbol*] ... PBeC
Beaver Creek, OH [*Radio station call letters*] ... WYMJ-FM
Beaver Dam, WI [*Radio station call letters*] ... WBEV
Beaver Dam, WI [*Radio station call letters*] ... WXRO
Beaver Defenders ... BD
Beaver Falls [*Pennsylvania*] [*Airport symbol*] ... BFP
Beaver Falls, PA [*Location identifier*] [*FAA*] ... BVI
Beaver Falls, PA [*Radio station call letters*] ... WBVP

Beaver Falls, PA [*Radio station call letters*] ... WGEV
Beaver Falls, PA [*Radio station call letters*] ... WWKS
Beaver Island Mormon Colony Library, St. James, Beaver Island, MI [*Library symbol*] [*Obsolete*] ... MiBeiM
Beaver, Meade, & Englewood [*AAR code*] ... BME
Beaver Memorial Library, Beaver, PA [*Library symbol*] ... PBe
Beaver, UT [*Radio station call letters*] ... KBBD
Beaverbrook Newspapers Ltd., London, United Kingdom [*Library symbol*] ... UkLB
Beaverton City Library, Beaverton, OR [*Library symbol*] ... OrB
Beaverton, MI [*Radio station call letters*] ... WGEO-FM
Beaverton, OR [*Radio station call letters*] ... KTJA
Beavertown Historical Society, Lincoln Park, NJ [*Library symbol*] ... NjLpBHi
Because ... BEC
Bechar [*Algeria*] [*Airport symbol*] ... CBH
Bechtel Group, Inc., San Francisco, CA [*Library symbol*] ... CSfBe
Bechtel Group, Inc., Technical Library, Houston, TX [*Library symbol*] ... TxHBec
Beck/Arnley Corporation [*NASDAQ symbol*] ... BACO
Beck Depression Inventory [*Psychology*] ... BDI
Beck Isoliertechnik [*A publication*] ... Beck Isoliertech
Beck [*A. S.*] **Shoe Corp.** [*American Stock Exchange symbol*] ... BEK
Becker [*Blood group*] ... Be
Becker & Hayes, Inc. [*Information service*] ... B & H
Becker Junior College, Worcester, MA [*OCLC symbol*] [*Inactive*] ... BQM
Becker Junior College, Worcester, MA [*Library symbol*] ... MWBe
Becket [*Bracket*] ... BCKT
Beckley [*West Virginia*] [*Airport symbol*] ... BKW
Beckley College, Beckley, WV [*Library symbol*] ... WvBC
Beckley-Raleigh County Library, Beckley, WV [*Library symbol*] ... WvB
Beckley, WV [*Radio station call letters*] ... WBKW
Beckley, WV [*Radio station call letters*] ... WCIR-FM
Beckley, WV [*Radio station call letters*] ... WJKK
Beckley, WV [*Radio station call letters*] ... WJLS
Beckley, WV [*Radio station call letters*] ... WVPB
Beckley, WV [*Radio station call letters*] ... WWNR
Becklin-Neugebauer [*Astronomy*] ... BN
Beckman Instruments, Inc. [*NYSE symbol*] [*Wall Street slang name: "Becky"*] [*Delisted*] ... BEC
Beckman Instruments, Inc., Fullerton, CA [*Library symbol*] ... CFIB
Beckman Instruments, Inc., Technical Library, Palo Alto, CA [*Library symbol*] ... CPaB
Beckman Report [*A publication*] ... Beckman Rep
Beckman Translation [*Computer language*] [*Beckman Instruments, Inc.*] ... BECKTRAN
Become ... BCM
Becoming One's Own Man [*Psychology*] ... BOOM
Becquerel [*Symbol*] [*SI unit of activity of ionizing radiation source*] ... Bq
Becton, Dickinson [*& Co.*] [*Initialism used in titles of a series of technical publications*] ... B-D
Becton, Dickinson, & Co. [*NYSE symbol*] ... BDX
Becton, Dickinson & Co., Paramus, NJ [*OCLC symbol*] ... JBD
Becton, Dickinson, & Co., Rutherford, NJ [*Library symbol*] ... NjRuB
Becton, Dickinson Research Center ... BDRC
Bed Bath [*Medicine*] ... BB
Bed and Breakfast [*Tourist accomodations*] ... B & B
Bed, Breakfast, and Bath [*Tourist accomodations*] ... BBB
Bed, Breakfast, and Evening Meal [*Tourist accommodations*] ... BB & EM
Bed Depth Service Time [*Wastewater treatment*] ... BDST
Bed Rest [*Medicine*] ... BR
Bedding ... BDNG
Bedding Plants, Incorporated [*An association*] ... BPI
Bedell Advertising Selling Improvement Corporation ... BASIC
Bedford [*Massachusetts*] [*Airport symbol*] ... BED
Bedford [*Borough and county in England*] ... BEDFD
Bedford Computer Corp. [*NASDAQ symbol*] ... BEDF
Bedford Free Library, Bedford, NY [*Library symbol*] ... NBed
Bedford Free Public Library, Bedford, MA [*Library symbol*] ... MBd
Bedford Hills Free Library, Bedford Hills, NY [*Library symbol*] ... NBedh
Bedford, IN [*Location identifier*] [*FAA*] ... BFR
Bedford, IN [*Radio station call letters*] ... WBIW
Bedford, MA [*Location identifier*] [*FAA*] ... SKR
Bedford, PA [*Radio station call letters*] ... WAYC
Bedford, PA [*Radio station call letters*] ... WBFD
Bedford Park Public Library District, Bedford Park, IL [*Library symbol*] ... IBpB
Bedford Public Library, Bedford, IN [*Library symbol*] ... InB
Bedford Public Library, Bedford, OH [*Library symbol*] ... OBed
Bedford Times-Press, Bedford, IA [*Library symbol*] ... IaBedTP
Bedford, VA [*Radio station call letters*] ... WBLT
Bedfordshire [*County in England*] ... BEDS
Bedi Karthlisa [*A publication*] ... Bedi Kart
Bedi Karthlisa [*A publication*] ... BK
Bedlington Terrier Club of America ... BTCA
Bedourie [*Australia*] [*Airport symbol*] [*Obsolete*] ... BEU
Bedpan ... BDPN
Bedpan ... BP
Bedrijfsontwikkeling. Editie Akkerbouw. Maandblad voor Agrarische Produktie. Verwerking en Afzet [*A publication*] ... Bedrijfsontwikkeling Ed Akkerbouw
Bedroom ... BR
Bedroom Steward [*In the first class aboard an ocean liner*] ... BR
Beds Occupied ... BEDOC
Beds and Patients Report ... BAPREPT
Bedside Network of the Veterans Hospital Radio and TV Guild [*Later, VBN*] ... BNVHRTVG
Bedspread Blanket ... BB
Bedtime ... BT
Bee County College, Beeville, TX [*Library symbol*] ... TxBeeC
Bee County Public Library, Beeville, TX [*Library symbol*] ... TxBee
Bee Industries Association ... BIA
Bee Keepers Association ... BKA
Bee Line Airlines [*Houston, TX*] [*FAA designator*] ... BLF
Bee Research Association ... BRA
Beebe Ranch [*California*] [*Seismograph station code, US Geological Survey*] ... BBR
Beech Aircraft Corporation ... BAC
Beech Aircraft Corp. [*NYSE symbol*] [*Delisted*] ... BCX
Beech Aircraft Corp. [*Wichita, KS*] [*FAA designator*] ... BEC
Beech Creek R. R. Co. [*NYSE symbol*] [*Delisted*] ... BCH
Beech Mountain Railroad Co. [*AAR code*] ... BEEM
Beech-Nut Life Savers, Inc. [*NYSE symbol*] [*Delisted*] ... BLS
Beecham Group plc ADR [*NASDAQ symbol*] ... BHAMY
Beecham Laboratories, White Hall, IL [*Library symbol*] ... IWhhB
Beecham Products-Western Hemisphere Research, Parsippany, NJ [*OCLC symbol*] ... BEE
Beecham Research Laboratories Ltd. [*Great Britain*] [*Research code symbol*] ... BRL
Beef Heart Infusion Broth [*Microbiology*] ... BHIB
Beef Improvement Federation ... BIF
BEEF [*Base Engineer Emergency Forces*] **Reporting, Analysis, and Status System** [*Air Force*] ... BRASS
Beefmaster Breeders Universal ... BBU
Beefsteak Charlie's [*American Stock Exchange symbol*] ... BCS
Beehive International [*American Stock Exchange symbol*] ... BHI
Beekman Community Library Reading Center, Poughquag, NY [*Library symbol*] ... NPoq
Beeler, J. L., Los Angeles CA [*STAC*] ... BJL
Beeline, Inc. [*NASDAQ symbol*] ... BLNE
Been ... BN
Been to America [*Slang*] [*British*] ... BTA
Beer Can Collectors of America ... BCCA
Beer Firkin ... BF
Beersheba [*Israel*] [*Airport symbol*] [*Obsolete*] ... BEV
Beet Sugar Development Foundation ... BSDF
Beet Yellows Virus ... BYV
Beethoven Jahrbuch [*A publication*] ... Be Jb
Beevers-Ross [*Beta-alumina crystallography*] ... BR
Beeville, TX [*Radio station call letters*] ... KCWW
Beeville, TX [*Radio station call letters*] ... KIBL
Befandriana [*Madagascar*] [*Airport symbol*] ... WBD
Before ... B
Before ... B4
Before ... BEF
Before ... BEFE
Before ... BFR
Before Bottom Center [*Valve position*] ... BBC
Before Bottom Dead Center ... BBDC
Before Business Clearance ... BBC
Before Casinos ... BC
Before Christ ... BC
Before the Common Era [*Jewish equivalent of BC*] ... BCE
Before Computer ... BC
Before the Crash [*i.e., before the 1929 stock market collapse*] [*Slang*] ... BC
Before Croonery [*Musical slang*] ... BC
Before Dark ... BFDK
Before Encountering Instrument Flight Rules Conditions ... BIFR
Before Flight ... BF
Before Flight Abort ... BFA
Before Flight Reliability ... BFR
Before Girls [*i.e., before women became part of armed forces*] [*Military*] ... BG
Before Marriage ... BM
Before the Present ... BP
Before Proceeding on Course [*Aviation*] ... BPOC
Before Queues [*Referring to pre-World War II period*] [*Slang*] [*British*] ... BQ
Before Top Center [*Valve position*] ... BTC
Before Top Dead Center ... BTDC
Before Touching [*Parapsychology*] ... BT
Befrienders International ... BI
Begin ... BGN
Begin Bracket Indicator [*Data processing*] ... BB
Begin Standard RADAR Refuel Orbit [*Later, BSRO*] [*Aviation*] ... BSRRO
Begin Standard Refuel Orbit [*Formerly, BSRRO*] [*Aviation*] ... BSRO
Begin Telemetry Cycle ... BTC
Begin Transmission, Break ... BT
Beginner's All-Purpose Symbolic Instruction Code [*Data processing*] ... BASIC
Beginning ... BEG
Beginning of Business ... BOB
Beginning Climb [*Aviation*] ... BC
Beginning of Cycle ... BOC

Beginning Descent [*Aviation*] ... BD
Beginning of Equilibrium Cycle [*Nuclear energy*] ... BEC
Beginning Evening Nautical Twilight ... BENT
Beginning of File ... BOF
Beginning of Information Marker [*Data processing*] ... BIM
Beginning of Life ... BOL
Beginning of Magnetic Tape [*Data processing*] ... BMT
Beginning of Month ... BOM
Beginning Morning Civil Twilight [*Navigation*] ... BMCT
Beginning Morning Nautical Twilight [*Navigation*] ... BMNT
Beginning Morning Nautical Twilight [*Navigation*] ... BMT
Beginning of Period ... BOP
Beginning Period ... BP
Beginning of Precipitation [*Meteorology*] ... B
Beginning Procedure Turn [*Aviation*] ... BPT
Beginning of Quarter ... BOQ
Beginning Standard Holding Procedure [*Aviation*] ... BSHP
Beginning Standard Range Approach [*Aviation*] ... BSRAP
Beginning Straight-In Approach [*Aviation*] ... BSIAP
Beginning of Tape [*Data processing*] ... BOT
Beginning Tape Label [*Data processing*] ... BTL
Beginning to Tape Test ... BTT
Begley Drug Co. [*NASDAQ symbol*] ... BGLY
Behavior-Based Personnel Systems ... BBPS
Behavior Cards [*Psychological testing*] ... BC
Behavior Classification Checklist [*Psychology*] ... BCC
Behavior Disorder ... BD
Behavior Evaluation Scale [*Educational testing*] ... BES
Behavior Genetics [*A publication*] ... Behav Genet
Behavior Genetics [*A publication*] ... BHGNA
Behavior Genetics Association ... BGA
Behavior Modification [*A publication*] ... Behav Modif
Behavior Modification [*Psychology*] ... B-MOD
Behavior Monitor System ... BMS
Behavior of Offshore Structures [*Conference*] ... BOSS
Behavior Rating Profile [*Educational testing*] ... BRP
Behavior Replication by Analog Instruction of the Nervous System [*Electrical stimulation of the brain*] ... BRAINS
Behavior Research Institute ... BRI
Behavior Research Methods and Instrumentation [*A publication*] ... Behav Res M
Behavior Research Methods and Instrumentation [*A publication*] ... Behav Res Methods & Instrum
Behavior Research Methods and Instrumentation [*A publication*] ... Behav Res Methods Instrum
Behavior Research Methods and Instrumentation [*A publication*] ... BRMIA
Behavior Research and Therapy [*A publication*] ... BRT
Behavior Research and Therapy [*A publication*] ... BRTHA
Behavior Science Notes [*A publication*] ... Behavior Sci Notes
Behavior Science Notes [*A publication*] ... Behav Sci N
Behavior Science Research [*A publication*] ... Behav Sci R
Behavior and Systems Research Laboratory [*Army*] ... BESERL
Behavior Therapy [*A publication*] ... Behavior Ther
Behavior Therapy [*A publication*] ... Behav Ther
Behavior Therapy and Research Society ... BTRS
Behavioral ... BEHAV
Behavioral ... BEHVL
Behavioral Approach Scale [*Psychology*] ... BAS
Behavioral Avoidance Test [*Psychometrics*] ... BAT
Behavioral Biology [*A publication*] ... Behav Biol
Behavioral Biology [*A publication*] ... Behavioral Bio
Behavioral Biology [*A publication*] ... BHBLA
Behavioral Characteristics Progression [*Scale*] ... BCP
Behavioral Checklist [*Psychology*] ... BCL
Behavioral Differential ... BD
Behavioral Ecology and Sociobiology [*A publication*] ... Behav Ecol Sociobiol
Behavioral Effects of Infectious Diseases [*Army*] ... BEID
Behavioral Engineering [*A publication*] ... BEJUA
Behavioral Kinesiology [*Book title*] ... BK
Behavioral and Neural Biology [*A publication*] ... Behav Neural Biol
Behavioral Neuropsychiatry [*A publication*] ... Behav Neuropsychiatry
Behavioral Pharmacology Society ... BPS
Behavioral Research Council [*for Scientific Inquiry into the Problems of Men in Society*] ... BRC
Behavioral Research Laboratories ... BRL
Behavioral Science [*A publication*] ... Behavioral Sci
Behavioral Science [*A publication*] ... Behav Sci
Behavioral Science [*A publication*] ... BEHSA
Behavioral Science [*A publication*] ... BSci
Behavioral Science Programing Language [*Data processing*] ... BSPL
Behavioral Science Research Laboratory [*Army*] ... BESRL
Behavioral Skills Training [*Navy*] ... BEST
Behavioral and Social Sciences ... BASS
Behavioral and Social Sciences ... BSS
Behavioral and Social Sciences Survey Committee ... BSSSC
Behaviorally Anchored Rating Scale ... BARS
Behaviorists for Social Action ... BFSA
Behaviour [*A publication*] ... Behav
Behaviour Research and Therapy [*A publication*] ... Behaviour Res & Ther
Behaviour Research and Therapy [*A publication*] ... Behav Res T
Behaviour Research and Therapy [*A publication*] ... Behav Res Ther
Behavioural Brain Research [*A publication*] ... Behav Brain Res
Behavioural Processes [*A publication*] ... Behav Processes
Behavioural Sciences and Community Development [*A publication*] ... BECD
Behavioural Sciences and Community Development [*A publication*] ... Behav Sci Com Dev
Behavioural Sciences and Community Development [*A publication*] ... Behav Sci Community Develop
Behcet's Disease [*Medicine*] ... BD
Behind ... BHND
Behind Completion Date ... BCD
Behind the Line [*Air Force*] ... BTL
Behind Schedule ... B/S
Behind Tape Reader ... BTR
Bei [*At, With*] [*German*] ... B
Beiblatt zur Anglia [*A publication*] ... Bei
Beiblatt zur Anglia [*A publication*] ... Beibl
Beiblatt zur Anglia [*A publication*] ... Beiblatt
Beica [*Ethiopia*] [*Airport symbol*] ... BEI
Beida [*Libya*] [*Airport symbol*] ... LAQ
Beifolgend [*Herewith*] [*German*] ... BEIF
Beiheft zur Internationalen Zeitschrift fuer Vitamin- und Ernaehrungsforschung [*A publication*] ... Beih Int Z Vitam-Ernaehrungsforsch
Beiheft du den Zeitschriften des Schweizerischen Forstvereins [*A publication*] ... Beih Z Schweiz Forstver
Beihefte zum Archiv fuer Schiffs und Tropen-Hygiene [*A publication*] ... Beihefte Arch Schiffs- u Tropen-Hyg
Beihefte zu den Berichten der Naturhistorischen Gesellschaft zu Hannover [*A publication*] ... Beih Ber Naturhist Ges Hannover
Beihefte zum Ja [*A publication*] ... BzJA
Beihefte zur Sydowia Annales. Mycologici. Ser II [*A publication*] ... Beih Sydowia Ann Mycol Ser II
Beihefte der Zeitschrift fuer Religions und Geistesgeschichte [*A publication*] ... BZR Gg
Beihefte zur Zeitschrift Wirkendes Wort [*A publication*] ... BZWW
Beijing [*China*] [*Airport symbol*] ... PEK
Beijing Proton Synchrotron [*China*] ... BPS
Beijing Review [*A publication*] ... Beijing R
Beilstein Unique Sequence [*Chemistry*] ... BUS
Beilstein Unique Sequence Number [*Chemistry*] ... BUSEN
Being ... BG
Beira [*Mozambique*] [*Airport symbol*] ... BEW
Beirut [*Lebanon*] [*Airport symbol*] ... BEY
Beitraege zur Alten Geschichte [*A publication*] ... BAG
Beitraege zur Analysis [*A publication*] ... Beitraege Anal
Beitraege zur Bayerischen Kirchengeschichte [*A publication*] ... BBKG
Beitraege zur Biblischen Landes-und Altertumskunde [*A publication*] ... BBLA
Beitraege zur Biblischen Landes-und Altertumskunde [*A publication*] ... BBLAK
Beitraege zur Biologie der Pflanzen [*A publication*] ... Beitr Biol Pflanz
Beitraege zur Deutschen Klassik [*A publication*] ... BDK
Beitraege zur Deutschen Klassik. Abhandlungen [*A publication*] ... BDKA
Beitraege zur Deutschen Philologie [*A publication*] ... BDP
Beitraege zur Deutschen Volks- und Altertumskunde [*A publication*] ... BDVA
Beitraege zur Deutschen Volks- und Altertumskunde [*A publication*] ... Beitr Deutsch Volks Altertumskunde
Beitraege zur Englischen Philologie [*A publication*] ... BEP
Beitraege zur Englischen Philologie [*A publication*] ... BEPh
Beitraege zur Entomologie [*A publication*] ... Beitr Entomol
Beitraege zur Entwicklungsmechanischen Anatomie der Pflanzen [*A publication*] ... Beitr Entwicklungsmech Anat Pflanz
Beitraege zur Erforschung der Sprache und Kultur Englands und Nordamerikas [*A publication*] ... Beitr Engl u Nordamerikas
Beitraege zur Forschungstechnologie [*A publication*] ... Beitr Forschungstechnol
Beitraege Geobotanischen Landesaufnahme der Schweiz [*A publication*] ... Beitr Geobot Landesaufn Schweiz
Beitraege zur Geologie der Schweiz. Geotechnische Serie [*A publication*] ... Beitr Geol Schweiz Geotech Ser
Beitraege zur Geologie der Schweiz. Kleinere Mitteilungen [*A publication*] ... Beitr Geol Schweiz Kleinere Mitt
Beitraege zur Geologie von Thueringen [*A publication*] ... Beitr Geol Thueringen
Beitraege zur Geophysik [*A publication*] ... Beitr Geoph
Beitraege zur Geophysik [*A publication*] ... Beitr Geophysik
Beitraege zur Gerichtlichen Medizin [*A publication*] ... Beitr Gerichtl Med
Beitraege zur Geschichte des Buchwesens [*A publication*] ... Beitraege Gesch Buchw
Beitraege zur Geschichte der Deutschen Sprache und Literatur [*Halle*] [*A publication*] ... Beitr
Beitraege zur Geschichte der Deutschen Sprache und Literatur [*Halle*] [*A publication*] ... BGDSL
Beitraege zur Geschichte der Deutschen Sprache und Literatur (Halle) [*A publication*] ... BGDSLH
Beitraege zur Geschichte der Deutschen Sprache und Literatur (Halle) [*A publication*] ... (Halle) Beitr

Beitraege zur Geschichte der Deutschen Sprache und Literatur (Tuebingen) [A publication].....................BGDSLT
Beitraege zur Geschichte der Pharmazie und Ihrer Nachbargebiete [A publication]......Beitr Gesch Pharm Ihrer Nachbargeb
Beitraege zur Geschichte der Philosophie und Theologie des Mittelalters [A publication].....................BGPTM
Beitraege zur Geschichte von Stadt und Stift Essen [A publication]..........................BGSSE
Beitraege zur Hygiene und Epidemiologie [A publication]......................Beitr Hyg Epidemiol
Beitraege zur Infusionstherapie und Klinische Ernaehrung [A publication].....................Beitr Infusionsther Klin Ernaehr
Beitraege zur Klinik und Erforschung der Tuberkulose und der Lungenkrankheiten [A publication]..........................Beitr Klin Erforsch Tuberk Lungenkr
Beitraege zur Klinik der Tuberkulose und Spezifischen Tuberkulose-Forschung [A publication].....................Beitr Klin Tuberk Spezif Tuber-Forsch
Beitraege zur Klinischen Chirurgie [A publication]..................Beitr Klin Chir
Beitraege zur Konfliktforschung [A publication]....................Beitr Konfl
Beitraege zur Konfliktforschung [A publication].............Beitr Konfliktforsch
Beitraege zur Kryptogamenflora der Schweiz [A publication].....................Beitr Kryptogamenflora Schweiz
Beitraege zur Kulturgeschichte des Mittelalters und der Renaissance [A publication] ....BKMR
Beitraege zur Linguistik und Informationsverarbeitung [A publication] ....BLI
Beitraege zum Mathematisch-Naturwissenschaftlichen Unterricht [A publication].................Beitr Math-Naturwiss Unterr
Beitraege zur Meereskunde [A publication]....................Beitr Meer
Beitraege zur Mineralogie und Petrographie [A publication].....................Beitr Mineralogie u Petrographie
Beitraege zur Mineralogie und Petrographie [A publication].....................Beitr Miner Petrogr
Beitraege zur Musikwissenschaft [A publication] ....B Mw
Beitraege zur Musikwissenschaft [A publication] ....BzMW
Beitraege zur Namenforschung [A publication]....................Beitraege Namen
Beitraege zur Namenforschung [A publication]....................BN
Beitraege zur Namenforschung [A publication] ....BNF
Beitraege zur Naturkundlichen Forschung in Suedwestdeutschland [A publication].....................Beitr Naturkd Forsch Suedwestdtsch
Beitraege zur Naturkundlichen Forschung in Suedwestdeutschland. Beihefte [A publication] ....Beitr Naturkd Forsch Suedwestdtsch Beih
Beitraege zur Neotropischen Fauna [A publication]........Beitr Neotrop Fauna
Beitraege zur Neueren Literaturgeschichte [A publication] ....BNL
Beitraege zur Neurochirurgie [A publication] ....Beitr Neurochir
Beitraege zur Numerischen Mathematik [A publication].....................Beitraege Numer Math
Beitraege zur Numerischen Mathematik [A publication] ....Beitr Numer Math
Beitraege zur Orthopaedie und Traumatologie [A publication].....................Beitr Orthop Traumatol
Beitraege zur Pathologie [A publication]....................Beitr Path
Beitraege zur Pathologie [A publication] ....Beitr Pathol
Beitraege zur Pathologischen Anatomie und zur Allgemeinen Pathologie [A publication]....................Beitr Path Anat u Allg Path
Beitraege zur Pathologischen Anatomie und zur Allgemeinen Pathologie [A publication]....................Beitr Pathol Anat Allg Pathol
Beitraege zur Physik der Atmosphaere [A publication].......Beitr Phys Atmos
Beitraege aus der Plasmaphysik [A publication]...................Beitr Plasmaphys
Beitraege aus der Plasmaphysik [A publication]....................Beitr Pl Physik
Beitraege suz Radioastronomie [A publication]..................Beitr Radioastron
Beitraege zur Rheumatologie [A publication]....................Beitr Rheumatol
Beitraege zur Romanischen Philologie [A publication]....................BRP
Beitraege zur Romanischen Philologie [A publication]....................BRPh
Beitraege zur Saechsischen Kirchengeschichte [A publication]..........BSKG
Beitraege zur Schweizerdeutschen Mundartforschungen [A publication].....................BSM
Beitraege zur Sexualforschung [A publication]................Beitr Sexualforsch
Beitraege zur Silikose-Forschung [A publication].........Beitr Silikose-Forsch
Beitraege zur Silikose-Forschung (Pneumokoniose) [A publication].....................Beitr Silikose-Forsch (Pneumokoniose)
Beitraege zur Tropischen Landwirtschaft und Veterinaermedizin [A publication].....................Beitr Trop Landwirtsch Veterinaermed
Beitraege zur Vogelkunde [A publication] ....Beitr Vogelkd
Beitrage zur Danziger Statistik [Danzig].....................BDS
Beitrage zur Statistik der Republik Osterreich [Austria].....................BSRO
Beja [MARC language code] [Library of Congress] ....bej
Bejaia [Algeria] [Airport symbol].....................BJA
Beke es Szocializmus [A publication] ....Beke es Szocial
Beker Industries Corp. [NYSE symbol].....................BKI
Beker Industries Corp. Wts [NASDAQ symbol].....................BKIWW
Bekesy Ascending Descending Gap Evaluation ....BADGE
Bekily [Madagascar] [Airport symbol].....................OVA
Bel [Ten decibels].....................B
Bel Air, MD [Radio station call letters].....................WHFC
Bel Air, MD [Radio station call letters].....................WHRF
Bel and the Dragon [Old Testament book] [Apocrypha]........Bel and Dr
Bel Fuse, Inc. [NASDAQ symbol].....................BELF

Bela Lyons Pratt [Designer's mark, when appearing on US coins].....................BLP
Belacker [France] [Seismograph station code, US Geological Survey].....BAF
Belady Optimum Replacement [Algorithm] [Data processing] ....BOR
Belaga [Malaysia] [Airport symbol].....................BLG
Belaruskaia Litaratura [A publication].....................BLL
Belaruskaia Medychnaia Dumka [A publication]..........Belarusk Med Dumka
Belaruskaja Linhvistyka [A publication].....................Bel L
Belco Petroleum Corporation [NYSE symbol] [Delisted].....................BPC
Belcourt, ND [Radio station call letters].....................KEYA
Belden Corp. [NYSE symbol] [Delisted].....................BEL
Belding Heminway Co., Inc. [NYSE symbol].....................BHY
Beleaguered.....................BEL
Beleid en Maatschappij [A publication].....................Beleid en Mij
Belem [Brazil] [Airport symbol].....................BEL
Belen, NM [Radio station call letters].....................KARS
Belen, NM [Radio station call letters].....................KMLW
Belep [New Caledonia] [Airport symbol].....................BMY
Belfagor [A publication].....................Bel
Belfast [Northern Ireland] [Airport symbol].....................BFS
Belfast [City in Northern Ireland].....................BLFST
Belfast [Northern Ireland] Harbour [Airport symbol].....................BHD
Belfast, ME [Radio station call letters].....................WBME
Belfast & Moosehead Lake Railroad Co. [AAR code].....................BML
Belfort [France] [Airport symbol].....................BOR
Belga [Monetary unit in Belgium] ....B
Belgarsko Muzikoznanie [A publication].....................B Muz
Belgaum [India] [Airport symbol].....................IXG
Belgian Air Force.....................BAF
Belgian Air Staff [NATO].....................BELAIR
Belgian American Educational Foundation.....................BAEF
Belgian American Trade Review [A publication] ....Belg Rev
Belgian Archives for the Social Sciences [Information service] ....BASS
Belgian Begonia Growers Association [Defunct].....................BBGA
Belgian Chamber of Commerce in the United States [Later, Belgian American Chamber of Commerce in the United States].....................BCCUS
Belgian Congo.....................CB
Belgian Draft Horse Corporation of America ....BDHCA
Belgian Educational Student Travel Service.....................BESTS
Belgian Engineers in North America [Defunct].....................BENA
Belgian Fourragere ....BF
Belgian Information and Dissemination Service.....................BELINDIS
Belgian International Air Services Cy. [ICAO designator].....................AP
Belgian Linen Association [Later, ILPC].....................BLA
Belgian Naval Staff [NATO].....................BELNAV
Belgian, Netherlands, Scandinavian, South African [Association of teachers and students].....................BENESCANSA
Belgian Plastics [A publication].....................Belg Plast
Belgian Reactor ....BR
Belgian Sheepdog Club of America.....................BSCA
Belgian Socialist Party.....................BSP
Belgique Medicale [A publication].....................Belgique Med
Belgisch Institut tot Verbetering van de Beit Driemaandelijkse Publikatie [A publication].......Belg Inst Verbetering Beit Driemaand Publ
Belgisch Tijdschrift voor Radiologie [A publication].......Belg Tijdschr Radiol
Belgisch Tijdschrift voor Reumatologie en Fysische Geneeskunde [A publication]........Belg Tijdschr Reumatol Fys Geneeskd
Belgische Radio en Televisie.....................BRT
Belgium.....................B
Belgium [MARC country of publication code] [Library of Congress]...........be
Belgium [Three-letter standard code].....................BEL
Belgium.....................BELG
Belgium [MARC geographic area code] [Library of Congress]..............e-be---
Belgium [Aircraft nationality and registration mark].....................OO
Belgium [Two-letter standard code].....................BE
Belgium-Luxembourg Economic Union ....BLEU
Belgium, Netherlands, Luxembourg [Economic union].....................BENELUX
Belgium Philatelic Society.....................BPS
Belgium. Service Geologique. Memoire [A publication].....................Belg Serv Geol Mem
Belgium. Service Geologique. Professional Paper [A publication].....................Belg Serv Geol Prof Pap
Belgium Standard Ltd. [NASDAQ symbol].....................BELGF
Belgrade [A publication].....................Be
Belgrade [Yugoslavia] [Airport symbol].....................BEG
Belgrade, MT [Radio station call letters].....................KGVW
Belgrade, MT [Radio station call letters].....................KMZK
Belgravia [A publication].....................Belgra
Belhaven College, Jackson, MS [Library symbol].....................MsJB
Belhaven, NC [Radio station call letters].....................WKJA
Belinfante-Swihart [Theory].....................BS
Belize [Three-letter standard code] ....BLZ
Belize [Two-letter standard code].....................BZ
Belize Airways Ltd. [ICAO designator].....................HB
Belize City [Belize] [Airport symbol].....................BZE
Belize Institute of Social Research and Action ....BISRA
Belknap, Inc. [NASDAQ symbol].....................BELP
Bell Aerospace Company ....BAC
Bell Aerospace Co., New Orleans, LA [Library symbol].....................LNBA
Bell Aerospace Textron, Technical Library, Niagara Falls, NY [Library symbol].....................NNiaB

Bell Aerosystems Co. ... BA
Bell Aerosystems Co., Buffalo, NY [*Library symbol*] ... NBuBA
Bell Alarm Switch ... BASW
Bell Atlantic Corp. [*NYSE symbol*] ... BEL
Bell Audit Relate System [*Bell Laboratories*] ... BARS
Bell Audit System [*Bell Laboratories*] ... BAS
Bell and Bell [*Technical drawings*] ... B & B
Bell Canada Enterprises ... BCE
Bell Canada Enterprises, Inc. [*NYSE symbol*] ... BCE
Bell [*W.*] **& Co., Inc.** [*NASDAQ symbol*] ... BLLW
Bell Cord [*Technical drawings*] ... BC
Bell Crank ... BELCRK
Bell Data Network [*Proposed*] ... BDN
Bell End ... BE
Bell and Flange [*Technical drawings*] ... B & F
Bell & Gossett Co. [*NYSE symbol*] [*Delisted*] ... BLG
Bell Helicopter Co., Fort Worth, TX [*Library symbol*] ... TxFBH
Bell & Howell Co. ... BH
Bell & Howell Co. [*NYSE symbol*] ... BHW
Bell & Howell Co., Research Laboratories, Pasadena, CA [*Library symbol*] ... CPBH
Bell & Howell/Mamiya Company ... BHMC
Bell Industries [*NYSE symbol*] ... BI
Bell Information Network ... BIN
Bell Intercontinental Corp. [*NYSE symbol*] [*Delisted*] ... BLL
Bell Jar System ... BJS
Bell Journal of Economics [*A publication*] ... Bell J Econ
Bell Journal of Economics [*A publication*] ... Bell J Econom
Bell Journal of Economics and Management Science [*A publication*] ... Bell J Econ Manage Sci
Bell Laboratories Automatic Design System ... BLADES
Bell Laboratories Automatic Design System ... BLADS
Bell Laboratories Automatic Device ... BLADE
Bell Laboratories FORTRAN Assembly Program [*Data processing*] ... BEFAP
Bell Laboratories Interpretive System [*Data processing*] ... BLIS
Bell Laboratories Library Real-Time Loan System ... BELLREL
Bell Laboratories Machine-Aided Technical Information Center ... BELLMATIC
Bell Laboratories Record [*A publication*] ... Bell Lab Re
Bell Laboratories Record [*A publication*] ... Bell Lab Rec
Bell Laboratories Record [*A publication*] ... BELR
Bell Little Electrodata Symbolic System for the Electrodata ... BLESSED
Bell Log System ... BLS
Bell Memorial Public Library, Mentone, IN [*Library symbol*] ... InMe
Bell National Corp. [*NASDAQ symbol*] ... BELL
Bell Northern Research, Bramalea, ON, Canada [*Library symbol*] ... CaOBramB
Bell Northern Research, Montreal, PQ, Canada [*Library symbol*] ... CaQMBNR
Bell Northern Research, Ottawa, ON, Canada [*Library symbol*] ... CaOONorE
Bell Northern Software Research, Toronto, ON, Canada [*Library symbol*] ... CaOTBNS
Bell Operating Company [*Also known as BSOC*] [*Post-divestiture division of American Telephone & Telegraph Co.*] ... BOC
Bell Petroleum Services [*NASDAQ symbol*] ... BPSI
Bell and Spigot [*Technical drawings*] ... B & S
Bell System Center for Technical Education ... BSCTE
Bell System Operating Company [*Also known as BOC*] [*Post-divestiture division of American Telephone & Telegraph Co.*] ... BSOC
Bell System Practices ... BSP
Bell System Technical Journal [*A publication*] ... Bell System Tech J
Bell System Technical Journal [*A publication*] ... Bell Syst T
Bell System Technical Journal [*A publication*] ... Bell Syst Tech J
Bell System Technical Journal [*A publication*] ... BSTJ
Bell Telephone ... BELLTEL
Bell Telephone Co. of Canada [*NYSE symbol*] [*Delisted*] ... BCA
Bell Telephone Co. of Canada, Law Department Library, Montreal, PQ, Canada [*Library symbol*] ... CaQMBL
Bell Telephone Co. of Canada, Montreal, PQ, Canada [*Library symbol*] ... CaQMB
Bell Telephone Laboratories, Inc. ... BTL
Bell Telephone Laboratories, Inc., Holmdel, NJ [*OCLC symbol*] ... BTL
Bell Telephone Laboratories, Inc., Murray Hill, NJ [*Library symbol*] ... NjMuB
Bell Telephone Laboratories, Inc., Technical Information Library, Holmdel, NJ [*Library symbol*] ... NjHolB
Bell Telephone Laboratories, Inc., Technical Information Library, Whippany, NJ [*Library symbol*] ... NjWhiB
Bell Telephone Magazine [*A publication*] ... Bell Telephone Mag
Bella Bella [*Canada*] [*Airport symbol*] ... ZEL
Bella Coola [*Canada*] [*Airport symbol*] ... QBC
Belladonna [*"Deadly-nightshade" plant, or medicinal extract from it*] ... BD
Belladonna and Opium [*Toxicology*] ... B & O
Bellaire City Library, Bellaire, TX [*Library symbol*] ... TxBl
Bellaire, MI [*Location identifier*] [*FAA*] ... ACB
Bellaire, MI [*Location identifier*] [*FAA*] ... CXK
Bellaire, OH [*Radio station call letters*] ... WBHR
Bellaire, OH [*Radio station call letters*] ... WOMP
Bellaire, OH [*Radio station call letters*] ... WOMP-FM
Bellaire Public Library, Bellaire, MI [*Library symbol*] ... MiBela
Bellaire, Zanesville, & Cincinnati Railroad [*Nickname: Bent, Zigzagged, and Crooked*] ... BZ & C
Bellar & Lichtenberg [*Device*] ... B & L
Bellarmine College, Louisville, KY [*OCLC symbol*] ... KBC
Bellarmine College, Louisville, KY [*Library symbol*] ... KyLoB
Bellarmine College, Plattsburgh, NY [*Library symbol*] ... NPlaB
Bellarmine College, Thomas Merton Studies Center, Louisville, KY [*Library symbol*] ... KyLoB-M
Belle Fourche Public Library, Belle Fourche, SD [*Library symbol*] ... SdBf
Belle Fourche, SD [*Radio station call letters*] ... KBFS
Belle Fourche, SD [*Radio station call letters*] ... KKEB
Belle Glade, FL [*Radio station call letters*] ... WSWN
Belle Glade, FL [*Radio station call letters*] ... WSWN-FM
Belle Plaine Union, Belle Plaine, IA [*Library symbol*] ... IaBepU
Belle W. Baruch Library in Marine Science [*A publication*] ... Belle W Baruch Libr Mar Sci
Belleek Collector's Society [*Commercial firm*] ... BCS
Bellefontaine, OH [*Location identifier*] [*FAA*] ... RUV
Bellefontaine, OH [*Radio station call letters*] ... WOHP
Bellefontaine, OH [*Radio station call letters*] ... WTOO-FM
Bellefonte Central Railroad Co. [*AAR code*] ... BFC
Bellefonte District Library Center [*Library network*] ... CPDLC
Bellefonte, PA [*Radio station call letters*] ... WBLF
Bellegarde, SK [*Television station call letters*] ... CBKFT-9
Belleten Tuerk Tarih Kurumu [*A publication*] ... Belleten
Belleville Area College, Belleville, IL [*Library symbol*] ... IBelC
Belleville Area College, Belleville, IL [*OCLC symbol*] ... IDF
Belleville Free Public Library, Belleville, NJ [*Library symbol*] ... NjBe
Belleville, IL [*Location identifier*] [*FAA*] ... BLV
Belleville, IL [*Location identifier*] [*FAA*] ... OXK
Belleville, IL [*Location identifier*] [*FAA*] ... RCC
Belleville, IL [*Location identifier*] [*FAA*] ... SKE
Belleville, IL [*Radio station call letters*] ... WIBV
Belleville, ON [*Radio station call letters*] ... CIGL-FM
Belleville, ON [*Radio station call letters*] ... CJBQ
Belleville Public Library, Belleville, IL [*Library symbol*] ... IBel
Belleville Public Library, Belleville, ON, Canada [*Library symbol*] ... CaOBE
Belleville Telegram, Belleville, NJ [*Library symbol*] ... NjBeT
Belleville Township High School District 201, Belleville, IL [*Library symbol*] ... IBelTSD
Bellevue Community College, Bellevue, WA [*Library symbol*] ... WaBB
Bellevue Herald-Leader, Bellevue, IA [*Library symbol*] ... IaBevHL
Bellevue, OH [*Radio station call letters*] ... WNRR
Bellevue Public Library, Bellevue, IA [*Library symbol*] ... IaBev
Bellevue Public Library, Bellevue, NE [*OCLC symbol*] ... BLL
Bellevue Public Library, Bellevue, NE [*Library symbol*] ... NbBe
Bellevue Public Library, Bellevue, OH [*Library symbol*] ... OBv
Bellevue School District, Instructional Materials Center, Bellevue, WA [*Library symbol*] ... WaBS
Bellevue, WA [*Location identifier*] [*FAA*] ... BVU
Bellevue, WA [*Radio station call letters*] ... KASB
Bellevue, WA [*Radio station call letters*] ... KBCS
Bellevue, WA [*Radio station call letters*] ... KJZZ
Bellevue, WA [*Radio station call letters*] ... KLSY
Bellevue, WA [*Radio station call letters*] ... KZAM-FM
Bellfield [*Australia*] [*Seismograph station code, US Geological Survey*] ... BFD
Bellin Memorial Hospital, Green Bay, WI [*Library symbol*] ... WGrB
Belling ... BLNG
Bellingham [*Washington*] [*Airport symbol*] ... BLI
Bellingham [*Washington*] [*Seismograph station code, US Geological Survey*] [*Closed*] ... BLL
Bellingham Public Library, Bellingham, WA [*Library symbol*] ... WaBe
Bellingham, WA [*Radio station call letters*] ... KBFW
Bellingham, WA [*Radio station call letters*] ... KGMI
Bellingham, WA [*Radio station call letters*] ... KISM
Bellingham, WA [*Radio station call letters*] ... KNWR
Bellingham, WA [*Radio station call letters*] ... KOQT
Bellingham, WA [*Radio station call letters*] ... KPUG
Bellingham, WA [*Radio station call letters*] ... KUGS
Bellingham, WA [*Television station call letters*] ... KVOS-TV
Bellingham, WA [*Location identifier*] [*FAA*] ... LUM
Bellmore Memorial Library, Bellmore, NY [*Library symbol*] ... NBellm
Bellmouth [*Design engineering*] ... BLMTH
Bellofram Rolling Diaphragm ... BRD
Bellona Island [*Solomon Islands*] [*Airport symbol*] ... BNY
Bellows ... BLWS
Bellows Falls, VT [*Radio station call letters*] ... WBFL
Bellows Tankage Module ... BTM
Bellows Valve ... BV
Bellport Memorial Library, Bellport, NY [*Library symbol*] ... NBel
BellSouth Corp. [*NYSE symbol*] ... BLS
Bellville, TX [*Radio station call letters*] ... KACO
Bellwether Explorations Co. [*NASDAQ symbol*] ... BELW
Bellwood, PA [*Radio station call letters*] ... WHGM
Bellwood Public Library, Bellwood, IL [*Library symbol*] ... IBelw
Belmar/Farmingdale, NJ [*Location identifier*] [*FAA*] ... BLM
Belmar Public Library, Belmar, NJ [*Library symbol*] ... NjBel
Belmond Independent, Belmond, IA [*Library symbol*] ... IaBelmI
Belmond Public Library, Belmond, IA [*Library symbol*] ... IaBelm
Belmont Abbey College [*North Carolina*] ... BAC
Belmont Abbey College, Belmont, NC [*Library symbol*] ... NcBe
Belmont College, Nashville, TN [*OCLC symbol*] ... TBC

Belmont College, Nashville, TN [*Library symbol*] .... TNBe
Belmont Memorial Library, Belmont, MA [*Library symbol*] .... MBelm
Belmont, NC [*Radio station call letters*] .... WCGC
Belmont Resources [*NASDAQ symbol*] .... BEOVF
Belmont Technical Institute, St. Clairsville, OH [*Library symbol*] .... OStcB
Belmonte [*Brazil*] [*Airport symbol*] .... BVM
Belmoral Mines Ltd. [*NASDAQ symbol*] .... BMRLF
Belo [*Madagascar*] [*Airport symbol*] .... BMD
Belo Horizonte [*Brazil*] [*Airport symbol*] .... BHZ
Beloit College, Beloit, WI [*Library symbol*] .... WBB
Beloit College Library, Beloit, WI [*OCLC symbol*] .... WII
Beloit/Janesville [*Wisconsin*] [*Airport symbol*] .... JVL
Beloit, KS [*Radio station call letters*] .... KVSV
Beloit, KS [*Radio station call letters*] .... KVSV-FM
Beloit Memorial Hospital, Beloit, WI [*Library symbol*] .... WBM
Beloit Poetry Journal [*A publication*] .... Beloit
Beloit Poetry Journal [*A publication*] .... Bel Po J
Beloit Poetry Journal [*A publication*] .... BPJ
Beloit, WI [*Radio station call letters*] .... WBCR-FM
Beloit, WI [*Radio station call letters*] .... WBEL
Beloit, WI [*Radio station call letters*] .... WGEZ
Belorussian [*MARC language code*] [*Library of Congress*] .... bel
Belorussian Review [*Munich*] [*A publication*] .... BLR
Belorussian Soviet Socialist Republic [*MARC country of publication code*] [*Library of Congress*] .... bwr
Belorussian Soviet Socialist Republic [*MARC geographic area code*] [*Library of Congress*] .... e-ur-bw
Below .... BLO
Below .... BLW
Below All Clouds [*Aviation*] .... BAC
Below Bridges [*Navigation*] .... BB
Below Clouds [*Aviation code*] .... BLO
Below the Detectable Limit .... BDL
Below Elbow [*Medicine*] .... BE
Below/Hook Lifters Section of the Material Handling Institute .... BHLS
Below Knee [*Medicine*] .... BK
Below Knee Amputation [*Medicine*] .... BKA
Below Layer Range .... BLR
Below Limit of Detection .... BLD
Below the Line [*Budget*] .... BTL
Below Lower Limit .... BLL
Below Minimum Standards [*TV ratings*] .... BMS
Below Proof .... BP
Below Threshold Change [*Air Force*] .... BTC
Below Waist [*Medicine*] .... BW
Below Watch .... BW
Below Water .... BW
Belpre, OH [*Radio station call letters*] .... WNUS
Belscot Retailers, Incorporated [*American Stock Exchange symbol*] [*Delisted*] .... BRI
Belsk [*Poland*] [*Geomagnetic observatory code*] .... BEL
Belsk [*Poland*] [*Seismograph station code, US Geological Survey*] [*Closed*] .... BEL
Belt Association .... BA
[*The*] **Belt Railway Co. of Chicago** .... BR of C
[*The*] **Belt Railway Co. of Chicago** [*AAR code*] .... BRC
Belt Work Line .... BWL
Belted Galloway Society .... BGS
Belting [*Freight*] .... BLTG
Belton Railroad Co. [*AAR code*] .... BRR
Belton, SC [*Radio station call letters*] .... WHPB
Belton, TX [*Television station call letters*] .... KNCT
Belton, TX [*Radio station call letters*] .... KTON
Belton, TX [*Radio station call letters*] .... KTON-FM
Beltran Corp. [*American Stock Exchange symbol*] .... BTN
Beltsville Agricultural Research Center [*Maryland*] [*Department of Agriculture*] .... BARC
Beltsville Human Nutrition Research Center [*Department of Agriculture*] .... BHNRC
Beltsville Space Center [*Later, Goddard Space Flight Center*] [*NASA*] .... BSC
Beltsville Symposia in Agricultural Research [*A publication*] .... Beltsville Symp Agric Res
Beluga, AK [*Location identifier*] [*FAA*] .... BLG
Belzoni, MS [*Radio station call letters*] .... WELZ
Bemba [*MARC language code*] [*Library of Congress*] .... bem
Bement Public Library, St. Johns, MI [*Library symbol*] .... MiStjo
Bemichi [*Guyana*] [*Airport symbol*] .... BCG
Bemidji [*Minnesota*] [*Airport symbol*] .... BJI
Bemidji, MN [*Television station call letters*] .... KAWE
Bemidji, MN [*Radio station call letters*] .... KBHP
Bemidji, MN [*Radio station call letters*] .... KBSB
Bemidji, MN [*Radio station call letters*] .... KBUN
Bemidji, MN [*Radio station call letters*] .... KCRB
Bemidji, MN [*Radio station call letters*] .... KKBJ-FM
Bemidji, MN [*Television station call letters*] .... KXBJ
Bemidji State College [*Later, Bemidji State University*] [*Minnesota*] .... BSC
Bemidji State College [*Later, Bemidji State University*], **Bemidji, MN** [*Library symbol*] .... MnBemS
Bemidji State University, Bemidji, MN [*OCLC symbol*] .... MNB
Bemis Co., Inc. [*NYSE symbol*] .... BMS
Ben Franklin Society .... BFS
Ben Hur Life Association .... BHLA
Benafuels, Inc. [*NASDAQ symbol*] .... BENF
Benard Convection Cell .... BCC
Benbecula [*Hebrides Islands*] [*Airport symbol*] .... BEB
Bence Jones [*As in Bence Jones protein, Bence Jones reaction, etc.*] [*Named for Henry Bence Jones, 19th century London physician*] .... BJ
Bench .... BNCH
Bench Check .... B/C
Bench Checkout Equipment .... BCE
Bench Checkout Equipment .... BCOE
Bench Craft, Inc. [*NASDAQ symbol*] .... SOFA
Bench Maintenance [*NASA*] .... BM
Bench Maintenance Equipment [*NASA*] .... BME
Bench Mark [*Control point*] [*Nautical charts*] .... BM
Bench Mark [*In surveying*] .... BM
Bench Mark Control Point .... BCP
Bench Order .... BO
Bench Replaceable Assembly .... BRA
Bench Scale Calorimeter .... BSC
Bench Test Console .... BTC
Bench Test Fixture .... BTF
Bench Test Specification .... BTS
Bench Welder Control Panel .... BWCP
Benchboard .... BNCHBD
Benchmark Papers on Energy [*A publication*] .... Benchmark Pap Energy
Benchmark Papers in Optics [*A publication*] .... Benchmark Pap Opt
Benchmark Soils Project [*University of Hawaii, University of Puerto Rico*] .... BSP
Bend .... BND
Bend Down .... BD
Bend Down .... BDN
Bend-Down Virginia [*A picked-up stub of a cigarette*] .... BDV
Bend Line .... BL
Bend, OR [*Radio station call letters*] .... KBND
Bend, OR [*Radio station call letters*] .... KGRL
Bend, OR [*Radio station call letters*] .... KICE
Bend, OR [*Television station call letters*] .... KOAB-TV
Bend, OR [*Television station call letters*] .... KTVZ
Bend, OR [*Radio station call letters*] .... KXIQ
Bend Radius .... BR
Bend Radius Template .... BRT
Bend Tangency Line .... BTL
Bend Up .... BU
Bend Up [*Technical drawings*] .... BUP
Bender-Gestalt Test [*Psychology*] .... B-G
Bender-Gestalt Test [*Psychology*] .... BGT
Bender Visual-Motor Gestalt Test [*Education*] .... BVMGT
Bending .... BNG
Bending Feedback Control .... BFC
Bending Form [*Tool*] .... BEFM
Bending Mode Filters .... BMF
Bending Moment [*Aerospace*] .... BM
Bending Moment [*Aerospace*] .... M
Bendix Aviation Corporation [*Later, Bendix Corp.*] .... BAC
Bendix Aviation Corp. [*Later, Bendix Corp.*], **Pacific Division, North Hollywood, CA** [*Library symbol*] .... CNhB
Bendix Corp. [*NYSE symbol*] .... BX
Bendix Corp., Baltimore, MD [*Library symbol*] .... MdBBR
Bendix Corp., Electrical Components Division, Engineering Library, Sidney, NY [*Library symbol*] .... NSidS
Bendix Corp., Technical Information Center, Kansas City, MO [*Library symbol*] .... MoKBen
Bendix Engineering Development Center, Southfield, MI [*OCLC symbol*] .... EEB
Bendix Field Engineering Corporation [*of Bendix Corp.*] .... BFEC
Bendix Integrated Data System .... BIDS
Bendix Optimum Configuration Satellite .... BOCS
Bendix Technical Journal [*A publication*] .... Bendix Tech J
Bendix-Westinghouse Automotive Air Brake Co. .... BW
Bene [*Well*] [*Pharmacy*] .... BEN
Bene Merenti [*To the Well-Deserving*] [*Latin*] .... BM
Bene Merenti [*To the Well-Deserving*] [*Latin*] .... BMT
Bene Merenti Fecit [*He Erected This to the Well-Deserving*] [*Latin*] .... BMF
Bene Quiescat [*May He, or She, Rest Well*] [*Latin*] .... BQ
Bene Vale [*Farewell*] [*Latin*] .... BV
Bene Vixit [*He Lived a Good Life*] [*Latin*] .... BV
Beneath .... BNTH
Benedict College, Columbia, SC [*OCLC symbol*] .... BDC
Benedict College, Columbia, SC [*Library symbol*] .... ScCoB
Benedict Nuclear Pharmaceuticals [*NASDAQ symbol*] .... BENE
Benedictina [*A publication*] .... Ben
Benedictine .... BENED
Benedictine and Brandy .... B & B
Benedictine College, Atchison, KS [*OCLC symbol*] .... KKA
Benedictine College, North Campus, Atchison, KS [*Library symbol*] .... KAS
Benedictine College, South Campus, Atchison, KS [*Library symbol*] .... KAM
Benedictine Heights College [*Oklahoma*] .... BHC
Benedictine High School, Cleveland, OH [*Library symbol*] .... OClBHS

Benedictine Hospital, Medical Library, Kingston, NY [*Library symbol*] ... NKiB
Benedictine Review [*A publication*] ... BR
Benedictiner Monatsschrift [*A publication*] ... BMS
Benediction ... B
Benedum Civic Center Public Library, Bridgeport, WV [*Library symbol*] ... WvBri
Beneficial Communications [*Computer system*] [*Beneficial Management Corp.*] ... BENCOM
Beneficial Corp. [*Wall Street slang name: "Big Nose Louie"*] [*NYSE symbol*] ... BNL
Beneficial Insects Research Laboratory [*Department of Agriculture*] ... BIRL
Beneficial Occupancy ... BO
Beneficial Occupancy Date ... BOD
Beneficial Rays of the Sun [*In reference to suntanning, supposedly occuring between 10am and 2pm*] [*See also SROTS*] ... BROTS
Beneficial Standard Corporation [*American Stock Exchange symbol*] ... BSC
Beneficial Standard Mortgage Investors [*NYSE symbol*] ... BSM
Beneficial Suggestion ... BS
Beneficial Suggestions [*Program*] ... BENNY SUGG
Beneficial Use Date ... BUD
Beneficiary ... BENEF
Beneficiary Data Exchange System [*between state welfare agencies and the Social Security Administration*] ... BENDEX
Beneficiary Developing Country [*Trade status*] ... BDC
Beneficiary Evaluation Survey Service [*LIMRA*] ... BESS
Beneficiary Government Production Program ... BGPP
Beneficiary Identification Records Location Subsystem ... BIRLS
Benefit-Cost [*Ratio*] ... B-C
Benefit Cost Analysis ... BCA
Benefit Rights Interview [*Unemployment insurance*] ... BRI
Benefit Service Series, Unemployment Insurance [*A publication*] ... BSUI
Benefit Year Ending [*Unemployment insurance*] ... BYE
Benelli Owner's Club of America ... BOCA
Benelux Countries [*MARC geographic area code*] [*Library of Congress*] ... el-----
BENELUX [*Belgium, Netherlands, Luxembourg*] **Subarea Channel** [*NATO*] ... BENECHAN
Benevento [*Italy*] [*Seismograph station code, US Geological Survey*] [*Closed*] ... BNV
Benevolent Association for Naming All Nonentities After Schools ... BANANAS
Benevolent and Protective Order of Elks [*Facetiously translated as "Best People on Earth"*] ... BPOE
Benevolent Protective Order - Wolves of the World [*Limited, not-too-serious order*] ... BPO-WOW
Benevolent Society of St. Patrick ... BSSP
Benevolenti Lectori Salutem [*Greeting to the Well-Wishing Reader*] [*Latin*] ... BLS
Bengal ... BENG
Bengal, Bay of [*MARC geographic area code*] [*Library of Congress*] ... ab-----
Bengal Civil Service ... BCS
Bengal Native Infantry ... BNI
Bengal Oil & Gas Co. [*NASDAQ symbol*] ... BGAL
Bengal Past and Present [*A publication*] ... BPP
Bengal Staff Corps ... BSC
Bengali [*MARC language code*] [*Library of Congress*] ... ben
Benghazi [*Libya*] [*Airport symbol*] ... BEN
Bengkulu [*Indonesia*] [*Airport symbol*] ... BKS
Benguela [*Angola*] [*Airport symbol*] ... BUG
Benguet Corp. [*NYSE symbol*] ... BE
Beni-Abbes [*Algeria*] [*Seismograph station code, US Geological Survey*] ... BAB
Benicia Free Public Library, Benicia, CA [*Library symbol*] ... CBen
Benign Essential Blepharospasm [*Medicine*] ... BEB
Benign Essential Blepharospasm Research Foundation ... BEBRF
Benign Intracranial Hypertension [*Medicine*] ... BIH
Benign Monoclonal Gammopathy [*Immunochemistry*] ... BMG
Benign Monoclonal Hypergammaglobulinemia [*Medicine*] ... BMH
Benign Prostatic Hyperplasia [*Medicine*] ... BPH
Benign Prostatic Hypertrophy [*Medicine*] ... BPH
Benign Symmetric Lipomatosis [*Medicine*] ... BSL
Benihana National Corp. [*NASDAQ symbol*] ... BNHN
Benin [*Three-letter standard code*] ... BEN
Benin [*Two-letter standard code*] ... BJ
Benin City [*Nigeria*] [*Airport symbol*] ... BNI
Benjamin Franklin High School Library, Rochester, NY [*OCLC symbol*] ... RVQ
Benjamin Franklin Junior Stamp Club ... BFJSC
Benjamin Franklin Literary and Medical Society ... BFLMS
Benjamin Franklin University [*Washington, DC*] ... BFU
Bennett College, Greensboro, NC [*OCLC symbol*] ... BEN
Bennett College, Greensboro, NC [*Library symbol*] ... NcGB
Bennett College, Millbrook, NY [*Library symbol*] ... NMbrB
Bennett County Library, Martin, SD [*Library symbol*] ... SdMa
Bennett, D. L., Wheeling WV [*STAC*] ... BDL
Bennett Junior College [*New York*] ... BJC
Bennett, Richard A., Stockton CA [*STAC*] ... BRA
Bennettsville, SC [*Radio station call letters*] ... WBSC
Bennington College, Bennington, VT [*OCLC symbol*] ... BNT
Bennington College, Bennington, VT [*Library symbol*] ... VtBennC
Bennington Free Library, Bennington, VT [*Library symbol*] ... VtBenn
Bennington Museum, Inc., Bennington, VT [*Library symbol*] ... VtBennM
Bennington, VT [*Radio station call letters*] ... WBTN
Bennington, VT [*Radio station call letters*] ... WHGC
Benny Goodman [*Clarinetist*] ... BG
Benrus Corp. [*American Stock Exchange symbol*] ... BEN
Bensbach [*Papua New Guinea*] [*Airport symbol*] ... BSP
Bensberg [*Federal Republic of Germany*] [*Seismograph station code, US Geological Survey*] ... BNS
Benson, AZ [*Radio station call letters*] ... KAVV
Benson, MN [*Radio station call letters*] ... KBMO
Benson, MN [*Radio station call letters*] ... KBMO-FM
Benson, NC [*Radio station call letters*] ... WPYB
Benson Needham Univas [*International advertising network*] ... BNU
Benson Public Library, Benson, AZ [*Library symbol*] ... AzBe
Bent ... BNT
Bent ... BT
Bent Logarithmically Periodic Zig-Zags ... BLPZZ
Bent-Mescalero School Library, Mescalero, NM [*Library symbol*] ... NmMeB
Bent Wire Antenna ... BWA
Benthic Metabolism Measurement ... BMM
Benthic Nepheloid Layer [*Oceanography*] ... BNL
Bentley College, Waltham, MA [*OCLC symbol*] ... BET
Bentley Drivers Club ... BDC
Bentley School, New York, NY [*Library symbol*] ... NNBeS
Bentley's Miscellany [*A publication*] ... Bentley
Bentley's Quarterly Review [*A publication*] ... Bent Q
Benton, AR [*Radio station call letters*] ... KAKI
Benton, AR [*Radio station call letters*] ... KBBA
Benton, AR [*Radio station call letters*] ... KGKO
Benton & Bowles [*Advertising agency*] ... B & B
Benton Harbor [*Michigan*] [*Airport symbol*] ... BEH
Benton Harbor, MI [*Radio station call letters*] ... WHFB
Benton Harbor, MI [*Radio station call letters*] ... WHFB-FM
Benton, IL [*Radio station call letters*] ... WQRL
Benton, KY [*Radio station call letters*] ... WCBL
Benton, KY [*Radio station call letters*] ... WCBL-FM
Benton, LA [*Radio station call letters*] ... KDKS
Benton, TN [*Radio station call letters*] ... WBIN
Benton Township - Potterville District Library, Potterville, MI [*Library symbol*] ... MiPot
Benton Visual Retention Time [*Psychiatry*] ... BVRT
Bentonite Flocculation [*Test*] ... BF
Bentonville, AR [*Radio station call letters*] ... KJEM
Bent's Old Fort National Historic Site ... BEOL
Benyzlimidazole [*Organic chemistry*] ... BZI
Benzalkonium Chloride [*Organic chemistry*] ... BAC
Benzanthracene [*Also, BzAnth*] [*Organic chemistry*] ... BA
Benzanthracene [*Also, BA*] [*Biochemistry*] ... BzAnth
Benzene Hexachloride [*Also, GBH, HCH*] [*Insecticide*] ... BHC
Benzene-Soluble Organics [*Pollutant*] ... BSO
Benzene, Toluene, and Xylene ... BTX
Benzenecarboxylic Acid [*Organic chemistry*] ... BCA
Benzenesulfonic Acid [*Organic chemistry*] ... BSA
Benzhydryl [*As substituent on nucleoside*] [*Biochemistry*] ... bh
Benzhydryl [*Biochemistry*] ... Bzh
Benzidine [*Carcinogen*] ... BENZ
Benzidine [*Carcinogen*] ... BZD
Benziger, Bruce, & Glencoe, Inc. ... BBG
Benzilic Acid Tropine Ester [*Also, BETE, BTE*] [*Pharmacology*] ... BAT
Benzilic Acid Tropine Ester [*Also, BAT, BTE*] [*Pharmacology*] ... BETE
Benzilic Acid Tropine Ester [*Also, BAT, BETE*] [*Pharmacology*] ... BTE
Benzimidazole [*Biochemistry*] ... Bza
Benzimidazolyl [*Biochemistry*] ... Bza
Benzimidazolylphenylmaleimide [*Organic chemistry*] ... BIPM
Benzodiazepine [*Organic chemistry*] ... BZ
Benzon [*Denmark*] [*Research code symbol*] ... U
Benzonia Public Library, Benzonia, MI [*Library symbol*] ... MiBen
Benzophenonetetracarboxylic Dianhydride [*Organic chemistry*] ... BTDA
Benzopyrene [*or Benzpyrene*] [*Also, BZ*] [*Carcinogen*] ... BP
Benzopyrene [*or Benzpyrene*] [*Also, BP*] [*Carcinogen*] ... BZ
Benzopyrenedihydrodiolepoxide [*Organic chemistry*] ... BPDE
Benzotriazole [*Organic chemistry*] ... BTA
Benzotrifuroxan [*Organic chemistry*] ... BTF
Benzoyl [*As substituent on nucleoside*] [*Biochemistry*] ... bz
Benzoyl [*Organic chemistry*] ... Bz
Benzoyl-para-aminosalicylate [*Pharmacology*] ... BPAS
Benzoyl Peroxide [*Organic chemistry*] ... BPO
Benzoylarginine Amide [*Biochemistry*] ... BAA
Benzoylarginine Ethyl Ester [*Biochemistry*] ... BAEE
Benzoylarginine Methyl Ester [*Biochemistry*] ... BAME
Benzoylarginine p-Nitroanilide [*Also, BAPNA*] [*Biochemistry*] ... BAPA
Benzoylarginine p-Nitroanilide [*Also, BAPA*] [*Biochemistry*] ... BAPNA
Benzoylargininenaphthylamide ... BANA
Benzoylated DEAE [*Diethylaminoethyl*] [*Organic chemistry*] ... BD
Benzoylated-Naphthoylated DEAE [*Diethylaminoethyl*] ... BND
Benzoylated-Naphthoylated (DEAE)-Cellulose [*Analytical biochemistry*] ... BNC
Benzoyloxime [*Organic chemistry*] ... BO
Benzoyltrifluoroacetone [*Organic chemistry*] ... BTA

Benzoyltyrosine [*Biochemistry*] ... BT
Benzoyltyrosine Ethyl Ester [*Biochemistry*] ... BTEE
Benzquinamide [*Pharmacology*] ... BZQ
Benzyl [*As substituent on nucleoside*] [*Biochemistry*] ... bzl
Benzyl [*Biochemistry*] ... Bzl
Benzyl-Aminophenol [*Organic chemistry*] ... BAP
Benzyl-Iso-Thiourea [*Organic chemistry*] ... BITU
Benzyladenine [*Biochemistry*] ... BA
Benzylaminopurine [*Biochemistry*] ... BAP
Benzylantiserotonin [*Pharmacology*] ... BAS
Benzyldimethylamine [*Organic chemistry*] ... BDMA
Benzylfurancarboxylic Acid [*Organic chemistry*] ... BFCA
Benzylfurylmethyl Alcohol [*Organic chemistry*] ... BFA
Benzylpenicilloyl [*Organic chemistry*] ... BPO
Benzylthiomethyl [*Biochemistry*] ... Btm
Benzyltrimethylammonium Chloride [*Also, TMBAC*] [*Organic chemistry*] ... BTM
Benzyl(vinyl)pyridinium Bromide [*Organic chemistry*] ... BVP
Beobachtung [*Observation*] [*German military*] ... BB
Beobachtungsstelle [*Observation post*] [*German military - World War II*] ... BST
Beograd [*Belgrade*] [*Yugoslavia*] [*Seismograph station code, US Geological Survey*] ... BEO
Beppu [*Japan*] [*Seismograph station code, US Geological Survey*] [*Closed*] ... BEP
Bequeathed ... BEQD
Bequeathed ... BEQTHD
Bequest ... BEQT
Berau [*Indonesia*] [*Airport symbol*] ... BEJ
Berber [*MARC language code*] [*Library of Congress*] ... ber
Berbera [*Somalia*] [*Airport symbol*] ... BBO
Berceo [*A publication*] ... Berc
Berea College, Berea, KY [*OCLC symbol*] ... KBE
Berea College, Berea, KY [*Library symbol*] ... KyBB
Berea, KY [*Radio station call letters*] ... WKXO
Berea, OH [*Radio station call letters*] ... WBWC
Berean Bible Society ... BBS
Bereaved Children's Program ... BCP
Bereina [*Papua New Guinea*] [*Airport symbol*] ... BEA
Bereitschaftsstellung [*Line of support*] [*German military - World War II*] ... BST
Berens River [*Canada*] [*Airport symbol*] ... YBV
Beresford Public Library, Beresford, SD [*Library symbol*] ... SdBer
Beretning fra Forsogslaboratoriet [*A publication*] ... Beret Forsogslab
Beretning fra Statens Husdyrbrugsforsog [*A publication*] ... Beret Statens Husdyrbrugsfors
Beretning fra Statsfrokontrollen (Denmark) [*A publication*] ... Beretn Statsfrokontr (Denmark)
Berg Enterprises, Inc. [*American Stock Exchange symbol*] ... BRG
Berg und Huettenmaennische Monatsheft [*A publication*] ... Berg Heuttenmaenn Monatsh
Berg und Huettenmaennische Zeitung [*A publication*] ... Berg u Huettenm Ztg
Bergamo [*Italy*] [*Airport symbol*] ... BGY
Bergbau Rohstoffe Energie [*A publication*] ... Bergbau Rohst Energ
Bergbauwissenschaften [*A publication*] ... Bergbauwiss
Bergen [*Norway*] [*Seismograph station code, US Geological Survey*] ... BER
Bergen [*Norway*] [*Airport symbol*] ... BGO
Bergen Brunswig Corporation [*American Stock Exchange symbol*] ... BBC
Bergen Citizen, Edgewater, NJ [*Library symbol*] ... NjEwB
Bergen Community College, Paramus, NJ [*OCLC symbol*] ... BER
Bergen Community College, Paramus, NJ [*Library symbol*] ... NjParB
Bergen County Historical Society, North Hackensack, NJ [*Library symbol*] ... NjNhBHi
Bergen Gazette, Inc., Garfield, NJ [*Library symbol*] ... NjGaB
Bergen News, Palisades Park, NJ [*Library symbol*] ... NjPalN
Bergen Reading Center, Bergen, NY [*Library symbol*] ... NBerR
Bergen Record, Hackensack, NJ [*Library symbol*] ... NjHackR
Bergenfield Free Public Library, Bergenfield, NJ [*Library symbol*] ... NjBer
Bergens Museums Aarbok [*A publication*] ... BMA
Bergerac [*France*] [*Airport symbol*] [*Obsolete*] ... EGC
Berggiesshubel [*German Democratic Republic*] [*Seismograph station code, US Geological Survey*] ... BRG
Bergonum [*A publication*] ... Berg
Bericht ueber die Ausgrabungen in Olympia [*1936-*] [*A publication*] ... Ol Ber
Bericht. Deutsche Gesellschaft fuer Holzforschung [*A publication*] ... Ber Dtsch Ges Holzforsch
Bericht. Ernst-Mach-Institut [*Freiburg*] [*A publication*] ... Ber Ernst-Mach-Inst
Bericht ueber das Geobotanische Forschungsinstitut Ruebel in Zuerich [*A publication*] ... Ber Geobot Forschungsinst Ruebel Zuerich
Bericht des Historischen. Vereins fuer des Fuestbistum (Bamberg) [*A publication*] ... BHVBamberg
Bericht des Historischen. Vereins fuer des Fuestbistum (Bamberg) [*A publication*] ... BHVFB
Bericht. Institut fuer Festkoerpermechanik der Fraunhofer-Gesellschaft [*A publication*] ... Ber Inst Festkoerpermech Fraunhofer-Ges
Bericht. Institut fuer Hochenergiephysik der Osterreichischen Akademie der Wissenschaften (Wien) [*A publication*] ... Ber Inst Hochenergiephys (Wien)
Bericht. Jyvaeskylae. Universitaet. Mathematisches Institut [*A publication*] ... Ber Univ Jyvaeskyla Math Inst
Bericht. Kernforschungszentrum Karlsruhe [*A publication*] ... Ber Kernforschungszentr Karlsruhe
Bericht. Max-Planck-Institut fuer Kernphysik (Heidelberg) [*A publication*] ... Ber MPI Kernphys (Heidelberg)
Bericht. Max-Planck-Institut fuer Physik und Astrophysik. Institut fuer Extraterrestrische Physik [*A publication*] ... Ber MPI Phys Astrophys Inst Extraterr Phys
Bericht. Max-Planck-Institut fuer Plasmaphysik. Garching bei Muenchen [*A publication*] ... Ber MPI Plasmaphys Garching
Bericht. Max-Planck-Institut fuer Stroemungsforschung [*A publication*] ... Ber MPI Stroemungsforsch
Bericht der Naturhistorischen Gesellschaft zu Hannover [*A publication*] ... Ber Naturhist Ges Hannover
Bericht over Rassenkeuze [*A publication*] ... Ber Rassenkeuze
Bericht der Romisch-Germanischen Kommission [*A publication*] ... BRGK
Bericht der Staatlichen Denkmalpflege in Saarland. Beitraege zur Archaeologie und Kunstgeschichte [*A publication*] ... Ber Staat Denkmaf Saarland
Bericht ueber die Zusammenkunft der Deutschen Ophthalmologischen Gesellschaft [*A publication*] ... Ber Zusammenkunft Dtsch Ophthalmol Ges
Berichte der Arbeitsgemeinschaft Saechsischer Botaniker [*A publication*] ... Ber Arbeitsgem Saechs Bot
Berichte der Bayerischen Botanischen Gesellschaft zur Erforschung der Heimischen Flora [*A publication*] ... Ber Bayer Bot Ges Erforsch Heim Flora
Berichte Biochemie und Biologie [*A publication*] ... Ber Biochem Biol
Berichte der Bunsengesellschaft fuer Physikalische Chemie [*A publication*] ... Ber Bun Ges
Berichte der Bunsengesellschaft fuer Physikalische Chemie [*A publication*] ... Ber Bunsen Ges
Berichte der Bunsengesellschaft fuer Physikalische Chemie [*A publication*] ... Ber Bunsenges Phys Chem
Berichte. Deutsche Botanische Gesellschaft [*A publication*] ... Ber Deut Bot Ges
Berichte der Deutsche Keramische Gesellschaft [*A publication*] ... Ber Deut Keram Gesell
Berichte des Deutschen Ausschusses fuer Stahlbau [*A publication*] ... Ber Deut Ausschusses Stahlbau
Berichte der Deutschen Botanischen Gesellschaft [*A publication*] ... Ber Deu Bot
Berichte der Deutschen Botanischen Gesellschaft [*A publication*] ... Ber Dtsch Bot Ges
Berichte der Deutschen Chemischen Gesellschaft [*A publication*] ... Ber Deut Chem Ges
Berichte der Deutschen Keramischen Gesellschaft [*A publication*] ... Ber Dtsch Keram Ges
Berichte des Deutschen Wetterdienstes [*A publication*] ... Ber Deut Wetterdienst
Berichte der Deutschen Wissenschaftlichen Kommission fuer Meeresforschung [*A publication*] ... Ber Dtsch Wiss Komm Meeresforsch
Berichte der Deutschen Wissenschaftlichen Kommission fuer Meeresforschung [*A publication*] ... Ber D W Meer
Berichte Eidgenoessische Anstalt fuer das Forstliche Versuchswesen [*A publication*] ... Ber Eidg Anst Forstl Versuchswes
Berichte und Informationen. Europaeische Gemeinschaften [*A publication*] ... Ber Inf Europ Gem
Berichte und Informationen. Kommission der Europaeischen Gemeinschaften [*A publication*] ... Ber Inf KEG
Berichte der Internationalen Gesellschaft fuer Getreidechemie [*A publication*] ... Ber Int Ges Getreidechem
Berichte der Kernforschungsanlage Juelich Gesellschaft mit Beschraenkter Haftung [*A publication*] ... Ber Kfa Juelich
Berichte ueber Landwirtschaft [*A publication*] ... Ber Landwirtsch
Berichte ueber Landwirtschaft. Sonderheft [*A publication*] ... Ber Landwirtsch Sonderh
Berichte Limnologischen Flussstation Freudenthal Munden [*A publication*] ... Ber Limnol Flussst Freudenthal Munden
Berichte der Naturforschenden Gesellschaft. Augsburg [*A publication*] ... Ber Naturforsch Ges Augsb
Berichte der Naturforschenden Gesellschaft zu Freiburg [*A publication*] ... Ber Naturforsch Ges Freiburg
Berichte der Naturforschenden Gesellschaft zu Freiburg im Breisgau [*A publication*] ... Ber Naturforsch Ges Freiburg Breisgau
Berichte des Naturwissenschaftlich-Medizinischen Vereins in Innsbruck [*A publication*] ... Ber Naturwiss-Med Ver Innsb
Berichte des Ohara Instituts fuer Landwirtschaftliche Biologie [*A publication*] ... Ber Ohara Inst Landw Biol
Berichte des Ohara Instituts fuer Landwirtschaftliche Biologie. Okayama Universitaet [*A publication*] ... Ber Ohara Inst Landwirtsch Biol Okayama Univ
Berichte der Physikalisch-Medizinischen Gesellschaft zu Wuerzburg [*A publication*] ... Ber Phys-Med Ges Wuerzb
Berichte [*Amtliche*] **der Preussischen Kunstsammlungen** [*A publication*] ... BPKS

Berichte der Schweizerischen Botanischen Gesellschaft [*A publication*] ... Ber Schweiz Bot Ges
Berichte ueber die Tagung in Nordwestdeutscher Forstverein [*A publication*] ... Ber Tag Nordwestdtsch Forstver
Berichte ueber die Verhandlungen der Saechsischen Akademie der Wissenschaften zu Leipzig [*A publication*] ... BVSAWL
Berichten van de Rijksdienst voor het Oudheidkundig Bodemonderzoek [*A publication*] ... BROB
Bering [*Komandorsky Islands*] [*USSR*] [*Seismograph station code, US Geological Survey*] ... BKI
Bering Sea Expedition [*or Experiment*] ... BESEX
Bering Sea Patrol [*Navy*] ... BERSEAPAT
Berita Biologi [*A publication*] ... Berita Biol
Berkeley [*A publication*] ... Berk
Berkeley-Byerly [*California*] [*Seismograph station code, US Geological Survey*] ... BKS
Berkeley, CA [*Location identifier*] [*FAA*] ... JBK
Berkeley, CA [*Radio station call letters*] ... KALX
Berkeley, CA [*Radio station call letters*] ... KBLX
Berkeley, CA [*Radio station call letters*] ... KPFA
Berkeley, CA [*Radio station call letters*] ... KPFB
Berkeley, CA [*Radio station call letters*] ... KRE
Berkeley-Haviland [*California*] [*Seismograph station code, US Geological Survey*] ... BRK
Berkeley Journal of Sociology [*A publication*] ... Ber J Soc
Berkeley Journal of Sociology [*A publication*] ... Berkeley J Sociol
Berkeley Nuclear Laboratories [*England*] ... BNL
Berkeley-Oakland Service System [*Library network*] ... BOSS
Berkeley Particle Data Center ... BPDC
Berkeley Particle Data Group [*Lawrence Radiation Laboratory*] ... BPDG
Berkeley Public Library, Berkeley, CA [*Library symbol*] ... CB
Berkeley Public Library, Berkeley, IL [*Library symbol*] ... IBerk
Berkeley Review [*A publication*] ... BeR
Berkeley Springs, WV [*Radio station call letters*] ... WCST
Berkeley Springs, WV [*Radio station call letters*] ... WCST-FM
Berkelium [*Chemical element*] ... Bk
Berkey Photo, Inc. [*NYSE symbol*] ... BKY
Berkley [*W. R.*] **Corp.** [*NASDAQ symbol*] ... BKLY
Berkley Heights Public Library, Berkley Heights, NJ [*Library symbol*] ... NjBh
[*The*] **Berkline Corp.** [*NASDAQ symbol*] ... BERK
Berks, Bucks, and Oxon. Archaeological Journal [*A publication*] ... BBOJ
Berks County Historical Society. Papers [*A publication*] ... BeCHS
Berks County Historical Society. Papers [*A publication*] ... BerksCoHS
Berkshire [*County in England*] ... BERKS
Berkshire Archaeological Journal [*A publication*] ... Berkshire Arch J
Berkshire Athenaeum, Pittsfield, MA [*Library symbol*] ... MPB
Berkshire Christian College, Lenox, MA [*Library symbol*] ... MLenB
Berkshire Community College [*Massachusetts*] ... BCC
Berkshire Community College, Pittsfield, MA [*Library symbol*] ... MPBC
Berkshire Gas Co. [*NASDAQ symbol*] ... BGAS
Berkshire Hathaway [*NASDAQ symbol*] ... BKHT
Berkshire Historical and Scientific Society [*A publication*] ... Berkshire Hist Sc Soc
Berkshire Law Library Association, Pittsfield, MA [*Library symbol*] ... MPBL
Berlevag [*Norway*] [*Airport symbol*] ... BVG
Berlin [*West Germany*] [*Airport symbol*] ... BER
Berlin [*New Hampshire*] [*Seismograph station code, US Geological Survey*] ... BNH
Berlin [*West Germany*] [*Seismograph station code, US Geological Survey*] ... BRN
Berlin [*East Germany*] [*Airport symbol*] ... SXF
Berlin [*West Germany*] [*Airport symbol*] ... TXL
Berlin Air Safety Center ... BASC
Berlin Airlift Device [*Military award*] ... BAD
Berlin Airlift Device [*Military award*] ... BerADev
Berlin Airlift Device [*Military award*] ... BERDEV
Berlin Border Guard [*East Germany*] ... BBG
Berlin Brigade ... BB
Berlin Brigade ... BBDE
Berlin Command [*Allied German Occupation Forces*] ... BC
Berlin Commission British [*Post-World War II*] ... BERCOMB
Berlin Contingency [*NATO*] ... BERCON
Berlin Control Zone [*Allied German Occupation Forces*] ... BCZ
Berlin, CT [*Radio station call letters*] ... WERB
Berlin District [*Allied German Occupation Forces*] ... BD
Berlin Document Center [*Allied German Occupation Forces*] ... BDC
Berlin - Free University [*West Germany*] [*Seismograph station code, US Geological Survey*] ... BRL
Berlin Freie Universitaet. FU Pressedienst Wissenschaft [*A publication*] ... Berl Freie Univ FU Pressedienst Wiss
Berlin Kommandatura ... BK
Berlin, MD [*Radio station call letters*] ... WOCQ
Berlin Mills [*AAR code*] ... BMS
Berlin, NH [*Location identifier*] [*FAA*] ... HXK
Berlin, NH [*Radio station call letters*] ... WBRL
Berlin, NH [*Radio station call letters*] ... WMOU
Berlin Philharmonic Orchestra ... BPO
Berlin Public Library, Berlin, WI [*Library symbol*] ... WBer
Berlin Sector [*Allied German Occupation Forces*] ... BS
Berlin, WI [*Radio station call letters*] ... WISS
Berlin, WI [*Radio station call letters*] ... WISS-FM
Berlin. Winckelmannsprogramm der Archaeologischen Gesellschaft [*A publication*] ... Berl Winck Prog
Berliner Beitraege zur Namenforschung [*A publication*] ... BBN
Berliner Beitraege zur Romanischen Philologie [*A publication*] ... BBRP
Berliner Byzantinistische Arbeiten [*A publication*] ... BBA
Berliner Byzantinistische Arbeiten. Deutsche Akademie der Wissenschaften zu Berlin [*A publication*] ... BByzA
Berliner Handels-und Frankfurter [*Bank*] ... BHF
Berliner Handelszentrale ... BHZ
Berliner Jahrbuch fuer Vor- und Fruehgeschichte [*A publication*] ... BJV
Berliner Klinische Wochenschrift [*A publication*] ... Berl Klin Wchnschr
Berliner und Muenchener Tieraerztliche Wochenschrift [*A publication*] ... Berl Muench Tieraerztl Wochenschr
Berliner Munzblaetter [*A publication*] ... BMBL
Berliner Museen [*A publication*] ... Berl Mus
Berliner Museen [*A publication*] ... BMus
Berliner Numismatische Zeitschrift [*A publication*] ... Berliner Num Z
Berliner Philologische Wochenschrift [*A publication*] ... BPhW
Berliner Philologische Wochenschrift [*A publication*] ... BPW
Berliner Tieraerztliche Wochenschrift [*A publication*] ... Berl Tieraerztl Wchnschr
Berliner Verkehrs-Gesellschaft [*Later, Berliner Verkehrs-Betriebe*] [*Berlin Transport*] [*West Berlin*] ... BVG
Berman Leasing Co. [*NYSE symbol*] [*Delisted*] ... BMA
Bermuda [*Airport symbol*] ... BDA
Bermuda [*MARC country of publication code*] [*Library of Congress*] ... bm
Bermuda [*Three-letter standard code*] ... BMU
Bermuda [*MARC geographic area code*] [*Library of Congress*] ... lnbm---
Bermuda [*Two-letter standard code*] ... BM
Bermuda Base Command [*World War II*] ... BBC
Bermuda Benevolent Association ... BBA
Bermuda Biological Station for Research. Special Publication [*A publication*] ... Bermuda Biol Stn Res Spec Publ
Bermuda-Columbia [*Bermuda*] [*Seismograph station code, US Geological Survey*] ... BEC
Bermuda Dunes, CA [*Location identifier*] [*FAA*] ... UDD
Bermuda Islands ... BI
Bermuda Library, Hamilton, Bermudas [*Library symbol*] ... BmuHB
Bermuda - Navy [*Bermuda*] [*Seismograph station code, US Geological Survey*] [*Closed*] ... BEN
Bermuda Range Safety Officer [*NASA*] ... BRSO
Bermuda Report of the Director of Agriculture and Fisheries [*A publication*] ... Bermuda Rep Dir Agric Fish
Bermuda Tracking Station [*NASA*] ... BDA
Bernadia [*Italy*] [*Seismograph station code, US Geological Survey*] ... BERI
Bernard Berenson [*American art critic, 1865-1959*] ... BB
Bernard Geis Associates [*Publisher*] [*Obsolete*] ... BGA
Bernard M. Baruch College of the City University of New York, New York, NY [*Library symbol*] ... NNBBC
[*The*] **Bernard Shaw Society** ... BSS
Bernard van Risenburgh [*Label stamped on works by the master ebeniste*] ... BVRB
Bernards Township Library, Inc., Basking Ridge, NJ [*Library symbol*] ... NjBas
Bernardsville Library Association, Bernardsville, NJ [*Library symbol*] ... NjBern
Bernardsville News, Bernardsville, NJ [*Library symbol*] ... NBernN
Bernardsville News, Bernardsville, NJ [*Library symbol*] ... NjBernN
Berne [*Switzerland*] [*Airport symbol*] ... BRN
Berne Public Library, Berne, IN [*OCLC symbol*] ... XBB
Berner Oberland-Bahnen [*Bernese Overland Railways*] ... BOB
Bernese Mountain Dog Club of America ... BMDCA
Bernice Pauahi Bishop Museum. Bulletin [*A publication*] ... Bernice Pauahi Bishop Museum Bull
Bernice Pauahi Bishop Museum. Bulletin. Special Publication [*A publication*] ... Bernice Pauahi Bishop Museum Bull Special Pub
Bernice Pauahi Bishop Museum, Honolulu, HI [*Library symbol*] ... HHB
Bernice Pauahi Bishop Museum. Occasional Papers [*A publication*] ... Bernice Pauahi Bishop Mus Oc P
Bernice Pauahi Bishop Museum. Special Publication [*A publication*] ... Bernice P Bishop Mus Spec Publ
Bernie [*Missouri*] [*Seismograph station code, US Geological Survey*] [*Closed*] ... BRM
Bernoulli [*Number*] ... B
Bernoulli Disk ... BD
Bernoulli Society for Mathematical Statistics and Probability ... BSMSP
BernzOmatic Corp. [*American Stock Exchange symbol*] [*Delisted*] ... BZO
Beroroha [*Madagascar*] [*Airport symbol*] ... WBO
Berrien Springs, MI [*Radio station call letters*] ... WAUS
Berry College, Mount Berry, GA [*OCLC symbol*] ... GBC
Berry College, Mount Berry, GA [*Library symbol*] ... GMtbC
Berry, Fruit, or Vegetable [*Freight*] ... BERRY F V
Berry Hill, TN [*Radio station call letters*] ... WVOL
Berry Industries Corp. [*American Stock Exchange symbol*] ... BYI
Berry, R. H., San Leandro CA [*STAC*] ... BRH
Berryman [*Missouri*] [*Seismograph station code, US Geological Survey*] [*Closed*] ... BRR
Berryville, AR [*Radio station call letters*] ... KSCC
Berryville, AR [*Radio station call letters*] ... KTHS
Berryville, VA [*Radio station call letters*] ... WWOO

Bertea Corp. [*American Stock Exchange symbol*] [*Delisted*] .... BTA
Berth .... BTH
Berth Terms [*Shipping*] .... BT
Bertha Hill [*Idaho*] [*Seismograph station code, US Geological Survey*] [*Closed*] .... BHI
Berthing .... BERTH
Berthoud Public Library, Berthoud, CO [*Library symbol*] .... CoBer
Bertoua [*Cameroon*] [*Airport symbol*] .... BTA
Bertrand Russell Peace Foundation .... BRPF
Bertrand Russell Society .... BRS
Beru [*Kiribati*] [*Airport symbol*] .... BEZ
Berufs-Dermatosen [*A publication*] .... Berufs-Derm
Berven Carpets Corp. [*American Stock Exchange symbol*] [*Delisted*] .... BVN
Berwick, PA [*Radio station call letters*] .... WBRX
Berwyn Public Library, Berwyn, IL [*Library symbol*] .... IBer
Beryllium [*Chemical element*] .... Be
Beryllium Oxide Reactor Experiment [*Formerly, EBOR*] [*Nuclear energy*] .... BORE
Beryllium Oxide Washer .... BOW
Beryllium Thrust Chamber .... BTC
Besalampy [*Madagascar*] [*Airport symbol*] .... BPY
Besancon [*France*] [*Seismograph station code, US Geological Survey*] .... BES
Besancon Universite Annales Scientifiques. Serie 3. Geologie [*A publication*] .... Besancon Univ Ann Sci Ser 3
Beschreibende Bibliographien [*A publication*] .... BBib
Besicorp Group, Inc. [*NASDAQ symbol*] .... BESI
Besonders [*Particularly*] [*German*] .... BSD
Bess Kaiser Foundation Hospital, Medical Library, Portland, OR [*Library symbol*] .... OrPK
Bessarione [*A publication*] .... Bess
Bessemer [*Metallurgy*] .... BESS
Bessemer, AL [*Radio station call letters*] .... WSMQ
Bessemer & Lake Erie Railroad Co. .... B & LE
Bessemer & Lake Erie Railroad Co. [*AAR code*] .... BLE
Best [*Moody's bond rating*] .... Aaa
Best Adaptive Path [*NASA*] .... BAP
Best Alternative Equally Effective Data System .... BAEDS
Best Asymptotically Normal [*Estimates*] [*Econometrics*] .... BAN
Best Available Control Technology [*Environmental Protection Agency*] .... BACT
Best Available Demonstrated Control Technology [*Environmental Protection Agency*] .... BADCT
Best Available Retrofit Technology [*Environmental Protection Agency*] .... BART
Best Available and Safest Technology .... BAST
Best Available Shelter Survey [*of fallout shelters*] [*Civil Defense*] .... BASS
Best Available Technology .... BAT
Best Available Technology Economically Achievable [*Wastewater treatment*] .... BATEA
Best Available True Heading .... BATH
Best Berlin Broadcast [*Radio program broadcast from Berlin by Robert H. Best, former South Carolina journalist*] [*World War II*] .... BBB
Best of Breed .... BB
Best Candidate Committee .... BCC
Best Commercial Flight Line Test Set .... BCFLS
Best & Co., Inc. [*NYSE symbol*] [*Delisted*] .... BST
Best Conventional Technology [*Environmental Protection Agency*] .... BCT
Best Copy Available .... BCA
Best Cruise Altitude .... BCA
Best Cruise Mach Number [*Aviation*] .... BCM
Best Delay [*Audiometry*] .... BD
Best Depth Range [*Military*] .... BDR
Best Dressed List .... BDL
Best Efficiency Point .... BEP
BEST [*Beneficial Employees Security Trust*] **Employers Association** .... BEA
Best Estimate Model .... BE
Best Estimate of Orbital Parameters .... BEOP
Best Estimate of Trajectory [*Apollo*] [*NASA*] .... BET
Best-Estimated Evaluation Trajectory [*NASA*] .... BEET
Best Ever Bottled [*Wines and spirits*] .... BEB
Best Excitatory Frequency [*Neurophysiology*] .... BEF
Best Execution Analysis Tabulation [*Data processing*] .... BEAT
Best and Final Offer .... BAFO
Best-Fit Central Y-Plane .... BFCY-P
Best-Fit Optic Z-Plane .... BFOZ-P
Best Fit Sphere .... BFS
Best Fixed-Sample Procedure [*Statistics*] .... BFSP
Best Foods, Inc. [*American Stock Exchange symbol*] .... BFX
Best in Group .... BIG
Best Inhibitory Frequency [*Neurophysiology*] .... BIF
Best Linear Unbiased Estimator [*Statistics*] .... BLUE
Best Loiter Mach Number [*Aviation*] .... BLM
Best Management Practice [*Environmental Protection Agency*] .... BMP
Best in Match .... BIM
Best Offer [*Classified advertising*] .... BO
Best Operational Capability .... BOC
Best Practicable Control Technology [*Wastewater treatment*] .... BPCT
Best Practicable Technology [*Environmental Protection Agency*] .... BPT
Best Preliminary Estimate .... BPE
Best Products Co., Inc. [*NYSE symbol*] .... BES
Best Professional Judgment [*Environmental Protection Agency*] .... BPJ
Best Range of Aging Verified Oscillator .... BRAVO
Best Sellers [*A publication*] .... Best
Best Sellers [*A publication*] .... Best Sell
Best Sellers [*A publication*] .... BS
Best in Show .... BIS
Best Speed Rating [*of a horse*] .... BSR
Best Straight Line [*Mathematics*] .... BSL
Best Technical Approach [*Military*] .... BTA
Best Times Available [*Television*] .... BTA
Best Western Motels [*Motel chain*] .... BWM
Beston, MA [*Radio station call letters*] .... WMJX
Best's Insurance News [*A publication*] .... Best's Ins N
Best's Review. Life/Health Edition [*A publication*] .... Best's Life
Best's Review. Life/Health Edition [*A publication*] .... BLH
Best's Review. Life/Health Insurance Edition [*A publication*] .... Best Life
Best's Review. Life/Health Insurance Edition [*A publication*] .... Best's Rev Life Health Insur Ed
Best's Review. Property/Liability Edition [*A publication*] .... Bests Prop
Best's Review. Property/Liability Edition [*A publication*] .... Best's R (Property Ed)
Bestwall Gypsum Co. [*NYSE symbol*] [*Delisted*] .... BWG
Bet Nahrain [*An association*] .... BN
Beta .... B
Beta Absorption Gauge .... BAG
Beta Alpha Psi .... BAP
Beta-Alumina Solid Electrolyte .... BASE
Beta-Aminopropionitrile [*Organic chemistry*] .... BAPN
Beta-Blocker Heart Attack Trial [*Cardiology*] .... BHAT
Beta Disintegration Energy .... BDE
Beta-Gamma .... BG
Beta Gamma Sigma .... BGS
Beta-Hydroxyethylhydrazine [*Plant growth compound*] .... BOH
Beta-Hydroxysteroid Dehydrogenase [*An enzyme*] .... BHD
Beta-Mercaptoethanol [*Organic chemistry*] .... BME
Beta-Naphthol [*Organic chemistry*] .... BN
Beta-Naphthoxyacetic Acid [*Plant growth compound*] .... BNOA
Beta-Naphthylamine [*Organic chemistry*] .... BNA
Beta-Nitropropionic Acid [*Organic chemistry*] .... BNPA
Beta-Oxynaphthoic Acid [*Organic chemistry*] .... BON
Beta-Propriolactone [*Organic chemistry*] .... BPL
Beta-Resorcylic Acid [*Organic chemistry*] .... BRA
Beta Spectrometer .... BS
Beta Thickness Gauge .... BTG
Beth Din of America .... BDA
Beth Hamikra. Bulletin of the Israel Society for Biblical Research and the World Jewish Biblical Society [*A publication*] .... Beth Hamikra
Beth Israel Hospital, Medical Library, Denver, CO [*Library symbol*] .... CoDBI-M
Beth Israel Medical Center, New York, NY [*Library symbol*] .... NNBI
Beth Israel Medical Center, New York, NY [*OCLC symbol*] VVI
Beth Mikra [*A publication*] .... BM
Bethalto Community Unit 8, Bethalto, IL [*Library symbol*] .... IBethCU
Bethalto Public Library, Bethalto, IL [*Library symbol*] .... IBeth
Bethany Beach, DE [*Radio station call letters*] .... WWTR-FM
Bethany College, Bethany, WV [*OCLC symbol*] .... WVB
Bethany College, Bethany, WV [*Library symbol*] .... WvBeC
Bethany College, Lindsborg, KS [*OCLC symbol*] .... KFB
Bethany College, Lindsborg, KS [*Library symbol*] .... KLindB
Bethany Lutheran College, Mankato, MN [*OCLC symbol*] .... MBE
Bethany Lutheran College, Mankato, MN [*Library symbol*] .... MnManBC
Bethany Lutheran Theological Seminary, Mankato, MN [*OCLC symbol*] .... MBS
Bethany Lutheran Theological Seminary, Mankato, MN [*Library symbol*] .... MnManBS
Bethany Medical Center, Kansas City, KS [*Library symbol*] .... KKcBM
Bethany Nazarene College [*Oklahoma*] .... BNC
Bethany Nazarene College, Bethany, OK [*OCLC symbol*] .... OKA
Bethany Nazarene College, Bethany, OK [*Library symbol*] .... OkBetC
Bethany and Northern Baptist Theological Seminaries Library, Oak Brook, IL [*OCLC symbol*] .... IDI
Bethany and Northern Baptist Theological Seminaries Library, Oak Brook, IL [*Library symbol*] .... IObT
Bethany, OK [*Radio station call letters*] .... KJIL
Bethany, WV [*Radio station call letters*] .... WVBC
Bethe-Salpeter Equation [*Physics*] .... BSE
Bethel [*Alaska*] [*Airport symbol*] .... BET
Bethel [*Alaska*] [*Seismograph station code, US Geological Survey*] [*Closed*] .... BET
Bethel, AK [*Location identifier*] [*FAA*] .... JBT
Bethel, AK [*Radio station call letters*] .... KJBA
Bethel, AK [*Radio station call letters*] .... KYUK
Bethel, AK [*Television station call letters*] .... KYUK-TV
Bethel, AK [*Location identifier*] [*FAA*] .... OSE
Bethel College, Learning Resources Center, St. Paul, MN [*OCLC symbol*] .... MNK
Bethel College, McKenzie, TN [*Library symbol*] .... TMckB
Bethel College, North Newton, KS [*Library symbol*] .... KNnB
Bethel College, St. Paul, MN [*Library symbol*] .... MnSB

Bethesda Base Hospital, Information Resource Center, Cincinnati, OH [*Library symbol*] ... OCBH
Bethesda Hospital, Medical Library, Denver, CO [*Library symbol*] ... CoDBH-M
Bethesda Lutheran Hospital, St. Paul, MN [*Library symbol*] ... MnSBH
Bethesda, MD [*Radio station call letters*] ... WGMS
Bethesda, MD [*Radio station call letters*] ... WGMS-FM
Bethesda, MD [*Radio station call letters*] ... WLTT
Bethesda, MD [*Radio station call letters*] ... WTKS
Bethesda Military Librarians Group [*Library network*] ... NMCLA
Bethlehem Corp. [*American Stock Exchange symbol*] ... BET
Bethlehem, PA [*Radio station call letters*] ... WGPA
Bethlehem, PA [*Radio station call letters*] ... WLVR-FM
Bethlehem, PA [*Radio station call letters*] ... WZZO
Bethlehem Public Library, Bethlehem, PA [*Library symbol*] ... PB
Bethlehem Public Library, Bethlehem, PA [*OCLC symbol*] ... PBL
Bethlehem Steel Corp. [*NYSE symbol*] [*Wall Street slang name: "Bessie"*] ... BS
Bethlehem Steel Corp., Charles H. Herty, Jr., Memorial Library, Bethlehem, PA [*Library symbol*] ... PBS
Bethlehem Steel Corp., Charles M. Schwab Memorial Library, Bethlehem, PA [*Library symbol*] ... PBSteel
Bethlehem, WV [*Radio station call letters*] ... WHLX
Bethpage Public Library, Bethpage, NY [*Library symbol*] ... NBet
Bethune-Cookman College [*Florida*] ... BCC
Bethune-Cookman College, Daytona Beach, FL [*OCLC symbol*] ... DBB
Bethune-Cookman College, Daytona Beach, FL [*Library symbol*] ... FDbBC
Betioky [*Madagascar*] [*Airport symbol*] ... BKU
Beton Herstellung Verwendung [*A publication*] ... Beton Herstellung Verwend
Betonstein Zeitung [*A publication*] ... Betonstein Zig
Betreffend [*Referring To*] [*German*] ... BETR
Betriebs- Berater [*Zeitschrift fuer Recht und Wirtschaft*] [*A publication*] ... Betr- Berat
Betriebs-Oekonom [*A publication*] ... Betr-Oekon
Betriebs-Technik [*A publication*] ... Betr-Tech
Betriebsberufsschule [*Factory Training School*] [*Germany*] ... BBS
Betriebsgewerkschaftsleitung [*Factory Union Headquarters*] [*Germany*] ... BGL
Betriebswirtschaftliche Forschung und Praxis [*A publication*] ... Betriebswirtsch Forsch Praxis
Betriebswirtschaftliche Mitteilungen fuer den Wirtschaftsberater [*A publication*] ... Betriebswirt Mitt Wirtberater
Betsie Valley District Library, Thompsonville, MI [*Library symbol*] ... MiTho
Bettendorf News, Bettendorf, IA [*Library symbol*] ... IaBetN
Better ... BTR
Better than Average ... BTA
Better Boys Foundation ... BBF
Better Business Bureau ... BBB
[*A*] **Better Chance** [*Scholarship program for the underprivileged*] ... ABC
Better Education thru Simplified Spelling [*An association*] ... BEtSS
Better Electronic Service Technicians ... BEST
Better than Expected [*Politics*] ... BTE
Better Fabrics Test Bureau ... BFTB
Better Farming [*A publication*] ... Better F
Better Government Association ... BGA
Better Hearing Institute ... BHI
Better Heating-Cooling Council ... BHC
Better Highways Information Foundation [*Later, ARTBA*] ... BHIF
Better Homes and Gardens [*A publication*] ... Bet Hom & Gard
Better Homes and Gardens [*A publication*] ... BH & G
Better Humanity League [*Commercial firm*] ... BHL
Better Kitchens Institute ... BKI
Better Lawn and Turf Institute ... BLTI
Better Light Better Sight Bureau [*Defunct*] ... BLBSB
Better on Lips than on Paper [*Put at the end of a letter with kisses*] [*British*] ... BOLTOP
Better Occupational Awareness Training ... BOAT
Better Packaging Advisory Council ... BPAC
Better Postcard Collectors' Club [*Later, D of A*] ... BPCC
Better Roads and Transportation Council ... BR & TC
Better Sleep Council ... BSC
Better Vision Institute ... BVI
Bettering Oregon's Opportunity for Saving Talent [*Educational project*] ... BOOST
Bettis Atomic Power Laboratory [*AEC*] ... BAPL
Bettles [*Alaska*] [*Airport symbol*] ... BTT
Bettles, AK [*Location identifier*] [*FAA*] ... EAV
[*The*] **Bettmann Archive** [*A publication*] ... TBA
Between ... BET
Between ... BETW
Between ... BTN
Between ... BTW
Between ... BTWN
Between Centers [*Technical drawings*] ... BC
Between Ischial Spines [*Pelvic measurement*] [*Gynecology*] ... BISp
Between Layers [*Aviation*] ... BL
Between Layers [*Aviation*] ... BTL
Between Librarians [*A publication*] ... Bet Libns
Between Librarians [*A publication*] ... Betw Libns
Between Perpendiculars [*Technical drawings*] ... BP
Between Worlds [*A publication*] ... BW
Betz Indicator [*A publication*] ... Betz Indic
Betz Laboratories, Inc. [*NASDAQ symbol*] ... BETZ
Betz Laboratories, Inc., Trevose, PA [*Library symbol*] ... PTrB
Beulah, ND [*Radio station call letters*] ... KHOL
Beulah Public Library, Beulah, MI [*Library symbol*] ... MiBeu
Beurre, Oeufs, Fromages [*Butter, Eggs, Cheese*] [*French*] ... BOF
Beva [*A prefix meaning multiplied by one billion; same as "giga"*] ... B
Bevatron ... BEV
Bevatron/Super-HILAC [*Combination of accelerators*] ... BEVALAC
Bevel ... BEV
Beveled Wood Siding [*Technical drawings*] ... BWS
Beverage ... BEV
Beverage ... BV
Beverage ... BVGE
Beverage Container Control Coalition [*Later, WCFR*] ... B3C
Beverage Industry [*A publication*] ... Beverage
Beverage Industry [*A publication*] ... Beverage Ind
Beverage Machinery Manufacturers Association [*Defunct*] ... BMMA
Beverage Manufacturers' Agents Association ... BMAA
Beverage World [*A publication*] ... Bev Wld
Beveren Rabbit Club [*Defunct*] ... BRC
Beverley [*Jamaica*] [*Seismograph station code, US Geological Survey*] [*Closed*] ... BEV
Beverly Enterprises [*NYSE symbol*] ... BEV
Beverly Hills Public Library, Beverly Hills, CA [*OCLC symbol*] ... BHP
Beverly Hills Public Library, Beverly Hills, CA [*Library symbol*] ... CBev
Beverly Hills Racquets Club [*Book title*] ... BHRC
Beverly Hills Savings & Loan [*NASDAQ symbol*] ... BHSL
Beverly Historical Society, Beverly, MA [*Library symbol*] ... MBevHi
Beverly, MA [*Location identifier*] [*FAA*] ... BVY
Beverly, MA [*Radio station call letters*] ... WBVD
Beverly Public Library, Beverly, MA [*Library symbol*] ... MBev
Beverly Springs [*Australia*] [*Airport symbol*] [*Obsolete*] ... BVZ
Beverly Times, Beverly, MA [*Library symbol*] ... MBevT
Bevier & Southern Railroad Co. [*AAR code*] ... BVS
Bevitron Orbit Code ... BOC
Bewani [*Papua New Guinea*] [*Airport symbol*] ... BWP
Bewusstein [*Consciousness*] [*Psychology*] ... BW
Bexar County Medical Library Association, San Antonio, TX [*Library symbol*] ... TxSaBM
Bexley Public Library, Columbus, OH [*Library symbol*] ... OCoBex
Beyer Aviation [*Dubuque, IA*] [*FAA designator*] ... BEY
Beyond ... BYD
Beyond Baroque [*A publication*] ... Bey B
Beyond Capacity of Intermediate Maintenance ... BCIM
Beyond Capacity of Maintenance ... BCM
Beyond Economical Repair ... BER
Beyond Fiction [*A publication*] ... BFF
Beyond the Horizon ... BTH
Beyond Infinity [*A publication*] ... BDI
Beyond Line of Sight ... BLOS
Beyond Local Repair [*Weaponry*] [*British*] ... BLR
Beyond Visual Range ... BVR
Beyond Visual Range Missile ... BVRM
Beziehungsweise [*Respectively*] [*German*] ... BEZW
Beziehungsweise [*Respectively*] [*German*] ... BZW
Beziers [*France*] [*Airport symbol*] ... BZR
Bezopasnost' Truda v Promyshlennosti [*A publication*] ... Bezop Tr Prom-st
Bezpartyjny Blok Wspolpracy z Rzadem [*Nonpartisan Bloc of Cooperation with the Government*] [*Poland*] ... BBWR
Bezueglich [*With Reference To*] [*German*] ... BEZ
BF Goodrich Co. Economic and Business Facts and Forecasts [*A publication*] ... Goodrich
BFI Communications [*NASDAQ symbol*] ... BFXC
BGS Systems, Inc. [*NASDAQ symbol*] ... BGSS
Bhabha Atomic Research Centre [*India*] ... BARC
Bhadrapur [*Nepal*] [*Airport symbol*] ... BDP
Bhairawa [*Nepal*] [*Airport symbol*] ... BWA
Bhakra [*India*] [*Seismograph station code, US Geological Survey*] ... BHK
Bhamo [*Burma*] [*Airport symbol*] ... BMO
Bharata Manisha Quarterly [*A publication*] ... Bhar Ma Q
Bharatiya Vidya [*A publication*] ... BhV
Bharatpur [*Nepal*] [*Airport symbol*] [*Obsolete*] ... BHR
Bhatnagar-Gross-Krook [*Equation*] ... BGK
Bhavan's Journal [*A publication*] ... Bhavan's J
Bhavnagar [*India*] [*Airport symbol*] ... BHU
BHM Berg-und Huttenmannische Monatshefte [*A publication*] ... BHM Berg u Huttenm Mh
Bhojpur [*Nepal*] [*Airport symbol*] ... BHP
Bhojpuri [*MARC language code*] [*Library of Congress*] ... bho
Bhopal [*India*] [*Airport symbol*] ... BHO
BHP [*Broken Hill Proprietary Co. Ltd.*] **Journal** [*A publication*] ... BHP J
BHP [*Broken Hill Proprietary Co. Ltd.*] **Technical Bulletin** [*A publication*] ... BHP Tech Bull
Bhubaneswar [*India*] [*Airport symbol*] ... BBI
Bhuj [*India*] [*Airport symbol*] ... BHJ
Bhumibol Dam [*Thailand*] [*Seismograph station code, US Geological Survey*] ... BDT
Bhutan [*MARC geographic area code*] [*Library of Congress*] ... a-bt---
Bhutan [*MARC country of publication code*] [*Library of Congress*] ... bt

Bhutan [*Three-letter standard code*]....BTN
Bhutan [*Two-letter standard code*]....BT
Bhutan Philatelic Society....BPS
Bi-Doppler Scoring System....BIDOPS
Bi-Drive Recreational All-Terrain Transporter [*Subaru automobile*]....BRAT
BI [*Bibliographisches Institut*] **Hochschultaschenbuecher** [*A publication*]....BI Hochschultaschenb
BI Inc. [*NASDAQ symbol*]....BIAC
Bi-Monthly Research Notes. Canada Department of Forestry [*A publication*]....Bi-M Res Notes Canada Dep For
Bi-State Academic Libraries [*Library network*]....BI-SAL
Biafra [*MARC geographic area code*] [*Library of Congress*]....f-by---
Biafra Relief Services Foundation....BRSF
Biafra Review [*A publication*]....Biafra R
Biak [*Indonesia*] [*Airport symbol*]....BIK
Bialla [*Papua New Guinea*] [*Airport symbol*]....BAA
Bianco e Nero [*A publication*]....Bian & Nero
Biarritz [*France*] [*Airport symbol*]....BIQ
Biaru [*Papua New Guinea*] [*Airport symbol*]....BRP
Bias Oscillator Frequency....BOF
Bias Telegraph Distortion....BTD
Biased Antiworld Paw Entry [*Testing of left and right laterality in mice*]....BAWPE
Biased World Paw Entry [*Testing of left and right laterality in mice*]....BWPE
Biaxial Shock Test Machine [*CERL*] [*Army*]....BSTM
Biaxially-Oriented Polypropylene [*Plastics technology*]....BOPP
Bibas in Christo [*May You Live in Christ*] [*Latin*]....BIC
Bibb Co. [*NASDAQ symbol*]....BIBB
Bibbia e Oriente [*A publication*]....Bib Or
Bibbia e Oriente [*A publication*]....B e O
Bibe [*Drink*] [*Pharmacy*]....BIB
Bible....B
Bible....BIB
Bible and the Ancient Near East [*A publication*]....BANE
Bible Club Movement....BCM
Bible Grove, IL [*Location identifier*] [*FAA*]....BIB
Bible Holiness Movement....BHM
Bible Institute of Los Angeles....BILA
Bible Literature International....BLI
Bible and Medical Missionary Fellowship [*Formerly, UFCS*] [*Later, BMMFI*]....BMMF
Bible Meditation League [*Later, BLI*]....BML
Bible Memory Association, International....BMA
Bible Protestant Missions....BPM
Bible Sabbath Association....BSA
Bible-Science Association....BSA
Bible Seminary in New York....BSNY
Bible Study League of America....BSLA
Bible Today [*A publication*]....Bible T
Bible Translator [*A publication*]....BT
Bible Version [*As opposed to the Prayer Book version of the Psalms*]....BV
Bibles for the World....BW
Biblica [*A publication*]....Bi
Biblica [*A publication*]....Bib
Biblical....BIBL
Biblical Archaeologist [*A publication*]....BA
Biblical Archaeologist [*A publication*]....BiA
Biblical Archaeologist [*A publication*]....Bib Arch
Biblical Archaeologist [*A publication*]....Bibl Arch
Biblical Archaeologist [*A publication*]....Bibl Archaeolo
Biblical Archaeology Review [*A publication*]....BAR
Biblical Archeologist [*A publication*]....Bib A
Biblical Archeologist [*A publication*]....Bibl Archeol
Biblical Colloquium....BC
Biblical Evangelism....BE
Biblical Numismatic Society....BNS
Biblical Research [*A publication*]....Bib Res
Biblical Research [*A publication*]....BR
Biblical Review [*A publication*]....Bib R
Biblical School of Theology, Hatfield, PA [*Library symbol*]....PHatfB
Biblical Seminary in New York, New York, NY [*Library symbol*]....NNBS
Biblical Theologians....BT
Biblical Theology Bulletin [*A publication*]....Bib Th Bul
Biblical Theology Bulletin [*A publication*]....BTB
Biblical Viewpoint [*A publication*]....BV
Biblical World [*A publication*]....Bib World
Biblio Service Informatique [*Informatics Biblio Service*] [*France*] [*Information service*]....BSI
Bibliofilia [*A publication*]....B
Bibliofilia [*A publication*]....BF
Bibliofilia [*A publication*]....Bi
Bibliofilia [*A publication*]....Biblio
Bibliografia Brasileira Odontologia [*A publication*]....Bibliogr Bras Odontol
Bibliografia Espanola [*A bibliographic publication*] [*Spain*]....BE
Bibliografia Filologica do Centro de Estudos Filologica de Lisboa [*A publication*]....Bibl Filol
Bibliografia General Espanola e Hispanoamericana [*A bibliographic publication*] [*Spain*]....BEH
Bibliografia Hispanica [*A publication*]....BH
Bibliografia Hispanica [*A publication*]....BHisp
Bibliografia Hispanica [*A publication*]....BiH
Bibliografia Italiana [*A publication*]....BI
Bibliografia Italiana sull'Educazione dei Sordi [*A publication*]....Biblio Ital Educ Sordi
Bibliographer [*A publication*]....Bibliog
Bibliographia Genetica [*A publication*]....Bibliogr Genet
Bibliographia Huntiana [*Computer-based bibliography*]....BH
Bibliographic Automation of Large Library Operations Using a Time-Sharing System [*Later, RLIN*] [*Stanford University*]....BALLOTS
Bibliographic Center for Research, Denver, CO [*OCLC symbol*]....TPS
Bibliographic Center for Research, Denver, CO [*OCLC symbol*]....TPT
Bibliographic Classification [*System of library classification devised by Henry Evelyn Bliss*]....BC
Bibliographic Data Processing Program [*For keyword indexing*]....BIDAP
Bibliographic Index [*A publication*]....Bibl
Bibliographic Index [*A publication*]....Bibl Ind
Bibliographic Information on Southeast Asia [*Australia*] [*Information service*]....BISA
Bibliographic and Library Information Search Service....BLISS
Bibliographic and Library Instruction for Secondary Schools....BLISS
Bibliographic Network [*Data processing*]....BIBNET
Bibliographic On-Line Display [*Data processing*]....BOLD
Bibliographic On-Line Organized Knowledge [*Data processing*]....BOOK
Bibliographic Retrieval Services [*Information service*]....BRS
Bibliographic Systems Center [*Case Western Reserve University*]....BSC
Bibliographica Genetica Medica [*A publication*]....Bibliogr Genet Med
Bibliographical Center for Research, Denver, CO [*OCLC symbol*]....BCR
Bibliographical Center for Research, Rocky Mountain Region, Inc. [*Library network*]....BCR
Bibliographical Center for Research, Rocky Mountain Region, Inc., Denver, CO [*Library symbol*]....CoDB
Bibliographical Series. Oregon State University. Forest Research Laboratory [*A publication*]....Bibliogr Ser Ore For Res Lab
Bibliographical Services Section [*of a library*]....BSS
Bibliographical Society [*British*]....BS
Bibliographical Society of America....BSA
Bibliographical Society of America. Papers [*A publication*]....Bibliog Soc Am Pa
Bibliographical Society of America. Papers [*A publication*]....Biblio Soc Am
Bibliographical Society of America. Papers [*A publication*]....Bibl Soc Am Pa
Bibliographical Society of America. Papers [*A publication*]....Bib Soc Am
Bibliographical Society of America. Papers [*A publication*]....BSAP
Bibliographical Society of America. Papers [*A publication*]....BSP
Bibliographical Society [*London*]. **Publications** [*A publication*]....BSP
Bibliographical Society of the University of Virginia....BSUV
Bibliographie Linguistique [*A publication*]....Bibl
Bibliographie Linguistique [*A publication*]....BL
Bibliographie Moderne [*A publication*]....BMod
Bibliographie der Pflanzenschutzliteratur [*A publication*]....Bibl Pflanz
Bibliographie de la Philosophie [*A publication*]....BPh
Bibliographien zur Deutsche Barockliteratur [*A publication*]....BzDB
Bibliographien zur Deutschen Literatur des Mittelalters [*A publication*]....BDLM
Bibliographien des Deutschen Wetterdienstes [*A publication*]....Biblphien Dt Wetterd
Bibliographien zum Studium der Deutschen Sprache und Literatur [*A publication*]....BSSL
Bibliographique Officiel des Imprimes Publies en Pologne. Bulletin [*A publication*]....BOP
Bibliography....BIBL
Bibliography....BIBLIOG
Bibliography of Agriculture [*A publication*]....BibAg
Bibliography of Agriculture [*A publication*]....BOA
Bibliography of American Literature [*A publication*]....BAL
Bibliography of Bioethics [*A publication*]....BOB
Bibliography on Cold Regions Science and Technology [*A publication*]....BCRST
Bibliography. Commonwealth Bureau of Soils [*A publication*]....Bibliogr Bur Soils
Bibliography of the Computer in Environmental Design [*A publication*]....BCED
Bibliography, Documentation, Terminology [*A publication*]....Bibl Docum Terminology
Bibliography, Documentation, Terminology [*A publication*]....Bibliog Doc Terminology
Bibliography of English Language and Literature [*A publication*]....Bibl Engl Lang & Lit
Bibliography on Incineration of Refuse and Waste [*Air Pollution Control Association*] [*A publication*]....BIR
Bibliography and Index of Geology [*A publication*]....BiblGeo
Bibliography and Index of Geology [*A publication*]....Bibl & Ind Geol
Bibliography and Index of Geology Exclusive of North America [*A publication*]....BIGENA
Bibliography of Medical Translations [*A publication*]....BMT
Bibliography of Old Norse-Icelandic Studies [*A publication*]....BONIS
Bibliography of Reproduction [*A publication*]....Bibl Repro
Bibliography of Research Studies in Education, 1926-1940 [*A publication*]....BRSE
Bibliography of Soil Science [*A publication*]....BSS
Biblionews and Australian Notes and Queries [*A publication*]....BANQ

Biblioteca Apostolica Vaticana, Vatican City, Vatican City [*Library symbol*] ... VatBA
Biblioteca dell'Archivum Romanicum [*A publication*] ... BAR
Biblioteca de Autores Cristianos [*A publication*] ... BAC
Biblioteca de Autores Espanoles [*A publication*] ... BAE
Biblioteca Benjamin Franklin, Guadalajara, Mexico [*Library symbol*] ... MxGuBF
Biblioteca Benjamin Franklin, Mexico City, Mexico [*Library symbol*] ... MxMBF
Biblioteca Berenson, Florence, Italy [*Library symbol*] ... ItFB
Biblioteca Centrala de Stat a R.S. Romania [*Central State Library of Romania*], **Bucharest, Romania** [*Library symbol*] ... RoBBC
Biblioteca Comunale "Angelillo", Servizio Prestito, Bari, Italy [*Library symbol*] ... ItBa
Biblioteca Comunale di Barletta, Barletta, Italy [*Library symbol*] ... ItBar
Biblioteca Hispana [*A publication*] ... BHis
Biblioteca della Liberta [*A publication*] ... Bibl Liberta
Biblioteca Marucelliana di Firenze, Servizio Prestito, Florence, Italy [*Library symbol*] ... ItFBM
Biblioteca Moderna Mondadori [*A publication*] ... BMM
Biblioteca Nacional de Agricultura [*National Library of Agriculture*] [*Brazil*] [*Information service*] ... BINAGRI
Biblioteca Nacional, Caracas, Venezuela [*Library symbol*] ... Ve
Biblioteca Nacional de Chile, Santiago, Chile [*Library symbol*] ... Chl
Biblioteca Nacional, Madrid, Spain [*Library symbol*] ... Sp
Biblioteca Nacional de Mexico, Mexico City, Mexico [*Library symbol*] ... MxMBN
Biblioteca Nacional, Rio De Janeiro, Brazil [*Library symbol*] ... Br
Biblioteca Nazional Universitaria di Torino, Servizio Prestito, Turin, Italy [*Library symbol*] ... ItTU
Biblioteca Nazionale Centrale Florence [*Italy*] ... BNCF
Biblioteca Nazionale Centrale, Rome, Italy [*Library symbol*] ... It
Biblioteca Publica, Palma De Mallorca, Spain [*Library symbol*] ... SpPm
Biblioteca Statale di Cremona, Cremona, Italy [*Library symbol*] ... ItCr
Bibliotek for Laeger [*A publication*] ... Bibl Laeger
Biblioteka Analiz Literackich [*A publication*] ... BALit
Biblioteka Juznoslovenskog Filologa [*A publication*] ... BJF
Biblioteka Matematyczna [*A publication*] ... Bibl Mat
Biblioteka Narodowa [*National Library*], **Warsaw, Poland** [*Library symbol*] ... PoWBN
Biblioteka Vracha [*A publication*] ... Bibliot Vrach
Bibliotekarz [*A publication*] ... B
Bibliotekernes Oplysningskontor, Centre de Pret International, Kobenhavn, Denmark [*Library symbol*] ... DnKBO
Bibliotekininkystes ir Bibliografijos Klausimai [*A publication*] ... BBK
Biblioteksbladet [*A publication*] ... BBL
Bibliotheca [*Library*] [*Latin*] ... BIBL
Bibliotheca Anatomica [*A publication*] ... Bibl Anat
Bibliotheca Anatomica [*A publication*] ... Bibl Anatom
Bibliotheca Arnamagnaeana [*A publication*] ... B Arn
Bibliotheca Biotheoretica [*A publication*] ... Bibl Biotheor
Bibliotheca Cardiologica [*A publication*] ... Bibl Cardio
Bibliotheca Cardiologica [*A publication*] ... Bibl Cardiol
Bibliotheca Celtica [*A publication*] ... BC
Bibliotheca Classica Orientalis [*A publication*] ... BCO
Bibliotheca Gastroenterologica [*A publication*] ... Bibl Gastro
Bibliotheca Gastroenterologica [*A publication*] ... Bibl Gastroenterol
Bibliotheca Gynaecologica [*A publication*] ... Bibl Gynaecol
Bibliotheca Haematologica [*A publication*] ... Bibl Haem
Bibliotheca Haematologica [*A publication*] ... Bibl Haematol
Bibliotheca Islamica [*A publication*] ... BI
Bibliotheca Medica Cassel [*A publication*] ... Biblioth Med Cassel
Bibliotheca Microbiologica [*A publication*] ... Bibl Microbiol
Bibliotheca Nutrito et Dieta [*A publication*] ... Bibl Nutr D
Bibliotheca Nutrito et Dieta [*A publication*] ... Bibl Nutr Dieta
Bibliotheca Ophthalmologica [*A publication*] ... Bibl Ophthalmol
Bibliotheca Orientalis [*A publication*] ... Bibl Orient
Bibliotheca Orientalis [*A publication*] ... BibO
Bibliotheca Orientalis [*A publication*] ... BiOr
Bibliotheca Orientalis [*A publication*] ... BO
Bibliotheca Oto-Rhino-Laryngologica [*A publication*] ... Bibl Oto-Rhino-Laryngol
Bibliotheca Paediatrica [*A publication*] ... Bibl Paediatr
Bibliotheca Parsoniana, New Orleans, LA [*Library symbol*] [*Obsolete*] ... LNP
Bibliotheca Philologica Classica [*A publication*] ... BPhC
Bibliotheca Phonetica [*A publication*] ... Bibl Phonet
Bibliotheca Phonetica [*A publication*] ... Bibl Phonetica
Bibliotheca Primatologica [*A publication*] ... Bibl Primatol
Bibliotheca Psychiatrica [*A publication*] ... Bibl Psych
Bibliotheca Psychiatrica [*A publication*] ... Bibl Psychiatr
Bibliotheca Psychiatrica et Neurologica [*A publication*] ... Bibl Psychiatr Neurol
Bibliotheca Radiologica [*A publication*] ... Bibl Radiol
Bibliotheca Romana [*A publication*] ... BR
Bibliotheca Sacra [*A publication*] ... Bibl Sac
Bibliotheca Sacra [*A publication*] ... Bib Sac
Bibliotheca Sacra [*A publication*] ... Bib Sacra
Bibliotheca Sacra [*A publication*] ... BS
Bibliotheca Tuberculosea [*A publication*] ... Bibl Tuberc
Bibliotheca Tuberculosea et Medicinae Thoracalis [*A publication*] ... Bibl Tuberc Med Thorac
Bibliotheca Tuberculosea et Medicinae Thoracalis [*A publication*] ... Bibl Tub Me T
Bibliotheca "Vita Humana" [*A publication*] ... Bibl "Vita Hum"
Bibliotheekleven [*A publication*] ... BL
Bibliothek des Literarischen Vereins (Stuttgart) [*A publication*] ... BLVS
Bibliotheque Archeologique et Historique de l'Institut Francais d'Archeologie d'Istanbul [*A publication*] ... BAHIFAI
Bibliotheque des Archives de la Province de Quebec, Quebec, PQ, Canada [*Library symbol*] ... CaQQA
Bibliotheque de l'Arsenal, Paris, France [*Library symbol*] ... FrPBA
Bibliotheque Battelle, Centre de Recherche, Geneve, Switzerland [*Library symbol*] ... SzGB
Bibliotheque Bonaventurienne. Series "Textes" [*A publication*] ... BBST
Bibliotheque Calvet, Avignon, France [*Library symbol*] ... FrAv
Bibliotheque Cantonal et Universitaire de Lausanne, Lausanne, Switzerland [*Library symbol*] ... SzLaCU
Bibliotheque Centrale de Prete de la Mauricie, Trois-Rivieres, PQ, Canada [*Library symbol*] ... CaQTBC
Bibliotheque des Centres d'Etudes Superieures Specialisees [*A publication*] ... BCESS
Bibliotheque des Centres d'Etudes Superieures Specialisees. Travaux du Centre d'Etudes Superieures Specialisees d'Histoire de Religions de Strasbourg [*A publication*] ... BCETCEHRS
Bibliotheque Deschatelets, Peres Oblats, Ottawa, ON, Canada [*Library symbol*] ... CaOOSJ
Bibliotheque de l'Ecole des Chartes [*A publication*] ... BEC
Bibliotheque de l'Ecole des Chartes [*A publication*] ... BECh
Bibliotheque de l'Ecole des Chartes [*A publication*] ... Bibl Ec Chartes
Bibliotheque de l'Ecole des Chartes [*A publication*] ... Bibl Ecole Chartes
Bibliotheque de l'Ecole des Hautes Etudes Belfagor [*A publication*] ... BEHE
Bibliotheque des Ecoles Francaises d'Athenes et de Rome [*A publication*] ... BEFAR
Bibliotheque de la Faculte Catholique de Theologie de Lyon [*A publication*] ... BFCTL
Bibliotheque de la Faculte de Philosophie et Lettres de l'Universite de Liege [*A publication*] ... BFPhLL
Bibliotheque de la Faculte de Philosophie et Lettres de l'Universite de Liege [*A publication*] ... BFPLUL
Bibliotheque Francaise et Romane [*A publication*] ... BFR
Bibliotheque Franciscaine, Quebec, PQ, Canada [*Library symbol*] ... CaQQF
Bibliotheque Gaspesienne, Cap Chat, PQ, Canada [*Library symbol*] ... CaQCC
Bibliotheque Generale et Archives, Rabat, Morocco [*Library symbol*] ... MorR
Bibliotheque Historique [*A publication*] ... BH
Bibliotheque Historique Vaudoise [*A publication*] ... Bibl Hist Vaudoise
Bibliotheque d'Humanisme et Renaissance [*A publication*] ... BHR
Bibliotheque d'Humanisme et Renaissance [*A publication*] ... BiblH & R
Bibliotheque d'Humanisme et Renaissance [*A publication*] ... BiHR
Bibliotheque de l'Institut de Droit Canonique de l'Universite de Strasbourg [*A publication*] ... BIDCUS
Bibliotheque des Instituteurs, Montreal, PQ, Canada [*Library symbol*] ... CaQMBI
Bibliotheque de la Legislature de la Province de Quebec, Quebec, PQ, Canada [*Library symbol*] ... CaQQL
Bibliotheque Municipale, Arthabaska, PQ, Canada [*Library symbol*] ... CaQArM
Bibliotheque Municipale, Asbestos, PQ, Canada [*Library symbol*] ... CaQAsB
Bibliotheque Municipale, Becancour, PQ, Canada [*Library symbol*] ... CaQBEC
Bibliotheque Municipale, Boucherville, PQ, Canada [*Library symbol*] ... CaQBO
Bibliotheque Municipale, Cap-De-La Madeleine, PQ, Canada [*Library symbol*] ... CaQCmM
Bibliotheque Municipale, Coaticook, PQ, Canada [*Library symbol*] ... CaQCB
Bibliotheque Municipale, Drummondville, PQ, Canada [*Library symbol*] ... CaQDM
Bibliotheque Municipale, Granby, PQ, Canada [*Library symbol*] ... CaQGM
Bibliotheque Municipale, Grand'Mere, PQ, Canada [*Library symbol*] ... CaQGmM
Bibliotheque Municipale, Hull, PQ, Canada [*Library symbol*] ... CaQH
Bibliotheque Municipale, La Salle, PQ, Canada [*Library symbol*] ... CaQLs
Bibliotheque Municipale, La Tuque, PQ, Canada [*Library symbol*] ... CaQLt
Bibliotheque Municipale, Laval, PQ, Canada [*Library symbol*] ... CaQLA
Bibliotheque Municipale, Levis, PQ, Canada [*Library symbol*] ... CaQLe
Bibliotheque Municipale, Longueuil, PQ, Canada [*Library symbol*] ... CaQLo
Bibliotheque Municipale de Lyon, Lyon, France [*Library symbol*] ... FrLy
Bibliotheque Municipale, Magog, PQ, Canada [*Library symbol*] ... CaQMgB
Bibliotheque Municipale, Montreal-Nord, PQ, Canada [*Library symbol*] ... CaQMn
Bibliotheque Municipale, Nantes, France [*Library symbol*] ... FrN
Bibliotheque Municipale, Plessisville, PQ, Canada [*Library symbol*] ... CaQPIM
Bibliotheque Municipale, Port Alfred, PQ, Canada [*Library symbol*] ... CaQPA
Bibliotheque Municipale, Princeville, PQ, Canada [*Library symbol*] ... CaQPrM

Bibliotheque Municipale, Quebec, PQ, Canada [*Library symbol*]..........CaQQ
Bibliotheque Municipale, Rock Island, PQ, Canada [*Library symbol*] .... CaQRIB
Bibliotheque Municipale, Saint-Jean, PQ, Canada [*Library symbol*] .... CaQStJB
Bibliotheque Municipale, St. Jerome, PQ, Canada [*Library symbol*] .... CaQStJe
Bibliotheque Municipale, Saint Laurent, PQ, Canada [*Library symbol*]............CaQStL
Bibliotheque Municipale, Saint-Leonard, PQ, Canada [*Library symbol*]............CaQStLe
Bibliotheque Municipale, Sept-Iles, PQ, Canada [*Library symbol*].......CaQSi
Bibliotheque Municipale de Sherbrooke, Sherbrooke, PQ, Canada [*Library symbol*]............CaQSherN
Bibliotheque Municipale, Sorel, PQ, Canada [*Library symbol*] ....CaQSo
Bibliotheque Municipale, Ste-Foy, PQ, Canada [*Library symbol*].......CaQSF
Bibliotheque Municipale, Trois-Rivieres, PQ, Canada [*Library symbol*] ....CaQT
Bibliotheque Municipale, Victoriaville, PQ, Canada [*Library symbol*] ....CaQV
Bibliotheque Nationale [*A publication*]............BN
Bibliotheque Nationale de Luxembourg, Service du Pret, Luxembourg, Luxembourg [*Library symbol*] .... LuxLBN
Bibliotheque Nationale, Paris, France [*Library symbol*] ....FrPBN
Bibliotheque Nationale du Quebec, Montreal, PQ, Canada [*Library symbol*] ....CaQMBN
Bibliotheque des Nations Unies, Geneve, Switzerland [*Library symbol*] ....SzGBNU
Bibliotheque Norbertine [*A publication*]............BN
Bibliotheque de la Pleiade [*A publication*]............B de P
Bibliotheque Regional du Haut Saint-Jean, Edmundston, NB, Canada [*Library symbol*]............CaNBEBR
Bibliotheque Royale d'Albert 1er, American Studies Center, Bruxelles, Belgium [*Library symbol*]............Be-Am
Bibliotheque Royale d'Albert 1er, Bruxelles, Belgium [*Library symbol*]..... Be
Bibliotheque de Sociologie Contemporaine [*A publication*]............BSC
Bibliotheque des Textes Philosophiques [*A publication*] ....BTP
Bibliotheque de Theologie [*A publication*]............BT
Bibliotheque de Theologie Historique [*A publication*]............BTH
Bibliotheque Universelle et Revue Suisse [*A publication*]............BURS
Bibliotheque de la Ville de Montreal, Montreal, PQ, Canada [*Library symbol*]............CaQMBM
Biblische Zeitschrift [*A publication*]............BiblZ
Biblische Zeitschrift [*A publication*]............Bib Z
Biblische Zeitschrift [*A publication*]............BiZ
Biblische Zeitschrift [*A publication*]............BZ
Biblischer Kommentar. Altes Testament [*A publication*]............BKAT
Biblos [*A publication*]............Bi
Biblos [*A publication*]............Bib
Bic Pen Corp. [*American Stock Exchange symbol*]............BIC
Bicarbonate............BICARB
Bicaz [*Romania*] [*Seismograph station code, US Geological Survey*]............BIZ
Bicentennial Council of the Thirteen Original States [*Later, CTOS*]............BCTOS
Bicentennial Information Network [*American Revolution Bicentennial Administration*]............BINET
Bicentennial Junior Committees of Correspondence [*American Revolution Bicentennial Administration, US Postal Service, and National Association of Elementary School Principals*]............BJCC
Bicentennial Youth Debates [*National Endowment for the Humanities program*]............BYD
Biceps Jerk [*Neurology*]............BJ
Biceps Tendon [*Anatomy*]............BT
Bichon Frise Club of America............BFCA
Biciklista Esperantista Movado Internacia [*International Movement of Esperantist Bicyclists - IMEB*]............BEMI
Bickel's Coin and Medal News. Munt en Medaljenuus [*A publication*]............Bickel C M N
Bickford Corp. [*American Stock Exchange symbol*]............BIK
Bicolor Guaiac [*Test*] [*Medicine*]............BCG
Bicolor Guaiac [*Test*] [*Medicine*]............BG
Bicomponent [*Laboratory tubing*]............BC
Biconditional............BICOND
Biconvex............BCVX
Biculturalism and Bilingualism [*Canada*]............B & B
Biculturalism and Bilingualism [*Canada*]............BI & BI
Bicuspid [*Dentistry*]............B
Bicycle............BCL
Bicycle Club of America............BCA
Bicycle Federation............BF
Bicycle Institute of America [*Defunct*]............BIA
Bicycle Manufacturers Association............BMA
Bicycle Motocross............BMX
Bicycle-Motocross Industrial Guild............BIG
Bicycle Network............BN
Bicycle Study Unit [*American Topical Association*]............BSU
Bicycle Touring Club [*British*]............BTC
Bicycle Wholesale Distributors Association............BWDA
Bicycles on Stamps [*Study unit*] [*American Topical Association*]............BOS
Bid [*or Buyer*] [*NYSE symbol*]............B
Bid Bond Service Undertaking............BBSU

Bid Opening Date............BOD
Bid and Proposal............B & P
Biddeford, ME [*Radio station call letters*]............WBSF
Biddeford, ME [*Radio station call letters*]............WBYC-FM
Biddeford, ME [*Radio station call letters*]............WIDE
Biddeford, ME [*Television station call letters*]............WMEG-TV
Bidders Master File Listing [*DoD*]............BMFL
Bide-A-Wee Home Association............BAWHA
Bidirectional Categorical Grammar............BCG
Bidirectional Category System............BCS
Bidirectional Reference Array, Internally Derived [*Data processing*]............BRAID
Bids Accepted for the Following Vacancies............BAFVC
Bids Solicited............BDSLD
Bids Solicited as Follows............BSAF
Bidston [*England*] [*Seismograph station code, US Geological Survey*] [*Closed*]............BID
Bie [*Angola*] [*Airport symbol*]............SVP
Biekorf [*A publication*]............B
Biel's Microfilm Company, West Seneca, NY [*Library symbol*]............BMC
Bienen-Zeitung [*A publication*]............Bienen Ztg
Biennial [*A publication*]............B
Biennial............BE
Biennial............BIENN
Biennial Report. Hawaii Agricultural Experiment Station [*A publication*]............Bien Rep Hawaii Agr Exp Sta
Biennial Report. Iowa. Book of Agriculture. Iowa State Department of Agriculture [*A publication*]............Bien Rep Iowa Book Agr
Biennial Report. Nevada State Department of Agriculture [*A publication*]............Bien Rep Nev State Dept Agr
Biennial Review of Anthropology [*A publication*]............Bienn Rev Anthropol
Bienville Parish Library, Arcadia, LA [*Library symbol*]............LArB
Biflyx [*NASDAQ symbol*]............BIFL
Big............BG
Big B, Inc. [*NASDAQ symbol*]............BIGB
Big Bands Collectors' Club............BBCC
Big Bear [*California*] [*Seismograph station code, US Geological Survey*] [*Closed*]............BBC
Big Bear, Inc. [*NASDAQ symbol*]............BGBR
Big Bear Lake, CA [*Radio station call letters*]............KBBV
Big Bear Lake, CA [*Radio station call letters*]............KTOT-FM
Big Ben Report [*World War II*]............BENREP
Big Bend [*Idaho*] [*Seismograph station code, US Geological Survey*]............BBI
Big Bend [*Montana*] [*Seismograph station code, US Geological Survey*] [*Closed*]............BBM
Big Bend Community College, Moses Lake, WA [*Library symbol*]............WaMIB
Big Bend National Park............BIBE
Big Big Gastrin [*Endocrinology*]............BBG
Big Bite, Inc. [*NASDAQ symbol*]............BGBT
Big Brand Names [*i.e., well-established writers*] [*Publishing slang*]............BBN
Big Brother [*From George Orwell's "Nineteen Eighty-Four"*]............BB
Big Brothers of America [*Later, BB/BSA*]............BBA
Big Brothers/Big Sisters of America............BB/BSA
Big Brothers League............BBL
Big Close-Up [*A photograph or motion picture sequence taken from a short distance*]............BCU
Big Creek [*Nevada*] [*Seismograph station code, US Geological Survey*] [*Closed*]............BGN
Big Creek Baldy [*Montana*] [*Seismograph station code, US Geological Survey*] [*Closed*]............BCB
Big Deal [*A publication*]............Big D
Big Dumb Booster............BDB
Big Dutch Hollow [*Utah*] [*Seismograph station code, US Geological Survey*]............BDU
Big Eight Council on Black Student Government............BECBSG
Big European Bubble Chamber [*Nuclear particle detector*]............BEBC
Big Fine Deal............BFD
Big Hole National Battlefield............BIHO
Big Horn County Public Library, Hardin, MT [*Library symbol*]............MtHar
Big, Intrusive Government............BIG
Big Lake, AK [*Location identifier*] [*FAA*]............BGQ
Big Lake, TX [*Radio station call letters*]............KWGH
Big Lake, TX [*Location identifier*] [*FAA*]............LUJ
Big Little Book [*of comic strips*]............BLB
Big Look Improvement Program............BLIP
Big Lost River [*Idaho*] [*Seismograph station code, US Geological Survey*] [*Closed*]............LRI
Big Machine on Campus [*Computer*]............BMOC
Big Mahogany Desk............BMD
Big Mama Rag [*A publication*]............Big Mama
Big Man on Campus [*Slang*]............BMOC
Big Maria Mountains [*California*] [*Seismograph station code, US Geological Survey*]............BMM
Big Mountain [*Alaska*] [*Seismograph station code, US Geological Survey*]............BIG
Big Name Fan [*of science fiction or fantastic literature*] [*See also LNF*]....BNF
Big Pine Key, FL [*Radio station call letters*]............WWUS
Big Piney Oil & Gas [*NASDAQ symbol*]............BPIN
Big Plasma Glucagon [*Endocrinology*]............BPG
Big Rapids Community Library, Big Rapids, MI [*Library symbol*]............MiBr
Big Rapids, MI [*Radio station call letters*]............WAAQ

Big Rapids, MI [*Radio station call letters*] .... WBRN
Big Sandy, TX [*Location identifier*] [*FAA*] .... ABG
Big Sky Airlines [*Billings, MT*] [*FAA designator*] .... BSY
Big Spring, TX [*Location identifier*] [*FAA*] .... BGS
Big Spring, TX [*Radio station call letters*] .... KBST
Big Spring, TX [*Radio station call letters*] .... KBYG
Big Spring, TX [*Radio station call letters*] .... KKIK
Big Spring, TX [*Television station call letters*] .... KWAB-TV
Big Spring, TX [*Radio station call letters*] .... KWKI
Big Stone Gap, VA [*Radio station call letters*] .... WLSD
Big Stone Gap, VA [*Radio station call letters*] .... WLSD-FM
Big Table [*A publication*] .... BT
Big Thicket Association .... BTA
Big Thicket Coordinating Committee .... BTCC
Big Three Industries, Inc. [*NYSE symbol*] .... BIG
Big-Time Operator [*Slang*] .... BTO
Big Trout Lake [*Canada*] [*Airport symbol*] .... YTL
Big Ugly Fat Fellow [*Nickname for B-52 bomber*] .... BUFF
Big V Supermarkets, Inc. [*American Stock Exchange symbol*] .... BIV
Big White Set [*Type of lush movie set used in 1930's musical-comedy films*] .... BWS
Big Woman on Campus [*Slang*] .... BWOC
Bigaku [*A publication*] .... B
Bigelow-Sanford, Inc. [*NYSE symbol*] [*Delisted*] .... BGS
Biggs Free Public Library, Biggs, CA [*Library symbol*] .... CBi
Bighorn Canyon National Recreation Area .... BICA
Bihar Academy of Agricultural Sciences. Proceedings [*A publication*] .... Bihar Acad Agr Sci Proc
Biharmonic Equation .... BHE
Bihorium [*During Two Hours*] [*Pharmacy*] .... BIHOR
Bijdragen [*A publication*] .... Bi
Bijdragen tot de Dierkunde [*A publication*] .... Bijdr Dierk
Bijdragen tot de Geschiedenis [*A publication*] .... BG
Bijdragen tot de Geschiedenis Bijzonderlijk van het Aloude Hertogdom Brabant [*A publication*] .... BGHB
Bijdragen voor de Geschiedenis van het Bisdom van Haarlem [*A publication*] .... BGBH
Bijdragen voor de Geschiedenis der Nederlanden [*A publication*] .... BGN
Bijdragen voor de Geschiedenis der Nederlanden [*A publication*] .... Bijdr Gesch Ndl
Bijdragen voor de Geschiedenis van de Provincie der Minderbroeders in de Nederlanden [*A publication*] .... BGPMN
Bijdragen en Mededeelingen der Dialectencommissie van de Koninklijke Akademie van Wetenschappen te Amsterdam [*A publication*] .... Bijdragen Dialectencommissie
Bijdragen en Mededeelingen der Dialectencommissie van de Koninklijke Akademie van Wetenschappen te Amsterdam [*A publication*] .... BMD
Bijdragen en Mededeelingen der Dialectencommissie van de Koninklijke Akademie van Wetenschappen te Amsterdam [*A publication*] .... BMDial
Bijdragen en Mededeelingen van het Genootschap voor de Joodsche Wetenschap in Nederland [*A publication*] .... BMGJW
Bijdragen en Mededeelingen van het Historisch Genootschap [*A publication*] .... BMHG
Bijdragen en Mededeelingen Uitgegeven door de Vereeniging Geire [*A publication*] .... BMGeire
Bijdragen van de Philosophische en Theologische Faculteiten der Nederlandsche Jezuieten [*A publication*] .... BP
Bijdragen tot de Taal-Land-en Volkenkunde [*A publication*] .... Bijdrag Taal-Land- Volkenk
Bijdragen tot de Taal-Land-en Volkenkunde [*A publication*] .... BijdrTLV
Bijdragen tot de Taal-Land-en Volkenkunde [*A publication*] .... BTLV
Bijdragen tot de Taal-Land-en Volkenkunde van Nederlandsche-Indie [*A publication*] .... Bijdragen Nederl-Indie
Bijdragen tot de Taal-Land-en Volkenkunde van Nederlandsche-Indie [*A publication*] .... BTLVNI
Bijdragen Uitgegeven door en Philosophische en Theologische Faculteiten der Noord-en Zuid-Nederlandse Jezuieten [*A publication*] .... BFNJ
Bijdragen voor Vaderlandsche Geschiedenis en Oudheidskunde [*A publication*] .... BVG
Bijdragen voor Vaderlandsche Geschiedenis en Oudheidskunde [*A publication*] .... BVGO
Biken Journal [*A publication*] .... Biken J
Bikini Photo Drone .... BPD
Bilateral .... BIL
Bilateral .... BILAT
Bilateral Agreements .... BLA
Bilateral Impedance Rheograph [*Instrumentation*] .... BR
Bilateral Iterative Network .... BITN
Bilateral Salpingo-Oophorectomy [*Gynecology*] .... BSO
Bilbao [*Spain*] [*Airport symbol*] .... BIO
Bild der Wissenschaft [*A publication*] .... Bild Wiss
Bild der Wissenschaft. Zeitschrift ueber die Wissenschaften und die Technik in Unserer Zeit [*A publication*] .... Bild der Wissenschaft
Bild Zeitung [*Picture newspaper*] [*German*] .... BZ
Bilderberg Continuum Atmosphere .... BCA
Bildudalur [*Iceland*] [*Airport symbol*] .... BIU
Bile [*Blood group*] .... Bi
Bile Duct [*Medicine*] .... BD
Bile Duct Examination [*Medicine*] .... BDE
Bile Esculin [*Medicine*] .... BE
Bile-Salt Limited Lipase [*An enzyme*] .... BSL
Bilevel .... BL
Bilevel Quality Assurance Program [*NASA*] .... BQAP
Bilevel Response Unit .... BRU
Bilevel Stimulus Unit .... BSU
Bilingual Foundation of the Arts .... BFA
Bilingual Review/La Revista Bilingue [*A publication*] .... BR/RB
Bill Blass [*Couturier*] .... BB
Bill Book [*Shipping*] .... BB
Bill for Collection .... B/C
Bill of Entry [*Business and trade*] .... B/E
Bill of Exchange [*Business and trade*] .... BE
Bill of Health .... BH
Bill of Lading .... BILDG
Bill of Lading .... BL
Bill of Lading .... BLADING
Bill of Material .... BM
Bill of Material Processor .... BOMP
Bill of Parcels .... BP
Bill of Rights .... BR
Bill of Sale .... BS
Bill of Sight .... BS
Bill of Sight .... B/ST
Bill of Store .... BS
Bill Tomorrow [*Business and trade*] .... BT
Bill of Work .... BOW
Billboard [*A publication*] .... BB
Billboard [*A publication*] .... BILLA
Billboard Information Network [*Billboard Publications, Inc.*] [*Information service*] .... BIN
Billerica Historical Society, Billerica, MA [*Library symbol*] .... MBilHi
Billet .... BIL
Billet .... BL
Billet Sequence Code .... BSC
Billet Split Lens .... BSL
Billet Steel .... BLSTL
Billeting and Accommodations Advisory [*Military communications*] .... BAA
Billeting and Inventory [*Military*] .... B & I
Billets a Payer [*Bills Payable*] [*French*] .... BAP
Billets a Recevoir [*Bills Receivable*] [*French*] .... BAR
Billiard [*s*] [*Freight*] .... BILLD
Billiard and Bowling Institute of America .... BBIA
Billiard Congress of America .... BCA
Billiard Players Association of America .... BPA
Billiards .... BILL
Billing, Accounts Receivable, Sales Analysis .... BARSA
Billing and Instruction Book .... B & IB
Billing, Inventory Control, Accounts Receivable, Sales Analysis .... BICARSA
Billings [*Montana*] [*Airport symbol*] .... BIL
Billings Corp. [*NASDAQ symbol*] .... BIEN
Billings, MT [*Radio station call letters*] .... KBMY
Billings, MT [*Radio station call letters*] .... KEMC
Billings, MT [*Radio station call letters*] .... KGHL
Billings, MT [*Radio station call letters*] .... KIDX
Billings, MT [*Radio station call letters*] .... KOOK
Billings, MT [*Radio station call letters*] .... KOOK-FM
Billings, MT [*Radio station call letters*] .... KOYN
Billings, MT [*Radio station call letters*] .... KRER
Billings, MT [*Television station call letters*] .... KTVQ
Billings, MT [*Television station call letters*] .... KULR
Billings, MT [*Radio station call letters*] .... KURL
Billings, MT [*Radio station call letters*] .... KYYA
Billings, MT [*Radio station call letters*] .... KZLS
Billings Public Library, Billings, MT [*Library symbol*] .... MtBil
Billion .... B
Billion .... BIL
Billion .... BN
Billion Barrels .... BB
Billion Cubic Feet .... BCF
Billion Cubic Meters .... BCM
Billion Electron Volts .... BeV
Billion Floating-Point Operations per Second [*Data processing*] .... BFLOPS
Billion Gallons per Day .... BGD
Billion Instructions per Second [*Data processing*] .... BIPS
Billion Liters per Day .... BLD
Billion Years .... BY
Billion Years .... BYR
Billions of Barrels of Oil Equivalent .... BBOE
Billions of Cubic Feet per Day [*of gas*] .... BCFD
Bills Discounted .... BD
Bills of Lading Act .... BLA
Bills of Materials .... BOM
Bills Payable .... BP
Bills Receivable .... BR
Billund [*Denmark*] [*Airport symbol*] .... BLL
Billy Graham Evangelistic Association .... BGEA
Biloxi, MS [*Location identifier*] [*FAA*] .... BIX
Biloxi, MS [*Television station call letters*] .... WLOX-TV

Biloxi, MS [*Television station call letters*] WMAH
Biloxi, MS [*Radio station call letters*] WMAH-FM
Biloxi, MS [*Radio station call letters*] WQID
Biloxi, MS [*Radio station call letters*] WVMI
Biloxi Public Library, Biloxi, MS [*Library symbol*] MsB
Bilten za Hematologiju i Transfuziju [*A publication*] Bilt Hematol Transfuz
Bilten za Hmelj i Sirak [*A publication*] Bilt Hmelj Sirak
Biltrite Corp. [*American Stock Exchange symbol*] BRL
Bilychnis [*A publication*] Bil
Bima [*Indonesia*] [*Airport symbol*] BMU
Bimetal Turbine Wheel BTW
Bimetallic BMTLC
Bimini [*Bahamas*] [*Airport symbol*] BIM
Bimini-North [*Bahamas*] [*Airport symbol*] NSB
Bimolecular Lipid Membrane [*or Bilayer Membrane*] BLM
Bimonthly BI-M
Bimonthly BM
Bimonthly Progress Report BMPR
Bimonthly Progress Report BPR
Binary B
Binary BIN
Binary Add BA
Binary-Analog Conversion [*Data processing*] BAC
Binary Asymmetric Channel BAC
Binary Asymmetric Dependent Channel BADC
Binary Asymmetric Independent Channel BAIC
Binary Automatic Computer BINAC
Binary Automatic Data Annotation System BADAS
Binary Code BC
Binary Code Box BCB
Binary Code Frequency Shift Keying [*SAGE*] BCFSK
Binary-Coded Data [*or Decimal*] [*Data processing*] BCD
Binary-Coded Decimal/Binary BCD/B
Binary-Coded Decimal Counter BCDC
Binary-Coded Decimal Interchange Code BCDIC
Binary-Coded Decimal/Quaternary BCD/Q
Binary-Coded Hexadecimal BCH
Binary-Coded Hollerith BCH
Binary-Coded Information BCI
Binary-Coded Octal [*Data processing*] BCO
Binary-Coded Range Time BCRT
Binary-Coded Range Time Signal BCRTS
Binary Constitution Information Service BCIS
Binary Counter BC
Binary Counting Unit BCU
Binary to Decimal [*Data processing*] B/D
Binary to Decimal [*Data processing*] BTD
Binary-to-Decimal Converter [*Data processing*] BIDEC
Binary Decimal Counter [*Data processing*] BDC
Binary-to-Decimal Decoder [*Data processing*] BDD
Binary Deck-to-Tape [*Data processing*] BDT
Binary Decode Scaler [*Data processing*] BDS
Binary Decoder [*Data processing*] BD
Binary Delta Modulation BDM
Binary Digit [*Data processing*] BIT
Binary Digital Data [*Data processing*] BDD
Binary Digital Multiplier [*Data processing*] BDM
Binary Digits [*Data processing*] BITS
Binary Discrete BD
Binary Discriminant Analysis [*Statistics*] BDA
Binary Divide BD
Binary Electromagnetic Signal Signature BESS
Binary Encounter Approximation [*Nuclear physics*] BEA
Binary Error Erasure Channel BEEC
Binary Floating-Point Digital Differential Analyzer BFPDDA
Binary Frequency Generator BFG
Binary to Hexadecimal BH
Binary Homing Device BHD
Binary Information Exchange BIX
Binary Intersystem Transmission Standard BITS
Binary Light Beam Deflector BLBD
Binary Logic Element [*Data processing*] BLE
Binary Magnetic Core BMC
Binary Metal and Metalloid Constitution Data Center [*Illinois Institute of Technology*] BMMCDC
Binary Multiply BM
Binary Number [*Data processing*] BN
Binary Number System [*Data processing*] BNS
Binary to Octal [*Data processing*] BO
Binary Order of Magnitude [*Data processing*] BOM
Binary Output Program BOP
Binary Oxide Film [*Memory*] BOF
Binary Pattern Detector BIPAD
Binary Phase-Shift Keying [*Data processing*] BPSK
Binary Ring Sequence BRS
Binary Run Tape [*Data processing*] BRT
Binary Scale BS
Binary to Seven Segment [*Data processing*] BINSS
Binary Subtract BS
Binary Symmetric Channel [*Data processing*] BSC
Binary Symmetric Dependent Channel [*Data processing*] BSDC
Binary Symmetric Independent Channel [*Data processing*] BSIC
Binary Synchronous Communication [*Data processing*] BSC
Binary Synchronous Communications Adapter [*Data processing*] BSCA
Binary Synchronous Transmission [*Data processing*] BISYNC
Binary Voltage Weigher BVW
Binational Science Foundation [*US and Israel*] BSF
Binaural Intensity Effect BIE
Binaural Phase Effect BPE
Binder BDR
Binder BNDR
Binder BR
Binder Control Subsystem BINCOS
Binders' Guild BG
Binding BDG
Binding Capacity BC
Binding Energy BE
Binding Head BDGH
Binding Industries of America BIA
Binding Post BP
Binding Unit BU
Bindings [*Publishing*] BDS
Bindley Western Industries [*NASDAQ symbol*] BIND
Bing Crosby Productions BCP
Bingham Oceanographic Collection BOC
Bingham Township Library, Suttons Bay, MI [*Library symbol*] MiSb
Binghamton [*New York*] [*Airport symbol*] BGM
Binghamton [*New York*] [*Seismograph station code, US Geological Survey*] BNY
Binghamton, NY [*Location identifier*] [*FAA*] AAJ
Binghamton, NY [*Radio station call letters*] WAAL
Binghamton, NY [*Television station call letters*] WBNG-TV
Binghamton, NY [*Radio station call letters*] WHRW
Binghamton, NY [*Television station call letters*] WICZ-TV
Binghamton, NY [*Radio station call letters*] WINR
Binghamton, NY [*Radio station call letters*] WKOP
Binghamton, NY [*Television station call letters*] WMGC-TV
Binghamton, NY [*Radio station call letters*] WNBF
Binghamton, NY [*Radio station call letters*] WQYT
Binghamton, NY [*Television station call letters*] WSKG
Binghamton, NY [*Radio station call letters*] WSKG-FM
Binghamton Public Library, Binghamton, NY [*Library symbol*] NBi
Bingo Clubs and Halls [*Public-performance tariff class*] [*British*] BO
Bingo King Co. [*NASDAQ symbol*] BNGO
Biniguni [*Papua New Guinea*] [*Airport symbol*] XBN
Binks Manufacturing Co. [*American Stock Exchange symbol*] BIN
Binnacle BNCL
Binnenschiffahrts-Nachrichten [*A publication*] Binnenschiffahrts-Nachr
Binney & Smith, Inc. [*NYSE symbol*] BYS
Binocular BNCLR
Binocular Deprivation [*Optics*] BD
Binocular Visual Efficiency BVE
Binomial Expansion [*Mathematics*] BINOMEXP
Binominal Proportion Test BITEST
Bintulu [*Malaysia*] [*Airport symbol*] BTU
Bintuni [*Indonesia*] [*Airport symbol*] NTI
Binza [*Leopoldville*] [*Zaire*] [*Geomagnetic observatory code*] BIN
Binza [*Leopoldville*] [*Zaire*] [*Seismograph station code, US Geological Survey*] BIN
Bio-Degradable Plastics, Incorporated BPI
Bio-Dynamic Farming and Gardening Association BDFGA
Bio-Dynamics, Inc., BMC Library, Indianapolis, IN [*Library symbol*] InIBio
Bio-Energy Council BEC
Bio-Feedback Research Society [*Later, BSA*] BFRS
Bio-Gas of Colorado, Inc. [*NASDAQ symbol*] BIOG
Bio-Logic Systems [*NASDAQ symbol*] BLSC
Bio Logicals, Inc. [*NASDAQ symbol*] BIOLF
Bio-Medical Purview [*A publication*] Bio-Med Purv
Bio-Medical Reports of the 406 Medical Laboratory [*A publication*] Bio-Med Rep 406 Med Lab
Bio-Medicus, Inc. [*NASDAQ symbol*] BMDS
Bio-Rad Laboratories, Inc. [*American Stock Exchange symbol*] BIO
Bio-Research Laboratories Ltd., Pointe-Claire, PQ, Canada [*Library symbol*] CaQMBR
Bio-Response, Inc. [*NASDAQ symbol*] BIOR
Bio-Sciences Information Exchange [*Smithsonian Institution*] BSIE
Bio Systems [*A publication*] Bio Syst
Bio-Technology General [*NASDAQ symbol*] BTGC
Bioaccumulation Factor [*Nuclear energy*] BAF
Bioanalytical Systems BAS
Bioassay Program BP
Bioassay Tank [*Spacecraft*] [*NASA*] BAT
Bioastronautic Orbiting Space Station [*or System*] BOSS
Bioastronautics Laboratory Research Tool BIOALRT
Bioastronautics Operational Support Unit BOSU
Bioastronautics Orbital Space Program [*Air Force*] BOSP
Biobreeding/Worcester [*Rat variety*] BB/W
Biocell Technology [*NASDAQ symbol*] BICL
Biochem International, Inc. [*NASDAQ symbol*] BIOC
Biochemical and Biophysical Perspectives in Marine Biology [*A publication*] Biochem Biophys Perspect Mar Biol

Biochemical and Biophysical Research Communications [*A publication*]....Bioc Biop R
Biochemical and Biophysical Research Communications [*A publication*]....Biochem Biophys Res Commun
Biochemical Genetics [*A publication*]....Biochem Gen
Biochemical Genetics [*A publication*]....Biochem Genet
Biochemical Journal [*A publication*]....Biochem J
Biochemical Medicine [*A publication*]....Biochem Med
Biochemical Modeling [*Data processing*]....BIOMOD
Biochemical Oxygen Demand....BOD
Biochemical Pharmacology [*A publication*]....Biochem Pharmacol
Biochemical Pharmacology [*A publication*]....Bioch Pharm
Biochemical Preparations [*A publication*]....Biochem Prep
Biochemical Reviews (Bangalore) [*A publication*]....Biochem Rev (Bangalore)
Biochemical Society....BS
Biochemical Society. Special Publications [*A publication*]....Biochem Soc Spec Publ
Biochemical Society. Symposia [*A publication*]....Biochem Soc Symp
Biochemical Society. Transactions [*A publication*]....Biochem Soc Trans
Biochemical Society. Transactions [*A publication*]....Bioch Soc T
Biochemical Systematics and Ecology [*A publication*]....Biochem Syst Ecol
Biochemie und Physiologie der Pflanzen [*A publication*]....Biochem Physiol Pflanz
Biochemie und Physiologie der Pflanzen [*A publication*]....Bioc Phy Pf
Biochemie und Physiologie der Pflanzen [*A publication*]....BPP
Biochemische Zeitschrift [*A publication*]....Biochem Z
Biochemistry [*A publication*]....Biochem
Biochemistry and Experimental Biology [*A publication*]....Biochem Exp Biol
Biochemistry-USSR [*A publication*]....Biochem SSR
Biochimica Applicata [*A publication*]....Biochim Appl
Biochimica e Biologia Sperimentale [*A publication*]....Biochim Biol Sper
Biochimica et Biophysica Acta [*A publication*]....Bioc Biop A
Biochimica et Biophysica Acta [*A publication*]....Biochim Biophys Acta
Biochimica et Biophysica Acta. B. Bioenergetics [*A publication*]....Biochim Biophys Acta B
Biochimica et Biophysica Acta. B. Bioenergetics [*A publication*]....Biochim Biophys Acta Bioenerg
Biochimica et Biophysica Acta. Biomembranes [*A publication*]....Biochim Biophys Acta Biomembranes
Biochimica et Biophysica Acta. BR. Reviews on Bioenergetics [*A publication*]....Biochim Biophys Acta BR
Biochimica et Biophysica Acta. Enzymology [*A publication*]....Biochim Biophys Acta Enzymol
Biochimica et Biophysica Acta. G. General Subjects [*A publication*]....Biochim Biophys Acta G
Biochimica et Biophysica Acta. Lipids and Lipid Metabolism [*A publication*]....Biochim Biophys Acta Lipids Lipid Metab
Biochimica et Biophysica Acta. M. Biomembranes [*A publication*]....Biochim Biophys Acta M
Biochimica et Biophysica Acta. MR. Reviews on Biomembranes [*A publication*]....Biochim Biophys Acta MR
Biochimica et Biophysica Acta. P. Protein Structure [*A publication*]....Biochim Biophys Acta P
Biochimica et Biophysica Acta. P. Protein Structure [*A publication*]....Biochim Biophys Acta Protein Struct
Bioclimat Numero Special [*A publication*]....Bioclimat Numero Spec
Bioconcentration Factor [*of chemicals by living organisms*]....BCF
Biocular Display Driver's Viewer....BDDV
Biodeterioration Information Centre [*British*]....BIC
Bioelectrochemistry....BEC
Bioelectrochemistry and Bioenergetics [*A publication*]....Bioelectr B
Bioelectrochemistry and Bioenergetics [*A publication*]....Bioelectrochem Bioenerg
Bioelectromagnetics Society....BEMS
Bioengineering....BIOENG
Biofeedback....BFB
Biofeedback Research Society [*Formerly, BFRS*] [*Later, BSA*]....BRS
Biofeedback and Self-Regulation [*A publication*]....BGGPB
Biofeedback and Self-Regulation [*A publication*]....Biofeedback Self-Regul
Biofeedback Society of America [*Formerly, BFRS, BRS*]....BSA
Biofeedback Training [*Physiology*]....BFT
Bioferm Corp., Research Library, Wasco, CA [*Library symbol*]....CWasB
Biofizika [*A publication*]....BIOFA
Biofizika [*A publication*]....Biofiz
Biogen NV [*NASDAQ symbol*]....BGENF
Biogenic Institutes of America [*Later, AHMI*]....BIA
Biogenic Silica [*In water sediments*]....BSI
Biographical Dictionaries and Related Works [*A publication*]....BD
Biographical Dictionaries and Related Works. Supplement [*A publication*]....BDS
Biographical Dictionary of Federal Judiciary [*A publication*]....BDFJ
Biographical Dictionary Master Index [*A publication*]....BDMI
Biographical Information Blank....BIB
Biographical Inventory Creativity....BIC
Biographical Inventory for Medicine....BIM
Biographical Inventory for Students [*Psychology*]....BIS
Biographical Memoirs. National Academy of Sciences [*A publication*]....Biogr Mem Natl Acad Sci
Biographics....BIO
Biographien Hervorragender Naturwissenschaftler, Techniker, und Mediziner [*A publication*]....Biogr Hervorragender Naturwiss Tech Med
Biography....BIOG
Biography and Genealogy Master Index [*A publication*]....BGMI
Biography Index [*A publication*]....Biog Ind
Biography Index [*A publication*]....Biol
Biography Master Index [*A publication*]....BMI
Biography News [*A publication*]....BN
Bioinorganic Chemistry [*A publication*]....Bioinorg Ch
Bioinorganic Chemistry [*A publication*]....Bioinorg Chem
Bioinstrumentation Advisory Council [*Defunct*]....BIAC
Bioinstrumentation Harness Assembly....BHA
Bioisolator Suit System....BISS
Biokhimiya [*A publication*]....Biokhim
Biokon Reports [*A publication*]....Biokon Rep
Biola College, La Mirada, CA [*OCLC symbol*]....CBC
Biola Library, La Mirada, CA [*Library symbol*]....CLamB
Biologia (Bratislava) [*A publication*]....Biol (Bratislava)
Biologia. Casopis Slovenskej Akademie vied Bratislava [*A publication*]....Biologia Bratisl
Biologia Culturale [*A publication*]....BioC
Biologia Culturale [*A publication*]....Biol Culturale
Biologia Gabonica [*A publication*]....Biol Gabonica
Biologia Gallo-Hellenica [*A publication*]....Biol Gallo-Hell
Biologia et Industria [*A publication*]....Biol Ind
Biologia Neonatorum [*Later, Biology of the Neonate*] [*A publication*]....Biol Neonatorum
Biologia Pesquera [*A publication*]....Biol Pesq
Biologia Plantarum [*A publication*]....Biologia Pl
Biologia Plantarum [*A publication*]....Biol Plant
Biologiai Koezlemenyek [*A publication*]....Biol Koezl
Biologiai Koezlemenyek [*A publication*]....Biol Koezlem
Biologica Latina [*A publication*]....Biol Lat
Biological Abstracts [*A publication*]....BA
Biological Abstracts [*A publication*]....BioAb
Biological Abstracts [*A publication*]....Biol Abs
Biological Abstracts/Reports, Reviews, Meetings [*Formerly, BIOI*] [*A publication*]....BA/RRM
Biological Abstracts' Subjects in Context [*A publication*]....BASIC
Biological Abstracts on Tape....BAT
Biological Aerosol Detection [*Army*]....BAD
Biological and Agricultural Index [*A publication*]....BAI
Biological and Agricultural Index [*A publication*]....BioAg
Biological and Agricultural Index [*A publication*]....Biol & Agr Ind
Biological Agricultural Reactor of the Netherlands....BARN
Biological Analysis Detection Instrumentation and Control....BADIC
Biological Assessment Laboratory....BAL
Biological, Behavioral, and Social Sciences [*Directorate*]....BBS
Biological Bulletin [*A publication*]....Biol B
Biological Bulletin [*A publication*]....Biol Bul
Biological Bulletin [*A publication*]....Biol Bull
Biological Bulletin. Department of Biology. College of Science. Tunghai University [*A publication*]....Biol Bull Dep Biol Coll Sci Tunghai Univ
Biological Bulletin (Woods Hole) [*A publication*]....Biol Bull (Woods Hole)
Biological/Chemical Attack Report....BIOREP/CHEMREP
Biological and Chemical Warfare....BC
Biological and Chemical Warfare....BCW
Biological and Chemical Warfare Division [*DoD*]....BCWD
Biological and Climatic Effects Research....BACER
Biological Conference "Oholo." Annual Meeting [*A publication*]....Biol Conf "Oholo" Annu Meet
Biological Conservation [*A publication*]....Biol Conser
Biological Conservation [*A publication*]....Biol Conserv
Biological Control of Insects Research Laboratory [*Department of Agriculture*]....BCIRL
Biological Control and Rearing of Insects Research Unit [*Department of Agriculture*]....BCRI
Biological Cybernetics [*A publication*]....BICYA
Biological Cybernetics [*A publication*]....Biol Cybern
Biological Damage Indicator....BDI
Biological Defense [*Military*]....BIODEF
Biological Defense [*Military*]....BIOLDEF
Biological Defense Research Laboratory....BDRL
Biological Defense System....BDS
Biological Detection System....BDS
Biological Effects of Atomic Radiation....BEAR
Biological Effects [*of Nonionizing*] **Electromagnetic Radiation**....BEER
Biological Effects of Ionizing Radiations....BEIR
Biological Electronics....BIONICS
Biological and Environmental Research Program [*Department of Energy*]....BER
Biological False Positive [*Clinical chemistry*]....BFP
Biological Half-Life....BHL
Biological Handbooks [*A publication*]....Biol Handb
Biological Hazard Potential [*Atomic energy*]....BHP
Biological Indicator [*Microbiology*]....BI
Biological Indicator Unit [*Food testing*]....BIU
Biological Information-Processing Organization [*Later, SIGBIO*]....BIO
Biological Inventory....BI

Biological Investigation of Space [*NASA*] .... BIOS
Biological Isolation Garment [*NASA*] .... BIG
Biological Journal of the Linnean Society [*A publication*] .... Biol J Linn
Biological Journal of the Linnean Society [*A publication*] .... Biol J Linn Soc
Biological Journal of Nara Women's University [*A publication*] .... Biol J Nara Women's Univ
Biological Journal of Okayama University [*A publication*] .... Biol J Okayama Univ
Biological Laboratory .... BL
Biological Laboratory, Brunswick, Georgia [*US Bureau of Commercial Fisheries; later, National Marine Fisheries Service*] .... BLBG
Biological Macromolecules [*A publication*] .... Biol Macromol
Biological Membranes [*A publication*] .... Biol Membr
Biological Nuclear Solvent [*Physiology*] .... BNS
Biological Operations [*Military*] .... BIOLOP
Biological Origin .... BO
Biological Oxygen Demand .... BOD
Biological Packs .... BIOPACK
Biological Papers. University of Alaska [*A publication*] .... Biol Pap Univ Alaska
Biological Papers. University of Alaska. Special Report [*A publication*] .... Biol Pap Univ Alaska Spec Rep
Biological Photographic Association .... BPA
Biological Psychiatry [*A publication*] .... Biol Psychi
Biological Psychiatry [*A publication*] .... Biol Psychiatry
Biological Psychiatry [*A publication*] .... BIPCB
Biological Psychology [*A publication*] .... Biol Psychol
Biological Psychology [*A publication*] .... BLPYA
Biological Radio Communications .... BRC
Biological Records Centre [*British*] [*Information service*] .... BRC
Biological Report .... BIOLREPT
Biological Report .... BIOREP
Biological Research .... BIOLRSCH
Biological Research .... BR
Biological Research Center [*Philippines*] .... BRC
Biological Research Institute .... BRI
Biological Research Module [*NASA*] .... BRM
Biological Research Resources .... BRR
Biological Resources Development Teams .... BIORED
Biological Response Modifiers Program .... BRMP
Biological Response Modulator .... BRM
Biological Reviews [*A publication*] .... Biol R
Biological Reviews [*A publication*] .... Biol Rs
Biological Reviews. Cambridge Philosophical Society [*A publication*] .... Biol Rev
Biological Reviews. Cambridge Philosophical Society [*A publication*] .... Biol Rev Camb Philos Soc
Biological Reviews. Cambridge Philosophical Society [*A publication*] .... Biol Rev Cambridge Phil Soc
Biological Safety Officer [*National Institutes of Health*] .... BSO
Biological Satellite .... BIOS
Biological Satellite .... BIOSAT
Biological Science [*A publication*] .... Biol Sci
Biological Sciences Communication Project [*American Institute of Biological Sciences*] .... BSCP
Biological Sciences Curriculum Study [*National Science Foundation*] .... BSCS
Biological Sciences Curriculum Study. Bulletin [*A publication*] .... Biol Sci Curriculum Study Bull
Biological, Social, Machine [*Combination*] .... BIOSOMA
Biological Society of Nevada. Memoirs [*A publication*] .... Biol Soc Nev Mem
Biological Society of Nevada. Occasional Papers [*A publication*] .... Biol Soc Nev Occas Pap
Biological Society of Pakistan. Monograph [*A publication*] .... Biol Soc Pak Monogr
Biological Society of Washington. Proceedings [*A publication*] .... Biol Soc Washington Proc
Biological Society of Washington. Proceedings [*A publication*] .... Biol Soc Wash Proc
Biological Stain Commission .... BSC
Biological Value .... BV
Biological Warfare .... BIOWAR
Biological Warfare .... BW
Biological Warfare/Chemical Warfare .... BW/CW
Biological Warfare Laboratory .... BWL
Biological Warfare Rapid Warning System [*Army*] .... BWRWS
Biological Weapon System .... BIOLWPNSYS
Biological Weapons [*Military*] .... BIOLWPN
Biological Weapons [*Military*] .... BW
Biological Weapons System [*Military*] .... BIOLWPNSYS
Biological Weapons System [*Military*] .... BWS
Biologicheskie Nauki [*Moscow*] [*A publication*] .... Biol Nauki
Biologicheskie Nauki (Moscow) [*A publication*] .... Biol Nauki (Mosc)
Biologicheskii Zhurnal Armenii [*A publication*] .... Biol Zh Arm
Biologicke Listy [*A publication*] .... Biol Listy
Biologicke Prace [*A publication*] .... Biol Pr
Biologie et Gastro-Enterologie [*A publication*] .... Biol Gastro
Biologie et Gastro-Enterologie [*A publication*] .... Biol Gastro-Enterol
Biologie Medical Milano. Edizione per l'Italia [*Milano*] [*A publication*] .... Biol Med Milano Ed Ital
Biologie Medicale (Paris) [*A publication*] .... Biol Med (Paris)
Biologie du Sol. Bulletin International d'Informations [*A publication*] .... Biol Sol
Biologie du Sol. Microbiologie [*A publication*] .... Biol Sol Microbiol
Biologie in Unserer Zeit [*A publication*] .... Biol Unserer Zeit
Biologisch Jaarboek [*A publication*] .... Biol Jaarb
Biologische Abhandlungen [*A publication*] .... Biol Abh
Biologische Rundschau [*A publication*] .... Biol Rdsch
Biologische Rundschau [*A publication*] .... Biol Rundsch
Biologische Rundschau [*A publication*] .... Biol Rundschau
Biologisches Zentralblatt [*A publication*] .... Biol Zbl
Biologisches Zentralblatt [*A publication*] .... Biol Zentralbl
Biologiske Meddelelser [*A publication*] .... Biol Meddr
Biologiske Meddelelser Kongelige Danske Videnskabernes Selskab [*A publication*] .... Biol Medd K Dan Vidensk Selsk
Biologiya Morya (Vladivostok) [*A publication*] .... Biol Morya (Vladivost)
Biologiya Vnutrennykh Vod Informatsionii Byulleten' [*A publication*] .... Biol Vnutr Vod Inf Byull
Biology [*or Biological*] .... BIO
Biology .... BIOL
Biology Bulletin of the Academy of Sciences of the USSR [*A publication*] .... Biol Bull Acad Sci USSR
Biology Digest [*A publication*] .... Biol Dig
Biology and Human Affairs [*A publication*] .... Biol Hum Aff
Biology of the Neonate [*A publication*] .... Biol Neonat
Biology of Reproduction [*A publication*] .... Biol Reprod
Biology Unit [*American Topical Association*] .... BU
Bioloski Glasnik [*A publication*] .... Biol Glas
Bioloski Vestnik [*A publication*] .... Biol Vestn
Bioluminescence .... BL
Biomass Energy Coordinating Committee [*Department of Energy*] .... BECC
Biomass Energy Research Association .... BERA
Biomass Energy Systems Program [*Department of Energy*] .... BES
Biomass Protein .... BMP
Biomaterials, Medical Devices, and Artificial Organs [*A publication*] .... Biomater Med Devices Artif Organs
Biomaterials, Medical Devices, and Artificial Organs [*A publication*] .... Biomat Med
Biomedical .... BIOMED
Biomedical .... BMD
Biomedical Application Teams [*NASA*] .... BAT
Biomedical Belt [*NASA*] .... BMB
Biomedical Communications [*A publication*] .... Biomed Commun
Biomedical Communications Inventory [*National Library of Medicine*] .... BCI
Biomedical Communications Network [*Proposed*] [*National Library of Medicine*] .... BCN
Biomedical Computing Council of California Universities .... BCCCU
Biomedical Computing Society [*Later, SIGBIO*] .... BCS
Biomedical Computing Technology Information Center [*Department of Energy*] .... BCTIC
Biomedical Data Analysis and Display System [*NASA*] .... BMDADS
Biomedical Display Unit .... BDU
Biomedical Electronics .... BME
Biomedical Engineering [*New York*] [*A publication*] .... Biomed Eng
Biomedical Engineering Current Awareness Notification [*A publication*] .... BECAN
Biomedical Engineering and Instrumentation Branch [*National Institutes of Health*] .... BEIB
Biomedical Engineering (London) [*A publication*] .... Biomed Eng (Lond)
Biomedical Engineering (New York) [*A publication*] .... Biomed Eng (NY)
Biomedical Engineering Research Corporation [*Illinois*] .... BERC
Biomedical Engineering Society .... BMES
Biomedical Equipment Technology .... BMET
Biomedical Experiment Scientific Satellite .... BESS
Biomedical Instrumentation Consultant .... BIC
Biomedical Interdisciplinary Curriculum Project [*National Science Foundation*] .... BICP
Biomedical Laboratory, Aberdeen Proving Grounds, MD [*OCLC symbol*] .... ADF
Biomedical Marketing Association .... BMA
Biomedical Mass Spectrometry [*A publication*] .... Biomed Mass
Biomedical Mass Spectrometry [*A publication*] .... Biomed Mass Spectrom
Biomedical Monitoring System .... BMS
Biomedical Recovery Capsule .... BRC
Biomedical Research Development Grants .... BRDG
Biomedical Research Support Grants .... BRSG
Biomedical Sciences Corps [*Air Force*] .... BSC
Biomedical Sciences Instrumentation [*A publication*] .... Biomed Sci Instrum
Biomedical Sciences Instrumentation [*A publication*] .... BMSIA
Biomedical Signal Conditioner .... BSC
Biomedical Studies Section [*Oak Ridge National Laboratory*] .... BMS
Biomedical Technology Transfer Team .... BATEAM
Biomedical Urine Sampling System .... BUSS
Biomedicine Express [*Paris*] [*A publication*] .... Biomed Expr
Biomedicine Express (Paris) [*A publication*] .... Biomed Express (Paris)
Biomedizinische Technik [*Berlin*] [*A publication*] .... Biomed Tech
Biomedizinische Technik (Berlin) [*A publication*] .... Biomed Tech (Berlin)
Biomedizinische Technik. Biomedical Engineering [*A publication*] .... Biomed Tech Biomed Eng
Biomet, Inc. [*NASDAQ symbol*] .... BMET
Biometric Society .... BS
Biometrical Journal [*A publication*] .... Biometrical J

Biometrical Journal [*A publication*] .... Biom J
Biometrics [*A publication*] .... Biom
Biometrie Humaine [*A publication*] .... Biometrie Hum
Biometrie-Praximetrie [*A publication*] .... Biomet-Praximet
Biometrika [*A publication*] .... Biom
Biometrische Zeitschrift [*A publication*] .... Biometr Z
Biometrische Zeitschrift [*A publication*] .... Biom Z
Biometrische Zeitschrift [*A publication*] .... Biom Zeit
Bionetics Research Laboratory .... BRL
Bionex Corp. [*NASDAQ symbol*] .... BIOXF
Bionics Adaptive Network .... BAN
Bionucleonics .... BIONUCL
Bioorganic Chemistry [*A publication*] .... Bioorg Chem
Bioorganicheskaya Khimiya [*A publication*] .... Bioorg Khim
Biopack [*NASA*] .... BP
Biopack Subsystem [*NASA*] .... BPSS
Biopharmaceutics and Drug Disposition [*A publication*] .... Biopharm Drug Dispos
Biophysical Chemistry [*A publication*] .... Biophys Ch
Biophysical Chemistry [*A publication*] .... Biophys Chem
Biophysical Journal [*A publication*] .... Biophys J
Biophysical Society .... BP
Biophysical Society .... BPS
Biophysical Society .... BS
Biophysical Society. Annual Meeting Abstracts [*A publication*] .... Biophys Soc Annu Meet Abstr
Biophysical Society. Symposium [*A publication*] .... Biophys Soc Symp
Biophysics [*A publication*] .... Biophys
Biophysics of Structure and Mechanism [*A publication*] .... Biophys Str
Biophysics of Structure and Mechanism [*A publication*] .... Biophys Struct & Mech
Biopsy [*Medicine*] .... BX
Bioradiotelemetric System .... BRTS
BioResearch Index [*Superseded by BA/RRM*] [*A publication*] .... BIOI
BioResearch Index [*Superseded by BA/RRM*] [*A publication*] .... BRI
BioResearch Titles .... BRT
Biorka [*Alaska*] [*Seismograph station code, US Geological Survey*] [*Closed*] .... BIO
BioScience [*A publication*] .... BioSci
Bioscience Program [*NASA*] .... BP
Bioscience Report. Abo Akademi [*A publication*] .... Biosci Rep Abo Akad
Bioscience Reports [*A publication*] .... Biosci Rep
Biosciences Communications [*A publication*] .... Biosci Commun
Biosciences Information Service [*Information service*] .... BIOSIS
Biosearch Medical Products [*NASDAQ symbol*] .... BMPI
Biosedra [*France*] [*Research code symbol*] .... B
Biosensor Corp. [*NASDAQ symbol*] .... BSNR
Bioshield Power Assembly [*NASA*] .... BPA
Bioshield Pyrotechnic Control Assembly [*for Mariner Venus-Mercury Project spacecraft*] [*NASA*] .... BPCA
BIOSIS Information Transfer Service .... BITS
Biosonics, Inc. [*NASDAQ symbol*] .... BIOS
Biosophical Institute, Incorporated [*Defunct*] .... BII
Biospherics, Inc. [*NASDAQ symbol*] .... BSPR
Biostatistics .... BIOSTAT
Biostim, Inc. [*NASDAQ symbol*] .... BIOZ
Biosynergy, Inc. [*NASDAQ symbol*] .... BSYN
Biosynthetic Human Insulin [*Medicine*] .... BHI
Biot [*Also, aA*] [*Unit of electric current*] .... Bi
Biot-Savart Law [*Physics*] .... BSL
Biotech Capital Corp. [*NASDAQ symbol*] .... BITC
Biotech Research Laboratories [*NASDAQ symbol*] .... BTRL
Biotechnia International, Inc. [*NASDAQ symbol*] .... BIOT
Biotechnology .... BT
Biotechnology and Bioengineering [*A publication*] .... Biotech Bio
Biotechnology and Bioengineering [*A publication*] .... Biotechnol Bioeng
Biotechnology and Bioengineering. Symposium [*A publication*] .... Biotechnol Bioeng Symp
Biotechnology Development [*NASDAQ symbol*] .... BIOD
Biotechnology and Human Research .... BHR
Biotechnology Orbital Laboratory .... BOL
Biotelemetry [*Later, Biotelemetry and Patient Monitoring*] [*A publication*] .... Biotelemetr
Biotelemetry and Patient Monitoring [*A publication*] .... Biotelem Patient Monit
Biotelemetry System .... BTS
Biotic Potential .... BP
Biotin Carboxyl Carrier Protein [*Biochemistry*] .... BCCP
Biparietal Diameter [*Gynecology*] .... BP
Biparietal Diameter [*Gynecology*] .... BPD
Biparting Door .... BIPD
Bipartite Board [*Post-World War II, Germany*] .... BIB
Bipartite Civil Aviation Panel [*Post-World War II, Germany*] .... BCAP
Bipartite Civil Service Advisors [*Post-World War II, Germany*] .... BICIV
Bipartite Communications Panel [*Post-World War II, Germany*] .... BICOM
Bipartite Control Office [*Post-World War II, Germany*] .... BICO
Bipartite Decartelization Commission [*Berlin*] [*Post-World War II, Germany*] .... BIDEC
Bipartite Decartelization Sub-Commission [*Minden*] [*Post-World War II, Germany*] .... BIDESC
Bipartite Economic Panel [*Post-World War II, Germany*] .... BIECO
Bipartite Economic Panel Railway Supplies Committee [*Post-World War II, Germany*] .... BIECO/RAIL
Bipartite Economics Control Group [*Post-World War II, Germany*] .... BECG
Bipartite Finance Panel [*Post-World War II, Germany*] .... BIFIN
Bipartite Food and Agriculture Panel [*Post-World War II, Germany*] .... BIF & A
Bipartite News Office [*Post-World War II, Germany*] .... BNO
Bipartite Secretariat [*Post-World War II, Germany*] .... BISEC
Bipartite Transport Control Group [*Post-World War II, Germany*] .... BTCG
Biphenylamine [*Organic chemistry*] .... BPA
(Biphenylyl)phenyloxazole [*Organic chemistry*] .... BPO
Bipiperidyl Mustard [*Pharmacology*] .... BPM
Biplane .... B
Biplane Experimental [*Aircraft*] [*World War I*] .... BE
Bipolar Active-Plastic Cell .... BAC
Bipolar Cell [*In the retina*] .... BC
Bipolar Insulated Gate Field-Effect Transistor [*Bell Laboratories*] .... BIGFET
Bipolar Junction Transistor [*Electronics*] .... BJT
Bipolar Metal-Oxide Semiconductor .... BiMOS
Bipolar Operational Amplifier .... BOA
Bipost .... BPT
Bipropellant .... BIP
Bipropellant Valve .... BPV
BIR [*British Institute of Radiology*] **Bulletin** [*A publication*] .... BIR Bull
Biratnagar [*Nepal*] [*Airport symbol*] .... BIR
Birbal Sahni Institute of Palaeobotany. Special Publication [*A publication*] .... Birbal Sahni Inst Palaeobot Spec Publ
Birch Creek [*Alaska*] [*Airport symbol*] .... KBC
Birch Hill [*Alaska*] [*Seismograph station code, US Geological Survey*] [*Closed*] .... BRH
Birch, Raymond Sr., Southampton PA [*STAC*] .... BRS
Birch Tree, MO [*Radio station call letters*] .... KBMV
Bird Association of California .... BAC
Bird-Banding [*A publication*] .... Bird-Band
Bird Effort [*A publication*] .... Bird E
Bird-Fanciers Lung [*Medicine*] .... BFL
Bird Friends Society .... BFS
Bird, Inc. [*NASDAQ symbol*] .... BIRD
Bird Island [*Seychelles Islands*] [*Airport symbol*] .... BDI
Bird Resistant [*Sorghum variety*] .... BR
Birdsville [*Australia*] [*Airport symbol*] .... BVI
Birdview Satllite [*NASDAQ symbol*] .... BVSC
Birger Sjoberg Sallskapet [*A publication*] .... BSS
Birkenhead [*British depot code*] .... BHD
Birmingham [*City, county borough, and university in England*] .... BHAM
Birmingham [*Alabama*] [*Airport symbol*] .... BHM
Birmingham [*England*] [*Airport symbol*] .... BHX
Birmingham [*City, county borough, and university in England*] .... BIRM
Birmingham, AL [*Location identifier*] [*FAA*] .... VUZ
Birmingham, AL [*Radio station call letters*] .... WAGG
Birmingham, AL [*Radio station call letters*] .... WAPI
Birmingham, AL [*Radio station call letters*] .... WAPI-FM
Birmingham, AL [*Radio station call letters*] .... WATV
Birmingham, AL [*Radio station call letters*] .... WBHM
Birmingham, AL [*Television station call letters*] .... WBMG-TV
Birmingham, AL [*Television station call letters*] .... WBRC-TV
Birmingham, AL [*Television station call letters*] .... WCAJ
Birmingham, AL [*Radio station call letters*] .... WCRT
Birmingham, AL [*Radio station call letters*] .... WDJC
Birmingham, AL [*Radio station call letters*] .... WENN-FM
Birmingham, AL [*Radio station call letters*] .... WERC
Birmingham, AL [*Radio station call letters*] .... WGIB
Birmingham, AL [*Radio station call letters*] .... WJSR
Birmingham, AL [*Radio station call letters*] .... WKXX
Birmingham, AL [*Radio station call letters*] .... WMJJ
Birmingham, AL [*Radio station call letters*] .... WRKK
Birmingham, AL [*Radio station call letters*] .... WSGN
Birmingham, AL [*Television station call letters*] .... WTTO-TV
Birmingham, AL [*Radio station call letters*] .... WTWG
Birmingham, AL [*Radio station call letters*] .... WVOK
Birmingham, AL [*Radio station call letters*] .... WVSU
Birmingham, AL [*Television station call letters*] .... WVTM-TV
Birmingham, AL [*Radio station call letters*] .... WYDE
Birmingham, AL [*Radio station call letters*] .... WZZK
Birmingham Belt R. R. [*AAR code*] .... BB
Birmingham Gauge .... BG
Birmingham-Jefferson Library, Birmingham, AL [*OCLC symbol*] .... ABJ
Birmingham, MI [*Radio station call letters*] .... WMJC
Birmingham [*England*] **Philosophical Society. Proceedings** [*A publication*] .... Birmingham Ph Soc Pr
Birmingham Post & Mail Ltd., Birmingham, United Kingdom [*Library symbol*] .... UkBP
Birmingham Public and Jefferson County Free Library, Birmingham, AL [*Library symbol*] .... AB
Birmingham Public Libraries, Birmingham, United Kingdom [*Library symbol*] .... UkB
Birmingham Revision [*of BNA*] [*Medicine*] [*British*] .... BR
Birmingham Small Arms, Inc. .... BSA
Birmingham & Southeastern R. R. [*AAR code*] .... BSE
Birmingham Southern College [*Alabama*] .... BSC
Birmingham Southern College, Birmingham, AL [*Library symbol*] .... ABS

Birmingham Southern Railroad Co. [*AAR code*] ..... BS
Birmingham University, Birmingham, United Kingdom [*Library symbol*] ..... UkBU
Birmingham University. Chemical Engineer [*A publication*] ..... Birmingham Univ Chem Eng
Birmingham University. Historical Journal [*A publication*] ..... Birmingham Univ Hist
Birmingham Wire Gauge ..... BWG
Biro Klasifikasi [*Indonesia*] ..... BKI
Biro Pengapalan, Indonesia ..... BIPALINDO
[*The*] **Birtcher Corp.** [*NASDAQ symbol*] ..... BIRT
Birth ..... B
Birth Control ..... BC
Birth Control Clinic ..... BCC
Birth Control Medication ..... BCM
Birth Defects Information System [*Tufts University*] ..... BDIS
Birth Defects. Original Article Series [*A publication*] ..... Birth Defects
Birth and the Family. Journal [*A publication*] ..... Birth Family J
Birth Weight [*Medicine*] ..... BW
Birth Weight [*Medicine*] ..... BWT
Birthday Honours [*Titles conferred on the sovereign's birthday*] [*British*] ..... BH
Birthplace ..... BP
Birthplace ..... BPL
Birthrate ..... BR
Births, Deaths, and Marriages ..... BDM
Birtle-Foxwarren, MB [*Television station call letters*] CKX-TV-1
Bis [*Twice*] [*Pharmacy*] ..... B
Bis-diazotized Benzidine [*Hematology*] ..... BDB
Bis in Die [*Twice a Day*] [*Pharmacy*] ..... BD
Bis in Die [*Twice a Day*] [*Pharmacy*] ..... BID
Bis in Die Sumendus [*To Be Taken Twice a Day*] [*Pharmacy*] ..... BDS
Bis in Noctus [*Twice a Night*] [*Pharmacy*] ..... BIN
Bis Terve in Die [*Two or Three Times a Day*] [*Pharmacy*] ..... BTID
Bis(amidino-benzimidazolyl)methane [*Biochemistry*] ..... BABIM
Bis(aminopropyl)piperazine [*Organic chemistry*] ..... BAPP
Bisbee [*Arizona*] [*Airport symbol*] ..... BSQ
Bisbee, AZ [*Radio station call letters*] ..... KBZB
Bisbee, AZ [*Radio station call letters*] ..... KZMK
Bis(biphenylyl)oxazole [*Organic chemistry*] ..... BBO
Bis(bromomethyl)oxetane [*Organic chemistry*] ..... BBMO
Bisbutoxybenzylidenebitoluidine [*Organic chemistry*] ..... BBBT
Biscayan ..... BISC
Biscayne Chemical Laboratories, Inc., Miami, FL [*Library symbol*] ..... FMB
Biscayne College, Miami, FL [*OCLC symbol*] ..... FBM
Biscayne College, Miami, FL [*Library symbol*] ..... FMBC
Biscayne Federal Savings & Loan Association [*NYSE symbol*] [*Delisted*] ..... BIS
Bis(chloroethyl)nitrosourea [*Carmustine*] [*Also, BiCNU*] [*Antineoplastic drug regimen*] ..... BCNU
Bis(chloroethyl)nitrosourea [*Carmustine*] [*Also, BCNU*] ..... BiCNU
Bis(chloromethyl)ether [*Organic chemistry*] ..... BCME
Bis(chloromethyl)oxetane [*Organic chemistry*] ..... BCMO
Biscuit Bakers Institute [*Later, B & CMA*] ..... BBI
Biscuit and Cracker Distributors Association ..... BCDA
Biscuit and Cracker Manufacturers' Association ..... B & CMA
Bis(dimethylsilyl)acetamide [*Organic chemistry*] ..... BDSA
Biserica Orthodoxa Romana [*A publication*] ..... BOR
Bis(ethylenedithiolo)tetrathiafulvalene [*Organic chemistry*] ..... BEDT-TTF
Bisexual Center ..... BC
Bisexual Person [*Pun on electricity's 'AC or DC' - alternating current or direct current*] ..... AC-DC
Bisexual White Male ..... BiWM
Bisha [*Saudi Arabia*] [*Airport symbol*] ..... BHH
Bishop [*Chess*] ..... B
Bishop ..... BHP
Bishop [*California*] [*Airport symbol*] ..... BIH
Bishop ..... BP
Bishop ..... BSHP
Bishop [*Ecclesiastical*] ..... B
Bishop Baraga Association ..... BBA
Bishop, CA [*Radio station call letters*] ..... KIBS
Bishop, CA [*Radio station call letters*] ..... KIOQ
Bishop of Carlisle [*British*] ..... CARIOL
Bishop of Chichester [*British*] ..... CICESTR
Bishop College, Dallas, TX [*OCLC symbol*] [*Inactive*] ..... BIS
Bishop College, Dallas, TX [*Library symbol*] ..... TxDaBC
Bishop of Durham [*British*] ..... DUNELM
Bishop Graphics, Inc. [*NASDAQ symbol*] ..... BGPH
Bishop Kearney High School Library, Rochester, NY [*OCLC symbol*] ..... RVR
Bishop and Martyr [*Church calendars*] ..... BM
Bishop of Salisbury [*British*] ..... SARUM
Bishop State Junior College, Mobile, AL [*Library symbol*] ..... AMobB
Bishop Suffragan ..... BS
Bishop, TX [*Radio station call letters*] ..... KFLZ
Bishopric ..... BHPRIC
Bishops' Committee for Ecumenical and Interreligious Affairs ..... BCEIA
Bishops' Committee on the Liturgy ..... BCL
Bishops' Committee on Priestly Formation ..... BCPF
Bishops' Committee for the Spanish Speaking [*Later, SHA*] ..... BCSS
Bishop's University, Department of Geography, Lennoxville, PQ, Canada [*Library symbol*] ..... CaQLBG
Bishop's University, Lennoxville, PQ, Canada [*Library symbol*] ..... CaQLB
Bishopville, SC [*Radio station call letters*] ..... WAGS
Bis(hydroxybenzyl)ethylenediaminediacetic Acid [*Organic chemistry*] ..... HBED
Bis(hydroxyethyl)aminoethanesulfonic Acid [*A buffer*] [*Organic chemistry*] ..... BES
Bis(hydroxyethyl)dimerate [*Organic chemistry*] ..... BHED
Bis(hydroxyethyl)glycine [*A buffer*] [*Organic chemistry*] ..... BICINE
Bis(hydroxyphenyl)trichloroethane [*Organic chemistry*] ..... HPTE
Biskra [*Algeria*] [*Airport symbol*] ..... BSK
Bislig [*Philippines*] [*Airport symbol*] ..... BPH
Bismarck [*North Dakota*] [*Airport symbol*] ..... BIS
Bismarck Hospital, School of Nursing Library, Bismarck, ND [*Library symbol*] ..... NdBH
Bismarck Junior College [*North Dakota*] ..... BJC
Bismarck Junior College, Bismarck, ND [*Library symbol*] ..... NdBC
Bismarck-Mandan, ND [*Radio station call letters*] ..... KLXX
Bismarck, ND [*Location identifier*] [*FAA*] ..... BZX
Bismarck, ND [*Radio station call letters*] ..... KBMR
Bismarck, ND [*Radio station call letters*] ..... KCND
Bismarck, ND [*Radio station call letters*] ..... KFYR
Bismarck, ND [*Television station call letters*] ..... KFYR-TV
Bismarck, ND [*Radio station call letters*] ..... KQDY
Bismarck, ND [*Television station call letters*] ..... KXMB-TV
Bismarck, ND [*Radio station call letters*] ..... KYYY
Bismarck [*Veterans Memorial*] **Public Library, Bismarck, ND** [*Library symbol*] ..... NdBV
Bismarck, TX [*Television station call letters*] ..... KBME
Bismorpholinecarbamylsulfenamide [*Organic chemistry*] ..... BCMS
Bismuth [*Chemical element*] ..... Bi
Bismuth Iodoform Paraffin [*Medicine*] ..... BIP
Bismuth Iodoform and Paraffin Paste [*Medicine*] ..... BIPP
Bismuth Subsalicylate [*Antidiarrhea agent*] ..... BS
Bispinous [*or Interspinous*] [*Gynecology*] ..... bisp
Bis(pyridiniumtrimethylene) [*Dichloride*] [*Biochemistry*] ..... BPT
Bissau [*Portuguese Guinea*] [*Airport symbol*] ..... BXO
Bistable Magnetic Core [*Data processing*] ..... BIMAC
Bistable Multivibrator ..... BMV
Bistable Multivibrator ..... BSM
Bistable Multivibrator ..... BSMV
Bistaple ..... BSTL
Bistatic RADAR Intelligence Generation and Analysis System ..... BRIGAND
Bis(tert-butylbenzoxazolyl)thiophene [*Organic chemistry*] ..... BBOT
Bis(tribromophenoxy)ethane [*Flame retardant*] [*Organic chemistry*] ..... BTBPE
Bis(trimethylsilyl)acetamide [*Organic chemistry*] ..... BSA
Bis(trimethylsilyl)acetylene [*Organic chemistry*] ..... BTMSA
Bis(trimethylsilyl)trifluoroacetamide [*Organic chemistry*] ..... BSTFA
Bis(trinitroethyl)carbonate [*An explosive*] ..... BTNEC
Bis(trinitroethyl)nitramine [*An explosive*] ..... BTNEN
Bit ..... B
BIT [*Binary Digit*] [*Data processing*] ..... B
BIT [*Binary Digit*] **Buffer Unit** [*Data processing*] ..... BBU
BIT [*Binary Digit*] **Control Block** [*Data processing*] ..... BCB
BIT [*Binary Digit*] **Control Panel** [*Data processing*] ..... BCP
BIT [*Binary Digit*] **Density** [*Data processing*] ..... BD
BIT [*Binary Digit*] **Error Probability** [*Data processing*] ..... BEP
BIT [*Binary Digit*] **Error Rate** [*Data processing*] ..... BER
BIT [*Binary Digit*] **Error-Rate-Test** [*Set*] [*Data processing*] ..... BERT
BIT [*Binary Digit*] **Image Memory** [*Data processing*] ..... BIM
Bit Nordisk Tidskrift fuer Informationsbehandling [*A publication*] ..... Bit Nord Tidskr Informationsbehandl
BIT [*Binary Digit*]**-Oriented Message** ..... BOM
BIT [*Binary Digit*]**-Plane Encoding** [*Data processing*] ..... BPE
BIT [*Binary Digit*] **Rate** [*Data processing*] ..... BR
BIT [*Binary Digit*] **Scan** [*Data processing*] ..... BSCN
BIT [*Binary Digit*] **Scan Command** [*Data processing*] ..... BSC
BIT [*Binary Digit*] **Slippage Rate** [*Data processing*] ..... BSR
BIT [*Binary Digit*] **Storage Density** [*Data processing*] ..... BSD
BIT [*Binary Digit*] **Sync** [*Data processing*] ..... BS
BIT [*Binary Digit*] **Sync Acquisition** [*Data processing*] ..... BSA
BIT [*Binary Digit*] **Sync Generator** [*Data processing*] ..... BSG
BIT [*Binary Digit*] **Sync Matched Filter** [*Data processing*] ..... BSMF
BIT [*Binary Digit*] **Time Counter** [*Data processing*] ..... BTC
Bitam [*Gabon*] [*Airport symbol*] ..... BMM
Bitch ..... B
Bitco Corp. [*NASDAQ symbol*] ..... BITU
BITE [*Built-In Test Equipment*] **Status Register** ..... BSR
Bithionol Sulfoxide [*Pharmacology*] ..... BTS
Bitki Koruma Bulteni [*A publication*] ..... Bitki Koruma Bul
BITS [*Binary Digits*] **per Inch** [*Data processing*] ..... BPI
BITS [*Binary Digits*] **per Minute** [*Data processing*] ..... BPM
BITS [*Binary Digits*] **per Second** [*Data processing*] ..... BPS
BITS [*Binary Digits*] **per Second** [*Data processing*] ..... B/S
Bitter National Magnet Laboratory ..... BNML
Bitterwater Creek [*California*] [*Seismograph station code, US Geological Survey*] ..... BTW
Bitumen ..... BITN

Bitumen-Teere-Asphalte-Peche und Verwandte Stoffe [*A publication*] ... Bitumen-Teere-Asphalte-Peche
Bituminized [*Freight*] ... BITUMD
Bituminous ... BITUM
Bituminous and Aggregate Equipment Bureau [*Formerly, BEMB*] ... BAEB
Bituminous Coal Institute [*Later, NCA*] ... BCI
Bituminous Coal Operators Association ... BCOA
Bituminous Coal Research, Inc. ... BCR
Bituminous Equipment Manufacturers Bureau [*Later, BAEB*] ... BEMB
Bituminous Pipe Institute [*Defunct*] ... BPI
Biuletyn Fonograficzny [*A publication*] ... BFo
Biuletyn Fonograficzny [*A publication*] ... B Fon
Biuletyn Historii Sztuki [*A publication*] ... BHS
Biuletyn Informacyjny. Institutu Zbozowego w Warszawie [*A publication*] ... Biul Inform Inst Zboz Warszawie
Biuletyn Informacyjny. Zakladu Narodowego Ossolinskich Biblioteki Polskiej Akademii Nauk [*A publication*] ... B Inf Zak Narod
Biuletyn. Instytutu Bibliograficznego [*A publication*] ... Biul IB
Biuletyn. Instytutu Energetyki [*A publication*] ... Biul Inst Energ
Biuletyn. Instytutu Gospodarstwa Spolecznego [*A publication*] ... Biul IGS
Biuletyn. Instytutu Hodowli i Aklimatyzacji Roslin [*A publication*] ... Biul Inst Hodowli Aklim Rosl
Biuletyn. Instytutu Medycyny Morskiej w Gdansku [*A publication*] ... Biul Inst Med Morsk Gdansk
Biuletyn. Instytutu Medycyny Morskiej i Tropikalne w Gdyni [*A publication*] ... Biul Inst Med Morsk Trop Gdyni
Biuletyn. Instytutu Naftowego [*A publication*] ... Biul Inst Naftowego
Biuletyn. Instytutu Ochrony Roslin [*Poznan*] [*A publication*] ... Biul Inst Ochr Rosl
Biuletyn. Instytutu Ochrony Roslin (Poznan) [*A publication*] ... Biul Inst Ochr Ros (Poznan)
Biuletyn. Instytutu Spawalnictwa [*A publication*] ... Biul Inst Spawalnictwa
Biuletyn. Instytutu Technologii Drewna [*A publication*] ... Biul Inst Tech Drewna
Biuletyn Lubeldkiego Towarzystwa Naukowego. Matematyka, Fizka, Chemia [*A publication*] ... Biul Lubel Towarz Nauk Mat Fiz Chem
Biuletyn Naukowy Instytutu Nauk Ekonomicznych Universytetu Warszawskiego [*A publication*] ... B Nauk Inst Nauk Ekon Univ Warszaw
Biuletyn Numizmatyczny [*A publication*] ... BN
Biuletyn Panstwowego Instytutu Ksiazki [*A publication*] ... Biul PIK
Biuletyn Peryglacjalny [*A publication*] ... Biul Peryglac
Biuletyn Polskiego Towarzystwa Jezykoznawczego [*A publication*] ... BPTJ
Biuletyn Producenta Pieczarek [*A publication*] ... Biul Prod Pieczarek
Biuletyn Sluzby Sanitarno Epidemiologiczej Wojewodztwa Katowickiego [*A publication*] ... Biul Sluzby Sanit Epidemiol Wojewodztwa Katowickiego
Biuletyn Warzywniczy [*A publication*] ... Biul Warzywniczy
Biuletyn Wojskowej Akademii Medycznej [*A publication*] ... Biul Wojsk Akad Med
Biuletyn Wojskowej Akademii Technicznej Imeni Jaroslawa Dabrowskiego [*A publication*] ... Biul Wojsk Akad Tech
Biuletyn Zydowskiego Instytutu Historycznego [*A publication*] ... Biul Zydowskiego Inst Hist
Biulleten Eksperimentalnoi Biologii i Meditsiny [*A publication*] ... BEBMA
Biulleten Eksperimentalnoi Biologii i Meditsiny [*A publication*] ... Biull Eksp Biol Med
Bivariant Function Generator ... BIVAR
Bivariate Exponential [*Distribution*] [*Statistics*] ... BVE
Bivariate Normal Mixture [*Statistics*] ... BVN
Bivouac ... BIV
BIW Cable Systems, Inc. [*NASDAQ symbol*] ... BIWC
Biweekly ... BI-W
Biweekly ... BW
Biweekly Report ... BWR
Biweekly Scientific and Technical Intelligence Summary [*A publication*] ... BSTIS
Bixby Memorial Free Library, Vergennes, VT [*Library symbol*] ... VtVe
Bizant [*Australia*] [*Airport symbol*] [*Obsolete*] ... BZP
Bizantion-Nea Hellas [*A publication*] ... BzNH
Bizarre Fantasy Tales [*A publication*] ... BFT
Bizarre Mystery Magazine [*A publication*] ... Biz
Bizarre People [*Extension of BP - Beautiful People*] [*Slang*] ... BP
BJ Aero Freight, Inc. [*Oskaloosa, IA*] [*FAA designator*] ... BAJ
Bjerrum Double Band [*Physics*] ... BDB
Bjulleten Akademiji Nauk Uzbekskoj SSR [*A publication*] ... Bjull Akad Nauk Uz SSR
Bjulleten Dialektologiceskogo Sektora Instituta Russkogo Jazyka [*A publication*] ... BDSekt
Bjulleten Glavnogo Botaniceskogo Sada [*A publication*] ... Bjull Glavn Bot Sada
Bjulleten Gosudarstvennogo Nikitskogo Botaniceskogo Sada [*A publication*] ... Bjull Gos Nikit Bot Sada
Bjulleten Inostrannoj Kommerceskoj Informacii Prilozenie [*A publication*] ... B Inostr Kommerc Inform Priloz
Bjulleten Instituta Teoreticeskoi Astronomii [*A publication*] ... Bjull Inst Teoret Astronom
Bjulleten' Moskovskogo Obscestva Ispytatelej Prirody. Otdel Biologiceskij [*A publication*] ... Bjull Mosk Obsc Ispyt Prir Otd Biol
BK Technical Review [*A publication*] ... BK Tech Rev
BKSTS [*British Kinematograph Sound and Television Society*] **Journal** [*A publication*] ... BKSTS J
BKW Inc. [*NASDAQ symbol*] ... BKWS
Black [*Buoy*] ... B
Black ... BK
Black ... BL
Black ... BLK
Black [*Pencils*] ... B
Black [*Thoroughbred racing*] ... BLK
Black Academy of Arts and Letters [*Defunct*] ... BAAL
Black Academy Review [*A publication*] ... BA Rev
Black Action Movement ... BAM
Black Affairs Center ... BAC
Black Affairs Council [*Unitarian-Universalist*] ... BAC
Black American Baptist Churchmen [*An association*] ... BABC
Black American Cinema Society ... BACS
Black American Law Students Association ... BALSA
Black American Literature Forum [*A publication*] ... BALF
Black American Travel Association [*Defunct*] ... BATA
Black Angus Systems [*NASDAQ symbol*] ... BLCK
Black Art [*London*] [*A publication*] ... BLA
Black Ball Transport, Inc. [*AAR code*] ... BBT
Black Body Radiator ... BBR
Black Books Bulletin [*A publication*] ... Bl Bks B
Black-Bordered [*Stationery*] ... BB
Black Butte [*New Mexico*] [*Seismograph station code, US Geological Survey*] [*Closed*] ... BBN
Black Butte [*Montana*] [*Seismograph station code, US Geological Survey*] [*Closed*] ... BLK
Black Canyon City, AZ [*Radio station call letters*] ... KUET
Black Canyon of the Gunnison National Monument ... BLCA
Black Caucus of the American Library Association ... BCALA
Black Child Development Institute [*Later, NBCDI*] ... BCDI
Black Christian Nationalist Church ... BCNC
Black Church [*A publication*] ... BlackCh
Black Citizens for a Fair Media ... BCFM
Black Code [*Law passed after the Civil War limiting the rights of Negroes in the South*] ... BC
Black Country Society ... BCS
Black Data Processing Associates ... DPA
Black Death [*1348-49*] ... BD
Black & Decker Manufacturing Co. ... B & D
Black & Decker Manufacturing Co. [*NYSE symbol*] ... BDK
Black Development Foundation ... BDF
Black Dome Energy Corporation [*NASDAQ symbol*] ... BDEC
Black Economic Research Center ... BERC
Black Economic Union ... BEU
Black Educational Resources Center [*Later, BMCERC*] ... BERC
Black Educational Services, Incorporated ... BESI
Black Efforts for Soul in Television ... BEST
Black Elected Official ... BEO
Black Employees of the Library of Congress ... BELC
Black Enamel Slate ... BES
Black Enamelled ... BE
Black English [*Dialect*] ... BE
Black Enterprise [*A publication*] ... B Ent
Black Entertainment Lawyers Association ... BELA
Black Entertainment Television [*Cable-television system*] ... BET
Black Executive Exchange Program [*of The National Urban League*] ... BEEP
Black, Female Republican ... BFR
Black Filmmaker Foundation ... BFF
Black Filmmakers Hall of Fame, Incorporated ... BFHFI
Black Forum [*A publication*] ... Black F
Black Fox Magazine [*A publication*] ... Black Fox Mag
Black Giant Oil Company [*NASDAQ symbol*] ... BGOC
Black Gold Cooperative Library System, Ventura, CA [*OCLC symbol*] ... BGC
Black Granite Gauge ... BGG
Black Hawk College, East Campus, Gustav E. Lundberg Learning Center, Kewanee, IL [*OCLC symbol*] ... ISY
Black Hawk College, Moline, IL [*Library symbol*] ... IMolB
Black Hill [*Scotland*] [*Seismograph station code, US Geological Survey*] ... EBH
Black Hills Army Depot ... BHAD
Black Hills Power & Light Co. [*NYSE symbol*] ... BHP
Black Hills State College, Spearfish, SD [*OCLC symbol*] ... BHS
Black Hills State College, Spearfish, SD [*Library symbol*] ... SdSpeT
Black Hills Teachers College [*Later, Black Hills State College*] [*South Dakota*] ... BHTC
Black Hole Ocarina ... BHO
Black I: A Canadian Journal of Black Expression [*A publication*] ... BlackIC
Black Images: A Critical Quarterly on Black Arts and Culture [*A publication*] ... BlackI
Black Industries, Inc. [*NASDAQ symbol*] ... BLAK
Black Intelligence Test of Cultural Homogeneity [*Sometimes facetiously translated "Black Intelligence Test to Counter Honkeyism"*] ... BITCH
Black Iron ... BI
Black, James F., Baltimore MD [*STAC*] ... BJF
Black-Jewish Information Center ... BJIC
Black Law Journal [*A publication*] ... Black L J

Black Legal Action for Soul in Television [*Student legal action organization*] .... BLAST
Black Leghorn [*Poultry*] .... BL
Black Letter [*Printing*] .... BKLR
Black Letter [*Printing*] .... BL
Black Liberation [*A publication*] .... Blk Lib
Black Liberation Army .... BLA
Black Librarians Caucus .... BCALA
Black Light .... BL
Black Light Blue [*Source for near ultraviolet radiation*] .... BLB
Black Liquor Oxidation [*For pollution control in paper mills*] .... BLO
Black Lung Association .... BLA
Black Lung Benefits Act [*1972*] .... BLBA
Black Male .... BM
Black Mesa Defense Fund .... BMDF
Black Mesa & Lake Powell [*AAR code*] .... BLKM
Black Mountain College [*1933-1956*] .... BMC
Black Mountain, NC [*Radio station call letters*] .... WFGW
Black Mountain, NC [*Radio station call letters*] .... WMIT
Black Mountain, NC [*Radio station call letters*] .... WONO
Black and Multiethnic Christian Education Resources Center .... BMCERC
Black Music Association .... BMA
Black Muslim .... BM
Black News Digest [*A publication*] .... Black N Dig
Black and Non-White YMCA Staffs [*An association*] .... BANWYS
Black Oil Finish Slate .... BOFS
Black Oracle [*A publication*] .... Bl Orcl
Black Ordinary Working People .... BOWP
Black Orpheus [*A publication*] .... BO
Black Panther [*A publication*] .... Blk Panth
Black Panther Party [*Defunct*] .... BPP
Black Peak [*Arizona*] [*Seismograph station code, US Geological Survey*] [*Closed*] .... BPK
Black Pigmented Bacteria [*Microbiology*] .... BPB
Black Political Women's Caucus .... BPWC
Black Powder .... BP
Black Psychiatrists of America .... BPA
Black Radical Action Group .... BRAG
Black Rapids [*Alaska*] [*Seismograph station code, US Geological Survey*] .... BLR
Black Resources Information Coordinating Services [*Information service*] .... BRICS
Black Review [*A publication*] .... BlackR
Black River [*Jamaica*] [*Seismograph station code, US Geological Survey*] [*Closed*] .... BRJ
Black River Falls, WI [*Radio station call letters*] .... WWIS
Black River & Western Corp. [*AAR code*] .... BRW
Black Rock Forest. Bulletin [*A publication*] .... Black Rock For Bull
Black Rock Forest. Papers [*A publication*] .... Black Rock For Pap
Black Scale .... BS
Black Scholar [*A publication*] .... BKSCA
Black Scholar [*A publication*] .... Black Sch
Black Scholar [*A publication*] .... Blk Schol
Black Scholar [*A publication*] .... BIS
Black Sea and Area [*MARC geographic area code*] [*Library of Congress*] .... mb-----
Black September Organization [*Israel*] .... BSO
Black Silent Majority Committee of the USA .... BSMC
Black Silk Suture [*Medicine*] .... BSS
Black Students Psychological Association .... BSPA
Black Students Union .... BSU
Black Stuntmen's Association .... BSA
Black, Syvalls, & Bryson, Inc., HOMCO Division, Houston, TX [*Library symbol*] .... TxHH
Black Theater Alliance .... BTA
Black-Top Delaine Merino Sheep Breeders' Association .... BTDMSBA
Black-Top and National Delaine Merino Sheep Association .... BLNDMSA
Black United Front .... BUF
Black Urban Professional [*Terminology used in "The Yuppie Handbook"*] .... Buppie
Black Varnish Cambric [*Insulation*] .... BVC
Black & Veatch Consulting Engineers, Central Library, Kansas City, MO [*Library symbol*] .... MoKBV
Black Veterans, Inc. [*An association*] .... BV
Black Void Reactor .... BVR
Black Watch [*Military unit*] [*British*] .... BW
Black and White [*Photography, television, etc.*] .... B
Black and White [*Photography, television, etc.*] .... B & W
Black and White [*Photography, television, etc.*] .... BW
Black and White Horizontal Bands [*Navigation markers*] .... BWHB
Black-White Infrared [*Film*] .... BWIR
Black and White Vertical Stripes [*Navigation markers*] .... BWVS
Black Widow Spider Toxin .... BWSTx
Black Widow Spider Venom .... BWSV
Black Women in Publishing .... BWIP
Black Women's Association .... BWA
Black Women's Educational Policy and Research Network .... BWEPRN
Black Women's Health Project .... BWHP
Black World [*A publication*] .... Black W
Black World [*A publication*] .... BL W
Black World Foundation .... BWF
Blackall [*Australia*] [*Airport symbol*] .... BKQ
Blackboard .... BBD
Blackboard .... BKD
Blackburn College, Carlinville, IL [*OCLC symbol*] .... IBN
Blackburn College, Carlinville, IL [*Library symbol*] .... ICarlB
Blacken .... BLKN
Blackening .... BLKNG
Blackfoot [*MARC language code*] [*Library of Congress*] .... bla
Blackfoot, ID [*Radio station call letters*] .... KBLI
Blackfoot, ID [*Radio station call letters*] .... KBLI-FM
Blackgold Energy Resources, Inc. [*NASDAQ symbol*] .... BLAU
Blackhawk Airways, Inc. [*Janesville, WI*] [*FAA designator*] .... BAK
Blackhawk Technical Institute, Janesville, WI [*Library symbol*] .... WJaB
Blackman's Volunteer Army of Liberation [*An association*] .... BVAL
Blackout .... BO
Blackout Door [*Military*] .... BOD
Blackout Exit Time .... BOE
Blackout Initiation Time .... BOI
Blackout Preparedness .... BP
Blackout Restrictions [*British*] [*World War II*] .... BR
Blackout Restrictions in Industrial Establishments [*British*] [*World War II*] .... BIE
Blackout Window [*Military*] .... BOW
Blackpool [*England*] [*Airport symbol*] .... BLK
Blackpool Central Library, Blackpool, United Kingdom [*Library symbol*] .... UkBl
Blackpool Gazette & Herald Ltd., Blackpool, United Kingdom [*Library symbol*] .... UkBlG
Blacks Against Nukes .... BAN
Blacks in Government .... BIG
Blacksburg [*Virginia*] [*Seismograph station code, US Geological Survey*] .... BAV
Blacksburg [*Virginia*] [*Seismograph station code, US Geological Survey*] .... BLA
Blacksburg, VA [*Radio station call letters*] .... WKEX
Blacksburg, VA [*Radio station call letters*] .... WQBX
Blacksburg, VA [*Radio station call letters*] .... WUVT
Blacksburg, VA [*Radio station call letters*] .... WVVV
Blackshear, GA [*Radio station call letters*] .... WIEZ
Blackshear, GA [*Radio station call letters*] .... WKUB
Blacksmith .... BSMITH
Blackstone, VA [*Location identifier*] [*FAA*] .... BKT
Blackstone, VA [*Radio station call letters*] .... WBBC
Blackstone, VA [*Radio station call letters*] .... WKLV
Blackstrap [*Freight*] .... BLKSTP
Blackwater [*Australia*] [*Airport symbol*] .... BLT
Blackwell, OK [*Location identifier*] [*FAA*] .... BWL
Blackwell, OK [*Radio station call letters*] .... KLTR
Blackwood, NJ [*Radio station call letters*] .... WDBK
Blackwood's Magazine [*A publication*] .... Black Mag
Blackwood's Magazine [*A publication*] .... Blackw
Blackwood's Magazine [*A publication*] .... Blackwood's Mag
Blackwood's Magazine [*A publication*] .... BM
Blacky Pictures [*Psychological testing*] .... BP
Bladder Tumor [*Medicine*] .... BT
Bladder Washout [*Urology*] .... BW
Blade .... BL
Blade Area Ratio .... BAR
Blade-Brake Clutch [*on lawn mowers*] .... BBC
Blade Inspection Method .... BIM
Blade Inspection Method System .... BIMS
Blade Loading Harmonics [*Helicopter*] .... BLH
Blade Rate .... BR
Blade Slap Factor [*Helicopter*] .... BSF
Bladen Technical Institute, Elizabethtown, NC [*Library symbol*] .... NcEB
Blaettchenpulver [*Flake powder*] [*German military - World War II*] .... BLP
Blaetter fuer das Bayerische Gymnasial-Schulwesen [*A publication*] .... BBG
Blaetter fuer Christliche Archaeologie und Kunst [*A publication*] .... BCA
Blaetter fuer Deutsche und Internationale Politik [*A publication*] .... Blaett Dtsche u Int Polit
Blaetter fuer Deutsche und Internationale Politik [*A publication*] .... Bl Dtsch Int Polit
Blaetter fuer Deutsche Landesgeschichte [*A publication*] .... BDLG
Blaetter fuer Deutsche Philosophie. Zeitschrift der Deutsche Philosophische Gesellschaft [*A publication*] .... BDPH
Blaetter fuer Kirchengeschichte Pommerns [*A publication*] .... BKGP
Blaetter fuer Munzfreunde [*A publication*] .... BMFR
Blaetter fuer Pfaelzische Kirchengeschichte [*A publication*] .... BPKG
Blaetter fuer Technikgeschichte [*A publication*] .... Blaett Technikgesch
Blaetter der Thomas Mann Gesellschaft [*A publication*] .... BTMG
Blaetter fuer Wuerttembergische Kirchengeschichte [*A publication*] .... BWKG
Blaine, WA [*Radio station call letters*] .... KARI
Blair [*John*] **& Co.** [*NYSE symbol*] .... BJ
Blair House Library Foundation .... BHLF
Blair and Ketchum's Country Journal [*A publication*] .... Blair & Ketchum's
Blair, NE [*Radio station call letters*] .... KBWH
Blair, NE [*Radio station call letters*] .... KDCV-FM
Blair Public Library, Blair, NE [*Library symbol*] .... NbBla
Blairmore, AB [*Radio station call letters*] .... CJPR
Blairstown, NJ [*Radio station call letters*] .... WFMV

Blairstown Press, Blairstown, NJ [*Library symbol*] ... NjBlaiP
Blairsville, PA [*Radio station call letters*] ... WCQO
Blairsville Public Library, Blairsville, PA [*Library symbol*] ... PBl
Blake, Cassels, & Graydon, Law Library, Toronto, ON, Canada [*Library symbol*] ... CaOTBCG
Blake Newsletter [*A publication*] ... BlakeN
Blake Studies [*A publication*] ... BlakeS
Blakely, GA [*Radio station call letters*] ... WBBK
Blakely Island [*Washington*] [*Airport symbol*] ... BYW
Blakesburg Public Library, Blakesburg, IA [*Library symbol*] ... IaBlak
Blalock-Taussig [*Cardiology*] ... BT
Blanc Sablon [*Canada*] [*Airport symbol*] ... YBX
Blanchard Community Library, Santa Paula, CA [*Library symbol*] ... CStp
Blanchester Public Library, Blanchester, OH [*Library symbol*] ... OBla
Blanding [*Utah*] [*Airport symbol*] ... BDG
Blanding Free Public Library, Rehoboth, MA [*Library symbol*] ... MReh
Blanding, UT [*Radio station call letters*] ... KUTA
Blaney, Pasternak, Smela, Eagleson, & Watson, Toronto, ON, Canada [*Library symbol*] ... CaOTBP
Blank ... B
Blank ... BLK
Blank Corrected Sample Data [*Data processing*] ... BCSD
Blank Die ... BLDI
Blank Film Door ... BFD
Blank Line [*Data processing*] ... BL
Blank Recording Disc ... BRD
Blank when Zero ... BZ
Blanked Picture Signal ... BPS
Blanket ... BLKT
Blanket ... BLNKT
Blanket Agreement ... BA
Blanket Bath [*Medicine*] ... BB
Blanket Crime Policy [*Insurance*] ... BCP
Blanket Delivery Date [*Military*] ... BDD
Blanket Position Bond ... BPB
Blanket Purchase Agreement ... BPA
Blanket Purchase Authority ... BPA
Blanking ... BL
Blanking ... BLKG
Blanking Die ... BLKGD
Blanking Input ... BI
Blantyre [*Malawi*] [*Airport symbol*] ... BLZ
Blaser [*Blower*] [*Wind instrument player*] ... BL
Blasius ... BL
Blasius Industries [*NASDAQ symbol*] ... BLAS
Blast ... BL
Blast Furnace [*Ironmaking*] ... BF
Blast Furnace Research, Inc. [*Defunct*] ... BFR
Blast Furnace and Steel Plant [*A publication*] ... Blast F & Steel Pl
Blast Furnace and Steel Plant [*A publication*] ... Blast Furn Steel Plant
Blast Gauge ... BG
Blast Propagation ... BP
Blast Suppression Device ... BSD
Blast Test Missile ... BTM
Blast Test Vehicle ... BTV
Blast Wave Yield ... BWY
Blasthole ... BH
Blastogenic Factor [*Immunochemistry*] ... BF
Blauvelt Free Library, Blauvelt, NY [*Library symbol*] ... NBla
Blaw-Knox Co. [*NYSE symbol*] [*Delisted*] ... BK
Bleach-Fix [*Photography*] ... BLIX
Bleachable Absorber LASER Amplifier and Detector ... BALAD
Bleached [*Freight*] ... BLCHD
Bleached Kraft Mill Effluent [*Pulp and paper processing*] ... BKME
Bleaching [*Freight*] ... BLCHG
Bleed ... BL
Bleed Hose Assembly ... BHA
Bleed Valve ... BLV
Bleeder ... BLDR
Bleeding Time [*Clinical chemistry*] ... BT
Bleeding [*or Bruising*] **of Undetermined Origin** [*Medicine*] ... BUO
Blend ... B
Blend ... BLN
Blended Credit Program [*Federal government*] ... BCP
Blending Octane Valve ... BOV
Blendkoerper [*Frangible-glass smoke grenade*] [*German military - World War II*] ... BK
Blenheim [*New Zealand*] [*Airport symbol*] ... BHE
Bleomycin [*Also, Bleo, BLM*] [*Antineoplastic drug*] ... B
Bleomycin [*Also, B, BLM*] [*Antineoplastic drug*] ... Bleo
Bleomycin [*Also, B, Bleo*] [*Antineoplastic drug*] ... BLM
Bleomycin, Adriamycin, CCNU [*Lomustine*]**, Oncovin** [*Vincristine*]**, Nitrogen Mustard** [*Antineoplastic drug regimen*] ... BACON
Bleomycin, Adriamycin, Cyclophosphamide, Oncovin [*Vincristine*]**, Prednisone** [*Antineoplastic drug regimen*] ... BACOP
Bleomycin, CCNU [*Lomustine*]**, Adriamycin, Velban** [*Vinblastine*] [*Antineoplastic drug regimen*] ... B-CAVe
Bleomycin, Cyclophosphamide, Dactinomycin [*Antineoplastic drug regimen*] ... BCD
Bleomycin, Dacarbazine, Oncovin [*Vincristine*]**, Prednisone, Adriamycin** [*Antineoplastic drug regimen*] ... B-DOPA
Bleomycin, Oncovin [*Vincristine*]**, Adriamycin, Prednisone** [*Antineoplastic drug regimen*] ... BOAP
Bleomycin, Vinblastine, Doxorubicin, Streptozocin [*Antineoplastic drug regimen*] ... BVDS
Blessed ... B
Blessed ... BL
Blessed Kateri Tekakwitha League ... BKTL
Blessed Sacrament ... BS
Blessed Sacrament Seminary, Cleveland, OH [*Library symbol*] ... OCIBS
Blessed Trinity Society [*Defunct*] ... BTS
Blessed Virgin ... BV
Blessings Corporation [*American Stock Exchange symbol*] ... BCO
Blimp Squadron [*Navy*] ... BLIMPRON
Blimp Squadron [*Later separated into BLIMPRON and Blimp-HEDRON*] [*Navy*] ... ZEDRON
Blind Approach [*Aviation*] ... BA
Blind Approach Beacon System [*Aviation*] ... BABS
Blind Approach Training [*Air Force*] ... BAT
Blind Fire Director ... BFD
Blind Landing Experimental Unit [*Aviation*] ... BLEU
Blind Learning Aptitude Test [*Education*] ... BLAT
Blind Loaded and Plugged [*Projectile*] ... BL & P
Blind Loaded and Traced [*Projectile*] ... BL & T
Blind-Made Products ... BMP
Blind Matching [*Parapsychology*] ... BM
Blind Mating Connector ... BMC
Blind Navigation ... BN
Blind Outdoor Leisure Development ... BOLD
Blind Persons Resettlement Officer [*Department of Employment*] [*British*] ... BPRO
Blind River, ON [*Radio station call letters*] ... CJNR
Blind Riveted Joint ... BRJ
Blind Service Association ... BSA
Blind Sports ... BS
Blind Toss ... BT
Blinded Veterans Association ... BVA
Blinder ... BLD
Blinker Tube ... BKT
Blinkers [*Horse racing*] ... B
Blinking Light Monitor ... BLM
Blinn College, Brenham, TX [*Library symbol*] ... TxBreB
Blip Counter System ... BCS
Blip/Frame ... B/F
Blip-Frame Ratio ... BFR
Blip/Scan ... B/S
Blip-Scan Counter ... BSC
Blip-Scan Counter System ... BSCS
Blip-Scan Ratio ... BSR
Bliss Classification Association ... BCA
Bliss [*A. T.*] **& Co.** [*NASDAQ symbol*] ... ATBL
Bliss [*E. W.*] **Co.** [*NYSE symbol*] [*Delisted*] ... EWB
Bliss & Laughlin Industries, Inc. [*NYSE symbol*] [*Delisted*] ... BLI
Blizzard [*Meteorology*] ... BLZD
BLJ London [*Great Britain*] [*ICAO designator*] ... BL
BLL [*British Library Lending Division*] **Review** [*A publication*] ... BLL Rev
Bloc Africain de Guinee [*African Bloc of Guinea*] ... BAG
Bloc Democratique Gabonais [*Gabonese Democratic Bloc*] [*Succeeded by PDG*] ... BDG
Bloc des Masses Senegalaises [*Bloc of the Senegalese Masses*] ... BMS
Bloc Populaire Senegalais [*Senegalese People's Bloc*] ... BPS
Block ... BL
Block ... BLCK
Block ... BLK
Block Automation System [*NYSE trading computer*] ... BAS
Block out of Balance [*Data processing*] ... BOOB
Block Check Character [*Data processing*] ... BCC
Block-Connected Graph [*Mathematics*] [*Used in GPRS*] ... BCG
Block Control Header [*Data processing*] ... BCH
Block Control Sheet [*Data processing*] ... BCS
Block Control Unit [*Data processing*] ... BCU
Block (Copolymerized) [*Organic chemistry*] ... b
Block Count [*Data processing*] ... BC
Block-Cutpoint-Tree [*Mathematics*] [*Used in ASAMS*] ... BCT
Block Decoder Assembly [*Space Flight Operations Facility, NASA*] ... BDA
Block Demultiplexer [*Ground Communications Facility, NASA*] ... BDXR
Block Design [*Psychometrics*] ... BD
Block Diagram Compiler ... BLODI
Block Diagram Compiler B ... BLODIB
Block Drug Cl A [*NASDAQ symbol*] ... BLOCA
Block Format Recording ... BFR
Block of Four [*Philately*] ... B4
Block Handler [*Data processing*] ... BH
Block Handler Routine [*Data processing*] ... BHR
Block Header Record [*Data processing*] ... BHR
Block [*H. & R.*]**, Inc.** [*NYSE symbol*] ... HRB
Block Input Length [*Data processing*] ... BIL
Block Island [*Rhode Island*] [*Airport symbol*] ... BID
Block and List Manipulator [*Data processing*] ... BALM
Block Multiplexer [*Ground Communications Facility, NASA*] ... BMXR
Block-Oriented Compiler ... BLOC
Block-Oriented Computer ... BOC

Block-Oriented Random-Access Memory [*Data processing*] .... BORAM
Block Proof List [*Data processing*] .... BPL
Block Proof Record [*Data processing*] .... BPR
Block Replacement .... BR
Block Tape Recorder .... BTR
Block Template .... BT
Blockade .... BLOC
Blockade Intelligence Department [*Ministry of Economic Warfare*] [*British*] [*World War II*] .... BID
Blockade Operations [*Military*] .... BLOKOPS
Blockage .... BLOC
Blocked .... BLKD
Blocker Energy [*American Stock Exchange symbol*] .... BLK
Blockhouse [*NASA*] .... BH
Blockhouse [*NASA*] .... BKHS
Blockhouse Battery Charger [*NASA*] .... BBC
Blockhouse Computer [*NASA*] .... BHC
Blockhouse Operation [*NASA*] .... BO
Blocking .... BLKG
Blocking Back [*Football*] .... BB
Blocking Oscillator .... BO
Blockout .... BO
Blocks [*Freight*] .... BLKS
Blodgett Memorial Library, Fishkill, NY [*Library symbol*] .... NFisk
Bloemfontein [*South Africa*] [*Airport symbol*] .... BFN
Bloemfontein [*South Africa*] [*Seismograph station code, US Geological Survey*] .... BLF
Blonduos [*Iceland*] [*Airport symbol*] .... BLO
Blood Agar [*Growth medium*] .... BA
Blood Agar Base [*Growth medium*] .... BAB
Blood Agar Plate [*Microbiology*] .... BAP
Blood Alcohol Concentration [*or Content*] [*Sobriety test*] .... BAC
Blood Alcohol Level .... BAL
Blood Bank .... BB
Blood Brain Barrier [*Neurology*] .... BBB
Blood Cell Separator .... BCS
Blood Color Analyzer .... BCA
Blood Culture [*Bacteriology*] .... BI C
Blood Glucose [*Medicine*] .... BG
Blood Group Class .... BGC
Blood Group Substances [*Hematology*] .... BGS
Blood Information Service [*Information service*] .... BLDIS
Blood and Lymphatic System .... BLS
Blood Precautions [*Isolation*] [*Medicine*] .... B/P
Blood Pressure .... BLP
Blood Pressure .... BP
Blood Pressure Assembly .... BPA
Blood Pressure Gauge .... BPG
Blood Pressure Measuring System .... BPMS
Blood Pressure Recorder .... BPR
Blood Program [*Red Cross*] .... BP
Blood Program Directives [*Red Cross*] .... BPD
Blood Research Foundation .... BRF
Blood Sedimentation Rate [*Medicine*] .... BSR
Blood Serological Test [*Medicine*] .... BST
Blood Sugar [*Medicine*] .... BI S
Blood Sugar [*Medicine*] .... BS
Blood Sugar Level [*Clinical chemistry*] .... BSL
Blood, Sweat, and Tears [*Rock music group*] .... BS & T
Blood Therapy Journal [*A publication*] .... Blood Ther J
Blood Transfusion Association .... BTA
Blood Transfusion Service [*Medicine*] .... BTS
Blood Type [*Medicine*] .... BI T
Blood Urea Nitrogen [*Medicine*] .... BUN
Blood Vessel [*Medicine*] .... BV
Blood Vessel of Branchial Filament .... BVBRF
Blood Vessel of Palp .... BVPP
Blood Vessel of Pinnule .... BVP
Blood Vessel Prostheses .... BVP
Blood Vessels [*A publication*] .... Blood Vess
Blood Volume .... BV
Blood Wassermann [*Medicine*] .... BW
Bloody Bastard [*British slang*] .... BB
Bloody Fool [*British slang*] .... BF
Bloody Hell [*British slang*] .... BH
Bloody Nuisance [*British slang*] .... BN
Bloody Public Nuisance [*British slang*] .... BPN
Bloom Syndrome [*Medicine*] .... BS
Bloomfield College, Bloomfield, NJ [*OCLC symbol*] .... BLO
Bloomfield College, Bloomfield, NJ [*Library symbol*] .... NjBIC
Bloomfield Democrat, Bloomfield, IA [*Library symbol*] .... IaBID
Bloomfield Hills, MI [*Radio station call letters*] .... WBFH
Bloomfield, IA [*Radio station call letters*] .... KXOF
Bloomfield Public Library, Bloomfield, IA [*Library symbol*] .... IaBI
Bloomfield Public Library, Bloomfield, IN [*Library symbol*] .... InBI
Bloomfield Public Library, Bloomfield, NJ [*Library symbol*] .... NjBI
Bloomfield Savings & Loan [*NASDAQ symbol*] .... BFCO
Bloomington [*Indiana*] [*Seismograph station code, US Geological Survey*] .... BLO
Bloomington [*Indiana*] [*Airport symbol*] .... BMG
Bloomington [*Illinois*] [*Airport symbol*] .... BMI
Bloomington, IL [*Television station call letters*] .... WBLN
Bloomington, IL [*Radio station call letters*] .... WBNQ
Bloomington, IL [*Radio station call letters*] .... WESN
Bloomington, IL [*Radio station call letters*] .... WJBC
Bloomington, IL [*Radio station call letters*] .... WRBA
Bloomington, IN [*Radio station call letters*] .... WBWB
Bloomington, IN [*Radio station call letters*] .... WFIU
Bloomington, IN [*Radio station call letters*] .... WGTC
Bloomington, IN [*Television station call letters*] .... WTIU
Bloomington, IN [*Radio station call letters*] .... WTTS
Bloomington, IN [*Television station call letters*] .... WTTV
Bloomsburg, PA [*Radio station call letters*] .... WCNR
Bloomsburg, PA [*Radio station call letters*] .... WHLM
Bloomsburg, PA [*Radio station call letters*] .... WHLM-FM
Bloomsburg State College, Bloomsburg, PA [*OCLC symbol*] .... PBB
Bloomsburg State College, Bloomsburg, PA [*Library symbol*] .... PBbS
Bloomsday Club .... BC
Blount, Inc. [*American Stock Exchange symbol*] .... BLT
Blountstown, FL [*Radio station call letters*] .... WKMK
Blountstown, FL [*Radio station call letters*] .... WRTM
Blow in Door .... BID
Blow-Down Valve [*Railroad term*] .... BDV
Blow Molding [*Bottle manufacturing*] .... BM
Blow Molding System .... BMS
Blow-Out Emergency Team [*British government*] .... BET
Blow Valve .... BV
Blowback .... BB
Blowdown [*Chemical engineering*] .... BLWDN
Blowdown Heat Transfer .... BDHT
Blower .... BL
Blower .... BLO
Blower .... BLR
Blower .... BLWR
Blower Access Cover .... BAC
Blower Wheel Housing .... BWH
Blowing Dust [*Meteorology*] .... BD
Blowing Rock, NC [*Radio station call letters*] .... WOIX
Blowing Sand [*Meteorology*] .... BN
Blowing Snow [*Meteorology*] .... BS
Blowing Spray [*Meteorology*] .... BY
Blowoff .... BO
Blowout .... BLWT
Blowout Coil .... BOC
Blowout Pipe System .... BPS
Blowout Preventer [*or Prevention*] .... BOP
Blowtorch .... BLWT
Blue [*Aviation*] .... B
Blue .... BL
Blue .... BLU
Blue .... Bu
Blue Affirmative Flag [*Navy*] [*British*] .... BF
Blue Anchor, Inc. [*Formerly, CFE*] [*Later, BAI*] [*An association*] .... BA
Blue Anchor, Incorporated [*Formerly, CFE, BA*] [*An association*] .... BAI
Blue Army of Our Lady of Fatima .... BALF
Blue Bell [*Pennsylvania*] [*Airport symbol*] .... BBX
Blue Bell, Inc. [*NYSE symbol*] .... BBL
Blue Bell, Inc. [*Greensboro, NC*] [*FAA designator*] .... WRN
Blue-Black .... BB
Blue Book [*Directory of proprietaries*] .... BB
Blue Card [*An association*] .... BC
Blue Cross [*Health insurance plan*] .... BC
Blue Cross Association .... BCA
Blue Cross Association, Chicago, IL [*Library symbol*] .... ICBC
Blue Cross Association. Research Series [*A publication*] .... Blue Cross Assoc Res Ser
Blue Cross/Blue Shield [*Health insurance plan*] .... BC/BS
Blue Cross & Blue Shield of Colorado, Denver, CO [*Library symbol*] .... CoDBCS
Blue Cross & Blue Shield of North Carolina, Durham, NC [*Library symbol*] .... NcDurBC
Blue Cross Interim Payment .... BIP
Blue Cross Plan [*Health insurance*] .... BCP
Blue Earth, MN [*Radio station call letters*] .... KBEW
Blue Earth, MN [*Radio station call letters*] .... KJLY
Blue Earth, MN [*Location identifier*] [*FAA*] .... SBU
Blue Grass Breeders [*NASDAQ symbol*] .... BLGR
Blue-Green Algae [*Water purification*] .... BGA
Blue Guitar [*A publication*] .... BG
Blue Hill Meteorological Observatory [*Harvard University*] .... BHMO
Blue Horizon Travel Club [*Cincinnati, OH*] [*FAA designator*] .... BLH
Blue Horizontal Branch .... BHB
Blue Indicator Light .... BIL
Blue Island Public Library, Blue Island, IL [*Library symbol*] .... IBi
Blue Jay Energy Corporation [*NASDAQ symbol*] .... BJEC
Blue-Johnnies [*Australian slang for "delirium tremens"*] .... BJ's
Blue Knights International Law Enforcement Motorcycle Club .... BK
Blue-Laid [*Paper*] .... BLD
Blue Line .... BL
Blue Line Copy .... BLC
Blue Line Print .... BLP

Blue Mountain [*Alaska*] [*Seismograph station code, US Geological Survey*] ....BLM
Blue Mountain College [*Mississippi*] ....BMC
Blue Mountain College, Blue Mountain, MS [*Library symbol*] ....MsBm
Blue Mountain Community College, Pendleton, OR [*Library symbol*] ....OrPeB
Blue Mountain Lake [*New York*] [*Seismograph station code, US Geological Survey*] [*Closed*] ....BML
Blue Mountain Seismological Observatory ....BMSO
Blue Mountains Array [*Oregon*] [*Seismograph station code, US Geological Survey*] [*Closed*] ....BMO
Blue Oyster Cult [*Rock music group*] ....BOC
Blue Pennant [*Navy*] [*British*] ....BL
Blue Print Files ....BPF
Blue Ribbon Defense Panel ....BRDP
Blue Ridge - Big Boulder Uts [*NASDAQ symbol*] ....BLRGU
Blue Ridge, GA [*Radio station call letters*] ....WPPL
Blue Ridge Parkway [*National Park Service designation*] ....BLRI
Blue Ridge Technical Institute, Hendersonville, NC [*Library symbol*] ....NcHvH
Blue Ridge, TX [*Location identifier*] [*FAA*] ....BUJ
Blue Shade [*Paper*] ....BS
Blue Shield [*Health insurance plan*] ....BS
Blue Shield Association [*Formerly, BSMCP*] ....BSA
Blue Shield Medical Care Plans [*Later, BSA*] [*An association*] ....BSMCP
Blue Sky Laws ....BSL
Blue Sky Oil & Gas [*NASDAQ symbol*] ....BLUSF
Blue Steel [*Guns*] ....BS
Blue Stellar Object [*Astronomy*] ....BSO
Blue Streak Request [*Military*] ....BSR
Blue Tetrazolium [*A dye*] ....BT
Blue Tool Steel ....BTS
Blue-Visual [*Color index*] ....B-V
Blue-Whale-Unit [*Whaling industry*] ....BWU
Blue Willow Collectors Society ....BWCS
Blue-Winged Olive [*Insect*] ....BWO
Bluebird, Inc. [*NYSE symbol*] ....BBX
Bluefield [*West Virginia*] [*Airport symbol*] ....BLF
Bluefield College, Bluefield, VA [*Library symbol*] ....ViBluC
Bluefield Public Library, Bluefield, WV [*Library symbol*] ....WvBl
Bluefield State College [*West Virginia*] ....BSC
Bluefield State College, Bluefield, WV [*Library symbol*] ....WvBlS
Bluefield Supply Co. [*NASDAQ symbol*] ....BFLD
Bluefield, VA [*Radio station call letters*] ....WBDY
Bluefield, VA [*Radio station call letters*] ....WBDY-FM
Bluefield, VA [*Television station call letters*] ....WRJK-TV
Bluefield, WV [*Radio station call letters*] ....WHAJ
Bluefield, WV [*Radio station call letters*] ....WHIS
Bluefield, WV [*Radio station call letters*] ....WKOY
Bluefield, WV [*Television station call letters*] ....WVVA-TV
Bluegrass [*A publication*] ....BLBIA
Bluegrass Army Depot ....BGAD
Bluegrass Depot Activity [*Army*] ....BGDA
Bluegrass Unlimited [*A publication*] ....BGU
Bluegrass Unlimited [*A publication*] ....Bluegrass
Bluejacket's Manual [*Navy*] ....BJM
Blueprint ....BP
Blueprints and Plans ....B & P
Blues Unlimited [*A publication*] ....Blues
Blues Unlimited [*A publication*] ....BU
Blues World [*A publication*] ....BW
Bluewater Oil & Gas [*NASDAQ symbol*] ....BWOGF
Bluff ....BLF
Bluff Creek Industries R. R. [*AAR code*] ....BCI
Bluffton College, Bluffton, OH [*OCLC symbol*] ....BLC
Bluffton College, Bluffton, OH [*Library symbol*] ....OBIC
Bluffton College, Mennonite Historical Library, Bluffton, OH [*Library symbol*] ....OBIC-M
Bluffton, IN [*Radio station call letters*] ....WCRD
Bluffton-Wells County Public Library, Bluffton, IN [*OCLC symbol*] ....IWM
Bluie East [*US air bases in Greenland*] [*World War II*] ....BE
Bluie West [*US air bases in Greenland*] [*World War II*] ....BW
Bluish Green ....BG
Blunt Conical Model ....BCM
Blunt Conical Reentry Vehicle ....BCRV
Blunt End Forward ....BEF
Blunt Leading Edge ....BLE
Blunt Trailing Edge ....BTE
Blunted Delta Wing ....BDW
Blunted Wedge ....BW
Blutkorpersenkung [*Blood Sedimentation Rate*] [*Medicine*] ....BKS
Blyn Mountain [*Washington*] [*Seismograph station code, US Geological Survey*] ....BLN
Blythe [*California*] [*Airport symbol*] ....BLH
Blythe, CA [*Radio station call letters*] ....KJMB
Blythe, CA [*Radio station call letters*] ....KJMB-FM
Blytheville, AR [*Location identifier*] [*FAA*] ....BYH
Blytheville, AR [*Location identifier*] [*FAA*] ....GOJ
Blytheville, AR [*Location identifier*] [*FAA*] ....HKA
Blytheville, AR [*Radio station call letters*] ....KHLS
Blytheville, AR [*Radio station call letters*] ....KLCN

Blyvooruitzicht Gold [*NASDAQ symbol*] ....BLYVY
BMC Industries [*NYSE symbol*] ....BMC
BMC International Corp. [*NASDAQ symbol*] ....LITE
BMEWS [*Ballistic Missile Early Warning System*] **Performance Test Outline** ....BPTO
BMEWS [*Ballistic Missile Early Warning System*] **Rearward Communications System** ....BRCS
BMEWS [*Ballistic Missile Early Warning System*] **Specification** ....BSP
BMEWS [*Ballistic Missile Early Warning System*] **System Program Office** ....BSPO
BMEWS [*Ballistic Missile Early Warning System*] **Test Procedure** ....BTP
BMEWS [*Ballistic Missile Early Warning System*] **Test Report** ....BTR
BMFT [*Bundesministerium fuer Forschung und Technologie*] **Mitteilungen** [*A publication*] ....BMFT Mitt
BMI: The Many Worlds of Music [*A publication*] ....BMI
BMMF [*Bible and Medical Missionary Fellowship*] **International** ....BMMFI
BMR [*Bureau of Mineral Resources*] **Journal of Australian Geology and Geophysics** [*A publication*] ....BMR J Aust Geol Geophys
BMW [*Bavarian Motor Works*] **Automobile Club of America** ....BMW-ACA
BMW [*Bavarian Motor Works*] **Car Club of America** ....BMWCCA
BMW [*Bavarian Motor Works*] **Vintage Club of America** ....BMWVCA
B'nai B'rith [*Later, BBI*] ....BB
B'nai B'rith Hillel Foundations ....BBHF
B'nai B'rith International [*Formerly, BB*] ....BBI
B'nai B'rith Vocational Service [*Later, B'nai B'rith Career and Counseling Services*] ....BBVS
B'nai B'rith Women ....BBW
B'nai B'rith Youth Organization ....BBYO
Bnai Zion ....BZ
Bnei Akiva of North America ....BA of NA
BNF [*British Nutrition Foundation*] **Nutrition Bulletin** [*A publication*] ....BNF Nutr Bull
BNIST [*Bureau National de l'Information Scientifique et Technique*] **Rapport Annuel** [*A publication*] ....BNIST Rapp Annu
Bo [*Sierra Leone*] [*Airport symbol*] [*Obsolete*] ....KBS
BO-S-AIRE Airlines, Inc. [*Anderson, SC*] [*FAA designator*] ....BAA
BO-S-AIRE Corp. [*Air carrier designation symbol*] ....BOSX
Boa Vista [*Brazil*] [*Airport symbol*] ....BVB
Boa Vista [*Cape Verde Islands*] [*Airport symbol*] ....BVC
Boaco [*Nicaragua*] [*Seismograph station code, US Geological Survey*] ....BOA
Boang [*Papua New Guinea*] [*Airport symbol*] ....BOV
Board ....BD
Board ....BRD
Board of Action on Letter of Intent Conversion [*Navy*] ....BALIC
Board of Action on Redetermination [*Navy*] ....BOAR
Board of Agriculture and Fisheries. Annual Reports of Proceedings under the Diseases of Animals Acts (London) [*A publication*] ....Bd Agric and Fish Ann Rep Proc Dis Anim Acts (London)
Board of Appeals and Review [*Later, ARB*] [*Civil Service Commission*] ....BAR
Board of the Army Council ....BAC
Board for Aviation Accident Research [*Army*] ....BAAR
Board of Broadcasting Governors ....BBG
Board of Certification in Anesthesiology ....BCA
Board of Certification in Surgery ....BCS
Board of Certified Hazard Control Management ....BCHCM
Board of Certified Product Safety Management ....BCPSM
Board of Certified Safety Professionals ....BCSP
Board of Contract Appeals [*Energy Research and Development Administration*] ....BCA
Board of Cooperative Educational Services, Nassau Education Resource Center, Westbury, NY [*Library symbol*] ....NWeBE
Board of Cooperative Educational Services, Regional Resource Center, Mexico, NY [*Library symbol*] ....NMxB
Board for Coordination of Civil Aviation [*NATO*] ....BOCCA
Board for Correction of Military Records ....BCMR
Board for Correction of Naval Records ....BCNR
Board of Customs and Excise [*British*] ....BCE
Board of Decorations and Medals [*Navy*] ....BD D & M
Board of Directors ....BOD
Board of Directors NATO Maintenance Supply Service System ....BDNMSSS
Board of Economic Warfare [*World War II*] ....BEW
Board of Education ....B of E
Board of Education ....BE
Board of Education ....BEd
Board of Education, Cleveland, OH [*Library symbol*] ....OCIBE
Board of Educational Development [*University of California, Berkeley*] ....BED
Board of Engineers for Rivers and Harbors [*Army*] ....BERH
Board of Engineers for Rivers and Harbors Resident Scholar Program [*Army*] ....BERH-RSP
Board of Examiners for the Foreign Service [*Department of State*] ....BEX
Board of Fire Underwriters of the Pacific [*Later, ISO*] ....BFUP
Board-Foot ....BD-FT
Board Foot ....BF
Board of Foreign Scholarships [*Department of State*] ....BFS
Board for Fundamental Education ....BFE
Board on Geographic Names [*Department of the Interior*] ....BGN
Board of Governors ....BG
Board of Governors, Federal Reserve System ....BGFRS

Board of Governors, Federal Reserve System, Washington, DC [Library symbol] .... DFR
Board of Health ....B of H
Board of Hospitals and Homes of the Methodist Church [Later, National Association of Health and Welfare Ministries of the United Methodist Church] .... BHHMC
Board of Immigration Appeals [Department of Justice] .... BIA
Board of Inland Revenue [British] .... BIR
Board of Inspection and Survey [Navy] .... BIS
Board of Inspection and Survey [Navy] .... B/S
Board of Inspection and Survey [Navy] .... INSURV
Board of Inspection and Survey, Instructions [Navy] .... INSURVINST
Board of Inspection and Survey, Preliminary Evaluation [Navy] .... BISPE
Board for International Broadcasting [Independent government agency] .... BIB
Board for International Food and Agricultural Development [Agency for International Development] .... BIFAD
Board of International Ministries .... BIM
Board of Investments [Philippines] .... BOI
Board Manufacture and Practice [A publication] .... Board Mfr
Board Measure [Lumber] .... BM
Board Measurement Feet .... BMF
Board on Medicine [of the National Academy of Sciences] [Later, IOM] .... BOM
Board of National Estimates [Terminated] [CIA] .... BNE
Board of National Ministries .... BNM
Board of Navy Commissioners [1815-1842] .... BNC
Board of Nephrology Examiners for Nursing and Technology .... BONENT
Board of Ordnance .... BO
Board of Parish Education, Lutheran Church in America .... BPE-LCA
Board of Parole [Abolished, 1976, functions transferred to United States Parole Commission] [Department of Justice] .... BP
Board of Patent Interferences [of Patent Office] .... BPI
Board President .... B/P
Board of Public Works .... BPW
Board of Rabbis .... BR
Board on Radioactive Waste Management [Formerly, CRWM] .... BRWM
Board of Registered Nursing .... BRN
Board of Review [Army] .... BOR
Board of Review [Army] .... BR
Board of Schools of Medical Technology [Later, NAACLS] .... BSMT
Board on Science and Technology for International Development [National Academy of Sciences] .... BOSTID
Board of Scientific Affairs .... BSA
Board of Standards Review [American National Standards Institute] .... BSR
Board of Supply, Executive Yuan [Responsible for removing surplus US war material to China from Guam] .... BOSEY
Board of Tax Appeals .... BTA
Board of Thoracic Surgery [Later, American Board of Thoracic Surgery] .... BTS
Board of Trade .... BOT
Board of Trade .... B of T
Board of Trade .... BT
Board of Trade of the City of Chicago .... B of TCC
Board of Trade Journals .... BTJ
Board of Trade of Kansas City [Missouri] .... B of TKC
Board of Trade of Kansas City, MO .... KCBT
Board of Trade Unit [British] .... BTU
Board of Trade of the Wholesale Seafood Merchants .... BTWSM
Board of Transport [NATO] .... BOT
Board of Underwriters of New York .... BUNY
Board of US Civil Service Examiners .... BCSE
Board of Veterans Appeals [Veterans Administration] .... BVA
Board of War Communications [World War II] .... BWC
Board of Works [British] .... BW
Board of Zoning Adjustment .... BZA
Boarding [Schools or pupils] .... B
Boardroom Reports [A publication] .... Boardroom
Boards .... BDS
Boards of Cooperative Educational Services .... BOCES
Boat .... B
Boat .... BT
Boat and Engine Repair Shop [Coast Guard] .... B & ERS
Boat Group Commander [Navy] .... BGC
Boat Harbor .... BHBR
Boat Inlet/High-Capacity [Analytical combustion system] .... BIHC
Boat Landing Team .... BLT
Boat Lanes .... BL
Boat Manufacturers Association [Later, NMMA] .... BMA
Boat Operating and Repair Unit [Navy] .... BORU
Boat Operating Unit [Navy] .... BOU
Boat Owners Association of the United States .... BOAT/US
Boat Owners Council of America [Defunct] .... BOCA
Boat Repair Unit [Navy] .... BRU
Boat Support Unit .... BSU
Boat Trailer Manufacturers Association [Later, TMA] .... BTMA
Boat Wave .... BTW
Boating Abstracts [A publication] .... BoAb
Boating Accident Reports System [Coast Guard] [Information service] .... BARS
Boating Anti-Pollution Council .... BAC

Boating Industry Association [Later, NMMA] .... BIA
Boating Safety Detachment [Coast Guard] .... BOSDET
Boating Writers International [An association] .... BWI
Boatmen's Bankshares, Inc. [NASDAQ symbol] .... BOAT
Boatswain .... B
Boatswain .... BOSN
Boatswain .... BOSUN
Boatswain .... BTSWN
Boatswain's Mate [Navy rating] .... BM
Boatswain's Mate, Chief [Navy rating] .... BMC
Boatswain's Mate, Construction Battalion, Boatswain [Navy rating] .... BMCBB
Boatswain's Mate, Construction Battalion, Stevedore [Navy rating] .... BMCBS
Boatswain's Mate, First Class [Navy rating] BM1
Boatswain's Mate, Master Chief [Navy rating] .... BMCM
Boatswain's Mate, Second Class [Navy rating] BM2
Boatswain's Mate, Senior Chief [Navy rating] .... BMCS
Boatswain's Mate, Ship Repair, Canvasman [Navy rating] .... BMSRS
Boatswain's Mate, Ship Repair, Crane Operator [Navy rating] .... BMSRC
Boatswain's Mate, Ship Repair, Rigger [Navy rating] .... BMSRR
Boatswain's Mate, Third Class [Navy rating] BM3
Boatyard [British Waterways Board sign] .... B
Boaz, AL [Radio station call letters] .... WBSA
Bob Jones University [South Carolina] [Library symbol] .... BJU
Bob Jones University, Greenville, SC [Library symbol] .... ScGBJ
Bob Oscar Plenty [Character in "Dick Tracy" comic strip] .... BO
Bobbie Brooks, Inc. [NASDAQ symbol] .... BBKS
Bobbin .... BOB
Bobbin Coil Winder .... BCW
Bobo Dioulasso [Upper Volta] [Airport symbol] .... BOY
Bobov in Israel [An association] .... BI
Boca Raton, FL [Radio station call letters] .... WKQS
Boca Raton, FL [Radio station call letters] .... WSBR
Boca Raton, FL [Radio station call letters] .... WWOG
Bocas Del Toro [Panama] [Airport symbol] .... BOC
BOCES [Boards of Cooperative Educational Services], Monroe 1, Penfield, NY [OCLC symbol] .... VBL
BOCES [Boards of Cooperative Educational Services], Monroe 2, Orleans, Spencerport, NY [OCLC symbol] .... VBM
Bochum [Federal Republic of Germany] [Seismograph station code, US Geological Survey] .... BOC
Bochum - University [Federal Republic of Germany] [Seismograph station code, US Geological Survey] .... BUG
Bochumer Anglistische Studien [A publication] .... BAS
Bochumer Arbeiten zur Sprach- und Literaturwissenschaft [A publication] .... BASL
Bockernas Varld [A publication] .... BoV
Bockus International Society of Gastroenterology .... BISG
Bodansky Unit [Also, BOD] [Clinical chemistry] .... BD
Bodansky Unit [Also, BD] [Clinical chemistry] .... BOD
Bodaybo [USSR] [Seismograph station code, US Geological Survey] .... BOD
Bodenbiologie Microbiologie [A publication] .... Bodenbiol Microbiol
Bodenstein Number .... Bo
Bodily Injury [Insurance] .... BI
Bodin Apparel, Inc. [American Stock Exchange symbol] [Delisted] .... BDN
Bodinumu [Papua New Guinea] [Airport symbol] .... BNM
Bodleian Library Record [A publication] .... BLR
Bodleian Library Record [A publication] .... Bodleian Lib Rec
Bodleian Library Record [A publication] .... Bodleian Libr Rec
Bodleian Quarterly Record [A publication] .... BQR
Bodo [Norway] [Airport symbol] .... BOO
Bodon [USSR] [Seismograph station code, US Geological Survey] .... BDN
Body .... B
Body .... BDY
Body Axis Coordinate System .... BACS
Body Bound Bolts .... BBB
Body Burden [of radiation] .... BB
Body Cell Mass .... BCM
Body-Centered [Crystallography] .... BC
Body-Centered Cubic [Crystallography] .... BCC
Body-Centered Tetragonal [Crystallography] .... BCT
Body-on-Chassis [Technical drawings] .... BOC
Body-Cooling Garment .... BCG
Body Count [Military] .... BC
Body Flap Control .... BFC
Body Mass Measurements Device .... BMMD
Body Mounted .... BM
Body-Mounted Accelerometer .... BMA
Body-Mounted Attitude Gyro .... BMAG
Body Odor [Slang] .... BO
Body Point .... BPT
Body Politic [A publication] .... Body Pol
Body or Roof [Freight] .... BDY or RF
Body Shell .... BS
Body Support Cradle .... BSC
Body Surface Area .... BSA
Body Temperature [Medicine] .... BT
Body Temperature Measuring System .... BTMS
Body Temperature, [Ambient] Pressure, Saturated [with water] [Medicine] .... BTPS

Body Water [*Medicine*] ... BW
Body Weight ... BW
Body Whorl ... BW
Body Wing ... BW
Boehm Test of Basic Concepts [*Psychology*] ... BTBC
Boehringer Mannheim Corporation [*Chemical industry supplier*] ... BMC
Boehringer Mannheim Corp., Indianapolis, IN [*OCLC symbol*] ... IBL
Boehringer Mannheim GmbH, Mannheim, Germany [*Library symbol*] ... GyMB
Boeing Air Transport ... BAT
Boeing Airplane Company [*later, Boeing Co.*] **Algebraic Interpretive Computing System** ... BACAIC
Boeing Associated Products ... BAP
Boeing Atlantic Test Center ... BATC
Boeing Commercial Airplane Group [*Seattle, WA*] [*FAA designator*] ... BOE
Boeing Co. [*NYSE symbol*] ... BA
Boeing Co., Aerospace Division, Technical Library, Kent, WA [*Library symbol*] ... WaSBo-A
Boeing Co., Commercial Airplane Group, Technical Libraries, Seattle, WA [*Library symbol*] ... WaSBo
Boeing Co., Wichita Division Library, Wichita, KS [*Library symbol*] ... KWiB
Boeing Computer Services ... BCS
Boeing on Dock ... BOD
Boeing Engineering Analog Computer ... BEAC
Boeing Ground Support ... BGS
Boeing Interface Surveillance Unit ... BISU
Boeing-Michigan Aeronautical Research Center ... BOMARC
Boeing Military Airplane Development Organization ... BMADO
Boeing Operational Supervisory System ... BOSS
Boeing Plastic Analysis Capability for Engines [*Data processing*] [*NASA*] ... BOPACE
Boeing Scientific Research Laboratories ... BSRL
Boeing Shaped Scan Correlator ... BOSSCO
Boeing Small Research Module [*NASA*] ... BSRM
Boeing Systems Coordinator ... BSC
Boeing Test Support [*NASA*] ... BTS
Boeing, Vega, Douglas ... BVD
Boeing Wind Tunnel ... BWT
Boekenschouw voor Godsdienst, Wetenschap en Kunst [*A publication*] ... BGWK
Boende [*Zaire*] [*Airport symbol*] ... BNB
Boergyogyaszati es Venerologiai Szemle [*A publication*] ... Boergyogy Venerol Sz
Boerne, TX [*Radio station call letters*] ... KNCI
Boersen-Zeitung [*A publication*] ... Boersen-Ztg
Bofors Spent Acid Concentration [*Chemical industry*] ... BOSAC
Bogalusa, LA [*Location identifier*] [*FAA*] ... BXA
Bogalusa, LA [*Radio station call letters*] ... WBOX
Bogalusa, LA [*Radio station call letters*] ... WIKC
Bogande [*Upper Volta*] [*Airport symbol*] ... XBG
Bogart-Brociner Associates, Inc. [*Information service*] ... BBA
Bogdanovka [*USSR*] [*Seismograph station code, US Geological Survey*] [*Closed*] ... BGD
Bogens Verden [*A publication*] ... BV
Bogert Oil Co. [*NASDAQ symbol*] ... BOGO
Bogoliubov-Born-Green-Kirkwood-Yvon [*Plasma kinetic theory hierarchy*] ... BBGKY
Bogong [*Victoria*] [*Seismograph station code, US Geological Survey*] [*Closed*] ... BOV
Bogoslovni Vestnik [*A publication*] ... BV
Bogoslovska Smotra [*A publication*] ... BS
Bogoslovski Glasnik [*A publication*] ... BG
Bogota [*Colombia*] [*Seismograph station code, US Geological Survey*] ... BOCO
Bogota [*Colombia*] [*Airport symbol*] ... BOG
Bogota [*Colombia*] [*Seismograph station code, US Geological Survey*] ... BOG
Bogota Public Library, Bogota, NJ [*Library symbol*] ... NjBo
Bogus Check ... BC
Bohack Corp. [*American Stock Exchange symbol*] ... BHK
Boheme, Butterfly, and Barber of Seville [*Frequently performed operas*] ... 3B's
Bohemia ... BOH
Bohemia, Inc. [*NASDAQ symbol*] ... BOHM
Bohemian Club, San Francisco, CA [*Library symbol*] ... CSfBo
Bohemian Free Thinking School Society ... BFTSS
Bohemian-Hungarian [*Slang*] ... BOHUNK
Bohn Aluminum & Brass Corp. [*NYSE symbol*] [*Delisted*] ... BHL
Bohr Frequency Condition ... BFC
Bohr and Mottleson Model [*of nuclear structure*] ... BMM
Bohr-Sommerfeld Atom ... BSA
Bohr-Wheeler Theory ... BWT
Boil-Off ... B-O
Boiled [*Linseed*] **Oil** ... BO
Boiler ... B
Boiler ... BLR
Boiler Design and Performance ... BODEPE
Boiler Feed [*Technical drawings*] ... BF
Boiler Feed Compound Tank [*Technical drawings*] ... BFCT
Boiler Feed Pump [*Technical drawings*] ... BFP
Boiler Feed Water [*Technical drawings*] ... BFW
Boiler Horsepower ... BHP
Boiler House [*Technical drawings*] ... BH
Boiler Inspection and Insurance ... BI & I
Boiler and Machinery ... B & M
Boiler Plate ... BP
Boiler Pressure ... BOPRESS
Boiler Pressure ... BP
Boiler and Pressure Vessel [*Nuclear energy*] ... B + PV
Boiler Room ... BR
Boiler Survey ... BS
Boiler Water ... BOWR
Boilermaker [*Navy*] ... B
Boilermaker ... BMKR
Boilermaker [*Navy rating*] ... BR
Boilermaker, Chief [*Navy rating*] ... BRC
Boilermaker, First Class [*Navy rating*] ... BR1
Boilermaker, Master Chief [*Navy rating*] ... BRCM
Boilermaker, Second Class [*Navy rating*] ... BR2
Boilermaker, Senior Chief [*Navy rating*] ... BRCS
Boilermaker, Ship Repair [*Navy rating*] ... BSR
Boilermaker, Third Class [*Navy rating*] ... BR3
Boilerman [*Navy rating*] ... BT
Boilerman, Chief [*Navy rating*] ... BTC
Boilerman, First Class [*Navy rating*] ... BT1
Boilerman, Master Chief [*Navy rating*] ... BTCM
Boilerman, Second Class [*Navy rating*] ... BT2
Boilerman, Senior Chief [*Navy rating*] ... BTCS
Boilerman, Third Class [*Navy rating*] ... BT3
Boilerwater/Feedwater Test and Treatment ... BFWTT
Boiling ... BOG
Boiling Heavy Water Reactor ... BHWR
Boiling Light Water [*Nuclear energy*] ... BLW
Boiling Liquid Expanding Vapor Explosion [*Chemical engineering*] ... BLEVE
Boiling Nuclear Superheat Critical Experiment ... BONUS-CX
Boiling Nuclear Superheat Reactor ... BONUS
Boiling Point ... BP
Boiling Point Elevation ... BPE
Boiling Point Rise ... BPR
Boiling Range ... BR
Boiling Reactor Experiments [*Nuclear energy*] ... BORAX
Boiling Springs, NC [*Radio station call letters*] ... WGWG
Boiling Water Reactor ... BWR
Boils At ... B
Bois et Forets des Tropiques [*A publication*] ... Bois Forets Trop
Bois et Forets des Tropiques [*A publication*] ... Bois For Trop
Boise [*Idaho*] [*Airport symbol*] ... BOI
Boise [*Idaho*] [*Seismograph station code, US Geological Survey*] ... BSE
Boise Cascade Corporation [*NYSE symbol*] ... BCC
Boise Cascade Corp., Research Library, International Falls, MN [*Library symbol*] ... MnIfBC
Boise, ID [*Television station call letters*] ... KAID
Boise, ID [*Radio station call letters*] ... KBBK
Boise, ID [*Television station call letters*] ... KBCI-TV
Boise, ID [*Radio station call letters*] ... KBOI
Boise, ID [*Radio station call letters*] ... KBOI-FM
Boise, ID [*Radio station call letters*] ... KBSU
Boise, ID [*Radio station call letters*] ... KGEM
Boise, ID [*Radio station call letters*] ... KIDQ
Boise, ID [*Radio station call letters*] ... KJOT
Boise, ID [*Radio station call letters*] ... KKIC
Boise, ID [*Radio station call letters*] ... KSPD
Boise, ID [*Radio station call letters*] ... KTOX
Boise, ID [*Television station call letters*] ... KTVB
Boise, ID [*Television station call letters*] ... KWHP
Boise Interagency Fire Center [*Boise, ID*] [*FAA designator*] ... BIN
Boise Interagency Fire Center, Boise, ID [*OCLC symbol*] ... UDF
Boise Junior College [*Idaho*] ... BJC
Boise Public Library, Boise, ID [*Library symbol*] ... IdB
Boise State College, Boise, ID [*Library symbol*] ... IdBB
Boissevain, MB [*Radio station call letters*] ... CJRB
Boissevain and Morton Regional Library, Boissevain, MB, Canada [*Library symbol*] ... CaMBoM
Boite Postale [*Post Office Box*] [*French*] ... BP
Bok og Bibliotek [*A publication*] ... Bo B
Bok og Bibliotek [*A publication*] ... Bok og Bibl
Bokaro [*India*] [*Seismograph station code, US Geological Survey*] ... BOK
Bokoudini [*Indonesia*] [*Airport symbol*] ... BUI
Boku [*Papua New Guinea*] [*Airport symbol*] [*Obsolete*] ... BOQ
Bolar Pharmaceutical [*American Stock Exchange symbol*] ... BLR
Bold Face [*Printing term*] ... BF
Bold Face Capitals [*Printing term*] ... BFC
Boletim. Academia Nacional de Medicina (Rio De Janeiro) [*A publication*] ... Bol Acad Nac Med (Rio De J)
Boletim. Academia Portuguesa do Ex-Libris [*A publication*] ... BAPE
Boletim. Academia Portuguesa do Ex-Libris [*A publication*] ... BAPEL
Boletim de Agricultura. Departmento de Producao Vegetal (Minas Gerais) [*A publication*] ... Bol Agr Dept Prod Veg (Minas Gerais)
Boletim de Agricultura. Diretoria de Publicidade Agricola (Sao Paulo) [*A publication*] ... Bol Agr Dir Publ Agr (Sao Paulo)
Boletim de Agricultura, Zootechnia, e Veterinaria. Bello Horizonte [*A publication*] ... Bol Agric Zootech e Vet Bello Horizonte

Boletim de Assistencia Medicaos Indigenas e da Luta Contra a Moleatia do Sono (Luanda) [*A publication*] .... Bol Assist Med Indigen (Luanda)
Boletim. Associacao de Filosofia Natural (Portugal) [*A publication*] .... Bol Assoc Filos Nat (Portugal)
Boletim de Bibliografia Portuguesa [*A bibliographic publication*] [*Portugal*] .... BBP
Boletim Bibliografico Brasileiro [*A publication*] .... BBBr
Boletim Biologica (Sao Paulo) [*A publication*] .... Bol Biol (S Paulo)
Boletim. Casa Regional da Beira-Douro [*A publication*] .... BCRBD
Boletim Cearense de Agronomia [*A publication*] .... Bol Cear Agron
Boletim. Centro de Estudos do Hospital dos Servidores do Estado (Rio De Janeiro) [*A publication*] .... Bol Cent Estud Hosp Servidores Estado (Rio De J)
Boletim de Ciencias do Mar [*A publication*] .... Bol Cienc Mar
Boletim Clinico dos Hospitals Civis de Lisboa [*A publication*] .... Bol Clin Hosp Civis Lisb
Boletim. Comissao Reguladora de'Cereais do Arquipelago dos Acores [*A publication*] .... BCRCA
Boletim Cultural [*A publication*] .... BCu
Boletim Cultural. Camara Municipal do Porto [*A publication*] .... BC
Boletim Cultural. Camara Municipal do Porto [*A publication*] .... BCCMP
Boletim Cultural da Guine Portuguesa [*A publication*] .... BCGuineP
Boletim Cultural da Guine Portuguesa [*A publication*] .... Bol Cult Guine Portug
Boletim. Divisao Nacional de Dermatologia Sanitaria [*A publication*] .... Bol Div Nac Dermatol Sanit
Boletim. Divisao Nacional de Lepra [*A publication*] .... Bol Div Nac Lepra
Boletim Epidemiologico (Rio De Janeiro) [*A publication*] .... Bol Epidemiol (Rio De J)
Boletim da Equipe de Odontologia Sanitaria [*A publication*] .... Bol Equipe Odontol Sanit
Boletim. Escola de Farmacia (Coimbra) [*A publication*] .... Bol Esc Farm (Coimbra)
Boletim. Escola de Farmacia. Universidade de Coimbra. Edicao Cientifica [*A publication*] .... Bol Esc Farm Univ Coimbra Ed Cien
Boletim. Escola de Farmacia. Universidade de Coimbra. Edicao Didactica. Noticias Farmaceuticas [*A publication*] .... Bol Esc Farm Univ Coimbra Ed Didact Not Farm
Boletim. Estacao de Biologia Marinha. Universidade Federal do Ceara [*A publication*] .... Bol Estac Biol Mar Univ Fed Ceara
Boletim de Estudos Classicos [*A publication*] .... BEC
Boletim de Estudos de Pesca [*A publication*] .... Bol Estud Pesca
Boletim. Faculdade de Ciencias Agrarias do Para [*A publication*] .... Bol Fac Cienc Agrar Para
Boletim. Faculdade de Direito (Coimbra) [*A publication*] .... Bol Fac Dir (Coimbra)
Boletim. Faculdade de Farmacia. Universidade de Coimbra. Edicao Cientifica [*A publication*] .... Bol Fac Farm Univ Coimbra Ed Cient
Boletim. Faculdade de Odontologia de Piracicaba. Universidade Estadual de Campinas [*A publication*] .... Bol Fac Odontol Piracicaba Univ Estadual Campinas
Boletim de Filologia [*A publication*] .... BdF
Boletim Fitossanitario [*A publication*] .... Bol Fitossanit
Boletim. Fundacao Goncalo Moniz [*A publication*] .... Bol Fund Goncalo Moniz
Boletim Geografico [*A publication*] .... Bol Geog
Boletim Geografico [*A publication*] .... Bol Geogr
Boletim. Hospital das Clinicas. Faculdade de Medicina. Universidade da Bahia [*A publication*] .... Bol Hosp Clin Fac Med Univ Bahia
Boletim de Industria Animal [*A publication*] .... Bol Ind Anim
Boletim Informativo. Instituto de Biologia Maritima [*A publication*] .... Bol Inf Inst Biol Marit
Boletim Informativo. Instituto de Cacau da Bahia [*A publication*] .... Bol Inform Inst Cacau Bahia
Boletim Informativo. Sociedade Brasileira de Radiologia [*A publication*] .... Bol Inf Soc Bras Radiol
Boletim. INPA [*Instituto Nacional de Pesquisas da Amazonia*]. **Botanica** [*A publication*] .... Bol INPA Bot
Boletim. INPA [*Instituto Nacional de Pesquisas da Amazonia*]. **Patologia Tropical** [*A publication*] .... Bol INPA Patol Trop
Boletim. INPA [*Instituto Nacional de Pesquisas da Amazonia*]. **Pesquisas Florestais** [*A publication*] .... Bol INPA Pesqui Florestais
Boletim. INPA [*Instituto Nacional de Pesquisas da Amazonia*]. **Tecnologia** [*A publication*] .... Bol INPA Tecnol
Boletim de Inseminacao Artificial [*A publication*] .... Bol Inseminacao Artif
Boletim. Instituto Agronomico Campinas [*A publication*] .... Bol Inst Agron Campinas
Boletim. Instituto Biologico da Bahia [*A publication*] .... Bol Inst Biol Bahia
Boletim. Instituto de Botanica (Sao Paulo) [*A publication*] .... Bol Inst Bot (Sao Paulo)
Boletim. Instituto Central de Biociencias. Serie Botanica [*A publication*] .... Bol Inst Cent Biocienc Ser Bot
Boletim. Instituto de Ecologia e Experimentacao Agricolas [*A publication*] .... Bol Inst Ecol Exp Agric
Boletim. Instituto de Historia Natural Curitiba Botanica [*A publication*] .... Bol Inst Hist Nat Curitiba Bot
Boletim. Instituto de Investigacao Cientifica de Angola [*A publication*] .... Bol Inst Invest Cient Angola
Boletim. Instituto de Investigacao Cientifica de Angola [*A publication*] .... Bol Inst Investig Cient Angola
Boletim. Instituto Luis de Camoes [*A publication*] .... BILC
Boletim. Instituto Oceanografico [*A publication*] .... Bol Inst Oceanogr
Boletim. Instituto de Pesquisas Cirurgicas (Rio De Janeiro) [*A publication*] .... Bol Inst Pesqui Cir (Rio De J)
Boletim. Instituto de Pesquisas Veterinarias "Desiderio Finamor" [*A publication*] .... Bol Inst Pesqui Vet "Desiderio Finamor"
Boletim. Instituto de Tecnologia de Alimentos [*A publication*] .... Bol Inst Tecnol Aliment
Boletim. Instituto de Tecnologia Rural. Universidade do Ceara [*A publication*] .... Bol Inst Tecnol Rural Univ Ceara
Boletim Internacional de Bibliografia Luso-Brasileira [*Lisboa*] [*A publication*] .... BIBLB
Boletim. IPA [*Instituto de Pesquisas Agronomicas*] **PSM** [*Programa de Sorgo e Milheto*] [*A publication*] .... Bol IPA PSM
Boletim. Junta Nacional da Cortica [*A publication*] ...... Bol Junta Nac Cortica
Boletim de Matematica, Estatistica, e Fisica [*A publication*] .... Bol Mat Estatist Fis
Boletim Mensal. Sociedade de Lingua Portuguesa [*A publication*].... BMSLP
Boletim de Minas (Portugal Direccao-Geral de Minas e Servicos Geologicos) [*A publication*] .... Bol Minas (Port Dir-Geral Minas Serv Geol)
Boletim. Museu Botanico Municipal (Curitiba) [*A publication*] .... Bol Mus Bot Munic (Curitiba)
Boletim. Museu de Historia Natural UFMG [*Universidade Federal de Minas Gerais*]. **Botanica** [*A publication*] .... Bol Mus Hist Nat UFMG Bot
Boletim. Museu de Historia Natural UFMG [*Universidade Federal de Minas Gerais*]. **Zoologia** [*A publication*] .... Bol Mus Hist Nat UFMG Zool
Boletim. Museu Municipal do Funchal [*A publication*] .... Bol Mus Munic Funchal
Boletim. Museu Nacional (Rio De Janeiro). Antropologia [*A publication*] .... Bol Mus Nac (Rio De J) Antropol
Boletim. Museu Nacional (Rio De Janeiro). Botanica [*A publication*] .... Bol Mus Nac (Rio De J) Bot
Boletim. Museu Nacional (Rio De Janeiro). Geologia [*A publication*] .... Bol Mus Nac (Rio De Janeiro) Geol
Boletim. Museu Nacional (Rio De Janeiro). Zoologia [*A publication*] .... Bol Mus Nac (Rio De J) Zool
Boletim. Museu Paraense Emilio Goeldi [*A publication*] .... Bol Mus Paraense Emilio Goeldi
Boletim. Museu Paraense Emilio Goeldi. Nova Serie. Geologia [*A publication*] .... Bol Mus Paraense Emilio Goeldi Nova Ser Geol
Boletim. Museu Paraense Emilio Goeldi. Nova Serie. Zoologia [*A publication*] .... Bol Mus Para Emilio Goeldi Nova Ser Zool
Boletim de Numismatica (Brasil) [*A publication*] .... Bol Num (Brasil)
Boletim de Oncologia [*A publication*] .... Bol Oncol
Boletim Paranaense de Geociencias [*A publication*] ...... Bol Parana Geocienc
Boletim Paranaense de Geografia [*A publication*] .... Bol Parana Geogr
Boletim Pecuario (Lisbon) [*A publication*] .... Bol Pecu (Lisb)
Boletim de Psicologia [*A publication*] .... Bol Psicol
Boletim de Psiquiatria [*A publication*] .... Bol Psiquiatr
Boletim do Sanatorio (Sao Lucas) [*A publication*] .... Bol Sanat (Sao Lucas)
Boletim. Sociedade Brasileira de Matematica [*A publication*] .... Bol Soc Brasil Mat
Boletim. Sociedade Broteriana [*A publication*] .... Bol Soc Broteriana
Boletim. Sociedade Cearense de Agronomia [*A publication*] .... Bol Soc Cear Agron
Boletim. Sociedade Cearense de Agronomia [*A publication*] .... Bol Soc Cearense Agron
Boletim. Sociedade de Estudios Filologicos [*A publication*] .... BSEF
Boletim. Sociedade Geologica de Portugal [*A publication*] .... Bol Soc Geol Port
Boletim. Sociedade de Medicina e Cirugia de Sao Paulo [*A publication*] .... Bol Soc Med e Cirug S Paulo
Boletim. Sociedade Paulista de Medicina Veterinaria [*A publication*] .... Bol Soc Paul Med Vet
Boletim. Sociedade Portuguesa de Ciencias Naturais [*A publication*] .... Bol Soc Port Cienc Nat
Boletim Tecnico. Centro de Pesquisas e Desenvolvimento (Estado da Bahia) [*A publication*] .... Bol Tec Cent Pesqui Desenvolvimento (Estado Bahia)
Boletim Tecnico. Centro de Tecnologia Agricola e Alimentar [*A publication*] .... Bol Tec Cent Tecnol Agric Aliment
Boletim Tecnico. Departamento Nacional de Obras Contra as Secas [*A publication*] .... Bol Tec Dep Nac Obras Contra Secas
Boletim Tecnico. Departamento de Producao Vegetal Secretaria de Agricultura do Parana [*A publication*] .... Bol Tec Dep Prod Veg Secr Agric Parana
Boletim Tecnico. Instituto Agronomico do Leste (Cruz Das Almas) [*A publication*] .... Bol Tec Inst Agron Leste (Cruz Das Almas)
Boletim Tecnico. Instituto Agronomico do Nordeste [*A publication*] .... Bol Tec Inst Agron Nordeste
Boletim Tecnico. Instituto Agronomico del Norte [*A publication*] .... Bolm Tec Inst Agron N
Boletim Tecnico. Instituto Agronomico do Norte Belem [*A publication*] .... Bol Tec Inst Agron Norte Belem
Boletim Tecnico. Instituto Agronomico do Sul [*A publication*] .... Bol Tec Inst Agron Sul

Boletim Tecnico. Instituto Agronomico do Sul (Pelotas) [*A publication*] .... Bol Tec Inst Agron Sul (Pelotas)
Boletim Tecnico. Instituto de Pesquisas e Experimentacao Agropecuarias do Norte [*A publication*] .... Bolm Tec Inst Pesq Exp Agropecuar N
Boletim Tecnico. Instituto de Pesquisas e Experimentacao Agropecuarias do Norte [*A publication*] .... Bol Tec IPEAN
Boletim Tecnico. Petrobras [*Centro de Pesquisas e Desenvolvimento*] [*A publication*] .... Bol Tec Petrobras
Boletim Trimestral Subcomissao Catarinense de Folclore da Comissao Nacional Brasileira de Folclore do Instituto Brasileiro de Educacao, Ciencia, e Cultura [*A publication*] .... BCF
Boletim. Universidade Federal do Parana. Botanica [*A publication*] .... Bol Univ Fed Parana Bot
Boletim. Universidade Federal do Parana. Zoologia [*A publication*] .... Bol Univ Fed Parana Zool
Boletim. Universidade do Parana. Farmacognosia [*A publication*] .... Bol Univ Parana Farm
Boletim. Universidade do Parana. Geologia [*A publication*] .... Bol Univ Parana Geol
Boletim de Zoologia [*A publication*] .... Bol Zool
Boletim de Zoologia e Biologia Marinha (Nova Serie) [*A publication*] .... Bol Zool Biol Mar (Nova Ser)
Boletin. Academia Aragonesa de Nobles y Bellas Artes de San Luis de Zaragoza [*A publication*] .... BANAZ
Boletin. Academia Argentina de Buenas Letras [*A publication*] .... BAABL
Boletin. Academia Argentina de Letras [*A publication*] .... BAAL
Boletin. Academia de Bellas Artes y Ciencias Historicas de Toledo [*A publication*] .... BABAT
Boletin. Academia de Bellas Artes de Cordoba [*A publication*] .... BABC
Boletin. Academia de Bellas Artes de Valladolid [*A publication*] .... BABA
Boletin. Academia de Ciencias, Bellas Letras, y Nobles Artes de Cordoba [*A publication*] .... BACBLNAC
Boletin. Academia de Ciencias Fisicas, Matematicas, y Naturales [*Caracas*] [*A publication*] .... Bol Acad Cienc Fis Mat Natur
Boletin. Academia de Ciencias Fisicas, Matematicas, y Naturales (Caracas) [*A publication*] .... Bol Acad Cienc Fis Mat Nat (Caracas)
Boletin. Academia Colombiana [*A publication*] .... BAC
Boletin. Academia Colombiana [*A publication*] .... BACol
Boletin. Academia Cubana de la Lengua [*A publication*] .... BACL
Boletin. Academia Gallega [*A publication*] .... BAG
Boletin. Academia de la Historia [*A publication*] .... BAH
Boletin. Academia Nacional de Ciencias (Cordoba) [*A publication*] .... Bol Acad Nac Cienc (Cordoba)
Boletin. Academia Nacional de la Historia (Quito) [*A publication*] .... BANHQ
Boletin. Academia Nacional de Medicina (Buenos Aires) [*A publication*] .... Bol Acad Nac Med (B Aires)
Boletin. Academia Norteamericana de la Lengua Espanola [*A publication*] .... BANLE
Boletin. Academia Venezolana [*A publication*] .... BAV
Boletin de Agricultura, Mineria, e Industrias [*A publication*] .... Bol Agr
Boletin Agro-Pecuario [*A publication*] .... Bol Agro-Pec
Boletin Argentino Forestal [*A publication*] .... Bol Argent For
Boletin Arqueologico de Tarragona [*A publication*] .... BAT
Boletin Arqueologico de Tarragona [*A publication*] .... Bol Arq
Boletin. Asociacion Argentina de Odontologia para Ninos [*A publication*] .... Bol Asoc Argent Odontol Ninos
Boletin. Asociacion Chilena de Proteccion de la Familia [*A publication*] .... Bol Asoc Chil Prot Fam
Boletin. Asociacion Europea de Profesores de Espanol [*A publication*] .... BAEPE
Boletin. Asociacion Folklorica (Argentina) [*A publication*] .... BAFA
Boletin. Asociacion Medica de Puerto Rico [*A publication*] .... Bol Asoc Med PR
Boletin. Asociacion Medica de Puerto Rico [*A publication*] .... Bol Asoc Med Puerto Rico
Boletin. Asociacion Mexicana de Geologos Petroleros [*A publication*] .... Bol Asoc Mex Geol Pet
Boletin. Asociacion Mexicana de Geologos Petroleros [*A publication*] .... Bol Asoc Mex Geol Petrol
Boletin. Asociacion Nacional de Ingenieros Agronomos [*A publication*] .... Bol Asoc Nac Ing Agron
Boletin. Asociacion Nacional de Ingenieros Agronomos [*A publication*] .... Bol Asoc Nac Ingen Agron
Boletin. Asociacion Tucumana de Folklore [*A publication*] .... BATF
Boletin. Asociacion Venezolana de Enfermeras Profesionales [*A publication*] .... Bol Asoc Venez Enferm Prof
Boletin Bibliografico de Antropologia Americana [*A publication*] .... BBAA
Boletin Bibliografico de Antropologia Americana [*A publication*] .... Bol Bibl Antropol Amer
Boletin Bibliografico. Facultad de Agronomia. Universidad Central de Venezuela [*A publication*] .... Bol Bibliogr Fac Agron Univ Cent Venez
Boletin Bibliografico Forestal [*Chile*] [*A publication*] .... Bol Bibl
Boletin Bibliografico Mexicano [*A publication*] .... BBM
Boletin Bibliografico (Peru) [*A publication*] .... Bol Biblio (Peru)
Boletin. Biblioteca de Menendez Pelayo [*A publication*] .... BBMP
Boletin. Biblioteca National (Lima) [*A publication*] .... BBNL
Boletin. Biblioteca National (Mexico) [*A publication*] .... BBNM
Boletin de Bibliotecas y Bibliografia [*A publication*] .... BBB
Boletin. Camara de Comercio (Caracas) [*A publication*] .... Bol Cam Com (Caracas)
Boletin. Centro de Estudios del Siglo XVIII, Oviedo [*A publication*] .... BOCES XVIII
Boletin. Centro de Investigaciones Biologicas. Universidad del Zulia [*A publication*] .... Bol Cent Invest Biol Univ Zulia
Boletin. Centro Naval [*A publication*] .... Bol Cent Nav
Boletin. Centro Panamericano de Fiebre Aftosa [*A publication*] .... Bol Cent Panam Fiebre Aftosa
Boletin Chileno de Parasitologia [*A publication*] .... Bol Chil Parasitol
Boletin. Clinica de Endocrinologia y Metabolismo [*A publication*] .... Bol Clin Endocrinol Metab
Boletin. Colegio de Profesionales de la Enfermeria de Puerto Rico [*A publication*] .... Bol Col Prof Enferm PR
Boletin. Colegio de Quimicos de Puerto Rico [*A publication*] .... Bol Col Quim PR
Boletin de Combustibles y Petroquimica [*A publication*] .... Bol Combust Petroquim
Boletin. Comision de Monumentos de Burgos [*A publication*] .... BCMB
Boletin. Comision de Monumentos de Lugo [*A publication*] .... BCML
Boletin. Comision de Monumentos de Valladolid [*A publication*] .... BCMV
Boletin. Comision Provincial de Monumentos de Navarra [*A publication*] .... BCPN
Boletin. Comision Provincial de Monumentos de Orense [*A publication*] .... BCPO
Boletin. Comision Provincial de Monumentos de Orense [*A publication*] .... BCPOrense
Boletin. Compania Administradora del Guano [*A publication*] .... Bol Cia Adm Guano
Boletin. Compania Administradora del Guano [*A publication*] .... Bol Comp Admin Guano
Boletin Cultural y Bibliografico [*Bogota*] [*A publication*] .... BCB
Boletin. Departamento Forestal (Montevideo, Uruguay) [*A publication*] .... Bol Dep For (Uruguay)
Boletin Dermatologico Sanitario [*A publication*] .... Bol Dermatol Sanit
Boletin de Dialectologia Espanola [*A publication*] .... BDE
Boletin. Direccion General de Archivos y Bibliotecas [*A publication*] .... BDGAB
Boletin. Direccion de Malariologia y Saneamiento Ambiental [*A publication*] .... Bol Dir Malariol Saneamiento Ambiental
Boletin. Direccion Nacional de Geologia y Mineria (Argentina) [*A publication*] .... Bol Dir Nac Geol Min (Argent)
Boletin de Divulgacion Tecnica Instituto de Patologia Vegetal (Buenos Aires) [*A publication*] .... Bol Divulg Tec Inst Patol Veg (B Aires)
Boletin Divulgativo. Instituto Nacional de Investigaciones Forestales (Mexico) [*A publication*] .... Bol Divulg Inst Nac Invest For (Mex)
Boletin de Documentacion. Fondo para la Investigacion Economica y Social [*A publication*] .... Bol Docum Fondo Invest Econ Soc
Boletin Eclesiastico de Filipinas [*A publication*] .... BEF
Boletin Eclesiastico de Filipinas [*A publication*] .... Bol Eclesias Fil
Boletin de Entomologia Venezolana [*A publication*] .... Bol Entomol Venez
Boletin Epidemiologico [*A publication*] .... Bol Epidemiol
Boletin. Escuela Nacional de Agricultura (Lima) [*A publication*] .... Bol Esc Nac Agr (Lima)
Boletin. Estacion Central de Ecologia [*A publication*] .... Bol Estac Cent Ecol
Boletin. Estacion Experimental Agricola "La Molina" [*A publication*] .... Bol Estac Exp Agric "La Molina"
Boletin. Estacion Experimental Agricola "La Molina" [*A publication*] .... Bol Estac Exp Agr "La Molina"
Boletin. Estacion Experimental Agricola "Tingo Maria" [*A publication*] .... Bol Estac Exp Agr "Tingo Maria"
Boletin. Estacion Experimental Agricola "Tingo Maria" [*A publication*] .... Boln Estac Exp Agric "Tingo Maria"
Boletin de Estudios Asturianos [*A publication*] .... BEA
Boletin de Estudios Economicos [*A publication*] .... Bol Estud Econ
Boletin de Estudios Geograficos de la Universidad Nacional de Cuyo [*A publication*] .... Bol Estud Geogr Univ Nac Cuyo
Boletin de Estudios Germanicos [*A publication*] .... BEG
Boletin de Estudios Latinoamericanos y del Caribe [*A publication*] .... Bol Estud Latinoamer
Boletin de Estudios Medicos y Biologicos [*A publication*] .... Bol Estud Med Biol
Boletin de Estudios Medicos y Biologicos. Universidad Nacional Autonoma de Mexico [*A publication*] .... Bol Estud Med Biol Univ Nac Auton Mex
Boletin. Experimental Servicio Agricola Interamericano (La Paz) [*A publication*] .... Bol Exp Serv Agric Interam (La Paz)
Boletin. Facultad de Derecho y Ciencias Sociales (Cordoba) [*A publication*] .... Bol Fac Der Cienc Soc (Cordoba)
Boletin. Facultad de Ingenieria y Agrimensura de Montevideo [*A publication*] .... Bol Fac Ing Agrimensura Montevideo
Boletin. Facultad de Ingenieria y Agrimensura. Universidad de la Republica [*A publication*] .... Bol Fac Ing Agrimens Univ Repub
Boletin de Filologia [*A publication*] .... BF
Boletin de Filologia Espanola [*A publication*] .... BFE
Boletin de Filologia. Instituto de Estudios Superiores del Uruguay [*A publication*] .... BFU
Boletin de Filologia. Instituto de Filologia de la Universidade de Chile [*A publication*] .... BFUCH
Boletin de Filologia (Montevideo) [*A publication*] .... BFM

Boletin de Filologia (Rio De Janeiro) [*A publication*]................................BFR
Boletin Forestal y de Industrias Forestales para America Latina. Oficina Forestal Regional de la FAO [*Food and Agriculture Organization*] [*A publication*].......................Bol For Ind For Amer Lat FAO
Boletin Genetico [*A publication*].................................. Bol Genet
Boletin de Geologia (Caracas) [*A publication*].................. Bol Geol (Caracas)
Boletin de Geologia (Caracas). Publicacion Especial [*A publication*]...................... Bol Geol (Caracas) Publ Espec
Boletin de Geologia. Direccion de Geologia (Venezuela) [*A publication*]...................................Bol Geo Dir Geol (Venez)
Boletin de Geologia. Direccion de Geologia (Venezuela) [*A publication*].................................Bol Geol Dir Geol (Venez)
Boletin de Geologia. Publicacion Especial. Direccion de Geologia (Venezuela) [*A publication*]............................ Bol Geol Publ Espec Dir Geol (Venez)
Boletin de Geologia. Universidad Industrial de Santander [*A publication*]....................Bol Geol Univ Ind Santander
Boletin Geologico y Minero (Espana) [*A publication*].........Bol Geol Min (Esp)
Boletin de Higiene y Epidemiologia [*A publication*] ....Bol Hig Epidemiol
Boletin de Historia Natural [*A publication*]........................... Bol Historia Nat
Boletin de Historia Natural. Sociedad "Felipe Poey" [*A publication*]...........................Bol Hist Nat Soc "Felipe Poey"
Boletin. Hospital Oftalmologico de Nuestra Senora de la Luz [*A publication*].........................Bol Hosp Oftalmol Nuestra Senora de la Luz
Boletin Indigenista Venezolano [*A publication*].............................BIV
Boletin de Informacion Dental (Madrid) [*A publication*] ... Bol Inf Dent (Madr)
Boletin de Informacion. Ministerio de Agricultura (Madrid) [*A publication*]........................... Bol Inform Minist Agric (Madrid)
Boletin. Informacion Tecnica. Asociacion de Investigacion Tecnica de las Industrias de la Madera y Corcho [*A publication*] .... Bol Inform Tec Asoc Invest Tec Ind Madera
Boletin Informativo. Instituto Forestal (Santiago-De-Chile) [*A publication*].. Bol Inform Inst For (Chile)
Boletin Informativo. Secretaria General del Movimiento [*A publication*]...BISGM
Boletin Informativo. Seminario de Derecho Politico [*A publication*]....BISDP
Boletin. Instituto de Antropologia. Universidad de Antioquia, Medellin [*A publication*] .... Bol Inst Antropol Univ Antioquia Medellin
Boletin. Instituto Bacteriologico de Chile [*A publication*] .... Bol Inst Bacteriol Chile
Boletin. Instituto de Biologia Marina. Mar Del Plata [*A publication*] .... Bol Inst Biol Mar Mar Del Plata
Boletin. Instituto Botanica. Universidad de Quito [*A publication*] .... Bol Inst Bot Univ Quito
Boletin. Instituto Caro y Curevo [*A publication*] ....BICC
Boletin. Instituto de Clinica Quirurgica [*A publication*]........ Bol Inst Clin Quir
Boletin. Instituto de las Espanas [*A publication*] ....BIE
Boletin. Instituto Espanol de Londres [*A publication*]..............................BIE
Boletin. Instituto Espanol de Oceanografia [*A publication*] .... Bol Inst Esp Oceanogr
Boletin. Instituto de Estudios Asturianos [*A publication*] .... BIEA
Boletin. Instituto de Estudios Helenicos [*A publication*] .... BIEH
Boletin. Instituto de Estudios Medicos y Biologicos [*A publication*] ....Bol Inst Estud Med Biol
Boletin. Instituto de Estudios Medicos y Biologicos. Universidad Nacional de Mexico [*A publication*] .... Bol Inst Estud Med Biol Univ Nac Mex
Boletin. Instituto de Estudios Politicos [*A publication*] .....Bol Inst Estud Polit
Boletin. Instituto Fernan Gonzalez [*A publication*] ....BIFG
Boletin. Instituto de Filologia de la Universidad de Chile [*A publication*]... BFC
Boletin. Instituto de Folklore [*A publication*]..................................BIFV
Boletin. Instituto de Folklore [*A publication*] .... Boletin IF
Boletin. Instituto de Folklore [*A publication*] ....Inst Folk
Boletin. Instituto Forestal de Investigaciones y Experiencias (Madrid) [*A publication*]............Bol Inst For Invest Exp (Madrid)
Boletin. Instituto Forestal Latino-Americano de Investigacion y Capacitacion [*A publication*] .... Bol Inst For Lat-Am Invest Capac
Boletin. Instituto Frances [*A publication*] ....BIF
Boletin. Instituto de Genetica. Sociedad Nacional Agraria (Lima) [*A publication*]........................ Bol Inst Genet Soc Nac Agrar (Lima)
Boletin. Instituto de Geologia (Mexico) [*A publication*] .... Bol Inst Geol (Mex)
Boletin. Instituto Geologico y Minero de Espana [*A publication*] .... Bol Inst Geol Min Esp
Boletin. Instituto de Investigacion de los Recursos Marinos (Callao) [*A publication*] ....Bol Inst Invest Recur Mar (Callao)
Boletin. Instituto de Investigaciones Folkloricas. Universidad Interamericana (Panama) [*A publication*].......................BIFP
Boletin. Instituto de Investigaciones Historicas [*A publication*]...............BIIH
Boletin. Instituto de Investigaciones Literarias [*A publication*]...............BIIL
Boletin. Instituto de Investigaciones Veterinarias (Maracay) [*A publication*].............................Bol Inst Invest Vet (Maracay)
Boletin. Instituto del Mar del Peru (Callao) [*A publication*]...................... Bol Inst Mar Peru (Callao)
Boletin. Instituto de Matematica, Astronomia, y Fisica [*A publication*]...........................Bol Inst Mat Astron Fis
Boletin. Instituto Nacional de Antropologia e Historia de Mexico [*A publication*]................ Bol Inst Nac Antropol Hist Mexico
Boletin. Instituto Nacional de Higiene (Caracas) [*A publication*] .... Bol Inst Nac Hig (Caracas)

Boletin. Instituto Nacional de Investigaciones Agronomicas (Madrid) [*A publication*] .... Bol Inst Nac Invest Agron (Madr)
Boletin. Instituto Nacional de Neumologia (Mexico) [*A publication*]...........................Bol Inst Nac Neumol (Mex)
Boletin. Instituto Oceanografico. Universidad de Oriente (Cumana) [*A publication*]......... Bol Inst Oceanogr Univ Oriente (Cumana)
Boletin. Instituto de Quimica. Universidad Nacional Autonoma de Mexico [*A publication*].................. Bol Inst Quim Mexico
Boletin. Instituto de Quimica. Universidad Nacional Autonoma de Mexico [*A publication*]..............Bol Inst Quim Univ Nac Auton Mex
Boletin. Instituto de Tonantzintla [*A publication*] .... Bol Inst Tonantzintla
Boletin Interamericano de Musica (Inter-American Music Bulletin) [*A publication*] .... Intam Mus B
Boletin. Laboratorio de la Clinica "Luis Razetti" [*A publication*]..................................... Bol Lab Clin "Luis Razetti"
Boletin. Laboratorio de Paleontologia de Vertebrados [*A publication*].....................Bol Lab Paleontol Vertebr
Boletin Latino-Americano de Musica [*A publication*]...........................BLAM
Boletin de Matematicas [*A publication*].................................Bol Mat
Boletin de Medicina, Cirugia, y Farmacia (Madrid) [*A publication*].......................... Bol Med Cirug y Farm (Madrid)
Boletin Medico. Hospital Infantil de Mexico [*A publication*]...................... Bol Med Hosp Infant Mex
Boletin Medico. Universidad Autonoma de Guadalajara [*A publication*]...................................Bol Med Univ Auton Guadalajara
Boletin Mensual de Estadistica [*A publication*] .... Bol Mens Estadist
Boletin Mexicano de Derecho Comparado [*A publication*] .... Bol Mexic Der Comp
Boletin Mexicano de Reumatologia [*A publication*]............Bol Mex Reumatol
Boletin de Minas y Petroleo [*A publication*] .... Bol Minas y Petroleo
Boletin Minero [*A publication*] ....Bol Minero
Boletin. Museo de Ciencias Naturales [*A publication*] ....Bol Mus Cienc Nat
Boletin. Museo de Motivos Populares Argentinos Jose Hernandez [*A publication*]....................................BMJH
Boletin. Museo Social Argentino [*A publication*] .... Bol Mus Soc Argent
Boletin de Musica y Artes Visuales [*A publication*] .... Mus y Artes
Boletin de Noticias. Instituto de Fomento Algodonero (Bogota) [*A publication*]...................... Bol Not Inst Fom Algodonero (Bogota)
Boletin Oficial. Asociacion de Tecnicos Azucareros de Cuba [*A publication*]................... Bol Of Asoc Tec Azucar Cuba
Boletin Oficial del Estado [*Spain*] [*A publication*]..................... Bol Of Estado
Boletin. Oficina Sanitaria Panamericana [*A publication*] .... B Of San Pa
Boletin. Oficina Sanitaria Panamericana [*A publication*] .... Bol Ofic Sanit Panamer
Boletin. Oficina Sanitaria Panamericana [*A publication*] .... Bol Of Sanit Panam
Boletin. Oficina Sanitaria Panamericana. English Edition [*A publication*]...............................Bol Ofic Sanit Panam Engl Ed
Boletin Paleontologico de Buenos Aires [*A publication*] .... Bol Paleontol B Aires
Boletin de Patologia Medica (Madrid) [*A publication*] .... Bol Patol Med (Madr)
Boletin de Patologia Vegetal y Entomologia Agricola [*A publication*].....................Boln Patol Veg Ent Agric
Boletin de Patologia Vegetal y Entomologia Agricola [*A publication*].....................Bol Patol Veg Entomol Agric
Boletin del Petroleo [*A publication*]....................................Bol Petroleo
Boletin Popular. Direccion General de Agricultura de Guatemala. Ministerio de Agricultura (Guatemala) [*A publication*]....................Bol Popular Min Agric (Guatemala)
Boletin de Produccion Animal [*A publication*]........................ Bol Prod Anim
Boletin de Produccion y Fomento Agricola [*A publication*] .... Bol Prod Fom Agric
Boletin. Publicaciones del Museo y de la Sociedad Arqueologica de la Serena [*A publication*]...................... Bol Mus Soc Arqueol la Serena
Boletin. Real Academia de Buenas Letras de Barcelona [*A publication*].................................. BABL
Boletin. Real Academia de Buenas Letras de Barcelona [*A publication*]..................................BABLB
Boletin. Real Academia de Buenas Letras de Barcelona [*A publication*].................................. BALB
Boletin. Real Academia de Buenas Letras de Barcelona [*A publication*]..................................BRABLB
Boletin. Real Academia de Cordoba [*A publication*] ....BAC
Boletin. Real Academia de Cordoba [*A publication*] ....BRAC
Boletin. Real Academia Espanola [*A publication*]................................BAE
Boletin. Real Academia Espanola [*A publication*]................................BRAE
Boletin. Real Academia de la Historia [*A publication*] ....BAHist
Boletin. Real Academia de la Historia [*A publication*] ....BRAH
Boletin. Real Academia de la Historia [*A publication*] ....B Real Acad
Boletin. Real Sociedad Espanola de Historia Natural [*A publication*].......................Bol R Soc Espan Hist Nat
Boletin. Real Sociedad Espanola de Historia Natural. Seccion Biologica [*A publication*]............Bol R Soc Esp Hist Nat Secc Biol
Boletin. Real Sociedad Espanola de Historia Natural. Seccion Geologica [*A publication*].....................Bol R Soc Esp Hist Nat Secc Geol
Boletin. Real Sociedad Geografica [*A publication*]...........................BRSG
Boletin. Real Sociedad Vascongada de Amigos del Pais [*A publication*].....................................BRSV

Boletin. Real Sociedad Vascongada de Amigos del Pais [*A publication*]......BSVasc
Boletin de Salud Publica [*A publication*]......Bol Salud Publica
Boletin. Seminario de Estudios de Arte y Arqueologia [*A publication*]......BSEA
Boletin. Seminario de Estudios de Arte y Arqueologia [*A publication*]......BSEAA
Boletin. Seminario de Estudios de Arte y Arqueologia. Universidad de Valladolid [*A publication*]......BSAAV
Boletin. Seminario de Estudios de Arte y Arqueologia. Universidad de Valladolid [*A publication*]......BSAV
Boletin. Servicio Geologico Nacional de Nicaragua [*A publication*]......Bol Serv Geol Nac Nicaragua
Boletin. Servicio de Plagas Forestales [*A publication*]......Bol Serv Plagas For
Boletin. Sociedad Argentina de Angiologia [*A publication*]......Bol Soc Argent Angiol
Boletin. Sociedad Argentina de Botanica [*A publication*]......Bol Soc Argent Bot
Boletin. Sociedad de Biologia de Concepcion [*A publication*]......Bol Soc Biol Concepcion
Boletin. Sociedad Botanica del Estado de Jalisco [*A publication*]......Bol Soc Bot Estado Jalisco
Boletin. Sociedad Botanica de Mexico [*A publication*]......Bol Soc Bot Mex
Boletin. Sociedad Castellonense de Cultura [*A publication*]......BSCC
Boletin. Sociedad de Cirugia de Chile [*A publication*]......Bol Soc Cirug Chile
Boletin. Sociedad de Cirugia del Uruguay [*A publication*]......Bol Soc Cir Urug
Boletin. Sociedad Espanola de Ceramica y Vidrio [*A publication*]......Bol Soc Esp Ceram Vidrio
Boletin. Sociedad Espanola de Historia de la Farmacia [*A publication*]......Bol Soc Esp Hist Farm
Boletin. Sociedad General de Autores de Espana [*A publication*]......BSGAE
Boletin. Sociedad Geologica del Peru [*A publication*]......Bol Soc Geol Peru
Boletin. Sociedad Matematica Mexicana [*A publication*]......Bol Soc Mat Mexicana
Boletin. Sociedad Nacional de Mineria y Petroleo [*A publication*]......Bol Soc Nac Mineria Petrol
Boletin. Sociedad Quimica del Peru [*A publication*]......Bol Soc Quim Peru
Boletin. Sociedad Venezolana de Ciencias Naturales [*A publication*]......Boln Soc Venez Cienc Nat
Boletin. Sociedad Venezolana de Ciencias Naturales [*A publication*]......Bol Soc Venez Cienc Nat
Boletin. Sociedad Venezolana de Cirugia [*A publication*]......Bol Soc Venez Cir
Boletin. Sociedad Venezolana de Espeleologia [*A publication*]......Bol Soc Venez Espeleol
Boletin. Sociedad Venezolana de Geologos [*A publication*]......Bol Soc Venez Geol
Boletin. Sociedade Brasileira de Matematica [*A publication*]......Bol Soc Bras Mat
Boletin. Sociedade do Estudos de Mocambique Byzantinoslavica [*A publication*]......BSEM
Boletin. Societe Espanola de Excursiones [*A publication*]......BSEE
Boletin sobre Suelos Derivados de Cenizas Volcanicas [*A publication*]......Bol Suelos Deriv Cenizas Volcanicas
Boletin Tecnico. Escuela de Ingenieria Forestal. Universidad de Chile [*A publication*]......Bol Tec Esc Ingen For Univ Chile
Boletin Tecnico. Escuela Nacional de Agricultura Chapingo [*A publication*]......Bol Tec Esc Nac Agr Chapingo
Boletin Tecnico. Federacion Nacional de Cafeteros (Colombia) [*A publication*]......Bol Tec Feder Nac Cafeteros (Colombia)
Boletin Tecnico. Instituto de Fomenta Algodonero (Bogota) [*A publication*]......Bol Tec Inst Fom Algodonero (Bogota)
Boletin Tecnico. Instituto Forestal. Santiago-De-Chile [*A publication*]......Bol Tec Inst For Chile
Boletin Tecnico. Instituto Nacional de Investigaciones Forestales (Mexico) [*A publication*]......Bol Tec Inst Nac Invest For (Mex)
Boletin Tecnico. Instituto Provincial Agropecuario (Mendoza) [*A publication*]......Bol Tec Inst Prov Agropecu (Mendoza)
Boletin Tecnico. Ministerio de Agricultura (Colombia) [*A publication*]......Bol Tec Min Agr (Colombia)
Boletin Tecnico. Ministerio de Agricultura (Guatemala) [*A publication*]......Bol Tec Min Agr (Guatemala)
Boletin Tecnico. Peru Servicio de Investigacion y Promocion Agraria [*A publication*]......Bol Tec Peru Serv Invest Promoc Agr
Boletin. Universidad de Chile [*A publication*]......Bol Univ Chile
Boletin. Universidad de Granada [*A publication*]......BUG
Boletin. Universidad de Madrid [*A publication*]......BUM
Boletin. Universidad de la Republica. Faculdad de Agronomia (Montevideo) [*A publication*]......Boln Univ Montevideo Fac Agron
Boletin. Universidad de Santiago de Compostela [*A publication*]......BUSC
Boletin Uruguayo de Sociologia [*A publication*]......Bol Urug Sociol
Boletines y Trabajos. Sociedad Argentina de Cirujanos [*A publication*]......Bol Trab Soc Argent Cir
Boletines y Trabajos. Sociedad de Cirugia de Buenos Aires [*A publication*]......Bol y Trab Soc Cirug Buenos Aires
Bolex Reporter [*A publication*]......Bolex Rep
Bolinger Road [*California*] [*Seismograph station code, US Geological Survey*]......BGC
Bolivar [*Monetary unit in Venezuela*]......B
Bolivar [*A publication*]......Bo
Bolivar [*A publication*]......Bol
Bolivar County Library, Cleveland, MS [*Library symbol*]......MsCle
Bolivar Free Library, Bolivar, NY [*Library symbol*]......NBo
Bolivar, MO [*Radio station call letters*]......KYOO
Bolivar, MO [*Radio station call letters*]......KYOO-FM
Bolivar, TN [*Radio station call letters*]......WBOL
Bolivar, TN [*Radio station call letters*]......WVST
Bolivarian Society of the United States......BSUS
Bolivia [*MARC country of publication code*] [*Library of Congress*]......bo
Bolivia......BOL
Bolivia [*Aircraft nationality and registration mark*]......CP
Bolivia [*MARC geographic area code*] [*Library of Congress*]......s-bo---
Bolivia [*Three-letter standard code*]......BOL
Bolivia [*Two-letter standard code*]......BO
Bolivian Air-Shower Joint Experiment......BASJE
Boliviano [*Monetary unit in Bolivia*]......B
Boll Weevil Research Laboratory [*Department of Agriculture*]......BWRL
Bollard Pull [*Shipping*] [*British*]......BP
Bolleti del Diccionari de la Llengua Catlana [*A publication*]......BDLIC
Bolleti. Societat Arqueologica Lubliana [*A publication*]......BSAL
Bolletini di Litteratura Moderna [*A publication*]......BLM
Bollettino. Accademia Medico-Chirurgica di Bologna [*A publication*]......Boll Accad Med-Chir Bologna
Bollettino. Accademia Svizzera delle Scienze Mediche [*A publication*]......Boll Accad Svizz Sci Med
Bollettino di Archeologia e Storia Dalmata [*A publication*]......BASD
Bollettino. Archivio Paleografico Italiano [*A publication*]......BAPI
Bollettino. Archivio Storico del Banco di Napoli [*A publication*]......BABN
Bollettino d'Arte [*A publication*]......BA
Bollettino d'Arte [*A publication*]......BDA
Bollettino d'Arte [*A publication*]......Boll Arte
Bollettino. Associazione degli Africanisti Italiani [*A publication*]......BAAI
Bollettino. Associazione degli Africanisti Italiani [*A publication*]......Boll Assoc African Ital
Bollettino. Associazione Archeologica Romana [*A publication*]......BAAR
Bollettino. Associazione Internazionale degli Studi Mediterranei [*A publication*]......BStM
Bollettino. Associazione Romana di Entomologia [*A publication*]......Boll Assoc Rom Entomol
Bollettino. Associazione per gli Studi Mediterranei [*A publication*]......BASM
Bollettino dell'Atlante Linguistico Italiano [*A publication*]......BALI
Bollettino dell'Atlante Linguistico Mediterraneo [*A publication*]......BALM
Bollettino ed Atti. Accademia Medica di Roma [*A publication*]......Boll Atti Accad Med Roma
Bollettino della Badia Greca di Grottaferrata [*A publication*]......BBGG
Bollettino della Capitale [*A publication*]......BC
Bollettino della Carta dei Dialetti Italiani [*A publication*]......BCDI
Bollettino. Centro Camuno di Studii Preistorici [*A publication*]......Boll Centro Camuno
Bollettino. Centro Internazionale per lo Studio dei Papiri Ercolanesi [*Cronache Ercolanesi*] [*Napoli*] [*A publication*]......BCPE
Bollettino. Centro di Studi Filologici e Linguistici Siciliani [*A publication*]......BCSFLS
Bollettino. Centro di Studi Filologici e Linguistici Siciliani [*A publication*]......BCSic
Bollettino. Centro di Studi Filologici e Linguistici Siciliani [*A publication*]......BCSS
Bollettino. Centro di Studi Onomastici [*G. D. Serra*] [*A publication*]......BCSO
Bollettino. Centro di Studi di Poesia Italiana e Straniera [*Roma*] [*A publication*]......BCSP
Bollettino. Centro di Studi Vichiani [*A publication*]......BCSV
Bollettino Chimico Farmaceutico [*A publication*]......Boll Chim Farm
Bollettino del Circolo Numismatico Napoletano [*A publication*]......Boll Circ Num Napoletano
Bollettino. Comitato per la Preparazione dell'Edizione Nazionale dei Classici Greci e Latini [*A publication*]......BPEC
Bollettino. Commemorazione del XVI Centenario del Concilio di Nicea [*A publication*]......BCCCN
Bollettino. Commissione Archeologica Comunale di Roma [*A publication*]......BCAC
Bollettino. Commissione Archeologica Comunale di Roma [*A publication*]......BCACR
Bollettino. Commissione Archeologica Comunale di Roma [*A publication*]......BCAR
Bollettino Critico di Cose Francescane [*A publication*]......BCCF
Bollettino. Deputazione di Storia Patria per l'Umbria [*A publication*]......BDSPU
Bollettino del Domus Mazziniana [*A publication*]......BDM
Bollettino di Filologia Classica [*A publication*]......BFC
Bollettino di Geofisica Teorica ed Applicata [*A publication*]......Boll Geofis Teor Appl
Bollettino Internazionale di Informazioni sul Latino [*A publication*]......BIL
Bollettino Internazionale delle Opere Scientifiche Medicina [*A publication*]......Boll Int Opere Sci Med
Bollettino. Istituto Centrale di Restauro [*A publication*]......BICR
Bollettino. Istituto di Diritto Romano [*A publication*]......BIDR
Bollettino. Istituto di Entomologia Agraria e dell'Osservatorio di Fitopatologia di Palermo [*A publication*]......Boll Ist Entomol Agrar Oss Fitopatol Palermo
Bollettino. Istituto dei Entomologia della Universita degli Studi di Bologna [*A publication*]......Boll Ist Entomol Univ Studi Bologna

Bollettino. Istituto di Filologia Greca. Universita di Padova [*A publication*] ... BIFG
Bollettino. Istituto di Lingue Estere [*Genova*] [*A publication*] ... BILE
Bollettino. Istituto di Lingue Estere (Genova) [*A publication*] ... BILEG
Bollettino. Istituto di Patologia del Libro [*A publication*] ... Bol Ist Pato Lib
Bollettino. Istituto di Patologia del Libro [*A publication*] ... Boll Ist Patol Libro
Bollettino. Istituto di Patologia del Libro [*A publication*] ... Boll Ist Patologia Lib
Bollettino. Istituto di Patologia del Libro Alfonso Gallo [*A publication*] ... Boll Ist Patol Libr
Bollettino. Istituto Sieroterapico Milanese [*A publication*] ... B Ist Sier
Bollettino. Istituto Sieroterapico Milanese [*A publication*] ... Boll Ist Sieroter Milan
Bollettino. Istituto di Storia della Societa e dello Stato Veneziano [*A publication*] ... BISV
Bollettino. Istituto Storico Italiano [*A publication*] ... BISI
Bollettino. Istituto Storico Italiano e Archivio Muratoriano [*A publication*] ... BISIAM
Bollettino. Istituto Storico Italiano per il Medioevo e Archivio Muratoriano [*A publication*] ... BISIMAM
Bollettino Italiano di Numismatica [*A publication*] ... BIN
Bollettino. Laboratori Chimici Provinciali [*A publication*] ... Boll Lab Chim Prov
Bollettino. Laboratorio di Entomologia Agraria [*A publication*] ... Boll Lab Entol Agr
Bollettino Linguistico per la Storia e la Cultura Regionale [*A publication*] ... BLSCR
Bollettino del Medici Svizzeri [*A publication*] ... Boll Med Svizz
Bollettino Mensile. Camera di Commercio Industria e Agricoltura (Perugia) [*A publication*] ... Boll Mens Cam Com Ind Agr (Perugia)
Bollettino Metallografico [*A publication*] ... Boll Metallogr
Bollettino di Meteorologia e di Idrologia Agraria [*A publication*] ... Boll Meteorol Idrol Agrar
Bollettino. Musei e Istituti Biologici. Universita di Genova [*A publication*] ... Boll Mus Ist Biol Univ Genova
Bollettino. Museo Civico di Storia Naturale di Venezia [*A publication*] ... Boll Mus Civ Stor Nat Ven
Bollettino. Museo Civico di Storia Naturale di Verona [*A publication*] ... Boll Mus Civ Stor Nat Verona
Bollettino. Museo della Civilta Romana [*A publication*] ... BMCR
Bollettino. Museo dell'Impero Romano [*A publication*] ... BMIR
Bollettino. Museo dell'Impero Romano [*A publication*] ... B Mus Imp
Bollettino. Museo di Zoologia. Universita di Torino [*A publication*] ... Boll Mus Zool Univ Torino
Bollettino Numismatico di Luigi Simonetti [*A publication*] ... BollN
Bollettino d'Oculistica [*A publication*] ... BOOCA
Bollettino Paleontologico Italiano [*A publication*] ... BPI
Bollettino di Pesca, Piscicoltura, e Idrobiologia [*A publication*] ... Boll Pesca Piscic Idrobiol
Bollettino di Psicologia Applicata [*A publication*] ... Boll Psicol App
Bollettino di Psicologia Applicata [*A publication*] ... Boll Psicol Appl
Bollettino di Psicologia Applicata [*A publication*] ... B Psic Appl
Bollettino di Psicologia Applicata. Inserto [*A publication*] ... Boll Psicol Appl Inserto
Bollettino delle Publicatione Italiane [*A publication*] ... BPI
Bollettino. R. Accademia de Scienze, Lettere, e Belle Arti di Palermo [*A publication*] ... BASP
Bollettino. R. Universita Italiana per Stranieri di Perugia [*A publication*] ... BRP
Bollettino. Reale Istituto di Archeologia e Storia dell'Arte [*A publication*] ... BIA
Bollettino. Reale Istituto di Archeologia e Storia dell'Arte [*A publication*] ... BIAA
Bollettino. Regia Deputazione di Storia Patria per la Liguria [*A publication*] ... BRDSPL
Bollettino. Regia Deputazione di Storia Patria per l'Umbria [*A publication*] ... BRDSPU
Bollettino. Regia Deputazione di Storia Patria per l'Umbria [*A publication*] ... BSPU
Bollettino delle Riviste [*A publication*] ... Boll Riv
Bollettino Scientifico [*A publication*] ... Boll Scient
Bollettino. Sedute della Accademia Gioenia di Scienze Naturali in Catania [*A publication*] ... Boll Sedute Accad Gioenia Sci Nat Catania
Bollettino Senese [*A publication*] ... BS
Bollettino Senese di Storia Patria [*A publication*] ... BSSP
Bollettino. Servizio Geologico d'Italia [*A publication*] ... Boll Serv Geol Ital
Bollettino della Sezione di Novara della R. Deputazione Subalpina di Storia Patria [*A publication*] ... BSNS
Bollettino Sistematico di Bibliografia Romana [*A publication*] ... BSBR
Bollettino. Societa Adriatica di Scienze Trieste [*A publication*] ... Boll Soc Adriat Sci Trieste
Bollettino. Societa Entomologica Italiana [*A publication*] ... Boll Soc Entomol Ital
Bollettino. Societa Filologica Friulana [*A publication*] ... BSFF
Bollettino. Societa Geografica Italiana [*A publication*] ... Boll Soc Geog
Bollettino. Societa Geografica Italiana [*A publication*] ... Boll Soc Geogr Ital
Bollettino. Societa Geologica Italiana [*A publication*] ... Boll Soc Geol Ital
Bollettino. Societa Italiana di Biologia Sperimentale [*A publication*] ... B Ital Biol
Bollettino. Societa Italiana di Biologia Sperimentale [*A publication*] ... Boll Soc Ital Biol Sper
Bollettino. Societa Italiana di Biologia Sperimentale [*A publication*] ... BSIBA
Bollettino. Societa Italiana di Cardiologia [*A publication*] ... Boll Soc Ital Cardiol
Bollettino. Societa Italiana di Farmacia Ospedaliera [*A publication*] ... Boll Soc Ital Farm Osp
Bollettino. Societa Italiana di Fisica [*A publication*] ... Boll Soc Ital Fis
Bollettino. Societa Italiana di Fisica [*A publication*] ... Bol Soc Ital Fis
Bollettino. Societa Italiana di Patologia [*A publication*] ... Boll Soc Ital Patol
Bollettino. Societa Medico-Chirurgica e Ospedali Provincia di Cremona [*A publication*] ... Boll Soc Med-Chir Osp Prov Cremona
Bollettino. Societa Medico-Chirurgica di Pavia [*A publication*] ... Boll Soc Med-Chir Pavia
Bollettino. Societa di Naturalisti di Napoli [*A publication*] ... Boll Soc Nat Napoli
Bollettino. Societa Paleontologica Italiana [*A publication*] ... Boll Soc Paleontol Ital
Bollettino. Societa Pavese di Storia Patria [*A publication*] ... BPSP
Bollettino. Societa Pavese di Storia Patria [*A publication*] ... BSPS
Bollettino. Societa Pavese di Storia Patria [*A publication*] ... BSPSP
Bollettino. Societa Piemontese di Archeologia [*A publication*] ... BSPA
Bollettino. Societa Piemontese di Archeologia e Belle Arti [*A publication*] ... BSPABA
Bollettino. Societa Romana per gli Studi Zoologici [*A publication*] ... Boll Soc Rom Stud Zool
Bollettino. Societa Zoologica Italiana [*A publication*] ... Boll Soc Zool Ital
Bollettino. Stazione di Patologia Vegetale di Roma [*A publication*] ... Boll Sta Patol Veg
Bollettino. Stazione di Patologia Vegetale di Roma [*A publication*] ... Boll Stn Patol Veg Roma
Bollettino di Storia Piacentina [*A publication*] ... BSPiac
Bollettino Storico Bibliographico Subalpino [*A publication*] ... BSBS
Bollettino Storico Catanese [*A publication*] ... Boll Stor Cat
Bollettino Storico Catanese [*A publication*] ... BSC
Bollettino Storico Catanese [*A publication*] ... BSCat
Bollettino Storico Cremonese [*A publication*] ... BSC
Bollettino Storico Livornese [*A publication*] ... BSL
Bollettino Storico Mantovano [*A publication*] ... BSM
Bollettino Storico Piacentino [*A publication*] ... Boll S P
Bollettino Storico Piacentino [*A publication*] ... BSP
Bollettino Storico Pisano [*A publication*] ... BSPis
Bollettino Storico Pistoiese [*A publication*] ... BSP
Bollettino Storico Pistoiese [*A publication*] ... BSPi
Bollettino Storico per la Provincia de Novara [*A publication*] ... BSPN
Bollettino Storico della Svizzera Italiana [*A publication*] ... BSSI
Bollettino degli Studi Inglesi in Italia [*A publication*] ... BSII
Bollettino do Studi Latini [*A publication*] ... BStud Lat
Bollettino di Studi Mediterranei [*A publication*] ... BSM
Bollettino di Studi Storici ed Archeologici di Tivoli e Regione [*A publication*] ... BSSAT
Bollettino Ufficiale. Camera di Commercio, Industria, e Agricoltura di Udine [*A publication*] ... Boll Uffic Cam Com Ind Agr Udine
Bollettino. Unione Matematica Italiana [*A publication*] ... Boll Un Mat Ital
Bollettino. Unione Matematica Italiana. A [*A publication*] ... Boll Un Mat Ital A
Bollettino. Unione Matematica Italiana. B [*A publication*] ... Boll Un Mat Ital B
Bollettino Universitario Italiano per Stranieri [*A publication*] ... Boll Stran
Bollettino di Zoologia [*A publication*] ... Boll Zool
Bollettino di Zoologia, Agraria, e di Bachicoltura [*A publication*] ... Boll Zool Agrar Bachic
Bollettino di Zoologia, Agraria, e di Bachicoltura [*A publication*] ... Boll Zool Agrar Bachicolt
Bollettino di Zoologia, Agraria, e di Bachicoltura [*A publication*] ... Boll Zool Agr Bachic
Bollettino di Zoologia, Agraria, e di Bachicoltura [*A publication*] ... Boll Zool Agr Bachicolt
Bollettino di Zoologia (Napoli) [*A publication*] ... Boll Zool (Napoli)
Bollingen Series [*A publication*] ... BS
Bologna [*Italy*] [*Airport symbol*] ... BLQ
Bologna [*Italy*] [*Seismograph station code, US Geological Survey*] ... BOL
Bolometric Correction ... BC
Bolometric Voltage and Current [*Voltage measurement*] [*National Bureau of Standards*] ... BOLOVAC
Bolster ... BOLS
Bolt ... BLT
Bolt ... BO
Bolt, Beranek, & Newman, Inc. [*NYSE symbol*] ... BBN
Bolt Circle [*Technical drawings*] ... BC
Bolt Installation and Removal Tool ... BIRT
Bolt and Nut ... BN
Bolt Out of the Blue [*Surprise nuclear attack*] ... BOOB
Bolt Removal Tool ... BRT
Bolt Technology Corp. [*NASDAQ symbol*] ... BOLT
Bolted-on-Base ... BO/BS
Bolted Plate [*Technical drawings*] ... BP
Bolted Separable Connector ... BSC
Bolton [*Craniometric point*] ... BO
Bolton Evening News, Bolton, United Kingdom [*Library symbol*] ... UkBoN

Bolton Institute for a Sustainable Future ..... BISF
Boltzmann Constant [*Symbol*] [*IUPAC*] ..... k
Boltzmann Transport Equation [*Physics*] ..... BTE
Bolus [*Large Pill*] [*Pharmacy*] ..... BOL
Bolworra [*Australia*] [*Airport symbol*] [*Obsolete*] ..... BCK
Bolyard Oil & Gas [*NASDAQ symbol*] ..... BOLY
Bolzano [*Italy*] [*Seismograph station code, US Geological Survey*] ..... BLZ
Bom Jesus Da Lapa [*Brazil*] [*Airport symbol*] ..... LAZ
Bomai [*Papua New Guinea*] [*Airport symbol*] ..... BMH
Bomaine Corporation [*NASDAQ symbol*] ..... BOMC
BOMARC [*Boeing-Michigan Aeronautical Research Center*] **Squadron Simulator** ..... BSS
Bomb ..... B
Bomb ..... BB
Bomb Alarm System [*Air Force*] ..... BAS
Bomb Assembly Spares ..... BAS
Bomb Bay [*of an aircraft*] ..... BB
Bomb Damage Assessment ..... BDA
Bomb Damage Repair ..... BDR
Bomb Damage Survey ..... BDS
Bomb Data Center [*International Association of Chiefs of Police*] ..... BDC
Bomb Director High-Speed Aircraft ..... BDHSA
Bomb Director Set [*or System*] ..... BDS
Bomb Disposal ..... BD
Bomb-Disposal Squad ..... BDS
Bomb-Disposal Unit ..... BDU
Bomb, Dummy Unit ..... BDU
Bomb Fall Line [*Military*] ..... BFL
Bomb LASER Directed ..... BOLD
Bomb LASER Tracking ..... BOLT
Bomb, Live Unit ..... BLU
Bomb Maintenance Spares ..... BMS
Bomb Mine ..... BOMINE
Bomb or Missile Optics ..... BOMO
Bomb Navigation Guidance System ..... BNGS
Bomb Nose Fuze ..... BNF
Bomb Orbital Strategic System ..... BOSS
Bomb Orbital Strategic System - Weapon Development Glide Entry ..... BOSS-WEDGE
Bomb Rack/Rocket Launcher ..... BR/RL
Bomb, Radio, Longitudinal, Generator-Powered ..... BRLG
Bomb Release Angle Computer ..... BRAC
Bomb Release Distance [*Army*] ..... BRD
Bomb Release Line ..... BRL
Bomb Release Line/End Exercise Point ..... BRL/EEP
Bomb Safety Officer [*Navy*] ..... BSO
Bomb Service ..... BS
Bomb Service Truck ..... BSTRK
Bomb Tail Fuse ..... BTF
Bomb Targets Information Committee [*Air Ministry*] [*British*] [*World War II*] ..... BTIC
Bomb Testing Device ..... BTD
Bomb-to-Warhead Conversion Components ..... BWCC
Bombardier ..... B
Bombardier ..... BDR
Bombardier ..... BMBDR
Bombardier ..... BMDR
Bombardier ..... BOM
Bombardier ..... BOMBDR
Bombardier-Navigator ..... BN
Bombardier's Information File ..... BIF
Bombardment ..... BBT
Bombardment ..... BOMB
Bombardment Control Unit ..... BCU
Bombardment Etch Rate ..... BEER
Bombardment-Induced Conductivity ..... BIC
Bombardment Liaison Officer [*Navy*] ..... BLO
Bombardment Rocket ..... BOMROC
Bombardon [*Musical instrument*] ..... BOMB
Bombay [*Colaba*] [*India*] [*Seismograph station code, US Geological Survey*] ..... BOM
Bombay [*India*] [*Airport symbol*] ..... BOM
Bombay [*India*] [*Later, ABG*] [*Geomagnetic observatory code*] ..... BOM
Bombay, Baroda, and Central India Railway ..... BB & CIRly
Bombay Hospital Journal [*A publication*] ..... Bombay Hosp J
Bombay Port Trust Employees' Union [*India*] ..... BPTEU
Bombay Technologist [*A publication*] ..... Bombay Technol
Bombenzielapparat [*Bomb sight*] [*German military - World War II*] ..... BZA
Bombenzielgeraet [*Bomb sight*] [*German military - World War II*] ..... BZG
Bomber [*Russian aircraft symbol*] ..... AR
Bomber [*Designation for US military aircraft*] ..... B
Bomber [*Russian aircraft symbol*] ..... BB
Bomber [*Air Force*] ..... BMBR
Bomber ..... BMR
Bomber [*Russian aircraft symbol*] ..... B-SCH
Bomber [*Russian aircraft symbol*] ..... DB
Bomber [*Russian aircraft symbol*] IL
Bomber [*Russian aircraft symbol*] ..... SB-RK
Bomber [*Russian aircraft symbol*] ..... ZKB
Bomber Command ..... BC
Bomber Command [*Army*] ..... BOMCOM
Bomber Command Intelligence Report ..... BCIR
Bomber Command Intelligence Summary ..... BCIS
Bomber Command Liaison Officer ..... BCLO
Bomber Command Operational Order ..... BCOO
Bomber Command Tactical Planning Committee ..... BCTPC
Bomber Defense Missile [*Air Force*] ..... BDM
Bomber Field ..... B
Bomber-Fighter Squadron [*Navy symbol*] ..... VBF
Bomber Operations [*Air Ministry*] [*British*] [*World War II*] ..... BOPS
Bomber Reconnaissance Aircraft ..... BR
Bomber Support ..... BS
Bomber Support Development Unit ..... BSDU
Bomber Transport [*Air Force*] ..... BT
Bombesin [*Biochemistry*] ..... BBS
Bombing ..... BOM
Bombing Analysis Unit [*Supreme Headquarters, Allied Expeditionary Force*] [*World War II*] ..... BAU
Bombing Computer Set ..... BCS
Bombing Development Unit ..... BDU
Bombing Encyclopedia ..... BE
Bombing Exercise [*Military*] ..... BOMBEX
Bombing-Fighting Aircraft [*Navy symbol*] ..... VBF
Bombing and Gunnery Range ..... BGR
Bombing and Gunnery School [*British*] ..... BGS
Bombing over the Horizon ..... BOTH
Bombing Landplane ..... BLP
Bombing/Navigation ..... B/N
Bombing and Navigation Inertial Reference ..... BANIR
Bombing-Navigation System ..... BNS
Bombing through Overcast [*By means of RADAR equipment*] ..... BTO
Bombing Plane [*Navy symbol*] ..... VB
Bombing RADAR Navigation Equipment ..... BRANE
Bombing and Reconnaissance Navigation ..... BARN
Bombing Report ..... BOMREP
Bombing Report ..... BOMREPT
Bombing Squadron ..... BOMRON
Bombing, Torpedo Plane [*Navy symbol*] ..... VBT
Bombline ..... BL
Bombsight ..... BOMST
Bome in Suid-Afrika [*A publication*] ..... Bome S-Afr
Bomed Medical Manufacturing [*NASDAQ symbol*] ..... BOMD
Bon Accord, NB [*Television station call letters*] CHSJ-TV-1
Bon pour Francs [*Value in Francs*] [*French*] ..... BPF
Bon Secours Medical Library, Baltimore, MD [*Library symbol*] ..... MdBBS
Bona Fide [*In Good Faith*] [*Latin*] ..... BF
Bona Fide Occupational Qualification ..... BFOQ
Bona Fide Purchaser for Value [*of a security, or other negotiable instrument*] [*Law*] ..... BFPV
Bonae Feminae [*To the Good Woman*] [*Latin*] ..... BF
Bonae Memoriae [*Of Happy Memory*] [*Latin*] ..... BM
Bonaire [*Netherland Antilles*] [*Airport symbol*] ..... BON
Bonanza Airlines Co. [*Torrance, CA*] [*FAA designator*] ..... BON
Bonanza International, Inc. [*NASDAQ symbol*] ..... BNZA
Bonaparte Record-Republican, Bonaparte, IA [*Library symbol*] ..... IaBonR
Bonaventure [*Canada*] [*Airport symbol*] ..... YVB
Bonavista Bay, NF [*Radio station call letters*] ..... CBGY
Bonavista, NF [*Radio station call letters*] ..... CJOZ-FM
Bond ..... B
Bond ..... BD
Bond Anticipation Notes ..... BANS
Bond and Burglary ..... B & BU
Bond Club of New York ..... BCNY
Bond County Community Unit, School District 2, De Land, IL [*Library symbol*] ..... IDelanSD
Bond Index to the Determination of Inorganic Crystal Structures [*McMaster University, Canada*] ..... BIDICS
Bond Industries, Inc. [*NYSE symbol*] [*Delisted*] ..... BND
Bond Maturity ..... BM
Bond Molecular Orbitals ..... BMO
Bond Number ..... Bo
Bond and Preferred [*Business and trade*] ..... BP
Bond Public Library, Wenona, IL [*Library symbol*] ..... IWen
Bond and Share Society ..... BSS
Bond Trade Analysis Program [*IBM Corp.*] ..... BTAP
Bondage and Discipline ..... B & D
Bonded ..... B
Bonded ..... BND
Bonded Double Cotton [*Wire insulation*] ..... BDC
Bonded Double Paper [*Wire insulation*] ..... BDP
Bonded Double Silk [*Wire insulation*] ..... BDS
Bonded Goods [*Business and trade*] ..... B/G
Bonded Phase Chromatography ..... BPC
Bonded Single Cotton [*Wire insulation*] ..... BC
Bonded Single Silk [*Wire insulation*] ..... BS
Bonded Warehouse ..... BW
Bonded Wine Cellar ..... BWC
Bonded Winery ..... BW
Bonderize ..... BNDZ
Bondi-Metzner-Sachs [*Physics*] ..... BMS
Bonding ..... BNDG
Bonding Tool ..... BNTO

Bondoukou [*Ivory Coast*] [*Airport symbol*] ... BDK
Bondsman ... BNDSMN
Bone Conduction [*Medicine*] ... BC
Bone-Derived Growth Factor [*Genetics*] ... BDGF
Bone Formation ... BF
Bone Greater Than Air [*Conduction*] ... B > A
Bone Injury [*Medicine*] ... BI
Bone and Joint [*Medicine*] ... B & J
Bone and Joint [*Medicine*] ... BJ
Bone Marker [*Aviation*] ... BM
Bone Marrow ... BM
Bone-Marrow Derived [*Hematology*] ... B
Bone-Marrow Derived Lymphocyte [*Hematology*] ... BL
Bone Marrow Transplant [*Medicine*] ... BMT
Bone Mineral Content ... BMC
Bone Morphogenetic Protein ... BMP
Bone Phosphate of Lime ... BPL
Bone Resorption ... BR
Bones, Joints, Muscles [*Medicine*] ... BJM
Bonesteel Public Library, Bonesteel, SD [*Library symbol*] ... SdBo
Bonham, TX [*Radio station call letters*] ... KFYN
Bonham, TX [*Radio station call letters*] ... KFYZ-FM
Bonhomie & Hattiesburg Southern R. R. [*AAR code*] ... BHS
Bonifay, FL [*Radio station call letters*] ... WTBB
Bonita Springs, FL [*Radio station call letters*] ... WLEQ
Bonn [*West Germany*] [*Airport symbol*] ... BNJ
Bonne Bay, NF [*Television station call letters*] ... CBYT-3
Bonner Arbeiten zur Deutschen Literatur [*A publication*] ... BADL
Bonner Beitraege [*A publication*] ... BB
Bonner Durchmusterung [*Star chart*] ... BD
Bonner Historische Forschungen [*A publication*] ... BHF
Bonner Jahrbuecher [*A publication*] ... BJ
Bonner Jahrbuecher [*A publication*] ... BJB
Bonner Jahrbuecher [*A publication*] ... Bonner Jb
Bonner Jahrbuecher [*A publication*] ... Bonn Jb
Bonner Mathematische Schriften [*A publication*] ... Bonn Math Schr
Bonner Orientalistische Studien [*A publication*] ... BOS
Bonner Studien zur Englischen Philologie [*A publication*] ... Bo Stud
Bonner Zeitschrift fuer Theologie und Seelsorge [*A publication*] ... BZTS
Bonner Zoologische Beitraege [*A publication*] ... Bonn Zool Beitr
Bonner Zoologische Monographien [*A publication*] ... Bonn Zool Monogr
Bonners Ferry, ID [*Radio station call letters*] ... KBFI
Bonnet ... BNT
Bonnet Valve ... BV
Bonneville Power Administration [*Department of Energy*] ... BPA
Bonneville Power Administration, Portland, OR [*Library symbol*] ... OrPB
Bonneville Power Administration Selective Dissemination of Information [*Department of the Interior*] ... BPA-SDI
Bonneville Regional Advisory Council [*Terminated, 1978*] [*Department of Energy*] ... BRAC
Bonneville, UT [*Location identifier*] [*FAA*] ... BVL
Bonney-Fessenden Sociograph [*Psychology*] ... BFS
Bonniers Litteraera Magasin [*A publication*] ... BLM
Bonniers Litteraera Magasin [*A publication*] ... BLMag
Bonniers Maenadstidning [*Stockholm*] [*A publication*] ... BM
Bonnyville, AB [*Television station call letters*] ... CBXFT-1
Bonnyville, AB [*Television station call letters*] ... CKSA-TV-2
Bonray Drilling Corp. [*NASDAQ symbol*] ... BNRY
Bons Vivants [*An association*] ... BV
Bonsai Clubs International ... BCI
Bonthe [*Sierre Leone*] [*Airport symbol*] ... BTE
Bonum Publicum [*The Public Good*] [*Latin*] ... BP
Bonus Expeditionary Force ... BEF
Bonus Points ... BP
Bonus Vacation Days [*United Auto Workers*] ... BVD
Boob and Bourgeoisie [*H. L. Mencken's portmanteau for the American middle class*] ... BOOBOISIE
Book ... B
Book ... BK
Book About Me [*Psychological testing*] ... BAM
Book Arts Guild ... BAG
Book Arts Review [*A publication*] ... BAR
Book Auction Records ... BAR
Book Buyer [*A publication*] ... Bk Buyer
Book Club of California, San Francisco, CA [*Library symbol*] ... CSfBk
Book Collecting and Library Monthly [*A publication*] ... Bk Collecting & Lib Mo
Book Collector [*A publication*] ... BC
Book Collector [*A publication*] ... BCol
Book Collector [*A publication*] ... Bk Coll
Book Collector [*A publication*] ... Bk Collec
Book Collector [*A publication*] ... Bk Collector
Book Collector's Market [*A publication*] ... BCM
Book Collector's Quarterly [*A publication*] ... BCQ
Book of Common Prayer [*Episcopalian*] ... BCP
Book Communications System [*Information service*] ... BCS
Book Development Council [*British*] ... BDC
Book Forum [*A publication*] ... BF
Book Forum [*A publication*] ... B Forum
Book Forum [*A publication*] ... Bk Forum
Book Indexing ... BINDEX
Book Indexing with Context and Entry Points from Text [*Data processing*] ... BICEPT
Book Industry Study Group ... BISG
Book Industry Systems Advisory Committee ... BISAC
Book League Monthly [*A publication*] ... BLM
Book-Library-Management [*System*] ... BLM
Book List [*Society for Old Testament Studies*] [*A publication*] ... BLOT
Book Manufacturers Institute ... BMI
Book-of-the-Month Club, Inc. [*NYSE symbol*] [*Delisted*] ... BOK
Book-of-the-Month Club, Inc. ... BOMC
Book-News [*A publication*] ... Bk-News
Book Notes [*A publication*] ... BN
Book Order and Selection [*Data processing*] ... BOS
Book - Physical Inventory Difference [*AEC*] ... B-PID
Book Production Industry [*A publication*] ... Book Prod
Book Production Industry [*A publication*] ... BPI
Book Publishing ... BP
Book Publishing Record ... BPR
Book Rack ... BR
Book of Reference ... BR
Book Review ... BR
Book Review Digest [*A publication*] ... Bk Rev Dig
Book Review Digest [*A publication*] ... BoRv
Book Review Index [*A publication*] ... Bk Rev Ind
Book Review Index [*A publication*] ... BRI
Book Reviews [*A publication*] ... Book R
Book Reviews of the Month [*A publication*] ... Bk Rev Mo
Book of the Season Scheme [*British*] ... BOSS
Book Supplement. Journal of Child Psychology and Psychiatry [*A publication*] ... Book Suppl J Child Psychol Psychiatr
Book Trolley [*A publication*] ... BKTLA
Book Trolley [*A publication*] ... Bk Trolley
Book Value [*Business and trade*] ... BV
Book Week [*A publication*] ... Bk Wk
[*A*] **Book of Weird Tales** [*A publication*] ... BKW
Book World [*A publication*] ... BkW
Book World [*A publication*] ... Bk World
Book World [*Chicago Tribune*] [*A publication*] ... BW
Book World (Washington Post) [*A publication*] ... BW (WP)
Bookbinding and Book Production [*A publication*] ... Bkbinding & Bk Production
Bookbird [*A publication*] ... Bkbird
Bookcase ... BC
Bookcase [*s*] [*Freight*] ... BK
Booker T. Washington Foundation ... BTWF
Booker T. Washington National Monument ... BOWA
Bookform Drawing ... BFD
Booking and Sampling for Indirect Standards [*British*] ... BASIS
Bookkeeping ... BKG
Bookkeeping ... BKPG
Booklegger Magazine [*A publication*] ... Bklegger
Booklet ... BKLT
Booklet. Forestry Commission (London) [*A publication*] ... Bookl For Comm (Lond)
Booklet Pane Society [*Defunct*] ... BPS
Bookline Alert: Missing Books and Manuscripts [*A publication*] ... BAMBAM
Booklist [*A publication*] ... Bkl
Booklist [*A publication*] ... BL
Booklist and Subscription Books Bulletin [*Later, Booklist*] [*A publication*] ... Bklist
Booklist and Subscription Books Bulletin [*Later, Booklist*] [*A publication*] ... Booklist
Booklist and Subscription Books Bulletin [*Later, Booklist*] [*A publication*] ... Booklist and SBB
Booklover's Magazine [*A publication*] ... Booklover's M
Bookman [*Published in US*] [*A publication*] ... Amer Bookman
Bookman [*A publication*] ... Bk
Bookman [*A publication*] ... Bookm
Bookman (London) [*A publication*] ... BkL
Bookman (London) [*A publication*] ... Bkman (Lond)
Bookman (London) [*A publication*] ... Bookm (Lond)
Bookman's Journal [*A publication*] ... BJ
Bookman's Price Index [*A reference publication listing rare books and their list prices*] ... BPI
Bookmark [*A publication*] ... Bkmark
Bookmark. New York State Library [*A publication*] ... Bookmark
Bookmark. University of Idaho [*A publication*] ... Bkmark (Idaho)
Bookplate [*Bibliography*] ... B/PL
Bookplates [*A publication*] ... BP
Books Abroad [*A publication*] ... BA
Books Abroad [*A publication*] ... Bk Abroad
Books Abroad [*A publication*] ... Bks Abroad
Books-Across-the-Sea [*Project*] ... BAS
Books and Bookmen [*A publication*] ... B & B
Books and Bookmen [*A publication*] ... BB
Books and Bookmen [*A publication*] ... Bk & Bkmen
Books and Bookmen [*A publication*] ... Bks & Bkmn
Books at Brown [*A publication*] ... BBr
Books in Canada [*A publication*] ... BIC
Books in Canada [*A publication*] ... Bks in Can
Books for College Libraries [*A publication of ALA*] ... BCL

Books for Equal Education [*An association*] [*Defunct*] .... BEE
Books from Finland [*A publication*] .... BF
Books at Iowa [*A publication*] .... BI
Books at Iowa [*A publication*] .... BkIA
Books-on-Japan-in-English [*A publication*] .... BJE
Books for Libraries [*Program*] .... BFL
Books for Libraries Micropublications, Freeport, NY [*Library symbol*] .... BFL
Books and Libraries at the University of Kansas [*A publication*] .... Bks & Libs
Books by Mail .... BBM
Books of the Month [*A publication*] .... B of M
Books for the People Fund .... BPF
Books in Print [*A publication*] .... BIP
Books in Series [*A publication*] .... BIS
Books on Tape .... BOT
Books of the Times (New York) [*A publication*] .... BOT (New York)
Books Today [*Sunday Chicago Tribune*] [*A publication*] .... Bks Today
Booksellers' Association Service House [*British*] .... BASH
Booksellers of Great Britain .... BGB
Boolean Algebra [*Mathematics*] .... BA
Boolean Array Identifier [*Mathematics*] .... BAID
Boolean Assignment Statement [*Mathematics*] .... BAS
Boolean Function Designator [*Mathematics*] .... BFD
Boolean Function Identifier [*Mathematics*] .... BFID
Boolean Normal Form [*Mathematics*] .... BNF
Boolean Simple Variable [*Mathematics*] .... BSV
Boolean Time Sequence [*Mathematics*] .... BTS
Boom Control Unit .... BCU
Boom Defense Officer .... BDO
Boone County Courthouse, Boone, IA [*Library symbol*] .... IaBoCoC
Boone and Crockett Club .... BCC
Boone, IA [*Radio station call letters*] .... KFGQ
Boone, IA [*Radio station call letters*] .... KFGQ-FM
Boone, IA [*Radio station call letters*] .... KWBG
Boone, IA [*Radio station call letters*] .... KWBG-FM
Boone Junior College [*Iowa*] .... BJC
Boone, NC [*Radio station call letters*] .... WASU-FM
Boone, NC [*Radio station call letters*] .... WATA
Booneville, AR [*Radio station call letters*] .... KJON
Booneville, MS [*Radio station call letters*] .... WBIP
Booneville, MS [*Radio station call letters*] .... WBIP-FM
Booneville, MS [*Television station call letters*] .... WMAE
Booneville, MS [*Radio station call letters*] .... WMAE-FM
Boonton Electronics [*NASDAQ symbol*] .... BOON
Boonville, IN [*Radio station call letters*] .... WBNL
Boonville, IN [*Radio station call letters*] .... WBNL-FM
Boonville, MO [*Radio station call letters*] .... KDBX
Boonville, MO [*Radio station call letters*] .... KWRT
Boonville, NY [*Radio station call letters*] .... WBRV
Boost Alcohol Consciousness Concerning the Health of University Students [*In association name BACCHUS of the US*] .... BACCHUS
Boost Glide Reentry Vehicle [*Air Force*] .... BGRV
Boost, Insertion, and Abort [*Aerospace*] .... BIA
Boost Phase Intercept .... BPHI
Boost Phase Intercept .... BPI
Boost Protective Cover [*Apollo*] [*NASA*] .... BPC
Boost Stage Discharge Pressure .... BSDP
Boosted Kinetic Energy Penetrator [*Proposed submunition*] .... BKEP
Booster .... B
Booster .... BST
Booster [*Military*] .... BSTR
Booster Assembly Building [*NASA*] .... BAB
Booster Assembly Contractor [*NASA*] .... BAC
Booster Change Assembly .... BCA
Booster Cutoff .... BCO
Booster Cutoff Backup .... BCOB
Booster Development .... BD
Booster-Distribution Amplifier .... BDA
Booster Engine [*Rocketry*] .... BE
Booster Engine Cutoff [*Rocketry*] .... BECO
Booster Exhaust Stream .... BES
Booster Exhaust Study Test [*NASA*] .... BEST
Booster Flight-Acceptance Composite Test [*NASA*] .... B-FACT
Booster Fuel Jacket .... BFJ
Booster Gas Generator .... BGG
Booster Inertial Guidance System [*Aerospace*] .... BIGS
Booster Interstage Assembly [*Aerospace*] .... BIA
Booster Jettison .... BOJ
Booster Lift-Off Mass [*NASA*] .... BLOM
Booster Lift-Off Weight [*NASA*] .... BLOW
Booster Orbiter .... B/O
Booster Press, Howell, NJ [*Library symbol*] .... NjHowB
Booster Pump [*Liquid gas carriers*] .... b
Booster-Regulator [*NASA*] .... BR
Booster Requirements Document .... BRD
Booster Separation Motors [*NASA*] .... BSM
Booster Situation Indicator .... BSI
Booster Solid Rocket Motor [*NASA*] .... BSRM
Booster and Sustainer .... B & S
Booster Systems Engineer [*NASA*] .... BSE
Booster Test Department [*NASA*] .... BST
Booster Umbilical Assembly .... BUA
Booster Vacuum Pump .... BVP
Booster Vacuum Pump System .... BVPS
Boot and Shoe Travelers Association of New York .... BSTANY
Boot and Shoe Workers' Union [*Later, UFCWIU*] .... BSW
Boot or Shoes, or Boot or Shoe Findings [*Freight*] .... BS BSF
Bootes [*Constellation*] .... Boo
Bootes [*Constellation*] .... Boot
Booth-Henry-Gorin [*Equations for calculation of net charge and valence of molecule*] .... BHG
Booth, Inc. [*NASDAQ symbol*] .... BOTH
Booth Library On-Line Circulation [*Data processing system*] [*Eastern Illinois University*] .... BLOC
Booth Memorial Hospital, Flushing, NY [*Library symbol*] .... NFB
[*Mask designed by*] **Boothby, Lovelace, and Bulbulian** [*of Mayo Clinic*] [*Medicine*] .... BLB
Boothe Financial Corp. [*NASDAQ symbol*] .... BCMP
Bootheville, LA [*Location identifier*] [*FAA*] .... BVE
Boots Pure Drug Co. [*Great Britain*] [*Research code symbol*] .... RD
Bootstrap Combined Programing Language [*Data processing*] .... BCPL
Bootstrap Commissioning Program [*Air Force*] .... BCP
Booue [*Gabon*] [*Airport symbol*] .... BGB
Booz-Allen Applied Research, Incorporated .... BAARINC
Booz, Allen & Hamilton, Inc., Chicago, IL [*Library symbol*] .... ICBAH
Bora-Bora [*French Polynesia*] [*Airport symbol*] .... BOB
Borabicyclononane [*Organic chemistry*] .... BBN
Borated Water Storage Tank [*Nuclear energy*] .... BWST
Bordano [*Italy*] [*Seismograph station code, US Geological Survey*] .... BORI
Bordeaux [*France*] [*Airport symbol*] .... BOD
Bordeaux-Hamburg Inclusive [*Shipping*] .... B/H
Bordeaux Medical [*A publication*] .... Bord Med
Borden, Inc. [*NYSE symbol*] [*Wall Street slang name: "Moo Moo"*] .... BN
Borden Museum, Borden, IN [*Library symbol*] [*Obsolete*] .... InBoM
Borden's Review of Nutrition Research [*A publication*] .... Borden's Rev Nutr Res
Bordentown Historical Society, Bordentown, NJ [*Library symbol*] .... NjBorHi
Border .... BDR
Border Boundary Police [*Thailand*] .... BBP
Border Patrol .... BOPAT
Border Patrol .... BP
Border Patrol Academy .... BPA
Border Patrol Police [*Thailand*] .... BPP
Border Patrol Sector Headquarters .... BPSH
Border Regiment [*British*] .... BR
Border Security Police [*NATO*] .... BSP
Border Surveillance [*Military*] .... BS
Border Terrier Club of America .... BTCA
Borderland Sciences Research Foundation .... BSRF
Borderlands of Neurology [*A publication*] .... Borderl Neurol
Borderline Dull [*Medicine*] .... BD
Borderline Left-Axis Deviation [*Cardiology*] .... BLAD
Bordet-Gengou [*Bacillus*] [*Microbiology*] .... BG
Bordetella Pertussis Vaccine .... BPV
Bordmechaniker [*Flight engineer*] [*German military - World War II*] .... BM
Bore [*Freight*] .... BRE
Bore Erosion Gauge Reading .... BEGR
Boreal Institute for Northern Studies. University of Alberta. Annual Report [*A publication*] .... Boreal Inst North Stud Univ Alberta Annu Rep
Boreal Institute for Northern Studies. University of Alberta. Occasional Publication [*A publication*] .... Boreal Inst North Stud Univ Alberta Occas Publ
Borehole .... BH
Borehole Capsule .... BHC
Borehole Seismometer .... BHS
Borescope .... BS
Boresight .... BRSIT
Boresight .... BS
Boresight Camera .... BC
Boresight Camera .... BSC
Boresight Datum Line [*Military*] .... BSDL
Boresight Fixture .... BSF
Boresight Tower .... BST
Borg-Warner Corp. [*NYSE symbol*] .... BOR
Borg-Warner Corp. .... BW
Borg-Warner Corp., B-J Electronics Division, Santa Ana, CA [*Library symbol*] .... CStaB-E
Borg-Warner Corp., Borg-Warner Chemicals Technical Center, Washington, WV [*Library symbol*] .... WvWaB
Borg-Warner Corp., Des Plaines, IL [*OCLC symbol*] .... IBW
Borg-Warner Corp., Ingersoll Research Center, Des Plaines, IL [*Library symbol*] .... IDesB
Borg-Warner Corp., York Division, York, PA [*Library symbol*] .... PYB
Borgarfjordur [*Iceland*] [*Airport symbol*] .... BGJ
Borge Priens Prover [*Danish intelligence test*] .... BPP
Borger, TX [*Location identifier*] [*FAA*] .... BGD
Borger, TX [*Radio station call letters*] .... KBBB
Borger, TX [*Radio station call letters*] .... KDKQ
Borger, TX [*Radio station call letters*] .... KQTY
Borgward Owners Club .... BOC

Borgyogyaszati es Venerologiai Szemle [*A publication*] .... Borgyogy Venerol Sz
Boric Acid [*Inorganic chemistry*] .... BA
Boring Bar .... BOBR
Boring Fixture .... BF
Boring Fixture .... BOFX
Borkum [*West Germany*] [*Airport symbol*] .... BMK
Borlange [*Sweden*] [*Airport symbol*] .... BLE
Borman's, Inc. [*Formerly, Borman Food Stores*] [*NYSE symbol*] .... BRF
Born .... B
Born .... BO
Born-Again Christian .... BAC
Born Again Pagans .... BAP
Born before Arrival [*of mother at hospital*] [*Medicine*] .... BBA
Born on Arrival [*of mother at hospital*] [*Medicine*] .... BOA
Born-Haber Cycle [*Physics*] .... BHC
Born-Infeld Theory [*Physics*] .... BIT
Born-Mayer Equation [*Physics*] .... BME
Born-Oppenheimer Method [*Physics*] .... BOM
Borneo Island [*MARC geographic area code*] [*Library of Congress*] .... a-bn---
Borneo Research Bulletin [*A publication*] .... Bor Res B
Bornholmske Samlinger [*A publication*] .... Bornholm Sam
Bornu Youth Movement - Action Group Alliance [*Nigeria*] .... BYM-AG
Borocarbon .... BC
Borocarbon Resistor .... BCR
Borok [*USSR*] [*Geomagnetic observatory code*] .... BOX
Boron [*Chemical element*] .... B
Boron-Aluminum .... BORAL
Boron-Based Fuel .... BBF
Boron Fiber Reinforced Plastics .... BFRP
Boron Metal Fiber .... BMF
Boron Neutron Capture Therapy .... BNCT
Boron Nitride [*Inorganic fiber*] .... BN
Boron Nitride Fiber [*Inorganic fiber*] .... BNF
Boron Plastic .... BP
Boron Pyrolytic Graphite .... BPG
Boron Recycle System [*Nuclear energy*] .... BRS
Borosilicate Crown .... BSC
Borough .... BO
Borough .... BOR
Borough Council .... BC
Borough of Manhattan Community College, New York, NY [*Library symbol*] .... NNBMC
Borough of Manhattan Community College, New York, NY [*OCLC symbol*] .... XMC
Borrego Springs [*California*] [*Airport symbol*] .... BXS
Borrego Springs, CA [*Radio station call letters*] .... KBSH
Borromeo Seminary of Ohio, Wickliffe, OH [*Library symbol*] .... OWicB
Borrowed Light .... BLT
Borrowed Military Manpower .... BMM
Borrowings .... BOR
Borrows, S. A., Detroit MI [*STAC*] .... BSA
Borsenblatt fuer den Deutschen Buchhandel [*A publication*] .... BDB
Borsodi Szemle [*A publication*] .... Borsod Szle
Borzhomi [*USSR*] [*Seismograph station code, US Geological Survey*] [*Closed*] .... BOR
Borzoi Club of America .... BCOA
Bosaso [*Somalia*] [*Airport symbol*] .... BSA
Bosbou in Suid-Afrika [*A publication*] .... Bosbou S-Afr
Bosbou in Suid-Afrika [*A publication*] .... Bosb Suid-Afr
Bosch Technische Berichte [*A publication*] .... Bosch Tech Ber
Bose-Chaudhuri-Hocquenguem [*Cyclic codes*] .... BCH
Bose-Einstein Statistics .... BES
Bosler Free Library, Carlisle, PA [*Library symbol*] .... PCarl
Bosque Alegre [*Argentina*] [*Seismograph station code, US Geological Survey*] [*Closed*] .... BOS
Bossche Bijdragen [*A publication*] .... BB
Bossier Parish Library, Benton, LA [*Library symbol*] .... LBeB
Boston [*Massachusetts*] [*Airport symbol*] .... BOS
Boston [*Massachusetts*] .... BOST
Boston & Albany Railroad .... B & A
Boston & Albany Railroad .... B & ARR
Boston & Albany Railroad [*AAR code*] .... BA
Boston Area Faculty Group on Public Issues .... BAFGOPI
Boston Athenaeum, Boston, MA [*OCLC symbol*] .... BAT
Boston Athenaeum, Boston, MA [*Library symbol*] .... MBAt
Boston Bar Association, Boston, MA [*Library symbol*] .... MBBA
Boston Bay, BC [*Radio station call letters*] CKGO-FM-1
Boston Biomedical Library Consortium [*Library network*] .... BBLC
Boston College [*Massachusetts*] .... BC
Boston College, Chestnut Hill, MA [*OCLC symbol*] .... BXM
Boston College, Chestnut Hill, MA [*Library symbol*] .... MChB
Boston College. Environmental Affairs Law Review [*A publication*] .... BC Environ Aff Law R
Boston College. Environmental Affairs Law Review [*A publication*] .... Boston Coll Environ Aff Law Rev
Boston College. Industrial and Commercial Law Review [*A publication*] .... BC Ind & Com L R
Boston College. Law Review [*A publication*] .... BCL Rev
Boston College Law School, Newton, MA [*OCLC symbol*] .... BXL
Boston College. Studies in Philosophy [*A publication*] .... Boston Col Stud Phil
Boston College, Weston Observatory, Weston, MA [*Library symbol*] .... MChB-WO
Boston Conservatory of Music .... BCM
Boston Diagnostic Aphasia Examination .... BDAE
Boston Digital Corp. [*NASDAQ symbol*] .... BOST
Boston Edison Co. [*NYSE symbol*] .... BSE
Boston Five Cents Savings Bank [*NASDAQ symbol*] .... BFCS
Boston Grain and Flour Exchange .... BGFE
Boston Irish .... BI
Boston Journal of Natural History [*A publication*] .... Boston J N H
Boston Journal of Philosophy and the Arts [*A publication*] .... Boston J Ph
Boston, MA [*Location identifier*] [*FAA*] .... LIP
Boston, MA [*Radio station call letters*] .... WBCN
Boston, MA [*Radio station call letters*] .... WBUR
Boston, MA [*Radio station call letters*] .... WBZ
Boston, MA [*Television station call letters*] .... WBZ-TV
Boston, MA [*Radio station call letters*] .... WCOZ
Boston, MA [*Television station call letters*] .... WCVB-TV
Boston, MA [*Radio station call letters*] .... WEEI
Boston, MA [*Radio station call letters*] .... WERS
Boston, MA [*Radio station call letters*] .... WEZE
Boston, MA [*Radio station call letters*] .... WGBH
Boston, MA [*Radio station call letters*] .... WGBH-FM
Boston, MA [*Television station call letters*] .... WGBH-TV
Boston, MA [*Television station call letters*] .... WGBX-TV
Boston, MA [*Radio station call letters*] .... WHDH
Boston, MA [*Radio station call letters*] .... WHTT
Boston, MA [*Radio station call letters*] .... WHUE
Boston, MA [*Radio station call letters*] .... WHUE-FM
Boston, MA [*Radio station call letters*] .... WILD
Boston, MA [*Radio station call letters*] .... WJIB
Boston, MA [*Radio station call letters*] .... WMRE
Boston, MA [*Television station call letters*] .... WNEV-TV
Boston, MA [*Television station call letters*] .... WQTV
Boston, MA [*Radio station call letters*] .... WRBB
Boston, MA [*Radio station call letters*] .... WRKO
Boston, MA [*Radio station call letters*] .... WROL
Boston, MA [*Radio station call letters*] .... WROR
Boston, MA [*Television station call letters*] .... WSBK-TV
Boston, MA [*Radio station call letters*] .... WUMB
Boston, MA [*Television station call letters*] .... WXNE-TV
Boston & Maine Corp. .... B & M
Boston & Maine Corp. [*AAR code*] .... BM
Boston & Maine Railroad [*Later, Boston & Maine Corp.*] [*NYSE symbol*] [*Delisted*] .... BMR
Boston & Maine Railroad [*Later, Boston & Maine Corp.*] .... B & MRR
Boston Medical and Surgical Journal [*A publication*] .... Boston Med and S J
Boston Monthly Magazine [*A publication*] .... Bost Mo
Boston Museum Bulletin [*A publication*] .... BMB
Boston Museum of Fine Arts .... BMFA
Boston Museum of Fine Arts. Bulletin [*A publication*] .... Boston Mus Bul
Boston Museum of Science, Boston, MA [*Library symbol*] .... MBN
Boston National Historic Sites Commission [*Government agency, discontinued, 1960*] .... BNHSC
Boston Naval Shipyard .... BNS
Boston Naval Shipyard .... BNSY
Boston Navy Yard [*Later, Boston Naval Shipyard*] .... BNYD
Boston, New York, Washington [*Proposed name for possible "super-city" formed by growth and mergers of other cities*] .... BOSNYWASH
Boston Ordnance District [*Military*] .... BOD
Boston Public Library and Eastern Massachusetts Regional Public Library System, Boston, MA [*Library symbol*] .... MB
Boston Public Library Quarterly [*A publication*] .... Boston Pub Lib Quar
Boston Public Library Quarterly [*A publication*] .... BPLQ
Boston Public Quarterly [*A publication*] .... BPQ
Boston Quarterly [*A publication*] .... Bost Q
Boston Red Sox [*Baseball team*] .... BOSOX
Boston Redevelopment Authority .... BRA
Boston Review [*A publication*] .... Bost R
Boston Shipping Association .... BSA
Boston Society of Civil Engineers. Journal [*A publication*] .... Boston Soc C E J
Boston Society of Natural History [*A publication*] .... Boston Soc N H
Boston Society of Natural History. Memoirs [*A publication*] .... Boston Soc of Nat Hist Memoirs
Boston Society of Natural History. Occasional Papers [*A publication*] .... Boston Soc of Nat Hist Occ Papers
Boston Society of Natural History. Occasional Papers [*A publication*] .... Bost Soc Natur Hist Occ Pa
Boston Society of Natural History. Proceedings [*A publication*] .... Boston Soc of Nat Hist Proc
Boston Society of Natural History. Proceedings [*A publication*] .... Bost Soc Natur Hist Proc
Boston State College, Boston, MA [*Library symbol*] .... MBSC
Boston State College Library, Boston, MA [*OCLC symbol*] .... BST
Boston Stock Exchange .... B
Boston Studies in the Philosophy of Science [*A publication*] .... Boston Stud Philos Sci

Boston Symphony Orchestra .... BSO
Boston Symphony Orchestra Concert. Bulletin [*A publication*] .... Bost Sym Concert Bul
Boston Symphony Orchestra. Program Notes [*A publication*] .... Bost Sym
Boston Tea Party II [*An association*] .... BTPII
Boston Terminal Company [*AAR code*] .... BTCO
Boston Terrier Club of America .... BTCA
Boston Theological Institute .... BTI
Boston Theological Institute, Cambridge, MA [*OCLC symbol*] .... BTI
Boston Theological Institute, Learning Development Program, Boston, MA [*Library symbol*] .... MBTI
Boston Theological Institute Library [*Library network*] .... BTI
Boston Transcript Book Section [*A publication*] .... BTBS
Boston University [*Massachusetts*] .... BU
Boston University, Boston, MA [*OCLC symbol*] .... BOS
Boston University, Boston, MA [*Library symbol*] .... MBU
Boston University Journal [*A publication*] .... Bos U J
Boston University Journal [*A publication*] .... BUJ
Boston University Law Review [*A publication*] .... Boston U LR
Boston University Law Review [*A publication*] .... BU L Rev
Boston University Marine Program .... BUMP
Boston University, School of Education, Boston, MA [*Library symbol*] .... MBU-E
Boston University, School of Law, Boston, MA [*Library symbol*] .... MBU-L
Boston University, School of Medicine, Boston, MA [*OCLC symbol*] .... MBU
Boston University, School of Medicine, Boston, MA [*Library symbol*] .... MBU-M
Boston University, School of Theology, Boston, MA [*OCLC symbol*] .... BZM
Boston University, School of Theology, Boston, MA [*Library symbol*] .... MBU-T
Boston University Studies in English [*A publication*] .... BUSE
Boston-Waltham, MA [*Radio station call letters*] .... WCRB
Boston to Washington [*Proposed name for possible "super-city" formed by growth and mergers between these two*] .... BOSWASH
Boston Wool Trade Association .... BWTA
Bostonian [*A publication*] .... Bost
Bostonian Society .... BS
Bostonian Society, Boston, MA [*Library symbol*] .... MBBS
Botanic Garden .... BG
Botanic Gardens (Singapore). Annual Report [*A publication*] .... Bot Gard (Singapore) Annu Rep
Botanica Marina [*A publication*] .... Botan Marin
Botanica Marina [*A publication*] .... Bot Mar
Botanica Rhedonica. Serie A [*A publication*] .... Bot Rhedonica Ser A
Botanical .... BOTAN
Botanical Bulletin. Academia Sinica [*A publication*] .... Botan B A S
Botanical Bulletin. Academia Sinica [*A publication*] .... Bot Bull Acad Sinica
Botanical Bulletin. Academia Sinica. Institute of Botany. New Series [*A publication*] .... Bot Bull Acad Sinica Inst Bot New Ser
Botanical Bulletin. Academia Sinica (Taipei) [*A publication*] .... Bot Bull Acad Sin (Taipei)
Botanical Gazette [*A publication*] .... Botan Gaz
Botanical Gazette [*A publication*] .... Bot Gaz
Botanical Journal. Linnean Society [*London*] [*A publication*] .... Botan J Lin
Botanical Journal. Linnean Society [*London*] [*A publication*] .... Bot J Linn Soc
Botanical Journal. Linnean Society (London) [*A publication*] .... Bot J Linn Soc (Lond)
Botanical Magazine [*Tokyo*] [*A publication*] .... Botan Mag
Botanical Magazine (Tokyo) [*A publication*] .... Bot Mag Tokyo
Botanical Monographs (New Delhi) [*A publication*] .... Bot Monogr (New Delhi)
Botanical Monographs (Oxford) [*A publication*] .... Bot Monogr (Oxf)
Botanical Museum Leaflets. Harvard University [*A publication*] .... Bot Mus Leafl
Botanical Museum Leaflets. Harvard University [*A publication*] .... Bot Mus Leafl Harv Univ
Botanical Origin .... BO
Botanical Review [*A publication*] .... Botan Rev
Botanical Review [*A publication*] .... Bot R
Botanical Review [*A publication*] .... Bot Rev
Botanical Society of America .... BSA
Botanical Society of the British Isles .... BSBI
Botanical Society of Edinburgh. Transactions [*A publication*] .... Bot Soc Edinb Trans
Botanical Society, London .... BSL
Botanical Survey of South Africa. Memoir [*A publication*] .... Bot Surv S Afr Mem
Botaniceskij Zurnal [*A publication*] .... Bot Z
Botanicheskie Materialy Gerbariya Instituta Botaniki. Akademii Nauk Kazakhskoi SSR [*A publication*] .... Bot Mater Gerb Inst Bot Akad Nauk Kaz SSR
Botanicheskii Zhurnal (Leningrad) [*A publication*] .... Bot Zh (Leningr)
Botanicheskii Zhurnal (Moscow) [*A publication*] .... Bot Zh (Moscow)
Botanicheskii Zhurnal (SSSR) [*A publication*] .... Bot Zh (SSSR)
Botanichnyi Zhurnal (Kiev) [*A publication*] .... Bot Zh (Kiev)
Botanico-Periodicum-Huntianum [*Book title*] .... B-P-H
Botanika. Issledovaniya. Belorusskoe Otdelenie Vsesoyuznogo Botanicheskogo Obshchestva [*A publication*] .... Bot Issled Beloruss Otd Vses Bot O-va
Botanikai Koezlemenyek [*A publication*] .... Bot Koezl
Botanikai Koezlemenyek [*A publication*] .... Bot Koezlem
Botanische Jahrbuecher fuer Systematik Pflanzengeschichte und Pflanzengeographie [*A publication*] .... Bot Jahrb Syst Pflanzengesch Pflanzengeogr
Botanische Studien [*A publication*] .... Bot Stud
Botanisches Archiv [*A publication*] .... Bot Arch
Botanisches Zentralblatt [*A publication*] .... Bot Zblt
Botanisk Haves Virksomhed Beretning [*A publication*] .... Bot Haves Virksomhed Beret
Botanisk Tidsskrift [*A publication*] .... Botan Tids
Botanisk Tidsskrift [*A publication*] .... Bot Tidsskr
Botaniska Notiser [*A publication*] .... Botan Notis
Botaniska Notiser [*A publication*] .... Bot Not
Botaniska Notiser [*A publication*] .... Bot Notis
Botaniska Notiser [*A publication*] .... Bot Notiser
Botany .... BOT
Botetourt Bibliographical Society Publications [*A publication*] .... BBSP
Both-to-Blame [*Shipping*] .... B/B
Both Bones [*With reference to fractures*] [*Medicine*] .... BB
Both Dates Inclusive [*Business and trade*] .... BDI
Both Faces [*Technical drawings*] .... BF
Both Hands [*Psychometrics*] .... BH
Both Sides [*Technical drawings*] .... BS
Both Way Trunk .... BWT
Both Ways [*Technical drawings*] .... BW
Botopasie [*Suriname*] [*Airport symbol*] .... BTO
Botswana [*MARC country of publication code*] [*Library of Congress*] .... bs
Botswana [*Two-letter standard code*] .... BW
Botswana [*Three-letter standard code*] .... BWA
Botswana [*MARC geographic area code*] [*Library of Congress*] .... f-bs---
Botswana Democratic Party .... BDP
Botswana. Geological Survey. District Memoir [*A publication*] .... Botswana Geol Surv Dist Mem
Botswana. Geological Survey and Mines Department. Annual Report [*A publication*] .... Botswana Geol Surv Mines Dep Annu Rep
Botswana Independence Party .... BIP
Botswana, Lesotho, Swaziland .... BLS
Botswana Notes and Records [*A publication*] .... BN & R
Botswana Notes and Records [*A publication*] .... Botswana Notes Rec
Botswana People's Party .... BPP
Botswana Protectorate Federal Party .... BPFP
Bottineau, ND [*Radio station call letters*] .... KBTO
Bottle .... BOT
Bottle .... BT
Bottle .... BTL
Bottle-Baby Meal [*Airline notation*] .... BBML
Bottled in Bond [*Wines and spirits*] .... B/B
Bottled in Bond [*Wines and spirits*] .... BIB
Bottom .... B
Bottom .... BO
Bottom .... BOT
Bottom .... BTM
Bottom Bounce [*SONAR propogation mode*] [*Navy*] .... BB
Bottom Bounce/Omnidirectional Transmission [*Navy*] .... BB/ODT
Bottom Bounce/Track [*Navy*] .... BB/T
Bottom Center [*Valve position*] .... BC
Bottom Chord .... BC
Bottom of Conduit .... BOC
Bottom Dead Center [*Engineering*] .... BDC
Bottom of Edge .... BOE
Bottom Environmental Sensing System .... BESS
Bottom Face [*Technical drawings*] .... BF
Bottom Finding Pinger .... BFP
Bottom of Hole [*Geology*] .... BOH
Bottom Hole Circulating Temperature [*Oil well borehole*] .... BHCT
Bottom Hole Static Temperature [*Oil well borehole*] .... BHST
Bottom Layer [*Technical drawings*] .... BL
Bottom Lead Left .... BTLL
Bottom Lead Right .... BTLR
Bottom Left Side .... BLS
Bottom-Loading Transfer Cask [*Nuclear energy*] .... BLTC
Bottom-Mounted Impact Locations System [*Missile technology*] .... BMILS
Bottom-Mounted Instrumentation System .... BOMIS
Bottom-Oriented Shrimp Harvester .... BOSH
Bottom Pressure Fluctuation .... BPF
Bottom [*or Beauty*] **(Quark)** [*Atomic physics*] .... b
Bottom Reflection [*Navy*] .... BR
Bottom Reflection Active SONAR System .... BRASS
Bottom Refraction Acoustic Telemetry System .... BRATS
Bottom Right Side .... BRS
Bottom Sediment [*Maps and charts*] .... BS
Bottom Sediment and Water .... BSW
Bottom Settlings [*of crude oil in storage*] .... BS
Bottom SONAR Marker .... BSM
Bottom Topography Survey System [*Naval Oceanographic Office*] .... BOTOSS
Bottom-Up Greedy .... BUG
Bottom Withdrawal [*Tube*] .... BW
Bottoming .... BOTMG
Bottu [*France*] [*Research code symbol*] .... BO
Botulinum Toxin .... BOT

Bouake [*Ivory Coast*] [*Airport symbol*] ... BYK
Bought ... BO
Bought ... BOT
Bought ... BT
Bouillon Filtre [*Bouillon Filtrate*] ... BF
Boulder [*Wyoming*] [*Seismograph station code, US Geological Survey*] ... BDW
Boulder [*Maps and charts*] ... Bld
Boulder [*Colorado*] [*Seismograph station code, US Geological Survey*] [*Closed*] ... BO1
Boulder [*Colorado*] [*Geomagnetic observatory code*] ... BOU
Boulder [*Colorado*] [*Airport symbol*] ... WBU
Boulder [*Colorado*] [*Seismograph station code, US Geological Survey*] [*Closed*] ... BOU
Boulder City [*Nevada*] [*Seismograph station code, US Geological Survey*] [*Closed*] ... BCN
Boulder City Library, Boulder City, NV [*Library symbol*] ... NvBc
Boulder City, NV [*Location identifier*] [*FAA*] ... BLD
Boulder City, NV [*Radio station call letters*] ... KRRI
Boulder, CO [*Radio station call letters*] ... KADE
Boulder, CO [*Radio station call letters*] ... KBCO
Boulder, CO [*Radio station call letters*] ... KBOL
Boulder, CO [*Radio station call letters*] ... KBVL
Boulder, CO [*Radio station call letters*] ... KGNU
Boulder, CO [*Television station call letters*] ... KTVJ
Boulder Dam [*Arizona*] [*Seismograph station code, US Geological Survey*] [*Closed*] ... BDA
Boulder Laboratory Macrosystem [*National Bureau of Standards*] ... BOUMAC
Boulder Public Library, Boulder, CO [*Library symbol*] ... CoB
Boulder Valley School District, Boulder, CO [*OCLC symbol*] ... BOA
Boulders [*Quality of the bottom*] [*Maps and charts*] ... Blds
Boulevard ... BD
Boulevard ... BLD
Boulevard ... BLVD
Boulevard ... BOUL
Boulia [*Australia*] [*Airport symbol*] ... BQL
Bouna [*Ivory Coast*] [*Airport symbol*] ... BQO
Bouncing-Ball Generator ... BBG
Bound ... BD
Bound ... BND
Bound Brook Chronicle, Bound Brook, NJ [*Library symbol*] ... NjBbC
Bound Brook Memorial Library, Bound Brook, NJ [*Library symbol*] ... NjBb
Bound to Stay Bound Books, Inc. ... BTSB
Boundary ... BDRY
Boundary ... BDY
Boundary ... BNDRY
Boundary 2 [*A publication*] ... Bound
Boundary, AK [*Location identifier*] [*FAA*] ... BYA
Boundary Estimate Message [*Aviation code*] ... EST
Boundary Layer ... BL
Boundary Layer Control ... BLC
Boundary Layer Flow ... BLF
Boundary Layer Instrumentation Package [*Meteorology*] ... BLIP
Boundary Layer Instrumentation System [*Meteorology*] ... BLIS
Boundary Layer Integral Matrix Procedure ... BLIMP
Boundary-Layer Meteorology [*A publication*] ... Boundary-Layer Meteorol
Boundary Layer Model ... BLM
Boundary Layer Profile [*Meteorology*] ... BLP
Boundary Layer Separation ... BLS
Boundary Layer Zone ... BLZ
Boundary Monument [*Control point*] [*Nautical charts*] ... Bdy Mon
Boundary Stimulus [*To light*] ... BS
Boundary Value Problem ... BVP
Boundary Waters Canoe Area [*Minnesota*] ... BWCA
Bounded Error Navigation System ... BENS
Boundiali [*Ivory Coast*] [*Airport symbol*] ... BXI
Boundji [*Congo*] [*Airport symbol*] ... BOE
Bountiful Peak [*Utah*] [*Seismograph station code, US Geological Survey*] [*Closed*] ... BPU
Bounty Information Service ... BIS
Bourdon Tube Element ... BTE
Bourgas [*Bulgaria*] [*Airport symbol*] ... BOJ
Bourjois, Inc. [*American Stock Exchange symbol*] ... BOJ
Bourke [*Australia*] [*Airport symbol*] ... BRK
Bournemouth [*England*] [*Airport symbol*] ... BOH
Bourns, Inc. [*NYSE symbol*] [*Delisted*] ... BOU
Bouton Corp. [*NASDAQ symbol*] ... BOTN
Bouvet Island [*MARC country of publication code*] [*Library of Congress*] ... bv
Bouvet Island [*MARC geographic area code*] [*Library of Congress*] ... lsbv---
Bouvetoya [*Two-letter standard code*] ... BV
Bouvetoya [*Three-letter standard code*] ... BVT
Bouwsteenen. Jaarboek der Vereeniging voor Nederlandsche Muziekgeschiedenis [*A publication*] ... Bouwsteenen J V N M
Bovine Capillary Endothelial [*Cytology*] ... BCE
Bovine Carbonic Anhydrase [*An enzyme*] ... BCA
Bovine Embryo Skeletal Muscle ... BESM
Bovine Gamma Globulin [*Immunology*] ... BGG
Bovine Growth Hormone [*Endocrinology*] ... BGH
Bovine Leukemia Virus ... BLV
Bovine Pancreatic Polypeptide ... BPP
Bovine Papillomavirus ... BPV
Bovine Parathyroid Hormone [*Endocrinology*] ... bPTH
Bovine Plasma Albumin ... BPA
Bovine Practitioner [*A publication*] ... Bovine Pract
Bovine Serum Albumin [*Immunology*] ... BSA
Bovine Thyroid-Stimulating Hormone [*Endocrinology*] ... BTSH
Bow Buoyancy ... BBYCY
Bow Diving ... BDVG
Bow Door ... BDO
Bow Light ... BWLT
Bow Plane ... BPLA
Bow Shock ... BS
Bow Tie Manufacturers Association ... BTMA
Bow Valley Industries Ltd. [*American Stock Exchange symbol*] ... BVI
Bowater Corp. plc ADR [*NASDAQ symbol*] ... BWTRY
Bowdock [*Navy symbol*] ... YBD
Bowdoin College, Brunswick, ME [*OCLC symbol*] ... BBH
Bowdoin College, Brunswick, ME [*Library symbol*] ... MeB
Bowdon College, Bowdon, GA [*Library symbol*] [*Obsolete*] ... GBowdC
Bowdon Railway Co. [*AAR code*] ... BODN
Bowel [*Medicine*] ... BO
Bowel Movement [*Medicine*] ... BM
Bowel Sounds [*Medicine*] ... BS
Bowel Sounds Normal [*Medicine*] ... BSN
Bowels Not Opened [*Medicine*] ... BNO
Bowels Opened [*Medicine*] ... BO
Bowen [*Australia*] [*Airport symbol*] [*Obsolete*] ... ZBO
Bowie State College, Bowie, MD [*Library symbol*] ... MdBo
Bowie State College Library, Bowie, MD [*OCLC symbol*] ... BCM
Bowie, TX [*Location identifier*] [*FAA*] ... GMZ
Bowie, TX [*Radio station call letters*] ... KBAN
Bowl America, Inc. [*American Stock Exchange symbol*] ... BWL
Bowled [*Cricket*] ... B
Bowled Out ... B
Bowles Engineering Corporation ... BEC
Bowline Corp. [*NASDAQ symbol*] ... BOLN
Bowling Apparel Manufacturers of America ... BAM
Bowling Green [*Ohio*] [*Seismograph station code, US Geological Survey*] ... BGO
Bowling Green College of Commerce [*Later, a division of Western Kentucky State College*] ... BGCC
Bowling Green, KY [*Location identifier*] [*FAA*] ... BWG
Bowling Green, KY [*Radio station call letters*] ... WBGN
Bowling Green, KY [*Radio station call letters*] ... WDNS
Bowling Green, KY [*Radio station call letters*] ... WKCT
Bowling Green, KY [*Television station call letters*] ... WKGB
Bowling Green, KY [*Radio station call letters*] ... WKYU-FM
Bowling Green, KY [*Radio station call letters*] ... WLBJ
Bowling Green, KY [*Radio station call letters*] ... WLBJ-FM
Bowling Green, KY [*Television station call letters*] ... WQQB
Bowling Green, MO [*Radio station call letters*] ... KPCR
Bowling Green, MO [*Radio station call letters*] ... KPCR-FM
Bowling Green, OH [*Radio station call letters*] ... WBGU
Bowling Green, OH [*Radio station call letters*] ... WJYM
Bowling Green, OH [*Radio station call letters*] ... WRQN
Bowling Green State University [*Ohio*] ... BGSU
Bowling Green State University, Bowling Green, OH [*OCLC symbol*] ... BGU
Bowling Green State University, Bowling Green, OH [*Library symbol*] ... OBgU
Bowling Green, VA [*Location identifier*] [*FAA*] ... APH
Bowling Proprietors' Association of America ... BPAA
Bowling Proprietors' Association of America - Duckpin Activities Department [*Defunct*] ... BPAA-DAD
Bowling Writers Association of America ... BWAA
Bowman [*South Carolina*] [*Seismograph station code, US Geological Survey*] ... BOW
Bowman Gray School of Medicine, Winston-Salem, NC [*OCLC symbol*] ... NBG
Bowman, ND [*Radio station call letters*] ... KPOK
Bowmar Canada Ltd., Ottawa, ON, Canada [*Library symbol*] ... CaOOBC
Bowmar Instrument Corp. [*American Stock Exchange symbol*] ... BOM
Bowne & Co., Inc. [*American Stock Exchange symbol*] ... BNE
Bowstring ... BWSTRN
Box ... BX
Box Core [*Marine geology*] ... BC
Box Diffusion [*Oceanography*] ... BD
Box External Data ... BED
Box Fin ... BXF
Box Office [*Theatrical slang*] ... BO
Box-Office Computer System ... BOCS
Box-Office Reservation and Information Service ... BORIS
Box Project [*An association*] ... BP
Boxboard Containers [*A publication*] ... Boxbrd Con
Boxboard Research and Development Association ... BRDA
Boxed ... BXD
Boxed or Tanked ... BX/TK
Boxes ... BXS
Boxes, Barrels, or Packages [*Freight*] ... BBP
Boxes or Crates [*Freight*] ... BC
Boxford, MA [*Radio station call letters*] ... WBMT

Boxing Writers Association ... BWA
Boxspring [*A publication*] ... Box
Boy Savior Youth Movement [*Defunct*] ... BSYM
Boy Scouts ... BS
Boy Scouts of America ... BSA
Boy Scouts of America Alumni Family ... BSAAF
Boy Scouts International Bureau ... BSIB
Boy Scouts World Bureau [*Later, WSB*] ... BSWB
Boyce, LA [*Radio station call letters*] ... KBCE
Boyce Thompson Institute. Contributions [*A publication*] ... Boyce Thompson Inst Contrib
Boyce Thompson Institute for Plant Research, Yonkers, NY [*Library symbol*] ... NYBT
Boyertown, PA [*Radio station call letters*] ... WBYO
Boyfriend [*Slang*] ... BF
Boyne City, MI [*Radio station call letters*] ... WCLX
Boyne City Public Library, Boyne City, MI [*Library symbol*] ... MiBoy
Boyne City Railroad Co. [*AAR code*] ... BCRR
Boyne Falls Public Library, Boyne Falls, MI [*Library symbol*] ... MiBoyf
Boyne Regional Library, Carman, MB, Canada [*Library symbol*] ... CaMCB
Boynton Beach, FL [*Radio station call letters*] ... WHRS
Boynton Beach, FL [*Radio station call letters*] ... WKAO
Boynton Beach, FL [*Radio station call letters*] ... WRMB
Boys' Apparel Buyers Association ... BABA
Boys Club Professional Association ... BCPA
Boys' Clubs of America ... BCA
Boys and Girls International Floor Hockey ... BGIFH
Boy's Life Brigade ... BLB
[*The*] **Boy's Own Paper** [*Late nineteenth- and early twentieth-century periodical*] [*British*] ... BOP
Boys Town Center for the Study of Youth Development, Omaha, NE [*OCLC symbol*] ... BTC
Boys Town Center for the Study of Youth Development, Omaha, NE [*Library symbol*] ... NbOB
Boy's Towns of Italy ... BTI
Boys of Woodcraft Sportsmen's Clubs [*Later, Woodmen Rangers and Rangerettes*] ... BWSC
Boys and Young Men's Apparel Manufacturers Association ... BAMA
Bozart and Contemporary Verse [*A publication*] ... Bozart
Bozeman [*Montana*] [*Seismograph station code, US Geological Survey*] [*Closed*] ... BOZ
Bozeman [*Montana*] [*Seismograph station code, US Geological Survey*] [*Closed*] ... BZE
Bozeman [*Montana*] [*Seismograph station code, US Geological Survey*] [*Closed*] ... BZM
Bozeman [*Montana*] [*Airport symbol*] ... BZN
Bozeman, MT [*Radio station call letters*] ... KBMN
Bozeman, MT [*Radio station call letters*] ... KBOZ
Bozeman, MT [*Television station call letters*] ... KCTZ
Bozeman, MT [*Radio station call letters*] ... KGLT
Bozeman, MT [*Radio station call letters*] ... KXXL
Bozzuto's, Inc. [*NASDAQ symbol*] ... BOZZ
BP [*Benzin und Petroleum A. G. Hamburg*] **Kurier** [*A publication*] ... BP Kur
BPI Resources Ltd. [*NASDAQ symbol*] ... BPIRF
BPI Systems, Incorporated [*NASDAQ symbol*] ... BPII
BR Communications [*NASDAQ symbol*] ... BRHF
Braathens South-American and Far East Airtransport [*Norway*] [*ICAO designator*] ... BU
Bracco Industria Chimica [*Italy*] [*Research code symbol*] ... H
Brace [*Medicine*] ... B
Brace ... BRC
Bracebridge Public Library, Bracebridge, ON, Canada [*Library symbol*] ... CaOBrac
Braced ... BRCD
Braced and Racked [*Freight*] ... BR
Brach [*E. J.*] **& Sons** [*NYSE symbol*] [*Delisted*] ... BRK
Brachial Artery Pressure [*Medicine*] ... BAP
Brachio [*To the Arm*] [*Pharmacy*] ... BRACH
Bracken Explorations Company [*NASDAQ symbol*] ... BXCO
Bracket ... BRKT
Bracket and Linkage Assembly ... BLA
Brada-Svejda [*Tumor*] [*Medicine*] ... BS
Braddock Heights, MD [*Radio station call letters*] ... WZYQ-FM
Braddock, PA [*Radio station call letters*] ... WHYH-FM
Braddock, PA [*Radio station call letters*] ... WJLY
Bradenton, FL [*Radio station call letters*] ... WBRD
Bradenton, FL [*Radio station call letters*] ... WDUV
Bradenton, FL [*Radio station call letters*] ... WOFN
Bradford [*Pennsylvania*] [*Airport symbol*] ... BFD
Bradford College [*Formerly, BJC*] [*Massachusetts*] ... BC
Bradford County Public Library, Starke, FL [*Library symbol*] ... FStaB
Bradford Durfee College of Technology [*Later, Southeastern Massachusetts Technical Institute*] ... BDCT
Bradford Junior College [*Later, BC*] [*Massachusetts*] ... BJC
Bradford Junior College [*Later, BC*], **Bradford, MA** [*Library symbol*] ... MBradJ
Bradford National Corp. [*American Stock Exchange symbol*] ... BDR
Bradford, PA [*Radio station call letters*] ... WESB
Bradford Public Library, Bradford, IL [*OCLC symbol*] ... IQX
Bradley Aberration Method ... BAM
Bradley Air Service [*Carp, ON*] [*FAA designator*] ... FAB
Bradley Fighting Vehicle Armament [*Army*] ... BFVA
Bradley Fighting Vehicle Systems [*Army*] ... BFVS
Bradley Infantry Fighting Vehicle ... BIFV
Bradley University, Peoria, IL [*OCLC symbol*] ... IBA
Bradley University, Peoria, IL [*Library symbol*] ... IPB
Brady Energy Corp. [*NASDAQ symbol*] ... BRAD
Brady, TX [*Radio station call letters*] ... KIXV
Brady, TX [*Radio station call letters*] ... KNEL
Brae Corp. [*NASDAQ symbol*] ... BRAE
Braganca [*Portugal*] [*Airport symbol*] ... BGC
Braid ... BRD
Braided Rug Manufacturers Association [*Defunct*] ... BRMA
Braided Trimming Manufacturers Association [*Later, EFMCNTA*] ... BTMA
Braided Tube Bundle ... BTB
Braided Wire Armor ... BW
Braille Authority of North America ... BANA
Braille Institute ... BI
Braille Institute of America [*Later, BI*] ... BIA
Braille Institute of America, Los Angeles, CA [*Library symbol*] ... CLBraille
Braille Revival League ... BRL
Braille Technical Press [*Defunct*] ... BTP
Brain, Behavior, and Evolution [*A publication*] ... Brain Behav
Brain, Behavior, and Evolution [*A publication*] ... Brain Behav Evol
Brain and Behavior Research Monograph Series [*A publication*] ... Brain Behav Res Monogr Ser
Brain and Development [*A publication*] ... Brain Dev
Brain Electrical Activity Mapping ... BEAM
Brain Evoked Potential [*Neurophysiology*] ... BEP
Brain-Heart Infusion [*Growth medium*] ... BHI
Brain-Heart Infusion [*Broth*] **with Acetone** [*Growth medium*] ... BHI-ac
Brain-Heart Infusion Blood Agar [*Growth medium*] ... BHIBA
Brain-Heart Infusion Supplemented [*Broth or agar*] [*Growth medium*] ... BHIS
Brain Hormone [*Endocrinology*] ... BH
Brain Information Service [*UCLA*] ... BIS
Brain. Journal of Neurology [*A publication*] ... BRAIA
Brain and Language [*A publication*] ... B & L
Brain and Language [*A publication*] ... Brain Lang
Brain and Language [*A publication*] ... BRLGA
Brain Mapping Technique ... BRAMATEC
Brain/Mind Bulletin [*A publication*] ... Brain/Mind
Brain Protein Solvent [*Biochemistry*] ... BPS
Brain Research [*A publication*] ... Brain Res
Brain Research [*A publication*] ... BRREA
Brain Research Bulletin [*A publication*] ... Brain Res Bull
Brain Research Bulletin [*A publication*] ... BRRAB
Brain Research Foundation ... BRF
Brain Research Institute [*UCLA*] ... BRI
Brain Research Reviews [*A publication*] ... Brain Res Rev
Brain Stimulation Reinforcement [*Electrophysiology*] ... BSR
Brain Tumor [*Medicine*] ... BT
Brain Tumor Study Group [*National Cancer Institute*] ... BTSG
Brain Uptake Index [*Physiology*] ... BUI
Brainerd [*Minnesota*] [*Airport symbol*] ... BRD
Brainerd Community College, Brainerd, MN [*Library symbol*] ... MnBrC
Brainerd, MN [*Radio station call letters*] ... KLIZ
Brainerd, MN [*Radio station call letters*] ... KLIZ-FM
Brainerd, MN [*Radio station call letters*] ... KQBR
Brainerd, MN [*Radio station call letters*] ... WJJY
Brains on Board [*Robot*] [*Androbot, Inc.*] ... BOB
Brainstem Auditory Evoked Potential [*Neurophysiology*] ... BAEP
Brainstem-Evoked Response [*Neurophysiology*] ... BSER
Brainstem Transmission Time [*Neurophysiology*] ... BTT
Braintech, Inc. [*NASDAQ symbol*] ... BEAM
Braj [*MARC language code*] [*Library of Congress*] ... bra
Brake ... BK
Brake Die ... BKDI
Brake Horsepower ... B
Brake Horsepower ... BHP
Brake Horsepower-Hour ... BHP-HR
Brake Mean Effective Pressure ... BMEP
Brake Mean Power ... BMP
Brake Relay ... BR
Brake Skid Control ... B/SC
Brake Specific Fuel Consumption ... BSFC
Brake System Parts Manufacturers Council ... BSPMC
Brakeband ... BRKBD
Braked Servomotor ... BSM
Braking Action [*Aviation*] ... BA
Braking Action Extremely Poor [*Aviation*] ... BRAXP
Braking Action Fair [*Aviation*] ... BRAF
Braking Action Good [*Aviation*] ... BRAG
Braking Action Nil [*Aviation*] ... BRAN
Braking Action Poor [*Aviation*] ... BRAP
Bralorne Resources Ltd. [*NASDAQ symbol*] ... BRALF
Bram Stoker Society ... BSS
Brampton Island [*Australia*] [*Airport symbol*] ... BMP
Brampton, ON [*Radio station call letters*] ... CKMW
Brampton Public Library, Brampton, ON, Canada [*Library symbol*] ... CaOBra

Bran and Multiple Vitamins and Minerals, B-Complex Vitamins, and Yogurt [*A nutritional plan*] .... BAMBY
Branch .... BR
Branch Arm Piping [*Nuclear energy*] .... BAP
Branch Arm Piping Enclosure [*Nuclear energy*] .... BAPE
Branch Arm Piping Shielding [*Nuclear energy*] .... BAPS
Branch Assistance Team [*Military*] .... BAT
Branch Aviation Supply Office [*Navy*] .... BRASO
Branch Back and Load [*Data processing*] .... BBL
Branch Bill .... BB
Branch-Bound Mixed Integer Programing [*Data processing*] .... BBMIP
Branch if Carry Set .... BCS
Branch Corp. [*NASDAQ symbol*] .... BNCH
Branch County Library, Coldwater, MI [*Library symbol*] .... MiCwB
Branch Cultural Affairs Officer [*United States Information Service*] .... BCAO
Branch of Fall Zero .... BFZ
Branch Hydrographic Office [*Navy*] .... BHO
Branch Hydrographic Office [*Navy*] .... BRANCHYDRO
Branch Immaterial .... BI
Branch Immaterial Officer Candidate Course .... BIOCC
Branch Industries, Incorporated [*American Stock Exchange symbol*] .... BII
Branch Intelligence Officer [*Military*] [*British*] .... BIO
Branch Material [*Military*] .... BM
Branch Memorandum .... BM
Branch No Group [*Data processing*] .... BNG
Branch Office .... BO
Branch Office London [*ONR*] .... BOL
Branch Office, Military Intelligence Division [*Army*] .... BOMID
Branch Office, Office of Naval Research .... ONR BR
Branch Operating Instruction [*Air Force*] .... BOI
Branch Operating Instruction [*Military*] .... BROI
Branch Output Interrupt [*Data processing*] .... BOI
Branch Public Affairs Officer [*United States Information Service*] .... BPAO
Branch Public Relations Office .... BPRO
Branch Report .... BR
Branch and Store Instruction [*Data processing*] .... BSI
Branch Technical Position [*Nuclear energy*] .... BTP
Branch Transportation Office [*or Officer*] [*Army*] .... BTO
Branch Warehouse Association .... BWA
Branched-Chain Amino Acid [*Biochemistry*] .... BAA
Branched-Chain Amino Acid [*Biochemistry*] .... BCAA
Branchial Filament .... BRF
Brand Insulations [*NASDAQ symbol*] .... BRAN
Brand Name Contract .... BNC
Brand Name Resale .... BNR
Brand Names Foundation .... BNF
Brand Rating Index Corp. .... BRI
Brandeis University, Waltham, MA [*OCLC symbol*] .... MBB
Brandeis University, Waltham, MA [*Library symbol*] .... MWalB
Brandenburg, KY [*Radio station call letters*] .... WMMG-FM
Brandl, H. R., Chicago IL [*STAC*] .... BHR
Brandon [*Canada*] [*Airport symbol*] .... YBR
Brandon Films, Inc. .... BF
Brandon Free Public Library, Brandon, VT [*Library symbol*] .... VtBran
Brandon General Hospital, School of Nursing, Brandon, MB, Canada [*Library symbol*] .... CaMBGH
Brandon, MB [*Television station call letters*] CBWFT-10
Brandon, MB [*Radio station call letters*] .... CJCM-FM
Brandon, MB [*Radio station call letters*] .... CKLQ
Brandon, MB [*Radio station call letters*] .... CKX
Brandon, MB [*Television station call letters*] .... CKX-TV
Brandon, MB [*Television station call letters*] .... CKYB-TV
Brandon Mental Health Centre, Brandon, MB, Canada [*Library symbol*] .... CaMBMH
Brandon, MS [*Radio station call letters*] .... WRJH
Brandon, MS [*Radio station call letters*] .... WRKN
Brandon University, Brandon, MB, Canada [*Library symbol*] .... CaMBC
Brandon University, Department of Geography, Brandon, MB, Canada [*Library symbol*] .... CaMBCG
Brandschutz Deutsche Feuerwehrzeitung [*A publication*] .... Brandschutz Dtsch Feuerwehrztg
Brandy and Soda .... B and S
Brandywine College of Widener University, Wilmington, DE [*OCLC symbol*] .... DLB
Brandywine Sports [*NASDAQ symbol*] .... BRDY
Branford Steam Railroad [*AAR code*] .... BRFD
Braniff Airways, Inc. [*of Braniff International Corp.*] .... BA
Braniff Airways, Inc. [*of Braniff International Corp.*] [*ICAO designator*] .... BN
Braniff International Corp. [*ICAO designator*] .... BNF
Braniff International Council [*Club for frequent flyers*] .... BIC
Branntweinwirtschaft [*A publication*] .... Branntweinwirt
Brans-Dicke-Jordan [*Scalar-tensor theory*] .... BDJ
Branson, MO [*Radio station call letters*] .... KLCO
Branson, MO [*Radio station call letters*] .... KRZK-FM
Branson, MO [*Location identifier*] [*FAA*] .... PLK
Brant County Historical Museum, Brantford, ON, Canada [*Library symbol*] .... CaOBrtBM
Brantford, ON [*Radio station call letters*] .... CKPC
Brantford, ON [*Radio station call letters*] .... CKPC-FM
Brantford Public Library, Brantford, ON, Canada [*Library symbol*] .... CaOBrt
Bras D'Or Mines Ltd. [*NASDAQ symbol*] .... BRASF
Brascan Ltd. [*American Stock Exchange symbol*] .... BRS
Brascon Resources Ltd., Calgary, AB, Canada [*Library symbol*] .... CaACB
Brasenose College [*Oxford*] .... BNC
Brashear-Hastings Prism .... BHP
Brasil Acucareiro [*A publication*] .... BrA
Brasil Acucareiro [*A publication*] .... Bras Acucareiro
Brasil Acucareiro [*A publication*] .... Brasil Acucar
Brasil [*Portuguese spelling*] **and Canada** [*In company name "Brascan Ltd."*] .... BRASCAN
Brasil. Instituto Brasileiro de Bibliographia e Documentacao. Noticias [*A publication*] .... Noticias
Brasil-Medico [*A publication*] .... Bras-Med
Brasilia [*Brazil*] [*Seismograph station code, US Geological Survey*] .... BAE
Brasilia [*Brazil*] [*Seismograph station code, US Geological Survey*] .... BDF
Brasilia [*A publication*] .... Bras
Brasilia [*Brazil*] [*Airport symbol*] .... BSB
Brasilia Array [*Brazil*] [*Seismograph station code, US Geological Survey*] .... BAO
Brass .... BR
Brass .... BRS
Brass or Bronze [*Top*] [*Freight*] .... B or B
Brass, Bronze, or Copper [*Freight*] .... BRBZC
Brass and Bronze Ingot Institute .... BBII
Brass Bulletin [*A publication*] .... Brass B
Brass Divider Strip [*Technical drawings*] .... BDS
Brass or Iron [*Freight*] .... B or I
Brass Pounders League [*Unit of American Radio Relay League*] .... BPL
Brass and Woodwind Quarterly [*A publication*] .... Brass & Wood Q
Brass World and Plater's Guide [*A publication*] .... Brass W
Brassboard Fault Tolerant Spaceborne Computer .... BFTSC
Braswell, J. V., Dallas TX [*STAC*] .... BJV
Bratislava [*Czechoslovakia*] [*Seismograph station code, US Geological Survey*] [*Closed*] .... BRA
Bratislava [*Czechoslovakia*] [*Airport symbol*] .... BTS
Bratislava [*Czechoslovakia*] [*Seismograph station code, US Geological Survey*] .... ZST
Bratislavske Lekarske Listy [*A publication*] .... Bratisl Lek Listy
Bratschen [*Viola*] .... BR
Bratsk [*USSR*] [*Airport symbol*] .... BTK
Brattleboro, VT [*Radio station call letters*] .... WKVT
Brattleboro, VT [*Radio station call letters*] .... WKVT-FM
Brattleboro, VT [*Radio station call letters*] .... WTSA
Braun [*C. F.*] **& Co.** [*NYSE symbol*] .... BRU
Braun Engineering Co. [*American Stock Exchange symbol*] .... BEX
Braunschweigische Wissenschaftliche Gesellschaft. Abhandlungen [*A publication*] .... Braunschweig Wiss Ges Abh
Brauwissenschaft [*A publication*] .... Brauwiss
Bravais-Miller Indices [*Physics*] .... BMI
Braverman-Chevigny Auditory Projective Test [*Psychology*] .... BCAPT
Bravo [*Phonetic alphabet*] .... B
Brawley, CA [*Location identifier*] [*FAA*] .... BWC
Brawley, CA [*Radio station call letters*] .... KROP
Brawley, CA [*Radio station call letters*] .... KSIQ
Brawley Public Library, Brawley, CA [*Library symbol*] .... CBr
Brayton Heat Exchanger Unit .... BHXU
Brayton Rotating Unit .... BRU
Brayton Turboelectric Engine .... BTE
Brayton Turboelectric Engine .... BTEE
Brazda [*A publication*] .... B
Braze .... BRZ
Brazier .... BRAZ
Brazier Head .... BRAZH
Brazil [*MARC country of publication code*] [*Library of Congress*] .... bl
Brazil [*Two-letter standard code*] .... BR
Brazil [*Three-letter standard code*] .... BRA
Brazil .... BRAZ
Brazil [*Aircraft nationality and registration mark*] .... PP
Brazil [*Aircraft nationality and registration mark*] .... PT
Brazil [*MARC geographic area code*] [*Library of Congress*] .... s-bl---
Brazil. Camara dos Deputados. Biblioteca. Boletim [*A publication*] .... Brazil Camara Deput Bibl Bol
Brazil. Conselho Nacional do Petroleo. Relatorio [*A publication*] .... Brazil Cons Nac Petrol Relat
Brazil Departamento Nacional da Producao Mineral. Anuario Mineral Brasileiro [*A publication*] .... Braz Dep Nac Prod Miner Anu Miner Bras
Brazil. Divisao de Geologia e Mineralogia. Boletim [*A publication*] .... Brazil Div Geol Mineral Bol
Brazil, IN [*Radio station call letters*] .... WBDJ-FM
Brazil, IN [*Radio station call letters*] .... WWCM
Brazil Labor Information and Resource Center .... BLI
Brazil-Medico [*A publication*] .... Brazil-Med
Brazil Ministerio das Minas e Energia. Departamento Nacional da Producao Mineral. Boletim [*A publication*] .... Brazil Minist Minas Energ Dep Nac Prod Miner Bol
Brazil Nut Advertising Fund [*Defunct*] .... BNAF
Brazil Nut Association .... BNA
Brazil Philatelic Association .... BPA
Brazil Public Library, Brazil, IN [*Library symbol*] .... InBra
Brazilian American Cultural Institute .... BACI
Brazilian-American Society [*Defunct*] .... BAS

Brazilian American Survey [*A publication*] .... BAS
Brazilian Business [*A publication*] .... Brazilian Bus
Brazilian Center of New York .... BCNY
Brazilian Coffee Institute .... BCI
Brazilian Expeditionary Force .... BEF
Brazilian Government Trade Bureau .... BGTB
Brazilian Infantry Division [*World War II*] .... BID
Brazilian International Airlines .... BIA
Brazilian Journal of Medical and Biological Research [*A publication*] .... Braz J Med Biol Res
Brazilian Navy .... BN
Brazilian Thorium Sludge .... BTS
Brazing .... BRZG
Brazing Accessory [*Tool*] .... BZAC
Brazing Fixture .... BZFX
Brazoria County Library, Angleton, TX [*Library symbol*] .... TxAng
Brazoria, TX [*Location identifier*] [*FAA*] .... BZT
Brazos Santiago, TX [*Location identifier*] [*FAA*] .... PIL
Brazosport College, Lake Jackson, TX [*Library symbol*] .... TxLjB
Brazosport Junior College, Freeport, TX [*Library symbol*] .... TxFrB
Brazzaville [*People's Republic of the Congo*] [*Airport symbol*] .... BZV
Breach of Peace .... BOP
Breach of Peace [*FBI standardized term*] .... B of P
Breach of Promise .... B of P
Bread Loaf Writers Conference .... BLWC
Bread and Roses [*An association*] .... B & R
Bread and Water .... B & W
Bread for the World [*An association*] .... BFW
Breadboard [*NASA*] .... BB
Breadboard of an Electrochemical Air Revitalization System [*NASA*] .... BEARS
Breadboard Kit [*NASA*] .... BBK
Breadboard Terminal Landing System [*NASA*] .... BTLS
Breadboard Verification Equipment [*NASA*] .... BVE
Breadboard Visual Reference System [*NASA*] .... BVRS
Breadth .... B
Breadth .... BRDTH
Breadth-Length .... BL
Break [*Electronics*] .... B
Break .... BRK
Break-Before-Make .... BBM
Break Bulk [*Transportation*] .... BB
Break Bulk Point [*Transportation*] .... BBP
Break Control Command Transducers .... BCCT
Break of Entry .... BOE
Break Even Analysis .... BEA
Break-Even Point [*Publishing*] .... B/E
Break-In Relay .... BIR
Break of Inspection .... BOI
Break of Integrity .... BOI
Break Jaw .... BJ
Break-Off Altitude [*Aviation*] .... BOA
Break-Off Height [*Aviation*] .... BOH
Break in Overcast [*Meteorology*] .... BINOVC
Break-Point Instruction .... BPI
Break Pulse Generator .... BPG
Break Request [*Data processing*] .... BR
Break Request Signal [*Data processing*] .... BRS
Break Signal [*Used to interrupt a transmission in progress*] [*Communications*] .... BK
Break Transmission .... BT
Break-Up Missile .... BUM
Breakdown .... BKDN
Breakdown [*Electronics*] .... B
Breakdown Air Traffic Control Services .... BATCS
Breakdown Control Number .... BCN
Breakdown Diode [*Electronics*] .... BKDNDIO
Breakdown Pulse Noise .... BPN
Breakdown of Recoverable Items .... BRI
Breakdown Truck [*British*] .... BT
Breakdown Voltage .... BV
Breaker .... BKR
Breaker .... BRKR
Breaker Block .... BB
Breaker End .... BE
Breakers [*Freight*] .... BRKS
Breakfast .... BRKF
Breakfast and Lunch [*Refers to a late morning or early afternoon meal*] .... BRUNCH
Breakfast Time [*Early morning television program*] [*BBC*] .... BT
Breaking [*FBI standardized term*] .... B
Breaking .... BRKG
Breaking and Entering .... B & E
Breaking and Entering and Auto Theft [*Police crime computer*] .... BEAT
Breaking and Entering in Nighttime and Petty Larceny .... B & ENT & PL
Breaking Strain [*Of fishing lines or casts*] .... BS
Breakover [*Electronics*] .... BO
Breakpoint .... BPT
Breaks Above .... BA
Breaks Below .... BB
Breaks in Higher Overcast [*Meteorology*] .... BRKHIC

Breakthrough .... BT
Breakthrough Bleeding [*Medicine*] .... BB
Breakthrough Bleeding [*Medicine*] .... BTB
Breakwater .... BKW
Breakwater Resources [*NASDAQ symbol*] .... BWRLF
Bream Fishermen Association .... BFA
Breast Biopsy [*Medicine*] .... BB
Breast Cancer Advisory Center .... BCAC
Breast Cancer Detection Demonstration Project [*NCI/ACS cosponsored project*] .... BCDDP
Breast Cancer Screening Indicator .... BCSI
Breast Cancer Task Force [*National Cancer Institute*] .... BCTF
Breast-Cyst Fluid Protein [*Immunochemistry*] .... BCFP
Breast Examination Bras, Incorporated .... BEBI
Breast Examination through Simultaneous Temperature Evaluation .... BEST
Breast Fed [*Medicine*] .... BF
Breast Self-Examination [*for cancer*] [*Medicine*] .... BSE
Breast Tumor [*Medicine*] .... BT
Breath [*Medicine*] .... BR
Breath Hydrogen Test .... BHT
Breath Rate per Minute .... BRPM
Breath Sounds [*Medicine*] .... BrS
Breath Sounds [*Medicine*] .... BS
Breath Test [*For determining whether or not an auto driver is legally drunk*] [*British*] .... B (Test)
Breathe .... BRTH
Breather .... BRTHR
Breather Hose/Mouthpiece .... BH/MP
Breathers for the Reduction of Atmospheric Hazards to the Environment [*Student legal action organization*] .... BREATHE
Breathers United to Stop Standing Time of Passenger-Buses [*Student legal action organization*] .... BUS STOP
Breathing Apparatus .... BA
Breathing Metabolic Simulator [*IBM Corp.*] .... BMS
Breaths per Minute .... BPM
Breaths per Second .... BPS
Brecht Heute - Brecht Today [*A publication*] .... BrechtH
Brecht-Jahrbuch [*A publication*] .... Brecht J
Breckenridge, CO [*Radio station call letters*] .... KLGT
Breckenridge, MN [*Radio station call letters*] .... KBMW
Breckenridge, MN [*Radio station call letters*] .... KKWB
Breckenridge, TX [*Location identifier*] [*FAA*] .... BKD
Breckenridge, TX [*Radio station call letters*] .... KROO
Breckenridge, TX [*Radio station call letters*] .... KSTB
Brecknockshire [*County in Wales*] .... BRKS
Brecon [*Welsh depot code*] .... BCN
Brecon and Merthyr Railway [*Wales*] .... BM
Breda News, Breda, IA [*Library symbol*] .... IaBreN
Breech-Loading [*Weapon*] .... BL
Breech-Loading Rifle .... BLR
Breech-Loading Rifled Guns .... BLRG
Breech Mechanism [*of a weapon*] .... BM
Breed of Sire .... BOS
Breeder Reactor .... BR
Breeder Reactor Corporation .... BRC
Breeder's Gazette [*A publication*] .... Breeder's Gaz
Breeze Corporations, Inc. [*American Stock Exchange symbol*] .... BRZ
Breezing [*Horse racing*] .... B
Breezy Point, MN [*Radio station call letters*] .... KLKS
Breguet Cruise [*SST*] .... BC
Breiddalsvik [*Iceland*] [*Airport symbol*] .... BXV
Breit-Wigner Formula .... BWF
Bremen [*West Germany*] [*Airport symbol*] .... BRE
Bremen, GA [*Radio station call letters*] .... WSLE
Bremen Port of Embarkation [*West Germany*] .... BPE
Bremer County Historical Society, Waverly, IA [*Library symbol*] .... IaWavBHi
Bremerhaven [*West Germany*] [*Airport symbol*] .... BRV
Bremerton Freight Car Ferry [*AAR code*] .... BFCF
Bremerton, WA [*Location identifier*] [*FAA*] .... CAN
Bremerton, WA [*Radio station call letters*] .... KBRO
Bremerton, WA [*Radio station call letters*] .... KWWA
Bremerton, WA [*Location identifier*] [*FAA*] .... PWT
Brenau College, Gainsville, GA [*Library symbol*] .... GGaB
Brenco, Inc. [*NASDAQ symbol*] .... BREN
Brenham, TX [*Radio station call letters*] .... KTTX
Brenham, TX [*Radio station call letters*] .... KWHI-FM
Brennan & Hargraves, Inc. [*Rocky Hill, CT*] [*FAA designator*] .... BHA
Brenner Companies, Inc. [*NASDAQ symbol*] .... BNER
Brenner-Studien [*A publication*] .... Bren-S
Brennstoff-Chemie [*A publication*] .... Brennst-Chem
Brennstoff-Waerme-Kraft [*Fuel, Heat, Power*] [*A publication*] .... Brennst-Waerme-Kraft
Brennstoff-Waerme-Kraft [*Fuel, Heat, Power*] [*A publication*] .... Brenns-Waerme-Kraft
Brennstoff-Waerme-Kraft [*Fuel, Heat, Power*] [*A publication*] .... Brenn-Waerme
Brennstoff-Waerme-Kraft [*Fuel, Heat, Power*] [*A publication*] .... BWK
Brenton Banks, Inc. [*NASDAQ symbol*] .... BRBK
Brentwood, NY [*Radio station call letters*] .... WXBA
Brentwood Public Library, Brentwood, MO [*Library symbol*] .... MoBr

Brentwood Public Library, Brentwood, NY [*Library symbol*] ... NBren
Brentwood, TN [*Radio station call letters*] ... WTBN
Brescia College, Owensboro, KY [*Library symbol*] ... KyOwB
Breslau [*Wroclaw*] [*Poland*] [*Seismograph station code, US Geological Survey*] [*Closed*] ... BRE
Brest [*France*] [*Airport symbol*] ... BES
Bretagne Air Services [*France*] [*ICAO designator*] ... VB
Brethren Life and Thought [*A publication*] ... BLT
Brethren Life and Thought [*A publication*] ... Breth Life
Brethren/Mennonite Council for Gay Concerns ... BMC
Brethren Peace Fellowship ... BPF
Brethren Service Commission [*Later, World Ministries Commission*] ... BSC
Brethren Volunteer Service ... BVS
Breton [*MARC language code*] [*Library of Congress*] ... bre
Brevard College, Brevard, NC [*Library symbol*] ... NcBreC
Brevard Community College [*Florida*] ... BCC
Brevard Community College, Cocoa, FL [*OCLC symbol*] ... EBC
Brevard Community College, Cocoa, FL [*Library symbol*] ... FCoaB
Brevard County Library System, Merritt Island, FL [*Library symbol*] ... FMiB
Brevard Engineering College [*Florida*] ... BEC
Brevard, NC [*Radio station call letters*] ... WPNF
Brevet [*Military*] ... BREV
Brevet [*Military*] ... BT
Brevete [*Patent*] [*French*] ... BREV
Brevete [*Patent*] [*French*] ... BTE
Brevete sans Garantie du Gouvernement [*Patent without Government Guarantee*] [*French*] ... BSGDG
Brevetoxin-B [*Biochemistry*] ... BTX-B
Brevier ... BREV
Brevig Mission [*Alaska*] [*Airport symbol*] ... KTS
Breviora Geologica Asturica [*A publication*] ... Breviora Geol Asturica
Brewarrina [*Australia*] [*Airport symbol*] ... BWQ
Brewer [*C.*] **& Co. Ltd.** [*American Stock Exchange symbol*] [*Delisted*] ... BRW
Brewer, ME [*Radio station call letters*] ... WGUY-FM
Brewers Association of America ... BAA
Brewers' Digest [*A publication*] ... Brew Dig
Brewers' Guardian [*A publication*] ... Brew Guardian
Brewers' Guild Journal [*A publication*] ... Brew Guild J
Brewers Hop Research Institute [*Later, USBA*] ... BHRI
Brewer's Spent Grain ... BSG
Brewer's Spent Grain Bran ... BSGB
Brewers Yeast Council [*Later, Brewers Yeast and Grains Council*] [*Defunct*] ... BYC
Brewing Industries Research Institute [*Defunct*] ... BIRI
Brewing Review [*A publication*] ... Brew Rev
Brewing Trade Review [*A publication*] ... Brew Trade Rev
Brewster [*Unit*] [*Physics*] ... B
Brewster, NY [*Radio station call letters*] ... WPUT
Brewster Public Library, Brewster, NY [*Library symbol*] ... NBre
Brewton, AL [*Radio station call letters*] ... WEBJ
Brewton, AL [*Radio station call letters*] ... WKNU
Brewton-Parker College, Mount Vernon, GA [*Library symbol*] ... GMtvB
BRH [*Bureau of Radiological Health*] **Bulletin** [*A publication*] ... BRH Bull
Briar Cliff College [*Iowa*] ... BCC
Briar Cliff College, Sioux City, IA [*Library symbol*] ... IaScB
Briar Cliff College, Sioux City, IA [*OCLC symbol*] ... IOB
Briarcliff College, Briarcliff Manor, NY [*Library symbol*] ... NBmB
Briarcliff Manor, NY [*Radio station call letters*] ... WZFM
Briarcliff Manor Public Library, Briarcliff Manor, NY [*Library symbol*] ... NBm
Briarcliff Quarterly [*A publication*] ... Briar Q
Briard Club of America ... BCA
Bribery [*FBI standardized term*] ... BRBY
Bribery-Labor [*FBI undercover investigation*] ... BRILAB
Brican Research Ltd. [*NASDAQ symbol*] ... BRIIF
Brices Crossroads National Battlefield Site ... BRCR
Brick ... BRK
Brick and Clay Record [*A publication*] ... B & C Rec
Brick and Clay Record [*A publication*] ... Brick Clay Rec
Brick Construction ... BR
Brick Institute of America ... BIA
Brick Protected [*Insurance classification*] ... BP
Brick Unprotected [*Insurance classification*] ... BU
Brickbuilder [*A publication*] ... Brickb
Bricklayers, Masons, and Plasterers' International of America [*Later, BAC*] ... BMP
Bricklin International ... BI
Bricks, Pottery, Glass, Cement [*Department of Employment*] [*British*] ... BPGC
Bricktown, NJ [*Radio station call letters*] ... WBGD
Bridal and Bridesmaids Apparel Association ... BBAA
Bridal Industry Association ... BIA
Bridge [*Shipping*] ... B
Bridge [*Board on Geographic Names*] ... BDG
Bridge ... BR
Bridge ... BRDG
Bridge ... BRG
Bridge ... BRI
Bridge Amplifier ... BA
Bridge and Building Supply Association [*Defunct*] ... BBSA
Bridge Construction Exercise [*Military*] ... BRIDGEX
Bridge Cutoff ... BCO
Bridge Display Console ... BDC
Bridge-Element Delay ... BED
Bridge Erection Boat ... BEB
Bridge Excitation ... BRDGSCIT
Bridge Plotting Room [*Navy*] ... BPR
Bridge Receiving Room [*Navy*] ... BRR
Bridge-Tunnel [*Proposed English Channel link between Britain and France*] ... BRUNNEL
Bridged Tap Isolator ... BTI
Bridgehead ... BRGHD
Bridgehead ... BRH
Bridgeport [*Connecticut*] [*Airport symbol*] ... BDR
Bridgeport [*Connecticut*] [*Seismograph station code, US Geological Survey*] [*Closed*] ... BPT
Bridgeport, AL [*Radio station call letters*] ... WBTS
Bridgeport City Normal School, Bridgeport, CT [*Library symbol*] [*Obsolete*] ... CtBN
Bridgeport, CT [*Television station call letters*] ... WBCT-TV
Bridgeport, CT [*Radio station call letters*] ... WDJZ
Bridgeport, CT [*Television station call letters*] ... WEDW
Bridgeport, CT [*Radio station call letters*] ... WEZN
Bridgeport, CT [*Radio station call letters*] ... WICC
Bridgeport, CT [*Radio station call letters*] ... WNAB
Bridgeport, CT [*Radio station call letters*] ... WPKN
Bridgeport Engineering Institute [*Connecticut*] ... BEI
Bridgeport Public Library, Bridgeport, CT [*OCLC symbol*] ... BPT
Bridgeport Public Library, Bridgeport, CT [*Library symbol*] ... CtB
Bridgeport, TX [*Radio station call letters*] ... KWCS
Bridgeton Evening News, Bridgeton, NJ [*Library symbol*] ... NjBN
Bridgeton Free Public Library, Bridgeton, NJ [*Library symbol*] ... NjB
Bridgeton, NC [*Radio station call letters*] ... WSFL
Bridgeton, NJ [*Radio station call letters*] ... WSNJ
Bridgeton, NJ [*Radio station call letters*] ... WSNJ-FM
Bridgettines [*Roman Catholic religious order*] ... BRIDG
Bridgeview Public Library, Bridgeview, IL [*Library symbol*] ... IBrv
Bridgewater College, Bridgewater, VA [*OCLC symbol*] ... VBC
Bridgewater College, Bridgewater, VA [*Library symbol*] ... ViBrC
Bridgewater, MA [*Radio station call letters*] ... WBIM-FM
Bridgewater, NS [*Radio station call letters*] ... CKBW
Bridgewater State College, Bridgewater, MA [*OCLC symbol*] ... BDR
Bridgewater State College, Bridgewater, MA [*Library symbol*] ... MBridT
Bridgewire ... BW
Bridgford Foods Corp. [*NASDAQ symbol*] ... BRID
Bridging Key [*on Dial Assistance Switchboard*] ... BR
Bridging Truck [*British*] ... BT
Brief ... BF
Brief ... BRF
Brief Intelligence Summary ... BINSUM
Brief Introduction ... BI
Brief Psychiatric Rating Scale ... BPRS
Brief Qualification Evaluation Program ... BQEP
Brief Stimulus Therapy [*Psychology*] ... BST
Brief Stop for Ammunition Lift [*Military*] ... BSA
Brief Stop for Cargo Lift [*or Delivery*] [*Military*] ... BSC
Brief Stop for Embarking or Debarking Personnel [*Military*] ... BSP
Brief Stop for Fuel [*Military*] ... BSF
Brief Systems Test [*NASA*] ... BST
Brief Task Description ... BTD
Brief Task Outline ... BTO
Brief and Time [*Photography*] ... B & T
Brief Vestibular Disorientation Test ... BVDT
Briefer ... BFR
Briefing ... BFG
Briefing ... BRFG
Briefing Room [*Navy*] ... BR
Brig ... BR
Brig [*Switzerland*] [*Seismograph station code, US Geological Survey*] [*Closed*] ... BRI
Brigade ... BDE
Brigade ... BGDE
Brigade ... BRIG
Brigade Administrative Area [*Military*] [*British*] ... BAA
Brigade Airborne Alert Force [*Military*] ... BAAF
Brigade Data Center [*Military*] ... BDC
Brigade Data Processing System ... BDPS
Brigade Engineer Group [*Marine Corps*] ... BEG
Brigade of Guards ... BOG
Brigade Headquarters [*Army*] ... BH
Brigade Headquarters [*Army*] ... BHQ
Brigade Headquarters [*Army*] ... BRIGHED
Brigade Landing Exercise [*Military*] ... BRIGLEX
Brigade Landing Team [*Army*] ... BDELT
Brigade Logistic Support Group [*Marine Corps*] ... BLSG
Brigade Major ... BM
Brigade Ordnance Officer [*British*] ... BOO
Brigade Ordnance Warrant Officer [*British*] ... BOWO
Brigade Quartermaster [*Marine Corps*] ... BRQM
Brigade Receiving Room ... BRR
Brigade Routine Order [*British*] ... BRO
Brigade Support Area [*Military*] ... BSA

Brigade Tactical Operations Center ... BTOC
Brigade Transport Officer [*British*] ... BTO
Brigadier ... BDR
Brigadier ... BRIG
Brigadier General ... BG
Brigadier General ... BGEN
Brigadier General ... BRIGEN
Brigadier General ... BRIG GEN
Brigadier, General Staff [*Army*] [*British*] ... BGS
Brigadier Royal Artillery [*British*] ... BRA
Brigantine [*Ship*] ... BGN
Brigantine Times, Brigantine, NJ [*Library symbol*] ... NjBrigT
Briggs-Lawrence County Public Library, Ironton, OH [*Library symbol*] ... OIB
Briggs Manufacturing Co. [*NYSE symbol*] [*Delisted*] ... BG
Briggs & Stratton Corp. [*NYSE symbol*] ... BGG
Brigham City, UT [*Radio station call letters*] ... KBUH
Brigham City, UT [*Radio station call letters*] ... KFRZ
Brigham Young University [*Utah*] ... BYU
Brigham Young University, Hawaii Campus, Laie, HI [*OCLC symbol*] ... BYU
Brigham Young University, Hawaii Campus, Laie, HI [*Library symbol*] ... HLaB
Brigham Young University, J. Reuben Clark Law Library, Provo, UT [*Library symbol*] ... UPB-L
Brigham Young University. Law Review [*A publication*] ... Brigham Young U L Rev
Brigham Young University Press ... BYUP
Brigham Young University, Provo, UT [*Library symbol*] ... UPB
Brigham Young University, School of Library and Information Science, Provo, UT [*OCLC symbol*] ... UUB
Brigham Young University. Science Bulletin. Biological Series [*A publication*] ... Brigham Young Univ Sci Bull Biol Ser
Brigham Young University. Studies [*A publication*] ... BYUS
Bright ... BRGT
Bright ... BRT
Bright Belt Warehouse Association ... BBWA
Bright Cathode-Ray Tube ... BCRT
Bright Display Equipment ... BDE
Bright Display RADAR Indicator ... BDRI
Bright Lights [*A publication*] ... Brt Lgts
Bright Object Sensor ... BOS
Bright Old Thing [*A member of established society in Washington, DC*] ... BOT
Bright RADAR Indicator-Tower Equipment ... BRITE
Bright RADAR Tube Display ... BRTD
Bright Source Protection [*Optics*] ... BSP
Bright Wire Goods Manufacturers Service Bureau [*Defunct*] ... BWGMSB
Brightness ... B
Brightness ... BRI
Brightness Contrast ... BC
Brightness Contrast Value ... BCV
Brightness Merit ... BM
Brighton [*County borough in England*] ... BRIGH
Brighton City Library, Brighton, MI [*Library symbol*] ... MiBrig
Brighton, CO [*Radio station call letters*] ... KLTT
Brighton Community Hospital, Medical Library, Brighton, CO [*Library symbol*] ... CoBriH-M
Brighton Enterprise-News, Brighton, IA [*Library symbol*] ... IaBrEN
Brighton High School Library, Rochester, NY [*OCLC symbol*] ... RVS
Brighton Memorial Library, Brighton, IL [*Library symbol*] ... IBri
Brigitte Bardot [*French actress*] ... BB
Brill, C. D., Washington DC [*STAC*] ... BCD
Brillante [*Brilliantly*] [*Music*] ... BRILL
Brilliance ... BRIL
[*A*] **Brilliant Career** ... ABC
Brilliant Cresyl Blue [*Biological stain*] ... BCB
Brilliant Green [*An indicator*] [*Chemistry*] ... BG
Brilliant Uncirculated [*Condition of coins*] [*Numismatics*] ... BU
Brillouin-Wentzel-Kramers [*Physics*] ... BWK
Brillouin Zone [*Physics*] ... BZ
Brilund Ltd. [*NASDAQ symbol*] ... BRILF
Brimstone R. R. [*AAR code*] ... BRM
Brindisi [*Italy*] [*Airport symbol*] ... BDS
Brinell Hardness Number [*Also, BHN, HB*] ... BH
Brinell Hardness Number [*Also, BH, HB*] ... BHN
Brinell Hardness Number [*Also, BH, BHN*] ... HB
Bring Your Own [*Liquor*] [*Party invitation notation*] ... BYO
Bring Your Own Beef [*Phrase popularized during 1973 beef shortage*] ... BYOB
Bring Your Own Booze [*or Bottle*] [*Party invitation notation*] ... BYOB
Bringham Memorial Library, Sharon, WI [*Library symbol*] ... WSha
Brinkley, AR [*Location identifier*] [*FAA*] ... BKZ
Brinkley, AR [*Radio station call letters*] ... KBRI
Brinkley, AR [*Radio station call letters*] ... KBRI-FM
Briquet ... BQ
Brisay, PQ [*Radio station call letters*] ... CHLG-FM-6
Brisbane [*Australia*] [*Airport symbol*] ... BNE
Brisbane [*Australia*] [*Seismograph station code, US Geological Survey*] ... BRS
Bristol [*Board/paper*] ... B
Bristol [*England*] [*Airport symbol*] ... BRS
Bristol [*City and county borough in England*] ... BRSTL
Bristol [*France*] [*Research code symbol*] ... B
Bristol Aero Engines Ltd., Montreal, PQ, Canada [*Library symbol*] ... CaQMBAE
Bristol Aeroplane Company ... BAC
Bristol Bay Oceanographic Processes ... B-BOP
Bristol Brass Corp. [*American Stock Exchange symbol*] [*Delisted*] ... BRB
Bristol Channel [*British*] ... BC
Bristol Channel [*British*] ... B/CH
Bristol Community College, Fall River, MA [*OCLC symbol*] ... BRC
Bristol Community College, Fall River, MA [*Library symbol*] ... MFB
Bristol Corp. [*NASDAQ symbol*] ... BRSL
Bristol County Law Library, Taunton, MA [*Library symbol*] ... MTaB
Bristol, CT [*Radio station call letters*] ... WBIS
Bristol Evening Post, Bristol, United Kingdom [*Library symbol*] ... UkBrP
Bristol Fighter [*Aircraft*] [*World War I*] ... BF
Bristol Gaming Corp. [*NASDAQ symbol*] ... BRST
Bristol Historical and Preservation Society, Bristol, RI [*Library symbol*] ... RBrHi
Bristol Independent School District Library, Bristol, SD [*Library symbol*] ... SdBrS
Bristol Laboratories ... BL
Bristol Laboratories [*Research code symbol*] ... BL-H
Bristol Laboratories [*Research code symbol*] ... P
Bristol Laboratories, Library, Syracuse, NY [*OCLC symbol*] ... ZUD
Bristol Laboratories, Syracuse, NY [*Library symbol*] ... NSyBL
Bristol Medico-Chirurgical Journal [*A publication*] ... Bristol Med-Chir J
Bristol-Myers Co. ... B-M
Bristol-Myers Co. [*NYSE symbol*] ... BMY
Bristol-Myers Co. [*Research code symbol*] ... NSC
Bristol-Myers Co. [*Research code symbol*] ... RP
Bristol Simplified Reheat [*Aircraft*] ... BSR
Bristol Social Adjustment Guides [*Psychology*] ... BSAG
Bristol, TN [*Location identifier*] [*FAA*] ... TRI
Bristol, TN [*Radio station call letters*] ... WBCV
Bristol, TN [*Radio station call letters*] ... WHCB
Bristol, TN [*Radio station call letters*] ... WOPI
Bristol United Press Ltd., Bristol, United Kingdom [*Library symbol*] ... BUP
Bristol. University. Spelaeological Society. Proceedings [*A publication*] ... Bristol Univ Spelaeol Soc Proc
Bristol, VA [*Television station call letters*] ... WCYB-TV
Bristol, VA [*Radio station call letters*] ... WFHG
Bristol, VA [*Radio station call letters*] ... WXBQ
Bristol, VA [*Radio station call letters*] ... WZAP
Bristow Helicopters Ltd. [*Great Britain*] [*ICAO designator*] ... UH
Bristow, OK [*Radio station call letters*] ... KREK
Bristow Public Library, Bristow, OK [*Library symbol*] ... OkBr
Britannia ... BRIT
Britannia Airways Ltd. [*ICAO designator*] ... BY
Britannia Petite Rabbit Fanciers Association ... BPRFA
Britannia Royal Naval College ... BritColl
Britannica ... BRIT
Britannica Book of the Year [*A publication*] ... BBY
Britannica Book of the Year [*A publication*] ... Brit Bk Yr
Britannica Junior Encyclopedia [*A publication*] ... BJE
Britannica Reading Achievement Center ... BRAC
Britannica Review of Foreign Language Education [*A publication*] ... Britannica R For Lang Educ
Brith Abraham Foundation [*Later, BZ*] ... BAF
Brith Sholom [*An association*] ... BS
Brith Trumpeldor of America ... BTA
Britische und Irische Studien zur Deutschen Sprache und Literatur [*A publication*] ... BISDSL
British ... B
British ... BR
British ... BRIT
British Absolute Unit ... BAU
British Academy ... BA
British Academy, London. Proceedings [*A publication*] ... Brit Acad Proc
British Acoustical Society ... BAS
British Acupuncture Association and Register ... BAAR
British Admiralty ... BA
British Admiralty Delegation [*to Washington*] ... BAD
British Admiralty Establishment ... BAE
British Admiralty Maintenance and Supply Representative ... BAMSR
British Admiralty Repair Mission ... BARM
British Admiralty Signal RADAR Establishment ... B/ASRE
British Admiralty Technical Mission [*World War II*] ... BATM
British Advisory Committee for Aeronautics ... BACA
British Aerial Transport Ltd. ... BAT
British Aeronautical Research Committee ... BARC
British Aerosol Manufacturers Association ... BAMA
British Aerospace ... BAe
British Aerospace Board ... BAB
British Agricultural Export Council ... BAEC
British Air Commission [*Washington*] ... BAC
British Air Ferries Ltd. ... BAF
British Air Ferries Ltd. ... VF
British Air Force ... BAF
British Air Forces in France [*World War II*] ... BAFF
British Air Forces of Occupation [*Military*] ... BAFO

British Air Line Pilots Association ... BALPA
British Air Ministry ... BAM
British Air Ministry Control Office ... BAMCO
British Aircraft Corporation ... BAC
British Aircraft Corporation Commercial Habitat under the Sea ... BACCHUS
British Airports Authority ... BAA
British Airports Information Retrieval [*System*] ... BAIR
British Airtours [*Airline*] ... BA
British Airways [*formerly, British European Airways and British Overseas Airways Corp.*] **European Division** [*ICAO designator*] ... BE
British Airways [*formerly, British European Airways and British Overseas Airways Corp.*] **Overseas Division** [*ICAO designator*] ... BA
British Airways [*formerly, British European Airways and British Overseas Airways Corp.*] **Regional Division (Cambrian Section)** [*ICAO designator*] [*Obsolete*] ... CS
British Airways [*formerly, British European Airways and British Overseas Airways Corp.*] **Regional Division (Northeast Section)** [*ICAO designator*] [*Obsolete*] ... NS
British Almanac Companion [*A publication*] ... Br Alma Comp
British Aluminium Co. Ltd. ... BA
British Amateur Athletic Board ... BAAB
British Amateur Tape Recording Society ... BATRS
British America ... BA
British American Arts Association ... BAAA
British-American Chamber of Commerce ... BACC
British-American Collectors' Club ... BACC
British-American Coordinating Committee [*Turkey*] ... BACC
British American Educational Foundation ... BAEF
British/American Light Opera Exchange ... BALOE
British American Repertory Company ... BARC
British-American Rhykenological Society ... B-ARS
British-American Scientific International Commercial English ... BASIC (English)
British-American Tobacco Co. ... BAT
British-American Tobacco Co. [*American Stock Exchange symbol*] ... BQB
British Angular Rate Bombsight ... BARB
British Antarctic Survey ... BAS
British Antarctic Survey. Bulletin [*A publication*] ... Br Antarct Surv Bull
British Antarctic Survey. Scientific Reports [*A publication*] ... Br Antarct Surv Sci Rep
British Antarctic Territory ... BAT
British Anti-Lewisite [*Also, DMP: Dimercapto, propanol*] [*Detoxicant*] ... BAL
British Antique Dealers' Association ... BADA
British Approvals Board for Telecommunications ... BABT
British Approved Name ... BAN
British Archaeological Abstracts [*A publication*] ... Br Archaeol Abstr
British Archaeological Abstracts [*A publication*] ... BritArchAb
British Archaeological Association. Journal [*A publication*] ... BAAJ
British Archives Council ... BAC
British Army ... BA
British Army Aid Group [*China*] [*World War II*] ... BAAG
British Army Forces Overseas ... BAFO
British Army of Occupation [*World War II*] ... BAO
British Army Review [*A publication*] ... BAR
British Army of the Rhine [*NATO/NORTHAG*] ... BAOR
British Army Staff ... BAS
British Association for the Advancement of Science ... BAAS
British Association for the Advancement of Science. Report [*A publication*] ... Brit As Rp
British Association for American Studies ... BAAS
British Association for American Studies. Bulletin [*A publication*] ... BAASB
British Association for American Studies. Bulletin [*A publication*] ... Brit Assoc Am Studies Bull
British Association of Chemists ... BAC
British Association of Consulting Engineers ... BACE
British Association for the Control of Airport Noise ... BACAN
British Association Screw Thread ... BA
British Astronomical Association ... BAA
British Atomic Energy Research Establishment ... B/AERE
British Automobile Manufacturers Association ... BAMA
British Automobile Racing Club ... BARC
British Bee Journal and Beekeepers' Adviser [*A publication*] ... Brit Bee J
British Beer-Mat Collectors' Society ... BB-CS
British Birds [*A publication*] ... Br Birds
British Birds [*A publication*] ... Brit Birds
British Bloodstock Agency ... BBA
British Blue [*A British sailor*] ... BB
British Board of Film Censors ... BBFC
British Board of Quality Control ... BBQC
British Bombing Research Mission [*World War II*] ... BBRM
British Bombing Survey Units [*World War II*] ... BBSU
British Book News [*A publication*] ... Brit Bk N
British Book News [*A publication*] ... Brit Bk News
British Book News. Children's Supplement [*A publication*] ... Brit Bk N C
British Books in Print [*A publication*] ... BBIP
British Borneo Civil Affairs Unit [*World War II*] ... BBCAU
British Boxing Board of Control ... BBBC
British Broadcasting Corporation [*State-operated radio and television*] ... BBC
British Broadcasting Corporation Scottish Symphony Orchestra ... BBCSSO
British Broadcasting Corporation Symphony Orchestra ... BBCSO
British Bryological Society ... BBS
British Bureau of Television Advertising ... BBTA
British Caledonian Airways ... BCA
British Caledonian Airways ... BCAL
British Caledonian Airways [*ICAO designator*] ... BR
British Calibration Service ... BCS
British Car Auctions ... BCA
British Cargo Ship ... BAK
British Caribbean Philatelic Study Group ... BCPSG
British Cast Iron Research Association ... BCIRA
British Catalogue of Music [*British National Bibliography*] ... BCM
British Central Office of Information ... BCOI
British Ceramic Abstracts [*A publication*] ... Br Ceram Abstr
British Ceramic Research Association. Special Publication [*A publication*] ... Br Cer Res Assoc Spec Publ
British Ceramic Society. Transactions [*A publication*] ... British Ceramic Soc Trans
British Chemical Engineering [*A publication*] ... Br Chem Eng
British Chemical Engineering [*A publication*] ... Br Chem Engng
British Chemical Engineering [*A publication*] ... Brit Chem Eng
British Chemical Engineering and Process Technology [*A publication*] ... Br Chem Engng Process Technol
British Chemical Engineering and Process Technology [*A publication*] ... Br Chem Eng Process Technol
British Chess Magazine ... BCM
British Chiefs of Staff ... BCOS
British Chiefs of Staff ... BCS
British Civil Airworthiness Requirements ... BCAR
British Clayworker [*A publication*] ... Br Claywkr
British Coal Utilisation Research Association ... BCURA
British Coal Utilisation Research Association. Monthly Bulletin [*A publication*] ... Br Coal Util Res Ass Mon Bull
British College of Aeronautics ... B/C of A
British Colonial Airlines, Inc. ... BCA
British Columbia [*Canadian province*] [*Postal code*] ... BC
British Columbia [*MARC country of publication code*] [*Library of Congress*] ... bcc
British Columbia [*MARC geographic area code*] [*Library of Congress*] ... n-cn-bc
British Columbia Barkerville Restoration Advisory Committee, Victoria, BC, Canada [*Library symbol*] ... CaBViB
British Columbia Bureau of Economics and Statistics, Business-Finance Library, Victoria, BC, Canada [*Library symbol*] ... CaBViBE
British Columbia Department of Mines. Annual Report. Bulletin [*A publication*] ... British Columbia Dept Mines Ann Rept Bull
British Columbia Department of Mines and Petroleum Resources. Bulletin [*A publication*] ... BC Dep Mines Pet Resour Bull
British Columbia Department of Recreation and Conservation. Annual Report [*A publication*] ... BC Dep Recreat Conserv Annu Rep
British Columbia Energy Commission, Vancouver, BC, Canada [*Library symbol*] ... CaBVaEC
British Columbia Forest Service. Annual Report [*A publication*] ... BC For Serv Annu Rep
British Columbia Forest Service. Forest Research Review [*A publication*] ... BC For Serv For Res Rev
British Columbia Forest Service. Research Notes [*A publication*] ... BC For Serv Res Notes
British Columbia Forest Service, Victoria, BC, Canada [*Library symbol*] ... CaBViFS
British Columbia Historical Quarterly [*A publication*] ... BC His Q
British Columbia Hydro Engineering Library, Vancouver, BC, Canada [*Library symbol*] ... CaBVaHE
British Columbia Hydro & Power Authority [*Formerly, British Columbia Electric Co. Ltd.*] [*AAR code*] ... BCE
British Columbia Hydro & Power Authority [*Formerly, British Columbia Electric Co. Ltd.*], **Vancouver, BC, Canada** [*Library symbol*] ... CaBVaH
British Columbia Institute of Technology, Burnaby, BC, Canada [*Library symbol*] ... CaBBIT
British Columbia Library, New Westminster, BC, Canada [*Library symbol*] ... CaBNWB
British Columbia Library Quarterly [*A publication*] ... BC Lib Q
British Columbia Library Quarterly [*A publication*] ... BCLQ
British Columbia Library Quarterly [*A publication*] ... Br Columb Libr Q
British Columbia Library Quarterly [*A publication*] ... Brit Columbia Lib Q
British Columbia Lumberman [*A publication*] ... BC Lumberm
British Columbia Medical Library Service, Vancouver, BC, Canada [*Library symbol*] ... CaBVaM
British Columbia Minister of Mines and Petroleum Resources. Annual Report [*A publication*] ... BC Minist Mines Pet Resour Annu Rep
British Columbia Ministry of Economic Development, Victoria, BC, Canada [*Library symbol*] ... CaBViED
British Columbia Ministry of Education, Victoria, BC, Canada [*Library symbol*] ... CaBViDE
British Columbia Ministry of the Environment, Environmental Protection, Pollution Control Branch, Victoria, BC, Canada [*Library symbol*] ... CaBViEP

British Columbia Ministry of the Environment, Victoria, BC, Canada [Library symbol] ...... CaBViLFW
British Columbia Ministry of Health, Health Information, Victoria, BC, Canada [Library symbol] ...... CaBViHI
British Columbia Ministry of Highways and Public Works, Victoria, BC, Canada [Library symbol] ...... CaBViH
British Columbia Ministry of Human Resources, Staff Development Division, Victoria, BC, Canada [Library symbol] ...... CaBViHRS
British Columbia Ministry of Mines and Petroleum Resources, Victoria, BC, Canada [Library symbol] ...... CaBViM
British Columbia Ministry of Recreation and Conservation, Fish and Game Branch, Victoria, BC, Canada [Library symbol] ...... CaBViRC
British Columbia Professional Engineer [A publication] ...... BC Prof Eng
British Columbia Provincial Museum, Ethnology Division, Victoria, BC, Canada [Library symbol] ...... CaBViPME
British Columbia Provincial Museum of Natural History and Anthropology. Report [A publication] ...... BC Prov Mus Nat Hist Anthropol Rep
British Columbia Railway Co. [AAR code] ...... BCOL
British Columbia Research Council, Vancouver, BC, Canada [Library symbol] ...... CaBVaR
British Columbia Teachers' Federation Resources Centre, Vancouver, BC, Canada [Library symbol] ...... CaBVaTF
British Columbia Telephone Co., Vancouver, BC, Canada [Library symbol] ...... CaBVaBT
British Columbia Union Catalogue, Burnaby, BC, Canada [Library symbol] ...... CaBBUC
British Columbia University. Department of Geology. Report [A publication] ...... BC Univ Dep Geol Rep
British Columbia University. Department of Geology. Report [A publication] ...... British Columbia Univ Dept Geology Rept
British Columbia and Yukon Chamber of Mines, Vancouver, BC, Canada [Library symbol] ...... CaBVaBY
British Commissioner [Salvation Army] ...... BC
British Commonwealth [MARC geographic area code] [Library of Congress] ...... b------
British Commonwealth ...... BC
British Commonwealth Air Training Plan [World War II] ...... BCATP
British Commonwealth and Empire ...... BCE
British Commonwealth Ex-Services League ...... BCEL
British Commonwealth of Nations ...... BCN
British Commonwealth Occupation Force [Military] ...... BCOF
British Commonwealth Pacific Airlines ...... BCPA
British Commonwealth Producers' Organization ...... BCPO
British Commonwealth Scientific Office [Washington, DC] ...... BCSO
British Commonwealth Scientific Office (North America) [Washington, DC] ...... BCSO(NA)
British Computer Society ...... BCS
British Conference on Automation and Computation ...... BCAC
British Constructional Steelworks Association. Publications [A publication] ...... Brit Constr Steelworks Ass Publ
British Control Supply Mission [World War II] ...... BCSM
British Corrosion Journal [A publication] ...... Br Corros J
British Corrosion Journal [A publication] ...... Brit Corros J
British Council ...... BC
British Council for Aid to Refugees ...... BCAR
British Council of Churches ...... BCC
British Crown Colony ...... BCC
British Deaf News [A publication] ...... Brit Deaf News
British Defence Coordination Committee, Middle East ...... BDCC/ME
British Defence Staff ...... BDS
British Defence Staff, Washington, DC [Also, BDSWASHDC] ...... BDSW
British Defence Staff, Washington, DC [Also, BDSW] ...... BDSWASHDC
British Dental Association ...... BDA
British Dental Journal [A publication] ...... BDJOA
British Dental Journal [A publication] ...... Br Dent J
British Dental Surgery Assistant [A publication] ...... Br Dent Surg Assist
British Destroyer Escort ...... BDE
British Double Summer Time ...... BDST
British Drug Houses Ltd. [Research code symbol] ...... BDH
British East Africa ...... BEA
British East Africa Protectorate [British government] ...... BEAP
British Ecological Society. Symposium [A publication] ...... Br Ecol Soc Symp
British Ecological Society. Symposium [A publication] ...... Brit Ecol Soc Symp
British Education Index [A publication] ...... BritEdI
British Electrical and Allied Manufacturers Association ...... BEAMA
British Electrical Approvals Board ...... BEAB
British Electricity Authority ...... BEA
British Electronic and Applied Research Association ...... BEARA
British Element ...... BE
British Embassy, Washington, DC [Library symbol] ...... DBE
British Empire ...... BE
British Empire and Commonwealth Weight-Lifting Council ...... BE & CWLC
British Empire Forces ...... BEF
British Empire Medal ...... BEM
British Empire Naturalist Association ...... BENA
British Empire Union ...... BEU
British Engine Technical Reports [A publication] ...... Br Engine Tech Rep
British Engine Technical Reports [A publication] ...... Br Eng Tech Rep
British Engineering Standards Association ...... BESA

British Engineers Association ...... BEA
British Engineers Club ...... BEC
British European Airways Corp. [Later, British Airways] ...... BEA
British European Airways Corporation [Later, British Airways] ...... BEAC
British European Airways Corp. [later, British Airways] Computerized Office Network ...... BEACON
British Expeditionary Force ...... BEF
British Experimental Pile Operation [Nuclear reactor] ...... BEPO
British Exports Marketing Advisory Committee [Defunct] ...... BEMAC
British Fern Gazette [A publication] ...... Br Fern Gaz
British Field Post Office [World War II] ...... BFPO
British Film Institute ...... BFI
British First Airborne Division ...... BFAD
British First Army ...... BFA
British Flight Battalion ...... BFB
British Food Mission [World War II] ...... BFM
British Forces Broadcasting Service ...... BFBS
British Forces Germany [NATO] ...... BFG
British Forces Network ...... BFN
British Forces Post Office ...... BFPO
British and Foreign Bible Society ...... BFBS
British and Foreign Evangelical Review [A publication] ...... Brit & For Evang R
British and Foreign Review [A publication] ...... Brit & For R
British Foundryman [A publication] ...... Br Foundryman
British Free Corps [Corps formed by Germans among POW's and civil internees] [World War II] ...... BFC
British Gallantry Medal ...... BGM
British Gas Corporation ...... BGC
British Gauge [Metal industry] ...... BG
British Gear Manufacturers Association ...... BGMA
British General Hospital ...... BGH
British Geologist [A publication] ...... Br Geol
British Granite and Whinstone Federation. Journal [A publication] ...... Brit Granite Whinstone Fed J
British Grassland Society. Journal [A publication] ...... Brit Grassland Soc J
British Grassland Society. Occasional Symposium [A publication] ...... Br Grassl Soc Occas Symp
British Grenadiers ...... BG
British Guiana ...... BG
British Guiana ...... BGU
British Guiana Airways Ltd. [A national airline] ...... BGAL
British Heart Journal [A publication] ...... Br Heart J
British Heart Journal [A publication] ...... Brit Heart J
British Heritage Society ...... BHS
British High Commissioner ...... BHC
British Honduras ...... BH
British Honduras [MARC geographic area code] [Library of Congress] ...... ncbh---
British Honduras [MARC country of publication code] [Library of Congress] ...... bh
British Honduras. Department of Agriculture. Annual Report [A publication] ...... Br Honduras Dep Agric Annu Rep
British Horsepower ...... BHP
British Hospital and Social Service Journal [A publication] ...... Brit Hosp Soc Serv J
British Hovercraft ...... BH
British Hovercraft Corporation ...... BHC
British Humanities Index [A publication] ...... BHI
British Humanities Index [A publication] ...... Brit Hum
British Hydromechanics Research Association ...... BHRA
British Imperial System ...... BIS
British Independent Air Transport Association ...... BIATA
British India ...... BI
British India Steam Navigation Company ...... BISNC
British Indian Ocean Territory [MARC country of publication code] [Library of Congress] ...... bi
British Indian Ocean Territory ...... BIOT
British Indian Ocean Territory [MARC geographic area code] [Library of Congress] ...... i-bi---
British Indian Ocean Territory [Two-letter standard code] ...... IO
British Indian Ocean Territory [Three-letter standard code] ...... IOT
British Industrial Biological Research Association ...... BIBRA
British Industrial Collaborative Exponential Program ...... BICEP
British Industrial Development Office [Through foreign branches, encourages investments in Britain from abroad] ...... BIDO
British Industrial Measuring and Control Apparatus Manufacturers' Association ...... BIMCAM
British Industrial and Scientific Film Association ...... BISFA
British Industrial Truck Association ...... BITA
British Industries Fair ...... BIF
British Industries Federation ...... BIF
British Information Services ...... BIS
British Information Services, New York, NY [Library symbol] ...... NNBLI
British Ink Maker [A publication] ...... Br Ink Mkr
British Ink Maker [A publication] ...... Brit Ink Maker
British Institute of Electrical Engineers ...... BIEE
British Institute of Industrial Art ...... BIIA
British Institute of International and Comparative Law ...... BIICL
British Institute of International and Comparative Law ...... BRICLAW
British Institute of Management ...... BIM
British Institute of Radio Engineers ...... BIRE

British Institute of Radiology	BIR
British Institute of Recorded Sound	BIRS
British Institute of Recorded Sound. Bulletin [*A publication*]	BIRS
British Institute of Sewage Purification	BISP
British Insulated Cables	BIC
British Insulated Callender's Cable [*ICAO designator*] [*Obsolete*]	BC
British Insulated Callender's Cable	BICC
British Insurance Association	BIA
British Intelligence Objectives Subcommittee	BIOS
British Internal Combustion Engine Manufacturers' Association	BICEMA
British and International Addressing Post [*A publication*]	BIA
British Interplanetary Society	BIS
British Iron and Steel Federation	BISF
British Iron and Steel Industry Translation Service	BISITS
British Iron and Steel Research Association	BISRA
British Island Airways Ltd.	BIA
British-Israel World Federation	BI
British-Israel World Federation	BIWF
British Jewish Cockney	BJC
British Joint Communications-Electronics Board [*Military*]	BJCEB
British Joint Communications Office	BJCO
British Joint Services	BJS
British Joint Services Mission [*Later, SUKLO*]	BJSM
British Joint Staff Mission [*World War II*]	BJSM
British Journal of Addiction [*A publication*]	Brit J Addict
British Journal of Addiction [*A publication*]	Br J Addict
British Journal of Aesthetics [*A publication*]	BJA
British Journal of Aesthetics [*A publication*]	BJEMA
British Journal of Aesthetics [*A publication*]	Brit J Aes
British Journal of Aesthetics [*A publication*]	Brit J Aesth
British Journal of Aesthetics [*A publication*]	Brit J Aesthetics
British Journal on Alcohol and Alcoholism [*A publication*]	Br J Alcohol Alcohol
British Journal of Anaesthesia [*A publication*]	BJANA
British Journal of Anaesthesia [*A publication*]	Br J Anaest
British Journal of Anaesthesia [*A publication*]	Br J Anaesth
British Journal of Applied Physics [*A publication*]	Brit J Ap Phys
British Journal of Applied Physics [*A publication*]	Br J Appl Phys
British Journal of Audiology [*A publication*]	Brit J Audiol
British Journal of Audiology [*A publication*]	Br J Audiol
British Journal of Audiology. Supplement [*A publication*]	Br J Audiol Suppl
British Journal of Cancer [*A publication*]	Br J Canc
British Journal of Cancer [*A publication*]	Br J Cancer
British Journal of Cancer. Supplement [*A publication*]	Br J Cancer Suppl
British Journal of Children's Diseases [*A publication*]	Brit J Child Dis
British Journal of Clinical Pharmacology [*A publication*]	Br J Clin Pharmacol
British Journal of Clinical Pharmacology [*A publication*]	Br J Cl Ph
British Journal of Clinical Practice [*A publication*]	Br J Clin P
British Journal of Criminology [*A publication*]	B J Criminology
British Journal of Criminology [*A publication*]	Brit J Crim
British Journal of Criminology [*A publication*]	Brit J Criminol
British Journal of Criminology [*A publication*]	Br J Crimin
British Journal of Criminology, Delinquency and Deviant Social Behavior [*A publication*]	Brit J Criminol
British Journal of Delinquency [*A publication*]	Brit J Delinq
British Journal of Dermatology [*A publication*]	Br J Derm
British Journal of Dermatology [*A publication*]	Br J Dermatol
British Journal of Dermatology. Supplement [*A publication*]	Br J Dermatol Suppl
British Journal of Diseases of the Chest [*A publication*]	Br J Dis Ch
British Journal of Diseases of the Chest [*A publication*]	Br J Dis Chest
British Journal of Disorders of Communication [*A publication*]	BJDEB
British Journal of Disorders of Communication [*A publication*]	B J Disorders of Communication
British Journal of Disorders of Communication [*A publication*]	Brit J Dis Commun
British Journal of Disorders of Communication [*A publication*]	Br J Dis Co
British Journal of Educational Psychology [*A publication*]	B J Ednl Psych
British Journal of Educational Psychology [*A publication*]	BJEP
British Journal of Educational Psychology [*A publication*]	BJESA
British Journal of Educational Psychology [*A publication*]	Brit J Ed Psychol
British Journal of Educational Psychology [*A publication*]	Brit J Educ Psychol
British Journal of Educational Psychology [*A publication*]	Br J Ed Psy
British Journal of Educational Psychology [*A publication*]	Br J Educ Psychol
British Journal of Educational Studies [*A publication*]	B J Ednl Studies
British Journal of Educational Studies [*A publication*]	BJES
British Journal of Educational Studies [*A publication*]	Brit J Ed Studies
British Journal of Educational Studies [*A publication*]	Brit J Educ Stud
British Journal of Educational Studies [*A publication*]	Br J Educ S
British Journal of Educational Technology [*A publication*]	B J Ednl Technology
British Journal of Educational Technology [*A publication*]	Br J Educ T
British Journal of Experimental Pathology [*A publication*]	Br J Ex Pat
British Journal of Experimental Pathology [*A publication*]	Br J Exp Pathol
British Journal of Guidance and Counseling [*A publication*]	B J Guidance & Counseling
British Journal of Haematology [*A publication*]	Br J Haem
British Journal of Haematology [*A publication*]	Br J Haematol
British Journal for the History of Science [*A publication*]	Brit J Hist Sci
British Journal for the History of Science [*A publication*]	Br J Hist S
British Journal for the History of Science [*A publication*]	Br J Hist Sci
British Journal of Hospital Medicine [*A publication*]	Brit J Hosp Med
British Journal of Hospital Medicine [*A publication*]	Br J Hosp Med
British Journal of In-Service Education [*A publication*]	B J In-Service Ed
British Journal of Industrial Medicine [*A publication*]	Brit J Industr Med
British Journal of Industrial Medicine [*A publication*]	Br J Ind Me
British Journal of Industrial Medicine [*A publication*]	Br J Ind Med
British Journal of Industrial Relations [*A publication*]	BJIR
British Journal of Industrial Relations [*A publication*]	Brit J Industr Relat
British Journal of International Studies [*A publication*]	Brit J Int Stud
British Journal of Law and Society [*A publication*]	Brit J L & Soc
British Journal of Mathematical and Statistical Psychology [*A publication*]	B J Ma St Ps
British Journal of Mathematical and Statistical Psychology [*A publication*]	B J Math & Stat Psych
British Journal of Mathematical and Statistical Psychology [*A publication*]	BJMSA
British Journal of Mathematical and Statistical Psychology [*A publication*]	Brit J Math & Stat Psychol
British Journal of Mathematical and Statistical Psychology [*A publication*]	Br J Math S
British Journal of Medical Education [*A publication*]	Br J Med Educ
British Journal of Medical Psychology [*A publication*]	BJMPA
British Journal of Medical Psychology [*A publication*]	BJMPs
British Journal of Medical Psychology [*A publication*]	Brit J Med Psychol
British Journal of Medical Psychology [*A publication*]	Br J Med Ps
British Journal of Medical Psychology [*A publication*]	Br J Med Psychol
British Journal of Mental Subnormality [*A publication*]	Brit J Ment Subnorm
British Journal of Mental Subnormality [*A publication*]	Br J Ment S
British Journal of Music Therapy [*A publication*]	BJMTD
British Journal of Non-Destructive Testing [*A publication*]	Brit J Non-Destruct Test
British Journal of Non-Destructive Testing [*A publication*]	Br J Non-Destr Test
British Journal of Nutrition [*A publication*]	Brit J Nutr
British Journal of Nutrition [*A publication*]	Br J Nutr
British Journal of Nutrition. Proceedings of the Nutrition Society [*A publication*]	Brit J Nutr Proc Nutr Soc
British Journal of Obstetrics and Gynaecology [*A publication*]	BJOGA
British Journal of Obstetrics and Gynaecology [*A publication*]	Br J Obstet Gynaecol
British Journal of Obstetrics and Gynaecology [*A publication*]	Br J Obst G
British Journal of Occupational Safety [*A publication*]	Br J Occup Saf
British Journal of Ophthalmology [*A publication*]	Br J Ophth
British Journal of Ophthalmology [*A publication*]	Br J Ophthalmol
British Journal of Oral Surgery [*A publication*]	Br J Oral S
British Journal of Oral Surgery [*A publication*]	Br J Oral Surg
British Journal of Orthodontics [*A publication*]	Br J Orthod
British Journal of Pharmacology [*A publication*]	BJPCB
British Journal of Pharmacology [*A publication*]	Brit J Pharmacol
British Journal of Pharmacology [*A publication*]	Br J Pharm
British Journal of Pharmacology [*A publication*]	Br J Pharmacol
British Journal of Pharmacology and Chemotherapy [*Later, British Journal of Pharmacology*] [*A publication*]	Brit J Pharmacol Chemother
British Journal of Pharmacology and Chemotherapy [*Later, British Journal of Pharmacology*] [*A publication*]	Br J Pharmacol Chemother
British Journal for the Philosophy of Science [*A publication*]	Brit J Philos Sci
British Journal for the Philosophy of Science [*A publication*]	Brit J Phil Sci
British Journal of Photography [*A publication*]	Br J Photogr
British Journal of Physical Education [*A publication*]	B J Physical Ed
British Journal of Physical Education [*A publication*]	Br J Phys Ed
British Journal of Physiological Optics [*A publication*]	Br J Physiol Opt
British Journal of Physiological Optics [*A publication*]	Br J Phys O
British Journal of Plastic Surgery [*A publication*]	Br J Plast Surg
British Journal of Plastic Surgery [*A publication*]	Br J Pl Sur
British Journal of Political Science [*A publication*]	Brit J Pol Sci
British Journal of Political Science [*A publication*]	Br J Poli S
British Journal of Preventive and Social Medicine [*A publication*]	Brit J Prev Soc Med
British Journal of Preventive and Social Medicine [*A publication*]	Br J Prev S
British Journal of Preventive and Social Medicine [*A publication*]	Br J Prev Soc Med
British Journal of Psychiatric Social Work [*A publication*]	Brit J Psych Soc Work
British Journal of Psychiatry [*A publication*]	BJPSB
British Journal of Psychiatry [*A publication*]	Brit J Psychiat
British Journal of Psychiatry [*A publication*]	Br J Psychi
British Journal of Psychiatry [*A publication*]	Br J Psychiatry
British Journal of Psychiatry. Special Publication [*A publication*]	Br J Psychiatry Spec Publ
British Journal of Psychology [*A publication*]	BJP
British Journal of Psychology [*A publication*]	BJPs

British Journal of Psychology [*A publication*] — B J Psych

British Journal of Psychology [*A publication*] — Brit J Psychol

British Journal of Psychology [*A publication*] — Br J Psycho

British Journal of Psychology [*A publication*] — Br J Psychol

British Journal of Psychology. General Section [*A publication*] — BJSGA

British Journal of Radiology [*A publication*] — Brit J Radiol

British Journal of Radiology [*A publication*] — Br J Radiol

British Journal of Radiology. Supplement [*A publication*] — Br J Radiol Suppl

British Journal of Social and Clinical Psychology [*A publication*] — BJCPB

British Journal of Social and Clinical Psychology [*A publication*] — BJSCP

British Journal of Social and Clinical Psychology [*A publication*] — B J Social and Clinical Psych

British Journal of Social and Clinical Psychology [*A publication*] — Brit J Social & Clin Psychol

British Journal of Social and Clinical Psychology [*A publication*] — Br J Soc Cl

British Journal of Social and Clinical Psychology [*A publication*] — Br J Soc Clin Psychol

British Journal of Social Psychiatry [*A publication*] — Brit J Social Psychiat

British Journal of Social Psychiatry [*A publication*] — Br J Soc Ps

British Journal of Social Work [*A publication*] — Br J Soc W

British Journal of Sociology [*A publication*] — BJOSA

British Journal of Sociology [*A publication*] — BJS

British Journal of Sociology [*A publication*] — B J Sociology

British Journal of Sociology [*A publication*] — Brit Jour Sociol

British Journal of Sociology [*A publication*] — Brit J Sociol

British Journal of Sociology [*A publication*] — Br J Sociol

British Journal of Sports Medicine [*A publication*] — Br J Sports Med

British Journal of Statistical Psychology [*A publication*] — B J Stat Psych

British Journal of Surgery [*A publication*] — Br J Surg

British Journal of Tuberculosis [*A publication*] — Br J Tuberc

British Journal of Tuberculosis and Diseases of the Chest [*A publication*] — Br J Tuberc Dis Chest

British Journal of Urology [*A publication*] — Br J Urol

British Journal of Venereal Diseases [*A publication*] — Br J Ven Dis

British Journal of Venereal Diseases [*A publication*] — Br J Vener Dis

British Kinematography Sound and Television [*A publication*] — Brit Kinematogr Sound Telev

British Kinematography Sound and Television [*A publication*] — Br Kinematogr

British Knitting Industry [*A publication*] — Br Knitting Ind

British Land of America [*NYSE symbol*] — BLA

British Leather Manufacturers Research Association — BLMRA

British Legion — BL

British Legion Headquarters — BLH

British Legion Village — BLV

British Leyland [*Later, BL Ltd.*] [*Auto manufacturing company*] — BL

British Liaison Officer — BLO

British Liberation Army [*Later, British Army of the Rhine*] — BLA

British Library [*Formerly, The British Museum Reading Room*] — BL

British Library Automated Information Service — BLAISE

British Library Journal [*A publication*] — Brit Lib J

British Library Lending Division — BLL

British Library Lending Division — BLLD

British Library, London, England [*OCLC symbol*] — BRI

British Library, London, United Kingdom [*Library symbol*] — Uk

British Library of Political and Economic Science [*London School of Economics*] — BLPES

British Library of Tape — BLOT

British Library of Wildlife Sound — BLOWS

British Life Assurance Trust — BLAT

British Light Aviation Center — BLAC

British Lighting Council [*Defunct*] — BLC

British Limbless Ex-Service Men's Association — BLESMA

British Lion [*Motion picture company*] — BL

British Maritime Law Association — BMLA

British Matchbox Label and Booklet Society — BML-BS

British Medical Association — BMA

British Medical Bulletin [*A publication*] — Br Med B

British Medical Bulletin [*A publication*] — Br Med Bull

British Medical Council — BMC

British Medical Journal [*A publication*] — BMJ

British Medical Journal [*A publication*] — BMJOA

British Medical Journal [*A publication*] — Brit Med J

British Medical Journal [*A publication*] — Br Med J

British Medical Research Council — BMRC

British Merchant Navy — BMN

British Merchant Shipping Mission — BMSM

British Metrication Board — BMB

British Middle East Office — BMEO

British Midland Airways [*ICAO designator*] — BD

British Midland Airways — BMA

British Military Administration — BMA

British Military Administration, British Borneo — BMA(BB)

British Military Authority — BMA

British Military Hospital — BMH

British Military Mission — BMM

British Military Supply Mission [*World War II*] — BMSM

British Ministry of Supply — B/MOS

British Ministry of Supply — BMS

British Ministry of Supply Research and Development Establishment — BMSRDE

British Ministry of War Transport [*World War II*] — BMWT

British Motor Corporation Ltd. — BMC

British Motor Holdings — BMH

British Movement [*Political party*] — BM

British Museum [*London*] — BM

British Museum Catalogue — BMC

British Museum Library [*London*] — BML

British Museum (Natural History) [*London*] — BMNH

British Museum (Natural History). Bulletin. Geology [*A publication*] — Br Mus (Nat Hist) Bull

British Museum (Natural History). Bulletin. Geology [*A publication*] — Br Mus (Nat Hist) Bull Geol

British Museum (Natural History). Bulletin. Zoology [*A publication*] — Br Mus (Nat Hist) Bull Zool

British Museum (Natural History). Economic Series [*A publication*] — Brit Mus (Nat Hist) Econom Ser

British Museum (Natural History). Economic Series [*A publication*] — Br Mus (Nat Hist) Econ Ser

British Museum (Natural History). Fossil Mammals of Africa [*A publication*] — Br Mus (Nat Hist) Fossil Mammals Afr

British Museum (Natural History). Mineralogy Leaflet [*A publication*] — Br Mus (Nat Hist) Mineral Leafl

British Museum (Natural History). Palaeontology Leaflet [*A publication*] — Br Mus (Nat Hist) Palaeontol Leafl

British Museum (Natural History). Publication [*A publication*] — Br Mus (Nat Hist) Publ

British Museum (Natural History). Report [*A publication*] — Br Mus (Nat Hist) Rep

British Museum Quarterly [*A publication*] — BM

British Museum Quarterly [*A publication*] — BMQ

British Music Society — BMS

British Mycological Society. Transactions [*A publication*] — Brit Mycol Soc Trans

British National Association of Perry Makers — BNAPM

British National Bibliographical Staff Association — BNBSA

British National Bibliography — BNB

British National Book Centre — BNBC

British National Committee on Data for Science and Technology — BNCDST

British National Committee on Space Research — BNCSR

British National Export Council — BNEC

British National Film Catalogue — BNFC

British National Formulary [*A publication*] — BNF

British National Oil Corporation [*Acronym pronounced "bee-knock"*] — BNOC

British National Opera Company — BNOC

British National Party — BNP

British Naval Air Service — BNAS

British Naval Air Staff — BNAS

British Naval Attache — BNA

British Naval Liaison Officer — BNLO

British Naval Liaison [*Office*] **US Navy** [*London*] — BNLUS

British Non-Ferrous Metals Research Association — BNFMRA

British Non-Ferrous Metals Research Association — BNMRA

British North Africa Force — BNAF

British North America — BNA

British North America Philatelic Society — BNAPS

British North American Act — BNAA

British-North American Committee — BNAC

British North Borneo — BNB

British Nuclear Ballistic Missile — BNBM

British Nuclear Design and Construction — BNDC

British Nuclear Energy Conference — BNEC

British Nuclear Energy Society — BNES

British Nuclear Export Executives [*Group to promote export of nuclear power stations of British design*] — BNX

British Nuclear Forum — BNF

British Nuclear Fuels — BNF

British Nuclear Fuels Limited — BNFL

British Numismatic Journal, Including the Proceedings of the British Numismatic Society [*A publication*] — BNJ

British Office for Training Exchange — BOTEX

British Olympic Association — BOA

British Optical Association, London, United Kingdom [*Library symbol*] — UkLBOA

British Order of Ancient Free Gardeners — BOAFG

British Ornithologists' Union — BOU

British Orthoptic Journal [*A publication*] — Br Orthopt J

British Overseas Airways [*Later, British Airways*] — BOA

British Overseas Airways Corporation [*Humorously interpreted as "Better on a Camel"*] [*Later, British Airways*] — BOAC

British Overseas Airways [*later, British Airways*] **Digital Information Computer for Electronic Automation** — BOADICEA

British Overseas Media Bureau — BOMB

British Overseas Trade Board — BOTB

British Oxygen Company — BOC

British Pacific Fleet — BPF

British Pacific Fleet Intelligence Liaison Officer — BPFILO

British Pacific Fleet Liaison Officer — BPFLO

British Paper and Board Industry Research Association .... BPBIRA
British Patent .... BP
British Penny [*Derived from Latin "denarius"*] .... d
British Petroleum Co. Ltd. [*NYSE symbol*] .... BP
British Pharmaceutical Codex [*A publication in pharmacy*] .... BPC
British Pharmacopoeia [*A publication in pharmacy*] .... BP
British Pharmacopoeia (Veterinary) .... BP(Vet)
British Phycological Bulletin [*Later, British Phycological Journal*] [*A publication*] .... Br Phycol Bull
British Phycological Journal [*A publication*] .... Br Phycol J
British Plain Spirits .... BPS
British Plastics [*A publication*] .... Brit Plast
British Plastics [*A publication*] .... Br Plast
British Plastics Federation .... BPF
British Plastics and Rubber [*A publication*] .... BP & R
British Plastics and Rubber [*A publication*] .... Br Plast Rubber
British Political Sociology. Yearbook [*A publication*] .... Brit Polit Sociol Yb
British Polymer Journal [*A publication*] .... Brit Polym J
British Polymer Journal [*A publication*] .... Br Polym J
British Post Office .... BPO
British Postmark Society .... BPS
British Poultry Science [*A publication*] .... Brit Poultry Sci
British Poultry Science [*A publication*] .... Br Poult Sc
British Poultry Science [*A publication*] .... Br Poult Sci
British Pound [*Monetary unit*] .... BP
British Printer [*A publication*] .... Brit Printer
British Printer [*A publication*] .... Br Print
British Printing & Communication Corporations [*Formerly, BPC*] .... BPCC
British Printing Corporation [*Later, BPCC*] .... BPC
British Productivity Council .... BPC
British Pteridological Society. Bulletin [*A publication*] .... Br Pteridol Soc Bull
British Public [*Slang*] .... BP
British Public Opinion [*A publication*] .... Br Public Opin
British Purchasing Commission .... BPC
British Quarterly Review [*A publication*] .... Brit Q
British Racing Motors .... BRM
British Racing and Sport Car Club .... BRSCC
British Radio Equipment Manufacturers Association .... BREMA
British Radio Valve Manufacturers' Association .... BRVMA
British Radiological Protection Association .... BRPA
British Railways .... BR
British Railways Board .... BRB
British Rate and Data .... BRAD
British Raw Materials Mission [*World War II*] .... BRMM
British Records Association .... BRA
British Red Cross Society .... BRCS
British Research Station .... BRS
British Revision [*of BNA*] [*Medicine*] .... BR
British Road Research Laboratory .... BRRL
British Routing Liaison Officer [*World War II*] .... BRLO
British Routing Office .... BRO
British Royal Marine Corps .... BRMC
British Rubber Products Research Association .... BRPRA
British Salonica Force .... BSF
British Savings Bond .... BSB
British School of Archaeology in Egypt. Publications [*A publication*] .... BSAE
British School of Archaeology at Rome. Papers [*A publication*] .... BSR
British School at Athens. Annual [*A publication*] .... Brit Sch Athens Ann
British School at Athens. Annual [*A publication*] .... BSA
British School of Osteopathy .... BSO
British School at Rome. Papers [*A publication*] .... Brit Sch at Rome Papers
British Schools Exploring Society News [*A publication*] .... BSES News
British Schools and Universities Club of New York .... BSUCNY
British Schools and Universities Foundation .... BSUF
British Scientific Instrument Research Association .... BSIRA
British Seafarers' Union .... BSU
British Ship Adoption Society .... BSAS
British Ship Research Association .... BSRA
British Shipbuilders .... BS
British Small Animal Veterinary Association. Congress. Proceedings [*A publication*] .... Br Small Anim Vet Assoc Congr Proc
British Socialist Party .... BSP
British Society for International Bibliography .... BSIB
British Society of Poster Designers .... BPD
British Society for Social Responsibility in Science .... BSSRS
British Solomon Islands [*MARC country of publication code*] [*Library of Congress*] .... bp
British Solomon Islands .... BSI
British Solomon Islands [*MARC geographic area code*] [*Library of Congress*] .... pobp---
British [*formerly, Birmingham*] **Sound Reproduction** [*Initialism is now name of company and brand name of its products*] .... BSR
British South Africa .... BSA
British South Africa Corps .... BSAC
British South Africa Police .... BSAP
British South American Airways .... BSAA
British South American Airways Corporation [*Later absorbed by BOAC*] .... BSAAC
British Space Development Company .... BSDC
British Space Fiction Magazine [*A publication*] .... BSP
British Standard .... BS
British Standard Beam [*Engineering*] .... BSB
British Standard Code of Practice .... BSCP
British Standard Data Code .... BSDC
British Standard Fine Thread .... BSF
British Standard Number .... BSN
British Standard Pipe Thread .... BSP
British Standard Specification [*A publication*] .... Brit Stand
British Standard Specification .... BSS
British Standard Time .... BST
British Standard Whitworth .... BSW
British Standards Institution [*Promulgates manufacturing standards and specifications*] .... BSI
British Standards Institution. British Standard [*A publication*] .... Brit Stand Inst Brit Stand
British Statistics Office .... BSO
British Steel [*A publication*] .... Br Steel
British Steel Castings Research Association .... BSCRA
British Steel Corporation .... BSC
British Steel Corporation Reports [*A publication*] .... Br Steel Corp Rep
British Steelmaker [*A publication*] .... Brit Steelmaker
British Steelmaker [*A publication*] .... Br Steelmaker
British Studies Monitor [*A publication*] .... BSM
British Sugar Beet Review [*A publication*] .... Br Sugar Beet Rev
British Sugar Beet Review [*A publication*] .... Br Sug Beet Rev
British Sugar Corporation .... BSC
British Sulphur Corporation Ltd. Statistical Supplement [*A publication*] .... BSC Stat
British Summer Time .... BST
British Supply Board [*Ottawa*] [*World War II*] .... BSB
British Supply Council .... BSC
British Supply Mission [*World War II*] .... BSM
British Supply Office .... BSO
British Tactical Air Force .... BTAF
British Tax Review [*A publication*] .... BTR
British Technical Council [*of the Motor and Petroleum Industries*] .... BTC
British Technology Group [*Formed by merger of NEB and NRDC*] .... BTG
British Technology Index [*A publication*] .... Brit Techl
British Technology Index [*A publication*] .... BTI
British Telecom [*or Telecommunications*] .... BT
British Telecom Phonecards [*Prepaid cards for use in noncoin pay telephones*] .... BTP
British Theatre Institute .... BTI
British Thermal Unit [*Also, BTU*] .... BTHU
British Thermal Unit [*Also, BTHU*] .... BTU
British Thermal Units per Hour .... BTU/h
British Thomson-Houston Co. .... BTH
British Tourist Authority [*Formerly, British Travel Association*] .... BTA
British Towing Tank Panel .... BTTP
British Trade Development Office .... BTDO
British Trade Mission .... BTM
British Trans-Atlantic Air Mail Service .... BTAMS
British Transport Commission .... BTC
British Transport Commission Police .... BTCP
British Transport Docks Board .... BTDB
British Travel and Holidays Association [*Later, British Travel Association*] .... BTHA
British Troops, Austria [*World War II*] .... BTA
British Troops in Egypt [*World War II*] .... BTE
British Troops in North Africa [*World War II*] .... BTNA
British Union Catalogue of Periodicals [*A publication*] .... BUCOP
British Union of Fascists .... BUF
British United Airways .... BUA
British United Island Airways .... BUIA
British United Press .... BUP
British-United States Agreement [*Signed May 17, 1943; formalized cooperation between the communications intelligence agencies of Great Britain and the United States*] .... BRUSA
British-United States Amateur Rocket Bureau .... BUSARB
British-United States Convoy Instructions .... BUSCI
British-United States Routing Agreement [*Shipping*] .... BUSRA
British Universities Annual [*A publication*] .... B Universities Annual
British Veterinary Journal [*A publication*] .... Br Vet J
British Virgin Islands .... BVI
British Virgin Islands [*Two-letter standard code*] .... VG
British Virgin Islands [*Three-letter standard code*] .... VGB
British Volunteer Programme .... BVP
British War Cabinet .... BWC
British War Medal .... BWM
British War Relief Society [*in US*] .... BWRS
British War Supplies Committee [*Combined Production and Resources Board*] [*World War II*] .... BWSC
British War Veterans of America .... BWVA
British Water Supply [*A publication*] .... Br Wat Supply
British Waterways Board .... BWB
British Waterworks Association .... BWA
British Welding Journal [*A publication*] .... Brit Weld J
British Welding Research Association [*Later, WI*] .... BWRA
British West Indian Airways Ltd. [*ICAO designator*] .... BW
British West Indian Airways Ltd. .... BWIA
British West Indies [*Later, WI*] .... BWI

British Wireless Marine Service .... BWMS
British Withdrawal from Northern Ireland Campaign .... BWNIC
British Wool Federation .... BWF
British Wool Marketing Board .... BWMB
British Yard Motor Minesweepers .... BYMS
British Yearbook of International Law [*A publication*] .... Brit Yb Int Law
British Yearbook of International Law [*A publication*] .... Brit Yearbook Int L
British Zone Petroleum Coordinating Authority [*Post-World War II, Germany*] .... BZPCA
Britt Airlines, Inc. [*Terre Haute, IN*] [*FAA designator*] .... BTA
Britt News-Tribune, Britt, IA [*Library symbol*] .... IaBriNT
Britt Technology Corp. [*NASDAQ symbol*] .... BRTT
Brittany Air International [*France*] [*ICAO designator*] .... BZ
Brittany Base Section [*World War II*] .... BBS
Brittany Oceanological Center .... BOC
Brittany Revolutionary Front [*France*] .... FLB
Brive-La-Gaillarde [*France*] [*Airport symbol*] .... BVE
Brixia Sacra [*A publication*] .... BS
Brno [*Czechoslovakia*] [*Airport symbol*] .... BRQ
Brno-Enfield [*Machine gun*] .... BREN
Brno Studies in English [*A publication*] .... BSE
Bro-Dart Industries [*American Stock Exchange symbol*] [*Delisted*] .... BD
Broach .... BRCH
Broach .... BRO
Broach Adapter .... BHAD
Broach Fixture .... BHFX
Broad-Flanged Beam .... BFB
Broad Ocean Area .... BOA
Broad Ocean Area - Missile Impact Locating System [*Navy*] .... BOA-MILS
Broad Ocean Deployment .... BOD
Broad Ocean Scoring System [*Missiles*] .... BOSS
Broad Pass [*Alaska*] [*Seismograph station code, US Geological Survey*] [*Closed*] .... BDP
Broad Street Pneumonia [*Center for Disease Control*] .... BSP
Broad System of Ordering .... BSO
Broadband .... BB
Broadband Acoustic Array Section .... BAAS
Broadband Active Analyzer .... BAA
Broadband Analysis SONAR Surveillance .... BASS
Broadband Antenna .... BBA
Broadband Antenna Kit .... BAK
Broadband Communication Network .... BCN
Broadband Conducted .... BBC
Broadband Exchange [*Western Union communication system*] .... BEX
Broadband Klystron Amplifier .... BKA
Broadband Latching Circulator .... BLC
Broadband Latching Switch .... BLS
Broadband Microwave Power Amplifier .... BMPA
Broadband Radiated .... BBR
Broadband Remote Oculometer .... BRO
Broadband Solid-State Preamplifier .... BSSP
Broadband Subsystem .... BRD
Broadband Waveguide Circulator .... BBWC
Broadband Waveguide Circulator .... BWC
Broadband X-Band Klystron .... BXK
Broadcast .... B/C
Broadcast .... BCST
Broadcast .... BRDCST
Broadcast .... BRST
Broadcast Advertisers Reports .... BAR
Broadcast to Allied Merchant Ships .... BAMS
Broadcast Audience Research Board [*British*] .... BARB
Broadcast Band .... BCB
Broadcast Bureau [*of FCC*] .... BB
Broadcast Communications System .... BCS
Broadcast Control .... BC
Broadcast Control Authority .... BCA
Broadcast Control Center .... BCC
Broadcast Designers Association .... BDA
Broadcast Education Association .... BEA
Broadcast Fighter Control [*Military*] .... BROFICON
Broadcast Financial Management Association [*Formerly, IBFM*] .... BFM
Broadcast Information Bureau, Inc. .... BIB
Broadcast Interference [*Communications*] .... BCI
Broadcast Keying Station .... BKS
Broadcast Listener [*Amateur radio*] .... BCL
Broadcast Management/Engineering [*A publication*] .... BM/E
Broadcast Measurement Bureau .... BMB
Broadcast Music, Incorporated .... BMI
Broadcast Net .... BRN
Broadcast Pioneers .... BP
Broadcast Radio Emergency Communication [*Air Force*] .... BRECOM
Broadcast Rating Council .... BRC
Broadcast Requested .... BCREQ
Broadcast Satellite [*Japan*] .... BS
Broadcast Station .... BCSTN
Broadcast and Television Receivers .... BTR
[*Weather*] **Broadcast Terminal Very-High-Frequency Omnirange** .... BTVOR
Broadcast Transmission Systems .... BTS
[*Weather*] **Broadcast Very-High-Frequency Omnirange** .... BVOR
Broadcasters Nonprofit Satellite Service [*Ford Foundation*] .... BNS
Broadcasters' Promotion Association .... BPA
Broadcasting .... B
Broadcasting .... BC
Broadcasting [*A publication*] .... Brdcstng
Broadcasting [*A publication*] .... B
Broadcasting [*A publication*] .... B/C
Broadcasting Amplitude Modulation .... BAM
Broadcasting Corporation of the Bahamas .... BCB
Broadcasting Corporation of China .... BCC
Broadcasting Corporation of New Zealand .... BCNZ
Broadcasting and Film Commission [*Later, Communication Commission*] .... BFC
Broadcasting Foundation of America .... BFA
Broadcasting Magazine [*A publication*] .... Broadcast
Broadcasting Organizations of Non-Aligned Countries .... BONC
Broadcasting Program [*Association of Independent Colleges and Schools specialization code*] .... BC
Broadcasting Satellite Experimental .... BSE
Broadcasting Station [*ITU designation*] .... BC
Broadcasting Station .... BS
Broadcasting Station, Television [*ITU designation*] .... BT
Broadened Opportunities for Officer Selection and Training [*Navy*] .... BOOST
Broader Term [*Cross-reference*] [*Indexing*] .... BT
Broadland Noise Generator .... BNG
Broadlaw [*Scotland*] [*Seismograph station code, US Geological Survey*] .... EBL
Broadside Series [*A publication*] .... Broad
Broadview Financial Corp. [*NASDAQ symbol*] .... BDVF
Broadview Public Library, Broadview, IL [*Library symbol*] .... IBrov
Broadway [*A street name*] .... BDWY
Broadway [*A street name*] [*British*] .... BDY
Broadway [*A publication*] .... Broadw
Broadway [*A street name*] .... B'WAY
Broadway Financial Corporation [*NASDAQ symbol*] .... BFCP
Broadway-Hale Stores, Inc. [*Later, Carter Hawley Hale Stores, Inc.*] [*NYSE symbol*] .... BHS
Broadway, VA [*Radio station call letters*] .... WBTX
Brocades-Stheeman [*Netherlands*] [*Research code symbol*] .... BS
Broche [*Sewn*] [*Of books*] .... BR
Brock Exploration Corp. [*NASDAQ symbol*] .... BKEX
Brock Hotel Corporation [*NYSE symbol*] .... BHC
Brock Township Public Library, Sunderland, ON, Canada [*Library symbol*] .... CaOSunB
Brock University, Department of Geography, Saint Catharines, ON, Canada [*Library symbol*] .... CaOStCBG
Brock University. Department of Geological Sciences. Research Report Series [*A publication*] .... Brock Univ Dep Geol Sci Res Rep Ser
Brock University, Saint Catharines, ON, Canada [*Library symbol*] .... CaOStCB
Brockport High School Library, Brockport, NY [*OCLC symbol*] .... RVT
Brockport, NY [*Radio station call letters*] .... WBKT
Brockport, NY [*Radio station call letters*] .... WBSU
Brockport, NY [*Radio station call letters*] .... WJBT
Brockton, MA [*Radio station call letters*] .... WAMK
Brockton, MA [*Radio station call letters*] .... WBET
Brockton, MA [*Radio station call letters*] .... WCAV
Brockton, MA [*Radio station call letters*] .... WMCI
Brockton, MA [*Radio station call letters*] .... WOKW
Brockton Public Library, Brockton, MA [*Library symbol*] .... MBrock
Brockville [*Canada*] [*Airport symbol*] .... XBR
Brockville, ON [*Radio station call letters*] .... CFJR
Brockville Public Library, Brockville, ON, Canada [*Library symbol*] .... CaOB
Brockway Glass Co., Inc. [*NYSE symbol*] [*Delisted*] .... BRK
Brodhead Memorial Public Library, Brodhead, WI [*Library symbol*] .... WBro
Brodmann's Areas [*Brain anatomy*] .... BA
Brodsky, David, New York NY [*STAC*] .... BDD
Brody [*B.*] **Seating Co.** [*American Stock Exchange symbol*] [*Delisted*] .... BDY
Broiler Producer [*A publication*] .... Broiler Prod
Brokaw Hospital Medical Center, Normal, IL [*Library symbol*] .... INBH
Broke [*Rough finish of paper*] .... B
Broken .... B
Broken .... BKN
Broken [*Quality of the bottom*] [*Nautical charts*] .... brk
Broken .... BRKN
Broken Arrow, OK [*Radio station call letters*] .... KNYD
Broken Arrow, OK [*Radio station call letters*] .... KSNE
Broken Bow Carnegie Library, Broken Bow, NE [*Library symbol*] .... NbBro
Broken Bow, NE [*Location identifier*] [*FAA*] .... CUZ
Broken Bow, NE [*Radio station call letters*] .... KCNI
Broken Bow, OK [*Radio station call letters*] .... KKBI
Broken Clouds or Better .... BCOB
Broken Corn and Foreign Material [*Quality measure for grain*] .... BCFM
Broken Hill [*Kabwe*] [*Zambia*] [*Seismograph station code, US Geological Survey*] .... BHA
Broken Hill [*Australia*] [*Airport symbol*] .... BHQ
Broken Hill Municipal Library, Broken Hill, NSW, Australia [*Library symbol*] .... AuBh
Broken Hill Property ADR [*NASDAQ symbol*] .... BRKNY
Broken Hill Proprietary [*Steel company*] [*Australia*] .... BHP
Broken Sea [*Navigation*] .... B

Broker Management Council ... BMC
Broker Services, Incorporated [*Information service*] ... BSI
Brokerage Accounting System Elements [*IBM computer program*] ... BASE
Brokers [*London Stock Exchange*] ... B
Broker's Order [*Finance*] ... BO
Bromacetylcellulose [*or Bromoacetycellulose*] [*Organic chemistry*] ... BAC
Bromatologia i Chemia Toksykologiczna [*A publication*] ... Bromatol Chem Toksykol
Bromcresol Green [*An indicator*] [*Chemistry*] ... BCG
Bromcresol Purple [*An indicator*] [*Chemistry*] ... BCP
Brome County Historical Society, Knowlton, PQ, Canada [*Library symbol*] ... CaQKB
Bromegrass Mosaic Virus ... BMV
Bromeliad Society ... BS
Brominated Vegetable Oil [*Soft drink additive*] ... BVO
Bromine [*Chemical element*] ... Br
Bromine Pentafluoride [*Corrosive compound*] ... BPF
Bromma Hembygds-Forenings Arsskrift [*A publication*] ... Bromma Hembygds-Foren Arsskr
Bromo [*As substituent on nucleoside*] [*Biochemistry*] ... br
Bromoacetone [*War gas*] ... BA
Bromoacetyl [*Organic chemistry*] ... BA
Bromoacetyl-DNP-Diamino-L-Butyric Acid [*Biochemistry*] ... BADB
Bromoacetyl-DNP-Ethylenediamine [*Biochemistry*] ... BADE
Bromoacetyl-DNP-L-Lysine [*Biochemistry*] ... BADL
Bromoacetyl-DNP-L-Ornithine [*Biochemistry*] ... BADO
Bromoacetylmono(azobenzenearsonic Acid)-L-tyrosine [*Biochemistry*] ... BAAT
Bromoamiloride [*Biochemistry*] ... Br-A
(Bromobenzoyl)methyladamantylamine [*Biochemistry*] ... BMA
Bromobenzyl Cyanide [*Tear gas*] ... BBC
Bromobenzylnitrile [*Toxic compound*] ... BBN
Bromodeoxyuridine [*Also, BDUR, BrDU*] [*Biochemistry*] ... BDU
Bromodeoxyuridine [*Also, BDU, BrDU*] [*Biochemistry*] ... BDUR
Bromodeoxyuridine [*Also, BDU, BDUR*] [*Biochemistry*] ... BrDU
Bromodiphenyl(ethylphenyl)ethylene [*Endocrinology*] ... BDPE
Bromoergocryptine [*Organic chemistry*] ... BEC
Bromoethanesulfonic Acid [*Organic chemistry*] ... BES
Bromoform-Triallyl Phosphate [*Flame retardant*] ... BAP
Bromoisovalerylurea [*Pharmacology*] ... BVU
Bromomercurihydroxypropane [*Clinical chemistry*] ... BMHP
Bromoperoxidase [*An enzyme*] ... BPO
Bromopyrogallol Red [*An indicator*] [*Chemistry*] ... BPR
Bromosulfophthalein [*Clinical chemistry*] ... BSP
Bromotrifluoroethylene [*Organic chemistry*] ... BFE
Bromouracil [*Biochemistry*] ... BU
Bromouracildeoxyriboside [*Antineoplastic drug*] ... BUdR
Bromouridine [*One-letter symbol; see BrUrd*] ... B
Bromouridine [*Also, B*] [*A nucleoside*] ... BrUrd
Bromovinyldeoxyuridine [*Biochemistry*] ... BVDU
Brompheniramine Maleate [*Antihistamine*] ... BPM
Bromphenol [*or Bromophenol*] **Blue** [*A dye*] ... BPB
Bromthymol [*or Bromothymol*] **Blue** [*A dye*] ... BTB
Bronchial ... BRON
Bronchial Asthma [*Medicine*] ... BA
Bronchial Carcinoid ... BC
Bronchial Provocation Test [*Medicine*] ... BPT
Bronchitis [*Medicine*] ... BR
Bronchoalveolar Cells [*Medicine*] ... BAC
Bronchoalveolar Lavage [*Medicine*] ... BAL
Bronchoalveolar Wash Fluids [*Medicine*] ... BAW
Bronchoesophagology [*Medicine*] ... BE
Bronchopleural [*Medicine*] ... BP
Bronchopulmonary Dysplasia [*Medicine*] ... BPD
Bronchoscopy [*Medicine*] ... BRON
Bronchoscopy [*Medicine*] ... BRONCH
Bronchospasm [*Medicine*] ... BSp
Broneje Transporter [*Soviet armored personnel carrier*] ... BTR
Bronnoysund [*Norway*] [*Airport symbol*] ... BNN
Bronsted Acid [*Biochemistry*] ... BA
Bronsted Base [*Biochemistry*] ... BB
Bronte Society ... BS
Bronte Society Transactions [*A publication*] ... BST
Bronx Community College [*New York*] ... BCC
Bronx Community College Library, Bronx, NY [*OCLC symbol*] ... VWB
Bronx Community College, New York, NY [*Library symbol*] ... NNBC
Bronxville Public Library, Bronxville, NY [*Library symbol*] ... NBron
Bronze ... BR
Bronze ... BRZ
Bronze ... BZ
Bronze Age ... BA
Bronze Floors [*On ships*] ... BF
Bronze Medal ... BM
Bronze Service Star [*Military award*] ... BSS
Bronze Star Medal ... BSM
Brooder [*s*] [*Freight*] ... BRD
Brook ... BRK
Brook-Iroquois Public Library, Brook, IN [*Library symbol*] ... InBro
Brookdale Community College, Lincroft, NJ [*OCLC symbol*] ... BCC
Brookdale Community College, Lincroft, NJ [*Library symbol*] ... NjLincB
Brooke Army Medical Center ... BAMC
Brooke General Hospital, Medical Library, Fort Sam Houston, TX [*Library symbol*] ... TxFshBH
Brookes Deflection Potentiometer ... BDP
Brookfield [*Connecticut*] [*Seismograph station code, US Geological Survey*] ... BCT
Brookfield, CT [*Radio station call letters*] ... WINE
Brookfield, CT [*Radio station call letters*] ... WRKI
Brookfield Free Public Library, Brookfield, IL [*Library symbol*] ... IBro
Brookfield, MO [*Location identifier*] [*FAA*] ... BZK
Brookfield, MO [*Radio station call letters*] ... KGHM
Brookfield, MO [*Radio station call letters*] ... KQMO
Brookhaven Area Office [*Energy Research and Development Administration*] ... BAO
Brookhaven Beam Research Reactor ... BBRR
Brookhaven Free Library, Brookhaven, NY [*Library symbol*] ... NBroo
Brookhaven Graphite Research Reactor ... BGRR
Brookhaven Linac Isotope Producer [*Nuclear energy*] ... BLIP
Brookhaven Medical Reactor ... BMR
Brookhaven Medical Research Center ... BMRC
Brookhaven Memorial Hospital, Patchogue, NY [*Library symbol*] ... NPatBH
Brookhaven, MS [*Location identifier*] [*FAA*] ... BVV
Brookhaven, MS [*Radio station call letters*] ... WCHJ
Brookhaven, MS [*Radio station call letters*] ... WJMB
Brookhaven, MS [*Radio station call letters*] ... WMRQ
Brookhaven National Laboratory [*Energy Research and Development Administration*] ... BNL
Brookhaven National Laboratory. Lectures in Science. Vistas in Research [*A publication*] ... Brookhaven Natl Lab Lect Sci Vistas Res
Brookhaven National Laboratory, Upton, NY [*OCLC symbol*] ... ZBN
Brookhaven Office [*AEC*] ... BH
Brookhaven Portable Cesium Developmental Irradiator Unit [*Nuclear energy*] ... BPCDI
Brookhaven Press, Washington, DC [*Library symbol*] ... BkP
Brookhaven Research Reactor ... BRR
Brookhaven Service Center [*IRS*] ... BSC
Brookhaven Symposia in Biology [*A publication*] ... Brookhaven Symp Biol
Brookhaven Symposia in Biology [*A publication*] ... Brook S Bio
Brookhaven Town Hall, Historical Collection, Patchogue, NY [*Library symbol*] ... NPatB
Brookings [*South Dakota*] [*Airport symbol*] ... BKX
Brookings Bulletin [*A publication*] ... Brookings Bull
Brookings Economics and Statistical Translator [*Data processing*] ... BEAST
Brookings Institution ... BI
Brookings Institution, Washington, DC [*Library symbol*] ... DBI
Brookings, OR [*Radio station call letters*] ... KURY
Brookings, OR [*Radio station call letters*] ... KURY-FM
Brookings Papers on Economic Activity [*A publication*] ... BPEA
Brookings Papers on Economic Activity [*A publication*] ... Brookings P
Brookings Papers on Economic Activity [*A publication*] ... Brookings Pa Econ Activ
Brookings Public Library, Brookings, SD [*Library symbol*] ... SdBro
Brookings, SD [*Radio station call letters*] ... KBRK
Brookings, SD [*Radio station call letters*] ... KESD
Brookings, SD [*Television station call letters*] ... KESD-TV
Brookings, SD [*Radio station call letters*] ... KGKG
Brookline, MA [*Radio station call letters*] ... WBOS
Brookline, MA [*Radio station call letters*] ... WUNR
Brooklyn ... BKLN
Brooklyn Academy of Music ... BAM
Brooklyn Army Terminal ... BART
Brooklyn Barrister [*A publication*] ... Brooklyn Bar
Brooklyn Botanic Garden (Annual Report) [*A publication*] ... Brooklyn Bot Gard (Annu Rep)
Brooklyn Botanic Garden, Brooklyn, NY [*Library symbol*] ... NBG
Brooklyn Botanic Garden Record. Plants and Gardens [*A publication*] ... Brooklyn Bot Gard Rec Plants Gard
Brooklyn, Bronx, and Queens [*New York City slang for nightclub or restaurant that has fallen out of favor with the pacesetters*] ... BBQ
Brooklyn Children's Museum, Brooklyn, NY [*Library symbol*] ... NBCMu
Brooklyn Chronicle, Brooklyn, IA [*Library symbol*] ... IaBroC
Brooklyn College, Brooklyn, NY [*Library symbol*] ... NBC
Brooklyn College, Brooklyn, NY [*OCLC symbol*] ... VDB
Brooklyn College of Pharmacy, Brooklyn, NY [*Library symbol*] ... NBCP
Brooklyn Eastern District Terminal [*AAR code*] ... BEDT
Brooklyn Friends School, New York, NY [*Library symbol*] ... NBF
Brooklyn Institute of Arts and Sciences ... BIAS
Brooklyn Institute of Arts and Sciences. Museum Bulletin [*A publication*] ... Brooklyn Mus Bul
Brooklyn Journal of International Law [*A publication*] ... Brooklyn J Intl L
Brooklyn Law Review [*A publication*] ... Brooklyn L Rev
Brooklyn Law School ... BLS
Brooklyn Law School, Brooklyn, NY [*Library symbol*] ... NBL
Brooklyn Law School, Brooklyn, NY [*OCLC symbol*] ... ZBL
Brooklyn Local Economic Development Corporation ... BLEDCO
Brooklyn-Manhattan Transit Corp. [*A New York City subway line*] ... BMT
Brooklyn Museum Annual [*A publication*] ... Brooklyn Mus Ann
Brooklyn Museum, Brooklyn, NY [*Library symbol*] ... NBB
Brooklyn Museum Quarterly [*A publication*] ... Brook Mus Q
Brooklyn Museum, Wilbour Library of Egyptology, Brooklyn, NY [*Library symbol*] ... NBB-E

Brooklyn, NY [*Location identifier*] [*FAA*] ... NOP
Brooklyn Public Library, Brooklyn, NY [*Library symbol*] ... NB
Brooklyn, Queens, Long Island [*Section of New York Times*] ... BQLI
Brooklyn-Queens-Staten Island Health Sciences Group [*Library network*] ... BQSI
Brooklyn Rapid Transit Co. [*A New York City subway line*] [*Became BMT*] ... BRT
Brooklyn Union Gas Co. [*Wall Street slang name: "Bug"*] [*NYSE symbol*] ... BU
Brooklyn Union Gas Co. ... BUG
Brookneal, VA [*Radio station call letters*] ... WODI
Brooks, AB [*Radio station call letters*] ... CIBQ
Brooks Art Gallery, Memphis, TN [*Library symbol*] ... TMBA
Brooks Bird Club ... BBC
Brooks Brothers [*Clothing store*] ... B^2
Brooks Fashion Stores [*NYSE symbol*] ... BKS
Brooks Memorial Library, Brattleboro, VT [*Library symbol*] ... VtBrt
Brooks & Perkins, Incorporated [*American Stock Exchange symbol*] [*Delisted*] ... BPI
Brooks Resources Corporation [*NASDAQ symbol*] ... BREC
Brooksville, FL [*Location identifier*] [*FAA*] ... BKV
Brooksville, FL [*Radio station call letters*] ... WWJB
Brookville, NY [*Radio station call letters*] ... WCWP
Brookville, PA [*Radio station call letters*] ... WMKX
Brookville Society of Natural History. Bulletin [*A publication*] ... Brookville Soc N H B
Brookwood Reservoir [*California*] [*Seismograph station code, US Geological Survey*] ... BKC
Broom Closet ... BCL
Broome [*Australia*] [*Airport symbol*] ... BME
Broome Technical Community College [*New York*] ... BTCC
Broome Technical Community College, Binghamton, NY [*Library symbol*] ... NBiBT
Broomfield, CO [*Television station call letters*] ... KBDI-TV
Broteria [*A publication*] ... Brot
Broteria. Serie Trimestral. Ciencias Naturais [*A publication*] ... Broteria Ser Trimest Cienc Nat
Broth Filtrate [*Microbiology*] ... BF
Brother [*or Brotherhood*] ... B
Brother ... BR
Brother ... BRO
Brotherhood of the American Lutheran Church [*Later, American Lutheran Church Men*] ... BALC
Brotherhood of Anglican Churchmen [*Canada*] ... BAC
Brotherhood of Associated Book Travelers ... BABT
Brotherhood Association of Military Airmen ... BAMA
Brotherhood of Book Travelers [*Later, ABT*] ... BBT
Brotherhood Commission [*of the Southern Baptist Convention*] ... BC
Brotherhood of the Holy Cross [*Anglican religious community*] ... BHC
Brotherhood of the Holy Name ... BHN
Brotherhood of the Holy Trinity ... BHT
Brotherhood of the Jungle Cock ... BJC
Brotherhood of the Knights of the Vine ... BKV
Brotherhood of Locomotive Engineers ... B of LE
Brotherhood of Locomotive Firemen and Enginemen [*Later, United Transportation Union*] [*AFL-CIO*] ... BLFE
Brotherhood of Locomotive Firemen and Enginemen [*Later, United Transportation Union*] [*AFL-CIO*] ... LFE
Brotherhood of Maintenance of Way Employees ... BMWE
[*The*] **Brotherhood of Man under the Fatherhood of God** [*Journalistic slang for political platitudes; said to be taken from a speech by Hubert H. Humphrey*] ... BOMFOG
Brotherhood of Marine Engineers [*Later merged with MEBA*] ... BME
Brotherhood of Marine Officers ... BMO
Brotherhood of Painters, Decorators, and Paperhangers of America [*Also known as B of PDPH of A*] [*Later, International Brotherhood of Painters and Allied Trades*] ... BPDP
Brotherhood of Painters, Decorators, and Paperhangers of America [*Also known as BPDP*] [*Later, International Brotherhood of Painters and Allied Trades*] ... B of PDPH of A
Brotherhood of Railroad Signalmen ... B of RS
Brotherhood of Railroad Signalmen ... BRS
Brotherhood of Railroad Trainmen [*Later, United Transportation Union*] ... BRT
Brotherhood of Railway, Airline, and Steamship Clerks, Freight Handlers, Express and Station Employees ... BRAC
Brotherhood of Railway, Airline, and Steamship Clerks, Freight Handlers, Express and Station Employees ... BRASC
Brotherhood of Railway Carmen of America [*Later, BRC of US & C*] [*AFL-CIO*] ... BRC
Brotherhood of Railway Carmen of America [*Later, BRC of US & C*] [*AFL-CIO*] ... BRC of A
Brotherhood of Railway Carmen of the United States and Canada [*Formerly, BRC, BRC of A*] [*AFL-CIO*] ... BRC of US & C
Brotherhood of Railway and Steamship Clerks, Freight Handlers, Express and Station Employees [*Later, BRAC*] ... BRSC
Brotherhood of St. Andrew ... BSA
Brotherhood of Shoe and Allied Craftsmen ... BSAC
Brotherhood of Sleeping Car Porters [*Later, BRAC*] ... SCP
Brotherhood of Utility Workers of New England ... UWNE
Brothers ... BROS
Brothers to All Men [*An association*] ... BAM
Brother's Brother Foundation ... BBF
Brothers of Charity of Spokane [*Roman Catholic religious order*] ... BCS
Brothers of the Good Shepherd [*Roman Catholic religious order*] ... BGS
[*From the Latin for*] **Brothers of the Holy Eucharist** [*Roman Catholic religious order*] ... FSE
[*From the Latin for*] **Brothers of the Holy Rosary** [*Roman Catholic religious order*] ... FSR
[*From the Latin for*] **Brothers of the Immaculate Heart of Mary** [*Roman Catholic religious order*] ... FICM
[*From the Latin for*] **Brothers of Mercy** [*Roman Catholic religious order*] ... FMM
Brothers of Our Lady of Mercy [*Roman Catholic religious order*] ... CFMM
[*From the Latin for*] **Brothers of St. Patrick** [*Patrician Brothers*] [*Roman Catholic religious order*] ... FSP
Brothers of St. Pius X [*Roman Catholic religious order*] ... CSPX
Brought in Dead [*Medicine*] ... BID
Brought Down [*Horse racing*] ... B
Brought Down [*Business and trade*] ... BD
Brought Forward [*Business and trade*] ... BF
Brought Over [*Business and trade*] ... B/O
Broughton [*Canada*] [*Airport symbol*] ... YVM
Brouwer General Perturbations Differential Correction Program ... BGPDC
Brouwer-Lyddane Orbit Generation Routine ... BROWRO
Broward Community College, Fort Lauderdale, FL [*OCLC symbol*] ... EDB
Broward Community College, Fort Lauderdale, FL [*Library symbol*] ... FFIB
Broward County Libraries Division, Fort Lauderdale, FL [*Library symbol*] ... FFIBL
Broward County Libraries Division, Pompano Beach, FL [*OCLC symbol*] ... FBR
Brower Flight Service [*Fort Madison, IA*] [*FAA designator*] ... BRO
Brown ... BR
Brown ... BRN
Brown [*Thoroughbred racing*] ... BR
Brown Adipose Tissue [*Physiology*] ... BAT
Brown American [*A publication*] ... Brown Am
Brown Bag Institute ... BBI
Brown & Bigelow ... B & B
Brown & Bigelow [*NYSE symbol*] ... BWB
Brown, Boveri, & Company Ltd. [*Switzerland*] ... BBC
Brown, Boveri-Krupp Reaktorbau [*Germany*] ... BB/KR
Brown Boveri Mitteilungen [*Brown Boveri Review*] [*A publication*] ... Brown Boveri Mitt
Brown Boveri Review [*A publication*] ... Brown Boveri Rev
Brown Boveri Review [*A publication*] ... Brown Bov R
Brown City Public Library, Brown City, MI [*Library symbol*] ... MiBrc
Brown Co. [*NYSE symbol*] [*Delisted*] ... BWN
Brown [*Robert C.*] **& Co.** [*NASDAQ symbol*] ... RCBI
Brown County Hospital, Green Bay, WI [*Library symbol*] ... WGrBC
Brown County Library, Green Bay, WI [*OCLC symbol*] ... GZG
Brown County Library, Green Bay, WI [*Library symbol*] ... WGr
Brown, Durbin, and Evans [*Statisticians*] ... BDE
Brown Engineering Company ... BEC
Brown Engineering Company ... BECO
Brown-Forman Distillers Corp. [*American Stock Exchange symbol*] ... BFD
Brown Group, Inc. [*NYSE symbol*] ... BG
Brown, James H., Atlanta GA [*STAC*] ... BJH
Brown Line Positive ... BR/L
Brown Lung Association ... BLA
Brown Norway [*Rat variety*] ... BN
Brown Oil of Vitriol ... BOV
Brown Public Library, Northfield, VT [*Library symbol*] ... VtN
Brown & Root, Inc., Technical Library, Houston, TX [*Library symbol*] ... TxHBR
Brown & Root-Northrop ... BRN
Brown and Sharpe [*Wire gauge*] ... B & S
Brown & Sharpe Manufacturing Co. [*NYSE symbol*] ... BNS
Brown Swiss Cattle Breeders Association of the USA ... BSCBA
Brown Trout Club ... BTC
Brown University [*Rhode Island*] ... BU
Brown University, Annmary Brown Memorial Library, Providence, RI [*Library symbol*] ... RPAB
Brown University Interpreter [*Data processing*] ... BRUIN
Brown University, John Hay Library of Rare Books annd Special Collections, Providence, RI [*Library symbol*] ... RPB-JH
Brown University, Providence, RI [*OCLC symbol*] ... RBN
Brown University, Providence, RI [*Library symbol*] ... RPB
Brown University Studies [*A publication*] ... BUS
Brown & Williamson Tobacco Corp. ... B & W
Brown & Williamson Tobacco Corp., Research Department Library, Louisville, KY [*Library symbol*] ... KyLoBW
Brownfield, TX [*Location identifier*] [*FAA*] ... BFE
Brownfield, TX [*Radio station call letters*] ... KKUB
Browning Aircraft Machine Gun ... BAMG
Browning Automatic Rifle ... BAR
Browning-Ferris Industries, Inc. [*NYSE symbol*] ... BFI
Browning Institute ... BI
Browning Institute. Studies [*A publication*] ... Browning Inst Stud
Browning Machine Gun ... BMG
Browning Newsletter [*A publication*] ... BN
Browning Society Notes [*A publication*] ... BSNotes

Brownish-Black .... BB
Brownson's Quarterly Review [*A publication*] .... Brownson
Brownstone Revival Committee .... BRC
Brownsville [*Texas*] [*Airport symbol*] .... BRO
Brownsville Historical Association, Brownsville, TX [*Library symbol*] .... TxBHi
Brownsville, PA [*Radio station call letters*] .... WASP
Brownsville, TN [*Radio station call letters*] .... WBHT
Brownsville, TN [*Radio station call letters*] .... WTBG
Brownsville, TX [*Radio station call letters*] .... KBOR
Brownsville, TX [*Radio station call letters*] .... KDUV
Brownsville, TX [*Radio station call letters*] .... KRIX
Brownsville, TX [*Location identifier*] [*FAA*] .... MIH
Brownwood [*Texas*] [*Airport symbol*] .... BWD
Brownwood Public Library, Brownwood, TX [*Library symbol*] .... TxBrd
Brownwood, TX [*Radio station call letters*] .... KBWD
Brownwood, TX [*Radio station call letters*] .... KOXE
Brownwood, TX [*Radio station call letters*] .... KPSM
Brownwood, TX [*Radio station call letters*] .... KXYL
Brownwood, TX [*Radio station call letters*] .... KXYL-FM
BRT Realty Trust SBI [*American Stock Exchange symbol*] .... BRT
Bruccoli-Clark Publishers .... BCP
Bruce County Public Library, Port Elgin, ON, Canada [*Library symbol*] .... CaOPteB
Bruce Trail Association .... BTA
Bruckner Society of America .... BSA
Bruel and Kjaer Technical Review [*A publication*] .... Bruel & Kjaer Tech Rev
Bruker Report [*A publication*] .... Bruker Rep
Brule, WI [*Radio station call letters*] .... WHSA
Brumado [*Brazil*] [*Airport symbol*] .... BMS
Brunauer-Emmett-Teller [*Adsorption equation*] .... BET
Brunei [*MARC geographic area code*] [*Library of Congress*] .... a-bx---
Brunei [*Two-letter standard code*] .... BN
Brunei [*Three-letter standard code*] .... BRN
Brunei [*MARC country of publication code*] [*Library of Congress*] .... bx
Brunei Broadcasting Service .... BBS
Brunei Museum Journal [*A publication*] .... Brun Mus J
Brunn-Bruckmann [*A publication*] .... Br Br
Bruno's, Inc. [*NASDAQ symbol*] .... BRNO
Bruns' Beitraege zur Klinischen Chirurgie [*A publication*] .... Bruns' Beitr Klin Chir
Brunswick [*Georgia*] [*Airport symbol*] .... BQK
Brunswick Corporation [*NYSE symbol*] .... BC
Brunswick, GA [*Radio station call letters*] .... WBGA
Brunswick, GA [*Radio station call letters*] .... WGIG
Brunswick, GA [*Radio station call letters*] .... WMOG
Brunswick, GA [*Radio station call letters*] .... WPIQ
Brunswick, GA [*Radio station call letters*] .... WYNR
Brunswick General Hospital, Amityville, NY [*Library symbol*] .... NAmiGH
Brunswick-Greensville Regional Library, Lawrenceville, VA [*Library symbol*] .... ViLaw
Brunswick Junior College, Brunswick, GA [*Library symbol*] .... GBruJC
Brunswick, MD [*Radio station call letters*] .... WTRI
Brunswick, ME [*Radio station call letters*] .... WBHS
Brunswick, ME [*Radio station call letters*] .... WBOR
Brunswick, ME [*Radio station call letters*] .... WCLZ
Brunswick, ME [*Radio station call letters*] .... WKXA
Brunswick Regional Library, Brunswick, GA [*Library symbol*] .... GBru
Brush .... BR
Brush Beryllium Company .... BBC
Brush Border [*of intestinal epithelial cell*] [*Cell physiology*] .... BB
Brush, CO [*Radio station call letters*] .... KCMP
Brush, CO [*Radio station call letters*] .... KCNQ
Brush Holder .... BRH
Brush-Off [*Slang*] .... BRO
Brush and Pencil [*A publication*] .... Brush & P
Brush Public Library, Brush, CO [*Library symbol*] .... CoBru
Brush Wellman, Inc. [*NYSE symbol*] .... BW
Brushless Torque Motor .... BTM
Brussels [*Belgium*] [*Airport symbol*] .... BRU
Brussels Community High School District 37, Brussels, IL [*Library symbol*] .... IBrusSD
Brussels. Musees Royaux d'Art et d'Histoire. Bulletin [*A publication*] .... Brussels Mus Roy Bul
Brussels. Musees Royaux des Beaux-Arts Belgiques. Bulletin [*A publication*] .... Brus Mus Roy Beaux Arts Bull
Brussels. Museum of Musical Instruments. Bulletin [*A publication*] .... Brus Museum
Brussels Nomenclature [*Standard customs nomenclature published by the Customs Cooperation Council*] .... BN
Brussels-Richwood Community Consolidated School District 41, Brussels, IL [*Library symbol*] .... IBrusRSD
Brussels Sprouts Marketing Program .... BSMP
Brussels Tariff Nomenclature [*Also known as CCCN*] [*EEC*] .... BTN
Brussels Treaty Organization [*Later, Western European Union*] .... BTO
Brussels Treaty Permanent Commission .... BTPC
Brussels. Universite Libre. Institut de Philologie et d'Histoire. Annuaire [*A publication*] .... Ann Phil Hist
Brute Force Gyro .... BFG
Bruttoregistertonne [*Gross Registered Ton*] [*German*] .... BRT
Bruxelles Medical [*A publication*] .... BRMEA
Bruxelles Medical [*A publication*] .... Brux Med
Bryan-Bennett Public Library, Salem, IL [*Library symbol*] .... ISal
Bryan, OH [*Location identifier*] [*FAA*] .... BWB
Bryan, OH [*Location identifier*] [*FAA*] .... BYN
Bryan, OH [*Radio station call letters*] .... WBNO
Bryan, OH [*Radio station call letters*] .... WBNO-FM
Bryan Public Library, Bryan, TX [*Library symbol*] .... TxBry
Bryan, TX [*Radio station call letters*] .... KAGC
Bryan, TX [*Television station call letters*] .... KBTX-TV
Bryan, TX [*Radio station call letters*] .... KORA
Bryan, TX [*Radio station call letters*] .... KTAM
Bryant College, Smithfield, RI [*OCLC symbol*] .... BRB
Bryant College, Smithfield, RI [*Library symbol*] .... RSmB
Bryant Library, Roslyn, NY [*Library symbol*] .... NRosl
Bryce Canyon National Park .... BRCA
Brymon Airways [*Great Britain*] [*ICAO designator*] .... PM
Bryn Mawr College [*Pennsylvania*] .... BMC
Bryn Mawr College, Bryn Mawr, PA [*OCLC symbol*] .... BMC
Bryn Mawr College, Bryn Mawr, PA [*Library symbol*] .... PBm
Bryology .... BRY
Bryson City, NC [*Radio station call letters*] .... WBHN
BSBI [*Botanical Society of the British Isles*] **Conference Reports** [*A publication*] .... BSBI Conf Rep
BSCP [*Biological Sciences Communication Project*] **Communique** [*A publication*] .... BSCP Commun
BSD Medical Corp. [*NASDAQ symbol*] .... BSDM
BSI [*British Standards Institution*] **News** [*A publication*] .... BSI News
BSN Corp. [*American Stock Exchange symbol*] .... BSN
BT Mortgage Investors SBI [*NYSE symbol*] [*Delisted*] .... BTM
BTK Industries [*Formerly, Billy the Kid*] [*American Stock Exchange symbol*] .... BTK
BTL Corp. [*Formerly, Butler Brothers*] .... BTL
BTL [*Bell Telephone Laboratories*] **Furnished Equipment** .... BFE
BTTA [*British Thoracic and Tuberculosis Association*] **Review** [*Scotland*] [*A publication*] .... BTTA Rev
BTU Engineering Corp. [*American Stock Exchange symbol*] [*Delisted*] .... BTU
Bua [*Fiji*] [*Airport symbol*] [*Obsolete*] .... BVF
Bubble .... BUB
Bubble Chamber .... BC
Bubble Chamber Experiment .... BCE
Bubble Column [*Engineering*] .... BC
Bubble Domain Memory .... BDM
Bubble-Gum Brigade [*Preteens*] .... BGB
Bubble Memory [*Data processing*] .... BM
Bubble Pulse Period .... BPP
Bucak [*Turkey*] [*Seismograph station code, US Geological Survey*] .... BCK
Bucaramanga [*Colombia*] [*Seismograph station code, US Geological Survey*] .... BCR
Bucaramanga [*Colombia*] [*Airport symbol*] .... BGA
Buccal [*Pertaining to the cheek*] .... B
Buccal Cartilage [*Dentistry*] .... BC
Buccal Commissure [*Dentistry*] .... BC
Buccal Ganglion [*Dentistry*] .... BUG
Buccal Mass [*Dentistry*] .... BM
Bucco-Occlusal [*Dentistry*] .... BO
Buccoaxial [*Dentistry*] .... BA
Buccoaxiocervical [*Dentistry*] .... BAC
Buccoaxiogingival [*Dentistry*] .... BAG
Buccocervical [*Dentistry*] .... BC
Buccodistal [*Dentistry*] .... BD
Buccogingival [*Dentistry*] .... BG
Buccolingual [*Dentistry*] .... BL
Buccomesial [*Dentistry*] .... BM
Buccopulpal [*Dentistry*] .... BP
Buch und Bibliothek [*A publication*] .... Buch und Bibl
Buchan [*Australia*] [*Seismograph station code, US Geological Survey*] [*Closed*] .... BUV
Bucharest [*Romania*] [*Later, SUR*] [*Geomagnetic observatory code*] .... BUC
Bucharest [*Romania*] [*Seismograph station code, US Geological Survey*] BUC1
Bucharest [*Romania*] [*Seismograph station code, US Geological Survey*] BUC2
Bucharest [*Romania*] [*Airport symbol*] .... BUH
Bucharest [*Romania*] [*Seismograph station code, US Geological Survey*] .... BUC
Bucharest [*Romania*] **Banesa Airport** [*Airport symbol*] .... BBU
Bucharest. Universitatea. Analele. Seria Stiintele Naturii [*A publication*] .... Buchar Univ An Ser Stiint Nat
Buchberg [*Switzerland*] [*Seismograph station code, US Geological Survey*] .... BUB
Bucherei und Bildung [*A publication*] .... BuB
Buchreihe Atomkernenergie [*A publication*] .... Buchr Atomkernenerg
Buck-Boost Transformer .... BBT
Buck Island Reef National Monument .... BUIS
Buck Memory Element .... BME
Bucket .... BKT
Bucket-Brigade Device [*Electronics*] .... BBD
Buckeye Air Freight [*Elyria, OH*] [*FAA designator*] .... BKI
Buckeye Airways International [*Air carrier designation symbol*] .... BAIX
Buckeye, AZ [*Location identifier*] [*FAA*] .... BXK

Buckeye Cellulose Corp., Technical Division Library, Memphis, TN [Library symbol] .... TMBC
Buckeye Financial Corp. [NASDAQ symbol].................... BCKY
Buckeye Pipe Line Co. [NYSE symbol] [Delisted] .... BKP
Buckeye Public Library, Buckeye, AZ [Library symbol].................... AzBu
Buckham Memorial Library, Faribault, MN [Library symbol] .... MnF
Buckhannon, WV [Radio station call letters].................... WBUC
Buckhannon, WV [Radio station call letters].................... WVPW
Buckhannon, WV [Radio station call letters].................... WVWC
Buckhorn, Inc. [American Stock Exchange symbol].................... BKN
Bucking Current Generator .... BCG
Buckingham Corp. [NYSE symbol] [Delisted] .... BHM
Buckinghamshire [County in England].................... BUCKS
Buckland [Alaska] [Airport symbol].................... BKC
Buckley Public Library, Poteau, OK [Library symbol].................... OkPot
Buckling of Shells of Revolution [Computer program] [NASA].................... BOSOR
Buckman Laboratories, Inc., Memphis, TN [Library symbol] .... TMBL
Buckminster Fuller Institute.................... BFI
Bucknell Review [A publication].................... BR
Bucknell Review [A publication].................... BuR
Bucknell University, Lewisburg, PA [OCLC symbol].................... PBU
Bucknell University, Lewisburg, PA [Library symbol].................... PLeB
Buckram [Fabric].................... BUCK
Bucks County Community College, Newtown, PA [OCLC symbol].................... BUC
Bucks County Free Library, Doylestown, PA [OCLC symbol].................... DPB
Bucks County Free Library, Doylestown, PA [Library symbol] .... PDoB
Bucks County Historical Society, Doylestown, PA [Library symbol].................... PDoBHi
Bucks County Historical Society. Papers [A publication] .... BuCHS
Bucks County Historical Society. Papers [A publication] .... BucksCoHS
Bucyrus-Erie Co..................... BE
Bucyrus-Erie Co. [NYSE symbol].................... BY
Bucyrus, OH [Radio station call letters] .... WBCO
Bucyrus, OH [Radio station call letters] .... WBCO-FM
Budakeszi [Hungary] [Later, TYH] [Geomagnetic observatory code] .... BUZ
Budapest [Hungary] [Airport symbol].................... BUD
Budapest [Hungary] [Seismograph station code, US Geological Survey].................... BUD
Budapest Regisegei [A publication].................... BR
Budapest Regisegei [A publication] .... Budapest Reg
Budavox Telecommunication Review [A publication].................... Budavox Telecommun Rev
Budd Co. [NYSE symbol].................... BF
Budd Co., Fort Washington, PA [Library symbol] .... PFwB
Buddhism .... BUDD
Buddhist Center of the United States of America.................... BCUSA
Buddhist Council for Refugee Rescue and Resettlement .... BCRRR
Buddhist Era.................... BE
Buddhist League of Esperantists .... BLE
Buddhist Peace Fellowship .... BPF
Buddhist Vihara Society .... BVS
Buddy Secondary Life Support System [Aerospace].................... BSLSS
Bude, MS [Television station call letters].................... WMAU
Bude, MS [Radio station call letters].................... WMAU-FM
Budget .... BUD
Budget, Accounting, and Finance .... BA & F
Budget Accounting Information System [IBM Corp.].................... BACIS
Budget and Accounting Officer [Military].................... BAO
Budget Activity [Navy].................... BA
Budget Activity Account [Army].................... BAA
Budget Adjustment Request .... BAR
Budget Advisory Board .... BAB
Budget Advisory Committee [Army].................... BAC
Budget Allocation Summary .... BAS
Budget Analysis Reporting System .... BARS
Budget Authority [Office of Management and Budget].................... BA
Budget Authorization [Air Force].................... BA
Budget Authorization Account Number [Air Force].................... BAAN
Budget Capital Corp. [NYSE symbol] [Delisted] .... BUG
Budget Center .... BC
Budget Change Proposal.................... BCP
Budget Change Request .... BCR
Budget Classification Code .... BCC
Budget at Completion .... BAC
Budget at Completion Variance .... BACV
Budget Estimates Presentation Instructions .... BEPI
Budget Execution [Army].................... BEXEC
Budget Execution Plan [Army].................... BEP
Budget Execution Review [Army].................... BER
Budget Executives Institute [Later, PEI].................... BEI
Budget and Finance Division [NATO].................... BUDFIN
Budget Fiscal Year .... BFY
Budget and Forecast Calendarization .... BFC
Budget Formulation [Army].................... BFORM
Budget Formulation Directive [Military].................... BFD
Budget Industries, Inc. [NYSE symbol] [Delisted].................... BGT
Budget and Manpower Guidance [Military].................... BMG
Budget Office [Army].................... BUD
Budget Office, War Department [World War II].................... BOWD
Budget Program .... BP
Budget Program Activity Code .... BPAC

Budget Project Account [Military].................... BPA
Budget Project Number [Navy].................... BPN
Budget Project Symbol Number .... BPSN
Budget and Reporting.................... B & R
Budget Review Committee .... BRC
Budget Workload Analysis Report [Navy].................... BWAR
Budget Workload Indicators.................... BWI
Budget Year .... BY
Budgetary and Planning .... B & P
Budgetary and Planning Quotations .... BPQ
Budgetary and Scheduling Information System .... BASIS
Budgeted Cost for Work Performed .... BCWP
Budgeted Cost for Work Scheduled .... BCWS
Budkov [Czechoslovakia] [Geomagnetic observatory code] .... BDV
Budoia [Papua New Guinea] [Seismograph station code, US Geological Survey].................... BDO
Buecherei des Augenarztes [A publication].................... Buech Augenarzt
Buehler Corp. [American Stock Exchange symbol] [Delisted] .... BLR
Buehlerhoehe [Federal Republic of Germany] [Seismograph station code, US Geological Survey].................... BUH
Buell Industries, Inc. [American Stock Exchange symbol].................... BUE
Buena Park, CA [Radio station call letters].................... KBPK
Buena Park Library District Library, Buena Park, CA [Library symbol] .... CBp
Buena Vista [Guatemala] [Seismograph station code, US Geological Survey].................... BVA
Buena Vista College [Iowa].................... BVC
Buena Vista College, Storm Lake, IA [Library symbol].................... IaSIB
Buena Vista College, Storm Lake, IA [OCLC symbol].................... IOE
Buena Vista Public Library, Buena Vista, CO [Library symbol].................... CoBue
Buena Vista, VA [Radio station call letters].................... WWZD
Buenos Aires [A publication].................... BA
Buenos Aires [Argentina] [Seismograph station code, US Geological Survey].................... BAA
Buenos Aires [Argentina] [Airport symbol].................... BUE
Buenos Aires [Argentina].................... BA
Buenos Aires [Argentina] Ezeiza [Airport symbol].................... EZE
Buenos Aires [Argentina] Jorge Newbery Airport [Airport symbol].................... AEP
Buenos Aires Literaria [A publication].................... BAL
Buenos Aires Musical [A publication].................... BAM
Buenos Aires Musical [A publication].................... Buenos Aires Mus
Buergerinitiativen [Citizens' action groups] [West Germany].................... BI's
Buerotechnik Automation und Organisation [A publication].................... Buerotech Autom & Organ
Buestenhalter [Brassiere] [German slang].................... BH
Buff and Polishing Wheel Manufacturers Association [Defunct].................... BPWMA
Buffalo [New York] [Airport symbol] .... BUF
Buffalo [New York] [Seismograph station code, US Geological Survey] [Closed] .... BUF
Buffalo [Rat variety].................... BUF
Buffalo Aeronautical Corporation [Buffalo, NY] [FAA designator].................... BAC
Buffalo Bill Historical Center.................... BBHC
Buffalo Bill Museum, Cody, WY [Library symbol].................... WyCoB
Buffalo Center Tribune, Buffalo Center, IA [Library symbol] .... IaBucCT
Buffalo Color Corp., Buffalo, NY [Library symbol].................... NBuCo
[The] Buffalo Creek Railroad Co. [Absorbed into Consolidated Rail Corp.] [AAR code].................... BCK
Buffalo and Erie County Historical Society, Buffalo, NY [Library symbol] .... NBuHi
Buffalo and Erie County Public Library, Buffalo, NY [Library symbol].................... NBu
Buffalo and Erie County Public Library, Buffalo, NY [OCLC symbol] .... VHB
Buffalo Fine Arts Academy. Albright Art Gallery. Notes [A publication].................... Buffalo Gal Notes
Buffalo Forge Company [NYSE symbol] [Delisted] .... BFC
Buffalo General Hospital, Buffalo, NY [Library symbol].................... NBuGH
Buffalo General Hospital, School of Nursing, Buffalo, NY [Library symbol] .... NBuGH-N
Buffalo Historical Society. Publications [A publication].................... Buffalo Hist Soc Publ
Buffalo, KY [Radio station call letters].................... WLCB
Buffalo - Larkin [New York] [Seismograph station code, US Geological Survey] [Closed].................... BFF
Buffalo Law Review [A publication].................... Buffalo L Rev
Buffalo Law Review [A publication].................... Buff Law R
Buffalo, MN [Radio station call letters].................... KRWC
Buffalo, MO [Radio station call letters].................... KBFL
Buffalo Narrows [Canada] [Airport symbol] [Obsolete].................... YVT
Buffalo, NY [Radio station call letters].................... WBEN
Buffalo, NY [Radio station call letters].................... WBEN-FM
Buffalo, NY [Radio station call letters].................... WBFO
Buffalo, NY [Radio station call letters].................... WBNY
Buffalo, NY [Radio station call letters].................... WBUF
Buffalo, NY [Radio station call letters].................... WDCX
Buffalo, NY [Radio station call letters].................... WEBR
Buffalo, NY [Radio station call letters].................... WGR
Buffalo, NY [Radio station call letters].................... WGRQ
Buffalo, NY [Television station call letters].................... WGRZ-TV
Buffalo, NY [Television station call letters].................... WIVB-TV
Buffalo, NY [Radio station call letters].................... WJYE
Buffalo, NY [Radio station call letters].................... WKBW
Buffalo, NY [Television station call letters].................... WKBW-TV

Buffalo, NY [*Radio station call letters*]...WNED-FM
Buffalo, NY [*Television station call letters*]...WNED-TV
Buffalo, NY [*Radio station call letters*]...WNYS
Buffalo, NY [*Radio station call letters*]...WNYS-FM
Buffalo, NY [*Radio station call letters*]...WPHD
Buffalo, NY [*Television station call letters*]...WUTV
Buffalo, NY [*Radio station call letters*]...WYRK
Buffalo, NY [*Radio station call letters*]...WYSL
Buffalo, OK [*Location identifier*] [*FAA*]...BFK
Buffalo Organization for Social and Technological Innovation, Inc. (BOSTI), Buffalo, NY [*Library symbol*]...NBuBO
Buffalo Philharmonic Program Notes [*A publication*]...Buffalo Phil
Buffalo Psychiatric Center, Buffalo, NY [*Library symbol*]...NBuPC
Buffalo Range [*Zimbabwe*] [*Airport symbol*]...BFO
Buffalo Rat Liver [*Cytology*]...BRL
Buffalo, Rochester, & Pittsburg Railway [*Terminated*]...BR & PRY
Buffalo, SD [*Location identifier*] [*FAA*]...BUA
Buffalo Society of Natural Sciences, Buffalo Museum of Science, Buffalo, NY [*Library symbol*]...NBuB
Buffalo Society of Natural Sciences. Bulletin [*A publication*]...Buffalo Soc Nat Sci Bull
Buffalo Society of Natural Sciences. Bulletin [*A publication*]...Buffalo Soc N Sc B
Buffalo, WY [*Location identifier*] [*FAA*]...BYG
Buffalo, WY [*Radio station call letters*]...KBBS
Buffalo, WY [*Radio station call letters*]...KLGM
Buffelsfontein Gold Mining Co. ADR [*NASDAQ symbol*]...BFELY
Buffer...BFR
Buffer Access Card [*Data processing*]...BAC
Buffer Address Register [*Data processing*]...BAR
Buffer Amplifier [*Data processing*]...BA
Buffer Control Junction Switch [*Data processing*]...BCJS
Buffer Control Unit [*Data processing*]...BCU
Buffer Control Word [*Data processing*]...BCW
Buffer Index [*Data processing*]...BI
Buffer Input-Output Memory [*Data processing*]...BIOM
Buffer Interface Unit [*Data processing*]...BIU
Buffer Map [*Data processing*]...BMAP
Buffer Module [*Data processing*]...BM
Buffer/Multiplexer [*Data processing*]...B/M
Buffer Register [*Data processing*]...BR
Buffer Stock Financing Facility [*International Monetary Fund*]...BSFF
Buffered [*Medicine*]...BF
Buffered Azide Glucose Glycerol [*Broth*] [*Microbiology*]...BAGG
Buffered Deoxycholate Glucose [*Broth*] [*Microbiology*]...BDG
Buffered Distilled Water [*Chemistry*]...BDW
Buffered Emitter Follower...BEF
Buffered FET [*Field Effect Transistor*] **Logic** [*Integrated circuitry*]...BFL
Buffered Filtered Seawater...BFSW
Buffered Flip-Flop [*Data processing*]...BFF
Buffered Ringer's Solution [*Medicine*]...BFR
Buffet and Bull [*Slang for a political dinner*]...B & B
Buffing...BFG
Buffoons of America...BA
Buffton Corp. [*NASDAQ symbol*]...BUFF
Buford, GA [*Radio station call letters*]...WDYX
Buford, GA [*Radio station call letters*]...WGCO
Bug-Eyed Monster [*Science fiction or fantastic literature which makes great use of monsters in its storyline or illustrations*]...BEM
Bug Off [*Slang*]...BO
Bugatti [*Automobile*]...BUG
Buggalo Nam Newsletter [*A publication*]...BNN
Buginarium [*Nasal Bougie*] [*Pharmacy*]...BUGINAR
Buglemaster [*Navy*]...BGM
Buglemaster...BGMSTR
Bugler...BGLR
Bugler...BR
Bugler [*Navy*]...BUG
Buia [*Italy*] [*Seismograph station code, US Geological Survey*]...BUII
Buick Club of America...BCA
Buick Collector's Club of America [*Defunct*]...BCCA
Buie's Creek, NC [*Radio station call letters*]...WCCE
Build and Blood Pressure Study [*Society of Actuaries*]...BBPS
Build International (English Edition) [*A publication*]...Build Int (Engl Ed)
Build Options, Renew Norms, Free Roles through Educational Equity [*National project to help students choose appropriate future careers*]...BORN FREE
Build-Up Control Organization [*Established to supervise flow of personnel and equipment to the Continent, immediately following Normandy invasion*] [*British*] [*World War II*]...BUCO
Builder...BLDR
Builder [*Navy rating*]...BU
Builder, Concrete [*Navy rating*]...BUR
Builder, First Class [*Navy rating*]...BU1
Builder, Heavy [*Navy rating*]...BUH
Builder, Light [*Navy rating*]...BUL
Builder, Second Class [*Navy rating*]...BU2
Builder, Third Class [*Navy rating*]...BU3
Builders Exchange of Detroit and Michigan...BEDM
Builders' Hardware Manufacturers Association [*Formerly, HMSA*]...BHMA
Builders Investment Group [*NYSE symbol*]...BSG
Builders Old Measurement...BOM
Builder's Risk [*Insurance*]...BR
Builders Transport [*NASDAQ symbol*]...TRUK
Builder's Trials [*Shipbuilding*]...BT
Buildex, Inc. [*American Stock Exchange symbol*]...BLX
Building...BLD
Building...BLDG
Building Advisor [*Red Cross Disaster Services*]...BA
Building Age and National Builder [*A publication*]...Bldg Age
Building Block...BB
Building Block Concept [*Army-ROAD concept*]...BBC
Building Block Monochromator...BBM
Building Block Principle...BBP
Building and Civil Engineer [*British*]...B & CE
Building and Construction Trades Department [*AFL-CIO*]...BCTD
Building and Contents [*Insurance*]...B & C
Building Energy Performance Standards...BEPS
Building Engineer...Bldg E
Building and Engineering [*British*]...B & E
Building Equipment Accessories and Materials [*Program*] [*Canada*]...BEAM
Building Industry Development Services...BIDS
Building Line [*Technical drawings*]...BL
Building and Loan [*Association*]...B & L
Building Maintenance Employers Association [*Later, SEA*]...BMEA
Building Material Exhibitors Association [*Defunct*]...BMEA
Building Material Series [*National Bureau of Standards*]...BMS
Building Materials [*A publication*]...Bldg Mater
Building Officials and Code Administrators International...BOCA
Building Operating Management [*A publication*]...Build Oper Manage
Building Optimization Program [*Data processing*]...BOP
Building Owners Federation of Mutual Insurance Companies [*Defunct*]...BOF
Building Owners and Managers Association International...BOMA
Building Owners and Managers Association International...BOMAI
Building Products Executives Conference...BPEC
Building Products Ltd., Montreal, PQ, Canada [*Library symbol*]...CaQMBP
Building Renovating Association...BRA
Building and Repair [*Red Cross Disaster Services*]...B and R
Building Research [*A publication*]...Build Res
Building Research Advisory Board [*Later, ABBE*] [*National Academy of Sciences*]...BRAB
Building Research Establishment (Station) Digest [*A publication*]...Build Res Estab (Sta) Digest
Building Research Institute [*Later, BRAB, ABBE*]...BRI
Building Research and Practice [*A publication*]...Build Res Pract
Building Research Station [*British*]...BRS
Building Research Station News [*A publication*]...BRS
Building Research (Washington, DC) [*A publication*]...Bldg Res (Washington DC)
Building and Safety Engineering...BSE
Building Science [*A publication*]...Bldg Sci
Building Science [*A publication*]...BS
Building Science [*A publication*]...Build Sci
Building Science Series [*National Bureau of Standards*]...BSS
Building Service Contractors Association International [*Formerly, NABSC*]...BSCA
Building Service Employees' International Union [*Later, SEIU*]...BSE
Building Service League [*Later, SEA*]...BSL
Building Services Engineer [*A publication*]...Bldg Serv Engr
Building Services Engineer [*A publication*]...Build Serv Eng
Building Stone Institute...BSI
Building Systems Design [*A publication*]...Bldg Systems Design
Building Systems Design [*A publication*]...Build Syst Des
Building Technology and Management [*A publication*]...Bldg Technol Mgmt
Building Waterproofers Association [*Defunct*]...BWA
Building Woodwork [*Freight*]...BLDG WDWRK
Building Workers' Industrial Union [*Australia*]...BWIU
Buildings, Antennas, Spans, and Earth Formations [*Fixed-object parachuting*]...BASE
Buildings: the Construction and Building Management Journal [*A publication*]...Bldgs
Buildings Control Officer...BUCO
Buildup [*Meteorology*]...BLDUP
Buildup...BU
Built...BLT
Built for British [*As suffix to plane designation*]...B
Built Environment [*A publication*]...Built Env
Built-In...BLTIN
Built-In Breathing System...BIBS
Built-In Cleaning Systems Institute...BCSI
Built-In Hold [*of countdown*] [*NASA*]...BIH
Built-In Light Beacon...BILB
Built-In Orderly Organized Knowledge [*Learning device*]...BOOK
Built-In Self-Test...BIST
Built-In Test [*or Testing*] [*Data processing*]...BIT
Built-In Test Equipment...BITE
Built-In Variance...BIV
Built-in-Place Component [*Electronics*]...BIPCO
Built-Up Roofing...BUR

Buin [*Papua New Guinea*] [*Airport symbol*] ... UBI
Buisson Ardent [*The Burning Bush*] [*Masonry*] ... BA
Bujumbura [*Burundi*] [*Airport symbol*] ... BJM
Buka Island [*Papua New Guinea*] [*Airport symbol*] ... BUA
Bukavu [*Zaire*] [*Airport symbol*] ... BKY
Bukhara [*USSR*] [*Airport symbol*] ... BHK
Bukoba [*Tanzania*] [*Airport symbol*] ... BKZ
Bul Bul Academy of Fine Arts [*Dacca, Pakistan*] ... BAFA
Bulawayo [*Zimbabwe*] [*Seismograph station code, US Geological Survey*] ... BUL
Bulawayo [*Zimbabwe*] [*Airport symbol*] ... BUQ
Bulb ... B
Bulb and Time [*Photography*] ... B & T
Bulbocavernosus Activity [*Physiology*] ... BCA
Buletin i Institutit te Schkecave [*A publication*] ... BISchk
Buletin per Shkencat Shoqerore [*A publication*] ... BSS
Buletin. Universiteti Shtereror te Tiranes. Seria Shkencat Shoqerore [*A publication*] ... BUT
Buletin. Universiteti Shteteror i Tiranes. Fakulteti i Shkencave te Natyres [*A publication*] ... Bul Univ Shteteror Tiranes Shk Nat
Buletinul Akademiei. Stiince a RSS Moldovenest [*A publication*] ... Bul Akad Stiince RSS Moldoven
Buletinul Bibliotecii Romane [*A publication*] ... BBR
Buletinul de Cercetari Piscicole [*A publication*] ... Bul Cercet Piscic
Buletinul. Comisiunii Monumentelor Istorice [*A publication*] ... BCM
Buletinul. Institutului Agronomic Cluj-Napoca [*A publication*] ... Bul Inst Agron Cluj-Napoca
Buletinul. Institutului de Cercetari si Proiectari Piscicole [*A publication*] ... Bul Inst Cercet Proiect Piscic
Buletinul. Institutului de Filologie Romaina. Alexandru Philippide [*Iasi*] [*A publication*] ... BIFR
Buletinul. Institutului de Filologie Romaina. Alexandru Philippide (Iasi) [*A publication*] ... BIFRI
Buletinul. Institutului Politehnic din Brasov. Seria A. Mecanica [*A publication*] ... Bul Inst Politeh Brasov A
Buletinul. Institutului Politehnic din Brasov. Seria B. Economie Forestiera [*A publication*] ... Bul Inst Polit Brasov Ser B Econ For
Buletinul. Institutului Politehnic Bucuresti [*A publication*] ... Bul Inst Politeh Bucur
Buletinul. Institutului Politehnic Bucuresti [*A publication*] ... Bul Inst Politeh Bucuresti
Buletinul. Institutului Politehnic "Gheorghe Gheorghiu-Dej" Bucuresti. Seria Mecanica [*A publication*] ... Bul Inst Politeh Bucuresti Ser Mec
Buletinul. Institutului Politehnic "Gheorghe Gheorghiu-Dej" Bucuresti. Seria Mecanica [*A publication*] ... Bul Inst Politeh (Mec)
Buletinul. Institutului Politehnic din Iasi [*A publication*] ... Bul Inst Politeh Iasi
Buletinul. Institutului Politehnic din Iasi. Sectia I. Matematica, Mecanica Teoretica, Fizica [*A publication*] ... Bul Inst Politeh Iasi I
Buletinul. Institutului Politehnic din Iasi. Sectia I. Matematica, Mecanica Teoretica, Fizica [*A publication*] ... Bul Inst Politeh Iasi Sect I
Buletinul. Institutului Politehnic din Iasi. Sectia II. Chimie [*A publication*] ... Bul Inst Politeh Iasi Sect II
Buletinul. Institutului Politehnic din Iasi. Sectia III. Electrotehnica, Electronica Automatizari [*A publication*] ... Bul Inst Politeh Iasi III
Buletinul. Institutului Politehnic din Iasi. Sectia III. Electrotehnica, Electronica Automatizari [*A publication*] ... Bul Inst Politeh Iasi Sect III
Buletinul. Institutului Politehnic din Iasi. Sectia IV. Mecanica Tehnica [*A publication*] ... Bul Inst Politeh Iasi Sect IV
Buletinul Institutului. Studii si Projectari Energetice [*A publication*] ... Bul Inst Stud & Proj Energ
Buletinul si Memorie. Societatii de Medicina Veterinaria din Bucuresti [*A publication*] ... Bul si Mem Soc Med Vet Bucuresti
Buletinul Monumentelor Istorica [*A publication*] ... Bul Mon Ist
Buletinul Societatii Numismatice Romane [*A publication*] ... BSNR
Buletinul Stiintific. Institutul de Constructii (Bucuresti) [*A publication*] ... Bul Stiint Inst Constr (Bucuresti)
Buletinul Stiintific. Institutului Politehnic Cluj [*A publication*] ... Bul Sti Inst Politehn Cluj
Buletinul Stiintific. Institutului Politehnic Cluj-Napoca [*A publication*] ... Bul Stiint Inst Politeh Cluj-Napoca
Buletinul Stiintific. Institutului Politehnic Cluj. Seria Constructii [*A publication*] ... Bul Sti Inst Politehn Cluj Ser Construc
Buletinul Stiintific. Institutului Politehnic Cluj. Seria Electromecanica [*A publication*] ... Bul Sti Inst Politehn Cluj Ser Electromec
Buletinul Stiintific. Institutului Politehnic Cluj. Seria Electromecanica [*A publication*] ... Bul Stiint Inst Politeh Cluj Ser Electromec
Buletinul Stiintific Tehnic. Institutului Politehnic "Traian Vuia" (Timisoara) [*A publication*] ... Bul Sti Tehn Inst Politehn "Traian Vuia" (Timisoara)
Buletinul. Universitatea din Brasov [*A publication*] ... Bul Univ Brasov
Buletinul. Universitatii din Brasov. Seria A. Mecanica Aplicata Constructii de Masini [*A publication*] ... Bul Univ Brasov Ser A Mec Apl
Buletinul. Universitatii din Brasov. Seria C. Matematica, Fizica, Chimie, Stiinte Naturale [*A publication*] ... Bul Univ Brasov Ser C Mat Fiz Chim Sti Natur
Bulgaria [*Two-letter standard code*] ... BG
Bulgaria [*Three-letter standard code*] ... BGR
Bulgaria ... BU
Bulgaria ... BULG
Bulgaria [*MARC geographic area code*] [*Library of Congress*] ... e-bu---
Bulgaria [*Aircraft nationality and registration mark*] ... LZ
Bulgaria [*MARC country of publication*] [*Library of Congress*] ... bu
Bulgarian [*MARC language code*] [*Library of Congress*] ... bul
Bulgarian Films [*A publication*] ... Bulg F
Bulgarian Journal of Physics [*A publication*] ... Bulgar J Phys
Bulgarian Journal of Physics [*A publication*] ... Bulg J Phys
Bulgarian National Committee ... BNC
Bulgarian National Front ... BNF
Bulgarian Socialist Labor Federation [*Defunct*] ... BSLF
Bulgarska Akademiya na Naukite. Doklady [*A publication*] ... Bulg Akad Nauk Dokl
Bulgarska Akademiya na Naukite. Geologicheski Institut. Izvestiya. Seriya Paleontologiya [*A publication*] ... Bulg Akad Nauk Geol Inst Izv Ser Paleontol
Bulgarska Akademiya na Naukite. Otdeleniye za Biologichni Nauki. Zoologicheski Institut si Muzey. Izvestiya [*A publication*] ... Bulg Akad Nauk Zool Inst Muz Izv
Bulgarska Komunisticheska Partiia [*Bulgarian Communist Party*] ... BKP
Bulgarska Muzika [*A publication*] ... Bulgar Muz
Bulgarska Telegrafna Agentsiya [*Bulgarian News Agency*] ... BTA
Bulgarski Tyutyun [*A publication*] ... Bulg Tyutyun
Bulgarsko Geologichesko Druzhestvo. Spisaniye [*A publication*] ... Bulg Geol Druzh Spis
Bulimba [*Australia*] [*Airport symbol*] [*Obsolete*] ... BIP
Bulk ... BLK
Bulk Airmail ... BAM
Bulk in Barrels [*Freight*] ... BLK B
Bulk Carriers Conference, Arlington VA [*STAC*] ... BLK
Bulk-Cohesion-Dipolarity-Elasticity [*Factor analysis of physical property data of liquid compounds*] ... BCDE
Bulk/Common Items List ... BCIL
Bulk Filtering Acquisition and Tracking System ... BATS
Bulk Head ... BH
Bulk Inland Petroleum, Oil, and Lubrication Transport ... BIPOLT
Bulk Items List ... BIL
Bulk Mail Center [*Postal Service*] ... BMC
Bulk Material Length ... BML
Bulk Modulus of Elasticity [*Symbol*] ... k
Bulk Molding Compound ... BMC
Bulk Packaging and Containerization Institute [*Later, CII*] ... BPCI
Bulk Petroleum Facilities and Systems ... BPFS
Bulk Polymerization Process [*Plastics technology*] ... BPP
Bulk Semiconductor Limiter ... BSL
Bulk Shielding Facility [*ORNL*] ... BSF
Bulk Shielding Reactor ... BSR
Bulk Store Memory Device ... BSMD
Bulk Tape Degausser ... BTD
Bulk Tape Eraser ... BTE
Bulk Transfer Hose ... BTH
Bulk Wet Density ... BWD
Bulked Continuous Fiber [*or Filament*] [*Textile*] ... BCF
Bulkhead ... BHD
Bulkhead ... Bkhd
Bulkhead ... BLKD
Bulkhead ... BLKHD
Bulkhead Connector ... BC
Bulkhead Jack ... BHJ
Bulkhead Jack ... BJ
Bulkhead Receptacle ... BHR
Bulkhead Receptacle ... BR
Bull & Bear Group Cl A [*NASDAQ symbol*] ... BNBGA
Bull Elephants [*An association*] ... BE
Bull General Electric ... BGE
Bull Nose ... BN
Bull Run Gold Mines [*NASDAQ symbol*] ... BULL
Bull Session [*Slang for a random conversation*] ... BS
Bull Terrier Club of America ... BTCA
Bullard Co. [*NYSE symbol*] [*Delisted*] ... BLD
Bullard-Sanford Public Library, Vassar, MI [*Library symbol*] ... MiVa
Bulldog Club of America ... BCA
Bulldozer [*Freight*] ... BDOZER
Bulldozer ... BDZR
Bullet Hit Indicator ... BHI
Bulleti. Associacio Catalana d'Antropologia [*A publication*] ... BACA
Bulleti de Dialectologia Catalana [*A publication*] ... BDC
Bulletin ... B
Bulletin ... BUL
Bulletin ... BULL
Bulletin. Aberdeen University African Studies Group [*A publication*] ... B Aberdeen Univ Afr Stud Group
Bulletin. Academie de Chirurgie Dentaire (Paris) [*A publication*] ... Bull Acad Chir Dent (Paris)
Bulletin. Academie Ebroicienne [*A publication*] ... Bull Acad Ebroic
Bulletin. Academie d'Hippone [*A publication*] ... BAH
Bulletin. Academie pour l'Histoire de la Culture Materielle [*A publication*] ... BACM

Bulletin. Academie Imperiale des Sciences de St. Petersbourg [*A publication*]....Bull Acad Imp Sc St Petersb
Bulletin. Academie des Inscriptions et Belles-Lettres [*A publication*]....BAIBL
Bulletin. Academie Malgache [*A publication*]....BAMalgache
Bulletin. Academie Malgache [*A publication*]....Bull Acad Malgache
Bulletin. Academie de Medecine (Paris) [*A publication*]....Bull Acad Med (Paris)
Bulletin. Academie de Medecine de Roumanie [*A publication*]....Bull Acad Med Roum
Bulletin. Academie Nationale de Medecine [*Paris*] [*A publication*]....Bull Acad Natl Med
Bulletin. Academie Nationale de Medecine (Paris) [*A publication*]....Bull Acad Natl Med (Paris)
Bulletin. Academie Polonaise de Cracovie [*A publication*]....BAPC
Bulletin. Academie Polonaise des Sciences [*A publication*]....Bull Acad Pol Sci
Bulletin. Academie Polonaise des Sciences et des Lettres [*A publication*]....BAPSL
Bulletin. Academie Polonaise des Sciences. Serie des Sciences Biologiques [*A publication*]....B Pol Biol
Bulletin. Academie Polonaise des Sciences. Serie des Sciences Biologiques [*A publication*]....Bull Acad Polon Sci Ser Sci Biol
Bulletin. Academie Polonaise des Sciences. Serie des Sciences Biologiques [*A publication*]....Bull Acad Pol Sci Biol
Bulletin. Academie Polonaise des Sciences. Serie des Sciences Biologiques [*A publication*]....Bull Acad Pol Sci Ser Sci Biol
Bulletin. Academie Polonaise des Sciences. Serie des Sciences Chimiques [*A publication*]....B Pol Chim
Bulletin. Academie Polonaise des Sciences. Serie des Sciences Chimiques [*A publication*]....Bull Acad Pol Sci Ser Sci Chim
Bulletin. Academie Polonaise des Sciences. Serie des Sciences Mathematiques, Astronomiques, et Physiques [*A publication*]....B Pol Math
Bulletin. Academie Polonaise des Sciences. Serie des Sciences Mathematiques, Astronomiques, et Physiques [*A publication*]....Bull Acad Polon Sci Ser Sci Math Astronom Phys
Bulletin. Academie Polonaise des Sciences. Serie des Sciences Techniques [*A publication*]....B Pol Techn
Bulletin. Academie Polonaise des Sciences. Serie des Sciences Techniques [*A publication*]....Bull Acad Polon Sci Ser Sci Tech
Bulletin. Academie Polonaise des Sciences. Serie des Sciences Techniques [*A publication*]....Bull Acad Pol Sci Ser Sci Tech
Bulletin. Academie Polonaise des Sciences. Serie des Sciences de la Terre [*A publication*]....B Pol Sci T
Bulletin. Academie Polonaise des Sciences. Serie des Sciences de la Terre [*A publication*]....Bull Acad Pol Sci Ser Sci Terre
Bulletin. Academie Royale d'Archeologie de Belgique [*A publication*]....BARAB
Bulletin. Academie Royale de Langue et de Litterature Francaises [*A publication*]....BALF
Bulletin. Academie Royale de Langue et de Litterature Francaises [*A publication*]....BARLLF
Bulletin. Academie Royale de Medecine de Belgique [*A publication*]....Bull Acad R Med Belg
Bulletin. Academie Royale de Medecine de Belgique [*A publication*]....Bull Acad Roy Med Belgique
Bulletin. Academie des Sciences Agricoles et Forestieres [*A publication*]....Bull Acad Sci Agric For
Bulletin. Academie des Sciences de Russie [*A publication*]....BASR
Bulletin. Academie des Sciences de l'URSS [*A publication*]....BASURSS
Bulletin. Academie Serbe des Sciences et des Arts. Classe des Sciences Mathematiques et Naturelles [*A publication*]....Bull Acad Serbe Sci Arts Cl Sci Math Nat
Bulletin. Academie Serbe des Sciences et des Arts. Classe des Sciences Mathematiques et Naturelles [*A publication*]....Bull Acad Serbe Sci Arts Cl Sci Math Natur
Bulletin. Academie et Societe Lorraines des Sciences [*A publication*]....Bull Acad Soc Lorraines Sci
Bulletin. Academie Suisse des Sciences Medicales [*A publication*]....Bull Acad Suisse Sci Med
Bulletin. Academie Veterinaire de France [*A publication*]....Bull Acad Vet Fr
Bulletin. Academie Veterinaire de France [*A publication*]....Bull Acad Vet France
Bulletin. Academy of Sciences of the USSR. Division of Chemical Science [*A publication*]....B Acad Sci
Bulletin. Academy of Sciences of the USSR. Division of Chemical Science [*A publication*]....Bull Acad Sci USSR Div Chem Sci
Bulletin. Academy of Sciences of the USSR. Geologic Series [*A publication*]....Bull Acad Sci USSR Geol Ser
Bulletin. Academy of Sciences of the USSR. Physical Sciences [*A publication*]....Bull Acad Sci USSR Phys Sci
Bulletin. Academy of Sciences of the USSR. Physical Series [*A publication*]....Bull Acad Sci USSR Phys Ser
Bulletin. Agence Internationale de l'Energie Atomique [*A publication*]....B Agenc Int Energie Atom
Bulletin Agricole du Congo [*A publication*]....Bull Agr Congo
Bulletin Agricole du Congo Belge [*A publication*]....Bull Agric Congo Belg
Bulletin Agricole du Rwanda [*A publication*]....Bull Agric Rwanda
Bulletin. Agricultural Chemical Society of Japan [*A publication*]....Bull Agr Chem Soc Jap
Bulletin. Agricultural Chemical Society of Japan [*A publication*]....Bull Agric Chem Soc Jpn
Bulletin. Agricultural Chemicals Inspection Station (Tokyo) [*A publication*]....Bull Agric Chem Insp Stn (Tokyo)
Bulletin. Agricultural Research Institute of Kanagawa Prefecture [*A publication*]....Bull Agric Res Inst Kanagawa Prefect
Bulletin. Agricultural Research Institute (Pusa) [*A publication*]....Bull Agr Res Inst (Pusa)
Bulletin. Agricultural Research Station (Rehovat) [*A publication*]....Bull Agr Res Sta (Rehovat)
Bulletin. Aichi Agricultural Experiment Station [*A publication*]....Bull Aichi Agr Exp Sta
Bulletin. Aichi Gakugei University [*A publication*]....Bull Aichi Gakugei Univ
Bulletin. Alabama Agricultural Experiment Station. Auburn University [*A publication*]....Bull Ala Agr Exp Sta
Bulletin. Alabama Agricultural Experiment Station. Auburn University [*A publication*]....Bull Ala Agric Exp Sta
Bulletin. Alabama Agricultural Experiment Station. Auburn University [*A publication*]....Bull Ala Agric Exp Stn
Bulletin. Alameda County Dental Society [*A publication*]....Bull Alameda Cty Dent Soc
Bulletin. Alaska Agricultural Experiment Station [*A publication*]....Bull Alaska Agr Exp Sta
Bulletin. Alaska Agricultural Experiment Station [*A publication*]....Bull Alaska Agric Exp Stn
Bulletin. Allyn Museum [*A publication*]....Bull Allyn Mus
Bulletin. American Academy of Psychiatry and the Law [*A publication*]....Bull Am Acad Psychiatry Law
Bulletin. American Anthropological Association [*A publication*]....B Am Anth A
Bulletin. American Astronomical Society [*A publication*]....Bull Am Astron Soc
Bulletin. American College of Surgeons [*A publication*]....Bull Am Coll Surg
Bulletin. American Game Protective Association [*A publication*]....Bull Am Game Protect Ass
Bulletin. American Group. International Institute for Conservation of Historic and Artistic Works [*A publication*]....Bull Am Group IIC
Bulletin. American Historical Collection [*A publication*]....B Am Hist Col
Bulletin. American Institute of Swedish Arts, Literature, and Science [*A publication*]....BAI
Bulletin. American Library Association [*A publication*]....BALA
Bulletin. American Malacological Union, Incorporated [*A publication*]....Bull Am Malacol Union Inc
Bulletin. American Mathematical Society [*A publication*]....B Am Math S
Bulletin. American Mathematical Society [*A publication*]....BAMS
Bulletin. American Mathematical Society [*A publication*]....Bull Am Math Soc
Bulletin. American Meteorological Society [*A publication*]....B Am Meteor
Bulletin. American Meteorological Society [*A publication*]....Bull Amer Meteorol Soc
Bulletin. American Meteorological Society [*A publication*]....Bull Am Meteorol Soc
Bulletin. American Museum of Natural History [*A publication*]....Bull Am Mus Nat Hist
Bulletin. American Musicological Society [*A publication*]....BAMS
Bulletin. American Physical Society [*A publication*]....B Am Phys S
Bulletin. American Physical Society [*A publication*]....Bull Am Phys Soc
Bulletin. American Physical Society [*A publication*]....Bull A Phys Soc
Bulletin. American Protestant Hospital Association [*A publication*]....Bull Am Prot Hosp Assoc
Bulletin. American School of Prehistoric Research [*A publication*]....BASPR
Bulletin. American School of Prehistoric Research [*A publication*]....Bull Am Sch Prehist Res
Bulletin. American Schools of Oriental Research [*A publication*]....B Amer School Orient
Bulletin. American Schools of Oriental Research [*A publication*]....BASOR
Bulletin. American Schools of Oriental Research in Jerusalem and Bagdad [*A publication*]....BASO
Bulletin. American Society of Bakery Engineers [*A publication*]....Bull Amer Soc Bakery Eng
Bulletin. American Society for Information Science [*A publication*]....Bull Am Soc Inf Sci
Bulletin. American Society of Papyrologists [*A publication*]....BASP
Bulletin. American Swedish Institute [*A publication*]....BASI
Bulletin Analytique de Bibliographie Hellenique [*A publication*]....BBH
Bulletin Analytique. Entomologie Medical et Veterinaire [*A publication*]....Bull Anal Ent Med Vet
Bulletin d'Ancienne Litterature et d'Archeologie Chretienne [*A publication*]....BALAC
Bulletin d'Ancienne Litterature et d'Archeologie Chretienne [*A publication*]....B Anc Lit
Bulletin des Anciens Eleves de l'Ecole Francaise de Meunerie [*A publication*]....Bull Anc Eleves Ec Fr Meun
Bulletin des Anciens Eleves de l'Ecole Francaise de Meunerie [*A publication*]....Bull Anciens Eleves Ecole Franc Meun
Bulletin of Animal Behavior [*A publication*]....Bull Anim Behav
Bulletin of Animal Health and Production in Africa [*A publication*]....Bull Anim Health Prod Afr
Bulletin et Annales. Societe Entomologique de Belgique [*A publication*]....Bull Ann Soc Entomol Belg

Bulletin et Annales. Societe Royale Belge d'Entomologie [*A publication*]....Bull Ann Soc R Belge Entomol
Bulletin et Annales. Societe Royale d'Entomologie de Belgique [*A publication*]....Bull Ann Soc R Entomol Belg
Bulletin et Annales. Societe Royale d'Entomologie de Belgique [*A publication*]....Bull Ann Soc Roy Entomol Belg
Bulletin Annuel. Musee d'Ethnographie de la Ville de Geneve [*A publication*]....BAMEG
Bulletin Annuel. Musee d'Ethnographie de la Ville de Geneve [*A publication*]....B Annu Mus Ethnogr Geneve
Bulletin. Anthropological Institute [*Nagoya*] [*A publication*]....B Anthropol Inst
Bulletin des Antiquites Luxembourgeoises [*A publication*]....BAL
Bulletin. Aomori Agricultural Experiment Station [*A publication*]....Bull Aomori Agr Exp Sta
Bulletin. Aomori Agricultural Experiment Station [*A publication*]....Bull Aomori Agric Exp Stn
Bulletin in Applied Statistics [*A publication*]....BIAS
Bulletin of Aquatic Biology [*A publication*]....Bull Aquat Biol
Bulletin d'Archeologie Algerienne [*A publication*]....BAA
Bulletin d'Archeologie Algerienne [*A publication*]....Bull Arch Alg
Bulletin d'Archeologie et d'Histoire Dalmate [*A publication*]....BAHD
Bulletin d'Archeologie Marocaine [*A publication*]....BAM
Bulletin d'Archeologie Marocaine [*A publication*]....Bul Arch Maroc
Bulletin Archeologique. Comite des Travaux Historiques [*A publication*]....BCTH
Bulletin Archeologique. Comite des Travaux Historiques et Archeologiques [*A publication*]....BAC
Bulletin Archeologique. Comite des Travaux Historiques et Scientifiques [*Paris*] [*A publication*]....BACTH
Bulletin Archeologique. Comite des Travaux Historiques et Scientifiques [*Paris*] [*A publication*]....BACTHS
Bulletin des Archives d'Anvers [*A publication*]....BAA
Bulletin. Arizona Agricultural Experiment Station [*A publication*]....Bull Ariz Agr Exp Sta
Bulletin. Arizona Agricultural Experiment Station. Cooperating Extension Service [*A publication*]....Bull Ariz Agr Exp Sta Coop Ext Serv
Bulletin. Arkansas Agricultural Experiment Station [*A publication*]....Bull Ark Agr Exp Sta
Bulletin. Arkansas Agricultural Experiment Station [*A publication*]....Bull Ark Agric Exp Stn
Bulletin Articles Information Subsystem [*Data processing*]....BAIS
Bulletin. Arts and Science Division. University of the Ryukyus. Mathematics and Natural Sciences [*A publication*]....Bull Arts Sci Div Univ Ryukyus Math Natur Sci
Bulletin. Association Amicale des Anciens Eleves de la Faculte des Lettres de Paris [*A publication*]....BAAFLP
Bulletin. Association des Amis des Eglises et de l'Art Coptes [*A publication*]....BAEC
Bulletin. Association des Amis de Flaubert [*A publication*]....BAF
Bulletin. Association des Amis de Rabelais et de la Deviniere [*A publication*]....BAARD
Bulletin. Association des Amis de Rabelais et de la Deviniere [*A publication*]....BAR
Bulletin. Association des Amis de Rabelais et de la Deviniere [*A publication*]....BARD
Bulletin. Association des Anatomistes [*A publication*]....Bull Assoc Anat
Bulletin. Association des Anatomistes (Nancy) [*A publication*]....Bull Assoc Anat (Nancy)
Bulletin. Association des Anciens Etudiants de l'Ecole Superieure de Brasserie de l'Universite de Louvain [*A publication*]....Bull Assoc Anc Etud Brass Univ Louv
Bulletin. Association des Anciens Etudiants de l'Ecole Superieure de Brasserie de l'Universite de Louvain [*A publication*]....Bull Assoc Anc Etud Ec Super Brass Univ Louv
Bulletin. Association de Cadres Dirigeants de l'Industrie pour le Progres Social et Economique [*A publication*]....B Assoc Cadres Dir Industr Progres Soc Econ
Bulletin. Association Canadienne des Bibliothecaires de Langue Francaise [*A publication*]....Bull Ass Can Bibliot Lang Fr
Bulletin. Association des Diplomes de Microbiologie de la Faculte de Pharmacie de Nancy [*A publication*]....Bull Ass Dipl Microbiol Nancy
Bulletin. Association des Diplomes de Microbiologie de la Faculte de Pharmacie de Nancy [*A publication*]....Bull Ass Diplomes Microbiol Fac Pharm Nancy
Bulletin. Association of Engineering Geologists [*A publication*]....Bull Assoc Eng Geol
Bulletin. Association Francaise pour l'Etude du Cancer [*A publication*]....Bull Assoc Fr Etude Cancer
Bulletin. Association Francaise pour l'Etude du Sol [*A publication*]....Bull Ass Fr Etude Sol
Bulletin. Association Francaise pour l'Etude du Sol [*A publication*]....Bull Assoc Fr Etude Sol
Bulletin. Association Francaise pour l'Etude du Sol [*A publication*]....Bull Assoc Fr Etud Sol
Bulletin. Association Francaise de Gemmologie [*A publication*]....Bull AFG
Bulletin. Association des Geographes Francais [*A publication*]....B Ass Geogr Franc
Bulletin. Association des Geographes Francais [*A publication*]....Bull Ass Geogr Fr
Bulletin. Association Guillaume Bude [*A publication*]....BAGB
Bulletin. Association Guillaume Bude [*A publication*]....BGB
Bulletin. Association Guillaume Bude. Supplement Critique [*A publication*]....BAGB SC
Bulletin. Association Lyonnaise de Recherches Archeologiques [*A publication*]....BALA
Bulletin. Association of Minnesota Entomologists [*A publication*]....Bull Assoc Minn Entomol
Bulletin. Association of Operative Millers [*A publication*]....Bull Ass Oper Millers
Bulletin. Association Philomathique d'Alsace et de Lorraine [*A publication*]....Bull Ass Philomath Alsace et Lorraine
Bulletin. Association Regionale pour l'Etude et la Recherche Scientifiques [*A publication*]....Bull ARERS
Bulletin. Association Royal des Anciens Etudiants en Brasserie de l'Universite de Louvain [*A publication*]....Bull Assoc R Anc Etud Brass Univ Louv
Bulletin. Association Suisse des Electriciens [*A publication*]....Bull Assoc Suisse Electr
Bulletin. Association Suisse des Electriciens [*A publication*]....Bull Ass Suisse Elec
Bulletin. Association for Tropical Biology [*A publication*]....Bull Assoc Trop Biol
Bulletin. Astronomical Institutes of Czechoslovakia [*A publication*]....B Astr I Cz
Bulletin. Astronomical Institutes of Czechoslovakia [*A publication*]....Bull Astron Inst Czech
Bulletin of the Atomic Scientists [*A publication*]....BAS
Bulletin of the Atomic Scientists [*A publication*]....B Atom Sci
Bulletin of the Atomic Scientists [*A publication*]....Bul Atomic Sci
Bulletin of the Atomic Scientists [*A publication*]....Bull Atom Sci
Bulletin of the Atomic Scientists [*A publication*]....Bull At Sci
Bulletin. Auckland Institute and Museum [*A publication*]....B Auckland Inst Mus
Bulletin. Auckland Institute and Museum [*A publication*]....Bull Auckl Inst Mus
Bulletin d'Audiophonologie [*A publication*]....Bull Audiophonol
Bulletin. Australasian Institute of Mining and Metallurgy [*A publication*]....Bull Australas Inst Min Metall
Bulletin. Australian Mathematical Society [*A publication*]....Bull Aust Math Soc
Bulletin. Australian Mathematical Society [*A publication*]....Bull Austral Math Soc
Bulletin. Australian Society of Exploration Geophysicists [*A publication*]....Bull Aust Soc Explor Geophys
Bulletin. Azabu Veterinary College [*A publication*]....Bull Azabu Vet Coll
Bulletin Balai Penelitian Perkebunan Medan [*A publication*]....Bull Balai Penelitian Perkebunan Medan
Bulletin of Baltic Studies [*A publication*]....BBS
Bulletin. Banque Nationale de Belgique [*A publication*]....B Banque Nat Belgique
Bulletin. Basrah Natural History Museum [*A publication*]....Bull Basrah Nat Hist Mus
Bulletin Baudelairien [*A publication*]....B Baud
Bulletin Belgicatom [*A publication*]....Bull Belgicatom
Bulletin. Bell Museum of Pathobiology [*A publication*]....Bull Bell Mus Pathobiol
Bulletin. Bernice P. Bishop Museum [*A publication*]....Bull Bernice P Bishop Mus
Bulletin Bibliographique de CREDIF [*Centre de Recherche et d'Etude pour la Diffusion du Francais*] **Service de Documentation** [*A publication*]....CREDIF
Bulletin Bibliographique. Musee Belge [*A publication*]....BBMB
Bulletin Bibliographique. Musee Belge [*A publication*]....BBPMB
Bulletin Bibliographique. Musee Belge [*A publication*]....BMB
Bulletin Bibliographique. Musee Belge [*A publication*]....MBBull
Bulletin Bibliographique de Pedologie. Office de la Recherche Scientifique et Technique d'Outre-Mer [*A publication*]....Bull Biblphique Pedol ORSTOM
Bulletin Bibliographique. Societe Internationale Arthurienne [*A publication*]....BBSIA
Bulletin of Bibliography [*A publication*]....BB
Bulletin of Bibliography [*A publication*]....Bul B
Bulletin of Bibliography [*A publication*]....Bul Bibliog
Bulletin of Bibliography [*A publication*]....Bull Bibl
Bulletin of Bibliography [*A publication*]....Bull Bibliog
Bulletin of Bibliography and Dramatic Index [*A publication*]....BBDI
Bulletin of Bibliography and Dramatic Index [*A publication*]....Bul of Bibliography
Bulletin du Bibliophile [*A publication*]....BBibl
Bulletin du Bibliophile et du Bibliothecaire [*A publication*]....BB
Bulletin du Bibliophile et du Bibliothecaire [*A publication*]....BBB
Bulletin des Bibliotheques de France [*A publication*]....BBF
Bulletin des Bibliotheques de France [*A publication*]....Bul Bibl de France
Bulletin des Bibliotheques de France [*A publication*]....Bull Bibl de France
Bulletin des Bibliotheques de France [*A publication*]....Bull Bibl France
Bulletin des Bibliotheques de France [*A publication*]....Bull Biblioth Fr
Bulletin Bimestriel. INACOL [*Institut National pour l'Amelioration des Conserves de Legumes*] [*A publication*]....Bull Bimest INACOL
Bulletin Bimestriel. Societe de Comptabilite de France [*A publication*]....B Bimestr Soc Comptabil France

Bulletin. Bingham Oceanographic Collection. Yale University [*A publication*].............................. Bull Bingham Oceanogr Collect Yale Univ

Bulletin. Biogeographical Society of Japan [*A publication*]....................... Bull Biogeogr Soc Jpn

Bulletin. Biological Research Centre (Baghdad) [*A publication*].................... Bull Biol Res Cent (Baghdad)

Bulletin. Biological Research Centre. Publication (Baghdad) [*A publication*]............................ Bull Biol Res Cent Publ (Baghdad)

Bulletin. Biological Society of Washington [*A publication*]....................... Bull Biol Soc Wash

Bulletin Biologique de la France et de la Belgique [*A publication*]....................... Bull Biol France et Belgique

Bulletin Biologique de la France et de la Belgique [*A publication*]....................... Bull Biol Fr Belg

Bulletin. Bismuth Institute [*A publication*] .... Bull Bismuth Inst

Bulletin of Black Theatre [*A publication*]...................BBT

Bulletin of Black Theatre [*A publication*]...................Bul Black Theatre

Bulletin Board.................................BB

Bulletin. Board of Celtic Studies [*A publication*] ....BBCS

Bulletin Board Systems .... BBS

Bulletin. Boris Kidric Institute of Nuclear Sciences. Biology [*A publication*]......................Bull Boris Kidric Inst Nucl Sci Biol

Bulletin. Boris Kidric Institute of Nuclear Sciences. Chemistry [*A publication*]................ Bull Boris Kidric Inst Nucl Sci Chem

Bulletin. Boris Kidric Institute of Nuclear Sciences. Electronics [*A publication*] .... Bull Boris Kidric Inst Nucl Sci Electron

Bulletin. Boris Kidric Institute of Nuclear Sciences. Nuclear Engineering [*A publication*] .... Bull Boris Kidric Inst Nucl Sci Nucl Eng

Bulletin. Boris Kidric Institute of Nuclear Sciences. Physics [*A publication*]................ Bull Boris Kidric Inst Nucl Sci Phys

Bulletin. Boris Kidric Institute of Nuclear Sciences. Supplement [*A publication*]................ Bull Boris Kidric Inst Nucl Sci Suppl

Bulletin. Botanic Gardens of Buitenzorg [*A publication*]........................ Bull Bot Gard Buitenzorg

Bulletin. Botanical Society of Bengal [*A publication*].......Bull Bot Soc Bengal

Bulletin. Botanical Society. College of Science (Nagpur) [*A publication*]......................Bull Bot Soc Coll Sci (Nagpur)

Bulletin. Botanical Society. University of Saugar [*A publication*]........................ Bull Bot Soc Univ Saugar

Bulletin. Botanical Survey of India [*A publication*] ....Bull Bot Surv India

Bulletin of Brewing Science [*A publication*]....................... Bull Brew Sci

Bulletin. British Museum (Natural History). Botany [*A publication*]...........................Bull Br Mus (Nat Hist) Bot

Bulletin. British Museum (Natural History). Entomology [*A publication*]................Bull Br Mus (Nat Hist) Entomol

Bulletin. British Museum (Natural History). Entomology. Supplement [*A publication*] .... Bull Br Mus (Nat Hist) Entomol Suppl

Bulletin. British Museum (Natural History). Geology [*A publication*]...........................Bull Br Mus (Nat Hist) Geol

Bulletin. British Museum (Natural History). Geology. Supplement [*A publication*] .... Bull Br Mus (Nat Hist) Geol Suppl

Bulletin. British Museum (Natural History). Historical Series [*A publication*] .... Bull Br Mus (Nat Hist) Hist Ser

Bulletin. British Museum (Natural History). Zoology [*A publication*] .... Bull Br Mus (Nat Hist) Zool

Bulletin. British Museum (Natural History). Zoology. Supplement [*A publication*] ....Bull Br Mus (Nat Hist) Zool Suppl

Bulletin. British Mycological Society [*A publication*] .... Bull Br Mycol Soc

Bulletin. British Ornithologists' Club [*A publication*] ..... Bull Br Ornithol Club

Bulletin. British Psychological Society [*A publication*] .... B Br Psycho

Bulletin. British Psychological Society [*A publication*] .... Bull B Psych Soc

Bulletin. British Society of Rheology [*A publication*]........... Bull Br Soc Rheol

Bulletin. Brooklyn Entomological Society [*A publication*] .... Bull Brooklyn Entomol Soc

Bulletin. Buddhist Cultural Institute. Ryukoku University [*A publication*]..........................B Buddhist Cult Inst Ryukoku Univ

Bulletin. Buffalo Society of Natural Sciences [*A publication*] .... Bull Buffalo Soc Nat Sci

Bulletin. Bureau of Animal Industry. United States Department of Agriculture [*A publication*].... Bull Bureau Animal Indust US Dept Agric

Bulletin. Bureau of Mineral Resources. Geology and Geophysics (Australia) [*A publication*]..... Bull Bur Miner Resour Geol Geophys (Aust)

Bulletin. Bureau de Recherches Geologiques et Minieres [*France*] [*A publication*] .... Bull Bur Rech Geol Minieres

Bulletin. Bureau de Recherches Geologiques et Minieres. Deuxieme Serie. Section 2. Geologie des Gites Mineraux [*A publication*]..........Bull Bur Rech Geol Minieres Deuxieme Ser Sect 2

Bulletin. Bureau de Recherches Geologiques et Minieres. Deuxieme Serie. Section 3. Hydrogeologie Geologie de l'Ingenieur [*A publication*]........................ Bull Bur Rech Geol Minieres Deuxieme Ser Sect 3

Bulletin. Byzantine Institute [*A publication*].............................. BByzI

Bulletin. Calcutta Mathematical Society [*A publication*]................................. Bull Calcutta Math Soc

Bulletin. Calcutta School of Tropical Medicine [*A publication*]...................... Bull Calcutta Sch Trop Med

Bulletin. California Agricultural Experiment Station [*A publication*]......................... Bull Calif Agr Exp Sta

Bulletin. California Agricultural Experiment Station [*A publication*]........................ Bull Calif Agric Exp Stn

Bulletin. California Department of Agriculture [*A publication*]....................... Bull Calif Dept Agr

Bulletin of the California Insect Survey [*A publication*]....................... Bull Calif Insect Surv

Bulletin of Canadian Petroleum Geology [*A publication*].... Bull Can Pet Geol

Bulletin. Canadian Wheat Board [*A publication*]..........Bull Can Wheat Board

Bulletin du Cancer [*Paris*] [*A publication*]........................B Cancer

Bulletin du Cancer [*Paris*] [*A publication*]........................Bull Cancer

Bulletin du Cancer (Paris) [*A publication*] ....Bull Cancer (Paris)

Bulletin du Cange [*A publication*]...............................BD

Bulletin. Carnegie Museum of Natural History [*A publication*]....................... Bull Carnegie Mus Nat Hist

Bulletin de la Carte et de la Vegetation de la Provence et des Alpes du Sud [*A publication*] ....Bull Carte Veg Provence Alpes Sud

Bulletin. Center for Children's Books [*A publication*] .... Bul Child Bks

Bulletin. Center for Children's Books [*A publication*] .... Bull CCB

Bulletin. Central Food Technological Research Institute (Mysore) [*A publication*].......... Bull Cent Food Technol Res Inst (Mysore)

Bulletin. Central Marine Fisheries Research Institute [*A publication*]....................... Bull Cent Mar Fish Res Inst

Bulletin. Central Mississippi Valley American Studies Association [*A publication*].............................BCMVASA

Bulletin. Central Research Laboratory. Osaka Institute of Technology [*A publication*].............................Bull Central Res Lab OIT

Bulletin. Centre de Documentation d'Etudes Juridiques, Economiques, et Sociales [*A publication*]....................... B Centre Docum Et Jur Econ Soc

Bulletin. Centre d'Etudes et de Discussion de Litterature Francaise. Universite de Bordeaux [*A publication*] .... BCEDLFB

Bulletin. Centre d'Etudes et de Recherches Scientifiques (Biarritz) [*A publication*].........................Bull Cent Etud Rech Sci (Biarritz)

Bulletin. Centre Europeen de la Culture [*A publication*]....................... B Centre Europ Cult

Bulletin. Centre d'Information et d'Etude du Credit [*A publication*].............................B Centre Inform Et Credit

Bulletin. Centre d'Information du Material et des Articles de Bureau [*A publication*]............................. Bull CIMAB

Bulletin. Centre de Physique Nucleaire. Universite Libre de Bruxelles [*A publication*] .... Bull Cent Phys Nucl Univ Lib Bruxelles

Bulletin. Centre Protestant d'Etudes [*A publication*] .... BCPE

Bulletin. Centre de Recherches de Pau [*A publication*] ....Bull Cent Rech Pau

Bulletin. Centres d'Etudes Techniques Agricoles [*A publication*]....................... Bull CETA

Bulletin. Centres de Recherches Exploration-Production ELF Aquitaine [*Formerly, Societe Nationale des Petroles d'Aquitaine. Centre de Recherches de Pau. Bulletin*] [*A publication*]....................Bull Cent Rech Explor ELF Aquitaine

Bulletin. Cercle Archeologique Hesbaye-Condroz [*A publication*] .... Bull Cerc Arch Hesbaye-Condroz

Bulletin. Cercle Archeologique, Litteraire, et Artistique de Malines [*A publication*]....................... BCAM

Bulletin. Cercle Belge de Linguistique [*A publication*]........................,....... BCBL

Bulletin. Cercle d'Etudes des Metaux [*A publication*]....................... Bull Cercle Etud Metaux

Bulletin. Cercle Historique et Archeologique de Courtrai [*A publication*]....................... BCHAC

Bulletin. Cercle Linguistique de Copenhague [*A publication*].............. BCLC

Bulletin. Chemical Society of Japan [*A publication*]....................B Chem S J

Bulletin. Chemical Society of Japan [*A publication*]...... Bull Chem Soc Japan

Bulletin. Chemists and Technologists of Macedonia [*A publication*]....................... Bull Chem Technol Macedonia

Bulletin. Chest Disease Research Institute. Kyoto University [*A publication*]....................Bull Chest Dis Res Inst Kyoto Univ

Bulletin. Chiba-ken Agricultural Experiment Station [*A publication*]....................... Bull Chiba-ken Agr Exp Sta

Bulletin. Chicago Academy of Sciences [*A publication*] .... Bull Chic Acad Sci

Bulletin. Chicago Herpetological Society [*A publication*]....................... Bull Chic Herpetol Soc

Bulletin. Chichibu Museum of Natural History [*A publication*]....................... Bull Chichibu Mus Nat Hist

Bulletin. Chinese Botanical Society [*A publication*]............ Bull Chin Bot Soc

Bulletin of Chinese Studies [*A publication*] .... BCS

Bulletin. Christian Institute of Islamic Studies [*A publication*].............. BCIIS

Bulletin. Chubu Institute of Technology [*A publication*]....................... Bull Chubu Inst Technol

Bulletin. Chugoku National Agricultural Experiment Station [*A publication*].............................Bull Chugoku Agr Exp Sta

Bulletin. Chugoku National Agricultural Experiment Station. Series A (Crop Division) [*A publication*]....................... Bull Chugoku Natl Agric Exp Stn Ser A

Bulletin. Chugoku National Agricultural Experiment Station. Series A (Crop Division) [*A publication*]....................... Bull Chugoku Natl Agric Exp Stn Ser A (Crop Div)

Bulletin. Chugoku National Agricultural Experiment Station. Series B (Livestock Division) [*A publication*]....................... Bull Chugoku Natl Agric Exp Stn Ser B

Bulletin. Chugoku National Agricultural Experiment Station. Series E (Environment Division) [*A publication*]....................... Bull Chugoku Natl Agric Exp Stn Ser E

Bulletin. Cincinnati Dental Society [*A publication*] ....Bull Cinci Dent Soc

Bulletin. Cincinnati Historical Society [*A publication*] ....BCHS

Bulletin. Classe des Lettres et des Sciences Morales et Politiques. Academie Royale de Belgique [A publication] .... B Acad Roy Belg

Bulletin. Classe des Sciences. Academie Royale de Belgique [A publication] .... B CSAR Belg

Bulletin. Classe des Sciences. Academie Royale de Belgique [A publication] .... Bull Classe Sci Acad Roy Belg

Bulletin. Classe des Sciences. Academie Royale de Belgique [A publication] .... Bull Cl Sci Acad R Belg

Bulletin. Classe des Sciences. Academie Royale de Belgique [A publication] .... Bull Cl Sci Acad Royale Belg

Bulletin. Classe des Sciences. Academie Royale de Belgique. 5e Serie [A publication] .... Bull Cl Sci Acad R Belg 5e Ser

Bulletin. Clemson Agricultural Experiment Station [A publication] .... Bull Clemson Agr Exp Sta

Bulletin. Cleveland Museum of Art [A publication] .... B Cleveland Mus Art

Bulletin. Cleveland Museum of Art [A publication] .... BCMA

Bulletin. Coconut Research Institute (Ceylon) [A publication] .... Bull Cocon Res Inst (Ceylon)

Bulletin. College of Agricultural Sciences (Mosonmagyarovar, Hungary) [A publication] ..... Bull Coll Agric Sci (Mosonmagyarovar Hung)

Bulletin. College of Agriculture and Forestry. University of Nanking [A publication] .... Bull Coll Agr Forest Univ Nanking

Bulletin. College of Agriculture. University of Teheran [A publication] .... Bull Coll Agric Univ Teheran

Bulletin. College of Agriculture. Utsunomiya University [A publication] .... Bull Coll Agric Utsunomiya Univ

Bulletin. College of Agriculture. Utsunomiya University [A publication] .... Bull Coll Agr Utsunomiya Univ

Bulletin. College of Agriculture and Veterinary Medicine. Nihon University [A publication] .... Bull Coll Agric Vet Med Nihon Univ

Bulletin. College of Foreign Studies. Yokohama. Natural Science [A publication] .... Bull Coll Foreign Stud Yokohama Nat Sci

Bulletin. College of General Education. Nagoya City University. Natural Science Section [A publication] .... Bull Coll Gen Educ Nagoya City Univ Nat Sci Sect

Bulletin. College of Science (Baghdad) [A publication] .... Bull College Sci (Baghdad)

Bulletin. College of Science. Part 1 [Baghdad] [A publication] .... Bull Coll Sci 1

Bulletin. College of Science. University of Baghdad [A publication] .... Bull Coll Sci Univ Baghdad

Bulletin. Colorado Agricultural Experiment Station [A publication] .... Bull Colo Agr Exp Sta

Bulletin. Colorado Agricultural Experiment Station [A publication] .... Bull Colo Agric Exp Stn

Bulletin. Colorado Department of Agriculture [A publication] .... Bull Colo Dept Agr

Bulletin. Colorado State University. Agricultural Experiment Station [A publication] .... Bull Colo State Univ Agr Exp Sta

Bulletin of the Comediantes [A publication] .... BC

Bulletin of the Comediantes [A publication] .... B Com

Bulletin. Comite Flamand de France [A publication] .... BCFF

Bulletin. Comite des Forets [A publication] .... Bull Com For

Bulletin. Commission Archeologique de Narbonne [A publication] ......BCAN

Bulletin. Commission Archeologique de Narbonne [A publication] .... Bull Comm Arch Narbonne

Bulletin. Commission Geologique de Finlande [A publication] .... Bull Comm Geol Finl

Bulletin. Commission Nationale de la Republique Populaire Roumaine pour l'UNESCO [A publication] ....BR UNESCO

Bulletin. Commission Royale d'Histoire [A publication] ....BCRH

Bulletin. Commission Royale de Toponymie et de Dialectologie [A publication] .... BCRTD

Bulletin. Commission Royale de Toponymie et de Dialectologie [A publication] .... BCTD

Bulletin. Commission Royale de Toponymie et de Dialectologie [A publication] .... BTD

Bulletin. Commissions Royales d'Art et d'Archeologie [A publication] .... BCRAA

Bulletin. Commonwealth Bureau of Pastures and Field Crops [A publication] ....Bull Commonw Bur Past Fld Crops

Bulletin. Commonwealth Scientific and Industrial Research Organization [A publication] .... Bull Commonw Scient Ind Res Org

Bulletin des Communautes Europeenes [A publication] ....B Commun Europ

Bulletin of Concerned Asian Scholars [A publication] .... Asian Sch

Bulletin of Concerned Asian Scholars [A publication] .... B Con As Sc

Bulletin of Concerned Asian Scholars [A publication] .... B Concern As Schol

Bulletin of Concerned Asian Scholars [A publication] .... B Concerned Asian Scholars

Bulletin de Conjoncture Regionale [A publication] .... B Conjonct Region

Bulletin de Conjoncture Regionale. Supplement [A publication] .... B Conjoncture Suppl

Bulletin. Connecticut Agricultural Experiment Station [A publication] .... Bull Conn Agr Exp Sta

Bulletin. Connecticut Agricultural Experiment Station [A publication] .... Bull Conn Agric Exp Sta

Bulletin pour la Conservation des Monuments Historiques d'Alsace [A publication] .... BMHA

Bulletin. Copyright Society of the USA [A publication] .... B Copyrgt S

Bulletin. Copyright Society of the USA [A publication] .... Bull Cr Soc

Bulletin. Cornell University Agricultural Experiment Station [A publication] .... Bull Cornell Univ Agric Exp Stn

Bulletin de Correspondance Hellenique [A publication] ....BCH

Bulletin de Correspondance Hellenique [A publication] .... Bul Corresp Hellenique

Bulletin de Correspondance Hellenique. Supplement [A publication] .... BCH Supp

Bulletin. Council for Research in Music Education [A publication] .... Bull Council Res Mus Educ

Bulletin Critique [A publication] .... BC

Bulletin Critique du Livre Francais [A publication] .... BCLF

Bulletin Critique du Livre Francais [A publication] .... BCr

Bulletin de Cultures Ethniques et de Civilisations Comparees [A publication] .... BCECC

Bulletin. Debating Association of Pennsylvania Colleges [A publication] .... BDAPC

Bulletin. Deccan College Research Institute [A publication] .... BDC

Bulletin. Deccan College Research Institute [A publication] .... B Deccan Coll Res Inst

Bulletin. Department of Agricultural Economics. University of Manchester [A publication] ....Bull Dept Agr Econ Univ Manchester

Bulletin. Department of Agricultural Technical Services (Republic of South Africa) [A publication] .... Bull Dept Agr Tech Serv (Repub S Afr)

Bulletin. Department of Agricultural Technical Services (Transvaal) [A publication] ....Bull Dep Agric Tech Serv (Transv)

Bulletin. Department of Agriculture and Industries (Western Australia) [A publication] ....Bull Dept Agric and Indust (West Australia)

Bulletin. Department of Agriculture. Mysore State. Entomology Series [A publication] .... Bull Dept Agr Mysore Entomol Ser

Bulletin. Department of Agriculture (Tanganyika) [A publication] .... Bull Dept Agr (Tanganyika)

Bulletin. Department of Agriculture (Trinidad and Tobago) [A publication] ....B Dept Ag (Trinidad)

Bulletin. Department of Archaeology and Anthropology [Taipei] [A publication] .... B Dept Archaeol Anthropol

Bulletin. Department of English (Calcutta) [A publication] ....BDEC

Bulletin. Department of Forestry (Pretoria, South Africa) [A publication] ....Bull Dep For (S Afr)

Bulletin. Department of Forestry. University of Ibadan [A publication] .... Bull Dep For Univ Ibadan

Bulletin. Department of General Education. Nagoya City University (Natural Science Section) [A publication] .... Bull Dept Gen Educ Nagoya City Univ (Nat Sci Sect)

Bulletin. Department of General Education. Tokyo Medical and Dental University [A publication] .... Bull Dep Gen Educ Tokyo Med Dent Univ

Bulletin. Department of Scientific and Industrial Research (New Zealand) [A publication] .... Bull Dep Sci Ind Res (NZ)

Bulletin. Department of Sociology (Okinawa) [A publication] .... B Dept Sociol (Okinawa)

Bulletin. Department of Zoology. University of the Punjab [A publication] ....Bull Dep Zool Univ Punjab

Bulletin du Dictionnaire Wallon [A publication] .... BDW

Bulletin. Direction des Etudes et Recherches. Serie A [A publication] ....Bull Dir Etud & Rech A

Bulletin. Direction des Etudes et Recherches. Serie A [A publication] .... Bull Dir Etud & Rech Ser A

Bulletin. Direction des Etudes et Recherches. Serie B [A publication] ....Bull Dir Etud & Rech B

Bulletin. Direction des Etudes et Recherches. Serie B [A publication] .... Bull Dir Etud & Rech Ser B

Bulletin. Direction des Etudes et Recherches. Serie C [A publication] ....Bull Dir Etud & Rech C

Bulletin. Direction des Etudes et Recherches. Serie C [A publication] .... Bull Dir Etud & Rech Ser C

Bulletin. Division of Human Relations [A publication] ....B Divis Hum Relat

Bulletin. Division of Mineral Resources (Virginia) [A publication].................... Bull Div Miner Resour (VA)

Bulletin. Division of Plant Industry. New South Wales Department of Agriculture [A publication].................... Bull Div Plant Ind NSW Dept Agr

Bulletin. Division of Silviculture. Department of Forests of Papua and New Guinea [A publication].................... Bull Div Silv Dep For Papua & N Guinea

Bulletin de Documentation. Association Internationale des Fabricants de Superphosphates [A publication] .... Bull Docum Ass Int Fabr Superphos

Bulletin de Documentation Bibliographique [A publication] .... Bul Doc Bibliog

Bulletin de Documentation Bibliographique [A publication] .... Bull Doc Bibliog

Bulletin de Documentation Pratique de Securite Sociale et de Legislation du Travail [A publication] .... B Docum Prat Secur Soc Legisl Trav

Bulletin: the Dolmetsch Foundation [A publication]....................Dolmetsch B

Bulletin. Dominion of Canada. Department of Agriculture [A publication]....................Bull Canada Dept Agric

Bulletin de Droit Nucleaire [A publication].............................. Bull Droit Nucl

Bulletin de Droit Tchecoslovaque [A publication] .... B Dr Tchecosl

Bulletin. Duke University School of Forestry [*A publication*] .... Bull Duke Univ Sch For
Bulletin. Earthquake Research Institute. University of Tokyo [*A publication*] .... Bull Earthquake Res Inst Univ Tokyo
Bulletin. Ecole Francaise d'Extreme-Orient [*A publication*] .... B Ecole Fr Ex Or
Bulletin. Ecole Francaise d'Extreme-Orient [*A publication*] .... BEFEO
Bulletin. Ecole Nationale Superieure d'Agronomie et des Industries Alimentaires [*A publication*] .... Bull Ec Natl Super Agron Ind Aliment
Bulletin. Ecole Nationale Superieure Agronomique de Nancy [*A publication*] .... Bull Ec Natl Super Agron Nancy
Bulletin. Ecole Nationale Superieure Agronomique de Nancy [*A publication*] .... Bull Ecole Nat Super Agron Nancy
Bulletin. Ecole Superieure d'Agriculture de Tunis [*A publication*] .... Bull Ecole Super Agr Tunis
Bulletin. Ecological Society of America [*A publication*] .... Bull Ecol Soc Amer
Bulletin d'Ecologie [*A publication*] .... Bull Ecol
Bulletin of Economic Research [*A publication*] .... B Econ Res
Bulletin Economique pour l'Europe [*A publication*] .... B Econ Europe
Bulletin Economique Mensuelle [*A publication*] .... Bull Econom
Bulletin Economique et Social du Maroc [*A publication*] .... B Econ Soc Maroc
Bulletin. Edinburgh School of Agriculture [*A publication*] .... Bull Edinburgh Sch Agr
Bulletin. Ehime Agricultural Experiment Station [*A publication*] .... Bull Ehime Agr Exp Sta
Bulletin. Ehime University Forest [*A publication*] .... Bull Ehime Univ For
Bulletin. Electrotechnical Laboratory (Tokyo) [*A publication*] .... Bull Electrotech Lab (Tokyo)
Bulletin of Endemic Diseases [*A publication*] .... Bull Endem Dis
Bulletin of Endemic Diseases (Baghdad) [*A publication*] .... Bull Endem Dis (Baghdad)
Bulletin des Engrais [*A publication*] .... Bull Engrais
Bulletin of Entomological Research [*A publication*] .... B Ent Res
Bulletin of Entomological Research [*A publication*] .... Bull Entomol Res
Bulletin of Entomological Research [*A publication*] .... Bull Ent Res
Bulletin. Entomological Society of America [*A publication*] .... Bull Entomol Soc Am
Bulletin. Entomological Society of America [*A publication*] .... Bull Entomol Soc Amer
Bulletin. Entomological Society of Egypt. Economic Series [*A publication*] .... Bull Entomol Soc Egypt Econ Ser
Bulletin. Entomological Society of Nigeria [*A publication*] .... Bull Entomol Soc Nigeria
Bulletin of Entomology [*A publication*] .... Bull Entomol
Bulletin of Environmental Contamination and Toxicology [*A publication*] .... B Envir Con
Bulletin of Environmental Contamination and Toxicology [*A publication*] .... Bull Environ Contam Toxicol
Bulletin of Environmental Education [*A publication*] .... BEE
Bulletin of Epizootic Diseases of Africa [*A publication*] .... Bull Epizoot Dis Afr
Bulletin de l'Etude en Commun de la Mediterranee [*A publication*] .... Bull Etud Commun Mediter
Bulletin des Etudes Arabes [*A publication*] .... BEA
Bulletin des Etudes Francaises [*A publication*] .... BEF
Bulletin d'Etudes Orientales [*A publication*] .... BEO
Bulletin d'Etudes Orientales [*A publication*] .... B Et Orient
Bulletin des Etudes Portugaises et de l'Institut Francais au Portugal [*A publication*] .... BEP
Bulletin des Etudes Portugaises et de l'Institut Francais au Portugal [*A publication*] .... BEPIF
Bulletin. European Society of Human Genetics [*A publication*] .... B Eur S Hum
Bulletin Europeen de Physiopathologie Respiratoire [*A publication*] .... Bull Eur Physiopathol Respir
Bulletin of the Experiment Forest. Tokyo University of Agriculture and Technology [*A publication*] .... Bull Exp For Tokyo Univ Agric Technol
Bulletin of Experimental Biology and Medicine [*A publication*] .... B Exp B Med
Bulletin of Experimental Biology and Medicine [*A publication*] .... Bull Exp Biol Med
Bulletin. Experimental Station for Horse Breeding (Slatinany) [*A publication*] .... Bull Exp Stn Horse Breed (Slatinany)
Bulletin. Faculte des Lettres de Lille [*A publication*] .... BFL
Bulletin. Faculte des Lettres de Strasbourg [*A publication*] .... BFLS
Bulletin. Faculte des Lettres de Strasbourg [*A publication*] .... BFS
Bulletin. Faculte de Medecine d'Istanbul [*A publication*] .... Bull Fac Med Istanbul
Bulletin. Facultes Catholiques de Lyon [*A publication*] .... BFCL
Bulletin. Faculty of Agricultural Sciences (Mosonmagyarovar, Hungary) [*A publication*] .... Bull Fac Agric Sci (Mosonmagyarovar Hung)
Bulletin. Faculty of Agriculture. Hirosaki University [*A publication*] .... Bull Fac Agric Hirosaki Univ
Bulletin. Faculty of Agriculture. Kagoshima University [*A publication*] .... Bull Fac Agric Kagoshima Univ
Bulletin. Faculty of Agriculture. Kagoshima University [*A publication*] .... Bull Fac Agr Kagoshima Univ
Bulletin. Faculty of Agriculture. Meiji University [*A publication*] .... Bull Fac Agric Meiji Univ
Bulletin. Faculty of Agriculture. Meiji University [*A publication*] .... Bull Fac Agr Meiji Univ
Bulletin. Faculty of Agriculture. Mie University [*A publication*] .... Bull Fac Agric Mie Univ
Bulletin. Faculty of Agriculture. Miyazaki University [*A publication*] .... Bull Fac Agric Miyazaki Univ
Bulletin. Faculty of Agriculture. Niigata University [*A publication*] .... Bull Fac Agric Niigata Univ
Bulletin. Faculty of Agriculture. Niigata University [*A publication*] .... Bull Fac Agr Niigata Univ
Bulletin. Faculty of Agriculture. Shimane University [*A publication*] .... Bull Fac Agric Shimane Univ
Bulletin. Faculty of Agriculture. Shimane University [*A publication*] .... Bull Fac Agr Shimane Univ
Bulletin. Faculty of Agriculture. Shizuoka University [*A publication*] .... Bull Fac Agric Shizuoka Univ
Bulletin. Faculty of Agriculture. Shizuoka University [*A publication*] .... Bull Fac Agr Shizuoka Univ
Bulletin. Faculty of Agriculture. Tamagawa University [*A publication*] .... Bull Fac Agric Tamagawa Univ
Bulletin. Faculty of Agriculture. Tokyo University of Agriculture and Technology [*A publication*] .... Bull Fac Agric Tokyo Univ Agric Technol
Bulletin. Faculty of Agriculture. Tottori University [*A publication*] .... Bull Fac Agric Tottori Univ
Bulletin. Faculty of Agriculture. University of Miyazaki [*A publication*] .... Bull Fac Agr Univ Miyazaki
Bulletin. Faculty of Agriculture. Yamaguchi University [*A publication*] .... Bull Fac Agr Yamaguchi Univ
Bulletin. Faculty of Agriculture. Yamaguti University [*A publication*] .... Bull Fac Agric Yamaguti Univ
Bulletin. Faculty of Arts. University of Egypt [*Cairo*] [*A publication*] .... BFA
Bulletin. Faculty of Arts. University of Egypt [*Cairo*] [*A publication*] .... BUE
Bulletin. Faculty of Arts. University of Egypt (Cairo) [*A publication*] .... BFAC
Bulletin. Faculty of Education. Hirosaki University [*A publication*] .... Bull Fac Educ Hirosaki Univ
Bulletin. Faculty of Education. Hiroshima University [*A publication*] .... Bull Fac Educ Hiroshima Univ
Bulletin. Faculty of Education. Hiroshima University. Part 3 (Science and Technology) [*A publication*] .... Bull Fac Educ Hiroshima Univ Part 3 (Sci Tech)
Bulletin. Faculty of Education. Kanazawa University. Natural Science [*A publication*] .... Bull Fac Educ Kanazawa Univ Nat Sci
Bulletin. Faculty of Education. Kobe University [*A publication*] .... Bull Fac Educ Kobe Univ
Bulletin. Faculty of Education. Kochi University. Series 3 [*A publication*] .... Bull Fac Educ Kochi Univ Ser 3
Bulletin. Faculty of Education. University of Kagoshima [*A publication*] .... Bull Fac Ed Univ Kagoshima
Bulletin. Faculty of Education. University of Kagoshima. Natural Science [*A publication*] .... Bull Fac Educ Univ Kagoshima Nat Sci
Bulletin. Faculty of Education. Utsunomiya University. Section 2 [*A publication*] .... Bull Fac Educ Utsunomiya Univ Sect 2
Bulletin. Faculty of Education. Utsunomiya University. Section 2 [*A publication*] .... Bull Fac Ed Utsunomiya Univ Sect 2
Bulletin. Faculty of Education. Wakayama University. Natural Science [*A publication*] .... Bull Fac Educ Wakayama Univ Nat Sci
Bulletin. Faculty of Education. Yamaguchi University [*A publication*] .... Bull Fac Educ Yamaguchi Univ
Bulletin. Faculty of Engineering. Hiroshima University [*A publication*] .... Bull Fac Eng Hiroshima Univ
Bulletin. Faculty of Engineering. Hiroshima University [*A publication*] .... Bull Fac Engrg Hiroshima Univ
Bulletin. Faculty of Engineering. Hokkaido University [*A publication*] .... Bull Fac Eng Hokkaido Univ
Bulletin. Faculty of Engineering. Ibaraki University [*A publication*] .... Bull Fac Eng Ibaraki Univ
Bulletin. Faculty of Engineering. Miyazaki University [*A publication*] .... Bull Fac Eng Miyazaki Univ
Bulletin. Faculty of Engineering. Miyazaki University [*A publication*] .... Bull Fac Engrg Miyazaki Univ
Bulletin. Faculty of Engineering. Tokushima University [*A publication*] .... Bull Fac Eng Tokushima Univ
Bulletin. Faculty of Engineering. Yokohama National University [*A publication*] .... Bull Fac Eng Yokohama Natl Univ
Bulletin. Faculty of Fisheries. Hokkaido University [*A publication*] .... Bull Fac Fish Hokkaido Univ
Bulletin. Faculty of Forestry. University of British Columbia [*A publication*] .... Bull Fac For Univ BC
Bulletin. Faculty of General Education. Utsunomiya University. Section 2 [*A publication*] .... Bull Fac Gen Educ Utsunomiya Univ Sect 2
Bulletin. Faculty of Liberal Arts. Ibaraki University (Natural Science) [*A publication*] .... Bull Fac Lib Arts Ibaraki Univ (Nat Sci)
Bulletin. Faculty of Pharmacy. Cairo University [*A publication*] .... Bull Fac Pharm Cairo Univ
Bulletin. Faculty of Pharmacy. Kinki University [*A publication*] .... Bull Fac Pharm Kinki Univ
Bulletin. Faculty of Science. Assiut University [*A publication*] .... Bull Fac Sci Assiut Univ
Bulletin. Faculty of Science (Cairo) [*A publication*] .... Bull Fac Sci (Cairo)

Bulletin. Faculty of Science. Cairo University [*A publication*] .... Bull Fac Sci Cairo Univ
Bulletin. Faculty of Science and Engineering. Chuo University [*A publication*] .... Bull Fac Sci Eng Chuo Univ
Bulletin. Faculty of Science and Engineering. Chuo University [*A publication*] .... Bull Fac Sci Engrg Chuo Univ
Bulletin. Faculty of Science. Ibaraki University. Series A. Mathematics [*A publication*] .... Bull Fac Sci Ibaraki Univ Series A
Bulletin. Far Seas Fisheries Research Laboratory (Shimizu) [*A publication*] .... Bull Far Seas Fish Res Lab (Shimizu)
Bulletin. Federal Ministry of Agriculture (Salisbury) [*A publication*] .... Bull Fed Min Agr (Salisbury)
Bulletin. Federation des Societes de Gynecologie et d'Obstetrique de Langue Francaise [*A publication*] .... Bull Fed Soc Gynecol Obstet Lang Fr
Bulletin. Federation des Societes d'Histoire Naturelle de Franche-Comte [*A publication*] .... Bull Fed Soc Hist Nat Franche-Comte
Bulletin. Fisheries Research Board of Canada [*A publication*] .... Bull Fish Res Board Can
Bulletin. Fisheries Research Station (Ceylon) [*A publication*] .... Bull Fish Res Stn (Ceylon)
Bulletin. Florida Agricultural Experiment Station [*A publication*] .... Bull Fla Agr Exp Sta
Bulletin. Florida Agricultural Experiment Station [*A publication*] .... Bull Fla Agric Exp Stn
Bulletin. Florida Department of Agriculture. Division of Plant Industry [*A publication*] .... Bull Fla Dept Agr Div Plant Ind
Bulletin. Florida State Museum. Biological Sciences [*A publication*] .... Bull Fla State Mus Biol Sci
Bulletin. Florida University Agricultural Experiment Station [*A publication*] .... Bull Fla Univ Agr Exp Sta
Bulletin. Fogg Art Museum [*A publication*] .... BFAM
Bulletin Folklorique d'Ile-de-France [*A publication*] .... BFIF
Bulletin. Fonds de Recherches Forestieres. Universite Laval [*A publication*] .... Bull Fonds Rech For Univ Laval
Bulletin. Food Industrial Experiment Station. Hiroshima Prefecture [*A publication*] .... Bull Food Ind Exp Stn Hiroshima Prefect
Bulletin. Ford Forestry Center [*A publication*] .... Bull Ford For Cent
Bulletin. Foreign Language Association of Virginia [*A publication*] .... BFLAV
Bulletin. Forest Department. Kampala (Uganda) [*A publication*] .... Bull For Dep (Uganda)
Bulletin. Forest Products Research. Ministry of Technology (London) [*A publication*] .... Bull For Prod Res (Lond)
Bulletin. Forestry Commission (London) [*A publication*] .... Bull For Comm (Lond)
Bulletin. Forestry Commission of Tasmania [*A publication*] .... Bull For Comm Tasm
Bulletin. Forestry and Timber Bureau (Canberra, Australia) [*A publication*] .... Bull For Timb Bur (Aust)
Bulletin. Forests Commission of Victoria [*A publication*] .... Bull For Comm Vict
Bulletin. Forests Department of Western Australia [*A publication*] .... Bull For Dep W Aust
Bulletin. Forests Department of Western Australia [*A publication*] .... Bull For Dep West Aust
Bulletin Francais de Pisciculture [*A publication*] .... Bull Fr Piscic
Bulletin. Freshwater Fisheries Research Laboratory (Tokyo) [*A publication*] .... Bull Freshw Fish Res Lab (Tokyo)
Bulletin. Friends Historical Association [*A publication*] .... BFHA
Bulletin. Fruit Tree Research Station. Series A (Hiratsuka) [*A publication*] .... Bull Fruit Tree Res Stn Ser A (Hiratsuka)
Bulletin. Fruit Tree Research Station. Series B (Okitsu) [*A publication*] .... Bull Fruit Tree Res Stn Ser B (Okitsu)
Bulletin. Fruit Tree Research Station. Series C (Morioka) [*A publication*] .... Bull Fruit Tree Res Stn Ser C (Morioka)
Bulletin. Fuji Women's College [*A publication*] .... Bull Fuji Women's Coll
Bulletin. Fukuoka Agricultural Experiment Station [*A publication*] .... Bull Fukuoka Agr Exp Stn
Bulletin. Fukuoka Prefectural Agricultural Experiment Station [*A publication*] .... Bull Fukuoka Pref Agr Exp Sta
Bulletin. Fukuoka University of Education. Part 3. Natural Sciences [*A publication*] .... Bull Fukuoka Univ Educ Part 3 Nat Sci
Bulletin. Fukuoka University of Education. Part III. Natural Sciences [*A publication*] .... Bull Fukuoka Univ Ed III
Bulletin. Fukuokaken Forest Experiment Station [*A publication*] .... Bull Fukuokaken For Exp Sta
Bulletin. Fukushima Prefectural Fisheries Experimental Station [*A publication*] .... Bull Fukushima Prefect Fish Exp Stn
Bulletin. Geisinger Medical Center [*A publication*] .... Bull Geisinger Med Cent
Bulletin General. Therapeutique Medicale, Chirurgicale, et Obstetricale (Paris) [*A publication*] .... Bull Gen Therap (Paris)
Bulletin Geodesique [*A publication*] .... Bull Geod
Bulletin. Geographical Survey Institute [*A publication*] .... Bull Geogr Surv Inst
Bulletin. Geological Institute. Bulgarian Academy of Sciences. Series Geotectonics [*A publication*] .... Bull Geol Inst Bulg Acad Sci Ser Geotecton
Bulletin. Geological Institutions of the University of Uppsala [*A publication*] .... Bull Geol Inst Univ Upps
Bulletin. Geological Society of Denmark [*A publication*] .... Bull Geol Soc Den
Bulletin. Geological Society of Finland [*A publication*] .... Bull Geol Soc Finl
Bulletin. Geological Society of Turkey [*A publication*] .... Bull Geol Soc Turk
Bulletin. Geological Survey of Canada [*A publication*] .... Bull Geol Surv Can
Bulletin. Geological Survey of Great Britain [*A publication*] .... Bull Geol Surv GB
Bulletin. Geological Survey of Greenland [*A publication*] .... Bull Geol Surv Greenland
Bulletin. Geological Survey of Guyana [*A publication*] .... Bull Geol Surv Guyana
Bulletin. Geological Survey of India. Series A. Economic Geology [*A publication*] .... Bull Geol Surv India A
Bulletin. Geological Survey of Israel [*A publication*] .... Bull Geol Surv Israel
Bulletin. Geological Survey of Japan [*A publication*] .... Bull Geol Surv Jpn
Bulletin. Geological Survey of Prague [*A publication*] .... Bull Geol Surv Prague
Bulletin. Geological Survey of Rhodesia [*A publication*] .... Bull Geol Surv Rhod
Bulletin. Geological Survey of South Australia [*A publication*] .... Bull Geol Surv S Aust
Bulletin. Geological Survey of Taiwan [*A publication*] .... Bull Geol Surv Taiwan
Bulletin. Geological Survey of Tanzania [*A publication*] .... Bull Geol Surv Tanz
Bulletin. Geological Survey of Western Australia [*A publication*] .... Bull Geol Surv West Aust
Bulletin. Geologiska Institut. Universitet Upsala [*A publication*] .... Bull Geol Inst Univ Ups
Bulletin de Geophysique [*A publication*] .... Bull Geophys
Bulletin. Georgia Academy of Science [*A publication*] .... Bull GA Acad Sci
Bulletin. Georgia Agricultural Experiment Station [*A publication*] .... Bull GA Agr Exp Sta
Bulletin. Georgia Agricultural Experiment Station [*A publication*] .... Bull GA Agric Exp Stn
Bulletin. Gifu College of Education [*A publication*] .... Bull Gifu College E
Bulletin. Government Forest Experiment Station [*Tokyo*] [*A publication*] .... Bull Govt Forest Expt Sta
Bulletin. Government Forest Experiment Station (Meguro) [*A publication*] .... Bull For Exp Sta (Meguro)
Bulletin. Government Forest Experiment Station (Tokyo) [*A publication*] .... Bull Gov For Exp Stn (Tokyo)
Bulletin. Government Industrial Research Institute (Osaka) [*A publication*] .... Bull Gov Ind Res Inst (Osaka)
Bulletin of Grain Technology [*A publication*] .... Bull Grain Technol
Bulletin. Groupe Francais des Argiles [*A publication*] .... Bull Grpe Fr Argiles
Bulletin. Groupe de Travail pour l'Etude de l'Equilibre Foret-Gibier [*A publication*] .... Bull Groupe Trav Etud Equilibre Foret-Gibier
Bulletin. Groupement International pour la Recherche Scientifique en Stomatologie [*A publication*] .... Bull Group Int Rech Sci Stomatol
Bulletin. Groupement International pour la Recherche Scientifique en Stomatologie et Odontologie [*A publication*] .... Bull Group Int Rech Sci Stomatol Odontol
Bulletin. Haffkine Institute [*A publication*] .... Bull Haffkine Inst
Bulletin. Hatano Tobacco Experiment Station [*A publication*] .... Bull Hatano Tob Exp Stn
Bulletin. Heart Institute of Japan [*A publication*] .... Bull Hear Inst Jpn
Bulletin. Hellenic Veterinary Medical Society [*A publication*] .... Bull Hell Vet Med Soc
Bulletin of High Points [*A publication*] .... B H Points
Bulletin. Highway Research Board [*A publication*] .... Bull Highw Res Bd
Bulletin. Hiroshima Agricultural College [*A publication*] .... Bull Hiroshima Agric Coll
Bulletin. Hiroshima Food Research Institute [*A publication*] .... Bull Hiroshima Food Res Inst
Bulletin. Hiroshima Jogakuin College [*A publication*] .... Bull Hiroshima Jogakuin Coll
Bulletin. Hiroshima Prefectural Agricultural Experiment Station [*A publication*] .... Bull Hiroshima Prefect Agric Exp Stn
Bulletin of Hispanic Studies [*A publication*] .... BHS
Bulletin Hispanique [*A publication*] .... BH
Bulletin Hispanique [*A publication*] .... BHi
Bulletin Hispanique [*A publication*] .... BHisp
Bulletin Hispanique [*A publication*] .... BIH
Bulletin Hispanique [*A publication*] .... Bull Hisp
Bulletin d'Histoire du Theatre Portugais [*A publication*] .... BHTP
Bulletin. Historical Metallurgy Group [*A publication*] .... Bull Hist Metal Group
Bulletin. Historical and Philosophical Society of Ohio [*A publication*] .... BHPSO
Bulletin. Historical Society of Montgomery County [*A publication*] .... BHSM
Bulletin. Historical Society of Montgomery County [*A publication*] .... BHSMCo
Bulletin Historique. Diocese de Lyon [*A publication*] .... BHDL
Bulletin Historique et Litteraire. Societe de l'Histoire du Protestantisme Francais [*A publication*] .... BHPF
Bulletin Historique et Philologique. Comite des Travaux Historiques et Scientifiques [*A publication*] .... BHPCTHS
Bulletin Historique. Societe des Antiquitaires de la Morinie [*A publication*] .... BHSAM
Bulletin of the History of Dentistry [*A publication*] .... Bull Hist Dent
Bulletin of the History of Medicine [*A publication*] .... B Hist Med
Bulletin of the History of Medicine [*A publication*] .... BHM

Bulletin of the History of Medicine [*A publication*] ..... Bull Hist Med
Bulletin. Hokkaido Forest Experiment Station [*A publication*] ..... Bull Hokkaido For Exp Stn
Bulletin. Hokkaido Prefectural Agricultural Experiment Station [*A publication*] ..... Bull Hokkaido Pref Agr Exp Sta
Bulletin. Hokkaido Prefectural Agricultural Experiment Station [*A publication*] ..... Bull Hokkaido Prefect Agric Exp Stn
Bulletin. Hokkaido Regional Fisheries Research Laboratories [*A publication*] ..... Bull Hokkaido Reg Fish Res Lab
Bulletin. Hokuriku National Agricultural Experiment Station [*A publication*] ..... Bull Hokuriku Natl Agric Exp Stn
Bulletin Horticole (Liege) [*A publication*] ..... Bull Hortic (Liege)
Bulletin. Hospital for Joint Diseases [*A publication*] ..... Bull Hosp Joint Dis
Bulletin. Hospital for Joint Diseases [*A publication*] ..... Bull Hosp Jt Dis
Bulletin. Hot Spring Research Institute. Kanagawa Prefecture [*A publication*] ..... Bull Hot Spring Res Inst Kanagawa Prefect
Bulletin. Hudson County Dental Society [*A publication*] ..... Bull Hudson Cty Dent Soc
Bulletin of Human Body Measurement [*A publication*] ..... Bull Hum Body Meas
Bulletin of Hygiene [*A publication*] ..... Bull Hyg
Bulletin de l'Hygiene Professionnelle [*A publication*] ..... Bull Hyg Prof
Bulletin. Hygienic Laboratory. United States Marine Hospital Service [*A publication*] ..... Bull Hyg Lab US Mar Hosp Serv
Bulletin. Hygienic Laboratory. United States Public Health and Marine-Hospital Service [*A publication*] ..... Bull Hyg Lab US Pub Health and Mar-Hosp Serv
Bulletin. Hygienic Laboratory. United States Public Health Service [*A publication*] ..... Bull Hyg Lab US Pub Health Serv
Bulletin. Hyogo Prefectural Agricultural Center for Experiment, Extension, and Education [*A publication*] ..... Bull Hyogo Prefect Agric Cent Exp Ext Educ
Bulletin. Hyogo Prefectural Agricultural Experiment Station [*A publication*] ..... Bull Hyogo Pref Agr Exp Sta
Bulletin. Hyogo Prefectural Forest Experiment Station [*A publication*] ..... Bull Hyogo Prefect For Exp Stn
Bulletin. Ibaraki Prefectural Forest Experiment Station [*A publication*] ..... Bull Ibaraki Prefect For Exp Stn
Bulletin. Idaho Agricultural Experiment Station [*A publication*] ..... Bull Idaho Agr Exp Sta
Bulletin. Idaho Bureau of Mines and Geology [*A publication*] ..... Bull Idaho Bur Mines Geol
Bulletin. Illinois Agricultural Experiment Station [*A publication*] ..... Bull Ill Agr Exp Sta
Bulletin. Illinois Foreign Language Teachers Association [*A publication*] ..... BIFLTA
Bulletin. Illinois State Laboratory of Natural History [*A publication*] ..... Bull Ill St Lab Nat Hist
Bulletin. Imperial Bureau of Pastures and Forage Crops [*A publication*] ..... Bull Imp Bur Pastures Forage Crops
Bulletin of Independent Biological Laboratories (Kefar-Malal) [*A publication*] ..... Bull Indep Biol Lab (Kefar-Malal)
Bulletin. Indian Council of Agricultural Research [*A publication*] ..... Bull Indian Coun Agric Res
Bulletin. Indian National Science Academy [*A publication*] ..... Bull Indian Natl Sci Acad
Bulletin. Indian Phytopathological Society [*A publication*] ..... Bull Indian Phytopathol Soc
Bulletin. Indian Society for Malaria and Other Communicable Diseases [*A publication*] ..... Bull Indian Soc Malar Commun Dis
Bulletin. Indian Society of Soil Science [*A publication*] ..... Bull Indian Soc Soil Sci
Bulletin of Indonesian Economic Studies [*A publication*] ..... B Indo Econ Stud
Bulletin of Indonesian Economic Studies [*A publication*] ..... B Indones Econ Stud
Bulletin of Indonesian Economic Studies [*Canberra*] [*A publication*] ..... IESB
Bulletin. Infirmieres Catholiques du Canada [*A publication*] ..... Bull Infirm Cathol Can
Bulletin. Information sur les Applications Industrielles des Radioelements [*A publication*] ..... Bull Inf Appl Ind Radioelem
Bulletin d'Information. Association Internationale pour l'Etude de la Mosaique Antique [*A publication*] ..... Bull AIEMA
Bulletin d'Information. Bureau National de Metrologie [*A publication*] ..... Bull Inf Bur Natl Metrol
Bulletin d'Information. Centre de Documentation pour l'Education en Europe [*A publication*] ..... B Inform Centre Docum Educ Europe
Bulletin d'Information. Centre National de la Cinematographie [*A publication*] ..... B Inform C N C
Bulletin d'Information et de Coordination. Association Internationale des Etudes Byzantines [*A publication*] ..... BICByz
Bulletin d'Information. Departement d'Economie et de Sociologie Rurales [*A publication*] ..... B Inform Dept Econ Sociol Rur
Bulletin d'Information sur les Generateurs Isotopiques [*A publication*] ..... Bull Inf Generateurs Isot
Bulletin d'Information. Institut National pour l'Etude Agronomique du Congo Belgique [*A publication*] ..... Bull Inf INEAC
Bulletin d'Information. Institut de Reboisement de Tunis [*A publication*] ..... Bull Inform Inst Rebois Tunis
Bulletin d'Information. Institut de Recherche et d'Histoire des Textes [*A publication*] ..... BIIRHT
Bulletin d'Information. Institut de Recherche et d'Histoire des Textes [*A publication*] ..... BIRT
Bulletin d'Information. Laboratoire d'Analyse Lexicologique [*A publication*] ..... BILAL
Bulletin d'Information et de Liaison. Association Internationale des Etudes Patristiques [*A publication*] ..... BILPatr
Bulletin d'Information. Ministere de l'Agriculture [*A publication*] ..... Bull Inf Minist Agric
Bulletin d'Information de la Region Parisienne [*A publication*] ..... B Inform Region Paris
Bulletin d'Information Regionale Champagne-Ardenne [*A publication*] ..... B Inform Region Champagne-Ardenne
Bulletin d'Information. Station Experimentale d'Aviculture de Ploufragan [*A publication*] ..... Bull Inf Stn Exp Avic Ploufragan
Bulletin d'Informations Economiques [*A publication*] ..... B Inform Econ
Bulletin d'Informations Scientifiques et Techniques [*A publication*] ..... Bull Inf Sci Tech
Bulletin d'Informations Scientifiques et Techniques. Commissariat a l'Energie Atomique [*A publication*] ..... B In Sci T
Bulletin d'Informations Scientifiques et Techniques (Paris) [*A publication*] ..... Bull Inf Sci & Tech (Paris)
Bulletin d'Informations Techniques. Centre Technique du Bois [*A publication*] ..... Bull Inform Tech Centre Tech Bois
Bulletin. Institut Agronomique et Stations de Recherches de Gembloux [*A publication*] ..... Bull Inst Agron Sta Rech Gembloux
Bulletin. Institut Agronomique et Stations de Recherches de Gembloux [*A publication*] ..... Bull Inst Agron Stn Rech Gembloux
Bulletin. Institut Archeologique Bulgare [*A publication*] ..... BIAB
Bulletin. Institut Archeologique Bulgare [*A publication*] ..... BIA Bulg
Bulletin. Institut Archeologique Liegeois [*A publication*] ..... BIAL
Bulletin. Institut Archeologique Liegeois [*A publication*] ..... Bull Inst Arch Liegeois
Bulletin. Institut d'Egypte [*A publication*] ..... BIE
Bulletin. Institut d'Egypte [*A publication*] ..... Bull Inst Egypt
Bulletin. Institut pour l'Etude de l'Europe Sud-Orientale [*A publication*] ..... BISO
Bulletin. Institut Fondamental d'Afrique Noire [*A publication*] ..... B Inst Fondam Afr Noire
Bulletin. Institut Fondamental d'Afrique Noire. Serie A. Sciences Naturelles [*A publication*] ..... Bull Inst Fondam Afr Noire Ser A Sci Nat
Bulletin. Institut Francais d'Afrique Noire [*A publication*] ..... BIFAN
Bulletin. Institut Francais d'Afrique Noire [*A publication*] ..... Bull Inst Fr Afr Noire
Bulletin. Institut Francais d'Afrique Noire. Serie A. Sciences Naturelles [*A publication*] ..... Bull Inst Fr Afr Noire Ser A Sci Nat
Bulletin. Institut Francais d'Archeologie Orientale [*A publication*] ..... BIAO
Bulletin. Institut Francais d'Archeologie Orientale [*A publication*] ..... BIFAO
Bulletin. Institut Francais d'Etudes Andines [*A publication*] ..... B Inst Franc Et Andines
Bulletin. Institut Historique Belge de Rome [*A publication*] ..... BIBR
Bulletin. Institut Historique Belge de Rome [*A publication*] ..... BIHBR
Bulletin. Institut International de l'Administration Publique [*A publication*] ..... B Inst Int Adm Publ
Bulletin. Institut International de Bibliographie [*A publication*] ..... BIB
Bulletin. Institut International du Froid [*A publication*] ..... Bull Inst Int Froid
Bulletin. Institut International de Statistique [*A publication*] ..... Bull Inst Internat Statist
Bulletin. Institut National d'Hygiene (Paris) [*A publication*] ..... Bull Inst Natl Hyg (Paris)
Bulletin. Institut National de la Sante et de la Recherche Medicale (Paris) [*A publication*] ..... Bull Inst Natl Sante Rech Med (Paris)
Bulletin. Institut National Scientifique et Technique d'Oceanographie et de Peche [*A publication*] ..... Bull Inst Natl Sci Rech Oceanogr Peche
Bulletin. Institut Oceanographie (Monaco) [*A publication*] ..... Bull Inst Oceanogr (Monaco)
Bulletin. Institut Pasteur [*Paris*] [*A publication*] ..... B I Pasteur
Bulletin. Institut Pasteur [*Paris*] [*A publication*] ..... Bull Inst Pasteur
Bulletin. Institut Pasteur (Paris) [*A publication*] ..... Bull Inst Pasteur (Paris)
Bulletin. Institut des Peches Maritimes du Maroc [*A publication*] ..... Bull Inst Peches Marit Maroc
Bulletin. Institut de Phonetique de Grenoble [*A publication*] ..... BIPG
Bulletin. Institut Provincial de Cooperation Agricole [*A publication*] ..... Bull Inst Prov Coop Agr
Bulletin. Institut de Recherches Economiques [*A publication*] ..... B Inst Rech Econ
Bulletin. Institut de Recherches Economiques et Sociales de l'Universite de Louvain [*A publication*] ..... BIRESUL
Bulletin. Institut de Recherches Scientifiques au Congo [*A publication*] ..... BIRSC
Bulletin. Institut Royal du Patrimoine Artistique [*A publication*] ..... BIRPA
Bulletin. Institut Royal des Sciences Naturelles de Belgique [*A publication*] ..... Bull Inst R Sci Nat Belg
Bulletin. Institut Royal des Sciences Naturelles de Belgique. Biologie [*A publication*] ..... Bull Inst R Sci Nat Belg Biol
Bulletin. Institut Royal des Sciences Naturelles de Belgique. Entomologie [*A publication*] ..... Bull Inst R Sci Nat Belg Entomol

Bulletin. Institut Royal des Sciences Naturelles de Belgique. Sciences de la Terre [*A publication*] ..... Bull Inst R Sci Nat Belg Sci Terre
Bulletin. Institute for Agricultural Research. Tohoku University [*A publication*]................................ Bull Inst Agric Res Tohoku Univ
Bulletin. Institute for Agricultural Research. Tohoku University [*A publication*]................................Bull Inst Agr Res Tohoku Univ
Bulletin. Institute of Archaeology. University of London [*A publication*]..BIAL
Bulletin. Institute of Archaeology. University of London [*A publication*]..B Inst Archaeol
Bulletin. Institute for Chemical Research. Kyoto University [*A publication*]...............................Bull Inst Chem Res Kyoto Univ
Bulletin. Institute of Classical Studies. University of London [*A publication*].. BICS
Bulletin. Institute of Communication Research [*A publication*]...................... B Inst Communication Res
Bulletin. Institute of Constitutional Medicine. Kumamoto University [*A publication*]................. Bull Inst Const Med Kumamoto Univ
Bulletin. Institute of Development Studies [*A publication*].. B Inst Develop Stud
Bulletin. Institute of Ethnology. Academia Sinica [*A publication*]..................... B Inst Ethnol Acad Sinica
Bulletin. Institute for Geological and Geophysical Research. Series A. Geology (English Translation) [*A publication*]....................... Bull Inst Geol Geophys Res Ser A (Engl Transl)
Bulletin. Institute for Geological and Geophysical Research. Series B. Engineering Geology and Hydrogeology (English Translation) [*A publication*] .... Bull Inst Geol Geophys Res Ser B (Engl Trans)
Bulletin. Institute for Geological and Geophysical Research. Series C. Applied Geophysics (English Translation) [*A publication*]........................Bull Inst Geol Geophys Res Ser C (Eng Trans)
Bulletin. Institute of Geological Sciences [*A publication*].... Bull Inst Geol Sci
Bulletin. Institute of Historical Research [*A publication*] .... BIHR
Bulletin. Institute of History of Medicine. Hyderabad [*A publication*]........................... B Inst Hist Med Hyderabad
Bulletin. Institute of History and Philology. Academia Sinica [*A publication*] .... BIHP
Bulletin. Institute of Immunological Science. Hokkaido University [*A publication*]................. Bull Inst Immunol Sci Hokkaido Univ
Bulletin. Institute of Jamaica. Science Series [*A publication*].. Bull Inst Jam Sci Ser
Bulletin. Institute of Marine Medicine in Gdansk [*A publication*] .... Bull Inst Mar Med Gdansk
Bulletin. Institute of Maritime and Tropical Medicine in Gdynia [*A publication*]................ Bull Inst Marit Trop Med Gdynia
Bulletin. Institute of Maritime and Tropical Medicine in Gdynia [*A publication*]................ Bull Inst Mar Trop Med Gdynia
Bulletin. Institute of Mathematics. Academia Sinica [*A publication*]......................... Bull Inst Math Acad Sinica
Bulletin. Institute of Mathematics and Its Applications [*A publication*].. Bull Inst Math Appl
Bulletin. Institute for Medical Research. Federated Malay States [*A publication*]........................Bull Inst Med Research FMS
Bulletin. Institute for Medical Research (Kuala Lumpur) [*A publication*]........................... Bull Inst Med Res (Kuala Lumpur)
Bulletin. Institute for Medical Research. University of Madrid [*A publication*]........................... Bull Inst Med Res Univ Madr
Bulletin. Institute of Natural Education in Shiga Heights [*A publication*]........................Bull Inst Nat Educ Shiga Heights
Bulletin. Institute of Oceanography and Fisheries [*A publication*]........................ Bull Inst Oceanogr Fish
Bulletin. Institute of Physical and Chemical Research [*A publication*]...................................... Bull Inst Phys Chem Res
Bulletin. Institute of Public Health (Tokyo) [*A publication*]........................ Bull Inst Public Health (Tokyo)
Bulletin. Institute of Space and Aeronautical Science. University of Tokyo [*A publication*] .... Bull Inst Space Aeronaut Sci Univ Tokyo
Bulletin. Institute of Space and Aeronautical Science. University of Tokyo. A [*A publication*] .... Bull Inst Space & Aeronaut Sci Univ Tokyo A
Bulletin. Institute of Space and Aeronautical Science. University of Tokyo. B [*A publication*] .... Bull Inst Space & Aeronaut Sci Univ Tokyo B
Bulletin. Institute for the Study of the USSR [*A publication*]....................BIS
Bulletin. Institute for the Study of the USSR [*A publication*]....................BSUSSR
Bulletin. Institute of Traditional Culture [*A publication*] .... B Inst Trad Cult
Bulletin. Institute of Vitreous Enamellers [*A publication*] .... Bull Inst Vitreous Enamellers
Bulletin. Institute of Zoology. Academia Sinica [*Taipei*] [*A publication*]..B I Zool AS
Bulletin. Institute of Zoology. Academia Sinica (Taipei) [*A publication*]............................... Bull Inst Zool Acad Sin (Taipei)
Bulletin. Institution of Engineers [*A publication*] .... Bull Inst Eng
Bulletin. Institution of Engineers (India) [*A publication*]........................ Bull Inst Eng (India)
Bulletin. Instrumentation Nucleaire [*A publication*] .... Bull Instrum Nucl
Bulletin Interministeriel pour la Rationalisation des Choix Budgetaires [*A publication*] .... B Interminist Rational Choix Budget
Bulletin International. Academie Polonaise des Sciences et des Lettres [*A publication*]... BIAP

Bulletin International. Academie Polonaise des Sciences et des Lettres [*A publication*]...BIAPSL
Bulletin International. Academie Yugoslave (Zagreb) [*A publication*]... Bull (Zagreb)
Bulletin. International Association for Educational and Vocational Guidance [*A publication*]........................ B Int Assoc Educ Vocat Guidance
Bulletin. International Association of Engineering Geology [*A publication*]................................ Bull Int Assoc Eng Geol
Bulletin. International Association of Medical Museums [*A publication*]................................ Bull Int Assoc Med Mus
Bulletin. International Association of Paper Historians [*A publication*]........................ Bull Intern Assocn Paper Hist
Bulletin. International Association of Scientific Hydrology [*A publication*]........................ Bull Int Assoc Sci Hydrol
Bulletin. International Association of Scientific Hydrology [*A publication*]........................ Bull Int Ass Sci Hydrol
Bulletin. International Association for Shell and Spatial Structures [*A publication*]........................ Bull Int Assoc Shell Spat Struct
Bulletin. International Association for Shell Structures [*A publication*]........................Bull Int Ass Shell Struct
Bulletin. International Association of Wood Anatomists [*A publication*]........................ Bull Int Ass Wood Anatomists
Bulletin. International Bureau of the American Republics [*A publication*]........................ Bul Am Repub
Bulletin. International Committee of Historical Sciences [*A publication*]... BICH
Bulletin. International Committee of Historical Sciences [*A publication*]...BICHS
Bulletin. International Committee on Urgent Anthropological and Ethnological Research [*A publication*]........................ BICAER
Bulletin for International Fiscal Documentation [*A publication*]........................ B Int Fisc Docum
Bulletin for International Fiscal Documentation [*A publication*].....B Int Fis D
Bulletin for International Fiscal Documentation [*A publication*]........................ Bul Int Fiscal Doc
Bulletin. International Institute of Refrigeration [*A publication*]........................ Bull Int Inst Refrig
Bulletin. International Peat Society [*A publication*]...............Bull Int Peat Soc
Bulletin. International Potash Institute [*A publication*] ..... Bull Int Potash Inst
Bulletin. International Railway Congress Association [*A publication*]........................Bull Int Ry Congr Ass
Bulletin. International Society for Tropical Ecology [*A publication*]........................Bull Int Soc Trop Ecol
Bulletin. International Union Against Tuberculosis [*A publication*]........................Bull Int Union Tuberc
Bulletin Interparlementaire [*A publication*]................................... B Interparl
Bulletin. Iowa Agricultural Experiment Station [*A publication*]........................ Bull Iowa Agr Exp Sta
Bulletin. Iowa Nurses Association [*A publication*]...... Bull Iowa Nurses Assoc
Bulletin. Iranian Institute [*A publication*].. B Iran Inst
Bulletin. Iranian Petroleum Institute [*A publication*] .... Bull Iran Pet Inst
Bulletin. Iraq Natural History Museum (University of Baghdad) [*A publication*]........................ Bull Iraq Nat Hist Mus (Univ Baghdad)
Bulletin. Ishikawa Prefecture College of Agriculture [*A publication*]........................ Bull Ishikawa Prefect Coll Agric
Bulletin. Israel Physical Society [*A publication*]................Bull Isr Phys Soc
Bulletin. Israel Society of Special Libraries and Information Centres [*A publication*] .... Bull Isr Soc Spec Libr & Inf Cent
Bulletin Italien [*A publication*].. BI
Bulletin Italien [*A publication*]... BItal
Bulletin. Iwate-ken Agricultural Experiment Station [*A publication*]........................ Bull Iwate-ken Agr Exp Sta
Bulletin. Iwate University Forests [*A publication*].............. Bull Iwate Univ For
Bulletin. Japan Electronic Materials Society [*A publication*]........................ Bull Jpn Electron Mater Soc
Bulletin. Japan Entomological Academy [*A publication*]........................ Bull Jpn Entomol Acad
Bulletin. Japan Institute of Metals [*A publication*].................Bull Jpn Inst Met
Bulletin. Japan Mining Industry Association [*A publication*]........................ Bull Jpn Min Ind Assoc
Bulletin. Japan Petroleum Institute [*A publication*]............... Bull Jap Pet Inst
Bulletin. Japan Petroleum Institute [*A publication*] .... Bull Jpn Pet Inst
Bulletin. Japan Sea Regional Fisheries Research Laboratories [*A publication*]........................Bull Jpn Sea Reg Fish Res Lab
Bulletin. Japan Society of Grinding Engineers [*A publication*]........................ Bull Jap Soc Grinding Eng
Bulletin. Japan Society of Mechanical Engineers [*A publication*]........................ Bull Jpn Soc Mech Eng
Bulletin. Japan Society of Precision Engineering [*A publication*]........................ Bull Jap Soc Precis Eng
Bulletin. Japanese Society of Phycology [*A publication*]........................ Bull Jpn Soc Phycol
Bulletin. Japanese Society of Scientific Fisheries [*A publication*]........................ B Jap S S F
Bulletin. Japanese Society of Scientific Fisheries [*A publication*]........................ Bull Jpn Soc Sci Fish
Bulletin. Jardin Botanique de Buitenzorg [*A publication*]........................ Bull Jard Bot Buitenzorg
Bulletin. Jardin Botanique de l'Etat a Bruxelles [*A publication*]........................ Bull Jard Bot Etat Brux

Bulletin. Jardin Botanique National de Belgique [A publication]..................... Bull Jard Bot Natl Belg
Bulletin des Jeunes Romanistes [A publication]..BJR
Bulletin. Jewish Palestine Exploration Society [A publication] ....BJewPES
Bulletin. Jewish Palestine Exploration Society [A publication] ....BJPES
Bulletin. John Rylands Library. University of Manchester [A publication]..BJR
Bulletin. John Rylands Library. University of Manchester [A publication]..BJRL
Bulletin. John Rylands Library. University of Manchester [A publication]..BJRLM
Bulletin. John Rylands Library. University of Manchester [A publication]..BRL
Bulletin. Johns Hopkins Hospital [A publication]..........Bull Johns Hopk Hosp
Bulletin. Johns Hopkins Hospital [A publication]..... Bull Johns Hopkins Hosp
Bulletin. Josai Dental University [A publication].............. Bull Josai Dent Univ
Bulletin. JSAE [Japan Society of Automotive Engineers] [A publication]..Bull JSAE
Bulletin. JSME [Japan Society of Mechanical Engineers] [A publication]..B JSME
Bulletin. JSME [Japan Society of Mechanical Engineers] [A publication]..Bull JSME
Bulletin. Kagawa Agricultural Experiment Station [A publication] .... Bull Kagawa Agr Exp Sta
Bulletin. Kagawa Agricultural Experiment Station [A publication] .... Bull Kagawa Agric Exp Sta
Bulletin. Kagoshima University Forest [A publication]...................... Bull Kagoshima Univ For
Bulletin. Kanagawa Agricultural Experiment Station [A publication]....................Bull Kanagawa Agric Exp Stn
Bulletin. Kanagawa Horticultural Experiment Station [A publication]........................ Bull Kanagawa Hortic Exp Stn
Bulletin. Kansas Agricultural Experiment Station [A publication] .... Bull Kans Agr Exp Sta
Bulletin. Kansas Agricultural Experiment Station [A publication] .... Bull Kans Agric Exp Sta
Bulletin. Kansas City Veterinary College Quarterly [A publication]....................Bull Kansas City Vet Coll Quart
Bulletin. Kansas Engineering Experiment Station [A publication] .... Bull Kans Eng Exp Stn
Bulletin. Kentucky Agricultural Experiment Station [A publication]....................Bull KY Agr Exp Sta
Bulletin. Kentucky Agricultural Experiment Station [A publication]....................Bull KY Agric Exp Sta
Bulletin. Kesennuma Miyagi Prefectural Fisheries Experiment Station [A publication]......... Bull Kesennuma Miyagi Prefect Fish Exp Stn
Bulletin. Kisarazu Technical College [A publication] .... Bull Kisarazu Tech Coll
Bulletin. Kobayasi Institute of Physical Research [A publication] .... Bull Kobayasi Inst Phys Res
Bulletin. Kobe Medical College [A publication] ....Bull Kobe Med Coll
Bulletin. Kochi Technical College [A publication] .... Bull Kochi Tech Coll
Bulletin. Konan Women's College [A publication] .... B Konan Women Coll
Bulletin van het Koninklijke Belgische Instituut voor Natuurwetenschappen. Aardwetenschappen [A publication].................. Bull K Belg Inst Natuurwet Aardwet
Bulletin van het Koninklijke Belgische Instituut voor Natuurwetenschappen. Biologie [A publication]...................................... Bull K Belg Inst Natuurwet Biol
Bulletin van het Koninklijke Belgische Instituut voor Natuurwetenschappen. Entomologie [A publication]...................................... Bull K Belg Inst Natuurwet Entomol
Bulletin. Korean Fisheries Society [A publication] .... Bull Korean Fish Soc
Bulletin. Korean Research Center [A publication].................................BKRC
Bulletin. Kyoto Prefectural University Forests [A publication] .... Bull Kyoto Prefect Univ For
Bulletin. Kyoto University of Education. Series B. Mathematics and Natural Science [A publication]....................Bull Kyoto Univ Ed Ser B
Bulletin. Kyoto University Forests [A publication].............Bull Kyoto Univ For
Bulletin. Kyushu Agricultural Experiment Station [A publication] .... Bull Kyushu Agr Exp Sta
Bulletin. Kyushu Agricultural Experiment Station [A publication] .... Bull Kyushu Agric Exp Stn
Bulletin. Kyushu Institute of Technology. Mathematics and Natural Science [A publication]...... Bull Kyushu Inst Tech Math Natur Sci
Bulletin. Kyushu Institute of Technology. Mathematics and Natural Science [A publication].... Bull Kyushu Inst Technol Math Nat Sci
Bulletin. Kyushu Institute of Technology. Science and Technology [A publication] .... Bull Kyushu Inst Technol Sci & Technol
Bulletin. Kyushu University Forests [A publication] .... Bull Kyushu Univ For
Bulletin. Laboratoire de Biologie Appliquee (Paris) [A publication]....................Bull Lab Biol Appl (Paris)
Bulletin. Laboratoire Maritime de Dinard [A publication] .... Bull Lab Marit Dinard
Bulletin. Landbouwproefstation in Suriname [A publication]...................................... Bull Landbproefstn Suriname
Bulletin des Lettres [A publication] .... BL
Bulletin. Liaison des Laboratoires des Ponts et Chaussees [A publication]...................................... Bull Liaison Lab Ponts Chaussees
Bulletin Linguistique et Ethnologique. Institut Granducal (Luxembourg) [A publication].. BLux

Bulletin Linguistique. Faculte des Lettres de Bucarest [A publication]..... BL
Bulletin Linguistique. Faculte des Lettres de Bucarest [A publication]..BLB
Bulletin de Litterature Chretienne [A publication] .... BLC
Bulletin de Litterature Ecclesiastique [A publication]..........................BLE
Bulletin. London Mathematical Society [A publication]...................................... Bull London Math Soc
Bulletin. Los Angeles County Museum of Natural History. Contributions in Science [A publication]...................................... Bull Los Ang Cty Mus Nat Hist Sci
Bulletin. Los Angeles Dental Society [A publication]...................................... Bull Los Angeles Dent Soc
Bulletin. Los Angeles Neurological Societies [A publication]...................................... Bull LA Neurol Soc
Bulletin. Los Angeles Neurological Societies [A publication]...................................... Bull Los Angeles Neurol Soc
Bulletin. Los Angeles Neurological Societies [A publication]...................................... Bull Los Ang Neurol Soc
Bulletin. Louisiana Agricultural Experiment Station [A publication]....................Bull LA Agr Exp Sta
Bulletin. Louisiana Agricultural Experiment Station [A publication]....................Bull LA Agric Exp Stn
Bulletin de Madagascar [A publication] ....BMadagascar
Bulletin. Madras Government Museum (Natural History Section) [A publication]....................Bull Madras Gov Mus (Nat Hist Sect)
Bulletin. Maine Forestry Department [A publication]............ Bull ME For Dep
Bulletin. Maine University Agricultural Experiment Station [A publication]...................................... Bull ME Agric Exp Sta
Bulletin. Maison Franco-Japonais [A publication]..............................BMFJ
Bulletin. Malaysian Mathematical Society [A publication]...................................... Bull Malaysian Math Soc
Bulletin. Manila Medical Society [A publication] .... Bull Manila Med Soc
Bulletin. Marine Biological Station of Asamushi [A publication]...................................... Bull Mar Biol Stn Asamushi
Bulletin of Marine Science [A publication].................................... B Marin Sci
Bulletin of Marine Science [A publication]............................... Bull Marine Sci
Bulletin of Marine Science [A publication].................................... Bull Mar Sci
Bulletin. Marine Science of the Gulf and Caribbean [Later, Bulletin of Marine Science] [A publication]...................................... Bull Marine Sci Gulf and Caribbean
Bulletin. Marine Science of the Gulf and Caribbean [Later, Bulletin of Marine Science] [A publication] ....Bull Mar Sci Gulf Caribb
Bulletin. Maryland Agricultural Experiment Station [A publication]....................Bull MD Agr Exp Sta
Bulletin. Maryland Agricultural Experiment Station [A publication]....................Bull MD Agric Exp Stn
Bulletin. Maryland Herpetological Society [A publication]...................................... Bull MD Herpetol Soc
Bulletin. Massachusetts Agricultural Experiment Station [A publication]....................Bull Mass Agr Exp Sta
Bulletin. Massachusetts Agricultural Experiment Station [A publication]....................Bull Mass Agric Exp Sta
Bulletin. Massachusetts Audubon Society [A publication]...................................... Bull Mass Audubon Soc
Bulletin. Massachusetts Nurses Association [A publication]...................................... Bull Mass Nurses Assoc
Bulletin of Mathematical Biology [A publication]..........................B Math Biol
Bulletin of Mathematical Biology [A publication]...........................BMTBA
Bulletin of Mathematical Biology [A publication]....................... Bull Math Biol
Bulletin of Mathematical Biology [A publication]............... Bull Math Biology
Bulletin of Mathematical Biophysics [A publication]........... Bull Math Biophys
Bulletin of Mathematical Statistics [A publication]........................ B Math Stat
Bulletin of Mathematical Statistics [A publication] ....Bull Math Statist
Bulletin of Mechanical Engineering Education [A publication] .... Bull Mech Eng Educ
Bulletin of Mechanical Engineering Education [A publication] .... Bull Mech Engng Educ
Bulletin. Mechanical Engineering Laboratory [A publication] .... Bull Mech Eng Lab
Bulletin. Mechanical Engineering Laboratory of Japan [A publication]...................................... BMEGA
Bulletin de Medecine Legale et de Toxicologie Medicale [A publication]....................Bull Med Leg Toxicol Med
Bulletin des Medecins Suisses [A publication].................... Bull Med Suisses
Bulletin. Medical Library Association [A publication] ....B Med Lib A
Bulletin. Medical Library Association [A publication] ....BMLA
Bulletin. Medical Library Association [A publication] .... Bull Med Libr Ass
Bulletin. Medical Library Association [A publication] ..... Bull Med Libr Assoc
Bulletin Medical du Nord [A publication] .... Bull Med Nord
Bulletin Medical (Paris) [A publication] .... Bull Med (Paris)
Bulletin. Medical Staff of Methodist Hospitals of Dallas [A publication]....................Bull Med Staff Methodist Hosp Dallas
Bulletin et Memoires. Academie Royale de Medecine de Belgique [A publication]....................Bull Mem Acad R Med Belg
Bulletin et Memoires. Institut des Fouilles de Provence et des Prealpes [A publication]....................BIFP
Bulletin et Memoires. Societe des Antiquaires de l'Ouest [A publication]....................BMSAO
Bulletin et Memoires. Societe Archeologique de Bordeaux [A publication]....................B Mem Soc Arch Bordeaux

Bulletin et Memoires. Societe des Chirurgiens de Paris [*A publication*].................................. Bull Mem Soc Chir Paris

Bulletin et Memoires. Societe de Medecine de Paris [*A publication*]............................... Bull Mem Soc Med Paris

Bulletin. Menninger Clinic [*A publication*] ....B Menninger

Bulletin. Menninger Clinic [*A publication*] .... Bull Menninger Clin

Bulletin Mensuel. Ecole Superieure d'Agriculture et de Viticulture d'Angers [*A publication*]
Bull Mens Ecole Super Agr Viticult Angers

Bulletin Mensuel des Naturalistes Belges [*A publication*] ....
Bull Mens Nat Belg

Bulletin Mensuel. Societe Linneenne de Lyon [*A publication*]
Bull Mens Soc Linn Lyon

Bulletin Mensuel. Societe des Sciences de Semur [*A publication*].......BSSS

Bulletin Mensuel. Societe Veterinaire Pratique de France [*A publication*]................... Bull Mens Soc Vet Prat France

Bulletin Mensuel des Statistiques du Travail. Supplement [*A publication*]......................... B Mens Statist Trav Suppl

Bulletin de Metrologie [*A publication*]..........................Bull Metrol

Bulletin. Metropolitan Museum of Art [*A publication*] ....BMM

Bulletin. Metropolitan Museum of Art [*A publication*] .... BMMA

Bulletin Meunerie Francaise [*A publication*] .... Bull Meun Fr

Bulletin. Michigan State Dental Society [*A publication*].......................
Bull Mich State Dent Soc

Bulletin de Microscopie Appliquee [*A publication*] ...... Bull Microscopie Appl

Bulletin. Millard Fillmore Hospital [*A publication*].......................
Bull Millard Fillmore Hosp

Bulletin. Mineral Research and Exploration Institute (Turkey) [*A publication*]..................Bull Miner Res Explor Inst (Turk)

Bulletin. Ministry of Agriculture, Fisheries, and Food [*A publication*].....................Bull Minist Agric Fish Fd

Bulletin. Ministry of Agriculture and Lands (Jamaica) [*A publication*] .... Bull Min Agr Land (Jamaica)

Bulletin. Misaki Marine Biological Institute. Kyoto University [*A publication*] .... Bull Misaki Mar Biol Inst Kyoto Univ

Bulletin. Mississippi State University. Agricultural Experiment Station [*A publication*] .... Bull Miss Agric Exp Sta

Bulletin. Mississippi State University. Agricultural Experiment Station [*A publication*] .... Bull Miss State Univ Agr Exp Sta

Bulletin. Missouri Academy of Science. Supplement [*A publication*] .... Bull MO Acad Sci Suppl

Bulletin. Miyagi Agricultural College [*A publication*] .... Bull Miyagi Agr Coll

Bulletin. Miyazaki Agricultural Experiment Station [*A publication*] .... Bull Miyazaki Agr Exp Sta

Bulletin. Montana Agricultural Experiment Station [*A publication*]..................................Bull Mont Agr Exp Sta

Bulletin. Montana Agricultural Experiment Station [*A publication*]........................... Bull Montana Agric Exp Stn

Bulletin. Montana State College. Cooperative Extension Service [*A publication*]........... Bull Mont State Coll Coop Ext Serv

Bulletin. Montgomery-Bucks Dental Society [*A publication*].......................
Bull Montg-Bucks Dent Soc

Bulletin Monumental [*A publication*] .... BM

Bulletin Monumental [*A publication*] .... B Mon

Bulletin Monumental [*A publication*] .... Bull Mon

Bulletin. Morioka Tobacco Experiment Station [*A publication*].......................
Bull Morioka Tob Exp Stn

Bulletin. Mount Desert Island Biological Laboratory [*A publication*]...................... Bull Mt Desert Isl Biol Lab

Bulletin de la Murithienne [*A publication*]................. Bull Murithienne

Bulletin. Musee d'Anthropologie Prehistorique [*A publication*].......................
B Mus Anthropol Prehist

Bulletin. Musee Basque [*A publication*]...........................BMB

Bulletin. Musee de Beyrouth [*A publication*].....................BMB

Bulletin. Musee de Beyrouth [*A publication*] .... BM Beyrouth

Bulletin. Musee d'Histoire Naturelle de Marseille [*A publication*].......................
Bull Mus Hist Nat Marseille

Bulletin. Musee Hongrois des Beaux Arts [*A publication*].................. BMHBA

Bulletin. Musee National de Burgas [*A publication*] .... BMNB

Bulletin. Musee National Hongrois des Beaux-Arts [*A publication*] .... Bull Mus Hong

Bulletin. Musees de France [*A publication*].......................BMF

Bulletin. Musees de France [*A publication*].......................BMusFr

Bulletin. Musees Royaux d'Art et d'Histoire [*A publication*] ....BMAH

Bulletin. Musees Royaux d'Art et d'Histoire [*A publication*] .... BMRAH

Bulletin. Musees Royaux d'Art et d'Histoire [*A publication*] .... B Mus Art

Bulletin. Musees Royaux des Beaux-Arts [*A publication*] ....BMRBA

Bulletin. Museum of Comparative Zoology [*A publication*].......................
Bull Mus Comp Zool

Bulletin. Museum of Comparative Zoology at Harvard University [*A publication*] .... Bull Mus Comp Zool Harv Univ

Bulletin. Museum of Far Eastern Antiquities [*Stockholm*] [*A publication*].......................
BMFEA

Bulletin. Museum of Far Eastern Antiquities [*A publication*].......................
B Mus Far East Antiq

Bulletin. Museum of Far Eastern Antiquities [*Stockholm*] [*A publication*]...................Bull Far Eastern Antiquities

Bulletin. Museum of Fine Arts [*Boston*] [*A publication*]........................BMFA

Bulletin. Museum of Fine Arts (Boston) [*A publication*].......................BMusB

Bulletin. Museum d'Histoire Naturelle de Marseille [*A publication*]..........................Bull Mus Hist Nat Mars

Bulletin. Museum d'Histoire Naturelle du Pays Serbe [*A publication*].......................... Bull Mus Hist Nat Pays Serbe

Bulletin. Museum of Mediterranean and Near Eastern Antiquities [*A publication*] .... BMNE

Bulletin. Museum National d'Histoire Naturelle [*Paris*] [*A publication*].......................... Bull Mus Natl Hist Nat

Bulletin. Museum National d'Histoire Naturelle. Botanique [*Paris*] [*A publication*]............Bull Mus Natl Hist Nat Bot

Bulletin. Museum National d'Histoire Naturelle. Ecologie Generale [*Paris*] [*A publication*]...............Bull Mus Natl Hist Nat Ecol Gen

Bulletin. Museum National d'Histoire Naturelle (Paris) [*A publication*].......................... Bull Mus Nat Hist Nat (Paris)

Bulletin. Museum National d'Histoire Naturelle. Sciences de la Terre [*Paris*] [*A publication*]..................Bull Mus Natl Hist Nat Sci Terre

Bulletin. Museum National d'Histoire Naturelle. Zoologie [*Paris*] [*A publication*]................. Bull Mus Natl Hist Nat Zool

Bulletin. Nagano Agricultural Experiment Station [*A publication*].......................
Bull Nagano Agr Exp Sta

Bulletin. Nagaoka Municipal Science Museum [*A publication*].......................
Bull Nagaoka Munic Sci Mus

Bulletin. Nagoya City University. Department of General Education. Natural Science Section [*A publication*].......................
Bull Nagoya City Univ Dep Gen Educ Nat Sci Sect

Bulletin. Nagoya Institute of Technology [*A publication*].......................
Bull Nagoya Inst Tech

Bulletin. Nansei Regional Fisheries Research Laboratories [*A publication*]....................Bull Nansei Reg Fish Res Lab

Bulletin. Nara University of Education. Natural Science [*A publication*].......................... Bull Nara Univ Ed Natur Sci

Bulletin. Nara University of Education. Natural Science [*A publication*]........................ Bull Nara Univ Educ Nat Sci

Bulletin on Narcotics [*A publication*]...............................B Narcotics

Bulletin on Narcotics [*A publication*].................................Bull Narc

Bulletin on Narcotics [*A publication*]...............................Bull Narcotics

Bulletin. National Association for Music Therapy [*A publication*] ..... BNAMC

Bulletin. National Association of Secondary-School Principals [*A publication*]..BNAP

Bulletin. National Botanic Garden [*Lucknow, India*] [*A publication*]........................... Bull Natl Bot Gard

Bulletin of National Fisheries. University of Busan (Natural Sciences) [*A publication*]....................Bull Natl Fish Univ Busan (Nat Sci)

Bulletin. National Geophysical Research Institute (India) [*A publication*].......................Bull Natl Geophys Res Inst (India)

Bulletin. National Grassland Research Institute [*Japan*] [*A publication*]............................Bull Natl Grassl Res Inst

Bulletin. National Hygienic Laboratory (Tokyo) [*A publication*].......................
Bull Natl Hyg Lab (Tokyo)

Bulletin. National Institute of Agricultural Sciences. Series B (Soils and Fertilizers) (Japan) [*A publication*].......................
Bull Natl Inst Agric Sci Ser B (Soils Fert) (Japan)

Bulletin. National Institute of Agricultural Sciences. Series D (Physiology and Genetics) (Japan) [*A publication*].......................
Bull Natl Inst Agric Sci Ser D (Physiol Genet) (Japan)

Bulletin. National Institute of Agricultural Sciences (Tokyo) [*A publication*]....................Bull Natn Inst Agric Sci (Tokyo)

Bulletin. National Institute of Animal Health (Japan) [*A publication*]....................Bull Natl Inst Anim Health (Jpn)

Bulletin. National Institute of Animal Industry [*A publication*].......................
Bull Nat Inst Anim Ind

Bulletin. National Institute of Animal Industry (Chiba) [*A publication*]..................Bull Natl Inst Anim Ind (Chiba)

Bulletin. National Institute of Hygienic Sciences [*A publication*].......................
Bull Nat Inst Hyg Sci

Bulletin. National Institute of Hygienic Sciences (Tokyo) [*A publication*]....................Bull Natl Inst Hyg Sci (Tokyo)

Bulletin. National Institute of Oceanography (India) [*A publication*]..................Bull Natl Inst Oceanogr (India)

Bulletin. National Institute of Sciences of India [*A publication*].......................
Bull Natl Inst Sci India

Bulletin. National Institute of Sciences of India [*A publication*].......................
Bull Natn Inst Sci India

Bulletin. National Museum (Singapore) [*A publication*].......................
Bull Natl Mus (Singapore)

Bulletin. National Pearl Research Laboratory [*Japan*] [*A publication*]...........................Bull Natl Pearl Res Lab

Bulletin. National Pearl Research Laboratory (Japan) [*A publication*]..................Bull Nat Pearl Res Lab (Jpn)

Bulletin. National Research Institute of History and Philology of the Academia Sinica [*A publication*]........................... BHPAS

Bulletin. National Research Institute of Tea [*Japan*] [*A publication*]............................... Bull Natl Res Inst Tea

Bulletin. National Research Laboratory of Metrology [*Japan*] [*A publication*]......................... Bull Natl Res Lab Metrol

Bulletin. National Research Laboratory of Metrology [*Japan*] [*A publication*].................... Bull Nat Res Lab Metrology

Bulletin. National Science Museum. Series A (Zoology) (Japan) [*A publication*]................. Bull Natl Sci Mus Ser A (Zool)

Bulletin. National Science Museum. Series B (Botany) (Japan) [*A publication*]................. Bull Natl Sci Mus Ser B (Bot)

Bulletin. National Science Museum. Series C (Geology) (Japan) [*A publication*]................. Bull Natl Sci Mus Ser C (Geol)

Bulletin. National Science Museum. Series D (Anthropology)
(Japan) [A publication]...................... Bull Natl Sci Mus Ser D (Anthropol)
Bulletin. National Science Museum (Tokyo) [A publication]..........................
Bull Natl Sci Mus (Tokyo)
Bulletin. National Speleological Society [United States] [A
publication]..Bull Natl Speleol Soc
Bulletin. Nationale Plantentuin van Belgie [A publication]..............................
Bull Natl Plant Belg
Bulletin. Natural History Museum in Belgrade. Series B.
Biological Sciences [A publication]...
Bull Nat Hist Mus Belgr Ser B Biol Sci
Bulletin. Natural History Research Center. University of
Baghdad [A publication].................. Bull Nat Hist Res Cent Univ Baghdad
Bulletin of Natural Sciences (Wellington) [A publication].............................
Bull Nat Sci (Wellington)
Bulletin. Nederlandse Oudheidkundige Bond [A publication].............. BNOB
Bulletin. New Hampshire Agricultural Experiment Station [A
publication]............................. Bull New Hamps Agric Exp Stn
Bulletin. New Hampshire Public Libraries [A publication]............... Bul NHPL
Bulletin. New Jersey Academy of Science [A publication].......... B NJ Acad S
Bulletin. New Jersey Academy of Science [A publication].... Bull NJ Acad Sci
Bulletin. New Jersey Agricultural Experiment Station [A
publication]............................Bull New Jers Agric Exp Stn
Bulletin. New Jersey Agricultural Experiment Station [A
publication]............................... Bull NJ Agr Exp Sta
Bulletin. New Mexico Agricultural Experiment Station [A
publication]............................Bull New Mex Agric Exp Stn
Bulletin. New Mexico Agricultural Experiment Station [A
publication]............................... Bull N Mex Agr Exp Sta
Bulletin. New York Academy of Medicine [A publication].......... B NY Ac Med
Bulletin. New York Academy of Medicine [A publication]..........................
Bull NY Acad Med
Bulletin. New York Agricultural Experiment Station [A
publication]............................... Bull NY Agr Exp Sta
Bulletin. New York Public Library [A publication]................................BNPL
Bulletin. New York Public Library [A publication]................................BNYPL
Bulletin. New York Public Library [A publication]................................ Bul NYPL
Bulletin. New York State Agricultural Experiment Station [A
publication]............................ Bull NY St Agric Exp Stn
Bulletin. New Zealand Department of Scientific and Industrial
Research [A publication]............................... Bull NZ Dep Scient Ind Res
Bulletin. New Zealand Department of Scientific and Industrial
Research [A publication]............................... Bull NZ Dept Sci Ind Res
Bulletin. New Zealand Geological Survey [A publication]............................
Bull NZ Geol Surv
Bulletin. New Zealand Society of Earthquake Engineering [A
publication]...............................Bull NZ Soc Earthquake Eng
Bulletin. New Zealand Society of Periodontology [A publication] ....
Bull NZ Soc Periodontol
Bulletin. Nigerian Forestry Departments [A publication]................................
Bull Niger For Dep
Bulletin. Niigata University Forests [A publication].........Bull Niigata Univ For
Bulletin. Nippon Dental College. General Education [A
publication]............................... Bull Nippon Dent Coll Gen Educ
Bulletin. Nippon Dental University. General Education [A
publication]............................... Bull Nippon Dent Univ Gen Educ
Bulletin. Nippon Veterinary and Zootechnical College [A
publication]............................... Bull Nippon Vet Zootech Coll
Bulletin. Norges Geologiske Undersokelse [A publication] ....
Bull Norg Geol Unders
Bulletin. North American Gladiolus Council [A publication]...........................
Bull N Am Gladiolus Counc
Bulletin. North Carolina Board of Health [A publication]................................
Bull North Carolina Bd Health
Bulletin. North Carolina Division of Mineral Resources [A
publication]................................Bull NC Div Miner Resour
Bulletin. North Carolina Division of Resource Planning and
Evaluation. Mineral Resources Section [A publication] ....
Bull NC Div Resour Plann Eval Miner Resour Sect
Bulletin. North Carolina Mineral Resources Section [A
publication]................................Bull NC Miner Resour Sect
Bulletin. North Dakota Agricultural Experiment Station [A
publication]............................... Bull N Dak Agr Exp Sta
Bulletin. North Dakota Agricultural Experiment Station [A
publication]................................Bull N Dak Agric Exp Stn
Bulletin. North of Scotland College of Agriculture [A publication]................
Bull N Scot Coll Agr
Bulletin. Northern Rhodesia Department of Agriculture [A
publication]................................Bull N Rhodesia Dept Agr
Bulletin de Numismatique [A publication] ....B Num
Bulletin. Ocean Research Institute. University of Tokyo [A
publication]............................... Bull Ocean Res Inst Univ Tokyo
Bulletin OEPP [Organisation Europeenne et Mediterraneenne
pour la Protection des Plantes] [A publication].........................Bull OEPP
Bulletin. Office of Experiment Stations. United States
Department of Agriculture [A publication]...
Bull Office Exper Stations US Dept Agric
Bulletin. Office International des Epizooties [A publication]..............................
Bull Off Int Epizoot
Bulletin. Office Internationale des Instituts d'Archeologie et
d'Histoire de l'Art [A publication] .... B Off Int

Bulletin. Office Internationale des Instituts d'Archeologie et
d'Histoire de l'Art [A publication] ....BOIA
Bulletin Officiel. Chambre de Commerce (Bruxelles) [A
publication]................................B Offic Ch Com (Bruxelles)
Bulletin Officiel. Propriete Industrielle [Berne] [A publication].........Bull Offic
Bulletin. Ohio Agricultural Experiment Station [A publication]........................
Bull Ohio Agr Exp Sta
Bulletin. Ohio Biological Survey [A publication] .... Bull Ohio Biol Surv
Bulletin de l'OIV [Office International de la Vigne et du Vin] [A
publication]................................ Bull OIV
Bulletin. Oji Institute for Forest Tree Improvement [A
publication]................................ Bull Oji Inst For Tree Impr
Bulletin. Okayama College of Science [A publication]......................................
Bull Okayama Coll Sci
Bulletin. Okayama Tobacco Experiment Station [A publication]......................
Bull Okayama Tob Exp Stn
Bulletin. Oklahoma Agricultural Experiment Station [A
publication]................................ Bull Okla Agric Exp Stn
Bulletin. Oklahoma Ornithological Society [A publication].............................
Bull Okla Ornithol Soc
Bulletin. Oklahoma State University. Agricultural Experiment
Station [A publication]........................... Bull Okla State Univ Agr Exp Sta
Bulletin. Ontario College of Pharmacy [A publication].....Bull Ont Coll Pharm
Bulletin. Operations Research Society of America [A
publication]................................Bull Oper Res Soc Am
Bulletin. Ophthalmological Society of Egypt [A publication] ....
Bull Ophthalmol Soc Egypt
Bulletin. Oregon Agricultural Experiment Station [A publication] ....
Bull Ore Agric Exp Stn
Bulletin. Oregon Agricultural Experiment Station [A publication] ....
Bull Oreg Agr Exp Sta
Bulletin. Oregon State University Forest Research Laboratory [A
publication]................................Bull Ore For Res Lab
Bulletin. Organisation Internationale de Metrologie Legale [A
publication]................................ Bull Organ Int Metrol Leg
Bulletin. Organisation Mondiale de la Sante [A publication].........................
Bull Org Mond Sante
Bulletin. Orton Society [A publication]................................Bull Orton Soc
Bulletin. Osaka Agricultural Research Center [A publication].........................
Bull Osaka Agric Res Cent
Bulletin. Osaka Medical School [A publication]............... Bull Osaka Med Sch
Bulletin. Osaka Museum of Natural History [A publication]............................
Bull Osaka Mus Nat Hist
Bulletin. Otago Catchment Board [A publication] ....Bull Otago Catchm Bd
Bulletin. Pacific Orchid Society of Hawaii [A publication].............................
Bull Pac Orchid Soc Hawaii
Bulletin. Pan American Health Organization [A publication].........................
Bull Pan Am Health Organ
Bulletin. Pan American Union [A publication]..BPAU
Bulletin. Pan American Union [A publication]..................... Bul Pan Am Union
Bulletin. Parenteral Drug Association [A publication].....................................
Bull Parenter Drug Assoc
Bulletin. Passaic County Dental Society [A publication]..................................
Bull Passaic Cty Dent Soc
Bulletin of Peace Proposals [A publication] ....B Peace Propos
Bulletin of Peace Proposals [A publication] ....Bull Peace Propos
Bulletin. Pennsylvania Agricultural Experiment Station [A
publication]................................ Bull PA Agr Exp Sta
Bulletin. Pennsylvania Agricultural Experiment Station [A
publication]................................Bull PA Agric Exp Stn
Bulletin. Pennsylvania State Modern Language Association [A
publication]................................BPSMLA
Bulletin. Pennsylvania State University. Agricultural Experiment
Station [A publication]................................ Bull PA State Univ Agr Exp Sta
Bulletin. Permanent International Association of Navigation
Congresses [A publication]..................... Bull Perma Int Ass Navig Congr
Bulletin. Permanent International Association of Navigation
Congresses [A publication].................... Bull Perm Int Assoc Navig Congr
Bulletin. Pharmaceutical Research Institute (Osaka) [A
publication]................................Bull Pharm Res Inst (Osaka)
Bulletin of Pharmacy (Istanbul) [A publication].............. Bull Pharm (Istanbul)
Bulletin. Philadelphia County Dental Society [A publication]........................
Bull Phila Cty Dent Soc
Bulletin. Philadelphia Herpetological Society [A publication]........................
Bull Phila Herpetol Soc
Bulletin. Philological Society of Calcutta [A publication]....................BPhSC
Bulletin. Philological Society of Calcutta [A publication]......................BPSC
Bulletin Philologique et Historique [A publication]................................ BPH
Bulletin Philologique et Historique [A publication]................................ BPHist
Bulletin Philologique et Historique. Comite des Travaux
Historiques et Scientifiques [Paris] [A publication] .... BPCTH
Bulletin Philologique et Historique. Comite des Travaux
Historiques et Scientifiques [Paris] [A publication]................BPHCTHS
Bulletin Philologique et Historique. Comite des Travaux
Historiques et Scientifiques (Paris) [A publication].....................BPHP
Bulletin. Phonetic Society of Japan [A publication]............................BPhSJ
Bulletin. Physical Fitness Research Institute [A publication] ....
Bull Phys Fitness Res Inst
Bulletin de Physiopathologie Respiratoire [A publication] .... B Physiopa
Bulletin de Physiopathologie Respiratoire (Nancy) [A
publication]................................ Bull Physiopathol Respir (Nancy)

Bulletin. Pittsburgh University [*A publication*]....Bull Pittsb Univ
Bulletin. Plankton Society of Japan [*A publication*]....Bull Plankton Soc Jpn
Bulletin. Postgraduate Institute of Medical Education and Research (Chandigarh) [*A publication*]....Bull Postgrad Inst Med Educ Res (Chandigarh)
Bulletin. Poznanskie Towarzystwo Przyjaciol Nauk. Serie D [*A publication*]....Bull Poznan Tow Przyjaciol Nauk Ser D
Bulletin. Presse- und Informationsamt der Bundesregierung [*A publication*]....Bull Presse- Informationsamt Bundesregier
Bulletin. Primary Tungsten Association [*A publication*]....Bull Primary Tungsten Assoc
Bulletin. Prince of Wales Museum of Western India [*A publication*]....B Prince of Wales Mus West India
Bulletin of Prosthetics Research [*A publication*]....BPR
Bulletin of Prosthetics Research [*A publication*]....Bull Prosthet Res
Bulletin du Protestantisme Francais [*A publication*]....BPF
Bulletin de Psychologie [*A publication*]....B Psychol
Bulletin. Psychonomic Society [*A publication*]....BPNSB
Bulletin. Psychonomic Society [*A publication*]....BPS
Bulletin. Psychonomic Society [*A publication*]....B Psychon S
Bulletin. Psychonomic Society [*A publication*]....Bull Psychon Soc
Bulletin. Public Health Institute of Hyogo Prefecture [*A publication*]....Bull Public Health Inst Hyogo Prefect
Bulletin. Pusan Fisheries College (Natural Sciences) [*A publication*]....Bull Pusan Fish Coll (Nat Sci)
Bulletin of Radiation Protection [*India*] [*A publication*]....Bull Radiat Prot
Bulletin. Raffles Museum [*A publication*]....Bull Raffles Mus
Bulletin. Ramakrishna Mission Institute of Culture [*A publication*]....B Rama Miss Inst Cult
Bulletin des Recherches Agronomiques de Gembloux [*A publication*]....Bull Rech Agron Gembloux
Bulletin. Regional Research Laboratory. Jammu [*A publication*]....Bull Reg Res Lab Jammu
Bulletin. Republic Institution for the Protection of Nature and the Museum of Natural History in Titograd [*A publication*]....Bull Repub Inst Prot Nat Mus Nat Hist Titograd
Bulletin of Research. College of Agriculture and Veterinary Medicine. Nihon University [*A publication*]....Bull Res Coll Agr Vet Med Nihon Univ
Bulletin of Research. College of Agriculture and Veterinary Science. Nihon University [*A publication*]....Bull Res Coll Agric Vet Sci Nihon Univ
Bulletin. Research Council of Israel [*A publication*]....Bull Res Counc Isr
Bulletin. Research Council of Israel. Section A. Chemistry [*A publication*]....Bull Res Counc Isr Sect A Chem
Bulletin. Research Council of Israel. Section A. Mathematics, Physics, and Chemistry [*A publication*]....Bull Res Counc Isr Sect A Math Phys Chem
Bulletin. Research Council of Israel. Section B. Biology and Geology [*A publication*]....Bull Res Counc Isr Sect B Biol Geol
Bulletin. Research Council of Israel. Section B. Zoology [*A publication*]....Bull Res Counc Isr Sect B Zool
Bulletin. Research Council of Israel. Section C. Technology [*A publication*]....Bull Res Counc Isr Sect C Technol
Bulletin. Research Council of Israel. Section D. Botany [*A publication*]....Bull Res Counc Isr Sect D Bot
Bulletin. Research Council of Israel. Section E. Experimental Medicine [*A publication*]....Bull Res Counc Isr Sect E Exp Med
Bulletin. Research Council of Israel. Section G. Geo-Sciences [*A publication*]....Bull Res Counc Isr Sect G Geo-Sci
Bulletin of Research in the Humanities [*A publication*]....BRH
Bulletin. Research Institute of Applied Electricity [*A publication*]....Bull Res Inst Appl Electr
Bulletin. Research Institute of Electronics. Shizuoka University [*A publication*]....Bull Res Inst Electron Shizuoka Univ
Bulletin. Research Institute for Food Science. Kyoto University [*A publication*]....Bull Res Inst Food Sci Kyoto Univ
Bulletin. Research Institute of Mineral Dressing and Metallurgy. Tohoku University [*A publication*]....Bull Res Inst Miner Dressing Metall Tohoku Univ
Bulletin. Research Institute for Polymers and Textiles [*A publication*]....Bull Res Inst Polymers Textiles
Bulletin. Research Institute for Scientific Measurements. Tohoku University [*A publication*]....Bull Res Inst Sci Meas Tohoku Univ
Bulletin. Research Laboratory for Nuclear Reactors (Tokyo Institute of Technology) [*A publication*]....Bull Res Lab Nucl React (Tokyo Inst Technol)
Bulletin. Research Laboratory of Precision Machinery and Electronics [*A publication*]....Bull Res Lab Precis Mach Electron
Bulletin. Research Laboratory of Precision Machinery and Electronics. (Tokyo Institute of Technology) [*A publication*]....Bull Res Lab Precis Mach Electron (Tokyo Inst Technol)
Bulletin on Rheumatic Diseases [*A publication*]....Bull Rheum Dis
Bulletin. Rhode Island Agricultural Experiment Station [*A publication*]....Bull Rhode Isl Agric Exp Stn
Bulletin. Rijksmuseum [*A publication*]....Bull Rijksmus
Bulletin. Rocky Mountain Modern Language Association [*A publication*]....BRMMLA
Bulletin. Saga Agricultural Experiment Station [*A publication*]....Bull Saga Agr Exp Sta
Bulletin. St. Marianna University. School of Medicine. General Education [*A publication*]....Bull St Marianna Univ Sch Med Gen Educ
Bulletin. Saitama Horticultural Experiment Station [*A publication*]....Bull Saitama Hortic Exp Stn
Bulletin. Salesian Polytechnic [*A publication*]....Bull Salesian Polytech
Bulletin des Sante et Production Animales en Afrique [*A publication*]....Bull Sante Prod Anim Afr
Bulletin. School of Engineering and Architecture of Sakarya [*A publication*]....Bull School Eng Archit Sakarya
Bulletin. School of Forestry. Montana State University [*A publication*]....Bull Sch For Mont St Univ
Bulletin. School of Forestry. Stephen F. Austin State College [*A publication*]....Bull Sch For S F Austin St Coll
Bulletin. School of Oriental and African Studies [*A publication*]....B Sch Orient Afr Stud
Bulletin. School of Oriental and African Studies [*A publication*]....BSOA
Bulletin. School of Oriental and African Studies [*A publication*]....BSOAS
Bulletin. School of Oriental and African Studies [*A publication*]....BSOS
Bulletin. School of Oriental Studies [*A publication*]....BSOS
Bulletin. Schweizerischen Akademie der Medizinischen Wissenschaften [*A publication*]....B Sc Ak Med
Bulletin. Schweizerischen Akademie der Medizinischen Wissenschaften [*A publication*]....Bull Schweiz Akad Med Wiss
Bulletin. Schweizerischen Gesellschaft fuer Anthropologie und Ethnologie [*A publication*]....Bull Schweiz Ges Anthropol Ethnol
Bulletin. Science and Engineering Research Laboratory. Waseda University [*A publication*]....Bull Sci Eng Res Lab Waseda Univ
Bulletin des Sciences Mathematiques [*A publication*]....B Sci Math
Bulletin des Sciences Mathematiques [*A publication*]....Bull Sci Math
Bulletin des Sciences Naturelles et de Geologie [*A publication*]....B Sc Nat
Bulletin des Sciences Pharmacologiques [*A publication*]....Bull Sci Pharmacol
Bulletin des Sciences. Societe Philomathique de Paris [*A publication*]....Bull Sc Soc Philomat Paris
Bulletin Scientifique. Association des Ingenieurs Electriciens Sortis de l'Institut Electrotechnique Montefiore [*A publication*]....Bul Sci AIM
Bulletin Scientifique. Conseil des Academies de la RSF de Yougoslavie [*A publication*]....Bull Sci Cons Acad RSF Yougosl
Bulletin Scientifique de la France et de la Belgique [*A publication*]....Bull Scient France et Belgique
Bulletin Scientifique. Institut Textile de France [*A publication*]....Bull Sci ITF
Bulletin Scientifique. Section A. Sciences Naturelles, Techniques, et Medicales [*A publication*]....Bull Sci Sect A
Bulletin. Scripps Institution of Oceanography of the University of California [*A publication*]....Bull Scripps Inst Oceanogr Univ Calif
Bulletin des Seances. Academie Royale des Sciences d'Outre-Mer [*A publication*]....B Seances Acad Roy Sci O-Mer
Bulletin des Seances. Academie Royale des Sciences d'Outre-Mer (Brussels) [*A publication*]....Bull Seances Acad R Sci Outre-Mer (Brussels)
Bulletin des Seances. Cercle Archeologique de Mons [*A publication*]....BSCAM
Bulletin. Section de Geographie. Actes du 96e Congres National des Societes Savantes [*A publication*]....B Sect Geogr Soc Sav
Bulletin. Section de Geographie. Comite des Travaux Historiques et Scientifiques [*A publication*]....BGCTH
Bulletin. Section Historique. Academie Roumaine [*A publication*]....BHAR
Bulletin. Seikai Regional Fisheries Research Laboratory [*A publication*]....Bull Seikai Reg Fish Res Lab
Bulletin. Seishin-Igaku Institute [*A publication*]....Bull Seishin-Igaku Inst
Bulletin. Seismological Society of America [*A publication*]....B Seis S Am
Bulletin. Seismological Society of America [*A publication*]....Bull Seismol Soc Am
Bulletin. Seismological Society of America [*A publication*]....Bull Seismol Soc Amer
Bulletin Seismologique (Warsaw) [*A publication*]....Bull Seismol (Warsaw)
Bulletin Semestriel. Association des Classiques de l'Universite de Liege [*A publication*]....BACILg
Bulletin. Sericultural Experiment Station (Tokyo) [*A publication*]....Bull Seric Exp Stn (Tokyo)
Bulletin. Service de la Carte Geologique de l'Algerie [*A publication*]....Bull Serv Carte Geol Alger
Bulletin. Service de la Carte Geologique d'Alsace et de Lorraine [*A publication*]....Bull Serv Carte Geol Als Lorr
Bulletin. Service de Culture et d'Etudes du Peuplier et du Saule [*A publication*]....Bull Serv Cult Etud Peuplier et Saule
Bulletin. Service Social des Caisses d'Assurance Maladie [*A publication*]....B Serv Soc Caisses Assur Malad
Bulletin. Shiga Prefectural Agricultural Experiment Station [*A publication*]....Bull Shiga Pref Agr Exp Sta
Bulletin. Shikoku Agricultural Experiment Station [*A publication*]....Bull Shikoku Agr Exp Sta
Bulletin. Shikoku Agricultural Experiment Station [*A publication*]....Bull Shikoku Agric Exp Stn
Bulletin. Shimane Agricultural College [*A publication*]....Bull Shimane Agr Coll
Bulletin. Shimane Agricultural College [*A publication*]....Bull Shimane Agric Coll

Bulletin. Shimane Agricultural Experiment Station [A publication].................................... Bull Shimane Agr Exp Sta

Bulletin. Shimane Agricultural Experiment Station [A publication].................................. Bull Shimane Agric Exp Stn

Bulletin. Shinshu University Forests [A publication]..... Bull Shinshu Univ For

Bulletin. Shizuoka Agricultural Experiment Station [A publication].................................... Bull Shizuoka Agr Exp Sta

Bulletin. Shizuoka Prefectural Agricultural Experiment Station [A publication]........................Bull Shizuoka Pref Agr Exp Sta

Bulletin. Shizuoka Prefectural Fisheries Experiment Station [A publication].................... Bull Shizuoka Prefect Fish Exp Stn

Bulletin. Shrimp Culture Research Center [A publication].......................... Bull Shrimp Cult Res Cent

Bulletin Signaletique [A publication]..................................... Bull Signal

Bulletin. Sinai Hospital of Detroit [A publication]........ Bull Sinai Hosp Detroit

Bulletin. Singapore National Institute of Chemistry [A publication]...................... Bulletin Singapore Natl Inst Chem

Bulletin. Sloane Hospital for Women in the Columbia-Presbyterian Medical Center [A publication]........................... Bull Sloane Hosp Women Columbia-Presbyt Med Cent

Bulletin. Slovenskej Pol'nohospodarskej Akademie. Vyskumneho Ustavu Potravinarskeho [A publication]............... Bull Slov Pol'nohospod Akad Vysk Ustavu Potravin

Bulletin. Societe des Amis de Montaigne [A publication].................... BSAM

Bulletin. Societe des Amis de Port-Royal [A publication].................... BSAPR

Bulletin. Societe des Amis des Sciences et des Lettres de Poznan. Serie C. Medecine [A publication]........................... Bull Soc Amis Sci Lett Poznan Ser C

Bulletin. Societe des Amis des Sciences et des Lettres de Poznan. Serie D. Sciences Biologiques [A publication]............... Bull Soc Amis Sci Lett Poznan Ser D Sci Biol

Bulletin. Societe Anatomique de Paris [A publication] .....Bull Soc Anat Paris

Bulletin. Societe des Antiquaires de Normandie [A publication] ....BSAN

Bulletin. Societe des Antiquaires de Normandie [A publication]............................ BSANormandie

Bulletin. Societe des Antiquaires de l'Ouest et des Musees de Poitiers [A publication].......................BSAO

Bulletin. Societe des Antiquaires de l'Ouest et des Musees de Poitiers [A publication]...........................BSAOuest

Bulletin. Societe d'Archeologie Copte [A publication]........................BSAC

Bulletin. Societe Archeologique d'Alexandrie [A publication]...............BSAA

Bulletin. Societe Archeologique de Bordeaux [A publication]................BSAB

Bulletin. Societe Archeologique Bulgare [A publication]...............B Soc Bulg

Bulletin. Societe Archeologique de la Correze [A publication]........................ BSACorreze

Bulletin. Societe Archeologique et Historique du Limousin [A publication]..............................BSAHLimousin

Bulletin. Societe Archeologique et Historique du Limousin [A publication].......................B Soc Archeol Hist Limousin

Bulletin. Societe Archeologique et Historique de Nantes et de Loire-Atlantique [A publication].................... BSAHNantes

Bulletin. Societe Archeologique du Limousin [A publication]............... BSAL

Bulletin. Societe Archeologique du Midi de la France [A publication]........................... BSAM

Bulletin. Societe Archeologique de Sens [A publication]...................... BSAS

Bulletin. Societe d'Archeologique et de Statistique de la Drome [A publication]........................... BSASD

Bulletin. Societe Archeologique de Touraine [A publication]............... BSAT

Bulletin. Societe d'Art et d'Histoire du Diocese de Liege [A publication]........................... BSAHDL

Bulletin. Societe Belge de Geologie, de Paleontologie, et d'Hydrologie [A publication] ....Bull Soc Belg Geol Paleontol Hydrol

Bulletin. Societe Belge d'Ophtalmologie [A publication]............................ Bull Soc Belge Ophtalmol

Bulletin. Societe Bibliographique des Publications Populaires [A publication]...........................BSBPP

Bulletin. Societe des Bibliolatres de France [A publication]................... BSBF

Bulletin. Societe des Bibliophiles Belges Seant a Mons [A publication]...........................BSBBM

Bulletin. Societe des Bibliophiles Liegeois [A publication]................... BSBL

Bulletin. Societe Botanique de France [A publication]........... Bull Soc Bot Fr

Bulletin. Societe Botanique de France [A publication].....Bull Soc Bot France

Bulletin. Societe Botanique de France. Premiere Partie [A publication]........................... B S Bot Fr I

Bulletin. Societe Botanique du Nord de la France [A publication]............................ Bull Soc Bot Nord Fr

Bulletin. Societe Botanique Suisse [A publication]........ Bull Soc Bot Suisse

Bulletin. Societe Centrale Forestiere de Belgique [A publication]............................ Bull Soc Cent For Belg

Bulletin. Societe Centrale de Medecine Veterinaire [A publication]............................Bull Soc Centr Med Vet

Bulletin. Societe de Chimie Biologique [A publication] .....Bull Soc Chim Biol

Bulletin. Societe de Chimie Biologique [France] [A publication]............................ Bull Soc Chim Biol

Bulletin. Societe Chimique (Beograd) [A publication]............................ Bull Soc Chim (Beograd)

Bulletin. Societe Chimique de France [A publication]..........Bull Soc Chim Fr

Bulletin. Societe Chimique de France [A publication]............................ Bull Soc Chim France

Bulletin. Societe Chimique de France. Deuxieme Partie [A publication]........................... B S Ch Fr II

Bulletin. Societe Chimique de France. Deuxieme Partie [A publication]............................Bull Soc Chim Fr II

Bulletin. Societe Chimique de France. Deuxieme Partie. Chimie Organique, Biochimie [A publication] ....Bull Soc Chim Fr Part 2

Bulletin. Societe Chimique de France. Premiere Partie [A publication]........................... B S Ch Fr I

Bulletin. Societe Chimique de France. Premiere Partie. Chimie Analytique, Chimie Minerale, Chimie Physique [A publication]............... Bull Soc Chim Fr I

Bulletin. Societe Chimique de France. Premiere Partie. Chimie Analytique, Chimie Minerale, Chimie Physique [A publication]............... Bull Soc Chim Fr Part 1

Bulletin. Societe de Chirurgie de Paris [A publication].....Bull Soc Chir Paris

Bulletin. Societe d'Emulation du Bourbonnais [A publication]........................... BSEBourbonnais

Bulletin. Societe Entomologique d'Egypte [A publication]............................ Bull Soc Entomol Egypte

Bulletin. Societe Entomologique de France [A publication]............................ Bull Soc Entomol Fr

Bulletin. Societe Entomologique Suisse [A publication]............................ Bull Soc Entomol Suisse

Bulletin. Societe d'Ethnographie du Limousin et de la Marche [A publication]............................ B Soc Ethnogr Limousin Marche

Bulletin. Societe d'Etudes Dantesques du Centre Universitaire Mediterraneen [A publication]............................BSED

Bulletin. Societe des Etudes Indochinoises [A publication]............................BSEIC

Bulletin. Societe des Etudes Indochinoises [A publication]............................ B Soc Et Indochinoises

Bulletin. Societe des Etudes de Lettres (Lausanne) [A publication]......BELL

Bulletin. Societe des Etudes Litteraires, Scientifiques, et Artistiques du Lot [A publication]............................BSELot

Bulletin. Societe d'Etudes Oceaniennes [A publication]........ B Soc Et Ocean

Bulletin. Societe d'Etudes de la Province de Cambrai [A publication]............................BSEPC

Bulletin. Societe d'Etudes Scientifiques de l'Aude [A publication]............................ B Soc Et Sci Aude

Bulletin. Societe Forestiere de Franche-Comte et Belfort [A publication]............................Bull Soc For Franche-Comte

Bulletin. Societe Francaise de Ceramique [A publication] ....B S Fr Cer

Bulletin. Societe Francaise de Ceramique [A publication]............................ Bull Soc Fr Ceram

Bulletin. Societe Francaise de Dermatologie et de Syphiligraphie [A publication] .... B S Fr D Sy

Bulletin. Societe Francaise de Dermatologie et de Syphiligraphie [A publication].................... Bull Soc Fr Dermatol Syphiligr

Bulletin. Societe Francaise d'Etudes Mariales [A publication]...........BSFEM

Bulletin. Societe Francaise d'Histoire de la Medecine [A publication]............................ BHM

Bulletin. Societe Francaise d'Hygiene [A publication] ......Bull Soc Franc Hyg

Bulletin. Societe Francaise de Mineralogie et de Cristallographie [A publication]............................B S Fr Min

Bulletin. Societe Francaise de Mineralogie et de Cristallographie [A publication] .... Bull Soc Fr Miner Cristallogr

Bulletin. Societe Francaise de Mycologie Medicale [A publication]............................ Bull Soc Fr Mycol Med

Bulletin. Societe Francaise de Numismatique [A publication] ....BSFN

Bulletin. Societe Francaise de Philosophie [A publication] ....B S Ph

Bulletin. Societe Francaise de Philosophie [A publication] .... Bull Soc Fr Phil

Bulletin. Societe Francaise de Photogrammetrie [A publication] .... Bull Soc Fr Photogramm

Bulletin. Societe Francaise de Physiologie Vegetale [A publication]............................ Bull Soc Franc Physiol Veg

Bulletin. Societe Francaise de Physiologie Vegetale [A publication]............................ Bull Soc Fr Physiol Veg

Bulletin. Societe Francaise de Sociologie [A publication]............................ B Soc Franc Sociol

Bulletin. Societe de Geographie et d'Archeologie d'Oran [A publication]............................BSGAO

Bulletin. Societe Geologique de France [A publication]........ Bull Soc Geol Fr

Bulletin. Societe Geologique et Mineralogique de Bretagne. Serie C [A publication] .... Bull Soc Geol Mineral Bretagne Ser C

Bulletin. Societe Geologique de Normandie [A publication]............................ Bull Soc Geol Normandie

Bulletin. Societe d'Histoire et d'Archeologie de Gand [A publication]............................ BHAG

Bulletin. Societe de l'Histoire de l'Art Francais [A publication]...........BSHAF

Bulletin. Societe pour l'Histoire des Eglises Wallonnes [A publication]............................BHEW

Bulletin. Societe pour l'Histoire des Eglises Wallonnes [A publication]............................BSHEW

Bulletin. Societe d'Histoire et de Geographie de la Region de Setif [A publication]............................BSHS

Bulletin. Societe d'Histoire de la Medecine [A publication]............................ BSHM

Bulletin. Societe d'Histoire Moderne [A publication]............................ BSHM

Bulletin. Societe d'Histoire Naturelle de l'Afrique du Nord [A publication]............................Bull Soc Hist Nat Afr Nord

Bulletin. Societe d'Histoire Naturelle de l'Afrique du Nord [A publication]............................ Bull Soc Hist Natur Afr Nord

Bulletin. Societe d'Histoire Naturelle du Doubs [A publication]........................ Bull Soc Hist Nat Doubs

Bulletin. Societe d'Histoire Naturelle de Toulouse [*A publication*]................
Bull Soc Hist Nat Toulouse
Bulletin. Societe de l'Histoire du Protestantisme Francais [*A publication*]...BSHPF
Bulletin. Societe de l'Histoire du Protestantisme Francais [*A publication*]... Bull SHPF
Bulletin. Societe Historique et Archeologique du Perigord [*A publication*]................................BSHAPerigord
Bulletin. Societe Historique de Paris et de l'Ile de France [*A publication*]................................BSHPIF
Bulletin. Societe Internationale de Chirurgie [*A publication*]......................
Bull Soc Int Chir
Bulletin. Societe Internationale pour l'Etude de la Philosophie Medievale [*A publication*]..................................BPhM
Bulletin. Societe de Langue et Litterature Wallonnes [*A publication*]................................... BSLLW
Bulletin. Societe de Linguistique de Paris [*A publication*]......................BSL
Bulletin. Societe de Linguistique de Paris [*A publication*]......................BSLP
Bulletin. Societe de Linguistique de Paris [*A publication*]......................
B Soc Linguist Paris
Bulletin. Societe Linneenne [*A publication*].................... B Soc Linn
Bulletin. Societe Linneenne de Bordeaux [*A publication*].................
Bull Soc Linn Bord
Bulletin. Societe Linneenne de Normandie [*A publication*]......................
Bull Soc Linn Normandie
Bulletin. Societe Linneenne de Provence [*A publication*]......................
Bull Soc Linn Provence
Bulletin. Societe Litteraire et Historique de la Brie [*A publication*]................................ B Soc Litt Hist Brie
Bulletin. Societe Lorraine des Etudes Locales dans l'Enseignement Public [*A publication*].....................BSLELEP
Bulletin. Societe Lorraine des Sciences [*A publication*]......................
Bull Soc Lorraine Sci
Bulletin. Societe des Mathematiciens et des Physiciens de la Republique Populaire de Macedoine [*A publication*].....................
Bull Soc Math Phys Macedoine
Bulletin. Societe Mathematique de Belgique [*A publication*]......................
Bull Soc Math Belg
Bulletin. Societe Mathematique de France [*A publication*].......... B S Math Fr
Bulletin. Societe Mathematique de Grece [*A publication*]......................
Bull Soc Math Grece
Bulletin. Societe Medicale d'Afrique Noire de Langue Francaise [*A publication*].................... Bull Soc Med Afr Noire Lang Fr
Bulletin. Societe Medico-Chirurgicale de l'Indo-Chine [*A publication*].................... Bull Soc Med-Chir Indo-Chine
Bulletin. Societe de Microscopie du Canada [*A publication*]......................
Bull Soc Microsc Can
Bulletin. Societe Nationale des Antiquaires de France [*A publication*]..................... B Ant Fr
Bulletin. Societe Nationale des Antiquaires de France [*A publication*]..................... BSAF
Bulletin. Societe Nationale des Antiquaires de France [*A publication*].....................BSAFrance
Bulletin. Societe Nationale des Antiquaires de France [*A publication*].....................BSNAF
Bulletin. Societe des Naturalistes et des Archeologues de l'Ain [*A publication*].................... Bull Soc Nat Archeol Ain
Bulletin. Societe Neuchateloise de Geographie [*A publication*].....................
B Soc Neuch Geogr
Bulletin. Societe Neuchatelloise des Sciences Naturelles [*A publication*].....................Bull Soc Neuchatel Sci Nat
Bulletin. Societe de Pathologie Exotique [*A publication*].....................
Bull Soc Pathol Exot
Bulletin. Societe de Pathologie Exotique et de ses Filiales [*A publication*].....................Bull Soc Pathol Exot Filiales
Bulletin. Societe de Pediatrie de Paris [*A publication*].....................
Bull Soc Pediat Paris
Bulletin. Societe de Pharmacie de Bordeaux [*A publication*].....................
Bull Soc Pharm Bord
Bulletin. Societe de Pharmacie de Lille [*A publication*].....................
Bull Soc Pharm Lille
Bulletin. Societe de Pharmacie de Marseille [*A publication*].....................
Bull Soc Pharm Mars
Bulletin. Societe de Pharmacie de Marseille [*A publication*].....................
Bull Soc Pharm Marseille
Bulletin. Societe de Pharmacie de Strasbourg [*A publication*].....................
Bull Soc Pharm Strasb
Bulletin. Societe Philomathique de Paris [*A publication*].....................
Bull Soc Philomat Paris
Bulletin. Societe Phycologique de France [*A publication*].....................
Bull Soc Phycol Fr
Bulletin. Societe Polonaise de Linguistique [*A publication*].................. BSPL
Bulletin. Societe Portugaise des Sciences Naturelles [*A publication*].................... Bull Soc Portugaise Sc Nat
Bulletin. Societe Prehistorique Francaise [*A publication*].................... BSPF
Bulletin. Societe Prehistorique Francaise [*A publication*].....................
Bull Soc Prehist Fr
Bulletin. Societe Prehistorique Francaise. Comptes Rendus Mensuels [*A publication*]........................ B Soc Prehist Franc C R Mens
Bulletin. Societe Royal d'Archeologie d'Alexandrie [*A publication*].....................BSRAA

Bulletin. Societe Royale Belge d'Anthropologie [*A publication*].....................
B Soc Roy Belge Anthropol
Bulletin. Societe Royale Belge des Electriciens [*A publication*].....................
Bull Soc R Belge Electr
Bulletin. Societe Royale Belge des Electriciens [*A publication*].....................
Bull Soc Roy Belg Elec
Bulletin. Societe Royale Belge de Gynecologie et d'Obstetrique [*A publication*]....................Bull Soc R Belge Gynecol Obstet
Bulletin. Societe Royale de Botanique de Belgique [*A publication*]....................Bull Soc Bot Belg
Bulletin. Societe Royale de Botanique de Belgique [*A publication*].................... Bull Soc R Bot Belg
Bulletin. Societe Royale Forestiere de Belgique [*A publication*].....................
Bull Soc For Belg
Bulletin. Societe Royale Forestiere de Belgique [*A publication*].....................
Bull Soc R For Belg
Bulletin. Societe Royale des Sciences de Liege [*A publication*].....................
Bull Soc Roy Sci Liege
Bulletin. Societe Royale des Sciences de Liege [*A publication*].....................
Bull Soc R Sci Liege
Bulletin. Societe Royale de Vieux-Liege [*A publication*].................... BSRV-L
Bulletin. Societe des Sciences Historiques et Naturelles de l'Yonne [*A publication*].....................BSSHNY
Bulletin. Societe des Sciences Historiques de l'Yonne [*A publication*].....................BSHY
Bulletin. Societe des Sciences Historiques de l'Yonne [*A publication*].....................BSSY
Bulletin. Societe des Sciences et des Lettres de Lodz [*A publication*].....................BSSL
Bulletin. Societe des Sciences et des Lettres de Lodz [*A publication*]....................Bull Soc Sci Lett Lodz
Bulletin. Societe des Sciences Medicales du Grand-Duche de Luxembourg [*A publication*]....................B S Sci Med
Bulletin. Societe des Sciences Medicales du Grand-Duche de Luxembourg [*A publication*]...... Bull Soc Sci Med Grand-Duche Luxemb
Bulletin. Societe des Sciences de Nancy [*A publication*].....................
Bull Soc Sci Nancy
Bulletin. Societe des Sciences Naturelles de l'Ouest de la France [*A publication*]....................Bull Soc Sci Nat Ouest Fr
Bulletin. Societe des Sciences Naturelles et Physiques du Maroc [*A publication*]....................Bull Soc Sci Nat Phys Maroc
Bulletin. Societe des Sciences Veterinaires de Lyon [*A publication*]....................Bull Soc Sc Vet Lyon
Bulletin. Societe des Sciences Veterinaires et de Medecine Comparee de Lyon [*A publication*]....... Bull Soc Sci Vet Med Comp Lyon
Bulletin. Societe Scientifique de Bretagne [*A publication*].....................
Bull Soc Sci Bretagne
Bulletin. Societe Scientifique d'Hygiene Alimentaire et d'Alimentation Rationnelle de l'Homme [*A publication*].....................
Bull Soc Sci Hyg Aliment Aliment Ration Homme
Bulletin. Societe Scientifique et Litteraire du Limbourg [*A publication*].....................BSL
Bulletin. Societe Scientifique et Litteraire du Limbourg [*A publication*].....................BSSLL
Bulletin. Societe Suisse des Americanistes [*A publication*].....................
B Soc Suisse American
Bulletin. Societe de Thanatologie [*A publication*].....................B Soc Thanatologie
Bulletin. Societe Toulousaine d'Etudes Classiques [*A publication*]....BSTEC
Bulletin. Societe Vaudoise des Sciences Naturelles [*A publication*].....................Bull Soc Vaudoise Sci Nat
Bulletin. Societe Vervietoise d'Archeologie et d'Histoire [*A publication*]..................... BSVAH
Bulletin. Societe Zoologique de France [*A publication*].................B S Zool Fr
Bulletin. Societe Zoologique de France [*A publication*].........Bull Soc Zool Fr
Bulletin. Societe Zoologique de France [*A publication*].....................
Bull Soc Zool France
Bulletin. Societes Archeologiques d'Eure-Et-Loir [*A publication*]....................
B Soc Arch Eure-Et-Loir
Bulletin. Societes Chimiques Belges [*A publication*].................... B S Chim Be
Bulletin. Societes Chimiques Belges [*A publication*]........Bull Soc Chim Belg
Bulletin. Societes d'Ophtalmologie de France [*A publication*].....................
Bull Soc Ophtalmol Fr
Bulletin. Society of Pharmacological and Environmental Pathologists [*A publication*].............. Bull Soc Pharmacol Environ Pathol
Bulletin. Society of Sea Water Science (Japan) [*A publication*].....................
Bull Soc Sea Water Sci (Jpn)
Bulletin. Society of Vector Ecologists [*A publication*].....Bull Soc Vector Ecol
Bulletin. Soil Bureau Department of Scientific and Industrial Research (New Zealand) [*A publication*]....................... Bull Soil Bur (NZ)
Bulletin. Soil Survey of Great Britain [*A publication*]....Bull Soil Surv Gt Br
Bulletin. Sommaires des Periodiques Francais et Etrangers [*A publication*].....................BS
Bulletin. South African Institute of Assayers and Analysts [*A publication*]....................Bull S Afr Inst Assayers Anal
Bulletin. South Carolina Academy of Science [*A publication*].....................
Bull SC Acad Sci
Bulletin. South Dakota Agricultural Experiment Station [*A publication*]....................Bull S Dak Agr Exp Sta
Bulletin. Southern California Academy of Sciences [*A publication*].................... Bull South Calif Acad Sci
Bulletin of Spanish Studies [*A publication*] ....BSS

Bulletin. Special Libraries Council of Philadelphia and Vicinity
[*A publication*]..................................Bull Spec Libr Coun Phila
Bulletin. Speleological Society of the District of Columbia [*A publication*] .... Bull Speleol Soc DC
Bulletin. Sport Fishing Institute [*A publication*]................. Bull Sport Fish Inst
Bulletin. State Biological Survey of Kansas [*A publication*]....................
Bull State Biol Surv Kans
Bulletin. State Plant Board of Florida [*A publication*]....................
Bull State Plant Board Fla
Bulletin. State University of Iowa [*A publication*] ..... Bull State Univ Iowa
Bulletin. Stations d'Experimentation Agricole Hongroises. A. Production Vegetale [*A publication*]............... Bull Stn Exp Agric Hong A
Bulletin. Stations d'Experimentation Agricole Hongroises. C. Horticulture [*A publication*]....................... Bull Stn Exp Agric Hong C
Bulletin de Statistique (Bruxelles) [*A publication*] .... B Statist (Bruxelles)
Bulletin de Statistique Suisse [*A publication*] .... BSS
Bulletin of Stomatology. Kyoto University [*A publication*]....................
Bull Stomatol Kyoto Univ
Bulletin des Stupefiants [*A publication*]....................B Stupefiants
Bulletin. Sugadaira Biological Laboratory [*A publication*] ....
Bull Sugadaira Biol Lab
Bulletin of Sugar Beet Research [*A publication*] .... Bull Sugar Beet Res
Bulletin of Sugar Beet Research. Supplement [*A publication*] ....
Bull Sugar Beet Res Suppl
Bulletin of Suicidology [*A publication*] ....Bull Suicidol
Bulletin of Suicidology [*A publication*] ....Bul Suicidol
Bulletin Suisse de Mycologie [*A publication*]....................... Bull Suisse Mycol
Bulletin. Suzugamine Women's College. Natural Science [*A publication*]................. Bull Suzugamine Women's Coll Nat Sci
Bulletin. Swaziland Department of Agriculture [*A publication*]....................
Bull Swazil Dep Agric
Bulletin. Taiwan Agricultural Research Institute [*A publication*]....................
Bull Taiwan Agric Res Inst
Bulletin. Taiwan Forestry Research Institute [*A publication*]....................
Bull Taiwan Forestry Res Inst
Bulletin. Taiwan Forestry Research Institute [*A publication*]....................
Bull Taiwan For Res Inst
Bulletin. Tall Timbers Research Station [*A publication*] ....
Bull Tall Timbers Res Stn
Bulletin. Tea Research Station. Ministry of Agriculture and Forestry [*Japan*] [*A publication*] ....Bull Tea Res Stn Minist Agric For
Bulletin. Technical University of Istanbul [*A publication*] ....
Bull Tech Univ Istanbul
Bulletin Technique Apicole [*A publication*]....................... Bull Tech Api
Bulletin Technique. Departement de Genetique Animale [*France*] [*A publication*] .... Bull Tech Dep Genet Anim
Bulletin Technique. Divisions des Sols. Province de Quebec - Ministere de l'Agriculture [*A publication*]...................
Bull Tech Div Sols Queb Minist Agric
Bulletin Technique d'Information [*A publication*]........................Bull Tech Inf
Bulletin Technique d'Information. Ministere de l'Agriculture (France) [*A publication*] .... Bull Tech Inform Min Agr (France)
Bulletin Technique de la Suisse Romande [*A publication*] ....
Bull Tech Suisse Romande
Bulletin. Technique Vevey [*A publication*] ....Bull Tech Vevey
Bulletin. Tennessee Agricultural Experiment Station [*A publication*]....................... Bull Tenn Agric Exp Stn
Bulletin. Tennessee Nurses Association [*A publication*]....................
Bull Tenn Nurses Assoc
Bulletin. Texas Agricultural Experiment Station [*A publication*]....................
Bull Tex Agr Exp Sta
Bulletin. Texas Agricultural Experiment Station [*A publication*]....................
Bull Tex Agric Exp Sta
Bulletin. Texas Memorial Museum [*A publication*] ....Bull Tex Mem Mus
Bulletin. Texas Ornithological Society [*A publication*]....................
Bull Tex Ornithol Soc
Bulletin de Theologie Ancienne et Medievale [*A publication*] .... BTAM
Bulletin de Theologie Ancienne et Medievale [*A publication*] .... BTh
Bulletin of Thermodynamics and Thermochemistry [*A publication*].....................Bull Thermodyn & Thermochem
Bulletin Thomiste [*A publication*] ....BThom
Bulletin of Tibetology [*A publication*] .... B Tibetol
Bulletin. Tobacco Research Institute [*A publication*] .... Bull Tob Res Inst
Bulletin. Tochigi Agricultural Experiment Station [*A publication*] ....
Bull Tochigi Agr Exp Sta
Bulletin. Tohoku Institute of Technology. Section B. Sciences [*A publication*]................. Bull Tohoku Inst Technol Sect B
Bulletin. Tohoku National Agricultural Experiment Station [*A publication*]................. Bull Tohoku Nat Agr Exp Sta
Bulletin. Tohoku National Agricultural Experiment Station (Morioka) [*A publication*] .... Bull Tohoku Natol Agr Exp Stn (Morioka)
Bulletin. Tohoku Regional Fisheries Research Laboratory [*A publication*]................. Bull Tohoku Reg Fish Res Lab
Bulletin. Tokai-Kinki National Agricultural Experiment Station [*A publication*]...............Bull-Tokai Kinki Agr Exp Sta
Bulletin. Tokai-Kinki National Agricultural Experiment Station [*A publication*]................. Bull Tokai-Kinki Nat Agr Exp Sta
Bulletin. Tokai-Kinki National Agricultural Experiment Station [*A publication*]....................Bull Tokai-Kinki Natl Agric Exp Stn
Bulletin. Tokai Regional Fisheries Research Laboratory [*A publication*]....................Bull Tokai Reg Fish Res Lab

Bulletin. Tokyo Dental College [*A publication*] ....Bull Tokyo Dent Coll
Bulletin. Tokyo Gakugei University [*A publication*] ....
Bull Tokyo Gakugei Univ
Bulletin. Tokyo Gakugei University. Series 4 [*A publication*]....................
Bull Tokyo Gakugei Univ Ser 4
Bulletin. Tokyo Institute of Technology [*A publication*]....................
Bull Tokyo Inst Technol
Bulletin. Tokyo Medical and Dental University [*A publication*]....................
Bull Tokyo Med Dent Univ
Bulletin. Tokyo Metropolitan Rehabilitation Center of the Physically and Mentally Handicapped [*A publication*]....................
Bull Tokyo Metro Rehab Cent Phys Ment Handcp
Bulletin. Tokyo Science Museum [*A publication*] ....Bull Tokyo Sci Mus
Bulletin. Tokyo University Forests [*A publication*] .... Bull Tokyo Univ For
Bulletin. Torrey Botanical Club [*A publication*]..............................B Tor Bot C
Bulletin. Torrey Botanical Club [*A publication*]...............Bull Torrey Bot Club
Bulletin. Tottori Agricultural Experiment Station [*A publication*]....................
Bull Tottori Agr Exp Sta
Bulletin. Tottori Tree Fruit Experiment Station [*A publication*]....................
Bull Tottori Tree Fruit Exp Stn
Bulletin. Tottori University Forests [*A publication*] .... Bull Tottori Univ For
Bulletin on Training [*A publication*]................................ Bull Train
Bulletin Trimestriel des Antiquites Africaines Recueillies par les Soins de la Societe de Geographie et d'Archeologie de la Province d'Oran [*A publication*]....................BOran
Bulletin Trimestriel. Banque de France [*A publication*] ....
B Trim Banque France
Bulletin Trimestriel. Ecole Nationale de la Sante Publique [*A publication*]....................B Trim Ecole Nat Sante Publ
Bulletin Trimestriel. Institut Archeologique du Luxembourg [*A publication*]....................... BTIAL
Bulletin Trimestriel. Institut Archeologique du Luxembourg [*A publication*]....................BTIALux
Bulletin Trimestriel. Institut National pour l'Amelioration des Conserves de Legumes (Belgium) [*A publication*]....................
Bull Trimest Inst Natl Amelior Conserves Legumes (Belg)
Bulletin Trimestriel. Societe Academique des Antiquaires de la Morinie [*A publication*].................... BSAM
Bulletin Trimestriel. Societe Academique des Antiquaires de la Morinie [*A publication*]....................BSAMorinie
Bulletin Trimestriel. Societe Academique des Antiquaires de la Morinie [*A publication*]....................BTSAAM
Bulletin Trimestriel. Societe des Antiquaires de Picardie [*A publication*]....................BSAP
Bulletin Trimestriel. Societe des Antiquaires de Picardie [*A publication*]....................BSAPicardie
Bulletin Trimestriel. Societe des Antiquaires de Picardie [*A publication*]....................BTSAP
Bulletin Trimestriel. Societe Forestiere de Franche-Comte et des Provinces de l'Est. Salinsles-Bains [*A publication*]....................
Bull Soc For Franche-Comte
Bulletin Trimestriel. Societe Mycologique de France [*A publication*] .... Bull Trimest Soc Mycol Fr
Bulletin. Tulane University Medical Faculty [*A publication*]....................
Bull Tulane Univ Med Fac
Bulletin. Union des Oceanographes de France [*A publication*]....................
Bull Union Oceanogr Fr
Bulletin. Union des Physiciens [*A publication*] .... Bull Union Physiciens
Bulletin. United Planters' Association of Southern India. Scientific Department [*A publication*]....................
Bull United Plant Assoc South Ind Sci Dep
Bulletin. United States Bureau of Mines [*A publication*] .... Bull US Bur Mines
Bulletin. United States Department of Agriculture [*A publication*]....................Bull US Dept Agric
Bulletin. United States Geological Survey [*A publication*]....................
Bull US Geol Surv
Bulletin. Universite de Strasbourg [*A publication*] .... BUS
Bulletin. Universite de Toulouse [*A publication*]..BUT
Bulletin. University of Alberta [*A publication*]...................... Bull Univ Alberta
Bulletin. University College of Medicine (Calcutta) [*A publication*]....................Bull Univ Coll Med (Calcutta)
Bulletin. University of Georgia. College of Agriculture. Cooperative Extension Service [*A publication*]....................
Bull Univ GA Coll Agr Coop Ext Serv
Bulletin. University of Idaho. College of Agriculture. Extension Service [*A publication*]....................Bull Univ Idaho Coll Agr Ext Serv
Bulletin. University of Illinois Agricultural Experiment Station [*A publication*]....................Bull Ill Agric Exp Sta
Bulletin. University of Iowa. Institute of Agricultural Medicine [*A publication*]....................Bull Univ Iowa Inst Agr Med
Bulletin. University of Maryland. Cooperative Extension Service [*A publication*]....................Bull Univ MD Coop Ext Serv
Bulletin. University of Missouri. College of Agriculture. Experiment Station [*A publication*]........... Bull Univ MO Coll Agr Exp Sta
Bulletin. University of Missouri at Rolla. Technical Series. [*A publication*]....................Bull Univ MO Rolla Tech Ser
Bulletin. University of Nebraska State Museum [*A publication*]....................
Bull Univ Nebr State Mus
Bulletin. University of Osaka Prefecture. Series A. Engineering and Natural Sciences [*A publication*]....................
Bull Univ Osaka Prefecture Ser A

Bulletin. University of Osaka Prefecture. Series B [*A publication*] ....
Bull Univ Osaka Pref Ser B
Bulletin. University of Osaka Prefecture. Series B. Agriculture and Biology [*A publication*] .... Bull Univ Osaka Prefect Ser B Agric Biol
Bulletin. University of Pittsburgh [*A publication*] .... BUP
Bulletin. University of the Ryukyus. Science and Engineering Division. Mathematics and Natural Science [*A publication*] ....
Bull Sci Engrg Div Univ Ryukyus Math Natur Sci
Bulletin. University of Tennessee. Agricultural Experiment Station [*A publication*] .... BlI Univ Tenn Agr Exp Sta
Bulletin. University of Wisconsin. Engineering Series [*A publication*] ....Wis U Bul Eng S
Bulletin Ustavu Russkeho Jazyka a Literatury [*A publication*] .... BURJL
Bulletin. Utah Agricultural Experiment Station [*A publication*] ....
Bull Utah Agr Exp Sta
Bulletin. Utah Agricultural Experiment Station [*A publication*] ....
Bull Utah Agric Exp Sta
Bulletin. Utah Engineering Experiment Station [*A publication*] ....
Bull Utah Eng Exp Sta
Bulletin. Utsunomiya Tobacco Experiment Station [*A publication*] .... Bull Utsunomiya Tob Exp Stn
Bulletin. Utsunomiya University Forests [*A publication*] ....
Bull Utsunomiya Univ For
Bulletin. Utsunomiya University. Section 2 [*A publication*] ....
Bull Utsunomiya Univ Sect 2
Bulletin. V. Luna General Hospital Medical Society [*A publication*] .... Bull V Luna Gen Hosp Med Soc
Bulletin. Vancouver Medical Association [*A publication*] ....
Bull Vancouver Med Assoc
Bulletin. Vegetable and Ornamental Crops Research Station. Series A [*A publication*] .... Bull Veg Ornamental Crops Res Stn Ser A
Bulletin. Vegetable and Ornamental Crops Research Station. Series C (Kurume) [*A publication*] ....
Bull Veg Ornamental Crops Res Stn Ser C (Kurume)
Bulletin van de Vereeniging tot Bevordering der Kennis van de Antike Beschaving [*A publication*] .... B A Besch
Bulletin van de Vereeniging tot Bevordering der Kennis van de Antike Beschaving [*A publication*] ....BVAB
Bulletin. Vereinigung der Schweizerischen Petroleum-Geologen und Ingenieure [*A publication*] ....
Bull Ver Schweiz Pet-Geol Ing
Bulletin Veterinaire (Lisbon) [*A publication*] .... Bull Vet (Lisb)
Bulletin. Veterinary Institute in Pulawy [*A publication*] .... Bull Vet Inst Pulawy
Bulletin. Virginia Agricultural Experiment Station [*A publication*] ....
Bull VA Agr Exp Sta
Bulletin. Virginia Agricultural Experiment Station [*A publication*] ....
Bull VA Agric Exp Stn
Bulletin. Virginia Geological Survey [*A publication*]..........Bull VA Geol Surv
Bulletin. Virginia Polytechnic Institute. Agricultural Extension Service [*A publication*] ....Bull VA Polytech Inst Agr Ext Serv
Bulletin. Virginia Sections of the American Chemical Society [*A publication*] ....Bull VA Sect Amer Chem Soc
Bulletin. Virginia Water Resources Research Center [*A publication*] ....Bull VA Water Resour Res Cent
Bulletin Volcanologique [*A publication*] .... Bull Volcanol
Bulletin. Vyskumneho Ustavu Potravinarskeho [*A publication*] ....
Bull Vysk Ustavu Potravin
Bulletin Vysoke Skoly Russkeho Jazyka a Literatury [*A publication*] ....BVSRJL
Bulletin. Wakayama Fruit Tree Experiment Station [*A publication*] .... Bull Wakayama Fruit Tree Exp Stn
Bulletin. Waseda Applied Chemical Society [*A publication*] ....
Bull Waseda Appl Chem Soc
Bulletin. Washington Agricultural Experiment Station [*A publication*] .... Bull Wash Agr Exp Sta
Bulletin. Washington Agricultural Experiment Station [*A publication*] .... Bull Wash Agric Exp Stn
Bulletin. West Virginia University. Agricultural Experiment Station [*A publication*] .... Bull W Va Agric Exp Sta
Bulletin. West Virginia University. Agricultural Experiment Station [*A publication*].........................Bull W Va Univ Agr Exp Sta
Bulletin. Wildlife Disease Association [*A publication*]......Bull Wildl Dis Assoc
Bulletin. Wisconsin Agricultural Experiment Station [*A publication*] .... Bull Wis Agr Exp Sta
Bulletin. Wood Research Laboratory. Virginia Polytechnic Institute [*A publication*].........................Bull Wood Res Lab VA Polyt Inst
Bulletin. Woods and Forests Department of South Australia [*A publication*] .... Bull Wds For Dep S Aust
Bulletin. World Health Organization [*A publication*].........................Bull WHO
Bulletin. World Health Organization [*A publication*].............Bull Wld Hlth Org
Bulletin. World Health Organization [*A publication*] ....
Bull World Health Organ
Bulletin. World Health Organization [*A publication*].........................B WHO
Bulletin. Wyoming Agricultural Experiment Station [*A publication*] .... Bull Wyo Agr Exp Sta
Bulletin. Wyoming Agricultural Experiment Station [*A publication*] .... Bull Wyo Agric Exp Stn
Bulletin. Wyoming Department of Agriculture. Division of Statistics and Information [*A publication*] ....
Bull Wyo Dept Agr Div Statist Inform

Bulletin Y. National Fertilizer Development Center (United States) [*A publication*]................................Bull Y Natl Fert Dev Cent (US)
Bulletin. Yale University School of Forestry [*A publication*] ....
Bull Yale Sch For
Bulletin. Yamagata University (Agricultural Science) [*A publication*]...............................Bull Yamagata Univ (Agric Sci)
Bulletin. Yamagata University (Engineering) [*A publication*] ....
Bull Yamagata Univ (Eng)
Bulletin. Yamagata University (Natural Science) [*A publication*]....................
Bull Yamagata Univ (Nat Sci)
Bulletin. Yamagata University (Natural Science) [*A publication*]....................
Bull Yamagata Univ (Natur Sci)
Bulletin. Yamaguchi Agricultural Experiment Station [*A publication*].........................Bull Yamaguchi Agric Exp Stn
Bulletin. Yamaguchi Medical School [*A publication*] ....
Bull Yamaguchi Med Sch
Bulletin. Yamaguchi Prefectural Poultry Breeding Station [*A publication*] .... Bull Yamaguchi Prefect Poult Breed Stn
Bulletin. Yamanashi Agricultural Experiment Station [*A publication*].........................Bull Yamanashi Agric Exp Stn
Bulletin. Yamanashi Prefectural Agricultural Experiment Station [*A publication*].........................Bull Yamanashi Pref Agr Exp Sta
Bulletin. Yamanashi Prefectural Forest Experiment Station [*A publication*].........................Bull Yamanashi For Exp Sta
Bulletin. Yokohama City University [*A publication*]......B Yokohama City Univ
Bulletin of the Zambia Language Group [*A publication*] ....
B Zambia Lang Group
Bulletin. Zoological Nomenclature [*A publication*]............ Bull Zool Nomencl
Bulletin. Zoological Society College of Science (Nagpur) [*A publication*].........................Bull Zool Soc Coll Sci (Nagpur)
Bulletin. Zoological Society of Egypt [*A publication*] .... Bull Zool Soc Egypt
Bulletins of American Paleontology [*A publication*].........................B Am Pal
Bulletins of American Paleontology [*A publication*]...........Bull Am Paleontol
Bulletins of American Paleontology [*A publication*]......Bull Am Paleontology
Bulletins of American Paleontology [*A publication*].... Bulls Am Paleontology
Bulletins of Marine Ecology [*A publication*] .... Bull Mar Ecol
Bulletins et Memoires. Faculte de Medecine et de Pharmacie de Dakar [*A publication*] .... Bull Mem Fac Med Pharm Dakar
Bulletins et Memoires. Societe Anatomique de Paris [*A publication*].........................Bull et Mem Soc Anat Paris
Bulletins et Memoires. Societe d'Anthropologie de Paris [*A publication*] .... B M S Anthr
Bulletins et Memoires. Societe d'Anthropologie de Paris [*A publication*] .... B Soc Anthropol Paris
Bulletins et Memoires. Societe d'Anthropologie de Paris [*A publication*] .... Bull Mem Soc Anthropol Paris
Bulletins et Memoires. Societe Centrale de Medecine Veterinaire [*A publication*] .... Bull et Mem Soc Centr Med Vet
Bulletins et Memoires. Societe de Chirurgie de Paris [*A publication*] .... Bull et Mem Soc Chir Paris
Bulletins et Memoires. Societe Francaise d'Ophtalmologie [*A publication*] .... Bull Mem Soc Fr Ophtalmol
Bulletins et Memoires. Societe Medicale des Hopitaux de Bucarest [*A publication*]................... Bull et Mem Soc Med Hop Bucarest
Bulletins et Memoires. Societe Medicale des Hopitaux de Paris [*A publication*] .... Bull et Mem Soc Med Hop Paris
Bulletins et Memoires. Societe Medicale des Hopitaux de Paris [*A publication*] .... Bull Soc Med Hop Paris
Bulletins et Memoires. Societe National de Chirurgie (Paris) [*A publication*] .... Bull et Mem Soc Nat Chir (Paris)
Bulletins et Memoires. Societe de Therapeutique [*A publication*] ....
Bull et Mem Soc Therap
Bulletins. Office of the Surgeon General. United States War Department [*A publication*]...................Bull Office Surg Gen US War Dept
Bulletins of Ordnance Information..BOI
Bulletins. Societe de Zoologie d'Anvers [*A publication*] ....
Bull Soc Zool Anvers
Bulletproof [*Army*]...BPRF
Bullettino di Archeologia Cristiana [*A publication*] .... B A Crist
Bullettino. Commissione Archeologica Comunale di Roma [*A publication*].........................Bull Comm
Bullettino. Commissione Archeologica de Governatorato di Roma [*A publication*].........................Bull Gov
Bullettino. Istituto di Corrispondenza Archeologica [*A publication*].........Bdl
Bullettino. Reale Accademia Medica di Roma [*A publication*].........................
Bull R Accad Med Roma
Bullettino delle Scienze Mediche [*A publication*]....................... Bull Sci Med
Bullettino. Scienze Mediche di Bologna [*A publication*] ....
Bull Sc Med Bologna
Bullhead City, AZ [*Radio station call letters*]..................................KBAS
Bullhead City, AZ [*Radio station call letters*]..................................KRHS
Bullhead City, AZ [*Radio station call letters*] .... KRHS-FM
Bullhead City [*Arizona*]/Laughlin [*Nevada*] [*Airport symbol*] .... BHC
Bulliat [*Let It Boil*] [*Pharmacy*]..BULL
Bullion Monarch Co. [*NASDAQ symbol*]......................................BMRK
Bullnose Morris Club .... BMC
Bullock's, Inc. [*NYSE symbol*] [*Delisted*] .... BUL
Bullous Pemphigoid [*Medicine*]...BP
Bullpup All-Weather Guidance System [*Naval Ordnance Systems Command*].........................BAGS
Bullseye Class Association .... BCA

Bullsling [*or Bullslinger*] [*Bowdlerized version*] .... BS
Bulolo [*Papua New Guinea*] [*Airport symbol*] .... BUL
Bulova Watch Co., Inc. [*NYSE symbol*] [*Delisted*] .... BVA
Bulwark .... BWK
Bulwer-Lytton Circle .... BLC
Bumazhnaya Promyshlennost [*A publication*] .... Bumazh Prom
Bumaznaja Promyslennost [*A publication*] .... Bumaz Prom
Bumba [*Zaire*] [*Airport symbol*] .... BMB
Bump Protection Hat .... BPH
Bumper Lift Jack .... BLJ
Bumper Recycling Association of North America .... BRANA
Bunbury [*Australia*] [*Airport symbol*] .... BUY
[*A*] **Bunch of Guys Sitting around a Table** [*Facetious description of a decision-making process*] .... BOGSAAT
Bunching .... BCHG
Bunching Block .... BB
Bundaberg [*Australia*] [*Airport symbol*] .... BDB
Bunder Jahrbuch [*A publication*] .... BundJb
Bundesanzeiger. Beilage [*A publication*] .... Bundesanzeiger Beil
Bundesgesetzblatt. Republik Oesterreich [*A publication*] .... Bundesgesetzbl Repub Oesterr
Bundesgrenzschutz [*Military*] [*West Germany*] .... BGS
Bundeskriminalamt [*West Germany's federal criminal police*] .... BKA
Bundesministerium fuer Bildung und Wissenschaft. Forschungsbericht [*A publication*] .... Bundesminist Bild Wiss Forschungsber
Bundesministerium fuer Forschung und Technologie. Forschungsbericht DV. Datenverabeitung [*A publication*] .... Bundesminist Forsch Technol Forschungsber DV
Bundesministerium fuer Forschung und Technologie. Forschungsbericht K. Kernforschung [*A publication*] .... Bundesminist Forsch Technol Forschungsber K
Bundesministerium fuer Forschung und Technologie. Forschungsbericht M. Meeresforschung [*A publication*] .... Bundesminist Forsch Technol Forschungsber M
Bundesministerium fuer Forschung und Technologie. Forschungsbericht T. Technologische Forschung und Entwicklung [*A publication*] .... Bundesminist Forsch Technol Forschungsber T
Bundesministerium fuer Forschung und Technologie. Forschungsbericht W. Weltraumforschung [*A publication*] .... Bundesminist Forsch Technol Forschungsber W
Bundesnachrichtendienst [*Intelligence-gathering agency of the Federal Republic of Germany*] .... BND
Bundesrepublik Deutschland [*Federal Republic of Germany*] .... BRD
Bundesstelle fuer Aussenhandelsinformation [*Foreign Trade Information Office*] [*Germany*] [*Information service*] .... BfA
Bundesstelle fur Aussenhandelsinformation [*West German Foreign Trade Information Office*] [*Information service*] .... BFAI
Bundesverband der Deutschen Industrie [*Federation of German Industry*] .... BDI
Bundi [*Papua New Guinea*] [*Airport symbol*] .... BNT
Bundle .... BD
Bundle .... BDL
Bundle .... BDLE
Bundle .... BNDL
Bundle Branch Block [*Cardiology*] .... BBB
Bundle Controlled Expansion .... BCEX
Bundle Drawing Process [*Metal fiber technology*] .... BDP
Bundles .... BDLS
Bundnerisches Monatsblatt [*A publication*] .... BUNDMB
Bundy Corp. [*NYSE symbol*] .... BNY
Bung-Hole [*i.e., cheese*] [*British slang*] .... BH
Bungaku [*A publication*] .... BG
Bungaku Ronshu [*Studies on Literature*] [*A publication*] .... BGRS
Bungarotoxin [*Also, BTX, BuTx*] [*Biochemistry*] .... BGT
Bungarotoxin [*Also, BGT, BuTx*] [*Biochemistry*] .... BTX
Bungarotoxin [*Also, BGT, BTX*] [*Biochemistry*] .... BuTx
Bunia [*Zaire*] [*Airport symbol*] .... BUX
Bunia-Ruampara [*Zaire*] [*Geomagnetic observatory code*] .... BNA
Bunker Hill Income Securities, Inc. [*NYSE symbol*] .... BHL
Bunker Hill Public Library, Bunker Hill, IL [*Library symbol*] .... IBun
Bunker-Ramo Corp. [*NYSE symbol*] [*Delisted*] .... BR
Bunnythorpe [*New Zealand*] [*Seismograph station code, US Geological Survey*] [*Closed*] .... BUN
Bunseki Kagaku [*A publication*] .... Bunseki Kag
Bunting, Inc. [*NASDAQ symbol*] .... BUNT
Buoy Boat .... BU
Buoy Boat, Stern Loading .... BUSL
Buoy Integrated Antenna Submarine .... BIAS
Buoy Messenger .... BMSS
Buoy Power Supply .... BPS
Buoy Underwater Sound Signal .... BUSS
Buoyancy .... B
Buoyancy Compensators .... BC
Buoyancy Transport Vehicle .... BTV
Buoyant .... BYNT
Buoyant Ballistic Inertial Missile .... BBIM
Buoyant Capsule .... BC
Buoyant Venus Station [*NASA*] .... BVS
Bur Oak Library System [*Library network*] .... BOLS
Burao [*Somalia*] [*Airport symbol*] .... BUO
Burbank [*California*] [*Airport symbol*] .... BUR
Burbank, CA [*Radio station call letters*] .... KROQ
Burbank Public Library, Burbank, CA [*Library symbol*] .... CBb
Burden Center .... BC
Bureau .... BU
Bureau .... BUR
Bureau of Accounts [*Department of the Treasury*] .... BA
Bureau of Administrative Management and Budget [*United Nations Development Program*] .... BAMB
Bureau for Adult Thalidomide Victims [*West Germany*] .... BATV
Bureau for the Advancement of Independent Retailing .... BAIR
Bureau of Aeronautics [*Later, Naval Air Systems Command*] .... B/A
Bureau of Aeronautics [*Later, Naval Air Systems Command*] .... BUAER
Bureau of Aeronautics General Representative [*Obsolete*] [*Navy*] .... BAGR
Bureau of Aeronautics General Representative, Eastern District [*Obsolete*] [*Navy*] .... BAGRED
Bureau of Aeronautics General Representative, Western District [*Obsolete*] [*Navy*] .... BAGRWD
Bureau of Aeronautics Industrial Reserve [*Obsolete*] [*Navy*] .... BAIR
Bureau of Aeronautics Maintenance Repair Officer [*Obsolete*] [*Navy*] .... BAMRO
Bureau of Aeronautics Maintenance Representative [*Obsolete*] [*Navy*] .... BAMR
Bureau of Aeronautics Maintenance Resident Representative Office [*Obsolete*] [*Navy*] .... BAMRRO
Bureau of Aeronautics Material Officer [*Obsolete*] [*Navy*] .... BAMO
Bureau of Aeronautics Representative [*Obsolete*] [*Navy*] .... BAR
Bureau of Aeronautics Resident Representative [*Obsolete*] [*Navy*] .... BARR
Bureau of Aeronautics Shipment Order [*Obsolete*] [*Navy*] .... BASO
Bureau of Aeronautics Training Unit [*Obsolete*] [*Navy*] .... BARTU
Bureau for Africa and Europe [*AID*] .... BAE
Bureau of African Affairs [*Department of State*] .... BAA
Bureau of Agricultural Economics [*Functions dispersed, 1953*] [*Department of Agriculture*] .... BAE
Bureau of Agricultural and Industrial Chemistry [*Department of Agriculture*] .... BAIC
Bureau on Agriculture and Renewable Resources .... BARR
Bureau of Air Commerce [*Later, Civil Aeronautics Authority*] .... BAC
Bureau of Air Commerce Type Certificate .... ACTC
Bureau of Air Pollution Sciences .... BAPS
Bureau of Air Traffic Management .... BATM
Bureau of Alcohol, Tobacco, and Firearms [*Department of the Treasury*] .... ATF
Bureau of Alcohol, Tobacco, and Firearms [*Department of the Treasury*] .... BATF
Bureau of Alcohol, Tobacco, and Firearms Laboratory, Washington, DC [*OCLC symbol*] .... ATF
Bureau of American Ethnology [*of the Smithsonian Institution*] .... BAE
Bureau of American Ethnology. Annual Report [*A publication*] .... Bur Am Ethnol Annual Report
Bureau of American Ethnology. Bulletin [*A publication*] .... Bur Am Ethn
Bureau d'Analyse et de Recherche Appliquees [*Bureau of Analysis and Applied Research*] .... BARA
Bureau of Animal Industry [*Department of Agriculture*] .... BAI
Bureau of Applied Social Research [*Columbia University*] .... BASR
Bureau of Apprenticeship and Training [*Department of Labor*] .... BAT
Bureau de l'Assistance Technique [*Technical Assistance Bureau*] .... BAT
Bureau of Automotive Regulation .... BAR
Bureau of Aviation Medicine .... BAM
Bureau of Biologics [*Also, BOB*] [*FDA*] .... BB
Bureau of Biologics [*Also, BB*] [*FDA*] .... BOB
Bureau of the Budget [*Later, OMB*] .... BB
Bureau of the Budget [*Later, OMB*] .... BOB
Bureau of the Budget [*Later, OMB*] .... BuB
Bureau of the Budget [*Later, OMB*] .... BUBUD
Bureau of the Budget Approval [*Obsolete*] .... BBA
Bureau for Careers in Jewish Service [*Defunct*] .... BCJS
Bureau of Catholic Indian Missions .... BCIM
Bureau of the Census [*Department of Commerce*] .... BC
Bureau of the Census, Field Division Library, Washington, DC [*OCLC symbol*] .... CBW
Bureau of the Census, Washington, DC [*OCLC symbol*] .... CBU
Bureau Central de Compensation [*Central Bureau of Compensation*] .... BCC
Bureau Central International de Seismologie [*International Central Seismological Bureau*] .... BCIS
Bureau Central de Renseignements et d'Action [*Free French*] .... BCRA
Bureau of Commercial Fisheries [*Later, National Marine Fisheries Service*] .... BCF
Bureau of Commercial Fisheries [*Later, National Marine Fisheries Service*] .... BOCF
Bureau of Community Environmental Management [*Terminated, 1973*] [*HEW*] .... BCEM
Bureau of Community Health Services [*Health Services Administration*] .... BCHS
Bureau of Competitive Assessment and Business Policy [*Department of Commerce*] .... BCABP
Bureau of Construction and Repair [*Until 1940*] [*Navy*] .... BUCON
Bureau of Construction and Repair [*Until 1940*] [*Navy*] .... BUC & R
Bureau of Construction and Repair [*Until 1940*] [*Navy*] .... C & R
Bureau of Consultation [*Federal Trade Commission*] .... BC

Bureau of Contract Information [Defunct] ....BCI
Bureau Control Activity Number........................BCAN
Bureau Control Number..............................BCN
Bureau County Historical Society, Princeton, IL [Library symbol].........IPriHi
Bureau of Customs [Later, US Customs Service] [Department of the Treasury]........................BC
Bureau of Customs [Later, US Customs Service] [Department of the Treasury]........................BOC
Bureau of Dairy Industry [Department of Agriculture] [Functions transferred to ARS, 1953]........................BDI
Bureau of Data Processing and Accounts [Social Security Administration]........................BDPA
Bureau de Developpement et de Promotion Industriels [Bureau of Industrial Promotion and Development] [Malagasy Republic].......BDPI
Bureau of Disability Insurance [Social Security Administration]..............BDI
Bureau of Disease Prevention and Environmental Control.............BDPEC
Bureau of Domestic Business Development [Department of Commerce]........................BDBD
Bureau of Domestic Commerce [Formerly, Business and Defense Services Administration and Office of Field Services] [Department of Commerce] [Terminated, 1977, functions transferred to Domestic and International Business Administration]........................BDC
Bureau of Drug Abuse Control [Absorbed by Bureau of Narcotics and Dangerous Drugs of Department of Justice]........................BDAC
Bureau of East Asian and Pacific Affairs [Formerly, Bureau of Far Eastern Affairs] [Department of State]........................BEAPA
Bureau of East-West Trade [Department of Commerce]........................BEWT
Bureau of Economic Affairs [Later, Bureau of Economic and Business Affairs] [Department of State]........................BEA
Bureau of Economic Analysis [Department of Commerce]........................BEA
Bureau of Economic and Business Affairs [Formerly, Bureau of Economic Affairs] [Department of State]........................BEBA
Bureau of Economic Regulation [of CAB]........................BER
Bureau of Economics [Federal Trade Commission]........................BE
Bureau of Education for Fair Trade........................BEFT
Bureau of Education for the Handicapped [Office of Education]...........BEH
Bureau d'Education Ibero-Americain........................BEIA
Bureau of Educational and Cultural Affairs [Later known as USIA, then as ICA or USICA, then again as USIA]........................BECA
Bureau of Educational Personnel Development [HEW]........................BEPD
Bureau Electronics Equipment Model [Navy]........................BEEM
Bureau of Elementary and Secondary Education [Office of Education]........................BESE
Bureau of Employees' Compensation [Later, OWCP] [Department of Labor]........................BEC
Bureau of Employment Security [Later, US Employment Service] [Department of Labor]........................BES
Bureau of Enforcement........................BOE
Bureau of Engineering [Obsolete] [Navy]........................BUENG
Bureau of Engraving and Printing [Department of the Treasury]...........BEP
Bureau pour l'Enseignement de la Langage et de la Civilisation Francaises a l'Etranger [France]........................BELC
Bureau of Entomology and Plant Quarantine [Department of Agriculture] [Functions transferred to ARS, 1953]........................BEPQ
Bureau of Equipment and Recruiting [Navy] [Abolished, 1914]..............BER
Bureau d'Etude de l'Energie Nucleaire [Belgium]........................BEEN
Bureau d'Etudes Industrielles et de Cooperation de l'Institut Francais du Petrole........................BEICIP
Bureau d'Etudes Nucleaires [Belgium]........................BEN
Bureau of European Affairs [Department of State]........................BEA
Bureau Europeen du Cafe [European Coffee Bureau]........................BEC
Bureau Europeen de Controle et d'Etudes Generales........................BECEG
Bureau Europeen de l'Education Populaire [European Bureau of Adult Education]........................BEEP
Bureau Europeen de la Jeunesse et de l'Enfance........................BEJE
Bureau Europeen des Unions de Consommateurs [European Bureau of Consumers' Unions] [Common Market]........................BEUC
Bureau of Executive Manpower [Civil Service Commission]........................BEM
Bureau of Explosives........................BE
Bureau of Export Development [Department of Commerce]........................BED
Bureau of Family Services [of SSA]........................BFS
Bureau of Far Eastern Affairs [Department of State]........................BFEA
Bureau Farmer [A publication]........................Bur Farmer
Bureau of Federal Credit Unions [Later, NCUA] [Social Security Administration]........................BFCU
Bureau of Finance and Administration [US Postal Service]........................BFA
Bureau of Flight Standards........................BFS
Bureau of Foods, Pesticides, and Product Safety [FDA]........................BFPPS
Bureau of Foreign Commerce [Abolished, 1961] [Department of Commerce]........................BFC
Bureau of Foreign and Domestic Commerce [Functions later dispersed] [Department of Commerce]........................BFDC
Bureau of Government Financial Operations [Department of Treasury]........................BGFO
Bureau Gravimetrique International [International Gravity Bureau].........BGI
Bureau of Health Insurance [Social Security Administration]........................BHI
Bureau of Health Manpower [Later, Health Resources Administration] [HEW]........................BHM
Bureau of Health Manpower Education [National Institutes of Health]........................BHME

Bureau of Health Planning and Resource Development [Later, Bureau of Health Planning] [HEW]........................BHPRD
Bureau of Health Professions Education and Manpower Training [HEW]........................BEMT
Bureau of Health Services [Public Health Service]........................BHS
Bureau of Hearings and Appeals [Social Security Administration].........BHA
Bureau of Higher Education [Later, Bureau of Higher and Continuing Education] [Office of Education]........................BHE
Bureau of Human Nutrition and Home Economics [Department of Agriculture] [Functions transferred to ARS, 1953]........................BHNHE
Bureau Hydrographique International [International Hydrographic Bureau]........................BHI
Bureau of Independent Publishers and Distributors........................BIPAD
Bureau of Indian Affairs [Department of the Interior]........................BIA
Bureau of Indian Affairs [Better known as BIA] [Department of the Interior]........................BOIA
Bureau of Industrial Economics [Department of Commerce]........................BIE
Bureau voor de Industriele Eigendom, Bibliotheek Octrooiraad, The Hague, Netherlands [Library symbol]........................NeHB
Bureau d'Information et de Presse [Circulated Allied propaganda in France and informed Allies of resistance activities] [World War II]........................BIP
Bureau d'Informations et de Previsions Economiques [France]........................BIPE
Bureau Inlichtingen [Netherlands Information Office] [World War II]...........BI
Bureau of Inspection and Survey........................BIS
Bureau of Institutional Development [Office of Education]........................BID
Bureau of Insular Affairs [Originally, part of War Department; functions transferred to Department of Interior, 1939]........................BIA
Bureau of Intelligence and Research [Department of State]........................BIR
Bureau of Intelligence and Research [Department of State]........................INR
Bureau of Inter-American Affairs [Department of State]........................BIAA
Bureau of Inter-Industrial Statistics and Multiple Regression Analysis........................BISMRA
Bureau Interafricain des Sols et de l'Economie Rurale [Inter-African Bureau of Soils and Rural Economy]........................BIS
Bureau of Intergovernmental Personnel Programs........................BIPP
Bureau of Internal Revenue [Department of the Treasury] [Later, Internal Revenue Service]........................BIR
Bureau of International Affairs........................BIA
Bureau International d'Anthropologie Differentielle [International Bureau of Differential Anthropology]........................BIAD
Bureau International d'Audiophonologie [International Bureau of Audiophonology]........................BIAP
Bureau International du Beton Manufacture [International Bureau for Precast Concrete]........................BIBM
Bureau of International Business Operations [Department of Commerce] [Abolished, 1963]........................BIBO
Bureau International Catholique de l'Enfance [International Catholic Child Bureau]........................BICE
Bureau International de la Chaussure et du Cuir........................BIC
Bureau International du Cinema [International Cinematograph Bureau]........................BIC
Bureau of International Commerce [Department of Commerce] [Functions transferred to Domestic and International Business Administration]........................BIC
Bureau International des Containers [International Container Bureau].....BIC
Bureau International de Documentation des Chemins de Fer [International Office of Railway Documentation]........................BDC
Bureau of International Economic Policy and Research [Department of Commerce]........................BIEPR
Bureau International de l'Edition Mecanique........................BIEM
Bureau International d'Education........................BIE
Bureau International des Expositions [International Bureau of Exhibitions]........................BIE
Bureau International du Film des Chemins de Fer [International Railway Film Bureau]........................BFC
Bureau International de l'Heure [International Time Bureau]........................BIH
Bureau International d'Information des Chambres de Commerce.......BIICC
Bureau of International Labor Affairs [Department of Labor]........................BILA
Bureau of International Labor Affairs [Department of Labor]........................ILAB
Bureau of International Organization Affairs [Department of State]......BIOA
Bureau International Permanent de Chimie Analytique pour les Matieres Destinees a l'Alimentation de l'Homme et des Animaux [Permanent International Bureau of Analytical Chemistry of Human and Animal Food]........................BIPCA
Bureau International des Poids et Mesures [International Bureau of Weights and Measures]........................BIPM
Bureau International des Producteurs d'Assurances et de Reassurances [International Bureau of Insurance and Reinsurance Brokers] [See also IAIRI]........................BIPAR
Bureau of International Programs [Department of Commerce]........................BIP
Bureau International de Recherche sur les Implications Sociales du Progres Technique........................BIRISPT
Bureau International de la Recuperation [International Reclamation Bureau]........................BIR
Bureau of International Scientific and Technological Affairs [Department of State]........................BISTA
Bureau International du Scoutisme........................BIS
Bureau International pour la Standardisation de la Rayonne et des Fibres Synthetiques [International Bureau for the Standardization of Man-Made Fibres]........................BISFA

Bureau International pour le Tourisme et les Echanges de la Jeunesse [*International Bureau for Tourism and Youth Exchanges*]..........BITEJ

Bureau International du Tourisme Social [*International Bureau of Social Tourism*] [*See also IBST*]..........BITS

Bureau International du Travail [*International Labour Office*]..........BIT

Bureau International des Universites..........BIU

Bureau of International Whaling Statistics..........BIWS

Bureau of Investigation [*Federal Trade Commission*]..........BI

Bureau Issues Association [*Philately*]..........BIA

Bureau of Jewish Education..........BJE

Bureau on Jewish Employment Problems..........BJEP

Bureau of Justice Statistics [*Department of Justice*]..........BJS

Bureau of Labor-Management Reports [*Department of Labor*]..........BLMR

Bureau of Labor Standards [*Absorbed by OSHA*] [*Department of Labor*]..........BLS

Bureau of Labor Statistics [*Department of Labor*]..........BLS

Bureau of Land Management [*Department of the Interior*]..........BLM

Bureau of Land Management [*Department of the Interior*]..........BOLM

Bureau of Land Management, Billings, MT [*Library symbol*]..........MtBilB

Bureau of Land Management, Billings, MT [*OCLC symbol*]..........UBD

Bureau of Land Management, Boise District Office, Boise, ID [*OCLC symbol*]..........UDL

Bureau of Land Management, Boise, ID [*Library symbol*]..........IdBLM-B

Bureau of Land Management, Denver, Denver, CO [*OCLC symbol*]..........UDD

Bureau of Land Management, Library, New Orleans, New Orleans, LA [*OCLC symbol*]..........UDQ

Bureau for Latin America [*Agency for International Development*]..........BLA

Bureau of Laundry and Dry Cleaning Standards..........BLDCS

Bureau de Liaison des Industries du Caoutchouc de la CEE [*Rubber Industries Liaison Bureau of the EEC*]..........BLIC

Bureau of Libraries and Educational Technology [*Later, BLLR*] [*HEW*]..........BLET

Bureau of Libraries and Learning Resources [*Formerly, BLET*] [*HEW*]..........BLLR

Bureau of Litigation [*Federal Trade Commission*]..........BL

Bureau of Manpower Utilization [*World War II*]..........BMU

Bureau of Medical Devices [*Food and Drug Administration*]..........BMD

Bureau of Medical Devices and Diagnostic Products [*FDA*]..........BMDDP

Bureau of Medical Services [*Public Health Service*]..........BMS

Bureau of Medicine [*of FDA*]..........BM

Bureau of Medicine and Supply Integrated Allowance List..........BM & SIAL

Bureau of Medicine and Surgery [*Later, Naval Medical Command*] [*Navy*]..........BMS

Bureau of Medicine and Surgery [*Navy*]..........BUMED

Bureau of Medicine and Surgery [*Navy*]..........BUM & S

Bureau of Medicine and Surgery [*Navy*]..........M & S

Bureau of Medicine and Surgery Hospital Corps Publication [*Later, NAVMED*] [*Navy*]..........NMSHC

Bureau of Medicine and Surgery Instructions [*Navy*]..........BUMEDINST

Bureau of Medicine and Surgery Publications [*Navy*]..........NM & S

Bureau Militaire de Standardisation [*Military Agency for Standardisation*] [*NATO*]..........BMS

Bureau of Military Application of Scientific Research..........BMASR

Bureau of Mines [*Department of the Interior*]..........BM

Bureau of Mines [*Department of the Interior*]..........BOM

Bureau of Mines [*Department of the Interior*]..........BuM

Bureau of Mines [*Department of the Interior*]..........BUMINES

Bureau of Mines Information Circular..........BMIC

Bureau of Mines Technical Paper..........BMTP

Bureau Minier de la France d'Outre-Mer [*Mining Bureau of Overseas France*]..........BUMIFOM

Bureau of the Mint [*Department of the Treasury*]..........BM

Bureau of Motor Carrier Safety [*Department of Transportation*]..........BMCS

Bureau of Motor Carriers [*ICC*]..........BMC

Bureau of Narcotics [*Department of the Treasury*] [*Absorbed by BNDD of Department of Justice*]..........BN

Bureau of Narcotics and Dangerous Drugs [*Formerly, Bureau of Narcotics and Bureau of Drug Abuse Control; later, Drug Enforcement Administration*] [*Department of Justice*]..........BNDD

Bureau of National Affairs [*Publisher*]..........BNA

Bureau of National Capital Airports [*of FAA*]..........BNCA

Bureau National des Donnees Oceaniques [*National Bureau for Ocean Data*] [*France*] [*Information service*]..........BNDO

Bureau National de l'Information Scientifique et Technique [*National Scientific and Technical Information Bureau*] [*France*] [*Information service*]..........BNIST

Bureau National Kamerunais pour la Conference des Peuples Africains [*Cameroonian National Bureau for African Peoples Conference*]..........BNKCPA

Bureau of Natural Gas [*of FPC*]..........BNG

Bureau of Naval Personnel [*Also, BUPERS, NAVPERS*]..........BNP

Bureau of Naval Personnel [*Also, BNP, NAVPERS*]..........BUPERS

Bureau of Naval Personnel [*Also, BNP, BUPERS*]..........NAVPERS

Bureau of Naval Personnel Circular Letters..........BNPCL

Bureau of Naval Personnel Controlled Instructor Billets..........BUPERSCONINSTRBIL

Bureau of Naval Personnel Instruction..........NAVPERSINST

Bureau of Naval Personnel Manual..........BNPM

Bureau of Naval Personnel - Personnel Research Division..........NAVPERS-PRD

Bureau of Naval Ships [*Obsolete*]..........BNS

Bureau of Naval Weapons [*Obsolete*]..........BNW

Bureau of Naval Weapons [*Obsolete*]..........BUWEPS

Bureau of Naval Weapons [*Obsolete*]..........NAVWEPS

Bureau of Naval Weapons Branch Representative [*Obsolete*]..........BWBR

Bureau of Naval Weapons Fleet Readiness [*Obsolete*]..........BUWEPS FR

Bureau of Naval Weapons Fleet Readiness Representative [*Obsolete*]..........BUWEPSFLTREADREP

Bureau of Naval Weapons Fleet Readiness Representative [*Obsolete*]..........BWFRR

Bureau of Naval Weapons Fleet Readiness Representative, Atlantic [*Obsolete*]..........BUWEPSFLEREADREPLANT

Bureau of Naval Weapons Fleet Readiness Representative, Atlantic [*Obsolete*]..........BWFRRLANT

Bureau of Naval Weapons Fleet Readiness Representative, Central [*Obsolete*]..........BUWEPSFLEREADREPCEN

Bureau of Naval Weapons Fleet Readiness Representative, Central [*Obsolete*]..........BWFRRCEN

Bureau of Naval Weapons Fleet Readiness Representative, Pacific [*Obsolete*]..........BUWEPSFLEREADREPPAC

Bureau of Naval Weapons Fleet Readiness Representative, Pacific [*Obsolete*]..........BWFRRPAC

Bureau of Naval Weapons Instruction [*Obsolete*]..........BUWEPSINST

Bureau of Naval Weapons Notice [*Obsolete*]..........BUWEPSNOTE

Bureau of Naval Weapons Representative [*Obsolete*]..........BUWEPSREP

Bureau of Naval Weapons Representative [*Obsolete*]..........BWR

Bureau of Naval Weapons Resident Representative [*Obsolete*]..........BUWEPSRESREP

Bureau of Naval Weapons Resident Representative [*Obsolete*]..........BWRR

Bureau of Naval Weapons Support Representative, Naval Air Training Command [*Obsolete*]..........BWSRT

Bureau of Naval Weapons Technical Liaison Office [*Obsolete*]..........BUWEPSTLO

Bureau of Naval Weapons Technical Representative [*Obsolete*]..........BUWEPSTECHREP

Bureau of Navigation [*Later, Bureau of Naval Personnel*] [*Navy*]..........BUNAV

Bureau of Navy Yards and Docks [*Later, NFEC*]..........BNYD

Bureau of Near Eastern and South Asian Affairs [*Department of State*]..........BNESAA

Bureau de Normalisation de la Mecanique [*France*]..........BNM

Bureau Number [*Aircraft identification*] [*Navy*]..........BUNO

Bureau of Occupational and Adult Education [*Office of Education*]..........BOAE

Bureau of Oceans, Fisheries, and Scientific Affairs [*Department of State*]..........BOFSA

Bureau of Old-Age and Survivors Insurance [*Social Security Administration*]..........BOASI

Bureau of Operating Rights [*ICC*]..........BOR

Bureau of Operations and Programming [*United Nations Development Program*]..........BOP

Bureau of Ordnance [*Functions transferred to Bureau of Naval Weapons, 1960, and later to Naval Ordnance Systems Command*] [*Navy*]..........BO

Bureau of Ordnance [*Functions transferred to Bureau of Naval Weapons, 1960, and later to Naval Ordnance Systems Command*] [*Navy*]..........BUORD

Bureau of Ordnance Design Unit [*Obsolete*] [*Navy*]..........BODU

Bureau of Ordnance Fleet Test Equipment [*Obsolete*] [*Navy*]..........B of TE

Bureau of Ordnance and Hydrography [*Obsolete*] [*Navy*]..........BOH

Bureau of Ordnance Instructions [*Later, NAVORDINST*]..........BUORDINST

Bureau of Ordnance Publication [*Later, NAVORD*] [*Navy*]..........NORD

Bureau of Ordnance Shipment Order [*Obsolete*] [*Navy*]..........BOSO

Bureau of Outdoor Recreation [*Terminated, 1978, functions transferred to Heritage Conservation and Recreation Service*] [*Department of the Interior*]..........BOOR

Bureau of Outdoor Recreation [*Terminated, 1978, functions transferred to Heritage Conservation and Recreation Service*] [*Department of the Interior*]..........BOR

Bureau of Pension Advocates [*Canada*]..........BPA

Bureau Permanent Interafricain de la Tse-Tse et de la Trypanosomiase..........BPITT

Bureau Permanent International des Constructeurs d'Automobiles [*International Permanent Bureau of Motor Manufacturers*]..........BPICA

Bureau Planned Procurement Guide [*Navy*]..........BPPG

Bureau of Plant Industry [*Later, BPISAE*] [*Department of Agriculture*]..........BPI

Bureau of Plant Industry, Soils, and Agricultural Engineering [*Formerly, BPI*] [*Functions transferred to ARS, 1953*] [*Department of Agriculture*]..........BPISAE

Bureau Politique National [*National Political Bureau*] [*of the Guinean PDG*]..........BPN

Bureau of Postsecondary Education [*Later, Bureau of Higher and Continuing Education*] [*Office of Education*]..........BPE

Bureau of Power [*of FPC*]..........BP

Bureau of Prisons [*Department of Justice*]..........BP

Bureau of Product Safety [*FDA*]..........BPS

Bureau of Professional Education of the American Osteopathic Association..........BPEAOA

Bureau of Provisions and Clothing [*See also BSA*] [*Navy*]..........BPC

Bureau of Public Assistance [*Later, BFS*] [*Social Security Administration*]..........BPA

Bureau of the Public Debt [*Department of the Treasury*]..........BPD

Bureau of Public Inquiries ... BPI
Bureau of Public Relations [*War Department*] [*World War II*] ... BPR
Bureau of Public Roads [*Department of Transportation*] ... BPR
Bureau of Public Roads Transport Highway Mobilization [*Federal emergency order*] ... BPR-THM
Bureau of Quality Assurance [*HEW*] ... BQA
Bureau of Radiological Health [*FDA*] ... BRH
Bureau of Radiological Health, Rockville, MD [*OCLC symbol*] ... BRH
Bureau of Railroad Safety [*Department of Transportation*] ... BRS
Bureau of Raw Materials for American Vegetable Oils and Fats Industries ... BORM
Bureau de Recherches Geologiques et Minieres [*France*] ... BRGM
Bureau de Recherches Geologiques et Minieres. Bulletin. Section 2. Geologie des Gites Mineraux (France) [*A publication*] ... Bur Rech Geol Min Bull Sect 2 Geol Gites Miner (Fr)
Bureau de Recherches et de Participations Minieres ... BRPM
Bureau of Reclamation [*Later, WPRS*] [*Department of the Interior*] ... BOR
Bureau of Reclamation [*Later, WPRS*] [*Department of the Interior*] ... BR
Bureau of Reclamation [*Later, WPRS*] [*Department of the Interior*] ... BUREC
Bureau of Recruiting and Examining [*Civil Service Commission*] ... BRE
Bureau for Reference and Loan Services [*Library network*] ... R & L
Bureau de Renseignements et d'Action, Londres [*Free French*] ... BRAL
Bureau of Research and Development ... BRAD
Bureau of Research and Development Center [*FAA*] ... BRDC
Bureau of Research and Engineering [*US Postal Service*] ... BRE
Bureau of Resource Assessment and Land Use Planning ... BRALUP
Bureau of Resources and Trade Assistance [*Department of Commerce*] ... BRTA
Bureau of Retirement and Insurance [*Civil Service Commission*] ... BRI
Bureau of Retirement Survivors Insurance [*Social Security Administration*] ... BRSI
Bureau of Safety and Supply Radio Services ... BSSRS
Bureau of Salesmen's National Associations ... BSNA
Bureau of School Systems [*Office of Education*] ... BSS
Bureau of Ships [*Later, Naval Sea Systems Command*] ... BS
Bureau of Ships [*Later, Naval Sea Systems Command*] ... BUSHIPS
Bureau of Ships Analog Computer [*Obsolete*] [*Navy*] ... BUSAC
Bureau of Ships Journal [*Obsolete*] [*Navy*] ... BSJ
Bureau of Ships Publications [*Obsolete*] [*Navy*] ... NBS
Bureau of Social Sciences Research, Inc. ... BSSR
Bureau Socialiste International [*Brussels*] ... BSI
Bureau of Solid Waste Management [*Environmental Protection Agency*] ... BSWM
Bureau of Sport Fisheries and Wildlife [*Replaced by US Fish and Wildlife Service*] [*Department of the Interior*] ... BOSFW
Bureau of Sport Fisheries and Wildlife [*Superseded by US Fish and Wildlife Service*] [*Department of the Interior*] ... BSFW
Bureau of Sport Fisheries and Wildlife, Eastern Fish Disease Laboratory, Kearneysville, WV [*Library symbol*] ... WvKeFW
Bureau of Standards ... B of S
Bureau of Standards ... BS
Bureau of Standards ... BUSTDS
Bureau of State Security [*Later, Department of National Security*] [*South Africa*] ... BOSS
Bureau of State Services [*of Public Health Service*] ... BSS
Bureau of Steam Engineering [*Navy*] ... BSE
Bureau of Student Support [*Office of Education*] ... BSS
Bureau of Sugar Experiment Stations (Brisbane). Annual Report [*A publication*] ... Bur Sugar Exp Stn (Brisbane) Annu Rep
Bureau of Supplies and Accounts [*Later, NSUPSC*] [*Navy*] ... BSA
Bureau of Supplies and Accounts [*Later, NSUPSC*] [*Navy*] ... BUSANDA
Bureau of Supplies and Accounts [*Later, NSUPSC*] [*Navy*] ... NAVSANDA
Bureau of Supplies and Accounts [*Later, NSUPSC*] [*Navy*] ... S & A
Bureau of Supplies and Accounts Shipment Order [*Obsolete*] [*Navy*] ... SANDASO
Bureau of Technical Assistance Operations [*UN*] ... BTAO
Bureau Township Consolidated School District 250, Princeton, IL [*Library symbol*] ... IPriBSD
Bureau of Trade Regulation [*Department of Commerce*] ... BTR
Bureau of Transportation and International Services [*US Postal Service*] ... BTIS
Bureau [*of Naval Personnel*] **Unit Identification Code** ... BUIC
Bureau Universitaire de Statistique [*France*] ... BUS
Bureau of University Travel [*Defunct*] ... BUT
Bureau Veritas [*International register for the classification of shipping and aircraft*] ... BV
Bureau of Veterans Reemployment Rights [*Department of Labor*] ... BVRR
Bureau of Veterinary Medicine [*FDA*] ... BVM
Bureau of Vital Statistics ... BVS
Bureau Voucher [*Army*] ... BV
Bureau of War Risk Litigation ... BWRL
Bureau Weather Control ... BWC
Bureau of Work-Training Programs [*Terminated, 1969*] [*Department of Labor*] ... BWTP
Bureau of Yards and Docks [*Later, NFEC*] [*Navy*] ... BUDOCKS
Bureau of Yards and Docks [*Later, NFEC*] [*Navy*] ... BUYARD
Bureau of Yards and Docks [*Later, NFEC*] [*Navy*] ... BUY & D
Bureau of Yards and Docks [*Later, NFEC*] [*Navy*] ... BUYDSDOCKS
Bureau of Yards and Docks [*Later, NFEC*] [*Navy*] ... BYD
Bureau of Yards and Docks [*Later, NFEC*] [*Navy*] ... Y & D
Bureau of Yards and Docks Publications [*Obsolete*] [*Navy*] ... NAVDOCKS
Bureau of Yards and Docks Publications [*Obsolete*] [*Navy*] ... NAVDOCSP
Bureaucratic Syndrome [*In book title "B.S.: The Bureaucratic Syndrome"*] ... BS
Bureaux Internationaux Reunis pour la Protection de la Propriete Intellectuelle [*United International Bureau for the Protection of Intellectual Property*] [*Later, WIPO*] ... BIRPI
Bureta [*Fiji*] [*Airport symbol*] ... LEV
Burg ... BG
Burg Eltz [*Federal Republic of Germany*] [*Seismograph station code, US Geological Survey*] ... BGG
Burgaw, NC [*Radio station call letters*] ... WVBS
Burgaw, NC [*Radio station call letters*] ... WVBS-FM
Burgenlaendische Heimatblaetter [*A publication*] ... BurgHb
Burgess ... BURG
Burgess Industries, Inc. [*American Stock Exchange symbol*] [*Delisted*] ... BGS
Burgess-Manning Co., Dallas, TX [*Library symbol*] ... TxDaBM
Burglar Alarm ... BA
Burgomaster ... BM
Buried ... BUR
Burien, WA [*Radio station call letters*] ... KQIN
Buring Food Group, Inc. [*American Stock Exchange symbol*] [*Delisted*] ... BFG
Burke Mills, Inc. [*NASDAQ symbol*] ... BMLS
Burke Public Library, Burke, SD [*Library symbol*] ... SdBu
Burke's Newsletter [*A publication*] ... BN
Burkesville, KY [*Radio station call letters*] ... WKYR
Burketown [*Australia*] [*Airport symbol*] ... BUC
Burkitt's Lymphoma [*Medicine*] ... BL
Burlap ... BRLP
Burlap and Jute Association ... BJA
Burlesque ... BURL
Burlesque Historical Society ... BHS
Burley Auction Warehouse Association ... BAWA
Burley and Dark Leaf Tobacco Export Association ... BDLTEA
Burley, ID [*Location identifier*] [*FAA*] ... BYI
Burley, ID [*Radio station call letters*] ... KBAR
Burley, ID [*Radio station call letters*] ... KMVC
Burley Leaf Tobacco Dealers Association ... BLTDA
Burley Stabilization Corporation ... BSC
Burley Tobacco Growers Cooperative Association ... BTGCA
Burlingame Public Library, Burlingame, CA [*Library symbol*] ... CBu
Burlington [*Iowa*] [*Airport symbol*] ... BRL
Burlington [*Vermont*] [*Airport symbol*] ... BTV
Burlington [*Vermont*] [*Seismograph station code, US Geological Survey*] [*Closed*] ... BUR
Burlington Airways [*Burlington, WI*] [*FAA designator*] ... BUR
Burlington Area Office [*Energy Research and Development Administration*] ... BAO
Burlington Atmospheric Density Model Evaluation Program [*IBM Corp.*] ... BADMEP
Burlington, CO [*Radio station call letters*] ... KNAB
Burlington, CO [*Radio station call letters*] ... KNAB-FM
Burlington Coat Factory [*NASDAQ symbol*] ... COAT
Burlington County Area Reference Library, Mount Holly, NJ [*Library symbol*] ... NjMhB
Burlington County Clerk, Mount Holly, NJ [*Library symbol*] ... NjMhCoC
Burlington County College, Pemberton, NJ [*Library symbol*] ... NjPeB
Burlington County Herald, Mount Holly, NJ [*Library symbol*] ... NjMhH
Burlington County Historical Society, Burlington, NJ [*Library symbol*] ... NjBuHi
Burlington County Lyceum [*Mount Holly Public Library*], **Mount Holly, NJ** [*Library symbol*] ... NjMhL
Burlington County Prison Museum, Mount Holly, NJ [*Library symbol*] ... NjMhPM
Burlington County Times, Willingboro, NJ [*Library symbol*] ... NjWiT
Burlington Free Public Library, Burlington, IA [*Library symbol*] ... IaB
Burlington-Graham, NC [*Radio station call letters*] ... WQRB
Burlington, IA [*Radio station call letters*] ... KBUR
Burlington, IA [*Radio station call letters*] ... KCPS
Burlington, IA [*Radio station call letters*] ... KDWD
Burlington, IA [*Radio station call letters*] ... KGRS
Burlington Industries, Inc. [*NYSE symbol*] ... BUR
Burlington Liars Club ... BLC
Burlington Magazine [*A publication*] ... BM
Burlington Magazine [*A publication*] ... Burl M
Burlington Magazine [*A publication*] ... Burl Mag
Burlington, NC [*Location identifier*] [*FAA*] ... BUY
Burlington, NC [*Radio station call letters*] ... WBAG-FM
Burlington, NC [*Radio station call letters*] ... WBBB
Burlington, NC [*Radio station call letters*] ... WPCM
Burlington, NC [*Television station call letters*] ... WRDG
Burlington Northern, Inc. [*AAR code*] ... BN
Burlington Northern, Incorporated [*NYSE symbol*] ... BNI
Burlington Northern (Manitoba) Limited [*AAR code*] ... BNML
Burlington, ON [*Radio station call letters*] ... CING-FM
Burlington Public Library, Burlington, CO [*Library symbol*] ... CoBur
Burlington Public Library, Burlington, ON, Canada [*Library symbol*] ... CaOBU
Burlington Public Library, Burlington, WI [*Library symbol*] ... WBur
Burlington-Rock Island Railroad Co. ... B-RI

Burlington, VT [*Television station call letters*] .... WCAX-TV
Burlington, VT [*Radio station call letters*] .... WDOT
Burlington, VT [*Television station call letters*] .... WETK
Burlington, VT [*Radio station call letters*] .... WEZF
Burlington, VT [*Radio station call letters*] .... WJOY
Burlington, VT [*Radio station call letters*] .... WQCR
Burlington, VT [*Radio station call letters*] .... WRUV
Burlington, VT [*Radio station call letters*] .... WVMT
Burlington, VT [*Television station call letters*] .... WVNY-TV
Burlington, VT [*Radio station call letters*] .... WVPS
Burlington, WI [*Location identifier*] [*FAA*] .... BUU
Burlington, WI [*Radio station call letters*] .... WBSD
Burma [*MARC geographic area code*] [*Library of Congress*] .... a-br---
Burma [*MARC country of publication code*] [*Library of Congress*] .... br
Burma [*Two-letter standard code*] .... BU
Burma [*Three-letter standard code*] .... BUR
Burma [*Aircraft nationality and registration mark*] .... XY
Burma [*Aircraft nationality and registration mark*] .... XZ
Burma-America Buddhist Association .... BABA
Burma Defense Army [*Later, BNA*] [*World War II*] .... BDA
Burma Independence Army [*Fighting on the side of the Japanese*] [*World War II*] .... BIA
Burma National Army [*Formerly, BDA*] .... BNA
Burma Socialist Programme Party .... BSPP
Burma Trade Union Congress .... BTUC
Burmah Oil Co. ADR [*NASDAQ symbol*] .... BURMY
Burmese [*MARC language code*] [*Library of Congress*] .... bur
Burmese Air Force .... BAF
Burmese Army .... BA
Burmese Communist Party .... BCP
Burmese Navy .... BN
Burn to Depletion [*NASA*] .... BTD
Burn-Dressing Change [*Medicine*] .... BDC
Burn-In/Aging Tester .... BIAT
Burn-In Screening .... BIS
Burn Time [*NASA*] .... BT
Burn Time Remaining .... BTR
Burn Unit [*Medicine*] .... BU
Burnable Poison Water Reactor .... BPWR
Burnaby Art Gallery, Burnaby, BC, Canada [*Library symbol*] .... CaBBA
Burnaby Public Library, Burnaby, BC, Canada [*Library symbol*] .... CaBB
Burndy Corporation [*NYSE symbol*] .... BDC
Burndy Corp., Technical Library, Norwalk, CT [*Library symbol*] .... CtNowaB
Burner .... BNR
Burner .... BRNR
Burnet, TX [*Radio station call letters*] .... KHLB
Burnet, TX [*Radio station call letters*] .... KMRB-FM
Burney, CA [*Radio station call letters*] .... KARZ-FM
Burney, CA [*Radio station call letters*] .... KAVA
Burnham City Hospital, Champaign, IL [*Library symbol*] .... IChamBH
Burnham, J. B., Chicago IL [*STAC*] .... BJB
Burnham Service Corporation [*NASDAQ symbol*] .... BSCO
Burnie High School [*Tasmania*] [*Seismograph station code, US Geological Survey*] .... BNE
Burning .... BRNG
Burning River News [*A publication*] .... Bur River
Burning Surface Area of Propellant [*Symbol*] [*Aerospace*] .... A
Burnish .... BNH
Burnish .... BNSH
Burnisher .... BRNSHR
Burnishing Tool .... BITO
Burnout .... BO
Burnout Proof .... BOP
Burnout Velocity .... BOV
Burns [*R. L.*] **Corp.** [*NYSE symbol*] [*Delisted*] .... RLB
Burns International Security Services, Inc. [*American Stock Exchange symbol*] [*Delisted*] .... BDA
Burns Lake, BC [*Radio station call letters*] .... CFLD
Burns, OR [*Radio station call letters*] .... KRNS
Burns & Roe, Inc., Branch Library, Hempstead, NY [*Library symbol*] .... NHemB
Burns & Roe, Inc., Oradell, NJ [*Library symbol*] .... NjOrdB
Burns and Schreiber Comedy Hour [*Television program*] [*Obsolete*] .... BS
Burns Society of the City of New York .... BSCNY
Burnside, KY [*Radio station call letters*] .... WKEQ
Burnside-Ott Aviation Training Center [*Florida*] .... BATC
Burnsville, NC [*Radio station call letters*] .... WKYK
Burnthrough .... BT
Burnup & Sims, Inc. [*NASDAQ symbol*] .... BSIM
Burr-Brown Corporation [*NASDAQ symbol*] .... BBRC
Burring Cutter .... BUCU
Burris Individuals, Inc. [*NASDAQ symbol*] .... BURS
Burritt Interfinancial Bancorp [*NASDAQ symbol*] .... BANQ
Burro Club [*Democratic political organization*] [*Defunct*] .... BC
Burro Red Blood Cells .... BRBC
Burroughs Advanced Statistical Inquiry System [*Data processing*] .... BASIS
Burroughs Algebraic Compiler .... BALGOL
Burroughs Clearing House [*A publication*] .... Burroughs Clear House
Burroughs Common Language [*Data processing*] .... BCL
Burroughs Computer Output to Microfilm .... BCOM
Burroughs Corporation .... BC
Burroughs Corp. [*NYSE symbol*] .... BGH
Burroughs Corporation .... BRC
Burroughs Corp., Western Region Central Technical Library, Pasadena, CA [*Library symbol*] .... CPB-E
Burroughs Data Link Control [*Data processing*] .... BDLC
Burroughs Distribution Scheduling System [*Data processing*] .... BURDS
Burrough's Electrographic Printer-Plotter for Ordnance Computing .... BEPOC
Burroughs Electronic Accounting Machine .... BEAM
Burroughs Hospital Administrative System [*Data processing*] .... BHAS
Burroughs Inventory Control System [*Data processing*] .... BICS
Burroughs Inventory Planning Analysis and Simulation System [*Data processing*] .... BIPASS
Burroughs Optical Lens Docking System .... BOLDS
Burroughs Scientific Processor [*Data processing*] .... BSP
Burroughs, UNIVAC, NCR, Control Data, Honeywell [*IBM competitors in computer manufacture*] .... BUNCH
Burroughs Wellcome & Co. .... BW
Burroughs Wellcome & Co., Research Triangle Park, NC [*OCLC symbol*] .... NRT
Burroughs Wellcome Research Institute [*Great Britain*] [*Research code symbol*] .... BW
Burry Port [*Welsh depot code*] .... BP
Burry Port & Gwendraeth Valley Railway [*Wales*] .... BPGV
Bursa [*Turkey*] [*Airport symbol*] [*Obsolete*] .... BTZ
Bursa Cells [*Of thymus or lymph nodes*] .... B
Bursal Dependent [*Cells*] [*Immunology*] .... BD
Bursar .... BURS
Burst .... BRST
Burst Agritech, Inc. [*NASDAQ symbol*] .... BRZT
Burst Delay Timer .... BDT
Burst Error Detection and Correlation .... BEDAC
Burst-Forming Unit erythroid [*Hematology*] .... BFUe
Burst-Height Indicator .... BHI
Burst Measuring System .... BMS
Burst Position Locator .... BPL
Burst-Promoting Factor [*Endocrinology; hematology*] .... BPF
Burst Slug Detection .... BSD
Burst-on-Target .... BOT
Burst Transmission Group .... BTG
Burst Waveform .... BWF
Burster .... BRSTR
Bursting Charge [*Military*] .... BC
Bursting Pacemaker Potential [*Electrophysiology*] .... BPP
Burton and Bitter [*Drink served in British public houses*] .... BB
Burton Energy & Solar Technology, Inc. [*NASDAQ symbol*] .... BEST
Burton/Hawks, Inc. [*NASDAQ symbol*] .... BURH
Burton-On-Trent Public Library, Burton-On-Trent, United Kingdom [*Library symbol*] .... UkBot
Burton Public Library, Burton, OH [*OCLC symbol*] .... BVP
Burton Public Library, Burton, OH [*Library symbol*] .... OBur
Burundi [*MARC country of publication code*] [*Library of Congress*] .... bd
Burundi [*Three-letter standard code*] .... BDI
Burundi [*Two-letter standard code*] .... BI
Burundi [*MARC geographic area code*] [*Library of Congress*] .... f-bd---
Burundi [*Aircraft nationality and registration mark*] 9U
Burwell, NE [*Location identifier*] [*FAA*] .... BUB
Bus Available [*Data processing*] .... BA
Bus-to-Bus Access Circuit [*Bell System*] .... BBAC
Bus Configuration Table .... BCT
Bus Control Electronics .... BCE
Bus Control Interface Unit .... BCIU
Bus Control Unit .... BCU
Bus Coupler [*Data processing*] .... BC
Bus-Earth Tracking Station Link [*NASA*] .... BEL
Bus History Association .... BHA
Bus Interface [*Data processing*] .... B/I
Bus Interface Circuit [*Data processing*] .... BIC
Bus Ion Mass Spectrometer [*Space science instrumentation*] .... BIMS
Bus Monitor Unit .... BMU
Bus Neutral Mass Spectrometer [*Space science instrumentation*] .... BNMS
Bus Selector [*Data processing*] .... BSLR
Bus Terminal Unit .... BTU
Bus Tie [*Technical drawings*] .... BT
Bus Tie Breaker .... BTB
Bus Tie Relay .... BTS
Bus Transfer .... BTR
Bus Transportation [*A publication*] .... Bus Transp
Buses International Association .... BIA
Buses and Trucks .... BAT
Bush Pilots Airways Ltd. [*Australia*] [*ICAO designator*] .... QN
Bush Terminal Buildings [*Later, BSH*] [*NYSE symbol*] .... BHB
Bush Terminal R. R. [*AAR code*] .... BUSH
Bush Universal, Inc. [*NYSE symbol*] [*Delisted*] .... BSH
Bushehr [*Iran*] [*Airport symbol*] .... BUZ
Bushel .... BSH
Bushel .... BU
Bushel .... BUS
Bushel .... BUSH
Bushing .... BSHG
Bushing .... BUSH

Bushing Current Transformer .... BCT
Bushing Potential Device .... BPD
Business .... BUS
Business Abroad [*A publication*] .... Bsns Abroad
Business Account Number File [*IRS*] .... BANF
Business Administration [*A publication*] .... Bus Adm
Business Administration, Management, and/or Marketing Programs [*Association of Independent Colleges and Schools specialization code*] .... BS
Business Advisory Committee on Procurement [*DoD*] .... BACP
Business Advisory Council [*Later, Business Council*] .... BAC
Business Air Service [*Airline*] [*Canada*] .... BAS
Business Air Transport Service .... BATS
Business Air Travel Ltd. [*Great Britain*] [*ICAO designator*] .... JW
Business Aircraft Corp. [*Stratford, CT*] [*FAA designator*] .... BSA
Business Alert to Nuclear War .... BANW
Business Alliance on Government Competition .... BAGC
Business America [*A publication*] .... Bus Am
Business Applications Programming Guide .... BAPG
Business Archives and History [*A publication*] .... BAH
Business Automation [*A publication*] .... Bsns Automation
Business Card Collectors International .... BCCI
Business Census .... BC
Business Coalition for Fair Competition .... BCFC
Business Committee for the Arts .... BCA
Business Computing [*NASDAQ symbol*] .... BCII
Business Conditions Digest [*A publication*] .... BCD
Business Conditions Digest [*A publication*] .... Bus Cond Dig
Business Corporation Board .... BCB
Business Corporation Law [*A publication*] .... BCL
Business Council .... BC
Business Council for Improved Transport Policies .... BCITP
Business Council for International Understanding .... BCIU
Business Cycle Developments [*A publication of Bureau of the Census*] .... BCD
Business Data Processing .... BDP
Business Data Processing Operation .... BDPO
Business and Defense Services Administration [*Later, BDC*] [*Department of Commerce*] .... BDSA
Business Economics [*A publication*] .... Bus Econ
Business Economics [*A publication*] .... Busin Econ
Business Economist [*A publication*] .... Busin Economist
Business EDP [*Electronic Data Processing*] **Systems Technique** .... BEST
Business Education Adminstrators Association [*Defunct*] .... BEAA
Business Education Council .... BEC
Business Education Forum [*A publication*] .... Bsns Ed Forum
Business Education Forum [*A publication*] .... Bus Ed Forum
Business Education Index [*A publication*] .... Bus Educ Ind
Business Education Journal [*A publication*] .... Bus Ed J
Business Education Research Associates .... BERA
Business Education Research Foundation .... BERF
Business Education World [*A publication*] .... Bsns Ed World
Business Education World [*A publication*] .... Bus Ed World
Business Efficiency Exhibition [*British*] .... BEE
Business Electronic Systems Techniques .... BEST
Business Electronics Computer [*Used in training*] .... BEC
Business Energy Investment Tax Credit [*IRS*] .... BEITC
Business, Engineering, Appropriate Technology, and Skilled Trades [*Peace Corps program*] .... BEAST
Business and Engineering Enriched FORTRAN [*UNIVAC*] .... BEEF
Business Equipment Manufacturers Association [*Later, CBEMA*] .... BEMA
Business Equipment Software Techniques [*Data processing*] .... BEST
Business Equipment Trade Association .... BETA
Business Exchange [*NASDAQ symbol*] .... BXBX
Business Executives Move for New National Priorities [*An association*] .... BEM
Business Executives for National Security .... BENS
Business Executives for National Security Educational Fund .... BENSE
Business Experience Training [*Program*] [*Chase Manhattan Bank*] .... BET
Business and Farm [*IRS*] .... B & F
Business Firms Master Index [*A publication*] .... BFMI
Business Flight Ltd. [*Canada*] [*ICAO designator*] .... CZ
Business Forecasting .... BIZFORC
Business Forms Institute [*Defunct*] .... BFI
Business Forms Management Association .... BFMA
Business Group for Latin America [*Later, COA*] .... BGLA
Business History [*A publication*] .... BH
Business History [*A publication*] .... Bus History
Business History Conference .... BHC
Business History Foundation [*Defunct*] .... BHF
Business History Review [*A publication*] .... BHR
Business History Review [*A publication*] .... Bsns Hist R
Business History Review [*A publication*] .... Bus Hist R
Business History Society. Bulletin [*A publication*] .... Bus Hist Soc Bull
Business Horizons [*A publication*] .... B Hor
Business Horizons [*A publication*] .... Bus Horiz
Business Horizons [*A publication*] .... Bus Horizons
Business Improvement Area .... BIA
Business and Industrial Coordinating Council .... BICC
Business and Industry Advisory Committee [*NATO*] .... BIAC
Business-Industry-Education [*Days*] [*Usually sponsored by chambers of commerce*] .... BIE
Business and Industry Management Abstracts .... BIMA
Business-Industry Political Action Committee .... BIPAC
Business Information Analysis and Integration Technique [*Data processing*] .... BIAT
Business Information Service [*Financial Times Business Information Ltd.*] [*British*] .... BIS
Business Information Systems [*Bell System*] .... BIS
Business Information Systems Analysis and Design [*Bell System*] .... BISAD
Business Information Systems Communications [*Bell System*] .... BISCOM
Business Information Systems Customer Service [*Bell System*] .... BISCUS
Business Information Systems Customer Service/Facilities Assignment and Control System [*Bell System*] .... BISCUS/FACS
Business Information Systems Modeling and Planning System [*Bell System*] .... BISMAPS
Business Information Systems Programs [*Bell System*] .... BISP
Business Input/Output Rerun .... BIOR
Business and Institutional Furniture Manufacturers Association .... BIFMA
Business Insurance [*A publication*] .... BI
Business Insurance [*A publication*] .... Binsurance
Business Insurance [*A publication*] .... Bus Insur
Business Intelligence Program [*SRI International*] [*Information service*] .... B-I-P
Business Intelligence Services Ltd. [*British*] .... BIS
Business International Corp. .... BI
Business Interruption [*Insurance*] .... BI
Business Interruption Insurance .... BII
Business Investment Game .... BIG
Business Japan [*A publication*] .... Bus Jap
Business Jet Flight Center [*Denmark*] [*ICAO designator*] .... JG
Business Jets Pty. Ltd. [*Australia*] [*ICAO designator*] .... BQ
Business Law Review [*A publication*] .... Bus L Rev
Business Lawyer [*A publication*] .... Bus Law
Business Leader Group .... BLG
Business Literature [*A publication*] .... Bsns Lit
Business Machine Computer .... BISMAC
Business Mail Foundation [*Later, DMMA*] .... BMF
Business Management [*A publication*] .... Bsns Mgt
Business Management Game .... BMG
Business Management (London) [*A publication*] .... Bsns Mgt (London)
Business Management System .... BMS
Business Master File .... BMF
Business Memo from Belgium [*A publication*] .... Belg Memo
Business Men's Assurance Company of America [*NASDAQ symbol*] .... BMAC
Business Men's League of the United States .... BMLUS
Business Name and Address File [*IRS*] .... BNAF
Business Name and Address Key Index File [*IRS*] .... BKIF
Business Office Force Administration Data System [*Bell System*] .... BOFADS
Business Office Must [*Copy that must be printed*] [*Publishing*] .... BOM
Business Opportunity Bank [*Institute for New Enterprise Development*] .... BOB
Business Organizations and Agencies Directory [*A publication*] .... BOAD
Business-Oriented Software System [*Data processing*] .... BOSS
Business Periodicals Circulation Services [*Harcourt Brace Jovanovich*] .... BPCS
Business Periodicals Index [*A publication*] .... BPI
Business Periodicals Index [*A publication*] .... BusI
Business Periodicals Index [*A publication*] .... Bus Period Index
Business/Professional Advertising Association [*Formerly, AIA, NIAA*] .... B/PAA
Business and Professional Women's Foundation .... BPW
Business Publications Audit of Circulation .... BPA
Business Publications Index and Abstracts [*A publication*] .... BPIA
Business Quarterly [*A publication*] .... Bus Q
Business Radio Service .... BRS
Business Records Manufacturers Association .... BRMA
Business Reply Card .... BRC
Business Review [*A publication*] .... Busin R
Business Review of Washington University [*A publication*] .... Bus Rev Wash Univ
Business Risk and Value of Operation in Space [*NASA*] .... BRAVO
Business Roundtable .... BR
Business Screen [*A publication*] .... Bus Scr
Business Service Center .... BSC
Business Service Checklist [*A publication*] .... BSCL
Business and Society Review [*A publication*] .... Busin Soc R
Business and Society Review [*A publication*] .... Bus & Soc R
Business and Society Review/Innovation [*A publication*] .... Bus & Soc R
Business Systems and Equipment [*A publication*] .... Bus Syst & Equip
Business Systems Planning .... BSP
Business Taxpayer Information File [*IRS*] .... BTIF
Business and Technology Sources [*A publication*] .... Bsns & Tech Sources
Business Training College .... BTC
Business User Groups [*Data processing*] .... BUG'S
Business as Usual .... BAU
Business Visit [*Program*] [*United States Travel Service*] .... BUSIVISIT
Business Week [*A publication*] .... Bsns W
Business Week [*A publication*] .... Bus W

Business Week [*A publication*] ... Bus Week
Business Week [*A publication*] ... BW
Business World [*A publication*] ... Bsns W
Businessland, Inc. [*NASDAQ symbol*] ... BUSL
Businessowners Policy [*Insurance*] ... BOP
Bust Bodice [*Early name for brassiere*] ... BB
Busted Aristocrat [*A cadet officer reduced to the ranks*] [*Military slang*] ... BA
Busulfan [*Also, BUS*] [*Antineoplastic drug*] ... BSF
Busulfan [*Also, BSF*] [*Antineoplastic drug*] ... BUS
Busy Hour Call Attempts [*Telephone technology*] ... BHCA
Busy Hour Model [*Data processing*] ... BHM
Busy Lamp Field [*Phone console*] [*Bell System*] ... BLF
Busy-Tone Start Lead ... BTST
But Less Than ... BLT
But Not ... BN
But Not Exceeding ... BNE
But Not Over ... BNOV
Buta [*Zaire*] [*Airport symbol*] ... BZU
Butadiene Extraction [*Chemical engineering*] ... BTX
Butadiene Rubber ... BR
Butane ... BUTN
Butane-Butene Fraction ... B-B
Butane Secondary Refrigerant ... BSR
Butanediol Diglycidyl Ether [*Organic chemistry*] ... BDGE
Butanediol Succinate [*Organic chemistry*] ... BDS
Butanetriol Trinitrate [*An explosive*] ... BTTN
Butanol-Extractable Iodine [*Clinical chemistry*] ... BEI
Butare [*Astrida*] [*Rwanda*] [*Seismograph station code, US Geological Survey*] [*Closed*] ... BTR
Butaritari [*Kiribati*] [*Airport symbol*] ... BBG
Butcher [*Navy*] ... B
Butcher ... BTCR
Butembo [*Zaire*] [*Seismograph station code, US Geological Survey*] ... BTC
Buthylethylmagnesium [*Organic chemistry*] ... BEM
Butler Air Transport Ltd. ... BAT
Butler, AL [*Radio station call letters*] ... WPRN
Butler, AL [*Radio station call letters*] ... WQGL
Butler Area Librarians [*Library network*] ... BAL
Butler College, Tyler, TX [*Library symbol*] ... TxTyB
Butler County Courthouse, Allison, IA [*Library symbol*] ... IaAlnBCo
Butler County Historical Society, Hamilton, OH [*Library symbol*] ... OHaBHi
Butler County Tribune-Journal, Allison, IA [*Library symbol*] ... IaAlnTJ
Butler Health Center, Providence, RI [*Library symbol*] ... RPBH
Butler High School, Augusta, GA [*Library symbol*] ... GAuBH
Butler International, Inc. [*NYSE symbol*] ... BTL
Butler Manufacturing [*NASDAQ symbol*] ... BTLR
Butler, MO [*Location identifier*] [*FAA*] ... BUM
Butler, MO [*Radio station call letters*] ... KMAM
Butler National Corp. [*NASDAQ symbol*] ... BUTL
Butler, PA [*Radio station call letters*] ... WBUT
Butler, PA [*Radio station call letters*] ... WISR
Butler, PA [*Radio station call letters*] ... WLER
Butler Public Library, Butler, PA [*Library symbol*] ... PBut
Butler University Botanical Studies [*A publication*] ... Butler Univ Bot Stud
Butler University, College of Pharmacy, Indianapolis, IN [*Library symbol*] ... InIB-P
Butler University, Indianapolis, IN [*OCLC symbol*] ... IIB
Butler University, Indianapolis, IN [*Library symbol*] ... InIB
Butoxyacetanilide [*Pharmacology*] ... BOA
Butoxycarbonyl [*Also, BOC*] [*Biochemistry*] ... Boc
Butoxycarbonyl [*or t-BOC*] [*Biochemistry*] ... t-Boc
Butoxycarbonyl [*Also, Boc*] [*Organic chemistry*] ... BOC
Butropium Bromide [*Pharmacology*] ... BHB
Butsuri. Physical Society of Japan [*A publication*] ... Butsuri Phys Soc Jap
Butt Line [*Technical drawings*] ... BL
Butt Plane ... BP
Butt Welded ... BTWLD
Butt Welded Filter ... BWF
Butt Welded Joint ... BWJ
Butte [*Montana*] [*Airport symbol*] ... BTM
Butte [*Montana*] [*Seismograph station code, US Geological Survey*] ... BUT
Butte, Anaconda, & Pacific Railway Co. [*AAR code*] ... BAP
Butte County Library, Oroville, CA [*Library symbol*] ... COroB
Butte Free Public Library, Butte, MT [*Library symbol*] ... MtBu
Butte, MT [*Radio station call letters*] ... KBOW
Butte, MT [*Radio station call letters*] ... KMSM-FM
Butte, MT [*Radio station call letters*] ... KOPR
Butte, MT [*Radio station call letters*] ... KQUY
Butte, MT [*Television station call letters*] ... KTVM-TV
Butte, MT [*Radio station call letters*] ... KXLF
Butte, MT [*Television station call letters*] ... KXLF-TV
Butter and Cheese Journal [*A publication*] ... Butter & Cheese J
Butter, Lard, and Salt Provisions ... BL & SP
Butterfield Equities [*NASDAQ symbol*] ... BUTR
Butterfly ... BTFL
Butterfly [*Stroke*] [*Swimming*] ... BUFLY
Buttermilk [*Freight*] ... BTRMLK
Butterworths Proprietory Ltd., Chatswood, NSW, Australia [*Library symbol*] ... AuBut
Buttes Gas & Oil Co. [*NYSE symbol*] ... BGO
Buttock Line [*Engineering*] ... BL
Button ... BTN
Button ... BUT
Button Cell Battery ... BCB
Button Head ... BTNHD
Butts Army Airfield [*Fort Carson, CO*] ... BAAF
Butuan [*Philippines*] [*Seismograph station code, US Geological Survey*] [*Closed*] ... BTN
Butuan [*Philippines*] [*Airport symbol*] ... BXU
Butyl [*Organic chemistry*] ... Bu
Butyl Acrylate [*Organic chemistry*] ... BA
Butyl Benzyl Phthalate [*Organic chemistry*] ... BBP
Butyl Ethyl Ketone [*Organic chemistry*] ... BEK
Butyl Glycidyl Ether [*Organic chemistry*] ... BGE
Butyl Isocyanate [*Organic chemistry*] ... BIC
Butyl Methacrylate [*Organic chemistry*] ... BMA
Butyl Vinyl Ether [*Organic chemistry*] ... BVE
Butylacetanilide [*Organic chemistry*] ... BAA
Butylated Hydroxyanisole [*Antioxidant*] ... BHA
Butylated Hydroxytoluene [*Also, DBPC*] [*Antioxidant*] ... BHT
Butylene Dimethacrylate [*Organic chemistry*] ... BDMA
Butyl(methoxy)azobenzene [*Organic chemistry*] ... BMAB
Butyl(octyl)magnesium [*Organic chemistry*] ... BOM
Butyrum [*Butter*] [*Diet order*] ... BUT
BUWEPS [*Bureau of Naval Weapons, now obsolete*] **Aviation Clothing and Survival Equipment Bulletin** ... BACSEB
BUWEPS [*Bureau of Naval Weapons, now obsolete*] **Evaluation** ... BWE
BUWEPS [*Bureau of Naval Weapons, now obsolete*] **- Industry Material Reliability Advisory Board** ... BIMRAB
Buxom Belle, International ... BBI
Buy a Car [*Slogan during automobile sales slump of 1974-75*] ... BAC
Buy-Off ... B-O
Buy-Off Date ... BOD
Buy United States Here [*Program to procure US-made supplies from overseas subsidiaries of US firms*] ... BUSH
Buyer Attitudes and Sales Experiences [*LIMRA*] ... BASE
Buyer Designated Equipment ... BDE
Buyer Has Seven Days to Take Up [*Securities brokerage*] ... B7D
Buyer Protection Plan [*American Motors*] ... BPP
Buyer's Option [*Business and trade*] ... BO
Buyers Screening Guide ... BSG
Buying [*Rate*] [*Value of the English pound*] ... BG
Buying Activity [*Air Force*] ... BUYAC
Buying Power Index ... BPI
Buying, Receiving, and Accounts Payable Integrated Data ... BRAID
Buys Ballot Law ... BBL
Buzzer ... BUZ
Buzzer [*RADAR*] ... BZR
BVD Co. [*Initials stand for Bradley, Voorhies, and Day, organizers of the company, and have come to be used as a generic term for underwear*] ... BVD
BVL Fund [*Formerly, Bowlers' Victory Legion*] ... BVL
BWPA [*British Wood Preserving Association*] **News Sheet** [*A publication*] ... BWPA News Sheet
By [*As in 9 x 12*] ... X
By Any Means Necessary ... BAMN
By Direction ... BYDIR
By Direction of the President ... DP
By Other Means ... BOM
By Visual Reference to the Ground [*Aviation*] ... VSA
Byblos Librairie Bookshop, Beirut, Lebanon [*Library symbol*] ... ByB
Bydgoszcz [*Poland*] [*Airport symbol*] [*Obsolete*] ... BZG
Bye [*Cricket*] ... B
Byelorussian-American Association in the USA ... BAZA
Byelorussian-American Veteran Association ... BAVA
Byelorussian-American Women Association ... BAWA
Byelorussian-American Youth Organization ... BAYO
Byelorussian Congress Committee of America ... BCCA
Byelorussian Institute of Arts and Science [*Formerly, WIAS*] ... BIAS
Byelorussian Liberation Front ... BLF
Byelorussian Literary Association ... BLA
Byelorussian Soviet Socialist Republic ... BelSSR
Byelorussian Soviet Socialist Republic ... BSSR
Byelorussian Youth Association of America [*Later, BAYO*] ... BYAA
Byers Communications [*NASDAQ symbol*] ... BYCM
Byers [*A. M.*] **Co.** [*NYSE symbol*] [*Delisted*] ... ABY
Bygningsstatiske Meddelelser [*A publication*] ... Bygnin Medd
Byk-Gulden Lomberg [*Germany*] [*Research code symbol*] ... C
Byk-Gulden Lomberg [*Germany*] [*Research code symbol*] ... Do
Bypass ... BP
Bypass ... BYP
Bypass Label Processing [*Data processing*] ... BLP
Bypass Monochrome Signal ... BMS
Bypass Ratio ... BPR
Bypass Turbojet Engine Noise ... BTJE
Bypass Valve ... BV
Byrd [*Antarctica*] [*Seismograph station code, US Geological Survey*] [*Closed*] ... BSA
Byrd [*Antarctica*] [*Seismograph station code, US Geological Survey*] [*Closed*] ... BYR
Byrd [*William*] **Press** [*NASDAQ symbol*] ... BYRD

Byrd - Stanford Research Institute [*Antarctica*] [*Seismograph station code, US Geological Survey*] [*Closed*].....................................BY1
Byrd Station, Antarctica ....BYA
Byron Journal [*A publication*]..Byron J
Byron Society ....BS
Bystander Dominates Initial Dominant [*Sociology*].................BDID
Byte [*Data processing*] ....B
Byte Control Protocol [*Data processing*]..............................BCP
Byte Input Control [*Data processing*] ....BIC
Byte Output Control [*Data processing*] ....BOC
Bytes per Inch [*Data processing*]..BPI
Bytes per Second [*Data processing*] ....BPS
Bytom [*Poland*] [*Seismograph station code, US Geological Survey*] ....BYT
Byulleten' Botanicheskogo Sada Akademii Nauk Armyanskoi SSR [*A publication*].................... Byull Bot Sada Akad Nauk Arm SSR
Byulleten' Eksperimental'noi Biologii i Meditsiny [*A publication*]....................
Byull Eksp Biol Med
Byulleten' po Fiziologii Rastenii [*A publication*] .... Byull Fiziol Rast
Byulleten' Glavnogo Botanicheskogo Sada [*Leningrad*] [*A publication*].. Byull Gl Bot Sada
Byulleten' Glavnogo Botanicheskogo Sada (Leningrad) [*A publication*]......................... Byull Glavn Bot Sada (Leningr)
Byulleten' Gosudarstvennogo Nikitskogo Botanicheskogo Sada [*A publication*] .... Byull Gos Nikitsk Bot Sada
Byulleten' Informatsionnogo Tsentral'nogo po Yadernym Dannym [*A publication*]..................Byull Inf Tsentra Yad Dannym
Byulleten'. Instituta Biologii Vodokhranilishcha [*A publication*] ....
Byull Inst Biol Vodokhran
Byulleten'. Instituta Biologiya Akademii Nauk Belorusskoi SSR [*A publication*]...................Byull Inst Biol Akad Nauk B SSR
Byulleten'. Instituta Teoreticheskoi Astronomii. Akademiya Nauk SSSR [*A publication*]..........Byull Inst Teor Astron Akad Nauk SSSR
Byulleten' Kirgizskogo Nauchno-Issledovatel'skogo Instituta Zemledeliya [*A publication*]........... Byull Kirgiz Nauch Issled Inst Zemled
Byulleten' Mezhdunarodnogo Obshchestva po Torfu [*A publication*]........................... Byull Mezhdunar O-va Torfu

Byulleten' Moskovskogo Obshchestva Ispytateley Prirody. Otdel Geologicheskiy [*A publication*].....................................
Moskov Obshch Ispytateley Prirody Byull Otdel Geol
Byulleten' Nauchno-Tekhnicheskoi Informatsii [*A publication*]....................
Byull Nauchno-Tekh Inf
Byulleten' Nauchno-Tekhnicheskoi Informatsii po Agronomicheskoi Fizike [*A publication*]....................
Byull Nauchno-Tekh Inf Agron Fiz
Byulleten' Nauchno-Tekhnicheskoi Informatsii (Sumskaya Gosudarstvennaya Sel'skokhozyaistvennaya Opytnaya Stantsiya) [*A publication*]....................
Byull Nauchno-Tekh Inf (Sumskaya Gos Skh Opytn Stn)
Byulleten'. Vsesoyuznogo Instituta Eksperimental'noi Veterinarii [*A publication*]..................Byull Vses Inst Eksp Vet
Byulleten'. Vsesoyuznogo Instituta Rastenievodstva [*A publication*]..................... Byull Vses Inst Rastenievod
Byzantina-Metabyzantina [*A publication*] ....Byz-Met
Byzantina-Metabyzantina [*A publication*] ....ByzMetabyz
Byzantine...BYZ
Byzantinisch-Neugriechische Jahrbuecher [*A publication*] ....BNJ
Byzantinisch-Neugriechische Jahrbuecher [*A publication*] .... ByJ
Byzantinisch-Neugriechische Jahrbuecher [*A publication*]...................
Byz-Neugr Jahrb
Byzantinisch-Neugriechische Jahrbuecher [*A publication*] ....BYZNGJB
Byzantinische Forschungen [*A publication*] ....Byz F
Byzantinische Forschungen [*A publication*] ....Byz Forsch
Byzantinische Zeitschrift [*A publication*] .... ByZ
Byzantinische Zeitschrift [*A publication*] ....ByzZ
Byzantinische Zeitschrift [*A publication*] ....BZ
Byzantinisches Archiv [*A publication*] ....Byz Arch
Byzantino-Bulgarica [*A publication*] ....Byz-Bulg
Byzantino-Slavica [*A publication*]..BSL
Byzantino-Slavica [*A publication*]..ByzS
Byzantino-Slavica [*A publication*]..ByzSl
Byzantion [*A publication*] ....Byz

C

Cabo Rojo, PR [*Radio station call letters*] .... WEKO
Cabo Verde [*A publication*] .... CaboV
Cabol, MO [*Location identifier*] [*FAA*] .... TVB
Cabool, MO [*Radio station call letters*] .... KVVC
Caboose [*Freight*] .... CBSE
Caborca [*Mexico*] [*Seismograph station code, US Geological Survey*] .... CBS
Cabot, AR [*Radio station call letters*] .... KBOT
Cabot, Cabot, & Forbes Land Trust [*NYSE symbol*] .... CFT
Cabot Corp. [*NYSE symbol*] .... CBT
Cabot Corp., Stellite Division, Kokomo, IN [*OCLC symbol*] .... ISD
Cabot Corp., Technical Information Center, Billerica, MA [*Library symbol*] .... MBilC
Cabramurra [*Australia*] [*Seismograph station code, US Geological Survey*] [*Closed*] .... CAB
Cabrillo College, Aptos, CA [*Library symbol*] .... CApC
Cabrillo National Monument .... CABR
Cabrini College, Library, Radnor, PA [*OCLC symbol*] .... PAB
Cacau Atualidades [*A publication*] .... Cacau Atual
Caceres [*Brazil*] [*Airport symbol*] CCX
Cache County Public Library, Logan, UT [*Library symbol*] .... ULC
Cache, Inc. [*NASDAQ symbol*] .... CACH
Cache Valley Historical Society, Logan, UT [*Library symbol*] .... ULCHi
Cachucha Ranch [*New Mexico*] [*Seismograph station code, US Geological Survey*] [*Closed*] .... CCN
CACI, Inc. [*NASDAQ symbol*] .... CACI
Cacquot Kite Balloon .... CKB
Cactaceas y Suculentas Mexicanas [*A publication*] .... Cact Suc Mex
Cactaceas y Suculentas Mexicanas [*A publication*] .... Cact Suculentas Mex
Cactus Journal [*A publication*] .... Cact J
Cactus and Succulent Journal [*A publication*] .... Cact Succ J
Cactus and Succulent Journal [*A publication*] .... Cactus Succulent J
Cactus and Succulent Society of America .... CSSA
Cadarache [*France*] [*Seismograph station code, US Geological Survey*] .... CDR
Cadaver [*Medicine*] .... Cad
Cadaver Donor [*Medicine*] .... CD
Caddo [*MARC language code*] [*Library of Congress*] .... cad
Caddo Mills, TX [*Location identifier*] [*FAA*] .... MII
Caddo Parish Library, Shreveport, LA [*Library symbol*] .... LShCa
Cadec Systems, Inc. [*NASDAQ symbol*] .... KDCK
Cadena Azul de Radiodifusion [*Radio network*] [*Spain*] .... CAR
Cadena Garcia Valseca [*Press agency*] [*Mexico*] .... CGV
Cadena de Ondas Populares Espanola [*Broadcasting organization*] .... COPE
Cadence Industries Corp. [*NYSE symbol*] [*Delisted*] .... CDE
Cadence Magazine [*A publication*] .... Cadence
Cadenza [*Cadence*] [*Music*] .... CAD
Cadernos Brasileiros [*A publication*] .... CadB
Cadernos Brasileiros [*A publication*] .... CBr
Cadernos Cientificos Instituto Pasteur de Lisboa [*A publication*] .... Cad Cient
Cadet .... CAD
Cadet Captain CC
Cadet Practice Squadron .... CADETRON
Cadillac Convertible Owners of America .... CCOA
Cadillac & Lake City Railway Co. [*AAR code*] .... CLK
Cadillac-LaSalle Club CLC
Cadillac, MI [*Location identifier*] [*FAA*] .... CAD
Cadillac, MI [*Radio station call letters*] .... WATT
Cadillac, MI [*Television station call letters*] .... WCMV
Cadillac, MI [*Radio station call letters*] .... WEVZ
Cadillac, MI [*Radio station call letters*] .... WKJF
Cadillac, MI [*Radio station call letters*] .... WKJF-FM
Cadillac, MI [*Television station call letters*] .... WWTV
Cadillac-Wexford Public Library, Cadillac, MI [*Library symbol*] .... MiCad
Cadiz, KY [*Radio station call letters*] .... WKDZ
Cadiz, KY [*Radio station call letters*] .... WKDZ-FM
Cadiz Public Library, Cadiz, OH [*Library symbol*] .... OCad
Cadiz Railroad Co. [*AAR code*] .... CAD
Cadmium [*Chemical symbol is Cd*] .... CAD
Cadmium [*Chemical element*] .... Cd
Cadmium Binding Protein .... CdBP
Cadmium Bronze .... CB
Cadmium Bronze Connector .... CBC
Cadmium Council CC
Cadmium Oxide - Ethylenediamine [*Cellulose solvent*] .... CADOXEN
Cadmium Red Line .... CRL
Cadmium-Sulfide Cell .... CSC
Cadres et Professions [*A publication*] .... Cadres et Profes
Caducee [*A publication*] .... Cad
Caduceus [*A publication*] .... Cad
Cady Mountains [*California*] [*Seismograph station code, US Geological Survey*] [*Closed*] .... CAD
Caecum C
Caeharris [*Cardiff*] [*Welsh depot code*] .... CH
Caelum [*Constellation*] .... Cae
Caelum [*Constellation*] .... Cael
Caen [*France*] [*Airport symbol*] .... CFR
Caernarvonshire [*County in Wales*] .... Caerns
Caesar C
Caesarean-Originated, Barrier-Sustained [*Rodent breeding*] .... COBS
Caesars New Jersey, Inc. [*American Stock Exchange symbol*] .... CJN
Caesars World, Inc. [*NYSE symbol*] .... CAW
Caesars World, Incorporated Wts [*NASDAQ symbol*] .... CAWIW
Cafe Solo [*A publication*] .... Cafe
Caffeic Acid [*Organic chemistry*] .... CA
Caffeine .... CAF
Cagayan De Oro [*Philippines*] [*Airport symbol*] .... CGY
Cage .... CG
CAGE [*Computerized Aerospace Ground Equipment*] **Test Language** [*Data processing*] .... CTL
Caging Amplifier Assembly .... CAA
Caging Retainer and Boresight [*Air Force*] .... CRAB
Cagle's, Inc. [*American Stock Exchange symbol*] .... CGL
Cagliari [*Italy*] [*Airport symbol*] .... CAG
Caguas [*Puerto Rico*] [*Seismograph station code, US Geological Survey*] .... CAG
Caguas, PR [*Television station call letters*] .... WKBM-TV
Caguas, PR [*Radio station call letters*] .... WNEL
Caguas, PR [*Television station call letters*] .... WUJA
Caguas, PR [*Radio station call letters*] .... WVJP
Caguas, PR [*Radio station call letters*] .... WVJP-FM
Cahier Canadien Claudel [*A publication*] .... CCanC
Cahier. Centre Technique du Bois [*A publication*] .... Cah Centre Tech Bois
Cahiers. Academie Luxembourgeoise [*A publication*] .... C A L
Cahiers d'Acoustique [*A publication*] .... Cah Acoust
Cahiers de l'Actualite Religieuse [*A publication*] .... Cah A R
Cahiers Africains d'Administration Publique [*A publication*] .... C Afr Adm Publ
Cahiers Africains de la Securite Sociale [*A publication*] .... C Afr Secur Soc
Cahiers Algeriens de Litterature Comparee [*A publication*] .... CALC
Cahiers Algeriens de la Sante [*A publication*] .... Cah Alg San
Cahiers Alsaciens d'Archeologie, d'Art, et d'Histoire [*A publication*] .... CAAH
Cahiers des Ameriques Latines [*A publication*] .... CAL
Cahiers des Ameriques Latines [*A publication*] .... C Amer Lat
Cahiers des Ameriques Latines. Serie Sciences de l'Homme [*A publication*] .... C Amer Lat Ser Sci Homme
Cahiers de l'Amitie Charles Peguy [*A publication*] .... CACP
Cahiers pour l'Analyse [*A publication*] .... Cah Anal
Cahiers d'Analyse Textuelle [*A publication*] .... Cah Anal Text
Cahiers d'Analyse Textuelle: les Belles Lettres [*Liege*] [*A publication*] .... CAT
Cahiers d'Anesthesiologie [*A publication*] .... Cah Anesth
Cahiers d'Anesthesiologie [*A publication*] .... Cah Anesthesiol
Cahiers d'Anthropologie et d'Ecologie Humaines [*A publication*] .... C Anthropol Ecol Hum
Cahiers d'Archeologie Biblique [*A publication*] .... CAB
Cahiers d'Archeologie et d'Histoire d'Alsace [*A publication*] .... CAHA
Cahiers d'Archeologie et d'Histoire du Berry [*A publication*] .... Cah Arch Hist Berry
Cahiers Archeologiques [*A publication*] .... Ca Ar
Cahiers Archeologiques [*A publication*] .... Cah Arch
Cahiers Archeologiques [*A publication*] .... CArch
Cahiers d'Art [*A publication*] .... Cah Art
Cahiers de Art Sacre [*A publication*] .... Cah Art Sacre
Cahiers de l'Asie du Sud-Est [*A publication*] .... Cah As Se
Cahiers. Association Internationale des Etudes Francaises [*A publication*] .... CAEF
Cahiers. Association Internationale des Etudes Francaises [*A publication*] .... Cah Ass Int Et Fr
Cahiers. Association Internationale des Etudes Francaises [*A publication*] .... CAIEF
Cahiers Benjamin Constant [*A publication*] .... CBC
Cahiers de la Biloque [*A publication*] .... Cah Biloque
Cahiers de Biologie Marine [*A publication*] .... Cah Biol Mar
Cahiers de Biologie Marine [*A publication*] .... Cah Bio Mar
Cahiers Bruxellois [*A publication*] .... Cah Brux
Cahiers de Byrsa [*A publication*] .... Byrsa
Cahiers. Centre d'Etudes des Coutumes [*A publication*] .... C Centre Et Coutumes
Cahiers. Centre d'Etudes Irlandaises [*A publication*] .... CCEI
Cahiers. Centre d'Etudes de Recherche Operationnelle [*A publication*] .... Cahiers Centre Etudes Recherche Oper
Cahiers. Centre Universitaire d'Histoire Contemporaine de Louvain [*A publication*] .... CCUHCL
Cahiers. CERBOM [*Centre d'Etudes et de Recherche de Biologie et d'Oceanographie Medicale*] [*A publication*] .... Cah CERBOM
Cahiers Cesairiens [*A publication*] .... Cahiers C
Cahiers de Chirurgie [*A publication*] .... Cah Chir
Cahiers du Cinema [*A publication*] .... Cahiers
Cahiers du Cinema [*A publication*] CC
Cahiers du Cinema [*A publication*] .... C Cinema
Cahiers du Cinema in English [*A publication*] .... Cahiers in Eng
Cahiers de Civilisation Medievale [*A publication*] .... Cah Civ Med
Cahiers de Civilisation Medievale [*A publication*] .... CCM
Cahiers de Civilisation Medievale [*A publication*] .... CCMe
Cahiers du Communisme [*A publication*] .... C Communisme
Cahiers de la Compagnie Madeleine Renaud-Jean Louis Barrault [*A publication*] .... CCRB
Cahiers de la Compagnie Madeleine Renaud-Jean Louis Barrault [*A publication*] .... CRB
Cahiers de la Documentation [*A publication*] .... Cah Docum

Cahiers de Documentation de la Chambre de Commerce et d'Industrie de Marseille [*A publication*]....... C Docum Ch Com Marseille
Cahiers de Droit [*A publication*]....C de D
Cahiers de Droit de l'Entreprise [*A publication*]....C Dr Entreprise
Cahiers de Droit Europeen [*A publication*]....C Dr Europ
Cahiers Economiques de Bruxelles [*A publication*]....Cah Econ Br
Cahiers Economiques de Bruxelles [*A publication*]....C Econ Bruxelles
Cahiers Economiques et Sociaux [*Kinshasa*] [*A publication*]....C Econ Soc
Cahiers Economiques et Sociaux (Kinshasa) [*A publication*].... C Econ Soc (Kinshasa)
Cahiers Elisabethains [*A publication*]....CahiersE
Cahiers de l'Enfrance [*A publication*]....Cah Enf
Cahiers d'Etudes Africaines [*A publication*]....Cah Et Afr
Cahiers d'Etudes Africaines [*A publication*]....Cah Etud Af
Cahiers d'Etudes Africaines [*A publication*]....CEAfr
Cahiers d'Etudes Africaines [*A publication*]....C Et Afr
Cahiers d'Etudes Anciennes [*A publication*]....CEA
Cahiers d'Etudes Biologiques [*A publication*]....Cah Etud Biol
Cahiers d'Etudes Cathares [*A publication*]....Cah Et Cath
Cahiers d'Etudes Cathares [*A publication*]....CEC
Cahiers d'Etudes Medievales [*A publication*]....CEM
Cahiers d'Etudes de Radio-Television [*A publication*]....CER-T
Cahiers Europeens [*A publication*]....C Europ
Cahiers Ferdinand de Saussure [*A publication*]....CFS
Cahiers Francais [*A publication*]....Cah Fr
Cahiers Francais [*A publication*]....C Franc
Cahiers Francophones [*A publication*]....CahiersF
Cahiers de Geographie Physique [*A publication*]....Cah Geogr Phys
Cahiers de Geographie de Quebec [*A publication*]....Cahiers Geog Quebec
Cahiers Geologiques [*A publication*]....Cah Geol
Cahiers Geologiques [*A publication*]....Cahiers Geol
Cahiers Geologiques de Thoiry [*A publication*]....Cah Geol Thoiry
Cahiers de Groupe Francais de Rheologie [*A publication*].... Cah Groupe Fr Rheol
Cahiers du Groupe Francois-Thureau-Dangin [*A publication*]....CGFTD
Cahiers de l'Herne [*A publication*]....Cahiers Herne
Cahiers d'Histoire [*A publication*]....Ca H
Cahiers d'Histoire [*A publication*]....Ca Hist
Cahiers d'Histoire [*A publication*]....CH
Cahiers d'Histoire et d'Archeologie [*A publication*]....Cah Hist Arch
Cahiers d'Histoire et d'Archeologie [*A publication*]....CHA
Cahiers d'Histoire Egyptienne [*A publication*]....Cah Hist Eg
Cahiers d'Histoire et de Folklore [*A publication*]....CHF
Cahiers d'Histoire de l'Institut Maurice Thorez [*A publication*].... C Hist Inst Maurice Thorez
Cahiers d'Histoire Mondiale/Journal of World History [*A publication*]....Cah Hist Mond
Cahiers d'Histoire Mondiale/Journal of World History [*A publication*]....CHM
Cahiers d'Histoire Publies par les Universites de Clermont-Lyon-Grenoble [*A publication*]....CHCLG
Cahiers d'Histoire de la Revolution Francaise [*A publication*]....CHRF
Cahiers d'Information du Chef de Personnel [*A publication*].... C Inform Chef Personnel
Cahiers d'Information Station de Biologie Marine de Grande-Riviere [*A publication*]....Cah Inf Stn Biol Mar Grande-Riviere
Cahiers des Ingenieurs Agronomes [*A publication*]....Cah Ing Agron
Cahiers des Ingenieurs Agronomes [*A publication*]....Cah Ingnrs Agron
Cahiers des Ingenieurs Agronomes [*A publication*]....C Ingen Agron
Cahiers. Institut d'Amenagement et d'Urbanisation de la Region Parisienne [*A publication*]....C Inst Amenag Urb Region Paris
Cahiers. Institut Francais d'Amerique Latine [*A publication*]....Cah I F A L
Cahiers. Institut du Moyen Age Grec et Latin [*A publication*]....CIMAGL
Cahiers Internacionaux [*A publication*]....Cah Int
Cahiers Internationaux de Sociologie [*A publication*]....Cah Int Soc
Cahiers Internationaux de Sociologie [*A publication*]....C Int Sociol
Cahiers Internationaux de Sociologie [*A publication*]....CIS
Cahiers Irlandais [*A publication*]....Cahiers I
Cahiers de l'Iroise [*A publication*]....Cah Iroise
Cahiers Jean Cocteau [*A publication*]....CJC
Cahiers Juridiques de l'Electricite et du Gaz [*A publication*].... Cah Juridiques Electr Gaz
Cahiers de Kinesitherapie [*A publication*]....Cah Kinesither
Cahiers de Lexicologie [*A publication*]....Cah Lex
Cahiers de Lexicologie [*A publication*]....CdL
Cahiers de Lexicologie [*A publication*]....CLe
Cahiers de Lexicologie [*A publication*]....CLex
Cahiers Ligures de Prehistoire et d'Archeologie [*A publication*].... C Ligures Prehist Archeol
Cahiers de Linguistique Asie Orientale [*A publication*]....Cah Ling As Or
Cahiers de Linguistique Theorique et Appliquee [*A publication*]....Cah Ling
Cahiers de Linguistique Theorique et Appliquee [*A publication*]....CLTA
Cahiers de Linguistique. Universite du Quebec [*A publication*]....CLUQ
Cahiers Linguistiques d'Ottawa [*A publication*]....CLO
Cahiers de Litterature et de Linguistique Appliquee [*A publication*]....CLLA
Cahiers de la Maboke [*A publication*]....Cah Maboke
Cahiers de Medecine Assises de Medecine [*A publication*].... Cah Med Assises Med
Cahiers de Medecine Europa Medica [*A publication*]....Cah Med Eur Med
Cahiers de Medecine Veterinaire [*A publication*]....Cah Med Vet
Cahiers Medicaux [*A publication*]....Cah Med
Cahiers Medicaux Lyonnais [*A publication*]....Cah Med Lyon
Cahiers du Monde Hispanique et Luso-Bresilien [*A publication*].... Cah Monde Hisp Luso-Bresil
Cahiers du Monde Hispanique et Luso-Bresilien [*A publication*].... C Monde Hisp Luso-Bresil
Cahiers du Monde Russe et Sovietique [*A publication*]....Cah Mon Rus
Cahiers du Monde Russe et Sovietique [*A publication*].... C Monde Russe Sov
Cahiers du Monde Russe et Sovietique [*A publication*]....CMRS
Cahiers des Naturalistes [*A publication*]....Cah Nat
Cahiers des Naturalistes [*A publication*]....CNat
Cahiers de Notes Documentaires [*A publication*]....Cah Notes Doc
Cahiers de Notes Documentaires. Securite et Hygiene du Travail [*A publication*]....Cah Notes Doc Secur Hyg Trav
Cahiers de la Nouvelle Journee [*A publication*]....Cah Nouv Journee
Cahiers Numismatiques [*A publication*]....CahN
Cahiers Numismatiques [*A publication*]....Cah Num
Cahiers de Nutrition et de Dietetique [*A publication*]....Cah Nutr Diet
Cahiers Oceanographiques [*A publication*]....Cah Oceanogr
Cahiers d'Odonto-Stomatologie [*A publication*]....Cah Odonto-Stomatol
Cahiers. ORSTOM [*Office de la Recherche Scientifique et Technique d'Outre-Mer*]. **Hydrobiologie** [*A publication*]....Cah ORST Hy
Cahiers. ORSTOM [*Office de la Recherche Scientifique et Technique d'Outre-Mer*]. **Oceanographie** [*A publication*].... Cah ORST Oc
Cahiers. ORSTOM [*Office de la Recherche Scientifique et Technique d'Outre-Mer*]. **Physiologie des Plantes Tropicales Cultivees** [*A publication*]....Cah ORSTOM Physiol Plant Trop Cult
Cahiers. ORSTOM [*Office de la Recherche Scientifique et Technique d'Outre-Mer*] **Serie Biologie** [*A publication*].... Cah ORSTOM Ser Biol
Cahiers. ORSTOM [*Office de la Recherche Scientifique et Technique d'Outre-Mer*] **Serie Entomologie Medicale** [*A publication*]....Cah ORSTOM Ser Entomol Med
Cahiers. ORSTOM [*Office de la Recherche Scientifique et Technique d'Outre-Mer*] **Serie Hydrobiologie** [*A publication*].... Cah ORSTOM Ser Hydrobiol
Cahiers. ORSTOM [*Office de la Recherche Scientifique et Technique d'Outre-Mer*] **Serie Hydrologie** [*A publication*].... Cah ORSTOM Ser Hydrol
Cahiers. ORSTOM [*Office de la Recherche Scientifique et Technique d'Outre-Mer*] **Serie Oceanographie** [*A publication*]....Cah ORSTOM Ser Oceanogr
Cahiers. ORSTOM [*Office de la Recherche Scientifique et Technique d'Outre-Mer*] **Serie Pedologie** [*A publication*].... Cah ORSTOM Ser Pedol
Cahiers. ORSTOM [*Office de la Recherche Scientifique et Technique d'Outre-Mer*] **Serie Sciences Humaines** [*A publication*]....Cah ORSTOM Ser Sci Hum
Cahiers. ORSTOM [*Office de la Recherche Scientifique et Technique d'Outre-Mer*] **Serie Sciences Humaines** [*A publication*]....C ORSTOM Ser Sci Hum
Cahiers de l'Ouest [*A publication*]....CO
Cahiers d'Outre-Mer [*A publication*]....Cah O-Mer
Cahiers d'Outre-Mer [*A publication*]....Cah Outre-Mer
Cahiers d'Outre-Mer [*A publication*]....C O-Mer
Cahiers du Pacifique [*A publication*]....Cah Pac
Cahiers Pedagogiques [*A publication*]....C Pedag
Cahiers Pedagogiques. Institut d'Etudes Occitanes [*A publication*]....C Pedag Inst Et Occitanes
Cahiers de Pedologie. Office de la Recherche Scientifique et Technique d'Outre-Mer [*A publication*]....Cah Pedol ORSTOM
Cahiers Pierre Loti [*A publication*]....Cah P L
Cahiers de la Pleiade [*A publication*]....CaPL
Cahiers Protestants [*A publication*]....Cah Prot
Cahiers de Prothese [*A publication*]....Cah Prothese
Cahiers de Psychiatrie [*A publication*]....Cah Psych
Cahiers Raciniens [*A publication*]....Cah Rac
Cahiers Raciniens [*A publication*]....CRa
Cahiers de la Recherche Agronomique [*A publication*]....Cah Rech Agron
Cahiers de la Recherche Agronomique. Institut National de la Recherche Agronomique (Morocco) [*A publication*].... Cah Rech Agron Inst Rech Agron (Morocco)
Cahiers de Recherches. Institut de Papyrologie et d'Egyptologie de Lille [*A publication*]....CRIPEL
Cahiers des Religions Africaines [*A publication*]....Cah Relig Afr
Cahiers Renaniens [*A publication*]....Cahiers R
Cahiers Rene de Lucinge [*A publication*]....Cah Rene de Lucinge
Cahiers de la Revue d'Histoire et de Philosophie Religieuses [*A publication*]....CRHPR
Cahiers Roumains d'Etudes Litteraires [*A publication*]....CREL
Cahiers de Science Appliquee [*A publication*]....Cah Sci Appl
Cahiers Scientifiques (Supplement to Bois et Forets des Tropiques) [*A publication*]....Cahiers Sci (Suppl Bois Forets Trop)
Cahiers du Seminaire d'Econometrie [*A publication*]....Cah Sem Econ
Cahiers Sextil Puscariu [*A publication*]....CSP
Cahiers. Societe Asiatique [*A publication*]....CSA
Cahiers de Sociologie et de Demographie Medicales [*A publication*]....Cah Sociol Demogr Med
Cahiers de Sociologie et de Demographie Medicales [*A publication*]....C Sociol Demogr Medic

Cahiers de Sociologie Economique [*A publication*] .... Cah Soc Ec
Cahiers Staeliens [*A publication*] .... Cahiers S
Cahiers van de Stichting Bio-Wetenschappen en Maatschappij [*A publication*] .... Cah Sticht Bio-Wet Maatsch
Cahiers du Sud [*A publication*] .... CS
Cahiers Techniques de l'Art [*A publication*] .... Cah Tech
Cahiers - Theatre Louvain [*A publication*] .... CTL
Cahiers Thomistes [*A publication*] .... CT
Cahiers de Topologie et Geometrie Differentielle [*A publication*] .... Cahiers Topologie Geom Differentielle
Cahiers de Tunisie [*A publication*] .... CAHT
Cahiers de Tunisie [*A publication*] .... Cah Tun
Cahiers de Tunisie [*A publication*] .... Cah Tunisie
Cahiers de Tunisie [*A publication*] .... CT
Cahiers de Tunisie [*A publication*] .... C Tunisie
Cahiers Universitaires Catholiques [*A publication*] .... CUC
Cahiers Victoriens et Edouardiens [*A publication*] .... CVE
Cahiers Vilfredo Pareto [*A publication*] .... Cah V Paret
Cahiers Zairois d'Etudes Politiques et Sociales [*A publication*] .... Cah Zair Et Polit Soc
Cahiers Zairois d'Etudes Politiques et Sociales [*A publication*] .... C Zair Et Polit Soc
Cahiers Zairois de la Recherche et du Developpement [*A publication*] .... C Zair Rech Develop
Cahners Books International, Inc. [*Later, CBI Publishing Co., Inc.*] .... CBI
Cahokia, IL [*Radio station call letters*] .... WRTE
CAIC [*Computer Assisted Instruction Center*] **Technical Memo. Florida State University** [*A publication*] .... CAI
Caicara [*Venezuela*] [*Airport symbol*] .... CXA
Caile Ferate Romane [*Roumanian State Railways*] .... CFR
Cain-Levine Social Competency Scale [*Psychology*] .... C-L
Cain-Levine Social Competency Scale [*Psychology*] .... CLSCS
Cairn Terrier Club of America .... CTCA
Cairns [*Australia*] [*Airport symbol*] .... CNS
Cairo [*Egypt*] [*Airport symbol*] .... CAI
Cairo, GA [*Location identifier*] [*FAA*] .... CYR
Cairo, GA [*Radio station call letters*] .... WGRA
Cairo, GA [*Radio station call letters*] .... WTGQ
Cairo, IL [*Location identifier*] [*FAA*] .... CIR
Cairo, IL [*Radio station call letters*] .... WKRO
Cairo Public Library, Cairo, IL [*Library symbol*] .... ICa
Cairo Studies in English [*A publication*] .... Cairo St Engl
Cairo Studies in English [*A publication*] .... CaiSE
Cairo University. Faculty of Science. Bulletin [*A publication*] .... Cairo Univ Fac Sci Bull
Caisse Centrale de Depots et Vriements de Titres .... CCDVT
Caisse Nationale de Credit Agricole [*France*] .... CNCA
Cajal Club CC
Cajamarca [*Peru*] [*Airport symbol*] .... CJA
Cajun Nike [*US Navy missile*] .... CAN
Cakavska Ric [*A publication*] .... CaR
Cake .... CK
Cal Dynamics Corp. [*NASDAQ symbol*] .... CYECF
Cal Federation, Inc. [*NASDAQ symbol*] .... CALF
Cal-Maine Foods, Inc. [*NASDAQ symbol*] .... CALM
Calabar [*Nigeria*] [*Airport symbol*] .... CBQ
Calabozo [*Venezuela*] [*Airport symbol*] .... CLZ
Calabria Nobilissima [*A publication*] .... CalN
Calabria Nobilissima [*A publication*] .... CaN
Calais, ME [*Radio station call letters*] .... WMED
Calais, ME [*Television station call letters*] .... WMED-TV
Calais, ME [*Radio station call letters*] .... WQDY
Calais, ME [*Radio station call letters*] .... WQDY-FM
Calama [*Chile*] [*Seismograph station code, US Geological Survey*] .... CAC
Calama [*Chile*] [*Airport symbol*] .... CJC
Calamus Length CL
Calamus Length Index CLI
Calando [*Dying Away*] [*Music*] .... CAL
Calaveras County Free Library, San Andreas, CA [*Library symbol*] .... CSadC
Calaveras Reservoir [*California*] [*Seismograph station code, US Geological Survey*] .... CVR
Calavo Growers of California .... CGC
Calbayog [*Philippines*] [*Airport symbol*] .... CYP
Calcareous [*Quality of the bottom*] [*Nautical charts*] .... Ca
Calcasieu Parish Public Library, Lake Charles, LA [*Library symbol*] LLcC
Calcified Tissue International [*A publication*] .... Calcif Tissue Int
Calcified Tissue Research [*Later, Calcified Tissue International*] [*A publication*] .... Calcif Tiss
Calcified Tissue Research [*Later, Calcified Tissue International*] [*A publication*] .... Calcif Tissue Res
Calcified Tissue Research [*Later, Calcified Tissue International*] [*A publication*] .... Calc Tiss Res
Calcified Tissues. Proceedings of the European Symposium [*A publication*] .... Calcif Tissues Proc Eur Symp
Calcined Gross Fission Product .... CGFP
Calcinosis, Raynaud's Phenomenon, Sclerodactyly, and Telangiectasis [*Medicine*] .... CRST
Calcite [*CIPW classification*] [*Geology*] cc
Calcite Compensation Depth [*Oceanography*] .... CCD
Calcitonin [*Also, TCA, TCT*] [*Endocrinology*] .... CT
Calcitonin Gene-Related Peptide [*Endocrinology*] .... CGRP
Calcium [*Chemical element*] .... Ca
Calcium-Activated Sarcoplasmic Factor [*A proteolytic enzyme*] .... CASF
Calcium-Based Minerals [*Inorganic chemistry*] .... CBM
Calcium Binding Protein [*Biochemistry*] .... CaBP
Calcium Chloride Institute [*Defunct*] CCI
Calcium Cyanamide Citrated [*or Citrated Calcium Carbimide*] [*Pharmacology*] CCC
Calcium Cyclamate [*Sweetener*] CC
Calcium Disodium Ethylenediaminetetraacetate [*Chelating agent*] .... CaEDTA
Calcium-Ion Dependent Regulator [*Biochemistry*] .... CDR
Calcium Magnesium Acetate .... CMA
Calcium- and Magnesium-Free .... CMF
Calcium- and Magnesium-Free Synthetic Seawater .... CMFSW
Calcium Pyrophosphate Dihydrate [*Inorganic chemistry*] .... CPPD
Calcium-Reduced Skim Milk .... CRSM
Calcoin News [*A publication*] .... CN
Calculated .... CALC
Calculated Air Speed .... CAS
Calculated Altitude .... CALALT
Calculated Average Life .... CAL
Calculated Colloidal Osmotic Pressure [*Clinical chemistry*] .... cCOP
Calculated Date of Confinement [*Medicine*] .... CDC
Calculated Particulate Organic Carbon [*Oceanography*] .... CPOC
Calculated Weight Report .... CWR
Calculation/Experiment .... C/E
Calculation of Indirect Resources and Conversion to Unit Staff [*Data processing*] .... CIRCUS
Calculations of Patient and Hospital Education Resources [*Data processing*] .... CIPHER
Calculator CC
Calculus of Variation [*NASA*] .... COV
Calcutta [*Alipore*] [*India*] [*Seismograph station code, US Geological Survey*] .... CAL
Calcutta [*India*] [*Airport symbol*] .... CCU
Calcutta Historical Journal [*A publication*] .... Calcutta Hist J
Calcutta Journal of Medicine [*A publication*] .... Calc J M
Calcutta Medical Journal [*A publication*] .... Calcutta Med J
Calcutta Medical Review [*A publication*] .... Calc Med Rev
Calcutta Port Shramik Union [*India*] .... CPSU
Calcutta Review [*A publication*] .... Calc Rev
Calcutta Review [*A publication*] .... Calcutta R
Calcutta Review [*A publication*] .... CalR
Calcutta Review [*A publication*] .... CR
Calcutta Sanskrit College Research Series [*A publication*] .... CSCRS
Calcutta Statistical Association. Bulletin [*A publication*] .... Calcut St
Caldera [*Chile*] [*Seismograph station code, US Geological Survey*] [*Closed*] .... CLD
Caldor, Inc. [*American Stock Exchange symbol*] [*Delisted*] .... CA
Caldwell College, Caldwell, NJ [*Library symbol*] .... NjCalC
Caldwell College for Women [*New Jersey*] .... CCW
Caldwell College for Women, Caldwell, NJ [*OCLC symbol*] .... CAL
Caldwell Community College and Technical Institute, Lenoir, NC [*Library symbol*] .... NcLeCT
Caldwell County Public Library, Lenoir, NC [*Library symbol*] .... NcLeC
Caldwell Free Public Library, Caldwell, NJ [*Library symbol*] .... NjCal
Caldwell, ID [*Radio station call letters*] .... KBGN
Caldwell, ID [*Radio station call letters*] .... KBXL
Caldwell, ID [*Radio station call letters*] .... KCID
Caldwell, ID [*Radio station call letters*] .... KCID-FM
Caldwell, ID [*Radio station call letters*] .... KQZQ
Caldwell Parish Library, Columbia, LA [*Library symbol*] .... LColC
Caldwell Progress, Caldwell, NJ [*Library symbol*] .... NjCalP
Caldwell Public Library, Caldwell, ID [*Library symbol*] .... IdCa
Caldwell Public Library, Caldwell, OH [*Library symbol*] .... OCal
Caledon Public Libraries, Bolton, ON, Canada [*Library symbol*] .... CaOBolC
Caledonia .... CALED
Caledonia [*Panama*] [*Airport symbol*] .... CDE
Caledonia, MN [*Location identifier*] [*FAA*] .... CHU
Caledonia-Mumford Junior/Senior High School Library, Caledonia, NY [*OCLC symbol*] .... RVU
Caledonia, NS [*Television station call letters*] CJCH-TV-6
Caledonian Railway [*Scotland*] .... CR
Calefiat [*Warm It*] [*Pharmacy*] .... CALEF
Calendae [*Calends*] [*The first day of the month*] [*Latin*] C
Calendar .... CAL
Calendar of Charter Rolls [*British*] .... CChR
Calendar of Close Rolls [*British*] .... CCR
Calendar Day .... CD
Calendar of Liberate Rolls [*British*] .... CLR
Calendar of Patent Rolls [*British*] .... CPR
Calendar Reform Foundation .... CRF
Calendar Reform Political Action Group .... CRPAG
Calendar Year .... CY
Calendarium Rotulorum Patentum [*Calendar of the Patent Rolls*] [*Latin*] .... CRP
Calendrier Republicain [*Republican Calendar*] .... CR
Calera, AL [*Radio station call letters*] .... WBYE
Calexico, CA [*Location identifier*] [*FAA*] CXL
Calexico, CA [*Radio station call letters*] .... KICO
Calexico, CA [*Radio station call letters*] .... KQVO

Calexico Public Library, Calexico, CA [*Library symbol*]....CCal
Calf....CF
Calf Certifying Officer [*Ministry of Agriculture, Fisheries, and Food*] [*British*]....CCO
Calgary [*Canada*] [*Airport symbol*]....YYC
Calgary, AB [*Radio station call letters*]....CBR
Calgary, AB [*Radio station call letters*]....CBR-FM
Calgary, AB [*Television station call letters*]....CBRT
Calgary, AB [*Radio station call letters*]....CFAC
Calgary, AB [*Television station call letters*]....CFAC-TV
Calgary, AB [*Radio station call letters*]....CFCN
Calgary, AB [*Television station call letters*]....CFCN-TV
Calgary, AB [*Radio station call letters*]....CHFM-FM
Calgary, AB [*Radio station call letters*]....CHQR
Calgary, AB [*Radio station call letters*]....CJAY-FM
Calgary, AB [*Radio station call letters*]....CKIK-FM
Calgary, AB [*Radio station call letters*]....CKO-FM-5
Calgary, AB [*Radio station call letters*]....CKRY-FM
Calgary, AB [*Radio station call letters*]....CKXL
Calgary Herald, Calgary, AB, Canada [*Library symbol*]....CaACCH
Calgary Library Service Centre, Calgary, AB, Canada [*Library symbol*]....CaACCL
Calgary Public Library, Calgary, AB, Canada [*Library symbol*]....CaAC
Calgary Public School Board, Calgary, AB, Canada [*Library symbol*]....CaACLS
Calgon Corp., Pittsburgh, PA [*OCLC symbol*]....PCA
Calhoun City, MS [*Radio station call letters*]....WJRL
Calhoun Community Unit, School District 40, Hardin, IL [*Library symbol*]....IHardCSD
Calhoun County Historical Society, Rockwell City, IA [*Library symbol*]....IaRcCHi
Calhoun Falls [*South Carolina*] [*Seismograph station code, US Geological Survey*]....CHF
Calhoun, GA [*Location identifier*] [*FAA*]....CZL
Calhoun, GA [*Radio station call letters*]....WEBS
Calhoun, GA [*Radio station call letters*]....WJTH
Cali [*Colombia*] [*Airport symbol*]....CLO
Cali Computer Systems [*NASDAQ symbol*]....CCSS
Caliber....CAL
Calibrate....CAB
Calibrate....CAL
Calibrate....CALIB
Calibrated Air Speed....CAS
Calibrated Altitude [*Navigation*]....CA
Calibrated Focal Length....CFL
Calibrated Magnification....CM
Calibrated Optical and Near Infrared Imaging System....CONIRIS
Calibrated Pressure Switch....CALIPS
Calibrated Sweep Delay....CSD
Calibrating, Amplitude-Variation, and Level-Correcting Analog-Digital Equipment....CAVALCADE
Calibration....CALBR
Calibration....CALIBN
Calibration....CLBR
Calibration Curve Data....CCD
Calibration Device....CD
Calibration Factor....CF
Calibration/Measurement Requirements Summary....CMRS
Calibration Procedure....CP
Calibration Procedure Status Report [*Polaris missile*]....CPSR
Calibration Procedures....CPC
Calibration Recall Information Systems....CRIS
Calibration Recall System [*Army*]....CRS
Calibration Requirements List....CARL
Calibration Requirements Summary....CRS
Calibration Rocket [*NASA*]....CALROC
Calibration Signal Generator....CSG
Calibration Technician....CT
Calibration Test Box....CTB
Calibration and Tracking Visible Sensor....CTVS
Calibration Vibration Exciter....CVE
Calibre Corp. [*NASDAQ symbol*]....CLBR
Caliche [*A publication*]....Cal
California [*Postal code*]....CA
California....CAL
California....CALIF
California [*MARC country of publication code*] [*Library of Congress*]....cau
California [*MARC geographic area code*] [*Library of Congress*]....n-us-ca
California Academy of Sciences [*A publication*]....Cal Ac Sc
California Academy of Sciences....CAS
California Academy of Sciences. Memoirs [*A publication*]....Cal Ac Sc Mem
California Academy of Sciences. Memoirs [*A publication*]....Calif Acad Sci Mem
California Academy of Sciences. Occasional Papers [*A publication*]....Cal Ac Sc Oc P
California Academy of Sciences. Occasional Papers and Proceedings [*A publication*]....Calif Acad Sci Occasional Paper Proc
California Academy of Sciences. Proceedings [*A publication*]....Cal Ac Sc Pr
California Academy of Sciences. Proceedings [*A publication*]....California Acad Sci Proc
California Academy of Sciences, San Francisco, CA [*Library symbol*]....CSfA
California Achievement Test....CAT
California Advocacy for Trollops [*Prostitute group*]....CAT
California Aeronautics Commission....CAC
California Agricultural Aircraft Association....CAAA
California Agricultural Experiment Station. Bulletin [*A publication*]....Calif Agric Exp Stn Bull
California Agricultural Extension Service. Circular [*A publication*]....Calif Agric Ext Serv Circ
California Agriculture [*A publication*]....Cal Agr
California Agriculture [*A publication*]....Calif Agr
California Agriculture [*A publication*]....Calif Agric
California Air Charter [*Burbank, CA*] [*FAA designator*]....CAC
California Air Commuter [*Novato, CA*] [*FAA designator*]....CLM
California Air Quality Data [*A publication*]....Calif Air Qual Data
California Air Resources Board....CARB
California Almond Growers Exchange....CAGE
California Amplifier, Inc. [*NASDAQ symbol*]....CAMP
California Anthropologist [*A publication*]....Calif Anthropol
California Apparel Industries Association [*Later, CFC*]....CAIA
California Apricot Advisory Board....CAAB
California Aqueduct Control System....CACS
California Artichoke Advisory Board....CAAB
California Asparagus Advisory Board [*Defunct*]....CAAB
California Association of Nurse Anesthetists [*A publication*]....CANA
California Association of Tiger-Owners....CAT
California Aviation Education Association....CAEA
California Avocado Advisory Board [*Later, CAC*]....CAAB
California Avocado Commission [*Formerly, CAAB*]....CAC
California Avocado Society....CAS
California Baptist Theological Seminary....CBTS
California Bearing Ratio [*Aviation*]....CBR
California Biotechnology [*NASDAQ symbol*]....CBIO
California Birds [*A publication*]....Calif Birds
California Brandy Advisory Board....CBAB
California Business [*A publication*]....Calif Bus
California Business Education Journal [*A publication*]....Calif Bus Ed J
California Cactus Growers Association....CCGA
California Canning Peach Association....CCPA
California Carvers Guild....CCG
California Central Airlines....CCA
California Citrograph [*A publication*]....Cal Citrograph
California Citrograph [*A publication*]....Calif Citrogr
California College of Arts and Crafts....CCAC
California College of Arts and Crafts, Oakland, CA [*Library symbol*]....COC
California College of Chiropody....CCC
California Computer Products, Incorporated [*American Stock Exchange symbol*] [*Delisted*]....CPI
California Concordia College, Oakland, CA [*Library symbol*]....COCC
California Cooperative Oceanic Fisheries Investigations. Atlas [*A publication*]....Calif Coop Oceanic Fish Invest Atlas
California Cooperative Oceanic Fisheries Investigations. Reports [*A publication*]....Calif Coop Oceanic Fish Invest Rep
California Cooperative Oceanic Fishery Investigations....CALCOFI
California Countryman [*A publication*]....Cal Countryman
California Cultivator [*A publication*]....Cal Cultivator
California Dairyman [*A publication*]....Cal Dairym
California Date Administrative Committee....CDAC
California Date Growers Association....CDGA
California Debris Commission [*Army*]....CDC
California Dental Association. Journal [*A publication*]....CDA J
California Department of Agriculture. Biennial Report [*A publication*]....Calif Dep Agric Bienn Rep
California Department of Agriculture. Bulletin [*A publication*]....Calif Ag Bul
California Department of Agriculture. Bulletin [*A publication*]....Calif Dep Agric Bull
California Department of Agriculture. Bureau of Entomology. Occasional Papers [*A publication*]....Calif Dep Agric Bur Entomol Occas Pap
California Department of Agriculture. Bureau of Entomology. Occasional Papers [*A publication*]....Calif Dept Agric Bur Entomol Occas Pap
California Department of Fish and Game. Fish Bulletin [*A publication*]....Calif Dep Fish Game Fish Bull
California Department of Fish and Game. Game Bulletin [*A publication*]....Calif Dep Fish Game Game Bull
California Department of Natural Resources. Division of Mines. Bulletin [*A publication*]....Calif Dep Nat Resour Div Mines Bull
California Department of Natural Resources. Division of Mines. Bulletin [*A publication*]....Calif Dept Nat Res Div Mines Bull
California Department of Natural Resources. Division of Mines. Economic Mineral Map [*A publication*]....Calif Dept Nat Res Div Mines Econ Mineral Map
California Department of Natural Resources. Division of Mines. Mineral Information Service [*A publication*]....Calif Dept Nat Res Div Mines Mineral Inf Service
California Department of Natural Resources. Division of Mines. Special Reports [*A publication*]....Calif Dep Nat Resour Div Mines Spec Rep

California Department of Natural Resources. Division of Mines. Special Report [*A publication*] .... Calif Dept Nat Res Div Mines Special Rept
California Department of Natural Resources. Division of Soil Conservation. Bulletin [*A publication*] .... Calif Dep Nat Resour Div Soil Conserv Bull
California Department of Parks and Recreation, Sacramento Area State Parks, Sacramento, CA [*Library symbol*] .... CSPR
California Department of Public Works. Division of Water Resources. Bulletin [*A publication*] .... Calif Dept Public Works Div Water Res Bull
California Department of Water Resources. Bulletin [*A publication*] .... Calif Dept Water Res Bull
California Department of Water Resources. Division of Resources. Planning Bulletin [*A publication*] .... Calif Dept Water Res Div Res Plan Bull
California Department of Water Resources. Report [*A publication*] .... Calif Dept Water Res Rept
California Depopulation Commission .... CALDEPOP
California Disaster Office .... CDO
California Distance Table Bureau, San Francisco CA [*STAC*] .... CDB
California Division of Forestry. Fire Control Notes [*A publication*] .... Calif Div For Fire Control Notes
California Division of Mines and Geology. Bulletin [*A publication*] .... California Div Mines and Geology Bull
California Division of Mines and Geology. Geologic Data Map [*A publication*] .... Calif Div Mines Geol Geol Data Map
California Division of Mines and Geology. Mineral Information Service [*A publication*] .... California Div Mines and Geology Mineral Inf Service
California Division of Mines and Geology. Report of the State Geologist [*A publication*] .... Calif Div Mines Geol Rep State Geol
California Division of Mines and Geology. Special Publication [*A publication*] .... Calif Div Mines Geol Spec Publ
California Division of Mines and Geology. Special Report [*A publication*] .... Calif Div Mines Geol Spec Rep
California Division of Mines and Geology. Special Report [*A publication*] .... California Div Mines and Geology Spec Rept
California Dried Fig Advisory Board .... CDFAB
California Dried Fruit Export Association .... CDFEA
California Dry Bean Advisory Board .... CDBAB
California Eastern Airways .... CEA
California Education [*A publication*] .... Calif Ed
California Elementary School Administrators Association. Monographs [*A publication*] .... Calif El Sch Adm Assn Mon
California Elementary School Administrators Association. Yearbook [*A publication*] .... Calif El Sch Adm Assn Yearbook
California Encephalitis [*Medicine*] .... CE
California English Journal [*A publication*] .... CEJ
California Fashion Creators .... CFC
California Feeders' Day [*A publication*] .... Calif Feeders Day
California Fig Institute .... CFI
California Financial Corp. [*NYSE symbol*] [*Delisted*] .... CFI
California Fire Control Notes. California Division of Forestry [*A publication*] .... Calif Fire Control Note Calif Div For
California Fire Prevention Notes. California Division of Forestry [*A publication*] .... Calif Fire Prev Note Calif Div For
California First Bank [*NASDAQ symbol*] .... CFBK
California Fish Canners Association [*Later, TRF*] .... CFCA
California Fish and Game [*A publication*] .... Calif Fish
California Fish and Game [*A publication*] .... Calif Fish Game
California Flyers School of Aeronautics .... CFSA
California Folklore Quarterly [*A publication*] .... Calif Folklore Qu
California Folklore Quarterly [*A publication*] .... CFQ
California Forestry and Forest Products. University of California. Forest Products Laboratory [*A publication*] .... Calif For & For Prod Calif For Prod Lab
California Freezers Association [*Later, AFFI*] .... CFA
California Fruit Exchange [*Later, BAI*] .... CFE
California Geology [*A publication*] .... Calif Geol
California Geology [*A publication*] .... California Geol
California Grape and Tree Fruit League .... CGTFL
California Highway Patrol [*Acronym used as title of TV series*] .... CHiPS
California Historical Quarterly [*A publication*] .... Calif Hist Q
California Historical Quarterly [*San Francisco*] [*A publication*] .... CHQ
California Historical Society. Quarterly [*San Francisco*] [*A publication*] .... Calif Hist Soc Q
California Historical Society. Quarterly [*San Francisco*] [*A publication*] .... Calif Hist Soc Quar
California Historical Society. Quarterly [*San Francisco*] [*A publication*] .... CHSQ
California Historical Society, San Francisco, CA [*Library symbol*] .... CHi
California History Nugget [*A publication*] .... Cali His Nugget
California Horticultural Journal [*A publication*] .... Calif Hortic J
California Iceberg Lettuce Commission CILC
California Information Network [*Library network*] .... CALINET
California Innovation Group .... CIG
California Institute of the Arts .... CIA
California Institute of the Arts, Valencia, CA [*OCLC symbol*] .... CIA
California Institute of the Arts, Valencia, CA [*Library symbol*] .... CValA
California Institute of Asian Studies [*An evening graduate school*] .... CIAS
California Institute of Asian Studies, San Francisco, CA [*Library symbol*] .... CSfCI
California Institute of Social Welfare .... CISW
California Institute of Technology [*Also, CALT, CALTECH, CIT*] .... CALIT
California Institute of Technology [*Also, CALIT, CALTECH, CIT*] .... CALT
California Institute of Technology [*Also, CALIT, CALT, CIT*] .... CALTECH
California Institute of Technology [*Also, CALIT, CALT, CALTECH*] .... CIT
California Institute of Technology. Division of Geological Sciences. Contributions [*A publication*] .... Calif Inst Technology Div Geol Sci Contr
California Institute of Technology. Earthquake Engineering Research Laboratory (Report) EERL [*A publication*] .... Calif Inst Technol Earthquake Eng Res Lab (Rep) EERL
California Institute of Technology. Jet Propulsion Laboratory. Technical Memorandum [*A publication*] .... Calif Inst Technol Jet Propul Lab Tech Memo
California Institute of Technology, Pasadena, CA [*OCLC symbol*] .... CIT
California Institute of Technology, Pasadena, CA [*Library symbol*] .... CPT
California Institution for Women .... CIW
California Jockey Club Paired Certificates [*NASDAQ symbol*] .... CJOCZ
California Journal of Educational Research [*A publication*] .... Calif J Ed Res
California Journal of Educational Research [*A publication*] .... Calif J Edu
California Journal of Elementary Education [*A publication*] .... Calif J El Ed
California Journal of Mines and Geology [*A publication*] .... Calif Jour Mines and Geology
California Journal of Secondary Education [*A publication*] .... Calif J Sec Ed
California Journal of Technology [*A publication*] .... Cal J Tech
California Kiwifruit Commission .... CKC
California Labor Federation AFL-CIO Library, San Francisco, CA [*Library symbol*] .... CSfSFL
California Law Enforcement Telecommunications System .... CLETS
California Law Review [*A publication*] .... Calif L Rev
California League Enlisting Action Now [*Antiobscenity group*] .... CLEAN
California Librarian [*A publication*] .... Calif Libn
California Librarian [*A publication*] .... Calif Librn
California Library Authority for Systems and Services [*Library network*] .... CLASS
California Life Corp. [*American Stock Exchange symbol*] [*Delisted*] .... CLQ
California Life Goals Evaluation Schedules [*Psychology*] .... CLGES
California Lutheran College, Thousand Oaks, CA [*OCLC symbol*] .... CCT
California Lutheran College, Thousand Oaks, CA [*Library symbol*] .... CToL
California Macadamia Society .... CMS
California Management Review [*A publication*] .... Calif Manag
California Management Review [*A publication*] .... Calif Manage Rev
California Management Review [*A publication*] .... Calif Manag R
California Management Review [*A publication*] .... Calif Mgt R
California Management Review [*A publication*] .... Cal Mgmt Rev
California Management Review [*A publication*] .... CMR
California Marijuana Initiative [*Proposition to legalize marijuana*] .... CMI
California Maritime Academy .... CMA
California Maritime Academy, Vallejo, CA [*Library symbol*] .... CVM
California Marriage Readiness Evaluation [*Psychology*] .... CMRE
California Mastitis Test .... CMT
California Medical Survey [*Psychology*] .... CMS
California Medicine [*A publication*] .... Calif Med
California Medicine [*A publication*] .... CAMEA
California Melon Research Board .... CMRB
California Mental Health Analysis [*Testing*] .... CMHA
California Microfilm Company, Fresno, CA [*Library symbol*] .... CmC
California Microwave, Inc. [*NASDAQ symbol*] .... CMIC
California Miners' Association [*A publication*] .... Cal M As
California, MO [*Radio station call letters*] .... KTAA
California, MO [*Radio station call letters*] .... KZMO-FM
California Mosquito Control Association. Proceedings and Papers of the Annual Conference [*A publication*] .... Calif Mosq Control Assoc Proc Pap Annu Conf
California Mosquito and Vector Control Association. Proceedings and Papers of the Annual Conference [*A publication*] .... Calif Mosq Vector Control Assoc Proc Pap Annu Conf
California National Fuchsia Society [*Later, NFS*] .... CNFS
California Natural Gas Association .... CNGA
California Nurse [*A publication*] .... Calif Nurs
California Occupational Preference Survey .... COPS
California Oil Fields [*A publication*] .... Calif Oil Fields
California Olive Association .... COA
California Olive Industry News .... COIN
California, PA [*Radio station call letters*] .... WVCS
California Packing Corp. [*NYSE symbol*] [*Delisted*] .... CFF
California Palace of the Legion of Honor. Museum Bulletin [*A publication*] .... Calif Pal Leg Hon Bul
California Palace of the Legion of Honor, San Francisco, CA [*Library symbol*] .... CSfLH
California Persimmon Growers Association .... CPGA
California Personality [*or Psychological*] **Inventory** .... CPI
California Physical Geography Club. Bulletin [*A publication*] .... Cal Phys Geog Club B
California Pistachio Association .... CPA
California Pistachio Commission .... CPC
California Polytechnic State University, Pomona, CA [*OCLC symbol*] .... CPO

California Polytechnic State University, Pomona, CA [*Library symbol*] ... CPomCP
California Polytechnic State University, San Luis Obispo, CA [*OCLC symbol*] ... CPS
California Polytechnic State University, San Luis Obispo, CA [*Library symbol*] ... CSluSP
California Portland Cement Co. [*American Stock Exchange symbol*] ... CPO
California Probation, Parole, and Correctional Association ... CPPCA
California Prune Advisory Board [*Later, CPB*] ... CPAB
California Prune and Apricot Growers Association [*Later, Sunsweet Growers*] ... CPAGA
California Prune Board ... CPB
California Q-Set [*Psychology*] ... CQS
California Quarterly [*A publication*] ... Calif Q
California Quarterly [*A publication*] ... Cal Q
California Quarterly [*A publication*] ... CaQ
California Quarterly of Secondary Education [*A publication*] ... Cal Q Sec Ed
California Raisin Advisory Board ... CALRAB
California Raisin Advisory Board ... CRAB
California Rare Fruit Growers ... CRFG
California Real Estate Investment Trust SBI [*American Stock Exchange symbol*] ... CT
California Redwood Association ... CRA
California Research Corp., Richmond, CA [*Library symbol*] ... CRicCR
California Resources Agency, Sacramento, CA [*Library symbol*] ... CSRes
California Rural Legal Assistance [*Antipoverty program*] ... CRLA
California School of Fine Arts ... CSFA
California School Libraries [*A publication*] ... Calif Sch Lib
California School Libraries [*A publication*] ... Calif Sch Libr
California School of Professional Psychology, Fresno, CA [*Library symbol*] ... CFSP
California Schools [*A publication*] ... Calif Sch
California Silver Ltd. [*NASDAQ symbol*] ... CALSF
California Slavic Studies [*A publication*] ... Calif Slavic Stud
California Slavic Studies [*A publication*] ... Cal SS
California Slavic Studies [*A publication*] ... CSS
California State College, Bakersfield, CA [*OCLC symbol*] ... CBA
California State College, Bakersfield, CA [*Library symbol*] ... CBaS
California State College, California, PA [*OCLC symbol*] ... CSC
California State College, California, PA [*Library symbol*] ... PCalS
California State College, Dominguez Hills [*Later, California State University, Dominguez Hills*], **Dominguez Hills, CA** [*Library symbol*] ... CDhS
California State College at Fresno ... CSCF
California State College, San Bernardino, San Bernardino, CA [*OCLC symbol*] ... CSB
California State College, San Bernardino, San Bernardino, CA [*Library symbol*] ... CSbC
California State College, Sonoma, Rohnert Part, CA [*Library symbol*] ... CRpS
California State College, Stanislaus, Turlock, CA [*OCLC symbol*] ... CTU
California State College, Stanislaus, Turlock, CA [*Library symbol*] ... CTurS
California State Commission of Horticulture. Monthly Bulletin [*A publication*] ... Cal State Comm Hort B
California State Department of Education. Bulletin [*A publication*] ... Calif State Dept Education Bull
California State Department of Fish and Game, Marine Technical Information Center, San Pedro, CA [*Library symbol*] ... C-F
California State Department of Mental Hygiene, Metropolitan State Hospital Professional Staff Library, Norwalk, CA [*Library symbol*] ... CNwMH
California State Division of Mines, San Francisco, CA [*Library symbol*] ... CSfCSM
California State [*University*], **Hayward** [*California*] [*Seismograph station code, US Geological Survey*] ... CSH
California State Journal of Medicine [*A publication*] ... Calif State J Med
California State Law Library, Sacramento, CA [*Library symbol*] ... C-L
California State Library, Sacramento, CA [*Library symbol*] ... C
California State Library, Sutro Branch, San Francisco, CA [*Library symbol*] ... C-S
California State Mining Bureau [*A publication*] ... Cal St M Bur
California State Mining Bureau. Annual Report. Bulletin [*A publication*] ... Cal St M Bur An Rp B
California State Polytechnic College [*Later, California Polytechnic State University*] ... CSPC
California State Psychological Association ... CSPA
California State University [*Formerly, San Francisco State College*] ... CSU
California State University, Chico, Chico, CA [*OCLC symbol*] ... CCH
California State University, Chico, Chico, CA [*Library symbol*] ... CChiS
California State University (Chico). Regional Programs Monograph [*A publication*] ... Calif State Univ (Chico) Reg Programs Monogr
California State University and Colleges [*System*] ... CSUC
California State University and Colleges, Tape Profile, Long Beach, CA [*OCLC symbol*] ... CAC
California State University, Dominguez Hills, Carson, CA [*OCLC symbol*] ... CDH
California State University, Fresno, Fresno, CA [*Library symbol*] [*OCLC symbol*] ... CFS
California State University, Fullerton, Fullerton, CA [*OCLC symbol*] ... CFI
California State University, Fullerton, Fullerton, CA [*Library symbol*] ... CFIS
California State University, Hayward, Hayward, CA [*Library symbol*] ... CHS
California State University, Hayward, Hayward, CA [*OCLC symbol*] ... CSH
California State University, Long Beach, Long Beach, CA [*OCLC symbol*] ... CLO
California State University, Long Beach, Long Beach, CA [*Library symbol*] ... CLobS
California State University, Los Angeles, Los Angeles, CA [*OCLC symbol*] ... CLA
California State University, Los Angeles, Los Angeles, CA [*Library symbol*] ... CLS
California State University, Northridge ... CSUN
California State University, Northridge, Northridge, CA [*OCLC symbol*] ... CNO
California State University, Northridge, Northridge, CA [*Library symbol*] ... CNoS
California State University, Sacramento, Sacramento, CA [*OCLC symbol*] ... CSA
California State University, Sacramento, Sacramento, CA [*Library symbol*] ... CSS
California State Water Pollution Control Board. Publication [*A publication*] ... Calif State Water Pollution Control Board Pub
California State Water Resources Board. Bulletin [*A publication*] ... Calif State Water Res Board Bull
California Strawberry Advisory Board ... CSAB
California Studies in Classical Antiquity [*A publication*] ... CSCA
California Supreme Court, San Francisco, CA [*Library symbol*] ... C-SC
California Table Grape Commission ... CTGC
California Teachers Association, Burlingame, CA [*Library symbol*] ... CBuCTA
California Terms [*Grain shipping*] ... CT
California Test of Basic Skills [*Education*] ... CTBS
California Test Bureau [*Psychology*] [*McGraw Hill, Inc.*] ... CTB
California Test of Mental Maturity ... CTMM
California Test of Personality [*Psychology*] ... CTP
California Texas Oil Co. ... CALTEX
California Tomorrow [*An association*] ... CT
California Traffic Safety Foundation [*Defunct*] ... CTSF
California Tumor Registry ... CTR
California Universities Council on Space Sciences ... CUCOSS
California University. Agricultural Experiment Station. Ground Water Studies [*A publication*] ... Calif Univ Agr Expt Sta Ground Water Studies
California University (Berkeley). Water Resources Center. Desalination Report [*A publication*] ... Calif Univ (Berkeley) Water Resour Cent Desalin Rep
California University. Chronicle [*A publication*] ... Calif Univ Chron
California University Cyclotron ... CALUTRON
California University. Institute of Transportation and Traffic Engineering. Information Circular [*A publication*] ... Calif Univ Inst Transp and Traffic Eng Inf Circ
California University. Memoirs [*A publication*] ... Calif Univ Mem
California University [*Berkeley*] **Publications in Agricultural Science** [*A publication*] ... Cal Univ Pub
California University. Publications in Astronomy [*A publication*] ... Calif Univ Pubs Astronomy
California University. Publications. Department of Geology. Bulletin [*A publication*] ... Cal Univ Dp G B
California University. Publications in Geography [*A publication*] ... Calif Univ Pubs Geography
California University. Publications in Geography [*A publication*] ... Cal Univ Pub Geog
California University. Publications in Geological Sciences [*A publication*] ... California Univ Pubs Geol Sci
California University. Publications in Geological Sciences [*A publication*] ... Calif Univ Publ Geol Sci
California University. Publications in Geological Sciences [*A publication*] ... Calif Univ Pubs Geol Sci
California University. Publications. Seismography Stations. Bulletin [*A publication*] ... Cal Univ Seism Sta B
California University. Publications in Zoology [*A publication*] ... Calif Univ Pubs Zoology
California University. Scripps Institution of Oceanography. Annual Report [*A publication*] ... Calif Univ Scripps Inst Oceanogr Annu Rep
California University. Scripps Institution of Oceanography. Bulletin [*A publication*] ... Calif Univ Scripps Inst Oceanography Bull
California University. Scripps Institution of Oceanography. Contributions [*A publication*] ... Calif Univ Scripps Inst Oceanogr Contrib
California University. Scripps Institution of Oceanography. Reference Series [*A publication*] ... Calif Univ Scripps Inst
California University. Scripps Institution of Oceanography. SIO Reference [*A publication*] ... Calif Univ Scripps Inst Oceanography SIO Reference
California University. Water Resources Center Report [*A publication*] ... California Univ Water Resources Center Rept
California University. Water Resources Center. Report [*A publication*] ... Calif Univ Water Resour Cent Rep
California Vector Views [*A publication*] ... Calif Vector Views
California Water Pollution Control Association. Bulletin [*A publication*] ... Calif Water Pollut Control Assoc Bull
California Water Service Co. [*NASDAQ symbol*] ... CWTR

California Western International Law Journal [*A publication*] .... Calif Western Int L J
California Western International Law Journal [*A publication*] .... Calif W Int Law J
California Western Law Review [*A publication*] .... Calif Western L Rev
California Western Railroad [*AAR code*] .... CWR
California Western School of Law Library, San Diego, CA [*OCLC symbol*] .... CWE
California Yoga Teachers Association .... CYTA
Californian Illustrated Magazine [*A publication*] .... Calif M
Californian Rabbit Specialty Club .... CRSC
California's Health [*A publication*] .... Calif Health
Californium [*Chemical element*] .... Cf
Calipatria, CA [*Location identifier*] [*FAA*] .... CLR
Caliper .... CLPR
Caliper Disk Brake .... CDB
Calistoga [*California*] [*Seismograph station code, US Geological Survey*] [*Closed*] .... CLS
Calistoga Free Public Library, Calistoga, CA [*Library symbol*] .... CCali
Calitatea Productiei si Metrologie [*A publication*] .... Calitatea Prod & Metrol
Calix Society .... CS
Call Accounting System [*Telecommunications*] .... CAS
Call for Action [*An association*] .... CFA
Call Aircraft Co. .... CAL
Call Back [*Word processing*] .... CB
Call Box Station .... CBS
Call Contract CC
Call Directing Code .... CDC
Call Director Unit .... CDU
Call Forward Directive [*World War II*] .... CFD
Call-In Time [*Military communications*] .... CIT
Call Indicator [*Data processing*] CI
Call to Quarters [*General call preceding transmission of radio signals*] .... CQ
Call Request .... CR
Call Sign [*or Signal*] [*Radio*] .... CS
Call Signs and/or Address Group Remain Same .... CADSAME
Call Time Adjustor [*Military communications*] .... CTA
Call-Us, Inc. .... CU
Callahan Mining Corp. [*NYSE symbol*] .... CMN
Callao Caves [*Philippines*] [*Seismograph station code, US Geological Survey*] .... CVP
Callaway Mills Co., Technical Library, LaGrange, GA [*Library symbol*] .... GLagCM
Called .... CLD
Called Output Image .... COI
Callier Center for Communication Disorders, Dallas, TX [*Library symbol*] .... TxDaCCD
Calling .... CLG
Calling Card Service [*Bell System*] .... CCS
Calling-On [*Railroad signal arm*] [*British*] C
Calling for Orders [*Shipping*] .... CFO
Callon Petroleum Co. [*NASDAQ symbol*] .... CLNP
Callose Platelets [*Botany*] .... CP
Calls Waiting [*Telephone communication*] .... CW
Calm [*i.e., no wind*] C
Calm Air International Ltd. [*Lynn Lake, MB*] [*FAA designator*] .... CAV
Calm Water Line .... CWL
Calmar, Incorporated [*NASDAQ symbol*] .... CLMI
Calmato [*More Calm*] [*Music*] .... CALM
Calmodulin [*Biochemistry*] .... CaM
Calny, Inc. [*NASDAQ symbol*] .... CLNY
Calomel, Rhubarb, Colocynth [*Medicine*] .... CRC
Calorie C
Calorie .... CAL
Calorie [*Diet order*] C
Calorie Control Council CCC
Calorific Recovery Anaerobic Process, Inc. [*Firm that manufactures gas from cow manure*] .... CRAP
Calorific Value [*of a fuel*] CV
Calorimetry Conference CC
Calorimetry and Thermal Analysis [*A publication*] .... Calorim Therm Anal
Caloundra [*Australia*] [*Airport symbol*] .... CUD
Calprop Corp. [*American Stock Exchange symbol*] .... CPP
Calspan Corp. [*Formerly, Cornell Aeronautical Laboratory*] .... CAL
Calspan On-Line Information Service [*Calspan Corp.*] [*Information service*] .... COINS
Caltech Political Military Exercise [*International relations simulation game*] .... PME
Caltech Population Program [*Agency for International Development*] .... CPP
Caltex Pacific Indonesia .... CPI
Calton, Inc. Uts [*NASDAQ symbol*] .... CATNU
Calumet City Public Library, Calumet City, IL [*Library symbol*] ICc
Calumet College, Whiting, IN [*OCLC symbol*] ICC
Calumet College, Whiting, IN [*Library symbol*] .... InWhC
Calumet & Hecla, Inc. [*NYSE symbol*] [*Delisted*] .... CAH
Calumet Industries, Inc. [*NASDAQ symbol*] .... CALI
Calvary Baptist School of Theology, Lansdale, PA [*Library symbol*] .... PLdaC
Calverton, NY [*Location identifier*] [*FAA*] .... PIC
Calvi [*Corsica*] [*Airport symbol*] .... CLY
Calvi [*Corsica*] [*Seismograph station code, US Geological Survey*] .... CVF
Calviac [*France*] [*Seismograph station code, US Geological Survey*] .... CAF
Calvin College and Seminary, Grand Rapids, MI [*OCLC symbol*] .... EXC
Calvin College and Seminary, Grand Rapids, MI [*Library symbol*] .... MiGrC
Calvin Coolidge Memorial Foundation .... CCMF
Calvin Explorations, Inc. [*NASDAQ symbol*] .... CLVN
Calvin Theological Journal [*A publication*] .... Cal Th J
Calvin Theological Journal [*A publication*] .... CTJ
Cam Action Wheel .... CAW
Cam Box .... CBX
Cam Case .... CMCS
Cam Follower .... CMFLR
Cam Limit Switch .... CLS
Cam-Operated Plunger .... COP
Cam-Or, Inc. [*NASDAQ symbol*] .... CAMO
Cam Plate Readout .... CPR
Cam Pocket .... CMPKT
Cam Ranh Bay [*Vietnam*] .... CRB
Cam Roller .... CMRLR
Cam Timing Contact .... CTC
Cam Wedge Clamp .... CWC
Cam Wedge Power Clamp .... CWPC
CAMAC [*Computer-Aided Measurement and Control*] **Input-Output Processor** [*Computer*] .... CIOP
Camaguey [*Cuba*] [*Airport symbol*] .... CMW
Camanachd Association .... CA
Camara Minera de Mexico .... CAMIMEX
Camarillo, CA [*Radio station call letters*] .... KZTR
Camarillo State Hospital, Camarillo, CA [*Library symbol*] .... CCamarH
Camaro Owners of America .... COA
Camas Prairie Railroad Co. [*AAR code*] .... CSP
Cambata Aviation Ltd. [*India*] [*ICAO designator*] [*Obsolete*] .... CZ
Camber [*Aerospace engineering*] .... CAM
Cambex Corp. [*NASDAQ symbol*] .... CBEX
Cambodia [*Democratic Kampuchea*] [*MARC geographic area code*] [*Library of Congress*] .... a-cb---
Cambodia [*Democratic Kampuchea*] [*MARC country of publication code*] [*Library of Congress*] .... cb
Cambodia [*Two-letter standard code*] .... KH
Cambodia [*Three-letter standard code*] .... KHM
Cambodia [*Aircraft nationality and registration mark*] .... XU
Cambodia Buddhist Society .... CBS
Cambodia Crisis Center [*Defunct*] CCC
Cambodian [*MARC language code*] [*Library of Congress*] .... cam
Cambodian Appeal .... CA
Cambria County Library System, Johnstown, PA [*OCLC symbol*] .... JOC
Cambria County Library System, Johnstown, PA [*Library symbol*] .... PJo
Cambria & Indiana Railroad Co. [*AAR code*] CI
Cambrian [*Period, era, or system*] [*Geology*] .... CAMB
Cambrian Airways Ltd. .... CAS
Cambrian Law Review [*A publication*] .... Cambrian Law R
Cambrian Law Review [*A publication*] .... Cambrian L Rev
Cambrian Railways [*Wales*] .... CAM R
Cambrian Systems, Inc. [*NASDAQ symbol*] .... CAMS
Cambridge [*Massachusetts*] [*Seismograph station code, US Geological Survey*] [*Closed*] .... CAM
Cambridge [*Municipal borough in England*] .... CAMB
Cambridge [*England*] [*Airport symbol*] [*Obsolete*] .... CBG
Cambridge [*Municipal borough in England*] .... CAM
Cambridge Abstracts [*A publication*] .... Cam Abs
Cambridge Acoustical Associates, Inc. .... CAA
Cambridge Algebraic System [*Data processing*] .... CAMAL
Cambridge Analog Simulator for Predicting Atomic Reactions [*British*] .... CASPAR
Cambridge Ancient History [*A publication*] .... CAH
Cambridge Anthropology [*A publication*] .... Cambridge Anthropol
Cambridge Automatic Digital Computer .... CADC
Cambridge Bay [*Canada*] [*Geomagnetic observatory code*] .... CBB
Cambridge Bay [*Canada*] [*Airport symbol*] .... YCB
[*The*] **Cambridge Bibliography of English Literature** [*A publication*] .... CBEL
Cambridge Bicycle Club [*British*] .... CBC
Cambridge Bio Science [*NASDAQ symbol*] .... CBCX
Cambridge Communication Corporation CCC
Cambridge Conference on School Mathematics [*National Science Foundation*] .... CCSM
Cambridge Crystallographic Database [*England*] .... CCD
Cambridge Econometrics [*British*] .... CE
Cambridge Electron Accelerator .... CEA
Cambridge Electron Accelerator Laboratories [*Massachusetts Institute of Technology*] .... CEAL
Cambridge Electronic Research Laboratory .... CERL
Cambridge Historical Journal [*A publication*] .... CHJ
Cambridge History of English Literature .... CHEL
Cambridge Institute of Education. Bulletin [*A publication*] .... Cambridge Inst Ed Bulletin
Cambridge Journal [*A publication*] .... Camb J
Cambridge Journal [*A publication*] .... CamJ
Cambridge Journal [*A publication*] .... CJ
Cambridge Journal of Economics [*A publication*] .... Cambridge J Econ
Cambridge Journal of Education [*A publication*] .... Cambridge J Ed
Cambridge Journal of Education [*A publication*] .... Cambridge J Educ
Cambridge Junior College [*Massachusetts*] .... CJC

Cambridge Language Research Unit ... CLRU
Cambridge Law Journal [*A publication*] ... Camb L J
Cambridge, MA [*Radio station call letters*] ... WCAS
Cambridge, MA [*Radio station call letters*] ... WHRB
Cambridge, MA [*Television station call letters*] ... WLVI-TV
Cambridge, MA [*Radio station call letters*] ... WMBR
Cambridge, MD [*Radio station call letters*] ... WCEM
Cambridge, MD [*Radio station call letters*] ... WESP
Cambridge Mediaeval History [*A publication*] ... CMH
Cambridge Medical Technology [*NASDAQ symbol*] ... CMTC
Cambridge Military Library, Halifax, NS, Canada [*Library symbol*] ... DaNSHC
Cambridge, MN [*Location identifier*] [*FAA*] ... CBG
Cambridge, MN [*Radio station call letters*] ... KXLV-FM
Cambridge Monitor System ... CMS
Cambridge Monographs in Experimental Biology [*A publication*] ... Camb Monogr Exp Biol
Cambridge, NY [*Location identifier*] [*FAA*] ... CAM
Cambridge, OH [*Radio station call letters*] ... WILE
Cambridge, OH [*Radio station call letters*] ... WILF-FM
Cambridge, OH [*Television station call letters*] ... WOUC-TV
Cambridge, ON [*Radio station call letters*] ... CFTJ
Cambridge Philosophical Society. Biological Reviews [*A publication*] ... Cambridge Philos Soc Biol Rev
Cambridge Philosophical Society. Proceedings [*A publication*] ... Cambridge Ph Soc Pr
Cambridge Philosophical Society. Transactions [*A publication*] ... Camb Philos Soc Trans
Cambridge Public Library, Cambridge, MA [*Library symbol*] ... MC
Cambridge Public Library, Cambridge, ON, Canada [*Library symbol*] ... CaOGal
Cambridge Quarterly [*A publication*] ... Cambridge Q
Cambridge Quarterly [*A publication*] ... CamQ
Cambridge Quarterly [*A publication*] ... CQ
Cambridge Radio Observatory Committee ... CAMROC
Cambridge Research Center [*Air Force*] ... CRC
Cambridge Research Institute, Inc., Cambridge, MA [*Library symbol*] ... MCRI
Cambridge Research Laboratory ... CRL
Cambridge Review [*A publication*] ... CamR
Cambridge Royalty Company [*NASDAQ symbol*] ... CRCO
Cambridge Scientific Abstracts [*Information service*] ... CSA
Cambridge Studies in Linguistics [*A publication*] ... CSL
Cambridge Studies in Medieval Life and Thought [*A publication*] ... CSMLT
Cambridge Technology, Incorporated ... CTI
Cambridge University [*England*] ... CAMB
Cambridge University [*England*] ... CU
Cambridge University Association Football Club ... CUAFC
Cambridge University Athletic Club ... CUAC
Cambridge University Boat Club ... CUBC
Cambridge University, Cambridge, United Kingdom [*Library symbol*] ... UkCU
Cambridge University Cricket Club ... CUCC
Cambridge University Mission ... CUM
Cambridge University Musical Society ... CUMS
Cambridge University Prayer Union ... CUPU
Cambridge University Press ... CUP
Cambridge University Press Limited Editions ... CUPLE
Cambridge University Rugby Union Football Club ... CURUFC
Cambridgeshire [*County in England*] ... CAMBS
Cambridgeshire and Huntingdonshire Archaeological Society [*A publication*] ... CHAS
Camco, Inc. [*American Stock Exchange symbol*] ... CAM
Camden [*Arkansas*] [*Airport symbol*] ... CDH
Camden, AL [*Location identifier*] [*FAA*] ... IWE
Camden, AL [*Radio station call letters*] ... WCOX
Camden, AL [*Radio station call letters*] ... WODB
Camden, AR [*Radio station call letters*] ... KAMD
Camden, AR [*Radio station call letters*] ... KJWH
Camden, AR [*Radio station call letters*] ... KWEH
Camden County College, Blackwood, NJ [*Library symbol*] ... NjBlaC
Camden County College, Voorhees, NJ [*OCLC symbol*] ... NCK
Camden County Historical Society, Camden, NJ [*Library symbol*] ... NjCaHi
Camden County Library, Voorhees, NJ [*OCLC symbol*] ... NCL
Camden County Times, Collingswood, NJ [*Library symbol*] ... NjCoT
Camden County Times, Westmont, NJ [*Library symbol*] ... NjWemT
Camden Free Public Library, Camden, NJ [*Library symbol*] ... NjCa
Camden-Gloucester Newspapers, Blackwood, NJ [*Library symbol*] ... NjBlaCG
Camden News, Camden, NJ [*Library symbol*] ... NjCaN
Camden, NJ [*Radio station call letters*] ... WKDN-FM
Camden, NJ [*Television station call letters*] ... WNJS
Camden, NJ [*Radio station call letters*] ... WSSJ
Camden, NJ [*Radio station call letters*] ... WTMR
Camden, SC [*Radio station call letters*] ... WCAM
Camden, SC [*Radio station call letters*] ... WPUB
Camden, SC [*Radio station call letters*] ... WPUB-FM
Camden, TN [*Radio station call letters*] ... WFWL
Camden, TN [*Radio station call letters*] ... WRJB
Camelopardalis [*Constellation*] ... Caml
Camelopardus [*Constellation*] ... Cam
Camera ... CAM
Camera ... CAMR
Camera Confederale del Lavoro [*Confederal Chamber of Labor*] [*Italy/Trieste*] ... CCDL
Camera Control System ... CCS
Camera Control Unit ... CCU
Camera Copy [*or Camera-Ready Copy*] ... C/C
Camera Electronic Unit ... CEU
Camera Evaluation Program ... CEP
Camera Gun ... CG
Camera Industries of West Germany [*Defunct*] ... CIWG
Camera Obscura [*A publication*] ... Cam Obs
Camera Override Control System [*NASA*] ... COCS
Camera Quality ... CQ
Camera-Ready Art [*Publishing*] ... CRA
Camera-Ready Mechanical ... CRM
Camera Rehearsal ... CR
Camera Repairman [*Navy rating*] ... CR
Camera Site [*NASA*] ... CS
Camera, Timing, and Control ... CTC
Camera Timing Indicator ... CTI
Camera Tube Evaluation Program ... CTEP
Camerino [*Italy*] [*Seismograph station code, US Geological Survey*] [*Closed*] ... CMR
Cameron-Brown Investment Group [*NYSE symbol*] ... CB
Cameron College, Medical Library Resource Center, Lawton, OK [*Library symbol*] ... OkLC-M
Cameron Iron Works, Inc. [*NYSE symbol*] ... CIW
Cameron Iron Works, Inc., Houston, TX [*Library symbol*] ... TxHCI
Cameron, MO [*Radio station call letters*] ... KMRN
Cameron Parish Library, Cameron, LA [*Library symbol*] ... LCaC
Cameron State Agricultural College [*Oklahoma*] ... CSAC
Cameron Station [*Virginia*] [*Army*] ... CAMSTA
Cameron, TX [*Radio station call letters*] ... KCRM
Cameron, TX [*Radio station call letters*] ... KMIL
Cameron University, Lawton, OK [*OCLC symbol*] ... OKC
Cameron University, Lawton, OK [*Library symbol*] ... OkLC
Cameroon [*MARC country of publication code*] [*Library of Congress*] ... cm
Cameroon [*Three-letter standard code*] ... CMR
Cameroon [*MARC geographic area code*] [*Library of Congress*] ... f-cm---
Cameroon [*Two-letter standard code*] ... CM
Cameroon Airlines [*ICAO designator*] ... UY
Cameroons People's National Congress ... CPNC
Cameroun [*Aircraft nationality and registration mark*] ... TJ
Cameroun. Direction des Mines et de la Geologie. Activites Minieres au Cameroun [*A publication*] ... Cameroun Dir Mines Geol Act Minieres Cameroun
Camilla, GA [*Location identifier*] [*FAA*] ... CXU
Camilla, GA [*Radio station call letters*] ... WCLB
Camilla, GA [*Radio station call letters*] ... WOFF
Camino, Placerville, & Lake Tahoe Railroad Co. [*AAR code*] ... CPLT
Camiri [*Bolivia*] [*Airport symbol*] ... CAM
Cammed-Gear Speed Variator ... CSV
Camosun College, Victoria, BC, Canada [*Library symbol*] ... CaBViC
Camouflage ... CAM
Camouflage ... CAMOF
Camouflage, Concealment, and Deception ... CCD
Camouflage Critical [*Designation*] [*Army*] ... CC
Camouflage Detection [*Often, in regard to a special photographic film, as, "CD film"*] [*Military*] ... CD
Camouflage Effectiveness Assessment Office [*Army*] ... CEAO
Camouflage Officer [*British*] ... CO
Camouflage-Sensitive [*Designation*] [*Army*] ... CS
Camouflage Signature Measurement [*Army*] ... CSM
Camouflage Unit [*Military*] ... CU
Camp ... CP
Camp de l'Arpa [*A publication*] ... CdA
Camp Atterbury, IN [*Location identifier*] [*FAA*] ... XAY
Camp Beverly Hills [*California clothing store*] ... CBH
Camp Century [*Greenland*] [*Seismograph station code, US Geological Survey*] [*Closed*] ... CCG
Camp Chair ... CC
Camp Coles Signal Laboratory [*Army*] ... CCSL
Camp Commandant ... CC
Camp Douglas, WI [*Location identifier*] [*FAA*] ... VOK
Camp Elliot [*California*] [*Seismograph station code, US Geological Survey*] ... CPE
Camp Evans Signal Laboratory [*Army*] ... CESL
Camp Fire Club of America ... CFCA
Camp Fire Girls [*Later, CFI*] ... CFG
Camp Fire, Incorporated [*Formerly, CFG*] [*An association*] ... CFI
Camp Horsemanship Association ... CHA
Camp Lejeune [*North Carolina*] [*Marine Corps*] ... CAMLEJ
Camp LeJeune, NC [*Radio station call letters*] ... WJIK
Camp Lejeune Railroad Co. [*AAR code*] ... CPLJ
Camp Manufacturing Co., Franklin, VA [*Library symbol*] ... ViFraC
Camp Newspaper Service ... CNS
Camp Parks, CA [*Location identifier*] [*FAA*] ... PNY
Camp Pendleton [*California*] [*Marine Corps*] ... CAMPEN
Camp Pendleton [*California*] [*Seismograph station code, US Geological Survey*] ... CPT

Camp Reception Station [*A kind of field hospital*] [*British*]....CRS
Camp Ripley/Little Falls, MN [*Location identifier*] [*FAA*]....MTK
Camp Sentinel RADAR [*Military*]....CRS
Camp Springs, MD [*Location identifier*] [*FAA*]....ADW
Camp Springs, MD [*Location identifier*] [*FAA*]....MXK
Camp Springs, MD [*Location identifier*] [*FAA*]....NSF
Camp Springs, MD [*Location identifier*] [*FAA*]....RWS
Camp Williams [*Utah*] [*Seismograph station code, US Geological Survey*]....CWU
Campaign Against Investment in South Africa....CAISA
Campaign Against Nuclear War....CANW
Campaign Against Pollution....CAP
Campaign for the Creation of the National Youth Advisor....CCNYA
Campaign for Economic Democracy....CED
Campaign Fund for Republican Women....CFRW
Campaign for Human Development [*US Catholic Conference*]....CHD
Campaign for Labour Party Democracy [*British*]....CLPD
Campaign for Nuclear Disarmament....CND
Campaign to Oppose Bank Loans to South Africa....COBLSA
Campaign for Peace and Democracy/East and West....CPDEW
Campaign for Political Rights [*Formerly, CSGS*]....CPR
Campaign for Real Ale....CAMRA
Campaign to Remove US Bases from the Philippines....CRUSBP
Campaign to Save the People of Palestine....CSPP
Campaign for Space Political Action Committee....CSPAC
Campaign to Stop Government Spying [*Later, CPR*]....CSGS
Campaign for Surplus Rosaries....CSR
Campaign for World Government....CWG
Campaigner [*A publication*]....Campaign
Campanelli Industries, Inc. [*American Stock Exchange symbol*]....CAP
Campanha da Mulher pela Democracia....CAMDE
Campbell Army Airfield [*Fort Campbell, Kentucky*]....CAAF
Campbell College, Buies Creek, NC [*Library symbol*]....NcBuC
Campbell Colpitts Bridge [*Electronics*]....CCB
Campbell-Ewald Co. [*Advertising agency*]....C-E
Campbell, Godfrey, & Lewtas, Toronto, ON, Canada [*Library symbol*]....CaOTCGL
Campbell Industries [*American Stock Exchange symbol*] [*Delisted*]....CMH
Campbell Island [*New Zealand*] [*Seismograph station code, US Geological Survey*]....CBZ
Campbell-Larsen Potentiometer....CLP
Campbell, OH [*Radio station call letters*]....WHOT
Campbell, OH [*Radio station call letters*]....WSRD
Campbell Red Lake Mines Ltd. [*NYSE symbol*]....CRK
Campbell Reproductions Ltd., Ottawa, ON, Canada [*Library symbol*]....CamR
Campbell Resources, Inc. [*Formerly, Campbell Chibougamau Mines Ltd.*] [*American Stock Exchange symbol*]....CCH
Campbell River [*Canada*] [*Airport symbol*]....YBL
Campbell River, BC [*Radio station call letters*]....CFWB
Campbell River, BC [*Television station call letters*]....CHEK-TV-5
Campbell Soup Co. [*NYSE symbol*]....CPB
Campbell Taggart, Incorporated [*NYSE symbol*]....CTI
Campbellford Public Library, Campbellford, ON, Canada [*Library symbol*]....CaOCam
Campbellpur [*Pakistan*] [*Seismograph station code, US Geological Survey*]....CBP
Campbell's Creek R. R. [*AAR code*]....CCK
Campbellsville College, Campbellsville, KY [*Library symbol*]....KyCambC
Campbellsville, KY [*Location identifier*] [*FAA*]....AAS
Campbellsville, KY [*Radio station call letters*]....WCKQ-FM
Campbellsville, KY [*Television station call letters*]....WGRB
Campbellsville, KY [*Radio station call letters*]....WKXJ
Campbellton Centennial Public Library, Campbellton, NB, Canada [*Library symbol*]....CaNBCa
Campbellton, NB [*Television station call letters*]....CHCR-TV
Campbellton, NB [*Television station call letters*]....CKCD-TV
Campbellton, NB [*Radio station call letters*]....CKNB
Campbeltown [*Scotland*] [*Airport symbol*]....CAL
Campeche [*Mexico*] [*Airport symbol*]....CPE
Camper Alert Team [*for missile sites*] [*Air Force*]....CAT
Campership Outdoor Program of Education [*Federal antipoverty program*]....COPE
Camphorsulfonic Acid [*Organic chemistry*]....CSA
Campina Grande [*Brazil*] [*Airport symbol*]....CPV
Campinas [*Brazil*] [*Airport symbol*]....CPQ
Camping Magazine [*A publication*]....Camp Mag
Camping Products Division [*of Industrial Fabrics Association International*]....CPD
Camping Trailer Manufacturers Association [*Later, RVIA*]....CTMA
Camping Women....CW
Campo Alegre [*Brazil*] [*Airport symbol*]....CMP
Campo, CA [*Location identifier*] [*FAA*]....CZZ
Campo Grande [*Brazil*] [*Airport symbol*]....CGR
Campo y Suelo Argentino [*A publication*]....Campo Suelo Argent
Campos [*Brazil*] [*Airport symbol*]....CAW
Campulung [*Romania*] [*Seismograph station code, US Geological Survey*]....CMP
Campus....CAM
Campus Americans for Democratic Action [*Defunct*]....CADA
Campus-Based Information System [*National Science Foundation*]....CBIS
Campus Crusade for Christ....CCC
Campus Crusade for Christ International....CCCI
Campus-Free College....CFC
Campus Life [*A publication*]....CaL
Campus Ministries of America....CMA
Campus Ministry Women....CMW
Campus Notre-Dame de Foy, Cap Rouge, PQ, Canada [*Library symbol*]....CaQCRCN
Campus Safety Association [*of the National Safety Council*]....CSA
Campus Safety Association of the National Safety Council....CSANSC
Campus Studies Institute....CSI
Camreco, Inc. [*NASDAQ symbol*]....CAMRF
Camrose, AB [*Radio station call letters*]....CFCW
Camrose Lutheran College, Camrose, AB, Canada [*Library symbol*]....CaACAL
Camseal, Inc. [*NASDAQ symbol*]....CMLC
Camshaft....CMSHFT
Camuy, PR [*Radio station call letters*]....WCHQ
Camuy, PR [*Radio station call letters*]....WCHQ-FM
Can [*Buoy*] [*Maps and charts*]....C
Can....CN
Can Do It [*Temporary-help agency*]....CDI
Can Go Over [*Newspapers*]....CGO
Can Manufacturers Institute....CMI
Can You Come and See Me?....UCM
Canada....C
Canada [*Two-letter standard code*]....CA
Canada [*Three-letter standard code*]....CAN
Canada....CDA
Canada [*Aircraft nationality and registration mark*]....CF
Canada [*MARC country of publication code*] [*Library of Congress*]....cn
Canada [*MARC geographic area code*] [*Library of Congress*]....n-cn---
Canada Arctic Gas Study Ltd., Toronto, ON, Canada [*Library symbol*]....CaOTCAG
Canada. Arctic Land Use Research Program Report [*A publication*]....Can Arct Land Use Res Prog Rep
Canada Art Council, Ottawa, ON, Canada [*Library symbol*]....CaOOCAC
Canada Cement Co. Ltd., Montreal, PQ, Canada [*Library symbol*]....CaQMCC
Canada Centre for Inland Waters....CCIW
Canada. Centre for Mineral and Energy Technology. Publications [*A publication*]....Can Cent Miner Energy Technol Publ
Canada. Centre de Terminologie. Bulletin de Terminologie [*A publication*]....Can Cent Terminol Bull Terminol
Canada Coast Guard College, Sydney, NS, Canada [*Library symbol*]....CaNSSCG
Canada College Library, Redwood City, CA [*OCLC symbol*]....CCG
Canada Commerce [*A publication*]....Can Commerce
Canada Defence Research Board. Handbook [*A publication*]....Canada Defence Research Board Handb
Canada Department of Agriculture, Animal Diseases Research Institute (West), Lethbridge, AB, Canada [*Library symbol*]....CaALADR
Canada. Department of Agriculture. Annual Report [*A publication*]....Can Dep Agric Annu Rep
Canada Department of Agriculture, Canadian Farm Management Data System, Guelph, ON, Canada [*Library symbol*]....CaOGCF
Canada Department of Agriculture, Canadian Grain Commission, Winnipeg, MB, Canada [*Library symbol*]....CaMWGR
Canada Department of Agriculture, Economics Branch, Regina, SK, Canada [*Library symbol*]....CaSRAgE
Canada Department of Agriculture, Entomological Society of British Columbia Library, Vancouver, BC, Canada [*Library symbol*]....CaBVaAg
Canada Department of Agriculture, Experimental Farm, La Pocatiere, PQ, Canada [*Library symbol*]....CaQPAg
Canada Department of Agriculture, Experimental Farm, L'Assomption, PQ, Canada [*Library symbol*]....CaQAsAg
Canada Department of Agriculture, Lethbridge, AB, Canada [*Library symbol*]....CaALAg
Canada Department of Agriculture, Ottawa, ON, Canada [*Library symbol*]....CaOOAg
Canada. Department of Agriculture. Publication [*A publication*]....Canada Ag
Canada. Department of Agriculture. Publication [*A publication*]....Can Dep Agric Publ
Canada. Department of Agriculture. Research Branch Monograph [*A publication*]....Can Dep Agric Res Branch Monogr
Canada. Department of Agriculture. Research Branch Report [*A publication*]....Can Dep Agric Res Branch Rep
Canada Department of Agriculture, Research Institute, Belleville, ON, Canada [*Library symbol*] [*Obsolete*]....CaOBP
Canada Department of Agriculture, Research Institute, London, ON, Canada [*Library symbol*]....CaOLAg
Canada Department of Agriculture, Research Station, Beaverlodge, AB, Canada [*Library symbol*]....CaABeAg
Canada Department of Agriculture, Research Station, Brandon, MB, Canada [*Library symbol*]....CaMBAg
Canada Department of Agriculture, Research Station, Charlottetown, PE, Canada [*Library symbol*]....CaPCAg

Canada Department of Agriculture, Research Station, Delhi, ON,
Canada [Library symbol] .... CaODeAg

Canada Department of Agriculture, Research Station,
Fredericton, NB, Canada [Library symbol] .... CaNBFAg

Canada Department of Agriculture, Research Station, Harrow,
ON, Canada [Library symbol] .... CaOHarAg

Canada Department of Agriculture, Research Station,
Kamloops, BC, Canada [Library symbol] .... CaBKAg

Canada Department of Agriculture, Research Station, Kentville,
NS, Canada [Library symbol] .... CaNSKR

Canada Department of Agriculture, Research Station, Morden,
MB, Canada [Library symbol] .... CaMMoAg

Canada Department of Agriculture, Research Station, Regina,
SK, Canada [Library symbol] .... CaSRAgR

Canada Department of Agriculture, Research Station,
Saanichton, BC, Canada [Library symbol] .... CaBSAg

Canada Department of Agriculture, Research Station, Saint-
Jean, PQ, Canada [Library symbol] .... CaQStJAg

Canada Department of Agriculture, Research Station,
Saskatoon, SK, Canada [Library symbol] .... CaSSAgR

Canada Department of Agriculture, Research Station, Ste-Foy,
PQ, Canada [Library symbol] .... CaQSFAg

Canada Department of Agriculture, Research Station,
Summerland, BC, Canada [Library symbol] .... CaBSuAg

Canada Department of Agriculture, Research Station, Swift
Current, SK, Canada [Library symbol] .... CaSSCAg

Canada Department of Agriculture, Research Station, Vineland
Station, ON, Canada [Library symbol] .... CaOVAgR

Canada Department of Agriculture, Research Station,
Winnipeg, MB, Canada [Library symbol] .... CaMWAG

Canada Department of Agriculture, Winnipeg, MB, Canada
[Library symbol] .... CaMWA

Canada Department of Communications, Communications
Research Centre, Ottawa, ON, Canada [Library symbol] .... CaOORPL

Canada Department of Communications, Ottawa, ON, Canada
[Library symbol] .... CaOOCO

Canada Department of Consumer and Corporate Affairs,
Ottawa, ON, Canada [Library symbol] .... CaOOCI

Canada Department of Energy, Mines, and Resources, Canada
Centre for Remote Sensing, Ottawa, ON, Canada [Library
symbol] .... CaOOCCR

Canada Department of Energy, Mines, and Resources, Earth
Physics Branch, Ottawa, ON, Canada [Library symbol] .... CaOOO

Canada Department of Energy, Mines, and Resources, Energy
Development Sector, Ottawa, ON, Canada [Library symbol]
[Obsolete] .... CaOOEME

Canada Department of Energy, Mines, and Resources, Map
Library, Ottawa, ON, Canada [Library symbol] .... CaOOSMM

Canada Department of Energy, Mines, and Resources, Physical
Metallurgy Division, Ottawa, ON, Canada [Library symbol] ...... CaOOMP

Canada Department of Energy, Mines, and Resources,
Resources Economic Library, Ottawa, ON, Canada [Library
symbol] .... CaOOMR

Canada Department of Energy, Mines, and Resources, Surveys
and Mapping Branch, Ottawa, ON, Canada [Library symbol] .... CaOOSM

Canada Department of the Environment, Atmospheric
Environment Service, Atlantic Region, Halifax, NS, Canada
[Library symbol] .... CaNSHW

Canada Department of the Environment, Atmospheric
Environment Service, Toronto, ON, Canada [Library symbol] ..... CaOTM

Canada Department of the Environment, Bedford Institute of
Oceanography, Dartmouth, NS, Canada [Library symbol] .... CaNSDB

Canada Department of the Environment, Canadian Wildlife
Service Edmonton, AB, Canada [Library symbol] .... CaAEECW

Canada Department of the Environment, Canadian Wildlife
Service, Ottawa, ON, Canada [Library symbol] .... CaOOECW

Canada Department of the Environment, Canadian Wildlife
Service, Prairie Migratory Bird Research Centre,
Saskatoon, SK, Canada [Library symbol] .... CaSSECW

Canada Department of the Environment, Canadian Wildlife
Service, Sackville, NB, Canada [Library symbol] .... CaNBSaCW

Canada Department of the Environment, Environmental
Protection Service, Vancouver, BC, Canada [Library symbol] ....
CaBVaEP

Canada Department of the Environment, Fisheries and Marine
Service, Research and Development Directorate, Pacific
Biological Station, Nanaimo, BC, Canada [Library symbol] .... CaBNP

Canada Department of the Environment, Fisheries and Marine
Service, Research and Development Directorate,
Vancouver Laboratory, Vancouver, BC, Canada [Library
symbol] .... CaBVaF

Canada Department of the Environment, Fisheries and Marine
Service, Ste.-Anne-De-Bellevue, PQ, Canada [Library symbol] ....
CaQMFR

Canada Department of the Environment, Fontaine Branch
Library, Ottawa, ON, Canada [Library symbol] .... CaOOEF

Canada Department of the Environment, Forest Fire Research
Institute, Ottawa, ON, Canada [Library symbol] .... CaOOFFR

Canada Department of the Environment, Forest Products
Laboratory, Vancouver, BC, Canada [Library symbol] .... CaBVaFP

Canada Department of the Environment, Forest Research
Laboratory, Victoria, BC, Canada [Library symbol] .... CaBViF

Canada Department of the Environment, Institute of Ocean
Sciences, Victoria, BC, Canada [Library symbol] .... CaBViEM

Canada Department of the Environment, Maritimes Forest
Research Centre, Fredericton, NB, Canada [Library symbol] ..... CaNBFE

Canada Department of the Environment, Northern Forest
Research Centre, Edmonton, AB, Canada [Library symbol] .... CaAEF

Canada Department of the Environment, Ottawa, ON, Canada
[Library symbol] .... CaOOFF

Canada Department of the Environment, Pacific Environment
Institute, Vancouver, BC, Canada [Library symbol] .... CaBVaPE

Canada Department of the Environment, Petawawa Forest
Experiment Station, Chalk River, ON, Canada [Library
symbol] .... CaOCkE

Canada Department of the Environment, Quebec Region, Ste-
Foy, PQ, Canada [Library symbol] .... CaQQE

Canada Department of the Environment, Research Station,
Sault Ste. Marie, ON, Canada [Library symbol] .... CaOStMF

Canada Department of the Environment, Resource and
Environmental Law Library, Ottawa, ON, Canada [Library
symbol] [Obsolete] .... CaOOERE

Canada Department of the Environment, Sea Lamprey Control
Centre, Sault Ste. Marie, ON, Canada [Library symbol] .... CaOStMEF

Canada Department of External Affairs, Legal Branch, Ottawa,
ON, Canada [Library symbol] .... CaOOELB

Canada Department of External Affairs, Ottawa, ON, Canada
[Library symbol] .... CaOOE

Canada Department of Finance, Ottawa, ON, Canada [Library
symbol] .... CaOOF

Canada. Department of Fisheries. Annual Report [A publication]...................
Can Dep Fish Annu Rep

Canada Department of Fisheries and the Environment,
Fisheries and Marine Service, Quebec, PQ, Canada [Library
symbol] .... CaQQPSM

Canada. Department of Fisheries and Forestry. Annual Report
[A publication].................................... Can Dep Fish For Annu Rep

Canada. Department of Fisheries and Forestry. Annual Report
of the Forest Insect and Disease Survey [A publication]...................
Can Dept Forestry Disease Surv

Canada. Department of Fisheries and Forestry. Bimonthly
Research Notes [A publication] .... Can Dep Fish For Bimon Res Notes

Canada. Department of Fisheries and Forestry. Bimonthly
Research Notes [A publication] .... Can Dept Forestry Bimo Res Note

Canada. Department of Fisheries and Forestry. Canadian
Forestry Service Information Report. FF-X [A publication].....................
Can Dep Fish For Can For Serv Inf Rep FF-X

Canada. Department of Fisheries and Forestry. Canadian
Forestry Service Publication [A publication] ....
Can Dep Fish For Can For Serv Publ

Canada. Department of Fisheries and Forestry. Departmental
Publications [A publication].................................Can Dept Forestry Publ

Canada. Department of Fisheries and Forestry. Forestry Branch
Departmental Publication [A publication].................................
Can Dep Fish For For Branch Dep Publ

Canada. Department of Fisheries and Forestry. Research News
[A publication].. Can Dept Forestry Res News

Canada Department of Fisheries and Oceans, St. Johns, NF,
Canada [Library symbol] .... CaNfSEC

Canada Department of Fisheries and Oceans, Vancouver, BC,
Canada [Library symbol] .... CaBVaFi

Canada. Department of Forestry and Rural Development.
Annual Report [A publication]...............Can Dep For Rural Dev Annu Rep

Canada. Department of Forestry and Rural Development. Bi-
Monthly Research Notes [A publication]...................................
Can Dep For Rural Dev Bi-Mon Res Notes

Canada. Department of Forestry and Rural Development.
Forestry Branch Department. Publication [A publication]....................
Can Dep For Rural Dev For Branch Dep Publ

Canada Department of Indian Affairs and Northern
Development, Parks Canada, Western Regional Office,
Calgary, AB, Canada [Library symbol] .... CaACIA

Canada Department of Indian Affairs and Northern
Development, Point Pelee National Park, Leamington, ON,
Canada [Library symbol] .... CaOLeI

Canada Department of Indian and Northern Affairs, Prince
Albert, SK, Canada [Library symbol] .... CaSPAIN

Canada Department of Indian and Northern Affairs, Yellowknife,
NT, Canada [Library symbol] .... CaNWYIM

Canada Department of Industry, Ottawa, ON, Canada [Library
symbol] [Obsolete] .... CaOOI

Canada Department of Industry, Trade, and Commerce, Ottawa,
ON, Canada [Library symbol] .... CaOOTC

Canada Department of Insurance, Ottawa, ON, Canada [Library
symbol] .... CaOOIn

Canada. Department of the Interior. Report of the Chief
Astronomer [A publication]............. Can Dp Interior Rp Chief Astronomer

Canada. Department of the Interior. Superintendent of Mines.
Report [A publication] ....Can Dp Interior Sup Mines Rp

Canada Department of Justice, Edmonton, AB, Canada [Library
symbol] .... CaAEJ

Canada Department of Justice, Halifax, NS, Canada [*Library symbol*] .... CaNSHJ
Canada Department of Justice, Montreal, PQ, Canada [*Library symbol*] .... CaQMJM
Canada Department of Justice, Occupational Analysis Library, Ottawa, ON, Canada [*Library symbol*] [*Obsolete*] .... CaOOOA
Canada Department of Justice, Ottawa, ON, Canada [*Library symbol*] .... CaOOJ
Canada Department of Justice, Toronto, ON, Canada [*Library symbol*] .... CaOTJ
Canada Department of Justice, Vancouver, BC, Canada [*Library symbol*] .... CaBVaJ
Canada Department of Justice, Winnipeg, MB, Canada [*Library symbol*] .... CaMWJ
Canada Department of Labour, Occupational Safety and Health Branch, Ottawa, ON, Canada [*Library symbol*] .... CaOOLAP
Canada Department of Labour, Ottawa, ON, Canada [*Library symbol*] .... CaOOL
Canada Department of Manpower and Immigration, Halifax, NS, Canada [*Library symbol*] [*Obsolete*] .... CaNSHMI
Canada Department of Manpower and Immigration, Prince Albert, SK, Canada [*Library symbol*] [*Obsolete*] .... CaSPAMI
Canada Department of Manpower and Immigration, Winnipeg, MB, Canada [*Library symbol*] .... CaMWMI
Canada. Department of Mines. Mines Branch. Summary Report [*A publication*] .... Can Mines Br Sum Rp
Canada Department of Mines and Resources, Centre for Inland Waters, Burlington, ON, Canada [*Library symbol*] .... CaOBUC
Canada. Department of Mines and Technical Surveys. Geographical Bulletin [*A publication*] .... Canada Dept Mines and Tech Surveys Geog Bull
Canada Department of Mines and Technical Surveys. Geographical Paper [*A publication*] .... Canada Dept Mines and Tech Surveys Geog Paper
Canada. Department of Mines and Technical Surveys. Memoir [*A publication*] .... Canada Dept Mines and Tech Surveys Mem
Canada Department of National Defence, Canadian Forces Staff School, Toronto, ON, Canada [*Library symbol*] .... CaOTRCS
Canada Department of National Defence, Defence Research Establishment, Esquimalt, BC, Canada [*Library symbol*] .... CaBEPN
Canada Department of National Defence, Defence Research Establishment, Ottawa, ON, Canada [*Library symbol*] .... CaOODRC
Canada Department of National Defence, Headquarters Mobile Command, St. Hubert, PQ, Canada [*Library symbol*] .... CaQStHuM
Canada Department of National Defence, Northern Region Information System, [*NORIS*], **Yellowknife, NT, Canada** [*Library symbol*] .... CaNWYND
Canada Department of National Defence, Ottawa, ON, Canada [*Library symbol*] [*Obsolete*] .... CaOOAM
Canada Department of National Defence, Reference and Recreational Library [*Stadacona*], **Halifax, NS, Canada** [*Library symbol*] .... CaNSHND
Canada Department of National Defense, Quality Assurance Division, Ottawa, ON, Canada [*Library symbol*] .... CaOOQA
Canada Department of National Health and Welfare, Food and Drug Directorate, Ottawa, ON, Canada [*Library symbol*] .... CaOOFD
Canada Department of National Health and Welfare, Health Protection Branch, Vancouver, BC, Canada [*Library symbol*] .... CaBVaNH
Canada Department of National Revenue, Customs and Excise Division, Ottawa, ON, Canada [*Library symbol*] .... CaOONR
Canada Department of National Revenue, Taxation Division, Ottawa, ON, Canada [*Library symbol*] .... CaOONRT
Canada Department of Public Works, Capital Region Library, Ottawa, ON, Canada [*Library symbol*] .... CaOOPWC
Canada Department of Public Works, Office of the Dominion Fire Commissioner, Ottawa, ON, Canada [*Library symbol*] [*Obsolete*] .... CaOOPWD
Canada Department of Public Works, Ottawa, ON, Canada [*Library symbol*] .... CaOOPW
Canada Department of Public Works, Research and Development Laboratories, Ottawa, ON, Canada [*Library symbol*] .... CaOOPWR
Canada Department of Regional Economic Expansion, Moncton, NB, Canada [*Library symbol*] .... CaNBMoRE
Canada Department of Regional Economic Expansion, Ottawa, ON, Canada [*Library symbol*] .... CaOOREx
Canada Department of Regional Economic Expansion, Prairie Farm Rehabilitation Administration, Regina, SK, Canada [*Library symbol*] .... CaSRREE
Canada Department of Regional Economic Expansion, Reference and Enquiries Unit, Ottawa, ON, Canada [*Library symbol*] [*Obsolete*] .... CaOORExR
Canada Department of Regional Economic Expansion, Toronto, ON, Canada [*Library symbol*] .... CaOTREx
Canada Department of Revenue, Canada Customs and Excise, Scientific and Technical Information Centre, Laboratory and Scientific Services Division, Ottawa, ON, Canada [*Library symbol*] .... CaOOSTI
Canada Department of the Secretary of State, Ottawa, ON, Canada [*Library symbol*] .... CaOOSS
Canada Department of the Secretary of State, Translation Bureau, Montreal, PQ, Canada [*Library symbol*] .... CaQMBD
Canada Department of the Secretary of State, Translation Bureau, Multilingual Services Division, Ottawa, ON, Canada [*Library symbol*] [*Obsolete*] .... CaOOSST
Canada Department of the Secretary of State, Translation Bureau, Terminology Centre Library, Ottawa, ON, Canada [*Library symbol*] .... CaOOSSTT
Canada Department of the Solicitor General, Ottawa, ON, Canada [*Library symbol*] .... CaOOSG
Canada Department of Supply and Services, Bureau of Management and Consulting, Ottawa, ON, Canada [*Library symbol*] .... CaOOBMC
Canada Department of Supply and Services, Compensation Branch, Superannuation Division, Ottawa, ON, Canada [*Library symbol*] .... CaOODPS
Canada Department of Supply and Services, Ottawa, ON, Canada [*Library symbol*] .... CaOODP
Canada Department of Veterans Affairs, Ottawa, ON, Canada [*Library symbol*] .... CaOOV
Canada Deposit Insurance Corporation .... CDIC
Canada Development Corporation .... CDC
Canada Dominion Observatory Contributions. Publications [*A publication*] .... Canada Dominion Observatory Contr Pub
Canada Dry Corp. [*NYSE symbol*] [*Delisted*] .... CD
Canada East .... CE
Canada Emergency Measures Organization [*Civil defense*] .... CEMO
Canada Employment and Immigration Department, Ottawa, ON, Canada [*Library symbol*] .... CaOOMI
Canada Employment and Immigration Department, Quebec Regional Office, Montreal, PQ, Canada [*Library symbol*] .... CaQMMIQ
Canada Employment and Immigration Department, Toronto, ON, Canada [*Library symbol*] .... CaOTMIO
Canada Employment and Immigration Department, Vancouver, BC, Canada [*Library symbol*] .... CaBVaMI
Canada. Environmental Protection Service. Economic and Technical Review Report [*A publication*] .... Can Environ Prot Serv Econ Tech Rev Rep
Canada. Environmental Protection Service. Technology Development Report [*A publication*] .... Can Environ Prot Serv Technol Dev Rep
Canada Farm Labor Pool .... CFLP
Canada. Fisheries and Marine Service. Data Report. Series Cen-D [*A publication*] .... Can Fish Mar Serv Data Rep Ser Cen-D
Canada. Fisheries and Marine Service. Miscellaneous Special Publication [*A publication*] .... Can Fish Mar Serv Misc Spec Publ
Canada. Fisheries and Marine Service. Technical Report [*A publication*] .... Can Fish Mar Serv Tech Rep
Canada. Fisheries Service Resource. Development Branch. Halifax Progress Report [*A publication*] .... Can Fish Serv Resour Dev Branch Halifax Prog Rep
Canada. Forest Entomology and Pathology Branch. Annual Report [*A publication*] .... Can For Entomol Pathol Branch Annu Rep
Canada. Forest Products Research Branch. Annual Report [*A publication*] .... Can For Prod Res Branch Annu Rep
Canada. Forest Research Branch. Annual Report [*A publication*] .... Can For Res Branch Annu Rep
Canada. Forestry Service. Bi-Monthly Research Notes [*A publication*] .... Can For Serv Bi-Mon Res Notes
Canada Francais [*A publication*] .... CF
Canada-France-Hawaii Telescope [*Mauna Kea, Hawaii*] .... CFHT
Canada Geographic Information System .... CGIS
Canada. Geological Survey [*A publication*] .... Can G S
Canada. Geological Survey. Annual Report [*A publication*] .... Can G S An Rp
Canada. Geological Survey. Bulletin [*A publication*] .... Canada Geol Survey Bull
Canada. Geological Survey. Bulletin [*A publication*] .... Can Geol Surv Bull
Canada. Geological Survey. Economic Geology Report [*A publication*] .... Canada Geol Survey Econ Geology Rept
Canada. Geological Survey. Geophysics Paper [*A publication*] .... Canada Geol Survey Geophysics Paper
Canada. Geological Survey. Map [*A publication*] .... Canada Geol Survey Map
Canada. Geological Survey. Map [*A publication*] .... Can Geol Surv Map
Canada. Geological Survey. Memoir [*A publication*] .... Canada Geol Survey Mem
Canada. Geological Survey. Memoir [*A publication*] .... Can Geol Surv Mem
Canada. Geological Survey. Memoir [*A publication*] .... Can G S Mem
Canada. Geological Survey. Miscellaneous Report [*A publication*] .... Can Geol Surv Misc Rep
Canada. Geological Survey. Museum Bulletin [*A publication*] .... Can G S Mus B
Canada. Geological Survey. Paper [*A publication*] .... Canada Geol Survey Paper
Canada. Geological Survey. Paper [*A publication*] .... Can Geol Surv Pap
Canada. Geological Survey. Preliminary Series. Map [*A publication*] .... Canada Geol Survey Prelim Ser Map
Canada. Geological Survey. Summary Report [*A publication*] .... Can G S Sum Rp
Canada Geological Survey, Vancouver, BC, Canada [*Library symbol*] .... CaBVaG
[*The*] **Canada & Gulf Terminal Railway Co.** [*AAR code*] .... CGT

Canada, Hungary, Indonesia, and Poland [*Countries comprising the International Commission of Control and Supervision, charged with supervising the cease-fire in Vietnam, 1973*] .... CHIP
Canada-India Reactor .... CIR
Canada. Inland Waters Branch. Report Series [*A publication*] .... Can Inland Waters Branch Rep Ser
Canada. Inland Waters Branch. Scientific Series [*A publication*] .... Can Inland Waters Branch Sci Ser
Canada Institute for Scientific and Technical Information .... CISTI
Canada Institute for Scientific and Technical Information, Administration Building Library, Ottawa, ON, Canada [*Library symbol*] .... CaOONAB
Canada Institute for Scientific and Technical Information, Aeronautical and Mechanical Engineering Branch, Ottawa, ON, Canada [*Library symbol*] .... CaOONAM
Canada Institute for Scientific and Technical Information, Chemistry Library, Ottawa, ON, Canada [*Library symbol*] .... CaOONC
Canada Institute for Scientific and Technical Information, Division of Building Research, Ottawa, ON, Canada [*Library symbol*] .... CaOONBR
Canada Institute for Scientific and Technical Information, National Research Council, Ottawa, ON, Canada [*Library symbol*] .... CaOON
Canada Institute for Scientific and Technical Information, Radio and Electrical Engineering Division, Ottawa, ON, Canada [*Library symbol*] .... CaOONRE
Canada Institute for Scientific and Technical Information, Sussex Library, Ottawa, ON, Canada [*Library symbol*] .... CaOONS
Canada Institute for Scientific and Technical Information, Uplands Library, Ottawa, ON, Canada [*Library symbol*] .... CaOONU
Canada Labour Relations Board .... CLRB
Canada Labour Relations Board, Ottawa, ON, Canada [*Library symbol*] .... CaOOLRB
Canada Manpower Centre .... CMC
Canada Manpower Industrial Training .... CMIT
Canada Manpower Training Program .... CMTP
Canada Medal .... CM
Canada Medical Journal and Monthly Record of Medical and Surgical Science [*A publication*] .... Canada Med J
Canada Ministry of State for Science and Technology, Ottawa, ON, Canada [*Library symbol*] .... CaOOMSS
Canada Ministry of State for Urban Affairs, Ottawa, ON, Canada [*Library symbol*] .... CaOOMUA
Canada Ministry of Transport, Canadian Air Transportation Administration, Ontario Region, Toronto, ON, Canada [*Library symbol*] .... CaOTTOA
Canada Ministry of Transport Executive Flight [*ICAO designator*] .... GO
Canada Ministry of Transport, Marine Library, Halifax, NS, Canada [*Library symbol*] .... CaNSHMT
Canada Ministry of Transport Training Institute, Ottawa, ON, Canada [*Library symbol*] .... CaOOTI
Canada Ministry of Transport, Transportation Development Agency, Montreal, PQ, Canada [*Library symbol*] .... CaQMTD
Canada Ministry of Transport, Waterways Development, Montreal, PQ, Canada [*Library symbol*] .... CaQMTR
Canada-Mongolia Review [*A publication*] .... Can-Mong R
Canada Music Book [*A publication*] .... Can Mus Bk
Canada. National Aeronautical Establishment. Mechanical Engineering Report [*A publication*] .... Can Natl Aeronaut Establ Mech Eng Rep
Canada Oil and Gas Lands Administration .... COGLA
Canada. Pacific Forest Research Centre. Report. BC X [*A publication*] .... Can Pac For Res Cent Rep BC X
Canada Pension Plan .... CPP
Canada Privy Council Office, Management Information, Ottawa, ON, Canada [*Library symbol*] .... CaOOPC
Canada Road [*California*] [*Seismograph station code, US Geological Survey*] .... CDC
Canada Savings Bond .... CSB
Canada Southern Railway [*Penn Central*] [*AAR code*] .... CASO
Canada Southern Railway [*Penn Central*] [*NYSE symbol*] [*Delisted*] .... CNS
Canada Steamship Lines .... CSL
Canada Steamship Lines [*AAR code*] .... CSSL
Canada-United Kingdom .... CAN-UK
Canada-United Kingdom-United States [*Agreement*] .... CANUKUS
Canada-United Kingdom-United States Joint Communications-Electronics Committees .... CANUKUS JCECS
Canada-United States .... CAN-US
Canada-United States Environmental Council .... CUSEC
Canada/United States Region .... CUSR
Canada-United States Regional Planning Group [*NATO*] .... CUSRPG
Canada. Victoria Memorial Museum. Bulletin [*A publication*] .... Can Victoria Mem Mus B
Canada West .... CW
Canada Wire & Cable Co. Ltd., Toronto, ON, Canada [*Library symbol*] .... CaOTCW
Canada and the World [*A publication*] .... Can & World
Canadair Limited [*Division of General Dynamics Corp.*] [*Montreal*] .... C-L
Canadair Ltd., Engineering Library, Montreal, PQ, Canada [*Library symbol*] .... CaQMCa
Canadair Ltd., Missiles and Systems Library, Montreal, PQ, Canada [*Library symbol*] .... CaQMCam
Canada's Mental Health [*A publication*] .... Can Ment He
Canada's Mental Health [*A publication*] .... Can Ment Health
Canada's Mental Health [*A publication*] .... Can Ment Hlth
Canadex Resources Ltd. [*NASDAQ symbol*] .... CDXOF
Canadian .... CANDN
Canadian .... CDN
Canadian .... CNDN
Canadian Academic Research Libraries .... CARL
Canadian Advertising Advisory Board .... CAAB
Canadian Advertising Rates and Data .... CARD
Canadian Aeronautical Institute .... CAI
Canadian Aeronautics and Space Institute .... CASI
Canadian Aeronautics and Space Journal [*A publication*] .... Can Aeronaut Space J
Canadian Aeronautics and Space Journal [*A publication*] .... Can Aer Spa
Canadian Agricultural Engineering [*A publication*] .... Can Agr Eng
Canadian Agricultural Engineering [*A publication*] .... Can Agric Eng
Canadian Agricultural Insect Pest Review [*A publication*] .... Can Agric Insect Pest Rev
Canadian Air Defence Identification Zone .... CADIZ
Canadian Air Division .... CAD
Canadian Air Division Headquarters [*Allied Air Forces in Europe*] .... CANAIRDIV
Canadian Air Force [*1920-1923*] .... CAF
Canadian Air-Ground Environment .... CAGE
Canadian Air Line Flight Attendants Association .... CALFAA
Canadian Air Lines Employees Association .... CALEA
Canadian Air Mail Collectors Club .... CAMCC
Canadian Air Publication .... CAP
Canadian Air Traffic Control Association .... CATCA
Canadian Air Training Command Headquarters .... CANAIRTRAIN
Canadian Air Transport Board .... CATB
Canadian Air Transport Command .... CATC
Canadian Air Transportation Administration .... CATA
Canadian Airline Pilots Association .... CALPA
Canadian Airways Limited .... CAL
Canadian Alpine Journal [*A publication*] .... Canadian Alpine Jour
Canadian Alpine Journal [*A publication*] .... Can Al J
Canadian Amateur Hockey Association .... CAHA
Canadian Amateur Speed Skating Association .... CASA
Canadian-American Committee [*of the National Planning Association and the C. D. Howe Research Institute*] .... CAC
Canadian-American Merchant Shipping Instructions .... CAMSI
Canadian-American Motor Carriers Association .... CAMCA
Canadian-American Review of Hungarian Studies [*A publication*] .... CARHS
Canadian-American Slavic Studies [*A publication*] .... Can-Am Slav
Canadian-American Slavic Studies [*A publication*] .... Can Slav Stud
Canadian-American Slavic Studies [*A publication*] .... CanSS
Canadian-American Slavic Studies [*A publication*] .... CASS
Canadian-American Women's Association, American Section .... CAWAAS
Canadian Anaesthetists Society .... CAS
Canadian Anaesthetists' Society. Journal [*A publication*] .... Can Anae S J
Canadian Anaesthetists' Society. Journal [*A publication*] .... Can Anaesth Soc J
Canadian Anaesthetists' Society. Journal [*A publication*] .... CANJA
Canadian Antiques Collector [*A publication*] .... Can Ant Coll
Canadian Architect [*A publication*] .... Can Arch
Canadian Arctic Gas Pipeline Limited .... CAGPL
Canadian Arctic Resources Committee .... CARC
Canadian Armament Research and Development Establishment .... CARDE
Canadian Armed Forces .... CAF
Canadian Armed Forces .... CANFORCE
Canadian Armoured Brigade .... CAB
Canadian Armoured Corps .... CAC
Canadian Army .... CA
Canadian Army .... CANA
Canadian Army Active Service Force .... CAASF
Canadian Army Liaison Executive .... CALE
Canadian Army Medical Corps .... CAMC
Canadian Army (Militia) .... CA(M)
Canadian Army Operational Research Establishment .... CAORE
Canadian Army Orders .... CAO
Canadian Army (Regular) .... CA(R)
Canadian Arsenals Limited .... CAL
Canadian Art [*A publication*] .... Can Art
Canadian Art Museum Directors Organization .... CAMDO
Canadian Association for Adult Education, Toronto, ON, Canada [*Library symbol*] .... CaOTCAE
Canadian Association for American Studies .... CAAS
Canadian Association for American Studies. Bulletin [*A publication*] .... CAAS Bull
Canadian Association of British Manufacturers and Agencies .... CABMA
Canadian Association of Chiefs of Police .... CACP
Canadian Association of Children's Librarians .... CACL
Canadian Association of College and University Libraries .... CACUL
Canadian Association for Health, Physical Education, and Recreation .... CAHPER
Canadian Association of Industrial, Mechanical, and Allied Workers .... CAIMAW

Canadian Association for Information Science ... CAIS
Canadian Association for Information Science/Association Canadienne des Sciences de l'Information ... CAIS/ACSI
Canadian Association of Law Libraries ... CALL
Canadian Association of Library Schools ... CALS
Canadian Association of Medical Students and Interns ... CAMSI
Canadian Association of Music Libraries ... CAML
Canadian Association of Pathologists ... CAP
Canadian Association of Public Libraries ... CAPL
Canadian Association of Special Libraries and Information Services ... CASLIS
Canadian Association in Support of the Native Peoples ... CASNP
Canadian Association in Support of the Native Peoples, Toronto, ON, Canada [Library symbol] ... CaOTCAS
Canadian Association of University Teachers ... CAUT
Canadian Astronautical Society ... CAS
Canadian Atlantic Subarea [Canadian Navy] ... CANLANT
Canadian Audubon [A publication] ... Can Aud
Canadian Audubon [A publication] ... Can Audubon
Canadian Australian Line ... CASCO
Canadian Author and Bookman [A publication] ... Can Auth & Book
Canadian Automobile Association ... CAA
Canadian Aviation [A publication] ... Can Av
Canadian Aviation Electronics ... CAE
Canadian Aviation Electronics, Montreal, PQ, Canada [Library symbol] ... CaQMCAE
Canadian Banker [A publication] ... Can Bank
Canadian Banker and ICB Review [A publication] ... Can Banker & ICB R
Canadian Bankers Association ... CBA
Canadian Bar Journal [A publication] ... Can B J
Canadian Bar Review [A publication] ... Can Bar R
Canadian Bar Review [A publication] ... Can B Rev
Canadian Bar Review [A publication] ... CBR
Canadian Barranca Corp. [NASDAQ symbol] ... CBRCF
Canadian Bee Journal [A publication] ... Can Bee J
Canadian Bible College, Regina, SK, Canada [Library symbol] ... CaSRCB
Canadian Book Exchange Centre ... CBEC
Canadian Book Publishers' Council ... CBPC
Canadian Bookman [A publication] ... Canad Bookm
Canadian Bookman [A publication] ... Can Bkman
Canadian Breweries Ltd. [NYSE symbol] [Delisted] ... CNB
Canadian Broadcasting Corporation [State-operated radio and television] ... CBC
Canadian Broadcasting Corp., Engineering Headquarters Library, Montreal, PQ, Canada [Library symbol] ... CaQMCBE
Canadian Broadcasting Corp., Montreal, PQ, Canada [Library symbol] ... CaQMCB
Canadian Broadcasting Corp., Music and Record Library, Halifax, NS, Canada [Library symbol] ... CaNSHCB
Canadian Broadcasting Corp., Music and Record Library, Winnipeg, MB, Canada [Library symbol] ... CaMWC
Canadian Broadcasting Corp., Ottawa, ON, Canada [Library symbol] ... CaOOAR
Canadian Broadcasting Corp., Program Archives, Toronto, ON, Canada [Library symbol] ... CaOTBCP
Canadian Broadcasting Corp., Toronto, ON, Canada [Library symbol] ... CaOTBC
Canadian Business [A publication] ... Can Bus
Canadian Business Magazine [A publication] ... Canada Bus
Canadian Business Magazine [A publication] ... Can Bus Mag
Canadian Business Periodicals Index [A publication] ... Can BPI
Canadian Business Periodicals Index [A publication] ... CBPI
Canadian Business Press ... CBP
Canadian Business Review [A publication] ... Can Bus R
Canadian Cable Television Association ... CCTA
Canadian Cancer Conference [A publication] ... Can Cancer Conf
Canadian Canners Ltd., Burlington, ON, Canada [Library symbol] ... CaOBUCC
Canadian Car Demurrage Bureau, The, Montreal PQ CDA [STAC] ... CCD
Canadian Cartographer [A publication] ... Can Cartogr
Canadian Catholic Conference ... CCC
Canadian Cattlemen [A publication] ... Can Cattlemen
Canadian Celanese Ltd., Drummondville, PQ, Canada [Library symbol] ... CaQDC
Canadian Centre for Films on Art, Ottawa, ON, Canada [Library symbol] ... CaOOCCFA
Canadian Centre for Folk Culture Studies Papers. National Museum of Man Mercury Series [A publication] ... CCFCSP
Canadian Centre for Remote Sensing ... CCRS
Canadian Ceramic Society. Journal [A publication] ... Canadian Ceramic Soc Jour
Canadian Chartered Accountant [Later, CA Magazine] [A publication] ... Can Chart Account
Canadian Chartered Accountant [Later, CA Magazine] [A publication] ... Can Chart Acct
Canadian Chemical Education [A publication] ... Can Chem Educ
Canadian Chemical Processing [A publication] ... Can Chem Process
Canadian Chemical Processing [A publication] ... Cdn Chem P
Canadian Chemistry and Metallurgy [A publication] ... Can Chem & Met
Canadian Chemistry and Process Industries [A publication] ... Can Chem & Process Ind
Canadian Chiefs of Staff Committee ... COSC
Canadian Children's Literature [A publication] ... Can Child Lit
Canadian Civil Liberties Association ... CCLA
Canadian Classification Research Group [International Federation for Documentation] ... CCRG
Canadian Clearinghouse for Ongoing Research in Nursing [University of Alberta] ... CORN
Canadian Club [A whiskey] ... CC
Canadian Club of New York ... CCNY
Canadian Coast Guard [Ottawa, ON, Canada] [FAA designator] ... CTG
Canadian Coastal Zone Atlantic ... CCZA
Canadian Coastal Zone Pacific ... CCZP
Canadian Colonial Airways ... CCA
Canadian Commander, Army, Pacific ... CANCOMARPAC
Canadian Commercial Corporation [Government-owned] ... CCC
Canadian Committee on Cataloguing [Librarianship] ... CCC
Canadian Communicable Disease Center ... CCDC
Canadian Communications and Transportation Commission ... CCTC
Canadian Composer [A publication] ... Can Comp
Canadian Composer [A publication] ... Can Composer
Canadian Computer-Based Reference Service [National Library of Canada] [Information service] ... CAN/CRS
Canadian Conference of Catholic Bishops ... CCCB
Canadian Consortium for Social Research ... CCSR
Canadian Construction Association ... CCA
Canadian Consumer [A publication] ... Can Consumer
Canadian Control System [For convoys in Canadian Coastal Zone] ... CANCON
Canadian Controls and Instrumentation [A publication] ... Can Controls & Instrum
Canadian Controls and Instrumentation [A publication] ... Cdn Contrl
Canadian Copper Refiners Ltd., Montreal, PQ, Canada [Library symbol] ... CaQMCR
Canadian Council for International Cooperation ... CCIC
Canadian Council of Professional Engineers ... CCPE
Canadian Council for Research in Education, Ottawa, ON, Canada [Library symbol] [Obsolete] ... CaOORE
Canadian Council of Resource Ministers, Montreal, PQ, Canada [Library symbol] ... CaQMCCR
Canadian Council on Social Development, Ottawa, ON, Canada [Library symbol] ... CaOOCW
Canadian Council on Urban and Regional Research ... CCURR
Canadian Credit Institute ... CCI
Canadian Cycling Association ... CCA
Canadian Daily Newspaper Publishers Association ... CDNPA
Canadian Dairy Commission ... CDC
Canadian Dairy and Ice Cream Journal [A publication] ... Can Dairy Ice Cream J
Canadian Datasystems [A publication] ... Can Datasyst
Canadian Datasystems [A publication] ... Cdn Data
Canadian Defence Liaison Staff (Washington) ... CDLS(W)
Canadian Defence Research Board ... CDRB
Canadian Dental Association ... CDA
Canadian Dental Association. Journal [A publication] ... Can Dent Assoc J
Canadian Dental Association, Ottawa, ON, Canada [Library symbol] ... CaOOCDA
Canadian Department of Agriculture ... CDA
Canadian Department of Defence Production ... CDDP
Canadian Department of Supply and Services ... CDSS
Canadian Destroyers Atlantic ... CANDESLANT
Canadian Destroyers Far East ... CANDESFE
Canadian Destroyers Pacific ... CANDESPAC
Canadian Deuterium Uranium [Family of nuclear reactors developed in Canada] ... CANDU
Canadian Deuterium Uranium Boiling Light-Water [Nuclear reactor] ... CANDU BLW
Canadian Diamond Drilling Association ... CDDA
Canadian Dimension [A publication] ... Can Dimen
Canadian Dimension [A publication] ... Dimension
Canadian Doctor [A publication] ... Can Doct
Canadian Documentation Centre, Fitness and Sport, Ottawa, ON, Canada [Library symbol] ... CaOOFS
Canadian Dollar [Monetary unit] ... CD
Canadian Dredge & Dock Co. Ltd. [American Stock Exchange symbol] ... CND
Canadian Education Association ... CEA
Canadian Education Association, Toronto, ON, Canada [Library symbol] ... CaOTCEA
Canadian Education Index [A publication] ... CanEdI
Canadian Education and Research Digest [A publication] ... Can Ed Res Digest
Canadian Electrical Association ... CEA
Canadian Electrical Code ... CEC
Canadian Electrical Manufacturers' Association ... CEMA
Canadian Electronic Sales Representatives ... CESR
Canadian Electronics Engineering [A publication] ... Can Electron Eng
Canadian Electronics Engineering [A publication] ... Cdn Elec E
Canadian Embassy, Washington, DC [Library symbol] ... DCaE
Canadian Engineer [A publication] ... Can Eng
Canadian Engineering Standards Association [Later, Canadian Standards Association] ... CESA

Canadian Entomologist [*A publication*] ....Canad Ent
Canadian Entomologist [*A publication*] ....Canad Entom
Canadian Entomologist [*A publication*] ....Can Entom
Canadian Entomologist [*A publication*] ....Can Entomol
Canadian Environmental Law Association....CELA
Canadian Equestrian Team....CET
Canadian Ethnic Studies [*A publication*] ....CEStudies
Canadian Executive Service Overseas....CESO
Canadian Expeditionary Forces....CEF
Canadian Export Association....CEA
Canadian Export Association, Montreal, PQ, Canada [*Library symbol*] ....CaQMCEA
Canadian Export Gas & Oil Ltd. [*American Stock Exchange symbol*] [*Delisted*]....CEX
Canadian Farm Economics [*A publication*]....Can Farm Ec
Canadian Federation of Agriculture ....CFA
Canadian Federation of Biological Societies ....CFBS
Canadian Federation of Engineers and Scientists ....CFES
Canadian Federation of Independent Business....CFIB
Canadian Federation of Labour ....CFL
Canadian Federation of Mayors and Municipalities ....CFMM
Canadian Federation of University Women....CFUW
Canadian Feed and Grain Journal [*A publication*]....Can Feed Grain J
Canadian Fiction Magazine [*A publication*] ....CFM
Canadian Field Artillery....CFA
Canadian Field-Naturalist [*A publication*]....Canad Fld-Nat
Canadian Field-Naturalist [*A publication*]....Can Field-Nat
Canadian Field-Naturalist [*A publication*]....Can Field-Natur
Canadian Film Development Corporation....CFDC
Canadian Film Institute, Ottawa, ON, Canada [*Library symbol*] ....CaOOCF
Canadian Fish Culturist [*A publication*] ....Can Fish Cult
Canadian Fisheries Reports [*A publication*] ....Can Fish Rep
Canadian Folk Music Journal [*A publication*] ....Can Folk Mus
Canadian Folk Music Journal [*A publication*] ....CFMJ
Canadian Food and Allied Workers ....CFAW
Canadian Food Industries [*A publication*]....Can Food Ind
Canadian Food Processors Association....CFPA
Canadian Football League....CFL
Canadian Force Communications System....CFCS
Canadian Forces ....CF
Canadian Forces Administrative Order....CFAO
Canadian Forces Attache....CFA
Canadian Forces Base....CFB
Canadian Forces College, Toronto, ON, Canada [*Library symbol*] ....CaOTRC
Canadian Forces Communication Command....CFCC
Canadian Forces Decoration....CD
Canadian Forces Dental Services Quarterly [*A publication*]....Can Forces Dent Serv Q
Canadian Forces in Europe ....CFE
Canadian Forces Headquarters [*NATO*]....CANFORCEHED
Canadian Forces Headquarters [*NATO*]....CFHQ
Canadian Forces Hospital ....CFH
Canadian Forces Publication ....CFP
Canadian Forces Station ....CFS
Canadian Forces Supplementary Order....CFSO
Canadian Forest Industries [*A publication*] ....Canad For Ind
Canadian Foresters Life Insurance Society [*Formerly, COF*] ....CFLIS
Canadian Forestry Journal [*A publication*]....Can For J
Canadian Forestry Magazine [*A publication*]....Can For M
Canadian Forestry Service. Annual Report of the Forest Insect and Disease Survey [*A publication*]....Can For Serv Annu Rep For Insect Dis Surv
Canadian Forestry Service. Chemical Control Research Institute. File Report [*A publication*]....Can For Serv Chem Control Res Inst File Rep
Canadian Forestry Service. Forest Fire Research Institute. Information Report FF-X [*A publication*]....Can For Serv For Fire Res Inst Inf Rep FF-X
Canadian Forestry Service. Forest Fire Research Institute. Miscellaneous Report FF-X [*A publication*]....Can For Serv For Fire Res Inst Misc Rep FF-X
Canadian Forestry Service. Forestry Technical Report [*A publication*]....Can For Serv For Tech Rep
Canadian Forestry Service. Northern Forest Research Centre. Forestry Report [*A publication*] ....Can For Serv North For Res Cent For Rep
Canadian Forestry Service. Pacific Forest Research Centre. Report BC-X [*A publication*].....Can For Serv Pac For Res Cent Rep BC-X
Canadian Forestry Service. Publication [*A publication*] .... Can For Serv Publ
Canadian Forum [*A publication*]....Canad Forum
Canadian Forum [*A publication*]....Can F
Canadian Forum [*A publication*]....Can Forum
Canadian Forum [*A publication*]....CF
Canadian Fourteenth Air Training Group Headquarters, Winnipeg....CANAIRPEG
Canadian Gas Association ....CGA
Canadian Gas Research Institute, Don Mills, ON, Canada [*Library symbol*]....CaOTCGR
Canadian General Electric Co., Peterborough, ON, Canada [*Library symbol*]....CaOPeTCG
Canadian General Electric Co., Toronto, ON, Canada [*Library symbol*] ....CaOTGE
Canadian General Standards Board [*Formerly, Canadian Government Specifications Board*] ....CGSB
Canadian Geographer [*A publication*]....Can Geog
Canadian Geographer [*A publication*]....Can Geogr
Canadian Geographic [*A publication*]....Can Geographic
Canadian Geographic [*A publication*] ....CG
Canadian Geographical Journal [*A publication*]....Canad Geog J
Canadian Geographical Journal [*A publication*]....Can Geog J
Canadian Geographical Journal [*A publication*]....CGJ
Canadian Geophysical Bulletin [*A publication*] ....Can Geophys Bull
Canadian Geotechnical Journal [*A publication*] .... Canadian Geotech Jour
Canadian Geotechnical Journal [*A publication*] ....Can Geotech J
Canadian Good Roads Association....CGRA
Canadian Government Photo Centre....CGPC
Canadian Government Travel Bureau, Reference Library, Ottawa, ON, Canada [*Library symbol*]....CaOOTB
Canadian Grain Research Laboratory. Annual Report [*A publication*]....Can Grain Res Lab Annu Rep
Canadian Historical Association. Annual Report [*A publication*] ....Can Hist Assoc Ann Rep
Canadian Historical Association. Historical Papers [*A publication*]....Can Hist Assn
Canadian Historical Association. Report [*A publication*] ....Can Hist Assn Rep
Canadian Historical Review [*A publication*]....Can His R
Canadian Historical Review [*A publication*]....Can Hist R
Canadian Historical Review [*A publication*]....CanHR
Canadian Historical Review [*A publication*]....CHR
Canadian Home Insulation Plan....CHIP
Canadian Homestead Oils Ltd. [*American Stock Exchange symbol*] [*Delisted*]....CHO
Canadian Horticulture and Home Magazine [*A publication*]....Can Hort
Canadian Hospital [*A publication*]....Canad Hosp
Canadian Hospital [*A publication*]....Can Hosp
Canadian Hospital Association, Toronto, ON, Canada [*Library symbol*]....CaOTCHA
Canadian Human Rights Commission, Ottawa, ON, Canada [*Library symbol*]....CaOOCHR
Canadian Hydrocarbons Ltd. [*American Stock Exchange symbol*] [*Delisted*]....CDH
Canadian Imperial Bank of Commerce....CIBC
Canadian Imperial Bank of Commerce, Toronto, ON, Canada [*Library symbol*]....CaOTCIB
Canadian Index to Geoscience Data [*A publication*]...... Can Ind Geosci Data
Canadian Industrial Traffic League....CITL
Canadian Industries Limited....CIL
Canadian Industries Limited, Central Research Laboratory, McMasterville, PQ, Canada [*Library symbol*]....CaQMCILR
Canadian Industries Limited, Legal Department, Montreal, PQ, Canada [*Library symbol*]....CaQMCILL
Canadian Industries Limited, Montreal, PQ, Canada [*Library symbol*]....CaQMCIL
Canadian Infantry Corps....CIC
Canadian Infantry Holding Unit....CIHU
Canadian Information Industry Association....CIIA
Canadian Information Processing Society....CIPS
Canadian Insect Pest Review [*A publication*] ....Can Insect Pest Rev
Canadian Institute of Adult Education, Montreal, PQ, Canada [*Library symbol*]....CaQMICE
Canadian Institute of Chartered Accountants ....CICA
Canadian Institute of Food Science and Technology. Journal [*A publication*]....Can I Food
Canadian Institute of Food Science and Technology. Journal [*A publication*]....Can Inst Food Sci Technol J
Canadian Institute of Food Technology. Journal [*A publication*]....Can Inst Food Technol J
Canadian Institute of Forestry....CIF
Canadian Institute of International Affairs....CIIA
Canadian Institute of International Affairs, Toronto, ON, Canada [*Library symbol*]....CaOTCIA
Canadian Institute of Mining and Metallurgy ....CIM
Canadian Institute of Mining and Metallurgy ....CIMM
Canadian Institute of Mining and Metallurgy, Montreal, PQ, Canada [*Library symbol*]....CaQMCIM
Canadian Institute of Mining and Metallurgy. Special Volume [*A publication*]....Can Inst Min Met Spec Vol
Canadian Institute of Mining and Metallurgy. Transactions [*A publication*]....Canadian Inst Mining and Metallurgy Trans
Canadian Institute Proceedings [*A publication*]....Can Inst Pr
Canadian Institute of Surveying and Photogrammetry ....CIS & P
Canadian Insurance [*A publication*] CI
Canadian Intelligence Corps....C Int C
Canadian Intercollegiate Athletic Union ....CIAU
Canadian Intercollegiate Sailing Association ....CISA
Canadian Intergovernmental Conference Secretariat ....CICS
Canadian International Development Agency [*Formerly, External Aid Office*]....CIDA
Canadian International Development Agency, Ottawa, ON, Canada [*Library symbol*]....CaOOCD

Canadian and International Education [*A publication*] .... Can Int Educ
Canadian International Power Co. Ltd. [*American Stock Exchange symbol*] [*Delisted*] CIV
Canadian Inventory of Historic Building [*Information service*] .... CIHB
Canadian Javelin Ltd. [*American Stock Exchange symbol*] [*Delisted*] .... CJV
Canadian Jewish Congress .... CJC
Canadian Jewish Congress Library, Montreal, PQ, Canada [*Library symbol*] .... CaQMCJ
Canadian Joint Staff .... CJS
Canadian Journal [*Toronto*] [*A publication*] .... Can J
Canadian Journal of African Studies [*A publication*] .... Canad J Afr Stud
Canadian Journal of African Studies [*A publication*] .... Can J Afr S
Canadian Journal of African Studies [*A publication*] .... Can J Afr Stud
Canadian Journal of African Studies [*A publication*] .... CJAS
Canadian Journal of Agricultural Economics [*A publication*] .... Can J Agr Econ
Canadian Journal of Agricultural Economics [*A publication*] .... Can J Agric Econ
Canadian Journal of Agricultural Science [*A publication*] .... Can J Ag Sci
Canadian Journal of Animal Science [*A publication*] .... Can J Anim
Canadian Journal of Animal Science [*A publication*] .... Can J Anim Sci
Canadian Journal of Applied Sport Sciences [*A publication*] .... Can J Appl Sport Sci
Canadian Journal of Behavioural Science [*A publication*] .... Can J Behav Sci
Canadian Journal of Behavioural Science [*A publication*] .... Can J Beh S
Canadian Journal of Biochemistry [*A publication*] .... Can J Bioch
Canadian Journal of Biochemistry [*A publication*] .... Can J Biochem
Canadian Journal of Biochemistry and Physiology [*A publication*] .... Canad J Biochem
Canadian Journal of Biochemistry and Physiology [*A publication*] .... Can J Biochem Physiol
Canadian Journal of Botany [*A publication*] .... Canad J Bot
Canadian Journal of Botany [*A publication*] .... Can J Bot
Canadian Journal of Chemical Engineering [*A publication*] .... Can J Chem Eng
Canadian Journal of Chemical Engineering [*A publication*] .... Can J Ch En
Canadian Journal of Chemistry [*A publication*] .... Canad J Chem
Canadian Journal of Chemistry [*A publication*] .... Can J Chem
Canadian Journal of Civil Engineering [*A publication*] .... Can J Civ Eng
Canadian Journal of Civil Engineering/Revue Canadienne de Genie Civil [*A publication*] .... Can J Civ Eng/Rev Can Genie Civ
Canadian Journal of Comparative Medicine [*A publication*] .... Can J Com M
Canadian Journal of Comparative Medicine [*A publication*] .... Can J Comp Med
Canadian Journal of Comparative Medicine and Veterinary Science [*A publication*] .... Can J Comp Med Vet Sci
Canadian Journal of Corrections [*A publication*] .... Can J Corr
Canadian Journal of Criminology and Corrections [*A publication*] .... Can J Crim
Canadian Journal of Earth Sciences [*A publication*] .... Can J Earth
Canadian Journal of Earth Sciences [*A publication*] .... Can J Earth Sci
Canadian Journal of Economics [*A publication*] .... Canad J Econ
Canadian Journal of Economics [*A publication*] .... Can J Ec
Canadian Journal of Economics [*A publication*] .... Can J Econ
Canadian Journal of Economics [*A publication*] .... CJ
Canadian Journal of Economics and Political Science [*A publication*] .... Can J Econ Polit Sci
Canadian Journal of Economics and Political Science [*A publication*] .... Can J Econ & Pol Sci
Canadian Journal of Economics and Political Science [*A publication*] .... CJE
Canadian Journal of Forest Research [*A publication*] .... Can J Forest Res
Canadian Journal of Forest Research [*A publication*] .... Can J For Res
Canadian Journal of Genetics and Cytology [*A publication*] .... Can J Genet
Canadian Journal of Genetics and Cytology [*A publication*] .... Can J Genet Cytol
Canadian Journal of History [*A publication*] .... Can J Hist
Canadian Journal of History [*A publication*] .... Can Jour Hist
Canadian Journal of History [*A publication*] .... CJH
Canadian Journal of Hospital Pharmacy [*A publication*] .... Can J Hosp Pharm
Canadian Journal of Industry [*A publication*] .... Canad J
Canadian Journal of Italian Studies [*A publication*] .... C J It S
Canadian Journal of Linguistics [*A publication*] .... Can J L
Canadian Journal of Linguistics [*A publication*] .... Can J Lingu
Canadian Journal of Linguistics [*A publication*] .... CJL
Canadian Journal of Mathematics [*A publication*] .... Can J Math
Canadian Journal of Mathematics [*A publication*] .... CDJM
Canadian Journal of Medical Science [*A publication*] .... Canad J Med Sc
Canadian Journal of Medical Science [*A publication*] .... Can J Med Sci
Canadian Journal of Medical Technology [*A publication*] .... Canad J Med Tech
Canadian Journal of Medical Technology [*A publication*] .... Canad J Med Technol
Canadian Journal of Medical Technology [*A publication*] .... Can J Med T
Canadian Journal of Medical Technology [*A publication*] .... Can J Med Technol
Canadian Journal of Microbiology [*A publication*] .... Canad J Microbiol
Canadian Journal of Microbiology [*A publication*] .... Can J Micro
Canadian Journal of Microbiology [*A publication*] .... Can J Microbiol
Canadian Journal of Neurological Science [*A publication*] .... Can J Neurol Sci
Canadian Journal of Occupational Therapy [*A publication*] .... Can J Occup Ther
Canadian Journal of Ophthalmology [*A publication*] .... Can J Ophth
Canadian Journal of Ophthalmology [*A publication*] .... Can J Ophthalmol
Canadian Journal of Otolaryngology [*A publication*] .... Can J Otolaryngol
Canadian Journal of Pharmaceutical Sciences [*A publication*] .... Can J Pharm Sci
Canadian Journal of Pharmaceutical Sciences [*A publication*] .... Can J Ph Sc
Canadian Journal of Philosophy [*A publication*] .... Can J Phil
Canadian Journal of Philosophy [*A publication*] .... CJPhil
Canadian Journal of Physics [*A publication*] .... Canad J Phys
Canadian Journal of Physics [*A publication*] .... Can J Phys
Canadian Journal of Physiology and Pharmacology [*A publication*] .... Can J Physiol Pharmacol
Canadian Journal of Physiology and Pharmacology [*A publication*] .... Can J Physl
Canadian Journal of Plant Science [*A publication*] .... Canad J Pl Sci
Canadian Journal of Plant Science [*A publication*] .... Can J Plant
Canadian Journal of Plant Science [*A publication*] .... Can J Plant Sci
Canadian Journal of Political Science [*A publication*] .... Canad J Polit Sci
Canadian Journal of Political Science [*A publication*] .... Can J Poli
Canadian Journal of Political Science [*A publication*] .... Can J Pol Sci
Canadian Journal of Psychiatric Nursing [*A publication*] .... Canad J Psychiatr Nurs
Canadian Journal of Psychiatric Nursing [*A publication*] .... Can J Psychiatr Nurs
Canadian Journal of Psychiatry [*A publication*] .... Can J Psychiatry
Canadian Journal of Psychology [*A publication*] .... Canad J Psychol
Canadian Journal of Psychology [*A publication*] .... Can J Psych
Canadian Journal of Psychology [*A publication*] .... Can J Psychol
Canadian Journal of Psychology [*A publication*] .... CJP
Canadian Journal of Psychology [*A publication*] .... CJPs
Canadian Journal of Psychology [*A publication*] .... CJPSA
Canadian Journal of Public Health [*A publication*] .... Canad J Public Health
Canadian Journal of Public Health [*A publication*] .... Can J Publ
Canadian Journal of Public Health [*A publication*] .... Can J Public Health
Canadian Journal of Radiography, Radiotherapy, Nuclear Medicine [*A publication*] .... Canad J Radiogr Radiother Nucl Med
Canadian Journal of Radiography, Radiotherapy, Nuclear Medicine (English Edition) [*A publication*] .... Can J Radiogr Radiother Nucl Med (Engl Ed)
Canadian Journal of Remote Sensing [*A publication*] .... Can J Remote Sens
Canadian Journal of Research [*A publication*] .... Can J Res
Canadian Journal of Research. Section C. Botanical Sciences [*A publication*] .... Can J Res Sect C Bot Sci
Canadian Journal of Research. Section D. Zoological Sciences [*A publication*] .... Can J Res Sect D Zool Sci
Canadian Journal of Research. Section E. Medical Sciences [*A publication*] .... Can J Res Sect E Med Sci
Canadian Journal of Soil Science [*A publication*] .... Canad J Soil Sci
Canadian Journal of Soil Science [*A publication*] .... Can J Soil
Canadian Journal of Soil Science [*A publication*] .... Can J Soil Sci
Canadian Journal of Spectroscopy [*A publication*] .... Can J Spect
Canadian Journal of Spectroscopy [*A publication*] .... Can J Spectrosc
Canadian Journal of Spectroscopy [*A publication*] .... Can J Spectry
Canadian Journal of Statistics [*A publication*] .... Canad J Statist
Canadian Journal of Statistics [*A publication*] .... Cand J St
Canadian Journal of Surgery [*A publication*] .... Can J Surg
Canadian Journal of Theology [*A publication*] .... Can J Th
Canadian Journal of Theology [*A publication*] .... CJT
Canadian Journal of Zoology [*A publication*] .... Canad J Zool
Canadian Journal of Zoology [*A publication*] .... Can J Zool
Canadian Journal of Zoology [*A publication*] .... CJZ
Canadian Kennel Club .... CKC
Canadian Labour [*A publication*] .... Can Lab
Canadian Labour Congress CLC
Canadian Labour Congress, Ottawa, ON, Canada [*Library symbol*] .... CaOOCLC
Canadian Land Forces Command and Staff College, Kingston, ON, Canada [*Library symbol*] .... CaOKF
Canadian Law Information Council CLIC
Canadian Library [*A publication*] .... Canad Lib
Canadian Library [*A publication*] .... Can Lib
Canadian Library Association [*Also known as ACB and CLA*] .... CANLA
Canadian Library Association [*Also known as ACB and CANLA*] .... CLA
Canadian Library Association. Bulletin [*A publication*] .... Canadian Lib Assn Bul
Canadian Library Association. Bulletin [*A publication*] .... Canad Lib Assn Bul
Canadian Library Association. Bulletin [*A publication*] .... Can Lib Assn Bul
Canadian Library Association. Feliciter [*A publication*] .... Canad Lib Assn Feliciter
Canadian Library Association, Ottawa, ON, Canada [*Library symbol*] .... CanLA
Canadian Library Bulletin [*A publication*] .... Can Lib Bull
Canadian Library Exhibitors' Association .... CLEA
Canadian Library Journal [*A publication*] .... Canad Lib J
Canadian Library Journal [*A publication*] .... Can Lib J
Canadian Library Journal [*A publication*] .... Can Libr J
Canadian Library Trustees' Association .... CLTA
Canadian Literature [*A publication*] .... Can L

Canadian Literature [*A publication*] .... Can Lit
Canadian Lumbermen's Association .... CLA
Canadian Machinery and Metalworking [*A publication*] .... Can Mach Metalwork
Canadian Machinery and Metalworking [*A publication*] .... Cdn Machin
Canadian Magazine [*A publication*] .... Canad M
Canadian Major Junior Hockey League .... CMJHL
Canadian Manufacturers Association .... CMA
Canadian Manufacturers of Chemical Specialties Association .... CMCSA
Canadian Marconi Co. [*American Stock Exchange symbol*] .... CMW
Canadian Marconi Co., Montreal, PQ, Canada [*Library symbol*] .... CaQMCM
Canadian Maritime Command .... CANMARCOM
Canadian Maritime Commander, Atlantic .... CANCOMARLANT
Canadian Mathematical Bulletin [*A publication*] .... Can Math B
Canadian Medical Association .... CMA
Canadian Medical Association. Journal [*A publication*] .... Canad Med Assoc J
Canadian Medical Association. Journal [*A publication*] .... Can Med A J
Canadian Medical Association. Journal [*A publication*] .... Can Med Assn J
Canadian Medical Association. Journal [*A publication*] .... Can Med Assoc J
Canadian Medical Association. Journal [*A publication*] .... CMAJ
Canadian Medical Association. Journal [*A publication*] .... CMAJA
Canadian Medical Protective Association .... CMPA
Canadian Member, Canadian Joint Staff, Washington, DC .... CANAVUS
Canadian Memorial Chiropractic College, Toronto, ON, Canada [*Library symbol*] .... CaOTCMC
Canadian Merchant Service Guild .... CMSG
Canadian Merrill Ltd. [*American Stock Exchange symbol*] [*Delisted*] .... CMJ
Canadian Metallurgical Quarterly [*A publication*] .... Can Metall Q
Canadian Metallurgical Quarterly [*A publication*] .... Can Metal Q
Canadian Metallurgical Quarterly [*A publication*] .... Can Met Quart
Canadian Metalworking/Machine Production [*A publication*] .... Can Metalwork/Mach Prod
Canadian Metalworking Production [*A publication*] .... Can Metalwork Prod
Canadian Metric Association .... CMA
Canadian Microfilming Co., Montreal, PQ, Canada [*Library symbol*] .... CanM
Canadian Micrographic Society .... CMS
Canadian Military Electronics Standards Agency .... CAMESA
Canadian Militia .... CM
Canadian Milling and Feed [*A publication*] .... Can Milling Feed
Canadian Mineral Industry. Review [*A publication*] .... Can Miner Ind Rev
Canadian Mineral Occurrence Index [*Information service*] .... CANMINDEX
Canadian Mineralogist [*A publication*] .... Can Mineral
Canadian Mining Journal [*A publication*] .... Can Min J
Canadian Mining and Metallurgical Bulletin [*A publication*] .... Can Mining Met Bul
Canadian Mining and Metallurgical Bulletin [*A publication*] .... Can Min Met
Canadian Mining and Metallurgical Bulletin [*A publication*] .... Can Min Metall Bull
Canadian Mining and Metallurgical Bulletin [*A publication*] .... Can Min & Metallurg Bull
Canadian Mining and Metallurgical Bulletin [*A publication*] .... Can Min & Met Bul
Canadian Mining Review [*A publication*] .... Can M Rv
Canadian Modern Language Review [*A publication*] .... CMLR
Canadian Monthly [*A publication*] .... Canad Mo
Canadian Mounted Rifles .... CMR
Canadian Music Journal [*A publication*] .... Can Mus J
Canadian Musician [*A publication*] .... Can Mus
Canadian Mutual Aid Board [*World War II*] .... CMAB
Canadian National Committee for Earthquake Engineering .... CANCEE
Canadian National Exhibition [*Held annually in Toronto*] .... CNE
Canadian National Institute for the Blind .... CNIB
Canadian National Railways [*AAR code*] .... CN
Canadian National Railways .... CNR
Canadian National Railways, Chemical Library, Montreal, PQ, Canada [*Library symbol*] .... CaQMCNC
Canadian National Railways, Montreal, PQ, Canada [*Library symbol*] .... CaQMCN
Canadian National Recreation Association .... CNRA
Canadian National Steamships [*AAR code*] .... CNSS
Canadian Natural Deuterium Uranium Pressurized Heavy-Water [*Nuclear reactor*] .... CANDU PHW
Canadian Naturalist and Geologist and Proceedings of the Natural History Society of Montreal [*A publication*] .... Can Nat
Canadian Naval Air Station .... CANAS
Canadian Naval Board .... CNB
Canadian Naval Commander Newfoundland .... CANCOMNEW
Canadian Naval Mission Overseas .... CNMO
Canadian Naval Service .... CNS
Canadian Network for Sampling Precipitation .... CANSAP
Canadian News Service .... CNS
Canadian Newspaper Index [*A publication*] .... CNI
Canadian Northeast Wideband Systems [*Air Force*] .... CNEWS
Canadian Northwest Atlantic Area .... CNA
Canadian NOTAM [*Notice to Airmen*] .... CANOT
Canadian Nuclear Association .... CNA
Canadian Nuclear Association. Annual International Conference (Proceedings) [*A publication*] .... Can Nucl Assoc Annu Int Conf (Pro)
Canadian Nuclear Society. Transactions [*A publication*] .... Can Nucl Soc Trans
Canadian Numismatic Journal [*A publication*] .... CNJ
Canadian Nurse [*A publication*] .... Canad Nurse
Canadian Nurse [*A publication*] .... Can Nurse
Canadian Nurse [*A publication*] .... CANUA
Canadian Nurses' Association, Ottawa, ON, Canada [*Library symbol*] .... CaOOCN
Canadian Occidental Petroleum Ltd. [*American Stock Exchange symbol*] .... CXY
Canadian Ocean Escort Vessel .... COEV
Canadian Oceanographic Data Centre .... CODC
Canadian Officers Training Corps .... COTC
Canadian Olympic Association .... COA
Canadian Olympic Regatta at Kingston .... CORK
Canadian On-Line Enquiry System [*Pronounced "can-olay"*] .... CAN/OLE
Canadian Operational Research Society .... CORS
Canadian Oral History Association. Journal/Societe Canadienne d'Histoire Orale. Journal [*A publication*] .... COHAJ
Canadian Order of Foresters [*Later, CFLIS*] .... COF
Canadian Overseas Telecommunications Corporation .... COTC
Canadian Owners and Pilots Association .... COPA
Canadian Pacific Airlines Ltd. [*ICAO designator*] .... CP
Canadian Pacific Airlines Ltd. .... CPA
Canadian Pacific Airlines Limited .... CPAL
Canadian Pacific Enterprises [*NYSE symbol*] .... ENT
Canadian Pacific Ltd. [*NYSE symbol*] .... CP
Canadian Pacific Railway .... CPR
Canadian Pacific Railway Co., Montreal, PQ, Canada [*Library symbol*] .... CaQMCP
Canadian Packaging [*A publication*] .... Can Pkg
Canadian Packaging [*A publication*] .... Cdn Pkg
Canadian Paper Money Journal [*A publication*] .... CPMJ
Canadian Paperworkers Union .... CPU
Canadian Passenger Transportation Corporation [*Proposed*] .... CPTC
Canadian Patent Office. Record [*A publication*] .... Can Pat Office Recd
Canadian Patents and Developments Limited .... CPDL
Canadian Peace Research Institute .... CPRI
Canadian Peat Society. Bulletin [*A publication*] .... Can Peat Soc B
Canadian Penitentiary Service .... CPS
Canadian Pension Commission .... CPC
Canadian Periodical Index [*A publication*] .... CanI
Canadian Periodical Index [*A publication*] .... Can Ind
Canadian Periodical Index [*Canadian Library Association*] [*Information service*] .... CPI
Canadian Periodical Reference Services, Ottawa, ON, Canada [*Library symbol*] [*Obsolete*] .... CaOOCAP
Canadian Personnel and Industrial Relations Journal [*A publication*] .... Canad Person Industr Relat J
Canadian Personnel and Industrial Relations Journal [*A publication*] .... Can Pers
Canadian Petroleum Association .... CPA
Canadian Petroleum Association, Calgary, AB, Canada [*Library symbol*] .... CaACCP
Canadian Pharmaceutical Association .... CPA
Canadian Pharmaceutical Journal [*A publication*] .... Can Pharm J
Canadian Plant Disease Survey [*A publication*] .... Can Plant Dis Surv
Canadian Plastics [*A publication*] .... Can Plastics
Canadian Plastics [*A publication*] .... Cdn Plast
Canadian Poetry [*A publication*] .... Can Po
Canadian Poetry [*A publication*] .... Can Poetry
Canadian Police Association .... CPA
Canadian Police College, Royal Canadian Mounted Police, Ottawa, ON, Canada [*Library symbol*] .... CaOOCPC
Canadian Police Information Centre .... CPIC
Canadian Political Science Association .... CPSA
Canadian Postal Corps [*Later, RCPC*] .... CPC
Canadian Postmaster's Association .... CPA
Canadian Potash Producers Association .... CPPA
Canadian Poultry Review [*A publication*] .... Can Poult Rev
Canadian Poultry Review [*A publication*] .... Can Poultry Rev
Canadian Power Squadrons [*Boating*] .... CPS
Canadian Practitioner [*A publication*] .... Canad Pract
Canadian Practitioner and Review [*A publication*] .... Canad Pract and Rev
Canadian Press .... CP
Canadian Prestressed Concrete Institute .... CPCI
Canadian Printer and Publisher [*A publication*] .... Can Printer Publ
Canadian Psychiatric Association .... CPA
Canadian Psychiatric Association. Journal [*A publication*] .... Canad Psychiat Ass J
Canadian Psychiatric Association. Journal [*A publication*] .... Can Psychi
Canadian Psychiatric Association. Journal [*A publication*] .... Can Psychiatr Assoc J
Canadian Psychiatric Association. Journal [*A publication*] .... CPAJA
Canadian Psychological Association .... CPA
Canadian Psychological Review [*A publication*] .... Can Psychol Rev
Canadian Psychological Review [*A publication*] .... Can Psych R
Canadian Psychologist [*A publication*] .... Can Psychol
Canadian Public Administration [*A publication*] .... Canad Publ Adm
Canadian Public Administration/Administration Publique du Canada [*A publication*] .... Can Pub Admin
Canadian Public Administration/Administration Publique du Canada [*A publication*] .... Can Publ Ad

Canadian Public Health Association ... CPHA
Canadian Public Relations Society ... CPRS
Canadian Pulp and Paper Association ... CPPA
Canadian Pulp and Paper Association, Montreal, PQ, Canada [*Library symbol*] ... CaQMNA
Canadian Pulp and Paper Industry [*A publication*] ... Can Pulp Paper Ind
Canadian Pulp and Paper Industry [*A publication*] ... Cdn P & P
Canadian Radio-Direction Finder ... CRDF
Canadian Radio-Television and Telecommunications Commission ... CRTC
Canadian Radio-Television and Telecommunications Commission, Ottawa, ON, Canada [*Library symbol*] ... CaOORT
Canadian Railway Labour Association ... CRLA
Canadian Real Estate Association ... CREA
Canadian Record of Natural History and Geology [*A publication*] ... Can Rec N H
Canadian Record of Science [*A publication*] ... Can Rec Sc
Canadian Red Cross, Ottawa, ON, Canada [*Library symbol*] ... CaOOCRC
Canadian Religious Conference ... CRC
Canadian Research [*A publication*] ... Can Res
Canadian Research and Development [*A publication*] ... Can Res Dev
Canadian Restaurant Association ... CRA
Canadian Review of American Studies [*A publication*] ... Can R Am St
Canadian Review of American Studies [*A publication*] ... C Rev AS
Canadian Review of Sociology and Anthropology [*A publication*] ... Canad R Sociol Anthropol
Canadian Review of Sociology and Anthropology [*A publication*] ... Can R Soc A
Canadian Review of Sociology and Anthropology [*A publication*] ... Can R Sociol Anth
Canadian Review of Sociology and Anthropology [*A publication*] ... Can R Sociol & Anthrop
Canadian Review of Studies in Nationalism [*A publication*] ... Can R Stud Nat
Canadian Risk Management and Business Insurance [*A publication*] ... RMBI
Canadian Sales Finance Long Form Report ... CANSAF
Canadian Schizophrenia Foundation ... CSF
Canadian School Library Association ... CSLA
Canadian School of Missions and Ecumenical Institute, Toronto, ON, Canada [*Library symbol*] ... CaOTCM
Canadian Science Monthly [*A publication*] ... Can Sc Mo
Canadian Selective Dissemination of Information ... CAN/SDI
Canadian Services College ... CANSERVCOL
Canadian Services Medical Journal [*A publication*] ... Can Serv Med J
Canadian Shipbuilding and Ship Repairing Association ... CSSRA
Canadian Siberian Expeditionary Force ... CSEF
Canadian Slavic Studies [*A publication*] ... CSS
Canadian Slavonic Papers [*A publication*] ... Canad Slavonic Pap
Canadian Slavonic Papers [*A publication*] ... Can Slav P
Canadian Slavonic Papers [*A publication*] ... CanSP
Canadian Slavonic Papers [*A publication*] ... CSLP
Canadian Slavonic Papers [*A publication*] ... CSP
Canadian Society for Chemical Engineering ... CSChE
Canadian Society for Electrical Engineers ... CSEE
Canadian Society of Laboratory Technologists. Bulletin [*A publication*] ... Canad Soc Lab Technol Bull
Canadian Society of New York ... CSNY
Canadian Society of Petroleum Geologists. Memoir [*A publication*] ... Can Soc Pet Geol Mem
Canadian Society of Wildlife and Fishery Biologists ... CSWFB
Canadian Socio-Economic Information Management System ... CANSIM
Canadian Soil Science Society ... CSSS
Canadian Spectroscopy [*A publication*] ... Can Spectrosc
Canadian Spectroscopy [*A publication*] ... Can Spectry
Canadian Sport Parachuting Association ... CSPA
Canadian Standards Association ... CSA
Canadian Standards Association. CSA Standard [*A publication*] ... Can Stand Ass CSA Stand
Canadian Standards Association, Toronto, ON, Canada [*Library symbol*] ... CaOTCSA
Canadian Structural Engineering Conference [*A publication*] ... Can Struct Eng Conf
Canadian Studies in German Language and Literature [*A publication*] ... CSGLL
Canadian Superior Oil Ltd. [*American Stock Exchange symbol*] [*Delisted*] ... CDS
Canadian Superior Oil Ltd., Calgary, AB, Canada [*Library symbol*] ... CaACCS
Canadian Surveyor [*A publication*] ... Can Surv
Canadian Symposium of Remote Sensing. Proceedings [*A publication*] ... Can Symp Remote Sensing Proc
Canadian Tactical Air Command Headquarters ... CANAIRTAC
Canadian Tax Foundation, Toronto, ON, Canada [*Library symbol*] ... CaOTCT
Canadian Tax Journal [*A publication*] ... Can Tax J
Canadian Teachers Federation ... CTF
Canadian Teachers Federation, Ottawa, ON, Canada [*Library symbol*] ... CaOOCT
Canadian Textile Journal [*A publication*] ... Can Text J
Canadian Tobacco Grower [*A publication*] ... Can Tob Grower
Canadian Tobacco Manufacturers Council, Montreal, PQ, Canada [*Library symbol*] ... CaQMCTM
Canadian Token [*A publication*] ... CT
Canadian Trade and Tariffs Committee ... CTTC
Canadian Transatlantic Telephone Cable ... CANTAT
Canadian Transport Commission ... CTC
Canadian Transport Commission, Air Transport Committee, Ottawa, ON, Canada [*Library symbol*] [*Obsolete*] ... CaOOAT
Canadian Transport Commission, Ottawa, ON, Canada [*Library symbol*] ... CaOOTT
Canadian Transportation Research Information Service ... CTRIS
Canadian, TX [*Location identifier*] [*FAA*] ... HHF
Canadian Underwriter [*A publication*] ... CU
Canadian Union College ... CUC
Canadian Union College, College Heights, AB, Canada [*Library symbol*] ... CaAChCU
Canadian Union of Jewish Students ... CUJS
Canadian Union of Postal Workers ... CUPW
Canadian Union of Public Employees ... CUPE
Canadian-United States Eastern Power Complex ... CANUSE
Canadian University Computer Network ... CANUNET
Canadian University Service Overseas ... CUSO
Canadian University Service Overseas, Ottawa, ON, Canada [*Library symbol*] ... CaOOCUS
Canadian Urban Transit Association ... CUTA
Canadian Veterinary Journal [*A publication*] ... Can Vet J
Canadian Veterinary Record [*A publication*] ... Canad Vet Rec
Canadian Veterinary Record [*A publication*] ... Can Vet Record
Canadian Vintage Wireless Association [*Defunct*] ... CVWA
Canadian War Museum, Ottawa, ON, Canada [*Library symbol*] ... CaOONMC
Canadian War Supplies Assignment Board [*World War II*] ... CWSAB
Canadian Weekly Bulletin [*A publication*] ... CWB
Canadian Welder and Fabricator [*A publication*] ... Can Welder Fabr
Canadian Welding Development Institute, Toronto, ON, Canada [*Library symbol*] ... CaOTCWB
Canadian Welfare [*A publication*] ... Can Wel
Canadian Welfare [*A publication*] ... CW
Canadian Western Approaches ... CWA
Canadian Westinghouse Library, Hamilton, ON, Canada [*Library symbol*] ... CaOHW
Canadian Wheat Board ... CWB
Canadian Wheat Board, Winnipeg, MB, Canada [*Library symbol*] ... CaMWCWB
Canadian Wildlife Service [*A publication*] ... Can Wildl Serv
Canadian Wildlife Service ... CWS
Canadian Wildlife Service. Occasional Papers [*A publication*] ... Can Wildl Serv Occas Pap
Canadian Wildlife Service. Progress Notes [*A publication*] ... Can Wildl Serv Prog Notes
Canadian Wildlife Service. Report Series [*A publication*] ... Can Wildl Serv Rep Ser
Canadian Women's Army Corps ... CWAC
Canadian Women's Press Club [*Later, Media Club of Canada*] ... CWPC
Canadian Woodmen of the World ... CWW
Canadian Yearbook of International Law [*A publication*] ... Canad Yb Int Law
Canadian Yearbook of International Law [*A publication*] ... Can Yearbook Int L
Canadian Youth Hostels Association ... CYHA
Canady, J. G., Charlotte NC [*STAC*] ... CJG
Canaima [*Venezuela*] [*Airport symbol*] ... CAJ
Canal [*Board on Geographic Names*] ... CNL
Canal Defense Light ... CDL
Canal Flats, BC [*Television station call letters*] ... CBUBT-1
Canal Fulton Public Library, Canal Fulton, OH [*Library symbol*] ... OCnf
Canal and Lake ... C and L
Canal, Lake, and Rail ... CL & R
Canal-Randolph Corp. [*NYSE symbol*] ... CRH
Canal Safe Transit System ... CASTS
Canal Society of New York State ... CSNYS
Canal Zone [*MARC country of publication code*] [*Library of Congress*] ... cz
Canal Zone [*MARC geographic area code*] [*Library of Congress*] ... nccz---
Canal Zone [*Three-letter standard code*] ... PCZ
Canal Zone [*Two-letter standard code*] ... PZ
Canal Zone [*Postal code*] ... CZ
Canal Zone Biological Area [*A preserve administered by the Smithsonian Institution*] [*Later, Smithsonian Tropical Research Institute*] ... CZBA
Canal Zone Government [*Superseded by Panama Canal Commission*] ... CZG
Canal Zone Junior College ... CZJC
Canal Zone Study Group ... CZSG
Canandaigua, NY [*Radio station call letters*] ... WCGR
Canandaigua, NY [*Radio station call letters*] ... WFLC
Canandaigua Veterans Administration Medical Center Library, Canandaigua, NY [*OCLC symbol*] ... VQC
Canandaigua Wine [*American Stock Exchange symbol*] ... CDG
Canarias [*Formerly, Tenerife*] [*Spain*] [*Geomagnetic observatory code*] ... TEN
Canary Islands ... CYI
Canary Islands [*MARC geographic area code*] [*Library of Congress*] ... lnca---

CanAtom Limited, Montreal, PQ, Canada [*Library symbol*] ...... CaQMCL
Canaveral [*Obsolete*] [*NASA*] ...... CAN
Canaveral Council of Technical Societies ...... CCTS
Canaveral District Office [*Obsolete*] [*NASA*] ...... CANDO
Canaveral International Corp. [*NASDAQ symbol*] ...... CANI
Canaveral International Corp. [*American Stock Exchange symbol*] [*Delisted*] CVL
Canaveral Test Report ...... CTR
Canavieiras [*Brazil*] [*Airport symbol*] ...... CNV
Canberra [*Australia*] [*Geomagnetic observatory code*] ...... CAA
Canberra [*Australia*] [*Seismograph station code, US Geological Survey*] ...... CAN
Canberra [*Australia*] [*Airport symbol*] ...... CBR
Canberra [*Australia*] ...... CNB
Canby Public Library, Canby, OR [*Library symbol*] ...... OrCan
Canby Union High School, Canby, OR [*Library symbol*] ...... OrCanHS
CANCAM Proceedings. Canadian Congress of Applied Mechanics [*A publication*] ...... CANCAM Proc Can Congr Appl Mech
Cancel ...... CAN
Cancel ...... CNCL
Cancel [*or Cancellation*] ...... CNL
Cancel ...... CNX
Cancel Approved Arrival [*Aviation*] ...... CXA
Cancel Approved Departure [*Aviation*] ...... CXD
Cancel on Back [*Deltiology*] ...... C/B
Cancel Back Order ...... CBO
Cancel Corridor Assignment [*Aviation*] ...... CCA
Cancel on Face [*Deltiology*] ...... C/F
Cancel Flight Plan On [*Aviation*] ...... CNLFP
Cancel IFR [*Instrument Flight Rules*] **Flight Plan** [*Aviation*] ...... CIFP
Cancel Instrument Flight Rules Clearance Previously Given [*Aviation*] ...... CIFR
Cancel Launch in Progress [*Air Force*] ...... CLIP
Cancel VFR [*Visual Flight Rules*] **Flight Plan** [*Aviation*] ...... CVFP
Cancel Visual Flight Rules Flight Plan [*Aviation*] ...... CVFR
Canceled C
Canceled ...... CANC
Canceled CX
Canceled Concurrent with Next Federal Register Amendment ...... CCFRA
Canceled Transmission ...... CANTRAN
Canceling Former Order ...... CFO
Cancellation Addendum Sales Order ...... CASO
Cancellation of Amplitude Modulation ...... CAM
Cancellation Ratio [*Aviation*] ...... CR
Cancelled to Order [*Philately*] ...... CTO
Cancer C
Cancer [*or Carcinoma*] [*Medicine*] ...... CA
Cancer [*Constellation*] ...... Canc
Cancer [*Constellation*] ...... Cnc
Cancer Assessment Group [*Environmental Protection Agency*] ...... CAG
Cancer Biochemistry Biophysics [*A publication*] ...... Canc Bioc B
Cancer Biochemistry Biophysics [*A publication*] ...... Cancer Biochem Biophys
Cancer Bulletin [*A publication*] ...... Cancer Bull
Cancer Care, Incorporated [*of the National Cancer Foundation*] CCI
Cancer of the Cervix [*Medicine*] ...... CACX
Cancer Chemotherapy Abstracts [*A publication*] ...... CCA
Cancer Chemotherapy Annual [*Elsevier Book Series*] [*A publication*] ...... CCA
Cancer Chemotherapy National Service Center [*National Institutes of Health*] ...... CCNSC
Cancer Chemotherapy and Pharmacology [*A publication*] ...... Cancer Chemother Pharmacol
Cancer Chemotherapy Reports [*A publication*] ...... Cancer Chemother Rep
Cancer Chemotherapy Reports [*A publication*] ...... Cancer Chem Rep
Cancer Chemotherapy Reports. Part 1 [*A publication*] ...... Canc Ch P 1
Cancer Chemotherapy Reports. Part 1 [*A publication*] ...... Cancer Chemother Rep Part 1
Cancer Chemotherapy Reports. Part 2 [*A publication*] ...... Canc Ch P 2
Cancer Chemotherapy Reports. Part 2 [*A publication*] ...... Cancer Chemother Rep Part 2
Cancer Chemotherapy Reports. Part 3 [*A publication*] ...... Canc Ch P 3
Cancer Chemotherapy Reports. Part 3 [*A publication*] ...... Cancer Chemother Rep Part 3
Cancer Chemotherapy Screening Data [*A publication*] ...... Cancer Chemother Screening Data
Cancer Clinical Trials [*A publication*] ...... Cancer Clin Trials
Cancer Connection CC
Cancer Control Society ...... CCS
Cancer Cytology [*A publication*] ...... Cancer Cytol
Cancer Cytology Foundation of America [*Later, National Cancer Cytology Center*] ...... CCF
Cancer Cytology Foundation of America [*Later, National Cancer Cytology Center*] ...... CCFA
Cancer Detection and Prevention [*A publication*] ...... Cancer Detect Prev
Cancer Federation, Incorporated ...... CFI
Cancer Free [*Medicine*] ...... CF
Cancer Genetics and Cytogenetics [*A publication*] ...... Cancer Genet Cytogenet
Cancer Guidance Institute ...... CGI
Cancer Hazards Ranking and Information System ...... CHRIS
Cancer Hopefuls United for Mutual Support ...... CHUMS
Cancer Hot Line [*of Cancer Connection*] ...... CH
Cancer Immunology and Immunotherapy [*A publication*] ...... Cancer Immunol Immunother
Cancer Information Dissemination and Analysis Center ...... CIDAC
Cancer Information Service [*HEW*] ...... CIS
Cancer International Research Cooperative ...... CANCIRCO
Cancer Journal for Clinicians [*A publication*] ...... Ca
Cancer Letters [*A publication*] ...... Cancer Lett
Cancer and Leukemia, Group B [*Medicine*] ...... CALGB
Cancer Literature [*Data base*] [*National Library of Medicine*] ...... CANCERLIT
Cancer Nursing [*A publication*] ...... Cancer Nurs
Cancer Nursing [*A publication*] ...... Ca Nurs
Cancer Potential Index ...... CPI
Cancer Research [*A publication*] ...... Cancer Res
Cancer Research Emphasis Grants ...... CREG
Cancer Research Projects [*Data base*] [*National Library of Medicine*] ...... CANCERPROJ
Cancer Serum Index ...... CSI
Cancer Supplement [*A publication*] ...... Cancer Suppl
Cancer Therapy Facility ...... CTF
Cancer Treatment Advisory Committee [*HEW*] ...... CTAC
Cancer Treatment Reports [*A publication*] ...... Cancer Treat Rep
Cancer Treatment Reviews [*A publication*] ...... Cancer T R
Cancer Treatment Reviews [*A publication*] ...... Cancer Treat Rev
Cancun [*Mexico*] [*Airport symbol*] ...... CUN
Candela [*A publication*] C
Candela [*Formerly, Candlepower*] [*Symbol*] [*SI unit of luminous intensity*] ...... cd
Candela [*Formerly, Candlepower*] [*See cd*] C
Candela per Steradian ...... CD/SR
Candelabra Prefocused ...... CPREF
Candelas per Square Foot ...... CD/FT²
Candid Quarterly Review of Public Affairs [*A publication*] ...... Candid
Candidate ...... CAND
Candidate Material ...... CM
Candidate/Nominee Protective Division [*US Secret Service*] ...... CNPD
Candidate Pass Generator [*NASA*] ...... CPG
Candidate of Pharmacy ...... Cand Pharm
Candidate in Philosophy ...... Fil Kand
Candidate of Science ...... C Sc
Candidate of Technical Science ...... Cand Techn Sci
Candidate of Theology ...... C Th
Candidate of Theology ...... Th C
Candidates Reply Date Agreement [*Education*] ...... CRDA
Candilejas [*Colombia*] [*Airport symbol*] ...... CJD
Candle [*Illumination*] C
Candle ...... Ca
Candle [*Illumination*] ...... CD
Candle-Hour [*Illumination*] ...... CH
Candle-Hour [*Illumination*] ...... C-HR
Candle Manufacturers Association [*Later, NCA*] ...... CMA
Candle Power [*Physics*] ...... CP
Candle Power/Square Foot ...... CPSF
Cando Public Library, Cando, ND [*Library symbol*] ...... NdCan
Candy Apple [*Bowdlerized version*] ...... CA
Candy Brokers Association of America [*Later, NCBSA*] ...... CBA
Candy, Chocolate and Confectionery Institute CCCI
Candy and Snack Industry [*A publication*] ...... Candy Ind
Candy and Snack Industry [*A publication*] ...... Candy Snack Ind
Cane Growers Quarterly Bulletin [*A publication*] ...... Cane Grow Q Bull
Canes Venatici [*Constellation*] ...... CVen
Canes Venatici [*Constellation*] ...... CVn
Canet Nordenfelt Gun ...... CN
Canever English History Club ...... CEHC
Canfield, Rodeman, Adams, and Preller [*Philadelphia law firm in Spiro Agnew's book, "The Canfield Decision"*] ...... CRAP
Canine [*Deciduous*] [*Dentistry*] C
Canine [*K9 Corps - Army Dogs*] [*World War II*] K9
Canine Behavior Institute ...... CBI
Canine Companions for Independence CCI
Canine Distemper [*Veterinary medicine*] ...... CD
Canine Distemper Encephalitis [*A disease*] ...... CDE
Canine Distemper Virus [*Veterinary medicine*] ...... CDV
Canine Dose [*Veterinary medicine*] ...... CD
Canine Home Protection Service [*Acronym is title of 1979 movie*] ...... CHOMPS
Canine Practice [*A publication*] ...... Canine Pract
Canis Major [*Constellation*] ...... CMa
Canis Major [*Constellation*] ...... CMaj
Canis Minor [*Constellation*] ...... CMi
Canis Minor [*Constellation*] ...... CMin
Canisius College, Buffalo, NY [*Library symbol*] ...... NBuCC
Canisius College, Buffalo, NY [*OCLC symbol*] ...... VKC
Canister ...... CAN
Canister ...... CSTR
Canister Harpoon Control and Launch System ...... CHCLS
Cannabidiol [*Organic chemistry*] ...... CBD
Cannabinol [*A component of marijuana*] ...... CBN
Cannan Electric Co., Los Angeles, CA [*Library symbol*] ...... CLCan
Canned Antiair Warfare Exercise ...... CAAWEX
Canned Chop Suey Foods Industry [*Defunct*] ...... CCSFI
Canned Salmon Institute [*Later, SI*] ...... CSI

Cannet Des Maures [France] [Seismograph station code, US Geological Survey] [Closed].....................CMF
Cannibalize.....................K-BALL
Canning Machinery and Supplies Association [Later, FPM & SA]......CMSA
Canning, NS [Television station call letters].....................CJCH-TV-1
Canning and Packing [A publication].....................Cann Pack
Canning Trade [A publication].....................Cann Trade
Cannon [Freight].....................CANN
Cannon Artillery Weapon Systems.....................CAWS
Cannon Aviation Co., Inc. [Hickory, NC] [FAA designator].....................CNV
[The] Cannon Group [NASDAQ symbol].....................CNON
Cannon House Office Building.....................CHOB
Cannon Hunters Association of Seattle.....................CHAOS
Cannon-Launched Beam Rider Projectile.....................CLBRP
Cannon-Launched Guided Projectile.....................CLGP
Cannon-Launched Precision Guided Munition.....................CL-PGM
Cannon Mills Co. [NYSE symbol] [Delisted].....................CAN
Cannon Nonlaunched Guided Projectile.....................CNLGP
Cannot Comply.....................CANTCO
Cannot Duplicate.....................CND
Cannot Find.....................CF
Cannot Hear Of [Bookselling].....................C/H/O
Canobie [Australia] [Airport symbol] [Obsolete].....................CBY
Canoe.....................C
Canoga Park Area Office [AEC].....................CPAO
Canoga Test Laboratory [NASA].....................CTL
Canon.....................C
Canon.....................CAN
Canon.....................CN
Canon City, CO [Radio station call letters].....................KRLN-FM
Canon City Public Library, Canon City, CO [Library symbol].....................CoCc
Canon, Inc. ADR [NASDAQ symbol].....................CANNY
Canon Law Abstracts [A publication].....................Canon Law
Canon Law Society of America.....................CLS
Canon Law Society of America.....................CLSA
Canonesses Regular of St. Augustine [Roman Catholic women's religious order].....................CRA
Canonical Unit of Length.....................CUL
Canonical Unit of Time.....................CUT
Canonici Regulares Immaculate Conceptionis [Canons Regular of the Immaculate Conception] [Roman Catholic men's religious order].....................CRIC
Canonici Regulares Lateranenses [Canons Regular of the Lateran].....................CRL
Canonici Regulares Ordinis Sanctae Crucis [Canons Regular of the Order of the Holy Cross] [Crosier Fathers] [Roman Catholic religious order].....................OSC
Canoniste [A publication].....................Can
Canoniste Contemporain [A publication].....................Can C
Canonsburg, PA [Radio station call letters].....................WARO
Canopus Acquisition Gate [NASA].....................CAG
Canopus Probe near Limb of Venus Angle [NASA].....................CPV
Canopy.....................CAN
Canopy Removal System [for helicopters].....................CRS
Canova Public Library, Canova, SD [Library symbol].....................SdCan
Canrad Hanovia, Inc. [NASDAQ symbol].....................CNRD
Cans or Cartons [Freight].....................CC
Cansurmount [An association].....................CS
Cant [or Canting] [Heraldry].....................CA
Can't Add, Doesn't Even Try [Data processing].....................CADET
Can't Manage a Rifle [Formed by reversing the initials of Royal Army Medical Corps] [British] [World War I].....................CMAR
Can't Tell What [Accounting slang].....................CTW
Cantabile [Flowing Style] [Music].....................CANT
Cantabile [Flowing Style] [Music].....................CANTAB
Cantabrigiensis [Of Cambridge University].....................CANTAB
Canted Fuselage Station.....................CFS
Canteras y Explotaciones [A publication].....................Canteras Explot
Canterbury [City in England].....................CANT
Canterbury Chamber of Commerce. Agricultural Bulletin [A publication].....................Canterbury Chamber Commer Agric Bull
Canterbury Engineering Journal [A publication].....................Canterbury Eng J
Canticles [Song of Solomon] [Old Testament book].....................Cant
Cantilever.....................CANTIL
Canto [Melody].....................CAN
Canto [Melody].....................CANT
Canto Fermo [Plain Song] [Music].....................CF
Canto Gregoriano [A publication].....................Canto Greg
Canton [Kwangchow] [Republic of China] [Seismograph station code, US Geological Survey].....................CNT
Canton [Republic of China] [Geomagnetic observatory code].....................CNT
Canton Carnegie Public Library, Canton, SD [Library symbol].....................SdCa
Canton and Enderbury Islands [MARC country of publication code] [Library of Congress].....................cp
Canton and Enderbury Islands [Two-letter standard code].....................CT
Canton and Enderbury Islands [Three-letter standard code].....................CTE
Canton and Enderbury Islands [MARC geographic area code] [Library of Congress].....................pocp---
Canton Free Library, Canton, NY [Library symbol].....................NCa
Canton, GA [Radio station call letters].....................WCHK
Canton, GA [Radio station call letters].....................WCHK-FM
Canton, IL [Radio station call letters].....................WBOD

Canton, IL [Radio station call letters].....................WBYS
Canton, IL [Radio station call letters].....................WBYS-FM
Canton Island Range Communications Control Center [Military].....................CRCCC
Canton, MO [Radio station call letters].....................KQCA
Canton, MS [Radio station call letters].....................WMGO
Canton, NC [Radio station call letters].....................WPTL
Canton, NC [Radio station call letters].....................WWIT
Canton, NJ [Radio station call letters].....................WNNN
Canton, NY [Radio station call letters].....................WSLU
Canton, OH [Television station call letters].....................WDLI
Canton, OH [Radio station call letters].....................WHBC
Canton, OH [Radio station call letters].....................WHBC-FM
Canton, OH [Radio station call letters].....................WINW
Canton, OH [Radio station call letters].....................WNYN
Canton, OH [Television station call letters].....................WOAC-TV
Canton, OH [Radio station call letters].....................WOOS
Canton, OH [Radio station call letters].....................WRCW
Canton, OH [Radio station call letters].....................WTOF
Canton, PA [Radio station call letters].....................WKAD
Canton Public Library Association, Canton, OH [Library symbol].....................OCan
Canton Public Library, Canton, MS [Library symbol].....................MsCa
Canton Railroad Co. [AAR code].....................CTN
Cantor.....................CANT
Cantoris [Of the Cantor] [Music].....................CAN
Cantors Assembly [Formerly, CAA].....................CA
Cantors Assembly of America [Later, CA].....................CAA
Cantrell and Cochrane [Initials used as brand name of soft drink].....................C & C
Cantrill's Filmnotes [A publication].....................Cantrill's Fmnts
Cantuaria [Canterbury] [Latin].....................CANTUAR
Cantus Firmus [Plain Chant] [Music].....................CF
Canvas.....................CANV
Canvas Awning Institute [Later, American Canvas Institute].....................CAI
Canvas-Covered Wire-Rope Handrail [Aerospace].....................CCWRH
Canvas-Covered Wire-Rope Handrail [Aerospace].....................CC WR HDR
Canvas Products Association International [Later, IFAI].....................CPAI
Canvasback Society.....................CS
Canyon.....................CYN
Canyon de Chelly National Monument.....................CACH
Canyon Cinema News [A publication].....................Cany C News
Canyon Diablo Troilite [Geophysics].....................CDT
Canyon Junction [Wyoming] [Seismograph station code, US Geological Survey] [Closed].....................CJW
Canyon Research Group, Inc., Westlake Village, CA [Library symbol].....................CWlvC
Canyon, TX [Radio station call letters].....................KHBJ
Canyon, TX [Radio station call letters].....................KHBQ
Canyon, TX [Radio station call letters].....................KWTS
Canyon View Group Home, East Wenatchee, WA [Library symbol].....................WaEawC
Canyonlands National Park.....................CANY
Cap Haitien [Haiti] [Airport symbol].....................CAP
Cap Screw and Special Threaded Products Bureau [Defunct].....................CSSTPB
Cap Skirring [Senegal] [Airport symbol].....................CSK
Capabilities and Procedures.....................C & P
Capability.....................CAPAB
Capability Categories.....................CAPCATS
Capability Design Specifications.....................CDS
Capability Evaluation Plan.....................CEP
Capability Inspection [Air Force].....................CI
Capability Objective Package.....................COP
Capability and Proficiency Evaluation.....................CAPE
Capability Support Plan.....................CASP
Capable [or Capability].....................CPBL
Capacitance [Symbol] [IUPAC].....................C
Capacitance.....................CAP
Capacitance Decode Box.....................CDB
Capacitance Electronic Disc [Videodisc system].....................CED
Capacitance Voltage Measurements.....................CVM
Capacitative Discharge [Voltage source].....................CD
Capacitive Loss Factor.....................CLF
Capacitive Read-Only Memory [Data processing].....................CROM
Capacitor.....................C
Capacitor.....................CAP
Capacitor Bank.....................CB
Capacitor Diode.....................CD
Capacitor Diode Gate.....................CDG
Capacitor Discharge Ignition.....................CDI
Capacitor Flashgun [Photography].....................CAPFG
Capacitor Input Filter.....................CIF
Capacitor Leakage Indicator.....................CLI
Capacitor Qualification Program.....................CQP
Capacitor Qualification Test.....................CQT
Capacitor Qualification Test Program.....................CQTP
Capacitor Rate-Integrating Gyroscope.....................CRIG
Capacitor-Resistor Diode.....................CRD
Capacitor Resonance Frequency.....................CRF
Capacitor-Start [Motor] [Electricity].....................CAPST
Capacitor Test Program.....................CTP
Capacity.....................CAP
Capacity.....................CPTY
Capacity.....................K

Capacity Coupling ... CC
Capacity Loading and Schedule System ... CLASS
Capacity Planning and Operations Sequencing System [*IBM Corp.*] ... CAPOSS
Capacity Planning and Operations Sequencing System-Extended [*IBM Corp.*] ... CAPOSS-E
Capacity Ships Force ... CAPSHIPFOR
Cape [*Maps and charts*] ... C
Cape ... CPE
Cape Ann Historical Association, Gloucester, MA [*Library symbol*] ... MGlHi
Cape Breton Island ... CB
Cape Breton Regional Library, Sydney, NS, Canada [*Library symbol*] ... CaNSSC
Cape Canaveral [*Florida*] ... CNV
Cape Canaveral Air Force Station ... CCAFS
Cape Canaveral Auxiliary Air Force Base [*Obsolete*] ... CCAAFB
Cape Canaveral, FL [*Location identifier*] [*FAA*] ... XMR
Cape Canaveral Forecast Facility [*NASA*] ... CCFF
Cape Canaveral Missile Test Annex [*Later, KSC*] ... CCMTA
Cape Canaveral Missile Test Center [*Later, KSC*] ... CCMTC
Cape Canaveral Public Library, Cape Canaveral, FL [*Library symbol*] ... FCa
Cape Canaveral Reference Atmosphere [*NASA*] ... CCRA
Cape Canaveral Test Annex [*Obsolete*] [*Aerospace*] ... CCTA
Cape Chelyuskin [*USSR*] [*Geomagnetic observatory code*] ... CCS
Cape Cod Community College [*Massachusetts*] ... CCCC
Cape Cod Community College, West Barnstable, MA [*Library symbol*] ... MWebaC
Cape Cod Direction Center [*Air Force*] ... CCDC
Cape Cod Experiment [*Oceanography*] ... CCE
Cape Cod National Seashore [*National Park Service designation*] ... CACO
Cape Cod System [*Air Force*] ... CCS
Cape Colony [*British Empire*] ... CC
Cape Communications Control [*NASA*] ... CCC
Cape Coral, FL [*Radio station call letters*] ... WRCC
Cape Dorset [*Canada*] [*Airport symbol*] ... YTE
Cape Douglas [*Alaska*] [*Seismograph station code, US Geological Survey*] ... CDA
Cape Fear Railways, Inc. [*AAR code*] ... CF
Cape Fear Technical Institute, Wilmington, NC [*Library symbol*] ... NcWCF
Cape Girardeau [*Missouri*] [*Airport symbol*] ... CGI
Cape Girardeau [*Missouri*] [*Seismograph station code, US Geological Survey*] ... CGM
Cape Girardeau, MO [*Television station call letters*] ... KBSI
Cape Girardeau, MO [*Radio station call letters*] ... KEWI
Cape Girardeau, MO [*Television station call letters*] ... KFVS-TV
Cape Girardeau, MO [*Radio station call letters*] ... KGIR
Cape Girardeau, MO [*Radio station call letters*] ... KGMO-FM
Cape Girardeau, MO [*Radio station call letters*] ... KRCU
Cape Girardeau, MO [*Radio station call letters*] ... KZYM
Cape Girardeau Public Library, Cape Girardeau, MO [*Library symbol*] ... MoCg
Cape Gloucester [*Papua New Guinea*] [*Airport symbol*] ... CGC
Cape of Good Hope ... C of GH
Cape of Good Hope ... CGH
Cape of Good Hope [*South Africa*] [*Seismograph station code, US Geological Survey*] [*Closed*] ... CGH
Cape Hatteras National Seashore [*National Park Service designation*] ... CAHA
Cape Kennedy [*NASA*] ... CK
Cape Kennedy Air Force Station ... CKAFS
Cape Kennedy Forecast Facility [*NASA*] ... CKFF
Cape Kennedy Missile Test Annex [*NASA*] ... CKMTA
Cape Kennedy Range Safety Officer [*NASA*] ... CKRSO
Cape Kennedy Space Network, Incorporated [*NASA*] ... CKSNI
Cape Librarian [*A publication*] ... Cape Librn
Cape Librarian [*A publication*] ... Cap Libn
Cape Lisburne [*Alaska*] [*Airport symbol*] ... LUR
Cape Lookout National Seashore [*National Park Service designation*] ... CALO
Cape May [*New Jersey*] [*Airport symbol*] ... WWD
Cape May County Clerk, Cape May Court House, NJ [*Library symbol*] ... NjCmCoC
Cape May County Gazette, Cape May Court House, NJ [*Library symbol*] ... NjCmG
Cape May County Library, Cape May Court House, NJ [*Library symbol*] ... NjCmCo
Cape May County Times and Seven Mile Beach Reporter, Sea Isle City, NJ [*Library symbol*] ... NjSicTR
Cape May, NJ [*Radio station call letters*] ... WSJL
Cape Mounted Rifles [*British*] ... CMR
Cape Mounted Rifles, Left Wing [*British*] ... CMRLW
Cape Mounted Rifles, Right Wing [*British*] ... CMRRW
Cape Newenham [*Alaska*] [*Airport symbol*] ... EHM
Cape Palmas [*Liberia*] [*Airport symbol*] ... CPA
Cape Province [*of South Africa*] ... CP
Cape Reinga [*New Zealand*] [*Seismograph station code, US Geological Survey*] ... CRZ
CAPE [*Capability and Proficiency Evaluation*] **Review Period** ... CRP
Cape Rodney [*Papua New Guinea*] [*Airport symbol*] ... CPN
Cape Romanzof [*Alaska*] [*Seismograph station code, US Geological Survey*] [*Closed*] ... CPR
Cape Romanzof [*Alaska*] [*Airport symbol*] ... CZF
Cape Romanzof, AK [*Location identifier*] [*FAA*] ... CZF
Cape San Juan [*Puerto Rico*] [*Seismograph station code, US Geological Survey*] ... CSJ
Cape Sarichef [*Alaska*] [*Seismograph station code, US Geological Survey*] [*Closed*] ... CSA
Cape Seppings, AK [*Location identifier*] [*FAA*] ... XCS
Cape Shipunski [*USSR*] [*Seismograph station code, US Geological Survey*] ... SPN
Cape Support Coordinator [*NASA*] ... CSC
Cape Town [*South Africa*] [*Airport symbol*] ... CPT
Cape Town [*South Africa*] [*Later, HER*] [*Geomagnetic observatory code*] ... CTO
Cape Town [*South Africa*] [*Seismograph station code, US Geological Survey*] [*Closed*] ... CTO
Cape Verde [*Islands*] [*MARC country of publication code*] [*Library of Congress*] ... cv
Cape Verde [*Islands*] [*MARC geographic area code*] [*Library of Congress*] ... lncv---
Cape Verde Islands ... CVI
Cape Vogel [*Papua New Guinea*] [*Airport symbol*] ... CVL
Capehart Corp. [*American Stock Exchange symbol*] [*Delisted*] ... CPE
Capiat [*Let Him Take*] [*Pharmacy*] ... CAP
Capiat Quantum Vult [*Let the Patient Take as Much as He Will*] [*Pharmacy*] ... CAP QUANT VULT
Capiendus [*To Be Taken*] [*Pharmacy*] ... CAPIEND
Capilano College, Vancouver, BC, Canada [*Library symbol*] ... CaBVaC
Capillary ... CPLRY
Capillary Column Gas Chromatography ... CCGC
Capillary Filtration Coefficient ... CFC
Capillary [*or Colloid*] **Osmotic Pressure** [*Physiology*] ... COP
Capillary Pressure [*Physiology*] ... CP
Capita [*Chapters*] [*Latin*] ... CC
Capita Zoologica [*A publication*] ... Capita Zool
Capital ... CAP
Capital Account [*Business and trade*] ... CA
Capital Airlines, Inc. ... CA
Capital Airlines, Inc. ... CAP
Capital Area, Personnel Service Office (Navy) ... CAPSO-N
Capital Area Regional Library, Raymond, MS [*Library symbol*] ... MsR
Capital Area Support Center [*Military*] ... CASC
Capital Asset ... CA
Capital-Asset Pricing Model ... CAPM
Capital Authorization Request ... CAR
Capital Cities Communications, Inc. [*Formerly, Capital Cities Broadcasting Corp.*] [*NYSE symbol*] ... CCB
Capital and Class [*A publication*] ... Capital
Capital Consumption Adjustment [*or Allowance*] ... CCA
Capital Cost Allowance ... CCA
Capital Development Fund [*United Nations*] ... CDF
Capital District Library Council for Reference and Research Resources [*Library network*] ... CDLC
Capital District Library Council, Schenectady, NY [*Library symbol*] ... NScHLC
Capital District Library Council, Troy, NY [*OCLC symbol*] ... VYD
Capital Expenditure Proposal ... CEP
Capital Expenditure Request ... CER
Capital Formation [*An association*] ... CF
Capital Gains Tax ... CGT
Capital Goods ... CAPG
Capital Holding Corp. [*NYSE symbol*] ... CPH
Capital Improvements Program ... CIP
Capital Industries [*NASDAQ symbol*] ... CIIC
Capital Investment Computer Program [*Economics*] ... CICP
Capital Investment Model [*Navy*] ... CIM
Capital Investment Program ... CIP
Capital Legal Foundation ... CLF
Capital Library Cooperative, Mason, MI [*OCLC symbol*] ... EEJ
Capital Market Services [*NASDAQ symbol*] ... CMSC
Capital Market Statistics ... CMS
Capital Military Assistance Command ... CMAC
Capital Military District [*Vietnam*] ... CMD
Capital Military Region ... CMR
Capital Mortgage Investments [*NYSE symbol*] ... CMU
Capital Needs Analysis ... CNA
Capital Planning Information Ltd. [*British*] [*Information service*] ... CPI
Capital Property Accounting and Control ... CAPPRO
Capital Recovery Factor ... CRF
Capital Recovery Schedule ... CRS
Capital Reserve Corp. [*American Stock Exchange symbol*] [*Delisted*] ... CIF
Capital ROK [*Republic of Korea*] **Infantry Division** ... CRID
Capital Ship [*Bomb*] ... CS
Capital Southwest Corporation [*NASDAQ symbol*] ... CSWC
Capital Speakers Club ... CSC
Capital Stock ... CS
Capital Systems Group, Inc. [*Information service*] ... CSG
Capital Transfer Tax [*British*] ... CTT
Capital University, Columbus, OH [*OCLC symbol*] ... CAU
Capital University, Columbus, OH [*Library symbol*] ... OCoC
Capital University, Law Library, Columbus, OH [*OCLC symbol*] ... CAV
Capital University Law Review [*A publication*] ... Capital U L Rev

Capital University, School of Law, Columbus, OH [Library symbol] .... OCoC-L
Capital Work Order .... CWO
Capitals [Printing] C
Capitals [Printing] .... CAPS
Capitals and Lower Case [Printing] .... C & LC
Capitals and Small Capitals [Printing] .... C & SC
Capitol .... CAP
Capitol Air, Inc. [NASDAQ symbol] .... CAIRC
Capitol Air Lines .... CAL
Capitol Air Service, Inc. [Manhattan, KS] [FAA designator] .... CPA
Capitol Area Health Consortium Libraries [Library network] .... CAHCL
Capitol Area Library Consortium, Inc. [Library network] .... CALCO
Capitol Area Motion Pictures Education Organization [Washington, DC] .... CAMEO
Capitol Bancorp [NASDAQ symbol] .... CAPB
Capitol Consortium Network [of CUMWA] [Information service] ..... CAPCON
Capitol Consortium Network, Washington, DC [OCLC symbol] .... TPU
Capitol Consortium Network, Washington, DC [OCLC symbol] .... TPV
Capitol Food Industries, Inc. [American Stock Exchange symbol] [Delisted] .... CFS
Capitol Hill Restoration Society .... CHRS
Capitol Hill Women's Political Caucus .... CHWPC
Capitol Historical Society [Washington, DC] ...... CHS
Capitol International Airways [Air carrier designation symbol] .... CAPX
Capitol International Airways [ICAO designator] CL
Capitol Peak [Washington] [Seismograph station code, US Geological Survey] .... CPW
Capitol Radio Engineering Institute [Now known only by initialism] ...... CREI
Capitol Reef National Monument .... CARE
Capitol Region Library Council [Library network] ...... CRLC
Capitol Services, Incorporated [Information service] ...... CSI
Capitol Studies [A publication] .... Capitol Stud
Capitol Studies [A publication] .... Cap Stud
Capitol Transamerica [NASDAQ symbol] .... CATA
Capitoli [A publication] .... Cap
Capitolium [A publication] .... Cap
Capitolium [A publication] .... Capit
Capitulum [Chapter] .... CAP
Capodimonte [Italy] [Seismograph station code, US Geological Survey] [Closed] .... CAP
Capped .... CPPD
Capper Military Occupational Specialty [Army] .... CMOS
Capri [Italy] [Geomagnetic observatory code] .... CPI
Capricornus [Constellation] .... Cap
Capricornus [Constellation] .... Capr
Caprine Arthritis-Encephalitis [Goat big-knee disease] ...... CAE
Capstan .... CPSN
Capsula [Capsule] [Pharmacy] .... CAP
Capsula [Capsule] [Pharmacy] .... CAPS
Capsula Amylacea [A Cachet] [Pharmacy] .... CAPS AMYLAC
Capsula Gelatina [A Gelatine Capsule] [Pharmacy] ..... CAPS GELAT
Capsula Mollis [Soft Capsule] [Pharmacy] ...... CAP MOLL
Capsule .... CAPS
Capsule .... CPSL
Capsule Communications [or Communicator] [NASA] ...... CAPCOM
Capsule Communications [or Communicator] [NASA] CC
Capsule Control [NASA] .... CAPCON
Capsule Drive Core [Aerospace] .... CDC
Capsule Elapsed Time [Aerospace] .... CET
Capsule End Cover [Aerospace] .... CEC
Capsule Escape and Survival Applied Research [Aerospace] .... CESAR
Capsule Integrated Test Equipment [Aerospace] .... CITE
Capsule Internal Programer [Aerospace] .... CIP
Capsule Mechanical Training Model [Aerospace] ...... CMTM
Capsule Observation Panel [Aerospace] .... COP
Capsule-Orbiting Bus Link [NASA] .... COL
Capsule Positioning Mechanism [Aerospace] .... CPM
Capsule Separation [Aerospace] .... CAPSEP
Capsule Systems Advanced Development [Aerospace] ...... CSAD
Capsule Systems Test [NASA] .... CST
Capsule Test Conductor [NASA] .... CTC
Capsule Test Unit [Aerospace] .... CTU
Captain C
Captain .... CAP
Captain .... CAPT
Captain [Military] .... CPT
Captain [Worn on captain's uniform] [Hockey] C
Captain, Coastal Forces [Navy] .... CCF
Captain, Coastal Forces, Eastern Theater [Navy] ...... CCFET
Captain Cook [Hawaii] [Seismograph station code, US Geological Survey] .... CPH
Captain Cook Study Unit [American Topical Association] ...... CCSU
Captain Crab's Take-Away [NASDAQ symbol] .... CRAB
Captain [Commanding] Escort Forces [Navy] .... CEF
Captain Future [A publication] .... CAF
Captain Future [A publication] .... CF
Captain-General .... CG
Captain of the Guard .... CG
Captain of Horse [British] .... CH
Captain-Instructor [Navy] [British] CI

Captain of the Port [Coast Guard] .... COTP
Captain of Royal Marines [Military] [British] .... RMC
Captain Theodore C. Freeman Memorial Library, Houston, TX [Library symbol] .... TxHF
Captain's Imperfect Entry [Shipping] .... CIE
Captive Air Bubble [Surface effect ship] .... CAB
Captive Air Spacecraft .... CASC
Captive European Nations .... CEN
Captive Firing Test Set [Aerospace] .... CFTS
Captive Flight .... C/FLT
Captive Flight Test Missiles .... CFTM
Captive Insurance Companies Association ...... CICA
Captive Insurance Concept [A publication] ...... Captv Insur
Captive Nations Committee .... CNC
Captive Test .... CT
Captive Test Unit .... CTU
Captive Test Vehicle .... CTV
Captive Trajectory System [Air Force] .... CTS
Capture .... CAP
Capture .... CPTR
Capture Orbit Vehicle Assembly Mode .... COVAM
Captured in Action [Military] .... CIA
Captured Air Bubble Boat [Navy] .... CABB
Captured Enemy Documents [Military] .... CED
Captured Enemy Documents Organization ...... CEDO
Captured Enemy Equipment [Military] .... CEE
Captured Enemy Material [Military] .... CEM
Captured Enemy Signal Equipment [Military] .... CESE
Captured Gamma Ray .... CGR
Captured Steam Bubble Nuclear .... CSBN
Capuchin Franciscan Friary .... CFF
Capuchin Theological Seminary, Garrison, NY [Library symbol] .... NGaC
Capulin Mountain National Monument [National Park Service designation] .... CAMO
Caput [Head] [Latin] C
Caput [Head] [Latin] .... CAP
Caquetania [Colombia] [Airport symbol] .... CQT
Car Care Council CCC
Car Deck .... CD
Car Department Officers Association .... CDOA
Car and Driver [A publication] .... Car & Dr
Car and Driver [A publication] .... C/D
Car Float [Non-self-propelled] [Navy symbol] .... YCF
Car Service [Railroads] .... CS
Car Service Section [Railroads] .... CSS
Car-Tours in Europe, Inc. .... CTE
Car and Truck Renting and Leasing Association ...... CATRALA
Car of the Year .... COY
Cara [Dear One] .... K
Caracas [Venezuela] [Seismograph station code, US Geological Survey] .... CAR
Caracas [Venezuela] [Airport symbol] .... CCS
Caraquet, NB [Radio station call letters] .... CJVA
Carat [Signifies a twenty-fourth part; i.e., 24-carat gold is pure gold, 12-carat gold is half gold, half other substances] C
Carat .... CAR
Carat [Metric] .... CM
Carat .... CT
Carat .... K
Carat .... KT
Carat [Unit of measure for precious stones equal to 200 milligrams; see also meaning re gold] C
Carat [Unit of weight] .... CAR
Caratage, Color, Clarity, and Shape [Factors in determining the value of a diamond] .... CCCS
Caravan of East and West .... CEW
Caravan House [An association] .... CH
Caraveli [Peru] [Seismograph station code, US Geological Survey] [Closed] .... CRV
Caravelle [A publication] .... Car
Carbamoylcyclopropene [Organic chemistry] .... CCP
Carbamoyldihydropyridine [Organic chemistry] ...... CDHP
Carbamyl Phosphate [Also, CP] [Organic chemistry] ...... CAP
Carbamyl Phosphate [Also, CAP] [Organic chemistry] ...... CP
Carbamyl-Phosphate Synthetase [An enzyme] .... CPS
Carbamylcholine [Organic chemistry] CC
Carbamylmethyl [Biochemistry] .... Cam
Carbazopropionyl - Phosphatidyl Ethanolamine [Organic chemistry] .... CPA-PE
Carbenicillin [Bactericide] .... CB
Carbide .... CARB
Carbide .... CBD
Carbide Journal [A publication] .... Carbide J
Carbide and Tool Journal [A publication] ...... Carbide Tool J
Carbine .... CBN
Carbobenzoxy [Also, CBZ] [Organic chemistry] .... Cb
Carbobenzoxy [Also, Cb] [Organic chemistry] .... CBZ
Carbodiimide Residue [As substituent on nucleoside] [Biochemistry] ...... cms
Carbohydrate [Diet order] C
Carbohydrate .... CARBO
Carbohydrate .... CHO

Carbohydrate ....COH
Carbohydrate-Induced Hyperglyceridemia [Medicine] ....CIH
Carbohydrate Metabolism Index [Biochemistry] ....CMI
Carbohydrate Research [A publication] ....Carbohyd Res
Carbohydrate Research [A publication] ....Carbohydr Res
Carbohydrate Research [A publication] ....Carbohy Res
Carbolfuchsin [A dye] ....CF
Carbolic Methylene Blue [Clinical chemistry] ....CMB
Carbon [Chemical element] C
Carbon ....CARB
Carbon-13 Nuclear Magnetic Resonance [Also, CMR] ....CNMR
Carbon Black Export ....CBE
Carbon Black Feedstock ....CBFS
Carbon Black Producers Traffic Committee ....CBPTC
Carbon-Carbon ....C-C
Carbon Copy CC
Carbon County Railway Company [AAR code] ....CBC
Carbon Dioxide Concentrating [or Concentrator] Module ....CDCM
Carbon Dioxide Economizer ....CDE
Carbon Dioxide Exchange Rate [Plant biochemistry] ....CER
Carbon Dioxide LASER ....CDL
Carbon Dioxide LASER Beam ....CDLB
Carbon Dioxide Therapy ....CDT
Carbon Electrode Equipment ....CEE
Carbon Equilibrium Loop ....CEL
Carbon Fiber Reinforced Composite ....CFC
Carbon Fiber Reinforced Plastic ....CFRP
Carbon Film ....CF
Carbon-Film Resistor ....CFR
Carbon Filtered ....CF
Carbon, Hydrogen, Nitrogen ....CHN
Carbon, Hydrogen, Nitrogen, Oxygen, Phosphorus, and Sulfur
[Compounds] ....CHNOPS
Carbon Magnetic Resonance [Also, CNMR] ....CMR
Carbon Molybdenum Steel ....CMOS
Carbon Monofluoride [Inorganic chemistry] ....CMF
Carbon Monoxide ....CO
Carbon Monoxide Measuring System ....CMMS
Carbon Monoxide Pollution Experiment [NASA/General Electric] ....COPE
Carbon-Nitrogen-Oxygen [Galactic molecular formation cycle] ....CNO
Carbon to Nitrogen Ratio ....C/N
Carbon Paper and Inked Ribbon Association [Defunct] ....CPIRA
Carbon Preference Index [Organic geochemistry] ....CPI
Carbon Rod Atomizer [Spectroscopy] ....CRA
Carbon Steel ....CS
Carbon Tetrachloride [Also, CTC] [Organic chemistry] ....CT
Carbon Tetrachloride [Also, CT] [Organic chemistry] ....CTC
Carbon Zinc Battery ....CZB
Carbonaceous Chondrite CC
Carbonaceous Chondrite Fission [Geophysics] ....CCF
Carbonaceous Chondrite Fission Xenon [Geophysics] ....CCFXe
Carbonaceous Chondrite Reference Standard [Geophysics] ....CCRS
Carbonate ....CARB
Carbonate ....CRBNT
Carbonate Compensation Depth [Oceanography] ....CCD
Carbonate Compensation Level [Oceanography] CCL
Carbonated ....CRBNATD
Carbonated Beverage Can Makers Committee [Division of
CBCMA] ....CBCMC
Carbonated Beverage Container Manufacturers Association
[Later, CMI] ....CBCMA
Carbonated Beverage Institute ....CBI
Carbondale [Illinois] [Airport symbol] ....MDH
Carbondale, CO [Radio station call letters] ....KDNK
Carbondale, IL [Radio station call letters] ....WCIL
Carbondale, IL [Radio station call letters] ....WCIL-FM
Carbondale, IL [Radio station call letters] ....WSIU
Carbondale, IL [Television station call letters] ....WSIU-TV
Carbondale Mining Technology Center [Department of Energy] ....CMTC
Carbondale, PA [Radio station call letters] ....WCDL
Carbondale, PA [Radio station call letters] ....WLSP
Carbonear, NF [Radio station call letters] ....CHVO
Carbonic Anhydrase [An enzyme] ....CA
Carbonic Dichloride [Phosgene] [Poison gas] [Army symbol] ....CG
Carbonylcyanide-meta-chlorophenylhydrazone [Also, CCP]
[Organic chemistry] ....CCCP
Carbonylcyanide-meta-chlorophenylhydrazone [Also, CCCP]
[Organic chemistry] ....CCP
Carborundum Co. [NYSE symbol] ....CBO
Carborundum Co., Niagara Falls, NY [Library symbol] ....NNiaCa
Carboxamidomethyl [Organic chemistry] ....CAM
Carboxy Nitroso Rubber [Organic chemistry] ....CNR
Carboxyfluorescein [Fluorophore] ....CF
Carboxyfluorescein Diacetate [Organic chemistry] ....CFDA
Carboxyl-Terminated Polybutadiene Binder [Organic chemistry] ....CTPB
Carboxylation Efficiency [Botany] ....CE
Carboxymethyl [Also, Cm, Cme] [Biochemistry] ....CM
Carboxymethyl [Also, CM, Cm] [Biochemistry] ....Cme
Carboxymethyl Hydroxyethyl Cellulose [Organic chemistry] ....CMHEC
Carboxymethylcellulose [Organic chemistry] ....CMC
Carboxymuconolactone Decarboxylase [An enzyme] ....CMD

Carboxypeptidase Inhibitor [in potatoes] ....CPI
Carboxypolymethylene [Organic chemistry] ....CARBOPOL
Carboxypyridine Disulfide [Biochemistry] ....CPDS
Carboy ....CB
Carboy ....CBY
Carburetor ....CARB
Carburetor Air Temperature [Aviation] ....CAT
Carcano Rifle ....CARC
Carcassonne [France] [Airport symbol] ....CCF
Carcinoembryonic Antigen [Immunochemistry] ....CEA
Carcinogen Bioassay in Small Rodents ....CBSR
Carcinogen Information Program ....CIP
Carcinogenesis Bioassay Data System [National Cancer Institute] ....CBDS
Carcinogenesis: A Comprehensive Survey [A publication]
..........Carcinog Compr Surv
Carcinogenic Index CI
Carcinoma Cell Line [Cytology] CCL
Carcinoma In Situ [Oncology] ....CIS
Card [Manuscript descriptions] C
Card ....CD
Card Assembly Program ....CAP
Card-Automated Reproduction and Distribution System [Library
of Congress] ....CARDS
Card Automatic Code System [IBM Corp.] ....CARDCODER
Card Capacitor Read-Only Storage [Data processing] ....CCROS
Card Clothing Manufacturers Association ....CCMA
Card Code CC
Card Column CC
Card Computer Interface [Data processing] CCI
Card Count [Data processing] CC
Card Distribution ....CD
Card Format Identifier ....CFI
Card Image Correction [Data processing] ....CIMCO
Card Input [Data processing] CI
Card Inventory Control CIC
Card-to-Magnetic Tape Conversion System [Data processing] ....CTS
Card Module Tester ....CMT
Card Packet System ....CARDPAC
Card Programed Calculator [Data processing] ....CPC
Card Punch [Data processing] ....CP
Card Punching Printer [Data processing] ....CPP
Card Random-Access Memory [Data processing] ....CRAM
Card Reader [Data processing] ....CR
Card Station [Data processing] ....CS
Card-to-Tape Tape [Data processing] ....CTT
Cardboard Illustrative Aid to Computation [Data processing] ....CARDIAC
Carded Packaging Institute ....CPI
Carded for Record Only ....CRO
Carded Yarn Association [Later, American Yarn Spinners
Association] ....CYA
Cardiac Accelerator Center [Physiology] ....CAC
Cardiac Adjustment Scale [Psychology] ....CAS
Cardiac Arrest Code [Medicine] ....CAC
Cardiac Care Unit [Medicine] ....CCU
Cardiac Enlargement [Medicine] ....CE
Cardiac Failure [Medicine] ....CF
Cardiac Index [Physiology] CI
Cardiac Inhibition Center [Physiology] CIC
Cardiac Minute Output [Physiology] ....CMO
Cardiac Output [Cardiology] ....CO
Cardiac Output Recorder [Physiology] ....COR
Cardiac Pulmonary Reserve [Physiology] ....CPR
Cardiac Resuscitation Team [Medicine] ....CRT
Cardiac Resuscitator [NASDAQ symbol] ....CARD
Cardiac Surgical Intensive Care Unit [Medicine] ....CSICU
Cardiac/Thoracic Unit [Medicine] ....CTU
Cardiac Work Index [Physiology] ....CWI
Cardiff [Welsh depot code] ....CDF
Cardiff [Wales] [Airport symbol] ....CWL
Cardiff Commercial, Inc. [NASDAQ symbol] ....CRDF
Cardiff East Docks [Welsh depot code] ....CED
Cardiff Equities [American Stock Exchange symbol] ....CEQ
Cardiff Railway [Wales] ....CAR R
Cardiff Valleys [Welsh depot code] CV
Cardigan Welsh Corgi Club of America ....CWCCA
Cardiganshire [County in Wales] ....CARDS
Cardillo Travel Systems, Inc. [Formerly, TraveLodge
International, Inc.] [American Stock Exchange symbol] ....TVL
Cardinal ....CARD
Cardinal ....CDL
Cardinal/Air Virginia [Lynchburg, VA] [FAA designator] ....FVA
Cardinal Distribution [NASDAQ symbol] ....CDIC
Cardinal Mindszenty Foundation ....CMF
Cardinal Mooney High School Library, Rochester, NY [OCLC
symbol] ....RVV
Cardinal Stritch College [Wisconsin] ....CSC
Cardio Search, Inc. [NASDAQ symbol] ....CSCH
Cardiolipin [Immunochemistry] CL
Cardiologia Hungarica [A publication] ....Cardil Hung
Cardiologia Pratica [A publication] ....Cardiol Prat
Cardiologisches Bulletin [A publication] ....Cardiol Bull

Cardiology .... CARDIO
Cardiomyography [*Cardiology*] .... CM
Cardiopulmonary .... CARDPLMNRY
Cardiopulmonary Bypass [*Medicine*] .... CPB
Cardiopulmonary Resuscitation [*Medicine*] .... CPR
Cardiorespiratory [*Medicine*] .... CR
Cardiotachometer [*Medicine*] .... CTM
Cardiothoracic Ratio [*Medicine*] .... CTR
Cardiothoracic Research and Education Foundation .... CREF
Cardiotocography [*Gynecology*] .... CTG
Cardiovascular [*Medicine*] CV
Cardiovascular Clinics [*A publication*] .... Cardiovasc Clin
Cardiovascular Conditioning Suit [*Medicine*] .... CVCS
Cardiovascular Disease [*Medicine*] .... CD
Cardiovascular Disease [*Medicine*] .... CVD
Cardiovascular Disease Study [*British*] .... CVDS
Cardiovascular Diseases Bulletin of the Texas Heart Institute [*A publication*] .... Cardiovasc Dis Bull Tex Heart Inst
Cardiovascular Flow Dynamics and Measurements (North Atlantic Treaty Organization. Advanced Study Institute on Cardiovascular Flow Dynamics) [*A publication*] .... Cardiovasc Flow Dyn Meas (NATO Adv Study Inst)
Cardiovascular In-Patient Care Unit .... CICU
Cardiovascular and Interventional Radiology [*A publication*] .... Cardiovasc Intervent Radiol
Cardiovascular Medicine [*A publication*] .... Cardiovasc Med
Cardiovascular Monitor [*Medicine*] .... CVM
Cardiovascular Nursing [*A publication*] .... Cardiovasc Nurs
Cardiovascular and Pulmonary Technology. Journal [*A publication*] .... CVP
Cardiovascular Radiology [*A publication*] .... Cardiovasc Radiol
Cardiovascular Reflex Conditioning [*Medicine*] .... CRC
Cardiovascular Reflex Conditioning System [*Medicine*] .... CRCS
Cardiovascular Renal Disease [*Medicine*] .... CVRD
Cardiovascular Research [*A publication*] .... Cardio Res
Cardiovascular Research [*A publication*] .... Cardiovasc Res
Cardiovascular Research Center. Bulletin [*Houston*] [*A publication*] .... Cardiovasc Res Cent Bull
Cardiovascular Research Center. Bulletin (Houston) [*A publication*] .... Cardiovasc Res Cent Bull (Houston)
Cardiovascular Respiratory [*System*] [*Medicine*] .... CVR
Cardiovascular Respiratory Disease [*Medicine*] .... CVRD
Cardiovascular Surgery [*Medicine*] .... CVS
Cardiovascular System [*Medicine*] .... CVS
Cards per Day [*Data processing*] .... CPD
Cards per Hour .... C/H
Cards per Hour .... CPH
Cards per Minute [*Data processing*] .... CPM
Cards per Second .... CPS
Care .... K
Care Centers, Inc. [*NASDAQ symbol*] .... CCEN
Care Corp. Cl A [*American Stock Exchange symbol*] .... KREA
Care Corp. Cl B [*American Stock Exchange symbol*] .... KREB
Care Custody and Control CCC
Care Enterprises [*NASDAQ symbol*] .... KARE
Care How Others Keep the Environment [*An association*] .... CHOKE
Care Logic Module .... CLM
Care Of .... C/O
Care-Oriented Medical Record [*University of Alabama*] .... COMREC
Care Plus, Inc. Uts [*NASDAQ symbol*] .... CPLSU
Care and Preservation [*Army*] .... C & P
Care of Supplies in Storage [*Military*] .... COSIS
Career Advancement Network .... CAN
Career Airmen Reenlistment Reservation System [*Air Force*] .... CAREERS
Career Analysis Procedure [*LIMRA*] .... CAP
Career Apparel Institute .... CAI
Career Area Rotation Model [*Air Force*] .... CAROM
Career Assistance Counseling [*Air Force*] .... CAC
Career Assistance Program [*Department of Labor*] .... CAP
Career Control CC
Career Counselor [*Military*] .... CARCSLR
Career Development Center .... CDC
Career Development Center, Shaker Heights, OH [*OCLC symbol*] .... SKS
Career Development Course .... CDC
Career Development Review .... CDR
Career Employment Experience [*Office of Youth Programs*] [*Department of Labor*] .... CEE
Career Executive Force [*Air Force*] .... CEF
Career Information and Counseling [*Air Force*] .... CIAC
Career Management and Assignment [*Department of State*] .... CMA
Career Management Field [*Military*] .... CMF
Career Management Information File [*Military*] .... CMIF
Career Minister [*Department of State*] .... CM
Career Motivation .... CM
Career Officer Candidate Development Course [*Air Force*] .... COCDC
Career Opportunities Program [*Office of Education*] .... COP
Career Opportunities for Youth .... COY
Career Orientation Program [*LIMRA*] .... COP
Career-Oriented Preparation for Employment [*Federal antipoverty program*] .... COPE
Career Placement Registry, Inc. [*Information service*] .... CPR
Career Planning and Adult Development Network .... CPADN
Career Planning Board [*Navy*] .... CPB
Career Reenlistment Objectives [*Navy*] .... CREO
Career Reserve Status [*Air Force*] .... CRS
Career Training Foundation .... CTF
Careers .... CARS
Careers Research and Advisory Centre [*British*] .... CRAC
Careers Services [*Navy*] [*British*] .... CS
Careless and Negligent Driving [*Traffic offense charge*] .... CN
Caressa, Inc. [*NYSE symbol*] .... CSA
Carey Foster Bridge [*Electronics*] .... CFB
Carey [*The Philip*] **Manufacturing Co.** [*NYSE symbol*] [*Delisted*] .... CAY
Carey's American Museum [*A publication*] .... Carey's Mus
Cargese Lectures in Physics [*A publication*] .... Cargese Lect Phys
Cargill Crop Bulletin [*A publication*] .... Cargill Crop Bull
Cargill Information Center, Wayzata, MN [*OCLC symbol*] .... CAR
Cargo .... CAR
Cargo .... CGO
Cargo Allocation and Load Control [*Aviation*] .... CALC
Cargo Apparent Good Order .... CAGO
Cargo Bay Module Personnel Provisions [*NASA*] .... CBMPP
Cargo Center of Gravity .... CCG
Cargo Container .... CACON
Cargo Data Interchange System .... CARDIS
Cargo Delivery Receipt .... CDR
Cargo Delivery System .... CDS
Cargo Disposition Instructions .... CDI
Cargo Drop Reel .... CDR
Cargo Glider [*Military*] .... CG
Cargo Handling Battalion [*Obsolete*] [*Army*] .... CHB
Cargo Handling Equipment [*Army*] .... CHE
Cargo Handling and Port Group [*Navy*] .... CHAPGRU
Cargo Handling Rig .... CHR
Cargo Helicopter .... CH
Cargo Integration Review .... CIR
Cargo Integration Test Equipment .... CITE
Cargo Left Trailer .... CLT
Cargo and Loading Analysis .... C & LA
Cargo Lunar Excursion Module .... CLEM
Cargo Module .... CAM
Cargo Outturn Report .... COR
Cargo Outturn Reporting System .... CORS
Cargo Processing Contract .... CPC
Cargo Processing Facility .... CPF
Cargo Processing Technician .... CPT
Cargo Propulsion Module [*NASA*] .... CPM
Cargo and Rescue Aircraft .... CARA
Cargo Security Advisory Standards [*Department of Transportation*] .... CSAS
Cargo Ship [*of any type*] [*Navy symbol*] .... AK
Cargo Ship .... CA
Cargo Ship [*Military Sea Transportation Service*] .... TAK
Cargo Ship and Aircraft Ferry [*Navy symbol*] .... AKV
Cargo Ship and Aircraft Ferry [*Military Sea Transportation Service*] .... TAKV
Cargo Ship, Dock [*Navy symbol*] .... AKD
Cargo Ship, Merchant Marine Manned .... XAK
Cargo Submarine [*Navy symbol*] .... AK(SS)
Cargo Submarine [*Navy symbol*] .... ASSA
Cargo Submarine [*Navy symbol*] .... SSA
Cargo Systems International [*A publication*] .... Cargo Syst Int
Cargo/Transport [*Designation for all US military aircraft*] C
Cargo/Transport Aircraft - Experimental CX
Cargo/Transport Aircraft Experimental - Heavy Logistics System .... CX-HLS
Cargolux Airlines International [*Luxembourg*] [*ICAO designator*] CV
Cargoman Ltd. [*Oman*] [*ICAO designator*] .... HC
Cargo's Proportion of (General) Average [*Business and trade*] .... CGA
Carhart Photo Cl A [*NASDAQ symbol*] .... CARPA
Carib [*MARC language code*] [*Library of Congress*] .... car
Carib Jet (Antigua) Ltd. [*Great Britain*] [*ICAO designator*] .... BV
Carib West Airways [*Barbados*] [*ICAO designator*] .... DQ
Caribair [*Airlines*] .... CB
Caribbean .... CAR
Caribbean .... CARIB
Caribbean Agriculture [*A publication*] .... Caribb Agr
Caribbean Agriculture [*A publication*] .... Caribb Agric
Caribbean Air Command [*Air Force*] .... CAC
Caribbean Air Command [*Air Force*] .... CAIRC
Caribbean Air Transport Co., Inc. [*Netherlands*] [*ICAO designator*] .... CJ
Caribbean Airways [*Barbados*] [*ICAO designator*] .... IQ
Caribbean American Intercultural Organization .... CAIO
Caribbean Area [*Services to the Armed Forces*] [*Red Cross*] .... CA
Caribbean Area [*MARC geographic area code*] [*Library of Congress*] .... cc-----
Caribbean Area Small Craft Project .... CASCP
Caribbean Atlantic Airlines [*Puerto Rico*] .... CARIBAIR
Caribbean Atlantic Airlines [*Puerto Rico*] [*ICAO designator*] .... CBA
Caribbean-Atlantic Geotraverse [*IDOE project*] .... CAG
Caribbean Basin Initiative [*Financial aid package proposed by President Reagan for Central American and Caribbean countries*] .... CBI
Caribbean Broadcasting Corporation .... CaBC
Caribbean Broadcasting Union .... CBU

Caribbean/Central American Action................C/CAA
Caribbean Command [*Military*]................CARIBCOM
Caribbean Commission [*Later, Caribbean Organization*]................CC
Caribbean Community [*Barbados, Jamaica, Trinidad-Tobago, Guyana, Belize, Dominica, Grenada, St. Kitts-Nevis-Anguilla, St. Lucia, St. Vincent*]................CARICOM
Caribbean Congress of Labor................CCL
Caribbean Conservation Association................CCA
Caribbean Conservation Corporation................CCC
Caribbean Defense Command [*or Commander*]................CDC
Caribbean Development Bank................CARIBANK
Caribbean Development Bank................CDB
Caribbean Division Naval Facilities Engineering Command................CARIBNAVFACENGCOM
Caribbean Division Naval Facilities Engineering Command................DIRCARIBDOCKS
Caribbean Educational Service................CES
Caribbean Food and Nutrition Institute................CFNI
Caribbean Forester [*A publication*]................Caribb For
Caribbean Free Trade Association................CARIFTA
Caribbean Gamefishing Association................CGA
Caribbean Hotel Association................CHA
Caribbean Industrial Research Institute................CARIRI
Caribbean Industrial Research Institute................CIRI
Caribbean Journal of Science [*A publication*]................Caribbean Jour Sci
Caribbean Journal of Science [*A publication*]................Caribb J Sci
Caribbean Journal of Science and Mathematics [*A publication*]................Caribbean J Sci Math
Caribbean Marine Biological Institute................CARMABI
Caribbean Medical Journal [*A publication*]................Caribb Med J
Caribbean Meteorological Institute................CMI
Caribbean Organization [*An international governmental body, of which the US was a member*] [*Terminated, 1965*]................CO
Caribbean Quarterly [*A publication*]................CQ
Caribbean Ready Group [*Navy*]................CARG
Caribbean Research Institute [*College of the Virgin Islands*]................CRI
Caribbean Sea Frontier [*Navy*]................CARIBSEAFRON
Caribbean Sea Frontier [*Navy*]................CSF
Caribbean Studies [*A publication*]................Caribbean S
Caribbean Studies [*A publication*]................Caribbean Stud
Caribbean Studies [*A publication*]................Carib Stud
Caribbean Studies Association................CSA
Caribbean Tourism Association................CTA
Caribbeana Council................CC
Cariboo College, Kamloops, BC, Canada [*Library symbol*]................CaBKCC
Caribou [*Maine*] [*Seismograph station code, US Geological Survey*]................CBM
Caribou, ME [*Location identifier*] [*FAA*]................CAR
Caribou, ME [*Radio station call letters*]................WFST
Caribou Performance Test................CPT
Caricaturists Society of America................CSA
Caries Research [*A publication*]................Caries Res
Carina [*Constellation*]................Car
Carina [*Constellation*]................Cari
Caring Relationship Inventory [*Psychology*]................CRI
Carissimus [*Dearest*]................K
Caritas Internationalis [*International Confederation of Catholic Organizations for Charitable and Social Action*]................CI
Carl H. Pforzheimer Library, New York, NY [*Library symbol*]................NNPf
Carl Hanser Verlag [*Publisher*]................CHV
Carl Karcher Enterprises [*NASDAQ symbol*]................CARL
Carl Sandburg Birthplace Association, Galesburg, IL [*Library symbol*]................IGS
Carl Sandburg College, Galesburg, IL [*Library symbol*]................IGSC
Carl Sandburg College, LRC, Galesburg, IL [*OCLC symbol*]................IHR
Carl Schurz Memorial Foundation [*Later, NCSA*]................CSMF
Carl Vinson Nuclear Powered Carrier [*DoD*]................CVN
Carle Foundation Hospital, Urbana, IL [*Library symbol*]................IUrCH
Carleton Board of Education, Ottawa, ON, Canada [*Library symbol*]................CaOOCBE
Carleton College, Northfield, MN [*OCLC symbol*]................MNN
Carleton College, Northfield, MN [*Library symbol*]................MnNC
Carleton Germanic Papers [*A publication*]................CGP
Carleton Miscellany [*A publication*]................Carleton Misc
Carleton Miscellany [*A publication*]................Carl Mis
Carleton Miscellany [*A publication*]................CM
Carleton Newsletter [*A publication*]................CarlN
Carleton Place Public Library, Carleton Place, ON, Canada [*Library symbol*]................CaOCp
Carleton, PQ [*Television station call letters*]................CHAU-TV
Carleton University, Department of Art History, Ottawa, ON, Canada [*Library symbol*]................CaOOCCAH
Carleton University. Department of Geology. Geological Paper [*A publication*]................Carleton Univ Dept Geology Geol Paper
Carleton University, Geography Department, Ottawa, ON, Canada [*Library symbol*]................CaOOCCG
Carleton University, Ottawa, ON, Canada [*Library symbol*]................CaOOCC
Carleton University, Social Sciences Division, Ottawa, ON, Canada [*Library symbol*] [*Obsolete*]................CaOOCCSS
Carling O'Keefe Ltd. [*NYSE symbol*]................CKB
Carlinville, IL [*Radio station call letters*]................WIBI
Carlinville Public Library, Carlinville, IL [*Library symbol*]................ICarl

[*Bishop of*] Carlisle [*British*]................CARLIOL
Carlisle [*England*] [*Airport symbol*]................CAX
Carlisle Citizen, Carlisle, IA [*Library symbol*]................IaCarlC
Carlisle Corp. [*NYSE symbol*]................CSL
Carlisle, PA [*Radio station call letters*]................WDCV-FM
Carlisle, PA [*Radio station call letters*]................WHYL
Carlisle, PA [*Radio station call letters*]................WHYL-FM
Carlisle, PA [*Radio station call letters*]................WIOO
Carlisle Public Library, Carlisle, IA [*Library symbol*]................IaCarl
Carlo Erba [*Italy*] [*Research code symbol*]................I
Carlo Erba [*Italy*] [*Research code symbol*]................K
Carload................CL
Carload Lot [*Commerce*]................CL
Carloforte [*Sardinia*] [*Seismograph station code, US Geological Survey*] [*Closed*]................CRL
Carlow College, Our Lady of Mercy Academy, Pittsburgh, PA [*Library symbol*]................PPiCa-O
Carlow College, Pittsburgh, PA [*OCLC symbol*]................CRC
Carlow College, Pittsburgh, PA [*Library symbol*]................PPiCa
Carlsbad [*California*] [*Airport symbol*]................CLD
Carlsbad [*New Mexico*] [*Seismograph station code, US Geological Survey*]................CLN
Carlsbad [*New Mexico*] [*Airport symbol*]................CNM
Carlsbad, CA [*Radio station call letters*]................KKOS
Carlsbad Caverns National Park................CACA
Carlsbad City Library, Carlsbad, CA [*Library symbol*]................CCarl
Carlsbad City Library, Carlsbad, CA [*OCLC symbol*]................CCP
Carlsbad, NM [*Location identifier*] [*FAA*]................CNM
Carlsbad, NM [*Radio station call letters*]................KAMQ
Carlsbad, NM [*Radio station call letters*]................KATK
Carlsbad, NM [*Television station call letters*]................KAVE-TV
Carlsbad, NM [*Radio station call letters*]................KBAD
Carlsbad, NM [*Radio station call letters*]................KCCC
Carlsbad, NM [*Television station call letters*]................KKSG
Carlsbad Public Library, Carlsbad, NM [*Library symbol*]................NmC
Carlsberg Corp. [*NASDAQ symbol*]................CRLS
Carlsberg Research Communications [*A publication*]................Carlsberg Res Commun
Carlyle Barton Laboratory................CBL
Carlyle Lake, SK [*Television station call letters*]................CIEW-TV
Carmarthen [*Welsh depot code*]................CARM
Carmarthenshire [*County in Wales*]................CARM
Carmarthenshire [*County in Wales*]................CARMS
Carme, Inc. [*NASDAQ symbol*]................CAME
Carmel, CA [*Radio station call letters*]................KRML
Carmel, CA [*Radio station call letters*]................KWST
Carmel Community [*Roman Catholic women's religious order*]................CC
Carmel, IN [*Radio station call letters*]................WHJE
Carmel, NY [*Location identifier*] [*FAA*]................CMK
Carmelite................CARM
Carmelite Brothers of the Holy Eucharist [*Roman Catholic religious order*]................CFSE
Carmelite Missionaries of St. Theresa [*Roman Catholic women's religious order*]................CMST
Carmelite Sisters of Charity [*Roman Catholic religious order*]................CaCh
Carmelite Sisters of the Divine Heart of Jesus [*Roman Catholic religious order*]................DCJ
Carmelite Sisters of St. Therese of the Infant Jesus [*Roman Catholic religious order*]................CST
Carmelus [*A publication*]................Car
Carmi, IL [*Location identifier*] [*FAA*]................CUL
Carmi, IL [*Radio station call letters*]................WROY
Carmi, IL [*Radio station call letters*]................WRUL
Carmichael, CA [*Radio station call letters*]................KFIA
Carnal Knowledge [*FBI standardized term*]................CK
Carnal Knowledge of Female Child [*FBI standardized term*]................CK of FC
Carnarvon [*Australia*] [*Airport symbol*]................CVQ
Carnarvon Tracking Station [*NASA*]................CRO
Carnarvonshire [*County in Wales*]................CARN
Carnasaw Mountain - Lookout Tower [*Oklahoma*] [*Seismograph station code, US Geological Survey*]................CRO
Carnation Co. [*NYSE symbol*]................CMK
Carnation Research Laboratories, Van Nuys, CA [*Library symbol*]................CVnCR
Carnegie Bookmobile Library, Grafton, ND [*Library symbol*]................NdGrC
Carnegie Center for Transnational Studies................CCTS
Carnegie College of Physical Education. Leeds. Research Papers in Physical Education [*A publication*]................Carnegie Coll Physical Ed Research Papers
Carnegie Commission on Higher Education................CCHE
Carnegie Corporation of New York................CCNY
Carnegie Corp. of New York, New York, NY [*Library symbol*]................NNCar
Carnegie Council of Policy Studies in Higher Education [*Defunct*]................CCPSHE
Carnegie Ellsworth Public Library, Iowa Falls, IA [*Library symbol*]................IaIf
Carnegie Endowment for International Peace................CEIP
Carnegie Endowment for International Peace, New York, NY [*Library symbol*]................NNCE
Carnegie Foundation for the Advancement of Teaching................CFAT
Carnegie Free Library, Beaver Falls, PA [*Library symbol*]................PBf
Carnegie Free Library, Braddock, PA [*Library symbol*]................PBra

Carnegie Free Library of McKeesport, McKeesport, PA [*Library symbol*] ... PMck
Carnegie Hall - Jeunesses Musicales [*Defunct*] ... CH-JM
Carnegie Hero Fund Commission ... CHFC
Carnegie Institute [*New York*] ... CI
Carnegie Institute of Technology [*Later, Carnegie-Mellon University*] [*Pennsylvania*] ... CIT
Carnegie Institution of Washington ... CIW
Carnegie Institution of Washington [*District of Columbia*] [*Seismograph station code, US Geological Survey*] [*Closed*] ... DTM
Carnegie Institution of Washington, Department of Terrestrial Magnetism, Washington, DC [*Library symbol*] ... DCI-T
Carnegie Institution of Washington, Geophysical Laboratory, Washington, DC [*Library symbol*] ... DCI-G
Carnegie Institution of Washington. Publication [*A publication*] ... Carnegie Inst Wash Publ
Carnegie Institution of Washington, Washington, DC [*Library symbol*] ... DCI
Carnegie Institution of Washington. Year Book [*A publication*] ... Carnegie Inst Wash Year Book
Carnegie Library of Parkersburg and Wood County, Parkersburg, WV [*Library symbol*] ... WvP
Carnegie Library of Pittsburgh, Allegheny Regional Branch, Monroeville, PA [*Library symbol*] ... PPi-A
Carnegie Library of Pittsburgh, Pittsburgh, PA [*OCLC symbol*] ... CPL
Carnegie Library of Pittsburgh, Pittsburgh, PA [*Library symbol*] ... PPi
Carnegie Library, Rockport, MA [*Library symbol*] ... MRp
Carnegie Library, Rome, GA [*Library symbol*] ... GR
Carnegie Magazine [*A publication*] ... Carnegie Mag
Carnegie Magazine [*A publication*] ... CarnM
Carnegie-Mellon University [*Pennsylvania*] ... CMU
Carnegie-Mellon University, Hunt Institute for Botanical Documentation, Pittsburgh, PA [*Library symbol*] ... PPiHB
Carnegie-Mellon University, Mellon Institute, Pittsburgh, PA [*Library symbol*] ... PPiM
Carnegie-Mellon University, Pittsburgh, PA [*OCLC symbol*] ... PMC
Carnegie-Mellon University, Pittsburgh, PA [*Library symbol*] ... PPiC
Carnegie-Mellon University, Pittsburgh. Transportation Research Institute. TRI Research Report [*A publication*] ... Carnegie-Mellon Univ TRI Res Rep
Carnegie Museum of Natural History. Annals [*A publication*] ... Carnegie Mus Annals
Carnegie Museum of Natural History. Annals. Memoirs [*A publication*] ... Carnegie Mus An Mem
Carnegie Museum of Natural History. Annual Report [*A publication*] ... Carnegie Mus Nat Hist Annu Rep
Carnegie Museum of Natural History. Special Publications [*A publication*] ... Carnegie Mus Nat Hist Spec Publ
Carnegie, PA [*Radio station call letters*] ... WPLW
Carnegie Public Library, Angola, IN [*OCLC symbol*] ... IIA
Carnegie Public Library, Angola, IN [*Library symbol*] ... InAng
Carnegie Public Library, Bradford, PA [*Library symbol*] ... PBr
Carnegie Public Library, Clarksdale, MS [*Library symbol*] ... MsCld
Carnegie Public Library, Conneaut, OH [*Library symbol*] ... OConC
Carnegie Public Library of Corning, Corning, CA [*Library symbol*] ... CCorn
Carnegie Public Library, Las Vegas, NM [*OCLC symbol*] ... LVN
Carnegie Public Library, Washington Court House, OH [*Library symbol*] ... OWas
Carnegie Public Library, Washington, IN [*Library symbol*] ... InWas
Carnegie-Rochester Conference Series on Public Policy [*Elsevier Book Series*] [*A publication*] ... CR
Carnegie Series in English [*A publication*] ... CaSE
Carnegie Southern Observatory [*Later, Las Campanas Observatory*] ... CARSO
Carnegie-Stout Free Public Library, Dubuque, IA [*Library symbol*] ... IaDu
Carnelian Bay, CA [*Radio station call letters*] ... KHTX
Carnet Musical [*A publication*] ... Carnet Mus
Carnets de l'Enfance [*A publication*] ... CARN
Carnets de l'Enfance [*A publication*] ... Carn Enfance
Carnets de l'Enfance [*A publication*] ... Carnets Enfance
Carnets de Zoologie [*A publication*] ... Carnets Zool
Carney, William L., Bresman IN [*STAC*] ... CWL
Carnivore Genetics Newsletter [*A publication*] ... Carnivore Genet Newsl
Caro, MI [*Radio station call letters*] ... WKYO
Caro, MI [*Radio station call letters*] ... WKYO-FM
Caro-Wings Flight Service, Inc. [*Rock Hill, SC*] [*FAA designator*] ... CWG
Carol Burnett Fund for Responsible Journalism ... CBFRJ
Carolin Mines Ltd. [*NASDAQ symbol*] ... CRLNF
Carolina Biology Readers [*A publication*] ... Carol Biol Readers
Carolina Casualty Insurance [*NASDAQ symbol*] ... CCIC
Carolina, Clinchfield & Ohio Railway [*NYSE symbol*] [*Delisted*] ... CCL
Carolina Discipliana Library, Wilson, NC [*Library symbol*] ... NcWilC
Carolina Energies, Incorporated [*American Stock Exchange symbol*] [*Delisted*] ... CEI
Carolina Freight Carriers Corp. [*NYSE symbol*] ... CAO
Carolina Library Services, Inc. ... CLS
Carolina & Northwestern Railway Co. [*AAR code*] ... CRN
Carolina Playbook [*A publication*] ... CarP
Carolina Population Center [*University of North Carolina*] ... CPC
Carolina Power & Light Co. [*NYSE symbol*] ... CPL
Carolina, PR [*Radio station call letters*] ... WIDA
Carolina, PR [*Radio station call letters*] ... WIDA-FM
Carolina, PR [*Radio station call letters*] ... WVOZ-FM
Carolina Quarterly [*A publication*] ... Carol Q
Carolina Quarterly [*A publication*] ... CAR Q
Carolina Quarterly [*A publication*] ... CQ
Carolina Regina [*Queen Caroline*] [*Latin*] ... CR
Carolina Southern Railway Co. [*AAR code*] ... CRS
Carolina Tips [*A publication*] ... Carol Tips
Carolina Western [*AAR code*] ... CARW
Carolinas-Virginia Nuclear Power Associates, Inc. ... CVNPA
Carolinas-Virginia Tube Reactor ... CVTR
Caroline County Public Library, Denton, MD [*Library symbol*] ... MdD
Caroline Islands [*MARC geographic area code*] [*Library of Congress*] ... poci---
Carolus Rex [*King Charles*] [*Latin*] ... CR
Carotid Artery System [*Medicine*] ... CAS
Carotid Compression Tomography ... CCT
Carotid Endarterectomy [*Medicine*] ... CE
Carousel Quarterly [*A publication*] ... Carousel Q
Carousel Transfer Tube ... CTT
Carovana [*A publication*] ... Car
Carpal Tunnel [*Medicine*] ... CT
Carpal Tunnel Decompression [*Medicine*] ... CTD
Carpal Tunnel Syndrome [*Medicine*] ... CTS
Carpenter [*or Carpentry*] ... CARP
Carpenter ... CPNTR
Carpenter ... CPTR
Carpenter Technology Corp. [*Formerly, Carpenter Steel Co.*] [*NYSE symbol*] ... CRS
Carpenters' Company ... CC
Carpenters' Company, Philadelphia, PA [*Library symbol*] ... PPCC
Carpenter's Mate ... CM
Carpenter's Mate, Construction Battalion ... CMCB
Carpenter's Mate, Construction Battalion, Builder ... CMCBB
Carpenter's Mate, Construction Battalion, Draftsman ... CMCBD
Carpenter's Mate, Construction Battalion, Excavation Foreman ... CMCBE
Carpenter's Mate, Ship Repair ... CMSR
Carpenter's Mate, Ship Repair, Boatbuilder-Wood ... CMSRB
Carpenter's Mate, Ship Repair, Carpenter ... CMSRC
Carpenter's Mate, Ship Repair, Caulker-Boat ... CMSRK
Carpenter's Mate, Ship Repair, Cement Worker-Concrete ... CMSRN
Carpenter's Mate, Ship Repair, Joiner ... CMSRJ
Carpenter's Mate, Ship Repair, Shipwright ... CMSRS
Carpet ... CARP
Carpet Cushion Council ... CCC
Carpet Manufacturers Marketing Association ... CMMA
Carpet Research, Engineering, Aesthetics, Technological Evaluation [*Dow Chemical Co.*] ... CREATE
Carpet and Rug Industry Consumer Action Panel [*Defunct*] ... CRICAP
Carpet and Rug Institute [*Formerly, ACI, TTMI*] ... CRI
Carpet Wool Council [*Defunct*] ... CWC
Carpeting Mats or Rugs [*Freight*] ... CPTNG MATS RGS
Carpinteria, CA [*Radio station call letters*] ... KGFT
Carpometacarpal [*Anatomy*] ... CMC
Carr-Purcell Spin-Echo ... CPSE
Carrel-Dakin [*Fluid*] ... CD
Carriacou [*Windward Islands*] [*Airport symbol*] ... CRU
Carriage ... CGE
Carriage ... CRG
Carriage Association of America ... CAA
Carriage Control ... CC
Carriage Control Character [*Data processing*] ... CCC
Carriage of Goods [*by sea*] ... C of G
Carriage of Goods by Sea Act ... COGSA
Carriage Paid ... CP
Carriage Return ... CR
Carriage Return Contact ... CRC
Carriage and Wagon Work [*British railroad term*] ... C and W
Carried Down ... CD
Carried Forward [*Accounting*] ... CF
Carried Over [*Accounting*] ... CO
Carrier [*Medicine*] ... C
Carrier ... CAR
Carrier ... CARR
Carrier ... CX
Carrier [*Telecommunications*] ... CXR
Carrier Air Group [*Navy*] ... CAG
Carrier Air Group [*Canadian military*] ... CANCARAIRGRP
Carrier Air Group [*Navy*] ... CARAIRGROUP
Carrier Air Group [*Navy*] ... CVG
Carrier Air Traffic Control Center [*Navy*] ... CATCC
Carrier Air Traffic Control Center - Direct Altitude Identity Readout [*Navy*] ... CATCC-DAIR
Carrier Air Traffic Control Officer [*Navy*] ... CATCO
Carrier Air Wing Reserve [*Navy*] ... CAWR
Carrier Air Wings ... CAW
Carrier Airborne Early Warning Squadron [*Navy*] ... CARAEWRON
Carrier Airborne Early Warning Squadron [*Navy symbol*] ... VAW
Carrier Airborne Early Warning Wing [*Navy*] ... CAEWW
Carrier Aircraft ... CA
Carrier Aircraft Deck Operations Control System [*Navy*] ... CADOCS

Carrier Aircraft Equipment ... CAE
Carrier Aircraft Inertial Navigation System ... CAINS
Carrier Aircraft Modification ... CAM
Carrier Aircraft Operational Compatibility System [*Navy*] ... CAOCS
Carrier Aircraft Service Detachment [*Marine Corps*] ... CASD
Carrier Aircraft Service Division [*Navy*] ... CASD
Carrier Aircraft Service Division [*Navy*] ... CASDIV
Carrier Aircraft Service Unit [*Navy*] ... CASU
Carrier Aircraft Squadron Effectiveness Evaluation ... CASEE
Carrier Aircraft Support Study [*Navy*] ... CASS
Carrier All-Weather Flying ... CAWF
Carrier Antisubmarine Air Group [*Navy*] ... COMCARANTISUBAIRGRU
Carrier Antisubmarine Air Group ... CVSG
Carrier Balloon/Omegasonde System [*National Center for Atmospheric Research*] ... CBO
Carrier-Based ... CB
Carrier-Based Airborne Tactical Data System ... CB/ATDS
Carrier-Based Tactical Support Center [*Navy*] ... CVTSC
Carrier Battle Group [*Navy*] ... CVBG
Carrier-Borne Air Liaison Section [*Navy*] ... CBALS
Carrier-Borne Air Liaison Section [*Navy*] ... CBLS
Carrier-Borne Ground Liaison Officer [*Military*] [*British*] ... CBGLO
Carrier Color Signal ... CCS
Carrier Controlled Approach [*Aircraft carrier RADAR landing system*] ... CCA
Carrier-Controlled Approach System ... CCAS
Carrier Corp. [*NYSE symbol*] [*Delisted*] ... CRR
Carrier Corp., Library, Syracuse, NY [*OCLC symbol*] ... ZUE
Carrier Corp., Syracuse, NY [*Library symbol*] ... NSyC
Carrier-on-Deck [*Navy carrier-based aircraft*] ... COD
Carrier Detector ... CD
Carrier Division [*Navy*] ... CARDIV
Carrier Elimination Filter ... CEF
Carrier Evaluation and Reporting System ... CERS
Carrier and Field Service Unit ... CAFSU
Carrier-Free [*Radioisotope*] ... CF
Carrier Frequency [*Radio*] ... CF
Carrier Frequency Pulse ... CFP
Carrier Frequency Shift ... CFS
Carrier Gas Fusion [*Chemistry*] ... CGF
Carrier Group Alarm [*Telephone communications*] ... CGA
Carrier Input ... CIN
Carrier-to-Interference Ratio [*Data processing*] ... C/I
Carrier-to-Interference Ratio ... CIR
Carrier Landing-Aid Stabilization System [*Navy*] ... CLASS
Carrier-to-Noise [*Ratio*] ... C/N
Carrier-to-Noise Density ... C/No
Carrier-to-Noise Density, Downlink ... C/No)d
Carrier-to-Noise Density, Intermodulation ... C/No)im
Carrier-to-Noise Density, Total ... C/No)t
Carrier-to-Noise Density, Uplink ... C/No)u
Carrier-to-Noise, Downlink ... C/N)d
Carrier-to-Noise, Intermodulation ... C/N)im
Carrier Noise Level ... CNL
Carrier-to-Noise Ratio ... CNR
Carrier-to-Noise Temperature ... C/T
Carrier-to-Noise Temperature, Downlink ... C/T)d
Carrier-to-Noise Temperature, Intermodulation ... C/T)im
Carrier-to-Noise Temperature, Total ... C/T)t
Carrier-to-Noise Temperature, Uplink ... C/T)u
Carrier-to-Noise, Total ... C/N)t
Carrier-to-Noise, Uplink ... C/N)u
Carrier Onboard Delivery [*Naval aviation*] ... COD
Carrier-Operated Device, Antinoise [*Radio*] ... CODAN
Carrier-Operated Noise Suppression ... CONS
Carrier-Operated Relay ... COR
Carrier Performance Rating ... CPR
Carrier Qualification [*Navy*] ... CARQUAL
Carrier Qualification Training Unit ... CQTU
Carrier Replacement Air Group [*Navy*] ... CRAG
Carrier Replacement Air Wing [*Navy*] ... CRAW
Carrier Sense Multiple Access with Collision Detection [*Data processing*] ... CSMA/CD
Carrier Stability ... CS
Carrier Striking Force [*Tactical Air Command*] ... CARSTRIKFOR
Carrier Striking Force [*Tactical Air Command*] ... CSF
Carrier Striking Group One [*NATO*] ... CARSTRIKGRUONE
Carrier Striking Group Two [*NATO*] ... CARSTRIKGRUTWO
Carrier Suitability ... CARSUIT
Carrier Supply ... CS
Carrier System for Control Approach of Naval Aircraft ... C-SCAN
Carrier Tactical Control Zone [*Military*] ... CTCZ
Carrier Task Force [*Navy*] ... CARTASKFOR
Carrier Telegraph Receiver ... CTR
Carrier Telephone Channel ... CT
Carrier Test Switch ... CTS
Carrier Tracking Loop ... CTL
Carrier Transfer Station ... CTS
Carrier Transmission Maintenance System [*Bell System*] ... CTMS
Carrier Vessel Reactor ... CVR
Carrier Wave [*A form of radio transmission in code*] ... CRW
Carrier Wave [*A form of radio transmission in code*] ... CW
Carriers & General Corp. [*NYSE symbol*] [*Delisted*] ... CGR
Carriers, Pacific Fleet [*Navy*] ... CARPAC
Carrier's Risk [*Shipping*] ... CR
Carrington, ND [*Radio station call letters*] ... KDAK
Carrington, ND [*Radio station call letters*] ... KDAK-FM
Carrizo [*California*] [*Seismograph station code, US Geological Survey*] ... CRR
Carrizo Springs, TX [*Location identifier*] [*FAA*] ... CZT
Carrizo Springs, TX [*Radio station call letters*] ... KBEN
Carrol, IA [*Radio station call letters*] ... KKRL
Carroll Center for the Blind ... CCB
Carroll College, Helena, MT [*Library symbol*] ... MtHC
Carroll College, Library, Helena, MT [*OCLC symbol*] ... MTC
Carroll College, Waukesha, WI [*OCLC symbol*] ... GZB
Carroll College, Waukesha, WI [*Library symbol*] ... WWauC
Carroll County Heritage Center, Berryville, AR [*Library symbol*] ... ArBerC
Carroll County Historical Society Museum, Carroll, IA [*Library symbol*] ... IaCarCH
Carroll County Public Library, Westminster, MD [*Library symbol*] ... MdWem
Carroll, IA [*Location identifier*] [*FAA*] ... CIN
Carroll, IA [*Radio station call letters*] ... KCIM
Carroll Public Library, Carroll, IA [*Library symbol*] ... IaCar
Carrollton, AL [*Radio station call letters*] ... WAQT
Carrollton, AL [*Radio station call letters*] ... WRAG
Carrollton Community Unit, District 1, Carrollton, IL [*Library symbol*] ... ICarrCD
Carrollton, GA [*Location identifier*] [*FAA*] ... GPQ
Carrollton, GA [*Radio station call letters*] ... WBTR
Carrollton, GA [*Radio station call letters*] ... WLBB
Carrollton, GA [*Radio station call letters*] ... WPPI
Carrollton, GA [*Radio station call letters*] ... WWGC
Carrollton, KY [*Radio station call letters*] ... WIKI
Carrollton, MO [*Radio station call letters*] ... KAOL
Carrollton, MO [*Radio station call letters*] ... KMZU
Carrollton, OH [*Location identifier*] [*FAA*] ... TSO
Carrollton Press, Inc., Washington, DC [*Library symbol*] ... CarP
Carrollton Public Library, Carrollton, IL [*Library symbol*] ... ICarr
[*The*] **Carrollton Railroad** [*AAR code*] ... CARR
Carrols Development Corp. [*American Stock Exchange symbol*] ... CRL
Carronade ... CAR
Carrow Elicited Language Inventory [*Education*] ... CELI
Carrville, AL [*Radio station call letters*] ... WACQ
Carry ... CY
Carry Forward ... C/F
Carry-On Box ... COB
Carry-On Laboratory [*NASA*] ... COL
Carry-On Oxygen System ... COS
Carry Out Remainder Basic Orders ... CARBASORD
Carry Propagate Adder [*Computer*] ... CPA
Carrying ... CRYG
Carrying [*Freight*] ... CRYNG
Carrying Capacity [*An association*] ... CC
Carrying Concealed Deadly Weapon [*Police term*] ... CCDW
Carrying Concealed Weapon [*Police term*] ... CCW
Carrying a Dangerous Weapon [*Police term*] ... CDW
Carson City [*Nevada*] [*Mint mark, when appearing on US coins*] [*Obsolete*] ... CC
Carson City, NV [*Radio station call letters*] ... KKBC
Carson City, NV [*Radio station call letters*] ... KNIS
Carson City, NV [*Radio station call letters*] ... KPTL
Carson City Public Library, Carson City, MI [*Library symbol*] ... MiCc
Carson Hill [*California*] [*Seismograph station code, US Geological Survey*] ... CRH
Carson-Newman College [*Tennessee*] ... CNC
Carson-Newman College, Jefferson City, TN [*OCLC symbol*] ... TCN
Carson-Newman College, Jefferson City, TN [*Library symbol*] ... TJefC
Carson Pirie Scott & Co. [*NYSE symbol*] ... CRN
Carson Times, Carson, IA [*Library symbol*] ... IaCarsT
Carson's Rule Bandwidth ... CRBW
Cartage ... CTG
Cartage ... CTGE
Cartagena [*Colombia*] [*Airport symbol*] ... CTG
Cartago [*Columbia*] [*Airport symbol*] ... CRC
Carte Blanche [*Credit card*] ... CB
Carte Blanche [*Freedom of Action*] [*French*] ... CBL
Carte Segrete [*A publication*] ... Carte
Carte de Visite [*Visiting Card*] [*French*] ... CDV
Carte de Visite [*Visiting Card*] [*French*] ... C de V
Cartel des Syndicats Caledoniens [*Federation of New Caledonian Trade Unions*] ... CSC
Carter & Burgess, Inc., Fort Worth, TX [*Library symbol*] ... TxFCB
Carter Hawley Hale Stores, Inc. [*NYSE symbol*] ... CHH
Carter-Wallace, Inc. [*NYSE symbol*] ... CAR
Carteret Savings & Loan Association [*NASDAQ symbol*] ... CFCC
Carteret Technical Institute, Morehead City, NC [*Library symbol*] ... NcMcC
Carters Dam [*Georgia*] [*Seismograph station code, US Geological Survey*] ... CDG
Cartersville, GA [*Radio station call letters*] ... WBHF
Cartersville, GA [*Radio station call letters*] ... WCCV
Cartersville, GA [*Radio station call letters*] ... WYXC

Cartesian Coordinate Grid ... CCG
Cartesian Mapping Function ... CMF
Cartesian to Polar ... C-P
Carthage ... CARTH
Carthage College, Kenosha, WI [*OCLC symbol*] ... GZC
Carthage College, Kenosha, WI [*Library symbol*] ... WKenC
Carthage, IL [*Radio station call letters*] ... WCAZ
Carthage, IL [*Radio station call letters*] ... WCAZ-FM
Carthage, MO [*Radio station call letters*] ... KDMO
Carthage, MO [*Radio station call letters*] ... KRGK
Carthage, MS [*Radio station call letters*] ... WECP
Carthage, MS [*Radio station call letters*] ... WWYN
Carthage, NY [*Radio station call letters*] ... WTOJ
Carthage, NY [*Television station call letters*] ... WWNY-TV
Carthage Public Library, Carthage, IL [*Library symbol*] ... ICart
Carthage Public Library, Carthage, SD [*Library symbol*] ... SdCar
Carthage, TN [*Radio station call letters*] ... WRKM
Carthage, TN [*Radio station call letters*] ... WRKM-FM
Carthage, TX [*Radio station call letters*] ... KGAS
Carthusian ... CARTH
Carti [*Panama*] [*Airport symbol*] ... CTE
Cartilla Electoral para el Plebiscito [*Colombia*] ... CARPLE
Carting to Shipside ... C to S
Carto-Philatelists ... CP
Cartographer [*or Cartography*] ... CRTOG
Cartographer [*Navy rating*] ... CT
Cartographic Assistant [*Ministry of Agriculture, Fisheries, and Food*] [*British*] ... CA
Cartographic Conversion Station ... CCS
Cartographic and Geodetic Processing Squadron [*Air Force*] ... CGPSq
Cartographic Journal [*A publication*] ... Cartogr J
Cartographic Test Standard [*Air Force*] ... CTS
Cartography ... CART
Cartography ... CARTOG
Carton ... C
Carton ... CRTN
Carton ... CT
Carton ... CTN
Cartoon Archetypical Slogan Theater [*London*] ... CAST
Cartoonists Guild ... CG
Cartophilic Society of Great Britain ... CSGB
Cartridge ... CRTG
Cartridge ... CTG
Cartridge-Actuated Device [*Military*] ... CAD
Cartridge-Actuated Devices [*Military*] ... CADS
Cartridge-Actuated Flame System [*Terminated*] [*Military*] ... CAFS
Cartridge Assembly Test ... CAT
Cartridge Storage Case ... CSC
Cartuja [*Granada*] [*Spain*] [*Seismograph station code, US Geological Survey*] ... CRT
Carupano [*Venezuela*] [*Airport symbol*] ... CUP
Carus ... K
Carus Chemical Co., Inc., LaSalle, IL [*Library symbol*] ... ILasC
Caruthersville, MO [*Radio station call letters*] ... KCRV
Caruthersville, MO [*Radio station call letters*] ... KCRV-FM
Carver County Library, Chaska, MN [*Library symbol*] ... MnCh
Carver, J. C., Neptune NJ [*STAC*] ... CJC
Carwash Operators Association ... COA
Cary Memorial Library, Lexington, MA [*OCLC symbol*] ... LEX
Cary Memorial Library, Lexington, MA [*Library symbol*] ... MLex
Casa de las Americas [*A publication*] ... CAm
Casa de las Americas [*A publication*] ... CasaA
Casa Editrice Dott. A. Milani [*Italian publisher*] ... CEDAM
Casa Grande, AZ [*Location identifier*] [*FAA*] ... CZG
Casa Grande, AZ [*Radio station call letters*] ... KPIN
Casa Grande, AZ [*Radio station call letters*] ... KSAA
Casa Grande, AZ [*Radio station call letters*] ... KWLL
Casa Grande Public Library, Casa Grande, AZ [*Library symbol*] ... AzCg
Casa Grande Ruins National Monument [*National Park Service designation*] ... CAGR
Casabella [*A publication*] ... CSBL-A
Casablanca [*Morocco*] [*Airport symbol*] ... CAS
CasaBlanca Industries [*American Stock Exchange symbol*] ... CAB
Casablanca-Mohamed V [*Morocco*] [*Airport symbol*] ... CMN
Casamari [*Italy*] [*Seismograph station code, US Geological Survey*] [*Closed*] ... CAS
Casamicciolo [*Isola D'Ischia*] [*Italy*] [*Seismograph station code, US Geological Survey*] [*Closed*] ... CSM
Casamino Acids [*Biochemistry*] ... CAA
Cascade ... CAS
Cascade Airways [*Spokane, WA*] [*FAA designator*] ... CCD
Cascade Amplifier ... CA
Cascade Charge Coupled Device [*Electronics*] ... C3D
Cascade College, Portland, OR [*Library symbol*] ... OrPC
Cascade Corp. [*NASDAQ symbol*] ... CASC
Cascade Improvement Program [*AEC*] ... CIP
Cascade Locks, OR [*Location identifier*] [*FAA*] ... CZK
Cascade Microfilm Systems, Inc., Portland, OR [*Library symbol*] ... CmI
Cascade Natural Gas Corporation [*NYSE symbol*] ... CGC
Cascade Orificial Restrictive Device ... CORD
Cascade Pioneer-Advertiser, Cascade, IA [*Library symbol*] ... IaCasPA
Cascade Steel Rolling Mills, Inc. [*NASDAQ symbol*] ... CSRL
Cascade Uprating Program [*AEC*] ... CUP
Cascadia Juvenile Diagnostic Center, Tacoma, WA [*Library symbol*] ... WaTCJ
Cascadian Regional Library [*A publication*] ... CAREL
Cascavel [*Brazil*] [*Airport symbol*] ... CAC
Case ... C
Case ... CS
Case Aide [*Red Cross*] ... CA
Case Assignment Control File [*IRS*] ... CACF
Case Collectors Club ... CCC
Case and Comment [*A publication*] ... Case & Com
Case [*J. I.*] **Co.** [*NYSE symbol*] [*Delisted*] ... JI
Case Fatality Ratio [*Medicine*] ... CFR
Case Handling Information Processing System [*National Labor Relations Board*] ... CHIPS
Case Harden [*Metal*] [*Technical drawings*] ... CH
Case Institute of Technology [*Later, Case Western Reserve University*] [*Ohio*] ... CIT
Case of Need ... CN
Case Of ... C/O
Case Oil ... C/O
Case-Oriented Studies Information Retrieval System [*Later, TISCA*] [*Navy*] ... COSIRS
Case Project [*IRS*] ... C/P
Case Project Master File [*IRS*] ... CPMF
Case Studies in Atomic Physics [*A publication*] ... Case Stud At Phys
Case Supervisor [*Red Cross*] [*Services to the Armed Forces; Disaster Services*] ... CS
Case Western Reserve Journal of International Law [*A publication*] ... Case West J Int Law
Case Western Reserve Journal of International Law [*A publication*] ... Case W Res
Case Western Reserve Journal of International Law [*A publication*] ... Case W Res J Int L
Case Western Reserve Law Review [*A publication*] ... Case W Reserve Law R
Case Western Reserve Law Review [*A publication*] ... Case W Reserve L Rev
Case Western Reserve Law Review [*A publication*] ... Cas W Res L Rev
Case Western Reserve University [*Ohio*] ... CWRU
Case Western Reserve University, Cleveland Health Sciences Library, Cleveland, OH [*Library symbol*] ... OCIW-H
Case Western Reserve University, Cleveland, OH [*OCLC symbol*] ... CWR
Case Western Reserve University, Cleveland, OH [*Library symbol*] ... OCIW
Case Western Reserve University Law Library, Cleveland, OH [*OCLC symbol*] ... CWL
Case Western Reserve University, School of Library Science, Cleveland, OH [*Library symbol*] ... OCIW-LS
Case Western Reserve University, Sears Library, Cleveland, OH [*Library symbol*] ... OCIW-S
Casein Hydrolyzate [*Cell growth medium*] ... CH
Casein Importers Association ... CIA
Caseless Ammunition Aerial Gun System ... CAAGS
Caseless Round Gun Program [*Military*] ... CRGP
Casement Aviation [*Painesville, OH*] [*FAA designator*] ... CMT
Casement Projected Transom [*Technical drawings*] ... CPT
Cases ... C/S
Cases and Cabinets [*JETDS nomenclature*] [*Military*] ... CY
Cases per Officer [*Term used by crime laboratories*] ... CPO
Cases of Settlements and Removals [*Legal*] [*British*] ... CASETT
Casework ... CW
Casework Supervisor [*Red Cross*] ... CWS
Caseworker ... CW
Casey [*Australia*] [*Geomagnetic observatory code*] ... CSY
Casey, IL [*Location identifier*] [*FAA*] ... CZB
Casey, IL [*Radio station call letters*] ... WKZI
Casey Jones Railroad Unit [*American Topical Association*] ... CJRRU
Casey's General Stores [*NASDAQ symbol*] ... CASY
Cash [*NYSE symbol*] ... C
Cash in Advance ... CIA
Cash Against Documents [*Banking*] ... CAD
Cash Against Policy [*Insurance*] ... CAP
Cash Before Delivery ... CBD
Cash Book ... CB
Cash Clothing Allowance ... CCA
Cash Credit ... CC
Cash on Delivery ... COD
Cash on Delivery Service ... CDS
Cash Discount ... CD
Cash Dispenser ... CD
Cash versus Documents ... CVD
Cash in Fist ... CIF
Cash Letter [*Banking*] ... C/L
Cash Management Account [*Merrill Lynch*] ... CMA
Cash Management Institute ... CMI
Cash Management Practitioners Association [*Later, NCCMA*] ... CMPA
Cash Order ... CO
Cash with Order ... CWO
Cash Purchasing Agent ... CPA
Cash on Receipt ... COR
Cash Register Tape ... CRT
Cash-on-Shipment ... COS

Cash Value Life Insurance CVLI
Cashier ....CASH
Cashiers' Automatic Processing System ....CAPS
Cashier's Check CC
CASI [Canadian Aeronautics and Space Institute] Transactions [A publication]..............................CASI Trans
Casing ....CSG
Casino [Australia] [Airport symbol]...........................CSI
Casitas Dam [California] [Seismograph station code, US Geological Survey]...BCD
Casitas Lake [California] [Seismograph station code, US Geological Survey] [Closed] ....BCL
Cask ....CK
Cask ....CSK
Cask Loading Station [Nuclear energy]......................CLS
Cask Support Structure [Nuclear energy]...................CSS
Cask Tilting Fixture [Nuclear energy].........................CTF
Casket Manufacturers Association of America ....CMA
Casopis Ceskenho Musea [A publication]..................CCM
Casopis Ceskoslovenske. Spolecnosti Entomologicke [A publication].......................Cas Cesk Spolecnosti Entomol
Casopis Katolickeko Duckovenstva a Prilohou [A publication]...............CKD
Casopis Lekaru Ceskych [A publication] .... Cas Lek Cesk
Casopis Lekaru Ceskych [A publication] ....CLCEA
Casopis Matice Moravske [A publication]...................CMM
Casopis pro Moderni Filologii [A publication]............CMF
Casopis pro Moderni Filologii [A publication]...........CpMF
Casopis pro Moderni Filologii a Literatury [A publication] ....CMFL
Casopis Moravskeho Muzea [A publication]........ Cas Morav Muz
Casopis Narodniho Muzea [Prague] [A publication] ....CNM
Casopis Narodniho Muzea. Historicke Muzeum Rocnik [Prague] [A publication].......................Cas Narod Muz
Casopis Narodniho Muzea. Oddil Priroddovedny [Prague] [A publication] .... Cas Nar Muz Oddil Priroddoved
Casopis Narodniho Muzea (Prague) [A publication] .... Cas Nar Muz (Prague)
Casopis Rodopisne Spolecnosti Ceskoslovenske [A publication]...........CRodSpol
Casopis Slezskeho Muzea [A publication] .... Cas Slezske Muz
Casopis Slezskeho Muzea. Series A. Scientiae Naturales [A publication]...........Cas Slezskeho Muz Ser A Sci Nat
Casopis pro Slovanske Jazyky, Literaturu, a Dejiny SSSR [A publication]...CSJ
Casopis pro Slovanske Jazyky, Literaturu, a Dejiny SSSR [A publication]..CSLJa
Casopis Vlasteveckseho Spolku Musejuiho v Olomouci [A publication]...........CVSMO
Caspair Ltd. [Kenya] [ICAO designator] ....QP
Casper [Wyoming] [Airport symbol]...........................CPR
Casper Air Service [Casper, WY] [FAA designator] ....CSP
Casper College, Casper, WY [Library symbol]..........WyCaC
Casper, WY [Radio station call letters]......................KATI
Casper, WY [Radio station call letters]....................KAWY
Casper, WY [Radio station call letters].................KAWY-FM
Casper, WY [Television station call letters]...........KCWY-TV
Casper, WY [Radio station call letters].....................KQLT
Casper, WY [Radio station call letters].....................KTRS
Casper, WY [Radio station call letters].....................KTWO
Casper, WY [Television station call letters]............KTWO-TV
Casper, WY [Radio station call letters].....................KVOC
Casper, WY [Location identifier] [FAA] ....SYD
Caspian Sea and Area [MARC geographic area code] [Library of Congress]...ak-----
Cass County Court House, Fargo, ND [Library symbol]..........NdFC
Cass County Library, Cassopolis, MI [Library symbol].............MiCassC
Cassa di Risparmio delle Provincie Lombarde [Italian savings bank]...........CARIPLO
Cassegrain Feed System..CFS
Cassegrain Reflector Antenna...................................CRA
Cassel Group Level of Aspiration Test [Psychology] ....CGLAT
Cassel Psychotherapy Progress Record [Psychology]............CPPR
Cassenne [France] [Research code symbol] C
Cassenne [France] [Research code symbol] ....CS
Cassette Information Services......................................CIS
Cassette Transport System...CTS
Cassier's Magazine [A publication] ....Cassier
Cassilandia [Brazil] [Airport symbol]........................CSS
Cassiopeia [Constellation]..Cas
Cassiopeia [Constellation]...Cass
Cassiopeia A [Constellation]......................................CasA
Cast C
Cast Brass ....CB
Cast Bronze Bearing Institute [Later, CBI].................CBBI
Cast Bronze Institute [Formerly, CBBI]......................CBI
Cast Bullet Association ....CBA
Cast Carbon Steel ....CCS
Cast Copper CC
Cast Double Base ....CDB
Cast Iron CI
Cast-Iron Pipe [Technical drawings]...........................CIP
Cast Iron Pipe Research Association [Later, DIPRA] ......CIPRA
Cast Iron Seat Collectors Association ....CISCA

Cast Iron Soil Pipe Foundation [Defunct]..................CISPF
Cast Iron Soil Pipe Institute.......................................CISPI
Cast Metal Part ....CMP
Cast Metals Federation..CMF
Cast-Out-Nines..CON
Cast Steel ....CS
Cast Stone ....CS
Castable Smoke Mix Grenade..................................CSMG
Castalia Foundation [Defunct].....................................CF
Castalia, OH [Radio station call letters].................WGGN
Castaway [Fiji] [Airport symbol]..................................CST
Castel Tesino [Italy] [Geomagnetic observatory code] ....CTS
Castellate ....CSTL
Caster and Floor Truck Manufacturers Association ....CFT
Caster and Floor Truck Manufacturers Association ....CFTMA
Casters and Towbar..CT
Castilejo-Dalitz-Dyson..CDD
Castillo de San Marcos National Monument.............CASA
Casting ....CSTG
Casting Engineering [A publication].....................Cast Eng
Castle C
Castle ....CAS
Castle Clinton National Monument...........................CACL
Castle [A. M.] & Co. [American Stock Exchange symbol] ....CAS
Castle Convertible Fund, Inc. [American Stock Exchange symbol]......CVF
Castle & Cooke, Inc. [NYSE symbol]..........................CKE
Castle Entertainment [NASDAQ symbol]................CPRQC
Castle Hill Museum, Cobham, VA [Library symbol]......ViCoC
Castle Industries [American Stock Exchange symbol] ....CSE
Castle Mountain [California] [Seismograph station code, US Geological Survey]...CTM
Castle Rock [California] [Seismograph station code, US Geological Survey]...CRC
Castle Rock [New York] [Seismograph station code, US Geological Survey]...CTR
Castle Rock, CO [Radio station call letters]............KRKY
Castlegar [Canada] [Airport symbol].........................YCG
Castlegar, BC [Radio station call letters].................CKQR
Castlepoint [New Zealand] [Seismograph station code, US Geological Survey]...CAZ
Castles Association ....CA
Castleton Industries, Incorporated [American Stock Exchange symbol] [Delisted].................................CII
Castleton State College, Castleton, VT [Library symbol]........VtCasT
Castleton, VT [Radio station call letters].................WIUV
Castor Oil...CO
Castroville, TX [Location identifier] [FAA]..................CVB
Castrovirreyna [Peru] [Seismograph station code, US Geological Survey]...CST
Castrum Peregrini [A publication]..................................C
Castrum Peregrini [A publication].................................CP
Castrum Peregrini [A publication]................................CPe
Casual ....CAS
Casual Disability Exclusion......................................CDEX
Casual Payment..CASPMT
Casualties Union ....CU
Casualty ....CAS
Casualty Actuarial Society.......................................CAS
Casualty Air Evacuation Unit [RAF] [British]............CAEU
Casualty Analysis for Determining Weapon System Effectiveness [Army]..................................CAWSE
Casualty Assistance Calls Officer.............................CACO
Casualty Assistance Calls Program...........................CACP
Casualty Branch [BUPERS] ....CB
Casualty Canceled [Navy].....................................CASCAN
Casualty Clearing Station [Military].........................CCS
Casualty Collecting-Post...CCP
Casualty Corrected [Navy]....................................CASCOR
Casualty Department [British police]...........................CD
Casualty Estimation Study [Military]..........................CES
Casualty Evacuation..CASEVAC
Casualty Evacuation and Control Ship [Navy]..........CECS
Casualty Evacuation Officer.....................................CEO
Casualty Evacuation Train [British]............................CET
Casualty Firing Panel..CFP
Casualty Officer ....CO
Casualty Receiving Hospital [British].......................CRH
Casualty Report [Navy]...CASREP
Casualty Report [Navy].......................................CASREPT
Casualty Situation Report.....................................CASSIT
Casualty Staging Facility [Military]...........................CSF
Casualty Staging Unit [Military].................................CSU
Casualty Underwriting Manual..................................CUM
Casualty Vulnerability Number.................................CVN
Casualty Weapon Director...CWD
Casualty Weapon Director Panel..............................CWDP
Cat Cay [Bahamas] [Airport symbol].........................CXY
Cat Collectors [Commercial firm] CC
Cat Fanciers' Association ....CFA
Cat Fanciers' Federation...CFF
Cat Fund ....CF

Cat Pack [*"Women's Wear Daily" slang for jetsetters*]..............CP
Cat Scratch Disease [*Medicine*]..............CSD
Catabolite Gene Activator Protein [*Biochemistry, genetics*]..............CAP
Cataclysmic Binary [*Data processing*]..............CB
Catafalque..............CAT
Catahoula Parish Library, Harrisonburg, LA [*Library symbol*]..............LHarC
Catalan [*Language, etc.*]..............CAT
Catalan [*MARC language code*] [*Library of Congress*]..............cat
Catalina Airlines, Incorporated [*Long Beach, CA*] [*FAA designator*]..............CAI
Catalina Island [*California*] [*Airport symbol*]..............AVX
Catalina Island [*California*] [*Seismograph station code, US Geological Survey*]..............CIS
Catalina Island [*California*] [*Airport symbol*] [*Obsolete*]..............TWH
Catalina Island [*California*] **Airport in the Sky** [*Airport symbol*]..............CIB
Catalina Marine Science Center..............CMSC
Catalog..............C
Catalog..............CAT
Catalog..............CATA
Catalog..............CATLG
Catalog Access System [*Project for automated library systems*]..............CATS
Catalog of American Portraits [*Smithsonian Institution*]..............CAP
Catalog of Approved Requirement Documents [*Army*]..............CARDS
Catalog of Available and Standard Hardware [*NASA*]..............CASH
Catalog Events [*Exhibition of US company product catalogs, etc., in foreign markets*] [*Department of Commerce*]..............CE
Catalog of Federal Domestic Assistance [*A publication*]..............CFDA
Catalog for Information Exchange and Message Standards..............CIEMS
Catalog Management Data Notification [*Army*]..............CMDN
Catalog of Navy Training Courses..............CANTRAC
Catalog Number..............CANO
Catalog On-Line [*Data base*] [*National Library of Medicine*]..............CATLINE
Catalog of the Public Documents [*A bibliographic publication*]..............CPD
Catalog Recovery Area [*Data processing*]..............CRA
Catalog Services Association [*Defunct*]..............CSA
Catalog Support System..............CATSS
Catalog Typing Worksheet [*for MT/ST typist*]..............CWS
Cataloging and Classification Section [*of ALA*]..............CCS
Cataloging and Classification Section's Descriptive Cataloging Committee [*of ALA*]..............CCS/DCC
Cataloging Code Revision Committee [*of ALA*]..............CCRC
Cataloging Distribution Service [*Library of Congress*]..............CDS
Cataloging and Indexing Number [*Later, AGRICOLA*] [*National Agricultural Library*]..............CAIN
Cataloging Management Data [*Army*]..............CMD
Cataloging in Publication [*Formerly, CIS*] [*Library science*]..............CIP
Cataloging Responsibility Code..............CRC
Cataloging Service Bulletin [*A publication*]..............CSB
Cataloging Services Department, OCLC [*Online Computer Library Center*], Inc., Columbus, OH [*OCLC symbol*]..............SER
Cataloging in Source [*Later, CIP*] [*Library science*]..............CIS
Catalogue of American Amphibians and Reptiles [*A publication*]..............Cat Am Amphib Reptiles
Catalogue Collectif des Periodiques [*A bibliographic publication*]..............CCP
Catalogue de l'Edition Francaise..............CEF
Catalogue and Index [*A publication*]..............Cat Index
Catalogue des Invertebres de la Suisse Museum d'Histoire Naturelle de Geneve [*A publication*]..............Cat Invertebres Suisse Mus Hist Nat Geneve
Catalogue Magazine..............CATAZINE
Catalogue des Theses de Doctorat [*A bibliographic publication*] [*France*]..............CTD
Catalogued..............CD
Cataloguing and Classification Quarterly [*A publication*]..............C & CQ
Catalogus Faunae Austriae [*A publication*]..............Cat Faunae Austriae
Catalogus Faunae Polonia [*A publication*]..............Cat Faunae Pol
Catalogus Fossilium Austriae [*A publication*]..............Cat Fossilium Austriae
Catalysis Reviews [*A publication*]..............Catal Rev
Catalysis Reviews. Science and Engineering [*A publication*]..............Catal Rev Sci Eng
Catalyst..............CTLST
Catalyst for Environmental Quality [*A publication*]..............Catal Environ Qual
Catalyst for Environmental Quality [*A publication*]..............Catalyst Envir Qual
Catalyst Resources for Women [*Bibliographic database*]..............CRFW
Catalysts in Chemistry [*A publication*]..............Catal Chem
Catalytic Coal Gasification [*Fuel technology*]..............CCG
Catalytic Coal Liquefaction..............CCL
Catalytic Construction Company..............CATCO
Catalytic Construction Company..............CCC
Catalytic Construction Company..............CCCO
Catalytic-Dow..............C-D
Catalytic Optimum Profit-Sharing..............COPS
Catalytic Oxidation..............CAT-OX
Catalytic Rich Gas..............CRG
Catamaran Mine Disposal System..............CATMDV
Catamarca [*Argentina*] [*Airport symbol*]..............CTC
Catania [*Italy*] [*Seismograph station code, US Geological Survey*]..............CAT
Catania [*Italy*] [*Airport symbol*]..............CTA
Catapilco [*Chile*] [*Seismograph station code, US Geological Survey*]..............CTP
Cataplasm [*Poultice*] [*Pharmacy*]..............CAT
Cataplasm [*Poultice*] [*Pharmacy*]..............CATAPLSM
Catapult..............CAT

Catapult Aircraft Merchantship [*Used by British RAF to catapult Hurricane fighter planes from ships to defend convoys from enemy bombers*] [*World War II*]..............CAM
Catapult Arresting Gear and Landing Aids Maintenance [*Aviation*]..............CALM
Catapult and Arresting Gear Pool [*Navy*]..............CAP
Catapult Bulletin..............CB
Catapult Hookup and Launch Surveillance..............CAHALS
Catapult Lighter [*Navy symbol*]..............YVC
Catarman [*Philippines*] [*Airport symbol*]..............CRM
Catarrhal Colds [*Medicine*]..............C (Colds)
Catastrophic Failure Rate..............CFR
Catastrophic Health Expense Protection Plan..............CHEPP
Catawba College, Salisbury, NC [*Library symbol*]..............NcSalC
Catawba County Library, Newton, NC [*Library symbol*]..............NcNt
Catawba Valley Technical Institute, Hickory, NC [*Library symbol*]..............NcHyC
Catboat Association..............CA
Catch Basin [*Technical drawings*]..............CB
Catch Phrase..............CP
Catch Society of America [*Defunct*]..............CSA
Catch per Standard Day of Fishing..............CPSDF
Catcher [*Baseball*]..............C
Catechism..............C
Catechism..............CAT
Catechol-O-Methyltransferase [*An enzyme*]..............CCMT
Catechol-O-Methyltransferase [*An enzyme*]..............COMT
Catecholamine [*or Catecholaminergic*] [*Biochemistry*]..............CA
Catecholamine [*Biochemistry*]..............CAT
Catecholamine Club..............CC
Catecholamines Radioenzymic Assay Kit [*Clinical chemistry*] [*Acronym is trademark*]..............CAT-A-KIT
Categorical Grammar..............CG
Category..............CAT
Category..............CTGY
Category Stimulus [*To light*]..............CS
Catequesis Latinoamericana [*A publication*]..............Cateques Latinoamer
Catering Industry Employee [*A publication*]..............CIE
Caterpillar Club..............CC
Caterpillar Tractor Co. [*Wall Street slang name: "Cat"*] [*NYSE symbol*]..............CAT
Caterpillar Tractor Co. [*NYSE symbol; later, CAT*] [*Wall Street slang name: "Cat"*]..............CTR
Caterpillar Tractor Co., Business Library, Peoria, IL [*Library symbol*]..............IPCT
Caterpillar Tractor Co., Peoria, IL [*OCLC symbol*]..............IDX
Caterpillar Tractor Co., Technical Information Center, Peoria, IL [*OCLC symbol*]..............ISH
Catfish Farmers of America..............CFA
Catfish Pond [*New Jersey*] [*Seismograph station code, US Geological Survey*] [*Closed*]..............CNJ
Catgut Acoustical Society..............CAS
Catgut Suture [*Medicine*]..............CGS
Cathartic [*Medicine*]..............CATH
Cathay Pacific Airways Ltd. [*ICAO designator*]..............CX
Cathays [*Cardiff*] [*Welsh depot code*]..............CYS
Cathedral..............CATH
Cathedral..............CATHL
Cathedral..............CD
Cathedral..............CTHDL
Cathedral City, CA [*Radio station call letters*]..............KWXY
Cathedral City, CA [*Radio station call letters*]..............KWXY-FM
Cathedral Organists' Association..............COA
Cathedral Peace Institute..............CPI
Cathedral Priory..............CDPR
Cathedral of Saint John the Divine, New York, NY [*Library symbol*]..............NNSJD
Catheter [*Medicine*]..............CATH
Catheter Corporation of America [*NASDAQ symbol*]..............CCAM
Catheter Specimen of Urine [*Medicine*]..............CSU
Catheterization and Cardiovascular Diagnosis [*A publication*]..............Cathet Cardiovasc Diagn
Catheterization and Cardiovascular Diagnosis [*A publication*]..............Catheterization Cardiovasc Diagn
Cathodal Closure Contraction [*Also, CCC*] [*Physiology*]..............CaCC
Cathodal Closure Contraction [*Also, CaCC*] [*Physiology*]..............CCC
Cathodal Closure Tetanus [*Physiology*]..............CCT
Cathodal Closure Tetanus [*Physiology*]..............CCTE
Cathodal Duration Tetanus [*Physiology*]..............CaDTe
Cathodal Opening Clonus [*Physiology*]..............COCL
Cathodal Opening Contraction [*Also, COC*] [*Physiology*]..............CaOC
Cathodal Opening Contraction [*Also, CaOC*] [*Physiology*]..............COC
Cathodal Opening Tetanus [*Physiology*]..............COT
Cathodal Opening Tetanus [*Physiology*]..............COTe
Cathode..............C
Cathode..............CA
Cathode..............CATH
Cathode Dark Space..............CDS
Cathode Flicker Effect..............CFE
Cathode Follower..............CF
Cathode Follower Mixer..............CFM
Cathode Grid Capacitance..............CGK
Cathode Heating Time..............CHT
Cathode Potential Stabilized..............CPS

Cathode Pulse Modulation	CPM
Cathode Ray	CR
Cathode-Ray Direction Finder [*RADAR*]	CRDF
Cathode-Ray Electron Tube	CRET
Cathode-Ray Furnace	CRF
Cathode-Ray Lamp	CRL
Cathode-Ray Oscillator	CO
Cathode-Ray Oscilloscope [*or Oscillograph*]	CRO
Cathode-Ray Screen [*Air Force*]	C-SCOPE
Cathode-Ray Tube	CRT
Cathode-Ray Tube Automatic Direction Finding	CADF
Cathode-Ray Tube Indicators [*JETDS nomenclature*] [*Military*]	IP
Cathode-Ray Tube Oscillograph	CRTO
Cathode-Ray Tube Shield	CRTS
Cathode-Ray Tube Tester	CRTT
Cathode-Ray Typesetting	CRT
Cathode Reaction	CR
Cathodic Protection Equipment	CPE
Cathodic Protection Industry Association	CPIA
Cathodic Protection Survey Kit	CPSK
Cathodic Stripping Voltammetry [*Analytical chemistry*]	CSV
Cathodic Survey Kit	CSK
Cathodochromic [*Cathode-ray tube*]	CC
Cathodoluminescence [*Geophysics*]	CL
Catholic	C
Catholic	CATH
Catholic	CATHOL
Catholic Accountants Guild	CAG
Catholic Actors Guild of America	CAG
Catholic Actors Guild of America	CAGA
Catholic Aid Association	CAA
Catholic Alumni Clubs International	CACI
Catholic Anthropological Association [*Defunct*]	CAA
Catholic Anthropological Conference	CAC
Catholic Archdiocese of Seattle, Archives, Seattle, WA [*Library symbol*]	WaSAA
Catholic Art Association [*Defunct*]	CAA
Catholic Association of Foresters	CAOF
Catholic Association for International Peace [*Defunct*]	CAIP
Catholic Audio-Visual Educators Association	CAVE
Catholic Aviation League of Our Lady of Loreto [*Defunct*]	CALOLL
Catholic Bible Society of America	CBSA
Catholic Biblical Association of America [*Superseded by Unda-USA*]	CBA
Catholic Biblical Quarterly [*A publication*]	Ca Bi Q
Catholic Biblical Quarterly [*A publication*]	Cath Bib Q
Catholic Biblical Quarterly [*A publication*]	CBQ
Catholic Big Brothers [*An association*]	CBB
Catholic Book Week	CBW
Catholic Broadcasters Association	CBA
Catholic Business Education Association [*Later, NCBEA*]	CBEA
Catholic Campus Ministry Association	CCMA
Catholic Central High School, London, ON, Canada [*Library symbol*]	CaOLC
Catholic Central Union [*Later, COF*]	CCU
Catholic Central Union of America	CCUA
Catholic Central Union of America, St. Louis, MO [*Library symbol*]	MoSV
Catholic Central Youth Union of America	CCYUA
Catholic Charismatic [*A publication*]	Cath Charis
Catholic Charismatic Renewal Movement	CCRM
Catholic Choirmaster [*A publication*]	Cath Choirmaster
Catholic Church Extension Society of the United States of America	CCESUSA
Catholic Church Extension Society of the USA [*Later, CCESUSA*]	CCES
Catholic Civics Clubs of America [*Defunct*]	CCCA
Catholic Clergyman	CC
Catholic College Admissions and Information Center	CCAIC
Catholic College of Oklahoma for Women, Guthrie, OK [*Library symbol*] [*Obsolete*]	OkGuC
Catholic Commission on Intellectual and Cultural Affairs	CCICA
Catholic Committee of Appalachia	CCA
Catholic Committee for Refugees	CCR
Catholic Committee on Scouting [*Later, NCCS*]	CCS
Catholic Committee on Urban Ministry	CCUM
Catholic Council on Civil Liberties [*Defunct*]	CCCL
Catholic Council on Working Life	CCWL
Catholic Curate	CC
Catholic Daughters of the Americas	CDA
Catholic Digest [*A publication*]	C Dgst
Catholic Economic Association [*Later, ASE*]	CEA
Catholic Educational Exhibitors Association [*Later, NCEE*]	CEEA
Catholic Educational Review [*A publication*]	Cath Ed R
Catholic Educational Review [*A publication*]	CER
Catholic Evidence Guild	CEG
Catholic Evidence Guild of New York [*Defunct*]	CEGNY
Catholic Family Life Insurance [*An association*]	CFLI
Catholic Family Missionary Alliance [*Later, MEW*]	CFMA
Catholic Fine Arts Society	CFAS
Catholic Foreign Mission Society of America	CFMSA
Catholic Fund for Overseas Development [*British*]	CAFOD
Catholic Golden Age [*An association*]	CGA

Catholic Guardian Society	CGS
Catholic Guild for All the Blind [*Later, CCB*]	CGFAB
Catholic Health Association of the US	CHA
Catholic High Schools Athletic Association	CHSAA
Catholic Historical Review [*A publication*]	Cath His R
Catholic Historical Review [*A publication*]	Cath Hist R
Catholic Historical Review [*A publication*]	CathHR
Catholic Historical Review [*A publication*]	C Hist
Catholic Historical Review [*A publication*]	CHR
Catholic Homiletic Society [*Later, CPC*]	CHS
Catholic Hospital [*A publication*]	Cath Hosp
Catholic Hospital [*A publication*]	Cathol Hosp
Catholic Information Society [*Defunct*]	CIS
Catholic Institute of the Food Industry	CIFI
Catholic Institute for International Relations	CIIR
Catholic Institute of the Press [*Later, Catholic Alliance for Communications*]	CIP
Catholic Inter-American Cooperation Program [*Defunct*]	CICOP
Catholic Intercontinental Press	CIP
Catholic International Education Office	CIEO
Catholic International Union for Social Service	CIUSS
Catholic Interracial Council of Chicago	CICC
Catholic Interracial Council of New York	CIC
Catholic Interracial Council of New York	CICNY
Catholic Irish Attorneys [*Fictional organization*]	CIA
Catholic Knights of America	CKA
Catholic Knights Insurance Society	CKIS
Catholic Knights of St. George	CKSG
Catholic Kolping Society of America	CKSA
Catholic Ladies Aid Society	CLAS
Catholic Ladies of Columbia	CLC
Catholic Lawyer [*A publication*]	Catholic Law
Catholic Lay Mission Corps	CLMC
Catholic League for Religious Assistance to Poland	CLRAP
Catholic League for Religious and Civil Rights	CLRCR
Catholic Library Association	CATLA
Catholic Library Association	CLA
Catholic Library World [*A publication*]	Cath Libr Wld
Catholic Library World [*A publication*]	Cath Lib W
Catholic Library World [*A publication*]	Cath Lib World
Catholic Library World [*A publication*]	CLW
Catholic Life Insurance Union	CLIU
Catholic Listener Library [*Later, Maynard Listener Library*]	CLL
Catholic Major Markets Newspaper Association	CMMNA
Catholic Media Council	CAMECO
Catholic Medical Mission Board	CMMB
Catholic Microfilm Center [*Defunct*]	CMC
Catholic Microfilm Center, Berkeley, CA [*Library symbol*] [*Obsolete*]	CathMC
Catholic Mind [*A publication*]	Cath M
Catholic Missionary Society	CMS
Catholic Near East Welfare Association	CNEWA
Catholic Negro-American Mission Board	CNAMB
Catholic Nurse (Wallsend) [*A publication*]	Cathol Nurse (Wallsend)
Catholic One Parent Organization	COPO
Catholic Order of Foresters	COF
Catholic Pamphlet Society of the United States	CPS
Catholic Peace Fellowship	CPF
Catholic Periodical and Literature Index [*A publication*]	Cathl
Catholic Periodical and Literature Index [*A publication*]	CPLI
Catholic Poetry Society of America [*Defunct*]	CPSA
Catholic-Presbyterian [*A publication*]	Cath-Presb
Catholic Press Association	CPA
Catholic Record Society	CRS
Catholic Record Society. Publications [*A publication*]	Cath Rec Soc Pub
Catholic Relief Services	CRS
Catholic Relief Services - National Catholic Welfare Conference [*Later, CRS-USCC*]	CRS-NCWC
Catholic Relief Services - US Catholic Conference [*Formerly, CRS-NCWC*]	CRS-USCC
Catholic Renascence Society [*Defunct*]	CRS
Catholic Russian Center, San Francisco, CA [*Library symbol*]	CSfCR
Catholic Scholarships for Negroes	CSN
Catholic School Commission, Montreal, PQ, Canada [*Library symbol*]	CaQMCEC
Catholic School Journal [*A publication*]	Cath Sch J
Catholic School Press Association [*Defunct*]	CSPA
Catholic Slovak Brotherhood	CSB
Catholic Sokol Printing Co., Passaic, NJ [*Library symbol*]	NjPasCS
Catholic Star Herald, Camden, NJ [*Library symbol*]	NjCaSH
Catholic Students' Mission Crusade [*Defunct*]	CSMC
Catholic Tape Recorders, International	CTRI
Catholic Teachers College [*Rhode Island*]	CTC
Catholic Television Network [*Cable TV programing service*]	CTN
Catholic Theological Society of America	CTSA
Catholic Theological Union, Chicago, IL [*Library symbol*]	ICTU
Catholic Theological Union, Chicago, IL [*OCLC symbol*]	IDJ
Catholic Total Abstinence Union of America	CTAUA
Catholic Traditionalist Movement	CTM
Catholic Union of the Sick in America	CUSA
Catholic University	CU

Catholic University of America [*Washington, DC*] ... CUA
Catholic University of America. Biological Studies [*A publication*] ... Cath Univ Am Biol Stud
Catholic University of America, Clementine Library, Washington, DC [*Library symbol*] ... DCU-C
Catholic University of America, Hyvernat Collection, Washington, DC [*Library symbol*] ... DCU-H
Catholic University of America, Ibero-American Collection, Washington, DC [*Library symbol*] ... DCU-IA
Catholic University of America. Law Review [*A publication*] ... Cath U Law
Catholic University of America. Law Review [*A publication*] ... Cath Univ Law Rev
Catholic University of America. Patristic Studies [*A publication*] ... CUAPS
Catholic University of America. Studies in Romance Languages and Literatures [*A publication*] ... CUASRL
Catholic University of America. Studies in Romance Languages and Literatures [*A publication*] ... CUASRLL
Catholic University of America, Washington, DC [*OCLC symbol*] ... CUA
Catholic University of America, Washington, DC [*Library symbol*] ... DCU
Catholic University. Bulletin [*A publication*] ... Cath Univ Bull
Catholic University. Bulletin [*A publication*] ... CUB
Catholic University. Law Review [*A publication*] ... Catholic U L Rev
Catholic University. Law Review [*A publication*] ... CULR
Catholic University of Puerto Rico ... CUPR
Catholic War Veterans of the USA ... CWV
Catholic War Veterans of the USA Ladies Auxiliary ... CWVA
Catholic Women for the ERA ... CWERA
Catholic Women's Benevolent Legion ... CWBL
Catholic Women's Seminary Fund ... CWSF
Catholic Worker [*A publication*] ... Cath Work
Catholic Worker Movement ... CWM
Catholic Workman [*An association*] ... CW
Catholic World [*A publication*] ... CathW
Catholic World [*A publication*] ... CaW
Catholic World [*A publication*] ... CW
Catholic World [*A publication*] ... Cwd
Catholic Writers Guild of America ... CWGA
Catholic Youth Adoration Society [*Defunct*] ... CYA
Catholic Youth Organization ... CYO
Catholicarum Universitatum Federatio [*Federation of Catholic Universities*] ... CUF
Catholics for Christian Political Action ... CCPA
Catholics for a Free Choice ... CFFC
Catholics for Latin America ... CFLA
Catholics United for the Faith ... CUF
Catholics United for Life ... CUL
Cation Exchange Capacity [*Chemical technology*] ... CEC
Cation-Responsive Electrode ... CRE
Cationic Asphalt-Neoprene Emulsion [*Dust control*] ... CANE
Catlettsburg, KY [*Radio station call letters*] ... WCAK
Catlin Aviation Co. [*Oklahoma City, OK*] [*FAA designator*] ... CLN
Cato Institute ... CI
Cato Township Public Library, Lakeview, MI [*Library symbol*] ... MiLakv
Catoctin Mountain Park [*National Park Service designation*] ... CATO
Catonsville Community College, Baltimore, MD [*OCLC symbol*] ... CAT
Catonsville, MD [*Radio station call letters*] ... WQSR
Catskill Airways [*Oneonta, NY*] [*FAA designator*] ... CSK
Catskill, NY [*Radio station call letters*] ... WCKL
Catskills [*FAA*] ... CTSKLS
Catskills/Sullivan County [*New York*] [*Airport symbol*] [*Obsolete*] ... MSV
Cattermole Memorial Library, Fort Madison, IA [*Library symbol*] ... IaFm
Cattle ... CAT
Cattle ... CTL
Cattle Hide ... CATLHD
Catwalk ... CTWALK
Cauayan [*Philippines*] [*Airport symbol*] ... CYZ
Caucasia [*Colombia*] [*Airport symbol*] ... CAQ
Caucasian ... CAU
Caucasian [*MARC language code*] [*Library of Congress*] ... cau
Caucasian Except as Otherwise Indicated [*Army*] ... CAUEOI
Caucasus [*MARC geographic area code*] [*Library of Congress*] ... e-urk--
Cauchy Boundary Condition [*Mathematics*] ... CBC
Cauchy Convergence Test [*Mathematics*] ... CCT
Cauchy-Riemann Equation [*Mathematics*] ... CRE
Caucus for a New Political Science ... CNPS
Caucus for Producers, Writers, and Directors ... CPWD
Caucus for Women in Statistics ... CWS
Caudal [*Medicine*] ... CD
Caudality Scale [*Psychology*] ... Ca
Caudate Nucleus [*Anatomy*] ... CN
Caudate-Putamen Complex [*Anatomy*] ... CPU
Caudill, Rowlett, & Scott [*Architectural firm*] ... CRS
Caught [*by*] [*In cricket*] ... C
Caught ... CAT
Caught ... CT
Caught and Bowled [*Cricket*] ... C & B
Caught Out ... C
Caught Stealing [*Baseball*] ... CS
Cauliflower Mosaic Virus [*Also, CLMV*] ... CaMV
Cauliflower Mosaic Virus [*Also, CaMV*] ... CLMV
Caulked Joint ... CAJ
Caulked Joint ... CLKJ
Caulking ... CLKG
Causa [*Case or Cause*] ... C
Causa Mortis [*On Occasion of Death*] [*Latin*] ... CM
Causapscal, PQ [*Radio station call letters*] ... CJBM
Causation ... CAUS
Cause ... C
Cause of Death [*Medicine*] ... COD
Cause-Effect Graph Language [*Data processing*] ... CEGL
Causeway ... CSWY
Caustic Boundary Layer [*Acoustics*] ... CBL
Caution ... CAUT
Caution ... CTN
Caution Advised until Further Notice [*Aviation*] ... CAUFN
Caution and Warning [*Aerospace*] ... C & W
Caution and Warning Annunciator ... CWA
Caution and Warning Electronics Assembly [*Apollo*] [*NASA*] ... CWEA
Caution and Warning Electronics Unit ... CWEC
Caution and Warning Equipment [*NASA*] ... CWE
Caution and Warning Status ... CWS
Caution and Warning System [*NASA*] ... C & WS
Caution and Warning Unit ... CWU
Cautious Hawk [*Description of President Reagan's position on foreign affairs, used in book "Gambling with History: Reagan in the White House"*] ... CAWK
Cavalier [*Knight title*] ... CAV
Cavalier King Charles Spaniel Club of America ... CKCSC
Cavalry ... CAV
Cavalry Brigade ... CB
Cavalry Fighting Vehicle ... CFV
Cavalry Navigation System ... CAVNAVS
Cavalry Replacement Training Center ... CRTC
Cavalry Transport [*Navy ship symbol*] [*Obsolete*] ... APC
Cavanagh Communities Corp. [*NYSE symbol*] [*Delisted*] ... CAA
Cavanagh Communities Corp. [*NASDAQ symbol*] ... CCAV
Cavco Industries, Inc. [*NASDAQ symbol*] ... CVCO
Cave City, AR [*Radio station call letters*] ... KZIG
Cave City, KY [*Radio station call letters*] ... WKVE
Cave Creek Public Library, Cave Creek, AZ [*Library symbol*] ... AzCc
Cave Geology [*A publication*] ... Cave Geol
Cave Junction, OR [*Radio station call letters*] ... KIVR
Cave Research Associates ... CRA
Cave Research Foundation ... CRF
Cave Research Group of Great Britain. Transactions [*A publication*] ... Cave Res Group Great Britain Trans
Cave Science [*A publication*] ... Cave Sci
Caveat [*A form of writ*] ... CAV
Caveat Emptor [*A publication*] ... Caveat
Caveat Emptor [*Let the Buyer Beware*] [*Latin*] ... CE
Cavedale Road [*California*] [*Seismograph station code, US Geological Survey*] ... CRD
Cavei Avir Lemitanim [*Israeli airline*] ... CAL
Cavei Avir Lemitanim [*Israel*] [*ICAO designator*] ... CH
Cavernous Sinus Thrombosis [*Medicine*] ... CST
Cavitation ... CAV
Cavitation Intensity Meter ... CIM
Cavitation Tendency Ratio ... CTR
Cavitron Corp. [*American Stock Exchange symbol*] [*Delisted*] ... CAV
Cavity ... CAV
Cavity Rim Cup [*A contraceptive device*] ... CRC
Cavity Tuned Oscillator ... CTO
Cavity Turnable Filter ... CTF
Cawcaw Swamp [*South Carolina*] [*Seismograph station code, US Geological Survey*] ... CCS
Cawkell Information & Technology Services, Ltd. [*British*] [*Information service*] ... CITECH
Cawthron Institute (Nelson, New Zealand). Report [*A publication*] ... Cawthron Inst (Nelson NZ) Rep
Cayce, SC [*Radio station call letters*] ... WLFF
Cayce, SC [*Radio station call letters*] ... WZLD
Cayenne [*French Guiana*] [*Airport symbol*] ... CAY
Cayey [*Puerto Rico*] [*Seismograph station code, US Geological Survey*] ... SJCC
Cayey, PR [*Radio station call letters*] ... WLEY
Cayley-Klein Parameter [*Mathematics*] ... CKP
Cayman Airways Ltd. [*ICAO designator*] ... KX
Cayman Brac [*West Indies*] [*Airport symbol*] ... CYB
Cayman Island Reinsurance Corporation [*NASDAQ symbol*] ... CIRCF
Cayman Islands ... CI
Cayman Islands [*MARC country of publication code*] [*Library of Congress*] ... cj
Cayman Islands [*Three-letter standard code*] ... CYM
Cayman Islands [*Two-letter standard code*] ... KY
Cayman Islands [*MARC geographic area code*] [*Library of Congress*] ... nwcj---
Cayuga County Community College, Auburn, NY [*Library symbol*] ... NAuC
Cayuga County Historical Society, Auburn, NY [*Library symbol*] ... NAuHi
Cazenovia College, Cazenovia, NY [*Library symbol*] ... NCazC
Cazenovia College, Witherill Learning Center, Cazenovia, NY [*OCLC symbol*] ... ZCZ
Cazenovia, NY [*Radio station call letters*] ... WITC

CB Radio Patrol ... CBRP
CB & T Bankshares, Inc. [*NASDAQ symbol*] ... CBTB
CBA Engineering Ltd., Vancouver, BC, Canada [*Library symbol*] ... CaBVaCBA
CBI [*Cement-och Betonginstitutet*] **Forskning** [*A publication*] ... CBI Forsk
CBI Industries [*Formerly, Chicago Bridge & Iron Co.*] [*NYSE symbol*] ... CBH
CBNU Learning Resources Center, Virginia Beach, VA [*OCLC symbol*] ... VCB
CBPO [*Consolidated Base Personnel Office*] **Strength Summary Card** ... CSS
CBPO [*Consolidated Base Personnel Office*] **Strength Summary Card** ... CSSC
CBS, Inc. [*Formerly, Columbia Broadcasting System, Inc.*] [*NYSE symbol*] ... CBS
CBT Corp. [*NASDAQ symbol*] ... CBCT
CCATS [*Communications, Command, and Telemetry Systems*] **Command Controller** [*NASA*] ... CCC
CCATS [*Communications, Command, and Telemetry Systems*] **Telemetry Controller** [*NASA*] ... CTC
CCB Financial Corp. [*NASDAQ symbol*] ... CCBF
CCCO [*Central Committee for Conscientious Objectors*]**/An Agency for Military and Draft Counseling** ... CCCO
CCI Corp. [*NYSE symbol*] [*Delisted*] ... CCI
CCNB Corporation [*NASDAQ symbol*] ... CCNC
CCNU [*Lomustine*], **Cyclophosphamide, Vincristine, Procarbazine, Prednisone** [*Antineoplastic drug regimen*] ... CCVPP
CCNU [*Lomustine*], **Oncovin** [*Vincristine*], **Procarbazine, Prednisone** [*Antineoplastic drug regimen*] ... COPP
CCNU [*Lomustine*], **Procarbazine, Methotrexate** [*Antineoplastic drug regimen*] ... CPM
CCNU [*Lomustine*], **Vinblastine, Bleomycin** [*Antineoplastic drug regimen*] ... CVB
CCR Video Corp. [*NASDAQ symbol*] ... CCCR
CCX, Inc. [*NYSE symbol*] ... CCX
CCX Network, Inc. [*NASDAQ symbol*] ... CCXN
CDI Corp. [*American Stock Exchange symbol*] [*Delisted*] ... CDI
CDX Corp. [*NASDAQ symbol*] ... CDXX
Ce Fastu? [*A publication*] ... CeF
Ce Fastu? [*A publication*] ... CF
CEA [*College English Association*] **Chap Book** [*A publication*] ... CEAC
CEA [*College English Association*] **Critic** [*A publication*] ... CEA
CEA [*College English Association*] **Critic** [*A publication*] ... CEACrit
CEA [*College English Association*] **Forum** [*A publication*] ... CEAF
Cebu [*Philippines*] [*Later, DAV*] [*Geomagnetic observatory code*] ... CCP
Cebu [*Philippines*] [*Airport symbol*] ... CEB
Cebu City [*Philippines*] [*Seismograph station code, US Geological Survey*] ... CCP
Cebu Stevedores Association [*Philippines*] ... CSA
Cecchetti Council of America ... CCA
Cechoslovakische Statistik [*Czechoslovakia*] ... CS
Cecidologia Indica [*A publication*] ... Cecidol Indica
Ceco Corporation [*NYSE symbol*] ... CCP
Cedar Breaks National Monument ... CEBR
Cedar City [*Utah*] [*Seismograph station code, US Geological Survey*] ... CCU
Cedar City [*Utah*] [*Airport symbol*] ... CDC
Cedar City, UT [*Radio station call letters*] ... KBRE
Cedar City, UT [*Radio station call letters*] ... KBRE-FM
Cedar City, UT [*Radio station call letters*] ... KGSU-FM
Cedar City, UT [*Radio station call letters*] ... KSUB
Cedar City, UT [*Radio station call letters*] ... KSUB-FM
Cedar County Historical Society, Clarence, IA [*Library symbol*] ... IaClarCHi
Cedar Creek Youth Camp, Littlerock, WA [*Library symbol*] ... WaLrC
Cedar Crest College [*Pennsylvania*] ... CCC
Cedar Crest College, Allentown, PA [*Library symbol*] ... PAtC
Cedar Crest and Muhlenberg Colleges, Allentown, PA [*OCLC symbol*] ... EVI
Cedar Falls Historical Society, Cedar Falls, IA [*Library symbol*] ... IaCfHi
Cedar Falls, IA [*Radio station call letters*] ... KCFI
Cedar Falls, IA [*Radio station call letters*] ... KHKE
Cedar Falls, IA [*Radio station call letters*] ... KUNI
Cedar Falls Public Library, Cedar Falls, IA [*Library symbol*] ... IaCf
Cedar Falls Record, Cedar Falls, IA [*Library symbol*] ... IaCfR
Cedar Grove Public Library, Cedar Grove, NJ [*Library symbol*] ... NjCg
Cedar Rapids Area Library Consortium [*Library network*] ... CRALC
Cedar Rapids Gazette, Cedar Rapids, IA [*Library symbol*] ... IaCrG
Cedar Rapids, IA [*Radio station call letters*] ... KCCK-FM
Cedar Rapids, IA [*Radio station call letters*] ... KCDR
Cedar Rapids, IA [*Radio station call letters*] ... KCOE
Cedar Rapids, IA [*Radio station call letters*] ... KCRG
Cedar Rapids, IA [*Television station call letters*] ... KCRG-TV
Cedar Rapids, IA [*Radio station call letters*] ... KHAK
Cedar Rapids, IA [*Radio station call letters*] ... KHAK-FM
Cedar Rapids, IA [*Radio station call letters*] ... KOJC
Cedar Rapids, IA [*Radio station call letters*] ... KQCR
Cedar Rapids, IA [*Radio station call letters*] ... KTOF
Cedar Rapids, IA [*Radio station call letters*] ... KWMR
Cedar Rapids, IA [*Radio station call letters*] ... WMT
Cedar Rapids, IA [*Radio station call letters*] ... WMT-FM
Cedar Rapids/Iowa City [*Iowa*] [*Airport symbol*] ... CID
Cedar Rapids & Iowa City Railway Co. [*AAR code*] ... CIC
Cedar Rapids Public Library, Cedar Rapids, IA [*Library symbol*] ... IaCr
Cedar Rapids Public Library, Cedar Rapids, IA [*OCLC symbol*] ... IWR
Cedar Rapids-Waterloo, IA [*Television station call letters*] ... KGAN-TV
Cedar Springs [*California*] [*Seismograph station code, US Geological Survey*] [*Closed*] ... CED
Cedar Springs [*California*] [*Seismograph station code, US Geological Survey*] ... CSP
Cedaredge Public Library, Cedaredge, CO [*Library symbol*] ... CoCe
Cedarholm, Bland, Havens, and Townes [*Ether drift experiment*] ... CBHT
Cedars of Lebanon Hospital ... CLH
Cedars-Sinai Medical Center, Los Angeles, CA [*Library symbol*] ... CLCLH
Cedartown, GA [*Radio station call letters*] ... WGAA
Cedarville College, Cedarville, OH [*OCLC symbol*] ... CDC
Cedarville College, Cedarville, OH [*Library symbol*] ... OCedC
Cedarville, OH [*Radio station call letters*] ... WCDR-FM
Ceduna [*Australia*] [*Airport symbol*] ... CED
Cefazolin [*Antibacterial compound*] ... CEZ
Cefazolin [*An antibiotic*] ... CZ
Cefotaxime [*An antibiotic*] ... CTX
Cefuroxime [*Antibacterial drug*] ... CXM
CEGB [*Central Electricity Generating Board*] **Research** [*A publication*] ... CEGB Res
CEGEP [*College d'Enseignement General et Professionel*] **de Limoilou, Quebec, PQ, Canada** [*Library symbol*] ... CaQQCE
CEGEP [*College d'Enseignement General et Professionel*] **Montmorency-Chomedy, Laval, PQ, Canada** [*Library symbol*] ... CaQLAC
CEGEP [*College d'Enseignement General et Professionel*] **de Shawinigan, Shawinigan, PQ, Canada** [*Library symbol*] ... CaQSHC
CEGEP [*College d'Enseignement General et Professionel*], **Trois-Rivieres, PQ, Canada** [*Library symbol*] ... CaQTCE
CEGS [*Council on Education in the Geological Sciences*] **Programs Publication** [*A publication*] ... CEGS Programs Publ
Ceiling [*Aviation*] ... CEIL
Ceiling [*Aviation*] ... CIG
Ceiling [*Aviation*] ... CLG
Ceiling and Visibility OK [*Aviation*] ... CAVOK
Ceiling and Visibility Unlimited [*Meteorology*] ... CAVU
Ceilings and Interior Systems Contractors Association ... CISCA
CEIP [*Communications-Electronics Implementation Plan*] **Implementation Directive** [*Air Force*] ... CID
Ceja Corp., Tulsa, OK [*Library symbol*] ... OkTC
Cela Zimes [*A publication*] ... CZ
Celanese Canada Ltd., Montreal, PQ, Canada [*Library symbol*] ... CaQMCE
Celanese Corp. [*NYSE symbol*] ... CZ
Celanese Corp., Clarkwood, TX [*Library symbol*] ... TxClwC
Celanese Corp., Narrows, VA [*Library symbol*] ... ViNarC
Celebrated ... CEL
Celescope Optical Package ... COP
Celestial ... CEL
Celestial ... CLST
Celestial Atomic Trajectile ... CAT
Celestial Equator ... CE
Celestial Infrared Mapping [*Air Force*] ... CIRM
Celestial Infrared Measurement System ... CIRMS
Celestial Mapping Program [*Air Force*] ... CMP
Celestial Mechanics [*A publication*] ... Celest Mech
Celestial Mechanics ... CM
Celestial Moving Target Indicator ... CMTI
Celestial Navigation ... CELNAV
Celestial Navigation Trainer ... CNT
Celestial Research Corporation ... CELESCO
Celestial Telescope [*OAO*] ... CELESCOPE
Celiac Axis [*Anatomy*] ... CA
Celiac, Superior Mesenteric Artery [*Anatomy*] ... CSMA
Celiac, Superior Mesenteric Vein [*Anatomy*] ... CSMV
Celibate ... CEL
Celina Financial Corp. Cl A [*NASDAQ symbol*] ... CELNA
Celina, OH [*Radio station call letters*] ... WCSM
Celina, OH [*Radio station call letters*] ... WCSM-FM
Celina, OH [*Radio station call letters*] ... WKKI
Celjabinskii Gosudarstvennyi Pedagogiceskii Institut. Trudy [*A publication*] ... Celjabinsk Gos Ped Inst Trudy
Cell ... C
Cell Adhesion Factor [*Cytochemistry*] ... CAF
Cell Adhesion Molecule [*Cytology*] ... CAM
Cell Associating Molecule [*Cytology*] ... CAM
Cell Atmosphere Processing System [*Nuclear energy*] ... CAPS
Cell Attachment Protein [*Cytochemistry*] ... CAP
Cell Biology International. Reports [*A publication*] ... Cell Biol Int Rep
Cell Biology Monographs [*A publication*] ... Cell Biol Monogr
Cell Biophysics [*A publication*] ... Cell Biophys
Cell Cover Arming Unit ... CCAU
Cell Culture and Nitrogen Fixation Laboratory [*Department of Agriculture*] ... CC & NF
Cell Current Density ... CCD
Cell Cycle Analyzer [*Instrumentation*] ... CCA
Cell Cycle Nonspecific [*Antitumor agent*] ... CCNS
Cell-Cycle Specific [*Antitumor agent*] ... CCS
Cell Differentiation [*A publication*] ... Cell Differ
Cell Division Cycle [*Cytology*] ... CDC
Cell Free Extract [*Microbiology*] ... CFE

Cell Kinetics Society ... CKS
Cell-Mediated Cytolysis ... CMC
Cell [*or Cellular*]**-Mediated Immunity** [*Immunochemistry*] ... CMI
Cell-Mediated Lympholysis [*Immunology*] ... CML
Cell Membrane ... CM
Cell Products [*NASDAQ symbol*] ... CELL
Cell Simulation [*Data processing*] ... CELLSIM
Cell Structure and Function [*A publication*] ... Cell Struct Funct
Cell Surface Antigens [*Immunology*] ... CSA
Cell Surface Protein [*Also known as LETS protein*] [*Cytochemistry*] ... CSP
Cell Surface Reviews [*A publication*] ... Cell Surf Rev
Cell Surface Reviews [*Elsevier Book Series*] [*A publication*] ... CSR
Cell and Tissue Kinetics [*A publication*] ... Cell Tiss K
Cell and Tissue Kinetics [*A publication*] ... Cell Tissue Kinet
Cell and Tissue Research [*A publication*] ... Cell Tis Re
Cell and Tissue Research [*A publication*] ... Cell Tissue Res
Cell and Tissue Research [*A publication*] ... CTSRC
Cell Volume [*Hematology*] ... CV
Cell Volume Profile [*Hematology*] ... CVP
Cell Wall ... CW
Cell Wall Defective [*Microbiology*] ... CWD
Cell Wall Material [*Biochemistry*] ... CWM
Cell Water Removal Mechanism ... CWRM
Cellophane ... K
Cells per Colony [*Microbiology*] ... CPC
Cellu-Craft, Inc. [*American Stock Exchange symbol*] ... CC
Cellular [*Freight*] ... CEUR
Cellular Absorbed Dose Spectrometer ... CADS
Cellular Cellulose Acetate [*Organic chemistry*] ... CCA
Cellular Concrete Association ... CCA
Cellular Immunology [*A publication*] ... Cell Immun
Cellular Immunology [*A publication*] ... Cell Immunol
Cellular and Molecular Biology [*A publication*] ... Cell Mol Biol
Cellular and Molecular Biology ... CMB
Cellular and Molecular Neurobiology [*A publication*] ... CMN
Cellular Neoprene Rubber ... CNR
Cellular Products [*NASDAQ symbol*] ... CELP
Cellular Radio Communications Association ... CRCA
Cellular Retinoic Acid-Binding Protein [*Biochemistry*] ... CRABP
Cellular Retinol-Binding Protein [*Biochemistry*] ... CRBP
Cellular Size Volume ... CSV
Cellular Technology [*NASDAQ symbol*] ... CTEK
Cellular Therapy [*Medicine*] ... CT
Celluloid ... CEL
Cellulosa e Carta [*A publication*] ... Cellul Carta
Cellulose [*Freight*] ... CEL
Cellulose Acetate [*Organic chemistry; plastics*] ... CA
Cellulose Acetate Butyrate [*Organic chemistry*] ... CAB
Cellulose Acetate Propionate [*Organic chemistry*] ... CAP
Cellulose, Chemistry and Technology [*A publication*] ... Cellulose Chem Technol
Cellulose Industry Standards Enforcement Program ... CISEP
Cellulose Manufacturers Association ... CMA
Cellulose Nitrate [*Organic chemistry*] ... CN
Cellulose Polyethylene [*Organic chemistry*] ... CPE
Cellulose Research Institute [*Syracuse University*] ... CRI
Cellulose Sponge Institute [*Defunct*] ... CSI
Cellulose Triacetate [*Organic chemistry*] ... CTA
Celoslovenska Geologicka Konferencia. Materialy [*A publication*] ... Celosloven Geol Konf Mater
Celostatna Konferencia o Termickej Analyze [*A publication*] ... Celostatna Konf Term Anal
Celotex Corp. [*NYSE symbol*] [*Delisted*] ... CLO
Celovek i Obscestvo [*A publication*] ... Celovek i Obsc
Celsius [*Centigrade*] [*Temperature scale*] ... C
Celsius [*Centigrade*] [*Temperature scale*] ... CEL
Celsius Temperature [*Symbol*] [*IUPAC*] ... t
Celtiberia [*A publication*] ... Celt
Celtic ... CEL
Celtic ... CELT
Celtic Group [*MARC language code*] [*Library of Congress*] [*Obsolete*] ... cel
Celtic League ... CL
Celtic League, American Branch ... CLAB
Celtic Review [*A publication*] ... Celtic R
Celtica [*A publication*] ... Ce
Celuloza si Hirtie [*A publication*] ... Celul Hirtie
Celuloza si Hirtie [*A publication*] ... Celuloza Hirt
Cembalo [*Cymbal*] [*Music*] ... CEMB
Cement ... CEM
Cement ... CEMT
Cement Base [*Technical drawings*] ... CB
Cement och Betong [*A publication*] ... Cem Betong
Cement-Coated Heavy Epoxy ... CCHEP
Cement-Coated Single Epoxy ... CCSEP
Cement-Coated Triple Epoxy ... CCTEP
Cement or Concrete [*Freight*] ... CMT CONC
Cement and Concrete Association. Research Report [*A publication*] ... Cem Concrete Ass Res Rep
Cement and Concrete Research [*A publication*] ... Cem Concr Res
Cement-Enamel Junction [*Dentistry*] ... CEJ
Cement Floor [*Technical drawings*] ... CF
Cement, Lime, and Gravel [*A publication*] ... Cem Lime Grav
Cement and Lime Manufacture [*A publication*] ... Cem Lime Mf
Cement Plaster ... CPL
Cement-Plaster Ceiling [*Technical drawings*] ... CPC
Cement Research Institute of India. Abstracts [*A publication*] ... CRI Abstr
Cement Riverine Assault Boat [*Navy*] ... CRAB
Cement Technology [*A publication*] ... Cem Technol
Cement Wapno Gips [*A publication*] ... Cem Wapno Gips
Cemented Carbide Producers Association ... CCPA
Cemented Only [*Of envelopes*] ... CO
Cementex [*Research code symbol*] ... N
Cemetery ... CEM
Cemetery Consumer Service Council ... CCSC
Cemetery Supply Association [*Later, ICSA*] ... CSA
Cenco, Inc. [*NYSE symbol*] ... CNC
Cencor, Inc. [*NASDAQ symbol*] ... CNCR
Cenobio [*A publication*] ... C
Cenozoic [*Period, era, or system*] [*Geology*] ... CEN
Cenozoic Paleoceanography Program ... CENOP
Censor [*or Censorship*] ... CENS
Censorship Policy Board [*World War II*] ... CPB
Censorship Records and Information [*Middle East*] [*Military*] ... CRIME
Census ... CS
Census Agglomeration [*Canada*] ... CA
Census Bureau [*Department of Commerce*] ... CB
Census County Division [*Bureau of Census*] ... CCD
Census Grievance Committee [*Vietnam*] ... CGC
Census Metropolitan Area [*Canada*] ... CMA
Census Registration Working Party [*US Military Government, Germany*] ... CRWP
Census Servomechanism and Tape Handler ... CENSER
Census User Guide ... CUG
Cent ... C
Cent ... CT
Cental [*100-pound weight*] ... CTL
Centare [*Unit of area in metric system*] ... CA
Centaur [*Rocket*] [*NASA*] ... CEN
Centaur [*Rocket*] [*NASA*] ... CENT
Centaur Sciences, Inc. [*NASDAQ symbol*] ... CTAR
Centaur Standard Shroud [*NASA*] ... CSS
Centaurus [*Constellation*] ... Cen
Centaurus [*Constellation*] ... Cent
Centavo [*Monetary unit in many Spanish-American countries*] ... C
Centel Corp. [*NYSE symbol*] ... CNT
Centenary College of Louisiana ... CCL
Centenary College of Louisiana, Magale Library, Shreveport, LA [*OCLC symbol*] ... CEN
Centenary College of Louisiana, Shreveport, LA [*Library symbol*] ... LShC
Centenary College for Women, Hackettstown, NJ [*Library symbol*] ... NjHaC
Centennial Centre of Science and Technology ... CCST
Centennial College of Applied Arts and Technology, Scarborough, ON, Canada [*Library symbol*] ... CaOTARC
Centennial Group [*American Stock Exchange symbol*] ... CEG
Centennial Legion of Historic Military Commands ... CLHMC
Centennial Museum, Vancouver, BC, Canada [*Library symbol*] ... CaBVaCM
Centennial Petroleum, Inc. [*NASDAQ symbol*] ... CPET
Centennial Review [*A publication*] ... CentR
Centennial Review [*A publication*] ... CR
Centennial Review of Arts and Sciences [*Later, Centennial Review*] [*A publication*] ... CRAS
Centennial Secondary School, Welland, ON, Canada [*Library symbol*] ... CaOWeC
Centennial Secondary School, Windsor, ON, Canada [*Library symbol*] ... CaOWC
Center [*A position in football, lacrosse, basketball*] ... C
Center [*or Central*] ... CEN
Center ... CNTR
Center ... CTR
Center for Accountability to the Public ... CAP
Center for Action on Endangered Species ... CAES
Center Ad Hoc Data Review Team [*NASA*] ... CAHDRT
Center for Administrative Justice [*Later, NCAJ*] ... CAJ
Center for Advanced Studies in International Business ... CASIB
Center for Advanced Study in the Behavioral Sciences ... CASBS
Center for Advanced Study in the Behavioral Sciences, Stanford, CA [*Library symbol*] ... CStC
Center for Advanced Study in the Developmental Sciences ... CASDS
Center for the Advanced Study of Educational Administration ... CASEA
Center for the Advancement of Human Service Practice ... CAHSP
Center for Aging Research ... CAR
Center Aiming Disc ... CAD
Center Airman Record File [*Air Force*] ... CARF
Center Aisle Connector Bracket ... CACB
Center of Alcohol Studies ... CAS
Center for the American Woman and Politics ... CAWP
Center for the Analysis of Public Issues [*Princeton, NJ*] ... CAPI
Center Apollo Data Manager [*NASA*] ... CADM
Center Apollo Document Description Standards [*NASA*] ... CADDS
Center Apollo Documentation Administration Instructions [*NASA*] ... CADAI
Center Apollo Program Offices [*NASA*] ... CAPO

Center for Application of Sciences and Technology ... CAST
Center for Applied Linguistics ... CAL
Center for Applied Linguistics, Arlington, VA [*Library symbol*] ... ViArAL
Center for Applied Research in the Apostolate ... CARA
Center for Applied Research in the Apostolate [*CARA*], **African Research and Information Center, Washington, DC** [*Library symbol*] ... DARI
Center for Arab-Islamic Studies ... CAIS
Center Area Discrete [*Channel*] ... CAD
Center for Arts Information ... CAI
Center for Assessment and Training [*Peace Corps*] ... CAST
Center for Astrophysics [*Harvard-Smithsonian*] ... CA
Center for Astrophysics [*Harvard-Smithsonian*] ... CFA
Center for Athletes' Rights and Education ... CARE
Center for Atomic Radiation Studies ... CARS
Center for Attitudinal Healing ... CAH
Center for Austrian Studies ... CAS
Center for Auto Safety ... CAS
Center Back [*Soccer*] ... CB
Center Back Stage [*A stage direction*] ... CBS
Center for the Biology of Natural Systems [*Washington University*] ... CBNS
Center for Book Arts ... CBA
Center on Budget and Policy Priorities ... CBPP
Center for Building Technology [*National Bureau of Standards*] ... CBT
Center of Buoyancy ... CB
Center for Business Information [*Information service*] ... CBI
Center to Center ... C-C
Center to Center [*Technical drawings*] ... C to C
Center for Children's Books. Bulletin [*A publication*] ... CCB
Center for Children's Books. Bulletin [*A publication*] ... CCB-B
Center for Children's Books. Bulletin [*A publication*] ... Center Child Bk Bull
Center for Chinese Research Materials ... CCRM
Center for Chinese Research Materials, Washington, DC [*Library symbol*] ... DCCRM
Center for Christian Studies ... CCS
Center City Transportation Program ... CCTP
Center for Climatic and Environmental Assessment [*National Oceanic and Atmospheric Administration*] ... CCEA
Center for Communications Ministry [*Formerly, NSCS*] ... CCM
Center for Communications Systems [*CADPL*] [*Army*] ... CENCOMS
Center for Community Change ... CCC
Center for Community Economic Development ... CCED
Center for Community Education Facility Planning ... CCEFP
Center for Community Justice ... CCJ
Center for Community Planning [*HEW*] ... CCP
Center for Comparative Sociology ... CCS
Center for Compliance Information ... CCI
Center for Computer-Assisted Legal Instruction ... CCALI
Center for Computer/Law ... CCL
Center for Computer Sciences and Technology [*Later, ICST*] [*National Bureau of Standards*] ... CCST
Center of Concern [*An association*] ... CC
Center for Conscious Evolution ... CCE
Center for Constitutional Rights ... CCR
Center for Consumer Affairs, University of Wisconsin-Extension ... CCA-UWEX
Center for Consumer Product Safety [*National Bureau of Standards*] ... CCPS
Center for Consumer Product Technology [*National Bureau of Standards*] ... CCPT
Center for Continuing Education for Women ... CCEW
Center for the Coordination of Foreign Manuscript Copying [*Library of Congress*] ... CCFMC
Center for Corporate Public Involvement ... CCPI
Center for Creative Leadership [*Greensboro, NC*] ... CCL
Center for Cuban Studies ... CCS
Center for Curriculum Design [*Defunct*] ... CCD
Center for Cybernetics Systems Synergism ... CYSYS
Center for Dance Medicine ... CDM
Center Data Descriptions Catalog ... CDDC
Center for Death Education and Research ... CDER
Center for the Defense of Free Enterprise ... CDFE
Center for Defense Information ... CDI
Center for Democratic Alternatives ... CDA
Center for Democratic Policy ... CDP
Center for Design Planning ... CDP
Center on Destructive Cultism ... CDC
Center for Development Planning, Projections, and Policies [*United Nations*] ... CDPPP
Center for Development Policy ... CDP
Center for Development Research, Koobenhavn, Denmark [*Library symbol*] ... DnKDR
Center for Disease Control, Atlanta, GA [*OCLC symbol*] ... HNC
Center for Disease Control, Family Planning Evaluation Division, Atlanta, GA [*Library symbol*] ... GACDC-FP
Center for Disease Control, Main Library, Atlanta, GA [*Library symbol*] ... GACDC
Center Distance ... CD
Center for Documentation and Communication Research [*Case Western Reserve University*] ... CDCR
Center for Early Adolescence ... CEA
Center for Editions of American Authors [*Later, CSE*] ... CEAA
Center for Editions of American Authors [*Later, CSE*] **Newsletter** [*A publication*] ... CEAAN
Center for Education and Research in Free Enterprise ... CERFE
Center for Educational Change [*University of California, Berkeley*] ... CEC
Center for Educational Policy and Management [*Department of Education*] ... CEPM
Center for Educational Policy Studies ... CEPS
Center for Educational Reform ... CER
Center for Educational Technology ... CET
Center for Energy and Environmental Information [*Department of Energy*] ... CEEI
Center for Energy and Environmental Research [*University of Puerto Rico*] ... CEER
Center for Energy Information [*Defunct*] ... CEI
Center for Energy and Mineral Resources [*Texas A & M University*] ... CEMR
Center for Energy Policy and Research ... CEPR
Center Engine Cutoff [*NASA*] ... CECO
Center for Entrepreneurial Development [*Carnegie-Mellon University*] ... CED
Center for Entrepreneurial Management ... CEM
Center for Environmental Assessment Services [*National Oceanic and Atmospheric Administration*] [*Information service*] ... CEAS
Center for Environmental Education ... CEE
Center for Environmental and Estuarian Studies [*University of Maryland*] ... CEES
Center for Environmental Intern Programs ... CEIP
Center for Experiment Design and Data Analysis [*National Oceanic and Atmospheric Administration*] ... CEDDA
Center for Experimental Studies in Business [*University of Minnesota*] ... CESB
Center for Family Business ... CFB
Center for Federal Policy Review ... CFPR
Center Field [*or Fielder*] [*Baseball*] ... CF
Center for Field Research ... CFR
Center of Filtering and Plotting ... CFP
Center for Financial Freedom and Accuracy in Financial Reporting ... CFFAFR
Center Fire ... CF
Center of Flotation ... CF
Center Focus [*Binoculars*] ... CF
Center for Foreign Policy Development ... CFPD
Center Forward [*Soccer*] ... CF
Center Frequency ... CF
Center Frequency Modulation ... CFM
Center Frequency Stabilization [*Radio*] ... CFS
Center for Governmental Research Library, Rochester, NY [*OCLC symbol*] ... VQD
Center of Gravity ... CG
Center of Gravity above Keel ... KG
Center-of-Gravity Locator ... CGL
Center for Growth Alternatives [*Defunct*] ... CGA
Center Halfback [*Soccer*] ... CH
Center Halfback [*Soccer*] ... CHB
Center for Health Resources Planning Information [*National Institutes of Health*] ... CHRPI
Center for Hellenic Studies, Harvard University, Washington, DC [*Library symbol*] ... DCHS
Center for High-Energy Forming. Proceedings. International Conference [*A publication*] ... Cent High-Energy Form Pro
Center for Highway Research. Research Report. University of Texas at Austin [*A publication*] ... Cent High Res Res Rep Tex Austin
Center for the History of American Needlework ... CHAN
Center for History of Chemistry [*American Chemical Society, University of Pennsylvania*] ... CHOC
Center for Holocaust Studies ... CHS
Center (Hospital and Domiciliary) [*Veterans Administration*] ... C(H & D)
Center for Housing, Building, and Planning [*United Nations*] ... UNCHBP
Center on Human Policy ... CHP
Center for Human Radiobiology ... CHR
Center for Humane Options in Childbirth Experiences ... CHOICE
Center of Impact ... CI
Center for Independent Action ... CFIA
Center for Independent Education [*Later, Cato Institute*] ... CIE
Center for Industrial Research and Service ... CIRAS
Center for Infectious Diseases [*Department of Health and Human Services*] ... CID
Center for Information on America ... CIOA
Center for Information and Numerical Data Analysis and Synthesis [*Purdue*] [*National Bureau of Standards*] ... CINDAS
Center for Information Research [*Drexel University*] ... CIR
Center for Information Sciences ... CIS
Center for Inquiry and Discovery [*Washington, DC, museum*] ... CID
Center for Integral Medicine ... CIM
Center for Inter-American Relations ... CIAR
Center for Inter-American Relations ... CIR
Center for International Economic Growth [*Defunct*] ... CIEG
Center for International Environment Information [*Later, WEC*] ... CIEI
Center for International Policy ... CIP
Center for International Private Enterprise ... CIPE
Center on International Race Relations [*University of Denver*] ... CIRR

Center for International Security .... CIS
Center of International Studies [*MIT*] .... CIS
Center for International Studies, Albany, NY [*Library symbol*] .... NAICI
Center for International Systems Research .... CISR
Center for Interreligious Affairs .... CIA
Center for Investigative Reporting .... CIR
Center Island [*Nuclear energy*] CI
Center Island Vessel [*Nuclear energy*] CIV
Center for Labor Education and Research [*University of Colorado*] .... CLEAR
Center for Lake Erie Area Research [*Ohio State University*] .... CLEAR
Center Landing Gear .... CLG
Center Launch and Flight Instrumentation Center [*NASA*] .... CLFIC
Center for Law and Education .... CLE
Center on Law and Pacifism .... CLP
Center for Law in the Public Interest .... CLIPI
Center for Law and Religious Freedom [*Christian Legal Society*] .... CLRF
Center for Law and Social Policy .... CLASP
Center for Libertarian Studies .... CLS
Center of Lift CL
Center Line CL
Center Line Average .... CLA
Center Line Bend .... CLB
Center-Line Plotting .... CLPLOT
Center for Local Tax Research .... CLTR
Center Magazine [*A publication*] .... Center
Center Magazine [*A publication*] .... Cn
Center for Management Development .... CMD
Center for Management Systems .... CMS
Center for Management Technology .... CMT
Center for Marine Affairs [*Scripps Institution of Oceanography*] .... CMA
Center for Marine Resources [*National Oceanic and Atmospheric Administration*] .... CMR
Center for Maritime Studies .... CMS
Center for Marketing Communications [*Later, Advertising Research Foundation*] .... CMC
Center for Marxist Research .... CMR
Center of Mass [*Atomic physics*] .... CM
Center for Mass Communication [*Columbia University*] .... CMC
Center Matched [*Technical drawings*] .... CM
Center Materials Representative [*NASA*] .... CMR
Center for Materials Science and Engineering [*MIT*] .... CMSE
Center for Medical Consumers and Health Care Information .... CMCHCI
Center for Medieval and Early Renaissance Studies .... CEMERS
Center for Medieval and Renaissance Studies .... CMRS
Center for Metric Education [*Western Michigan University*] .... CME
Center for Migration Studies [*City University of New York*] .... CMS
Center of Military History .... CMH
Center Moriches Free Public Library, Center Moriches, NY [*Library symbol*] .... NCm
Center for Multinational Studies [*International Economic Policy Association*] .... CMS
Center on National Labor Policy .... CNLP
Center for National Policy .... CNP
Center for National Policy Review .... CNPR
Center for National Security Studies [*of the Fund for Peace and the American Civil Liberties Union Foundation*] .... CNSS
Center for Natural Areas .... CNA
Center for Naval Analyses .... CNA
Center for Neo-Hellenic Studies .... CNHS
Center for New Corporate Priorities [*Defunct*] .... CNCP
Center for New National Security .... CNNS
Center for New Schools .... CNS
Center for Non-Broadcast Television [*Formerly, AFAE*] .... CNB-TV
Center for Nonprofit Organizations .... CNO
Center for Nursing Education, Spokane, WA [*Library symbol*] .... WaSpCN
Center for Occupational Hazards .... COH
Center Operations Directorate .... COD
Center for Operations Research [*MIT*] .... COR
Center for Optimum Environments .... COE
Center Overage Pending Assignment .... COPA
Center for Overseas Program Analysis [*Department of State*] .... COPA
Center for Packaging Education .... CPE
Center for Parapsychological Research [*Defunct*] .... CPR
Center for Peace Studies .... CPS
Center for Philosophy, Law, Citizenship .... CPLC
Center for Philosophy and Public Policy .... CPPP
Center of Pillar .... CPLR
Center for Plutonium Production [*France*] .... CPP
Center for Policy Process [*Defunct*] .... CPP
Center for Policy Research .... CPR
Center for Political Research [*Later, Government Research Corporation*] .... CPR
Center for Popular Economics .... CPE
Center for Population Options .... CPO
Center for Population Research [*National Institutes of Health*] .... CPR
Center of Pressure .... CP
Center of Pressure Back .... CPB
Center for Prevention of Premature Arterial Sclerosis .... CPPA
Center for Process Studies .... CPS
Center Program Director [*NASA*] .... CPD
Center Program Manager [*NASA*] .... CPM
Center of Programed Instruction .... CPI
Center for Public Representation .... CPR
Center for Public Resources .... CPR
Center Punch .... CP
Center for Radiation Research [*National Bureau of Standards*] .... CRR
Center for Radiophysics and Space Research [*Cornell University*] .... CRSR
Center Range Control Station [*NASA*] .... CRCS
Center for Rate Controlled Recordings [*Defunct*] .... CRCR
Center for Reformation Research .... CRR
Center for Reformation Research, St. Louis, MO [*Library symbol*] .... MoSCRR
Center (Regional Office and Hospital) [*Veterans Administration*] .... C(RO & H)
Center (Regional Office and Insurance) [*Veterans Administration*] .... C(RO & INS)
Center for Renewable Resources .... CRR
Center for Reproductive and Sexual Health .... CRASH
Center for Research in Ambulatory Health Care Administration .... CRAHCA
Center for Research in College Instruction of Science and Mathematics .... CRICISAM
Center for Research in Engineering Science [*University of Kansas*] .... CRES
Center for Research and Evaluation in Applications of Technology in Education [*Palo Alto, CA*] .... CREATE
Center for Research in the Hospitality Service Industries .... CRHSI
Center for Research on Language and Language Behavior [*University of Michigan*] .... CRLLB
Center for Research Libraries [*Library network*] .... CRL
Center for Research Libraries, Chicago, IL [*OCLC symbol*] [*Inactive*] .... CRL
Center for Research Libraries, Chicago, IL [*Library symbol*] .... ICRL
Center for Research in Management Science [*University of California*] .... CRMS
Center for Research for Mothers and Children [*National Institutes of Health*] .... CRMC
Center for Research in Scientific Communication [*Johns Hopkins University*] .... CRSC
Center for Research in Security Prices [*University of Chicago*] [*Information service*] .... CRSP
Center for Research in Social Change [*Emory University, Atlanta, GA*] .... CRSC
Center for Research in Social Systems [*American Institutes for Research*] .... CRESS
Center for Research in Social Systems of the American University .... CRESS/AU
Center for Research on Utilization of Scientific Knowledge [*University of Michigan*] .... CRUSK
Center of Resistance .... CR
Center for Responsive Governance .... CRG
Center for Responsive Psychology .... CRP
Center for the Rights of Campus Journalists .... CRCJ
Center for Russian and East European Jewry .... CFRJ
Center for Scholarly Editions [*Formerly, CEAA*] .... CSE
Center for Science in the Public Interest [*Formed by consumer-advocate Ralph Nader*] .... CSPI
Center Section .... CS
Center for Self-Sufficiency .... CSS
Center for Settlement Studies. Research Reports. University of Manitoba [*A publication*] .... Cent SS RR
Center for Short-Lived Phenomena [*Cambridge, MA*] .... CFSLP
Center for Short-Lived Phenomena [*Cambridge, MA*] .... CSLP
Center for Sickle Cell Disease .... CSCD
Center for Social Organization of Schools [*Department of Education*] .... CSOS
Center for Social Research and Education .... CSRE
Center for Social Science Research and Documentation for the Arab Region [*UNESCO*] [*Information service*] .... ARCSS
Center on Social Welfare Policy and Law .... CSWPL
Center for Socialist History .... CSH
Center for Southern Folklore .... CSF
Center for Space Research [*MIT*] .... CSR
Center Special Slotted Container [*Packaging*] .... CSSC
Center Stage [*A stage direction*] .... CS
Center Stage Back [*A stage direction*] .... CSB
Center Stage Front [*A stage direction*] .... CSF
Center Standards Officer [*Job Corps*] .... CSO
Center for State Employment Security Automated Systems .... CSESAS
Center for Strategic and International Studies [*Georgetown University*] .... CSIS
Center for Studies in Criminal Justice .... CSCJ
Center for Studies in Criminology and Criminal Law .... CSCCL
Center for Studies of Mental Health of the Aging [*National Institute of Mental Health*] .... CSMHA
Center for Studies of Suicide Prevention [*National Institute of Mental Health*] .... CSSP
Center for the Study of Aging .... CSA
Center for the Study of Democratic Institutions [*Later, Robert Maynard Hutchins Center for the Study of Democratic Institutions*] .... CSDI
Center for the Study of Democratic Societies .... CSDS
Center for the Study of Drug Policy .... CSDP
Center for the Study of Economics .... CSE

Center for the Study of Evaluation [*Department of Education*]....CSE
Center for the Study of the Evaluation of Instructional Programs....CSEIP
Center for the Study of Foreign Affairs....CSFA
Center for the Study of the Future....CSF
Center for the Study of Human Rights....CSHR
Center for the Study of Information and Education [*Syracuse University*]....CSIE
Center for the Study of Instruction [*of NEA*]....CSI
Center for the Study of Legal Authority and Mental Patient Status....LAMP
Center for the Study of Liberal Education for Adults....CSLEA
Center for Study of Multiple Birth [*Formerly, CSMG*]....CSMB
Center for the Study of Multiple Gestation [*Later, CSMB*]....CSMG
Center for the Study of Non-Medical Drug Use [*Later, CSDP*]....CSNMDU
Center for the Study of Parent Involvement....CSPI
Center for the Study of Power [*Later, SPI*]....CSP
Center for the Study of the Presidency....CSP
Center for the Study of Private Enterprise [*American University*]....CSPE
Center for Study of Responsive Law....CSRL
Center for the Study of Social Policy....CSSP
Center for Supplying Services by Redemptorists for North America....CSSRNA
Center for Surface Coatings Research [*Lehigh University*]....CSCR
Center Surveillance RADAR....CASR
Center for the Survival of Western Democracies....CSWD
Center for Sustainable Agriculture....CSA
Center for Systems Engineering and Integration [*Army*]....CENSEI
Center for Tactical Computer Systems [*CADPL*] [*Army*]....CENTACS
Center Tap [*Technical drawings*]....CT
Center for Teaching about China....CTAC
Center on Transnational Corporations [*United Nations*]....CTC
Center, TX [*Location identifier*] [*FAA*]....CZJ
Center, TX [*Radio station call letters*]....KDET
Center, TX [*Radio station call letters*]....KLCR
Center for UFO [*Unidentified Flying Object*] **Studies** [*Information service*]....CUFOS
Center for Urban Black Studies....CUBS
Center for Urban Environmental Studies....CUES
Center for Urban and Regional Studies....CURS
Center for the Utilization of Federal Technology [*Department of Commerce*]....CUFT
Center for Vocational and Technical Education, Ohio State University, Columbus, OH [*OCLC symbol*] [*Inactive*]....CVT
Center for Vocational and Technical Education, Ohio State University, Columbus, OH [*Library symbol*]....OCoV
Center for a Voluntary Society [*Defunct*]....CVS
Center for War/Peace Studies....CW/PS
Center for Water Resources Research [*University of Nevada*]....CWRR
Center Weather Service Unit....CWSU
Center for the Well-Being of Health Professionals....CWBHP
Center for a Woman's Own Name [*An association*]....CWON
Center for Women Policy Studies....CWPS
Center for Women and Sport....CWS
Center for Women's Studies and Services....CWSS
Center Work System [*NASA*]....CWS
Centerbanc Savings Association [*NASDAQ symbol*]....CBNK
Centerboard....CNTBRD
Centering....CTRG
Centerline....CNTRLN
Centerline Vertical Keel....CVK
Centerre Bancorp [*NASDAQ symbol*]....CTBC
Centers for Disease Control [*Formerly, Communicable Disease Center*] [*Atlanta*] [*Public Health Service*]....CDC
Centers for Disease Control. Publications [*A publication*]....CDC
Centers and Regional Associations....CARA
Centerville Community College [*Iowa*]....CCC
Centerville, IA [*Radio station call letters*]....KCOG
Centerville, IA [*Radio station call letters*]....KMGO
Centerville, IN [*Radio station call letters*]....WHON
Centerville, MS [*Radio station call letters*]....WSLL
Centerville, OH [*Radio station call letters*]....WCWT-FM
Centerville, TN [*Location identifier*] [*FAA*]....GHM
Centerville, TN [*Radio station call letters*]....WHLP
Centerville, TN [*Radio station call letters*]....WHLP-FM
Centerville, UT [*Radio station call letters*]....KBBX
Centerville, UT [*Radio station call letters*]....KCGL
Centex Corp. [*NYSE symbol*]....CTX
Centi [*A prefix meaning divided by 100*] [*SI symbol*]....c
Centigrade [*Celsius*] [*Temperature scale*]....C
Centigrade [*Celsius*] [*Temperature scale*]....CEN
Centigrade [*Celsius*] [*Temperature scale*]....CENT
Centigrade Heat Unit....CHU
Centigrade Thermal Unit....CTU
Centigram....C
Centigram....cg
Centigram....CGM
Centiliter....CL
Centime [*Monetary unit in France*]....C
Centime [*Monetary unit in France*]....CENT
Centimeter....C
Centimeter....cm
Centimeter-Candle....CM C
Centimeter-Gram-Second [*System of units*]....CGS
Centimeter-Gram-Second-Biot [*System of units*]....cm-g-s-Bi
Centimeter-Gram-Second-Electromagnetic....CGSM
Centimeter-Gram-Second-Electrostatic....CGSE
Centimeter-Gram-Second-Franklin [*System of units*]....cm-g-s-Fr
Centimeter Height-Finder [*RADAR*]....CMH
Centimeters per Second....CMPS
Centipoise....CP
Centistere [*Metric*]....CS
Centistoke [*Also, cSt*] [*Unit of kinematic viscosity*]....cs
Centistoke [*Also, cs*] [*Unit of kinematic viscosity*]....cSt
Cento [*Composition compiled from other works*]....C
CENTO [*Central Treaty Organization*] **Conference on Land Classification for Non-Irrigated Lands** [*A publication*]....CENTO Conf Ld Classif Non-Irrig Lds
CENTO [*Central Treaty Organization*] **Institute of Nuclear Science**....CINS
CENTO [*Central Treaty Organization*] **Military Communications System**....CMCS
Centocor, Inc. [*NASDAQ symbol*]....CNTO
Centraal Economisch Plan [*A publication*]....Centr Econ Plan
Centraal Sociaal Werkgevers Verbond [*Employers' organization*] [*Netherlands*]....CSWV
Centrafic Charter Airlines [*Central African Empire*] [*ICAO designator*]....QH
Centrafrique Air [*Empire Centrafricain*] [*ICAO designator*]....QR
Centraide, Montreal, PQ, Canada [*Library symbol*]....CaOMCCS
Centrais Eletricas Brasileiras SA [*Brazil*]....ELETROBRAS
Centrais Eletricas de Goias....CELG
Centrais Eletricas de Sao Paulo SA [*Brazil*]....CESP
Centrais Eletricas do Sul do Brasil SA....ELETROSUL
Central....C
Central [*Alaska*] [*Airport symbol*]....CEM
Central....CENT
Central....CNTL
Central....CNTRL
Central....CTL
Central....CTRL
Central Abstracting and Indexing Service [*American Petroleum Institute*] [*Information service*]....CAIS
Central Accounting Office [*Military*]....CAO
Central Address Memory [*Data processing*]....CAM
Central Advisory Committee [*British*]....CAC
Central Advisory Council for Science and Technology [*British*]....CACST
Central Aero-Hydrodynamical Institute [*USSR*]....CAHI
Central Africa Party [*Southern Rhodesia*]....CAP
Central Africa Protectorate [*British government*]....CAP
Central African Airways Corp.....CAA
Central African Empire [*Later, CAR*]....CAE
Central African Empire [*Later, CAR*] [*Three-letter standard code*]....CAF
Central African Empire [*Later, CAR*] [*Two-letter standard code*]....CF
Central African Federation [*Disbanded Dec. 31, 1963*]....CAF
Central African Journal of Medicine [*A publication*]....Cent Afr J Med
Central African Republic [*Formerly, Ubangi-Shari, Central African Empire*]....CAR
Central African Republic [*Central African Empire*] [*MARC country of publication code*] [*Library of Congress*]....cx
Central African Republic [*Central African Empire*] [*MARC geographic area code*] [*Library of Congress*]....f-cx---
Central African Republic [*Aircraft nationality and registration mark*]....TL
Central Aguirre Sugar Co. [*NYSE symbol*] [*Delisted*]....CEG
Central Air Conditioning [*Classified advertising*]....CAC
Central Air Data Computer....CADC
Central Air Data System [*Air Force*]....CADS
Central Air Defense Force....CADF
Central Air Documents Office [*Air Force*]....CADO
Central Air Materiel Area, Europe....CAMAE
Central Air Procurement District....CEAPD
Central Air Transport....CATR
Central Air Transport, Inc. [*Nashville, TN*] [*FAA designator*]....TCR
Central Airborne Performance Analyzer....CAPA
Central Aircraft Dispatch....CAD
Central Aircrew Medical Review Board....CAMRB
Central Airlines, Inc.....CEN
Central Airlines, Inc.....CN
Central Airlines, Inc. [*Kansas City, KS*] [*FAA designator*]....CTL
Central Airways....CA
Central Altitude Reservation Facility [*or Function*]....CARF
Central America....CA
Central America [*MARC geographic area code*] [*Library of Congress*]....nc-----
Central American Airways [*Louisville, KY*] [*FAA designator*]....CAA
Central American Airways [*Air carrier designation symbol*]....CAAX
Central American Bank for Economic Integration....CABEI
Central American Club of New York....CAC
Central American Common Market....CACM
Central American Common Market....CACOM
Central American Economics Association....CAEA
Central American Free Trade Area....CAFTA
Central American Indian [*MARC language code*] [*Library of Congress*]....cai
Central American International [*Air carrier designation symbol*]....CAIX
Central American Mission [*Later, CAM International*]....CAM
Central American Refugee Center....CARECEN

Central Ammunition Depot ... CAD

Central Ammunition Management Office - Pacific [*Army*] ... CAMO-PAC

Central Ammunition Supply Status Point ... CASSP

Central Analog Data Distributing and Computing System ... CADDAC

Central Annunciator Display Panel ... CADP

Central Apollo Data Index [*NASA*] ... CADI

Central Apparatus Room ... CAR

Central Archives of Fiji, Suva, Fiji [*Library symbol*] ... Fj-Ar

Central Area ... CA

Central Area, Military Traffic Management and Terminal Service ... CAMTMTS

Central Arizona College, Instructional Materials Center, Coolidge, AZ [*Library symbol*] ... AzCoC

Central Arizona Project [*Federal water-and-power project, similar to TVA*] ... CAP

Central Arizona Project Association ... CAPA

Central Arkansas Library System, Little Rock, AR [*OCLC symbol*] ... AKD

Central [*European*] **Army Group** [*NATO*] ... CENTAG

Central Asian Review [*A publication*] ... CAR

Central Asian Review [*A publication*] ... CAsR

Central Asiatic Journal [*A publication*] ... CAJ

Central Asiatic Journal [*A publication*] ... CAsJ

Central Asiatic Journal [*A publication*] ... Cent Asia J

Central Asiatic Journal [*A publication*] ... Centr Asiat J

Central Asiatic Studies [*A publication*] ... CAS

Central Association of the Miraculous Medal ... CAMM

Central Association of Science and Mathematics Teachers [*Later, SSMA*] ... CASMT

Central Atlantic Regional Ecological Test Site [*Department of the Interior*] ... CARETS

Central Atlantic Regional Educational Laboratory ... CAREL

Central Automated Inventory and Referral Activity [*Organization for operation of CAIRS*] [*Air Force*] ... CAIRA

Central Automated Inventory and Referral System [*Air Force*] ... CAIRS

Central Automated Personnel Security Transaction or Notification Exchange [*DoD*] ... CAPSTONE

Central Automated Replenishment Technique ... CART

Central Automatic Digital Data Encoder [*NASA*] ... CADDE

Central Automatic Message Accounting System ... CAMAS

Central Automatic Reliability Tester ... CART

Central Bancorp, Inc. [*NASDAQ symbol*] ... CBAN

Central Bancshares of the South [*NASDAQ symbol*] ... CBSS

Central Bank of Ireland. Annual Report [*A publication*] ... Centr Bank Ireland Annu Rep

Central Bank of Ireland. Quarterly Bulletin [*A publication*] ... Centr Bank Ireland Quart B

Central Bank Money ... CBM

Central Banking Systems [*NASDAQ symbol*] ... CSYS

Central Baptist Theological Seminary, Kansas City, KS [*Library symbol*] ... KKcB

Central Battery ... CB

Central Battery Signaling ... CBS

Central Bible Institute [*Missouri*] ... CBI

Central Bibliographic System [*Library of Congress*] ... CBS

Central Bidder's List ... CBL

Central Black Soil Region, RSFSR [*MARC geographic area code*] [*Library of Congress*] ... e-urc--

Central Board ... CB

Central Bureau of Astronautical Telegrams ... CBAT

Central Bureau, Catholic Central Union of America ... CBCCUA

Central Bureau for the Jewish Aged ... CBJA

Central Bureau of Nuclear Measurements [*European Atomic Energy Community*] ... CBNM

Central Business District ... CBD

Central California Traction Co. [*AAR code*] ... CCT

Central Canada Broadcasting Association ... CCBA

Central Canal [*Anatomy*] ... CC

Central Cardiac Monitoring System ... CCMS

Central Carolina Technical Institute, Sanford, NC [*Library symbol*] ... NcSaC

Central Certificate Service [*NYSE symbol*] ... CCS

Central Certificate System [*Stock exchange automation program*] ... CCS

Central Circulating Blood Volume [*Physiology*] ... CCBV

Central Citroen Club ... CCC

Central City, KY [*Radio station call letters*] ... WKYA

Central City, KY [*Radio station call letters*] ... WMTA

Central City, KY [*Radio station call letters*] ... WNES

Central City, PA [*Radio station call letters*] ... WWZE

Central Civilian Personnel Office [*Military*] ... CCPO

Central Classification Committee [*International Federation for Documentation*] ... CCC

Central College of Kentucky ... CCK

Central College, Pella, IA [*Library symbol*] ... IaPeC

Central College, Pella, IA [*OCLC symbol*] ... IOP

Central Colorado Regional Library Service System [*Library network*] ... CCLS

Central Command Decoder [*Spacecraft assembly*] ... CCD

Central Command Network ... CCN

Central Commissioning Detail [*Navy*] ... CCD

Central Committee ... CC

Central Committee on Communications Facilities ... CCCF

Central Committee of Lithuanian Jurists ... CCLJ

Central Communications Region [*Air Force*] ... CCR

Central Communications Region [*Military*] ... CENCOMMRGN

Central Composite Design [*Statistical design of experiments*] ... CCD

Central Computer ... CC

Central Computer Accounting ... CCA

Central Computer Accounting Corporation ... CCAC

Central Computer Center ... CCMPTC

Central Computer Complex ... CCC

Central Computer and Display Facility [*Air Force*] ... CC & DF

Central Computer and Sequencer [*NASA*] ... CC & S

Central Computer and Telecommunications Agency [*British*] ... CCTA

Central Computer Unit ... CCU

Central Computing Facility [*NASA*] ... CCF

Central Conference of American Rabbis ... CCAR

Central Connecticut State College ... CCSC

Central Connecticut State College, New Britain, CT [*Library symbol*] ... CtNbT

Central Console ... CC

Central Contract Management Region [*Air Force*] ... CCMR

Central Control ... CC

Central Control Computer System ... CCCS

Central Control and Display Console ... CCDC

Central Control Evaluation and Warning Team ... CCEWT

Central Control Facility [*Military*] ... CCF

Central Control Room ... CCR

Central Control Section ... CCS

Central Control Ship [*Navy*] ... CCS

Central Control Station ... CCS

Central Control Unit ... CCU

Central Cooperative Society [*United Arab Republic*] ... CCS

Central Coordinating Staff, Canada ... CCS-C

Central Council for Agricultural and Horticultural Co-operation [*British*] ... CCAC

Central Council of Ceylon Trade Unions ... CCCTU

Central Council for Education and Training in Social Work [*British*] ... CCETSW

Central Council of National Retail Associations ... CCNRA

Central Criminal Court [*Old Bailey*] [*British*] ... CCC

Central Cultural Movement [*China*] ... CCM

Central Data Acquisition System ... CDAS

Central Data Analysis Area ... CDAA

Central Data Bank ... CDB

Central Data Buffer [*Data processing*] ... CDB

Central Data and Cataloging Center ... CD & CC

Central Data Collection System ... CDCS

Central Data-Conversion Equipment ... CDCE

Central Data Display ... CDD

Central Data Distribution Facility [*National Oceanic and Atmospheric Administration*] ... CDDF

Central Data Facility [*NASA*] ... CDF

Central Data Flow Control ... CFC

Central Data Management ... CDM

Central Data Processing Computer ... CDPC

Central Data Processing Facility [*NASA*] ... CDPF

Central Data Processor ... CDP

Central Data Station ... CDS

Central Data Subsystem ... CDS

Central Data and Switching Center [*NASA*] ... CD & SC

Central Datum ... CEN

Central Daylight Saving Time ... CDST

Central Daylight Time ... CDT

Central Defence Staff [*British*] ... CDS

Central Dental Laboratories [*Army*] ... CDL

Central Differential Analyzer Control ... CEDAC

Central Digital Computer ... CDC

Central Display Unit ... CDU

Central Distribution Panel ... CDP

Central Distribution System [*Publications*] [*Navy*] ... CDS

Central District ... CD

Central Dockyard Laboratory [*British*] ... CDL

Central Document Control [*Jet Propulsion Laboratory, NASA*] ... CDC

Central Drafting Officer [*Navy*] ... CENDRAFT

Central Drug Research Institute [*India*] [*Research code symbol*] ... X

Central East Pacific [*Region*] ... CEP

Central Eastern Personnel Organization [*Computerized scouting combine for professional football teams*] ... CEPO

Central Economic Committee ... CEC

Central Economic Information Service [*British*] ... CEIS

Central Educational Network [*Television*] ... CEN

Central Electric Railfans' Association ... CERA

Central Electricity Authority [*British*] ... CEA

Central Electricity Board [*British*] ... CEB

Central Electricity Generating Board [*British*] ... CEGB

Central Electricity Research Laboratories [*British*] ... CERL

Central Electrochemical Research Institute ... CERI

Central Electronic Management System ... CEMS

Central Electronics System ... CES

Central Engine Room Control ... CERC

Central Engineering Projects Office [*NATO*] ... CEPO

Central Europe ... CE

Central Europe Inland Waterways Transport [*NATO*]....CE/IWT
Central Europe Joint Emergency Defense Plan [*NATO*]....CEJEDP
Central Europe Operating Agency [*NATO*]....CEOA
Central Europe Pipeline Agency [*Later, CEOA*] [*NATO*]....CEPA
Central Europe Pipeline Office [*NATO*]....CEPO
Central Europe Pipeline Policy Committee [*NATO*]....CEPPC
Central Europe Pipeline System [*NATO*]....CEPS
Central Europe Railroad Transport [*NATO*]....CE/RRT
Central Europe Road Transport [*NATO*]....CE/RT
Central European....CENEUR
Central European Communication Region [*Air Force*]....CECR
Central European Federal Youth Movement....CEFYM
Central European Federalist [*A publication*]....Cent Eur Fed
Central European Federation of Christian Trade Unions....CEFCTU
Central European Forces Distribution Agency [*NATO*]....CEFDA
Central European History [*A publication*]....CEH
Central European History [*A publication*]....Cen Eur Hist
Central European History [*A publication*]....Cent Eur H
Central European History [*A publication*]....Cent Eur Hist
Central European Line [*Oil pipeline*]....CEL
Central European Time....CET
Central Evidence of Research and Development Reports....CERD
Central Exchange....CENTREX
Central Exchange....CX
Central [*Nervous System*] **Excitatory State**....CES
Central Experimental and Proving Establishment [*Canada*]....CEPE
Central External Liaison Department [*Chinese Secret Service*]....CELD
Central Fidelity Bank [*NASDAQ symbol*]....CFBS
Central Fighter Establishment [*British*]....CFE
Central Fighter Weapons Instructor School....CFWIS
Central Files....CF
Central Files Repository....CFR
Central Financial Management Activities [*Military*]....CFMA
Central Fire Control [*Military*]....CFC
Central Firing Unit....CFU
Central Flight Status Selection Board [*Air Force*]....CFSSB
Central Florida Community College, Ocala, FL [*Library symbol*]....FOcC
Central Florida Regional Library, Ocala, FL [*Library symbol*]....FOc
Central Flow Control Facility [*or Function*]....CFCF
Central Flow Weather Service Unit....CFWSU
Central Flying School [*RAF*] [*British*]....CFS
Central Flying Service, Inc. [*Little Rock, AR*] [*FAA designator*]....CNT
Central Flying Training Command [*AAFCFTC*]....CFTC
Central Food Preparation Facility [*Military*]....CFPF
Central Food Preparation System [*Military*]....CFPS
Central Food Technology Research Institute [*India*]....CFTRI
Central Forms Committee [*Defunct*]....CFC
Central Foundry Co. [*Later, GBI*] [*NYSE symbol*]....FD
Central Frequency Synthesizer....CFS
Central Gear Box....CGB
Central General Hospital, Plainview, NY [*Library symbol*]....NPICH
Central Georgia Associated Libraries [*Library network*]....CGAL
Central of Georgia Railroad Co.....CG
Central of Georgia Railroad Co.....C of GA
Central of Georgia Railroad Co.....CGARY
Central of Georgia Railroad Co. [*NYSE symbol*] [*Delisted*]....GEO
Central of Georgia Railroad Co. [*AAR code*]....CGA
Central German Administrative Department [*Economic Committee*] [*US Military Government, Germany*]....CADM
Central Glass and Ceramic Research Institute. Bulletin [*A publication*]....Cent Glass Ceram Res Inst Bull
Central Government Borrowing Requirement [*British*]....CGBR
Central Gray [*Brain anatomy*]....CG
Central Gray Matter [*Physiology*]....CGM
Central Grounding Point....CGP
Central Gyro Reference System....CGRS
Central Heating....CH
Central Heating Plant....CHP
Central Hockey League....CHL
Central Hudson Gas & Electric Corp. [*NYSE symbol*]....CNH
Central [*Atom*] **Hyperfine Structure**....CHFS
Central Illinois Light Co. [*NYSE symbol*]....CER
Central Illinois Public Service Co. [*NYSE symbol*]....CIP
Central Index File....CIF
Central Index File - Europe....CIFE
Central Indiana Railway Co. [*Absorbed into Consolidated Rail Corp.*] [*AAR code*]....CIND
Central Inertial Guidance Test Facility [*Air Force*]....CIGTF
Central Inertial Reference Instrumentation System....CIRIS
Central Information File....CIF
Central Information, Library, and Editorial Section [*CSIRO*] [*Information service*]....CILES
Central Information Processor....CIP
Central Information Reference and Control....CIRC
Central [*Nervous System*] **Inhibitory State**....CIS
Central Initial Zone [*in inflorescence*] [*Botany*]....CIZ
Central Input-Output Multiplexer [*Data processing*]....CIO
Central Installation Supply [*Air Force*]....CIS
Central Institute for the Deaf....CID
Central Institute of Foreign Affairs Research....CIFAR
Central Institute for Industrial Research....CIIR
Central Institute for Nutrition and Food Research [*Netherlands*]....CINFR
Central Institute of Physics. Institute for Physics and Nuclear Engineering. Report (Romania) [*A publication*]....Cent Inst Phys Inst Phys Nucl Eng Rep (Romania)
Central Instructor School....CIS
Central Instrumentation Facility [*NASA*]....CIF
Central Integrated Checkout System....CICS
Central Integrated Test System....CITS
Central Integration Facility....CIF
Central Integration Site....CIS
Central Intelligence Agency [*of the US*]....CIA
Central Intelligence Agency, McLean, VA [*Library symbol*]....ViMcC
Central Intelligence Board....CIB
Central Intelligence Organizations [*South Vietnam*]....CIO
Central Intelligence Retirees Association....CIRA
Central Intelligence Retrieval Center....CIRC
Central Intercollegiate Athletic Association....CIAA
Central Interface Converter Unit....CICU
Central Interpretation Unit [*Military*]....CIU
Central Interval....CI
Central Inventory of Production Equipment Records [*Army*]....CIPER
Central Iowa Railway Company [*AAR code*]....CIRC
Central Iowa Regional Library [*Library network*]....CIRL
Central Islip Public Library, Central Islip, NY [*Library symbol*]....NCi
Central Islip State Hospital, Central Islip, NY [*Library symbol*]....NCiSH
Central Issue Facility [*Military*]....CIF
Central Jersey Bank [*NASDAQ symbol*]....CJER
Central Juvenile Index....CJI
Central Kansas Library System [*Library network*]....CKLS
Central Kansas Library System, Book Processing Center, Great Bend, KS [*OCLC symbol*]....KKV
Central Kansas Library System, Great Bend, KS [*Library symbol*]....KGbLS
Central Kansas Medical Center, Great Bend, KS [*Library symbol*]....KGbMC
Central Labor Relations Commission [*Japan*]....CLRC
Central Laboratory....CL
Central Laboratory Equipment Management....CLEM
Central Lake Township Library, Central Lake, MI [*Library symbol*]....MiCenl
Central Latinoamerica de Trabajadores....CLAT
Central Leather Research Institute [*British*]....CLRI
Central Library and Documentation Branch [*International Labor Organization*]....CLD
Central Library Network [*Library network*]....CLN
Central Limit Theorem [*Statistics*]....CLT
Central Line....CL
Central Liquidity Facility [*National Credit Union Administration*]....CLF
Central Load Dispatching Office [*US Military Government, Germany*]....CLDO
Central Logic Unit....CLU
Central Logistics Command [*Republic of Vietnam Armed Forces*]....CLC
Central Logistics Management Center....CLMC
Central London Underground Railway....CLR
Central Louisiana Electric Co. [*NYSE symbol*]....CNL
Central Louisiana Energy Corp. [*NYSE symbol*] [*Delisted*]....CEL
Central Louisiana State Hospital, Medical Library, Pineville, LA [*Library symbol*]....LPiC
Central Lutheran Theological Seminary, Fremont, NE [*Library symbol*]....NbFC
Central Machine Gun....CMG
Central Maine Power Co. [*NYSE symbol*]....CTP
Central Maintenance Facility....CMF
Central Management Army Commissaries....CMAC
Central Marine Chamber of Commerce [*Defunct*]....CMCC
Central Marine Fisheries Research Institute [*India*]....CMFRI
Central Marine Fisheries Research Institute. Bulletin [*A publication*]....Cent Mar Fish Res Inst Bull
Central Marketing & Realty Trust [*NASDAQ symbol*]....CMRTS
Central Massachusetts Regional Public Library System [*Library network*]....CMRLS
Central Master Control....CMC
Central Materiel Service Team [*Military*]....CMS
Central Meat Processing Facility [*Army*]....CMPF
Central Mechanical Engineering Research Institute....CMERI
Central Medical Establishment, Aviation [*Air Force*]....CMEA
Central Medical Journal. Seminar Reports (Moscow) [*A publication*]....Cent Med J Semin Rep (Moscow)
Central Mediterranean....MEDCENT
Central Mediterranean Force [*Later, AAI*] [*British*] [*World War II*]....CMF
Central Memory [*Data processing*]....CM
Central Meridian Distance [*NASA*]....CMD
Central Meteorological Observatory [*Japan*]....CMO
Central Methodist College, Fayette, MO [*Library symbol*]....MoFC
Central Michigan Library System [*Library network*]....CMLS
Central Michigan University, Mount Pleasant, MI [*OCLC symbol*]....EZC
Central Michigan University, Mount Pleasant, MI [*Library symbol*]....MiMtpT
Central Microfilm Service Corp., St. Louis, MO [*Library symbol*]....CeM
Central Midwest Regional Educational Laboratory....CEMREL
Central Midwives Board....CMB
Central Milk Distributive Committee [*British*]....CMDC
Central Minnesota Seismic Array [*Minnesota*] [*Seismograph station code, US Geological Survey*]....CM6
Central Mississippi Library Council [*Library network*]....INFO PASS

Central Missouri State College [*Later, Central Missouri State University*] .... CMSC
Central Missouri State University, Warrensburg, MO [*OCLC symbol*] .... MCW
Central Missouri State University, Warrensburg, MO [*Library symbol*] .... MoWarbT
Central Mortgage & Housing Corporation [*Canadian government*] .... CMHC
Central Mortgage & Housing Corp., Children's Environments Advisory Service, Ottawa, ON, Canada [*Library symbol*] .... CaOOCMC
Central Mortgage & Housing Corp., Ottawa, ON, Canada [*Library symbol*] .... CaOOCM
Central Mortgage & Housing Corp., Standards Information Centre, Ottawa, ON, Canada [*Library symbol*] .... CaOOCMS
Central Nacional de Informaciones [*Supersedes DINA*] .... CNI
Central Naval Ordnance Management Information System .... CENO
Central Navigation Computer .... CNC
Central Nervous System [*Physiology*] .... CNS
Central Neuropsychiatric Association .... CNA
Central New York Library Resources Council [*Library network*] .... CENTRO
Central New York Library Resources Council, Syracuse, NY [*OCLC symbol*] .... SRR
Central New York Railroad Corp. [*AAR code*] .... CNYK
Central New York Union List of Serials, Syracuse, NY [*OCLC symbol*] .... ZUA
Central Night Vision Training School [*Military*] [*British*] .... CNVTS
Central Normal College, Danville, IN [*Library symbol*] [*Obsolete*] .... InDanN
Central North Carolina Regional Library, Burlington, NC [*Library symbol*] .... NcBur
Central NOTAM [*Notice to Airmen*] **Facility** [*Military*] .... CNF
Central Obrera Boliviana .... COB
Central Office .... CO
Central Office to Central Office [*Bell System*] .... CO-CO
Central Office for Environmental Protection [*Basle, Switzerland*] .... COEP
Central Office Equipment [*Bell System*] .... COE
Central Office Equipment Estimation System [*Bell System*] .... COEES
Central Office of the Industrial Tribunal [*Department of Employment*] [*British*] .... COIT
Central Office of Information [*British*] .... COI
Central Office of Record [*DoD*] .... COR
Central Office of South Vietnam [*North Vietnamese high command in the South*] .... COSVN
Central Officers' Training School .... COTS
Central Ohio Interlibrary Network [*Library network*] .... COIN
Central Ontario Regional Library, Richmond Hill, ON, Canada [*Library symbol*] .... CaORhCO
Central Opera Service .... COS
Central Opera Service. Bulletin [*A publication*] .... Central Opera
Central Operating Agency .... COA
Central Oregon Community College, Bend, OR [*Library symbol*] .... OrBeC
Central Oregon Community College, Library, Bend, OR [*OCLC symbol*] .... CEO
Central Organization of Liaison for Allocation of Circuit .... COLAC
Central Organization of Trade Unions .... COTU
Central Pacific Area [*Navy*] .... CENPAC
Central Pacific Area [*Hawaiian area*] [*World War II*] .... CPA
Central Pacific Base Command [*Navy*] .... CENTPACBACOM
Central Pacific Base Command [*Hawaiian Islands*] [*World War II*] .... CPBC
Central Pacific Combat Air Transport Service .... CENCATS
Central Pacific Communications Instructions .... CENTCOM
Central Pacific Corporation [*NASDAQ symbol*] .... CPCO
Central Pacific Fisheries Research Center [*National Oceanic and Atmospheric Administration*] .... CPFRC
Central Pacific Forces .... CENPACFOR
Central Pacific Hurricane Center [*Honolulu*] [*National Weather Service*] .... CPHC
Central Pacific Minerals ADR [*NASDAQ symbol*] .... CPMNY
Central Pastry Kitchen [*Army*] .... CPK
Central Patents Index [*A publication*] .... CPI
Central Path Method [*Data processing*] .... CPM
Central Pattern Generator [*Neurochemistry*] .... CPG
Central Pay Accounts Division [*Navy*] .... CPAD
Central Pennsylvania District Library Center, Bellefonte, PA [*OCLC symbol*] .... PCB
Central Pennsylvania Medical Librarians [*Library network*] .... CPHSLA
Central Perfusion Pressure [*Medicine*] .... CPP
Central Personnel Data File [*DoD*] .... CPDF
Central Personnel Directorate [*British*] .... CPD
Central Personnel Security Clearance Index [*Nuclear energy*] .... CPSCI
Central Pharmaceutical Journal [*A publication*] .... Cent Phar J
Central Physical Evaluation Board [*Navy*] .... CPEB
Central Piedmont Community College, Charlotte, NC [*Library symbol*] .... NcCCP
Central Plains Turfgrass Foundation .... CPTF
Central Planning Center .... CPC
Central Planning Office [*NASA*] .... CPO
Central Planning Team .... CPT
Central Point .... CP
Central Point, OR [*Radio station call letters*] .... KCHC
Central Policy Review Staff [*British*] .... CPRS
Central Pontine Myelinolysis [*Medicine*] .... CPM
Central Port Call Office [*Army*] .... CPCO
Central Post Fund [*Army*] .... CPF
Central Post, South Brunswick, NJ [*Library symbol*] .... NjSobC
Central Postal Directory [*Army*] .... CPD
Central Power & Light Co. [*American Stock Exchange symbol*] [*Delisted*] .... CEW
Central Power System .... CPS
Central Powerhouse .... CPH
Central Premonitions Registry .... CPR
Central Press .... CP
Central Problem [*Psychometrics*] .... CP
Central Processing Element [*Data processing*] .... CPE
Central Processing Facility .... CPF
Central Processing Modules [*Data processing*] .... CPM
Central Processing Point [*Data processing*] .... CPP
Central Processing Subsystem [*Data processing*] .... CPSS
Central Processing System [*Data processing*] .... CPS
Central Processing Unit [*Data processing*] .... CPU
Central Processor [*Data processing*] .... CP
Central Processor Subunit [*Data processing*] .... CPSU
Central Processor Test Console [*Data processing*] .... CPTC
Central Procurement [*or Centrally Procured*] .... CP
Central Procurement Division [*Marine Corps*] .... CPD
Central Procurement Office .... CPO
Central Professional Hockey League .... CPHL
Central Programer and Evaluator .... CPE
Central Project Office [*of ARS, Department of Agriculture*] .... CPO
Central Property Control .... CPC
Central Property Control System .... CPCS
Central Provinces [*Later, Madhya Pradesh, India*] .... CP
Central Provision Office [*World War II*] .... CPO
Central Psi Research Institute .... CPRI
Central Purchasing Authority [*Military*] .... CPA
Central R. R. of Pennsylvania [*AAR code*] .... CRP
Central Radio Propagation Laboratory [*Later, ITS*] .... CRPL
Central Railroad Co. of New Jersey [*Absorbed into Consolidated Rail Corp.*] [*AAR code*] .... CNJ
Central Railroad Co. of New Jersey [*Absorbed into Consolidated Rail Corp.*] .... CRR of NJ
Central Rappahannock Regional Library, Fredericksburg, VA [*Library symbol*] .... ViFre
Central Real Estate Office [*Military*] .... CREO
Central Receiver Test Facility [*Department of Energy*] .... CRTF
Central Record, Medford, NJ [*Library symbol*] .... NjMedR
Central Recorder Subsystem [*NASA*] .... CR
Central Recorder Subsystem [*NASA*] .... CRS
Central Records Facility, United States Army Intelligence Center .... CRFUSAIC
Central Records Office .... CRO
Central Recruiting Division [*Military*] .... CRD
Central Reference Library [*British*] .... CRL
Central Reference Supply .... CRS
Central Region [*FAA*] .... ACE
Central Region Interface Working Group [*NATO*] .... CRIWG
Central Region, RSFSR [*MARC geographic area code*] [*Library of Congress*] .... e-url--
Central Region SEATO [*Southeast Asia Treaty Organization*] **Field Forces** .... CRSFF
Central Registry [*of the Ordnance Survey*] [*British*] .... CR
Central Registry of Charities [*British*] .... CRC
Central Registry of Magazine Subscription Solicitors [*Defunct*] .... CRMSS
Central Registry of War Criminals and Security Suspects [*Organization that used crime detection methods to ferret out German war criminals*] [*World War II*] .... CROWCASS
Central Registry of World Dancers .... CROWD
Central Regulatory Electronic Stenographic System .... CRESS
Central Repair Depot .... CRD
Central Repair Facility .... CRF
Central Repeater System .... CRS
Central Requirements Committee .... CRC
Central Research Agency [*Cuc Nghien-Chu Trung-Uong*] [*North Vietnamese intelligence agency*] .... CRA
Central Research Laboratory of Tashiba .... CRLT
Central Reserve Life [*NASDAQ symbol*] .... CRLC
Central Retinal Artery .... CRA
Central Retinal Artery Occlusion [*Ophthalmology*] .... CRAO
Central Rhine Commission [*Post-World War II*] .... CRC
Central Rice Research Institute [*India*] .... CRRI
Central Rural Construction Command [*Military*] .... CRCC
Central Securities Corp. [*American Stock Exchange symbol*] .... CET
Central Security Control [*Military*] .... CSC
Central Security Service [*Obsolete*] [*National Security Agency*] .... CSS
Central Selling Organization [*London diamond exchange*] .... CSO
Central Sephardic Jewish Community of America .... CSJCA
Central Servicing Development Establishment .... CSDE
Central Ships Alignment Console [*Navy*] .... CSAC
Central Sierra Snow Laboratory [*Norden, CA*] .... CSSL
Central Sign Off .... CSO
Central Signal Processor .... CSP
Central Signals Establishment [*Military*] [*British*] .... CSE
Central Society for Clinical Research .... CSCR
Central & South West Corp. [*NYSE symbol*] .... CSR

Central and Southern Line Islands [*gb (Gilbert Islands) used in records cataloged after October 1978*] [*MARC country of publication code*] [*Library of Congress*]....In
Central and Southern Line Islands [*MARC geographic area code*] [*Library of Congress*].... poln---
Central & Southern Motor Freight Tariff Association, Inc., Louisville KY [*STAC*].... CSA
Central & Southern Motor Freight Tariff Association, Inc..... CSMFTA
Central Soya Co., Inc. [*NYSE symbol*].... CSY
Central Square, NY [*Radio station call letters*]....WCSQ
Central Standard Time.... C
Central Standard Time.... CST
Central State Airline [*Green Bay, WI*] [*FAA designator*].... CSE
Central State College [*Ohio, Oklahoma*].... CSC
Central State Hospital, Waupun, WI [*Library symbol*].... WWpC
Central State University, Edmond, OK [*Library symbol*].... OkEdT
Central State University, Edmond, OK [*OCLC symbol*].... OKX
Central State University, Wilberforce, OH [*OCLC symbol*].... CNC
Central State University, Wilberforce, OH [*Library symbol*].... OWibfC
Central States College Association [*Defunct*]....CSCA
Central States Football League.... CSFL
Central States Motor Freight Bureau....CSMFB
Central States Motor Freight Bureau, Chicago IL [*STAC*].... CMB
Central States Roller Canary Breeders Association....CSRCBA
Central States Speech Journal [*A publication*].... Cent St Spe
Central States Speech Journal [*A publication*].... CSSJ
Central Station [*NASA*].... C/S
Central Station Electrical Protection Association....CSEPA
Central Statistical Board [*Functions taken over by Bureau of the Budget, 1940*].... CSB
Central Statistical Office [*British government*]....CSO
Central Statistical Unit [*of VLRL*].... CSU
Central Suffolk Hospital, Riverhead, NY [*Library symbol*]....NRvCH
Central Supplies Agency.... CSA
Central Supply....CS
Central Supply Association [*Later, ASA*].... CSA
Central Supply Support Activity....CSSA
Central Switching Concept.... CSC
Central Switching Facility....CSF
Central Switching Unit.... CSU
Central System Maintenance Support.... CSMS
Central Systems Design Agency.... CSDA
Central Tactical System [*RAF*].... CTS
Central Tactical Unit [*Drug Enforcement Administration*].... CENTAC
Central Target Simulator [*Navy*].... CTS
Central Task Force....CTF
Central Technical Community College, Hastings, NE [*Library symbol*].... NbHCC
Central Technical Documents Office [*Naval Ordnance Systems Command*]....CTDO
Central Technical Institute [*Netherlands*]....CTI
Central Technical Manual Management Activity [*Navy*].... CTMMA
Central Technical Order Control [*or Coordination*] **Unit**.... CTOCU
Central Telephone Pfd [*NASDAQ symbol*].... CTELP
Central Telephone & Utilities Corp. [*NYSE symbol*] [*Delisted*].... CTU
Central Terminal Unit.... CTU
Central Territory Railroad Tariff Bureau.... CTR
Central Texas College, Killeen, TX [*Library symbol*]....TxKiC
Central Texas Library System [*Library network*].... CTLS
Central Time....CT
Central Time and Frequency Control.... CTFC
Central Timing Equipment....CTE
Central Timing Signal Generator [*Air Force*]....CTSG
Central Timing System.... CTS
Central Timing Unit.... CTU
Central Tool Room.... CTR
Central Torpedo Office.... CTO
Central Tracing Bureau [*Post-World War II*].... CTB
Central Tracing Policy Board [*Post-World War II*].... CTPB
Central Trade Test Board [*British*].... CTTB
Central Trade Union Council [*Czechoslovakia*]....CTUC
Central Traffic Control.... CTC
Central Training Council [*Department of Employment*] [*British*].... CTC
Central Training Facility....CTF
Central Training Section [*Air Force*].... CTS
Central Transfer Point.... CTP
Central Translation Evidence....CTE
Central Treaty Organization [*Also, CTO*] [*Formerly, Baghdad Pact*].... CENTO
Central Treaty Organization [*Also, CENTO*] [*Formerly, Baghdad Pact*].... CTO
Central Treaty Organization Allied Military Publication.... CENTAMP
Central Trunk Terminals.... CTT
Central Unit-Memory.... CUM
Central Unit-Memory Programer.... CUMP
Central Unit for Scientific Photography [*Royal Aircraft Establishment*] [*British*]....CUSP
Central United States Registry [*Army*]....CUSR
Central Vacuum Loading System.... CVLS
Central Vehicle Index [*Record of cars lost or stolen in London*]....CVI
Central Venous Pressure [*Medicine*].... CVP
Central Verband der Siebenburger Sachsen of the United States [*Later, Alliance of Transylvanian Saxons*].... CVSSUS
Central Vermont Public Service Corp. [*NYSE symbol*]....CV
Central Vermont Railway, Inc. [*AAR code*]....CV
Central Vermont Railway, Inc..... CVT
Central Virginia Community College, Lynchburg, VA [*Library symbol*].... ViLCV
Central Visual Field [*Optics*]....CVF
Central Washington State College, Ellensburg, WA [*Library symbol*]....WaEIC
Central Welsh Board.... CWB
Central Wireless Station [*Air Force*] [*British*].... CWS
Central Wisconsin Bankshares [*NASDAQ symbol*]....CWCB
Central Wisconsin Colony, Staff Library, Madison, WI [*Library symbol*]....WMaC
Central Wyoming Community College, Riverton, WY [*Library symbol*]....WyRiC
Central Yiddish Culture Organization.... CYCO
Central YMCA Community College, Chicago, IL [*Library symbol*].... ICCYM
Central Youth Employment Executive [*Department of Employment*] [*British*].... CYEE
Centrala Filmarkivet Ab, Stockholm, Sweden [*Library symbol*].... CeF
Centralblatt fuer Allgemeine, Pathologie, und Pathologische Anatomie [*A publication*].... Centralbl Allg Path u Path Anat
Centralblatt fuer Bakteriologie und Parasitenkunde [*A publication*].... Centralbl Bakteriol
Centralblatt fuer Bibliothekwesen [*A publication*].... CBW
Centralblatt fuer Chirurgie [*A publication*].... Centralbl Chir
Centralblatt fuer das Gesamte Forstwesen [*A publication*].... Cbl Ges Forstw
Centralblatt fuer das Gesamte Forstwesen [*A publication*].... Centralbl Gesamte Forstwes
Centralblatt fuer Innere Medicin [*A publication*].... Centralbl Innere Med
Centralblatt fuer Mineralogie, Geologie, und Palaeontologie [*A publication*].... Centralbl Miner
Centrale des Bibliotheques, Centre Documentaire, Montreal, PQ, Canada [*Library symbol*].... CaQMCD
Centrale Generale des Syndicats Liberaux de Belgique [*General Federation of Liberal Unions of Belgium*].... CGSLB
Centrale van Hogere Ambtenaren....CHA
Centrale Nationale des Travailleurs Croyants de Cote d'Ivoire [*National Union of Believing Workers of the Ivory Coast*].... CNTCCI
Centrale Nationale des Travailleurs Croyants de Senegal [*National Believing Workers of Senegal*]....CNTC
Centrale Nucleaire des Ardennes....CNA
Centrale Nucleaire Belge [*Nuclear reactor*]....CNB
Centrale Nucleaire Interescaut [*A nuclear power station*] [*Belgium*].... CNI
Centralia-Chehalis, WA [*Radio station call letters*].... KELA
Centralia-Chehalis, WA [*Radio station call letters*]....KITI
Centralia College, Centralia, WA [*Library symbol*].... WaCeC
Centralia Correctional Center, Centralia, IL [*Library symbol*]....ICenC
Centralia District High School, District 200, Centralia, IL [*Library symbol*]....ICenHS
Centralia, IL [*Location identifier*] [*FAA*]....ENL
Centralia, IL [*Radio station call letters*]....WILY
Centralia, IL [*Radio station call letters*].... WRXX
Centralia Public Library, Centralia, IL [*Library symbol*]....ICen
Centralia Township Junior College [*Illinois*].... CTJC
Centralia, WA [*Radio station call letters*]....KCED
Centralia, WA [*Television station call letters*]....KCKA
Centralia, WA [*Radio station call letters*].... KMNT
Centralization of Supply Management Operations [*DoD*]....COSMOS
Centralized Accounting for Local Management [*Veterans Administration*].... CALM
Centralized Army Passenger Port Call System.... CAPPS
Centralized Asset Visibility and Management Program for Vietnam [*Army*].... CAVAMP-V
Centralized Assignment Procedures Computer System [*Military*].... CAP III
Centralized Attendants Service [*Bell System*].... CAS
Centralized Authorized File [*IRS*].... CAF
Centralized Automated Military Pay System....CAMPS
Centralized Automatic Message Accounting [*Bell System*]....CAMA
Centralized Automatic Recorder and Tester.... CART
Centralized Automatic Recording on Trunks [*Bell System*].... CAROT
Centralized Automatic Test System [*Navy*]....CATES
Centralized Automatic Test System [*Navy*]....CATS
Centralized Automatic Testing.... CAT
Centralized Cancer Patient Data System.... CCPDS
Centralized COMINT Communications Center [*National Security Agency*].... CCCC
Centralized Control Facility.... CENTCON
Centralized Data Processing....CDP
Centralized Digital Communications System....CDTS
Centralized Electronic Control [*Navy*].... CEC
Centralized Expenditure/Reimbursement Processing System....CERPS
Centralized Information Reference and Control.... CIRC
Centralized Integrated Technical Information System....CITIS
Centralized Intercept Bureau [*Bell System*]....CIB
Centralized Intermediate Logistics Concept.... CILC
Centralized Intermediate Logistics System....CILS
Centralized Maintenance System [*Telecommunications*].... CMS
Centralized Message Data System [*Bell System*]....CMDS

Centralized Receiving Point..CRP
Centralized Referral Activity [*Military*]............................CRA
Centralized Referral System [*Military*]............................CRS
Centralized Requisitioning Accounting and Billing..........CRAB
Centralized Ships Force Management System..................CSFMS
Centralized Status, Alarm, and Control System [*Bell System*]..........CSACS
Centralized Supervisory and Control..............................CSC
Centralized Ticket Investigation [*AT & T*].....................CTI
Centralized Title Service [*A publication*].......................CTS
Centralized Translation System [*Communications*]..........CTS
Centrally Funded...CF
Centrally Planned Economy...CPE
Centrally Procured Items..CPI
Centralna Rada Zwiazkow Zawodowych [*Central Council of Trade Unions*] [*Poland*]..CRZZ
Centran Corp. [*NASDAQ symbol*]..................................CENB
Centre d'Action Europeenne Federaliste [*European Center for Federalist Action*]..AEF
Centre d'Actualisation Scientifique et Technique..............CAST
Centre Africain de Formation et de Recherche Administratives pour la Developpement [*African Training and Research Center in Administration for Development*]....................CAFRAD
Centre for Agricultural Publications and Documents, Wageningen, Netherlands [*OCLC symbol*]..................NET
Centre, AL [*Radio station call letters*].........................WAGC
Centre, AL [*Radio station call letters*].........................WEIS
Centre d'Analyse Documentaire pour l'Archeologie...........CADA
Centre d'Analyse et de Recherche Documentaires pour l'Afrique Noire..CARDAN
Centre d'Animation de Developpement et de Recherche en Education, Montreal, PQ, Canada [*Library symbol*]..........CaQMCAD
Centre Antonien, Quebec, PQ, Canada [*Library symbol*]..........CaQQCA
Centre for Applied Research and Engineering Design [*McMaster University, Hamilton, ON*]..CARED
Centre d'Assistance Technique et de Documentation [*Center for Technical Assistance and Documentation*] [*France*] [*Information service*]..CATED
Centre College of Kentucky, Danville, KY [*OCLC symbol*]..........KCC
Centre College of Kentucky, Danville, KY [*Library symbol*]..........KyDC
Centre Commun de Recherches Nucleaires [*Joint Nuclear Research Center*] [*EURATOM*]................................CCRN
Centre de Compilation de Donnees Neutroniques [*Neutron Data Compilation Center*] [*France*] [*Information service*]..........CCDN
Centre de Controle Mixte [*Joint Control Center*] [*NATO*]..........CCM
Centre de Controle Tactique Aerien [*Air Tactical Control Center*] [*NATO*]..CCTA
Centre de Cooperation pour les Recherches Scientifiques Relatives au Tabac [*Cooperation Centre for Scientific Research Relative to Tobacco*]....................................CORESTA
Centre County Court House, Bellefonte, PA [*Library symbol*]..........PBelC
Centre County Library, Bellefonte, PA [*Library symbol*]..........PBel
Centre Culturel, Verdun, PQ, Canada [*Library symbol*]..........CaQVeC
Centre for Curriculum Renewal and Educational Development Overseas..CREDO
Centre for Development of Instructional Technology..........CENDIT
Centre de Documentation de la Direction Generale de l'Energie du Ministere des Richesses Naturelles du Quebec, Quebec, PQ, Canada [*Library symbol*] [*Obsolete*]..................CaQQRNC
Centre de Documentation Internationale des Industries Utilisatrices de Produits Agricoles [*International Documentation Center for Industries Using Agricultural Products*] [*France*] [*Information service*]....................CDIUPA
Centre de Documentation de la Mecanique [*Documentation Center for Mechanics*] [*France*] [*Information service*]..........CDM
Centre de Documentation de Musique Internationale. Bulletin [*A publication*]..CDMI Bul
Centre de Documentation Sciences Humaines [*Documentation Center for Human Sciences*] [*France*] [*Information service*]..........CDSH
Centre de Documentation Siderurgique. Circulaire d'Information Techniques [*A publication*].....Cent Doc Sider Cir Inf Tech
Centre de Documentation en Theatre Quebecois, Trois-Rivieres, PQ, Canada [*Library symbol*]..................CaQTUTH
Centre de Documentation Universitaire [*A publication*]..........CDU
Centre de Donnees Stellaires [*Stellar Data Center*] [*France*] [*Information service*]..CDS
Centre for Economic and Social Information [*United Nations*]..........CESI
Centre Economique de Secours Europeens [*European Economic Relief Committee*] [*NATO*]..CESE
Centre for Educational Development Overseas..................CEDO
Centre for Educational Research and Innovation [*OECD*]..........CERI
Centre for Educational Television Overseas [*British*]..........CETO
Centre d'Essais Regional Europeen [*European Regional Test Center*] [*NATO*]..CERE
Centre d'Essais en Vol [*France*]....................................CEV
Centre d'Etude de l'Azote [*A publication*]..................Cent Etude Azote
Centre d'Etude de l'Energie Nucleaire [*Also known as NERC or SCK*] [*Belgium*]..CEEN
Centre d'Etude des Litteratures d'Expression Graphique..........CELEG
Centre d'Etudes pour les Applications de l'Energie Nucleaire [*Belgium*]..CEAN

Centre d'Etudes des Consequences Generales des Grands Techniques Nouvelles [*Center for the Study of the General Results of New Technologies*]....................................CTN
Centre d'Etudes et de Documentation Europeennes [*Montreal*]..........CEDE
Centre d'Etudes et de Documentation Sociales (Liege) [*A publication*]................................Centre Et Docum Soc (Liege)
Centre d'Etudes de l'Energie Nucleaire [*Belgium*]..........CEN
Centre d'Etudes Internationales de la Propriete Industrielle..........CEIPI
Centre d'Etudes pour le Monde Arabe Moderne [*Beirut*]..........CEMAM
Centre d'Etudes Nord-Americaines, Aix-En-Provence, France [*Library symbol*]..FrAipNA
Centre d'Etudes Nucleaires de Cadarache [*France*]..........CENC
Centre d'Etudes Nucleaires de Saclay [*France*]..............CENS
Centre d'Etudes Phylosociologiques et Ecologiques [*France*]..........CEPE
Centre d'Etudes et de Recherches de Biologie et d'Oceanographie Medicale..CERBOM
Centre d'Etudes et Recherches des Charbonnages de France ....CERCHAR
Centre d'Etudes et de Recherches Documentaires [*France*]..........CERDOC
Centre d'Etudes et de Recherches Documentaires sur l'Afrique Centrale..CERDAC
Centre d'Etudes et de Recherches de Medecine Aeronautique [*France*]..CERMA
Centre d'Etudes Sociales [*Belgium*]..............................CES
Centre d'Etudes des Supports de Publicite [*Center for the Study of Advertising Support*] [*France*]..............................CESP
Centre d'Etudes Theoriques de la Detection et des Communications..CETHEDEC
Centre Europeen d'Aviation Agricole..............................CEAA
Centre Europeen du Commerce de Detail [*European Center of the Retail Trade*] [*Common Market*]..........................CECODE
Centre Europeen de la Culture [*European Cultural Center*]..........CEC
Centre Europeen de Documentation et de Compensation..........CEDEC
Centre Europeen d'Etudes de Population [*European Center for Population Studies*]..CEEP
Centre Europeen des Federations de l'Industrie Chimique [*European Center of Chemical Manufacturers' Federations*]..........CEFIC
Centre Europeen de Formation des Statisticiens-Economistes des Pays en Voie de Developpement [*France*]..............CESD
Centre Europeen de Recherches Mauvernay [*France*] [*Research code symbol*]..CERM
Centre Europeen de Traduction [*European Translation Center*]..........CET
Centre Europeen de Traitement de l'Information Scientifique [*EURATOM*]..CETIS
Centre of Forensic Sciences, Ontario Solicitor General, Toronto, ON, Canada [*Library symbol*]..................................CaOTCF
Centre de Formation en Aerodynamique Experimentale..........CFAE
Centre Francais de la Corrosion..................................CEFRACOR
Centre de Geomorphologie de Caen. Bulletin [*A publication*]..........Cent Geomorphol Caen Bull
Centre de Hautes Etudes Administratives sur l'Afrique et l'Asie Modernes [*Center for Advanced Administrative Study on Modern Africa and Asia*]..CHEAM
Centre des Hautes-Etudes Americaines [*Paris*]..............HEA
Centre Hospitalier Hotel Dieu, Sherbrooke, PQ, Canada [*Library symbol*]..CaQSherHD
Centre Hospitalier Jacques Viger, Montreal, PQ, Canada [*Library symbol*]..CaQMHM
Centre Hospitalier de Lachine, Montreal, PQ, Canada [*Library symbol*]..CaQMCHL
Centre Hospitalier Pierre Janet, Hull, PQ, Canada [*Library symbol*]..CaQHPJ
Centre Hospitalier du Sacre-Coeur, Hull, PQ, Canada [*Library symbol*]..CaQHSC
Centre Hospitalier St. Vincent-de-Paul, Sherbrooke, PQ, Canada [*Library symbol*]..CaQSherSV
Centre Hospitalier de Verdun, Montreal, PQ, Canada [*Library symbol*]..CaQMHGC
Centre of Indian Trade Unions......................................CITU
Centre d'Information des Chemins de Fer Europeens [*Information Center of the European Railways*]............CICE
Centre d'Information du Chrome Dur. Bulletin de Documentation [*A publication*]..........Cent Inf Chrome Dur Bull Doc
Centre d'Information du Chrome Dur. Bulletin de Documentation [*A publication*]..........Centre Inform Chrome Dur Bull Doc
Centre for Information and Documentation [*EURATOM*]..........CID
Centre d'Information et de Documentation Atlantique [*Brussels, Belgium*]..CIDA
Centre d'Information des Nations Unies..........................CINU
Centre d'Information de Presse [*Press agency*] [*Belgium*]..........CIP
Centre d'Information Spectroscopique et Physico-Chimique d'Analyse [*Information Center for Spectroscopic and Physicochemical Analysis*] [*France*] [*Information service*]..........CIS
Centre d'Information en Temps Reel pour l'Europe [*European Center for Information in Real Time*] [*France*] [*Information service*]..CITERE
Centre d'Informations Catholiques pour la France et l'Etranger..........CIC
Centre d'Informatique et Documentation Automatique [*Center for Automated Information and Documentation*] [*France*] [*Information service*]..CIDA
Centre Interamericain d'Education Rurale..........................CIER
Centre Intercontinental d'Etudes de Techniques Biologiques..........CIETB

Centre International de l'Actualite Fantastique et Magique ....CIAFMA
Centre International des Antiparasitaires ....CIA
Centre International d'Aviation Agricole [*International Agricultural Aviation Center*] ....CIAA
Centre International du Commerce de Gros [*International Center for Wholesale Trade*] ....CICG
Centre International de Coordination pour la Celebration des Anniversaires ....CICCA
Centre International pour la Coordination des Recherches en Agriculture ....CICRA
Centre International de Developpement de l'Aluminium ....CIDA
Centre International de Documentation [*International Center for Documentation*] ....CID
Centre International de Documentation Arachnologique [*International Centre for Arachnological Documentation*] ....CIDA
Centre International de Documentation Concernant les Expressions Plastiques ....CIDEP
Centre International de Documentation Economique et Sociale Africaine [*International Center for African Social and Economic Documentation*] ....CIDESA
Centre International de Documentation et d'Information ....CIDI
Centre International de Documentation de l'Inspection Technique des Vehicules Automobiles ....CIDITVA
Centre International de Documentation Parlementaire [*International Center for Parliamentary Documentation*] [*Switzerland*] [*Information service*] ....CIDP
Centre International de l'Enfance [*International Children's Center*] ....CIE
Centre International des Engrais Chimiques [*International Center of Fertilizers*] ....CIEC
Centre International pour l'Etude de la Marionnette Traditionnelle [*International Center for Research on Traditional Marionettes*] ....CIPEMAT
Centre International des Etudes de la Musique Ancienne [*International Center of Studies on Early Music*] ....CIEMA
Centre International d'Etudes et de Recherches en Socio-Economie de la Sante [*International Health Centre of Socio-Economics Researches and Studies - IHCSERS*] ....CIERSES
Centre International d'Etudes des Textiles Anciens [*International Research Centre on Ancient Textiles*] ....CIETA
Centre International du Film pour l'Enfance et la Jeunesse [*International Center of Films for Children and Young People*] ....CIFEJ
Centre International de Formation Europeenne ....CIFE
Centre International de Gerontologie Sociale [*International Center of Social Gerontology*] ....CIGS
Centre International de Hautes Etudes Agronomiques Mediterraneennes ....CIHEAM
Centre International d'Information de la Mutualite ....CIIM
Centre International d'Information et de Recherche sur la Formation Professionnelle ....CIRF
Centre International d'Informations de Securite et d'Hygiene du Travail [*International Occupational Safety and Health Information Center*] ....CIS
Centre International de Liaison des Ecoles de Cinema et de Television [*International Liaison Center for Cinema and Television Schools*] ....CILECT
Centre International Provisoire de Calcul ....CIPC
Centre International de Recherche sur le Cancer [*International Agency for Research on Cancer*] ....CIRC
Centre International de Recherches sur l'Anarchisme [*International Research Centre on Anarchism*] ....CIRA
Centre International de Recherches sur les Communautes Cooperatives Rurales [*International Research Center on Rural Cooperative Communities*] ....CIRCOM
Centre International de Recherches et d'Information sur l'Economie Collective [*International Center of Research and Information on Public and Cooperative Economy*] ....CIRIEC
Centre International pour le Reglement des Differends Relatifs aux Investissements [*International Center for Settlement of Investment Disputes*] ....CIRDI
Centre International des Sciences Mecaniques ....CISM
Centre International des Syndicalistes Libres en Exil [*International Center of Free Trade Unionists in Exile*] ....CISLE
Centre International de la Tapisserie Ancienne et Moderne ....CITAM
Centre for Internationalising the Study of English ....CIE
Centre d'Investigation sur le Colonialisme Portugais ....CISCOP
Centre Italien pour les Relations Universitaires avec l'Etranger [*Italy*] ....CRUEI
Centre de Liaison des Etudes et Recherches Economiques et Sociales [*France*] ....CLERES
Centre de Liaison des Industries de Traitement des Algues Marines de la CEE [*Liaison Center of the Industries for the Treatment of Seaweeds in the European Economic Community*] ....CLITAM
Centre de Liaison des Industries Transformatrices de la CEE [*Liaison Center of the Meat Processing Industries of the EEC*] ....CLITRAVI
Centre de Liaison International des Marchands de Machines Agricoles et Reparateurs [*International Liaison Center for Agricultural Machinery Distributors and Maintenance*] [*Common Market*] ....CLIMMAR
Centre for Library and Information Management [*Loughborough University of Technology*] [*British*] [*Information service*] ....CLAIM
Centre Lyonnais d'Applications Atomiques [*France*] ....CLAA
Centre Mondiale de Donnees [*World Data Center*] ....CMD
Centre National de Documentation [*National Documentation Center*] [*Morocco*] [*Information service*] ....CND
Centre National de Documentation Scientifique et Technique [*National Scientific and Technical Documentation Center*] [*Senegal*] [*Information service*] ....CNDST
Centre National de Documentation Scientifique et Technique. Rapport d'Activite [*A publication*] ....Cent Natl Doc Sci Tech Rap Act
Centre National d'Etudes et d'Experimentation du Machinisme Agricole ....CNEEMA
Centre National d'Etudes Scientifiques [*National Center for Scientific Studies*] [*France*] ....CNES
Centre National d'Etudes Spatiales [*National Center for Space Studies*] [*France*] ....CNES
Centre National d'Etudes des Telecommunications [*France*] ....CNET
Centre National pour l'Exploitation des Oceans [*France*] ....CNEXO
Centre National pour l'Exploitation des Oceans. Publications. Serie. Rapports Scientifiques et Techniques (France) [*A publication*] ....Cent Nat Exploit Oceans Publ Ser Rapp Sci Tech (Fr)
Centre National des Expositions et Concours Agricoles ....CENECA
Centre National de l'Information Chimique de France [*National Center for Chemical Information of France*] [*Information service*] ....CNIC
Centre National des Oeuvres Universitaires et Scolaires [*France*] ....CNOUS
Centre National de Prevention et de Traitement des Intoxications [*National Poison Control Center*] [*Information service*] ....CNPTI
Centre National de la Recherche Scientifique [*National Center of Scientific Research*] [*France*] ....CNRS
Centre National de la Recherche Scientifique. Groupe Francais des Argiles. Bulletin [*A publication*] ....CNRS Groupe Fr Argiles Bull
Centre National de Recherches Metallurgiques [*Belgium*] ....CNRM
Centre National de Recherches Scientifique et Techniques pour l'Industrie Cimentiere. Rapport de Recherche [*A publication*] ....Cent Natl Rech Sci Tech Ind Cimentiere Rapp Rech
Centre for Natural Resources, Energy, and Transport [*United Nations*] ....CNRET
Centre for Overseas Pest Research [*England*] ....COPR
Centre for Overseas Pest Research. Miscellaneous Report [*A publication*] ....Cent Overseas Pest Res Misc Rep
Centre for Overseas Pest Research. Report [*A publication*] ....Cent Overseas Pest Res Rep
Centre de Perfectionnement pour le Developpement et la Cooperation Economique et Technique [*France*] ....CPDCET
Centre for Policy Studies [*British*] ....CPS
Centre de Preparation Documentaire a la Traduction [*Center for Translation Documentation*] [*France*] [*Information service*] ....CPDT
Centre de Recherche et d'Etude pour la Diffusion du Francais [*France*] ....CREDIF
Centre de Recherche, d'Etude, et de Documentation sur la Consommation [*France*] ....CREDOC
Centre du Recherche et l'Information Socio-Politiques ....CRISP
Centre de Recherches sur l'Afrique Mediterraneenne ....CRAM
Centre de Recherches pour Combustibles Atomiques [*France*] ....CERCA
Centre de Recherches et de Documentation des Institutions Chretiennes [*Christian Institutions Research and Documentation Center*] [*France*] [*Information service*] ....CERDIC
Centre de Recherches Ecologiques et Phytosociologiques de Gembloux. Communication [*A publication*] ....Cent Rech Ecol Phytosociol Gembloux Commun
Centre des Recherches Historiques, Quebec, PQ, Canada [*Library symbol*] [*Obsolete*] ....CaQQCRH
Centre de Recherches Industrielles en Afrique Centrale ....CRIAC
Centre de Recherches. Institut d'Etudes Hispaniques [*A publication*] ....CRIEH
Centre de Recherches et d'Irradiations [*France*] ....CRI
Centre de Recherches Oceanographiques Abidjan. Documents Scientifiques [*A publication*] ....Cent Rech Oceanogr Abidjan Doc Sci
Centre de Recherches de Pau. Bulletin [*A publication*] ....Centre Recherches Pau Bull
Centre de Recherches en Relations Humaines, Montreal, PQ, Canada [*Library symbol*] ....CaQMRH
Centre de Recherches Routieres [*Brussels*] ....CRR
Centre de Reflexion sur le Monde Non Occidental [*Center for the Study of the Non-Occidental World*] ....CRM
Centre de Regroupement Africain [*Center for African Regroupment*] [*Congo - Leopoldville*] ....CEREA
Centre for Scientific and Technological Information ....CSTI
Centre Scientifique et Technique du Batiment [*Building research*] [*France*] ....CSTB
Centre de Services Sociaux, Trois-Rivieres, PQ, Canada [*Library symbol*] ....CaQTCSS
Centre for Social Development and Humanitarian Affairs [*United Nations*] ....CSDHA
Centre Technique International de l'Embouteillage [*International Technical Center of Bottling*] ....CETIE
Centre pour le Traitement de l'Information ....CENTI
Centres Regionaux d'Action Pedagogique [*France*] ....CRAP
Centreville, AL [*Location identifier*] [*FAA*] ....CKL

Centreville, AL [*Radio station call letters*] .... WBIB
Centreville, MI [*Radio station call letters*] .... WZZB
Centrex [*Bell System*] .... CTX
Centric Occlusion [*Dentistry*] .... CO
Centric Relation [*Dentistry*] .... CR
Centric Relation Occlusion [*Dentistry*] .... CRO
Centrifugal C
Centrifugal .... CENT
Centrifugal .... CENTF
Centrifugal .... CNTFGL
Centrifugal .... CNTRF
Centrifugal [*Freight*] .... CNTRFUGL
Centrifugal Barrel Finishing [*of metal surfaces*] .... CBF
Centrifugal Coating CC
Centrifugal Countercurrent Chromatography CCCC
Centrifugal Fast Analyzer [*Analytical chemistry*] .... CFA
Centrifugal Fluidized Bed [*Chemical engineering*] .... CFB
Centrifugal Force .... CF
Centrifugal Spraying .... CS
Centrifugal Urine Separator Assembly [*Aerospace*] .... CUSA
Centrifugation Extractable Fluid .... CEF
Centrifuge Moisture Equivalent .... CME
Centrifuge Plant Demonstration Facility [*Department of Energy*] .... CPDF
Centripetal Force .... CF
Centripetal Rub [*Medicine*] .... CPR
Centro Academico de Democracia Crista [*Coimbra*] [*A publication*] .... CADC
Centro Agricola [*A publication*] .... Cent Agric
Centro Agronomico Tropical de Investigacion y Ensenanza [*Tropical Agriculture Research and Training Center*] [*Costa Rica*] .... CATIE
Centro Anglo-Espanol .... CAE
Centro Argentino de Informacion Cientifica y Tecnologica [*Argentine Center for Scientific and Technological Information*] [*Information service*] .... CAICYT
Centro Autonomo Militaire Energia Nucleare [*Italy*] .... CAMEN
Centro di Azione e Documentazione sull'America Latina .... CADAL
Centro Brasileiro de Pesquisas Fisicas [*Brazilian Center for Physics Research*] .... CBPF
Centro de Cultura Valenciana [*A publication*] CCV
Centro Didattico Telefonico [*Telephone Teaching Center*] [*Italy*] .... CEDIT
Centro de Documentacao Cientifica e Tecnica [*Scientific and Technical Documentation Center*] [*Portugal*] [*Information service*] .... CDCT
Centro Editor de America Latina [*A publication*] .... CEAL
Centro de Esploro kaj Dokumentado pri la Monda Lingvo-Problemo [*Center for Research and Documentation on International Language Problems*] .... CED
Centro Estadual de Abastecimento SA [*State Central Supply Company*] [*Brazil*] .... CEASA
Centro de Estudios Democraticos de America Latina .... CEDAL
Centro de Estudios para el Desarrollo e Integracion de America Latina .... CEDIAL
Centro de Estudios y Documentacion Latinoamericanos .... CEDLA
Centro de Estudios Mayas-Cuadernos [*A publication*] .... CEMC
Centro de Estudios Monetarios Latinoamericanos [*Center for Latin-American Monetary Studies*] .... CEMLA
Centro de Estudios Puertorriquenos, New York, NY [*Library symbol*] .... NNCEP
Centro de Estudios Puertorriquenos, New York, NY [*OCLC symbol*] .... VXY
Centro de Estudos Franciscanos e Pastorais para a America Latina .... CEFEPAL
Centro Filatelico Internazionale .... CFI
Centro Hispano Catolico [*Catholic Spanish Center*] .... CHC
Centro de Informacion Cientifica/Humanistica [*Center for Scientific and Humanistic Information*] [*Mexico*] [*Information service*] .... CICH
Centro de Informacion, Documentacion, y Analisis Latinoamericano .... CIDAL
Centro de Informacoes Nucleares [*Center for Nuclear Information*] [*Brazil*] [*Information service*] .... CIN
Centro de Informativo y Documentacion [*Press agency*] [*Argentina*] .... CID
Centro Interamericano de Documentacion, Informacion, y Communicacion Agricola [*Inter-American Agricultural Documentation, Information, and Communication Center*] .... CIDIA
Centro Interamericano de Ensenanza de Estadistica .... CIENES
Centro Interamericano de Fotointerpretacion [*Bogota, Colombia*] .... CIAF
Centro Interamericano de Investigacion y Documentacion sobre Formacion Profesional [*Interamerican Research and Documentation Center on Vocational Training*] .... CINTERFOR
Centro Interamericano de Libros Academicos [*Inter-American Scholarly Book Center*] .... CILA
Centro Interamericano de Promocion de Exportaciones [*Interamerican Export Promotion Center*] .... CIPE
Centro Interamericano de Vivienda .... CINVA
Centro Intercultural de Documentacion [*Center for Intercultural Documentation*] [*Cuernavaca, Mexico*] .... CIDOC
Centro Intercultural de Documentacion Sondeos [*A publication*] .... CIDS
Centro Internacional de Agricultura Tropical [*International Center for Tropical Agriculture*] [*Colombia*] .... CIAT
Centro Internacional de Agricultura Tropical. Annual Report [*A publication*] .... Cent Int Agric Trop Annu Rep
Centro Internacional de Agricultura Tropical. Series CE [*A publication*] .... Cent Int Agric Trop Ser CE
Centro Internacional de Agricultura Tropical. Series EE [*A publication*] .... Cent Int Agric Trop Ser EE
Centro Internacional de Agricultura Tropical. Series FE [*A publication*] .... Cent Int Agric Trop Ser FE
Centro Internacional de Agricultura Tropical. Series GE [*A publication*] .... Cent Int Agric Trop Ser GE
Centro Internacional de Agricultura Tropical. Series Seminars [*A publication*] .... Cent Int Agric Trop Ser Semin
Centro Internacional de Agricultura Tropical. Technical Bulletin [*A publication*] .... Cent Int Agric Trop Tech Bull
Centro Internacional de Arreglo de Diferencias Relativas a Inversiones [*International Center for Settlement of Investment Disputes*] .... CIADI
Centro Internacional de Estudios Superiores de Periodisma para America Latina [*Press agency*] [*Ecuador*] .... CIESPAL
Centro Internacional de Formacion en Ciencias Ambientales para Paises de Habla Espanol [*International Center for the Preparation of Personnel in Environmental Sciences in Spanish-Speaking Countries*] [*Spain*] .... CIFCA
Centro Internacional de la Infancia [*International Children's Center*] CII
Centro Internacional de Informacion Economica .... CIDIE
Centro Internacional de Investigaciones sobre el Cancer [*International Agency for Research on Cancer*] CIIC
Centro Internacional de Mejoramiento de Maiz y Trigo [*International Maize and Wheat Improvement Center*] [*Mexico*] .... CIMMYT
Centro Internacional de Mejoramiento de Maiz y Trigo. News [*A publication*] .... CIMMYT News
Centro Internacional de la Papa [*International Potato Center*] [*Peru*] .... CIP
Centro Internazionale Radio-Medico [*International Radio Medical Center; gives emergency medical advice to ships at sea*] .... CIRM
Centro de Investigacion de Biologia Marina. Contribucion Tecnica [*A publication*] .... Cent Invest Biol Mar Contrib Tec
Centro de Investigacion y de Estudios Avanzados, Instituto Politecnico Nacional, Mexico City, Mexico [*Library symbol*] .... MxMC
Centro de Investigaciones Agronomicas Maracay. Monografia [*A publication*] .... Cent Invest Agron Maracay Monogr
Centro de Investigaciones Sociales [*Social Research Center*] [*Colombia*] .... CIS
Centro de Investigaciones Tecnologicas (Pando, Uruguay). Informe de Investigacion [*A publication*] .... Cent Invest Tecnol (Pando Urug) Inf Invest
Centro Latinoamericana de Demografia [*Latin American Demographic Center*] .... CELADE
Centro Latinoamericano de Administracion para el Desarrollo .... CLAD
Centro Latinoamericano de Documentacion Economica y Social [*Latin American Center for Economic and Social Documentation*] [*United Nations*] [*Information service*] .... CLADES
Centro Latinoamericano de Venezuela .... CLAVE
Centro Nacional de Desenvolvimento Micrografico [*National Center for Micrographic Development*] [*Brazil*] [*Information service*] .... CENADEM
Centro Nacional de Informacion y Documentacion [*National Center for Information and Documentation*] [*Information service*] [*Chile*] .... CENID
Centro Nacional de Informacion y Documentacion en Salud [*National Center for Health Information and Documentation*] [*Mexico*] [*Information service*] .... CENIDS
Centro Nacional de Microfilm, Madrid, Spain [*Library symbol*] .... CnM
Centro Nazionale per il Catalogo Unico delle Biblioteche Italiane [*Italy*] .... CUBI
Centro Operacional del Desarrollo [*Operational Center for Development*] [*Colombia*] .... CODESA
Centro de Pesquisas e Desenvolvimento. Boletim Tecnico (Estado da Bahia) [*A publication*] .... Cent Pesqui Desenvolvimento Bol Tec (Estado Bahia)
Centro de Preparacao de Oficiais de Reserva [*Brazil*] .... CPOR
Centro Regional de Education Fundamental para la America Latina [*Mexico*] .... CREFAL
Centro Regional para el Fomento del Libro en America Latina .... CERLAL
Centro Richerche Aerospaziali [*Italy*] .... CRA
Centro di Riferimento Italiano DIANE [*Italian Reference Center for EURONET DIANE*] [*Information service*] .... CRID
Centro Studi e Documentazione sull'Italia Romana [*A publication*] .... CSDIR
Centro di Studi Nucleari Enrico Fermi [*Italy*] .... CESNEF
Centro Studi Politica Economica [*of the Italian Communist Party*] .... CESPE
Centromeric Indices [*Chromosomes*] CI
Centronics Data Computer Corp. [*NYSE symbol*] .... CEN
Centrum voor Informatie Beleid [*Netherlands Center for Information Policy*] [*Information service*] .... CIB
Cents .... CTS
Cents per Available Seat Statute Mile [*Aviation*] .... C/ASSM
Cents-Off Coupon [*Coupon redemption*] .... C/O
Centum [*Hundred*] C
Centum [*Hundred*] .... CENT
Centum [*Hundred*] .... CT
Centuri, Inc. [*NASDAQ symbol*] .... CENT

Centuries ... CC
Centurion Colidar System ... CCS
Centurion LASER Range-Finder ... CLR
Century ... C
Century ... CEN
Century ... CENT
Century [*A publication*] ... C
Century Airlines [*Eureka, CA*] [*FAA designator*] ... CNY
Century Association, New York, NY [*Library symbol*] ... NNCenC
Century Electric Co. [*NYSE symbol*] ... CEY
Century Energy Corporation Ltd. [*NASDAQ symbol*] ... CECRF
Century Factors, Inc. [*American Stock Exchange symbol*] ... CTY
Century Magazine [*A publication*] ... Cent
Century Oil/Gas Cl A [*NASDAQ symbol*] ... COGCA
Century Papers, Inc. [*NASDAQ symbol*] ... CPAP
Century Publishing Company ... CPC
Century Sports Network ... CSN
Century Telephone Enterprises, Inc. [*NYSE symbol*] ... CTL
Centus [*Constellation*] ... Cet
Centus [*Constellation*] ... Ceti
Cenvill Development CTFS [*NASDAQ symbol*] ... CNVLZ
Cenvill Investors [*NYSE symbol*] ... CVI
Ceol. Journal of Irish Music [*A publication*] ... Ceol
CEPEC [*Centro de Pesquisas do Cacau*] **Informe Tecnico** [*A publication*] ... CEPEC Inf Tec
Cephalic Artery ... CA
Cephalic Index ... CI
Cephalic Sinus ... CS
Cephalin Cholesterol Antigen [*Immunochemistry*] ... CCA
Cephalin-Cholesterol Flocculation [*Clinical chemistry*] ... CCF
Cephalo Pedal Sinus ... CPS
Cephalopelvic Disproportion [*Gynecology*] ... CPD
Cepheus [*Constellation*] ... Cep
Cepheus [*Constellation*] ... Ceph
CEPLAC [*Comissao Executiva do Plano da Lavoura Cacaueira*] **Boletim Tecnico** [*A publication*] ... CEPLAC Bol Tec
CEPLAC [*Comissao Executiva do Plano da Lavoura Cacaueira*] **Comunicacao Tecnica** [*A publication*] ... CEPLAC Comun Tec
Ceramic ... CER
Ceramic Abstracts [*A publication*] ... Ceram Abstr
Ceramic Abstracts [*A publication*] ... Ceramic Abstr
Ceramic Age [*A publication*] ... Ceram Age
Ceramic and Alloy [*NASA*] ... CERAMAL
Ceramic Art Federation International ... CAFI
Ceramic Awareness Bulletin [*Defense Ceramic Information Center*] [*A publication*] ... CAB
Ceramic-Based Microcircuit ... CBM
Ceramic Beam Pentode ... CBP
Ceramic Delay Line ... CDL
Ceramic Disk Capacitor ... CDC
Ceramic Educational Council ... CEC
Ceramic Engineer ... Cer E
Ceramic Fiber Optics ... CFO
Ceramic Foam Insulation ... CFI
Ceramic [*or Clear*] **Glazed Structural Facing Units** [*Technical drawings*] ... CGSFU
Ceramic [*or Clear*] **Glazed Structural Unit Base** [*Technical drawings*] ... CGSUB
Ceramic Glazed Units [*Technical drawings*] ... CGU
Ceramic Gold Coating ... CGC
Ceramic and Graphite Information Center [*Air Force*] ... C & G
Ceramic-Heated Tunnel [*Langley Research Center*] ... CHT
Ceramic Hotform Die ... CHFD
Ceramic Industry [*A publication*] ... Ceram Ind
Ceramic Industry [*A publication*] ... Cer Ind
Ceramic Insulated Wire ... CIW
Ceramic-to-Metal [*Seal*] ... CERMET
Ceramic Metal Element [*NASA*] ... CERMET
Ceramic to Metal Seal ... CTMS
Ceramic Oceanographic Buoy ... COB
Ceramic Planar Tube ... CPT
Ceramic Refraction Coating ... CRC
Ceramic Reusable Surface Insulation ... CRSI
Ceramic Tile [*Technical drawings*] ... CT
Ceramic-Tile Base [*Technical drawings*] ... CTB
Ceramic-Tile Floor [*Technical drawings*] ... CTF
Ceramic Tile Marketing Federation ... CTMF
Ceramic Tube Fabrication ... CTF
Ceramic Vacuum Relay ... CVR
Ceramic-Wafer Printed Circuit ... CPC
Ceramica y Cristal [*A publication*] ... Ceram Crist
Ceramics Distributors of America ... CDA
Ceramics, Glass, and Solid State Science Division [*National Bureau of Standards*] ... CGSS
Ceramics and Graphite Branch [*Air Force*] ... CGB
Ceramics and Graphite Information Center [*Air Force*] ... CGIC
Ceramics Industries Journal [*A publication*] ... Ceram Ind J
Ceramics International Association ... CIA
Ceramics Japan [*A publication*] ... Ceram Jap
Ceramics Japan [*A publication*] ... Ceram Jpn
Ceramics Monthly [*A publication*] ... Ceramics Mo
Ceramics Monthly [*A publication*] ... Ceram Mo
Ceramide [*Biochemistry*] ... Cer
Ceramurgia International [*A publication*] ... Ceramurgia Int
Ceramurgia International [*A publication*] ... Ceramurg Int
Ceramurgia, Tecnologia Ceramica [*A publication*] ... Ceramurgia Tec Ceram
Ceratum [*Wax Ointment*] [*Pharmacy*] ... CERAT
Cerberonics, Inc. Cl A [*NASDAQ symbol*] ... CRBRA
Cerberus Elektronik [*A publication*] ... Cerberus Elektron
CERBOM [*Centre d'Etudes et de Recherches de Biologie et d'Oceanographie Medicale*] **Rapport d'Activite** [*France*] [*A publication*] ... CERBOM Rapp Act
Cercarienhullen Reaktion [*Medicine*] ... CHR
Cercetari Arheologice [*A publication*] ... CA
Cercetari de Linguistica [*A publication*] ... CLin
Cercetari de Linguistica [*A publication*] ... C Ling
Cercetari Metalurgice [*A publication*] ... Cercet Metal
Cercle Archeologique d'Enghien. Annales [*A publication*] ... CAE
Cercle Archeologique d'Enghien. Annales [*A publication*] ... CAEAn
Cercle Archeologique de Malines. Bulletin [*A publication*] ... CAMBull
Cercle Archeologique de Mons. Annales [*A publication*] ... CAMAn
Cercle Archeologique du Pays de Waes. Annales [*A publication*] ... CAPWAn
Cercle Culturel Camerounais ... CCC
Cercle d'Etudes Numismatiques. Bulletin [*A publication*] ... CENB
Cercle Historique et Archeologique de Courtrai. Bulletin [*A publication*] ... CHAC
Cercle Historique et Archeologique de Courtrai. Bulletin [*A publication*] ... CHACBull
Cereal Chemistry [*A publication*] ... Cereal Chem
Cereal Crop Series. Indian Council of Agricultural Research [*A publication*] ... Cereal Crop Ser Indian Counc Agr Res
Cereal Foods World [*A publication*] ... Cereal F W
Cereal Institute [*Defunct*] ... CI
Cereal Research Communications [*A publication*] ... Cereal Res Commun
Cereal Rust Laboratory [*Department of Agriculture*] ... CRL
Cereal Science Today [*A publication*] ... Cereal Sci Today
Cerebellar Model Articulation Control [*System*] [*National Bureau of Standards*] ... CMAC
Cerebellopontine Angle [*Brain anatomy*] ... CPA
Cerebral Aqueduct [*Brain anatomy*] ... CA
Cerebral Blood Flow [*Medicine*] ... CBF
Cerebral Commissure [*Brain anatomy*] ... CC
Cerebral Ganglion [*Medicine*] ... CG
Cerebral Metabolic Rate [*Medicine*] ... CMR
Cerebral Metabolic Rate of Glucose ... CMRG
Cerebral Metabolic Rate for Oxygen ... $CMRO_2$
Cerebral Palsy [*Medicine*] ... CP
Cerebral Palsy Association of Quebec, Inc., Quebec, PQ, Canada [*Library symbol*] ... CaQQAPC
Cerebral Palsy Bulletin [*A publication*] ... CEPBA
Cerebral Palsy Clinic ... CPC
Cerebral Palsy International Sports and Recreation Association ... CPISRA
Cerebral Palsy Review [*A publication*] ... CBPRA
Cerebral Peduncle [*Brain anatomy*] ... CP
Cerebral Perfusion Pressure [*Medicine*] ... CPP
Cerebral Ridge [*Medicine*] ... CR
Cerebral Thrombosis [*Medicine*] ... CT
Cerebral Tumor [*Medicine*] ... CT
Cerebral Vascular Diseases [*A publication*] ... Cereb Vas Dis
Cerebral Vascular Diseases. International Conference [*A publication*] ... Cereb Vas Dis Int Conf
Cerebro-Buccal Commissure [*Medicine*] ... CBC
Cerebro-Pedal Commissure [*Medicine*] ... CPC
Cerebrospinal [*Medicine*] ... CS
Cerebrospinal Fluid [*Medicine*] ... CSF
Cerebrospinal Meningitis [*Medicine*] ... CSM
Cerebrotendinous Xanthomatosis [*Medicine*] ... CTX
Cerebrovascular [*Medicine*] ... CV
Cerebrovascular Accident [*Medical term for stroke*] ... CVA
Cerebrovascular Diseases [*A publication*] ... Cerebrovasc Dis
Cerebrovascular Insufficiency [*Medicine*] ... CVI
Cerebrovascular Resistance [*Medicine*] ... CVR
Ceredo, WV [*Radio station call letters*] ... WCKV
Cereolus [*An urethral bougie*] [*Pharmacy*] ... CEREOL
Ceres [*South Africa*] [*Seismograph station code, US Geological Survey*] ... CER
Ceres, CA [*Radio station call letters*] ... KLOC
Cerf-Volant [*A publication*] ... CV
Ceric Ammonium Nitrate [*Inorganic chemistry*] ... CAN
Cerium [*Chemical element*] ... Ce
Cerium Magnesium Nitrate [*Inorganic chemistry*] ... CMN
Cerknica [*Yugoslavia*] [*Seismograph station code, US Geological Survey*] ... CEY
CERMET [*Ceramic Metal Element*] **Hybrid Integrated Circuit** ... CHIC
CERMET [*Ceramic Metal Element*] **Resistor Network** ... CRN
Cermetek Microelectronics [*NASDAQ symbol*] ... CRMK
Cerprobe Corp. [*NASDAQ symbol*] ... CRPB
Cerre Les Noroy [*France*] [*Seismograph station code, US Geological Survey*] [*Closed*] ... CNF
Cerritos Junior College, Artesia, CA [*Library symbol*] ... CArtC
Cerro Corp. [*NYSE symbol*] [*Delisted*] ... CDP

Cerro De Punta [*Puerto Rico*] [*Seismograph station code, US Geological Survey*] ..... CDP
Cerro Del Durzno [*New Mexico*] [*Seismograph station code, US Geological Survey*] ..... CDN
Cerro La Pandura [*Puerto Rico*] [*Seismograph station code, US Geological Survey*] ..... CPD
Cerro-Marmon Corp. [*American Stock Exchange symbol*] [*Delisted*] ..... CDM
Cerro-Negro [*Argentina*] [*Seismograph station code, US Geological Survey*] ..... CEN
Cerro-Tololo Inter-American Observatory [*Chile*] [*National Science Foundation*] ..... CTIO
Certain Boroughs [*British*] ..... CBs
Certain Submarine [*Navy*] ..... CERTSUB
Certain-teed Corp. [*NYSE symbol*] ..... CRT
[*A*] **Certainty** ..... CERT
Certificat d'Etudes Litteraires Generales [*France*] ..... CELG
Certificate [*or Certification*] ..... CERT
Certificate ..... CERTIF
Certificate [*NYSE symbol*] ..... CT
Certificate ..... CTF
Certificate of Accrual on Treasury Securities ..... CATS
Certificate of Advanced Graduate Study ..... CAGS
Certificate of Airworthiness ..... C of A
Certificate of Airworthiness ..... CA
Certificate of Assignment of Quarters [*Navy*] ..... C/Q
Certificate of Beneficial Ownership ..... CBO
Certificate of Competency [*Education*] ..... C of C
Certificate of Competency [*Small Business Administration*] ..... COC
Certificate of Conformance [*DoD*] ..... COC
Certificate in Data Education ..... CDE
Certificate in Data Processing ..... CDP
Certificate of Deposit [*Banking*] ..... C of D
Certificate of Deposit [*Banking*] ..... CD
Certificate of Deposit [*Banking*] ..... CDS
Certificate Depository [*New York Stock Exchange*] ..... CEDE
Certificate of Destruction ..... CD
Certificate of Disability for Discharge [*Military*] ..... CDD
Certificate of Disposition of Classified Documents ..... CDCD
Certificate of Eligibility [*Navy*] ..... COE
Certificate of Flight Readiness [*NASA*] ..... COFR
Certificate of Flight Worthiness [*NASA*] ..... COFW
Certificate of Industrial Health ..... CIH
Certificate in Industrial Relations ..... CI Rel
Certificate of Insurance CI
Certificate in Lieu [*of*] CIL
Certificate of Management Accounting ..... CMA
Certificate of Merit ..... C of M
Certificate of Need ..... C of N
Certificate of Need ..... CON
Certificate of Origin ..... C/O
Certificate of Prior Submission [*Navy*] ..... CPS
Certificate in Public Administration ..... CP Adm
Certificate of Public Convenience and Necessity ..... CPC & N
Certificate in Public Health [*British*] ..... CPH
Certificate of Qualification ..... COQ
Certificate as a Qualified Social Worker [*British*] ..... CQSW
Certificate of Reasonable Value [*Veterans Administration*] ..... CRV
Certificate of Retirement ..... C/R
Certificate of the Royal College of Physicians [*British*] ..... CRCP
Certificate of the Royal College of Surgeons [*British*] ..... CRCS
Certificate in Sales Engineering ..... CS En
Certificate of Sanitary Science [*British*] ..... CSS
Certificate of Secondary Education [*British*] ..... CSE
Certificate of Security Clearance ..... CSC
Certificate of Service [*Military*] ..... CS
Certificate of Tax Deposit [*British*] ..... CTD
Certificate of War Necessity [*World War II*] ..... CWN
Certificated Engineer [*A publication*] ..... Certifd Engr
Certificated Engineer [*A publication*] ..... Certif Eng
Certificated Master [*or Mistress*] [*British*] ..... CM
Certificated Teacher [*British*] ..... CT
Certificates of Deposit [*Banking*] ..... COD
Certification Analysis Network ..... CAN
Certification Approval Request ..... CAR
Certification of Completion ..... COC
Certification of Computer Professionals [*Institute for the Certification of Computer Professionals*] ..... CCP
Certification for Emergency Nursing ..... CEN
Certification Evaluation Review ..... CER
Certification Inspection CI
Certification of Nonavailability [*DoD*] ..... C/NA
Certification as Professional Contract Manager ..... CPCM
Certification of Purchase ..... CP
Certification Status Report ..... CSR
Certification Test Network [*NASA*] ..... CTN
Certification Test Requirement [*NASA*] ..... CTR
Certification Test Specification [*NASA*] ..... CTS
Certification Test System ..... CERTS
Certified C
Certified ..... CERTD
Certified Administration Manager ..... CAM
Certified Advertising Agency Practitioner ..... CAAP
Certified Assistant Export Manager [*Designation given by American Society of International Executives*] ..... CAEM
Certified Automotive Repairmen's Society [*Defunct*] ..... CARS
Certified Ballast Manufacturers Association ..... CBM
Certified Ballast Manufacturers Association ..... CBMA
Certified Bank Examiner ..... CBE
Certified Biomedical Equipment Technician ..... CBET
Certified Cell Line [*ATCC*] CCL
Certified Chamber Executive [*Designation awarded by American Chamber of Commerce Executives*] ..... CCE
Certified Check [*Banking*] CC
Certified Claims Professional Accreditation Council ..... CCPAC
Certified Cold Fur Storage Association ..... CCFSA
Certified Collateral [*NASDAQ symbol*] ..... CARX
Certified Color Manufacturers Association ..... CCMA
Certified Commercial Investment Member [*Realtors National Marketing Institute*] ..... CCIM
Certified Consultants International CCI
Certified Consumer Credit Executive [*Designation awarded by International Consumer Credit Association*] ..... CCCE
Certified Corp. [*American Stock Exchange symbol*] [*Delisted*] ..... CTF
Certified Corrective Therapist ..... CCT
Certified Data Processor ..... CDP
Certified Decal Manufacturers ..... CDM
Certified Dental Assistant ..... CDA
Certified Dental Technician ..... CDT
Certified Dental Technician [*A publication*] ..... Certif Dent Tec
Certified Documentary Specialist [*Designation given by American Society of International Executives to persons in international trade*] ..... CDS
Certified Employee Benefit Specialist ..... CEBS
Certified Engineer [*A publication*] ..... Certif Eng
Certified Flight Instructor [*Aviation*] ..... CFI
Certified Fund-Raising Executive ..... CFRE
Certified General Accountant ..... CGA
Certified Graphoanalyst ..... CGA
Certified Herbalist ..... CH
Certified Industrial Manager ..... CIM
Certified Information Systems Auditor ..... CISA
Certified Institution for the Mental Defective [*British*] ..... CIMD
Certified Internal Auditor ..... CIA
Certified International Executive - Air Forwarding [*Designation given by American Society of International Executives*] ..... CIE-AF
Certified International Executive - Export Management [*Designation given by American Society of International Executives*] ..... CIE-EM
Certified International Executive - Forwarding [*Designation given by American Society of International Executives*] ..... CIE-F
Certified International Executive - Traffic Management [*Designation given by American Society of International Executives*] ..... CIE-TM
Certified International Traffic Manager [*Designation given by American Society of International Executives*] ..... CITM
Certified Kitchen Designer ..... CKD
Certified Kosher [*Food labeling*] ..... K
Certified Laundry Manager ..... CLM
Certified Life Underwriter [*Insurance*] ..... CLU
Certified Livestock Marketing Association [*Later, Livestock Marketing Association*] ..... CLMA
Certified Medical Assistant ..... CMA
Certified Medical Representatives Institute ..... CMRI
Certified Milk Producers Association of America ..... CMPAA
Certified Nurse Midwife ..... CNM
Certified Occupational Therapy Assistant ..... COTA
Certified Office Administrator ..... COA
Certified Official Government Business ..... COGB
Certified Operating Room Technician ..... CORT
Certified Orthotist ..... CO
Certified Patient [*British*] ..... CP
Certified Pedorthist ..... CPed
Certified Personnel Consultant [*Designation awarded by National Association of Personnel Consultants*] ..... CPC
Certified Professional Logistician ..... CPL
Certified Professional Secretary [*Designation given by National Secretaries Association*] ..... CPS
Certified Property Manager [*Designation given by Institute of Real Estate Management*] ..... CPM
Certified Prosthetist ..... CP
Certified Prosthetist and Orthotist ..... CPO
Certified Public Accountant ..... CPA
Certified Record Librarian ..... CRL
Certified Records Manager ..... CRM
Certified Reference Materials ..... CRM
Certified Registered Nurse Anesthetist ..... CRNA
Certified Rehabilitation Counselor ..... CRC
Certified Residential Broker [*Realtors National Marketing Institute*] ..... CRB
Certified Residential Specialist [*Realtors National Marketing Institute*] ..... CRS
Certified Respiratory Therapy Technician ..... CRTT
Certified Safety Professional ..... CSP

Certified Shorthand Reporter ... CSR
Certified Speaking Professional ... CSP
Certified Test Data ... CTD
Certified Test Results ... CTR
Certified Tool List ... CTL
Certified Travel Counselor [*Designation given by Institute of Certified Travel Agents*] ... CTC
Certified Vendor Information ... CVI
Certify ... CRTFY
Certron Corp. [*NASDAQ symbol*] ... CRTN
Certron Corp. [*American Stock Exchange symbol*] [*Delisted*] ... CT
Cervical [*Medicine*] ... C
Cervical Intraepithelial Neoplasia [*Medicine*] ... CIN
Cervical Orthosis [*Medicine*] ... CO
Cervical Vertebra [*Medicine*] ... CV
Cervicoaxial [*Dentistry*] ... CA
Cervicolinguoaxial [*Dentistry*] ... CLA
Cervicothoracic Orthosis [*Also, CTO*] [*Medicine*] ... CER
Cervicothoracic Orthosis [*Also, CER*] [*Medicine*] ... CTO
Cervicothoracolumbar Orthosis [*Medicine*] ... CTLO
Cervicothoracolumbosacral Orthosis [*Medicine*] ... CTLSO
Cervix [*Anatomy*] ... CERV
Cervix [*Medicine*] ... CX
Cesare Barbieri Courier [*A publication*] ... CBC
[*The*] **Cesarean Connection** ... TCC
Cesarean Delivered [*Medicine*] ... CD
Cesarean Prevention Movement ... CPM
Cesarean Section [*Medicine*] ... C (Section)
Cesarean Section [*Medicine*] ... CS
Cesareans/Support, Education, and Concern [*An association*] ... C/SEC
Cesium [*Chemical element*] ... Cs
Cesium Beam Time Standard ... CBTS
Cesium Beam Tube ... CBT
Cesium Bombardment Engine ... CBE
Cesium Chloride Polymerizable [*Analytical chemistry*] ... CCP
Cesium Contact Engine ... CCE
Cesium Contact Thruster ... CCT
Cesium Dihydrogen Arsenate ... CDA
Cesium Feed System ... CFS
Cesium Ion Emission ... CIE
Cesium Ion Propulsion System ... CIPS
Cesium Ion Source ... CIS
Cesium Time Standard ... CTS
Cesium Trifluoroacetate [*Reagent*] ... CsTFA
Cesium Vapor Cathode ... CVC
Cesium Vapor Feed System ... CVFS
Ceska Literatura [*A publication*] ... CL
Ceska Literatura [*A publication*] ... CLit
Ceska Mykologie [*A publication*] ... Ceska Mykol
Ceskoslovenska Akademie Ved [*A publication*] ... CSAV
Ceskoslovenska Biologie [*A publication*] ... Cesk Biol
Ceskoslovenska Dermatologie [*A publication*] ... Cesk Dermatol
Ceskoslovenska Epidemiologie, Mikrobiologie, Immunologie [*A publication*] ... Cesk Epidemiol Mikrobiol Immunol
Ceskoslovenska Farmacie [*A publication*] ... Cesk Farm
Ceskoslovenska Fysiologie [*A publication*] ... Cesk Fysiol
Ceskoslovenska Gastroenterologie a Vyziva [*A publication*] ... Cesk Gastroenterol Vyz
Ceskoslovenska Gynekologie [*A publication*] ... CEGYA
Ceskoslovenska Gynekologie [*A publication*] ... Cesk Gynekol
Ceskoslovenska Hygiena [*A publication*] ... Cesk Hyg
Ceskoslovenska Informatika. Teorie a Praxe [*A publication*] ... Cesk Inf
Ceskoslovenska Mikrobiologie [*A publication*] ... Cesk Mikrobiol
Ceskoslovenska Morfologie [*A publication*] ... Cesk Morfol
Ceskoslovenska Neurologie [*Later, Ceskoslovenska Neurologie a Neurochirurgie*] [*A publication*] ... Cesk Neurol
Ceskoslovenska Neurologie [*Later, Ceskoslovenska Neurologie a Neurochirurgie*] [*A publication*] ... CSKNA
Ceskoslovenska Neurologie a Neurochirurgie [*A publication*] ... Cesk Neurol Neurochir
Ceskoslovenska Obec Sokolska [*Czechoslovakia*] ... COS
Ceskoslovenska Oftalmologie [*A publication*] ... CEOFA
Ceskoslovenska Oftalmologie [*A publication*] ... Cesk Oftalmol
Ceskoslovenska Otolaryngologie [*A publication*] ... CEOTA
Ceskoslovenska Otolaryngologie [*A publication*] ... Cesk Otolaryngol
Ceskoslovenska Parasitologie [*A publication*] ... Cesk Parasitol
Ceskoslovenska Patologie [*A publication*] ... Cesk Patol
Ceskoslovenska Pediatrie [*A publication*] ... CEPEA
Ceskoslovenska Pediatrie [*A publication*] ... Cesk Pediatr
Ceskoslovenska Psychiatrie [*A publication*] ... CEPYA
Ceskoslovenska Psychiatrie [*A publication*] ... Cesk Psychiatr
Ceskoslovenska Psychologie [*A publication*] ... CEPSB
Ceskoslovenska Psychologie [*A publication*] ... Cesk Psycho
Ceskoslovenska Psychologie [*A publication*] ... Cesk Psychol
Ceskoslovenska Radiologie [*A publication*] ... Cesk Radiol
Ceskoslovenska Rusistika [*A publication*] ... CRu
Ceskoslovenska Rusistika [*A publication*] ... CRus
Ceskoslovenska Rusistika [*A publication*] ... CsR
Ceskoslovenska Standardizace [*A publication*] ... Cesk Stand
Ceskoslovenska Stomatologie [*A publication*] ... CES A
Ceskoslovenska Stomatologie [*A publication*] ... Cesk Stomatol
Ceskoslovenska Stomatologie [*A publication*] ... Ce Sta
Ceskoslovenska Tiskova Kancelar [*Czechoslovak News Agency*] ... CTK
Ceskoslovenske Aerolinie [*Czechoslovak Airline*] ... CSA
Ceskoslovenske Aerolinie [*Czechoslovakia*] [*ICAO designator*] ... OK
Ceskoslovenske Zdravotnictvi [*A publication*] ... Cesk Zdrav
Ceskoslovensky Casopis pro Fysiku. Sekce A [*A publication*] ... Cesk Cas Fys A
Ceskoslovensky Casopis pro Fysiku. Sekce A [*A publication*] ... Cesk C Fys
Ceskoslovensky Casopis Historicky [*A publication*] ... Cesk Cas Hist
Ceskoslovensky Casopis Historicky [*A publication*] ... CSCH
Ceskoslovensky Spisovatel [*A publication*] ... CSp
Ceskoslovensky Svaz Mladeze [*Czechoslovakia*] ... CSM
Ceskoslovensky Terminologicky Casopis [*A publication*] ... CSTC
Ceskoslovensky Terminologicky Casopis [*A publication*] ... CTC
Cesky Casopis Filologicky [*A publication*] ... CCF
Cesky Casopis Historicky [*A publication*] ... CCH
Cesky Jazyk a Literatura [*A publication*] ... CJL
Cesky Jazyk a Literatura [*A publication*] ... CJLit
Cesky Lid [*A publication*] ... CLid
CESRL Report. University of Texas at Austin. Department of Civil Engineering. Structures Research Laboratory [*A publication*] ... CESRL Rep Univ Tex Austin Dep Civ Eng Struct Res Lab
Cessna Aircraft Company ... CAC
Cessna Aircraft Co. [*NYSE symbol*] ... CEA
Cessnock [*Australia*] [*Airport symbol*] ... CES
Cesspool ... CP
C'Est-a-Dire [*That Is to Say*] [*French*] ... C-A-D
Cetane Number ... CN
Cetec Corporation [*American Stock Exchange symbol*] ... CEC
Ceteris Paribus [*Other Things Being Equal*] [*Latin*] ... CET PAR
Cetus Corp. [*NASDAQ symbol*] ... CTUS
Cetyldimethylbenzylammonium Chloride [*Surfactant*] ... CDAC
Cetylpyridinium Chloride [*Organic chemistry*] ... CPC
Cetyltrimethylammonium [*Organic chemistry*] ... CTA
Cetyltrimethylammonium Bromide [*Also, CTAB*] [*Antiseptic*] ... CETAB
Cetyltrimethylammonium Bromide [*Also, CETAB*] [*Antiseptic*] ... CTAB
Cetyltrimethylammonium Toluenesulfonate [*Organic chemistry*] ... CETATS
Ceylon [*Sri Lanka*] [*MARC geographic area code*] [*Library of Congress*] ... a-ce---
Ceylon [*Sri Lanka*] [*MARC country of publication code*] [*Library of Congress*] ... ce
Ceylon [*Sri Lanka*] ... CL
Ceylon [*Sri Lanka*] [*Aircraft nationality and registration mark*] ... 4R
Ceylon Association for the Advancement of Science. Proceedings of the Annual Session [*A publication*] ... Ceylon Assoc Adv Sci Proc Annu Sess
Ceylon Civil Service [*Obsolete*] ... CCS
Ceylon Coconut Planters' Review [*A publication*] ... Ceylon Coconut Plant Rev
Ceylon Coconut Quarterly [*A publication*] ... Ceylon Coconut Q
Ceylon Dental Journal [*A publication*] ... Ceylon Dent J
Ceylon Economist [*A publication*] ... CE
Ceylon Federation of Labor [*Obsolete*] ... CFL
Ceylon Forester [*A publication*] ... Ceylon For
Ceylon Journal of Historical and Social Studies [*A publication*] ... Cey J Hist Soc Stud
Ceylon Journal of Medical Science [*A publication*] ... Ceylon J Med Sci
Ceylon Journal of Science. Anthropology [*A publication*] ... Ceylon J Sci Anthropol
Ceylon Journal of Science. Biological Sciences [*A publication*] ... Ceylon J Sci Biol Sci
Ceylon Journal of Science. Section A. Botany [*A publication*] ... Ceylon J Sci Sect A Bot
Ceylon Journal of Science. Section B. Zoology [*A publication*] ... Ceylon J Sci Sect B Zool
Ceylon Journal of Science. Section C. Fisheries [*A publication*] ... Ceylon J Sci Sect C Fish
Ceylon Journal of Science. Section D. Medical Science [*A publication*] ... Ceylon J Sci Sect D Med Sci
Ceylon Labor Union [*Obsolete*] ... CLU
Ceylon Medical Journal [*A publication*] ... Ceylon Med J
Ceylon Mercantile Union [*Obsolete*] ... CMU
Ceylon National Museums. Ethnographic Series [*A publication*] ... Ceylon Natl Mus Ethnogr Ser
Ceylon Plantation Workers' Union [*Obsolete*] ... CPWU
Ceylon Railway Clerical Service Union [*Obsolete*] ... CRCSU
Ceylon Rubber Research Scheme. Quarterly Circular [*A publication*] ... Ceylon Rubber Res Scheme Q Circ
Ceylon Trade Union Federation [*Obsolete*] ... CTUF
Ceylon Veterinary Journal [*A publication*] ... Ceylon Vet J
Ceylon Workers' Congress [*Obsolete*] ... CWC
CF & I Steel Corp. [*Formerly, Colorado Fuel & Iron Corp.*] [*NYSE symbol*] ... CF
CFEM [*Comision Forestal del Estado de Michoacan*] **Serie Tecnica** [*A publication*] ... CFEM Ser Tec
CFO [*Colorado Field Ornithologists*] **Journal** [*A publication*] ... CFO J
CFS Continental, Inc. [*NASDAQ symbol*] ... CFSC
CFU [*Croatian Fraternal Union of America*] **Junior Cultural Federation** [*Affiliated with CFU*] ... CFUJCF
CGA Computer Association [*NASDAQ symbol*] ... CGAC
Cha-Pa [*Vietnam*] [*Geomagnetic observatory code*] ... CPA

Chabot College, Hayward, CA [*Library symbol*]..................CHC
Chabot Observatory, Oakland, CA [*Library symbol*] ....COCh
Chacarita [*Argentina*] [*Seismograph station code, US Geological Survey*] [*Closed*]..................CCR
Chaco Canyon National Monument ....CHCA
Chad [*MARC country of publication code*] [*Library of Congress*]..................cd
Chad [*MARC geographic area code*] [*Library of Congress*] ....f-cd---
Chad [*Three-letter standard code*]..................TCD
Chad [*Two-letter standard code*]..................TD
Chad [*Aircraft nationality and registration mark*]..................TT
Chad Therapeutics [*NASDAQ symbol*]..................CDTX
Chadbourn, Incorporated [*Later, SNW*] [*NYSE symbol*]..................CGI
Chadbourn, NC [*Radio station call letters*]..................WVOE
Chadron [*Nebraska*] [*Airport symbol*]..................CDR
Chadron, NE [*Location identifier*] [*FAA*]..................HIN
Chadron, NE [*Radio station call letters*]..................KCSR
Chadron, NE [*Radio station call letters*]..................KQSK
Chadron Public Library, Chadron, NE [*Library symbol*]..................NbCh
Chadron State College, Chadron, NE [*Library symbol*]..................NbChS
Chadron State College, Chadron, NE [*OCLC symbol*]..................NCC
Chadwell, Kayser, Ruggles, McGee, & Hastings, Chicago, IL [*OCLC symbol*]..................ILQ
Chadwick-Goldhaber Effect [*Physics*]..................CGE
Chadwick-Miller, Inc. [*American Stock Exchange symbol*]..................CWK
Chadwyck-Healey Ltd., Bishops Stortford, Herts, United Kingdom [*Library symbol*]..................ChaH
Chaff Rocket [*Military*]..................CHAFFROC
Chaffey College, Alta Loma, CA [*Library symbol*]..................CAltaC
Chagan-Uzun [*USSR*] [*Seismograph station code, US Geological Survey*]..................CUR
Chagrin Falls Public Library, Chagrin Falls, OH [*Library symbol*]..................OCf
Chah-Bahar [*Iran*] [*Airport symbol*]..................ZBR
Chain..................CH
Chain..................CHN
Chain Belt Co. [*NYSE symbol*] [*Delisted*]..................CHB
Chain of Command..................CHACOM
Chain Grate..................CG
Chain Home [*Aviation*]..................CH
Chain Home Beamed [*Aviation*]..................CHB
Chain Home Extra Low [*Aviation*]..................CHEL
Chain Home Low [*Aviation*]..................CHL
Chain Ignition Hazard..................CIH
Chain Link Fence Manufacturers Institute..................CLFMI
Chain Operator..................CO
Chain Overseas..................CO
Chain Overseas Extremely Low [*Aviation*]..................COEL
Chain Overseas Low [*Aviation*]..................COL
Chain RADAR System..................CRS
Chain Saw Manufacturers Association..................CSMA
Chain Store Age [*A publication*]..................Chn Store
Chain Store Age (Administration Edition) [*A publication*]..................Chain Store Age (Adm Ed)
Chain Store Age. Executive Edition [*A publication*]..................Chain Store Age Exec
Chained File Management System [*IBM Corp.*]..................CFMS
Chained Sequential Operation..................CSO
Chair..................CH
Chairman [*or Chairwoman or Chairperson*]..................C
Chairman..................CH
Chairman..................CHAIR
Chairman..................CHM
Chairman..................CHMN
Chairman..................CHRM
Chairman..................CHRMN
Chairman, Communications-Electronics Committee [*NATO*]..................CCEC
Chairman of Defense Committee..................CODEF
Chairman, Joint Chiefs of Staff..................CJCS
Chairman of Military Committee..................COMIL
Chairman Military Committee Memorandum [*NATO*]..................CMCM
Chairman, Special Studies Group [*Joint Chiefs of Staff*]..................CSSG
Chairman of Volunteers [*Red Cross*]..................CV
Chairman's Memorandum..................CM
Chairperson..................CHRPRSN
Chaix Hill [*Alaska*] [*Seismograph station code, US Geological Survey*]..................CHX
Chakcharan [*Afghanistan*] [*Airport symbol*] [*Obsolete*]..................CCN
Chala [*Peru*] [*Seismograph station code, US Geological Survey*] [*Closed*]..................CLA
Chalco Industrials, Inc. [*NASDAQ symbol*]..................CLCO
Chaldea..................CHALD
Chaldron [*Unit of measure*] [*Obsolete*]..................CH
Chaldron [*Unit of measure*] [*Obsolete*]..................CHAL
Chaleur et Climats [*A publication*]..................Chal Clim
Chaleur et Climats [*A publication*]..................Chal Climats
Chaleur Library Region, Campbellton, NB, Canada [*Library symbol*]..................CaNBCaC
Chalk [*Quality of the bottom*] [*Nautical charts*]..................Ck
Chalk River Nuclear Laboratories [*Atomic Energy of Canada Ltd.*] [*Information service*]..................CRNL
Chalk River Unidentified Deposit..................CRUD
Chalkyitsik [*Alaska*] [*Airport symbol*]..................CIK
Challenge..................CHAL
Challenge Position [*Dancing*]..................CH-P

Challenge Test Plan..................CTP
Challenges to Montana Agriculture [*A publication*]..................Challenges Mont Agr
Chalmers Tekniska Hoegskola. Doktorsavhandlingar [*A publication*]..................Chalmers Tek Hogsk Doktorsavh
Chalmers Tekniska Hoegskola. Handlingar [*A publication*]..................Chalmers Tek Hoegsk Handl
Chalmette National Historical Park..................CHAL
Chalumeau [*Reed*] [*Music*]..................CHAL
Chama [*New Mexico*] [*Seismograph station code, US Geological Survey*] [*Closed*]..................CNM
Chamaeleon [*Constellation*]..................Cha
Chamaeleon [*Constellation*]..................Cham
Chamber..................CHAMB
Chamber..................CHM
Chamber..................CHMBR
Chamber of Commerce..................C of C
Chamber of Commerce..................CC
Chamber of Commerce..................COC
Chamber of Commerce of the Apparel Industry..................CCAI
Chamber of Commerce of the United States..................CCUS
Chamber of Commerce of the United States..................COCUSA
Chamber of Commerce of the United States, Washington, DC [*Library symbol*]..................DCC
Chamber Coolant Valve..................CCV
Chamber of Destination of Ships..................CDS
Chamber of Mines Journal [*A publication*]..................Chamber Mines J
Chamber Music America [*An association*]..................CMA
Chamber Music Society of Lincoln Center..................CMS/LC
Chamber Orchestra of Europe..................COE
Chamber Pressure..................CP
Chamberlain [*California*] [*Seismograph station code, US Geological Survey*]..................CBC
Chamberlain Public Library, Chamberlain, SD [*Library symbol*]..................SdCh
Chambers..................CHAS
Chamber's Edinburgh Journal [*A publication*]..................Chamb J
Chambersburg, PA [*Location identifier*] [*FAA*]..................EQB
Chambersburg, PA [*Radio station call letters*]..................WCBG
Chambersburg, PA [*Radio station call letters*]..................WCHA
Chambersburg, PA [*Radio station call letters*]..................WIKZ
Chambery [*France*] [*Airport symbol*]..................CMF
Chambon-La-Foret [*France*] [*Geomagnetic observatory code*]..................CLF
Chambon-La-Foret [*France*] [*Seismograph station code, US Geological Survey*] [*Closed*]..................CLF
Chambre de Commerce Internationale [*International Chamber of Commerce*] [*See also ICC*]..................CCI
Chambre des Ingenieurs - Conseils de France..................CICF
Chambres d'Agriculture [*A publication*]..................Ch Agric
Chameleon Micro Implementation Language [*Data processing*]..................CHAMIL
Chamfer [*Design engineering*]..................CHAM
Chamizal National Memorial..................CHAM
Champ Du Feu [*France*] [*Seismograph station code, US Geological Survey*]..................CDF
Champagne d'Argent Federation..................CDF
Champaign [*Illinois*] [*Airport symbol*]..................CMI
Champaign, IL [*Radio station call letters*]..................WBGL
Champaign, IL [*Television station call letters*]..................WCIA
Champaign, IL [*Radio station call letters*]..................WDWS
Champaign, IL [*Radio station call letters*]..................WDWS-FM
Champaign, IL [*Radio station call letters*]..................WEFT
Champaign, IL [*Radio station call letters*]..................WERU
Champaign, IL [*Television station call letters*]..................WICD
Champaign, IL [*Radio station call letters*]..................WLRW
Champaign, IL [*Radio station call letters*]..................WPCD
Champaign Public Library, Champaign, IL [*Library symbol*]..................ICham
Champaign Public Library, Champaign, IL [*OCLC symbol*]..................IKG
Champaign/Urbana, IL [*Location identifier*] [*FAA*]..................CMI
Champaign-Urbana, IL [*Television station call letters*]..................WILL-TV
Champion..................CH
Champion Aircraft Company..................CAC
Champion Fleet Owners Association..................CFOA
Champion Home Builders Co. [*American Stock Exchange symbol*]..................CHB
Champion International Corp. [*NYSE symbol*]..................CHA
Champion Papers, Inc. [*Later, CHA*] [*NYSE symbol*]..................CPP
Champion Papers, Inc., Pasadena, TX [*Library symbol*]..................TxPC
Champion Parts Rebuilders, Inc. [*NASDAQ symbol*]..................CREB
Champion Products [*American Stock Exchange symbol*]..................CH
Champion Spark Plug Co. [*NYSE symbol*]..................CHM
Championship..................CHP
Championship Auto Racing Teams..................CART
Champlain College, Burlington, VT [*Library symbol*]..................VtBC
Champlain College, Plattsburgh, NY [*Library symbol*] [*Obsolete*]..................NPlaC
Champlain Regional College, Campus 1, St-Lambert, PQ, Canada [*Library symbol*]..................CaQSlCR
Champlain Society..................CS
Champlain Valley Physicians Hospital, Plattsburgh, NY [*Library symbol*]..................NPlaP
Champlain Valley School of Nursing, Plattsburgh, NY [*Library symbol*]..................NPlaCN
Champlin Oil & Refining Co. [*NYSE symbol*] [*Delisted*]..................CHI
Chanaral [*Chile*] [*Seismograph station code, US Geological Survey*]..................CAA
Chance..................CHC

Chance Vought Aircraft, Inc. [*Obsolete*]	CVA
Chancellor	C
Chancellor	CHANC
Chancellor Computer [*NASDAQ symbol*]	CHCC
Chancellor Corp. [*NASDAQ symbol*]	CHCR
Chancellor of the Duchy of Lancaster [*British*]	CDL
Chancellor of the Exchequer [*British*]	CE
Chancery	C
Chancery [*British*]	CH
Chancery	CHAN
Chancery	CHY
Chancery Division	CD
Chances Accepted [*Baseball*]	CA
Chandalar [*Alaska*] [*Airport symbol*]	WCR
Chandalar Lake, AK [*Location identifier*] [*FAA*]	WCR
Chandigarh [*India*] [*Airport symbol*]	IXC
Chandler, AZ [*Radio station call letters*]	KMLE
Chandler Evans Corporation	CECO
Chandler Flyers [*Chandler, AZ*] [*ICAO designator*]	CRR
Chandler Public Library, Chandler, AZ [*Library symbol*]	AzCh
Changalane [*Mozambique*] [*Seismograph station code, US Geological Survey*]	CNG
Changchun [*China*] [*Airport symbol*]	CGQ
Changchun [*Republic of China*] [*Seismograph station code, US Geological Survey*]	CNH
Change [*Army*] [*Used in combinations only*]	C
Change	CH
Change	CHG
Change	CHNG
Change [*A publication*]	CNG
Change of Address	COA
Change Administration	CA
Change Administration Conference	CAC
Change Administration Cover Sheet	CA/CS
Change Analysis Board	CAB
Change Analysis Group	CAG
Change Analysis Section	CAS
Change of Appointing Office [*Aviation*]	CAO
Change [*or Changing*] to Approach Control [*Aviation*]	CAC
Change of Assignment	COA
Change Board	CB
Change Board Register	CBR
Change Bulletin	CB
Change [*or Changing*] to Center Control [*Aviation*]	CTCC
Change for Children [*An association*]	CC
Change Code	CC
Change of Command	COC
Change of Contract	COC
Change Control Board	CCB
Change Control Board	CHGCB
Change Control Board Directive	CCBD
Change Control Board Summary	CCBS
Change Control Determine	CCD
Change Control Engineer	CCE
Change Control Group	CCG
Change Control System	CCS
Change Course	CC
Change of Course [*Aviation*]	C/C
Change in Design	CID
Change Design Order [*Navy*]	CDO
Change Directive	CD
Change in Drawing Authorization	CIDA
Change in Drawing Notice	CIDN
Change Evaluation	CE
Change Flight Plan	CFP
Change in Formula	CF
Change [*or Changing*] to Frequency [*Followed by number*] [*Communications*]	CF
Change Identification Control [*Number*]	CIC
Change Identification Control Schedule Analysis	CICSA
Change Identification Control Schedule Summary	CIC-SS
Change Impact Board	CIB
Change Impact Summary	CIS
Change Implementation Board	CIB
Change Incorporation Notice	CIN
Change to Initial Release	CIR
Change Initiation Requests	CIR
Change Instrumentation Notice	CIN
Change Letter Control	CLC
Change List	CL
Change to Lower Grade [*Army*]	CLG
Change Management/Tracking [*IBM Corp.*]	CM/T
Change My Operation Order [*Military*]	CHORD
Change My Operation Plan [*Military*]	CHOPLN
Change My Operation Schedule [*Military*]	CHSKED
Change to Navy Regulations	CNR
Change Notice	CN
Change Notice Request	CNR
Change of Operational Control [*Military*]	CHOP
Change of Operational Control of Air Cover [*Military*]	CHOPAIR
Change of Operational Control Summary [*Military*]	CHOPSUM
Change Order	C/O
Change [*of*] Order	CO
Change Order Account	COA
Change Order (Aircraft)	CO(A)
Change Order Board	COB
Change Order Conference	COC
Change Order (Electronic)	CO(E)
Change Order Modification	COM
Change Over	CHGOV
Change Over	CO
Change Package	CP
Change Package Identification	CPI
Change Package Identification Number	CPIN
Change Planning Group	CPG
Change of Plaster [*Medicine*]	COP
Change Point [*Surveying*]	CP
Change Processing Station	CPS
Change Proposal	CP
Change of Rating	C/R
Change Recommendation	CR
Change Release [*Military*]	CR
Change Request	CR
Change Request Forms	CRF
Change Request Material	CRM
Change Review Board	CRB
Change Review Committee	CRCOM
Change Review Panel	CRP
Change Schedule Chart	CSC
Change Sheet [*Marine Corps*]	CS
Change of Status	CS
Change [*or Changing*] to Tower Frequency [*Aviation*]	CTF
Change Weight Manifest [*Aviation*]	CWM
Changeable Type-Plate Style	CT-PS
Changed Particle Research Laboratory	CPRL
Changeout	C/O
Changeover	CHOVR
Changeover Panel	COP
Changeover Point [*Aviation*]	CHOP
Changeover Point [*Aviation*]	COP
Changeover Switch	COS
Changes Improvement Plan	CIP
Changes in Itinerary to Proceed to Additional Places [*Military*]	CIPAP
Changes Socialist Monthly [*A publication*]	Changes
Changes and Specifications	C & S
Changing Education [*A publication*]	Chang Ed
Changing Path of Operation	CPO
Changing Radio Automatic Frequency Transmission	CRAFT
Changing Times [*A publication*]	Changing T
Changing Times [*A publication*]	Chang Times
Changing Times [*A publication*]	Cha Ti
Changsha [*China*] [*Airport symbol*]	CSX
Changuinola [*Panama*] [*Airport symbol*]	CHX
Changzhi [*China*] [*Airport symbol*]	CIH
Chania [*Greece*] [*Airport symbol*]	CHQ
Channel	CH
Channel [*Maps and charts*]	CHAN
Channel	CHNL
Channel Adapter [*Data processing*]	CA
Channel Address Register [*Data processing*]	CAR
Channel Address Word [*Data processing*]	CAW
Channel Allocation and Routing Data	CARD
Channel Aviation Ltd. [*Great Britain*] [*ICAO designator*]	GD
Channel Base Section [*World War II*]	CBS
Channel-to-Channel Adapter [*Data processing*]	CTCA
Channel-Check Handler	CCH
Channel Command [*Refers to English Channel*] [*Military*]	CC
Channel Command [*or Control*] Word [*Data processing*]	CCW
Channel Committee [*NATO*]	CHANCOM
Channel Committee [*NATO*]	CHANCOMTEE
Channel Committee Secretary [*NATO*]	CHANSEC
Channel Continuity Check Transmission [*Communications*]	CH
Channel Control	CHC
Channel Electron Multiplier	CEM
Channel End	CHE
Channel Evaluation and Call	CHEC
Channel Identification	CID
Channel Indirect Data Addressing	CIDA
Channel Industries [*NASDAQ symbol*]	CHNN
Channel Island Aviation [*Oxnard, CA*] [*FAA designator*]	CHN
Channel Islands	CI
Channel Islands National Monument	CHIS
Channel Multiplier Array	CMA
Channel for Orders [*Business and trade*]	CFO
Channel Oscilloscope	C/O
Channel Port Index	CPI
Channel Program Block [*Data processing*]	CPB
Channel Status	CS
Channel Status Indicator [*Data processing*]	CST
Channel Status Word	CSW
Channel Synchronizer Unit [*Data processing*]	CSU

Channel and Technical Control Facility [*In a tape-relay station in the AIRCOMNET*] ... CTCF
Channel and Traffic Control Agency [*of AACS*] ... CTCA
Channel and Traffic Control Unit [*Subordinate unit of the Channel and Traffic Control Agency*] ... CTCU
Channel Transmission and Engineering Activation ... CTEA
Channel Tunnel [*Joint British-French project in English Channel*] ... CHUNNEL
Channel Verification Signal Generator ... CVSG
Channeling Effect Factor ... CEF
Channels Ratio ... CR
Chanoyu Quarterly [*A publication*] ... Chanoyu Q
Chanute Air Force Base [*Illinois*] ... CHAFB
Chanute, KS [*Location identifier*] [*FAA*] ... CNU
Chanute, KS [*Radio station call letters*] ... KKOY
Chanute, KS [*Radio station call letters*] ... KQSM
Chanute Technical Training Center [*Air Force*] ... CTTC
Chapais, PQ [*Radio station call letters*] ... CFED
Chaparral Airlines [*Abilene, TX*] [*FAA designator*] ... CPL
Chaparral Aviation, Inc. [*Reno, NV*] [*FAA designator*] ... MAV
Chaparral/Forward Area Alert RADAR [*Military*] ... CHAP/FAAR
Chaparral Resources [*NASDAQ symbol*] ... CHAR
Chapeau, PQ [*Television station call letters*] ... CIVP-TV
Chapeco [*Brazil*] [*Airport symbol*] ... XAP
Chapel ... C
Chapel ... CHAP
Chapel of Ease [*Church of England*] ... CHE
Chapel Hill [*North Carolina*] [*Seismograph station code, US Geological Survey*] ... CEH
Chapel Hill [*North Carolina*] [*Seismograph station code, US Geological Survey*] [*Closed*] ... CHC
Chapel Hill, NC [*Radio station call letters*] ... WCHL
Chapel Hill, NC [*Radio station call letters*] ... WRBX
Chapel Hill, NC [*Radio station call letters*] ... WUNC
Chapel Hill, NC [*Television station call letters*] ... WUNC-TV
Chapel Hill, NC [*Radio station call letters*] ... WXYC
Chapelco [*Argentina*] [*Airport symbol*] ... CPC
Chapelry [*Geographical division*] [*British*] ... CHAP
Chapin Social Insight Test [*Psychology*] ... CSIT
Chaplain ... CH
Chaplain ... CHAP
Chaplain ... CHAPL
Chaplain ... CHPLN
Chaplain Area Representative [*Air Force*] ... CHAPAR
Chaplain-in-Chief [*British*] ... CH-in-C
Chaplain Corps ... CHC
Chaplain of the Fleet [*Navy*] [*British*] ... C of F
Chaplain of the Fleet [*Navy*] [*British*] ... CF
Chaplain of the Fleet [*Navy*] [*British*] ... CH of F
Chaplain of the Fleet [*Navy*] [*British*] ... ChF
Chaplain to the Forces [*British*] ... CF
Chaplain to the Forces - Emergency Commission [*British*] ... CF(EC)
Chaplain to the Forces (Jewish) [*British*] ... CF(J)
Chaplain to the Forces - Reserve of Officers [*British*] ... CF(R of O)
Chaplain to the Forces (Territorial Army) [*British*] ... CF(TA)
Chaplain of the Order of St. John of Jerusalem [*Later, Ch St J*] ... Chap St J
Chaplain of the Order of St. John of Jerusalem [*Formerly, Chap St J*] ... Ch St J
Chaplain of the Order of St. John of Jerusalem ... CHSTJJ
Chaplain Service Personnel [*Air Force*] ... CSP
Chaplain of the Territorial Army [*British*] ... CTA
Chaplain to the Territorial Forces [*British*] ... CTF
Chaplains' Aid Association ... CAA
Chaplains' Relevance to the Emerging Drug Order [*Navy*] ... CREDO
Chapleau [*Canada*] [*Airport symbol*] ... YLD
Chaplin [*Connecticut*] [*Seismograph station code, US Geological Survey*] [*Closed*] ... CPL
Chapman [*One who sells in a cheaping or market*] [*Said to be origin of "chap," meaning "fellow"*] ... CHAP
Chapman Chemical Co., Memphis, TN [*Library symbol*] ... TMCC
Chapman College Library, Orange, CA [*OCLC symbol*] ... CCX
Chapman College, Orange, CA [*Library symbol*] ... COrC
Chapman Energy, Inc. [*NASDAQ symbol*] ... CHPN
Chapman-Jouquet [*Pressures*] ... CJ
Chappaqua Library, Chappaqua, NY [*Library symbol*] ... NChap
Chappell, NE [*Location identifier*] [*FAA*] ... CNP
Chapter ... C
Chapter ... CH
Chapter ... CHAP
Chapter ... CP
Chapter Director ... CD
Chapter Liaison Officer ... CLO
Char-Oil-Energy-Development [*Process*] [*Project of Office of Coal Research*] ... COED
Char-Swiss Breeders Association ... CSBA
Characato [*Formerly, Arequipa*] [*Peru*] [*Later, FRD*] [*Geomagnetic observatory code*] ... ARE
Character ... C
Character ... CH
Character ... CHAR
Character ... CHR
Character, Capacity, Capital [*Economics*] ... 3C's
Character Control Block [*Data processing*] ... CCB
Character Count [*Typography*] ... CC
Character Disorder Sign [*Psychology*] ... CdS
Character Generator [*Telecommunications*] ... CG
Character Guidance [*Army*] ... CHARGUID
Character-Oriented Message ... COM
Character Position in Frame ... CPIF
Character Printer [*Data processing*] ... CP
Character Register ... CHR
Character Scan or Alternate [*Data processing*] ... CSA
Character Scan Command [*Data processing*] ... CSCN
Character Scan or Fail [*Data processing*] ... CSF
Character Set Computer Development ... CSCD
Character String Scanner [*Computer program*] ... CSS
Characteristic ... CHAR
Characteristic ... CHARC
Characteristic ... CHRST
Characteristic Frequency [*Acoustics*] ... CF
Characteristic Independence ... CI
Characteristic Item Description ... CID
Characteristic Relief ... CR
Characteristic Slope ... CS
Characteristic Statistical Value ... CSV
Characteristics of Materials ... COMAT
Characteristics of Transportation Resources File ... CHSTR
Characters per Column [*Typesetting*] ... CPC
Characters per Hour [*Data processing*] ... CPH
Characters per Inch [*Typesetting*] ... CPI
Characters per Line [*Typesetting*] ... CPL
Characters per Minute [*Data processing*] ... CPM
Characters per Second [*Data processing*] ... CPS
Charactron Tube ... CHT
Charactron Tube ... CRT
Charan Industries [*NASDAQ symbol*] ... CHRN
Charcoal, Ink, Oil, Pencil, and Watercolor [*Acronym is used as title of 1931 volume containing art works by e.e. cummings*] ... CIOPW
Charcoal Viral Transport [*Medium*] [*Microbiology*] ... CVTR
Charcoal Yeast Extract [*Agar medium*] [*Microbiology*] ... CYE
Chardon, OH [*Location identifier*] [*FAA*] ... CXR
Chardon, OH [*Radio station call letters*] ... WBKC
Charge ... CGE
Charge ... CHG
Charge ... CHGE
Charge ... CHRG
Charge Account Bankers Association [*Later, ABA*] ... CABA
Charge d'Affaires [*Department of State Foreign Service*] ... CA
Charge d'Affaires [*Foreign Service*] ... CHG
Charge Conjugation [*Atomic physics*] ... C
Charge Conjugation - Parity - Time-Reversal [*Theorem*] [*Atomic physics*] ... CPT
Charge-Coupled Device [*Electronics*] ... CCD
Charge-Coupled Devices [*Electronics*] ... CCDS
Charge-Coupled Imager ... CCI
Charge-Density Wave [*Physics*] ... CDW
Charge Exchange ... CEX
Charge Exchange Cross Section ... CECS
Charge-Free Anticontamination System ... CFAS
Charge-Injection Device [*Electronics*] ... CID
Charge Material Allocation Processor ... CMAP
Charge Number of a Cell Reaction [*Symbol*] [*Electrochemistry*] ... z
Charge Number Grouping ... CNG
Charge Parity [*Atomic physics*] ... CP
Charge of Quarters [*Army*] ... CQ
Charge-Transfer [*Intermolecular electron transfer*] ... CT
Charge-Transfer Device [*Electronics*] ... CTD
Charge-Transfer Photography ... CTP
Charge-Transfer Spectrum ... CTS
Charge Transforming Operator ... CTO
Charge Transforming Parameter ... CTP
Charged Particle Beam [*Weapon*] [*DoD*] ... CPB
Charged Particle Electrostatic Thruster ... CPET
Charged Particle Equilibrium ... CPE
Charged Particle Lunar Environment Experiment [*NASA*] ... CPLEE
Charged Particles Information Center [*ORNL*] ... CPIC
Charged and Reactive Polymers [*A publication*] ... Charged React Polym
Charged Tape Detection [*Fuel-failure monitor*] [*Nuclear energy*] ... CTD
Charger ... CHGR
Charger-Battery-Regulator Module [*NASA*] ... CBRM
Charger Battery Relay ... CBR
Chargit, Inc. [*NASDAQ symbol*] ... CHGT
Charismatic Renewal Services ... CRS
Charitable/Employee Stock Ownership Plan [*Tax plan*] ... CHESOP
Charities [*A publication*] ... Char
Charities Review [*A publication*] ... Char R
Chariton Herald-Patriot, Chariton, IA [*Library symbol*] ... IaChHP
Chariton, IA [*Location identifier*] [*FAA*] ... CNC
Chariton, IA [*Radio station call letters*] ... KYRS
Chariton Leader, Chariton, IA [*Library symbol*] ... IaChL
Charity ... CHAR
Charity ... CHY

Charity Commission [*British*] CC
Charity Organization Society [*British*] .... COS
Charleroi, PA [*Radio station call letters*] .... WESA
Charleroi, PA [*Radio station call letters*] .... WESA-FM
Charles A. Lindbergh Association [*Defunct*] .... CALA
Charles A. Lindbergh Collectors Club .... CALCC
Charles A. Ransom Public Library, Plainwell, MI [*Library symbol*] ...... MiPl
Charles Babbage Institute for the History of Information Processing ......CBI
Charles Bruning Reproduction Processes ....CB
Charles City, IA [*Radio station call letters*] .... KCHA
Charles City, IA [*Radio station call letters*] .... KCHA-FM
Charles City Public Library, Charles City, IA [*Library symbol*] .... IaChc
Charles City Western Railway Co. [*AAR code*] .... CCW
Charles County Community College [*Maryland*] CCCC
Charles County Community College, La Plata, MD [*Library symbol*] ....MdLapC
Charles Darwin Foundation for the Galapagos Isles ....CDFGI
Charles De Gaulle Airport [*France*] .... CDG
Charles E. Frosst & Co., Montreal, PQ, Canada [*Library symbol*] .....CaQMCF
Charles E. Stevens American Atheist Library and Archives, Inc., Austin, TX [*Library symbol*] ....TxAuA
Charles Edison Memorial Youth Fund .... CEMYF
Charles F. Kettering Foundation, Dayton, OH [*OCLC symbol*] ....OKK
Charles F. Kettering Foundation, Kettering, OH [*Library symbol*].........OKetK
Charles F. Kettering Foundation, Research Laboratory Library, Yellow Springs, OH [*Library symbol*] ....OYesK
Charles H. Roth High School Library, Henrietta, NY [*OCLC symbol*] ..... RVW
Charles H. Taylor Memorial Library, Hampton, VA [*Library symbol*].......ViHa
Charles Ives Society ....CIS
Charles Lamb Bulletin [*A publication*]........................Ch L B
Charles Lamb Society [*British*] .... CLS
Charles Lamb Society. Bulletin [*A publication*] .... CLS
Charles Lamb Society. Bulletin [*A publication*] .... CLSB
Charles Pfizer & Co. [*Research code symbol*] ....CP
Charles River Associates Library, Boston, MA [*OCLC symbol*]...............CRA
Charles River Breeding Laboratories .... CRBL
Charles River Breeding Laboratories [*NASDAQ symbol*] ...... CRIV
Charles S. Peirce Society .... CPS
Charles Stark Draper Laboratory [*MIT*] .... CSDL
Charles Stark Draper Laboratory, Inc., Technical Information Center, Cambridge, MA [*Library symbol*] ..... MCCSD
Charles Stewart Mott Community College [*Formerly, Genesee Community College*] [*Michigan*] .... CSMCC
Charles Town, WV [*Radio station call letters*] .... WXVA
Charles Town, WV [*Radio station call letters*]....... WXVA-FM
Charles Williams Society.. CWS
Charlesbourg [*Quebec*] [*Seismograph station code, US Geological Survey*]....................................CHQ
Charleston [*South Carolina*] [*Airport symbol*] .... CHS
Charleston [*West Virginia*] [*Airport symbol*] .... CRW
Charleston Air Force Base [*South Carolina*] .... CAFB
Charleston Army Depot [*South Carolina*] [*Closed*] .... CHAD
Charleston Community Memorial Hospital, Charleston, IL [*Library symbol*].......................ICharH
Charleston County Library, Charleston, SC [*Library symbol*] ....ScCF
Charleston Diocesan Archives, Roman Catholic Church, Charleston, SC [*Library symbol*] ....ScCRC
Charleston General Hospital, Charleston, WV [*Library symbol*]........WvCGH
Charleston-Huntington, WV [*Television station call letters*] .... WVAH-TV
Charleston, IL [*Radio station call letters*] .... WEIC
Charleston, IL [*Radio station call letters*] .... WEIC-FM
Charleston Library Society, Charleston, SC [*Library symbol*]...............ScC
Charleston, MO [*Radio station call letters*] .... KCHR
Charleston Museum Library, Charleston, SC [*Library symbol*]...............ScCMu
Charleston Naval Shipyard [*South Carolina*] .... CHASNAVSHIPY
Charleston Naval Shipyard [*South Carolina*] .... CHNSY
Charleston Naval Shipyard [*South Carolina*] .... CNSY
Charleston Naval Shipyard [*South Carolina*] .... CNSYD
Charleston Naval Station [*South Carolina*] .... CNAVSTA
Charleston Naval Weapons Annex [*South Carolina*] .....CNWA
Charleston, SC [*Location identifier*] [*FAA*] .... NAO
Charleston, SC [*Television station call letters*] .... WCBD-TV
Charleston, SC [*Radio station call letters*] .... WCEW
Charleston, SC [*Television station call letters*] .... WCIV
Charleston, SC [*Radio station call letters*] .... WCSC
Charleston, SC [*Television station call letters*] ...... WCSC-TV
Charleston, SC [*Radio station call letters*] .... WEZL
Charleston, SC [*Radio station call letters*] .... WGCA
Charleston, SC [*Television station call letters*] .... WITV
Charleston, SC [*Radio station call letters*] .... WOKE
Charleston, SC [*Radio station call letters*] .... WPAL
Charleston, SC [*Radio station call letters*] .... WSCI
Charleston, SC [*Radio station call letters*] .... WSSX
Charleston, SC [*Radio station call letters*] .... WTMA
Charleston, SC [*Radio station call letters*] .... WXTC
Charleston Submarine Training Center [*South Carolina*]......................CSTC
Charleston Training Center [*South Carolina*] .... CTC
Charleston & Western Carolina Railway Co. [*Seaboard Coast Line Railroad*].................................C & WC
Charleston & Western Carolina Railway Co. [*Seaboard Coast Line Railroad*] [*AAR code*] ....CWC

Charleston, WV [*Radio station call letters*] .... WBES
Charleston, WV [*Radio station call letters*] .... WCAW
Charleston, WV [*Radio station call letters*] .... WCHS
Charleston, WV [*Television station call letters*]....... WCHS-TV
Charleston, WV [*Radio station call letters*] .... WQBE
Charleston, WV [*Radio station call letters*] .... WQBE-FM
Charleston, WV [*Radio station call letters*] .... WTIP
Charleston, WV [*Radio station call letters*] .... WVAF
Charleston, WV [*Radio station call letters*] .... WVPN
Charleston, WV [*Radio station call letters*] .... WVSR
Charleston, WV [*Radio station call letters*] .... WXIT
Charleville [*Australia*] [*Airport symbol*] .... CTL
Charlevoix, MI [*Location identifier*] [*FAA*] CVX
Charlevoix, MI [*Radio station call letters*] .... WKHQ
Charlevoix, MI [*Radio station call letters*] .... WVOY
Charlevoix Public Library, Charlevoix, MI [*Library symbol*].................. MiChv
Charley [*Nevada*] [*Seismograph station code, US Geological Survey*] [*Closed*] ....NYC
Charlie [*Phonetic alphabet*]..C
Charlie Hammond's Flying Service, Inc. [*Houma, LA*] [*FAA designator*].................................... HMD
Charlo [*Canada*] [*Airport symbol*] ....YCL
Charlotte [*North Carolina*] [*Mint mark, when appearing on US coins*]...........C
Charlotte [*North Carolina*] [*Airport symbol*] .... CLT
Charlotte Amalie, VI [*Television station call letters*] ..... WBNB-TV
Charlotte Amalie, VI [*Radio station call letters*]........... WIBS
Charlotte Amalie, VI [*Radio station call letters*]........... WSTA
Charlotte Amalie, VI [*Radio station call letters*]...........WSTT
Charlotte Amalie, VI [*Television station call letters*] ..... WTJX-TV
Charlotte Amalie, VI [*Radio station call letters*].......... WVWI
Charlotte Charles, Inc. [*NASDAQ symbol*] ....CAKE
Charlotte County Historical Society, Inc., St. Andrews, NB, Canada [*Library symbol*]...........CaNBACCH
Charlotte-Glades Library System, Port Charlotte, FL [*Library symbol*].........................FPoCG
Charlotte Junior/Senior High School Library, Rochester, NY [*OCLC symbol*] ....RVX
Charlotte Medical Journal [*A publication*] ....Charlotte Med J
Charlotte, MI [*Radio station call letters*] .... WGWY
Charlotte, MI [*Radio station call letters*] .... WMMQ
Charlotte, NC [*Location identifier*] [*FAA*] .... DQG
Charlotte, NC [*Radio station call letters*] .... WAME
Charlotte, NC [*Radio station call letters*] .... WAYS
Charlotte, NC [*Radio station call letters*] .... WBCY
Charlotte, NC [*Radio station call letters*] .... WBT
Charlotte, NC [*Television station call letters*] .... WBTV
Charlotte, NC [*Television station call letters*] .... WCCB-TV
Charlotte, NC [*Radio station call letters*] .... WEZC
Charlotte, NC [*Radio station call letters*] .... WFAE
Charlotte, NC [*Radio station call letters*] .... WGIV
Charlotte, NC [*Radio station call letters*] .... WHVN
Charlotte, NC [*Radio station call letters*] .... WIST
Charlotte, NC [*Television station call letters*] .... WPCQ-TV
Charlotte, NC [*Radio station call letters*] .... WQCC
Charlotte, NC [*Radio station call letters*] .... WROQ
Charlotte, NC [*Radio station call letters*] .... WSOC-FM
Charlotte, NC [*Television station call letters*] .... WSOC-TV
Charlotte, NC [*Television station call letters*] .... WTVI
Charlotte Ordnance Missile Plant................................COMP
Charlotte Public Library, Charlotte, MI [*Library symbol*] .... MiChar
Charlottesville [*Virginia*] [*Airport symbol*] .... CHO
Charlottesville [*Virginia*] [*Seismograph station code, US Geological Survey*] [*Closed*] ....CLT
Charlottesville [*Virginia*] [*Seismograph station code, US Geological Survey*] [*Closed*] ....CTV
Charlottesville [*Virginia*] [*Seismograph station code, US Geological Survey*] CVV
Charlottesville, VA [*Radio station call letters*] .... WCHV
Charlottesville, VA [*Radio station call letters*] .... WINA
Charlottesville, VA [*Radio station call letters*] ..... WQMC-FM
Charlottesville, VA [*Radio station call letters*] .... WTJU
Charlottesville, VA [*Radio station call letters*] .... WUVA
Charlottesville, VA [*Television station call letters*] ..... WVIR-TV
Charlottesville, VA [*Radio station call letters*] .... WWWV
Charlottesville, VA [*Radio station call letters*] .... WXAM
Charlottetown [*Canada*] [*Airport symbol*] .... YYG
Charlottetown, PE [*Television station call letters*] .... CBCT
Charlottetown, PE [*Radio station call letters*] .... CBCT-FM
Charlottetown, PE [*Radio station call letters*] .... CFCY
Charlottetown, PE [*Radio station call letters*] .... CHLQ-FM
Charlottetown, PE [*Radio station call letters*] .... CHTN
Charlottetown, PE [*Television station call letters*] CKCW-TV-1
Charlton, MA [*Radio station call letters*] .... WBPV-FM
Charmed (Quark) [*Atomic physics*] c
Charming Shoppes, Inc. [*NASDAQ symbol*] .... CHRS
Charnwood Forest [*England*] [*Seismograph station code, US Geological Survey*].................................CWF
Charring Ablation Program [*NASA*] .... CHAP
Charriot Resources Ltd. [*NASDAQ symbol*] .... CIORF
Chart..CT
Chart Comparison Unit...CCU

Chart Distribution Data.......CDD
Chart Updating Manual [*Air Force*].......CHUM
Charta [*Paper*] [*Pharmacy*].......CHART
Charta Bibula [*Blotting Paper*] [*Latin*].......CHART BIB
Charta Cerata [*Waxed Paper*] [*Pharmacy*].......CHART CERAT
Chartair, Inc. [*Los Angeles, CA*] [*FAA designator*].......ALS
Charter.......CHAR
Charter.......CHTR
Charter Co. [*NYSE symbol*].......CHR
Charter of Economic Rights and Duties of States [*United Nations*]... CERDS
Charter Long Term.......CHLT
Charter Medical Corp. [*American Stock Exchange symbol*].......CMD
Charter New York Corp. [*NYSE symbol*] [*Delisted*].......CN
Charter Oak Times, Charter Oak, IA [*Library symbol*].......IaChoT
Charter Party [*Transportation*].......CP
Charter Rolls [*British*].......CH
Chartercorp [*NASDAQ symbol*].......CHCP
Chartered Accountant.......CA
Chartered Accountant.......CHARTAC
Chartered Association Executive [*Designation given by American Society of Association Executives*].......CAE
Chartered Bank Auditor [*Designation*].......CBA
Chartered Cartographer.......CC
Chartered Chemist [*British*].......CChem
Chartered Engineer [*British*].......CE
Chartered Engineer [*British*].......C Eng
Chartered Engineer (Melbourne) [*A publication*].......Chart Eng (Melbourne)
Chartered Financial Analyst [*Designation given by Institute of Chartered Financial Analysts*].......CFA
Chartered Institute of Marine Engineers.......CIME
Chartered Institute of Public Finance and Accountancy [*Formerly, IMTA*] [*British*].......CIPFA
Chartered Insurance Broker.......CIB
Chartered Insurance Institute [*British*].......CII
Chartered Librarian [*British*].......CL
Chartered Life Underwriter.......CLU
Chartered Life Underwriters Journal [*A publication*].......CLU J
Chartered Mechanical Engineer [*A publication*].......Chart Mech Eng
Chartered Mechanical Engineer [*A publication*].......Chart Mech Engr
Chartered Mechanical Engineer [*A publication*].......CME
Chartered Municipal Engineer [*A publication*].......Chart Munic Eng
Chartered Patent Agent.......CPA
Chartered Property and Casualty Underwriter.......CPCU
Chartered Public Accountant.......CPA
Chartered Society of Physiotherapy [*British*].......CSP
Chartered Stenographic Reporter.......CSR
Chartered Surveyor [*A publication*].......Chart Surv
Charterers Pay Dues.......CPD
Charters Towers [*Australia*] [*Seismograph station code, US Geological Survey*].......CTA
Charters Towers [*Australia*] [*Seismograph station code, US Geological Survey*].......CTAO
Charters Towers [*Australia*] [*Airport symbol*].......CXT
Chartiers Aero-Maritime de la Seine [*France*].......CAMS
Charting.......CHTG
Charts.......CH
Charvoz-Carsen Corp. [*NASDAQ symbol*].......CHZC
Chase Aircraft Company.......CAC
Chase City, VA [*Location identifier*] [*FAA*].......CXE
Chase City, VA [*Radio station call letters*].......WMEK
Chase Convertible Fund of Boston, Inc. [*NYSE symbol*] [*Delisted*].......CFB
Chase Econometrics Associates, Incorporated [*Information service*]... CEAI
Chase Economic Bulletin [*A publication*].......Chase Econ Bul
Chase Manhattan Bank. International Finance [*A publication*].......Chase Fin
Chase Manhattan Bank, New York, NY [*OCLC symbol*].......ZCB
Chase Manhattan Corp. [*NYSE symbol*].......CMB
Chase Manhattan Mortgage & Realty Trust [*NYSE symbol*] [*Delisted*].......CMR
Chase Public Library, Chase, MI [*Library symbol*].......MiCha
Chase Ranch [*California*] [*Seismograph station code, US Geological Survey*].......CSR
Chase World Information Corporation [*Information service*].......CWIC
Chasmogamous [*Botany*].......CH
Chassis.......CHA
Chassis.......CHAS
Chassis Marking Kit.......CMK
Chasti Osobogo Naznacheniia [*Elements of Special Designation*] [*Political police units attached to the armed forces*] [*USSR*].......ChON
Chateau [*New Zealand*] [*Seismograph station code, US Geological Survey*].......CNZ
Chateau De Ville [*NASDAQ symbol*].......CDEV
Chatham [*Canada*] [*Airport symbol*].......YCH
Chatham, AK [*Location identifier*] [*FAA*].......CYM
Chatham College, Pittsburgh, PA [*OCLC symbol*].......HHC
Chatham College, Pittsburgh, PA [*Library symbol*].......PPiCC
Chatham Courier, Chatham, NJ [*Library symbol*].......NjCC
Chatham Division Royal Marines [*Military unit*] [*British*].......CDRM
Chatham Islands [*New Zealand*] [*Seismograph station code, US Geological Survey*].......CIZ
Chatham-Kent Museum, Chatham, ON, Canada [*Library symbol*].......CaOChaK
Chatham Manufacturing Co. [*NASDAQ symbol*].......CHAT
Chatham, NJ [*Location identifier*] [*FAA*].......CAT
Chatham, ON [*Radio station call letters*].......CBEE-FM
Chatham, ON [*Radio station call letters*].......CFCO
Chatham, ON [*Television station call letters*].......CICI-TV-59
Chatham Public General Hospital, Chatham, ON, Canada [*Library symbol*].......CaOChaH
Chatham Public Library, Chatham, NJ [*Library symbol*].......NjC
Chatham Public Library, Chatham, NY [*Library symbol*].......NCha
Chatham Public Library, Chatham, ON, Canada [*Library symbol*].......CaOCha
Chatham Township Echoes, Chatham, NJ [*Library symbol*].......NjCE
Chatham, VA [*Radio station call letters*].......WKBY
Chatra [*Nepal*] [*Seismograph station code, US Geological Survey*].......CHA
Chatsworth, GA [*Television station call letters*].......WCLP-TV
Chatsworth, GA [*Radio station call letters*].......WQMT
Chattahoochee, FL [*Radio station call letters*].......WENO
Chattahoochee Industrial Railroad [*AAR code*].......CIRR
Chattahoochee Valley Railway Co. [*AAR code*].......CHV
Chattahoochee Valley Regional Library, Columbus, GA [*OCLC symbol*].......GCV
Chattanooga [*Tennessee*] [*Airport symbol*].......CHA
Chattanooga-Hamilton County Bicentennial Library, Chattanooga, TN [*Library symbol*].......TC
Chattanooga-Hamilton County Bicentennial Library, Chattanooga, TX [*OCLC symbol*].......TCH
Chattanooga State Technical Community College, Chattanooga, TN [*Library symbol*].......TCST
Chattanooga State Technical Institute [*Tennessee*].......CSTI
Chattanooga, TN [*Radio station call letters*].......WDEF
Chattanooga, TN [*Radio station call letters*].......WDEF-FM
Chattanooga, TN [*Television station call letters*].......WDEF-TV
Chattanooga, TN [*Radio station call letters*].......WDOD
Chattanooga, TN [*Radio station call letters*].......WDOD-FM
Chattanooga, TN [*Television station call letters*].......WDSI-TV
Chattanooga, TN [*Radio station call letters*].......WDXB
Chattanooga, TN [*Radio station call letters*].......WDYN-FM
Chattanooga, TN [*Radio station call letters*].......WGOW
Chattanooga, TN [*Radio station call letters*].......WMBW
Chattanooga, TN [*Radio station call letters*].......WNOO
Chattanooga, TN [*Television station call letters*].......WRCB-TV
Chattanooga, TN [*Radio station call letters*].......WSKZ
Chattanooga, TN [*Television station call letters*].......WTCI
Chattanooga, TN [*Television station call letters*].......WTVC
Chattanooga, TN [*Radio station call letters*].......WUTC
Chattanooga, TN [*Radio station call letters*].......WZRA
Chattem, Inc. [*NASDAQ symbol*].......CHTT
Chaucer Review [*A publication*].......Chaucer R
Chaucer Review [*A publication*].......ChauR
Chaucer Society [*A publication*].......Chaucer Soc
Chaurjahari [*Nepal*] [*Airport symbol*].......CJR
Chautauqua Airlines [*Jamestown, NY*] [*FAA designator*].......CHQ
Chautauqua-Cattaraugus Library System [*Library network*].......CCLS
Chautauqua-Cattaraugus Library System, Jamestown, NY [*Library symbol*].......NJamC
Chautauqua-Cattaraugus Library System, Jamestown, NY [*OCLC symbol*].......VXU
Chautauqua County Historical Society, Westfield, NY [*Library symbol*].......NWefHi
Chautauqua Literary and Scientific Circle.......CLSC
Chautauquan [*A publication*].......Chaut
Chavis, KY [*Location identifier*] [*FAA*].......DUF
CHB Foods, Inc. [*American Stock Exchange symbol*].......CBF
CHC Corp. [*American Stock Exchange symbol*] [*Delisted*].......CYH
Cheb [*Eger*] [*Czechoslovakia*] [*Seismograph station code, US Geological Survey*] [*Closed*].......CHE
Cheboygan Area Public Library, Cheboygan, MI [*Library symbol*].......MiChe
Cheboygan, MI [*Radio station call letters*].......WCBY
Cheboygan, MI [*Radio station call letters*].......WQLZ-FM
Cheboygan, MI [*Television station call letters*].......WTOM-TV
Chebychev Trajectory Optimization Program.......CHEBYTOP
Chechen [*MARC language code*] [*Library of Congress*].......che
Check.......CH
Check.......CHK
Check.......CK
Check Air [*Milwaukee, WI*] [*FAA designator*].......CHA
Check Area Airports.......CARA
Check Authorization Method.......CAM
Check Authorization Record.......CAR
Check Bit.......CHKB
Check Coil.......CHC
Check Collectors Round Table.......CCRT
Check Digit [*IRS*].......CD
Check Digit Verifier.......CDG
Check Form [*Tool*].......CKFM
Check Gauge [*Tool*].......CKGA
Check Operator.......CKO
Check Processing Control System.......CPCS
Check Signal Return.......CSR
Check Sorter.......CS
Check Status Reply.......CSR
Check Technology Corp. [*NASDAQ symbol*].......CTCQ

Check Template ... CKT
Check Valve ... CHV
Check Valve ... CV
Checker ... CHKR
Checker Club ... CC
Checker Motors Corporation [*NYSE symbol*] [*Delisted*] ... CHC
Checkered [*Navigation markers*] ... CHEC
Checking ... CHKG
Checklist ... C/L
Checkmate ... CHM
Checkout ... CKOUT
Checkout ... CO
Checkout and Automatic Monitoring ... CAM
Checkout Command Decoder ... CCD
Checkout Control and Monitor Subsystem [*NASA*] ... CCMS
Checkout Data Processor [*RADAR*] ... CDP
Checkout Equipment for Onboard Automatic Maintenance ... CEFOAM
Checkout and Fault Isolation [*NASA*] ... COFI
Checkout Interpreter Module ... COIM
Checkout Language [*NASA*] ... COL
Checkout and Maintenance ... CAM
Checkout Operating System ... COSY
Checkout Operations Manual ... COM
Checkout-Oriented Language [*Data processing*] ... COOL
Checkout Test Language [*Data processing*] ... CTL
Checkout Test Set ... COTS
Checkout Time ... COT
Checkout Valve ... COV
Checkpoint [*Data processing*] ... CHKPT
Checkpoint ... CKPT
Checkpoint ... CP
Checkpoint Systems, Inc. [*NASDAQ symbol*] ... CHEK
Checks Anonymous ... CA
Chediak-Higashi Disease [*Medicine*] ... CHD
Chediak-Higashi Syndrome [*Medicine*] ... CHS
Cheektowaga, NY [*Radio station call letters*] ... WECK
Cheese Importers Association of America ... CIAA
Cheese Whey Powder ... CWP
Cheezem Development Corp. [*NASDAQ symbol*] ... CHZM
Chef des Generalstabs des Heeres [*Chief of General Staff of the Army*] [*German military - World War II*] ... CGS
Chef der Zivilverwaltung [*Chief of Civil Affairs Section*] [*German military - World War II*] ... CDZ
Chefornak [*Alaska*] [*Airport symbol*] ... CYF
Chefornak, AK [*Location identifier*] [*FAA*] ... CYF
Chefs de Cuisine Association of America ... CCAA
Chefs de Cuisine Association of America ... CDCA
Chefs International, Inc. [*NASDAQ symbol*] ... CHEF
Cheguitti [*Mauritania*] [*Airport symbol*] ... CGT
Chehalis, WA [*Location identifier*] [*FAA*] ... CLS
Cheju [*South Korea*] [*Airport symbol*] ... CJU
Chekhoslovatskaya Biologiya [*A publication*] ... Chekhoslov Biol
Chekiang Province [*China, Mainland*] [*MARC geographic area code*] [*Library of Congress*] ... a-cc-ch
Chekok [*Alaska*] [*Seismograph station code, US Geological Survey*] ... CKK
Chelan Butte [*Washington*] [*Seismograph station code, US Geological Survey*] ... CBW
Chelan, WA [*Radio station call letters*] ... KOZI
Chelan, WA [*Radio station call letters*] ... KOZI-FM
Chelmsford Library, Chelmsford, United Kingdom [*Library symbol*] ... UkCh
Chelovek i Biosfera [*A publication*] ... Chel Biosfera
Chelsea [*A publication*] ... Chel
Chelsea Industries, Inc. [*NYSE symbol*] ... CHD
Chelsea, London, Islington, Office [*Denoting a location where a manuscript was written*] [*Acronym used as pseudonym of Joseph Addison, British author, 1672-1719*] ... CLIO
Chelsea Public Library, Chelsea, MA [*Library symbol*] ... MChels
Cheltenham [*Maryland*] [*Seismograph station code, US Geological Survey*] [*Closed*] ... CLH
Cheltenham [*United States of America*] [*Geomagnetic observatory code*] ... CLH
Chem. Fabr. Tempelhof [*Germany*] [*Research code symbol*] ... CFT
Chem-Tronics, Inc. [*NASDAQ symbol*] ... CTRN
Chem. Werke Albert [*Germany*] [*Research code symbol*] ... HA
Chemagro, Kansas City, MO [*Library symbol*] ... MoKChe
Chemcell Ltd., Montreal, PQ, Canada [*Library symbol*] ... CaQMCh
Chemed Corp. [*NYSE symbol*] ... CHE
Chemehuevi Mountains [*California*] [*Seismograph station code, US Geological Survey*] ... CMH
Chemeketa Community College, Salem, OR [*OCLC symbol*] ... CHK
Chemeketa Community College, Salem, OR [*Library symbol*] ... OrSaC
Chemeketa Cooperative Regional Library Service [*Library network*] ... CCRLS
Chemetron Corp. [*NYSE symbol*] [*Delisted*] ... CTN
Chemex Pharmaceuticals [*NASDAQ symbol*] ... CHMX
Chemfix Technologies [*NASDAQ symbol*] ... CFIX
Chemia Analityczna [*Warszawa*] [*A publication*] ... Chemia Analit
Chemia Analityczna (Warszawa) [*A publication*] ... Chem Anal (Warszawa)
Chemia Stosowana [*A publication*] ... Chem Stosow
Chemia Stosowana. Seria A [*A publication*] ... Chem Stosow Ser A
Chemia Stosowana. Seria B [*A publication*] ... Chem Stosow Ser B
Chemica Scripta [*A publication*] ... Chem Scr
Chemica Scripta [*A publication*] ... Chem Scripta
Chemical [*or Chemistry*] ... CHEM
Chemical ... CHEML
Chemical [*Freight*] ... CHM
Chemical ... CML
Chemical Abstracts [*A publication*] ... CA
Chemical Abstracts [*A publication*] ... ChemAb
Chemical Abstracts [*A publication*] ... Chem Abstr
Chemical Abstracts Condensates [*A publication*] ... CAC
Chemical Abstracts, Even-Numbered Issue ... CAE
Chemical Abstracts Integrated Subject File [*A publication*] ... CAISF
Chemical Abstracts, Odd-Numbered Issue ... CAO
Chemical Abstracts, Ohio State University, Columbus, OH [*Library symbol*] ... OUCA
Chemical Abstracts Service ... CAS
Chemical Abstracts Service, Columbus, OH [*OCLC symbol*] ... CAS
Chemical Abstracts Service Source Index [*A publication*] ... CASSI
Chemical Abstracts Service. Source Index Quarterly [*A publication*] ... C A Source Index
Chemical Abstracts Subject Index Alert [*A publication*] ... CASIA
Chemical Accident/Incident Control Officer [*Military*] ... CAICO
Chemical Advertisers Group of New York ... CAGNY
Chemical Age [*A publication*] ... C A
Chemical Age [*A publication*] ... Chem Age
Chemical Age of India [*A publication*] ... Chem Age India
Chemical Age International [*A publication*] ... Chem Age Int
Chemical Age (London) [*A publication*] ... Chem Age (Lond)
Chemical Age Survey [*A publication*] ... Chem Ag Sv
Chemical Agent Identification Training Set ... CAITS
Chemical Agent Munition Disposal System [*Army*] ... CAMDS
Chemical and Allied Industries [*Department of Employment*] [*British*] ... CAI
Chemical Analysis Detection Instrumentation Control ... CADIC
Chemical Analysis Facility ... CAF
Chemical Analysis: A Series of Monographs on Analytical Chemistry and Its Applications (New York) [*A publication*] ... Chem Anal (New York)
Chemical Analysis: A Series of Monographs on Analytical Chemistry and Its Applications [*A publication*] ... Chem Anal Ser Monogr Anal Chem Appl
Chemical Automated Search Terminal [*Computer Corp. of America*] [*Information service*] ... CAST
Chemical Binding Effect ... CBE
Chemical and Biological [*Warfare*] [*Formerly, CBR, CEBAR*] [*Military*] ... CB
Chemical and Biological Accident and Incident Control [*Army*] ... CBAIC
Chemical and Biological Accident and Incident Control Plan [*Army*] ... CBAICP
Chemical-Biological Activities [*A publication*] ... CBAC
Chemical-Biological Computer System ... CBCS
Chemical-Biological Coordination Center [*NAS/NRC*] ... CBCC
Chemical and Biological Information Handling [*National Institutes of Health*] ... CBIH
Chemical-Biological Munitions ... CBM
Chemical, Biological, and Radiological [*Warfare*] [*Later, CB*] [*Military*] ... CBR
Chemical, Biological, Radiological Agency [*Military*] ... CBRA
Chemical, Biological, and Radiological Center [*Military*] ... CBRC
Chemical, Biological, Radiological Control Center ... CBRCC
Chemical, Biological, and Radiological Element [*Military*] ... CBRE
Chemical-Biological-Radiological Engineering Group [*Army*] ... CBREG
Chemical, Biological, Radiological, and Nuclear [*Army*] ... CBRN
Chemical, Biological, Radiological Officer [*Army*] ... CBRO
Chemical, Biological, and Radiological Section [*Military*] ... CBRS
Chemical, Biological, Radiological Warfare [*Later, CB*] [*Military*] ... CEBAR
Chemical and Biological Warfare [*Military*] ... CBW
Chemical and Biological Weapons [*Military*] ... CBW
Chemical, Biomedical, and Environmental Instrumentation [*A publication*] ... Chem Biomed Environ Inst
Chemical Blowing Agent [*Plastics technology*] ... CBA
Chemical Bond Approach ... CBA
Chemical Bond Approach Study ... CBAS
Chemical Bulletin [*A publication*] ... Chem Bull
Chemical Business [*A publication*] ... Chem Bus
Chemical Coaters Association ... CCA
Chemical Communications [*Journal of the Chemical Society. Section D*] [*A publication*] ... Chem Commun
Chemical Communications Association ... CCA
Chemical Composition [*Of precious stones*] ... CC
Chemical Compound Registry (System) ... CCR(S)
Chemical Concepts [*A publication*] ... Chem Concepts
Chemical Corps [*Army*] ... CM
Chemical Corps [*Army*] ... CMLC
Chemical Corps Biological Laboratories [*Army*] ... CMLCBL
Chemical Corps Engineering Command [*Army*] ... CMLCENCOM
Chemical Corps Historical Office [*Army*] ... CMLHO
Chemical Corps Material Command [*Army*] ... CMLCMATCOM
Chemical Corps Proving Ground [*Army*] ... CCPG
Chemical Corps Research and Development Command [*Army*] ... CCRDC
Chemical Corps Research and Development Command [*Army*] ... CMLCRDCOM

Chemical Corps Research and Engineering Command [*Army*] ... CMLCRECOM

Chemical Corps Technical Command [*Army*] ... CCTC

Chemical Corps Training Command [*Army*] ... CMLCTNGCOM

Chemical Data Center, Inc. [*Information service*] ... CDC

Chemical Data System ... CDS

Chemical Defence Establishment [*British*] ... CDE

Chemical Defence Experimental Establishment [*British*] ... CDEE

Chemical Defence Experimental Station [*British*] [*World War II*] ... CDES

Chemical Defence Research Establishment [*British*] ... CDRE

Chemical Defense ... CMLDEF

Chemical Dependencies [*A publication*] ... Chem Depend

Chemical Development Corporation [*Geneva, Switzerland*] ... CDC

Chemical Dictionary On-Line [*Data base*] [*National Library of Medicine*] ... CHEMLINE

Chemical Discriminator System ... CDS

Chemical Economics Handbook [*Database*] ... CEH

Chemical Economy and Engineering Review [*A publication*] ... CEER

Chemical Economy and Engineering Review [*A publication*] ... Chem Econ

Chemical Education Material Study ... CHEMS

Chemical Education Planning and Coordinating Committee [*American Chemical Society*] ... CEPACC

Chemical Effects Information Center [*Department of Energy*] ... CEIC

Chemical Energy ... CE

Chemical Engineer ... CE

Chemical Engineer ... Ch E

Chemical Engineer ... Chem E

Chemical Engineer ... Chem Eng

Chemical Engineer [*A publication*] ... Chem Engr

Chemical Engineer [*A publication*] ... Chem Eng

Chemical Engineer (London) [*A publication*] ... Chem Eng (London)

Chemical Engineer (London) [*A publication*] ... Chem Engr (Lond)

Chemical Engineer (Rugby) [*A publication*] ... Chem Eng (Rugby)

Chemical Engineering [*A publication*] ... Chem Eng

Chemical Engineering Catalog [*A publication*] ... CEC

Chemical Engineering Communications [*A publication*] ... Chem Eng Commun

Chemical Engineering Education [*A publication*] ... Chem Eng Educ

Chemical Engineering Information Processing System ... CHIPS

Chemical Engineering Investigation of Reaction Paths [*Data processing*] ... CHIRP

Chemical Engineering Journal [*A publication*] ... Chem Eng J

Chemical Engineering Journal [*A publication*] ... Chem Engrg J

Chemical Engineering and Mining Review [*A publication*] ... Chem Eng and Min Rev

Chemical Engineering Modular Instruction [*Project*] ... CHEMI

Chemical Engineering Monographs [*Elsevier Book Series*] [*A publication*] ... CEM

Chemical Engineering (New York) [*A publication*] ... Chem Eng (NY)

Chemical and Engineering News [*A publication*] ... C & EN

Chemical and Engineering News [*A publication*] ... C & E News

Chemical and Engineering News [*A publication*] ... Chem & Eng N

Chemical and Engineering News [*A publication*] ... Chem Eng News

Chemical Engineering Operations [*MIT*] ... CEO

Chemical Engineering Progress [*A publication*] ... CEP

Chemical Engineering Progress [*A publication*] ... Chem Eng Pr

Chemical Engineering Progress [*A publication*] ... Chem Eng Prog

Chemical Engineering Progress [*A publication*] ... Chem Eng Progr

Chemical Engineering Progress. Symposium Series [*A publication*] ... Chem Eng Progr Symp Ser

Chemical Engineering Progress. Symposium Series [*A publication*] ... Chem Eng Prog Symp Ser

Chemical Engineering Science [*A publication*] ... Chem Engng Sci

Chemical Engineering Science [*A publication*] ... Chem Eng Sc

Chemical Engineering Science [*A publication*] ... Chem Eng Sci

Chemical Engineering World [*A publication*] ... Chem Eng World

Chemical Era [*India*] [*A publication*] ... Chem Era

Chemical Express Co. [*American Stock Exchange symbol*] [*Delisted*] ... CX

Chemical Fabrics [*NASDAQ symbol*] ... CMFB

Chemical Fabrics and Film Association ... CFFA

Chemical Farming [*A publication*] ... Chem Farming

Chemical Gas ... CG

Chemical Geology [*A publication*] ... Chem Geol

Chemical Geology [*A publication*] ... Chem Geology

Chemical Hazard Information Profile [*Environmental Protection Agency*] ... CHIP

Chemical Hazards ... CH

Chemical Hazards Response Information System [*Coast Guard*] ... CHRIS

Chemical Industries [*A publication*] ... Chem Ind

Chemical Industry in Basle ... CIBA

Chemical Industry Council ... CIC

Chemical Industry Developments [*A publication*] ... Chem Ind Dev

Chemical Industry Institute of Toxicology ... CIIT

Chemical Industry for Minorities in Engineering ... ChIME

Chemical Industry Notes [*A publication*] ... CIN

Chemical Information Center [*Indiana University*] ... CIC

Chemical Information and Computer Sciences. Journal [*A publication*] ... Chem Info

Chemical Information and Data System [*Army*] ... CIDS

Chemical Information Management, Incorporated [*Information service*] ... CIMI

Chemical Information Retrieval System [*Army*] ... CIRS

Chemical Information Services [*Stanford Research Institute*] ... CIS

Chemical Information System [*NIH-EPA*] ... CIS

Chemical Inspectorate [*British*] ... CI

Chemical Institute of Canada ... CIC

Chemical Institute of Canada. Joint Conference with the American Chemical Society. Abstracts of Papers [*A publication*] ... Chem Inst Can J Conf Am Chem Soc Abstr Pap

Chemical Instrumentation [*A publication*] ... Chem Instr

Chemical Instrumentation [*A publication*] ... Chem Instrum

Chemical International Information Center ... CIIC

Chemical Ion Generator ... CIG

Chemical Ionization [*Spectrometry*] ... CI

Chemical Ionization/Electron Impact [*Spectroscopy*] ... CI/EI

Chemical Ionization Mass Spectrometry ... CIMS

Chemical Kinetics Information Center [*National Bureau of Standards*] ... CKIC

Chemical Laboratory ... CL

Chemical Laboratory Technician [*or Technology*] [*Navy*] ... LBT

Chemical LASER ... CL

Chemical LASER Mode Control ... CLMC

Chemical LASER Study [*or System*] ... CLS

Chemical LASER System Code ... CLASYC

Chemical Leaman, Inc. [*NASDAQ symbol*] ... CLEA

Chemical Literature [*A publication*] ... CL

Chemical Low-Altitude Missile Puny ... CLAMP

Chemical Machining Template ... CMT

Chemical Machining Template Line ... CMTL

Chemical Manufacture [*Department of Employment*] [*British*] ... CM

Chemical Manufacturers Association [*Formerly, MCA*] ... CMA

Chemical Marketing and Economics ... CM & E

Chemical Marketing and Economics ... CMEC

Chemical Marketing Reporter [*A publication*] ... Chem Market Reptr

Chemical Marketing Reporter [*A publication*] ... Chem Mktg Rep

Chemical Marketing Research Association ... CMRA

Chemical Mass Balance ... CMB

Chemical Materials Catalog ... CMC

Chemical and Metallurgical Engineering [*A publication*] ... Chem & Met Eng

Chemical Milling ... CM

Chemical Milling Machine ... CMM

Chemical Monograph Referral Center [*Consumer Product Safety Commission*] [*Information service*] ... CHEMRiC

Chemical Mutagens [*A publication*] ... Chem Mutagens

Chemical New York Corp. [*NYSE symbol*] ... CHL

Chemical On-Line Data Analyzer [*Interactive Elements, Inc.*] ... CODA

Chemical Operations [*Army*] ... CMLOPS

Chemical Operations System ... CHEOPS

Chemical Orbit-to-Orbit Shuttle [*NASA*] ... COOS

Chemical Oxygen Demand ... COD

Chemical Oxygen Iodine LASER ... COIL

Chemical and Petroleum Engineering [*A publication*] ... Chem Pet Eng

Chemical and Pharmaceutical Bulletin [*A publication*] ... Chem Pharm

Chemical and Pharmaceutical Bulletin (Tokyo) [*A publication*] ... Chem Pharm Bull (Tokyo)

Chemical Physics [*A publication*] ... Chem Phys

Chemical Physics Letters [*A publication*] ... Chem Phys Lett

Chemical Physics Letters [*A publication*] ... Chem P Lett

Chemical Physics of Solids and Their Surfaces [*A publication*] ... Chem Phys Solids Their Surf

Chemical Pigment Co., Metals Division, Baltimore, MD [*Library symbol*] ... MdBCPM

Chemical and Process Engineering [*A publication*] ... Chem & Process Eng

Chemical and Process Engineering [*A publication*] ... Chem Process Eng

Chemical and Process Engineering (London) [*A publication*] ... Chem Process Eng (London)

Chemical Processing [*A publication*] ... Chem Process

Chemical Processing and Engineering (Bombay) [*A publication*] ... Chem Process Eng (Bombay)

Chemical Processing (London) [*A publication*] ... Chem Process (London)

Chemical Progress [*A publication*] ... Chem Progr

Chemical Propulsion Division [*NASA*] ... CPD

Chemical Propulsion Information Agency [*Applied Physics Laboratory, Johns Hopkins University*] ... CPIA

Chemical Public Relations Association [*Later, CCA*] ... CPRA

Chemical, Radiological, Biological Warfare ... CRB

Chemical and Radiological Laboratories [*Army*] ... CRLR

Chemical Reaction Engineering ... CRE

Chemical Reactions Documentation Service [*Derwent Publications Ltd.*] ... CRDS

Chemical Record-Age [*A publication*] ... Chem Rec-Age

Chemical Regulations and Guidelines System [*CRC Systems, Inc.*] [*Information service*] ... CRGS

Chemical Release and Radiation Effects Satellite [*NASA*] ... CRRES

Chemical Remanent Magnetization [*Meteorite*] ... CRM

Chemical Report ... CR

Chemical Research Applied to World Need [*IUPAC*] ... CHEMRAWN

Chemical Research Consultants, Inc. ... CRC

Chemical Research and Development Center [*Army*] ... CRDC

Chemical Research and Development Laboratories [*Army*] ... CRDL

Chemical Research Project [*Military*] ... CRP

Chemical Resistant Coating ... CRC

Chemical Reviews [*A publication*] ... Chem R
Chemical Reviews [*A publication*] ... Chem Rev
Chemical Rubber Company ... CRC
Chemical Rust-Inhibiting ... CRI
Chemical Selection Working Group [*National Cancer Institute*] ... CSWG
Chemical Senses and Flavor [*A publication*] ... Chem Senses
Chemical Society [*Later, RSC*] [*British*] ... CS
Chemical Society. Journal [*London*] [*A publication*] ... Chem Soc J
Chemical Society, London, United Kingdom [*Library symbol*] ... UkLC
Chemical Society Research Unit in Information Dissemination and Retrieval [*British*] ... CSRUIDR
Chemical Society. Reviews [*London*] [*A publication*] ... Chem Soc Re
Chemical Society. Reviews [*London*] [*A publication*] ... Chem Soc Rev
Chemical Society. Special Publication [*London*] [*A publication*] ... Chem Soc Spec Publ
Chemical Specialties Manufacturers Association ... CSMA
Chemical Structure and Nomenclature System [*Environmental Protection Agency*] ... CSNS
Chemical Substances Information Network [*Federal Interagency Toxic Substances Data Committee*] ... CSIN
Chemical Substructure Index [*Trademark*] ... CSI
Chemical System Laboratory, Aberdeen Proving Grounds, MD [*OCLC symbol*] ... ADE
Chemical Systems Laboratory [*Later, CRDC*] [*Army*] ... CSL
Chemical Take-Off [*A publication*] ... Chem Take-Off
Chemical Technicians Curriculum [*Project*] ... ChemTeC
Chemical Technology [*A publication*] ... Chem Tech
Chemical Technology [*A publication*] ... Chem Technol
Chemical Thermodynamics Data Center [*National Bureau of Standards*] ... CTDC
Chemical Thermodynamics and Energy Hazard Evaluation [*American Society for Testing and Materials*] ... CHETAH
Chemical Titles [*A publication*] ... Chem Titles
Chemical Titles [*A publication*] ... CT
Chemical Toilet Association ... CTA
Chemical Transfer ... CT
Chemical Transportation Emergency Center [*Chemical Manufacturers Association*] ... CHEMTREC
Chemical Transportation Industry Advisory Committee ... CTIAC
Chemical Vapor Deposition ... CVD
Chemical Vapor Plating ... CVP
Chemical Vapor Transport ... CVT
Chemical and Volume Control System ... CVCS
Chemical Warfare ... CW
Chemical Warfare - Bacteriological Warfare ... CWBW
Chemical Warfare/Chemical Biological Defense ... CW/CBD
Chemical Warfare Laboratories [*Army*] ... CWL
Chemical Warfare Service [*Army*] ... CWS
Chemical Warfare Service Officer [*Army*] ... CWSO
Chemical Warfare Specialist, Medical [*Navy rating*] ... CWT
Chemical Warfare Technical Committee ... CWTC
Chemical Weapons ... CW
Chemical Week [*A publication*] ... Chem W
Chemical Week [*A publication*] ... Chem Week
Chemical Workers' Union ... CWU
Chemical World Index Key ... CWIK
Chemical Zoology [*A publication*] ... Chem Zool
Chemically [*Freight*] ... CHEMLY
Chemically Active Fluidized Bed [*Fuel gas*] ... CAFB
Chemically Fueled Low-Altitude Missile [*Air Force program*] ... CLAM
Chemically Induced Dynamic Electron Polarization [*Spectrometry*] ... CIDEP
Chemically Induced Dynamic Nuclear Polarization [*Spectrometry*] ... CIDNP
Chemically Initiated Electron Exchange Luminescence ... CIEEL
Chemically-Powered Interorbital Space Shuttle ... CIS
Chemically Pure [*Chemistry*] ... CP
Chemically Rigidized Space Structure ... CRSS
Chemically Sensitive Field Effect Transistor ... CHEMFET
Chemically Sensitive Semiconductor Devices ... CSSD
Chemically Stable Oxide ... CSO
Chemicals in Commerce Information System [*Environmental Protection Agency*] ... CICIS
Chemicals and Petro-Chemicals Journal [*A publication*] ... Chem Petro-Chem J
Chemicals, Plastic Research ... CPR
Chemicals, Runoff, and Erosion from Agricultural Management Systems [*Agricultural Research Service*] ... CREAMS
Chemicals Selected for Equal, Analogous, or Related Character ... CHEMSEARCH
Chemicke Listy [*A publication*] ... Chem Listy
Chemicke Zvesti [*A publication*] ... Chem Zvesti
Chemicky Prumysl [*A publication*] ... Chem Prum
Chemico-Biological Interactions [*A publication*] ... Chem-Bio In
Chemico-Biological Interactions [*A publication*] ... Chem-Biol Interact
Chemie-Anlagen und Verfahren [*A publication*] ... Chem-Anlagen Verfahren
Chemie der Erde [*A publication*] ... Chem Erde
Chemie. Experiment und Didaktik [*A publication*] ... Chem Exp Didakt
Chemie. Experiment und Technologie [*A publication*] ... Chem Exp + Technol
Chemie. Experiment und Technologie [*A publication*] ... Chem Exp Technol
Chemie Gruenenthal GmbH [*Germany*] [*Research code symbol*] ... CG
Chemie-Information und Dokumentation Berlin [*Chemical Information and Documentation-Berlin*] [*Germany*] ... CIDB
Chemie-Ingenieur-Technik [*A publication*] ... Chem-Ing-T
Chemie-Ingenieur-Technik [*A publication*] ... Chem-Ing-Tech
Chemie fuer Labor und Betrieb [*A publication*] ... Chem Lab Betr
Chemie, Mikrobiologie, Technologie der Lebensmittel [*A publication*] ... Chem Mikrobiol Technol Lebensm
Chemie en Techniek (Amsterdam) [*A publication*] ... Chem Tech (Amsterdam)
Chemie und Technik in der Landwirtschaft [*A publication*] ... Chem Tech Landwirt
Chemie in Unserer Zeit [*A publication*] ... Chem Unserer Zeit
Chemiefasern und Textil-Anwendungstechnik [*A publication*] ... Chemiefasern Text-Anwendungstech
Chemiefasern/Textil-Industrie [*A publication*] ... Chemiefasern/Text-Ind
Chemiewerke Homburg [*Germany*] [*Research code symbol*] ... D
Chemiker-Zeitung [*A publication*] ... Chem-Zeitun
Chemiker-Zeitung [*A publication*] ... Chem-Ztg
Chemiluminescence ... CL
Chemisch Weekblad [*Later, Chemisch Weekblad Magazine*] [*A publication*] ... Chem Weekbl
Chemisch Weekblad Magazine [*A publication*] ... Chem Weekb Mag
Chemische Berichte [*A publication*] ... Chem Ber
Chemische Industrie AKU [*Algemene Kunstzidie Unie*]**-Goodrich** [*Belgium*] ... CIAGO
Chemische Industrie (Duesseldorf) [*A publication*] ... Chem Ind (Duesseldorf)
Chemische Produktion [*A publication*] ... Chem Prod
Chemische Reihe [*A publication*] ... Chem Reihe
Chemische Rundschau fuer Mitteleuropa und der Balkan [*A publication*] ... Chem Rdsch Mitteleur
Chemische Technik [*A publication*] ... Chem Tech
Chemische Technik (Leipzig) [*A publication*] ... Chem Tech (Leipzig)
Chemischer Informationsdienst [*A publication*] ... Chem Infd
Chemischer Informationsdienst [*A publication*] ... ChemInform
Chemischer Ingenieur [*Chemical Engineer*] [*German*] ... Chem Ing
Chemisches Zentralblatt [*A publication*] ... C
Chemist and Druggist ... C & D
Chemistry in Australia [*A publication*] ... Chem Aust
Chemistry and Biochemistry of Amino Acids, Peptides, and Proteins [*A publication*] ... Chem Biochem Amino Acids Pept Proteins
Chemistry in Britain [*A publication*] ... Chem in Br
Chemistry in Britain [*A publication*] ... Chem Br
Chemistry in Britain [*A publication*] ... Chem Brit
Chemistry in Canada [*A publication*] ... Chem Can
Chemistry in Ecology [*A publication*] ... CE
Chemistry and Industry [*A publication*] ... Chem Ind
Chemistry and Industry [*A publication*] ... Chem & Ind
Chemistry and Industry [*A publication*] ... Chemy Ind
Chemistry and Industry (London) [*A publication*] ... Chem Ind (Lond)
Chemistry and Industry (London) [*A publication*] ... Chem Ind (London)
Chemistry Letters [*A publication*] ... Chem Lett
Chemistry and Life [*A publication*] ... Chemy Life
Chemistry of Natural Compounds [*A publication*] ... Chem Nat Compd
Chemistry in New Zealand [*A publication*] ... Chem NZ
Chemistry and Physics of Lipids [*A publication*] ... Chem Phys L
Chemistry and Physics of Lipids [*A publication*] ... Chem Phys Lipids
Chemistry Records and Grading System [*Data processing*] ... CRAGS
Chemistry Study Unit [*American Topical Association*] ... CSU
Chemistry Teaching Information Processing System ... CHEMTIPS
Chemistry and Technology of Fuels and Oils [*A publication*] ... Chem Technol Fuels Oils
Chemists' Club (of New York) ... CCNY
Chemists' Club, New York, NY [*Library symbol*] ... NNCC
Chemithermomechanical Pulp [*Papermaking*] ... CTMP
Chemlawn Corp. [*NASDAQ symbol*] ... CHEM
Chemoreceptor Trigger Zone ... CTZ
Chemotactic Factor ... CF
Chemotactic Factor Inactivator [*Immunology*] ... CFI
Chemotaxis-Generating Factor ... CGF
Chemotherapeutic Index [*Medicine*] ... CI
Chemotherapy [*A publication*] ... Chemothera
Chemotherapy. Proceedings of the International Congress of Chemotherapy [*A publication*] ... Chemother Pro Int Congr Chemother
Chemotherapy Research Bulletin ... CRIB
Chemplast, Inc. [*American Stock Exchange symbol*] [*Delisted*] ... CMP
Chemstrand Research Center, Inc., Durham, NC [*Library symbol*] ... NcDurCR
Chemtech (United States) [*Formerly, Chemical Technology*] [*A publication*] ... Chemtech (US)
Chemung County Historical Society, Elmira, NY [*Library symbol*] ... NElmHi
Chemurgic Digest [*A publication*] ... Chem Digest
Chemurgic Digest [*A publication*] ... Chemurgic Dig
Chemway Corp. [*NYSE symbol*] [*Delisted*] ... CMY
Cheney, WA [*Radio station call letters*] ... KEWC-FM
Chengou [*China*] [*Airport symbol*] ... CTU
Chengtu [*Republic of China*] [*Seismograph station code, US Geological Survey*] ... CNU
Chenodeoxycholic [*Biochemistry*] ... CHENIC
Chenodeoxycholic Acid [*Also, CDC, CDCA*] [*Biochemistry*] ... CDA
Chenodeoxycholic Acid [*Also, CDA, CDCA*] [*Biochemistry*] ... CDC

Chenodeoxycholic Acid [*Also, CDA, CDC*] [*Biochemistry*] ... CDCA
Cheque [*British*] ... CHQ
Cheque and Document Personalising [*British*] ... CDP
Cheraw, SC [*Radio station call letters*] ... WCRE
Cheraw, SC [*Radio station call letters*] ... WPDZ
Cherbourg [*France*] [*Airport symbol*] ... CER
Chernovtsy [*USSR*] [*Seismograph station code, US Geological Survey*] [*Closed*] ... CRA
Chernovtsy [*USSR*] [*Seismograph station code, US Geological Survey*] [*Closed*] ... CRB
Cherokee [*MARC language code*] [*Library of Congress*] ... chr
Cherokee County Courthouse, Cherokee, IA [*Library symbol*] ... IaCheCoC
Cherokee County Historical Society, Cherokee, IA [*Library symbol*] ... IaCheCHi
Cherokee County Public Library, Gaffney, SC [*Library symbol*] ... ScGa
Cherokee Group [*NASDAQ symbol*] ... CHKE
Cherokee, IA [*Location identifier*] [*FAA*] ... CKP
Cherokee, IA [*Radio station call letters*] ... KCHE
Cherokee, IA [*Radio station call letters*] ... KCHE-FM
Cherokee National Historical Society ... CNHS
Cherokee, OK [*Location identifier*] [*FAA*] ... CKA
Cherokee Public Library, Cherokee, IA [*Library symbol*] ... IaChe
Cherokee Village, AR [*Location identifier*] [*FAA*] ... CVK
Cherokee Village, AR [*Radio station call letters*] ... KFCM
Cherokee, WY [*Location identifier*] [*FAA*] ... CKW
Cherry-Burrel Corp. [*American Stock Exchange symbol*] ... CHY
Cherry Electronic Products Corp. [*NASDAQ symbol*] ... CHER
Cherry Growers and Industries Foundation ... CGIF
Cherry Hill Free Public Library, Cherry Hill, NJ [*OCLC symbol*] ... CHF
Cherry Hill Free Public Library, Cherry Hill, NJ [*Library symbol*] ... NjCh
Cherry Hill Medical Center, Cherry Hill, NJ [*Library symbol*] ... NjChM
Cherry Hill, NJ [*Radio station call letters*] ... WBEK
Cherry Point [*North Carolina*] [*Seismograph station code, US Geological Survey*] [*Closed*] ... CPC
Cherry Point, North Carolina [*Marine Corps*] ... CPNC
Cherry School District 92, Cherry, IL [*Library symbol*] ... ICherSD
Cherry Valley, NY [*Radio station call letters*] ... WJIV
Cherryville, NC [*Radio station call letters*] ... WCSL
Chesaning Public Library, Chesaning, MI [*Library symbol*] ... MiChes
Chesapeake [*Bay*] [*Virginia and Maryland*] ... CHES
Chesapeake Bay Annex [*Navy*] ... CBA
Chesapeake Bay Center for Environmental Studies [*Smithsonian Institution*] ... CBCES
Chesapeake Bay Institute [*Johns Hopkins University*] ... CBI
Chesapeake Biological Laboratories [*University of Maryland*] ... CBL
Chesapeake Corp. of Virginia [*NYSE symbol*] ... CSK
Chesapeake Division Naval Facilities Engineering Command ... CHES/NAVFAC
Chesapeake Division Naval Facilities Engineering Command ... CHESNAVFACENGCOM
Chesapeake Division Naval Facilities Engineering Command ... DIRCHESDOCKS
Chesapeake Industries [*NASDAQ symbol*] ... CHES
Chesapeake Information Retrieval Service ... CIRS
Chesapeake, OH/Huntington, WV [*Location identifier*] [*FAA*] ... HTW
Chesapeake and Ohio Canal National Monument ... CHOH
Chesapeake and Ohio Historical Society ... COHS
[*The*] **Chesapeake & Ohio Railway Co.** [*Later, Chessie System, Inc.*] ... C & O
[*The*] **Chesapeake & Ohio Railway Co. (Pere Marquette District)** [*AAR code*] ... PM
Chesapeake Research Consortium ... CRC
Chesapeake Science [*A publication*] ... Chesapeake Sci
Chesapeake Seafood Packers Association ... CSPA
Chesapeake Utilities Corp. [*NASDAQ symbol*] ... CHPK
Chesapeake, VA [*Radio station call letters*] ... WCPK
Chesapeake, VA [*Radio station call letters*] ... WFOS
Chesapeake Western Railway [*AAR code*] ... CHW
Chesbro Reservoir [*California*] [*Seismograph station code, US Geological Survey*] ... CBO
Chesebrough-Pond's, Inc. [*NYSE symbol*] ... CBM
Cheshire [*County in England*] ... CHES
Chess Club ... CC
Chess Journalists of America [*Formerly, AUSCJ*] ... CJA
Chess on Stamps Unit [*American Topical Association*] ... CSU
Chess Wing Ltd. [*Great Britain*] [*ICAO designator*] ... DU
Chessco Industrials [*NASDAQ symbol*] ... CHSS
Chessie System, Inc. [*Formerly, The Chesapeake & Ohio Railway Co.*] [*Later, CSX*] [*NYSE symbol*] [*AAR code*] ... CO
Chest [*Medicine*] ... C
Chest [*Medicine*] ... CH
Chest [*Shipping*] ... CHT
Chest-Back [*Medicine*] ... CB
Chest of Drawers ... CDWR
Chest, Heart, and Stroke Journal [*A publication*] ... Chest Heart Stroke J
Chest and Left Arm [*Cardiology*] ... CL
Chest Pain of Unknown Etiology [*Medicine*] ... CPUE
Chest and Right Arm [*Cardiology*] ... CR
Chest Roentgenogram [*Radiology*] ... CR
Chest Strap [*Medicine*] ... CS
Chest, Training [*Parachute*] ... CT
Chest Wall [*Medicine*] ... CW
Chest Wall Stimulation [*Medicine*] ... CWS
Chest X-Ray [*Medicine*] ... CX
Chest X-Ray [*Medicine*] ... CXR
Chestatee Regional Library [*Library network*] ... NGAL
Chester [*British depot code*] ... CHS
Chester Beatty Research Institute [*Great Britain*] [*Research code symbol*] ... CB
Chester, CA [*Location identifier*] [*FAA*] ... CBD
Chester County District Library Center, Exton, PA [*OCLC symbol*] ... PWC
Chester County District Library Center, West Chester, PA [*Library symbol*] ... PWcC
Chester County Historical Society, West Chester, PA [*Library symbol*] ... PWcHi
Chester Free Public Library, Chester, NJ [*Library symbol*] ... NjChe
Chester, IL [*Radio station call letters*] ... KSGM
Chester, PA [*Radio station call letters*] ... WDNR
Chester, PA [*Radio station call letters*] ... WQIQ
Chester, PA [*Radio station call letters*] ... WVCH
Chester, SC [*Radio station call letters*] ... WDZK
Chester, SC [*Radio station call letters*] ... WGCD
Chester, VA [*Radio station call letters*] ... WDYL
Chester, VA [*Radio station call letters*] ... WGGM
Chester White Swine Record Association ... CWSRA
Chesterfield, VA [*Location identifier*] [*FAA*] ... HYU
Chesterton, IN [*Radio station call letters*] ... WDSO
Chesterton Review [*A publication*] ... C Rev
Chestertown, MD [*Radio station call letters*] ... WCTR
Chestnut [*Thoroughbred racing*] ... CH
Chestnut [*Horse racing*] ... CHSTNT
Chestnut Hill College [*Pennsylvania*] ... CHC
Chestnut Hill College, Philadelphia, PA [*OCLC symbol*] ... CHE
Chestnut Hill College, Philadelphia, PA [*Library symbol*] ... PPCCH
Chestnut Ridge Railway Co. [*AAR code*] ... CHR
Cheswick & Harmar [*AAR code*] ... CHH
Cheswick Historical Society ... CHS
Chetham Society [*A publication*] ... Chet Soc
Cheticamp, NS [*Television station call letters*] ... CBHFT-4
Cheticamp, NS [*Television station call letters*] ... CBIT-2
Chetumal [*Mexico*] [*Airport symbol*] ... CTM
Chetvertichnyi Period [*A publication*] ... Chetvertichn Period
Chetwynd [*British Columbia*] [*Seismograph station code, US Geological Survey*] [*Closed*] ... CTC
Chetwynd, BC [*Radio station call letters*] ... CHET
Chevak [*Alaska*] [*Airport symbol*] ... VAK
Cheval-Vapeur [*Horsepower*] [*French*] ... CH-V
Cheval-Vapeur [*Horsepower*] [*French*] ... CV
Chevalier [*Knight title*] ... CHEV
Chevron ... CHEV
Chevron Oil Field Research Company ... COFRC
Chevron Oil Field Research Co., La Habra, CA [*Library symbol*] ... CLhC
Chevron Research Co., Technical Information Center, Richmond, CA [*Library symbol*] ... CRicC
Chewing, Sucking, Swallowing [*Medicine*] ... CSS
Chewings Fescue and Creeping Red Fescue Commission ... CFCRFC
Chexchange Network ... CN
Cheyenne [*MARC language code*] [*Library of Congress*] ... chy
Cheyenne [*Wyoming*] [*Airport symbol*] ... CYS
Cheyenne Airways, Inc. [*Cheyenne, WY*] [*FAA designator*] ... CYA
Cheyenne Mountain Complex [*NORAD*] ... CMC
Cheyenne, OK [*Television station call letters*] ... KWET
Cheyenne Resources [*NASDAQ symbol*] ... CHYN
Cheyenne, WY [*Location identifier*] [*FAA*] ... CYS
Cheyenne, WY [*Radio station call letters*] ... KFBC
Cheyenne, WY [*Radio station call letters*] ... KFBQ
Cheyenne, WY [*Radio station call letters*] ... KKAZ
Cheyenne, WY [*Television station call letters*] ... KLWY
Cheyenne, WY [*Radio station call letters*] ... KRAE
Cheyenne, WY [*Radio station call letters*] ... KSHY
Cheyenne, WY [*Radio station call letters*] ... KUUY
Cheyenne, WY [*Television station call letters*] ... KYCU-TV
Cheyne-Stokes Respiration [*Medicine*] ... CSR
Cheyney State College, Cheyney, PA [*OCLC symbol*] ... PCH
Cheyney State College, Cheyney, PA [*Library symbol*] ... PCheS
Chi Chi's, Inc. [*NASDAQ symbol*] ... CHIC
Chi-Squared Function ... CSF
Chiake Epitheoresis [*A publication*] ... ChE
Chian Federation of America ... CFA
Chiang Ching-kuo [*Son of Nationalist Chinese leader Chiang Kai-shek*] ... CCK
Chiang Kai-shek ... CKS
Chiang Mai [*Thailand*] [*Seismograph station code, US Geological Survey*] ... CHG
Chiang Mai [*Thailand*] [*Seismograph station code, US Geological Survey*] ... CHTO
Chiang Mai [*Thailand*] [*Airport symbol*] ... CNX
Chiang Rai [*Thailand*] [*Airport symbol*] ... CEI
Chiavari [*Italy*] [*Seismograph station code, US Geological Survey*] [*Closed*] ... CHV
Chiayi [*Republic of China*] [*Seismograph station code, US Geological Survey*] ... CHY
Chiayi [*Taiwan*] [*Airport symbol*] ... CYI

Chiba Medical Journal [A publication] .... Chiba Med J
Chibcha [MARC language code] [Library of Congress] .... chb
Chibougamau [Canada] [Airport symbol] .... YMT
Chibougamau, PQ [Radio station call letters] .... CHIB
Chibougamau, PQ [Radio station call letters] .... CJMD
Chicago [Illinois] .... CHI
Chicago [Illinois] .... CHIC
Chicago [Illinois] [Seismograph station code, US Geological
   Survey] [Closed] .... CHK
Chicago [Illinois] [Airport symbol] .... CHI
Chicago Academic Library Council [Library network] .... CALC
Chicago Academy of Fine Arts .... CAFA
Chicago Academy of Science .... CAS
Chicago Academy of Sciences. Bulletin. Natural History
   Miscellanea [A publication] .... Chicago Acad Sci Bull Nat History Misc
Chicago Alliance of Businessmen .... CAB
Chicago & Alton Railroad Co. .... C & A
Chicago Area Transportation Study .... CATS
Chicago Art Institute. Bulletin [A publication] .... Chicago Art Inst Bul
Chicago Art Institute. Calendar [A publication] .... Chicago Art Inst Cal
Chicago Art Institute. Quarterly [A publication] .... Chicago Art Inst Q
Chicago, Aurora, & Elgin Railroad Corp. [AAR code] .... CAE
Chicago Bar Record [A publication] .... Chi B Rec
Chicago Board Options Exchange [Stock options] .... CBOE
Chicago Board of Trade [A futures exchange] .... CBOT
Chicago Board of Trade .... CBT
Chicago Board of Trade, Chicago, IL [OCLC symbol] .... IEY
Chicago Book Clinic .... CBC
Chicago Bridge & Iron Co. [Later, CBI Industries] .... CB & I
Chicago Bridge & Iron Co., Oak Brook, IL [Library symbol] ..... IObC
Chicago, Burlington & Quincy Railroad .... CB & Q
Chicago, Burlington, & Quincy Railroad [Slang] .... Q
Chicago, Burlington, & Quincy Railroad [AAR code] .... CBQ
Chicago City Junior College [Illinois] .... CCJC
Chicago Clinical Chemist [A publication] CCC
Chicago Cluster of Theological Schools [Library network] .... CCTS
Chicago College of Osteopathic Medicine .... CCOM
Chicago College of Osteopathic Medicine, Chicago, IL [Library
   symbol] .... ICCO
Chicago Daily News [A publication] .... CDN
Chicago Daily Tribune, Chicago, IL [Library symbol] .... ICDT
Chicago Dental Society. Review [A publication] .... CDS Rev
Chicago & Eastern Illinois Railroad Co. [Absorbed into Missouri
   Pacific System] .... C & EI
Chicago & Eastern Illinois Railroad Co. [Absorbed into Missouri
   Pacific System] [AAR code] .... CEI
Chicago & Eastern Illinois Railroad Co. [Absorbed into Missouri
   Pacific System] [NYSE symbol] [Delisted] .... CGE
Chicago Envelope Manufacturers Association .... CEMA
Chicago & Erie Railroad Co. .... C & E
Chicago Evangelistic Institute .... CEI
Chicago Gorilla [Slang for a desperado gunman] .... CHICAGORILLA
Chicago Great Western Railway [NYSE symbol] [Delisted] ..... CGW
Chicago Great Western Railway .... C & GWRY
Chicago Heights Free Public Library, Chicago Heights, IL
   [Library symbol] .... ICh
Chicago Heights, IL [Radio station call letters] .... WCGO
Chicago Heights, IL [Radio station call letters] .... WMPP
Chicago Heights Terminal Transfer Railroad Co. [AAR code] .... CHTT
Chicago Helicopter Airways, Inc. [ICAO designator] [Obsolete] .... CH
Chicago Helicopter Airways, Inc. .... CHA
Chicago Helicopter Airways, Inc. [Air carrier designation symbol] .... CHP
Chicago Historical Society, Chicago, IL [Library symbol] ...... ICHi
Chicago, IL [Location identifier] [FAA] .... HKH
Chicago, IL [Location identifier] [FAA] .... IAC
Chicago, IL [Location identifier] [FAA] .... IDN
Chicago, IL [Location identifier] [FAA] .... JAV
Chicago, IL [Location identifier] [FAA] .... MXT
Chicago, IL [Location identifier] [FAA] .... NOH
Chicago, IL [Location identifier] [FAA] .... PYN
Chicago, IL [Location identifier] [FAA] .... RVG
Chicago, IL [Location identifier] [FAA] .... RXZ
Chicago, IL [Location identifier] [FAA] .... TSL
Chicago, IL [Radio station call letters] .... WAIT
Chicago, IL [Radio station call letters] .... WBBM
Chicago, IL [Radio station call letters] .... WBBM-FM
Chicago, IL [Television station call letters] .... WBBM-TV
Chicago, IL [Television station call letters] .... WBBS-TV
Chicago, IL [Radio station call letters] .... WBEZ
Chicago, IL [Radio station call letters] .... WBHI
Chicago, IL [Television station call letters] .... WCFC-TV
Chicago, IL [Radio station call letters] .... WCFL
Chicago, IL [Television station call letters] .... WCIU-TV
Chicago, IL [Radio station call letters] .... WCRW
Chicago, IL [Radio station call letters] .... WCRX
Chicago, IL [Radio station call letters] .... WCYC
Chicago, IL [Radio station call letters] .... WEDC
Chicago, IL [Television station call letters] .... WFLD-TV
Chicago, IL [Radio station call letters] .... WFMT-FM
Chicago, IL [Radio station call letters] .... WFYR
Chicago, IL [Radio station call letters] .... WGCI

Chicago, IL [Radio station call letters] .... WGCI-FM
Chicago, IL [Radio station call letters] .... WGN
Chicago, IL [Television station call letters] .... WGN-TV
Chicago, IL [Radio station call letters] .... WHPK-FM
Chicago, IL [Radio station call letters] .... WIND
Chicago, IL [Radio station call letters] .... WJEZ
Chicago, IL [Radio station call letters] .... WJJD
Chicago, IL [Radio station call letters] .... WJPC
Chicago, IL [Radio station call letters] .... WKKC
Chicago, IL [Radio station call letters] .... WKQX
Chicago, IL [Radio station call letters] .... WLAK
Chicago, IL [Radio station call letters] .... WLOO
Chicago, IL [Radio station call letters] .... WLS
Chicago, IL [Radio station call letters] .... WLS-FM
Chicago, IL [Television station call letters] .... WLS-TV
Chicago, IL [Radio station call letters] .... WLUP
Chicago, IL [Radio station call letters] .... WLUW
Chicago, IL [Radio station call letters] .... WMAQ
Chicago, IL [Television station call letters] .... WMAQ-TV
Chicago, IL [Radio station call letters] .... WMBI
Chicago, IL [Radio station call letters] .... WMBI-FM
Chicago, IL [Radio station call letters] .... WMET
Chicago, IL [Radio station call letters] .... WNIB
Chicago, IL [Radio station call letters] .... WOUI
Chicago, IL [Radio station call letters] .... WSBC
Chicago, IL [Television station call letters] .... WSNS-TV
Chicago, IL [Radio station call letters] .... WSSD
Chicago, IL [Television station call letters] [Letters stand for
   "Windows to the World"] .... WTTW
Chicago, IL [Radio station call letters] .... WUSN
Chicago, IL [Radio station call letters] .... WXRT
Chicago, IL [Television station call letters] .... WYCC
Chicago, IL [Radio station call letters] .... WZRD
Chicago & Illinois Midland Railway Co. .... C & IM
Chicago & Illinois Midland Railway Co. [AAR code] .... CIM
Chicago & Illinois Western Railroad [AAR code] .... CIW
Chicago, Indianapolis, & Louisville [Louisville & Nashville
   Railroad Co.] [AAR code] CIL
Chicago Jewish Forum [A publication] .... CJF
Chicago-Joliet Livestock Marketing Center .... CJLMC
Chicago Journalism Review [A publication] .... Chi Jrl R
Chicago Journalism Review [A publication] .... CJR
Chicago, Kalamazoo, & Saginaw Railway [AAR code] .... CKS
Chicago-Kent College of Law .... CKCL
Chicago-Kent Law Review [A publication] .... Chi-Kent L Rev
Chicago Law Institute, Chicago, IL [Library symbol] .... ICLaw
Chicago Linear Music Language .... CLML
Chicago Livestock Exchange .... CLE
Chicago - Loyola [Illinois] [Seismograph station code, US
   Geological Survey] .... CHI
Chicago Lutheran Theological Seminary .... CLTS
Chicago Medical Examiner [A publication] .... Chicago Med Exam
Chicago Medical School .... CMS
Chicago Medical School Quarterly [A publication] .... Chic Med Sch Q
Chicago [Illinois] Meigs Field [Airport symbol] .... CGX
Chicago Mercantile Exchange .... CME
Chicago Mercantile Exchange, Chicago, IL [OCLC symbol] ...... IHU
Chicago [Illinois] Midway [Airport symbol] .... MDW
Chicago [Illinois] Midway Airport [Airport symbol] .... MDW
Chicago Midway Laboratory [Army] .... CML
Chicago and Midwest Envelope Manufacturers Association
   [Defunct] .... CMEMA
Chicago Milwaukee Corp. [NYSE symbol] .... CHG
Chicago, Milwaukee, & Gary Railroad [Nickname: Cold,
   Miserable, and Grouchy] .... CM & G
Chicago, Milwaukee, St. Paul, & Pacific Railroad Co. ...... CM ST P & P
Chicago, Milwaukee, St. Paul, & Pacific Railroad Co. [AAR code] .... MILW
Chicago, Milwaukee, St. Paul & Pacific Railroad Co. [NYSE
   symbol] [Delisted] .... ST
Chicago Municipal Reference Library, Chicago, IL [OCLC symbol] .... IBF
Chicago Municipal Reference Library, Chicago, IL [Library symbol] .... ICMR
Chicago Natural History Museum .... CNHM
Chicago Natural History Museum. Annual Report [A publication] ....
   .... Chic Nat Hist Mus Annu Rep
Chicago North Shore & Milwaukee R. R. [AAR code] .... CNSM
Chicago & North Western Railway Co. [NYSE symbol] [Delisted] .... NW
Chicago & North Western Transportation Co. [AAR code] [NYSE
   symbol] .... CNW
Chicago & North Western Transportation Co. [Nicknames: Can't
   and Never Will, Cheap and Nothing Wasted] .... C & NW
Chicago & Northern Pacific Railroad .... C & NPRR
Chicago [Illinois] O'Hare Airport [Airport symbol] [Derived from
   former name: Orchard Field] .... ORD
Chicago Open Board of Trade .... COBT
Chicago Operations Office [Energy Research and Development
   Administration] .... COO
Chicago Operations and Regional Office [Department of Energy] .... CORO
Chicago Outer Belt R. R. [AAR code] .... EJE
Chicago Pile [Nuclear reactor] .... CP
Chicago Pile-5 [Nuclear heavy-water-research reactor] CP-5

Chicago-Pittsburgh [*Proposed name for possible "super-city" formed by growth and mergers of other cities*] CHIPITTS
Chicago Playing Card Collectors CPCC
Chicago Pneumatic Tool Co. [*NYSE symbol*] CGG
Chicago Produce Terminal Co. [*Later, CPTC*] [*AAR code*] CPT
Chicago Produce Terminal Company [*Formerly, CPT*] [*AAR code*] CPTC
Chicago Psychoanalytic Literature Index [*A publication*] Chicago Psychoanal Lit Ind
Chicago Public Library, Chicago, IL [*OCLC symbol*] CGP
Chicago Public Library, Chicago, IL [*Library symbol*] IC
Chicago Public Library System [*Library network*] CLS
Chicago Railroad Terminal Information System [*Pronounced "Curtis"*] CRTIS
Chicago Reactor CR
Chicago Review [*A publication*] Chicago R
Chicago Review [*A publication*] Chic R
Chicago Review [*A publication*] ChiR
Chicago Ridge Public Library, Chicago Ridge, IL [*Library symbol*] ICr
[*The*] **Chicago River & Indiana Railway Co.** [*Absorbed into Consolidated Rail Corp.*] CR & I
[*The*] **Chicago River & Indiana Railway Co.** [*Absorbed into Consolidated Rail Corp.*] [*AAR code*] CRI
Chicago Rivet & Machine Co. [*American Stock Exchange symbol*] CVR
Chicago, Rock Island, & Pacific Railroad Co. [*Nickname: The Baby Road*] CRI & P
Chicago, Rock Island, & Pacific Railroad Co. [*NYSE symbol*] [*AAR code*] RI
Chicago, St. Paul, Minneapolis, & Omaha R. R. [*AAR code*] CMO
Chicago, St. Paul, Minneapolis, & Omaha R. R. CSTPM & O
Chicago School of Professional Psychology, Chicago, IL [*OCLC symbol*] JAX
Chicago Schools Journal [*A publication*] Chicago Sch J
Chicago Short Line Railway Co. [*AAR code*] CSL
Chicago and South Consortium [*Library network*] C & SC
Chicago South Shore & South Bend Railroad [*AAR code*] CSS
Chicago State University, Chicago, IL [*OCLC symbol*] IAA
Chicago State University, Chicago, IL [*Library symbol*] ICSU
Chicago Studies [*A publication*] Chicago Studs
Chicago Suburban Motor Carriers Association, Inc., Homewood IL [*STAC*] CHS
Chicago Sun Book Week [*A publication*] CSBW
Chicago Sun-Times and Chicago Daily News, Chicago, IL [*Library symbol*] ICSN
Chicago Sunday Tribune [*A publication*] CST
Chicago Symphony Orchestra CSO
Chicago Symphony Orchestra. Program Notes [*A publication*] Chi Sym
Chicago Teachers College [*Later, Chicago State University*] CTC
Chicago Technical College CTC
Chicago, Terre Haute, & Southeastern R. R. [*AAR code*] CTSE
Chicago Theological Seminary CTS
Chicago Theological Seminary, Chicago, IL [*Library symbol*] ICT
Chicago Theological Seminary, Chicago, IL [*OCLC symbol*] IDG
Chicago Transit Authority CTA
Chicago Transit Authority, Chicago, IL [*OCLC symbol*] IBB
Chicago Transit Authority, Chicago, IL [*Library symbol*] ICTA
Chicago Tribune Magazine [*A publication*] Chi T M
Chicago Union Station Co. [*AAR code*] CUST
Chicago. University. Department of Geography. Research Paper [*A publication*] Chicago Univ Dept Geography Research Paper
Chicago. University. Department of Geography. Research Paper [*A publication*] Chic Univ Dep Geogr Res Pap
Chicago-University of Illinois [*RADAR system*] CHILL
Chicago/West Chicago, IL [*Location identifier*] [*FAA*] DPA
Chicago, West Pullman, & Southern Railroad Co. [*AAR code*] CWP
Chicago & Western Indiana Railroad Co. [*AAR code*] CWI
Chicago White Sox [*Baseball team*] CHISOX
Chicago Yellow Cab Co., Inc. [*NYSE symbol*] [*Delisted*] CYC
Chicana Rights Project CRP
Chicano Education Project CEP
Chicano Press Association CPA
Chicano Training Center CTC
Chichen Itza [*Mexico*] [*Airport symbol*] CZA
Chichibu [*Japan*] [*Seismograph station code, US Geological Survey*] CHJ
Chichijima [*Bonin Islands*] [*Seismograph station code, US Geological Survey*] CBI
Chichijima [*Japan*] [*Geomagnetic observatory code*] CBI
Chick Cell Agglutination [*Vaccine potency test*] CCA
Chick Embryo Fibroblast CEF
Chick Embryo Origin CEO
Chick Embryonic Skin CES
Chick Fibroblast [*Cytology*] CF
Chick Heart Fibroblast [*Cytology*] CHF
Chick-Martin [*Test*] [*Microbiology*] CM
Chick Red Blood Cells CRBC
Chickamauga and Chattanooga National Military Park CHCH
Chickasaw, AL [*Radio station call letters*] WJQY
Chickasaw Horse Association CHA
Chickasaw Library System, Ardmore, OK [*OCLC symbol*] CKL
Chickasaw Library System, Ardmore, OK [*Library symbol*] OkArC
Chickasha Cotton Oil Co. [*NYSE symbol*] [*Delisted*] CIK
Chickasha, OK [*Radio station call letters*] KWCO
Chickasha, OK [*Radio station call letters*] KXXK
Chicken CHKN
Chicken, AK [*Location identifier*] [*FAA*] CKX
Chicken Embryo CE
Chicken Embryo Lethal Orphan [*Virus*] CELO
Chicken Gamma-Globulin [*Immunology*] CGG
Chicken Thymidine Kinase [*An enzyme*] ChTK
Chicken Unlimited Enterprises, Inc. [*American Stock Exchange symbol*] [*Delisted*] CUE
Chickenpox [*Also, Cp*] [*Medicine*] CHPX
Chickenpox [*Also, CHPX*] [*Medicine*] Cp
Chickering House, Dover, MA [*Library symbol*] MDovC
Chiclayo [*Peru*] [*Airport symbol*] CIX
Chico [*California*] [*Seismograph station code, US Geological Survey*] CCO
Chico [*California*] [*Airport symbol*] CIC
Chico, CA [*Radio station call letters*] KCHO
Chico, CA [*Radio station call letters*] KFMF
Chico, CA [*Radio station call letters*] KHSL
Chico, CA [*Television station call letters*] KHSL-TV
Chico, CA [*Radio station call letters*] KPAY
Chico, CA [*Radio station call letters*] KPAY-FM
Chico Public Library, Chico, CA [*Library symbol*] CChi
Chicopee, MA [*Radio station call letters*] WACE
Chicopee Public Library, Chicopee, MA [*Library symbol*] MChi
Chicoutimi, PQ [*Radio station call letters*] CBJ
Chicoutimi, PQ [*Radio station call letters*] CBJE-FM
Chicoutimi, PQ [*Television station call letters*] CBJET
Chicoutimi, PQ [*Radio station call letters*] CBJ-FM
Chicoutimi, PQ [*Television station call letters*] CIVV-TV
Chicoutimi, PQ [*Radio station call letters*] CJMT
Chicoutimi, PQ [*Television station call letters*] CJPM-TV
Chief C
Chief CH
Chief CHF
Chief Accountant CA
Chief Accountant Officer [*RAF*] [*British*] CAO
Chief Activation Engineer CAE
Chief Administrative Engineer CAE
Chief Administrative Officer CAO
Chief Advisor CA
Chief Advisor, International District Office [*FAA*] CAIDO
Chief Advisor, International Field Office [*FAA*] CAIFO
Chief, Aerial Reconnaissance Coordination, All Hurricanes [*National Hurricane Center*] CARCAH
Chief Aerographer [*Navy rating*] [*Obsolete*] CAER
Chief Aerographer [*Navy rating*] [*Obsolete*] CHAER
Chief Aerographer's Mate [*Navy rating*] [*Obsolete*] CAERM
Chief Agency Officer [*Insurance*] CAO
Chief of Air Corps [*World War II*] C of AC
Chief of Air Corps [*World War II*] CAC
Chief of Air Defense CAD
Chief, Air Force Advisory Group CHAFAG
Chief of Air Force Chaplains C of AFCH
Chief of Air Force Chaplains COFAFCH
Chief, Air Force Section CHAFSEC
Chief of Air Staff [*World War II*] C of AS
Chief of Air Staff [*World War II*] CAS
Chief, Aircraft Maintenance CAM
Chief Aircrew Survival Equipmentman [*Formerly, Chief Parachute Rigger*] [*Navy rating*] PRC
Chief, Airport District Office [*FAA*] CADO
Chief Airship Rigger [*Navy rating*] [*Obsolete*] CAR
Chief Airways Technical District Office CATDO
Chief Airways Technical Field Office CATFO
Chief of the Army Air Forces [*World War II*] C of AAF
Chief of the Army Air Forces [*World War II*] CAAF
Chief of Army Audit Agency CAAA
Chief of Army Aviation CAA
Chief, Army Reserve CAR
Chief, Army Reserve and Reserve Officers Training Corps Affairs CARROTC
Chief Artillery Controller CAC
Chief Aviation Machinist's Mate (Reciprocating) [*Navy rating*] ADC
Chief Aviation Pilot [*Navy, Coast Guard*] CAP
Chief Baron [*British*] CB
Chief Boatswain [*Navy rating*] [*Obsolete*] CHBOSN
Chief Boatswain's Mate [*Navy rating*] [*Obsolete*] CBM
Chief Boatswain's Mate, A [*Master-at-Arms*] [*Navy rating*] [*Obsolete*] CBMM
Chief Boatswain's Mate, Acting [*Navy rating*] [*Obsolete*] CBMA
Chief Boatswain's Mate, Construction Battalion, Boatswain [*Navy rating*] [*Obsolete*] CBMCBB
Chief Boatswain's Mate, Construction Battalion, Stevedore [*Navy rating*] [*Obsolete*] CBMCBS
Chief Boatswain's Mate, Ship Repair, Canvasman [*Navy rating*] [*Obsolete*] CBMSRS
Chief Boatswain's Mate, Ship Repair, Crane Operator [*Navy rating*] [*Obsolete*] CBMSRC
Chief Boatswain's Mate, Ship Repair, Rigger [*Navy rating*] [*Obsolete*] CBMSRR
Chief Boilermaker [*Navy rating*] [*Obsolete*] CB

Chief Boilermaker [*Coast Guard*] ... CBMKR
Chief Boilermaker, Ship Repair [*Navy*] ... CBSR
Chief Bombardment Liaison Officer [*Navy*] ... CBLO
Chief of Budget and Finance Division [*Supreme Headquarters Allied Powers Europe*] ... CBUDFIN
Chief of Budget and Finance Division [*Supreme Headquarters Allied Powers Europe*] ... CCM
Chief Builder [*Navy rating*] ... BUC
Chief of the Bureau of Aeronautics [*Obsolete*] [*Navy*] ... CHBUAER
Chief of the Bureau of Medicine and Surgery [*Navy*] ... CHBUMED
Chief of the Bureau of Naval Personnel ... CHBUPERS
Chief of the Bureau of Ordnance [*Obsolete*] [*Navy*] ... CHBUORD
Chief of the Bureau of Ships [*Obsolete*] [*Navy*] ... CHBUSHIPS
Chief of the Bureau of Supplies and Accounts [*Obsolete*] [*Navy*] ... CHBUSANDA
Chief of the Bureau of Yards and Docks [*Obsolete*] [*Navy*] ... CHBUDOCKS
Chief Cable Censor [*Navy rating*] [*Obsolete*] ... CCC
Chief Carpenter [*Navy rating*] [*Obsolete*] ... CHCARP
Chief Carpenter's Mate [*Navy rating*] [*Obsolete*] ... CCM
Chief Carpenter's Mate, Construction Battalion, Builder [*Navy rating*] [*Obsolete*] ... CCMCBB
Chief Carpenter's Mate, Construction Battalion, Draftsman [*Navy rating*] [*Obsolete*] ... CCMCBD
Chief Carpenter's Mate, Construction Battalion, Excavation Foreman [*Navy rating*] [*Obsolete*] ... CCMCBE
Chief Carpenter's Mate, Construction Battalion, Surveyor [*Navy rating*] [*Obsolete*] ... CCMCBS
Chief Carpenter's Mate, Ship Repair, Boatbuilder, Wood [*Navy rating*] [*Obsolete*] ... CCMSRB
Chief Carpenter's Mate, Ship Repair, Joiner [*Navy rating*] [*Obsolete*] ... CCMSRJ
Chief of Cavalry ... C of CAV
Chief of Chaplains [*Later, CCH*] [*Army*] ... CC
Chief of Chaplains [*Formerly, CC, C of CH, COFCH*] [*Army*] ... CCH
Chief of Chaplains [*Navy*] ... COC
Chief of Chaplains [*Later, CCH*] [*Army*] ... COFCH
Chief of Chaplains [*Later, CCH*] [*Army*] ... C of CH
Chief Chemical Officer [*Army*] ... CCMLO
Chief Chemical Officer [*Army*] ... CCO
Chief of the Chemical Warfare Service [*World War II*] ... C of CWS
Chief of the Chemical Warfare Service [*World War II*] ... CCWS
Chief of Civil Affairs [*Army*] ... CCA
Chief Civil Affairs Officer [*Navy*] ... CCAO
Chief Civil Affairs Officer (Burma) [*British*] ... CCAO(B)
Chief of Civil Engineers [*Army*] ... CHCIVENGS
Chief Clerk ... CC
Chief Clerk of the Admiralty [*British*] ... CCA
Chief of Coast Artillery ... C of CA
Chief of Combined Operations ... CCO
Chief Commanding Officer ... CCO
Chief Commissary Steward [*Navy rating*] [*Obsolete*] ... CCS
Chief Commissary Steward [*Navy rating*] [*Obsolete*] ... CCSTD
Chief Commissaryman [*Later, MSC*] [*Navy rating*] ... CSC
Chief of Communications - Electronics ... CCE
Chief Complaint [*Medicine*] ... CC
Chief Constable [*Scotland Yard*] ... CC
Chief Controller ... CC
Chief Controller [*Air Force*] ... CCNT
Chief Controller [*Aviation*] ... CCTLR
Chief Cook [*Navy rating*] [*Obsolete*] ... CCK
Chief Cook [*Navy rating*] [*Obsolete*] ... CHCK
Chief Cook (Baker) [*Navy rating*] [*Obsolete*] ... CCK(B)
Chief Cook (Commissary) [*Navy rating*] [*Obsolete*] ... CCK(C)
Chief, Corps of Engineers [*Army*] ... CCE
Chief Counsel ... CC
Chief Damage Controlman [*Navy*] ... DCC
Chief Data Processing Technician [*Formerly, MAC*] [*Navy rating*] ... DPC
Chief Decision Makers ... CDM
Chief of Defence Procurement [*British*] ... CDP
Chief of Defence Staff [*British*] ... CDS
Chief of Defense ... CHOD
Chief, Defense Liaison Group ... CHDLG
Chief of Detectives ... CD
Chief of Division ... CD
Chief Draftsman ... CD
Chief Draftsman's Instructions ... CDI
Chief Electoral Officer [*Canada*] ... CEO
Chief Electrician [*Navy rating*] [*Obsolete*] ... CHELEC
Chief Electrician's Mate [*Navy rating*] [*Obsolete*] ... CEM
Chief Electrician's Mate, Construction Battalion, Communications [*Navy rating*] [*Obsolete*] ... CEMCBC
Chief Electrician's Mate, Construction Battalion, Draftsman [*Navy rating*] [*Obsolete*] ... CEMCBD
Chief Electrician's Mate, Construction Battalion, General [*Navy rating*] [*Obsolete*] ... CEMCBG
Chief Electrician's Mate, Construction Battalion, Line and Station [*Navy rating*] [*Obsolete*] ... CEMCBL
Chief Electrician's Mate, Ship Repair, General Electrician [*Navy rating*] [*Obsolete*] ... CEMSRG
Chief Electrician's Mate, Ship Repair, IC Repairman [*Navy rating*] [*Obsolete*] ... CEMSRT
Chief Electrician's Mate, Ship Repair, Shop Electrician [*Navy rating*] [*Obsolete*] ... CEMSRS
Chief Engineer [*Navy*] ... CE
Chief of Engineers [*Later, COE*] [*Army*] ... C of E
Chief of Engineers [*Later, COE*] [*Army*] ... CE
Chief of Engineers [*Later, COE*] [*Army*] ... C of ENGRS
Chief of Engineers [*Formerly, CE, C of E, C of ENGRS, COFENGS*] [*Army*] ... COE
Chief of Engineers [*Later, COE*] [*Army*] ... COFENGS
Chief Executive Dockyard [*Navy*] [*British*] ... CED
Chief Executive Officer ... CEO
Chief Executives Forum ... CEF
Chief of Field Artillery ... CFA
Chief of Finance [*Army*] ... C of F
Chief of Finance [*Army*] ... CF
Chief of Finance [*Army*] ... COFF
Chief of Finance and Accounting [*Army*] ... CF & A
Chief Financial Officer ... CFO
Chief Fire Controlman [*Navy rating*] [*Obsolete*] ... CFC
Chief Fire Controlman, Operator [*Navy rating*] [*Obsolete*] ... CFCO
Chief Fire Controlman, Submarines [*Navy rating*] [*Obsolete*] ... CFCS
Chief of Fleet Support [*Navy*] [*British*] ... CFS
Chief Flying Instructor [*RAF*] [*British*] ... CFI
Chief of the General Staff [*in the field*] [*Formerly, CIGS*] [*Military*] [*British*] ... CGS
Chief of Government ... COG
Chief Gunner [*Navy rating*] [*Obsolete*] ... CHGUN
Chief Gunner's Mate [*Navy rating*] [*Obsolete*] ... CGM
Chief Gunner's Mate, Construction Battalion, Armorer [*Navy rating*] [*Obsolete*] ... CGMCBG
Chief Gunner's Mate, Construction Battalion, Powderman [*Navy rating*] [*Obsolete*] ... CGMCBP
Chief Gunner's Mate, Technician [*Navy rating*] ... GMTC
Chief Illustrator Draftsman [*Navy rating*] ... DMC
Chief of the Imperial General Staff [*Later, CGS*] [*British*] ... CIGS
Chief Industrial Property ... CIP
Chief of Information [*Also, CINFO*] [*Navy*] ... CHINFO
Chief of Information [*Army*] ... CI
Chief of Information [*Also, CHINFO*] [*Navy*] ... CINFO
Chief Inspector ... CI
Chief Inspector of Armaments ... CIA
Chief Inspector of Engineering and Signal Stores [*Military*] [*British*] ... CIESS
Chief Inspector of Land Service Ammunition ... CILSA
Chief Inspector of Naval Ordnance [*British*] ... CINO
Chief Instructor ... CI
Chief Instrumentman [*Navy rating*] ... IMC
Chief, Intelligence Corps ... CINTC
Chief Intercept Director ... CIND
Chief Japanese Maritime Staff Office ... CMSO
Chief of the Joint General Staff [*Vietnam*] ... CJGS
Chief, Joint United States Military Advisory Group [*Followed by name of country*] ... CHJUSMAG
Chief Journalist [*Navy rating*] ... JOC
Chief Judge [*Sports*] ... CJ
Chief Justice [*Various supreme courts*] ... CJ
Chief, Korea Military Assistance Group ... CHKMAG
Chief Labour Management Officer [*Ministry of Supply*] [*British*] ... CLMO
Chief Launch Vehicle Test Conductor [*NASA*] ... CLTC
Chief of Legislative Liaison [*Army*] ... CLL
Chief Lithographer [*Navy rating*] ... LIC
Chief, Logistics Data Management Office [*Army*] ... C/LDMO
Chief Machine Accountant [*Later, DPC*] [*Navy rating*] ... MAC
Chief Machinist [*Navy rating*] [*Obsolete*] ... CHMACH
Chief Machinist's Mate [*Navy rating*] [*Obsolete*] ... CMM
Chief Machinist's Mate, Construction Battalion, Equipment Operator [*Navy rating*] [*Obsolete*] ... CMMCBE
Chief Machinist's Mate, Industrial Gas Generating Mechanic [*Navy rating*] [*Obsolete*] ... CMMG
Chief Machinist's Mate, Refrigeration [*Navy rating*] [*Obsolete*] ... CMMR
Chief Machinist's Mate, Ship Repair, Outside Machinist [*Navy rating*] [*Obsolete*] ... CMMSRO
Chief Machinist's Mate, Shop [*Navy rating*] [*Obsolete*] ... CMMS
Chief Mailman [*Navy rating*] [*Obsolete*] ... CMAM
Chief Maintenance Officer ... CMO
Chief Marine Gunner [*Navy rating*] ... CMG
Chief Marketing Officer [*Insurance*] ... CMO
Chief Master at Arms [*Navy rating*] ... CMAA
Chief Master Sergeant ... CMSGT
Chief Master Sergeant of the Air Force ... CMSAF
Chief Mechanical and Electrical Engineer [*Air Force*] [*British*] ... CMEE
Chief Mechanical Engineer [*Military*] [*British*] ... CME
Chief Medical Officer [*Military*] ... CMO
Chief Mess Management Specialist [*Formerly, CSC, CST, SDC*] [*Navy rating*] ... MSC
Chief Metalsmith [*Navy rating*] [*Obsolete*] ... CM
Chief Metalsmith, Ship Repair, Blacksmith [*Navy rating*] [*Obsolete*] ... CMSRB
Chief Metalsmith, Ship Repair, Coppersmith [*Navy rating*] [*Obsolete*] ... CMSRC

Chief Metalsmith, Ship Repair, Sheet Metal Worker [*Navy rating*] [*Obsolete*] ... CMSRS
Chief, Military Assistance Advisory Group [*Followed by name of country*] ... CHMAAG
Chief, Military Assistance Advisory Group, Korea (Provisional) ... CHPROVMAAGK
Chief, Military Equipment Delivery Team ... CHMEDT
Chief of Military History [*Army*] ... CMH
Chief, Military Planning Office ... CHMPO
Chief, Military Technical Advisory Group ... CHMILTAG
Chief of Mission Operations [*NASA*] ... CMO
Chief Motor Machinist's Mate [*Navy rating*] [*Obsolete*] ... CMOMM
Chief Motor Machinist's Mate, Ship Repair, Diesel Engineering Mechanic [*Navy rating*] [*Obsolete*] ... CMOMSRD
Chief Motor Machinist's Mate, Ship Repair, Gasoline Engineering Mechanic [*Navy rating*] [*Obsolete*] ... CMOMSRG
Chief Moulder [*Navy rating*] [*Obsolete*] ... CML
Chief Musician [*Navy rating*] [*Obsolete*] ... CMUS
Chief, National Guard Bureau [*Army*] ... CNGB
Chief, Naval Advanced Air Training ... CNAAT
Chief Naval Adviser [*British*] ... CNA
Chief, Naval Advisory Group ... CHNAVADGP
Chief, Naval Advisory Group [*Followed by name of country*] ... CHNAVADGRU
Chief, Naval Advisory Group ... CHNAVGP
Chief of Naval Air ... CNA
Chief of Naval Air Advanced Training [*Also, CNAVANTRA*] [*Formerly, CNAOPTRA, CNAOT*] ... CNAADRA
Chief of Naval Air Advanced Training [*Also, CNAADTRA*] [*Formerly, CNAOPTRA, CNAOT*] ... CNAVANTRA
Chief of Naval Air Basic Training [*Formerly, CNAINTERMTRA, CNAIT*] ... CNABATRA
Chief, Naval Air Basic Training ... CNABT
Chief of Naval Air Intermediate Training [*Later, CNABATRA*] ... CNAINTERMTRA
Chief of Naval Air Intermediate Training [*Later, CNABATRA*] ... CNAIT
Chief of Naval Air Operational Training [*Later, CNAADTRA, CNAVANTRA*] ... CNAOPTRA
Chief of Naval Air Operational Training [*Later, CNAADTRA, CNAVANTRA*] ... CNAOT
Chief of Naval Air Pacific ... CNAP
Chief of Naval Air Primary Training [*Later, CNARFSTRA*] ... CNAPRIMTRA
Chief of Naval Air Primary Training [*Later, CNARFSTRA*] ... CNAPT
Chief of Naval Air Primary Training [*Formerly, CNAPRIMTRA, CNAPT*] ... CNARFSTRA
Chief of Naval Air Reserve Training ... CNARESTRA
Chief of Naval Air Services [*British*] ... CNAS
Chief of Naval Air Technical Training ... CNATECHTRA
Chief of Naval Air Technical Training ... CNATT
Chief of Naval Air Training ... CNAT
Chief of Naval Air Training ... CNATRA
Chief, Naval Airships Training ... CHNAVAIRSHIPTRA
Chief of Naval Airships Training and Experimentation ... CNATE
Chief of Naval Aviation Logistics ... CNAL
Chief Naval Censor [*Navy rating*] [*Obsolete*] ... CNC
Chief of Naval Communications [*Formerly, DNC*] ... CNC
Chief of Naval Development ... CND
Chief of Naval Education and Training ... CNET
Chief Naval Engineering Officer [*British*] ... CNEO
Chief of Naval Information [*British*] ... CNI
Chief of Naval Intelligence ... CNI
Chief Naval Judge Advocate [*British*] ... CNJA
Chief of Naval Material ... CHNAVMAT
Chief of Naval Material ... CNM
Chief, Naval Mission ... CHNAVMIS
Chief of Naval Operations [*Also, CNO*] ... CNAVOP
Chief of Naval Operations [*Also, CNAVOP*] ... CNO
Chief of Naval Operations Budget Office ... CNOBO
Chief of Naval Operations Command/Management Information System ... CNOCOM/MIS
Chief of Naval Operations Communications Center ... CNOCC
Chief of Naval Operations Memorandum ... CNOM
Chief of Naval Operations Memorandum and Commandant of the Marine Corps Memorandum [*Joint*] ... CNOM/CMCM
Chief of Naval Personnel ... CHNAVPERS
Chief of Naval Personnel [*The Second Sea Lord*] [*British*] ... CNP
Chief Naval Representative [*British*] ... CNR
Chief of Naval Research ... CNR
Chief, Naval Reserve Forces ... CNRF
Chief, Naval Reserve Training ... CNRT
Chief of the Naval Staff [*Canada*] ... CNS
Chief Naval Supply and Secretariat Officer [*British*] ... CNSSO
Chief of Naval Technical Services [*Canada*] ... CNTS
Chief of Naval Technical Training ... CNTT
Chief of Naval Training ... CHNAVTRA
Chief of Naval Training ... CNT
Chief of Naval Transportation Service ... CNTS
Chief Navy Disbursing Officer ... CNDO
Chief, Navy Section ... CHNAVSEC
Chief, Navy Section, Military Assistance Advisory Group ... CHNAVSECMAAG
Chief Nursing Officer [*British*] ... CNO
Chief Observer [*Navy*] ... CHOBS
Chief, Office of Personnel Operations [*Army*] ... COPO
Chief of Office of Research and Inventions [*Navy*] ... CHORI
Chief, Office of Reserve Components [*Army*] ... CORC
Chief Officer [*Women's Royal Naval Service*] [*British*] ... C/O
Chief Officers of State Library Agencies ... COSLA
Chief Operating Officer ... COO
Chief Operating Officer of Business Affairs [*Proposed alternative to the hiring of a baseball commissioner*] ... COOBA
Chief of Operations ... CHOPS
Chief of Operations Analysis ... COA
Chief Operator ... CHOP
Chief Operator ... CO
Chief Opticalman [*Navy rating*] ... OMC
Chief of Ordnance [*Army*] ... CO
Chief of Ordnance [*Army*] ... COFORD
Chief of Ordnance [*Army*] ... C of ORD
Chief of Ordnance [*Army*] ... CORD
Chief Ordnance Officer ... COO
Chief Ordnance Officer ... CORDO
Chief Painter [*Navy rating*] [*Obsolete*] ... CPTR
Chief Painter, Aircraft [*Navy rating*] [*Obsolete*] ... CPTRV
Chief Patriarch ... CP
Chief Patrol Inspector [*Immigration and Naturalization Service*] ... CPI
Chief Patternmaker [*Navy rating*] [*Obsolete*] ... CPM
Chief Patternmaker [*Navy rating*] ... PMC
Chief Pay Clerk [*Navy rating*] [*Obsolete*] ... CHPCLK
Chief Pay Clerk [*Navy rating*] [*Obsolete*] ... CPC
Chief of Personnel and Logistics [*Navy*] [*British*] ... CPL
Chief Personnelman [*Navy rating*] ... PNC
Chief Petty Officer [*Navy*] ... CPO
Chief Petty Officer of the Watch [*Navy*] ... CPOW
Chief Pharmacist [*Navy rating*] [*Obsolete*] ... CHPHAR
Chief Pharmacist's Mate [*Navy rating*] [*Obsolete*] ... CPHM
Chief Pharmacist's Mate, Dental Prosthetic Technician [*Navy rating*] [*Obsolete*] ... CPHMDP
Chief Pharmacist's Mate (Radium Plaque Adaptometer Operator) [*Navy rating*] [*Obsolete*] ... CPHM(RPA)
Chief Photographer [*Navy rating*] [*Obsolete*] ... CHPHOT
Chief Photographer [*Navy rating*] [*Obsolete*] ... CPHO
Chief Photographer's Mate [*Navy rating*] [*Obsolete*] ... CPHOM
Chief Photographer's Mate [*Navy rating*] ... PHC
Chief Photographic Intelligenceman [*Navy rating*] ... PTC
Chief Planning and Control Staff [*Coast Guard*] ... CPC
Chief Polaris Executive [*Missiles*] ... CPE
Chief of Police ... COP
Chief of Police ... CP
Chief Political Officer [*British Military Administration*] ... CPO
Chief Postal Clerk [*Navy rating*] ... PCC
Chief Printer [*Navy rating*] [*Obsolete*] ... CPRTR
Chief Printer, Lithographer [*Navy rating*] [*Obsolete*] ... CPRTRL
Chief Printer, Offset Process [*Navy rating*] [*Obsolete*] ... CPRTRM
Chief Program Engineer [*NASA*] ... CPE
Chief of Public Affairs ... CPA
Chief of Public Information [*Army*] ... CPI
Chief of Public Information Division [*NATO*] ... CPUBINFO
Chief Quartermaster [*Navy rating*] [*Obsolete*] ... CQM
Chief Quartermaster [*Navy rating*] ... QMC
[*The*] **Chief Quartermaster** [*Military*] ... TCQM
Chief Quartermaster Clerk [*Coast Guard*] ... CHQMCLK
Chief Quartermaster Clerk [*Navy rating*] [*Obsolete*] ... CQMC
Chief RADARman [*Navy rating*] [*Obsolete*] ... CRDM
Chief RADARman [*Navy rating*] ... RDC
Chief Radio Electrician [*Navy rating*] [*Obsolete*] ... CHRELE
Chief Radio Electrician [*Navy rating*] [*Obsolete*] ... CRE
Chief Radio Technician [*Navy rating*] [*Obsolete*] ... CRT
Chief Radioman [*Navy rating*] [*Obsolete*] ... CRM
Chief Radioman [*Navy rating*] ... RMC
Chief Ranger ... CR
Chief Registrar's Reports [*Legal*] [*British*] ... CRR
Chief Regulating Officer [*Southwest Pacific Area, World War II*] [*Army*] ... CREGO
Chief of Research and Development [*Army*] ... CR & D
Chief of Research and Development [*Army*] ... CRD
Chief of Research, Development, and Acquisition [*Army*] ... CRDA
Chief of Reserve Components [*Army*] ... CRC
Chief Scientific Adviser [*British*] ... CSA
Chief Scientific Officer [*Also, CSO*] [*Ministry of Agriculture, Fisheries, and Food*] [*British*] ... CScO
Chief Scientific Officer [*Also, CScO*] [*Ministry of Agriculture, Fisheries, and Food*] [*British*] ... CSO
Chief Scientist (Royal Air Force) [*British*] ... CS(RAF)
Chief, SEATO [*Southeast Asia Treaty Organization*] **Military Planning Office** ... CMPO
Chief of Section ... COS
Chief of Section ... C of S
Chief of Section ... CS
Chief Shipfitter [*Navy rating*] [*Obsolete*] ... CSF
Chief Shipfitter [*Navy rating*] ... SFC

Chief Shipfitter, Construction Battalion, Mechanical Draftsman [Navy rating] [Obsolete]............CSFCBM
Chief Shipfitter, Construction Battalion, Pipe Fitter and Plumber [Navy rating] [Obsolete] .... CSFCBP
Chief Shipfitter, Construction Battalion, Rigger [Navy rating] [Obsolete] ....CSFCBR
Chief Shipfitter, Construction Battalion, Steel Worker [Navy rating] [Obsolete]............CSFCBS
Chief Shipfitter, Construction Battalion, Welder [Navy rating] [Obsolete]............CSFCBW
Chief Shipfitter, Ship Repair [Navy rating] [Obsolete]............CSFSR
Chief Shipfitter, Ship Repair, Pipe Fitter and Plumber [Navy rating] [Obsolete] ....CSFSRP
Chief Shipfitter, Ship Repair, Welder [Navy rating] [Obsolete]........ CSFSRW
Chief Ship's Clerk [Navy rating] [Obsolete] ....CHSCLK
Chief Ship's Clerk [Navy rating] [Obsolete] ....CSCLK
Chief Ship's Service Man [Navy rating] [Obsolete]............CSSM
Chief Ship's Service Man, Barber [Navy rating] [Obsolete]............CSSMB
Chief Ship's Service Man, Cobbler [Navy rating] [Obsolete] ....CSSMC
Chief Ship's Service Man, Laundryman [Navy rating] [Obsolete]........CSSML
Chief Ship's Service Man, Tailor [Navy rating] [Obsolete]............CSSMT
Chief Ship's Serviceman [Navy rating]............SHC
Chief, Signal Corps [Army]............CSIGC
Chief Signal Officer [Army]............CSIGO
Chief Signal Officer [Army]............CSO
Chief Signalman [Navy rating] [Obsolete]............ CSM
Chief Signalman [Navy rating]............SMC
Chief Skipper [Navy] [British]............ChSkr
Chief SONAR Technician [Navy rating]............STC
Chief SONARman [Navy rating] [Obsolete]............CSOM
Chief SONARman [Navy rating] [Obsolete]............SOC
Chief SONARman, Harbor Defense [Navy rating] [Obsolete]............CSOMH
Chief Special Artificer [Navy rating] [Obsolete]............CSA
Chief Special Artificer, Instruments [Navy rating] [Obsolete]............CSAI
Chief Special Artificer, Instruments, Typewriter and Office Equipment Repairman [Navy rating] [Obsolete]............CSAITR
Chief Special Artificer, Instruments, Watch Repairman [Navy rating] [Obsolete]............CSAIWR
Chief Special Artificer, Optical [Navy rating] [Obsolete]............ CSAO
Chief Special Artificer, Synthetic Training Devices [Navy rating] [Obsolete]............CSAD
Chief Specialist [Navy rating] [Obsolete]............ CSP
Chief Specialist, All Designators [Navy rating] [Obsolete]............CSPX
Chief Specialist, Chaplain's Assistant [Navy rating] [Obsolete]............CSPW
Chief Specialist, Control Tower Operator [Navy rating] [Obsolete] ......CSPY
Chief Specialist, Identification [Navy rating] [Obsolete]............CSPR
Chief Specialist, Laboratory [Navy rating] [Obsolete]............CSPPLB
Chief Specialist, Link Trainer Instructor [Navy rating] [Obsolete].....CSPTLT
Chief Specialist, Motion Picture Production [Navy rating] [Obsolete]............CSPMP
Chief Specialist, Personnel Supervisor [Navy rating] [Obsolete]..........CSPS
Chief Specialist, Petroleum Inspector [Navy rating] [Obsolete]............CSPO
Chief Specialist, Photogrammetry [Navy rating] [Obsolete]............CSPPPG
Chief Specialist, Physical Training Instructor [Navy rating] [Obsolete]............CSPA
Chief Specialist, Recruiter [Navy rating] [Obsolete]............CSPR
Chief Specialist, Shore Patrol and Security [Navy rating] [Obsolete]............CSPS
Chief Specialist, Teacher [Navy rating] [Obsolete]............CSPT
Chief Specialist, Transport Airman [Navy rating] [Obsolete]............CSPV
Chief Specialist, V-Mail [Navy rating] [Obsolete]............CSPPVM
Chief of Staff [Military]............COFS
Chief of Staff [Military]............COS
Chief of Staff [Military]............CS
Chief of Staff [Military]............C of S
Chief of Staff Air Force Memorandum............CSAFM
Chief of Staff, Army Memorandum [Air Force]............CSAM
Chief of Staff Memorandum [Military]............CSM
Chief of Staff, Military Intelligence Committee............COSMIC
Chief Staff Officer............CSO
Chief of Staff Regulations............CSR
Chief of Staff to Supreme Allied Commander [Europe] [World War II]............COSSAC
Chief of Staff Supreme Headquarters [British]............CSSH
Chief of Staff, United States Air Force............COFSAF
Chief of Staff, United States Air Force............CSAF
Chief of Staff, United States Army [Later, CSA]............COFSA
Chief of Staff, United States Army [Formerly, COFSA, C of SA]............COFSA
Chief of Staff, United States Army [Later, CSA]............C of SA
Chief of State............COS
Chief of Station [CIA country team]............COS
Chief Steelworker [Navy rating]............SWC
Chief Steward [Later, MSC] [Navy rating]............CST
Chief Steward [Later, MSC] [Navy rating]............SDC
Chief Storekeeper [Navy rating] [Obsolete]............CSK
Chief Storekeeper, Aviation [Navy rating] [Obsolete]............CSKV
Chief Storekeeper, Construction Battalion, Stevedore [Navy rating] [Obsolete]............CSKCB
Chief Storekeeper, Disbursing [Navy rating] [Obsolete]............CSKD
Chief Storekeeper, Technical [Navy rating] [Obsolete]............CSKT
Chief Superintendent of Hydrographic Supplies............CSHS

Chief Superintendent of Naval Meteorology [British] ....CSNM
Chief Superintendent of Ordnance Factories [British] [World War II] ....CSOF
Chief, Superintendent Range Operations [NASA] ....CSRO
Chief of Supplies and Transport [Navy] [British] ....CST
Chief of Support Services [Army] ....COFSPTS
Chief of Support Services [Army] ....C of SptS
Chief of Support Services [Army] ....CSS
Chief of Tariff Bureau ....CTB
Chief, Technical Services ....CTS
Chief Telegrapher [Navy rating] [Obsolete] ....CT
Chief Test Conductor ....CTC
Chief Torpedoman [Navy rating] [Obsolete] ....CHTORP
Chief Torpedoman [Navy rating] [Obsolete] ....CTORP
Chief Torpedoman's Mate [Navy rating] [Obsolete] ....CTM
Chief Torpedoman's Mate [Navy rating] ....TMC
Chief Torpedoman's Mate, Aviation [Navy rating] [Obsolete] ....CTMV
Chief Torpedoman's Mate, Electrical [Navy rating] [Obsolete] ....CTME
Chief TRADEVMAN [Training Devices Man] [Navy rating] ....TDC
Chief of Transportation [Army] ....COFT
Chief of Transportation [Army] ....CT
Chief of Transportation [Army] ....C of T
Chief Turret Captain [Obsolete] [Navy] ....CTC
Chief, United States Army Overseas Supply Agency, San Francisco ....CHUSAOSASF
Chief, United States Army Reserve and Reserve Officers Training Corps Affairs ....CUSARROTC
Chief, United States Military Supply Mission, India............CHUSMSI
Chief Value............CV
Chief Veterinary Officer [Ministry of Agriculture, Fisheries, and Food] [British]............CVO
Chief Warrant Officer [Army]............CWO
Chief Warrant Officer 2 [Army]............CW2
Chief Warrant Officer 3 [Army]............CW3
Chief Warrant Officer 4 [Army]............CW4
Chief Warrant Officer, W-2............CWO-2
Chief Warrant Officer, W-3............CWO-3
Chief Warrant Officer, W-4............CWO-4
Chief Warrant and Warrant Officers Association, United States Coast Guard............CW & WOA
Chief Watch Officer [Navy]............CWO
Chief Water Tender [Navy rating] [Obsolete]............CWT
Chief, Western Pacific Transportation Office............CHWTO
Chief Yeoman [Navy rating] [Obsolete]............CY
Chiefland, FL [Radio station call letters]............WLQH
Chiefs of Staff, Mediterranean [Military]............COSMED
Chiefs of Staff, Washington [Military]............COS(W)
Chieftain Development Co. Ltd. [American Stock Exchange symbol] ...... CID
Chifeng [China] [Airport symbol]............CIF
Chiffonier............ CH
Chigorodo [Colombia] [Airport symbol]............IGO
Chihuahua [Mexico] [Seismograph station code, US Geological Survey]............CHH
Chihuahua [Mexico] [Airport symbol]............CUU
Chihuahua Club of America............CCA
Chikungunya Virus............CV
Child............C
Child [or Children]............CH
Child Abuse Listening Mediation [An association]............CALM
Child Abuse and Neglect............CA/N
Child Attitudes Survey [Education]............ CAS
Child Behavior Rating Scale [Psychology]............CBRS
Child Care Action Campaign............CCAC
Child Care Employee Project............CCEP
Child Care Health and Development [A publication]....Child Care Health Dev
Child Care Quarterly [A publication] .... Child Care
Child Care Quarterly [A publication] ....Child Care Q
Child Care Worker............CCW
Child Development [A publication]............ CD
Child Development [A publication]............CHDEA
Child Development [A publication]............Child Dev
Child Development [A publication]............Child Devel
Child Development Abstracts [A publication] ....ChildDevAb
Child Development Abstracts and Bibliography [A publication]............Child Developm Absts Biblio
Child Development Associate Consortium [Defunct]............CDAC
Child Development Center............CDC
Child Development Consultant............CDC
Child Development Research Unit [Nigeria]............CDRU
Child Education Foundation, New York, NY [Library symbol] [Obsolete]............NNCEF
Child Evangelism Fellowship............CEF
Child Evangelism Fellowship International [Later, CEF]............CEFI
Child Find [An association]............CF
Child Health Assessment Program............CHAP
Child Health Associate Program............CHAP
Child Neurology............CHN
Child Neurology Society............CNS
Child Nutrition............CN
Child Nutrition Forum............CNF
Child Of [Genealogy]............CH/O

Child-Operated Mobile Electric Transport .... COMET
Child Protection Report [*A publication*] .... CPR
Child Psychiatry .... CP
Child Psychiatry and Human Development [*A publication*] .... Child Psych
Child Psychiatry and Human Development [*A publication*] .... Child Psych & Human Devel
Child Psychiatry and Human Development [*A publication*] .... Child Psychiatry Hum Dev
Child Psychiatry Quarterly [*A publication*] .... Child Psy Q
Child Psychology .... CP
Child Rearing Study .... CRS
Child Resistant .... CR
Child-Resistant Closure [*Medicine containers, etc.*] .... CRC
Child Safety Council [*Later, NCSC*] .... CSC
Child Sexual Assault Victim Assistance Project .... CSAVAP
Child Study Association of America [*Defunct*] .... CSAA
Child Study Association of America, New York, NY [*Library symbol*] .... NNCS
Child Study Journal [*A publication*] .... Child St J
Child Study Journal [*A publication*] .... Child Stud J
Child Study Journal [*A publication*] .... CHSTA
Child Study Team [*Education*] .... CST
Child Support Enforcement [*Department of Health and Human Services*] .... CSE
Child Welfare [*A publication*] .... Child Wel
Child Welfare .... CW
Child Welfare League of America .... CWLA
Child Welfare Service .... CWS
Child World, Incorporated [*American Stock Exchange symbol*] [*Delisted*] .... CWI
Child and Youth Centered Information Systems .... CYCIS
Childbearing Hips .... CBH
Childbirth Education Foundation .... CEF
Childbirth Without Pain .... CWOP
Childbirth Without Pain Education Association .... CWPEA
Childhood Disease [*Medicine*] .... CHD
Childhood Education [*A publication*] .... CE
Childhood Education [*A publication*] .... C Ed
Childhood Education [*A publication*] .... Child Ed
Childhood Education [*A publication*] .... Childh Educ
Childhood Muscular Dystrophy .... CMD
Childhood in Poetry [*A publication*] .... CIP
Childhood in Poetry Supplement [*A publication*] .... CIPS
Childhood Sensuality Circle .... CSC
Children of Ageing Parents .... CAPS
Children of Alcoholics Foundation .... CAF
Children of the Americas .... CA
Children Before Dogs .... CBD
Children with Behavioral and Emotional Difficulty .... CBED
Children of the Confederacy CC
Children in Contemporary Society [*A publication*] .... Child Contemp Soc
Children of Gays/Lesbians .... CGL
Children of the Green Earth .... CGE
Children Have a Potential [*Program for handicapped or disturbed children of Air Force personnel*] .... CHAP
Children in Hospitals .... CIH
Children, Incorporated CI
Children with Learning Disabilities .... CLD
Children in Need of Supervision [*Classification for delinquent children*] .... CHINS
Children in Need of Supervision .... CINS
Children of the Night .... CN
Children: the Parents' Magazine [*A publication*] .... Child Par M
Children Today [*A publication*] .... Child Today
Children Today [*A publication*] .... CT
Children in the Tropics (English Edition) [*A publication*] .... Child Trop (Engl Ed)
Children of the Universe [*Defunct*] .... CU
Children and Young Persons Act [*British*] .... CYPA
Children's Advocacy Center .... CAC
Children's Aid International .... CAI
Children's Art Foundation .... CAF
Children's Asthma Research Institute and Hospital [*Denver, CO*] .... CARIH
Children's Blood Foundation [*New York Hospital - Cornell Medical Center*] .... CBF
Children's Book Council .... CBC
Children's Book Review Index [*A publication*] .... CBRI
Children's Book Review Service [*A publication*] .... CBRS
Children's Bureau [*of SSA*] .... CB
Children's Campaign for Nuclear Disarmament .... CCND
Children's Cancer Fund of America .... CCFA
Children's Committee CC
Children's Creative Response to Conflict Program .... CCRC
Children's Defense Fund .... CDF
Children's Dress, Cotton Dress, and Sportswear Contractors Association [*Later, Metropolitan Area Apparel Association*] .... CDCDSCA
Children's Embedded Figures Test [*Psychology*] .... CEFT
Children's Eye Care Foundation .... CECF
[*The*] **Children's Foundation** .... TCF
Children's Health Care [*A publication*] .... Child Health Care
Children's Health Services Division [*HEW*] .... CHSD
Children's Home of Kingston, Kingston, NY [*Library symbol*] .... NKiC
Children's Hospital, Buffalo, NY [*Library symbol*] .... NBuCH
Children's Hospital Medical Center [*Ohio*] .... CHMC
Children's Hospital, Medical Library, Denver, CO [*Library symbol*] .... CoDCH-M
Children's Hospital of Michigan, Detroit, MI [*Library symbol*] .... MiDCh
Children's Hospital, Ottawa, ON, Canada [*Library symbol*] .... CaOOCH
Children's Hospital of Pittsburgh, Pittsburgh, PA [*OCLC symbol*] .... PHC
Children's Hospital Research Foundation, Research Library, Cincinnati, OH [*Library symbol*] .... OCCH
Children's Hospital, St. Paul, MN [*Library symbol*] .... MnSCH
Children's Hospital Society, Doctor's Library, Los Angeles, CA [*Library symbol*] .... CLCH
Children's Hypnotic Susceptibility Scale [*Psychology*] .... CHSS
Children's International Summer Villages International Association .... CISV
Children's Legal Rights Information and Training [*An association*] .... CLRIT
Children's Literature [*A publication*] .... ChildL
Children's Literature [*A publication*] .... Child Lit
Children's Literature Association .... ChLA
Children's Literature in Education [*A publication*] .... Child Lit Educ
Children's Literature Review [*A publication*] .... CLR
Children's Liver Foundation .... CLF
Children's Medical Relief International [*Defunct*] .... CMRI
Children's Memorial Hospital, Joseph Brennemann Medical Library, Chicago, IL [*Library symbol*] .... ICChH
Children's Mercy Hospital, Kansas City, MO [*Library symbol*] .... MoKCH
Children's Museum of Indianapolis, Indianapolis, IN [*OCLC symbol*] .... IIM
Children's Museum of Indianapolis, Indianapolis, IN [*Library symbol*] .... InICM
Children's Nutrition Laboratory [*Baylor College of Medicine*] .... CNL
Children's Organization for Peace and Brotherhood [*Defunct*] .... COPB
Children's Peace Union [*Defunct*] .... CPU
Children's Personality Questionnaire [*Psychology*] .... CPQ
Children's Plea for Peace [*Later, World Pen Pals*] .... CPP
Children's Public Policy Network .... CPPN
Children's Rights Group .... CRG
Children's Rights, Incorporated .... CRI
Children's Self-Conceptions Test .... CSC
Children's Services Division [*American Library Association*] [*Later, ALSC*] .... CSD
Children's Special Service Mission [*British*] .... CSSM
Children's Television Workshop .... CTW
Children's Theatre Association of America [*Formerly, CTC*] .... CTA
Children's Theatre Association of America [*Formerly, CTC*] .... CTAA
Children's Theatre Conference [*Later, CTA, CTAA*] .... CTC
Children's Treatment Center, Madison, WI [*Library symbol*] .... WMaCT
Children's Village, USA [*of International Orphans Inc.*] .... CVUSA
Children's Ward [*of a hospital*] .... CW
Children's Wear Association .... CWA
Children's and Young Adult Services .... CAYAS
Childrenswear Manufacturers Association .... CMA
Childress [*Texas*] [*Seismograph station code, US Geological Survey*] .... CEC
Childress [*Texas*] [*Seismograph station code, US Geological Survey*] .... CNE
Childress [*Texas*] [*Seismograph station code, US Geological Survey*] .... CNO
Childress [*Texas*] [*Seismograph station code, US Geological Survey*] .... CNW
Childress [*Texas*] [*Seismograph station code, US Geological Survey*] .... CSE
Childress [*Texas*] [*Seismograph station code, US Geological Survey*] .... CSW
Childress [*Texas*] [*Seismograph station code, US Geological Survey*] .... CWT
Childress, TX [*Radio station call letters*] .... KCTX
Child's Apperception Test [*Psychology*] .... CAT
Chile [*Aircraft nationality and registration mark*] CC
Chile .... CHIL
Chile [*Three-letter standard code*] .... CHL
Chile [*MARC country of publication code*] [*Library of Congress*] cl
Chile [*MARC geographic area code*] [*Library of Congress*] .... s-cl---
Chile [*Two-letter standard code*] CL
Chile-American Association .... CAA
Chile Committee for Human Rights [*Institute for Policy Studies*] .... CCHR
Chile Democratico [*An association*] .... ChD
Chile-Ecuador-Peru .... CEP
Chile Legislative Center [*An association*] CLC
Chilean Iodine Educational Bureau [*Defunct*] .... CIEB
Chilean Nitrate Agricultural Service Information [*A publication*] .... Chil Nitrate Agric Serv Inf
Chilecito [*Argentina*] [*Seismograph station code, US Geological Survey*] [*Closed*] .... CCT
Chileka [*Malawi*] [*Seismograph station code, US Geological Survey*] .... CLK
Chili Appreciation Society International .... CASI
Chilik [*USSR*] [*Seismograph station code, US Geological Survey*] [*Closed*] .... CHL
Chillagoe [*Australia*] [*Airport symbol*] [*Obsolete*] .... LLG
Chillan, Chile. Estacion Experimental. Boletin Tecnico [*A publication*] .... Chillan Chile Estac Exp Bol Tec
Chilldown [*NASA*] .... CD
Chilldown Flow Meter .... CFM
Chilled .... CHLD
Chilled Drinking Water [*Aerospace*] .... CDW
Chilled Drinking Water Return [*Aerospace*] .... CDWR
Chilled Water [*Aerospace*] .... CHW
Chilled Water Supply [*Aerospace*] .... CWS

Chillicothe, IL [Radio station call letters].................. WTXR
Chillicothe, MO [Location identifier] [FAA]....................... CHT
Chillicothe, MO [Radio station call letters].................. KCHI
Chillicothe, MO [Radio station call letters].............. KCHI-FM
Chillicothe, OH [Location identifier] [FAA]......................RZT
Chillicothe, OH [Radio station call letters]..................WBEX
Chillicothe, OH [Radio station call letters]..................WCHI
Chillicothe, OH [Radio station call letters]..................WFCB
Chillicothe, OH [Radio station call letters]..................WKKJ
Chillicothe and Ross County Public Library, Chillicothe, OH
   [Library symbol]... OCh
Chillicothe Township Free Public Library, Chillicothe, IL [OCLC
   symbol].. ISI
Chilliwack, BC [Radio station call letters]..................CHWK
Chilliwack Public Library, Chilliwack, BC, Canada [Library
   symbol].. CaBCh
Chilton Corp. [American Stock Exchange symbol]...............CHN
Chilton, WI [Radio station call letters]....................WMBE
Chimachoy [Guatemala] [Seismograph station code, US
   Geological Survey]... CIM
Chimbote [Peru] [Airport symbol] [Obsolete]..................CHM
Chimica [A publication].....................................Chim
Chimica Acta Turcica [A publication]............... Chim Acta Turc
Chimica Didactica [A publication]..................Chim Didact
Chimica e l'Industria [A publication]............... Chim Ind
Chimica e l'Industria (Milano) [A publication] ....Chimica Ind (Milano)
Chimica e l'Industria (Milano) [A publication] ....Chim Ind (M)
Chimica e l'Industria (Milano) [A publication] ....Chim Ind (Milano)
Chimica Therapeutica [A publication].................Chim Ther
Chimie Actualites [A publication].....................Chimie Act
Chimie Analytique [A publication]...................Chim Analyt
Chimie Analytique (Paris) [A publication]..............Chim Anal (Paris)
Chimie et Industrie [A publication]..................Chimie & Ind
Chimie et Industrie - Genie Chimique [A publication]..................
                                       Chim Ind - Genie Chim
Chimie et Industrie (Paris) [A publication]..............Chim Ind (Paris)
Chimie, Microbiologie, Technologie Alimentaire [A publication]...
                                 Chim Microbiol Technol Aliment
Chimie Pure et Appliquee [A publication].............Chim Pure Appl
Chimie Therapeutique [A publication]..................Chim Ther
Chimika Chronika (Athens) [A publication]..............Chim Chron (Athens)
Chimizarea Agriculturii [A publication]..................Chim Agric
Chimkent [USSR] [Seismograph station code, US Geological
   Survey] [Closed].. CHM
Chimney...CHY
Chimney Sweep Guild [Later, NCSG]..........................CSG
Chimney Sweeps of America...................................CSA
Chimpanzee Coryza Agent [A virus]..........................CCA
Chin National Organization [Burma].........................CNO
China [Aircraft nationality and registration mark]............ B
China...CHI
China...CHIN
China [Three-letter standard code]..........................CHN
China [Two-letter standard code]............................ CN
China Airlines...CAL
China American Petrochemical Company Ltd....................CAPCO
China Association of Standardization [INFOTERM]..............CAS
China-Burma-India Hump Pilots Association ....CBIHPA
China-Burma-India Theater [World War II].....................CBI
China-Burma-India Theater [World War II].....................CBIT
China-Burma-India Veterans Association.......................CBIVA
China Business Review [A publication]..................China Bus R
China Central Television [The national Chinese network].......CCTV
China Clay Producers Trade Association.......................CCP
China Council for the Promotion of International Trade ....CCPIT
China Defense Supplies, Inc.................................CDS
China External Trade Development Council [Taiwan]............CETDC
China Geographer [Los Angeles] [A publication]......... China Geog
China, Glass, and Giftware Association ....CGGA
China, Glass, Giftware Board of Trade [Later, CGGA] ....CGGBT
China, Glass, and Pottery Association of America [Later, China,
   Glass, and Giftware Association)..........................CGPAA
China Grove, NC [Radio station call letters].................WRNA
China, India, Burma...CIB
China Inland Mission...CIM
China Inland Mission Overseas Missionary Fellowship [Later,
   Overseas Missionary Fellowship] ....CIM-OMF
China Institute in America..................................CIA
China Institute of New Jersey, Montclair State College, Upper
   Montclair, NJ [Library symbol]...........................NjUpM-C
China International Foundation [Later, TIF]...................CIF
China Lake [California] [Seismograph station code, US Geological
   Survey]..CLC
China, Mainland [MARC geographic area code] [Library of
   Congress].. a-cc---
China Man-Made Fiber Corporation [Taiwan]...................CMFC
China Medical Board of New York.............................CMBNY
China Medical Journal [A publication]................. China Med J
China Medical Missionary Journal [A publication] .... China Med Miss J
China National Aviation Corps...............................CNAC
China National Publications Import Corporation................CNPIC

China News Analysis [Hong Kong] [A publication] ....China News Anal
China News Service..CNS
China Ocean Shipping Company...............................COSCO
China Philatelic Study Group................................CPSG
China Pictorial [A publication].............................CP
China Pottery and Glassware Association ....CPGA
China Quarterly [London] [A publication]..............China Q
China Quarterly [A publication] ....China Q
China Quarterly [A publication] ....China Quart
China Quarterly [A publication] ....CQ
China Reconstructs [A publication]..................China Reconstr
China Reconstructs [A publication]..........................CR
China Report [A publication].........................China Rep
China, Republic of [Taiwan] [MARC geographic area code]
   [Library of Congress].................................... a-ch---
China, Republic of [Taiwan] [MARC country of publication code]
   [Library of Congress]....................................ch
China Research Associates...................................CRA
China Service Medal...CHSM
China Shipbuilding Corporation..............................CSBC
China Society of America....................................CSA
China Stamp Society...CSS
China Surface-to-Surface Experimental Number 4 [Rocket]...........CSS-X-4
China Technical Consultants, Incorporated ....CTCI
China Theater [World War II].................................CT
China Theater of Operations [World War II]...................CTO
China Weekly Review [A publication].....................China W R
China's Foreign Trade [Peking] [A publication] .... China For Tr
China's Medicine (Peking) [A publication]......... China's Med (Peking)
Chinchina [Colombia] [Seismograph station code, US Geological
   Survey].. CHN
Chincoteague Island, VA [Location identifier] [FAA] ....VWU
Chincoteague, VA [Location identifier] [FAA].................WAL
Chinese [MARC language code] [Library of Congress]..........chi
Chinese Academy of Sciences.................................CAS
Chinese for Affirmative Action..............................CAA
Chinese Air Force [Nationalist].............................CAF
Chinese Air Task Force......................................CATF
Chinese American Citizens Alliance ....CACA
Chinese American Civic Council..............................CACC
Chinese-American Composite Wing [Air Force].................CACW
Chinese-American Educational Foundation ....CAEF
Chinese-American Librarians Association ....CALA
Chinese American Restaurant Association......................CARA
Chinese Army..CA
Chinese Army in India.......................................CAI
Chinese Art Society of America [Later, AS]..................CASA
Chinese Art Society of America. Archives [A publication]......ACAS
Chinese Art Society of America. Archives [A publication]......ACASA
Chinese Association for the Advancement of Science ....CAAS
Chinese Astronomy [Later, Chinese Astronomy and
   Astrophysics] [A publication]..................... Chin Astron
Chinese Astronomy and Astrophysics [A publication].........CAA
Chinese Banknote Collectors Society ....CBCS
Chinese Christian Mission...................................CCM
Chinese Communist...CHICOM
Chinese Communist Air Force.................................CCAF
Chinese Communist Army......................................CCA
Chinese Communist Forces....................................CCF
Chinese Communist Navy......................................CCN
Chinese Communist Party.....................................CCP
Chinese Consolidated Benevolent Association.................CCBA
Chinese Cooperative Catalog [Library of Congress] [A publication] CCC
Chinese Culture [A publication].........................C Cul
Chinese Culture [A publication].........................ChC
Chinese Culture [A publication].................... Chinese Cult
Chinese Culture Association.................................CCA
Chinese Culture Foundation of San Francisco ....CCFSF
Chinese Development Council.................................CDC
Chinese Economic Studies [A publication]....................CES
Chinese Economic Studies [A publication]............... Chin Econ S
Chinese Education [A publication].................... Chin Educ
Chinese-English Translation Assistance Group ....CETA
Chinese Exclusion Act.......................................CEA
Chinese Expeditionary Force.................................CEF
Chinese Federation of Industrial Associations ....CFIA
Chinese Federation of Labor [Nationalist China].............CFL
Chinese Foreign Missionary Union ....CFMU
Chinese Hamster Embryo Fibroblast [Cytology]...............CHEF
Chinese Hamster Ovarian [or Ovary] [Cytology]...............CHO
Chinese Historical Society of America ....CHHS
Chinese Institute of Engineers - USA ....CIE-USA
Chinese Journal of Archaeology [A publication]......... Chin J Archaeol
Chinese Journal of Mathematics [A publication]...........Chinese J Math
Chinese Journal of Microbiology [A publication]......... Chin J Microbiol
Chinese Journal of Physics [A publication].................Chin J Phys
Chinese Journal of Physics (New York) [A publication]...........
                                       Chin J Phys (New York)
Chinese Journal of Physics (Peking) [A publication] ....
                                       Chinese J Phys (Peking)
Chinese Journal of Physics (Taipei) [A publication]......... Chin J Phys (Taipei)

Chinese Journal of Physiology [*A publication*] .... Chin J Physiol
Chinese Journal of the Science of Agriculture [*A publication*] .... Chin J Sci Agr
Chinese Language Computer Society .... CLCS
Chinese Language Encoder .... CHICODER
Chinese Language Teachers Association .... CLTA
Chinese Laundry Association .... CLA
Chinese Law and Government [*A publication*] .... Chinese Law Gvt
Chinese Law and Government [*A publication*] .... Chin Law G
Chinese Law and Government [*New York*] [*A publication*] .... Chin Law Govt
Chinese Librarians Association .... CLA
Chinese Linguistics Bibliography on Computer .... CLIBOC
Chinese Literature [*A publication*] .... ChinL
Chinese Literature [*Peking*] [*A publication*] .... Chin Lit
Chinese Literature [*A publication*] .... ChLit
Chinese Literature Monthly [*A publication*] .... CLM
Chinese Materials and Research Aids Service Center, Inc., Taipei, Taiwan, China [*Library symbol*] .... CiTCM
Chinese Medical Journal [*A publication*] .... Chin Med J
Chinese Merchants Association .... CMA
Chinese Music Society of North America .... CMSNA
Chinese Musical and Theatrical Association .... CMTA
Chinese Nationalist .... CHINAT
Chinese Navy .... CN
Chinese-Oriented Antiballistic Missile System .... C-ABM
Chinese Pen [*Taipei*] [*A publication*] .... Chin Pen
Chinese People's Political Consultative Conference .... CPPCC
Chinese People's Republic .... CPR
Chinese Refugee Relief [*Defunct*] .... CRR
Chinese Republic Studies. Newsletter [*A publication*] .... Chin Repub Stud
Chinese Restaurant Asthma .... CRA
Chinese Restaurant Syndrome [*Malady affecting some people while eating in Chinese restaurants*] .... CRS
Chinese Social and Political Science Review [*A publication*] .... Chin Social & Pol Sci R
Chinese Sociology and Anthropology [*A publication*] .... Chin Soc A
Chinese Sociology and Anthropology [*New York*] [*A publication*] .... Chin Sociol Anthro
Chinese Studies in History [*New York*] [*A publication*] .... Chin Stud Hist
Chinese Studies in Philosophy [*A publication*] .... Chin Stud Phil
Chinese Studies in Philosophy [*New York*] [*A publication*] .... Chin Stud Philo
Chinese Women's Association .... CWA
Chinese Women's Benevolent Association .... CWBA
Chinese World, San Francisco, CA [*Library symbol*] .... CSfCWL
Chinese Youth Council [*Later, CDC*] .... CYC
Ching Feng [*A publication*] .... CFeng
Chinguacousy Township Public Library, Bramalea, ON, Canada [*Library symbol*] .... CaOBram
Chinle High School Library, Chinle, AZ [*Library symbol*] .... AzCH
Chino, CA [*Location identifier*] [*FAA*] .... CNO
Chinook Jargon [*MARC language code*] [*Library of Congress*] .... chn
Chinook, MT [*Radio station call letters*] .... KRYK
Chinook Regional Library, Swift Current, SK, Canada [*Library symbol*] .... CaSCR
Chios [*Greece*] [*Airport symbol*] .... JKH
Chip Hermeticity in Plastic [*Electronics*] .... CHIP
Chip Select .... CSE
Chipata [*Zambia*] [*Airport symbol*] .... CIP
Chipley, FL [*Radio station call letters*] .... WBGC
Chipola Junior College [*Florida*] .... CJC
Chipola Junior College, Marianna, FL [*Library symbol*] .... FMaC
Chippewa Air Commuter, Inc. [*Manistee, MI*] [*FAA designator*] .... CPW
Chippewa County Library System, Montevideo, MN [*Library symbol*] .... MnMov
Chippewa Falls Public Library, Chippewa Falls, WI [*Library symbol*] .... WCf
Chippewa Falls Public Library, Chippewa Falls, WI [*Library symbol*] [*Obsolete*] .... WCh
Chippewa Falls, WI [*Radio station call letters*] .... WAYY
Chippewa Falls, WI [*Radio station call letters*] .... WCFW
Chippewa Library League [*Library network*] CLL
Chippewa Valley Museum, Eau Claire, WI [*Library symbol*] .... WECV
Chiredzi [*Rhodesia*] [*Seismograph station code, US Geological Survey*] .... CIR
Chiricahua National Monument and Fort Bowie National Historic Site .... CHIR
Chiro-Xylographic [*Type of block book*] .... CHX
Chiron Corp. [*NASDAQ symbol*] .... CHIR
Chiropody Bibliographical Research Society .... CBRS
Chirurgia [*Surgery*] [*Latin*] .... CH
Chirurgia Gastroenterologica (English Edition) [*A publication*] .... Chir Gastroenterol (Engl Ed)
Chirurgia Italiana [*A publication*] .... Chir Ital
Chirurgia Maxillofacialis et Plastica [*A publication*] .... Chir Maxillofac Plast
Chirurgia Narzadow Ruchu i Ortopedia Polska [*A publication*] .... Chir Narzadow Ruchu Ortop Pol
Chirurgia degli Organi di Movimento [*A publication*] .... Chir Organi Mov
Chirurgia degli Organi di Movimento [*A publication*] .... Chir Org Movimento
Chirurgia e Patologia Sperimentale [*A publication*] .... Chir Patol Sper
Chirurgia Plastica [*A publication*] .... Chir Plast
Chirurgia Plastica et Reconstructiva [*A publication*] .... Chir Plast Reconstr
Chirurgia Veterinaria Referate. Abstracts [*A publication*] .... Chir Vet Ref Abstr
Chirurgiae Baccalaureus [*Bachelor of Surgery*] .... CB
Chirurgiae Baccalaureus [*Bachelor of Surgery*] .... Ch B
Chirurgiae Doctor [*Doctor of Surgery*] .... ChD
Chirurgiae Doctor [*Doctor of Surgery*] .... Chir Doct
Chirurgiae Doctor [*Doctor of Surgery*] .... D Ch
Chirurgiae Magister [*Master of Surgery*] .... Ch M
Chirurgiae Magister [*Master of Surgery*] .... CM
Chirurgicalis [*Surgical*] [*Pharmacy*] .... CHIRURG
Chirurgie Pediatrique [*A publication*] .... Chir Pediatr
Chirurgien-Dentiste de France [*A publication*] .... Chir-Dent Fr
Chirurgisches Forum fuer Experimentelle und Klinische Forschung [*A publication*] .... Chir Forum Exp Klin Forsch
Chisana [*Alaska*] [*Airport symbol*] .... CZN
Chisana, AK [*Location identifier*] [*FAA*] .... CZN
Chistochina, AK [*Location identifier*] [*FAA*] .... CZO
Chita [*USSR*] [*Seismograph station code, US Geological Survey*] .... CIT
Chitato [*Angola*] [*Airport symbol*] [*Obsolete*] .... PGI
Chitina, AK [*Location identifier*] [*FAA*] CXC
Chitral [*Pakistan*] [*Airport symbol*] [*Obsolete*] .... CJL
Chittagong [*Bangladesh*] [*Airport symbol*] .... CGP
Chittagong [*Bangladesh*] [*Seismograph station code, US Geological Survey*] .... CHT
Chittenden Corp. [*NASDAQ symbol*] .... CNDN
Chitty's Law Journal [*A publication*] .... Chitty's L J
Chlor-Alkali-Market Model .... CAMM
Chlorambucil [*Also, CHL, CMB*] [*Antineoplastic drug*] C
Chlorambucil [*Also, C, CMB*] [*Antineoplastic drug*] .... CHL
Chlorambucil [*Also, C, CHL*] [*Antineoplastic drug*] .... CMB
Chlorambucil, Vinblastine, Procarbazine, Prednisone [*Antineoplastic drug regimen*] .... CHL VPP
Chloramphenicol [*Also, CAP, CM*] [*Antimicrobial compound*] C
Chloramphenicol [*Also, C, CM*] [*Antimicrobial compound*] .... CAP
Chloramphenicol [*Also, C, CAP*] [*Antimicrobial compound*] .... CM
Chloramphenicol Acetyltransferase [*An enzyme*] .... CAT
Chloramphetamine [*Neurochemistry*] .... CA
Chlorate Oxygen Candle .... COC
Chlordan [*or Chlordane*] [*Insecticide*] .... CD
Chlordecone (Kepone) [*Pesticide*] .... CD
Chlorella International Union [*Later, MIU*] .... CIU
Chlorendic Acid [*Organic chemistry*] .... CA
Chlorendic Aldehyde [*Organic chemistry*] .... CEA
Chlorendic Anhydride [*Also, CAN*] [*Organic chemistry*] .... CA
Chlorendic Anhydride [*Also, CA*] [*Organic chemistry*] .... CAN
Chlorinated [*Freight*] .... CHLOR
Chlorinated Dibenzo-para-dioxin [*Organic chemistry*] .... CDD
Chlorinated Naphthalene [*Organic chemistry*] .... CN
Chlorinated Organics in Wastewater .... COW
Chlorinated Paraffin [*Organic chemistry*] .... CP
Chlorinated Polyethylene [*Organic chemistry*] .... CPE
Chlorinated Poly(vinyl Chloride) [*Organic chemistry*] .... CPVC
Chlorine [*Chemical element*] Cl
Chlorine Emergency Plan [*Chlorine Institute*] .... CHLOREP
Chlorine Institute CI
Chlorine Pentafluoride [*Inorganic chemistry*] .... CLPF
Chlorine Pentafluoride [*Inorganic chemistry*] .... CPF
Chlorine Trifluoride [*Inorganic chemistry*] .... CTF
Chlornaltrexamine [*Narcotic antagonist*] [*Pharmacochemistry*] .... CNA
Chloro [*As substituent on nucleoside*] [*Biochemistry*] cl
Chloro-deoxy-glucose [*Biochemistry*] .... CDG
Chloroacetaldehydedinitrophenylhydrazone [*Fungicide*] .... CADNPH
Chloroacetate Esterase [*An enzyme*] .... CAE
Chloroacetophenone [*Also, CN*] [*Tear gas*] .... CAP
Chloroacetophenone [*Also, CAP*] [*Tear gas*] [*Army symbol*] .... CN
Chloroacetyl Chloride [*Organic chemistry*] .... CAC
Chloroallyl Diethyldithiocarbamate [*Herbicide*] .... CDEC
Chlorobenzalmalononitrile [*Tear gas*] [*Army symbol*] .... CS
Chlorobenzotrifluoride [*Organic chemistry*] .... CBTF
Chlorobromomethane [*Organic chemistry*] .... CBM
Chlorocetophenone Solution .... CNS
Chlorocholine Chloride [*Organic chemistry*] CCC
Chlorodiallylacetamide [*Herbicide*] .... CDAA
(Chloroethyl)cyclohexylnitrosourea [*Lomustine*] [*Antineoplastic drug regimen*] .... CCNU
Chloroethylnitrosourea [*A class of antineoplastic agents*] .... CENU
Chloroethylphosphonic Acid [*Maturation compound for fruits*] .... CEPA
Chlorofluorocarbon [*Organic chemistry*] .... CFC
Chlorofluoromethane [*Propellant*] .... CFM
Chloroform and Ether [*Mixture*] .... CE
Chlorogenic Acid [*Organic chemistry*] .... CGA
Chloromercuribenzoate [*Biochemistry*] .... ClHgBzO
Chloromercuribenzoic [*Organic chemistry*] .... CMB
Chloromethyl Methyl Ether [*Organic chemistry*] .... CMME
Chloromethylfurfuraldehyde [*Organic chemistry*] .... CMF
Chloro(methyl)phenol [*Organic chemistry*] .... CMP
Chloronitroaniline [*Organic chemistry*] .... CNA
Chlorophenoxyacetic Acid [*Plant growth hormone*] .... CPA
Chlorophenoxyisobutyrate [*Pharmacology*] .... CPIB
Chlorophenyl Red [*A dye*] .... CPR
Chlorophenylalanine [*Biochemistry*] .... CPA

Chlorophenyldimethylurea [Herbicide]..............CMU
(Chlorophenyl)methylcarbamate [Organic chemistry]..............CPMC
Chloropicolinic Acid [Organic chemistry]..............CPA
Chloropicrin [Poison gas] [Army symbol]..............PS
Chloropicrin Stannic Chloride [Inorganic chemistry]..............NC
Chloroplasts to Nuclei per Cell [Botany]..............C/N
Chloroprene Rubber..............CR
Chloroquine [Antimalarial drug]..............CQ
Chlorosulfonyl Isocyanate [Organic chemistry]..............CSI
Chlorotrifluoroethylene [Organic chemistry]..............CTFE
Chloroxymorphamine [Narcotic agonist] [Pharmacochemistry]..............COA
Chlorpheniramine Maleate [Antihistamine]..............CPM
Chlorpromazine [Sedative]..............CPZ
Chlorpropamide-Alcohol Flushing [Medicine]..............CPAF
Chlortetracycline [Antibiotic]..............CTC
Choay [France] [Research code symbol]..............CY
Chochma, Bina, Daat [Wisdom, Understanding, Knowledge] [Philosophy of the Lubarich Movement, a Hasidic sect]..............CHABAD
Chock Full O'Nuts Corp. [NYSE symbol] [Wall Street slang name: "Nuts"]..............CHF
Chocolate..............ch
Chocolate..............CHOC
Chocolate-Colored Tablet [Pharmacy]..............CCT
Chocolate Manufacturers Association of the USA..............CMA
Chocolate Milk Foundation [Defunct]..............CMF
Choctaw [MARC language code]..............cho
Choctaw Nation Multi-County Library, McAlester, OK [OCLC symbol]..............OKI
Choctaw Nation Multi-County Library, McAlester, OK [Library symbol]..............OkMcC
Choctawhatchee Regional Library [Library network]..............CRL
Choice [A publication]..............CHO
Choice Magazine Listening [An "aural magazine" for the blind and visually handicapped]..............CML
Choice Old Marsala..............COM
Choir..............CHOR
Choir Organ..............CH
Choirmaster..............CM
Choiseul Bay [Solomon Islands] [Airport symbol]..............CHY
Choke..............CH
Choke Coil..............CHC
Cholame Valley [California] [Seismograph station code, US Geological Survey]..............CVC
((Cholamidopropyl)dimethylammonio)propanesulfonate [Biochemistry]..............CHAPS
Cholecystokinin [Also, PZ] [Endocrinology]..............CCK
Cholecystokinin-Pancreozymin [Endocrinology]..............CCK-PZ
Cholera Research Laboratory [Bangladesh]..............CRL
Cholera Toxin..............CT
Cholera Vaccine..............CHO/VAC
Cholera Vaccine Immunization..............CVI
Cholesterol [Clinical chemistry]..............CHOL
Cholesterol Epoxide [Biochemistry]..............CAE
Cholesterol Ester Storage Disease [Medicine]..............CESD
Cholesterol Lowering Lipid [Biochemistry]..............CLL
Cholesterol/Phospholipid Ratio [Clinical chemistry]..............C/P
Cholesteryl Iopanoate [Biochemistry]..............CI
Cholesteryl Oleate-Triglyceride [Biochemistry]..............COT
Choline [Also, Cho] [Biochemistry]..............Ch
Choline [Also, Ch] [Biochemistry]..............Cho
Choline Acetylase [An enzyme]..............ChA
Choline Acetylase [An enzyme]..............ChAc
Choline Acetyltransferase [An enzyme]..............CAT
Choline-Adrenalin [Test] [Medicine]..............CA
Choline Kinase [An enzyme]..............CK
Choline Oxidase [An enzyme]..............CO
Cholinesterase [An enzyme]..............ChE
Chomerics, Inc. [NASDAQ symbol]..............CHOM
Chonco [Nicaragua] [Seismograph station code, US Geological Survey]..............CNR
Chondritic Uniform Reservoir [Geology]..............CHUR
Chondroitin Sulfate [Biochemistry]..............CS
Chondroitin Sulfate A [Biochemistry]..............CSA
Chondromyxoid Fibroma [Medicine]..............CMF
Chongqing [China] [Airport symbol]..............CKG
Chonnam Medical Journal [A publication]..............Chonnam Med J
Chopped Meat [Medium] [Microbiology]..............CM
Chopped Meat Glucose [Medium] [Microbiology]..............CMG
Chopped Meat Glucose Broth with Digoxin [Medium] [Microbiology]..............CMCD
Chopper..............CHP
Chopper Stabilized Amplifier..............CSA
Choppy, Short, or Cross Sea [Navigation]..............C
Choral..............CHO
Choral..............CHOR
Choral Conductors Guild..............CCG
Choral Journal [A publication]..............Choral J
Choral Journal [A publication]..............CJ
Choral and Organ Guide [A publication]..............Choral G
Chord..............CD
Chord..............CHD
Chord Plane Line..............CPL

Chorda Chirurgicalis [Surgical Catgut] [Pharmacy]..............CHORD CHIRURG
Choreograph..............CHOR
Choreographers Guild..............CG
Choreographers Theatre..............CT
Chorioallantoic Membrane [Embryology]..............CAM
Choriocarcinoma [Medicine]..............CC
Chorionic Gonadotrophin [Endocrinology]..............CG
Chorionic Gonadotrophin, Human [Endocrinology]..............CGH
Chorionic Growth Hormone - Prolactin [Also, HCS, HPL] [Endocrinology]..............CGP
Chorionic Somatomammotrophin [Endocrinology]..............CS
Chorionic Villi Biopsy [Obstetrics]..............CVB
Chorionic Villi Sampling [Gynecology]..............CVS
Chorismic Acid [Biochemistry]..............Chr
Choristers Guild..............CG
Chorus..............CHOR
Chorzow [Poland] [Seismograph station code, US Geological Survey]..............CHZ
Chosen Gakuno [A publication]..............CSGH
Choshi [Japan] [Seismograph station code, US Geological Survey]..............CHO
Chosonminhang - CAA of DPR of Korea [ICAO designator]..............JS
Choteau, MT [Location identifier] [FAA]..............CHX
Chow Chow Club..............CCC
Chowan College, Murfreesboro, NC [Library symbol]..............NcMfC
Chowder Review [A publication]..............Chowder
Chowiet Island [Alaska] [Seismograph station code, US Geological Survey]..............CHW
Choya [Argentina] [Seismograph station code, US Geological Survey]..............CYA
CHRA [Canadian Health Record Association] Recorder [A publication]..............CHRA Rec
Chrezvychainaya Komissiya po Borbe s Kontrrevolutsiei i Sabotazhem [Extraordinary Commission for Combating Counterrevolution and Sabotage; Soviet secret police organization, 1917-1921]..............CHEKA
Chripa [Costa Rica] [Seismograph station code, US Geological Survey]..............AR6
Chris-Craft Antique Boat Club..............CCABC
Chris-Craft Industries, Inc. [NYSE symbol]..............CCN
Christ..............CH
Christ [or Christian]..............CHR
Christ..............XT
Christ Church..............CHCH
Christ Hospital Institute of Medical Research, Research Library, Cincinnati, OH [Library symbol]..............OCCIM
Christ Hospital, Oak Lawn, IL [Library symbol]..............IOIC
Christ the King..............CHK
Christ the King Foundation [Defunct]..............CKF
Christ the King Seminary, East Aurora, NY [Library symbol]..............NEAuC
Christ the King Seminary, East Aurora, NY [OCLC symbol]..............VYK
Christ Seminary-Seminex, St. Louis, MO [Library symbol]..............MoSCEx
Christchurch [New Zealand] [Airport symbol]..............CHC
Christchurch [New Zealand] [Later, EYR] [Geomagnetic observatory code]..............CHR
Christchurch [New Zealand] [Seismograph station code, US Geological Survey]..............CHR
Christchurch Chromosome..............Ch'c
Christelijk Oosten en Hereniging [A publication]..............COH
Christened..............CHR
Christentum und Wissenschaft [A publication]..............C & W
Christian..............CHRSTN
Christian..............XN
Christian..............XTIAN
Christian Action Council..............CAC
Christian Action for Development in the Eastern Caribbean..............CADEC
Christian Action Party [Puerto Rico]..............CAP
Christian Airmen's Fellowship International [Defunct]..............CAS
Christian-Albrechts-Universitat Kiel, Kiel, Germany [Library symbol]..............GyKiU
Christian Amendment Movement [Later, CGM]..............CAM
Christian Anti-Communism Crusade..............CACC
Christian Anti-Narcotic Association [Later, SFM]..............CANA
Christian Appalachian Project..............CAP
Christian Association for Psychological Studies..............CAPS
Christian Beacon, Collingswood, NJ [Library symbol]..............NjCoB
Christian Bodybuilding Association..............CBA
Christian Booksellers Association..............CBA
Christian Bookstall Managers Association..............CBMA
Christian Broadcasting Network..............CBN
Christian Brothers Boys Association..............CBBA
Christian Brothers College [Tennessee]..............CBC
Christian Brothers College, Memphis, TN [Library symbol]..............TMCBC
Christian Brothers Education Association [Later, RECCB]..............CBEA
Christian Business Men's Committee International [Later, CBMC]..............CBMCI
Christian Business Men's Committee of USA [Formerly, CBMCI]..............CBMC
Christian Camping International..............CCI
Christian Century [A publication]..............CC
Christian Century [A publication]..............C Cent
Christian Century [A publication]..............ChC
Christian Century [A publication]..............ChCen
Christian Century [A publication]..............Chr C
Christian Century [A publication]..............Chr Cent
Christian Century [A publication]..............Christ Cen

Christian Century Foundation .... CCF
Christian Children's Fund .... CCF
Christian Chiropractors Association .... CCA
Christian Citizens' Crusade CCC
Christian College Coalition CCC
Christian College, Columbia, MO [*Library symbol*] .... MoCoC
Christian College Consortium CCC
Christian College News [*A publication*] .... CCN
Christian College of the Southwest, Dallas, TX [*Library symbol*] .... TxDaCC
Christian Communications, Incorporated CCI
Christian Crusade CC
Christian Democratic Alliance [*Political party*] [*The Netherlands*] .... CDA
Christian Democratic Party [*Political party*] .... CDP
Christian Democratic Union of Central Europe .... CDUCE
Christian Democratic World Union .... CDWU
Christian Democrats .... ChrDem
Christian Dental Society .... CDS
Christian Dior [*Couturier*] .... CD
Christian Disciple [*A publication*] .... Chr Disc
Christian East [*A publication*] .... CE
Christian Educators Fellowship [*Formerly, NEF*] .... CEF
Christian Educators Journal [*A publication*] .... CEJ
Christian Endeavor Union .... CEU
Christian Era .... CE
Christian Examiner [*A publication*] .... Chr Exam
Christian Family Life .... CFL
Christian Family Movement .... CFM
Christian Family Renewal .... CFR
Christian Feminists .... CF
Christian Focus on Government .... CFG
Christian Forum Reserch Foundation .... CFRF
Christian Freedom Foundation .... CFF
Christian Government Movement [*Defunct*] .... CGM
Christian Herald Association .... CHA
Christian Heritage College [*California*] .... CHC
Christian Heritage Library, El Cajon, CA [*Library symbol*] .... CEcajC
Christian Heritage Year [*1984*] [*British*] .... CHY
Christian Holiness Association .... CHA
Christian Home [*A publication*] .... C Home
Christian Homesteading Movement .... CHM
Christian Knowledge Society [*Also known as Society for Promoting Christian Knowledge*] .... CKS
Christian Labor Association of the United States of America .... CLA
Christian Labour Association of Canada .... CLAC
Christian Law Association .... CLA
Christian Law Institute CLI
Christian Legal Society .... CLS
Christian Liberty [*A publication*] .... ChL
Christian Liberty Association .... CLA
Christian Librarian [*A publication*] CLi
Christian Librarians' Fellowship .... CLF
Christian Life [*A publication*] .... C Life
Christian Life Movement .... CLM
Christian Literacy Associates .... CLA
Christian Literature [*A publication*] .... Chr Lit
Christian Medical Commission .... CMC
Christian Medical Council [*Defunct*] .... CMC
Christian Medical Society .... CMS
Christian Methodist Episcopal [*Church*] .... CME
Christian Methodist Episcopal Church .... CMEC
Christian Mission .... CM
Christian and Missionary Alliance .... CMA
Christian Missionary Fellowship .... CMF
Christian Missions in Many Lands .... CMML
Christian Monthly Spectator [*A publication*] .... Chr Mo Spec
Christian Motorcyclists Association .... CMA
Christian Movement for Peace .... CMP
Christian Nurse [*A publication*] .... Christ Nurse
Christian Observer [*A publication*] .... Chr Obs
Christian Peace Conference .... CPC
Christian Periodical Index [*A publication*] .... Chr Per Ind
Christian Perspectives [*A publication*] .... ChrPer
Christian Preaching Conference [*Defunct*] .... CPC
Christian Quarterly [*A publication*] .... Chr Q
Christian Quarterly Review [*A publication*] .... Chris Q
Christian Quarterly Spectator [*A publication*] .... Chr Q Spec
Christian Record Benevolent Association [*Later, CRBF*] .... CRBA
Christian Record Braille Foundation [*Formerly, CRBA*] .... CRBF
Christian Reformed World Relief Committee .... CRWRC
Christian Remembrance [*A publication*] .... Chr Rem
Christian Renewal Ministry .... CRM
Christian Rescue Effort for the Emancipation of Dissidents [*Acronym now used as organization name*] .... CREED
Christian Research Institute .... CRI
Christian Restoration Association .... CRA
Christian Review [*A publication*] .... Chr R
Christian Rural Fellowship [*Defunct*] .... CRF
Christian Rural Overseas Program [*Acronym is now the official name of organization*] .... CROP
Christian Scholar [*A publication*] .... ChS
Christian Scholar's Review [*A publication*] .... Chr Sch R
Christian Scholar's Review [*A publication*] .... CSR
Christian Schools International [*Formerly, NUCS*] .... CSI
Christian Science .... CS
Christian Science Monitor [*A publication*] .... Chris Sc Mon
Christian Science Monitor [*A publication*] .... Christ Sci Mon
Christian Science Monitor [*A publication*] .... Chr Sci Mon
Christian Science Monitor [*A publication*] .... Chr Sci Monitor
Christian Science Monitor [*A publication*] .... CSM
Christian Science Monitor. Magazine Section [*A publication*] .... Christian Sci Mon Mag
Christian Science Monitor. Magazine Section [*A publication*] .... CSMMS
Christian Science Monitor. Magazine Section [*A publication*] .... C S Mon Mag
Christian Science Publishing Society .... CSPS
Christian Science Reading Room, Cleveland, OH [*Library symbol*] .... OClCh
Christian Science Reading Room, Montreal, PQ, Canada [*Library symbol*] .... CaQMCS
Christian Scientist .... SC
Christian Service Brigade .... CSB
Christian Service Club .... CSC
Christian Service Corps .... CSC
Christian Socialist .... ChrSoc
Christian Solidarity International .... CSI
Christian Theological Seminary, Indianapolis, IN [*Library symbol*] .... InIT
Christian Theological Seminary, Indianapolis, IN [*OCLC symbol*] .... IXT
Christian Union [*A publication*] .... Chr Un
Christian Voice CV
Christian Welfare Hospital, East St. Louis, IL [*Library symbol*] .... IEsCH
Christian Women's Fellowship .... CWF
Christian Women's National Concerns .... CWNC
Christian Yellow Pages [*A publication*] .... CYP
Christiana Companies, Inc. [*NYSE symbol*] .... CST
Christianity .... XNTY
Christianity .... XTY
Christianity and Crisis [*A publication*] .... C & C
Christianity and Crisis [*A publication*] .... Chr & Cr
Christianity and Crisis [*A publication*] .... Chr Cris
Christianity and Crisis [*A publication*] .... Chr & Crisis
Christianity Today [*A publication*] .... Chr T
Christianity Today [*A publication*] .... Chr Today
Christianity Today [*A publication*] .... CT
Christians Concerned for Israel [*Superseded by NCLCI*] CCI
Christians Heeding Righteousness Instead of Satanic Tyranny [*Conservative organization*] .... CHRIST
Christians United for Responsible Entertainment .... CURE
Christiansburg, VA [*Radio station call letters*] .... WJJJ
Christiansted National Historic Site .... CHRI
Christiansted, VI [*Radio station call letters*] .... WIVI-FM
Christiansted, VI [*Radio station call letters*] .... WJKC
Christiansted, VI [*Radio station call letters*] .... WSTX
Christiansted, VI [*Television station call letters*] .... WSVI-TV
Christic Institute CI
Christie, Atkins, Munch-Peterson Test [*Bacteriology*] .... CAMP
Christler Flying Service, Inc. [*Thermopolis, WY*] [*FAA designator*] .... CHR
Christlich-Demokratische Union [*Christian Democratic Union*] [*West German political party*] .... CDU
Christlich-Nationaler Gewerkschaftsbund der Schweiz [*Swiss Federation of National-Christian Trade Unions*] .... CNGS
Christlich-Soziale Union [*Political party in Bavaria connected with the CDU*] [*West Germany*] .... CSU
Christliche Gewerkschaftsbewegung Deutschlands [*Christian Trade Union Movement of Germany*] [*West Germany*] .... CGD
Christliche Vereine Junger Manner [*Young Men's Christian Associations*] [*Germany*] .... CVJM
Christlicher Gewerkschaftsbund Deutschlands [*Confederation of German Christian Trade Unions*] [*West Germany*] .... CGB
Christlijk Nationaal Vakverbond in Nederland [*National Federation of Christian Workers*] [*Protestant*] [*Netherlands*] .... CNV
Christman Air System [*Washington, PA*] [*FAA designator*] .... CAS
Christmas .... XM
Christmas .... XMAS
Christmas Club CC
Christmas Factor [*Also, PTC*] [*Hematology*] .... CF
Christmas Island [*Two-letter standard code*] CX
Christmas Island [*Kiribati*] [*Airport symbol*] CXI
Christmas Island [*Three-letter standard code*] .... CXR
Christmas Island [*Indian Ocean*] [*MARC geographic area code*] [*Library of Congress*] .... i-xa---
Christmas Island [*Indian Ocean*] [*MARC country of publication code*] [*Library of Congress*] .... xa
Christmas Island [*Seismograph station code, US Geological Survey*] .... XMI
Christmas Philatelic Club .... CPC
Christmas Seal and Charity Stamp Society .... CS & CSS
Christmas Study Unit [*American Topical Association*] .... CSU
[*A*] **Christmas Trains and Trucks Program** [*Marine Corps program in Vietnam*] .... ACTT
Christmas Tree Growers Journal [*A publication*] .... Christmas Tree Grow J
Christmas Tree Pattern .... CTP
Christopher Columbus Philatelic Society .... CCPS
Christopher Morley Knothole Association .... CMKA
Christopher Newport College, Newport News, VA [*OCLC symbol*] .... VCN

Christopher Newport College, Newport News, VA [*Library symbol*] .... ViNeC
Christopher Street [*A publication*] .... CS
Christos Lavatus [*An association*] CL
Christus X
Christus .... XPC
Christus .... XS
Chrom-Moly .... CM
Chromalloy American Corp. [*NYSE symbol*] .... CRO
Chromated Copper Arsenate [*Wood preservative*] .... CCA
Chromatic Aberation-Free [*Optics*] .... CF
Chromatin and Chromosomal Protein Research [*A publication*] .... Chromatin Chromosomal Protein Res
Chromatogram Automatic Soaking Scanning and Digital Recording Apparatus .... CASSANDRA
Chromatographia [*A publication*] .... Chromatogr
Chromatographic Reviews [*A publication*] .... Chromatogr Rev
Chromatographic Reviews [*A publication*] .... Chromat Rev
Chromatographic Science [*A publication*] .... Chromatogr Sci
Chromatographic Separation .... CGS
Chromatography Control Module [*Instrumentation*] .... CCM
Chromatography of Environmental Hazards [*Elsevier Book Series*] [*A publication*] .... CEH
Chromatography Laboratory Automatic Software .... CLAS
Chromatopyrography [*for polymer characterization*] .... CPG
Chrome .... CRM
Chrome Card Collectors Club [*Later, D of A*] CCCC
Chrome Plated [*Freight*] .... CHRO PLTD
Chrome Vanadium .... CRV
Chrome Vanadium .... CRVAN
Chromite [*CIPW classification*] [*Geology*] .... cm
Chromium [*Chemical symbol is Cr*] .... CHR
Chromium [*Chemical symbol is Cr*] .... CHROM
Chromium [*Chemical element*] .... Cr
Chromium Plate [*Metallurgy*] .... CRPL
Chromographic Mode Sequencing [*Chromatography*] .... CMS
Chromosoma [*A publication*] .... Chromos
Chromosomal Fraction .... CF
Chromosome Information Service (Tokyo) [*A publication*] .... Chromos Inform Serv (Tokyo)
Chromosome Information Service (Tokyo) [*A publication*] .... Chromosome Inf Serv (Tokyo)
Chromosome Variations in Human Evolution [*A publication*] .... Chromosome Var Hum Evol
Chronar Corp. [*NASDAQ symbol*] .... CRNR
Chronic .... CH
Chronic [*Medicine*] .... CHR
Chronic Active Hepatitis [*Medicine*] .... CAH
Chronic Active Liver Disease [*Medicine*] .... CALD
Chronic Airflow Limitation [*Medicine*] .... CAL
Chronic Airway Obstruction [*Medicine*] .... CAO
Chronic Atrophic Gastritis [*Medicine*] .... CAG
Chronic Benign Mucous Membrane Pemphigoid [*Medicine*] .... CBMMP
Chronic Brain Syndrome [*Medicine*] .... CBS
Chronic Brain Syndrome [*Medicine*] .... CHRBRSYN
Chronic Bronchitis [*Medicine*] .... CB
Chronic Bronchitis and Asthma [*Medicine*] .... CBA
Chronic Cerebellar Stimulation [*Medicine*] .... CCS
Chronic Coronary Insufficiency [*Medicine*] CCI
Chronic Disabling Dermatoses [*Medicine*] .... CDD
Chronic Disease Facility [*Medicine*] .... CDF
Chronic Endstage Renal Disease [*Nephrology*] .... CERD
Chronic Glomerulonephritis [*Medicine*] .... CGN
Chronic Granulocytic Leukemia [*Medicine*] .... CGL
Chronic Granulomatous Disease [*Medicine*] .... CGD
Chronic Hemodialysis [*Nephrology*] .... CHD
Chronic Hemolytic Anemia [*Medicine*] .... CHA
Chronic Infectious Neuropathic Agents [*Medicine*] .... CHINA
Chronic Lymphatic [*or Lymphocytic*] **Leukemia** [*Medicine*] CLL
Chronic Lymphocytic Thyroiditis [*Medicine*] .... CLT
Chronic Mesenteric Ischemia [*Medicine*] .... CMI
Chronic Myelocytic [*or Myeloid or Myelogenous*] **Leukemia** [*Medicine*] .... CML
Chronic Nervous Exhaustion [*Medicine*] .... CNE
Chronic Obstruction of Biliary Tract [*Medicine*] .... COBT
Chronic Obstructive Airway Disease [*Medicine*] .... COAD
Chronic Obstructive Lung Disease [*Medicine*] .... COLD
Chronic Obstructive Outflow Disease [*Medicine*] .... COOD
Chronic Obstructive Pulmonary Disease [*Medicine*] .... COPD
Chronic Obstructive Pulmonary Emphysema [*Medicine*] .... COPE
Chronic Passive Congestion [*Medicine*] .... CPC
Chronic Progressive Coccidioidal Pneumonitis [*Medicine*] .... CPCP
Chronic Pulmonary Emphysema [*Medicine*] .... CPE
Chronic Pyelonephritis [*Urology*] .... CP
Chronic Rejection [*Medicine*] .... CR
Chronic Renal Disease [*Medicine*] .... CRD
Chronic Renal Failure [*Medicine*] .... CRF
Chronic Respiratory Disease [*Medicine*] .... CRD
Chronic Subclinical Scurvy [*Medicine*] .... CSS
Chronic Suppurative Otitus Media [*Otolaryngology*] .... CSOM
Chronic Ulcerative Colitis [*Medicine*] .... CUC
Chronica Botanica [*A publication*] .... Chron Bot
Chronica Horticulturae [*A publication*] .... Chron Hortic
Chronicle .... CHRON
Chronicle of Higher Education [*A publication*] .... CHE
Chronicle of Higher Education [*A publication*] .... C H Ed
Chronicle of Higher Education [*A publication*] .... Chron Higher Educ
Chronicles [*Old Testament book*] .... Chr
Chronicles [*Old Testament book*] .... Chron
Chronicles of Oklahoma [*A publication*] .... Chronicles Okla
Chronicles of Oklahoma [*A publication*] .... ChronOkla
Chronicles of Oklahoma [*A publication*] .... CO
Chronicles of Oklahoma [*A publication*] .... COO
Chronicles of Oklahoma [*A publication*] .... Okla Chronicles
Chronik Wiener Goetheverein [*A publication*] .... CWGV
Chronique Aluminum [*A publication*] .... Chron Alum
Chronique Archeologique du Pays de Liege [*A publication*] .... CAPL
Chronique d'Egypte [*A publication*] .... CdE
Chronique d'Egypte [*A publication*] .... CE
Chronique d'Egypte [*A publication*] .... ChrE
Chronique d'Egypte [*A publication*] .... Chr Eg
Chronique d'Egypte [*A publication*] .... Chron Egypte
Chronique des Lettres Francaises [*A publication*] .... CLF
Chronique. Organisation Mondiale de la Sante [*A publication*] .... Chron OMS
Chronique de Politique Etrangere [*A publication*] .... Chron Polit Etr
Chronique Sociale de France [*A publication*] .... Chron Soc France
Chronique. Societe Vervietoise d'Archeologie et d'Histoire [*A publication*] .... CSVAH
Chroniques d'Actualite [*A publication*] .... Chron Actual
Chronological .... CHRON
Chronological .... CHRONO
Chronological Age [*Psychology*] .... CA
Chronometer .... CHRON
Chronometer .... CRNMTR
Chronometer Correction [*Navigation*] CC
Chronometer Error [*Navigation*] .... CE
Chronometer Time [*Navigation*] C
Chronometer Time Minus Watch Time [*Navigation*] .... C-W
Chronometric .... CRNMTC
Chrysanthemum Chlorotic Mottle Viroid .... ChCMV
Chrysanthemum Stunt Viroid .... CSV
Chrysler Corp. [*NYSE symbol*] C
Chrysler Corporation CC
Chrysler Corp., Engineering Division, Detroit, MI [*Library symbol*] .... MiDChryE
Chrysler Corporation Missile Division .... CCMD
Chrysler Corporation Space Division .... CCSD
Chrysler Improved Numerical Differencing Analyzer [*Data processing*] .... CINDA
Chrysler Improved Numerical Differencing Analyzer for Third-Generation Computers [*Data processing*] CINDA-3G
Chrysler Optical Processing Scanner .... COPS
Chrysler Products Restorers Club [*Later, CRC*] .... CPRC
Chrysler Restorers Club [*Formerly, CPRC*] .... CRC
Chrysler Town and Country Owners Registry .... CTCR
Chrysler Town and Country Owners Registry .... TCOR
Chualar, CA [*Radio station call letters*] .... KUBO
Chub Cay [*Bahamas*] [*Airport symbol*] .... CCZ
Chuban Kenkyu [*Studies on Chinese Language and Literature*] [*A publication*] .... CBKK
[*The*] **Chubb Corp.** [*NASDAQ symbol*] .... CHUB
Chubbuck, ID [*Radio station call letters*] .... KKLB
Chuchupate [*California*] [*Seismograph station code, US Geological Survey*] [*Closed*] .... CHP
Chuck Jaws [*Tools*] .... CCJW
Chugoku Bungaku Ho [*A publication*] .... C Bun H
Chugoku Gogaku [*A publication*] .... CG
Chugoku No Bunka To Shakai [*Chinese Culture and Society*] [*A publication*] .... CBS
Chuian-Garon [*USSR*] [*Seismograph station code, US Geological Survey*] [*Closed*] .... CGT
Chula Vista Public Library, Chula Vista, CA [*Library symbol*] .... CChu
Ch'ung Chi Hsueh-Pao [*A publication*] .... CCHP
Chung Chi Journal [*A publication*] .... CCJ
Chung-Hau Min Kuo [*Republic of China*] .... CHMK
Chung-Kuo Yu-Wen [*A publication*] .... CKYW
Chung-wai Literary Monthly [*A publication*] .... CWLM
Chur [*Coire*] [*Switzerland*] [*Seismograph station code, US Geological Survey*] [*Closed*] .... CHU
Church C
Church .... CH
Church [*Alaska*] [*Seismograph station code, US Geological Survey*] .... CHB
Church .... CHR
Church .... CHU
Church Architectural Guild of America [*Later, IFRAA*] .... CAGA
Church Army [*British*] .... CA
Church Army Society .... CA
Church Army Society .... CAS
Church Association [*British*] .... CA
Church Association for Seamen's Work [*Later, SCI*] .... CASW
[*The*] **Church of the Brethren Homes and Hospitals Association** .... TCBHHA
Church Building Society [*British*] .... CBS

Church Center for the United Nations .... CCUN
Church of Christ, Scientist .... CCS
Church Coalition for Human Rights in the Philippines .... CCHRP
Church Committee on Human Rights in Asia .... CCHRA
Church Defence Institution [*British*] .... CDI
Church & Dwight Co. [*NASDAQ symbol*] .... CRCH
Church Employed Women .... CEW
Church of England .... C of E
Church of England .... CE
Church of England Children's Society .... CECS
Church of England Men's Society .... CEMS
Church of England Newspaper .... CEN
Church of England Soldiers', Sailors', and Airmen's Clubs .... CESSAC
Church of England Sunday School Institute .... CESSI
Church of England Temperance Society .... CETS
Church of England Working Men's Society .... CEWMS
Church of England Young Men's Society .... CEYMS
Church Evangelism Association [*Later, Masterkey Association*] .... CEA
Church Executive Development Board .... CEDB
Church Extension Association [*British*] .... CEA
Church Furniture Manufacturers Association .... CFMA
Church of God Peace Fellowship .... CGPF
Church Guilds Union [*British*] .... CGU
Church Hill, TN [*Radio station call letters*] .... WMCH
Church Historical Society [*Later, Historical Society of the
    Episcopal Church*] .... CHS
Church Historical Society, Austin, TX [*Library symbol*] .... TxAuCH
Church History [*A publication*] .... CH
Church History [*A publication*] .... ChH
Church History [*A publication*] .... CHist
Church History [*A publication*] .... Church Hist
Church Information Office [*British*] .... CIO
Church of Ireland .... C of I
Church of Ireland .... C of IRE
Church of Jesus Christ of Latter-Day Saints, Genealogical
    Society Library, Huntsville Branch, Huntsville, AL [*Library
    symbol*] .... AHGS
Church of Jesus Christ of Latter-Day Saints, Genealogical
    Society Library, Anchorage Branch, Anchorage, AK [*Library
    symbol*] .... AkAGS
Church of Jesus Christ of Latter-Day Saints, Genealogical
    Society Library, Fairbanks Alaska District Branch, Fairbanks,
    AK [*Library symbol*] .... AkFGS
Church of Jesus Christ of Latter-Day Saints, Genealogical
    Society Library, Adelaide Stake Branch, Firle, SA, Australia
    [*Library symbol*] .... AuFirGS
Church of Jesus Christ of Latter-Day Saints, Genealogical
    Society Library, Sydney South Branch, Sutherland Ward
    Chapel, Kirrawee, NSW, Australia [*Library symbol*] .... AuKirGS
Church of Jesus Christ of Latter-Day Saints, Genealogical
    Society Library, Melbourne Branch, Northcote, V, Australia
    [*Library symbol*] .... AuNocGS
Church of Jesus Christ of Latter-Day Saints, Genealogical
    Society Library, Sydney Branch, Sydney, NSW, Australia
    [*Library symbol*] .... AuSGS
Church of Jesus Christ of Latter-Day Saints, Genealogical
    Society Library, Flagstaff Branch, Flagstaff, AZ [*Library
    symbol*] .... AzFGS
Church of Jesus Christ of Latter-Day Saints, Genealogical
    Society Library, Holbrook Branch, Holbrook, AZ [*Library
    symbol*] .... AzHGS
Church of Jesus Christ of Latter-Day Saints, Genealogical
    Society Library, Mesa Branch, Mesa, AZ [*Library symbol*] .... AzMGS
Church of Jesus Christ of Latter-Day Saints, Genealogical
    Society Library, Phoenix Arizona North Branch, Phoenix, AZ
    [*Library symbol*] .... AzPhGS
Church of Jesus Christ of Latter-Day Saints, Genealogical
    Society Library, Phoenix Arizona West Branch, Phoenix, AZ
    [*Library symbol*] .... AzPhWGS
Church of Jesus Christ of Latter-Day Saints, Genealogical
    Society Library, Prescott Branch, Prescott, AZ [*Library
    symbol*] .... AzPrGS
Church of Jesus Christ of Latter-Day Saints, Genealogical
    Society Library, Safford Branch, Safford, AZ [*Library symbol*] ....
                                                                    AzSafGS
Church of Jesus Christ of Latter-Day Saints, Genealogical
    Society Library, Show Low Branch, Show Low, AZ [*Library
    symbol*] .... AzShGS
Church of Jesus Christ of Latter-Day Saints, Genealogical
    Society Library, St. Johns Branch, Stake Center, St. Johns,
    AZ [*Library symbol*] .... AzSjGS
Church of Jesus Christ of Latter-Day Saints, Genealogical
    Society Library, Snowflake Branch, Snowflake, AZ [*Library
    symbol*] .... AzSnGS
Church of Jesus Christ of Latter-Day Saints, Genealogical
    Society Library, St. David Arizona Stake Branch, St. David,
    AZ [*Library symbol*] .... AzStdGS
Church of Jesus Christ of Latter-Day Saints, Genealogical
    Society Library, Tucson Branch, Tucson, AZ [*Library symbol*] ..... AzTGS
Church of Jesus Christ of Latter-Day Saints, Genealogical
    Society Library, Yuma Branch, Yuma, AZ [*Library symbol*] .... AzYGS

Church of Jesus Christ of Latter-Day Saints, Genealogical
    Society Library, Cardston Branch, Cardston, AB, Canada
    [*Library symbol*] .... CaACaCJC
Church of Jesus Christ of Latter-Day Saints, Genealogical
    Society Library, Calgary Branch, Calgary, AB, Canada
    [*Library symbol*] .... CaACCJC
Church of Jesus Christ of Latter-Day Saints, Genealogical
    Society Library, Edmonton Branch, Edmonton, AB, Canada
    [*Library symbol*] .... CaAECJC
Church of Jesus Christ of Latter-Day Saints, Genealogical
    Society Library, Lethbridge Branch, Stake Center,
    Lethbridge, AB, Canada [*Library symbol*] .... CaALCJC
Church of Jesus Christ of Latter-Day Saints, Genealogical
    Society Library, Vancouver Branch, Stake Center, Burnaby,
    Vancouver, BC, Canada [*Library symbol*] .... CaBBCJC
Church of Jesus Christ of Latter-Day Saints, Genealogical
    Society Library, Anaheim Branch, Anaheim, CA [*Library
    symbol*] .... CAnaGS
Church of Jesus Christ of Latter-Day Saints, Genealogical
    Society Library, Toronto Branch, Etobicoke, ON, Canada
    [*Library symbol*] .... CaOTCJC
Church of Jesus Christ of Latter-Day Saints, Genealogical
    Society Library, Bakersfield Branch, Bakersfield, CA [*Library
    symbol*] .... CBaGS
Church of Jesus Christ of Latter-Day Saints, Genealogical
    Society Library, Barstow Branch, Barstow, CA [*Library
    symbol*] .... CBarGS
Church of Jesus Christ of Latter-Day Saints, Genealogical
    Society Library, Chico Branch, Stake Center, Chico, CA
    [*Library symbol*] .... CChiGS
Church of Jesus Christ of Latter-Day Saints, Genealogical
    Society Library, Covina Branch, Covina, CA [*Library symbol*] ....
                                                                    CCovGS
Church of Jesus Christ of Latter-Day Saints, Genealogical
    Society Library, Eureka Branch, Eureka, CA [*Library symbol*] .... CEGS
Church of Jesus Christ of Latter-Day Saints, Genealogical
    Society Library, Fresno Branch, Fresno, CA [*Library symbol*] .... CFGS
Church of Jesus Christ of Latter-Day Saints, Genealogical
    Society Library, Santa Barbara Branch, Goleta, CA [*Library
    symbol*] .... CGoGS
Church of Jesus Christ of Latter-Day Saints, Genealogical
    Society Library, Gridley Branch, Gridley, CA [*Library symbol*] .... CGrlGS
Church of Jesus Christ of Latter-Day Saints, Genealogical
    Society Library, Los Angeles Temple, Los Angeles, CA
    [*Library symbol*] .... CLGL
Church of Jesus Christ of Latter-Day Saints, Genealogical
    Society Library, Los Angeles East Branch, Los Angeles, CA
    [*Library symbol*] .... Cl.GLE
Church of Jesus Christ of Latter-Day Saints, Genealogical
    Society Library, Long Beach East Branch, Stake Center,
    Long Beach, CA [*Library symbol*] .... CLobGS
Church of Jesus Christ of Latter-Day Saints, Genealogical
    Society Library, Santa Maria Branch, Lompoc, CA [*Library
    symbol*] .... CLomGS
Church of Jesus Christ of Latter-Day Saints, Genealogical
    Society Library, Modesto, CA [*Library symbol*] .... CMG
Church of Jesus Christ of Latter-Day Saints, Genealogical
    Society Library, Arvada Branch, Arvada, CO [*Library symbol*] ....
                                                                    CoArGS
Church of Jesus Christ of Latter-Day Saints, Genealogical
    Society Library, Boulder Stake Branch, Boulder, CO [*Library
    symbol*] .... CoBGS
Church of Jesus Christ of Latter-Day Saints, Genealogical
    Society Library, Colorado Springs Branch, Colorado Springs,
    CO [*Library symbol*] .... CoCGS
Church of Jesus Christ of Latter-Day Saints, Genealogical
    Society Library, Durango Stake Branch, Cortez, CO [*Library
    symbol*] .... CoCoGS
Church of Jesus Christ of Latter-Day Saints, Genealogical
    Society Library, Denver Branch, Stake Center, Denver, CO
    [*Library symbol*] .... CoDGL
Church of Jesus Christ of Latter-Day Saints, Genealogical
    Society Library, Fort Collins Branch, Fort Collins, CO [*Library
    symbol*] .... CoFGS
Church of Jesus Christ of Latter-Day Saints, Genealogical
    Society Library, Grand Junction Branch, Stake Center,
    Grand Junction, CO [*Library symbol*] .... CoGjGS
Church of Jesus Christ of Latter-Day Saints, Genealogical
    Society Library, Oakland Branch, Oakland, CA [*Library
    symbol*] .... COGS
Church of Jesus Christ of Latter-Day Saints, Genealogical
    Society Library, Littleton Branch, Littleton, CO [*Library
    symbol*] .... CoLiGS
Church of Jesus Christ of Latter-Day Saints, Genealogical
    Society Library, LaJara Branch, Stake Center, LaJara, CO
    [*Library symbol*] .... CoLjaGS
Church of Jesus Christ of Latter-Day Saints, Genealogical
    Society Library, Denver North Branch, Northglenn, CO
    [*Library symbol*] .... CoNgGS

Church of Jesus Christ of Latter-Day Saints, Genealogical Society Library, Redding Branch, Redding, CA [*Library symbol*] .... CRedGS
Church of Jesus Christ of Latter-Day Saints, Genealogical Society Library, Riverside Branch, Riverside, CA [*Library symbol*] .... CRivGS
Church of Jesus Christ of Latter-Day Saints, Genealogical Society Library, Riverside West Branch, Riverside, CA [*Library symbol*] .... CRivGS-W
Church of Jesus Christ of Latter-Day Saints, Genealogical Society Library, San Bernardino Branch, San Bernardino, CA [*Library symbol*] .... CSbGS
Church of Jesus Christ of Latter-Day Saints, Genealogical Society Library, San Diego Branch, San Diego, CA [*Library symbol*] .... CSdGS
Church of Jesus Christ of Latter-Day Saints, Genealogical Society Library, Monterey Branch, Seaside, CA [*Library symbol*] .... CSeaGS
Church of Jesus Christ of Latter-Day Saints, Genealogical Society Library, Sacramento Branch, Sacramento, CA [*Library symbol*] .... CSGS
Church of Jesus Christ of Latter-Day Saints, Genealogical Society Library, San Jose Branch, San Jose, CA [*Library symbol*] .... CSjGS
Church of Jesus Christ of Latter-Day Saints, Genealogical Society Library, San Luis Obispo Branch, San Luis Obispo, CA [*Library symbol*] .... CSluGS
Church of Jesus Christ of Latter-Day Saints, Genealogical Society Library, Santa Clara Branch, Santa Clara, CA [*Library symbol*] .... CStclGS
Church of Jesus Christ of Latter-Day Saints, Genealogical Society Library, Stockton Branch, Stockton, CA [*Library symbol*] .... CStoGS
Church of Jesus Christ of Latter-Day Saints, Genealogical Society Library, Hartford Branch, Manchester, CT [*Library symbol*] .... CtManGS
Church of Jesus Christ of Latter-Day Saints, Genealogical Society Library, Ventura Branch, Ventura, CA [*Library symbol*] .... CVtGS
Church of Jesus Christ of Latter-Day Saints, Genealogical Society Library, Jacksonville Branch, Jacksonville, FL [*Library symbol*] .... FJGS
Church of Jesus Christ of Latter-Day Saints, Genealogical Society Library, Miami Branch, Miami, FL [*Library symbol*] .... FMGS
Church of Jesus Christ of Latter-Day Saints, Genealogical Society Library, Orlando Branch, Orlando, FL [*Library symbol*] .... FOGS
Church of Jesus Christ of Latter-Day Saints, Genealogical Society Library, Pensacola Branch, Pensacola, FL [*Library symbol*] .... FPeGS
Church of Jesus Christ of Latter-Day Saints, Genealogical Society Library, Tampa Branch, Tampa, FL [*Library symbol*] .... FTGS
Church of Jesus Christ of Latter-Day Saints, Genealogical Society Library, Macon Branch, Columbus, GA [*Library symbol*] .... GColuGS
Church of Jesus Christ of Latter-Day Saints, Genealogical Society Library, Sandy Springs Georgia Branch, Dunwoody, GA [*Library symbol*] .... GDunGS
Church of Jesus Christ of Latter-Day Saints, Genealogical Society Library, Laie Branch, Laie, HI [*Library symbol*] .... HLaGS
Church of Jesus Christ of Latter-Day Saints, Genealogical Society Library, Des Moines Branch, West Des Moines, IA [*Library symbol*] .... IaWdmGS
Church of Jesus Christ of Latter-Day Saints, Genealogical Society Library, Champaign Stake Branch, Champaign, IL [*Library symbol*] .... IChamGS
Church of Jesus Christ of Latter-Day Saints, Genealogical Society Library, Chicago Heights Branch, Chicago Heights, IL [*Library symbol*] .... IChGS
Church of Jesus Christ of Latter-Day Saints, Genealogical Society Library, Blackfoot West Branch, Stake Center, Blackfoot, ID [*Library symbol*] .... IdBfGS
Church of Jesus Christ of Latter-Day Saints, Genealogical Society Library, Burley Branch, Burley, ID [*Library symbol*] .... IdBurGS
Church of Jesus Christ of Latter-Day Saints, Genealogical Society Library, Driggs Branch, Driggs, ID [*Library symbol*] .... IdDrGS
Church of Jesus Christ of Latter-Day Saints, Genealogical Society Library, Idaho Falls Branch, Idaho Falls, ID [*Library symbol*] .... IdIfGS
Church of Jesus Christ of Latter-Day Saints, Genealogical Society Library, Lewiston Branch, Stake Center, Lewiston, ID [*Library symbol*] .... IdLGS
Church of Jesus Christ of Latter-Day Saints, Genealogical Society Library, Malad Stake Branch, Malad City, ID [*Library symbol*] .... IdMaGS
Church of Jesus Christ of Latter-Day Saints, Genealogical Society Library, Moore Branch, Lost River Stake Center, Moore, ID [*Library symbol*] .... IdMoGS
Church of Jesus Christ of Latter-Day Saints, Genealogical Society Library, Pocatello Branch, Pocatello, ID [*Library symbol*] .... IdPGS
Church of Jesus Christ of Latter-Day Saints, Genealogical Society Library, Salmon Branch, Salmon River Stake Center, Salmon, ID [*Library symbol*] .... IdSulGS
Church of Jesus Christ of Latter-Day Saints, Genealogical Society Library, Twin Falls Branch, Twin Falls, ID [*Library symbol*] .... IdTfGS
Church of Jesus Christ of Latter-Day Saints, Genealogical Society Library, Naperville Branch, Naperville, IL [*Library symbol*] .... INapGS
Church of Jesus Christ of Latter-Day Saints, Genealogical Society Library, Fort Wayne Branch, Fort Wayne, IN [*Library symbol*] .... InFwGS
Church of Jesus Christ of Latter-Day Saints, Genealogical Society Library, Wilmette Branch, Wilmette, IL [*Library symbol*] .... IWilGS
Church of Jesus Christ of Latter-Day Saints, Genealogical Society Library, Wichita Branch, Wichita, KS [*Library symbol*] .... KWiGS
Church of Jesus Christ of Latter-Day Saints, Genealogical Society Library, Baton Rouge Branch, Baton Rouge, LA [*Library symbol*] .... LBrGS
Church of Jesus Christ of Latter-Day Saints, Genealogical Society Library, Silver Spring Branch, Silver Spring, MD [*Library symbol*] .... MdSsGS
Church of Jesus Christ of Latter-Day Saints, Genealogical Society Library, Augusta Branch, Farmingdale, ME [*Library symbol*] .... MeFarGS
Church of Jesus Christ of Latter-Day Saints, Genealogical Society Library, Bloomfield Hills Branch, Bloomfield Hills, MI [*Library symbol*] .... MiBloGS
Church of Jesus Christ of Latter-Day Saints, Genealogical Society Library, Dearborn Stake Branch, LDS Chapel, Dearborn, MI [*Library symbol*] .... MiDbGS
Church of Jesus Christ of Latter-Day Saints, Genealogical Society Library, Lansing Branch, Stake Center, Lansing, MI [*Library symbol*] .... MiLGS
Church of Jesus Christ of Latter-Day Saints, Genealogical Society Library, Midland Stake Branch, Midland, MI [*Library symbol*] .... MiMidGS
Church of Jesus Christ of Latter-Day Saints, Genealogical Society Library, Minneapolis Branch, Minneapolis, MN [*Library symbol*] .... MnMGS
Church of Jesus Christ of Latter-Day Saints, Genealogical Society Library, Columbia Missouri Branch, Columbia, MO [*Library symbol*] .... MoCoGS
Church of Jesus Christ of Latter-Day Saints, Genealogical Society Library, Kansas City Branch, Kansas City, MO [*Library symbol*] .... MoKGS
Church of Jesus Christ of Latter-Day Saints, Genealogical Society Library, St. Louis Branch, St. Louis, MO [*Library symbol*] .... MoSGS
Church of Jesus Christ of Latter-Day Saints, Genealogical Society Library, Billings Branch, Billings, MT [*Library symbol*] .... MtBilGS
Church of Jesus Christ of Latter-Day Saints, Genealogical Society Library, Butte Stake Branch, Dillon Chapel, Dillon, MT [*Library symbol*] .... MtDiGS
Church of Jesus Christ of Latter-Day Saints, Genealogical Society Library, Great Falls Branch, Great Falls, MT [*Library symbol*] .... MtGrGS
Church of Jesus Christ of Latter-Day Saints, Genealogical Society Library, Helena Branch, Helena, MT [*Library symbol*] .... MtHGS
Church of Jesus Christ of Latter-Day Saints, Genealogical Society Library, Kalispell Branch, Kalispell, MT [*Library symbol*] .... MtKGS
Church of Jesus Christ of Latter-Day Saints, Genealogical Society Library, Missoula Branch, Missoula, MT [*Library symbol*] .... MtMisGS
Church of Jesus Christ of Latter-Day Saints, Genealogical Society Library, Boston Branch, Weston, MA [*Library symbol*] .... MWestonGS
Church of Jesus Christ of Latter-Day Saints, Genealogical Society Library, Colonia Juarez Branch, Chihuahua, Mexico [*Library symbol*] .... MxChGS
Church of Jesus Christ of Latter-Day Saints, Genealogical Society Library, Omaha Branch, Omaha, NE [*Library symbol*] .... NbOGS
Church of Jesus Christ of Latter-Day Saints, Genealogical Society Library, Charlotte North Carolina Branch, Charlotte, NC [*Library symbol*] .... NcCGS
Church of Jesus Christ of Latter-Day Saints, Genealogical Society Library, Raleigh Branch, Raleigh, NC [*Library symbol*] .... NcRGS
Church of Jesus Christ of Latter-Day Saints, Genealogical Society Library, East Brunswick Stake Branch, East Brunswick, NJ [*Library symbol*] .... NjEbGS
Church of Jesus Christ of Latter-Day Saints, Genealogical Society Library, Caldwell Branch, Summit, NJ [*Library symbol*] .... NjSGS
Church of Jesus Christ of Latter-Day Saints, Genealogical Society Library, Albany New York Stake Branch, Loudonville, NY [*Library symbol*] .... NLouvGS

Church of Jesus Christ of Latter-Day Saints, Genealogical
Society Library, Albuquerque Branch, Albuquerque, NM
[*Library symbol*] .... NmAGS

Church of Jesus Christ of Latter-Day Saints, Genealogical
Society Library, Farmington Branch, Farmington, NM [*Library
symbol*] ....NmFGS

Church of Jesus Christ of Latter-Day Saints, Genealogical
Society Library, New York Branch, New York, NY [*Library
symbol*] .... NNGS

Church of Jesus Christ of Latter-Day Saints, Genealogical
Society Library, Plainview Branch, Plainview, NY [*Library
symbol*] ....NPIGS

Church of Jesus Christ of Latter-Day Saints, Genealogical
Society Library, Rochester Branch, Rochester, NY [*Library
symbol*] .... NRGS

Church of Jesus Christ of Latter-Day Saints, Genealogical
Society Library, Ithaca Branch, Vestal, NY [*Library symbol*] ....NVeGS

Church of Jesus Christ of Latter-Day Saints, Genealogical
Society Library, Ely Branch, Ely, NV [*Library symbol*] ....NvElGS

Church of Jesus Christ of Latter-Day Saints, Genealogical
Society Library, Fallon Branch, Fallon, NV [*Library symbol*] ....NvFGS

Church of Jesus Christ of Latter-Day Saints, Genealogical
Society Library, Las Vegas Branch, Las Vegas, NV [*Library
symbol*] .... NvLGS

Church of Jesus Christ of Latter-Day Saints, Genealogical
Society Library, Reno Branch, Reno, NV [*Library symbol*] ....NvRGS

Church of Jesus Christ of Latter-Day Saints, Genealogical
Society Library, Auckland Branch, Auckland, New Zealand
[*Library symbol*] ....NzAGS

Church of Jesus Christ of Latter-Day Saints, Genealogical
Society Library, Canterbury Branch, Christchurch, New
Zealand [*Library symbol*] ....NzCGS

Church of Jesus Christ of Latter-Day Saints, Genealogical
Society Library, Temple View Branch, Temple View, New
Zealand [*Library symbol*] ....NzTvGS

Church of Jesus Christ of Latter-Day Saints, Genealogical
Society Library, Wellington Stake Branch, Wellington, New
Zealand [*Library symbol*] ....NzWGS

Church of Jesus Christ of Latter-Day Saints, Genealogical
Society Library, Cincinnati Branch, Cincinnati, OH [*Library
symbol*] .... OCGS

Church of Jesus Christ of Latter-Day Saints, Genealogical
Society Library, Columbus Branch, Columbus, OH [*Library
symbol*] .... OCoGS

Church of Jesus Christ of Latter-Day Saints, Genealogical
Society Library, Dayton Ohio Branch, Dayton, OH [*Library
symbol*] .... ODaGL

Church of Jesus Christ of Latter-Day Saints, Genealogical
Society Library, Oklahoma City Branch, Oklahoma City, OK
[*Library symbol*] ....OkOkGS

Church of Jesus Christ of Latter-Day Saints, Genealogical
Society Library, Tulsa Branch, Tulsa, OK [*Library symbol*] ....OkTGS

Church of Jesus Christ of Latter-Day Saints, Genealogical
Society Library, Beaverton Branch, Beaverton, OR [*Library
symbol*] .... OrBGS

Church of Jesus Christ of Latter-Day Saints, Genealogical
Society Library, Corvallis Branch, Corvallis, OR [*Library
symbol*] .... OrCGS

Church of Jesus Christ of Latter-Day Saints, Genealogical
Society Library, Eugene Branch, Eugene, OR [*Library symbol*] .... OrEGS

Church of Jesus Christ of Latter-Day Saints, Genealogical
Society Library, Gresham Branch, Gresham, OR [*Library
symbol*] .... OrGrGS

Church of Jesus Christ of Latter-Day Saints, Genealogical
Society Library, La Grande Branch, La Grande, OR [*Library
symbol*] .... OrLgGS

Church of Jesus Christ of Latter-Day Saints, Genealogical
Society Library, Medford Branch, Medford, OR [*Library
symbol*] .... OrMeGS

Church of Jesus Christ of Latter-Day Saints, Genealogical
Society Library, Coos Bay Stake Branch, North Bend, OR
[*Library symbol*] ....OrNbGS

Church of Jesus Christ of Latter-Day Saints, Genealogical
Society Library, Nyssa Branch, Nyssa, OR [*Library symbol*] .... OrNyGS

Church of Jesus Christ of Latter-Day Saints, Genealogical
Society Library, Portland Branch, Portland, OR [*Library
symbol*] .... OrPGS

Church of Jesus Christ of Latter-Day Saints, Genealogical
Society Library, Portland East Branch, Portland, OR [*Library
symbol*] .... OrPGSE

Church of Jesus Christ of Latter-Day Saints, Genealogical
Society Library, Salem Branch, Salem, OR [*Library symbol*] ...... OrSaGS

Church of Jesus Christ of Latter-Day Saints, Genealogical
Society Library, Cleveland Branch, Westlake, OH [*Library
symbol*] .... OWlGS

Church of Jesus Christ of Latter-Day Saints, Genealogical
Society Library, Philadelphia Branch, Broomall, PA [*Library
symbol*] .... PBroGS

Church of Jesus Christ of Latter-Day Saints, Genealogical
Society Library, Gettysburg Branch, York, PA [*Library symbol*].....PYGS

Church of Jesus Christ of Latter-Day Saints, Genealogical
Society Library, Columbia Branch, Columbia, SC [*Library
symbol*] ....ScCoGS

Church of Jesus Christ of Latter-Day Saints, Genealogical
Society Library, Knoxville Branch, Knoxville, TN [*Library
symbol*] .... TKGS

Church of Jesus Christ of Latter-Day Saints, Genealogical
Society Library, Memphis Branch, Memphis, TN [*Library
symbol*] .... TMGS

Church of Jesus Christ of Latter-Day Saints, Genealogical
Society Library, Tennessee South District Branch, Tullahoma,
TN [*Library symbol*] .... TTuGS

Church of Jesus Christ of Latter-Day Saints, Genealogical
Society Library, Austin Branch, Austin, TX [*Library symbol*]...... TxAuGS

Church of Jesus Christ of Latter-Day Saints, Genealogical
Society Library, Corpus Christi Branch, Corpus Christi, TX
[*Library symbol*] ....TxCcGS

Church of Jesus Christ of Latter-Day Saints, Genealogical
Society Library, Dallas Branch, Dallas, TX [*Library symbol*] ....TxDaGS

Church of Jesus Christ of Latter-Day Saints, Genealogical
Society Library, El Paso Branch, El Paso, TX [*Library symbol*] ..... TxEGS

Church of Jesus Christ of Latter-Day Saints, Genealogical
Society Library, Fort Worth Branch, North Richland Hills,
Fort Worth, TX [*Library symbol*].................................... TxFGS

Church of Jesus Christ of Latter-Day Saints, Genealogical
Society Library, Longview Branch, Gilmer, TX [*Library
symbol*] ....TxGilGS

Church of Jesus Christ of Latter-Day Saints, Genealogical
Society Library, Houston Branch, Houston, TX [*Library
symbol*] ....TxHGS

Church of Jesus Christ of Latter-Day Saints, Genealogical
Society Library, Odessa Stake Branch, Odessa, TX [*Library
symbol*] ....TxOGS

Church of Jesus Christ of Latter-Day Saints, Genealogical
Society Library, San Antonio Branch, San Antonio, TX
[*Library symbol*] ....TxSaGS

Church of Jesus Christ of Latter-Day Saints, Genealogical
Society Library, Beaumont Branch, Vidor, TX [*Library symbol*] ....
TxVidGS

Church of Jesus Christ of Latter-Day Saints, Genealogical
Society Library, Brigham City South Branch, Brigham City, UT
[*Library symbol*] ....UBcGS

Church of Jesus Christ of Latter-Day Saints, Genealogical
Society Library, Beaver Branch, Beaver, UT [*Library symbol*] .....UBeGS

Church of Jesus Christ of Latter-Day Saints, Genealogical
Society Library, Duchesne Branch, Stake Center, Duchesne,
UT [*Library symbol*] ....UDucGS

Church of Jesus Christ of Latter-Day Saints, Genealogical
Society Library, Kanab Branch, Stake Center, Kanab, UT
[*Library symbol*] ....UKaGS

Church of Jesus Christ of Latter-Day Saints, Genealogical
Society Library, Cache Branch, Logan, UT [*Library symbol*] ....ULGS

Church of Jesus Christ of Latter-Day Saints, Genealogical
Society Library, Mount Pleasant Branch, Stake Center,
Mount Pleasant, UT [*Library symbol*] ....UMpGS

Church of Jesus Christ of Latter-Day Saints, Genealogical
Society Library, Ogden Branch, Ogden, UT [*Library symbol*] .... UOGS

Church of Jesus Christ of Latter-Day Saints, Genealogical
Society Library, Utah Valley Branch, Provo, UT [*Library
symbol*] ....UPGS

Church of Jesus Christ of Latter-Day Saints, Genealogical
Society Library, Price Branch, Price, UT [*Library symbol*] ....UPrGS

Church of Jesus Christ of Latter-Day Saints, Genealogical
Society Library, Richfield Branch, Richfield, UT [*Library
symbol*] ....URifGS

Church of Jesus Christ of Latter-Day Saints, Genealogical
Society Library, Santaquin Stake Branch, Santaquin, UT
[*Library symbol*] ....USanGS

Church of Jesus Christ of Latter-Day Saints, Genealogical
Society Library, Salt Lake City, UT [*Library symbol*].....................USlGS

Church of Jesus Christ of Latter-Day Saints, Genealogical
Society Library, Springville Branch, Springville, UT [*Library
symbol*] ....USpGS

Church of Jesus Christ of Latter-Day Saints, Genealogical
Society Library, St. George Branch, St. George, UT [*Library
symbol*] .... UStgGS

Church of Jesus Christ of Latter-Day Saints, Genealogical
Society Library, Uintah Basin Branch, Vernal, UT [*Library
symbol*] ....UVGS

Church of Jesus Christ of Latter-Day Saints, Genealogical
Society Library, Annandale Branch, Annandale, VA [*Library
symbol*] ....ViAnGS

Church of Jesus Christ of Latter-Day Saints, Genealogical
Society Library, Richmond Stake Branch, Richmond, VA
[*Library symbol*] ....ViRGS

Church of Jesus Christ of Latter-Day Saints, Genealogical
Society Library, Norfolk Virginia Stake Branch, Virginia
Beach, VA [*Library symbol*].................................... ViVbGS

Church of Jesus Christ of Latter-Day Saints, Genealogical
Society Library, Bellevue Branch, Bellevue, WA [*Library
symbol*] ....WaBGS

Church of Jesus Christ of Latter-Day Saints, Genealogical Society Library, Everett, Washington Stake Branch, Everett, WA [*Library symbol*] ... WaEGS
Church of Jesus Christ of Latter-Day Saints, Genealogical Society Library, Longview Stake Branch, Longview, WA [*Library symbol*] ... WaLoGS
Church of Jesus Christ of Latter-Day Saints, Genealogical Society Library, Moses Lake Branch, Moses Lake, WA [*Library symbol*] ... WaMlGS
Church of Jesus Christ of Latter-Day Saints, Genealogical Society Library, Mount Vernon Branch, Mount Vernon, WA [*Library symbol*] ... WaMtvGS
Church of Jesus Christ of Latter-Day Saints, Genealogical Society Library, Olympia Branch, Olympia, WA [*Library symbol*] ... WaOGS
Church of Jesus Christ of Latter-Day Saints, Genealogical Society Library, Pasco Branch, Pasco, WA [*Library symbol*] ... WaPaGS
Church of Jesus Christ of Latter-Day Saints, Genealogical Society Library, Quincy Branch, Quincy, WA [*Library symbol*] ... WaQGS
Church of Jesus Christ of Latter-Day Saints, Genealogical Society Library, Richland Branch, Richland, WA [*Library symbol*] ... WaRiGS
Church of Jesus Christ of Latter-Day Saints, Genealogical Society Library, Seattle North Branch, Seattle, WA [*Library symbol*] ... WaSGS
Church of Jesus Christ of Latter-Day Saints, Genealogical Society Library, Spokane Branch, Spokane, WA [*Library symbol*] ... WaSpGL
Church of Jesus Christ of Latter-Day Saints, Genealogical Society Library, Tacoma Branch, Tacoma, WA [*Library symbol*] ... WaTGS
Church of Jesus Christ of Latter-Day Saints, Genealogical Society Library, Yakima Branch, Yakima, WA [*Library symbol*] ... WaYGS
Church of Jesus Christ of Latter-Day Saints, Genealogical Society Library, Milwaukee Branch, Hales Corners, WI [*Library symbol*] ... WHcGS
Church of Jesus Christ of Latter-Day Saints, Genealogical Society Library, Wisconsin East District Branch, Shawano, WI [*Library symbol*] ... WShawGS
Church of Jesus Christ of Latter-Day Saints, Genealogical Society Library, Afton Branch, Afton, WY [*Library symbol*] ... WyAGS
Church of Jesus Christ of Latter-Day Saints, Genealogical Society Library, Casper Branch, Casper, WY [*Library symbol*] ... WyCaGS
Church of Jesus Christ of Latter-Day Saints, Genealogical Society Library, Cheyenne Branch, Cheyenne, WY [*Library symbol*] ... WyCGS
Church of Jesus Christ of Latter-Day Saints, Genealogical Society Library, Cody Branch, Cody, WY [*Library symbol*] ... WyCoGS
Church of Jesus Christ of Latter-Day Saints, Genealogical Society Library, Evanston Branch, Evanston, WY [*Library symbol*] ... WyEvGS
Church of Jesus Christ of Latter-Day Saints, Genealogical Society Library, Lovell Branch, Lovell, WY [*Library symbol*] ... WyLoGS
Church of Jesus Christ of Latter-Day Saints, Historian's Office, Salt Lake City, UT [*Library symbol*] ... USIC
Church Lads' Brigade [*Church of England*] ... CLB
Church League of America ... CLA
Church of the Lutheran Confession ... CLC
Church Missionary College [*Church of England*] ... CMCOLL
Church Missionary Society [*British*] ... CMS
Church Missionary Union [*British*] ... CMU
Church of Monday Night Football ... CMNFB
Church Music Association of America ... CMAA
Church Music (London) [*A publication*] ... Church Mus (London)
Church Music Publishers Association ... CMPA
Church Music (St. Louis) [*A publication*] ... Church Mus (St L)
Church Pastoral Aid Society [*British*] ... CPAS
Church Peace Union [*Later, CRIA*] ... CPU
Church Penitentiary Association [*British*] ... CPA
Church Pennant [*Navy*] [*British*] ... CH
Church Pension Fund ... CPF
Church Pensions Conference ... CPC
Church Periodical Club ... CPC
Church Quarterly [*A publication*] ... Ch Q
Church Quarterly Review [*A publication*] ... Ch Q R
Church Quarterly Review [*A publication*] ... Church Q R
Church Quarterly Review [*A publication*] ... CQR
Church Record [*Genealogy*] ... CR
Church Research and Information Projects ... CRIPS
Church of Scientology of California ... CSC
Church of Scotland ... C of S
Church of Scotland ... C of SCOT
Church of Scotland and Free Churches Chaplain [*Navy*] [*British*] ... CSFCh
Church Slavic [*MARC language code*] [*Library of Congress*] ... chu
Church and Society [*A publication*] ... Ch Soc
Church Society for College Work ... CSCW
Church of South India ... CSI
Church Sunday School Union [*British*] ... CSSU
Church and Synagogue Libraries [*A publication*] ... C & SLib
Church and Synagogue Library Association ... CSLA
Church of What's Happening Now ... CWHN
Church Women United ... CWU
Church Women's Missionary Association [*Episcopalian*] ... CWMA
Church World Service [*of the National Council of Churches of Christ in the USA*] ... CWS
Churches' Center for Theology and Public Policy ... CCTPP
Churchill [*Canada*] [*Airport symbol*] ... YYQ
Churchill Falls [*Canada*] [*Airport symbol*] ... ZUM
Churchill Falls, NF [*Radio station call letters*] ... CFLC-FM
Churchill, MB [*Radio station call letters*] ... CHFC
Churchill Public Library, Churchill, MB, Canada [*Library symbol*] ... CaMCh
Churchill Research Range [*Air Force*] ... CRR
Churchman [*A publication*] ... Chmn
Churchmen's Commission for Decent Publications [*Defunct*] ... CCDP
Church's Fried Chicken, Inc. [*NYSE symbol*] ... CHU
Church's Ministry among Jews [*Church of England*] ... CMJ
Churchville-Chili Senior High School Library, Rochester, NY [*OCLC symbol*] ... RVY
Churchville, VA [*Radio station call letters*] ... WNLR
Churchwarden ... C
Churchwarden ... CHWDN
Churchwarden ... CW
Churchyard ... CHYD
Churdan City Library, Churdan, IA [*Library symbol*] ... IaChu
Chusal [*USSR*] [*Seismograph station code, US Geological Survey*] [*Closed*] ... CHS
Chute ... CHT
Chuvash [*MARC language code*] [*Library of Congress*] ... chv
Chymotrypsin [*An enzyme*] ... CT
Chymotrypsin Inhibitor Activity ... CIA
Chymotrypsin Unit ... CU
Chymotrypsin Units Inhibited ... CUI
Chymotrypsinogen [*Biochemistry*] ... ChTg
Chymotrypsinogen B [*Biochemistry*] ... CTRB
Chyron Corporation [*NASDAQ symbol*] ... CHYC
CI Mortgage Group SBI [*NYSE symbol*] [*Delisted*] ... CI
CI Realty Investors SBI [*NYSE symbol*] ... CIX
CIAT [*Centro Internacional de Agricultura Tropical*] **Annual Report** [*A publication*] ... CIAT Annu Rep
CIAT [*Centro Internacional de Agricultura Tropical*] **Series Seminars** [*A publication*] ... CIAT Ser Semin
Ciba Clinical Symposia [*A publication*] ... Ciba Clin Symp
Ciba Collection of Medical Illustrations [*A publication*] ... Ciba Collect Med Illus
Ciba Co. Ltd., Montreal, PQ, Canada [*Library symbol*] ... CaQMCi
Ciba Foundation. Colloquia on Endocrinology [*A publication*] ... Ciba Found Colloq Endocrinol
Ciba Foundation. Study Group [*A publication*] ... Ciba Found Study Group
Ciba Foundation. Symposia [*A publication*] ... Ciba Found Symp
Ciba-Geigy [*France*] [*Research code symbol*] ... AP
Ciba-Geigy AG [*Switzerland*] [*Research code symbol*] ... Ba
Ciba-Geigy AG [*Switzerland*] [*Research code symbol*] ... C
Ciba-Geigy AG [*Switzerland*] [*Research code symbol*] ... G
Ciba-Geigy AG [*Switzerland*] [*Research code symbol*] ... GP
Ciba-Geigy Canada Ltd., Dorval, PQ, Canada [*Library symbol*] ... CaQMCG
Ciba-Geigy Corp. [*Research code symbol*] ... GPA
Ciba-Geigy Corp. [*Research code symbol*] ... Su
Ciba-Geigy Technical Notes [*A publication*] ... Ciba-Geigy Tech Notes
Ciba Pharmaceutical Co., Research Library, Summit, NJ [*Library symbol*] ... NjSC
Ciba Review [*A publication*] ... Ciba R
Ciba Symposia [*A publication*] ... CBASA
Ciba Symposia [*A publication*] ... Ciba Symp
Cibachrome-Print [*Color photography*] ... CCP
Cibola Energy Corp. [*NASDAQ symbol*] ... CBLA
Cibus [*Meal*] [*Latin*] ... C
Cibus [*Meal*] [*Latin*] ... CIB
CIC Informations. Bulletin d'Informations Generales [*A publication*] ... CIC Inform B Inform Gen
Cicero [*Roman orator and author, 106-43 BC*] ... CIC
Cicero, IL [*Radio station call letters*] ... WCEV
Cicero, IL [*Radio station call letters*] ... WXOL
Cicero Public Library, Cicero, IL [*Library symbol*] ... ICic
Cicia [*Fiji*] [*Airport symbol*] ... ICI
CID [*Consortium on International Development*] **Information Network** ... CIDNET
Cidra, PR [*Radio station call letters*] ... WBRQ
Cidra, PR [*Television station call letters*] ... WCNT
Cie Internationale des Wagons-Lits et du Tourisme [*International Sleeping Car Company*] ... CIWLT
CIEA [*Central Institute for Experimental Animals*] **Preclinical Reports** [*A publication*] ... CIEA Preclin Rep
Ciencia [*A publication*] ... Cienc
Ciencia Agronomica [*A publication*] ... Cienc Agron
Ciencia Biologica: Biologia Molecular e Cellular [*A publication*] ... Cienc Biol: Biol Mol Cel
Ciencia Biologica, Ecologia, e Sistematica [*A publication*] ... Cienc Biol Ecol Sist
Ciencia e Cultura (Sao Paulo) [*A publication*] ... Cienc Cult (Sao Paulo)

Ciencia Interamericana [*A publication*]....Cienc Interam
Ciencia e Investigacion [*A publication*]....Cienc Invest
Ciencia e Investigacion (Buenos Aires) [*A publication*]....Cienc Invest (B Aires)
Ciencia y Naturaleza [*A publication*]....Cienc Nat
Ciencia y Tecnica [*A publication*]....Cienc & Tec
Ciencia y Tecnica en el Mundo [*A publication*]....Cienc Tec Mundo
Ciencia Tomista [*A publication*]....Cien Tom
Ciencia Tomista [*A publication*]....CiT
Ciencia Tomista [*A publication*]....CT
Ciencias Administrativas [*A publication*]....Cienc Adm
Ciencias Biologicas (Luanda) [*A publication*]....Cienc Biol (Luanda)
Ciencias Neurologicas [*A publication*]....Cienc Neurol
Ciencias. Serie 1. Matematica [*Havana*] [*A publication*]....Ciencias Ser 1 Mat
Ciencias. Serie 4. Ciencias Biologicas (Havana) [*A publication*]....Cienc Ser 4 Cienc Biol (Havana)
Ciencias. Serie 8. Investigaciones Marinas (Havana) [*A publication*]....Cienc Ser 8 Invest Mar (Havana)
Ciencias. Serie 10. Botanica (Havana) [*A publication*]....Cienc Ser 10 Bot (Havana)
Ciencias Veterinarias [*A publication*]....Cienc Vet
Ciencias Veterinarias y Alimentas y Nutricion Animal [*A publication*]....Cienc Vet Aliment Nutr Anim
Cienfuegos [*Cuba*] [*Airport symbol*] [*Obsolete*]....CFG
CIG, Cryogenics and Industrial Gases [*A publication*]....CIG Cryog Indus Gases
Cigar Association of America....CAA
Cigar Box Manufacturers [*Defunct*]....CBM
Cigar Institute of America [*Later, CAA*]....CIA
Cigar Makers' International Union of America [*Later, Retail, Wholesale, and Department Store Union*]....CMIU of A
Cigar Manufacturers Association of America [*Later, CAA*]....CMA
Cigar Manufacturers Association of America [*Later, CAA*]....CMAA
Cigar Manufacturers Association of Tampa....CMAT
Cigar Smokers of America [*Defunct*]....CSA
Cigarette Advertising Code, Inc.....CAC
Cigarette Advertising Normally Directed to Youth [*Student legal action organization*]....CANDY
Cigarette Lighter Manufacturers Association....CLMA
Cigarette Pack Collectors Association....CPCA
Cigarette Smoke Condensate....CSC
CIGNA Corp. [*NYSE symbol*]....CI
Ciguatoxin....CT
CIIG [*Construction Industry Information Group*] **Bulletin** [*A publication*]....CIIG Bull
CILA [*Centre Internationale de Linguistique Appliquee*] **Bulletin** [*A publication*]....CILA B
Cilag-Chemie AG [*Switzerland*] [*Research code symbol*]....C
Cilag-Chemie AG [*Switzerland*] [*Research code symbol*]....R
Ciliary Particle Transport Activity....CPTA
Ciliated Epithelial Cells [*Medicine*]....CEC
Ciliated Groove to Mouth....CGM
Ciliated Groove to Ventral Sac....CGVS
Cilicap [*Indonesia*] [*Airport symbol*]....CXP
Ciliocytopathoria [*Medicine*]....CCP
CIM [*Canadian Institute of Mining and Metallurgy*] **Bulletin** [*A publication*]....CIM Bull
Cimarron Corp. [*NASDAQ symbol*]....CIMN
Cimarron Investment [*NASDAQ symbol*]....CINV
Cimarron, NM [*Location identifier*] [*FAA*]....CIM
Cimarron Review [*A publication*]....CimR
Cimbebasia. Memoir [*A publication*]....Cimbebasia Mem
Cimbebasia. Series A [*A publication*]....Cimbebasia Ser A
Cimber Air [*Denmark*] [*ICAO designator*]....QI
Cimitarra [*Colombia*] [*Airport symbol*]....CIM
Cincinnati [*Ohio*]....CIN
Cincinnati [*Ohio*] [*Seismograph station code, US Geological Survey*] [*Closed*]....CNN
Cincinnati [*Ohio*] [*Airport symbol*]....CVG
Cincinnati Area Health Sciences Library Association [*Library network*]....CAHSLA
Cincinnati Art Museum. Bulletin [*A publication*]....Cincinnati Mus Bull
Cincinnati Art Museum. Bulletin. New Series [*A publication*]....Cincinnati Mus Bul ns
Cincinnati Art Museum, Cincinnati, OH [*Library symbol*]....OCA
Cincinnati Art Museum. News [*A publication*]....Cincinnati Mus N
Cincinnati Bell, Inc. [*NYSE symbol*]....CSN
Cincinnati Bible Seminary, Cincinnati, OH [*OCLC symbol*]....BSC
Cincinnati Bible Seminary, Cincinnati, OH [*Library symbol*]....OCB
Cincinnati Board of Trade....CBT
Cincinnati [*Ohio*] **- Covington** [*Kentucky*] [*Airport symbol*]....CVG
Cincinnati Electronics Corporation, Cincinnati, OH [*Library symbol*]....OCEleC
Cincinnati Financial Corp. [*NASDAQ symbol*]....CINF
Cincinnati Gas & Electric Co. [*NYSE symbol*]....CIN
Cincinnati General Hospital, Medical Library, Cincinnati, OH [*Library symbol*]....OCG
Cincinnati Historical Society. Bulletin [*A publication*]....CHSB
Cincinnati Historical Society, Cincinnati, OH [*Library symbol*]....OCHP
Cincinnati Law Library Association, Cincinnati, OH [*Library symbol*]....OCLaw
Cincinnati Masonic Temple, Cincinnati, OH [*Library symbol*]....OCM
Cincinnati Microwave [*NASDAQ symbol*]....CNMW
Cincinnati Milacron, Inc. [*NYSE symbol*]....CMZ
Cincinnati Milacron, Inc., Corporate Information Center, Cincinnati, OH [*OCLC symbol*]....CML
Cincinnati Milacron, Inc., Research Library, Cincinnati, OH [*Library symbol*]....OCMil
Cincinnati Milacron, Inc., Technical Information Center, Cincinnati, OH [*Library symbol*]....OCMil-T
Cincinnati, New Orleans, & Texas Pacific Railway Co.....CNO & TP
Cincinnati, New Orleans, & Texas Pacific Railway Co. [*AAR code*]....CNTP
Cincinnati Northern [*AAR code*]....CNOR
Cincinnati, OH [*Location identifier*] [*FAA*]....LUK
Cincinnati, OH [*Radio station call letters*]....WAIF
Cincinnati, OH [*Radio station call letters*]....WAKW
Cincinnati, OH [*Television station call letters*]....WBTI
Cincinnati, OH [*Television station call letters*]....WCET
Cincinnati, OH [*Radio station call letters*]....WCIN
Cincinnati, OH [*Radio station call letters*]....WCKY
Cincinnati, OH [*Television station call letters*]....WCPO-TV
Cincinnati, OH [*Radio station call letters*]....WEBN
Cincinnati, OH [*Radio station call letters*]....WGUC
Cincinnati, OH [*Radio station call letters*]....WJVS
Cincinnati, OH [*Radio station call letters*]....WKRC
Cincinnati, OH [*Television station call letters*]....WKRC-TV
Cincinnati, OH [*Radio station call letters*]....WKRQ
Cincinnati, OH [*Radio station call letters*]....WLW
Cincinnati, OH [*Television station call letters*]....WLWT
Cincinnati, OH [*Radio station call letters*]....WMLX
Cincinnati, OH [*Radio station call letters*]....WSAI
Cincinnati, OH [*Radio station call letters*]....WSAI-FM
Cincinnati, OH [*Radio station call letters*]....WTSJ
Cincinnati, OH [*Radio station call letters*]....WUBE-FM
Cincinnati, OH [*Radio station call letters*]....WVXU-FM
Cincinnati, OH [*Radio station call letters*]....WWEZ
Cincinnati Service Center [*IRS*]....CSC
Cincinnati Symphony Orchestra. Program Notes [*A publication*]....Cinc Sym Prog Notes
Cincinnati Symphony Orchestra. Program Notes [*A publication*]....Cin Sym
Cincinnati Technical College, Cincinnati, OH [*Library symbol*] [*OCLC symbol*]....OCT
CINCPAC [*Commander-in-Chief, Pacific*] **Operation Center**....COC
CINCPAC [*Commander-in-Chief, Pacific*] **Route Slip**....CPRS
CINCPAC [*Commander-in-Chief, Pacific*] **Supplement to DoD** [*Department of Defense*] **Basic Planning**....CSBPD
CINCPAC [*Commander-in-Chief, Pacific*] **Supplement to the Military Assistance Manual**....CSMAM
CINCPAC [*Commander-in-Chief, Pacific*] **Teletype Automated Net**....CTAN
CINCPAC [*Commander-in-Chief, Pacific*] **Voice Automated Net**....CVAN
Cinders [*Quality of the bottom*] [*Nautical charts*]....Cn
Cindy's, Inc. [*NASDAQ symbol*]....CNDY
Cine [*Turkey*] [*Seismograph station code, US Geological Survey*]....CIN
Cine Cubano [*A publication*]....C Cubano
Cine Revue [*A publication*]....C Revue
Cine Tracts [*A publication*]....C Tracts
Cinefantastique [*A publication*]....C Fantas
Cineforum [*A publication*]....C Forum
Cinegram Magazine [*A publication*]....Cinegram
Cinegraphic Scoring System....CSS
Cinema 5 Ltd. [*American Stock Exchange symbol*] [*Delisted*]....CNE
Cinema 77 [*A publication*]....C77
Cinema Canada [*A publication*]....C Can
Cinema Center Films....CCF
Cinema Journal [*A publication*]....Cinema J
Cinema Journal [*A publication*]....CJ
Cinema Nuovo [*A publication*]....C Nuovo
Cinema Papers [*A publication*]....C Papers
Cinema Pratique [*A publication*]....C Pratiq
Cinema Quebec [*A publication*]....C Quebec
Cinema (Romania) [*A publication*]....C (Romania)
Cinema Societa [*A publication*]....C Societa
Cinema Television Digest....CTVD
Cinema (United States) [*A publication*]....C (US)
Cinema (Zurich) [*A publication*]....C (Zurich)
Cinemanews [*A publication*]....C News
Cinemas [*Public-performance tariff class*] [*British*]....C
Cinemascope....CS
Cinemasud [*A publication*]....Csud
Cinematheque Scientifique Internationale [*International Scientific Film Library*]....CSI
Cinematographic....CINE
Cinemists 63....C63
Cinerama, Inc. [*American Stock Exchange symbol*] [*Delisted*]....CNM
Cineschedario-Letture Drammatiche [*A publication*]....C Let Dram
Cinetheodolite Orientation Target Array....COTA
Cinnaminson Little Paper, Cinnaminson, NJ [*Library symbol*]....NjCiL
Cintas Corp. [*NASDAQ symbol*]....CTAS
Cipher Data Products [*NASDAQ symbol*]....CIFR
Cipher and Telephony Equipment [*Military*]....CIPHONY
Cipher Text Auto Key [*Data processing*]....CTAK

Cipolletti [*Argentina*] [*Seismograph station code, US Geological Survey*] [*Closed*] ... CIP
Ciprico, Incorporated [*NASDAQ symbol*] ... CPCI
CIRC [*Central Information Reference and Control*] **On-Line Experiment** ... COLEX
Circa [*About*] [*Latin*] ... C
Circa [*About*] [*Latin*] ... Ca
Circa [*About*] [*Latin*] ... CIR
Circa [*About*] [*Latin*] ... CIRC
Circadian Data System ... CDS
Circadian Pacemaker [*Neurophysiology*] ... CP
Circadian Periodicity Experiment [*Skylab*] [*NASA*] ... CPE
Circimus [*Constellation*] ... Cir
Circimus [*Constellation*] ... Circ
Circle ... CIR
Circle ... CIRC
Circle ... CRC
Circle [*Alaska*] [*Airport symbol*] ... IRC
Circle Bed [*Medicine*] ... CB
Circle of Companions ... COC
Circle Cutting ... CCT
Circle End Point ... CEP
Circle of Equal Probability ... CEP
Circle Fine Art Corp. [*NASDAQ symbol*] ... CFNE
Circle Hot Springs [*Alaska*] [*Airport symbol*] [*Obsolete*] ... CHP
Circle Income Shares [*NASDAQ symbol*] ... CINS
Circle K Corp. [*American Stock Exchange symbol*] ... CKP
Circle Repertory Theater Company ... CRTC
Circle Seven Oil [*NASDAQ symbol*] ... CSOG
Circleville, OH [*Location identifier*] [*FAA*] ... CYO
Circleville, OH [*Radio station call letters*] ... WNRE
Circleville, OH [*Radio station call letters*] ... WNRE-FM
Circling [*Approach and landing charts*] [*Aviation*] ... C
Circolo Speleologico Romano. Notiziario [*A publication*] ... Circ Speleol Rom Not
Circon Corp. [*NASDAQ symbol*] ... CCON
Circuit ... C
Circuit ... CCT
Circuit ... CIR
Circuit ... CIRC
Circuit ... CKT
Circuit ... CRCT
Circuit ... CT
Circuit Activation Order ... CAO
Circuit Analysis [*Data processing*] ... CIRCAL
Circuit Board Card ... CBC
Circuit Board Card Tester ... CBCT
Circuit Board Extractor ... CBE
Circuit Board Holder ... CBH
Circuit Board Rack ... CBR
Circuit Breaker ... CB
Circuit Card Assembly ... CCA
Circuit Closing ... CC
Circuit Concentration Bay ... CCB
Circuit Condition Indicator ... CCI
Circuit Control ... C/C
Circuit Control Office [*Automatic Digital Information Network*] ... CCO
Circuit Court ... CC
Circuit Court of Appeals ... CCA
Circuit Court Library, Birmingham, AL [*Library symbol*] ... ABCC
Circuit Data Sheet ... CDS
Circuit Description ... CD
Circuit Design Fabrication ... CDF
Circuit Design, Fabrication, and Test Data Systems ... CDF & TDS
Circuit Diagrams ... CD
Circuit Distribution Assembly [*Ground Communications Facility, NASA*] ... CDA
Circuit Distribution Assembly [*Ground Communications Facility, NASA*] ... CDSA
Circuit Finder ... CF
Circuit Interrupter ... CI
Circuit Layout [*AT & T*] ... CL
Circuit Line Up ... CLU
Circuit Maintenance System [*AT & T*] ... CMS
Circuit Net Loss ... CNL
Circuit Notice [*Aviation*] ... CIRNOT
Circuit Order Preparation [*or Processing*] **System** [*AT & T*] ... COPS
Circuit Package ... CP
Circuit Package Schematic ... CPS
Circuit Protection Device ... CPD
Circuit Provision System [*AT & T*] ... CPS
Circuit Reliability Improvement ... CRI
Circuit Requirement Table ... CRT
Circuit Research Laboratories [*NASDAQ symbol*] ... CRLI
Circuit Switched Digital Capability [*AT & T*] ... CSDC
Circuit Switching Magnetic Tape ... CSMT
Circuit Switching Network ... CSN
Circuit Switching Station ... CSS
Circuit Switching Unit ... CSU
Circuit Terminating Arrangement ... CTA
Circuit under Test ... CUT
Circuit Test Set ... CTS
Circuit Theory ... CT
Circuits Manufacturing [*A publication*] ... Circuits Mfg
Circuits and Systems [*IEEE*] ... CAS
Circuits and Systems [*A publication*] ... Circuits Syst
Circuits, Systems, and Signal Processing [*A publication*] ... CSSP
Circular ... C
Circular ... CIR
Circular ... CIRC
Circular. Alabama Agricultural Experiment Station [*A publication*] ... Circ Ala Agr Exp Sta
Circular. Alabama Polytechnic Institute. Extension Service [*A publication*] ... Circ Ala Polytech Inst Ext Serv
Circular Aperture Antenna ... CAA
Circular Arc [*Aviation*] ... CA
Circular Arc ... CIRCARC
Circular Area Method ... CAM
Circular. Association of Mine Managers of South Africa [*A publication*] ... Circ Assoc Mine Managers S Afr
Circular. Auburn University. Agricultural Extension Service [*A publication*] ... Circ Auburn Univ Agr Ext Serv
Circular. California Agricultural Extension Service [*A publication*] ... Circ Calif Agr Ext Serv
Circular. Centro de Investigaciones Agricolas de El Bajio (CIAB) [*A publication*] ... Circ Cent Invest Agr El Bajio (CIAB)
Circular. Centro de Investigaciones Agricolas del Noroeste (CIANO) [*A publication*] ... Circ Cent Invest Agr Noroeste (CIANO)
Circular. Centro de Investigaciones Agricolas del Sudeste [*A publication*] ... Circ Cent Invest Agr Sudeste
Circular. Centro de Investigaciones del Basicas (CIB) [*A publication*] ... Circ Cent Invest Basicas (CIB)
Circular. Clemson Agricultural College. Extension Service [*A publication*] ... Circ Clemson Agr Coll Ext Serv
Circular. Comision de Parasitologia Agricola (Mexico) [*A publication*] ... Circular Com Parasitol Agric (Mexico)
Circular Crystal Facet ... CCF
Circular Cylindrical Shell ... CCS
Circular Dichroism ... CD
Circular Diffraction Grating ... CDG
Circular Dispersion ... CD
Circular Electric Mode ... CEM
Circular Electric Wire ... CEW
Circular Error [*Military*] ... CE
Circular Error Average [*Military*] ... CEA
Circular Error Probability [*Military*] ... CEP
Circular Farmaceutica [*A publication*] ... Circ Farm
Circular. Florida Agricultural Experiment Station [*A publication*] ... Circ Fla Agric Exp Stn
Circular. Florida University. Agricultural Extension Service [*A publication*] ... Circ Fla Univ Agr Ext Serv
Circular. Georgia Agricultural Experiment Stations [*A publication*] ... Circ GA Agr Exp Sta
Circular Hollow Section [*Metal industry*] ... CHS
Circular. Illinois Agricultural Experiment Station [*A publication*] ... Circular Illinois Agric Exper Station
Circular. Illinois Natural History Survey [*A publication*] ... Circ Ill Nat Hist Surv
Circular. Illinois Natural History Survey [*A publication*] ... Circ Ill Natur Hist Surv
Circular of Information. Oregon State College. Agricultural Experiment Station [*A publication*] ... Circ Inform Oreg State Coll Agr Exp Sta
Circular. Instituto Agronomico do Sul (Pelotas) [*A publication*] ... Circ Inst Agron Sul (Pelotas)
Circular. Instituto de Pesquisa Agropecuarias do Norte [*A publication*] ... Circ Inst Pesqui Agropecu Norte
Circular. Instituto de Pesquisa Agropecuarias do Sul [*A publication*] ... Circ Inst Pesqui Agropecu Sul
Circular. Instituto de Pesquisas e Experimentacao Agropecuarias do Norte [*A publication*] ... Circ Inst Pesq Exp Agropecuar N
Circular Intensity Difference [*Spectrometry*] ... CID
Circular. Kansas Agricultural Experiment Station [*A publication*] ... Circ Kans Agr Exp Sta
Circular. Kansas State University of Agriculture and Applied Science. Extension Service [*A publication*] ... Circ Kans State Univ Agr Appl Sci Ext Serv
Circular. Kentucky Agricultural Experiment Station [*A publication*] ... Circ KY Agric Exp Stn
Circular. Kentucky University. Agricultural Extension Service [*A publication*] ... Circ KY Univ Agr Ext Serv
Circular Letter ... CILET
Circular Letter [*Military*] ... CIRCLTR
Circular Letter ... CL
Circular. Line Elevators Farm Service [*A publication*] ... Circ Line Elevators Farm Serv
Circular. Louisiana Agricultural Experiment Station [*A publication*] ... Circ LA Agr Exp Sta
Circular Magnetic Wave ... CMW
Circular Measure ... CM
Circular Mil [*Wire measure*] ... CM

Circular Mil [*Wire measure*] ..... CMIL
Circular Mil Area ..... CMA
Circular Mil Foot ..... CMF
Circular Mils, Thousands ..... MCM
Circular. Missouri University. College of Agriculture. Extension Service [*A publication*] ..... Circ MO Univ Coll Agr Ext Serv
Circular. Montana Agricultural Experiment Station [*A publication*] ..... Circ Mont Agr Exp Sta
Circular. Montana State College. Cooperative Extension Service [*A publication*] ..... Circ Mont State Coll Coop Ext Serv
Circular Muscle [*Anatomy*] ..... CM
Circular. New Jersey Agricultural Experiment Station [*A publication*] ..... Circ New Jers Agric Exp Stn
Circular. New Jersey Agricultural Experiment Station [*A publication*] ..... Circ NJ Agr Exp Sta
Circular. New Mexico State Bureau of Mines and Mineral Resources [*A publication*] ..... Circ New Mex St Bur Mines Miner Resour
Circular. New Mexico State University. Agricultural Extension Service [*A publication*] ..... Circ N Mex State Univ Agr Ext Serv
Circular. North Dakota Agricultural College. Agricultural Extension Service [*A publication*] ..... Circ N Dak Agr Coll Agr Ext Serv
Circular Note [*Business and trade*] ..... CN
Circular. Oklahoma State University of Agriculture and Applied Science. Agricultural Extension Service [*A publication*] ..... Circ Okla State Univ Agr Appl Sci Agr Ext Serv
Circular. Oregon State College. Engineering Experiment Station [*A publication*] ..... Circ Oreg State Coll Eng Exp
Circular. Oregon State University. Engineering Experiment Station [*A publication*] ..... Circ Oreg State Univ Eng Exp St
Circular Parking Orbit [*Aerospace*] ..... CPO
Circular. Pennsylvania Agricultural Experiment Station [*A publication*] ..... Circ PA Agric Exp Stn
Circular. Pennsylvania State University. Earth and Mineral Sciences Experiment Station [*A publication*] ..... Circ PA State Univ Earth Miner Sci Exp St
Circular Pitch [*Technical drawings*] ..... CP
Circular Polarization ..... CP
Circular Probable Error ..... CPE
Circular Radio Beacon ..... RC
Circular of Requirements ..... COR
Circular Series. Oregon State College. Engineering Experiment Station [*A publication*] ..... Cir Ser Oreg State Coll Eng Exp Stn
Circular. South Dakota Agricultural Experiment Station [*A publication*] ..... Circ S Dak Agr Exp Sta
Circular Terminal Orbit [*Aerospace*] ..... CTO
Circular. University of Georgia. College of Agriculture. Cooperative Extension Service [*A publication*] ..... Circ Univ GA Coll Agr Coop Ext Serv
Circular. University of Illinois. College of Agriculture. Cooperative Extension Service [*A publication*] ..... Circ Univ Ill Coll Agr Coop Ext Serv
Circular. University of Kentucky. Agricultural Extension Service [*A publication*] ..... Circ Univ KY Agr Ext Serv
Circular. University of Wisconsin. College of Agriculture. Extension Service [*A publication*] ..... Circ Univ Wis Coll Agr Ext Serv
Circular Variable Filter [*Instrumentation*] ..... CVF
Circular Variable Filter Spectrometer ..... CVFS
Circular Vection [*Optics*] CV
Circular Velocity VC
Circular. Virginia Polytechnic Institute. Agricultural Extension Service [*A publication*] ..... Circ VA Polytech Inst Agr Ext Serv
Circular. Washington Agriculture Experiment Station [*A publication*] ..... Circ Wash Agr Exp Sta
Circular. West Virginia Agricultural Experiment Station [*A publication*] ..... Circular West Virginia Agric Exper Station
Circularly Disposed Antenna Array [*Radio receiver*] ..... CDAA
Circularly Polarized Antenna [*or Array*] ..... CPA
Circulars. Electrotechnical Laboratory (Tokyo) [*A publication*] ..... Circ Electrotech Lab (Tokyo)
Circulars. Electrotechnical Laboratory (Tokyo, Japan) [*A publication*] ..... Circ Electrotech Lab (Tokyo Japan)
Circulate ..... CRCLT
Circulate ..... CRLC
Circulating Copy CC
Circulating Fuel Reactor Experiment [*Nuclear energy*] ..... CFRE
Circulating Granulocyte Pool [*Hematology*] ..... CGP
Circulating Immune Complexes [*Medicine*] CIC
Circulating Platelet Aggregate [*Hematology*] ..... CPA
Circulating Water Pump ..... CWP
Circulation ..... CIRC
Circulation Control Point ..... CCP
Circulation Control Rotor [*Navy*] ..... CCR
Circulation Control Wing ..... CCW
Circulation Input Recording Center [*Data processing system*] ..... CIRC
Circulation Library Automated System for Inventory Control [*Cincinnati Electronics Corp.*] [*Information service*] ..... CLASSIC
Circulation Lift Limit CLL
Circulation, Motor Ability, Sensation, and Swelling [*Medicine*] ..... CMSS
Circulation Research [*A publication*] ..... Circ Res
Circulation Research [*A publication*] ..... Circulation Res
Circulation Research. Supplement [*A publication*] ..... Circ Res Suppl
Circulation. Supplement [*A publication*] ..... Circ Suppl
Circulatory Shock [*A publication*] ..... Circ Shock
Circulatory Shock (Supplement) [*A publication*] ..... Circ Shock (Suppl)
Circulo de Escritores y Poetas Iberoamericanos [*An association*] ..... CEPI
Circum C
Circum-Pacific Energy and Mineral Resources Conference ..... CPEMRC
Circumcaribbean [*MARC geographic area code*] [*Library of Congress*] ..... cr-----
Circumcision [*Medicine*] ..... CIRC
Circumference C
Circumference ..... CIRC
Circumference ..... CIRCM
Circumference ..... CIRCUM
Circumference ..... CRCMF
Circumference of Head [*Medicine*] ..... C of H
Circumferential Pneumatic Compression [*Medicine*] ..... CPC
Circumflex ..... CFX
Circumlunar Mission ..... CLM
Circumnavigate ..... CIRNAV
Circumnavigators Club CC
Circumpolar Deep Water [*Oceanography*] ..... CDW
Circumstance ..... CIRC
Circumstance ..... CIRCE
Circumstances Undetermined Pending Police Investigation ..... CUPPI
Circus ..... CIR
Circus Circus Enterprises [*NYSE symbol*] ..... CIR
Circus Fans Association of America ..... CFA
Circus Historical Society ..... CHS
Circus Model Builders, International ..... CMB
Circus Saints and Sinners Club of America ..... CSSCA
Circus World Museum, Baraboo, WI [*Library symbol*] ..... WBaraC
Circuses [*Public-performance tariff class*] [*British*] ..... K
Cirebon [*Indonesia*] [*Airport symbol*] ..... CBN
Cirfico Holdings Corp. [*NASDAQ symbol*] ..... CRFC
Ciro, Incorporated [*NASDAQ symbol*] ..... CIRI
Cirpho Review [*A publication*] ..... Cirpho
Cirripedia [*Quality of the bottom*] [*Nautical charts*] ..... Cir
Cirrocumulus [*Meteorology*] CC
Cirrocumulus [*Meteorology*] ..... CICU
Cirrostratus [*Meteorology*] ..... CS
Cirrus [*Meteorology*] C
Cirrus [*Meteorology*] CI
Cirugia Bucal [*A publication*] ..... Cir Bucal
Cirugia y Cirujanos [*A publication*] ..... Cir Cir
Cirugia Espanola [*A publication*] ..... Cir Esp
Cirugia del Uruguay [*A publication*] ..... Cir Urug
CIS [*Congressional Information Service*] **Abstracts on Cards** [*A publication*] ..... CIS Abstr
cis-Dichlorodiammineplatinum [*Cisplatin*] [*Also, DDP, CPDD*] [*Antineoplastic drug regimen*] ..... cis-DDP
CIS [*Congressional Information Service*] **Index** [*A publication*] ..... CISI
CIS [*Congressional Information Service*] **Index** [*A publication*] ..... CIS Ind
cis-Platinum Diammine Dichloride [*Cisplatin*] [*Also, DDP, cis-DDP*] [*Antineoplastic drug*] ..... cPDD
Cisco Junior College [*Texas*] ..... CJC
Cisco Junior College, Cisco, TX [*Library symbol*] ..... TxCiC
Cislennye Metody Mehaniki Splosnoi Stredy [*A publication*] ..... Cisl Metody Meh Splosn Stredy
Cislunar Space ..... CLS
Cistercian Studies [*A publication*] ..... Cist Stud
Cistercienserchronik [*A publication*] ..... CistC
CIT Financial Corp. [*NYSE symbol*] [*Delisted*] ..... CIT
Citadel Capital Corp. [*American Stock Exchange symbol*] ..... CDL
Citadel, Charleston, SC [*Library symbol*] ..... ScCCit
Citadel, Daniel Library, Charleston, SC [*OCLC symbol*] ..... SCN
Citadel Gold Mines [*NASDAQ symbol*] ..... CIGFC
Citation ..... CIT
Citation ..... CITA
Citation Abstract Procurement ..... CAP
Citation Companies, Inc. [*American Stock Exchange symbol*] [*Delisted*] ..... TCC
Cite de la Sante de Laval, Laval, PQ, Canada [*Library symbol*] ..... CaQLACS
Citeaux [*A publication*] ..... Cit
Citeaux. Commentarii Cistercienses [*A publication*] CCC
Citeaux. Commentarii Cistercienses [*A publication*] ..... CCCist
Citeaux in de Nederlande [*A publication*] ..... CitN
Citel, Inc. [*NASDAQ symbol*] ..... CITL
Citibank Economic Database [*Citibank, NA*] [*Information service*] ..... CITIBASE
Citicorp [*Formerly, First National City Corp.*] [*NYSE symbol*] ..... FNC
Cities Service Co. [*NYSE symbol*] [*Delisted*] ..... CS
Cities Service Co., Corporate Library, New York, NY [*Library symbol*] ..... NNCit
Cities Service Co., Energy Resources Group, E & P Library, Tulsa, OK [*Library symbol*] ..... OkTCS
Cities Service Co., Technical Center - Energy Resources Group, Research Library, Tulsa, OK [*OCLC symbol*] ..... OCS
Citinskii Gosudarstvennyi Pedagogiceskii Institut. Ucenye Zapiski [*A publication*] ..... Citin Gos Ped Inst Ucen Zap
Citizen ..... CIT
Citizen Action Group [*Defunct*] ..... CAG

Citizen Education Association [*Formerly, SCEWA*] ... CEA
Citizen Exchange Council ... CEC
Citizen Involvement Training Project ... CITP
Citizen/Labor Energy Coalition ... C/LEC
Citizen Military Forces [*New Guinea*] ... CMF
Citizen Mobilization Campaign ... CMC
Citizen of Morris County, Denville, NJ [*Library symbol*] ... NjDeC
Citizen Soldier [*An association*] ... CS
Citizen Utility Board Campaign ... CUBC
Citizens' Advice Bureau [*British*] ... CAB
Citizens Advisory Committee on Environmental Quality ... CACEQ
Citizens' Advisory Council on the Status of Women ... CACSW
Citizens Advocate Center [*Antipoverty organization*] [*Defunct*] ... CAC
Citizens Against the Concorde Here ... CATCH
Citizens Against Legalized Murder [*Opposes death penalty for criminals*] [*Defunct*] ... CALM
Citizens Against Military Injustice ... CAMI
Citizens Against Noise ... CAN
Citizens Against Nuclear War ... CAN
Citizens Against Trident/ELF ... CATE
Citizens Against UFO Secrecy ... CAUS
Citizens Against Unneccessary Tax Increases and Other Nonsense [*St. Louis organization*] ... CAUTION
Citizens Alarm System ... CAS
Citizens Alliance for Self-Help ... CASH
Citizens Alliance for VD Awareness ... CAVDA
Citizens for America ... CFA
Citizens for Animals ... CA
Citizens Assessment Administration ... CAA
Citizens Association for the Care of Animals ... CACA
Citizens Association for Sound Energy ... CASE
Citizens Bancorp of Maryland [*NASDAQ symbol*] ... CIBC
Citizens Bancorp of Wisconsin [*NASDAQ symbol*] ... CZBN
Citizens Band [*A radio frequency band for limited-range, two-way voice communications by persons without technical training or standard operator licenses*] ... CB
Citizens Band Operating Area ... CBOA
Citizens for Better Care in Nursing Homes, Homes for the Aged, and Other After-Care Facilities ... CBC
Citizens for Better Driving Records [*Later, CSD*] ... CBDR
Citizens for a Better Environment ... CBE
Citizens Cable Communications [*NASDAQ symbol*] ... CITI
Citizen's Call [*An association*] ... CC
Citizen's Choice [*An association*] ... CC
Citizens for Clean Air ... CCA
Citizen's Clearinghouse for Hazardous Wastes ... CCHW
Citizens Commission on Civil Rights ... CCCR
Citizens' Committee for Children of New York ... CCC
Citizens Committee for Constitutional Liberties [*Defunct*] ... CCCL
Citizens Committee on the El Salvador Crisis ... CCESC
Citizens Committee on the Fair Labor Standards Act ... CCFLSA
Citizens Committee for a Free Cuba ... CCFC
Citizens' Committee for Immigration Reform ... CCIR
Citizens Committee on Natural Resources [*Defunct*] ... CCNR
Citizens Committee for the Right to Keep and Bear Arms ... CCRKBA
Citizens Committee for Victim Assistance ... CCVA
Citizens for Common Sense ... CCS
Citizens Communication Center of the Institute for Public Representation [*Georgetown University*] ... CCCIPR
Citizens Conference on State Legislatures [*Later, Legis 50/The Center for Legislative Improvement*] ... CCSL
Citizens for Constitutional Concerns ... CCC
Citizens Council of America for Segregation ... CCAS
Citizens' Council Forum [*Defunct*] ... CCF
Citizens' Councils of America ... CCA
Citizens Crusade Against Poverty ... CCAP
Citizens for a Debt Free America ... CDFA
Citizens for Decency through Law ... CDL
Citizens for Decent Literature [*Later, Citizens for Decency through Law*] ... CDL
Citizens in Defense of Civil Liberties ... CDCL
Citizens' Defense Corps ... CDC
Citizens Educational Advisory Committee ... CEAC
Citizens for Educational Freedom ... CEF
Citizens for Energy Conservation and Solar Development ... CECSD
Citizens Energy Corporation [*Nonprofit*] ... CEC
Citizen's Energy Council ... CEC
Citizens' Energy Project ... CEP
Citizens for Farm Labor ... CFL
Citizens Fidelity Corp. [*NASDAQ symbol*] ... CFDY
Citizens Financial [*NASDAQ symbol*] ... CTZN
Citizens First Bancorporation, Inc. [*American Stock Exchange symbol*] ... CFB
Citizens First National Bank of New Jersey [*American Stock Exchange symbol*] [*Delisted*] ... CFN
Citizens Foreign Aid Committee [*Defunct*] ... CFAC
Citizens Freedom Foundation ... CFF
Citizens for Good Government [*Political fund of Ling-Temco-Vought, Inc.*] ... CITIGO
Citizens for Governmental Restraint ... CGR
Citizens Growth Properties [*NASDAQ symbol*] ... CITGS
Citizens for Highway Safety ... CHS
Citizens Honest Elections Foundation ... CHEF
Citizens for Improved Education ... CIE
Citizens for Informed Choices on Marijuana ... CICOM
Citizens Insurance Co. of America Cl A [*NASDAQ symbol*] ... CINNA
Citizens Law and Research Association ... CLARA
Citizens League Against the Sonic Boom [*Defunct*] ... CLASB
Citizens for a Lebanon-Grenada National Memorial ... CLGNM
Citizens Legal Protective League ... CLPL
Citizens Library, Washington, PA [*Library symbol*] ... PW
Citizen's Library, Washington, PA [*OCLC symbol*] ... WWC
Citizens Military Training Corps ... CMTC
Citizens Mortgage Investment Trust [*NYSE symbol*] ... CZM
Citizens for a Nuclear Freeze ... CNF
Citizens for Ocean Law ... COL
Citizens Organized to Defend the Environment ... CODE
Citizens for Parental Control [*Group opposing sex education in schools*] ... CPC
Citizens for Parents' Rights [*Group opposing sex education in schools*] ... CPR
Citizen's Party ... CIP
Citizen's Party ... CP
Citizens in Politics ... CIP
Citizens for a Quieter City [*New York City*] ... CQC
Citizens Radio UFO [*Unidentified Flying Object*] **Network** ... CRUFON
Citizens for Reagan ... CFR
Citizens to Reduce Airline Smoking Hazards [*Student legal action organization*] ... CRASH
Citizens for the Republic ... CFTR
Citizens' Research Foundation ... CRF
Citizens Research and Investigative Committee [*California*] ... CRIC
Citizens Responsible Action for Safety on the Highways ... CRASH
Citizens for Safe Drivers [*Formerly, CBDR*] ... CSD
Citizens Savings Financial Corporation Cl A [*NASDAQ symbol*] ... CSFCA
Citizens Savings & Loan FA [*NASDAQ symbol*] ... CSFA
Citizens' Scholarship Foundation of America ... CSFA
Citizens' Service Corps ... CSC
Citizens & Southern Corp. [*NASDAQ symbol*] ... CITS
Citizens & Southern Georgia Corp. [*NASDAQ symbol*] ... CSGA
Citizens & Southern Realty Investors SBI [*NYSE symbol*] [*Delisted*] ... SM
Citizens for Space Demilitarization ... CFSD
Citizens Stamp Advisory Committee [*US Postal Service*] ... CSAC
Citizens for Tax Justice ... CTJ
Citizens' Training Corps ... CTC
Citizens for the Treatment of High Blood Pressure ... CTHBP
Citizens Trust Co. [*NASDAQ symbol*] ... CTBT
Citizens United for Racial Equality ... CURE
Citizens United for Research and Education ... CURE
Citizens United for Responsible Energy ... CURE
Citizens Utilities Cl A [*NASDAQ symbol*] ... CITUA
Citizenship Clearing House ... CCH
Cito Dispensetur [*Dispense Quickly*] [*Pharmacy*] ... CITO DISP
Citrate ... CIT
Citrate-Extractable Heavy Metal ... cxHM
Citrate-Phosphate-Dextrose [*Anticoagulant*] [*Hematology*] ... CPD
Citrate-Phosphate-Dextrose-Adenine [*Anticoagulant*] [*Hematology*] ... CPDA
Citrate Synthase [*An enzyme*] ... CS
Citric Acid Fermenter [*Microbiology*] ... CAF
Citroen Car Club ... CCC
Citrovorum Factor [*Physiology*] ... CF
Citrovorum-Factor Rescue [*Cancer treatment*] ... CFR
Citrus College, Azusa, CA [*Library symbol*] ... CAzC
Citrus College, Azusa, CA [*OCLC symbol*] ... CCI
Citrus Country Land Bureau, Inc. [*NASDAQ symbol*] ... CCLB
Citrus Exocortis Viroid ... CEV
Citrus Grower [*A publication*] ... Citrus Grow
Citrus Grower and Sub-Tropical Fruit Journal [*A publication*] ... Citrus Grow Sub-Trop Fruit J
Citrus Industry [*A publication*] ... Citrus Ind
Citrus Junior College [*California*] ... CJC
Citrus Label Society ... CLS
Citrus Magazine [*A publication*] ... Citrus Mag
Citta di Vita [*A publication*] ... CV
City [*Maps and charts*] ... C
City ... CTY
City ... CY
City Administrative Office ... CAO
City Air Defense Evaluation Tool ... CADET
City of Alamosa-Southern Peaks Library, Alamosa, CO [*Library symbol*] ... CoAl
City Art Museum of St. Louis, St. Louis, MO [*Library symbol*] ... MoSR
City Center Arts [*A publication*] ... CCA
City [*or County*] **Civil Defense Director** ... CCD
City College of City University of New York ... CCCUNY
City College of City University of New York, New York, NY [*Library symbol*] ... NNR
City College of New York [*Later, City University of New York*] ... CCNY
City College of New York [*New York*] [*Seismograph station code, US Geological Survey*] ... CNY
City College of New York, New York, NY [*OCLC symbol*] ... ZXC

City College of San Francisco [*California*] .... CCSF
City College of San Francisco, San Francisco, CA [*OCLC symbol*] .... CCS
City College of San Francisco, San Francisco, CA [*Library symbol*] .... CSfCiC
City Corporation [*of London*] CC
City Council [*or Councillor*] CC
City-County Memorial Library, Bay St. Louis, MS [*Library symbol*] .... MsBs
City-County Public Library, Moundsville, WV [*Library symbol*] .... WvMo
City Demonstration Agency .... CDA
City of Edmonton Archives, Edmonton, AB, Canada [*Library symbol*] .... CaAEEA
City Federal Savings & Loan [*NASDAQ symbol*] .... CTYF
City-Flug GmbH [*West Germany*] [*ICAO designator*] .... WH
City Gas Co. of Florida [*American Stock Exchange symbol*] .... CGF
City and Guilds of London Insignia Award [*British*] .... CGIA
City Home Corp. [*NYSE symbol*] [*Delisted*] .... CTH
City of Hope [*Medical facility*] .... CH
City of Hope Medical Center, Duarte, CA [*Library symbol*] .... CDuH
City of Hope Medical Center, Duarte, CA [*OCLC symbol*] .... CHM
City Hospital at Elmhurst, Elmhurst, NY [*Library symbol*] .... NElmhC
City Hostess International .... CHI
City of Houston Legal Department, Houston, TX [*Library symbol*] .... TxHLD
City Imperial Volunteers [*Military unit*] [*British*] CIV
City Investing Co. [*NYSE symbol*] .... CNV
City Invincible [*A publication*] CI
City of Lincoln Public Library, Lincoln, United Kingdom [*Library symbol*] .... UkLin
City of London [*British*] .... C of L
City of London [*British*] CL
City of London Rifles [*British*] .... CLR
City National Corp. [*NASDAQ symbol*] .... CTYN
City Normal School, Syracuse, NY [*Library symbol*] [*Obsolete*] .... NSyN
City of Prineville Railway [*AAR code*] .... COP
City Products Corp. [*NYSE symbol*] [*Delisted*] .... CY
City of Refuge National Historic Park .... CIRE
City and Regional Magazine Association .... CRMA
City & Suburban Homes Co. [*American Stock Exchange symbol*] .... CBU
City of Sydney Public Library, Sydney, NSW, Australia [*Library symbol*] .... AuS
City University of New York .... CUNY
City University of New York, Division of Teacher Education, New York, NY [*Library symbol*] .... NNCU-T
City University of New York, Graduate Center, New York, NY [*Library symbol*] .... NNCU-G
City University of New York, Graduate School, New York, NY [*OCLC symbol*] .... ZGM
City Urban Renewal Management Corporation [*New York City*] .... CURMCO
Citytrust Bancorp [*NASDAQ symbol*] .... CITR
Ciudad Bolivar [*Venezuela*] [*Airport symbol*] .... CBL
Ciudad Del Carmen [*Mexico*] [*Airport symbol*] .... CME
Ciudad de Dios [*A publication*] .... CD
Ciudad de Dios [*A publication*] .... CdD
Ciudad Juarez [*Mexico*] [*Airport symbol*] .... CJS
Ciudad Obregon [*Mexico*] [*Airport symbol*] .... CEN
Ciudad Victoria [*Mexico*] [*Airport symbol*] .... CVM
Civic Action .... CA
Civic Action Centers [*Military*] .... CAC
Civic Action Group [*Military*] .... CAG
Civic Action Group [*Military*] .... CIVACTGP
Civic Action Institute .... CAI
Civic Club of Philadelphia, Philadelphia, PA [*Library symbol*] [*Obsolete*] .... PPCiC
Civic Issues Voluntary Information Council [*Michigan*] CIVIC
Civic Leaders for Ecological Action and Responsibility [*Connecticut*] .... CLEAR
Civil CIV
Civil Action Team .... CAT
Civil Administration Committee [*US Military Government, Germany*] .... CAC
Civil Administrator .... CIVAD
Civil Aero-Medical Institute [*FAA*] .... CAMI
Civil Aeromedical Institute [*FAA*] .... CAI
Civil Aeromedical Research Institute [*FAA*] .... CARI
Civil Aeronautics Administration [*Later, part of FAA*] .... CAA
Civil Aeronautics Administration Journal [*A publication*] .... CAA J
Civil Aeronautics Administration Journal [*A publication*] .... Civil Aero J
Civil Aeronautics Administration Manual .... CAAM
Civil Aeronautics Administration Type Certificate .... CAATC
Civil Aeronautics Authority [*Later, Civil Aeronautics Administration*] .... CAA
Civil Aeronautics Board [*Independent government agency*] .... CAB
Civil Aeronautics Board Air Transport Mobilization Standby Order .... CAB-ATM
Civil Aeronautics Bulletin .... CAB
Civil Aeronautics Manual .... CAM
Civil Affairs .... CA
Civil Affairs Association .... CAA
Civil Affairs Division [*Military*] .... CAD
Civil Affairs Inland Depot [*for relief supplies to liberated territory*] [*British*] [*World War II*] .... CAID
Civil Affairs/Military Government .... CA/MG
Civil Affairs Mobile Training Team .... CAMTT
Civil Affairs Officer [*Navy*] .... CAO
Civil Affairs Officer [*Army*] S5
Civil Affairs Police Officer [*British*] [*World War II*] .... CAPO
Civil Affairs Section .... CAS
Civil Affairs Section [*of an Army division or brigade general staff; the officer in charge of this section*] G-5
Civil Affairs Service (Burma) [*British*] .... CAS(B)
Civil Affairs Service (Malaya) [*British*] .... CAS(M)
Civil Affairs Staff Center [*Wimbledon, England*] .... CCSC
Civil Affairs Staff Officer [*British*] .... CASO
Civil Affairs Staging Area [*World War II*] .... CASA
Civil Affairs Summary [*Navy*] .... CASUM
Civil Affairs Team .... CAT
Civil Affairs Training Center [*World War II*] .... CATC
Civil Affairs Training School [*Navy*] .... CATS
Civil Affairs Unit [*British*] .... CAU
Civil Agency .... CA
Civil Air Attache [*British*] .... CAA
Civil Air Branch [*Air Force*] .... CAB
Civil Air Carrier Turbojet .... CACT
Civil Air Defense Services .... CADS
Civil Air Defense Warning .... CADW
Civil Air Guard [*British*] .... CAG
Civil Air Movement .... CAM
Civil Air Patrol .... CAP
Civil Air Patrol Coastal Patrol [*Wartime*] .... CAPCP
Civil Air Patrol Guard .... CAPG
Civil Air Patrol, South Carolina Wing [*Columbia, SC*] [*FAA designator*] .... BKR
Civil Air Publication [*British*] .... CAP
Civil Air Regulation [*of FAA*] .... CAR
Civil Air Reserve .... CAR
Civil Air Surgeon [*of FAA*] .... CAS
Civil Air Transport [*Free China's international airline*] .... CAT
Civil Aircraft Airworthiness Data Recording Program [*British*] .... CAADRP
Civil Assistant to Medical Director-General [*Navy*] [*British*] .... CAMDG
Civil Assistant Personal Services [*Navy*] [*British*] .... CAPS
Civil Authorities .... CA
Civil Aviation .... CA
Civil Aviation Administration of China .... CAAC
Civil Aviation Advisory [*or Assistance*] **Group** .... CAAG
Civil Aviation Authority [*British*] .... CAA
Civil Aviation Authority - War Training Service .... CAA-WTS
Civil Aviation Chaplains International .... CACI
Civil Aviation Communication Center [*Canada*] .... CACC
Civil Aviation Medical Association .... CAMA
Civil Aviation Planning Committee .... CAPC
Civil Aviation Research and Development [*NASA*] .... CARD
Civil Aviation Security Service [*FAA*] .... ACS
Civil Budget Committee [*NATO*] .... CBC
Civil Censorship Division [*US Military Government, Germany*] .... CCD
Civil Censorship Study Group [*American Philatelic Society*] .... CCSG
Civil Commotion CC
Civil Communication Planning Committee .... CCPC
Civil Communications-Electronics Working-Group .... CCEWG
Civil Communications Element [*Military*] .... CCE
Civil Coordination Detachment [*General Air Traffic Element at Operational Traffic and Defense Centers*] [*NATO*] .... CCD
Civil Coordination Detachment General [*NATO*] .... CCDG
Civil Court CC
Civil Damage Assessment Program [*Army*] .... CDAP
Civil Defence Bulletin [*A publication*] .... Civ Def Bull
Civil Defense .... CD
Civil Defense Adult Education [*Program*] .... CDAE
Civil Defense Adult Education Program .... CDAEP
Civil Defense Advisory Council .... CDAC
Civil Defense Agency .... CDA
Civil Defense Career Development Program .... CDCDP
Civil Defense Committee .... CDC
Civil Defense Coordinator .... CDC
Civil Defense Countermeasures System .... CDCS
Civil Defense Director/Coordinator .... CD D/C
Civil Defense Education Program .... CDEP
Civil Defense Emergency Operations System .... CDEOS
Civil Defense Exercise .... CDEX
Civil Defense Management .... CDM
Civil Defense Organization [*United Nations*] .... CDO
Civil Defense Receiver .... CDR
Civil Defense Report .... CIDERE
Civil Defense Research Associates .... CDRA
Civil Defense Support Detachments .... CDSD
Civil Defense, United States of America [*Home study course*] .... CD-USA
Civil Defense University Extension Program .... CDUEP
Civil Defense Warning .... CDW
Civil Defense Warning System .... CDWS
Civil Direction of Shipping .... CDS
Civil Director of Economics .... CDE
Civil Disturbance Group [*Department of Justice intelligence unit*] .... CDG
Civil Disturbance Readiness Conditions .... CIDCON
Civil Disturbance Status Reporting [*Army*] .... CIDSTAT
Civil Effects Exercise [*NASA*] .... CEX
Civil Effects Experiments [*DASA and AEC*] .... CEX

Civil Effects Test Group [*DASA and AEC*] ... CETG
Civil Effects Test Operations [*DASA and AEC*] ... CETO
Civil Emergency Information Room [*NATO*] ... CEIR
Civil Emergency Planning [*NATO*] ... CEP
Civil Emergency Planning Bureau [*NATO*] ... CEPB
Civil Emergency Planning Committee [*US/Canada*] ... CEPC
Civil Engineer ... CE
Civil Engineer ... CENGR
Civil Engineer Automated Specification Retrieval System [*Air Force*] ... CEASRS
Civil Engineer Construction Operations Group [*Air Force*] ... CECOGp
Civil Engineer Corps [*Army*] ... CEC
Civil Engineer Management System ... CEMS
Civil Engineer Preventive Maintenance [*Air Force*] ... CEPM
Civil Engineer Support Equipment [*Army*] ... CESE
Civil Engineer Support Office [*Navy*] ... CESO
Civil Engineer Support Plan ... CESP
Civil Engineering [*A publication*] ... Civ Eng
Civil Engineering [*A publication*] ... Civil Eng
Civil Engineering Computer Laboratory [*MIT*] ... CECL
Civil Engineering Contractor [*A publication*] ... Civ Eng Contract
Civil Engineering and Evaluation Laboratory [*Navy*] ... CEREL
Civil Engineering in Japan [*A publication*] ... Civ Eng Jpn
Civil Engineering Laboratory [*Also, CIVENGRLAB*] [*Navy*] ... CEL
Civil Engineering Laboratory [*Also, CEL*] [*Navy*] ... CIVENGRLAB
Civil Engineering Maintenance, Inspection, Repair, and Training Team [*Air Force*] ... CEMIRT
Civil Engineering (New York) [*A publication*] ... Civ Eng (NY)
Civil Engineering Package ... CEP
Civil Engineering Problems ... CEPS
Civil Engineering Program Applications [*Later, SCAEPA*] ... CEPA
Civil Engineering and Public Works Review [*A publication*] ... Civ Engng Publ Wks Rev
Civil Engineering and Public Works Review [*A publication*] ... Civ Eng Public Works Rev
Civil Engineering and Public Works Review [*A publication*] ... Civ Eng Pub Works Rev
Civil Engineering Report ... CER
Civil Engineering Report of Performance ... CERP
Civil Engineering Research Association ... CERA
Civil Engineering in South Africa [*A publication*] ... Civ Eng S Afr
Civil Engineering Systems Laboratory [*University of Illinois*] ... CESL
Civil Engineers Corps Officers School [*Navy*] ... CECOS
Civil and Environmental Engineering Development Office [*Air Force*] ... CEEDO
Civil Guard [*Air Force*] ... CG
Civil Imprisonment ... CI
Civil Information and Education Section of Allied Headquarters [*World War II*] ... CIANDE
Civil Investigative Demand [*Department of Justice*] ... CID
Civil Jet Transport ... CJT
Civil Law ... CL
Civil Liability Convention [*British*] ... CLC
Civil Liaison Division [*Army*] ... CLD
Civil Liaison Officer [*Army*] ... CLO
Civil Liberties Bureau [*Forerunner of the American Civil Liberties Union*] ... CLB
Civil Liberties Educational Foundation [*Defunct*] ... CLEF
Civil Liberties Legal Defense Fund ... CLLDF
Civil Liberties Review [*A publication*] ... Civil Liberties Rev
Civil Member for Development and Production [*British*] ... CMDP
Civil-Military Affairs ... CMA
Civil-Military Operations ... CMO
Civil and Mining Engineer ... C & ME
Civil Navigation Aids System ... CNAS
Civil Operations Revolutionary Development Support ... CORDS
Civil Pilot Training Program ... CPTP
Civil Post Office ... CPO
Civil Power ... CP
Civil Practice Law and Rules [*A publication*] ... CPLR
Civil Preparedness Guide [*Civil Defense*] ... CPG
Civil Procedure [*Legal*] ... CP
Civil Procedures, Quebec ... CPQ
Civil and Public Services Association [*British*] ... CPSA
Civil Readjustment Officer ... CRO
Civil Reserve Air Fleet [*Department of Commerce*] ... CRAF
Civil Reserve Air Fleet Summary Report [*Department of Commerce*] ... CRAFREP
Civil Rights ... CR
Civil Rights Act [*1957, 1964, 1968*] ... CRA
Civil Rights Association [*Northern Ireland*] ... CRA
Civil Rights Commission ... CRC
Civil Rights Congress ... CRC
Civil Rights Digest [*A publication*] ... Civ Rights Digest
Civil Rights Division [*Department of Justice*] ... CRD
Civil Rights Documentation Project ... CRDP
Civil and Sanitary Engineering ... CSE
Civil Service ... CS
Civil Service Arbitration Tribunal [*British*] ... CSAT
Civil Service Association of Canada ... CSAC
Civil Service Benevolent Fund [*British*] ... CSBF
Civil Service Board ... CSB
Civil Service Building Society [*British*] ... CSBS
Civil Service Catering Organization [*British*] ... CISCO
Civil Service Club [*British*] ... CSC
Civil Service College [*British*] ... CSC
Civil Service Commission [*Later, MSPB*] ... CSC
Civil Service Commission - Investigations ... CSC-I
Civil Service Commission of Ontario, Toronto, ON, Canada [*Library symbol*] ... CaOTCSC
Civil Service Cooperative Society [*British*] ... CSCS
Civil Service Council for Further Education [*British*] ... CSCFE
Civil Service Department [*British*] ... CSD
Civil Service Employees Association ... CSEA
Civil Service Foreign Service Allowances Committee [*British*] ... CSFSAC
Civil Service Forum ... CSF
Civil Service Housing Association [*British*] ... CSHA
Civil Service Insurance Society [*British*] ... CSIS
Civil Service Journal [*A publication*] ... Civ Serv J
Civil Service Journal [*A publication*] ... CSJ
Civil Service Legal Society [*British*] ... CSLS
Civil Service National Whitley Council [*British*] ... CSNWC
Civil Service Pensioners Alliance [*British*] ... CSPA
Civil Service Reform Act ... CSRA
Civil Service Retirement ... CSR
Civil Service Retirement and Disability Fund ... CSRDF
Civil Service Retirement Fellowship [*British*] ... CSRF
Civil Service Rifle Volunteers [*British*] ... CSRV
Civil Service Rule ... CSR
Civil Service Selection Board [*Pronounced "sissby"*] [*British*] ... CSSB
Civil Service Supply Association [*British*] ... CSSA
Civil Service Union [*British*] ... CSU
Civil Service Working Party [*US Military Government, Germany*] ... CSWP
Civil Situation Reporting System ... CIVSITREP
Civil Society ... CS
Civil War Centennial Association ... CWCA
Civil War Centennial Commission [*Terminated, 1966*] ... CWCC
Civil War History [*A publication*] ... Civil War Hist
Civil War History [*A publication*] ... CWH
Civil War Philatelic Society [*Later, AHPS*] ... CWPS
Civil War Press Corps ... CWPC
Civil War Round Table Associates ... CWRTA
Civil War Times Illustrated [*A publication*] ... CWTI
Civil War Token Society ... CWTS
Civil Works Administration [*1933-1934*] ... CWA
Civil Works Program ... CWP
Civilian ... CIV
Civilian Acquired Skills Program [*Military*] ... CASP
Civilian Actress Technician [*Term for professional actresses who worked under Army Special Services Division in soldier shows*] [*World War II*] ... CAT
Civilian Aviation Advisory Committee [*Air Defense Planning Board*] ... CAAC
Civilian Bachelor Quarters [*Air Force*] ... CBQ
Civilian Clothing ... CIVCLO
Civilian Clothing Maintenance Allowance [*Army*] ... CCMA
Civilian Complaint Review Board ... CCRB
Civilian Congress ... CC
Civilian Conservation Centers [*Job Corps*] ... CCC
Civilian Conservation Corps [*Created, 1937; liquidated, 1943*] ... CCC
Civilian Control Agency ... CCA
Civilian Defense Volunteer Office ... CDVO
Civilian Electronics Technician Afloat [*Navy*] ... CETA
Civilian Employee Health Service ... CEHS
Civilian Employment Projection ... CEP
Civilian Engineering Technical Service [*Navy*] ... CETS
Civilian Enterprise ... CE
Civilian Extraction [*Nuclear energy*] ... CIVEX
Civilian Goods (Supply) Committee [*British*] [*World War II*] ... CG(S)C
Civilian Health and Medical Program of the Uniformed Services [*Military*] ... CHAMPUS
Civilian Health and Medical Program of the Veterans Administration [*Military*] ... CHAMPVA
Civilian Information Manpower Management System [*Navy*] ... CIMMS
Civilian Instruction Program ... CIP
Civilian Irregular Defense Group [*Military*] ... CIDG
Civilian Jeep ... CJ
Civilian Labor Group Center [*Army*] ... CLGC
Civilian Labor Group Special Orders [*Army*] ... CLGSO
Civilian Man-Years [*Military*] ... CMY
Civilian Manpower Management Guides [*Navy*] ... CMMG
Civilian Manpower Management Instruction [*Navy*] ... CMMI
Civilian Manpower Management Letters [*Navy*] ... CMML
Civilian Marine Personnel Instructions [*Navy*] ... CMPI
Civilian-Military Contingency Hospital System [*DoD*] ... CMCHS
Civilian Military Cooperation ... CIMIC
Civilian/Military Liaison Committee ... CMLC
Civilian Mobilization Manpower Allocation/Requirements Plan ... CIV-M-MARP
Civilian Occupational Specialty ... COS
Civilian Payroll Circular ... CPRC
Civilian Personnel Accounting System [*Military*] ... CPAS

Civilian Personnel Advisor [*Military*] .... CPA
Civilian Personnel Branch [*BUPERS*] .... CPB
Civilian Personnel Career Plan [*Air Force*] .... CPCP
Civilian Personnel Circular [*Army*] .... CPC
Civilian Personnel Division .... CPD
Civilian Personnel Division [*Coast Guard*] .... PC
Civilian Personnel Information System [*Army*] .... CIVPERSINS
Civilian Personnel Letter .... CPL
Civilian Personnel Letters and Dispatches .... CPL & D
Civilian Personnel Management Information System .... CPMIS
Civilian Personnel Occupational Standards [*Military*] .... CPOS
Civilian Personnel Office [*or Officer*] .... CPO
Civilian Personnel Pamphlet [*Military*] .... CPP
Civilian Personnel and Payroll Letter [*Military*] .... CPPL
Civilian Personnel Procedures Manual [*Military*] .... CPPM
Civilian Personnel Records [*Military*] .... CPR
Civilian Personnel Regulation [*Military*] .... CPR
Civilian Pilot Training [*Became War Training Service*] [*World War II*] .... CPT
Civilian Production Administration [*Became part of Office of Temporary Controls, 1946*] .... CPA
Civilian Property Agent .... CPA
Civilian Public Service .... CPS
Civilian Repair Organization [*Aircraft*] .... CRO
Civilian Research, Interplanetary Flying Objects .... CRIFO
Civilian Science Systems Administration [*Proposed for National Science Foundation*] .... CSSA
Civilian Screening Center .... CSC
Civilian Service Unit .... CSU
Civilian Substitution Program [*Navy*] .... CIVSUB
Civilian Supervisory Selection Battery .... CSSB
Civilian Supply Branch [*Army Service Forces*] [*World War II*] .... CSB
Civilian Supply Division [*Allied Military Government*] [*World War II*] .... CSD
Civilian War Dead .... CWD
Civilian Wartime Injuries .... CWTI
Civilian Welfare Fund .... CWF
Civilian Welfare and Recreation Committee .... CWRC
Civilians in Foreign Communications Operations [*Military*] .... CIFCO
Civilta Cattolica [*A publication*] CC
Civilta Cattolica [*A publication*] .... CCa
Civilta Cattolica [*A publication*] .... CCatt
Civilta Cattolica [*A publication*] .... Civilta Catt
Civilta Fascista [*A publication*] CV
Civilta Moderna [*A publication*] .... CM
Civis Romanus [*Roman Citizen*] [*Latin*] .... CR
Civitan International CI
Civvies in Disguise [*Facetious translation of the initialism for Criminal Investigation Department, q.v. Used by British conscripts to describe themselves during World War II*] .... CID
Cizi Jazyky ve Skole [*A publication*] .... CJa
Cizi Jazyky ve Skole [*A publication*] .... CJS
Cizi Jazyky ve Skole [*A publication*] .... CJVS
CL Assets, Inc. [*NASDAQ symbol*] .... CLAS
CLA [*College Language Association*] **Journal** [*A publication*] .... CLAJ
Clabir Corp. [*NYSE symbol*] .... CLG
Clackamas Community College Library, Oregon City, OR [*OCLC symbol*] .... CCK
Clackamas Community College, Oregon City, OR [*Library symbol*] .... OrOCC
Clackamas Cooperative County-Wide Library Services [*Library network*] .... CCCLS
Clackamas County Public Library, Oregon City, OR [*Library symbol*] .... OrOC
Clackamas High School, Media Center, Milwaukie, OR [*Library symbol*] .... OrMiCHS
Clackamas, OR [*Location identifier*] [*FAA*] .... CWY
Clackmannanshire [*County in Scotland*] .... CLACK
Clad Controlled Expansion .... CCEX
Claflin College, Orangeburg, SC [*OCLC symbol*] .... CFC
Claflin College, Orangeburg, SC [*Library symbol*] .... ScOrC
Claflin College Review [*A publication*] .... CCR
Claim Agent [*Insurance*] .... CA
Claimant Advisory Service Program [*Unemployment insurance*] .... CLASP
Claimant Procurement Planning Officer .... CPPO
Claiming Race [*Horse racing*] .... CLM
Claims Representative Exam for Social Security [*Federal job exam*] .... CRESS
Clairborne Parish Library, Homer, LA [*Library symbol*] .... LHoC
Clamp .... CLP
Clamped Dielectric Constant .... CDC
Clamped Speed Regulator .... CSR
Clamping Fixture .... CF
Clamshell Alliance .... CA
Clandestine Underwater Nuclear Explosion .... CUNE
Clann Ltd., Sydney, NSW, Australia [*OCLC symbol*] .... CLN
Clanton, AL [*Location identifier*] [*FAA*] .... GGY
Clanton, AL [*Radio station call letters*] .... WEZZ
Clanton, AL [*Radio station call letters*] .... WKLF
Clapeyron-Clausius Equation [*Physics*] .... CCE
Clapper [*Electricity*] .... CLPR
Clara Peak [*New Mexico*] [*Seismograph station code, US Geological Survey*] .... CLP
Clara Rhodos [*A publication*] .... ClRh
Clare, MI [*Radio station call letters*] .... WRNN-FM
Clare, MI [*Radio station call letters*] .... WSDM
Claremont, CA [*Radio station call letters*] .... KSPC
Claremont Capital Corp. [*American Stock Exchange symbol*] .... CCM
Claremont & Concord Railway Co., Inc. [*AAR code*] .... CLCO
Claremont Men's College [*California*] .... CMC
Claremont Men's College, Claremont, CA [*OCLC symbol*] .... HDC
Claremont, NH [*Location identifier*] [*FAA*] .... CNH
Claremont, NH [*Radio station call letters*] .... WECM
Claremont, NH [*Radio station call letters*] .... WTSV
Claremont Public Library, Claremont, SD [*Library symbol*] .... SdCla
Claremont Quarterly [*A publication*] .... Clare Q
Claremore, OK [*Radio station call letters*] .... KNGX
Claremore, OK [*Radio station call letters*] .... KOKN
Claremore, OK [*Radio station call letters*] .... KWPR
Clarendon College, Clarendon, TX [*Library symbol*] .... TxClaC
Clarendon Hills Public Library, Clarendon Hills, IL [*Library symbol*] .... IClh
Clarendon Laboratory [*Oxford University*] CL
Clarendon Medieval and Tudor Series [*A publication*] .... CMTS
[*The*] **Clarendon & Pittsford Railroad Co.** [*AAR code*] .... CLP
Clarendon, TX [*Location identifier*] [*FAA*] .... CNZ
Clarenville, NF [*Radio station call letters*] .... CKVO
Claretian Fathers Library, Washington, DC [*Library symbol*] .... DCF
Clarification [*or Clarify*] .... CLAR
Clarify .... CFY
Clarinda Herald-Journal, Clarinda, IA [*Library symbol*] .... IaCladHJ
Clarinda, IA [*Location identifier*] [*FAA*] ICL
Clarinda, IA [*Radio station call letters*] .... KQIS
Clarinda Public Library, Clarinda, IA [*Library symbol*] .... IaClad
Clarinet CL
Clarinet .... CLAR
Clarinet [*A publication*] .... CLAWA
Clarino [*Clarion*] [*Music*] .... CLARO
Clarion Free Library, Clarion, PA [*Library symbol*] .... PCl
Clarion, IA [*Location identifier*] [*FAA*] .... CAV
Clarion, IA [*Radio station call letters*] .... KRIT
Clarion Music Society .... CMS
Clarion, PA [*Location identifier*] [*FAA*] .... CIP
Clarion, PA [*Radio station call letters*] .... WCUC-FM
Clarion, PA [*Radio station call letters*] .... WWCH
Clarion Public Library, Clarion, IA [*Library symbol*] .... IaCla
Clarion State College, Clarion, PA [*Library symbol*] .... PClS
Clarion State College, Clarion, PA [*OCLC symbol*] .... REC
Clarion State College, Oil City, PA [*Library symbol*] .... POC
Clarion State College, School of Library Media, Clarion, PA [*OCLC symbol*] .... CSI
Clarissima Femina [*Most Illustrious Woman*] [*Latin*] .... CF
Clarissima Puella [*Most Illustrious Maiden*] [*Latin*] .... CP
Clarissimus Vir [*Most Illustrious Man*] [*Latin*] CLV
Claritas Corporation [*Information service*] CLC
Clark Aviation Corp. [*New Cumberland, PA*] [*FAA designator*] .... CLK
Clark College, Atlanta, GA [*OCLC symbol*] CLC
Clark College, Atlanta, GA [*Library symbol*] .... GAC
Clark College, Library, Vancouver, WA [*OCLC symbol*] CCV
Clark College, Vancouver, WA [*Library symbol*] .... WaVC
Clark Consolidated Industries, Inc. [*American Stock Exchange symbol*] .... CLK
Clark County Library, Las Vegas, NV [*Library symbol*] .... NvLC
Clark County Technical Institute, Springfield, OH [*Library symbol*] .... OSC
Clark Equipment Co. [*NYSE symbol*] .... CKL
Clark Free Public Library, Clark, NJ [*Library symbol*] .... NjCl
Clark Hill Reservoir [*Georgia*] [*Seismograph station code, US Geological Survey*] CH5
Clark Hill Reservoir [*Georgia*] [*Seismograph station code, US Geological Survey*] CH6
Clark [*J. L.*] **Manufacturing Co.** [*NASDAQ symbol*] .... CLRK
Clark Memorial College [*Mississippi*] .... CMC
Clark Oil Refining Corp. [*NYSE symbol*] [*Delisted*] .... CKO
Clark Public Library, Clark, SD [*Library symbol*] .... SdCl
Clark Road Secondary School, London, ON, Canada [*Library symbol*] .... CaOLCR
Clark Technical College, Library Resource Center, Springfield, OH [*OCLC symbol*] .... CLT
Clark University, Worcester, MA [*OCLC symbol*] .... CKM
Clark University, Worcester, MA [*Library symbol*] .... MWC
Clarke College, Dubuque, IA [*Library symbol*] .... IaDuCl
Clarke College, Dubuque, IA [*OCLC symbol*] .... IOC
Clarke Institute of Psychiatry. Monograph Series [*A publication*] .... Clarke Inst Psychiatry Monogr Ser
Clarke Memorial College, Newton, MS [*Library symbol*] .... MsNeC
Clarke, W. H., New York NY [*STAC*] .... CWH
Clarkesville, GA [*Radio station call letters*] .... WIAF
Clarks Point [*Alaska*] [*Airport symbol*] .... CLP
Clarks Point, AK [*Location identifier*] [*FAA*] .... CLP
Clarksburg [*West Virginia*] [*Airport symbol*] .... CKB
Clarksburg Public Library, Clarksburg, WV [*Library symbol*] .... WvCl
Clarksburg, WV [*Location identifier*] [*FAA*] .... CKB
Clarksburg, WV [*Television station call letters*] .... WBOY-TV
Clarksburg, WV [*Radio station call letters*] .... WHAR
Clarksburg, WV [*Radio station call letters*] .... WKKW

Clarksburg, WV [*Television station call letters*] WLYJ
Clarksburg, WV [*Radio station call letters*] WPDX
Clarksburg, WV [*Radio station call letters*] WPDX-FM
Clarksburg, WV [*Radio station call letters*] WPQZ
Clarksburg, WV [*Radio station call letters*] WVHF
Clarksdale, MS [*Location identifier*] [*FAA*] CKM
Clarksdale, MS [*Radio station call letters*] WAID
Clarksdale, MS [*Radio station call letters*] WJBI
Clarksdale, MS [*Radio station call letters*] WROX
Clarkson College of Technology [*New York*] CCT
Clarkson College of Technology, Potsdam, NY [*Library symbol*] NPotC
Clarkson College of Technology, Potsdam, NY [*OCLC symbol*] VYT
Clarkson, Gordon, & Co.: Woods, Gordon, & Co., Toronto, ON, Canada [*Library symbol*] CaOTCGW
Clarkson Industries, Inc. [*American Stock Exchange symbol*] [*Delisted*] CJS
Clarkston, WA [*Radio station call letters*] KCLK
Clarkston, WA [*Radio station call letters*] KCLK-FM
Clarksville [*Tennessee*] [*Airport symbol*] CKV
Clarksville, AR [*Location identifier*] [*FAA*] CZE
Clarksville, AR [*Radio station call letters*] KLYR
Clarksville, AR [*Radio station call letters*] KLYR-FM
Clarksville Branch Office [*AEC*] CBO
Clarksville Star, Clarksville, IA [*Library symbol*] IaClvS
Clarksville, TN [*Location identifier*] [*FAA*] CKV
Clarksville, TN [*Radio station call letters*] WDXN
Clarksville, TN [*Radio station call letters*] WJZM
Clarksville, TX [*Radio station call letters*] KCAR
Claro [*Light-colored cigar*] CCC
Clarostat Manufacturing Co., Inc. [*American Stock Exchange symbol*] CLR
Clasp CLP
Class [*Used with number for Navy rating as: 1c; i.e., first class*] C
Class CL
Class [*Freight*] CLA
Class Action Study and Survey [*Student legal action organization*] CLASS
Class Convening CLCVN
Class Determination and Finding CD & F
Class Determination and Finding CDF
Class Improvement Plan [*Navy*] CIP
Class Interval [*Statistics*] i
Class of Material CM
Class-Oriented Ring-Associative Language [*Data processing*] CORAL
Class Rate CR
Class for Retarded in Mental Development CRMD
Class Work Planning Document [*Navy ship overhauls*] CWPD
Classic AMX Club International CACI
Classic Car Club of America CCCA
Classic Chevy Club International CCCI
Classic Comet Club of America CCCA
Classic Corp. [*NASDAQ symbol*] WBED
Classic Film Collector [*A publication*] Classic F Col
Classic Jaguar Association CJA
Classic Racing Motorcycle Club CRUC
Classic Stage Company CSC
Classic Thunderbird Association CTA
Classic Thunderbird Club International CTCI
Classic Yacht Association CYA
Classica et Mediaevalia [*A publication*] Cl Med
Classica et Mediaevalia [*A publication*] C & M
Classica et Mediaevalia [*A publication*] CM
Classical C
Classical CL
Classical America CA
Classical Analytic Technique CAT
Classical Anaphylatoxin [*Immunology*] CAT
Classical Bulletin [*A publication*] CB
Classical Conditioning CC
Classical Folia [*A publication*] CF
Classical Folia [*A publication*] CFol
Classical General Linear Model [*Statistics*] CGLM
Classical Journal [*A publication*] CJ
Classical Journal [*A publication*] Classic Jnl
Classical Journal [*A publication*] Class J
Classical Journal [*A publication*] CLJ
Classical Journal (Malta) [*A publication*] CJ(Malta)
Classical Outlook [*A publication*] CO
Classical Philology [*A publication*] Class Philol
Classical Philology [*A publication*] CLP
Classical Philology [*A publication*] CP
Classical Philology [*A publication*] CPh
Classical Quarterly [*A publication*] Class Q
Classical Quarterly [*A publication*] Cl Q
Classical Quarterly [*A publication*] CQ
Classical Review [*A publication*] Class R
Classical Review [*A publication*] Cl R
Classical Review [*A publication*] CR
Classical Review. New Series [*A publication*] Class R ns
Classical Scattering Aerosol Spectrometer [*Aerosol measurement device*] CSASP
Classical Scattering Spectrometer Probe [*Aerosol measurement device*] CSSP
Classical Weekly [*A publication*] Cl Weekly
Classical Weekly [*A publication*] CW
Classical World [*A publication*] Classic World
Classical World [*A publication*] Class World
Classical World [*A publication*] CW
Classification CLASS
Classification CLASSN
Classification and Audit C & A
Classification Change Notice CCN
Classification of Characteristics [*Navy*] CC
Classification Code [*IRS*] CC
Classification Decimale Universelle [*Universal Decimal Classification*] CDU
Classification of Defects CD
Classification of Identification of Covert Satellites CLASSICS
Classification and Index [*Air Force*] C & I
Classification Inventory [*Military*] CI
Classification of Occupations and Directory of Occupational Titles [*Formerly, MOLOC*] [*British*] CODOT
Classification Order Watch Service [*Research Publications, Inc.*] COWS
Classification and Rating Administration [*For movies*] CARA
Classification Research CR
Classification Research Group [*British*] CRG
Classification Research Study Group CRSG
Classification on Science and Technology CST
[*The*] **Classification Society** TCS
Classification Society. Bulletin [*A publication*] Class Soc Bull
Classification and Testing [*Air Force*] C & T
Classified Abstract Archive of the Alcohol Literature CAAAL
Classified Area Term Pass CATP
Classified Control Clerk [*Army*] CCC
Classified Control Officer CCO
Classified Defense Information [*Military*] CDI
Classified Document Control CDC
Classified Entries in Lateral Transposition [*Indexing*] CELT
Classified Financial [*NASDAQ symbol*] CLSS
Classified Mail Address CMA
Classified Material Receipt CMR
Classified Matter Control Center CMCC
Classified Message CM
Classified Ministry Lists of Types of Educational Establishments [*British*] CMLTEE
Classified Register CR
Classified Scientific and Technical Aerospace Reports [*NASA*] CSTAR
Classify CLAS
Classify CLS
Classiques Francais du Moyen Age [*A publication*] CFMA
Classiques Garnier [*A publication*] CG
Classiques du XX Siecle [*A publication*] CVS
Classroom Adjustment Rating Scale CARS
Classroom-Aided Dynamic Educational Time-Sharing System CADETS
Classroom Assembly Program CAP
Classroom Periodical Publishers Association [*Later, CPA*] CPPA
Classroom Publishers Association CPA
Clathrin-Associated Protein [*Cytology*] CAP
Clatsop Community College, Astoria, OR [*Library symbol*] OrAstC
Claudel Studies [*A publication*] ClaudelS
Clause CL
Clausen, Miller, Gorman, Caffrey, Witous, Chicago, IL [*OCLC symbol*] ILP
Clausing Corp. [*American Stock Exchange symbol*] CLA
Clauson Rolling Platform CRP
Clausthal [*Federal Republic of Germany*] [*Seismograph station code, US Geological Survey*] CLZ
Clausthaler Geologische Abhandlungen [*A publication*] Clausthaler Geol Abh
Clavicle [*Anatomy*] CL
Clavier [*A publication*] Cl
Clavier [*Keyboard*] [*Music*] CLAV
Clavier [*A publication*] CLAVA
Clavileno [*A publication*] Cl
Clavileno [*A publication*] Clav
Claw Plate [*Technical drawings*] CP
Claxton, GA [*Radio station call letters*] WCLA
Claxton, GA [*Radio station call letters*] WCLA-FM
Clay [*Quality of the bottom*] [*Nautical charts*] Cl
Clay Center, KS [*Location identifier*] [*FAA*] CYW
Clay Center, KS [*Radio station call letters*] KCLY
Clay County Public Library, Green Cove Springs, FL [*Library symbol*] FGcC
Clay County Public Library, Manchester, KY [*Library symbol*] KyMan
Clay Flue Lining Institute [*Defunct*] CFLI
Clay Minerals [*A publication*] Clay Miner
Clay Minerals. Bulletin [*Later, Clay Minerals*] [*A publication*] Clay Miner Bull
Clay Minerals Society CMS
Clay Pigmented Organic Coating CPOC
Clay Pipe [*Technical drawings*] CP
Clay Pipe Institute CPI
Clay Products Association CPA

Clay Products Haulers Bureau, Inc., Worthington OH [*STAC*]................CPH
Clay Science (Tokyo) [*A publication*]..Clay Sci (Tokyo)
Clay Sewer Pipe Association..CSPA
Clay or Terra Cotta [*Freight*]..CLY T C
Claymont Public Library, Claymont, DE [*Library symbol*]........................DeC
Clays and Clay Minerals [*A publication*]......................................CCM
Clays and Clay Minerals [*A publication*]......................................Clay Clay M
Clays and Clay Minerals [*A publication*]......................................Clays Clay Miner
Clayton College, Denver, CO [*Library symbol*]................................CoDC
Clayton Corp. [*NASDAQ symbol*]...CLAY
Clayton, GA [*Radio station call letters*]....................................WGHC
Clayton Homes, Inc. [*NASDAQ symbol*]...CLHO
Clayton, MO [*Radio station call letters*]....................................KFUO
Clayton, MO [*Radio station call letters*]....................................KFUO-FM
Clayton, MO [*Radio station call letters*]....................................KHRU
Clayton, MO [*Radio station call letters*]....................................KSIV
Clayton, MO [*Radio station call letters*]....................................KWUR
Clayton, NC [*Radio station call letters*]....................................WHPY
Clayton, NM [*Location identifier*] [*FAA*]...................................CAO
Clayton, NM [*Radio station call letters*]....................................KLMX
Clayton Silver Mines [*NASDAQ symbol*]..CLSM
Clayton, W. G., III, Buffalo NY [*STAC*].......................................CWG
CLC of America, Inc. [*Formerly, Consolidated Leasing Corporation of America*] [*NYSE symbol*]........CLC
Clean..CLN
Clean Air Act [*1963*]...CAA
Clean Air Car Race...CACR
Clean Air. Journal [*A publication*]...Clean Air J
Clean Air Movement...CAM
Clean Air Package..CAP
Clean Air Projector..CAP
Clean Air Scientific Advisory Committee [*Environmental Protection Agency*].....CASAC
Clean Air. Special Edition [*A publication*]...................................Clean Air Spec Ed
Clean Assembly Facility..CAF
Clean Catch [*of urine*] [*Medicine*]..CC
Clean Catch Midstream [*Medicine*]...CCMS
Clean Catch Midstream Urine [*Medicine*].......................................CCMSU
Clean Coal Coalition...CCC
Clean Community System [*Waste management program*]...........................CCS
Clean Energy Research Institute..CERI
Clean Fuel Oil Tank..CFT
Clean Fuels from Biomass and Wastes. Symposium Papers [*A publication*]........Clean Fuels Biomass Wastes Symp Pap
Clean Harbors Cooperative..CHC
Clean Identification Decal [*Aerospace*]......................................CID
Clean Lube Oil...CLO
Clean-in-Place [*Food processing*]..CIP
Clean Room Kit...CRK
Clean and Sober [*Slang*]..C and S
Clean Sweep Generator..CSG
Clean Tanks, Gas Free..CTGF
Clean Up Buck..CUB
Clean Urban River Environments [*Project*].....................................CURE
Clean Voided Specimen [*Medicine*]...CVS
Clean Water Act [*Environmental Protection Agency*]...........................CWA
Clean Water Action Project...CWAP
Clean Work Area [*NASA*]...CWA
Clean World International..CWI
Cleaning...CLNG
Cleaning Equipment Manufacturers Association...................................CEMA
Cleaning Gear Locker...CGLKR
Cleaning Management Station...CMS
Cleanliness Identification [*Label*] [*Aerospace*].............................CID
Cleanly Designed Cigar...CDC
Cleanout...CO
Cleanout Flush with Finished Floor...FCO
Clear [*Calculators*]..C
Clear..CL
Clear..CLR
Clear and Add..CA
Clear and Add..CLA
Clear Air Dot Angle..CADA
Clear Air Mass...CLAM
Clear Air Temperature..CAT
Clear Air Turbulence [*Aviation*]..CAT
Clear, AK [*Location identifier*] [*FAA*]......................................CLF
Clear All Channels...CAC
Clear Aperture...CA
Clear Both [*Data processing*]...CLB
Clear Carry..CLC
Clear-Cell Carcinoma of Endometrium [*Medicine*]...............................CCE
Clear Channel Broadcasting Service...CCBS
Clear of Clouds [*Aviation*]...CCLDS
Clear Creek Butte [*Alaska*] [*Seismograph station code, US Geological Survey*] [*Closed*]........CCB
Clear-Entry [*Calculators*]..CE
Clear Glazed Structural Facing Units [*Technical drawings*]....................CLGSFU
Clear Glazed Structural Unit Base [*Technical drawings*].......................CLGSUB
Clear Indicating Light...CIL
Clear Lake City [*Texas*] [*Airport symbol*]...................................CLC
Clear Lake City, TX [*Location identifier*] [*FAA*]............................CLC
Clear Lake City, TX [*Radio station call letters*].............................KMJQ
Clear Lake, IA [*Radio station call letters*]..................................KZEV
Clear Lake Public Library, Clear Lake, IA [*Library symbol*]...................IaCll
Clear Lane Marking System [*Army*]...CLAMS
Clear Language for Expressing Orders [*Data processing*].......................CLEO
Clear Line-of-Sight..CLOS
Clear Liquid [*Medicine*]..CL
Clear Mews [*Alaska*] [*Seismograph station code, US Geological Survey*] [*Closed*]........CMA
Clear Only if Known [*Buzz words, acronyms, etc., that are clear in context only if already known to the reader*]........COIK
Clear to Send..CTS
Clear and Smooth [*Meteorology*]...CLRS
Clear and Subtract...CLS
Clear and Subtract...CS
Clear Type of Ice Formation [*Aviation code*]..................................CLA
Clear Wire Glass [*Technical drawings*]..CLWG
Clear Write Condition..CWC
Clearance..C
Clearance..CL
Clearance..CLN
Clearance..CLNC
Clearance..CLR
Clearance [*Physiology*]...Cx
Clearance Delivery...CD
Clearance Diving [*Navy*] [*British*]..CD
Clearance Not Delivered [*Aviation*]...N
Clearance Required [*Civil Service*]...CR
Cleared..CLD
Cleared to Airport [*Point of intended landing*] [*Aviation*]..................A
Cleared for Approach [*Aviation*]..CFA
Cleared for Approach [*Aviation*]..CFAP
Cleared Bidder's List..CBL
Cleared Customs [*Aviation*]...CCUS
Cleared to Depart from the Fix [*Aviation*]....................................D
Cleared as Filed...CAF
Cleared to the Fix [*Aviation*]..F
Cleared to Land [*Aviation*]...L
Cleared to the Outer Marker [*Aviation*].......................................O
Cleared as Planned [*Aviation*]..CLRAP
Cleared Through for Landing and Takeoff [*Aviation*]...........................T
Cleared To...CLR
Clearfield Chronicle, Clearfield, IA [*Library symbol*]........................IaClfC
Clearfield, PA [*Radio station call letters*]..................................WCPA
Clearfield, PA [*Television station call letters*].............................WPSX-TV
Clearfield, PA [*Radio station call letters*]..................................WQYX
Clearing House [*A publication*]...Clear H
Clearing House [*A publication*]...Clearing H
Clearing House Interbank Payment System..CHIPS
Clearinghouse [*Banking*]..CH
Clearinghouse Announcements in Science and Technology [*of CFSTI*] [*Later, WGA*]........CAST
Clearinghouse for Augmenting Resources for Training [*DoD*].....................CHART
Clearinghouse Committee for Information on the Arts and Humanities..............CCIAH
Clearinghouse for Community Based Free Standing Educational Institutions.......CBFSEI
Clearinghouse on Counseling and Personnel Services [*ERIC*]....................CAPS
Clearinghouse on Educational Administration [*ERIC*]...........................CEA
Clearinghouse on Educational Facilities [*ERIC*]...............................CEF
Clearinghouse on Election Administration [*Federal Election Commission*]........CEA
Clearinghouse for Federal Scientific and Technical Information [*Later, NTIS*] [*National Bureau of Standards*]........CFSTI
Clearinghouse for Innovation in Scientific Communication........................CISC
Clearinghouse International of the Women's Forum................................CIWF
Clearinghouse and Laboratory for Census Data [*Defunct*]........................CLCD
Clearinghouse for Library and Information Sciences..............................CLIS
Clearinghouse on Migration Issues [*Australia*]................................CHOMI
Clearinghouse for Occupational Safety and Health Information [*HEW*]............COSHI
Clearinghouse for Research in Child Life [*Federal Security Administration*]....CRCL
Clearinghouse on Rural Education and Small Schools [*ERIC*]....................CRESS
Clearinghouse for Scientific and Technical Information [*Later, NTIS*] [*National Bureau of Standards*]........CSTI
Clearinghouse on Women's Issues in Congress.....................................CWIC
Clearinghouse on Women's Studies...CWS
Clearwater, BC [*Radio station call letters*]..................................CHNL-1
Clearwater Correctional Center, Resident Library, Forks, WA [*Library symbol*]........WaForC-R
Clearwater Correctional Center, Staff Library, Forks, WA [*Library symbol*]........WaForC
Clearwater, FL [*Location identifier*] [*FAA*].................................CLW
Clearwater, FL [*Radio station call letters*]..................................WAMA
Clearwater, FL [*Radio station call letters*]..................................WCKX
Clearwater, FL [*Television station call letters*].............................WCLF
Clearwater, FL [*Radio station call letters*]..................................WMGG
Clearwater, FL [*Radio station call letters*]..................................WQXM
Clearwater, FL [*Radio station call letters*]..................................WTAN

Clearwater Public Library, Clearwater, FL [*Library symbol*] FCl
Clearwater Publishing Co., Inc., New York, NY [*Library symbol*] CpCo
Clearway [*Aviation code*] CWY
Cleary College, Ypsilanti, MI [*Library symbol*] MiYCC
Cleat CLT
Clebsch-Gordan Coefficients [*Mathematics*] CGC
Cleburne Public Library, Cleburne, TX [*Library symbol*] TxCle
Cleburne, TX [*Radio station call letters*] KCLE
Cleft Palate [*Medicine*] CL PAL
Cleft Palate [*Medicine*] CP
Cleft Palate Journal [*A publication*] Clef Pal J
Cleft Palate Journal [*A publication*] CLPJA
Cleistogamous [*Botany*] CL
CLEM [*Closed-Loop Ex-Vessel Machine*] **Maintenance Pit** [*Nuclear energy*] CMP
CLEM [*Closed-Loop Ex-Vessel Machine*] **Transporter** [*Nuclear energy*] CT
Clemency Review Board [*for Vietnam War draft dodgers and defectors*] CRB
Clemson, SC [*Radio station call letters*] WCCP
Clemson, SC [*Radio station call letters*] WSBF-FM
Clemson University, Clemson, SC [*Library symbol*] ScCleU
Clemson University, Clemson, SC [*OCLC symbol*] SEA
Clemson University. Department of Forestry. Forest Research Series [*A publication*] Clemson Univ Dep For For Res Ser
Clemson University. Department of Forestry. Forestry Bulletin [*A publication*] Clemson Univ Dep For For Bull
Clemson University. Department of Forestry. Technical Paper [*A publication*] Clemson Univ Dep For Tech Pap
Clemson University. Review of Industrial Management and Textile Science [*A publication*] Clemson Univ Rev Ind Manage Text Sci
Cleobury, Mortimer, and Ditton Prior Light Railway [*Wales*] CMDP
Clergy CL
Clergy CLER
Clergy Counseling Service for Problem Pregnancies [*Defunct*] CCSPP
Clergy Economic Education Foundation [*Later, EEFC*] CEEF
Clergy and Laymen Concerned [*Formerly, CALCAV*] CALC
Clergy and Laymen Concerned about Vietnam [*Later, CALC*] CALCAV
Clergy Mutual Assurance Society [*British*] CMAS
Clergy Orphan Corporation [*British*] COC
Clergy Review [*A publication*] Clergy R
Clergyman CLERG
Clerical CLER
Clerical, Administrative, and Fiscal [*Used with number, as, CAF-6, to indicate grade of position*] [*Civil Service*] CAF
Clerical and Administrative Workers Union [*British*] CAWU
Clerical Aptitude [*Test*] CA
Clerical Aptitude Area CL
Clerical Aptitude Test CAT
Clerical Assistant [*Civil Service*] [*British*] CA
Clerical Officer [*Civil Service*] [*British*] CO
Clerical Support CLS
Clerical Technician, Medical [*Navy*] CLT
Clerical Test [*Military*] CLER
Clerical Work Evaluation [*British*] CWE
Clerical Work Improvement Program [*British*] CWIP
Clerici Regulares Congregationis Somaschae [*Somaschi Fathers*] [*Roman Catholic religious order*] CRCS
Clerici Regulares Matris Dei [*Clerics Regular of the Mother of God*] [*Roman Catholic religious order*] CRMD
Clerici Regulares Ministrantes Infirmis [*Clerics Regular Attendant on the Sick, Camillini, Camilliani*] [*Roman Catholic religious order*] CRMI
Clerici Regulares Minores [*Clerics Regular Minor*] [*Adorno Fathers*] [*Roman Catholic religious order*] CRM
Clerici Regulares Pauperum Matris Dei Scholarum Piarum [*Clerics Regular of the Poor Men of the Mother of God for Pious Schools*] [*Piarists*] [*Roman Catholic religious order*] CRSP
Clerici Regulares Sancti Pauli [*Clerics Regular of St. Paul*] [*Barnabites*] [*Also, Barn*] [*Roman Catholic men's religious order*] CRSP
Clerici Regulares Theatini [*Theatines*] [*Roman Catholic religious order*] CRT
Clerici Sancti Viatoris [*Clerics of St. Viator*] [*Viatorian Fathers*] [*Roman Catholic religious order*] CSV
Clericorum Regularium Somaschensium [*Somascan Fathers*] [*Roman Catholic religious order*] CRS
Clerk CL
Clerk CLK
Clerk of the [*Privy*] **Council** [*British*] CC
Clerk of the Crown [*British*] CC
Clerk of Monmouth County, Freehold, NJ [*Library symbol*] NjFrCoC
Clerk in Orders [*Church of England*] CLKO
Clerk of the Peace CP
Clerk of the Privy Council [*British*] CPC
Clerk to the Signet [*British*] CS
Clerk and Steward [*British*] C & S
Clermont [*Australia*] [*Airport symbol*] CMQ
Clermont County Public Library, Batavia, OH [*Library symbol*] OBat
Clermont-Ferrand [*France*] [*Airport symbol*] CFE
Clermont-Ferrand [*France*] [*Seismograph station code, US Geological Survey*] CFF
Clermont, FL [*Radio station call letters*] WWFL
Clermont General and Technical College, Batavia, OH [*Library symbol*] OBatC
Clermont. Universite. Annales Scientifiques. Geologie et Mineralogie [*A publication*] Clermont Univ Ann Sci Geol Mineral
Cleve [*Australia*] [*Seismograph station code, US Geological Survey*] CLV
Cleveland [*Ohio*] [*Airport symbol*] CLE
Cleveland [*Ohio*] [*Seismograph station code, US Geological Survey*] CLE
Cleveland Area Metropolitan Library System [*Library network*] CAMLS
Cleveland Bar Association. Journal [*A publication*] Clev B A J
Cleveland Bay Association of America [*Later, Cleveland Bay Society of America*] CBAA
Cleveland Bay Society of America CBSA
Cleveland [*Ohio*] **Burke Lakefront** [*Airport symbol*] BKL
Cleveland, Cincinnati, Chicago, & St. Louis Railway [*AAR code*] CCCL
Cleveland-Cliffs Iron Co. [*NYSE symbol*] CLF
Cleveland Clinic. Cardiovascular Consultations [*A publication*] Cleveland Clin Cardiovasc Consult
Cleveland Clinic Educational Foundation, Cleveland, OH [*Library symbol*] OCIC
Cleveland Clinic. Quarterly [*A publication*] Cleve Clin Q
Cleveland County Memorial Library, Shelby, NC [*Library symbol*] NcSh
Cleveland County Technical Institute, Shelby, NC [*Library symbol*] NcShC
Cleveland Electric Illuminating Co. [*NYSE symbol*] CVX
Cleveland, GA [*Radio station call letters*] WRWH
Cleveland Health Sciences Library, Cleveland, OH [*OCLC symbol*] CHS
Cleveland Heights, OH [*Radio station call letters*] WRQC
Cleveland Heights-University Heights Public Library, Cleveland Heights, OH [*Library symbol*] OClh
Cleveland Heights-University Heights Public Library, Cleveland Heights, OH [*OCLC symbol*] OZC
Cleveland Institute of Art, Cleveland, OH [*OCLC symbol*] OAC
Cleveland Institute of Art, Cleveland, OH [*Library symbol*] OCISA
Cleveland Institute of Electronics [*Ohio*] CIE
Cleveland Institute of Music [*Ohio*] CIM
Cleveland Institute of Music, Cleveland, OH [*Library symbol*] OCICIM
Cleveland-Marshall College of Law, Cleveland, OH [*OCLC symbol*] LMC
Cleveland-Marshall College of Law, Cleveland State University, Cleveland, OH [*Library symbol*] OCIU-L
Cleveland-Marshall Law Review [*A publication*] Clev-Mar L Rev
Cleveland Metropolitan General Hospital, Cleveland, OH [*Library symbol*] OCIMGH
Cleveland, MS [*Radio station call letters*] WCLD
Cleveland, MS [*Radio station call letters*] WCLD-FM
Cleveland, MS [*Radio station call letters*] WQAZ
Cleveland, MS [*Radio station call letters*] WRDC
Cleveland. Museum of Art. Bulletin [*A publication*] Cleveland Mus Bull
Cleveland Museum of Art, Cleveland, OH [*Library symbol*] OCIMA
Cleveland Museum of Natural History, Cleveland, OH [*Library symbol*] OCIMN
Cleveland. Museum of Natural History. Museum News [*A publication*] Cleveland Mus Nat History Mus News
Cleveland. Museum of Natural History. Science Publications [*A publication*] Cleveland Mus Nat History Sci Pubs
Cleveland, OH [*Location identifier*] [*FAA*] BFT
Cleveland, OH [*Location identifier*] [*FAA*] LVJ
Cleveland, OH [*Radio station call letters*] WABQ
Cleveland, OH [*Radio station call letters*] WBBG
Cleveland, OH [*Television station call letters*] WCLQ-TV
Cleveland, OH [*Radio station call letters*] WCLV
Cleveland, OH [*Radio station call letters*] WCPN
Cleveland, OH [*Radio station call letters*] WCRF
Cleveland, OH [*Radio station call letters*] WCSB
Cleveland, OH [*Radio station call letters*] WDMT
Cleveland, OH [*Radio station call letters*] WDOK
Cleveland, OH [*Radio station call letters*] WERE
Cleveland, OH [*Television station call letters*] WEWS
Cleveland, OH [*Radio station call letters*] WGAR
Cleveland, OH [*Radio station call letters*] WGCL
Cleveland, OH [*Radio station call letters*] WHK
Cleveland, OH [*Television station call letters*] WJKW-TV
Cleveland, OH [*Radio station call letters*] WJMO
Cleveland, OH [*Radio station call letters*] WJW
Cleveland, OH [*Radio station call letters*] WKSW
Cleveland, OH [*Television station call letters*] WKYC-TV
Cleveland, OH [*Radio station call letters*] WMJI
Cleveland, OH [*Radio station call letters*] WMMS
Cleveland, OH [*Radio station call letters*] WQAL
Cleveland, OH [*Radio station call letters*] WRUW-FM
Cleveland, OH [*Television station call letters*] WVIZ-TV
Cleveland, OH [*Radio station call letters*] WWWE
Cleveland, OH [*Radio station call letters*] WWWM
Cleveland, OH [*Radio station call letters*] WZAK
Cleveland, OH [*Radio station call letters*] WZZP
Cleveland, OK [*Location identifier*] [*FAA*] EVL
Cleveland Orchestra. Program Notes [*A publication*] Clev Orch
Cleveland & Pittsburgh R. R. Co. [*NYSE symbol*] [*Delisted*] PTT
Cleveland Plain Dealer [*A publication*] Pln Dealr

Cleveland Public Library, Cleveland, OH [*OCLC symbol*]....CLE
Cleveland Public Library, Cleveland, OH [*Library symbol*]....OCl
Cleveland Public Library, Cleveland, TN [*Library symbol*]....TCle
Cleveland Public [*Charles O. Austin Memorial*] **Library, Cleveland, TX** [*Library symbol*]....TxClv
Cleveland State Community College, Cleveland, TN [*Library symbol*]....TCleC
Cleveland State. Law Review [*A publication*]....Clev St L R
Cleveland State University, Cleveland, OH [*OCLC symbol*]....CSU
Cleveland State University, Cleveland, OH [*Library symbol*]....OClU
Cleveland Symposium on Macromolecules [*A publication*]....Cleveland Symp Macromol
Cleveland, TN [*Location identifier*] [*FAA*]....HDI
Cleveland, TN [*Radio station call letters*]....WALV
Cleveland, TN [*Radio station call letters*]....WBAC
Cleveland, TN [*Radio station call letters*]....WCLE
Cleveland, TN [*Radio station call letters*]....WQLS
Cleveland, TN [*Radio station call letters*]....WQNE
Cleveland, TN [*Radio station call letters*]....WUSY
Cleveland Trust Company....CTC
Cleveland, TX [*Radio station call letters*]....KJCH
Clevepak Corp. [*NYSE symbol*]....CLV
Cleverness Factor [*Psychology*]....C
Clevetrust Realty SBI [*NASDAQ symbol*]....CTRIS
Clevis [*Metal shackle*]....CLV
Clevite Corp. [*NYSE symbol*] [*Delisted*]....CGH
Clewiston, FL [*Radio station call letters*]....WAFC
Client-Centered Counseling Progress Record [*Psychology*]....CCCPR
Client-Oriented Data Acquisition Process [*FDA*]....CODAP
Clients Lifetime Advisory Service Program [*Insurance*]....CLASP
Clifford, Arlington, Buckingham, Ashley, Lauderdale [*Ministers of Charles II of England*] [*Some claim that the word "cabal" is derived from this acronym; others, that it comes from the Hebrew "cabala"*]....CABAL
Cliffs....CLFS
Cliffside [*Montana*] [*Seismograph station code, US Geological Survey*] [*Closed*]....CFM
Cliffside Park Public Library, Cliffside Park, NJ [*Library symbol*]....NjClp
Cliffside Railroad Co. [*AAR code*]....CLIF
Clifton, AZ [*Radio station call letters*]....KCUZ
Clifton-Essex-Franklin Library [*Library network*]....C-E-F L
Clifton Forge, VA [*Radio station call letters*]....WXCF
Clifton Forge, VA [*Radio station call letters*]....WXCF-FM
Clifton Hills [*Australia*] [*Airport symbol*] [*Obsolete*]....CFH
Clifton Independent Prospector, Clifton, NJ [*Library symbol*]....NjClifI
Clifton Leader, Clifton, NJ [*Library symbol*]....NjClifL
Clifton Park, NY [*Radio station call letters*]....WCSF
Clifton Public Library, Clifton, NJ [*Library symbol*]....NjClif
Clifton Publishing Co., Clifton, NJ [*Library symbol*]....NjClifP
Climactic....CLIM
Climate - Altitude Chamber....CAC
Climate Control [*India*] [*A publication*]....Clim Control
Climate: Long-Range Investigation, Mapping, and Prediction [*National Science Foundation*]....CLIMAP
Climate Test Chamber....CTC
Climate, Vegetation, Productivity....CVP
Climatic Change [*A publication*]....Clim Change
Climatic Data Analysis Program....CDAP
Climatic Data for the World [*A publication*]....W
Climatic Impact Assessment Program [*for high altitude aircraft*]....CIAP
Climatic Impact Committee [*National Academy of Sciences - National Academy of Engineering*]....CIC
Climatic Index Monitoring Program....CIMP
Climatic Laboratory [*Military*]....CL
Climatic Laboratory Instrumentation System....CLINS
Climatic Modeling and Applications Program....CMAP
Climatological....CLTGL
Climatological Data [*A publication*]....CD
Climatological Data [*A publication*]....Climat Data
Climatological Data Sheet [*Air Force*]....CDS
Climatology....CLIMATOL
Climatology Mission Success Indicators....CMSI
Climatology and Persistence....CLIPER
Climax Mine [*Nevada*] [*Seismograph station code, US Geological Survey*] [*Closed*]....NYM
Climax Molybdenum Company, Technical Library, Climax, CO [*Library symbol*]....CoCxC
Climb [*Aviation*]....C
Climb [*Aviation*]....CLB
Climb on Course [*Aviation*]....COC
Climb and Cross [*Aviation*]....CATX
Climb so as to Cross [*Aviation*]....CSATC
Climb to and Cross [*Aviation*]....CTAX
Climb to and Cruise [*Aviation*]....CCRZ
Climb Enroute [*Aviation*]....CER
Climb Immediately [*Aviation*]....CLBI
Climb to and Maintain [*Aviation*]....CTAM
Climb so as to Reach [*Aviation*]....CSATR
Climb Well to Right [*Aviation*]....CWTR
Climb Well to Right of Course [*Aviation*]....CWRC
Climbing Fiber [*Cytology*]....CF
Clin-Byla [*France*] [*Research code symbol*]....CB
Clin-Byla [*France*] [*Research code symbol*]....FH
Clinch River Breeder Reactor....CRBR
Clinch River Breeder Reactor Plant [*Department of Energy*]....CRBRP
Clinch River Mile [*Energy Research and Development Administration*]....CRM
Clinch Valley College of the University of Virginia, Wise, VA [*OCLC symbol*]....VCV
Clinch Valley College of the University of Virginia, Wise, VA [*Library symbol*]....ViWisC
Clinchfield Railroad Company [*AAR code*]....CCO
Cling Peach Advisory Board....CPAB
Clini-Therm Corp. [*NASDAQ symbol*]....CLIN
Clinica Chimica Acta [*A publication*]....Clin Chim A
Clinica Chimica Acta [*A publication*]....Clin Chim Acta
Clinica Europa [*A publication*]....Clin Eur
Clinica Geral (Sao Paulo) [*A publication*]....Clin Geral (Sao Paulo)
Clinica Ginecologica [*A publication*]....Clin Ginecol
Clinica y Laboratoria [*A publication*]....Clin Lab
Clinica Medical Italiana [*A publication*]....Clin Med Ital
Clinica Ortopedica [*A publication*]....Clin Ortop
Clinica Otorinolaringoiatrica [*A publication*]....COURA
Clinica Otorinolaringoiatrica (Catania) [*A publication*]....Clin Otorinolaringoiatr (Catania)
Clinica Pediatrica [*A publication*]....Clin Pediat
Clinica Terapeutica [*A publication*]....Clin Ter
Clinica Veterinaria (Milan) [*A publication*]....Clin Vet (Milan)
Clinical....CLIN
Clinical and Administrative Record [*System*]....CARE
Clinical Allergy [*A publication*]....Clin Allergy
Clinical Anesthesia [*A publication*]....Clin Anesth
Clinical Approaches to Problems of Childhood [*A publication*]....Clin Approaches Probl Child
Clinical Behavior Therapy Review [*A publication*]....CBTR
Clinical and Biochemical Analysis [*A publication*]....Clin Biochem Anal
Clinical Biochemistry [*A publication*]....Clin Bioch
Clinical Biochemistry [*A publication*]....Clin Biochem
Clinical Bulletin [*A publication*]....Clin Bull
Clinical Bulletin (Memorial Sloan-Kettering Cancer Center) [*A publication*]....Clin Bull (Mem Sloan-Kettering Cancer Cent)
Clinical Cancer Protocols [*Data base*] [*National Library of Medicine*]....CLINPROT
Clinical Cardiology [*A publication*]....Clin Cardiol
Clinical Center [*National Institutes of Health*]....CC
Clinical Center Blood Bank....CCBB
Clinical Chemistry [*A publication*]....Clin Chem
Clinical Cytology: A Series of Monographs [*A publication*]....Clin Cytol Ser Monogr
Clinical Data, Inc. [*NASDAQ symbol*]....CLDA
Clinical Diagnostics [*NASDAQ symbol*]....CLND
Clinical Electroencephalography [*A publication*]....Clin EEG
Clinical Electroencephalography [*A publication*]....Clin Electr
Clinical Electroencephalography [*A publication*]....Clin Electroencephalogr
Clinical Endocrinology [*A publication*]....Clin Endocr
Clinical Endocrinology [*A publication*]....Clin Endocrinol
Clinical Endocrinology and Metabolism [*A publication*]....Clin Endocrinol Metab
Clinical Engineering [*A publication*]....Clin Eng
Clinical and Experimental Dermatology [*A publication*]....Clin Exp Dermatol
Clinical and Experimental Hypertension [*A publication*]....Clin Exp Hypertens
Clinical and Experimental Immunology [*A publication*]....Clin Exp Im
Clinical and Experimental Immunology [*A publication*]....Clin Exp Immunol
Clinical and Experimental Immunoreproduction [*A publication*]....Clin Exp Immunoreprod
Clinical and Experimental Neurology [*A publication*]....Clin Exp Neurol
Clinical and Experimental Obstetrics and Gynecology [*A publication*]....Clin Exp Obstet Gynecol
Clinical and Experimental Pharmacology and Physiology [*A publication*]....Clin Exp Ph
Clinical and Experimental Pharmacology and Physiology [*A publication*]....Clin Exp Pharmcol Physiol
Clinical and Experimental Pharmacology and Physiology. Supplement [*A publication*]....Clin Exp Pharmacol Physiol Suppl
Clinical Genetics [*A publication*]....Clin Genet
Clinical Immunology and Immunopathology [*A publication*]....Clin Immun
Clinical Immunology and Immunopathology [*A publication*]....Clin Immunol Immunopathol
Clinical Information Was Not Provided [*Medicine*]....CIWNP
Clinical Investigation Center....CIC
Clinical and Investigative Medicine [*A publication*]....Clin Invest Med
Clinical Laboratory Data Acquisition System [*Data processing*]....CLDAS
Clinical and Laboratory Haematology [*A publication*]....Clin Lab Haematol
Clinical Laboratory Improvement Act....CLIA
Clinical Laboratory Management Association....CLMA
Clinical Laboratory Management System [*Data processing*]....CLMS
Clinical Laboratory Technician....CLT
Clinical Ligand Assay Society....CLAS
Clinical Literature Untoward Effects [*Service published by International Information Institute*]....CLUE
Clinical Medical Librarian....CML

Clinical Medical Officer [*British*] ..... CMO
Clinical Medicine [*A publication*] ..... Clin Med
Clinical Nephrology [*A publication*] ..... Clin Nephrol
Clinical Nephrology [*A publication*] ..... CN
Clinical Neurology Information Center ..... CNIC
Clinical Neurology and Neurosurgery [*A publication*] ..... Clin Neurol
Clinical Neurology (Tokyo) [*A publication*] ..... Clin Neurol (Tokyo)
Clinical Neuropharmacology [*A publication*] ..... Clin Neuropharmacol
Clinical Neurosurgery [*A publication*] ..... Clin Neurosurg
Clinical Notes on Respiratory Diseases [*A publication*] ..... Clin Notes Respir Dis
Clinical Nuclear Medicine [*A publication*] ..... Clin Nucl Med
Clinical Nursing ..... CN
Clinical Nutrition [*A publication*] ..... Clin Nutr
Clinical Obstetrics and Gynecology [*A publication*] ..... Clin Obstet Gynecol
Clinical Obstetrics and Gynecology [*A publication*] ..... CO & G
Clinical Oncology [*A publication*] ..... Clin Oncol
Clinical Orthopaedic Society ..... COS
Clinical Orthopaedics and Related Research [*A publication*] ..... Clin Orthop
Clinical Orthopaedics and Related Research [*A publication*] ..... Clin Orthop Relat Res
Clinical Otolaryngology [*A publication*] ..... Clin Otolaryngol
Clinical Pathology ..... CLP
Clinical Pathology ..... CP
Clinical Pathology Conference ..... CPC
Clinical Pediatrics [*Philadelphia*] [*A publication*] ..... Clin Pediat
Clinical Pediatrics [*Philadelphia*] [*A publication*] ..... CPEDA
Clinical Pediatrics (Philadelphia) [*A publication*] ..... Clin Pediatr (Phila)
Clinical Pediatrics (Philadelphia) [*A publication*] ..... Clin Pediatr (Philadelphia)
Clinical Pharmacokinetics [*A publication*] ..... Clin Pharmacokinet
Clinical Pharmacology and Drug Epidemiology [*Elsevier Book Series*] [*A publication*] ..... CPDE
Clinical Pharmacology and Therapeutics [*A publication*] ..... Clin Pharm
Clinical Pharmacology and Therapeutics [*A publication*] ..... Clin Pharmacol Ther
Clinical Physics and Physiological Measurement [*A publication*] ..... CPPM
Clinical Physiology [*A publication*] ..... CP
Clinical Proceedings. Children's Hospital of the District of Columbia [*Later, Children's Hospital National Medical Center*] [*A publication*] ..... Clin Proc Child Hosp DC
Clinical Proceedings. Children's Hospital National Medical Center [*A publication*] ..... Clin Proc Child Hosp Natl Med Cent
Clinical Radiology [*A publication*] ..... Clin Radiol
Clinical Record [*Medicine*] ..... CR
Clinical Record Cover Sheet [*Army medical*] ..... CRCS
Clinical Reproductive Neuroendocrinology. International Seminar on Reproductive Physiology and Sexual Endocrinology [*A publication*] ..... Clin Reprod Neuroendocrinol Int Semin
Clinical Research [*A publication*] ..... Clin Res
Clinical Research Unit ..... CRU
Clinical Science [*Oxford*] [*Later, Clinical Science and Molecular Medicine*] [*A publication*] ..... Clin Sci
Clinical Science and Molecular Medicine [*Oxford*] [*A publication*] ..... Clin Sci Mol Med
Clinical Science and Molecular Medicine [*Oxford*] [*A publication*] ..... Clin Sc Mol
Clinical Science and Molecular Medicine (Supplement) [*A publication*] ..... Clin Sci Mol Med (Suppl)
Clinical Science (Oxford) [*Later, Clinical Science and Molecular Medicine (Oxford)*] [*A publication*] ..... Clin Sci (Oxf)
Clinical Science. Supplement [*A publication*] ..... Clin Sci Suppl
Clinical Social Work Journal [*A publication*] ..... Clin S Work
Clinical Society of Genito-Urinary Surgeons ..... CSGUS
Clinical Sociology Association ..... CSA
Clinical State ..... CS
Clinical Studies [*Elsevier Book Series*] [*A publication*] ..... CS
Clinical Symposia [*A publication*] ..... Clin Symp
Clinical Therapeutics [*A publication*] ..... Clin Ther
Clinical Toxicology [*A publication*] ..... Clin Toxic
Clinical Toxicology [*A publication*] ..... Clin Toxicol
Clinical Toxicology. Bulletin [*A publication*] ..... Clin Toxicol Bull
Clinical Toxicology of Commercial Products [*A publication*] ..... CTCP
Clinical Trials Monitoring System ..... CTMS
Clinical Unit ..... CU
Clinically Important Adverse Drug Interactions [*Elsevier Book Series*] [*A publication*] ..... CIADI
Clinically Undetectable Primary Malignancy [*Oncology*] ..... CUPM
Clinician Full Time [*Chiropody*] [*British*] ..... CF
Clinics in Chest Medicine [*A publication*] ..... Clin Chest Med
Clinics in Endocrinology and Metabolism [*A publication*] ..... Clin End Me
Clinics in Gastroenterology [*A publication*] ..... Clin Gastro
Clinics in Haematology [*A publication*] ..... Clin Haemat
Clinics in Haematology [*A publication*] ..... Clin Haematol
Clinics in Perinatology [*A publication*] ..... Clin Perinatol
Clinics in Plastic Surgery [*A publication*] ..... Clin Plast Surg
Clinics in Rheumatic Diseases [*A publication*] ..... Clin Rheum Dis
Clinique d'Aide a l'Enfance, Ste-Foy, PQ, Canada [*Library symbol*] ..... CaQSFCAE
Clinique Ophtalmologique [*A publication*] ..... Clin Ophtalmol
Clinoenstatite [*A mineral*] ..... CE
Clinometer [*Engineering*] ..... CLN
Clinton [*Iowa*] [*Airport symbol*] ..... CWI
Clinton, AR [*Radio station call letters*] ..... KGFL
Clinton, AR [*Radio station call letters*] ..... KHPQ
Clinton Community College, Clinton, IA [*Library symbol*] ..... IaCliCC
Clinton Community College, Plattsburgh, NY [*Library symbol*] ..... NPlaCC
Clinton Community College, Plattsburgh, NY [*OCLC symbol*] ..... YLC
Clinton Corn Processing Co., Clinton, IA [*Library symbol*] ..... IaCliC
Clinton Corners Reading Center, Clinton Corners, NY [*Library symbol*] ..... NClinc
Clinton County Historical Society, Clinton, IA [*Library symbol*] ..... IaCliCHi
Clinton-Essex-Franklin Library, Plattsburgh, NY [*OCLC symbol*] ..... VZC
Clinton-Essex-Franklin Library System, Plattsburgh, NY [*Library symbol*] ..... NPlaCEF
Clinton Herald, Clinton, IA [*Library symbol*] ..... IaCliH
Clinton, IA [*Location identifier*] [*FAA*] ..... CWI
Clinton, IA [*Location identifier*] [*FAA*] ..... FNO
Clinton, IA [*Radio station call letters*] ..... KLNT
Clinton, IA [*Radio station call letters*] ..... KNJY
Clinton, IA [*Radio station call letters*] ..... KROS
Clinton, IA [*Radio station call letters*] ..... KSAY
Clinton, IL [*Radio station call letters*] ..... WHOW
Clinton, IL [*Radio station call letters*] ..... WHOW-FM
Clinton, LA [*Radio station call letters*] ..... WQCK
Clinton, MO [*Location identifier*] [*FAA*] ..... GLY
Clinton, MO [*Radio station call letters*] ..... KDKD
Clinton, MO [*Radio station call letters*] ..... KDKD-FM
Clinton, MS [*Radio station call letters*] ..... WHJT
Clinton, MS [*Radio station call letters*] ..... WTWZ
Clinton, NC [*Radio station call letters*] ..... WCLN
Clinton, NC [*Radio station call letters*] ..... WRRZ
Clinton, NC [*Radio station call letters*] ..... WRRZ-FM
Clinton, NY [*Radio station call letters*] ..... WHCL-FM
Clinton, OK [*Location identifier*] [*FAA*] ..... BFV
Clinton, OK [*Location identifier*] [*FAA*] ..... BZF
Clinton, OK [*Location identifier*] [*FAA*] ..... CLK
Clinton, OK [*Radio station call letters*] ..... KCLI
Clinton, OK [*Radio station call letters*] ..... KKCC
Clinton, OK [*Radio station call letters*] ..... KKCC-FM
Clinton Public Library, Clinton, IA [*Library symbol*] ..... IaCli
Clinton Public Library, Clinton, MI [*Library symbol*] ..... MiClin
Clinton Public Library, Clinton, OK [*Library symbol*] ..... OkCl
Clinton, SC [*Radio station call letters*] ..... WPCC
Clinton, TN [*Radio station call letters*] ..... WNKX
Clinton, TN [*Radio station call letters*] ..... WYSH
Clintonville, WI [*Location identifier*] [*FAA*] CLI
Clintonville, WI [*Radio station call letters*] ..... WFCL
Clintonville, WI [*Radio station call letters*] ..... WFCL-FM
Clintwood, VA [*Radio station call letters*] ..... WDIC
Clio Medica [*A publication*] ..... Clio Med
Clio Medica [*A publication*] ..... CM
Clip CL
Clipper Club [*Pan American Airlines' club for frequent flyers*] CC
Clipper Negative ..... CLN
Clipper Positive ..... CLP
Clipping Amplifier ..... CA
CLIRA [*Closed-Loop In-Reactor Assembly*] **Backup Plug Tool** [*Nuclear energy*] ..... CBPT
CLIRA [*Closed-Loop In-Reactor Assembly*] **Holddown Assembly Tool** [*Nuclear energy*] ..... CHAT
Cloak and Suit Trucking Association ..... CSTA
Clock ..... CLK
Clock Assemblers and Importers Association ..... CAIA
Clock Coercion ..... C/C
Clock Coercion Signal ..... CCS
Clock Delay ..... CDL
Clock Driver ..... CD
Clock Hour ..... CH
Clock Oscillator ..... CO
Clock Phase ..... CP
Clock, Programing, and Timing [*NASA*] ..... CPT
Clock Pulse ..... CP
Clock Pulse Generator ..... CPG
Clock Pulse Interval ..... CPI
Clock Pulse Repeater ..... CPR
Clock Pulsed Control ..... CPC
Clock Start Command ..... CSC
Clock Subsystem ..... CSS
Clock-Sync Receiver Assembly [*Deep Space Instrumentation Facility, NASA*] ..... CSR
Clock Synchronization ..... CS
Clock Time ..... CT
Clock and Watch Manufacturers Association of America [*Defunct*] ..... CWMAA
Clockwise C
Clockwise ..... CLKWS
Clockwise ..... CLKWZ
Clockwise ..... CW
Clockwise ..... CWS
Clockwise Orbit [*Aviation*] ..... CLKOB
Cloncurry [*Australia*] [*Airport symbol*] ..... CNJ

Cloning Inhibiting Factor .... CIF
Clopay Corp. [*American Stock Exchange symbol*] .... CPY
Cloquet, MN [*Radio station call letters*] .... WKLK
Cloquet, MN [*Radio station call letters*] .... WKLK-FM
Clorox Co. [*NYSE symbol*] CLX
Clorox Co. [*Later, CLX*] [*NYSE symbol*] CXC
Close CL
Close .... CLO
Close .... CLS
Close Air Support [*Military*] .... CAS
Close Air Support Aircraft [*Military*] .... CASA
Close Air Support Control [*Military*] .... CASCON
Close Air Support Exercise [*Military*] .... CASEX
Close Air Support Gun Program [*Military*] .... CASGP
Close Air Support Gun System [*Military*] .... CASGS
Close Air Support Missile [*Military*] .... CASM
Close Air Support Request Processing [*Military*] .... CASRP
Close Air Support System [*Military*] .... CLASS
Close Air Support Weapon [*Military*] .... CASW
Close Air Support Weapon [*Military*] .... CLAW
Close Air Support Weapon System [*Military*] .... CASWS
Close Annealed [*Metal industry*] .... CA
Close Assault Weapon .... CAW
Close-Binding-Intimate .... CBI
Close Boundary Sentry [*Military*] .... CBS
Close of Business [*With date*] .... COB
Close Combat LASER Assault Weapon .... C-CLAW
Close Combat Weapon System [*Army*] .... CCW
Close Control Bombing [*Air Force*] .... CCB
Close-Coupled [*Electricity*] CC
Close Encounters of the Third Kind [*Movie title*] CE3
Close Focus Lens .... CFL
Close-In CI
Close-In Automatic Route Restoral System [*NORAD*] .... CARRS
Close-In Improvement Program [*to increase torpedo effectiveness*] .... CLIP
Close-In Support [*Military*] .... CIS
Close-In Weapon System .... CIWS
Close Lunar Satellite .... CLS
Close Medium Shot [*A photograph or motion picture sequence taken from a relatively short distance*] .... CMS
Close-Open .... CO
Close-Open-Close .... COC
Close Packed .... CP
Close-Packed Hexagonal [*Metallography*] .... CPH
Close-Packed Structure .... CPS
Close-Pair Interstitial Atom .... CPIA
Close Reconnaissance Zone [*Army*] .... CRZ
Close Rolls [*British*] CL
Close Shot [*Photography*] .... CS
Close to Shoulder .... CTS
Close Support [*Army*] .... CS
Close Support Artillery Rocket System .... CSARS
Close Support Artillery Weapon System .... CSAWS
Close Support Assault Weapon [*Obsolete*] [*Navy*] .... CSAW
Close Support Missile [*Air Force*] .... CSM
Close Surveillance Contractor List [*DoD*] .... CSCL
Close Talking Microphone .... CTM
Close This Office .... CLOTO
Close Tolerance .... CT
Close Type Control Circuit Contact .... CTCCC
Close-Up [*A photograph or motion picture sequence taken from a short distance*] .... CU
Closed .... CLSD
Closed Bladder Drainage [*Medicine*] .... CBD
Closed Captioned [*Refers to captioning of television programs for the deaf*] CC
Closed Chest Cardiac Massage and Mouth-to-Mouth [*Resuscitation*] .... CCCMMM
Closed Chest Cardiac Resuscitation .... CCCR
Closed Circuit [*Transmission*] CC
Closed Circuit Loop CCL
Closed-Circuit Radio .... CCR
Closed-Circuit Television .... CCTV
Closed-Cycle Cooler CCC
Closed-Cycle Cryogenic Equipment .... CCCE
Closed-Cycle Gas-Cooled Reactor .... CCGCR
Closed-Cycle Refrigerator .... CCR
Closed Ecological System .... CES
Closed End .... CLE
Closed Entry Socket Insulator .... CESI
Closed Flux Memory [*Data processing*] .... CFM
Closed Line Assembly for Single Particles .... CLASP
Closed Loop CL
Closed Loop Accounting for Stores Sales .... CLASS
Closed-Loop Aeronautical Management Programs .... CLAMP
Closed-Loop Approach Control .... CLAC
Closed-Loop Bandwidth .... CLBW
Closed-Loop Continuity Check [*Aerospace*] CLCC
Closed-Loop Control and Instrumentation System [*Nuclear energy*] .... CLCIS
Closed-Loop Cover Gas Monitor [*Nuclear energy*] .... CLCGM
Closed-Loop Ecological Cycle [*Aerospace*] .... CLEC
Closed-Loop Evaluation and Reporting System .... CLEAR
Closed-Loop Ex-Vessel Machine [*Formerly, EVHM*] [*Nuclear energy*] .... CLEM
Closed-Loop Fire Control [*Army*] .... CLFC
Closed-Loop Gain .... CLG
Closed-Loop In-Reactor Assembly [*Nuclear energy*] .... CLIRA
Closed-Loop Jumper Assembly [*Nuclear energy*] .... CLJA
Closed-Loop Support [*Army*] .... CLS
Closed-Loop Support Extended .... CLSX
Closed-Loop System [*Nuclear energy*] .... CLS
Closed-Loop System Melt-Down Accident [*Nuclear energy*] .... CLSMDA
Closed-Loop Telemetry .... CLT
Closed-Loop Television .... CLTV
Closed Pore Insulation .... CPI
Closed Position [*Dancing*] .... CP
Closed Shell .... CS
Closed System Respirator Evaluator .... CSRE
Closed Waveguide .... CWG
Closed, Well-Formed Formula [*Logic*] .... CWFF
Closely Spaced Basing [*Proposed plan for protecting MX missiles from enemy attack*] .... CSB
Closeout Door System .... CDS
Closeout System Installation .... COSI
Closest Approach [*Aerospace*] .... CA
Closest Point of Approach [*Navigation*] .... CPA
Closet CL
Closet .... CLO
Closing .... CLSG
Closing .... CLSNG
Closing Capacity CC
Closing Coil CC
Closing Date .... CLODA
Closing Station CL
Closing Volume [*Physiology*] CV
Closure [*Physiology*] CL
Closure .... CLOS
Closure .... CLSR
Closure Manufacturers Association .... CMA
Clot Lysis Time [*Hematology*] .... CLT
Clot Retraction [*Medicine*] .... CR
Cloth CL
Cloth Assistance Factor [*Textiles*] .... CAF
Cloth Elongation Factor [*Textiles*] .... CEF
Cloth Sides [*Bookbinding*] .... CS
Clothes .... CLTH
Clothespin Manufacturers of America .... CMA
Clothestime, Inc. [*NASDAQ symbol*] .... CTME
Clothing .... CLO
Clothing .... CLTHG
Clothing Articles Require Explanation [*Student legal action organization*] .... CARE
Clothing and Equipage .... C & E
Clothing and Equipment Development Branch [*Army*] .... C/ED
Clothing, Equipment, and Materials Engineering Laboratory [*Army*] .... CEMEL
Clothing and Equipment Test Facility [*Army*] .... CETF
Clothing and Footwear [*Department of Employment*] [*British*] .... CF
Clothing and Housing Research Division [*of ARS, Department of Agriculture*] .... CH
Clothing Initial Issue Point [*Military*] .... CIIP
Clothing Maintenance Allowance .... CMA
Clothing Maintenance [*or Monetary*] **Allowance, Basic** [*Army*] .... CMAB
Clothing Maintenance Allowance, Standard [*Air Force*] .... CMAS
Clothing Manufacturers Association of the USA .... CMA
Clothing Monetary Allowance .... CLMA
Clothing Monetary Allowance, Initial Issue [*Army*] .... CMAIISS
Clothing Monetary Allowance, Initial (Women's Army Corps) .... CMAIWAC
Clothing Monetary Allowance List [*Military*] .... CMAL
Clothing Monetary Allowance, Standard [*Army*] .... CMAS
Clothing Monetary Maintenance Allowance [*Military*] .... CMMA
Clothing and Organic Materials [*Army*] .... C & OM
Clothing and Organic Materials Laboratory [*Army*] .... C/OM
Clothing Pattern Repository [*DoD*] .... CPR
Clothing and Personal Life Support Equipment Laboratory [*Army*] .... C/PLSEL
Clothing Sales Store .... CSS
Clothing and Small Stores Account .... CSSA
Clothing and Small Stores Fund .... CSSF
Clothing Supply Office [*Military*] .... CSO
Clothing and Survival Equipment Bulletin .... CSEB
Clothing and Survival Equipment Change [*Navy*] .... CSC
Clothing and Survival Equipment Change [*Naval Air Systems Command*] .... CSEC
Clothing and Textile Materiel [*Army*] .... C & TM
Clothing and Textiles .... C & T
Clotting [*or Coagulation*] **Time** [*Hematology*] .... CT
Cloud .... CLD
Cloud Camera Multiplexer .... CCM
Cloud in Cell CIC
Cloud Chamber Analysis .... CCA

Cloud Chamber Photographic Analysis ... CCPA
Cloud Condensation Nuclei [*Fog*] ... CCN
Cloud Cover ... CC
Cloud-Croft Radiation Measurement ... CRM
Cloud-Free Line of Sight [*Meteorology*] ... CFLOS
Cloud-to-Ground Lightning ... CGLTG
Cloud Physics Observatory [*University of Hawaii*] ... CPO
Cloud Physics Radiometer ... CPR
Cloud Processing Equipment ... CPE
Cloud-Top Altitude Radiometer ... CAR
Cloudiness-Temperature [*Hypothesis*] [*Meteorology*] ... C-T
Cloudy [*Meteorology*] ... C
Cloudy ... CLDY
Clover Aero, Inc. [*Friendswood, TX*] [*FAA designator*] ... CLV
Cloverdale Public Library, Cloverdale, CA [*Library symbol*] ... CCl
Cloverland Processing Center, Escanaba, MI [*OCLC symbol*] ... EZB
Clovis [*New Mexico*] [*Airport symbol*] ... CVN
Clovis, CA [*Radio station call letters*] ... KXQR
Clovis-Carver Public Library, Clovis, NM [*OCLC symbol*] ... CVC
Clovis-Carver Public Library, Clovis, NM [*Library symbol*] ... NmCl
Clovis, NM [*Location identifier*] [*FAA*] ... CVN
Clovis, NM [*Location identifier*] [*FAA*] ... CVS
Clovis, NM [*Location identifier*] [*FAA*] ... GLO
Clovis, NM [*Radio station call letters*] ... KCLV
Clovis, NM [*Radio station call letters*] ... KCLV-FM
Clovis, NM [*Radio station call letters*] ... KICA
Clovis, NM [*Radio station call letters*] ... KICA-FM
Clovis, NM [*Television station call letters*] ... KMCC
Clovis, NM [*Radio station call letters*] ... KTQM
Clovis, NM [*Radio station call letters*] ... KWKA
Clow Corp. [*NASDAQ symbol*] ... CLOW
Clown Club of America [*Superseded by Clowns of America*] ... CCA
Clowns of America [*Supersedes Clown Club of America*] ... CA
Clozapine [*A drug*] ... CLZ
Club ... C
Club ... CLB
Club de las Americas ... CLA
Club of Channel Islands Collectors ... CCIC
Club Delahaye ... CD
Club Elite of North America ... CE
Club Francais du Livre [*French Book Club*] ... CFL
Club Francais de la Medaille [*A publication*] ... CFM
Club of the Friends of Ancient Smoothing Irons ... CFASI
Club des Lecteurs d'Expression Francaise ... CLEF
Club du Livre Francais [*A publication*] ... CLF
Club Magazine [*Generic term for a publication covering the activities of a science-fiction fan club*] ... CLUBZINE
Club Managers Association of America ... CMAA
Club Mediterranee ... CM
Club du Meilleur Livre [*A publication*] ... CML
Club for Philately in Gerontology ... CPG
Club of Printing Women of New York ... CPW
Club of Rome ... CoR
Clubmart of America [*NASDAQ symbol*] ... CLBT
Clubs [*Public-performance tariff class*] [*British*] ... J
Cluett, Peabody & Co., Inc. [*NYSE symbol*] ... CLU
Cluj [*Kolozvar*] [*Romania*] [*Seismograph station code, US Geological Survey*] [*Closed*] ... CLU
Cluj-Napoca [*Romania*] [*Airport symbol*] ... CLJ
Clujul Medical [*A publication*] ... Cluj Med
Clumber Spaniel Club of America ... CSCA
Clumping Inducing Agent [*Bacteriology, genetics*] ... CIA
Cluster [*Data processing*] ... CLU
Cluster Activation Systems Specialist [*NASA*] ... CAS
Cluster Activation Systems Specialist [*NASA*] ... CASS
Cluster Bomb [*Military*] ... CLSTBB
Cluster Bomb Unit [*Military*] ... CBU
Cluster Control Unit ... CCU
Cluster Mission Simulator [*NASA*] ... CLMS
Cluster Systems Description Document ... CSDD
Clustered Airfield Defeat Munition ... CADM
Clustered Atomic Warhead ... CLAW
Clutch ... CL
Clutch Release Bearing ... CRB
Clutter Automatic Gain Control ... CAGC
Clutter Doppler Error ... CDE
Clutter Gate ... CG
Clutter Gate Amplifier ... CGA
Clutter-Locked Airborne Moving Target Indicator [*Air Force*] ... CLAMTI
Clutter Mapper Card ... CMC
Clutter-Operated Anticlutter ... COAC
Clutter Rejection RADAR ... CRR
Clutter on Target ... COT
Clutter Threshold Detector ... CTD
Clyde Mood Scale [*Psychology*] ... CMS
Clyde, OH [*Radio station call letters*] ... WMEX
Clyde River [*Canada*] [*Airport symbol*] ... YCY
Clyden Airways [*Great Britain*] [*ICAO designator*] ... CN
Clydesdale Breeders Association of the United States [*Later, CBUS*] ... CBA
Clydesdale Breeders of the United States ... CBUS
Clymer System ... CS
CMC International [*NASDAQ symbol*] ... CMCI
CME-SAT, Inc. [*NASDAQ symbol*] ... CSAT
CMFRI [*Central Marine Fisheries Research Institute*] **Bulletin** [*A publication*] ... CMFRI Bull
CMI Corp. [*American Stock Exchange symbol*] ... CMX
CMI [*Commonwealth Mycological Institute*] **Descriptions of Pathogenic Fungi and Bacteria** [*A publication*] ... CMI Descr Pathog Fungi Bact
CMI Investment Corp. [*NYSE symbol*] ... CML
CML Group [*NASDAQ symbol*] ... CMLI
CMP Newsletter [*A publication*] ... CMP
CMT Industries, Inc. [*American Stock Exchange symbol*] [*Delisted*] ... CMT
CMT Investment [*NASDAQ symbol*] ... CMTI
CMV [*Cucumber Mosaic Virus*] **Associated Ribonucleic Acid** [*Biochemistry, genetics*] ... CARNA
CNA Financial Corp. [*NYSE symbol*] ... CAF
CNA Financial Corp., Chicago, IL [*Library symbol*] ... ICCNA
CNA Financial Corp., Library, Chicago, IL [*OCLC symbol*] [*Inactive*] ... IBG
CNA Income Shares, Inc. [*NYSE symbol*] ... CNN
CNA Larwin Investment Co. [*NYSE symbol*] ... CNL
CNARESTRA [*Chief of Naval Air Reserve Training*] **Fleet Operating Squadrons** ... CFOS
CNE Communication/Navigation Electronics [*A publication*] ... CNE Commun Navig Electron
CNEP [*Comision Nacional para la Erradicacion del Paludismo*] **Boletin** [*A publication*] ... CNEP Bol
CNL Financial Corp. [*NASDAQ symbol*] ... CNLF
CNO [*Chief of Naval Operations*] **Advisory Board** ... CAB
CNO [*Chief of Naval Operations*] **Executive Board** ... CEB
CNO [*Chief of Naval Operations*] **Industry Advisory Committee for Telecommunications** [*DoD*] ... CIACT
CNO [*Chief of Naval Operations*] **Policy and Planning Guidance** ... CPPG
CNO [*Chief of Naval Operations*] **Program Analysis Memorandum** ... CPAM
CNRM (Centre National de Recherches Metallurgiques). Metallurgical Reports (Belgium) [*A publication*] ... CNRM (Cent Natl Rech Metall) Metall Rep
CNRM [*Centre National de Recherches Metallurgiques*]**. Metallurgical Reports** [*A publication*] ... CNRM
Co-Build Companies, Inc. [*American Stock Exchange symbol*] [*Delisted*] ... BLD
Co-Editor ... CO-ED
Co-Operative Bulletin. Taiwan Forestry Research Institute [*A publication*] ... Co-Op Bull Taiwan For Res Inst
Co-Operative Wholesale Society [*British*] ... CWS
Coach House ... CH
Coach Lace Institute [*Defunct*] ... CLI
Coachella [*California*] [*Seismograph station code, US Geological Survey*] ... COA
Coachella, CA [*Radio station call letters*] ... KCHV
Coachella, CA [*Radio station call letters*] ... KVIM
Coachella Municipal Public Library, Coachella, CA [*Library symbol*] ... CCoac
Coaches [*Freight*] ... COCH
Coaching Clinic [*A publication*] ... Coach Clin
Coaching Club ... CC
Coaching Women's Athletics [*A publication*] ... Coach Women's Athletics
Coachmen Industries, Inc. [*NYSE symbol*] ... COA
Coagulation [*Test*] ... CA
Coagulation ... COAG
Coahoma Junior College [*Mississippi*] ... CJC
Coahuila & Zacatecas Railway [*AAR code*] ... CZ
Coal and Coke ... C & C
Coal Employment Project ... CEP
Coal and Energy Quarterly [*A publication*] ... Coal Energy Q
Coal Equivalent ... CE
Coal Experts Committee [*Allied German Occupation Forces*] ... CEC
Coal Exporters Association of the United States ... CEA
Coal Fluid Flow Facility ... CFFF
Coal Fuel Mixtures Association ... CFMA
Coal [*into*] **Gas** [*Process*] ... COGAS
Coal, Gold, and Base Minerals of Southern Africa [*A publication*] ... Coal Gold Base Miner South Afr
Coal Industry Advisory Board ... CIAB
Coal Management Techniques Symposia [*A publication*] ... Coal Manage Tech Symp
Coal Mine Drainage Research Symposia [*A publication*] ... Coal Mine Drain Res Symp
Coal and Mining ... C & M
Coal Mining Institute of America [*Later, PCMIA*] ... CMIA
Coal Mining and Processing [*A publication*] ... Coal Min Process
Coal Mining and Quarrying ... CMQ
Coal-Oil Mixture ... COM
Coal-Oil-Water Mixture [*Fuel*] ... COWM
Coal and Petroleum Products [*Department of Employment*] [*British*] ... CPP
Coal Preparation [*A publication*] ... Coal Prep
Coal Preparation Symposia [*A publication*] ... Coal Prep Symp
Coal Processing Technology [*A publication*] ... Coal Process Technol
Coal Production Committee ... COPROD
Coal Science and Technology [*Elsevier Book Series*] [*A publication*] ... CST
Coal and Steel ... CS

Coal and Steel Planning Committee [*NATO*] .... CSPC
Coal Tar Pitch Emulsion Council [*Defunct*] .... CTPEC
Coal Utilisation Council [*British*] .... CUC
Coal Utilization Symposia [*A publication*] .... Coal Util Symp
Coal-Water Mixture [*Fuel*] .... CWM
Coal-Water Slurry .... CWS
Coal Workers' Pneumoconiosis [*Medicine*] .... CWP
Coalesce .... CLSC
Coaling Station [*As part of a symbol*] .... CS
Coalinga, CA [*Location identifier*] [*FAA*] .... CLG
Coalinga, CA [*Radio station call letters*] .... KOLI
Coalinga Unified School District Library, Coalinga, CA [*Library symbol*] .... CCoa
Coalition for the Abolition of Marijuana Prohibition .... CAMP
Coalition of Adult Education Organizations .... CAEO
Coalition Against Sexist-Racist Hiring [*Student legal action organization*] .... CASH
Coalition for Alternatives in Jewish Education .... CAJE
Coalition of American Pro-Life University Students .... CAMPUS
Coalition of American Public Employees .... CAPE
Coalition for the Apostolic Ministry [*Later, ECM*] .... CAM
Coalition for Asian Peace and Security .... CAPS
Coalition of Asians to Nix Charlie Chan .... CAN Charlie Chan
Coalition for Better Television .... CBTV
Coalition of Black Trade Unionists .... CBTU
Coalition on Block Grants and Human Needs .... CBGHN
Coalition for Common Sense in Government Procurement .... CCSGP
Coalition for Decency .... CFD
Coalition for a Decent USA [*Defunct*] .... CDUSA
Coalition for a Democratic Majority .... CDM
Coalition of Digestive Disease Organizations .... CDDO
Coalition for Drug-Free Horse Racing .... CDFHR
Coalition of Eastern Native Americans [*Defunct*] .... CENA
Coalition to End Grand Jury Abuse [*Later, CPR*] .... CEGJA
Coalition for Equitable Truck Taxes .... CEET
Coalition to Free Petkus and Gajauskas .... CFPG
Coalition to Halt Auto Theft .... CHAT
Coalition for Health and the Environment .... CHE
Coalition for Health Funding .... CHF
Coalition of Higher Education Assistance Organizations .... CHEAO
Coalition for International Cooperation and Peace .... CICP
Coalition of Labor Union Women .... CLUW
Coalition for Literacy CL
Coalition for the Medical Rights of Women .... CMRW
Coalition Mondiale pour l'Abolition de la Vivisection [*World Coalition for the Abolition of Vivisection*] .... CMAV
Coalition for National Dance Week .... CNDW
Coalition for a National Health Service [*Formerly, HSA*] .... CNHS
Coalition for a Non-Nuclear World [*Defunct*] .... CNNW
Coalition of Northeastern Governors .... CONEG
Coalition for Peace Through Strength .... CPTS
Coalition to Preserve the American Copyright .... CPAC
Coalition to Protect Social Security .... SOS
Coalition of Public Employee Organizations .... CPEO
Coalition for Responsible Mining Law .... CRML
Coalition for Safe Food [*Defunct*] .... CSF
Coalition to Save America's Music .... CSAM
Coalition to Save Our Documentary Heritage .... CSDH
Coalition on Sensible Transport .... COST
Coalition of Service Industries .... CSI
Coalition on Sexuality and Disability .... CSD
Coalition of Spanish Speaking Mental Health Organizations [*Later, National Coalition of Hispanic Mental Health and Human Services Organizations*] .... COSSMHO
Coalition for State Prompt Pay .... CSPP
Coalition to Stop Draize Rabbit Blinding Tests .... CSDRBT
Coalition for Strategic Stability in the Middle East .... CSSME
Coalition Unity Party [*British*] .... CoU
Coalition for Women in the Humanities and Social Sciences [*Defunct*] .... CWHSS
Coalition for Women in International Development .... CWID
Coalition of Women in National and International Business .... CWNIB
Coalition on Women and Religion .... CWR
Coalition for Women's Appointments .... CWA
Coalition of Women's Art Organizations .... CWAO
Coalitions for Health Care .... CHC
Coaming [*Naval architecture*] .... COAM
Coamo [*Puerto Rico*] [*Seismograph station code, US Geological Survey*] .... CCA
Coamo, PR [*Radio station call letters*] .... WCPR
Coarctation [*Cardiology*] .... COARC
Coarse [*Appearance of bacterial colony*] C
Coarse .... CRS
Coarse Alignment .... CA
Coarse Alignment Servo .... CAS
Coarse Alignment Subsystem .... CASS
Coarse Alignment Unit .... CAU
Coarse Bearing Servo .... CBS
Coarse Control [*Nuclear energy*] CC
Coarse Control Damper [*Nuclear energy*] .... CCD
Coarse Diffraction Pattern Analysis .... CDPA
Coarse Erection .... CE
Coarse-Fine/Pulse Code Modulator .... C-F/PCM
Coarse Glass Frit .... CGF
Coarse Grains, Pulses, Roots, and Tubers .... CGPRT
Coarse Optical Alignment Sight .... COAS
Coarse Particulate Organic Matter .... CPOM
Coast [*Board on Geographic Names*] .... CST
Coast African People's Union [*Kenya*] .... CAPU
Coast Alliance [*Defunct*] .... CA
Coast and Antiaircraft Experimental Establishment [*British*] [*World War II*] .... CAAEE
Coast Artillery .... CA
Coast Artillery Antiaircraft .... CAAA
Coast Artillery Corps [*Army*] .... CAC
Coast Artillery Reserve Corps .... CARC
Coast Artillery School [*British*] .... CAS
Coast Artillery Training Battalion .... CATB
Coast Community College District, Orange Coast College, Costa Mesa, CA [*OCLC symbol*] .... CRG
Coast Defense .... CD
Coast Federal Savings & Loan [*NASDAQ symbol*] .... CFSF
Coast and Geodetic Magnetic Observatory .... CGMO
Coast and Geodetic Survey [*Later, NOAA*] .... C & GS
Coast and Geodetic Survey [*Later, NOAA*] .... CGS
Coast and Geodetic Tide Station .... CGTS
Coast Guard [*Military flight identification prefix*] C
Coast Guard .... CG
Coast Guard .... COGARD
Coast Guard Academy .... CGA
Coast Guard Activities Europe .... CGACTEUR
Coast Guard Air Base .... CGAB
Coast Guard Air Detachment .... CGAIRDET
Coast Guard Air Station .... CGAS
Coast Guard Auxiliary .... CGA
Coast Guard Base .... CGBASE
Coast Guard Commandant .... COMDTCOGARD
Coast Guard Cutter .... CGC
Coast Guard District .... CGD
Coast Guard District .... CGDIST
Coast Guard District Office .... CGDO
Coast Guard Docket .... CGD
Coast Guard Good Conduct Medal .... CGGCM
Coast Guard League .... CGL
Coast Guard Lifeboat Station .... CGLBSTA
Coast Guard Light Attendant Station .... CGLASTA
Coast Guard Light Station .... CGLTSTA
Coast Guard LORAN Station .... CGLS
Coast Guard LORAN Transmitting Station .... CGLORSTA
Coast Guard Oceanographic Unit .... CGOU
Coast Guard Operating Base .... CGOB
Coast Guard Procurement Regulations .... CGPR
Coast Guard Publication [*Formerly, NCG*] .... NAVCG
Coast Guard Publication [*Later, NAVCG*] .... NCG
Coast Guard Radio .... CGRDO
Coast Guard Radio Station .... CGRADSTA
Coast Guard Recruiting Station .... CGCRUITSTA
Coast Guard Research and Development Center .... CGR/DC
Coast Guard Reserve .... CGR
Coast Guard Ship [*When precedes vessel classification*] [*Navy symbol*] .... W
Coast Guard Specification .... CGS
Coast Guard Station .... CGSTA
Coast Guard Supply Center .... CGSUPCEN
Coast Guard Teletype .... CGTEL
Coast Guard Training Station .... CGTRASTA
Coast Guard Training Station .... CGTS
Coast Guard Yard .... CGYD
Coast [*R. V.*] **Incorporated** [*NASDAQ symbol*] .... CRVI
Coast Manufacturing Co., Inc. [*NASDAQ symbol*] .... CMFG
Coast Orbital Insertion .... COI
Coast for Orders [*Chartering*] .... CFO
Coast-Out Point .... COP
Coast Phase Control System [*Army*] .... CPCS
Coast-in-Point .... CIP
Coast RADAR Station [*Maps and charts*] .... RA
Coast Star, Manasquan, NJ [*Library symbol*] .... NjManS
Coast Station [*ITU designation*] .... FC
Coast Survey Marine Observation System .... COSMOS
Coast Torpedo Boat [*Navy symbol*] .... CTB
Coastal .... CSTL
Coastal Air Force [*British*] .... CAF
Coastal Airways [*Gulfport, MS*] [*FAA designator*] .... CNG
Coastal AMOS [*Automated Meteorological Observing Station*] **Experiment** .... CAMEX
Coastal Antimissile System .... CAMS
Coastal Base Section [*Name changed to Continental Advance Section*] [*World War II*] .... CBS
Coastal Carolina Community College, Jacksonville, NC [*Library symbol*] .... NcJaC
Coastal Command [*Air Force*] [*British*] CC
Coastal Command Defence Unit [*British*] .... CCDU
Coastal Command Development Unit [*British*] .... CCDU

Coastal Corp. [*Formerly, Coastal States Gas Producing Co.*] [*NYSE symbol*]....CGP
Coastal Defense RADAR....CD
Coastal Defense RADAR for Detecting U-Boats....CDU
Coastal District Surveillance Center [*Military*]....CDSC
Coastal Energy Impact Program [*National Oceanic and Atmospheric Administration*]....CEIP
Coastal Engineering [*A publication*]....Coastal Eng
Coastal Engineering Information Analysis Center [*NASA*]....CEIAC
Coastal Engineering in Japan [*A publication*]....Coastal Eng Japan
Coastal Engineering in Japan [*A publication*]....Coastal Eng Jpn
Coastal Engineering Research Board [*Army*]....CERB
Coastal Engineering Research Center [*Army*]....CERC
Coastal Engineering Research Council....CERC
Coastal Escort [*Ship symbol*]....PC
Coastal Escort Medium [*200-500 tons*] [*Ship symbol*]....PCM
Coastal Frontier [*Military*]....CF
Coastal Frontier [*Coast Guard*]....COFRON
Coastal, Harbor, and Inland....CHI
Coastal Helicopter Aircraft Carrier [*Ship symbol*]....CVHC
Coastal International Ltd. [*NASDAQ symbol*]....CSTIF
Coastal Minelayer [*Navy symbol*]....CMC
Coastal Minesweepers [*Navy symbol*]....AMC
Coastal Motorboat....CMB
Coastal-Nonrigid Airship [*Royal Naval Air Service*] [*British*]....C
Coastal Offshore Stratigraphic Tests [*Geology*]....COST
Coastal Patrol Boat [*Navy symbol*]....CPC
Coastal Patrol and Interdiction Craft [*Navy symbol*]....CPIC
Coastal Plains Experiment Station, Tifton, GA [*Library symbol*]....GTiE
Coastal Plains Regional Commission [*FAA*]....CPRC
Coastal Plains Regional Library, Tifton, GA [*Library symbol*]....GTi
Coastal Research Notes [*A publication*]....Coastal Res Notes
Coastal River Squadron [*Navy*]....COSRIVRON
Coastal Sentry Quebec....CSQ
Coastal Society....CS
[*The*] **Coastal Society**....TCS
Coastal States Organization....CSO
Coastal Studies Institute [*Louisiana State University*]....CSI
Coastal Surveillance Center....CSC
Coastal Surveying Ship [*Navy symbol*] [*Obsolete*]....AGSC
Coastal Telegraph Station [*ITU designation*]....CT
Coastal Upwelling Ecosystems Analysis....CUEA
Coastal Upwelling Experiment....CUE
Coastal Watching RADAR....CWR
Coastal Zone Color Scanner....CZCS
Coastal Zone Management....CZM
Coastal Zone Management Act [*1972*]....CZMA
Coastal Zone Management Journal [*A publication*]....Coastal Zone Manage J
Coastal Zone Management Journal [*A publication*]....Coast Zone Manage J
Coasting Flight....CF
Coastland Corp. of Florida [*NASDAQ symbol*]....CLFL
Coastwise-Great Lakes and Inland Hull Association [*Defunct*]....CGLIHA
Coat of Arms....C/A
Coat of Arms [*A publication*]....CoA
Coat Hook....CH
Coated....CTD
Coated Abrasives Fabricators Association....CAFA
Coated Abrasives Manufacturers Institute....CAMI
Coated on the Back Side [*Carbonless paper*]....CB
Coated Compressed Tablet [*Pharmacy*]....CCT
Coated Foam Tape....CFT
Coated Front and Back [*Carbonless paper*]....CFB
Coated on the Front Side [*Carbonless paper*]....CF
Coated Metal....CMET
Coated Paper Copier [*Reprography*]....CPC
Coated Polycarbonate Visor....CPV
Coated and Processed Paper Association [*Defunct*]....CPPA
Coated Tablet [*Pharmacy*]....CT
Coatesville, PA [*Location identifier*] [*FAA*]....CVE
Coatesville, PA [*Location identifier*] [*FAA*]....VZO
Coatesville, PA [*Radio station call letters*]....WCOJ
Coating....CTG
Coating and Chemical Laboratory [*Army*]....C & CL
Coating and Chemical Laboratory [*Army*]....CCL
Coaxial....CA
Coaxial....COAX
Coaxial Adapter Waveguide....CAWG
Coaxial Diode Limiter....CDL
Coaxial Directional Coupler....CDC
Coaxial Line Attenuator....CLA
Coaxial Power Divider....CPD
Coaxial Single-Pole Relay....CSR
Coaxial Slotted Line....CSL
Coaxial Switch and Alternator Panel....COSWAP
Coaxial Switching Matrix....CSM
Coaxial Thermal Voltmeter....CTV
Coaxial Triple-Stud Tuner....CTST
Cobalamin [*Biochemistry*]....Cbl
Cobalt [*Chemical symbol is Co*]....C
Cobalt [*Chemical element*]....Co
Cobalt Base Alloy Foil....CBAF
Cobalt Bomb [*Nuclear*]....C (Bomb)
Cobalt Bomb [*Nuclear*]....CB
Cobalt-Chrome....COBCRM
Cobalt Information Center [*Battelle Memorial Institute*]....CIC
Cobalt Thiocyanate Active Substance [*Organic analysis*]....CTAS
Cobaltiprotoporphyrin [*Medicine*]....COPP
Cobamide [*Biochemistry*]....Cba
Cobar [*Australia*] [*Airport symbol*]....CAZ
Cobb [*New Zealand*] [*Seismograph station code, US Geological Survey*]....COB
Cobb County-Marietta Public Library, Marietta, GA [*Library symbol*]....GMarC
Cobb Resources Corp. [*NASDAQ symbol*]....COBB
Cobbler....COBB
Cobbler Shop....CBSHP
Cobe Laboratories [*NASDAQ symbol*]....COBE
Cobe Laboratories, Denver, CO [*Library symbol*]....CoDCo
Cobelda RADAR Automatic Preflight Analyzer....CORAPRAN
Cobija [*Bolivia*] [*Airport symbol*]....CIJ
Cobinamide [*Biochemistry*]....Cbi
Coblentz Society....CS
Cobleskill, NY [*Radio station call letters*]....WSCM
COBOL [*Common Business-Oriented Language*] **Automatic Language Modifier** [*Data processing*]....CALM
COBOL-to-COBOL Translator....COTRAN
COBOL [*Common Business-Oriented Language*] **Compiler Validation System** [*Data processing*]....CCVS
COBOL [*Common Business-Oriented Language*] **Conversion** [*Data processing*]....COCO
COBOL [*Common Business-Oriented Language*] **Element Subtype** [*Data processing*]....COB
COBOL [*Common Business-Oriented Language*] **Information Bulletin** [*Air Force*]....CIB
COBOL [*Common Business-Oriented Language*] **Instrumentation Package** [*Data processing*]....CIP
COBOL [*Common Business-Oriented Language*] **Library** [*Data processing*]....COBLIB
Cobourg, ON [*Radio station call letters*]....CFMX-FM
Cobourg, ON [*Radio station call letters*]....CHUC
Cobourg Public Library, Cobourg, ON, Canada [*Library symbol*]....CaOCo
Cobra Club [*Later, SAAC*]....CC
Cobra Factor....CoF
Cobra Night Fire Control System [*Military*]....CONFICS
Cobra Owners Club of America....COCOA
Cobra Venom Factor [*Immunochemistry*]....CoVF
Cobyric Acid [*Biochemistry*]....Cby
Coca [*Ecuador*] [*Airport symbol*]....OCC
Coca-Cola Bottling Co. Consolidated [*NASDAQ symbol*]....COKE
Coca-Cola Bottling Co. of New York, Inc. [*NYSE symbol*] [*Delisted*]....KNY
Coca-Cola Co. [*NYSE symbol*]....KO
Coca-Cola Co., Business Information, Atlanta, GA [*OCLC symbol*]....GCC
Coca-Cola Co., Law Library, Atlanta, GA [*OCLC symbol*]....GCW
Coca-Cola Co., Marketing Information Center, Atlanta, GA [*Library symbol*]....GACo
Coca-Cola Company, Technical Information Services, Atlanta, GA [*Library symbol*]....GACCC
Coca-Cola Co., Technical Information Services, Atlanta, GA [*OCLC symbol*]....GCT
Cocaine [*Slang*]....C
Cocaine Anonymous....CA
Cocaine and Heroin....C & H
Coccygeal [*Anatomy*]....COC
Cochabamba [*Bolivia*] [*Airport symbol*]....CBB
Cochabamba [*Bolivia*] [*Seismograph station code, US Geological Survey*]....CCH
Cochin [*India*] [*Airport symbol*]....COK
Cochise Airlines [*Tucson, AZ*] [*FAA designator*]....CAZ
Cochise, AZ [*Location identifier*] [*FAA*]....CIE
Cochise College, Douglas, AZ [*Library symbol*]....AzDC
Cochiti [*New Mexico*] [*Seismograph station code, US Geological Survey*]....COH
Cochlear Microphonics [*Response*] [*Auditory testing*]....CM
Cochlear Nuclei [*Brain anatomy*]....CN
Cochlear Potential [*Otolaryngology*]....CP
Cochleare [*Spoonful*] [*Pharmacy*]....COCH
Cochleare [*Spoonful*] [*Pharmacy*]....COCHL
Cochleare Amplum [*Tablespoonful*] [*Pharmacy*]....COCH AMP
Cochleare Infantum [*Teaspoonful*] [*Pharmacy*]....COCH INFANT
Cochleare Magnum [*Tablespoonful*] [*Pharmacy*]....COCH MAG
Cochleare Maximum [*Tablespoonful*] [*Pharmacy*]....COCH MAX
Cochleare Medium [*Dessertspoonful*] [*Pharmacy*]....COCH MED
Cochleare Minimum [*Teaspoonful*] [*Pharmacy*]....COCH MIN
Cochleare Modicum [*Dessertspoonful*] [*Pharmacy*]....COCH MOD
Cochleare Parvum [*Teaspoonful*] [*Pharmacy*]....COCH PARV
Cochleare Plenum [*Tablespoonful*] [*Pharmacy*]....COCH PLEN
Cochran, GA [*Radio station call letters*]....WDCO-FM
Cochran, GA [*Television station call letters*]....WDCO-TV
Cochran, GA [*Radio station call letters*]....WVMG
Cochran, GA [*Radio station call letters*]....WVMG-FM
Cochrane [*Canada*] [*Airport symbol*]....YCN

Cochrane Furniture [*NASDAQ symbol*] ... CFUR
Cochrane Public Library, Cochrane, ON, Canada [*Library symbol*] ... CaOCoc
Cockcroft-Walton Accelerator [*Physics*] ... CWA
Cockcroft-Walton Experiment [*Physics*] ... CWE
Cockpit ... CKPT
Cockpit Geometry Evaluation [*Computer program*] [*Boeing Co.*] ... CGE
Cockpit Orientation Trainer [*Aviation*] ... COT
Cockpit Orientation Trainer [*Aviation*] ... COTR
Cockpit Procedures Trainer [*Air Force*] ... CPT
Cockpit Television Sensor ... CTV
Cockpit Voice Recorder ... CVR
Coco Solo, Canal Zone ... CS
Cocoa Beach Apollo [*NASA*] ... CBA
Cocoa Beach, FL [*Radio station call letters*] ... WCKS
Cocoa Beach, FL [*Radio station call letters*] ... WRKT
Cocoa Beach, FL [*Radio station call letters*] ... WRKT-FM
Cocoa Beach Public Library, Cocoa Beach, FL [*Library symbol*] ... FCb
Cocoa, FL [*Location identifier*] [*FAA*] ... PKC
Cocoa, FL [*Location identifier*] [*FAA*] ... RDX
Cocoa, FL [*Radio station call letters*] ... WEZY
Cocoa, FL [*Radio station call letters*] ... WEZY-FM
Cocoa, FL [*Radio station call letters*] ... WKKO
Cocoa, FL [*Radio station call letters*] ... WMIE
Cocoa, FL [*Television station call letters*] ... WTGL-TV
Cocoa, FL [*Radio station call letters*] ... WWBC
Cocoa Merchants' Association of America ... CMAA
Cocoa Producers' Alliance ... COPAL
Cocoa Public Library, Cocoa, FL [*Library symbol*] ... FCoa
Cocoa Research Institute (Council for Scientific and Industrial Research). Annual Report [*A publication*] ... Cocoa Res Inst (CSIR) Annu Rep
Cocoa Research Institute (Ghana Academy of Sciences). Annual Report [*A publication*] ... Cocoa Res Inst (Ghana Acad Sci) Annu Rep
Coconut Bulletin [*A publication*] ... Coconut Bull
Coconut Cadang-Cadang Viroid [*Also, CCV*] ... CCCV
Coconut Cadang-Cadang Viroid [*Also, CCCV*] ... CCV
Coconut Grove [*Florida*] ... CG
Coconut Grove and Coral Gables [*Florida*] ... CG²
Coconut Research Institute. Bulletin [*A publication*] ... Coconut Res Inst Bull
COCORP Extended Research Project [*Geology*] ... CERP
Cocos [*Keeling*] **Islands** [*Two-letter standard code*] ... CC
Cocos [*Keeling*] **Islands** [*Seismograph station code, US Geological Survey*] [*Closed*] ... CCK
Cocos [*Keeling*] **Islands** [*MARC geographic area code*] [*Library of Congress*] ... i-xb---
Cocos [*Keeling*] **Islands** [*MARC country of publication code*] [*Library of Congress*] ... xb
Cocos [*Keeling*] **Islands** [*Three-letter standard code*] ... CCK
Coctio [*Boiling*] ... COCT
Cod Liver Oil ... CLO
CODAP [*Control Data Assembly Program*] **Language Block-Oriented Compiler** ... COBLOC
CODATA [*Committee on Data for Science and Technology*] **Bulletin** [*A publication*] ... CODATA Bull
Code ... CD
Code ... CDE
Code Actuated Random Load Apparatus ... CARLA
Code of Advertising Practices [*British*] ... CAP
Code Book ... CB
Code Clock Transfer Loop ... CCTL
Code of Conduct [*Military*] ... COC
Code Control ... CC
Code Converter ... CC
Code Directing Character [*Data processing*] ... CDC
Code Division Multiple Access ... CDMA
Code of Federal Regulations ... CFR
Code to Handle Angular Data ... CHAD
Code Identification Number ... CIN
Code Inserter Verifier [*Air Force*] ... CIV
Code for Magnetic Characters ... CMC
Code Matching Technique ... CMT
Code Names Dictionary [*A publication*] ... CND
Code Napoleon ... CN
Code Not Allocated ... CNA
Code Operations Coordinator ... COC
Code of Practice ... CP
Code Practice Oscillator ... CPO
Code of Procedure [*Legal*] ... CP
Code of Professional Responsibility [*American Bar Association*] ... CPR
Code Proficiency [*Amateur radio*] ... CP
Code Relations Index ... CRI
Code Selection Language [*Data processing*] ... CSL
Code Ship Parametric Model ... CSPM
Code Telegram ... CT
Code Translation Data System [*Air Force*] ... CTDS
Code Variante [*Codification*] ... CV
Code and Visual Entry Authorization Technique [*Closed-circuit TV*] ... CAVEAT
Coded Acoustic Interrogator ... CAI
Coded Address Private Radio Intercommunications ... CAPRI
Coded Analysis [*Navy*] ... CODAN
Coded Armaments System ... CAS
Coded Automatic Gain Control ... CAGC
Coded Automatic Reading Device ... CARD
Coded Biphase ... COBI
Coded Command ... CCMD
Coded Decimal Digit ... CDD
Coded Decimal Notation ... CDN
Coded Division Multiplex ... CDM
Coded Doppler RADAR Command ... CODORAC
Coded Integrated Armament Control System ... CIACS
Coded Optical Character [*Data processing*] ... COC
Coded Pulse Anticlutter System ... CPACS
Coded Switch System [*To permit or deny the ability to arm nuclear weapons in strategic aircraft*] ... CSS
Coded Telemetry Processor ... CTP
Codenoll Technology [*NASDAQ symbol*] ... CODN
Coder-Decoder Group [*Army*] ... CDG
Coder-Decoders ... CODEC
Coder and Random Access Switch ... CRAS
Coder Sequential Pulse ... CSP
Codex ... C
Codex Iuris Canonici [*Code of Canon Law*] [*Latin*] ... CIC
Codices Manuscripti [*A publication*] ... Cod Man
Codicil ... COD
Codicil ... CODL
Coding ... COD
Coding Board Officer ... CBO
Coding Room Watch Officer [*Navy*] ... CRWO
Codling Moth Granulosis Virus ... CMGV
Codrul Cosminului [*A publication*] ... CC
Cody [*Wyoming*] [*Airport symbol*] ... COD
Cody, WY [*Radio station call letters*] ... KODI
Cody, WY [*Radio station call letters*] ... KTAG
Cody, WY [*Radio station call letters*] ... KYDZ
Coe College, Cedar Rapids, IA [*Library symbol*] ... IaCrC
Coe College, Cedar Rapids, IA [*OCLC symbol*] ... ION
Coe Ranch [*California*] [*Seismograph station code, US Geological Survey*] ... COE
Coeducational ... COED
Coefficient ... C
Coefficient ... COEF
Coefficient ... COEFF
Coefficient of Association [*Statistics*] ... Q
Coefficient of Contingency [*Statistics*] ... CC
Coefficient of Correlation [*Statistics*] ... CC
Coefficient of Drag ... CD
Coefficient of Haze [*Environment*] ... COH
Coefficient of Heat Transfer [*Symbol*] [*Thermodynamics*] ... h
Coefficient of Intelligence ... CI
Coefficient of Lift ... CL
Coefficient of Luminous Intensity ... CLI
Coefficient of Performance ... COP
Coefficient of Performance ... CP
Coefficient of Retraction ... CR
Coefficient of Thermal Expansion ... CTE
Coefficient of Utilization ... CU
Coefficient of Variation [*Mathematics*] ... COV
Coefficient of Variation [*Mathematics*] ... CV
Coelliptic Rendezvous Sequence ... CRS
Coelliptic Sequence Initiation [*Aerospace*] ... CSI
Coen [*Australia*] [*Airport symbol*] ... CUQ
Coenzyme [*Biochemistry*] ... Co
Coenzyme A [*Biochemistry*] ... CoA
Coenzyme Q [*Ubiquinone*] [*Also, Q, U, UQ*] [*Biochemistry*] ... CoQ
Coenzyme Q [*Ubiquinone*] [*Also, CoQ, U, UQ*] [*Biochemistry*] ... Q
Coercion ... CORCN
Coeur D'Alene [*Idaho*] [*Airport symbol*] ... COE
Coeur D'Alene, ID [*Location identifier*] [*FAA*] ... AUC
Coeur D'Alene, ID [*Location identifier*] [*FAA*] ... HYD
Coeur D'Alene, ID [*Radio station call letters*] ... KVNI
Coeur D'Alene Mines [*NASDAQ symbol*] ... COUR
Coeur D'Alene Public Library, Coeur D'Alene, ID [*Library symbol*] ... IdC
Coeur et Medecine Interne [*A publication*] ... Coeur Med I
Coeur et Medecine Interne [*A publication*] ... Coeur Med Interne
Coevolution Quarterly [*A publication*] ... Coevolutn
CoEvolution Quarterly [*A publication*] ... CoEv Q
Coffee Berry Disease ... CBD
Coffee Brewing Center ... CBC
Coffee Brewing Institute ... CBI
Coffee and Cacao Journal [*A publication*] ... Coffee Cacao J
Coffee Growers' Association of El Salvador [*Defunct*] ... CGAES
Coffee Mill ... COFML
Coffee Research Foundation. Kenya. Annual Report [*A publication*] ... Coffee Res Found Kenya Annu Rep
Coffee, Sugar, and Cocoa Exchange ... CSCE
Coffee Table Book [*Large, extensively illustrated book designed for display and browsing*] ... CTB
Cofferdam [*Engineering*] ... COFF
Coffeyville, KS [*Radio station call letters*] ... KGGF

Coffeyville, KS [*Radio station call letters*]........KQQF-FM
Coffin [*Missile launch environment symbol*]........C
Coffin Ground-Attack Missile........CGM
Coffin Intercept Missile........CIM
Coffin Strategic Missile........CSM
Coffs Harbour [*Australia*] [*Airport symbol*]........CFS
Cofield, NC [*Location identifier*] [*FAA*]........CVI
Cogenic Energy Systems [*NASDAQ symbol*]........CESI
Coggan Monitor, Coggan, IA [*Library symbol*]........IaCogM
Cognate........C
Cognition [*A publication*]........CGSTB
Cognition [*The Hague*] [*A publication*]........Cog
Cognitive Abilities Test [*Education*]........CAT
Cognitive Hybrid Intelligent Learning Device........CHILD
Cognitive Operating System [*NASA*]........COGNOSYS
Cognitive Psychology [*A publication*]........Cognitive Psychol
Cognitive Psychology [*A publication*]........Cog Psyc
Cognitive Psychology [*A publication*]........Cog Psychol
Cognitive Psychology [*A publication*]........CPsy
Cognitive Science [*A publication*]........C Sc
Cognitive Science Society........CSS
Cognitive Stimulation [*Experimental psychology*]........CS
Cognitronics Corp. [*American Stock Exchange symbol*]........CGN
Cognizance Symbol........CS
Cognizant........COG
Cognizant Development Engineer........CDE
Cognizant Engineer........CE
Cognizant Field Activity........CFA
Cognizant Operating Authority........COA
Cognizant Operations Engineer........COE
Cognizant Operations Engineer's Parts List........COEPL
Cognizant Quality Engineer........CQE
Cognizant Security Office [*Controls industrial security at government facilities*] [*Military*]........CSO
Cognizant Sustaining Engineer........CSE
Cognizant Technical Manager........CTM
Cognizant Transportation Office [*or Officer*] [*Air Force*]........CTO
Cognizant User Engineer [*Deep Space Network, NASA*]........CUE
Coheir [*Joint heir*] [*Genealogy*]........COH
Cohen-Hatfield Industries, Inc. [*American Stock Exchange symbol*] [*Delisted*]........CHJ
Coherent Acceleration and Velocity Observations in Real Time........CAVORT
Coherent Acoustic Torpedo System........CATS
Coherent Anti-Stokes Raman Spectroscopy........CARS
Coherent Anti-Stokes Resonance Raman Scattering [*Spectrometry*]........CARRS
Coherent Cloud Physics RADAR........CCPR
Coherent Digital Phased Array System [*ARPA*]........CODIPHASE
Coherent Doppler Measurement System........CDMS
Coherent Echo Modulation and Detection........CEMAD
Coherent Electromagnetic Energy Transmission........COMET
Coherent Event [*Trademark*]........COHVENT
Coherent Frequency-Hopping Signal........CFHS
Coherent Frequency Shift Keying........CFSK
Coherent Frequency Synthesizer........CFS
Coherent Imaging RADAR........CIR
Coherent, Inc. [*NASDAQ symbol*]........COHR
Coherent Infrared Energy........CIE
Coherent LASER Illumination........CLI
Coherent Light Detecting and Ranging [*RADAR*] [*Hughes Aircraft*]........COLIDAR
Coherent Light Detector........COLD
Coherent Light Detector System........COLIDS
Coherent Master Oscillator........COMO
Coherent Memory Filter........CMF
Coherent Microwave Memory........CMM
Coherent Monopulse Doppler RADAR........CMDR
Coherent Optical Adaptive Techniques........COAT
Coherent Optical Array........COA
Coherent Optical Device........COD
Coherent Optical Fingerprint Identification System........COFIDS
Coherent Optical LASER........COL
Coherent Optical Processing System........COPS
Coherent Optical Processor........COP
Coherent Optical RADAR Laboratory........CORAL
Coherent Optical Receiver........COR
Coherent Oscillator [*RADAR*]........COHO
Coherent Phase Shift Keyed [*System*] [*Data processing*]........CPSK
Coherent Potential Approximation [*Physics*]........CPA
Coherent Processing Interval [*Data processing*]........CPI
Coherent RADAR Array........CORA
Coherent-on-Receive........CORE
Coherent-on-Receive Doppler System [*RADAR*]........CORDS
Coherent Side-Lobe Cancellation........CSLC
Coherent Signal Processing System [*Army*]........CSPS
Coherent Signal Processor........CSP
Coherent Stokes Raman Spectroscopy........CSRS
Cohesion, Operational Readiness, and Training [*Army*]........COHORT
Cohesive Energy Density [*Solubility parameter*]........CED
Cohesive Intermolecular Force........CIF
Cohesive Unit Program [*Army*]........CUP
Cohlmia Aviation [*Dallas, TX*] [*FAA designator*]........CHL
Cohort Research Development Program........CORD
Cohu, Inc. [*American Stock Exchange symbol*]........COH
Coil........CL
Coil Finish........CF
Coil Sketch........CS
Coil Stock Cradle........CSC
Coil Winding Equipment........CWE
Coil Winding International [*A publication*]........Coil Winding Int
Coil Winding Machine........CWM
Coiled [*Freight*]........COIL
Coils [*Freight*]........CLS
Coils per Slot [*Technical drawings*]........CPS
Coimbatore [*India*] [*Airport symbol*]........CJB
Coimbra [*A publication*]........C
Coimbra [*Portugal*] [*Geomagnetic observatory code*]........COI
Coimbra [*Portugal*] [*Seismograph station code, US Geological Survey*]........COI
Coimbra Medica [*A publication*]........Coimbra Med
Coin Dimple........CD
Coin Level Indicator [*Telephone communications*]........CLI
Coin Monthly [*A publication*]........CMonth
Coin-Op Car Wash Association........COCWA
Coin-Operated Amusement Device........COAD
Coin Operated Self-Service Laundry Owners' Association........COSSLOA
Coin, Stamp, and Antique News [*A publication*]........CSAN
Coin World [*A publication*]........CW
Coincidence Gate........CG
Coincidence Guidance........C/G
Coincident-Current Magnetic Core........CCMC
Coincident Light Information Photographic Strips........CLIPS
Coins and Antiquities Ltd. Fixed Price List [*London*] [*A publication*]........C Antiq FPL
Coins, Incorporating Coins and Medals [*A publication*]........CM
Coins, Medals, and Currency Digest and Monthly Catalogue [*A publication*]........CMCD
Coins, Medals, and Currency Weekly [*A publication*]........CMC
Coins, Stamps, and Collecting [*A publication*]........CSC
Coins on Stamps Unit [*American Topical Association*]........COSSU
Coinsurance........CO
Coinsurance........COINS
Coinvestigator........Co-I
Coit International, Inc. [*American Stock Exchange symbol*] [*Delisted*]........CNI
Coke and Chemistry (USSR) [*A publication*]........Coke Chem R
Coke and Chemistry (USSR) [*A publication*]........Coke Chem (USSR)
Coke Oven........CO
Coke Oven Gas........COG
Coker College, Hartsville, SC [*Library symbol*]........ScHaC
Col Basso [*With the Bass*] [*Music*]........CB
Col Canto [*With the Melody*] [*Music*]........COL C
Col Legno [*With the Back of the Bow*] [*Music*]........CL
Cola [*or Colatus*] [*Strain*] [*Pharmacy*] [*See also COLAT*]........COL
[*The*] **Cola Clan** [*An association*]........TCC
Colatitude [*Navigation*]........CO-L
Colatus [*Strained*] [*See also COL*] [*Pharmacy*]........COLAT
Colburn's New Monthly Magazine [*A publication*]........Colburn
Colby College. Monographs [*A publication*]........CCM
Colby College. Monographs [*A publication*]........ColCM
Colby College, Waterville, ME [*OCLC symbol*]........CBY
Colby College, Waterville, ME [*Library symbol*]........MeWC
Colby Community College, Colby, KS [*Library symbol*]........KColC
Colby Junior College for Women [*Later, CSC*] [*New Hampshire*]........CJCW
Colby Junior College for Women [*Later, CSC*], **New London, NH** [*OCLC symbol*] [*Inactive*]........CYC
Colby Junior College for Women [*Later, CSC*], **New London, NH** [*Library symbol*]........NhNelC
Colby, KS [*Location identifier*] [*FAA*]........CBK
Colby, KS [*Television station call letters*]........KBOM
Colby, KS [*Radio station call letters*]........KQLS
Colby, KS [*Radio station call letters*]........KTCC
Colby, KS [*Radio station call letters*]........KXXX
Colby Library. Quarterly [*A publication*]........CLQ
Colby Resources Corp. [*NASDAQ symbol*]........CLBMF
Colby-Sawyer College [*Formerly, CJCW*] [*New Hampshire*]........CSC
Colcemid [*Demecolcine*] [*Antineoplastic drug*]........CMD
Colchester [*Vermont*] [*Seismograph station code, US Geological Survey*]........COV
Colchester-East Hants Regional Library, Truro, NS, Canada [*Library symbol*]........CaNSTC
Colchester, VT [*Radio station call letters*]........WWPV-FM
Colchicine [*Biochemistry*]........CCH
Colchicine-Binding Protein [*Biochemistry*]........CBP
Cold........C
Cold [*Air mass*]........K
Cold Agglutination [*Test*] [*Clinical chemistry*]........CA
Cold Air........CA
Cold Bay [*Alaska*] [*Seismograph station code, US Geological Survey*] [*Closed*]........CBA
Cold Bay [*Alaska*] [*Airport symbol*]........CDB
Cold Brine Pump........CBPMP
Cold Cathode Discharge........CCD
Cold Cathode Electron Beam LASER........CCEBL

Cold Cathode Gauge Experiment [Apollo] [NASA] .... CCGE
Cold Cathode Ion Gauge .... CCIG
Cold Cathode Ion Source .... CCIS
Cold Cranking Ampere .... CCA
Cold-Drawn [Metal] .... CD
Cold-Drawn Steel .... CDS
Cold-Extractable Copper .... cxCu
Cold-Finished [Metal] .... CF
Cold-Finished Steel .... CFS
Cold Finished Steel Bar Institute .... CFSBI
Cold Flow Development Test System [AEC] .... CFDTS
Cold Flow Laboratory [Martin Marietta Corp.] .... CFL
Cold Flow Test .... CFT
Cold Fluctuating Temperature .... CFT
Cold Fog Dissipation [System] .... CFD
Cold Front [Meteorology] .... CDFNT
Cold Front [Meteorology] .... CF
Cold Front [or Frontal] Passage [Meteorology] .... CFP
Cold Heading Wire .... CHW
Cold and Hot Water .... CHW
Cold, Hungry, and Dry [Slang] .... CH and D
Cold-Induced Vasodilation .... CIVD
Cold-Insoluble Fibrinogen [Hematology] .... CIF
Cold-Insoluble globulin [Cytochemistry] .... CIg
Cold Lake [Canada] [Airport symbol] .... YOD
Cold Leg [Nuclear energy] .... COLG
Cold Leg Check Valve [Nuclear energy] CLCV
Cold Leg Isolation Valve [Nuclear energy] CLIV
Cold Molecular Weld .... CMW
Cold to the Opposite and Warm to the Same Side [Audiometry] .... COWS
Cold Pack [Medicine] .... CP
Cold Pressor Response [Test] .... CPR
Cold Protective Response [Physiology] .... CPR
Cold-Punched [Metal] .... CP
Cold Regions Engineering Laboratory .... CREL
Cold Regions Research Company .... CRRC
Cold Regions Research and Engineering Laboratory [Army] .... CRREL
Cold Regions Test Center [Army] .... CRTC
Cold Rocket Instrument Carrying Kit .... CRICKET
Cold-Rolled [Metal] .... CR
Cold-Rolled Close-Annealed [Metal] .... CRCA
Cold-Rolled Half Hard [Metal] .... CRHH
Cold-Rolled Steel .... CRS
Cold-Rolled and Tempered [Metal] .... CRT
Cold Side .... CSD
Cold Spring Harbor Biological Laboratory, Cold Spring Harbor, NY [Library symbol] .... NCshB
Cold Spring Harbor Conference on Cell Proliferation [A publication] .... Cold Spring Harbor Conf Cell Proliferation
Cold Spring Harbor Public Library, Cold Spring Harbor, NY [Library symbol] .... NCsh
Cold Spring Harbor Symposia on Quantitative Biology [A publication] .... Cold S Harb
Cold Spring Harbor Symposia on Quantitative Biology [A publication] .... Cold Spr Harb Symp
Cold Spring Harbor Symposia on Quantitative Biology [A publication] .... Cold Spring Harbor Symp Quant Biol
Cold Spring Harbor Symposia on Quantitative Biology [A publication] .... Cold Spring Harbor Symp Quantit Biol
Cold Start Entry [Data processing] .... CSE
Cold Type Composition [Selection of Printing Industries of America] ...... CTC
Cold Vapor Atomic Absorption [Spectrometry] .... CVAA
Cold War .... CW
Cold War Activities Group .... CWAG
Cold War Council .... CWC
Cold Water [Technical drawings] .... CW
Cold-Water Detergent .... CWD
Cold Water Reactor Test Assembly .... CWTA
Cold-Water Soluble .... CWS
Cold Water Treatment [Medicine] .... CWT
Cold Weather Exercise [Military] .... COWEAEX
Cold Weather Injury [Military] .... CWINJ
Cold Weather Landing Exercise [Military] .... COWLEX
Cold Weather Materiel Test Unit [Military] .... CWMTU
Cold Weather Operations [Military] .... CWOP
Cold-Worked [Nuclear energy] .... CW
Coldfoot, AK [Location identifier] [FAA] .... CXF
Coldplate .... CP
Coldplate Clamp .... CPC
Coldstream Guards [British] .... CG
Coldwater, MI [Radio station call letters] .... WNWN
Coldwater, MI [Radio station call letters] .... WTVB
Coldwater, MS [Radio station call letters] .... WVIM-FM
Coldwater Public Library, Coldwater, MI [Library symbol] ...... MiCw
Coldwell, Banker & Company [NYSE symbol] [Delisted] ...... CBC
Cole National Corp. [NYSE symbol] .... CLE
Colecao Documentos Brasileiros [A publication] .... CDB
Colecao Ensaio [A publication] .... CEn
Colecao General Benicio [A publication] .... CGB
Colecao Poetas de Hoje [A publication] .... CPH
Colecao Studium [A publication] .... CSt

Coleco Industries, Inc. [NYSE symbol] .... CLO
Colegio de Mexico, Mexico, Mexico City, Mexico [Library symbol] .... MxMCM
Colegio Quimico-Farmaceutico [A publication] ...... Col Quim-Farm
Colegio de Quimicos e Ingenieros Quimicos de Costa Rica. Revista [A publication] .... Col Quim Ing Quim Costa Rica Rev
Colegio Universitario de Cayey, Cayey, PR [Library symbol] ...... PrCaC
Colegio Universitario de Gerona. Seccion de Ciencias. Anales [A publication] .... Col Univ Gerona Secc Cien An
Colegio Universitario del Sagrado Corazon [College of the Sacred Heart], Santurce, PR [Library symbol] .... PrSaC
Colel Hibath Jerusalem [Society of the Devotees of Jerusalem] ...... CHJ
Coleman [Alberta] [Seismograph station code, US Geological Survey] [Closed] .... CLM
Coleman Air Transport Corp. [Winnetka, IL] [FAA designator] ...... CAT
Coleman Co., Inc. [NYSE symbol] .... CLN
Coleman Prop Jet Sales Corp. [Winnetka, IL] [FAA designator] ...... CCA
Coleman, TX [Radio station call letters] .... KSTA
Coleman, TX [Radio station call letters] .... KSTA-FM
Coleopterists' Bulletin [A publication] .... Coleopt Bull
Coleopterists' Society .... CS
Coles Signal Laboratory [Army] .... CSL
Coletanea. Instituto de Tecnologia de Alimentos [A publication] .... Colet Inst Tecnol Aliment
Coletur [Let It Be Strained] [Pharmacy] .... COLET
Colfax Free Public Library, Colfax, IA [Library symbol] ...... IaCol
Colfax, WA [Radio station call letters] .... KCLX
Colgan Airways Corp. [Manassas, VA] [FAA designator] ..... CJC
Colgate-Palmolive Co. [NYSE symbol] CL
Colgate-Palmolive Co., Technical Information Center, Piscataway, NJ [Library symbol] .... NjPwC
Colgate-Rochester Divinity School [New York] .... CRDS
Colgate-Rochester Divinity School, Library, Rochester, NY [OCLC symbol] .... VQE
Colgate-Rochester Divinity School, Rochester, NY [Library symbol] .... NRCR
Colgate, SK [Television station call letters] CKCK-TV-1
Colgate University, Hamilton, NY [Library symbol] .... NHC
Colgate University, Hamilton, NY [OCLC symbol] VVC
Colicine Factor [Immunology] .... CF
Colistimethate-Nystatin-Vancomycin [Antibiotic mixture] ...... CNV
Colistin [Also, CO] [Generic form] [An antibiotic] CL
Colistin [Also, CL] [Generic form] [An antibiotic] .... CO
Colistin [or Colimycin] - Nalidixic Acid [Antibacterial combination] [Clinical chemistry] .... CNA
Colla Destra [With the Right Hand] [Music] .... CD
Colla Parte [With the Solo Part] [Music] .... CP
Colla Sinistra [With the Left Hand] [Music] .... CS
Colla Voce [With the Voice] [Music] .... COL VO
Colla Voce [With the Voice] [Music] CV
Colla Voce [With the Voice] [Music] .... C VOC
Collaboration .... COLLAB
Collaborative International Pesticides Analytic Council [See also CIMAP] .... CIPAC
Collaborative Library System Development .... CLSD
Collaborative Perinatal Project .... CPP
Collaborative Radiological Health Laboratory [Colorado State University and Department of Health and Human Services] ...... CRHL
Collaborative Research, Inc. .... CR
Collaborative Research, Incorporated [NASDAQ symbol] ...... CRIC
Collaborative Research Support Program [Agency for International Development] .... CRSP
Collagen Corp. [NASDAQ symbol] .... CGEN
Collagen Sponge Contraceptive .... CSC
Collagen Vascular Disease [Medicine] .... CVD
Collagenase-Digestible Protein .... CDP
Collana Accademica. Accademia Patavina di Scienze, Lettere, ed Arti [A publication] .... Collana Accad Accad Patav Sci Lett Arti
Collana di Monografie. Ateneo Parmense [A publication] .... Collana Monogr Ateneo Parmense
Collapse .... COLPS
Collapsed [Freight] .... COLSPD
Collapsible Airborne Military Equipment Lifter .... CAMEL
Collapsible Maintenance Hangar .... CMH
Collapsible Maintenance Shelter .... CMS
Collapsible Rollup Antenna Mast .... CRAM
Collar .... CLR
Collar .... COL
Coll'arco [With the Bow] [Music] .... CA
Collate .... COL
Collateral .... COLL
Collateral .... COLLAT
Collateral Action Officer [Army] .... CAO
Collateral Damage Distance .... CDD
Collateral Duty Alcoholism Counselor [Navy] .... CODAC
Collateral Duty Inspector .... CDI
Collateral Trust [Bond] .... CLT
Collateral Trust Bond .... CTB
Collateralized Mortgage Obligation [Federal Home Loan Mortgage Corporation] .... CMO
Collating and Binding .... CAB

Collationes Brugenses et Gandavenses [*A publication*] ... CBG
Collatis Pecuniis Poni Curaverunt [*They Collected the Money and Had Put in Position*] [*Latin*] ... CPPC
Collato [*Collated*] [*Latin*] ... COLL
Collator ... COLL
Collbran Public Library, Collbran, CO [*Library symbol*] ... CoCol
Colleague ... COLL
Collect ... COL
Collect [*or Collection*] ... COLL
Collect Adapter ... CLAD
Collect on Delivery ... COD
Collectanea Botanica (Barcelona) [*A publication*] ... Collect Bot (Barc)
Collectanea Cisterciensa [*A publication*] ... CCist
Collectanea Cisterciensa [*A publication*] ... Coll Cist
Collectanea Commissionis Synodalis [*Peking*] [*A publication*] ... CCS
Collectanea Franciscana [*A publication*] ... CF
Collectanea Franciscana [*A publication*] ... Coll Fran
Collectanea Mathematica [*A publication*] ... Collect Math
Collectanea Ordinis Cisterciensium Reformatorum [*A publication*] ... COCR
Collectanea Theologica [*A publication*] ... CT
Collected Algorithm for Learning Machines [*Data processing*] ... CALM
Collected Alongside Ship [*Business and trade*] ... CAS
Collected [*or Delivered*] **by Barge** [*Business and trade*] ... C by B
Collected or Delivered by Truck or Barge [*Business and trade*] ... C or D by T or B
Collected Papers on Earth Sciences. Nagoya University. Department of Earth Sciences [*A publication*] ... Collect Pap Earth Sci Nagoya Univ Dep Earth Sci
Collected Papers. Lister Institute of Preventive Medicine [*A publication*] ... Collect Papers Lister Inst Prevent Med
Collected Papers. Mathematical Society. Wakayama University [*A publication*] ... Collect Papers Math Soc Wakayama Univ
Collected Papers on Medical Science. Fukuoka University [*A publication*] ... Collect Pap Med Sci Fukuoka Univ
Collected Papers in Medicine. Mayo Clinic and Mayo Foundation [*A publication*] ... Collect Pap Med Mayo Clin Mayo Found
Collected Papers in Surgery. Mayo Clinic and Mayo Foundation [*A publication*] ... Collect Pap Surg Mayo Clin Mayo Found
Collected Papers on Technological Sciences. Fukuoka University [*A publication*] ... Collect Pap Technol Sci Fukuoka Univ
Collected Reports. Natural Science Faculty. Palacky University (Olomouc) [*A publication*] ... Collect Rep Nat Sci Fac Palacky Univ (Olomouc)
Collected [*or Delivered*] **by Truck** [*Business and trade*] ... C by T
Collected Works on Cardio-Pulmonary Disease [*A publication*] ... Collect Works Cardio-Pulm Dis
Collected Works on Cardio-Pulmonary Disease [*A publication*] ... Coll Works Cardio-Pulm Dis
Collecting ... CLTG
Collecting and Breeding [*A publication*] ... Collect Breed
Collection ... COLLN
Collection Activity Reports [*IRS*] ... CAR
Collection Agency Practices ... CAP
Collection Agency Project [*Student legal action organization*] ... CAP
Collection. Amis de l'Histoire [*A publication*] ... Coll Amis Hist
Collection of Czechoslovak Chemical Communications [*A publication*] ... Coll Czech
Collection of Czechoslovak Chemical Communications [*A publication*] ... Collec Czechosl Chem Commun
Collection of Czechoslovak Chemical Communications [*A publication*] ... Collect Czech Chem Commun
Collection of Czechoslovak Chemical Communications [*A publication*] ... Collect Czechoslovak Chem Commun
Collection and Delivery [*Business and trade*] ... C & D
Collection and Distribution [*Transportation*] ... C & D
Collection Entry [*Banking*] ... CL
Collection Holding Transfer [*Shipboard waste disposal*] ... CHT
Collection de l'Institut Pasteur [*France*] ... CIP
Collection Intelligence Requirements ... CIR
Collection Langues et Litteratures de l'Afrique Noire [*A publication*] ... CLLAN
Collection Latomus [*A publication*] ... ColLat
Collection Latomus [*A publication*] ... Coll Latomus
Collection "Les Grands Problemes de la Biologie." Monographie [*A publication*] ... Collect Grands Probl Biol Monogr
Collection Management System [*IRS*] ... CMS
Collection de Monographies de Botanique et de Biologie Vegetale [*A publication*] ... Colect Monogr Bot Biol Veg
Collection de Monographies de Botanique et de Biologie Vegetale [*A publication*] ... Collect Monogr Bot Biol Veg
Collection Nelson Rockefeller [*Identifying mark on art reproductions from the collection of Nelson Rockefeller*] ... CNR
Collection Operation Potential Yield System [*IRS*] ... COPYS
Collection of Papers Presented at the Annual Symposium on Fundamental Cancer Research [*A publication*] ... Collect Pap Annu Symp Fundam Cancer Res
Collection/Requirements ... C/R
Collection Statute Expiration Date [*IRS*] ... COLSED
Collection Statute Expiration Date [*IRS*] ... CSED
Collection of Theses. Kwang Woon Institute of Technology [*Republic of Korea*] [*A publication*] ... Collect Theses Kwang Woon Inst Technol
Collection Voucher ... CV
Collectionneur Francais [*A publication*] ... Coll Fr
Collections Litteratures Africaines [*A publication*] ... CLA
Collections de Statistique Agricole. Etudes [*A publication*] ... Coll Statist Agric Et
Collective ... CLTV
Collective Address Directory [*Navy*] ... CAD
Collective Address Group [*Navy*] ... CAG
Collective Bargaining Institute [*New York City*] ... CBI
Collective Bargaining Organization ... CBO
Collective Bargaining Unit ... CBU
Collective Black Artists ... CBA
Collective Call Sign [*Radio*] ... CCS
Collective Consciousness Society [*Vocal and instrumental group*] ... CCS
Collective Negotiations ... CN
Collective Phenomena [*A publication*] ... Collect Phenom
Collective Pitch Lever ... CPL
Collective Protection Equipment ... CPE
Collective Protection Unit ... CPU
Collective Protective System [*Navy*] ... CPS
Collective Reserve Unit [*International finance*] ... CRU
Collective Security [*Army*] ... COLSEC
Collective Training [*Army*] ... CT
Collective Training Plan [*Army*] ... CTP
Collector [*Electronics*] ... C
Collector [*s*] [*Freight*] ... CLCT
Collector [*Business and trade*] ... COLLR
Collector Circle ... CC
Collector Diffusion Isolation [*Electronics*] ... CDI
Collector Platemakers Guild ... CPG
Collector Ring [*Electricity*] ... CLRG
Collectors of American Art ... CAA
Collectors, Artists, and Dealers for Responsible Equity ... CADRE
Collector's Chronicle [*A publication*] ... CC
Collectors Club ... CC
Collectors Club, New York, NY [*Library symbol*] ... NNCo
Collectors' Guild [*NASDAQ symbol*] ... CGII
Collectors of Numismatic Errors ... CONE
Collectors Record Club ... CRC
Collectors of Religion on Stamps ... COROS
College ... C
College ... CLG
College ... COL
College [*or Collegiate*] ... COLL
College [*Alaska*] [*Geomagnetic observatory code*] ... COL
College Ability Test ... CAT
College Admissions Assistance Center [*Defunct*] ... CAAC
College Admissions Center ... CAC
College Advanced Technology [*British technical colleges*] ... CAT
College of Aeronautics [*British*] ... COA
College of Agriculture (Nagpur). Magazine [*A publication*] ... Coll Agric (Nagpur) Mag
College of the Albemarle, Elizabeth City, NC [*Library symbol*] ... NcElcA
College d'Alma, Lac St. Jean, PQ, Canada [*Library symbol*] ... CaQALC
College of American Pathologists ... CAP
College Andre Grasset, Montreal, PQ, Canada [*Library symbol*] ... CaQMCAG
College Art Association of America ... CAA
College Art Association of America ... CAAA
College Art Journal [*A publication*] ... CAJ
College Art Journal [*A publication*] ... Coll Art J
College Assistance Migrant Program ... CAMP
College de l'Assomption, L'Assomption, PQ, Canada [*Library symbol*] ... CaQLASC
College Athletic Business Managers Association ... CABMA
College Band Directors National Association ... CBDNA
[*The*] **College Board** [*An association*] ... TCB
College Board Review [*A publication*] ... Coll Bd R
College Bois de Boulogne, Montreal, PQ, Canada [*Library symbol*] ... CaQMBB
College Bourchemin (CEGEP) [*College d'Enseignement General et Professionel*]**, Drummondville, PQ, Canada** [*Library symbol*] ... CaQDCE
College Bourget, Rigaud, PQ, Canada [*Library symbol*] ... CaQRCB
College of Cape Breton, Archives and General Library, Sydney, NS, Canada [*Library symbol*] ... CaNSSXA
College of Cape Breton, Sydney, NS, Canada [*Library symbol*] ... CaNSSX
College Center of the Finger Lakes, Corning, NY [*Library symbol*] ... NCorniFL
College of Chaplains [*of APHA*] ... COC-APHA
College Characteristics Analysis ... CCA
College Characteristics Index [*A questionnaire*] ... CCI
College of Charleston, Charleston, SC [*OCLC symbol*] ... SBM
College of Charleston, Charleston, SC [*Library symbol*] ... ScCC
College Chemistry Consultants Service ... C3S
College Communautaire de New Brunswick, Bathurst, NB, Canada [*Library symbol*] ... CaNBBCC
College Composition and Communication [*A publication*] ... CCC

College Composition and Communication [*A publication*]............... Col Comp & Comm

College Composition and Communication [*A publication*]............... Coll Comp & Comm

College Composition and Communication [*A publication*]............... Coll Composition & Commun

College Discovery [*Educational project for disadvantaged youngsters*] .... CD

College Dominicain de Philosophie et de Theologie, Ottawa, ON, Canada [*Library symbol*]...................... CaOOCDP

College of Du Page, Glen Ellyn, IL [*OCLC symbol*]................. IBI

College of Du Page, Glen Ellyn, IL [*Library symbol*]............... IGleD

College d'Eastern Utah, Price, UT [*Library symbol*]................. UPrE

College Edouard-Montpetit, Longueuil, PQ, Canada [*Library symbol*]...................... CaQLoCE

College of Emporia, Emporia, KS [*Library symbol*]................. KEmC

College of Engineers of Puerto Rico .... CEPR

College English [*A publication*]................................... CE

College English [*A publication*]............................... Co Engl

College English [*A publication*].............................. ColEng

College English [*A publication*]............................. CollE

College English [*A publication*].......................... Coll Eng

College English Association .... CEA

College d'Enseignement General et Professional de l'Outaouais, Hull, PQ, Canada [*Library symbol*]...................... CaQHC

College d'Enseignement General et Professional de Regional Cote Nord, Hauterive, PQ, Canada [*Library symbol*].... CaQHaC

College d'Enseignement, Ste.-Foy, PQ, Canada [*Library symbol*].... CaQSFC

College d'Enseignement Secondaire [*France*]...................... CES

College Entrance Examination Board [*Known as The College Board; acronym no longer used*]...................... CEEB

College Eye Data Processing System [*Air Force*]................. CEDPS

College - Fairbanks [*Alaska*] [*Seismograph station code, US Geological Survey*] [*Closed*]...................... CMO

College Fiord [*Alaska*] [*Seismograph station code, US Geological Survey*]...................... CFI

College Football Association .... CFA

College Fraternity Editors Association .... CFEA

College Fraternity Scholarship Officers Association .... CFSOA

College Fraternity Secretaries Association [*Later, FEA*]........ CFSA

College of Great Falls [*Montana*]............................ CGF

College of Great Falls, Great Falls, MT [*Library symbol*]...... MtGrCE

College of Health Sciences [*Iran*].......................... CHS

College of the Holy Cross [*Massachusetts*].................... CHC

College of the Holy Cross, Worcester, MA [*OCLC symbol*]........ HCD

College of the Holy Cross, Worcester, MA [*Library symbol*]..... MWH

College for Human Services [*Formerly, WTC*].................. CHS

College of Idaho, Caldwell, ID [*Library symbol*]............. IdCaC

College of Insurance, New York, NY [*Library symbol*]......... NNCI

College International de Podologie [*International College of Podology*]...................... CIP

College Internationale pour l'Etude Scientifique des Techniques de Production Mecanique [*International Institute for Production Engineering Research*] [*Formerly, College Internationale de Recherches pour la Production*]............ CIRP

College Inventory of Academic Adjustment [*Psychology*]......... CIAA

College Jean-de-Brebeuf, Montreal, PQ, Canada [*Library symbol*]...................... CaQMDB

College Jesus-Marie de Sillery, Sillery, PQ, Canada [*Library symbol*]...................... CaQSilC

College de Joliette, Joliette, PQ, Canada [*Library symbol*]..... CaQJC

College de Jonquiere, Jonquiere, PQ, Canada [*Library symbol*]... CaQJoC

College Lafleche, Trois-Rivieres, PQ, Canada [*Library symbol*]... CaQTCL

College Language Association.................................. CLA

College Language Association. Journal [*A publication*]......... CLA

College Letter [*British*].................................... CL

College-Level Examination Program [*Trademark/service mark of the College Entrance Examination Board*]............... CLEP

College de Levis, Levis, PQ, Canada [*Library symbol*]......... CaQLeC

College Literature [*A publication*]......................... Col Lit

College Literature [*A publication*]......................... Coll L

College of the Mainland, Texas City, TX [*Library symbol*]...... TxTCM

College de Maisonneuve, Montreal, PQ, Canada [*Library symbol*]...................... CaQMCDM

College Management [*A publication*]......................... Coll Mgt

College Management [*A publication*]......................... Col Mgt

College Marguerite d'Youville, Ste.-Foy, PQ, Canada [*Library symbol*]...................... CaQSFCM

College of Marin, Kentfield, CA [*Library symbol*]............ CKenM

College of Marin, Kentfield, CA [*OCLC symbol*]............... CMK

College Mathieu, Gravelbourg, SK [*Library symbol*]........... CaSGM

College of Medical Evangelists [*Los Angeles, CA*]............ CME

College of Medicine and Dentistry of New Jersey................ CMDNJ

College of Medicine and Dentistry of New Jersey, Newark, NJ [*OCLC symbol*]...................... NJN

College Merici, Quebec, PQ, Canada [*Library symbol*]......... CaQQCM

College Militaire Royal [*Canada*]........................... CMR

College Militaire Royal de Saint-Jean, Saint-Jean, PQ, Canada [*Library symbol*]...................... CaQStJ

College Misericordia, Dallas, PA [*Library symbol*]........... PDalCM

College de Montreal, Montreal, PQ, Canada [*Library symbol*]... CaQMC

College of Mount St. Joseph-on-the-Ohio, Mount St. Joseph, OH [*OCLC symbol*]...................... CMJ

College of Mount St. Joseph-on-the-Ohio, Mount St. Joseph, OH [*Library symbol*]...................... OMtsjC

College of Mount Saint Vincent, New York, NY [*Library symbol*] ..... NNMtSV

College of Mount Saint Vincent, New York, NY [*OCLC symbol*].... VZV

College Music Society .... CMS

College Music Symposium [*A publication*].................... CLMBB

College Music Symposium [*A publication*].................... College Mus

College of New Caledonia, Prince George, BC, Canada [*Library symbol*]...................... CaBPGC

College of New Rochelle [*New York*]......................... CNR

College of New Rochelle, New Rochelle, NY [*Library symbol*].... NNerC

College of New Rochelle, New Rochelle, NY [*OCLC symbol*]....... VZCN

College du Nord Ouest, Rouyn, PQ, Canada [*Library symbol*]..... CaQRCN

College of Notre Dame, Belmont, CA [*Library symbol*]......... CBelmN

College of Optometrists in Vision Development................ COVD

College of Optometry of Ontario............................. COO

College of Osteopathic Medicine............................. COM

College of Osteopathic Medicine and Surgery, Des Moines, IA [*Library symbol*]...................... IaDmS

College of Osteopathic Physicians and Surgeons.............. COPS

College of Our Lady of the Elms [*Massachusetts*]............ COLE

College of Our Lady of the Elms, Chicopee, MA [*Library symbol*]........ MChiL

College of Our Lady of Mount Carmel, Washington, DC [*Library symbol*]...................... DOLM

College Outpost [*Alaska*] [*Seismograph station code, US Geological Survey*]...................... COL

College of the Ozarks, Clarksville, AR [*Library symbol*]...... ArCIC

College Park, GA [*Radio station call letters*].............. WREE

College Park, MD [*Radio station call letters*]............. WMUC-FM

College of Petroleum and Minerals [*Dhahran, Saudi Arabia*]... CPM

College Physical Education Association [*Later, NAPEHE*]...... CPEA

College Physical Education Association [*Later, NAPEHE*] Proceedings [*A publication*]...................... Col Phys Ed Assn Proc

College of Physicians of Philadelphia, Philadelphia, PA [*Library symbol*] [*OCLC symbol*]...................... PPC

College of Physicians and Surgeons, and School of Dentistry, San Francisco, CA [*Library symbol*]................ CSfCPS

College Place, WA [*Radio station call letters*]............ KGTS

College Placement Council................................. CPC

College of Police Science, New York, NY [*Library symbol*].... NNCPL

College of Preceptors [*British*]......................... CP

College Press Service [*A publication*]................... Coll Press

College Press Service.................................... CPS

College Publishers Group................................. CPG

College Qualification Tests.............................. CQU

College Republican National Committee.................... CRNC

College and Research Libraries [*A publication*] .... College & Research Lib

College and Research Libraries [*A publication*] .... Coll Res Li

College and Research Libraries [*A publication*] .... Coll & Res Lib

College and Research Libraries [*A publication*] .... Coll Res Libr

College and Research Libraries [*A publication*] .... Col & Res Lib

College and Research Libraries [*A publication*] .... CRL

College and Research Library News [*A publication*] .... Coll & Res Lib N

College Retirement Equities Fund........................ CREF

College de Rouyn, Rouyn, PQ, Canada [*Library symbol*] [*Obsolete*]...................... CaQRC

College du Sacre-Coeur, Sherbrooke, PQ, Canada [*Library symbol*]...................... CaQSherSC

College of the Sacred Heart [*Puerto Rico*]............... CSH

College of St. Benedict [*Minnesota*].................... CSB

College of St. Benedict, St. Joseph, MN [*OCLC symbol*] ..... MNF

College of St. Benedict, St. Joseph, MN [*Library symbol*]... MnStjoS

College de St. Boniface, St. Boniface, MB, Canada [*Library symbol*]...................... CaMSC

College of St. Catherine [*Minnesota*].................... CSC

College of St. Catherine, St. Paul, MN [*OCLC symbol*]...... MNE

College de St. Catherine, St. Paul, MN [*Library symbol*]... MnSSC

College of Saint Elizabeth [*New Jersey*]................. CSE

College of Saint Elizabeth, Convent Station, NJ [*OCLC symbol*] ...... CSE

College of Saint Elizabeth, Convent Station, NJ [*Library symbol*]...... NjConC

College of Saint Francis [*Illinois*].................... CSF

College of Saint Francis, Joliet, IL [*OCLC symbol*]....... ICD

College of Saint Francis, Joliet, IL [*Library symbol*].... IJolStF

College Saint-Jean-sur-Richelieu, Saint-Jean, PQ, Canada [*Library symbol*]...................... CaQStJC

College Saint-Louis-Maillet, Edmundston, NB, Canada [*Library symbol*]...................... CaNBESLM

College of Saint Mary [*Nebraska*]....................... CSM

College of Saint Mary of the Springs [*Ohio*]............ CSMS

College of Saint Mary-of-the-Wasatch, Salt Lake City, UT [*Library symbol*] [*Obsolete*]...................... USIStM

College of Saint Rose [*New York*]....................... CSR

College of Saint Rose, Albany, NY [*Library symbol*]...... NAICSR

College of Saint Scholastica [*Minnesota*]............... CSS

College of Saint Scholastica, Duluth, MN [*Library symbol*]... MnDuStS

College of Saint Scholastica Library, Duluth, MN [*OCLC symbol*] ...... MNS

College of Saint Teresa [*Minnesota*].................... CST

College of Saint Teresa, Winona, MN [*Library symbol*] ..... MnWinoCT

College of Saint Teresa, Winona, MN [*OCLC symbol*]........ MNZ

College of St. Thomas [*Minnesota*] ... CST
College of St. Thomas, St. Paul, MN [*Library symbol*] ... MnSST
College of St. Thomas, St. Paul, MN [*OCLC symbol*] ... MNT
College de Sainte-Anne, La Pocatiere, PQ, Canada [*Library symbol*] ... CaQPC
College Sainte-Croix, Montreal, PQ, Canada [*Library symbol*] ... CaQMStC
College Sainte-Marie, Montreal, PQ, Canada [*Library symbol*] ... CaQMSM
College of San Mateo [*California*] ... CSM
College of San Mateo Library, San Mateo, CA [*OCLC symbol*] ... CMT
College of San Mateo, San Mateo, CA [*Library symbol*] ... CSmatC
College of Santa Fe, Santa Fe, NM [*Library symbol*] ... NmSC
College Scholarship Service [*Service mark of the College Entrance Examination Board*] ... CSS
College Science Improvement Program [*National Science Foundation*] [*Defunct*] ... COSIP
College Selection Service [*Peterson's Guides*] [*Information service*] ... CSS
College & Seminary Library, Inc., Naperville, IL [*Library symbol*] [*Obsolete*] ... INapC
College Senior Engineering Program [*Air Force*] ... CSEP
College of the Sequoias, Visalia, CA [*Library symbol*] ... CViCS
College Service Bureau ... CSB
College de Sherbrooke (CEGEP) [*College d'Enseignement General et Professionel*]**, Sherbrooke, PQ, Canada** [*Library symbol*] ... CaQSherE
College of the Siskiyous Library, Weed, CA [*OCLC symbol*] ... CIS
College of the Southwest, Hobbs, NM [*Library symbol*] ... NmHoSW
College Sports Information Directors of America ... COSIDA
College of Staten Island, St. George Campus Library, Staten Island, NY [*OCLC symbol*] ... VSI
College of Staten Island, St. George Campus, Staten Island, NY [*Library symbol*] ... NSiCS
College Station [*Texas*] [*Airport symbol*] ... CLL
College Station, TX [*Location identifier*] [*FAA*] ... CLL
College Station, TX [*Radio station call letters*] ... KAMU-FM
College Station, TX [*Television station call letters*] ... KAMU-TV
College Station, TX [*Radio station call letters*] ... KTAW-FM
College Station, TX [*Radio station call letters*] ... WTAW
College of Steubenville, Steubenville, OH [*Library symbol*] ... OSteC
College Stores Association ... CSA
College Student Journal [*A publication*] ... Coll Stud J
College Student Personnel Abstracts [*A publication*] ... Coll Stud Pers Abstr
College Student Personnel Abstracts [*A publication*] ... ColStuAb
College Student Personnel Institute [*Defunct*] ... CSPI
College Student Questionnaires [*Psychology*] ... CSQ
College Swimming Coaches Association of America ... CSCAA
College Theology Society ... CTS
College of Trades and Technology, Medical Sciences Library, St. John's, NF, Canada [*Library symbol*] ... CaNfSCTM
College Training Detachment ... CTD
College de Travaux. Academie Internationale d'Histoire des Sciences [*A publication*] ... CTAIHS
College and University [*A publication*] ... Coll & Univ
College and University [*A publication*] ... Col & Univ
College and University [*A publication*] ... Col Univ
College and University [*A publication*] ... C & U
College and University Business [*A publication*] ... Coll & Univ Bus
College and University Business [*A publication*] ... Col & Univ Bsns
College and University Environment Scales [*Psychology*] ... CUES
College and University Journal [*A publication*] ... Coll & Univ J
College and University Journal [*A publication*] ... Col & Univ J
College and University Machine Records Conference ... CUMREC
College and University Personnel Association ... CUPA
College and University Systems Exchange [*Acronym is now used as name of association*] ... CAUSE
College de Victoriaville, Victoriaville, PQ, Canada [*Library symbol*] ... CaQVC
College of the Virgin Islands ... CVI
College of the Virgin Islands, St. Thomas, VI [*Library symbol*] ... VnStC
College of White Plains, White Plains, NY [*Library symbol*] ... NWhpG
College of White Plains, White Plains, NY [*OCLC symbol*] ... VZW
College of William and Mary, Law School, Williamsburg, VA [*Library symbol*] ... ViW-L
College of William and Mary, Law School, Williamsburg, VA [*OCLC symbol*] ... VWL
College of William and Mary, Williamsburg, VA [*Library symbol*] ... ViW
College of William and Mary, Williamsburg, VA [*OCLC symbol*] ... VWM
College Women's Volunteer Service [*World War II*] ... CWVS
College of Wooster, Wooster, OH [*Library symbol*] ... OWoC
College of Wooster, Wooster, OH [*OCLC symbol*] ... WOO
College Work-Study [*Program*] ... CW-S
College Work-Study Program ... CWSP
Collegedale, TN [*Radio station call letters*] ... WSMC-FM
Colleges of Mid-America [*An association*] ... CMA
Collegeville, MN [*Radio station call letters*] ... KSJR-FM
Collegeville, MN [*Radio station call letters*] ... KSJU
Collegiate Basketball Officials Bureau [*Later, Eastern College Basketball Association*] ... CBOB
Collegiate Commissioners Association ... CCA
Collegiate Council for the United Nations ... CCUN
Collegiate News and Views [*A publication*] ... Coll N & V
Collegium Internationale Activitatis Nervosae Superioris ... CIANS
Collegium Internationale Activitatis Nervosae Superioris ... CINS
Collegium Internationale Allergologicum ... CIA
Collegium Internationale Neuro-Psychopharmacologicum ... CINP
Collegium Medicorum Theatri [*An association*] ... COMET
Colles et Resines Adhesives du Midi [*France*] ... CORAM
Collett Dickenson Pearce [*British advertising agency*] ... CDP
Colliding Beam Accelerator [*High-energy physics*] ... CBA
Collie Club of America ... CCA
Collier [*Navy symbol*] ... AC
Collier County Free Public Library, Naples, FL [*Library symbol*] ... FNaC
Collier's [*A publication*] ... C
Collier's Encyclopedia Yearbook [*A publication*] ... Collier's Yrbk
Collier's National Weekly [*A publication*] ... Collier's
Collierville, TN [*Radio station call letters*] ... WMSO
Colliery ... COLL
Colliery Guardian [*A publication*] ... Colliery Guard
Colliery Mazdoor Union [*India*] ... CMU
Collimated Monochromatic Light ... CML
Collimator ... COLIM
Collingswood Free Public Library, Collingswood, NJ [*Library symbol*] ... NjCo
Collingswood Publishing Co., Collingswood, NJ [*Library symbol*] ... NjCoC
Collingwood, ON [*Radio station call letters*] ... CKCB
Collingwood Public Library, Collingwood, ON, Canada [*Library symbol*] ... CaOCol
Collins & Aikman Corp. [*NYSE symbol*] ... CK
Collins Foods International Corp. [*NYSE symbol*] ... CF
Collins Industries [*NASDAQ symbol*] ... COLL
Collins, MS [*Radio station call letters*] ... WKNZ
Collins [*Keith*] **Petroleum** [*NASDAQ symbol*] ... KCPC
Collins Public Library, Collins, IA [*Library symbol*] ... IaColn
Collins Radio Company ... CRC
Collins Radio Co. [*NYSE symbol*] [*Delisted*] ... CRI
Collins Radio Co., Dallas, TX [*Library symbol*] ... TxDaCR
Collinsville [*Australia*] [*Airport symbol*] ... KCE
Collinsville Community Unit 10, Collinsville, IL [*Library symbol*] ... IColCU
Collinsville Public Library, Collinsville, IL [*Library symbol*] ... ICol
Collinsville, VA [*Radio station call letters*] ... WFIC
Collision [*Automobile insurance*] ... COLL
Collision Avoidance, Proximity Warning, Station Keeping Equipment [*Military*] ... CAPWSK
Collision Avoidance RADAR Simulator [*Maritime*] ... CARS
Collision Avoidance System [*Aviation*] ... CAS
Collision Avoidance System Technical Evaluation ... CASTE
Collision Damage Waiver [*Insurance*] ... CDW
Collision Diameter of a Molecule [*Symbol*] [*IUPAC*] ... d
Collision-Dominated Quiescent Discharge ... CDQD
Collision-Imparted Velocity Method ... CIVM
Collision-Induced Dissociation [*Spectrometry*] ... CID
Collision Number [*Symbol*] [*IUPAC*] ... Z
Collision and Obstacle/Terrain Avoidance Warning System ... COTAWS
Collision Prevention Advisory Group [*US*] ... COPAG
Collision Warning System ... CWS
Collisionally Activated Dissociation ... CAD
Collmberg [*German Democratic Republic*] [*Seismograph station code, US Geological Survey*] ... CLL
Collocated Operating Bases ... COB
Collocation Flutter Analysis ... CFA
Collocation Flutter Analysis ... COFA
Colloid ... COLL
Colloid Antigen [*Immunology*] ... CA
Colloid and Interface Science. Proceedings of the International Conference on Colloids and Surfaces [*A publication*] ... Colloid Interface Sci Pro Int Conf
Colloid Journal [*USSR*] [*A publication*] ... Colloid J
Colloid Journal (USSR) [*A publication*] ... Colloid J (USSR)
Colloid Microthruster Experiment ... CME
Colloid and Polymer Science [*A publication*] ... Colloid Polym Sci
Colloid and Polymer Science [*A publication*] ... Colloid P S
Colloid Science [*A publication*] ... Colloid Sci
Colloid Surface Science Symposium [*A publication*] ... Colloid Surf Sci Symp
Colloidal Iron Hydroxide ... CIH
Colloidal Osmotic Pressure [*Analytical biochemistry*] ... COP
Colloidal System Test ... CST
Colloids and Surfaces [*A publication*] ... Colloids Surf
Colloque. Club Jules Gonin [*A publication*] ... Colloq Club Jules Gonin
Colloque International sur la Blennorragie. Comptes Rendus [*A publication*] ... Colloq Int Blennorragie
Colloque International sur l'Electricite Solaire. Comptes Rendus [*A publication*] ... Colloq Int Electr Sol
Colloques Internationaux. Centre National de la Recherche Scientifique [*A publication*] ... Colloq Int Cent Natl Rech Sci
Colloques Internationaux. Centre National de la Recherche Scientifique [*A publication*] ... Colloq Int CNRS
Colloquia Germanica [*A publication*] ... ColGer
Colloquia Germanica [*A publication*] ... Coll G
Colloquia Mathematica. Societatis Janos Bolyai [*Elsevier Book Series*] [*A publication*] ... CM
Colloquia Mathematica. Societatis Janos Bolyai [*A publication*] ... Colloq Math Soc Janos Bolyai

Colloquia for Presidents and Academic Administrators [*Formerly, ICUA*] ... CPAA
Colloquial ... COLL
Colloquial ... COLLOQ
Colloquium. Freien Universitaet [*A publication*] ... Col
Colloquium. Gesellschaft fuer Biologische Chemie in Mosbach [*A publication*] ... Colloq Ges Biol Chem Mosbach
Colloquium. Gesellschaft fuer Physiologische Chemie [*A publication*] ... Colloq Ges Physiol Chem
Colloquium. International Potash Institute [*A publication*] ... Colloq Int Potash Inst
Colloquium Mathematicum [*A publication*] ... Coll Math
Colloquium Spectroscopicum Internationale. Acta [*A publication*] ... Colloq Spectrosc Int Acta
Colloquium Spectroscopicum Internationale. Proceedings [*A publication*] ... Colloq Spectro Int Pro
Colloredo [*Italy*] [*Seismograph station code, US Geological Survey*] ... COLI
Coll'Ottava [*With the Octave*] [*Music*] ... COLL'OTTA
Collunarium [*Nose Wash*] [*Pharmacy*] ... COLLUN
Collurania [*Italy*] [*Seismograph station code, US Geological Survey*] [*Closed*] ... CLR
Collutorium [*Mouthwash*] [*Pharmacy*] ... COLLUT
Collyrium [*Eye Wash*] [*Pharmacy*] ... COLLYR
Colmar [*France*] [*Airport symbol*] ... CMR
Cologarithm [*Mathematics*] ... COLOG
Cologne [*West Germany*] [*Seismograph station code, US Geological Survey*] ... CLG
Cologne/Bonn [*West Germany*] [*Airport symbol*] ... CGN
Cologne/Bonn-Main RR [*West Germany*] [*Airport symbol*] ... QKL
Colombia [*ucu (United States Miscellaneous Caribbean Islands) used in records cataloged before January 1978*] [*MARC country of publication code*] [*Library of Congress*] ... ck
Colombia [*Two-letter standard code*] ... CO
Colombia ... COL
Colombia [*Aircraft nationality and registration mark*] ... HK
Colombia [*MARC geographic area code*] [*Library of Congress*] ... s-ck---
Colombia [*Three-letter standard code*] ... COL
Colombia. Ministro de Minas y Energia. Memoria [*A publication*] ... Colomb Minist Minas Energ Mem
Colombia, SC [*Location identifier*] [*FAA*] ... VYK
Colombian-American Chamber of Commerce ... CACC
Colombo [*Sri Lanka*] [*Airport symbol*] ... CMB
Colombo [*Sri Lanka*] [*Seismograph station code, US Geological Survey*] ... COC
Colome Public Library, Colome, SD [*Library symbol*] ... SdCo
Colon [*Monetary unit in Costa Rica, El Salvador*] ... C
Colon ... CLN
Colon [*Panama*] [*Airport symbol*] ... ONX
Colon Classification [*Library science*] ... CC
Colon Mucoprotein Antigen [*Immunochemistry*] ... CMA
Colon and Rectal Surgery [*Medicine*] ... CRS
Colon Resection [*Medicine*] ... CR
Colon Township Library, Colon, MI [*Library symbol*] ... MiColo
Colonel [*Military*] ... COL
Colonel By Secondary School, Ottawa, ON, Canada [*Library symbol*] ... CaOOCB
Colonel Coon Collectors Club ... CCCC
Colonel, Royal Artillery Training [*British*] ... CRAT
Colonel's Island [*AAR code*] ... COLI
Colonia Sabana [*Puerto Rico*] [*Seismograph station code, US Geological Survey*] ... CSB
Colonial ... COLON
Colonial Air Lines ... CAL
Colonial Aircraft Company ... CAC
Colonial American Bankshares [*NASDAQ symbol*] ... CABK
Colonial BancGroup A [*NASDAQ symbol*] ... CLBGA
Colonial Bancorp [*NASDAQ symbol*] ... CBCN
Colonial Bird Register [*Cornell University*] [*Information service*] ... CBR
Colonial Bishoprics' Fund [*British*] ... CBF
Colonial Commercial Corp. [*NASDAQ symbol*] ... CCOM
Colonial Commercial Corp. [*American Stock Exchange symbol*] [*Delisted*] ... COL
Colonial [*or Commonwealth*] **and Continental Church Society** [*British*] ... CCCS
Colonial Corp. of America [*NYSE symbol*] [*Delisted*] ... CLA
Colonial Development Corporation ... CDC
Colonial Gas Co. [*NASDAQ symbol*] ... CGES
Colonial Geology and Mineral Resources [*A publication*] ... Colonial Geology and Mineral Res
Colonial Heights, VA [*Radio station call letters*] ... WYNT
Colonial Life & Accident [*NASDAQ symbol*] ... CACCB
Colonial Medical Department [*British*] ... CMD
Colonial Military Forces [*British*] ... CMF
Colonial National Historic Park ... COLO
Colonial Newsletter [*A publication*] ... ColN
Colonial Office [*British*] ... CO
Colonial Order of the Acorn ... COA
Colonial Penn Group, Inc. [*NYSE symbol*] ... CPG
Colonial Penn Group, Inc., Marketing Research Library, Philadelphia, PA [*Library symbol*] ... PPColP
Colonial Plant and Animal Products [*A publication*] ... Colon Plant Anim Prod
Colonial Police Medal [*British*] ... CPM
Colonial Research Publications [*A publication*] ... Colonial Research Pub
Colonial Society of Massachusetts ... CSM
Colonial Society of Massachusetts. Publications [*A publication*] ... Col Soc Mass Publ
Colonial Society of Massachusetts. Transactions [*A publication*] ... Col Soc Mass Trans
Colonial Society of Pennsylvania ... CSP
Colonial Stores, Incorporated [*NYSE symbol*] [*Delisted*] ... CSI
Colonial Williamsburg, Inc., Williamsburg, VA [*Library symbol*] ... ViWC
Colonial X-Ray Corp. [*NASDAQ symbol*] ... XRAY
Colony ... COL
Colony Forming [*Cytology*] ... CF
Colony-Forming Ability [*Microbiology*] ... CFA
Colony-Forming Cell [*Cytology*] ... CFC
Colony-Forming Unit [*Cytology*] ... CFU
Colony-Forming Unit - Culture [*Cytology*] ... CFU-C
Colony-Forming Unit/Erythroid [*Cytology*] ... CFU-E
Colony-Forming Unit/Granulocyte Macrophage [*Cytology*] ... CFU-GM
Colony-Forming Unit/Lymphoid [*Cytology*] ... CFU-L
Colony-Forming Unit/Megakaryocyte [*Cytology*] ... CFU-M
Colony-Forming Unit - Single Cell [*Cytology*] ... CFU-S
Colony-Forming Unit Spleen [*Cytology*] ... CFUS
Colony Overlay Test [*Microbiology*] ... COT
Colony-Stimulating Activity [*Genetics*] ... CSA
Colony-Stimulating Factor [*Hematology*] ... CSF
Coloquio Artes [*A publication*] ... ColA
Coloquio Letras [*A publication*] ... Coloquio
Coloquio (Lisbon) [*A publication*] ... ColL
Color ... C
Color ... CLR
Color ... COL
Color Association of the United States ... CAUS
Color Changing Unit [*Medical technology*] ... CCU
Color Code [*as, for types of wire*] [*Technical drawings*] ... CC
Color Compensation [*Photography*] ... CC
Color Computer ... COCO
Color Contrast ... CC
Color Contrast Value ... CCV
Color Correction [*Color printing*] ... CC
Color Data Display ... CDD
Color Data System ... CDS
Color Detail [*Rorschach*] [*Psychology*] ... C
Color Diaposition Plate ... CDP
Color Difference Computer ... CODIC
Color Difference Meter ... CDM
Color Difference Signal ... CDS
Color Engineering [*A publication*] ... Color Eng
Color Evaluation Program ... CEP
Color Excess [*Astronomy*] ... E
Color Exterior Film ... CX
Color Forming Ability [*Food technology*] ... CFA
Color Forming Units [*Food technology*] ... CFU
Color Guild Associates ... CGA
Color Index ... C
Color Index ... CI
Color Infrared [*Image*] ... CIR
Color Interior Film ... CI
Color Marketing Group ... CMG
Color Mat Processor ... CMP
Color Mixture Curve ... CMC
Color Mixture Function ... CMF
Color Pack Camera ... CPC
Color Perception [*Medicine*] ... CP
Color Phase Alternation ... CPA
Color Picture Signal ... CPS
Color Printing [*Filter*] [*Photography*] ... CP
Color Pyramid Test [*Psychology*] ... CPT
Color Rendition Index [*Measure of color distortion*] ... CRI
Color Research and Application [*A publication*] ... Color Res Appl
Color Specification ... CS
Color Sync Signal ... CSS
Color Television ... CTV
Color Tile, Inc. [*NASDAQ symbol*] ... TILE
Color Trade Journal and Textile Chemist [*A publication*] ... Color Tr J
Color Video Tape ... CVT
Color Vision [*Medicine*] ... CV
Color Vision [*Ophthalmology*] ... VC
Color Vision Deviate [*Medicine*] ... CVD
Color Word Test ... CWT
Colorado [*Dark-colored cigar*] ... C
Colorado [*Postal code*] ... CO
Colorado ... COL
Colorado ... COLO
Colorado [*MARC country of publication code*] [*Library of Congress*] ... cou
Colorado [*MARC geographic area code*] [*Library of Congress*] ... n-us-co
Colorado Academy, Englewood, CO [*Library symbol*] ... CoEnCA
Colorado Agricultural Experiment Station. Annual Report [*A publication*] ... Colo Agric Exp Stn Annu Rep

Colorado Agricultural Experiment Station. Bulletin [*A publication*]....Colo Agric Exp Stn Bull
Colorado Agricultural Experiment Station. Publications [*A publication*]....Colo Ag Exp
Colorado Alliance of Research Libraries [*Library network*]....CARL
Colorado Bureau of Mines. Annual Report [*A publication*]....Colo Bur Mines Ann Rept
Colorado City, TX [*Radio station call letters*]....KVMC
Colorado-Claro [*Medium-colored cigar*]....CC
Colorado College, Colorado Springs, CO [*OCLC symbol*]....COC
Colorado College, Colorado Springs, CO [*Library symbol*]....CoCC
Colorado Department of Game, Fish, and Parks. Special Report [*A publication*]....Colo Dep Game Fish Parks Spec Rep
Colorado Division of Game, Fish, and Parks. Fisheries Research Review [*A publication*]....Colo Div Game Fish Parks Fish Res Rev
Colorado Division of Game, Fish, and Parks. Game Research Review [*A publication*]....Colo Div Game Parks Game Res Rev
Colorado Division of Game, Fish, and Parks. Special Report [*A publication*]....Colo Div Game Fish Parks Spec Rep
Colorado Division of State Archives, Denver, CO [*Library symbol*]....CoDAr
Colorado Division of Wildlife. Division Report [*A publication*]....Colo Div Wildl Div Rep
Colorado Division of Wildlife. Special Report [*A publication*]....Colo Div Wildl Spec Rep
Colorado Division of Wildlife. Technical Publication [*A publication*]....Colo Div Wildl Tech Publ
Colorado Energy Corp. [*NASDAQ symbol*]....CRDO
Colorado Engineer [*A publication*]....Colo Engineer
Colorado Farm and Home Research [*A publication*]....Colo Farm & Home Res
Colorado Field Ornithologist [*A publication*]....Colo Field Ornithol
Colorado Fisheries Research Review [*A publication*]....Colo Fish Res Rev
Colorado Fuel & Iron Co., Pueblo, CO [*Library symbol*]....CoPC
Colorado Game, Fish, and Parks Department. Special Report [*A publication*]....Colo Game Fish Parks Dep Spec Rep
Colorado Game Research Review [*A publication*]....Colo Game Res Rev
Colorado Gasahol, Inc. [*NASDAQ symbol*]....CGAS
Colorado Genealogical Society....CGS
Colorado General Hospital, Residents' Library, Denver, CO [*Library symbol*]....CoDGH
Colorado. Geological Survey. Bulletin [*A publication*]....Colo Geol Surv Bull
Colorado. Geological Survey. Map Series [*A publication*]....Colo Geol Surv Map Ser
Colorado Gold & Silver, Incorporated [*NASDAQ symbol*]....CGSI
Colorado Journal of Pharmacy [*A publication*]....Colo J Pharm
Colorado Journal of Research in Music Education [*A publication*]....Colo J Res Mus Ed
Colorado Library Association. Bulletin [*A publication*]....CLA Bull
Colorado Library Association. Bulletin [*A publication*]....Colo Lib Assn Bul
Colorado Library Network [*Library network*]....COLONET
Colorado-Maduro [*Very dark-colored cigar*]....CM
Colorado Magazine [*A publication*]....CM
Colorado Magazine [*A publication*]....ColM
Colorado Magazine [*A publication*]....ColoM
Colorado Magazine [*A publication*]....Colo Mag
Colorado Medicine [*A publication*]....Colo Med
Colorado Medicine [*A publication*]....Colorado Med
Colorado Mining Association....CMA
Colorado Motor Carriers' Association, Denver CO [*STAC*]....COA
Colorado Motor Tariff Bureau, Inc., Denver CO [*STAC*]....COB
Colorado Mountain College, Eastern Campus, Leadville, CO [*Library symbol*]....CoLeC
Colorado Mountain College, Western Campus, Glenwood Springs, CO [*Library symbol*]....CoGsC
Colorado National Bankshares [*NASDAQ symbol*]....COLC
Colorado National Monument....COLM
Colorado Northwestern Community College, Rangely, CO [*Library symbol*]....CoRaC
Colorado Nurse [*A publication*]....Colo Nurse
Colorado Potato Beetle....CPB
Colorado Potato Beetle Spiroplasma [*Insect pathogen*]....CPBS
Colorado Psychiatric Hospital, Residents' Library, Denver, CO [*Library symbol*]....CoDPH
Colorado Quarterly [*A publication*]....ColoQ
Colorado Quarterly [*A publication*]....ColQ
Colorado Ranger Horse Association....CRHA
Colorado Research Corporation....CRC
Colorado Research in Linguistics [*A publication*]....CRIL
Colorado River Association....CRA
Colorado River Basin Project....CRBP
Colorado River Board of California, Los Angeles, CA [*Library symbol*]....CLCol
Colorado River Indian Tribes Public Library, Parker, AZ [*Library symbol*]....AzPa
Colorado River Municipal Water District....CRMWD
Colorado River Storage Project [*Department of the Interior*]....CRSP
Colorado School for the Deaf and Blind, Colorado Springs, CO [*Library symbol*]....CoCD
Colorado School of Mines....CSM
Colorado School of Mines, Golden, CO [*Library symbol*]....CoG
Colorado School of Mines, Golden, CO [*OCLC symbol*]....COP
Colorado School of Mines. Mineral Industries Bulletin [*A publication*]....Colo Sch Mines Miner Ind Bull
Colorado School of Mines. Professional Contributions [*A publication*]....Colorado School Mines Prof Contr
Colorado School of Mines. Quarterly [*A publication*]....Colo Sch Mines Q
Colorado Scientific Society. Proceedings [*A publication*]....Colo Sci Soc Proc
[*The*] **Colorado & Southern Railway Co.**....C & S
[*The*] **Colorado & Southern Railway Co.** [*NYSE symbol*] [*Delisted*]....CX
[*The*] **Colorado & Southern Railway Co.** [*AAR code*]....CS
Colorado Springs [*Colorado*] [*Airport symbol*]....COS
Colorado Springs, CO [*Location identifier*] [*FAA*]....AFF
Colorado Springs, CO [*Radio station call letters*]....KCMN
Colorado Springs, CO [*Radio station call letters*]....KEPC
Colorado Springs, CO [*Radio station call letters*]....KILO
Colorado Springs, CO [*Radio station call letters*]....KKCS-FM
Colorado Springs, CO [*Radio station call letters*]....KKFM
Colorado Springs, CO [*Television station call letters*]....KKTV
Colorado Springs, CO [*Radio station call letters*]....KPIK
Colorado Springs, CO [*Radio station call letters*]....KRCC
Colorado Springs, CO [*Radio station call letters*]....KRDO
Colorado Springs, CO [*Radio station call letters*]....KRDO-FM
Colorado Springs, CO [*Television station call letters*]....KRDO-TV
Colorado Springs, CO [*Radio station call letters*]....KSPZ
Colorado Springs, CO [*Radio station call letters*]....KSSS
Colorado Springs, CO [*Radio station call letters*]....KVOR
Colorado Springs, CO [*Radio station call letters*]....KYSN
Colorado Springs Fine Arts Center, Fine Arts and Anthropology of the Southwest, Library, Colorado Springs, CO [*Library symbol*]....CoCF
Colorado Springs Maintenance and Operations System [*Space Defense Center*]....COSMOS
Colorado State College [*Later, University of Northern Colorado*]....CSC
Colorado State Department of Highways, Denver, CO [*Library symbol*]....CoDCDH
Colorado State Department of Social Services, Denver, CO [*Library symbol*]....CoDSS
Colorado State Historical Society, Denver, CO [*Library symbol*]....CoHi
Colorado State Home for the Aged, Trinidad, CO [*Library symbol*]....CoTA
Colorado State Home and Training School, Grand Junction, CO [*Library symbol*]....CoGjT
Colorado State Home and Training School, Medical Library, Wheatridge, CO [*Library symbol*]....CoWeT-M
Colorado State Home and Training School, Residents' Library, Pueblo, CO [*Library symbol*]....CoPT
Colorado State Home and Training School, Staff Library, Grand Junction, CO [*Library symbol*]....CoGjTS
Colorado State Home and Training School, Staff Library, Pueblo, CO [*Library symbol*]....CoPTS
Colorado State Home and Training School, Wheatridge, CO [*Library symbol*]....CoWeT
Colorado State Hospital, Children's Center, Pueblo, CO [*Library symbol*]....CoPCS-C
Colorado State Hospital, Hospital Community Library, Pueblo, CO [*Library symbol*]....CoPCS
Colorado State Hospital, Professional Library, Pueblo, CO [*Library symbol*]....CoPCS-M
Colorado State Library for the Blind and Physically Handicapped, Denver, CO [*Library symbol*]....Co-B
Colorado State Library, Denver, CO [*Library symbol*]....Co
Colorado State Library, Denver, CO [*OCLC symbol*]....COZ
Colorado State Library, Western Slope Clearinghouse, Grand Junction, CO [*Library symbol*]....CoGjW
Colorado State Penitentiary, Canon City, CO [*Library symbol*]....CoCcP
Colorado State Penitentiary, Colorado Women's Correctional Institution, Residents' Library, Canon City, CO [*Library symbol*]....CoCcPW
Colorado State Penitentiary, Colorado Women's Correctional Institution, Staff Library, Canon City, CO [*Library symbol*]....CoCcPWS
Colorado State Penitentiary, Law Library, Canon City, CO [*Library symbol*]....CoCcPL
Colorado State Penitentiary, Medium Security Law Library, Canon City, CO [*Library symbol*]....CoCcPML
Colorado State Penitentiary, Medium Security Residents' Library, Canon City, CO [*Library symbol*]....CoCcPM
Colorado State Penitentiary, Medium Security Staff Library, Canon City, CO [*Library symbol*]....CoCcPMS
Colorado State Penitentiary, Staff Library, Canon City, CO [*Library symbol*]....CoCcPS
Colorado State Publications Depository and Distribution Center, Denver, CO [*OCLC symbol*]....DDB
Colorado State Reformatory, Buena Vista, CO [*Library symbol*]....CoBueR
Colorado State Reformatory, Law Library, Buena Vista, CO [*Library symbol*]....CoBueRL
Colorado State Reformatory, Staff Library, Buena Vista, CO [*Library symbol*]....CoBueRS
Colorado State University....CSU
Colorado State University. Annual Report [*A publication*]....Colo State Univ Annu Rep
Colorado State University. Experiment Station. Bulletin [*A publication*]....Colo State Univ Exp Stn Bull

Colorado State University. Experiment Station. Bulletin [A publication]................................Colo State Univ Expt Sta Bull
Colorado State University. Experiment Station. Technical Bulletin [A publication]....Colo State Univ Exp Stn Tech Bull
Colorado State University, Fort Collins, CO [OCLC symbol].................COF
Colorado State University, Fort Collins, CO [Library symbol]..............CoFS
Colorado State University. Range Science Department. Range Science Series [A publication]...................
Colo State Univ Range Sci Dep Range Sci Ser
Colorado State Veterans Center, Homelake, CO [Library symbol].......CoHIV
Colorado State Veterans Nursing Home, Florence, CO [Library symbol]..................CoFloV
Colorado Supreme Court, Denver, CO [Library symbol]....Co-SC
Colorado Supreme Court Library, Denver, CO [OCLC symbol]....DVJ
Colorado Technical Reference Center [University of Colorado] [Information service]................CTRC
Colorado Union Catalog, Denver Public Library, Denver, CO [OCLC symbol]................CLF
Colorado-Utah-Wyoming Committee, Chicago IL [STAC]....CUW
Colorado Venture Capital [NASDAQ symbol]................COVC
Colorado Video, Incorporated....................CVI
Colorado Weights and Measures Laboratory [National Bureau of Standards]................CWML
Colorado Women's College [Formerly, Temple Buell College]..............CWC
Colorado Women's College, Denver, CO [Library symbol].................CoDCW
Colorado-Wyoming Academy of Science. Journal [A publication]...................
Colorado-Wyoming Acad Sci Jour
Colorado-Wyoming Academy of Science. Journal [A publication]...................
Colo-Wyo Acad Sci Jour
[The] **Colorado & Wyoming Railway Co.** [AAR code]...................CW
Colorado Youth Center, Denver, CO [Library symbol]..................CoDYC
Colorant Mixture Computer [Du Pont trademark]................COMIC
Colored...................CLD
Colored...................COL
Colored Female...................C-F
Colored People's Time [Slang]...................CPT
Colorimetric Solution...................CS
Colosseum of Motion Picture Salesmen...................CMPS
Colossians [New Testament book]...................Col
Colour Index [Numerical listing of dyes] [British]...................CI
Colour Printed Pottery Collectors Association...................CPPCA
Colour-Sergeant [Army] [British]...................COL-SERGT
Coloured Progressive Matrices...................CPM
Colquitt-Thomas Regional Library, Moultrie, GA [Library symbol]......GMoC
Colson Canyon [California] [Seismograph station code, US Geological Survey]...................BCC
Colt...................C
Colt [Thoroughbred racing]...................C
Colt Industries, Inc. [NYSE symbol]...................COT
Coltivatore e Giornale Vinicolo Italiano [A publication]..........Colt G Vinic Ital
Colton High School, Colton, OR [Library symbol]...................OrColHS
Colton Public Library, Colton, CA [Library symbol]...................CCol
Columba [Constellation]...................Col
Columba [Constellation]...................Colm
Columba House Fund...................CHF
Columbia [South Carolina] [Airport symbol]...................CAE
Columbia [Missouri] [Airport symbol]...................COU
Columbia [South Carolina] [Seismograph station code, US Geological Survey] [Closed]...................CSC
Columbia Basin College, Pasco, WA [Library symbol]...................WaPaC
Columbia Bible College [South Carolina]...................CBC
Columbia Bible College, Columbia, SC [OCLC symbol]...................SBI
Columbia Broadcasting System, Inc., New York, NY [Library symbol]...................NNCBS
Columbia, CA [Location identifier] [FAA]...................CUF
Columbia City, IN [Radio station call letters]...................WKSY
Columbia College, Chicago, IL [OCLC symbol] [Inactive]...................IBZ
Columbia College, Chicago, IL [Library symbol]...................ICCC
Columbia College, Columbia, SC [Library symbol]...................ScCoC
Columbia College Library, Columbia, CA [OCLC symbol]...................CCY
Columbia County Historical Library, Valatie, NY [Library symbol]......NValHi
Columbia County Historical Society, Bloomsburg, PA [Library symbol]...................PBbChi
Columbia & Cowlitz Railway Co. [AAR code]...................CLC
Columbia Essays on Modern Writers [A publication]...................CEMW
Columbia Forum [A publication]...................ColF
Columbia Forum [A publication]...................Colum Forum
Columbia Gas System, Inc. [NYSE symbol]...................CG
Columbia Gas System Service Corporation [of Columbia Gas System, Inc.]...................CGSSC
Columbia General Corp. [NASDAQ symbol]...................CLGN
Columbia-Greene Community College, Athens, NY [Library symbol]...................NAtC
Columbia Gulf Transmission Co., Houston, TX [Library symbol]........TxHCG
Columbia Historical Society...................CHS
Columbia Historical Society. Records [A publication].........Col Hist Soc Rec
Columbia Historical Society. Records [A publication]...................
Columbia Hist Soc Rec
Columbia Historical Society. Records [A publication]...................Colum His S
Columbia Historical Society, Washington, DC [Library symbol]..............DCHi

Columbia Hospital School of Nursing, Milwaukee, WI [Library symbol]...................WMCH
Columbia Human Rights Law Review [A publication]...................
Colum Human Rights L Rev
Columbia, IL [Radio station call letters]...................WCBW
Columbia Journal of Law and Social Problems [A publication].... Columb J L
Columbia Journal of Law and Social Problems [A publication]...................
Colum J L & Soc Prob
Columbia Journal of Transnational Law [A publication]...................
Columbia J Transnat Law
Columbia Journal of Transnational Law [A publication].............Columb J Tr
Columbia Journal of Transnational Law [A publication]...................
Colum J Transnat L
Columbia Journal of World Business [A publication]...................
Columbia J Wld Busin
Columbia Journal of World Business [A publication]...................
Columbia J World Bus
Columbia Journal of World Business [A publication]............ Columb J W
Columbia Journal of World Business [A publication]........Colum J World Bus
Columbia Journalism Review [A publication]...................CJR
Columbia Journalism Review [A publication]...................ColJR
Columbia Journalism Review [A publication]......... Columbia J-ism R
Columbia Journalism Review [A publication].........Columbia Journalism Rev
Columbia Journalism Review [A publication]......... Colum Journalism R
Columbia Junior College, Columbia, CA [Library symbol]..............CColumC
Columbia, KY [Radio station call letters]...................WAIN
Columbia, KY [Radio station call letters]...................WAIN-FM
Columbia, LA [Radio station call letters]...................KCTO
Columbia, LA [Radio station call letters]................... KCTO-FM
Columbia Law Review [A publication]................... Columbia Law Rev
Columbia Law Review [A publication]...................Columb Law
Columbia Law Review [A publication]................... Colum L Rev
Columbia Library. Columns [A publication]...................CLC
Columbia Library. Columns [A publication]...................Columbia Lib C
Columbia Library. Columns [A publication]................... Columbia Libr Col
Columbia Mental Maturity Scale [Psychology]................... CMMS
Columbia & Millstadt R. R. [AAR code]...................COML
Columbia, MO [Location identifier] [FAA]...................CBI
Columbia, MO [Radio station call letters]...................KARO-FM
Columbia, MO [Radio station call letters]................... KBIA
Columbia, MO [Television station call letters]................... KCBJ-TV
Columbia, MO [Radio station call letters]...................KCMQ
Columbia, MO [Radio station call letters]...................KCOU
Columbia, MO [Radio station call letters]...................KFMZ
Columbia, MO [Radio station call letters]...................KFRU
Columbia, MO [Television station call letters]...................KOMU-TV
Columbia, MO [Radio station call letters]...................KOPN
Columbia, MO [Radio station call letters]...................KTGR
Columbia, MO [Radio station call letters]...................KWWC-FM
Columbia, MS [Location identifier] [FAA]...................FOH
Columbia, MS [Radio station call letters]...................WCJU
Columbia, MS [Radio station call letters]...................WFFF
Columbia, MS [Radio station call letters]................... WFFF-FM
Columbia National Fisheries Research Laboratory [Department of the Interior]...................CNFRL
Columbia National Fisheries Research Laboratory, Columbia, MO [OCLC symbol]...................FZX
Columbia, NC [Television station call letters]...................WUND-TV
Columbia, NC [Radio station call letters]...................WWOK
Columbia, Newberry, & Laurens Railroad Co. [AAR code]...................CNL
Columbia Pacific Airlines [Richland, WA] [FAA designator]...................CPC
Columbia Pictures Industries, Inc. [NYSE symbol] [Delisted]...................CPS
Columbia Research and Development Corporation...................CRDC
Columbia River Conservation League...................CRCL
Columbia River Datum...................CRD
Columbia River Fisheries Development Program...................CRFDP
Columbia River Salmon and Tuna Packers Association...................CRSTPA
Columbia, SC [Location identifier] [FAA]...................CUB
Columbia, SC [Location identifier] [FAA]...................EOV
Columbia, SC [Location identifier] [FAA]...................MMT
Columbia, SC [Television station call letters]...................WCCT-TV
Columbia, SC [Radio station call letters]...................WCOS
Columbia, SC [Radio station call letters]...................WCOS-FM
Columbia, SC [Radio station call letters]...................WDPN
Columbia, SC [Radio station call letters]...................WIS
Columbia, SC [Television station call letters]...................WIS-TV
Columbia, SC [Radio station call letters]...................WLTR
Columbia, SC [Television station call letters]...................WLTX-TV
Columbia, SC [Radio station call letters]...................WMHK
Columbia, SC [Radio station call letters]...................WNOK
Columbia, SC [Radio station call letters]...................WNOK-FM
Columbia, SC [Radio station call letters]...................WOIC
Columbia, SC [Television station call letters]...................WOLO-TV
Columbia, SC [Radio station call letters]...................WQXL
Columbia, SC [Television station call letters]...................WRLK-TV
Columbia, SC [Radio station call letters]...................WUSC-FM
Columbia Scholastic Press Advisers Association...................CSPAA
Columbia Scholastic Press Association...................CSPA
Columbia Sheep Breeders Association of America...................CSBA
Columbia Theological Seminary, Decatur, GA [OCLC symbol]...................GCL
Columbia Theological Seminary, Decatur, GA [Library symbol]............GDC

Columbia, TN [*Radio station call letters*]	WKOM
Columbia, TN [*Radio station call letters*]	WKRM
Columbia, TN [*Radio station call letters*]	WMCP
Columbia Township Library, Unionville, MI [*Library symbol*]	MiUnv
Columbia Union College, Takoma Park, MD [*OCLC symbol*]	CUC
Columbia Union College, Takoma Park, MD [*Library symbol*]	DColU
Columbia University [*New York*]	CU
Columbia University, American Typefounders' Library, New York, NY [*Library symbol*]	NNC-Typ
Columbia University, Avery Library of Architecture, New York, NY [*Library symbol*]	NNC-A
Columbia University, Biological Sciences Library, New York, NY [*Library symbol*]	NNC-B
Columbia University, College of Pharmacy, New York, NY [*Library symbol*]	NNC-P
Columbia University, Division of War Research	CUDWR
Columbia University. East Asian Institute. Studies [*A publication*]	EAIS
Columbia University, East Asiatic Library, New York, NY [*Library symbol*]	NNC-EA
Columbia University. Forum [*A publication*]	CUF
Columbia University. Germanic Studies [*A publication*]	CUGS
Columbia University Hudson Laboratory	CUHL
Columbia University, International Institute for the Study of Human Reproduction, Center for Population and Family Health, New York, NY [*Library symbol*]	NNC-Pop
Columbia University, Lamont-Doherty Geological Observatory, Palisades, NY [*Library symbol*]	NNC-G
Columbia University, Law Library, New York, NY [*Library symbol*]	NNC-L
Columbia University, Medical Library, New York, NY [*Library symbol*]	NNC-M
Columbia University, New York, NY [*Library symbol*]	NNC
Columbia University Press	CUP
Columbia University, Psychology Library, New York, NY [*Library symbol*]	NNC-Ps
Columbia University. Quarterly [*A publication*]	Columbia U Q
Columbia University. Quarterly [*A publication*]	Colum Univ Q
Columbia University. Quarterly [*A publication*]	CUQ
Columbia University, Teachers College, New York, NY [*Library symbol*]	NNC-T
Columbia University. Working Papers in Linguistics [*A publication*]	CUWPL
Columbia Valley Authority	CVA
Columbia, Yale, Harvard [*Used to refer to a project involving the medical libraries of these universities*]	COLYAHAR
Columbian Carbon Co. [*NYSE symbol*]	CBN
Columbian Squires [*An association*]	CS
Columbiana County Court House, Lisbon, OH [*Library symbol*]	OLiC
Columbine Explorations Corp. [*NASDAQ symbol*]	COLX
Columbium [*A chemical element; modern name is niobium, see Nb*]	Cb
Columbus [*Ohio*] [*Airport symbol*]	CMH
Columbus [*Georgia*] [*Airport symbol*]	CSG
Columbus [*Mississippi*] [*Airport symbol*]	GTR
Columbus [*Nebraska*] [*Airport symbol*]	OLU
Columbus Air Transport, Inc. [*Columbus, OH*] [*FAA designator*]	KLR
Columbus Army Depot [*Ohio*]	COAD
Columbus City School, Columbus, OH [*OCLC symbol*]	CSS
Columbus College, Columbus, GA [*Library symbol*]	GColuC
Columbus College, Library, Columbus, GA [*OCLC symbol*]	GCO
Columbus [*Georgia*] Fort Benning [*Airport symbol*]	QFE
Columbus, GA [*Radio station call letters*]	WCGQ
Columbus, GA [*Radio station call letters*]	WCLS
Columbus, GA [*Radio station call letters*]	WDAK
Columbus, GA [*Radio station call letters*]	WFXE
Columbus, GA [*Radio station call letters*]	WHYD
Columbus, GA [*Television station call letters*]	WJSP-TV
Columbus, GA [*Television station call letters*]	WLTZ
Columbus, GA [*Radio station call letters*]	WOKS
Columbus, GA [*Radio station call letters*]	WPNX
Columbus, GA [*Television station call letters*]	WRBL-TV
Columbus, GA [*Radio station call letters*]	WRCG
Columbus, GA [*Television station call letters*]	WTVM
Columbus, GA [*Radio station call letters*]	WVOC
Columbus, GA [*Television station call letters*]	WXTX
Columbus, GA [*Location identifier*] [*FAA*]	XLE
Columbus Gazette & Columbus Safeguard, Columbus Junction, IA [*Library symbol*]	IaCjGS
Columbus & Greenville Railway Co. [*AAR code*]	CAGY
Columbus & Greenville Railway Co.	C & G
Columbus Hospital, Health Sciences Library, Great Falls, MT [*Library symbol*]	MtGrCH
Columbus, IN [*Radio station call letters*]	WCSI
Columbus, IN [*Radio station call letters*]	WCSI-FM
Columbus, IN [*Radio station call letters*]	WWWY
Columbus, KS [*Radio station call letters*]	KCCU
Columbus Mills [*NASDAQ symbol*]	COLM
Columbus, MO [*Radio station call letters*]	WACR-FM
Columbus, MS [*Location identifier*] [*FAA*]	CBM
Columbus, MS [*Location identifier*] [*FAA*]	TBB
Columbus, MS [*Location identifier*] [*FAA*]	UBS
Columbus, MS [*Radio station call letters*]	WACR
Columbus, MS [*Radio station call letters*]	WCBI

Columbus, MS [*Television station call letters*]	WCBI-TV
Columbus, MS [*Radio station call letters*]	WJWF
Columbus, MS [*Radio station call letters*]	WLNK
Columbus, MS [*Radio station call letters*]	WMBC
Columbus, MS [*Radio station call letters*]	WMUW
Columbus, NE [*Radio station call letters*]	KOXI
Columbus, NE [*Radio station call letters*]	KTLX
Columbus, NE [*Radio station call letters*]	KTTT
Columbus, NE [*Radio station call letters*]	KTTT-FM
Columbus, NE [*Location identifier*] [*FAA*]	PLT
Columbus, NM [*Location identifier*] [*FAA*]	CUS
Columbus, OH [*Location identifier*] [*FAA*]	BUZ
Columbus, OH [*Location identifier*] [*FAA*]	IVX
Columbus, OH [*Location identifier*] [*FAA*]	LCK
Columbus, OH [*Location identifier*] [*FAA*]	OSU
Columbus, OH [*Location identifier*] [*FAA*]	OYY
Columbus, OH [*Radio station call letters*]	WBNS
Columbus, OH [*Radio station call letters*]	WBNS-FM
Columbus, OH [*Television station call letters*]	WBNS-TV
Columbus, OH [*Television station call letters*]	WCBE
Columbus, OH [*Television station call letters*]	WCMH
Columbus, OH [*Radio station call letters*]	WCOL
Columbus, OH [*Radio station call letters*]	WLVQ
Columbus, OH [*Radio station call letters*]	WMNI
Columbus, OH [*Radio station call letters*]	WNCI
Columbus, OH [*Radio station call letters*]	WOSU
Columbus, OH [*Radio station call letters*]	WOSU-FM
Columbus, OH [*Television station call letters*]	WOSU-TV
Columbus, OH [*Radio station call letters*]	WRMZ
Columbus, OH [*Radio station call letters*]	WSNY
Columbus, OH [*Television station call letters*]	WTTE
Columbus, OH [*Radio station call letters*]	WTVN
Columbus, OH [*Television station call letters*]	WTVN-TV
Columbus, OH [*Radio station call letters*]	WVKO
Columbus, OH [*Radio station call letters*]	WXGT
Columbus, Ohio. Columbus Gallery of Fine Arts. Bulletin [*A publication*]	Columbus Gal Bul
Columbus Public Library, Columbus, NE [*Library symbol*]	NbCo
Columbus Public Library, Columbus, OH [*Library symbol*]	OCo
Columbus & Southern Ohio Electric Company [*NYSE symbol*]	COC
Columbus State Hospital, Columbus, OH [*Library symbol*]	OCoSH
Columbus Technical Institute, Columbus, OH [*OCLC symbol*]	CTI
Columbus Technical Institute, Columbus, OH [*Library symbol*]	OCoCT
Columbus, TX [*Radio station call letters*]	KULM
Columbus-Worthington, OH [*Radio station call letters*]	WRFD
Columellar Muscle	CM
Column	COL
Column	COLM
Column	COLN
Column Chromatography [*Analytical chemistry*]	CC
Column Chromatography - High-Performance [*or Pressure*] Liquid Chromatography [*Analytical chemistry*]	CC-HPLC
Column-Digit Binary Network	CDBN
Column Gap [*Army*]	COLMGP
Column Position Counter	CPC
Column Research Council [*Later, SSRC*]	CRC
Column Valve Diaphragm	CVD
Colusa County Free Library, Colusa, CA [*Library symbol*]	CColu
Colville [*Washington*] [*Seismograph station code, US Geological Survey*] [*Closed*]	CLW
Colville River, AK [*Location identifier*] [*FAA*]	CVL
Colville, WA [*Radio station call letters*]	KCRK-FM
Colville, WA [*Radio station call letters*]	KCVL
Colwell Co. [*American Stock Exchange symbol*] [*Delisted*]	CLW
Colwell Mortgage Trust [*NYSE symbol*]	CLM
Com Vu Corp. [*NASDAQ symbol*]	CMVU
Comair, Inc. [*Cincinnati, OH*] [*FAA designator*]	COM
Comair, Inc. [*NASDAQ symbol*]	COMR
Comanche Oil Explorations [*NASDAQ symbol*]	COMO
Comanche, OK [*Radio station call letters*]	KHME
Comanche, TX [*Radio station call letters*]	KCOM
Comandacia General de Aeronautica [*Peru*]	CGA
Comando Geral do Ar [*Brazilian Air Force*]	COMGAR
Comarco, Inc. [*NASDAQ symbol*]	CMRO
Combat [*In unit designations and symbols only*]	C
Combat	CBT
Combat	CMBT
Combat	COMBT
Combat Activity Report [*Navy*]	COACT
Combat Air Crew	CAC
Combat Air Delivery Division [*Air Force*]	CADD
Combat Air Operations Center	CAOC
Combat Air Patrol	CAP
Combat Air Patrol Mission [*Air Force*]	CAPM
Combat Air Vehicle Navigation and Vision	CAVNAV
Combat Aircraft Recording and Data System	CARDS
Combat Aircraft Service Unit [*Navy*]	CASU
Combat Aircraft Technology	CAT
Combat Aircrew [*or Aircrewman*]	CA
Combat Aircrew Recovery Aircraft [*Later, ARRS, ARS*]	CARA
Combat Aircrew Training Unit [*Navy*]	CATU

Combat Airlift Support Unit [*Air Force*] ... CALSU
Combat Alert Aircrew [*Air Force*] ... CAAC
Combat Analysis Group [*Joint Chiefs of Staff*] ... CAG
Combat Applications Group ... CAG
Combat Aptitude Area ... CO
Combat Arms Enlistment Bonus [*Military*] ... CAEB
Combat Arms Group [*Army*] ... CAG
Combat Arms Regimental System [*Army*] ... CARS
Combat Artist Team ... CAT
Combat Assault ... CA
Combat Aviation Battalion ... CAB
Combat Aviation Group ... CAG
Combat Brigade Air Cavalry ... CBAC
Combat Cargo Command ... CCC
Combat Cargo Group ... CCG
Combat Cargo Mission [*Air Force*] ... CCM
Combat Cargo Officer [*Military*] ... CCO
Combat Center [*Military*] ... CC
Combat Center Director ... CCD
Combat Center Remoted [*Military*] ... CCR
Combat Clothing and Equipment Working Party [*NATO*] ... CCEWP
Combat Command [*Initialism may be followed by a number as, CC2, to indicate a specific, numbered command*] [*Army*] ... CC
Combat Command A ... CCA
Combat Command B ... CCB
Combat Command C ... CCC
Combat Command D ... CCD
Combat Command L ... CCL
Combat Command Reserve ... CCR
Combat Command V ... CCV
Combat Communications Equipment [*Military*] ... CCE
Combat Consumption Support from D-Day to P-Day [*Military*] ... DPSPT
Combat Control [*Army*] ... CC
Combat Control [*Army*] ... COMCON
Combat Control Elements [*Army*] ... CCE
Combat, Control, Support [*Army*] ... COMCONSUP
Combat Control Team ... CCT
Combat Correspondent ... CC
Combat Crew [*Air Force*] ... CCr
Combat Crew Replacement Center [*World War II*] ... CCRC
Combat Crew Training [*Air Force*] ... CCT
Combat Crew Training School [*Air Force*] ... CCTS
Combat Crew Training Wing [*Air Force*] ... CCTWg
Combat Data Information Center [*Army*] ... CDIC
Combat Defense Force ... CDF
Combat Development ... CD
Combat Development Branch ... CDB
Combat Development Command [*Terminated, 1973*] [*Army*] ... CDC
Combat Development Command Experimentation Center [*Terminated*] [*Army*] ... CDCEC
Combat Development Command Infantry Agency [*Terminated*] [*Army*] ... CDCIA
Combat Development Command - Intelligence Agency [*Terminated*] [*Army*] ... CDC-INTA
Combat Development Command Maintenance Agency [*Terminated*] [*Army*] ... CDCMA
Combat Development Command Transportation Agency [*Terminated*] [*Army*] ... CDCTA
Combat Development Objective Guide [*CDC*] ... CDOG
Combat Development Office ... CDO
Combat Development Project [*Army*] ... CDP
Combat Development Technical Evaluation Center ... CDTEC
Combat Development Test Center ... CDTC
Combat Development Test Center - Vietnam ... CDTC-V
Combat Developments Experimentation Command [*Army*] ... CDEC
Combat Developments and Material Evaluation [*Program*] [*Army*] ... CD & ME
Combat Direction Center ... CDC
Combat Direction Systems ... CDS
Combat Documentation ... COMDOC
Combat Effectiveness Report ... CER
Combat Electronic Warfare Intelligence ... CEWI
Combat Elevation Launch ... CEL
Combat Emplacement Excavator ... CEE
Combat Engineer Tractor [*British*] ... CET
Combat Engineer Vehicle [*Army*] ... CEV
Combat Essential Items List [*Army*] ... CEIL
Combat Fitness Badge [*Army*] ... CFB
Combat Group ... CG
Combat Gunnery Officers School [*Army Air Forces*] ... CGOS
Combat Identification System ... CIS
Combat Ineffective [*Military*] ... CI
Combat Infantryman's Badge ... CIB
Combat Information Center [*Navy*] ... CIC
Combat Information Center Office [*or Officer*] [*Navy*] ... CICO
Combat Information Center Watch Officer [*Navy*] ... CICWO
Combat Information and Detection ... CID
Combat Intelligence ... CBTI
Combat Intelligence Center ... CIC
Combat Intelligence Officer [*Navy*] ... CIO
Combat Intelligence Plot ... CIP
Combat Intercept Control ... CIC
Combat Interviews ... CI
Combat Launch and Recovery Kit ... CLARK
Combat Lessons Bulletin ... CLB
Combat and Liaison ... CL
Combat Logistic Support System ... CLSS
Combat Logistics Network [*DoD*] ... COMLOGNET
Combat Loss ... C/L
Combat Loss and Expenditure Data ... COLED
Combat Loss and Expenditure Data - Vietnam ... COLED-V
Combat Maneuver Battalion [*Army*] ... CMB
Combat Maneuver Battalion [*Army*] ... COMANBAT
Combat Material ... CM
Combat Medical Badge ... CMB
Combat Mission Failure ... CMF
Combat Mission Folder ... CMF
Combat Operational Reserve Group ... CORG
Combat Operational Support Aircraft ... COSA
Combat Operations Center [*Air Force*] ... COC
Combat Operations Report ... COR
Combat Operations Specialist Course [*Air Force*] ... COSC
Combat Optimization and Analysis Program [*Air Force*] ... COAP
Combat-Oriented General Support [*Army*] ... COGS
Combat Outpost ... COP
Combat Outpost Line ... COPL
Combat Potential Display [*SAGE*] [*Air Force*] ... CPD
Combat Radius Capability [*Military*] ... COMRAC
Combat Rated Thrust [*Navy*] ... CRT
Combat Reaction ... CR
Combat Reaction Time ... CRT
Combat Readiness Air Wing ... CRAW
Combat Readiness Assessment Exercise [*Obsolete*] [*Navy*] ... CRAE
Combat Readiness Categories [*Navy*] ... CRCAT
Combat Readiness by Electronic Service Testing [*Army*] ... CREST
Combat Readiness Evaluation [*Army*] ... CRE
Combat Readiness Evaluation Criteria [*Navy*] ... CREC
Combat Readiness Medal ... CRM
Combat Readiness Rating System [*Air Force*] ... CRRS
Combat Readiness Trainer [*or Training*] ... CRT
Combat Ready ... CR
Combat Ready Rate ... CRR
Combat Reconnaissance Platoon ... CRP
Combat Reporting Center ... CRC
Combat Reporting Post ... CRP
Combat Reporting System [*Air Force*] ... CREST
Combat Reserve [*Military*] ... CR
Combat Resource Allocation Model ... CRAM
Combat Search and Rescue [*Aviation*] ... CSAR
Combat Search and Rescue [*Aviation*] ... CSR
Combat-Service to the Army ... CO-STAR
Combat Service Group [*Army*] ... CSG
Combat Service Support [*DoD*] ... CSS
Combat Service Support Area [*Army*] ... CSSA
Combat Service Support Group [*Army*] ... CSSG
Combat Service Support System [*Army*] ... CS3
Combat Service Support System [*Army*] ... CSSS
Combat Store Ship [*Navy symbol*] ... AFS
Combat Studies Institute [*Command and General Staff College, Fort Leavenworth*] [*Army*] ... CSI
Combat Support ... CS
Combat to Support Balance Study ... CSBS
Combat Support Company [*Army*] ... CSC
Combat Support Coordination Center ... CSCC
Combat Support Force ... CSF
Combat Support Group [*Army*] ... CSG
Combat Support Group [*Air Force*] ... CSGp
Combat Support Hospital ... CSH
Combat Support Liaison ... CSL
Combat Support Training [*Military*] ... CST
Combat Support Units [*Army*] ... COMSUP
Combat Support Units [*Army*] ... CSU
Combat Surveillance Agency [*Signal Corps*] ... CSA
Combat Surveillance Laboratory ... CSL
Combat Surveillance Night Vision and Target Acquisition Laboratories [*Army*] ... CSNVTAL
Combat Surveillance RADAR ... CSR
Combat Surveillance and Target Acquisition [*Army*] ... CSTA
Combat Surveillance and Target Acquisition Equipment [*Army*] ... CS & TAE
Combat Surveillance and Target Acquisition Laboratory [*Army*] ... CSTAL
Combat Surveillance and Target Acquisition Training Command [*Army*] ... CSTATC
Combat System Alignment Document ... CSAD
Combat System Alignment Test ... CSAT
Combat System Engineering Authorization ... CSEA
Combat System Engineering Development Site ... CSEDS
Combat System Interface Test Tool ... CSITT
Combat System Tactical Operation Manual [*Navy*] ... CSTOM
Combat System Training Unit ... CSTU
Combat Systems Certification Site [*Navy*] ... CONCERTS
Combat Systems Operability Test ... CSOT

Combat Systems Readiness Review [Navy].................CSRR
Combat Systems Readiness Test ....CSRT
Combat Systems Training...............................CST
Combat Team...CT
Combat Theater Communications Program [Air Force].......CTCP
Combat Tracking Team..................................CTT
Combat Training Launch................................CTL
Combat Training Launch Instrumentation [Minuteman] ....CTLI
Combat Training Unit..................................CTU
Combat Unit Training Center [Army]....................CUTC
Combat Using Price Incentives Doctrine ....CUPID
Combat Vehicle [Army]...................................CV
Combat Vehicle [Army].................................CVEH
Combat Vehicle Reconnaissance Tracked [British]......CVR(T)
Combat Vehicle Simulator..............................CVS
Combat Vehicle Weapons System.......................CVWS
Combat Vehicle Weapons System (Long Range) ....CVWS(LR)
Combat Water Survival Test [Army] ....CWST
Combat Wing Command Post...........................CWCP
Combat Zone..CZ
Combed Yarn Spinners Association [Later, American Yarn
    Spinners Association].............................CYSA
Combinatio Nova [New Combination] [Biology, taxonomy].............comb nov
Combination [or Combine] ....COMB
Combination Companies [Insurance] CC
Combination Die.......................................CNDI
Combination Drug..CD
Combination Export Management [Small Business Administration].......CEM
Combination of Forward Combustion and Waterflooding
    [Commercial oil production process] ....COFCAW
Combination Inventory [LIMRA]............................CI
Combination Network [Graph theory]....................CNW
Combination [Type] Oral Contraceptive.................COC
Combination Publication Authority ....CPA
Combined...CMBD
Combined Acceptance Trials............................CAT
Combined Accident Reduction Effort...................CARE
Combined Account Number File [IRS]...................CANF
Combined Acquisition and Tracking RADAR [NASA] ....CATRADAR
Combined Action Company [Formerly, Joint Action Company]
    [Military]...CAC
Combined Action Group [Senior command of all Combined
    Action Companies] [Military]........................CAG
Combined Action Platoon ....CAP
Combined Active/Passive Emitter Rangings ....CAPER
Combined Activities System [Vietnam] [Air Force] ....CAS
Combined Additional Coverage [Insurance] ....CAC
Combined Administrative Committee.....................CADC
Combined Administrative Liquidating Agency [Microfilmed
    SHAEF documents for each participating country after
    SHAEF was disbanded] [Post-World War II]..........CALA
Combined Agencies Field Team [US Military Government,
    Germany]..CAFT
Combined Agency for Middle East Supplies [World War II]..............CAMES
Combined Agricultural and Food Machinery Committee [World
    War II]...CAFMC
Combined Air Documents Research Center ....CADRC
Combined Air Force Operating Base....................CAFOB
Combined Air Transport Operations Room [Allied office, World
    War II]...CATOR
Combined Airborne Surveillance and Control for Aerospace
    Defense...CASCADE
Combined Aircraft Submarine Exercise ....CASEX
Combined Allied Air Forces.............................CAAF
Combined Allied Land Forces...........................CALF
Combined Allied Naval Forces..........................CANF
Combined Allied Naval Forces, Southwest Pacific Area...........CANFSWPA
Combined Allied Naval Forces, Southwest Pacific Ocean Area
    Operating Plan.............................CANFSWPAOPPLAN
Combined Allowance for Logistics and Maintenance Support
    System [Coast Guard]..............................CALMS
Combined Altitude RADAR Altimeter [Electronic defense system]......CARA
Combined Amphibious Task Force........................CATF
Combined Amplitude Phase Shift Keying................CAPSK
Combined Analog-Digital Systems Simulator [Data processing].......CADSS
Combined Annual Wage Reporting [IRS].................CAWR
Combined Approach Control/International Station [Aviation] ....CAP/IS
Combined Arms...CA
Combined Arms Army.....................................CAA
Combined Arms Center...................................CAC
Combined Arms Combat Development Activity [Army].................CACDA
Combined Arms Group [Army]..............................CAG
Combined Arms Live Fire Exercises....................CALFEX
Combined Arms Research Office.........................CARO
Combined Arms and Services Staff School [Army]........CAS3
Combined Arms Simulation Model........................CASM
Combined Arms and Support [Army]......................CAAS
Combined Arms and Support Research Office.............CASRO
Combined Arms Tactical Training Simulator [Army].......CATTS
Combined Arms Training [Military]...................CMBARMTNG
Combined Arms Training Center [Army]..................CATC

Combined Arms Training Developments Activity [Army] ....CATRADA
Combined Army Air Transport Organization [World War II].............CAATO
Combined Black Publishers [Defunct]...................CBP
Combined Bomber Offensive [World War II] ....CBO
Combined Book Exhibit..................................CBE
Combined Cadet Force [British equivalent of US ROTC].........CCF
Combined Case Control [IRS]............................CCC
Combined Center/RAPCON [RADAR Approach Control]
    [Aviation]...CERAP
Combined Center/Tower [Aviation]......................CC/T
Combined Chiefs of Staff...............................CCOS
Combined Chiefs of Staff [DoD].........................CCS
Combined Cipher Machine...............................CCM
Combined Civil Affairs Committee [World War II] ....CCAC
Combined Civil Affairs Committee, London Subcommittee
    [World War II].....................................CCAC/L
Combined Civil Affairs Committee, Supply Subcommittee
    [World War II].....................................CCAC/S
Combined Civil Affairs Liquidating Agency [World War II].............CCALA
Combined Coding Machine...............................CCM
Combined Command for Reconnaissance Activities in Korea........CCRAK
Combined Committee on Air Training in North America.........CCATNA
Combined Committee for North Africa [World War II].......CCNA
Combined Communications Board [World War II]..........CCB
Combined Communications Board Publications............CCBP
Combined Communications Corp. [NYSE symbol].........CCA
Combined Contaminants, Oxygen, and Humidity.........CCOH
Combined Coordinating Committee CCC
Combined Cos. [NASDAQ symbol].......................COMB
Combined Defense Improvement Projects ....CDIP
Combined Development Agency [Anglo-American uranium
    procurement]......................................CDA
Combined Diesel and Gas [Turbine].....................CODAG
Combined Displaced Persons Executive [World War II].......CDPX
Combined Distribution Frame [RADAR]...................CDF
Combined Distribution Function........................CDF
Combined Economic Warfare Agencies..................CEWA
Combined Effects Bomb.................................CEB
Combined Effects Munition.............................CEM
Combined Effects Submissile...........................CES
Combined Electrolysis and Catalytic Exchange [CANDU-reactor
    advantage]...CECE
Combined Environmental Reliability Testing [Air Force] ....CERT
Combined Environmental, Vibration, Acceleration,
    Temperature [Aerospace]...........................CEVAT
Combined Exercise [Military]..........................COMBEX
Combined Exports Market Committee [World War II].......CEMC
Combined Federal Campaign [Federal government].........CFC
Combined Field Maintenance Shop [Army] ....CFMS
Combined File Search [Data processing]................CFS
Combined File Search Strategy [Data processing] ....CFSS
Combined Filter and Plot...............................CFP
Combined Food Board [United States, United Kingdom, and
    Canada] [World War II].............................CFB
Combined-Heat-and-Power Station [Energy production]......CHP
Combined Helmholtz Integral Equation Formulation......CHIEF
Combined Immunodeficiency Disease [Immunology].......CID
Combined In-Port Tactical Exercise [Navy].............CINTEX
Combined Instrument Panel.............................CIP
Combined Intelligence Center, Iraq [World War II].......CICI
Combined Intelligence Center, Vietnam.................CICV
Combined Intelligence Committee [World War II] CIC
Combined Intelligence Objectives Subcommittee [World War II].........CIOS
Combined Intelligence Priorities Committee [Later, CIU] [US
    and British] [London, World War II].................CIPC
Combined Intelligence Staff [World War II].............CIS
Combined Intelligence Unit [Formerly, CIPC] [RAF] [British] ....CIU
Combined International Corp. [NYSE symbol]............PMA
Combined International Corp. Conv Pfd [NASDAQ symbol].........PMAPP
Combined Jewish Philanthropies........................CJP
Combined LASER Instrumentation Package ....CLIP
Combined Lease Plan...................................CLP
Combined Liberated Areas Committee [World War II]......CLAC
Combined Liberated Areas Committee, Supply Subcommittee
    [World War II].....................................CLAC(S)
Combined Limit [Insurance]............................C/L
Combined Line and Recording Trunk...................CLR
Combined Loads Orbiter Tests.........................CLOTS
Combined Map and Electronic Display ....COMED
Combined Master File [Data processing]................CMF
Combined Meteorological Committee....................CMC
Combined Military Exploitation Center.................CMEC
Combined Military Interrogation Center................CMIC
Combined Military Transportation [British].............CMT
Combined Military Transportation Committee............CMTC
Combined Miniature Deterrent Forces [Organization in film
    "Fantastic Voyage"].................................CMDF
Combined Munitions Assignments Board [World War II]......CMAB
Combined Name and Address File [IRS]................CNAF
Combined National Veterans Association of America ....CNVAA
Combined Office Material Procurement and Distribution............COMPAD

Combined Officer of Merchant Navy Operations [*British*] .... COMNO
Combined Oil and Tanker Group .... COT
Combined Operational Intelligence Center [*Navy*] .... COIC
Combined Operational Planning Committee [*Royal Air Force and US 8th Air Force*] [*World War II*] .... COPC
Combined Operational Service Command .... COSC
Combined Operations .... CO
Combined Operations Command [*British*] .... COC
Combined Operations Experimental Wing [*World War II*] .... COEW
Combined Operations Headquarters [*World War II*] .... COHQ
Combined Operations Material Liaison Officer .... COMLO
Combined Operations Personnel [*Navy*] [*British*] .... COP
Combined Operations Pilotage Party .... COPP
Combined Operations Repair Organization [*For invasion of France*] [*World War II*] .... COREP
Combined Operations Scout Unit .... COSU
Combined Operations Signal Maintenance Depot .... COSMD
Combined Operations Signal Maintenance Officer .... COSMO
Combined Operations Signal Officer .... COSO
Combined Operations Supply Depot .... COSD
Combined Operations Tug Organization [*For invasion of France*] [*World War II*] .... COTUG
Combined Optical [*Photography*] .... COMOPT
Combined Orbital Maneuvering and Abort System [*NASA*] .... COMAS
Combined Over-the-Beach Terminal Unit .... COBTU
Combined Overload Repair Control .... COREP
Combined Passive Active Detection [*RADAR*] .... COMPACT
Combined Personnel Recovery Center .... CPRC
Combined Photographic Interpretation Center .... CPIC
Combined Planning Staff [*Military*] [*British*] .... CPS
Combined Policy Committee [*NATO*] .... CPC
Combined Principles Simulator [*Nuclear engine*] .... CPS
Combined Procurement Processing Series .... CPPS
Combined Production and Resources Board [*World War II*] .... CPRB
Combined Programing Language [*Data processing*] .... CPL
Combined Quarantine Force [*US/Venezuela/Dominican Republic/Argentina*] .... COMBQUARFOR
Combined Radiation Test .... CRT
Combined Raw Materials Board [*US and Britain*] [*World War II*] .... CRMB
Combined Receiving and Transmitting Unit .... CRTU
Combined Reentry Effort in Small Systems .... CRESS
Combined Reference Frequency System .... CRFS
Combined Registered Publication Memoranda .... CRPM
Combined Removal Interval [*Engine*] .... CMRI
Combined Resources Allocation Board [*World War II*] .... CRAB
Combined Retrospective Index Sets [*Carrollton Press, Inc.*] [*Information service*] .... CRIS
Combined Rocket Warhead .... CROW
Combined Rotating Unit [*Nuclear energy*] .... CRU
Combined Rubber Committee .... CRC
Combined S-Band .... CSB
Combined Sensor Tracking Exercise [*Military*] .... COMSENEX
Combined Service Territory [*Red Cross*] .... CST
Combined Services Detailed Interrogation Center [*World War II*] .... CSDIC
Combined Services Detailed Interrogation Center - Nonoperational Intelligence [*World War II*] .... CSDICNOI
Combined Services Support Program [*Navy*] .... CSSP
Combined Setter Clubs of America .... CSCA
Combined Shaft Unit .... CSU
Combined Shipbuilding Committee [*World War II*] .... CSC
Combined Shipping Adjustment Board [*World War II*] .... CSAB
Combined Signal Board [*North Africa*] [*World War II*] .... CSB
Combined Single Limit [*Insurance*] .... CSL
Combined Special Forces Operational Detachment .... CSFOD
Combined Staff Planners .... CSP
Combined Station/Center [*Aviation*] .... CS/C
Combined Station/Tower [*Aviation*] .... CS/T
Combined Steam and Gas .... COSAG
Combined Strategic Targets Committee [*World War II*] .... CSTC
Combined Stratospheric Measuring Program [*Army*] .... COSMEP
Combined Studies Group [*Central Intelligence Agency operation in Southeast Asia*] .... CSG
Combined System Test Stand .... CSTS
Combined Systems Acceptance Test .... CSAT
Combined Systems Test .... CST
Combined Systems Test Unit .... CSTU
Combined Target Area .... CTA
Combined Task Force .... CTF
Combined Task Group .... CTG
Combined Test Team .... CTT
Combined Training Center .... CTC
Combined Transportation Equipment Committee [*Combined Production and Resources Board*] [*World War II*] .... CTEC
Combined Travel Board [*Allied German Occupation Forces*] .... CTB
Combined Travel Security Board [*Allied German Occupation Forces*] .... CTSB
Combined Trials [*Shipbuilding*] .... CT
Combined Unconventional Warfare Task Force .... CUWTF
Combined VHF [*Very-High-Frequency*]**-Band** .... CVB
Combined Wage Claim [*Unemployment insurance*] .... CWC
Combined Welfare Administration Fund .... CWAF
Combined Wheat Control Section [*Allied German Occupation Forces*] .... CWCS
Combining Power .... CP
Combs Airways, Inc. [*Billings, MT*] [*FAA designator*] .... CMB
Combustibili per Reattori Nucleari [*A nuclear power company*] [*Italy*] .... COREN
Combustible .... COMBL
Combustible Metals [*Fire classification*] .... D
Combustible Storage Building .... CSB
Combustion .... COMB
Combustion .... COMBN
Combustion Chamber CC
Combustion Engineering [*Navy*] .... CE
Combustion Engineering [*A publication*] .... Comb Eng
Combustion Engineering, Inc. [*NYSE symbol*] .... CSP
Combustion Engineering Nuclear Division [*AEC*] .... CEND
Combustion Equipment Associates, Inc. [*NYSE symbol*] [*Delisted*] .... CE
Combustion, Explosion, and Shock Waves [*USSR*] [*A publication*] .... Combust Explos Shock Waves
Combustion, Explosion, and Shock Waves (USSR) [*A publication*] .... Comb Expl R
Combustion and Explosives Research .... C & ER
Combustion and Flame [*A publication*] .... Comb Flame
Combustion and Flame [*A publication*] .... Combust Flame
Combustion Institute CI
Combustion Research Facility [*Department of Energy*] .... CRF
Combustion Science and Technology [*A publication*] .... Comb Sci T
Combustion Science and Technology [*A publication*] .... Combust Sci Technol
Combustion Science and Technology. Book Series [*A publication*] .... Combust Sci Technol Book Ser
Combustion Stability Monitor .... CSM
Combustor .... CMBSTR
Comcast Corp. Class A [*NASDAQ symbol*] .... CMCSA
Comcoa, Inc. [*NASDAQ symbol*] .... CCOA
Comdata Network [*NASDAQ symbol*] .... CASH
Comdial Corp. [*NASDAQ symbol*] .... CMDL
Comdisco, Inc. [*NYSE symbol*] .... CDO
Come from Away [*Term used by Newfoundlanders to denote visitors or non-native residents of their province*] .... CFA
Come, Let Us Reason Together [*Labor mediators' slogan*] .... CLURT
Come Off Your Old Tired Ethics [*Prostitutes' lobbying group*] .... COYOTE
Come Quick - Danger [*International distress signal, used before SOS*] .... CQD
Come Sopra [*As Above*] [*Music*] .... CO SO
Come Sopra [*As Above*] [*Music*] .... CS
Come-Up .... C/U
Come-Up Time [*Time required for a retort to reach operating conditions*] .... CUT
Comedian Society for Amateurs and Professionals [*Defunct*] .... CSAP
Comedy .... COM
[*The*] **Comedy of Errors** [*Shakespearean work*] .... C of E
[*The*] **Comedy of Errors** [*Shakespearean work*] .... Err
Comedy Store [*Nightclub in which inexperienced comedians appear free in return for exposure to an audience*] .... CS
Comenius-Blaetter fuer Volkserziehung [*A publication*] .... CBV
Comenius World Council .... CWC
Comercio Exterior de Mexico [*A publication*] .... Com Ext Mexico
Comerica, Inc. [*NASDAQ symbol*] .... CMCA
Comet and Asteroid Rendezvous Docking .... CARD
Comet Rendezvous Mission .... CRM
Comet Stories [*A publication*] .... COM
Cometary Feasibility Study Group [*European Space Research Organization*] .... CFSG
Cometary-Mass-to-Planets [*Astronomy*] .... CMTP
Comfort Index CI
Comgen Technology [*NASDAQ symbol*] .... COMG
Comhaltas Ceoltoiri Eireann [*An organization promoting traditional Irish music*] .... CCE
Comhuriyet Halk Partisi [*Turkey*] .... CHP
Comic .... COM
Comic Crusader [*A publication*] CC
Comics Amateur Press Alliance .... CAPA
Comics Code Authority [*Regulatory body for comic book and comic magazine publishing industry*] .... CCA
Comics Magazine Association of America .... CMAA
Cominco Ltd. [*American Stock Exchange symbol*] .... CLT
Cominco Ltd., Toronto, ON, Canada [*Library symbol*] .... CaOTCom
Cominco Ltd., Vancouver, BC, Canada [*Library symbol*] .... CaBVaCOM
COMINT Receiver Test System .... CRTS
Comision Asesora Regional de Pesca el Atlantico Sud-Occidental [*Southwest Atlantic Fishery Commission*] .... CARPAS
Comision Ejecutiva Permanente del Consejo Interamericano Economico y Social [*Permanent Executive Committee of the Inter-American Economic and Social Council*] .... CEPCIES
Comision Especial de Coordinacion Latinoamericana .... CECLA
Comision de Estudios de Historia de la Iglesia en Latinoamerica .... CEHILA
Comision Femenil Mexicana Nacional .... CFM
Comision Ibero-Americano de Navigacion Aerea [*Spain*] .... CIANA
Comision Interamericana del Atun Tropical [*Interamerican Tropical Tuna Commission*] .... CIAT

Comision Interamericana del Atun Tropical. Boletin [*A publication*].................................. Com Interam Atun Trop Bol

Comision Interamericana de Mujeres [*Inter-American Commission of Women*]..CIM

Comision de Inversiones y Desarrollo Economico [*Uruguay*] .... CIDE

Comision de Investigaciones Cientificas de la Provincia de Buenos Aires. Informes [*A publication*].
Com Invest Cient Prov Buenos Aires Inf

Comision Nacional de Energia Atomica [*National Commission for Atomic Energy*] [*Mexico, Argentina*]........................CNEA

Comision Nacional de Energia Nuclear [*National Commission for Nuclear Energy*] [*Mexico*]......................CNEN

Comision Nacional del Espacio Exterior [*National Commission for Outer Space*] [*Mexico*]........................CNEE

Comision Nacional de Investigacion Cientifica y Tecnologica [*Chile*]..CONICYT

Comision Nacional de Investigacion del Espacio [*Spanish space commission*]..CONIE

Comision Nacional de Investigaciones Espaciales [*Argentina*] .... CNIE

Comision Panamericana de Normas Tecnicas [*Pan American Standards Commission*] [*See also PASC*]........................COPANT

Comissao Nacional de Atividades Espaciais [*Later, INPE*] [*Brazil*].......CNAE

Comission Internationale de l'Organisation Scientifique du Travail [*International Committee of Work Study and Labour Management in Agriculture*]........................IOSTA

Comitan [*Mexico*] [*Seismograph station code, US Geological Survey*]....COM

Comitato Elettrotechnico Italiano..CEI

Comitato Glaciologico Italiano. Bollettino. Serie Seconda [*A publication*]................................ Com Glaciol Ital Boll Ser 2

Comitato di Liberazione Nazionale per l'Alta Italia........................CLNAI

Comitato Nazionale per l'Energia Nucleare [*National Nuclear Energy Committee*] [*Italy*]........................CNEN

Comitato Nazionale per l'Energia Nucleare. Notiziario [*A publication*]................................ Com Naz Energ Nucl Not

Comitato Nazionale per l'Energia Nucleare. Reprints [*A publication*]................................ Com Naz Energ Nucl Repr

Comitato Nazionale per le Ricerche Nucleari [*Later, CNEN*] [*Italy*]...... CNRN

Comite d'Action pour la Defense de la Legalite [*Committee for Legal Defense*] [*Dahomey*] ....CADEL

Comite d'Action en France..COMDAC

Comite d'Action Lyceen [*France*]..CAL

Comite d'Action Musulman [*Mauritian political party*] .... CAM

Comite d'Action Politique et Sociale pour l'Independance de Madagascar [*Political and Social Committee for Malagasy Independence*]..CAPISM

Comite d'Action de l'Union Nationale des Cabindais [*Action Committee for the National Association of the People of Cabinda*] ....CAUNC

Comite Administratif de Coordination [*des Nations Unies*] [*Aviation*] ....CAC

Comite d'Aide au Developpement [*OCDE*]........................CAD

Comite des Applications Militaires de l'Energie Atomique [*France*]..CAMEA

Comite Arctique International ....CAI

Comite Asesor sobre Investigaciones de Recursos Marinos [*Advisory Committee on Marine Resources Research*] [*FAO*] ....CAIRM

Comite Catholique International de Coordination Aupres de l'UNESCO..CCIC

Comite Central Permanent de l'Opium .... CCPO

Comite Central de la Propriete Forestiere de la CEE [*Central Committee on Forest Property for the EEC*]........................CCPF

Comite du Commerce des Cereales et des Aliments du Betail de la Communaute Economique Europeenne [*Committee of the Cereals and Animal Feed Trade of the European Economic Community*] ....COCERAL

Comite Commun pour la Promotion de l'Aide aux Cooperatives [*Joint Committee for the Promotion of Aid to Cooperatives*] [*UN Food and Agriculture Organization*] ....COPAC

Comite de Compradores de Material Aeronautico de America Latina..CCMA

Comite des Constructeurs Europeens de Materiel Alimentaire [*Committee of European Manufacturers of Plant for the Food Industry*] [*Common Market*]........................COCEMA

Comite des Constructeurs de Materiel Frigorifique de la CEE [*Committee of Manufacturers of Refrigeration Equipment of the EEC*]..COMAF

Comite Consultatif International du Coton [*International Cotton Advisory Committee*]........................CCIC

Comite Consultatif International des Radiocommunications [*International Radio Consultative Committee*] ....CCIR

Comite Consultatif International Telephonique des Frequences [*International Telephone Consultative Committee*] ....CCIF

Comite Consultatif de la Recherche sur les Resources de la Mer [*Advisory Committee on Marine Resources Research*] [*FAO*] ...... CCRRM

Comite de Cooperacion Economica del Istmo Centroamericano [*Central American Economic Cooperation Committee*]........................CCE

Comite de Coordination de l'Assistance Technique [*ONU*]................CCAT

Comite de Coordination Camerounaise [*Committee for Cameroonese Coordination*]........................COCOCAM

Comite de Coordination des Experts Budgetaires Gouvernementaux [*Coordinating Committee of Government Budget Experts*] [*NATO*]........................CCG

Comite de Coordination des Plans Civils d'Urgence [*Civil Emergency Coordinating Committee*] [*NATO*]........................CCPC

Comite de Coordination des Plans de Transport [*Coordinating Committee for Transport Planning*] [*NATO*]........................CCPT

Comite de Coordination des Telecommunications [*Coordinating Committee for Communications*] [*NATO*]........................CCT

Comite des Demenageurs du Marche Commun .... CODEMAC

Comite Economique et Social [*Economic and Social Committee*] [*of CEE*]..CES

Comite Electrotechnique Belge..CEB

Comite d'Entente et d'Action Politique [*Committee for Understanding and Political Action*]........................CEAP

Comite d'Etude des Producteurs de Charbon d'Europe Occidentale [*West European Coal Producers' Association*] ....CEPCEO

Comite d'Etudes des Consequences des Vols Stratospheriques .....COVOS

Comite d'Etudes Economiques de l'Industrie du Gaz [*Economic Research Committee of the Gas Industry*]........... COMETEC-GAZ

Comite d'Etudes Regionales Economiques et Sociales........................CERES

Comite Europeen des Assurances [*European Insurance Committee*] ..... CEA

Comite Europeen du Beton [*European Committee for Concrete*] .... CEB

Comite Europeen de la Chaudronnerie et de la Tolerie [*European Committee for Boilermaking and Kindred Steel Structures*]..CECT

Comite Europeen du Commerce des Produits Amylaces et Derives [*European Center for Trade in Starch Products and Derivatives*] [*Common Market*]........................CECPA

Comite Europeen de Controle Laitierbeurrier ....CECLB

Comite Europeen de Coordination des Normes [*European Committee for Coordination of Standards*]........................CEN

Comite Europeen de Coordination des Normes Electriques [*European Electrical Standards Coordinating Committee*]........................CENEL

Comite Europeen de la Culture du Houblon [*European Hop Growers Committee*]........................CECH

Comite Europeen d'Etudes de Zoologie Agricole........................CEZA

Comite Europeen des Fabricants d'Appareils de Chauffage et de Cuisine Domestiques [*European Committee of Manufacturers of Domestic Heating and Cooking Appliances*] ... CEFACD

Comite Europeen des Fabricants de Sucre [*European Committee of Sugar Manufacturers*] [*Common Market*] .... CEFS

Comite Europeen des Groupements de Constructeurs du Machinisme Agricole [*European Committee of Associations of Manufacturers of Agricultural Machinery*] [*Common Market*] .... CEMA

Comite Europeen de Liaison des Commerces Agro-Alimentaires [*European Liaison Committee for Agricultural and Food Trades*] [*Common Market*]........................CELCAA

Comite Europeen de Liaison des Industries de la Machine a Coudre [*European Liaison Committee for the Sewing Machine Industries*]..CELIMAC

Comite Europeen de Liaison des Negociants et Utilisateurs de Combustibles [*European Liaison Committee of Fuel Merchants and Users*]........................ CELNUCO

Comite Europeen de Normalisation [*European Committee for Standardization*].. CEN

Comite Europeen Permanent de Recherches sur la Protection des Populations contre les Risques de Toxicite a Long Terme [*Permanent European Research Committee for the Protection of the Population against the Hazards of Chronic Toxicity*] ...... EUROTOX

Comite Europeen pour les Problemes Criminels [*Conseil de l'Europe*] ....CEPC

Comite Europeen pour le Progres Economique et Social [*European Committee for Economic and Social Progress*]............CEPES

Comite Europeen pour les Relations Economiques .... CERE

Comite Europeen des Syndicats de l'Alimentation, du Tabac, et de l'Industrie Hoteliere [*European Trade Union Committee of Food and Allied Workers*] [*Common Market*]........................CESA

Comite des Fabricants de Levure de Panification de la CEE [*Committee of Bread Yeast Manufacturers of the EEC*]............COFALEC

Comite de Familiares de Presos Politicos Uruguayos [*Relatives' Committee for Uruguayan Political Prisoners*]........................CFPPU

Comite Flamand de France. Annales [*A publication*]........................ CFFAn

Comite Francais Liberation Nationale ....CFLN

Comite General de la Cooperation Agricole des Pays de la CEE [*General Committee for Agricultural Cooperation of the EEC*] ... COGECA

Comite des Industries des Mayonnaises et Sauces Condimentaires de la CEE [*Committee of the Industries of Mayonnaises and Table Sauces of the European Economic Community*]..CIMSCEE

Comite des Industries de la Moutarde de la CEE [*EEC Committee for the Mustard Industries*] ....CIMCEE

Comite d'Information et de Defense de l'Union Nationale des Artisans et Travailleurs Independents........................CIDUNATI

Comite d'Initiative pour le Congres du Peuple Europeen ....CICPE

Comite Interallie des Officiers Medecins de Reserve [*Interallied Committee of Medical Reserve Officers*]........................CIOMR

Comite Interamericano de la Alianza para el Progreso [*Inter-American Committee of the Alliance for Progress*]........................CIAP

Comite Interamericano de Desarrollo Agricola [*Inter-American Committee for Agricultural Development*]........................CIDA

Comite Interamericano Permanente Antiacridiana........................CIPA

Comite Interamericano de Proteccion Agricola [*Interamerican Committee for Crop Protection*]........................CIPA

Comite Intergouvernemental du Droit d'Auteur [*See also IGC*] .... CIDA
Comite Intergouvernemental pour les Migrations Europeennes [*Intergovernmental Committee for European Migration*] .... CIME
Comite International d'Aide aux Intellectuels .... CIAI
Comite International des Associations Techniques de Fonderie [*International Committee of Foundry Technical Associations*] .... CIATF
Comite International d'Auschwitz [*International Auschwitz Committee*] .... CIA
Comite International Catholique des Infirmieres et Assistantes Medico-Sociales [*International Committee of Catholic Nurses*] [*See also ICCN*] .... CICIAMS
Comite International de la Conserve CIC
Comite International pour le Controle de la Productivite Laitiere du Betail [*International Committee for Recording the Productivity of Milk Animals - ICRPMA*] .... CICPLB
Comite International de Coordination pour l'Initiation a la Science et le Developpement des Activites Scientifiques Extra-Scolaires [*International Coordinating Committee for the Presentation of Science and the Development of Out-of-School Scientific Activities*] [*See also ICC*] CIC
Comite International de la Croix-Rouge [*International Committee of the Red Cross*] .... CICR
Comite International de la Croix-Rouge [*International Committee of the Red Cross*] [*ICAO designator*] .... RX
Comite International de la Culture du Houblon [*International Hop Growers Convention*] .... CICH
Comite International de Dachau .... CID
Comite International des Derives Tensio-Actifs [*International Committee of Tensio-Active Derivatives*] .... CID
Comite International pour la Diffusion des Arts et des Lettres par le Cinema [*International Committee for the Diffusion of Arts and Literature through Cinema*] .... CIDALC
Comite International des Echanges pres la Chambre de Commerce Internationale .... CIE
Comite International d'Enregistrement des Frequences [*International Frequency Registration Board*] .... CIEF
Comite International des Entreprises a Succursales [*International Association of Chain Stores*] .... CIES
Comite International d'Esthetique et de Cosmetologie [*International Committee for Esthetics and Cosmetology*] .... CIDESCO
Comite International pour l'Etude des Bauxites de l'Alumine et d'Aluminium. Travaux [*A publication*] .... Com Int Etude Bauxites Alumine Alum Trav
Comite International pour l'Etude des Bauxites, des Oxydes, et des Hydroxydes d'Aluminium. Travaux [*A publication*] .... Com Int Etude Bauxites Oxydes Hydroxydes Alum Trav
Comite International pour les Etudes Myceniennes [*Standing International Committee for Mycenaean Studies*] .... CIPEM
Comite International pour le Fair Play [*International Fair Play Committee*] .... CIFP
Comite International des Federations Theatrales d'Amateurs de Langue Francaise .... CIFTA
Comite International du Film Ethnographique .... CIFE
Comite International de Geophysique [*International Geophysical Committee*] .... CIG
Comite International d'Histoire de l'Art [*International Committee on the History of Art*] .... CIHA
Comite International pour l'Information et Documentation des Sciences Sociales [*International Committee for Social Sciences Documentation*] .... CIDSS
Comite International de l'Inspection Technique Automobile [*International Motor Vehicle Inspection Committee*] .... CITA
Comite International de Liaison des Gynecologues et Obstetriciens .... CILOPGO
Comite International de Liaison pour la Navigation de Plaisance [*Pleasure Navigation International Joint Committee - PNIC*] .... CINP
Comite International de Medecine et de Pharmacie Militaires [*International Committee of Military Medicine and Pharmacy*] .... CIMPM
Comite International des Mouvements d'Enfants et d'Adolescents [*International Committee of Children's and Adolescents' Movements*] .... CIMEA
Comite International Olympique [*International Olympic Committee*] .... CIO
Comite International de l'Organisation Scientifique [*International Committee for Scientific Management*] .... CIOS
Comite International Permanent de la Conserve [*International Permanent Committee on Canned Foods*] .... CIPC
Comite International Permanent des Linguistes [*Permanent International Committee of Linguists*] .... CIPL
Comite International des Pharmaciens Homeopathiques [*International Committee of Homeopathic Pharmacists*] .... CIPH
Comite International de Photobiologie [*International Committee of Photobiology*] .... CIP
Comite International des Plastiques en Agriculture [*International Committee of Plastics in Agriculture*] .... CIPA
Comite International des Poids et Mesures [*International Committee on Weights and Measures*] .... CIPM
Comite International Radio Maritime [*International Maritime Radio Committee*] .... CIRM
Comite International Radioaeronautique .... CIRA
Comite International de la Rayonne et des Fibres Synthetiques [*International Rayon and Synthetic Fibres Committee*] .... CIRFS
Comite International de Recherche et d'Etude de Facteurs de l'Ambiance [*International Committee for Research and Study on Environmental Factors*] .... CIFA
Comite International des Sciences Historiques [*International Committee of Historical Sciences*] .... CISH
Comite International des Sciences Onomastiques [*International Committee of Onomastic Sciences*] .... CISO
Comite International de Solidarite avec la Jeunesse Algerienne .... CISJA
Comite International de Soutien aux Antifascistes Iberiques .... CISAI
Comite International Special des Perturbations Radioelectriques [*International Special Committee on Radio Interference*] .... CISPR
Comite International des Sports Silencieux [*International Committee of the Silent Sports*] [*Later, Comite International des Sports des Sourds*] .... CISS
Comite International des Sports des Sourds [*International Committee of Sports for the Deaf*] [*Formerly, Comite International des Sports Silencieux*] .... CISS
Comite International de Standardisation en Biologie Humaine [*International Committee for Standardization in Human Biology*] .... CISBH
Comite International Technique d'Experts Juridiques Aeriens [*International Technical Committee of Aerial Legal Experts*] .... CITEJA
Comite International de la Teinture et du Nettoyage [*International Committee for Dyeing and Dry Cleaning*] .... CITEN
Comite International des Telecommunications de Presse [*International Press Telecommunications - IPTC*] .... CIPT
Comite International de Television [*International Television Committee*] .... CIT
Comite International de Thermodynamique et de Cinetique Electro-Chimiques [*International Committee of Electro-Chemical Thermodynamics and Kinetics*] .... CITCE
Comite International des Transports par Chemins de Fer [*International Rail Transport Committee*] .... CIT
Comite International Tzigane [*International Gypsy Committee*] .... CIT
Comite Juridique International de l'Aviation .... CJIA
Comite Latinoamericano de Textos Teologicos .... CLATT
Comite de Liaison de l'Agrumiculture Mediterraneenne [*Liaison Committee for Mediterranean Citrus Fruit Culture*] [*See also LCMCFC*] .... CLAM
Comite de Liaison de la Construction de Carrosseries et de Remorques [*Liaison Committee of Coachwork and Trailer Builders*] .... CLCCR
Comite de Liaison de la Construction d'Equipements et de Pieces d'Automobile [*Liaison Committee of Manufacturers of Motor Vehicle Parts and Equipment*] .... CLEPA
Comite de Liaison des Etudiants Revolutionnaires [*French student group*] .... CLER
Comite de Liaison des Industries Metalliques Europeennes .... COLIME
Comite de Liaison International des Broderies, Rideaux, et Dentelles [*International Liaison Committee for Embroideries, Curtains, and Laces*] .... CELIBRIDE
Comite Maritime International [*International Maritime Committee*] .... CMI
Comite Meteorologique International .... CMI
Comite de Mexico y Aztlan .... COMEXAZ
Comite National pour la Liberation de la Cote d'Ivoire [*National Committee for the Liberation of the Ivory Coast*] .... CNLCI
Comite pour l'Organisation et le Developpement des Investissements Intellectuels en Afrique et a Madagascar .... CODIA
Comite des Organisations de la Boucherie-Charcuterie de la CEE [*Committee of Butchery and Cooked Meats Organizations of the EEC*] .... COBCCEE
Comite des Organisations Commerciales des Pays de la CEE [*Committee of Commercial Organizations in the EEC Countries*] .... COCCEE
Comite des Organisations Familiales aupres des Communautes Europeennes [*Committee of Family Organizations in the European Communities*] [*Common Market*] .... COFACE
Comite des Organisations Professionnelles Agricoles de la CEE [*Committee of Professional Agricultural Organizations in the EEC*] .... COPA
Comite Permanent des Congres Internationaux pour l'Apostolat des Laics .... COPECIAL
Comite Permanent des Congres Internationaux de Zoologie .... CPCIZ
Comite Permanent International des Techniques et de l'Urbanisme Souterrains [*Permanent and International Committee of Underground Town Planning and Construction*] .... CPITUS
Comite Permanent International d'Urbanisme Souterrain .... CPIUS
Comite Permanent International du Vinaigre [*Permanent International Committee on Vinegar*] [*Common Market*] .... CPIV
Comite Permanent des Secretaires Generaux [*Standing Committee of Secretaries General*] [*NATO*] .... CSG
Comite de Politique Economique [*OCDE*] .... CPE
Comite Regional d'Afrique Centrale pour la Conservation et l'Utilisation du Sol .... CRACCUS
Comite Regional Ouest-Africain pour la Conservation et l'Utilisation du Sol .... CROACUS
Comite de Relevement du Peuple Bassa [*Committee for the Aid of the Bassa People*] .... CRPB
Comite pour la Reunification du Camaroon [*Committee for the Reunification of the Cameroons*] .... CORECA

Comite Revolucionario de Mocambique [*Mozambique*] ....COREMO
Comite de la Science et de la Technologie dans les Pays en Voie de Developpement [*Committee on Science and Technology in Developing Countries*] ....COSTED
Comite Scientifique pour l'Etude des Effets des Radiations Ionisantes ....CSEERI
Comite Scientifique International de Recherches sur les Trypanosomiases ....CSIRT
Comite Scientifique pour les Recherches Antarctiques [*Scientific Committee on Antarctic Research*] ....CSRA
Comite Scientifique pour les Recherches Oceaniques [*Scientific Committee on Oceanic Research*] ....CSRO
Comite des Semences du Marche Commun [*Seed Committee of the Common Market*] ....COSEMCO
Comite de Solidarite de Madagascar [*Madagascar Solidarity Committee*] ....COSOMA
Comite Special de l'Annee Geophysique Internationale [*Special Committee for the International Geophysical Year*] [*Superseded by CIG*] ....CSAGI
Comite Special du Katanga ....CSK
Comite Special du Programme Biologique International [*Special Committee for the International Biological Program*] ....CSPBI
Comite Sportif International du Travail [*International Workers Sport Committee*] ....CSIT
Comite Syndical International du Tourisme Social et des Loisirs [*International Trade Unions Committee of Social Tourism and Leisure - ITUCSTL*] ....CSITSL
Comite Technique International de Prevention et d'Extinction du Feu [*International Technical Committee for the Prevention and Extinction of Fire*] ....CTIF
Comite de Travail des Malteries de la CEE [*Working Committee of European Economic Community Malters*] ....EUROMALT
Comite des Travaux Historiques et Scientifiques. Bulletin Archeologique [*A publication*] ....CTHBAr
Comite des Travaux Historiques et Scientifiques. Bulletin Archeologique [*A publication*] ....CTHBull
Comite des Travaux Historiques et Scientifiques. Bulletin Historique et Philologique [*A publication*] ....CTHBullH
Comite d'Union Nationale des Cabindais [*Cabindan Committee of National Union*] ....CUNC
Comite de l'Unite Togolaise [*Committee for Togolese Unity*] [*Defunct*] ....CUT
Comite pour l'Utilisation des Resultats de l'Annee Geophysique Internationale [*IGY completion committee*] ....CURAGI
Comma ....CMA
Comma ....CMM
Commack Public Library, Commack, NY [*Library symbol*] ....NCo
Command ....CD
Command ....CM
Command ....CMD
Command ....CMND
Command ....COM
Command ....COMD
Command Accountant [*Military*] [*British*] ....CA
Command Accounting and Finance Office ....CAFO
Command Acknowledge ....CAK
Command Acquisition Unit ....CAU
Command Action ....CA
Command Action Plan ....CAP
Command Activation Unit ....CAU
Command Active Sonobuoy System [*Navy*] ....CASS
Command and Administration ....C & A
Command and Administration System [*Army*] ....COADS
Command Advisory Board ....CAB
Command Aerospace Maintenance Manpower Information System ....CAMMIS
Command Airways, Inc. [*Wappingers Falls, NY*] [*FAA designator*] ....CMD
Command Airways, Inc. [*NASDAQ symbol*] ....COMD
Command Analysis Center ....CAC
Command Analysis Pattern ....CAP
Command Arithmetic Unit ....CAU
Command Assessment Review ....CAR
Command Augmentation System ....CAS
Command Authorization List ....CAL
Command Automated Budget System [*Army*] ....CABS
Command Automated Procurement System ....CAPS
Command Automatic Card Tester ....CACT
Command Budget Estimates [*Military*] ....CBE
Command Center CC
Command Center Processing and Display System [*Military*] ....CCPDS
Command Chaplain [*AFSC*] ....HC
Command Classified Control Register ....CCCR
Command Code [*IRS*] CC
Command Communications Boat ....CCB
Command Communications Service Designator ....CCSD
Command and Communications System [*NASA*] ....CCS
Command Comply Current Instructions ....PLYINST
Command Computer ....CD
Command Computer Console ....CMDCC
Command Computer Input Multiplexer ....CCIM
Command Conference [*Viking lander mission*] [*NASA*] CC

Command Confirmation ....CCN
Command Confirmation Buffer ....COMB
Command and Control [*Pronounced "see-squared"*] ....C^2
Command and Control ....CAC
Command and Control ....C & C
Command and Control Alert/Conferencing Network ....CCACN
Command Control Block [*Data processing*] ....CCB
Command and Control Boat [*Navy symbol*] ....CCB
Command and Control Center [*Air Force*] CCC
Command, Control, and Communications [*Pronounced "see-cubed"*] ....C^3
Command, Control, and Communications [*Air Force*] ....CC & C
Command, Control, Communications, and Computer Systems ....C^4
Command, Control, Communications, Computing/Information and Intelligence ....C^4I^2
Command Control and Communications Program [*Air Force*] ....CC & CP
Command, Control, and Communications System ....CCCS
Command Control Console CCC
Command and Control Defense Systems Office ....CCDSO
Command Control/Destruct ....CC/D
Command Control Destruct System ....CCDS
Command and Control Development Division [*Air Force*] ....CCDD
Command Control Dial Panel ....CCDP
Command and Control Director [*Air Force*] ....CCD
Command and Control Division [*SHAPE Technical Center*] ....CCD
Command Control Equipment ....CCE
Command Control Information System ....CCIS
Command Control Interactive Display Experimentation System [*Army*] ....CCIDES
Command Control Interface [*Army*] CCI
Command Control and Monitor System [*NASA*] ....CCMS
Command Control Number [*Air Force*] ....CCN
Command Control Operations Center [*Army*] ....CCOC
Command Control Order ....CCO
Command Control Panel ....CCP
Command Control Post ....CCP
Command Control Receiver ....CCR
Command Control Room ....CCR
Command, Control, Support [*Army*] ....CCS
Command and Control System ....C & CS
Command and Control Technical Center [*DoD*] ....CCTC
Command and Control Technical Center WWMCCS [*Worldwide Military Command and Control System*] ADP [*Automatic Data Processing*] Directorate [*DoD*] ....CCTC-WAD
Command and Control Test Facility ....CCTF
Command and Control Voice Communications System [*Defense Supply Agency*] ....CCVCS
Command and Data Acquisition ....CDA
Command and Data Acquisition Station [*Aerospace*] ....CDAS
Command Data Buffer [*Air Force*] ....CDB
Command Data Format Control Handbook [*NASA*] ....CDFCHB
Command and Data Handling ....CDH
Command and Data-Handling Console ....CDC
Command and Data-Handling Console ....CDHC
Command Data Management Routine [*Data processing*] ....CDMR
Command Data Management System ....CDMS
Command, Data Processing, and Instrumentation [*NASA*] ....CDPI
Command, Data Processing, and Instrumentation System [*NASA*] ....CDPIS
Command Data Processing Interface Equipment ....CDPIE
Command Data Processor ....CDP
Command and Data Simulator ....CADS
Command and Data Simulator ....C & DS
Command Decision and Movement Control Charts ....COMDEC
Command and Decision Sensor Interface Data System ....CDSIDS
Command Decoder ....CD
Command Decoder Coaxial ....CDC
Command Decoder Filter ....CDF
Command Dental Service Report [*Air Force*] ....COMD DSR
Command Descriptor Table ....CDT
Command Destruct ....C/D
Command Destruct Control ....CDC
Command Destruct Decoder ....CDD
Command-Destruct Epoxy [*A plastic resin*] ....CDE
Command Destruct Receiver ....CDR
Command Destruct System ....CDS
Command Destruct Transmitter ....CDT
Command Destruct Unit ....CDU
Command Disable System [*Air Force*] ....CDS
Command Display and Control Processor ....CDCP
Command Display Indicator ....CDI
Command Display Unit ....CDU
Command Distribution Rack ....CDR
Command Duty Officer [*Navy*] ....CDO
Command and Edit Program [*Data processing*] ....CANDE
Command Education Officer [*Military*] [*British*] ....CEO
Command Entertainments Officer [*Military*] [*British*] ....CEO
Command Equipment Management Office [*Military*] ....CEMO
Command Equipment Management Team [*Military*] ....CEMT
Command and Expenditure Report ....CER
Command and General Staff [*Military*] ....C & GS
Command and General Staff College [*Military*] ....C & GSC
Command and General Staff College [*Military*] ....CGSC

Command and General Staff School [Military]....................C & GSS
Command Generation Program [Mariner] [NASA]....................COMGEN
Command Guidance [Aerospace]....................CG
Command Guidance Computer....................CGC
Command Guidance Test Vehicle....................CGTV
Command Guided Tactical Missile....................CGTM
Command Indicator Performance Review....................CIPR
Command Information Bureau [Military]....................CIB
Command Information Center [Military]....................CIC
Command Information Program [Military]....................CIP
Command Information Systems [Army]....................CIS
Command Input Block [Data processing]....................CIB
Command Input Buffer [Data processing]....................CIB
Command Input Coupler....................CIC
Command Inspection [Military]....................CMDINSP
Command Interface Control....................CIC
Command Interface Test....................CIT
Command Interface Unit....................CIU
Command Issuing Office [or Officer]....................CIO
Command Language for Interrogating Computers....................CLIC
Command Language Processor....................CLP
Command and Launch Subsystem....................CLS
Command to Line of Sight [Military] [British]....................CLOS
Command Load Acceptance Message....................CLAM
Command Load Controller....................CLC
Command Logic Unit....................CLU
Command Maintenance [Military]....................COMAINT
Command Maintenance Inspection [Army]....................CMI
Command Maintenance Management Inspection [Army]....................CMMI
Command Maintenance Readiness Inspection [Army]....................CMRI
Command Management Center [Military]....................CMC
Command Management Control List....................CMCL
Command Management Information System [Air Force]....................CMIS
Command Management Information System [Air Force]....................COMIS
Command Management Inventory Accounting [Army]....................CMIA
Command and Management Presentation [Marine Corps]....................CAMP
Command Management Review and Analysis [Army]....................CAMERA
Command Manpower Data System....................CMDS
Command Message....................CMDMSG
Command Model for Analysis and Design....................COMMAND
Command Modulator Assembly [NASA]....................CMA
Command Module [NASA]....................CM
Command Module Computer [NASA]....................CMC
Command Module Electrical Power System [NASA]....................CEPS
Command Module Multiple Docking Assembly [NASA]....................CMMDA
Command Module Pilot [Apollo] [NASA]....................CMP
Command Module Procedures Simulator [NASA]....................CMPS
Command Module - Service Module [Combined] [NASA]....................CM-SM
Command Module Simulator [NASA]....................CMS
Command Not Operationally Ready [Navy]....................CNOR
Command Objective Plan [Air Force]....................COP
Command Observation Post....................COP
Command Off the Line of Sight [Military] [British]....................COLOS
Command Operating Budget [Army]....................COB
Command Operating Program [Army]....................COP
Command Operating Program/Budget [DoD]....................COP/B
Command Operationally Ready [Navy]....................COR
Command Operations [Army]....................CO
Command Operations Center [Military]....................COC
Command Operations Priority Requirements List [Air Force]....................COPRL
Command Orders....................CO
Command Paper....................C
Command Patrol Plane Replacement Squadrons Pacific....................COMPATPLANEREPRONSPAC
Command Personnel Management Inspections....................CPMI
Command Personnel Summary....................CPS
Command Pilot....................CP
Command Post [Military]....................CP
Command Post Alerting Network [Military]....................COPAN
Command Post Digital Display [SAGE] [Air Force]....................CPDD
Command Post Exercise [Military]....................CPEx
Command Post Exercise [Military]....................CPX
Command Post Officer [Military]....................CPO
Command Post Record Capability [Military]....................COPREC
Command Pouch [Air Force]....................CP
Command Processor [Data processing]....................CP
Command Processor Distributor Control....................CPDC
Command Processor Module....................CPM
Command Pulse....................CP
Command Pulse Output....................CPO
Command Radio Link....................CORAL
Command Read Pulse....................CRP
Command Receiver....................C/R
Command Receiver Equipment....................CRE
Command Receiver Monitor....................CRM
Command Register....................CR
Command Relationship Agreements [Army]....................CRA
Command Relay Driver Unit....................CRDU
Command Reporting Center....................CRC
Command Representative....................CR
Command Retrieval Information System....................CRIS

Command Retrieval System....................CRS
Command Scheduling Control Block [Data processing]....................CSCB
Command Selector....................CS
Command Selector Control....................CSC
Command Sergeant Major....................COMDSGTMAJ
Command Sergeant Major [Army]....................CSM
Command Sergeant Major....................E9
Command Service Module [NASA]....................CSM
Command Ship [Navy symbol]....................CC
Command Ship Data System [Navy]....................CSDS
Command Signal Decoder....................CSD
Command Signal Generator....................CSG
Command Signal Limiter....................CSL
Command Software Subsystem [Space Flight Operations Facility, NASA]....................CMDSW
Command and Staff....................C & S
Command and Staff College [Air Force]....................CSC
Command Subsystem Group....................CSG
Command Supply Discipline Program [Army]....................CSDP
Command Support Control Console....................CSCC
Command Surgeon [AFSC]....................SG
Command Surveillance and Weather....................CSW
Command System....................CS
Command System Operations Analysis Group Area [Space Flight Operations Facility, NASA]....................CAG
Command Systems Support Activity....................COSSACT
Command Tactical [Navy]....................COMTAC
Command Technical Inspection [Army]....................CTI
Command Telemetry Buoy....................CTB
Command and Telemetry Data Handling....................CTDH
Command and Telemetry System....................CTS
Command Translator and Programer....................CTP
Command Transmitter....................C/T
Command and Triangulation....................CAT
Command Uplink [NASA]....................CUL
Command Uplink Request [NASA]....................CUR
Command Vehicle....................CV
Command Verification [NASA]....................CV
Command Verification....................CVR
Command Verification/Drop....................CVR/D
Command Verify/Transmit....................CVT
Command Voltage Regulator....................CVR
Command Word [Data processing]....................CW
Commandable Audio Engine Detector....................CAEDET
Commandant [Coast Guard]....................C
Commandant [Military]....................COM
Commandant [Air Force]....................COMDT
Commandant....................COMMDT
Commandant....................COMT
Commandant Assistant [Coast Guard]....................CA
Commandant, Civil Affairs Branch [British] [World War II]....................CCAB
Commandant of the Coast Guard....................CCG
Commandant, Eleventh Naval District....................COMELEVEN
Commandant, Fifth Naval District....................COMFIVE
Commandant, First Naval District....................COMONE
Commandant of the Marine Corps....................CMC
Commandant of the Marine Corps....................COMDTMARCORPS
Commandant of the Marine Corps Memorandum....................CMCM
Commandant, Marine Corps Schools [Quantico, VA]....................CMCS
Commandant, Naval Base, San Diego....................COMNAVBASEDIEGO
Commandant, Naval District, Washington, DC....................COMNAVDIST WASHDC
Commandant, Naval District, Washington, DC....................COMNDW
Commandant, Naval Operating Base....................COMDTNOB
Commandant, Navy Yard....................COMDTNY
Commandant, Ninth Naval District....................COMNINE
Commandant Nucleus Department [Military] [British]....................CND
Commandant, Third Naval District....................COMTHREE
Commandant, Thirteenth Naval District....................COMTHIRTEEN
Commandant, Twelfth Naval District....................COMTWELVE
Commandant, United States Coast Guard....................COMDTUSCG
Commandant, United States Marine Corps....................COMDTUSMC
Commandant's Instruction....................COMDTINST
Commandant's Training Strategy [Military]....................CTS
Commandement Aerien des Forces de Defense Aerienne [Air Defense Forces Air Command]....................CAFDA
Commandement Allie des Approches de la Baltique [Baltic Approaches Allied Command] [NATO]....................CAAB
Commandement des Transports Aeriens Militaires Francais [France] [ICAO designator]....................FM
Commander [Usually in combination, as: CNAB for Commander, Naval Air Bases]....................C
Commander....................CDR
Commander....................CMDR
Commander....................COM
Commander....................COMDR
Commander....................COMM
Commander....................COMMDR
Commander [Navy] [British]....................Cr
Commander, Aegean Defense Sector....................COMAEGEANBASE
Commander Air Center....................CAC
Commander, Air Defense Command....................COMADC

Commander, Air Force, Atlantic Fleet ....COMAIRLANT
Commander, Air Force Forces .... COMAFFOR
Commander, Air Force, Pacific Fleet ....COMAIRPAC
Commander, Air Forces [Navy] .... COMAIR
Commander, Air Forces, Solomons ....COMAIRSOLS
Commander, Air Forces, South Pacific Force ....COMAIRSOPAC
Commander, Air Group [Navy] .... CAG
Commander, Air Transport ....COMAIRTRANS
Commander, Air Transport Squadron.................. COMAIRTRANSRON
Commander, Aircraft Support Control Unit [Navy].......................CASCU
Commander, Airship Group ....COMAIRSHIPGR
Commander, Alameda Group ....COMALAMGRU
Commander, Alaskan Sea Frontier......................COMALSEAFRON
Commander, Alaskan Sector .... COMALSEC
Commander, All Forces, Aruba-Curacao ....CAFAC
Commander, Allied Air Forces, Baltic Approaches ...........COMAIRBALTAP
Commander, Allied Air Forces, Central Europe ....COMAIRCENT
Commander, Allied Air Forces, North Norway ....COMAIRNON
Commander, Allied Air Forces, Northern Europe ....COMAIRNORTH
Commander, Allied Air Forces, Northern Europe ..........COMALAIRNOREUR
Commander, Allied Air Forces, South Norway ....COMAIRSONOR
Commander, Allied Air Forces, Southern Europe ....COMAIRSOUTH
Commander, Allied Forces, North Norway................................COMNON
Commander, Allied Land Forces, Central Europe ....COMLANDCENT
Commander, Allied Land Forces, Denmark ................COMLANDENMARK
Commander, Allied Land Forces, Denmark ....COMLANDMARK
Commander, Allied Land Forces, Norway................COMLANDNORWAY
Commander, Allied Land Forces, Schleswig-Holstein ....
COMLANDSCHLESWIG
Commander, Allied Land Forces, Schleswig-Holstein and
Jutland...COMLANDJUT
Commander, Allied Land Forces, Southeastern Europe.........................
COMLANDSOUTHEAST
Commander, Allied Land Forces, Southern Europe ........COMLANDSOUTH
Commander, Allied Land Forces, Zealand ..................COMLANDZEALAND
Commander, Allied Maritime Air Force Channel [NATO]....COMMAIRCHAN
Commander, Allied Naval Forces, Baltic Approaches.......COMNAVBALTAP
Commander, Allied Naval Forces, Central Europe ....COMNAVCENT
Commander, Allied Naval Forces, North Norway....................COMNAVNON
Commander, Allied Naval Forces, Northern Europe.... COMALNAVNOREUR
Commander, Allied Naval Forces, Northern Europe ....COMNAVNORTH
Commander, Allied Naval Forces, Scandinavian Approaches ....
COMNAVSCAP
Commander, Allied Naval Forces, South Norway ....COMNAVSONOR
Commander, Allied Tactical Air Force, North Norway .......COMTAFNORNOR
Commander, Allied Tactical Air Force, South Norway ....COMTAFSONOR
Commander, Allied Tactical Air Forces, Southern Norway.........................
COMATAFSONOR
Commander, Allied Task Forces, North Norway ...........COMTASKFORNON
Commander, Amphibious Force.....................................COMPHIB
Commander, Amphibious Force .... COMPHIBFOR
Commander, Amphibious Force, Atlantic Fleet....................CAFAF
Commander, Amphibious Force, Atlantic Fleet....................COMPHIBLANT
Commander, Amphibious Force, Europe ....COMPHIBEU
Commander, Amphibious Force, Northwest African Waters.....................
COMPHIBNAW
Commander, Amphibious Force, Pacific Fleet ..............COMPHIBFORPAC
Commander, Amphibious Force, Pacific Fleet ....COMPHIBPAC
Commander, Amphibious Group...COMPHIBGRU
Commander Amphibious Ready Group [Navy] ....CARG
Commander, Amphibious Squadron ....COMPHIBRON
Commander, Amphibious Task Force ....CATF
Commander, Amphibious Task Force .... COMATF
Commander, Amphibious Training Command, Atlantic ....
COMPHIBTRALANT
Commander, Amphibious Training Command, Pacific.........................
COMPHIBTRAPAC
Commander, Amphibious Training Command, United States
Atlantic Fleet ....CATCUSAF
Commander, Amphibious Troops.....................................CAT
Commander, Antarctic Support Activities........ COMANTARCTICSUPPACT
Commander, Antilles Defense Command ........................COMANTDEFCOM
Commander, Antisubmarine Warfare Force....................COMASWFOR
Commander, Antisubmarine Warfare Forces, Atlantic ....
COMASWFORLANT
Commander, Antisubmarine Warfare Forces, Pacific ..... COMASWFORPAC
Commander, Antisubmarine Warfare Group ....COMASWGRU
Commander at Arms [Navy] [British] ....CrAA
Commander, Army Forces ....COMARFOR
Commander, Atlantic Approaches Gibraltar ....COMGIBLANT
Commander, Atlantic Fleet Bases, Antilles.................COMFLTBASTILLES
Commander, Atlantic Fleet Weapons Range .... COMLANTFLTWPNRNGE
Commander, Attack Carrier Air Wing................COMATKCARAIRWING
Commander, Attack Carrier Striking Force .......COMATKCARSTRIKEFOR
Commander, Australian Army Forces, Vietnam ....COMAAFV
Commander, Australian Forces, Vietnam ....COMAFV
Commander, Barrier Forces, Atlantic ....................COMBARFORCLANT
Commander, Barrier Pacific ....COMBARPAC
Commander, Battleship Division .... COMBATDIV
Commander, Battleships, Atlantic Fleet ....COMBATLANT
Commander, Battleships-Cruisers, Atlantic Fleet......... COMBATCRULANT

Commander, Battleships, Pacific Fleet ....COMBATPAC
Commander, Bay of Biscay Atlantic Subarea [NATO]............ COMBISLANT
Commander, BENELUX Subarea Channel ....COMBENECHAN
Commander, Black Sea Defense Sector .........................COMBLACKBASE
Commander, Bombing Squadron ....COMBOMRON
Commander, Bosphorus Fortifications ....COMBOSFORT
Commander, Boston Group ....COMBSNGRU
Commander, Bremerhaven Naval Group ....COMNAVBREM
Commander, Bremerton Group ....COMBREMGRU
Commander, Brest Subarea Channel .........................COMBRESTCHAN
Commander of the [Order of the] British Empire ....CBE
Commander, British Forces, Caribbean Area ....CBFCA
Commander, British Naval Elbe Squadron.........................COMBRITELBE
Commander, British Naval Rhine Squadron ....COMBRITRHIN
Commander, British Naval Staff ....CBNS
Commander, Canadian Atlantic Subarea [NATO] .... COMCANLANT
Commander, Canadian Destroyers, Atlantic ................CANCOMDESLANT
Commander, Canadian Destroyers, Far East ....CANCOMDESFE
Commander, Canadian Destroyers, Pacific ................CANCOMDESPAC
Commander, Caribbean Sea Frontier....................................CCSF
Commander, Caribbean Sea Frontier....................... COMCARIBSEAFRON
Commander, Carrier Air Wing [Navy] ....COMCVW
Commander, Carrier Aircraft Service Unit...............................COMCASU
Commander, Carrier Antisubmarine Air Group........COMCARASWAIRGRU
Commander, Carrier Division ....COMCARDIV
Commander, Carrier Striking Force ...............................COMCARSTRIKFOR
Commander, Carrier Striking Group ...............................COMCARSTRIKGRU
Commander, Carrier Striking Group One ............COMCARSTRIKGRUONE
Commander, Carrier Striking Group Two ..........COMCARSTRIKGRUTWO
Commander, Carrier Training Squadron, Pacific Fleet............................
COMTRAINCARRONPAC
Commander, Central Army Group, Central Europe................COMCENTAG
Commander, Central Atlantic Subarea [NATO]................... COMCENTLANT
Commander, Central Mediterranean ....COMEDCENT
Commander, Central Pacific ....COMCENPAC
Commander, Central Region SEATO [Southeast Asia Treaty
Organization] Field Forces ....CCRSFF
Commander, Central Region SEATO Field Forces (Designate) ....
CCRSFF(D)
Commander, Charleston Group ....COMCHASNGRU
Commander, Cherbourg Subarea Channel.......................COMCHERCHAN
Commander-in-Chief...C-in-C
Commander-in-Chief [Air Force] CIC
Commander-in-Chief.. CINC
Commander-in-Chief [US fleet].............................. COMINCH
Commander-in-Chief, Aerospace Defense ....CINCAD
Commander-in-Chief, Air Force Atlantic Command................ CINCAFLANT
Commander-in-Chief, Air Force Strike Command.................CINCAFSTRIKE
Commander-in-Chief, Air Forces, Europe...............................CINCAFE
Commander-in-Chief, Alaskan Command............................ CINCAL
Commander-in-Chief, Allied Air Forces, Central Europe..........................
CINCALAIRCENEUR
Commander-in-Chief, Allied Forces....................................CINCAF
Commander-in-Chief, Allied Forces, Central Europe [NATO] ..... CINCCENT
Commander-in-Chief, Allied Forces, Mediterranean [NATO]... CINCAFMED
Commander-in-Chief, Allied Forces, Northern Europe [NATO].........................
CINCNORTH
Commander-in-Chief, Allied Forces, Southern Europe [NATO].........................
CINCSOUTH
Commander-in-Chief, America West Indies Station [British] .... CINCAWI
Commander-in-Chief, [US] Army Forces, Atlantic ....CINCARLANT
Commander-in-Chief, [US] Army Forces in the Pacific.............. CINCAFPAC
Commander-in-Chief, [US] Army Forces, Pacific ....CINCARPAC
Commander-in-Chief, Army Strike Command .....................CINCARSTRIKE
Commander-in-Chief, [US] Asiatic Fleet ....CINCAF
Commander-in-Chief, Atlantic..CINCLANT
Commander-in-Chief, Atlantic Fleet ....CINCLANTFLT
Commander-in-Chief, Atlantic and West Indies ....CINCA & WI
Commander-in-Chief, British Pacific Fleet ....CINCBPF
Commander-in-Chief, Canadian Northwest Atlantic [World War
II]... C in C CNA
Commander-in-Chief, Caribbean ....CINCARIB
Commander-in-Chief Channel and Southern North Sea ....CINCHAN
Commander-in-Chief, Continental Air Command.......................CINCAC
Commander-in-Chief, Continental Air Defense Command ...... CINCCONAD
Commander-in-Chief, Continental Air Defense Command ......CINCONAD
Commander-in-Chief, [US Fleet], Convoy and Routing Section ....
COMROUTE
Commander-in-Chief, East Indies Station [British] ....CINCEI
Commander-in-Chief, Eastern Atlantic Area [NATO].......... CINCEASTLANT
Commander-in-Chief, Europe...CINCEUR
Commander-in-Chief, Far East ....CINCFE
Commander-in-Chief, Far East Station [British] ....CINCFES
Commander-in-Chief, Far East Station [British] ....CINCFESTA
Commander-in-Chief, Home Forces [British]........................... C-in-CHF
Commander-in-Chief, Iberian Atlantic Area ...................CINCIBERLANT
Commander-in-Chief, Japan Area [World War II] ....CINCJAPA
Commander-in-Chief, Mediterranean ....CINCMED
Commander-in-Chief, Middle East Land Forces ....CINCMELF
Commander-in-Chief, Middle East/Southern Asia and Africa
South of the Sahara [Military]...............................CINCMEAFSA

Commander-in-Chief, Naval Forces, Eastern Atlantic and Mediterranean.................CINCNAVEASTLANTMED
Commander-in-Chief, Naval Forces, Eastern Atlantic and Mediterranean..................CINCNELM
Commander-in-Chief, Netherlands Forces in the East .... CINCNEDE
Commander-in-Chief, North American Air Defense................. CINCNORAD
Commander-in-Chief, [US] Northeast Command.....................CINCNE
Commander-in-Chief, Northern Europe...........................CINCNOREUR
Commander-in-Chief, Pacific ....CINCPAC
Commander-in-Chief, Pacific Air Forces ....CINCPACAF
Commander-in-Chief, Pacific Fleet ....CCPF
Commander-in-Chief, Pacific Fleet ....CINCPACFLT
Commander-in-Chief, [US] Pacific Fleet Headquarters, Pearl Harbor..................................CINCPACHEDPEARL
Commander-in-Chief, [US] Pacific Fleet and Pacific Ocean Areas.................................CINCPAC-CINCPOA
Commander-in-Chief, Pacific Ocean Areas ....CINCPOA
Commander-in-Chief, Pacific Ocean Areas Headquarters, Pearl Harbor.............................CINCPOAHEDPEARL
Commander-in-Chief, Pacific Representative ....CINCPACREP
Commander-in-Chief, Pacific Representative, Philippines .............................CINCPACREPPHIL
Commander-in-Chief, Pacific Staff Instruction .........CINCPACSTAFFINSTR
Commander-in-Chief, [US] Readiness Command.................CINCREDCOM
Commander-in-Chief, Royal Danish Air Force...................CINCRDAF
Commander-in-Chief, Royal Danish Navy......................CINCRDN
Commander-in-Chief, Royal Norwegian Air Force ....CINCRNAF
Commander-in-Chief, Royal Norwegian Navy ....CINCRNORN
Commander-in-Chief, South Atlantic Station [British]............CINCSA
Commander-in-Chief, [US] Southern Command.................CINCSO
Commander-in-Chief, Southwest Pacific Area [World War II] .... CINCSWPA
Commander-in-Chief, Specified Command, Middle East .............................CINCSPECOMME
Commander-in-Chief, Strategic Air Command...................CINCSAC
Commander-in-Chief, [US] Strike Command ....CINCSTRIKE
Commander-in-Chief, Tactical Air Command..................CINCTAC
Commander-in-Chief, United Kingdom Air Force ....CINCUKAIR
Commander-in-Chief, United Kingdom Home Fleet [Also, CINCHOMEFLT] .... CINCHF
Commander-in-Chief, United Kingdom Home Fleet [Also, CINCHF].................................CINCHOMEFLT
Commander-in-Chief, United Nations Command .... CINCUNC
Commander-in-Chief, United Nations Command, Korea .............................CINCUNCKOREA
Commander-in-Chief, United States Air Force, Atlantic..... CINCUSAFLANT
Commander-in-Chief, United States Air Force Strike......CINCUSAFSTRIKE
Commander-in-Chief, United States Air Forces in Europe........ CINCUSAFE
Commander-in-Chief, United States Army, Europe ....CINCUSAREUR
Commander in Chief, United States Army Forces, Naval Supply Center, Oakland [California] ..............CINCUSAFNSCO
Commander-in-Chief, United States Army, Pacific...........CINCUSARPAC
Commander-in-Chief, United States Fleet [Obsolete]...........CINCUS
Commander-in-Chief, United States Naval Forces, Europe .............................CINCUSNAVEUR
Commander-in-Chief, United States/Thai Forces.............CINCUSTAF
Commander-in-Chief, Vietnamese Navy ....CINCVNN
Commander-in-Chief, Western Approaches [British][World War II] .... C in C WA
Commander-in-Chief, Western Atlantic Area [NATO]........CINCWESTLANT
Commander-in-Chief, Western Pacific [World War II] ....CINCWESPAC
Commander, Coast Defenses ....CCD
Commander, Coast Guard District ....CCGD
Commander, Coast Guard District ....COMCOGARD
Commander, Columbia River Group ....COMCOLUMGRU
Commander, Combined Amphibious Task Force [Military] ....CCATF
Commander, Composite Squadron............................COMCOMRON
Commander Corps Medium Artillery [British].....................CCMA
Commander Corps Royal Artillery [British].......................CCRA
Commander, Cruiser-Destroyer Flotilla [Acronym always followed by a number] [Navy] .... COMCRUDESFLOT
Commander, Cruiser-Destroyer Force ....COMCRUDES
Commander, Cruiser-Destroyer Forces, Atlantic [Navy].............................COMCRUDESLANT
Commander, Cruiser-Destroyer Forces, Pacific [Navy] ... COMCRUDESPAC
Commander, Cruiser Division.................................COMCRUDIV
Commander, Cruiser Forces, Atlantic Fleet.....................COMCRULANT
Commander, Cruiser Forces, Pacific Fleet.....................COMCRUPAC
Commander, Cruiser Scouting Squadron......................COMCRUSCORON
Commander, Dardanelles Fortifications....................COMDARFORT
Commander, Destroyer Development Group [Navy] .......COMDESDEVGRU
Commander, Destroyer Development Group, Pacific [Navy]............CDDGP
Commander, Destroyer Division................................COMDESDIV
Commander, Destroyer Flotilla............................COMDESFLOT
Commander, Destroyer Group ....COMDESGRU
Commander, Destroyer Squadron..............................CDS
Commander, Destroyer Squadron ....COMDESRON
Commander, Destroyers ....COMDES
Commander, Destroyers, Atlantic Fleet....................COMDESLANT
Commander, Destroyers, Pacific Fleet.....................COMDESPAC
Commander, Disaster Control Element ....CDCE
Commander, Disaster Control Force...........................CDCF

Commander, Disaster Control Group.............................CDCG
Commander of the Dockyard at [place].......................COMYARD
Commander, Eastern Atlantic Forces ....COMEASTLANT
Commander, Eastern Mediterranean ....COMEDEAST
Commander, Eastern Sea Frontier [Navy] ....CESF
Commander, Eastern Sea Frontier [Navy] ....COMEASTFRON
Commander, Eastern Sea Frontier [Navy] ..................COMEASTSEAFRON
Commander, Emergency Recovery Force........................CERF
Commander, Emergency Recovery Group ....CERG
Commander, Emergency Recovery Section ....CERS
Commander, Emergency Recovery Unit ....CERU
Commander, Experimental Division [Navy]...................COMEXDIV
Commander of Federal Republic of Nigeria ....CFR
Commander, Field Command, Defense Atomic Support Agency .............................COMFLDCOMDASA
Commander, Fifth Allied Tactical Air Force....................COMFIVEATAF
Commander, Fighting Squadron ....COMFIGHTRON
Commander, First Canadian Destroyer Flotilla .... CANCOMDESFLOT 1
Commander, [US] First Fleet..................................COMFIRSTFLEET
Commander, [US] First Fleet.................................COMFIRSTFLT
Commander, Fleet Air ....COMFAIR
Commander, Fleet Air, Adak, Alaska ....COMFAIRADAK
Commander, Fleet Air, Alameda............................COMFAIRALAMEDA
Commander, Fleet Air, Bermuda ...........................COMFAIRBERMUDA
Commander, Fleet Air, Brunswick .......................COMFAIRBRUNSWICK
Commander, Fleet Air Defense ....CFAD
Commander, Fleet Air Detachment ....CFAD
Commander, Fleet Air, Eastern Atlantic and Mediterranean.............................COMFAIRELM
Commander, Fleet Air, Hawaii ............................COMFAIRHAWAII
Commander, Fleet Air, Jacksonville, Florida ....COMFAIRJAX
Commander, Fleet Air, Japan .... COMFAIRJAPAN
Commander, Fleet Air, Keflavik, Iceland .....................COMFAIRKEFLAVIK
Commander, Fleet Air, Mediterranean ....COMFAIRMED
Commander, Fleet Air, Norfolk, Virginia ...................COMFAIRNORFOLK
Commander, Fleet Air, Quonset Point, Rhode Island ....COMFAIRQUONSET
Commander, Fleet Air, San Diego, California .............COMFAIRSANDIEGO
Commander, Fleet Air, Southwest Pacific ...................COMFAIRSOWESTPAC
Commander, Fleet Air, Western Pacific .....................COMFAIRWESTPAC
Commander, Fleet Air Wing ....CFAW
Commander, Fleet Air Wing ....COMFAIRWING
Commander, Fleet Air Wing, Atlantic ....CFAWL
Commander, Fleet Air Wing, Atlantic .... COMFAIRWINGLANT
Commander, Fleet Air Wing, Northern Atlantic ... COMFAIRWINGNORLANT
Commander, Fleet Air Wing, Pacific ....CFAWP
Commander, Fleet Logistic Air Wing..........................COMFLOGWING
Commander, Fleet Operational Training Command ....COTC
Commander, Fleet Operational Training Command, Atlantic Fleet..................................COTCLANT
Commander, Fleet Operational Training Command, Pacific Fleet.................................. COTCPAC
Commander, Fleet Operational Training Command, Pacific Subordinate Command ..........................COTCPACSUBCOM
Commander, Fleet Train..COFT
Commander, Fleet Training Group .........................COMFLETRAGRU
Commander, Fleet Training Group and Underway Training Element..............................COMFLETRAGRUWATE
Commander, Florida Group...................................COMFLAGRU
Commander, Fourth Allied Tactical Air Force, Central Europe.............................COMFOURATAF
Commander, French Rhine River Squadron [NATO].............COMSURFRHIN
Commander, German Naval Forces, Baltic ...............COMNAVGERBALT
Commander, German North Sea Subarea ................COMGERNORSEA
Commander, Gibraltar [Navy] ....COMGIB
Commander, Gibraltar-Mediterranean Command ....COMGIBMED
Commander, Greenland Patrol ....COMGREPAT
Commander of the Guard [Military].............................. COG
Commander, Hawaiian Sea Frontier [Navy] ...............COMHAWSEAFRON
Commander, Headquarters Squadron ....COMHEDRON
Commander, Hunter-Killer Force, Atlantic Fleet .... COMHUKFORLAN
Commander, Iberian Atlantic Area ....COMIBERLANT
Commander, Iceland Antisubmarine Warfare Group .... COMICEASWGRU
Commander, Iceland Defense Force ....COMICEDEFOR
Commander-Instructor [Navy] [British] CI
Commander, Joint Expeditionary Force..........................COMJEF
Commander, Joint Task Force ....COMJTF
Commander, Joint Task Force ....COMJTF
Commander, Joint Task Group ....CJTG
Commander, Joint Unconventional Warfare Task Force..........COMJUWATF
Commander, Land Forces [Army]..............................COMLANDFOR
Commander, Land Forces, North Norway ....COMLANDNON
Commander, Landing Force [Navy]................................CLF
Commander, Light Attack Wing - Pacific Fleet ....COMLAWP
Commander, Long Beach Group ...........................COMLBEACHGRU
Commander, Mare Island Group ....COMAREGRU
Commander, Marianas ....COMMARIANAS
Commander, Marine Air Reserve Training ....COMART
Commander, Marine Forces..................................COMMARFOR
Commander, Maritime Air Central Subarea [NATO].............................COMMAIRCENTLANT

Commander, Maritime Air Eastern Atlantic Area [NATO]....................COMMAIREASTLANT
Commander, Maritime Air Gibraltar Subarea [NATO]....COMMAIRGIBLANT
Commander, Maritime Air Northeast Subarea Channel [NATO] ...................COMMAIRNORECHAN
Commander, Maritime Air Northern Subarea [NATO]...................COMMAIRNORLANT
Commander, Maritime Air Plymouth Subarea Channel [NATO]...................COMMAIRPLYMCHAN
Commander, Maritime Forces, Morocco............................COMOROCLANT
Commander, Maritime Rhine...................................COMARRHIN
Commander, Marshalls-Carolines Area.........................COMARCARAREA
Commander, Mediterranean Defense Sector....................COMEDBASE
Commander, Mediterranean Operations Center.................COMEDOC
Commander, Middle East Force.................................COMIDEASTFOR
Commander, Military Air Transport Service [Later, COMAC].........COMATS
Commander, Military Airlift Command [Formerly, COMATS]...........COMAC
Commander, Military Assistance Group, Republic of China, Vietnam.......................COMMAGROCV
Commander, Military Sea Transportation Service [Obsolete].........COMSTS
Commander, Military Sea Transportation Service, Atlantic Area.......................COMSTSLANTAREA
Commander, Military Sea Transportation Service, Eastern Atlantic and Mediterranean Area...................COMSTSELMAREA
Commander, Military Sea Transportation Service, Far East.......COMSTSFE
Commander, Military Sea Transportation Service, Gulf Subarea.......................COMSTSGULFSUBAREA
Commander, Military Sea Transportation Service, Management Information System...................COMSTS/MIS
Commander, Military Sea Transportation Service, Mid-Pacific Subarea...................COMSTSMIDPACSUBAREA
Commander, Military Sea Transportation Service, Northern Pacific Subarea...................COMSTSNORPACSUBAREA
Commander, Military Sea Transportation Service, Pacific Area.......................COMSTSPACAREA
Commander, Military Sea Transportation Service, Southeast Asia...................COMSTSSEA
Commander, Military Sea Transportation Service, West Pacific Area...................COMSTSWESTPACAREA
Commander, Military Sealift Command.........................COMMSC
Commander, Military Sealift Command.........................COMSC
Commander, Military Sealift Command, Atlantic...............COMSCLANT
Commander, Military Sealift Command, Eastern Atlantic and Mediterranean...................COMSCELM
Commander, Military Sealift Command, Far East...............COMSCFE
Commander, Military Sealift Command, Gulf Subarea..........COMSCGULF
Commander, Military Sealift Command, Mediterranean.........COMSCMED
Commander, Military Sealift Command, Pacific................COMSCPAC
Commander, Mine Flotilla.....................................COMINFLOT
Commander, Mine Force, Atlantic Fleet [Navy]...............COMINELANT
Commander, Mine Force, Atlantic Fleet [Navy]...............COMINLANT
Commander, Mine Force, Pacific Fleet [Navy]................COMINEPAC
Commander, Mine Group.......................................COMINGRP
Commander, Mine Group, Okinawa.............................COMINGRPOK
Commander, Mine Squadron....................................COMINRON
Commander, Minecraft [Navy].................................COMIN
Commander, Minecraft Division [Navy]........................COMINDIV
Commander, Minecraft, Pacific Fleet [Navy].................COMINPAC
Commander, Moroccan Sea Frontier Forces....................COMORSEAFRON
Commander, Motor Torpedo Boat Flotilla......................COMTBFLOT
Commander, Motor Torpedo Boat Squadron.....................COMTBRON
Commander, Motor Torpedo Boat Squadron Training Center.......................COMTBRONTRACENT
Commander, Naval Activities, Japan.........................COMNAVJAP
Commander, Naval Air Bases..................................CNAB
Commander, Naval Air Bases..................................COMNAB
Commander, Naval Air Force..................................COMNAVAIR
Commander, Naval Air Force, Atlantic........................CNAL
Commander, Naval Air Force, Atlantic Fleet..................COMNAVAIRLANT
Commander, Naval Air Force, Pacific Fleet...................COMNAVAIRPAC
Commander, Naval Air Technical Training (Lighter Than Air).......................CNATEC (LTA)
Commander, Naval Base.......................................CNB
Commander, Naval Base.......................................COMNAVBASE
Commander, Naval Base, Los Angeles..........................CNBLA
Commander, Naval Communications............................COMNAVCOMM
Commander, Naval Construction Battalions, Atlantic Fleet....COMCBLANT
Commander, Naval Construction Battalions, Pacific Fleet......COMCBPAC
Commander, Naval Defense Forces, Eastern Pacific.......................COMNAVDEFOREEASTPAC
Commander, [US] Naval Forces................................CNF
Commander, [US] Naval Forces................................COMNAVFOR
Commander, [US] Naval Forces, Azores........................COMNAVZOR
Commander, Naval Forces, Central Army Group Area and Bremerhaven.......................COMNAVCAG
Commander, [US] Naval Forces, Continental Air Defense Command.......................COMNAVFORCONAD
Commander, [US] Naval Forces, Eastern Atlantic and Mediterranean...................COMNAVEASTLANTMED
Commander, [US] Naval Forces, Europe........................COMNAVEU
Commander, [US] Naval Forces, Far East......................COMNAVFE

Commander, [US] Naval Forces, Germany.......................COMNAVFORGER
Commander, [US] Naval Forces, Germany.......................COMNAVGER
Commander, [US] Naval Forces, Iceland.......................COMNAVFORICE
Commander, [US] Naval Forces, Iceland.......................COMNAVICE
Commander, [US] Naval Forces, Japan.........................COMNAVFORJAPAN
Commander, [US] Naval Forces, Korea.........................COMNAVFORKOREA
Commander, Naval Forces, Marianas..........................COMNAVFMARIANAS
Commander, [US] Naval Forces, Marianas.....................COMNAVMARIANAS
Commander, [US] Naval Forces, Northwest African Waters.......................COMNAVNAW
Commander, [US] Naval Forces, Philippines..................COMNAVFORPHIL
Commander, Naval Forces, Southern Europe...................COMNAVSOUTH
Commander, [US] Naval Forces, Vietnam......................COMNAVFORV
Commander, Naval Inshore Warfare Command, Atlantic.......................COMNAVINSWARLANT
Commander, Naval Missile Center............................COMNMC
Commander, Naval Operating Base............................CNOB
Commander, Naval Reserves..................................CNAVRES
Commander, Naval Special Warfare Task Group................CNSWTG
Commander, Naval Support Activity..........................COMNAVSUPPACT
Commander, Naval Support Force.............................COMNAVSUPPFOR
Commander, Naval Support Force, Antarctic.......................COMNAVSUPPFORANTARCTIC
Commander, Naval Surface Forces, Atlantic..................COMNAVSURFLA
Commander, Naval Telecommunications Command.......COMNAVTELCOM
Commander, Navy Military Personnel Command.......................COMNAVMILPERSCOM
Commander, New London Group................................COMNEWLONGRU
Commander, New York Group..................................COMNYKGRU
Commander, New Zealand Army Forces, Far East...............COMNZAFFE
Commander, New Zealand Assistance Detachment, Vietnam.......................COMNEWZEDV
Commander, Norfolk Group...................................COMNORVAGRU
Commander, North American Antisubmarine Defense Force, Atlantic [NATO]...................COMNORASDEFLANT
Commander, North American Defense Force, Atlantic [NATO].......................COMNADEFLANT
Commander, North Pacific Force.............................COMNORPAC
Commander, North Sea Subarea, Central Europe..........COMNORSEACENT
Commander, Northeast Atlantic..............................COMNEATLANT
Commander, Northeast Mediterranean.........................COMEDNOREAST
Commander, Northeast Subarea Channel.......................COMNORECHAN
Commander, Northern Area Forces, Central Europe....COMNAVNORCENT
Commander, Northern Army Group, Central Europe...........COMNORTHAG
Commander, Northern Atlantic Subarea [NATO]................COMNORLANT
Commander, Northern Group..................................CNG
Commander of a Numbered Group..............................COMGRU
Commander, Ocean Atlantic Subarea [NATO]..................COMOCEANLANT
Commander, Ocean Subarea...................................COMOCEANSUBAREA
Commander, Oceanographic Surveillance Systems, Atlantic.......................COMOCEANSYSLANT
Commander, Oceanographic Surveillance Systems, Pacific.......................COMOCEANSYSPAC
Commander, Operational Control Center......................COMOPCONCEN
Commander, Operational Development Force [Navy].........COMOPDEVFOR
Commander, Operational Test and Evaluation Force [Navy].......................COMOPTEVFOR
Commander, Orange, Texas, Group; Inactive Reserve Fleet, Atlantic...................COMORTEXGRU
Commander of the Order of Distinction [Jamaica]............CD
Commander of the Order of Leopold..........................CL
Commander of the Order of Military Merit...................CMM
Commander of the Order of the Niger [Nigeria]..............CON
Commander, Order of St. John of Jerusalem [British]........CStJ
Commander of the Order of St. Lazarus of Jerusalem.........CLJ
Commander, Pacific Air Fleet...............................COMPAF
Commander, Pacific Missile Range...........................COMPACMISRAN
Commander, Pacific Missile Range...........................COMPMR
Commander, Pacific Missile Range Instruction...............COMPMRINST
Commander, Pacific Missile Range Notice....................COMPMRNOTE
Commander, Panama Sea Frontier.............................COMPASEAFRON
Commander, Patrol Aircraft Service Unit....................COMPASU
Commander, Patrol Forces...................................COMPATFOR
Commander, Patrol Forces, Northern Subarea, Atlantic.......................COMPATFORNORLANT
Commander, Patrol Squadron.................................COMPATRON
Commander, Philadelphia Group..............................COMPHILAGRU
Commander, Philippine Military Assistance Group, Vietnam.......................COMPHILMAGV
Commander, Plymouth Subarea Channel........................COMPLYMCHAN
Commander, [US] Ports and Bases, France....................COMBASFRANCE
Commander, Republic of Korea Forces, Vietnam...............COMROKFV
Commander, Republic of Korea Military Assistance Group, Vietnam...................COMROKMAGV
Commander, Reserve Destroyer Squadron......................COMRESDESRON
Commander, River Division..................................COMRIVDIV
Commander, River Flotilla..................................COMRIVFLOT
Commander, River Flotilla One..............................COMRIVFLOTONE
Commander, River Patrol Force..............................COMRIVPATFOR
Commander, River Support Squadron..........................COMRIVSUPPRON
Commander, Riverine Division [Navy]........................COMRNDN

Commander, Riverine Flotilla [*Navy*] .... COMRNFLOT
Commander, Riverine Squadron [*Navy*] .... COMRNRON
Commander, Royal Army Service Corps [*British*] .... CRASC
Commander, Royal Artillery [*Division level*] [*British*] .... CRA
Commander, Royal Engineers [*British*] .... CRE
Commander, Royal Thai Military Assistance Group, Vietnam .... COMRTMAGV
Commander of the Royal Victorian Order [*British*] .... CVO
Commander, San Diego Group .... COMDIEGOGRU
Commander, San Francisco Group .... COMSANFRANGRU
Commander, Scouting Squadron .... COMSCORON
Commander, Sea Frontier .... COMSEAFRON
Commander, SEATO [*Southeast Asia Treaty Organization*] **Field Forces** .... CSFF
Commander, Second Allied Tactical Air Force .... COMTWOATAF
Commander, Second Fleet .... COMSECONDFLT
Commander, Service Force .... COMSERV
Commander, Service Force, Atlantic Fleet .... COMSERVLANT
Commander, Service Force, Pacific Fleet .... COMSERVPAC
Commander, Service Force, South Pacific Subordinate Command .... COMSERFORSOPACSUBCOM
Commander, Service Force, Southwest Pacific .... COMSERVSOWESPAC
Commander, Service Group Two [*Navy*] CSG2
Commander, Service Squadron .... COMSERVRON
Commander, Seventh Fleet .... COMSEVENTHFLT
Commander, Sixth Allied Tactical Air Force .... COMSIXATAF
Commander, Sixth Fleet .... COMSIXFLT
Commander, Sixth Fleet .... COMSIXTHFLT
Commander, South Atlantic Force .... COMSOLANT
Commander, South Atlantic Maritime Area .... CAMAS
Commander, South Pacific .... COMSOPAC
Commander, Southeast Mediterranean .... COMEDSOUEAST
Commander, Southeast Pacific Force .... COMSOEASTPAC
Commander, Southern Sector, Western Sea Frontier .... COMSOSECWESTSEAFRON
Commander, Southwest Pacific Force .... COMSOWESPAC
Commander, Stockton Group .... COMSTOCKGRU
Commander, Straits and Marmara Defense Sector .... COMSAMAR
Commander, Strategic Reserve, Allied Land Forces, Central Europe .... COMSTRATRESCENT
Commander, Striking Fleet, Atlantic .... COMSTRIKFLANT
Commander, Striking Fleet, Atlantic .... COMSTRIKFLTLANT
Commander, Striking Fleet, Atlantic Representative in Europe .... COMSTRIKFLANTREPEUR
Commander, Striking and Support Forces, Southern Europe .... COMSTRIKFORSOUTH
Commander, Submarine Allied Command, Atlantic .... COMSUBACLANT
Commander, Submarine Base .... COMSUBASE
Commander, Submarine Development Group .... COMSUBDEVGRU
Commander, Submarine Division .... COMSUBDIV
Commander, Submarine Flotilla .... COMSUBFLOT
Commander, Submarine Force, Atlantic .... COMSUBLANT
Commander, Submarine Force, Eastern Atlantic .... COMSUBEASTLANT
Commander, Submarine Force, Mediterranean .... COMSUBMED
Commander, Submarine Force, Northeast Mediterranean .... COMSUBMEDNOREAST
Commander, Submarine Force, Pacific .... COMSUBPAC
Commander, Submarine Force, Western Atlantic Area .... COMSUBWESTLANT
Commander, Submarine Squadron .... COMSUBRON
Commander, Submarine Training Facilities .... COMSUBTRAFAC
Commander, Submarines .... COMSUBS
Commander, Submarines, Northeast Mediterranean .... COMSUBLEDNOREAST
Commander, Submarines, Southwest Pacific Force .... COMSUBSSOWESPAC
Commander, Subordinate Command, [*US*] **Atlantic Fleet** .... COMSUCOMLANTFLT
Commander, Subordinate Command, Service Force Pacific Fleet [*Navy*] .... CSFPSC
Commander, Support Operations Task Force, Europe .... COMSOTFE
Commander, Tactical Air Command .... COMTAC
Commander, Tactical Air Control Group .... COMTACGRU
Commander, Tactical Air Control Squadron .... COMTACRON
Commander, Tactical Air Force, Denmark .... COMTAFDEN
Commander, Taiwan Defense Command .... COMTAIWANDEFCOMD
Commander, Taiwan Patrol Force .... COMTAIWANPATFOR
Commander, Task Element .... CTE
Commander, Task Force .... CTF
Commander, Task Group .... CTG
Commander, Task Unit .... CTU
Commander, Texas Group .... COMTEXGRU
Commander, Tongue Point Group, Inactive Reserve Fleet, Pacific .... COMTONGRU
Commander, Torpedo Squadron .... COMTORPRON
Commander, Training Command, Atlantic .... COMTRALANT
Commander, Training Command, Pacific .... COMTRAPAC
Commander, Transport Division .... COMTRANSDIV
Commander, Transport Group .... COMTRANSGR
Commander, Transport Group, South Pacific Force .... COMTRANSGRSOPAC
Commander, Transportation Division .... CTD
Commander, Transports, Amphibious Force .... COMTRANSPHIB
Commander, Transports, Amphibious Force, Atlantic Fleet .... COMTRANSPHIBLANT
Commander, Transports, Amphibious Force, Pacific Fleet .... COMTRANSPHIBPAC
Commander of Troops [*for a parade or review*] [*Military*] .... COT
Commander, United Kingdom Air Defense Region .... COMUKADR
Commander, United States Air Force Forces .... COMUSAFFOR
Commander, United States Air Force Southern Command .... COMUSAFSO
Commander, United States Air Force Task Force .... COMUSAFTF
Commander, United States Army Forces .... COMUSARFOR
Commander, United States Army Forces Southern Command .... COMUSARSO
Commander, United States Army, Japan .... COMUSARJAPAN
Commander, United States Army Task Force .... COMUSARTF
Commander, United States Atlantic Subarea .... COMUSLANT
Commander, United States Fleet Air Wing, Mediterranean .... COMUSFAIRWINGMED
Commander, United States Forces .... COMUS
Commander, United States Forces, Azores .... COMUSFORAZ
Commander, United States Forces, Japan .... COMUSJAPAN
Commander, United States Forces, Korea .... COMUSKOREA
Commander, United States Forces, Marianas .... COMUSMARIANAS
Commander, United States Forces, Southeast Asia .... COMUSSEASIA
Commander, United States Joint Task Force .... COMUSJTF
Commander, United States Joint Unconventional Warfare Task Force .... COMUSJUWTF
Commander, United States Land Forces .... COMUSLANDFOR
Commander, United States Marine Forces .... COMUSMARFOR
Commander, United States Marine Task Force .... COMUSMARTF
Commander, United States Military Assistance Command, Thailand .... COMUSMACTHAI
Commander, United States Military Assistance Command, Vietnam .... COMUSMACV
Commander, United States Military Group .... COMUSMILGP
Commander, United States Naval Advanced Base [*Weser River, West Germany*] .... COUSNAB
Commander, United States Naval Forces .... COMUSNAVFOR
Commander, United States Naval Forces, Southern Command .... COMUSNAVSO
Commander, United States Naval Task Force .... COMUSNAVTF
Commander, United States Ports and Bases, France .... COMUSBASFRANCE
Commander, United States Rhine River Patrol .... COMUSRHIN
Commander, United States Special Advisory Group .... COMUSSAG
Commander, United States Taiwan Defense Command .... COMUSTDC
Commander, Utility Squadron .... COMUTRON
Commander, Utility Wing .... COMUTWING
Commander, Utility Wing, Service Force, Atlantic .... COMUTWINGSERVLANT
Commander, Utility Wing, Service Force, Pacific .... COMUTWINGSERVPAC
Commander, Western Sea Frontier .... COMWESTSEAFRON
Commander, Western Sea Frontier .... CWSF
Commander, Western Transport Air Force [*Travis AFB*] .... COMWESTAF
Commanderie de Bordeaux .... CB
Commanders Availability Report .... CAR
Commander's Critical Item List [*Army*] CCIL
Commander's Digest [*A publication*] .... CDI
Commander's Digest [*A publication*] .... Comman Dig
Commander's Distinguished Visitors [*Program*] [*Air Force*] .... CDV
Commanders Evaluation Report [*Army*] .... CER
Commanders' Internal Management Conference [*Air Force*] .... CIMC
Commanders' Internal Management Review [*Also known as Black Saturday*] [*Military*] .... CIMR
Commander's Manual [*Military*] .... CM
Commanding .... CMDG
Commanding .... COMDG
Commanding .... COMMDG
Commanding Army Audit Agency - Midwestern District .... CAAA-MWD
Commanding General .... CG
Commanding General .... COMDGEN
Commanding General .... COMGEN
Commanding General, Air Defense Command .... CGADC
Commanding General, Aircraft Fleet Marine Force, Atlantic .... CGAIRFMLANT
Commanding General, Aircraft Fleet Marine Force, Pacific .... CGAIRFMFPAC
Commanding General, Army Air Forces .... CGAAF
Commanding General, Army Forces, Mid-Pacific [*World War II*] .... COMGENAFMIDPAC
Commanding General, Continental Army Command .... CGCARC
Commanding General, Continental Army Command .... CGCONARC
Commanding General, European Command .... COMGENEUCOM
Commanding General, Fleet Marine Force, Atlantic .... CGFMFLANT
Commanding General, Fleet Marine Force, Pacific .... CGFMFPAC
Commanding General, Ground Forces [*World War II*] .... CCGN
Commanding General, India-Burma Theater [*World War II*] .... CGIBT
Commanding General, Marine Aircraft Group .... CGMAG
Commanding General, Marine Aircraft Wing .... CGMAW
Commanding General, Marine Base .... CGMB

Commanding General, Marine Brigade ... CGMARBRIG
Commanding General, Mediterranean Theater of Operations [*World War II*] ... CGMTO
Commanding General, Mediterranean Theater of Operations [*World War II*] ... COMGENMED
Commanding General, Pacific Ocean Areas [*World War II*] ... COMGENPOA
Commanding General, South Pacific Area [*World War II*] ... COMGENSOPAC
Commanding General, Strategic Air Command ... CGSAC
Commanding General, Tactical Air Command ... CGTAC
Commanding General, Tenth Army ... COMGENTEN
Commanding General, Third Air Division ... COMGENTHIRDAIR
Commanding General, Third Marine Air Wing ... CGTHIRDMAW
Commanding General, United States Air Forces, Europe ... COMGENUSAFE
Commanding General, United States Army Air Defense Command ... CGARADCOM
Commanding General, United States Army Air Defense Command ... CGUSARADCOM
Commanding General, United States Army, Alaska ... CGUSARAL
Commanding General, United States Army Combat Developments Command ... CGUSADC
Commanding General, United States Army Combat Developments Command ... CGUSARCDC
Commanding General, United States Army Communications Zone, Europe ... CGUSACOMZEUR
Commanding General, United States Army, Europe ... COMGENUSAREUR
Commanding General, United States Army Forces ... CGUSARF
Commanding General, United States Army Material Command ... CGUSAMC
Commanding General, United States Army Material Command ... CGUSARMAC
Commanding General, United States Army Material Command ... CGUSARMC
Commanding General, United States Army, Ryukyu Islands ... CGUSARYIS
Commanding General, United States Continental Army Command [*Obsolete*] ... CGUSCONARC
Commanding General, United States Forces, European Theater [*World War II*] ... CGUSFET
Commanding General's Management Information System [*Army*] ... CGMIS
Commanding Officer ... C
Commanding Officer ... CO
Commanding Officer ... COMDG OF
Commanding Officer [*Military slang*] ... KO
Commanding Officer, Air Evacuation Squadron ... COAIREVACRON
Commanding Officer, Atlantic Coast ... COAC
Commanding Officer, Landing Force Air Support Control Unit ... COLANFORASCU
Commanding Officer, Naval Advanced Base ... CONAB
Commanding Officer, Naval Air Base ... CONAB
Commanding Officer, Naval Air Station ... CONAS
Commanding Officer, Naval Air Wing ... CONAIR
Commanding Officer, Naval Divisions [*Canada*] ... COND
Commanding Officer, Naval Supply Depot ... CONSD
Commanding Officer, Observation Squadron ... COOBSRON
Commanding Officer, Pacific Coast [*Navy*] [*Canada*] ... COPC
Commanding Officer, Port of Embarkation ... COPOE
Commanding Officer, Section Base [*Navy*] ... COSECTBASE
Commanding Officer, Submarine Chaser Training Center ... COSCTRACEN
Commanding Officer, United States Ship ... COUSS
Commanding Officer, United States Special Forces (Provisional) ... COUSSF(P)
Commanding Officer's Narrative Report ... CONAR
Commanding Officer's Tactical Display System [*Navy*] ... COTDS
Commanding Officer's Tactical Plan [*or Plot*] [*Navy*] ... COTP
Commando ... CDO
Commando ... CMDO
Commando ... COMDO
Commando Forces, Royal Marines [*British*] ... CdoFcsRM
Commando Logistics Regiment, Royal Marines [*British*] ... CdoLogRegtRM
Commando Operacional do Continente [*Continental Operations Command*] [*Portuguese security force*] ... COPCON
Commando Shackle Relay [*Intelligence gathering*] [*Vietnam*] ... CSR
Commando Training Centre [*British*] ... CTC
Commemorate ... COMMEM
Commemorating ... COMMEMG
Commemorative Stamp Posters ... CSP
Commence ... CMNC
Commence Exercise [*Military*] ... COMEX
Commencement of Rifling ... CR
Commencement and Termination [*British railroad term*] ... C and T
Commencing at a Point ... CAP
Commendation ... CMD
Commendation Ribbon ... CR
Commendation Ribbon with Metal Pendant ... CRMPT
Commendation Ribbon with Metal Pendant ... CRWMP
Comment ... CMT
Comment Issue ... CI
Comment Recevez-Vous? [*French*] ... CRV
Commentari. Accademia di Brescia [*A publication*] ... C A Brescia
Commentarii Mathematici Helvetici [*A publication*] ... Comment Math Helv
Commentarii Mathematici Helvetici [*A publication*] ... Comm Math H
Commentarii Mathematici. Universitatis Sancti Pauli [*A publication*] ... Comment Math Univ St Paul
Commentary ... COM
Commentary ... COMM
Commentary [*A publication*] ... Commen
Commentary [*A publication*] ... Comt
Commentary [*A publication*] ... Ctary
Commentary [*A publication*] ... COM
Commentationes Balticae [*A publication*] ... CB
Commentationes Balticae [*A publication*] ... CBalt
Commentationes Biologicae [*A publication*] ... Commentat Biol
Commentationes Biologicae. Societas Scientiarum Fennica [*A publication*] ... Commentat Biol Soc Sci Fenn
Commentationes Humanarum Litterarum. Societas Scientiarum Fennica [*A publication*] ... CHLSSF
Commentationes Mathematicae. Universitatis Carolinae [*A publication*] ... CMUC
Commentationes Mathematicae. Universitatis Carolinae [*A publication*] ... Comment Math Univ Carolinae
Commentationes Physico-Mathematicae [*A publication*] ... Commentat Phys-Math
Commentationes Physico-Mathematicae [*A publication*] ... Comm Phys-M
Commentationes Physico-Mathematicae. Supplement [*A publication*] ... Commentat Phys-Math Suppl
Commentationes Pontificiae. Academiae Scientiarum [*A publication*] ... Commentat Pontif Acad Sci
Commentationes Vindobonenses [*A publication*] ... CV
Commentationes Vindobonenses [*A publication*] ... C Vind
Comments on Astrophysics and Space Physics [*A publication*] ... Comments Astrophys Space Phys
Comments on Atomic and Molecular Physics [*A publication*] ... Comments At Mol Phys
Comments on Contemporary Psychiatry [*A publication*] ... Com Con Psy
Comments on Contemporary Psychiatry [*A publication*] ... Comments Contemp Psychiatry
Comments on Earth Sciences. Geophysics [*A publication*] ... Comments Earth Sci Geophys
Comments on Molecular and Cellular Biophysics [*A publication*] ... CMCB
Comments on Nuclear and Particle Physics [*A publication*] ... Comments Nucl & Part Phys
Comments on Nuclear and Particle Physics [*A publication*] ... Comments Nucl Part Phys
Comments on Nuclear and Particle Physics. Supplement [*A publication*] ... Comments Nucl Part Phys Suppl
Comments on Plasma Physics and Controlled Fusion [*A publication*] ... C Pl Phys C Fus
Comments on Solid State Physics [*A publication*] ... Comments Solid State Phys
Comments on Solid State Physics [*A publication*] ... C Sol St Phys
Commerce ... COM
Commerce ... COMM
Commerce Action Group for the Near East ... CAGNE
Commerce America [*A publication*] ... Com Amer
Commerce Bancshares [*NASDAQ symbol*] ... CBSH
Commerce Business Daily [*A publication*] ... CBD
Commerce Business Daily [*A publication*] ... COBD
Commerce Canada [*A publication*] ... Com Canada
Commerce Clearing House [*A publishing company*] ... CCH
Commerce Clearing House [*NASDAQ symbol*] ... CCLR
Commerce Clearing House, Washington, DC [*Library symbol*] ... DCCH
Commerce et Cooperation [*A publication*] ... Commerce et Coop
Commerce Department ... C
Commerce Department ... CD
Commerce Department Procurement Regulations ... COMPR
Commerce Exterieur Tchecoslovaque [*A publication*] ... Com Ext Tchecosl
Commerce and Finance ... C & F
Commerce and Finance [*A publication*] ... Comm & Fin
Commerce, GA [*Radio station call letters*] ... WJJC
Commerce Group Corp. [*American Stock Exchange symbol*] [*Delisted*] ... CJG
Commerce and Industry ... C & I
Commerce Moderne [*A publication*] ... Com Mod
Commerce Monthly [*A publication*] ... Comm M
Commerce Productivity Center ... CPC
Commerce Reports [*A publication*] ... Comm Rep
Commerce Southwest [*NYSE symbol*] [*Delisted*] ... CSI
Commerce Technical Advisory Board [*Department of Commerce*] ... CTAB
Commerce Today [*A publication*] ... Comm Today
Commerce Today [*A publication*] ... Com Today
Commerce, TX [*Radio station call letters*] ... KEMM
Commerce, TX [*Radio station call letters*] ... KETR
Commerce Union Corp. [*NASDAQ symbol*] ... COMU
Commercial [*Rate*] [*Value of the English pound*] ... CM
Commercial ... CML
Commercial ... COML
Commercial ... COMM
Commercial Agent ... CA
Commercial Air ... CA
Commercial Air Freight Movement ... CAFM
Commercial Air Movement ... CAM

Commercial Air Service [*Pty.*] Ltd. ....COMAIR
Commercial Air Services [*South Africa*] [*ICAO designator*].....................MN
Commercial Alliance Corporation [*American Stock Exchange symbol*] ....CAC
Commercial and Allied Workers' Union [*Somali Republic*].................CAWU
Commercial Art Program [*Association of Independent Colleges and Schools specialization code*] ....CA
Commercial Artists' Guild ....CAG
Commercial, Automatic Test System [*Military*]..................CATE
Commercial Bancorp of Colorado [*NASDAQ symbol*]..................CBOCA
Commercial Bancshares of New Jersey [*NASDAQ symbol*].................CBNJ
Commercial Bank ....CB
Commercial Bank Address File [*IRS*]..................CBAF
Commercial Bank of Australia ....CBA
Commercial Bank of Korea ....CBK
Commercial Banking Company of Sydney [*Australia*]..................CBC
Commercial Bill of Lading ....CBL
Commercial Breeder Reactor ....CBR
Commercial Cable Company ....COMCABCO
Commercial Carrier CC
Commercial Casualty Products [*Insurance*]..................CCP
Commercial Casualty Underwriting [*Insurance*]..................CCU
Commercial Chemical Development Association [*Later, CDA*]..................CCDA
Commercial Commodity Acquisition Program [*DoD*]..................CCAP
Commercial Communications Satellite [*Japan*]..................CCS
Commercial Communications Work Order [*Air Force*]..................CCWO
Commercial Construction Equipment [*Plan*] [*Army*]..................CCE
Commercial Construction Equipment and Military Adaptation of Commercial Items ....CCE/MACI
Commercial Construction and Selected Materials Handling Equipment ....CCE/SMHE
Commercial Consumables..................CC
Commercial Contract Change CCC
Commercial Contracting Officer ....CCO
Commercial Contractor-Furnished Equipment..................CCFE
Commercial Credit Co. [*NYSE symbol*] [*Delisted*] CC
Commercial Data Processing Center ....CDPC
Commercial Decal, Inc. [*NASDAQ symbol*]..................COME
Commercial Demonstration Fast Reactor ....CDFR
Commercial Development Association ....CDA
Commercial Dock ....CD
Commercial Earth Station ....CES
Commercial Education [*A publication*]..................Comm Ed
Commercial Engineer..................CE
Commercial Enterprise ....CE
Commercial Equipment Requirement List..................CERL
Commercial Exchange of Philadelphia ....CEP
Commercial Fast Reactor [*British*] ....CFR
Commercial Fertilizer [*A publication*]..................Comm Fert
Commercial Fertilizer and Plant Food Industry [*A publication*] ....Commer Fert Plant Food Ind
Commercial and Financial Chronicle [*A publication*]........Comm & Fin Chron
Commercial Fisheries Abstracts [*A publication*]..............Commer Fish Abstr
Commercial Fisheries Research and Development Act..................CFRDA
Commercial Fisheries Review..................CFRV
Commercial Fisheries Review [*A publication*] ....Commer Fish Rev
Commercial Food Equipment Service Agencies of America..............CFESA
Commercial and General Workers' Union [*Rhodesia and Nyasaland*]..................CGWU
Commercial Import Division [*Vietnam*]..................CID
Commercial Import Program ....CIP
Commercial Index [*A publication*]..................Commer Ind
Commercial or Industrial and Control Service Data System ....CICS
Commercial Industrial Services Program [*Navy*]..................CIS
Commercial and Industrial-Type Activity ....CITA
Commercial and Industrial-Type Functions [*Army*]..................CITF
Commercial Instrument Landing CIL
Commercial International Corporation [*NASDAQ symbol*] ....CMMC
Commercial Item Description ....CID
Commercial Item Drawing..................CID
Commercial Item Support Program [*DoD*]..................CISP
Commercial Law Journal [*A publication*]..................Com L J
Commercial Law League of America ....CLLA
Commercial Loan Insurance Corporation CLIC
Commercial Market Appraisal ....CMA
Commercial Metals Company [*NYSE symbol*]..................CMC
Commercial/Military Spares Release ....CMSR
Commercial Motor [*A publication*] ....Comm Mot
Commercial Multi-Peril [*Insurance*] ....CMP
Commercial Museum, Philadelphia, PA [*Library symbol*] [*Obsolete*]..................PPComm
Commercial Nondevelopment Items [*Military*]..................CNDI
Commercial Practices Program [*Air Force*]..................CPP
Commercial Printing Co., Trenton, NJ [*Library symbol*]..................NjTCP
Commercial Product Development..................CPD
Commercial Production of Electronic Solid State Systems ....COMPRESS
Commercial Program Development ....CPD
Commercial Projected Window [*Technical drawings*]..................CPW
Commercial Property Products ....CPP
Commercial Property Underwriting [*Insurance*] ....CPU
Commercial Quality ....CQ

Commercial Refrigerator Manufacturers Association..................CRMA
Commercial Satellite Communications System ....COMSATCOM
Commercial Service Area [*Military*] ....CSA
Commercial-Service Authorization [*Military*]..................CSA
Commercial Shearing, Inc. [*NASDAQ symbol*]..................CSHR
Commercial Solvents Corporation ....CSC
Commercial Solvents Corp. [*NYSE symbol*] [*Delisted*] CV
Commercial Solvents Corp., Terre Haute, IN [*Library symbol*] [*Obsolete*] ....InTCS
Commercial Standard [*A publication*]..................CS
Commercial Steamship Company ....CSC
Commercial Subroutine Package [*IBM Corp.*] ....CSP
Commercial Synchronous Communication Satellite ....CSCSAT
Commercial Telegraphers' Union [*Later, UTW*]..................CTU
Commercial Television ....CTV
Commercial Test Equipment ....CTE
Commercial Traffic Bulletin ....CTB
Commercial Translator ....COMTRAN
Commercial Translator ....CT
Commercial Transport Navigation Display System ....CTNDS
Commercial Transportation Officer ....CTO
Commercial Traveler ....CT
Commercial Travelers Insurance Federation ....CTIF
Commercial Type Property ....CTP
Commercial Utility Cargo Vehicle [*Army*]..................CUCV
Commercial Value..................CV
Commercial Vehicles [*A publication*]..................Comm Veh
Commercial Warehouse Field Officer [*Military*]..................CWFO
Commercial Water Movement Number ....CWM
Commercial Weight..................CW
Commercially Available/Fabricated Training Device ....CAFTD
Commercially Available/Fabricated Training Device Requirement..................CAFTDR
Commercially Available Organic Chemicals Index [*Data processing*] [*British*] ....CAOCI
Commercially Important Person..................CIP
Commercium Litterarium ad Rei Medicae et Scientiae Naturali Incrementum Institutum [*A publication*]
..................Commercium Lit Rei Med et Sc Nat
Commissar ....COMR
Commissariat ....COMRT
Commissariat a l'Energie Atomique [*Atomic Energy Commission*] [*France*] ....CEA
Commissariat for Montagnard Affairs ....CMA
Commissary [*Marine Corps*]..................C
Commissary ....COM
Commissary ....COMMY
Commissary ....COMSRY
Commissary [*Air Force*] ....COMSY
Commissary Civilian Career Enhancement Program [*Air Force*]..................CCCEP
Commissary General ....CG
Commissary-General of Subsistence [*Army*] [*British*] ....CGS
Commissary Operating Manual ....COM
Commissary Operating Program [*Air Force*] ....COP
Commissary Resale Division of the Army Stock Fund ....CORDASF
Commissary Store [*Army*]..................COMSYSTR
Commissary Store [*Navy*]..................CS
Commissary Technician, Medical ....CMT
Commissaryman [*Navy rating*]..................CS
Commissaryman, First Class [*Navy rating*]..................CS1
Commissaryman, Master Chief [*Navy rating*]..................CSCM
Commissaryman, Second Class [*Navy rating*]..................CS2
Commissaryman, Third Class [*Navy rating*]..................CS3
Commissie voor Bibliografie en Documentatie [*Netherlands Bibliographical and Documentary Committee*] [*Information service*] ....COBIDOC
Commission ....CMSN
Commission [*or Commissioner*] ....COM
Commission ....COMM
Commission ....COMMN
Commission ....COMSN
Commission for Acceleration of Black Participation in Psychology ....CABPP
Commission on Accreditation of Rehabilitation Facilities..................CARF
Commission on Accreditation of Service Experiences [*Later, OECC*]..................CASE
Commission on Administrative Review [*House of Representatives*]..................CAR
Commission for the Advancement of Public Interest Organizations..................CAPIO
Commission for Aeronautical Meteorology [*WMO*]..................CAeM
Commission for Agricultural Meteorology [*WMO*]..................CAgM
Commission on American Shipbuilding ....CAS
Commission on Archives and History of the United Methodist Church [*Formerly, HSEUBC, AMHS*]..................CAHUMC
Commission on Art and Antiquities ....CAA
Commission on Asian and Far Eastern Affairs of the International Chamber of Commerce..................CAFEA-ICC
Commission on Asian and Pacific Affairs [*International Chamber of Commerce*]..................CAPA
Commission on Atmospheric Chemistry and Global Pollution [*IAMAP*]..................CACGP

Commission for Atmospheric Sciences [*WMO*] .... CAS
Commission for Basic Systems [*WMO*] .... CBS
Commission on Biochemical Nomenclature [*IUPAC*] .... CBN
Commission Centrale pour la Navigation du Rhin [*Central Commission for the Navigation of the Rhine*] .... CCR
Commission Certified [*Bacteriology*] CC
Commission of the Churches on International Affairs [*of the World Council of Churches*] .... CCIA/WCC
Commission on Civil Rights .... CCR
Commission on College Physics .... CCP
Commission du Commerce International des Produits de Base [*United Nations*] .... CCIP
Commission Consultative des Employes et des Travailleurs Intellectuels [*de l'OIT*] .... CCETI
Commission Consultative des Etudes Postales [*de l'Union Postale Universelle*] .... CCEP
Commission Consultative Universitaire de Pedagogie [*Belgium*] .... CCUP
Commission on Critical Choices for Americans .... CCCA
Commission du Danube [*Danube Commission*] .... CD
Commission du Droit International [*United Nations*] .... CDI
Commission Economique pour l'Afrique [*United Nations*] .... CEA
Commission Economique pour l'Amerique Latine [*United Nations*] .... CEPAL
Commission Economique pour l'Asie et l'Extreme-Orient [*United Nations*] .... CEAEO
Commission Economique pour l'Europe [*United Nations*] .... CEE
Commission of Editors of Biochemical Journals .... CEBJ
Commission on Education in Agriculture and Natural Resources [*National Research Council*] [*Defunct*] .... CEANAR
Commission on Education for Mission [*National Council of Churches*] .... CEM
Commission for Educational Exchange between the United States of America and Afghanistan .... CEEUSA
Commission Electrotechnique Internationale [*International Electrotechnical Commission*] [*See also IEC*] .... CEI
Commission on English of the College Entrance Examination Board .... CECEEB
Commission Episcopale de Cooperation Apostolique Canada-Amerique Latine .... CECAL
Commission pour l'Etude des Nuages [*OMI*] .... CEN
Commission of the European Communities .... CEC
Commission Europeenne de l'Aviation Civile [*European Civil Aviation Commission*] .... CEAC
Commission Europeenne des Forets .... CEF
Commission Europeenne du Tourisme .... CET
Commission for the Exploration and Utilization of Space [*USSR*] .... CEUS
Commission on Federal Paperwork [*Terminated, 1978*] .... CFP
Commission on Financial Structure and Regulation [*White House*] .... CFSR
Commission of Fine Arts [*Independent government agency*] .... CFA
Commission for Fisheries Research in the West Pacific .... WPFC
Commission for the Geological Map of the World .... CGMW
Commission on Government Procurement [*Terminated, 1973*] .... CGP
Commission on Government Procurement [*Office of Management and Budget*] .... COGP
Commission on Government Security [*Terminated, 1957*] .... CGS
Commission on Health and Healing [*Formerly, CCMW*] .... CHH
Commission on Highway Beautification .... CHB
Commission on Human Resources [*National Research Council*] .... CHR
Commission for Hydrology [*WMO*] .... CHy
Commission on Increased Industrial Use of Agricultural Products .... CIIUAP
Commission on Independent Colleges and Universities [*Pennsylvania*] .... CICU
Commission on Industrial Relations [*Department of Employment*] [*British*] .... CIR
Commission on Instructional Technology .... CIT
Commission des Instruments et des Methodes d'Observation [*Commission for Instruments and Methods of Observation*] [*OMI*] .... CIMO
Commission Interamericaine d'Energie Nucleaire [*Inter-American Nuclear Energy Commission*] .... CIEN
Commission on Intergovernmental Relations .... CIR
Commission on International Commodity Trade .... CICT
Commission for International Development .... CID
Commission for International Due Process of Law .... CIDPL
Commission for International Educational Reconstruction .... CIER
Commission Internationale d'Analyses .... CIA
Commission Internationale de la Baleine [*International Whaling Commission*] .... CIB
Commission Internationale Catholique pour les Migrations [*International Catholic Migration Commission*] [*See also ICMC*] .... CICM
Commission Internationale du Chataignier CIC
Commission Internationale pour la Conservation des Thonides de l'Atlantique [*International Commission for the Conservation of Atlantic Tunas*] .... CICTA
Commission Internationale Contre le Regime Concentrationnaire ... CICRC
Commission Internationale de l'Eclairage [*International Commission on Illumination*] .... CIE
Commission Internationale de l'Enseignement de la Physique [*International Commission on Physics Education - ICPE*] .... CIEP
Commission Internationale de l'Etat Civil [*International Commission on Civil Status*] [*See also ICCS*] .... CIEC
Commission Internationale pour l'Etude Scientifique de la Famille [*International Scientific Commission on the Family*] .... COMIFA
Commission Internationale d'Etudes de la Police de Circulation [*International Study Commission for Traffic Police*] .... CIEPC
Commission Internationale pour l'Exploration Scientifique de la Mer Mediterranee [*International Commission for the Scientific Exploration of the Mediterranean Sea*] .... CIESM
Commission Internationale du Genie Rural [*International Commission of Agricultural Engineering*] .... CIGR
Commission Internationale des Grands Barrages [*International Commission on Large Dams*] [*See also ICOLD*] .... CIGB
Commission Internationale d'Histoire Militaire [*International Commission of Military History*] .... CIHM
Commission Internationale des Industries Agricoles [*International Commission for Agricultural Industries*] .... CIIA
Commission Internationale des Irrigations et du Drainage [*International Commission on Irrigation and Drainage - ICID*] .... CIID
Commission Internationale de Juristes [*International Commission of Jurists*] .... CIJ
Commission Internationale de Lutte Biologique Contre les Ennemis des Cultures .... CILB
Commission Internationale de Meteorologie Aeronautique [*OMI*] ..... CIMAe
Commission Internationale des Methodes d'Analyse des Pesticides [*Collaborative International Pesticides Analytic Commission*] [*See also CIPAC*] .... CIMAP
Commission Internationale de la Navigation Aerienne [*International Air Navigation Commission*] .... CINA
Commission Internationale de la Nomenclature Anatomique Veterinaire [*International Committee on Veterinary Anatomical Nomenclature - ICVAN*] .... CINAV
Commission Internationale de Numismatique [*International Numismatic Commission*] .... CIN
Commission Internationale d'Optique [*International Commission for Optics*] [*See also ICO*] .... CIO
Commission Internationale pour l'Organisation Scientifique du Travail en Agriculture [*International Committee of Scientific Management in Agriculture*] .... CIOSTA
Commission Internationale des Peches de l'Atlantique du Nord-Ouest [*International Commission for the Northwest Atlantic Fisheries*] .... CIPAN
Commission Internationale des Peches de l'Atlantique Sud-Est [*International Commission for the Southeast Atlantic Fisheries - ICSAF*] .... CIPASE
Commission Internationale du Peuplier [*International Poplar Commission*] .... CIP
Commission Internationale de Protection Contre les Radiations .... CIPR
Commission Internationale pour la Protection des Regions Alpines .... CIPRA
Commission Internationale pour le Sauvetage Alpin [*International Commission for Alpine Rescue*] .... CISA
Commission Internationale Technique de Sucrerie [*International Commission of Sugar Technology*] .... CITS
Commission Internationale de Tourisme Aerien .... CITA
Commission Internationale du Verre [*International Commission on Glass*] [*See also ICG*] CIV
Commission Intersyndicale des Deshydrateurs Europeens [*European Dehydrators' Association*] [*Common Market*] .... CIDE
Commission on Law Enforcement and Criminal Justice, Criminal Justice Information System, Baton Rouge, LA [*Library symbol*] .... LBrCJIS
Commission on Law and Public Affairs .... COLPA
Commission pour le Marche Commun du Commerce International de Bulbes a Fleurs et de Plantes [*Common Market Commission for International Trade in Flower Bulbs and Plants*] .... CIBEP
Commission for Marine Geology [*International Union of Geological Sciences*] .... CMG
Commission on Marine Science, Engineering, and Resources .... CMSER
Commission for Maritime Meteorology [*World Meteorological Organization*] .... CMM
Commission on Marriage and Family Life [*of NCC*] [*Defunct*] .... CMFL
Commission on Missionary Education [*Later, Department of Education for Missions*] .... CME
Commission Mixte Internationale pour les Experiences Relatives a la Protection des Lignes de Telecommunication et des Canalisations Souterraines .... CMI
Commission on Molecular Structure and Spectroscopy .... CMSS
Commission Mondiale d'Action Professionnelle [*World Committee for Trade Action - WCTA*] .... CMAP
Commission on National Parks and Protected Areas .... CNPPA
Commission Nationale pour l'Amenagement du Territoire .... CNAT
Commission Nationale pour l'Etude de l'Utilisation Pacifique de l'Energie Nucleaire [*Belgium*] .... CNEUPEN
Commission des Nations Unies pour l'Inde et le Pakistan .... CNUIP
Commission des Nations Unies pour l'Unification et le Relevement de la Coree .... CNUURC
Commission on Natural Resources [*National Research Council*] .... CNR
Commission to New Towns [*British*] .... CNT
Commission on the Nomenclature of Organic Chemistry [*IUPAC*] .... CON

Commission Oceanographique Intergouvernementale [*Intergovernmental Oceanographic Commission*] [*See also IOC*] .... COI
Commission on Ore-Forming Fluid in Inclusions .... COFFI
Commission on Organization of the Executive Branch of the Government .... COEBG
Commission on the Patent System .... CPS
Commission Permanente de la Convention Internationale des Peches [*Permanent Commission of the International Fisheries Convention*] .... CPCIP
Commission Permanente Internationale de l'Acetylene, de la Soudure Autogene, et des Industries qui S'y Rattachent [*Permanent International Committee on Acetylene, Oxy-Acetylene Welding, and Allied Industries*] .... CPI
Commission Permanente Internationale Europeenne des Gaz Industriels et du Carbure de Calcium [*Permanent International European Committee on Industrial Gases and Calcium Carbide*] .... CPI
Commission Permanente du Pacifique Sud [*Permanent Commission for the South Pacific*] .... CPPS
Commission on Personnel Interchange [*Presidential*] .... CPI
Commission Phytosanitaire Interafricaine .... CPI
Commission on Population Growth and the American Future [*Presidential commission*] .... CPGAF
Commission Preparatoire Europeenne de Recherches Spatiales .... COPERS
Commission on Private Philanthropy and Public Needs [*Defunct*] .... CPPPN
Commission on Professional and Hospital Activities .... CPHA
Commission on Professional Rights and Responsibilities of the NEA [*Defunct*] .... CPRR-NEA
Commission of Professors of Adult Education .... CPAE
Commission for Racial Equality [*British*] .... CRE
Commission for Racial Justice .... CRJ
Commission on Reform of Undergraduate Education and Living [*University of Illinois*] .... CRUEL
Commission Regionale Europeenne du Tourisme .... CRET
Commission on Religion in Appalachia .... CORA
Commission des Reparations [*Reparation Commission*] .... CDR
Commission de Representants Permanents [*Committee of Permanent Representatives*] [*EEC*] .... COREPER
Commission Royale d'Histoire. Bulletin [*A publication*] .... CRHBull
Commission on Rural Water [*Defunct*] .... CRW
Commission on Science Education .... CSE
Commission Scolaire Regionale des Vieilles-Forges, Trois-Rivieres, PQ, Canada [*Library symbol*] .... CaQTCSRV
Commission on Security and Cooperation in Europe .... CSCE
Commission Sericicole Internationale [*International Sericultural Commission*] .... CSI
Commission on Social Action of Reform Judaism .... CSARJ
Commission for Social Justice .... CSJ
Commission on Software Issues in the 80s .... COSIE
Commission for Special Applications of Meteorology and Climatology [*WMO*] .... COSAMC
Commission Sportive Internationale [*Auto racing*] .... CSI
Commission on Standards and Accreditation of Services for the Blind [*Superseded by NAC*] .... COMSTAC
Commission on the Status of Jewish War Orphans in Europe, American Section .... CSJWOE
Commission on the Status of Women in Adult Education .... CSWAE
Commission to Study the Organization of Peace .... CSOP
Commission for Synoptic Meteorology .... CSM
Commission for Teacher Preparation and Licensing .... CTPL
Commission for Technical Cooperation for Africa .... CTCA
Commission de Toponymie et Dialectologie [*A publication*] .... CTD
Commission de Transport de la Communaute Urbaine de Montreal, Montreal, PQ, Canada [*Library symbol*] .... CaQMCT
Commission on Undergraduate Education in the Biological Sciences .... CUEBS
Commission of United States Latin American Relations .... CUSLAR
Commission on Voluntary Service and Action .... CVSA
Commission on World Mission and Evangelism of the World Council of Churches [*Later, CWME*] .... CWMEWCC
Commissioned .... CD
Commissioned .... CMSND
Commissioned .... COMMND
Commissioned .... COMND
Commissioned Corps Personnel Manual .... CCPM
Commissioned Loss to Enlisted Status [*Revocation of an officer's appointment*] .... CLTE
Commissioned Officer Corps [*National Oceanic and Atmospheric Administration*] .... COC
Commissioned Officer Residency Deferment [*Program of Public Health Service*] .... CORD
Commissioned Officer Student Training and Extern Program [*Public Health Service*] .... COSTEP
Commissioned Officers Association of the United States Public Health Service .... COA
Commissioned Officers Mess [*Navy*] .... COM
Commissioned Royal Marine Gunner [*British*] .... CdRMG
Commissioned Signals Boatswain [*British*] .... CdSB
Commissioned Supply Officer [*British*] .... CdSO
Commissioned Warrant Officer .... CWO
Commissioned Warrant Officer Hospital Corps .... CWOHC
Commissioner .... CMSNR
Commissioner .... COMMR
Commissioner .... COMR
Commissioner .... COMSNR
Commissioner of Accounts .... CA
Commissioner of Crown Lands [*British*] CCL
Commissioner of Election Expenses [*Canada*] .... CEE
Commissioner for Oaths .... CO
Commissioner of Official Languages [*Canada*] .... COL
Commissioner of Official Languages, Ottawa, ON, Canada [*Library symbol*] .... CaOOCOL
Commissioner's Decisions [*US Patent and Trademark Office*] .... CD
Commissioners Disability Table [*Insurance*] .... CDT
Commissioners of District of Columbia .... CDC
Commissioners Industrial Extended Mortality Table [*Insurance*] .... CIET
Commissioners of Inland Revenue [*British*] .... CIR
Commissioner's Office [*Scotland Yard*] .... CO
Commissioners Standard Industrial Mortality Table [*Insurance*] .... CSI
Commissioners Standard Ordinary Table [*Insurance*] .... CSO
Commissioning Detail .... COMMDET
Commissioning and Fitting Out .... CFO
Commissions Board of Trade .... CBOT
Commissions Royales d'Art et d'Archeologie. Bulletin [*A publication*] .... CRAABull
Commissural Gastric Driver [*Neurology*] .... CGD
Commit .... COMT
Commit Sequence Summary .... CSS
Commit Start .... CST
Commit Stop .... CS
Commitment .... COMM
Commitment Authorization .... CA
Commitment Control System .... CCS
[*A*] **Commitment to Improve Our Nation** [*Canada*] .... ACTION
Commitment and Payment System .... CAPS
Committed Change Incorporation Record .... CCIR
Committed to Scheduled Programs [*Military*] .... CSP
Committed Stem Cell [*Hematology*] .... CSC
Committee .... CMTE
Committee .... CMTTEE
Committee .... COM
Committee .... COMM
Committee .... COMTE
Committee .... CTEE
Committee .... CTTEE
Committee to Abolish Sport Hunting .... CASH
Committee for the Absorption of Soviet Emigres .... CASE
Committee on Academic Science and Engineering [*Federal Council for Science and Technology*] .... CASE
Committee on Accreditation [*American Library Association*] .... COA
Committee on the Acquisition and Use of Scientific and Technical Information in Pesticide Regulatory Decision Making at the Federal and State Levels [*National Research Council*] .... CPRDM
Committee of the Acta Endocrinologica Countries .... CAEC
Committee on Administrative Services of Hospitals .... CASH
Committee Against the Political Misuse of Psychiatry .... CAPMP
Committee Against Registration and the Draft .... CARD
Committee on Agriculture [*Food and Agricultural Organization*] [*United Nations*] .... COAG
Committee to Aid Cold War Veterans .... CACWV
Committee to Aid Democratic Dissidents in Yugoslavia .... CADDY
Committee on Air and Water Conservation [*Later, Committee for Environmental Affairs*] [*American Petroleum Institute*] .... CAWC
Committee for the Alliance for Progress [*Commerce Department*] .... COMAP
Committee on Allied Health Education and Accreditation .... CAHEA
Committee on American East Asian Relations [*Defunct*] .... AEAR
Committee on American Library Resources on South Asia [*Later, CALROSEA, CORMOSEA*] .... CALROSA
Committee on American Library Resources on Southeast Asia [*Formerly, CALROSA*] [*Later, CORMOSEA*] .... CALROSEA
Committee for American Principles .... CFAP
Committee of American Steamship Lines [*Later, AIMS*] .... CASL
Committee of Americans for Peace in the Middle East [*Defunct*] ...... CAPME
Committee on Appeal for Human Rights .... COAHR
Committee for the Application of the Behavioral Sciences to the Strategies of Peace .... ABSSOP
Committee on Application of Polarized Headlights [*OECD*] .... CAPH
Committee on Army and Navy Religious Activities [*National Jewish Welfare Board*] .... CANRA
Committee for Artistic and Intellectual Freedom in Iran .... CAIFI
Committee on Assessing the Progress of Education [*Later, NAEP*] ..... CAPE
Committee to Assure the Availability of Casein .... CAAC
Committee on the Atlantic Salmon Emergency .... CASE
Committee on Atlantic Studies [*of the Atlantic Council of the United States and the Atlantic Institute for International Affairs*] .... CAS
Committee on Atmospheric Problems of Aerospace Vehicles [*American Meteorological Society*] .... CAPAV
Committee of Atomic Bomb Survivors in the US .... CABSUS
Committee for Automobile Reform .... CAR

Committee on Autonomous Groups .... CAG
Committee on Aviation Medicine [*NAS/NRC*] .... CAM
Committee to Award Miss Piggy the Oscar [*Defunct*] .... CAMPO
Committee on Basic Research in Education .... COBRE
Committee for Better Transit .... CBT
Committee on Biological Information [*British*] .... CBI
Committee on Biological Sciences Information [*NAS/NRC*] .... COBSI
Committee of Black Americans for Truth about the Middle-East [*Defunct*] .... COBATAME
Committee of Black Gay Men .... CBGM
Committee to Bridge the Gap .... CBG
Committee on Captured Enemy Electronics Equipment .... COCEEE
Committee for the Care of the Diabetic .... CCD
Committee of Catholics Who Care .... CCWC
Committee on the Challenges of Modern Society [*NATO*] .... CCMS
Committee on the Challenges of Modern Society. Air Pollution [*A publication*] .... Com Challenges of Mod Soc Air Pollution
Committee on Changing International Realities .... CIR
Committee on Christian Literature for Women and Children in Mission Fields .... CCLWCMF
Committee for Collective Security [*Defunct*] .... CCS
Committee for the Collegiate Education of Black Students .... CCEBS
Committee to Combat Huntington's Disease .... CCHD
Committee of Combined Boards .... COB
Committee on Commodity Problems [*UN Food and Agriculture Organization*] .... CCP
Committee of Common Market Automobile Constructors [*EEC*] .... CCMAC
Committee for Common Sense Speed Laws [*California*] [*Defunct*] .... CCSSL
Committee on Comparative Urban Economics .... CCUE
Committee of Concern .... COC
Committee of Concerned Africans .... CCA
Committee of Concerned Artists and Professionals .... CCAP
Committee of Concerned Scientists .... CCS
Committee for Congested Production Areas [*1943-1944*] .... CCPA
Committee for Constitutional Government .... CCG
Committee on Constitutional and Legal Matters [*UN Food and Agriculture Organization*] .... CCLM
Committee on the Constitutional System .... CCS
Committee for Consumers No-Fault .... CCNF
Committee on Contamination of Extra-Terrestrial Exploration [*NASA*] .... CETEX
Committee on Contributions for Elective State Officials .... CCESO
Committee of Control of the International Zone of Tangier .... CCIZT
Committee for Conventional Armaments .... CCA
Committee on Cooperation in Latin America [*of The National Council of Churches of Christ in the USA*] .... CCLA
Committee for Coordination of Emergency Economic Planning [*US/Canada*] .... CCEEP
Committee for the Coordination of National Bibliographic Control [*Defunct*] .... CCNBC
Committee for Corporate Support of American Universities [*Later, Committee for Corporate Support of Private Universities*] .... CCSAU
Committee for Corporate Support of Private Universities .... CCSPU
Committee on Cosmic Humanism .... CCH
Committee on Data for Science and Technology [*ICSU*] .... CODATA
Committee on Data for Science and Technology. Special Report (International Council of Scientific Unions) [*A publication*] .... Comm Data Sci Technol Spec Rep (ICSU)
Committee on Decentralization of Controls after V-E Day [*War Production Board*] .... CODCAVE
Committee to Defend America by Aiding the Allies [*Active prior to US entry into World War II*] .... CDAAA
Committee to Defend the First Amendment .... CDFA
Committee for Defense of Human Rights in Morocco .... CDHRM
Committee for the Defense National Interest .... CDNI
Committee in Defense of the Palestinian and Lebanese Peoples .... CDPLP
Committee for the Defense of Persecuted Orthodox Christians .... CDPOC
Committee for the Defense of Political Prisoners in Vietnam .... CDPPV
Committee in Defense of the Revolution [*Cuba*] .... CDR
Committee for Defense of Soviet Political Prisoners .... CDSPP
Committee for the Development of Art in Negro Colleges [*Later, CAA*] .... CDANC
Committee on the Development of Engineering Faculties .... CDEF
Committee on Diagnostic Reading Tests .... CDRT
Committee on Domestic Technology Transfer [*Federal Council for Science and Technology*] .... CDTT
Committee on Donor Enlistment [*Superseded by Organ Recovery*] .... CODE
Committee on Drugs and Alcohol .... CODA
Committee on East Asian Libraries .... CEAL
Committee for Economic Development .... CED
Committee for the Economic Growth of Israel .... CEG-I
Committee on the Economic Impact of Defense and Disarmament .... CEIDD
Committee on Economic Security [*Terminated as formal agency, 1936, but continued informally for some time thereafter*] .... CES
Committee on Education Needs for Teen-Age Unwed Mothers .... CENTAUM
Committee on Educational Policy in Agriculture [*National Academy of Sciences*] .... CEPA
Committee on Educational Reconstruction .... CER
Committee for Effective Capital Recovery .... CECR
Committee to Eliminate Premature Christmas Advertising and Display [*Defunct*] .... CEPCAD
Committee for Elimination of Death [*Later, CEL*] .... CFED
Committee on Emergency Medical Identification .... CEMI
Committee to End Pay Toilets in America [*Defunct*] .... CEPTIA
Committee for Energy Awareness .... CEA
Committee on Energy and the Environment [*National Research Council*] .... CEE
Committee for Enlisted Classification Selection and Testing [*Navy*] .... CECSET
Committee on Environmental Decision Making [*National Research Council*] .... CEDM
Committee for Environmental Information .... CEI
Committee on Equal Opportunities in Science and Technology [*National Science Foundation*] .... CEOST
Committee for Equality of Citizens Before the Courts .... CO-EQUAL
Committee for Equitable Access to Crude Oil .... CEACO
Committee to Eradicate Syphilis [*Defunct*] .... CES
Committee to Establish the Gold Standard .... CEGS
Committee for European Airspace Coordination [*NATO*] .... CEAC
Committee for European Airspace Coordination [*NATO*] .... CEASC
Committee for European Economic Cooperation [*Marshall Plan*] [*Post-World War II*] .... CEEC
Committee for European Marine Biological Symposia [*European Marine Biological Association*] .... CEMBS
Committee for Evaluating the Feasibility of Space Rocketry [*Navy Bureau of Aeronautics*] [*Obsolete*] .... CEFSR
Committee for an Extended Lifespan [*Defunct*] .... CEL
Committee on Extension to the Standard Atmosphere .... COESA
Committee on Fair Employment Practices [*World War II*] .... CFEP
Committee on Federal Laboratories [*Federal Council for Science and Technology*] .... CFL
Committee on Federal Laboratories [*Federal Council for Science and Technology*] .... COFL
Committee on Fisheries [*Food and Agriculture Organization*] .... COFI
Committee on Foreign Investment in the United States .... CFIUS
Committee on Foreign Resistance [*War Cabinet*] [*British*] [*World War II*] .... CFR
Committee on Foreign Resistance, Economic Policy [*Ministry of Supply*] [*British*] [*World War II*] .... CFR(EP)
Committee on Forestry [*Food and Agricultural Organization*] [*United Nations*] .... COFO
Committee to Form a US-Albania Friendship Association .... CFUSAFA
Committee for a Free Afghanistan .... CFA
Committee for a Free China .... CFC
Committee for a Free Estonia [*Defunct*] .... CFE
Committee for a Free Gold Market .... CFGM
Committee for a Free Latvia .... CFL
Committee for a Free Lithuania .... CFL
Committee for a Free Mozambique [*Defunct*] .... CFM
Committee for a Free Namibia .... CFN
Committee on Free Press and Fair Trial [*of the American Newspaper Publishers Association*] .... CFPFT
Committee for the Free World .... CFW
Committee for Freedom of Choice in Cancer Therapy .... CFCCT
Committee of French American Wives .... CFAW
Committee of French Speaking Societies .... CFSS
Committee on Friendly Relations among Foreign Students [*Later, ISS*] .... CFR
Committee for Full Funding of Education Programs .... CFFEP
Committee for the Furtherance of Torah Observance .... CFTO
Committee for the Future of America .... CFA
Committee on Genetic Experimentation [*ICSU*] .... COGENE
Committee for the Global Atmospheric Research Program .... CGARP
Committee on Government Operations .... CGO
Committee to Halt Indoctrination and Demoralization in Education [*Group opposing sex education in schools*] .... CHIDE
Committee to Halt Useless College Killings .... CHUCK
Committee for Handgun Control .... CHC
Committee of Heads of Administration [*NATO*] .... CHA
Committee on the Health Services Industry [*Cost of Living Council*] [*Abolished, 1973*] .... CHSI
Committee on Hearing and Bio-Acoustics .... CHABA
Committee for Hispanic Arts and Research .... CHAR
Committee for Human Rights and Democracy in Turkey .... CHRDT
Committee on Human Rights in Malaysia and Singapore .... COHRIMS
Committee on Human Rights for Nicaragua .... CHRN
Committee for Human Rights in Rumania .... CHRR
Committee for Human Rights in Syria .... CHRS
Committee for Humane Legislation .... CHL
Committee on Imagery Requirements and Exploitation [*United States Intelligence Board*] .... COMIREX
Committee for Imperial Defence [*British*] .... CID
Committee for the Implementation of Textile Agreements .... CITA
Committee on Improvement of National Statistics [*Inter-American*] .... COINS
Committee for an Independent Canada CIC
Committee for Independent Political Action .... CIPA
Committee for Industrial Development [*United Nations*] .... CID
Committee on Information Needs .... COIN

Committee for Inland Fisheries of Africa [*UN Food and Agriculture Organization*] .... CIFA
Committee on Institutional Cooperation [*Big Ten universities and University of Chicago*] CIC
Committee on Instruction in the Use of Libraries [*American Library Association*] .... IULC
Committee Insuring and Guaranteeing Anyone's Right to Smoke .... CIGARS
Committee to Integrate the Elks .... CITE
Committee for the Inter-American Telecommunications .... CITEL
Committee on Interest and Dividends [*Terminated, 1974*] [*Federal Reserve Board*] .... CID
Committee for International Co-operation in Information Retrieval Among Examining Patent Offices .... CICIREPATO
Committee for International Collaborative Activities [*An association*] .... CICA
Committee for International Coordination of National Research in Demography .... CICRED
Committee on International Environmental Affairs [*Department of State*] .... CIEA
Committee on International Exchange of Persons .... CIEP
Committee on International Exchange of Persons Conference Board of Associated Research Councils [*Later, Council for International Exchange of Scholars*] .... CIEPCBC
Committee on International Freedom to Publish .... CIFP
Committee for International Municipal Cooperation .... CIMC
Committee for an International Program in Atmospheric Sciences and Hydrology [*United Nations*] .... CIPASH
Committee on International Reference Atmosphere .... CIRA
Committee on International Scientific and Technical Information Programs [*National Academy of Sciences - National Research Council*] .... CISTIP
Committee of Interns and Residents .... CIR
Committee on Interpretation of the Nation-Wide Marine Definition [*Later, COI*] .... CINWMD
Committee to Investigate Assassinations .... CTIA
Committee to Investigate Copyright Problems .... CICP
Committee on Invisibles and Financing Related to Trade [*United Nations Conference on Trade and Development*] .... CIFT
Committee for Italic Handwriting [*Defunct*] .... CIH
Committee on Jobs, Environment, and Technology .... CJET
Committee on Joint Support of Air Navigation Services [*International Civil Aviation Organization*] .... CJSANS
Committee for Leaving the Environment of America Natural .... CLEAN
Committee of Liberal Exiles .... CLE
Committee on Library Automation [*American Library Association*] .... COLA
Committee for Liquidation of German War Potential [*Allied German Occupation Forces*] .... CLWP
Committee for the Maintenance of Jewish Standards .... CMJS
Committee on Manpower Opportunities in Israel [*Later, IAC*] .... COMOI
Committee on Manpower Resources for Science and Technology .... CMR
Committee on Man's Underwater Activities .... CMU/WA
Committee on Materials [*Federal Council for Science and Technology*] .... COMAT
Committee on Medical Research [*Subdivision of OSRD*] [*World War II*] .... CMR
Committee on Mediterranean Neogene Stratigraphy .... CMNS
Committee Meeting Information System .... COMIS
Committee on the Meteorological Effects of Stratospheric Aircraft .... COMESA
Committee on Migration and Resettlement [*Department of State*] [*World War II*] .... CMR
Committee on Militarism in Education [*Defunct*] .... CME
Committee on Mineral Resources and the Environment [*National Research Council*] .... COMRATE
Committee on Missionary Evangelism .... COME
Committee for Modern Courts .... CMC
Committee for the Monument of Garibaldi .... CMG
Committee for Mother and Child Rights .... CMCR
Committee on Motor Vehicle Emissions [*National Academy of Sciences*] .... CMVE
Committee on a Multimedium Approach to Sludge Management [*National Research Council*] .... CMSM
Committee for National Arbor Day .... CNAD
Committee for National Health Insurance .... CNHI
Committee of National Institutes of Patent Agents .... CNIPA
Committee for National Land Development Policy [*Defunct*] .... CNLDP
Committee on National Library Information Systems .... CONLIS
Committee for a National Peace Academy [*Later, N-PAC*] .... NPA
Committee for National Security .... CNS
Committee on National Statistics .... CNSTAT
Committee on National Student Citizenship in Every National Case of Emergency .... CONSCIENCE
Committee for a National Trade Policy [*Defunct*] .... CNTP
Committee on Nationwide Television Audience Measurement .... CONTAM
Committee on New Alternatives in the Middle East [*Later, FOR*] .... CONAME
Committee for Nonviolent Action [*Later, WRL*] .... CNVA
Committee on Nuclear and Alternative Energy Systems [*National Research Council*] [*Defunct*] .... CONAES

Committee for Nuclear Information [*Later, Committee for Environmental Information*] .... CNI
Committee for Nuclear Responsibility .... CNR
Committee for Oil Pipe Lines [*Later, AOPL*] .... COPL
Committee for Oil Shale Development [*Defunct*] .... COSHD
Committee on Organization [*American Library Association*] .... COO
Committee on Original People's Entitlement [*Eskimo claim to Canadian land*] .... COPE
Committee on Overhead Reconnaissance [*Later, COMIREX*] .... COMOR
Committee on Paperless Entries .... COPE
Committee on Parenthood Education [*Defunct*] .... COPE
Committee on the Peaceful Uses of Outer Space [*United Nations*] .... COPUOS
Committee on Peaceful Uses of the Sea-Bed and Ocean Floor Beyond Limits of National Jurisdiction [*United Nations*] .... CPUSOFBLNJ
Committee for Pedestrian Tolls .... CPT
Committee on Period One [*US committee concerned with the period between the end of the German War and the end of the Japanese War*] [*World War II*] .... CPO
Committee on Persistent Pesticides .... CPP
Committee on Physics and Society [*of American Institute of Physics*] .... COMPAS
Committee on Planetary and Lunar Exploration [*National Research Council*] .... COMPLEX
Committee on Polar Research [*Later, PRB*] [*US*] .... CPR
Committee on Policy Implementation [*American Library Association*] .... COPI
Committee on Political Education [*AFL-CIO*] .... COPE
Committee on Political Parties .... CPP
Committee for Positive Education .... CPE
Committee on Power Plant Siting [*National Academy of Engineering*] .... COPPS
Committee on the Present Danger .... CPD
Committee for the Preservation of the Tule Elk .... CPTE
Committee to Preserve American Color Television .... COMPACT
Committee of Presidents of Statistical Societies .... COPSS
Committee of Presidents of Statistical Societies .... CPSS
Committee for Prisoner Humanity and Justice .... CPHJ
Committee on Problems of Drug Dependence. Proceedings of the Annual Scientific Meeting. United States National Research Council [*A publication*] .... Comm Probl Drug Depend Proc Annu Sci Meet US Nat Res Counc
Committee on Procedure and Valuation of Reparations [*Allied German Occupation Forces*] .... CPVR
Committee on Professional Ethics, Rights, and Freedom [*of the American Political Science Association*] .... CPERF
Committee for Program and Coordination [*Economic and Social Council*] [*United Nations*] .... CPC
Committee on Program Evaluation and Support [*American Library Association*] .... COPES
Committee to Promote Action [*Poverty program*] .... COMPACT
Committee to Promote Science and Technology .... CPST
Committee to Promote the Study of Austrian History .... CPSAH
Committee to Promote Uniformity in the Regulation of Motor Carriers .... CPURMC
Committee on Propagation [*National Defense Research Committee*] .... CP
Committee on Prosthetics Research and Development [*National Research Council*] .... CPRD
Committee to Protect Journalists .... CPJ
Committee to Protect Our Children's Teeth [*Defunct*] .... CPCT
Committee on Public Doublespeak .... CPD
Committee for Public Education and Religious Liberty .... PEARL
Committee on Public Engineering Policy [*National Academy of Engineering*] .... COPEP
Committee on Public Engineering Policy [*National Academy of Engineering*] .... CPEP
Committee for Public Justice .... CPJ
Committee of Publicly Owned Companies .... COPOC
Committee for Purchase of Products and Services of the Blind and Other Severely Handicapped [*Later, Committee for Purchase from the Blind and Other Severely Handicapped*] .... CPPSBOSH
Committee on Radio Frequencies [*National Academy of Sciences*] .... CORF
Committee on Radioactive Waste Management [*Later, BRWM*] .... CRWM
Committee to Re-Elect the President [*Also, CRP*] [*1972*] .... CREEP
Committee to Re-Elect the President [*Also, CREEP*] [*1972*] .... CRP
Committee on Reactor Safety Technology .... CREST
Committee for Real Ale .... CRA
Committee on Reciprocal Deliveries [*Allied German Occupation Forces*] .... CRD
Committee for Reciprocity Information [*A federal government body*] .... CRI
Committee for the Recovery of Archaeological Remains .... CRAR
Committee for Rejection of Obnoxious Commercials .... CROC
Committee of Religion and Art of America [*Later, FAAR*] .... CRAA
Committee of Religious Concern for Peace .... CRCP
Committee on Remote Sensing Programs for Earth Resource Survey [*Formerly, COSPEAR*] [*National Academy of Sciences*] .... CORSPERS
Committee to Remove Unnatural Deposits from the Environment [*Student legal action organization*] .... CRUDE

Committee to Rescue Italian Art.....CRIA
Committee on Research Evaluation [*US*].....CORE
Committee on Research Materials on Southeast Asia.....CORMOSEA
Committee to Resist Abortion.....CRA
Committee to Resist Acronym Proliferation.....CRAP
Committee to Resist the Efforts of the Ex-President [*Opposed Richard Nixon's visit to Oxford University, 1978*].....CREEP
Committee of Responsibility.....COR
Committee for a Responsible Federal Budget.....CRFB
Committee to Restore the Constitution.....CRC
Committee to Retain Our Segregated Schools [*Group in Arkansas, organized to oppose STOP*].....CROSS
Committee of Returned Volunteers [*Defunct*].....CRV
Committee for Review of Our China Policy [*Defunct*].....CROCP
Committee for the Revision of the Criminal Code [*Allied German Occupation Forces*].....CRICO
Committee on Rhetoric, Administration, and Perspicacity [*Satirical bureaucracy term*].....CRAP
Committee on Rural Economic and Social Trends.....CREST
Committee for Safe Bicycling [*Defunct*].....CSB
Committee on the Safety of Machines [*British*].....CSM
Committee on Safety of Medicines [*British*].....CSM
Committee on Sane Telephone Service.....COSTS
Committee to Save the Peace Symbol [*Student legal action organization*].....CSPS
Committee on Scholarly Communications with the People's Republic of China.....CSCPRC
Committee for Science, Engineering, and Public Policy [*Formerly, COSPUP*] [*National Academy of Sciences*].....COSEPUP
Committee on Science and Public Policy [*Later, COSEPUP*] [*National Academy of Sciences*].....COSPUP
Committee on Science and Technology [*EEC*].....COST
Committee on Scientific Information [*Federal Council for Science and Technology*].....COSI
Committee for the Scientific Investigation of Claims of the Paranormal.....CSICOP
Committee for the Scientific Survey of Air Defence [*British*] [*World War II*].....CSSAD
Committee for the Scientific Survey of Air Offence [*British*] [*World War II*].....CSSAO
Committee for the Scientific Survey of Air Warfare [*British*] [*World War II*].....CSSAW
Committee on Scientific and Technical Information [*Defunct*] [*Federal Council for Science and Technology*].....COSATI
Committee on Scientific and Technical Information.....CSTI
Committee of Security Experts [*Military*].....CSE
Committee for Single Adoptive Parents.....CSAP
Committee of Singled-Out Taxpayers [*Later, American Council of Taxpayers*].....COST
Committee for Small Business Exports.....CSBE
Committee of Small Magazine Editors and Publishers.....COSMEP
Committee on Societal Consequences of Transportation Noise Abatement [*National Research Council*].....CTNA
Committee on Society, Development, and Peace [*of the Roman Catholic Church and the World Council of Churches*] [*Defunct*].....SODEPAX
Committee on Solar-Terrestrial Research [*National Academy of Sciences*].....CSTR
Committee for Solidarity with the Bolivian People.....CSBP
[*US*] **Committee in Solidarity with the People of El Salvador**.....CISPES
Committee in Solidarity with the People of Guatemala.....CSPG
Committee in Solidarity with the People of Iran.....CSPI
Committee on SONAR Model Standards [*Navy*].....COSMOS
Committee of Southern Churchmen [*Formerly, FSC*].....CSC
Committee on Space Programs for Earth Observation [*Later, CORSPERS*] [*National Academy of Sciences*].....COSPEAR
Committee on Space Research [*of the International Council of Scientific Unions*].....COSPAR
Committee on Special Educational Projects [*Cornell University*].....COSEP
Committee on the Standardization of Hospital Graphics [*Defunct*].....CSHG
Committee on State and Local Government Cooperation.....CSLGC
Committee on State Sovereignty.....CSS
Committee on Statistics of Drilling [*American Association of Petroleum Geologists*].....CSD
Committee on the Status of Women in Anthropology.....COSWA
Committee on the Status of Women in the Archival Profession.....CSWAP
Committee on the Status of Women in the Economics Profession.....CSWEP
Committee on the Status of Women in Linguistics.....CSWL
Committee on Status of Women Microbiologists.....CSWM
Committee on the Status of Women in Sociology.....CSWS
Committee to Stop Chemical Atrocities.....CSCA
Committee to Stop Children's Murder [*Defunct*].....CSCM
Committee on Storage, Automatic Processing, and Retrieval of Geological Data [*International Union of Geological Sciences*] [*Information service*].....COGEODATA
Committee for the Study of the American Electorate.....CSAE
Committee for the Study of Environmental Manpower [*National Research Council*].....CSEM
Committee for the Study of Handgun Misuse.....CSHM
Committee for the Suit Against Government Misconduct.....CSAGM
Committee on Supply Questions in Liberated Areas (Official) [*World War II*].....SLAO
Committee to Support Nicaragua.....CSN
Committee on Support of Research in the Mathematical Sciences [*National Academy of Sciences*].....COSRIMS
Committee in Support of Solidarity.....CSS
Committee for the Survey of Chemistry [*National Academy of Sciences*].....CSC
Committee on the Survey of Materials Science and Engineering [*Obsolete*] [*National Academy of Sciences*].....COSMAT
Committee for the Survival of a Free Congress.....CSFC
Committee on the Teaching of Science of the International Council of Scientific Unions.....ICSU-CTS
Committee of Ten Million.....COTM
Committee for Thorough Agricultural Political Education [*Associated Milk Producers, Inc.*].....C-TAPE
Committee on Thrombolytic Agents.....CTA
Committee on Tidal Hydraulics [*Army*].....CTH
Committee for Time Uniformity [*Defunct*].....CTU
Committee to Review Generic Requirements [*Nuclear Regulatory Commission*].....CRGR
Committee of Transylvania.....CT
Committee on Tunneling and Underground Construction.....CTUC
Committee on Undersea Warfare.....CUW
Committee on Uniform Crime Records.....UCR
Committee on Uniform Security Identification Procedures [*Banking*].....CUSIP
Committee on Uniform Traffic Accident Statistics [*Later, Traffic Records Committee*].....CUTAS
Committee on the Unisex Military.....CUM
[*The*] **Committee to Unite America**.....TCUA
Committee of University Industrial Relations Librarians.....CUIRL
Committee of Urban Program Universities.....CUPU
Committee Urging Regulatory Reform for Efficient National Trucking [*Later, BCIPT*].....CURRENT
Committee on Valuation of Securities.....CVS
Committee on Veterans Medical Problems [*US*].....CVMP
Committee for the Visual Arts [*Later, CVAAS*].....CVA
Committee for a Voluntary Census.....CVC
Committee on Water Research [*International Council of Scientific Unions*].....COWAR
Committee on Water Resources Research [*US*].....COWRR
Committee of the Whole [*United Nations*].....COW
Committee for Wildlife on the Last Frontier.....WOLF
Committee on Women in Asian Studies.....CWAS
Committee for Women in Geophysics.....CWG
Committee for Women in Public Administration.....CWPA
Committee for World Development and World Disarmament [*Defunct*].....CWDWD
Committee on the World Food Crisis [*Defunct*].....WFC
Committee on World Literacy and Christian Literature [*Later, Intermedia*].....LIT-LIT
Committee for Zero Automobile Growth.....CZAG
Committees of Correspondence.....COC
Commode [*Medicine*].....COM
Commodities - Coal and Steel.....C/CS
Commodities Data Information Service [*MJK Associates*] [*Information service*].....CDIS
Commodities - Food and Agriculture.....C/FA
Commodities Import Program [*Military*].....CIP
Commodities Research Unit Ltd. [*British*] [*Information service*].....CRU
Commodity.....CMDTY
Commodity Class Manager.....CCM
Commodity Command Management Information System [*Army*].....CCMIS
Commodity Command Standard System.....CCSS
Commodity Control List [*Office of Export Administration*].....CCL
Commodity Coordination Groups.....CCG
Commodity Credit Corporation [*Department of Agriculture*].....CCC
Commodity Exchange.....COMEX
Commodity Exchange Act.....CEA
Commodity Exchange Authority [*Later, CFTC*] [*Department of Agriculture*].....CEA
Commodity Exchange Commission [*Functions transferred to CFTC*].....CEC
Commodity Futures Trading Commission [*Formerly, CEA*] [*Independent government agency*].....CFTC
Commodity Information Services Company.....CISCO
Commodity Integrated Materiel Manager.....CIMM
Commodity Letters of Credit.....CLOC
Commodity Management Master Plan.....CMMP
Commodity Master Plan [*Army*].....CMP
Commodity News Services, Inc. [*Information service*].....CNS
Commodity-Oriented Digital Label Input System.....CODILS
Commodity Policy and Relief [*British*].....CPR
Commodity Pool Operator.....CPO
Commodity Prices [*A publication*].....CP
Commodity Rate.....CR
Commodity Stabilization Service [*Name changed to Agricultural Stabilization and Conservation Service, 1961*].....CSS
Commodity Supplemental Food Program [*Food and Nutrition Service*].....CSFP
Commodity Systems, Incorporated [*Information service*].....CSI

Commodity Trading Advisor ... CTA
Commodity Transportation Survey [*Census Bureau*] ... CTS
Commodo [*Easily*] [*Music*] ... COM
Commodore ... CDRE
Commodore ... COM
Commodore ... COMM
Commodore ... COMMO
Commodore ... COMO
Commodore Air Train [*Navy*] ... COMAT
Commodore Commanding Newfoundland Force [*Navy*] [*Canada*] [*World War II*] ... CCNF
Commodore Corporation [*American Stock Exchange symbol*] ... CCT
Commodore, (Destroyers) Western Approaches [*British*] ... COM(D) WA
Commodore Hotel, Inc. [*NYSE symbol*] [*Delisted*] ... COH
Commodore International Ltd. [*NYSE symbol*] ... CBU
Commodore, Naval Air Stations, East Africa [*British*] ... COMNAS(EA)
Commodore, Royal Canadian Navy Barracks at [*Place*] ... COMBRAX
Commodore Superintendent Contract Built Ships [*Navy*] [*British*] ... CSCBS
Commodore Thomas ap Catesby Jones Society [*Defunct*] ... CTAPCJS
Common ... CMN
Common ... COM
Common ... COMM
Common ... COMN
Common Access Security Terminal ... CAST
Common Access Switching Equipment ... CASE
Common Acute Lymphoblastic Leukemia Antigen [*or Antiserum*] [*Immunochemistry*] ... CALLA
Common Agricultural Policy [*Common Market*] ... CAP
Common Aperture Multifunction Array RADAR ... CAMAR
Common Aperture Multispectrum Seeker [*Army*] ... CAMS
Common Aperture Technique for Imaging Electro-Optical Sensors ... CATIES
Common Attitude Pointing System ... CAPS
Common Aviation Weather Subsystem ... CAWS
Common Base [*Data processing*] ... CB
Common Battery [*Electronics; or in technical drawings*] ... CB
Common Beam Former ... CBF
Common Bench [*Legal*] [*British*] ... CB
Common Bench, New Series [*Legal*] [*British*] ... CBNS
Common Bias, Common Control ... CBCC
Common Bias, Single Control ... CBSC
Common Bile Duct [*Medicine*] ... CBD
Common and Bulk Items List ... CBIL
Common Bulkhead Joint ... CBJ
Common Business-Oriented Language [*Data processing*] ... COBOL
Common Carrier ... CC
Common Carrier Bureau [*of FCC*] ... CCB
Common Carrier Motor Freight Association, Dallas TX [*STAC*] ... CCA
Common Cause [*An association*] ... CC
Common Channel Interoffice Signaling [*System*] [*Bell System*] ... CCIS
Common Cold Foundation [*Defunct*] ... CCF
Common Cold Research Unit [*British Medical Council*] ... CCRU
Common Collector [*Amplifier*] ... CC
Common Communication Adapter [*Data processing*] ... CCA
Common Control Switching Arrangement [*AT & T*] ... CCSA
Common Control Unit [*Army*] ... CCU
Common Council [*or Councilman*] ... CC
Common Customs Tariff [*Common Market*] ... CCT
Common Data Buffer ... CDBFR
Common Data Bus [*Data processing*] ... CDB
Common Defense Installation ... CDI
Common Denominator ... CD
Common Depth Point [*Seismology*] ... CDP
Common Digitizer [*FAA*] ... CD
Common Display Logic [*Data processing*] ... CDL
Common Electronic Parts ... CEP
Common Emitter ... CE
Common Entrance [*Examination for entry into public school*] [*British*] ... C
Common Entrance [*Examination for entry into public school*] [*British*] ... CE
Common Era ... CE
Common External Tariff [*for EEC countries*] ... CET
Common External Tariff [*for EEC countries*] ... CXT
Common Fisheries Policy [*EEC*] ... CFP
Common Fund ... CF
Common Fund for Nonprofit Organizations ... CFNO
[*The*] **Common Fund for Nonprofit Organizations** [*Ford Foundation*] ... TCFNO
Common Ground [*A publication*] ... CG
Common Ground Support Equipment ... CGSE
Common Ground Support Equipment List ... CGSEL
Common ICAO [*International Civil Aviation Organization*] **Data Interchange Network** ... CIDIN
Common IFR [*Instrument Flight Rules*] **Room** [*Aviation*] ... CIR
Common-Impression Cylinder ... CIC
Common Input Processor ... CIP
Common Instrument Flight Rules Room [*Aviation*] ... CIFRR
Common Interactive Graphics Application Routine [*Army*] ... CIGAR
Common Interest Network ... CIN
Common Ion Effect ... CIE
Common Item Order ... CIO
Common Language System [*Data processing*] ... CLS
Common Law ... CL
Common Law Reports [*British*] ... CLR
Common Logistic Support Group [*Military*] ... CLSG
Common Machine Language [*Data processing*] ... CML
Common Main Objective [*Stereomicroscope optical element*] ... CMO
[*The*] **Common Man in the Street** [*The average man*] [*See also MITS*] ... T C MITS
Common Manpower Standards ... CMS
Common Market News [*London*] [*A publication*] ... CMN
Common Meter [*Music*] ... C
Common Meter [*Music*] ... CM
Common Meter Double [*Music*] ... CMD
Common Military Intelligence Skills ... CMIS
Common Mode Error ... CME
Common Mode Input Resistance ... CMIR
Common Mode Rejection ... CMR
Common Mode Rejection Ratio ... CMRR
Common Mode Signal ... CMS
Common Mode Voltage ... CMV
Common Mode Voltage Range ... CMVR
Common Number System ... CNS
Common Operational Research Equipment ... CORE
Common Particular Meter [*Music*] ... CPM
Common Payload Support Equipment [*NASA*] ... CPSE
Common Personal Hygiene Equipment ... CPHE
Common Pleas [*Legal*] ... CP
Common Pleas Division ... CPD
Common Pool ... COMPOOL
Common Power Supply Group ... CPSG
Common Prayer ... CP
Common Program Control Station [*Emergency Broadcast System*] ... CPCS
Common Program Language [*Data processing*] ... CPL
Common Program Support System ... CPSS
Common Pulse Line ... CPL
Common Radio and Electronic Test Equipment [*Navy*] [*British*] ... CRETE
Common Register of Development Projects [*United Nations*] ... CORE
Common/See Individual Components List ... COMSICL
Common Service Area [*Data processing*] ... CSA
Common Set ... CS
Common Signaling Channel ... CSC
Common Slavic [*Language, etc.*] ... CS
Common Source Noise Figure ... CSNF
Common Source Power Gain ... CSPG
Common Source Spot Noise ... CSSN
Common Source Spot Noise Figure ... CSSNF
Common Specialist Training ... CST
Common Specification Language ... CSL
Common Specifications Statements Generator ... COMGEN
Common and Standard [*Items*] ... CS
Common Steel [*Projectile*] ... CS
Common Strategic Doppler ... CSD
Common Supply Support ... CSSPT
Common Supply Support Overseas [*Military*] ... COMSOS
Common Support Equipment ... CSE
Common Support Module [*NASA*] ... CSM
Common Systems Main Interconnecting [*Frame system*] [*Bell System*] ... COSMIC
Common Table of Allowances [*Army*] ... CTA
Common Terminal RADAR Approach Control [*Aviation*] ... CTRAC
Common Test Facility ... CTF
Common Time ... C
Common Usage Equipment ... CUE
Common Usage Item List ... CUIL
Common Usage Radio Frequency Checkout Equipment ... CURFCOE
Common User Data Terminal [*Military*] ... CUDAT
Common User Digital Information Exchange ... CUDIX
Common User Digital Information Exchange System [*or Subsystem*] [*Satellite communication*] ... CUDIXS
Common User Group [*SAGE*] ... CUG
Common User Land Transportation [*Military*] ... CULT
Common User Radio Transmission Sounding System ... CURTS
Common Variable Immunodeficiency [*Medicine*] ... CVI
Common Version [*Bible*] ... CV
Common Video System ... CVS
Commonality Candidate List [*NASA*] ... CCL
Commonality Usage Board ... CUB
Commonality Usage Proposal ... CUP
Commons Expenditure Committee [*British*] ... CEC
Commonweal [*A publication*] ... C
Commonweal [*A publication*] ... Comm
Commonweal [*A publication*] ... Comw
Commonweal [*A publication*] ... Cweal
Commonwealth ... COM
Commonwealth ... COMM
Commonwealth [*A publication*] ... Cwealth
Commonwealth ... CWLTH
Commonwealth Advisory Aeronautical Research Council [*British*] ... CAARC
Commonwealth Agricultural Bureaux [*British*] ... CAB
Commonwealth Air Transport Council [*British*] ... CATC
Commonwealth Aircraft Corporation Ltd. [*Australia*] ... CAC

Commonwealth Association of Architects ... CAA
Commonwealth Association of Museums ... CAM
Commonwealth Association of Planners ... CAP
Commonwealth Association of Science, Technology, and Mathematics Educators ... CASTME
Commonwealth Association of Surveying and Land Economy ... CASLE
Commonwealth of Australia ... COA
Commonwealth Bancshares [*NASDAQ symbol*] ... CBKS
Commonwealth Board of Architectural Education ... CBAE
Commonwealth Board of Surveying Education ... CBSE
Commonwealth Broadcasting Association ... CBA
Commonwealth Bureau of Animal Breeding and Genetics. Technical Communication [*A publication*] ... Commonw Bur Anim Breed Genet Tech Commun
Commonwealth Bureau of Animal Health. Review Series [*A publication*] ... Commonw Bur Anim Health Rev Ser
Commonwealth Bureau of Animal Nutrition. Technical Communications [*A publication*] ... Commonw Bur Anim Nutr Tech Commun
Commonwealth Bureau of Nutrition. Technical Communications [*A publication*] ... Commonw Bur Nutr Tech Commun
Commonwealth Bureau of Pastures and Field Crops. Bulletin [*A publication*] ... Commonw Bur Pastures Field Crops Bull
Commonwealth Bureau of Soils. Special Publications [*A publication*] ... Commonw Bur Soils Spec Publ
Commonwealth Bureau of Soils. Technical Communications [*A publication*] ... Commonw Bur Soils Tech Commun
Commonwealth Club of California, San Francisco, CA [*Library symbol*] ... CSfCCL
Commonwealth Communications Council [*British*] [*World War II*] ... CCC
Commonwealth Countries' League ... CCL
Commonwealth Development Finance Company Ltd. [*Joint government and private agency in London established to aid businesses elsewhere in British Commonwealth*] ... CDFC
Commonwealth Economic Committee [*British*] ... CEC
Commonwealth Economic Consultative Council [*British*] ... CECC
Commonwealth Edison Co. [*NYSE symbol*] ... CWE
Commonwealth Edison Co., Chicago, IL [*Library symbol*] ... ICComE
Commonwealth Education Liaison Committee [*British*] ... CELC
Commonwealth and Empire Radio for Civil Aviation [*British*] ... CERCA
Commonwealth Energy System [*NYSE symbol*] ... CES
Commonwealth Engineers Council ... CEC
Commonwealth Essays and Studies [*A publication*] ... CE & S
Commonwealth Expedition [*British*] ... COMEX
Commonwealth Federal Savings Bank [*NASDAQ symbol*] ... CMFL
Commonwealth Financial Group REIT [*NASDAQ symbol*] ... CFGRS
Commonwealth Forestry Association ... CFA
Commonwealth Forestry Bureau. Technical Communications [*A publication*] ... Commonw For Bur Tech Commun
Commonwealth Forestry Institute [*British*] ... CFI
Commonwealth Forestry Review [*A publication*] ... Com For Rev
Commonwealth Forestry Review [*A publication*] ... Commonw For Rev
Commonwealth Fund, New York, NY [*Library symbol*] ... NNCF
Commonwealth Fund for Technical Cooperation [*British*] ... CFTC
Commonwealth Games Federation ... CGF
Commonwealth Human Ecology Council ... CHEC
Commonwealth Institute of Biological Control [*Trinidad*] ... CIBC
Commonwealth Institute of Biological Control. Miscellaneous Publication [*A publication*] ... Commonw Inst Biol Control Misc Publ
Commonwealth Institute of Entomology [*British*] ... CIE
Commonwealth International Philatelic Society ... CIPS
Commonwealth Law Enforcement Assistance Network [*Pennsylvania*] ... CLEAN
Commonwealth Legal Education Association ... CLEA
Commonwealth Library Association [*British*] ... CLA
Commonwealth Magistrates' Association ... CMA
Commonwealth Microfilm Library Ltd., Calgary, AB, Canada [*Library symbol*] ... CmL
Commonwealth Military Forces [*British*] ... CMF
Commonwealth Mycological Institute. Mycological Papers [*A publication*] ... Commonw Mycol Inst Mycol Pap
Commonwealth Mycological Institute. Phytopathological Papers [*A publication*] ... Commonw Mycol Inst Phytopathol Pap
Commonwealth Mycology Institute [*British*] ... CMI
Commonwealth Nation ... CN
Commonwealth National Financial [*NASDAQ symbol*] ... CNHC
Commonwealth National Library, Parliament House, Canberra, ACT, Australia [*Library symbol*] ... AuCNL
Commonwealth Office [*Formerly, CRO*] [*British*] ... CO
Commonwealth Oil Refining Co., Inc. [*NYSE symbol*] [*Delisted*] ... CWO
Commonwealth Parliamentary Association ... CPA
Commonwealth Pharmaceutical Association ... CPA
Commonwealth Phytopathological News [*A publication*] ... Commonwealth Phytopathol
Commonwealth Phytopathological News [*A publication*] ... Commonw Phytopath News
Commonwealth Phytopathological News [*A publication*] ... Comm Phytopathol News
Commonwealth Preference Area ... CPA
Commonwealth Press Union [*British*] ... CPU
Commonwealth Quarterly [*A publication*] ... ComQ
Commonwealth Realty Trust Cl B [*NASDAQ symbol*] ... CRTYZ
Commonwealth Regional Renewable Energy Resources Information System ... CRRERIS
Commonwealth Relations Office [*Later, CO*] [*British*] ... CRO
Commonwealth Savings & Loan of FLorida [*NASDAQ symbol*] ... COMW
Commonwealth Scientific Committee [*British*] ... CSC
Commonwealth Scientific and Industrial Research Organisation [*Australia*] ... CSIRO
Commonwealth Service Corps [*British*] ... CSC
Commonwealth Sugar Agreement [*British*] ... CSA
Commonwealth Supply Council [*British*] [*World War II*] ... CSC
Commonwealth Telecommunications Board [*British*] ... CTB
Commonwealth Telecommunications Organization ... CTO
Commonwealth Telephone Enterprises, Inc. [*NASDAQ symbol*] ... CWTE
Commonwealth Trading Bank of Australia ... CTBA
Commonwealth Transpacific [*Submarine cable in Pacific*] ... COMPAC
Commonwealth War Graves Commission [*British*] ... CWGC
Commonwealth Weightlifting Federation ... CWF
Commonwealth of World Citizens ... CWC
Communaute Economique de l'Afrique de l'Ouest [*West African Economic Community*] [*Formerly, UDEAO*] ... CEAO
Communaute Economique des Etats de l'Afrique de l'Ouest ... CEDEAO
Communaute Economique Europeenne [*European Economic Community*] ... CEE
Communaute Europeenne [*European Community*] ... CE
Communaute Europeenne des Associations du Commerce de Gros de Biere des Pays Members de la CEE [*European Community of Associations of the Wholesale Beer Trade of the EEC*] ... CEGROB
Communaute Europeenne du Charbon et de l'Acier [*European Coal and Steel Community*] ... CECA
Communaute Europeenne des Cooperatives de Consommateurs [*European Consumers' Cooperation Committee*] [*Common Market*] ... EURO COOP
Communaute Europeenne de Credit Communal [*European Municipal Credit Community*] ... CECC
Communaute Europeenne de Defense [*European Defense Community*] ... CED
Communaute Europeenne de l'Energie Atomique ... CEEA
Communaute Europeenne des Etudiants en Sciences Economiques ... CEDESE
Communaute Europeenne des Organisations de Publicitaires [*European Community of Advertising Organizations*] ... CEOP
Communaute Financiere Africaine ... CFA
Communaute Internationale des Associations de la Librairie [*International Community of Booksellers Associations*] ... CIAL
Communaute Internationale Baha'ie [*Baha'i International Community*] ... CIB
Communaute Radiophonique des Programmes de Langue Francaise [*Community of French-Language Radio Programmes*] ... CRPLF
Communaute de Travail des Brasseurs du Marche Commun [*Working Committee of Common Market Brewers*] ... CBMC
Commune ... COM
Communicable Disease [*or a patient with such a disease*] [*Medicine*] ... CD
Communicable Disease Report [*A publication*] ... CD
Communicate ... CMCT
Communicate [*or Communications*] ... COM
Communicating for Agriculture ... CA
Communicating Nursing Research [*A publication*] ... Commun Nurs Res
Communicating Word Processors ... CWPS
Communication ... COMM
Communication ... COMN
Communication Analysis Section ... CAS
Communication Arts [*A publication*] ... CA
Communication Association of the Pacific ... CAP
Communication Automatic Processing Equipment ... CAPE
Communication and Broadcasting [*A publication*] ... Comm Broadc
Communication Carrier Assembly [*Spaceship*] ... CCA
Communication Center ... CC
Communication Center Console ... CCC
Communication Central Facility [*Air Force*] ... CCF
Communication. Centre de Recherches Zootechniques. Universite de Louvain [*A publication*] ... Commun Cent Rech Zootech Univ Louv
Communication and Command Control Requirements ... CCCR
Communication Commission [*Formerly, BFC*] ... CC
Communication Comptroller ... CC
Communication Computer Programing Center ... CCPC
Communication Control Number ... CCN
Communication Control Program ... CCP
Communication Control Unit ... CCU
Communication Countermeasures ... COMCM
Communication Countermeasures Evaluation Facility [*Air Force*] ... CCEF
Communication and Cybernetics [*A publication*] ... Commun Cybern
Communication and Data Subsystem ... C & DSS
Communication. Department of Agricultural Research. Royal Tropical Institute (Amsterdam) [*A publication*] ... Commun Dep Agric Res R Trop Inst (Amst)
Communication Desk ... CDK
Communication Disorders Specialist ... CDS

Communication Education [*A publication*] ... Comm Educ
Communication Electronic Instructions ... CEI
Communication-Electronic-Meteorological Board [*Air Force*] ... CEMB
Communication and Electronics [*A publication*] ... Com & Electronics
Communication Electronics Element [*Army*] ... CEE
Communication Engineering [*A publication*] ... Commun Eng
Communication with Extraterrestrial Intelligence [*Later, SETI*] [*Radioastronomy*] ... CETI
Communication Facilities Mediterranean and Middle East ... COMMFACMEDME
Communication Identification Navigation ... CIN
Communication Identifier [*Data processing*] ... CID
Communication Implementation Directive [*Air Force*] ... CID
Communication Improvement Program ... CIP
Communication Industrial Services ... CIS
Communication Information ... CI
Communication Information System ... CIS
Communication Instructions for Reporting Enemy Sightings [*Navy*] ... CIRES
Communication and Instrumentation ... C & I
Communication and Instrumentation ... CI
Communication and Instrumentation Support Services ... CISS
Communication and Instrumentation System [*CIS is preferred*] [*NASA*] ... C & IS
Communication and Instrumentation System [*See C & IS*] [*NASA*] ... CIS
Communication Interrupt Control Program [*Data processing*] ... CICP
Communication et Langages [*A publication*] ... Communic et Lang
Communication Line Adapters ... CLA
Communication Line Adapters for Teletype ... CLAT
Communication Line Terminal [*Data processing*] ... CLT
Communication Line Terminator ... COLT
Communication Link Analyzer ... CLA
Communication Link Subsystem ... CLSS
Communication Management System [*Data processing*] ... CMS
Communication Managers Association ... CMA
Communication Monographs [*A publication*] ... Com M
Communication Monographs [*A publication*] ... Comm Monogr
Communication and Navigation ... C & N
Communication, Navigation, and Identification ... CNI
Communication and Navigation Research Laboratory ... CNRL
Communication Net Control Station [*Navy*] ... NECOS
Communication Operation Station ... COS
Communication Optimization Program Translator [*NASA*] ... COPTRAN
Communication Personnel [*Marine Corps*] ... CP
Communication Prediction Program [*NASA*] ... CPPM
Communication Quarterly [*A publication*] ... Comm Q
Communication Quarterly [*A publication*] ... Commun Quart
Communication-Quebec, Trois-Rivieres, PQ, Canada [*Library symbol*] ... CaQTCO
Communication and RADAR Assignment Coordinating Committee ... CRACC
Communication, Range, and Azimuth Unit [*Data processing*] ... COMRAZ
Communication Registered Publication Memoranda ... CRPM
Communication Representative ... CR
Communication Research [*A publication*] ... Comm Res
Communication Research and Development Satellite [*NASA*] ... COMR & DSAT
Communication Scanner Base ... CSB
Communication Science Research Center [*Battelle Memorial Institute*] ... CSRC
Communication Sciences Laboratory [*University of Florida*] ... CSL
Communication Security Activity ... COMMSECACT
Communication Security Publication Memorandum [*Army*] ... CSPM
Communication Signal Distribution System ... CSDS
Communication Skills Corporation [*British*] ... CSC
Communication and Social Science Information Service [*Canadian research collection network*] ... CASSIS
Communication Standing Order ... CSO
Communication Station ... CS
Communication Supplementary Activity ... COMMSUPACT
Communication Supplementary Detachment ... COMMSUPDET
Communication System Control Element [*of TCCF*] ... CSCE
Communication System Simulation Language [*Data processing*] ... COMSL
Communication Systems Engineering Laboratory [*NASA*] ... CSEL
Communication Technical Evaluation Console ... CTEC
Communication and Tracking [*NASA*] ... C & T
Communication Trench [*Military*] ... CT
Communication Valve Development [*British*] ... CVD
Communication Vector Table ... CVT
Communication Watch Officer ... CWO
Communication Workers Alliance [*Philippines*] ... CWA
Communication Workers of Canada ... CWC
Communicationes. Bibliotheca Historiae Medicae Hungarica [*A publication*] ... Comm Bibl Hist Med Hungar
Communicationes de Historia Artis Medicinae [*A publication*] ... Comm Hist Art Med
Communicationes. Instituti Forestalis Cechosloveniae [*A publication*] ... Commun Inst For Cech
Communicationes. Instituti Forestalis Cechosloveniae [*A publication*] ... Commun Inst For Csl
Communicationes. Instituti Forestalis Fenniae [*A publication*] ... Commun Inst For Fenn
Communicationes Veterinariae [*A publication*] ... Commun Vet
Communications ... C
Communications ... COMMS
Communications ... COMMUN
Communications Access Device ... CAD
Communications. ACM [*Association for Computing Machinery*] [*A publication*] ... CACM
Communications. ACM [*Association for Computing Machinery*] [*A publication*] ... Comm ACM
Communications. ACM [*Association for Computing Machinery*] [*A publication*] ... Commun ACM
Communications Advisory Committee ... COMAC
Communications Afloat Program ... CAP
Communications Afloat Work Study ... CAWS
Communications in Algebra [*A publication*] ... Comm Algeb
Communications in Algebra [*A publication*] ... Commun Algebra
Communications Allocation Order ... CAO
Communications on Alternatives in Education [*Defunct*] ... KOA
Communications, Analysis, Simulation, and Evaluation [*Army*] ... CASE
Communications Antenna Sleeve ... CAS
Communications Area Local Station ... CALS
Communications Area Master Station ... CAMS
Communications Assist Team ... CAT
Communications/Automatic Data Processing Laboratory [*Army*] ... CADPL
Communications in Behavioral Biology. Part A. Original Articles [*A publication*] ... Commun Behav Biol Part A Orig Artic
Communications Branch, National Research Council ... CBNRC
Communications Buffer Memory [*Data processing*] ... CBM
Communications and Cable [*NASDAQ symbol*] ... CCAB
Communications Center ... COMCEN
Communications Center ... COMMCEN
Communications Central [*Military*] ... CC
Communications Circular Letter [*Navy*] ... CCL
Communications, Command, Control, and Intelligence [*Pronounced "see-cubed eye"*] ... C^3I
Communications Command Technical Manual [*Army*] ... CCTM
Communications, Command, and Telemetry Systems ... CCATS
Communications Concentrator Software Package [*Data processing*] ... CCSP
Communications and Configuration Console ... CACC
Communications Control ... CC
Communications Control Applications Program ... CCAP
Communications Control Center ... CCC
Communications Control Equipment ... CCE
Communications Control Field ... CCF
Communications Control Group Assembly [*Ground Communications Facility, NASA*] ... CCGA
Communications Control Language ... CCL
Communications Control Package ... CCP
Communications Control Panel ... CCP
Communications and Control Systems Laboratory ... CCSL
Communications Control Team [*Military*] ... CCT
Communications Controller Multichannel [*Data processing*] ... CCM
Communications Corporation of America [*NASDAQ symbol*] ... CCPA
Communications Council ... CC
Communications Countermeasures [*Military*] ... COMMCM
Communications Coupling Unit ... CCU
Communications and Data ... C & D
Communications Data Base [*Canada*] [*Information service*] ... COMBASE
Communications-Data Field ... CDF
Communications and Data Link ... CADL
Communications/Data Manager ... CDM
Communications and Data Processing Operation ... CADPO
Communications Data Processing System ... CDPS
Communications Data Processor [*Electronics*] ... CDP
Communications and Data Subsystems ... CDS
Communications and Data Systems Integration ... CADSI
Communications Digital Control Unit ... CDCU
Communications, Distribution, and Switching Center [*NASA*] ... CD & SC
Communications, Distribution, and Switching Center [*NASA*] ... CDSC
Communications. Dublin Institute for Advanced Studies. Series A [*A publication*] ... Comm Dublin Inst Adv Studies Ser A
Communications. Dublin Institute for Advanced Studies. Series A [*A publication*] ... Commun Dublin Inst Adv Stud A
Communications. Dublin Institute for Advanced Studies. Series D. Geophysical Bulletin [*A publication*] ... Commun Dublin Inst Adv Stud Ser D
Communications Duty Officer ... CDO
Communications Editing Unit ... COMED
Communications and Electronics [*SHAPE*] ... CANDE
Communications and Electronics ... C & E
Communications-Electronics ... C-E
Communications-Electronics ... COMMEL
Communications-Electronics Agency [*Army*] ... C-EA
Communications-Electronics Board ... CEB
Communications and Electronics Command [*Formerly, ASC*] [*Army*] ... CEC
Communications-Electronics Command [*Army*] ... CECOM
Communications-Electronics Committee ... CEC

Communications-Electronics Consolidated Mobilization Reserve List ... CECMRL
Communications-Electronics Coordinating Section [*NATO*] ... CECS
Communications-Electronics Doctrinal Projects Office [*Air Force*] ... CEDPO
Communications-Electronics Doctrine [*Series of Air Force manuals*] ... CED
Communications-Electronics Document ... CED
Communications-Electronics Engineering Installation Agency [*DoD*] ... CEEIA
Communications-Electronics Engineering Installation Agency-National Communications Command [*DoD*] ... CEEIA-NCC
Communications-Electronics Facility Inoperative for Parts ... CEFIP
Communications-Electronics Implementation Plan [*For major air command requirements within the communications-electronics area*] [*Air Force*] ... CEIP
Communications-Electronics Implementation Plan Amendment [*See CEIP*] [*Air Force*] ... CEIPA
Communications and Electronics Maintenance Squadron ... CEMSq
Communications and Electronics Materiel Readiness Command [*Army*] ... CERCOM
Communications-Electronics-Meteorological [*Equipment*] ... CEM
Communications-Electronics-Meteorological Program Aggregate Code [*Air Force*] ... CEMPAC
Communications-Electronics-Meteorological Program Implementation Management System [*Air Force*] ... CEMPIMS
Communications-Electronics Officer [*Air Force*] ... CEO
Communications-Electronics Operating Instruction ... CEOI
Communications-Electronics Policy Directives [*NATO*] ... CEPD
Communications-Electronics Scheme Accounting and Control [*Air Force*] ... CESAC
Communications-Electronics Section [*of a joint military staff; also, the officer in charge of this section*] ... J-6
Communications-Electronics Standing Instruction ... CESI
Communications-Electronics Survivability and Vulnerability ... CESV
Communications Engineering and Installation Agency ... CEIA
Communications Engineering and Installation Department [*Army*] ... CEI
Communications Equipment ... CE
Communications Equipment and Systems Design [*A publication*] ... Commun Equip & Syst Des
Communications Era Task Force ... CERATF
Communications Facilities in Support of DA [*Department of the Army*] **Continuity of Operations Plan** ... COOPCOMM
Communications. Faculte de Medecine Veterinaire. Universite de l'Etat Gand [*A publication*] ... Commun Fac Med Vet Univ Etat Gand
Communications. Faculte des Sciences. Universite d'Ankara [*A publication*] ... Commun Fac Sci Univ Ankara
Communications. Faculte des Sciences. Universite d'Ankara. Serie A. Mathematiques-Physique-Astronomie [*A publication*] ... Comm Fac Sci Univ Ankara Ser A
Communications. Faculte des Sciences. Universite d'Ankara. Serie A2. Physique [*A publication*] ... Commun Fac Sci Univ Ankara Ser A2
Communications. Faculte des Sciences. Universite d'Ankara. Serie C. Sciences Naturelles [*A publication*] ... Commun Fac Sci Univ Ankara Ser C
Communications. Faculty of Veterinary Medicine. State University (Ghent) [*A publication*] ... Commun Fac Vet Med State Univ (Ghent)
Communications-Failure Detecting and Switching Equipment ... COMMSWITCH
Communications Field Exercise [*Military*] ... COMMFEX
Communications Group [*NASDAQ symbol*] ... CMGI
Communications Identification Directory [*Air Force*] ... CID
Communications Improvement Memorandum [*Military*] ... CIM
Communications Industries, Inc. [*NASDAQ symbol*] ... COMM
Communications and Information Handling Equipment and Services ... CO IN HES
Communications Input and Output Control System ... CIOCS
Communications Instructions [*Navy*] ... COMINST
Communications Instructions for Merchant Ships [*Navy*] ... CIMS
Communications Instructions for Reporting Vital Intelligence Sightings [*Military*] ... CIRVIS
Communications Instructor Console ... CIC
Communications Integrated Control Engineering, Reporting, and Operations ... CICERO
Communications Intelligence [*Military*] ... COMINT
Communications Interface Assembly [*Data processing*] ... CIA
Communications Interface Modules [*Data processing*] ... CIM
Communications Interface System ... CIS
Communications International [*A publication*] ... Comm Intnl
Communications International [*A publication*] ... Commun Int
Communications. International Association of Theoretical and Applied Limnology [*A publication*] ... Commun Int Assoc Theor Appl Limnol
Communications Interrupt Analysis ... CIA
Communications Jamming [*Military*] ... COMJAM
Communications Jamming Operator [*Military*] ... CJO
Communications Junction Module Assembly [*Ground Control Facility, NASA*] ... CJMA
Communications. Kamerlingh Onnes Laboratory. University of Leiden [*A publication*] ... Commun Kamerlingh Onnes Lab Univ Leiden
Communications Link Analyzer System ... CLAS
Communications Link Characterization Experiment [*Communications Technology Satellite*] ... CLCE
Communications Logistics Network ... COMLOGNET
Communications. Lunar and Planetary Laboratory [*A publication*] ... Commun Lunar & Planet Lab
Communications Maintenance and Storage ... CM & S
Communications Market Association ... CMA
Communications in Mathematical Physics [*A publication*] ... Comm Math P
Communications in Mathematical Physics [*A publication*] ... Commun Math Phys
Communications Message Traffic Control Unit [*Air Force*] ... CMTCU
Communications Mode Control ... CMC
Communications Monitoring and Control Subsystem ... CMCS
Communications Monitoring Report ... CMR
Communications Moon Relay [*System*] [*NASA*] ... CMR
Communications Multiplexer [*Data processing*] ... CM
Communications. Musee National de l'Ermitage [*A publication*] ... ComErm
Communications Need ... COMNEED
Communications Network ... COMNET
Communications Network Control Element ... CNCE
Communications Network Design Program ... CNDP
Communications, Networks, and Information Processing Theory Group [*MIT*] ... CNIPTG
Communications News [*A publication*] ... Comm News
Communications Office Building ... COB
Communications Officer [*Navy*] ... CO
Communications Officer ... COMMO
Communications Officer ... COMO
Communications Operating Directive ... COD
Communications Operations Instructions [*Air Force*] ... COI
Communications Operations Report [*Air Force*] ... COR
Communications-Oriented Automatic Test ... COATS
Communications-Oriented Processing Equipment ... COPE
Communications-Oriented Production Information and Control System [*IBM Corp.*] ... COPICS
Communications Outage Restoral Section [*ADC*] ... COORS
Communications in Partial Differential Equations [*A publication*] ... Comm Partial Differential Equations
Communications in Partial Differential Equations [*A publication*] ... Commun Part Differ Equ
Communications on Physics [*A publication*] ... Commun Phys
Communications Plan ... COMPLAN
Communications Planning and Development ... CPD
Communications Pool ... COMPOOL
Communications Procedure-Oriented Language [*Data processing*] ... CPOL
Communications Processing Center ... CPC
Communications Processing System ... CPS
Communications Processing Unit ... CPU
Communications Processor ... COM
Communications Processor ... CP
Communications Processor Assembly [*Ground Control Facility, NASA*] ... CPRA
Communications Processor Conversion Center ... CPCC
Communications Programs [*NASA*] ... CP
Communications Project ... CP
Communications in Psychopharmacology [*A publication*] ... Commun Psychopharmacol
Communications on Pure and Applied Mathematics [*A publication*] ... Comm Pure Appl Math
Communications on Pure and Applied Mathematics [*A publication*] ... Commun Pure Appl Math
Communications on Pure and Applied Mathematics [*A publication*] ... Com P A Math
Communications Relay Center [*Air Force*] ... CRC
Communications Requirements Systems Configuration and Equipment List ... CORESCEL
Communications Research Centre [*Defunct*] [*Canada*] ... CRC
Communications Research and Development Command [*Army*] ... CORADCOM
Communications Research Establishment ... CRE
Communications Research Institute ... CRI
Communications/Research/Machines, Inc. [*Publisher*] ... CRM
Communications Resources Data System [*Defense Communications Agency*] ... CREDATA
Communications Routing Indicator ... COMRI
Communications. Royal Society of Edinburgh. Physical Sciences [*A publication*] ... Commun R Soc Edinburgh Phys Sci
Communications Satellite ... COMMUNICAT
Communications Satellite [*Japan*] ... CS
Communications Satellite Advanced Research [*AFSC*] ... CSAR
Communications Satellite Corp. [*Assignee of operational and developmental responsibilities for Telstar and other international communications space devices*] ... COMSAT
Communications Satellite Corporation [*See also COMSAT*] ... COMSATCORP
Communications Satellite Corp. [*See also COMSAT*] [*NYSE symbol*] ... CQ
Communications Satellite Corp. [*See also COMSAT*] ... CSC
Communications Satellite Program [*NASA*] ... CSP
Communications Satellite Project Office ... CSPO
Communications Satellite Relay ... CSR

Communications Security [*Military*] .... COMSEC
Communications Security Control Group [*Navy*] .... CSCG
Communications Security Education Program .... CSEP
Communications Security Equipment Engineering Bulletin .... CSEEB
Communications Security Equipment Systems Document [*National Security Agency*] .... CSESD
Communications Security Material Sub-Issuing Office [*Military*] .... CMSIO
Communications Security Material Van-Issuing Office [*Military*] .... CMVIO
Communications Security Mobile Issuing Office [*Military*] .... CMMIO
Communications Security Publication .... CSP
Communications Security System .... CSS
Communications Service Authorization [*Obsolete*] .... CSA
Communications with and Service to the Public [*Army*] .... CWSP
Communications Soft Hat [*NASA*] .... CSH
Communications in Soil Science and Plant Analysis [*A publication*] .... Comm Soil S
Communications in Soil Science and Plant Analysis [*A publication*] .... Commun Soil Sci Plant Anal
Communications Spacecraft Operation Center [*NASA*] .... COMSOC
Communications Speaker .... COMSPK
Communications Squadron [*Marine Corps*] .... COMSQN
Communications in Statistics [*A publication*] .... Comm Statis
Communications in Statistics. A. Theory and Methods [*A publication*] .... Comm St A
Communications in Statistics. A. Theory and Methods [*A publication*] .... Commun Stat A
Communications in Statistics. B. Simulation and Computation [*A publication*] .... Comm St B
Communications in Statistics. B. Simulation and Computation [*A publication*] .... Commun Stat B
Communications Status Report [*Military*] .... COMSTATRPT
Communications Subcommittee [*Allied German Occupation Forces*] .... CSC
Communications Subsystem .... CSS
Communications Support .... COMS
Communications Support Element [*Military*] .... CSE
Communications Surveillance Transistor .... CST
Communications Switch Operating System .... CSOS
Communications Switchboard Console .... CSC
Communications Switcher .... CS
Communications System .... CS
Communications System Control Console .... CSCC
Communications System Status Display .... CSSD
Communications Systems [*NASDAQ symbol*] .... CSII
Communications Systems Agency [*Army*] .... CSA
Communications Systems Center .... CSC
Communications Systems Engineer .... CSE
Communications Systems Engineering Program [*Army*] .... CSEP
Communications Systems, Incorporated .... CSI
Communications Systems Management Association .... CSMA
Communications and Tactical [*Publications*] [*Navy*] .... COMTAC
Communications Tag Pool .... COMPOOL
Communications Technical Operations Center [*Air Force*] .... CTOC
Communications Technician [*Navy rating*] .... CT
Communications Technician, Chief [*Navy rating*] .... CTC
Communications Technician, First Class [*Navy rating*] CT1
Communications Technician, Master Chief [*Navy rating*] .... CTCM
Communications Technician, Second Class [*Navy rating*] CT2
Communications Technician, Senior Chief [*Navy rating*] .... CTCS
Communications Technician, Third Class [*Navy rating*] CT3
Communications Technology Satellite .... CTS
Communications and Telemetry .... CMTM
Communications Terminal [*Data processing*] .... CT
Communications Terminal Module [*Data processing*] .... CTM
Communications Terminal Module Controller [*Data processing*] .... CTMC
Communications Terminal Synchronous [*Data processing*] .... CTS
Communications Test Station [*NASA*] .... CTS
Communications Timing Procedure .... CTP
Communications and Tracking System [*or Subsystem*] .... CATS
Communications and Tracking System [*or Subsystem*] .... CTS
Communications Unit Executor .... CUE
Communications User Program .... CUP
Communications User Radio Transmission Sounding [*Navy*] .... CURTS
Communications Validating Office .... CVO
Communications Workers of America [*Formerly, NFTW*] .... CWA
Communications Yeoman [*Navy rating*] .... CYN
Communications Zone .... COMMZ
Communications Zone .... COMZ
Communications Zone .... CZ
Communications Zone Indicator [*Air Force*] .... COZI
Communicative .... COMMUNV
Communicative Ability in Daily Living .... CADL
Communicative Disorders .... CD
Communicator of Scientific and Technical Information [*A publication*] .... Commun Sci & Tech Inf
Communicators for Nuclear Disarmament .... CFND
Communio Viatorum [*A publication*] .... Com Via
Communion [*A publication*] .... Commun
Communiquer a Toutes Adresses [*To Be Circulated to All Addresses*] [*French*] .... CTA
Communis [*Common*] [*Latin*] .... CS
Communist .... COM
Communist Activities [*British*] .... CA
Communist Bloc Intelligence Service .... CBIS
Communist China Digest [*A publication*] .... Communist China Dig
Communist Information .... COMINFORM
Communist International .... COMINTERN
Communist Labor Party .... CLP
Communist Party .... COMM
Communist Party .... CP
Communist Party of Argentina .... CPA
Communist Party of Belgium .... CPB
Communist Party (Bolsheviks) .... CP (b)
Communist Party of Canada .... CPC
Communist Party of China .... CPC
Communist Party of Colombia .... CPC
Communist Party of Denmark .... CPD
Communist Party of Ecuador .... CPE
Communist Party of Finland .... CPF
Communist Party of India .... CPI
Communist Party of Ireland .... CPI
Communist Party of Lesotho [*Basutoland*] .... CPL
Communist Party of Luxembourg .... CPL
Communist Party of Malaya .... CPM
Communist Party of Malta .... CPM
Communist Party Marxist .... CPM
Communist Party of Norway .... CPN
Communist Party of the Philippines .... CPP
Communist Party of the Philippines/Marxist-Leninist .... CPP/ML
Communist Party of South Africa .... CPSA
Communist Party of the Soviet Union .... CPSU
Communist Party of Thailand .... CPT
Communist Party of the United States of America .... CPUSA
Communist Party of the USA/Marxist Leninist .... CPUSA/ML
Communist Party of Venezuela .... CPV
Communist Rebel Combat Captives .... CRCC
Communist Suppression Operations Command [*Thailand*] .... CSOC
Communist Sympathizer .... COMSYMP
Communist Terrorist [*Rhodesia*] .... CT
Communist Workers Party .... CWP
Communist Youth League .... CYL
Communist Youth League [*From the Russian*] .... KOMSOMOL
Communita Internazionale [*A publication*] .... Com Internaz
Communitatis Europeae Lex [*European Community Law*] [*Information service*] .... CELEX
Communities Organization of People .... COOP
Community .... CMTY
Community .... COM
Community .... COMMUN
Community Action Agencies [*Community Services Administration*] .... CAA
Community Action to Control High Blood Pressure [*HEW*] .... CATCH
Community Action on Latin America .... CALA
Community Action Program [*Community Services Administration*] .... CAP
Community Action Team [*Department of Labor*] .... CAT
Community Adaptation Schedule [*Psychology*] .... CAS
Community/Airport Economic Development Model [*FAA*] .... CAEDM
Community Alert Patrol .... CAP
Community of All Hallows [*Anglican religious community*] .... CAH
Community Antenna Relay [*Service*] [*FCC*] .... CAR
Community Antenna Relay Service [*FCC*] .... CARS
Community Antenna Television [*Later, CTV*] .... CATV
Community Antenna Television Association .... CATA
Community Arts Councils, Incorporated [*Later, American Council for the Arts*] .... CACI
Community Associations Institute .... CAI
Community Automatic Exchange [*Telephone*] .... CAEX
Community Automatic Exchange [*Telephone*] .... CAX
Community Based Organization [*Organization which provides employment and training services*] [*CETA*] .... CBO
Community of the Blessed Virgin Mary [*Anglican religious community*] .... CBVM
Community Broadcasters Association .... CBA
Community College CC
Community College of the Air Force .... CCAF
Community College of Allegheny County, Boyce Campus, Monroeville, PA [*OCLC symbol*] [*Inactive*] .... AIB
Community College of Allegheny County, Boyce Campus, Monroeville, PA [*Library symbol*] .... PMvAC
Community College of Allegheny County, Center North, Pittsburgh, PA [*OCLC symbol*] .... AIN
Community College of Allegheny County, Pittsburgh, PA [*OCLC symbol*] .... AIC
Community College of Allegheny County, Pittsburgh, PA [*Library symbol*] .... PPiAC
Community College of Allegheny County, South Campus, West Mifflin, PA [*OCLC symbol*] .... AIS
Community College of Allegheny County, South Campus, West Mifflin, PA [*Library symbol*] .... PWesAC
Community College Association for Instruction and Technology .... CCAIT
Community College of Baltimore, Baltimore, MD [*Library symbol*] .... MdBBJC
Community College of Denver, Auraria Campus, Denver, CO [*Library symbol*] .... CoDCC-A

Community College of Denver, Denver, CO [*Library symbol*] .... CoDCC
Community College of Denver, North AEC Project, Westminster, CO [*OCLC symbol*] .... DVE
Community College of Denver, North Campus, Denver, CO [*Library symbol*] .... CoDCC-N
Community College of Denver, North Campus, Westminster, CO [*OCLC symbol*] .... DVC
Community College of Denver, North Campus, Westminster, CO [*OCLC symbol*] .... DVN
Community College of Denver, Red Rocks Campus, Golden, CO [*OCLC symbol*] .... DVR
Community College of Denver, Red Rocks Campus, Lakewood, CO [*Library symbol*] .... CoDCC-R
Community College of the Finger Lakes, Canandaigua, NY [*Library symbol*] .... NCanC
Community College of the Finger Lakes, Canandaigua, NY [*OCLC symbol*] .... ZFM
Community College Frontiers [*A publication*] .... Com Coll Front
Community College Journalism Association .... CCJA
Community College of Philadelphia, Philadelphia, PA [*OCLC symbol*] .... PDC
Community College of Philadelphia, Philadelphia, PA [*Library symbol*] .... PPCoC
Community College Review [*A publication*] .... Com Coll R
Community College Social Science Association .... CCSSA
Community College Unit [*Office of Education*] .... CCU
Community Communications [*Independent Local Radio*] [*British*] CC
Community of the Companions of Jesus the Good Shepherd [*Anglican religious community*] .... CJGS
Community Coordinated Child Care Program [*Also, CCCC*] 4C
Community Coordinated Child Care Program [*Also, 4C*] CCCC
Community Dentistry and Oral Epidemiology [*A publication*] .... Comm Den Or
Community Dentistry and Oral Epidemiology [*A publication*] .... Community Dent Oral Epidemiol
Community Design Center Directors Association .... CDCDA
Community Development .... CD
Community Development Administration [*HUD*] .... CDA
Community Development Block Grant [*HUD*] .... CDBG
Community Development Bulletin [*A publication*] .... CDB
Community Development Corporation [*Later, NCDC*] .... CDC
Community Development Foundation [*Later, SCF*] .... CDF
Community Development Journal [*A publication*] .... Com Develop J
Community Development Journal [*A publication*] .... Com Dev J
Community Development Journal [*A publication*] .... Comm Dev J
Community Development Journal [*A publication*] .... Community Devel J
Community Development Journal [*A publication*] .... Community Develop J
Community Development Journal [*A publication*] .... Community Dev J
Community Development and Panchayati Raj Digest [*A publication*] .... Com Dev Pancha Raj D
Community Development Society .... CDS
Community Dial Office .... CDO
Community Dispute Services .... CDS
Community Economics, Incorporated [*An association*] .... CEI
Community Educational Resources .... CER
Community Electronic Teller System .... COMETS
Community Employment Development [*Department of Labor*] .... CED
Community Energy Program [*Office of Volunteer Liaison*] [*ACTION*] .... CEP
Community Enterprise Program [*British*] .... CEP
Community Environmental Council .... CEC
Community of the Epiphany [*Anglican religious community*] .... CE
Community Facilities Administration [*of HHFA*] [*Terminated*] .... CFA
Community Fellows Program .... CFP
Community Food and Nutrition Programs [*Community Services Administration*] .... CFNP
Community Free Library, Holley, NY [*Library symbol*] .... NHoll
Community-General Hospital, Staff Library, Syracuse, NY [*OCLC symbol*] .... ZUG
Community-General Hospital, Syracuse, NY [*Library symbol*] .... NSyGH
Community of the Glorious Ascension [*Anglican religious community*] .... CGA
Community Guidance Service .... CGS
Community Health [*A publication*] .... CH
Community Health [*A publication*] .... Comm Health
Community Health Action Planning Service .... CHAPS
Community Health Air Monitoring Program [*Environmental Protection Agency*] .... CHAMP
Community Health Association .... CHA
Community Health Center .... CHC
Community Health Computing .... CHC
Community Health Council [*British*] .... CHC
Community Health Education Project .... CHEP
Community Health and Environmental Surveillance System [*Environmental Protection Agency project*] .... CHESS
Community Health Information Network [*Library network*] .... CHIN
Community Health Service [*HEW*] .... CHS
Community Helps in Life Development .... CHILD
Community of the Holy Cross [*Anglican religious community*] .... CHC
Community of the Holy Family [*Anglican religious community*] .... CHF
Community of the Holy Name of Jesus [*Anglican religious community*] .... CHN
Community of the Holy Rood [*Anglican religious community*] .... CHR
Community Hospital of Ottawa, Ottawa, IL [*Library symbol*] .... IOtCH
Community Hospital of Springfield, Springfield, OH [*Library symbol*] .... OSH
Community Human and Industrial Development, Inc. [*Office of Economic Opportunity*] [*Terminated*] .... CHID
Community Hypertension Evaluation Clinic [*New Jersey*] .... CHEC
Community Improvement Program .... CIP
Community Improvement Scale [*Psychology*] .... CIS
Community Industry Scheme [*Department of Employment*] [*British*] .... CIS
Community Information Network [*Cable TV programing service*] .... CIN
Community Information Services .... CIS
Community Information Utility .... CIU
Community of Interest [*DoD*] .... COI
Community Investment Officer [*Federal Home Loan Bank Board*] .... CIO
Community of Jesus of Nazareth [*Anglican religious community*] .... CJN
Community Junior College .... CJC
Community and Junior College Journal [*A publication*] .... CMJPB
Community and Junior College Journal [*A publication*] .... Com & Jr Coll
Community and Junior College Journal [*A publication*] .... Com & Jr Coll J
Community and Junior College Journal [*A publication*] .... Community Jr Coll J
Community Land Use Game [*Urban-planning game*] .... CLUG
Community Law Offices .... CLO
Community Living Arrangement [*For the handicapped*] .... CLA
Community Market Catalog .... CM
Community Medicine [*A publication*] .... Community Med
Community Memorial Hospital, Health Science Library, Menomonee Falls, WI [*Library symbol*] .... WMenofH
Community Mental Health Center .... CMHC
Community Mental Health Centers Act [*1975*] .... CMHCA
Community Mental Health Journal [*A publication*] .... Com Ment Health J
Community Mental Health Journal [*A publication*] .... Comm Ment H
Community Mental Health Journal [*A publication*] .... Community Ment Health J
Community Mental Health Journal [*A publication*] .... Community Ment Hlth J
Community Mental Health Program .... CMHP
Community Mental Health Review [*A publication*] .... Community Ment Health Rev
Community National Bank & Trust Co. of New York [*NASDAQ symbol*] .... CNBT
Community Newspapers [*A publication*] .... Comnty
Community Noise Equivalent Level .... CNEL
Community Noise Rating .... CNR
Community of the Nursing Sisters of St. John the Divine [*Anglican religious community*] .... NSSJD
Community Nutrition Institute .... CNI
Community On-Line Intelligence Network System [*Computer network*] [*National Science Administration and Central Intelligence Agency*] .... COINS
Community Organization for Full Employment Economy .... COFFEE
Community-Oriented Police .... COP
Community-Oriented Primary Care [*Medicine*] .... COPC
Community-Oriented Programs Environment Scale [*Psychosocial assessment test*] .... COPES
Community Patent Convention [*European Common Market*] .... CPC
Community Planning Association of Canada .... CPAC
Community Planning Association of Canada, Ottawa, ON, Canada [*Library symbol*] .... CaOOCP
Community Planning and Management [*HUD*] .... CPM
Community Planning Review [*A publication*] .... Com Plan R
Community Post Office .... CPO
Community of the Presentation [*Anglican religious community*] .... CP
Community Products, Incorporated .... CPI
Community Psychiatric Centers [*NYSE symbol*] .... CMY
Community Public Service Co. [*NYSE symbol*] [*Delisted*] .... CMM
Community Radio Watch .... CRW
Community Recreation and Skill Development Activities .... CRSDA
Community Redevelopment Agency .... CRA
Community Reinvestment Act [*Requires banks to list credit facilities available to the communities they serve*] .... CRA
Community Relations [*Military*] .... COMREL
Community Relations .... CR
Community Relations Advisory Council [*Military*] .... CRAC
Community Relations Commission [*British*] .... CRC
Community Relations Service [*Terminated*] [*Department of Justice*] .... CRS
Community for Religious Research and Education .... CRRE
Community Renewal Program .... CRP
Community of Reparation to Jesus in the Blessed Sacrament [*Anglican religious community*] .... CRJBS
Community Research Associates .... CRA
Community Residential Facility [*For the handicapped*] .... CRF
Community Resources Workshop Association [*Later, NAIEC*] .... CRWA
Community of the Resurrection [*Anglican religious community*] .... CR
Community of St. Clare [*Anglican religious community*] .... CSCl
Community of St. Denys [*Anglican religious community*] .... CSD
Community of St. Francis [*Anglican religious community*] .... CSF
Community of St. John the Baptist [*Anglican religious community*] .... CSJB
Community of St. John the Evangelist [*Anglican religious community*] .... CSJE
Community of St. Katharine of Egypt [*Anglican religious community*] .... CSK

Community of St. Laurence [*Anglican religious community*] ..... CSL
Community of St. Mary the Virgin [*Anglican religious community*] ..... CSMV
Community of St. Michael and All Angels [*Anglican religious community*] ..... CSM and AA
Community of St. Peter [*Anglican religious community*] ..... CSP
Community of St. Wilfrid [*Anglican religious community*] ..... CSW
Community Security ..... COMSEC
Community of the Servants of the Cross [*Anglican religious community*] ..... CSC
Community Service ..... CS
Community Service Activities [*AFL-CIO*] ..... CSA
Community Service Grant [*Corporation for Public Broadcasting*] ..... CSG
Community Service Newsletter [*A publication*] ..... Cmmty Serv
Community Service Volunteers [*British*] ..... CSV
Community Services [*Formerly, DWS*] ..... CS
Community Services Administration [*Superseded Office of Economic Opportunity*] [*HEW*] ..... CSA
Community Services Block Grant ..... CSBG
Community Shelter Plan [*Civil Defense*] ..... CSP
Community Shelter Planning Officer, State [*Civil Defense*] ..... CSPOS
Community of the Sisters of the Church [*Anglican religious community*] ..... CSC
Community of the Sisters of the Love of God [*Anglican religious community*] ..... SLG
Community for Social Justice in the Middle East and North Africa ..... CSJMENA
Community Systems Foundation ..... CSF
Community Task Force [*British*] ..... CTF
Community and Technical College Libraries ..... CTCL
Community Training and Development [*An association*] ..... CTD
Community War Services [*of FSA*] [*World War II*] ..... CWS
Community Welfare Planning Association, Social Research Library, Houston, TX [*Library symbol*] ..... TxHCS
Community of the Whole Person ..... CWP
Community of the Will of God [*Anglican religious community*] ..... CWG
Community Work and Training Program [*Department of Labor*] ..... CWTP
Commutaire International [*Miami, FL*] [*FAA designator*] ..... CMA
Commutated Aerial Direction ..... CAD
Commutated Antenna Direction Finder ..... CADF
Commutating Detection System ..... CODES
Commutation et Electronique [*A publication*] ..... Commutat & Electron
Commutation et Electronique [*A publication*] ..... Commutation Electron
Commutation Factor ..... CF
Commutation Rate ..... C/R
Commutation of Rations and Quarters [*Military*] ..... CRQ
Commutative Principle for Addition [*New math*] ..... CPA
Commutative Principle for Multiplication [*New math*] ..... CPM
Commutator ..... COMM
Commutator Assemblies [*SONAR*] ..... CA
Commutator End ..... CE
Commuted Rations [*Acronym refers to married Marine living off base and receiving these special pay dispensations*] ..... COMRAT
Commuter Airline Association of America [*Later, RAA*] ..... CAAA
Commuter Airlines [*Airline code*] ..... CB
Commuter Airlines [*Binghamton, NY*] [*FAA designator*] ..... CRA
Commuter Services Corporation [*Formerly, ACSC*] ..... CSC
Commuters Air Transport, Inc. ..... CAT
Commuting Area Candidates [*Civil Service*] ..... CAC
Comodoro Rivadavia [*Argentina*] [*Airport symbol*] ..... CRD
Comoro Islands [*MARC country of publication code*] [*Library of Congress*] ..... cq
Comoro Islands [*MARC geographic area code*] [*Library of Congress*] ..... i-cq---
Comoros [*Three-letter standard code*] ..... COM
Comoros [*Two-letter standard code*] ..... KM
Comox [*Canada*] [*Airport symbol*] ..... YQQ
Comp-U-Card International [*NASDAQ symbol*] ..... CUCD
Comp-U-Check, Inc. [*NASDAQ symbol*] ..... CMUC
Compac Corp. [*American Stock Exchange symbol*] [*Delisted*] ..... CPK
Compact [*Car size*] C
Compact ..... CMPCT
Compact All-Purpose Range Instrument [*RADAR*] ..... CAPRI
Compact Automatic Retrieval Device [*Data processing*] ..... CARD
Compact Automatic Retrieval Display [*Data processing*] ..... CARD
Compact Blazing Combustion Axiom [*Auto engineering*] ..... COMBAX
Compact Buoy System ..... CBS
Compact Disc Group ..... CDG
Compact Disk [*Audio/video technology*] ..... CD
Compact Electronic Components Inspection Laboratory ..... CECIL
Compact Gamma Ray Spectrometer ..... CGRS
Compact High-Performance Aerial Gun ..... CHAG
Compact Nuclear Brayton System ..... CONUBS
Compact Orbital Gears Ltd. ..... COG
Compact Periscope ..... COP
Compact Sounder ..... CDS
Compact Video, Incorporated [*NASDAQ symbol*] ..... CVSI
Compactor Company, Incorporated CCI
Compagnia Edizioni Internazionali SPA ..... CEI
Compagnia d'Exploitation de Lignes Aeriennes Interieures - Royal Air Inter [*Morocco*] [*ICAO designator*] ..... RN
Compagnia Italiana Autoservizi Turistici ..... CIAT
Compagnia Italiana del Grandi Alberghi [*Italian hotel chain*] ..... CIGA
Compagnia Tecnica Industrie Petroli [*Italy*] ..... CTIP
Compagnie [*Company*] [*French*] ..... CIE
Compagnie Aerienne du Languedoc [*France*] [*ICAO designator*] ..... WL
Compagnie Aeromaritime [*France*] [*ICAO designator*] ..... QK
Compagnie Africaine des Ingenieurs-Conseils ..... CADIC
Compagnie d'Applications Mecaniques a l'Electronique au Cinema et a l'Atomistique [*French company that invented Scopitone, a coin-operated machine that projects musical movies in places of entertainment*] ..... CAMECA
Compagnie d'Applications et de Recherches Atomiques [*France*] ..... CARA
Compagnie d'Applications et de Recherches Atomiques [*France*] ..... CARATOM
Compagnie du Congo pour le Commerce et l'Industrie [*Congo Commerce and Industry Company*] CCCI
Compagnie Electromecanique [*Swiss-German electrical equipment company*] ..... CEM
Compagnie Europeenne d'Automatisme [*Became part of Compagnie Internationale d'Informatique*] ..... CAE
Compagnie Europeenne de la Jeunesse ..... CEJ
Compagnie de Financement de l'Industrie Atomique [*France*] ..... COFINATOME
Compagnie Francaise de l'Afrique Occidentale ..... CFAO
Compagnie Francaise pour le Developpement des Fibres Textiles [*Ivory Coast*] ..... CFDT
Compagnie Francaise Industrielle et Miniere du Pacifique [*French commercial firm*] ..... COFIMPAC
Compagnie Francaise des Minerais d'Uranium ..... CFMU
Compagnie Francaise des Petroles [*France*] ..... CFP
Compagnie Francaise des Petroles. Notes et Memoires [*A publication*] ..... Cie Fr Pet Notes Mem
Compagnie Francaise de Raffinage ..... CFR
Compagnie Francaise Thomson Houston ..... CFTH
Compagnie Gabonaise d'Affretement Aerien [*Airline*] ..... AFFETAIR
Compagnie Gabonaise d'Affretement Aerien [*ICAO designator*] ..... DG
Compagnie Generale d'Electricite [*General Electric Company*] ..... CGE
Compagnie Generale de Transport Aerien [*Algeria*] ..... CGTA
Compagnie Industrielle de Combustibles Atomiques Frittes [*France*] ..... CICAF
Compagnie Internationale pour l'Informatique [*Formed by merger of SEA and CAE*] CII
Compagnie Internationale de Services en Informatique [*International Information Services Co.*] [*France*] [*Information service*] ..... CISI
Compagnie Libanaise Television [*Television network*] [*Lebanon*] ..... CLT
Compagnie Luxembourgeoise Telediffusion - Radio Television Luxemburg ..... CLT-RTL
Compagnie Maritime Belge ..... CMB
Compagnie Maritime du Zaire ..... CMZ
Compagnie Miniere de l'Ogooue [*Ogooue Mining Company*] [*Gabon*] ..... COMILOG
Compagnie Nationale Algerienne de Navigation [*National shipping line of Algeria*] ..... CNAN
Compagnie Nationale de Transports Aeriens-Royal Air Maroc [*Morocco*] [*ICAO designator*] ..... AT
Compagnie Orientale des Petrole d'Egypte [*Egyptian-Italian oil company*] ..... COPE
Compagnie du Polyisoprene Francais ..... CPF
Compagnie Senegalaise [*Senegal*] [*ICAO designator*] ..... DS
Compagnie de Telegraphie Sans Fil [*Electronics concern*] [*France*] ..... CSF
Compagnie de Transport Aerien [*Switzerland*] [*ICAO designator*] ..... RU
Compagnies Republicaines de Securite [*France*] ..... CRS
Companhia Agricola de Sergipe [*State of Sergipe, Brazil*] ..... COMASE
Companhia de Diamantes de Angola ..... DIAMANG
Companhia de Eletricidade do Estado da Bahia ..... COELBA
Companhia Hidro Eletrica do Sao Francisco [*State-owned utility*] [*Brazil*] ..... CHESF
Companhia de Pesquisas de Recursos Minerais [*Brazil*] ..... CPRM
Companhia Siderurgica Nacional [*Steel producer*] [*Brazil*] ..... CSN
Companhia Telefonica Brasileira [*A telecommunications company*] [*Brazil*] ..... CTB
Compania [*Company*] [*Spanish*] ..... CIA
Compania Aeronautics Uruguaya, Sociedad Anonima ..... CAUSA
Compania de Alumbrado [*NASDAQ symbol*] ..... ELSAY
Compania Amazonia Textil de Aniagem [*Commercial firm*] [*Brazil*] ..... CATA
Compania de Aviacion Trans-Europa [*Spain*] [*ICAO designator*] ..... TR
Compania Boliviana de Energia Electrica [*NASDAQ symbol*] ..... BPWRF
Compania de Desarrollo Turistico, Residencial, e Industrial, Sociedad Anonima [*Dominican Republic resort development company*] ..... CODDETREISA
Compania Dominicana de Aviacion, SA [*Dominican Republic airline*] ..... CDA
Compania Dominicana de Aviacion, SA [*ICAO designator*] ..... DO
Compania Ecuatoriana de Aviacion [*Ecuador*] [*ICAO designator*] ..... EU
Compania de Electronica y Comunicaciones, Sociedad Anonima [*Spain*] ..... CECSA
Compania Espanola de Petroleos, Sociedad Anonima ..... CEPSA
Compania Internacional Editora, Sociedad Anonima ..... CIESA
Compania Mexicana de Aviacion [*Mexican airline*] ..... CMA
Compania Mexicana de Aviacion [*ICAO designator*] ..... MX
Compania Nacional de Turismo Aereo [*Chilean airline*] ..... CINTA
Compania Panamena de Aviacion, SA [*Panama*] [*ICAO designator*] ..... CM

Compania Panamena de Aviacion, SA [*Panamanian airline*]	COPA
Compania Peruana de Vapores [*Peruvian airline*]	CPV
Compania Sud America de Vapores [*Chilean airline*]	CSAV
Compania Telefonica Nacionale de Espana	CTNE
Companion	C
Companion	COMP
Companion of the [*Order of the*] **Star of India**	CSI
Companion of the [*Order of the*] **Bath** [*British*]	CB
Companion of the Distinguished Service Order	CDS
Companion of the Distinguished Service Order	CDSO
Companion Dog [*Degree of obedience training*]	CD
Companion Dog, Excellent [*Degree of obedience training*]	CDX
Companion of Honour [*British*]	CH
Companion of the [*Order of the*] **Indian Empire** [*British*]	CIE
Companion of the Institute of Marine Engineers [*British*]	CIMarE
Companion of the Institute of Personnel Management [*Formerly, FIPM*] [*British*]	CIPM
Companion of the Institution of Agricultural Engineers [*British*]	CIAgrE
Companion of the Institution of Electrical Engineers [*British*]	CIEE
Companion of the Institution of Electrical Engineers [*British*]	CompIEE
Companion of the Institution of Electronic and Radio Engineers [*British*]	CompIERE
Companion of the Institution of Mechanical Engineers [*British*]	CI Mech E
Companion of Literature [*Royal Society of Literature award*] [*British*]	CLit
Companion of the Order of Australia	AC
Companion of the Order of Canada	CC
Companion of the Order of St. Michael and St. George [*Facetiously translated "Call Me God"*] [*British*]	CMG
Companion Service Cross	CSC
Companion of the Textile Institute [*British*]	CompTI
Companion Trainer Aircraft	CTA
Companions	COM
Companions of the Forest of America	CFA
Companions of the Forest of America	COFOA
Company	CO
Company	COMP
Company	COY
Company Buyer Study [*LIMRA*]	CBS
Company Commander	CC
Company-to-Company Agreement	CCA
Company Data Coordinator	CDC
Company Distributing Point [*Army*]	CDP
Company of Fifers and Drummers	CFD
Company First [*A mealtime whimsicality for use when guests are present*]	CF
Company Fiscal Year	CFY
Company Lightweight Mortar System [*Army*]	CLMS
Company Lightweight Mortar System [*Army*]	CLWM
Company of Mary [*Roman Catholic women's religious order*]	ODN
Company of Military Collectors and Historians [*Later, CMH*]	CMCH
Company of Military Historians [*Formerly, CMCH*]	CMH
Company-Owned and Maintained	COAM
Company Persistency Rater [*LIMRA*]	CPR
Company Policy	CP
Company [*or Corporate*] **Policy Statement**	CPS
Company Quartermaster-Sergeant	CQMS
Company of the Savior [*Roman Catholic women's religious order*]	CS
Company Sergeant-Major [*Army*] [*British*]	CSM
Company Sergeant-Major Instructor [*Army*] [*British*]	CSMI
Company Source Inspection	CSI
Company Standard Form Instruction	CSFI
Company Standard Practice	CSP
Company Technical Document Center	CTDC
Company's Risk [*Insurance*]	CR
Compaq Computer Corp. [*NASDAQ symbol*]	CMPQ
Comparable Worth Project	CWP
Comparative	COMP
Comparative	COMPAR
Comparative Administration Research Institute [*Kent State University, Ohio*]	CARI
Comparative Animal Nutrition [*A publication*]	Comp Anim Nutr
Comparative Animal Research Laboratory [*Department of Energy*]	CARL
Comparative Biochemistry and Physiology [*A publication*]	Comp Biochem Physiol
Comparative Biochemistry and Physiology. A [*A publication*]	Comp Bioc A
Comparative Biochemistry and Physiology. A. Comparative Physiology [*A publication*]	Comp Biochem Physiol A Comp Physiol
Comparative Biochemistry and Physiology. B [*A publication*]	Comp Bioc B
Comparative Biochemistry and Physiology. B. Comparative Biochemistry [*A publication*]	Comp Biochem Physiol B
Comparative Biochemistry and Physiology. B. Comparative Biochemistry [*A publication*]	Comp Biochem Physiol B Comp Biochem
Comparative Biochemistry and Physiology. C [*A publication*]	Comp Bioc C
Comparative Biochemistry and Physiology. C. Comparative Pharmacology [*A publication*]	Comp Biochem Physiol C
Comparative Biochemistry and Physiology. C. Comparative Pharmacology [*A publication*]	Comp Biochem Physiol C Comp Pharmacol
Comparative Civilization Review [*A publication*]	C C Rev
Comparative Criticism [*A publication*]	C Crit
Comparative Drama [*A publication*]	CD
Comparative Drama [*A publication*]	CompD
Comparative Drama [*A publication*]	CompDr
Comparative Drama [*A publication*]	Comp Drama
Comparative Education [*A publication*]	Comparative Ed
Comparative Education [*A publication*]	Comp Ed
Comparative Education [*A publication*]	Comp Educ
Comparative Education Review [*A publication*]	CER
Comparative Education Review [*A publication*]	Comp Ed R
Comparative Education Review [*A publication*]	Comp Educ R
Comparative Education Review [*A publication*]	Comp Edu Re
Comparative Education Society [*Later, CIES*]	CES
Comparative and General Pharmacology [*A publication*]	Comp Gen Pharmacol
Comparative Guidance and Placement Program [*College Entrance Examination Board*]	CGPP
Comparative Immunology, Microbiology, and Infectious Diseases [*A publication*]	Comp Immunol Microbiol Infect Dis
Comparative and International Education Society [*Formerly, CES*]	CIES
Comparative and International Law Journal of Southern Africa [*A publication*]	Comp Int Law J South Afr
Comparative Literature [*A publication*]	CL
Comparative Literature [*A publication*]	CoLi
Comparative Literature [*A publication*]	Comp L
Comparative Literature [*A publication*]	Comp Lit
Comparative Literature Association	CLA
Comparative Literature News-Letter [*A publication*]	CLNL
Comparative Literature Studies [*A publication*]	CLS
Comparative Literature Studies [*A publication*]	Comp Lit Stud
Comparative Medicine East and West [*A publication*]	CMEW
Comparative Medicine East and West [*A publication*]	Comp Med East West
Comparative Pathology Bulletin [*A publication*]	Comp Pathol Bull
Comparative Physiology and Ecology [*A publication*]	Comp Physiol Ecol
Comparative Political Studies [*A publication*]	Compar Pol Stud
Comparative Political Studies [*A publication*]	Comp Poli S
Comparative Political Studies [*A publication*]	Comp Polit Stud
Comparative Political Studies [*A publication*]	Comp Pol Stud
Comparative Political Studies [*A publication*]	CPS
Comparative Politics [*A publication*]	Comp Pol
Comparative Politics [*A publication*]	Comp Polit
Comparative Romance Linguistics Newsletter [*A publication*]	CRLN
Comparative Studies in Society and History [*A publication*]	Comp Stud S
Comparative Studies in Society and History [*A publication*]	Comp Stud Soc & Hist
Comparative Studies in Society and History [*A publication*]	Comp Stud Soc Hist
Comparative Studies in Society and History [*A publication*]	CSSH
Comparative Systems Laboratory	CSL
Comparative Urban Research [*A publication*]	Comp Urb Res
Comparator	COMP
Comparator [*Data processing*]	COMPTR
Comparator Buffer [*Data processing*]	CB
Comparator Systems [*NASDAQ symbol*]	CSCO
Comparators [*JETDS nomenclature*] [*Military*]	CM
Compare	CMPR
Compare	COMP
Compare	COMPR
Compare	CP
Comparing Political Experiences [*National Science Foundation project*]	CPE
Comparing Reading Approaches in First Grade Teaching	CRAFT
Comparison of Recognition Algorithms [*US Postal Service*]	CORAL
Compartment	COMP
Compartment	COMPRT
Compartment	COMPT
Compartment and Access [*Technical drawings*]	C & A
Compartment Checkoff List [*Navy*]	CCOL
Compass	C
Compass	CMPS
Compass	COMP
Compass [*A publication*]	Comp
Compass Bearing [*Navigation*]	CB
Compass Control Alarm	CCA
Compass Control System	CCS
Compass Course	CC
Compass Equal Target Acquisition System	CETAS
Compass Error [*Navigation*]	CE
Compass Failure Annunciator	CFA
Compass Heading	CH
Compass Integrated System Compiler	CISCO
Compass Locator	COMLO
Compass Locator of Inner Marker Site	LIM
Compass North	CN
Compass Operation Alarm	COA
Compass System Controller	CSC
Compass Tilt Signal	CTS
Compassion International	CI
Compassionate [*Army*]	COMPATE

Compassionate Case [Airline notation]................................CM
[The] Compassionate Friends ....TCF
Compassionate Reassignment Not Favorably Considered
   [Army] ....COMPATENFC
Compatibility...COMPAT
Compatibility...CPT
Compatibility Engineering Change Proposal [NASA]..........CECP
Compatibility-Integration Mock-Up...........................CIMU
Compatibility and Interoperability ....C & I
Compatibility of Materials ....COMAT
Compatibility Mock-Up.......................................CMU
Compatibility Operating System [Data processing]............COS
Compatibility Test Area [NASA]...............................CTA
Compatibility Test Capsule..................................CTC
Compatibility Test Unit......................................CTU
Compatible...COMP
Compatible Algebraic Compiler and Translator...........COMPACT
Compatible Duplex System....................................CDS
Compatible Expansion [Noise-reduction system for
   manufacturing phonograph records] [CBS]....................CX
Compatible Hardware and Milestone Program for Integrating
   Organizational Needs [AFSC]..........................CHAMPION
Compatible Independent Peripherals ....CIP
Compatible Instrument Landing System [Aviation]............CILS
Compatible LASER System.....................................CLS
Compatible Materials List...................................CMAT
Compatible On-Board Ranging...............................COBRA
Compatible Sidelobe Suppression Technique ....CSST
Compatible Single Sideband.................................CSSB
Compatible Time-Sharing System [Data processing]..........CTSS
Compendium of Copyright Office Practices [A publication].....CCP
Compendium of Plausible Materiel Options [Army]...........CPMO
Compendium of Technical Papers. Annual Meeting. Institute of
   Transportation Engineers [A publication]........................
                     Compend Tech Pap Annu Meet Inst Transp Eng
Compensate [or Compensating]...............................COMP
Compensate [or Compensator].............................COMPEN
Compensated Avalanche Diode.................................CAD
Compensated Ion Chamber.....................................CIC
Compensated Work Therapy....................................CWT
Compensating...COMPSG
Compensating Air Supply......................................CAS
Compensation Act [Forms]......................................CA
Compensation Fee..CF
Compensation and Pension....................................C & P
Compensation Review [A publication] ....Compens Rev
Compensation System Analyst.................................CSA
Compensation System Review.................................CSR
Compensator Design [Data processing] ....COMPDES
Compensator Improvement Program............................CIP
Compensators [JETDS nomenclature] [Military].................CN
Compensatory Financing Facility [International Monetary Fund]..CFF
Competence in Clearing Bacilli [Test for leprosy bacilli].......CCB
Competence Level Unit [Education].............................CLU
Competency-Based Adult Education..........................CBAE
Competency-Based Instruction.................................CBI
Competency-Based Learning [Education].......................CBL
Competency-Based Teacher Education........................CBTE
Competent Reliability History Survey [Navy] ....CRHS
Competing Risks...CR
Competition Evaluation Exercise ....COMPEX
Competition with Industrial Cooperation.....................CWIC
Competitive..COMPET
Competitive Aircraft Data Summary Sheets...............COMPASS
Competitive Design..CD
Competitive Development Phase...............................CDP
Competitive Health and Medical Plan [Proposed] ....CHAMP
Competitive Industrial Concept Formulation..................CICF
Competitive Medical Plans....................................CMP
Competitive Operational Readiness Evaluation [Air Force].....CORE
Competitive Protein Binding [Clinical chemistry]..............CPB
Competitive Protein-Binding Analysis ....CPBA
Competitive Prototype Phase..................................CPP
Competitive Research Grants Office [for federal research in
   agriculture]..CRGO
Competitive Study Engineer...................................CSE
Competitive Voluntary Indefinite [Status] [Army].............CVI
Compile, Load, and Go [Data processing]......................CLG
Compile On-Line and Go [Data processing]................COLINGO
Compile and Test...CAT
Compiler...COMP
Compiler-Assembler.......................................COMPASS
Compiler and Assembler by General Electric.................CAGE
Compiler for Automatic Machine Programing................CAMP
Compiler for Automatic Teaching Operation..................CATO
Compiler, Executive Program, Assembler Routines ....CLEAR
Compiler and Generalized Translator......................COGENT
Compiler Language...CL
Compiler Language for Information Processing................CLIP
Compiler, Los Alamos Scientific Laboratories ....COLASL
Compiler/Massachusetts Institute of Technology............COMIT

Compiler Monitor System ....CMS
Compiler Oriented for Multiprograming and Multiprocessing
   Environments...COMMEN
Complainant...COMPLT
Complains Of [Medicine]......................................C/O
Complaint..COMP
Complaint Type Investigation [Army]..........................CTI
Complaints Investigation Branch [Scotland Yard]..............CIB
Complement [Immunochemistry]..................................C
Complement..CMPLM
Complement...COM
Complement...COMP
Complement...COMPL
Complement..CPL
Complement 3 Degradation Product [Immunology]............C3DP
Complement Accumulator.....................................CMA
Complement Carry...CMC
Complement-Fixation [Immunology]..............................CF
Complement-Fixation for Avian Leucosis Virus [Immunology]..COFAL
Complement Fixation Inhibition [Test] [Immunology]...........CFI
Complement-Fixation for Murine Leukemia [Test] [Immunology].....COMUL
Complement-Fixation Test [Immunology].......................CFT
Complement-Fixing Antibody [Immunology] ....CFA
Complement-Fixing Islet Cell Antibodies [Immunochemistry]..CF-ICA
Complement Hemolyzing 50 [Immunology]......................CH50
Complement Receptor [Immunology]............................CR
Complement Receptor Lymphocyte [Immunology]...............CRL
Complement Requiring Neutralizing............................CRN
Complementarity-Determining Residue [Genetics].............CDR
Complementary Analysis Team [NASA].........................CAT
Complementary Constant Current Logic [Data processing] CCCL
Complementary Constant Current Logic......................C^3L
Complementary Emitter Follower..............................CEF
Complementary Instruction Book [Military]....................CIB
Complementary Magnetic Oxide on Silicone [Data processing]..CMOS
Complementary Manual [Military]...............................CM
Complementary Metal-Oxide Semiconductor [Electronics]......CMOS
Complementary Metal-Oxide Semiconductor/Silicon-on-
   Sapphire [Electronics]..............................CMOS/SOS
Complementary Metal-Oxide Semiconductor Transistor
   [Electronics]..CMOST
Complementary Pair Switch Element ....CPSE
Complementary Semiconductor.............................CSCR
Complementary Technical Report [Military] ....COMTECHREP
Complementary Transistor Logic [Data processing] ....CTL
Complementary Unijunction Transistor........................CUJT
Complete..C
Complete...CMPL
Complete...CMPLT
Complete...COMPL
Complete...CPL
Complete Address Constant...................................CAC
Complete ADR [Applied Data Research, Inc.] Environment.....CADRE
Complete Assembly for Ferry [Air Force].......................CAF
Complete Assembly for Strike.................................CAS
Complete Background Investigation............................CBI
Complete Basis of Issue [Military]...........................CBOI
Complete Basis of Issue Plan [Military].....................CBOIP
Complete Bed Rest [Medicine].................................CBR
Complete Blood Count [Medicine]..............................CBC
[A] Complete Computerized Examination System [Anatomy and
   physiology]..ACCESS
Complete Controlled Quick Release ....CQR
Complete Crew..CCRU
Complete Deal [Coupon redemption]...........................C/D
Complete Design Release [Navy]..............................CDR
Complete Engine Repair......................................CER
Complete Engine Repair Requirements Card [DoD] ....CERRC
Complete Engineering Release................................CER
Complete Fabrication..CF
Complete Freund's Adjuvant [Immunology].....................CFA
Complete Games [Baseball]....................................CG
Complete Heart Block [Medicine]..............................CHB
Complete Help and Assistance Necessary for College
   Education [Project]..................................CHANCE
Complete Matched Set [Philately]............................CMS
Complete Medium [Microbiology]...............................CM
Complete Minimum Essential Medium ....CMEM
Complete Missile Container..................................CMC
Complete Mixing Activated Sludge ....CMAS
Complete Neglect of Differential Overlap [Quantum mechanics]..CNDO
Complete Operating Equipment................................COE
Complete Operating Information [Data processing].............COIN
Complete Operational Capability.............................COC
Complete Power Failure [Aviation]............................CPF
Complete Provisions Only....................................CPO
Complete Reaction of Degeneration [Physiology].............CRD
Complete Remission [Medicine].................................CR
Complete Responders [to medication].........................CR's
Complete Response [Medicine]..................................CR
Complete Right Bundle Branch Block [Cardiology]...........CRBBB

Complete Round [*Technical drawings*] CR
Complete Round Ammunition Shipment CRAMSHIP
Complete Round Chart CRC
Complete Service Life CSL
Complete Utter Monumental Foul-Up [*Military slang*] [*Bowdlerized version*] CUMFU
Complete Utter Monumental Military Foul-Up [*Slang*] [*Bowdlerized version*] CUMMFU
Complete Verification Record CVE
Completed Active Duty Requirements, Enlisted [*Military*] CADRE
Completed Discharge CODIS
Completed Loading [*Navy*] COLOD
Completed Procedure Turn [*Aviation*] COPT
Completely Automatic Operational System CAOS
Completely Denatured CD
Completely Denatured Alcohol CDA
Completely Finished Sets CFS
Completely Integrated Range Instrumentation System [*NASA*] CIRIS
Completely Knocked Down [*i.e., disassembled, as a toy or piece of furniture which must be assembled before use*] CKD
Completely Knocked Down [*i.e., disassembled, as a toy or piece of furniture which must be assembled before use*] [*Freight*] COMKD
Completely Reliable Source for Intelligence Information A
Completion, Arithmetic, Vocabulary, Directions [*Psychology*] CAVD
Completion of Bed Occupancy Care [*Veterans Administration*] CBOC
Completion Fitting-Out Period CFP
Completion and Ready for Test CART
Completion Tour of Duty CTD
Completions COM
Complex C
Complex CMPLX
Complex CMPX
Complex CPLX
Complex CX
Complex Atmospheric Energetics Experiment [*National Science Foundation and USSR*] CAENEX
Complex Behavior Simulator CBS
Complex Chemical Reaction CCR
Complex Conjugate CC
Complex Control Center CCC
Complex Control Room [*NASA*] CCR
Complex Control Set CCS
Complex Coordination Test CCT
Complex Effluent Toxicity Information System [*Environmental Protection Agency*] CETIS
Complex Energetics Experiment CENEX
Complex Equipment Contract CEC
Complex Facility Console [*Aerospace*] CFC
Complex Facility Operator [*Aerospace*] CFO
Complex Fourier Transform CFT
Complex Integrated Circuit CIC
Complex Maintenance Facility [*Deep Space Instrumentation Facility, NASA*] CMF
Complex Modulus Apparatus CMA
Complex Overhaul COH
Complex Refraction Index CRI
Complex Safety Officer [*Air Force*] CSO
Complex Safety Technician [*Air Force*] CST
Complex Spikes CS
Complex Support Controller [*NASA*] CSC
Complex Support Office [*NASA*] CSO
Complex Utility Routine CUR
Complex Vehicle Erector CVE
Complex Wiring System CWS
Compliance C
Compliance COMPL
Compliance COMPLI
Compliance Data System [*Environmental Protection Agency*] CDS
Compliance with Requirements CWR
Compliance Safety and Health Officer [*Occupational Safety and Health Administration*] CSHO
Complications [*Medicine*] COMPL
Compliment COMPL
Complimentary Technical Manual CTM
Compline CP
Compo Industries, Inc. [*American Stock Exchange symbol*] CEM
Component CMPNT
Component CMPT
Component COMP
Component Action List [*NASA*] CAL
Component Auto-Programed Checkout Equipment [*Aerospace*] CAPCHE
Component Board CB
Component Board Assembly CBA
Component Change Control [*Navy*] CCC
Component Change Control Board [*DoD*] CCCB
Component Change Request CCR
Component Characteristics Record CCR
Component Check Test [*Nuclear energy*] CC (Test)
Component Checkout Area CCA
Component Control Section CCS
Component Cooling Service Water [*Nuclear energy*] CCSW
Component Cooling Water [*Nuclear energy*] CCW
Component Cooling Water System [*Nuclear energy*] CCWS
Component Cost Index CCI
Component Development and Integration Facility [*Energy Research and Development Administration*] CDIF
Component Disassembly Station [*Nuclear energy*] CDS
Component Engineering Request CER
Component Error Propagation CEP
Component Failure Impact Analysis [*IBM Corp.*] CFIA
Component Failure Summary CFS
Component Handling and Cleaning Facility [*Energy Research and Development Administration*] CHCF
Component Identification CID
Component Improvement Program CIP
Component List [*DoD*] CL
Component Maintenance Manual CMM
Component Maintenance and Mock-Up Facility [*Nuclear energy*] CMMF
Component Manufacturers Council of the Truss Plate Institute CMC
Component and Material Engineering Request CMER
Component and Material Evaluation Loop [*Nuclear energy*] CAMEL
Component Meantime Between Removals CMBR
Component Open/Short Monitor COSMON
Component Operational Data Notice [*NASA*] CODN
Component to Part Record CPR
Component Parts CP
Component Percentage Shipment Schedule CPSS
Component Pilot Overhaul [*Navy*] CPO
Component Pilot Rework [*Navy*] CPR
Component Pilot Rework/Repair [*Navy*] CPR/R
Component Preparation Laboratory [*Oak Ridge*] [*Energy Research and Development Administration*] CPL
Component Quality Assurance CQA
Component Quality Assurance Program CQAP
Component Record Intensive Management CRIM
Component Reliability Prediction CRP
Component Repair CR
Component Repair Data Sheets CRDS
Component Repair Squadron CRS
Component Reword Analyst CRA
Component Selection Board CSB
Component Selection Review Board CSR
Component Specification CS
Component Technology [*A publication*] Component Technol
Component Technology [*NASDAQ symbol*] CTEC
Component Test CT
Component Test Area CTA
Component Test Equipment CTE
Component Test Laboratory CTL
Component Test Set CTS
Components Life Evaluation and Reliability CLEAR
Components and Materials Laboratory CML
Components Only CO
Components Report [*A publication*] Components Rep
Components Response Information Center CRIC
Components Test Unit CTU
Compool Look-Up Memory Print CLUMP
Composer Recordings, Incorporated [*Recording label*] CRI
Composers, Authors, and Artists of America CAAA
Composers-Authors Guild CAG
Composers, Authors, and Publishers Association of Canada CAPAC
Composers' Autograph Publications [*An association*] [*Defunct*] CAP
Composers Cooperative Society [*Later, Composers Theatre*] CCS
Composers' Forum for Catholic Worship [*Defunct*] CFCW
Composers and Lyricists Guild of America CLGA
Composers News-Record [*A publication*] Comp News-Rec
Composers Theatre [*Formerly, Composers Cooperative Society*] CT
Composite CMPST
Composite COMP
Composite CX
Composite Aeronautical Load List CALL
Composite Air Strike Force [*Air Force*] CASF
Composite Aircraft Program CAP
Composite Aircraft Squadron [*Navy symbol*] VC
Composite Analog Video CAV
Composite Army-Marine CAM
Composite Can and Tube Institute CCTI
Composite Cell Logic CCL
Composite Checkout [*Aerospace*] CC/O
Composite Cutoff [*Aerospace*] CC-O
Composite Electrical Readiness Test CERT
Composite Engineering Change Memo [*NASA*] CECM
Composite External Symbol Dictionary CESD
Composite Feed System CFS
Composite Flight Data Processing CFAD
Composite Ganglioneuroblastoma [*Oncology*] CGNB
Composite Launch and Spacecraft Program CLASP
Composite for the Lunar Excursion Module [*NASA*] CLEM
Composite Maneuver Augmentation COMMA
Composite Materials [*A publication*] Compos Mater

Composite Mechanized Information and Document Retrieval System ... COMEINDORS
Composite Medical Facility ... CMF
Composite Merge ... CM
Composite-Modified Double Base [*Propellants*] ... CMDB
Composite Mood Adjective Check List [*FAA*] ... CMACL
Composite Noise Rating [*Aviation*] ... CNR
Composite Operational Mission Profiles ... COMP
Composite Primary Structures ... CPS
Composite Professional Performance Score ... CPPS
Composite RADAR Data Processing ... CRAD
Composite Reactor Components Test Activity ... CRCTA
Composite Readiness Test ... CRT
Composite Reentry Test Vehicle ... CRTV
Composite Research Aircraft ... CRA
Composite Service [*Army*] ... CS
Composite Signal Mixer ... CSM
Composite Squadron ... COMPORON
Composite Station Rate ... CSR
Composite Structures for Advanced Aircraft ... CSAA
Composite Teacher Rating ... CTR
Composite Training Unit [*Military*] ... COMPTU
Composite Training Unit Exercise [*Military*] ... COMPTUEX
Composite Warfare Commander [*Military*] ... CWC
Composite Wave ... CW
Composite Wave Filter ... CWF
Composite Weighted Work Unit ... CWU
Compositio Mathematica [*A publication*] ... Comp Math
Compositio Mathematica [*A publication*] ... Compositio Math
Composition ... CMPSN
Composition ... COMP
Composition ... COMPN
Composition ... COMPOS
Composition ... COMPSN
Composition-4 [*Explosive*] ... C-4
Composition and Editing Display [*Later, MRTT*] ... COED
Composition of Ending Inventory ... COEI
Composition Floor ... COMPF
Composition Information Services [*Commercial firm*] ... CIS
Composition Reduction Printing ... CRP
Composition Roof ... COMPR
Composition Technology, Incorporated ... CTI
Compositus [*Compound*] [*Pharmacy*] ... C
Compositus [*Compound*] [*Pharmacy*] ... CO
Compositus [*Compound*] [*Pharmacy*] ... COMP
Compost Science [*A publication*] ... Compost Sci
Compost Science/Land Utilization [*A publication*] ... Compost Sci Land Util
Compound [*Engines*] [*Lloyd's Register*] [*Shipping*] ... C
Compound ... CMPD
Compound ... COMP
Compound ... COMPD
Compound [*Medicine*] ... CP
Compound ... CPD
Compound Action Potential [*Biology*] ... CAP
Compound Batch Identification [*Data processing*] ... CBI
Compound Card Terminal ... CCT
Compound Cathartic [*Pills*] ... CC
Compound Diffraction Projector ... CDP
Compound Fracture [*Medicine*] ... FC
Compound Handling Machine ... CHM
Compound Hypermetropic Astigmatism [*Ophthalmology*] ... H + Hm
Compound Inserting Machine ... CIM
Compound Myopic Astigmatism [*Ophthalmology*] ... M + Am
Compound Parabolic Concentrator [*Solar energy research*] ... CPC
Compound Pressure ... CPRESS
Compound Valve Hemispherical Head [*Engine*] ... CVH
Compound Vortex Combustion Chamber [*Auto engine*] ... CVCC
Comprehensive ... COMP
Comprehensive Aircraft Support Effectiveness Evaluation ... CASEE
Comprehensive Airship Sizing and Performance Computer Program ... CASCOMP
Comprehensive Analytical Chemistry [*A publication*] ... Compr Anal Chem
Comprehensive Analytical Method of Planning in the University Sphere [*Cost simulation technique*] ... CAMPUS
Comprehensive Analytical Methods of Planning ... CAMP
Comprehensive Analytical Test System ... CATS
Comprehensive Areal Rainfall Program [*British*] ... CARP
Comprehensive Assembler System [*Data processing*] ... COMPASS
Comprehensive Assistance to Undergraduate Science Education [*National Science Foundation*] ... CAUSE
Comprehensive Automation of the Hydrometeorological Service ... CAHS
Comprehensive Cancer Center Program [*National Cancer Institute*] ... CCCP
Comprehensive Care [*NASDAQ symbol*] ... CMPH
Comprehensive Close Air Support [*Military*] ... CCAS
Comprehensive College Test ... CCT
Comprehensive and Coordinated Scientific Program [*Intergovernmental Oceanographic Commission*] ... COSPR
Comprehensive Country Programing System [*Department of State*] ... CCPS
Comprehensive Data Handling System [*Environmental Protection Agency*] ... CDHS
Comprehensive Dishonesty, Disappearance, and Destruction Policy [*Insurance*] ... DDD
Comprehensive Display System ... CDS
Comprehensive Dissertation Index [*A publication*] ... CDI
Comprehensive Dwelling Policies [*Insurance*] ... CDP
Comprehensive Education [*A publication*] ... Comprehensive Ed
Comprehensive Electronic Office ... CEO
Comprehensive Employment and Training Act [*1973*] [*Formerly, MDTA*] [*Expired, 1982*] [*Department of Labor*] ... CETA
Comprehensive Employment and Training Plan [*Department of Labor*] ... CETP
Comprehensive Environmental Response, Compensation, and Liability Act [*1980*] ... CERCLA
Comprehensive Export Schedule [*US*] ... CES
Comprehensive General and Automobile Liability [*Insurance*] ... CGAL
Comprehensive General Liability [*Insurance*] ... CGL
Comprehensive Health Assessments and Primary Care for Children [*Proposed*] ... CHAP
Comprehensive Health Insurance Act ... CHIA
Comprehensive Health Insurance Plan [*or Proposal*] ... CHIP
Comprehensive Health Manpower Training Act [*1971*] ... CHMA
Comprehensive Health Planning [*A requirement for HEW grants to local agencies*] ... CHP
Comprehensive Health Planning Service [*Federal government*] ... CHPS
Comprehensive Human Resources Data System ... CHRDS
Comprehensive Immunology [*A publication*] ... Compr Immunol
Comprehensive Index to the Publications [*A bibliographic publication*] ... CIP
Comprehensive Industrywide Program of Communication [*Defunct*] ... CIPC
Comprehensive Information Service ... COMPIS
Comprehensive Information System and Data Base ... CIS & DB
Comprehensive Inorganic Chemistry [*A publication*] ... CIC
Comprehensive Medical Society [*Defunct*] ... CMS
Comprehensive Migrant Program [*Department of Labor*] ... CMP
Comprehensive Model ... COMO
Comprehensive Nursing Quarterly [*A publication*] ... Compr Nurs Q
Comprehensive Occupational Data Analysis Program [*Military*] ... CODAP
Comprehensive Offender Program Effort [*Department of Labor*] ... COPE
Comprehensive Organic Chemistry [*A publication*] ... COC
Comprehensive Pediatric Nursing [*A publication*] ... Compr Pediatr Nurs
Comprehensive Personal Liability [*Insurance*] ... CPL
Comprehensive Plan, South Vietnam ... CPSVN
Comprehensive Psychiatry [*A publication*] ... Comp Psychi
Comprehensive Psychiatry [*A publication*] ... Compr Psychiatry
Comprehensive Psychiatry [*A publication*] ... COPYA
Comprehensive Psychopathological Rating Scale ... CPRS
Comprehensive Radiance Profile Synthesizer ... CORPS
Comprehensive School Improvement Project ... CSIP
Comprehensive School Mathematics Program ... CSMP
Comprehensive Schools Committee ... CSC
Comprehensive Self-Check [*Computer*] ... CSC
Comprehensive Sickle Cell Center [*HEW*] ... CSCC
Comprehensive System of Personnel Development [*Education*] ... CSPD
Comprehensive Test Ban [*of nuclear testing*] ... CTB
Comprehensive Test Ban Treaty ... CTBT
Comprehensive Tests of Basic Skills ... CTBS
Comprehensive Therapy [*A publication*] ... Compr Ther
Comprehensive Work Training Program [*Employment and Training Administration*] [*Department of Labor*] ... CWTP
Compress ... CPRS
Compressed ... COMP
Compressed Air ... CA
Compressed Air ... COMPA
Compressed Air [*A publication*] ... Compres Air
Compressed Air [*A publication*] ... Compress Air
Compressed Air Accumulator Rocket ... CAAR
Compressed Air Circuit Breaker ... CACB
Compressed Air Energy Storage ... CAES
Compressed Air and Gas Institute ... CAGI
Compressed Air Institute ... CAI
Compressed Air Loudspeaker ... CAL
Compressed Air Magazine [*A publication*] ... Comp Air Mag
Compressed Air Spraying ... CAS
Compressed Air Tunnel [*British*] ... CAT
Compressed Citation File ... CCF
Compressed Coherency Detection [*RADAR technique*] ... COCODE
Compressed Data Storage ... CDS
Compressed Data Storage System ... CDSS
Compressed Data Tape ... CDT
Compressed Gas Association ... CGA
Compressed-Gas-Insulated Cable ... CGIC
Compressed-Gas-Insulated Transmission Line ... CGIT
Compressed Medical Gas [*Food and Drug Administration*] ... CMG
Compressed Natural Gas ... CNG
Compressed Pulse RADAR Altimeter ... CPRA
Compressed Symbolic ... COSY
Compressed Tablet [*Pharmacy*] ... CP
Compressed Tablet [*Pharmacology*] ... CT

Compressed Tablet Triturate [*Pharmacology*] .... CTT
Compressible Cell and Maker .... COMCAM
Compressible Flow Facility [*NASA*] .... CFF
Compression .... CMP
Compression .... COMPR
Compression .... CPRSN
Compression Bonding Encapsulation .... CBE
Compression of Earth C
Compression Engine .... CE
Compression Factor [*Symbol*] [*Thermodynamics*] .... Z
Compression Ignition [*Engine*] CI
Compression Ignition and Turbine Engine .... CITE
Compression Mold Dies .... CMD
Compression Ratio .... CR
Compression Scanning Array RADAR [*Raytheon*] .... COSAR
Compression in Transit .... CIT
Compressional Heating and Linear Injection Cusp Experiment .... CHALICE
Compressive Load Cell CLC
Compressor .... CPRSR
Compressor Discharge Pressure .... CDP
Compressor End Seal .... CES
Compressor Endurance Loops .... CEL
Compressor Expander .... COMPANDER
Compressor Inlet Pressure .... CIP
Compressor Inlet Temperature .... CIT
Compressor Inlet Variable Vane CIVV
Compromised Pulmonary Functions [*Medicine*] .... CPF
Compromising Emanations .... CEM
Compte Courant [*Current Account*] [*French*] CC
Compte Ouvert [*Open Account*] [*Business and trade*] .... CO
Compte Rendu. Association Lyonnaise de Recherches Archeologiques [*A publication*] .... CRAL
Compte Rendu. Commission Imperiale Archeologique (St. Petersbourg) [*A publication*] .... C R (Petersb)
Compte Rendu des Seances. Societe de Biogeographie [*A publication*] .... C R Seances Soc Biogeogr
Compte Rendu des Seances. Societe de Physique et d'Histoire Naturelle de Geneve [*A publication*] .... C R Seances Soc Phys Hist Nat Geneve
Comptek Research, Inc. [*NASDAQ symbol*] .... CMTK
Comptes Rendus [*A publication*] .... CR
Comptes Rendus. Academie Agricole Georgi Dimitrov [*A publication*] .... C R Acad Agric Georgi Dimitrov
Comptes Rendus. Academie d'Agriculture de France [*A publication*] .... Compt Rend Acad Agr France
Comptes Rendus. Academie Bulgare des Sciences [*A publication*] .... Compt Rend Acad Bulg Sci
Comptes Rendus. Academie Bulgare des Sciences [*A publication*] .... C R Acad Bulgare Sci
Comptes Rendus. Academie Bulgare des Sciences [*A publication*] .... C R Acad Bulg Sci
Comptes Rendus. Academie des Inscriptions et Belles Lettres [*A publication*] .... CRAI
Comptes Rendus. Academie des Inscriptions et Belles Lettres [*A publication*] .... CRAIBL
Comptes Rendus. Academie Polonaise des Sciences et des Lettres [*A publication*] .... CRAP
Comptes Rendus. Academie des Sciences [*A publication*] .... Compt Rend Acad Sci
Comptes Rendus. Academie des Sciences Agricoles en Bulgaria [*A publication*] .... C R Acad Sci Agric Bulg
Comptes Rendus. Academie de Sciences (Paris) [*A publication*] .... C R Acad Sci (Paris)
Comptes Rendus. Academie des Sciences de Russie [*A publication*] .... CRASR
Comptes Rendus. Academie des Sciences (Union des Republiques Sovietiques Socialistes) [*A publication*] .... CASURSS
Comptes Rendus. Association des Anatomistes [*A publication*] .... C R Assoc Anat
Comptes Rendus. Association Internationale d'Essais de Semences [*A publication*] .... C R Assoc Int Essais Semences
Comptes Rendus. Congres International de Medecine Tropicale et d'Hygiene [*A publication*] .... Compt Rend Cong Internat Med Trop et Hyg
Comptes Rendus. Congres International de Psychotherapie [*A publication*] .... C R Congr Int Psychother
Comptes Rendus. Congres de l'Union Phytopathologique Mediterraneenne [*A publication*] .... C R Congr Union Phytopathol Mediterr
Comptes Rendus Hebdomadaires des Seances. Academie d'Agriculture de France [*A publication*] .... C R Acad Agric France
Comptes Rendus Hebdomadaires des Seances. Academie d'Agriculture de France [*A publication*] .... C R Hebd Seances Acad Agric Fr
Comptes Rendus Hebdomadaires des Seances. Academie des Sciences [*A publication*] .... C R Acad Sci
Comptes Rendus Hebdomadaires des Seances. Academie des Sciences [*A publication*] .... C R Hebd Seances Acad Sci
Comptes Rendus Hebdomadaires des Seances. Academie des Sciences (Paris) [*A publication*] .... Compt Rend Acad Sc (Paris)
Comptes Rendus Hebdomadaires des Seances. Academie des Sciences. Serie A [*A publication*] .... C R Ac Sci A
Comptes Rendus Hebdomadaires des Seances. Academie des Sciences. Serie B [*A publication*] .... C R Ac Sci B
Comptes Rendus Hebdomadaires des Seances. Academie des Sciences. Serie C [*A publication*] .... C R Ac Sci C
Comptes Rendus Hebdomadaires des Seances. Academie des Sciences. Serie D [*A publication*] .... C R Ac Sci D
Comptes Rendus Hebdomadaires des Seances. Academie des Sciences. Vie Academique (Paris) [*A publication*] .... C R Acad Sci Paris Vie Academique
Comptes Rendus de Recherches et Bibliographie sur l'Immigration [*A publication*] .... C R Rech Bibl Immigr
Comptes Rendus des Seances. Academie d'Agriculture de France [*A publication*] .... C R Seances Acad Agric Fr
Comptes Rendus des Seances. Academie des Inscriptions et Belles-Lettres [*A publication*] .... Compt Rend Acad
Comptes Rendus des Seances. Academie des Inscriptions et Belles-Lettres [*A publication*] .... CRSAIBL
Comptes Rendus des Seances Mensuelles. Societe des Sciences Naturelles et Physiques du Maroc [*A publication*] .... C R Seances Mens Soc Sci Nat Phys Maroc
Comptes Rendus des Seances. Societe de Biologie et des Filiales [*A publication*] .... CRSBA
Comptes Rendus des Seances. Societe de Biologie (Paris) [*A publication*] .... C R Soc Biol (Paris)
Comptes Rendus des Seances. Societe de Biologie et de Ses Filiales [*A publication*] .... C R Seances Soc Biol Fil
Comptes Rendus des Seances. Societe de Biologie et de Ses Filiales [*A publication*] .... C R Soc Biol
Comptes Rendus des Seances. Societe de Biologie et de Ses Filiales et Associees (Paris) [*A publication*] .... Compt Rend Soc Biol (Paris)
Comptes Rendus. Societe Francais de Gynecologie [*A publication*] .... C R Soc Fr Gynecol
Comptes Rendus. Societe des Sciences et des Lettres de Lodz [*A publication*] .... CRSL
Comptes Rendus. Societe des Sciences et des Lettres de Poznan [*A publication*] .... CRSP
Comptes Rendus. Societe des Sciences et des Lettres. Universite Catholique de Lublin [*A publication*] .... CRSLub
Comptes Rendus. Societe des Sciences et des Lettres de Varsovie [*A publication*] .... CRSVa
Comptes Rendus. Societe des Sciences et des Lettres de Wroclaw [*A publication*] .... CRSW
Comptes Rendus Sommaire des Seances. Societe Geologique de France [*A publication*] .... C R Som Seances Soc Geol Fr
Comptes Rendus. Symposium International sur les Jets Moleculaires [*A publication*] .... C R Symp Int Jets Mol
Comptes Rendus des Travaux du Laboratoire Carlsberg [*A publication*] .... C R Trav Lab Carlsberg
Comptes Rendus des Travaux du Laboratoire Carlsberg [*A publication*] .... C R Tr Lab C
Comptes Rendus des Travaux du Laboratoire Carlsberg. Serie Chimique [*A publication*] .... C R Trav Lab Carlsberg Ser Chim
Comptes Rendus des Travaux du Laboratoire Carlsberg. Serie Physiologique [*A publication*] .... C R Trav Lab Carlsberg Ser Physiol
Comptes Rendus Trimestriels. Academie des Sciences d'Outre-Mer [*A publication*] .... C R Trim Acad Sci O-Mer
Comptes Rendus Trimestriels des Seances. Academie des Sciences d'Outre-Mer [*A publication*] .... Compt Rend Acad Sci Outre-Mer
Comptoir Guineen du Commerce Exterieur [*Guinean Foreign Trade Agency*] .... CGCE
Compton, CA [*Radio station call letters*] .... KJLH
Compton College, Compton, CA [*Library symbol*] .... CComC
Compton Recoil Electron .... CRE
Compton Recoil Particle .... CRP
Comptroller C
Comptroller .... COMP
Comptroller .... COMPT
Comptroller of Accounts .... CA
Comptroller of the Army .... CA
Comptroller of the Army .... COA
Comptroller and Auditor General .... CAG
Comptroller-Director of Programs [*Army*] .... C-DP
Comptroller General .... CG
Comptroller General .... COMPGEN
Comptroller General Decisions [*Navy*] .... COMPGENDEC
Comptroller General Opinion .... CGO
Comptroller General's Decision .... CGD
Comptroller General's Procurement Decisions [*A publication*] .... CPD
Comptroller of the Navy .... COMPT
Compu-Plan, Inc. [*NASDAQ symbol*] .... NSUR
Compucare, Inc. [*NASDAQ symbol*] .... CMPC
Compucom Development [*NASDAQ symbol*] .... CMDC
Compucorp [*NASDAQ symbol*] .... CCUP
CompuDyne Corporation [*American Stock Exchange symbol*] .... CDC
Compugraphic Corp. [*NYSE symbol*] .... CPU
Compugraphics Users Association .... CUA
Compulsory C

Compulsory Censorship [British] [World War II]................CC
Compulsory Insurance CI
Compulsory Purchase Order [British].........................CPO
Compuscan, Inc. [NASDAQ symbol].........................CSCN
Compuserve Information Service [Compuserve, Inc.] ....CIS
CompuShop, Inc. [NASDAQ symbol].........................CSHP
Computation...COMP
Computation and Analysis Division [NASA]................CAD
Computation Center CC
Computation and Communication Trade-Off Study [ARPA] ....CACTOS
Computation and Data Flow Integrated Subsystem ......CADFISS
Computation and Data Processing Center....................CDPC
Computation of Miss Between Orbits [Air Force]........COMBO
Computation Subsystem [Space Flight Operations Facility, NASA] ....COMP
Computational ....CMP
Computational Arithmetic Program ....CAP
Computational Linguistics CL
Computational Linguistics [A publication]..................CompL
Computational Linguistics [A publication]..................Comput L
Computational Requirements for Engineering and Simulation, Training and Education [Time-sharing computer complex] [Air Force].........CREATE
Computations and Data Reduction Division [NASA] ....CDRD
Compute [or Computer]..C
Compute [or Computer]..CMPT
Compute Air-Trans Systems, Inc..............................CATS
Compute Parallel ....COMPEL
Computed...CMPTD
Computed Air-Release Point..CARP
Computed Ephemeris Position ....CEP
Computed Point [Navigation] ....CP
Computed Slant Detection Range ....CSDR
Computed Tomographic Metrizamide Myelography..........CTMM
Computer ....CMP
Computer ....CMPTR
Computer ....COMP
Computer [A publication]...Comput
Computer Abstracts [A publication].............................ComAb
Computer Abstracts [A publication].............................Comput Abstr
Computer Access Device ....CAD
Computer Access Device Input ....CADI
Computer Access Device Output ....CADO
Computer-Accessed [or-Aided] Telemetry System..........CATS
Computer Achievement Monitoring ....CAM
Computer Adaptor Display...CAD
Computer Address Matrix ....CAM
Computer-Administered Instruction ....CAI
Computer Administered Instructional System ....CAIS
Computer Administrative Instruction ....CADMINI
Computer, Aerial Reconnaissance ....COMAR
Computer Aid..CAID
Computer-Aided Analysis and Information Recovery Systems..........CAIRS
Computer-Aided Approach Spacing [Aviation] ....CAAS
Computer-Aided Chartroom ....COACH
Computer-Aided Circuit Analysis [Electronics] ....CACA
Computer-Aided Data Management Procedure ....CADMP
Computer-Aided Design..CAD
Computer Aided Design [A publication] ....Comput Aided Des
Computer-Aided Design and Analysis ....CADA
Computer-Aided Design, Analysis, and Reliability ....CADAR
Computer-Aided Design/Computer-Aided Manufacturing ....CAD/CAM
Computer-Aided Design and Drafting ....CADD
Computer-Aided Design and Electrical Test ....CADET
Computer-Aided Design of Electronic Circuit ....CADEC
Computer-Aided Design of Electronic Circuits [Elsevier Book Series] [A publication]..........CADEC
Computer-Aided Design of Electronic Products ....CADEP
Computer-Aided Design Engineering ....CADE
Computer-Aided Design Environment ....COMRADE
Computer-Aided Design Experiment Translator............CADET
Computer-Aided Design of Integrated Circuits ....CADIC
Computer-Aided Design/Numerical Control ....CD/NC
Computer-Aided Design and Numerical Control Effort [General Motors Corp.]..........CADENCE
Computer-Aided Design and Test [System]..................CADAT
Computer-Aided Detection..CAD
Computer-Aided Drafting...CAD
Computer-Aided Education ....CAE
Computer-Aided Engineering ....CAE
Computer-Aided Engineering and Architectural Design System .....CAEDS
Computer-Aided Film Editor..CAFE
Computer-Aided Flight Operations Center...................CAFOC
Computer-Aided Function Allocation and Evaluation System ......CAFES
Computer-Aided [or -Assisted] Instruction ....CAI
Computer-Aided Instruction ....CAIS
Computer-Aided Instruction System ....CAISYS
Computer-Aided [or -Assisted] Learning ....CAL
Computer-Aided Line Balance......................................CALB
Computer-Aided Loads Analysis ....CALA
Computer-Aided [or -Assisted] Makeup [Graphic arts].......... CAM

Computer-Aided Manufacturing....................................CAM
Computer Aided Manufacturing International [An association]..........CAM-I
Computer-Aided Measurement and Control [NASA] ....CAMAC
Computer-Aided Mechanical Drafting ....CAMD
Computer-Aided Missile Synthesis [Army]..................CAMS
Computer-Aided Operations Research Facility [National Maritime Research Center].........CAORF
Computer-Aided Patient Management ....CAPM
Computer-Aided Pattern Evaluation and Recognition ....CAPER
Computer-Aided Pipe Sketching [System] [Du Pont]..........CAPS
Computer-Aided Piping Design and Construction..........CAPDAC
Computer-Aided Process Design ....CAPD
Computer-Aided Process Planning ....CAPP
Computer-Aided Processing and Terminal Access Information Network [Library computer network]..........CAPTAIN
Computer-Aided [or Assisted] Production ....CAP
Computer-Aided Programing System..........................CAPS
Computer-Aided Quality Assurance ....CAQA
Computer-Aided RADAR Design ....CARD
Computer-Aided Railway Engineering System ....CARES
Computer-Aided Reference Service [Information service] ....CARS
Computer-Aided Reliability Data Systems [Bell System] ....CARDS
Computer-Aided Reorder Trap Analysis [Bell Laboratories]..........CARTA
Computer-Aided Research into Stock Market Applications..........CARISMA
Computer-Aided Routing System ....CARS
Computer-Aided Ship Design and Construction..........CASDAC
Computer-Aided Ship Design and Construction..........CASDC
Computer-Aided Structural Design..............................CASD
Computer-Aided Structural Technology.......................CAST
Computer-Aided System Design ....CASD
Computer-Aided System Evaluation ....CASE
Computer-Aided Teaching..CAT
Computer-Aided Teaching System ....CATS
Computer-Aided Technology..CAT
Computer-Aided Translation ....CAT
Computer-Aided Troubleshooting ....CATS
Computer-Aided Typesetting Process..........................CATP
Computer-Aided Work Sampling ....CAWS
Computer Aids for Chemical Engineering Education [National Academy of Engineering]..........CACHE
Computer Amplifier Alarm ....CAA
Computer Analog Input ....CAI
Computer Analog Input/Output ....CAI/O
Computer Analog Input/Output....................................CAIOP
Computer Analysis of Thermochemical [Data tables] ....CATCH
Computer Analyzed Newspaper Data On-Line [Newspaper Advertising Bureau, Inc.] [Information service]..........CAN DO
Computer Animation Language ....CAL
Computer Annunciation Matrix ....CAM
Computer Application Control Code..............................CACC
Computer Applications [A publication]..........................Comput Appl
Computer Applications Digest [A publication]..............CAD
Computer Applications for the Graphic Arts ....CAFGA
Computer Applications Group [Air Force].....................CAG
Computer Applications, Incorporated...........................CAI
Computer Applications of Military Problems [Computer users' group]..........CAMP
Computer Applications in the Minerals Industry [Title of a series of conferences]..........APCOM
Computer Applications Service [A publication] ....Comput Appl Serv
Computer Applications in Shipping and Shipbuilding [Elsevier Book Series] [A publication]..........CASS
Computer Applications Support and Development Office [Navy].....CASDO
Computer Architecture Specification Language..........CASL
Computer Assembly ....CA
Computer-Assisted Accounting ....CAA
Computer-Assisted Action Information System [British]..........CAAIS
Computer-Assisted Area Source Emissions [Environmental Protection Agency]..........CAASE
Computer-Assisted Audit Techniques ....CAAT
Computer-Assisted Axial Tomography [Also, CAT, CT] [Roentgenography]..........CAAT
Computer-Assisted Classification and Assignment System........COMPASS
Computer-Assisted Counseling [Proposed for Air Force] ....CAC
Computer-Assisted Design ....CAD
Computer-Assisted Detailing of Ships........................CASDOS
Computer-Assisted Development Aids.........................CADA
Computer-Assisted Diagnosis ....CAD
Computer-Assisted Dialog ....CAD
Computer-Assisted Dispatching System [IBM Corp.]..........CADS
Computer-Assisted Disposal Simulation [Game]..........CADISIM
Computer-Assisted Distribution and Assignment ....CADA
Computer-Assisted Enrollment [IBM Corp.]..................CAE
Computer-Assisted Entry...CAE
Computer-Assisted Estimating ....CAE
Computer-Assisted Estimating and Management Information Systems..........CAE/MIS
Computer-Assisted Fault Isolation Test ....CAFIT
Computer-Assisted Industrial Simulation [Army]..........CAISIM
Computer-Assisted Instruction Center........................CAIC
Computer-Assisted Instruction Study Management System ....CAISMS

Computer-Assisted Interactive Resources Scheduling System	CAIRS
Computer-Assisted Learning Network	CALN
Computer-Assisted Legislative Liaison; On-Line Political Evaluation	CALLIOPE
Computer-Assisted Library Mechanization	CALM
Computer-Assisted Logistics Simulation [Navy]	CALOGSIM
Computer-Assisted Logistics Simulation [Navy]	CALS
Computer-Assisted Maintenance	CAM
Computer-Assisted Maintenance Planning and Control System	CAMCOS
Computer-Assisted Maintenance Simulation [Army]	CAMSIM
Computer-Assisted Makeup	CAM
Computer-Assisted Makeup and Imaging Systems	CAMIS
Computer-Assisted/Managed Instructional Language	CAMIL
Computer-Assisted Management of Portfolios	CAMP
Computer-Assisted Mapping and Records Activities System	CAMRAS
Computer-Assisted Mathematics Program	CAMP
Computer-Assisted Menu Planning	CAMP
Computer-Assisted Method Assembly [Analytical method writing]	CAMA
Computer-Assisted Movie Production	CAMP
Computer-Assisted Network Scheduling System	CANS
Computer-Assisted Placement Service [British]	CAPS
Computer-Assisted Printing	CAP
Computer-Assisted Prisoner Transportation Index Service [National Sheriffs' Association]	CAPTIS
Computer-Assisted Problem Solving	CAPS
Computer-Assisted Program Evaluation Review-Technique Simulation [Army]	CAPERTSIM
Computer-Assisted Reliability and Maintainability Simulation [Game]	CARMSIM
Computer-Assisted Repair Simulation [Game]	CARESIM
Computer-Assisted Research	CAR
Computer-Assisted Retrieval	CAR
Computer-Assisted Scanning Techniques	CAST
Computer-Assisted Search Planning	CASP
Computer-Assisted Simulation of Supply and Related Systems	CASSARS
Computer-Assisted Surveillance Subsystem	COMPASS
Computer-Assisted System for Theater Level Engineering [Military]	CASTLE
Computer-Assisted Technique for Numerical Indexing Purposes	CATNIP
Computer-Assisted Test Shop	CATS
Computer-Assisted Testing	CAT
Computer-Assisted Total Value Assessment [Army]	CATVA
Computer-Assisted Trading System	CATS
Computer-Assisted Training	COMAT
Computer-Assisted Training System [IRS]	CATS
Computer-Associated [or -Assisted] Device	CAD
Computer-Associated Self-Assessment [British]	CASA
Computer Associates International [NASDAQ symbol]	CASI
Computer Audit Retrieval System	CARS
Computer Audit Specialist [IRS]	CAS
Computer-Augmented Design and Manufacturing [Aviation]	CADAM
Computer-Augmented Loft Lines [Graphics]	CALL
Computer-Automated Real-Time Betting Information Network	CARBINE
Computer-Automated Social Simulation	CASS
Computer-Automated Support Equipment	CASE
Computer and Automated Systems Association	CASA
Computer and Automated Systems Association [Later, CASA/SME]	CASE
Computer and Automated Systems Association of SME [Formerly, CASE]	CASA/SME
Computer-Automated Test System [AT & T]	CATS
Computer-Automated Transit Systems	CATS
Computer Automatic Scheduling System	CASS
Computer Automation [NASDAQ symbol]	CAUT
Computer of Average Transients	CAT
Computer-Based Behavioral Studies	CBBS
Computer-Based Bibliographic Search Service	CBBS
Computer-Based Case Tracing [Medicine]	COMTRAC
Computer-Based Education [Project]	C-BE
Computer-Based Education Research Laboratory [University of Illinois]	CERL
Computer-Based Estimating Technique for Contractors	COBESTCO
Computer-Based Financial Management System [Harper & Shuman, Inc.] [Information service]	CFMS
Computer-Based Instruction [Education]	CBI
Computer-Based Instruction System	COBIS
Computer-Based Instructional System	CBIS
Computer-Based Laboratory for Automated School Systems	CLASS
Computer-Based Learning	CBL
Computer-Based Message System	CBMS
Computer-Based Message Systems	CBMS
Computer-Based Optimization Routines and Techniques for Effective X	CORTEX
Computer-Based Recruit Assignment	COBRA
Computer-Based Reference Service [Information service]	CBRS
Computer-Based Resource Units [Education]	CBRU
Computer-Based Terminal	CBT
Computer-Based Training	CBT

Computer Bulletin [A publication]	Comp Bul
Computer Bulletin [A publication]	Comput Bull
Computer Burst Order	CBO
Computer and Business Equipment Manufacturers Association	CBEMA
Computer Calculator	CC
Computer Campaign Services [Data processing firm in field of politics]	CCS
Computer Center	CMPCTR
Computer Character Recognition	CCR
Computer Command Control [General Motors Corp.]	CCC
Computer Command Engineer	CCE
Computer Command Subsystem [NASA]	CCS
Computer & Commercial Technology [NASDAQ symbol]	CCTC
Computer Communications [A publication]	Comp Comm
Computer Communications [A publication]	Comput Commun
Computer Communications Console	CCC
Computer Communications Converter	CCC
Computer and Communications Industry Association	CCIA
Computer Communications Networks Group [University of Waterloo] [Canada] [Information service]	CCNG
Computer Community	CC
[The] Computer Company, Inc. [Information service]	TCC
Computer-Compatible Tape	CCT
Computer Complex	CC
Computer Components and System Group	CCSG
Computer Composition Corporation	CCC
Computer-to-Computer	C-to-C
Computer Conference	COMPCON
Computer Consoles, Inc. [American Stock Exchange symbol]	CCS
Computer Consulting Service	CCS
Computer Contributions [A publication]	Comput Contrib
Computer and Control Abstracts [A publication]	CCA
Computer and Control Abstracts [A publication]	Comput & Contr Abstr
Computer and Control Abstracts [A publication]	Comput Control Abstr
Computer Control Communication	CCC
Computer Control Corporation	CCC
Computer Control Loading	CCL
Computer Control Panel	CCP
Computer Control Unit	CCU
Computer-Controlled Area Sterilization Multisensor System	CASMS
Computer-Controlled Automated Cargo Handling Envelope	CACHE
Computer-Controlled Automatic Test Equipment	CATE
Computer-Controlled Catalytic Converter [General Motors Corp.]	C-4
Computer-Controlled Coil Ignition	C^3I
Computer-Controlled Display	CCD
Computer-Controlled Interconnect System	CCIS
Computer-Controlled Launch Set [NASA]	CCLS
Computer-Controlled Microfilm Search System	CCMSS
Computer-Controlled X-Ray Diffractometer	CCXD
Computer Controller Multiplexer Unit	CCMU
Computer Core Segment	CCS
Computer Corporation of America	CCA
Computer Craft, Inc. [NASDAQ symbol]	CRFT
Computer Cross Select Unit	CCSU
Computer Data [A publication]	Comp Data
Computer Data Entry Keyboard	CDEK
Computer Data Recording System	CDRS
Computer Data Switchboard	CDS
Computer Data System	CDS
Computer Data Systems, Incorporated [Information service]	CDSI
Computer Data Systems, Inc. [NASDAQ symbol]	CPTD
Computer Data Word	CDW
Computer Dealer Exposition	COMDEX
Computer Dealers and Lessors Association	CDLA
Computer Decisions [A publication]	Comp Dec
Computer Decisions [A publication]	Comp Decisions
Computer Decisions [A publication]	Comput Decis
Computer Description Language	CDL
Computer Design [A publication]	Comp Des
Computer Design [A publication]	Comput Des
Computer Design and Architecture Series [Elsevier Book Series] [A publication]	CDAS
Computer Design and Evaluation System	CODES
Computer Design Language	CDL
Computer Designed Systems [NASDAQ symbol]	CDSI
Computer-Developed Instruction	CDI
Computer Development Center	CDC
Computer Development Center	CDEVC
Computer Developments Limited Automatic Coding System	CODEL
Computer Devices, Incorporated [NASDAQ symbol]	CDITQ
Computer Dialysis Systems [NASDAQ symbol]	CODI
Computer Direct to Telegraph	CODIT
Computer-Directed Communications	CODIC
Computer-Directed Drawing	CDD
Computer-Directed Drawing Instrument	CDDI
Computer-Directed Instrument	CDI
Computer-Directed Training Lesson Building System	CDTLBS
Computer-Directed Training System	CDTS
Computer Directions Advisors, Inc. [Information service]	CDA
Computer Directions Corporation	CDC
Computer Display Channel	CDC

Computer Display Unit ... CDU
Computer-Driven Simulation Environment [*FAA*] ... CDSE
Computer Duplex System ... CDS
Computer Education Conference [*A publication*] ... Computer Ed
Computer Election Systems ... CES
Computer Electroencephalogram ... CEEG
Computer Elements and Systems [*A publication*] ... Comput Elem Syst
Computer Engineer ... CE
Computer Engineering Service ... CES
Computer Entry Keyboard ... CEK
Computer Entry Punch ... CEP
Computer Entry and Readout Equipment ... CERE
Computer Entry Systems [*NASDAQ symbol*] ... CESC
Computer Equipment System for Surface-to-Air Missiles ... CESSAM
Computer Evaluation of Scanning Electron Microscope Image ... CESEMI
Computer Execute Function ... CEF
Computer-Extended Instruction ... CEI
Computer Facilities Management ... CFM
Computer Factory, Inc. [*American Stock Exchange symbol*] ... CFA
Computer Format Control Buffer ... CFCB
Computer-Generated Hologram ... CGH
Computer-Generated Imagery ... CGI
Computer-Generated Purchase Request ... CGPR
Computer Graphics ... CG
Computer Graphics Display System [*Army*] ... CGDS
Computer Graphics and Image Processing [*A publication*] ... Comput Graphics Image Process
Computer Graphics Structural Analysis ... CGSA
Computer Guidance Corporation ... CGC
Computer Hardware Description Language ... CHDL
Computer Horizons Corp. [*NASDAQ symbol*] ... CHRZ
Computer and Human-Assisted Organization of a Technical Information Center [*National Bureau of Standards*] ... CHAOTIC
Computer Human Interaction ... CHI
Computer Identics Corp. [*NASDAQ symbol*] ... CIDN
Computer Image Generator ... CIG
Computer Index of Neutron Data ... CIND
Computer Index of Neutron Data ... CINDA
Computer Indicator ... CI
Computer Information [*A publication*] ... Comput Inf
Computer Information Center ... COPIC
Computer/Information/Library Sciences [*Abstracts*] ... C/I/L
Computer and Information Science Research Center [*Ohio State University*] ... CISRC
Computer and Information Sciences ... COINS
Computer and Information Services [*Corporation for Public Broadcasting*] ... CIS
Computer and Information Systems [*A publication*] ... Comput & Info Sys
Computer-Informationsdienst Graz [*Graz Computer-Information Service*] [*Austria*] ... CIG
Computer Input Matrix ... CIM
Computer Input Microfilming ... CIM
Computer Input Multiplexer ... CIM
Computer Inquiries ... CI
Computer Institute for Applications in Science and Engineering ... CIASE
Computer Instruction and Training Assistance for the Blind ... CITAB
Computer Instruments Corporation ... CIC
Computer Instruments Corp. [*American Stock Exchange symbol*] [*Delisted*] ... CUI
Computer-Integrated Factory ... CIF
Computer-Integrated Instruction ... CII
Computer-Integrated Manufacturing ... CIM
Computer-Integrated Test Equipment ... CITE
Computer Interface Adaptor ... CIA
Computer Interface Conditioning Unit ... CICU
Computer Interface Control [*Part of digital television computer*] ... CIC
Computer Interface Device ... CID
Computer Interface for Television ... CINTEL
Computer Interface Terminal ... CIT
Computer Interface Unit ... CIU
Computer Investors Group, Inc. [*American Stock Exchange symbol*] [*Delisted*] ... CIG
Computer Journal [*A publication*] ... Comp J
Computer Journal [*A publication*] ... Computer J
Computer Journal [*A publication*] ... Comput J
Computer Laboratory of Harvard University ... CLHU
Computer Laboratory for Instruction in Psychological Research [*University of Colorado*] ... CLIPR
Computer Language for Aeronautics and Space Programing [*NASA*] ... CLASP
Computer Language to Aid and Stimulate Scientific, Mathematical, and Technical Education ... CLASSMATE
Computer Language Recorder ... CLR
Computer Language Research ... CLR
Computer Language Research, Incorporated [*NASDAQ symbol*] ... CLRI
Computer Language Translator ... CLT
Computer Languages [*A publication*] ... Comput Lang
Computer Launch Interference Problems ... CLIP
Computer Launch and Separation Problem ... CLASP
Computer Law and Tax Report [*A publication*] ... Comp Law
Computer Lessors Association [*Later, CDLA*] ... CLA
Computer Library Services, Incorporated ... CLSI
Computer Load and Resource Analysis ... CLARA
Computer Lock-On ... CLO
Computer Logic Demonstrator ... CLD
Computer Logic Unit Tester ... CLUT
Computer Maintenance Test Set ... CMTS
Computer-Managed Instruction ... CMI
Computer-Managed Laboratory ... CML
Computer Management [*A publication*] ... Comp Mgmt
Computer Management [*A publication*] ... Comput Manage
Computer Management System ... CMS
Computer-Marked Assignment [*Education*] [*British*] ... CMA
Computer Marketing [*Standard & Poor's*] ... COMPMARK
Computer Memories [*NASDAQ symbol*] ... CMIN
Computer Memory Element ... CME
Computer Memory Tester ... CMT
Computer Method of Sequencing Operations for Assembly Lines ... COMSOAL
Computer Methods in Applied Mechanics and Engineering [*A publication*] ... Comp Methods Appl Mech Eng
Computer Methods in Applied Mechanics and Engineering [*A publication*] ... Comput Methods Appl Mech Eng
Computer Methods in Applied Mechanics and Engineering [*A publication*] ... Comput Methods Appl Mech & Eng
Computer Microfilm Corp. [*NASDAQ symbol*] ... COMI
Computer Microfilm International Corporation [*Information service*] ... CMIC
Computer Micrographics Technology [*An association*] ... CMT
Computer Micrographics Technology [*An association*] ... COMTEC
Computer Module ... CM
Computer Music Journal [*A publication*] ... Computer Mus J
Computer Negotiations Report [*A publication*] ... C N Report
Computer Network Corp. [*NASDAQ symbol*] ... CNET
Computer Network Corp. [*Information service*] ... COMNET
Computer Networks [*A publication*] ... Comp Net
Computer Networks [*A publication*] ... Comput Networks
Computer Numerical Control [*Data processing*] ... CNC
Computer On-Line Real-Time Applications Language [*Data processing*] ... CORAL
Computer with On-Line Remote Devices [*National Bureau of Standards*] ... CORD
Computer-Operated [*or -Oriented*] **Electronic Display** ... COED
Computer-Operated Machine Evaluation Technique [*Air Force*] ... COMET
Computer-Operated Management Evaluation Technique [*AEC-Army*] ... COMET
Computer-Operated Multifunction Electronic Test System ... COMETS
Computer-Operated Universal Test ... COUNT
Computer Operations Facility ... COF
Computer Operations Group ... COG
Computer Operator Handbook ... COH
Computer Operators' Course ... COC
Computer Optimization Package [*or Program*] ... COP
Computer Optimized Fabrication [*Sheet metal*] [*Raytheon Co.*] ... COF
Computer Optimized Sheetmetal Technology [*Raytheon Co.*] ... COST
Computer Oriented Classicists ... COC
Computer-Oriented Design of Electronic Devices ... CODED
Computer-Oriented Language [*Data processing*] ... COL
Computer-Oriented Language Translator ... COLT
Computer-Oriented Mechanical Design ... COMMEND
Computer-Oriented Modal Control and Appraisal System ... COMCAS
Computer-Oriented Partial Sum ... COPS
Computer-Oriented Programed Instruction ... COPI
Computer-Oriented Reference System for Automatic Information Retrieval ... CORSAIR
Computer-Oriented Reporting Efficiency ... CORE
Computer-Oriented Retrieval of Auto Larcenists ... CORRAL
Computer-Oriented System for Management Order Synthesis [*IBM Corp.*] ... COSMOS
Computer-Oriented System - Newly Organized Storage-to-Retrieval Apparatus ... COSNOSTRA
Computer Output Microfilm [*or Microfiche or Microform*] ... COM
Computer Output Microform Catalog ... COMCAT
Computer Packages ... COMPAC
Computer Paragraph ... CP
Computer Payroll ... COMPAY
Computer Performance Evaluation ... CPE
Computer Performance Evaluation Users Group ... CPEUG
Computer Peripheral Equipment ... CPE
Computer Peripheral Manufacturers Association ... CPMA
Computer Peripheral Products [*NASDAQ symbol*] ... CPPI
Computer Peripheral Unit ... CPU
Computer Personnel [*A publication*] ... Comp Pers
Computer Personnel [*A publication*] ... Comput Pers
Computer Personnel Research Group [*Later, Special Interest Group for Computer Personnel Research*] ... CPRG
Computer Personnel Research Proceedings [*A publication*] ... CPR Proc
Computer and Photographic Assisted Learning ... CAPAL
Computer Physics Communications [*A publication*] ... Comp Phys Comm
Computer Physics Communications [*A publication*] ... Computer Ph
Computer Physics Communications [*A publication*] ... Comput Phys Commun

Computer-Planning and Aircraft-Weighing Scales ... CPAWS
Computer Planning and Control Technique ... COMPACT
Computer Pneumatic Input Panel ... CPIP
Computer Power Supply ... CPS
Computer Praxis [*A publication*] ... Comput Prax
Computer-Prescribed Instruction ... CPI
Computer Printer Unit ... CPU
Computer Process Control ... CPC
Computer Products [*NASDAQ symbol*] ... CPRD
Computer Program ... COMPROG
Computer Program Abstracts [*NASA*] [*A publication*] ... CPA
Computer Program Associated Contractor ... CPAC
Computer Program for Automatic Control ... COMPAC
Computer Program Book ... CPB
Computer Program Change Request ... CPCR
Computer Program Components ... CPC
Computer Program Configured Item ... CPCI
Computer Program Contract End Item ... CPCEI
Computer Program Design [*or Development*] **Specification** [*NASA*] ... CPDS
Computer Program Development Center [*Air Force*] ... CPDC
Computer Program End Item ... CPEI
Computer Program Identification Numbers ... CPIN
Computer Program Implementation Process ... CPIP
Computer Program Integration Contractor ... CPIC
Computer Program Library ... CPL
Computer Program Module ... CPM
Computer Program Specification ... CPS
Computer Program System [*Boeing Co.*] ... CPS
Computer Program Tapes ... CPT
Computer Program Update ... CPU
Computer-Programed Automatic Checkout and Test System ... COMPACT
Computer Programing Concepts ... CPC
Computer Programing Performance Specification ... CPPS
Computer Programing Service ... CPS
Computer Programing and Testing Activity ... CPTA
Computer Programs in Biomedicine [*A publication*] ... Computer Pr
Computer Programs in Biomedicine [*A publication*] ... Comput Programs Biomed
Computer Research [*NASDAQ symbol*] ... CORE
Computer Research, Systems, and Software ... COMPRESS
Computer Reset Pulse ... CRP
Computer Resource Unit ... CRU
Computer Resources [*NASDAQ symbol*] ... CRII
Computer Response Corporation ... CRC
Computer Retrieval Editor [*Used to manage CORKIPER file family*] ... COREDITOR
Computer Retrieval of Information on Scientific Projects ... CRISP
Computer Retrieval of Kinetic Parameters of Electrode Reactions ... CORKIPER
Computer Retrieval of Organic Structures Based on Wiswesser ... CROSSBOW
Computer Review and Orientation Course ... CROC
Computer Run Report ... CRR
Computer Science ... CS
Computer Sciences Corporation [*NYSE symbol*] ... CSC
Computer Sciences Corp., Technical Library, El Segundo, CA [*Library symbol*] ... CEsC
Computer Search Center [*Illinois Institute of Technology*] ... CSC
Computer Search Services ... CSS
Computer Security Evaluation Center ... CSEC
Computer Security Institute ... CSI
Computer Sensitive Language ... CSL
Computer Sequence Number ... CSN
Computer Service Center ... CSC
Computer Service Corp. ADR [*NASDAQ symbol*] ... CSKKY
Computer Services - Long Beach ... CSLB
Computer Sharing Services, Inc. [*Information service*] ... CSS
Computer Simulation ... CS
Computer Simulation Language ... CSL
Computer Simulation Program ... CSP
Computer Software Analysis Conference [*IEEE*] ... COMPSAC
Computer Software Data Tapes ... CSDT
Computer Software Management and Information Center [*NASA facility at University of Georgia*] ... COSMIC
Computer Software and Peripheral Show ... COMPSO
Computer for Special Small Tactical Application ... COSSTA
Computer Status Lights ... CSL
Computer Status Matrix ... CSM
Computer Stock Inventory Control ... CSIC
Computer Stock Timing and Analysis Technique ... COM-STAT
[*The*] **Computer Store** [*NASDAQ symbol*] ... TCS
Computer-Stored Ambulatory Record ... COSTAR
Computer Structure Language ... CSL
Computer Studies in the Humanities and Verbal Behavior [*A publication*] ... Comput Stud Hum & Verbal Behav
Computer Studies in the Humanities and Verbal Behavior [*A publication*] ... CSHVB
Computer Subsystem ... CSS
Computer Subsystem Controller ... CSC
Computer Support Equipment ... CSE
Computer Support in Military Psychiatry [*Project*] ... COMPSY
Computer Survey [*A publication*] ... Comput Surv
Computer System Analyst ... CSA
Computer System Interface Circuits ... CSIC
Computer System Language ... CSL
Computer System for Main Frame Operations [*Bell System*] ... COSMOS
Computer System Manual ... CSM
Computer System for Medical Information Services ... COSMIS
Computer System Science Training [*IBM Corp.*] ... CSST
Computer System Simulator ... CSS
Computer Systems Command [*Also, ACSC*] [*Army*] ... CSC
Computer Systems Director ... CSD
Computer Systems Integration Review ... CSIR
Computer Systems Support and Evaluation Command ... CSSEC
Computer Tape Recorder ... CTR
Computer Task Group [*NASDAQ symbol*] ... CTSK
Computer Technology ... CT
Computer Technology Center ... CTC
Computer Telewriter Systems ... CTS
Computer Terminal Systems [*NASDAQ symbol*] ... CTML
Computer Test Set ... CTS
Computer Transceiver [*NASDAQ symbol*] ... CTRC
Computer Translation, Incorporated [*Information service*] ... CTI
Computer Transponder ... CT
Computer Typing System ... CTS
Computer Unit [*American Topical Association*] ... CU
Computer Update Equipment ... CUE
Computer for Uprange Point-of-Impact Determination [*NASA*] ... CUPID
Computer Usage Co. [*NASDAQ symbol*] ... CUSE
Computer Usage Control ... CUC
Computer Usage List Processor ... CULP
Computer Usage's Business-Oriented Language [*Data processing*] ... CUBOL
Computer Use in the Health Service [*British*] ... CUHS
Computer User Education [*An association*] ... CUE
Computer Utility Educational System ... CUES
Computer Utilization Accounting System ... CUAS
Computer Utilization Reporting System ... CURES
Computer Utilized Turning System [*Warner & Swasey*] ... CUTS
Computer Weekly [*A publication*] ... Computer Wkly
Computer Weekly [*A publication*] ... Comput Wkly
Computer Weekly International [*A publication*] ... Comput Wkly Int
Computerimmunoelectrophoresis [*Medicine*] ... CIE
Computerised Information from National Criminological Holdings [*Australian Institute of Criminology Library*] [*Information service*] ... CINCH
Computerised Instrumented Residential Audit [*Energy auditing*] ... CIRA
Computerised Library of Analysed Igneous Rocks [*Australia*] [*Information service*] ... CLAIR
Computerization of Army Movement Schedules ... COAMS
Computerization of World Facts ... COMPACT
Computerized Acquisitions Systems Series [*A publication*] ... Comput Acquis Syst Ser
Computerized Advance Personnel Requirements Information [*or Inventory*] [*Navy*] ... CAPRI
Computerized Aerospace Ground Equipment ... CAGE
Computerized Agricultural Research Information System ... CARIS
Computerized Aircraft Maintenance Program ... CAMP
Computerized Algorithmic Satellite Scheduler [*NASA*] ... CASS
Computerized Anatomical Man [*NASA*] ... CAM
Computerized Annotated Bibliography System ... CABS
Computerized Assignment of Personnel [*Military*] ... CAP
Computerized, Automated, Bus Spacing and Dispatching System ... CABSADS
Computerized Automatic Inertial Test Set ... CAITS
Computerized Automatic Rating Technique ... CART
Computerized Automatic Systems Tester ... CAST
Computerized Automotive Replacement Scheduling [*Bell System*] ... CARS
Computerized Automotive Reporting Service ... CARS
Computerized Axial Tomography [*Also, CAAT, CT*] [*Roentgenography*] [*Usually used in combination, as CATscan*] ... CAT
Computerized Axial Tomography Scanner [*Roentgenography*] ... CATscan
Computerized Biomechanical Man-Model [*Air Force*] ... COMBIMAN
Computerized Boolean Reliability Analysis [*Boeing*] ... COBRA
Computerized Branch Exchange [*Telecommunications*] ... CBX
Computerized Cable Upkeep Administrative Program [*Bell System*] ... CCUAP
Computerized Cataloging Systems Series [*A publication*] ... Comput Cat Syst Ser
Computerized Circulation Systems Series [*A publication*] ... Comput Circ Syst Ser
Computerized Criminal History [*FBI*] ... CCH
Computerized Dispersive Spectroscopy ... CDS
Computerized Distribution and Control of Microfilm [*American Motors Corp.*] ... CODICOM
Computerized Documentation System [*UNESCO*] ... CDS
Computerized Documentation System/Integrated Set of Information Systems [*UNESCO*] ... CDS/ISIS
Computerized Drawing Electrical Information ... CODEIN
Computerized Electro Neuro-Ophthalmograph ... CENOG
Computerized Engineering Index [*of Engineering Index, Inc.*] ... COMPENDEX

Computerized Environmental Legislative Data System [*Army*] .... CELDS
Computerized Evaluation of the Logistics System [*Army*] .... COMPELS
Computerized Freight Remittance System [*Pronounced "coffers"*] .... COFRS
Computerized Hierarchy and Relationship Table .... CHART
Computerized Hospital Information System .... CHICS
Computerized Industrial Tomography [*Nondestructive testing method*] .... CIT
Computerized Interactive Graphics .... CIG
Computerized Library Acquisitions System [*Lukac Data Systems*] [*Information service*] .... CLAS
Computerized Link Analysis System .... CLANS
Computerized Literature Access Search Service .... CLASS
Computerized Literature Searching Service .... CLSS
Computerized Logic-Oriented Design System [*Air Force*] .... CLODS
Computerized Lubrication Control [*Sun Oil Co.*] CLC
Computerized Medical Information Support System [*Veterans Administration*] .... COMISS
Computerized Moment Stability System [*Navy*] .... CMSS
Computerized Movement Planning and Status System [*Military*] .... COMPASS
Computerized National Range Documentation .... CONRAD
Computerized Officer Planning System [*Navy*] .... COPS
Computerized On-Line Testing .... COLT
Computerized Operational Audit Routine .... COPAR
Computerized Optimization of Elastic Booster Autopilot .... COEBRA
Computerized Performance and Analysis Response Evaluator .... COMPARE
Computerized Performance Rating [*of a horse*] .... CPR
Computerized Reader Enquiry Service System .... CRESS
Computerized Rearrangements of Special Subjects [*or Subject Specialties*] .... CROSS
Computerized Recall Identification System [*Automobile industry*] .... CRIS
Computerized Register of Voice Research [*Southern Illinois University at Carbondale*] [*Information service*] .... CRVR
Computerized Relationship Layout Planning .... CORELAP
Computerized Relative Allocation of Facilities Technique [*IBM Corp.*] .... CRAFT
Computerized Reliability Analysis Method .... CRAM
Computerized Reliability Organization System .... CROS
Computerized Resources Information Bank [*United States Geological Survey*] .... CRIB
Computerized Retrieval Service .... CRS
Computerized Scientific Management Planning System .... CSMPS
Computerized Serials Systems Series [*A publication*] .... Comput Ser Syst Ser
Computerized Spot Television Evaluation and Processing [*Advertising*] .... COM-STEP
Computerized Tomography [*A publication*] .... Comput Tomogr
Computerized Tomography [*Also, CAAT, CAT*] [*Roentgenography*] .... CT
Computerized Tomography Society .... CTS
Computerized Topographic Scanner [*Medicine*] .... CTS
Computerized Training System [*Army*] .... CTS
Computerized Transaxial Tomograms .... CTT
Computerized Travel Aid [*Mobility device for the blind*] .... CTA
Computerized Vocational Information System [*Guidance program*] .... CVIS
Computerizing Medical Examination [*IBM Corp.*] .... CME
Computers [*JETDS nomenclature*] [*Military*] .... CP
Computers and Automation .... CA
Computers and Automation [*Later, Computers and People*] [*A publication*] .... Comp & Automation
Computers and Automation [*Later, Computers and People*] [*A publication*] .... Comput Autom
Computers and Automation Universal Mailing List .... CAUML
Computers in Biology and Medicine [*A publication*] .... Comput Biol Med
Computers and Biomedical Research [*A publication*] .... Comput Biom
Computers and Biomedical Research [*A publication*] .... Comput Biomed Res
Computers in Cardiology [*A publication*] .... Comput Cardiol
Computers in Chemical and Biochemical Research [*A publication*] .... Comput Chem Biochem Res
Computers and Chemical Engineering [*A publication*] .... Comput & Chem Eng
Computers and Chemical Engineering [*A publication*] .... Comput Chem Eng
Computers and Chemistry [*A publication*] .... Comp Chem
Computers and Chemistry [*A publication*] .... Comput Chem
Computers and Communications .... C & C
Computers and Education [*A publication*] .... Comp & Educ
Computers and Electrical Engineering [*A publication*] .... Comput & Electr Eng
Computers and Electrical Engineering [*A publication*] .... Comput Electr Eng
Computers and Fluids [*A publication*] .... Comp Fluids
Computers and Fluids [*A publication*] .... Comput & Fluids
Computers and Fluids [*A publication*] .... Comput Fluids
Computers and Geosciences [*A publication*] .... Comput & Geosci
Computers and Geosciences [*A publication*] .... Comput Geosci
Computers and Graphics [*A publication*] .... Comput Graphics
Computers and the Humanities [*A publication*] .... CHUM
Computers and the Humanities [*A publication*] .... Computer Hu
Computers and the Humanities [*A publication*] .... Comput & Humanities
Computers and the Humanities [*A publication*] .... CPHCC
Computers and Industrial Engineering [*A publication*] .... Comput Ind Eng
Computers Lawyers Association .... CLA
Computers and Mathematics with Applications [*A publication*] .... Comput Math Appl
Computers and Medicine [*A publication*] .... Comp & Med
Computers and Operations Research [*A publication*] .... Comp Oper Res
Computers and Operations Research [*A publication*] .... Comput Oper Res
Computers and Operations Research [*A publication*] .... Comput & Oper Res
Computers at Oregon State University, North Carolina Educational Computing Service, Dartmouth College, and the Universities of Iowa and Texas at Austin [*An educational consortium*] .... CONDUIT
Computers and People [*A publication*] .... Comp & People
Computers and People [*A publication*] .... Computer Pe
Computers and Software Review Panel [*NASA*] .... CSRP
Computers and Structures [*A publication*] .... Comput Struct
Computers and Systems .... C & S
Computers and Systems .... CS
Computers Users' Committee [*United Nations Development Program*] .... CUC
ComputerTown, USA! [*An association*] .... CTUSA
Computervision Corp. [*NYSE symbol*] .... CVN
Computerworld [*A publication*] .... Computwrld
Computerworld [*A publication*] .... CW
Computing .... CMPTG
Computing. Archiv fuer Elektronisches Rechnen [*A publication*] .... Comput Arch Elektron Rechn
Computing. Archiv fuer Informatik und Numerik [*A publication*] .... Comput Arch Inf Num
Computing Assistance Program [*Taylor University*] [*Information service*] .... CAP
Computing Devices of Canada, Ottawa, ON, Canada [*Library symbol*] .... CaOOCDC
Computing Media .... CM
Computing Reviews [*A publication*] .... Comp Rev
Computing Reviews [*A publication*] .... Comput Rev
Computing Reviews [*A publication*] .... ComRev
Computing Reviews [*A publication*] .... CR
Computing & Software, Inc. [*NYSE symbol*] [*Delisted*] .... CSW
Computing South Africa [*A publication*] .... Comput S Afr
Computing Surveys [*A publication*] .... Comp Surv
Computing Surveys [*A publication*] .... Comput Surv
Computing Surveys [*A publication*] .... Comput Survey
Computone Systems [*NASDAQ symbol*] .... CTON
Computrac, Inc. [*NASDAQ symbol*] .... CTTX
Computrac Instruments [*NASDAQ symbol*] .... CTII
Comrey Personality Scales .... CPS
COMSAT [*Communications Satellite Corp.*] **Maritime Communications Satellite** .... CMCS
COMSAT [*Communications Satellite Corp.*] **Nonreflecting** [*Solar cell*] .... CNR
COMSAT [*Communications Satellite Corp.*] **Technical Review** [*A publication*] .... COMSAT Tech Rev
COMSAT [*Communications Satellite Corp.*] **Technical Review** [*A publication*] .... CTR
COMSAT [*Communications Satellite Corp.*]**, Washington, DC** [*OCLC symbol*] .... CLD
COMSAT [*Communications Satellite Corp.*]**, Washington, DC** [*OCLC symbol*] .... CMD
COMSEC [*Communications Security*] **Field Office of Record** [*Army*] .... CFOR
COMSEC [*Communications Security*] **Logistic Support Center** [*Army*] .... CLSC
COMSEC [*Communications Security*] **Logistic Support Unit** [*Army*] .... CLSU
COMSEC Logistics Data Center .... CLDC
COMSEC [*Communications Security*] **Material Issuing Office** [*Military*] .... CMIO
COMSEC [*Communications Security*] **Regional Issuing Office** [*Army*] .... CRIO
COMSEC [*Communications Security*] **Repair Center** [*Army*] .... CRC
COMSEC [*Communications Security*] **Research and Engineering Coordinating Group** [*Army*] .... CREC
COMSEC [*Communications Security*] **Resources Program** [*Army*] .... CRP
Comserv Corp. [*NASDAQ symbol*] .... CMSV
Comshare, Inc. [*NASDAQ symbol*] .... CSRE
Comstock Township Library, Comstock, MI [*Library symbol*] .... MiCom
Comsystems, Incorporated [*NASDAQ symbol*] .... CMSI
Comtech Telecommunications [*NASDAQ symbol*] .... CMTL
Comten, Inc. [*NASDAQ symbol*] .... CMTN
Comtex Scientific Corp. [*NASDAQ symbol*] .... CMTX
Comtrol Systems [*NASDAQ symbol*] .... CSIS
Comunicacion y Cultura [*A publication*] .... Comun y Cult
Comunicacion. Instituto Forestal de Investigaciones y Experiencias (Madrid) [*A publication*] .... Comun Inst For Invest Exp (Madrid)
Comunicacion, Intercambio, y Desarrollo Humano en America Latina .... CIDHAL
Comunicaciones Botanicas. Museo de Historia Natural de Montevideo [*A publication*] .... Comun Bot Mus Hist Nat Montev
Comunicaciones. INIA [*Instituto Nacional de Investigaciones Agrarias*] **Serie Produccion Vegetal** [*A publication*] .... Comun INIA Ser Prod Veg

Comunicaciones. INIA [*Instituto Nacional de Investigaciones Agrarias*] **Serie Proteccion Vegetal** [*A publication*] .... Comun INIA Ser Prot Veg

Comunicaciones. INIA [*Instituto Nacional de Investigaciones Agrarias*] **Serie Proteccion Vegetal (Spain)** [*A publication*]...................... Comun INIA Ser Pro Veg (Spain)

Comunicaciones. INIA [*Instituto Nacional de Investigaciones Agrarias*] **Serie Recursos Naturales** [*A publication*] .... Comun INIA Ser Recur Nat

Comunicaciones. Instituto Nacional de Investigacion de las Ciencias Naturales. Ciencias Botanicas [*A publication*] .... Comun Inst Nac Invest Cienc Nat Cienc Bot

Comunicaciones. Instituto Tropical de Investigaciones Cientificas [*A publication*]......................... Comun Inst Trop Invest Cient

Comunicaciones Paleontologicas. Museo de Historia Natural de Montevideo [*A publication*].......... Comun Paleontol Mus Hist Nat Montev

Comunicaciones. Sociedad Malacologica del Uruguay [*A publication*].................................. Comun Soc Malacol Urug

Comunicaciones Zoologicas. Museo de Historia Natural de Montevideo [*A publication*]................. Comun Zool Mus Hist Nat Montev

Comunicacoes. Servicos Geologicos de Portugal [*A publication*] .... Comun Serv Geol Port

Comunicado. Instituto Agronomico do Sul [*A publication*] .... Com Inst Agron Sul

Comunicados Tecnicos. Instituto de Ecologia e Experimentacao Agricolas [*A publication*] .... Comun Tec Inst Ecol Exp Agric

Comunicari de Botanica [*A publication*] .... Comun Bot

Comunicari Stiintifice. Simpozion de Biodeteriorare si Climatizare [*A publication*] .... Comun Stiint Simp Biodeterior Clim

Comunicari de Zoologie [*A publication*].............................Comun Zool

Comunicarile. Academiei Republicii Populare Romine [*A publication*].................................... Comun Acad Rep Pop Romine

Comunidad Latinoamericana de Escritores. Boletin [*A publication*] .... CLEB

Comunita Internazionale [*A publication*]......................Comunita Int

Comut Aire of Michigan, Inc. [*Pontiac, MI*] [*FAA designator*].................. CTA

Con Espressione [*With Expression*] [*Music*].....................CON ESP

CONAD [*Continental Air Defense Command*] **Operational Employment Concept**.................................. COEC

ConAgra, Inc. [*NYSE symbol*] .... CAG

Conair [*Denmark*] [*ICAO designator*]................................OY

Conair Corp. [*NYSE symbol*] .... CAA

Conakry [*Guinea*] [*Airport symbol*]...................................CKY

CONARC [*Continental Army Command*] **Alternate Headquarters Plan** [*Obsolete*].................................. CONALT

CONARC [*Continental Army Command*] **Automated System Support Agency** [*Obsolete*]................. CASSA

CONARC [*Continental Army Command*] **Class One Automated System** [*Later, BASOPS*].................. COCOAS

CONARC [*Continental Army Command*] **Education Data System** [*Obsolete*] ....CONEDS

CONARC [*Continental Army Command*] **Emergency Relocation Plan** [*Obsolete*].................................CONREP

CONARC [*Continental Army Command*] **Intelligence Center** [*Obsolete*]................................ CONTIC

CONARC [*Continental Army Command*] **Logistics Operations - Streamline** [*Obsolete*].................................CONLOS

CONARC [*Continental Army Command*] **Operating Program** [*Obsolete*].................................CONOPPR

Concanavalin A [*Biochemistry*]................................Con A

Concave Cc

Concave ....CNCV

Concealed ....CNCL

Concealed Target Detection ....CONTAD

Concealed Weapon Detector .... CWD

Concealed Weapons ....CW

Conceicao Do Arguaia [*Brazil*] [*Airport symbol*] ....CDJ

Concentracion de Fuerzas Populares [*Concentration of Popular Forces*] [*Political party in Ecuador*] ....CFP

Concentrated ....CONCD

Concentrated .... CONCTD

Concentrated Employment Program [*Also known as CIEP*] [*Department of Labor*] .... CEP

Concentrated Impact Employment Program [*Also known as CEP*] [*Department of Labor*]................................ CIEP

Concentrated Oil of Vitriol.....................................COV

Concentrated Orange Juice for Manufacturing ....COJM

Concentrated Phosphate Export Association.................CPEA

Concentrated Rust-Inhibiting ....CRI

Concentrated Strength [*of solutions*] [*Pharmacy*]..................CS

Concentrated Urban Enforcement [*Bureau of Alcohol, Tobacco, and Firearms*]................................... CUE

Concentrated Urban Placement Service [*Department of Labor*]..........CUPS

Concentrating ....CONCTG

Concentration C

Concentration .... CON

Concentration .... CONC

Concentration ....CONCN

Concentration ....CONTRTN

Concentration Camp CC

Concentration Camp Syndrome [*Psychiatry*]...................CCS

Concentration - Dependent Regulation of Oxygen ....CDRO

Concentration on Engineering Design .... COED

Concentration Length...CL

Concentration Stress Test [*Psychical stress*] .... CST

Concentration by volume [*Chemistry*]............................c

Concentrator Terminal Buffer [*Data processing*] .... CTB

Concentric..CNCTRC

Concentric... CONC

Concentric Flight Plan...CFP

Concentric Line Oscillator ....CLO

Concentric-Orbit Rendezvous [*NASA*]...........................COR

Concentric Sequence Initiation [*Aerospace*]...................CSI

Concepcion [*Chile*] [*Airport symbol*] ....CCP

Concepcion [*Bolivia*] [*Airport symbol*] ....CEP

Concepcion [*Chile*] [*Seismograph station code, US Geological Survey*]..CON

Concept Definition .... CD

Concept Definition Proposal .... CDP

Concept Development .... CD

Concept Development [*NASDAQ symbol*]........................CDII

Concept Development Plan .... CDP

Concept Evaluation Program [*Army*] .... CEP

Concept Evaluation Technique [*Psychometrics*]...............CET

Concept Exploration ....CE

Concept of a Family of Army Divisions.......................CONFAD

Concept Feasibility .... CF

Concept Feasibility Analysis .... CFA

Concept Formation Test [*Psychology*].........................CFT

Concept Formulation [*DoD*] .... CF

Concept Formulation/Contract Definition [*Procurement procedure*] .... CF/CD

Concept Formulation Package [*Military*] ....CFP

Concept Formulation Package - Technical Development Plan [*Air Force*]...CFP/TDP

Concept Formulation Program Plan .... CFPP

Concept Formulation Studies ....CFS

Concept Game [*A war game*] .... CONGA

Concept Identification [*Psychology*] CI

Concept, Inc. [*NASDAQ symbol*] ....CCPT

Concept Learning System [*Data processing*] ....CLS

Concept for Low-Cost Air-to-Air Weapon ....CLAW

Concept Plan ....CONPLAN

Concept for a Radiological Detection System ....CCRDES

Concept Resources [*NASDAQ symbol*].......................CNCPF

Concept Verification Test .... CVT

Conception Abbey and Seminary, Conception, MO [*Library symbol*] .... MoConA

Concepts Analysis Agency [*Military*] .... CAA

Concepts Analysis Agency, Bethesda, MD [*Library symbol*]...........MdBeCA

Concepts Analysis Group [*Army*] .... CAG

Concepts of Postal Economics [*A series of newsletters of Mail Advertising Corp.*]....................................COPE

Concepts, Trends, Relationships, Issues, Problems, Solutions.........CTRIPS

Conceptual Design for the Army in the Field ....CONAF

Conceptual Design Requirement..............................CDR

Conceptual Design Study......................................CDS

Conceptual Operational System ....COS

Conceptual Organization [*Psychometrics*] .... CO

Conceptual Project Design Description ....CPDD

Conceptual Quotient [*Psychology*] .... CQ

Conceptual Reference Mission [*NASA*] ....CRM

Conceptual Satellite Surveillance System ....CS³

Conceptual Satellite Surveillance System ....CSSS

Conceptual System Design Description ....CSDD

Conceptual Systems Test .... CST

Conceptual Thought Random Net Simulation ....CONTRANS

Conceptually Oriented Mathematics Program ....COMP

Conceptually Oriented Program in Elementary Science ....COPES

Concern for Dying [*An association*] ....CFD

Concern for Health Options: Information, Care and Education ....CHOICE

Concerned Broadcasters Using Inter-City Video Transmission Facilities ....CBUIVTF

Concerned Broadcasters Using Inter-City Video Transmission Facilities ....CON-VID

Concerned Citizens Information Council [*Group opposing sex education in schools*]..................................CCIC

Concerned Citizens for the Nuclear Breeder ....CCNB

Concerned Educators Against Forced Unionism ....CEAFU

Concerned Guatemala Scholars ....CGS

Concerned Persons for Adoption ....CPFA

Concerned Relatives of Nursing Home Patients ....CRNHP

Concerned Senators for the Arts ....CSA

Concerned Seniors for Better Government ....CSBG

Concerned Theatre Japan [*A publication*] ....CTJ

Concerned about Trident [*Ecology group*].....................CAT

Concerned United Birthparents ....CUB

Concerned Women for America ....CWA

Concerning Poetry [*A publication*] ....ConcPo

Concerning Poetry [*A publication*] .... CP

Concerns of Motherhood.......................................CM

Concert Artists Guild ....CAG

Concert Music Broadcasters Association .... CMBA
Concerto [*Music*] .... CON
Concerto [*Music*] .... CTO
Concerts and Recitals of Serious Music (Annual Licence) [*Public-performance tariff class*] [*British*] .... LA
Concerts and Recitals of Serious Music (Permits) [*Public-performance tariff class*] [*British*] L
Concession .... CSN
Conch Review of Books [*A publication*] .... C Rev B
Conchemco, Inc. [*American Stock Exchange symbol*] .... CKC
Conchology .... CONCH
Conciliation Commission for Palestine [*of the UN*] .... CCP
Conciliation Officer (Tribunal) [*British*] .... COT
Concimi e Concimazione [*A publication*] .... Concimi Concimaz
Concise Oxford Dictionary [*A publication*] .... COD
Concise Oxford English Dictionary [*A publication*] .... COED
Conciseness, Lively Details, Action Relationship, Intelligence, Talk, Youthfulness .... CLARITY
Concisus [*Cut*] [*Medicine*] C
Concisus [*Cut*] [*Medicine*] .... CONCIS
Conclusion .... CON
Conclusion .... CONCL
Concora Medium Test .... CMT
Concord, CA [*Television station call letters*] .... KFCB
Concord, CA [*Radio station call letters*] .... KVHS
Concord, CA [*Radio station call letters*] .... KWUN
Concord College, Athens, WV [*Library symbol*] .... WvAC
Concord - Diablo Valley College [*California*] [*Seismograph station code, US Geological Survey*] [*Closed*] .... CNC
Concord Fabrics, Inc. [*American Stock Exchange symbol*] .... CIS
Concord Free Public Library, Concord, MA [*Library symbol*] .... MCo
Concord Grape Association .... CGA
Concord, MA [*Radio station call letters*] .... WIQH
Concord, NC [*Radio station call letters*] .... WEGO
Concord, NC [*Radio station call letters*] .... WPEG
Concord, NC [*Television station call letters*] .... WUNG-TV
Concord, NH [*Location identifier*] [*FAA*] .... EPP
Concord, NH [*Radio station call letters*] .... WEVO
Concord, NH [*Radio station call letters*] .... WJYY
Concord, NH [*Radio station call letters*] .... WKXL
Concord, NH [*Radio station call letters*] .... WKXL-FM
Concord, NH [*Television station call letters*] .... WNHT
Concord, NH [*Radio station call letters*] .... WSPS
Concord Public Library, Concord, NC [*Library symbol*] .... NcCo
Concordance Words in Titles [*Indexing*] .... CWIT
Concordia [*Brazil*] [*Airport symbol*] [*Obsolete*] CCI
Concordia [*Argentina*] [*Airport symbol*] .... COC
Concordia College, Bronxville, NY [*Library symbol*] .... NBronC
Concordia College, Conover, NC [*Library symbol*] [*Obsolete*] .... NcConC
Concordia College, Edmonton, AB, Canada [*Library symbol*] .... CaAEC
Concordia College, Milwaukee, WI [*Library symbol*] .... WMC
Concordia College, Moorhead, MN [*Library symbol*] .... MnMohC
Concordia College, Portland, OR [*Library symbol*] .... OrPCC
Concordia College, St. Paul, MN [*OCLC symbol*] .... MNC
Concordia College, St. Paul, MN [*Library symbol*] .... MnSCC
Concordia College, Seward, NE [*OCLC symbol*] .... NBC
Concordia Collegiate Institute [*New York*] CCI
Concordia Historical Institute .... CHI
Concordia Historical Institute Quarterly [*A publication*] .... CHIQ
Concordia Historical Institute, St. Louis, MO [*Library symbol*] .... MoSCH
Concordia Hospital, Winnipeg, MB, Canada [*Library symbol*] .... CaMWCH
Concordia, KS [*Location identifier*] [*FAA*] .... CNK
Concordia, KS [*Radio station call letters*] .... KCKS
Concordia, KS [*Radio station call letters*] .... KNCK
Concordia, KS [*Radio station call letters*] .... KVCO
Concordia Lutheran College, Ann Arbor, MI [*Library symbol*] .... MiAaC
Concordia Lutheran College, Austin, TX [*Library symbol*] .... TxAuC
Concordia Mutual Life Association .... CML
Concordia Parish Library, Ferriday, LA [*Library symbol*] .... LFC
Concordia Seminary, St. Louis, MO [*Library symbol*] .... MoSCS
Concordia Senior College, Fort Wayne, IN [*Library symbol*] .... InFwC
Concordia Teachers College [*Illinois, Nebraska*] .... CTC
Concordia Teachers College, River Forest, IL [*OCLC symbol*] .... ICE
Concordia Teachers College, River Forest, IL [*Library symbol*] .... IRivfT
Concordia Teachers College, Seward, NE [*Library symbol*] .... NbSeT
Concordia Theological Monthly [*A publication*] .... Concor
Concordia Theological Monthly [*A publication*] .... ConTM
Concordia Theological Monthly [*A publication*] .... CTM
Concordia Theological Seminary [*Later, Concordia Seminary*] [*Missouri*] .... CTS
Concordia Theological Seminary, Fort Wayne, IN [*Library symbol*] .... InFwCT
Concordia Theological Seminary, Fort Wayne, IN [*OCLC symbol*] .... ITC
Concordia Theological Seminary, Springfield, IL [*Library symbol*] [*Obsolete*] .... ISC
Concordia Tract Mission .... CTM
Concordia University, Loyola Campus, Montreal, PQ, Canada [*Library symbol*] .... CaQML
Concordia University, Sir George Williams Campus, Department of Geography, Montreal, PQ, Canada [*Library symbol*] .... CaQMGG
Concordia University, Sir George Williams Campus, Department of Geography, University Map Collection, Montreal, PQ, Canada [*Library symbol*] .... CaQMGGM
Concordia University, Sir George Williams Campus, Montreal, PQ, Canada [*Library symbol*] .... CaQMG
Concours Medical [*A publication*] .... Concours Med
Concrete .... CON
Concrete .... CONC
Concrete .... CONCR
Concrete Arch [*Bridges*] .... KA
Concrete Block .... CCB
Concrete Cancer [*Refers to weathering and resultant disintegration of concrete*] CC
Concrete Ceiling CCC
Concrete Construction [*A publication*] .... Concr Constr
Concrete Deep Water Structure [*Oil platform*] .... CONDEEP
Concrete Floor .... CCF
Concrete Industries Council CIC
Concrete Industry Board .... CIB
Concrete Joint Institute [*Defunct*] .... CJI
Concrete Piercing .... CP
Concrete Pipe Association .... CPA
Concrete Plant Manufacturers Bureau .... CPMB
Concrete Products [*A publication*] .... Concrete P
Concrete Reinforcing Steel Institute .... CRSI
Concrete Sawing and Drilling Association .... CSDA
Concrete Society .... CS
Concrete Society. Technical Report [*A publication*] .... Concr Soc Tech Rep
Concrete Splash Block [*Technical drawings*] .... CSB
Concrete Technology Information Analysis Center [*Army Corps of Engineers*] .... CTIAC
Concurrent C
Concurrent .... CNCR
Concurrent with Aircraft Delivery .... CWAD
Concurrent Algorithmic Programing Language [*Data processing*] .... CAP
Concurrent Concession CC
Concurrent with Design Release .... CWDR
Concurrent Operating System [*UNIVAC*] [*Data processing*] .... COS
Concurrent Peripheral Operations .... CPO
Concurrent Photon Amplification [*Air Force*] .... CPA
Concurrent Planometric [*A discrimination task*] .... CP
Concurrent Spare Parts .... CSP
Concurrent Stereometric [*A discrimination task*] .... CS
Concurrently .... CNCNT
Condec Corp. [*American Stock Exchange symbol*] .... CDT
Condemned C
Condemned .... CND
Condemned or Suppressed .... COS
Condemno [*I Condemn*] [*Used by Romans in criminal trials*] [*Latin*] C
Condensate .... CNDS
Condensate Heat Exchanger .... CH-X
Condensation Nuclei .... CN
Condensation Nuclei Counter .... CNC
Condensation Pressure Spread .... CPS
Condensation Trail [*in the air*] .... CONTRAIL
Condensed .... COND
Condensed Chemical Dictionary [*A publication*] .... CCD
Condensed or Dried .... COD
Condensed Nearest Neighbor [*Mathematics*] .... CNN
Condensed Negative Binomial Distribution [*Statistics*] .... CNBD
Condenser .... CONDR
Condenser Absolute Pressure .... CAP
Condensing .... CONDG
Condition .... CND
Condition .... COND
Condition .... CONDTN
Condition BIT [*Binary Digit*] [*Data processing*] .... CB
Condition Code CC
Condition of Detail .... CD
Condition Monitored Maintenance .... CMM
Condition Monitoring .... COM
Condition and Recommendation .... CAR
Condition Reservation Code [*Army*] .... CRC
Conditional Amount of Sample Information [*Statistics*] .... CASI
Conditional Breakpoint Instruction .... CBI
Conditional Breakpoint Instruction .... CBPI
Conditional Instability of the Second Kind .... CISK
Conditional Peak Flow [*Biology*] .... CPF
Conditional Proof [*Method in logic*] .... CP
Conditional Reflex [*A publication*] .... Cond Reflex
Conditional Relaxation Analysis Method .... CRAM
Conditional Release Violator [*FBI standardized term*] .... CRV
Conditional Response Analog Machine .... CORA
Conditional Value of Sample Information [*Statistics*] .... CVSI
Conditional Variable Incremental Computer CVIC
Conditionally Accepted Tag .... CAT
Conditionally Qualified .... CQ
Conditioned Avoidance Response [*Psychometrics*] .... CAR
Conditioned Emotional Response [*Psychology*] .... CER
Conditioned Medium Reconstituting Factor [*Immunochemistry*] .... CMRF
Conditioned Orientation Reflex .... COR

Conditioned Reflex [Machine] ....CONFLEX
Conditioned Reflex [or Response] [Psychometrics]..............CR
Conditioned Reflex Analog ....CORA
Conditioned Stimulus [Psychometrics].........................CS
Conditioner ....CONDTR
Conditioning [Neurophysiology] C
Conditioning Container CC
Conditions [A publication]..............................Condition
Conditions of Assembly and Release Transfer ....CART
Conditions, Covenants, and Restrictions [On condominiums]......CC & R
Condobolin [Australia] [Airport symbol].......................CBX
Condominium Research and Education Society ....CRES
Condon, Kinzua, & Southern Railroad Co. [AAR code] ......CKSO
Condon Public Library, Condon, OR [Library symbol]........OrCon
Condor Data Link ....CDL
Condor Data Link System.....................................CDLS
Condor Flugdienst [Germany] [ICAO designator]..................DF
Condor Missile System ....CMS
Condoto [Colombia] [Airport symbol].........................COG
Condotta Medica [A publication]...................Condotta Med
Conduct ....CDT
Conduct ....CNDCT
Conduct of Fire Trainer [Army] ....COFT
Conduct and Utilization of Research in Nursing ....CURN
Conductance [Symbol] [IUPAC]...................................G
Conductance Increase Mechanism ....CIM
Conducted Emission ....CE
Conducted Susceptibility....................................CS
Conduction Analysis Program Using Eigenvalues [NASA] ....CAPE
Conduction Band [Electronics] ....CB
Conduction Electron Polarization ....CEP
Conduction Electron Spin Resonance ....CESR
Conductive Coating CC
Conductive Plastic ....CP
Conductive Plastic Potentiometer ....CPP
Conductivity C
Conductivity Cell Volume [Hematology] CCV
Conductivity, Temperature, and Depth [Oceanography] ....CTD
Conductor...C
Conductor...COND
Conductor..CONDR
Conductor Head ....CH
Conductron Corp. [NASDAQ symbol] ....COND
Conduit ....CDT
Conduit ....CND
Cone ....CE
Cone Angle [NASA]...CA
Cone Mills Corp. [NYSE symbol] ....COE
Cone Peak [Hawaii] [Seismograph station code, US Geological
   Survey]...CPK
Cone Point ....CP
Conemaugh & Black Lick Railroad Co. [AAR code] ....CBL
Conesco Industries [NASDAQ symbol]........................CNSC
Conestoga Society..CS
Confectio [Confection] [Pharmacy]..........................CONF
Confectionary..CONFCTY
Confederacao Nacional do Comercio [A publication].........Confed Nac Com
Confederacion Evangelica Mundial [World Evangelical Fellowship]........CEM
Confederacion General Economica de la Republica Argentina.............CGE
Confederacion Interamericana de Ganaderos ....CIAGA
Confederacion Internacional de Organizaciones Sindicales
   Libres [International Confederation of Free Trade Unions] ....CIOSL
Confederacion Latinoamericana de Sindicalistas Cristianos
   [Latin American Federation of Christian Trade Unionists]........CLASC
Confederacion Nacional de Trabajo [National Confederation of
   Labor] [In Exile] [Spain] ....CNT
Confederacion Obrera Argentina..............................COA
Confederacion de Organizaciones Turisticas de la America
   Latina [Confederation of Tourist Organizations of Latin
   America] ....COTAL
Confederacion de Trabajadores de America Latina
   [Confederation of Latin-American Workers] ....CTAL
Confederacion de Trabajadores de Mexico [Workers'
   Confederation of Mexico].................................CTM
Confederacion de Trabajadores de Venezuela [Venezuelan
   Workers' Confederation].................................CTV
Confederate Air Force [Group of ex-WW II fliers] ....CAF
Confederate Army...CA
Confederate High Command, International [Later, AT] [An
   association]..CHC
Confederate Memorial Association ....CMA
Confederate Memorial Library, Hillsboro, NC [Library symbol].............NcHil
Confederate Memorial Literary Society ....CMLS
Confederate Stamp Alliance ....CSA
Confederate States of America ....CSA
Confederate States Army ....CSA
Confederate States Navy ....CSN
Confederate States Ship ....CSS
Confederated Spanish Societies [Defunct] ....CSS
Confederated Unions of America [Later, NFIU].............CUA
Confederation ....CONFED

Confederation for the Advancement of State Education ......CASE
Confederation Africaine des Syndicats Libres de Cote d'Ivoire
   [African Confederation of Free Trade Unions of the Ivory
   Coast] ....CASL-CI
Confederation Africaine des Syndicats Libres - Force Ouvriere
   [African Confederation of Free Trade Unions - Workers'
   Force] [Cameroon, Chad, Gabon]...................CASL-FO
Confederation Africaine des Syndicats Libres - Force Ouvriere -
   Republique Centafricaine [African Confederation of Free
   Trade Unions - Workers' Force - Central African Republic]...............
                                         CASL-FO-RC
Confederation Africaine des Syndicats Libres de la Haute Volta
   [African Confederation of Free Trade Unions of the Upper
   Volta] ....CASL-HV
Confederation Africaine des Travailleurs Croyants [African
   Confederation of Believing Workers] ....CATC
Confederation of All Type Canaries...........................CATC
Confederation of Arab Trade Unions ....CATU
Confederation Art Gallery and Museum, Charlottetown, PE,
   Canada [Library symbol]...............................CaPCCA
Confederation des Associations du Katanga [Confederation of
   Katangan Associations].............................CONAKAT
Confederation Autonome de Travail [Autonomous Confederation
   of Labor]...CAT
Confederation of British Industry [Formerly, FBI]............CBI
Confederation Camerounaise des Syndicats Chretiens
   [Confederation of Believing Workers of the Cameroon]....................CCSC
Confederation of Canadian Unions...........................CCU
Confederation of Central Government Employees' Unions [India]....CCGEU
Confederation Centre Library, Charlottetown, PE, Canada
   [Library symbol] ....CaPCL
Confederation Chretienne des Syndicats Malgaches [Christian
   Confederation of Malagasy Unions].....................CCSM
Confederation of Citizens Labor Union [Philippines] ....CCLU
Confederation College, Thunder Bay, ON, Canada [Library
   symbol]...CaOTBCC
Confederation Congolaise des Syndicats Libres [Congolese
   Confederation of Free Unions] [Brazzaville]...........CCSL
Confederation des Educateurs Americains [Confederation of
   American Educators]....................................CEA
Confederation Europeenne de l'Agriculture [European
   Confederation of Agriculture].........................CEA
Confederation Europeenne de Billard ....CEB
Confederation Europeenne des Categories Auxiliaires des
   Activites Viti-Vinicole [European Confederation of Auxiliary
   Occupations in the Wine Trade] [Common Market]...........CECAVI
Confederation Europeenne d'Etudes Phytosanitaires [European
   Confederation for Plant Protection Research] ....CEP
Confederation Europeenne des Industries du Bois [European
   Confederation of Woodworking Industries] ....CEIBOIS
Confederation Francaise de la Cooperation Agricole ....CFCA
Confederation Francaise et Democratique du Travail [French
   trade union] ....CFDT
Confederation Francaise des Syndicats Independents [French
   Confederation of Independent Unions]...................CFSI
Confederation Francaise des Travailleurs Chretiens [French
   Confederation of Christian Workers]....................CFTC
Confederation of Free Trade Unions [India] ....CFTU
Confederation Generale Africaine du Travail [African General
   Confederation of Labor]...............................CGAT
Confederation Generale de l'Agriculture [France]............CGA
Confederation Generale des Cadres [General Confederation of
   Supervisory Employees] [France]........................CGC
Confederation Generale Camerounaise du Travail [Cameroonian
   General Confederation of Workers].....................CGCT
Confederation Generale Kamerounaise du Travail [Cameroonian
   General Confederation of Workers].....................CGKT
Confederation Generale des Syndicats [General Confederation
   of Trade Unions] [Congo - Leopoldville]................CGS
Confederation Generale des Syndicats Independents [General
   Confederation of Independent Unions] [Algeria] ....CGSI
Confederation Generale du Travail [General Confederation of
   Labor] [France].......................................CGT
Confederation Generale du Travail - Force Ouvriere [General
   Confederation of Labor - Workers' Force] ....CGT-FO
Confederation Generale des Travailleurs [South Vietnam] ....CGT
Confederation Generale des Travailleurs Africains [General
   Confederation of African Workers] [Former French Equatorial
   Africa]...CGTA
Confederation Interalliee des Officers de Reserve [Interallied
   Confederation of Reserve Officers - ICRO].............CIOR
Confederation Interamericaine d'Education Catholique [Inter-
   American Confederation of Catholic Education].........CIEC
Confederation of International Contractors' Associations ....CICA
Confederation International des Fabricants de Tapis et de
   Tissus d'Ameublement [International Confederation of
   Manufacturers of Carpets and Furnishing Fabrics].......CITTA
Confederation of International Trading Houses Associations ....CITHA
Confederation Internationale des Accordeonistes [International
   Confederation of Accordionists].......................CIA

Confederation Internationale des Anciens Prisonniers de Guerre [*International Confederation of Former Prisoners of War*] ... CIAPG
Confederation Internationale des Associations de Diplomes en Sciences Economiques et Commerciales [*International Confederation of Associations of Graduates in Economic and Commercial Sciences*] ... CIADEC
Confederation Internationale des Associations d'Experts et de Conseils [*International Confederation of Associations of Experts and Consultants*] ... CIDADEC
Confederation Internationale des Betteraviers Europeens [*International Confederation of European Sugar Beet Growers*] [*Common Market*] ... CIBE
Confederation Internationale de la Boucherie et de la Charcuterie [*International Federation of Meat Traders' Associations*] ... CIBC
Confederation Internationale des Cadres [*International Confederation of Executive Staffs*] ... CIC
Confederation Internationale Catholique des Institutions Hospitalieres [*International Catholic Confederation of Hospitals*] ... CICIH
Confederation Internationale des Cinemas d'Art et d'Essai [*International Experimental and Art Film Theatres Confederation*] ... CICAE
Confederation Internationale de la Coiffure [*International Conference of the Hairdressing Trade*] ... CIC
Confederation Internationale des Corps de Fonctionnaires [*International Confederation of Public Service Officers*] ... CICF
Confederation Internationale du Credit Agricole [*International Confederation for Agricultural Credit*] ... CICA
Confederation Internationale du Credit Populaire [*International Confederation for Popular Credit*] ... CICP
Confederation Internationale pour le Desarmement et la Paix [*International Confederation for Disarmament and Peace*] ... CIDP
Confederation Internationale des Fonctionnaires [*International Confederation of Public Service Officers*] ... CIF
Confederation Internationale de Genealogie et d'Heraldique [*International Confederation of Genealogy and Heraldry - ICGH*] ... CIGH
Confederation Internationale des Industries Techniques du Cinema ... CIITC
Confederation Internationale des Ingenieurs Agronomes [*International Confederation of Technical Agricultural Engineers*] ... CITA
Confederation Internationale des Instituts Catholiques d'Education des Adultes Ruraux [*International Confederation of Catholic Rural People's Schools*] ... CIEPRC
Confederation Internationale du Lin et du Chanvre [*International Linen and Hemp Confederation*] ... CILC
Confederation Internationale des Negociants en Oeuvres d'Art [*International Confederation of Art Dealers*] ... CINOA
Confederation Internationale de la Representation Commerciale de la Communaute Europeenne [*International Confederation of Commercial Representation in the European Community*] ... CIRCCE
Confederation Internationale des Sages Femmes ... CISF
Confederation Internationale des Societes d'Auteurs et Compositeurs [*International Confederation of Societies of Authors and Composers*] ... CISAC
Confederation Internationale des Societes Populaires de Musique ... CISPM
Confederation Internationale des Syndicats Chretiens [*International Federation of Christian Trade Unions*] ... CISC
Confederation Internationale des Syndicats Libres [*International Confederation of Free Trade Unions*] ... CISL
Confederation Internationale des Travailleurs Intellectuels [*International Confederation of Professional and Intellectual Workers*] ... CITI
Confederation of Labor in the Philippines ... CLP
Confederation of Latin-American Teachers ... CLAT
Confederation of Lebanese Labor ... CLL
Confederation Life Association, Toronto, ON, Canada [*Library symbol*] ... CaOTCLA
Confederation Luxembourgeoise des Syndicats Chretiens [*Confederation of Christian Trade Unions of Luxembourg*] ... CLSC
Confederation Mondiale des Activites Subaquatiques [*World Underwater Federation*] ... CMAS
Confederation Mondiale des Organisations de la Profession Enseignante [*World-Confederation of Organizations of the Teaching Profession*] [*Also known as WCOTP*] ... CMOPE
Confederation Mondiale du Travail [*World Confederation of Labour*] [*See also WCL*] ... CMT
Confederation of National Educational Associations ... CONEA
Confederation of National Trade Unions ... CNTU
Confederation National des Travailleurs de Guinee [*National Confederation of Guinean Workers*] ... CNTG
Confederation Nationale Independante des Travailleurs [*National Independent Confederation for Workers*] [*Belgium*] ... CNIT
Confederation Nationale des Instituteurs Malagaches [*National Confederation of Malagascan Teachers*] ... CNIM
Confederation Nationale des Syndicats du Mali [*National Confederation of Malian Unions*] ... CNSM
Confederation Nationale du Travail [*National Confederation of Labor*] [*France*] ... CNT
Confederation of Shipbuilding and Engineering Unions [*British*] ... CSEU
Confederation Syndicale Africaine [*African Trade Union Confederation*] ... CSA
Confederation Syndicale Mondiale des Enseignants [*World Confederation of Teachers*] [*See also WCT*] ... CSME
Confederation des Syndicats Chretiens de Belgique [*Confederation of Christian Trade Unions*] [*Belgium*] ... CSC
Confederation des Syndicats Chretiens du Congo [*Confederation of Christian Syndicates of the Congo*] [*Leopoldville*] ... CSCC
Confederation des Syndicats Libres du Congo [*Leopoldville*] [*Merger of FGTK, APIC, SNTC*] [*Congolese Free Trade Union Federation*] ... CSLC
Confederation des Syndicats des Travailleurs du Viet-Nam [*Confederation of Workers' Trade Unions of Viet-Nam*] [*South Vietnam*] ... CSTV
Confederation des Travailleurs des Madagascar et Comores [*Confederation of Workers of Madagascar and the Comores*] ... CTMC
Confederation of Unions in Government Corporations and Offices [*Philippines*] ... CUGCO
Confederation Vietnamienne du Travail Chretien [*Vietnamese Confederation of Christian Labor*] [*South Vietnam*] ... CVTC
Confederazione Generale Italiana del Lavoro [*Italian General Confederation of Labor*] ... CGIL
Confederazione Generale Somala dei Lavoratori [*Somali General Confederation of Workers*] ... CGSL
Confederazione Italiana Sindacati Lavoratori [*Italian Confederation of Labor Unions*] ... CISL
Confederazione Italiana di Sindacati Liberi [*Italian Confederation of Free Workers*] ... CISL
Confederazione Italiana Sindacati Nazionali Lavoratori [*Italian Confederation of National Workers' Unions*] ... CISNAL
Confederazione Somala dei Lavoratori [*Somali Workers Confederation*] ... CSL
Confer [*Compare*] [*Latin*] ... CF
Confer [*Compare*] [*Latin*] ... CONF
Conference [*A publication*] ... Co
Conference ... CONF
Conference of Actuaries in Public Practice ... CAPP
Conference of Administrators of College and University Counseling Services ... CACUCS
Conference for the Advancement of Private Practice [*in social work*] ... CAPP
Conference on Advances in Magnetic Materials and Their Applications [*A publication*] ... Conf Adv Magn Mater Their Appl
Conference Aeronautique Internationale [*International Aeronautical Conference*] ... CAI
Conference on Alternative State and Local Policies [*Formerly, CASLPP*] ... CASLP
Conference on Alternative State and Local Public Policies [*Later, CASLP*] ... CASLPP
Conference of American Renting and Leasing Associations ... CARALA
Conference of American Small Business Organizations ... CASBO
Conference of Americans of Central and Eastern European Descent [*Defunct*] ... CACEED
Conference on the Application of Science and Technology to the Development of Africa ... CASTAFRICA
Conference on the Application of Science and Technology to the Development of Latin America ... CASTALA
Conference on Asian Affairs [*Later, AS*] ... CAA
Conference on Asian History ... CAH
Conference on the Atlantic Community ... CONTAC
Conference of Baltic Oceanographers ... CBO
[*The*] **Conference Board** [*Formerly, National Industrial Conference Board*] ... CB
[*The*] **Conference Board** [*Formerly, National Industrial Conference Board*] ... TCB
Conference Board of Associated Research Councils ... CBARC
Conference Board. Business Management Record [*A publication*] ... Conf Bd Bsns Mgt Rec
Conference Board. Business Record [*A publication*] ... Conf Bd Bsns Rec
Conference Board. Information Bulletin [*A publication*] ... CB Bul
Conference Board of Major Printers ... CBMP
Conference Board of the Mathematical Sciences ... CBMS
Conference Board. Record [*A publication*] ... Conf Bd Rec
Conference Board. Record [*A publication*] ... Conf Board Rec
Conference on British Studies ... CBS
Conference of Business Economists ... CBE
Conference of California Historical Societies ... CCHS
Conference on Capturing the Sun through Bioconversion. Proceedings [*A publication*] ... Conf Capturing Sun Bioconver Pro
Conference of Casualty Insurance Companies [*Formerly, CMCC*] ... CCIC
Conference of Catholic Schools of Nursing ... CCSN
Conference of Central and East African States ... CCEAFS
Conference of Chief Justices ... CCJ
Conference for Chinese Oral and Performing Literature ... CHINOPERL
Conference on Christianity and Literature ... CCL
Conference of Church Workers Among the Deaf [*Later, ECD*] ... CCWAD

Conference Circompolaire sur l'Ecologie du Nord. Compte Rendu [*A publication*] ... Conf Circompolaire Ecol Nord R
Conference on College Composition and Communication ... CCCC
Conference of College Teachers of English of Texas. Proceedings [*A publication*] ... CCTE
Conference and Commission on World Mission and Evangelism [*of the World Council of Churches*] [*Formerly, CWMEWCC*] ... CWME
Conference of the Committee on Disarmament [*Formerly, ENDC*] [*NATO*] ... CCD
Conference Committee for Refugee Rabbis ... CCRR
Conference on Compatibility of Propellants, Explosives, and Pyrotechnics with Plastics and Additives [*A publication*] ... Conf Compat Propellants Explos Pyrotech Plast Addit
Conference on Computers in Undergraduate Science Education ... COMUSE
Conference on Conceptual and Terminological Analysis in the Social Sciences [*1981*] ... CONTA
Conference on Confidence and Security-Building Measures and Disarmament in Europe ... CDE
Conference of Consumer Organizations ... COCO
Conference on the Control of Gaseous Sulphur and Nitrogen Compound Emission [*A publication*] ... Conf Control Gaseous Sulphur Nitrogen Comp Emiss
Conference on Culture of Marine Invertebrate Animals. Proceedings [*A publication*] ... Conf Cult Mar Invertebr Anim Proc
Conference on Data Systems Languages [*Data processing*] ... CODASYL
Conference of Directors of State University Librarians of Illinois [*Library network*] ... CODSULI
Conference on Disarmament in Europe ... CDE
Conference on Dual Distribution ... CDD
Conference on Early American History ... CEAH
Conference of Eastern College Librarians ... CECL
Conference on Economic Progress ... CEP
Conference of Educational Administrators Serving the Deaf ... CEASD
Conference on Electrical Insulation and Dielectric Phenomena [*National Academy of Sciences*] ... CEIDP
Conference on English Education ... CEE
Conference on Environmental Chemicals. Human and Animal Health. Proceedings [*A publication*] ... Conf Environ Chem Hum Anim Health Proc
Conference on European Security and Cooperation ... CESC
Conference Europeenne des Administrations des Postes et des Telecommunications [*Conference of European Postal and Telecommunications Administrations*] ... CEPT
Conference Europeenne des Experts Meteorologistes de l'Aeronautique ... CEEMA
Conference Europeenne des Experts Radiotelegraphistes de l'Aeronautique ... CEERA
Conference Europeenne des Horaires des Trains de Voyageurs [*European Passenger Timetable Conference*] ... CEH
Conference Europeenne sur la Microcirculation [*A publication*] ... Conf Eur Microcirc
Conference Europeenne des Ministres des Transports [*European Conference of Ministers of Transport*] ... CEMT
Conference Europeenne des Pouvoirs Locaux ... CEPL
Conference Europeenne des Telecommunications par Satellite [*European Conference on Satellite Communications*] ... CETS
Conference of Executives of State Associations of Counties [*Later, National Council of County Association Executives*] ... CESAC
Conference to Explore Machine Readable Bibliographic Interchange ... CEMBI
Conference on Faith and History ... CFH
Conference of Funeral Service Examining Boards of the United States ... CFSEB
Conference Generale des Poids et Mesures [*General Conference on Weights and Measures*] ... CGPM
Conference on Great Lakes Research. Proceedings [*A publication*] ... Conf Great Lakes Res Proc
Conference Group on French Politics and Society ... CGFPS
Conference Group on German Politics ... CGGP
Conference Group on Italian Politics ... CGIP
Conference for Health Council Work [*Later, Conference on Community Health Planning*] ... CHCW
Conference of Independent African States ... CIAS
Conference on Industrial Robot Technology ... CIRT
Conference of Insurance Legislators ... COIL
Conference on Interlibrary Communications and Information Networks ... CICIN
Conference on International Economic Cooperation ... CIEC
Conference Internationale Administrative des Radiocommunications Aeronautiques ... CIARA
Conference Internationale des Africanistes de l'Ouest ... CIAO
Conference Internationale des Charites Catholiques [*International Conference of Catholic Charities*] ... CICC
Conference Internationale pour l'Enseignement Universitaire des Relations Publiques [*International Conference on University Education for Public Relations*] ... CIEURP
Conference Internationale du Goudron [*International Tar Conference - ITC*] ... CIG
Conference Internationale des Grands Reseaux Electriques [*International Conference on Large High Voltage Electric Systems*] ... CIGRE
Conference Internationale de Liaison entre Producteurs d'Energie Electrique [*International Conference of Producers of Electrical Energy*] ... CILPE
Conference Internationale de la Mutualite et des Assurances Sociales ... CIMAS
Conference Internationale du Scoutisme Catholique [*International Conference of Catholic Scouting*] ... CISC
Conference Internationale de Service Social [*International Conference of Social Service*] ... CISS
Conference Internationale de Sociologie Religieuse [*International Conference of Sociology of Religion*] ... CISR
Conference Internationale pour l'Unite Technique des Chemins de Fer ... UT
Conference of Internationally-Minded Schools ... CIS
Conference of Jesuit Student Personnel Administrators [*Later, JASPA*] ... CJSPA
Conference of Jewish Communal Service [*Formerly, NCJCS*] ... CJCS
Conference on Jewish Material Claims Against Germany ... CJMCAG
Conference on Jewish Social Studies ... CJSS
Conference of the Labour Party [*British*] ... CLP
Conference on LASERs and Electro-Optics ... CLEO
Conference on Latin American History ... CLAH
Conference of Latin Americanist Geographers ... CLAG
Conference of Liberal Arts Colleges for Women ... CLACW
Conference of Local Environmental Health Administrators [*Later, NCLEHA*] ... CLEHA
Conference of Major Religious Superiors of Women's Institutes of the United States of America [*Later, LCWR*] ... CMSW
Conference of Major Superiors of Men's Institutes ... CMSM
Conference of Ministers of Education [*World War II*] ... CME
Conference Mondiale de l'Energie [*World Energy Conference*] [*See also WEC*] ... CME
Conference Mondiale des Experts Radiotelegraphistes de l'Aeronautique ... CMERA
Conference of Motion Picture and Television Unions ... COMPTU
Conference of Municipal Public Health Engineers [*Later, CLEHA, NCLEHA*] ... CMPHE
Conference of Mutual Casualty Companies [*Later, CCIC*] ... CMCC
Conference of National Armaments Directors [*NATO*] ... CNAD
Conference of National Park Concessioners ... CNPC
Conference of New Emerging Forces [*Indonesia*] ... CONEFO
Conference of New Law Librarians ... CONELL
Conference of Officers of Affiliated States and Territorial Associations ... COASTA
Conference des Organisations Nationales des Colonies Portugaises [*Conference of National Organizations of Portuguese Colonies*] ... CONCP
Conference on Oriental-Western Literary Relations [*Later, ALD*] ... COWLR
Conference Paper ... CP
Conference Papers Index [*A publication*] ... CPI
Conference Papers. International Cosmic Ray Conference [*A publication*] ... Conf Pap Int Cosmic Ray Conf
Conference on Peace Research in History ... CPRH
Conference Permanente de l'Industrie Europeenne de Produits Emailles ... EUREMAIL
Conference on Personal Finance Law ... CPFL
Conference on Personal Finance Law. Quarterly Report [*A publication*] ... Conf Pers Fin L Q Rep
Conference of Philosophical Societies ... CPS
Conference des Plenipotentiaires ... CPNU
Conference of Podiatry Executives ... COPE
Conference on Precision Electromagnetic Measurements ... CPEM
Conference of Presidents of Major American Jewish Organizations ... CPMAJO
Conference of Presidents and Officers of State Medical Associations [*Later, FMA*] ... CPOSMA
Conference of Prince Hall Grand Masters ... CPHGM
Conference Proceedings. Annual Symposium on Computer Architecture [*A publication*] ... Conf Proc Annu Symp Comput Archit
Conference Proceedings. International Conference on Fire Safety [*A publication*] ... Conf Proc Int Conf Fire Saf
Conference Proceedings. Intersociety Energy Conversion Engineering Conference [*A publication*] ... Conf Proc Intersoc Energy Convers Eng Conf
Conference on the Production, Properties, and Testing of Aggregates. Papers [*A publication*] ... Conf Prod Prop Test Aggregates Pap
Conference for Progressive Labor Action ... CPLA
Conference for Progressive Political Action ... CPPA
Conference on Psychoanalytic Education and Research ... COPER
Conference of Public Health Lab Directors ... CPHLD
Conference of Public Health Veterinarians ... CPHV
Conference on the Public Service ... CPS
Conference Publications. Institution of Mechanical Engineers [*A publication*] ... Conf Publ Inst Mech Eng
Conference of Radiation Control Program Directors [*Bureau of Radiological Health*] ... CRCPD

Conference on Reading (University of Chicago). Proceedings [A publication]............................Conf Read (Univ Chicago)
Conference on Reading (University of Pittsburgh). Report [A publication]........................Conf on Read (Univ Pittsburgh) Rep
Conference for Reconciliation, Restitution Fund.............CONREC
Conference Record. Annual Pulp and Paper Industry Technical Conference [A publication]........Conf Rec Annu Pulp Pap Ind Tech Conf
Conference Record. IAS [IEEE Industry Applications Society] Annual Meeting [A publication]..............Conf Rec IAS Annu Meet
Conference des Recteurs et des Principaux des Universites du Quebec, Montreal, PQ, Canada [Library symbol]..........CaQMCRP
Conference on Remote Systems Technology. Proceedings [A publication]..................Conf Remote Syst Technol Proc
Conference Report...CR
Conference on Research in Peace History...............CRPH
Conference of Research Workers in Animal Diseases.......CRWAD
Conference on Science, Philosophy, and Religion.......CSPR
Conference on Science and Religion [Later, UDC].........CSR
Conference on Science and World Affairs................COSWA
Conference for Secondary School English Department Chairpersons...CSSEDC
[United States] Conference of Secular Institutes..........CSI
Conference sur la Securite Europeene [Conference on Security in Europe]..CSE
Conference on Security and Cooperation in Europe [NATO].......CSCE
Conference on Self-Operating Systems [Data processing]...COSOS
Conference of Small Private Colleges....................CSPC
Conference des Societes d'Ingenieurs de l'Europe Occidental et des Etats-Unis d'Amerique [Conference of Engineering Societies of Western Europe and the United States of America]..EUSEC
Conference of Societies for the History of Pharmacy.......CSHP
Conference on the Sociology of the Languages of American Women [1976]...SLAW
Conference de Solidarite des Pays Afro-Asiatiques.........CSPAA
Conference of Southeast Asian Librarians................CONSAL
Conference Spatiale Europeenne [European Space Conference]......CSE
Conference of State Bank Supervisors....................CSBS
Conference of State Cable Agencies.....................CSCA
Conference of State Cemetery Association Secretaries.....CSCAS
Conference of State Court Administrators................COSCA
Conference of State and Provincial Health Authorities of North America [Defunct].....................................CSPHA
Conference of State and Provincial Public Health Laboratory Directors..CSPPHLD
Conference of State Sanitary Engineers.................CSSE
Conference of State Societies [Later, National Conference of State Societies]......................................CSS
Conference of State and Territorial Directors of Public Health Education...CSTDPHE
Conference of State and Territorial Epidemiologists......CSTE
Conference of State and Territorial Health Officers with Public Health Service..CSTHOPHS
Conference of State Utility Commission Engineers [Later, NCRUCE]..CSUCE
Conference for the Study of Political Thought...........CSPT
Conference on Superionic Conductors. Chemistry, Physics, and Applications. Proceedings [A publication]...........Conf Superionic Conduct Chem Phys Appl Pro
Conference on Transportation Unity [Defunct]............CTU
Conference of UN Representatives, UNA [United Nations Association]-USA.....................................CUNR
Conference for Universal Reason and Ethics [Founded by motion picture actor Lew Ayres]............................CURE
Conference Upon Research and Education in World Government.......CURE
Conferences. Institut de Linguistique de Paris [A publication]........CILP
Conferences on Research on International Peace and Security [Founded International Peace Research Association].........COROIPAS
Conferencia [A publication]...............................Conf
Conferencia Interamericana de Agricultura (Caracas) [A publication].........................Conf Interam Agric (Caracas)
Conferencia Interamericana de Bienestar Social [Interamerican Social Welfare Conference]...............................CIBS
Conferencia Interamericana de Seguridad Social [Interamerican Conference on Social Security]........................CISS
Conferenze. Seminario di Matematica. Universita di Bari [A publication]........................Confer Sem Mat Univ Bari
Confessions..CF
Confessor..C
Confidence-Building Measures [for European military security].......CBM's
Confidence Development Plan.............................CDP
Confidence Firing Kit......................................CFK
Confidence Interval [Psychometrics].......................CI
Confidence Limits..CL
Confidence Test Program [NASA]..........................CTP
Confidence Training Launch................................CTL
Confidential...C
Confidential...COFI
Confidential...CONF
Confidential Admiralty Merchant Shipping Instructions......CAMSI
Confidential Book [Navy] [British].........................CB

Confidential Bulletin.......................................CB
Confidential Bulletin [Navy]...............................CONFBUL
Confidential Business Information [Environmental Protection Agency]..CBI
Confidential Cover Sheet..................................CCS
Confidential Document [Navy]..............................CD
Confidential Employment Listing [American Chemical Society].......CELACS
Confidential, Formerly Restricted Data.....................CFRD
Confidential Hydrographic Office [later, Naval Oceanographic Office] Reports - Atlantic [Navy]................CONHYDROLANT
Confidential Informant [Department of Justice]..............CI
Confidential Memorandum...................................CM
Confidential - Modified Handling [Army]...................CONF-MH
Confidential - Modified Handling Authorized [Military]........C-MHA
Confidential - Modified Handling Authorized [Army]........CONFMOD
Confidential Restricted Data...............................CRD
Confidential and Secret Weekly Orders [Naval Air Stations].......CASWO
Configuration..CONF
Configuration..CONFIG
Configuration..CONFIGN
Configuration Acceptance Inspection........................CAI
Configuration and Acceptance Review.......................CAR
Configuration Accounting and Management Report...........CAMR
Configuration Accounting Number...........................CAN
Configuration Analysis and Performance....................CAPER
Configuration Audit Inspection [Army]......................CAI
Configuration Audit Review................................CAR
Configuration Baseline.....................................CB
Configuration Breakdown List..............................CBL
Configuration Change Control Board [NASA].................CCCB
Configuration Change Directive.............................CCD
Configuration Change Order................................CCO
Configuration Change Plan.................................CCP
Configuration Change Point.................................CCP
Configuration Control......................................CC
Configuration Control Action...............................CCA
Configuration Control Board [DoD]..........................CCB
Configuration Control Board Data [or Directive] [DoD].......CCBD
Configuration Control Number..............................CCN
Configuration Control Panel.................................CCP
Configuration Control Phase................................CCP
Configuration Control Reporting System [Navy]..............CCRS
Configuration Control Secretariat...........................CCS
Configuration Control and Sensing Unit.....................CCSU
Configuration Data Control.................................CDC
Configuration Data Table...................................CDT
Configuration Deviation List................................CDL
Configuration Identification Control and Accounting..........CICA
Configuration Identification Index...........................CII
Configuration Identification Tables..........................CIT
Configuration Index and Status Report......................CISR
Configuration Information System...........................CIS
Configuration Inspection....................................CI
Configuration [or Contract] Inspection Log..................CIL
Configuration Interaction [Quantum mechanics]...............CI
Configuration Item..CI
Configuration Item Data List................................CIDL
Configuration Item Specification.............................CISPEC
Configuration Item Verification Review......................CIVR
Configuration Management..................................CM
Configuration Management Accounting.......................CMA
Configuration Management Branch [NASA]....................CMB
Configuration Management Operating Systems Manual.......CMOSM
Configuration Management Plan [or Program]................CMP
Configuration Management Review...........................CMR
Configuration Management System..........................CMS
Configuration Selection Register............................CSR
Configuration Standardization Document [Deep Space Instrumentation Facility, NASA]........................CSD
Configuration Status Accounting.............................CSA
Configuration Status Accounting Report.....................CSAR
Configuration Status Accounting System.....................CSAS
Configuration Switch Controller.............................CSC
Configuration and Traceability..............................CAT
Configuration and Tuning Module [Data processing].........CTM
Configuration Utilization Efficiency.........................CUE
Configuration Verification and Accounting System............CVAS
Configuration Verification Index.............................CVI
Configuration Verification List..............................CVL
Configuration Verification Test..............................CVT
Configuration Work Package Item [Army].....................CWPI
Confine..CFN
Confine..CNF
Confine [or Confinement]...................................CONF
Confined to Camp [Military].................................CC
Confined Detonating Cord..................................CDC
Confined Detonating Fuze..................................CDF
Confined to Post..C to P
Confinement to Barracks [A military punishment]............CB
Confinement Factor [Nuclear energy]........................CF
Confinement at Hard Labor [Army]..........................CHL

Confinia Neurologica [*A publication*]....Confin Neurol
Confinia Psychiatrica [*A publication*]....CFPSA
Confinia Psychiatrica....Confin Psychiatr
Confinia Psychiatrica [*A publication*]....Conf Psych
Confirm....CFM
Confirmation of Balance [*Banking*]....C of B
Confirmatory Test [*Army*]....CT
Confirmed Exposure but Unconscious [*Advertising*]....CEBUS
Confirmed and Made a Matter of Record [*Army*]....CMMR
Confirming Requisition Follows [*Aviation*]....COREQ
Confirming Telephone [*or message*] **Authority Of**....COTA
Conflict Alert [*Aircraft control*]....CA
Conflict Alert System [*Aviation*]....CAS
Conflict Resolution Center....CRC
Conflict Resolution Inventory [*Psychology*]....CRI
Confluence [*A publication*]....Cfl
Confluence [*A publication*]....Conf
Confluent Education Development and Research Center....CEDARC
Confoederatio Internationalis ad Qualitates Plantarum Edulium Perquirendas [*International Association for Quality Research on Food Plants*]....CIQ
Conformal Fuel Tank....CFT
Conformal Tactical Array....CONTACT
Conformal Wire Grating....CWG
Conformance....CONF
Conformational Analysis. Scope and Present Limitations Papers Presented at the International Symposium [*A publication*]....Conform Anal Pap Int Symp
Conforms to Copyright Guidelines....CCG
Conforms to Copyright Law....CCL
Confraternity of the Blessed Sacrament....CBS
Confraternity of Christian Doctrine....CCD
Confrontation [*A publication*]....Confr
Confused Artificial Insemination....CAI
Confusion Reflector Material....CRM
Congenital [*Medicine*]....CONGEN
Congenital Absence of Vagina [*Medicine*]....CAV
Congenital Adrenal Hyperplasia [*Medicine*]....CAH
Congenital Adrenal Virilism [*Medicine*]....CAV
Congenital Central Hypoventilation Syndrome [*Medicine*]....CCHS
Congenital Dislocation of the Hip [*Medicine*]....CDH
Congenital Dyserythropoietic Anemia [*Hematology*]....CDA
Congenital Erythropoietic Porphyria [*Medicine*]....CEP
Congenital Heinz Body Hemolytic Anemia [*Medicine*]....CHBA
Congenital Hypoplastic Anemia [*Hematology*]....CHA
Congenital Malformation [*Medicine*]....CM
Congenital Malformation of Heart [*Medicine*]....CMH
Congenital Nonspherocytic Hemolytic Anemia [*Medicine*]....CNSHA
Congenital Pulmonary Cystic Lymphangiectasis [*Medicine*]....CPCL
Congenital Rubella Syndrome [*Medicine*]....CRS
Congenital Syphilis [*Medicine*]....CS
Congested Freeway Driving Schedule [*For vehicle emission measurements*]....CFDS
Congestion [*Aviation*]....CGSTN
Congestive Cardiac Failure [*Medicine*]....CCF
Congestive Heart Failure [*Medicine*]....CHF
Congestive Myocardiopathy [*Medicine*]....CM
Congiuntura Economica Lombarda [*A publication*]....Congiunt Econ Lombarda
Congius [*Gallon*] [*Pharmacy*]....C
Congius [*Gallon*] [*Pharmacy*]....CONG
Conglomerate [*Lithology*]....CGL
Conglomerate....CONGL
Conglutinating Complement Absorption Test [*Immunochemistry*]....CCAT
Congo [*MARC country of publication code*] [*Library of Congress*]....cf
Congo [*Two-letter standard code*]....CG
Congo [*Three-letter standard code*]....COG
Congo [*MARC geographic area code*] [*Library of Congress*]....f-cf---
Congo-Afrique [*A publication*]....CAfr
Congo (Brazzaville) [*Aircraft nationality and registration mark*]....TN
Congo (Kinshasa) [*Zaire*] [*MARC country of publication code*] [*Library of Congress*]....cg
Congo (Kinshasa) [*Zaire*] [*MARC geographic area code*] [*Library of Congress*]....f-cg---
Congo (Leopoldville) [*Aircraft nationality and registration mark*]....9Q
Congo Military Mission - United States....COMISH-US
Congo Protestant Relief Agency [*Defunct*]....CPRA
Congo Red [*A dye*]....CoR
Congo-Red Millipore Filter....CRMF
Congo River and Basin [*MARC geographic area code*] [*Library of Congress*]....fg-----
Congoleum Corp. [*NYSE symbol*]....COG
Congregate Housing Services Program [*HUD*]....CHSP
Congregatio Clericorum Regularium Marianorum sub titulo Immaculatae Conceptionis Beatae Mariae Virginis [*Marian Fathers*] [*Roman Catholic religious order*]....MIC
Congregatio Filiorum Sacratissimi Cordis Jesu [*Sons of the Sacred Heart*] [*Verona Fathers*] [*Roman Catholic religious order*]....FSCJ
Congregatio Fratrum Caritate [*Brothers of Charity*] [*Roman Catholic religious order*]....FC
Congregatio Fratrum Cellitarum seu Alexianorum [*Alexian Brothers*] [*Roman Catholic religious order*]....CFA
Congregatio Fratrum Pauperum [*Brothers of the Poor of St. Francis*] [*Roman Catholic religious order*]....CFP
Congregatio Fratrum Sancti Francisci Xaverii [*Brothers of St. Francis Xavier*] [*Xaverian Brothers*] [*Roman Catholic religious order*]....CFX
Congregatio Immaculati Cordis Mariae [*Congregation of the Immaculate Heart of Mary*] [*Roman Catholic men's religious order*]....CICM
Congregatio Iosephitarum [*Josephite Fathers*] [*Roman Catholic religious order*]....CJ
Congregatio Jesu et Mariae [*Congregation of Jesus and Mary*] [*Eudist Fathers*] [*Roman Catholic religious order*]....CJM
Congregatio Mariae [*Fathers of the Company of Mary*] [*Roman Catholic religious order*]....CM
Congregatio Missionariorum Filiorum Immaculati Cordis Beatae Maria Virginia [*Congregation of Missionary Sons of the Immaculate Heart of the Blessed Virgin Mary*] [*Claretians*] [*Roman Catholic religious order*]....CMF
Congregatio Missionariorum de Mariannhill [*Congregation of Mariannhill Missionaries*] [*Mariannhill Fathers*] [*Roman Catholic religious order*]....CMM
Congregatio Missionariorum a Sancta Familia [*Congregation of the Missionaries of the Holy Family*] [*Roman Catholic men's religious order*]....MSF
Congregatio Missionariorum a Sancto Carlo [*Congregation of the Missionary Fathers of St. Charles*] [*Formerly, PSSC*] [*Roman Catholic religious order*]....CS
Congregatio Missionis Sancti Vicentii a Paulo [*Congregation of the Mission of St. Vincent de Paul*] [*Vincentians*] [*Roman Catholic men's religious order*]....CM
Congregatio Passionis [*Congregation of the Passion*] [*Passionists*] [*Roman Catholic religious order*]....CP
Congregatio Pretiosissimi Sanguinis [*Society of the Most Precious Blood*] [*Roman Catholic religious order*]....CPPS
Congregatio Reformatorium Praemonstratensium [*Premonstratensians*] [*Roman Catholic men's religious order*]....CRP
Congregatio Resurrectionis [*Congregation of the Resurrection*] [*Roman Catholic religious order*]....CR
Congregatio Sacerdotum a Corde Jesu [*Congregation of the Priests of the Sacred Heart of Jesus*] [*Roman Catholic religious order*]....SCJ
Congregatio Sacratissimorum Cordium [*Missionaries of the Sacred Hearts of Jesus and Mary*] [*Roman Catholic religious order*]....CSSCC
Congregatio a Sacro Corde Jesu [*Congregation of the Priests of the Sacred Heart*] [*Roman Catholic religious order*]....CCV
Congregatio Sacrorum Cordium [*Fathers of the Sacred Heart*] [*Picpus Fathers*] [*Roman Catholic religious order*]....SSCC
Congregatio a Sancta Cruce [*Congregation of Holy Cross*] [*Roman Catholic religious order*]....CSC
Congregatio Sancti Basilii [*Congregation of the Priests of St. Basil*] [*Basilians*] [*Roman Catholic men's religious order*]....CSB
Congregatio Sancti Joseph [*Congregation of St. Joseph*] [*Roman Catholic religious order*]....CSJ
Congregatio Sancti Pauli [*Paulists*] [*Roman Catholic men's religious order*]....CSP
Congregatio Sancti Spiritus [*Congregation of the Holy Ghost*] [*Holy Ghost Fathers*] [*Roman Catholic religious order*]....CSSP
Congregatio Sanctissimi Redemptoris [*Congregation of the Most Holy Redeemer*] [*Redemptionists*] [*Roman Catholic men's religious order*]....CSSR
Congregation....C
Congregation of Christian Brothers [*Formerly, Christian Brothers of Ireland*] [*Roman Catholic religious order*]....CFC
Congregation of Clerics Regular [*Theatine Fathers*] [*Roman Catholic religious order*]....CR
Congregation of Daughters of Jesus [*Roman Catholic religious order*]....FJ
Congregation of the Divine Spirit [*Roman Catholic women's religious order*]....CDS
Congregation of Humility of Mary [*Roman Catholic women's religious order*]....CHM
Congregation of the Incarnate Word and the Blessed Sacrament [*Roman Catholic women's religious order*]....IWBS
Congregation of the Incarnate Word and the Blessed Sacrament [*Roman Catholic women's religious order*]....SIW
Congregation of the Incarnate Word and the Blessed Sacrament [*Roman Catholic women's religious order*]....VI
Congregation of Notre Dame de Sion [*Roman Catholic women's religious order*]....NDS
Congregation of Oblates of Bethany [*Roman Catholic women's religious order*]....COB
Congregation of the Oratory [*Oratorians*] [*Roman Catholic men's religious order*]....CO
Congregation of the Oratory [*Oratorians*] [*Roman Catholic men's religious order*]....CongOrat
Congregation Organized by United Genial Hackers....COUGH
Congregation of Our Lady, Help of the Clergy [*Roman Catholic women's religious order*]....CLHC

Congregation of Our Lady of the Holy Rosary [*Roman Catholic women's religious order*] ... RSR
Congregation of Our Lady of the Retreat in the Cenacle [*Roman Catholic women's religious order*] ... RC
Congregation of Priests of Mercy [*Fathers of Mercy*] [*Roman Catholic religious order*] ... CPM
Congregation of the Sacred Stigmata [*Stigmatine Fathers and Brothers*] [*Roman Catholic religious order*] ... CSS
Congregation of St. Brigid [*Roman Catholic women's religious order*] ... CSB
Congregation of the Servants of Christ [*Anglican religious community*] ... SC
Congregation of the Sisters of Charity of the Incarnate Word [*Roman Catholic religious order*] ... CCVI
Congregation of the Sisters of the Family [*Roman Catholic religious order*] ... SSF
Congregation of the Sisters Marianites of Holy Cross [*Roman Catholic religious order*] ... MSC
Congregation of the Sisters of St. Felix [*Felician Sisters*] [*Roman Catholic religious order*] ... CSSF
Congregation of Sisters of St. Louis [*Roman Catholic religious order*] ... SSL
Congregation of Sisters of St. Thomas of Villanova [*Roman Catholic religious order*] ... SSTV
Congregation Sons of Israel and David, Temple Beth-El, Providence, RI [*Library symbol*] ... RPT
Congregational ... CONG
Congregational ... CONGL
Congregational ... CONGR
Congregational Christian Historical Society ... CCHS
Congregational Christian Service Committee [*Superseded by UCBWM*] ... CCSC
Congregational Magazine [*A publication*] ... Cong M
Congregational Publishing Society ... CPS
Congregational Quarterly [*A publication*] ... Cong Q
Congregational Review [*A publication*] ... Cong R
Congregational Union ... CU
Congregationalist [*A publication*] ... Cong
Congres Archeologique de France [*A publication*] ... Congres Archeol
Congres Archeologique de France [*A publication*] ... Congres Archeol de France
Congres. Association Francaise pour l'Avancement des Sciences (Nancy) [*A publication*] ... Congr Assoc Fr Av Sci (Nancy)
Congres. Association Geologique Carpatho-Balkanique. Bulletin [*A publication*] ... Congr Assoc Geol Carpatho-Balkan Bull
Congres International de Cybernetique. Actes [*A publication*] ... Congr Int Cybern Actes
Congres International des Editeurs [*International Congress of Publishers*] ... CIE
Congres International des Fabrications Mecaniques [*International Mechanical Engineering Congress*] ... CIM
Congres International des Jus de Fruits [*A publication*] ... Congr Int Jus Fruits
Congres International de Medecine. Comptes Rendus [*A publication*] ... Cong Internat Med C R
Congres International de Reproduction Animale et Insemination Artificielle [*A publication*] ... Congr Int Reprod Anim Insemination Artif
Congres International de Stratigraphie et de Geologie du Carbonifere. Compte Rendu [*A publication*] ... Congr Int Stratigr Geol Carbonifere C R
Congres International de la Vigne du Vin [*A publication*] ... Congr Int Vigne Vin
Congres Internationaux de Medecine Tropicale et de Paludisme [*International Congresses on Tropical Medicine and Malaria*] ... CIMTP
Congres Islamique Mondial ... CIM
Congres Juif Mondial [*World Jewish Congress*] ... CJM
Congres National. Societes Savantes. Section des Sciences. Comptes Rendus [*A publication*] ... Congr Natl Soc Savantes Sect Sci C R
Congres du Peuple Europeen ... CPE
Congres Pomologique [*A publication*] ... Congres Pomol
Congres des Relations Industrielles. Universite Laval. Rapport [*A publication*] ... Congres des Rel Ind
Congresboek. Wereldcongres voor Oppervlaktebehandeling van Metalen [*A publication*] ... Congresb Wereldcongr Oppervlaktebehandel Met
Congreso Geologico Argentino. Relatorio [*A publication*] ... Congr Geol Argent Relat
Congreso Ibero-Americano de Geologia Economica [*A publication*] ... Congr Ibero-Am Geol Econ
Congreso Internacional de Filosofia. Anais (Sao Paulo) [*A publication*] ... CIF-SP
Congreso Nacional de Tuberculosis y Enfermedades Respiratorias [*A publication*] ... Congr Nac Tuberc Enferm Respir
Congreso Venezolano de Cirugia [*A publication*] ... Congr Venez Cir
Congress ... C
Congress [*or Congressman*] ... CON
Congress ... CONG
Congress of African Peoples ... CAP
Congress of American Unions ... CAU
Congress of Arabic and Islamic Studies ... CAIS
Congress of Astrological Organizations [*Defunct*] ... CAO
Congress of County Medical Societies ... CCMS
Congress. Hungarian Pharmacological Society. Proceedings [*A publication*] ... Congr Hung Pharmacol Soc Pro
Congress of Independent Unions ... CIU
Congress of Independent Unions ... COIU
Congress of Industrial Organizations [*Later, AFL-CIO*] ... CIO
Congress of Industrial Organizations, Political Action Committee [*Later, COPE*] ... CIOPAC
Congress. International Potash Institute [*A publication*] ... Congr Int Potash Inst
Congress of the International Theater Institute ... CITI
Congress of Irish Unions ... CIU
Congress of Italian-American Organizations ... CIAO
Congress for Jewish Culture ... CJC
Congress of Joke-Abused Cities ... COJAC
Congress Liberation Party [*Nyasaland*] ... CLP
Congress of Lung Association Staff ... CLAS
Congress of National Black Churches ... CNBC
Congress of Neurological Surgeons ... CNS
Congress of Organizations of the Physically Handicapped ... COPH
Congress Party [*India*] ... CP
Congress of Racial Equality ... CORE
Congress on Research in Dance ... CORD
Congress of Russian Americans ... CRA
Congress of Scientists on Survival [*Inactive*] ... SOS
Congress Task Force [*of the Anti-Martial Law Coalition and the Friends of the Filipino People*] ... CTF
Congress of Unions of Employees in the Public and Civil Services [*Malaya*] ... CUEPACS
Congress for the Unity of Black Students ... CUBS
Congress of Unrepresented People ... COUP
Congress Watch [*An association*] ... CW
Congress of World Unity ... CWU
Congressional ... CONGL
Congressional Action Fund ... CAF
Congressional Alcohol Fuels Caucus ... CAFC
Congressional Arts Caucus ... CAC
Congressional Arts Caucus Education Program ... CACEP
Congressional Automotive Caucus ... CAC
Congressional Black Caucus ... CBC
Congressional Budget Office ... CBO
Congressional Caucus for Women's Issues ... CC
Congressional Clearinghouse on the Future ... CCF
Congressional Club ... CC
Congressional Delegate [*or Delegation*] ... CODEL
Congressional Descriptive Summaries ... CDS
Congressional Digest [*A publication*] ... Cong Dig
Congressional Digest [*A publication*] ... Cong Digest
Congressional Digest [*A publication*] ... Congr Dig
Congressional Digest, Washington, DC [*Library symbol*] ... DCD
Congressional District ... CD
Congressional District Data [*Bureau of the Census*] ... CDD
Congressional Fact Paper [*Army*] ... CFP
Congressional Friends of Human Rights Monitors ... CFHRM
Congressional Hispanic Caucus ... CHC
Congressional Information Service [*Information service*] ... CIS
Congressional Information Service, Bethesda, MD [*Library symbol*] ... MdBeCI
Congressional Information Sources, Inventories, and Directories ... CISID
Congressional Interference ... CI
Congressional Liaison ... CL
Congressional Liaison Office ... CLO
Congressional Management Foundation ... CMF
Congressional Medal of Honor ... CMH
Congressional Medal of Honor Society ... CMHS
Congressional Monitoring Group on Southern Africa ... CMGSA
Congressional Office of the Budget ... COB
Congressional Office of Science and Technology ... COST
Congressional Presentation Document ... CPD
Congressional Quarterly, Inc. ... CQ
Congressional Record ... CR
Congressional Record On-Line [*Data processing*] ... CRECORD
Congressional Research Service [*Formerly, Legislative Reference Service*] [*Library of Congress*] ... CRS
Congressional Research Service, Washington, DC [*OCLC symbol*] ... CRS
Congressional Rural Caucus ... CRC
Congressional Space Caucus ... CSC
Congressional Staff Club ... CSC
Congressional Steel Caucus ... CSC
Congressional Textile Caucus ... CTC
Congressional Underwater Explorers Club ... CUEC
Congressional Union ... CU
Congressionally Mandated Mobility Study [*DoD*] ... CMMS
Congresso Internacional de Hematologia. Conferencias [*A publication*] ... Congr Int Hematol Conf
Congruent ... CONGR
Congruent Melting Point ... CMP
Conical Alignment Kit ... CAK
Conical Fin ... COF
Conical Flow Field ... CFF
Conical Monopole Antenna ... CMA
Conical Monopole Antenna Kit ... CMAK

Conical Scan ... CONSCAN
Conical Scan Antenna ... CSA
Conical Scan-on-Receive Only ... COSRO
Conical Scan-on-Receive Only ... CSORO
Conical Shaped Charge ... CSC
Conical Shell Vibration ... CSV
Conical Shock Tube ... CST
Conical Tank [*Liquid gas carriers*] ... co
Conifer/Essex Group, Inc. [*NASDAQ symbol*] ... CNFG
Coniferous Forest Biome [*Ecological biogeographic study*] ... CFB
Conjugata Vera [*Conjugate diameter of pelvic inlet*] [*Anatomy*] ... CV
Conjugata Vera Obstetrica [*Conjugate diameter of pelvic inlet*] [*Anatomy*] ... CVO
Conjugate Acid-Base Pair [*Chemistry*] ... CABP
Conjugate Filter Data Link ... CONFIDAL
Conjugated Estrogens [*Endocrinology*] ... CE
Conjugation ... CONJ
Conjugation-Parity [*Physics*] ... CP
Conjugation-Parity Asymmetry [*Physics*] ... CPA
Conjugi [*To My Spouse*] [*Latin*] ... COI
Conjugi Optimo [*To My Most Excellent Spouse*] [*Latin*] ... CO
Conjunction ... CJ
Conjunction ... CONJ
Conjunctive Alteration File ... CAF
Conjunctive Alteration Indicator ... CAI
Conjunctive Normal Formula ... CNF
Conjunctivitis [*Medicine*] ... CONJ
Conjunctura Economica [*A publication*] ... Conjunct Econ
Conjux [*Consort, Spouse*] [*Genealogy*] ... CON
Conn Water Service [*NASDAQ symbol*] ... CTWS
Conna Corp. [*NASDAQ symbol*] ... CONA
Connaissance de la Loire [*A publication*] ... Connaiss Loire
Connaissement [*Bill of Lading*] [*French*] ... CONNT
Connaught Medical Research Laboratories, Toronto, ON, Canada [*Library symbol*] ... CaOTCL
Connaught Rangers [*Military*] [*British*] ... CR
Conneaut, OH [*Radio station call letters*] ... WGOJ
Conneaut, OH [*Radio station call letters*] ... WWOW
Connect ... CNCT
Connected Replenishment [*Military*] ... CONREP
Connecticut ... CONN
Connecticut [*Postal code*] ... CT
Connecticut [*MARC country of publication code*] [*Library of Congress*] ... ctu
Connecticut [*MARC geographic area code*] [*Library of Congress*] ... n-us-ct
Connecticut Academy of Arts and Sciences. Transactions [*A publication*] ... Conn Acad Arts & Sci Trans
Connecticut Advanced Nuclear Engineering Laboratory ... CANEL
Connecticut Agricultural Experiment Station ... CAES
Connecticut Agricultural Experiment Station. Bulletin [*New Haven*] [*A publication*] ... Conn Agr Expt Sta Bull
Connecticut Agricultural Experiment Station. Bulletin (New Haven) [*A publication*] ... Conn Agric Exp Stn Bull (New Haven)
Connecticut Agricultural Experiment Station. Department of Entomology. Special Bulletin [*A publication*] ... Conn Agric Exp Stn Dep Entomol Spec Bull
Connecticut Agricultural Experiment Station (New Haven) Circular [*A publication*] ... Conn Agric Exp Stn (New Haven) Circ
Connecticut Agricultural Experiment Station, New Haven, CT [*Library symbol*] ... CtNhAS
Connecticut Association of Health Sciences Libraries [*Library network*] ... CAHSL
Connecticut Bar Journal [*A publication*] ... Conn B J
Connecticut College, New London, CT [*OCLC symbol*] ... CTL
Connecticut College, New London, CT [*Library symbol*] ... CtNlC
Connecticut Energy Corp. [*NYSE symbol*] ... CNE
Connecticut Film Circuit [*Library network*] ... CFC
Connecticut General Insurance Corp. [*NYSE symbol*] [*Delisted*] ... CGN
Connecticut General Mortgage & Realty Investments [*NYSE symbol*] [*Delisted*] ... CGM
Connecticut. Geological and Natural History Survey [*A publication*] ... Conn G S
Connecticut. Geological and Natural History Survey. Bulletin [*A publication*] ... Conn Geol Natur Hist Surv Bull
Connecticut Historical Society. Bulletin [*A publication*] ... CHSB
Connecticut Historical Society. Bulletin [*A publication*] ... Conn Hist Soc Bull
Connecticut Historical Society. Bulletin [*A publication*] ... ConnHSB
Connecticut Historical Society. Collections [*A publication*] ... Conn His S
Connecticut Historical Society. Collections [*A publication*] ... Conn Hist Soc Coll
Connecticut Historical Society, Hartford, CT [*Library symbol*] ... CtHi
Connecticut Industry [*A publication*] ... Conn Ind
Connecticut Law Review [*A publication*] ... Conn L Rev
Connecticut Libraries [*A publication*] ... Conn Lib
Connecticut Library Association. Bulletin [*A publication*] ... Conn Lib Assn Bul
Connecticut Light & Power Co. ... CL & P
Connecticut Medicine [*A publication*] ... Conn Med
Connecticut Mental Health Center, New Haven, CT [*Library symbol*] ... CtNhMH
Connecticut. Mineral Folios [*A publication*] ... Conn Mineral Folio
Connecticut Natural Gas Corp. ... CNG
Connecticut Natural Gas Corp. [*NYSE symbol*] ... CTG
Connecticut On-Line Law-Enforcement Communications and Teleprocessing [*Computer law-enforcement system*] ... COLLECT
Connecticut Review [*A publication*] ... Conn R
Connecticut River Watershed Council ... CRWC
Connecticut. State Agricultural Experiment Station. Publications [*A publication*] ... Conn State Ag Exp
Connecticut State Department of Health, Hartford, CT [*Library symbol*] ... Ct-H
Connecticut State Library, Hartford, CT [*Library symbol*] ... Ct
Connecticut State Library, Hartford, CT [*OCLC symbol*] ... CZL
Connecticut State Medical Journal [*A publication*] ... Conn State Med J
Connecticut. Storrs Agricultural Experiment Station. Bulletin [*A publication*] ... Conn Storrs Agric Exp Stn Bull
Connecticut. Storrs Agricultural Experiment Station. Research Report [*A publication*] ... Conn Storrs Agric Exp Stn Res Rep
Connecticut Valley Historical Museum, Springfield, MA [*Library symbol*] ... MSCV
Connecticut Water Resources Bulletin [*A publication*] ... Connecticut Water Resources Bull
Connecticut Water Resources Bulletin [*A publication*] ... Conn Water Resour Bull
Connecticut Water Resources Commission. Connecticut Water Resources Bulletin [*A publication*] ... Conn Water Res Comm Conn Water Res Bull
Connecticut Woodlands [*A publication*] ... Conn Woodl
Connecticut Woodlands [*A publication*] ... Conn Woodlands
Connecticutensis Academiae Socius [*Fellow of the Connecticut Academy of Arts and Sciences*] ... CAS
Connecting Carrier ... CC
Connecting Line ... CL
Connecting-Rod ... CONNROD
Connecting-Rod ... CONROD
Connection ... CON
Connection ... CONEC
Connection Conversion ... CONVERS
Connection Fitting Out [*Navy*] ... CFO
Connection Naval Air Reserve Training Program ... CONARESTRAPROG
Connection Point [*Data processing*] ... CP
Connection Reactivation ... CONVATE
Connective Tissue ... CT
Connective Tissue Massage [*Medicine*] ... CTM
Connective Tissue Research [*A publication*] ... Connect Tis
Connective Tissue Research [*A publication*] ... Connect Tissue Res
Connectivity Table [*Data processing*] ... CT
Connector ... CONN
Connector Backing Shell ... CBS
Connector Bracket (Power) ... CBP
Connector Circuit ... CC
Connector for Networked Information Center [*MIT*] ... CONIT
Connector for Networked Information Transfer [*Massachusetts Institute of Technology*] [*Information service*] ... CONIT
Connector Panel ... CP
Connector Replacement ... CR
Connector Symposium. Proceedings [*A publication*] ... Connector Symp Proc
Connel [*Washington*] [*Seismograph station code, US Geological Survey*] ... CNL
Connellan Airways Ltd. ... CONN
Connellsville, PA [*Location identifier*] [*FAA*] ... VVS
Connellsville, PA [*Radio station call letters*] ... WCVI
Connelly Containers, Inc. [*American Stock Exchange symbol*] ... CON
Conner Homes Corp. [*American Stock Exchange symbol*] ... CNR
Connersville, IN [*Radio station call letters*] ... WCNB-FM
Connersville Public Library, Connersville, IN [*Library symbol*] ... InCo
Connetquot Public Library, Bohemia, NY [*Library symbol*] ... NBoh
Conning Director [*Navy*] ... CD
Conning Tower [*Naval architecture*] ... CONTWR
Connoisseur [*A publication*] ... Conn
Connors State Agricultural College [*Oklahoma*] ... CSAC
Connotation ... CONN
Connotation [*A publication*] ... Conn
Connradh na Gaedhilge [*The Gaelic League, founded in 1893*] ... CG
Conoco, Inc. [*Formerly, Continental Oil Co.*] [*NYSE symbol*] [*Delisted*] ... CLL
Conococheague District Library, Chambersburg, PA [*Library symbol*] ... PChCo
Conococheague District Library, Chambersburg, PA [*OCLC symbol*] ... PCO
Conolog Corp. [*NASDAQ symbol*] ... CNLG
Conoseal Pipe Joint ... CPJ
Conquering Hero [*British, for returning soldiers*] ... CH
Conquest Exploration Co. [*American Stock Exchange symbol*] ... CQX
Conquest of Hunger Program [*Rockefeller Foundation*] ... CHP
Conquista [*Brazil*] [*Airport symbol*] ... COQ
Conrac Corp. [*NYSE symbol*] ... CAX
Conrad Record, Conrad, IA [*Library symbol*] ... IaConR
CONRAIL [*Consolidated Rail Corp.*] **Analysis Model** [*Data processing*] ... CRAM
Conrock Co. [*American Stock Exchange symbol*] ... CRZ
Conroe, TX [*Location identifier*] [*FAA*] ... CXO

Conroe, TX [*Radio station call letters*] ... KIKR
Conroe, TX [*Radio station call letters*] ... KJOJ
Conroe, TX [*Radio station call letters*] ... KSKS
Conroy, Inc. [*American Stock Exchange symbol*] ... CRY
Conscience and Military Tax Campaign ... CMTC
Conscientious Objector ... CO
Conscientious Objector ... CONOBJTR
Conscientious Objectors' News [*British*] ... CON
Consciousness ... CS
Consciousness-Raising ... CR
Consciousness Research and Training Project ... CRTP
Consco Enterprises [*NASDAQ symbol*] ... CNSO
Consecrated ... CONS
Consecutive Duty Tour [*Air Force*] ... CDT
Consecutive Number Printer ... CNP
Consecutive Oversea Tour [*Military*] ... COT
Conseil d'Assistance Economique Mutuelle [*Mutual Economic Aid Council*] ... CAEM
Conseil des Communes d'Europe [*Council of European Municipalities*] ... CCE
Conseil de Cooperation Douaniere [*Customs Co-Operation Council - CCC*] ... CCD
Conseil Episcopal Latino-Americain [*Latin American Episcopal Council*] ... CELAM
Conseil Europeen du "Codex Alimentarius" ... CODEXAL
Conseil Europeen du Comite International de l'Organisation Scientifique [*European Council of International Committee of Scientific Management*] ... CECIOS
Conseil Europeen du Cuir Brut [*European Untanned Leather Council*] ... CECB
Conseil Europeen des Jeunes Agriculteurs [*European Committee of Young Farmers*] [*Common Market*] ... CEJA
Conseil Europeen des Recherches Nucleaires [*Later, Organisation Europeenne pour la Recherche Nucleaire*] ... CERN
Conseil des Federations Commerciales d'Europe [*Council of European Commercial Federations*] ... CFCE
Conseil des Federations Industrielles d'Europe [*Council of European Industrial Federations*] ... CFIE
Conseil des Federations Industrielles d'Europe [*Council of European Industrial Federations*] ... CIFE
Conseil General des Peches pour la Mediterranee [*General Fisheries Council for the Mediterranean*] ... CGPM
Conseil Indo-Pacifique des Peches [*Indo-Pacific Fisheries Council*] ... CIPP
Conseil Inter-Americain de Securite [*Inter-American Safety Council*] ... CIAS
Conseil Interamericain du Commerce et de la Production ... CICEP
Conseil Intergouvernemental des Pays Exportateurs de Cuivre [*Intergovernmental Council of Copper-Exporting Countries*] [*Chile, Peru, Zaire, and Zambia*] ... CIPEC
Conseil International des Archives [*International Council on Archives*] ... CIA
Conseil International du Batiment pour la Recherche, l'Etude, et la Documentation [*International Council for Building Research, Studies, and Documentation*] ... CIB
Conseil International du Ble [*International Wheat Council*] [*See also IWC*] ... CIB
Conseil International de la Chasse et de la Conservation du Gibier [*International Council for Game and Wildlife Conservation*] ... CIC
Conseil International du Cinema et de la Television [*International Film and Television Council*] ... CICT
Conseil International des Compositeurs [*International Council of Composers*] ... CIC
Conseil International pour le Developpement du Cuivre [*International Copper Development Council*] ... CIDEC
Conseil International de l'Education Physique et Sportive [*International Council of Sport and Physical Education*] ... CIEPS
Conseil International des Employeurs du Commerce [*International Council of Commerce Employers*] ... CIEC
Conseil International de l'Etain [*International Tin Council - ITC*] ... CIE
Conseil International pour l'Exploration de la Mer [*International Council for the Exploration of the Sea*] ... CIEM
Conseil International pour l'Exploration de la Mer. Zooplankton Sheet [*A publication*] ... Cons Int Explor Mer Zooplankton Sheet
Conseil International des Femmes [*International Council of Women*] ... CIF
Conseil International du Film d'Enseignement [*International Council for Educational Films*] ... CIFE
Conseil International des Infirmieres [*International Council of Nurses*] ... CII
Conseil International de la Langue Francaise [*International Council of the French Language - ICFL*] ... CILF
Conseil International des Machines a Combustion [*International Council of Combustion Engines*] ... CIMAC
Conseil International de la Musique [*International Music Council*] ... CIM
Conseil International de la Musique Populaire [*International Folk Music Council*] ... CIMP
Conseil International des Organismes de Travailleuses Familiales [*International Council of Home-Help Services*] ... CIOTF
Conseil International de la Philosophie et des Sciences Humaines [*International Council for Philosophy and Humanistic Studies*] ... CIPSH
Conseil International des Praticiens du Plan Comptable International [*International Council of Practitioners of the International Plan of Accounts*] ... CIPCI
Conseil International de la Preparation a l'Enseignement [*International Council on Education for Teaching*] ... CIPE
Conseil International pour la Preservation des Oiseaux [*International Council for Bird Preservation*] ... CIPO
Conseil International des Radios-Televisions d'Expression Francaise [*International Council of French-Speaking Radio and Television*] ... CIRTEF
Conseil International des Sciences Sociales [*International Social Science Council*] [*See also ISSC*] ... CISS
Conseil International des Services d'Aide Familiale [*International Council of Homehelp Services - ICHS*] ... CISAF
Conseil International du Sport Militaire [*International Military Sports Council*] ... CISM
Conseil International des Tanneurs [*International Council of Tanners*] [*See also ICT*] ... CIT
Conseil International des Telecommunications de Press [*International Press Telecommunications Council*] ... CITP
Conseil International des Unions Scientifiques [*International Council of Scientific Unions*] ... CIUS
Conseil Interprofessionel du Vin de Bordeaux [*France*] ... CIVB
Conseil de la Jeunesse [*Youth Council*] [*Senegal, Mali, Upper Volta, Niger, and Dahomey*] ... CJ
Conseil de la Jeunesse d'Afrique [*African Youth Council*] [*Senegal*] ... CJA
Conseil de la Jeunesse de Cote d'Ivoire [*Ivory Coast Youth Council*] ... CJCI
Conseil Mondial pour l'Assemblee Constituante des Peuples [*World Council for the Peoples World Convention*] ... CMACP
Conseil Mondial de la Paix [*World Council of Peace*] ... CMP
Conseil National du Patronat Francais [*France*] ... CNPF
Conseil National de Recherches Canada [*National Research Council Canada*] ... CNRC
Conseil National de la Resistance [*France*] ... CNR
Conseil National de la Revolution Algerienne [*National Council of the Algerian Revolution*] ... CNRA
Conseil National de la Revolution de la Guinee Dite Portugaise [*National Revolutionary Council of So-called Portuguese Guinea*] ... CNRG
Conseil Oecumenique des Eglises [*World Council of Churches*] ... COE
Conseil des Organisations Internationales Directement Interessees a l'Enfance et a l'Adolescence [*Council of International Organizations Directly Interested in Children and Youth*] ... COIDIEA
Conseil des Organizations Syndicales d'Union Francaise [*Council of Labor Unions of the French Union*] ... COSOF
Conseil Parlementaire du Mouvement Europeen ... CPME
Conseil de la Recherche et du Developpement Forestiers du Quebec Etude [*A publication*] ... Cons Rech Dev For Que Etude
Conseil Regional de Developpement, Trois-Rivieres, PQ, Canada [*Library symbol*] ... CaQTCRD
Conseil Scientifique pour l'Afrique au Sud de Sahara [*Scientific Council for Africa South of the Sahara*] ... CSA
Conseil Scientifique International de Recherches sur les Trypanosomiases [*A publication*] ... Cons Sci Int Rech Trypanosomiases
Conseil Superieur de Livre [*Canada*] ... CSL
Conseiller du Commerce Exterieur [*A publication*] ... Cons Com Ext
Conseiller de la Reine [*Queen's Counsel*] [*Canada*] ... CR
Consejo Estatal de Azucar [*Sugar Council*] [*Dominican Republic*] ... CEA
Consejo Interamericano de Comercio y Produccion [*Interamerican Council of Commerce and Production*] ... CICYP
Consejo Interamericano Economico-Social [*Inter-American Economic and Social Council*] ... CIES
Consejo Interamericano para la Educacion, la Ciencia, y la Cultura [*Inter-American Council for Education, Science, and Culture*] ... CIECC
Consejo Interamericano de Musica [*Inter-American Music Council*] ... CIDEM
Consejo Internacional de Buena Vecindad [*International Good Neighbor Council - IGNC*] ... CIBV
Consejo Internacional de Mujeres [*International Council of Women*] ... CIM
Consejo Internacional de la Pelicula de Ensenanza [*International Council for Educational Films*] ... CIPE
Consejo Latinamericano de Escuelas de Administracion [*Latin American Council of Schools of Administration*] ... CLADEA
Consejo Mundial de Artes y Oficios [*World Crafts Council*] ... CMAO
Consejo Nacional de Ciencia y Tecnologia [*Mexico*] ... CONACYT
Consejo Nacional de Investigaciones Cientificas y Tecnicas [*Argentina*] ... CNICT
Consejo Oleicola Internacional [*International Olive Oil Council*] ... COI
Consejo Superior de Investigaciones Cientificas [*Madrid*] [*A publication*] ... CSIC
Consejo Superior de Investigaciones Cientificas. Biblioteca General. Boletin [*Madrid*] [*A publication*] ... Consejo Sup Invest Cient Bibl Bol
Consejo Superior de Investigaciones Cientificas. Estudios Geologicos [*Madrid*] [*A publication*] ... CSIC Estud Geol
Conselho de Desenvolvimento Economico de Sergipe [*State of Sergipe, Brazil*] ... CONDESE
Conselho de Desenvolvimento do Estado [*Brazil*] ... CDE
Conselho Estadual de Agricultura [*Brazil*] ... CEAGRI
Conselho Estadual de Cultura [*A publication*] ... CEC
Conselho Nacional de Pesquisas [*Brazil*] ... CNPq
Conselho Nacional do Trabalho [*Brazil*] ... CNT

Consensus Voluntary Reference Compound [*Environmental science*] .... CVRC
Consequence .... CONS
Conserva [*Conserve*] [*Pharmacy*] .... CONS
Conservation .... CON
Conservation .... CONSERV
Conservation Analytical Laboratory [*Smithsonian Institution*] .... CAL
Conservation Education Association .... CEA
Conservation, Exploration, Diving, Archeology, Museums [*Acronym is used as name of an international organization interested in these five subjects*] .... CEDAM
Conservation Foundation .... CF
Conservation Law Society of America [*Defunct*] .... CLSA
Conservation League CL
Conservation Materials and Services .... CMS
Conservation and Recycling [*A publication*] .... Conserv & Recycling
Conservation and Renewable Energy Inquiry and Referral Service .... CAREIRS
Conservation and Renewable Energy Program [*Department of Energy*] .... C & RE
Conservation Reporting and Evaluation System [*Department of Agriculture*] .... CRES
Conservation and Research Foundation .... CRF
Conservation Research Report [*A publication*] .... CRR
Conservation Research Report. United States Department of Agriculture. Agricultural Research Service [*A publication*] .... Conserv Res Rep US Dep Agric Agric Res Serv
Conservation Reserve Program .... CRP
Conservation Voltage Reduction [*Public Utilities Commission*] .... CVR
Conservation Volunteer [*A publication*] .... Conserv Volunteer
Conservationist [*A publication*] .... Conserv
Conservative [*Politics*] C
Conservative .... CONS
Conservative Baptist Association of America .... CBAA
Conservative Baptist Foreign Mission Society .... CBFMS
Conservative Baptist Home Mission Society .... CBHMS
Conservative Baptist Theological Seminary, Denver, CO [*Library symbol*] .... CoDCB
Conservative Baptist Theological Seminary, Englewood, CO [*OCLC symbol*] .... CBS
Conservative Book Club .... CBC
[*The*] **Conservative Caucus** [*An association*] .... TCC
[*The*] **Conservative Caucus Research, Analysis, and Education Foundation** .... TCCRAEF
Conservative Clubs of America .... CCA
Conservative Democratic Forum .... CDF
Conservative Judaism [*A publication*] .... CJ
Conservative Library Association [*Defunct*] .... CLA
Conservative and National Liberal Party [*British*] .... CNL
Conservative Nationalist Party [*British*] .... CN
Conservative Party .... CP
Conservative Party's Defense Committee [*British*] .... CPDC
Conservative Political Centre [*British*] .... CPC
Conservative Review [*A publication*] .... Conserv R
Conservative Society of America .... CSA
Conservative Trade Unionists [*British*] .... CTU
Conservatives Against Liberal Legislation .... CALL
Conservatives for a Constitutional Convention CCC
Conservatoire d'Art Dramatique du Quebec, Montreal, PQ, Canada [*Library symbol*] .... CaQMCADQ
Conservatoire de Musique du Quebec, Quebec, PQ, Canada [*Library symbol*] .... CaQQCMQ
Conservatory .... CONSERV
Conservatory .... CONSV
Conserve .... CONSV
Conserve e Derivati Agrumari [*A publication*] .... Conserve Deriv Agrum
Conserved Vector Current CVC
Conservez Taxe Payee [*Retain Charge Paid*] [*French*] .... CTP
Consider .... CONS
Consider .... CSDR
Consider Yourself Kissed [*Correspondence*] .... CYK
Considerable .... CSDRBL
Consideration .... CON
Consideration .... CONSON
Consiglio Nazionale delle Ricerche [*National Research Council*] [*Italy*] .... CNDR
Consiglio Nazionale delle Ricerche [*National Research Council*] [*Italy*] .... CNR
Consiglio Nazionale delle Ricerche, Rome, Italy [*Library symbol*] .... ItRC
Consign .... CONS
Consigna [*A publication*] .... Cons
Consignment .... CONSGT
Consignment Item Request .... CIR
Consignment Note [*Business and trade*] .... CN
Consiliul Central al Sindicatelor [*Central Council of Trade Unions*] [*Romania*] .... CCS
Consist .... CONS
Consist Of .... C/O
Consistency .... CNSISTY
Consistency Recording Controller .... CRC
Consistent .... CNSIST
Consistent .... CNSTNT
Consisting Of [*Freight*] .... CON OF
Consociatio Internationalis Musicae Sacrae .... CIMS
Consoer, Townsend & Associates, Chicago, IL [*Library symbol*] .... ICCT
Consol Synthetic Fuel [*Coal liquefaction process*] .... CSF
Consolan Facility [*Aviation*] .... CONSO
Consolata Missionary Sisters [*Roman Catholic religious order*] .... MC
Console .... CNSL
Console [*Data processing*] .... CONS
Console .... CSL
Console Action Processor .... CAP
Console Communication System .... CCS
Console to Computer Buffer .... CCB
Console Computer Interface Adapter .... CCIA
Console Digital Display Programer .... CDDP
Console Intelligence Unit .... CIU
Console Message Processor [*Data processing*] .... CMP
Console Operating System .... COS
Console Operator Proficiency Examination .... COPE
Console for Optical Measurement and Precise Analysis of Radiation from Electronics .... COMPARE
Console-Oriented Model Building [*Data processing*] .... COMB
Console-Oriented Statistical Matrix Operator System [*Data processing*] .... COSMOS
Console Processor .... CP
Console Set Group .... CSG
Console Simulator [*Data processing*] .... CONSIM
Consolidate .... CNSLD
Consolidate .... CONS
Consolidate .... CONSOL
Consolidate .... CSLDT
Consolidate Time Rate .... CTR
Consolidated .... CON
Consolidated Accelerated Navy Documentation Organization .... CAN DO
Consolidated Administrative Management Organization [*AID*] .... CAMO
Consolidated Advance Field Teams .... CAFT
Consolidated Aerospace Equipment List .... CAEL
Consolidated Aerospace Ground Equipment List .... CAGEL
Consolidated Aerospace Supplier Evaluation .... CASE
Consolidated Air Mission Results Analysis .... CAMRA
Consolidated Air Target Material Notices [*NOO*] .... CATMN
Consolidated Air Tour Manual [*Air travel term*] .... CATM
Consolidated Aircraft Corporation [*Later, General Dynamics Corp.*] .... CAC
Consolidated Aircraft Maintenance .... CAM
Consolidated Airways, Inc. [*Houston, TX*] [*FAA designator*] .... CLD
Consolidated Analysis Centers, Incorporated .... CACI
Consolidated Antijam Equipment .... CAJE
Consolidated Aquanauts Vital Equipment .... CAVE
Consolidated Army System for Processing Entitlements to Reservists .... CASPER
Consolidated Assistance and Relocation Efforts .... CARE
Consolidated Athletic Commission .... CAC
Consolidated Atomic Time .... CAT
Consolidated Balance Sheet .... CBS
Consolidated Base Personnel Office [*Air Force*] .... CBPO
Consolidated Base Personnel Office Letter [*Air Force*] .... CBPOL
Consolidated Capital Income Trust [*NASDAQ symbol*] .... CCITS
Consolidated Capital Realty Investors [*NASDAQ symbol*] .... CCPLS
Consolidated Capital Special Trust [*NASDAQ symbol*] .... CCSTS
Consolidated Carriers Tariff Bureau .... CCTB
Consolidated Cigar Corp. [*NYSE symbol*] [*Delisted*] .... CDR
Consolidated Cinola Mines [*NASDAQ symbol*] .... CCIMF
Consolidated Communications Recording Facility .... CCRF
Consolidated Computer and Control Center CCCC
Consolidated Cryptologic Program [*DoD*] .... CCP
Consolidated Defense Intelligence Program .... CDIP
Consolidated Defense Supply Material .... CDSM
Consolidated Delivery Status Report .... CDSR
Consolidated Delivery Status Report System .... CDSRS
Consolidated Edison Co., Inc., New York, NY [*Library symbol*] .... NNConE
Consolidated Edison Co. of New York, Inc. [*NYSE symbol*] .... ED
Consolidated Edison Thorium Reactor .... CETR
Consolidated Eglin Real-Time System .... CERTS
Consolidated Electrodynamics Corporation .... CEC
Consolidated Electronics Corporation .... CEC
Consolidated Electronics Industries Corp. [*NYSE symbol*] [*Delisted*] .... CEI
Consolidated Engineering Technology Corporation .... CETEC
Consolidated Equities [*NASDAQ symbol*] .... CNEG
Consolidated Facilities Corp. [*Railroads*] .... CONFAC
Consolidated Federal Law Enforcement Training Center [*Later, FLETC*] [*Department of the Treasury*] .... CFLETC
Consolidated Fibres, Inc. [*NASDAQ symbol*] .... CFIB
Consolidated Flight Record Custodian [*Air Force*] .... CFRC
Consolidated Foods Corp. [*NYSE symbol*] .... CFD
Consolidated Freight Classification .... CFC
Consolidated Freight Classification [*A publication*] .... Consol Frt Classif
Consolidated Freightways, Inc. [*NYSE symbol*] .... CNF
Consolidated Function Ordinary [*IBM Corp.*] .... CFO
Consolidated Funds Ordinary [*Insurance*] .... CFO
Consolidated Gas Supply Corp., Chelyan, WV [*Library symbol*] .... WvCheC
Consolidated Gas Supply Corp., Clarksburg, WV [*Library symbol*] .... WvClC

Consolidated Gold Fields [*British*] .... CGF
Consolidated Gold Fields [*British*] .... CONSGOLD
Consolidated Guidance .... CG
Consolidated Hazardous Item List .... CHIL
Consolidated Index of Translations into English .... CITE
Consolidated Industrial Relations Office .... CIRO
Consolidated Instrument Package [*Atmospheric research*] .... CIP
Consolidated Intelligence Program .... CIP
Consolidated Intelligence Resource Information System [*Air Force*] .... CIRIS
Consolidated Interchangeable and Substitute Item List .... CISIL
Consolidated Labor Union of the Philippines .... CLUP
Consolidated Limit Order Book [*Stock market*] .... CLOB
Consolidated Listing CL
Consolidated Logistics Information Planning and Programing Requirements .... CLIPPR
Consolidated Mail Room [*Air Force*] .... CMR
Consolidated Management Office [*Military*] .... CMO
Consolidated Master Cross-Reference List [*Defense Supply Agency*] .... CMCRL
Consolidated Master Cross Reference List [*A publication*] .... CMRL
Consolidated Material Distribution Objectives [*Air Force*] .... CMDO
Consolidated Material List .... CML
Consolidated Metropolitan Statistical Area [*Census Bureau*] .... CMSA
Consolidated Mining & Smelting Co., Central Technical Library, Trail, BC, Canada [*Library symbol*] .... CaBTC
Consolidated National Interveners [*An association*] .... CNI
Consolidated Natural Gas Co. [*NYSE symbol*] .... CNG
Consolidated Nuclear Steam Generator .... CNSG
Consolidated Oil & Gas, Inc. [*American Stock Exchange symbol*] .... CGS
Consolidated Operability Test [*or Trial*] .... COT
Consolidated Ordnance Allowance List [*Navy*] .... COAL
Consolidated Papers, Inc. [*NASDAQ symbol*] .... CPER
Consolidated Pilot Training Program [*Air Force*] .... CPT
Consolidated Professor Mines [*NASDAQ symbol*] .... CPFTF
Consolidated Programing Document .... CPD
Consolidated Progress Report .... CPR
Consolidated Rail Corp. [*Also, CR, CRC*] .... CONRAIL
Consolidated Rail Corp. [*AAR code*] [*Also, CONRAIL, CRC*] .... CR
Consolidated Rail Corporation [*Also, CR, CONRAIL*] .... CRC
Consolidated Rail Corp. (Eastern District) [*AAR code*] .... CRE
Consolidated Record Communications Center [*Army*] .... CRCC
Consolidated Refining Co., Inc. [*American Stock Exchange symbol*] [*Delisted*] .... CDR
Consolidated Repairable Item List .... CRIL
Consolidated Report .... CR
Consolidated Reporting and Evaluating System, Tactical [*Computer program*] [*Air Force*] .... CREST
Consolidated Reserve Components Reporting System .... CORCAPS
Consolidated Reserve Personnel Office [*Air Force*] .... CRPO
Consolidated RVNAF [*Republic of Vietnam Armed Forces*] **Improvement and Modernization Program** .... CRIMP
Consolidated Ship Electronic Design [*Navy*] .... CSED
Consolidated Site Base Loading .... CSBL
Consolidated Space Operations Center [*Military*] .... CSOC
Consolidated Special Information Dissemination Office [*Proposed for military intelligence gathering, late 1940's, but never activated*] .... CONSIDO
Consolidated Spot [*TV*] **Buying** [*General Foods advertising*] .... CSB
Consolidated Standing Route Order [*Army*] .... CSRO
Consolidated Stock Status Report .... CSSR
Consolidated Surplus Sales Office [*Military - Merged with Defense Supply Agency*] .... CSSO
Consolidated Tape Association .... CTA
Consolidated Telecommunications Program .... CTP
Consolidated Telemetry Checkout System [*Air Force*] .... CTCS
Consolidated Tenants League .... CTL
Consolidated Textile Co. [*NYSE symbol*] [*Delisted*] .... CTX
Consolidated Tomoka Land [*NASDAQ symbol*] .... CTLC
Consolidated Translation Survey [*CIA*] .... CTS
Consolidated Unit Personnel Section .... CUPS
Consolidated Vacuum Corp., Rochester, NY [*Library symbol*] .... NRCV
Consolidated-Vultee Aircraft Corp. [*Later, General Dynamics Corp.*] .... CONVAIR
Consolidated-Vultee Aircraft Corporation [*Later, General Dynamics Corp.*] .... CVAC
Consolidated Western Steel .... CWS
Consolidating Station .... CSTA
Consolidation Above Battalion Level [*Army*] .... CABL
Consolidation Coal - Bethlehem Steel - National Steel - Republic Steel [*Coke pellet process developed by four-company group of steel and coke producers*] .... CONSOL-BNR
Consolidation Coal Co. [*NYSE symbol*] [*Delisted*] .... CSC
Consolidation Exercise [*Military*] .... CONSOLEX
Consolidation of Military Pay Services [*Strategic Air Command proposal*] .... COMPS
Consolidation of Military Personnel Activities at Fixed Installations .... COMPACT
Consolidation of Pay and Personnel Functions [*Military*] .... COPPER
Consolidation of Supply and Maintenance Regulations [*Military*] .... COSAMREG
Consonant .... CONS
Consonant-Vowel CV
Consonant-Vowel-Consonant [*Form used in verbal learning and conditioning studies involving meaningfulness of nonsense syllables*] CVC
Consort Coarse Servo .... CCS
Consort Observation Time .... COT
Consort Parallax Servo .... CXS
Consort Speed Servo .... CSS
Consortia of London Boroughs [*British*] .... CLB
Consortium C
Consortium of Academic and Special Libraries in Montana [*Library network*] .... CASLIM
Consortium for an Advanced Silent Transport .... CAST
Consortium for the Advancement of Physics Education .... CAPE
Consortium of Central Massachusetts Health Related Libraries [*Library network*] .... CCMHRL
Consortium on Chemical Information [*British*] .... COCI
Consortium for Continental Reflection Profiling .... COCORP
Consortium for Continuing Higher Education - Librarians' Networking Committee [*Library network*] .... CCHENV-LNC
Consortium on Financing Higher Education .... COFHE
Consortium of Graduate Liberal Studies Programs .... CGLSP
Consortium for Graduate Study in Business for Negroes [*Later, CGSM*] .... CGSBN
Consortium for Graduate Study in Management [*Formerly, CGSBN*] .... CGSM
Consortium for Health Information and Library Sciences [*Library network*] .... CHI
Consortium for Information Resources, Framingham, MA [*OCLC symbol*] .... CIR
Consortium for International Cooperation in Higher Education .... CICHE
Consortium on International Development .... CID
Consortium of Jazz Organizations and Artists [*Later, AJA*] .... CJOA
Consortium of Latin American Studies Programs .... CLASP
Consortium on Peace Research, Education, and Development .... COPRED
Consortium for Peaceful Coexistence .... CPC
Consortium Perfectae Caritatis [*Association of Perfect Love*] .... CPC
Consortium of Professional Associations to Supervise Studies of Special Programs for the Improvement of Instruction in American Education .... CONPASS
Consortium of Publishers for Employment .... COPE
Consortium of Regional Environmental Education Councils .... CREEC
Consortium Research Development [*Office of Education*] .... CORD
Consortium of Rhode Island Academic and Research Libraries [*Library network*] .... CRIARL
Consortium for Sharing Instructional Materials [*Library network*] .... CSIM
Consortium of Social Science Associations .... COSSA
Consortium on Soils of the Tropics .... CST
Consortium for the Study of Intelligence .... CSI
Consortium of Universities of the Metropolitan Washington Area .... CUMWA
Consortium of University Film Centers [*Library network*] .... CUFC
Consorzio Interuniversitario Lombardo per l'Elaborazione Automatica [*Lombard Interuniversity Consortium for Data Processing*] [*Italy*] [*Information service*] .... CILEA
Conspergere [*Dust or Sprinkle*] [*Pharmacy*] .... CONSPERG
Conspicuity Enhancement [*Aviation*] .... CE
Conspicuous .... conspic
Conspicuous Gallantry Medal [*British*] .... CGM
Conspicuous Service Cross [*British*] .... CSC
Conspicuously .... CNSP
Constable C
Constable .... CONS
Constable .... CONST
Constable on Patrol .... COP
Constabulary .... CONSTAB
Constant C
Constant .... CONST
Constant .... K
Constant Absolute Vorticity Trajectory .... CAVT
Constant-Adjustment Matrix, Flexible-Accelerator Path [*Economic theory*] .... CFAP
Constant Alert Cycle .... CAC
Constant Altitude Glide .... CAG
Constant Altitude Plan Position Indicator [*Aviation*] .... CAPPI
Constant Amplitude .... CA
Constant Angular Velocity .... CAV
Constant Axial Offset Control .... CAOC
Constant Bandwidth .... CB
Constant Bandwidth .... CBW
Constant BIT [*Binary Digit*] **Density** [*Control feature of magnetic tape recorders*] [*Data processing*] .... CBD
Constant Boiling Mixture .... CBM
Constant Boiling Point .... CBP
Constant-Choice Perceptual Maze Test .... CCPM
Constant-Control Oil Pressure .... CCOP
Constant Current Flux Reset .... CCFR
Constant Current Fringes .... CDF
Constant Current Generator .... CCG
Constant Current Modulation .... CCM

Constant Current Transformer ... CCT
Constant Delay Line ... CDL
Constant Delta Height [*Aerospace*] ... CDH
Constant-Depth Temperature Sensor [*Oceanography*] ... CDTS
Constant Deviation Prism ... CDP
Constant Differential Height [*Aerospace*] ... CDH
Constant Dose Range [*Radiation in atmosphere*] ... CDR
Constant Elasticity of Substitution [*Industrial production*] ... CES
Constant Energy Differences ... CED
Constant False Alarm Probability [*Military*] ... CFAP
Constant False Alarm Rate [*Military*] ... CFAR
Constant Feed Lubricator ... CFL
Constant-Flow/High Pressure [*Oxygen system*] ... CF/HP
Constant Frequency [*Electronics*] ... CF
Constant Frequency Variable Dot ... CFVD
Constant Hazard Ratio ... CHR
Constant Heat Summation ... CHS
Constant Hot Water [*British*] ... CHW
Constant Impedance Mechanical Modulation ... CIMM
Constant Level Balloon ... CLB
Constant Level Speech ... CLS
Constant Misery [*Slang*] ... CM
Constant-Output Amplifier ... COA
Constant-Output Level Adapter ... COLA
Constant Potential ... CP
Constant Potential Accelerator ... CPA
Constant Pressure ... CP
Constant Property ... CP
Constant Purchasing Power ... CPP
Constant Rate of Heating ... CRH
Constant Rate Injector [*Instrumentation*] ... CRI
Constant Ratios of Elasticities of Substitution-Homothetic [*Statistics*] ... CRESH
Constant Region [*Immunochemistry*] ... C
Constant Returns to Scale [*Econometrics*] ... CRTS
Constant Ringing Drop [*Alarm system*] ... CRD
Constant Ringing Relay [*Alarm system*] ... CRR
[*The*] **Constant Society** ... TCS
Constant-Speed Drive/Starter ... CSDS
Constant-Speed Drives ... CSD
Constant Stimulus Difference [*Pair comparison*] [*Aircraft noise*] ... CSD
Constant Tangential Velocity ... CTV
Constant Temperature Anemometer System ... CTAS
Constant Temperature Circulator [*Instrumentation*] ... CTC
Constant Torque Compensation ... CTC
Constant Velocity Recording ... CVR
Constant-Viscosity [*Rubber*] ... CV
Constant Voltage/Constant Current ... CV/CC
Constant Voltage and Constant Frequency ... CVCF
Constant Voltage Reference ... CVR
Constant Voltage Transformer ... CVT
Constant Voltage Unit ... CVU
Constant Volume ... CV
Constant Volume Sampling [*ACF Industries*] ... CVS
Constant Wear ... CW
Constant-Wear Garment [*Apollo*] [*NASA*] ... CWG
Constanta [*Romania*] [*Airport symbol*] ... CND
Constantian Society ... CS
Constantine [*Algeria*] [*Airport symbol*] ... CZL
Constantinople [*Later, Istanbul*] [*Province in Turkey*] ... CPLE
Constants Board Assembly ... CBA
Constants Change Display ... CCD
Constituency ... CONST
Constituency ... CONSTIT
Constituency Proportion Distribution ... CPD
Constituent Assembly [*Vietnam*] ... CA
Constitution ... CONS
Constitution [*or Constitutional*] ... CONST
Constitution ... CONSTN
Constitution Parties of the United States [*An association*] ... CPUS
Constitutional ... CONSTL
Constitutional Aplastic Anemia [*Medicine*] ... CAA
Constitutional Convention ... CON-CON
Constitutional Educational League ... CEL
Constitutional Psychopathic Inferior ... CPI
Constitutional Psychopathic State ... CPS
Constitutional Revival [*An association*] ... CR
Constitutional Rights Foundation ... CRF
Constitutive Transcript [*Genetics*] ... CT
Constitutive Transcription Unit [*Genetics*] ... CTU
Constrained Optimal Design [*Data processing*] ... COD
Constrained Procedure ... CP
Constrained Structure Generation ... CONGEN
Constraint ... CONSTR
Constraint Control ... C/C
Construcciones Aeronauticas, Sociedad Anonima [*Spain*] ... CASA
Construct ... CONST
Constructeurs Europeens de Locomotives Thermiques et Electriques [*European Diesel and Electric Locomotive Manufacturers' Association*] ... CELTE
Constructia de Masini [*A publication*] ... Constru Masini
Constructing Contractor ... CC
Constructing Quartermaster [*Army*] ... CQM
Construction ... CONS
Construction ... CONSTR
Construction ... CONSTRN
Construction of Aircraft and Related Procurement ... CARP
Construction-Amenagement [*A publication*] ... Construct-Amenag
Construction Apprentice ... CP
Construction Assistance Vehicle [*Navy*] ... CAV
Construction Authorization ... CA
Construction Battalion [*Navy*] ... CB
Construction Battalion [*Navy*] ... CBN
Construction Battalion [*CB*] [*Acronym is a phonetic reference to a member of this Naval unit*] ... SEABEE
Construction Battalion [*USNR classification*] ... VCB
Construction Battalion Base Unit [*Obsolete*] [*Navy*] ... CBBU
Construction Battalion Center [*Navy*] ... CBC
Construction Battalion Detachment [*Navy*] ... CBD
Construction Battalion Maintenance Unit [*Navy*] ... CBMU
Construction Battalion Replacement Depot [*Navy*] ... CBRD
Construction Battalion Unit [*Navy*] ... CBU
Construction Battalions, Atlantic [*Navy*] ... CBLANT
Construction Battalions, Pacific [*Navy*] ... CBPAC
Construction Completion Date ... CCD
Construction Coordination Group ... CCG
Construction Corps ... CC
Construction Corps of the Philippines [*World War II*] ... CONCOR
Construction and Development ... C & D
Construction-Differential Subsidy [*Authorized by Merchant Marine Act of 1936*] ... CDS
Construction Discrepancy Report ... CDR
Construction Dollar Control System [*AT & T*] ... CDCS
Construction Dollar Spreading [*System*] [*AT & T*] ... CDS
Construction Electrician [*Navy rating*] ... CE
Construction Electrician, Chief [*Navy rating*] ... CEC
Construction Electrician, First Class [*Navy rating*] ... CE1
Construction Electrician, Master Chief [*Navy rating*] ... CECM
Construction Electrician Power [*Navy rating*] ... CEP
Construction Electrician, Second Class [*Navy rating*] ... CE2
Construction Electrician, Senior Chief [*Navy rating*] ... CECS
Construction Electrician Shop [*Navy rating*] ... CES
Construction Electrician Telephone [*Navy rating*] ... CET
Construction Electrician, Third Class [*Navy rating*] ... CE3
Construction Electrician Wiring [*Navy rating*] ... CEW
Construction Engineer ... CRENGR
Construction and Engineering [*Philippines*] [*A publication*] ... CE
Construction Engineering Research Laboratory [*Army*] ... CERL
Construction and Equipment ... C & E
Construction Equipment Advertisers [*Later, CEAPRC*] ... CEA
Construction Equipment Advertisers and Public Relations Council [*Formerly, CEA*] ... CEAPRC
Construction of Facilities [*NASA*] ... COF
Construction Financial Management Association ... CFMA
Construction Industry Collective Bargaining Commission [*Terminated, 1978*] [*Department of Labor*] ... CICBC
Construction Industry Commission [*Canada*] ... CIC
Construction Industry Development Council [*Canada*] ... CIDC
Construction Industry Foundation [*Defunct*] ... CIF
Construction Industry Joint Conference ... CIJC
Construction Industry Management Board ... CIMB
Construction Industry Manufacturers Association ... CIMA
Construction Industry Research and Information Association [*British*] ... CIRIA
Construction Industry Stabilization Committee [*Abolished, 1974*] ... CISC
Construction Industry Training Board ... CITB
Construction Industry Training Center ... CITC
Construction Industry Translation and Information Services [*Dublin, Ireland*] ... CITIS
Construction/Inspection Procedure ... C/IP
Construction Joint [*Technical drawings*] ... CJ
Construction and Machinery ... C & M
Construction and Machinery ... CM
Construction Machinery and Equipment [*A publication*] ... Constr Mach Equip
Construction Maintenance Supervisor ... CMS
Construction Management ... CM
Construction Management [*A publication*] ... CM
Construction Management Association of America ... CMAA
Construction Management Control System [*General Services Administration*] ... CMCS
Construction Mechanic [*Navy rating*] ... CM
Construction Mechanic, Automotive [*Navy rating*] ... CMA
Construction Mechanic, Chief [*Navy rating*] ... CMC
Construction Mechanic Construction [*Navy rating*] ... CMH
Construction Mechanic, First Class [*Navy rating*] ... CM1
Construction Mechanic, Master Chief [*Navy rating*] ... CMCM
Construction Mechanic, Second Class [*Navy rating*] ... CM2
Construction Mechanic, Senior Chief [*Navy rating*] ... CMCS
Construction Mechanic, Third Class [*Navy rating*] ... CM3
Construction Metallique [*A publication*] ... Constr Met
Construction Metallique [*A publication*] ... Constr Metal

Construction Methods [*A publication*] ... Constr Meth
Construction Methods and Equipment [*A publication*] ... Constr Methods Equip
Construction and Overhaul Testing ... COT
Construction Permit [*FCC*] ... CP
Construction Plant and Equipment [*A publication*] ... Constr Plant Equip
Construction Products Manufacturers Council [*Formerly, PC*] ... CPMC
Construction Project Alternative Selection Program [*Bell System*] ... CONPASP
Construction Recruit [*Navy*] ... CR
Construction and Repair ... CANDR
Construction and Repair [*Coast Guard*] ... C and R
Construction and Repair, Alteration [*Coast Guard*] ... CONALT
Construction Report, Building Permits [*A publication*] ... CRBP
Construction Report, Construction Activity [*A publication*] ... CRCA
Construction Report, Housing Starts [*A publication*] ... CRHS
Construction Requirements Review Committee ... CRRC
Construction Review [*A publication*] ... Constr R
Construction Review [*A publication*] ... CORE
Construction Scheduling and Coordination [*AT & T*] ... CSC
Construction Specifications Institute ... CSI
Construction Specifier [*A publication*] ... Constr Specifier
Construction Superintendent ... CRSUPT
Construction Supervisor ... CRSUPVR
Construction Surveyors Institute ... CSI
Construction Test Procedure ... CTP
Construction Training Unit ... CTU
Construction Unit [*Data processing*] ... CU
Construction Work in Progress ... CWIP
Construction Writers Association ... CWA
Constructional Review [*A publication*] ... Constr Rev
Constructionman [*Nonrated enlisted man*] [*Navy*] ... CN
Constructionman, Apprentice [*Navy rating*] ... CA
Constructionman, Apprentice Builder, Striker [*Navy rating*] ... BUCA
Constructionman Apprentice, Construction Electrician, Striker [*Navy rating*] ... CECA
Constructionman Apprentice, Construction Mechanic, Striker [*Navy rating*] ... CMCA
Constructionman Apprentice, Engineering Aid, Striker [*Navy rating*] ... EACA
Constructionman Apprentice, Equipment Operator, Striker [*Navy rating*] ... EOCA
Constructionman Apprentice, Steelworker, Striker [*Navy rating*] ... SWCA
Constructionman Apprentice, Utilitiesman, Striker [*Navy rating*] ... UTCA
Constructionman, Construction Electrician, Striker [*Navy rating*] ... CECN
Constructionman, Construction Mechanic, Striker [*Navy rating*] ... CMCN
Constructionman, Engineering Aid, Striker [*Navy rating*] ... EACN
Constructionman, Equipment Operator, Striker [*Navy rating*] ... EOCN
Constructionman Recruit [*Navy*] ... CR
Constructionman, Steelworker, Striker [*Navy rating*] ... SWCN
Constructionman, Utilitiesman, Striker [*Navy rating*] ... UTCN
Constructive Action, Incorporated ... CAI
Constructive Dilemma [*Rule of inference*] [*Logic*] ... CD
Constructive Placement [*Railcar*] ... CP
Constructive Quarterly [*A publication*] ... Constr Q
Constructive Republican Alternative Programs [*Position papers on legislative issues prepared for Republican House leaders during Lyndon Johnson administration*] ... CRAP
Constructive Total Loss [*Business and trade*] ... CTL
Constructive Total Loss Only [*Business and trade*] ... CTLO
Constructores Navales Espanoles ... CONSTRUNAVES
Construtora e Incorporadora Eldorado ... CIEL
Consul ... C
Consul [*or Consulate*] ... CON
Consul ... CONS
Consul ... CS
Consul Corp. [*NASDAQ symbol*] ... CNSL
Consul General ... CG
Consul General ... CGEN
Consul General ... CONGEN
Consul-General ... CONS-GEN
Consular Agent ... CA
Consular Corps ... CC
Consular Declaration ... CD
Consular Invoice ... CI
Consular Law Society ... CLS
Consular Liaison Officer ... CLO
Consular Security Officer ... CSO
Consular Shipping Adviser ... CSA
Consular Shipping Advisor ... CONSA
Consulate ... C
Consules [*Consuls*] ... CC
Consules [*Consuls*] ... COSS
Consult [*Medicine*] ... CONS
Consultant ... CONSLTNT
Consultant ... CONSULT
Consultant-Adviser ... CA
Consultant Agreement ... CA
Consultant in Dental Surgery [*Medical Officer designation*] [*British*] ... C
Consultant-Initiated Activity [*LIMRA*] ... CIA
Consultant Report ... CR
Consultants and Consulting Organizations Directory [*A publication*] ... CCO
Consultation [*Medicine*] ... C
Consultation ... CONSULTN
Consultation on Church Union ... COCU
Consultative Committee on Administrative Questions [*United Nations*] ... CCAQ
Consultative Committee on the Definition of the Meter [*International Bureau of Weights and Measures*] ... CCDM
Consultative Committee for the Definition of the Second ... CCDS
Consultative Committee on Electricity [*International Bureau of Weights and Measures*] ... CCE
Consultative Committee on International Telegraphy and Telephony [*ITU*] ... CCITT
Consultative Committee on International Telephony [*Later, CCITT*] ... CCIT
Consultative Committee for Photometry and Radiometry [*International Committee on Weights and Measures*] ... CCPR
Consultative Committee for Postal Studies [*UPU*] ... CCPS
Consultative Committee for Public Information [*United Nations*] ... CCPI
Consultative Committee for the Standards of Measurement of Ionizing Radiations [*International Bureau of Weights and Measures*] ... CCEDMRI
Consultative Committee on Substantive Questions [*United Nations*] ... CCSQ
Consultative Committee on Thermometry [*International Bureau of Weights and Measures*] ... CCT
Consultative Committee for Units [*International Bureau of Weights and Measures*] ... CCU
Consultative Council of Jewish Organizations ... CCJO
Consultative Group [*NATO*] ... CG
Consultative Group on Food Production and Investment in Developing Countries [*United Nations*] ... CGFPI
Consultative Group for International Agricultural Research [*World Bank, UN Development Programme, and UN Food and Agriculture Organization*] ... CGIAR
Consultative Group on Potentially Harmful Effects of Space Experiments ... CGOPHEOSE
Consultative Political Council [*Laos*] ... CPC
Consulting Chemists and Chemical Engineers ... CCCE
Consulting Engineer (London) [*A publication*] ... Consult Eng (London)
Consulting Engineer (St. Joseph, Michigan) [*A publication*] ... Consult Eng (St Joseph Mich)
Consulting Engineers Council [*Later, ACEC*] ... CEC
Consulting Teacher ... CT
Consumable Case Rocket ... CCR
Consumable-Electrode Vacuum-Arc Remelt [*Nuclear energy*] ... CEVAR
Consumable Electrode Vacuum Melting ... CEVM
Consumable Maintenance and Overhaul List ... CMOL
Consumable Maintenance and Overhaul Material List [*Navy*] ... CMOML
Consumable Vacuum Melt [*Steel*] ... CVM
Consumables Management ... CM
Consumables Status ... CS
Consumer ... CNSMR
Consumer ... CNSR
Consumer Action Now ... CAN
Consumer Affairs Clearinghouse ... CACH
Consumer Affairs Office [*Federal Energy Administration*] ... CAO
Consumer Aid Series [*National Highway Traffic Safety Administration*] ... CAS
Consumer Alert, Incorporated [*An association*] ... CAI
Consumer Bankers Association ... CBA
Consumer Briefing Summary [*A publication*] ... Consum Brief Summ
Consumer Buying Expectations Survey [*Formerly, Quarterly Survey of Intentions*] [*Bureau of the Census*] ... CBE
Consumer Buying Prospects [*A publication*] ... Consumer Buying Prosp
Consumer Choice Health Plan ... CCHP
Consumer Coalition for Health ... CCH
Consumer Commission on the Accreditation of Health Services ... CCAHS
Consumer Complaint Guide ... CCG
Consumer Confidence Index [*Conference Board*] ... CCI
Consumer and Corporate Affairs Department [*Canada*] ... CCA
Consumer Council [*American National Standards Institute*] ... CC
Consumer Credit Counselors ... CCC
Consumer Credit Insurance Association ... CCIA
Consumer Credit Project ... CCP
Consumer Credit Protection Act [*1969*] ... CCPA
Consumer Demographics, Incorporated [*Information service*] ... CDI
Consumer Economic Study Report [*Department of Agriculture*] ... CESR
Consumer Education and Information Liaison [*Federal interagency group*] ... CEIL
Consumer Education Research Center [*Formerly, CERG*] ... CERC
Consumer Education Research Group [*Later, CERC*] ... CERG
Consumer Education Resource Network ... CERN
Consumer Energy Council of America ... CECA
Consumer and Environmental Health Services Administration [*HEW*] ... CEHSA
Consumer Expenditure Survey ... CESR
Consumer Federation of America ... CFA
Consumer Goods System [*Data processing*] ... COGS
Consumer Health Information Program and Services [*LSCA*] ... CHIPS
Consumer Health Perspectives [*A publication*] ... Consum Health Perspect

Consumer Help on the Individual's Conservation of Energy [Student legal action organization]............CHOICE
Consumer Information Association............CIA
Consumer Information Center [of the General Services Administration]............CIC
Consumer Information Regulation [National Highway Traffic Safety Administration]............CIR
Consumer Information Series [National Bureau of Standards]............CIS
Consumer Interests Foundation............CIF
Consumer Level Quality Audit Program............COLEQUAP
Consumer Level Quality Audit Program............COLQUAP
Consumer and Marketing Service [Later, AMS] [Department of Agriculture]............C & MS
Consumer and Marketing Service [Later, AMS] [Department of Agriculture]............CMS
Consumer and Marketing Service, Service and Regulatory Announcements [Later, AMS] [Department of Agriculture]............C & MSSRA
Consumer News [A publication]............Cons N
Consumer Price Index [Economics]............CPI
Consumer Price Index for Services............CPIS
Consumer Product Information Center............CPIC
Consumer Product Safety Act............CPSA
Consumer Product Safety Commission [Federal agency]............CPSC
Consumer Product Safety Commission, Washington, DC [OCLC symbol]............CPR
Consumer Products Information Index [National Bureau of Standards]............CPII
Consumer and Professional Relations Division [of HIAA] [Formerly, HIC]............CPRD
Consumer Protection Act............CPA
Consumer Protection Agency............CPA
Consumer Protection Center............CPC
Consumer Protection and Environmental Health Service [Later, Environmental Health Service] [US government]............CPEHS
Consumer Purchasing Service............CPS
Consumer Reports [A publication]............Consmr Rpt
Consumer Reports [A publication]............Cons Rep
Consumer Reports [A publication]............Consumer Rep
Consumer Reports [A publication]............Consum Rep
Consumer Research Bulletin [A publication]............CR
Consumer Safety Glazing Committee............CSGC
Consumer Services Organization............CSO
Consumer Sourcebook [A publication]............CS
Consumer Survival Kit [Program on public TV]............CSK
Consumer Value Stores............CVS
Consumers' Advisory Board............CAB
Consumer's Advisory Council............CAC
Consumers' Association of Canada............CAC
Consumers' Association of Jamaica............CAJ
Consumers' Association of Trinidad and Tobago............CATT
Consumers Cooperative Association [Later, Farmland Industries]............CCA
Consumers Education and Protective Association International............CEPA
Consumers Financial Corp. [NASDAQ symbol]............CFIN
Consumer's Index [A publication]............Consum Ind
Consumers Opposed to Inflation in the Necessities............COIN
Consumers Organization for the Hearing Impaired............COHI
Consumers Power Co. [NYSE symbol]............CMS
Consumers Public Power District............CPPD
Consumer's Reliability Risk............CRR
Consumers' Research [Service reporting results of tests on consumers' goods]............CR
Consumers' Research Magazine [A publication]............Con Res Mag
Consumers and Taxpayers............CONTAX
Consumers Union of United States............CU
Consumers Water Co. [NASDAQ symbol]............CONW
Consumers for World Trade............CWT
Consumption Data Exchange............CDE
Consumption Entry [Business and trade]............CE
Consumption Levels Enquiry [British]............CLE
Contact............C
Contact [A publication]............CNTA
Contact............CNTC
Contact [A publication]............Con
Contact............CONT
Contact............CTC
Contact Analog [Submarine instrumentation]............CONALOG
Contact Analog Flight Display............CAFD
Contact Approach [Aviation]............CT
Contact Approach Control [Aviation]............CAC
Contact Area Commander............CAC
Contact Area Summary Position Estimate Report [Military]............CASPER
Contact Center [Aviation]............CTCEN
Contact Center Control [Aviation]............CTCC
Contact Closure............CC
Contact Conversion Exercise [Military]............CONVERSIONEX
Contact Dermatitis [Medicine]............CD
Contact Evaluation Plot............CEP
Contact Flight Rules [Same as VFR] [Meteorology]............CFR
Contact Glow Discharge Electrolysis............CGDE

Contact and Intraocular Lens Medical Journal [A publication]............Contact Intraocul Lens Med J
Contact Ion Thruster............CIT
Contact. Journal of Urban and Environmental Affairs [A publication]............Contact J Urban Environ Aff
Contact Karate............C-K
Contact Lens Association of Ophthalmologists............CLAO
Contact Lens Association for Optometry............CLAO
Contact-Lens-Induced Keratoconjunctivitis [Ophthalmology]............CLK
Contact Lens Manufacturers Association............CLMA
Contact Lens Medical Bulletin [A publication]............Contact Lens Med Bull
Contact Lens Society of America............CLSA
Contact Lens Society of America. Journal [A publication]............Contact Lens Soc Am J
Contact Lost [RADAR]............CL
Contact Maker............CM
Contact-Making Ammeter............CMA
Contact-Making Clock............CMC
Contact-Making Voltmeter............CMVM
Contact Party [Army]............CONPY
Contact Party............CP
Contact Personality Factor Test [Psychology]............CPFT
Contact Potential Difference............CPD
Contact Soil Sampling Device [Aerospace]............CSSD
Contact Teleministries USA [An association]............CTUSA
Contact Tension............CT
Contactair Flugdienst & Co. [ICAO designator]............KI
Contactless Vacuum Controller............CVC
Contactor............CNTOR
Contactor Control Relay............CCR
Contactor, Running............COR
Contactor, Starting............COS
Contadora [Panama] [Airport symbol]............OTD
Contagious............CONTAG
Contagious Diseases............CD
Contagious Diseases Act [British]............CDA
Contagious Equine Metritis............CEM
Contagious Pustular Dermatitis [Dermatology]............CPD
Contain............CNTN
Contained............CNTD
Contained............CONTD
Container............CNTNR
Container............CNTR
Container............CO
Container............CONT
Container............CONTNR
Container............CONTR
Container Anchorage Terminal............CAT
Container Automated Marking Systems............CAMS
Container and Chassis Identification and Reporting System [Military]............CCIRS
Container Consolidation Point............CCP
Container Corporation of America [Later, Marcor, Inc.]............CCA
Container Corp. of America [Later, Marcor, Inc.] [NYSE symbol]............CNR
Container Delivery System [Military]............CDS
Container Design Retrieval System............CDRS
Container for Export............CONEX
Container Express [Army]............CONEX
Container on Flatcar [Railroad]............COFC
Container Freight Station [Shipping]............CFS
Container Handling in Terminal Operations [Army study]............CHITO
Container Offloading and Transfer System............COTS
Container Over-the-Shore............COTS
Container Repair Building............CRB
Container Tariff............CT
Container Terminal [Shipping]............CT
Containerization Institute [Later, CII]............CI
Containerization and Intermodal Institute [Formerly, BPCI, CI]............CII
Containerized Ammunition Distribution System............CADS
Containerized Avionics Maintenance System............CAMS
Containers in Barrels or Boxes [Freight]............CNTRS BB
Containers and Packaging [A publication]............Cont & Packag
Containing............CONT
Containing............CONTG
Containment Atmosphere Dilution [Nuclear energy]............CAD
Containment Atmospheric Monitoring [Nuclear energy]............CAM
Containment Building [Nuclear energy]............CB
Containment Cooling System [Nuclear energy]............CCS
Containment Isolation A [Nuclear energy]............CIA
Containment Isolation B [Nuclear energy]............CIB
Containment Isolation System [Nuclear energy]............CIS
Containment Spray System [Nuclear energy]............CSS
Containment Support Fixture [Nuclear energy]............CSF
Containment Systems Experiment [Nuclear energy]............CSE
Contaminacion y Prevencion [A publication]............CyP
Contaminant Control Cartridge............CCC
Contaminant Control System............CCS
Contaminated............CONTAM
Contaminated Normal [Statistics]............CN
Contaminated Oil Settling Tank............COST
Contamination Control [A publication]............Contam Control

Contamination Control. Biomedical Environments [*A publication*] .... Contam Control Biomed Environ
Contamination-Decontamination Experiment [*Nuclear energy*] .... CDE
Contamination Index [*Medicine*] CI
Contamination Mode [*NASA*] .... CM
Contamination/Overpressure .... C/O
Contano [*Parts so marked to rest*] [*Music*] .... CONT
Conte Corrente [*Running Account*] .... C/C
Contemplate .... CONTEM
Contemplative Review [*A publication*] .... Contemp Rev
Contemporaneo [*A publication*] .... Contemp
Contemporaneous Reserve Requirements [*Banking*] .... CRR
Contemporary .... CONTEMP
Contemporary Agriculture [*A publication*] .... Contemp Agric
Contemporary Anesthesia Practice [*A publication*] .... Contemp Anesth Pract
Contemporary Asia Review [*A publication*] .... Contemp As R
Contemporary Authors [*A biographical reference book*] .... CA
Contemporary Authors: Permanent Series [*A publication*] .... CAP
Contemporary China [*A publication*] CC
Contemporary China [*A publication*] .... Contemp China
Contemporary Civilization [*University course*] CC
Contemporary Crisis [*A publication*] .... Contemp Crisis
Contemporary Drug Problems [*A publication*] .... Cont Drug P
Contemporary Drug Problems [*A publication*] .... Contemp Drug
Contemporary Drug Problems [*A publication*] .... Contemp Drug Prob
Contemporary Education [*A publication*] .... Cont Ed
Contemporary Education [*A publication*] .... Cont Educ
Contemporary Education [*A publication*] .... Contemp Ed
Contemporary Education [*A publication*] .... Contemp Educ
Contemporary Educational Psychology [*A publication*] .... Contemp Educ Psychol
Contemporary Entertainment Services [*Air carrier designation symbol*] .... CESX
Contemporary Evaluation Form [*Army*] .... CEF
Contemporary French Civilization [*A publication*] .... CFC
Contemporary Games [*A publication*] .... CG
Contemporary Historical Examination Current Operations [*Air Force*] .... CHECO
Contemporary Historical Vehicle Association .... CHVA
Contemporary Indian Literature [*A publication*] CIL
Contemporary Issues Clearinghouse CIC
Contemporary Issues Criticism [*A publication*] CIC
Contemporary Japan [*A publication*] .... CJap
Contemporary Jewish Record [*A publication*] .... Contemp Jewish Rec
Contemporary Jewish Record [*A publication*] .... Cont Jew Rec
Contemporary Keyboard [*A publication*] .... Cont Keybd
Contemporary Literary Criticism [*Reference publication; often pronounced "click"*] CLC
Contemporary Literature [*A publication*] .... ConL
Contemporary Literature [*A publication*] .... ConLit
Contemporary Literature [*A publication*] .... Contemp Lit
Contemporary Marxism [*A publication*] .... Contemp M
Contemporary Music Project [*Defunct*] .... CMP
Contemporary Music Society .... CMS
Contemporary Neurology Series [*A publication*] .... Contemp Neurol Ser
Contemporary Pharmacy Practice [*A publication*] .... Contemp Pharm Pract
Contemporary Physics [*A publication*] .... Contemp Phys
Contemporary Physics [*A publication*] .... Cont Phys
Contemporary Poetry [*A publication*] .... Con P
Contemporary Poetry [*A publication*] .... Cont P
Contemporary Poland [*A publication*] .... Contemp Poland
Contemporary Politics [*A publication*] .... Contemp Polit
Contemporary Problems in Cardiology [*A publication*] .... Contemp Probl Cardiol
Contemporary Psychoanalysis [*A publication*] .... Contemp Psychoanal
Contemporary Psychoanalysis [*A publication*] .... Cont Psycha
Contemporary Psychology [*A publication*] .... Contemp Psychol
Contemporary Psychology [*A publication*] .... Cont Psycho
Contemporary Religions in Japan [*A publication*] .... CRJ
Contemporary Review [*A publication*] .... ConR
Contemporary Review [*A publication*] .... Contemp
Contemporary Review [*A publication*] .... Contemp R
Contemporary Review [*A publication*] .... Cont R
Contemporary Review [*A publication*] .... CoR
Contemporary Review [*A publication*] .... CR
Contemporary Sociology [*A publication*] .... Contemp Sociol
Contemporary Sociology [*A publication*] .... Contemp Sociology
Contemporary Sociology [*A publication*] .... Cont Sociol
Contemporary Sociology [*A publication*] .... CS
Contemporary Surgery [*A publication*] .... Contemp Surg
Contemporary Theatre [*A publication*] .... CT
Contemporary Topics in Analytical and Clinical Chemistry [*A publication*] .... Contemp Top Anal Clin Chem
Contemporary Topics in Immunobiology [*A publication*] .... Contemp Top Immunobiol
Contemporary Topics in Molecular Immunology [*A publication*] .... Contemp Top Mol Immunol
Contemporary Writers in Christian Perspective [*A publication*] .... CWCP
Contempt [*FBI standardized term*] .... CMPT
Contempt of Court .... COC
Content-Addressable Memory [*Data processing*] .... CAM
Content-Addressable Parallel Processor [*Data processing*] .... CAPP
Content Indication Codes CIC
Contention Priority-Oriented Demand Assignment [*Protocol*] [*Data processing*] .... CPODA
Contents .... CONT
Contents of Contemporary Mathematical Journals [*A publication*] .... CCMJ
Contents of Current Legal Periodicals [*A publication*] .... CCLP
Contents of Recent Economics Journals [*A publication*] .... CREJ
Contents of Recent Economics Journals [*A publication*] .... Econ Cont
Contents of Selected Periodicals [*A publication*] .... CSP
Contents of Selected Periodicals - Technical [*A publication*] .... CSP-T
Contere [*Rub Together*] [*Pharmacy*] .... CONTER
Conterminous US Mineral Assessment Program [*Department of the Interior*] .... CUSMAP
Context Free .... CF
Context Free Language .... CFL
Context Free Syntactical Translator .... CFST
Context Industries, Inc. [*NASDAQ symbol*] .... CTEX
Context, Input, Process, Product [*Data processing*] .... CIPP
Contiguous Fisheries Zone [*Offshore*] .... CFZ
Contiguous Node Group Restoral Supervision and Switching .... CONGRESS
Continent .... CONT
Continent between Bordeaux and Hamburg [*Business and trade*] .... CB & H
Continent between Havre and Hamburg [*Business and trade*] .... CH & H
Continental [*Air mass*] C
Continental .... CON
Continental .... CONTL
Continental Advance Section [*Originally called Coastal Base Section*] [*World War II*] .... CONAD
Continental Advertising Agency Network [*Later, Advertising and Marketing International Network*] .... CAAN
Continental Africa Chamber of Commerce .... CACC
Continental Africa Project [*National Academy of Sciences*] .... CAP
Continental Air Command .... CAC
Continental Air Command .... CONAC
Continental Air Defense Command [*Discontinued, 1975*] .... CADC
Continental Air Defense Command [*Discontinued, 1975*] .... CONAD
Continental Air Defense Integration, North .... CADIN
Continental Air Defense Objectives Plan .... CADOP
Continental Air Defense System .... CADS
Continental Air Forces .... CAF
Continental Air Lines, Inc. [*ICAO designator*] .... CAL
Continental Air Lines, Inc. [*CAB official abbreviation*] .... CO
Continental Air Services .... CAS
Continental Airborne Reconnaissance for Damage Assessment [*Air Force*] .... CARDA
Continental Aircraft Control and Warning .... CAC & W
Continental Airways .... CA
Continental Airways and Communications Service [*Air Force*] .... CACS
Continental Army .... CONAR
Continental Army Command [*See CONARC*] .... CAC
Continental Army Command [*Responsible for induction, processing, training of active duty personnel*] [*Superseded by FORSCOM*] .... CONARC
Continental Army and Major Overseas Commands Systems [*Later, ASMIS*] .... CARMOCS
Continental Association of Funeral and Memorial Societies .... CAFMS
Continental Association of Resolute Employers .... CARE
Continental Assurance Co. .... CA
Continental Aviation & Engineering Corp. .... CAE
Continental Baking Co. [*NYSE symbol*] [*Wall Street slang name: "Coney Island"*] [*Delisted*] CI
Continental Ballistic Missile .... CBM
Continental Bancorp, Inc. [*NASDAQ symbol*] .... CBRP
Continental Base Section .... CBS
Continental Basketball Association .... CBA
Continental Carbon Co., Houston, TX [*Library symbol*] .... TxHCC
Continental Comment [*A publication*] .... Continentl
Continental Confederation of Adopted Indians .... CCAI
Continental Connector Corp. [*American Stock Exchange symbol*] [*Delisted*] .... CCE
Continental Control Area [*FAA*] .... CCA
Continental Corporation [*NYSE symbol*] CIC
Continental Divide [*FAA*] .... CONTDVD
Continental Divide Trail Society .... CDTS
Continental Division, Transport Control Center [*Military*] .... CTCC
Continental Dorset Club .... CDC
Continental Electronics Manufacturing Company .... CEMCO
Continental Entry Charts [*Air Force*] .... CEC
Continental Exercise [*Military*] .... CONEX
Continental Federal Savings & Loan [*NASDAQ symbol*] .... CONF
Continental Flood Basalt [*Geology*] .... CFB
Continental Football League .... CFL
Continental Group Co., Inc. [*Formerly, Continental Can Company*] [*NYSE symbol*] CCC
Continental Group Co., Inc., Chicago, IL [*Library symbol*] .... ICCon
Continental Health Affiliates [*NASDAQ symbol*] .... CTHL
Continental Health Care [*NASDAQ symbol*] .... CHSI
Continental Illinois Corp. [*NYSE symbol*] CIL
Continental Illinois Properties [*NYSE symbol*] .... CIE

Continental Illinois Realty [*NYSE symbol*] [*Delisted*]....CIR
Continental Information Systems Corp. [*NASDAQ symbol*]....CISY
Continental Insurance Co. [*NYSE symbol*] [*Wall Street slang name: "Coney Island Sand"*] [*Delisted*]....CIS
Continental Intelligence Data Processing System....CIDPS
Continental Investment Corp. [*NYSE symbol*] [*Delisted*]....COI
Continental Jet, Inc. [*Palm Springs, CA*] [*FAA designator*]....COJ
Continental Land Masses Air Traffic Control [*NASA*]....COLM/ATC
Continental Limits, United States....CLUS
Continental Limits, United States of America [*Navy*]....CLUSA
Continental Marines....CM
Continental Mark II Owner's Association....CMOA
Continental Materials Corp. [*American Stock Exchange symbol*]....CUO
Continental [*United States*] **Meteorological Teletype System** [*Navy*]....COMET
Continental Monthly [*A publication*]....Contin Mo
Continental Mortgage Investors [*NYSE symbol*] [*Delisted*]....CMI
Continental Motors Corp. [*NYSE symbol*] [*Delisted*]....CMR
Continental National America [*Insurance group*]....CNA
Continental-Oceanic [*Crust*] **Boundary** [*Geology*]....COB
Continental Offshore Stratigraphic Test [*Offshore oil technology*]....COST
Continental Oil, Atlantic Refining, Tidewater Oil, and Cities Service [*Group of companies joined together for mutual drilling ventures*]....CATC
Continental Oil Co. [*Ponca City, OK*] [*FAA designator*]....CON
Continental Oil Company....CONOCO
Continental Oil Co., R and D Technical Information Service, Ponca City, OK [*Library symbol*]....OkPoC
Continental Operations Range....COR
Continental Organization of Distributor Enterprises, Inc.....CODE
Continental Pharma [*Belgium*] [*Research code symbol*]....CP
Continental Polar Air Mass....CP
Continental Polar Air Mass....CPAM
Continental Service Corps....CSC
Continental Shelf....CONSHELF
Continental Shelf Crawler....CSC
Continental Shelf Mining....CSM
Continental Shelf Submersible [*Undersea exploration vehicle*]....CONSUB
Continental Shelf Wave....CSW
Continental Silver Corp. [*NASDAQ symbol*]....CTLSF
Continental Steel Corporation [*NASDAQ symbol*]....CSCS
Continental Steel Corp. [*NYSE symbol*] [*Delisted*]....CTL
Continental Telecom [*Formerly, Continental Telephone Corporation*] [*NYSE symbol*]....CTC
Continental Transportation Association....CTA
Continental Tropical Air Mass....CTAM
Continental, Union, Shell, and Superior [*Ocean drilling barge; named after oil companies that financed its development*]....CUSS I
Continental United States....CONUS
Continental United States....CUS
Continental United States Intelligence [*Domestic intelligence project*] [*Army*]....CONUS INTEL
Continental United States and the Military District of Washington [*Refers to the numbered armies in that area*]....CONUSAMDW
Continental United States Operations [*Army*]....CONOPS
Continental United States Over-the-Horizon [*RADAR system*]....CONUS OTH
Continental United States Over-the-Horizon-Backscatter [*RADAR system*]....CONUS OTH-B
Continental Wage Schedule [*Military*]....CWS
Contingencies of the Army....CA
Contingency....CNTGCY
Contingency....CONT
Contingency....CONTG
Contingency Amphibious Plan [*NATO*]....CAP
Contingency Analysis Model....CAM
Contingency and Confidential Intelligence....C & CI
Contingency Extravehicular Transfer [*NASA*]....CEVT
Contingency Landing Area [*NASA*]....CLA
Contingency Landing Site [*NASA*]....CLS
Contingency Landing Support Officer....CLSO
Contingency Lines of Communication, Europe [*Military*]....CLOCE
Contingency for Movement....CFM
Contingency Operations Plans Report....COPS
Contingency Orbit Insertion [*NASA*]....COI
Contingency Planning Aid....CPA
Contingency Planning Facilities Lists....CPFL
Contingency Planning Support Capability....CPSC
Contingency Relief Force [*Military*]....CRF
Contingency Rerouting of Communications [*NATO*]....CRDCS
Contingency Reserve [*British*]....CR
Contingency Response Program [*DoD*]....CORE
Contingency Sample [*NASA*]....CS
Contingency Support Center....CSC
Contingency Support Staff....CSS
Contingency Support Stocks [*Army*]....CONSSTOCS
Contingency Support Stocks [*Military*]....CONSTOCS
Contingency and Training [*Army*]....C & T
Contingency Transfer System [*Aerospace*]....CTS
Contingent Aftereffects [*Visual*]....CAE
Contingent Employee Liability Insurance....CELI
Contingent Liability Ledger [*DoD*]....CLL
Contingent Negative Variation [*Electrocortical measurement*]....CNV
Continuance....CONTCE
Continuation....CONTN
Continuation Clause....CC
Continuation Incentive Pay [*Proposed*] [*Army*]....COIN
Continuation-in-Part [*Patent application*]....CIP
Continue....CONT
Continue-Any [*Mode*] [*Data processing*]....CA
Continue Calling Until....CONCA
Continue to Hold [*Aviation*]....CONTH
Continue Present Duty [*Military*]....CONPRESDU
Continue-Specific [*Mode*] [*Data processing*]....CS
Continue Treatment [*Navy*]....CONTREAT
Continue Treatment [*Medicine*]....CT
Continued....CON
Continued....CONTD
Continued on Active Duty....COAD
Continued Lymphocyte Culture [*Immunology*]....CLC
Continuentur Remedia [*Continue the Medicines*] [*Pharmacy*]....CONT REM
Continuetur [*Let It Be Continued*] [*Pharmacy*]....CONTIN
Continuing Action Maintenance Instruction....CAMI
Continuing Balance System [*Army*]....CBS
Continuing Balance System - Expanded....CBS-X
Continuing Committee on Muslim-Christian Cooperation....CCMCC
Continuing Committee of the National Women's Conference [*Later, NW*]....CCNWC
Continuing Education....CE
Continuing Education Council [*Later, CNCE*]....CEC
Continuing Education Delivery Systems....CEDS
Continuing Education for Laboratory Technicians [*Union Carbide Co.*]....CELT
Continuing Education Learning Laboratory [*of Youth Pride, Inc.*]....CELL
Continuing Education Lectures (Society of Nuclear Medicine. Southeastern Chapter) [*A publication*]....Contin Edu Lect (Soc Nucl Med Southeast Chapter)
Continuing Education in Nursing Focus [*A publication*]....CE Focus
Continuing Education Program....CEP
Continuing Education Recognition Program [*For nurses*]....CERP
Continuing Education Service for State and Local Government Officials....CESSLGO
Continuing Education Unit [*American Management Association*]....CEU
Continuing Education for Young Women....CEYW
Continuing Legal Education....CLE
Continuing Library Education Network and Exchange [*Information service*]....CLENE
Continuing Library Education Planning and Advisory Project....COLEPAC
Continuing Medical Education....CME
Continuing Numerical Data Projects....CNDP
Continuing Property Records....CPR
Continuing Resolution Authority [*Military*]....CRA
Continuity Accept Limit....CAL
Continuity Check....CCHK
Continuity and Logic [*Unit*]....CONALOC
Continuity of Operations, Alaskan Air Command....COPAAC
Continuity of Operations Plan [*Army*]....COOP
Continuity of Operations Plan [*Navy*]....COOPLAN
Continuity of Operations Plan [*Military*]....COP
Continuity of Operations Plan, Department of the Air Force....COPDAF
Continuity of Operations Plan of the Joint Chiefs of Staff....COOP-JCS
Continuity Test Current....CTC
Continuous [*Aviation code*]....CNS
Continuous Acceleration Device....CAD
Continuous Accumulation of Coriolis Acceleration [*Bioscience*]....CACA
Continuous Action [*Acronym is brand of decongestant capsule*]....CONTAC
Continuous Air Monitor [*Nuclear energy*]....CAM
Continuous Air Monitoring Program [*or Project*] [*Environmental Protection Agency*]....CAMP
Continuous Air Patrol [*Proposed defense for missiles*] [*Military*]....CAP
Continuous Airworthiness Visit....CAV
Continuous Ambulatory Peritoneal Dialysis [*Medicine*]....CAPD
Continuous Automated Placement Survey [*Department of Labor*]....CAPS
Continuous Automated Single Base Line [*Automated control system*]....CASBL
Continuous Automatic Line Monitoring System....CALMS
Continuous Blowdown....CB
Continuous Boresight Correction....CBC
Continuous Butt-Weld [*Metal industry*]....CBW
Continuous until Cancelled [*Insurance*]....CUC
Continuous Casting [*Metalworking*]....CC
Continuous Casting Machine [*Metalworking*]....CCM
Continuous Commercial Service [*Equipment specifications*]....CCS
Continuous Correlation Processing....CCP
Continuous Current....CC
Continuous Current-Monitoring Device....CCMD
Continuous Duty Target....CDT
Continuous Duty Target Source....CDTS
Continuous Dynamical System....CDS
Continuous Electrical Stimulation....CES
Continuous Electrocardiogram in Ambulatory Patients [*Medicine*]....CELIA

Continuous Estimation Program ... CEP
Continuous Explosion-Puffing System [*Food technology*] ... CEPS
Continuous Fiber Reinforcing Mat [*Fiberglass*] ... CFRM
Continuous Flow ... CF
Continuous Flow Analysis ... CFA
Continuous-Flow Centrifuging [*Clinical chemistry*] ... CFC
Continuous Flow Electrophoresis System [*Chemical separation*] ... CFES
Continuous Flow Hypersonic Tunnel [*NASA*] ... CFHT
Continuous Flow Stirred Tank Reactor ... CFSTR
Continuous-Flow Tub ... CT
Continuous Fourier Transport ... CFT
Continuous Fuel Injection ... CFI
Continuous Gas LASER ... CGL
Continuous Gradient Ray Tracing System ... CONGRATS
Continuous Grinding Gauge ... CGG
Continuous Image Microfilm ... CIM
Continuous Interlock ... CI
Continuous Learning [*A publication*] ... Cont Learning
Continuous Level of Production Plan ... CLOPP
Continuous Lightweight Exterior ... CLX
Continuous Line Bucket [*Deep mining system*] ... CLB
Continuous Line Plotter ... CLP
Continuous Liner [*Fitting for a propeller shaft*] ... CL
Continuous Longitudinal Manpower Survey [*Department of Labor*] ... CLMS
Continuous Maximum Rating [*of equipment*] ... CMR
Continuous Monitor ... CM
Continuous Motion Assembly Machine ... COMAM
Continuous Multiple Access Collator [*Data processing*] ... COMAC
Continuous National Survey [*National Opinion Research Center*] ... CNS
Continuous Negative Pressure Breathing ... CNPB
Continuous Noise ... CN
Continuous Operation during Hours Shown [*Broadcasting*] ... C
Continuous Operation Production Allocation and Control [*Data processing*] ... COPAC
Continuous Operation Program [*Data processing*] ... COP
Continuous Orbital Guidance System ... COGS
Continuous Page Facsimile Recorder ... CPFR
Continuous Particle Electrophoresis ... CPE
Continuous Patrol Aircraft ... CPA
Continuous Performance Test [*Psychology*] ... CPT
Continuous Positive Airway Pressure [*Resuscitation system*] [*Medicine*] ... CPAP
Continuous Positive Pressure Breathing [*Physiology*] ... CPPB
Continuous Positive Pressure Ventilation ... CPPV
Continuous Random Analog to Frequency Transmission ... CRAFT
Continuous-Reading Meter Relay ... CRMR
Continuous Ream Discharge [*Papermaking*] ... CRD
Continuous Receiver On [*Electronic device*] ... CRO
Continuous Reinforcement [*Psychometrics*] ... CRF
Continuous, Remote, Unobstructive Monitoring of Biobehavioral Systems ... CRUMBS
Continuous Rod ... CR
Continuous Sampler Monitor [*Radioactivity*] ... CSM
Continuous Sampling Plan ... CSP
Continuous Seam Diffusion Bonding ... CSDB
Continuous Service Certificate [*Navy*] ... CSC
Continuous Sheet Memory [*Data processing*] ... CSM
Continuous Sheet Music ... CSM
Continuous Slowing Down Models [*Physics*] ... CSM
Continuous Stirred Tank Biological Reactor ... CSTBR
Continuous Stratification Profiler ... CSP
Continuous Subcarrier Barrage ... CSB
Continuous Subcutaneous Insulin Infusion [*Medicine*] ... CSII
Continuous Survey of Machinery ... CSM
Continuous System Modeling Program [*Computer*] ... CSMP
Continuous Systems Simulation Language [*Data processing*] ... CSSL
Continuous Thymus-Cell [*Cell line*] ... CTC
Continuous Tone [*Color printing*] ... CT
Continuous-Transmission Frequency-Modulated [*SONAR*] ... CTFM
Continuous Update Memory Display ... CUMD
Continuous Variable Slope Delta ... CVSD
Continuous Vent System ... CVS
Continuous Vulcanization ... CV
Continuous Wage and Benefit History [*Unemployment insurance*] ... CWBH
Continuous Wave [*A form of radio transmission*] ... CW
Continuous Wave Acquisition RADAR [*Military*] ... CWAR
Continuous Wave Acquisition and Track ... CWAT
Continuous Wave Frequency-Modulated ... CWFM
Continuous Wave Gas ... CWG
Continuous Wave Illuminator ... CWI
Continuous Wave Illuminator RADAR [*Military*] ... CWIR
Continuous Wave Intermediate Frequency ... CWIF
Continuous Wave LASER ... CWL
Continuous-Wave Oscillator ... CWO
Continuous Wave Space Duplexed ... CWSD
Continuous Wave Surface-to-Air Missile ... CWSAM
Continuous Wave Tactical Detection Console ... CWTDC
Continuous Wave Target Detection ... CWTD
Continuous Wave Traveling Wave Tube ... CWTWT
Continuous Wave Video ... CWV
Continuous Window ... CONTW
Continuous Work History Sample [*Department of Labor*] ... CWHS
Continuous-Wound ... CW
Continuously Advertised Nutritionally Deficient Yummies [*In cookbook title, "The Taming of the CANDY Monster"*] ... CANDY
Continuously Airborne Missile Launching and Low-Level [*Penetration*] [*Air Force*] ... CAMAL
Continuously Computed Impact Point [*Type of bombing sighting system*] [*Air Force*] ... CCIP
Continuously Displayed Impact Point ... CDIP
Continuously Stirred Tank ... CST
Continuously Stirred Tank Reactor [*Chemical engineering*] ... CSTR
Continuously Updated Dynamic Optimizing Systems ... CUDOS
Continuously Variable ... CV
Continuously Variable, for Emergency ... CVE
Continuously Variable Filter [*Spectrometry*] ... CVF
Continuously Variable Mechanical Advantage Shifter ... CVMAS
Continuously Variable Transmission [*Of engines*] ... CVT
[*The*] **Continuum Company** [*NASDAQ symbol*] ... CTUC
Contour [*A publication*] ... Con
Contour ... CTR
Contour Check Template ... CCT
Contour Check Template Set ... CCTS
Contour Rolls ... CRRL
Contour Template ... CT
Contra [*Against*] [*Latin*] ... C
Contra [*Against*] [*Latin*] ... CON
Contra [*Against*] [*Latin*] ... CONT
Contra Bonos Mores [*Contrary to Good Manners*] [*Latin*] ... CONT BON MOR
Contra Costa College, San Pablo, CA [*Library symbol*] ... CSpaW
Contra Costa County Library, Pleasant Hill, CA [*Library symbol*] ... CPlhC
Contra Costa Historical Society, Martinez, CA [*Library symbol*] ... CMartCH
Contra Credit [*Banking*] ... CC
Contraband ... CONTBD
Contraband Control [*Navy*] ... CBC
Contraband Control Base [*Navy*] ... CCB
Contrabass [*Music*] ... CB
Contracap, Inc. [*NASDAQ symbol*] ... CAPS
Contraception [*A publication*] ... Contracept
Contraception-Fertilite-Sexualite [*A publication*] ... Contracept-Fertil-Sex
Contraceptive Technique [*Gynecology*] ... CT
Contraceptive Vaginal Ring [*Gynecology*] ... CVR
Contract ... CONT
Contract ... CONTR
Contract ... CONTT
Contract [*Navy*] ... KT
Contract Accounting Standard ... CAS
Contract Administration [*or Administrator*] [*DoD*] ... CA
Contract Administration Advisory Board [*DoD*] ... CAAB
Contract Administration Data [*DoD*] ... CAD
Contract Administration Data File [*DoD*] ... CADF
Contract Administration Office [*or Officer*] [*Navy*] ... CAO
Contract Administration Panel [*Military*] ... CAP
Contract Administration Report [*DoD*] ... CAR
Contract Administration Services [*DoD*] ... CAS
Contract Administration Southeast Area (Office of Naval Research) ... CASEAREA(ONR)
Contract Air Mail ... CAM
Contract Appeals Board [*Veterans Administration*] ... CAB
Contract Appraisal Report ... CAR
Contract Audit Manual ... CAM
Contract Auditor Coordinator ... CAC
Contract Authorization ... CA
Contract Authorization Request ... CAR
Contract Award ... CA
Contract Award Date ... CAD
Contract Award Rates Delivery Study [*Army*] ... CARDS
Contract Baseline Report ... CBR
Contract Brief ... CB
Contract Bulk Inclusive Tour [*Airline fare*] ... CBIT
Contract Carrier Conference ... CCC
Contract Change Authorization ... CCA
Contract Change Board ... CCB
Contract Change Estimate ... CCE
Contract Change Identification ... CCI
Contract Change Mass Estimate ... CCME
Contract Change Negotiation ... CCN
Contract Change Notification ... CCN
Contract Change Order ... CCO
Contract Change Proposal ... CCP
Contract Change Release ... CCR
Contract Change Request ... CCR
Contract Completion Notices [*DoD*] ... CCN
Contract Data Change Notice ... CDCN
Contract Data Coordinator ... CDC
Contract Data List ... CDL
Contract Data Management Officer ... CDMO
Contract Data Requirement ... CDR
Contract [*or Contractor*] **Data Requirements List** ... CDRL
Contract Deficiency Listing ... CDL
Contract Definition [*Military*] ... CD
Contract Definition ... CONDEF

Contract Definition Phase [DoD]	CDP
Contract Definition Test	CDT
Contract Design	CD
Contract Document Change Notice	CDCN
Contract Documentation Requirements Records [NASA]	CDRR
Contract End Item	CEI
Contract End Item Number	CEIN
Contract Engineers	CE
Contract [or Contractor] Field Service	CFS
Contract Field Technician	CFT
Contract Finance Committee [Military]	CFC
Contract Financial Reporting Manual	CFRM
Contract Financial Requirements Estimate [NASA]	CFRE
Contract Financial Status	CFS
Contract Formulation	CF
Contract Formulation	CONFORM
Contract Fund Status Report [Army]	CFSR
Contract Furnishings Council	CFC
Contract Information Processor	CIP
Contract Information Subsystem	CISS
Contract Interiors [A publication]	Contract Int
Contract Interiors [A publication]	Contract Inter
Contract Item Material List	CIML
Contract Item Number	CIN
Contract Items	CI
Contract Items Specification and Schedule	CISS
Contract Labour Branch [Admiralty] [British]	CLB
Contract Law	CL
Contract Liaison and Master Planning Office [Military]	CLIMPO
Contract Line Item Number [Army]	CLIN
Contract Line Item Status	CLIS
Contract Lineage Equivalent [Formula used by certain publications for calculating number of lines of advertising copy]	CLE
Contract Maintenance Activity	CMA
Contract Management	CM
Contract Management Assistance Officer [NASA]	CMAO
Contract Management District	CMD
Contract Management Network	CMN
Contract Management Office [Jet Propulsion Laboratory, NASA]	CMO
Contract Management Region	CMR
Contract Management Review [DoD]	CMR
Contract Modification	CM
Contract Monitoring Point	CMP
Contract Number [Data processing]	CN
Contract Operations Data [DoD]	COD
Contract Parts Material Order	CPMO
Contract Pilot School	CPS
Contract [or Contractor] Plant Services	CPS
Contract Potential Difference	CPD
Contract Price	C/P
Contract Price of Items Terminated [Business and trade]	CPIT
Contract Procurement Request	CPR
Contract Program Manager	CPM
Contract Progress Control	CPC
Contract Regarding an Interim Supplement to Tanker Liability for Oil Pollution [Oil industry]	CRISTAL
Contract Repair Service	CRS
Contract [or Contractor] Report	CR
Contract Report. US Army Engineer Waterways Experiment Station [A publication]	Contract Rep US Army Eng Waterw Exp Stn
Contract Requirement	C/R
Contract Requirement Card	CRC
Contract Research and Development	CRAD
Contract Review and Selection Criteria [DoD]	CRSC
Contract Revision Number	CRN
Contract Serial Number	CSN
Contract Service Rework Orders	CSRO
Contract Status Report	CSR
Contract Strategy Paper	CSP
Contract Subline Item Number	CSLIN
Contract Supplemental Tooling	CST
Contract Supply Facility	CSF
Contract Support Detachment	CSD
Contract Surgeon [Military]	CS
Contract Surgeon [Military]	CSN
Contract Task Change Proposal	CTCP
Contract Technical Compliance	CTC
Contract Technical Compliance Inspection	CTCI
Contract Technical Instructor [Army]	CTI
Contract Technical Manager	CTM
Contract Technical Representative	CTR
Contract [or Contractor] Technical Services [Air Force]	CTS
Contract Technical Services Personnel	CTSP
Contract Termination and Completion	CTC
Contract Termination Inventory [DoD]	CTI
Contract Termination Manual	CTM
Contract Termination Settlement	CTS
Contract War Service	CWS
Contract Work Breakdown Structure	CWBS
Contract Work Hours and Safety Standards Act	CWHSSA
Contract Work Notification	CWN
Contracted Gaussian-Type Orbital [Atomic physics]	CGTO
Contractile Element [of skeletal muscle]	CE
Contracting Officer [Also, CONTRO, KO]	CO
Contracting Officer [Also, CO, KO]	CONTRO
Contracting Officer [Also, CO, CONTRO]	KO
Contracting Officer	KOR
Contracting Officer's Representative [Army]	COR
Contracting Officers' Technical Representative [Army]	COTR
Contracting Plasterers' and Lathers' International Association [Later, IAWCC]	CPLIA
Contraction	C
Contraction Stress Test [Obstetrics]	CST
Contractions Handbook	CTH
Contractor	CONTR
Contractor	COR
Contractor [Navy]	KR
Contractor Acceptance Test	CAT
Contractor-Acquired Materiel	CAM
Contractor-Acquired Operational Equipment	CAOE
Contractor-Acquired Property	CAP
Contractor All-Risk Incentive Contract [Air Force]	CARIC
Contractor-Assisted	CA
Contractor Attention List	CAL
Contractor Change Evaluation	CCE
Contractor Cost Data Reporting	CCDR
Contractor Cost Reduction	CCR
Contractor Developed Material	CDM
Contractor Employee Compensation System Review [DoD]	CECSR
Contractor Engineer - Furnish and Install	CEFI
Contractor Engineering and Technical Services	CETS
Contractor Estimating Methods Review [DoD]	CEMR
Contractor Experience List [DoD]	CEL
Contractor Field Team	CFT
Contractor Fin Opener Crank	CFOC
Contractor Functional Demonstration	CFD
Contractor-Furnished Aeronautical Equipment	CFAE
Contractor-Furnished Equipment	CFE
Contractor-Furnished Material	CFM
Contractor-Furnished Property [Air Force]	CFP
Contractor-Held Air Force Property	CHAP
Contractor Independent Technical Effort [DoD]	CITE
Contractor Independent Technical Effort	CITEC
Contractor Installation Make or Buy Authorization	CIMBA
Contractor Insurance and Pension Review [DoD]	CIPR
Contractor Inventory	CI
Contractor Inventory Utilization Group	CIUG
Contractor Line Item	CLI
Contractor Logistics Support [DoD]	CLS
Contractor Maintenance Engineering Support	CMES
[A] Contractor Managed Account	ACMA
Contractor-Managed Base Supply [Facility]	COMBS
Contractor Material Review Board [NASA]	CMRB
Contractor-Operated Civil Engineer Supply Store	COCESS
Contractor-Operated Parts Stores [Military]	COPARS
Contractor-Oriented Data Abstract Modules [Air Force]	CODAM
Contractor Overhaul Facility	COF
Contractor-Owned, Contractor-Operated	COCO
Contractor Packaging Capability Review [DoD]	CPCR
Contractor Performance Evaluation	CPE
Contractor Performance Evaluation Group	CPEG
Contractor Performance Evaluation Plan [or Program] [Military]	CPEP
Contractor Performance Evaluation System	CPES
Contractor Performance Record [DoD]	CPR
Contractor Personnel Employment Report	CPER
Contractor Procurement List	CPL
Contractor Procurement System Review [DoD]	CPSR
Contractor Property Management System	CPMS
Contractor-Recommended Change List	CRCL
Contractor-Recommended Coding	CRC
Contractor Relations Specialist [DoD]	CRS
Contractor Reports Register	CRR
Contractor Required Shipment Date	CRSD
Contractor Resident Office	CRO
Contractor Responsible Action	KRA
Contractor Standard Item	CSI
Contractor Standard Parts	CSP
Contractor Storage Site	CSS
Contractor Support Area	CSA
Contractor Support Facility	CSF
Contractor Support Material List	CSML
Contractor Technical Assistance	CTA
Contractor Technical Manual Plan [DoD]	CTMP
Contractor Technical Meeting	CTM
Contractor Technical Support	CTS
Contractor Test and Evaluation	CTE
Contractor Work Authorization	CWA
Contractor Work Plan	CWP
Contractor's Demonstration Inspection	CDI
Contractor's Development Testing	CDT
Contractor's Identification Number	CIDNO

Contractor's Manual Prepared after Negotiated Authorization for Contract .... CMA
Contractors Mutual Association [*Defunct*] .... CMA
Contractors' Operational Representative .... COR
Contractors Panel [*Aerospace*] .... CN/PNL
Contractors Pump Bureau .... CPB
Contractor's Weighted Average Share [*in Cost Risk*] [*Accounting*] .... CWAS
Contractor's Work Estimate [*Military*] .... CWE
Contracts Compliance Regional Office [*DoD*] .... CCO
Contracts Group Office .... CGO
Contracts Maintenance Log .... CML
Contracts Station .... CS
Contractual Data Status Reporting System .... CDSR
Contractual Nontechnical Report .... CNR
Contractual Requirements, Recording, Analysis, and Management [*Air Force*] .... CRAM
Contractual Technical Report .... CTR
Contraindicated [*Medicine*] .... CONTRA
Contralateral Optic Tectum .... COT
Contralateral Routing of Signal [*Audiometry*] .... CROS
Contralto C
Contralto .... CONTR
Contrary .... CONTR
Contrast .... CONTR
Contrast .... CTRS
Contrast Contour Seeker .... CCS
Contrast Gate .... CG
Contrast Gate Amplifier .... CGA
Contrast Media [*Radiology*] .... CM
Contrast Media Appearance Picture [*Also known as coronary arteriography*] [*Radiology*] .... CMAP
Contrast Optical LASER Tracking Subsystem [*Missile guidance*] .... COLTS
Contrast Sensitivity Function [*of the retina*] .... CSF
Contrast Value CV
Contre Complications Bronchiques [*Vaccine for "bronchial complaints"*] [*Medicine*] .... CCB
Contribuciones del Instituto Antartico Argentino [*A publication*] .... Contrib Inst Antart Argent
Contribuicoes Avulsas do Instituto Oceanografico Sao Paulo [*A publication*] .... Contrib Avulsas Inst Oceanogr Sao Paulo
Contribuicoes para o Estudo da Antropologia Portuguesa [*A publication*] .... Contrib Estudo Antropol Port
Contribute .... CNTR
Contributi dell'Istituto di Filologia Moderna [*A publication*] .... CIFM
Contributi dell'Istituto di Ricerche Agrarie Milano [*A publication*] .... Contrib Ist Ric Agrar Milano
Contributi Scientifico. Pratici per una Migliore Conoscenza ed Utilizzazione del Legno [*A publication*] .... Contr Sci Prat Migl Conosc Util Legno
Contributing to Delinquency of Minor [*FBI standardized term*] .... C to D of M
Contributing Value [*Shipping*] CV
Contribution .... CONTR
Contribution .... CONTRIB
Contribution. Canada Department of Forestry. Forest Research Branch [*A publication*] .... Contr Canada Dep For Forest Res Brch
Contribution. Fonds de Recherches Forestieres. Universite Laval [*A publication*] .... Contr Fonds Rech For Univ Laval
Contribution. Institute of Forest Products. University of Washington. College of Forest Resources [*A publication*] .... Contr Inst For Prod Univ Wash
Contribution to Music Education [*A publication*] .... Con Mus Ed
Contribution. Welder Wildlife Foundation [*A publication*] .... Contrib Welder Wildl Found
Contributions of the American Entomological Institute (Ann Arbor) [*A publication*] .... Contrib Am Entomol Inst (Ann Arbor)
Contributions to Applied Statistics [*A publication*] .... Cont Appl St
Contributions of the Arctic Institute. Catholic University of America [*A publication*] .... Contrib Arct Inst Cathol Univ Am
Contributions to Asian Studies [*A publication*] .... Contrib As Stud
Contributions to Atmospheric Physics [*A publication*] .... Contrib Atmos Phys
Contributions from Bears Bluff Laboratories [*A publication*] .... Contrib Bears Bluff Lab
Contributions from Boyce Thompson Institute for Plant Research [*A publication*] .... Contr Boyce Thompson Inst Pl Res
Contributions from Boyce Thompson Institute for Plant Research [*A publication*] .... Contrib Boyce Thompson Inst
Contributions to Canadian Economics [*A publication*] .... CCE
Contributions from the Central Research Institute for Agriculture (Bogor) [*A publication*] .... Contrib Cent Res Inst Agric (Bogor)
Contributions to Current Research in Geophysics [*A publication*] .... Contrib Curr Res Geophys
Contributions. Cushman Foundation for Foraminiferal Research [*A publication*] .... Contrib Cushman Found Foraminiferal Res
Contributions. Department of Geology and Mineralogy. Niigata University [*A publication*] .... Contrib Dep Geol Mineral Niigata Univ
Contributions from the Department of Limnology. Academy of Natural Sciences of Philadelphia [*A publication*] .... Contrib Dep Limnol Acad Nat Sci Phila

Contributions from the Dudley Herbarium [*A publication*] .... Contrib Dudley Herb
Contributions from the Dudley Museum [*A publication*] .... Contrib Dudley Mus
Contributions to Economic Analysis [*Elsevier Book Series*] [*A publication*] .... CEA
Contributions. Faculty of Science. Haile Selassie I University. Series C. Zoology [*A publication*] .... Contrib Fac Sci Haile Selassie I Univ Ser C Zool
Contributions from the General Agricultural Research Station (Bogor) [*A publication*] .... Contrib Gen Agric Res Stn (Bogor)
Contributions to Geology. Special Paper [*A publication*] .... Contrib Geol Spec Pap
Contributions to Geology. University of Wyoming [*A publication*] .... Contrib Geol Univ Wyo
Contributions. Geophysical Institute. Kyoto University [*A publication*] .... Contrib Geophys Inst Kyoto Univ
Contributions. Geophysical Institute. Slovak Academy of Sciences [*A publication*] .... Contrib Geophys Inst Slovak Acad Sci
Contributions from the Gray Herbarium of Harvard University [*A publication*] .... Contrib Gray Herb Harv Univ
Contributions to Gynecology and Obstetrics [*A publication*] .... Contrib Gynecol Obstet
Contributions from Herbarium Australiense [*A publication*] .... Contrib Herb Aust
Contributions to Human Development [*A publication*] .... Cont Hum De
Contributions to Human Development [*A publication*] .... Contrib Hum Dev
Contributions to Indian Sociology [*A publication*] .... Contrib Ind Sociol
Contributions. Institut de Botanique. Universite de Montreal [*A publication*] .... Contrib Inst Bot Univ Montreal
Contributions. Institut de Botanique. Universite de Montreal [*A publication*] .... Contr Inst Bot Univ Montreal
Contributions. Institute of Geology and Paleontology. Tohoku University [*A publication*] .... Contrib Inst Geol Paleontol Tohoku Univ
Contributions. Institute of Low Temperature Science. Hokkaido University. Series B [*A publication*] .... Contrib Inst Low Temp Sci Hokkaido Univ B
Contributions. Institute of Low Temperature Science. Series A [*A publication*] .... Contrib Inst Low Temp Sci A
Contributions d'Istanbul a la Science Clinique [*A publication*] .... Contrib Istanbul Sci Clin
Contributions from the Laboratory of Vertebrate Biology of the University of Michigan [*A publication*] .... Contrib Lab Vertebr Biol Univ Mich
Contributions. Lunar Science Institute [*A publication*] .... Contrib Lunar Sci Inst
Contributions in Marine Science [*A publication*] .... Contrib Mar Sci
Contributions in Marine Science [*A publication*] .... Contr Marine Sci
Contributions in Marine Science [*A publication*] .... Contr Mar S
Contributions to Microbiology and Immunology [*A publication*] .... Contrib Microbiol Immunol
Contributions to Mineralogy and Petrology [*A publication*] .... Contrib Mineral & Petrol
Contributions to Mineralogy and Petrology [*A publication*] .... Contrib Mineral Petrol
Contributions to Mineralogy and Petrology [*A publication*] .... Contr Min P
Contributions from the Museum of Paleontology. University of Michigan [*A publication*] .... Contrib Mus Paleontol Univ Mich
Contributions to Music Education [*A publication*] .... CMUED
Contributions to Nepalese Studies [*A publication*] .... Contrib Nepal Stud
Contributions to Nephrology [*A publication*] .... Contrib Nephrol
Contributions from the New South Wales National Herbarium [*A publication*] .... Contrib NSW Natl Herb
Contributions from the New South Wales National Herbarium. Flora Series [*A publication*] .... Contrib NSW Natl Herb Flora Ser
Contributions to Primatology [*A publication*] .... Contrib Primatol
Contributions to Primatology [*A publication*] .... Contr Prim
Contributions to Science [*A publication*] .... Contr Sc
Contributions to Sensory Physiology [*A publication*] .... Contrib Sens Physiol
Contributions to Sensory Physiology [*A publication*] .... CSPHA
Contributions from the United States National Herbarium [*A publication*] .... Contrib US Natl Herb
Contributions from the University of Michigan Herbarium [*A publication*] .... Contrib Univ Mich Herb
Contributions to Vertebrate Evolution [*A publication*] .... Contrib Vertebr Evol
Contributor .... CTR
[*A*] **Contrived Reduction of Nomenclature Yielding Mnemonics** [*Humorous interpretation of the term*] .... ACRONYM
Contro-clusive Magnetism [*Pest control concept*] .... CCM
Control C
Control .... CNTL
Control .... CNTRL
Control .... CON
Control .... CONT
Control .... CONTL
Control .... CONTR
Control .... CONTRL
Control .... CTL
Control .... CTRL
Control Access Manager .... CAM

Control and Acquisition Interface ... CAI
Control Adjustment Strap ... CAS
Control Air Force Specialty Code ... CAFSC
Control of Aircraft Maintenance and Servicing ... CAMS
Control and Analysis Centers [*ERADCOM*] ... CAC
Control Area [*Aviation*] ... CTA
Control Area [*Aviation*] ... CTLA
Control Assembly ... CA
Control Assembly ... CONTA
Control Assembly Program ... CAP
Control and Assessment Team ... CAT
Control Attenuator Timer ... CAT
Control Augmentation ... CA
Control Augmentation System ... CAS
Control and Authorization Process ... CAP
Control and Auxiliary Power Supply System ... CAPS
Control Booth ... CB
Control Boundary [*Aviation*] ... CTLB
Control Branch [*Military*] ... CB
Control Break ... CB
Control Cabin ... CC
Control Card Listing [*Data processing*] ... CCL
Control Center ... CC
Control Center Programing Center [*NASA*] ... CCPC
Control Center Rack ... CCR
Control Chamber [*Diving apparatus*] ... CC
Control Channel Information Demodulator ... CCID
Control Cibernetica y Automatizacion [*A publication*] ... Control Cibern & Autom
Control Circuit ... CC
Control Circuit Resistance ... CCR
Control Circuits Design Section ... CCDS
Control and Command Systems Support Agency [*NATO*] ... CCSSA
Control Commission for Germany [*World War II*] ... CCG
Control Commission Military Section [*British*] [*World War II*] ... CCMS
Control Commission Shipping Bureau [*Allied German Occupation Forces*] ... CCSB
Control, Communication, and Display Subsystem ... CCDS
Control and Computation System [*Navy*] ... CCS
Control Computer ... CC
Control Configured Propulsion ... CCP
Control Configured Vehicle [*Air Force*] ... CCV
Control Console ... CC
Control Contactor ... CCR
Control and Coordination [*Army*] ... CAC
Control Current Impedance ... CCI
Control and Cybernetics [*A publication*] ... Control & Cybern
Control and Cybernetics [*A publication*] ... Control Cybern
Control Data Assembly Program ... CODAP
Control Data Corp. [*NYSE symbol*] ... CDA
Control Data Corporation ... CDC
Control Data Education Institutes ... CDEI
Control Data Institute ... CDI
Control Data Panel ... CDP
Control and Data Retrieval System [*Formerly, DCDRS*] [*Air Force*] ... CDRS
Control Data System ... CDS
Control Data Terminal ... CDT
Control Data Unit ... CDU
Control of Destination of Ships ... CDS
Control Detonating Fuses ... CDF
Control and Diagnostic Unit [*Data processing*] ... CDU
Control Diagram Language [*Data processing*] ... CODIL
Control Diet ... CD
Control Differential Transformer ... CDT
Control Differential Transmitter ... CDX
Control Director Intercept ... CDI
Control and Display Panel ... CDP
Control and Display Subsystem ... CDS
Control and Display Unit ... CADU
Control and Display Unit ... CDU
Control Distribution Center ... CDC
Control Distribution System ... CDS
Control Drawing Change Request ... CDCR
Control of Electromagnetic Radiations [*Purpose is to deny the enemy aircraft the use of electromagnetic radiations for navigation, while still providing essential services*] ... CONELRAD
Control Electronics Assembly [*Aerospace*] ... CEA
Control Electronics Section [*Apollo*] [*NASA*] ... CES
Control Electronics Unit ... CEU
Control Element ... CE
Control Element Assembly [*Nuclear energy*] ... CEA
Control Element Test Stand [*Nuclear energy*] ... CETS
Control Encoder Coupler ... CEC
Control Engineering ... CE
Control Engineering [*A publication*] ... Contr Eng
Control Engineering [*A publication*] ... Control Eng
Control Escort Vessel [*Navy symbol*] ... DEC
Control of Feeding Behavior and Biology of the Brain in Protein-Calorie Malnutrition [*A publication*] ... Control Feed Behav Biol Brain Protein-Calorie Malnutr
Control Filter Post ... CFP
Control Flight Test Bed ... CFTB
Control Flow Jet ... CFJ
Control Fragmentation Munitions ... COFRAM
Control Functional Diagram ... CFD
Control Functional Unit [*Data link*] ... CFU
Control Group ... CG
Control and Guidance ... C & G
Control Heading ... CH
Control Hole ... CH
Control and Indication ... C & I
Control Indicator ... CI
Control Indicator Set ... CIS
Control and Information Center ... CIC
Control in Information Systems ... COINS
Control Inlet Panel [*Aerospace*] ... CIP
Control and Instrumentation [*A publication*] ... Contr Instr
Control and Instrumentation [*A publication*] ... Contr Instrum
Control and Instrumentation [*A publication*] ... Control Instrum
Control Interface Assembly ... CIA
Control Interval Definition Field [*Data processing*] ... CIDF
Control Joint ... CLJ
Control Language [*Data processing*] ... CL
Control Language Translator ... COLT
Control Laser Corp. [*NASDAQ symbol*] ... CLSR
Control Launch Center ... CLC
Control Leader [*Data processing*] ... CL
Control Level Item ... CLI
Control and Line ... C & L
Control Logic ... CL
Control Logic Array ... CLA
Control Logic and Drive Assembly ... CLDA
Control Magnetization Curve ... CMC
Control Mark ... CM
Control Message Automation [*Aviation*] ... CMA
Control Moment Gyro [*Aerospace*] ... CMG
Control Moment Gyro Assembly [*Aerospace*] ... CMGA
Control Moment Gyro Electrical Assembly [*Aerospace*] ... CMGEA
Control Moment Gyro Inverter Assembly [*Aerospace*] ... CMGIA
Control Moment Gyro System [*or Subsystem*] [*Aerospace*] ... CMGS
Control Monitor ... CM
Control Monitor Group ... CMG
Control and Monitor Panel ... CAMP
Control and Monitoring ... C & M
Control Net System [*Chiefly British*] ... CNS
Control Number ... CN
Control Officers' Console ... COC
Control of Official Histories [*British*] ... COH
Control of Operation Programs ... COP
Control Orbitron Gauge ... COG
Control-Oriented Language [*Data processing*] ... COOL
Control Panel ... CP
Control Panel Subassembly ... CPS
Control Parameter Assembly Program ... CPAP
Control Phasing Unit [*for aircraft*] ... CPU
Control Point ... CP
Control of Pollution Act [*British*] ... CPA
Control Post [*RADAR*] ... CP
Control Power Supply ... CPS
Control Power Transformer ... CPT
Control Pressure System ... CPS
Control Procedures ... CP
Control Processes in Multicellular Organisms ... CPMO
Control Processing Unit ... CPU
Control Processor ... CP
Control Program [*Data processing*] ... CP
Control Program Facility ... CPF
Control Program for Microcomputers ... CP/M
Control and Protection Panel ... CPP
Control and Protection of Transoceanic Air Lanes of Communication ... CAPTALC
Control Purchasing Authority ... CPA
Control Quality Monitor ... CQM
Control of Radio Transmission [*British*] [*World War II*] ... CRT
Control Rate Gyro [*Aerospace*] ... CRG
Control Read-Only Memory [*Data processing*] ... CROM
Control Record Listing [*IRS*] ... CRL
Control Relay ... CR
Control Relay Automatic ... CRA
Control Relay Forward ... CRF
Control Relay Hand ... CRH
Control Relay Latch ... CRL
Control Relay Master ... CRM
Control Relay Unlatch ... CRU
Control of Rents and Furnished Lets [*British*] ... FRC
Control Repeater Amplifier ... CRA
Control and Reporting ... C and R
Control and Reporting Center [*Air Force*] ... CRC
Control and Reporting Center/Post ... CRC/P
Control and Reporting Post [*RADAR*] [*Air Force*] ... CRP
Control and Reporting System ... CRS
Control and Reproducibility Monitor ... CRM

Control Rod [*Nuclear energy*]...CR
Control Rod Analysis...CORONA
Control Rod Assembly [*Nuclear energy*]...CRA
Control Rod Drive [*Nuclear energy*]...CRD
Control Rod Drive Mechanism Study...CRDM
Control Room...CR
Control Room Patching and Labeling...CORPAL
Control Route Tag...CRT
Control Scanner...CS
Control of Sea Ice Information...ICECON
Control Section...CSECT
Control Section Report [*NATO*]...CSR
Control Segment...CS
Control Servo Input...CSI
Control Set...CS
Control Shift Register...CSR
Control by Ship...CONSHIP
Control from Shore...CONSHORE
Control Signal...CS
Control Signal Processor [*for spacecraft*]...CSP
Control and Simulation Language [*Data processing*]...CSL
Control Slip...CS
Control Station...CS
Control Station Manual Operating Level...CSMOL
Control and Status Logic...CSL
Control Stick Boost and Pitch Compensator...CSBPC
Control Stick Maneuver...CSM
Control Stick Sensor Assembly...CSSA
Control Stick Steering [*Aviation*]...CSS
Control Stick Tie-In [*Aviation*]...CSTI
Control Submarine Chaser [*136 feet*] [*Navy symbol*]...PCSC
Control Subroutine Language [*Data processing*]...CONSUL
Control Subsystem...CSS
Control and Surveillance of Friendly Forces...CASOFF
Control Switch...CS
Control Switch...CSW
Control Switching Assembly...CSA
Control and Switching Equipment [*RADAR*]...CSE
Control Switching Point...CSP
Control Symbol Number...CSN
Control Synthetic Gas [*Process*]...CSG
Control System Development...CSD
Control System Jet...CSJ
Control System Simulation Equipment...CSSE
Control System Test...CST
Control Systems [*A publication*]...Control Sys
Control Systems...CS
Control Systems Development Division [*NASA*]...CSDD
Control Systems Engineering...CSE
Control Systems Laboratory [*University of Illinois*]...CSL
Control Systems Society...CSS
Control Techniques Guidelines [*Environmental Protection Agency*]...CTG
Control Test Bed...CTB
Control Test Vehicles...CTV
Control Tower [*For chart use only*] [*Aviation*]...CT
Control Tower Operator [*Army*]...CTO
Control Track Direction Computer...CTDC
Control Transformer...CT
Control Translator [*Honeywell Information Systems*] [*Data processing*]...CONTRAN
Control Transmitter...CX
Control Unit [*Data processing*]...CU
Control Unit Tester [*Data processing*]...CUT
Control Users Handbook...CUH
Control Valve...CV
Control Valve Primary Coolant...CVPC
Control Valve Secondary Coolant...CVSC
Control Van [*Diving apparatus*]...CV
Control Van Connecting Room...CVCR
Control Variable Valve...CVV
Control Wheel Steering...CWS
Control Word...CW
Control Zone [*Aviation*]...CTLZ
Control Zone [*Aviation code*]...CTR
Control Zone [*Aviation*]...CTZ
Control Zone [*For chart use only*] [*Aviation*]...CTR
Controllability and Observability...C & O
Controllable Pitch Propeller [*For ships*]...CPP
Controllable RADAR Target Simulator...CRTS
Controllable and Reversible Pitch Propeller [*For ships*]...CRP
Controllable Twist Rotor [*Aviation*]...CTR
Controlled American Source [*Military*]...CAS
Controlled Assembly Parts List [*Aerospace*]...CAPL
Controlled Atmosphere...CA
Controlled Atmosphere Protected [*Army*]...CONAP
Controlled Avalanche Transit Time [*Electronics*]...CATT
Controlled Barrier System...CBS
Controlled Blip Scan...CBS
Controlled Carrier Modulation...CCM
Controlled-Circulation [*Boiler*]...C/C

Controlled Circulation Audit [*Name changed to Business Publications Audit of Circulation*]...CCA
Controlled Clinical Trials [*A publication*]...Controlled Clin Trials
Controlled Combustion System [*Antipollution device for automobiles*]...CCS
Controlled Cord Traction [*Medicine*]...CCT
Controlled Current Feedback Transfer...CCFT
Controlled Data Analysis Workshops [*Magnetospheric physics*]...CDAW
Controlled Date of Separation [*Military*]...CDOS
Controlled Delivery System...CDS
Controlled Deployment Specular Reflector [*Army*]...CDSR
Controlled Drug...CD
Controlled Dynamic Range...CDR
Controlled Ecosystem Pollution Experiment [*National Science Foundation project*]...CEPEX
Controlled Element Computer...CEC
Controlled Energy Flow Forming...CEFF
Controlled Energy Relief Valve...CERV
Controlled Environment Agriculture...CEA
Controlled Environment Testing...CET
Controlled Environmental Forestry...CEF
Controlled Environmental System [*NASA*]...CES
Controlled Experimental Ecosystem [*Study technique*]...CEE
Controlled Facility [*Aerospace*]...CF
Controlled Flash Evaporation...CFE
Controlled Flight into Terrain...CFIT
Controlled Force Circulation [*Boilers*]...CFC
Controlled Foreign Company...CFC
Controlled Fusion Atomic Data Center [*Department of Energy*]...CFADC
Controlled Ground Landing...CGL
Controlled Handling of Internal Executive Functions [*UNIVAC*]...CHIEF
Controlled Impulse...CIMP
Controlled Interceptor Trainer [*Aerospace*]...CIT
Controlled Internal Extension...CIE
Controlled Interval Inspection...CII
Controlled Item...CI
Controlled Large Aperture Wavefront Sampling...CLAWS
Controlled Letter Contract Reduction...CLCR
Controlled Materials Officer...CMO
Controlled Materials Plan [*of War Production Board*] [*World War II*]...CMP
Controlled Materials Production [*Nuclear energy*]...CMP
Controlled Mechanical Ventilation...CMV
Controlled Minefield [*Navy*]...CM
Controlled Mission Equipment...CME
Controlled Multiple Address Letter...CMAL
Controlled Multivibrator...CMV
Controlled Overhead Management Performance and Standard System...COMPASS
Controlled-Pore Glass [*Corning*]...CPG
Controlled Precision Oscillator...CPO
Controlled Production Planning Officer...CPPO
Controlled Products Area...CPA
Controlled Range Air Burst Fuze...CRAB
Controlled Range Network...CORN
Controlled Recirculation Boiling Water Reactor...CRBR
Controlled Rectifier...CR
Controlled Referral Plan...CRP
Controlled Release Device...CRD
Controlled Residual Element [*Nuclear energy*]...CRE
Controlled Retracting Injection Port [*System for underground coal burning*]...CRIP
Controlled Rupture Accuracy...CRA
Controlled Short Takeoff and Landing [*Acronym used for a type of aircraft*]...C-STOL
Controlled-Slip Differentials...CSD
Controlled Solid Rocket Motors...CSRM
Controlled Supply Rate...CSR
Controlled Surface Porosity...CSP
Controlled Surface Process...CSP
Controlled Temperature...CT
Controlled Temperature Bath...CTB
Controlled Temperature Furnace...CTF
Controlled Temperature Profile [*Vapor trap*] [*Nuclear energy*]...CTP
Controlled Thermolytic Dissociation...CTD
Controlled Thermonuclear Fusion...CTF
Controlled Thermonuclear Fusion...CTNF
Controlled Thermonuclear Reaction [*or Reactor*] [*National Bureau of Standards*]...CTR
Controlled Thrust Assembly...CTA
Controlled Tornado Research...CTR
Controlled Tuning Fork Oscillator...CTFO
Controlled Variable Time [*Fuze*]...CVT
Controlled Visual Flight...CVF
Controlled Visual Rules [*FAA*]...CVR
Controlled Work Area...CWA
Controller...CON
Controller...CONT
Controller [*Aviation*]...CTLR
Controller of Accounts...CA
Controller of American Supplies and Repair [*Ministry of Aircraft Production*] [*British*] [*World War II*]...CASR

Controller/Attitude-Direct Electronics ....CADE
Controller Central Operating Authority ....CCOA
Controller-in-Charge [*Aviation*] CIC
Controller Checkout Console CCC
Controller of Chemical Defence Department [*Ministry of Supply*] [*British*] ....CCDD
Controller of Chemical Research and Development [*Ministry of Supply*] [*British*] ....CCRD
Controller of Communications [*RAF*] [*British*] ....C of C
Controller of Communications Equipment Overseas [*British*] ....CCEO
Controller Decision Evaluation ....CODE
Controller Defence Communications Network [*Navy*] [*British*] ....CDCN
Controller/Director Information File ....CDIF
Controller Error ....CONE
Controller General of Civil Aviation [*British*] ....CGCA
Controller General of Economy [*Military*] [*British*] ....CGE
Controller General of Machine Tools [*Ministry of Supply*] [*British*] ....CGMT
Controller General of Munitions Production [*Ministry of Supply*] [*British*] ....CGMP
Controller Input Test Equipment ....CITE
Controller Interface Unit ....CIU
Controller of Merchant Shipbuilding and Repairs [*Navy*] [*British*] ....CMSR
Controller of the Navy [*British*] ....C of N
Controller of Physical Research and Signals Development [*Ministry of Supply*] [*British*] ....CPRSD
Controller of Projectile Development [*Ministry of Supply*] [*British*] [*World War II*] ....CPD
Controller of Research and Development [*Ministry of Aircraft Production*] [*British*] ....CRD
Controller of Research and Development Establishments and Research [*British*] ....CER
Controllers Institute of America [*Later, FEI*] ....CIA
Controllers' Operations/Procedures Committee [*FAA*] ....COPCOM
Controls [*JETDS nomenclature*] [*Military*] C
Controls Assembly Set ....CAS
Controls Company of America [*NYSE symbol*] [*Delisted*] ....CTC
Controls and Displays [*Aerospace*] ....C & D
Controls and Displays [*Aerospace*] ....CD
Controls and Displays System [*or Subsystem*] [*Aerospace*] ....C & DS
Controls Mock-Up ....CMU
Controls and Monitoring Processor ....CAMP
Contusus [*Bruised*] [*Medicine*] C
Contusus [*Bruised*] [*Medicine*] ....CONT
Contusus [*Bruised*] [*Medicine*] ....CONTUS
CONUS [*Continental United States*] **Air Defense Effectiveness Model** ....CADEM
CONUS [*Continental United States*] **Air Defense Modernization** ....CADM
CONUS, Inc. [*Jonesboro, AR*] [*FAA designator*] ....COS
CONUS [*Continental United States*] **Meteorological Data** [*or Distribution*] **System** ....COMEDS
CONUS [*Continental United States*] **Net Depot Method** ....CND
CONUS [*Continental United States*] **and Overseas Microfilm User Tests** ....COMUT
CONUS [*Continental United States*] **Sustaining Increment** [*Army*] ....CSI
CONVAIR [*Consolidated-Vultee Aircraft Corp.; later, General Dynamics Corp.*] **Astronautics** ....CVA
CONVAIR [*Consolidated-Vultee Aircraft Corp.*] **Astronautics Corporation** [*Later, General Dynamics Corp.*] ....CAC
CONVAIR [*Consolidated-Vultee Aircraft Corp.*] **Daingerfield** [*Later, General Dynamics/Daingerfield*] ....C-D
CONVAIR [*Consolidated-Vultee Aircraft Corp.*] **Fort Worth** [*Later, General Dynamics/Fort Worth*] ....CFW
CONVAIR [*Consolidated-Vultee Aircraft Corp.; later, General Dynamics Corp.*] **Government-Owned Facilities and Equipment** ....CGOFE
Convalescent ....CONV
Convalescent Camp [*Military*] CVC
Convalescent Hospital for Children, Library, Rochester, NY [*OCLC symbol*] ....VQF
Convalescent and Rehabilitation [*Military*] ....C & R
Convalescent Status [*Medicine*] ....CS
Convalescent Training Depot ....CTD
Convalescent Unit [*of a hospital*] ....CU
Convection ....CNV
Convection Suppression Device [*for energy collectors*] ....CSD
Convective ....CNVTV
Convective Condensation Level [*Meteorology*] CCL
Convective Heat Transfer ....CHT
Convective Storms Division [*National Center for Atmospheric Research*] ....CSD
Convegno Internazionale sulle Acque Sotterranee. Atti. Ente Sviluppo Agricolo in Sicilia [*Palermo*] [*A publication*] ....Conv Int Acque Sotterranee Atti
Convene ....CVN
Convenience ....CNVC
Convenience of the Government ....C of G
Convenience of the Government ....COG
Convenience Store ....C-STORE
Convenient ....CONV
Convenient ....CONVN
Convenient Food Mart [*NASDAQ symbol*] ....CFMI
Convening Authority ....CA
Convenio IICA-ZN-ROCAP [*Instituto Interamericano de Ciencias Agricolas-Zona Norte-Regional Organization for Central America and Panama*] **Bibliografia** [*A publication*] ....Conv IICA-ZN-ROCAP Bibliogr
Convenio IICA-ZN-ROCAP [*Instituto Interamericano de Ciencias Agricolas-Zona Norte-Regional Organization for Central America and Panama*] **Publication Miscelanea** [*A publication*] ....Conv IICA-ZN-ROCAP Publ Misc
Convent ....CONV
Convent of Immaculate Conception Sisters of St. Benedict, Ferdinand, IN [*OCLC symbol*] XIC
Convention [*or Conventional*] ....CONV
Convention Africaine [*African Covenant*] ....CA
Convention African National Union [*Nyasaland*] ....CANU
Convention of American Instructors of the Deaf ....CAID
Convention II CII
Convention on International Trade in Endangered Species [*Treaty*] ....CITES
Convention Internationale Concernant le Transport des Marchandises par Chemins de Fer [*International Convention Concerning the Carriage of Goods by Rail*] ....CIM
Convention Internationale Concernant le Transport des Voyageurs et des Bagages par Chemins de Fer [*International Convention Concerning the Carriage of Passengers and Luggage by Rail*] CIV
Convention Liaison Council CLC
Convention Magazine [*Generic term for a publication covering science-fiction fans' conventions*] ....CONZINE
Convention People's Party [*1949-1966*] [*Ghana*] ....CPP
Convention Relative au Contrat de Transport de Marchandises en Navigation Interieure [*Convention on the Carriage of Goods by Inland Waterways*] ....CMN
Convention-Seminar Cassettes [*Commercial firm*] ....CSC
Conventional ....CONVL
Conventional CV
Conventional ....CVNTL
Conventional Airfield Attack Missile ....CAAM
Conventional Ammunition Integrated Management System ....CAIMS
Conventional Ammunition Working Capital Fund [*DoD*] ....CAWCF
Conventional Arms Transfers ....CAT
Conventional District [*Church of England*] ....CD
Conventional Friend Virus ....CFV
Conventional Instruction CI
Conventional International Origin ....CIO
Conventional Military Fuels ....CMF
Conventional Mortgage-Backed Security ....CMBS
Conventional Ordnance Release Computer ....CORC
Conventional Oxidation Catalysis [*of gasoline engine exhausts*] ....COC
Conventional Polyethylene ....CPE
Conventional Standoff Weapon ....CSW
Conventional Takeoff [*Aviation*] ....CTO
Conventional Takeoff and Landing [*Aviation*] ....CTOL
Conventional-Transmission Electron Microscope ....CEM
Conventional-Transmission Electron Microscope ....CTEM
Conventional [*Non-Nuclear*] **War Capability** ....CWC
Conventional Weighted Least Square ....CWLS
Conventions, Meetings, Incentive Travel [*Of CMI World, a publication aimed at those markets*] ....CMI
Converge ....CNVG
Convergence ....CONVG
Convergence Source-Image Distortion [*Crystal*] ....CSID
Convergence Zone [*Military*] ....CZ
Convergence Zone Propagation [*Military*] ....CZP
Convergent Beam Electron Diffraction [*Analytical chemistry*] ....CBED
Convergent-Divergent Nozzle ....CDN
Convergent Exhaust Nozzle Control ....CENC
Convergent Stereoscopic [*Photography*] ....CS
Convergent Technology [*NASDAQ symbol*] ....CVGT
Converging-Diverging ....CD
Conversation ....CON
Conversation ....CONV
Conversational Algebraic Language [*Adaptation of JOSS language*] [*Data processing*] ....CAL
Conversational Compiling System [*Xerox Corp.*] ....CCS
Conversational Extensible Language [*Data processing*] ....CEL
Conversational File Information Retrieval and Management System [*Data processing*] ....CONFIRM
Conversational Interactive Digital/Analog Simulator [*IBM Corp.*] ....CIDAS
Conversational Mode Terminal [*Friden Inc.*] ....CMT
Conversational Modeling Language [*Data processing*] ....CML
Conversational Monitor System [*Data processing*] ....CMS
Conversational Parts Programing Language [*Data processing*] ....CAPT
Conversational Programing System [*Data processing*] ....CPS
Conversational Remote Batch Entry [*Data processing*] ....CRBE
Conversational Remote Job Entry [*Data processing*] ....CRJE
Conversational Statistical Analysis ....COSAN
Conversational System with On-Line Remote Terminals [*Data processing*] ....CONSORT
Conversational Terminal System [*Data processing*] ....CTS
Conversational Time-Sharing [*Data processing*] ....CTS

Conversational Traffic Analysis .... COTRAN
Conversational Voice [*Medicine*] CV
Converse .... CNV
Converse College, Spartanburg, SC [*OCLC symbol*] .... SCO
Converse College, Spartanburg, SC [*Library symbol*] .... ScSpC
Converse County Library, Douglas, WY [*Library symbol*] .... WyDo
Converse, Inc. [*NASDAQ symbol*] .... CVRS
Conversion .... CNVSN
Conversion .... CONV
Conversion .... CVRSN
Conversion, Alteration, and Repair [*Navy*] .... CAR
Conversion Computer Unit .... CCU
Conversion Control Officer [*Army*] .... CCO
Conversion Electron Mossbauer Spectroscopy .... CEMS
Conversion Factor .... CF
Conversion in Lieu of Procurement [*Military*] .... CILOP
Conversion Loss CL
Conversion in Place [*Aerospace*] .... CIP
Conversion Process Controller System .... CPCS
Conversion of Production System [*Engineering Index, Inc.*] .... COPS
Conversion Program System .... CPS
Conversion of Range Telemetry Systems .... CORTS
Conversion of Serials [*Council on Library Resources*] .... CONSER
Convert .... CNVRT
Convert .... CONVT
Convert Gray to Binary .... CGB
Convert Makers of America [*Later, CMOA*] .... CMA
Convert Movement Our Apostolate [*An association*] .... CMOA
Converted Aerial Targets .... CAT
Converted Destroyer .... CONVDD
Converter .... CONV
Converter Amplifier Unit .... CAU
Converter Compressor Facility .... CCF
Converter Display Group .... CDG
Converter, Frequency to DC [*Direct Current*] **Voltage** .... CFD
Converter/Programer .... C/P
Converter Simulator Signal Unit .... CSSU
Converter, Voltage, AC [*Alternating Current*] **to DC** [*Direct Current*] .... CVAD
Converters [*Electronic*] [*JETDS nomenclature*] [*Military*] CV
Convertible [*Rate*] [*Value of the English pound*] .... CN
Convertible .... CONV
Convertible [*NYSE symbol*] CV
Convertible .... CVT
Convertible Circuit Breaker .... CCB
Convertible Lens [*Photography*] CL
Converting-Enzyme Inhibitor [*Biochemistry*] .... CEI
Convest Energy Corp. [*NASDAQ symbol*] .... CVST
Convex CVX
Convex CX
Convexity, Symmetry, Maximum [*Statistics*] .... CSM
Conveyance .... CONVCE
Conveyancer and Property Lawyer [*A publication*] .... Convey
Conveying .... CNVYG
Conveyor .... CNVR
Conveyor .... CNVYR
Conveyor Control System .... CCS
Conveyor Equipment Manufacturers Association .... CEMA
Conveyor Equipment Manufacturers Association .... ConEMA
Conveyor Section of the Material Handling Institute .... CS
Conveyorized Automatic Tube Tester [*Data processing*] .... CATT
Convict .... CNVT
Convict .... CONV
Conviction by Civil Court .... CBCC
Convicts' Association for a Good Environment [*Defunct*] .... CAGE
Convivium [*A publication*] .... Con
Convivium [*A publication*] .... Conv
Convivium (New Series) [*A publication*] .... Con(NS)
Convocation .... CONV
Convocation .... CONVOC
Convolutional Coding Unit .... CCU
Convolutional Decoder Assembly .... CDA
Convorbiri Literare [*A publication*] .... CLit
Convorbiri Literare [*A publication*] .... ConLit
Convorbiri Literare [*A publication*] .... ConvLit
Convoy .... CONV
Convoy Commodore [*Navy*] CC
Convoy Commodore [*Navy*] .... CONCOMO
Convoy Control Officer [*Navy*] .... CCO
Convoy Escort Vessel .... CEV
Convoy Exercise [*Military*] .... CONVEX
Convoy and Routing [*Section*] [*US Fleet*] .... CANDR
Convoy and Routing [*Section*] [*US Fleet*] .... CONROUTE
Convoy and Routing [*Section*] [*US Fleet*] .... C & R
Convulsive Disorder [*Medicine*] .... CD
Convulsive Dose .... CD
Convulsive Shock Therapy .... CST
Conway, AR [*Location identifier*] [*FAA*] .... CWS
Conway, AR [*Radio station call letters*] .... KCON
Conway, AR [*Radio station call letters*] .... KHDX
Conway, AR [*Radio station call letters*] .... KMJX
Conway, AR [*Radio station call letters*] .... KTOD
Conway, AR [*Radio station call letters*] .... KVCA
Conway, NH [*Radio station call letters*] .... WBNC
Conway, NH [*Radio station call letters*] .... WMWV
Conway, SC [*Location identifier*] [*FAA*] .... HYW
Conway, SC [*Television station call letters*] .... WHMC
Conway, SC [*Radio station call letters*] .... WJXY
Conway, SC [*Radio station call letters*] .... WLAT
Conway, SC [*Radio station call letters*] .... WLAT-FM
Conwed Corp. [*NASDAQ symbol*] .... CWED
Conwood Corp. [*NYSE symbol*] .... CWD
Conyers, GA [*Radio station call letters*] .... WCGA
Coober Pedy [*Australia*] [*Airport symbol*] .... CPD
Cook County Hospital, Dr. Frederick Tice Memorial Library, Chicago, IL [*Library symbol*] .... ICCH
Cook County Law Library, Chicago, IL [*Library symbol*] ICCL
Cook County School of Nursing, Chicago, IL [*Library symbol*] .... ICCN
Cook Data Services [*NASDAQ symbol*] .... CDSG
Cook Inlet Aviation, Inc. [*Homer, AK*] [*FAA designator*] .... CKA
Cook International, Inc. [*American Stock Exchange symbol*] .... CKI
Cook Island [*MARC geographic area code*] [*Library of Congress*] .... pocw---
Cook Island Airways Ltd. [*New Zealand*] [*ICAO designator*] .... KH
Cook Islands [*Two-letter standard code*] .... CK
Cook Islands [*Three-letter standard code*] .... COK
Cook Islands [*MARC country of publication code*] [*Library of Congress*] .... cw
Cook Paint & Varnish Co. [*American Stock Exchange symbol*] .... COK
Cook Transit R. R. [*AAR code*] .... COOK
Cook United, Inc. [*NYSE symbol*] .... CCF
Cooke Air Force Base [*Later, VAFB*] .... CAFB
Cooke County Junior College, Gainsville, TX [*Library symbol*] .... TxGaiC
Cooked .... CKD
Cooker Control Unit .... CCU
Cookery Officer [*Navy*] [*British*] .... CK
Cookeville, TN [*Location identifier*] [*FAA*] .... CJE
Cookeville, TN [*Television station call letters*] .... WCTE
Cookeville, TN [*Radio station call letters*] .... WGSQ
Cookeville, TN [*Radio station call letters*] .... WHUB
Cookeville, TN [*Radio station call letters*] .... WHUB-FM
Cookeville, TN [*Television station call letters*] .... WKWR-TV
Cookeville, TN [*Radio station call letters*] .... WPTN
Cookeville, TN [*Radio station call letters*] .... WTTU
Cookie Cutter Collectors Club CCCC
Cookie and Snack Bakers Association .... CSBA
Cooking for Survival Consciousness .... CSC
Cooktown [*Australia*] [*Airport symbol*] .... CTN
Cookware Manufacturers Association [*Formerly, AWA, MCMA*] .... CMA
Cool Down .... CLDWN
Cool-Down Facility .... CDF
Cool Room .... CLRM
Coolant .... CLNT
Coolant .... COOL
Coolant Control Valve CCV
Coolant Pump Power Inverters .... CPPI
Cooled .... CLD
Cooled-Anode Transmitting [*Valve*] .... CAT
Cooler .... CLR
Cooley's Anemia Foundation .... CAF
Coolidge, AZ [*Radio station call letters*] .... KCKY
Coolidge, AZ [*Radio station call letters*] .... KQEZ
Coolidge High School Library, Sioux Falls, SD [*Library symbol*] .... SdSifH
Coolidge Public Library, Coolidge, AZ [*Library symbol*] .... AzCo
Cooling .... CLG
Cooling .... COOLG
Cooling Coil CC
Cooling Effect Detection and Control .... CEDAC
Cooling Fan .... CF
Cooling-Induced Luminescence [*In glass containing rare earth salts*] CIL
Cooling Tower Institute .... CTI
Cooling Water System [*Nuclear energy*] .... CWS
Cooma [*Australia*] [*Airport symbol*] .... OOM
Coomassie Brilliant Blue [*A stain*] .... CBB
Coombs' Test [*for the presence of globulin on the surface of red cells*] [*Hematology*] .... CT
Coon Peak [*Utah*] [*Seismograph station code, US Geological Survey*] .... CPU
Coonabarabran [*Australia*] [*Airport symbol*] .... COJ
Coonamble [*Australia*] [*Airport symbol*] .... CNB
Cooney Tunnel [*Armidale*] [*Australia*] [*Seismograph station code, US Geological Survey*] .... COO
Coop Grain Quarterly [*A publication*] .... Coop Grain Quart
Cooper Biomedical [*NASDAQ symbol*] .... BUGS
Cooper-Harper Rating [*NASA*] .... CHR
Cooper Industries, Inc. [*Formerly, Cooper-Bessemer Corp.*] [*NYSE symbol*] .... CBE
Cooper-Jarrett, Inc. [*American Stock Exchange symbol*] [*Delisted*] .... CJT
Cooper Laboratories, Inc. [*NYSE symbol*] .... COO
Cooper Landing, AK [*Location identifier*] [*FAA*] .... JLA
Cooper Medical Center, Camden, NJ [*Library symbol*] .... NjCaC
Cooper Ornithological Society .... COS
Cooper Resources & Energy [*NASDAQ symbol*] .... CPEN
Cooper Tire & Rubber Co. [*NYSE symbol*] .... CTB
Cooper Union for the Advancement of Science and Art, New York, NY [*Library symbol*] .... NNCoo

Cooper Union Museum Chronicle [*A publication*] .... Cooper Union Chron
Cooperage [*Freight*] .... COOPG
Cooperating Individual [*FBI*] CI
Cooperating Libraries in Consortium [*Library network*] CLIC
Cooperating Libraries of Greater Springfield [*Library network*] .... CLGS
Cooperating Teachers' Attitude Questionnaire .... CTAQ
Cooperating Users of Burroughs Equipment [*Data processing*] .... CUBE
Cooperating Users' Exchange .... CUE
Cooperation [*A publication*] .... Coop
Cooperation Agricole [*A publication*] .... Coop Agr
Cooperation Agricole [*A publication*] .... Coop Agric
Cooperation and Conflict [*A publication*] .... Coop and Conflict
Cooperation and Coordination .... CAC
Cooperation-Distribution-Consommation [*A publication*] .... Coop-Distrib-Consom
Cooperation in Documentation and Communication [*An association*] .... CODOC
Cooperation Information [*A publication*] .... Coop Inf
Cooperation Internationale pour le Developpement Socio-Economique [*International Cooperation for Socio-Economic Development*] .... CIDSE
Cooperation Internationale en Matiere de Documentation sur l'Economie des Transports [*International Co-Operation in the Field of Transport Economics Documentation*] [*France*] [*Information service*] .... CIDET
Cooperation Mediterraneenne pour l'Energie Solaire .... COMPLES
Cooperation in Space [*USSR*] .... COSPAS
Cooperation via Televised Instruction in Education [*Colorado State University*] .... CO-TIE
Cooperative .... COOP
Cooperative Africana Microform Project, Archives-Libraries Committee, African Studies Association, Center for Research Libraries, Chicago, IL [*Library symbol*] .... ICRL(CAMP)
Cooperative Agricole des Producteurs de Cereales de la Region d'Arras .... CAPCRA
Cooperative for American Relief Everywhere [*Formerly, Cooperative for American Remittances to Europe and Cooperative for American Remittances to Everywhere*] .... CARE
Cooperative Analysis of Broadcasting [*Term used in TV rating*] .... CAB
Cooperative Applications Satellite [*France*] [*NASA*] .... CAS
Cooperative Area Manpower Planning System [*Environmental Protection Agency*] .... CAMPS
Cooperative Assessment of Experiential Learning [*Project*] .... CAEL
Cooperative Association of Professional Salespeople .... CAPS
Cooperative Atomic Migration .... CAM
Cooperative Awards in Pure Science [*British*] .... CAPS
Cooperative Bibliographic Center for Indiana Libraries .... COBICIL
Cooperative Bureau for Teachers [*Superseded by IES*] .... CBT
Cooperative College of Canada, Saskatoon, SK, Canada [*Library symbol*] .... CaSSC
Cooperative College Development Program .... CCDP
Cooperative College Library Center [*Library network*] CCLC
Cooperative College Library Center, Atlanta, GA [*OCLC symbol*] CCL
Cooperative College Registry [*Defunct*] .... CCR
Cooperative College-School Science [*Program*] [*Defunct*] [*National Science Foundation*] .... CCSS
Cooperative Commonwealth Federation [*Former Canadian political party; later, NDP*] .... CCF
Cooperative Computing System [*Echo detection*] .... CCS
Cooperative Convection Precipitation Experiment [*Meteorology*] .... CCOPE
Cooperative Education Association .... CEA
Cooperative Educational Enterprises .... CEE
Cooperative Educational Research Laboratory, Incorporated .... CERLI
Cooperative Educational Service Agency [*National Science Foundation*] .... CESA
Cooperative English Test .... CET
Cooperative Expendable Jammer .... CEJ
Cooperative Extension Service [*Department of Agriculture*] .... CES
Cooperative Finance Association of America .... CFAA
Cooperative Finance Corporation [*of National Rural Utilities*] .... CFC
Cooperative Financing Facility [*Export-Import Bank*] .... CFF
Cooperative Food Distributors of America .... CFDA
Cooperative Forest Fire Prevention [*Forest Service, Department of Agriculture*] .... CFFP
Cooperative Fuels Research [*Committee*] .... CFR
Cooperative Generic Technology [*Centers for cooperative government and industry work*] .... COGENT
Cooperative Health Statistics System [*Medicine*] .... CHSS
Cooperative Housing Foundation [*Formerly, FCH*] .... CHF
Cooperative Immunoassay .... CIA
Cooperative Industrial and Commercial Reference and Information Service .... CICRIS
Cooperative Information Network [*Library network*] .... CIN
Cooperative Institute for Research in Environmental Sciences .... CIRES
Cooperative Intelligence Network System [*Proposed*] [*Navy*] .... COINS
Cooperative International Pupil-to-Pupil Program .... CIPPP
Cooperative International Pupil-to-Pupil Program .... CIPTPP
Cooperative Investigation of the Caribbean and Adjacent Regions [*UNESCO*] .... CICAR
Cooperative Investigation of the Mediterranean .... CIM
Cooperative Investigation of the Northern Part of the Eastern Central Atlantic .... CINECA
Cooperative Investigations of a Large Ocean Gyre [*Proposed*] .... CILOG
Cooperative League of the United States of America .... CLUSA
Cooperative Libraries in Central Connecticut [*Library network*] CLICC
Cooperative Logistic Support Arrangement [*Military*] .... CLSA
Cooperative Logistics CL
Cooperative Logistics Support Program [*Air Force*] .... CLSP
Cooperative Machine-Readable Cataloging Program [*Library of Congress*] .... COMARC
Cooperative Management Housing Insurance Fund [*Federal Housing Administration*] .... CMHIF
Cooperative Manager and Farmer [*A publication*] .... Coop Manager & F
Cooperative Meteorological Rocket Network [*NASA*] .... CMRN
Cooperative Observational Week .... COW
Cooperative Preservation of Architectural Records .... COPAR
Cooperative Program in Educational Administration .... CPEA
Cooperative Program for Educational Opportunity .... CPEO
Cooperative Program of Research on Aquaculture [*UN Food and Agriculture Organization*] .... COPRAQ
Cooperative Project for Educational Development [*Office of Education*] .... COPED
Cooperative Publication Association .... CPA
Cooperative Recreation Service [*Later, World Around Songs*] .... CRS
Cooperative Research [*in agriculture*] .... COR
Cooperative Research Act .... CRA
Cooperative Research Council .... CRC
Cooperative Research and Development Program .... CR & DP
Cooperative Research Institute [*Defunct*] .... CORE
Cooperative Research Program [*Military and Office of Education*] .... CRP
Cooperative School Program [*US Employment Service*] [*Department of Labor*] .... CSP
Cooperative Society .... CS
Cooperative State Research Service [*Department of Agriculture*] .... CSRS
Cooperative Statistical Program [*For IUD data*] .... CSP
Cooperative Study of the Kuroshio [*UNESCO*] .... CSK
Cooperative Upper-Air Unit [*National Weather Service*] .... CUA
Cooperative Users of Equimatics Financial Systems .... CUEFS
Cooperative Weapons Data Indexing Committee [*AEC and DoD*] .... CWDIC
Cooperative Wind Tunnel .... CWT
Cooperative Work Experience Education Association .... CWEEA
Coopers' International Union of North America .... CIU
Coopers' International Union of North America .... CIUNA
Coopers Lake [*Montana*] [*Seismograph station code, US Geological Survey*] [*Closed*] .... CKM
Cooperstown & Charlotte Valley Railway Corp. [*AAR code*] .... CACV
Cooperstown Public Library, Cooperstown, ND [*Library symbol*] .... NdCo
Coopersville District Library, Coopersville, MI [*Library symbol*] .... MiCoop
CooperVision, Inc. [*NYSE symbol*] .... EYE
Coorbital Interceptor Scoring Technique .... CIST
Coordinate .... COOR
Coordinate [*or Coordination*] .... COORD
Coordinate Conversion Computer CCC
Coordinate Conversion Routine .... COCO
Coordinate Converter CC
Coordinate Data Transmission .... CDT
Coordinate Geometry [*Computer language*] .... COGO
Coordinate Index CI
Coordinate Indexing Group [*ASLIB*] .... CIG
Coordinate Measuring Machine .... CMM
Coordinate Rotation Digital Computer .... CORDIC
Coordinate Transformation System .... CTS
Coordinated Activity Allowance List [*Military*] .... COAAL
Coordinated Activity List [*Navy*] .... COOAL
Coordinated Agency-Wide Research Activities [*National Science Foundation*] .... CARA
Coordinated Aircraft/Stores Program [*Obsolete*] [*Navy*] .... COASP
Coordinated ASW [*Antisubmarine Warfare*] **Services and Training** [*Navy*] .... CAST
Coordinated Atomic Operations .... CAO
Coordinated Commentary Programing [*Data processing*] .... CCP
Coordinated Design Data Required .... CDDR
Coordinated Electronic Countermeasures Exercise [*Military*] .... COREX
Coordinated Evaluation System [*National Bureau of Standards*] .... CES
Coordinated Experimental Research [*Program*] [*National Science Foundation*] .... CER
Coordinated Federal Wage System .... CFWS
Coordinated Financial Planning .... CFP
Coordinated Fire Line .... CFL
Coordinated Hungarian Relief [*Defunct*] .... CHR
Coordinated Joint Outline Emergency Plan [*Military*] .... CJOEP
Coordinated Management of Meaning [*Communications theory*] .... CMM
Coordinated Manual Control .... CMC
Coordinated Navy Total Acquisition Control [*System*] .... CONTAC
Coordinated Occupational Information Network [*Bell & Howell Co.*] .... COIN
Coordinated Operability Test .... COT
Coordinated Procurement Program Appraisal [*DoD*] .... COPPA
Coordinated Reconnaissance Plan .... CRP
Coordinated Science Laboratory [*University of Illinois*] .... CSL
Coordinated Ship Development Plan [*Navy*] .... CSDP
Coordinated Ship Electronic Design .... CSED

Coordinated Shipboard [*or Shorebased*] **Allowance List** [*Navy*]........ COSAL
Coordinated Shipboard [*or Shorebased*] **Allowance List** [*Navy*]...... COSBAL
Coordinated Situation System........ CSS
Coordinated Test Plan [*Obsolete*]........ CTP
Coordinated Test Program........ CTP
Coordinated Transfer Application System [*For medical students*]........ COTRANS
Coordinated Universal Time........ CUT
Coordinated Vocational-Academic Education........ CVAE
Coordinates Computed........ CC
Coordinateur Automatique de Traffic........ CAUTRA
Coordinating Area Production Urgency Committee........ CAPUC
Coordinating Authority........ COORAUTH
Coordinating Board of Jewish Organizations........ CBJO
Coordinating Board of Tobacco Trade Associations [*Later, NATD*]........ CBTTA
Coordinating Committee........ COCOM
Coordinating Committee on Great Lakes Basic Hydraulic and Hydrologic Data [*US, Canada*]........ CCGLBHHD
Coordinating Committee of Independent Trade Unions........ CCITU
Coordinating Committee for International Voluntary Service........ CCIVS
Coordinating Committee on Materials Research and Development [*Executive Office of the President*]........ CCMRD
Coordinating Committee on Oceanography........ CCO
Coordinating Committee of Overseas Students Organization [*British*]........ CCOSO
Coordinating Committee for Slavic and East European Library Resources........ COCOSEERS
Coordinating Committee of Technical Assistance........ CCTA
Coordinating Committee of Trade Union Organizations [*Ceylon*]..... CCTUO
Coordinating Committee on Women in the Historical Profession.... CCWHP
Coordinating Council for Higher Education........ CCHE
Coordinating Council of Literary Magazines........ CCLM
Coordinating Council on Manufactured Housing Finance........ CCMHF
Coordinating Council on Medical Education [*Superseded by CFMA*]........ CCME
Coordinating Council of National Archaeological Societies........ CCONAS
Coordinating Council for North American Affairs........ CCNAA
Coordinating Council of Private Educational Associations........ COCOPEA
Coordinating Council of South African Trade Unions........ CCSATU
Coordinating Equipment Research Committee........ CER
Coordinating Fuel Research........ CFR
Coordinating Lubricant and Equipment Research Committee [*Coordinating Research Council*]........ CLR
Coordinating Organization of Book Associations........ COBA
Coordinating Panel [*NATO*]........ CP
Coordinating Research Council........ CRC
Coordinating Research Council. CRC Report [*A publication*]........ Coord Res Counc CRC Rep
Coordinating Research Council of the Petroleum Industry........ CRCPI
Coordinating of Research and Development [*Navy*]........ CORD
Coordinating Secretariat of National Unions of Students [*in Africa*]........ COSEC
Coordinating Working Party on Atlantic Fishery Statistics........ CWP
Coordination........ COORDN
Coordination of Allied Supplies [*World War II*]........ CAS
Coordination of Atomic Operations - Standard Operating Procedures........ CAO-SOP
Coordination of Benefits [*Insurance*]........ COB
Coordination Chemistry Reviews [*A publication*]........ Coord Ch Re
Coordination Committee for Transport Planning [*NATO*]........ CCTP
Coordination and Contract Summary Sheet........ CCSS
Coordination Control Board........ CCB
Coordination in Development [*International consortium of church-related and private voluntary service organizations*]........ CODEL
Coordination in Direct Support........ CIDS
Coordination Document........ CD
Coordination and Equipment........ C & E
Coordination and Information Center [*Department of Energy*] [*Information service*]........ CIC
Coordination Line........ CL
Coordination Message [*Aviation code*]........ CDN
Coordination Number [*Chemistry*]........ CN
Coordination of Operating Data by Automatic Computer........ CODAC
Coordination of Recent and Projected System Efforts [*DoD*]........ CORPSE
Coordination of Systems, Integrated Goals, and Networks [*DoD*]........ COSIGN
Coordinative Retrieval of Selectively Sorted Permuted Analogue-Title Entries [*Data processing*]........ CROSSPATE
Coordinator of Army Studies........ CAS
Coordinator for Industrial Cooperation [*Functions ceased, 1937*]........ CIC
Coordinator of Information........ COI
Coordinator of Inter-American Affairs........ CIAA
Coordinator and Liaison Maintenance Officer........ CLMO
Coors [*Adolph*] **Cl B** [*NASDAQ symbol*]........ ACCOB
Coos Bay, OR [*Television station call letters*]........ KCBY-TV
Coos Bay, OR [*Radio station call letters*]........ KHSN
Coos Bay, OR [*Radio station call letters*]........ KYNG
Coos Bay, OR [*Radio station call letters*]........ KYNG-FM
Coos Bay, OR [*Radio station call letters*]........ KYTT-FM
Coos Bay Public Library, Coos Bay, OR [*OCLC symbol*]........ BAY
Coos Bay Public Library, Coos Bay, OR [*Library symbol*]........ OrCb
Coos Bay Wagon Road [*Lands*] [*Department of the Interior*]........ CBWR
Coos County Library Association [*Library network*]........ CCLA
Coosa Valley Librarians Association [*Library network*]........ CVLA
Cootamundra [*Australia*] [*Airport symbol*]........ CMO
Copeland Corp. [*NYSE symbol*] [*Delisted*]........ CRF
Copenhagen [*Denmark*] [*Later, RSV*] [*Geomagnetic observatory code*]........ COP
Copenhagen [*Denmark*] [*Airport symbol*]........ CPH
Copenhagen [*Denmark*] [*Seismograph station code, US Geological Survey*]........ COP
Copenhagen, Brussels, and Amsterdam [*Refers to a group of expressionist artists based in these three cities*]........ COBRA
Copenhagen School of Economics and Business Administration. Language Department Publications [*A publication*]........ CEBAL
Copi-Elgot-Wright [*Electronics*]........ CEW
Copiague Memorial Public Library, Copiague, NY [*Library symbol*]..... NCop
Copiah-Jefferson Regional Library, Hazelhurst, MS [*Library symbol*]........ MsHz
Copiah-Lincoln Junior College [*Mississippi*]........ CLJC
Copiapo [*Chile*] [*Seismograph station code, US Geological Survey*]........ CPP
Copier Dealers Association........ CDA
Copilot........ CP
Copilot........ CPLT
Copilot/Gunner Stabilized Sight........ CGSS
Coping with Medical Issues [*Elsevier Book Series*] [*A publication*]........ CMI
Coplanar Waveguide........ CPW
Copley News Service........ CNS
Copley Newspapers, Inc., James S. Copley Library, La Jolla, CA [*Library symbol*]........ CLjC
Copolyester Elastomer [*Plastics technology*]........ COPE
Copolymerized with [*Organic chemistry*]........ co
Copper [*Chemical symbol is Cu*]........ C
Copper [*Chemical symbol is Cu*]........ COP
Copper [*Chemical symbol is Cu*]........ COPR
Copper [*Chemical symbol is Cu*]........ CPR
Copper Abstracts [*A publication*]........ Copper Abstr
Copper Alloy Tubing........ CAT
Copper Band [*Dentistry*]........ CuB
Copper and Brass Fabricators Council [*Formerly, CBFFTA*]........ CBFC
Copper and Brass Fabricators Foreign Trade Association [*Later, CBFC*]........ CBFFTA
Copper and Brass Research Association [*Superseded by CDA*]........ CABRA
Copper and Brass Research Association [*Superseded by CDA*]........ CBRA
Copper and Brass Servicenter Association [*Formerly, CBWA*]........ CBSA
Copper and Brass Warehouse Association [*Later, CBSA*]........ CBWA
Copper Center, AK [*Location identifier*] [*FAA*]........ CZC
Copper Chromite........ CC
Copper Data Center [*Battelle Memorial Institute*] [*Information service*]........ CDC
Copper Development Association [*Supersedes CABRA, CBRA*]........ CDA
Copper in Disguise [*Facetious translation of the initialism for Criminal Investigation Department, q.v.*]........ CID
Copper Fastened........ CF
Copper Jacketed Steel........ CJS
Copper Lake Explorations [*NASDAQ symbol*]........ CLEXF
Copper, Lead, or Zinc [*Freight*]........ CLZ
Copper Mine [*Northwest Territories*] [*Seismograph station code, US Geological Survey*] [*Closed*]........ CMC
Copper Nickel Alloy........ CNA
Copper Oxide........ CUO
Copper Oxide Modulator........ COM
Copper Oxide Rectifier........ COR
Copper Products Development Association [*Later, INCRA*]........ CPDA
Copper Queen Library, Bisbee, AZ [*Library symbol*]........ AzB
Copper Range Co. [*NYSE symbol*] [*Delisted*]........ CPX
Copper Range R. R. [*AAR code*]........ COPR
Copper Recovery Corporation........ CRC
Copper Shielding Braid........ CSB
Copper or Steel [*Freight*]........ CS
Copper, Steel, or Zinc [*Freight*]........ CSZ
Copper Sulfate Treated Sorbeads........ CSTS
Copper Sulfide Rectifier........ CSR
Copper Trade Association........ CTA
Copper Weld........ CW
Copperas Cove, TX [*Radio station call letters*]........ KOOV
Coppered........ C
Coppered........ COPD
Copperhill, TN [*Radio station call letters*]........ WLSB
Coppermine [*Canada*] [*Airport symbol*]........ YCO
Copperopolis, CA [*Radio station call letters*]........ KZDO
Coppersmith........ CSMITH
Copperweld Corp. [*Formerly, Copperweld Steel Co.*] [*NYSE symbol*]...... COS
Coppin State College, Baltimore, MD [*Library symbol*]........ MdBCS
Coppin State College, Parlett L. Moore Library, Baltimore, MD [*OCLC symbol*]........ MDP
Coprecipitation X-Ray Fluorescence Spectroscopy........ COPREX
Coproduction for Security Program [*US and Italy*]........ CSP
Coproporphyrin [*Also, CP*] [*Clinical chemistry*]........ COPRO
Coproporphyrin [*Also, COPRO*] [*Clinical chemistry*]........ CP

Coptic ... COP
Coptic ... COPT
Coptic [*MARC language code*] [*Library of Congress*] ... cop
Copulative ... COP
Copulatory Mechanism [*Medicine*] ... CM
Copy ... C
Copy ... CP
Copy ... CPY
Copy ... CY
Copy and Add Logical Word ... CAL
Copy Furnished [*Army*] ... CF
Copy Payments Center [*for copyrighted material*] ... CPC
Copy Processing System [*Photocomposition*] ... CPS
Copy of Reply Be Furnished This Office [*Army*] ... CORBFUS
Copy Research Council ... CRC
Copyright ... C
Copyright [*Deltiology*] ... CPY
Copyright Clearance Center [*of Association of American Publishers*] ... CCC
Copyright Law Symposium. American Society of Composers, Authors, and Publishers [*A publication*] ... Copyright L Sym (ASCAP)
Copyright Office [*US*] ... CO
Copyright Office Publication and Interactive Cataloging System [*Library of Congress*] ... COPICS
Copyright Royalty Tribunal [*Library of Congress*] ... CRT
Copyright Society of the United States of America ... CSUSA
Copyrighted ... COP
CopyTele, Inc. [*NASDAQ symbol*] ... COPY
Coque [*Boil*] [*Pharmacy*] ... COQ
Coquille, OR [*Radio station call letters*] ... KSHR
Coquille, OR [*Radio station call letters*] ... KSHR-FM
Coquille Public Library, Coquille, OR [*Library symbol*] ... OrCo
Cor Anglais [*English Horn*] ... CA
Coracoid Process [*Anatomy*] ... CP
Coradian Corp. [*American Stock Exchange symbol*] ... CDN
Coral [*Quality of the bottom*] [*Nautical charts*] ... Co
Coral Gables [*Florida*] ... CG
Coral Gables, FL [*Radio station call letters*] ... WRHC
Coral Gables, FL [*Radio station call letters*] ... WVCG
Coral Gables, FL [*Radio station call letters*] ... WVUM
Coral Gables, FL [*Radio station call letters*] ... WYOR
Coral Harbour [*Canada*] [*Airport symbol*] ... YZS
Coral Head [*Quality of the bottom*] [*Nautical charts*] ... Co Hd
Coralta Resources Ltd. [*NASDAQ symbol*] ... CORRF
Coralville Public Library, Coralville, IA [*Library symbol*] ... IaCorv
Coras Iompair Eireann [*Irish Transport Company*] ... CIE
Coratomic, Inc. [*NASDAQ symbol*] ... CORT
Corazon De Jesus [*Panama*] [*Airport symbol*] ... CZJ
Corbin [*Virginia*] [*Seismograph station code, US Geological Survey*] ... CBN
Corbin, KY [*Radio station call letters*] ... WCTT
Corbin, KY [*Radio station call letters*] ... WCTT-FM
Corbin, KY [*Radio station call letters*] ... WYGO
Corbin, KY [*Radio station call letters*] ... WYGO-FM
Corbit-Calloway Memorial Library, Odessa, DE [*OCLC symbol*] ... CRB
Corcom, Inc. [*NASDAQ symbol*] ... CORC
Corcoran Art Gallery, Washington, DC [*Library symbol*] ... DCA
Cord ... C
Cord ... CD
Cord-Air [*Pavilion, NY*] [*FAA designator*] ... CDS
Cord [*Umbilical*] **Blood Leukocytes** [*Hematology*] ... CBL
Cord Welt ... CDWT
Cordage Institute ... CI
Cordatum, Inc. [*NASDAQ symbol*] ... CDAT
Cordele, GA [*Radio station call letters*] ... WFAV
Cordele, GA [*Radio station call letters*] ... WMJM
Cordell Hull Foundation for International Education ... CHFIE
Cordi-Marian Missionary Sisters [*Roman Catholic religious order*] ... MCM
Cordis Corp. [*NASDAQ symbol*] ... CORD
Cordoba [*Monetary unit in Nicaragua*] ... C
Cordoba [*Argentina*] [*Airport symbol*] ... COR
Cordoba [*Spain*] [*Airport symbol*] ... ODB
Cordoba Durchmusterung [*Star chart*] ... CD
Cordon International Corp. [*American Stock Exchange symbol*] [*Delisted*] ... CD
Cordon and Search [*Military*] ... C & S
Cordova [*Alaska*] [*Airport symbol*] ... CDV
Cordova [*Alaska*] [*Seismograph station code, US Geological Survey*] ... CVA
Cordova Airlines, Inc. ... COA
Cordova, AK [*Location identifier*] [*FAA*] ... CKU
Cordova, AK [*Radio station call letters*] ... KLAM
Cordura Corp. [*NYSE symbol*] ... CDU
Corduroy [*A publication*] ... Cord
Corduroy Council of America [*Defunct*] ... CCA
Core ... CR
Core Auxiliary Cooling Water [*Nuclear energy*] ... CACW
Core Auxiliary Cooling Water System [*Nuclear energy*] ... CACWS
Core Auxiliary Heat Exchanger [*Nuclear energy*] ... CAHE
Core Component Cleaning System [*Nuclear energy*] ... CCCS
Core Component Conditioning Station [*Nuclear energy*] ... CCCS
Core Component Pot [*Nuclear energy*] ... CCP
Core Component Receiving Container [*Nuclear energy*] ... CCRC
Core Component Test Loop [*Nuclear energy*] ... CCTL
Core Current Driver ... CCD
Core Disruptive Accident [*Nuclear energy*] ... CDA
Core and Drum Corrector ... CADCO
Core File ... COFIL
Core Image Converter [*Data processing*] ... CIC
Core Industries, Inc. [*NYSE symbol*] ... CRI
Core Laboratories, Inc. [*American Stock Exchange symbol*] ... CLB
Core Laboratories, Inc., Dallas, TX [*Library symbol*] ... TxDaCL
Core Logic Intervalometer ... CLI
Core Logic Intervalometer ... CLIV
Core Maximum Fraction of Limiting Power Density [*Nuclear energy*] ... CMFLPD
Core Mechanical Mock-Up [*Nuclear energy*] ... CMM
Core Memory ... CM
Core Memory Driver ... CMD
Core Memory Unit ... CMU
Core Protection Computer [*Nuclear energy*] ... CPC
Core Restraint Mechanism [*Nuclear energy*] ... CRM
Core Sample Vacuum Container [*NASA*] ... CSVC
Core Segment ... CS
Core Segment Development Facility [*Nuclear energy*] ... CSDF
Core Segment Interface Unit ... CSIU
Core Segment Processing Unit ... CSPU
Core Segment Simulator ... CSS
Core Shift ... CS
Core Shift Driver ... CSD
Core Standby Cooling System [*Nuclear energy*] ... CSCS
Core Storage Element ... CSE
Core Storage Terminal Table [*Data processing*] ... CSTT
Core Support Structure [*Nuclear energy*] ... CSS
Core Test Facility ... CTF
Core Transistor Logic [*Data processing*] ... CTL
Core Transistor Register ... CTR
Corenco Corporation [*American Stock Exchange symbol*] [*Delisted*] ... CCR
CoreStates Financial [*NASDAQ symbol*] ... CSFN
Corey-Pauling-Koltun [*Molecular models*] ... CPK
Corfu [*Greece*] [*Airport symbol*] ... CFU
Corfu [*Washington*] [*Seismograph station code, US Geological Survey*] ... CRF
Corfu Free Library, Corfu, NY [*Library symbol*] ... NCorf
Corinaldo [*Italy*] [*Seismograph station code, US Geological Survey*] ... CRN
[*The*] **Corinth & Counce Railroad Co.** [*AAR code*] ... CCR
Corinth, MS [*Radio station call letters*] ... WADI
Corinth, MS [*Radio station call letters*] ... WALP
Corinth, MS [*Radio station call letters*] ... WCMA
Corinth, MS [*Radio station call letters*] ... WKCU
Corinth, MS [*Radio station call letters*] ... WKCU-FM
Corinthians [*New Testament book*] ... Cor
Coriolanus [*Shakespearean work*] ... Cor
Coriolis Absorber ... CA
Coriolis Acceleration Platform ... CAP
Coriolis Correction ... Z
Coriolis Sickness Susceptibility Index [*Orientation*] ... CSSI
Cork ... CK
Cork ... CRK
Cork [*Ireland*] [*Airport symbol*] ... ORK
Cork Base ... CKB
Cork Board ... CKBD
Cork Floor ... CKF
Cork Institute of America [*Defunct*] ... CIA
Cork Insulation Material ... CIM
Cormosea Newsletter [*A publication*] ... Cormosea Newsl
Corn Annual [*A publication*] ... Corn Ann
Corn, Beans, Miami [*Tongue-in-cheek description of a crop rotation system. Modern time-saving equipment allegedly allows farmers to rotate corn and soybeans in summer, spend winter in Miami*] ... CBM
Corn Belt Library System [*Library network*] ... CBLS
Corn Belt Library System, Bloomington, IL [*Library symbol*] ... IBloC
Corn Belt Library System, Normal, IL [*OCLC symbol*] ... JAF
Corn Belt Livestock Feeders Association [*Later, NCA*] ... CBLFA
Corn-Equivalent Feed Unit ... CFU
Corn Exchange Bank [*NYSE symbol*] ... CEX
Corn Industries Research Foundation [*Later, CRA*] ... CIRF
Corn Refiners Association ... CRA
Corn, Soybean, and Milk [*Products*] [*Main ingredients of a formulated food*] ... CSM
Corn Stunt [*Plant pathology*] ... CS
Corn Stunt Organism [*Plant pathology*] ... CSO
Corn Syrup Solids ... CSS
Corn Trade Clauses [*Shipping*] ... CTC
Corneal Transplant [*Medicine*] ... CT
Corned Beef [*Restaurant slang*] ... CB
Cornelia, GA [*Radio station call letters*] ... WCON
Cornelia, GA [*Radio station call letters*] ... WCON-FM
Cornelia de Lange Parents Group [*Later, Cornelia de Lange Syndrome Foundation*] ... CLPG
Cornelio Procopio [*Brazil*] [*Airport symbol*] ... CKO
Cornelius Corp. [*American Stock Exchange symbol*] [*Delisted*] ... L
Cornell Aeronautical Laboratory ... CAL
Cornell Aeronautical Laboratory, Buffalo, NY [*Library symbol*] ... NBuCA

Cornell College, Mount Vernon, IA [*Library symbol*] .... IaMvC
Cornell College, Mount Vernon, IA [*OCLC symbol*] .... IMV
Cornell Computing Language .... CORC
Cornell Dubilier Electronics .... CDE
Cornell Electron Storage Ring [*Atomic physics*] .... CESR
Cornell Engineer [*A publication*] .... Cornell Eng
Cornell Extension Bulletin [*A publication*] .... Cornell Ext Bull
Cornell Feed Service. New York State College of Agriculture. Extension Service [*Cornell University*] [*A publication*] .... Cornell Feed Serv NY State Coll Agr Ext Serv
Cornell High-Energy Synchrotron Source [*Laboratory*] .... CHESS
Cornell Hotel Administration Simulation Exercise [*Computer-programed management game*] .... CHASE
Cornell Hotel and Restaurant Administration Quarterly [*A publication*] .... Cornell Hotel & Rest Adm Q
Cornell Hotel and Restaurant Administration Quarterly [*A publication*] .... Cornell Hotel & Restau Adm Q
Cornell Hotel and Restaurant Administration Quarterly [*A publication*] .... Cornell Hotel Restaur Adm Q
Cornell Index [*Psychology*] CI
Cornell International Law Journal [*A publication*] .... Cornell I J
Cornell International Law Journal [*A publication*] .... Cornell Int L J
Cornell International Symposium and Workshop on the Hydrogen Economy [*A publication*] .... Cornell Int Symp Workshop Hydrogen Econ
Cornell Journal of Social Relations [*A publication*] .... Cornell J S
Cornell Journal of Social Relations [*A publication*] .... Cornell J Soc Relat
Cornell Law Quarterly [*A publication*] .... Cornell L Q
Cornell Law Review [*A publication*] .... Cornell Law Rev
Cornell Law Review [*A publication*] .... Cornell L R
Cornell Law Review [*A publication*] .... Cornell L Rev
Cornell Learning and Recognizing Automation .... CLARA
Cornell Learning and Recognizing Automaton .... CLARA
Cornell Library Journal [*A publication*] .... CLJ
Cornell Library Journal [*A publication*] .... Cornell Lib J
Cornell List Processor [*Data processing*] .... CLP
Cornell Medical Index [*Psychology*] .... CMI
Cornell Plantations [*A publication*] .... Cornell Plant
Cornell Plantations [*A publication*] .... Cornell Plantat
Cornell Studies in Classical Philology [*A publication*] .... CSPh
Cornell Studies in English [*A publication*] .... CSE
Cornell University. Agricultural Experiment Station. Publications [*A publication*] .... Cornell Ag Exp
Cornell University. Department of Structural Engineering. Report [*A publication*] .... Cornell Univ Dep Struc Eng Rep
Cornell University, Ithaca, NY [*OCLC symbol*] .... COO
Cornell University, Ithaca, NY [*Library symbol*] .... NIC
Cornell University Laboratory of Ornithology .... CULO
Cornell University Libraries. Bulletin [*A publication*] .... Cornell Univ Lib Bull
Cornell University, Medical College, New York, NY [*Library symbol*] .... NNCorM
Cornell University, Medical College, New York, NY [*OCLC symbol*] .... VYC
Cornell University, Medical College, Oskar Diethelm Historical Library, New York, NY [*Library symbol*] .... NNCorM-D
Cornell Veterinarian [*A publication*] .... Cornell Vet
Cornell Veterinarian. Supplement [*A publication*] .... Cornell Vet Suppl
Cornell, WI [*Radio station call letters*] .... WOGO
Cornell Word Form 2 [*Psychology*] CWF2
Corner .... COR
Corner Brook City Library, Corner Brook, NF, Canada [*Library symbol*] .... CaNfCB
Corner Brook, NF [*Radio station call letters*] .... CBY
Corner Brook, NF [*Television station call letters*] .... CBYT
Corner Brook, NF [*Radio station call letters*] .... CFCB
Corner Brook, NF [*Television station call letters*] .... CJWN-TV
Corner Brook, NF [*Radio station call letters*] .... CKOZ-FM
Corner Wear [*Deltiology*] .... COR/WR
Cornerback [*Football*] .... CB
Cornet .... COR
Cornet .... CORT
Cornhill Magazine [*A publication*] .... CM
Cornhill Magazine [*A publication*] .... Cornh
Cornhusker Army Ammunition Plant .... CAAP
Corning, AR [*Radio station call letters*] .... KCCB
Corning Community College, Corning, NY [*Library symbol*] .... NCorniCC
Corning Community College, Corning, NY [*OCLC symbol*] .... ZDG
Corning Free Public Library, Corning, IA [*Library symbol*] .... IaCorn
Corning Glass Works .... CGW
Corning Glass Works [*NYSE symbol*] [*Wall Street slang name: "Glow Worm"*] .... GLW
Corning Glass Works, Corning, NY [*Library symbol*] .... NCorniC
Corning Museum of Glass, Corning, NY [*Library symbol*] .... NCorniM
Corning Museum of Glass, Corning, NY [*OCLC symbol*] .... YKM
Corning, NY [*Radio station call letters*] .... WCBA
Corning, NY [*Radio station call letters*] .... WCLI
Corning, NY [*Radio station call letters*] .... WZKZ
Corning Public Library, Corning, NY [*Library symbol*] .... NCorni
Corning Uniformity Limit Level .... CULL
Cornish [*MARC language code*] [*Library of Congress*] .... cor
Cornish Archaeology [*A publication*] .... Cornish Arch
Cornish Studies [*A publication*] .... CS
Corno Emplumado [*A publication*] .... CE
Cornu Double Prism .... CDP
Cornu-Jellet Prism .... CJP
Cornwall [*County in England*] .... CORN
Cornwall [*County in England*] .... CRNWL
Cornwall, CT [*Radio station call letters*] .... WKKA
Cornwall, NY [*Radio station call letters*] .... WCRR
Cornwall, ON [*Radio station call letters*] .... CFLG-FM
Cornwall, ON [*Radio station call letters*] .... CFML
Cornwall, ON [*Television station call letters*] CJOH-TV-8
Cornwall, ON [*Radio station call letters*] .... CJSS
Cornwall Public Library, Cornwall, NY [*Library symbol*] .... NCorn
Cornwall Public Library, Cornwall, ON, Canada [*Library symbol*] .... CaOC
Cornwall R. R. [*AAR code*] .... CWL
Cornwell-Weisskopf Formula .... CWF
Coro [*Venezuela*] [*Airport symbol*] .... CZE
Coro Foundation .... CF
Corolla C
Corollary .... COROL
Corollary Discharge Neuron [*Neurophysiology*] .... CD
Corona [*A publication*] .... Co
Corona Australis [*Constellation*] .... CorA
Corona Australis [*Constellation*] .... CrA
Corona Borealis [*Constellation*] .... CorB
Corona Borealis [*Constellation*] .... CrB
Corona, CA [*Television station call letters*] .... KBSC-TV
Corona, CA [*Radio station call letters*] .... KWRM
Corona Current Detector .... CCD
Corona, Eddy Current, Beta Ray, Microwave .... CEBM
Corona Extinction Voltage .... CEV
Corona, NM [*Location identifier*] [*FAA*] .... CNX
Corona Onset Voltage .... COV
Corona Public Library, Corona, CA [*Library symbol*] .... CCoro
Corona Starting Voltage .... CSV
Coronado National Memorial .... CORO
Coronado Public Library, Coronado, CA [*Library symbol*] .... CCoron
Coronary Arteriosclerotic Heart Disease .... CASHD
Coronary Arteriovenous Fistula [*Cardiology*] .... CAVF
Coronary Artery [*Medicine*] .... CA
Coronary Artery Bypass [*Medicine*] .... CAB
Coronary Artery Bypass Graft [*Medicine*] .... CABG
Coronary Artery Bypass Graft Surgery [*Medicine*] .... CABGS
Coronary Artery Disease [*Medicine*] .... CAD
Coronary Artery Risk Evaluation Program [*Air Force*] .... CARE
Coronary Artery Surgery Study [*Medicine*] .... CASS
Coronary Artery Surgery Trial [*Medicine*] .... CAST
Coronary Care Team [*Medicine*] .... CCT
Coronary Care Unit [*of a hospital*] .... CCU
Coronary Club CC
Coronary Drug Project .... CDP
Coronary Flow [*Medicine*] .... CF
Coronary Heart Disease [*Medicine*] .... CHD
Coronary Insufficiency [*Medicine*] CI
Coronary Intensive Care Unit [*of a hospital*] .... CICU
Coronary Sclerosis [*Medicine*] .... CS
Coronary Sinus [*Cardiology*] .... CS
Coronary Status [*Cardiology*] .... CS
Coronary Thrombosis [*Medicine*] .... CT
Coronation, AB [*Television station call letters*] CKRD-TV-1
Coronel Fontana [*Argentina*] [*Seismograph station code, US Geological Survey*] .... CFA
Coroner .... COR
Coroners' Rolls [*British*] .... COR
Corozal [*Belize*] [*Airport symbol*] .... CZH
Corozal, PR [*Radio station call letters*] .... WORO
Corpora Amylacea [*Neurology*] .... CA
Corpora Cardiaca [*Endocrinology*] CC
Corporacion del Cobre de Chile [*Chilean government copper corporation*] .... CODELCO
Corporacion Dominicana de Empresas Estatales [*Dominican Republic*] .... CORDE
Corporacion de Fomento de la Produccion [*Industrial promotion agency*] [*Chile*] .... CORFO
Corporacion de Investigaciones Economicas para Latinoamerica .... CIEPLAN
Corporacion Minera de Bolivia .... COMIBOL
Corporacion Venezolana de Fomento [*Venezuelan Development Corporation*] .... CVF
Corporal .... CORP
Corporal .... CORPL
Corporal [*Military*] .... CPL
Corporal E4
Corporal-Major of Horse [*British*] .... CMH
Corporate Accountability Research Group [*Formed by consumer-advocate Ralph Nader*] .... CARG
Corporate Action Project [*Defunct*] .... CAP
Corporate Administrative Contracting Officer [*DoD*] .... CACO
Corporate Air, Inc. [*Hartford, CT*] [*FAA designator*] .... CPR
Corporate Air Travel, Inc. [*Tallahassee, FL*] [*FAA designator*] .... CRP
Corporate Angel Network [*An association*] .... CAN
Corporate Average Fuel Economy [*Automobile industry*] .... CAFE

Corporate Capital Charge CCC
Corporate Capital Resources [*NASDAQ symbol*] .... CCRS
Corporate Committee of Telecommunications Users .... CCTU
Corporate Communications System [*Bell-Northern Research Ltd.*] [*Data processing*] .... COCOS
Corporate Consolidated Data Network [*IBM Corp.*] .... CCDN
Corporate Contract Officer .... CCO
Corporate Control Procedure .... CCP
Corporate Data Base .... CDB
Corporate Data Exchange [*An association*] .... CDE
Corporate Democracy [*An association*] .... CD
Corporate Emergency Response Center [*Nuclear emergency planning*] .... CERC
Corporate Engineering and Sales Directive .... CEASD
Corporate Income Tax [*Economics*] .... CIT
Corporate Industrial Preparedness Representative [*Military*] .... CIPR
Corporate Information Center [*Later, ICCR*] CIC
Corporate Information Processing Standards .... CIPS
Corporate Mountaineers Cult .... CMC
Corporate Office .... CO
Corporate Planning Office [*AFSC*] CCX
Corporate Practice Commentator [*A publication*] .... Corp Prac Comm
Corporate Purchasing Agreements .... COPA
Corporate Research and Development .... CRD
Corporate Source [*Data processing*] .... CS
Corporate Technical Information Center .... CTIC
Corporate Transfer Agents Association .... CTAA
Corporation .... CORP
Corporation .... CORPN
Corporation Commission CC
Corporation for Economics and Industrial Research [*Subsidiary of Control Data Corp.*] .... CEIR
Corporation des Instituteurs et Institutrices Catholiques du Quebec CIC
Corporation Journal [*A publication*] .... Corp J
Corporation of London [*The City of London as opposed to Greater London*] .... C of L
Corporation Network [*Telephone communications*] .... CORNET
Corporation Pierre-Boucher, Trois-Rivieres, PQ, Canada [*Library symbol*] .... CaQTCPB
Corporation for Public Broadcasting .... CPB
Corporation Standard Practice .... CSP
Corporation Tax [*British*] .... CT
Corporations and Labor Union Returns Act .... CALURA
Corporeal Pin [*Method of tuberculin and histoplasmin testing*] [*Medicine*] .... CORPPIN
Corpori [*To the Body*] [*Pharmacy*] .... CORP
Corps C
Corps Advisory Detachment .... CAD
Corps d'Afrique .... C d'A
Corps Area Communications System [*Vietnam*] .... CACS
Corps d'Armee [*Army Corps*] [*France*] .... CA
Corps Automation Requirements [*Army*] .... CAR
Corps Brandenburgia .... CB
Corps of Cadets .... COC
Corps Commander Coast Artillery [*British*] .... CCCA
Corps Contingency Force [*Army*] .... CCF
Corps Diplomatique [*Diplomatic Corps*] .... CD
Corps of Engineers [*Army*] .... C of E
Corps of Engineers [*Army*] .... CE
Corps of Engineers [*Army*] .... COE
Corps of Engineers [*Army*] .... COREN
Corps of Engineers Ballistic Missile Construction Agency [*Army*] .... CEBMCA
Corps of Engineers Ballistic Missile Construction Office [*Army*] .... CEBMCO
Corps of Engineers Board of Contract Appeals [*Army*] .... ENGBCA
Corps of Engineers (Civil Works) [*Army*] .... COE(CW)
Corps of Engineers Guide Specifications for Emergency Type Construction [*Army*] .... CE-E
Corps of Engineers Manual for Military Construction [*Army*] .... EMMC
Corps of Engineers Office of Appalachian Studies [*Army*] .... CEOAS
Corps of Engineers Reserve Fleet .... CERF
Corps of Engineers Technical Committee [*Army*] .... CETC
Corps of Engineers Waterborne Commerce Statistics Center [*Army*] .... CEWCSC
Corps Epidemiological Reference Office [*Military*] .... CERO
Corps Expeditionaire Francais .... CEF
Corps Front Luxembourgeois [*Resistance organization in Luxembourg*] [*World War II*] .... CFL
Corps Headquarters [*Army*] .... CHQ
Corps Maintenance Area .... CMA
Corps of Military Police [*British*] .... CMP
Corps Movement Control Organization [*Royal Corps of Transport*] [*British*] .... CMCO
Corps Observation .... CO
Corps Phase Line .... CPL
Corps Service Area [*Army*] .... COSA
Corps Specifications Revision .... CSR
Corps Storage Area [*Military*] .... CSA
Corps Support Brigade .... CSB
Corps Support Command [*Army*] .... COSCOM
Corps Support Missile System .... CSMS
Corps Support Weapon System .... CSWS
Corps Tactical Operations Center .... CTOC
Corps Tactical Zone [*Military*] .... CTZ
Corps of Transportation [*Army*] .... CT
Corps Wanita Angkatan Darat [*Indonesia*] .... COWAD
Corpus [*Body*] [*Latin*] .... COR
Corpus Allatum .... CA
Corpus Callosum [*Brain anatomy*] CC
Corpus Christi [*Texas*] [*Airport symbol*] .... CRP
Corpus Christi Army Depot .... CCAD
Corpus Christi Campaign CCC
Corpus Christi College [*Cambridge and Oxford*] CCC
Corpus Christi Geological Society. Bulletin [*A publication*] .... Corpus Christi Geol Soc Bull
Corpus Christi Public Library, Corpus Christi, TX [*OCLC symbol*] .... CCA
Corpus Christi State University, Corpus Christi, TX [*OCLC symbol*] .... TXF
Corpus Christi, TX [*Location identifier*] [*FAA*] .... CUX
Corpus Christi, TX [*Radio station call letters*] .... KCCT
Corpus Christi, TX [*Radio station call letters*] .... KCTA
Corpus Christi, TX [*Television station call letters*] .... KEDT
Corpus Christi, TX [*Radio station call letters*] .... KEXX
Corpus Christi, TX [*Radio station call letters*] .... KEYS
Corpus Christi, TX [*Radio station call letters*] .... KFLB-FM
Corpus Christi, TX [*Television station call letters*] .... KIII
Corpus Christi, TX [*Radio station call letters*] .... KIOU
Corpus Christi, TX [*Radio station call letters*] .... KKED-FM
Corpus Christi, TX [*Television station call letters*] .... KORO-TV
Corpus Christi, TX [*Television station call letters*] .... KRIS-TV
Corpus Christi, TX [*Radio station call letters*] .... KRYS
Corpus Christi, TX [*Radio station call letters*] .... KSIX
Corpus Christi, TX [*Radio station call letters*] .... KUNO
Corpus Christi, TX [*Radio station call letters*] .... KZFM
Corpus Christi, TX [*Television station call letters*] .... KZTV
Corpus Christi, TX [*Location identifier*] [*FAA*] .... NPJ
Corpus Christi, TX [*Location identifier*] [*FAA*] .... OYC
Corpus Christianorum [*A publication*] CC
Corpus Inscriptionum Atticarum [*A publication*] .... CIA
Corpus Inscriptionum Etruscarum [*A publication*] .... CIE
Corpus Inscriptionum Graecarum [*A publication*] .... CIG
Corpus Inscriptionum Latinarum [*A publication*] CIL
Corpus Inscriptionum Semiticarum [*A publication*] .... CIS
Corpus Juris [*Body of Law*] [*Latin*] .... CJ
Corpus Juris Secundum [*A publication*] .... CJS
Corpus Luteum [*Endocrinology*] CL
Corpus Scriptorum Christianorum Orientalium [*A publication*] .... CSCO
Corpus Scriptorum Ecclesiasticorum Latinorum [*A publication*] .... CSEL
Corpus Vasorum Antiquorum [*A publication*] .... CVA
Corpuscular Volume [*Hematology*] CV
Corrales, NM [*Radio station call letters*] .... KXAK
Correct [*or Corrected or Correction*] .... CORR
Correct .... CQ
Correct .... CRT
Correct Age Stocking and Height [*Inventory*] [*Forestry*] .... CASH
Correct [*an error*] **or Amplify** [*information*] [*US Copyright Office form*] .... CA
Correct Code CC
Correct Copy [*A printing direction*] CX
Correct End Item .... CEI
Correct Seating Institute .... CSI
Correct Selection [*Statistics*] .... CS
Correct Words per Minute [*Typewriting, etc.*] .... CWPM
Correctable Gate [*Data processing*] .... CORREGATE
Corrected Count Increment [*Hematology*] CI
Corrected Effective Temperature .... CET
Corrected Geomagnetic Latitude .... CGL
Corrected Geomagnetic Time .... CGT
Corrected Head Count .... CHC
Corrected Mean Temperature .... CMT
Corrected Sedimentation Rate [*Medicine*] .... CSR
Corrected Unpostable [*IRS*] .... CU
CorRecTerm [*Mergenthaler typesetting*] .... CRT
Correcting Computer .... CORCOM
Correction C
Correction .... CO
Correction .... COR
Correction .... CRTN
Correction Action Committee .... CAC
Correction of Deficiency .... COD
Correction Factor .... CF
Correction to Follow .... CTF
Correction Memo .... CM
Correction Notice .... CN
Correctional Administrators Association of America [*Later, ASCA*] .... CAA
Correctional Custody Facility [*Military*] .... CCF
Correctional Custody Unit [*Navy*] .... CCU
Correctional Education Association .... CEA
Correctional Facilities Association .... CFA
Correctional Health Care Program .... CHCP
Correctional Holding Detachment [*Military*] .... CHD
Correctional Industries Association .... CIA
Correctional Service Associates .... CSA

Correctional Service Federation - USA ... CSF/USA
Correctional Services of Ontario, Toronto, ON, Canada [*Library symbol*] ... CaOTCS
Correctional Training Facility [*Army*] ... CTF
Corrections to Applied Research Laboratories Ion-Sputtering Mass Analyzers [*Data processing*] ... CARISMA
Corrections Magazine [*A publication*] ... Correct Mag
Corrective ... CORREC
Corrective Action ... CA
Corrective Action Board ... CAB
Corrective Action Directive [*or Disposition*] ... CAD
Corrective Action Reply ... CAR
Corrective Action Report ... CAR
Corrective Action Request ... CAR
Corrective Eye Care Foundation ... CECF
Corrective Lens [*Freight*] ... C LN
Corrective Maintenance ... CM
Corrective Maintenance Burden ... CMB
Corrective Maintenance System ... CMS
Corrective and Social Psychiatry [*A publication*] ... Corr Soc Ps
Corrective Therapist ... CT
Corregidor-Bataan Memorial Commission [*Government agency*] [*Terminated, 1967*] ... CBMC
Correio Agricola [*A publication*] ... Correio Agric
Correlated Color Temperature ... CCT
Correlated Data Processor ... CDP
Correlated RADAR Data Printout [*Electronics*] ... CORDPO
Correlated RADAR Data Printout - Separation of RADAR Data [*Electronics*] ... CORDPO-SORD
Correlated Spectroscopy ... COSY
Correlation ... CORR
Correlation Air Navigation ... CAN
Correlation Bombing System [*Air Force*] ... CBS
Correlation Cancellation System ... CCS
Correlation Detection and Ranging ... CODAR
Correlation Display Analyzing and Recording ... CODAR
Correlation Echo Sound Processor [*Oceanography*] ... CESP
Correlation Factor ... CF
Correlation-Protected Instrument Landing System ... CP-ILS
Correlation RADAR ... CORAD
Correlation Radio Link ... CORAL
Correlation Spectrometer ... COSPEC
Correlation Tracking and Ranging [*System*] [*Satellite and missile tracking term*] [*RADAR*] ... COTAR
Correlation Tracking and Ranging Angle Measuring Equipment [*RADAR*] ... COTAR-AME
Correlation Tracking and Ranging Data Acquisition System [*RADAR*] ... COTAR-DAS
Correlation Tracking and Ranging Data Measuring Equipment [*RADAR*] ... COTAR-DME
Correlation Tracking and Triangulation ... COTAT
Correlative ... COR
Correlative ... CORR
Correlative ... CORREL
Correo Erudito [*A publication*] ... CE
Correo Literario [*A publication*] ... CLit
Correo Literario [*A publication*] ... CorL
Correspond ... CORRES
Correspondance d'Orient. Etudes [*A publication*] ... Corresp Orient Et
Correspondence ... COR
Correspondence ... CORR
Correspondence Aid [*A publication*] ... CA
Correspondence Chess League of America ... CCLA
Correspondence Course ... CC
Correspondence Factor Analysis ... CFA
Correspondence Review Group [*NASA*] ... CRG
Correspondence Routing Form ... CRF
Correspondence and Service Branch [*BUPERS*] ... C & SB
Correspondent [*A publication*] ... C
Correspondent [*A publication*] ... Cor
Correspondent Validity File [*IRS*] ... CVF
Correspondenzblatt des Naturforscher-Vereins zu Riga [*A publication*] ... Cor-Bl Naturf-Ver Riga
Corresponding ... CORRESP
Corresponding Fellow ... CF
Corresponding Member ... CM
Corresponding Member of the International Institute of Arts and Letters ... CIAL
Corresponding Member of the Zoological Society [*British*] ... CMZS
Corresponding States Equation [*Physics*] ... CSE
Corridor ... COR
Corridor [*Board on Geographic Names*] ... CRDR
Corridor Assignment [*Aviation*] ... CORAS
Corrientes [*Argentina*] [*Airport symbol*] ... CNQ
Corriere della Sera [*A publication*] ... CdS
Corrin [*Biochemistry*] ... Crn
Corris, Machynlleth, & River Dovey Tramway [*Wales*] ... CM & RDT
Corris Railway [*Wales*] ... COR R
Corroon & Black Corp. [*NYSE symbol*] ... CBL
Corrosion ... CORR
Corrosion ... CRSN
Corrosion Abstracts [*A publication*] ... Corros Abstr
Corrosion Engineering (Tokyo) [*A publication*] ... Corros Eng (Tokyo)
Corrosion Evaluation and Test Area [*NASA*] ... CETA
Corrosion Interception Sleeve ... CIS
Corrosion Prevention and Control [*A publication*] ... Corros Pre Contr
Corrosion Prevention and Control [*A publication*] ... Corros Prev Control
Corrosion Prevention Panel ... CPP
Corrosion y Proteccion [*A publication*] ... Corros Prot
Corrosion and Protection Association ... CAPA
Corrosion Resistant ... CRE
Corrosion-Resistant Steel ... CRES
Corrosion Science [*A publication*] ... Corrosion Sci
Corrosion Science [*A publication*] ... Corros Sci
Corrosion, Traitements, Protection, Finition [*A publication*] ... Corros Trait Prot Finition
Corrosive ... COR
Corrosive ... CRSV
Corrugated ... CORR
Corrugated ... CORU
Corrugated Container Institute [*Defunct*] ... CCI
Corrugated or Cupped [*Freight*] ... CC
Corrugated, Cupped, or Indented [*Freight*] ... CCI
Corrugated Galvanized Iron ... CGI
Corrugated-Laminated Coaxial [*Cable*] ... CLOAX
Corrugated Metal Pipe [*Technical drawings*] ... CMP
Corrugated Newsletter [*A publication*] ... Corrugated Newsl
Corrugated TEFLON Tubing ... CTT
Corrugated Wire Glass [*Technical drawings*] ... CWG
Corrupt ... COR
Corrupt ... CORR
Corrupt Commissioners [*Federal operation investigating illegal practices by Oklahoma's county commissioners*] ... CORCOM
Corry, PA [*Location identifier*] [*FAA*] ... ORJ
Corry, PA [*Radio station call letters*] ... WWCB
CORS [*Canadian Operational Research Society*] **Journal** [*A publication*] ... CORS J
Corse Historique [*A publication*] ... CHist
Corse Historique. Etudes et Documents [*A publication*] ... Corse Hist
Corset and Brassiere Association of America [*Later, AAMA*] ... CBAA
Corset and Brassiere Council [*Defunct*] ... CBC
Corset and Brassiere Women's Club [*Later, Underfashion Club of New York*] ... CBWC
Corsi di Cultura sull'Arte Ravennate e Bizantina [*A publication*] ... CCAB
Corsica ... CORS
Corsican National Liberation Front [*France*] ... FLNC
Corsicana, TX [*Radio station call letters*] ... KAND
Corsicana, TX [*Radio station call letters*] ... KXCL
Cortex [*Anatomy*] ... C
Cortex [*Bark*] [*Pharmacy*] ... CORT
Cortex [*A publication*] ... CRTXA
Cortez [*Colorado*] [*Airport symbol*] ... CEZ
Cortez, CO [*Radio station call letters*] ... KISZ
Cortez, CO [*Radio station call letters*] ... KVFC
Cortez Public Library, Cortez, CO [*Library symbol*] ... CoCo
Cortical Blood Flow [*Urology*] ... CBF
Cortical Evoked Potential [*Neurophysiology*] ... CEP
Cortical Magnification Factor ... CMF
Cortical Spreading Depression [*Medicine*] ... CSD
Cortically Induced Movement [*Medicine*] ... CIM
Cortically Originating Extra-Pyramidal System [*Physiology*] ... COEPS
Corticoliberin-Like Immunoreactivity ... CLI
Corticosteroid [*Endocrinology*] ... CS
Corticosteroid-Binding Globulin [*Transcortin*] [*Endocrinology*] ... CBG
Corticosterone Methyl Oxidase [*An enzyme*] ... CMO
Corticotrophin-Like Intermediate-Lobe Peptide [*Endocrinology*] ... CLIP
Corticotrophin-Releasing Factor [*Also, CRH*] [*Endocrinology*] ... CRF
Corticotrophin-Releasing Hormone [*Also, CRF*] [*Endocrinology*] ... CRH
Cortisone [*Endocrinology*] ... COR
Cortisone Acetate [*Endocrinology*] ... CA
Cortisone [*Primed*] **Oral Glucose Tolerance Test** [*Medicine*] ... COGTT
Cortland County Historical Society, Cortland, NY [*Library symbol*] ... NCortHi
Cortland Free Library, Cortland, NY [*Library symbol*] ... NCort
Cortland, NY [*Radio station call letters*] ... WKRT
Cortland, NY [*Radio station call letters*] ... WSUC-FM
Corumba Mato Grosso [*Brazil*] [*Airport symbol*] ... CMG
Corundum [*CIPW classification*] [*Geology*] ... C
Corvair Society of America ... CORSA
Corvallis [*Oregon*] [*Seismograph station code, US Geological Survey*] ... COR
Corvallis Clinic, Corvallis, OR [*Library symbol*] ... OrCC
Corvallis Environmental Research Laboratory [*Environmental Protection Agency*] ... CERL
Corvallis, OR [*Location identifier*] [*FAA*] ... CVO
Corvallis, OR [*Radio station call letters*] ... KBVR
Corvallis, OR [*Radio station call letters*] ... KEJO
Corvallis, OR [*Radio station call letters*] ... KFLY
Corvallis, OR [*Radio station call letters*] ... KLOO
Corvallis, OR [*Radio station call letters*] ... KLOO-FM
Corvallis, OR [*Radio station call letters*] ... KOAC
Corvallis, OR [*Television station call letters*] ... KOAC-TV

Corvallis, OR [*Location identifier*] [*FAA*]....LWG
Corvallis Public Library, Corvallis, OR [*Library symbol*]....OrC
Corvette [*Navy symbol*]....DDC
Corvus [*Constellation*]....Corv
Corvus [*Constellation*]....Crv
Corvus Systems, Inc. [*NASDAQ symbol*]....CRVS
Corydon, IN [*Radio station call letters*]....WJDW
Coryza [*Medicine*]....CZ
COSAL [*Coordinated Shipboard Allowance List*] **Processing Point**....COPP
Cosco, Inc. [*American Stock Exchange symbol*] [*Delisted*]....CSO
Cosecant....COSEC
Cosecant [*Mathematics*]....CSC
Cosecant, Hyperbolic....CSCH
Coshocton, OH [*Radio station call letters*]....WTNS
Coshocton, OH [*Radio station call letters*]....WTNS-FM
Cosiguina [*Nicaragua*] [*Seismograph station code, US Geological Survey*]....COS
Cosine [*Mathematics*]....COS
Cosine of the Amplitude....CN
Cosine Emission Law....CEL
Cosine, Hyperbolic....COSH
Cosine Integral....Ci
Cosite Analysis Model [*Data processing*]....COSAM
Cosmetic Career Women [*Later, CEW*]....CCW
Cosmetic Chemists. Journal of the Society [*A publication*]....Cos Chem
Cosmetic Executive Women [*Formerly, CCW*]....CEW
Cosmetic Industry Buyers and Suppliers Association....CIBS
Cosmetic Ingredient Review [*Program*] [*Cosmetic, Toiletry, and Fragrance Association*]....CIR
Cosmetic Sciences [*NASDAQ symbol*]....COSS
Cosmetic, Toiletry, and Fragrance Association [*Formerly, TGA*]....CTFA
Cosmetics for the Community of Tomorrow [*Acronym used as brand name*]....KOSCOT
Cosmetics and Toiletries [*A publication*]....Cosmet & Toiletries
Cosmetics and Toiletries [*A publication*]....Cos & Toil
Cosmetology Accrediting Commission [*Later, NACCAS*]....CAC
Cosmetology Program [*Association of Independent Colleges and Schools specialization code*]....CS
Cosmic Background Explorer [*NASA*]....COBE
Cosmic Dust Detector....CDD
Cosmic Electrodynamics [*A publication*]....Cosmic Electrodyn
Cosmic Noise Absorption....CNA
Cosmic Ray....CR
Cosmic Ray Albedo Neutron Decay [*Geophysics*]....CRAND
Cosmic Ray Altimeter....CRA
Cosmic Ray Detector [*NASA*]....CRD
Cosmic Ray Emulsion Plastic Equipment [*NASA*]....CREPE
Cosmic Ray Flux....CRF
Cosmic Ray Gas....CRG
Cosmic Ray Ionization Program [*NASA*]....CRISP
Cosmic Ray Isotope Experiment....CRIE
Cosmic Ray Nuclear Experiment....CRANE
Cosmic Ray Particle....CRP
Cosmic Ray Physics Laboratory....CRPL
Cosmic Ray Satellite [*Japan*]....CORSA
Cosmic Ray Shower....CRS
Cosmic-Ray Subsystem [*Astrophysics*]....CRS
Cosmic Ray Telescope....CRT
Cosmic Research [*A publication*]....Cosmic Res
Cosmic Science Fiction [*A publication*]....Cosm
Cosmic Stories [*A publication*]....Cos
Cosmic Top Secret....CTS
Cosmic X-Ray Background....CXB
Cosmo Communications [*NASDAQ symbol*]....CSMO
Cosmo Dog....CD
Cosmography....COSMOG
Cosmopolitan [*A publication*]....Cosmop
Cosmopolitan [*A publication*]....Cosmopol
Cosmopolitan Associates [*Later, OC*]....CA
Cosmopolitan Aviation Corp. [*Farmingdale, NY*] [*FAA designator*]....CMO
Cosmopolitan International....CI
Cosmopolitan Soccer League [*Formerly, GAFA*]....CSL
Cosmos Club, Washington, DC [*Library symbol*]....DCos
Cosmos Science Fiction and Fantasy Magazine [*A publication*]....Cos
Coso Basin North [*California*] [*Seismograph station code, US Geological Survey*]....CBHM
Coso Springs South [*California*] [*Seismograph station code, US Geological Survey*]....CSSM
COSPAR [*Committee on Space Programs for Earth Observation*] **International Reference Atmosphere**....CIRA
Cosponsor....COSP
Cossack-American Citizens Committee....CACC
Cost....C
Cost Account....CA
Cost Account Code....CAC
Cost Account Number....CAN
Cost Account Package....CAP
Cost Account Performance Status Report....CAPSR
Cost Accountant....CA
Cost Accounting Standards....CAS
Cost Accounting Standards Board [*US*] [*Terminated*]....CASB
Cost Analysis Improvement Group....CAIG
Cost Analysis Information Report [*Air Force*]....CAIR
Cost Analysis of LASER Investment, Production, Engineering, and Research Cost Mode....CALIPER
Cost Analysis Monthly Exchange [*Army*]....CAME
Cost Analysis Office [*Army*]....CAO
Cost of Analysis Organization [*Navy*]....CAO
Cost Analysis Plan....CAP
Cost Analysis Task Force [*NASA*]....CATF
Cost Analysis Technical Manual....CATEM
Cost of Arms [*Army*]....C/A
Cost Audit Board....CAB
Cost-Benefit Analysis [*Accounting*]....CBA
Cost/Burden Reduction....C/BR
Cost Center....CC
Cost Center Determination....CCD
Cost Center Performance Measurement System....CCPMS
Cost Change Commitment Notice....CCCN
Cost Charge Number....CCN
Cost Code....CC
Cost Control Item....CCI
Cost Control Program....CCP
Cost Data Bank Index....CDBI
Cost Data Plan....CDP
Cost and Economic Information System [*DoD*]....CEIS
Cost-Effective Ratio [*Economics*]....CER
Cost Effective Surface Torpedo....CEST
Cost Effectiveness....CE
Cost-Effectiveness Analysis....CEA
Cost Effectiveness Analysis of Bonuses and Reenlistment Policies....CEABREP
Cost-Effectiveness Analysis Methodology....CEAM
Cost Effectiveness Index....CEI
Cost Effectiveness Study....CES
Cost Element Monitor [*Air Force*]....CEM
Cost Engineering [*A publication*]....Cost Eng
Cost Estimate Change Order....CECO
Cost Estimate Control Data Center....CECDC
Cost Estimate Dispersion....CED
Cost Estimate Error Report....CEER
Cost Estimate Input Sheet [*Jet Propulsion Laboratory, NASA*]....CEIS
Cost Estimating Relationship....CER
Cost Estimating Techniques for System Acquisition [*Army*]....CETSA
Cost of Facilities....C of F
Cost-Factoring System for Force Readiness Projection....COFACTS
Cost per Flight [*NASA*]....CPF
Cost and Freight [*Business and trade*]....CAF
Cost and Freight [*Business and trade*]....C & F
Cost and Freight [*Business and trade*]....CF
Cost and Freight [*Business and trade*] [*"INCOTERM," International Chamber of Commerce official code*]....CFR
Cost, Freight, Assurance [*Business and trade*]....CFA
Cost, Freight, and Insurance [*Business and trade*]....CF & I
Cost, Freight, and Insurance [*Business and trade*]....CFI
Cost Improvement Program....CIP
Cost Information Reporting Data Plan....CRDP
Cost Information Reports [*DoD*]....CIR
Cost Information System....CIS
Cost per Inquiry....CPI
Cost Inspection Service [*Navy*]....CIS
Cost Inspector....CI
Cost per Instruction [*Data processing*]....CPI
Cost and Insurance [*Business and trade*]....C & I
Cost and Insurance [*Business and trade*]....CI
Cost, Insurance, and Freight [*Business and trade*] [*"INCOTERM," International Chamber of Commerce official code*]....CIF
Cost, Insurance, Freight, and Commission [*Business and trade*]....CIF & C
Cost, Insurance, Freight, and Commission [*Business and trade*]....CIFC
Cost, Insurance, Freight, Commission, and Exchange [*Business and trade*]....CIFCE
Cost, Insurance, Freight, Commission, and Interest [*Business and trade*]....CIFC & I
Cost, Insurance, Freight, Commission, and Interest [*Business and trade*]....CIFCI
Cost, Insurance, Freight, and Exchange [*Business and trade*]....CIF & E
Cost, Insurance, Freight, and Exchange [*Business and trade*]....CIFE
Cost, Insurance, Freight, Free Out [*Business and trade*]....CIFFO
Cost, Insurance, Freight, and Interest [*Business and trade*]....CIFI
Cost, Insurance, Freight, and Interest [*Business and trade*]....CIF & I
Cost, Insurance, Freight, Interest, and Exchange [*Business and trade*]....CIFI & E
Cost, Insurance, Freight, London Terms [*Business and trade*]....CIFLT
Cost of Knowing....CoK
Cost Laid Down....CLD
Cost, Life, Interchangeability, Function, and Safety [*Navy*]....CLIFS
Cost of Living....C of L
Cost of Living....CL
Cost of Living....COL
Cost of Living Allowance....COLA
Cost of Living Council [*Also, COLC*] [*Terminated, 1974*] [*Acronym pronounced "click"*]....CLC

Cost of Living Council [*Also, CLC*] [*Terminated, 1974*] ... COLC
Cost-of-Living Index ... CLI
Cost and Management [*A publication*] ... Cost and Man
Cost and Management [*A publication*] ... Cost Manage
Cost Management Improvement Program ... CMIP
Cost and Material Position System ... CAMPS
Cost Measurement Technique ... COMET
Cost and Operational Effectiveness Analysis [*Military*] ... COEA
Cost Operations Management Information Center ... COMIC
Cost-Oriented Models Built to Analyze Tradeoffs ... COMBAT
Cost-Oriented Systems Technique ... COST
Cost-of-Ownership ... COO
Cost and Performance ... CP
Cost and Performance Effectiveness Ratios ... CAPERS
Cost Performance Index ... CPI
Cost Performance Report ... CPR
Cost and Performance Summary Report [*Army*] ... CPSR
Cost Planning and Appraisal ... CPA
Cost Planning and Control System ... CPCS
Cost Plus Award Fee [*Business and trade*] ... CPAF
Cost Plus Fixed Fee [*Business and trade*] ... CPFF
Cost Plus Incentive [*Business and trade*] ... CPI
Cost-Plus-Incentive-Award Fee [*Business and trade*] ... CPIAF
Cost-Plus-Incentive Fee [*Business and trade*] ... CIF
Cost-Plus-Incentive Fee [*Business and trade*] ... CPIF
Cost Plus No Fee [*Business and trade*] ... CPNF
Cost Plus a Percentage of Cost [*Business and trade*] ... CPPC
Cost Price of the Items Canceled [*Business and trade*] ... CPIC
Cost Progress Evaluation ... COPE
Cost Proposal ... CP
Cost Proposal Outline ... CPO
Cost Quote Request ... CQR
Cost Reduction Alternative Study ... CRAS
Cost Reduction Curve ... CRC
Cost Reduction Early Decision Information Techniques [*Hughes Aircraft Co.*] ... CREDIT
Cost Reduction Journal ... CRJO
Cost Reduction Program ... CRP
Cost Reduction Report ... CRR
Cost Reimbursement ... CR
Cost Reimbursement Contract ... CRC
Cost Reimbursement Incentive Contracting [*Business and trade*] ... CRIC
Cost of Sale ... C/S
Cost Schedule and Control System ... CSCS
Cost/Schedule Control System Criteria ... C/SCSC
Cost and Schedule Planning and Control ... CSPC
Cost/Schedule Planning and Control Specification [*Air Force*] ... C/SPCS
Cost Schedule Status Report ... C/SSR
Cost Schedule Technical Control System ... CSTCS
Cost Sensitivity Factor ... CSF
Cost of Service Indexing ... COSI
Cost Sharing ... CS
Cost per Thousand [*Advertising*] ... CPM
Cost and Training Effectiveness Analysis ... COTA
Cost and Training Effectiveness Analysis ... CTEA
Cost Travel Chargeable ... TRAVCHAR
Cost per Unit ... CPU
Cost Variance ... CV
Costa [*Rib*] [*Anatomy*] ... C
Costa Rica [*MARC country of publication code*] [*Library of Congress*] ... cr
Costa Rica [*Three-letter standard code*] ... CRI
Costa Rica [*MARC geographic area code*] [*Library of Congress*] ... nccr---
Costa Rica [*Aircraft nationality and registration mark*] ... TI
Costa Rica [*Two-letter standard code*] ... CR
Costa Rica. Boletin de Fomento [*A publication*] ... Costa Rica B Fomento
Costa Rica. Centro de Estudios Sismologicos. Anales [*A publication*] ... Costa Rica Centro de Estudios Sismologicos An
Costa Rica. Ministerio de Agricultura y Ganaderia. Boletin Miscelaneo [*A publication*] ... Costa Rica Minist Agric Ganad Bol Misc
Costa Rica. Ministerio de Agricultura y Ganaderia. Boletin Tecnico [*A publication*] ... Costa Rica Minist Agric Ganad Bol Tec
Costal Margin [*Medicine*] ... CM
Costilla County Library, San Luis, CO [*Library symbol*] ... CoSl
Costing and Data Management System ... CADMS
Costovertebral Angle [*Medicine*] ... CVA
Costruzioni Metalliche [*A publication*] ... Costr Met
Costs, Budgeting, and Economics ... CBE
Costs Chargeable to Fund Authorization [*Army*] ... CHGFA
Costs Chargeable to Purchase Authorization Advice ... CHGPAA
Costume Designers Guild ... CDG
Costume Jewelry Board of Trade of New York ... CJBT
Costume Jewelry Salesmen's Association ... CJSA
Costume Jewelry Trade Association [*Defunct*] ... CJTA
Costume Society of America ... CSA
Cosumnes River College, Sacramento, CA [*OCLC symbol*] ... CCR
Cosworth Vega Owner's Association ... CVOA
Cotabato [*Philippines*] [*Airport symbol*] ... CBO
Cotangent [*Mathematics*] ... COT
Cotangent ... CTN
Cotangent, Hyperbolic ... COTH
Cotangent, Hyperbolic ... CTGH
Cotati, CA [*Television station call letters*] ... KRCB-TV
Coto 47 [*Costa Rica*] [*Airport symbol*] ... OTR
Coton et Fibres Tropicales [*A publication*] ... Coton Fibres Trop
Cotonou [*Benin*] [*Airport symbol*] ... COO
Cotswold Personality Assessment [*Psychology*] ... CPA
Cott Corp. [*American Stock Exchange symbol*] [*Delisted*] ... CTT
Cottage Grove, OR [*Radio station call letters*] ... KNND
Cottages ... COTTS
Cotter ... COT
Cottey College, Nevada, MO [*Library symbol*] ... MoNvC
Cotton ... C
Cotton ... COT
Cotton ... CTN
Cotton Council International ... CCI
Cotton Digest [*A publication*] ... Cotton Dig
Cotton Equalization Program ... CEP
Cotton Export Market Acreage Program ... CEMAP
Cotton Growing Review [*A publication*] ... Cotton Grow Rev
Cotton Importers Association ... CIA
Cotton Incorporated [*An association*] ... CI
Cotton Insurance Association [*Defunct*] ... CIA
Cotton, Jute, or Sisal [*Freight*] ... CJS
Cotton. Monthly Review of the World Situation [*A publication*] ... Cotton Rev
Cotton Piece Goods ... CPG
Cotton Plant - Fargo Railway Co. [*AAR code*] ... CPF
Cotton Research Corporation ... CRC
Cotton Research Corporation. Cotton Research Reports [*A publication*] ... Cotton Res Corp Cotton Res Rep
Cotton Research Corporation. Progress Reports from Experiment Stations [*A publication*] ... Cotton Res Corp Prog Rep Exp Stn
Cotton Research Institute. Sindos Science Bulletin. New Series [*A publication*] ... Cotton Res Inst Sindos Sci Bull New Ser
Cotton Seed ... CS
Cotton States Life & Health Insurance [*NASDAQ symbol*] ... CSLH
Cotton Warehouse Association of America [*Formerly, NCCCWA*] ... CWAA
Cotton Warehouse Inspection Service [*Defunct*] ... CWIS
Cotton or Wool [*Freight*] ... CW
Cottonseed [*Freight*] ... COTNSD
Cottonseed Flour ... CF
Cottonseed Meal ... CSM
Cottonseed Protein Isolate ... CI
Cottonwood [*California*] [*Seismograph station code, US Geological Survey*] ... CWC
Cottonwood, AZ [*Radio station call letters*] ... KSMK-FM
Cottonwood, AZ [*Radio station call letters*] ... KVRD
Cottonwood Mountains [*California*] [*Seismograph station code, US Geological Survey*] ... CTW
Cottonwood Public Library, Cottonwood, AZ [*Library symbol*] ... AzCot
Coty, Inc. [*NYSE symbol*] [*Delisted*] ... COT
Coty International Corp. [*NYSE symbol*] [*Delisted*] ... CYI
Couch ... COU
Couch Potatoes [*An association*] ... CP
Coudersport, PA [*Radio station call letters*] ... WFRM
Coudersport & Port Allegany [*AAR code*] ... CPA
Cougar Club of America ... CCA
Cough [*Medicine*] ... C
Cough [*Medicine*] ... CGH
Cough and Deep-Breathe [*Medicine*] ... C & DB
Could ... CD
Couldn't Be Cuter [*Slang*] ... CBC
Coulee Dam National Recreation Area ... CODA
Coulomb [*Symbol*] [*SI unit of electric charge*] ... C
Coulomb [*Quantity of electricity*] ... CB
Coulomb ... COUL
Coulombs per Cubic Meter ... C/M^3
Coulombs per Kilogram ... C/KG
Coulombs per Volt ... C/V
Coulsdon Library, Croydon, United Kingdom [*Library symbol*] ... UkCrC
Coulter Diagnostics, Inc., Hialeah, FL [*Library symbol*] ... FHiaC
Council ... COUN
Council of 1890 College Presidents ... CCP
Council on Abandoned Military Posts - USA ... CAMP
Council Accepted [*Medicine*] ... CA
Council of Active Independent Oil and Gas Producers ... CAIOGP
Council of Administrators of Special Education ... CASE
Council on Adoptable Children ... COAC
Council of Adult Stutterers [*Later, NCS*] ... CAS
Council on Advanced Programing ... CAP
Council for the Advancement of Citizenship ... CAC
Council for the Advancement of Consumer Policy ... CACP
Council for the Advancement of Experiential Learning ... CAEL
Council for the Advancement of Hospital Recreation [*Defunct*] ... CAHR
Council for the Advancement of the Psychological Professions and Sciences [*Later, AAP*] ... CAPPS
Council for the Advancement of Science Writing ... CASW
Council for Advancement of Secondary Education [*Defunct*] ... CASE
Council for the Advancement of Small Colleges [*Later, CIC*] ... CASC
Council for the Advancement and Support of Education ... CASE
Council of Affiliated Associations of Jewelers of America ... CAAJA

Council of AFL-CIO Unions for Scientific, Professional, and Cultural Employees [*Later, Department for Professional Employees, AFL-CIO*] ....SPACE
Council Against Communist Aggression [*Later, CDF*] ....CACA
Council for Agricultural and Chemurgic Research ....CACR
Council for Agricultural Science and Technology ....CAST
Council of Air-Conditioning and Refrigeration Industry ....CARI
Council, AK [*Location identifier*] [*FAA*] CIL
Council of the Alleghenies ....CA
Council for Alternatives to Stereotyping in Entertainment ....CASE
Council of American Artist Societies ....CAAS
Council of American Building Officials ....CABO
Council of American Chambers of Commerce in Europe [*Later, Council of American Chambers of Commerce - Europe and Mediterranean*] ....CACCE
Council of American-Flag Ship Operators ....CASO
Council of American Indian Arts ....CAIA
Council of American Maritime Museums ....CAMM
Council of American Official Poultry Tests ....CAOPT
Council for American Private Education ....CAPE
Council of American Survey Research Organizations ....CASRO
Council of the Americas ....COA
Council of the Americas/Fund for Multinational Management Education ....CoA/FMME
Council on Anthropology and Education ....CAE
Council on Anthropology and Education Quarterly [*A publication*] ....Council Anthropol Educ Qu
Council of Arab Economic Unity ....CAEU
Council of Archives and Research Libraries in Jewish Studies ....CARLJS
Council on Arteriosclerosis of the American Heart Association ....CAAHA
Council of Association Attorneys ....CAA
Council on Atmospheric Sciences ....COAS
Council on Atmospheric Studies ....CAS
Council for Basic Education ....CBE
Council of Better Business Bureaus ....CBBB
Council for Better Hearing and Speech Month ....CBHSM
Council on Biological Sciences Information ....CBSI
Council of Biology Editors ....CBE
Council for Biology in Human Affairs ....CBHA
Council of Black Architectural Schools ....COBAS
Council Bluffs Free Public Library, Council Bluffs, IA [*Library symbol*] ....IaCb
Council Bluffs Free Public Library, Council Bluffs, IA [*OCLC symbol*] ....IWB
Council Bluffs, IA [*Location identifier*] [*FAA*] ....CBF
Council Bluffs, IA [*Television station call letters*] ....KBIN
Council Bluffs, IA [*Radio station call letters*] ....KIWR
Council Bluffs, IA [*Radio station call letters*] ....KLNG
Council Bluffs, IA [*Radio station call letters*] ....KQKQ
Council on Botanical and Horticultural Libraries ....CBHL
Council of the Brass and Bronze Ingot Industry ....CBBII
Council for British Archaeology ....CBA
Council of Canning Association Executives [*Later, CFPAE*] ....CCAE
Council for Career Planning [*Formerly, AAC*] ....CCP
Council of Chemical Associations ....CCA
Council for Chemical Research ....CCR
Council of Chief State School Officers ....CCSSO
Council for Children with Behavioral Disorders ....CCBD
Council on Chiropractic Education ....CCE
Council on Chiropractic Orthopedics ....CCO
Council for Christian Medical Work [*Later, CHH*] ....CCMW
Council for Christian Social Action [*Later, OCIS*] [*United Church of Christ*] ....CCSA
Council on Christian Unity ....CCU
Council of Churches CC
Council of Citizens with Low Vision CCLV
Council on Clinical Optometric Care [*American Optometric Association*] ....CCOC
Council for Clinical Training [*Later, ACPE*] ....CCT
Council of Colleges of Arts and Sciences ....CCAS
Council of Communication Societies ....CCS
Council of Community Blood Centers ....CCBC
Council of Community Churches [*Later, National Council of Community Churches*] CCC
Council for a Competitive Economy ....CCE
Council for Computerized Library Networks ....CCLN
Council of Conservationists CC
Council of Construction Employers [*Defunct*] ....CCE
Council of Consumer Advisers ....CCA
Council on Consumer Information [*Later, ACCI*] CCI
Council of Container Carriers CCC
Council on the Continuing Education Unit ....CCEU
Council on Cooperation in Teacher Education [*Defunct*] ....CCTE
Council on Cooperative College Projects [*Later, CCP*] ....CCCP
Council for Cultural Cooperation [*Council of Europe*] CCC
Council for the Defense of Freedom ....CDF
Council of Defense and Space Industry Associations ....CODSIA
Council for Democracy in Korea ....CDK
Council for Democratic and Secular Humanism ....CODESH
Council for a Department of Peace ....CODEP
Council Deputies ....CD
Council for the Development of Economic and Social Research in Africa ....CODESRIA
Council for the Development of French in Louisiana ....CODOFIL
Council for Distributive Teacher Education ....CDTE
Council on Documentation Research [*Defunct*] ....CDR
Council of Eastern Orthodox Youth Leaders of the Americas ....CEOYLA
Council of Economic Advisers [*to the President*] ....CEA
Council on Economic and Cultural Affairs [*Later, ADC*] [*Rockefeller Brothers Fund, Ford Foundation activity*] ....CECA
Council for Economic Growth and Security [*Defunct*] ....CEGS
Council for Economic Mutual Assistance [*Also known as CMEA, COMECON*] [*Communist-bloc nations: Poland, Russia, East Germany, Czechoslovakia, Romania, Bulgaria, Hungary*] ....CEMA
Council on Economic Policy [*Inactive*] ....CEP
Council on Economic Priorities ....CEP
Council on Education of the Deaf ....CED
Council on Education in the Geological Sciences ....CEGS
Council for the Education of the Partially Seeing [*Later, Division for the Visually Handicapped*] ....CEPS
Council on Education in Professional Responsibility [*Later, CLEPR*] ....CEPR
Council on Education for Public Health ....CEPH
Council for Educational Advance [*British*] ....CEA
Council for Educational Development and Research ....CEDAR
Council of Educational Facility Planners ....CEFP
Council for Educational Freedom in America ....CEFA
Council on Electrolysis Education ....CEE
Council for Elementary Science International ....CESI
Council on Employee Benefits ....CEB
Council for the Encouragement of Music and the Arts [*Later, Arts Council*] ....CEMA
Council on Energy Policy [*Proposed Presidential council*] ....CEP
Council of Energy Resource Tribes [*American Indian organization*] ....CERT
Council of Engineering Institutions [*British*] ....CEI
Council on Engineering Laws [*Defunct*] ....CEL
Council of Engineering and Scientific Society Executives ....CESSE
Council of Engineering Society Secretaries [*Later, CESSE*] ....CESS
Council of Engineers and Scientists Organizations ....CESO
Council on Environmental Alternatives ....CEA
Council on Environmental Pollutants ....CEP
Council on Environmental Quality [*of Federal Council on Science and Technology*] ....CEQ
Council of Europe ....CE
Council of Europe ....COE
Council of European-American Associations [*Later, FEAO*] ....CEAA
Council of the European Communities ....CEC
Council of European Industrial Federations ....CEIF
Council of European Municipalities ....CEM
Council for European Studies ....CES
Council for Exceptional Children ....CEC
Council for Export Trading Companies ....CETC
Council on Family Health ....CFH
Council of Fashion Designers of America ....CFDA
Council of Federated Jewish Organizations [*Defunct*] ....CFJO
Council of Federated Organizations [*Also, CFO*] [*Defunct*] ....COFO
Council on Fertilizer Application [*Defunct*] ....CFA
Council of Film Organizations ....CFO
Council for Financial Aid to Education ....CFAE
Council of Fleet Specialists ....CFS
Council of Food Processors Association Executives ....CFPAE
Council on Foreign Economic Policy [*Functions transferred to Secretary of State, 1961*] ....CFEP
Council of Foreign Ministers ....CFM
Council on Foreign Relations ....CFR
Council on Foreign Relations, New York, NY [*Library symbol*] ....NNCFR
Council of Forest Industries of British Columbia, Vancouver, BC, Canada [*Library symbol*] ....CaBVaCF
Council on Foundations ....CF
Council on Foundations, New York, NY [*Library symbol*] ....NNCFo
Council of General Motors Credit Unions ....CGMCU
Council on Governmental Relations ....COGR
Council of Governments [*Voluntary organizations of municipalities and counties*] ....COG
Council of Graduate Schools in the United States ....CGS
Council of Graduate Schools in the United States ....CGSUS
Council of Graphological Societies ....COGS
Council of the Great City Schools ....CGCS
Council on Health Information and Education ....CHIE
Council of Health Organizations ....COHO
Council for Health and Welfare Services, United Church of Christ ....CHWS
Council on Hemispheric Affairs ....COHA
Council on Higher Education in the American Republics [*Later, ICHE*] ....CHEAR
Council for Holocaust Survivors with Disabilities [*Formerly, NCJISN*] ....CHSD
Council on Hotel, Restaurant, and Institutional Education ....CHRIE
Council of Housing Producers [*Defunct*] ....CHP
Council of Independent Colleges [*Formerly, CASC*] CIC
Council for Independent Distribution [*Later, CPDA*] ....CID
Council of Independent Managers ....CIM
Council for Independent School Aid ....CISA

Council of Industrial Boiler Owners ... CIBO
Council of Industrial Design [*British*] ... COID
Council of Institute of Telecommunication Engineers ... CITE
Council for Inter-American Cooperation [*Later, NFTC*] ... CIAC
Council for Inter-American Security ... CIS
Council for Intercultural Studies and Programs ... CISP
Council for Interdisciplinary Communication in Medicine ... CIDCOMED
Council of Intergovernmental Coordinators ... CIC
Council for Interinstitutional Leadership ... CIL
Council of International Civil Aviation ... CICA
Council on International Economic Policy [*Terminated, 1977*] ... CIEP
Council on International Educational Exchange ... CIEE
Council for International Exchange of Scholars ... CIES
Council of International Investigators ... CII
Council of International Lay Associations [*Defunct*] ... CILA
Council on International Nontheatrical Events ... CINE
Council for International Organizations of Medical Sciences ... CIOMS
Council of International Programs for Youth Leaders and Social Workers [*Also known as Council of International Programs*] ... CIP
Council for International Progress in Management ... CIPM
Council on International and Public Affairs ... CIPA
Council on International Scientific and Technological Cooperation ... CISTC
Council for International Urban Liaison ... CIUL
Council on Interracial Books for Children ... CIBC
Council for Intersocietal Studies ... CIS
Council on Islamic Affairs ... CIA
Council for Jewish Education [*Formerly, NCJE*] ... CJE
Council of Jewish Federations [*Formerly, CJFWF*] ... CJF
Council of Jewish Federations and Welfare Funds [*Later, CJF*] ... CJFWF
Council of Jewish Organizations in Civil Service ... CJO
Council of Jewish Organizations in Civil Service ... CJOCS
Council of Jews from Germany ... CJG
Council of Landscape Architectural Registration Boards ... CLARB
Council for Languages and Other International Studies ... CLOIS
Council for Latin America [*Later, COA*] ... CLA
Council for Lay Life and Work ... CLLW
Council for Learning Disabilities ... CLD
Council on Legal Education Opportunity ... CLEO
Council on Legal Education for Professional Responsibility ... CLEPR
Council of Library Association Executives ... CLAE
Council on Library-Media Technical-Assistants ... COLT
Council on Library Resources ... CLR
Council on Library Resources. Recent Developments [*A publication*] ... CLR Recent Devt
Council for a Livable World ... CLW
Council for Livestock Protection ... CLP
Council of the Living Theatre [*Defunct*] ... CLT
Council of Lutheran Church Men [*Defunct*] ... CLCM
Council on Marine Resources and Engineering Development ... CMRED
Council of Mechanical Specialty Contracting Industries [*Later, ASC*] ... CMSCI
Council for Medical Affairs ... CFMA
Council on Medical Education [*of the American Medical Association*] ... CME-AMA
Council on Medical Television [*Later, HESCA*] ... CMT
Council of Mennonite Colleges ... CMC
Council for Microphotography and Document Reproduction [*British*] ... CMDR
Council for Microphotography and Document Reproduction [*British*] ... MICRODOC
Council for Middle Eastern Affairs [*Defunct*] ... CMEA
Council for Military Aircraft Propulsion Standards ... CMAPS
Council for Military Aircraft Standards ... CMAS
Council of Mining and Metallurgical Institutions ... CMMI
Council of Motion Picture Organizations ... COMPO
Council on Multiemployer Pension Security ... COMPS
Council on Municipal Performance ... CMP
Council on Municipal Performance ... COMP
Council for Mutual Economic Assistance [*Also known as CEMA, COMECON*] [*Communist-bloc nations: Poland, Russia, East Germany, Czechoslovakia, Romania, Bulgaria, Hungary*] ... CMEA
Council for Mutual Economic Assistance [*Also known as CEMA, CMEA*] [*Communist-bloc nations: Poland, Russia, East Germany, Czechoslovakia, Romania, Bulgaria, Hungary*] ... COMECON
Council of Mutual Savings Institutions ... CMSI
Council for National Academic Awards [*British*] ... CNAA
Council for National Cooperation in Aquatics ... CNCA
Council of National Library Associations [*Later, CNLIA*] ... CNLA
Council of National Library and Information Associations [*Formerly, CNLA*] ... CNLIA
Council on National Literatures ... CNL
Council of National Organizations for Adult Education ... CNO-AE
Council of National Organizations for Children and Youth [*Later, NCOCY*] ... CNOCY
Council for Native American Indian Progress ... CNAIP
Council for Noncollegiate Continuing Education ... CNCE
Council of North Atlantic Shipping Associations [*Also, CONASA*] ... CNASA
Council of North Atlantic Shipping Associations [*Also, CNASA*] ... CONASA
Council for a Nuclear Weapons Freeze ... CNWF
Council on Occupational Licensing [*Later, NCOL*] ... COL
Council of Oil-Importing Nations ... COIN
Council for Old World Archaeology [*Defunct*] ... COWA
Council of Ontario Universities, Toronto, ON, Canada [*Library symbol*] ... CaOTCOU
Council Operations and Exercise Committee [*NATO*] ... COEC
Council for Opportunity in Graduate Management Education [*Minority student program*] ... COGME
Council on Optical Radiation Measurement ... CORM
Council on Optometric Education [*American Optometric Association*] ... COE
Council of the Organization of American States [*OAS*] ... COAS
Council of Organizations Serving the Deaf [*Defunct*] ... COSD
Council of Oriental Organizations ... COO
Council for Overseas Colleges of Arts, Sciences, and TETOC [*British*] ... COCAST
Council of Pennsylvania State College and University Library Directors [*Library network*] ... COPSCAULD
Council for Periodical Distributors Associations ... CPDA
Council of Philatelic Organizations ... COPO
Council for Philosophical Studies ... CPS
Council of Planning Librarians ... CPL
Council on Podiatry Education ... CPE
Council of Pollution Control Financing Agencies ... CPCFA
Council on Population and Environment ... COPE
Council on Postal Suppression ... COPS
Council on Postsecondary Accreditation ... COPA
Council for the Preservation of Rural England ... CPRE
Council of Professional Associations on Federal Statistics ... COPAFS
Council on Professional Certification ... CPC
Council for Professional Education for Business [*Later, AACSB*] **n**] ... CPEB
Council for Research in Music Education. Bulletin [*A publication*] ... CRME
Council for Research on Turkish History ... CRTH
Council on Resident Education in Obstetrics and Gynecology ... CREOG
Council of Resident Stock Theatres ... CORST
Council for Responsible Nutrition ... CRN
Council of Review Board [*Army*] ... CRB
Council Rock High School, Newtown, PA [*Library symbol*] ... PNtC
Council on Roentgenology of the American Chiropractic Association ... CRACA
Council for Rural Housing and Development ... CRHD
Council for Safe Transportation of Hazardous Articles ... COSTHA
Council of Sales Promotion Agencies ... CSPA
Council to Save the Postcard ... CSP
Council of Savings and Loan Financial Corporations ... CSLFC
Council for Science and Society [*British*] ... CSS
Council on Science and Technology for Development ... CSTD
Council for Sciences of Indonesia. Publication [*A publication*] ... Counc Sci Indones Publ
Council for Scientific and Industrial Research [*South Africa*] ... CSIR
Council for Scientific Policy ... CSP
Council of Scientific Society Presidents ... CSSP
Council of Scottish Clan Associations ... COSCA
Council of Scottish Clan Associations ... CSCA
Council for the Securities Industry [*British*] ... CSI
Council for Sex Information and Education [*Formerly, SICAM*] ... CSIE
Council Situation Room [*NATO*] ... CSR
Council for Small Industries in Rural Areas [*British*] ... CoSIRA
Council for Social and Economic Studies ... CSES
Council of Social Science Data Archives [*Defunct*] ... CSSDA
Council of Social Service [*British*] ... CSS
Council on Social Work Education ... CSWE
Council of Societies in Dental Hypnosis ... CSDH
Council on Soil Testing and Plant Analysis ... CSTPA
Council of the Southern Mountains ... CSM
Council of Specialized Accrediting Agencies ... CSAA
Council of Spokane Area Libraries [*Library network*] ... COSAL
Council of State Administrators of Vocational Rehabilitation ... CSAVR
Council of State Chambers of Commerce ... CSCC
Council of State Community Affairs Agencies ... COSCAA
Council of State Governments ... CSG
Council of State Governments, Lexington, KY [*OCLC symbol*] ... KSC
Council of State Governments, State Information Center, Lexington, KY [*Library symbol*] ... KyLxCS
Council of State Housing Agencies ... CSHA
Council of State Planning Agencies ... CSPA
Council of Stock Theatres ... COST
Council of Student Personnel Associations in Higher Education [*Defunct*] ... COSPA
Council on Student Travel [*Later, CIEE*] ... CST
Council for the Study of Mankind [*Defunct*] ... CSM
Council on the Study of Religion ... CSR
Council on the Study of Religion. Bulletin [*A publication*] ... C S R Bul
Council on Tall Buildings and Urban Habitat ... CTBUH
Council of Teaching Hospitals ... COTH
Council for Technical Education and Training for Overseas Countries [*British*] ... TETOC
Council for Technological Advancement ... CTA
Council for Television Development [*Defunct*] ... CTD
Council on Thai Studies ... COTS
Council of the Thirteen Original States ... CTOS
Council for Tobacco Research - USA ... CTR-USA

Council of Tree and Landscape Appraisers .... CTLA
Council for UHF [*Ultrahigh Frequency*] **Broadcasting** .... CUB
Council on Undergraduate Research .... CUR
Council for Understanding Mental Illness .... CUMI
Council for Unified Research and Education .... CURE
Council of United States Universities for Rural Development in India .... CUSURDI
Council of United States Universities for Soil and Water Development in Arid and Sub-Humid Areas .... CUSUSWASH
Council of University Institutes for Urban Affairs [*Later, UAA*] .... CUIUA
Council of University Teaching Hospitals [*Defunct*] .... CUTH
Council for Urban Affairs [*Terminated, 1970*] .... CUA
Council of Urban Health Providers .... CUHP
Council of Urban Rebuilding Enterprises .... CURE
Council for a Volunteer Military [*Defunct*] .... CVM
Council on Wage and Price Stability [*Also, CWPS*] [*Abolished, 1981*] .... COWPS
Council on Wage and Price Stability [*Also, COWPS*] [*Abolished, 1981*] .... CWPS
Council of Women Chiropractors [*Formerly, NCWC, ACWC*] .... CWC
Council on Women and the Church .... COWAC
Council of Women Citizens .... CWC
Council of World Organizations Interested in the Handicapped .... CWOIH
Council on World Tensions [*Later, Institute on Man and Science*] .... CWT
Council of Writers Organizations .... CWO
Council of Young Israel Rabbis .... CYIR
Council on Youth Opportunity [*Disbanded 1971; functions taken over by Domestic Council and OMB*] .... CYO
Councillor .... CLLR
Counsel [*or Counseling or Counselor*] .... CNSL
Counsel .... COL
Counseling and Assistance Center [*Military*] .... CAAC
Counseling at the Local Level [*Small Business Administration*] .... CALL
Counseling Psychologist [*A publication*] .... Couns Psych
Counseling Satisfaction Inventory [*Education*] .... CSI
Counseling and Values [*A publication*] .... Counsel Val
Counseling and Values [*A publication*] .... Counsel & Values
Counselor .... COUNS
Counselor Activity Inventory [*Guidance*] .... CAI
Counselor Advisor University Summer Education [*Department of Labor program*] .... CAUSE
Counselor Education and Supervision [*A publication*] .... Couns Ed Su
Counselor Education and Supervision [*A publication*] .... Counsel Ed & Sup
Counselor Education and Supervision [*A publication*] .... Counsel Educ & Superv
Counselor Structured .... CS
Counselor-in-Training [*for summer camps*] .... CIT
Count C
Count .... CT
Count Clock [*NASA*] .... CTCL
Count - Double Count .... CDC
Count Dracula Fan Club .... CDFC
Count Dracula Society .... CDS
Count Forward [*Data processing*] .... CF
Count Rate Meter .... CRM
Count Reduction Technique [*Food bacteriology*] .... CRT
Count Reverse [*Data processing*] .... CR
Count Routine Applied to Zero Input [*Computer program*] .... CRAZI
Count/Time Data System .... C/TDS
Countdown [*Aerospace*] .... CD
Countdown [*NASA*] .... CTDN
Countdown [*Credit card*] [*British*] .... CD
Countdown Clock [*Aerospace*] .... CDC
Countdown Demonstration Test [*NASA*] .... CDDT
Countdown Demonstration Test [*NASA*] .... CDT
Countdown Deviation Request [*Aerospace*] .... CDR
Countdown Modification Request [*Aerospace*] .... CMR
Countdown and Status Receiving Station [*or System*] [*NASA*] .... CASRS
Countdown and Status Transmission System [*NASA*] .... CASTS
Countdown Time [*Aerospace*] .... CDT
Countdown Working Group [*NASA*] .... CDWG
Counted Thread Society of America .... CTSA
Counter .... CNT
Counter .... CNTR
Counter .... CTR
Counter Accelerometer Unit .... CAU
Counter-Air and Interdiction .... CAINT
Counter Battery .... CB
Counter-Battery Officer .... CBO
Counter-C^3 [*Command, Control, and Communications*] [*Pronounced "see-see-cubed"*] .... CC^3
Counter-Countermeasures [*Military*] .... CCM
Counter Display Unit .... CDU
Counter-Double-Current Distribution [*Analytical chemistry*] .... CDCD
Counter Electromotive Cell .... CEM
Counter Electromotive Cell .... CEMC
Counter Electromotive Force .... CEMF
Counter Filling System .... CFS
Counter Flip-Flop [*Data processing*] .... CFF
Counter Infiltration - Counter Guerilla Concept and Requirement Plan .... CIGCOREP
Counter Intelligence Center Corps School, Fort Holabird, Baltimore, MD [*Library symbol*] .... MdBCIC
Counter Intelligence, Combat [*World War II*] CIC
Counter, n Stages [*Electronics*] .... CT/N
Counter-Operating Voltage .... COV
Counter-Propaganda Directorate [*British*] .... CPD
Counter-Racism, Equal Opportunity [*Military*] .... CREO
Counter Recovery Time .... CRT
Counter-Rotating Optical Wedge .... CROW
Counter-Sabotage .... CS
Counter-Target-Acquisition .... CTA
Counter-Tenor [*Music*] C
Counter Timer .... CT
Counter-Timer Control .... CTC
Counter Voltage CV
Counterattack .... CATK
Counterbalance .... CBAL
Counterbattery .... CBTRY
Counterbattery Intelligence Officer [*Army*] .... CBIO
Counterbore .... CBORE
Counterbore Arbor [*Tool*] .... CBAR
Counterbore Cutter [*Tool*] .... CBCU
Counterbore Other Side .... CBOREO
Counterclockwise CC
Counterclockwise .... CCLKWS
Counterclockwise .... CCW
Counterclockwise .... CNTCLKWS
Counterclockwise .... CNTCLKWZ
Counterclockwise Orbit .... CCLKOB
Countercurrent Chromatography CCC
Countercurrent Digestion [*Ore leach process*] .... CCD
Countercurrent Distribution [*Analytical chemistry*] .... CCD
Countercurrent Electrophoresis [*Also, CE*] [*Analytical chemistry*] .... CCE
Countercurrent Electrophoresis [*Also, CCE*] [*Analytical chemistry*] .... CE
Countercurrent Immunoelectrophoresis [*Analytical chemistry*] .... CIE
Counterdrill .... CDRILL
Counterdrill Other Side .... CDRILLO
Counterelectrophoresis [*Analytical chemistry*] .... CEP
Counterespionage .... CE
Counterfeit [*FBI standardized term*] .... CTFT
Counterfeiting [*FBI standardized term*] .... CTFG
Counterfire [*Military*] .... CF
Counterfire Reference Grid .... CRG
Counterflashing .... CFLG
Counterflow Film Cooling .... CFFC
Counterimmunoelectrophoresis .... CIEP
Counterinsurgency CI
Counterinsurgency .... CINSGCY
Counterinsurgency .... COIN
Counterinsurgency Operations .... COINOPS
Counterinsurgency Plan .... CIP
Counterinsurgency Research and Development System .... CIRADS
Counterintelligence CI
Counterintelligence Analysis Division [*DoD*] .... CIAD
Counterintelligence Corps [*Military*] CIC
Counterintelligence Group [*Military*] .... CIG
Counterintelligence Interrogation Center [*Military*] CIIC
Counterintelligence Program [*FBI program carried out against political activists from 1956 to 1971*] .... COINTELPRO
Counterintelligence Records Information System [*Army*] .... CRIS
Counterintelligence Team .... CIT
Counterintelligence Working Party [*US Military Government, Germany*] .... CIWP
Countermarked .... CM
Countermeasure .... CM
Countermeasure Office [*of Harry Diamond Laboratories*] [*Military*] .... CMO
Countermeasures .... CTMS
Countermeasures, Airborne Infrared .... CAIR
Countermeasures/Counter Countermeasures [*Army*] .... CM/CCM
Countermeasures and Deception [*RADAR*] .... CM & D
Countermeasures Dispenser .... CMD
Countermeasures Dispenser Set .... CMDS
Countermeasures Evaluation - Infrared and Optical .... CERFIRO
Countermeasures Homing .... CMH
Countermeasures Penetrating Antiarmor Munitions .... CPAM
Countermeasures Receiving Set .... CRS
Countermeasures Receiving System .... CMRS
Countermeasures Related to Alcohol Safety on the Highways [*Vermont*] .... CRASH
Countermeasures Set, Acoustic .... CSA
Countermine/Counterintrusion Department [*Army*] .... CCID
Countermortar .... CM
Countermortar Fire .... CMF
Countermortar RADAR .... CMR
Counterpart .... COPART
Counterpoint [*A publication*] .... Counterpt
Counterpoise .... CPSE
Counterpunch .... CPUNCH
CounterRADAR Measures .... CRM
CounterRADAR Missile .... CRM
Counterreconnaissance [*Army*] .... CRECON

Counterrevolutionary Organization on Salvation and Service .... CROSS
Countershaft .... CTSHFT
Countersink .... CSK
Countersink Cutter .... CSCU
Countersink Other Side .... CSKO
Counterstamped [*Numismatics*] .... CS
Countersunk .... CTSK
Countersunk Head .... CSKH
Counterterrorist Joint Task Force [*Military*] .... CTJTF
Counterweight .... CNTRWT
Counterweight .... CTW
Counterweight .... CTWT
Counterweight .... C/W
Countess .... CTS
Countess .... CTSS
Counties (Wales) .... CW
Counting .... CTG
Counting Fingers [*Also, FC*] .... CF
Counting Switch .... CS
Countries of the World [*A publication*] .... CW
Countries of the World and Their Leaders Yearbook [*A publication*] ..... COW
Country .... CO
Country Analysis Strategy Paper [*Bureau of Inter-American Affairs*] [*Department of State*] .... CASP
Country Assistance Strategy Statement [*Military*] .... CASS
Country Bluegrass Blues [*Initialism used in name of New York City nightclub*] .... CBGB
Country Calendar [*A publication*] .... Country Cal
Country Club CC
Country Club Hills Public Library District, Country Club Hills, IL [*Library symbol*] .... ICch
Country Code CC
Country Dance Society of America [*Later, CDSSA*] .... CDSA
Country Dance and Song [*A publication*] .... CDS
Country Dance and Song Society of America [*Formerly, CDSA*] .... CDSSA
Country Dance and Song Society. News [*A publication*] .... CDSS N
Country Day School Headmasters Association of the US .... CDSHA
Country Demographic Profiles [*A publication*] .... Ctry Demogr Profiles
Country Development Strategy Statement [*Agency for International Development*] .... CDSS
Country Gentleman [*A publication*] .... Country Gent
Country Joe and the Fish [*Pop music group*] .... CJF
Country Joe and His All Star Band [*Pop music group*] .... CJASB
Country Landowner [*A publication*] .... Ctry Landowner
Country Life in America [*A publication*] .... Ctry Life Am
Country Logistics Improvement Program [*Air Force*] .... CLIP
Country Music Association .... CMA
Country Music Disk Jockeys Association [*Defunct*] .... CMDJA
Country Music Foundation .... CMF
Country Music Foundation Library and Media Center, Nashville, TN [*Library symbol*] .... TNC
Country Profiles [*A publication*] .... Ctry Profiles
Country and Regional Specialist [*Navy*] .... CARS
Country Standard Technical Order .... CSTO
Country Team [*Military*] .... CT
Country and Western [*Music*] .... C & W
Country Women [*A publication*] .... Cntry Wom
Country Women [*A publication*] .... Ctry Women
Country Women's Association .... CWA
Country Women's Council, USA .... CWC
Country Workshops, Incorporated [*An association*] .... CWI
Countryside Commission [*British*] CC
Countryside Magazine [*A publication*] .... Countryside M
Countryside Magazine and Suburban Life [*A publication*] ...... Countryside M
Countrywide Credit Industries [*American Stock Exchange symbol*] .... CCR
Counts per Hour .... CPH
Counts per Minute .... C/M
Counts per Minute .... C/MIN
Counts per Minute .... CPM
Counts per Second .... CPS
Counts per Second .... C/S
Countway Library of Medicine, Boston, MA [*Library symbol*] .... MBCo
County C
County .... CO
County .... CT
County [*Board on Geographic Names*] .... CTY
County .... CY
County Alderman [*British*] .... CA
County Architect [*British*] .... CA
County Attorney .... CA
County Borough .... CB
County Borough of Wigan Public Libraries, Central Library, Wigan, United Kingdom [*Library symbol*] .... UkWg
County Business Patterns [*A publication*] .... CBP
County Circuit [*As in "CC Rider," i.e., a traveling preacher*] CC
County Commissioner CC
County Council [*or Councillor*] [*British*] CC
County Court CC
County Courts [*Legal*] [*British*] .... COCTS
County Courts Chronicle [*Legal*] [*British*] .... CCCHRON
County of Henrico Public Library, Richmond, VA [*OCLC symbol*] .... VHP
County Intermediate Unit Superintendents [*of NEA*] [*Later, AASA*] ...... CIUS
County Law Enforcement Applied Regionally .... CLEAR
County of London Yeomanry [*British*] .... CLY
County Newsletter [*A publication*] .... County Newsl
County Office Manager .... COM
County Tower Corporation [*NASDAQ symbol*] .... CYTC
Coupeville, WA [*Location identifier*] [*FAA*] .... NRA
Couple .... CPL
Couple to Couple League CCL
Coupled .... CPD
Coupled .... CPLD
Coupled Breeding Superheating Reactor .... CBSR
Coupled Channel [*Electronics*] CC
Coupled Electron Pair Approximation [*Physics*] .... CEPA
Coupled General Circulation Model .... CGCM
Coupled Global Climate Model .... CGCM
Coupled Impedance Synthesis .... CIS
Coupled Microwave Plasma [*Spectrometry*] .... CMP
Coupled Oscillator .... CO
Coupled Range-Finders .... CR
Coupled States [*Physics*] .... CS
Coupled Vibration Dissociation .... CVD
Coupled Vibration-Dissociation Process .... CVDP
Coupled Vibration Dissociation Vibration .... CVDV
Coupler .... CPLR
Coupler Cut-Through .... CCT
Coupler Electronics Unit .... CEU
Couplers [*JETDS nomenclature*] [*Military*] .... CU
Coupling .... CPLG
Coupling Capacitor Voltage Transformer .... CCVT
Coupling Control Unit .... CCU
Coupling Data Unit .... CDU
Coupling Display Optical Hand Controller .... CDOH
Coupling Display Unit .... CDU
Coupling Factor [*Cytology*] .... CF
Coupon C
Coupon .... CP
Coupons Attached [*Business and trade*] .... CA
Cour Internationale de Justice [*International Court of Justice*] .... CIJ
Cour Permanente de Justice Internationale [*Permanent Court of International Justice*] [*Later, CIJ*] .... CPJI
Courant [*Of the Current Month*] [*French*] .... COUR
Courant [*Of the Current Month*] [*French*] .... CT
Courant Alternatif [*Alternating Current*] [*French*] .... CA
Courant Continu [*Direct Current*] [*French*] CC
Courant-Isaacson-Rees [*Method*] .... CIR
Courchevel [*France*] [*Airport symbol*] .... CVF
Courier .... COUR
Courier Air Service .... CAS
Courier Corporation [*NASDAQ symbol*] .... CRRC
Courier Dispatch Group [*NASDAQ symbol*] .... CDGI
Courier Forschungsinstitut Senckenberg [*A publication*] .... Cour Forschungsinst Senckenb
Courier-Journal & Louisville Times Co., Inc., Louisville, KY [*Library symbol*] .... KyLoC
Courier, Middletown, NJ [*Library symbol*] .... NjMiC
Courier Post, Cherry Hill, NJ [*Library symbol*] .... NjChCP
Courier Transfer Office [*or Officer*] .... CTO
Courier Transfer Station .... CTS
Courrier du Centre International pour l'Enfance [*A publication*] .... Courr Centre Int Enfance
Courrier de l'Extreme-Orient [*A publication*] .... CEO
Courrier de l'Extreme-Orient/Berichten uit het Verre Oosten [*A publication*] .... Courr Extr-Orient
Courrier Graphique [*A publication*] .... CG
Courrier Musical de France [*A publication*] .... Cour Mus France
Courrier de la Nature [*A publication*] .... Courr Nat
Courrier de la Normalisation [*A publication*] .... Courr Norm
Courrier des Pays de l'Est [*A publication*] .... Courr Pays Est
Courrier Revue Medico-Sociale de l'Enfance [*A publication*] .... Courrier
Courrier de l'UNESCO [*A publication*] .... Courr UNESCO
Cours et Documents de Biologie [*A publication*] .... Cours Doc Bil
Cours de Perfectionnement en Pediatrie pour le Practicien [*A publication*] .... Cours Perfect Pediatr Prat
Cours de Perfectionnement de la Societe Suisse de Psychiatrie [*A publication*] .... Cours Perfect Soc Suisse Psychiatr
Course .... CO
Course .... CRS
Course .... CSE
Course [*Ships*] .... CUS
Course Alignment .... CA
Course Angle [*Navigation*] C
Course Author Language [*Data processing*] .... CAL
Course of Construction .... C of C
Course Content Improvement CCI
Course Deviation Indicator [*Aviation*] .... CDI
Course and Distance Calculator .... CDC
Course Generator .... CG
Course per Gyro Compass [*Navigation*] .... CPGC
Course of Instruction [*Military*] .... COI
Course Line [*Aviation*] CL

Course-Line Computer [Aviation] CLC
Course Made Good over the Ground .... COG
Course Made Good through the Water .... CTW
Course Ordered Transmitter .... COT
Course Pennant [Navy] [British] .... CO
Course Setting Bombsight .... CSBS
Course and Speed Calculator .... CSC
Course and Speed Made Good over the Ground .... CSG
Course and Speed Made Good through the Water .... CSW
Course Training Standard [Air Force] .... CTS
Course Winner [Horse racing] C
Coursewriter [IBM Corp. computer language] .... CW
Court C
Court .... CRT
Court .... CT
Court of Appeal .... CA
Court of Bankruptcy, Undischarged [British] .... CBU
Court of Civil Appeals, Dallas, TX [Library symbol] .... TxDaCiA
Court of Claims .... CCLS
Court of Claims .... CTCLS
Court of Claims Reports .... CCLSR
Court of Common Pleas .... CCP
Court of Customs and Patent Appeals .... CCPA
Court Employment Project .... CEP
Court House .... CH
Court House Library, West Point, MS [Library symbol] .... MsWpCt
Court of Industrial Relations [Philippines] .... CIR
Court Interpreters and Translators Association .... CITA
Court of Justice .... COJ
Court of Justice of the European Communities [Common Market] .... CJ
Court-Martial .... CM
Court Martial Appeal Court of Canada .... CMAC
Court-Martial Appointing Order .... CMAO
Court-Martial Forfeiture .... CMF
Court-Martial Officer .... CMO
Court-Martial Orders [Navy] .... CMO
Court-Martial Report .... CMR
Court of Military Appeals .... CMA
Court of Military Appeals .... COMA
Court of Military Review .... CMR
Court of Military Review .... COMR
Court of Probate .... CP
Court Reporter .... CTREPTR
Court Reporting Program [Association of Independent Colleges and Schools specialization code] .... CR
Court Rolls [British] .... CT
Court of Session .... CS
Courtauld's All-Purpose Simulator .... CAPS
Courtaulds Ltd. [American Stock Exchange symbol] .... COU
Courtaulds Ltd., Cornwall, ON, Canada [Library symbol] [Obsolete] .... CaOCC
Courtauld's Rapid Extract, Sort, and Tabulate System .... CRESTS
Courtenay, BC [Radio station call letters] .... CFCP
Courtenay, BC [Television station call letters] CHAN-TV-4
Courtenay and District Museum, Courtenay, BC, Canada [Library symbol] .... CaBCoM
Courtesy Air Service, Inc. [Glens Falls, NY] [FAA designator] .... CTS
Courtesy Flight [Aviation] .... CFLT
Courthouse .... Ct Ho
Courtier .... CRTR
Courtship Analysis [Psychology] .... CA
Coushatta, LA [Radio station call letters] .... KRRP
Cousin C
Cousin .... COUS
Cousins Home Furnishings [NASDAQ symbol] .... CUZZ
Cousins Mortgage & Equity Investments [NYSE symbol] [American Stock Exchange symbol] [Delisted] .... CUZ
Cousins Properties [NASDAQ symbol] .... COUS
[The] Cousteau Society .... TCS
Cout, Assurance, Fret [Cost, Insurance, Freight] [French] .... CAF
Couvent des Ursulines, Quebec, PQ, Canada [Library symbol] .... CaQQU
Covariance Analysis Program for the Study of Augmented Inertial Navigators .... CAPTAIN
Cove [Maps and charts] C
Cove CV
Covefort [Utah] [Seismograph station code, US Geological Survey] .... CFU
Covelo, CA [Radio station call letters] .... KPAU
Covenant .... COV
Covenant Theological Seminary, St. Louis, MO [Library symbol] .... MoSCT
Covenant Young Adults [Defunct] .... CYA
Coventry [City in England] .... COV
Coventry [England] [Airport symbol] .... CVT
Coventry Corp., Coventry, United Kingdom [Library symbol] .... UkCov
Coventry, RI [Radio station call letters] .... WCVY
Cover .... COV
Cover .... CVR
Cover Aft .... CA
Cover Collectors Circuit Club CCCC
Cover Collectors Club .... CoCo
Cover and Deception .... C & D
Cover Forward .... CF

Cover Gas Evaluation Loop [Nuclear energy] .... CGEL
Cover Layer Assembly .... CLA
Cover Note [Insurance] .... CN
Cover Point [Lacrosse position] .... CP
Cover Your Anatomy [Military, government slang] [Bowdlerized version] .... CYA
Cover Your Anatomy with Paper [Military, government slang] [Bowdlerized version] .... CYAWP
Coverage .... CVGE
Coverage Exercise .... COVEX
Covered .... COVD
Covered Button Association of New York .... CBANY
Covered Carriage Trucks [British railroad term] .... CCT
Covered Hopper [Freight] .... CVRD HPR
Covered Lighter [Self-propelled] [Navy symbol] .... YF
Covered Lighter [Non-self-propelled] [Navy symbol] .... YFN
Covered Lighter (Range Tender) [Self-propelled] [Navy symbol] .... YFRT
Covered Lighter (Repair) [Navy symbol] .... YRL
Covered Lighter (Special Purpose) [Later, YFNX] [Navy symbol] .... YFNG
Covered Pedestrian Space .... CPS
Covered Radio Teletype .... CRATT
Covered Threads Association [Defunct] .... CTA
Covering Fire Mine .... CFM
Covering Force Area .... CFA
Coverings, Facing, or Floor [Freight] .... COVFF
Covers [JETDS nomenclature] [Military] .... CW
Covert Action [A publication] .... Covrt Act
Covert Active Modular Electro-Optical System .... CAMEO
Covert All-Weather Gun System .... CAWGS
Covert Camera Spy [System] .... CCS
Covert Communications .... COCO
Covert Investigation [Police term] CI
Covert Submarine Transmitter and Receiver .... CO-STAR
Covert Viewing System .... CVS
Covina Public Library, Covina, CA [Library symbol] .... CCov
Covina Public Library, Covina, CA [OCLC symbol] .... CVP
Covington & Burling, Washington, DC [OCLC symbol] .... DCO
Covington/Cincinnati, OH [Location identifier] [FAA] .... JDP
Covington, GA [Location identifier] [FAA] .... VOF
Covington, GA [Radio station call letters] .... WGFS
Covington, IN [Radio station call letters] .... WVWV
Covington, KY [Radio station call letters] .... WCLU
Covington, KY [Television station call letters] .... WCVN
Covington, KY/Cincinnati, OH [Location identifier] [FAA] .... CVG
Covington, LA [Radio station call letters] .... WARB
Covington Technology [NASDAQ symbol] .... COVT
Covington, TN [Radio station call letters] .... WKBL
Covington, TN [Radio station call letters] .... WKBL-FM
Covington, VA [Radio station call letters] .... WIQO
Covington, VA [Radio station call letters] .... WKEY
Cow Castle Creek [South Carolina] [Seismograph station code, US Geological Survey] .... COW
Cowan, TN [Radio station call letters] .... WZYX
Cowboy Artists of America .... CAA
Cowl-Flap Angle [Air Force] .... CFA
Cowles Broadcasting, Inc. [NYSE symbol] .... CWL
Cowles Communications, Inc., New York, NY [Library symbol] Ccl
Cowley/Lovell/Byron, WY [Location identifier] [FAA] .... HCY
Cowling Number [IUPAC] .... Co
Cowpens National Battlefield Site .... COWP
Cowra [Australia] [Airport symbol] .... CWT
Cox Cable Communications, Inc. [of Cox Broadcasting Corp.] [American Stock Exchange symbol] [Delisted] CXC
Cox Communications, Inc. [NYSE symbol] .... COX
Cox Coronary Heart Institute, Dayton, OH [Library symbol] .... ODaCox
Cox Resources Corporation [NASDAQ symbol] .... CXRC
Cox's Bazar [Bangladesh] [Airport symbol] .... CXB
Coxswain .... COX
Coxswain, Construction Battalion, Stevedore .... COXCBS
Coxswain, Ship Repair, Canvasman .... COXSRS
Coxswain, Ship Repair, Rigger .... COXSRR
Coyle, NJ [Location identifier] [FAA] .... CYN
Coyote Hills [California] [Seismograph station code, US Geological Survey] .... CYH
Coyotepe [Nicaragua] [Seismograph station code, US Geological Survey] .... CYN
Coyote's Journal [A publication] .... CJ
Cozad, NE [Location identifier] [FAA] .... CZD
Cozad, NE [Radio station call letters] .... KAMI
Cozad, NE [Radio station call letters] .... KOOC
Cozumel [Mexico] [Airport symbol] .... CZM
CP-17 [Nevada] [Seismograph station code, US Geological Survey] [Closed] .... CPN
CP National Corp. [NYSE symbol] .... CPN
CP Rail (Canadian Pacific Ltd.) [NYSE symbol] [Delisted] [AAR code] .... CP
CP Rehabilitation Corp. [NASDAQ symbol] .... CRHB
CP1 [Nevada] [Seismograph station code, US Geological Survey] .... CPX
CPA [Certified Public Accountant] Associates .... CPAA
CPA [American Institute of Certified Public Accountants] Journal [A publication] .... CPAJ
CPAC, Inc. [NASDAQ symbol] .... CPAK

CPC International, Inc. [*Formerly, Corn Products Company*] [*NYSE symbol*] ... CPC
CPC International, Inc., Argo, IL [*Library symbol*] ... IArgoC
CPI Corporation [*NASDAQ symbol*] ... CPIC
CPI [*Current Physics Index*] **Management Service** [*A publication*] ... CPI Mgmt
CPPA [*Canadian Pulp and Paper Association*] **Monthly Newsprint Report** [*A publication*] ... CPPA Newsprint Rept
CPPA [*Canadian Pulp and Paper Association*] **Newsprint Data** [*A publication*] ... CPPA Newsprint Data
CPPA [*Canadian Pulp and Paper Association*] **Press Digest** [*A publication*] ... CPPA Press Dig
CPPA [*Canadian Pulp and Paper Association*] **Reference Tables** [*A publication*] ... CPPA Ref Tables
CPPA [*Canadian Pulp and Paper Association*] **Technical Section Proceedings** [*A publication*] ... CPPA Tech Sect Proc
CPS Chemical Co., Inc. [*NASDAQ symbol*] ... CPSC
CPT Corporation [*NASDAQ symbol*] ... CPTC
CQ Radio Amateur's Journal [*A publication*] ... CQ Radio Amat J
Crab Angle Sensing System ... CASS
[*The*] **Crab House, Inc.** [*NASDAQ symbol*] ... CRHO
Crab Orchard & Egyptian Railroad [*American Rail Heritage Ltd.*] ... CO & E
Crab Orchard & Egyptian Railroad [*American Rail Heritage Ltd.*] [*AAR code*] ... COER
Crack Opening Displacement ... COD
Crack Propagation ... CP
Cracker Barrel Old Country Store [*NASDAQ symbol*] ... CBRL
Craddock-Terry Shoe [*NASDAQ symbol*] ... CDCK
Cradle ... CRDL
Craft ... CFT
Craft Horizons [*A publication*] ... Craft Horiz
Craft Horizons [*A publication*] ... Cr H
Craft House Corp. [*NASDAQ symbol*] ... CRFH
Craft Inclination [*Aerospace*] ... CI
Craft Loss [*Shipping*] ... C/L
Craft Union Department [*AFL-CIO*] ... CUD
Craftsman [*Military*] [*British*] ... CFN
Craftsman ... CFTMN
Craig [*Alaska*] [*Airport symbol*] ... CGA
Craig [*Colorado*] [*Seismograph station code, US Geological Survey*] [*Closed*] ... CGC
Craig, CO [*Location identifier*] [*FAA*] ... CAG
Craig, CO [*Radio station call letters*] ... KRAI
Craig, CO [*Radio station call letters*] ... KXRC
Craig Corp. [*NYSE symbol*] ... CRA
Craig Cove [*Vanuata*] [*Airport symbol*] ... CCV
Craig House Technoma Workshop, Pittsburgh, PA [*OCLC symbol*] ... PIC
Craig-Moffat County Public Library, Craig, CO [*Library symbol*] ... CoCra
Craig Mountain Railway [*AAR code*] ... CMT
Craik-Leibovich [*Physics*] ... CL
Craiova [*Romania*] [*Airport symbol*] ... CRA
Cramer Electronics, Inc. [*American Stock Exchange symbol*] [*Delisted*] ... CRM
Cramer, Inc. [*NASDAQ symbol*] ... CRMR
Cramer - von Mises Test [*Statistics*] ... CVM
Cranberry Institute ... CI
Cranbrook [*Canada*] [*Airport symbol*] ... YXC
Cranbrook Academy of Art, Bloomfield Hills, MI [*Library symbol*] ... MiBloA
Cranbrook, BC [*Television station call letters*] ... CBUBT-7
Cranbrook, BC [*Radio station call letters*] ... CKEK
Cranbrook Institute of Science, Bloomfield Hills, MI [*Library symbol*] ... MiBloC
Cranbrook Institute of Science Bulletin [*A publication*] ... Cranbrook Inst Sci Bull
Cranbury Press, Cranbury, NJ [*Library symbol*] ... NjCrbP
Crandall Library, Glens Falls, NY [*Library symbol*] ... NGlf
Crandell Feline Kidney [*Cytology*] ... CRFK
Crane ... CRN
Crane Army Ammunition Activity ... CAAA
Crane Co. [*NYSE symbol*] ... CR
Crane Co., Chicago, IL [*Library symbol*] ... ICCra
Crane Engines [*Trains*] [*British*] ... C
Crane Load ... CL
Crane Manufacturers Association of America [*Formerly, EOCI*] ... CMAA
Crane Review [*A publication*] ... CraneR
Crane Ship [*Navy symbol*] ... AB
Crane, TX [*Radio station call letters*] ... KXOI
Cranfield Institute of Technology [*California*] ... CIT
Cranfield Institute of Technology, Cranfield, Bedfordshire, United Kingdom [*Library symbol*] ... UkCraT
Cranford Citizen & Chronicle, Cranford, NJ [*Library symbol*] ... NjCrC
Cranford Historical Society, Cranford, NJ [*Library symbol*] ... NjCrHi
Cranford Public Library, Cranford, NJ [*Library symbol*] ... NjCr
Cranial ... CR
Cranial Academy ... CA
Cranial Nerve [*Anatomy*] ... CN
Craniofacial Biology Group [*of the International Association for Dental Research*] ... CBG
Craniology ... CRAN
Crank ... CRK
Crankcase ... CRK
Crankcase ... CRKC
Crankpin ... CPIN
Crankshaft ... CRKSFT
Crankshaft ... CSHAFT
Crankshaft Rate ... CSR
Ranksheave ... CRKSHV
Cras [*Tomorrow*] [*Pharmacy*] ... CR
Cras Mane [*Tomorrow Morning*] [*Pharmacy*] ... CM
Cras Mane Sumendus [*To Be Taken Tomorrow Morning*] [*Pharmacy*] ... CMS
Cras Nocte [*Tomorrow Night*] [*Pharmacy*] ... CN
Cras Nocte Sumendus [*To Be Taken Tomorrow Night*] [*Pharmacy*] ... CNS
Cras Vespere [*Tomorrow Evening*] [*Pharmacy*] ... CR VESP
Cras Vespere [*Tomorrow Evening*] [*Pharmacy*] ... CV
Crash Boat ... CB
Crash Damage Material List ... CDML
Crash Data Position Indication Recorder ... CDPIR
Crash Fire Rescue [*Aviation*] ... CFR
Crash Injury Research Organization [*Cornell University*] ... CIRO
Crash Locator Beacon [*Air Force*] ... CLB
Crash Locator Beacon [*Aviation*] ... CLBN
Crash Phone Activated [*Aviation*] ... CPA
Crash Position Indicator [*Air Force*] ... CPI
Crash Position Indicator/Flight Data Recorder [*Air Force*] ... CPI/FDR
Crash-Resistant Fuel System ... CRFS
Crashworthy Fuel Systems [*Aviation*] ... CWFS
Crassulacean Acid Metabolism [*Biochemistry*] ... CAM
Crastinus [*Of Tomorrow*] [*Pharmacy*] ... CRAST
Crate ... CRT
Crater [*Costa Rica*] [*Seismograph station code, US Geological Survey*] ... A10
Crater [*Constellation*] ... Crat
Crater [*Constellation*] ... Crt
Crater Lake National Park ... CRLA
Crater-Lamp Recorder ... CLR
Cratering Demolition Device ... CDD
Craters of the Moon National Monument ... CRMO
Crates ... CTS
Crating ... CTG
Crating, Packaging Instructions ... CPI
Craven-Pamlico-Carteret Regional Library [*Library network*] ... C-P-C
Craven-Pamlico-Carteret Regional Library, New Bern, NC [*Library symbol*] ... NcNbCP
Craven Technical Institute, New Bern, NC [*Library symbol*] ... NcNbC
Cravo Norte [*Colombia*] [*Airport symbol*] ... RAV
Crawdaddy [*A publication*] ... Cy
Crawford Bay, BC [*Radio station call letters*] ... CBTE-FM
Crawford & Co. [*NASDAQ symbol*] ... CRAW
Crawford County Historical Society, Meadville, PA [*Library symbol*] ... PMCHi
Crawford County Library, Grayling, MI [*Library symbol*] ... MiGray
Crawford Energy [*American Stock Exchange symbol*] ... CE
Crawford Small Parts Dexterity Test [*Education*] ... CSPDT
Crawford W. Long Memorial Hospital, Atlanta, GA [*Library symbol*] ... GACL
Crawfordsville District Public Library, Crawfordsville, IN [*Library symbol*] ... InC
Crawfordsville, IN [*Radio station call letters*] ... WCVL
Crawfordsville, IN [*Radio station call letters*] ... WLFQ
Crawfordsville, IN [*Radio station call letters*] ... WNDY
Crawler/Transporter ... C/T
Crawler/Transporter Intercom System ... CTIS
Crawler/Transporter/Mobile Service Structure ... CT/MSS
Crawlerway [*NASA*] ... CW
Cray Research [*NYSE symbol*] ... CYR
Crayon, Water Color, and Craft Institute ... CWCCI
Crazy Horse Memorial Foundation ... CHMF
Crazy Woman, WY [*Location identifier*] [*FAA*] ... CZI
CRC [*Chemical Rubber Company*] **Critical Reviews in Analytical Chemistry** [*A publication*] ... CRC Crit Rev Anal Chem
CRC [*Chemical Rubber Company*] **Critical Reviews in Biochemistry** [*A publication*] ... CRC Crit Rev Biochem
CRC [*Chemical Rubber Company*] **Critical Reviews in Bioengineering** [*A publication*] ... CRC Crit Rev Bioeng
CRC [*Chemical Rubber Company*] **Critical Reviews in Clinical Laboratory Sciences** [*A publication*] ... CRC Crit Rev Clin Lab Sci
CRC [*Chemical Rubber Company*] **Critical Reviews in Clinical Radiology and Nuclear Medicine** [*A publication*] ... CRC Crit Rev Clin Radiol Nucl Med
CRC [*Chemical Rubber Company*] **Critical Reviews in Environmental Control** [*A publication*] ... CRC Crit Rev Environ Control
CRC [*Chemical Rubber Company*] **Critical Reviews in Food Science and Nutrition** [*A publication*] ... CRC Crit Rev Food Sci Nutr
CRC [*Chemical Rubber Company*] **Critical Reviews in Food Technology** [*A publication*] ... CRC Crit Rev Food Technol
CRC [*Chemical Rubber Company*] **Critical Reviews in Microbiology** [*A publication*] ... CRC Crit R Microbiol
CRC [*Chemical Rubber Company*] **Critical Reviews in Toxicology** [*A publication*] ... CRC Crit Rev Toxicol
Cream Received in Separating Cottonseed Oil ... CRISCO
Cream Shade [*Paper*] ... CS
Cream of Tartar Substitute ... CTS
Crease [*Deltiology*] ... CR
Crease Clinic Library, Essondale, BC, Canada [*Library symbol*] ... CaBEC

Created ... C
Created [*or Creation*] ... CR
Creatine Kinase [*Also, CPK*] [*An enzyme*] ... CK
Creatine Phosphate [*Phosphocreatine; see PC*] [*Biochemistry*] ... CP
Creatine Phosphokinase [*Preferred form is CK*] [*An enzyme*] ... CPK
Creatinine [*Biochemistry*] ... Cr
Creation-Evolution ... CREVO
Creation Facilities Program [*Data processing*] ... CFP
Creation Research ... CR
Creation Research Society ... CRS
Creation Research Society Quarterly [*A publication*] ... Creation Res Soc Q
Creation Research Society Quarterly [*A publication*] ... CRSQ
Creative Artists Public Service Program ... CAPS
Creative Audio and Music Electronics Organization ... CAMEO
Creative Computer Applications [*NASDAQ symbol*] ... CCAI
Creative Consulting [*NASDAQ symbol*] ... CCCI
Creative Crafts [*A publication*] ... Cr Crafts
Creative Crafts [*A publication*] ... Creat Crafts
Creative Education Foundation ... CEF
Creative Guitar International [*A publication*] ... CGI
Creative Initiative [*An association*] ... CI
Creative Initiative Foundation ... CIF
Creative Moment [*A publication*] ... CMo
Creative Music Foundation ... CMF
Creative Playthings Foundation [*Defunct*] ... CPF
Creative Printers of America ... CPA
Creative Time [*Formerly, CTP*] [*An association*] ... CT
Creative Times Project [*Later, CT*] ... CTP
Creative Tour Operators Association ... CTOA
Creative Use of Leisure Time under Restrictive Environments [*Federally funded prison program*] ... CULTURE
Creative Writing [*A publication*] ... Cr Wtg
Creativity Quotient [*Testing term*] ... CQ
Credentialing Commission ... CC
Credit ... CR
Credit ... CRED
Credit Account [*Business and trade*] ... CA
Credit Authorization Terminal ... CAT
Credit Balance ... CB
Credit Card Purchase ... CCP
Credit Card Reader ... CCR
Credit Card Service Bureau [*Formerly, CCSBA*] ... CCSB
Credit Card Service Bureau of America [*Later, CCSB*] ... CCSBA
Credit Commercial de France ... CCF
Credit and Financial Management [*A publication*] ... C F Mgmt
Credit and Financial Management [*A publication*] ... Credit & Fin Mgt
Credit Memo ... CM
Credit Monthly [*A publication*] ... Credit M
Credit Note [*Business and trade*] ... CN
Credit Officers Group ... COG
Credit Requisition ... CR
Credit Research Foundation ... CRF
Credit Suisse. Bulletin [*A publication*] ... Cred Suisse B
Credit Systems Incorporated ... CSI
Credit Transfer ... CT
Credit Union ... CRU
Credit Union ... CU
Credit Union Central of Manitoba, Winnipeg, MB, Canada [*Library symbol*] ... CaMWCU
Credit Union National Association ... CUNA
Credit Women - International ... CW-I
Credit Women's Breakfast Clubs of North America [*Later, Credit Women - International*] ... CWBCNA
Credit World [*A publication*] ... Credit Wld
Creditable Record ... CR
Credithrift Financial, Inc. [*NYSE symbol*] [*Delisted*] ... CRD
Credito Industriale Sardo [*Sardinia*] ... CIS
Credito Rural [*A publication*] ... Cred Rur
Credo Petroleum Corp. [*NASDAQ symbol*] ... CRED
Cree [*MARC language code*] [*Library of Congress*] ... cre
Cree Questionnaire [*Psychology*] ... CQ
Creed Taylor, Incorporated [*Recording label*] ... CTI
Creede Public Library, Creede, CO [*Library symbol*] ... CoCre
Creedence Clearwater Revival [*Rock music group*] ... CCR
Creedmore Psychiatric Center, Queens Village, New York, NY [*Library symbol*] ... NNCre
Creek [*Maps and charts*] ... CR
Creek ... CRK
Creek Indian Memorial Association ... CIMA
Creem Magazine [*A publication*] ... CRCMC
Creep in Axisymmetric Shells ... CRASH
Creighton Law Review [*A publication*] ... Creighton L Rev
Creighton University, Alumni Library, Omaha, NE [*OCLC symbol*] ... OCA
Creighton University, Health Sciences Library, Omaha, NE [*OCLC symbol*] ... OCM
Creighton University Law Library, Omaha, NE [*OCLC symbol*] ... CLL
Creighton University, Omaha, NE [*Library symbol*] ... NbOC
Creighton University, School of Dentistry, Omaha, NE [*Library symbol*] ... NbOC-D
Creighton University, School of Law, Omaha, NE [*Library symbol*] ... NbOC-L
Creighton University, School of Medicine and School of Pharmacy, Omaha, NE [*Library symbol*] ... NbOC-M
Cremation Association of America [*Later, CANA*] ... CAA
Cremation Association of North America [*Formerly, CAA*] ... CANA
Creoles and Pidgins [*MARC language code*] [*Library of Congress*] ... crp
Crepitus [*Crepitation*] [*Medicine*] ... CREP
Crescendo ... CRES
Crescendo ... CRESC
Crescendo ... CRESO
Crescendo International [*A publication*] ... CRCFA
Crescendo International [*A publication*] ... Crescendo Int
Crescent ... CRES
Crescent Air Transport Ltd. [*Pakistan*] [*ICAO designator*] [*Obsolete*] ... KJ
Crescent Airways, Inc. [*Hollywood, FL*] [*FAA designator*] ... CRS
Crescent City [*California*] [*Airport symbol*] ... CEC
Crescent City, CA [*Radio station call letters*] ... KCRE
Crescent City, CA [*Radio station call letters*] ... KCRE-FM
Crescent City, CA [*Radio station call letters*] ... KPOD
Crescent City, FL [*Radio station call letters*] ... WBAS
Crescent City Public Library, Crescent City, CA [*Library symbol*] ... CCc
Crescent Heights High School, Medicine Hat, AB, Canada [*Library symbol*] ... CaAMCH
Crescent Oil & Gas Uts [*NASDAQ symbol*] ... CRESU
Crescent Petroleum Corporation [*NYSE symbol*] [*Delisted*] ... CRC
Cresco, IA [*Location identifier*] [*FAA*] ... CJJ
Cresco Public Library, Cresco, IA [*Library symbol*] ... IaCresco
Cresolphthalein Complexone [*Analytical chemistry*] ... CPC
Cresset [*A publication*] ... Cres
Cresson, PA [*Radio station call letters*] ... WBXQ
Crest-Foam Corp. [*American Stock Exchange symbol*] ... CFO
Crest Hill, IL [*Radio station call letters*] ... WCCQ
Crested Butte Air Service, Inc. [*Crested Butte, CO*] [*FAA designator*] ... CBA
Crested Butte Silver Mining, Inc. [*NASDAQ symbol*] ... CBAG
Crested Fowl Club of America [*Later, CFFA*] ... CFCA
Crested Fowl Fanciers' Association [*Formerly, CFCA*] ... CFFA
Cresterea Colectiilor. Caiet Selectiv de Informare Bibliotecii Academii Republicii Socialiste Romania [*A publication*] ... Crest Colect
Crestmont Oil & Gas Co. [*American Stock Exchange symbol*] [*Delisted*] ... CRE
Creston, BC [*Radio station call letters*] ... CFKC
Creston, IA [*Radio station call letters*] ... KITR
Creston, IA [*Radio station call letters*] ... KSIB
Crestview, FL [*Radio station call letters*] ... WAAZ
Crestview, FL [*Radio station call letters*] ... WCNU
Crestview, FL [*Radio station call letters*] ... WJSB
Crestwood Library District, Crestwood, IL [*Library symbol*] ... ICw
Crestwood, MO [*Radio station call letters*] ... KSHE
Cresyl Diphenylphosphate ... CDP
Cresyl Violet [*Biological stain*] ... CV
Cretaceous [*Period, era, or system*] [*Geology*] ... CRET
Cretans' Association Omonoia ... CAO
Crete, IL [*Radio station call letters*] ... WTAS
Crete, NE [*Radio station call letters*] ... KTAP
Crete Public Library, Crete, IL [*Library symbol*] ... ICre
Crete Public Library, Crete, NE [*Library symbol*] ... NbCr
Creutzfeldt-Jakob [*Neurological disorder*] ... CJ
Creutzfeldt-Jakob Disease [*Neurological disorder*] ... CJD
Crew ... CR
Crew Activities Scheduling Program [*NASA*] ... CASP
Crew Activity Plan ... CAP
Crew Boat ... CB
Crew Cargo Module [*NASA*] ... CCM
Crew Chief ... CC
Crew Chief ... CRC
Crew Chief ... CRCH
Crew Chief ... CRCHF
Crew [*or Crewman*] **Communications Umbilical** [*Apollo*] [*NASA*] ... CCU
Crew Compartment ... CC
Crew Compartment Cooling Unit [*NASA*] ... CCCU
Crew Compartment Fit and Function [*NASA*] ... CCFF
Crew Compartment Fit and Function [*NASA*] ... C2F2
Crew Equipment Interface Test ... CEIT
Crew Escape and Rescue Techniques [*Air Force*] ... CREST
Crew Escape System ... CES
Crew Habitability and Protection [*NASA*] ... CH & P
Crew-Initiated Automatic Test ... CIAT
Crew Interface ... CI
Crew Life-Support Monitor [*NASA*] ... CLSM
Crew Loose Equipment [*Aerospace*] ... CLE
Crew Loose Equipment Nomenclature [*Aerospace*] ... CLENOM
Crew Member ... CR/M
Crew Member Identification ... CM-ID
Crew Module [*NASA*] ... CM
Crew Module Computer ... CMC
Crew [*or Crewman*] **Optical Alignment Sight** [*or Subsystem*] [*NASA*] ... COAS
Crew Passive Dosimeter [*NASA*] ... CPD
Crew Personal Equipment ... CPE
Crew Personal Hygiene Equipment ... CPHE
Crew Procedures Change Request ... CPCR
Crew Procedures Division [*NASA*] ... CPD

Crew Procedures Documentation System .... CPDS
Crew Procedures Evaluation Simulator .... CPES
Crew Procedures Management Plan [*NASA*] .... CPMP
Crew Procedures Simulator .... CPS
Crew Procedures Trainer .... CPT
Crew Provisioning Report .... CPR
Crew Public Library, Salem, IA [*Library symbol*] .... IaSal
Crew Quarters .... CQ
Crew Reception Area [*Apollo*] [*NASA*] .... CRA
Crew Research Laboratory [*Air Force*] .... CRL
Crew Reserve Status [*Military*] .... CRS
Crew Rest [*Military*] .... CR
Crew Safety System .... CSS
Crew Scheduling and Training Plan .... CSTP
Crew-Served Weapon .... C/S
Crew-Served Weapon Sight .... CSWS
Crew-Served Weapons Captured .... CSWC
Crew Software Interface .... CSI
Crew Software Training Aid .... CSTA
Crew Station [*NASA*] .... CS
Crew Station Review [*NASA*] .... CSR
Crew Station Trainer [*NASA*] .... CST
Crew Systems .... CS
Crew Systems Division [*NASA*] .... CSD
Crew Systems Operating Procedures .... CSOP
Crew Task Demand .... CTD
Crew Task Detail .... CTD
Crew Training Air Force .... CREWTAF
Crew Training Air Force .... CTAF
Crew Transfer Tunnel [*NASA*] .... CTT
Crew Weapons Sight .... CWS
Crewe, VA [*Radio station call letters*] .... WSVS
Crewe, VA [*Radio station call letters*] .... WSVS-FM
Crewman .... CM
Crewman .... CRMN
Cricket Club CC
Crime Abatement Team .... CAT
Crime Aboard Aircraft .... CAA
Crime Control, Inc. [*NASDAQ symbol*] .... CRIM
Crime and Delinquency [*A publication*] .... Crime Delin
Crime and Delinquency [*A publication*] .... Crime & Delinq
Crime and Delinquency Abstracts [*A publication*] .... CDAB
Crime and Delinquency Abstracts [*A publication*] .... Crime Delinq Abstr
Crime on Government Reservation .... CGR
Crime on High Seas .... CHS
Crime on Indian Reservation .... CIR
Crime and Social Justice [*A publication*] .... Crim Just
Crime Stoppers .... CS
Crimean Astrophysical Observatory .... CAO
Criminal .... CRIM
Criminal Headquarters for Underworld Master Plan [*Organization in TV series "Lancelot Link"*] .... CHUMP
Criminal Identification and Investigation CII
Criminal, Immoral, and Narcotic .... CIN
Criminal Informant CI
Criminal Injuries Compensation Board [*British*] .... CICB
Criminal Intelligence [*Branch of the Metropolitan Police, London*] CI
Criminal Intelligence Bureau .... CIB
Criminal Investigation [*or Investigator*] [*Military*] CI
Criminal Investigation Department [*Often loosely referred to as Scotland Yard*] [*British*] .... CID
Criminal Investigation Detachment .... CID
Criminal Investigation Division [*Army*] .... CID
Criminal Investigation Field Office [*Military*] .... CIFO
Criminal Justice and Behavior [*A publication*] .... Crim Just B
Criminal Justice and Behavior [*A publication*] .... Crim Just & Behav
Criminal Justice Information System .... CJIS
Criminal Justice Periodical Index [*A publication*] .... CJPI
Criminal Justice Reference Library [*University of Texas*] .... CJRL
Criminal Justice Statistics Association .... CJSA
Criminal Law Bulletin [*A publication*] .... Crim Law Bul
Criminal Law Bulletin [*A publication*] .... Crim L Bull
Criminal Law and Procedure .... CLP
Criminal Law Quarterly [*A publication*] .... Crim Law Q
Criminal Law Quarterly [*A publication*] .... Crim L Q
Criminal Law Review [*A publication*] .... Crim Law R
Criminal Law Review [*A publication*] .... Crim L R
Criminal Matters .... CM
Criminal Offence [*British*] .... CO
Criminal Office .... CO
Criminal Record Office [*Scotland Yard*] .... CRO
Criminal Sexual Psychopath .... CSP
Criminalistic Laboratory Information Systems .... CLIS
Criminally Receiving Stolen Property .... CRSP
Criminally Uttering and Publishing False [*or Forged*] **Check** .... CU & PFC
Criminology [*A publication*] .... Crim
Crimp [*Engineering*] .... CRP
Crimp-On Snap-In Contacts .... COSI-KON
Crimping Tool Kit .... CTK
Crinkled Single Aluminized Mylar .... CSAM
Cripple Creek Public Library, Cripple Creek, CO [*Library symbol*] .... CoCri
Crippled Leap-Frog Test .... CLFT
Crippled Leap-Frog Test .... CLT
Crisciuma [*Brazil*] [*Airport symbol*] .... CCM
Crisis Action Team .... CAT
Crisis Assessment Group [*NATO*] .... CAG
Crisis Confrontation .... CRICON
Crisis Home Alert Technique .... CHAT
Crisis on Location [*Psychological test*] .... COL
Crisis Management Information Report .... CRIMREP
Crisis Management Organization [*DoD*] .... CMO
Crisis-Oriented Program .... COP
Crisis Relocation Plans [*Federal Emergency Management Agency*] .... CRP
Criss-Cross Art Communications [*A publication*] .... Criss-Cross
Crista Terminalis [*Cardiology*] .... CT
Cristianismo y Sociedad [*A publication*] .... Crist y Soc
Cristobalite-Tridymite [*A form of silica*] .... CT
Criterion [*A publication*] .... Cr
Criterion [*A publication*] .... Cri
Criterion .... CRIT
Criterion [*A publication*] .... Crit
Criterion-Referenced Instruction .... CRI
Criterion-Referenced Measurement [*Education*] .... CRM
Criterion-Referenced Test [*or Testing*] [*Education*] .... CRT
Critic [*A publication*] .... Crit
Critica [*A publication*] C
Critica [*A publication*] .... Crit
Critica d'Arte [*A publication*] .... CA
Critica Hispanica [*A publication*] .... CH
Critica Marxista [*A publication*] .... Crit Marx
Critica Sociologica (Roma) [*A publication*] .... Crit Sociol (Roma)
Critica Storica [*A publication*] .... CrS
Critica Storica [*A publication*] .... CS
Critical .... CRIT
Critical Aeronautical Material and Equipment List .... CAMEL
Critical Air Blast [*Test*] .... CAB
Critical Angle Prism Sensor .... CAPS
Critical Area Flag .... CAF
Critical Assembly [*Nuclear energy*] .... CA
Critical Assembly Fuel Element Exchange [*AEC*] .... CAFEE
Critical Bandwidth [*of noise*] .... CBW
Critical Carbohydrate Level [*Nutrition*] CCL
Critical Care [*Medicine*] CC
Critical Care Manual .... CCM
Critical Care Medicine [*A publication*] .... CCM
Critical Care Medicine [*A publication*] .... Crit Care Med
Critical Care Quarterly [*A publication*] .... CCQ
Critical Care Registered Nurse .... CCRN
Critical Care Unit [*Medicine*] .... CCU
Critical Care Update [*A publication*] .... Crit Care Update
Critical Collection Problems Committee [*United States Intelligence Board*] [*Obsolete*] .... CCPC
Critical Communications System [*Military*] .... CRITCOM
Critical Components List CCL
Critical Compression Pressure .... CCP
Critical Compression Ratio .... CCR
Critical Condition [*Medicine*] CC
Critical Damping Resistance External .... CDRX
Critical Decision Point .... CDP
Critical Design and Qualification Review .... CDQR
Critical Design Review .... CDR
Critical Design Review Commercial .... CDRC
Critical Experiment Laboratory .... CEL
Critical Experiment Pulsed Fast Reactor .... CEPFR
Critical Experiment Reactor .... CER
Critical Experiment Tank .... CET
Critical Field Strength .... CFS
Critical Flicker [*or Fusion*] **Frequency** [*Psychophysical test*] .... CFF
Critical Frequency .... FC
Critical Grid Current .... CGC
Critical Grid Voltage .... CGV
Critical Health Manpower Shortage Areas .... CHMSA
Critical Heat Flux [*Nuclear*] .... CHF
Critical Housing Shortage at [*named place*] [*Army*] .... CRITHOUS
Critical Human Performance and Evaluation .... CHPAE
Critical Influence CI
Critical Inquiry [*A publication*] .... Crit I
Critical Inquiry [*A publication*] .... Crit Inq
[*A*] **Critical Insight into Israel's Dilemmas** [*Jewish student newspaper*] .... ACIID
Critical Intelligence Communications System [*Later, DIN/DSSCS*] .... CRITICOMM
Critical Intelligence Report .... CRITIC
Critical Intermediate Design Review .... CIDR
Critical Isotope Reactor, General Atomics .... CIRGA
Critical Issues Council [*Defunct*] CIC
Critical Item Code CIC
Critical Item List CIL
Critical Link Factor .... CLF
Critical List [*Medicine*] CL
Critical Load Level CLL
Critical Mass [*Later, CMEP*] [*An association*] .... CM

Critical Mass Energy Project [*Consumer group*] ... CMEP
Critical Mass Laboratory ... CML
Critical Materials Parts List ... CMPL
Critical Micelle Concentration ... CMC
Critical Nuclear Weapons Design Information ... CNWDI
Critical Officer Personnel Requirement [*Air Force*] ... COPR
Critical Path Analysis ... CPA
Critical Path Length ... CPL
Critical Path Method [*Graph theory*] ... CPM
Critical Path Planning ... CPP
Critical Path Planning and Scheduling ... CPPS
Critical Path Scheduling [*or System*] ... CPS
Critical Path Technique ... CPT
Critical Phase System Software [*NASA*] ... CPSS
Critical Pigment Volume Concentration [*of paint*] ... CPVC
Critical Power Ratio [*Nuclear energy*] ... CPR
Critical Problem Report [*NASA*] ... CPR
Critical Qualification Design Review ... CQDR
Critical Quarterly [*A publication*] ... CQ
Critical Quarterly [*A publication*] ... Crit Q
Critical Quarterly [*A publication*] ... CrQ
Critical Ratio ... CR
Critical Ratio of the Difference ... CRD
Critical Reactor Component ... CRC
Critical Reliability Action Report ... CRAR
Critical Requirements Review ... CRR
Critical Resolved Shear Stress ... CRSS
Critical Review [*A publication*] ... CR
Critical Review [*A publication*] ... Crit R
Critical Reviews in Analytical Chemistry [*A publication*] ... Crit Rev Anal Chem
Critical Reviews in Biochemistry [*A publication*] ... Crit Rev Biochem
Critical Reviews in Bioengineering [*A publication*] ... Crit Rev Bioeng
Critical Reviews in Clinical Laboratory Sciences [*A publication*] ... Crit Rev Clin Lab Sci
Critical Reviews in Clinical Radiology and Nuclear Medicine [*A publication*] ... Crit Rev Clin Radiol Nucl Med
Critical Reviews in Environmental Control [*A publication*] ... Crit Rev Environ Control
Critical Reviews in Food Science and Nutrition [*A publication*] ... Crit Rev Food Sci Nutr
Critical Reviews in Food Technology [*A publication*] ... Crit Rev Food Technol
Critical Reviews in Microbiology [*A publication*] ... Crit Rev Microbiol
Critical Reviews in Solid State Sciences [*A publication*] ... Crit Rev Solid State Sci
Critical Reviews in Toxicology [*A publication*] ... Crit Rev Toxicol
Critical Sensitive ... CS
Critical Shear Stress ... CSS
Critical Shortage Report ... CSR
Critical Solution Temperature ... CST
Critical Success Factor [*Management tool*] ... CSF
Critical Survey [*A publication*] ... CritS
Critical Temperature ... CT
Critical Terrain; Obstacles; Cover and Concealment; Observation and Fields of Fire; Avenues of Approach [*Military*] ... COCOA
Critical Thermal Maximum ... CTM
Critical Tool Service ... CTS
Critical Tracking Task [*System for preventing drunken driver from starting car*] ... CTT
Criticality ... CRTL
Criticality Analysis ... CA
Criticallity Data Center ... CDC
Criticism ... CRIT
Criticism [*A publication*] ... Critm
Critique [*A publication*] ... C
Critique [*A publication*] ... Critiq
Critique [*A publication*] ... Critq
Critique of Anthropology [*A publication*] ... Critique of Anthropol
Critique Socialiste (Paris) [*A publication*] ... Crit Social (Paris)
Critique: Studies in Modern Fiction [*A publication*] ... Crit
Critiques de l'Economie Politique [*A publication*] ... Crit Econ Polit
Critisch Bulletin [*A publication*] ... CrB
Criton Corp. [*NYSE symbol*] [*Delisted*] ... CN
Crkoven Vestnik [*A publication*] ... CV
Croatia Sacra [*A publication*] ... CS
Croatian Academy of America ... CAA
Croatian Catholic Union of the USA ... CCU
Croatian Fraternal Union of America [*Affiliated with CFUJCF*] ... CFU
Croatian National Congress ... CNC
Croatian Philatelic Society ... CPS
Croatian Workers Association of America ... CWAA
Croatica Chemica Acta [*A publication*] ... Croat Chem
Croatica Chemica Acta [*A publication*] ... Croat Chem Acta
Croce Rossa Italiana [*Italian Red Cross*] ... CRI
Crochet ... CR
Crochet Association International ... CAI
Crocker National Bank, San Francisco, CA [*Library symbol*] ... CSfCAB
Crocker National Corp. [*NYSE symbol*] ... CKN
Crockery Township Library, Nunica, MI [*Library symbol*] ... MiNun
Crockett Public Library, Crockett, TX [*Library symbol*] ... TxCr
Crockett, TX [*Radio station call letters*] ... KCKR
Crockett, TX [*Radio station call letters*] ... KIVY
Crockett, TX [*Radio station call letters*] ... KIVY-FM
Croes Newydd [*Welsh depot code*] ... CNYD
Croghan [*New York*] [*Seismograph station code, US Geological Survey*] ... CROG
Crohn's Disease [*Medicine*] ... CD
Crohn's Disease Activity Index [*Medicine*] ... CDAI
Croix des Evades [*Belgian military decoration*] ... CDE
Croix de Guerre [*French military decoration*] ... CDG
Croix de Guerre [*French military decoration*] ... C de G
Cromaine Library, Hartland, MI [*Library symbol*] ... MiHal
Crompton Company, Inc. [*American Stock Exchange symbol*] ... CRC
Crompton & Knowles Corp. [*NYSE symbol*] ... CNK
Cromwell Association ... CA
Cronaca delle Belle Arti [*A publication*] ... CBA
Cronache di Archeologia e di Storia dell'Arte. Universita de Catania [*A publication*] ... Cron Catania
Cronache Culturali [*A publication*] ... CCult
Cronache Economiche [*A publication*] ... Cron Econ
Cronache Ercolanesi [*A publication*] ... Cron Erc
Cronache Farmaceutiche [*A publication*] ... Cron Farm
Cronar Dot Litho [*Du Pont*] ... CDL
Cronar Halftone Litho [*Du Pont*] ... CHL
Cronholm-Ottosson Rating Scale [*Psychopathology*] ... CORS
Cronica Medica (Lima) [*A publication*] ... Cron Med (Lima)
Cronica Medica Mexicana [*A publication*] ... Cron Med Mexicana
Cronica Medico-Quirurgica de la Habana [*A publication*] ... Cron Med-Quir Habana
Cronos [*A publication*] ... Cron
Cronus Industries, Inc. [*NASDAQ symbol*] ... CRNS
Crook Community Library, Crook, CO [*Library symbol*] ... CoCroo
Crook County Library, Prineville, OR [*Library symbol*] ... OrPr
Crooked Creek [*Alaska*] [*Airport symbol*] ... CKD
Crooked Creek, AK [*Location identifier*] [*FAA*] ... CKD
Crooked Island [*Bahamas*] [*Airport symbol*] ... CRI
Crookston, MN [*Location identifier*] [*FAA*] ... CKN
Crookston, MN [*Radio station call letters*] ... KCUM-FM
Crookston, MN [*Radio station call letters*] ... KDEZ
Crookston, MN [*Radio station call letters*] ... KROX
Crookston, MN [*Radio station call letters*] ... KYCK
Crookston, NE [*Radio station call letters*] ... KINI
Crop Bulletin. Grain Research Laboratory (Canada) [*A publication*] ... Crop Bull Grain Res Lab (Can)
Crop Condition Assessment ... CCA
Crop Dryer Manufacturers Council ... CDMC
Crop-Hail Insurance Actuarial Association ... CHIAA
Crop Husbandry Adviser [*Ministry of Agriculture, Fisheries, and Food*] [*British*] ... CHA
Crop Identification Technology Assessment for Remote Sensing [*NASA*] ... CITARS
Crop Improvement [*A publication*] ... Crop Improv
Crop Production [*A publication*] ... Crop Prod
Crop Protection Chemicals Reference ... CPCR
Crop Protection Institute ... CPI
Crop Quality Council ... CQC
Crop Reporting Board ... CRB
Crop Science [*A publication*] ... Crop Sci
Crop Science Society of America ... CSSA
Crop Soils. North Carolina State University [*A publication*] ... Crop Soil NC State Univ
Cropland Adjustment Program ... CAP
Cropland Conversion Program ... CCP
Crops Research ARS [*Agricultural Research Service*] [*A publication*] ... Crop Res ARS
Crops Research Division [*of ARS, Department of Agriculture*] ... CR
Croquet Foundation of America ... CFA
Crosby Memorial Library, Picayune, MS [*Library symbol*] ... MsPi
Crosby, Stills, and Nash [*Rock music group*] [*Later, CSN & Y*] ... CSN
Crosby, Stills, Nash, and Young [*Rock music group*] [*Formerly, CSN*] ... CSN & Y
Crosier Fathers' Library, Hastings, NE [*Library symbol*] ... NbHCro
Crosier Heritage Association ... CHA
Crosier Theological Seminary [*Minnesota*] ... CTS
Crosley Automobile Club ... CAC
Cross [*As in X-roads*] ... X
Cross Air [*Switzerland*] [*ICAO designator*] ... LX
Cross Arm ... XARM
Cross Channel ... CC
Cross-Channel Coordination Center [*NATO*] ... CCCC
Cross-Channel Rejection ... CCR
Cross-Check Procedure ... CCP
Cross City, FL [*Radio station call letters*] ... WDKA
Cross [*A. T.*] **Co.** [*American Stock Exchange symbol*] ... ATX
Cross Connection ... XCO
Cross Connection ... XCONN
Cross Correlation ... CC
Cross-Correlation Function ... CCF
Cross Country [*Also, XCY*] ... XC
Cross Country [*Also, XC*] ... XCY

Cross-Country Movement [*Maps*] ... CCM
Cross-Country Skiing ... XCS
Cross Couple ... CC
Cross and Crown [*A publication*] ... Cross & Cr
Cross Currents [*A publication*] ... CC
Cross Currents [*A publication*] ... Cross C
Cross Currents [*A publication*] ... Cross Cur
Cross Currents [*A publication*] ... Cross Curr
Cross Deck Pendant ... CDP
Cross-Field Acceleration ... XFA
Cross-Field Jammer ... CFJ
Cross Front [*Photography*] ... CF
Cross-Guide Coupler ... CGC
Cross Hair ... XHAIR
Cross, Iddings, Pirsson, and Washington [*Norms*] [*Geology*] ... CIPW
Cross Lake [*Canada*] [*Airport symbol*] ... YCR
Cross-Lines Alternative School ... CLAS
Cross-Linked Dextran Polymer [*Organic chemistry*] ... CDP
Cross-Linked Polyethylene [*Organic chemistry*] ... CLP
Cross-Linked Polyethylene [*Organic chemistry*] ... XLPE
Cross-Linked Polyethylene [*Organic chemistry*] ... XLT
Cross-Linking Agent ... CLA
Cross-Modulation Factor ... CMF
Cross of the Order of the Niger ... CON
Cross-Pointer Course Indicator ... CPCI
Cross Pointer Indicator ... CPI
Cross Polarization [*Atomic physics*] ... CP
Cross-Polarization Discrimination ... XPD
Cross Polarization Magic Angle Spinning [*Spectroscopy*] ... CPMAS
Cross Pollinated [*Genetics*] ... CP
Cross-Power Spectral Density ... CPSD
Cross-Question [*Transcripts*] ... XQ
Cross-Range Error ... CRE
Cross-Range Error Function ... CEF
Cross-Range Velocity Correlator ... CRVC
Cross-Reacting Material [*Immunology*] ... CRM
Cross-Reactive Idiotype [*Genetics*] ... CRI
Cross Reference ... CREF
Cross Reference ... CRREF
Cross Reference ... X-REF
Cross-Reference File ... CRF
Cross-Reference List ... XL
Cross-Reference Project ... CRP
Cross Reference Utility [*Data processing*] ... CULL
Cross-Scan Terrain-Avoidance Displays ... CRAN
Cross Section ... CS
Cross Section ... XS
Cross Section ... XSECT
Cross-Section Data Reduction ... CSDR
Cross-Section Information Storage and Retrieval System [*Nuclear energy*] ... CSISRS
Cross-Section Measurement System ... CMS
Cross-Sectional Area [*Cardiology*] ... XSA
Cross-Sectional Sensitivity [*Aviation*] ... CSS
Cross-Service Agreement [*Obsolete*] [*Military*] ... CSA
Cross-Service Order [*Military*] ... CSO
Cross-Spin Stabilization Systems ... CSSS
Cross Tabulation of Frequencies ... CTAB
Cross Talk ... XT
Cross Talk [*Aviation*] ... XTLK
Cross-Talk Unit ... CU
Cross Tell ... XTEL
Cross-Tell Simulator ... XTS
Cross-Track Contiguous ... CTC
Cross-Track Error ... CTE
Cross-Track Noncontiguous ... CTNC
Cross & Trecker Corporation [*NASDAQ symbol*] ... CTCO
Cross of Valour [*Military award*] [*Canada*] ... CV
Crossbar [*Bell System*] ... XB
Crossbar ... XBAR
Crosscurrents International Institute ... CII
Crosscurrents/Modern Critiques [*A publication*] ... CMC
Crosscurrents/Modern Fiction [*A publication*] ... CMF
Crossed Electroimmunodiffusion [*Analytical biochemistry*] ... CEID
Crossed-Field Amplifier [*Air Force*] ... CFA
Crossed-Field Output Tube ... CFOT
Crossed-Field Plasma Sheath ... CFPS
Crossed-Field Tube ... CFT
Crossed-Film Cryotron ... CFC
Crossed Olivocochlear Bundles [*Hearing*] ... COCB
Crossed Olivocochlear Potential [*Hearing*] ... COCP
Crossed Yogi Antenna ... CYA
Crossett, AR [*Radio station call letters*] ... KAGH
Crossett, AR [*Radio station call letters*] ... KAGH-FM
Crossfeed ... XFD
Crossfire ... CFR
Crosshatch Generator ... CHG
Crosshead ... CRSHD
Crossing ... XING
Crossing Protective Device ... CPD
Crossover [*Genetics*] ... CO
Crossover [*Technical drawings*] ... CRSVR
Crossover Value [*Genetics*] ... COV
Crosspoint ... XPT
Crossroads [*Maps and charts*] ... CR
Crossroads ... XRDS
Crossroads Joint Task Force [*Atomic weapons testing*] ... CJTF
Crossroads Technical Instrumentation [*Atomic weapons testing*] ... CTI
Crosstell Input ... CXI
Crosstell Output ... CXO
Crosstrail [*Military*] ... CT
Crossville, TN [*Location identifier*] [*FAA*] ... HCH
Crossville, TN [*Radio station call letters*] ... WAEW
Crossville, TN [*Radio station call letters*] ... WCSV
Crossville, TN [*Television station call letters*] ... WINT-TV
Crosswind Force ... CWF
Crosyton, TX [*Location identifier*] [*FAA*] ... CZX
Croton Free Library, Croton-On-Hudson, NY [*Library symbol*] ... NCroh
Croton Public Library, Newaygo, MI [*Library symbol*] ... MiNew-C
Croup-Associated [*Virus*] ... CA
Crouse-Hinds Company ... CHC
Crouse-Hinds Co. [*NYSE symbol*] [*Delisted*] ... CHI
Crouse-Irving Hospital, School of Nursing, Library, Syracuse, NY [*OCLC symbol*] ... ZUZ
Crouse-Irving Hospital, Syracuse, NY [*Library symbol*] ... NSyCH
Crow Canyon [*California*] [*Seismograph station code, US Geological Survey*] ... CYC
Crow River Regional Library, Willmar, MN [*Library symbol*] ... MnWilRL
Crowd, Lift, Actuate, Swing [*Backhoe controls for tractors*] ... CLAS
Crowell-Collier & Macmillan, Inc. [*Later, Macmillan, Inc.*] [*Publishers*] ... CCM
Crowell-Collier & Macmillan, Inc. [*Later, MLL*] [*NYSE symbol*] ... CRW
Crowfoot ... CRFT
Crowley, LA [*Radio station call letters*] ... KAJN
Crowley, LA [*Radio station call letters*] ... KAJN-FM
Crowley, LA [*Radio station call letters*] ... KSIG
Crowley, Milner, & Co. [*American Stock Exchange symbol*] ... COM
Crown ... CR
Crown ... CRN
Crown [*Paper size*] ... CR
Crown Agent ... CA
Crown Agents for the Colonies [*British*] ... CAC
Crown Agents for Overseas Governments [*British*] ... CAOG
Crown Airways, Inc. [*DuBois, PA*] [*FAA designator*] ... CRO
Crown America, Inc. [*NASDAQ symbol*] ... CRNA
Crown Asset Disposal Corporation [*Canada*] ... CADC
Crown Aviation, Inc. [*Texico, NM*] [*FAA designator*] ... HPS
Crown Books Corp. [*NASDAQ symbol*] ... CRWN
Crown Cases [*Legal*] [*British*] ... CC
Crown Cases Reserved [*Legal*] [*British*] ... CCR
Crown Cat Fanciers Federation ... CCFF
Crown Central Petroleum Corp. [*American Stock Exchange symbol*] ... CNP
Crown Colony ... CC
Crown Cork & Seal Co., Inc. [*NYSE symbol*] ... CCK
Crown Crafts, Inc. [*American Stock Exchange symbol*] ... CRW
Crown Estate Commissioner [*British*] ... CEC
Crown Estate Commissioner [*British*] ... CREST
Crown-Heel [*Length of fetus*] [*Medicine*] ... CH
Crown Industries, Inc. [*American Stock Exchange symbol*] ... KRO
Crown Mine [*Nevada*] [*Seismograph station code, US Geological Survey*] [*Closed*] ... CMN
Crown Office [*British*] ... CO
Crown Point Community Schools, Crown Point, IN [*Library symbol*] ... InCrpCS
Crown Point Community Schools, Crown Point, IN [*OCLC symbol*] ... IPO
Crown Point, IN [*Radio station call letters*] ... WWJY
Crown Resource Corp. [*NASDAQ symbol*] ... CRRS
Crown-Rump [*Length of fetus*] [*Medicine*] ... CR
Crown-Rump Length [*Medicine*] ... CRL
Crown Victoria Association ... CVA
Crown Zellerbach Corp. ... CZ
Crown Zellerbach Corp. [*NYSE symbol*] ... ZB
Crown Zellerbach Corp., San Francisco, CA [*Library symbol*] ... CSfCZ
Crownair Flygtjanst [*ICAO designator*] ... EH
Crowned ... C
Crownsville State Hospital, Crownsville, MD [*Library symbol*] ... MdCvH
Crows Landing, CA [*Location identifier*] [*FAA*] ... NRC
Croydon [*Australia*] [*Airport symbol*] [*Obsolete*] ... CDQ
Croydon [*Borough of London*] ... CROYD
Croydon Advertiser, Croydon, United Kingdom [*Library symbol*] ... UkCrA
Croydon Library, Croydon, United Kingdom [*Library symbol*] ... UkCr
Crozet, VA [*Radio station call letters*] ... WPED
Crozet, VA [*Radio station call letters*] ... WPED-FM
CRS/Sirrine, Inc. [*Formerly, CRS Group, Inc.*] [*American Stock Exchange symbol*] ... DA
CRT [*Cathode-Ray Tube*] **Display Unit** ... CDU
Crucible Institute [*Formerly, CMA*] ... CI
Crucible Manufacturers Association [*Later, CI*] ... CMA
Crucible Melt Extraction [*Metal fiber technology*] ... CME
Crucible Steel Co. of America [*NYSE symbol*] [*Delisted*] ... XA
Cruciform Wing Module ... CWM
Cruciform Wing Weapon ... CWW

Crude Barrel Equivalent [*Oil*] ... CBE
Crude Birth Rate [*Medicine*] ... CBR
Crude Fiber ... CF
Crude Magazine [*Generic term for a one-person science-fiction fan magazine, produced by an inexperienced publisher*] ... CRUDZINE
Crude Marijuana Extract ... CME
Crude Myosin [*Food technology*] ... CM
Crude Oil Equalization Tax [*Proposed, 1978*] ... COET
Crude Oil Processing Plant ... COPP
Crude Oil Washing [*of cargo tank*] ... COW
Crude Protein ... CP
Cruisair Ltd. [*Kenya*] [*ICAO designator*] ... KB
Cruise ... CRU
Cruise ... CRZ
Cruise ... CSE
Cruise Altitude [*Aviation*] ... CA
Cruise/Entry Data Acquisition Unit [*NASA*] ... CEDAU
Cruise Guidance Control [*Aviation*] ... CGC
Cruise Guide Indicator [*Aviation*] ... CGI
Cruise Lines International Association ... CLIA
Cruise and Maintain [*Aviation*] ... CAM
Cruise Missile ... CM
Cruise Missile Carrier [*Aircraft*] ... CMC
Cruise Missile Carrier Aircraft ... CMCA
Cruise Missile Guidance Set ... CMGS
Cruise Missile Guidance System ... CMGS
Cruise Passengers Club International ... CPCI
Cruise Speed [*Aviation*] ... VC
Cruise Vehicle [*Military*] ... CV
Cruise Well to Right [*Aviation*] ... CRZWTR
Cruiser ... C
Cruiser ... CR
Cruiser-Destroyer Flotilla [*Navy symbol*] ... CRUDESFLOT
Cruiser-Destroyer Force, Atlantic Fleet [*Navy symbol*] ... CRUDESLANT
Cruiser-Destroyer Force, Pacific Fleet [*Navy symbol*] ... CRUDESPAC
Cruiser Division [*Navy*] ... CRUDIV
Cruiser Flag [*Navy*] [*British*] ... CR
Cruiser Minelayer ... CM
Cruiser Olympia Association ... COA
Cruiser-Scouting Aircraft Squadron [*Navy symbol*] ... VCS
Cruiser-Scouting Force [*Navy*] ... CRUSCOFOR
Cruiser-Scouting Squadron [*Navy*] ... CRUSCORON
Cruiser Squadron [*Navy*] ... CS
Cruiser Submarine [*Navy symbol*] [*Obsolete*] ... SC
Cruiser Submarine [*Navy symbol*] ... SSC
Cruisers ... CC
Cruisers, Atlantic Fleet [*Navy*] ... CRULANT
Cruisers, Atlantic Fleet [*Navy*] ... CRULANTFLT
Cruisers, Battle Force [*Navy*] ... CRUBATFOR
Cruisers, Pacific Fleet [*Navy*] ... CRUPAC
Cruisers, Pacific Fleet [*Navy*] ... CRUPACFLT
Cruising ... CRUIS
Cruising Club of America ... CCA
Cruising Speed ... CSPD
Crum & Forster [*NYSE symbol*] [*Delisted*] ... CMF
Crump [*E. H.*] **Cos.** [*NASDAQ symbol*] ... CRMP
Crusade to Abolish War and Armaments by World Law ... CAWAWL
Crusade for a Cleaner Environment [*Defunct*] ... CCE
Crusade for Decency ... CD
Crushed or Ground ... CG
Crusher and Portable Plant Association ... CAPPA
Crusher and Portable Plant Association ... CPPA
Crustacean Society ... CS
Crustaceana Supplement (Leiden) [*A publication*] ... Crustaceana Suppl (Leiden)
Crutch Walking [*Medicine*] ... CW
Crutcher Resources Corp. [*American Stock Exchange symbol*] ... CTR
Crutchfield [*Kentucky*] [*Seismograph station code, US Geological Survey*] ... CRU
Crux [*A publication*] ... Cr
Crux [*Constellation*] ... Cru
Cruz Alta [*Brazil*] [*Airport symbol*] ... CZB
Cruz y Raya [*A publication*] ... CyR
Cruzeiro Do Sul [*Brazil*] [*Airport symbol*] ... CZS
Cryderman Air Service [*Air carrier designation symbol*] ... CASX
Cryderman Air Service [*Drayton Plains, MI*] [*FAA designator*] ... CTY
Cryogenic ... CRYO
Cryogenic ... CRYOG
Cryogenic Continuous Film Memory [*Data processing*] ... CCFM
Cryogenic Data Center [*National Bureau of Standards*] ... CDC
Cryogenic Electrically Suspended Gyroscope ... CESG
Cryogenic Engineering Laboratory [*National Bureau of Standards*] ... CEL
Cryogenic Engineering News [*A publication*] ... Cryog Eng News
Cryogenic Explosive Valve ... CEV
Cryogenic Expulsive Bladder ... CEB
Cryogenic Fluid Storage ... CFS
Cryogenic Fluid Storage Container ... CFSC
Cryogenic Gas Storage System ... CGSS
Cryogenic Inertial Navigating System ... CINS
Cryogenic Instrumentation System ... CIS
Cryogenic Insulation Program ... CIP
Cryogenic Positive Expulsion Bladder ... CPEB
Cryogenic Pressure Transducer ... CPT
Cryogenic Quartz Crystal Microbalance ... CQCM
Cryogenic Refrigerator Program ... CRP
Cryogenic Society of America ... CSA
Cryogenic Storage Container ... CSC
Cryogenic Storage System [*Apollo project*] [*NASA*] ... CSS
Cryogenic Technology [*A publication*] ... Cryog Technol
Cryogenic Temperature Sensor [*or Source*] ... CTS
Cryogenic Vacuum Calorimeter ... CVC
Cryogenics [*A publication*] ... Cryog
Cryogenics Engineering Conference ... CEC
Cryogenics and Industrial Gases [*A publication*] ... Cryog & Ind Gases
Cryogenics. Supplement [*A publication*] ... Cryog Suppl
Cryoglobulin [*Clinical medicine*] ... CG
Cryostatic Switching-Avalanche and Recombination ... CRYOSAR
Cryotron Associative Processor ... CAP
Cryptanalysis [*Air Force*] ... CRYPTA
Crypto Access Authorization [*Military*] ... CAA
Crypto-Communication Network ... CRYPTONET
Crypto Radio Service ... CRS
Cryptoancillary Unit ... CAU
Cryptocenter Watch Officer ... CCWO
Cryptofacility Security Questionnaire [*Army*] ... CSQ
Cryptograph ... CTGH
Cryptographer [*Navy rating*] ... CR
Cryptographic [*or Cryptography*] ... CRYPTO
Cryptographic Aid, General Publication ... KAG
Cryptographic Repair Facilities ... CRF
Cryptographic Supplement to the Industrial Security Manual [*DoD*] ... CSISM
Cryptologic Communications ... CRITICOM
Cryptologic Support Group ... CSG
Crystal ... CRYS
Crystal [*s*] [*or Crystalline or Crystallize or Crystallography*] ... CRYST
Crystal ... XL
Crystal ... XTAL
Crystal Can Relay ... CCR
Crystal Chemistry of Non-Metallic Materials [*A publication*] ... Cryst Chem Non-Met Mater
Crystal City, TX [*Radio station call letters*] ... KHER
Crystal Control ... CC
Crystal-Controlled Oscillator ... CCO
Crystal-Controlled Transmitter ... CCT
Crystal Current ... CC
Crystal Cut [*Symbol*] ... X
Crystal Data Center [*National Bureau of Standards*] ... CDC
Crystal Diffusion Reflection ... CDR
Crystal Diode ... CD
Crystal Driver ... CD
Crystal Field Effects in Metals and Alloys (Proceedings of the International Conference on Crystal Field Effects in Metals and Alloys) [*A publication*] ... Cryst Field Eff Met Alloys (Proc Int Conf)
Crystal Field Stabilization Energy ... CFSE
Crystal Field Surface Orbital-Bond Energy Bond Order [*Model for chemisorption*] ... CFSO-BEBO
Crystal Field Theory [*Chemistry*] ... CFT
Crystal Frequency Multiplier ... CFM
Crystal Holder [*JETDS nomenclature*] [*Military*] ... HC
Crystal Impedance Meter ... CIM
Crystal-Induced Chemotactic Factor [*Immunology*] ... CCF
Crystal Kit ... CK
Crystal Lake [*New York*] [*Seismograph station code, US Geological Survey*] ... CLY
Crystal Lake, IL [*Radio station call letters*] ... WIVS
Crystal Lattice Defects [*A publication*] ... Crys Lattice Defects
Crystal Lattice Defects [*A publication*] ... Cryst Latt
Crystal Lattice Defects [*A publication*] ... Cryst Lattice Defects
Crystal Marker Oscillator ... CMO
Crystal Oil Co. [*American Stock Exchange symbol*] ... COR
Crystal Oscillator ... CO
Crystal Oscillator ... XO
Crystal Oscillator ... XTLO
Crystal Palace, Sydenham [*British*] ... CP
Crystal Pressure Transducer ... CPT
Crystal Quartz Modern ... CQM
Crystal Rectifier ... CR
Crystal Research and Technology [*A publication*] ... Cryst Res Technol
Crystal River, FL [*Radio station call letters*] ... WRYO
Crystal Shamrock [*Minneapolis, MN*] [*FAA designator*] ... CYT
Crystal Size Distribution ... CSD
Crystal Springs Library, Crystal Springs, MS [*Library symbol*] ... MsCs
Crystal Springs, MS [*Radio station call letters*] ... WCSP
Crystal Unit [*Piezoelectric*] ... CU
Crystal Unit Cell ... CUC
Crystal Video Receiver ... CVR
Crystal Violet [*An indicator*] [*Chemistry*] ... CV
Crystalline Insulin ... CI
Crystalline or Powdered ... CP
Crystalline Style ... CST
Crystalline Transitional Material ... CTM

Crystalline Zinc Insulin [*Medicine*] .... CZI
Crystallographic [*Origin*] [*Of precious stones*] .... CRST
Crystallographic Computing Network [*AEC*] .... CRYSNET
Crystallographic Computing Techniques. Proceedings of an International Summer School [*A publication*] .... Crystallogr Comput Tech Proc Int Summer Sch
Crystallographic Laboratory [*MIT*] CL
Crystallography (Soviet Physics) [*A publication*] .... Crystallogr (Sov Phys)
Crystals [*JETDS nomenclature*] [*Military*] .... CR
Crystals [*or Crystallography*] .... CRY
CS Group [*American Stock Exchange symbol*] [*Delisted*] .... CSG
Csatornamue Informacio [*A publication*] .... Csatornamue Inf
CSE Aviation Ltd. [*Great Britain*] [*ICAO designator*] .... NR
CSE Corp. [*American Stock Exchange symbol*] [*Delisted*] .... CSE
CSELT [*Centro Studi e Laboratori Telecomunicazioni*] **Rapporti Tecnici** [*A publication*] .... CSELT Rappo Tec
CSIO [*Central Scientific Instruments Organisation*] **Communications** [*India*] [*A publication*] .... CSIO Commun
CSIR [*Council for Scientific and Industrial Research*] **News (India)** [*A publication*] .... CSIR News (India)
CSIR [*Council for Scientific and Industrial Research*] **Special Report FIS** [*A publication*] .... CSIR Spec Rep FIS
CSIR [*Council for Scientific and Industrial Research*] **Zoological Monograph** [*A publication*] .... CSIR Zool Monogr
CSIRO [*Commonwealth Scientific and Industrial Research Organisation*] **Abstracts** [*A publication*] .... CSIRO Abstr
CSIRO [*Commonwealth Scientific and Industrial Research Organisation*] **Annual Report** [*A publication*] .... CSIRO Annu Rep
CSIRO [*Commonwealth Scientific and Industrial Research Organisation*] **Australia. Division of Tropical Crops and Pastures. Technical Paper** [*A publication*] .... CSIRO Aust Div Trop Crops Pastures Tech Pap
CSIRO [*Commonwealth Scientific and Industrial Research Organisation*] **Division of Chemical Physics. Annual Report** [*A publication*] .... CSIRO Div Chem Phys Annu Rep
CSIRO [*Commonwealth Scientific and Industrial Research Organisation*] **Division of Entomology. Annual Report** [*A publication*] .... CSIRO Div Entomol Annu Rep
CSIRO [*Commonwealth Scientific and Industrial Research Organisation*] **Division of Fisheries and Oceanography. Report (Australia)** [*A publication*] .... CSIRO Div Fish Oceanogr Rep (Aust)
CSIRO [*Commonwealth Scientific and Industrial Research Organisation*] **Division of Forest Products. Technological Papers** [*A publication*] .... CSIRO Div Forest Prod Technol Paper
CSIRO [*Commonwealth Scientific and Industrial Research Organisation*] **Division of Tropical Agronomy. Annual Report** [*A publication*] .... CSIRO Div Trop Agron Annu Rep
CSIRO [*Commonwealth Scientific and Industrial Research Organisation*] **Food Preservation Quarterly** [*A publication*] .... CSIRO Food Preserv Q
CSIRO [*Commonwealth Scientific and Industrial Research Organisation*] **Food Research Quarterly** [*A publication*] .... CSIRO Food Res Q
CSIRO [*Commonwealth Scientific and Industrial Research Organisation*] **Forest Products Newsletter** [*A publication*] .... CSIRO Forest Prod Newsl
CSIRO [*Commonwealth Scientific and Industrial Research Organisation*] **Marine Biochemistry Unit. Annual Report** [*A publication*] .... CSIRO Mar Biochem Unit Annu Rep
CSIRO [*Commonwealth Scientific and Industrial Research Organisation*] **Minerals Research Laboratories. Annual Report** [*A publication*] .... CSIRO Miner Res Lab Annu Rep
CSIRO [*Commonwealth Scientific and Industrial Research Organisation*] **Minerals Research Laboratories. Investigation Report** [*A publication*] .... CSIRO Miner Res Lab Invest Rep
CSIRO [*Commonwealth Scientific and Industrial Research Organisation*] **National Measurement Laboratory. Biennial Report** [*A publication*] .... CSIRO Natl Meas Lab Bienn Rep
CSIRO [*Commonwealth Scientific and Industrial Research Organisation*] **National Standards Laboratory. Biennial Report** [*A publication*] .... CSIRO Natl Stand Lab Bienn Rep
CSIRO [*Commonwealth Scientific and Industrial Research Organisation*] **Wheat Research Unit. Annual Report** [*A publication*] .... CSIRO Wheat Res Unit Annu Rep
CSIRO [*Commonwealth Scientific and Industrial Research Organisation*] **Wildlife Research** [*A publication*] .... CSIRO Wildl Res
CSM [*Command and Service Module*] **and ATM** [*Apollo Telescope Mount*] **Communications Specialist** [*NASA*] .... CATCO
CSM [*Command and Service Module*] **Environmental and Electrical Systems Engineer** [*NASA*] .... EECOM
CSM [*Command and Service Module*] **Navigation Update** [*NASA*] .... CNU
CSM Systems, Inc. [*NASDAQ symbol*] .... CSMS
CSP Incorporated [*NASDAQ symbol*] .... CSPI
CSPG [*Canadian Society of Petroleum Geologists*] **Memoir** [*A publication*] .... CSPG Mem
CSSA [*Crop Science Society of America*] **Special Publication** [*A publication*] .... CSSA Spec Publ
CSTA [*Canadian Society of Technical Agriculturists*] **Review** [*A publication*] .... CSTA R
CSX Corp. [*Formed by merger of Chessie System, Inc. and Seaboard Coast Line Railroad*] [*Formerly, CO*] [*NYSE symbol*] .... CSX
CT Exploranda Ltd. [*NASDAQ symbol*] .... CXPVF
CTA [*Cine Technicians' Association*] **Journal** [*India*] [*A publication*] .... CTA J
Ctenidial Analog [*Biology*] .... CA
Ctenidial Nerve [*Biology*] .... CTN
Ctenidial Sinus [*Biology*] .... CS
CTFA [*Cosmetic, Toiletry, and Fragrance Association*] **Cosmetic Journal** [*A publication*] .... CTFA Cosmet J
CTG Inc. Uts [*NASDAQ symbol*] .... CTGUF
CTS Corp. [*NYSE symbol*] .... CTS
Cuadernos Americanos [*A publication*] .... CA
Cuadernos Americanos [*A publication*] .... Cuad Amer
Cuadernos Bibliograficos [*Madrid*] [*A publication*] .... CB
Cuadernos Canarios de Investigacion [*A publication*] .... CuCanI
Cuadernos de la Catedra de Unamuno [*A publication*] .... CCU
Cuadernos de Ciencias Biologicas. Universidad de Granada [*A publication*] .... Cuad Cienc Biol Univ Granada
Cuadernos del Congreso por la Libertad de la Cultura [*A publication*] CCLC
Cuadernos de la Corporacion Venezolana de Fomento [*A publication*] .... Cuad CVF
Cuadernos de Cultura Espanola [*A publication*] .... CCE
Cuadernos de Cultura Teatral [*A publication*] .... CCT
Cuadernos para el Dialogo [*A publication*] .... CD
Cuadernos de Economia (Barcelona) [*A publication*] .... Cuad Econ (Barcelona)
Cuadernos de Estudios Gallegos [*A publication*] .... CEG
Cuadernos de Estudios Manchegos [*A publication*] .... CEM
Cuadernos de Filologia [*A publication*] .... CdF
Cuadernos de Filologia Clasica [*A publication*] .... CFC
Cuadernos de Filosofia [*A publication*] .... Cuad Filosof
Cuadernos de Geologia. Universidad de Granada [*A publication*] .... Cuad Geol Univ Granada
Cuadernos Hispanoamericanos [*Madrid*] [*A publication*] .... CH
Cuadernos Hispanoamericanos [*Madrid*] [*A publication*] .... CHA
Cuadernos Hispanoamericanos [*Madrid*] [*A publication*] .... CuH
Cuadernos de Historia de Espana [*A publication*] .... CHE
Cuadernos de Historia de la Salud Publica [*A publication*] .... Cuad Hist Salud Publica
Cuadernos del Idioma [*A publication*] CI
Cuadernos del Instituto Nacional de Antropologia [*A publication*] .... Cuad Inst Nac Antropol
Cuadernos de Literatura [*A publication*] CL
Cuadernos de Literatura [*A publication*] CLi
Cuadernos de Literatura Contemporanea [*A publication*] CLC
Cuadernos Oceanograficos. Universidad de Oriente Cumana [*A publication*] .... Cuad Oceanogr Univ Oriente Cumana
Cuadernos de Ruedo Iberico [*A publication*] .... Cuad Ruedo Iber
Cuajimalpa [*Mexico*] [*Later, TEO*] [*Geomagnetic observatory code*] .... CUA
Cub Master [*Scouting*] .... CM
Cuba C
Cuba [*Aircraft nationality and registration mark*] .... CU
Cuba [*Three-letter standard code*] .... CUB
Cuba [*MARC geographic area code*] [*Library of Congress*] .... nwcu
Cuba [*MARC country of publication code*] [*Library of Congress*] .... cu
Cuba [*Two-letter standard code*] .... CU
Cuba Bibliotecologica [*A publication*] .... Cuba Bibl
Cuba. Direccion de Montes y Minas. Boletin de Minas [*A publication*] .... Cuba Dir Montes B Minas
Cuba, MO [*Radio station call letters*] .... KBCC
Cuba, MO [*Location identifier*] [*FAA*] .... UBX
Cuba Resource Center .... CRC
Cuban-American National Foundation .... CANF
Cuban Journal of Agricultural Science [*A publication*] .... Cuban J Agric Sci
Cuban National Planning Council .... CNPC
Cuban Nationalist Movement .... CNM
Cuban Navy .... CN
Cuban Philatelic Society of America .... CPSA
Cuban Refugee Program [*HEW*] .... CRP
Cuban Refugee Program Staff [*HEW*] .... CRPS
Cube .... CU
Cube Alignment Kit .... CAK
Cube Corner Holder .... CCH
Cube Corner Reflector .... CCR
Cube-On-Edge [*Metal grain structure*] .... COE
Cubic C
Cubic .... CU
Cubic .... CUB
Cubic Boron Nitride [*Cutting tool edges*] .... CBN
Cubic Centimeter cc
Cubic Centimeter .... CUCM
Cubic Centimeters at Standard Temperature and Pressure [*Also, CSTP*] .... CCSTP
Cubic Centimeters at Standard Temperature and Pressure [*Also, CCSTP*] .... CSTP
Cubic Contents CC
Cubic Corp. [*American Stock Exchange symbol*] .... CUB
Cubic Corp., San Diego, CA [*Library symbol*] .... CSdCu
Cubic Decameters per Day .... DAM^3/D
Cubic Feet .... CF

Cubic Feet per Day ... CFD
Cubic Feet per Foot Day ... $FT^3/(FT\ D)$
Cubic Feet per Hour ... CFH
Cubic Feet per Minute ... CFM
Cubic Feet per Minute/Second ... CFM/S
Cubic Feet per Second ... CFS
Cubic Feet per Second ... CUSEC
Cubic Feet per Second ... FT^3/S
Cubic Feet per Square Foot Day ... $FT^3/(FT^2\ D)$
Cubic Foot ... CUFT
Cubic Inch ... CI
Cubic Inch ... CUIN
Cubic Inch Displacement [*in engines*] ... CID
Cubic Inches per Revolution ... CIPR
Cubic Meter ... CUM
Cubic Meters per Day ... M^3/D
Cubic Meters per Joule ... M^3/J
Cubic Meters per Kilogram ... M^3/KG
Cubic Meters per Meter Day ... $M^3/(M\ D)$
Cubic Meters per Meter Year ... $M^3/(M\ A)$
Cubic Meters per Minute ... M^3/MIN
Cubic Meters per Second ... CUMECS
Cubic Meters per Second ... M^3/S
Cubic Meters per Square Meter Day ... $M^3/(M^2\ D)$
Cubic Meters per Square Meter Second ... $M^3/(M^2\ S)$
Cubic Meters per Square Meter Year ... $M^3/(M^2\ A)$
Cubic Micron ... CUMU
Cubic Millimeter ... CMM
Cubic Millimeter ... CUMM
Cubic Spline Regression [*Statistics*] ... CRS
Cubic Tonnage [*Shipping*] ... CT
Cubic Weight ... CW
Cubic Yard ... CUYD
Cubic Yard ... CY
Cubicle ... CUB
Cubicle ... CUBE
Cubitainer ... CU
Cucos, Inc. [*NASDAQ symbol*] ... CUCO
Cucumber Mosaic Virus ... CMV
Cucumber Pale Fruit Viroid ... CPFV
Cucurbita Cruenta [*Cupping Glass*] [*Medicine*] ... CC
Cucuta [*Colombia*] [*Airport symbol*] ... CUC
Cudahy Co. [*NYSE symbol*] [*Delisted*] ... CUD
Cudahy Public Library, Cudahy, WI [*Library symbol*] ... WC
Cue Indexing System ... CIS
Cuenca [*Ecuador*] [*Airport symbol*] ... CUE
Cuenta Abierta [*Open Account*] [*Business and trade*] [*Spanish*] ... CA
Cuenta y Riesgo [*For Account and Risk of*] [*Business and trade*] [*Spanish*] ... C/R
Cuero, TX [*Radio station call letters*] ... KEWS
Cuesta College, San Luis Obispo, CA [*Library symbol*] ... CSluCu
Cuget Romanesc [*A publication*] ... CRom
Cuglieri [*Italy*] [*Seismograph station code, US Geological Survey*] ... CUG
Cuiaba [*Brazil*] [*Airport symbol*] ... CGB
Cuirassed [*Numismatics*] ... CUIR
Cujus [*Of Which*] [*Latin*] ... CUJ
Cujus Libet [*Of Any You Please*] [*Pharmacy*] ... CUJ LIB
Culbro Corporation [*NYSE symbol*] ... CUC
Culebra [*Puerto Rico*] [*Airport symbol*] ... CPX
Culebra [*Puerto Rico*] [*Seismograph station code, US Geological Survey*] ... CUP
Culebra de Aviacion, Inc. [*San Juan, PR*] [*FAA designator*] ... CDC
Culegere de Studii si Cercetari (Brasov) [*A publication*] ... Cul Stud Cerc (Brasov)
Culham Laboratory Reports [*United Kingdom Atomic Energy Authority*] ... CLM
Culiacan [*Mexico*] [*Airport symbol*] ... CUL
Culiacan [*Mexico*] [*Seismograph station code, US Geological Survey*] [*Closed*] ... CUL
Culinary Arts Program [*Association of Independent Colleges and Schools specialization code*] ... CU
Culinary and Fine Arts Club ... C & FA
Culinary Institute of America ... CIA
Cullen/Frost Bankers, Incorporated [*NASDAQ symbol*] ... CFBI
Culligan International Co. [*NYSE symbol*] [*Delisted*] ... CUL
Cullinet Software [*NYSE symbol*] ... CUL
Cullman, AL [*Radio station call letters*] ... WFMH
Cullman, AL [*Radio station call letters*] ... WFMH-FM
Cullman, AL [*Radio station call letters*] ... WKLN
Cullman, AL [*Radio station call letters*] ... WXXR
Cullman County Library [*Library network*] ... CCPL
Cullowhee, NC [*Radio station call letters*] ... WWCU
Cullum Cos., Inc. [*NASDAQ symbol*] ... CULL
Culp, Inc. [*NASDAQ symbol*] ... CULP
Culpeper, VA [*Radio station call letters*] ... WCUL
Culpeper, VA [*Radio station call letters*] ... WCVA
Cultivador Moderno [*A publication*] ... Cult Mod
Cultivar [*Cultural Variety*] [*Biology*] ... cv
Cultivated Mushroom Institute of America ... CMIA
Cultivator ... CULTVR
Cultura [*A publication*] ... Cult
Cultura Biblica [*A publication*] ... CB
Cultura Medica Moderna [*A publication*] ... Cultura Med Mod
Cultura Neolatina [*A publication*] ... CN
Cultura Neolatina [*A publication*] ... Cult Neol
Cultura Neolatina [*A publication*] ... Cult Neolat
Cultura Politica [*Rio De Janeiro*] [*A publication*] ... CP
Cultura e Scuola [*A publication*] ... CeS
Cultura e Scuola [*A publication*] ... C & S
Cultura Universitaria (Caracas) [*A publication*] ... CUC
Cultura Universitaria de la Universidad Central de Venezuela [*A publication*] ... CUUCV
Cultural ... CULT
Cultural Affairs Officer [*United States Information Service*] ... CAO
Cultural Auction of Many Extraordinary Lots of Treasure [*St. Louis, Missouri*] ... CAMELOT
Cultural Events in Africa [*A publication*] ... CulEA
Cultural Exchange Officer [*United States Information Service*] ... CEO
Cultural Exchange Society of America ... CESA
Cultural Forum [*New Delhi*] [*A publication*] ... CForum
Cultural Hermeneutics [*A publication*] ... Cult Hermen
Cultural [*formerly, Counterinsurgency*] **Information Analysis Center** [*Discontinued*] ... CINFAC
Cultural Information Service ... CIS
Cultural Integration Fellowship ... CIF
Cultural and Recreational Education Achieved through Investigations Ordinarily Neglected [*University course*] ... CREATION
Cultural Survival [*An association*] ... CS
Culture [*A publication*] ... Clt
Culture [*Microbiology*] ... CULT
Culture [*Montreal*] [*A publication*] ... Cult
Culture Francaise [*A publication*] ... Cult Franc
Culture, Medicine, Psychiatry [*A publication*] ... Cult Med Psychiatry
Culture and Sensitivity ... C & S
Culture and Tradition [*A publication*] ... C & T
Cultured Dairy Products Journal [*A publication*] ... Cul Dair Prod J
Cultured Marble Institute ... CMI
Cultured Pearl Association of America ... CPAA
Cultured Thymic Epithelium [*Immunochemistry*] ... CTE
Cultures et Developpement [*A publication*] ... Cult et Devel
Cultuur-en Ontspanningscentrum [*Center for Culture and Recreation, an association of homosexuals*] [*Holland*] ... COC
Culver City, CA [*Location identifier*] [*FAA*] ... CVR
Culver-Stockton College [*Missouri*] ... CSC
Culver-Stockton College, Canton, MO [*Library symbol*] ... MoCanC
Culvert ... CULV
Cum [*With*] [*Latin*] ... C
Cum Correction [*With lenses*] [*Ophthalmology*] ... cc
Cum Dividendo [*With Dividend*] [*Business and trade*] ... CD
Cum Laude Society ... CLS
Cum Omnibus Bonis Quiescat [*May He, or She, Repose with All Good Souls*] [*Latin*] ... COBQ
Cum Tanto [*With the Same Amount Of*] [*Pharmacy*] ... C TANT
Cum Testamento Annexo [*With the Will Annexed*] [*Latin*] ... CTA
Cumana [*Venezuela*] [*Airport symbol*] ... CUM
Cumana [*Venezuela*] [*Seismograph station code, US Geological Survey*] ... CUM
Cumberland [*Maryland*] [*Airport symbol*] ... CBE
Cumberland [*County in England*] ... CUMB
Cumberland College of Tennessee, Lebanon, TN [*Library symbol*] ... TLebC
Cumberland College, Williamsburg, KY [*Library symbol*] ... KyWilC
Cumberland County Advertiser-Press, Inc., Bridgeton, NJ [*Library symbol*] ... NjBAP
Cumberland County Clerk, Bridgeton, NJ [*Library symbol*] ... NjBCoC
Cumberland County College, Vineland, NJ [*Library symbol*] ... NjVC
Cumberland County Historical Society, Greenwich, NJ [*Library symbol*] ... NjGrHi
Cumberland County Historical Society and Hamilton Library Association, Carlisle, PA [*Library symbol*] ... PCarlH
Cumberland County Public Library, Fayetteville, NC [*Library symbol*] ... NcFayC
Cumberland Gap National Historical Park [*National Park Service designation*] ... CUGA
Cumberland, KY [*Radio station call letters*] ... WCPM
Cumberland Law Review [*A publication*] ... Cumb L Rev
Cumberland, MD [*Location identifier*] [*FAA*] ... RYP
Cumberland, MD [*Radio station call letters*] ... WALI
Cumberland, MD [*Radio station call letters*] ... WCBC
Cumberland, MD [*Radio station call letters*] ... WKGO
Cumberland, MD [*Radio station call letters*] ... WROG
Cumberland, MD [*Radio station call letters*] ... WTBO
Cumberland Plateau [*Tennessee*] [*Seismograph station code, US Geological Survey*] ... CPO
Cumberland Plateau Seismological Observatory ... CPSO
Cumberland Presbyterian Quarterly Review [*A publication*] ... Cumb Q
Cumberland Presbyterian Theological Seminary, Bethel College, McKenzie, TN [*Library symbol*] ... TMckB-C
Cumberland Public Library, Cumberland, WI [*Library symbol*] ... WCu
Cumberland Railway & Coal Company [*AAR code*] ... CDC
Cumberland Regional Library, Amherst, NS, Canada [*Library symbol*] ... CaNSAMC
Cumberland Resources [*NASDAQ symbol*] ... CRIG

Cumberland-Samford Law Review [*A publication*] ....Cumber-Sam L Rev
Cumberland Trail Library System [*Library network*] ....CTLS
Cumberland Trail Library System, Flora, IL [*OCLC symbol*] ....IEZ
Cumberland Trail Library System, Flora, IL [*Library symbol*] ....IFICL
Cumming, GA [*Radio station call letters*] ....WHNE
Cumming, GA [*Radio station call letters*] ....WWEV
Cummins Engine Co., Inc. [*NYSE symbol*] ....CUM
Cumo Resources Ltd. [*NASDAQ symbol*] ....CUMOF
Cumulated Index Medicus [*A publication*] ....CIM
Cumulated Summaries ....CUMS
Cumulative ....CUM
Cumulative Audience [*Telecommunications*] ....CUME
Cumulative Book Index [*A publication*] ....CBI
Cumulative Book List [*A publication*] ....CBL
Cumulative Bulletin [*US Internal Revenue Service*] [*A publication*]............CB
Cumulative Changes CC
Cumulative Computer Abstracts [*A publication*] .... Cum Comput Abstr
Cumulative Damage Function [*Nuclear energy*] ....CDF
Cumulative Data Report ....CDR
Cumulative Data Statistics ....CUDS
Cumulative Distribution Function [*Statistics*] ....CDF
Cumulative Elapsed Time ....CET
Cumulative Failure Rate ....CFR
Cumulative Frequency ....CF
Cumulative Frequency Distribution ....CFD
Cumulative Index to Nursing and Allied Health Literature [*A publication*] ....CINL
Cumulative List [*Internal Revenue code with names of exempt organizations*] ...CL
Cumulative List Indicator [*IRS*] ....CU
Cumulative Monthly Issue [*Material*] ....CMI
Cumulative Mortality [*Radiology*] ....CM
Cumulative Paperback Index 1939-1959 [*A publication*] ....CPI
Cumulative Percentage Frequency ....CPF
Cumulative Population Doubling ....CPD
Cumulative Population Doubling Level ....CPDL
Cumulative Preferred [*A class of stock*] ....CMPF
Cumulative Probability Distribution ....CPD
Cumulative Quality Point Ratio ....CQPR
Cumulative Radiation Effect ....CRE
Cumulative Results Criterion ....CRC
Cumulative Sum ....CUSUM
Cumulative Sum Diagram [*Statistics*] ....CSD
Cumulative Weight Percent ....CWP
Cumuliform [*Meteorology*] ....CUF
Cumulonimbus [*Meteorology*] ....CB
Cumulonimbus [*Meteorology*] ....CN
Cumulonimbus [*Meteorology*] ....CUN
Cumulonimbus Mammatus [*Meteorology*] ....CBMAM
Cumulonimbus Mammatus [*Meteorology*] ....CM
Cumulus [*Meteorology*] ....CU
Cumulus [*Meteorology*] ....K
Cumulus and Cumulonimbus [*Meteorology*] ....CUCB
Cumulus Fractus [*Meteorology*] ....CUFR
Cumulus Fractus [*Meteorology*] ....CUFRA
CUNA [*Credit Union National Association*] **Retirement Savings Fund** ......CRSF
Cuneo Press, Inc. [*NYSE symbol*] [*Delisted*] ....CUN
Cunnamulla [*Australia*] [*Airport symbol*] ....CMA
Cunningham Drug Stores, Inc. [*NYSE symbol*] [*Delisted*] ....CDD
Cunningham & Walsh [*Advertising agency*] ....C & W
Cuore e Circolazione [*A publication*] ....Cuore Circ
Cup C
Cupboard ....CUP
Cupertino, CA [*Radio station call letters*] ....KKUP
Cupola ....CUP
Cupro Nickel ....CN
Cuprum [*Copper*] [*Chemical element*] ....Cu
Curacao [*Netherlands Antilles*] ....CU
Curacao [*Netherlands Antilles*] [*Airport symbol*] ....CUR
Curacao Group [*MARC geographic area code*] [*Library of Congress*] ....nwco---
Curacao Tourist Board ....CTB
Curacy [*or Curate*] C
Curate-in-Charge [*Church of England*] ....C-in-C
Curates' Alliance [*British*] ....CA
Curates' Augmentation Fund [*British*] ....CAF
Curatio [*A Dressing*] [*Pharmacy*] ....CURAT
Curative [*Medicine*] ....CUR
Curative Dose [*Medicine*] ....CD
Curd Firmness Tester [*For milk products*] ....CFT
Curecanti Recreation Area [*National Park Service designation*] ....CURE
Curia Advisari Vult [*The Court Wishes to Consider*] [*Legal*] ....CAV
Curia Regis Rolls [*British*] ....CUR
Curie [*Unit of radioactivity*] [*See Ci*] C
Curie [*Unit of radioactivity*] [*Preferred unit is Bq, Becquerel*] Ci
Curing Agent ....CA
Curious to Know [*An inquisitive customer*] [*Merchandising slang*] ....C to K
Curitiba [*Brazil*] [*Airport symbol*] ....CWB
Curium [*Chemical element*] ....Cm
Curling Club CC

Currant [*Nevada*] [*Seismograph station code, US Geological Survey*] .....CND
Currency C
Currency ....CUR
Currency ....CURR
Currency ....CY
Currency Bond ....CB
Currency Collector [*A publication*] CC
Currency Overprinting and Processing Equipment [*Bureau of Printing and Engraving*] ....COPE
Currency Regulation ....CR
Currency Technology Corp. [*NASDAQ symbol*] ....BUCK
Currency Transaction Report [*IRS*] ....CTR
Current C
Current ....CT
Current ....CUR
Current ....CURR
Current ....CURT
Current Abstracts of Chemistry [*A publication*] ....CAC
Current Abstracts of Chemistry and Index Chemicus [*A publication*] ....CAC & IC
Current Account ....CA
Current Actions Center ....CAC
Current Actions Duty Officer [*Air Force*] ....CADO
Current Adjusting Type ....CAT
Current Advances in Plant Science [*A publication*] ......Current Adv Plant Sci
Current Aerospace Research Activities ....CARA
Current Affairs Bulletin [*A publication*] ....Curr Aff B
Current Affairs Bulletin [*A publication*] ....Curr Aff Bull
Current Agricultural Research Information System [*United Nations*] [*Information service*] ....CARIS
Current Antarctic Literature [*A publication*] ....CAL
Current Anthropology [*A publication*] ....CAnth
Current Anthropology [*A publication*] ....CAnthr
Current Anthropology [*A publication*] ....Cur Anthrop
Current Anthropology [*A publication*] ....Cur Anthropol
Current Anthropology [*A publication*] ....Curr Anthr
Current ARDC [*Air Research and Development Command*] **Technical Efforts** [*DoD program*] ....CATE
Current Assessment Plan ....CAP
Current Assets [*Business and trade*] ....CA
Current Australian and New Zealand Legal Literature Index [*A publication*] ....Curr Aus NZ Leg Lit Ind
Current Awareness Bulletin [*A publication*] ....CAB
Current Awareness and Document Retrieval for Engineers ....CADRE
Current Awareness. Library Literature [*A publication*] ....CALL
Current Awareness Literature Service [*Agricultural Research Service*] ......CALS
Current Awareness Service [*Cryogenic literature bibliography*] [*Cryogenic Data Center*] ....CAS
Current Awareness System in Coordination Chemistry ....CASCC
Current Bibliographic Directory of the Arts and Sciences [*A publication*] ....CBD
Current Bibliography on African Affairs [*A publication*] ....CBAA
Current Bibliography on African Affairs [*A publication*] ....Cur Bibliog African Affairs
Current Bibliography for Aquatic Sciences and Fisheries [*A publication*] ....CBASF
Current Bibliography for Aquatic Sciences and Fisheries [*A publication*] ....Curr Bibl Aquatic Sci & Fish
Current Biography [*A publication*] ....Cur Biog
Current Biography Yearbook [*A publication*] ....Cur Biog Yrbk
Current BIT [*Binary Digit*] **Monitor Unit** [*Data processing*] ....CBMU
Current Book Review Citations [*A publication*] ....CBRC
Current Cancer Research Project Analysis Center ....CCRESPAC
Current Chemical Reactions [*A publication*] ....CCR
Current Chemical Translations [*A publication*] ....Current Chem Transl
Current Complaints [*Medicine*] CC
Current Concepts of Cerebrovascular Disease-Stroke [*A publication*] ....Curr Concepts Cerebrovasc Dis-Stroke
Current Concepts in Emergency Medicine [*A publication*] .....Curr Concepts Emerg Med
Current Concepts in Nutrition [*A publication*] ....Curr Concepts Nutr
Current Contents [*A publication*] CC
Current Contents [*A publication*] ....CurrCont
Current Contents/Agriculture, Biology, and Environmental Sciences [*A publication*] ....CC/AB & ES
Current Contents/Arts and Humanities [*A publication*] ....CC/A & H
Current Contents/Chemical Sciences [*A publication*] ....CC/CS
Current-Controlled Oscillator ....CCO
Current Cost CC
Current Cost Accounting ....CCA
Current Data BIT [*Binary Digit*] [*Data processing*] ....CDB
Current Density ....CD
Current Design Expendable [*Refers to payload type*] [*NASA*] ....CDE
Current Design Reusable [*Refers to payload type*] [*NASA*] ....CDR
Current Developments in Psychopharmacology [*A publication*] ....Curr Dev Psychopharmacol
Current Digest of the Soviet Press [*A publication*] ....CDSP
Current Digest of the Soviet Press [*A publication*] ....Curr Dig Sov Press
Current Directional Relay ....CDR
Current Domestic Value [*of goods in the country of origin*] ....CDV

Current Driver ... CD
Current Economic Reporting Program [*Department of State*] ... CERP
Current Economics and Business Aspects of the Wine Industry. Symposium [*A publication*] ... Curr Econ Bus Aspects Wine Ind Symp
Current Efficiency [*Electrochemistry*] ... CE
Current Endocrinology [*Elsevier Book Series*] [*A publication*] ... CE
Current Energy Patents [*A publication*] ... CEP
Current Engineering Practice [*A publication*] ... Curr Eng Pract
Current Enlistment Date [*Military*] ... CED
Current Expendable ... CE
Current Files Area ... CFA
Current Fiscal Year ... CFY
Current Flight Plan Message [*Aviation code*] ... CPL
Current Gain ... CG
Current Gate Tube ... CGT
Current Geographical Publications [*A publication*] ... CGP
Current Good Manufacturing Practice [*Food and Drug Administration*] ... CGMP
Current History [*A publication*] ... CH
Current History [*A publication*] ... Cu H
Current History [*A publication*] ... Cur Hist
Current History [*A publication*] ... Curr Hist
Current History Magazine of the New York Times [*A publication*] ... Cur Hist M NY Times
Current Hogging Injection Logic ... CHIL
Current-Hogging Logic [*Electronics*] ... CHL
Current Housing Reports [*A publication*] ... CHR
Current Income Shares, Inc. [*NYSE symbol*] ... CUR
Current Index to Commonwealth Legal Periodicals [*A publication*] ... Curr Ind Commonw Leg Per
Current Index to Journals in Education [*US Office of Education*] [*A publication*] ... CIJE
Current Indicator and Integrator ... CII
Current Industrial Reports [*Census Bureau*] ... CIR
Current Industrial Reports [*A publication*] ... Current Ind Rept
Current Information Selection [*IBM Corp.*] ... CIS
Current Information Tapes for Engineering ... CITE
Current Injection Probe ... CIP
Current Inquiry into Language and Linguistics [*A publication*] ... CILL
Current Instruction Register ... CIR
Current Intelligence Bulletin [*A publication*] ... CIB
Current Intelligence Digest [*A publication*] ... CIDG
Current Intelligence, Group ... CIG
Current Intelligence Indication Center ... CIIC
Current Intelligence Targets Groups [*Military*] ... CITG
Current Issues in Higher Education [*A publication*] ... Cur Issues Higher Ed
Current Issues in Higher Education. Annual Series [*A publication*] ... Cur Issues Higher Educ Ann Ser
Current Laboratory Practice [*A publication*] ... CLP
Current Law and Social Problems [*A publication*] ... Current Law
Current Law Year Book [*A publication*] ... CLYB
Current Leather Literature [*A publication*] ... Curr Leather Lit
Current Legal Problems [*A publication*] ... Curr Leg Probl
Current-Limiting Device [*Short-circuit limiter*] ... CLD
Current-Limiting Resistor ... CLR
Current Line Pointer [*Data processing*] ... CLP
Current List of Medical Literature ... CLML
Current Literature [*A publication*] ... Cur Lit
Current Literature Alerting Search Service [*of BIOSIS*] ... CLASS
Current Literature of Blood [*A publication*] ... Curr Lit Blood
Current-Logic-Current-Switching [*Electronics*] ... CLCS
Current Market Appraisal ... CMA
Current Mathematical Publications [*A publication*] ... Current Math Publ
Current Medical Information and Terminology ... CMIT
Current Medical Practice [*A publication*] ... Curr Med Pract
Current Medical Practice (India) [*A publication*] ... Curr Med Pract (India)
Current Medical Research and Opinion [*A publication*] ... Curr Med Res Opin
Current Medical Terminology ... CMT
Current Medicine for Attorneys [*A publication*] ... Current Med
Current Mode Complementary Transistor Logic ... CMCTL
Current-Mode Digital-to-Analog Converter [*Data processing*] ... CMDAC
Current-Mode Logic [*Data processing*] ... CML
Current-Mode Switching [*Data processing*] ... CMS
Current Municipal Problems [*A publication*] ... Curr Mun Pr
Current Musicology [*A publication*] ... C Mc
Current Musicology [*A publication*] ... Current Mus
Current Nephrology [*A publication*] ... Curr Nephrol
Current NOTAM [*Notice to Airmen*] **Indicator** ... CNI
Current Notes on International Affairs [*A publication*] ... Curr Notes Int Aff
Current Operating Allowances ... COA
Current Operating Budget Year ... COBY
Current Operating Procedure ... COP
Current Operational Data System ... CODAS
Current Operational Group [*NATO*] ... COG
Current Operations ... COPS
Current Operations Division [*Tactical Air Command*] ... COD
Current Operator - Next Operator [*Data processing*] ... CO/NO
Current Opinion [*A publication*] ... Cur Opinion
Current Paper ... CP
Current Papers on Computers and Control [*A publication*] ... CPC
Current Papers in Electrical and Electronics Engineering [*A publication*] ... CPE
Current Papers in Physics [*A publication*] ... CPP
Current Papers in Physics [*A publication*] ... Curr Pap Phys
Current and Past Psychopathology Scales [*Psychology*] ... CAPPS
Current Period ... CP
Current Physics Advance Abstracts [*A publication*] ... CPAA
Current Physics Bibliographies [*A publication*] ... CPB
Current Physics Index [*A publication*] ... CPI
Current Physics Information [*American Institute of Physics*] [*Information service*] ... CPI
Current Physics Microform [*A publication*] ... CPM
Current Physics Selected Articles [*A publication*] ... CPSA
Current Physics Titles [*A publication*] ... CPT
Current Population Reports [*A publication*] ... CPR
Current Population Reports. Consumer Income. Series P-60 (United States) [*A publication*] ... Curr Popul Rep (Consum Income)
Current Population Reports. Population Characteristics. Series P-20 (United States) [*A publication*] ... Curr Popul Rep (Popul Charact)
Current Population Reports. Population Estimates and Projections. Series P-25 (United States) [*A publication*] ... Curr Popul Rep (Popul Estim Proj)
Current Population Reports. Special Censuses. Series P-28 (United States) [*A publication*] ... Curr Popul Rep (Spec Censuses)
Current Population Reports. Special Studies. Series P-23 (United States) [*A publication*] ... Curr Popul Rep (Spec Stud)
Current Population Survey [*Census Bureau*] ... CPS
Current Practice in Gerontological Nursing [*A publication*] ... Curr Pract Gerontol Nurs
Current Practice in Obstetric and Gynecologic Nursing [*A publication*] ... Curr Pract Obstet Gynecol Nurs
Current Practice in Orthopaedic Surgery [*A publication*] ... Curr Pract Orthop Surg
Current Practices ... CP
Current Problems in Cancer [*A publication*] ... Curr Probl Cancer
Current Problems in Cardiology [*A publication*] ... Curr Probl Cardiol
Current Problems in Clinical Biochemistry [*A publication*] ... Curr Probl Clin Biochem
Current Problems in Dermatology [*A publication*] ... Curr Prob Dermatol
Current Problems in Dermatology [*A publication*] ... Curr Probl Dermatol
Current Problems in Diagnostic Radiology [*A publication*] ... Curr Probl Diagn Radiol
Current Problems in Pediatrics [*A publication*] ... Curr Probl Pediatr
Current Problems in Surgery [*A publication*] ... Curr Probl Surg
Current Procedural Terminology [*American Medical Association*] ... CPT
Current Property Law [*British*] ... CPL
Current Psychiatric Therapies [*A publication*] ... CPSTB
Current Psychiatric Therapies [*A publication*] ... Curr Psychiatr Ther
Current Purchasing Power [*Accounting*] ... CPP
Current Rate ... CR
Current Relay ... CR
Current Report. West Virginia University. Agricultural Experiment Station [*A publication*] ... Curr Rep W Va Univ Agr Exp Sta
Current Requirements ... CRQ
Current Research and Development in Scientific Documentation [*A publication*] ... CRDSD
Current Research Information System [*Department of Agriculture*] ... CRIS
Current Research in the Netherlands. Biology [*A publication*] ... Curr Res Neth Biol
Current Researches in Anesthesia and Analgesia [*A publication*] ... Curr Res Anesth Analg
Current Retail Trade Reports ... CRTR
Current Review of Agricultural Conditions in Canada [*A publication*] ... Curr Rev Agr Cond Can
Current Scene [*Hong Kong*] [*A publication*] ... CS
Current Scene [*A publication*] ... Cur Scene
Current Science [*Bangalore, India*] [*A publication*] ... Curr Sci
Current Science (Bangalore, India) [*A publication*] ... Curr Sci (Bangalore)
Current Science (Bangalore, India) [*A publication*] ... Curr Sci (India)
Current Series [*Army*] ... CS
Current Ship's Maintenance Project ... CSMP
Current Sociology [*A publication*] ... Curr Sociol
Current Source ... CS
Current Source Amplifier ... CSA
Current Steering Switch ... CSS
Current Strength ... CS
Current Surgery [*A publication*] ... Curr Surg
Current Switch Logic ... CSL
Current Technology Index [*A publication*] ... CTI
Current, Temperature, Density ... CTD
Current Theory and Research in Motivation. Nebraska Symposium on Motivation [*A publication*] ... Curr Theory Res Motiv Nebr Symp Motiv
Current Therapeutic Research. Clinical and Experimental [*A publication*] ... Curr Ther R
Current Therapeutic Research. Clinical and Experimental [*A publication*] ... Curr Ther Res Clin Exp
Current Titles in Electrochemistry [*A publication*] ... Curr Tit Electrochem
Current Topics in Bioenergetics [*A publication*] ... Curr Top Bioenerg
Current Topics in Cellular Regulation [*A publication*] ... Curr Top Cell Regul
Current Topics in Clinical Chemistry [*A publication*] ... Curr Top Clin Chem

Current Topics in Comparative Pathobiology [*A publication*] ... Curr Top Comp Pathobiol
Current Topics in Critical Care Medicine [*A publication*] ... Curr Top Crit Care Med
Current Topics in Developmental Biology [*A publication*] ... Curr Top Dev Biol
Current Topics in Experimental Endocrinology [*A publication*] ... Curr Top Exp Endocrinol
Current Topics in Eye Research [*A publication*] ... Curr Top Eye Res
Current Topics in Hematology [*A publication*] ... Curr Top Hematol
Current Topics in Immunology Series [*A publication*] ... Curr Top Immunol Ser
Current Topics in Materials Science [*Elsevier Book Series*] [*A publication*] ... CTMS
Current Topics in Membranes and Transport [*A publication*] ... Curr Top Membranes Transp
Current Topics in Microbiology and Immunology [*A publication*] ... Curr Top Microbiol Immunol
Current Topics in Molecular Endocrinology [*A publication*] ... Curr Top Mol Endocrinol
Current Topics in Neurobiology [*A publication*] ... Curr Top Neurobiol
Current Topics in Nutrition and Disease [*A publication*] ... Curr Top Nutr Dis
Current Topics in Pathology [*A publication*] ... Curr Top Pathol
Current Topics in Radiation Research [*Elsevier Book Series*] [*A publication*] ... CTRR
Current Topics in Radiation Research [*A publication*] ... Curr Top Radiat Res
Current Topics in Radiation Research. Quarterly [*A publication*] ... Curr Top Radiat Res Q
Current Topics in Surgical Research [*A publication*] ... Curr Top Surg Res
Current Topics in Thyroid Research. Proceedings of the International Thyroid Conference [*A publication*] ... Curr Top Thyroid Res Proc Int Thyroid Conf
Current Transactions ... CT
Current Transfer Ratio [*Bell System*] ... CTR
Current Transformer ... CRT
Current Transformer ... CT
Current US Government Periodicals on Microfiche [*A publication*] ... Curr US Gov Per Mfiche
Current Variable Attenuator ... CVA
Current Variable Inductor ... CVI
Current Viewing Resistor ... CVR
Current or Voltage ... CURTAGE
Current-Voltage Diagram ... CVD
Current Wage Developments [*A publication*] ... CWD
Current Working Estimate [*Military*] ... CWE
Current Year [*Obsolete*] ... CY
Currentis [*Of the Current Month or Year*] [*Latin*] ... C
Currentis [*Of the Current Month or Year*] [*Latin*] ... CUR
Currents in Alcoholism [*A publication*] ... Curr Alcohol
Currents in Modern Biology [*A publication*] ... Curr Mod Biol
Currents in Modern Biology. Biosystems [*A publication*] ... Curr Mod Biol Biosyst
Currents in Theology and Mission [*A publication*] ... CuTM
Curriculum ... CURR
Curriculum ... CURRIC
Curriculum Adaptation Network for Bilingual, Bicultural Education ... CANBBE
Curriculum Inquiry [*A publication*] ... Curric Inquiry
Curriculum and Instruction Development [*Program*] [*National Science Foundation*] ... CID
Curriculum Resource Materials ... CRM
Curriculum Review [*A publication*] ... Cur R
Curriculum Review [*A publication*] ... Curric R
Curriculum Study and Educational Research Bulletin [*A publication*] ... Curric Stud and Ed Res B
Curriculum Theory Network [*A publication*] ... Curric Theo
Curriculum Vitae [*Job applications*] ... CV
Currie, Coopers, & Lybrand Ltd., Montreal, PQ, Canada [*Library symbol*] ... CaQMCCL
Currie, Coopers, & Lybrand Ltd., Toronto, ON, Canada [*Library symbol*] ... CaOTCCL
Curry College, Milton, MA [*OCLC symbol*] ... CUM
Curry College, Milton, MA [*Library symbol*] ... MMiltC
Cursor Control [*Data processing*] ... CC
Cursos y Conferencias [*A publication*] ... CuCo
Cursos y Conferencias [*A publication*] ... CyC
Cursos e Conferencias da Biblioteca de Universidade de Coimbra [*A publication*] ... CCBUC
Curtain ... CURT
Curtice-Burns, Inc. [*American Stock Exchange symbol*] ... CBI
Curtis Bay Railroad Co. [*AAR code*] ... CURB
Curtis Completion Form [*Psychology*] ... CCF
Curtis [*Helene*] **Industries, Inc.** [*NYSE symbol*] ... HC
Curtis Institute of Music [*Pennsylvania*] ... CIM
Curtis Institute of Music, Philadelphia, PA [*Library symbol*] ... PPCI
Curtis Mathes Corp. [*American Stock Exchange symbol*] [*Delisted*] ... CM
Curtis Memorial Public Library, Meriden, CT [*Library symbol*] ... CtMer
Curtis, Milburn, & Eastern Railroad Co. [*AAR code*] ... CMER
Curtis Publishing Company [*NYSE symbol*] [*Delisted*] ... CPC
Curtis Publishing Co., Research Library, Philadelphia, PA [*Library symbol*] [*Obsolete*] ... PPCuP
Curtiss-Wright Corp. [*NYSE symbol*] ... CW
Curtiss-Wright Corporation ... CWC
Curtiss-Wright Research Reactor ... CWRR
Curuzu Cuatia [*Argentina*] [*Airport symbol*] ... UZU
Curve ... CRV
Curved Dash Olds Owners Club ... CDOOC
Curved Motion Cutter ... CMC
Curvilinear Body [*in Batten disease*] ... CLB
[*The*] **Curwood Collector** [*A publication*] ... TCC
Cusac Industries Ltd. [*NASDAQ symbol*] ... CUSIF
Cusco [*Peru*] [*Seismograph station code, US Geological Survey*] ... CUS
Cushing, OK [*Location identifier*] [*FAA*] ... CUH
Cushing, OK [*Radio station call letters*] ... KUSH
Cushion ... CSHN
Cushion ... CUSH
Cushion Air Tread Articulate [*Vehicle*] [*Army*] ... CATA
Cushion Craft ... CC
Cushion Lift ... C
Cushioning Pads ... CP
Cushitic [*MARC language code*] [*Library of Congress*] ... cus
Cushman Electronics [*NASDAQ symbol*] ... CUSH
Cushman Foundation for Foraminiferal Research ... CFFR
Cushman Foundation for Foraminiferal Research. Contributions [*A publication*] ... Cushman Found Foram Research Contr
Cushman Foundation for Foraminiferal Research. Special Publication [*A publication*] ... Cushman Found Foraminiferal Res Spec Publ
Cusp Creek [*British Columbia*] [*Seismograph station code, US Geological Survey*] [*Closed*] ... CCC
Cuspidore Hitters Association Worldwide ... CHAW
Custer Battlefield National Monument [*National Park Service designation*] ... CUST
Custer County Junior College [*Montana*] ... CCJC
Custer County Library, Custer, SD [*Library symbol*] ... SdCu
Custer County Public Library, Westcliffe, CO [*Library symbol*] ... CoWc
Custodial, Protective, and Crafts [*US government workers*] ... CPC
Custodian ... CUST
Custodian of Allied and Enemy Property [*British*] [*World War II*] ... CAEP
Custodian Contractor ... CC
Custodian of Fund ... C of F
Custodian of Postal Effects [*Military*] ... COPE
Custody ... CUST
Custody Action for Lesbian Mothers [*An association*] ... CALM
Custody Pending Completion of Use ... CPCU
Custom Automotive Sound Association ... CASA
Custom Computer System ... CCS
Custom Contract Service [*IBM Corp.*] ... CCS
Custom Creamery Systems [*NASDAQ symbol*] ... CCSI
Custom Energy Services, Inc. [*American Stock Exchange symbol*] ... CUS
Custom House ... CH
Custom Input/Output Unit [*Data processing*] ... CIOU
Custom Interest Profile ... CIP
Custom Laboratories [*NASDAQ symbol*] ... CLAB
Custom Metallized Multigate Array [*NASA*] ... CMMA
Custom Microfilm Systems, Inc., Riverside, CA [*Library symbol*] ... CusM
Custom of the Port [*Shipping*] ... COP
Custom and Port [*Business and trade*] ... C/P
Custom Spherical Resins ... CSR
Custom Tailors and Designers Association of America ... CTDA
Custom, Tradition, and Usage ... CTU
Customary Behavior [*Psychology*] ... CUB
Customary Quick Dispatch ... CQD
Customer ... CUST
Customer ... CUSTR
Customer Acceptance Readiness Review [*Apollo*] [*NASA*] ... CARR
Customer Acceptance Review Item Disposition ... CARID
Customer Account Representative ... CAR
Customer Acquisition Unit ... CAU
Customer Assistance Office ... CAO
Customer Authorization for Additional Work ... CAAW
Customer-Bank Communication Terminal [*Computerized banking*] ... CBCT
Customer Communications Exchange [*Bell System*] ... CCX
Customer Engineer [*Data processing*] ... CE
Customer Engineering Monitor [*IBM Corp.*] ... CEMON
Customer-Furnished Material ... CFM
Customer Identification Code ... CIC
Customer Information Control System [*IBM Corp.*] [*Acronym pronounced "kicks"*] ... CICS
Customer Information Control System Virtual Storage [*Data processing*] ... CICS/VS
Customer Information File [*Data processing*] ... CIF
Customer Information Squawk Sheet ... CIS
Customer Information System [*IBM Corp.*] ... CIS
Customer-Integrated Automated Procurement System ... CIAPS
Customer Material Return ... CMR
Customer-Operated Terminal [*Data processing*] ... COT
Customer Order Processing ... COP
Customer Order Processing System ... COPS
Customer-Oriented Data System ... CODAS
Customer-Orienting Program ... COP
Customer-Originated Change ... COC

Customer-Owned and Maintained [*Equipment*] ... COAM
Customer-Owned Property ... COP
Customer Premise ... CU
Customer Premises Equipment [*Telecommunications*] ... CPE
Customer Premises System [*Bell System*] ... CPS
Customer Provided Equipment [*Telecommunications*] ... CPE
Customer Reaction Survey ... CRS
Customer Records and Billing [*Bell System*] ... CRB
Customer Requirements List ... CRL
Customer Satisfaction ... CUSAT
Customer Service ... CS
Customer Service Department Procedure ... CSDP
Customer Service Representative ... CSR
Customer Set-Up [*Data processing*] ... CSU
Customer Supply Assistance [*Military*] ... CSA
Customer Supply Assistance Office [*Military*] ... CSAO
Customer Support ... CS
Customer-Vended Equipment ... CVE
Customer Work Authorization ... CWA
Customhouse ... Cus Ho
Customized Processor [*IBM Corp.*] ... CP
Customs ... CSTMS
Customs ... CUST
Customs Accelerated Passenger Inspection System [*US Customs Service*] ... CAPIS
Customs Assigned Number [*Shipping*] [*British*] ... CAN
Customs Automatic Data Processing Intelligence Network [*US Customs Service*] ... CADPIN
Customs Cooperation Council [*See also CCD*] ... CCC
Customs Cooperation Council Nomenclature [*Also known as BTN*] ... CCCN
Customs Court ... CUSTCT
Customs Declaration ... C/D
Customs and Economic Union of Central Africa ... CEUCA
Customs Enforcement Officer [*US Customs Service*] ... CEO
Customs and Excise ... CE
Customs and Excise Laboratory [*Canada*] ... CEL
Customs Form ... CF
Customs Has Been Notified [*Aviation*] ... CUSNO
Customs Information Exchange [*An arm of US Customs Service*] ... CIE
Customs and International Trade Bar Association [*Formerly, ACB*] ... CITBA
Customs Optical Reader Passport Systems [*A scanning device capable of reading the latest US passports*] ... CORPS
Customs Port Investigator [*US Customs Service*] ... CPI
Customs Regulations of the United States ... CRUS
Custos Privati Sigilli [*Keeper of the Privy Seal*] [*British*] ... CPS
Custos Rotulorum [*Keeper of the Rolls*] [*British*] ... CR
Custos Sigilli [*Keeper of the Seal*] [*Latin*] ... CS
Cut Bank, MT [*Radio station call letters*] ... KCTB
Cut, Carat, Clarity, Color [*Factors in determining the value of a diamond*] ... 4C's
Cut, Carat, Clarity, Color [*Factors in determining the value of a diamond*] ... CCCC
Cut Film [*Photography*] ... CF
Cut Holes and Sink 'Em [*Navy ammunition disposal project*] ... CHASE
Cut In ... CI
Cut Off [*Military*] ... COFF
Cut Out ... CO
Cut Paraboloidal Reflector ... CPR
Cut Stone ... CUTS
Cutaneous T-Cell Lymphoma [*Medicine*] ... CTCL
Cutaneous Water Loss ... CWL
Cutco Industries, Inc. [*NASDAQ symbol*] ... CUTC
Cuthbert, GA [*Radio station call letters*] ... WCUG
Cuticle ... C
Cuticular Plate [*Biology*] ... CP
Cutie Pie [*Survey meter for radiation*] ... CP
Cutler Federal, Inc. [*NASDAQ symbol*] ... CFED
Cutler-Hammer, Inc. [*Later, CH*] [*NYSE symbol*] ... CEH
Cutler-Hammer, Inc. [*NYSE symbol*] [*Delisted*] ... CH
Cutlery ... CTLRY
Cutoff ... CO
Cutoff Frequency ... COF
Cutoff Shear [*Tool*] ... COSR
Cutoff Signal ... COS
Cutoff Velocity and Range ... COVER
Cutoff Voltage ... COV
Cutout Valve ... COV
Cutral-Co [*Argentina*] [*Airport symbol*] ... CUT
Cutter ... CTR
Cutter [*Ship*] ... CUT
Cutter Laboratories [*Research code symbol*] ... CL
Cutter Laboratories, Berkeley, CA [*Library symbol*] ... CBCL
Cutting ... CTG
Cutting ... CUTG
Cutting Die Institute ... CDI
Cutting Fluid Manufacturers Association ... CFMA
Cutting with Intent to Kill ... CWIK
Cutting or Molding Machine ... CMM
Cutting Needle Biopsy [*Medicine*] ... CNB
Cutting Specification ... CS
Cutting Tool Engineering [*A publication*] ... Cut Tool En
Cutting Tool Manufacturers Association ... CTMA
Cutting and Welding Permit ... CWP
Cuvee Extra ... CE
Cuyahoga Community College, Cleveland, OH [*Library symbol*] ... OCICC
Cuyahoga Community College, Learning Resource Center, Cleveland, OH [*OCLC symbol*] ... CUL
Cuyahoga County Public Library, Cleveland, OH [*OCLC symbol*] ... CXP
Cuyahoga County Public Library, Cleveland, OH [*Library symbol*] ... OCICo
Cuyahoga Falls, OH [*Radio station call letters*] ... WCUE
[*The*] **Cuyahoga Valley Railway Co.** [*AAR code*] ... CUVA
Cuzco [*Peru*] [*Airport symbol*] ... CUZ
CVB Financial Corp. [*NASDAQ symbol*] ... CVBF
CVP. Journal of Cardiovascular and Pulmonary Technology [*A publication*] ... CVP J Cardiovasc Pulm Technol
CW-Canadian Welfare [*A publication*] ... CW-Can Welf
CW Transport, Inc. [*American Stock Exchange symbol*] [*Delisted*] ... CWM
Cyanamid Magazine [*A publication*] ... Cyanamid Mag
Cyanamid, Niagara Falls, ON, Canada [*Library symbol*] ... CaONfCy
Cyanide ... CYN
Cyanoacrylate Adhesive ... CAA
Cyanocobalamin [*Biochemistry*] ... CNCbl
Cyanoethylsucrose ... CES
Cyanoethylurea [*Immunochemistry*] ... CEU
Cyanogen [*Toxic compound*] ... CY
Cyanogen Chloride [*Poison gas*] [*Army symbol*] ... CK
Cyathus [*Glassful*] [*Pharmacy*] ... CYATH
Cyathus Amplus [*Tumblerful*] [*Pharmacy*] ... CYATH AMP
Cyathus Vinosus [*Wineglassful*] [*Pharmacy*] ... CYATH VIN
[*The*] **Cybele Society** ... TCS
Cybermatics, Inc. [*NASDAQ symbol*] ... CYBR
Cybermedic, Inc. [*NASDAQ symbol*] ... CMED
Cybernetic Anthropomorphous Machine [*Army*] ... CAM
Cybernetic Anthropomorphous Machine System [*Robot*] [*Army*] ... CAMS
Cybernetic Logistics Planning, Control, and Management Information System [*Military*] ... CYBERLOG
Cybernetic Organism [*Concept of machine to alter man's bodily functions for space environment*] ... CYBORG
Cybernetics Research Institute ... CRI
Cycad Society ... CS
Cycare Systems, Inc. [*NASDAQ symbol*] ... CYCR
Cyclazocine [*Morphine antagonist*] ... Cyc
Cycle [*Electricity*] ... C
Cycle ... CY
Cycle ... CYC
Cycle Control Unit [*IRS*] ... CCU
Cycle Count ... CC
Cycle Engineers' Institute ... CEI
Cycle Parts and Accessories Association ... CPA
Cycle Parts and Accessories Association ... CPAA
Cycle Pressure Ratio ... CPR
Cycle Program Control ... CPC
Cycle Program Counter ... CPC
Cycle Proof Listing [*IRS*] ... CPL
Cycle Shift ... CS
Cycle-Significant Items ... CSI
Cycle Time ... CT
Cycles per Day ... CPD
Cycles per Hour ... C/H
Cycles per Minute ... C/MIN
Cycles per Minute ... CPM
Cycles between Overhaul ... CBO
Cycles between Scheduled Visits ... CBSV
Cycles per Second ... CC/S
Cycles per Second [*See also Hz*] ... CPS
Cycles per Second [*See also Hz*] ... C/S
Cycles per Second Alternating Current ... CPSAC
Cyclic [*Biochemistry*] ... c
Cyclic Adenosine Monophosphate [*Also, cAMP*] [*Biochemistry*] ... CAMP
Cyclic Air Sampling Monitor ... CASM
Cyclic-AMP [*Adenosine Monophosphate*] **Receptor Protein** [*Genetics*] ... CRP
Cyclic Check Character [*Data processing*] ... CCC
Cyclic Code ... CC
Cyclic Cytidine Monophosphate [*Biochemistry*] ... cCMP
Cyclic Data Management Routine [*Data processing*] ... CDMR
Cyclic Error Detection Code ... CEDC
Cyclic Guanosine Monophosphate [*Biochemistry*] ... cGMP
Cyclic Multilayered Alloy [*Electroplating technology*] ... CMA
Cyclic Permutation Code ... CPC
Cyclic Pitch Control Stick ... CPCS
Cyclic Program Control ... CPC
Cyclic Redundancy Check [*Data processing*] ... CRC
Cyclic Redundancy Check Character ... CRCC
Cyclic Strain Attenuator ... CSA
Cyclic Time Processor ... CTP
Cyclic Voltammetry [*Analytical electrochemistry*] ... CV
Cycling Club ... CC
Cycling Fibroblast [*Cytology*] ... CF
Cycling Oiler [*Navy*] ... CO
Cycling Strength Test ... CST
Cyclists' Touring Club ... CTC

Cyclododecatriene [*Organic chemistry*]......................CDT
Cyclododectriene [*Organic chemistry*]......................CDDT
Cyclogenesis [*Meteorology*]......................CYCLGN
Cyclohexadiene [*Organic chemistry*]......................CHD
Cyclohexenedicarboxylic Acid [*Organic chemistry*]......................CHDC
(Cyclohexenyl)cyclohexanone [*Organic chemistry*]......................CHCH
Cyclohexamide [*Fungicide*] [*Also, CHX, CXM*]......................CH
Cyclohexamide [*Also, CH, CXM*] [*Fungicide*]......................CHX
Cyclohexamide [*Also, CH, CHX*] [*Fungicide*]......................CXM
Cyclohexyl Methacrylate [*Organic chemistry*]......................CHMA
Cyclohexyladenosine [*Biochemistry*]......................CHA
Cyclohexylamine [*Organic chemistry*]......................CHA
Cyclohexylamine Carbonate [*Corrosion prevention*]......................CHC
Cyclohexylaminoethanesulfonic Acid [*A buffer*]......................CHES
Cyclohexylaminopropanesulfonic Acid [*A buffer*]......................CAPS
(Cyclohexylenedinitrilo)tetraacetic Acid [*Organic chemistry*]......................CDTA
Cyclohexyllinoleic Acid [*Organic chemistry*]......................CHLA
Cyclohexylthiophthalimide [*Organic chemistry*]......................CTP
Cyclone......................CYC
Cyclonite [*Organic chemistry*]......................RDX
Cyclooctadiene [*Organic chemistry*]......................COD
Cyclooctatetraene [*or Cyclooctatetraenyl*] [*Organic chemistry*]......................COT
Cyclopaedia of Anatomy and Physiology [*A publication*]......................
Cycl Anat and Physiol
Cyclopedia......................CYC
Cyclopedia......................CYCL
Cyclopedia......................CYCLO
Cyclopedia of Portraits......................CYP
Cyclopenta(alpha)phenanthrene [*Organic chemistry*]......................CPAP
Cyclopentadiene [*Organic chemistry*]......................CPD
Cyclophosphamide [*Cytoxan*] [*Also, CP, CPM, CTX, CY, CYC, CYP, CYT*] [*Antineoplastic drug*]......................C
Cyclophosphamide [*Cytoxan*] [*Also, CPM, CTX, CY, CYC, CYP, CYT*] [*Antineoplastic drug*]......................CP
Cyclophosphamide [*Cytoxan*] [*Also, C, CP, CTX, CY, CYC, CYP, CYT*] [*Antineoplastic drug*]......................CPM
Cyclophosphamide [*Cytoxan*] [*Also, C, CP, CPM, CTX, CYC, CYP, CYT*] [*Antineoplastic drug*]......................CY
Cyclophosphamide [*Cytoxan*] [*Also, C, CP, CPM, CTX, CY, CYP, CYT*] [*Antineoplastic drug*]......................CYC
Cyclophosphamide [*Cytoxan*] [*Also, C, CP, CPM, CTX, CY, CYC, CYT*] [*Antineoplastic drug*]......................CYP
Cyclophosphamide, Adriamycin, Fluorouracil [*Antineoplastic drug regimen*]......................CAF
Cyclophosphamide, Adriamycin, Fluorouracil, Vincristine, Prednisone [*Antineoplastic drug regimen*]......................CAFVP
Cyclophosphamide, Adriamycin, Prednisone [*Antineoplastic drug regimen*]......................CAP
Cyclophosphamide, Adriamycin [*Doxorubicin*]**, Vincristine** [*Antineoplastic drug regimen*]......................CAV
Cyclophosphamide (Cytoxan) [*Also, CP, CPM, CYT*] [*Antineoplastic drug*]......................CYC
Cyclophosphamide, Fluorouracil, Prednisone [*Antineoplastic drug regimen*]......................CFP
Cyclophosphamide, Hydroxydaunomycin [*Adriamycin*]**, Oncovin** [*Vincristine*]**, Prednisone** [*Antineoplastic drug regimen*]......................CHOP
Cyclophosphamide, Hydroxydaunomycin [*Adriamycin*]**, Oncovin** [*Vincristine*]**, Procarbazine, Prednisone** [*Antineoplastic drug regimen*]......................CHOPP
Cyclophosphamide, Methotrexate, Fluorouracil [*Antineoplastic drug regimen*]......................CMF
Cyclophosphamide, Methotrexate, Fluorouracil, Vincristine, Prednisone [*Antineoplastic drug regimen*]......................CMFVP
Cyclophosphamide, Oncovin [*Vincristine*] [*Antineoplastic drug regimen*]......................CO
Cyclophosphamide, Oncovin [*Vincristine*]**, ara-C, Prednisone** [*Antineoplastic drug regimen*]......................COAP
Cyclophosphamide, Oncovin [*Vincristine*]**, Methotrexate** [*Antineoplastic drug regimen*]......................COM
Cyclophosphamide, Oncovin [*Vincristine*]**, Methotrexate, ara-C** [*Antineoplastic drug regimen*]......................COMA
Cyclophosphamide, Oncovin [*Vincristine*]**, Methotrexate, Prednisone** [*Antineoplastic drug regimen*]......................COMP
Cyclophosphamide, Oncovin [*Vincristine*]**, Prednisone** [*Antineoplastic drug regimen*]......................COP
Cyclophosphamide, Oncovin [*Vincristine*]**, Procarbazine, Prednisone** [*Antineoplastic drug regimen*]......................COPP
Cyclophosphamide, Vinblastine, Prednisone [*Antineoplastic drug regimen*]......................CVP
Cyclophosphamide, Vinblastine, Procarbazine, Prednisone [*Antineoplastic drug regimen*]......................CVPP
Cyclophosphamide, Vincristine, Adriamycin, Actinomycin D [*Antineoplastic drug regimen*]......................CYVADACT
Cyclophosphamide, Vincristine, Adriamycin, Dacarbazine [*Antineoplastic drug regimen*]......................CYVADIC
Cyclophosphamide, Vincristine, Fluorouracil, Methotrexate [*Antineoplastic drug regimen*]......................CVFM
Cyclopropanecarboxylic Acid [*Organic chemistry*]......................CPCA
Cyclopropenoid Fatty Acid [*Biochemistry*]......................CPFA
Cyclops Corp. [*Formerly, UCS*] [*NYSE symbol*]......................CYL
Cyclosporin A [*See CYA*] [*An immunosuppressant drug*]......................CSA

Cyclosporin A [*See CSA*] [*An immunosuppressant drug*]......................CYA
Cyclotron Laboratory......................CL
Cyclotron Wave Device......................CWD
Cygnus [*Constellation*]......................Cyg
Cygnus [*Constellation*]......................Cygn
Cylinder......................C
Cylinder......................CL
Cylinder......................CY
Cylinder......................CYL
Cylinder-Cylinder-Head-Sector [*Data processing*]......................CCHS
Cylinder or Drum [*Freight*]......................CYL DRM
Cylinder-Head Temperature......................CHT
Cylinder Lock......................CYLL
Cylinder Manufacturers Association......................CMA
Cylinder-Pressure Monitoring and Conditioning Detection System......................CYLDET
Cylinder Rate......................CR
Cylinder Stroke Control......................CSC
Cylindrical......................CYLNDL
Cylindrical Electrostatic Probe [*NASA*]......................CEP
Cylindrical Electrostatic Probe Experiment [*NASA*]......................CEPE
Cylindrical Horizontal Tank [*Liquid gas carriers*]......................ch
Cylindrical Internal Reflection [*Spectroscopy*]......................CIR
Cylindrical LASER Plasma......................CLASP
Cylindrical Lens [*Ophthalmology*]......................CYL
Cylindrical Magnetic Film......................CMF
Cylindrical Perforated......................CP
Cylindrical Vertical Tank [*Liquid gas carriers*]......................cv
Cylindrical Vibration Mount......................CVM
Cylindrically Symmetrical Field......................CSF
Cymbeline [*Shakespearean work*]......................Cym
Cymbidium Society of America......................CSA
Cynthiana, KY [*Radio station call letters*]......................WCYN
Cynthiana, KY [*Radio station call letters*]......................WCYN-FM
Cypher Policy Board [*British*] [*World War II*]......................CPB
Cypher Security Committee [*British*] [*World War II*]......................CSC
Cyphernetics Text Processing Language [*Data processing*]......................
CYPHERTEXT
Cyprair Tours Ltd. [*Cyprus*] [*ICAO designator*]......................CB
Cypress Gardens, FL [*Radio station call letters*]......................WGTO
Cypress Hills, SK [*Television station call letters*]......................CBCP-TV-2
Cypress Junior College, Cypress, CA [*Library symbol*]......................CCyC
Cypress Savings Association CI A [*NASDAQ symbol*]......................CYPSA
Cypriot Liberation Army......................CLA
Cyproterone Acetate [*Endocrinology*]......................CA
Cyprus [*MARC geographic area code*] [*Library of Congress*]......................a-cy---
Cyprus [*Aircraft nationality and registration mark*]......................5B
Cyprus [*MARC country of publication code*] [*Library of Congress*]......................cy
Cyprus [*Three-letter standard code*]......................CYP
Cyprus......................CYPR
Cyprus [*Two-letter standard code*]......................CY
Cyprus Agricultural Research Institute. Annual Report [*A publication*]......................Cyprus Agric Res Inst Annu Rep
Cyprus Agricultural Research Institute. Miscellaneous Publications [*A publication*]......................Cyprus Agric Res Inst Misc Publ
Cyprus Agricultural Research Institute. Progress Report [*A publication*]......................Cyprus Agric Res Inst Prog Rep
Cyprus Agricultural Research Institute. Technical Bulletin [*A publication*]......................Cyprus Agric Res Inst Tech Bull
Cyprus Agricultural Research Institute. Technical Paper [*A publication*]......................Cyprus Agric Res Inst Tech Pap
Cyprus Airways Ltd. [*ICAO designator*]......................CY
Cyprus Airways Ltd.......................CYP
Cyprus Broadcasting Corporation......................CyBC
Cyprus Corporation [*American Stock Exchange symbol*]......................CYC
Cyprus Department of Agriculture. Annual Report [*A publication*]......................Cyprus Dep Agric Annu Rep
Cyprus Federation of America......................CFA
Cyprus Mines Corp. [*NYSE symbol*] [*Delisted*]......................CYM
Cyrillic Union Catalog [*Library of Congress*]......................CUC
Cysteamine-S-Phosphate [*Biochemical analysis*]......................CASP
Cysteine [*One-letter symbol*] [*Also, Cys, CySH*]......................C
Cysteine [*Also, C, CySH*] [*An amino acid*]......................Cys
Cysteine [*Also, C, Cys*] [*An amino acid*]......................CySH
Cystic Duct [*Medicine*]......................CD
Cystic Fibrosis [*Medicine*]......................CF
Cystic Fibrosis Foundation......................CFF
Cystic Fibrosis of the Pancreas [*Medicine*]......................CFP
Cystic Fibrosis Society......................CFS
Cystic Medial Necrosis [*of aorta*] [*Medicine*]......................CMN
Cystine [*or CyS*] [*An amino acid*]......................Cys
Cystine-Lactose-Electrolyte Deficient [*Clinical chemistry*]......................CLED
Cystine-Tellurite [*Medium*] [*Microbiology*]......................CT
Cystine Trypticase Agar [*Microbiology*]......................CTA
Cystometrography [*Urology*]......................CMG
Cystoscopy [*Medicine*]......................CYS
Cystoscopy and Pyelogram [*Medicine*]......................C & P
Cystourethrogram [*Medicine*]......................CUG
Cystylaminopeptidase [*An enzyme*]......................CAP
Cytarabine [*Cytosine arabinoside*] [*Also, ara-C, CAR*] [*Antineoplastic drug*]......................CA

Cytarabine [*Cytosine arabinoside*] [*Also, ara-C, CA*]
  [*Antineoplastic drug*] .... CAR
Cytidine [*One-letter symbol; see Cyd*] C
Cytidine [*Also, C*] [*A nucleoside*] .... Cyd
Cytidine Diphosphate [*Biochemistry*] .... CDP
Cytidine Diphosphoabequose [*Biochemistry*] .... CDPAbe
Cytidine Monophosphate [*Biochemistry*] .... CMP
Cytidine Triphosphate [*Biochemistry*] .... CTP
Cytochalasin B [*Cytology*] .... CB
Cytogenetics and Cell Genetics [*A publication*] .... Cytog C Gen
Cytogenetics and Cell Genetics [*A publication*] .... Cytogenet Cell Genet
Cytokinin [*Biochemistry*] .... CK
Cytologia [*A publication*] .... Cytol
Cytological and Neurological Studies. Faculty of Medicine.
  University of Kanazawa [*A publication*] ....
                    Cytol Neurol Stud Fac Med Univ Kanazawa
Cytology .... CYT
Cytology .... CYTOL
Cytology and Genetics [*A publication*] .... Cytol Genet
Cytology and Genetics (English Translation of Tsitologiya i
  Genetika) [*A publication*] .... Cytol Genet (Engl Transl Tsitol Genet)
Cytolytic Thymus-Dependent Lymphocyte [*Cell biology*] .... CTL
Cytomegalic Inclusion Disease [*Medicine*] .... CID
Cytomegalovirus .... CMV
Cytopathic Effect [*Medicine*] .... CE
Cytopathogenic [*or Cytopathic*] **Effect** [*Microbiology*] .... CPE
Cytophotometric Data Converter [*Instrumentation*] .... CYDAC
Cytoplasmic Immunoglobulin [*Immunology*] .... C-Ig
Cytoproct [*Protozoology*] .... CYP
Cytosine [*Also, Cyt*] [*Biochemistry*] C
Cytosine [*Also, C*] [*Biochemistry*] .... Cyt
Cytosine Arabinoside [*ara-C*], **Adriamycin, Thioguanine**
  [*Antineoplastic drug regimen*] .... CAT
Cytosine arabinoside [*ara-C*], **L-Asparaginase, Rubidomycin**
  [*Daunorubicin*], **Thioguanine** [*Antineoplastic drug regimen*] .... CART
Cytosine Arabinoside Monophosphate [*Biochemistry*] .... ara-CMP
Cytosine Arabinoside Triphosphate [*Biochemistry*] .... ara-CTP
Cytosine Diphosphate [*Biochemistry*] .... CDP
Cytosine Monophosphate [*Biochemistry*] .... CMP
Cytosine Triphosphate [*Biochemistry*] .... CTP
Cytotechnologist .... CT
Cytotechnology .... CYTECH
Cytotoxic Factor .... CTF
Cytotoxic Index [*Cytochemistry*] CI
Cytotoxic T Lymphocyte [*Hematology*] .... CTL
Cytotoxicity Negative - Absorption Positive [*Immunology*] .... CYNAP
Cytox Corp. [*NASDAQ symbol*] .... CYTX

Cytoxan [*Cyclophosphamide*] [*Also, C, CP, CPM, CY, CYC, CYP,*
  CYT] [*Antineoplastic drug*] .... CTX
Cytoxan (Cyclophosphamide) [*Also, CP, CPM, CYC*]
  [*Antineoplastic drug*] .... CYT
CZ Chemie-Technik [*A publication*] .... CZ Chem-Tech
Czasopismo Stomatologiczne [*A publication*] .... Czas Stomatol
Czasopismo Techniczne (Krakow) [*A publication*] .... Czas Tech (Krakow)
Czech .... CZE
Czech [*MARC language code*] [*Library of Congress*] .... cze
Czech American National Alliance .... CANA
Czech Catholic Union .... CCU
Czech Heritage Foundation .... CHF
Czechoslovak Christian Democracy [*An association*] .... CCD
Czechoslovak Congress of Gastroenterology [*A publication*] ......
                                                Czech Congr Gastroenterol
Czechoslovak Economic Papers [*A publication*] .... CEP
Czechoslovak Economic Papers [*A publication*] .... Czechosl Econ Pap
Czechoslovak Film [*A publication*] .... Czech F
Czechoslovak Heavy Industry [*A publication*] .... Czech Heavy Ind
Czechoslovak Journal of Physics [*A publication*] .... Czech J Phys
Czechoslovak Journal of Physics. Section B [*A publication*] .... Czec J Phys
Czechoslovak Mathematical Journal [*A publication*] .... CMJ
Czechoslovak Mathematical Journal [*A publication*] .... Czec Math J
Czechoslovak Medicine [*A publication*] .... Czech Med
Czechoslovak National Council .... CNC
Czechoslovak Philatelic Society [*Later, SCP*] .... CZPS
Czechoslovak Rationalist Federation of America .... CRFA
Czechoslovak Red Cross .... CRC
Czechoslovak Socialist Republic .... CSSR
Czechoslovak Society of America .... CSA
Czechoslovak Society of Arts and Sciences [*Formerly, CSASA*] ..... CSAS
Czechoslovak Society of Arts and Sciences in America [*Later,*
  CSAS] .... CSASA
Czechoslovakia [*MARC country of publication code*] [*Library of*
  Congress] .... cs
Czechoslovakia [*Three-letter standard code*] .... CSK
Czechoslovakia .... CZ
Czechoslovakia .... CZECH
Czechoslovakia .... CZS
Czechoslovakia [*MARC geographic area code*] [*Library of*
  Congress] .... e-cs---
Czechoslovakia [*Aircraft nationality and registration mark*] .... OK
Czechoslovakia [*Two-letter standard code*] .... CS
Czechoslovakia Research Institutes for Crop Production.
  Annual Report [*A publication*] .... Czech Res Inst Crop Prod Annu Rep
Czechoslovakian Kronen [*Monetary unit*] .... CZKR
Czytelnik [*A publication*] .... Cz

D

(D-Ala, D-Leu) Enkephalin [*Biochemistry*]..............................DADL
(D-Ala, D-Leu) Enkephalin [*Biochemistry*].........................DADLE
(D-Ala²)-Met-enkephalinamide [*Analgesic peptide*]................DALA
D-Amino Acid Oxidase [*An enzyme*] ....DAAO
D. H. Lawrence Review [*A publication*]................D H Lawrence R
D. H. Lawrence Review [*A publication*].............................DHLR
D. J. Crowther Ltd. Fixed Price List [*A publication*]...........Crowther FPL
D-Pantothenyl Alcohol [*Biochemistry*].................................DPA
D-Penicillamine [*Pharmacology*]......................................DPCN
D. R. Moon Memorial Library, Stanley, WI [*Library symbol*].............WSt
D-Related [*Antigen*] [*Immunology*].....................................DR
D. T. Watson Home for Crippled Children, Leetsdale, PA [*OCLC
    symbol*]..PID
Da [*Give*] [*Pharmacy*]..D
Da Capo [*Return to Beginning*] [*Music*]..................................DC
Da Nang East Yard [*Vietnam*] [*Navy*]..................................DNEY
DAB Industries, Inc. [*NASDAQ symbol*]..................................DABI
Dabrowa Gornicza [*Poland*] [*Seismograph station code, US
    Geological Survey*]..DGP
Dacca University Studies [*A publication*].............................DUS
Dacca University Studies. Part B [*A publication*]........Dacca Univ Stud Part B
Daohshund Club of America ....DCA
Dacia [*A publication*] ....Dac
Dacoromania [*A publication*] ....D
Dacoromania [*A publication*] ....Dac
Dacoromania [*A publication*] ....Dacor
Dacotah Territory [*A publication*] ....Dac Terr
Dacro-Cysto-Rhinostomy [*Medicine*] ....DCR
Dacron Braid Lacquered..DL
Dacron and Nylon ....DACRYLON
Dactinomycin (Actinomycin-D) [*Also, act-D, AMD*]
    [*Antineoplastic drug*]...DACT
Dada-Surrealism ....D-S
Daddy's Little Girl ....DLG
Dade City, FL [*Radio station call letters*]............................WDCF
Dadeville, AL [*Radio station call letters*]...........................WDLK
Daedalian Foundation ....DF
Daemen College, Buffalo, NY [*Library symbol*].........................NBuDa
Daemen College, Buffalo, NY [*OCLC symbol*]..............................VVH
Dafare [*Djibouti*] [*Seismograph station code, US Geological Survey*].......DAF
Dagens Nyheter [*A publication*] ....DN
Daggett, CA [*Location identifier*] [*FAA*]............................DAG
Dahl-Kirkam Telescope ....DKT
Dahlberg Electronics [*NASDAQ symbol*]..................................DESI
Dahlgren Rifle..DR
Dahlgren Smoothbore ....DSB
Dahlonega [*Georgia*] [*Mint mark, when appearing on US coins*]...............D
Dahlonega, GA [*Radio station call letters*]..........................WDRG
Dahomey [*Benin*] [*MARC country of publication code*] [*Library of
    Congress*]..dm
Dahomey [*Benin*] [*MARC geographic area code*] [*Library of
    Congress*]..f-dm---
Dahomey [*Aircraft nationality and registration mark*]....................TY
Dai-Ichi Kangyo Bank [*Japan*]...DKB
Dai'Ei, Inc. ADR [*NASDAQ symbol*]....................................DAIEY
Daiichi Seiyaku Co. Ltd. [*Japan*] [*Research code symbol*] ....DJ
Daily...D
Daily...DLY
Daily Activity Report [*Military*].......................................DAR
Daily Advance, Dover, NJ [*Library symbol*]............................NjDA
Daily Air Activity Report ....DAAR
Daily Ambient Photophase [*Biochronometry*]...........................DAPP
Daily Automatic Rescheduling Technique [*Data processing*].............DART
Daily Bulletin [*Military*]...DB
Daily Communication Report ....DCR
Daily Delinquency Penalty ....DDP
Daily Demand Rate..DDR
Daily Double [*Horse racing*]...DD
Daily Encephalic Photophase [*Biochronometry*] ....DEPP
Daily Equipment Status Report [*Army*]...............................DESPORT

Daily Estimated Position Location [*Navy*]...........................DEPLOC
Daily Estimated Position Summary [*Navy*]............................DEPSUM
Daily Express Film Award [*British*].....................................DEFA
Daily Fetal Movements Record ....DFMR
Daily Field Activity Report ....DFAR
Daily Flight Log [*Aviation*]..DFL
Daily Inspection Call Record ....DICR
Daily Intelligence Digest ....DID
Daily Intelligence Summary [*Air Force*]..............................DISUM
Daily Journal, Elizabeth, NJ [*Library symbol*].......................NjEliJ
Daily Journal of the Supreme Court....................................DJSC
Daily JUMPS [*Joint Uniform Military Pay System*] Update Output
    Listing...DJUOL
Daily Mail National Film Award [*British*]............................DMNFA
Daily Mechanical Report..DMR
Daily Mercury, Mackay, QLD, Australia [*Library symbol*] ....AuMacD
Daily Missouri-Mississippi River Bulletin [*A publication*] ....DMMRB
Daily Observer, Beachwood, NJ [*Library symbol*]...................NjBeacO
Daily Official List [*London Stock Exchange prices*]...................DOL
Daily Operating Log ....DOL
Daily Operational Report ....DOR
Daily Planet [*A publication*].......................................DI Planet
Daily Princetonian, Princeton, NJ [*Library symbol*]..................NjPD
Daily Receipt of Obligation [*Military*]...............................DRO
Daily Register, Red Bank, NJ [*Library symbol*].......................NjRbR
Daily Replacement Factor [*Of lymphocytes*] [*Medicine*]...............DRF
Daily Report...DR
Daily Report of Obligation [*Navy*]...................................DRO
Daily Reports Notice [*Air Force*].....................................DRN
Daily Review...DR
Daily Routine Order..DRO
Daily Status Report..DSR
Daily Summary of Enemy Intelligence [*World War II*].................DSEI
Daily Systems Operability Test [*for surface-to-air missiles*] ....DSOT
Daily Telegraph [*A publication*]...DT
Daily Times-Herald, Carroll, IA [*Library symbol*] ....IaCarTH
[*The*] Daily Times of Nigeria [*A publication*].........................DTN
Daily Traffic Assignment Model [*Aviation*] ....DTAM
Daily Transaction File ....DTF
Daily Transaction Register File [*Data processing*]..................DTRF
Daily Transaction Registering [*or Reporting*] [*Data processing*]......DTR
Daily Weather and River Bulletin [*A publication*]..................DW & RB
Daily and Weekly till Forbidden [*Advertising*].....................D & WTF
Daily and Weekly till Forbidden [*Advertising*].......................DWTF
Daimler-Benz [*Name of German engine factory*] [*World War II*]...........DB
Daimler and Lanchester Owners' Club ....DLOC
Daimler and Lanchester Owners Club of North America ....DLOC of NA
Daingerfield, TX [*Radio station call letters*].......................KEGG
Dainippon Pharmaceutical Co. [*Japan*] [*Research code symbol*].........AB
Dainippon Pharmaceutical Co. [*Japan*] [*Research code symbol*]..........P
Dairen [*Republic of China*] [*Seismograph station code, US
    Geological Survey*] [*Closed*]......................................DAI
Dairy Farmer [*A publication*].......................................Dairy F
Dairy and Food Industries Supply Association [*Formerly, DISA*].......DFISA
Dairy Forage Research Center [*Department of Agriculture*]............DFRC
Dairy Goat Journal [*A publication*]............................Dairy Goat J
Dairy Herd Improvement Association [*Later, AIPL*]...................DHIA
Dairy Herd Improvement Registry ....DHIR
Dairy Herd Management [*A publication*] ....Dairy Herd Manage
Dairy Herd Management [*A publication*] ....Dairy Herd Mgt
Dairy Husbandry Adviser [*Ministry of Agriculture, Fisheries, and
    Food*] [*British*]...DHA
Dairy Indemnity Payment Program [*Department of Agriculture*] ....DIPP
Dairy Industries [*Later, Dairy Industries International*] [*A
    publication*]..Dairy Indus
Dairy Industries International [*A publication*]..................Dairy Ind
Dairy Industries International [*A publication*].............Dairy Ind Int
Dairy Industries Supply Association [*Later, DFISA*]................DISA
Dairy Industry Committee ....DIC
Dairy Mart Convenience Stores [*NASDAQ symbol*]...................DMCV

Dairy Products Improvement Institute .... DPII
Dairy Remembrance Fund .... DRF
Dairy Research, Incorporated .... DRINC
Dairy Science Abstracts [*A publication*] .... Dairy Sci Abstr
Dairy Shrine [*An association*] .... DS
Dairy Society International .... DSI
Dairy Suppliers Foundation [*Defunct*] .... DSF
Dairy Training and Merchandising Institute .... DTMI
Dairyfarming Annual [*A publication*] .... Dairyfarm Annu
Dairylea Cooperative [*Formerly, DLCA*] .... DC
Dairymen's League Cooperative Association [*Later, DC*] .... DLCA
Daisetta, TX [*Location identifier*] [*FAA*] .... DAS
"Daisy Cutter" [*A type of World War II bomb*] .... DC
Daisy Systems Corp. [*NASDAQ symbol*] .... DAZY
Daito Bunka Daigaku Kangakkaishi [*A publication*] .... DBDKK
Daito Bunka Daigaku Kiyo [*A publication*] .... DBDK
Dakar [*Senegal*] [*Seismograph station code, US Geological Survey*] [*Closed*] .... DAK
Dakar [*Senegal*] [*Airport symbol*] .... DKR
Dakhla [*Mauritania*] [*Airport symbol*] VIL
Dakota .... DAK
Dakota [*MARC language code*] [*Library of Congress*] .... dak
Dakota Clinic, Fargo, ND [*Library symbol*] .... NdFD
Dakota County Library, West St. Paul, MN [*Library symbol*] .... MnWspD
Dakota Farmer [*A publication*] .... Dakota F
Dakota Microfilm Service, Inc., Denver, CO [*Library symbol*] .... DmS
Dakota Minerals, Inc. [*NASDAQ symbol*] .... DKMN
Dakota State College, Madison, SD [*Library symbol*] .... SdMadT
Dakota Wesleyan University [*South Dakota*] .... DWU
Dakota Wesleyan University, Layne Library, Mitchell, SD [*OCLC symbol*] .... SDW
Dakota Wesleyan University, Mitchell, SD [*Library symbol*] .... SdMW
Dakota Wowapipahi Library, Marty, SD [*Library symbol*] .... SdMar
Dakotas [*FAA*] .... DKTS
Dal Segno [*Repeat from the Sign*] [*Music*] .... DAL S
Dal Segno [*Repeat from the Sign*] [*Music*] .... DAL SEG
Dal Segno [*Repeat from the Sign*] [*Music*] .... DS
Dalaman [*Turkey*] [*Airport symbol*] .... DLM
Dalby [*Australia*] [*Airport symbol*] .... DBY
Dalcho Historical Society of the Episcopal Diocese of South Carolina, Charleston, SC [*Library symbol*] .... ScCDHHi
Dale .... DL
Dale Electronics [*American Stock Exchange symbol*] .... DLE
Daler [*Numismatics*] .... D
Dalhart, TX [*Radio station call letters*] .... KXIT
Dalhart, TX [*Radio station call letters*] .... KXIT-FM
Dalhousie [*India*] [*Seismograph station code, US Geological Survey*] [*Closed*] .... DLH
Dalhousie Law Journal [*A publication*] .... Dalhousie L J
Dalhousie Review [*A publication*] .... Dal R
Dalhousie Review [*A publication*] .... DR
Dalhousie University, Halifax, NS, Canada [*Library symbol*] .... CaNSHD
Dalhousie University, Institute of Public Affairs, Halifax, NS, Canada [*Library symbol*] .... CaNSHDIP
Dalhousie University, Law School, Halifax, NS, Canada [*Library symbol*] .... CaNSHDL
Dalhousie University, Map Library, Halifax, NS, Canada [*Library symbol*] .... CaNSHDMA
Dalhousie University, W. K. Kellog Health Sciences Library, Halifax, NS, Canada [*Library symbol*] .... CaNSHDM
Dalien [*China*] [*Airport symbol*] .... DLC
Dallas [*Texas*] [*Seismograph station code, US Geological Survey*] .... DAL
Dallas [*Texas*] [*Seismograph station code, US Geological Survey*] [*Closed*] .... DLS
Dallas Area Media Project [*Library network*] .... DAMP
Dallas Baptist College, Dallas, TX [*OCLC symbol*] .... IDA
Dallas Baptist College, Dallas, TX [*Library symbol*] .... TxDaB
Dallas, CA [*Radio station call letters*] .... KWIP
Dallas Center Public Library, Dallas Center, IA [*Library symbol*] .... IaDc
Dallas Christian College, Dallas, TX [*OCLC symbol*] .... TDC
Dallas Christian College, Dallas, TX [*Library symbol*] .... TxDaDC
Dallas Cotton Exchange .... DCE
Dallas County Community College District, Dallas, TX [*OCLC symbol*] .... TDJ
Dallas County Courthouse, Adel, IA [*Library symbol*] .... IaAdeCoC
Dallas County News, Adel, IA [*Library symbol*] .... IaAdeN
Dallas Cowboys Cheerleaders .... DCC
Dallas Federal Savings & Loan [*NASDAQ symbol*] .... DFSL
Dallas/Fort Worth [*Texas*] [*Airport symbol*] .... DFW
Dallas/Fort Worth [*Texas*] **Love** [*Airport symbol*] .... DAL
Dallas-Fort Worth, TX [*Location identifier*] [*FAA*] .... BXN
Dallas-Fort Worth, TX [*Location identifier*] [*FAA*] .... FLQ
Dallas-Fort Worth, TX [*Location identifier*] [*FAA*] .... PKQ
Dallas-Fort Worth, TX [*Location identifier*] [*FAA*] .... VYN
Dallas, GA [*Radio station call letters*] .... WKRP
Dallas Historical Society, Dallas, TX [*Library symbol*] .... TxDaHi
Dallas [*Texas*] **Love Field** [*Airport symbol*] .... DAL
Dallas Museum of Fine Arts, Dallas, TX [*Library symbol*] .... TxDaMF
Dallas, NC [*Radio station call letters*] .... WAAK
Dallas, NC [*Radio station call letters*] .... WSGE-FM
Dallas Oil & Minerals, Inc. [*NASDAQ symbol*] .... DOIL
Dallas Power & Light Co. .... DP & L
Dallas Power & Light Co., Dallas, TX [*Library symbol*] .... TxDaP
Dallas Public Library, Dallas, OR [*Library symbol*] .... OrDal
Dallas Public Library, Dallas, TX [*OCLC symbol*] .... IGA
Dallas Public Library, Dallas, TX [*Library symbol*] .... TxDa
Dallas Symphony Orchestra Program Notes [*A publication*] .... Dallas Sym
Dallas Theological Seminary and Graduate School, Dallas, TX [*Library symbol*] .... TxDaTS
Dallas, TX [*Location identifier*] [*FAA*] .... ADS
Dallas, TX [*Radio station call letters*] .... KAAM
Dallas, TX [*Radio station call letters*] .... KAFM
Dallas, TX [*Radio station call letters*] .... KCBI
Dallas, TX [*Television station call letters*] .... KDFW-TV
Dallas, TX [*Radio station call letters*] .... KERA-FM
Dallas, TX [*Television station call letters*] .... KERA-TV
Dallas, TX [*Radio station call letters*] .... KKDA-FM
Dallas, TX [*Radio station call letters*] .... KLIF
Dallas, TX [*Radio station call letters*] .... KLVU
Dallas, TX [*Radio station call letters*] .... KMEZ
Dallas, TX [*Radio station call letters*] .... KMEZ-FM
Dallas, TX [*Radio station call letters*] .... KMGC
Dallas, TX [*Television station call letters*] .... KNBN-TV
Dallas, TX [*Radio station call letters*] .... KNON
Dallas, TX [*Radio station call letters*] .... KOAX
Dallas, TX [*Radio station call letters*] .... KPBC
Dallas, TX [*Radio station call letters*] .... KRLD
Dallas, TX [*Radio station call letters*] .... KRQX
Dallas, TX [*Radio station call letters*] .... KRSM
Dallas, TX [*Radio station call letters*] .... KSKY
Dallas, TX [*Television station call letters*] .... KTWS-TV
Dallas, TX [*Radio station call letters*] .... KVTT
Dallas, TX [*Television station call letters*] .... KXTX
Dallas, TX [*Radio station call letters*] .... KZEW
Dallas, TX [*Location identifier*] [*FAA*] .... LUE
Dallas, TX [*Location identifier*] [*FAA*] .... LVF
Dallas, TX [*Location identifier*] [*FAA*] .... NBE
Dallas, TX [*Location identifier*] [*FAA*] .... RBD
Dallas, TX [*Television station call letters*] .... WFAA-TV
Dallas, TX [*Radio station call letters*] .... WRR
Dallas Union Terminal [*AAR code*] .... DUTC
Dalmatian Club of America .... DCA
Dal'Nevostocyni Matematiceskii Sbornik [*A publication*] .... Dal'Nevostocn Mat Sb
Daloa [*Ivory Coast*] [*Airport symbol*] .... DJO
Dalton [*Australia*] [*Seismograph station code, US Geological Survey*] [*Closed*] .... DLN
Dalton [*California*] [*Seismograph station code, US Geological Survey*] [*Closed*] .... DLT
Dalton-Dalton-Newport, Cleveland, OH [*OCLC symbol*] .... ODN
Dalton, GA [*Radio station call letters*] .... WBLJ
Dalton, GA [*Radio station call letters*] .... WRCD
Dalton, GA [*Radio station call letters*] .... WTTI
Dalton, MA [*Location identifier*] [*FAA*] .... DXT
Daly City Public Library, Daly City, CA [*Library symbol*] .... CDc
Dam .... D
Dam .... DM
Damage .... DAM
Damage .... DMG
Damage Assessment and Casualty Report [*Military*] .... DACAS
Damage Assessment Routines .... DAR
Damage Before Launch .... DBL
Damage Control [*or Controlman*] [*Navy*] .... DC
Damage Control Assistant [*Military*] .... DCA
Damage Control Center .... DCC
Damage Control Diagrams [*Naval Ship Systems Command*] .... DCD
Damage Control In-Port Training .... DCIPT
Damage Control School [*Navy*] .... DCS
Damage Control Suit [*Navy*] .... DCS
Damage Control Suit System [*Navy oxygen sensor*] .... DCSS
Damage Control System .... DCS
Damage Control Texts [*Naval Ship Systems Command*] .... DCT
Damage Controlman, Fireman [*Navy*] .... DCFN
Damage Controlman, Fireman Apprentice [*Navy*] .... DCFA
Damage Expectancy .... DE
Damage Free .... DF
Damage Limitation [*Strategy*] [*in a war*] .... DL
Damage Limiting Program .... DLP
Damage-Risk Criteria [*Tolerable limits for noise exposure*] .... DRC
Damage Tolerant/Easy Repair Structures .... DETERS
Damage and Vulnerability .... DV
Damaged .... DA
Damaged Goods .... DG
Damaged Vehicle Assessment Program .... DVAP
Damascus [*Syria*] [*Airport symbol*] .... DAM
Dame .... D
Dame Commander of the [*Order of the*] **British Empire** .... DBE
Dame Commander of the Royal Victorian Order [*British*] .... DCVO
Dame Commander of St. Michael and St. George [*British*] .... DCMG
Dame of Grace, Order of St. John of Jerusalem [*Later, D St J*] [*British*] .... DGStJ

Dame of Justice/Grace of the Order of St. John of Jerusalem [*British*] ... D St J
Dame of Justice of St. John of Jerusalem [*Later, D St J*] [*British*] ... DJStJ
Dames of the Loyal Legion of the United States ... DLL
Dames of Malta ... D of M
Damien Dutton Society for Leprosy Aid ... DDS
Damien Dutton Society for Leprosy Aid ... DDSLA
Damn ... D
Damned Average Raiser [*A diligent student*] [*Slang*] ... DAR
Damned Bad ... DB
Damned Old Fool About Books [*Acronym created by Eugene Field*] ... DOFAB
Damned Young Fools [*Officers under the age of thirty*] [*British naval slang*] ... DYF
Damon Biotech [*NASDAQ symbol*] ... DBIO
Damon Corp. [*NYSE symbol*] ... DMN
Damon Creations, Incorporated [*American Stock Exchange symbol*] ... DNI
Damon and Pythias [*Fourth-century BC Greek philosophers renowned for their loyalty to one another*] ... D & P
Damon Runyon Memorial Fund for Cancer Research [*Later, DRWWCF*] ... DRMF
Damon Runyon-Walter Winchell Cancer Fund [*Formerly, DRMF*] ... DRWWCF
Damp-Proofing ... DP
Damp Rag [*Decontamination method*] [*Nuclear energy*] ... D-R
Damper ... DMPR
Damping ... DPG
Damping Factor ... DF
Damping Structural Vibrations ... DSV
Damson Oil Corp. [*American Stock Exchange symbol*] ... DAM
Dan-Air Services Ltd. [*Great Britain*] [*ICAO designator*] ... DA
Dan River Mills Co., Danville, VA [*Library symbol*] ... ViDR
Dana College, Blair, NE [*Library symbol*] ... NbBlaD
Dana College, C. A. Dana-Life Library, Blair, NE [*OCLC symbol*] ... DAN
Dana Corporation [*NYSE symbol*] ... DCN
Dana Hall School Library, Wellesley, MA [*Library symbol*] ... MWelD
Dana-Report. Carlsberg Foundation [*A publication*] ... Dana-Rep Carlsberg Found
Danang [*North Vietnam*] [*Airport symbol*] ... DAD
Danbury [*Connecticut*] [*Airport symbol*] [*Obsolete*] ... DXR
Danbury, CT [*Radio station call letters*] ... WFAR
Danbury, CT [*Radio station call letters*] ... WLAD
Danbury, CT [*Radio station call letters*] ... WLAD-FM
Danbury, CT [*Radio station call letters*] ... WXCI
Danbury Public Library, Danbury, CT [*Library symbol*] ... CtDab
Dance [*A publication*] ... D
Dance Critics Association ... DCA
Dance and Dancers [*A publication*] ... DD
Dance Educators of America ... DEA
Dance Films Association ... DFA
Dance Halls (Commercial) [*Public-performance tariff class*] [*British*] ... D
Dance History Scholars ... DHS
Dance Magazine [*A publication*] ... Dance Mag
Dance Magazine [*A publication*] ... DM
Dance Masters of America ... DMA
Dance News [*A publication*] ... Dance N
Dance News [*A publication*] ... DN
Dance Notation Bureau ... DNB
Dance Observer [*A publication*] ... DO
Dance Perspectives [*A publication*] ... Dance Per
Dance Perspectives [*A publication*] ... DP
Dance Theater of Harlem ... DTH
Dance Theatre Workshop ... DTW
Dance Touring Program [*National Endowment for the Arts*] ... DTP
Dance Tuition Schools [*Public-performance tariff class*] [*British*] ... DS
Dancer-Fitzgerald-Sample [*Advertising agency*] ... DFS
Dancers for Disarmament ... DFD
Dandie Dinmont Terrier Club of America ... DDTCA
Dandke Folkemaal [*A publication*] ... DF
Dandus [*To Be Given*] [*Pharmacy*] ... DAND
Dane [*Ontario*] [*Seismograph station code, US Geological Survey*] [*Closed*] ... DAN
Dane County Hospital, Verona, WI [*Library symbol*] ... WVD
Danfoss Journal [*A publication*] ... Danfoss J
Dang [*Nepal*] [*Airport symbol*] ... DNP
Danger ... DGR
Danger ... DNG
Danger Area [*Aviation*] ... D
Danger Areas in the Pacific ... DAPAC
Danger List [*Medicine*] ... DL
Dangerous [*FBI standardized term*] ... DANG
Dangerous Articles Tariff ... DAT
Dangerous Defective [*British*] ... DD
Dangerous Drug Cabinet [*Lockable auxiliary to bathroom medicine chest*] ... DDC
Dangerous Drugs [*British*] ... DD
Dangerous Drugs Act [*British*] ... DDA
Dangerous Goods [*Shipping*] ... DG
Dangerous and Suspicious ... D & S
Dangerous Weapon ... DW
Dangling, at Bedside [*Medicine*] ... d
Dangling Construction [*Used in correcting manuscripts, etc.*] ... DGL
Dangriga [*Belize*] [*Airport symbol*] ... DGA
Daniel [*Old Testament book*] ... Dan
Daniel [*Old Testament book*] ... Danl
Daniel [*Old Testament book*] ... Dn
Daniel Industries, Inc. [*NYSE symbol*] ... DAN
Daniels Canyon [*Utah*] [*Seismograph station code, US Geological Survey*] ... DAU
Danish ... DA
Danish ... DAN
Danish [*MARC language code*] [*Library of Congress*] ... dan
Danish American Chamber of Commerce ... DACC
Danish American Women's Association [*Defunct*] ... DAWA
Danish Arctic Research [*A publication*] ... Dan Arct Res
Danish Army ... DA
Danish Atomic Energy Commission ... DAEC
Danish Atomic Energy Commission. Research Establishment. Riso Report [*A publication*] ... Dan AEC Res Establ Riso Rep
Danish Brotherhood in America ... DBA
Danish Building Research Institute ... DBRI
Danish Defense Research Board ... DDRB
Danish Defense Research Establishment ... DDRE
Danish International Development Agency ... DANIDA
Danish Krone [*Monetary unit*] ... DK
Danish Krone [*Monetary unit*] ... D KR
Danish Medical Bulletin [*A publication*] ... Dan Med B
Danish Medical Bulletin [*A publication*] ... Dan Med Bull
Danish Pest Infestation Laboratory. Annual Report [*A publication*] ... Dan Pest Infest Lab Annu Rep
Danish Reactor ... DR
Danish Review of Game Biology [*A publication*] ... Dan Rev Game Biol
Danish Sailors' and Firemen's Union ... DSFU
Danish West Indies ... DWI
Danish Yearbook of Philosophy [*A publication*] ... Dan Yrbk Phil
Danker Laboratories, Inc. [*NASDAQ symbol*] ... DANK
Danmarks Gamle Folkeviser [*A publication*] ... DGF
Danmarks Geologiske Undersoegelse [*A publication*] ... Danmarks Geol Undersoegelse
Danmarks Geologiske Undersoegelse. Arbog [*A publication*] ... Dan Geol Unders Arbog
Danmarks Geologiske Undersoegelse. II Raekke [*A publication*] ... Dan Geol Unders II Raekke
Danmarks Geologiske Undersoegelse. III Raekke [*A publication*] ... Dan Geol Unders III Raekke
Danmarks Geologiske Undersoegelse. IV Raekke [*A publication*] ... Dan Geol Unders IV Raekke
Danmarks Geologiske Undersoegelse. Raekke 2 [*A publication*] ... Dan Geol Unders Raekke 2
Danmarks Geologiske Undersoegelse. Raekke 3 [*A publication*] ... Dan Geol Unders Raekke 3
Danmarks Geologiske Undersoegelse. Rapport [*A publication*] ... Dan Geol Unders Rapp
Danmarks Geologiske Undersoegelse. Serie A [*A publication*] ... Dan Geol Unders Ser A
Danmarks Geologiske Undersoegelse. Serie B [*A publication*] ... Dan Geol Unders Ser B
Danmarks Laererhojskole [*Royal Danish School of Educational Studies*]**, Kobenhavn, Denmark** [*Library symbol*] ... DnKL
Danmarks Naturfredningsforenings Arsskrift [*A publication*] ... Dan Naturfredningsforen Arsskr
Danmarks Paedagogiske Bibliotek [*Danish National Library of Education*]**, Kobenhavn, Denmark** [*Library symbol*] ... DnKP
Danmarks Radio ... DSR
Danmarks Statistik [*Denmark*] ... DS
Danmarks Tekniske Bibliotek [*National Technological Library of Denmark*] [*Information service*] ... DTB
Danmarkshavn [*Greenland*] [*Seismograph station code, US Geological Survey*] ... DAG
Dannemiller, Lawrence B., Columbus OH [*STAC*] ... DLB
Dannemora [*New York*] [*Seismograph station code, US Geological Survey*] ... DANY
Danners, Inc. [*NASDAQ symbol*] ... DNNR
Dannevirke [*New Zealand*] [*Seismograph station code, US Geological Survey*] [*Closed*] ... DNN
Dansk Astronautisk Forening [*Danish Astronautical Society*] ... DAF
Dansk Audiologopaedi [*A publication*] ... Dansk Audiol
Dansk Botanisk Arkiv [*A publication*] ... Dan Bot Ark
Dansk Botanisk Arkiv [*A publication*] ... Dansk Botan
Dansk Dendrologisk Arsskrift [*A publication*] ... Dan Dendrol Arsskr
Dansk Forening til Fremme af Opfindelser [*Danish Society for Furthering Inventions*] ... DAFFO
Dansk Geologisk Forening Meddelelser [*A publication*] ... Dansk Geol Foren Medd
Dansk Geologisk Forening Meddelelser [*A publication*] ... Dansk Geol Foren Meddel
Dansk Historisk Tidskrift [*A publication*] ... HTD
Dansk Ingeniorforening Spildevandskomiteen Skrift [*A publication*] ... Dan Ingeniorforen Spildevandskom Skr
Dansk Kemi [*A publication*] ... Dan Kemi
Dansk Musiktidsskrift [*A publication*] ... Dansk Mus
Dansk Naturfredning [*A publication*] ... Dan Naturfredning

Dansk Normal Nul [*Oceanography*] ... DNN
Dansk Ornithologisk Forening. Feltornithologen [*A publication*] ... Dan Ornithol Foren Feltornithol
Dansk Ornithologisk Forening. Fuglevaern [*A publication*] ... Dan Ornithol Foren Fuglevaern
Dansk Ornithologisk Forening. Tidsskrift [*A publication*] ... Dan Ornithol Foren Tidsskr
Dansk Skovforenings Tidsskrift [*A publication*] ... Dan Skovforen Tidsskr
Dansk Teologisk Tidsskrift [*A publication*] ... Dteol T
Dansk Teologisk Tidsskrift [*A publication*] ... DTTid
Dansk Tidsskrift foer Farmaci [*A publication*] ... Dan Tdsskr Farm
Dansk Udsyn [*A publication*] ... DanU
Danske Boghandleres Importrfrening [*Danish Booksellers Import Association*] ... DANBIF
Danske Folkemaal [*A publication*] ... DanF
Danske Magazin [*A publication*] ... DM
Danske Sprog-og Literaturselskab [*A publication*] ... DSL
Danske Statsbaner [*Danish State Railways*] ... DSB
Danske Studier [*A publication*] ... DS
Danske Studier [*A publication*] ... DSt
Danske Videnskabernes Selskabs Historishfilologiske Meddelelser [*A publication*] ... DVSM
Danske Videnskabernes Selskabs Skrifter [*A publication*] ... DVSS
[*The*] **Dansville & Mount Morris Railroad Co.** [*AAR code*] ... DMM
Dansville, NY [*Location identifier*] [*FAA*] ... DSV
Dansville, NY [*Radio station call letters*] ... WDNY
Dansville Senior High School Library, Dansville, NY [*OCLC symbol*] ... RVZ
Dansyl [*As substituent on nucleoside*] [*Biochemistry*] ... dns
Dansyl Glutamate [*Biochemistry*] ... DG
Dansylaspartate [*Biochemistry*] ... DA
Dansylcadaverine [*Biochemistry*] ... DACAD
Dante Alighieri Society of Southern California ... DASSC
Dante Society of America ... DSA
Dante Studies [*A publication*] ... DaSt
Dante Studies with the Annual Report of the Dante Society [*A publication*] ... DSARDS
Danube [*River in central Europe*] ... DAN
Danube River and Basin [*MARC geographic area code*] [*Library of Congress*] ... eo-----
Danube River Field Organization [*Allied German Occupation Forces*] ... DRFO
Danvers State Hospital, Hathorne, MA [*Library symbol*] ... MHathD
Danville [*Virginia*] [*Airport symbol*] ... DAN
Danville [*Illinois*] [*Airport symbol*] ... DNV
Danville, IL [*Radio station call letters*] ... WDAN
Danville, IL [*Radio station call letters*] ... WDNL
Danville, IL [*Radio station call letters*] ... WIAI
Danville, IL [*Radio station call letters*] ... WITY
Danville, IN [*Radio station call letters*] ... WGRT
Danville Junior College [*Illinois*] ... DJC
Danville Junior College, Danville, IL [*Library symbol*] ... IDanviC
Danville, KY [*Location identifier*] [*FAA*] ... DVK
Danville, KY [*Television station call letters*] ... WDKY-TV
Danville, KY [*Radio station call letters*] ... WHIR
Danville, KY [*Radio station call letters*] ... WKLO
Danville, KY [*Radio station call letters*] ... WMGE
Danville, PA [*Radio station call letters*] ... WPGM
Danville, PA [*Radio station call letters*] ... WPGM-FM
Danville Public Library, Danville, IL [*Library symbol*] ... IDanvi
Danville Public Library, Danville, VA [*Library symbol*] ... ViD
Danville Quarterly Review [*A publication*] ... Danv Q
Danville State Hospital, Danville, PA [*Library symbol*] ... PDanSH
Danville State Hospital, Danville, PA [*OCLC symbol*] ... PHJ
Danville, VA [*Location identifier*] [*FAA*] ... DAN
Danville, VA [*Radio station call letters*] ... WAKG
Danville, VA [*Radio station call letters*] ... WBTM
Danville, VA [*Radio station call letters*] ... WDVA
Danville, VA [*Radio station call letters*] ... WILA
Danygraig [*Welsh depot code*] ... DG
Danzig Study Group [*German Philatelic Society*] ... DSG
Danziger Statistische Mitteilungen [*Danzig*] ... DSM
Dar Es Salaam [*Tanzania*] [*Airport symbol*] ... DAR
Dar Es Salaam [*Tanzania*] [*Geomagnetic observatory code*] ... DRS
Dar Es Salaam Medical Journal [*A publication*] ... Dar Es Salaam Med J
Darband [*Pakistan*] [*Seismograph station code, US Geological Survey*] ... DBP
DARCOM Announcement Distribution System ... DADS
Darcy [*Physics*] ... D
D'Arcy-MacManus & Masius [*Advertising agency*] ... DM & M
Dardanelle, AR [*Radio station call letters*] ... KCAB
Dardanelle, AR [*Radio station call letters*] ... KWKK
Dardanelle & Russellville Railroad Co. [*AAR code*] ... DR
Dardo de Investigacion Meteorologica [*Argentina*] ... DIM
Daremberg and Saglio, Dictionnaire des Antiquites Grecques et Romaines [*A publication*] ... Dar Sag
Daresbury Nuclear Physics Laboratory. Report [*A publication*] ... Daresbury Nucl Phys Lab Rep
Daresbury Nuclear Physics Laboratory. Technical Memorandum [*A publication*] ... Daresbury Nucl Phys Lab Tech Memo
Dari de Seama ale Sedintelor. Republica Populara Romana Comitetul Geologic [*A publication*] ... Dari Seama Sedint RPR Com Geol
Darien Library, Darien, CT [*Library symbol*] ... CtD
Darien Public Library, Darien, WI [*Library symbol*] ... WDar
Dark ... DK
Dark Agouti [*Rat strain*] ... DA
Dark Field Illumination ... DFI
Dark Ignition ... DI
Dark on Light ... DL
Dark Mantling Material [*Lunar surface*] ... DMM
Darkroom [*Photography*] ... DR
Darlington County Library, Darlington, SC [*OCLC symbol*] ... SCD
Darlington, SC [*Radio station call letters*] ... WDAR-FM
Darlington, SC [*Radio station call letters*] ... WKGE
Darmstaedter Beitraege zur Neuen Musik [*A publication*] ... DBNM
Darned Insulting, Rotten, Terrible Yarns [*Book title*] ... DIRTY
Darnell Army Hospital, Medical Library, Fort Hood, TX [*Library symbol*] ... TxFhH
Darshana International [*A publication*] ... Darshana Int
Dart Drug Corp. Cl A [*NASDAQ symbol*] ... DRUGA
Dart Industries, Inc. [*NYSE symbol*] ... D
Dart & Kraft, Incorporated [*NYSE symbol*] ... DKI
Dartmouth Alumni Magazine [*A publication*] ... Dartmouth Alumni Mag
Dartmouth Bi-Monthly [*A publication*] ... Dart Bi-Mo
Dartmouth College, Business Administration and Engineering Library, Hanover, NH [*Library symbol*] ... NhD-BE
Dartmouth College, Dana Biomedical Library, Hanover, NH [*Library symbol*] ... NhD-D
Dartmouth College, Hanover, NH [*OCLC symbol*] ... DRB
Dartmouth College, Hanover, NH [*Library symbol*] ... NhD
Dartmouth College, Kresge Physical Sciences Library, Hanover, NH [*Library symbol*] ... NhD-K
Dartmouth, NS [*Radio station call letters*] ... CFDR
Dartmouth Regional Library, Dartmouth, NS, Canada [*Library symbol*] ... CaNSD
Dartmouth Time-Sharing System [*Data processing*] ... DTSS
Daru [*Papua New Guinea*] [*Airport symbol*] ... DAU
Daru [*Papua New Guinea*] [*Seismograph station code, US Geological Survey*] [*Closed*] ... DNG
Darwin [*California*] [*Seismograph station code, US Geological Survey*] ... DAC
Darwin [*Australia*] [*Seismograph station code, US Geological Survey*] [*Closed*] ... DAR
Darwin [*Australia*] [*Airport symbol*] ... DRW
Darwin, MN [*Location identifier*] [*FAA*] ... DWN
Darwin R. Barker Library Association, Fredonia, NY [*Library symbol*] ... NFred
Das Heisst [*That Is*] [*German*] ... DH
Das Ist [*That Is*] [*German*] ... DI
Das Kleine Wunder [*Initialism used as name of German automobile, manufactured by Auto Union*] ... DKW
DASD [*Direct Access Storage Device*] **Dump Restore** [*Data processing*] ... DDR
Dash Automatic Test Equipment ... DATE
Dash Industries, Inc. [*NASDAQ symbol*] ... DASH
Dash Pot [*Relay*] ... DP
Dashboard ... DBD
Dasher Owners of America ... DOA
Dashpot Cup Retention Nut [*Nuclear energy*] ... DCRN
Dasika Chronika [*A publication*] ... Das Chron
Dat, Dicat, Dedicat [*He Gives, Devotes, and Dedicates*] [*Latin*] ... DDD
Data Acceptance Tests ... DAT
Data Access Arrangement [*Data processing*] ... DAA
Data Access Line ... DAL
Data Access Protocol ... DAP
Data Access Register [*Data processing*] ... DAR
Data Access Systems, Inc. [*American Stock Exchange symbol*] [*Delisted*] ... DAC
Data Accession List ... DAL
Data Accountability System ... DAS
Data Accumulating and Reporting Sheet ... DARS
Data Accumulation and Distribution Units [*Navy*] ... DADU
Data Accumulation and Transfer Sheet ... DATS
Data Acquisition ... DA
Data Acquisition Camera ... DAC
Data Acquisition Center ... DAQC
Data Acquisition Chassis ... DAC
Data Acquisition Computer ... DAC
Data Acquisition and Control ... DAC
Data Acquisition Control and Buffer ... DACB
Data Acquisition and Control Buffer Unit ... DACBU
Data Acquisition Control System ... DACS
Data Acquisition and Control Unit ... DACU
Data Acquisition Controller ... DAC
Data Acquisition and Decommutation Equipment ... DADE
Data Acquisition and Display System ... DADS
Data Acquisition Division [*National Weather Service*] ... DATAC
Data Acquisition Equipment ... DAE
Data Acquisition Facility [*of STADAN*] ... DAF
Data Acquisition and Interpretation System ... DAISY
Data Acquisition List ... DAL
Data Acquisition Logging System ... DALS
Data Acquisition and Monitoring Equipment [*Electronics*] ... DAME

Data Acquisition Multiprograming System [*Data processing*] .... DAMPS
Data Acquisition Plan .... DAP
Data Acquisition and Processing .... DA & P
Data Acquisition and Processing in Biology and Medicine [*A publication*] .... Data Acquis Process Biol Med
Data Acquisition and Processing Program [*Later, DMSP*] [*Air Force*] .... DAPP
Data Acquisition and Processing System .... DAPS
Data Acquisition and Processing Unit [*Viking orbiter system*] [*NASA*] .... DAPU
Data Acquisition Recorder .... DAR
Data Acquisition Recording System .... DARS
Data Acquisition and Reduction System .... DARS
Data Acquisition and Reports Control [*Army*] .... DARC
Data Acquisition Requirements Document .... DARD
Data Acquisition Station .... DAS
Data Acquisition Statistical Recorder .... DASR
Data Acquisition Subsystem Group .... DASG
Data Acquisition Support Document .... DASD
Data Acquisition System .... DAS
Data Acquisition System, Correlation Tracking and Ranging [*Air Force*] .... DASCOTAR
Data Acquisition Test [*Later, DST*] .... DAT
Data Acquisition and Transmission System .... DATS
Data Acquisition Unit .... DAU
Data Adapter .... DA
Data Adapter Unit .... DAU
Data Adaptive Evaluator and Monitor .... DAEMON
Data Addressed Memory [*Data processing*] .... DAM
Data Administration Section .... DAS
Data from Aeromechanics' Test and Analytics-Management and Analysis Package .... DATAMAP
Data-Aided Loop [*NASA*] .... DAL
Data-Aided Receiver [*NASA*] .... DAR
Data Aids for Training, Operations, and Maintenance .... DATOM
Data for Allotments Transmitted Electronically .... DATE
Data Amplification Sheet .... DAS
Data Analog Computer .... DATAC
Data Analysis .... DA
Data Analysis .... DATAN
Data and Analysis Center for Software [*Illinois Institute of Technology*] [*Information service*] .... DACS
Data Analysis Computer .... DAC
Data Analysis Console .... DAC
Data Analysis Control .... DAC
Data Analysis Facility .... DAF
Data Analysis Information Memo .... DAIM
Data Analysis Laboratory .... DAL
Data Analysis [*Program*] **of Massachusetts Institute of Technology** .... DAMIT
Data Analysis and Processing Facility .... DAPF
Data Analysis Program .... DAP
Data Analysis Recording Tape .... DART
Data Analysis and Reduction System .... DARES
Data Analysis Station .... DAS
Data Analysis System .... DASY
Data Analysis and Technique Development Center .... DATDC
Data Aquisition Language [*Data processing*] .... DAL
Data Architects, Inc. [*NASDAQ symbol*] .... DRCH
Data Article Requirements .... DAR
Data Assembler .... DA
Data Association Message .... DAM
Data Automatic Reduction Equipment .... DARE
Data Automation .... DA
Data Automation Activity .... DAA
Data Automation Design Office [*Air Force*] .... ADO
Data Automation Design Office [*Air Force*] .... DADO
Data Automation Digest [*A publication*] .... DAD
Data Automation Equipment .... DAE
Data Automation Proposal .... DAP
Data Automation Requirement .... DAR
Data Automation Research and Experimentation .... DARE
Data Automation System [*or Subsystem*] [*NASA*] .... DAS
Data Available .... DA
Data Bank .... D (Bank)
Data Bank .... DB
Data Bank .... DBK
Data Bank .... DBNK
Data Bank Release Notice .... DBRN
Data Bank Update Request .... DBUR
Data Base [*Data processing*] .... DB
Data Base Administration [*or Administrator*] [*Data processing*] .... DBA
Data Base Computer .... DBC
Data Base/Data Communications [*IBM Corp.*] .... DB/DC
Data Base Description [*Data processing*] .... DBD
Data Base Design Aid [*Data processing*] .... DBDA
Data Base File [*Military*] .... DBF
Data Base File Numbers .... DBFN
Data Base Generation [*Data processing*] .... DBGEN
Data Base Handling System .... DBHS
Data Base Input Languages [*Data processing*] .... DBIL
Data Base List .... DBL
Data Base Load [*Data processing*] .... DBL
Data Base Management [*or Manager*] [*Data processing*] .... DBM
Data Base Management System [*Data processing*] .... DBMS
Data Base Organization and Maintenance Processor .... DBOMP
Data Base System .... DBS
Data Base and Transaction Management System [*IBM Corp.*] .... DTMS
Data Base Update Time .... DBUT
Data Bibliography Card .... DBC
Data Buffer Module .... DBM
Data Buoy Project Office [*Later, NDBC*] [*National Oceanic and Atmospheric Administration*] .... DBPO
Data Bus [*Data processing*] .... DB
Data Bus Control [*Data processing*] .... DBC
Data Bus Control Unit [*Data processing*] .... DBCU
Data Bus Coupler [*Data processing*] .... DBC
Data Bus Enable [*Data processing*] .... DBE
Data Bus Generation and Maintenance Package [*Data processing*] .... DBGMP
Data Bus Group [*Data processing*] .... DBG
Data Bus In [*Data processing*] .... DBIN
Data Bus Interface Adapter [*Data processing*] .... DBIA
Data Bus Interface Unit [*Data processing*] .... DBIU
Data Bus Interface Unit-Launch [*Data processing*] .... DBI
Data Bus Isolation Amplifier [*Data processing*] .... DBIA
Data Bus Monitor [*Data processing*] .... DBM
Data Bus Network [*Data processing*] .... DBN
Data Call .... DC
Data Camera .... DC
Data Card Corp. [*NASDAQ symbol*] .... DATC
Data Cell [*Data processing*] .... DC
Data Center .... DC
Data Center for Atomic and Molecular Ionization Processes .... DCAMIP
Data Change Notice .... DCN
Data Channel [*Data processing*] .... DC
Data Channel Filter [*Data processing*] .... DCF
Data Check .... DC
Data Checklist .... DCL
Data Chief .... DCH
Data Circuit-Terminating Equipment [*Data processing*] .... DCE
Data Classifier .... DC
Data Code .... DC
Data Collection .... DATACOL
Data Collection .... DC
Data Collection and Analysis System [*NASA*] .... DCAS
Data Collection Center [*Army Infantry Board*] .... DCC
Data Collection and Distribution Units [*Military*] .... DCDU
Data Collection and Evaluation System .... DCES
Data Collection Form [*Civil Defense*] .... DCF
Data Collection Module, High Speed .... DCMH
Data Collection Module, Low Speed .... DCML
Data Collection Order .... DCO
Data Collection Platform [*National Weather Service*] .... DCP
Data Collection and Reduction System .... DCRS
Data Collection/Relay .... DC/R
Data Collection System [*Data processing*] .... DCS
Data Collection Unit .... DCU
Data Command Unit .... DCU
Data Communication [*Data processing*] .... DC
Data Communication Equipment .... DCE
Data Communication Input Buffer .... DCIB
Data Communication Network Architecture .... DCNA
Data Communication Output Selector .... DCOS
Data Communication Processing System .... DCPS
Data Communication Processor [*Data processing*] .... DCP
Data Communication System .... DCS
Data Communications [*A publication*] .... Data C
Data Communications .... DATACOM
Data Communications [*A publication*] .... Data Comm
Data Communications Channel .... DCC
Data Communications Control Unit .... DCCU
Data Communications Corporation [*Information service*] .... DCC
Data Communications Equipment Monitoring and Switching .... DACEMS
Data Communications, Inc. [*Information service*] .... Da-Com
Data Communications Terminal .... DCT
Data Compendium .... DATCOM
Data Computation Subsystem Group .... DCSG
Data Concentrator [*Data processing*] .... DC
Data Condition Code .... DCC
Data Conditioning System [*NASA*] .... DCS
Data Consistency Orbit .... DACO
Data Control .... DC
Data Control Block [*Data processing*] .... DCB
Data Control Group .... DCG
Data Control Multiplex System .... DCMS
Data Control Office .... DCO
Data Control Panel Submodule .... DCPS
Data Control Services .... DCS
Data Control System .... DCS
Data Control Unit .... DCU
Data Controller .... DACON

Data Conversion [*Data processing*] ... D/C
Data Conversion Equipment [*Data processing*] ... DCE
Data Conversion Receiver [*Data processing*] ... DCR
Data Conversion System [*Data processing*] ... DCS
Data Conversion Transmitter [*Data processing*] ... DCT
Data Coordinator ... DC
Data Coordinator and Retriever [*Data processing*] ... DCR
Data Correction [*IBM Corp.*] ... DACOR
Data Correction Amplifier ... DCA
Data Correction Indicator Panel ... DCIP
Data Correlation Control Unit ... DCCU
Data Correlation Facility ... DCF
Data Correlation and Transfer System ... DATACORTS
Data Correlator ... DACOR
Data Count Printout [*Data processing*] ... DACPO
Data Definition [*Data processing*] ... DD
Data Demand Module ... DDM
Data Description ... DD
Data Description Language [*Data processing*] ... DAD
Data Description Language ... DDL
Data Description Table ... DDT
Data-Design Laboratories [*NASDAQ symbol*] ... DDES
Data for Development International Association [*See also DD*] ... DFD
Data Dialog System ... DDS
Data Dictionary ... DADIC
Data Dictionary [*Data processing*] ... DD
Data Dictionary/Directory System ... DD/DS
Data Directed Programing System [*British*] ... DDPS
Data Direction Register [*Microcomputer*] ... DDR
Data Discrepancy Report ... DDR
Data Display ... DDIS
Data Display Board ... DDB
Data Display Buffer ... DDB
Data Display Central ... DDC
Data Display Generator ... DDG
Data Display Indicator ... DDI
Data Display Module ... DDM
Data Display Set ... DDS
Data Display System ... DDS
Data Display Unit ... DDU
Data Distribution Center ... DDC
Data Distribution List ... DDL
Data Distribution Panel ... DDP
Data Distribution Point [*NATO*] ... DDP
Data Distribution System [*or Subsystem*] ... DDS
Data Documentation Costs ... DDC
Data Down Link [*Data processing*] ... DDL
Data Drawing List ... DDL
Data Drawing and Parts List ... DDPL
Data Education [*A publication*] ... Data Ed
Data Element [*Data processing*] ... DE
Data Element Description List [*Data processing*] ... DEDL
Data Element Dictionary [*A publication*] [*Army*] ... DED
Data Element Management Accounting/Reporting ... DELMAR
Data Element Management Accounting and Reporting ... DEMAR
Data Element Number ... DEN
Data Encoder ... DE
Data Encoder Unit ... DEU
Data Encoder Unit Transmitter ... DEUT
Data Encryption Standard [*National Bureau of Standards*] ... DES
Data Encrypton Standard [*National Bureau of Standards*] ... DES
Data Engineering Section ... DES
Data Entry Aboard Ship [*Navy*] ... DEAS
Data Entry and Display Assembly [*Apollo*] [*NASA*] ... DEDA
Data Entry and Display Panel ... DEDP
Data Entry Keyboard [*Data processing*] ... DEK
Data Entry Management Association ... DEMA
Data Entry Panel ... DEP
Data Entry/Separation ... DE/S
Data Event Control Block [*Data processing*] ... DECB
Data Exchange Agreement ... DEA
Data Exchange Annex ... DEA
Data Exchange Auxiliary Consoles ... DEACS
Data Exchange Control ... DXC
Data Exchange Control Unit ... DECU
Data Exchange Optimization Study [*DoD*] ... DEOS
Data Exchange Program ... DEP
Data Exchange System ... DES
Data Exchange Unit ... DEU
Data Extent Block ... DEB
Data Extraction and Analysis Group ... DEAG
Data Facility Data Set Services ... DFDSS
Data Facility Extended ... DFE
Data Facility Product ... DFP
Data File Utility [*Data processing*] ... DFU
Data Flow Control ... DFC
Data Flow Diagrams ... DFD
Data Flow Engineer ... DFE
Data Folder ... DF
Data Format Converter ... DFC
Data Function Information Book ... DFIB
Data Gathering Monitoring [*System*] ... DGM
Data Gathering System ... DGS
Data General Corp. [*NYSE symbol*] ... DGN
Data General Corp., Westboro, MA [*OCLC symbol*] ... DAT
Data Generating Program ... DGP
Data Generation ... DGEN
Data Graphics Corporation ... DGC
Data Ground Station [*NASA*] ... DGS
Data Handling Center ... DHC
Data Handling and Control Unit ... DHCU
Data Handling and Display Subsystem ... DHDS
Data Handling Equipment ... DHE
Data Handling Subsystem ... DHSS
Data Handling System ... DHS
Data Hardware Project Engineer [*NASA*] ... DHPE
Data I/O Corp. [*NASDAQ symbol*] ... DAIO
Data Identification ... DID
Data Identification Number ... DIN
Data Identification Table ... DIT
Data Information System for Management Control [*Military*] ... DISC
Data Information Test Material Checkout ... DITMCO
Data Input [*Data processing*] ... DI
Data Input Bus [*Data processing*] ... DIB
Data Input Clerk [*Data processing*] ... DIC
Data Input Consoles [*Data processing*] ... DIC
Data Input/Data Output [*Data processing*] ... DI/DO
Data Input Display [*Data processing*] ... DID
Data Input Display Console [*Data processing*] ... DIDC
Data Input Processor [*Data processing*] ... DIP
Data Input System [*Data processing*] ... DIS
Data Input Voice Output Telephone System ... DIVOTS
Data Inquiry Terminal ... DIT
Data Inserter ... DATIN
Data Insertion Converter ... DIC
Data Inspection Station ... DIS
Data Integrator ... DI
Data Interchange Format ... DIF
Data Interface ... DI
Data Interface Unit ... DIU
Data Interfile Transfer, Testing, and Operations Utility [*IBM program product*] ... DITTO
Data Item Category ... DIC
Data Item Description [*DoD*] ... DID
Data Item Requirement ... DIR
Data Language ... DL
Data Language Version 1 [*Data processing*] ... DL/1
Data-Line Concentration System [*Bell System*] ... DLCS
Data Line Flight Direction Unit ... DLFDU
Data Link ... DL
Data Link ... DLK
Data Link Address ... DLA
Data Link Control [*Data processing*] ... DLC
Data Link Control Field [*Data processing*] ... DLCF
Data Link Control Panel [*Data processing*] ... DLCP
Data Link Decoder ... DLD
Data Link Equipment ... DLE
Data Link Escape [*Data processing*] ... DLE
Data Link Processor [*Data processing*] ... DLP
Data Link Programs ... DLP
Data Link Receiver [*Data processing*] ... DLR
Data Link Reference Point ... DLRP
Data Link Set ... DLS
Data Link Simulator ... DLS
Data Link Summary Message ... DLSM
Data Link Terminal ... DLT
Data Link Terminal Repeater ... DLTR
Data Link Test Message ... DLTM
Data Link Test Set ... DALTS
Data Link Translator ... DLT
Data Link Transmission Repeater ... DLTR
Data List File ... DLF
Data Listing Programs ... DLP
Data Lists [*DoD*] ... DL
Data Logging System ... DLS
Data Logging and Transmission System ... DALATS
Data Loop Transceiver [*Data processing*] ... DLT
Data Maintenance Diagnostic Program ... DMDP
Data Management [*A publication*] ... Data Mgmt
Data Management [*A publication*] ... Data Mgt
Data Management ... DM
Data Management Analysis ... DMA
Data Management Channel ... DMC
Data Management Computer ... DMC
Data Management Group ... DMG
Data Management Information System [*DoD*] ... DMIS
Data Management Office [*or Officer*] [*Air Force*] ... DMO
Data Management Plan [*Jet Propulsion Laboratory, NASA*] ... DMP
Data Management Policy Office [*Army*] ... DMPO
Data Management and Retrieval System ... DMRS
Data Management Routine ... DMR
Data Management Service ... DMS

Data Management Summary Processor	DMSP
Data Management System [*Data processing*]	DATAMAN
Data Management System [*Data processing*]	DMS
Data Management System/Computer Subsystem [*Data processing*]	DMS/CS
Data Management System Problem Specification Model [*Air Force*]	DMSPSM
Data Management System Simulator [*NASA*]	DMSS
Data Management Unit [*Data processing*]	DMU
Data Manager	DMAN
Data Manipulation Language [*Data processing*]	DML
Data Master	DM
Data Material Required, Increasing Urgency [*Navy*]	DMRI
Data Measuring System	DMS
Data Microfilming Corp., Whittier, CA [*Library symbol*]	DmC
Data Monitoring System	DMS
Data Multiplex [*Computer*]	DMX
Data Multiplex Subsystem [*Data processing*]	DMSS
Data Multiplex System [*Data processing*]	DMS
Data Name	DN
Data Name Card	DNC
Data Net Control Unit	DNCU
Data Network	DATANET
Data Number	DN
Data Observing Testing Console	DOTC
Data Operational Requirements Board [*NATO Military Committee*]	DATOR
Data, Operations, and Control	DOC
Data Optimizing Computer	DOC
Data Output [*Data processing*]	DO
Data Output Multiplexer [*Data processing*]	DOM
Data Packaging Corp. [*NASDAQ symbol*]	DPKG
Data-Phone Digital Service [*Trademark of the American Telephone & Telegraph Co.*]	DDS
Data [*or Digital*] Phone Line Formatter	DPLF
Data Plotting Board	DPB
Data Present Signal	DPS
Data Printer	DP
Data Printout Program	DROP
Data Process Work Request	DPWR
Data Processing [*A publication*]	Data Proc
Data Processing [*A publication*]	Data Proces
Data Processing	DP
Data Processing Activities	DPA
Data Processing Agency	DPA
Data Processing Algorithm	DPA
Data Processing Area	DPA
Data Processing Assembly	DPA
Data Processing Automatic Publication Service	DAPS
Data Processing Automatic Record Standardization	DPARS
Data Processing Branch	DPB
Data Processing Center	DPC
Data Processing Central	DPC
Data Processing and/or Computer Programing Programs [*Association of Independent Colleges and Schools specialization code*]	DP
Data Processing Control	DPC
Data Processing Control Area [*Space Flight Operations Facility, NASA*]	DPCA
Data Processing Control Center [*or Console*] [*Space Flight Operations Facility, NASA*]	DPCC
Data Processing Department	DPD
Data Processing Detachment	DPD
Data Processing Digest [*A publication*]	Data Process
Data Processing for Education [*A publication*]	Data Process Educ
Data Processing Equipment	DPE
Data Processing Facility	DPF
Data Processing Group [*Army*]	DPG
Data Processing Group [*Air Force*]	DPGp
Data Processing and Information Retrieval	DPIR
Data Processing Installation	DPI
Data Processing Machine	DPM
Data Processing Magazine [*A publication*]	Data Process Mag
Data Processing Management Association [*Formerly, NMAA*]	DPMA
Data Processing in Medicine [*A publication*]	Data Process Med
Data Processing Operation	DPO
Data Processing Practitioner [*A publication*]	Data Process Pract
Data Processing Products Contract	DPPC
Data Processing Project Engineer	DPPE
Data Processing Request	DPR
Data Processing Service Center	DPSC
Data Processing Service Request	DPSR
Data Processing and Software	DP & S
Data Processing and Software	DPS
Data Processing Standards [*NASA*]	DPS
Data Processing Subsystem	DPSS
Data Processing Supplies Association [*Later, IOSA*]	DPSA
Data Processing Switching System [*Space Flight Operations Facility, NASA*]	DPSS
Data Processing System	DPS
Data Processing System Simulator	DPSS

Data Processing Systems Office [*Military*]	DPSO
Data Processing Technician [*Navy rating*]	DP
Data Processing Technician, First Class [*Navy rating*]	DP1
Data Processing Technician, Second Class [*Navy rating*]	DP2
Data Processing Technician, Third Class [*Navy rating*]	DP3
Data Processing Unit	DPU
Data Processor and Computer Test Equipment	DPCTE
Data Project Directive	DPD
Data Project Management System	DPMS
Data Publishing International [*Netherlands*] [*Information service*]	DPI
Data Quality Control	DQC
Data Quality Control Monitor	DQCM
Data Quality Monitors	DQM
Data Rate Changer	DRC
Data Rate Indicator	DRI
Data Rate Selector	DRS
Data Reaction System	DRS
Data Readout [*Navy*]	DRO
Data Ready Queue	DRQ
Data Receiver [*or Recorder*]	DR
Data Receiving Station	DRS
Data Record Number	DRN
Data Record of Oceanographic Observations and Exploratory Fishing (Hokkaido) [*A publication*]	Data Rec Oceanogr Obs Explor Fish (Hokkaido)
Data Recorder/Reproducer	DRR
Data Recording	DATREC
Data Recording Camera	DRC
Data Recording Controller [*Data processing*]	DRC
Data Recording Device [*Data processing*]	DRD
Data Recording Interface	DRI
Data Recording and Processing Equipment	DRAPE
Data Recording Set	DRS
Data Recording System	DRS
Data Recording System Analyst	DRSA
Data Records Management	DRM
Data Recovery Vehicle	DRV
Data Reduction	DR
Data Reduction	DRON
Data Reduction and Analysis	DR & A
Data Reduction and Analysis System	DRANS
Data Reduction Analysis Tape	DRAT
Data Reduction Center [*or Complex*]	DRC
Data Reduction Compiler	DRC
Data Reduction and Computing Group [*Range Commanders Council*] [*NASA*]	DR-CG
Data Reduction and Computing Working Group [*Range Commanders Council*] [*NASA*]	DR-CWG
Data Reduction Equipment	DRE
Data Reduction Input Program [*Data processing*]	DRIP
Data Reduction Interpreter	DRI
Data Reduction Laboratory	DRL
Data Reduction Procedure [*or Program*]	DRP
Data Reduction System [*Data processing*]	DRS
Data Reduction Translator	DART
Data Reduction Working Group	DRWG
Data Redundancy Removal	DRR
Data Reference Number	DRN
Data Reformatter Assembly	DRA
Data Regulations	DREG
Data Relay Satellite [*NASA*]	DRS
Data Relay Satellite System [*NASA*]	DRSS
Data Relay Station	DRS
Data Reorganization Utility [*Data processing*]	DRU
Data Report [*A publication*]	Data Rep
Data Report	DR
Data Reporting and Accounting	DR & A
Data Reporting Form	DRF
Data Request Keyboard	DRK
Data Requirement Description [*NASA*]	DRD
Data Requirement Form	DRF
Data Requirement List	DRL
Data Requirements [*NASA*]	DR
Data Requirements and Analysis	DR & A
Data Requirements/Change Request	DR/CR
Data Requirements Justification [*Military*]	DRJ
Data Requirements Review Board [*DoD*]	DRRB
Data Requirements Specification	DRS
Data Resources, Incorporated [*Information service*]	DRI
Data Resources Series [*Elsevier Book Series*] [*A publication*]	DRS
Data Retrieval Language [*National Bureau of Standards*]	DRL
Data Retrieval System [*Data processing*]	DRS
Data Return Capsule [*or Container*]	DRC
Data Review Technician	DRT
Data Routing and Error Detecting	DRED
Data Routing Indicator	DRI
Data Sampling Automatic Receiver	DSAR
Data Scanning	DS
Data Scanning and Formatting	DSF
Data Scanning and Routing	DSR
Data Selector and Tagger	DASAT

Data Self-Test Program	DSTP
Data Service Unit	DSU
Data Services Center [*International City Management Association*] [*Information service*]	DSC
Data Services Operations [*Informatics, Inc.*]	DSO
Data Services Planning Form	DSPF
Data Set [*Data processing*]	DS
Data Set Control Block [*Data processing*]	DSCB
Data Set Definition	DSD
Data Set Extension [*Data processing*]	DSE
Data Set Identification	DSID
Data Set Identifier	DSI
Data Set Label [*Data processing*]	DSL
Data Set Name	DSN
Data Set Ready	DSR
Data Sheet	DS
Data Source Panel	DSP
Data Source Terminal	DST
Data Specification Request	DSR
Data Standardization Project [*DoD*]	DSP
Data Status Display	DSD
Data Status Messages	DSM
Data Status Word	DSW
Data Storage [*Data processing*]	DS
Data Storage Device	DSD
Data Storage Distribution Unit	DSDU
Data Storage Electronics Assembly [*Apollo*] [*NASA*]	DSEA
Data Storage Equipment	DSE
Data Storage Memory	DSM
Data Storage and Retrieval	DSR
Data Storage and Retrieval	DS & R
Data Storage System	DSS
Data Storage Unit	DSU
Data and Structure Definition Language [*Data processing*]	DASDL
Data Structure Diagram	DSD
Data Structures Language [*Data processing*]	DSL
Data Submitted Information	DSI
Data Summary Sheets	DSS
Data Support Command [*Army*]	DATCOM
Data Survey Report	DSR
Data Switch Corp. [*NASDAQ symbol*]	DASW
Data Switching and Data Handling	DS & DH
Data Synchronization	DS
Data Synchronization [*or Synchronizer*] Unit	DSU
Data Synchronizer Channel	DSC
Data System	DS
Data System Development Plan	DSDP
Data System Integration [*NASA*]	DSI
Data Systems [*A publication*]	Data Sys
Data Systems [*A publication*]	Data Syst
Data Systems Administration	DSA
Data Systems and Analysis Directorate	DSAD
Data Systems Application Division [*Agricultural Research Service*]	DSAD
Data Systems Automation Office [*Columbus, Ohio*] [*Military*]	DSAO
Data Systems Automation Program	DSAP
Data Systems Design Center [*Air Force*]	DSDC
Data Systems Designator	DSD
Data Systems Engineering	DSE
Data Systems Environment Functions and Application Design [*Course*] [*Data processing*]	DSE/FAD
Data Systems Inquiry	DSI
Data Systems and Mathematics Staff [*Bureau of Radiological Health*]	DSMS
Data Systems Modernization	DSM
Data Systems News [*A publication*]	Data Systems N
Data Systems Office	DSO
Data Systems Specification	DSS
Data Systems and Statistics	DS & S
Data Systems Supervisor	DSS
Data Systems Support Office	DASSO
Data Systems Technician [*Navy rating*]	DS
Data Systems Technician, Chief [*Navy rating*]	DSC
Data Systems Technician, First Class [*Navy rating*]	DS1
Data Systems Technician, Master Chief [*Navy rating*]	DSCM
Data Systems Technician, Second Class [*Navy rating*]	DS2
Data Systems Technician, Senior Chief [*Navy rating*]	DSCS
Data Systems Technician, Third Class [*Navy rating*]	DS3
Data Systems Test [*Formerly, DAT*]	DST
Data Takeoff [*Air Force*]	DTO
Data Telemetering Register	DTR
Data Telemetry Exploitation Aid	DTEA
Data Terminal Equipment [*Data processing*]	DTE
Data Terminal Ready	DTR
Data Terminal Set	DTS
Data Terminal Systems, Inc. [*NYSE symbol*] [*Delisted*]	DTS
Data Test Station	DTS
Data Transcriber	DT
Data Transfer and Certification Record	DTCR
Data Transfer Command Word	DTCW
Data Transfer Rate	DTR
Data Transfer System [*Army*]	DTS
Data Transfer Timing	DTT
Data Transfer Unit	DTU
Data-Transition Tracking Loop	DTTL
Data Translator	DT
Data Transmission	DT
Data Transmission Center	DTC
Data Transmission Co.	DATRAN
Data Transmission and Control System	DTCS
Data Transmission Factor	DTF
Data Transmission Feature	DTF
Data Transmission Function	DTF
Data Transmission Generator	DTG
Data Transmission and Processing	DATAP
Data Transmission/Recording Subsystem	DT/RSS
Data Transmission and Switching	DTAS
Data Transmission System	DATS
Data Transmission System [*Air Force*]	DTS
Data Transmission Unit	DTU
Data Transmittal Form	DTF
Data Transmittal and Routing Form	DTRF
Data Transmitting Equipment	DTE
Data Under Voice [*Bell System*]	DUV
Data Universal Numbering System	DUNS
Data Update Edit Language [*Data processing*]	DUEL
Data Use and Access Laboratories [*Information service*]	DUALABS
Data Use Identifier	DUI
Data Users' Note [*NASA*]	DUN
Data Utilization Center [*Navy*]	DUC
Data Utilization Station	DUS
Data Valid	DAV
Data Validation Program [*NASA*]	DVP
Data Vetting	DV
Data/Voice Data	D/VD
Data Word Buffer [*Data processing*]	DW
Databank of Program Evaluations [*UCLA*]	DOPE
Database Acquisition for Student Health	DASH
Database Journal [*A publication*]	Database Jrnl
Database Reference [*A publication*]	D/R
Datacopy Corp. [*NASDAQ symbol*]	DCPY
Dataflex Corp. [*NASDAQ symbol*]	DFLX
Dataflow Systems, Inc. [*Information service*]	DfS
Datakey, Inc. [*NASDAQ symbol*]	DKEY
Datamarine International [*NASDAQ symbol*]	DMAR
Datamation Industry Directory	DID
Dataphone Switched Digital Service [*AT & T*]	DSDS
Datapoint Corp. [*NYSE symbol*]	DPT
Datapower, Inc. [*NASDAQ symbol*]	DPWR
Dataproducts Corporation [*American Stock Exchange symbol*]	DPC
Dataram Corp. [*American Stock Exchange symbol*]	DTM
Datascope Computer Output Microfilmer	DACOM
Datascope Corp. [*NASDAQ symbol*]	DSCP
Datasouth Computer [*NASDAQ symbol*]	DSCC
Dataspeed, Inc. [*NASDAQ symbol*]	DTSP
Datatab Inc. [*NASDAQ symbol*]	DTAB
Datatrak, Inc. [*NASDAQ symbol*]	DTRK
Datatron Assembly System	DAS
Datatron, Inc. [*NASDAQ symbol*]	DTRN
Datatron Users' Organization	DUO
Datavision, Inc. [*NASDAQ symbol*]	DVIS
Date	D
Date	DT
Date Arrived Station [*Military*]	DAS
Date of Availability [*Military*]	DOA
Date of Birth	DOB
Date of Change	DOC
Date of Change of Accountability [*Military*]	DOCA
Date of Current Appointment [*Military*]	DOCA
Date of Current Enlistment [*Military*]	DOCE
Date Deficiency [*or Discrepancy*] Discovered	DDD
Date Departed Continental United States [*Military*]	DDCONUS
Date Departed Last Duty Station [*Military*]	DDLDS
Date Departed United States [*Military*]	DDUS
Date of Departure [*Military*]	DODPRT
Date Draft [*Business and trade*]	D/D
Date Eligible for Return from Overseas [*Military*]	DEROS
Date of Enlistment [*Military*]	DOE
Date of Entering Office	EOD
Date of Entry [*Military*]	DE
Date of Estimated Return from Overseas [*Military*]	DEROS
Date Expected Delivery [*Medicine*]	DED
Date of Extension [*Military*]	DE
Date Filed [*IRS*]	DF
Date of Full Availability	DOFA
Date Growers' Institute	DGI
Date of Initial Appointment	DIA
Date Material Required	DMR
Date Number	DN
Date of Permanent Grade	DPG
Date and Place of Birth	DPOB
Date of Rank [*Air Force*]	DOR
Date of Rank [*Air Force*]	DR

Date of Rank, Current Grade [*Air Force*] ..... DORCG
Date of Rank, Permanent Grade [*Air Force*] ..... DORPG
Date of Request ..... DOR
Date Required to Load ..... DRL
Date Returned from Overseas [*Military*] ..... DROS
Date of Separation [*Military*] ..... DOS
Date of Service [*Military*] ..... DS
Date-Time Group [*Group of figures at head of radio or Teletype message indicating filing time*] ..... DTG
Dated ..... D/D
Dated ..... DTD
Dated Forecast Authorization Equipment Data ..... DFAED
Datenbank fuer Wassergefahrdende Stoffe [*Data Bank on Substances Harmful to Water*] [*West Germany*] [*Information service*] ..... DABAWAS
Datenverarbeitung in der Medizin [*A publication*] ..... Datenverarb Med
DATICO [*Digital Automatic Tape Intelligence Checkout*] **Missile Interface Simulator** ..... DMIS
Dating Problems Checklist [*Psychology*] ..... DPC
Dative ..... DAT
Datricon Corp. [*NASDAQ symbol*] ..... DATN
Datron Corp. [*NASDAQ symbol*] ..... DATR
Datsun Owners Club ..... DOC
Datum ..... D
Datum ..... DAT
Datum Collection of Tokai Regional Fisheries Research Laboratory [*A publication*] ..... Datum Collect Tokai Reg Fish Res Lab
Datum, Inc. [*NASDAQ symbol*] ..... DATM
Datur Omnibus Mori [*It Is Allotted unto All to Die*] [*Latin*] ..... DOM
Daughter ..... D
Daughter ..... DA
Daughter ..... DAU
Daughter ..... DAUGR
Daughter ..... DT
Daughter [*Citizens band radio slang*] ..... XYD
Daughter and Co-Heiress [*Genealogy*] ..... D & COH
Daughter and Heiress [*Genealogy*] ..... D & H
Daughter Of [*Genealogy*] ..... D/O
[*National Council*] **Daughters of America** ..... D of A
Daughters of the American Revolution, Hendrick Hudson Chapter, Hudson, NY [*Library symbol*] ..... NHudDAR
Daughters of the American Revolution, Washington, DC [*Library symbol*] ..... DNDAR
Daughters of Bilitis [*Superseded by United Sisters*] ..... DOB
Daughters of Bosses ..... DOB
Daughters of Charity of the Sacred Heart [*Roman Catholic religious order*] ..... FCSCJ
Daughters of Charity of St. Vincent de Paul [*Roman Catholic religious order*] ..... DC
Daughters of the Cincinnati ..... DC
Daughters of the Confederacy ..... D of C
Daughters of the Cross [*Roman Catholic religious order*] ..... DC
Daughters of the Cross of Liege [*Roman Catholic religious order*] ..... FC
Daughters of the Defenders of the Republic, USA ..... DDR
Daughters of Divine Charity [*Roman Catholic religious order*] ..... FDC
Daughters of the Divine Redeemer [*Roman Catholic religious order*] ..... DDR
Daughters of the Elderly Bridging the Unknown Together ..... DEBUT
Daughters of Evrytania ..... DE
Daughters of the Heart of Mary [*Roman Catholic religious order*] ..... DHM
Daughters of the Holy Spirit [*Roman Catholic religious order*] ..... DHS
Daughters of the Immaculate Heart of Mary [*Roman Catholic religious order*] ..... IHM
Daughters of Isabella, International Circle ..... DIIC
Daughters of Jesus [*Roman Catholic religious order*] ..... FI
Daughters of the King ..... DK
Daughters of Mary Help of Christians [*Salesian Sisters of St. John Bosco*] [*Roman Catholic religious order*] ..... FMA
Daughters of Mary Immaculate [*Marianist Sisters*] [*Roman Catholic religious order*] ..... FMI
Daughters of Mary of the Immaculate Conception [*Roman Catholic religious order*] ..... DM
Daughters of Mary and Joseph [*Roman Catholic religious order*] ..... DMJ
Daughters of the Most Holy Redeemer [*Roman Catholic religious order*] ..... DMHR
Daughters of the Nile, Supreme Temple ..... DNST
Daughters of Our Lady of Mercy [*Roman Catholic religious order*] ..... DM
Daughters of Penelope ..... DP
Daughters of the Republic of Texas ..... DRT
Daughters of the Republic of Texas Museum, Austin, TX [*Library symbol*] ..... TxAuDR
Daughters of the Revolution ..... DR
Daughters of the Sacred Heart of Jesus [*Bethlemita Sisters*] [*Roman Catholic religious order*] ..... SCIF
Daughters of St. Francis of Assisi [*Roman Catholic religious order*] ..... DSF
Daughters of St. Mary of Providence [*Roman Catholic religious order*] ..... DSMP
Daughters of St. Paul, Missionary Sisters of the Catholic Editions [*Roman Catholic religious order*] ..... DSP
Daughters of St. Rita of the Immaculate Heart [*Roman Catholic religious order*] ..... DSR
Daughters of Scotia ..... D of S
Daughters and Sons United ..... D & SU
Daughters of Union Veterans of the Civil War ..... DUV
Daughters of Utah Pioneers Museum Library, Salt Lake City, UT [*Library symbol*] ..... USID
Daughters of Wisdom [*Montfort Sisters*] [*Roman Catholic religious order*] ..... DW
Daunorubicin [*Daunomycin, Rubidomycin*] [*Also, DNR, DRB, R*] [*Antineoplastic drug*] ..... D
Daunorubicin [*Daunomycin*] [*Also, D, DRB, R*] [*Antineoplastic drug*] ..... DNR
Daunorubicin [*Daunomycin*] [*Also, D, DNR, R*] [*Antineoplastic drug*] ..... DRB
Daunorubicin, Oncovin [*Vincristine*], **ara-C, Prednisone** [*Antineoplastic drug regimen*] ..... DOAP
Dauphin [*Canada*] [*Airport symbol*] ..... YDN
Dauphin County Library System, Harrisburg, PA [*OCLC symbol*] ..... HBP
Dauphin County Library System, Harrisburg, PA [*Library symbol*] ..... PHarD
Dauphin Deposit Corp. [*NASDAQ symbol*] ..... DAPN
Dauphin, MB [*Television station call letters*] ..... CBWST
Dauphin, MB [*Radio station call letters*] ..... CKDM
Dauphin Public Library, Dauphin, MB, Canada [*Library symbol*] [*Obsolete*] ..... CaMDa
Davao [*Philippines*] [*Geomagnetic observatory code*] ..... DAV
Davao [*Philippines*] [*Airport symbol*] ..... DVO
Davao [*Philippines*] [*Seismograph station code, US Geological Survey*] ..... DAV
Davenport [*Washington*] [*Seismograph station code, US Geological Survey*] ..... DVW
Davenport, IA [*Location identifier*] [*FAA*] ..... CVA
Davenport, IA [*Location identifier*] [*FAA*] ..... DVN
Davenport, IA [*Radio station call letters*] ..... KALA
Davenport, IA [*Television station call letters*] ..... KDAV
Davenport, IA [*Radio station call letters*] ..... KIIK
Davenport, IA [*Television station call letters*] ..... KLJB
Davenport, IA [*Radio station call letters*] ..... KRVR
Davenport, IA [*Radio station call letters*] ..... KSTT
Davenport, IA [*Radio station call letters*] ..... KXRK
Davenport, IA [*Radio station call letters*] ..... WOC
Davenport, IA [*Television station call letters*] ..... WOC-TV
Davenport Library, Bath, NY [*Library symbol*] ..... NBa
Davenport Public Library, Davenport, IA [*Library symbol*] ..... IaDa
Davenport Public Library, Davenport, IA [*OCLC symbol*] ..... IOS
Davenport Public Museum, Davenport, IA [*Library symbol*] ..... IaDaM
Davenport, Rock Island, & North Western Railway Co. [*AAR code*] ..... DRI
David [*Panama*] [*Airport symbol*] ..... DAV
David A. Howe Public Library, Wellsville, NY [*Library symbol*] ..... NWel
David Herbert Lawrence [*British novelist, 1885-1930*] ..... DHL
David Jamison Carlyle [*NASDAQ symbol*] ..... DJCC
David Lipscomb College [*Tennessee*] ..... DLC
David Lipscomb College, Nashville, TN [*OCLC symbol*] ..... TDL
David Lipscomb College, Nashville, TN [*Library symbol*] ..... TNL
David Minerals Ltd. [*NASDAQ symbol*] ..... DAMIF
David Sarnoff Research Center [*RCA*] ..... DSRC
David Syme & Co. Ltd., Melbourne, V, Australia [*Library symbol*] ..... AuMDS
David Thompson University Centre [*Formerly, Notre Dame University of Nelson*], **Nelson, BC, Canada** [*Library symbol*] ..... CaBNND
David W. Taylor Model Basin [*Also, DTMB, TMB*] [*Later, DTNSRDC, NSRDC*] ..... DATMOBAS
David W. Taylor Model Basin [*Also, DATMOBAS, TMB*] [*Later, DTNSRDC, NSRDC*] ..... DTMB
David W. Taylor Model Basin [*Also, DATMOBAS, DTMB*] [*Later, DTNSRDC, NSRDC*] ..... TMB
David W. Taylor Naval Ship Research and Development Center [*Also, NSRDC*] ..... DTNSRDC
Davidon-Fletcher-Powell [*Method*] ..... DFP
Davidson College, Davidson, NC [*Library symbol*] ..... NcDaD
Davidson College, Davidson, NC [*OCLC symbol*] ..... NNM
Davidson County Community College, Lexington, NC [*Library symbol*] ..... NcLxDC
Davidson County Public Library, Lexington, NC [*Library symbol*] ..... NcLxD
Davidson Laboratory [*Stevens Institute of Technology*] ..... DL
Davidson, NC [*Radio station call letters*] ..... WDAV
Davie, FL [*Radio station call letters*] ..... WAVS
Davis [*Australia*] [*Geomagnetic observatory code*] ..... DVS
Davis Airlines [*Bryan, TX*] [*FAA designator*] ..... DVA
Davis-Bacon Act [*1921*] ..... DBA
Davis, CA [*Radio station call letters*] ..... KDVS
Davis, CA [*Radio station call letters*] ..... KYLO
Davis Computer Systems, Inc. ..... DCS
Davis County Genealogical Society, Bloomfield, IA [*Library symbol*] ..... IaBlGen
Davis County Library, Farmington, UT [*Library symbol*] ..... UFD
Davis County Republican, Bloomfield, IA [*Library symbol*] ..... IaBlDR
Davis and Elkins College [*West Virginia*] ..... DEC
Davis and Elkins College, Elkins, WV [*OCLC symbol*] ..... WVD
Davis and Elkins College, Elkins, WV [*Library symbol*] ..... WvED
Davis Polk & Wardwell Library, New York, NY [*OCLC symbol*] ..... DPW
Davis Water & Waste [*NASDAQ symbol*] ..... DWWS
Davison United States Army Airfield ..... DUSAA
Davisson-Germer Experiment [*Physics*] ..... DGE
Davy Crockett [*A tactical atomic weapon*] [*Army*] ..... DC
Daw [*New Britain*] [*Seismograph station code, US Geological Survey*] [*Closed*] ..... DAW

Dawe Digest [*A publication*] ... Dawe Dig
Dawn Bible Students Association ... DBSA
Dawn and Dusk Combat Air Patrol ... DADCAP
Dawson College, Glendive, MT [*Library symbol*] ... MtGD
Dawson County Junior College [*Montana*] ... DCJC
Dawson Creek [*Canada*] [*Airport symbol*] ... YDQ
Dawson Creek, BC [*Radio station call letters*] ... CJDC
Dawson Creek, BC [*Television station call letters*] ... CJDC-TV
Dawson Creek Public Library, Dawson Creek, BC, Canada [*Library symbol*] ... CaBDC
Dawson, GA [*Television station call letters*] ... WACS-TV
Dawson, GA [*Radio station call letters*] ... WAZE
Dawson, GA [*Radio station call letters*] ... WHIA
Dawson Geophysical [*NASDAQ symbol*] ... DWSN
Dawson Public Library, Dawson, YT, Canada [*Library symbol*] ... CaYDaw
Daxor Corp. [*NASDAQ symbol*] ... DAXR
Day [*Approach and landing charts*] [*Aviation*] ... D
Day ... DA
Day [*SI symbol*] ... d
Day-After Recall [*Advertising*] ... DAR
Day of Ammunition ... DOA
Day Book ... DB
Day Care Center ... DCC
Day Care and Early Education [*A publication*] ... Day Care & Early Educ
Day Frequency ... DFQ
Day Hospital ... DH
Day Letter [*Telegraphy*] ... DL
[*A*] **Day in the Life of Hawaii** [*Coffee-table book by Workman Publishing*] ... DITLOHA
Day Mines, Incorporated [*American Stock Exchange symbol*] [*Delisted*] ... DMI
Day and Night [*Approach and landing charts*] [*Aviation*] ... DN
Day-Night Capability [*Aerospace*] ... DNC
Day and Night Television System [*Army*] ... DANTS
Day-Old ... DO
Day Plane Guard [*Military*] ... DPLG
Day Room Orderly [*Army*] ... DRO
Day Sailer Association ... DSA
Day-Second-Foot [*Measurement*] ... DSF
Day of Supply [*Military*] ... DOFS
Day of Supply [*Military*] ... D of S
Day of Year ... DOY
Daybreak ... DABRK
Dayco Corp. [*NYSE symbol*] ... DAY
Daydream Island [*Australia*] [*Airport symbol*] ... DDI
Daylight ... DALGT
Daylight ... DL
Daylight Impression [*Psychical research*] ... DI
Daylight Opening ... DLO
Daylight Saving Time ... DST
Daylight Time ... DT
Daylight View Plan Position Indicator ... DVPPI
Daylin, Inc. [*American Stock Exchange symbol*] [*Delisted*] ... DLN
Days after Acceptance [*Business and trade*] ... DA
Days before Anthesis [*Botany*] ... DBA
Days after Contract [*Business and trade*] ... DAC
Days after Contract Award [*Business and trade*] ... DACA
Day's Date ... DD
Days after Date [*Business and trade*] ... DD
Days Delay at Address within CONUS [*Continental United States*] **Authorized Chargeable as Leave** [*Military*] ... DDALVAHP
Days Delay Enroute Authorized Chargeable as Leave [*Military*] ... DDALV
Days after Delivery ... DD
Days before Launch [*Usually followed by a number*] [*NASA*] ... L-
Days Lost [*Military*] ... DL
Days before Move Operation [*Usually followed by a number*] [*NASA*] ... M-
Days of Our Lives [*NBC-TV daytime serial*] ... DOOL
Days' Purposes [*Shipping*] ... DP
Days after Sight [*Business and trade*] ... DS
Days of Supply [*Rations*] ... DOS
Days a Week [*Classified advertising*] ... DAW
Daystrom Analog-to-Digital Integrating Translator ... DADIT
Daytime Broadcasters Association [*Defunct*] ... DBA
Dayton [*Ohio*] [*Airport symbol*] ... DAY
Dayton Air Force Depot ... DAFD
Dayton Area Office [*Energy Research and Development Administration*] ... DAO
Dayton Art Institute, Dayton, OH [*Library symbol*] ... ODaA
Dayton-Hudson Corp. [*NYSE symbol*] ... DH
Dayton-Miami Valley Library Consortium - Library Division [*Library network*] ... DMVC
Dayton and Montgomery County Public Library, Dayton, OH [*OCLC symbol*] ... DMM
Dayton and Montgomery County Public Library, Dayton, OH [*Library symbol*] ... ODa
Dayton Museum of Natural History, Dayton, OH [*Library symbol*] ... ODaMNH
Dayton, OH [*Location identifier*] [*FAA*] ... ATD
Dayton, OH [*Location identifier*] [*FAA*] ... DAY
Dayton, OH [*Location identifier*] [*FAA*] ... JQC
Dayton, OH [*Location identifier*] [*FAA*] ... VUQ
Dayton, OH [*Radio station call letters*] ... WAVI
Dayton, OH [*Radio station call letters*] ... WDAO
Dayton, OH [*Radio station call letters*] ... WDPS
Dayton, OH [*Television station call letters*] ... WDTN
Dayton, OH [*Radio station call letters*] ... WGXM
Dayton, OH [*Radio station call letters*] ... WHIO
Dayton, OH [*Radio station call letters*] ... WHIO-FM
Dayton, OH [*Television station call letters*] ... WHIO-TV
Dayton, OH [*Radio station call letters*] ... WING
Dayton, OH [*Television station call letters*] ... WKEF
Dayton, OH [*Radio station call letters*] ... WONE
Dayton, OH [*Radio station call letters*] ... WSMR-FM
Dayton, OH [*Radio station call letters*] ... WTUE
Dayton, OH [*Radio station call letters*] ... WWSU
Dayton Power & Light Co. [*NYSE symbol*] ... DPL
Dayton, TN [*Location identifier*] [*FAA*] ... DTE
Dayton, TN [*Radio station call letters*] ... WDNT
Dayton, TN [*Radio station call letters*] ... WKOE
Dayton, TN [*Radio station call letters*] ... WLCX
Daytona Beach [*Florida*] [*Airport symbol*] ... DAB
Daytona Beach, FL [*Radio station call letters*] ... WDAT
Daytona Beach, FL [*Radio station call letters*] ... WDOQ
Daytona Beach, FL [*Television station call letters*] ... WESH-TV
Daytona Beach, FL [*Radio station call letters*] ... WMFJ
Daytona Beach, FL [*Radio station call letters*] ... WNDB
Daytona Beach, FL [*Radio station call letters*] ... WROD
Daytona Beach, FL [*Radio station call letters*] ... WWLV
DB-Panhard Registry ... DBPR
DB, Sound Engineering Magazine [*A publication*] ... DB Sound Eng Mag
DBA Systems, Inc. [*NASDAQ symbol*] ... DBAS
DBH [*Dopamine Beta-Hydroxylase*] **Index** ... DBHI
DC Bar Journal [*A publication*] ... DCB J
DC Trading & Development [*NASDAQ symbol*] ... DCTR
DCAS [*Defense Contract Administration Services*] **Quality Assurance Staff Development Office** ... DQADO
DCASR [*Defense Contract Administration Services Region*], **Atlanta** ... DCRA
DCASR [*Defense Contract Administration Services Region*], **Boston** ... DCRB
DCASR [*Defense Contract Administration Services Region*], **Chicago** ... DCRI
DCASR [*Defense Contract Administration Services Region*], **Cleveland** ... DCRO
DCASR [*Defense Contract Administration Services Region*], **Dallas** ... DCRT
DCASR [*Defense Contract Administration Services Region*], **Detroit** ... DCRD
DCASR [*Defense Contract Administration Services Region*], **Los Angeles** ... DCRL
DCASR [*Defense Contract Administration Services Region*], **New York** ... DCRN
DCASR [*Defense Contract Administration Services Region*], **Philadelphia** ... DCRP
DCASR [*Defense Contract Administration Services Region*], **St. Louis** ... DCRS
DCASR [*Defense Contract Administration Services Region*], **San Francisco** ... DCRC
DCL, Inc. [*American Stock Exchange symbol*] [*Delisted*] ... DCL
DCNY Corp. [*NASDAQ symbol*] ... DCNY
DCSLOG [*Deputy Chief of Staff for Logistics*] **Data Processing Center** [*Military*] ... DDPC
DDC [*Defense Documentation Center*] **Retrieval and Indexing Terminology** [*DoD*] ... DRIT
DDL Foodshow [*Food emporium which derives its name from its creator, movie producer Dino DeLaurentiis*] ... DDL
De Andreis Seminary, Lemont, IL [*Library symbol*] ... ILeD
De Badande Vannerna [*Sweden*] ... DBV
De Bilt [*Netherlands*] [*Later, WIT*] [*Geomagnetic observatory code*] ... DBN
De Bilt [*Netherlands*] [*Seismograph station code, US Geological Survey*] ... DBN
De Bonis Non [*Of the Goods Not Yet Administered*] ... DBN
De Bow's Commercial Review [*A publication*] ... De Bow
De Dato [*Of Today's Date*] [*Latin*] ... DD
De Die [*Daily*] [*Pharmacy*] ... DD
De Die in Diem [*From Day to Day*] [*Latin*] ... DD in D
De Die in Diem [*From Day to Day*] [*Latin*] ... DE D in D
DE, Domestic Engineering [*Formerly, DE Journal*] [*A publication*] ... DE Dom Eng
De Economist [*A publication*] ... DeEc
De-Evolution [*Acronym is name of musical group*] ... DEVO
De Funiak Springs, FL [*Radio station call letters*] ... WGTX
De Funiak Springs, FL [*Radio station call letters*] ... WQUH
De Funiak Springs, FL [*Radio station call letters*] ... WZEP
De Gids [*A publication*] ... Gids
De Graff, OH [*Radio station call letters*] ... WDEQ-FM
De Haas-van Alphen [*Effect*] ... DHVA
De Havilland Aircraft of Canada Ltd., Downsview, Toronto, ON, Canada [*Library symbol*] ... CaOTDHA
De Homine [*A publication*] ... DeH
DE Journal [*Later, DE, Domestic Engineering*] [*A publication*] ... DE/J
DE. Journal of Dental Engineering [*A publication*] ... DE
DE. Journal of Dental Engineering [*A publication*] ... DE J Dent Eng
De Kalb, IL [*Radio station call letters*] ... WDEK
De Kalb, IL [*Radio station call letters*] ... WLBK
De Kalb, IL [*Radio station call letters*] ... WNIU-FM
De Kalb & Western Transportation R. R. [*AAR code*] ... DKWT

De Katholick [*A publication*] .... DKath
De La Rue Automatic Cash System [*Banknote-disbursing equipment*] [*British*] .... DACS
De Land, FL [*Radio station call letters*] .... WELE-FM
De Land, FL [*Radio station call letters*] .... WXVQ
De Luxe Check Print [*NYSE symbol*] .... DLX
De Maasgouw. Orgaan voor Limbrugsche Geschiedenis, Taal- en Letterkunde [*A publication*] .... DMG
De Navorscher [*A publication*] .... DNav
De Nieuwe Taglalgids [*A publication*] .... DNT
De Odeon Kring [*The Odeon Club, for homosexuals*] [*Holland*] .... DOK
De Paul Law Review [*A publication*] .... De Paul L Rev
De Paul University [*Illinois*] .... DEPU
De Paul University, Chicago, IL [*OCLC symbol*] .... IAC
De Paul University, Chicago, IL [*Library symbol*] .... ICD
De Paul University, Law Library, Chicago, IL [*OCLC symbol*] .... IBC
De Paul University, Law Library, Chicago, IL [*Library symbol*] .... ICD-L
De Pauw University, Archives, Greencastle, IN [*Library symbol*] .... InGrD-Ar
De Pauw University, Greencastle, IN [*OCLC symbol*] .... IDU
De Pauw University, Greencastle, IN [*Library symbol*] .... InGrD
De Pere, WI [*Radio station call letters*] .... WJLW
De Profundis .... DP
De Proprietatibus Litterarum [*A publication*] .... DPL
De Queen, AR [*Radio station call letters*] .... KDQN
De Queen, AR [*Radio station call letters*] .... KDQN-FM
De Queen & Eastern Railroad Co. [*AAR code*] .... DQE
De-Rating Appeals [*Legal*] [*British*] .... DRA
De Ridder, LA [*Location identifier*] [*FAA*] .... DRI
De Ridder, LA [*Location identifier*] [*FAA*] .... DSR
De Ridder, LA [*Radio station call letters*] .... KDLA
De Ridder, LA [*Radio station call letters*] .... KEAZ
De Rose Industries, Inc. [*American Stock Exchange symbol*] .... DRI
De Ruyter, NY [*Radio station call letters*] .... WOIV
De Sales Hall School of Theology, Hyattsville, MD [*Library symbol*] .... MdHyD
De Smet Public Library, De Smet, SD [*Library symbol*] .... SdDs
De Soto, Inc. [*NYSE symbol*] .... DSO
De Soto, Inc., Des Plaines, IL [*Library symbol*] .... IDesD
De Soto, MO [*Radio station call letters*] .... KHAD
De Soto National Memorial .... DESO
De Tour Area School and Public Library, De Tour Village, MI [*Library symbol*] .... MiDet
[*Don Juan*] **De Tro y Ortolano** [*Acronym identifies manuscript discovered in library of Don Juan De Tro y Ortolano in 1866*] .... TROANO
De Vrije Fries [*A publication*] .... VF
De Witt, AR [*Radio station call letters*] .... KDEW
De Witt, AR [*Radio station call letters*] .... KDEW-FM
Deacon .... D
Deacon .... DEA
Deacon .... DEAC
Deacon Air Ballistic .... DAB
Deacon and Martyr [*Church calendars*] .... DM
Deacon and Nike [*Research rocket*] .... DAN
Deaconess Community of St. Andrew [*Anglican religious community*] .... DssCSA
Deaconess Hospital, Medical Library, Cleveland, OH [*Library symbol*] .... OClDe
Deaconess Hospital, Milwaukee, WI [*Library symbol*] .... WMDe
Deaconess Hospital, Oklahoma City, OK [*Library symbol*] .... OkOkD
Deaconess Hospital, School of Nursing, Spokane, WA [*Library symbol*] .... WaSpD
Deactivate .... DACT
Deactivation .... DEACT
Dead [*or Deceased*] .... D
Dead Air Space .... D
Dead Air Space [*Physiology*] .... DS
Dead on Arrival [*Medicine*] .... DOA
Dead Band .... DB
Dead Cat Lying in the Road [*Traffic report*] .... DCLIR
Dead, Dying, Diseased, Disabled [*Food processors' classification of animals unfit for use*] 4-D
Dead Freight [*Shipping*] .... DF
Dead Heat .... DH
Dead Indian [*Careless man*] [*Army slang*] .... DI
Dead Letter Office [*US Postal Service*] .... DLO
Dead Light .... DL
Dead Load .... DL
Dead Reckoning [*Navigation*] .... DR
Dead Reckoning .... DREK
Dead Reckoning Analog [*or Analyzer*] **Indicator** .... DRAI
Dead Reckoning Analyzer .... DRA
Dead Reckoning Automatic Computer [*Obsolete*] .... DRACO
Dead Reckoning Equipment .... DRE
Dead Reckoning Indicator .... DRI
Dead Reckoning Own Ship .... DROS
Dead Reckoning Plotter .... DRP
Dead Reckoning Tracer [*RADAR*] .... DRT
Dead Reckoning Trainer .... DRT
Dead Reckoning Trainer .... DRTR
Dead Time .... DT
Dead Time Correction .... DTC
Dead Time Log .... DTL
Dead in the Water [*Navy*] .... DIW
Deadhead [*Freight*] .... DH
Deadhorse [*Alaska*] [*Airport symbol*] .... SCC
Deadhorse, AK [*Location identifier*] [*FAA*] .... SCC
Deadhorse, AK [*Location identifier*] [*FAA*] .... SKO
Deadline .... DL
Deadline Date .... DD
Deadline Date [*Air Force*] .... DLD
Deadline Delivery Date .... DDD
Deadly Weapon Act .... DWA
Deadman's Cay [*Bahamas*] [*Airport symbol*] .... LGI
Deadweight .... DW
Deadweight .... DWT
Deadweight All Told [*Shipping*] .... DWAT
Deadweight Capacity .... DWC
Deadweight Cargo Capacity [*Shipping*] .... DWCC
Deadweight Gauge .... DWG
Deadweight Tester .... DWT
Deadweight Tons [*Shipping*] .... DWT
Deadwood, SD [*Radio station call letters*] .... KDSJ
Deadwood, SD [*Radio station call letters*] .... KSQY
Deaerating .... DEARTG
Deaerating Cold Weather Oil System .... DCWOS
Deaerating Feed Tank .... DFT
Deaf Communicating Terminal [*Telephone for the deaf*] .... DCT
Deaf Sons of Master Masons .... DESOMS
Deafness Research Foundation .... DRF
Deafness Research and Training Center [*A publication*] .... Deafness Res & Train Cent
Deal-Cased Frame [*Carpentry*] .... DCF
Deal Proneness Index [*Marketing*] .... DPI
Dealer Bank Association .... DBA
Dealer Election Action Committee [*Campaign funding*] .... DEAC
Dealer Tankwagon [*Gasoline*] .... DTW
Dealers Art Exchange .... DAE
Deals and Battens [*Business and trade*] .... DB
Deals, Battens, and Boards [*Business and trade*] .... DBB
Deamino [*As substituent on nucleoside*] [*Biochemistry*] .... o
Deamino-D-arginine Vasopressin [*Antidiuretic*] .... DDAVP
Deaminophenylalaninedehydroproline [*Biochemistry*] .... DPD
Dean .... D
Dean and Chapter [*Anglican Church*] .... D & C
Dean of the Faculty .... DF
Dean of the Faculty, Aeronautics [*Air Force Academy*] .... DFAN
Dean Foods Co. [*NYSE symbol*] .... DF
Dean Witter Organization, Inc. [*Later, DWR*] [*NYSE symbol*] .... DW
Dean Witter Reynolds Organization, Inc. [*Formerly, DW*] [*NYSE symbol*] [*Delisted*] .... DWR
Dearborn Historical Museum, Dearborn, MI [*Library symbol*] .... MiDbHi
Dearborn, MI [*Radio station call letters*] .... WHFR
Dearborn, MI [*Radio station call letters*] .... WNIC
Dearborn, MI [*Radio station call letters*] .... WNIC-FM
Dearborn Public [*Henry Ford Centennial*] **Library, Dearborn, MI** [*Library symbol*] .... MiDb
Deargentur Pilulae [*Let The Pills Be Silverized*] [*Pharmacy*] .... DEARG PIL
Death .... D
Death from Accidental Injuries [*Military*] .... DAI
Death Certificate .... DC
Death from Disease [*Military*] .... DD
Death and Dying [*Medical course*] .... D & D
Death Education [*A publication*] .... Death Educ
Death Gratuity Payment [*Army*] .... DGRTP
Death Row .... DR
Death Valley [*California*] [*Airport symbol*] .... DTH
Death Valley National Monument .... DEVA
Deaurentur Pilulae [*Let The Pills Be Gilded*] [*Pharmacy*] .... DEAUR PIL
Deauretur [*Let It Be Gilded*] [*Pharmacy*] .... DEAUR
Deaza [*As substituent on nucleoside*] [*Biochemistry*] c
Deb Shops, Inc. [*NASDAQ symbol*] .... DEBS
Deballasted Test Vehicle .... DBT
Debark .... DEBK
Debarred Bidder's List .... DBL
Debater's Magazine [*A publication*] .... DM
Debbie Fox Foundation .... DFF
Debden-Pascal, SK [*Television station call letters*] CBKFT-3
DeBeers Consolidated Mines ADR [*NASDAQ symbol*] .... DBRSY
Debenture .... DB
Debenture .... DEB
Debility, Dependency, and Dread [*Factors producing compliance in hostages, prisoners, etc.*] .... DDD
Debit .... DB
Debit .... DEB
Debit Accounting Information Retrieval .... DAIR
Debit Collection .... DC
Debit Memo .... DM
Debit Note .... DN
Debit Request .... DR
Debita Spissitudo [*Proper Consistence*] [*Pharmacy*] .... DEB SPISS
Debrecen [*Hungary*] [*Seismograph station code, US Geological Survey*] [*Closed*] .... DEB

Debreceni Agrartudomanyi Egyetem, Debrecen, Hungary [*Library symbol*]..HuDeAgE

Debreceni Orvostudomanyi Egyetem, Debrecen, Hungary [*Library symbol*]..HuDeOE

Debreceni Reformatus Kollegium Nagykonyvtara, Debrecen, Hungary [*Library symbol*]...............................HuDeK

Debt Collection Agency ....DC

Debt and Correspondence Branch [*BUPERS*]..........D & CB

Debt Liquidation Schedule ....DLS

Debtor ....DR

Debtor Reporting System [*World Bank*].................DRS

Debtors Anonymous ....DA

Debugging Mode ....DM

Debutanized Pyrolysis Gasoline ....DPG

Debutante ....DEB

Debye [*Unit of electric moment*]..........................D

Debye Dipole Theory [*Physics*]............................DDT

Debye-Falkenhagen Effect [*Physics*].....................DFE

Debye-Hueckel Equation [*Physics*]........................DHE

Debye-Sears Cell [*Physics*]..................................DSC

Debye-Sears Effect [*Physics*]...............................DSE

Deca [*A prefix meaning multiplied by 10*] [*SI symbol*]......da

Deca [*or Deka*] [*A prefix meaning multiplied by 10*]......DK

Deca Energy Corp. [*NASDAQ symbol*]....................DCAS

Decabromodiphenyl Oxide [*Flame retardant*] [*Organic chemistry*].....DBDPO

Decade Counter ....DC

Decade Counting Assembly ....DCA

Decade Counting Unit..DCU

Decade Ratio Transformer ....DRT

Decade Resolver Bridge ....DRB

Decade of Short Stories [*A publication*].................Dec

Decade Synchro Bridge ....DSB

Decalcomania...DECAL

Decalitre ....DCL

Decalogue Society of Lawyers ....DSL

Decameter ....DAM

Decameter ....DM

Decametre ....DCM

Decamired ....DM

Decani [*Of the Dean*] [*Music*] ....DEC

Decanning Scuttle ....DS

Decanta [*Pour Off*] [*Pharmacy*]...........................DEC

Decanus Ruralis [*Rural Dean*]..............................DR

Decapacitation Factor [*with reference to sperm*] [*Medicine*]......DF

Decapitation, Disembowelment, and Dismemberment [*Types of movies*].............................3-D

Decarboxylase Base Moeller [*Medium*] [*Microbiology*]............DBM

Decathalon Association [*Acronym is used as name of association*]......DECA

Decatur [*Illinois*] [*Airport symbol*]........................DEC

Decatur, AL [*Radio station call letters*] ....WAJF

Decatur, AL [*Radio station call letters*] ....WBQM

Decatur, AL [*Radio station call letters*] ....WDRM

Decatur, AL [*Radio station call letters*] ....WHOS

Decatur, AL [*Radio station call letters*] ....WMSL

Decatur, AL [*Radio station call letters*] ....WRSA

Decatur Baptist College [*Iowa*]...........................DBC

Decatur Daily, Decatur, AL [*Library symbol*]...........ADeD

Decatur, GA [*Radio station call letters*].................WAVO

Decatur, GA [*Radio station call letters*].................WXLL

Decatur, IL [*Television station call letters*].............WAND

Decatur, IL [*Radio station call letters*]...................WDZ

Decatur, IL [*Radio station call letters*]...................WDZQ

Decatur, IL [*Radio station call letters*]...................WJMU

Decatur, IL [*Radio station call letters*]...................WSOY

Decatur, IL [*Radio station call letters*]...................WSOY-FM

Decatur, IN [*Radio station call letters*]...................WADM

Decatur, IN [*Radio station call letters*]...................WADM-FM

Decatur Memorial Hospital, Medical Staff and Nursing School Library, Decatur, IL [*Library symbol*].............IDecH

Decatur Public Library, Decatur, IL [*Library symbol*] ......IDec

Decatur Township Library, Webster Memorial Library Building, Decatur, MI [*Library symbol*]................MiDecD

Decay in Flight [*Nuclear physics*]..........................DIF

Decay Heat Removal System [*Nuclear energy*].......DHRS

Decay Rate Meter ....DRM

Decay Time ....DT

Decayed [*Quality of the bottom*] [*Nautical charts*]......dec

Decayed, Extracted, and Filled [*Teeth*] [*Dentistry*]......DEF

Decayed, Missing, Filled [*Dentistry*].....................DMF

Decayed, Missing, or Filled Surfaces [*of teeth*]......DMFS

Decayed, Missing, and Filled Teeth [*Dentistry*]......DMFT

Decaying Extrastellar Body [*Astronomy*]................DEB

Decca Integrated Airborne Navigator ....DIAN

Decca Records, Inc. [*NYSE symbol*] [*Delisted*].........DKA

Deccan College Monograph Series [*A publication*]......DCMS

Deceased ....D

Deceased ....DEC

Deceased ....DECD

Decelerate ....DCLR

Decelerate ....DCLRT

Deceleration ....DECEL

Deceleration Units of Gravity versus Time...............G vs T

Deceleration Units of Gravity Versus Velocity ....G vs V

Decelerator and Aileron [*NASA*]............................DECELERON

December ....D

December ....DEC

December ....DECR

Decennie Hydrologique Internationale [*International Hydrological Decade*] ....DHI

Decennie Internationale d'Exploration des Oceans [*International Decade of Ocean Exploration*]..........DIEO

Decent Suit of Civvies [*British slang military decoration*] [*World War I*] ....DSC

Decentralized Automated Service Support System [*Army*]................DAS3

Decentralized Data Processing Network System ......DNS

Decentralized Hospital Computer Program [*Veterans Administration*]..DHCP

Decentralized Open Network Architecture..............DONA

Decentralized Printing Program [*Army*] ....DPP

Deception Island [*Antarctica*] [*Seismograph station code, US Geological Survey*] [*Closed*].........................DEC

Deception Jamming System ....DJS

Deceptive Self-Screening Jammer ....DSSJ

Decessit [*Died*] [*Latin*] ....D

Decessit Sine Prole [*Died Without Issue*] [*Latin*]......DSP

Decessit Sine Prole Legitima [*Died Without Legitimate Issue*] [*Latin*] ... DSPL

Decessit Sine Prole Mascula [*Died Without Male Issue*] [*Latin*] ....DSPM

Decessit Sine Prole Mascula Superstita [*Died Without Surviving Male Issue*] [*Latin*].............DSPMS

Decessit Sine Prole Superstita [*Died Without Surviving Issue*] [*Latin*]..DSPS

Decessit Vita Matris [*Died during the Lifetime of the Mother*] [*Latin*]......DVM

Decessit Vita Patris [*Died during the Lifetime of the Father*] [*Latin*]........DVP

DECHEMA [*Deutsche Gesellschaft fuer Chemisches Apparatewesen*] Monographien [*A publication*]......DECHEMA Monogr

DECHEMA [*Deutsche Gesellschaft fuer Chemisches Appartewesen*] Stoffdaten Dienst [*DECHEMA Data Service*] [*West Germany*] [*Information service*].........DSD

Decheniana Beihefte [*A publication*] ....Decheniana Beih

Deci [*A prefix meaning divided by ten*] [*SI symbol*]......d

Decibel [*Symbol*] [*SI unit of sound level*]................dB

Decibel A-Weighted ....dB(A)

Decibel Above the Reference Coupling ....DBX

Decibel Meter ....DBM

Decibel Unit ....dBU

Decibels on the A Scale ....dba

Decibels, Adjusted ....dBA

Decibels Expanded [*Initialism is name of electronics company and brand name of its products*] ....dbx

Decibels above Milliwatt per Square Meter ....DB/M²

Decibels above One Carrier ....dBc

Decibels above One Kilowatt ....dBK

Decibels above One Milliwatt...............................dBM

Decibels above One Milliwatt, Referred to or Measured at a Point of Zero Transmission Level, Psophometrically Weighted dBm0p

Decibels above One Picowatt...............................dBP

Decibels above One Volt.....................................dBV

Decibels above One Watt....................................dBW

Decibels above Reference Acoustic Power ....dBRAP

Decibels above Reference Noise...........................dBRN

Decibels above Reference Noise, C-Message Weighted ......dBRNC

Decibels per Square Meter ....DBSM

Deciduous..D

Deciduous..DECID

Deciduous Fruit Grower [*A publication*]................Deciduous Fruit Grow

Decigram ....DCG

Decigram ....DG

Deciliter ....DL

Decimal ....D

Decimal ....DEC

Decimal Add ....DA

Decimal Adjust Accumulator ....DAA

Decimal-to-Analog ....DA

Decimal to Binary [*Data processing*].....................D/B

Decimal to Binary [*Data processing*].....................DTB

Decimal Classification ....DC

Decimal Code Binaire [*Binary Coded Decimal*] [*Data processing*]......DCB

Decimal Code Translator ....DCT

Decimal Counting Unit ....DCU

Decimal Digit ....DECIT

Decimal Digital Differential Analyzer ....DDDA

Decimal Divide ....DD

Decimal Equivalent Chart ....DEC

Decimal Factor ....DF

Decimal Fraction ....DF

Decimal to Hexadecimal ....D-H

Decimal Index of Art in the Lowlands [*A publication*] ......DIAL

Decimal Keyboard [*Data processing*].....................DKB

Decimal Multiply ....DM

Decimal Number ....DN

Decimal Number System.....................................DNS

Decimal to Octal [*Data processing*] ... D-O
Decimal to Octal Conversion ... DOC
Decimal Register Binary ... DRB
Decimal Subtract ... DS
Decimal Voltage Output ... DVO
Decimalisation Day [*February 15, 1971, day English money was decimalized*] ... D (Day)
Decimeter ... DE
Decimeter ... DECIM
Decimeter ... DM
Decimeter Height-Finder [*RADAR*] ... DMH
Decinem [*One-tenth of a NEM*] [*See NEM*] ... dn
Decineper ... dN
Decision ... DEC
Decision ... DECN
Decision [*A publication*] ... Decs
Decision Acknowledge ... DAK
Decision Aiding Information System ... DAISY
Decision Aids for Resource Expenditure ... DARE
Decision Circuit Reception ... DCR
Decision Coordinating Paper ... DCP
Decision Data Computer Corporation [*NASDAQ symbol*] ... DDCC
Decision, Design, and the Computer [*Symposium*] ... DDC
Decision Element ... DE
Decision Error ... DE
Decision Evaluation and Logic ... DEAL
Decision Expediting [*Graphic Sciences, Inc., copying machine*] ... DEX
Decision Height [*Aviation*] ... DH
Decision Information Distribution System ... DIDS
Decision Information Distribution System - Civil Defense ... DIDS-CD
Decision Information Services Ltd. [*Information service*] ... DIS
Decision Leaflets [*US Patent Office*] ... DL
Decision Logic Table [*DoD*] ... DLT
Decision Maker ... DM
Decision/Making/Information [*Information service*] ... D/M/I
Decision Making System ... DMS
Decision Mapping via Optimum Go-No Networks ... DEMON
Decision-Oriented Evaluation System ... DOES
Decision-Oriented Scheduling System ... DOSS
Decision Outstanding ... DOS
Decision Package Sets ... DPS
Decision Process Pattern ... DPP
Decision Response Time ... DRT
Decision Sciences Corporation ... DSC
Decision Sheet ... DS
Decision Support System ... DSS
Decision and Switching ... DS
Decision Systems, Inc. [*NASDAQ symbol*] ... DCSNC
Decision Table [*Data processing*] ... DETAB
Decision Table [*Data processing*] ... DT
Decision Table to COBOL Processor [*Data processing*] ... DETOC
Decision Table Experimental [*Data processing*] ... DETAB-X
Decision Table Processor [*IBM Corp.*] ... DETAP
Decision Table Processor [*IBM Corp.*] ... DTABL
Decision Table Translator [*Data processing*] ... DETRAN
Decision Threshold Computer ... DTC
Decision Unit [*Management*] ... DU
Decisions of the Comptroller General ... DCG
Decisions Lost [*Boxing*] ... LD
Decisions Won [*Boxing*] ... WD
Deck ... DK
Deck of Cards ... DOC
Deck Cargo ... DC
Deck Court ... DC
Deck Decompression Chamber [*Undersea technology*] ... DDC
Deck Drain Valve ... DDV
Deck Edge ... DKE
Deck Edge Light ... DELT
Deck Edge Outlet [*Navy*] ... DEO
Deck and Engineering Duties, General Service [*USNR officer designation*] ... DE
Deck Landing Control Officer [*British*] ... DLCO
Deck Landing Training ... DLT
Deck Landing Training School ... DLTS
Deck-Launched Intercept ... DLI
Deck Motion Compensator ... DMC
Deck Piercing ... DP
Deck Surface Light ... DSLT
Deck Watch [*A small chronometer*] [*Navy*] ... DW
[*Qualified for*] **Deck Watch** [*USNR officer classification*] ... WD
Deck Watch Time [*Navigation*] ... DWT
Deck Working Space ... DWS
Deckerville, MI [*Location identifier*] [*FAA*] ... DQV
Deckerville Public Library, Deckerville, MI [*Library symbol*] ... MiDeck
Deckle-Edged [*Paper*] ... DE
Declaration ... DEC
Declaration of Atlantic Unity [*Defunct*] ... DAU
Declaration of Independence House and Library [*An association*] ... DIHL
Declaration of Independence Second Centennial Commemorative National Committee ... DISCCNC
Declare ... DECL
Declared ... DECD
Declared Excess [*Military*] ... DE
Declared Excess Personal Property Catalog [*Military*] ... DEPPC
Declared National Program [*to share oceanographic data with other nations*] ... DNP
Declassified Documents Reference System ... DDRS
Declassify [*Military*] ... DECL
Declension ... DECL
Declension ... DECN
Declination ... D
Declination ... DEC
Declination of Launch Asymptote [*NASA*] ... DLA
Decline ... DECL
Declines Appointment ... DAP
Declines Transfer [*as offered*] ... DCLTR
Declining Error Rate ... DER
Declutch ... DCLU
Decoctum [*Decoction*] [*Pharmacy*] ... DECOCT
Decode ... DCD
Decoder ... DCDR
Decoder Driver ... DD
Decoder Switching Unit ... DSU
Decoding Memory Drive [*Data processing*] ... DE-ME-DRIVE
Decom Systems, Incorporated [*NASDAQ symbol*] ... DSII
Decommission ... DCMSN
Decommissioned ... DCMSND
Decommissioned ... DECOM
Decommissioning [*Date*] [*Navy*] ... DECOMG
Decommissioning [*Date*] [*Navy*] ... DECOMM
Decommutation ... DECOMM
Decommutation and Readout System [*Data processing*] ... DARS
Decommutator ... DECOM
Decommutator Conditioning Unit ... DCCU
Decommutator Distribution Unit ... DDU
Decompose ... DEC
Decomposed Ammonia Radioisotope Thruster [*Aerospace*] ... DART
Decomposition ... DECOMP
Decomposition Mathematical Programing System ... DECOMP
Decomposition Sintering ... DS
Decompression ... DECOMPN
Decompression ... DECOMPR
Decontaminate ... DECON
Decontaminate and Decommission [*Nuclear energy*] ... D & D
Decontaminating Agent, Noncorrosive ... DANC
Decontamination ... DC
Decontamination ... DECN
Decontamination ... DECONTN
Decontamination Factor ... DF
Decontrolled Defense Supply Material ... DDSM
Decor Corp. [*NASDAQ symbol*] ... DCOR
Decorah, IA [*Radio station call letters*] ... KDEC
Decorah, IA [*Radio station call letters*] ... KLCD
Decorah, IA [*Radio station call letters*] ... KWLC
Decoration ... DCR
Decoration ... DECRTN
Decoration and Design [*Building*] [*New York City*] ... D & D
Decoration for Exceptional Civilian Service [*Army civilian employee award*] ... DECS
Decorative ... DEC
Decorative Arts Trust ... DAT
Decorative Fabrics Institute [*Defunct*] ... DFI
Decorative Furniture Manufacturers Association [*Defunct*] ... DFM
Decorator Industries, Incorporated [*American Stock Exchange symbol*] ... DII
Decorators Club ... DC
Decoy [*Missile mission symbol*] ... D
Decoy Discrimination Group ... DDG
Decoy Discrimination RADAR ... DDR
Decoy Dispensing Set ... DDS
Decoy Ejection Mechanism ... DEM
Decrease ... DCR
Decrease ... DEC
Decrease ... DECR
Decrease Feedback ... Dec-FB
Decreased ... DECD
Decreased Fuel Ingestion ... DFI
Decreasing Consumption of Oxygen [*Endocrinology*] ... DECO
Decreasing Failure Rate ... DFR
Decreasing Failure Rate Average ... DFRA
Decreasing Mean Residual Life ... DMRL
Decrement ... DECR
Decrement Accumulator ... DAC
Decrescendo [*Decreasing in Loudness*] [*Music*] ... DECRES
Decrescendo [*Decreasing in Loudness*] [*Music*] ... DECRESC
Decretum [*Decree*] [*Latin*] ... D
Decubitus [*Lying Down*] [*By extension, the medical term for bedsores*] ... DECUB
Dedalo [*A publication*] ... Ded
Dedendum [*Design engineering*] ... DED
Dederunt [*They Gave*] [*Latin*] ... DD
Dedham Historical Society, Dedham, MA [*Library symbol*] ... MDedHi

Dedicated Display and Control Subsystem................DD & CS
Dedicated Displays...DD
Dedicated to Eliminating Acronymic Designations [An association]....DEAD
Dedicated Man/Months [Jet Propulsion Laboratory, NASA].............DMM
Dedicated Signal Conditioner...............................DSC
Dedicated Wooden Money Collectors...........................DWMC
Dedication..DEDIC
Dedit [or Dedicavit] [Gave, Dedicated] [Latin]..............DD
Deduct..DDT
Deduct..DED
Deductible Average Clause [Insurance].......................DAC
Deduction Theorem [Logic]....................................DT
Deductive Analysis of Missile Systems.........................DAMS
Deductive Communicator....................................DEDUCOM
Dee Scofield Awareness Program................................DSAP
Deed Poll..DP
Deel Mobile Target..DMT
Deep..D
Deep...DP
Deep Airborne Expendable Bathythermograph [Naval
　Oceanographic Office]......................................DAXBT
Deep Basing [Underground placement of missiles]...............DB
Deep Battle Area...DBA
Deep Breathe [Medicine]......................................DB
Deep Case Hardened..DCH
Deep Chlorophyll Maximum [Oceanography]......................DCM
Deep-Diving Research Vehicles.................................DRV
Deep-Diving System...DDS
Deep-Diving Vehicle..DDV
Deep-Drawn [Metals]...DD
Deep-Drawn Metal Part..DDMP
Deep Earth Penetrating Projectile.............................DEPP
Deep Electric Research Investigation [Navy]....................DERI
Deep Etch [Lithography term].................................DE
Deep Experimental Torpedo [Also, DSWS] [Later, EXTOR].......DEXTOR
Deep Foundations Institute....................................DFI
Deep Level Transient Spectroscopy.............................DLTS
Deep Ocean Environment......................................DOE
Deep Ocean Floor...DOF
Deep Ocean Installation......................................DOI
Deep Ocean Mining Environmental Study [National Oceanic and
　Atmospheric Administration].................................DOMES
Deep Ocean Object Location and Recovery......................DOOLAR
Deep Ocean Optical Measurement..............................DOOM
Deep Ocean Ordnance...DOO
Deep Ocean Research Vehicle..................................DORV
Deep Ocean Technology.......................................DOT
Deep Ocean Technology Project................................DOTP
Deep Ocean Test-in-Place and Observation System [Navy].......DOTIPOS
Deep Ocean Transponder......................................DOT
Deep Oceanic Turbulence......................................DOT
Deep Oceanographic Survey Vehicle [Naval Oceanographic Office]....DOSV
Deep Operating Work Board....................................DOWB
Deep Passive Sensors...DPS
Deep Passive Sonobuoy System.................................DPSS
Deep Penetration [Air Force].................................DP
Deep Pulse [Medicine].......................................DP
Deep Quest..DQ
Deep Reconnaissance Zone [Army].............................DRZ
Deep Research Vehicle [or Vessel] [NOO]......................DRV
Deep Scattering Layer [Undersea populations].................DSL
Deep Sea Drilling Project [Later, IPOD] [National Science
　Foundation]..DSDP
Deep Sea Drilling Project. Initial Reports [A publication]........
　　　　　　　　　　　Deep Sea Drill Proj Initial Rep
Deep Sea Research [A publication]......................Deep Sea Re
Deep Sea Research [A publication].....................Deep Sea Res
Deep Sea Research and Oceanographic Abstracts [A
　publication]................................Deep Sea Res & Oceanogr Abstr
Deep Sea Research and Oceanographic Abstracts [A
　publication]................................Deep Sea Res Oceanogr Abstr
Deep-Sea System for Evaluating Acoustic Transducers [Navy]........
　　　　　　　　　　　　　　　　　　　DEEPSEAT
Deep Sea Winch..DSW
Deep Space Communications Complex...........................DSCC
Deep Space Instrumentation Facility...........................DSIF
Deep Space Measurement......................................DSM
Deep Space Network [NASA]...................................DSN
Deep Space Probe..DSP
Deep Space Station [NASA]...................................DSS
Deep Space Surveillance RADAR...............................DSSR
Deep Springs College, Deep Springs, CA [Library symbol]........CDs
Deep Submergence Device.....................................DSD
Deep Submergence Group......................................DSG
Deep Submergence Program....................................DSP
Deep Submergence Rescue System [Navy].......................DSRS
Deep Submergence Rescue Vehicle [Navy]......................DSRV
Deep Submergence Research Vessel.............................DSRV
Deep Submergence Search Vehicle [Research submarine] [Navy].....DSSV
Deep Submergence Systems [Navy].....................DEEPSUBSYS
Deep Submergence Systems [Navy].............................DSS

Deep Submergence Systems Project [Navy]......................DSSP
Deep Submergence Systems Project Office [Navy].....DEEPSUBSYSPROJO
Deep Submergence Systems Project Office [Navy]................DSSPO
Deep Submergence Systems Project Technical Office [Navy].......DSSPTO
Deep Submergence Systems Review Group [Navy]................DSSRG
Deep Submergence Vehicle [Navy symbol]......................DSV
Deep Submergence Weapon System [Also, DEXTOR]..............DSWS
Deep Tank...DT
Deep Tendon Reflex [Physiology].............................DTR
Deep Underground Communications System......................DUCS
Deep Underground Missile Basing..............................DUMB
Deep Underground Mountain Basing [Proposed defense for
　missiles] [Military].......................................DUMB
Deep Underground Sanguine System [Navy].....................DUSS
Deep Underground Support Center [Air Force]..................DUSC
Deep Underwater Muon and Neutrino Detection.................DUMAND
Deep Underwater Nuclear Counting............................DUNC
Deep Unmanned Submersibles..................................DUMS
Deep Venous Thrombosis [Medicine]............................DVT
Deep Water [Nautical charts]................................DW
Deep Water Dump...DWD
Deep Water Environmental Survival Training [Navy]............DWEST
Deep Water Isotopic Current Analyzer [TVA]..................DWICA
Deep X-Ray..DXR
Deep X-Ray Therapy..DXRT
Deep X-Ray Therapy..DXT
Deepening...DPNG
Deepest Working Depth.......................................DWD
Deepsea Ventures, Inc., Gloucester Point, VA [Library symbol]........ViGpD
Deepstar [A manned, self-propelled submersible vehicle built by
　Western Electric Corp.].....................................DS
Deepwater Escort Hydrofoil [Also, DBH].......................DEH
Deepwater Motion Picture System.............................DMPS
Deepwater Port..DWP
Deepwell Pump [Liquid gas carriers]..........................d
Deer Creek Reservoir [Utah] [Seismograph station code, US
　Geological Survey]...DCU
Deer Environment Ecology and Resources [An association].......DEER
Deer Kidney Virus...DKV
Deer Lake [Canada] [Airport symbol].........................YDF
Deer Lodge Hospital, Winnipeg, MB, Canada [Library symbol].......CaMWDL
Deer Lodge, MT [Radio station call letters]..................KDRG
Deer Park Consolidated Community School District 82, Ottawa,
　IL [Library symbol].......................................IOtDSD
Deer Park, NY [Location identifier] [FAA]....................DPK
Deer Park Public Library, Deer Park, NY [Library symbol].......NDp
Deer Park, WA [Radio station call letters]..................KNOI
Deer Trail, CO [Radio station call letters].................KTMG
Deer Unlimited of America....................................DUA
Deere & Co. [NYSE symbol]...................................DE
Deere & Company [Moline, IL] [FAA designator]...............JDC
Deere & Co., Moline, IL [OCLC symbol].......................IEJ
Deere & Co., Moline, IL [Library symbol]....................IMolD
Deerfield Academy, Deerfield, MA [Library symbol]............MDeeD
Deerfield, MA [Radio station call letters]..................WGAJ
Deering [Alaska] [Airport symbol]...........................DRG
Defamation, Identification, and Publication...................DIP
Defatted Peanut Flour [Food industry].......................DPF
[In] Default [Standard & Poor's bond rating].................D
Defeat Opiate Addiction [An association].....................DOA
Defeated..D
Defeated..DEF
Defecation..DEF
Defecation-Collection Device [Apollo] [NASA].................DCD
Defect Action Level [FDA]...................................DAL
Defect Information and Servicing Control [Aviation]...........DISC
Defect Prevention Reports....................................DPR
Defection Intercept-Passive Submarine........................DIPS
Defective...DEF
Defective Equipment Repair Program [Telephone company].......DERP
Defective Equipment Review...................................DER
Defective-Interfering [Virology].............................DI
Defective Material Notice....................................DMN
Defective Materiel Report [Air Force].......................DMR
Defective Parts and Components Control Program...............DPCCP
Defects in Crystalline Solids [Elsevier Book Series] [A publication]........DCS
Defects in Solids [Elsevier Book Series] [A publication].....DSOL
Defektologija [A publication]...............................Defektol
Defektoskopiya [A publication].............................Defektosk
Defence Adviser [British]...................................DA
Defence Aid Supply Committee [Later, ISC] [World War II].....DASC
Defence of Airfields [British] [World War II]...............DA
Defence Arrangements for Indian Ocean [British] [World War II]........DIO
Defence Automatic Data Processing Training Centre [British].....DADPTC
Defence Chemical, Biological, and Radiation Establishment
　[Canada]..DCBRE
Defence Chemical, Biological, and Radiation Laboratories
　[Canada]..DCBRL
Defence and Civil Institute of Environmental Medicine [Canada]......DCIEM
Defence Communication Network [British].....................DCN
Defence Construction [1951] Limited [Canada]................DCL

Defence Equipment Policy Committee [British]..............DEPC
Defence Fellowship [British]..DF
Defence Intelligence [British]......................................DI
Defence Intelligence Staff [British]..............................DIS
Defence Journal [A publication]..............................Def J
Defence Operational Analysis Establishment [British]........DOAE
Defence Operational Analysis Organisation [Far East]......DOAO(FE)
Defence Operations [British] [World War II]....................DO
Defence Planning Committee [NATO]...........................DPC
Defence Planning Working Group [NATO]....................DPWG
Defence Policy Staff [British]......................................DPS
Defence Production Board [NATO]..............................DPB
Defence Production Chief [British]..............................DPC
Defence Production Committee [NATO]........................DPC
Defence Production Supply Board [NATO]....................DPSB
Defence Quality Assurance Board [British]....................DQAB
Defence of the Realm Act [British] [World War I]............DORA
Defence Research Analysis Establishment [Canada].........DRAE
Defence Research Board [Canada]...............................DRB
Defence Research Chemical Laboratories [Canada]..........DRCL
Defence Research Committee [British]..........................DRC
Defence Research Directors [NATO]............................DRD
Defence Research Establishment [Canada]....................DRE
Defence Research Establishment, Atlantic [Canada].........DREA
Defence Research Establishment, Atlantic Defence Research
   Board, Halifax, NS, Canada [Library symbol]............CaNSHN
Defence Research Establishment, Ottawa [Canada].........DREO
Defence Research Establishment, Pacific [Canada]..........DREP
Defence Research Establishment, Suffield [Canada].........DRES
Defence Research Establishment, Suffield, Test Centre [British]....DRESTC
Defence Research Establishment, Toronto [Canada].........DRET
Defence Research Establishment, Valcartier [Canada].......DREV
Defence Research Establishment, Valcartier, Canada
   Department of National Defence, Quebec, PQ, Canada
   [Library symbol]..CaQQC
Defence Research Information Centre [Great Britain]........DRIC
Defence Research Kingston Laboratory [Canada]............DRKL
Defence Research Medical Laboratory [Canada]..............DRML
Defence Research Northern Laboratory [Canada]............DRNL
Defence Research Policy Committee [British]..................DRPC
Defence Research Telecommunication Establishment [Canada]........DRTE
Defence Review Committee [NATO].............................DRC
Defence Science Journal [A publication].....................Def Sci J
Defence Science and Technology Organization [Australia]........DSTO
Defence Scientific Information Service [Canada] [Information
   service]...DSIS
Defence Signal Board [British]....................................DSB
Defence Standards Laboratories [British]......................DSL
Defence Studies Methodology [British].........................DSM
Defence Systems Analysis Group [Canada]....................DSAG
Defence Telecommunications Research Establishment [British]........DTRE
Defencively Armed Merchant Ship [British] [World War I]........DAMS
Defendant..DEF
Defendant..DEFT
Defendant..DFT
Defended Area Model [Army]....................................DAM
Defended Area Model II Engagement Evaluation [Army]........DAM II-EE
Defended Area Model II Engagement Planning [Army]........DAM II-EP
Defender of the Faith..DF
Defenders of the American Constitution.......................DAC
Defenders of the Christian Faith [Superseded by CCI]........DCF
Defenders of Furbearers [Later, Defenders of Wildlife]......DOF
Defenders of Wildlife [A publication].................Defenders Wildl
Defenders of Wildlife International [A publication]......Defenders Wildl Int
Defenders of Wildlife News [A publication]......Defenders Wildl News
Defense [Men's lacrosse position].................................D
Defense..DEF
Defense Acquisition Executive..................................DAE
Defense Acquisition RADAR......................................DAR
Defense Acquisition Regulation.................................DAR
Defense Acquisition Regulatory System [DoD]..................DARS
Defense Activity for Nontraditional Education Support [Military]........DANE
Defense Activity for Nontraditional Education Support [Military]....DANTES
Defense Activity North Carolina................................DAN
Defense ADPE [Automatic Data Processing Equipment]
   Reutilization Office......................................DARO
Defense Advanced Disposal Management Course [Army]........DADMC
Defense Advanced Inventory Management Course [Army]........DAIMC
Defense Advanced Procurement Management Course [Army]........DAPMC
Defense Advanced Research Projects Agency [DoD]............DARPA
Defense Advisory Committee on Women in the Services........DACOWITS
Defense Against Methods of Entry [Military intelligence]........DAME
Defense Against Missiles Systems...............................DAMS
Defense Against Sound Equipment [Military intelligence]........DASE
Defense Against Underwater Swimmers [Military]..............DAUS
Defense Aid [Lend-Lease] [World War II]..........................DA
Defense Aid [Lend-Lease] Administration Expenses [World War II].....DAAE
Defense Aid [Lend-Lease] Agricultural, Industrial, and Other
   Commodities [World War II]...........................DAAI & OC
Defense Aid [Lend-Lease] Aircraft and Aeronautical Material
   [World War II]...DAA & AM

Defense Aid [Lend-Lease] Facilities and Equipment [World War
   II]..DAF & E
Defense Aid [Lend-Lease] Ordnance and Ordnance Stores
   [World War II]..DAO & OS
Defense Aid [Lend-Lease] Services and Expenses [World War II]....DAS & E
Defense Aid [Lend-Lease] Special Fund [World War II]........DASF
Defense Aid [Lend-Lease] Tanks and Other Vehicles [World War
   II]..DAT & OV
Defense Aid [Lend-Lease] Testing, Reconditioning, etc., of
   Defense Articles [World War II]........................DATRDA
Defense Aid [Lend-Lease] Vessels and Other Watercraft [World
   War II]..DAV & OW
Defense Air Transportation Administration [Abolished 1962,
   functions transferred to Office of the Under Secretary of
   Commerce for Transportation]..........................DATA
Defense of Airborne Vehicles in Depth.........................DAVID
Defense Area Communications Control Center.................DACCC
Defense Area Communications Control Center, Alaska........DACCC-AL
Defense Area Communications Control Center, CONUS........DACCC-CON
Defense Area Communications Control Center, Europe........DACCEUR
Defense Atomic Research Facility...............................DARF
Defense Atomic Support Agency [Later, DNA]..................DASA
Defense Atomic Support Agency Data Center...................DASA-DC
Defense Atomic Support Agency Information and Analysis
   Center...DASIAC
Defense Atomic Support Agency Technical Letters............DASTL
Defense Atomic Support Agency Technical Publications........DASA-TP
Defense Attache...DAT
Defense Attache...DATT
Defense Attache Liaison Officer................................DALO
Defense Attache Office...DAO
Defense Attache System [Department of State]................DAS
Defense Audiovisual Agency [DoD]..............................DAVA
Defense Audiovisual Booking and Distribution System........DAVBADS
Defense Audiovisual Depository System.........................DADS
Defense Audiovisual Information System........................DAVIS
Defense Audiovisual Support Activity...........................DAVSA
Defense Audit Service [Abolished 1982, functions transferred to
   Office of the Inspector General (DoD)].....................DAS
Defense Automatic Addressing System Office...................DAASO
Defense Automatic Integrated Switch [Army communications
   system]..DAIS
Defense Automotive Supply Center.............................DASC
Defense Base Act..DBA
Defense Center Control Building [Army].........................DCCB
Defense Center Data Processing [Army].........................DCDP
Defense Central Index of Investigations........................DCII
Defense Ceramic Information Center [Later, MCIC] [Battelle
   Memorial Institute]....................................DCIC
Defense Civil Disturbance Facility List.........................DCDFL
Defense Civil Preparedness Agency [FEMA].....................DCPA
Defense Clothing and Textile Supply Center [Later, Defense
   Personnel Support Center] [DoD]......................DC & TSC
Defense Clothing and Textile Supply Center [Later, Defense
   Personnel Support Center] [DoD].......................DCTSC
Defense Clothing and Textile Supply Center [Later, Defense
   Personnel Support Center] [DoD]........DEFCLOTH & TEXSUPCEN
Defense Combat Evaluation....................................DCE
Defense Combat Maneuvers.....................................DCM
Defense Command...DEFCOM
Defense Commercial Communications Activity [Military]........DECCA
Defense Commercial Communications Center [Military]........DECCC
Defense Commercial Communications Office [Military]........DECCO
Defense Committee..DC
Defense Committee on Research [Air Force].....................DCOR
Defense Communication Engineering Agency...................DECEA
Defense Communications Agency...............................DCA
Defense Communications Agency Circular......................DCAC
Defense Communications Agency, Europe.......................DCAEUR
Defense Communications Agency Instruction...................DCAI
Defense Communications Agency/MILSATCOM Systems Office........
   ....DCA/MSO
Defense Communications Agency Note [or Notice]..............DCAN
Defense Communications Agency Operations Center............DCAOC
Defense Communications Agency Operations Center Complex........DOCC
Defense Communications Agency Systems Engineering Facility........
   ....DCASEF
Defense Communications Agency, Technical Library,
   Washington, DC [Library symbol].......................DDCA
Defense Communications Board.................................DCB
Defense Communications Control Center........................DCCC
Defense Communications Control System [Air Force]...........DCCS
Defense Communications Engineering Center [Army]............DCEC
Defense Communications Engineering Office [Army]............DCEO
Defense Communications Engineering Office [Army]............DECEO
Defense Communications Planning Group........................DCPG
Defense Communications Satellite Project [or Program]........DCSP
Defense Communications System [DoD].........................DCS
Defense Communications System Air Operational Network........
   ....DCSAIROPNET

Defense Communications System Automatic Digital Information Network .... DCS/AUTODIN
Defense Communications System Automatic Digital Network [*DoD*] .... DCSADN
Defense Communications System Data Network .... DCSDATANET
Defense Communications System Operations Center .... DCSOC
Defense Communications System - Personnel Emergency Actions Book .... DCS/PEAB
Defense Communications System Teletype Network .... DCSTTYNET
Defense Communications Systems Configuration Items .... DCSCI
Defense Computer Institute .... DCI
Defense Concept Paper [*Military*] .... DCP
Defense Concessions Committee .... DCC
Defense Construction Service .... DCS
Defense Construction Supply Center [*Defense Supply Agency*] .... DCSC
Defense Construction Supply Center [*Defense Supply Agency*] .... DEFCONTRSUPCEN
Defense Contract Administration Services [*DoD*] .... DCAS
Defense Contract Administration Services District [*DoD*] .... DCASD
Defense Contract Administration Services Management Area [*DoD*] .... DCASMA
Defense Contract Administration Services Office [*DoD*] .... DCASO
Defense Contract Administration Services Plant Representative Office [*DoD*] .... DCASPRO
Defense Contract Administration Services Region [*DoD*] .... DCASR
Defense Contract Audit Agency [*DoD*] .... DCAA
Defense Contract Audit Agency Pamphlets [*DoD*] .... DCAAP
Defense Contract Management Agency .... DCMA
Defense Contract Services Administration Region .... DCSAR
Defense Contractor Planning Report .... DCPR
Defense Contre Aeronefs [*Antiaircraft Defense*] [*French*] .... DCA
Defense Control Administration .... DCA
Defense Control Center .... DCC
Defense Counsel .... DC
Defense Credit Union Council .... DCUC
Defense Criminal Investigation Service .... DCIS
Defense Customer Supply Assistance Office [*DoD*] .... DCSAO
Defense Data Network .... DDN
Defense Department [*US government*] .... D
Defense Department [*US government*] .... DD
Defense Department Form .... DDF
Defense Depot [*DoD*] .... DD
Defense Depot - Mechanicsburg, Pennsylvania [*DoD*] .... DDMP
Defense Depot - Memphis, Tennessee [*DoD*] .... DDMT
Defense Depot - Ogden, Utah [*DoD*] .... DDOU
Defense Depot Operations Management Course [*DoD*] .... DDOMC
Defense Depot - Tracy, California [*DoD*] .... DDTC
Defense Development and Engineering Laboratories [*Military*] .... DDEL
Defense Development Exchange Program .... DDEP
Defense Development Research and Engineering .... DDR & E
Defense Development Sharing Program [*US and Canada*] .... DDSP
Defense Development Sharing Program [*US and Canada*] .... DSP
Defense Disposal Executive Development Seminar [*DoD*] .... DDEDS
Defense Dissemination Program .... DDP
Defense Documentation Center [*Later, DTIC*] [*DoD*] .... DDC
Defense Eastern Regional Audit Office [*DoD*] .... DERA
Defense Economic Analysis Council .... DEAC
Defense Electric Power Administration [*Department of the Interior*] [*Terminated, 1977*] .... DEPA
Defense Electric Supply Center .... DEFELECSUPCEN
Defense Electronic Countermeasures .... DECM
Defense Electronic Products .... DEP
Defense Electronics, Incorporated .... DEI
Defense Electronics Supply Center [*DSA*] .... DESC
Defense Emergency .... DE
Defense Energy Information System [*DoD*] .... DEIS
Defense Engineering Data Office .... DEDO
Defense Enrollment Eligibility Reporting System [*DoD*] .... DEERS
Defense Exchange Agreement .... DEA
Defense Family Housing [*Army*] .... DFH
Defense Finance Economic Committee .... DFEC
Defense Fisheries Administration [*Abolished, 1953*] .... DFA
Defense Force Section Base [*Navy*] .... DFSB
Defense Foreign Disclosure Coordinating Office .... FDCO
Defense Freight Railway Interchange Fleet [*Army*] .... DFRIF
Defense Fuel Quality Assurance Office [*DoD*] .... DFQAO
Defense Fuel Region [*DoD*] .... DFR
Defense Fuel Supply Center [*DoD*] .... DFSC
Defense Fuel Support Point [*DoD*] .... DFSP
Defense Fuels Automated Management System [*DoD*] .... DFAMS
Defense General Supply Center .... DEFGENSUPCEN
Defense General Supply Center .... DGSC
Defense Guidance .... DG
Defense Guidance Memorandum .... DGM
Defense Homes Corporation [*World War II*] .... DHC
Defense Identification Code .... DIC
Defense Identification Zone .... DIZ
Defense Improved Management Engineering System [*Military*] .... DIMES
Defense Inactive Item Program .... DIIP
Defense Industrial Facilities Protection Program [*DoD*] .... DIFPP
Defense Industrial Fund .... DIF
Defense Industrial and Management Engineering Office [*DoD*] .... DIMEO
Defense Industrial Plant Equipment Center [*DoD*] .... DEFINDPLANTEQUIPCEN
Defense Industrial Plant Equipment Center [*DoD*] .... DIPEC
Defense Industrial Plant Equipment Facility [*DoD*] .... DIPEF
Defense Industrial Reserve [*DoD*] .... DIR
Defense Industrial Security Clearance Office .... DISCO
Defense Industrial Security Education and Training Office .... DISTO
Defense Industrial Security Institute [*DoD*] .... DISI
Defense Industrial Security Program [*DoD*] .... DISP
Defense Industrial Supply Center .... DEFINDSUPCEN
Defense Industrial Supply Center .... DISC
Defense Industrial Supply Depot .... DEFINDSUPDEP
Defense Industrial Supply Depot .... DISD
Defense Industry Advisory Council [*Later, IAC*] .... DIAC
Defense Industry Advisory Group Europe [*Terminated, 1977*] .... DIAGE
Defense Industry Bulletin [*A publication*] [*DoD*] .... DIB
Defense Industry Bulletin [*A publication*] [*DoD*] .... DIBtn
Defense Industry Export Advisory Group .... DIEAG
Defense Industry Studies Program .... DISP
Defense Information .... DI
Defense Information Analysis Center [*DoD*] .... DIAC
Defense Information Automated Locator System .... DIALS
Defense Information Distribution System [*Proposed in-home disaster warning system*] .... DIDS
Defense Information Memorandum .... DIM
Defense Information School .... DINFOS
Defense Institute of Security Assistance Management .... DISAM
Defense Institute of Security Assistance Management, Wright-Patterson AFB, OH [*OCLC symbol*] .... DIS
Defense Integrated Data System .... DIDS
Defense Integrated Data System Program Management Office [*DoD*] .... DIDSO
Defense Integrated Management Engineering System [*Military*] .... DIMES
Defense Intelligence Agency [*Formerly, JJ-2*] .... DEFINTELAGCY
Defense Intelligence Agency [*Formerly, JJ-2*] .... DIA
Defense Intelligence Agency Instruction .... DIAI
Defense Intelligence Agency Manual .... DIAM
Defense Intelligence Agency On-Line Information System .... DIAOLS
Defense Intelligence Agency Regulation .... DIAR
Defense Intelligence Agency, Washington, DC [*OCLC symbol*] .... DIA
Defense Intelligence Projection for Planning .... DIPP
Defense Intelligence Relay Center .... DIRC
Defense Intelligence Requirement Manual .... DIRM
Defense Intelligence School .... DIS
Defense Intelligence School, Washington, DC [*Library symbol*] .... DN-IS
Defense Intercontinental Ballistic Missile .... DICBM
Defense International Logistics Management Course [*DoD*] .... DILMC
Defense Inventory Management Course [*DoD*] .... DIMC
Defense Investigative Service [*DoD*] .... DIS
Defense Item Data Utilization .... DIDU
Defense Item Entry Control Office [*Military*] .... DIECO
Defense Item Entry Control Program [*Military*] .... DIECP
Defense Language Aptitude Test [*Army*] .... DLAT
Defense Language Institute .... DLI
Defense Language Institute, East Coast Center .... DLIEC
Defense Language Institute, English Language Center .... DLIEL
Defense Language Institute, Foreign Language Center .... DLIFLC
Defense Language Institute, Southwest Branch .... DLISW
Defense Language Institute, Support Command - El Paso .... DLISC-EP
Defense Language Institute, Systems Development Agency .... DLISDA
Defense Language Institute, West Coast Branch .... DLIWC
Defense Language Institute, West Coast Branch, Presidio of Monterey, CA [*Library symbol*] .... CPmD
Defense Language Proficiency Tests [*Military*] .... DLPT
Defense Language Program .... DLP
Defense Law Journal [*A publication*] .... Defense L J
Defense Law Journal [*A publication*] .... Def Law J
Defense Legal Services Agency [*DoD*] .... DLS
Defense Legal Services Agency .... DLSA
Defense Liaison Group .... DLG
Defense Liaison Officer to the White House .... DEFLOWH
Defense Logistics Agency .... DLA
Defense Logistics Agency, Alexandria, VA [*OCLC symbol*] .... DLO
Defense Logistics Area .... DLA
Defense Logistics Instructor Development Course [*Army*] .... DLIDC
Defense Logistics Management Training Board .... DLMTB
Defense Logistics Services Center [*Military*] .... DLSC
Defense Logistics Standards Systems Office .... DLSSO
Defense Logistics Studies Information Exchange [*Army*] .... DLSIE
Defense Logistics Support Center [*Military*] .... DLSC
Defense Management Educating and Training [*DoD*] .... DMET
Defense Management Education and Training Board [*DoD*] .... DMETB
Defense Management Journal [*A publication*] .... Def Man J
Defense Management Journal [*A publication*] .... DMJ
Defense Management Journal Office [*DoD*] .... DMJO
Defense Management System .... DMS
Defense Manpower Administration [*Department of Labor*] [*Superseded by Office of Manpower Administration, 1953*] .... DMA
Defense Manpower Commission .... DMC
Defense Manpower Policy .... DMP

Defense Mapping Agency ... DMA
Defense Mapping Agency Aerospace Center [*Formerly, ACIC*] ... DMAAC
Defense Mapping Agency Aerospace Center Technical Translation Section ... DMAAC-TC
Defense Mapping Agency Hydrographic Center [*Later, DMAHTC*] ... DMAHC
Defense Mapping Agency Hydrographic/Topographic Center [*Formerly, DMAHC, DMATC*] ... DMAHTC
Defense Mapping Agency Topographic Center [*Later, DMAHTC*] ... DMATC
Defense Mapping School [*Army*] ... DMS
Defense Marketing Group [*AMA*] ... DMG
Defense Marketing Survey ... DMS
Defense Material Item ... DMI
Defense Materials Procurement Agency [*Abolished 1953, functions transferred to General Services Administration*] ... DMPA
Defense Materials Service [*of GSA*] ... DMS
Defense Materials System ... DMS
Defense Materials Systems Office ... DMSO
Defense Materiel Council [*DoD*] ... DMC
Defense Materiel Interservicing Program [*DoD*] ... DMIP
Defense Materiel Specifications and Standards Office [*DoD*] ... DMSSO
Defense Materiel Utilization Program [*DoD*] ... DMUP
Defense Mechanism Test [*Psychometrics*] ... DMT
Defense Mechanisms Inventory [*Psychology*] ... DMI
Defense Medical Material Board ... DMMB
Defense Medical Purchase Description [*Defense Supply Agency*] ... DMPD
Defense Medical Supply Center [*Later, Defense Personnel Support Center*] ... DMSC
Defense Metals Information Center [*Later, MCIC*] ... DMIC
Defense Meteorological Satellite Program [*Formerly, DAPP*] [*Air Force*] ... DMSP
Defense Meteorological Satellite System [*Air Force*] ... DMSS
Defense Minerals Exploration Administration [*Department of the Interior*] ... DMEA
Defense Missile Systems ... DMS
Defense Mobilization Board [*Terminated, 1958*] ... DMB
Defense Mobilization Order ... DMO
Defense National Agency Check Center [*DoD*] ... DNACC
Defense National Communications Control Center ... DNCCC
Defense Nationale [*A publication*] ... Def Nat
Defense Nationale [*A publication*] ... Def Natl
Defense Navigation Planning Group [*DoD*] ... DNPG
Defense Navigation Satellite Development Program ... DNSDP
Defense Navigation Satellite System [*Formerly, SSPN*] ... DNSS
Defense Notice [*Classification given to British news items which are considered harmful to national security and which are voluntarily censored by the press*] ... D
Defense Nuclear Agency ... DNA
Defense Nuclear Agency Technical Publications ... DNA-TP
Defense de l'Occident [*A publication*] ... Def Occident
Defense Occupational Specialties [*Army*] ... DOS
Defense Officer Personnel Management Act ... DOPMA
Defense Officer Personnel Management Study ... DOPMS
Defense Order ... DO
Defense Organization Entity Standards [*DoD*] ... DOES
Defense Organization Entity System [*DoD*] ... DOES
Defense Orientation Conference Association ... DOCA
Defense Orthopedic Footwear Clinic [*Military*] ... DOFC
Defense Personnel Support Center ... DEFPERSUPPCEN
Defense Personnel Support Center ... DPSC
Defense Personnel Support Center, Directorate of Medical Material Library, Philadelphia, PA [*Library symbol*] ... PPDef-M
Defense Petroleum Supply Center ... DPSC
Defense Planning Council ... DPC
Defense Planning Programing Category ... DPPC
Defense Planning Staff [*Military*] ... DPS
Defense Plant Corporation [*Obsolete*] [*Subsidiary of Reconstruction Finance Corp.*] ... DPC
Defense Plant Installation ... DPI
Defense Point ... DP
Defense Policy Planning Guidance ... DPPG
Defense Printing Service ... DPS
Defense Priorities System [*DoD*] ... DPS
Defense Procurement Circular [*DoD*] ... DPC
Defense Procurement Management Course [*DoD*] ... DPMC
Defense Procurement Program [*DoD*] ... DPP
Defense Production Act [*Obsolete*] ... DPA
Defense Production Administration [*Functions transferred to Office of Defense Mobilization*] ... DPA
Defense Program Management Office [*DoD*] ... DPMO
Defense Program Memorandum ... DPM
Defense Program Operation ... DPO
Defense Projects Support Office [*NASA*] ... DPSO
Defense Property Disposal Office [*DoD*] ... DPDO
Defense Property Disposal Precious Metals Recovery Office - Earle [*New Jersey*] [*DoD*] ... DPDPMRO-E
Defense Property Disposal Region [*DoD*] ... DPDR
Defense Property Disposal Service [*DoD*] ... DPDS
Defense Race Relations Institute [*Air Force*] ... DRRI
Defense RDT & E [*Research, Development, Test, and Evaluation*] **On-Line System** ... DROL
Defense Readiness Condition [*Army*] ... DEFCON
Defense Readiness Posture [*Army*] ... DEFREP
Defense Reconnaissance Support Program ... DRSP
Defense Regional Communications Control Center ... DRCCC
Defense Regional Communications Control Center, Far East ... DRCCC-FE
Defense Regional Communications Control Center, Southeast Asia ... DRCCC-SEA
Defense Reorganization Act ... DRA
Defense Representative, North Atlantic and Mediterranean Area ... DEFREPNAMA
Defense Research Advisory Committee ... DRAC
Defense Research and Engineering [*DoD*] ... DR & E
Defense Research and Engineering Office [*DoD*] ... DREO
Defense Research Establishment [*Israel*] ... DRE
Defense Research Group [*NATO*] ... DRG
Defense Research Institute ... DRI
Defense Research Laboratory ... DRL
Defense Research Laboratory/University of Texas ... DRL/UT
Defense Research Office, Latin America [*Army*] ... DRO-LA
Defense Research Sciences ... DRS
Defense Resources Board ... DRB
Defense Resources Planning Operation ... DRPO
Defense Retail Interservice Logistic Support [*Military*] ... DRILS
Defense Retail Interservice Support [*Military*] ... DRIS
Defense SAAMS [*Special Airlift Assignment Missions*] **Program Management Office** [*DoD*] ... DSPMO
Defense Satellite Communications Program ... DSCP
Defense Satellite Communications System [*DoD*] ... DSCS
Defense Science Board [*DoD*] ... DSB
Defense Science Board Subcommittee [*DoD*] ... DSBS
Defense Science Journal [*A publication*] ... Defense Sci J
Defense Scientists Immigration Program ... DEFSIP
Defense Sector [*Navy*] ... DEFSEC
Defense Security Assistance Agency ... DSAA
Defense Security Assistance Program ... DSAP
Defense Sensor Interpretation and Application Training Program ... DSIATP
Defense Shipping Authority ... DSA
Defense Shipping Council ... DSC
Defense Shipping Executive Board ... DSEB
Defense Signals Staff ... DSS
Defense Small Business Advanced Technology Program ... DESAT
Defense Solid Fuels Administration [*Terminated, 1954*] ... DSFA
Defense Special Missile and Astronautic Center ... DEFSMAC
Defense Special Missile and Astronautics Center [*Pronounced "deff-smack"*] [*National Security Agency*] ... DEFSMAC
Defense Special Projects Group ... DSPG
Defense Special Security Communications System [*Pronounced "discus"*] ... DSSCS
Defense Specification Management Course [*Army*] ... DSMC
Defense Standard Contract Administration Procedure ... DEFSCAP
Defense Standardization Manual [*DoD*] ... DSM
Defense Standardization Program [*DoD*] ... DSP
Defense Standardization and Specification Program [*DoD*] ... DSSP
Defense Stock Fund [*DoD*] ... DSF
Defense Subsistence Office [*DoD*] ... DSO
Defense Subsistence Region [*DoD*] ... DSR
Defense Subsistence Region - Europe ... DSRE
Defense Subsistence Supply Center [*Later, Defense Personnel Support Center*] ... DEFSUBSUPCEN
Defense Subsistence Supply Center [*Later, Defense Personnel Support Center*] ... DSSC
Defense Subsystem Development and Demonstration ... DSDD
Defense Supply Agency [*Later, Defense Logistics Agency*] [*DoD*] ... DSA
Defense Supply Agency Administrative Support Center [*DoD*] ... DSASC
Defense Supply Agency Contract Administration Services [*DoD*] ... DSACAS
Defense Supply Agency Contractor Experience List [*DoD*] ... DSACEL
Defense Supply Agency Handbook [*DoD*] ... DSAH
Defense Supply Agency Handbook [*DoD*] ... DSAHBK
Defense Supply Agency Industrial Equipment Reserve [*DoD*] ... DSAIER
Defense Supply Agency Manual [*DoD*] ... DSAM
Defense Supply Agency Poster [*DoD*] ... DSAP
Defense Supply Agency Regulation [*DoD*] ... DSAR
Defense Supply Agency - Western Regional Audit Office [*DoD*] ... DSA-WRAO
Defense Supply Association [*Later, ALA*] ... DSA
Defense Supply Center ... DSC
Defense Supply Corporation [*World War II*] ... DSC
Defense Supply Management Agency ... DSMA
Defense Supply Procurement Regulation [*Military*] ... DSPR
Defense Supply Service [*DoD*] ... DSS
Defense Supply Service - Washington [*DoD*] ... DSS-W
Defense Support ... DS
Defense Support Program ... DSP
Defense Suppression Expendable Drone ... DSED
Defense Suppression Group [*DoD*] ... DSG
Defense Suppression Missile ... DSM
Defense Suppression Rocket ... DSR
Defense Surplus Bidders Control Office ... DSBCO
Defense Surplus Sales Office ... DSSO

Defense Switched Network ... DSN
Defense System Operator [*ECM operator*] ... DSO
Defense System Terminal Equipment ... DSTE
Defense Systems Acquisition Review Council ... DSARC
Defense Systems Analysis [*DoD*] ... DSA
Defense Systems Application Program [*DoD*] ... DSAP
Defense Systems Evaluation Squadron [*Air Force*] ... DSES
Defense Systems Management College [*Army*] ... DSMC
Defense Systems Management Course [*Air Force*] ... DSMC
Defense Systems Management Review [*A publication*] ... Def Syst Man Rev
Defense Systems Management School ... DSMS
Defense and Tactical Armament Control ... DATAC
Defense Technical Center ... DTC
Defense Technical Information Center [*Formerly, DDC*] ... DTIC
Defense Technical Information Center, Alexandria, VA [*OCLC symbol*] ... DTI
Defense Technical Review Activity [*or Agency*] [*Military*] ... DTRA
Defense Telephone Service [*DoD*] ... DTS
Defense Telephone Service - Washington [*DoD*] ... DTS-W
Defense Teleprinter Network ... DTN
Defense Traffic Management Service ... DTMS
Defense Transport Administration [*Terminated, functions transferred to Interstate Commerce Commission*] ... DTA
Defense Transportation Order [*Department of Commerce*] ... DTO
Defense Transportation System [*DoD*] ... DTS
Defense Unit Classification System ... DUCS
Defense Value Engineering Services Officer ... DVEO
Defense des Vegetaux [*A publication*] ... Defense Veg
Defense des Vegetaux [*A publication*] ... Def Veg
Defense Visual Flight Rules ... DVFR
Defense Vocational Aptitude Battery [*Military*] ... DVAB
Defense Waste Processing Facility [*Department of Energy*] ... DWPF
Defense Weapons System ... DWS
Defense Weapons System Management Center ... DEFWEAPSYSMGTCEN
Defense Weapons System Management Center ... DWSMC
Defense Western Regional Audit Office [*DoD*] ... DWRA
Defense Western Regional Telecommunications Office [*DoD*] ... DWRTO
Defense Work Measurement Standard Time Data Program [*Air Force*] ... DWMSTDP
Defensive Back [*Football*] ... DB
Defensive Concentration ... DEFCON
Defensive Driving Course [*National Safety Council*] ... DDC
Defensive End [*Football*] ... DE
Defensive Fire ... DF
Defensive Guard [*Football*] ... DG
Defensive Radio Warfare ... DRW
Defensive Response [*Psychology*] ... DR
Defensive Satellite ... DSAT
Defensive Tackle [*Football*] ... DT
Defensive Target [*Military*] ... DT
Defensively-Equipped Merchant Ship ... DEMS
Defensively-Equipped Merchant Ship School ... DEMSS
Defensiveness Scale for Children [*Psychology*] ... DSC
Defer ... DFR
Deferoxamine [*Chelating agent*] ... DF
Deferoxamine Methanesulfonate [*or Desferrioxamine Mesylate*] [*Pharmacology*] ... DFOM
Deferred ... DEF
Deferred Adverse Tax Consequences Implementation Group [*IRS*] ... DATCIG
Deferred Commercial Annuity ... DCA
Deferred Delivery [*Especially, of securities*] ... DD
Deferred Delivery ... DFDEL
Deferred Nesting Program ... DNP
Deferred Organic Supply ... DOS
Deferred Pay Fund ... DPF
Deferred Telegram ... DT
Defiance College, Defiance, OH [*OCLC symbol*] ... DEF
Defiance College, Defiance, OH [*Library symbol*] ... ODefC
Defiance, OH [*Radio station call letters*] ... WONW
Defiance Public Library, Defiance, OH [*Library symbol*] ... ODef
Defibrillate [*Cardiology*] ... DEFIB
Deficiencies in Allowance List [*Military*] ... DIAL
Deficiency ... DEFN
Deficiency Action Report ... DAR
Deficiency in Allowance [*Military*] ... DIA
Deficiency Analysis Summary ... DAS
Deficiency Corrective Action Program [*Surface missile systems*] ... DCAP
Deficiency and Replacement ... DFRP
Deficiency Report [*Air Force*] ... DR
Deficient Equippage Reporting Procedures ... DERP
Deficit ... DEF
Define ... DEF
Define Area ... DA
Define Constant ... DC
Define Constant with Wordmark ... DCW
Define Device Table ... DDT
Define the File [*Data processing*] ... DTF
Define File Processor [*Data processing*] ... DFP
Define Symbol ... DS
Definite ... DEF
Definite ... DFNT
Definite Quantity ... DQ
Definite Quantity Control ... DQC
Definite-Time [*Relay*] ... DEFT
Definite-Time Relay ... DTR
Definitely Dull [*Medicine*] ... DD
Definition ... DEF
Definition, Analysis, and Mechanization ... DAM
Definition Phase Review ... DPR
Definitive Contract ... DC
Definitive Orbit Determination System [*NASA*] ... DODS
Definitized Spare Parts List ... DSPL
Deflagration to Detonation Transition ... DDT
Deflating ... DFL
Deflect ... DEFL
Deflect ... DEFLT
Deflect ... DFL
Deflectable Photomultiplier ... DPM
Deflected Jet Exhaust ... DJE
Deflected Nasal Septum [*Medicine*] ... DNS
Deflection ... DEFLTN
Deflection Coil Amplifier ... DCA
Deflection Coil Drive ... DCD
Deflection Coil Set ... DCS
Deflection Error [*Military*] ... DE
Deflection Error Average [*Military*] ... DEA
Deflection Error Probable [*Military*] ... DEP
Deflection Factor ... DF
Deflection Plate [*Technical drawings*] ... DP
Deflection Temperature under Load [*Plastics technology*] ... DTUL
Deflection of the Vertical ... V
Deflection Yoke ... DY
Deflection Yoke Amplifier ... DYA
Deflector ... DEFLTR
Deflector ... DFTR
Defogging ... DF
Defoliation ... DEFOL
Deformation of Aligned Phase ... DAP
Deformographic Storage Display Tube [*IBM Corp.*] ... DSDT
Defraction Limited Thermograph System ... DLTS
Defrauding [*FBI standardized term*] ... DEFR
Defrost ... DFR
Defruiter [*Aviation*] ... DEF
Deganawidah-Quetzalcoatl University [*Initials preferred to spelled-out name*] [*California*] ... DQU
Degasifier ... DGSFR
Degaussing ... DEGUSG
Degaussing ... DG
Degaussing Calibration ... DEG
Degaussing Calibration ... DEGCALB
Degaussing Compass ... DCMPS
Degaussing Computer ... DCMPTR
Degaussing and Deperming [*Navy*] ... D & D
Degaussing and Deperming [*Navy*] ... DEG and DEP
Degaussing Officer [*Navy*] ... DGO
Degaussing Range Officer [*Navy*] ... DGRO
Degaussing Services [*Navy*] ... DEGSVC
Degaussing Ship [*Navy symbol*] ... ADG
Degaussing System ... DGS
Degaussing Technical Officer [*Navy*] ... DGTO
Degaussing Wiping Officer [*Navy*] ... DGWO
Degenerate Electron Gas ... DEG
Degenerate Oscillating System ... DOS
Degeneration ... DEG
Degeneration Reaction ... DR
Degenerative Arthritis ... DA
Degenerative Diseases Research Foundation ... DDRF
Degenerative Joint Disease ... DJD
Deglutiatur [*Swallow*] [*Pharmacy*] ... DEGLUT
DeGoyler Foundation, Dallas, TX [*Library symbol*] ... TxDaDF
DeGoyler and MacNaughton Library, Dallas, TX [*Library symbol*] ... TxDaDM
Degradation Products [*Hematology*] ... DP
Degradation of RADAR Defense System ... DRADS
Degradation of RADAR Defense System ... DRDS
Degraded Amyloid [*Medicine*] ... DAM
Degraded Mission Assessment ... DMA
Degraded Mission Capability ... DMC
Degraduation Effects Program ... DEP
Degrease ... DGR
Degree ... D
Degree ... DEG
Degree of Cell Rupture ... DCR
Degree Celsius [*British Standards Institution*] ... degC
Degree of Conjugation [*Analytical biochemistry*] ... DC
Degree of Cooperation [*Military*] ... DOC
Degree Fahrenheit [*British Standards Institution*] ... degF
Degree of Freedom ... DOF
Degree of Honor Protective Association ... DHPA
Degree Kelvin [*British Standards Institution*] ... degK
Degree of Pocahontas ... D of P
Degree of Polymerization ... DP

Degree Rankine [*British Standards Institution*] ... degR
Degree of Substitution ... DS
Degrees Baume ... °B
Degrees Celsius ... °C
Degrees Celsius ... DC
Degrees Fahrenheit ... DF
Degrees Fahrenheit ... DGF
Degrees Fahrenheit ... °F
Degrees of Freedom [*of movement*] ... DF
Degrees Kelvin ... DK
Degrees Kelvin ... °K
Degrees Rankine ... DR
Degrees per Revolution ... DPR
Degrees per Second ... DPS
DeGroot, Dr. A. T., Texas Christian University, Fort Worth, TX [*Library symbol*] ... Deg
DeHavilland [*Aircraft Co.*] ... DH
DeHavilland Aircraft Company, Canada ... DACC
Dehra Dun [*India*] [*Later, SAB*] [*Geomagnetic observatory code*] ... DDI
Dehra Dun [*India*] [*Seismograph station code, US Geological Survey*] ... DDI
Dehumidify ... DHMY
Dehydrated ... DEHYD
Dehydrated and Convenience Foods Council [*Defunct*] ... DCFC
Dehydrated Foods Industry Council [*Later, DCFC*] ... DFIC
Dehydrator ... DYHR
Dehydroabietic Acid [*Organic chemistry*] ... DHA
Dehydroacetic Acid [*Pharmacology*] ... DHA
Dehydroascorbic Acid [*Also, DHA*] [*Oxidized form of Vitamin C*] [*Biochemistry*] ... DAA
Dehydroascorbic Acid [*Also, DAA*] [*Oxidized form of Vitamin C*] [*Biochemistry*] ... DHA
Dehydrocholesterol [*Organic chemistry*] ... DHC
Dehydrocholic Acid [*Organic chemistry*] ... DHC
Dehydroepiandrosterone [*Also, DHEA, DHIA*] [*Endocrinology*] ... DHA
Dehydroepiandrosterone [*Also, DHA, DHIA*] [*Endocrinology*] ... DHEA
Dehydroepiandrosterone Sulfate [*Also, DHEA*] [*Endocrinology*] ... DHAS
Dehydroepiandrosterone Sulfate [*Biochemistry*] ... DHEAS
Dehydrogenase [*An enzyme*] ... DH
Dehydroisoandrosterone [*Also, DHA, DHEA*] [*Endocrinology*] ... DHIA
Dehydroproline [*Biochemistry*] ... DHP
Dei Gratia [*By the Grace of God*] [*Latin*] ... DG
Deicing ... DI
Deionization-Filtration ... DF
Deir Ezzor [*Syria*] [*Airport symbol*] ... DEZ
Dejur-Amsco Corp. [*American Stock Exchange symbol*] [*Delisted*] ... DEJ
Dekagram ... DAG
Dekagram ... DEKAG
Dekagram ... DKG
DeKalb AgReseach, Inc. Cl B [*NASDAQ symbol*] ... DKLBB
DeKalb Community College, Clarkston, GA [*OCLC symbol*] ... GCD
DeKalb County Library System, Regional Service-Rockdale and Newton Counties, Decatur, GA [*Library symbol*] ... GD
DeKalb General Hospital, Decatur, GA [*Library symbol*] ... GDH
DeKalb Historical Society, Decatur, GA [*Library symbol*] ... GDD
DeKalb Literary Arts Journal [*A publication*] ... DeKalb
DeKalb Literary Arts Journal [*A publication*] ... DLAJ
Dekaliter ... DAL
Dekaliter ... DKL
Dekameter ... DKM
Dekanem [*Ten NEM*] [*See NEM*] ... DN
Dekanewton ... daN
Dekeleia [*Greece*] [*Later, PEN*] [*Geomagnetic observatory code*] ... DEK
Dekker & Nordemann [*Publisher*] ... D & N
Dekoratie voor Trouwe Dienst [*Decoration for Devoted Service*] [*South Africa*] ... DTD
Dekorativnoe Iskusstvo SSSR [*A publication*] ... Dek Iskusstvo
Dekorativnoe Iskusstvo SSSR [*A publication*] ... Dekor Isk SSSR
DeKoven Foundation for Church Work, Racine, WI [*Library symbol*] ... WRacD
Del Electronics Corp. [*NASDAQ symbol*] ... DELE
Del Laboratories, Incorporated [*American Stock Exchange symbol*] ... DLI
Del Mar College, Corpus Christi, TX [*Library symbol*] ... TxCcD
Del Monte Corp. [*NYSE symbol*] [*Delisted*] ... DEL
Del Monte Properties Company [*American Stock Exchange symbol*] [*Delisted*] ... PBC
Del Rio [*Texas*] [*Airport symbol*] [*Obsolete*] ... DRT
Del Rio, TX [*Radio station call letters*] ... KDLK
Del Rio, TX [*Radio station call letters*] ... KLKE
Del Rio, TX [*Radio station call letters*] ... KWMC
Del-Val Financial Corp. [*American Stock Exchange symbol*] ... DVL
Delactonized Ascorbate [*Biochemistry*] ... DELA
Delafield, WI [*Radio station call letters*] ... WHAD
Delalande [*France*] [*Research code symbol*] ... MD
DeLancey Divinity School, Buffalo, NY [*Library symbol*] [*Obsolete*] ... NBuDD
DeLand, FL [*Radio station call letters*] ... WDLF
Delano, CA [*Radio station call letters*] ... KCHJ
Delano, CA [*Radio station call letters*] ... KDNO
Delary [*Sweden*] [*Seismograph station code, US Geological Survey*] ... DEL
Delavan, WI [*Location identifier*] [*FAA*] ... LVV
Delaware [*Postal code*] ... DE
Delaware ... DEL
Delaware [*MARC country of publication code*] [*Library of Congress*] ... deu
Delaware [*Ontario*] [*Seismograph station code, US Geological Survey*] ... DLA
Delaware [*MARC geographic area code*] [*Library of Congress*] ... n-us-de
Delaware [*MARC language code*] [*Library of Congress*] ... del
Delaware Academy of Medicine, Wilmington, DE [*OCLC symbol*] ... DLF
Delaware Agricultural Experiment Station. Bulletin [*A publication*] ... Del Agric Exp Stn Bull
Delaware Agricultural Experiment Station. Publications [*A publication*] ... Del Ag Exp
Delaware County District Library, Delaware, OH [*Library symbol*] ... OD
Delaware County Historical Society, Chester, PA [*Library symbol*] ... PCDHi
Delaware County Institute of Science, Media, PA [*Library symbol*] ... PMedS
Delaware County Institute of Science. Proceedings [*A publication*] ... Delaware Co Inst Sc Pr
Delaware Department of State, Division of Historical and Cultural Affairs, Hall of Records, Dover, DE [*Library symbol*] ... De-Ar
Delaware Division of Libraries, Dover, DE [*OCLC symbol*] ... DWA
Delaware Historical Society. Papers [*A publication*] ... Delaware Hist Soc Papers
Delaware History [*A publication*] ... DelH
Delaware History [*A publication*] ... Del Hist
Delaware History [*A publication*] ... DH
Delaware & Hudson Railway Co. [*AAR code*] ... DH
Delaware & Hudson Railway Co. [*Nickname: Delay and Hesitate*] ... D & H
Delaware, Lackawanna & Western Railroad [*AAR code*] ... DLW
Delaware, Lackawanna & Western Railroad ... DL & WRR
Delaware, Lackawanna & Western Railroad [*Nicknames: Delay, Linger & Wait; Darn Long & Winding; Dirty, Long & Weary*] ... DL & W
Delaware Law School of Widener College, Wilmington, DE [*OCLC symbol*] ... DLA
Delaware, Maryland, Virginia ... DELMARVA
Delaware Medical Journal [*A publication*] ... Del Med J
Delaware Medical Journal [*A publication*] ... DSMJA
Delaware Notes [*A publication*] ... DelN
Delaware Notes [*A publication*] ... Del Notes
Delaware Nurse [*A publication*] ... Del Nurs
Delaware, OH [*Radio station call letters*] ... WDLR
Delaware, OH [*Radio station call letters*] ... WSLN
Delaware Rapid Interlibrary Loan Project [*Library network*] ... DRILL
Delaware River Basin Commission [*Successor to INCODEL*] ... DELRIBACO
Delaware River Basin Commission [*Successor to INCODEL*] ... DRBC
Delaware River Port Authority ... DRPA
Delaware State College ... DSC
Delaware State College, Dover, DE [*Library symbol*] ... DeDS
Delaware State Hospital, New Castle, DE [*Library symbol*] ... DeNcD
Delaware Technical and Community College, Dover, DE [*Library symbol*] ... DeDT
Delaware Technical and Community College, Northern Campus, Wilmington, DE [*Library symbol*] ... DeWT
Delaware Technical and Community College, Southern Campus, Georgetown, DE [*Library symbol*] ... DeGeT
Delaware Technical and Community College, Southern Campus, Georgetown, DE [*OCLC symbol*] ... DTS
Delaware Technical and Community College, Stanton Campus, Newark, DE [*Library symbol*] ... DeST
Delaware Technical and Community College, Stanton Campus, Newark, DE [*OCLC symbol*] ... DLE
Delaware Technical and Community College, Wilmington, DE [*OCLC symbol*] ... DLD
Delaware Valley College of Science and Agriculture, Doylestown, PA [*Library symbol*] ... PDoN
Delaware Valley News, Frenchtown, NJ [*Library symbol*] ... NjFrtD
Delaware Water Gap National Recreation Area ... DEWA
Delay [*Electronics*] ... D
Delay ... DEL
Delay ... DLA
Delay ... DLY
Delay Account of_____ [*Aviation*] ... DLAC
Delay in Arriving at Port of Embarkation [*Navy*] ... DELRIVEPOE
Delay/Capacity [*Airport terminal*] [*FAA*] ... DELCAP
Delay Driver ... DD
Delay Enroute Authorized as Ordinary Leave Provided It Does Not Interfere with Reporting Date [*Military*] ... DALVP
Delay Fuse ... DF
Delay Indefinite [*Aviation*] ... DI
Delay Key On ... DKO
Delay Line ... DL
Delay Line Assembly ... DLA
Delay Line Case ... DLC
Delay Line Memory ... DLM
Delay Line Register ... DLR
Delay Line Time Compression ... DELTIC
Delay Message [*Aviation code*] ... DEL
Delay Message [*Aviation code*] ... DLA
Delay Multivibrator ... DMV
Delay-On-Pull-In ... DPOI
Delay in Separation Code [*Military*] ... DISC
Delay Study Analysis ... DSA
Delay Timer Multiplier ... DTM

Delayed [*Indicates delayed meteorological message*] .... RTD
Delayed Action .... DA
Delayed Action Bomb .... DAB
Delayed Action Tablet [*Pharmacy*] .... DAT
Delayed Alpha Particle .... DAP
Delayed Arming [*of explosive device*] .... DA
Delayed Auditory Feedback [*Audiology*] .... DAF
Delayed Automatic Gain Control .... DAGC
Delayed Automatic Volume Control .... DAVC
Delayed Breeder or Alternative [*Nuclear energy*] .... DBOA
Delayed Broadcast [*Television*] .... DB
Delayed Clearance [*Aviation*] .... DLC
Delayed Coincidence Spectroscopy .... DCS
Delayed Contact Closure .... DCC
Delayed Delivery .... DD
Delayed Echo RADAR Marker .... DERM
Delayed Enlistment [*or Entry*] **Program** [*Military*] .... DEP
Delayed Free Recall .... DFR
Delayed Hypersensitivity [*Immunology*] .... DH
Delayed Hypersensitivity Reaction [*Medicine*] .... DHR
Delayed Jam on Target .... DJOT
Delayed Light Emission [*Green plant phenomenon*] .... DLE
Delayed Merge Package .... DMP
Delayed Neutron .... DN
Delayed Neutron Monitor .... DNM
Delayed Opening Chaff .... DOC
Delayed Opening Leaflet System [*Military propaganda*] .... DOLLS
Delayed Output [*Data processing*] .... DLO
Delayed Printer Simulator .... DPS
Delayed Procurement .... DP
Delayed Procurement Item .... DPI
Delayed Procurement Program .... DPP
Delayed Range on Target [*Air Force*] .... DROT
Delayed Readout Detector [*Satellite instrument*] .... DROD
Delayed Reenlistment Program [*Air Force*] .... DRP
Delayed Sleep Phase Syndrome .... DSPS
Delayed Sound Reinforcement .... DSR
Delayed on Target .... DOT
Delayed Time .... DT
Delayed Time/Telemetry .... DT/TM
Delayed-Type Hypersensitivity [*Immunology*] .... DTH
Delayed Weather .... DW
Delchamps, Inc. [*NASDAQ symbol*] .... DLCH
Delco Electronics Division, General Motors Corp., Technical Library, Kokomo, IN [*OCLC symbol*] .... IKN
Delcommune [*Zaire*] [*Seismograph station code, US Geological Survey*] .... DCC
Delegate .... DEL
Delegate .... DELEG
Delegate [*or Delegation*] **to Western Union** [*NATO*] .... DELWU
Delegated Engineering Representative .... DER
Delegation for Afro-American and Caribbean Cultural Affairs .... DAACA
Delegation a l'Amenagement du Territoire et a l'Action Regionale [*France*] .... DATAR
Delegation for Assistance to Jewish Emigrants [*World War II organization*] .... DELASEM
Delegation Generale a la Recherche Scientifique et Technique [*France*] .... DGRST
Delegation Ministerielle a l'Armement [*France*] .... DMA
Delete .... DEL
Delete .... DELE
Delete .... DELT
Delete .... DLT
Delete in Its Entirety .... DELENT
Deleted .... D
Deleted Quality Review Transaction [*IRS*] .... DQ
Deleted Unpostable [*IRS*] .... DU
Deleted Unpostable from Cards [*IRS*] .... DC
Deletion Reason/Supply History Code .... DRSHC
Deletions/Deferments [*Military*] .... D/D
Delft Progress Report [*A publication*] .... Delft Prog Rep
Delft Progress Report. Series A. Chemistry and Physics. Chemical and Physical Engineering [*A publication*] .... Delft Prog Rep Ser A
Delft Progress Report. Series B. Electrical. Electronic and Information Engineering [*A publication*] .... Delft Prog Rep Ser B
Delft Progress Report. Series C. Mechanical and Aeronautical Engineering and Shipbuilding [*A publication*] .... Delft Prog Rep Ser C
Delft Progress Report. Series E. Geosciences [*A publication*] .... Delft Prog Rep Ser E
Delft Progress Report. Series F. Mathematical Engineering. Mathematics and Information Engineering [*A publication*] .... Delft Prog Rep Ser F
Delhi [*India*] [*Airport symbol*] .... DEL
Delhi, CA [*Radio station call letters*] .... KNTO
Delhi International Oil Corp. [*American Stock Exchange symbol*] [*Delisted*] .... DLH
Delhi Public Library, Delhi, ON, Canada [*Library symbol*] .... CaODe
Delicatamente [*With Delicacy*] [*Music*] .... DELIC
Delicatessen .... DELI
Delineation .... DEL
Delineator [*A publication*] .... Delin
Delineavit [*He, or She, Drew It*] [*Latin*] .... DEL
Delineavit [*He Drew It*] [*Latin*] .... DELT
Delinquency .... DELNQY
Delinquency Delivery Report .... DDR
Delinquency Investigation Inventory Profile [*IRS*] .... DIIP
Delinquency Item Summary and Forecast .... DISAF
Delinquent .... DEL
Delinquent .... DELINQ
Delinquent .... DELQ
Delinquent Account .... DELACCT
Delinquent Accounts and Returns [*IRS*] .... DAR
Delinquent Investigation Research File [*IRS*] .... DIRF
Delinquent Year [*IRS*] .... DY
Deliquency Account Inventory Profile [*IRS*] .... DAIP
Deliquescent .... DELIQ
Delirium Tremens [*Also, DT's*] [*Hallucinatory condition of advanced alcoholism*] .... DT
Delirium Tremens [*Also, DT*] [*Hallucinatory condition of advanced alcoholism*] .... DT's
Delius Society .... DS
Delius Society Journal [*A publication*] .... Delius
Deliver .... DEL
Deliver .... DLVR
Deliver by Telephone [*Message handling*] .... DELPHO
Deliverable Contract Item .... DCI
Deliverable Items List .... DIL
Delivered .... DD
Delivered .... DELD
Delivered .... DLD
Delivered .... DLVD
Delivered Alongside Ship .... DAS
Delivered at Docks .... DD
Delivered Duty Paid [*"INCOTERM," International Chamber of Commerce official code*] .... DDP
Delivered at Frontier [*Seller's responsibility is fulfilled when goods have arrived at frontier, but before "customs border," of country named*] [*"INCOTERM," International Chamber of Commerce official code*] .... DAF
Delivered Sound [*Shipping*] .... DD/S
Delivered with Standard Wiring .... DSW
Delivery .... D
Delivery .... DELY
Delivery .... DLVY
Delivery .... DY
Delivery with Equipment .... DWE
Delivery on Field .... DOF
Delivery Indicator Group .... DIG
Delivery Lead Time [*Army*] .... DLT
Delivery Order .... DO
Delivery Point .... DP
Delivery Room [*Medicine*] .... DR
Delivery Schedule .... DS
Dell Rapids Carnegie Public Library, Dell Rapids, SD [*Library symbol*] .... SdDel
Dellwood Foods, Inc. [*American Stock Exchange symbol*] [*Delisted*] .... DLD
Delmarva Power & Light Co. [*NYSE symbol*] .... DEW
Delmed, Inc. [*American Stock Exchange symbol*] .... DMD
Delorean Motor Club of America [*Commercial firm*] .... DMCA
DeLorean Motor Company [*Initials used as name of its cars*] .... DMC
Delphian Society .... DS
Delphinium Society .... DS
Delphinus [*Constellation*] .... Del
Delphinus [*Constellation*] .... Delph
Delphos, OH [*Radio station call letters*] .... WDOH
Delphos Public Library, Delphos, OH [*Library symbol*] .... ODelp
Delray Beach, FL [*Radio station call letters*] .... WDBF
Delray Beach Library, Delray Beach, FL [*Library symbol*] .... FDlb
Delray Connecting Railroad Co. [*AAR code*] .... DC
Delta [*Phonetic alphabet*] .... D
Delta Air Lines, Inc. .... DA
Delta Air Lines, Inc. [*NYSE symbol*] [*Air carrier designation symbol*] .... DAL
Delta Air Lines, Inc. [*ICAO designator*] .... DL
Delta Air Lines, Inc. .... DLT
Delta Air Lines Special Handling [*for small packages*] .... DASH
Delta Air Regionalluftverkehr GmbH & Co. [*Germany*] [*ICAO designator*] .... BO
Delta Air Transport [*ICAO designator*] .... DE
Delta-Aminolevulinic Acid [*Biochemistry*] .... DALA
Delta-Aminovaleric Acid [*Organic chemistry*] .... DAV
Delta Amplitude .... DA
Delta, CO [*Radio station call letters*] .... KDTA
Delta, CO [*Radio station call letters*] .... KDTA-FM
Delta College, University Center, MI [*Library symbol*] .... MiUcD
Delta Community Library, Delta Junction, AK [*Library symbol*] .... AkDj
Delta Data Systems Corporation [*NASDAQ symbol*] .... DDSC
Delta Dental Plans Association .... DDPA
Delta Downs [*Australia*] [*Airport symbol*] [*Obsolete*] .... DDN
Delta Drilling Co. [*NASDAQ symbol*] .... DLTA
Delta Epsilon Sigma Bulletin [*A publication*] .... DESB
Delta Honor Camp, Delta, CO [*Library symbol*] .... CoDelC

Delta [or Digital] Inertial Guidance System [NASA] ....DIGS
Delta Junction/Fort Greely, AK [Location identifier] [FAA] ....BIG
Delta Kappa Epsilon [Society] ....DKE
Delta Kappa Gamma Bulletin [A publication] ....Delta Kappa Gamma Bull
Delta Milliohm Sensor ....DMS
Delta Ministry ....DM
Delta Modulation ....DM
Delta Modulation System ....DMS
Delta Natural Gas Co. [NASDAQ symbol] ....DGAS
Delta Nu Alpha Transportation Fraternity ....DNA
Delta Pressure/Delta Time ....DP/DT
Delta Psi Kappa [Society] ....DPK
Delta Public Library, Delta, CO [Library symbol] ....CoDel
Delta Queen Steamboat Company [NASDAQ symbol] ....DQSC
Delta Regional Primate Research Center, Science Information
    Service, Covington, LA [Library symbol] ....LCovD
Delta-Sleep-Inducing Peptide ....DSIP
Delta Society ....DS
Delta State College, Cleveland, MS [Library symbol] ....MsCleD
Delta Teen-Lift [An association] ....DTL
Delta, UT [Location identifier] [FAA] ....DTA
Delta, UT [Radio station call letters] ....KNAK
Delta Valley & Southern Railway Co. [AAR code] ....DVS
Delta Velocity ....DV
Delta Velocity Display ....DVD
Delta Velocity Launch ....DVL
Delta Velocity On/Off ....DVO
Delta Velocity Planet ....DVP
Delta Velocity Ullage ....DVU
Delta Waterfowl Research Station, Delta, MB, Canada [Library
    symbol] ....CaMDW
Delta Wing Orbiter ....DWO
Deltak Corp. [NASDAQ symbol] ....DLTK
Deltec International Limited [NYSE symbol] [Delisted] ....DTL
Deltiologists of America ....D of A
Deltion Agrotikes Trapezes [A publication] ....Delt Agrotikes Trapezes
Deltion tes Hellenikes Kteniatrikes Hetaireias [A publication] ....
    Delt Hell Kteniatr Hetair
Delton District Library, Delton, MI [Library symbol] ....MiDelD
Deltona Corp. [NYSE symbol] ....DLT
Delusion ....DEL
Deluxe ....DLX
Demag Nachrichten [A publication] ....Demag Nachr
Demagnetize ....DMGZ
Demagnetizer ....DMTZR
Demand ....DEM
Demand-Assignment Multiple Access ....DAMA
Demand-Assignment Signaling and Switching Unit ....DASS
Demand Deposited Accounting [Banking] ....DDA
Demand Draft ....DD
Demand Forecasting Program ....DFP
Demand History File [DoD] ....DHF
Demand Indicator ....DI
Demand Loan ....D/L
Demand Meter ....DM
Demand Meter, Printing ....DP
Demand Mode Integral Rocket Ramjet ....DMIRR
Demand Order Number [Army] ....DON
Demand Return Disposal ....DRD
Demand Totalizing Relay ....DTR
Demanding Equal Access to Facts and Warnings Aired on TV
    for Citizens Who are Hearing-Impaired [Student legal action
    organization] ....DEAFWATCH
Dembidollo [Ethiopia] [Airport symbol] ....DEM
Demeclocycline [Also, DMCT] [Antimicrobial compound] ....DMC
Dementia Praecox [or a patient with this condition] [Medical slang] ....DP
(Demethoxy)daunorubicin [Antineoplastic drug] ....DMDR
Demethylchlortetracycline [Obsolete name] [Antimicrobial
    compound] [See DMC] ....DMCT
Demi Official [Military] [British] ....DO
Demijohn [Freight] ....DEM
Demijohn ....DJN
Demilitarization Protective Ensemble ....DPE
Demilitarize ....DEMIL
Demilitarized Zone ....DMZ
Demineralized Water ....DMW
Demineralized Water Storage Tank [Nuclear energy] ....DWST
Demineralizer ....DMNRLZR
Deming, NM [Radio station call letters] ....KDEM
Deming, NM [Radio station call letters] ....KOTS
Deming Public Library, Deming, NM [Library symbol] ....NmD
Demirkoy [Turkey] [Seismograph station code, US Geological
    Survey] ....DMK
Demobilize ....DEMOB
Democracy International ....DI
Democracy Project ....DP
Democrat [or Democratic] ....D
Democrat [or Democratic] ....DEM
Democrat-Farmer-Labor [Party] [Minnesota] ....DFL
Democrat Socialist Party [Japan] ....DSP
Democratic Action Party [Malaysia] ....DAP

Democratic Agenda [An association] ....DA
Democratic Business Council ....DBC
Democratic Congress Alliance [Gambia] ....DCA
Democratic Congressional Campaign Committee ....DCCC
Democratic Governors Conference ....DGC
Democratic Kampuchea [Pol Pot's regime in Cambodia] ....DK
Democratic Labor Association [Philippines] ....DLA
Democratic Labor Party [Australia] ....DLP
Democratic Left [A publication] ....Demo Left
Democratic Movement for Change [Political party] [Israel] ....DMC
Democratic National Committee ....DNC
Democratic National Committee - Women's Affairs Division
    [Later, DNCWD] ....DNCWAD
Democratic National Committee - Women's Division [Formerly,
    DNCWAD] ....DNCWD
Democratic National Strategy Council ....DNSC
Democratic Non-Party Nationalist Party [British] ....DemNPN
Democratic Party [Slang] ....DEMP
Democratic Party [Suspended] [Uganda] ....DP
Democratic Party of Nigeria and the Cameroons ....DPNC
Democratic Peoples Republic of Korea ....DPRK
Democratic Peoples Republic of Korea ....DRK
Democratic Peoples Republic of Korea [Two-letter standard code] ....KP
Democratic Peoples Republic of Korea [Three-letter standard code] ....PRK
Democratic Policy Committee ....DPC
Democratic Republic of China ....DRC
Democratic Republic of the Congo [Later, Zaire] ....DRC
Democratic Republic of Vietnam [North Vietnam] ....DRV
Democratic Republic of Vietnam [North Vietnam] ....DRVN
Democratic Republican Party [Political party] [Korea] ....DRP
Democratic Review [A publication] ....Dem R
Democratic Senatorial Campaign Committee ....DSCC
Democratic Socialist Organizing Committee [Later, DSA] ....DSOC
Democratic Socialists of America ....DSA
Democratic Study Group ....DSG
Democratic Turnhalle Alliance [Political party] [Namibia] ....DTA
Democratic Unionist Party [Ireland] ....DUP
Democratic Workers' Congress [Ceylon] ....DWC
Democrazia e Diritto [A publication] ....Democr e Dir
Democritus Nuclear Research Center [Greece] ....DNRC
Demodulate/Modulate ....D/M
Demodulator ....DEM
Demodulator ....DEMOD
Demodulator Band Filter ....DBF
Demodulator Neon Driver ....DND
Demografia y Economia [A publication] ....Demogr y Econ
Demographic Data Retrieval System [Census Bureau]
    [Information service] ....DDRS
Demographic Research Company [Information service] ....DRC
Demographics Laboratory [Information service] ....DEM/LAB
Demography [A publication] ....DEMO
Demokratie und Recht [A publication] ....Demokr Recht
Demokratische Bauernpartei Deutschlands [Democratic
    Peasants' Party] [East Germany] ....DBD
Demolition ....DEMO
Demolition ....DEMOL
Demolition ....DML
Demolition Bomb ....DEMBOMB
Demolition Firing Device ....DFD
Demolition Research Unit ....DRU
Demolition Rocket ....DR
Demonstrate ....DMST
Demonstratio Mathematica [A publication] ....Demonstratio Math
Demonstration ....DEM
Demonstration ....DMSTN
Demonstration Air Force ....DAF
Demonstration Cities and Metropolitan Development Act ....DCMDA
Demonstration Detail Test Objectives ....DDTO
Demonstration Flight Rating Test ....DFRT
Demonstration Flight Satellite ....DFS
Demonstration of Operational Feasibility ....DOF
Demonstration Programs Administration [HUD] ....DPA
Demonstration Reliability Acceptance Test ....DRAT
Demonstration and Research Center for Early Education
    [George Peabody College, Nashville] ....DARCEE
Demonstration and Shakedown Operation Piggyback [Kit]
    [Military] ....DASOP
Demonstration and Shakedown Operations [Military] ....DASO
Demonstration Site Operational Test Series ....DSOTS
Demonstration and Training ....D & T
Demonstration and Validation ....DV
Demonstrative ....DEMON
Demonstrator ....DEMO
Demonstrator ....DEMONST
Demonstrators Association of Illinois ....DAI
Demopolis, AL [Location identifier] [FAA] ....RZO
Demopolis, AL [Television station call letters] ....WIIQ
Demopolis, AL [Radio station call letters] ....WNAN
Demopolis, AL [Radio station call letters] ....WXAL
DeMorgans Theorems [Rules of replacement] [Logic] ....DeM
Demos D Scale [Psychology] ....DDS

Demote ... DEM
Demountable Cathode Lamp ... DCL
Demultiplexer [*Data processing*] ... DEMUX
Demultiplexer [*Data processing*] ... DMUX
Demurrage ... DEM
Demy [*Size of paper*] ... DEM
Demystify the Established Standardized Tests [*Project*] ... DETEST
Den-Tal-Ez, Inc. [*American Stock Exchange symbol*] [*Delisted*] ... DTZ
Denarius [*or Denarii*] [*Silver coin in Ancient Rome; gold coin in Roman Empire*] ... D
Denatured ... DENAT
Denatured ... DNTRD
Denatured Uranium [*Nuclear reactor technology*] ... DU
Denbighshire [*County in Wales*] ... DENB
Denbighshire [*County in Wales*] ... DENBIGHS
Denbighshire [*County in Wales*] ... DENBS
Dencor Energy Cost Controls, Inc. [*NASDAQ symbol*] ... DENC
Dendrite Arm Spacing ... DAS
Dendritic Algorithm [*Organic molecules*] ... DENDRAL
Denelcor, Inc. [*NASDAQ symbol*] ... DENL
Den'gi i Kredit [*A publication*] ... Den'gi i Kred
Dengue Hemorrhagic Fever ... DHF
Dengue Hemorrhagic Fever Syndrome [*Medicine*] ... DHFS
Denham [*Australia*] [*Airport symbol*] ... DNM
Denham Springs, LA [*Radio station call letters*] ... WLBI
Denial [*Psychology*] ... Dn
Denied-Boarding Compensation [*Airlines*] ... DBC
Denier [*Later, tex*] ... den
Deniliquin [*Australia*] [*Airport symbol*] ... DNQ
Denis Island [*Seychelles Islands*] [*Airport symbol*] ... DEI
Denison Carnegie Library, Denison, IA [*Library symbol*] ... IaDen
Denison, IA [*Radio station call letters*] ... KDSN
Denison, IA [*Radio station call letters*] ... KDSN-FM
Denison Mines Ltd. [*NASDAQ symbol*] ... DENIF
Denison & Pacific Suburban Railway Co. [*AAR code*] ... DPS
Denison Public Library, Denison, TX [*Library symbol*] ... TxDeni
Denison, TX [*Radio station call letters*] ... KALK-FM
Denison, TX [*Radio station call letters*] ... KDSQ
Denison, TX [*Radio station call letters*] ... KDSX
Denison, TX [*Radio station call letters*] ... KGCC
Denison, TX [*Television station call letters*] ... KOAV
Denison University, Granville, OH [*OCLC symbol*] ... DNU
Denison University, Granville, OH [*Library symbol*] ... OGraD
Denison University. Scientific Laboratories. Bulletin [*A publication*] ... Denison Univ Sc Lab B
Denison University. Scientific Laboratories. Journal [*A publication*] ... Denison Univ Sci Lab Jour
Denki Kagaku [*A publication*] ... Denki Kag
Denkschriften der Oesterreichischen Akademie der Wissenschaften. Philosophisch-Historische Klasse [*A publication*] ... OAW PHKD
Denkschriften der Schweizerischen Naturforschenden Gesellschaft [*A publication*] ... Denkschr Schweiz Naturforsch Ges
Denmark ... D
Denmark ... DE
Denmark ... DEN
Denmark [*MARC country of publication code*] [*Library of Congress*] ... dk
Denmark [*Three-letter standard code*] ... DNK
Denmark [*MARC geographic area code*] [*Library of Congress*] ... e-dk---
Denmark [*Aircraft nationality and registration mark*] ... OY
Denmark [*Three-letter standard code*] ... DK
Denmark-America Foundation ... DAF
Denmark Cheese Association ... DCA
Denmark. Research Establishment Risoe. Report [*A publication*] ... Den Res Establ Risoe Rep
Denmark. Research Establishment Risoe. Risoe Report [*A publication*] ... Den Res Establ Risoe Risoe Rep
Denmark. Technical University. Structural Research Laboratory. Report [*A publication*] ... Den Tech Univ Struct Res Lab Rep
Denning Mobile Robot [*NASDAQ symbol*] ... GARD
Dennis Memorial Library, Newton, NJ [*Library symbol*] ... NjNet
Dennis R. Williams [*Designer's mark on US bicentennial dollar*] ... DRW
Dennison Manufacturing Co. [*NYSE symbol*] ... DSN
Denniston [*New Zealand*] [*Seismograph station code, US Geological Survey*] [*Closed*] ... DNS
Denny's, Inc. [*NYSE symbol*] ... DEN
Denomination ... DENOM
Denominational Executives of Christian Education ... DECE
Denominator [*In formulas for life annuities and life insurance premiums*] ... D
Denominazione di Origine Controllata [*Italian wine designation*] ... DOC
Denote ... DEN
Denote Chassis ... DCH
Denpasar [*Indonesia*] [*Seismograph station code, US Geological Survey*] ... DNP
Denpasar [*Indonesia*] [*Airport symbol*] ... DPS
Dense ... DNS
Dense-Cored Vesicles [*Anatomy*] ... DCV
Dense Electronic Population ... DEP
Dense Flint ... DF
Dense Plasma Focus ... DPF
Dense-Staining Material [*Cytology*] ... DSM
Dense Tubular System ... DTS
Dense Upper Cloud ... DUC
Densely Packaged Encased Standard Element ... DPESE
Densest Random Packing [*Solid state physics*] ... DRP
Densified Refuse-Derived Fuel ... DRDF
Density ... D
Density ... DEN
Density ... DENS
Density ... DY
Density Altitude [*Navigation*] ... DA
Density Altitude [*Computer*] ... DENALT
Density Dependent Inhibition [*of cell growth*] ... DDI
Density-Depth ... DEDE
Density Gradient ... DG
Density Gradient Electrophoresis ... DGE
Density Gradient Sedimentation [*Analytical biochemistry*] ... DGS
Density Manipulation Subsystem ... DMS
Density Meter [*Instrumentation*] ... DM
Density Phenomena [*Japan*] ... DENPA
Density Probe ... DENPRE
Density of Water ... DOW
Dent [*Idaho*] [*Seismograph station code, US Geological Survey*] [*Closed*] ... DEI
Dental ... D
Dental ... DEN
Dental ... DENTL
Dental ... DNTL
Dental Abstracts [*A publication*] ... Dent Abstr
Dental Activity ... DENTAC
Dental Admission Test [*Education*] ... DAT
Dental Amalgamator ... DAMLG
Dental Anaesthesia and Sedation [*A publication*] ... Dent Anaesth Sedat
Dental Anesthetic [*Medicine*] ... DA
Dental Apprentice ... DA
Dental Assistant ... DA
Dental Assistant [*A publication*] ... Dent Assist
Dental Assisting National Board ... DANB
Dental Auxiliary Utilization ... DAU
Dental Cadmos [*A publication*] ... DECAA
Dental Cadmos [*A publication*] ... Dent Cadmos
Dental Civic Action Program [*Vietnam*] ... DENTCAP
Dental Clinics of North America [*A publication*] ... Dent Clin N
Dental Clinics of North America [*A publication*] ... Dent Clin North Am
Dental Company [*Marine Corps*] ... DENCO
Dental Continuation Pay [*Military*] ... DCP
Dental Corps [*Navy*] ... DC
Dental Corps [*Air Force*] ... DENTCORPS
Dental Corps, General Service [*USNR officer designation*] ... DCR
Dental Cosmos Library, Philadelphia, PA [*Library symbol*] [*Obsolete*] ... PPDC
Dental Dealers of America ... DDA
Dental Dialogue [*A publication*] ... Dent Dialogue
Dental Dimensions [*A publication*] ... Dent Dimens
Dental Discourse [*A publication*] ... Dent Discourse
Dental Documentary Foundation ... DDF
Dental Echo [*A publication*] ... Dent Echo
Dental Economics [*A publication*] ... Dent Econ
Dental Examining Board ... DEB
Dental Gold Institute ... DGI
Dental Group Management Association ... DGMA
Dental Guidance Council for Cerebral Palsy ... DGCCP
Dental Health International ... DHI
Dental Health (London) [*A publication*] ... Dent Health (Lond)
Dental Hygiene [*A publication*] ... Dent Hyg
Dental Images [*A publication*] ... Dent Images
Dental Journal [*A publication*] ... Dent J
Dental Labor (Munich) [*A publication*] ... Dent Labor (Munch)
Dental Laboratory Conference ... DLC
Dental Laboratory Review [*A publication*] ... Dent Lab Rev
Dental Literature Index [*A publication*] ... Dent Ind
Dental Management [*A publication*] ... Dent Manage
Dental Manufacturers of America ... DMA
Dental Officer ... DO
Dental Pay ... DENPAY
Dental Practitioner's Formulary ... DPF
Dental Press [*A publication*] ... Dent Press
Dental Progress [*A publication*] ... Dent Prog
Dental Prosthetic Technician ... DP
Dental Radiography and Photography [*A publication*] ... Dent Radiogr Photogr
Dental Recruit ... DR
Dental Repair Technician [*Navy*] ... DRM
Dental Research Information Center ... DRIC
Dental Student [*A publication*] ... Dent Stud
Dental Suction Apparatus ... DSCAPRS
Dental Surgery [*Medical Officer designation*] [*British*] ... DS
Dental Surgery Assistant [*British*] ... DSA
Dental Survey [*A publication*] ... Dent Surv
Dental Technician [*A publication*] ... Dent Tech
Dental Technician [*Navy rating*] ... DT
Dental Technician, Chief [*Navy rating*] ... DTC

Dental Technician, First Class [*Navy rating*]........................DT1
Dental Technician, Master Chief [*Navy rating*]...................DTCM
Dental Technician, Second Class [*Navy rating*].................DT2
Dental Technician, Senior Chief [*Navy rating*]..................DTCS
Dental Technician, Third Class [*Navy rating*]....................DT3
Dental Therapy Assistant .... DTA
Dental Update [*A publication*]..............................Dent Update
Dental World Center [*NASDAQ symbol*].......................DWLD
Dental X-Ray Teaching and Training Replica................DEXTER
Dentalman [*Nonrated enlisted man*] [*Navy*]..................... DN
Dentistry ....DENT
Dentistry in Japan (Tokyo) [*A publication*] .... Dent Jpn (Tokyo)
Dentition [*Medicine*]..DENT
Dento-Enamel Junction [*Dentistry*]................................DEJ
Dento-Med Industries [*NASDAQ symbol*].......................DTMD
Denton [*Texas*] [*Seismograph station code, US Geological
    Survey*] [*Closed*] .... DNT
Denton, TX [*Location identifier*] [*FAA*]...........................DTO
Denton, TX [*Radio station call letters*].........................KDNT
Denton, TX [*Radio station call letters*].........................KIXK
Denton, TX [*Radio station call letters*].........................KNTU
Dentsply International, Inc. [*Formerly, Dentists' Supply Co. of
    NY*] [*NYSE symbol*] .... DSP
Dentur [*Give*] [*Pharmacy*]..D
Dentur [*Give*] [*Pharmacy*]...DENT
Dentur Tales Doses [*Give in Such Doses*] [*Pharmacy*]...........DENT TAL DOS
Dentur Tales Doses [*Give of Such Doses*] [*Pharmacy*].............DTD
Denver [*Colorado*] [*Mint mark, when appearing on US coins*]................D
Denver [*Colorado*] [*Airport symbol*]..............................DEN
Denver [*Colorado*] [*Seismograph station code, US Geological Survey*]....DEN
Denver Area Project, Denver, CO [*OCLC symbol*]...........DVX
Denver Art Museum, Denver, CO [*Library symbol*]..........CoDA
Denver Botanic Gardens, Inc., Denver, CO [*Library symbol*] ....CoDDB
Denver, CO [*Location identifier*] [*FAA*] .... APA
Denver, CO [*Location identifier*] [*FAA*] ....BJC
Denver, CO [*Location identifier*] [*FAA*] ....BKF
Denver, CO [*Location identifier*] [*FAA*] ....CHY
Denver, CO [*Location identifier*] [*FAA*] ....GQW
Denver, CO [*Radio station call letters*] .... KAZY
Denver, CO [*Radio station call letters*] .... KBNO
Denver, CO [*Radio station call letters*] .... KBPI
Denver, CO [*Radio station call letters*] .... KBRQ
Denver, CO [*Television station call letters*] .... KBTV
Denver, CO [*Radio station call letters*] .... KCFR
Denver, CO [*Television station call letters*] ....KCNC-TV
Denver, CO [*Radio station call letters*] .... KDEN
Denver, CO [*Television station call letters*] .... KDVR
Denver, CO [*Radio station call letters*] .... KEZW
Denver, CO [*Radio station call letters*] .... KHOW
Denver, CO [*Radio station call letters*] .... KHUM
Denver, CO [*Radio station call letters*] .... KIMN
Denver, CO [*Radio station call letters*] .... KJJZ
Denver, CO [*Radio station call letters*] .... KKBB
Denver, CO [*Radio station call letters*] .... KLDR
Denver, CO [*Radio station call letters*] .... KLIR
Denver, CO [*Radio station call letters*] .... KLZ
Denver, CO [*Television station call letters*] ....KMGH-TV
Denver, CO [*Radio station call letters*] .... KNUS
Denver, CO [*Radio station call letters*] .... KOA
Denver, CO [*Radio station call letters*] .... KOAQ
Denver, CO [*Radio station call letters*] .... KOSI-FM
Denver, CO [*Radio station call letters*] .... KPKE
Denver, CO [*Radio station call letters*] .... KPOF
Denver, CO [*Radio station call letters*] .... KRKS
Denver, CO [*Television station call letters*] ....KRMA-TV
Denver, CO [*Radio station call letters*] .... KVOD
Denver, CO [*Television station call letters*] .... KWGN
Denver, CO [*Radio station call letters*] .... KYGO
Denver Developmental Screening Test [*For mental development
    of infants*] ....DDST
Denver Federal Records Center, Denver, CO [*Library symbol*] ....CoDFR
Denver Journal of International Law and Policy [*A publication*].....................
    Denver J Int L & Pol
Denver Laboratories [*Great Britain*] [*Research code symbol*] ....R
Denver Law Center Journal [*A publication*] ....Denver LCJ
Denver Law Journal [*A publication*]....................... Denver Law
Denver Law Journal [*A publication*].......................Denver L J
Denver Law Librarians Group, Denver, CO [*OCLC symbol*]...............COY
Denver Medical Times [*A publication*].............. Denver Med Times
Denver Museum of Natural History, Denver, CO [*Library symbol*]..................
    CoDMNH
Denver Museum of Natural History. Museum Pictorial Popular
    Series. Proceedings [*A publication*] ....
    Denver Mus Nat History Mus Pictorial Pop Ser Proc
Denver Post, Inc., Denver, CO [*Library symbol*] ....CoDDP
Denver Public Library, Denver, CO [*Library symbol*].............CoD
Denver Public Library, Denver, CO [*OCLC symbol*].............DPL
Denver Public Library, Denver General Hospital Library, Denver,
    CO [*Library symbol*]...CoD-H
Denver Public Library, Denver, IA [*Library symbol*]................. IaDv

Denver Public Schools, Professional Library, Denver, CO
    [*Library symbol*]...CoDPS
Denver Quarterly [*A publication*] .... Den Q
Denver Quarterly [*A publication*] .... DenverQ
Denver Quarterly [*A publication*] .... DQ
Denver Research Institute ....DRI
[*The*] Denver & Rio Grande Western Railroad Co. .... D & RGW
[*The*] Denver & Rio Grande Western Railroad Co. [*AAR code*] .... DRGW
Denver & Salt Lake Railroad..................................... D & SL
Denver & Salt Lake Railroad [*AAR code*]........................DSL
Denver Special Librarians, Denver, CO [*OCLC symbol*] .... DVS
Denver Western Petroleum [*NASDAQ symbol*]................DENW
Denver Wildlife Research Center [*Department of the Interior*]........DWRC
Denville Free Public Library, Denville, NJ [*Library symbol*]............NjDe
Denying ....DENYG
Deo Dedit [*He Gave to God*] [*Latin*].............................. DD
Deo Gratias [*Thanks Be to God; or God Be Thanked*] [*Latin*]................. DG
Deo Optimo Maximo [*To God, Most Good, Most Great*] [*Latin*]........ DOM
Deo Volente [*God Willing*] [*Latin*].................................DV
Deorbit, Entry, and Landing ....DEL
Deorbit/Landing.. D/L
Deoxidized High-Residual Phosphorus [*Copper*].............DHP
Deoxidized Low-Residual Phosphorus [*Copper*]..............DLP
Deoxophylloerythroetioporphyrin [*Biochemistry*]............DPEP
Deoxy [*or Desoxy*] [*Biochemistry*]................................. d
Deoxy-d-glucose [*Also, DG, DOG*] [*Biochemistry*]............DDG
Deoxy-D-glucose [*Also, DDG, DOG*] [*Biochemistry*]............ DG
Deoxy-D-glucose [*Also, DDG, DG*] [*Biochemistry*]............ DOG
Deoxyadenosine Diphosphate [*Biochemistry*].................dADP
Deoxyadenosine Monophosphate [*Biochemistry*]..............dAMP
Deoxyadenosine Triphosphate [*Biochemistry*].................dATP
Deoxycholate [*Biochemistry*].....................................DOC
Deoxycholate-Citrate Agar [*Microbiology*].....................DCA
Deoxycholate-Citrate-Lactose-Sucrose [*Agar*] [*Microbiology*]......DCLS
Deoxycholic Acid [*Biochemistry*]................................DCA
Deoxycoformycin [*Also, dCF*] [*Antileukemia drug*] ....DCF
Deoxycorticosterone [*Endocrinology*]............................DOC
Deoxycorticosterone [*or Desoxycorticosterone*] Acetate [*Also,
    DOCA*] [*Endocrinology*]...DCA
Deoxycorticosterone [*or Desoxycorticosterone*] Acetate [*Also,
    DCA*] [*Endocrinology*]...DOCA
Deoxycorticosterone Glucoside [*Also, DOCG*] [*Endocrinology*]............DCG
Deoxycorticosterone Glucoside [*Also, DCG*] [*Endocrinology*]............DOCG
Deoxycorticosterone Trimethylacetate [*Endocrinology*] ....DCTMA
Deoxycytidine Diphosphate [*Biochemistry*]....................dCDP
Deoxycytidine Monophosphate [*Biochemistry*]................dCMP
Deoxycytidinetriphosphatase [*An enzyme*]...................dCTPase
Deoxycytidinetriphosphate [*Organic chemistry*] ....DCTP
Deoxyephedrine [*or Desoxyephedrine*] [*Pharmacology*] .... D-O-E
Deoxyglucose-Phosphate [*Biochemistry*].......................DGP
Deoxyguanosine Diphosphate [*Biochemistry*].................dGDP
Deoxyguanosine Monophosphate [*Biochemistry*]..............dGMP
Deoxyguanosine Triphosphate [*Biochemistry*].................DGTP
Deoxyguanylate [*Biochemistry*]................................... dG
Deoxyheptulosonic Acid [*Biochemistry*]......................dHpuA
Deoxyinosine Diphosphate [*Biochemistry*].....................dIDP
Deoxyinosine Monophosphate [*Biochemistry*]..................dIMP
Deoxyinosine Triphosphate [*Biochemistry*].....................dITP
Deoxynorlaudanosolinecarboxylic Acid [*Biochemistry*] ....DNLCA
Deoxyribonuclease [*Preferred form, DNase*] [*An enzyme*] .... DNAase
Deoxyribonuclease [*An enzyme*]................................DNase
Deoxyribonucleic Acid [*Biochemistry, genetics*]................DNA
Deoxyribonucleic Acid - Chloroplast [*Biochemistry, genetics*]
    [*Also, ctDNA*] .... Chl-DNA
Deoxyribonucleic Acid, Chloroplast [*Biochemistry, genetics*]
    [*Also, Chl-DNA*] ....ctDNA
Deoxyribonucleic Acid, Cloned [*Biochemistry, genetics*]...............cDNA
Deoxyribonucleic Acid, Complementary [*Biochemistry, genetics*]........cDNA
Deoxyribonucleic Acid, Double-Stranded [*Biochemistry; genetics*]....dsDNA
Deoxyribonucleic Acid, Histone [*Biochemistry, genetics*]..............hDNA
Deoxyribonucleic Acid - Kinetoplast [*Biochemistry, genetics*]............ K-DNA
Deoxyribonucleic Acid, Mitochondrial [*Biochemistry, genetics*] ....mtDNA
Deoxyribonucleic Acid, Nuclear [*Biochemistry, genetics*]...............nDNA
Deoxyribonucleic Acid Polymerase [*An enzyme*]...............DNAp
Deoxyribonucleic Acid, Recombinant [*Biochemistry; genetics*] ....rDNA
Deoxyribonucleic Acid, Ribosomal [*Biochemistry; genetics*]...............rDNA
Deoxyribonucleic Acid, Ribosomal - Chloroplast [*Biochemistry,
    genetics*] ....Chl-rDNA
Deoxyribonucleic Acid, Single-Stranded [*Biochemistry, genetics*] ..... ssDNA
Deoxyribonucleic Acid, Traditional Form [*DNA with right-handed
    helix*] [*Biochemistry, genetics*]...............................B DNA
Deoxyribonucleic Acid, Zigzag [*DNA with left-handed helix*]
    [*Biochemistry, genetics*] ....Z DNA
Deoxyribosylthymine Diphosphate [*Biochemistry*]............dTDP
Deoxyribosylthymine Monophosphate [*Biochemistry*] ....dTMP
Deoxyribosylthymine Triphosphate [*Biochemistry*]............dTTP
Deoxystreptamine [*Organic chemistry*]..........................DOS
Deoxythymidine [*Organic chemistry*]............................... DT
Deoxythymidine Diphosphate [*Biochemistry*]..................DTDP
Deoxythymidine Monophosphate [*Biochemistry*].............. DTMP
Deoxythymidine Triphosphate [*Biochemistry*] .... DTTP

Deoxyuridine Diphosphate [*Biochemistry*] .... dUDP
Deoxyuridine Monophosphate [*Biochemistry*] .... dUMP
Deoxyuridine Triphosphate [*Biochemistry*] .... dUTP
Deoxyxanthosine Diphosphate [*Biochemistry*] .... dXDP
Deoxyxanthosine Monophosphate [*Biochemistry*] .... dXMP
Deoxyxanthosine Triphosphate [*Biochemistry*] .... dXTP
DEP Corporation [*NASDAQ symbol*] .... DEPC
Depart .... D
Depart .... DEP
Depart .... DEPT
Depart .... DPRT
Depart .... DPT
Departamento Administrativo do Servico Publico [*Administrative Department of Public Service*] [*Brazil*] .... DASP
Departamento de Imprensa e Propaganda [*Brazil*] .... DIP
Departamento Nacional do Cafe [*Brazil*] .... DNC
Departamento Nacional de Estradas de Ferro [*National Railways Department*] [*Brazil*] .... DNEF
Departamento Nacional de Saude Publica [*Brazil*] .... DNSP
Departement des Archives et Statistiques de la Ville de Quebec, Quebec, PQ, Canada [*Library symbol*] .... CaQQCH
Departement de Biologie du College Bourget Rigaud Bulletin. [*A publication*] .... Dep Biol Coll Bourget Rigaud Bull
Departement Etranger Hachette .... DEH
Departement d'Etudes et de Recherches en Technologie Spatiale .... DERTS
Department .... D
Department .... DEP
Department .... DEPART
Department .... DEPT
Department .... DPT
Department of Aboriginal Affairs, Darwin, NT, Australia [*Library symbol*] .... AuDDa
Department of Aeronautics and Astronautics [*MIT*] .... DAA
Department of Aeronautics, State of Nebraska [*Lincoln, NE*] [*FAA designator*] .... NEB
Department of Agriculture [*Hyattsville, MD*] [*FAA designator*] .... AGR
Department of Agriculture .... D of A
Department of Agriculture .... DA
Department of Agriculture .... DOA
Department of Agriculture, Animal Disease Research Institute, Ottawa, ON, Canada [*Library symbol*] .... CaOOAgA
Department of Agriculture, Animal Research Institute, Ottawa, ON, Canada [*Library symbol*] .... CaOOAgAR
Department of Agriculture, Central Experimental Farm Reference Library, Ottawa, ON, Canada [*Library symbol*] [*Obsolete*] .... CaOOAgC
Department of Agriculture, Chemistry Division, Ottawa, ON, Canada [*Library symbol*] [*Obsolete*] .... CaOOAgCh
Department of Agriculture, Engineering Research Service, Ottawa, ON, Canada [*Library symbol*] .... CaOOAgER
Department of Agriculture, Entomology Research Institute, Ottawa, ON, Canada [*Library symbol*] .... CaOOAgE
Department of Agriculture and Fisheries [*Scotland*] .... DAF
Department of Agriculture and Fisheries for Scotland .... DAFS
Department of Agriculture, Food Production and Marketing Branch, Laboratory Services Section, Ottawa, ON, Canada [*Library symbol*] .... CaOOAgFP
Department of Agriculture, Horticultural Division, Ottawa, ON, Canada [*Library symbol*] [*Obsolete*] .... CaOOAgH
Department of Agriculture, Legal Library, Ottawa, ON, Canada [*Library symbol*] [*Obsolete*] .... CaOOAgL
Department of Agriculture, Neatby Library, Ottawa, ON, Canada [*Library symbol*] .... CaOOAGCH
Department of Agriculture, Plant Research Institute, Ottawa, ON, Canada [*Library symbol*] .... CaOOAgB
Department of Agriculture, Research Station, Ottawa, ON, Canada [*Library symbol*] .... CaOOAgO
Department of Agriculture, Soil Research Institute, Ottawa, ON, Canada [*Library symbol*] .... CaOOAgSR
Department of the Air Force .... DAF
Department of the Air Force Command and Control System .... DAFCCS
Department of the Air Force Integrated Command and Control Systems .... DAFICCS
Department of the Air Force Special Order .... DAFSO
Department of the Air Member for Personnel [*British*] .... DAMP
Department of the Air Member for Supply and Organization [*British*] .... DAMSO
Department of the Air Member for Training [*British*] .... DAMT
Department of Antiquities in Palestine. Quarterly [*A publication*] .... QAP
Department of the Army .... DA
Department of the Army .... DEPTAR
Department of the Army .... DOA
Department of the Army Administrative Area .... DAAA
Department of the Army Air Traffic Coordinating Officer .... DAATCO
Department of the Army Allocation Committee, Ammunition .... DAACA
Department of the Army Alternate Command and Control Element .... DAACCE
Department of the Army Alternate Command and Control Element .... DACE
Department of the Army Audiovisual Media Production Program .... DAAVMPP
Department of the Army Audiovisual Program .... DAAP
Department of the Army Avionics Master Plan .... DAAMP
Department of the Army Certificate of Achievement .... DACA
Department of the Army Civilian .... DAC
Department of the Army Command and Control Reporting System .... DAXREP
Department of the Army Command and Control System .... DACCS
Department of the Army Communication Resources Plan .... DACRP
Department of the Army Communications Center .... DACC
Department of the Army Compassionate Review Board .... DACRB
Department of the Army Decoration for Meritorious Civilian Service .... DADMCS
Department of the Army, Deputy Chief of Staff for Logistics .... DADCSLOG
Department of the Army Distribution/Allocation Committee .... DADAC
Department of the Army Equipment Data Review Committee .... DAEDARC
Department of the Army Field Manuals .... DAFM
Department of the Army Forward Depot .... DAFD
Department of the Army Forward-Floating Depot .... DAFFD
Department of the Army Historical Advisory Committee .... DAHAC
Department of the Army Inspector General .... DAIG
Department of the Army Integrated Materiel Support .... DAIMS
Department of the Army Intelligence Plan .... DAIP
Department of the Army Liaison Team .... DALT
Department of the Army Logistics Readiness Liaison Visits .... DALRLV
Department of the Army Long-Range Technological Forecast .... DALRTF
Department of the Army/Main .... DEPTAR/MAIN
Department of the Army Management Information System .... DAMIS
Department of the Army Management Review and Improvement Program .... DAMRIP
Department of the Army Master Priority List .... DAMPL
Department of the Army Materiel Annex .... DAMA
Department of the Army Materiel Program .... DAMP
Department of the Army Military Personnel Management Team .... DAMPMT
Department of the Army Modification Work Order .... DAMWO
Department of the Army Motion Picture/Television Production Board .... DAMP/TVPB
Department of the Army Motion Picture/Television Production Program .... DAMP/TVPP
Department of the Army, Office of the Chief, Army Reserve .... DAAR
Department of the Army Pamphlet .... DAP
Department of the Army Pamphlet .... DA PAM
Department of the Army Panel on Environmental Physiology .... DAPEP
Department of the Army Plan for Assistance in Department of Health, Education, and Welfare .... DA-AHEW
Department of the Army Plan for [*Possession, Control, and*] **Operation of Railroads** .... DA-OPRR
Department of the Army Policy for Disclosure of Classified Military Information [*to foreign government*] .... DADCMI
Department of the Army Program Report .... DAPR
Department of the Army Program Review .... DAPR
Department of the Army Regional Representative .... DARR
Department of the Army Relocation Sites .... DARS
Department of the Army Requisitioning, Receipt, and Issue System .... DARRIS
Department of the Army Secure Facsimile .... DARFAX
Department of the Army Shipping Document .... DASD
Department of the Army Special Order .... DASO
Department of the Army Special Photographic Office .... DASPO
Department of the Army Standard Port System .... DASPS
Department of the Army Strategic Logistics [*Study*] .... DASL
Department of the Army Suitablility Evaluation Board .... DASEB
Department of the Army System Coordinator .... DASC
Department of the Army Systems Staff Officer .... DASSO
Department of the Army Technical Manual .... DATM
Department of the Army Training and Support Committee .... DATSC
Department of the Army Vocabulary of Information Elements .... DAVIE
Department of the Attorney General and of Justice, Sydney, NSW, Australia [*Library symbol*] .... AuSAJ
Department of Audiovisual Instruction [*of NEA*] [*Later, AECT*] .... DAVI
Department of Bantu Administration and Development [*An agency of South African government*] .... BAD
Department Bulletin. United States Department of Agriculture [*A publication*] .... Dept Bull US Dept Agric
Department of Central Intelligence [*Thailand*] .... DCI
Department of City and Regional Planning [*MIT*] .... DCRP
Department of Civil Aviation [*Australia*] .... DCA
Department of Classroom Teachers [*of NEA*] .... DCT
Department of the Commandant-General, Royal Marines [*British*] .... CGRM
Department of Commerce .... COMM
Department of Commerce .... D of C
Department of Commerce .... DC
Department of Commerce .... DOC
Department of Commerce Board of Contract Appeals .... COMMBCA
Department of Commerce Library .... DOCL
Department of Communications [*Canada*] .... DOC
Department of Community Development [*Proposed government department*] .... DCD

Department of Conservation and Environment [*Proposed name for US Department of the Interior*].................DCE
Department of Data Management [*Veterans Administration*]..............DDM
Department of Defence. Aeronautical Research Laboratories. Mechanical Engineering Report (Australia) [*A publication*].................... Dep Def Aeronaut Res Lab Mech Eng Rep (Aust)
Department of Defense.................DD
Department of Defense.................DoD
Department of Defense Activity Address Code.................DODAAC
Department of Defense Activity Address Directory.................DODAAD
Department of Defense Activity Address File.................DODAAF
Department of Defense Aircraft Ground Fire Suppression and Rescue Office.................DOD-AGFSRS
Department of Defense Ammunition Code.................DODAC
Department of Defense Authorized Data List.................DODADL
Department of Defense Central Automated Personnel System.................DODCAPS
Department of Defense Claimant Program.................DDCP
Department of Defense Computer Institute.................DODCI
Department of Defense Consolidated List of Principal Military Items.................DODCLPMI
Department of Defense Damage Assessment Center.................DODDAC
Department of Defense Dependents Schools.................DODDS
Department of Defense Directive.................DODD
Department of Defense Emergency Plans.................DODEP
Department of Defense Exercise Planning.................DODEP
Department of Defense Explosives Safety Board.................DDESB
Department of Defense Foreign Counterintelligence Program.................DODFCI
Department of Defense Foreign Disclosure Coordinating Office.................DODFDCO
Department of Defense Gravity Experiment [*Satellite*].................DODGE
Department of Defense Gravity Experiment, Multipurpose [*Satellite*].................DODGE-M
Department of Defense Handbook.................DODH
Department of Defense Handbook.................DODHBK
Department of Defense High School Newspaper Service.................DODHSNS
Department of Defense Household Goods Commercial Storage Office.................DODHGCSO
Department of Defense Household Goods Field Office.................DODHGFO
Department of Defense Identification Badge.................DODIDENTBAD
Department of Defense Identification Code.................DODIC
Department of Defense Index of Specifications and Standards.................DIS
Department of Defense Index of Specifications and Standards.................DODISS
Department of Defense Industrial Equipment Reserve.................DODIER
Department of Defense Industrial Security Bulletin.................DODISB
Department of Defense Industrial Security Letter.................DODISL
Department of Defense Industrial Security Manual.................DODISM
Department of Defense Industrial Security Regulation.................DODISR
Department of Defense Instruction.................DODI
Department of Defense Instruction.................DODINST
Department of Defense Inventory Manager.................DODIM
Department of Defense Item Code.................DODIC
Department of Defense Item Entry Control.................DODIEC
Department of Defense Item Standardization Code.................DODISC
Department of Defense Management Information System.................DOD/MIS
Department of Defense Manned Space Flight.................DDMS
Department of Defense Manual.................DODM
Department of Defense Manual.................DODMNL
Department of Defense Master Urgency List.................DODMUL
Department of Defense Medical Examination Review Board.................DODMERB
Department of Defense Military Pay and Allowance Committee.................DODMPAC
Department of Defense Military Pay and Allowance Entitlements Manual.................DODPM
Department of Defense Military Personnel Records Center.................DODMPRC
Department of Defense Military Traffic Management Agency.................DDMTMA
Department of Defense National Agency Check Center.................DODNACC
Department of Defense, Pacific Research Office.................DODPRO
Department of Defense Poster.................DODPSTR
Department of Defense Precious Metals Recovery Program.................DODPMRP
Department of Defense Production.................DDP
Department of Defense Regulation.................DODR
Department of Defense Research and Engineering.................DODRE
Department of Defense Resource Management System.................DRMS
Department of Defense Single Stock Point.................DOD-SSP
Department of Defense Small Arms Serialization Program.................DODSASP
Department of Defense Surplus Property Bidders List.................DODSPBL
Department of Defense Systems Management Center.................DESMC
Department of the Director, Women's Royal Naval Service [*British*].................DWRNS
Department of Economic Affairs [*Department of Agriculture*].................DEA
Department of Economic Affairs of the United Nations.................ECA
Department of Economic and Social Affairs of the United Nations [*Later, Department of Social Affairs*].................ESA (UN)
Department of Economics and Social Science [*MIT*].................DESS
Department of Education [*Generic*].................DE
Department of Education [*Cabinet department*].................Ed
Department of Education and Science [*British*].................DES
Department of Education and Science: Reports on Education [*London*] [*A publication*].................Dept of Ed and Science Repts

Department of Elementary, Kindergarten, and Nursery Education [*of NEA*] [*Later, American Association of Elementary, Kindergarten, Nursery Educators*].................EKNE
Department of Elementary School Principals [*of NEA*].................DESP
Department of Elementary School Principals. Bulletin [*A publication*].................Dept El Sch Prin B
Department of Employment [*Formerly, DEP, MOL*] [*British*].................DE
Department of Employment and Productivity [*Later, DE*] [*British*].................DEP
Department of Energy [*British*].................DEn
Department of Energy.................DOE
Department of Energy/Assistant Secretary for Energy Technology.................DOE/ET
Department of Energy, Bartlesville Energy Technology Center, Bartlesville, OK [*OCLC symbol*].................DOB
Department of Energy, Mines, and Resources [*Canada*].................DEMR
Department of Energy, Mines, and Resources, Canada Center for Mineral and Energy Technology, Ottawa, ON, Canada [*Library symbol*].................CaOOM
Department of the Environment [*Formerly, MPBW, MT*] [*British*].................DOE
Department of the Environment. Fire Research Station. Fire Research Technical Paper (United Kingdom) [*A publication*].................Dep Environ Fire Res St Fire Res Tech Pap (UK)
Department of Environmental and Drug-Induced Pathology [*of the Armed Forces Institute of Pathology*].................DEDIP
Department of Family Life [*Later, Commission on Marriage and Family Life*] [*of NCC*].................DFL
Department of the Financial Secretary of the War Office [*British*].................DFSWO
Department of Foreign Affairs.................DFA
Department of Foreign Affairs and Information [*South Africa*].................DFAI
Department of Geology and Geophysics [*MIT*].................DGG
Department of Harbours and Marine. Queensland Fisheries Notes [*A publication*].................Dep Harbours Mar Queensl Fish Notes
Department of Health, Education, and Welfare [*Later, HHS*].................DHEW
Department of Health, Education, and Welfare [*Sometimes facetiously translated "Halls of Eternal Warfare"*] [*Later, HHS*].................HEW
Department of Health, Education, and Welfare. National Institutes of Health. Publication [*A publication*].................Dep Health Educ Welfare Natl Inst Health Publ
Department of Health, Education, and Welfare [*Later, HHS*] Procurement Regulations.................HEWPR
Department of Health, Education, and Welfare. Publication (Health Services Administration) (United States) [*A publication*].................Dep Health Educ Welfare Publ (Health Serv Adm) (US)
Department of Health, Education, and Welfare Publications [*A publication*].................HEW
Department of Health, Education, and Welfare, Washington, DC [*OCLC symbol*].................HEW
Department of Health and Human Services.................DHHS
Department of Health and Human Services.................HHS
Department of Health and Social Security [*British*].................DHSS
Department of Home Economics [*of NEA*] [*Later, HEEA*].................DHE
Department of Housing and Urban Development.................DHUD
Department of Housing and Urban Development.................HUD
Department of Indian Affairs and Northern Development [*Canada*].................DIAND
Department of Information and Broadcasting [*India*].................DIB
Department Information Bulletin.................DIB
Department Instrument Equipment Reserve.................DIER
Department of the Interior.................D of I
Department of the Interior.................DI
Department of the Interior.................DOI
Department of Interior Board of Contract Appeals.................IBCA
Department of Internal Security.................DIS
Department of Justice.................D of J
Department of Justice.................DOJ
Department of Labor.................D of L
Department of Labor.................DL
Department of Labor.................DOL
Department of Labor International Technical Assistance Corps.................DOLITAC
Department of Labor, Manpower Administration.................DLMA
Department of Labor Recreation Association.................DLRA
Department of Legal Affairs of the United Nations.................LEG (UN)
Department of the Master General of the Ordnance [*British*].................DMGO
Department of the Medical Director-General [*Navy*] [*British*].................DMDG
Department of Medicine.................DOM
Department of Medicine and Surgery [*Veterans Administration*].................DMS
Department of Mental Health [*or Hygiene*].................DMH
Department of Mines and Technical Survey [*Canada*].................DMTS
Department of Motor Vehicles.................DMV
Department of National Defence [*Canada*].................DND
Department of National Defence, Chief Computer Services, Ottawa, ON, Canada [*Library symbol*].................CaOONDC
Department of National Defence, Chief Construction and Properties, Ottawa, ON, Canada [*Library symbol*].................CaOONDCP
Department of National Defence, Chief Engineering and Maintenance, Ottawa, ON, Canada [*Library symbol*].................CaOONDEM
Department of National Defence, Defence and Civil Institute of Environmental Medicine, Toronto, ON, Canada [*Library symbol*].................CaOTDR
Department of National Defence, Directorate of Information Services, Ottawa, ON, Canada [*Library symbol*].................CaOONDIS

Department of National Defence, General Engineering and Maintenance, Directorate of Clothing, Ottawa, ON, Canada [*Library symbol*] ... CaOONDCG
Department of National Defence, Historical Section, Ottawa, ON, Canada [*Library symbol*] ... CaOONDH
Department of National Defence, Judge Advocate General's Library, Ottawa, ON, Canada [*Library symbol*] ... CaOONDJ
Department of National Defence, Land Technical Library, Ottawa, ON, Canada [*Library symbol*] ... CaOONDLT
Department of National Defence, Mapping and Charting Establishment, Ottawa, ON, Canada [*Library symbol*] ... CaOONDMC
Department of National Defence, Marine Technical Library, Ottawa, ON, Canada [*Library symbol*] ... CaOONDMT
Department of National Defence, Medical Library, Ottawa, ON, Canada [*Library symbol*] ... CaOONDM
Department of National Defence, Operational Research and Analysis Establishment, Ottawa, ON, Canada [*Library symbol*] ... CaOONDORAE
Department of National Defence, Ottawa, ON, Canada [*Library symbol*] ... CaOOND
Department of National Savings [*British*] ... DNS
Department of Natural Resources [*Department of Agriculture*] [*Sometimes facetiously referred to as Department of Nuts with Rifles*] ... DNR
Department of Naval Architecture and Marine Engineering [*MIT*] ... DNAME
Department of the Navy ... DN
Department of the Navy ... DON
Department of the Navy Five-Year Program ... DNFYP
Department of the Navy Management Information Control System ... DONMICS
Department of the Navy Program Information Center ... DONPIC
Department of the Navy System Acquisition Review Council ... DNSARC
Department of Nuclear Engineering [*MIT*] ... DNE
Department of Nutrition, Food Science, and Technology [*MIT*] ... DNFST
Department of the Army International Rationalization Office ... DAIRO
Department Operating Instruction ... DOI
Department of Organization and Field Services, AFL-CIO ... DOFS
Department of Overseas Trade [*British*] ... DOT
Department of the Pacific [*Marine Corps*] ... DP
Department Performance Rating ... DPR
Department Personnel Manual ... DPM
Department of Physical Research [*British*] ... DPR
Department of Prices and Consumer Protection [*British*] ... DPCP
Department for Professional Employees [*AFL-CIO*] ... DPE
Department of Public Health ... DPH
Department of Public Information [*United Nations*] ... DPI
Department of Public Instruction, Division for Library Services, Cooperative Children's Book Center, Madison, WI [*Library symbol*] ... WMaPI-CC
Department of Public Instruction, Division for Library Services, Professional Library, Madison, WI [*Library symbol*] ... WMaPI
Department of Public Instruction, Division for Library Services, Public Library Services, Madison, WI [*Library symbol*] ... WMaPI-PL
Department of Public Instruction, Division for Library Services, Reference and Loan Library, Madison, WI [*Library symbol*] ... WMaPI-RL
Department of Public Libraries and Information, City of Virginia Beach, Reference Department, Virginia Beach, VA [*Library symbol*] ... ViVb
Department of Public Social Services ... DPSS
Department of Public Welfare ... DPW
Department of Public Works ... DPW
Department of Regional Economic Expansion [*Canada*] ... DREE
Department of Rural Education [*of NEA*] [*Later, REA*] ... DRE
Department of Science, Technology, Energy, and Materials [*Proposed Cabinet department*] ... STEAM
Department of Scientific and Industrial Research [*of the Privy Council for Scientific and Industrial Research*] [*Later, SRC*] [*British*] ... DSIR
Department of Secondary School Principals. Bulletin [*A publication*] ... Dept Sec Sch Prin B
Department of Security Council Affairs of the United Nations ... SCA(UN)
Department of Social Services [*in various governmental agencies*] ... DSS
Department Standardization Office [*Navy*] ... DEPSO
Department of State ... DOS
Department of State ... D of S
Department of State ... DS
Department of State Bulletin [*A publication*] ... Dept Sta Bul
Department of State Bulletin [*A publication*] ... Dept State Bul
Department of State Bulletin [*A publication*] ... Dept State Bull
Department of State Bulletin [*A publication*] ... DSB
Department of State Correspondents Association ... DOSCA
Department of State Correspondents Association ... DSCA
Department of State Newsletter [*A publication*] ... Dept Sta Nl
Department of State Newsletter [*A publication*] ... SNL
Department of State Procurement Regulations ... DOSPR
Department of State, Washington, DC [*OCLC symbol*] ... DOS
Department Summary Schedule [*NASA*] ... DSS
Department of Supply and Services, Canadian Government Expositions Centre, Ottawa, ON, Canada [*Library symbol*] ... CaOOGE
Department Supply Storage Point/Stock Storage Depot [*DoD*] ... DSSP/SSD
Department of Surgery ... DOS
Department of Tank Design [*British*] ... DTD
Department of Technical Cooperation [*British*] ... DTC
Department of Technology and Society ... DTS
Department of Tourism, Recreation, and Cultural Affairs, Public Library Services, Winnipeg, MB, Canada [*Library symbol*] ... CaMWPL
Department of Trade [*British*] ... DoT
Department of Trade and Industry [*British*] ... DTI
Department Training ... DT
Department of Transport [*Canada*] ... DOT
Department of Transport (Canada) ... DOTC
Department of Transportation ... DOT
Department of Transportation/Climatic Impact Assessment Program ... DOT/CIAP
Department of Transportation Continuity of Operations Plan [*Federal emergency plan*] ... DOTCOOP
Department of Transportation Contract Appeals Board ... DOTCAB
Department of Transportation and Development, Aviation Office, Baton Rouge, LA [*Library symbol*] ... LBrTD-Av
Department of Transportation and Development, Office of Highways, Research and Development Library, Baton Rouge, LA [*Library symbol*] ... LBrTD-H
Department of Transportation and Development, Office of Public Works, Baton Rouge, LA [*Library symbol*] ... LBrTD-Pw
Department of Transportation's Emergency Organization ... DOTEO
Department of the Treasury ... DOT
Department of the Treasury [*Commonly TD, Treasury Department*] ... D of T
Department of Trusteeship and Information from Non-Self-Governing Territories of the United Nations ... TRIUN
Department of Urban and Community Affairs, Office of Planning and Technical Assistance, Baton Rouge, LA [*Library symbol*] ... LBrUC
Department of Veterans Affairs [*Canada*] ... DVA
Department of Veterans Benefits [*Veterans Administration*] ... DVB
Department of Wildlife and Fisheries, Louisiana Stream Control Commission, Baton Rouge, LA [*Library symbol*] ... LBrWF-S
Department Work Order ... DWO
Department of Works [*Military*] [*British*] ... D of W
Departmental Circulars ... DC
Departmental Civilian Personnel Branch ... DCPB
Departmental Data Coordinator ... DDC
Departmental Data Processing Center [*Department of Labor*] ... DDPC
Departmental Estimate ... DE
Departmental Industrial Plant Reserve [*Army*] ... DIPR
Departmental Industrial Reserve System ... DIRS
Departmental Instruction ... DI
Departmental Management System [*Department of Labor*] ... DMS
Departmental Materiel Requisition ... DMR
Departmental Notice ... DN
Departmental Property Management System ... DPMS
Departmental Records Branch [*Military*] ... DRB
[*A*] **Departmental Reporting System** [*IBM Corp.*] ... ADRS
Departmental Science Development [*National Science Foundation*] ... DSD
Departmental Square Feet ... DSF
Departmentalized Billing ... DB
Departmente de Aeronautica Civil [*Peru*] ... DAC
Departure ... P
Departure Airfield ... DAF
Departure Airfield Control ... DAFC
Departure Airfield Control Group [*Military*] ... DACG
Departure Airfield Control Group ... DAFCG
Departure Approval Request for IFR [*Instrument Flight Rules*] **Flight** [*Aviation*] ... DI
Departure Approved [*Aviation*] ... DA
Departure Control ... DEPCON
Departure Control ... DPT
Departure Date ... DD
Departure Locator ... DL
Departure Message [*Aviation code*] ... DEP
Departure from Nucleate Boiling ... DNB
Departure from Nucleate Boiling Ratio ... DNBR
Departure Point ... DP
Departure Procedure ... DPCR
DePaul Rehabilitation Hospital Medical Library, Milwaukee, WI [*Library symbol*] ... WMDR
Dependency [*Psychology*] ... Dy
Dependency Certificate Filed ... DCF
Dependency and Indemnity Compensation [*Military*] ... D & IC
Dependency and Indemnity Compensation [*Military*] ... DIC
Dependent ... DEPN
Dependent Drainage [*Medicine*] ... DD
Dependent Housing Area [*Army*] ... DHA
Dependent Meteorological Office ... DMO
Dependent Overseas Territory ... DOT
Dependent Political Entity [*Board on Geographic Names*] ... PCLD
Dependent Vehicle ... DV
Dependents ... DEP
Dependents Assistance Act ... DAA
Dependents' Daylight Cruise [*Navy*] ... DEPCRU
Dependents Evacuation Pay [*Military*] ... DEPEVACPAY

Dependents' Medical Care Act [*HEW*] ..... DMCA
Dependents Not Authorized Overseas Duty Station [*Military*] ..... DEPNOTAUTH
Dependents Overseas [*Military*] ..... DOS
Dependents Rate [*Air Force*] ..... DR
Dependents Schooling Office [*Military*] ..... DSO
Deperming and Flashing Station [*Navy*] ..... DEPERMSTA
Depew, NY [*Radio station call letters*] ..... WBLK
Depilatorium [*Depilatory*] [*Pharmacy*] ..... DEPILAT
Depletion ..... DEPL
Depletion-Layer Transistor ..... DLT
Depletion Metal-Oxide Semiconductor ..... DMOS
Deploy ..... DEPL
Deploy ..... DPL
Deploy ..... DPLY
Deployable Automatic Relay Terminal [*Air Force*] ..... DART
Deployable Defense System ..... DDS
Deployable Solar Array ..... DSA
Deployable Solar Panel ..... DSP
Deployment ..... DEP
Deployment Adjustment Notification [*Military*] ..... DAN
Deployment Adjustment Request [*Military*] ..... DAR
Deployment Area Location Code [*Army*] ..... DALC
Deployment Assembly [*Skylab*] [*NASA*] ..... DA
Deployment Data File ..... DEPDA
Deployment Manning Document ..... DMD
Deployment Mobilization Troop Basis ..... DMTB
Deployment Model [*Army*] ..... DEMOD
Deployment Pennant [*Navy*] [*British*] ..... DP
Deployment Position RADAR ..... DPR
Deployment Readiness Assistance Program [*Military*] ..... DRAP
Deployment Readiness Condition [*Army*] ..... DRC
Deployment Reporting System ..... DEPREP
Deployment Status of Army Units ..... DEPSTAR
Deployment Summary Report [*Air Force*] ..... DEPSUM
Depo-Provera [*Contraceptive*] [*The Upjohn Co.*] ..... D-P
Depolarization Shift [*Electrophysiology*] ..... DS
Depolarizing After-Potential [*Neurochemistry*] ..... DAP
Depolarizing Bipolar Cell [*In the retina*] ..... DPBC
Depolymerized Rubber ..... DPR
Depomedroxyprogesterone Acetate [*Contraceptive*] ..... DMPA
Deponent ..... DEP
Deponent ..... DPT
Deportation [*FBI standardized term*] ..... DEP
Deposed ..... DEP
Deposit ..... DEP
Deposit ..... DPST
Deposit Account [*Banking*] ..... DA
Deposit Account Number ..... DAN
Deposit Administration ..... DA
Deposit Book ..... D/B
Deposit Fund Account ..... DFA
Deposit Guaranty Corp. [*NASDAQ symbol*] ..... DEPS
Deposit Liquidation Board ..... DLB
Deposit Passbook [*Banking*] ..... DPB
Deposit Receipt ..... DR
Deposit Ticket/Debit Voucher [*Data processing*] ..... DT/DV
Depositary ..... DEPOS
Deposited Carbon ..... DC
Deposition ..... DEPOSN
Depositors Corp. [*American Stock Exchange symbol*] ..... DEP
Depository Institutions Deregulation Committee [*Congress*] ..... DIDC
Depository Library Council to the Public Printer ..... DLCPP
Depositus [*Laid to Rest*] [*Latin*] ..... D
Depot ..... DEP
Depot ..... DPO
Depot ..... DPT
Depot Acceptance Procedures ..... DAP
Depot Activity ..... DEPACTV
Depot Automatic Rescheduling Technique ..... DART
Depot Command Management System ..... DCMS
Depot Component/Equipment Rework Report [*Navy*] ..... DCERR
Depot Condemnation Percent ..... DCP
Depot Control Number ..... DCN
Depot Fixed ..... DF
Depot Inspection and Repair ..... DIR
Depot Installation Management Information System [*Army*] ..... DIMIS
Depot-Installed Maintenance Automatic Test Equipment ..... DIMATE
Depot Integrated Maintenance Support Agreement [*Air Force*] ..... DIMSA
Depot Level Activity ..... DLA
Depot Level Inspection Auto Repair ..... DLIR
Depot Level Maintenance [*Air Force*] ..... DLM
Depot Level Repairable ..... DLR
Depot Maintenance Activity ..... DMA
Depot Maintenance Control [*or Coordinator*] **Center** [*Army*] ..... DMCC
Depot Maintenance Industrial Fund ..... DMIF
Depot Maintenance Industrial Funding Customer ..... DMIFCUS
Depot Maintenance Interservice Support Agreement [*Military*] ..... DMISA
Depot Maintenance Level ..... DML
Depot Maintenance Production Report ..... DMPR
Depot Maintenance Support ..... DMS
Depot Maintenance Support Plan [*Air Force*] ..... DMSP
Depot Maintenance Work Request [*or Requirement*] [*Army*] ..... DMWR
Depot Management Information System [*Army*] ..... DEPMIS
Depot Manufacture ..... DM
Depot Master Item Data File [*Army*] ..... DMIDF
Depot Materiel Maintenance and Support Activities [*Army*] ..... DMM & SA
Depot Operation Management System [*Army*] ..... DOMS
Depot Overhaul ..... D/O
Depot Property Officer ..... DPO
Depot Purchased Equipment Management [*DoD*] ..... DPEM
Depot Quartermaster [*Marine Corps*] ..... DQM
Depot Quartermaster, Norfolk, Virginia [*Marine Corps*] ..... DQN
Depot Quartermaster, Pearl Harbor, Hawaii [*Marine Corps*] ..... DQPH
Depot Quartermaster, Philadelphia, Pennsylvania [*Marine Corps*] ..... DQP
Depot Quartermaster, Quantico, Virginia [*Marine Corps*] ..... DQQ
Depot Quartermaster, Richmond, Virginia [*Marine Corps*] ..... DQR
Depot Quartermaster, San Francisco, California [*Marine Corps*] ..... DQSF
Depot Recovery Factor ..... DRF
Depot Repair Cycle ..... DRC
Depot Repair Cycle Time ..... DRCT
Depot of Supplies [*Marine Corps*] ..... DOFS
Depot of Supplies [*Marine Corps*] ..... D of S
Depot Supply Center ..... DSC
Depot Supply System [*Army*] ..... DSS
Depot Systems Command [*Army*] ..... DESCOM
Depot Training Center ..... DTC
Depot Turn-Around Time ..... DTAT
Depot Vehicle Automatic Tester ..... DEVAT
Depot Working Standards ..... DWS
Depreciation ..... DEPR
Depreciation, Depletion, and Amortization ..... DD & A
Depressed ..... DPRSD
Depressed Sight Line ..... DSL
Depressed-Trajectory Intercontinental Ballistic Missile ..... DICBM
Depression ..... D
Depression [*Board on Geographic Names*] ..... DEPR
Depression Adjective Check Lists [*Psychology*] ..... DACL
Depression Deviation Indicator ..... DDI
Depression Obvious [*Psychology*] ..... DO
Depression Position-Finder ..... DPF
Depression Proneness Sentence Stems [*Navy*] ..... DPSS
Depression Sine Depression [*Psychology*] ..... DSD
Depression Subtle [*Psychology*] ..... DS
Depressives Anonymous ..... DA
Deprived Eye [*Optics*] ..... DE
Deptford [*Region of London*] ..... DPFD
Depth ..... D
Depth ..... DEP
Depth ..... DP
Depth ..... DPT
Depth ..... DPTH
Depth Bomb [*Military*] ..... DB
Depth of Burial [*of explosives*] ..... DOB
Depth of Burst ..... DOB
Depth Charge [*Aerial*] ..... DC
Depth-Charge Projector ..... DCP
Depth-Charge Thrower ..... DCT
Depth-Charges Track ..... DCT
Depth Control Tank ..... DCT
Depth Cut Out [*Navy*] ..... DCO
Depth Deviation Indicator ..... DDI
Depth of Discharge ..... DOD
Depth-Duration-Area ..... DDA
Depth of Field [*or Focus*] [*Photography*] ..... DF
Depth-First Search ..... DFS
Depth of Flash Optical Landing System [*Navy*] ..... DFOLS
Depth Gauge ..... DEGA
Depth of Hold ..... DPH
Depth Keeping ..... DKPG
Depth of Modulation ..... DOM
Depth of Ship ..... D
Depth Sounder ..... DS
Depth Telemetering Pinger ..... DTP
DePue Public Library, DePue, IL [*Library symbol*] ..... IDep
DePue Unit, School District 103, DePue, IL [*Library symbol*] ..... IDepSD
Deputation ..... DEPUTN
Deputatus [*Purified*] [*Pharmacy*] ..... DEP
Deputy ..... D
Deputy ..... DEP
Deputy ..... DEPT
Deputy ..... DEPY
Deputy ..... DPTY
Deputy ..... DY
Deputy Adjutant-General [*Military*] ..... DAG
Deputy Adjutant and Quartermaster General [*British*] ..... DA & QMG
Deputy Administrator [*NASA*] ..... AD
Deputy Administrator ..... DA
Deputy of the Air Member for Supply and Organization [*British*] ..... DAMSO
Deputy Assistant Adjutant-General [*British*] ..... DAAG
Deputy Assistant-Adjutant and Quartermaster-General [*British*] ..... DAA & QMG

Deputy Assistant Chaplain-General [*British*] ... DACG
Deputy Assistant Chief of Staff ... DACOS
Deputy Assistant Director ... DAD
Deputy Assistant Director of Army Dental Services [*British*] ... DADADS
Deputy Assistant Director, Army Veterinary Services ... DADAVS
Deputy Assistant Director of Artillery [*British*] ... DADA
Deputy Assistant Director of Labor [*Allied Control Commission*] [*World War II*] ... DADL
Deputy Assistant Director for Management Support Division [*Vietnam*] ... DAD/MSD
Deputy Assistant Director of Medical Services ... DADMS
Deputy Assistant Director of Ordnance Services (Engineering) [*British*] ... DADOS(E)
Deputy Assistant Director of Ordnance Stores [*Military*] ... DADOS
Deputy Assistant Director for Plans and Evaluation [*Vietnam*] ... DAD/PE
Deputy Assistant Director for the Psychological Operations Division [*Vietnam*] ... DAD/POD
Deputy Assistant Director of Quartering [*British*] ... DADQ
Deputy Assistant Director of Remounts [*British*] ... DADR
Deputy Assistant Director of Supplies and Transport [*British*] ... DADST
Deputy Assistant Director of Transportation [*British*] ... DADT
Deputy Assistant Master-General of Ordnance [*British*] ... DAMGO
Deputy Assistant Military Secretary [*British*] ... DAMS
Deputy Assistant Provost-Marshall [*British*] ... DAPM
Deputy Assistant Quartermaster General ... DAQMG
Deputy Assistant Secretary of Defense ... DASD
Deputy Assistant Secretary for Employment and Training [*Department of Labor*] ... DASET
Deputy Associate Administrator [*NASA*] ... AAD
Deputy Associate Regional Administrator ... DARA
Deputy Base Manager ... DBM
Deputy Brigade Commander [*Army*] ... DBC
Deputy Censorship Office [*London*] [*World War II*] ... DCO
Deputy Chaplain-General [*British*] ... DCG
Deputy Chief ... DC
Deputy Chief ... DCF
Deputy Chief ... DEPCH
Deputy Chief of the Air Staff [*British*] ... DCAS
Deputy Chief Architect [*British*] ... DCA
Deputy Chief, Chemical Warfare Service [*Army*] ... DCCWS
Deputy Chief Civil Affairs Officer [*US and Britain*] ... DCCAO
Deputy Chief Constable ... DCC
Deputy Chief of Defence Staff (Operational Requirements) [*British*] ... DCDS(OR)
Deputy Chief of the General Staff in the Field [*Military*] [*British*] ... DCGS
Deputy Chief of the Imperial General Staff [*Military*] [*British*] ... DCIGS
Deputy Chief for Intelligence ... DCI
Deputy Chief of Maintenance ... DCM
Deputy Chief of the Military Planning Office ... DCMPO
Deputy Chief of Mission [*Diplomatic corps*] ... DCM
Deputy Chief Naval Adviser [*British*] ... DCNA
Deputy Chief Naval Engineering Officer [*British*] ... DCNEO
Deputy Chief of Naval Material ... DCNM
Deputy Chief of Naval Material, Development ... DCNM(D)
Deputy Chief of Naval Material, Management and Organization ... DCNM(M & O)
Deputy Chief of Naval Material, Material and Facilities ... DCNM(M & F)
Deputy Chief of Naval Material, Programs and Financial Management ... DCNM(P & FM)
Deputy Chief of Naval Operations ... DCNO
Deputy Chief of Naval Operations, Administration ... DCNOA
Deputy Chief of Naval Operations (Air) ... DCNO(AIR)
Deputy Chief of Naval Operations (Development) ... DCNO(D)
Deputy Chief of Naval Operations, Fleet Operations and Readiness ... DCNOFOR
Deputy Chief of Naval Operations (Logistics) ... DCNO(L)
Deputy Chief of Naval Operations (Manpower and Naval Reserve) ... DCNO(M & NR)
Deputy Chief of Naval Operations (Personnel and Naval Reserve) ... DCNO(P & R)
Deputy Chief of Naval Operations (Plans and Policies) ... DCNO(P & P)
Deputy Chief of Naval Staff [*Marine Corps; also, British Navy*] ... DCNS
Deputy Chief Patrol Inspector [*Immigration and Naturalization Service*] ... DCPI
Deputy Chief of Personnel Operations ... DCOPO
Deputy Chief Political Officer [*British Military Administration*] ... DCPO
Deputy Chief Quartermaster ... DCQM
Deputy Chief Scientific Officer [*British*] ... DCSO
Deputy Chief of Staff ... DCOFS
Deputy Chief of Staff ... DCOS
Deputy Chief of Staff ... DC of S
Deputy Chief of Staff ... DCS
Deputy Chief of Staff for Administration ... DCA
Deputy Chief of Staff, Air Force ... DC/SAF
Deputy Chief of Staff, Army ... DC of SA
Deputy Chief of Staff for Combat Developments ... DCSCD
Deputy Chief of Staff, Communications-Electronics [*Army*] ... DCSC-E
Deputy Chief of Staff, Comptroller ... DCS/C
Deputy Chief of Staff, Comptroller ... DCSCOMPT
Deputy Chief of Staff, Development [*Air Force*] ... AFDDC
Deputy Chief of Staff, Development ... DCS/D
Deputy Chief of Staff, Force Development ... DCSFOR
Deputy Chief of Staff for Intelligence [*Army*] ... DCSI
Deputy Chief of Staff, Intelligence [*Air Force*] ... DCS/INT
Deputy Chief of Staff, Logistics [*Army*] ... DCSL
Deputy Chief of Staff, Logistics [*Army*] ... DCSLOG
Deputy Chief of Staff, Logistics and Administration [*NATO*] ... DCLA
Deputy Chief of Staff, Management Information System ... DCSMIS
Deputy Chief of Staff, Materiel ... DCSM
Deputy Chief of Staff for Military Government [*World War II*] ... DCSMG
Deputy Chief of Staff, Military Operations [*Army*] ... DC/SMO
Deputy Chief of Staff, Operations [*Air Force*] ... AFODC
Deputy Chief of Staff, Operations [*NATO*] ... DCO
Deputy Chief of Staff, Operations ... DCSO
Deputy Chief of Staff, Operations and Administration ... DCSOA
Deputy Chief of Staff for Operations and Intelligence ... DCSOI
Deputy Chief of Staff for Operations and Plans [*Army*] ... DCSOPS
Deputy Chief of Staff, Operations and Training ... DCSO & T
Deputy Chief of Staff, Personnel [*Air Force*] ... AFPDC
Deputy Chief of Staff, Personnel ... DCS/P
Deputy Chief of Staff, Personnel [*Army*] ... DCSPER
Deputy Chief of Staff, Personnel and Administration ... DCSPA
Deputy Chief of Staff, Personnel and Organization [*NATO*] ... DCPO
Deputy Chief of Staff for Plans and Operations ... DCS/P & O
Deputy Chief of Staff, Plans and Policy [*NATO*] ... DCPANDP
Deputy Chief of Staff for Plans and Programs ... DCS/P & P
Deputy Chief of Staff for Plans and Research ... DCPR
Deputy Chief of Staff for Plans and Research [*Army*] ... DCSPR
Deputy Chief of Staff for Programs and Resources ... DCS/P & R
Deputy Chief of Staff, Research and Development [*Army*] ... DCSR & D
Deputy Chief of Staff for Research, Development, and Acquisition [*Army*] ... DCSRDA
Deputy Chief of Staff, Research and Technology ... DCS/R & T
Deputy Chief of Staff, Reserve Components [*Army*] ... DCS/RC
Deputy Chief of Staff for Reserve Officers' Training Corps ... DCSROTC
Deputy Chief of Staff for Resource Management ... DCSRM
Deputy Chief of Staff, Systems and Logistics ... DCS/S & L
Deputy Chief of Staff for Training [*Army*] ... DCST
Deputy Chief of Staff for Training and Schools ... DCSTS
Deputy Clerk of Session [*British*] ... DCS
Deputy Commandant ... DC
Deputy Commandant Royal Engineers [*British*] ... DCRE
Deputy Commander of Aerospace System [*Air Force*] ... DCAS
Deputy Commander for Logistics ... DCL
Deputy Commander, Military Sea Transport Service [*Obsolete*] [*Navy*] ... DEPCOMSTS
Deputy Commander, Naval Striking and Support Forces, Southern Europe ... DEPCOMSTRIKFORSOUTH
Deputy Commander, Operational Test and Evaluation Force, Pacific [*Navy*] ... DCOTFP
Deputy Commander, Operational Test and Evaluation Force, Pacific [*Navy*] ... DECOMOPTEVFORPAC
Deputy Commander, Operational Test and Evaluation Force, Pacific [*Navy*] ... DEPCOMOPTEVFORPAC
Deputy Commander for Research and Development [*Navy*] ... DEPCDR(R & D)
Deputy Commander for Ship Acquisitions [*Navy*] ... DEPCDR(SA)
Deputy Commander, United States Military Assistance Command, Thailand ... DEPCOMUSMACTHAI
Deputy Commander, United States Military Assistance Command, Vietnam ... DEPCOMUSMACV
Deputy Commanding General ... DCG
Deputy Commanding General, Continental Army Command [*Later, DCG/T*] [*Army*] ... DCG/CONARC
Deputy Commanding General, Training [*Formerly, DCG/CONARC*] [*Army*] ... DCG/T
Deputy Commanding Officer ... DCO
Deputy Commissary-General ... DCG
Deputy Consul ... DC
Deputy for Contract Financing [*Air Force*] ... DCF
Deputy Controller (Polaris) [*Navy*] [*British*] ... DCPolaris
Deputy Controller of Property [*World War II*] ... DCP
Deputy County Architect [*British*] ... DCA
Deputy Director ... DD
Deputy Director ... DEPDIR
Deputy Director for Administration [*National Security Agency*] ... DDA
Deputy Director of Armament Supply (Eastern Theater) ... DDAS (ET)
Deputy Director of Armaments [*British*] ... DDA
Deputy Director of Bomber Operations [*Air Ministry*] [*British*] [*World War II*] ... DDBOps
Deputy Director of Civil Affairs [*War Office*] [*British*] [*World War II*] ... DDCA
Deputy Director of Combined Operations (India) ... DDCO (I)
Deputy Director, Contract Administration Services [*DoD*] ... DDCAS
Deputy Director, Contract Administration Services Memorandum [*DoD*] ... DDCASM
Deputy Director of Dental Services [*Military*] [*British*] ... DDDS
Deputy Director of Design [*British*] ... DDD
Deputy Director of Equipment [*Air Force*] [*British*] ... DDE
Deputy Director for Field Management and Evaluation [*National Security Agency*] ... DDF
Deputy Director-General [*British*] ... DDG

Deputy Director-General of Ordnance Factories [*Ministry of Supply*] [*British*] [*World War II*].................DDGOF
Deputy Director-General of Ordnance Factories, Engineering Factories [*Ministry of Supply*] [*British*] [*World War II*]...............DDGOF(E)
Deputy Director-General of Ordnance Factories, Filling Factories [*Ministry of Supply*] [*British*] [*World War II*]...............DDGOF(F)
Deputy Director-General of Production [*Ministry of Aircraft Production*] [*British*] [*World War II*].................DDGP
Deputy Director of Home Operations [*Air Ministry*] [*British*] [*World War II*].................DDHO
Deputy Director of Hygiene and Pathology [*Military*] [*British*].................DDHP
Deputy Director of Intelligence [*Air Ministry*] [*British*] [*World War II*].......DDI
Deputy Director of Labour [*British*].................DDL
Deputy Director of Manpower Planning [*Military*] [*British*].......DDMP
Deputy Director of Mechanical Engineering [*British*].................DDME
Deputy Director of Medical Organization for War [*Military*] [*British*].................DDMOW
Deputy Director of Medical Services [*British*].................DDMS
Deputy Director of Military Intelligence [*British*].................DDMI
Deputy Director of Military Operations and Intelligence [*British*].......DDMOI
Deputy Director of Military Training [*British*].................DDMT
Deputy Director of Movements and Quartering [*Military*] [*British*].......DDMQ
Deputy Director, National Security Agency.................D/DIRNSA
Deputy Director of Naval Construction [*British*].................DDNC
Deputy Director of Naval Intelligence [*British*].................DDNI
Deputy Director of Operations [*Air Force*].................DDO
Deputy Director of Operations Division [*Air Ministry*] [*British*]...........DDOD
Deputy Director of Operations and Intelligence [*Air Ministry*] [*British*].................DDOI
Deputy Director of Ordnance Factories, Explosives Factories [*Ministry of Supply*] [*British*] [*World War II*].................DDOF(X)
Deputy Director of Organization [*Air Ministry*] [*British*].................DDO
Deputy Director Pacific Division, Bureau of Yards and Docks [*Navy*] [*Later, NFEC*] [*Navy*].................DEPDIRPACDOCKS
Deputy Director of Personal Services [*Navy*] [*British*].................DDPS
Deputy Director of Plans [*CIA*].................DDP
Deputy Director for Plans and Policy [*National Security Agency*].........DDPP
Deputy Director of Post-Hostilities Plans [*Military*] [*British*]...............DDPHP
Deputy Director of Prisoners of War [*British*].................DDPOW
Deputy Director for Programs and Resources [*National Security Agency*].................DDPR
Deputy Director of Public Relations [*Military*] [*British*].................DDPR
Deputy Director of Quartering [*Military*] [*British*].................DDQ
Deputy Director of Recruiting and Demobilization [*Military*] [*British*].................DDRD
Deputy Director of Royal Artillery [*Military*] [*British*].................DDRA
Deputy Director of Science [*Military*] [*British*].................DDS
Deputy Director of Selection of Personnel [*Military*] [*British*].................DDSP
Deputy Director of Staff Duties [*Military*] [*British*].................DDSD
Deputy Director of Supply and Transport [*British*].................DDST
Deputy Director of Tactical Investigation [*Military*] [*British*].................DDTI
Deputy Director of Technical Administration [*Ministry of Supply*] [*British*].................DDTA
Deputy Director for Test and Evaluation [*NASA*].................DD-T & E
Deputy Director of Works, Electrical and Mechanical [*British*].....DDWE & M
Deputy Directorate of Weapons, Polaris [*Navy*] [*British*].................DDWP
Deputy Educators Against Narcotics [*Defunct*].................DEAN
Deputy for Flight Operations [*NASA*].................DFO
Deputy General Manager [*AEC*].................DGM
Deputy General Purchasing Agent [*Military*].................DGPA
Deputy Grand Director of Ceremonies [*Masonry*].................DGDC
Deputy Grand Master [*Masonry*].................DGM
Deputy Inspector-General.................DIG
Deputy Inspector-General for Safety [*Air Force*].................DIGS
Deputy Inspector of Naval Ordnance.................DINO
Deputy for Intelligence.................DI
Deputy Judge Advocate General.................DJAG
Deputy for Launch Operations [*NASA*].................DLO
Deputy Lieutenant [*British*].................DL
Deputy Local Naval Commander.................DLNC
Deputy Master-General [*Military*] [*British*].................DMG
Deputy for Materiel.................DM
Deputy Military Governor [*US Military Government, Germany*].................DMG
Deputy Military Secretary [*British*].................DMS
Deputy Missile Combat Crew Commander.................DMCCC
Deputy for Nuclear Affairs.................DNA
Deputy for Operations.................DO
Deputy Paymaster in Chief.................DPIC
Deputy Prime Minister [*British*].................DPM
Deputy Principal Officer [*Foreign Service*].................DPO
Deputy Project Manager.................DPM
Deputy Provincial Grand Master [*Masonry*].................DProGM
Deputy Provost Marshal [*British*].................DPM
Deputy Public Affairs Officer [*United States Information Service*].................DPAO
Deputy Quartermaster General.................DQMG
Deputy Quartermaster-Sergeant [*British*].................DQMS
Deputy Regional Administrator.................DRA
Deputy Regional Commander.................DRC
Deputy Registrar-General [*British*].................DR-G
Deputy Safeguard [*Missile defense*] **System Manager**.................DSAFSM
Deputy Scientific Adviser [*British*].................DSA

Deputy and Scientific Director of Army Research.................DSDAR
Deputy-Secretary [*British*].................DS
Deputy-Secretary to the Admiralty [*British*].................DSA
Deputy Secretary of Defense.................DEPSECDEF
Deputy Secretary General.................DSG
Deputy Secretary General.................DSYG
Deputy Secretary of the General Staff (Coordination and Reports) [*Army*].................DSGS(CAR)
Deputy Sector Advisor.................DSA
Deputy Senior Advisor.................DSA
Deputy of Space Systems [*Air Force*].................DSS
Deputy Supreme Allied Commander.................DSAC
Deputy Supreme Allied Commander, Atlantic.................DEPSACLANT
Deputy Supreme Allied Commander, Europe.................DSACEUR
Deputy Supreme Commander, Allied Expeditionary Force.................DSCAEF
Deputy System Manager [*Army*].................DSAFSM
Deputy Under Secretary of the Army.................DUSA
Deputy Under Secretary of Defense.................DUSD
Deputy Undersecretary for Field Coordination [*HUD*].................DUSFC
Dequincy, LA [*Location identifier*] [*FAA*].................DQU
Der Alte Orient [*A publication*].................Alt O
Der Altsprachliche Unterricht [*A publication*].................AU
Der Herold. Vierteljahrsschrift fuer Heraldik, Genealogie, und Verwandte Wissenschaften [*A publication*].................Herold
Der Islam. Zeitschrift fuer Geschichte und Kultur des Islamischen Orients [*A publication*].................Islam
Der Neue Weg [*A publication*].................DNW
Dera Ismail Khan [*Pakistan*] [*Airport symbol*].................DSK
Derby [*Colorado*] [*Seismograph station code, US Geological Survey*] [*Closed*].................DER
Derby [*Australia*] [*Airport symbol*].................DRB
Derby, CT [*Radio station call letters*].................WLNV
Derby, KS [*Radio station call letters*].................KYMG
Derby Public Library, Derby, CT [*Library symbol*].................CtDe
Derby Public Library, Derby, KS [*Library symbol*].................KDe
Derbyshire [*County in England*].................DERB
Derbyshire [*County in England*].................DERBY
Derbyshire [*County in England*].................DERBYS
Derbyshire Archaeological Journal [*A publication*].................DAJ
Derbyshire Archaeological Journal [*A publication*].................Derbyshire Arch J
Derbyshire England Red Cap Club of America.................DERCCA
Derecho de la Integracion [*A publication*].................Der Integr
Dereco, Inc. [*NYSE symbol*] [*Delisted*].................DER
Derevoobrabatyvajuscaja Promyslennost [*A publication*].................Derev Prom
Deri Muzeum Evkoenyve [*A publication*].................Deri Muz Ev
Derim [*Papua New Guinea*] [*Airport symbol*].................DER
Deringer Duell Head Process.................DDHP
Derivation [*or Derivative*].................DER
Derivation [*or Derivative*].................DERIV
Derivation & Tabulation Associates, Inc. [*Information service*].................DATA
Derivative Cyclic Voltammetry [*Analytical electrochemistry*].................DCV
Derivative Thermogravimetry.................DTG
Derived Delta Modulation.................DDM
Derjaguin-Landau-Verwey-Overbeek [*Theory in cytology*].................DLVO
Derma-Lock Medical Corp. [*Norwegian*].................DERM
Dermatan Sulfate [*Biochemistry*].................DS
Dermatine.................DER
Dermatitis [*Medicine*].................DERM
Dermatitis Herpetiformis [*Medicine*].................DH
Dermato-Venerologia [*A publication*].................Derm Venerol
Dermatofibrosarcoma Protuberans [*Oncology*].................DFSP
Dermatologia Internationalis [*A publication*].................Dermatol Int
Dermatologia Tropica et Ecologia Geographica [*A publication*].................Dermatol Trop Ecol Geogr
Dermatologica [*A publication*].................Dermatolog
Dermatologische Monatsschrift [*A publication*].................Dermatol Monatsschr
Dermatologische Wochenschrift [*A publication*].................Dermatol Wochenschr
Dermatologische Wochenschrift [*A publication*].................Dermat Wochnschr
Dermatologiya i Venerologiya [*A publication*].................Dermatol Venerol
Dermatology.................DERM
Dermatology.................DERMATOL
Dermatology Foundation.................DF
Dermatology Nurses Association.................DNA
Dermatology and Syphilology Technician [*Navy*].................DST
Dermatosen in Beruf und Umwelt [*A publication*].................Derm Beruf Umwelt
Dermatoses Professionnelles [*A publication*].................Dermatoses Prof
Dermo-Optical Perception [*Parapsychology*].................DOP
Dermott, AR [*Radio station call letters*].................KAKA
Dernier [*Of the Last Month*] [*French*].................DER
Derrick.................DRK
Derry, NH [*Radio station call letters*].................WDER
Derry, NH [*Television station call letters*].................WNDS
Dersam [*New York*] [*Seismograph station code, US Geological Survey*].................DNY
Des Laufenden Monats [*Of the Current Month*] [*German*].................DLM
Des Moines [*Iowa*] [*Seismograph station code, US Geological Survey*] [*Closed*].................DMI
Des Moines [*Iowa*] [*Airport symbol*].................DSM
Des Moines Area Community College, Ankeny, IA [*Library symbol*].................IaAnkD
Des Moines & Central Iowa Railway Co. [*AAR code*].................DCI

Des Moines County Historical Society, Burlington, IA [Library symbol] ..... IaBDHi
Des Moines, IA [Radio station call letters] ..... KCBC
Des Moines, IA [Television station call letters] ..... KCBR
Des Moines, IA [Television station call letters] ..... KCCI-TV
Des Moines, IA [Television station call letters] ..... KDIN-TV
Des Moines, IA [Radio station call letters] ..... KDMI
Des Moines, IA [Radio station call letters] ..... KDPS
Des Moines, IA [Radio station call letters] ..... KGGO
Des Moines, IA [Radio station call letters] ..... KIOA
Des Moines, IA [Radio station call letters] ..... KLYF
Des Moines, IA [Radio station call letters] ..... KMGK
Des Moines, IA [Radio station call letters] ..... KRNQ
Des Moines, IA [Radio station call letters] ..... KRNT
Des Moines, IA [Radio station call letters] ..... KSO
Des Moines, IA [Radio station call letters] ..... KUCB-FM
Des Moines, IA [Radio station call letters] ..... KWKY
Des Moines, IA [Radio station call letters] ..... WHO
Des Moines, IA [Television station call letters] ..... WHO-TV
Des Moines Metropolitan Service Area Library Cooperative, Des Moines, IA [Library symbol] ..... IaDmMet
Des Moines Public Library, Des Moines, IA [Library symbol] ..... IaDm
Des Moines Union Railway Co. [AAR code] ..... DMU
Des Plaines, IL [Radio station call letters] ..... WYEN
Desaguadero [Bolivia] [Seismograph station code, US Geological Survey] [Closed] ..... DSG
Desalination [A publication] ..... Desalinatn
Desalkylflurazepam [Sedative] ..... DAF
Desalter ..... DSLTR
Desarrollo Economico [A publication] ..... Desarr Econ
Desarrollo Indoamericano [A publication] ..... Desarr Indoamer
Desarrollo Quimico Industrial, SA [Spain] ..... DEQUISA
Desarrollo Rural en las Americas [A publication] ..... Desarr Rur Amer
Desaturated ..... DESAT
Desaturated Phosphatidylcholine [Biochemistry] ..... DPC
Desbromoleptophos [Insecticide] ..... DBL
Descend [Aviation] ..... D
Descend ..... DESC
Descend [Aviation] ..... DSND
Descend so as to Cross [Aviation] ..... DSATC
Descend to and Cross [Aviation] ..... DTAX
Descend to and Cruise [Aviation] ..... DCRZ
Descend Immediately [Aviation] ..... DSNDI
Descend to and Maintain [Aviation] ..... DTAM
Descend so as to Reach [Aviation] ..... DSATR
Descend To [Aviation] ..... DES
Descend Well to Right [Aviation] ..... DWTR
Descend Well to Right of Course [Aviation] ..... DWRC
Descendant ..... DESCDT
Descendants of the New Jersey Settlers ..... DNJS
Descendants of the Signers of the Declaration of Independence ..... DSDI
Descending Medial Longitudinal Fasciculus ..... DMLF
Descending Node Orbit ..... DNO
Descent ..... DES
Descent ..... DSCNT
Descent ..... DSNT
Descent Battery Pack ..... DBP
Descent through Cloud [Procedure] [Aviation code] ..... PP
Descent Engine [NASA] ..... DE
Descent Engine Control Assembly [Apollo] [NASA] ..... DECA
Descent Orbit Insertion [Aerospace] ..... DOI
Descent Performance Test ..... DPT
Descent Power [or Propulsion] System [NASA] ..... DPS
Descent Rate RADAR ..... DRR
Descent Stage [NASA] ..... DS
Descent State [NASA] ..... D/S
Descent System ..... DS
Deschutes County Library, Bend, OR [Library symbol] ..... OrBe
Describe ..... DB
Describe ..... DESCR
Describing Function ..... DF
Describing Function Analyzer [NASA] ..... DFA
Description ..... DESC
Description ..... DESCRON
Description, Installation, and Maintenance ..... DIM
Description and Instructions ..... DI
Description, Operation, and Maintenance ..... DOM
Description Pattern ..... DP
Description of Underwater Contacts Hastily and Exactly [Navy slang] ..... DOUCHE
Descriptive and Applied Linguistics [A publication] ..... Descrip Appl Ling
Descriptive Item File ..... DIF
Descriptive Method ..... DM
Descriptive Method Item Identification [DoD] ..... DMII
Descriptor [Data processing] ..... DE
Descriptor Attribute Matrix ..... DAM
Descriptor Justification Form [ERIC] ..... DJF
Descriptor Word Index ..... DWI
Desensitization Test [Allergy] ..... DST
Desensitize ..... DSNTZ
Deseronto, ON [Television station call letters] CJOH-TV-6

Desert [Hawaii] [Seismograph station code, US Geological Survey] ..... DES
Desert [Board on Geographic Names] ..... DSRT
Desert Air Force [British] ..... DAF
Desert Air, Inc. [Seattle, WA] [FAA designator] ..... DSA
Desert Air Service [Mesa, AZ] [FAA designator] ..... MTA
Desert Arabian Bloodstock [NASDAQ symbol] ..... DABS
Desert Bighorn Council ..... DBC
Desert Biome [Ecological biogeographic study] ..... DB
Desert Botanical Garden [An association] ..... DBG
Desert Field Exercise [Military] ..... DESFEX
Desert Firing Exercise [Military] ..... DESFIREX
Desert Fishes Council ..... DFC
Desert Hot Springs [California] [Seismograph station code, US Geological Survey] [Closed] ..... DHS
Desert Institute Bulletin [A publication] ..... Desert Inst Bull
Desert Locust Control Organization for East Africa [UN Food and Agriculture Organization] ..... DLCO-EA
Desert Locust Control Organization for Eastern Africa. Technical Report [A publication] ..... Desert Locust Control Organ E Afr Tech Rep
Desert Magazine [A publication] ..... Desert Mag
Desert Pacific Airlines [Sedona, AZ] [FAA designator] ..... DSP
Desert Pacific Airways [Oxnard, CA] [FAA designator] ..... DPA
Desert Protective Council ..... DPC
Desert Research Institute [University of Nevada] ..... DRI
Desert Test Center [Army] ..... DTC
Desert Tortoise Council ..... DTC
Desert Training Center [Army] ..... DTC
Deserted Medieval Village [British] ..... DMV
Deserter [Military] ..... D
Deserter [Military] ..... DSTR
Deserter's Effects [Military] ..... DESEFF
Desertion ..... DES
Deservicing, Maintenance, and Checkout Facility [NASA] ..... DMCF
Desglycinamide-Arginine-Vasopressin [Antidiuretic] ..... DGAVP
Desi-Lucille Arnaz Co. ..... DESILU
Desialylated Ovine Submaxillary Mucin [Biochemistry] ..... DOSM
Desiccant [Chemistry] ..... DSCC
Design ..... D
Design ..... DES
Design ..... DGN
Design ..... DSGN
Design Acceptance [or Approval] Test ..... DAT
Design Acceptance [or Approval] Test Report ..... DATR
Design Action Request ..... DAR
Design of Aircraft Wing Structures [Computer program] ..... DAWNS
Design Approval Data ..... DAD
Design, Architecture, Software, and Testing ..... DAST
Design Augmented by Computer ..... DAC
Design Authorization ..... DA
Design Automation ..... DA
Design Bandwidth ..... DBW
Design Baseline ..... DB
Design Baseline Program ..... DBP
Design Basis Accident [Nuclear energy] ..... DBA
Design Basis Depressurization Accident [Nuclear energy] ..... DBDA
Design Basis Earthquake [Nuclear energy] ..... DBE
Design Basis Fault [Nuclear energy] ..... DBF
Design Basis Tornado [Nuclear energy] ..... DBT
Design Burst ..... DB
Design Capability Line [Army] ..... DCL
Design Certificate Board ..... DCB
Design Certification Review [NASA] ..... DCR
Design Change ..... DC
Design Change Authorization ..... DCA
Design Change Clearance Sheet ..... DCCS
Design Change Control ..... DCC
Design Change Control Program ..... DCCP
Design Change Document ..... DCD
Design Change Listing ..... DCL
Design Change Notice ..... DCN
Design Change Proposal ..... DCP
Design Change Request ..... DCR
Design Change Request Engineering Order ..... DCREO
Design Change Request Serial Engineering Order ..... DCRSEO
Design Change Review Board ..... DCRB
Design Change Schedule ..... DCS
Design Change Summary ..... DCS
Design Change Work Order ..... DCWO
Design Characteristic Review ..... DCR
Design and Components in Engineering [A publication] ..... Des Compon Engn
Design Concept Change ..... DCC
Design Concern Report ..... DCR
Design Contractor ..... DC
Design Control Specification ..... DCS
Design Corrective Action Form ..... DCAF
Design Corrective Action Report ..... DCAR
Design to Cost ..... DTC
Design Criteria Plan ..... DCP
Design Criteria Specification ..... DCS

Design Data Book	DDB
Design Data Package	DDP
Design Data Sheet [Naval Ship Engineering Center]	DDS
Design Data Transmittal	DDT
Design Decision Memo	DDM
Design, Development, Fabrication, Testing	DDFT
Design Development Plan	DDP
Design Development Record	DDR
Design Development Test	DDT
Design, Development, Test, and Evaluation	DDT & E
Design Deviation [Aerospace]	DD
Design Discharge Format	DDF
Design Disclosure Formats [Naval Applied Science Laboratory]	DDF
Design Disclosure Standard	DDS
Design Disclosure for Systems and Equipment	DDSE
Design and Drafting Management Council	DDMC
Design Drafting Reference Information	DDRI
Design and Drafting Techniques	DDT
Design Effect [Ratio used in statistics]	DEFT
Design Electronics [A publication]	Des Electron
Design Engine Inspection	DEI
Design Engineer	DGE
Design Engineering	DE
Design Engineering [A publication]	Des Eng
Design Engineering Directorate	DED
Design Engineering Identification	DEI
Design Engineering Inspection Simulation	DEIS
Design Engineering (Toronto) [A publication]	Des Eng (Toronto)
Design Evaluation	DE
Design Evaluation Inspection Simulator	DEIS
Design Evaluation/Qualification	DE/Q
Design Evaluation Test	DET
Design Evaluation Vehicle	DEV
Design Expansion System	DES
Design of Experiments [Conference] [Army]	DOE
Design External Pressure	DEP
Design Eye Point [Cockpit visibility]	DEP
Design Fabrication Assembly	DFA
Design Failure-Mode Analysis	DFMA
Design Feasibility Test	DFT
Design Field Change	DFC
Design Handbook	DH
Design Hourly Volume [Transportation]	DHV
Design Improvement Program	DIP
Design Improvement Study	DIS
Design for Industry [A publication]	Design Ind
Design for Industry [A publication]	Design for Ind
Design Information Bulletin	DIB
Design Information Manual	DIM
Design Information Worksheet	DIW
Design Institute for Physical Property Data [AIChE]	DIPPR
Design Interface Meeting	DIM
Design Internal Pressure [Nuclear energy]	DIP
[A] Design Language for Indicating Behavior [Data processing]	ADLIB
Design Limit and Endurance	DL & E
Design Limit Load Factor	DLLF
Design Load Limit	DLL
Design, Manage, Construct	DMC
Design Management Institute	DMI
Design Manual	DM
Design Margin Evaluation	DME
Design Memorandum	DM
Design Mission Effect	DME
Design News [A publication]	Des News
Design Objective Reliability	DOR
Design Operation Capability	DOC
Design Option Decision Tree	DODT
Design Performance Optimization	DESPOT
Design and Performance Specification	D & PS
Design Point Vehicle	DPV
Design to Price	DTP
Design-to-Price Electronic Warfare Suite [Navy]	DTPEWS
Design-to-Price Electronics Warfare System [Military]	DPEWS
Design and Procedure Standard [NASA]	DPS
Design and Production	D & P
Design Professions Technical Specialty Index [National Society of Professional Engineers] [Information service]	DPTSI
Design Proof	DP
Design Proof Tests	DPT
Design Proof Unit	DPU
Design Proposal	DP
Design Qualification	DQ
Design Qualification Requirement	DQR
Design Qualification Test Plan	DQTP
Design Quarterly [A publication]	Design Q
Design Quarterly [A publication]	DQ
Design Quarterly [A publication]	DSNQ
Design Reference Mission [NASA]	DRM
Design Reference Model	DRM
Design Release Engineering Change Proposal	DRECP
Design Release [or Request] Review	DRR
Design Requirement	DR
Design Requirement Drawing	DRD
Design Requirements Baseline	DRB
Design Review	DR
Design Review and Acceptance Group [Reviews nuclear weapon designs for DoD]	DRAAG
Design Review Agreement	DRA
Design Review Board	DRB
Design Review List	DRL
Design Rule Checker [For integrated circuitry]	DRC
Design Safety Criteria [Nuclear energy]	DSC
Design Safety Factor	DSF
Design Schedule Analysis	DSA
Design Science Institute	DSI
Design Section Drawing Record	DSDR
Design Sheet	DS
Design Simulator	DESSIM
Design Specification	DS
Design Specification	DSPEC
Design Standards	DS
Design Standards Manual	DSM
Design Studies Evaluation Group [NATO]	DSEG
Design Technical Information [or Instruction]	DTI
Design/Test Contractor	DTC
Design [or Development], Test, and Mission Operations [NASA]	DTMO
Design Test Model	DTM
Design Thermal Transient [Nuclear energy]	DTT
Design to Unit Production Cost [Army]	DTUPC
Design Verification Demonstration	DVD
Design Verification Period	DVP
Design Verification Program	DVP
Design Verification Rig	DVR
Design Verification Specification	DVS
Design Verification Test	DVT
Design Work Study	DWS
Designate	DESG
Designate [or Designation]	DESIG
Designate	DSG
Designate	DSGN
Designate Command Line [Data processing]	DCL
Designated	DSGND
Designated Aircraft Maintenance Inspector	DAMI
Designated Engineer Representative [FAA title]	DER
Designated Field Activity [DoD]	DFA
Designated Ground Zero	DGZ
Designated Hitter [Baseball]	DESI
Designated Hitter [Formerly, DPH] [Baseball]	DH
Designated Inspection Points	DIP
Designated Manufacturing Inspection Representative	DMIR
Designated Marketing Area [Television ratings term used by A. C. Nielsen Co.]	DMA
Designated National Agency [for exchange of oceanographic data]	DNA
Designated as Naval Aviation Pilot [Marine Corps]	DESIGNAP
Designated Overhaul Point	DOP
Designated Pinch Hitter [Later, DH] [Baseball]	DPH
Designated Processing Agency	DPA
Designated Project Manager	DPM
Designated for Prompt Mobilization	DPM
Designated Qualified Person [Department of Agriculture]	DQP
Designated Security Agency	DSA
Designated Special Disbursing Agent	DESIGDISBAGENT
Designated Special Emphasis Engineering	DSEE
Designated Stock Point	DSP
Designated Student Naval Aviator	DESNAVAV
Designated Subsystems Project Manager [NASA]	DSPM
Designated Systems Management Group [Military]	DSMG
Designated Systems Management Group [Military]	DSMGP
Designating Optical Tracker [Telescope]	DOT
Designation Accuracy Test Equipment	DATE
Designation Equipment	DE
Designation Indicator	DI
Designator	DES
Designator Register [Data processing]	DR
Designatronics, Inc. [American Stock Exchange symbol]	DSG
Designatus [Named] [Latin]	DES
Designcraft Jewel Industries, Inc. [American Stock Exchange symbol]	DJI
Designed Water Line [Technical drawings]	DWL
Designer Choice Logic	DCL
Designer Shoe Guild	DSG
Designers Lighting Forum	DLF
Designhouse International, Inc. [NASDAQ symbol]	DHIN
Designing Out Maintenance	DOM
Designs for Change [An association]	DC
Designs for Change [An association]	DFC
Desinfektion und Gesundheitswesen [A publication]	Desinfekt Gesundheitswes
Desirable Body Weight [Medicine]	DBW
Desirable Objective	DO
Desire	DES
Desire	DSR
Desired Delivery Date	DDD

Desired Ground Zero [*Bombing*] ... DGZ
Desired Image Distribution Using Orthogonal Constraints [*Illinois Institute of Technology*] ... DIDOC
Desired Learner Outcomes [*Education*] ... DLO
Desired Mean Point of Impact [*Military*] ... DMPI
Desired Point of Impact [*Military*] ... DPI
Desired Work Load ... DWL
Desires to Transfer ... DESTR
Desk, Combination Flat Top and Typewriter ... FT & TW
Desk and Derrick [*Oil industry*] ... D & D
Desk, Double-Pedestal Flat-Top ... DPFT
Desk, Double-Pedestal Typewriter ... DPTW
Desk Side Computer System [*GE*] ... DSCS
Desk Side Time Shared [*Data processing*] [*GE*] ... DSTS
Desk Top ... DT
Desk Top Computer ... DTC
Desktop Analysis Tool [*A publication*] ... DAT
Desmethylimipramine [*Antidepressant*] ... DMI
Desmethylmetoxuron [*Organic chemistry*] ... DMM
Desorption Chemical Ionization ... DCI
Desorption Ionization ... DI
DeSoto Club of America ... DCA
DeSoto, MO [*Radio station call letters*] ... KOLS
DeSoto Parish Library, Mansfield, LA [*Library symbol*] ... LMaD
Despatch ... DESP
Despatch Rider [*Military*] [*British*] ... DR
Despatch-Rider Letter-Service [*Military*] [*British*] ... DRLS
Despeciated Bovine Serum ... DBS
Despin Control Electronics [*Aerospace*] ... DCE
Despin Control Subsystem [*Aerospace*] ... DCS
Despun Antenna Test Satellite [*Air Force*] ... DATS
Despun Heat Shield ... DHS
Desquamative Interstitial Pneumonia [*Medicine*] ... DIP
Dessau, Inscriptiones Latinae Selectae [*A publication*] ... ILS
Dessie [*Ethiopia*] [*Airport symbol*] ... DSE
Destainer Power Supply [*Electrophoresis*] ... DPS
Destillo [*Distill*] [*Pharmacy*] ... DEST
Destin, FL [*Radio station call letters*] ... WMMK
Destination ... DEST
Destination ... DESTN
Destination ... DSTN
Destination Address Field [*Data processing*] ... DAF
Destination Change [*Military*] ... DESCHA
Destination Queues [*Data processing*] ... DQ
Destiny Research Foundation ... DRF
Destra [*Right*] [*Italian*] ... D
Destra [*Right*] [*Italian*] ... DEST
Destra Mano [*Right Hand*] [*Italian*] ... DM
Destratification Impeller Unit ... DIU
Destratification Motor Impeller ... DMI
Destratification Motor Impeller Unit ... DMIU
Destratification Motor Unit ... DMU
Destroy ... DEST
Destroyed ... D
Destroyed [*or Destructor*] ... DESTR
Destroyer [*Navy*] [*British*] ... D
Destroyer [*Navy symbol*] ... DD
Destroyer ... DES
Destroyer [*Navy*] [*British*] ... DEST
Destroyer Advisory Board [*Navy*] ... DAB
Destroyer Antisubmarine Helicopter ... DASH
Destroyer Antisubmarine Transportable Array Detector ... DASTARD
Destroyer Battle Force [*Navy*] ... DESBATFOR
Destroyer Development Group [*Navy*] ... DESDEVGRU
Destroyer Division [*Navy*] ... DESDIV
Destroyer Engineered Operating Cycle ... DDEOC
Destroyer Escort ... DE
Destroyer Escort Experimental ... DEX
Destroyer Experimental ... DX
Destroyer Flag [*Navy*] [*British*] ... DR
Destroyer Flotilla [*Navy*] ... DESFLOT
Destroyer Flotilla [*Navy*] ... DF
Destroyer Force, Atlantic Fleet [*Navy symbol*] ... DESLANT
Destroyer Force, Pacific Fleet [*Navy symbol*] ... DESPAC
Destroyer Helicopter System ... DHS
Destroyer Leader [*Navy*] ... DL
Destroyer Minelayer [*Navy symbol*] ... DM
Destroyer Minesweeper [*Navy symbol*] [*Obsolete*] ... DMS
Destroyer Repair [*Navy*] ... DESREP
Destroyer Representative [*Navy*] ... DESREP
Destroyer Rocket ... DESROC
Destroyer Schoolship [*Navy*] ... DESS
Destroyer Scouting Force [*Navy*] ... DESCOFOR
Destroyer SONAR Analysis Center [*Navy*] ... DESAC
Destroyer Squadron [*Navy*] ... DESRON
Destroyer/Submarine Antisubmarine Warfare Exercise [*Military*] ... DESUBEX
Destroyer Surface-Effect Ship ... DS
Destroyer Tactical Bulletin [*Navy*] ... DTB
Destroyer Tender [*Navy symbol*] ... AD
Destroyers, Asiatic Fleet [*Navy*] ... DESAF
Destroyers/Cruisers, Pacific Fleet [*Navy*] ... DESCRUPAC
Destroyers, Disbursing Office [*Navy*] ... DDO
Destroyers, Southwest Pacific Fleet [*Navy*] ... DESSOWESPAC
Destruct ... DEST
Destruct Charge ... DC
Destruct Command Receiver ... DCR
Destruct Command System ... DCS
Destruct Safe Arm Device ... DSAD
Destruction of Aircraft or Motor Vehicles ... DAMV
Destruction of Government Property ... DGP
Destruction of Interstate Property ... DIP
Destruction and Removal Efficiency [*Of waste incinerators*] ... DRE
Destructive Dilemma [*Rule of inference*] [*Logic*] ... DD
Destructive Lot Acceptance Testing ... DLAT
Destructive Readout ... DRO
Destructively Distilled ... DEST-DIST
Destructor [*Military*] ... DST
Destructor ... DSTR
Desuperheater ... DSUPHTR
Det Danske Luftfartselskab A/S [*Danish airline*] ... DDL
Det Kongelige Danske Videnskabernes Selskab Matematisk-Fysiske Meddelelser [*A publication*] ... Danske Vid Selsk Mat-Fys Medd
Det Kongelige Norske Videnskabers Selbskabs Forhandlinger [*A publication*] ... NoVidSF
Det Kongelige Videnskapers Selskap [*A publication*] ... DKVS
Det Norske Luftfartselkap [*Norwegian airline*] ... DNL
Det Norske Sprak-og Litteraturselskap [*A publication*] ... NSL
Det Norske Videnskapers Selskap [*A publication*] ... DNVS
Detach ... DET
Detachable Container Association ... DCA
Detached ... DTCH
Detached from Duty Indicated and from All Other Duty Assigned ... DETALL
Detached Enlisted Men's List [*Army*] ... DEML
Detached Officer's List [*Army*] ... DOL
Detached Service [*Army*] ... DS
Detachment d'Armee des Alpes ... DAALPS
Detachment d'Armee de l'Atlantique ... DAATL
Detachment Equipment Authorization List [*Military*] ... DEAL
Detachment of Patients ... DOP
Detachments Left in Contact [*Military*] ... DLIC
Detail ... D
Detail ... DET
Detail ... DTL
Detail Assembly Panel ... DAP
Detail Assembly Template ... DAT
Detail Checkout Specifications ... DCS
Detail Condition ... DC
Detail Condition Register ... DCR
Detail Design Review ... DDR
Detail Finish Specification ... DFS
Detail Networks ... DN
Detail Program Interrelationships ... DPI
Detail Specification ... DS
Detail Velocity Display ... DVD
Detailed Acceptance Test Procedure ... DATP
Detailed Acceptance Test Specification ... DATS
Detailed Budget Decision ... DBD
Detailed Checklist ... DCL
Detailed Checkout Procedures ... DCOP
Detailed Data Display ... DDD
Detailed Design Review and Evaluation ... DDR & E
Detailed Design Specification ... DDS
Detailed Elementary Wiring Diagrams ... DEWD
Detailed Experimental Computer-Assisted Language ... DECAL
Detailed Forecast ... DF
Detailed Function System Requirement ... DFSR
Detailed Human Engineering Plan ... DHEP
Detailed Individual Test Plan ... DITP
Detailed Interrogation Center [*Navy*] ... DIC
Detailed Issue Depot [*Military supply organization for Allied armies in Europe*] [*World War II*] ... DID
Detailed Labor and Time Analysis [*PERT*] ... DELTA
Detailed Maneuver Table ... DMT
Detailed Operating Procedure ... DOP
Detailed Performance Analysis [*Bell System*] ... DPA
Detailed Project Plan ... DPP
Detailed Report ... DR
Detailed Requirements Document ... DRD
Detailed Routing Instructions ... DETRINS
Detailed Ship Loading ... DSL
Detailed Supplementary Objective ... DSO
Detailed System Functional Requirements ... DSFR
Detailed System Test ... DST
Detailed Test Description ... DTD
Detailed Test Objective [*NASA*] ... DTO
Detailed Test Plan [*or Procedure*] ... DTP
Detailed Test Specification ... DTS
Detailed Type Specification ... DTS
Detailed Work Statement ... DWS
Details of Agreement [*NATO*] ... DOFA

Detain .... DTN
Detained on Board [*Referring to seamen*] .... DOB
Detained Pay .... D/P
Detainee .... DET
Detectability of Yes-No .... DYN
Detected Pulse Interference .... DPI
Detecting Heads [*JETDS nomenclature*] [*Military*] .... DT
Detection .... DET
Detection .... DETEC
Detection, Action, and Response Technique .... DART
Detection, Classification, and Targeting .... DCT
Detection and Control Unit .... DCU
Detection and Mapping [*Package*] [*NASA*] .... DAM
Detection RADAR .... DR
Detection RADAR Automatic Monitoring .... DRAM
Detection RADAR Data Processing .... DRDP
Detection RADAR Data Takeoff [*Air Force*] .... DRDTO
Detection RADAR Electronic Component .... DREC
Detection RADAR Environmental Display [*Air Force*] .... DRED
Detection and Range [*Early name for RADAR*] .... DERAX
Detection Scheme with Fixed Thresholds [*Communication signal*] .... DSFT
Detection Scheme with Learning of Thresholds [*Communication signal*] .... DSLT
Detection Systems [*NASDAQ symbol*] .... DETC
Detection Track Evaluation and Assignment Systems [*Navy*] .... DTEAS
Detection/Tracker .... D/T
Detection and Tracking of Satellites .... DATOS
Detection of Unauthorized Equipment [*Bell Laboratories*] .... DUE
Detection and Warning .... D & W
Detective .... D
Detective .... DET
Detective - Agents - Science Fiction - Thriller [*Acronym used as title of magazine*] .... DAST
Detective Constable [*Scotland Yard*] .... DC
Detective Inspector [*Scotland Yard*] .... DI
Detective Quantum Efficiency [*Photon device*] .... DQE
Detective Sergeant [*Scotland Yard*] .... DS
Detective Superintendent .... D-SUPT
Detector .... DETR
Detector Assembly .... DA
Detector Back Bias .... DBB
Detector Balanced Bias .... DBB
Detector Dependent Response [*Measurement*] .... DDR
Detector Electronics [*NASDAQ symbol*] .... DETX
Detector Mosaic .... DM
Detector, Selector, and Effector [*Social science*] .... DSE
Detector Tracker Switch .... DTS
Detent [*Mechanical engineering*] .... DTT
Detention .... DETN
Detention Clause [*Insurance*] .... D/C
Detention of Pay .... DP
Detergent Aid .... DA
Deteriorate .... DTRT
Deterioration Control .... DC
Deterioration Index [*Index of intellectual impairment on intelligence test*] .... DI
Deterioration Quotient [*Medicine*] .... DQ
Determination .... DET
Determination .... DETER
Determination .... DETN
Determination of Air-Launched Missile Environment .... DAME
Determination of Dependency .... DD
Determination Effective Levels of Task Automation [*Data processing*] .... DELTA
Determination and Findings .... D & F
Determination of Organic Structures by Physical Methods [*A publication*] .... Determ Org Struct Phys Methods
Determine .... DETM
Determine .... DTRM
Determined .... DETD
Determined .... DTMD
Detonator .... DET
Detonator Inspection Gauge .... DIG
Detrex Chemical Industries [*NASDAQ symbol*] .... DTRX
Detrimental .... DETR
Detroit [*Michigan*] [*Airport symbol*] .... DTT
Detroit [*Michigan*] [*Airport symbol*] .... DTW
Detroit Academy of Natural Sciences. Occasional Papers [*A publication*] .... Detroit Acad Nat Sci Occasional Paper
Detroit Adjustment Inventory [*Psychology*] .... DAI
Detroit Air Defense Sector [*ADS*] .... DEADS
Detroit Area Consortium of Catholic Colleges [*Library network*] .... DACCC
Detroit Arsenal [*Michigan*] [*Army*] .... DA
Detroit Arsenal [*Michigan*] [*Army*] .... DAR
Detroit Baptist Divinity School, Allen Park, MI [*Library symbol*] .... MiApDB
Detroit Bar Association, Detroit, MI [*Library symbol*] .... MiDB
Detroit & Canada Tunnel [*NASDAQ symbol*] .... DTUN
Detroit Chancery [*Catholic Church*] **Archives, Detroit, MI** [*Library symbol*] .... MiDC
Detroit [*Michigan*] **City Airport** [*Airport symbol*] .... DET
Detroit College of Law [*Michigan*] .... DCL
Detroit College of Law. Review [*A publication*] .... Det Coll L Rev
Detroit Cooperative Cataloging Center, Detroit, MI [*OCLC symbol*] .... EYQ
Detroit Data Center [*IRS*] .... DDC
Detroit Diesel Allison Division, General Motors Corp., Indianapolis, IN [*OCLC symbol*] .... IDD
Detroit Edison Co. [*NYSE symbol*] .... DTE
Detroit Edison Co., Detroit, MI [*Library symbol*] .... MiDEd
Detroit Edison Co., Information Services, Detroit, MI [*OCLC symbol*] .... EEE
Detroit Fast Food Workers' Union .... DFWU
Detroit General Hospital, Medical Library, Detroit, MI [*Library symbol*] .... MiDGH
Detroit Historical Society, Detroit, MI [*Library symbol*] .... MiDHi
Detroit Institute of Arts. Bulletin [*A publication*] .... Detroit Inst Bul
Detroit Institute of Arts, Detroit, MI [*Library symbol*] .... MiDA
Detroit Institute of Arts, Research Library, Detroit, MI [*OCLC symbol*] .... EYT
Detroit Institute of Technology .... DIT
Detroit Institute of Technology, Detroit, MI [*Library symbol*] .... MiDIT
Detroit Jazz Center [*Formerly, DJC/JRI*] .... DJC
Detroit Jazz Center/Jazz Research Institute [*Later, DJC*] .... DJC/JRI
Detroit Lakes [*Minnesota*] [*Airport symbol*] [*Obsolete*] .... DTL
Detroit Lakes, MN [*Radio station call letters*] .... KDLM
Detroit Lakes, MN [*Radio station call letters*] .... KVLR
Detroit Lawyer [*A publication*] .... Detroit Law
Detroit & Mackinac Railway Co. .... D & M
Detroit & Mackinac Railway Co. .... D & MRR
Detroit & Mackinac Railway Co. [*AAR code*] .... DM
Detroit, MI [*Location identifier*] [*FAA*] .... DWC
Detroit, MI [*Location identifier*] [*FAA*] .... DXP
Detroit, MI [*Location identifier*] [*FAA*] .... HUU
Detroit, MI [*Location identifier*] [*FAA*] .... NOI
Detroit, MI [*Location identifier*] [*FAA*] .... VQM
Detroit, MI [*Radio station call letters*] .... WABX
Detroit, MI [*Radio station call letters*] .... WCXI
Detroit, MI [*Radio station call letters*] .... WCXI-FM
Detroit, MI [*Radio station call letters*] .... WCZY-FM
Detroit, MI [*Radio station call letters*] .... WDET-FM
Detroit, MI [*Television station call letters*] .... WDIV
Detroit, MI [*Radio station call letters*] .... WDRQ
Detroit, MI [*Radio station call letters*] .... WDTR
Detroit, MI [*Radio station call letters*] .... WGPR
Detroit, MI [*Television station call letters*] .... WGPR-TV
Detroit, MI [*Radio station call letters*] .... WHYT-FM
Detroit, MI [*Television station call letters*] .... WJBK-TV
Detroit, MI [*Radio station call letters*] .... WJLB
Detroit, MI [*Radio station call letters*] .... WJOI
Detroit, MI [*Radio station call letters*] .... WJR
Detroit, MI [*Radio station call letters*] .... WJZZ
Detroit, MI [*Television station call letters*] .... WKBD-TV
Detroit, MI [*Radio station call letters*] .... WLQV
Detroit, MI [*Radio station call letters*] .... WMUZ
Detroit, MI [*Radio station call letters*] .... WNIC
Detroit, MI [*Radio station call letters*] .... WOMC
Detroit, MI [*Radio station call letters*] .... WQBH
Detroit, MI [*Radio station call letters*] .... WQRS
Detroit, MI [*Radio station call letters*] .... WRIF
Detroit, MI [*Television station call letters*] .... WTVS
Detroit, MI [*Radio station call letters*] .... WTWR
Detroit, MI [*Radio station call letters*] .... WWJ
Detroit, MI [*Radio station call letters*] .... WWWW
Detroit, MI [*Television station call letters*] .... WXON-TV
Detroit, MI [*Radio station call letters*] .... WXYZ
Detroit, MI [*Television station call letters*] .... WXYZ-TV
Detroit News [*A publication*] .... DN
Detroit Ordnance District [*Army*] .... DOD
Detroit Public Library, Burton Historical Collection, Detroit, MI [*Library symbol*] .... MiD-B
Detroit Public Library, Detroit, MI [*OCLC symbol*] .... EYP
Detroit Public Library, Detroit, MI [*Library symbol*] .... MiD
Detroit Review of Medicine and Pharmacy [*A publication*] .... Detroit Rev Med and Pharm
Detroit Signal Laboratory [*Army*] .... DSL
Detroit Steel Corp. [*NYSE symbol*] [*Delisted*] .... DES
Detroit Suburban Network [*Radio*] .... DSN
Detroit Symphony Orchestra. Program Notes [*A publication*] .... Detroit Sym
Detroit Terminal Railroad Co. [*AAR code*] .... DT
Detroit Tests of Learning Aptitude [*Education*] .... DTLA
Detroit-Texas Gas Gathering [*NASDAQ symbol*] .... DTXG
Detroit, Toledo & Ironton Railroad Co. [*AAR code*] .... DTI
Detroit, Toledo & Ironton Railroad Co. [*Nickname: Damned Tough and Independent*] .... DT & I
[*The*] **Detroit & Toledo Shore Line Railroad Co.** [*AAR code*] .... DTS
[*The*] **Detroit & Toledo Shore Line Railroad Co.** .... D & TSL
Detroit Tooling Association .... DTA
Detroit Waldhorn Society .... DWS
Detroit & Western [*Later, DW*] [*AAR code*] .... DETW
Detroit & Western [*AAR code*] .... DW
Detrucking Point .... DP
Detskaya Literatura [*A publication*] .... DL
Detur [*Give*] [*Pharmacy*] .... DET

Detur Ad [*Let It Be Given To*] [*Pharmacy*].................... DD
Detur in Duplo [*Give Twice as Much*] [*Pharmacy*]........... D in DUP
Detur in Duplo [*Let Twice as Much Be Given*] [*Pharmacy*].........DET in DUP
Detur et Signatur [*Let It Be Given and Labeled*] [*Pharmacy*]...............D et S
DEU [*Display Electronics Unit*] **Control Program End Item** [*NASA*].......DCPEI
Deus [*God*] [*Latin*]....................... D
Deus Loci [*A publication*]....................... DL
Deuterated Hydrogen Y [*Type of zeolite*]................DHY
Deuterated Polyethylene [*Organic chemistry*] ....DPE
Deuterium [*Also, H²*] [*Radioisotope of hydrogen*]....................D
Deuterium [*Also, D*] [*Radioisotope of hydrogen*]......................H²
Deuterium-Deuterium Reaction [*Nuclear energy*]....................D-D
Deuterium Moderated Pile Low Energy [*Reactor*] ....DIMPLE
Deuterium-Tritium Reaction [*Fusion program*] ....D-T
Deutero [*Chemistry*]....................... d
Deuteronomy [*Old Testament book*] ....Deut
Deuteronomy [*Old Testament book*] ....Dt
[*Otto Erich*] **Deutsch** [*When used in identifying Schubert's
    compositions, refers to cataloging of his works by
    musicologist Deutsch*] .... D
Deutsch-Amerikanische Petroleum Gesellschaft [*German-
    American Petroleum Society*] ....DAPG
Deutsch-Amerikanischer National-Kongress [*German-American
    National Congress*] ....DANK
Deutsch-Dominikanisches Tropenforschungsinstitut
    Veroeffentlichungen [*A publication*]
            Deutsch-Dominikan Tropenforschungsinstitut Veroeff
Deutsch-Franzoesische Monatshefte [*A publication*] ....DFMhe
Deutsch-Franzoesische Rundschau [*A publication*] ....DFR
Deutsch als Fremdsprache [*A publication*] ....DaF
Deutsch Shakespeare Gesellschaft West. Jahrbuch [*A
    publication*]...............Deutsch Shakespeare Ges West Jahrb
Deutsch-Sowjetische-Freundschaft [*German-Soviet Friendship*]
    [*Common street name in East Germany*]...............DSF
Deutsch-Taschenbuecher [*A publication*] ....Deutsch-Taschenb
Deutsche Adels-Gesellschaft in Nord Amerika [*Association of
    the German Nobility in North America*] ....DAGNA
Deutsche Aerztezeitung [*A publication*] ....Deutsche Aerzte-Ztg
Deutsche Agrartechnik [*A publication*]...............Deut Agrartech
Deutsche Akademie fuer Sprache und Dichtung. Darmstadt.
    Jahrbuch [*A publication*]...............DASD
Deutsche Akademie fuer Sprache und Dichtung. Darmstadt.
    Jahrbuch [*A publication*]...............DASDJ
Deutsche Akademie der Wissenschaften zu Berlin [*A publication*] .....DAWB
Deutsche Akademie der Wissenschaften zu Berlin. Institut fuer
    Deutsche Sprache und Literatur [*A publication*]...............DAWBIDSL
Deutsche Akademie der Wissenschaften zu Berlin. Institut fuer
    Orientforschung. Mitteilungen [*A publication*] ....MIODAWB
Deutsche Akademie der Wissenschaften zu Berlin. Institut fuer
    Orientforschung. Veroeffentlichungen [*A publication*]...........VIODAWB
Deutsche Akademie der Wissenschaften zu Berlin. Schriften
    der Sektion fuer Vor- und Fruehgeschichte [*A publication*]...............
            Deutsche Akad Wissen Berlin Schr
Deutsche Allgemeine Nachrichten Agentur [*German general
    news agency, sponsored by US newspapermen as a
    successor to the NAZI-controlled DNB*] [*Post-World War II*] ....DANA
Deutsche Allgemeine Zeitung [*A publication*] ....DAZ
Deutsche Angestellten Gewerkschaft [*German Salaried
    Employees' Union*] [*West Germany*]....................DAG
Deutsche Annalen [*A publication*]...............Dtsche A
Deutsche Apotheker [*A publication*] ....Dtsch Apoth
Deutsche Apotheker-Zeitung [*A publication*]...............Dtsch Apoth-Ztg
Deutsche Arbeiten der Universitaet Koeln [*A publication*]...............DAUK
Deutsche Arbeitgemeinschaft fuer Rechen-Anlagen [*A data
    processing association*]...............DARA
Deutsche Arbeitsfront [*German Workers Front*] [*Post-World War II*] ......DAF
Deutsche Atomkommission [*Germany*]...............DAK
Deutsche Aussenpolitik [*A publication*] ....Dtsche Aussenpolit
Deutsche Babcock Wilcox Werke ....DBW
Deutsche Baumschule [*A publication*] ....Dtsch Baumsch
Deutsche Bauzeitschrift. Fachblatt fuer Entwurf und
    Ausfuehrung [*A publication*]...............Dtsch Bauz
Deutsche Bauzeitung [*A publication*]...............DBZT-A
Deutsche Beitraege zur Geistigen Ueberlieferung [*A publication*].......DBGU
Deutsche Beitraege zur Geotechnik [*A publication*] ....Dtsch Beitr Geotech
Deutsche Bibliographie [*A bibliographic publication*] [*Germany*] ....DB
Deutsche Bibliothek, Zeppelinallee, Frankfurt am Main,
    Germany [*Library symbol*]...............GyFmDB
Deutsche Bienenwirtschaft [*A publication*] ....Dtsch Bienenwirtsch
Deutsche Bundesbahn [*German Federal Railway*] [*Since 1949*]...............DB
Deutsche Bundesbahn [*German Federal Railway*] [*Since 1949*]...............DBB
Deutsche Demokratische Republik [*German Democratic
    Republic*] [*East Germany*] [*Three-letter standard code*]...............DDR
Deutsche Dendrologische Gesellschaft Kurzmitteilungen [*A
    publication*]...............Dtsch Dendrol Ges Kurzmitt
Deutsche Dialektgeographie [*A publication*] ....DD
Deutsche Dialektgeographie [*A publication*]...............DDG
Deutsche Edelstahlwerke Aktiengesellschaft [*West Germany*]...........DEW
Deutsche Entomologische Zeitschrift [*A publication*] ....Deut Entomol Z
Deutsche Entomologische Zeitschrift [*A publication*] ....Dtsch Entomol Z

Deutsche Entomologische Zeitschrift "Iris" [*A publication*]...............
            Deutsche Entom Ztschr "Iris"
Deutsche Entwicklungsdienst [*German Development Service*]...............DED
Deutsche Farben Zeitschrift [*A publication*]...............Dtsch Farben Z
Deutsche Fischerei Zeitung [*A publication*]...............Dtsch Fisch Ztg
Deutsche Fischereirundschau [*A publication*] ....Dtsch Fischereirundsch
Deutsche Forschungs- und Versuchsanstalt fuer Luft- und
    Raumfahrt [*West Germany*] ....DFVLR
Deutsche Forschungsanstalt fuer Luft- und Raumfahrt [*West
    Germany*] ....DFLR
Deutsche Forschungsgemeinschaft [*German Research Association*]..... DFG
Deutsche Gartenbau [*A publication*]...............Dtsch Gartenbau
Deutsche Geographische Blaetter [*A publication*] .... Deut Geog Blaetter
Deutsche Geologische Gesellschaft Zeitschrift [*A publication*]...............
            Deutsche Geol Gesell Zeitschr
Deutsche Gesellschaft fuer Amerikastudien [*German
    Association for American Studies*] ....DGA
Deutsche Gesellschaft fuer Arbeitsmedizin. Jahrestagung [*A
    publication*] .... Dtsch Ges Arbeitsmed Jahrestag
Deutsche Gesellschaft fuer Klinischen Chemie ....DGKC
Deutsche Gesellschaft fuer Luft- und Raumfahrt [*West Germany*].......DGLR
Deutsche Gesellschaft fuer Ortung und Navigation [*West
    Germany*]...............DGON
Deutsche Gesellschaft fuer Photographie [*West Germany*] ....DGPH
Deutsche Gesellschaft fuer Raketentechnik und Raumfahrt
    [*German Society for Rocket Research and Space Flight*]...............DGRR
Deutsche Gesundheitswesen [*A publication*]...............Dtsch Gesundheitsw
Deutsche Gesundheitswesen [*A publication*]...............Dtsch Gesundheitswes
Deutsche Gewaesserkundliche Mitteilungen [*A publication*]...............
            Dtsch Gewaesserkd Mitt
Deutsche Girozentrale - Deutsche Kommunalbank [*West
    German bank*]...............DGZ
Deutsche Grammophon Gesellschaft [*Phonograph recording
    company*]...............DGG
Deutsche Hebe und Foerdertechnik [*A publication*]...............
            Dtsch Hebe Foerdertech
Deutsche Hoehere Schule [*A publication*]...............DDHS
Deutsche Hydrographische Zeitschrift [*A publication*]........ Dtsch Hydrogr Z
Deutsche Kameramann [*A publication*] ....Deutsch Kam
Deutsche Keramische Gesellschaft. Berichte [*A publication*]...............
            Deutsche Keramische Gesell Ber
Deutsche Kommunistische Partei ....DKP
Deutsche Krankenpflegezeitschrift [*A publication*] ..... Dtsch Krankenpflegez
Deutsche Kunst und Denkmalpflege [*A publication*] ....DKDP
Deutsche Landwirtschaft [*A publication*]...............Deut Landwirt
Deutsche Landwirtschaft [*A publication*]...............Dt Landwirt
Deutsche Lebensmittel Rundschau [*A publication*]...............
            Deut Lebensm Rundsch
Deutsche Lebensmittel Rundschau [*A publication*]...............
            Dtsch Lebensm Rundsch
Deutsche Literatur [*A publication*] ....DLit
Deutsche Literatur und Sprachstudien [*A publication*]...............DLS
Deutsche Literaturzeitung [*A publication*]...............DL
Deutsche Literaturzeitung [*A publication*]...............DLtz
Deutsche Literaturzeitung [*A publication*]...............DLZ
Deutsche Luft- und Raumfahrt. Forschungsbericht [*A
    publication*]...............Deut Luft Raumfahrt Forschungsber
Deutsche Luft- und Raumfahrt. Forschungsbericht [*A
    publication*]...............Dtsch Luftfahrt Raumfahrt Forschungsber
Deutsche Luft- und Raumfahrt. Mitteilung [*A publication*]...............
            Dtsch Luftfahrt Raumfahrt Mitt
Deutsche Luft- und Raumfahrt. Mitteilung [*A publication*]...............
            Dtsch Luft Raumfahrt Mitt
Deutsche Lufthansa AG [*Germany*] [*ICAO designator*] ....LH
Deutsche Mark [*Monetary unit in Germany*]...............DM
Deutsche Medizinal-Zeitung [*A publication*] .... Deutsche Med-Ztg
Deutsche Medizinische Wochenschrift [*A publication*] .... Deut Med Wo
Deutsche Medizinische Wochenschrift [*A publication*]...............
            Deutsche Med Wochenschr
Deutsche Medizinische Wochenschrift [*A publication*]...............
            Dtsch Med Wochenschr
Deutsche Medizinische Wochenschrift [*A publication*]...............Dtsch Med Wschr
Deutsche Mineralogische Gesellschaft. Fortschritte der
    Mineralogie [*A publication*]...............
            Deutsche Mineralog Gesell Fortschr Mineralogie
Deutsche Molkerei-Zeitung [*A publication*] ....Dtsch Molkerei Ztg
Deutsche Morgenlaendische Gesellschaft [*A publication*] ....DMG
Deutsche Motorrader Register ....DMR
Deutsche Mueller Zeitung [*A publication*]...............Deut Mueller Ztg
Deutsche Nationalbibliographie [*A bibliographic publication*]
    [*Germany*]...............DNB
Deutsche Oper am Rhein [*A publication*] .... Deutsche Oper
Deutsche Ophthalmologische Gesellschaft. Bericht [*A
    publication*]...............Dtsch Ophthalmol Ges Ber
Deutsche Papierwirtschaft [*A publication*] ....Deut Papierwirtsch
Deutsche Philologie [*A publication*] ....DP
Deutsche Presse-Agentur [*Press agency*] [*West Germany*] ....DPA
Deutsche Reichsbahn [*German State Railway*] [*Pre-1945*] ....DRB
Deutsche Revue [*A publication*] ....DeutR
Deutsche Revue [*A publication*]...............DRev
Deutsche Rundschau [*A publication*] ....Deut Rundschau

Deutsche Rundschau [*A publication*] ... DR
Deutsche Rundschau [*A publication*] ... DRs
Deutsche Rundschau [*A publication*] ... DRu
Deutsche Rundschau [*A publication*] ... D Rund
Deutsche Schlacht-und Viehhof-Zeitung [*A publication*] ... Deutsche Schlacht-u Viehhof-Ztg
Deutsche Sex Partei [*Political party*] [*Germany*] ... DSP
Deutsche-Slawische Forschungen zur Namenkunde und Siedlungsgeschichte [*A publication*] ... DSFNS
Deutsche Sprache [*A publication*] ... DSp
Deutsche Stomatologie [*A publication*] ... DESTA
Deutsche Stomatologie [*A publication*] ... Dtsch Stomatol
Deutsche Studien [*A publication*] ... DS
Deutsche Studien [*A publication*] ... DSt
Deutsche Studien zur Geistesgeschichte [*A publication*] ... DSG
Deutsche Studien. Vierteljahreshefte fuer Vergleichende Gegenwartskunde [*A publication*] ... Dtsche Stud
Deutsche Texte des Mittelalters [*A publication*] ... DTM
Deutsche Tieraerztliche Wochenschrift [*A publication*] ... Deutsche Tieraerztl Wochenschr
Deutsche Tieraerztliche Wochenschrift [*A publication*] ... Dtsch Tieraerztl Wochenschr
Deutsche Universitaetszeitung [*A publication*] ... DUZ
Deutsche Verlags-Anstalt [*Publishing company*] ... DVA
Deutsche Versicherungsanstalt [*German Insurance Institute*] ... DVA
Deutsche Vierteljahrsschrift [*A publication*] ... DV
Deutsche Vierteljahrsschrift fuer Literaturwissenschaft und Geistesgeschichte [*A publication*] ... Deut Vier Lit
Deutsche Vierteljahrsschrift fuer Literaturwissenschaft und Geistesgeschichte [*A publication*] ... Deu Viertel
Deutsche Vierteljahrsschrift fuer Literaturwissenschaft und Geistesgeschichte [*A publication*] ... DtVis
Deutsche Vierteljahrsschrift fuer Literaturwissenschaft und Geistesgeschichte [*A publication*] ... Dt Vischr
Deutsche Vierteljahrsschrift fuer Literaturwissenschaft und Geistesgeschichte [*A publication*] ... DVJS
Deutsche Vierteljahrsschrift fuer Literaturwissenschaft und Geistesgeschichte [*A publication*] ... DVLG
Deutsche Vierteljahrsschrift fuer Literaturwissenschaft und Geistesgeschichte [*A publication*] ... VL
Deutsche Waffen- und Munitionsfabriken [*Name of German armament company*] [*World War II*] ... DWM
Deutsche Waffen Stillstandkommission [*German Armistice Commission, in France*] [*World War II*] ... DWStK
Deutsche Warande en Belfort [*A publication*] ... DWB
Deutsche Weinbau [*A publication*] ... Dtsch Weinbau
Deutsche Welle [*Radio network*] [*West Germany*] ... DW
Deutsche Wissenschaft, Erziehung, und Volksbildung [*A publication*] ... DWEV
Deutsche Wissenschaftliche Zeitschrift fuer Polen [*A publication*] ... DWZP
Deutsche Wissenschaftlicher Dienst [*A publication*] ... DWD
Deutsche Woche [*A publication*] ... DW
Deutsche Zahn- Mund- und Kieferheilkunde [*A publication*] ... Dtsch Zahn- Mund- Kieferheilkd
Deutsche Zahnaerztliche Zeitschrift [*A publication*] ... Dtsch Zahnaerztl Z
Deutsche Zahnaerztliche Zeitschrift [*A publication*] ... DZZEA
Deutsche Zeitschrift fuer Chirurgie [*A publication*] ... Deutsche Ztschr Chir
Deutsche Zeitschrift fuer die Gesamte Gerichtliche Medizin [*A publication*] ... Dtsch Z Gesamte Gerichtl Med
Deutsche Zeitschrift fuer Kirchenrecht [*A publication*] ... DZKR
Deutsche Zeitschrift fuer Nervenheilkunde [*A publication*] ... Deutsche Ztschr Nervenh
Deutsche Zeitschrift fuer Nervenheilkunde [*A publication*] ... Dtsch Z Nervenheilkd
Deutsche Zeitschrift fuer Philosophie [*A publication*] ... Deut Z Phil
Deutsche Zeitschrift fuer Philosophie [*A publication*] ... Dtsche Z Philos
Deutsche Zeitschrift fuer Verdauungs und Stoffwechselkrankheiten [*A publication*] ... Dtsch Z Verdau Stoffwechselkr
Deutsche Zoologische Gesellschaft. Verhandlungen [*A publication*] ... Deutsch Zool Ges Verh
Deutschen Gesellschaft fuer Geologische Wissenschaften. Berichte [*A publication*] ... Deutsch Gesell Geol Wiss Ber
Deutscher Akademischer Austauschdienst [*German Academic Exchange Service*] ... DAAD
Deutscher Ausschuss fuer Stahlbeton [*A publication*] ... Deut Ausschuss Stahlbeton
Deutscher Beamtenbund [*Federation of German Civil Service Officials*] [*West Germany*] ... DBB
Deutscher Depeschen-Dienst [*Press agency*] [*West Germany*] ... DDD
Deutscher Geographentag Verhandlungen [*A publication*] ... Deutscher Geographentag Verh
Deutscher Gewerkschaftsbund fuer das Gebiet der Bundesrepublik Deutschland und Berlin [*German Trade Union Federation for the Area of the Federal Republic and Berlin*] [*West Germany*] ... DGB
Deutscher Handels- und Industrieangestellten-Verband [*Association of Clerical Employees of Germany*] [*West Germany*] ... DHV
Deutscher Kaelte und Klimatechnischer Verein. Abhandlungen [*A publication*] ... Dtsch Kaelte Klimatech Ver Abh
Deutscher Kaeltetechnischer Verein. Abhandlungen [*A publication*] ... Dtsch Kaeltetech Ver Abh
Deutscher Kongress fuer Perinatale Medizin [*A publication*] ... Dtsch Kongr Perinat Med
Deutscher Normenausschuss [*German Standards Association*] [*Later, DIN*] ... DNA
Deutscher und Oesterreichischer Alpen-Verein. Zeitschrift [*A publication*] ... Deut Oesterr Alpen-Ver Zs
Deutscher Orden der Harugari [*German Order of Harugari*] ... DOH
Deutscher Sportausschuss [*German Sports Commission*] ... DSA
Deutscher Taschenbuch Verlag [*Publisher*] ... DTV
Deutscher Verein von Gas- und Wasserfachmaennern. Schriftenreihe. Gas [*A publication*] ... Dtsch Ver Gas Wasserfachmaennern Schriften Gas
Deutscher Verein fuer Kunstwissenschaft. Zeitschrift [*A publication*] ... Deutsch Verein Kunstwis Z
Deutsches Aerzteblatt. Aerztliche Mitteilungen [*A publication*] ... Dtsch Aerztebl
Deutsches Afrika Korps [*World War II*] ... DAK
Deutsches Archaeologisches Institut. Jahrbuch [*A publication*] ... Deutch Archaeol Inst Jahrb
Deutsches Archaeologisches Institut. Mitteilungen. Roemische Abteilung [*A publication*] ... Deutsch Archaeol Inst Roem Mitt
Deutsches Archiv [*A publication*] ... DA
Deutsches Archiv fuer die Erforschung des Mittelalters [*A publication*] ... DAEM
Deutsches Archiv fuer Geschichte des Mittelalters [*A publication*] ... DAGM
Deutsches Archiv fuer Klinische Medizin [*A publication*] ... Deutsches Arch Klin Med
Deutsches Archiv fuer Klinische Medizin [*A publication*] ... Dtsch Arch Klin Med
Deutsches Archiv fuer Landes und Volksforschung [*A publication*] ... DALV
Deutsches Arzneibuch [*Medicine*] ... DAB
Deutsches Bucherverzeichnis [*A bibliographic publication*] [*Germany*] ... DBV
Deutsches Dante Jahrbuch [*A publication*] ... DDJ
Deutsches Dante Jahrbuch [*A publication*] ... Deutsch Dante Jahrb
Deutsches Elektronen-Synchrotron [*West Germany*] ... DESY
Deutsches Geodaetisches Forschungsinstitut [*Munich, West Germany*] ... DGFI
Deutsches Hydrographisches Institut [*Hamburg, West Germany*] ... DHI
Deutsches Hydrographisches Institut. Jahresbericht [*A publication*] ... Dtsch Hydrogr Inst Jahresber
Deutsches Institut fuer Medizinische Dokumentation und Information [*German Institute for Medical Documentation and Information*] [*Information service*] ... DIMDI
Deutsches Institut fuer Normung [*German Standards Institute*] [*Formerly, DNA*] ... DIN
Deutsches Institut fuer Wirtschaftsforschung Wochenbericht [*A publication*] ... Dtsch Inst Wirtschaftsforsch Wochenber
Deutsches Jahrbuch fuer Musikwissenschaft [*A publication*] ... Deutsch Jahrb Musikw
Deutsches Jahrbuch fuer Numismatik [*A publication*] ... DJbN
Deutsches Jahrbuch fuer Volkskunde [*A publication*] ... DjbVk
Deutsches Jahrbuch fuer Volkskunde [*A publication*] ... DJV
Deutsches Kunststoff-Institut, Darmstadt, Germany [*Library symbol*] ... GyDaD
Deutsches Medizinisches Journal [*A publication*] ... Dtsch Med J
Deutsches Mozartfest der Deutschen Mozart-Gesellschaft [*A publication*] ... DMG
Deutsches Museum. Abhandlungen und Berichte [*A publication*] ... Dtsch Mus Abh Ber
Deutsches Nachrichtenburo [*German news agency*] ... DNB
Deutsches Paedagogisches Zentralinstitut [*German Pedagogical Central Institute*] ... DPZI
Deutsches Reich [*German Empire*] ... DR
Deutsches Reichs-Patent [*German patent*] ... DRP
Deutsches Reichsbahn [*East German railway system*] ... DR
Deutsches-Reichsgebrauchsmuster [*German-Registered Design*] ... DRGM
Deutsches Roheisen [*A publication*] ... Dtsch Roheisen
Deutsches Verwaltungsblatt und Verwaltungsarchiv [*A publication*] ... Dtsch Verwaltungsbl Verwaltungsarch
Deutschkundliche Arbeiten [*A publication*] ... DkA
Deutschland [*Germany*] ... D
Deutschland-Union-Dienst [*A publication*] ... Dtschl Union Dienst
Deutschlandfunk [*Radio network*] [*West Germany*] ... DLF
Deutschnationale Volkspartei [*German National People's Party*] ... DNVP
Deutschoesterreichische Tieraerztliche Wochenschrift [*A publication*] ... Deutschoesterr Tieraerztl Wchnschr
Deutschunterricht [*A publication*] ... DU
Deutschunterricht fuer Auslaender [*A publication*] ... DUA
Deva [*Romania*] [*Seismograph station code, US Geological Survey*] ... DEV
Devco Railway [*Cape Breton Development Corp. - Coal Div.*] [*AAR code*] ... DVR
Develet Hava Yollari [*Airline*] ... DHY
Develop [*or Development*] ... DEV
Develop ... DVL
Develop and Qualify ... DAQ
Developed Country ... DC
Developed Horsepower ... DHP
Developed Length ... DL

Developed Pressure [*Cardiology*] ... DP
Developed Template ... DT
Developed Width ... DW
Developer Demonstrator ... DD
Developing Economies [*A publication*] ... DE
Developing Economies [*A publication*] ... Dev Econ
Developing Economies [*A publication*] ... Develop Eco
Developing Economies [*A publication*] ... Develop Econ
Developing Learning Readiness ... DLR
Developing Nations Tractor [*Ford Motor Co.*] ... DNT
Developing-Out Paper ... DOP
Developing and Printing ... D & P
Developing Proboscis ... DP
Developing Systems Training and Devices Directorate [*Army*] ... DST & DD
Developing Understanding of Self and Others [*Educational tool*] ... DUSO
Development ... D
Development ... DEVEL
Development ... DEVT
Development ... DVLP
Development Acceptance ... DEVA
Development Acceptance in Process Review ... DEVAIPR
Development Acceptance Test [*Army*] ... DAT
Development of Advanced Rate Techniques ... DART
Development Assist Test ... DAT
Development Assistance ... DA
Development Assistance Committee [*of the Organization for Economic Cooperation and Development*] ... DAC
Development Assistance Group ... DAG
Development Big Hydrofoil [*Also, DEH*] ... DBH
Development at Birth Index [*Medicine*] ... DBI
Development Change [*Aerospace*] ... DEVC
Development and Change [*A publication*] ... Dev Change
Development and Change [*A publication*] ... Develop Cha
Development and Change [*A publication*] ... Develop and Change
Development Change Notice [*Aerospace*] ... DCN
Development Characteristic ... DC
Development Commission [*British*] ... DC
Development Concept Paper ... DCP
Development Contract Officer ... DCO
Development Control Center ... DCC
Development Corporation of America [*American Stock Exchange symbol*] ... DCA
Development Cost Plan ... DCP
Development Costs ... DC
Development Council for Research ... DCR
Development Data Sheet ... DDS
Development Dialogue [*A publication*] ... Develop Dialogue
Development Digest [*A publication*] ... DD
Development Digest [*A publication*] ... Devel Dig
Development Directive ... DD
Development Discrepancy Report ... DDR
Development Display Assembly ... DDA
Development Economics Group ... DEG
Development and Education Command ... DEC
Development Engineering ... DE
Development, Engineering, and Acquisition [*Directorate*] [*Army*] ... DEA
Development and Engineering Directorate [*Army*] ... DRCDE
Development Engineering Inspection ... DEI
Development Engineering Management System [*Air Force*] ... DEMS
Development Engineering Review ... DER
Development Ephemeris ... DE
Development Estimate ... DE
Development and Evaluation of a Firearms Training Facility ... DEFT
Development Field Office [*Air Force*] ... AFDFO
Development Finance Companies [*Independent financial institutions in developing countries*] ... DFC's
Development Fixture ... DF
Development Flight ... DF
Development Forum [*A publication*] ... Dev Forum
Development-Forward ... DF
Development Fund ... DF
Development Group for Alternative Policies ... DGAP
Development, Growth, and Differentiation [*A publication*] ... Develop Gr
Development, Growth, and Differentiation [*A publication*] ... Dev Growth Differ
Development, Growth, and Differentiation (Nagoya) [*A publication*] ... Dev Growth Differ (Nagoya)
Development of Improved Management Engineering Systems [*Military*] ... DIMES
Development Information Processing System ... DIPS
Development-Inhibitor-Releasing [*Photography*] ... DIR
Development of Integrated Logistics ... DEVIL
Development of Integrated Management Engineering Systems [*Military*] ... DIMES
Development Investigation in Military Orbiting Systems ... DEIMOS
Development Laboratory Unit ... DLU
Development Land Tax [*British*] ... DLT
Development-Left ... DL
Development Loan Committee [*Department of State*] ... DLC
Development Loan Fund [*Abolished 1961, functions redelegated to Agency for International Development*] ... DLF
Development in Mammals [*A publication*] ... Dev Mamm
Development Management System [*IBM Corp.*] ... DMS
Development Milestone [*Aerospace*] ... DM
Development of Minicomputers in an Environment of Scientific and Technological Information Centers [*Data processing*] ... DOMESTIC
Development of Operational Reasoning Skills ... DOORS
Development Operations Division [*NASA*] ... DOD
Development of Opportunities through Meaningful Education [*Project*] ... DOME
Development Phase ... DP
Development Plan ... DP
Development Planning Memo ... DPM
Development Planning Objective ... DPO
Development Planning Reports ... DPR
Development Program Plan ... DPP
Development Project Engineer ... DPE
Development Project Office for Selected Ammunition [*Army*] ... DPO-SA
Development Project Officer ... DPO
Development Project Team ... DPT
Development and Proof Services ... DPS
Development Proposal ... DP
Development Prototype ... DP
Development Prototype ... DPT
Development Prototype Launcher ... DPL
Development Quotient ... DQ
Development Reactor Mock-Up ... DRM
Development and Readiness Command [*Formerly, AMC*] [*See also MDRC*] [*Army*] ... DARCOM
Development and Readiness Command Automated Logistics Management Systems Agency [*Army*] ... DARCOMALMSA
Development and Readiness Command Facilities and Services Center [*Army*] ... DARCOMFASC
Development and Readiness Command Field Safety Agency [*Army*] ... DARCOMFSA
Development and Readiness Command Installations and Service Agency [*Army*] ... DARCOMI & SA
Development and Readiness Command Logistics Data Center [*Army*] ... DARCOMLDC
Development and Readiness Command Logistics Systems Support Agency [*Army*] ... DARCOMLSSA
Development of Reasoning in Science ... DORIS
Development Reference Service [*Society for International Development*] ... DRS
Development of Regional Impact [*Land use*] ... DRI
Development Release Order ... DRO
Development Report ... DR
Development Research Associates, Inc., Institute for New Enterprise Development ... DRA/INED
Development Resources Panel [*United Nations Development Program*] ... DRP
Development Revision Record ... DRR
Development-Right ... DR
Development in Science Education [*National Science Foundation*] ... DISE
Development Sciences Information System [*Canada*] [*Information service*] ... DEVSIS
Development Signature Approval ... DSA
Development Signature Approval - Fabrication Order ... DSA/FO
Development Student Engineer ... DSE
Development of Substitute Materials ... DSM
Development Support Equipment ... DSE
Development Support and Integration Program ... DSIP
Development and Technical Assistance International ... DATA
Development Test [*or Testing*] ... DT
Development Test Article ... DTA
Development, Test, and Evaluation ... DT & E
Development Test Instrumentation ... DTI
Development Test/Operational Test ... DT/OT
Development Test Requirement Specification ... DTRS
Development Test Requirements Document [*NASA*] ... DTRD
Development Test Satellite ... DTS
Development and Training Center [*Navy*] ... DATC
Development Type ... DT
Development Verification Testing ... DVT
Development Work Order ... DWO
Development Work Request ... DWR
Development Work Statement ... DWS
Developmental ... DEVLPMTL
Developmental Activities Screening Inventory [*Psychology*] ... DASI
Developmental Age ... DA
Developmental Basis of Issue [*Military*] ... DBOI
Developmental Biology [*A publication*] ... Dev Biol
Developmental Biology [*A publication*] ... Develop Bio
Developmental Biology [*A publication*] ... Develop Biol
Developmental Biology. Supplement [*A publication*] ... Dev Biol Suppl
Developmental and Cell Biology [*A publication*] ... Dev Cell Biol
Developmental and Comparative Immunology [*A publication*] ... Dev Comp Immunol
Developmental Cycle Research Plan ... DCRP
Developmental Disabilities [*Federally funded program*] ... DD

Developmental Disabilities Office [*Department of Health and Human Services*] ..... DDO
Developmental Disabilities Services ..... DDS
Developmental Economic Education Program ..... DEEP
Developmental Engineering Inspection Board ..... DEIB
Developmental Fast Hydrofoil ..... DFH
Developmental Flight Instrumentation [*NASA*] ..... DFI
Developmental Indicators for the Assessment of Learning [*Education*] ..... DIAL
Developmental Medicine and Child Neurology [*A publication*] ..... Develop Med
Developmental Medicine and Child Neurology [*A publication*] ..... Dev Med Child Neurol
Developmental Medicine and Child Neurology [*A publication*] ..... DMCNA
Developmental Medicine and Child Neurology. Supplement [*A publication*] ..... Dev Med Child Neurol Suppl
Developmental Neuroscience [*A publication*] ..... Dev Neurosci
Developmental Pharmacology and Therapeutics [*A publication*] ..... Dev Pharmacol Ther
Developmental Potential of Preschool Children [*Psychology*] ..... DPPC
Developmental Psychobiology [*A publication*] ..... DEPBA
Developmental Psychobiology [*A publication*] ..... Develop Psy
Developmental Psychobiology [*A publication*] ..... Dev Psychobiol
Developmental Psychology [*A publication*] ..... Develop Psychol
Developmental Psychology [*A publication*] ..... DEVPA
Developmental Psychology [*A publication*] ..... Dev Psychol
Developmental Psychology [*A publication*] ..... DP
Developmental Psychology. Monograph [*A publication*] ..... Dev Psychol Monogr
Developmental Sentence Analysis [*Education*] ..... DSA
Developmental Tactical Operations Systems ..... DEVTOS
Developmental Technician Team ..... DTT
Developmental Test Model ..... DTM
Developmental Test of Visual Perception ..... DTVP
Developments in Agricultural and Managed-Forest Ecology [*Elsevier Book Series*] [*A publication*] ..... DAME
Developments in Animal and Veterinary Sciences [*Elsevier Book Series*] [*A publication*] ..... DAVS
Developments in Applied Spectroscopy [*A publication*] ..... Dev Appl Spectrosc
Developments in Atmosphere Science [*Elsevier Book Series*] [*A publication*] ..... DAS
Developments in Biochemistry [*Elsevier Book Series*] [*A publication*] ..... DB
Developments in Biochemistry [*A publication*] ..... Dev Biochem
Developments in Bioenergetics and Biomembranes [*Elsevier Book Series*] [*A publication*] ..... DBB
Developments in Biological Standardization [*A publication*] ..... Dev Biol Stand
Developments in Cancer Research [*Elsevier Book Series*] [*A publication*] ..... DCR
Developments in Cell Biology [*Elsevier Book Series*] [*A publication*] ..... DCB
Developments in Cell Biology (Amsterdam) [*A publication*] ..... Dev Cell Biol (Amsterdam)
Developments in Civil Engineering [*Elsevier Book Series*] [*A publication*] ..... DCE
Developments in Crop Science [*Elsevier Book Series*] [*A publication*] ..... DC
Developments in Crop Science [*A publication*] ..... Dev Crop Sci
Developments in Diabetes Research [*Elsevier Book Series*] [*A publication*] ..... DDR
Developments in Economic Geology [*Elsevier Book Series*] [*A publication*] ..... DEG
Developments in Economic Geology [*A publication*] ..... Dev Econ Geol
Developments in Endocrinology [*Elsevier Book Series*] [*A publication*] ..... DIE
Developments in Environmental Modelling [*Elsevier Book Series*] [*A publication*] ..... DEM
Developments in Food Science [*Elsevier Book Series*] [*A publication*] ..... DFS
Developments in Genetics [*Elsevier Book Series*] [*A publication*] ..... DIG
Developments in Geochemistry [*Elsevier Book Series*] [*A publication*] ..... DGC
Developments in Geomathematics [*Elsevier Book Series*] [*A publication*] ..... DGM
Developments in Geotechnical Engineering [*A publication*] ..... Dev Geotech Eng
Developments in Geotechnical Engineering [*Elsevier Book Series*] [*A publication*] ..... DGE
Developments in Geotectonics [*A publication*] ..... Dev Geotectonics
Developments in Geotectonics [*Elsevier Book Series*] [*A publication*] ..... DG
Developments in Halophilic Microorganisms [*Elsevier Book Series*] [*A publication*] ..... DHM
Developments in Immunology [*Elsevier Book Series*] [*A publication*] ..... DI
Developments in Industrial Microbiology [*A publication*] ..... Dev Ind Microbiol
Developments in Neurology [*Elsevier Book Series*] [*A publication*] ..... DIN
Developments in Nutrition and Metabolism [*Elsevier Book Series*] [*A publication*] ..... DINM
Developments in Ophthalmology [*A publication*] ..... Dev Ophthalmol
Developments in Palaeontology and Stratigraphy [*Elsevier Book Series*] [*A publication*] ..... DPAS
Developments in Petroleum Science [*Elsevier Book Series*] [*A publication*] ..... DPS
Developments in Petrology [*Elsevier Book Series*] [*A publication*] ..... DP
Developments in Plant Biology [*Elsevier Book Series*] [*A publication*] ..... DPB
Developments in Precambrian Geology [*Elsevier Book Series*] [*A publication*] ..... DPG
Developments in Psychiatry [*Elsevier Book Series*] [*A publication*] ..... DIP
Developments in Sedimentology [*A publication*] ..... Dev Sedimentol
Developments in Sedimentology [*Elsevier Book Series*] [*A publication*] ..... DS
Developments in Soil Science [*A publication*] ..... Dev Soil Sci
Developments in Soil Science [*Elsevier Book Series*] [*A publication*] ..... DSS
Developments in Solar System and Space Science [*Elsevier Book Series*] [*A publication*] ..... DSSSS
Developments in Solid Earth Geophysics [*Elsevier Book Series*] [*A publication*] ..... DSEG
Developments in Toxicology and Environmental Science [*A publication*] ..... Dev Toxicol Environ Sci
Developments in Toxicology and Environmental Science [*Elsevier Book Series*] [*A publication*] ..... DT
Developpement et Civilisations [*A publication*] ..... Develop et Civilis
Developpement Industriel et Scientifique [*A publication*] ..... Dev Ind Sci
Dever Explorations [*NASDAQ symbol*] ..... DEVR
Devereux Adolescent Behavior [*Rating scale*] [*Also, ABRS*] [*Psychology*] ..... DAB
Devereux Child Behavior [*Rating scale*] [*Psychology*] ..... DCB
Devereux Elementary School Behavior [*Rating scale*] [*Psychology*] ..... DESB
Deviant Flight Plan ..... DFP
Deviating Oscillator ..... DO
Deviation ..... D
Deviation ..... DEV
Deviation ..... DEVN
Deviation Approval Request [*NASA*] ..... DAR
Deviation Authorization ..... DA
Deviation Clause [*Business and trade*] ..... DC
Deviation Difficulty [*Aerospace*] ..... DD
Deviation for Failure Location ..... DFL
Deviation Indicator ..... DI
Deviation Intelligence Quotient [*Education*] ..... DIQ
Deviation from Mean Standard ..... DMS
Deviation Range ..... DR
Deviation Ratio ..... DR
Deviation for Replacement Time ..... DRT
Deviation Test Bridge ..... DTB
Device ..... DEV
Device ..... DV
Device ..... DVC
Device for Automatic Remote Data Collection [*National Weather Service*] ..... DARDC
Device for Automatic Word Identification and Discrimination [*Data processing*] ..... DAWID
Device Base Control Block [*Data processing*] ..... DVB
Device Characteristics Table [*Data processing*] ..... DCT
Device Control ..... DC
Device Control Character ..... DCC
Device Independent Display Operator Console Support ..... DIDOCS
Device Mount Unit ..... DMU
Device Multiplexing Nonsynchronized Inputs [*Data processing*] ..... DMNI
Device Multiplexing Nonsynchronized Outputs [*Data processing*] ..... DMNO
Device Selector ..... DS
Device Status Byte [*Data processing*] ..... DSB
Device-Switching Unit ..... DSU
Device under Test ..... DUT
Devices ..... DVCS
Devil Mountain [*Alaska*] [*Seismograph station code, US Geological Survey*] ..... DMA
Devil Pups [*An association*] ..... DP
Devilbiss Co. [*NYSE symbol*] [*Delisted*] ..... DEV
Devil's Advocate ..... DA
Devil's Box [*A publication*] ..... DevB
Devils Lake [*North Dakota*] [*Airport symbol*] ..... DVL
Devils Lake Carnegie Library, Devils Lake, ND [*Library symbol*] ..... NdDe
Devils Lake, ND [*Radio station call letters*] ..... KDLR
Devils Lake, ND [*Radio station call letters*] ..... KDVL
Devils Lake, ND [*Radio station call letters*] ..... KZZY-FM
Devils Lake, ND [*Television station call letters*] ..... WDAZ-TV
Devils Postpile National Monument ..... DEPO
Devils Tower National Monument ..... DETO
Devin Register [*An association*] ..... DR
Devine, TX [*Location identifier*] [*FAA*] ..... HHH
Devine, TX [*Radio station call letters*] ..... KDCI
Devon Cattle Association [*Formerly, ADCC*] ..... DCA
Devon and Cornwall. Notes and Queries [*A publication*] ..... DCNQ
Devon Group, Inc. [*American Stock Exchange symbol*] [*Delisted*] ..... DEV
Devon Stores Corp. [*NASDAQ symbol*] ..... DVON
Devonian [*Period, era, or system*] [*Geology*] ..... DEV
Devonian Group of Charitable Foundations, Calgary, AB, Canada [*Library symbol*] ..... CaACDG
Devonian Period [*Geology*] ..... D
Devonport [*Tasmania*] [*Airport symbol*] ..... DPO
Devonshire [*County in England*] ..... DEVON
Devotions ..... DEVS
DeVry, Inc. [*NASDAQ symbol*] ..... DVRY
Devteron [*A nuclear particle*] ..... d
DEW [*Distant Early Warning*] **East Military Identification Zone** ..... DEMIZ

Dew Point ... DP
Dew Point ... DWPNT
Dew Point Sensing Device ... DPSD
Dew-Point Temperature [*Measure of humidity*] ... DPT
Dew Point Tester ... DPT
DEW [*Deutsche Edelstahlwerke*] **Technische Berichte** [*A publication*] ... DEW Tech Ber
Dewan Bahasa Dan Pustaka, Kuala Lumpur, Malaysia [*Library symbol*] ... DbP
Dewan Pengurus Sementara [*Provisional Management Board Section*] [*Indonesia*] ... DPS
Dewar Cryogenic Refrigerator ... DCR
Dewey Decimal ... DD
Dewey Decimal Classification [*Also, DDC*] ... DC
Dewey Decimal Classification [*Also, DC*] ... DDC
Dewey Electronics Corp. [*NASDAQ symbol*] ... DEWY
DeWitt Historical Society of Tompkins County, Ithaca, NY [*Library symbol*] ... NIHi
DeWitt State Hospital, Auburn, CA [*Library symbol*] ... CAuD
Dewoitine [*French aircraft type*] [*World War II*] ... D
Dewsbury Central Library, Dewsbury, United Kingdom [*Library symbol*] ... UkDw
Dexamethasone [*Also, DXM*] [*Clinical chemistry, endocrinology*] ... DEX
Dexamethasone [*Also, DEX*] [*Clinical chemistry, endocrinology*] ... DXM
Dexamethasone Suppression Test [*Clinical chemistry*] ... DST
Dexedrine ... DEX
Dexedrine ... DEXIE
Dexon, Inc. [*NASDAQ symbol*] ... DEXO
Dexter [*Right*] [*Latin*] ... D
Dexter [*Right*] [*Latin*] ... DEXT
Dexter Corp. [*NYSE symbol*] ... DEX
Dexter District library, Dexter, MI [*Library symbol*] ... MiDex
Dexter Free Library, Dexter, NY [*Library symbol*] ... NDex
Dexter, MO [*Location identifier*] [*FAA*] ... DXE
Dexter, MO [*Radio station call letters*] ... KDEX
Dexter, MO [*Radio station call letters*] ... KDEX-FM
Dexter Museum, Dexter, IA [*Library symbol*] ... IaDexM
Dextro [*Configuration in chemical structure*] ... D
Dextro-Levo(rotary) [*Also, r, rac*] [*Chemistry*] ... dl
Dextro-Tubocurarine [*Organic chemistry*] ... DTC
Dextroamphetamine Sulfate [*CNS stimulant*] ... DAS
Dextromethorphan [*Antitussive compound*] ... DM
Dextro(rotatory) [*Chemistry*] ... d
Dextrose [*Freight*] ... DXT
Dextrose Equivalent [*Food technology*] ... DE
Dextrose-Gelatin-Veronal [*Solution*] [*Microbiology*] ... DGV
Dextrose [*5%*] **in Hartman's Solution** [*Medicine*] ... D/5HS
Dextrose : Nitrogen Ratio ... D : N
Dextrose and Saline [*Medicine*] ... D/S
Dextrose [*5%*] **in Saline** [*Medicine*] ... D5/S
Dextrose [*5%*] **in Water** [*Medicine*] ... D5/W
Dezimal-Klassifikation ... DK
DFBO [*Deutsche Forschungsgesellschaft fuer Blechverarbeitung und Oberflaechenbehandlung*] **Mitteilungen** [*A publication*] ... DFBO Mitt
DFG Mitteilungen. Deutsche Forschungsgemeinschaft [*A publication*] ... DFG Mitt
Dhahran [*Saudi Arabia*] [*Airport symbol*] ... DHA
Dhaka [*Bangladesh*] [*Airport symbol*] ... DAC
Dhangarhi [*Nepal*] [*Airport symbol*] ... DHI
DHL Island Airways [*Honolulu, HI*] [*FAA designator*] ... DHL
Di-An Controls, Inc. [*NASDAQ symbol*] ... DICC
Di-isopropyl Phosphorofluoridase [*An enzyme*] ... DFPase
Di-normal-butylamine [*Organic chemistry*] ... DNBA
Di-normal-Butylmagnesium [*Organic chemistry*] ... DNBM
Di-normal-Hexylmagnesium [*Organic chemistry*] ... DNHM
Di-normal-propylamine [*Organic chemistry*] ... DNPA
Di-ortho-toylguanidine [*Organic chemistry*] ... DOTG
Di-tert-butyl-m-cresol [*Organic chemistry*] ... DBMC
Di-tert-butyl-p-cresol [*Also, BHT*] [*Antioxidant*] ... DBPC
Di-tert-butyl Peroxide [*Organic chemistry*] ... DTBP
Di-tert-butylcresol [*Organic chemistry*] ... DTBC
Di-tert-butylhydroquinone [*Organic chemistry*] ... DTBHQ
Di-tert-butylnaphthalene [*Organic chemistry*] ... DTBN
DIA [*Division de Investigaciones Agropecuarias*] **Boletin de Divulgacion** [*A publication*] ... DIA Bol Divulg
DIA [*Division de Investigaciones Agropecuarias*] **Boletin Tecnico** [*A publication*] ... DIA Bol Tec
DIA [*Division de Investigaciones Agropecuarias*] **Medico** [*A publication*] ... DIA Med
Diabete et Metabolisme [*A publication*] ... Diabete Met
Diabete et Metabolisme [*A publication*] ... Diabete Metab
Diabetes Foundation, Incorporated [*Later, JDC*] ... DFI
Diabetes Insipidus ... DI
Diabetes Literature Index [*A publication*] ... Diab Lit Ind
Diabetes Literature Index [*A publication*] ... DLI
Diabetes Mellitus [*Medicine*] ... DM
Diabetes Personalized Alerting Service ... DIAPAS
Diabetes Retrieval Element Generator and Executor ... DREGE
Diabetic ... DIAB
Diabetic Management [*Medicine*] ... DBM
Diabetic Retinopathy [*Medicine*] ... DR
Diabetic Ulcer Meal [*Airline notation*] ... DUML
Diabetologia [*A publication*] ... Diabetolog
Diablo Oil Co. [*NASDAQ symbol*] ... DBLO
Diablo Valley College, Concord, CA [*Library symbol*] ... CConE
Diacetone Acrylamide [*Organic chemistry*] ... DAA
Diacetoxydiphenylmethylpyridine [*Pharmacology*] ... DAMP
Diacetoxyscirpenol [*Fungal toxin*] ... DAS
Diacetyl Monooxime [*Organic chemistry*] ... DAM
Diacetyldiaminodiphenylsulfone [*Antibacterial compound*] ... DADDS
Diacetylferrocene [*Organic chemistry*] ... DAF
Diacetylmorphine [*Pharmacology*] ... DAM
Diademed [*Numismatics*] ... DIAD
Diagnon Corp. [*NASDAQ symbol*] ... DIGN
Diagnosis ... D
Diagnosis ... DG
Diagnosis ... DIAG
Diagnosis ... DX
Diagnosis, Objectives, Method, Evaluation [*Formula*] [*LIMRA*] ... DOME
Diagnosis-Rework Action ... DRA
Diagnosis Undetermined [*or Unknown*] [*Medicine*] ... DU
Diagnostek, Inc. [*NASDAQ symbol*] ... DXTK
Diagnostic ... DGNSTC
Diagnostic Achievement Battery ... DAB
Diagnostic Center ... DC
Diagnostic Connector Assembly ... DCA
Diagnostic Controlled MODEM [*Data processing*] ... DCM
Diagnostic Data [*NASDAQ symbol*] ... DIAG
Diagnostic Decision Logic Table [*Data processing*] ... DDLT
Diagnostic Decision Table [*Data processing*] ... DDT
Diagnostic Display Unit ... DDU
Diagnostic Educational Grouping ... DEG
Diagnostic Flow Chart [*Data processing*] ... DFC
Diagnostic FORTRAN [*Data processing*] ... DITRAN
Diagnostic Function Test [*Data processing*] ... DFT
Diagnostic Gynecology and Obstetrics [*A publication*] ... Diagn Gynecol Obstet
Diagnostic Histopathology [*A publication*] ... Diagn Histopathol
Diagnostic Imaging [*A publication*] ... Diagn Imaging
Diagnostic Machine Aids/Digital [*Raytheon Co.*] ... DMAD
Diagnostic Mathematics Inventory ... DMI
Diagnostic Medicine [*A publication*] ... Diagn Med
Diagnostic Monitor [*Data processing*] ... DIAMON
Diagnostic Monitor Executive [*Data processing*] ... DME
Diagnostic Prescriptive Teaching ... DPT
[*A*] **Diagnostic and Prescriptive Technique** [*Education*] ... ADAPT
Diagnostic Products Corporation [*NASDAQ symbol*] ... DPCZ
Diagnostic Radiology [*Medicine*] ... DR
Diagnostic Reading Scales [*Education*] ... DRS
Diagnostic Related Group [*Medicine*] ... DRG
Diagnostic Retrieval Systems Cl B [*American Stock Exchange symbol*] ... DRSB
Diagnostic Retrieval Systems Cv A [*American Stock Exchange symbol*] ... DRSA
Diagnostic Rework Sheets ... DRS
Diagnostic Rhyme Test ... DRT
Diagnostic Rifle Marksmanship Simulator ... DRIMS
Diagnostic Roentgenology [*Medicine*] ... DRNT
Diagnostic Simulation System ... DSS
Diagnostic and Statistical Manual of Mental Disorders [*A publication*] ... DSM
Diagnostic Test of Arithmetic Strategies ... DTAS
Diagnostik und Intensivtherapie [*A publication*] ... Diagn Intensivther
Diagnostiyka Laboratorynja [*A publication*] ... Diagn Lab
Diagonal ... DGNL
Diagonal ... DIAG
Diagonal Bands [*Navigation markers*] ... Diag
Diagonal Braked Vehicle [*FAA*] ... DBV
Diagonal Proof Line [*Technical drawings*] ... DPL
Diagram ... D
Diagram ... DIAG
Diagrammatic ... DIAGR
Diakonia of the Americas [*An association*] ... DOTA
Dial ... DL
Dial-A-Ride Transportation ... DART
Dial Access Information Retrieval System ... DAIRS
Dial Assist Operator ... DAO
Dial Assistance Switchboard ... DAS
Dial (Chicago) [*A publication*] ... Dial (Ch)
Dial Corporation [*Formerly, Dial Financial Corporation*] [*NYSE symbol*] [*Delisted*] ... DFC
Dial Depth Gauge ... DDG
Dial Drive Belt ... DDB
Dial Illumination ... DLILMN
Dial Indicating ... DLINDG
Dial Lock ... DLOCK
Dial Long Line [*Bell System*] ... DLL
Dial Marking Kit ... DMK
Dial Pulse [*Telecommunications*] ... DP
Dial Service Assistance ... DSA
Dial Service Assistance Switchboard ... DSAS
Dial System ... DS

Dial a Teacher Assistance [*Telephone service*] DATA
Dial Teletypewriter Exchange DTWX
Dial Test Indicator DTI
Dialdehyde Starch [*Wet-strength agent*] DAS
Dialect DIAL
Dialect of Algorithmic Language DIALGOL
Dialect Notes [*A publication*] DN
Dialectes Belgo-Romans [*A publication*] DBR
Dialectes Belgo-Romans [*A publication*] Dial Belg-Rom
Dialectes de Wallonie [*A publication*] D d W
Dialectic Problem Solver DPS
Dialectica [*A publication*] D
Dialectica [*A publication*] Dialec
Dialectical Anthropology [*A publication*] Dial Anthro
Dialectics and Humanism [*A publication*] Dialec Hum
Dialektischer Materialismus DIAMAT
Dialektolohicnyi Bjuleten [*A publication*] DialB
Dialing Code Information [*Telecommunications*] [*British*] DCI
Diallyl Chlorendate [*Fire retardant*] DAC
Diallyl Maleate [*Organic chemistry*] DAM
Diallyl Phthalate [*Organic chemistry*] DAP
Diallyl Tetrabromophthalate [*Organic chemistry*] DATBP
Diallylmelamine [*Organic chemistry*] DAM
Diallyltartardiamide [*Also, DATDA*] [*Organic chemistry*] DATD
Diallyltartardiamide [*Also, DATD*] [*Organic chemistry*] DATDA
Dialog [*Warsaw*] [*A publication*] Dg
Dialog [*A publication*] Di
Dialog [*Minneapolis*] [*A publication*] Dial
Dialog. Fairleigh Dickinson University. School of Dentistry [*A publication*] Dialog Fairleigh Dickinson Univ Sch Dent
Dialog: Teatertidskrift (Stockholm) [*A publication*] DialS
Dialog (Warsaw) [*A publication*] Dialog W
Dialoghi [*A publication*] Di
Dialoghi [*A publication*] Dia
Dialoghi [*A publication*] Dial
Dialoghi di Archeologia [*A publication*] D Arch
Dialoghi di Archeologia [*A publication*] Dial Ar
Dialoghi di Archeologia [*A publication*] Dial Arch
Dialogue DIAL
Dialogue: Canadian Philosophical Review [*A publication*] Dialogue (Canada)
Dialogue Foundation [*Latter-Day Saints*] DF
Dialogue in Instrumental Music Education [*A publication*] DIME
Dialogue (Phi Sigma Tau) [*A publication*] Dialogue (PST)
Dialogues d'Historie Ancienne [*A publication*] DHA
Dialysis Disequilibrium Syndrome DDS
Dialysis-Related Muscle Cramps [*Medicine*] DMC's
Dialysis and Transplantation [*A publication*] Dial Transplant
Dialysis and You [*of the DAY Association*] [*Defunct*] DAY
Diamant [*France*] [*Research code symbol*] SD
Diameter D
Diameter DI
Diameter DIA
Diameter DIAM
Diameter [*Symbol*] [*IUPAC*] d
Diameter Bolt Circle [*Technical drawings*] DBC
Diameter at Breast Height [*Of trees*] DBH
Diameter of Driving-Wheel in Inches [*Railroad term*] W
Diametrical Pitch DP
Diamidinophenylindole [*A dye*] [*Organic chemistry*] DAPI
Diamine Oxidase [*Also, DO*] [*An enzyme*] DAO
Diamine Oxidase [*Also, DAO*] [*An enzyme*] DO
Diamineanisole Sulfate [*Organic chemistry*] DAAS
Diaminoacetanilide [*Organic chemistry*] DAA
Diamino(adamantyl)ethylpyrimidine [*Biochemistry*] DAEP
Diaminoanisole [*A dye*] [*Organic chemistry*] DAA
Diaminobenzanilide [*Organic chemistry*] DABA
Diaminobenzene [*Organic chemistry*] DAB
Diaminobenzidine [*Organic chemistry*] DAB
Diaminobenzoic Acid [*Organic chemistry*] DABA
Diaminocyclohexanetetraacetic Acid [*Also, OCTA*] [*Organic chemistry*] DCTA
Diamino(diethoxyphosphinyl)triazine [*Organic chemistry*] DAPT
Diaminodiphenyl Ether [*Organic chemistry*] DADPE
Diaminodiphenyl Methane [*Organic chemistry*] DADPM
Diaminodiphenyl Sulfone [*Also, DAPSONE, DDS*] [*Pharmacology*] DADPS
Diaminodiphenyl Sulfone [*Also, DADPS, DDS*] [*Pharmacology*] DAPSONE
Diaminodiphenyl Sulfone [*Also, DADPS, DAPSONE*] [*Pharmacology*] DDS
Diaminodiphenylmethane [*Also, DDM, MDA*] DAPM
Diaminodiphenylmethane [*Also, DAPM, MDA*] [*Organic chemistry*] DDM
Diaminohydroxypropanetetraacetic Acid [*Also, DTA, DPTA*] [*Organic chemistry*] DHPTA
Diaminomaleonitrile [*Organic chemistry*] DAMN
Diaminophenylthiazole [*Pharmacology*] DAPT
Diaminopimelic Acid [*Also, DAPA*] [*Organic chemistry*] DAP
Diaminopimelic Acid [*Also, DAP*] [*Organic chemistry*] DAPA
Diaminopropanol Tetraacetic Acid [*Also, DTA, DHPTA*] [*Organic chemistry*] DPTA
Diaminopropanoltetraacetic Acid [*Also, DPTA, DHPTA*] [*Organic chemistry*] DTA
Diaminopurine [*Biochemistry*] DAP
Diaminopyridine [*Organic chemistry*] DAP
Diaminostilbenedisulfonic Acid [*Also, DASD*] [*Organic chemistry*] DAS
Diaminostilbenedisulfonic Acid [*Also, DAS*] [*Organic chemistry*] DASD
Diamino(tribromopropyl)triazine [*Flame retardant*] [*Organic chemistry*] DABT
Diaminotrinitrobenzene [*An explosive*] DATB
Diaminovaleric Acid [*Biochemistry*] DAV
Diammonium Phosphate [*Inorganic chemistry*] DAP
Diamond DIA
Diamond DMD
Diamond Anvil Cell [*Spectrometry*] DAC
Diamond-B Industries [*NASDAQ symbol*] DIAB
Diamond Bathurst [*American Stock Exchange symbol*] DBH
Diamond Core Drill Manufacturers Association DCDMA
Diamond Council of America DCA
Diamond Crystal Salt [*NASDAQ symbol*] DSLT
Diamond Dealers Club DDC
Diamond Flap [*Envelopes*] DF
Diamond and Gemstone Remarketing Association DGRA
Diamond International Corp. [*NYSE symbol*] [*Delisted*] DN
Diamond Locking Knurl DLK
Diamond M Co. [*Formerly, Diamond M Drilling Co.*] [*NYSE symbol*] DMD
Diamond Manufacturers and Importers Association of America DMI
Diamond Manufacturers and Importers Association of America DMIAA
Diamond Ordnance Fuze Laboratory [*Later, Harry Diamond Laboratories*] [*AMC*] DOFL
Diamond Ordnance Radiation Facility [*Nuclear reactor*] DORF
Diamond Pyramid Hardness DPH
Diamond Pyramid Hardness Number DPN
Diamond Radiation Facility DRF
Diamond Ranch [*California*] [*Seismograph station code, US Geological Survey*] DIR
Diamond Research [*A publication*] Diamond Res
Diamond Setters Fraternal Guild DSFG
Diamond Shamrock Corp. [*Formerly, Diamond Alkali Co.*] [*NYSE symbol*] DIA
Diamond Shamrock Corp., Harrison, NJ [*Library symbol*] NjHarN
Diamond Shamrock Corp., Research Library, Painesville, OH [*Library symbol*] OPaD
Diamond-Square-Diamond [*Lipscomb polyhedral rearrangement in borane anion and carborane series*] dsd
Diamond T Register DTR
Diamond Tool Engineering Co. DTE
Diamond Trade Association of America DTAA
Diamond Walnut Growers DWG
Diamond West Energy [*NASDAQ symbol*] DMND
Diamond Wheel Manufacturers Institute DWMI
Diamonds, Emeralds, Amethysts, and Rubies DEAR
Diana Stores Corp. [*NYSE symbol*] [*Delisted*] DIN
Diapaga [*Upper Volta*] [*Airport symbol*] DIP
Diapason [*A publication*] Diap
Diapason [*Octave*] [*Music*] DIAP
Diapause Hormone [*In insects*] [*Endocrinology*] DH
Diaper Service Accreditation Council DSAC
Diaper Service Industry Association [*Later, National Institute of Infant Services*] DSIA
Diaphone [*Fog signal*] DIA
Diaphragm DIAPH
Diaphragm Gland DGLD
Diaphragm Nerve Stimulation DNS
Diaphragm Operated Valve DOV
Diario de Noticias (Lisbon, Portugal) [*A publication*] DNAL
Diario Oficial del Ministerio de Marina [*A publication*] Diario Of Minist Mar
Diarrhea and Vomiting [*Medicine*] D & V
Diasonics, Inc. [*NASDAQ symbol*] DNIC
Diastatic Power DP
Diastematic Club of America DCA
Diastolic [*Medicine*] DIAS
Diastolic Blood Pressure [*Medicine*] DBP
Diastolic Filling Period [*Medicine*] DFP
Diastolic Murmur [*Medicine*] DM
Diathermy [*Medicine*] D
Diathermy [*Medicine*] DIA
Diathermy [*Medicine*] DIATH
Diatomic Molecule Spectra and Energy Levels Center DMSELC
Diatomic Research Bulletin [*A publication*] Diatomic Research Bull
Diatoms [*Quality of the bottom*] [*Nautical charts*] Di
Diazabicycloheptene [*Organic chemistry*] DBH
Diazabicyclooctane [*Organic chemistry*] DABCO
Diazabutadiene [*Organic chemistry*] DAB
Diazepam [*Pharmacology*] DAP
Diazepam Binding Inhibitor [*Biochemistry*] DBI
Diazo Print DPR
Diazobicyclononene [*Organic chemistry*] DBN
Diazobicycloundecane [*Organic chemistry*] DBU
Diazodicyanoimidazole [*Organic chemistry*] DDI
Diazodinitrophenol [*Organic chemistry*] DDNP
Diazooxo-L-norleucine [*Antineoplastic drug*] DON
Diazouracil [*Pharmacology*] DU
Dibasic Ester [*Organic chemistry*] DBE
Dibenzanthracene [*Carcinogen*] DBA

Dibenzothiophene [*Organic chemistry*]........DBT
Dibenzyl Ether [*Organic chemistry*]........DBE
Dibenzylamine [*Organic chemistry*]........DBA
Dibenzylethylenediamine [*Organic chemistry*]........DBED
Dibenzylmethylamine [*Organic chemistry*]........DBMA
Dibenzylphosphoryl Chloride [*Organic chemistry*]........DBPCl
Diboll, TX [*Radio station call letters*]........KIPR
Diboll, TX [*Radio station call letters*]........KIPR-FM
Dibrell Brothers [*NASDAQ symbol*]........DBRL
Dibromochloropropane [*Nematocide*]........DBCP
Dibromodulcitol [*Mitolactol*] [*Antineoplastic drug*]........DBD
Dibromoethane [*Same as EB, EDB*] [*Organic chemistry*]........DBE
Dibromohydroxymercurifluorescein [*Antiseptic*]........DOMF
Dibromomannitol [*Mitobronitol*] [*Antineoplastic drug*]........DBM
Dibromomethyl(isopropyl)benzoquinone [*Organic chemistry*]........DBMIB
Dibromoneopentyl Glycol [*Flame retardant*] [*Organic chemistry*]........DBNPG
Dibromonitrilopropionamide [*Organic chemistry*]........DBNPA
Dibromosalicil [*Germicide*]........DBS
Dibrugarh [*India*] [*Airport symbol*]........DIB
Dibucaine Number [*Anesthesiology*]........DN
Di(butoxyethyl) Phthalate [*Organic chemistry*]........DBOEP
Dibutyl Hyponitrite [*Organic chemistry*]........DBHN
Dibutyl Maleate [*Organic chemistry*]........DBM
Dibutyl Phthalate [*Organic chemistry*]........DBP
Dibutyl Sebacate [*Organic chemistry*]........DBS
(Dibutylaminosulfenyl)methylcarbamate [*Insecticide*]........DBSC
Dibutylmagnesium [*Organic chemistry*]........DBM
Dibutylnitrosamine [*Also, DBNA*] [*Organic chemistry*]........DBN
Dibutylnitrosamine [*Also, DBN*] [*Organic chemistry*]........DBNA
Dibutylphosphoric Acid [*Organic chemistry*]........DBP
Dibutyltin Dilaurate [*Organic chemistry*]........DBTL
Dibutyryl CAMP [*Cyclic Adenosine Monophosphate*] [*Biochemistry*]........DAMP
Dicalcium Phosphate [*Inorganic chemistry*]........DCP
Dicalcium Phosphate Dihydrate [*Inorganic chemistry*]........DCPD
Dicarbethoxydihydrocollidine [*Biochemistry*]........DDC
Dicarbethoxy(dimethyl)(ethyl)dihydropyridine [*Biochemistry*]........DDEP
Dicarbethoxythiamine [*Pharmacology*]........DCET
Dicarboxylic Aciduria [*Medicine*]........DCA
Diccionario de la Real Academia Espanola [*A publication*]........DRAE
Diceon Electronics [*NASDAQ symbol*]........DICN
Dichloro Analog of Zomepirac [*Biochemistry*]........DCZ
Dichloro-bis(trifluoromethyl)diphenylurea [*Insectproofing agent for wool*]........DTDU
Dichloroacetate [*Organic chemistry*]........DCA
Dichloroacetic Acid [*Organic chemistry*]........DCAA
Dichloroallyl Diisopropylthiocarbamate [*Di-allate*] [*Herbicide*]........DATC
Dichloroaniline [*Dye intermediate*]........DCA
Dichlorobenzidine [*Organic chemistry*]........DCB
Dichlorobenzophenone [*Also, DCBP*] [*Organic chemistry*]........DBP
Dichlorobenzophenone [*Also, DBP*] [*Organic chemistry*]........DCBP
Dichlorodiammineplatinum [*Cisplatin*] [*Also, cis-DDP, CPDD*] [*Antineoplastic drug*]........DDP
Dichlorodibenzodioxin [*Also, DDD*] [*Organic chemistry*]........DCDD
Dichlorodibenzodioxin [*Also, DCDD*] [*Organic chemistry*]........DDD
Dichlorodicyanobenzoquinone [*Organic chemistry*]........DDQ
Dichlorodiphenyl Disulfide [*Insecticide*]........DDDS
Dichlorodiphenyldichloroethane [*Also, TDE*] [*Insecticide*]........DDD
Dichlorodiphenyldichloroethylene [*Pesticide residue*]........DDE
Dichlorodiphenylmethane [*Organic chemistry*]........DDM
Dichlorodiphenylmethylcarbinol [*Also, DMC*] [*Insecticide*]........DCPC
Dichlorodiphenylmethylcarbinol [*Also, DCPC*] [*Insecticide*]........DMC
Dichlorodiphenylsulfone [*Organic chemistry*]........DCDPS
Dichlorodiphenyltrichloroethane [*Insecticide*]........DDT
Dichloroethyl Ether [*Organic chemistry*]........DCEE
Dichloroisocyanuric Acid [*Organic chemistry*]........DCCA
Dichloroisoprenaline........DCI
Dichloroisoproterenol [*Pharmacology*]........DCI
Dichloromaleic Acid [*Organic chemistry*]........DCM
Dichloromethane [*Anesthetic*] [*Organic chemistry*]........DCM
Dichloromethotrexate [*Antineoplastic drug*]........DCM
Dichloronitroaniline [*Also, DICHLORAN*] [*Fungicide*]........DCNA
Dichloronitroaniline [*Also, DCNA*] [*Fungicide*]........DICHLORAN
Dichloronitrosalicylanilide [*Economic poison*] [*Organic chemistry*]........DCN
Dichlorophenol [*Organic chemistry*]........DCP
Dichlorophenol-Indophenol [*Also, DCPI, DPIP*] [*Analytical reagent*]........DCIP
Dichlorophenolindophenol [*Also, DCIP, DPIP*] [*Analytical reagent*]........DCPI
Dichlorophenolindophenol [*Also, DCIP, DCPI*] [*Analytical reagent*]........DPIP
(Dichlorophenoxy)triethylamine [*Herbicide*]........DCPTA
(Dichlorophenyl) Methyl Isopropylphosphoramidothioate [*Herbicide*]........DMPA
(Dichlorophenyl)dimethylurea [*Herbicide*]........DCMU
(Dichlorophenyl)methylurea [*Organic chemistry*]........DCPMU
Dichloropropene-Dichloropropane [*Pesticide*]........DD
Dichloropropionanilide [*Also, DPA*] [*Herbicide*]........DCPA
Dichloropropionanilide [*Also, DCPA*] [*Herbicide*]........DPA
Dichloropropyl Acrylate [*Organic chemistry*]........DCOPA
Dichlororibofuranosylbenzimidazole [*Biochemistry*]........DRB
(Dichlorotriazinyl)aminofluorescein [*Also, DTAF*] [*Analytical biochemistry*]........DCTAF
(Dichlorotriazinyl)aminofluorescein [*Also, DCTAF*] [*Analytical biochemistry*]........DTAF
Dichroic Microspectrophotometer........DMSP
Dichroic Parametric Mirror........DPM
Dichtung und Erkenntnis [*A publication*]........DuE
Dichtung und Volkstum [*A publication*]........Dicht u Volkst
Dichtung und Volkstum [*A publication*]........DuV
Dichtung und Volkstum [*A publication*]........DV
Dichtung und Wirklichkeit [*A publication*]........DuW
Dicionario Bibliografico Portugues [*A bibliographic publication*] [*Portugal*]........DBP
Dick [*A. B.*] **Co.** [*NYSE symbol*]........ABD
Dicke-Fix [*Electronics*]........DF
Dicke-Fix [*Electronics*]........DFX
Dickens Society........DS
Dickens Studies [*A publication*]........DiS
Dickens Studies. Annual [*A publication*]........DSA
Dickens Studies. Newsletter [*A publication*]........DSN
Dickensian [*A publication*]........D
Dickensian [*A publication*]........Dick
Dickenson Mines Cl A [*NASDAQ symbol*]........DKNFA
Dickey [*Maine*] [*Seismograph station code, US Geological Survey*]........D1A
Dickey [*Maine*] [*Seismograph station code, US Geological Survey*]........D2A
Dickey [*Maine*] [*Seismograph station code, US Geological Survey*]........D3A
Dickey-John Corporation [*NASDAQ symbol*]........DKJC
Dickinson [*North Dakota*] [*Airport symbol*] [*Obsolete*]........DIK
Dickinson Air Service [*Dickinson, ND*] [*FAA designator*]........DKN
Dickinson College, Carlisle, PA [*OCLC symbol*]........DKC
Dickinson College, Carlisle, PA [*Library symbol*]........PCarlD
Dickinson Law Review [*A publication*]........Dick L Rev
Dickinson Library, Deerfield, MA [*Library symbol*]........MDee
Dickinson Memorial Library, Orange City, FL [*Library symbol*]........FOrD
Dickinson, ND [*Radio station call letters*]........KDIX
Dickinson, ND [*Television station call letters*]........KDSE
Dickinson, ND [*Radio station call letters*]........KLTC
Dickinson, ND [*Television station call letters*]........KNDX
Dickinson, ND [*Television station call letters*]........KQCD-TV
Dickinson, ND [*Radio station call letters*]........KRRB
Dickinson Public Library, Dickinson, ND [*Library symbol*]........NdDi
Dickinson Review [*A publication*]........DickinsonR
Dickinson School of Law [*Pennsylvania*]........DSL
Dickinson School of Law, Sheely-Lee Law Library, Carlisle, PA [*OCLC symbol*]........DKL
Dickinson State College, Dickinson, ND [*Library symbol*]........NdDiS
Dickinson State College, Dickinson, ND [*OCLC symbol*]........NDI
Dickinson Studies [*A publication*]........Dic S
Dickman Aviation Service [*Rolla, MO*] [*FAA designator*]........DKM
Dickson, TN [*Radio station call letters*]........WDKN
Dicomed Corp. [*NASDAQ symbol*]........DCOM
Dicrotic Notch [*Cardiology*]........DN
Dictaphone........DICT
Dictaphone Corporation [*NYSE symbol*] [*Delisted*]........DC
Dictaphone Machine Transcriber........DMT
Dictation........DICT
Dictation Equipment........DE
Dictator........DICT
Dicti Anni [*Of the Said Year*] [*Latin*]........DA
Dictionary........DIC
Dictionary........DICT
Dictionary of Abbreviations in Medicine [*A publication*]........DAM
Dictionary of American Biography [*A publication*]........DAB
Dictionary of American English [*A publication*]........DAE
Dictionary of American English [*A publication*]........DAME
Dictionary of American History [*A publication*]........DAH
Dictionary of American Library Biography [*A publication*]........DALB
Dictionary of American Naval Fighting Ships [*A publication*]........DANFS
Dictionary of American Regional English [*A publication*]........DARE
Dictionary of American Slang [*A publication*]........DAS
Dictionary of Americanisms [*A publication*]........DA
[*The*] **Dictionary of Biographical Quotation** [*A publication*]........DBQ
Dictionary of Canadian Biography [*More correctly, DCB/DBC*] [*A publication*]........DCB
Dictionary of Canadian Biography/Dictionnaire Biographique du Canada [*A publication*]........DCB/DBC
Dictionary of Carribean English Usage [*A publication*]........DCEU
Dictionary of Computer and Control Systems Abbreviations, Signs, and Symbols [*A publication*]........DCCSA
Dictionary of Electrical Abbreviations, Signs, and Symbols [*A publication*]........DEIA
Dictionary of Electronics Abbreviations, Signs, and Symbols [*A publication*]........DEA
Dictionary of Folklore, Mythology, and Legend [*A publication*]........DFML
[*A*] **Dictionary of Forces' Slang** [*A publication*]........DFS
Dictionary of the History of Ideas [*A publication*]........DHI
Dictionary of Industrial Engineering Abbreviations [*A publication*]........DIEA
Dictionary of International Biography [*A publication*]........DIB
Dictionary of Jamaican English [*A publication*]........DJE
Dictionary of Literary Biography [*A publication*]........DLB
Dictionary of National Biography [*A publication*]........DNB
Dictionary of Naval Abbreviations [*A publication*]........DICNAVAB
Dictionary of Occupational Titles [*Department of Labor*] [*A publication*]........DOT
Dictionary of the Older Scottish Tongue [*A publication*]........DOST

Dictionary of Organic Compounds [*A publication*] .... DOC
Dictionary of Organic Compounds [*A publication*] .... DOCS
Dictionary of Physics and Mathematics Abbreviations, Signs, and Symbols [*A publication*] .... DPMA
Dictionary of Scientific Biography [*A publication*] .... DSB
[*A*] **Dictionary of Slang and Unconventional English** [*A publication*] .... DSUE
Dictionary Society of North America .... DSNA
Dictionary of South African Biography [*A publication*] .... DSAB
[*A*] **Dictionary of the Underworld** [*A publication*] .... DU
Dictionnaire d'Archeologie et de Liturgie [*A publication*] .... DACL
Dictionnaire Biographique du Canada [*More correctly, DCB/DBC*] [*A publication*] .... DBC
Dictionnaire Classique d'Histoire Naturelle [*A publication*] .... Dict Class Hist Nat
Dicyanobenzene [*Organic chemistry*] .... DCNB
Dicyanodiamide [*Organic chemistry*] .... DICY
Dicyanomethylenetrinitrofluorene [*Organic chemistry*] .... DTF
Dicyclohexyl [*Organic chemistry*] .... DCH
Dicyclohexyl Phthalate [*Organic chemistry*] .... DCHP
Dicyclohexylcarbodiimide [*Also, DCCD, DCCI*] [*Organic chemistry*] .... DCC
Dicyclohexylcarbodiimide [*Also, DCC, DCCI*] [*Organic chemistry*] .... DCCD
Dicyclohexylcarbodiimide [*Also, DCC, DCCD*] [*Organic chemistry*] .... DCCI
Dicyclopentadiene [*Also, DCPD*] [*Organic chemistry*] .... DCP
Dicyclopentadiene [*Also, DCP*] [*Organic chemistry*] .... DCPD
Did Not Attend .... DNA
Did Not Come .... DNC
Did Not Finish .... DNF
Did Not Keep Appointment [*Medicine*] .... DNKA
Did Not Play .... DNP
Did Not Receive Questionnaire .... DNRQ
Did Not Suit .... DNS
Didactic .... DID
Didaskaleion [*A publication*] .... Di
Didaskaleion [*A publication*] .... Did
Didcot [*British depot code*] .... DID
Didecyl Glutarate [*Organic chemistry*] .... DDG
Diderot Studies [*A publication*] .... Did S
Diderot Studies [*A publication*] .... DS
Didicyclohexylammonium Naphthylthiolphosphate [*Organic chemistry*] .... DDNTP
Dido and Pluto Handmaiden for Nuclear Experiments [*Nuclear reactor at Harwell, England*] .... DAPHNE
Die Cast Zinc .... DCZ
Die Casting Engineer [*A publication*] .... Die Cast Eng
Die Casting Federation .... DCF
Die Casting Mold .... DCM
Die Casting Research Foundation .... DCRF
Die Forged Aluminum .... DFA
Die Griechische Christliche Schriftsteller der Ersten Drei Jahrhunderte [*A publication*] .... GCS
Die Haghe. Bijdragen en Mededeelingen [*A publication*] .... HBM
Die Kultur [*A publication*] .... DK
Die Literatur [*A publication*] .... DL
Die Lock .... DLX
Die Neue Literatur [*A publication*] .... DNL
Die Neuren Sprachen [*A publication*] .... DNS
Die Template .... DT
Die Welt des Islam [*A publication*] .... Welt Isl
Die Weltliteratur [*A publication*] .... DW
Diebold Generator for Statistical Tabulation .... DIGEST
Diebold, Inc. [*NYSE symbol*] .... DBD
Diebus Alternis [*Every Other Day*] [*Pharmacy*] .... DIEB ALT
Diebus Secundis [*Every Second Day*] [*Pharmacy*] .... DIEB SECUND
Diebus Tertiis [*Every Third Day*] [*Pharmacy*] .... DIEB TERT
Diecasting and Metal Moulding [*A publication*] .... Diecasting Met Moulding
Died .... D
Died of Disease .... DOD
Died with Disease [*Medicine*] .... DWD
Died of Injuries [*Military*] .... DOI
Died of Wounds .... DOW
Died of Wounds Resulting from Action with Enemy .... DWA
Diego [*Blood group*] .... Di
Diego Suarez [*Madagascar*] [*Airport symbol*] .... DIE
Diehlektriki i Poluprovodniki [*A publication*] .... Diehlektr Poluprovodn
Dielectric Constant .... DC
Dielectric Constant Indicator .... DCI
Dielectric Dissipation Factor .... DDF
Dielectric Heating Equipment .... DHE
Dielectric Infrared Beamsplitter .... DIB
Dielectric Isolation .... DI
Dielectric Loading Factor [*Electronics*] .... DL
Dielectric and Optical Aspects of Intermolecular Interactions [*A publication*] .... Dielectr Opt Aspects Intermol Interact
Dielectric Rod Antenna .... DRA
Dielectric Spectroscopy .... DS
Dielectric Strength Test .... DST
Dielectrophoresis .... DEP
Diemakers and Diecutters Association [*Later, NADD*] .... DDA
Dienstanweisung [*Service regulations*] [*German military - World War II*] .... DAW
Dieppe [*France*] [*Airport symbol*] [*Obsolete*] .... DPE
Dies [*Day*] [*Latin*] .... D
Diesel [*British Waterways Board sign*] .... D
Diesel .... DIES
Diesel .... DSL
Diesel Automobile Association .... DAA
Diesel Belt Drive .... DBD
Diesel Direct .... DD
Diesel Direct Drive .... DDD
Diesel Electric .... DE
Diesel Electric .... DIEL
Diesel Electric Direct Drive .... DEDD
Diesel Electric Reduction Drive .... DERD
Diesel Electric Tandem Motor Drive .... DET
Diesel Engine Driven .... DED
Diesel Engine Manufacturers Association .... DEMA
Diesel Engine, Reduction Drive .... DER
Diesel Engined Road Vehicle .... DERV
Diesel Engineers and Users Association. Publication [*A publication*] .... Diesel Eng Users Ass Publ
Diesel Equipment Superintendent [*A publication*] .... Diesel Equip Supt
Diesel Fruit Vessel .... DIFR
Diesel Fuel .... DF
Diesel Fuel with an Antarctic Additive .... DFA
Diesel Fuel, Marine .... DFM
Diesel and Gas Turbine Progress [*A publication*] .... Diesel Gas Turbine Prog
Diesel and Gas Turbine Progress [*A publication*] .... Diesel Gas Turbine Progr
Diesel and Gas Turbine Progress Worldwide [*A publication*] .... Diesel Gas Turb Prog Worldwide
Diesel Geared Drive .... DGD
Diesel Geared - Motor Geared .... DG-MG
Diesel Generator .... DG
Diesel Mechanical .... DM
Diesel Oil .... D
Diesel Oil .... DESOIL
Diesel Oil .... DO
Diesel Particulate .... DP
Diesel Radial [*Aircraft engine*] .... DR
Diesel Reduction Drive .... DRD
Diesel Tank Vessel .... DITA
Diesel V-Belt Drive .... DVBD
Diet Beverage .... DB
Diet Institute, Inc. [*NASDAQ symbol*] .... DYET
Diet as Tolerated [*Medicine*] .... DAT
Dietary Fiber [*Nutrition*] .... DF
Dietetics .... DIET
Diethanolamine [*Also, DIOLAMINE*] [*Organic chemistry*] .... DEA
Diethanolamine [*Also, DEA*] [*USAN*] [*Organic chemistry*] .... DIOLAMINE
Diethoxyanthracene [*Organic chemistry*] .... DEA
Diethoxyethylene [*Organic chemistry*] .... DEE
Diethyl Dicarbocyanine Iodide [*Organic chemistry*] .... DDI
Diethyl Hydrogen Phosphite [*Organic chemistry*] .... DEHP
Diethyl Ketone [*Organic chemistry*] .... DEK
Diethyl-m-toluamide [*Insect repellent*] .... DEET
Diethyl Maleate [*Biochemistry*] .... DEM
Diethyl Nitrophenyl Phosphorothioate [*Insecticide*] .... DNTP
Diethyl Pyrocarbonate [*Chemical preservative*] .... DEP
Diethyl Succinate [*Organic chemistry*] .... DES
Diethyl Sulfate [*Organic chemistry*] .... DES
Diethyl Zinc [*Organic chemistry*] .... DEZ
Diethylamine [*Organic chemistry*] .... DEA
Diethylamine Analog of Ethmozine [*Biochemistry*] .... DAAE
Diethylaminoethanol [*Organic chemistry*] .... DEAE
Diethylaminoethyl [*Organic chemistry*] .... DEAE
Diethylaminoethyl Chloride [*Organic chemistry*] .... DEC
Diethylaminoethyl Dextran [*Organic chemistry*] .... DEAE-D
Diethylaminoethyl Mercaptan [*Organic chemistry*] .... DEAEM
Diethylaminopropylamine [*Organic chemistry*] .... DEAPA
Diethylaminosulfur Trifluoride [*Organic chemistry*] .... DAST
Diethylcarbamazine [*Anthelmintic drug*] .... DEC
Diethylcarbamazine Citrate [*Biochemistry*] .... DECC
Diethylcyclohexane [*Organic chemistry*] .... DECH
Diethyldithiocarbamate [*Organic chemistry*] .... DDC
Diethyldithiocarbonate [*Analytical chemistry*] .... DIECA
Diethyldithiophosphate [*Organic chemistry*] .... dtp
Diethylene Glycol [*Organic chemistry*] .... DEG
Diethylene Glycol Adipate [*Organic chemistry*] .... DEGA
Diethylene Glycol Dimethyl Ether [*Organic chemistry*] .... DIGLYME
Diethylene Glycol Dinitrate [*Explosive*] .... DEGN
Diethylene Glycol Succinate [*Organic chemistry*] .... DEGS
Diethylenediamine [*Organic chemistry*] .... dien
Diethylenetriamine [*Also, DTA*] [*Organic chemistry*] .... DETA
Diethylenetriamine [*Also, DETA*] [*Organic chemistry*] .... DTA
Diethylenetriaminepentaacetic Acid [*Also, DETPA, DTPA*] [*Chelating agent*] .... DETP
Diethylenetriaminepentaacetic Acid [*Also, DETP, DTPA*] [*Chelating agent*] .... DETPA
Diethylenetriaminepentaacetic Acid [*Also, DETP, DETPA*] [*Chelating agent*] .... DTPA
Di(ethylhexyl) Adipate [*Organic chemistry*] .... DEHA
Di(ethylhexyl)phosphoric Acid [*Organic chemistry*] .... DEHPA

Di(ethylhexyl)phthalate [*Also, DOP*] [*Organic chemistry*] ... DEHP
Diethylhydroxylamine [*Organic chemistry*] ... DEHA
Diethylnitrosamine [*Also, DENA*] [*Carcinogen*] ... DEN
Diethylnitrosamine [*Also, DEN*] [*Carcinogen*] ... DENA
Diethyloxadicarbocyanine Iodide [*A dye*] ... DODCI
Diethylpropanediol [*Biochemistry*] ... DEP
Diethylpyrocarbonate [*Antiseptic for wines*] ... DEPC
Diethylstilbestrol [*Endocrinology*] ... DES
Diethylstilbestrol Adenosis [*Oncology*] ... DESAD
Diethylthiacarbocyanine [*Organic chemistry*] ... DETC
Diethylthiatricarbocyanine [*Organic chemistry*] ... DTTC
Diethyltoluamide [*Also, DETA*] [*Insect repellant*] [*Organic chemistry*] ... DET
Diethyltoluamide [*Also, DET*] [*Insect repellant*] [*Organic chemistry*] ... DETA
Diethyltryptamine [*Hallucinogenic drug*] ... DET
Dietitian ... D
Dietrich, AK [*Location identifier*] [*FAA*] ... DTK
Dietrich Resources Corp. [*NASDAQ symbol*] ... DTRH
Dietskaia Meditsina [*A publication*] ... Dietsk Med
DIFAR Triangular Tactic ... TRITAC
Difference ... D
Difference ... DIF
Difference ... DIFCE
Difference ... DIFF
Difference, Center ... DC
Difference in Conditions ... DIC
Difference in Depth of Modulation ... DDM
Difference Figure of Merit ... DFOM
Difference Index [*Protein calculation*] [*Biochemistry*] ... DI
Difference of Latitude [*Navigation*] ... DL
Difference of Latitude [*Navigation*] ... DLAT
Difference of Latitude [*Navigation*] ... L
Difference Limen [*Physiology, psychology*] ... DL
Difference of Longitude [*Navigation*] ... DLO
Difference of Longitude [*Navigation*] ... DLONG
Difference, Port [*Navigation*] ... DP
Difference in Pressure ... DP
Difference Pressure Control Switch ... DPCS
Difference of Rate ... DRATE
Difference Sensation [*Psychology*] ... DS
Difference, Starboard [*Navigation*] ... DS
Differenced-Range Doppler ... DRD
Differenced-Range Versus Integrated Doppler [*Charged particle measurement*] ... DRVID
Differencial'nye Uravnenija i Vycislitelnaja Matematika [*A publication*] ... Differencial'nye Uravnenija i Vycisl Mat
Different ... DIFT
Different Orbitals for Different Spins [*Atomic physics*] ... DODS
Differential ... DFRN
Differential ... DIF
Differential ... DIFF
Differential-Absorption LIDAR [*Spectroscopy*] ... DIAL
Differential-Absorption Remote Sensing [*LASER*] ... DARS
Differential Absorption and Scattering [*Remote sensing technique*] ... DAS
Differential Agglutination Titer [*Hematology*] ... DAT
Differential Amplifier ... DA
Differential Analyzer ... DA
Differential Analyzer Replacement [*Data processing*] ... DARE
Differential Aptitude Test [*Psychology*] ... DAT
Differential Ballistic Wind ... DBW
Differential Ballistic Wind Computer ... DBWC
Differential Ballistic Wind Offset ... DBWO
Differential Base Current Drift ... DBCD
Differential Bearing Indicator ... DBI
Differential Blood Count ... DIFF
Differential Calculus ... DC
Differential Coefficient ... D
Differential Coherent Phase Shift Keyed [*System*] [*Data processing*] ... DCPSK
Differential Corrected Spectral Unit [*Spectrometry*] ... DCSU
Differential Correction ... DC
Differential Current Density ... DCD
Differential Diagnosis [*Medicine*] ... DD
Differential Distribution Law [*Meteorology*] ... DDL
Differential Electronically-Locking Test Accessory ... DELTA
Differential Encoding Phase Shift Keying ... DEPSK
Differential Energy Spectrum ... DES
Differential Equation Solver ... DES
Differential Equations [*A publication*] ... Differ Equations
Differential Equations Pseudocode Interpreter [*Jet Propulsion Laboratory, NASA*] ... DEPI
Differential Generator ... DG
Differential Interference Contrast [*Microscope*] ... DIC
Differential LASER Gyro ... DILAG
Differential Leukocyte Counts [*Hematology*] ... DLC
Differential Light Scattering ... DLS
Differential Logistics Services Center [*AEC*] ... DLSC
Differential Long-Baseline Interferometer [*Radio interferometry*] ... DLBI
Differential Maneuvering Simulator [*Aviation*] ... DMS
Differential (of) ... D
Differential Orbit Improvement ... DOI
Differential Paramagnetic Effect [*Low-temperature physics*] ... DPE
Differential Phase Shift Keying ... DPSK
Differential Power Switch ... DPS
Differential Pressure ... DP
Differential Pressure Control ... DPC
Differential Pressure Feedback ... DPF
Differential Pressure Seawater ... DPSW
Differential Pulse Anodic Stripping Voltametry [*Electrochemistry*] ... DPASV
Differential Pulse Code Modulation ... DPCM
Differential Pulse Polarography [*Analytical chemistry*] ... DPP
Differential Pulse Voltammetry [*Analytical chemistry*] ... DPV
Differential Rate ... DR
Differential Reactive Current Project Relay ... DRCPR
Differential Reinforcement [*Psychometrics*] ... DRF
Differential Reinforcement of Low Rate [*Psychometrics*] ... DRL
Differential Reinforcement of Other [*Psychometrics*] ... DRO
Differential Relay ... DFRL
Differential Scanning Calorimeter [*or Calorimetry*] [*Instrumentation*] ... DSC
Differential Scatter [*Remote sensing technique*] ... DISC
Differential Signal Control ... DSC
Differential Spacing [*Typography*] ... DS
Differential Temperature Measuring Device ... DTMD
Differential Thermal Analysis [*or Analyzer*] ... DTA
Differential Thermocouple Voltmeter ... DTVM
Differential Throttle Control ... DTC
Differential Time ... DT
Differential Time Relay ... DIFFTR
Differential Value Profile [*Psychology*] ... DVP
Differential Vector Equation ... DVE
Differential Velocity ... DV
Differential Voltage ... DV
Differential Voltage Amplifier ... DVA
Differential Wave Impedance ... DWI
Differentially (Expressed) Gastrula [*Genetics*] ... DG
Differentiation [*Calculus*] ... D
Differentiation [*A publication*] ... Differentia
Differentiation with Asymmetrical Reinforcement ... DAR
Differentiation with Symmetrical Reinforcement ... DSR
Differentsial'nye Uravneniya [*A publication*] ... Differ Uravn
Differentsial'nye Uravneniya i Ikh Primenenie [*A publication*] ... Differ Uravn Primen
Differs ... DFRS
Difficult ... DFCLT
Difficult ... DIFCLT
Difficulty ... DIFCLTY
Difficulty-Importance-Frequency ... DIF
Diffraction ... DIFFR
Diffraction Limited ... DL
Diffraction Limited Focusing ... DLF
Diffraction Limited Modulation Transfer Function ... DMTF
Diffraction Limited Raman LASER ... DLRL
Diffuse ... DFUS
Diffuse ... DIF
Diffuse Esophageal Spasm [*Medicine*] ... DES
Diffuse Histiocytic Lyphoma [*Medicine*] ... DHL
Diffuse Idiopathic Skeletal Hyperostosis [*Medicine*] ... DISH
Diffuse Infiltrative Lung Disease [*Medicine*] ... DILD
Diffuse Intravascular Coagulation [*Hematology*] ... DIC
Diffuse Mixed Lymphoma [*Oncology*] ... DML
Diffuse Poorly Differentiated Lymphocytic (Lymphoma) [*Oncology*] ... DPDL
Diffuse Process Such as Pericarditis [*Cardiology*] ... DPSP
Diffuse Undifferentiated Lymphoma [*Oncology*] ... DUL
Diffused Alloy Power ... DAP
Diffused Base ... DB
Diffused Junction ... DJ
Diffused Mesa ... DM
Diffused Planar ... DP
Diffuser ... DFSR
Diffuser [*s*] [*Freight*] ... DIF
Diffusing ... DIFFUS
Diffusing Capacity ... D
Diffusing Capacity of the Lungs for Carbon Monoxide ... DLCO
Diffusion Coefficient [*Symbol*] [*IUPAC*] ... D
Diffusion Data [*A publication*] ... Diffus Data
Diffusion and Defect Monograph Series [*A publication*] ... Diffus Defect Monogr Ser
Diffusion Destainer [*Electrophoresis*] ... DD
Diffusion under [*Epitaxial*] **Film** ... DUF
Diffusion Formed Coating ... DFC
Diffusion in Metals and Alloys Data Center [*National Bureau of Standards*] ... DIMADC
Diffusion in Metals and Alloys Data Center [*National Bureau of Standards*] ... DMDC
Diffusion Pressure Deficit ... DPD
Diffusion Self-Aligned Metal-Oxide Semiconductor ... DSAMOS
Diffusion Transfer Processing System ... DTPS
Difluorodiphenyldichloroethane [*Insecticide*] ... DFDD
Difluorodiphenyltrichloroethane [*Insecticide*] ... DFDT
Difluoromethylarginine [*Organic chemistry*] ... DFMA
Difluoromethylornithine [*Organic chemistry*] ... DFMO
Difluorophosphate [*Inorganic chemistry*] ... DFP

Difluorourea [*Organic chemistry*]....DFU
Difurfurylideneacetone [*Organic chemistry*]....DIFA
Dig-In Angle....DIA
Digby, NS [*Radio station call letters*]....CKDY
Digest....DIG
Digest of Decisions of the National Labor Relations Board [*A publication*]....DLRB
Digest of Literature on Dielectrics [*A publication*]....Dig Lit Dielec
Digest of Neurology and Psychiatry [*A publication*]....Dig Neurol Psychiat
Digest of Papers. IEEE Computer Society International Conference [*A publication*]....Dig Pap IEEE Comput Soc Int Conf
Digest of Papers. Semiconductor Test Symposium [*A publication*]....Dig Pap Semicond Test Symp
Digest of Public General Bills [*Library of Congress*] [*A publication*]....D
Digest of Public General Bills [*Library of Congress*] [*A publication*]....DPGB
Digest of Selected Health and Insurance Plans [*A publication*]....DSHIP
Digest of Selected Pension Plans [*Bureau of Labor Statistics*] [*A publication*]....DSPP
Digest of Technical Papers. IEEE International Solid State Circuits Conference [*A publication*]....Dig Tech Pap IEEE Int Solid State Circuits Conf
Digest of Technical Papers. IEEE MTTS International Microwave Symposium [*A publication*]....Dig Tech Pap IEEE MTTS Int Microwave Symp
Digestion and Metabolism in the Ruminant. Proceedings of the International Symposium on Ruminant Physiology [*A publication*]....Dig Metab Ruminant Proc Int Symp
Digestive Anlage....DA
Digestive Diseases and Sciences [*A publication*]....Dig Dis Sci
Digestive Gland....DG
Digicon, Inc. [*American Stock Exchange symbol*]....DGC
Digilog, Inc. [*NASDAQ symbol*]....DILO
DiGiorgio Corp. [*NYSE symbol*]....DIG
DiGiorgio Corp. Debs [*NASDAQ symbol*]....DIGXG
Digit [*or Digital*]....D
Digit....DGT
Digit Copying [*Psychiatry*]....DC
Digit Plane Driver [*Data processing*]....DPD
Digit Present....DP
Digit/Record Mark....DIGRM
Digit/Record Mark Group/Mark....DIGRMGM
Digit Select....DS
Digit Storage Relay....DSR
Digit Symbol [*Psychometrics*]....DS
Digit-Symbol Substitution Test [*Psychiatry*]....DST
Digital....DGTL
Digital....DIG
Digital....DIGI
Digital....DIGTL
Digital Acoustic Simulation System....DASS
Digital Acoustic Target....DAT
Digital Acquisition and Documentation Equipment....DADE
Digital Adaptive Area Correlation....DAAC
Digital Adaptive Recording System....DARS
Digital Adaptive Technique for Efficient Communications....DATEC
Digital Address System....DAS
Digital Air Data Computer....DADC
Digital Airborne Computer....DIGITAR
Digital Aircraft Simulator....DAS
Digital Alternator....DA
Digital Altimeter Scanner....DAS
Digital Altimeter Setting Indicators [*Aviation*]....DASI
Digital-to-Analog [*Converter*] [*Data processing*]....D-to-A
Digital-to-Analog [*Converter*] [*Data processing*]....D-A
Digital Analog [*Data processing*]....DIAN
Digital-to-Analog Converter [*Data processing*]....DAC
Digital-to-Analog Converter [*Data processing*]....DACON
Digital-to-Analog Converter Unit [*Data processing*]....DACU
Digital-to-Analog Deck Angle Converter [*Data processing*] [*Navy*]....DADAC
Digital-to-Analog Function Table [*Data processing*]....DAFT
Digital-to-Analog Interface Unit [*Data processing*]....DAIU
Digital-to-Analog Multiplier....DAM
Digital Analog Simulator [*Data processing*]....DAS
Digital Angle Data....DAD
Digital Angle Data Recorder....DADR
Digital Angle Recorder....DAR
Digital Angular Readout by LASER Interferometry....DARLI
Digital Angular Torquing Equipment....DATE
Digital Animated Control System....DACS
Digital Applique Unit....DAU
Digital Arithmetic Center....DAC
Digital Assembly Program....DAP
Digital Attenuator System....DAS
Digital Attitude and Rate System....DARS
Digital Attitude Reference System....DARS
Digital Audio Disc [*Audio/video technology*]....DAD
Digital Audio for Television [*System to improve sound*] [*Public Broadcasting Service*]....DATE
Digital Automatic Acquisition....DAA
Digital Automatic Frequency Control....DAFC
Digital Automatic Gain Control....DAGC
Digital Automatic Multiple Pressure Recorder [*Lewis Research Center*]....DAMPR
Digital Automatic Pattern Recognition....DAPR
Digital Automatic Tape Intelligence Checkout....DATICO
Digital Automatic Tester and Classifier....DATAC
Digital Automatic Tracking and Ranging [*or Remoting*] [*Air Force*]....DATAR
Digital Automatic Weather Network....DAWN
Digital Autopilot....DAP
Digital Autopilot Flight Director System....DAFDS
Digital Autopilot Requirements....DAR
Digital Autotransducer and Recorder....DATAR
Digital Avionics Information System [*Air Force*]....DAIS
Digital Avionics System....DAS
Digital Azimuth Range Tracking System....DARTS
Digital Bargraph Display....DBD
Digital Bargraph Display Unit....DBDU
Digital-to-Binary Converter [*Data processing*]....DBC
Digital Block [*Data processing*]....DB
Digital Block And-Or Gate [*Data processing*]....DBAO
Digital Block Clock Oscillator [*Data processing*]....DBCO
Digital Block Flip-Flop [*Data processing*]....DBFF
Digital Block Inverter Amplifier [*Data processing*]....DBIA
Digital Block Multivibrator [*Data processing*]....DBMV
Digital Block Noninverting Amplifier [*Data processing*]....DBNA
Digital Block Schmitt Trigger [*Data processing*]....DBST
Digital Block Slave Clock [*Data processing*]....DBSC
Digital Camera Control System....DCCS
Digital Capacitance Measuring System....DCMS
Digital Card And-Or Gate [*Data processing*]....DCAO
Digital Card Clock Oscillator [*Data processing*]....DCCO
Digital Card Flip-Flop [*Data processing*]....DCFF
Digital Card Inverting Amplifier [*Data processing*]....DCIA
Digital Card Multivibrator [*Data processing*]....DCMV
Digital Card Noninverting Amplifier [*Data processing*]....DCNA
Digital Card Schmitt Trigger [*Data processing*]....DCST
Digital Card Slave Clock [*Data processing*]....DCSC
Digital Central Office [*Also known as DEO*] [*Telecommunications*]....DCO
Digital Circuit Module [*Data processing*]....DCM
Digital Circuit Quality Monitor [*Data processing*]....DCQM
Digital Clock....DC
Digital Clock Indicator....DCI
Digital Clock Pulse....DCP
Digital Clock Pulse Generator....DCPG
Digital Code....DC
Digital Coefficient Unit [*Data processing*]....DCU
Digital Color Television....DCTV
Digital Command Assembly [*NASA*]....DCA
Digital Command Communications System....DCCS
Digital Command System [*or Subsystem*]....DCS
Digital Communication through Orbiting Needles....DICON
Digital Communication System [*Data processing*]....DCS
Digital Communications....DIGICOM
Digital Communications Associates, Incorporated [*NASDAQ symbol*]....DCAI
Digital Communications and Control Unit....DCCU
Digital Communications Experimental Facility [*Air Force*]....DICEF
Digital Communications System Evaluator....DICOSE
Digital Comparator....DC
Digital Computer....DC
Digital Computer....DIGCOM
Digital Computer Association....DCA
Digital Computer Control Panel....DCCP
Digital Computer Laboratory [*MIT*]....DCL
Digital Computer Processor....DCP
Digital Computer Programing [*Data processing*]....DCP
Digital Computer Switching Unit....DCSU
Digital Concentration Readout [*Data processing*]....DCR
Digital Control Computer....DCC
Digital Control Design Language [*Data processing*]....DCDL
Digital Control Design System....DCDS
Digital Control and Interface Unit....DCIU
Digital Control Signal Processor....DCSP
Digital Control Station [*Data processing*]....DCS
Digital Control System....DCS
Digital Control Unit....DCU
Digital Control and Vector Generator....DCVG
Digital Conversion Receiver....DCR
Digital Coordinate Transformation System....DCTS
Digital Correlation Demonstrator....DICODE
Digital Countdown Display [*Data processing*]....DCD
Digital Countdown Display System [*Data processing*]....DCDS
Digital Countdown System [*Data processing*]....DCS
Digital Counting Unit....DCU
Digital Daily System Operability Test....DDSOT
Digital Data....DD
Digital Data Acquisition System....DDAS
Digital Data Archives System....DDAS
Digital Data, Auxiliary Storage, Track Display, Outputs, and RADAR Display....DATOR
Digital Data Buffer....DDB
Digital Data Calibration System....DDCS

Digital Data Communications Message Protocol ... DDCMP
Digital Data Communications System ... DIDACS
Digital Data Computer ... DIDAC
Digital Data Conversion Equipment ... DDCE
Digital Data Converter ... DDC
Digital Data Display ... DIDAD
Digital Data Display System ... DDDS
Digital Data Distributor ... DDD
Digital Data Down Link [*Data processing*] ... DDDL
Digital Data Generator ... DDG
Digital Data Group ... DDG
Digital Data Handling ... DDH
Digital Data Handling and Display System ... DDH & DS
Digital Data Link ... DDL
Digital Data Logger ... DDL
Digital Data Measuring System ... DDMS
Digital Data Network ... DDN
Digital Data Output Conversion Equipment ... DDOCE
Digital Data Processing Center [*or Complex*] ... DDPC
Digital Data Processing Equipment ... DDPE
Digital Data Processing System ... DDPS
Digital Data Processing Unit ... DDPU
Digital Data Processor ... DDP
Digital Data Processor ... DIDAP
Digital Data Receiver ... DDR
Digital Data Recording Head ... DDRH
Digital Data Recording System ... DDRS
Digital Data Satellite Service [*Communications Satellite Corp.*] ... DIGISAT
Digital Data Servo ... DDS
Digital Data Storage Unit ... DDSU
Digital Data Switching Matrix ... DDSM
Digital Data System ... DDS
Digital Data Terminal ... DDT
Digital Data Terminal Equipment ... DDTE
Digital Data Terminal Equipment Service Module ... DDTESM
Digital Data Transmission System ... DDTS
Digital Data Transmitter ... DDT
Digital Data Unit ... DDU
Digital Datacom, Incorporated [*NASDAQ symbol*] ... DDII
Digital Debugging Tape ... DDT
Digital Decoder Driver Unit ... DDDU
Digital Demodulation Technique ... DDT
Digital Design Language [*Air Force*] [*Data processing*] ... DDL
Digital Differencing Junction ... DDJ
Digital Differential Analyzer ... DDA
Digital-to-Digital ... D-to-D
Digital Display ... DD
Digital Display Converter ... DDC
Digital Display Driver ... DDD
Digital Display Generator ... DDG
Digital Display Generator Element ... DDGE
Digital Display Indicator ... DDI
Digital Display Machine ... DDM
Digital Display Makeup ... DDM
Digital Display Scope ... DDS
Digital Display Unit ... DDU
Digital Distributing Unit ... DDU
Digital Doppler System ... DIGIDOPS
Digital Drafting System ... DDS
Digital Drive Amplifier ... DDA
Digital Dynamics Simulator ... DDS
Digital Electric Monitor ... DEMON
Digital Electron Beam Scanner ... DEBS
Digital Electronic Continuous Ranging ... DECOR
Digital Electronic Countermeasures Analyzer ... DECA
Digital Electronic Engine Control ... DEEC
Digital Electronic Message Systems ... DEMS
Digital Electronic Universal Calculating Engine ... DEUCE
Digital Electrophysiological Data Acquisition and Analysis System [*Neurometrics*] ... DEDAAS
Digital Element ... DE
Digital Element Test Set ... DETS
Digital Elevation Data Base ... DEDB
Digital Encoder Handbook ... DEH
Digital Encoder Handbook ... DEHB
Digital End Office [*Also known as DCO*] [*Telecommunications*] ... DEO
Digital Equation-Solving Computer ... DESC
Digital Equipment Computer Users Society ... DECUS
Digital Equipment Corporation [*NYSE symbol*] ... DEC
Digital Equipment Corp. [*Maynard, MA*] [*FAA designator*] ... DGT
Digital Equipment Corporation Author Language [*Data processing*] ... DECAL
Digital Equipment Corp., Colorado Springs, Colorado Springs, CO [*OCLC symbol*] ... DCX
Digital Equipment Corporation, Corporate Library, Maynard, MA [*OCLC symbol*] ... DEC
Digital Equipment Corp., Hudson, Westboro, MA [*OCLC symbol*] ... DHL
Digital Equipment Corp., Marlboro, Marlboro, MA [*OCLC symbol*] ... DMR
Digital Equipment Corp., Merrimack, Merrimack, NH [*OCLC symbol*] ... DMK
Digital Equipment Corp., Salem, Salem, NH [*OCLC symbol*] ... DNI
Digital Equipment Corp., Spit Brook, Nashua, NH [*OCLC symbol*] ... DTN
Digital Equipment Corp., Tewkesbury, Tewkesbury, MA [*OCLC symbol*] ... DTW
Digital Equipment Corp., Westminster, Westminster, MA [*OCLC symbol*] ... WMD
Digital Equipment's Business-Oriented Language [*Data processing*] ... DIBOL
Digital Error Detection Subsystem [*Data processing*] ... DEDS
Digital Error Monitoring System ... DEMS
Digital European Backbone [*System*] ... DEB
Digital Evaluation Computer ... DEC
Digital Evaluation Equipment ... DEE
Digital Evaluation Unit ... DEU
Digital Event Timer ... DET
Digital Events Evaluator ... DEE
Digital Expansion System ... DES
Digital Experimental Airborne Navigator ... DEXAN
Digital Facsimile Interface System ... DFIS
Digital Fault Analysis ... DFA
Digital Ferrite Phase Shifter ... DFPS
Digital Field System ... DFS
Digital Filtering Technique ... DFT
Digital Flight Control and Landing System ... DFCLS
Digital Flight Control Software [*NASA*] ... DFCS
Digital Flight Control System ... DFCS
Digital Flight Controller ... DFC
Digital Flight Data Recorder ... DFDR
Digital Flight Display ... DFD
Digital Fly by Wire [*Aviation*] ... DFBW
Digital Force Balance Pressure Transducer ... DFBPT
Digital Frequency Analyzer ... DFA
Digital Frequency Display ... DFD
Digital Frequency Meter [*or Monitor*] ... DFM
Digital Frequency Synthesizer ... DFS
Digital Function Generator ... DFG
Digital Gas Turbine Engine Control ... DIGATEC
Digital Geoballistic Computer ... DGBC
Digital Geoballistic Computer ... DGC
Digital Ground Bus ... DGBUS
Digital Ground System ... DGS
Digital Group Multiplexer ... DGM
Digital Guidance and Control Computer ... DIGACC
Digital Hardware Voter Monitor ... DHVM
Digital High Definition Display ... DHDD
Digital High-Speed Standard Eastern Automatic Computer ... DYSEAC
Digital Image Analysis and Display System [*Data processing*] ... DIADS
Digital Image Analysis Laboratory ... DIAL
Digital Image Manipulation and Enhancement Systems ... DIMES
Digital Incremental Plotter ... DIP
Digital Information Display [*Data processing*] ... DID
Digital Information Display System [*Data processing*] ... DIDS
Digital Input [*Data processing*] ... DI
Digital Input [*Data processing*] ... DIN
Digital Input [*or Integrating*] **Computer** [*Data processing*] ... DIC
Digital Input Module [*Data processing*] ... DIM
Digital Input/Output Buffer [*Data processing*] ... DIOB
Digital Input/Output Interface [*Data processing*] ... DIOI
Digital Input/Output Package [*Data processing*] ... DIOP
Digital Input Simulator [*Data processing*] ... DISIM
Digital Input Unit [*Data processing*] ... DIU
Digital Inquiry - Voice Answerback [*Touch-tone*] [*Bell System*] ... DIVA
Digital Insertion Unit [*Data processing*] ... DIU
Digital Instrumentation Programer ... DIP
Digital Instrumentation RADAR ... DIR
Digital Instrumentation Subsystem ... DIS
Digital Integral Ballistic Analyzer ... DIBA
Digital Integrated Attack and Navigation Equipment ... DIANE
Digital Integrated Avionics System ... DIAS
Digital Integrated Circuit [*Data processing*] ... DIC
Digital Integrated Circuit Element [*Data processing*] ... DICE
Digital Integrated Design Language [*Data processing*] ... DIDL
Digital Interactive Complex for Image Feature Extraction and Recognition [*Air Force*] ... DICIFER
Digital Intercontinental Conversion Equipment ... DICE
Digital Interface Adapter [*Data processing*] ... DIA
Digital Interface Code Converter [*Data processing*] ... DICC
Digital Interface and Control Unit ... DICU
Digital Interface Countermeasures Equipment [*Air Force*] ... DICE
Digital Interface Test Unit [*Data processing*] ... DITU
Digital Interface Unit [*Data processing*] ... DIU
Digital Interface Weapon Aiming Computer ... DIWAC
Digital Isolation Amplifier ... DIA
Digital Land Mass Simulation ... DLMS
Digital Linear Slide Switch ... DLSS
Digital Linear Slide Switch Assembly ... DLSSA
Digital Logic Circuit ... DLC
Digital Logic Module ... DLM
Digital Logic System ... DLS
Digital Magnetic Tape Plotting System ... DMTPS
Digital Magnetic Tape Unit ... DMTU
Digital Major Alarm ... DMA

Digital Management Unit	DMU
Digital Map Display	DMD
Digital Message Device	DMD
Digital Message Entry Device	DMED
Digital Message Entry System	DMES
Digital Message Terminal	DMT
Digital Message Terminal Computer	DMTC
Digital Message Unit	DMU
Digital Microcircuit	DMC
Digital Missile Autopilot	DMAP
Digital Module Automatic Tester	DMAT
Digital Module Test Set	DMTS
Digital Monitor Computer	DMC
Digital Monitor Unit	DMU
Digital Motor Electronics	DME
Digital Multibeam Steering	DIMUS
Digital Multibeam Steering System	DMSS
Digital Multimeter	DMM
Digital Multimeter Control	DMMC
Digital Multiplexing and Formatting [Data processing]	DMF
Digital Multiplexing Synchronizer [Data processing]	DMS
Digital Network Analyzer	DINA
Digital Network Architecture [Data processing]	DNA
Digital Network-Defense Special Security Communications System [National Security Agency]	DIN/DCSS
Digital Network Simulation System	DIGINESS
Digital Noise Reduction [Television]	DNR
Digital Nonsecure Voice Terminal	DNVT
Digital Null Command Generator	DNCG
Digital Oceanographic Data Acquisition System	DODAS
Digital Off-Line Automatic Recording System	DOLARS
Digital Ohmmeter	DOM
Digital On-Line Cryptographic Equipment	DOLCE
Digital Operation System	DOS
Digital Optical Projection System	DOPS
Digital Optical Technology System [3-D television system]	DOTS
Digital Output [Data processing]	DO
Digital Output/Input Translator [Data processing]	DO/IT
Digital Output Timer [Data processing]	DOT
Digital Oxygen Metering Device [Aerospace]	DOMD
Digital Panel Meter [Data processing]	DPM
Digital Parallel Processing Array	DIPPA
Digital Pattern Generator	DPG
Digital Phase Comparator	DPC
Digital Phase Difference	DPD
Digital Phase-Locked Loop [Space communication]	DPLL
Digital Phase Shifter	DPS
Digital Plotter Map [Military] [British]	DPM
Digital Plotter System	DPS
Digital Power Supply	DPS
Digital Pressure Converter	DPC
Digital Process Controller	DPC
Digital Processes [A publication]	Digit Process
Digital Processing and Control Unit	DPCU
Digital Processing Oscilloscope	DPO
Digital Processing Unit	DPU
Digital Products Corporation [NASDAQ symbol]	DIPC
Digital Propellant Level Control System	DPLCS
Digital Pseudorandom Inspection	DPI
Digital Quadrature Detection [Instrumentation]	DQD
Digital Quality Monitor	DQM
Digital RADAR Altimeter	DIGIRALT
Digital RADAR Landmass Simulator	DRLMS
Digital RADAR Relay	DRR
Digital RADAR Relay Link	DRRL
Digital RADAR Signal Processor	DRSP
Digital RADAR Simulator	DRS
Digital RADAR System	DRS
Digital Radio and Multiplexer Acquisition	DRAMA
Digital Range Machine	DIRAM
Digital Range Machine	DRM
Digital Range Safety	DRS
Digital Range Safety Command Receiver [NASA]	DRSCR
Digital Range Safety Command System [NASA]	DRSCS
Digital Range Unit	DRU
Digital Ranging Generator [Apollo] [NASA]	DRG
Digital Rate-Integrating Gyro	DRIG
Digital Ratiometer	DRM
Digital Ray and Intensity Projector	DRIP
Digital Read-In Assembly [Data processing]	DRA
Digital Read-In Subsystem [Data processing]	DRISS
Digital Readout [Data processing]	DIGRO
Digital Readout [Data processing]	DRO
Digital Readout Head [Data processing]	DRH
Digital Readout Light [Data processing]	DRL
Digital Readout Oscilloscope [Data processing]	DRO
Digital Readout Oscilloscope [Data processing]	DROO
Digital Readout System [Data processing]	DRS
Digital Readout Timer [Data processing]	DRT
Digital Receiver Station [Data processing]	DRS
Digital Recorder Analyzer [Data processing]	DRA

Digital Recorder Signal Generator [Data processing]	DRSG
Digital Recording [NASDAQ symbol]	DRSO
Digital Recording and Measuring System	DRAMS
Digital Recording and Playback Equipment	DRAPE
Digital Recording Process	DRP
Digital Recording System	DRS
Digital Rectal [Proctoscopy]	DR
Digital Register Unit	DRU
Digital Remote Unit [Data processing]	DRU
Digital Remote Unit Buffer [Data processing]	DRUB
Digital Resolver	DR
Digital Rotary Transducer	DRT
Digital Scan Converter	DSC
Digital Scan Converter Group	DSCG
Digital Scene Matching Area Correlator	DIGISMAC
Digital Select Matrix	DSM
Digital Select Module	DSM
Digital Selective Communications	DISCOM
Digital Shaft Encoder	DSE
Digital Shift Register	DSR
Digital Signal Analyzer	DSA
Digital Signal Conditioner	DSC
Digital Signal Generator	DSG
Digital Signal Processing System	DSPS
Digital Signal Synchronizer	DSS
Digital Simulated Analog Computer	DYSAC
Digital Simulation Language [Data processing]	DSL
Digital Simulation Model	DSM
Digital Simulator and Computer	DISAC
Digital Simulator Computer System	DSCS
Digital Simulator System	DSS
Digital Space Trajectory Measurement System [Raytheon Co.]	DISTRAM
Digital Spectrum Analyzer	DSA
Digital Speech Interpolation [Telephone channels]	DSI
Digital Stabilization Console	DSC
Digital Stepping Recorder	DSR
Digital Storage System	DSS
Digital Storage Unit	DSU
Digital Strain Indicator	DSI
Digital Strip Printer	DSP
Digital Subscriber Terminal	DST
Digital Subscriber Terminal Equipment	DSTE
Digital Subset [or Subsystem]	DSS
Digital Subtraction Angiography [Medicine]	DSA
Digital Switch Corp. [NASDAQ symbol]	DIGI
Digital Synchro Data Source	DSDS
Digital System Design	DSD
Digital Tactical Automatic Control	DIGITAC
Digital Tandem Switch	DTS
Digital Tape Conversion	DTC
Digital Tape Recorder	DTR
Digital Tape Unit	DTU
Digital Tape Unit Test Facility [NASA]	DTUTF
Digital Technique	DT
Digital Telemetering Register	DTR
Digital Telemetry Analog Recording	DITAR
Digital Telemetry System	DTS
Digital Telemetry Unit	DTU
Digital-to-Teletype	DTTY
Digital-to-Television	D/TV
Digital Television Camera	DITEC
Digital Television Camera	DTC
Digital Television Display System	DTDS
Digital Television Encoder	DTE
Digital Television Encoding	DITEC
Digital Television Equipment	DTE
Digital Television Monitor	DTM
Digital Television Spectrometer	DITS
Digital Termination Systems [Telecommunications]	DTS
Digital Test Command System	DTCS
Digital Test Measurement [or Monitor] System	DTMS
Digital Titration System	DTS
Digital to Tone Converter	DTC
Digital Tracker	DT
Digital Tracking System [or Subsystem]	DTS
Digital Transmission System	DTSY
Digital Transmission Unit	DTU
Digital Transmission and Verification Converter	DTVC
Digital Transmitting and Routing System	DTARS
Digital Unit	DU
Digital Universal Test Equipment	DUTE
Digital Uplink Assembly	DUA
Digital Variable-Frequency Oscillator	DVFO
Digital Variable Increment Computer	DIVIC
Digital Vascular Imaging [Roentgenology]	DVI
Digital Velocity Meter	DVM
Digital Video	DV
Digital Video Bandwidth	DVB
Digital Video Display System	DVDS
Digital Video Generator [Data processing]	DVG
Digital Video Integrator and Processor	DVIP

Digital Voice Communications..DVC
Digital Voice System..DVS
Digital-to-Voice Translator..DIVOT
Digital Volt-Ohmmeter..DVOM
Digital Voltage Source..DVS
Digital Voltmeter...DVM
Digital Watch Association...DWA
Digital Waveform Generator...DWG
Digital Wired Recorder...DWR
Digitally Controlled Delta Modulator...............................DCDM
Digitally Controlled Power Source....................................DCPS
Digitally Implemented Communications Experiment.....DICE
Digitally Integrated Fleet Air Defense............................DIFAD
Digitally Scanned Image Display...............................DIGISPLAY
Digitech, Inc. [NASDAQ symbol]..DGTC
Digitized Message Link..DML
Digitized Moving Target Indicator....................................DMTI
Digitized RADAR Experiment..D/RADEX
Digitized Shipboard Expandable Bathythermograph [Naval
    Oceanographic Office]...DSXBT
Digitizer Logic Unit...DLU
Digitronics Users Association [Later, IUA].......................DUA
Diglyceride [Clinical chemistry]..DG
Diglycidyl Ether of Bisphenol A [Monomer] [Organic chemistry]........DGEBA
Diglycidyl Ether of Methylolresorcinol [Organic chemistry]............DGEMER
Diglycolamine [Organic chemistry].....................................DGA
Dignitary Protective Division [US Secret Service]..........DPD
Dignity after Death [An association]....................................DAD
Digoxin Reduction Products [Clinical chemistry]............DRP
Dihaloacetonitrile [Organic chemistry]............................DHAN
Dihydralazine [Antihypertensive agent]..............................DHZ
Dihydrate..DIHY
Dihydro [As substituent on nucleoside] [Biochemistry].........h
Dihydro-Dimethyl-Benzopyranbutyric Acid.....................DBA
Dihydroalprenolol [Pharmacochemistry]..........................DHA
Dihydroanthracene [Organic chemistry].........................DHA
Dihydrochalcone [Sweetening agent]..................................DHC
Dihydrodeoxycorticosterone [Endocrinology]............DH-DOC
Dihydroepiandrosterone Loading Test [Endocrinology]......DLT
Dihydroergocornine [Endocrinology]..................................DHE
Dihydroergocryptine [Organic chemistry].....................DHEC
Dihydroergotamine [Pharmacology]....................................DHE
Dihydrofolate [Biochemistry]..DHF
Dihydrofolate Reductase [An enzyme].............................DHFR
Dihydroisocodeine [Pharmacology]...................................DHIC
Dihydrolevobunolol [Biochemistry]...................................DHLB
Dihydromorphine [Analgesic compound] [Organic chemistry].......DHM
Dihydropteridine Reductase [An enzyme]........................DHPR
Dihydrostreptomycin [Also, DST] [Antimicrobial agent]..........DHSM
Dihydrostreptomycin [Also, DHSM] [Antimicrobial agent].........DST
Dihydrostreptomycin Sulfate [Antimicrobial agent]......DHSS
Dihydrotachysterol [Same as ATL-IO] [Biochemistry].....DHT
Dihydroteleocidin B [Biochemistry].................................DHTB
Dihydrotestosterone [Endocrinology].................................DHT
Dihydrotestosterone Propionate [Endocrinology].........DHTP
Dihydrouridine [One-letter symbol; see H₂Urd].....................D
Dihydrouridine [Two-letter symbol; see H₂Urd]....................hU
Dihydrouridine [Also, D, hU] [A nucleoside]..................H_2Urd
Dihydroxyacetone [Organic chemistry].............................DHA
Dihydroxyacetone Phosphate [Also, DHAP] [Organic chemistry].......DAP
Dihydroxyacetone Phosphate [Also, DAP] [Organic chemistry].....DHAP
Dihydroxyborylaminoethyl [Organic chemistry]............DBAE
(Dihydroxybutyl)guanine [Biochemistry].........................DHBG
Dihydroxycholecalciferol [Vitamin D₃].............................DHCC
Dihydroxycholestanoic Acid [Biochemistry]..................DHCA
Dihydroxydichlorodiphenylmethane [Fungicide]..........DDDM
Dihydroxydinaphthyl Disulfide [Analytical chemistry].......DDD
Dihydroxydiphenyl [Antioxidant] [Organic chemistry]........DOD
Di(hydroxyethyl)glycinate [Organic chemistry]..............DHG
Di(hydroxyethyl)glycine [Organic chemistry]................DHEG
Dihydroxy(hydroxydisulfonaphthylazo)naphthalenedisulfonic
    Acid [An indicator] [Chemistry]....................................DSNADNS
Dihydroxyindol..DHI
Dihydroxymandelic Acid [Organic chemistry].............DOMA
Dihydroxymethoxybenzoxazinone [Organic chemistry].....DIMBOA
Dihydroxyphenol [Organic chemistry].................................DHP
Dihydroxyphenylacetic Acid [Biochemistry]...............DOPAC
Dihydroxyphenylalanine [Biochemistry]..........................DOPA
Dihydroxyphenylethanol [Organic chemistry]............DOPET
Dihydroxyphenylglycol [Organic chemistry]...............DOPEG
(Dihydroxyphenylimino)imidazolidine [Biochemistry].......DPI
Dihydroxyphenylserine [Biochemistry]...........................DOPS
(Dihydroxypropoxymethyl)guanine [Biochemistry]......DHPG
Dihydroxypropyl Methacrylate [Organic chemistry]....DHPMA
Dihydroxypropyladenine [Biochemistry].........................DHPA
Dihydroxytryptamine [Biochemistry]..................................DHT
Diiminosuccinonitrile [Organic chemistry].....................DISN
Diiodonitrophenol [Pharmacology]......................................DNP
Diiodothyroacetic Acid [Biochemistry]............................DIAC
Diiodotyrosine [Biochemistry]..DIT
Diis Manibus [To the Manes, i.e., Departed Souls] [Latin]........DM

Diis Manibus Sacrum [Sacred to the Manes, i.e., Departed Souls]
    [Latin]..DMS
Di(isoamyloxy)thiocarbanilide [Pharmacology]..............DAT
Diisobutyl Adipate [Organic chemistry]..........................DIBA
Diisobutyl Ketone [Organic chemistry]............................DIBK
Diisobutylaluminum Hydride [Also, DIBAH] [Organic chemistry]......DBAH
Diisobutylaluminum Hydride [Also, DBAH] [Organic chemistry]....DIBAH
Diisobutylamine [Organic chemistry]................................DIBA
Diisodecyl Adipate [Organic chemistry]..........................DIDA
Diisodecyl Glutarate [Organic chemistry].......................DIDG
Diisodecyl Phthalate [Organic chemistry].......................DIDP
Diisooctyl Adipate [Organic chemistry]...........................DIOA
Diisooctyl Phthalate [Organic chemistry]........................DIOP
Diisooctyl Sebacate [Organic chemistry].........................DIOS
Diisopropanolamine [Organic chemistry].........................DIPA
Diisopropyl Fluorophosphate [or Diisopropyl
    Fluorophosphonate] [Also, DIFP] [Toxic compound]......DFP
Diisopropyl Fluorophosphonate [Also, DFP] [Toxic compound]......DIFP
Diisopropyl Methylphosphonate [Organic chemistry].....DIMP
Diisopropyl Percarbonate [Organic chemistry]..............DIPP
Diisopropylamine [Organic chemistry].............................DIPA
Diisopropylamine [or Diisopropylammonium] Dichloroacetate
    [Pharmacology]...DADA
Diisopropylaminoethyl Chloride [Organic chemistry].....DIC
Diisopropylbenzene [Organic chemistry].........................DIPB
Diisopropylbenzene Hydroperoxide [Organic chemistry].....DIBHP
(Diisopropyl)ethylamine [Organic chemistry].................DIEA
Diisothiocyano (Disulfonic Acid) Stilbene [Organic chemistry].....DIDS
Dikalium Phosphate [Pharmacology]..................................DKP
Diketogulonic Acid [Organic chemistry]...........................DKA
Diketopiperazine [Organic chemistry]................................DKP
Dilatation and Evacuation [Medicine].................................D & E
Dilation [Medicine]..DILAT
Dilation and Curettage [of the uterus] [Obstetrics].......D & C
Dilauryl Thiodipropionate [Also, DLTDP, DLTP] [Food preservative].....DLT
Dilauryl Thiodipropionate [Also, DLT, DLTP] [Food preservative].....DLTDP
Dilauryl Thiodipropionate [Also, DLT, DLTDP] [Food preservative].....DLTP
Dili [Indonesia] [Airport symbol]...DIL
Diliman Review [A publication]..DilR
Diliman Review [A publication]...DR
Dillard Department Stores, Inc. [American Stock Exchange symbol]......DDS
Dillard University, New Orleans, LA [OCLC symbol]..........DIL
Dillard University, New Orleans, LA [Library symbol]......LND
Dillingham [Alaska] [Airport symbol]..................................DLG
Dillingham, AK [Radio station call letters]....................KDLG
Dillingham Corp. [NYSE symbol] [Delisted]......................DHM
Dillingham Public Library, Dillingham, AK [Library symbol]......AkDil
Dillon Companies, Inc. [NYSE symbol] [Delisted].............DLL
Dillon, MT [Radio station call letters].............................KDBM
Dillon, MT [Radio station call letters].............................KDLN
Dillon Ranch [California] [Seismograph station code, US
    Geological Survey]...DIL
Dillon, SC [Radio station call letters]...........................WDSC
Dillon, SC [Radio station call letters]....................WDSC-FM
Dillons Bay [Vanuata] [Airport symbol]............................DLY
Diluculo [At Daybreak] [Pharmacy]..................................DILUC
Dilute...DIL
Dilute Homogeneous Charge...DHC
Dilute Strength [Chemistry]..DS
Dilute Volume [Chemistry]...DV
Diluted...DILD
Dilution..DILN
Dilutions to Threshold [Olfactory].......................................D/T
Dilutus [Dilute] [Pharmacy]...DILUT
Dimapur [India] [Airport symbol]..DMU
Dime..D
Dimension...DIM
Dimension..DIMEN
Dimension...DMN
Dimensional..D
Dimensional Control Drawing...DCD
Dimensional Control Standard..DCS
Dimensional Motion Time...DMT
Dimensional Special Tooling..DST
Dimensionality of Nations Project [Hawaii]....................DON
Dimensionally Stabilized Anode..DSA
Dimensionless Power Spectral Density............................DPSD
Dimensions of Critical Care Nursing [A publication].....DCCN
Dimensions Description Questionnaire..............................DDQ
Dimensions Economiques de la Bourgogne [A publication]....
    Dim Econ Bourgogne
Dimensions in Health Service [A publication].............DMNHA
Dimensions in Health Services [A publication]......Dimens Health Serv
Dimensions. [US] National Bureau of Standards [A publication]....
    Dimen NBS
Dimensions. [US] National Bureau of Standards [A publication]....
    Dimensions NBS
Dimercaptopropanesulfonate [Salt] [Organic chemistry]....DMPS
Dimercaptopropanol [Also, BAL: British Anti-Lewisite]
    [Detoxicant] [Organic chemistry]...................................DMP
Dimercaptosuccinic Acid [Organic chemistry].................DMS

Dimethoxy(amino)stilbene [Organic chemistry] ... DMBAS
Dimethoxyanthracene Sulfonate [Organic chemistry] ... DAS
Dimethoxybenzene [Organic chemistry] ... DMB
Dimethoxyethane [Also known as GLYME] [Organic chemistry] ... DME
Dimethoxymethane [Organic chemistry] ... DMM
Dimethoxymethylamphetamine [A hallucinogenic drug, more commonly known as STP] ... DOM
(Dimethoxyphenyl)ethylamine [Also, DMPE, DMPEA] [Psychomimetic compound] ... DIMPEA
(Dimethoxyphenyl)ethylamine [Also, DIMPEA, DMPEA] [Psychomimetic compound] ... DMPE
(Dimethoxyphenyl)ethylamine [Also, DIMPEA, DMPE] [Psychomimetic compound] ... DMPEA
Dimethoxyphenylisopropylamine [Organic chemistry] ... DMPIA
Dimethoxytrityl [As substituent on nucleoside] [Biochemistry] ... dmt
Dimethoxytryptamine [Possible central nervous system neuroregulator] ... DMT
Dimethyl Adipimidate [Biochemistry] ... DMA
Dimethyl Aminoethyl Acetate [Organic chemistry] ... DAEA
Dimethyl Aminoethyl Methacrylate [Organic chemistry] ... DMAM
Dimethyl Carbinol [Organic chemistry] ... DMC
Dimethyl Dichlorovinyl Phosphate [Insecticide] ... DDVP
Dimethyl Disulfide [Organic chemistry] ... DMDS
Dimethyl Ether [Organic chemistry] ... DME
Dimethyl-gamma-butyrolactone [Biochemistry] ... DMGBL
Dimethyl Isosorbide [Organic chemistry] ... DMI
Dimethyl Methylphosphonate [Organic chemistry] ... DMMP
Dimethyl Phthalate [Organic chemistry] ... DMP
Dimethyl Silicone [Organic chemistry] ... DMS
Dimethyl Sulfate-Hydrazine [Organic chemistry] ... DMS-HZ
Dimethyl Sulfide [Organic chemistry] ... DMS
Dimethyl Sulfoxide [Also, DMSO] [Organic chemistry] ... DMS
Dimethyl Sulfoxide [Also, DMS] [Organic chemistry] ... DMSO
Dimethyl Terephthalate [Organic chemistry] ... DMT
Dimethyl Tetrachloroterephthalate [Herbicide] ... DCPA
Dimethyl Trisulfide [Organic chemistry] ... DMTS
Dimethylacetamide [Also, DMAC] [Organic chemistry] ... DMA
Dimethylacetamide [Also, DMA] [Organic chemistry] ... DMAC
Dimethylacetylenedicarboxylate [Organic chemistry] ... DMAD
Dimethylallyl Pyrophosphate [Organic chemistry] ... DMAPP
Dimethylamine [Organic chemistry] ... DMA
Dimethylaminoazobenzene [Organic chemistry] ... DAB
Dimethylaminobenzaldehyde [Ehrlich's reagent] [Analytical chemistry] ... DMAB
Dimethylaminoethanol [Antidepressant] ... DMAE
Dimethylaminoethyl Chloride [Organic chemistry] ... DMC
Dimethylaminoethyl Methacrylate [Organic chemistry] ... DMAEMA
Dimethylaminomethylcoumarin [Organic chemistry] ... DAMC
(Dimethylamino(methyl)coumarinyl)maleimide [Organic chemistry] ... DACM
Dimethylamino(methyl)propanol [Organic chemistry] ... DMAMP
Dimethylaminonaphthalenesulfonyl [Also, Dns, DNS] [Biochemical analysis] ... Dansyl
Dimethylaminonaphthalenesulfonyl [Also, Dansyl, dns] [Biochemical analysis] ... DNS
Dimethylaminonaphthalenesulfonyl Chloride [Also, DNSC] [Fluorescent reagent] ... DANS
Dimethylaminonaphthalenesulfonyl Chloride [Also, DANS] [Fluorescent reagent] ... DNSC
Dimethylaminonaphthalenesulfonyl Phosphatidylserine [Biochemistry] ... DNS-PS
Dimethylaminopropionitrile [Organic chemistry] ... DMAPN
Dimethylaminopropyl Chloride [Organic chemistry] ... DMPC
Dimethylaminopropyl Methacrylamide [Organic chemistry] ... DMAPMA
Dimethylaminopropylamine [Also, DMAPA] [Organic chemistry] ... DIMAPA
Dimethylaminopropylamine [Also, DIMAPA] [Organic chemistry] ... DMAPA
Di(methylamyl) Maleate [Organic chemistry] ... DMAM
Dimethylaniline [Organic chemistry] ... DMA
Dimethylarginine [Biochemistry] ... DMA
Dimethylarsenonic Acid [Organic chemistry] ... DMAA
Dimethylbenzanthracene [Carcinogen] ... DMBA
Dimethylbenzanthraceneoxide [Organic chemistry] ... DMBAO
Dimethylbenzimidazole [Organic chemistry] ... DMBZ
Dimethylbenzimidazolylcobamide [Biochemistry] ... DBC
Dimethylbenzylcarbinol [Organic chemistry] ... DMBC
Dimethylbenzylcarbinol Acetate [Organic chemistry] ... DMBCA
Dimethyl(butyl)amine [Organic chemistry] ... DMBA
Dimethylcarboxypsoralen [Metabolite of TMeP] ... DMeCP
Dimethylcetylbenzylammonium Chloride [Antiseptic] [Organic chemistry] ... DMCBAC
Dimethylcyclohexamine [Organic chemistry] ... DMCHA
Dimethylcyclohexanedione [Analytical chemistry] ... DIMEDONE
Dimethylcyclooctadiene [Organic chemistry] ... DMCOD
Dimethylcysteine (Penicillamine) [Pharmacology] ... DMC
Dimethyldichlorosilane [Organic chemistry] ... DMCS
Dimethyldiethyllead [Organic chemistry] ... DMDEL
Dimethyldithiocarbamate [Organic chemistry] ... DMDC
Dimethylethanolamine [Organic chemistry] ... DME
Dimethylformamide [Also, DMFA] [Organic chemistry] ... DMF
Dimethylformamide [Also, DMF] [Organic chemistry] ... DMFA
Dimethylglycine [Biochemistry] ... DMG
Dimethylhydrazine [Rocket fuel base, convulsant poison] ... DMH
Dimethylmercury [Toxicology] ... DMM
Dimethyl(methylthio)sulfonium Fluoroborate [Organic chemistry] ... DMTSF
Dimethylmonochlorosilane [Organic chemistry] ... DMMCS
Dimethylmuconic Acid [Organic chemistry] ... DMMA
Dimethylnaphthalene [Organic chemistry] ... DMN
Dimethylnitrosamine [Also, DMNA, NDMA] [Organic chemistry] ... DMN
Dimethylnitrosamine [Also, DMN, NDMA] [Organic chemistry] ... DMNA
Dimethyloctadecanamine N-Oxide [Organic chemistry] ... DONO
Dimethyloctadiene [Organic chemistry] ... DMOD
Dimethyloctatriene [Organic chemistry] ... DMOT
Dimethylol Dihydroxyethyleneurea [Used to provide durable press finish in fabrics] ... DMDHEU
Dimethylol dimethylhydantoin [Organic chemistry] ... DMDMH
Dimethylolpropionic Acid [Organic chemistry] ... DMPA
Dimethylolpropyleneurea [Organic chemistry] ... DMPU
Dimethylolurea [Organic chemistry] ... DMU
Dimethyloxazolidinedione [Pharmacology] ... DMO
Dimethylphenol [Organic chemistry] ... DMP
Dimethylphenylenediamine [Organic chemistry] ... DMPD
Dimethylphosphorodithioate [Organic chemistry] ... DMPDT
Dimethylpiperazine [Also, DMPP] [Organic chemistry] ... DMP
Dimethylpiperazine [Also, DMP] [Organic chemistry] ... DMPP
Dimethylsilapentane Sulfonate [Organic chemistry] ... DSS
Dimethylsuberimidate [Organic chemistry] ... DMS
Dimethyltetrahydrothiadiazinethione [Pesticide] [Organic chemistry] ... DMTT
(Dimethyltriazenyl)imidazolecarboxamide [Dacarbazine] [Also, DTIC] [Antineoplastic drug] ... DIC
(Dimethyltriazenyl)imidazolecarboxamide [Dacarbazine] [Also, DIC] [Antineoplastic drug] ... DTIC
Dimethyltryptamine [Hallucinogenic agent] ... DMT
Dimethyluracil [Biochemistry] ... DMU
Dimethynaphthidine [An indicator] [Chemistry] ... DMN
Dimidius [One-Half] [Pharmacy] ... DIM
Dimidius [One-Half] [Pharmacy] ... DIMID
Diminish ... DMSH
Diminished ... DIM
Diminishing Error Method of Optimization for Networks [Data processing] ... DEMON
Diminishing Manufacturing Sources and Material Shortages ... DMSM
Diminuendo [Getting Softer] [Music] ... DIM
Diminutive ... DIM
Dimis, Inc. [NASDAQ symbol] ... DMIS
Dimitrovgrad [Bulgaria] [Seismograph station code, US Geological Survey] ... DIM
Dimitrovski Komunisticheski Mladezhki Suiuz [Bulgaria] ... DKMS
Dimitrovski Suiuz na Narodnata Mladesh [Bulgaria] ... DSNM
Dimmer ... DIM
Dimmer ... DMR
Dimmitt, TX [Radio station call letters] ... KDHN
Dimondale, MI [Radio station call letters] ... WDTB
Dimple Die ... DPDI
DIMUS [Digital Multibeam Steering] **Narrow-Band Accelerated** ... DNA
Dimyristoyl-Lecithin [Biochemistry] ... DML
Dimyristoylphosphatidylcholine [Biochemistry] ... DMPC
Dinamika Sploshnoj Sredy [A publication] ... Din Sploshn Sredy
Di(naphthyl)phenylenediamine [Organic chemistry] ... DNPD
Dinar [Monetary unit in Bahrain] ... BD
Dinar [Monetary unit in Tunisia] ... D
Dinar [Monetary unit in Algeria] ... DA
Dinar [Monetary unit in Yugoslavia] ... DIN
Dinar [Monetary unit in Iraq] ... ID
Dinar [Monetary unit in Jordan] ... JD
Dinar [Monetary unit in Kuwait] ... KD
Dinard [France] [Airport symbol] ... DNR
Dine Bizaad Nanil' lih/Navajo Language Review [A publication] ... NLR
Dinero Contante [Cash] [Spanish] ... DC
Diners Club, Inc. [NYSE symbol] [Delisted] ... DCL
Dining ... DNG
Dining Permit [Slang] ... DP
Dining Room ... DR
Dinitro-ortho-Cresol [Also, DNOC] [Herbicide] ... DN
Dinitro-ortho-Cresol [Also, DN] [Herbicide] ... DNOC
Dinitro-ortho-secondary-butylphenol [Also, DNOSBP, DNSBP] [Herbicide] ... DNBP
Dinitro-ortho-secondary-butylphenol [Also, DNBP, DNSBP] [Herbicide] ... DNOSBP
Dinitro-ortho-secondary-butylphenol [Also, DNBP, DNOSBP] [Herbicide] ... DNSBP
Dinitrobenzenesulfonic [Organic chemistry] ... DNBS
Dinitrobenzidine [Organic chemistry] ... DNB
Dinitrobenzoic Acid [Organic chemistry] ... DNBA
Dinitrocarbanilide [Organic chemistry] ... DNC
Dinitrocellulose [Organic chemistry] ... DNC
Dinitrochlorobenzene [Organic chemistry] ... DNCB
Dinitrocyclohexylphenol [Insecticide] ... DNOCHP
Dinitrodiphenyl Disulfide [Organic chemistry] ... DNDS
Dinitrofluorobenzene [Also, DNFB, FDNB] [Organic chemistry] ... DFB
Dinitrofluorobenzene [Also, DFB, FDNB] [Organic chemistry] ... DNFB
Dinitronaphtholsulfonic Acid [Organic chemistry] ... DNNS

Dinitrophenyl [*Biochemistry*] ... Dnp
Dinitrophenyl [*Organic chemistry*] ... DNP
Dinitrophenylated Keyhole Limpet Hemocyanin [*Immunology*] ... DNP-KLK
(Dinitrophenylazo)phenol [*Organic chemistry*] ... DNAP
Dinitrophenylhydrazine [*Also, DNPH*] [*Organic chemistry*] ... DNP
Dinitrophenylhydrazine [*Also, DNP*] [*Organic chemistry*] ... DNPH
Dinitropropyl Acrylate [*An explosive*] ... DNPA
Dinitrosalicylate [*Organic chemistry*] ... DNSA
Dinitrosalicylic [*Organic chemistry*] ... DNS
Dinitrosopentamethylenetetramine [*Organic chemistry*] ... DNPT
Dinitrosopiperazine [*Animal carcinogen*] ... DNPZ
Dinitrosoterephthalamide [*Organic chemistry*] ... DNTA
Dinitrotoluene [*Organic chemistry*] ... DNT
Dinitrotrifluoromethyl [*Organic chemistry*] ... DNT
Dinka [*MARC language code*] [*Library of Congress*] ... din
Dinking Die [*Tool*] ... DKDI
Dinner Bell Foods [*NASDAQ symbol*] ... DINB
Dinner Theater ... D-T
Dinonyl Sebacate [*Organic chemistry*] ... DNS
Dinosaur National Monument ... DINO
Dinuba, CA [*Radio station call letters*] ... KOJY
Dinuba, CA [*Radio station call letters*] ... KRDU
Diocesan Home Missionary ... DHM
Diocesan Library, Boston, MA [*Library symbol*] ... MBDio
Diocesan Library, Milwaukee, WI [*Library symbol*] [*Obsolete*] ... WMDio
Diocesan Library, Philadelphia, PA [*Library symbol*] [*Obsolete*] ... PPDio
Diocesan Travelling Mission [*Roman Catholic*] ... DTM
Diocese ... DIO
Diocese [*or Diocesan*] ... DIOC
Diocese of Central New York, Syracuse, NY [*Library symbol*] ... NSYDCN
Dioceses ... DIOS
Dioctyl Adipate [*Organic chemistry*] ... DOA
Dioctyl Azelate [*Organic chemistry*] ... DOZ
Dioctyl Fumarate [*Organic chemistry*] ... DOF
Dioctyl Isophthalate [*Organic chemistry*] ... DOIP
Dioctyl Phosphate [*Organic chemistry*] ... DOP
Dioctyl Phthalate [*Also, DEHP*] [*Organic chemistry*] ... DOP
Dioctyl Sebacate [*Organic chemistry*] ... DOS
Dioctyl Sodium Sulfosuccinate [*Organic chemistry*] ... DSS
Dioctyl Terephthalate [*Organic chemistry*] ... DOTP
Diode ... D
Diode ... DIO
Diode Array Rapid Scan Spectrometer ... DARSS
Diode-Capacitor-Diode ... DCD
Diode-Capacitor-Diode Gate ... DCDG
Diode-Capacitor Gate ... DCG
Diode Curve Tracer ... DCT
Diode-Diode Logic [*Physics*] ... DDL
Diode Flat Pack ... DFP
Diode Function Generator ... DFG
Diode Gate ... DG
Diode Ion Injector ... DII
Diode Ion Source Injector ... DISI
Diode Logic ... DL
Diode Microwave Oscillator ... DMO
Diode Phase Shifter ... DPS
Diode Phase Shifter Module ... DPSM
Diode Qualification Program ... DQP
Diode Qualification Test ... DQT
Diode Qualification Test Program ... DQTP
Diode Recovery Tester ... DRT
Diode Resistor Transistor Logic ... DRTL
Diode Semiconductor Device ... DSD
Diode Switch ... DS
Diode Test Program ... DTP
Diode-Transistor Logic ... DTL
Diodes, Inc. [*American Stock Exchange symbol*] ... DIO
Dionex Corp. [*NASDAQ symbol*] ... DNEX
Dionics, Inc. [*NASDAQ symbol*] ... DION
Dioniso [*A publication*] ... Dion
Diopside [*CIPW classification*] [*Geology*] ... di
Diopter [*Also, DIOPT*] [*Optics*] ... D
Diopter [*Also, D*] [*Optics*] ... DIOPT
Dioptre Spherical ... DSPH
Dioptric Strength ... DS
Dioxane-Methanol [*Scintillation solvent*] [*Bray solution*] ... DM
Dioxide [*Freight*] ... DIOX
Dip ... D
Di(p-chlorophenyl)trichloromethylcarbinol [*Miticide*] ... DTMC
Dip Coating ... DC
Dipalmitoyl Lecithin [*Biochemistry*] ... DPL
Dipalmitoyl Phosphatidylcholine [*Biochemistry*] ... DPPC
Dipentamethylenethiuram Hexasulfide [*Organic chemistry*] ... DPTH
Dipeptidyl-aminopeptidase [*An enzyme*] ... DAP
Dipeptidyl Carboxypeptidase [*An enzyme*] ... DCP
Diphenolic Acid [*Organic chemistry*] ... DPA
Diphenyl [*Organic chemistry*] ... DP
Diphenyl Carbonate [*Organic chemistry*] ... DPC
Diphenyl Oxide [*Organic chemistry*] ... DPO
Diphenyl Phosphorochloridate [*or Diphenylphosphoric Acid Monochloride*] [*Organic chemistry*] ... DPPC
Diphenyl Phthalate [*Organic chemistry*] ... DPP
Diphenyl Sulfone [*Organic chemistry*] ... DPS
Diphenylamine [*Organic chemistry*] ... DPA
Diphenylaminechloroarsine [*Tear gas*] [*Army symbol*] ... DM
Diphenylanthracene [*Organic chemistry*] ... DPA
Diphenylanthracene Endoperoxide [*Organic chemistry*] ... DAE
Diphenylcarbazide [*Organic chemistry*] ... DPC
Diphenylchloroarsine [*Tear gas*] [*Army symbol*] ... DA
Diphenylcyanoarsine [*A war gas*] ... DC
Diphenylguanidine [*Organic chemistry*] ... DPG
Diphenylhexatriene [*A fluorophore*] [*Organic chemistry*] ... DPH
Diphenylhydantoin [*Anticonvulsant*] ... DPH
Diphenylphenylenediamine [*Organic chemistry*] ... DPPD
Diphenylpicrylhydrazyl [*Analytical chemistry*] ... DPPH
Diphenylstilbene [*Organic chemistry*] ... DPS
Diphenylthiohydantoin [*Organic chemistry*] ... DPTH
Diphenyltrichloroethane [*Also, DPT*] [*Organic chemistry*] ... DPE
Diphenyltrichloroethane [*Also, DPE*] [*Organic chemistry*] ... DPT
Diphosgene [*Poison gas*] [*Army symbol*] ... DP
Diphosphoglycerate [*Also, DPGA*] [*Biochemistry*] ... DPG
Diphosphoglycerate [*Also, DPG*] [*Biochemistry*] ... DPGA
Diphosphoglyceromutase [*An enzyme*] ... DPGM
Diphosphoinositide [*Biochemistry*] ... DPI
Diphosphopyridine Nucleotide [*Also, ARPPRN, NAD*] [*Biochemistry*] ... DPN
Diphosphopyridine Nucleotide Glycohydrolase [*Also, NaDase*] [*An enzyme*] ... DPNase
Diphosphopyridine Nucleotide, Reduced Form [*Biochemistry*] ... DPNH
Diphosphothiamine [*Also, TDP, TPP*] [*Biochemistry*] ... DPT
Diphtheria [*Medicine*] ... DIP
Diphtheria [*Medicine*] ... DIPH
Diphtheria Pertussis Prophylactic [*Medicine*] ... DPP
Diphtheria, Pertussis, and Tetanus [*Also, DTP*] [*Immunology*] ... DPT
Diphtheria/Tetanus [*Immunology*] ... DIPH/TET
Diphtheria, Tetanus [*Medicine*] ... DT
Diphtheria, Tetanus, Pertussis [*Also, DPT*] [*Immunology*] ... DTP
Diphtheria, Tetanus, Poliovirus [*Vaccine*] [*Medicine*] ... DTP
Diphtheria-Tetanus Toxoid [*Medicine*] ... DTT
Diphtheria-Tetanus Vaccine [*Medicine*] ... DT/VAC
Diphtheria Toxin Normal [*Medicine*] ... DTN
Diphtheria Toxoid [*Immunology*] ... DIPH TOX
Diphtheria Toxoid, Alum Precipitated [*Immunology*] ... DIPH TOX AP
Dipicolinic Acid [*Organic chemistry*] ... DPA
Diplexer [*Electronics*] ... DIPLXR
Diploid Number [*Genetics*] ... 2N
Diploma ... DIP
Diploma ... DIPL
Diploma in Advanced Engineering [*British*] ... DAE
Diploma in Agriculture ... DipAgr
Diploma in Anesthetics [*British*] ... DA
Diploma in Applied Mechanics [*British*] ... Dip AM
Diploma in Applied Parasitology and Entomology [*British*] ... DAP & E
Diploma of the Architectural Association School of Architecture [*British*] ... AA Dip
Diploma in Architecture [*British*] ... D Arch
Diploma in Architecture [*British*] ... Dip Arch
Diploma in Art ... DA
Diploma in Art and Design [*British*] ... Dip AD
Diploma in Automobile Engineering [*British*] ... D Au E
Diploma in Aviation Medicine [*British*] ... D Av Med
Diploma in Bacteriology [*British*] ... Dip Bact
Diploma of British Orthoptics ... DBO
Diploma in Business Administration [*British*] ... Dp BA
Diploma in Chemistry [*British*] ... Dipl Chem
Diploma in Chest Diseases [*British*] ... DCD
Diploma in Child Health [*British*] ... DCH
Diploma of Choir Master of the Royal College of Organists [*British*] ... CHM
Diploma in Civic Design [*British*] ... DipCD
Diploma in Clinical Medicine of the Tropics [*British*] ... DCMT
Diploma in Clinical Pathology [*British*] ... DCP
Diploma in Clinical Pathology [*British*] ... Dip Clin Path
Diploma in Clinical Psychology [*British*] ... DCP
Diploma of the College of Aeronautics [*British*] ... DCAe
Diploma of College of Obstetricians and Gynecologists ... DCOG
Diploma of the College of Optics [*British*] ... DCO
Diploma of the College of Pathologists [*British*] ... DC Path
Diploma in Commerce ... Dipl Kaufm
Diploma in Commerce ... Dipl Kfm
Diploma in Commerce ... Dkfm
Diploma of Curative Education [*British*] ... DCE
Diploma in Dental Health [*British*] ... DDH
Diploma in Dental Orthopaedics [*British*] ... DDO
Diploma in Dental Public Health [*British*] ... DDPH
Diploma in Dental Public Health, Royal College of Surgeons of England ... DDPHRCS Eng
Diploma in Dermatological Medicine [*British*] ... DDM
Diploma of Designer, Royal College of Art [*British*] ... Des RCA
Diploma in Diagnostic Radiology [*British*] ... DDR
Diploma of Education [*British*] ... DipEd
Diploma in Education Administration and Supervision ... D Ed AS
Diploma in Elementary Education ... D El Ed
Diploma in Engineering [*British*] ... Dip Eng

Diploma in Engineering [*British*] ... Dipl Eng
Diploma of the Faculty of Homoeopathy [*British*] ... DF Hom
Diploma of Fine Art [*British*] ... DFA
Diploma in Government Administration [*British*] ... DGA
Diploma in Graduate Studies [*British*] ... DGS
Diploma in Gynecology and Obstetrics [*British*] ... DGO
Diploma of Higher Education ... DipHE
Diploma in Industrial Chemistry [*British*] ... Dip Ind Chem
Diploma in Industrial Health [*British*] ... DIH
Diploma of the Institute of Engineering [*British*] ... DIE
Diploma in Laryngology and Otolaryngology [*British*] ... DLO
Diploma of Loughborough College [*British*] ... DLC
Diploma in Management Studies [*British*] ... DMS
Diploma in Mathematics [*British*] ... Dipl Math
Diploma in Medical Jurisprudence [*British*] ... DMJ
Diploma in Medical Jurisprudence (Clinical) [*British*] ... DMJ (Clin)
Diploma in Medical Jurisprudence (Pathological) [*British*] ... DMJ (Path)
Diploma in Medical Radio-Diagnosis [*British*] ... DMRD
Diploma in Medical Radio-Therapy [*British*] ... DMRT
Diploma in Medical Radiology [*British*] ... DMR
Diploma in Medical Radiology and Electrology [*British*] ... DMRE
Diploma in Medical Services Administration [*British*] ... DMSA
Diploma of Membership of Imperial College of Science and Technology, University of London [*British*] ... DIC
Diploma in Microbiology [*British*] ... Dip Microbiol
Diploma in Municipal Administration [*British*] ... DMA
Diploma in Musical Education, Royal Scottish Academy of Music and Drama ... Dip (Mus Ed) RSAM
Diploma in Natural Therapeutics [*British*] ... DNTh
Diploma in Naturopathy [*British*] ... ND
Diploma in Nursing ... DN
Diploma in Nutrition [*British*] ... DN
Diploma in Obstetrics, Royal College of Obstetricians and Gynaecologists [*British*] ... D Obst RCOG
Diploma in Occupational Hygiene [*British*] ... DO Hyg
Diploma in Occupational Therapy ... DipOT
Diploma of Occupational Therapy ... DOT
Diploma in Ophthalmic Medicine and Surgery [*British*] ... DOMS
Diploma in Ophthalmology [*British*] ... DO
Diploma in Opthalmic Surgery [*British*] ... D Ch O
Diploma in Orthodontics [*British*] ... DOrth
Diploma in Orthoptics [*British*] ... D Orth
Diploma in Osteopathy [*British*] ... DO
Diploma in Pathology [*British*] ... D Path
Diploma in Physical Education [*British*] ... Dip PE
Diploma in Physical Education [*British*] ... DPE
Diploma in Physical Medicine [*British*] ... D Phys Med
Diploma in Physics [*British*] ... Dipl Phys
Diploma of Physio-Therapy [*British*] ... DPT
Diploma of Physiotherapy [*British*] ... DPhys
Diploma of Practitioners in Advertising [*British*] ... DipPA
Diploma in Psychiatry [*British*] ... D Psych
Diploma in Psychological Medicine [*British*] ... DPM
Diploma in Psychology [*British*] ... Dip Psych
Diploma in Public Administration [*British*] ... Dipl PA
Diploma in Public Administration [*British*] ... DPA
Diploma in Public Dentistry [*British*] ... DPD
Diploma in Public Dentistry, University of Dundee [*British*] ... DPDU Dund
Diploma in Public Health [*British*] ... DPH
Diploma in Radiology [*British*] ... DR
Diploma of Royal Academy of Dramatic Art [*British*] ... DipRADA
Diploma of the Royal College of Obstetrics and Gynaecology [*British*] ... DRCOG
Diploma of the Royal College of Pathologists [*British*] ... DRC Path
Diploma of the Royal College of Science and Technology, Glasgow [*British*] ... DRC
Diploma of the Royal Scottish Academy of Music and Drama ... DRSAM
Diploma of the Royal Technical College [*British*] ... DRTC
Diploma in Sanitary Science [*British*] ... DSSc
Diploma Scam [*FBI investigation of mail-order colleges*] ... DIPSCAM
Diploma in Social Administration [*British*] ... Dip Soc Ad
Diploma in Social Administration [*British*] ... DSA
Diploma in Social Medicine [*British*] ... Dip Soc Med
Diploma in Social Medicine [*British*] ... DSM
Diploma in Social Studies [*British*] ... Dip Soc Studies
Diploma of Teacher of Physiotherapy ... DipTP
Diploma in Technology [*British*] ... Dip Tech
Diploma of Technology (Engineering) [*British*] ... Dip Tech (Eng)
Diploma in Theology [*British*] ... D Theol
Diploma in Theory and Practice of Teaching [*British*] ... DipTPT
Diploma in Theory and Practice of Teaching (Durham University) [*British*] ... DThPT
Diploma in Therapeutic Radiology [*British*] ... DTR
Diploma in Town Planning [*British*] ... DipTP
Diploma in Tropical Child Health [*British*] ... DTCH
Diploma in Tropical Hygiene [*British*] ... DTH
Diploma in Tropical Medicine [*British*] ... DTM
Diploma in Tropical Medicine and Hygiene [*British*] ... DTM & H
Diploma in Tropical Public Health [*British*] ... DTPH
Diploma in Tropical Veterinary Medicine [*British*] ... DTVM
Diploma in Tuberculosis and Chest Diseases [*British*] ... DTCD
Diploma in Tuberculous Diseases [*British*] ... DTD
Diploma of the University of Paris ... DUP
Diploma of the University of Southampton [*British*] ... DUS
Diploma in Venereology [*British*] ... Dip Ven
Diploma in Veterinary Anaesthesia [*British*] ... DVA
Diploma in Veterinary Hygiene [*British*] ... DVH
Diploma in Veterinary State Medicine ... DVSM
Diplomacy Test of Empathy [*Psychology*] ... DTE
Diplomate ... DIPT
Diplomate in Dental Orthoptics of the Royal College of Physicians and Surgeons of Glasgow [*British*] ... DDORCPS Glas
Diplomate in Orthodontics, Royal College of Surgeons of England ... D Orth RCS Eng
Diplomatic Conference of International Maritime Law ... DCML
Diplomatic and Consular Officers, Retired ... DACOR
Diplomatic Corps ... DC
Diplomatic History [*A publication*] ... Dipl Hist
Diplomatic Protection Group [*of the London Metropolitan Police*] ... DPG
Diplomatic Service Administration Office [*British*] ... DSAO
Diplomatic Telecommunications Service ... DTS
Diplome d'Etudes Universitaires Generales [*France*] ... DEUG
Dipole ... DP
Dipole ... DPL
Dipole Antenna System ... DAS
Dipole Flat Plate ... DFP
Dipole Xerography ... DIXY
Dipolog [*Philippines*] [*Airport symbol*] ... DPL
Dipropylacetic Acid [*Also, VPA*] [*Valproic acid*] [*Anticonvulsant compound*] ... DPA
Dipropylamine [*Organic chemistry*] ... DPA
Dipropylene Glycol Dibenzoate [*Organic chemistry*] ... DGDB
Dipropylnitrosamine [*Also, DPNA, NDPA*] [*Organic chemistry*] ... DPN
Dipropylnitrosamine [*Also, DPN, NDPA*] [*Organic chemistry*] ... DPNA
Dipropyltryptamine [*Hallucinogenic agent*] ... DPT
Dipstick ... DPSTK
Dipyridyl [*Also, DIPY*] [*Organic chemistry*] ... DIP
Dipyridyl [*Also, DIP*] [*Organic chemistry*] ... DIPY
Dire Dawa [*Ethiopia*] [*Airport symbol*] ... DIR
Direccao Geral de Seguranca [*Secret police*] [*Portugal*] ... DGS
Direccion de Aviacion Comercial y Civil [*Peru*] ... DAC
Direccion General de Archivos y Bibliotecas. Boletin [*A publication*] ... Dir Gen Bol
Direccion General de Normas [*Mexico*] [*National standards organization*] ... DGN
Direccion de Inteligencia Nacional [*Chilean secret police*] [*Superseded by CNI*] ... DINA
Direct [*In relation to flight plan clearances and type of approach*] [*Aviation*] ... DCT
Direct ... DRCT
Direct Access ... DA
Direct Access Beacon System ... DABS
Direct Access Communications Channels ... DACC
Direct Access Computing ... DAC
Direct Access Device Space Management ... DADSM
Direct Access Memory ... DAM
Direct Access Method [*Data processing*] ... DAM
Direct Access Programing System [*Data processing*] ... DAPS
Direct-Access RADAR Channel [*System*] [*Aviation*] ... DARC
Direct Access to Reference Information [*Xerox*] ... DATRIX
Direct Access Storage Device [*Acronym pronounced "daz-dee"*] [*Data processing*] ... DASD
Direct Access Storage Facility [*Data processing*] ... DASF
Direct Access Terminal Application [*Data processing*] ... DATA
Direct Acting ... DACT
Direct Acting Steam ... DAS
Direct Action [*Bomb or shell fuze*] ... DA
Direct Adjacent Channel Interference ... DACI
Direct Advertising [*Later, Printing Paper Quarterly*] [*A publication*] ... d/a
Direct Advisory of Recorded Transactions ... DART
Direct Aerial Fire Support [*Military*] ... DAFS
Direct Aid for Full Yaw ... DAFFY
Direct Air Cycle ... DAC
Direct Air Support [*Military*] ... DAS
Direct Air Support Center [*Military*] ... DASC
Direct Air Support Flight [*Military*] ... DASF
Direct Air Support Squadron [*Military*] ... DASq
Direct Air Support Squadron [*Military*] ... DASSQ
Direct Air Support Team [*Military*] ... DAST
Direct Altitude and Identification Readout [*Aviation*] ... DAIR
Direct Altitude and Identification Readout Equipment [*Aviation*] ... DAIRE
Direct Ascent ... DA
Direct-Ascent Powered-Flight Simulation [*NASA*] ... DAPFS
Direct Assistance and Training Command [*Navy*] ... DATC
Direct Automotive Support ... DAS
Direct Billing ... DB
Direct Broadcast Satellite [*Television transmission system in which signals are transmitted by satellite directly to individual locations*] ... DBS
Direct Carbon Transfer ... DCT
Direct Carrier Injection ... DCI
Direct Centrifugal Flotation [*Parasitology*] ... DCF

Direct Command ... DC
Direct Commissary Support System [*DoD*] ... DICOMSS
Direct Communications Link [*US/USSR*] ... DCL
Direct Computer Input ... DCI
Direct Computer Input Load Module ... DCILM
Direct Connection Module [*Data processing*] ... DCM
Direct-to-Consumer [*Sales*] ... DTC
Direct Contact Evaporator [*Chemical engineering*] ... DCE
Direct Conversion Reactor ... DCR
Direct Coombs' Test ... DCT
Direct Cortical Response ... DCR
Direct Couple Operating System ... DCOS
Direct Couple System ... DCS
Direct Coupled ... DC
Direct-Coupled FET [*Field Effect Transistor*] **Logic** [*Integrated circuitry*] ... DCFL
Direct Coupled Loop Network [*Data processing*] ... DCLN
Direct-Coupled Transistor Logic ... DCTL
Direct-Coupled Unipolar Transistor Logic ... DCUTL
Direct from Cuba [*A publication*] ... Dir fr Cu
Direct Current ... DC
Direct Current [*A publication*] ... Direct Curr
Direct-Current Amplifier ... DCA
Direct-Current Analog Input ... DCAI
Direct-Current Arc ... DCA
Direct-Current Circuit Analysis Program [*Data processing*] ... DICAP
Direct-Current Differential Transformer ... DCDT
Direct-Current Dump ... DCD
Direct-Current Electroluminescence ... DCEL
Direct-Current Experiments [*Nuclear energy*] ... DCX
Direct-Current Free Gyro ... DCFG
Direct-Current Generator ... DCG
Direct-Current Key Pulsing ... DCKP
Direct-Current Plasma [*Spectrometry*] ... DCP
Direct-Current Plasma Torch ... DCPT
Direct Current and Power Electronics [*A publication*] ... Direct Curr & Power Electron
Direct-Current Power Supply Panel ... DCPSP
Direct-Current Restorer ... DCR
Direct-Current Sensor ... DCS
Direct-Current Servo Amplifier ... DCSA
Direct-Current Test Volts ... VDCT
Direct-Current Torque Motor ... DCTM
Direct-Current Voltage Reference ... DCVR
Direct-Current Voltage Regulator ... DCVR
Direct-Current Volts ... DCV
Direct-Current Working Volts ... DCWV
Direct-Current Working Volts ... VDCW
Direct Cycle ... DC
Direct Cycle Diphenyl Reactor ... DCDR
Direct Data Channel ... DDC
Direct Data Entry [*Data processing*] ... DDE
Direct Data Entry Replacement System ... DDERS
Direct Data Entry System ... DDES
Direct Dial In ... DDI
Direct Dial Telephone System ... DDTS
Direct Digital Control ... DDC
Direct Digital Control System ... DDCS
Direct Digital Encoder ... DDE
Direct Digital Interface ... DDI
Direct Digital Numerical Controller ... DDNC
Direct Distance Dialing [*of telephone numbers for toll calls*] ... DDD
Direct and Distribution [*Postal Service*] ... D & D
Direct Drawing Change ... DDC
Direct Drive ... DDR
Direct Electrical Linkage ... DEL
Direct Electronic Fourier Transform [*Camera*] ... DEFT
Direct Encounter ... DE
Direct Energy Conversion ... DEC
Direct Energy Conversion Laboratory [*Johnson Space Center*] [*NASA*] ... DECL
Direct Energy Conversion Operation ... DECO
Direct Energy Transfer ... DET
Direct Energy Weapon ... DEW
Direct Engineering Estimate ... DEE
Direct Engineering Hours ... DEH
Direct English Access and Control [*Data processing*] ... DEACON
Direct Exchange [*Army*] ... DX
Direct Exchange Activity ... DXA
Direct Exchange Item [*Army*] ... DXI
Direct Fire Antitank Weapon ... DFAW
Direct Fire Simulator ... DFS
Direct Fire System ... DFS
Direct Flight ... DF
Direct Flight Mode ... DFM
Direct Flight Test ... DFT
Direct Flow ... DF
Direct Flow Sampler [*Meteorology*] ... DFS
Direct Fluorescence ... DF
Direct Fluorescent Antibody (Stain) [*Clinical medicine*] ... DFA
Direct Fluorescent Antibody Technique [*Clinical chemistry*] ... DFAT
Direct Forces Support [*Military*] ... DFS
Direct Foreign Investment ... DFI
Direct Grant ... DG
Direct Imaging Mass Analyzer ... DIMA
Direct Immunofluorescent Assay [*Analytical biochemistry*] ... DFA
Direct-Induced High-Explosive Simulation Technique ... DIHEST
Direct Information Access Network for Europe [*Commission of the European Communities*] [*Information service*] ... DIANE
Direct-Injected Stratified Charge [*Engine*] ... DISC
Direct Injection Enthalpimetry ... DIE
Direct Instant Response Electronic Composition ... DIREC
Direct Instructional System for Teaching Arithmetic and Reading ... DISTAR
Direct Internal Noise Amplification ... DINA
Direct Investor ... DI
Direct Inward Dialing [*Telecommunications*] ... DID
Direct Keying System ... DKS
Direct Labor ... DL
Direct Labor Charges by Organization ... DLCO
Direct Labor Man-Hours ... DLMH
Direct Labor Organization ... DLO
Direct Labor Time ... DLT
Direct Laboratories Estimate ... DLE
Direct Latex Agglutination Pregnancy [*Test*] [*Medicine*] ... DAP
Direct Least Squares [*Econometrics*] ... DLS
Direct Letter Perfect [*Actors' slang*] ... DLP
Direct Liaison Authorized [*Military*] ... DIRLAUTH
Direct to Licensee ... DTL
Direct Lift Control ... DLC
Direct Line [*Followed by telephone number*] ... DL
Direct Logistical Support ... DLS
Direct Lytic Factor [*Polypeptide from cobra venom*] ... DLF
Direct Magnification Radiography ... DMR
Direct Mail Advertising Association [*Later, DMMA*] ... DMAA
Direct Mail Fundraisers Association ... DMFA
Direct Mail/Marketing Association ... DMMA
Direct Mail/Marketing Educational Foundation ... DMMEF
Direct Mail Shelter Development System [*Civil Defense*] ... DMSDS
Direct Maintenance Cost ... DMC
Direct Maintenance Man-Hours per Flight Hour [*Navy*] ... DMMH/FH
Direct Man-Hours ... DMH
Direct Marketing [*A publication*] ... DM
Direct Marketing Computer Association ... DMCA
Direct Marketing Creative Guild [*Formerly, DMWG*] ... DMCG
Direct Marketing Credit Association ... DMCA
Direct Marketing Market Place [*A publication*] ... DMMP
Direct Marketing Writers Guild [*Later, DMCG*] ... DMWG
Direct Match Screening ... DMS
Direct Matrix Abstraction Process ... DMAP
Direct Measurements Explorer [*Satellite*] ... DME
Direct Measurements Explorer A [*Satellite*] ... DME-A
Direct Memory Access [*Data processing*] ... DMA
Direct Memory Access Control [*Data processing*] ... DMAC
Direct Metal Mastering [*System for manufacturing phonograph records*] ... DMM
Direct Microscopic Clump Counts ... DMCC
Direct Microscopic Count ... DMC
Direct Mission Support Equipment ... DMSE
Direct Modulation Technique ... DMT
Direct Molded Sole [*Boot*] [*Military*] ... DMS
Direct Multiplexor Channel ... DMC
Direct Notice of Cancellation [*Insurance*] ... DNC
Direct Numerical Control [*Data processing*] ... DNC
Direct Obligation ... DO
Direct Operating Cost ... DOC
Direct Order ... DO
Direct Order Recording and Invoicing System [*A computer-based system of British petroleum companies*] ... DORIS
Direct Outward Dialing [*Telecommunications*] ... DOD
Direct Path ... DP
Direct Patient Care [*Medicine*] ... DPC
Direct Payroll Deposit ... DPD
Direct Plaque-Forming Cell [*s*] [*Immunology*] ... dPFC
Direct Port [*Transportation*] ... DP
Direct Power Conversion [*Nuclear energy*] ... DPC
Direct Procurement Method [*Personal property*] ... DPM
Direct Procurement Petty Officer ... DPPO
Direct Product Actual Hours ... DPAH
Direct Program Control ... DPC
Direct Question [*Legal testimony*] ... DQ
Direct RADAR Scope Camera ... DRSC
Direct RADAR Scope Recorder ... DRSR
Direct-Reaction Calculation ... DRC
Direct Reading Azimuth Protractor [*Bureau of Mines*] ... DRAP
Direct Reading Emission Spectrograph ... DRES
Direct Reading Encoder ... DRE
Direct Reading Pocket Chamber ... DRPC
Direct Reading Receiver ... DRR
Direct Reading Totalizer ... DRT
Direct Readout Equatorial Weather Satellite ... DREWS
Direct Readout Ground Station ... DRGS

Direct Readout Image Dissector [Camera system]............DRID
Direct Readout Infrared Radiometer................DRIR
Direct Readout Miss Distance Indicator ....DROMDI
Direct Readout Satellite................DROS
Direct Readout Weather Satellite................DROWS
Direct Reckoning Analyzer................DRA
Direct Recording Oscillograph................DRO
Direct Reduction [Ironmaking process]................DR
Direct Reduction Iron [Ironmaking process] ....DRI
Direct Reentry Telemetry [Air Force]................DRET
Direct Reentry Telemetry System [Air Force]................DRETS
Direct Relief Foundation................DRF
Direct/Reverse................D/R
Direct Route................DR
Direct Satellite Communications................DSC
Direct Scope Recording System................DSRS
Direct Selling Association................DSA
Direct Selling Educational Foundation................DSEF
Direct Ship................D/S
Direct Ship Release................DSR
Direct Ship Requirements................DSR
Direct Shipment Order................DSO
Direct Side Force Control [Aviation]................DSFC
Direct Space Refinement................DSR
Direct Stage Recorder................DSR
Direct Station Selection................DSS
Direct Steamer................DS
Direct-Step-on-the-Wafer [Microelectronics]................DSW
Direct Suggestion under Hypnosis................DSUH
Direct Supply Support [Military]................DSS
Direct Supply Support Activity [Army]................DSSA
Direct Supply Support Depot [Military]................DSSD
Direct Supply Support Point [Military]................DSSP
Direct Support [Army]................DS
Direct Support Aviation Section [Army]................DSAS
Direct Support Element................DSE
Direct Support Group [Army]................DSG
Direct Support Item [Army]................DSI
Direct Support Maintenance [Army]................DSM
Direct Support Operations................DSOPS
Direct Support System [Army]................DSS
Direct Support Unit [Army]................DSU
Direct Support Unit/General Support Unit [Computer system]......DSU/GSU
Direct Support Unit Standard Supply System [Army]................DS4
Direct System Output [Data processing]................DSO
Direct Turn-Over................DTO
Direct Variable Cost................DVC
Direct Vendor Delivery [DoD]................DVD
Direct-View Device [Night vision]................DVD
Direct-View Navigation Aid................DVNA
Direct View Optics................DVO
Direct-Viewing Storage Tube................DVST
Direct Voice Line................DVL
Direct Wire Burglar Alarm................DWBA
Direct Writing................D/W
Direct Writing Oscillograph................DWO
Directed Audit Program................DAP
Directed Drawing Instrument................DDI
Directed Duty Assignment [Military]................DDA
Directed Energy [Weaponry]................DE
Directed Fan Engine................DFE
Directed Proliferation................DP
Directed Reading Activity [Education]................DRA
Directed to Request Termination of Inactive Duty Training
    Orders [Navy]................TERMINACTRAORD
Directed Studies Group [Air Force]................DSG
Directed Studies Group [Air Force]................DSGp
Directing Ordnance Officer [Military] [British]................DOO
Directing Point................DP
Directing Staff................DISTAFF
Directing Staff................DS
Direction................DIR
Direction [A publication]................Direc
Direction................DIRON
Direction................DRCTN
Direction Action [Bomb fuze]................DA
Direction of Arrival................DOA
Direction of Arrival/Time of Arrival ....DOA/TOA
Direction Center [SAGE] [RADAR]................DC
Direction Center Active [SAGE] [RADAR]................DCA
Direction Center - Ground Controlled Intercept [SAGE] [RADAR]....DC/GCI
Direction Center Standby [SAGE] [RADAR]................DCS
Direction Cosine................DC
Direction Cosine Linkage................DIRCOL
Direction Cosine Matrix................DCM
Direction Cycle................DC
Direction de l'Environnement, Hydro-Quebec, Montreal, PQ,
    Canada [Library symbol]................CaQMHDE
Direction Finder [or Finding] [Radio aid to navigation]................DF
Direction Finder [or Finding] [Radio aid to navigation]................DIF
Direction Finding Antenna................DFA

Direction Finding Equipment................DFE
Direction Finding Receiver................DFR
Direction Finding Set [or System]................DFS
Direction Finding Station [Aviation]................DFSTN
Direction of Fire [Weaponry]................DOF
Direction of Flight................DOF
Direction et Gestion [A publication]................Dir Gestion
Direction et Gestion des Entreprises [A publication]............Dir Gestion Entr
Direction of President................DP
Direction and Range Acquisition System................DARAS
Direction des Recherches et Moyens d'Essais [France]................DRME
Direction of Relative Movement [Navigation]................DRM
Direction de Service de Securite Militaire [France]................DSM
Direction Sports [An association]................DS
Direction de la Surveillance du Territoire [French security
    organization]................DST
Direction of Systems Management................DSM
Directional Aerial Disposal [Insecticide spray]................DAD
Directional Antenna Phasing Network................DAPN
Directional Arm Lock................DAL
Directional Automatic Realignment of Trajectory................DART
Directional Command Activated Sonobuoy [System] [Navy]................DICAS
Directional Command Activated Sonobuoy System [Navy]............DICASS
Directional Control [Rocket]................DC
Directional Control Valve................DCV
Directional Controlled Rocket-Assisted Projectile................DICORAP
Directional Coupler................DC
Directional Coupler Synthesis................DICOSY
Directional Discontinuity Ring Radiator................DDRR
Directional Doppler................DIDO
Directional Emittance Measurement................DEM
Directional Explosive Echo Ranging................DEER
Directional Frequency Analysis and Recording System................DIFAR
Directional Gyro................DG
Directional Gyro Mode................DGM
Directional Gyro Operation................DGO
Directional Gyro Unit................DGU
Directional Horizon Indicator................DHI
Directional Infrared Intrusion Detector................DIRID
Directional Radio................D/R
Directional Radio Beacon [ITU designation]................RD
Directional Reference Locator................DRL
Directional Variable Microphone................DVM
Directional Warhead Fuze................DWF
Directionally-Controlled Rocket-Assisted Projectile................DISCORAP
Directionally Solidified [Metallurgy]................DS
Directione Propria [With Proper Direction] [Pharmacy]................DIR PROP
Directione Propria [With Proper Direction] [Pharmacy]................DP
Directions for Education in Nursing via Technology................DENT
Directive................DIR
Directive Antenna with Reflector................DR
Directive Coordinated and Approved by Budget Director [Air
    Force]................DICAB
Directive-Organic [Designation for biologically oriented,
    authoritarian psychiatrists]................D-O
Directive Parental Counseling................DPC
Directives Control [Employment and Training Administration]
    [Department of Labor]................DC
Directives Documentation [NASA]................DD
Directives Management Officer [FAA]................DMO
Directivity Index................DI
Directly................DRCTY
Directly Executable Test-Oriented Language [Data processing]........DETOL
Directly Heated................DH
Director [Films, television, etc.]................D
Director [or Directorate]................DIR
Director of Administrative Services [US Military Government,
    Germany]................DAS
Director, Advanced Base Logistics Control [Navy]................DABLC
Director, Advanced Base Office, Atlantic [Navy]................DABOA
Director, Advanced Base Office, Pacific [Navy]................DABOP
Director of Advanced Systems Management................DASM
Director of Advanced Systems Planning................DASP
Director [or Directorate] of Advanced Technology [Air Force]................DAT
Director of Aeronautical Inspection [British]................DAI
Director of Aeroplane Production [Air Ministry] [British] [World
    War II]................DAP
Director of Air Material [Navy] [British]................DAM
Director of Air Ministry Factories [British] [World War II]................DAMF
Director of Air Personnel [Air Force] [British]................DAP
Director of Air Training Corps [British]................DATC
Director of Aircraft................DA
Director aircraft capable of controlling drones or missiles
    [Designation for all US military aircraft]................D
Director of Aircraft Equipment [Ministry of Aircraft Production]
    [British]................DAE
Director of Aircraft Maintenance and Repair [Navy] [British]................DAMR
Director of Aircraft Maintenance and Repair (Washington)
    [Navy]................DAMR(W)
Director of Airfield and Carrier Requirements [British]................DACR
Director of Allied Air Cooperation [World War II]................DAAC

Director of Ammunition Production [*Ministry of Supply*] [*British*] [*World War II*]..DAP
Director of Anti-U-Boat Division [*British*] [*World War II*].......................DAUD
Director of Antisubmarine Material [*British*] ....DA/SM
Director of Antisubmarine Warfare [*British*] ....DA/SW
Director of Armament Engineering [*Military*] [*Canada*]................DARME
Director of Armament Supplies [*British*] [*World War II*]................DAS
Director of Army Dental Services [*British*] ....DADS
Director of Army Education [*British*] ....DAE
Director of Army Fire Services [*British*] ....DAFS
Director [*or Directorate*] of Army Legal Services [*British*]................DALS
Director of Army Postal Services [*British*] ....DAPS
Director of Army Programs ....DAP
Director of Army Psychiatry [*British*] ....DAP
Director of Army Requirements [*British*] ....DAR
Director of Army Staff Duties [*British*] ....DASD
Director of Army Technical Information ....DATI
Director of Army Training [*British*] ....DAT
Director of Army Transportation.................DAT
Director of Army Veterinary and Remount Services [*British*]...........DAVRS
Director of Army Welfare Services [*British*] ....DAWS
Director of Artillery [*British*] ....D of A
Director Assignment Console ....DAC
Director, Atlantic Division, Bureau of Yards and Docks [*Obsolete*] ...............DIRLANTDOCKS
Director Attack Mine [*Air Force*]................DAM
Director [*or Directorate*] of Audiovisual Activities [*Army*]................DAVA
Director of Base Medical Services ....DBMS
Director of Biological Research [*Military*] [*British*] ....DBR
Director Bomber [*Air Force*] ....DB
Director of Bombing Operations [*Air Ministry*] [*British*] [*World War II*] ....DBOps
[*Term of reference for the*] Director of Britain's Secret Intelligence Service [*Said to date from the desire for anonymity on the part of the department's first director, Sir Mansfield Cumming*] C
Director of Camouflage [*British*]................DOC
Director of Central Intelligence................DCI
Director of Central Intelligence Directive................DCID
Director of Civil Affairs [*Military*] [*British*] ....DCA
Director for Civil Disturbance Planning and Operations ....CDPO
Director [*or Directorate*] of Civil Engineering [*Air Force*]................DCE
Director of Civilian Marksmanship [*Army*] ....DCM
Director of Civilian Personnel [*Navy*] ....DCP
Director of Clothing and Stores [*Military*] [*British*] ....DCS
Director of Coastal Forces Material Department [*British*] ....DCFMD
Director of Combat Development [*British*] ....DCD
Director of Combat Developments [*Army*] ....DCD
Director of Combat Operations................DCO
Director of Combined Operations (India)................DCO(I)
Director of Combined Operations (Middle East) ....DCO(ME)
Director to Commissary Operations [*Military*] ....DOCO
Director of Communications Development [*Ministry of Aircraft Production*] [*British*] ....DCD
Director [*or Directorate*] of Communications - Electronics [*ADC*]................DCE
Director Comptroller Systems ....DCS
Director of Contract Labour [*Admiralty*] [*British*] ....DCL
Director of Contracts [*Military*] [*British*]................DOC
Director, Defense Communications Agency ....DDCA
Director [*or Directorate*] of Defense Research and Engineering [*DoD*]................DDR & E
Director [*or Directorate*] of Defense Research and Engineering [*DoD*]................DDRE
Director, Defense Test and Evaluation [*Army*] ....DDTE
Director of Dental Services [*British*]................DDS
Director Design Engineering................DDE
Director, Development and Operations................DDO
Director [*or Directorate*] of Development Planning [*Air Force*]................DDP
Director of Dockyards [*Admiralty*] [*British*]................D of D
Director of Dockyards [*Admiralty*] [*British*]................DOD
Director of Economics, Civil Affairs [*War Office*] [*British*] [*World War II*]................DE(CA)
Director of the Education Department [*Navy*] [*British*] ....DED
Director of Educational Services [*Air Force*] [*British*] ....DES
Director of Engine Development [*Ministry of Aircraft Production*] [*British*] ....DED
Director of Engineer Stores Service [*British*] ....DES
Director of Engineering [*Navy*] [*British*]................DE
Director of Engineering and Industrial Services................DEIS
Director of Equal Employment Opportunity [*Department of Labor*]......DEEO
Director Error [*Military*]................DE
Director [*or Directorate*] of Evaluation [*Army*] ....DEV
Director of Facilities and Engineering [*Military*] ....DFAE
Director Field Maintenance [*Army*]................DIRFM
Director, Field Support Activity ................DIRFLDSUPPACT
Director Fire Control System [*Air Force*]................DFCS
Director of Fleet Maintenance [*Navy*] [*British*]................DFM
Director of Fleet Management Services [*Navy*] [*British*]................DFManS
Director, Fleet Training................DFT
Director, Flight Operations [*NASA*]................DFO
Director of Flight Safety [*Air Force*]................DFS

Director [*or Directorate*] of Flight Safety Research [*Air Force*]................DFSR
Director, Food Management [*Army*]................DFM
Director of Fortifications and Works [*British*]................DFW
Director-General [*British*]................DG
Director-General [*United Nations*]................D-G
Director-General of Aircraft Equipment [*Ministry of Aircraft Production*] [*British*]................DGAE
Director-General of Armoured Vehicles [*British*]................DGAV
Director-General of Army Education [*British*]................DGAE
Director-General of Army Medical Services [*British*]................DGAMS
Director-General of Army Requirements [*British*]................DGAR
Director-General of Civil Aviation [*British*]................DGCA
Director-General of Civilian Clothing [*British*]................DGCC
Director-General of Engine Production [*British*]................DGEP
Director-General of Equipment [*Air Force*] [*British*]................DGE
Director-General of Explosives Production [*Ministry of Supply*] [*British*] [*World War II*]................DGX
Director-General of Fighting Vehicles and Engineer Equipment [*British*]................DGFVE
Director-General of Filling Factories [*Formerly, DGOF(F)*] [*Ministry of Supply*] [*British*] [*World War II*]................DGFF
Director-General of Ground Defence [*Military*] [*British*]................DGGD
Director-General of Guided Weapons and Electronics [*British*]................DGGWL
Director-General of Internal Audit [*British*]................DGIA
Director-General of Manpower [*Ministry of Labour*] [*British*]................DGM
Director-General of Mechanical Engineering, Supply [*Ministry of Supply*] [*British*]................DGMechE(S)
Director-General of Medical Services [*British*]................DGMS
Director-General of Military Training [*British*]................DGMT
Director-General of Munitions Production [*Ministry of Supply*] [*British*] [*World War II*]................DGMP
Director-General of Naval Manpower and Training [*British*] ....DGNMT
Director-General of Naval Personnel Services [*British*]................DGNPS
Director-General of Ordnance Factories [*Ministry of Supply*] [*British*] [*World War II*]................DGOF
Director-General of Ordnance Factories (Filling) [*Later, DGFF*] [*Ministry of Supply*] [*British*] [*World War II*]................DGOF(F)
Director-General, Ordnance Systems [*Canada*] ....DGOS
Director-General of Organization [*RAF*] [*British*] ....DGO
Director-General of Personnel [*British*]................DGP
Director-General of Production [*British Air Ministry*]................DGP
Director-General of Quality Assurance [*British*]................DGQA
Director-General of Raw Materials [*Ministry of Supply*] [*British*] ....DGRM
Director-General of Royal Air Force Medical Services [*British*]....DGRAFMS
Director-General of Scientific Research and Development [*Ministry of Supply*] [*British*]................DGSRD
Director-General of Servicing and Maintenance [*RAF*] [*British*] ....DGSM
Director-General, Ships [*Navy*] [*British*]................DGShips
Director-General of Small Arms Ammunition Production [*Ministry of Supply*] [*British*] [*World War II*]................DGSAA
Director-General of Statistics and Planning [*Ministry of Supply*] [*British*]................DGSP
Director-General of Supplies and Transport (Naval) [*British*]................DGST(N)
Director-General of the Territorial Army [*British*]................DGTA
Director-General of Transportation Services [*British*]................DG Tn
Director-General of Weapons [*Army*] [*British*]................DGW(A)
Director-General of Weapons Department (Naval) [*British*]................DGW(N)
Director-General of Weapons and Instruments Production [*Military*] [*British*]................DGWIP
Director-General of Works [*RAF*] [*British*]................DGW
Director of Graves Registration [*British*]................DGR
Director of Ground Defence [*Military*] [*British*]................DGD
Director of Ground Safety [*Air Force*]................DGS
Director of Health Services [*Army*]................DHS
Director of Home Operations [*Air Ministry*] [*British*] [*World War II*] ....DHO
Director of Industrial Operations [*Military*]................DIO
Director of Industrial Planning [*War Office*] [*British*] [*World War II*] ....DIP
Director of Infantry [*Military*] [*British*]................DI
Director of Inland Water Transport Service [*British*]................DIWT
Director [*or Directorate*] of Installations [*Air Force*] [*Abolished 1953, functions transferred to Department of Defense*]................DI
Director of Intelligence [*RAF*] [*British*]................D of I
Director of Intelligence, Division of the Admiralty [*British*]................DIDA
Director of International Logistics [*Military*]................DIL
Director International Military Staff Memorandum [*NATO*]................DIMS
Director, Joint Staff [*Military*]................DJS
Director, Joint Staff Memorandum [*Military*]................DJM
Director, Joint Staff Memorandum [*Military*]................DJSM
Director of Laboratories [*AFSC*]................DL
Director of Laboratories ....DOL
Director of Laboratory Programs [*Navy*]................DLP
Director of Labour [*Military*] [*British*]................DL
Director, Launch Operations [*NASA*]................DLO
Director of Liaison and Munitions [*Military*] [*British*]................DLM
Director of Machine Tools [*Ministry of Aircraft Production and Ministry of Supply*] [*British*]................DMT
Director, Management Information Systems [*Army*]................DMIS
Director of Manpower and Organization [*Air Force*]................DMO
Director of Manpower Planning [*British*]................DMP
Director, Marine Corps Reserve................DMCR
Director of Maritime Operations [*RAF*] [*British*]................DMO

Director of Materiel Readiness [*Army*] DMR
Director of Mechanical Engineering [*War Office*] [*British*] [*World War II*] DME
Director of Medical Activities DMEDA
Director of Medical Education DME
Director of Medical and Health Services [*British*] DMHS
Director of Medical and Sanitary Services [*British*] DMSS
Director of Medical Services [*British*] DMS
Director Meteorological Officer, Ministry of Defence, London [*British*] DMO
Director for Military Assistance DFMA
Director of Military Assistance DMA
Director of Military Intelligence [*US, British*] DMI
Director [*or Directorate*] **of Military Operations** DMO
Director of Military Operations and Intelligence DMOI
Director of Military Personnel [*Air Force*] DMP
Director of Military Training DMT
Director of Missile Safety Research [*Air Force*] DMSR
Director of Movements and Quartering [*British*] DMQ
Director for Mutual Security DMS
Director, National Security Agency [*Pronounced "dern-za"*] DIRNSA
Director of Naval Accounts DNA
Director of Naval Air Division DNAD
Director of Naval Air Organization [*British*] DNAO
Director of Naval Air Warfare and Flying Training [*British*] DAWT
Director, Naval Audit Service NAVAUDSVC
Director, Naval Communications Instruction DNCINST
Director, Naval Communications Notice DNCNOTE
Director of Naval Construction [*British*] DNC
Director of Naval Equipment DNE
Director of Naval Guided Weapons [*British*] DNGW
Director of Naval History DIRNAVHIST
Director of Naval Intelligence [*US, British*] DNI
Director of Naval Laboratories DNL
Director of Naval Manning and Training [*British*] DNMT
Director of Naval Medical Services [*Royal Australian Navy*] DNMS
Director of Naval Oceanography and Meteorology [*British*] DNOM
Director of Naval Officer Procurement DNOP
Director of Naval Operations DNO
Director of Naval Ordnance [*Admiralty*] [*British*] DNO
Director of Naval Ordnance, Torpedoes, and Mines [*Royal Australian Navy*] DOTM
Director of Naval Physical Training and Sport [*British*] DNPTS
Director of Naval Records and History DNRH
Director of Naval Recruiting [*British*] D of NR
Director of Naval Recruiting [*British*] DNR
Director of the Naval Service [*Canada, 1910-1926*] DNS
Director of Naval Service Conditions [*British*] DNSC
Director, Naval Transportation Service [*Later, CNTS*] DNTS
Director of Naval Weather Service, Ministry of Defence [*British*] DNWS
Director of Navy Communications DNC
Director, Navy Petroleum Reserves DNPR
Director, Navy Program Planning DNPP
Director, Navy Publication and Printing Service DIRNAVPUBPRINTSERV
Director of Nuclear Safety [*Air Force*] DNS
Director of Nuclear Safety Research [*Air Force*] DNSR
Director of Nursing DON
Director of Nursing Education DNE
Director, Office of Civil Defense DIROCD
Director, Office of Oceanography [*UNESCO*] DOO
Director, Office of Transport and Communications [*Department of State*] DOTC
Director of Operational Requirements [*Air Ministry*] [*British*] DOR
Director of Operational Training [*RAF*] [*British*] DOT
Director of Operations DO
Director of Operations Division [*Navy*] [*British*] DOD
Director of Operations Division (Foreign) [*Navy*] [*British*] DOD(F)
Director of Operations Division (Home) [*Navy*] [*British*] DOD(H)
Director of Operations Narcotics Control Reports [*CIA*] DONCS
Director of Operations, Operational Plans Officer DOOPO
Director of Operations, Training and Intelligence [*Army*] DOTI
Director of Ordnance Factories [*Ministry of Supply*] [*British*] [*World War II*] DOF
Director of Ordnance Factories, Engineering Factories [*Ministry of Supply*] [*British*] [*World War II*] DOF(E)
Director of Ordnance Factories, Explosives Factories [*Ministry of Supply*] [*British*] [*World War II*] DOF(X)
Director of Ordnance Services [*Military*] [*British*] DOS
Director of Overseas Civil Aviation [*British*] DOCA
Director, Pacific and Alaskan Divisions, Bureau of Yards and Docks [*Obsolete*] DIRPACALDOCKS
Director, Pacific Division, Bureau of Yards and Docks [*Obsolete*] DIRPACDOCKS
Director of Pathology DP
Director of Personal Services [*Navy*] [*British*] DPS
Director of Personnel and Administration [*Army*] DIRPA
Director of Personnel and Community Activities [*Army*] DPCA
Director, Personnel Department [*Marine Corps*] DPD
Director of Personnel, Marine Corps DPMC
Director of Personnel Planning [*Air Force*] DPP
Director of Personnel Procurement and Training [*Air Force*] DPPT
Director of Personnel and Training [*Army*] D/P & T
Director of Personnel and Training [*Army*] DPT
Director of Physical Training and Sports [*Navy*] [*British*] DPTS
Director of Planes [*Admiralty*] [*British*] D of P
Director of Planning of War Production [*Air Ministry*] [*British*] [*World War II*] DPWP
Director of Plans Division [*Navy*] [*British*] DPD
Director of Plans Division (Quartering) [*Navy*] [*British*] D of PD(Q)
Director of Plans and Programs [*Army*] DP & P
Director of Plans and Training [*Military*] DPT
Director, Polaris Technical [*Missiles*] DPT
Director of Postal Services [*British*] DPS
Director of Postings [*RAF*] [*British*] DP
Director of Printing and Stationery Services [*Military*] [*British*] DPSS
Director of Prisoners of War [*British*] [*World War II*] DPW
Director of Procurement and Production [*Army*] DPP
Director of Program Analysis and Evaluation DPAE
Director of Programs [*Air Force, Army*] DP
Director of Public Instruction DPI
Director of Public Prosecutions [*British*] DPP
Director of Public Relations DPR
Director of Public Service D of PS
Director of Radio Equipment [*Navy*] [*British*] DRE
Director of Radio Production [*Air Ministry*] [*British*] [*World War II*] DRP
Director of Recruiting and Organization [*Military*] [*British*] DRO
Director of Religious Education DRE
Director of Remounts [*Military*] [*British*] D of R
Director [*or Directorate*] **of Research and Development** [*Air Force*] DRD
Director [*or Directorate*] **of Research and Engineering** [*Military*] DRE
Director and Response Tester DART
Director of the Royal Armoured Corps [*British*] DRAC
Director of Royal Artillery [*British*] DRA
Director of Salvage Department [*Navy*] [*British*] DS/VD
Director of Scientific Research [*British*] DSR
Director of Security DSEC
Director of Selection and Personnel [*British*] DSP
Director Selector Panel DSP
Director of Services [*Air Force*] DS
Director of Signal Department [*Navy*] [*British*] DSD
Director of Small Vessels Pool [*Admiralty*] [*British*] DSVP
Director of Special Weapons [*Army*] DSW
Director of Special Weapons and Vehicles [*Military*] [*British*] DSWV
Director of Staff Duties [*Military*] [*British*] DSD
Director Standing Group Memorandum [*NATO*] DSGM
Director [*or Directorate*] **of Statistical Services** [*Air Force*] DSS
Director of Stores [*Navy*] [*British*] DOS
Director of Stores (Washington) [*Navy*] D of S (W)
Director, Strategic Systems Project Office [*Navy*] DIRSSP
Director of Strategic Target Planning [*Military*] DSTP
Director of Strategic Target Planning Staff [*Offutt AFB*] [*Military*] DSTPS
Director of Supplies and Transport [*British*] DST
Director of Supply and Maintenance [*Army*] DSM
Director [*or Directorate*] **of Support** [*Army*] DOS
Director of Surveillance and Reconnaissance [*Army*] DSR
Director of Tactical Division [*Navy*] [*British*] D of TD
Director of Tactical Investigation [*Military*] [*British*] DTI
Director/Telecommunications and Command and Control System DTACCS
Director of Telecommunications Management [*Air Force*] [*Abolished, 1970*] DTM
Director of Traffic D of T
Director Train Indicator DTI
Director [*or Directorate*] **of Training** [*Army*] DOT
Director of Training and Staff Duties Division [*Navy*] [*British*] DTSD
Director of Undersea Warfare, Ministry of Defence, London DUSW
Director of Underwater Weapons [*British*] DUW
Director of Unexploded Bomb Disposal Department [*Navy*] [*British*] DUBDD
Director, United States Naval Weather Service DUSNWS
Director, Vehicle and Field Engineering [*Military*] [*Canada*] DVFE
Director of Veterinary Services [*Military*] [*British*] DVS
Director of War Archives [*British*] DWA
Director of Weapon Systems Analysis [*Army*] DWSA
Director of Weapons Surface Projects (Naval) [*British*] DWSP(N)
Director, Weapons Systems Evaluation Group DIRWSEG
Director of Women Marines DIRW
Director, Women's Army Corps DWAC
Director of Women's Auxiliary Air Force [*British*] DWAAF
Director of Works [*Air Ministry*] [*British*] DW
Director of Works and Buildings [*British*] DOWB
Director of Wreck Disposal DWD
Directorate of Accident Prevention [*RAF*] [*British*] DAP
Directorate of Advanced Systems Technology DAST
Directorate of Aeronautical Inspection Services [*British*] DAIS
Directorate of Aerospace Studies [*Air Force*] DAS
Directorate of Air Force Welfare [*British*] DAFW
Directorate of Aircraft Production Development [*British*] DAPD
Directorate of Airlift [*Air Force*] DOAL
Directorate of Ammunition [*Military*] [*Canada*] DAMMO
Directorate of Armament Development [*Ministry of Aircraft Production*] [*British*] [*World War II*] DArmD

Directorate of Armament Requirements [*RAF*] [*British*] .... DAR
Directorate for Armed Forces Information and Education [*Military*] ... DAFIE
Directorate, Army MAP [*Military Assistance Program*] **Logistics** .... DAML
Directorate of Army Research .... DAR
Directorate for Astronomical, Atmospheric, Earth, and Ocean Sciences [*National Science Foundation*] .... AAEO
Directorate of Atomic Warfare .... DAW
Directorate of Ballistic Missiles .... D/BM
Directorate of Biological Operations .... DBO
Directorate of Civil Aviation .... DCA
Directorate for Civil Disturbance Planning and Operations [*Army*] .... DCDPO
Directorate for Classification Management [*DoD*] .... DCM
Directorate of Combat Developments [*Army*] .... DCD
Directorate of Design Engineering [*NASA*] .... DE
Directorate of Fleet Supply Duties [*Navy*] [*British*] .... DFSD
Directorate of Flight and Missile Safety Research [*Air Force*] .... DFMSR
Directorate for the Freedom of Information [*Formerly, Directorate for Security Review*] [*DoD*] .... DFI
Directorate General of Highways [*Vietnam*] .... DGOH
Directorate of Geophysics Research [*Air Research and Development Command*] .... DGR
Directorate for Inspection Services [*Assistant Secretary of Defense for Administration*] .... DINS
Directorate of Intelligence (Operations) [*RAF*] [*British*] .... DI(O)
Directorate of Intelligence (Research) [*RAF*] [*British*] .... DI(R)
Directorate of Intelligence (Security) [*RAF*] [*British*] .... DI(S)
Directorate of Internal Affairs and Communications [*Allied German Occupation Forces*] .... DIAC
Directorate of Logistic Support Management [*or Manager*] .... D/LSM
Directorate of Materials and Structures Research and Development [*British*] .... DMSRD
Directorate of Materiel Management .... DMM
Directorate of Medical Research [*Army*] .... DMR
Directorate of Microgram Services [*RAF*] [*British*] .... DMS
Directorate of Military Satellite Systems .... DMSS
Directorate of Military Support .... DOMS
Directorate of Missile Captive Test .... DMCT
Directorate of National Coordination .... DNC
Directorate of Naval Administration Planning [*British*] .... DNAP
Directorate of Naval Air Warfare [*British*] .... DNAW
Directorate of Naval Operational Requirements [*British*] .... DNOR
Directorate of Naval Operations and Trade [*British*] .... DNOT
Directorate of Naval Plans [*British*] .... DNPlans
Directorate of Naval Security [*British*] .... DNSy
Directorate of Naval Signals [*British*] .... DNS
Directorate of Naval Warfare [*British*] .... DNW
Directorate Notice .... DN
Directorate Office Instruction .... DOI
Directorate of Policy [*Air Ministry*] [*British*] .... DPA
Directorate of Public Relations (Naval) [*British*] .... DPR(N)
Directorate of Quartering (Navy) [*British*] .... D of Q(N)
Directorate for Resource Management [*CIA*] .... DRM
Directorate of Scientific Information Service [*Canada*] .... DSIS
Directorate of Scientific Information Service, Defence Research Board, Ottawa, ON, Canada [*Library symbol*] .... CaOONDR
Directorate of Scientific and Technical Intelligence [*British*] .... DSTI
Directorate of Stores and Clothing Development [*British*] .... DSCD
Directorate of Systems Engineering .... DSE
Directorate of Technical Development .... DTD
Directorate of Technical Research [*Navy*] [*Canada*] .... DTR
Directorate of Training Developments [*Army*] .... DTD
Directorate of War Organization [*RAF*] [*British*] .... DWO
Directorate of Weapons Effect Tests .... DWET
Directorate of Weapons and Engineering Research [*Canada*] .... DWER
Directorio Revolucionario Iberico de Liberta [*Revolutionary Directorate for Iberian Liberation*] .... DRIL
Directors Advisory Committee [*National Institutes of Health*] .... DAC
Directors and Boards [*A publication*] .... Dir Boards
Director's Discretionary Fund .... DDF
Directors-in-Exile [*British*] .... DIE
Directors Guild of America .... DGA
Director's Instant Reversible Talkback [*Device enabling contact between director in control room and crew in studio*] .... DIRT
Director's Office .... DO
Directors' and Officers' [*Liability insurance*] .... D & O
Directory .... DIR
Directory .... DRCTY
Directory of American Book Workers [*A publication*] .... DABW
Directory Assistance System/Microfilm [*Bell System*] .... DAS/M
Directory of Automated Information Systems .... DAIS
Directory of Computerized Information in Science and Technology .... DCIST
Directory Development Study .... DDS
Directory of Directories [*A publication*] .... DOD
Directory of Engineering Document Services [*A publication*] .... DEDS
Directory of Environmental Documentation Centres [*Information service*] [*EURONET*] .... ENDOC
Directory of Environmental Research Projects in the European Communities [*Information service*] [*EURONET*] .... ENREP
Directory. Indiana Crop Improvement Association. Seed Certification Service [*A publication*] .... Dir Indiana Crop Impr Ass Seed Certif Serv
Directory of International Mail [*A publication*] .... DIM
Directory of International Mail [*A publication*] .... DOIM
Directory of Mortuary Operations [*Army*] .... DMO
Directory of Opportunities for Graduates [*A publication*] .... DOG
Directory of Post Office .... DPO
Directory Project [*Bell Laboratories*] .... DIR/ECT
Directory Scope Analysis Program [*Bell System*] .... DSAP
Directory of Special Libraries and Information Centers [*A publication*] .... DSL
Directory Tape Processor .... DTP
Directory Verification Processor [*Data processing*] .... DIRVIR
DirectVision [*Home-information service of KPIX-TV*] .... DV
Dirham [*Monetary unit in Morocco*] .... DH
Dirham [*Monetary unit in Iraq*] .... DIRH
Diritto Ecclesiastico [*A publication*] .... DE
Dirranbandi [*Australia*] [*Airport symbol*] [*Obsolete*] .... DRN
Dirt [*Gossip*] [*Theatre slang*] .... D
Dirt [*or Dust*] **Collector** .... DC
Dirty Book .... DB
Dirty Lubricating Oil .... DLO
Dirty Old Man [*Slang*] .... DOM
Dirty Word Remover [*Graffiti-removing chemical*] .... DWR
Dirty Writers of America [*Satirical*] .... DWA
DISA [*Danske Industri Syndikat A/S*] **Information** [*A publication*] .... DISA Inf
Disability .... DIS
Disability .... DSBLTY
Disability Assistance .... DA
Disability Benefit Law .... DBL
Disability Income [*Insurance*] .... DI
Disability Insurance .... DI
Disability Insurance Sales Course [*LUTC*] .... DISC
Disability Insurance Training Council .... DITC
Disability Policy Board [*Veterans Administration*] .... DPB
Disability Retirement Branch [*BUPERS*] .... DRB
Disability Review Council [*Military*] .... DRC
Disability Rights Center .... DRC
Disability Rights Education and Defense Fund .... DREDF
Disability Severance Pay .... DSABLSEVP
Disable .... DSABL
Disable .... DSBL
Disabled American Veterans .... DAV
Disabled American Veterans Auxiliary .... DAVA
Disabled List [*Athletics*] .... DL
Disabled Officers Association .... DOA
Disabled People's International .... DPI
Disabled Veterans Outreach Program .... DVOP
Disablement Advisory Committee [*Department of Employment*] [*British*] .... DAC
Disablement Resettlement Office [*or Officer*] [*Department of Education*] [*British*] .... DRO
Disaccharide Repeating Unit [*Biochemistry*] .... DRU
Disaccommodation Factor .... DF
Disadvantaged Children Series [*A publication*] .... DCS
Disalicylidenepropanediamine [*Organic chemistry*] .... DSPD
Disappearance of Single Cell [*Assay*] [*Cytology*] .... DSC
Disappearing .... DISAPG
Disappearing Automatic Retaliatory Target .... DART
Disapprove .... DISAP
Disarm Education Fund .... DEF
Disarmament [*A publication*] .... Disarm
Disarmament and Arms Control [*A publication*] .... Disarm & Arms Control
Disarmament Commission [*Also, DC (UN), UNDC*] .... DC
Disarmament Commission of the United Nations [*Also, DC, UNDC*] .... DC (UN)
Disarmament Resource Center .... DRC
Disarmed Military Personnel .... DMP
Disassemble .... DA
Disassemble .... DISASSM
Disassembly .... DISASSY
Disassembly Inspection Report .... DIR
Disassembly/Reassembly Equipment [*Nuclear energy*] .... D/RE
Disassembly/Reassembly Station [*Nuclear energy*] .... D/RS
Disaster Action Team [*Red Cross*] .... DAT
Disaster Assistance Centers [*Federal Emergency Management Agency*] .... DAC
Disaster Assistance Recovery Teams [*Military*] .... DART
Disaster Control .... DC
Disaster Control Center .... DCC
Disaster Control Force .... DCF
Disaster Control Group .... DCG
Disaster Control Officer .... DCO
Disaster Control Plan .... DCP
Disaster Control Recovery Plan .... DCRP
Disaster Control Team .... DCT
Disaster Loan Corporation [*Dissolved 1945, functions transferred to Reconstruction Finance Corporation*] .... DLC
Disaster Nursing Chairman [*Red Cross*] .... DNC
Disaster Preparedness .... DP

Disaster Preparedness Planning Board ... DPPB
Disaster Representative [*Red Cross*] ... DR
Disaster Research Group [*National Academy of Sciences*] ... DRG
Disaster Research Institute ... DRI
Disaster Services [*Red Cross*] ... DS
Disaster Unemployment Assistance [*Disaster Relief Act*] ... DUA
Disaster Warning System [*National Weather Service*] ... DWS
Disaster Welfare Inquiry Center [*Federal disaster planning*] ... DWIC
Disbandment Control Unit [*Allied Military Government of Occupied Territory*] [*Post-World War II*] ... DCU
Disburse ... DISB
Disbursement ... DISBMT
Disbursement Voucher ... DV
Disbursing ... DSBG
Disbursing Clerk [*Navy rating*] ... DK
Disbursing Clerk, Chief [*Navy rating*] ... DKC
Disbursing Clerk, First Class [*Navy rating*] ... DK1
Disbursing Clerk, Master Chief [*Navy rating*] ... DKCM
Disbursing Clerk, Second Class [*Navy rating*] ... DK2
Disbursing Clerk, Senior Chief [*Navy rating*] ... DKCS
Disbursing Clerk, Third Class [*Navy rating*] ... DK3
Disbursing Office Serial Number ... DOSN
Disbursing Officer ... DISBOFF
Disbursing Officer ... DO
Disbursing Officers Liaison Office ... DOLO
Disbursing Officer's Voucher ... DOV
Disbursing Order ... DO
Disbursing Station Symbol Number [*Military*] ... DSSN
Disbursing and Transportation Office ... DATO
Disc Data Unit ... DDU
Disc Diameter ... DD
Disc Grind [*Technical drawings*] ... DG
Disc Issuer and Assistant [*Sports*] ... D
Disc Jockey ... DJ
Disc Jockeys (Mobile) [*Public-performance tariff class*] [*British*] ... DJ
Disc Storage Device ... DSD
Discard at Failure ... DAF
Discard-at-Failure Maintenance ... DAFM
Discard Message ... DM
Discarding Sabot ... DS
Discharge ... DIS
Discharge ... DISCH
Discharge and Advise [*Medicine*] ... D/A
Discharge Afloat ... DA
Discharge Gratuity [*Military*] ... DISGRAT
Discharge [*from Military Service*] **under Honorable Conditions, under Age of Authorized Enlistment** ... HCMU
Discharge [*from Military Service*] **under Honorable Conditions, Convenience of Government** ... HCCG
Discharge [*from Military Service*] **under Honorable Conditions, Convenience of Man** ... HCCM
Discharge [*from Military Service*] **under Honorable Conditions, Dependency Existing Prior to Enlistment** ... HCDP
Discharge [*from Military Service*] **under Honorable Conditions, Expiration of Enlistment** ... HCEE
Discharge [*from Military Service*] **under Honorable Conditions, Medical Survey** ... HCMS
Discharge [*from Military Service*] **under Honorable Conditions, Minor Enlisted Without Consent, under 18 at Time of Discharge** ... HCMW
Discharge [*from Military Service*] **under Honorable Conditions, Unsuitable** ... HCUS
Discharge Multimedia Environmental Goals [*Environmental Protection Agency*] ... DMEG
Discharge Ringing Frequency ... DRF
Discharged ... D
Discharged [*Medicine*] ... DC
Discharged Dead [*On a serviceman's papers*] ... DD
Discharged Patient [*British*] ... DP
Discharged Prisoners' Aid [*British*] ... DPA
Discharged Prisoners' Aid Society [*British*] ... DPAS
Discharged to Sick Quarters ... DSQ
Discharged on Visit [*Psychiatry*] ... DOV
Disciple ... DIS
Disciple ... DP
Disciples of Christ ... DC
Disciples of Christ Historical Society ... DCHS
Disciples of Christ Historical Society, Nashville, TN [*Library symbol*] ... TNDC
Disciples of the Divine Master [*Roman Catholic women's religious order*] ... PDDM
Disciples Peace Fellowship ... DPF
Disciplinary ... DSPL
Disciplinary Barracks ... DB
Disciplinary Training Center ... DTC
Discipline ... DIS
Discipline ... DSPLN
Disclosure of Classified Military Information [*to foreign governments*] ... DCMI
Discographical Forum [*A publication*] ... Disco Forum
Discoid Lupus Erythematosus [*Medicine*] ... DLE
Discolored ... Discol
Discomfiture Index [*Weather*] ... DI
Discone Antenna ... DSC
Disconnect ... DIS
Disconnect ... DISC
Disconnect ... DISCON
Disconnect Actuating Tools [*Nuclear energy*] ... DAT
Disconnect at Lift-Off [*NASA*] ... DALO
Disconnect Switch ... DS
Disconnecting Device ... DD
Disconnecting Manhole ... DM
Discontinue ... DC
Discontinue ... DISC
Discontinue ... DISCON
Discontinue ... DS
Discontinue ... DSCONT
Discontinue Previous Medication [*Pharmacology*] ... DPM
Discontinued ... DIS
Discontinued ... discontd
Discontinued Post Office [*Deltiology*] ... DPO
Discontinuous Variational Method ... DVM
Discount ... DIS
Discount ... DISC
Discount ... DISCT
Discount Fabrics, Incorporated [*American Stock Exchange symbol*] [*Delisted*] ... DFI
Discount Merchandiser [*A publication*] ... Discount M
Discounted Cash Flow ... DCF
Discourse Processes [*A publication*] ... DP
Discover ... DISC
Discover America Travel Organizations, Inc. [*Formerly, National Association of Travel Organizations, and Discover America, Inc.*] [*Later, TIA*] ... DATO
Discoverer Recovery Capsule [*NASA*] ... DRC
Discovery [*A publication*] ... Disc
Discovery and Excavation (Scotland) [*A publication*] ... Disc Excav (Scot)
Discovery [*or Dissemination*] **of Information through Cooperative Organization** ... DICO
Discovery Oil Ltd. [*NASDAQ symbol*] ... DISV
Discovery Reports [*A publication*] ... Discovery Rep
Discrepancy ... DISCRP
Discrepancy Check ... DC
Discrepancy and Corrective Action Report ... DCAR
Discrepancy Notice [*NASA*] ... DN
Discrepancy Record [*or Report*] ... DR
Discrepancy Report ... DISCREP
Discrepancy Report Squawk Sheet [*NASA*] ... DRSS
Discrepancy Reporting System [*NASA*] ... DRS
Discrepancy in Shipment Confirmation [*DoD*] ... DISCON
Discrepancy in Shipment Report [*DoD*] ... DISREP
Discrete ... DIS
Discrete ... DISC
Discrete Activity Indicator [*NASA*] ... DAI
Discrete Address ... DA
Discrete Address Beacon System ... DABS
Discrete Address Communications System ... DACS
Discrete Autoregressive-Moving Average Model [*Statistics*] ... DARMA
Discrete Command ... DC
Discrete Data Input ... DDI
Discrete Data Output ... DDO
Discrete Depth Plankton Sampler ... DDPS
Discrete Digital Input ... DDI
Discrete Elastic System ... DES
Discrete Event Evaluator ... DEE
Discrete Fourier Transform ... DFT
Discrete Frequency Generator ... DFG
Discrete Horizon Sensor ... DHS
Discrete Input [*Data processing*] ... DI
Discrete Input High ... DIH
Discrete Input Low ... DIL
Discrete Mathematics [*A publication*] ... Discr Math
Discrete Memoryless Channel [*Data processing*] ... DMC
Discrete Network Simulation ... DNS
Discrete Network Simulation ... DNWS
Discrete Ordinate Transport ... DOT
Discrete Orthonormal Sequence ... DOS
Discrete Out Blockhouse [*NASA*] ... DOB
Discrete Out Vehicle [*NASA*] ... DOV
Discrete Output [*Data processing*] ... DO
Discrete Output High ... DOH
Discrete Rate Command ... DRC
Discrete Recovery Area ... DRA
Discrete Register ... DR
Discrete Sample Analyzer ... DSA
Discrete Sonic Jet ... DSJ
Discrete Space and Discrete Time ... DSDT
Discrete Subaortic Stenosis [*Medicine*] ... DSAS
Discrete System Concept ... DSC
Discretion ... DISCRON
Discretionary Capital Expenditure System [*Bell System*] ... DCES

Discretionary Population Effects for Riot and Stability Employment [*Crowd control*] DISPERSE
Discriminate DISCR
Discriminate DISCRM
Discriminate Function DIF
Discriminate Function Analysis DFAn
Discriminating Selector Repeater DSR
Discrimination Analysis Technique Adapted and Refined at Kwajalein [*Army*] DARK
Discrimination and Control Computer DCC
Discrimination Data Processing System DDPS
Discrimination Difficulty [*Psychometrics*] DD
Discrimination Filter DF
Discrimination RADAR DR
Discrimination RADAR Control Group DRCG
Discrimination Reversal [*Neurophysiology*] DR
Discriminator DSCRM
Discussion sur l'Alphabetisation [*A publication*] Discuss Alphabet
Discussion in Groups DIG
Discussion Paper DP
Discussions of the Faraday Society [*A publication*] Discn Faraday Soc
Discussions of the Faraday Society [*A publication*] Discuss Faraday Soc
Disease D
Disease DIS
Disease-Free Intervals DFI
Disease-a-Month [*A publication*] DM
Disease and Nonbattle Injury [*Military*] DNBI
Disease Variable [*Medicine*] DV
Disease Vector Ecology and Control Center [*Military*] DVECC
Diseases of the Chest [*A publication*] Dis Chest
Diseases of the Colon and Rectum [*A publication*] Dis Colon Rectum
Diseases of the Colon and Rectum [*A publication*] Dis Col Rec
Diseases of the Nervous System [*A publication*] Dis Ner Sys
Diseases of the Nervous System [*A publication*] Dis Nerv Syst
Diseases of the Nervous System [*A publication*] DNSYA
Disembark DISEMB
Disengage DISENG
Disengaging DSENGA
Disestablish DISESTAB
Disestablish DISTAB
Disgruntled Old Graduate [*West Point*] DOG
Dish-Rinsing DSHR
Dishekimligi Dergisi [*A publication*] Dishekim Derg
Dishonest John [*In TV series "Time for Beany"*] DJ
Dishonorable Discharge DD
Dishonorable Discharge, General Court-Martial, after Confinement in Prison [*Navy*] DDGC
Dishonorable Discharge, General Court-Martial, Immediate [*Navy*] DDGI
Dishonorable Discharge, General Court-Martial, after Violation of Probation [*Navy*] DDGP
Dishonored Check [*IRS*] DC
Dishonored Check File [*IRS*] DCF
Dishonored Check Name File [*IRS*] DCNF
Dishwasher [*Classified advertising*] DW
Disinfected Mail Study Circle DMSC
Disintegration DIS
Disintegration per Second DPS
Disintegrations per Hour DPH
Disintegrations per Minute D/M
Disintegrations per Minute D/MIN
Disintegrations per Minute DPM
Disintegrations per Minute/Second DPM/S
Disintegrations per Second DIS/SEC
Disintegrations per Second D/S
Disjunctive Normal Formula DNF
Disjunctive Syllogism [*Rule of inference*] [*Logic*] DS
Disjunctively Linear DL
Disk Allocation Table [*Data processing*] DAT
Disk, Balls, and Roller DBR
Disk-Based Operating System DBOS
Disk Controller [*Data processing*] DC
Disk Diameter [*Ophthalmology*] dd
Disk Electrophoresis DE
Disk File [*Data processing*] DF
Disk File Control [*Data processing*] DFC
Disk File Descriptor Control [*Data processing*] DFDC
Disk File Optimizer [*Data processing*] DFO
Disk Gap Band [*Parachute*] DGB
Disk Island [*Alaska*] [*Seismograph station code, US Geological Survey*] DSK
Disk Memory Controller [*Data processing*] DMC
Disk Monitor System [*Data processing*] DMS
Disk Operating System [*Data processing*] DOS
Disk Operating System/Virtual Storage [*Data processing*] DOS/VS
Disk-Oriented Computer System DOCS
Disk-Oriented Engineering System [*Data processing*] DOES
Disk Pack [*Data processing*] DP
Disk Preparation Processor [*Data processing*] DPREP
Disk Programing System [*Data processing*] DPS
Disk Recorder DR
Disk Resident Operating System [*Data processing*] DROS
Disk Storage [*Data processing*] DS
Disk Storage Unit [*Data processing*] DSU
Disk Tape [*Data processing*] D/T
Disk Turbine Assembly DTA
Disk Utility Program [*Data processing*] DUP
Diskretnyi Analiz. Sbornik Trudov [*A publication*] Diskret Analiz
Dislocation [*Medicine*] DISLOC
Dislocation Allowance [*Military*] DA
Dislocation Allowance [*Military*] DLA
Dislocations in Solids [*Elsevier Book Series*] [*A publication*] DIS
Dismantle DISM
Dismiss DISM
Dismounted DSMTD
Disney [*Walt*] **Productions** [*NYSE symbol*] [*Wall Street slang name: "Mickey Mouse"*] DIS
Disodium DISOD
Disodium Cromoglycate [*Also, DSCG*] [*Pharmacology*] DSC
Disodium Cromoglycate [*Also, DCG*] [*Pharmacology*] DSCG
Disodium Hydrophosphate [*Inorganic chemistry*] [*Also, DSP*] DSHP
Disodium Methyl Arsonate [*Herbicide*] DSMA
Disodium Phosphate [*or Dibasic Sodium Phosphate*] [*Also, DSHP*] [*Inorganic chemistry*] DSP
Disordered Action of the Heart [*Medicine*] DAH
Disorderly [*FBI standardized term*] DIS
Disorderly Conduct DC
Disorderly House DH
Disorderly Person DP
Disorders DSORDRS
Dispatch DSPCH
Dispatch Critical System DCS
Dispatch Inoperative List DIL
Dispatch Loading Only DLO
Dispatch, New Providence, NJ [*Library symbol*] NjNpD
Dispatch Note [*Business and trade*] D/N
Dispatch Point DP
Dispatch Reliability DR
Dispatch Rider [*Marine Corps*] D/R
Dispatch, Union City, NJ [*Library symbol*] NjUcD
Dispatcher DISP
Dispensary DISP
Dispensation DISP
Dispense as Directed [*Pharmacy*] DAD
Dispenser D
Dispenser DISP
Dispensetur [*Dispense*] [*Pharmacy*] DISP
Dispensing DISPNSG
Dispensing DSPNSG
Dispensing Precaution DP
Dispersal DSPRL
Dispersal Anchorage [*Navy*] DSA
Dispersal Base [*Military*] DB
Dispersal Point DP
Disperse DISP
Dispersed Emergency Station DES
Dispersed Operating Base [*Air Force*] DOB
Dispersion Against Concealed Targets [*Experiment*] [*Army*] DACTS
Dispersion Coated Fabric [*Plastics technology*] DCF
Dispersion Strengthened [*Metallurgy*] DS
Dispersion Time DT
Dispersive Delay Line DDL
Dispersive Mechanism Test DMT
Displace DSPLC
Displaced DSPLCD
Displaced Business Loan [*Small Business Administration*] DBL
Displaced Employee Program [*Department of Labor*] DEP
Displaced Homemakers Network DHN
Displaced Person [*Post-World War II*] DP
Displaced Persons Assembly Center Camp Staffs [*Allied Military Government of Occupied Territory*] [*Post-World War II*] DPACCS
Displaced Persons' Camps DPC
Displaced Persons Commission [*Terminated, 1952*] DPC
Displaced Persons Executive [*Allied Military Government detachments, Red Cross teams, and UN Relief and Rehabilitation Administration Corps*] [*Post-World War II*] DPX
Displaced Phase Center Antenna DPCA
Displaced Virtual Machine DVM
Displacement DISPL
Displacement DP
Displacement Cardiograph DCG
Displacement Gyro [*Aerospace*] DG
Displacement Method Matrix Generator DMMG
Displacement Transducer DT
Displacement Water Line DWL
Display D
Display DIS
Display DISP
Display DSPL
Display/AGAP [*Attitude Gyro Accelerometer Package*] **Electronic Control Assembly** DECA
Display Analysis Console DAC
Display Attention BITS [*Binary Digits*] [*Data processing*] DAB

Display Automated Telemetry Analyzer ... DATA
Display Buffer [*Data processing*] ... DB
Display Channel Complex ... DCC
Display Compartments [*Freight*] ... DC
Display Computer ... DC
Display Computer Control Unit ... DCCU
Display Console ... DC
Display and Control ... D & C
Display Control Console ... DCC
Display and Control Module ... DCM
Display Control Panel ... DCP
Display and Control Subsystem ... D & CS
Display and Control Unit ... DCU
Display Coupler ... DC
Display and Debriefing Subsystem ... DDS
Display and Debug Unit [*Data processing*] ... DDU
Display and Decision Area ... DDA
Display Decoder Drive ... DDD
Display Driver Unit ... DDU
Display Electronics ... DE
Display Electronics Assemblies ... DEA
Display Electronics Unit ... DEU
Display Evaluation Flight Testing ... DEFT
Display Evaluation Index ... DEI
Display Format Generator ... DFG
Display Formatting Language ... DFL
Display Formatting System ... DFS
Display Generation System ... DGS
Display Generator ... DG
Display Hold ... DH
Display Information Processor [*Air Force*] ... DIP
Display Initial Program Load ... DIPL
Display Integrated Software System and Plotting Language [*Data processing*] ... DISSPLA
Display Interactive Assembly Language [*Data processing*] ... DIAL
Display Interface Processing ... DIP
Display/Keyboard ... DK
Display and Keyboard [*Data processing*] ... DSKY
Display Logic Unit ... DLU
Display Maintenance Program ... DMP
Display Management System [*IBM Corp.*] ... DMS
Display Observer Performance Study ... DOPS
Display, Oral, Printed, and Electronic [*Media*] ... DOPE
Display-Oriented Computer Usage System ... DOCUS
Display-Oriented Language [*Data processing*] ... DOL
Display Panel ... DP
Display Power Control ... DPC
Display Power Supply ... DPS
Display Racks [*Freight*] ... DR
Display Request Keyboard ... DRK
Display Simulation Program ... DSP
Display and Storage ... D & S
Display Storage Tube ... DST
Display Switching Oscilloscope ... DSO
Display of Synoptic Data ... DISYNDA
Display System Computer Input Multiplexer ... DCIM
Display Test Chamber ... DTC
Display Timing Control ... DTC
Display Transmission Generator ... DTG
Display Unit ... DU
Display Unit Test Assembly ... DUTA
Display, Upper ... DU
Displayed Impact Line ... DIL
Displayed Impact Point ... DIP
Displayed under Program Control ... DUPC
Displays, Controls, and Operation Procedures ... DCOP
Disposable Absorption Collection Trunk ... DACT
Disposable Barrel Cartridge Area Target Ammunition [*Weapon launcher*] ... DBCATA
Disposable Personal Income ... DPI
Disposable Seismic Intrusion Detector ... DSID
[*The*] **Disposables Association** ... TDA
Disposables International and Nonwoven Fabric Review [*A publication*] ... Dispos Intern
Disposal ... DISP
Disposal ... DSPL
Disposal Accounting Management System [*DoD*] ... DAMS
Disposal Release Order [*DoD*] ... DRO
Dispose [*or Destroy*] [*Routing slip*] ... D
Dispose ... DSPO
Disposition ... DISPN
Disposition ... DSPN
Disposition and Findings ... D & F
Disposition Form [*Army*] ... DF
Disposition of Inactive Parts List ... DIP
Disposition One Only ... DOO
Disposition Pennant [*Navy*] [*British*] ... DN
Disposition Record ... DR
Disqualified [*Horse racing*] ... D
Disqualified ... DQ
Disqualify ... DISQUAL
Disraeli Newsletter [*A publication*] ... DN
Disregard ... DISRE
Disregard Previous Assignment Instructions and Assign as Indicated [*Army*] ... DPAIAI
Dissatisfied Peugeot Owners of America ... DPOA
Dissector Camera Tube ... DCT
Disseminate ... DISEM
Disseminated ... DISSEM
Disseminated Gonococcal Infection [*Clinical chemistry*] ... DGI
Disseminated Histoplasmosis [*Medicine*] ... DH
Disseminated Intravascular Coagulation [*Hematology*] ... DIC
Disseminated Lupus Erythematosus [*Hematology*] ... DLE
Disseminated Sclerosis [*Medicine*] ... DS
Dissent [*A publication*] ... Dis
Dissenter ... DISS
Dissertation ... DISS
Dissertation ... DISSERT
Dissertation Abstracts [*A publication*] ... DA
Dissertation Abstracts [*A publication*] ... DAb
Dissertation Abstracts [*A publication*] ... DisA
Dissertation Abstracts [*A publication*] ... Dis Abst
Dissertation Abstracts [*A publication*] ... Diss Abs
Dissertation Abstracts [*A publication*] ... Diss Abstr
Dissertation Abstracts. B. Sciences and Engineering [*A publication*] ... Diss Abstr B Sci Eng
Dissertation Abstracts International [*A publication*] ... DAI
Dissertation Abstracts International [*A publication*] ... Dissert Abs Internat
Dissertation Abstracts International [*A publication*] ... Dissert Abstr Int
Dissertation Abstracts International. A [*A publication*] ... DABAA
Dissertation Abstracts International. B [*A publication*] ... DABBB
Dissertation Abstracts International. Retrospective Index [*A publication*] ... DAIRI
Dissertation Abstracts International. Section B. Sciences and Engineering [*A publication*] ... Diss Abstr Int B Sci Eng
Dissertation Abstracts International. Section B. Sciences and Engineering [*A publication*] ... Diss Abstr Int Sec B
Dissertation. Hohenheim Landwirtschaftliche Hochschule [*A publication*] ... Diss Hohenheim Landwirt Hochsch
Dissertation Inquiry Service [*Xerox Corp.*] ... DIS
Dissertationen der Universitaet Wien [*A publication*] ... DissUW
Dissertationes Mathematicae (Rozprawy Matematyczny) [*A publication*] ... Dissertationes Math (Rozprawy Mat)
Dissertationes Pannonicae [*A publication*] ... Diss Pan
Dissertationes Pharmaceuticae [*A publication*] ... Diss Pharm
Dissertationes Pharmaceuticae et Pharmacologicae [*A publication*] ... Diss Pharm Pharmacol
Dissertations on Chemical Oceanography ... DISCO
Dissertazioni della Pontificia Accademia Roman di Archeologia [*A publication*] ... DPAA
Dissimilar Air Combat Tactics [*Navy*] ... DACT
Dissimilar Air Combat Training ... DACT
Dissimilarity Coefficient [*Numerical taxonomy*] ... DC
Dissimulation [*Psychology*] ... Ds
Dissipate ... DSIPT
Dissipation Factor ... DF
Dissociate ... DISSOC
Dissociator [*Genetics*] ... DS
Dissolve ... DISS
Dissolved ... DISLVD
Dissolved ... DSLV
Dissolved Acetylene ... DA
Dissolved Adenosine Triphosphate [*Oceanography*] ... DATP
Dissolved Air Flotation ... DAF
Dissolved Free Amino Acids ... DFAA
Dissolved Inorganic Carbon [*Also, DIOC*] ... DIC
Dissolved Inorganic Carbon [*Also, DIC*] ... DIOC
Dissolved Organic Carbon ... DOC
Dissolved Organic Matter [*Oceanography*] ... DOM
Dissolved Organic Phosphorus ... DOP
Dissolved Oxygen ... DO
Dissolved Oxygen Deficit [*Water pollution*] ... DOD
Dissolved Oxygen Electrode ... DOE
Dissolved Reactive Phosphorus [*Environmental science*] ... DRP
Dissolved Solids ... DS
Disston, Inc. [*NYSE symbol*] [*Delisted*] ... DST
Distal [*Medicine*] ... D
Distal [*Medicine*] ... DIST
Distal Accessory Flexor Muscle [*of a lobster*] ... DAFM
Distal Convoluted Tubule [*Nephrology*] ... DCT
Distal Interphalangeal [*Joint*] [*Anatomy*] ... DIP
Distal Over-Shoulder Strap ... DOSS
Distal Palmar Crease [*Anatomy*] ... DPC
Distal Radioulnar Joint [*Anatomy*] ... DRUJ
Distal Tingling on Percussion [*Medicine*] ... DTP
Distance ... D
Distance ... DIS
Distance [*or Distant*] ... DIST
Distance ... DSTC
Distance [*Radio term*] ... DX
Distance and Angularity Measurement Equipment [*Navy*] ... DAME
Distance Azimuth Measuring Equipment [*Navy*] ... DAME

Distance in Error .....DIE
Distance Finding Station .....DFS
Distance Indicating Automatic Navigation Equipment .....DIANE
Distance Measuring Equipment [*Navigation*] .....DME
Distance Measuring Equipment-Collocated with VOR .....DMEV
Distance Measuring Equipment Command and Navigation .....DECAN
Distance Measuring Equipment/Correlation Tracking and Ranging .....DME/COTAR
Distance Measuring Equipment TACAN .....DMET
Distance Measuring Equipment Terminal .....DMET
Distance Measuring Instrument .....DMI
Distance Measuring System .....DMS
Distance Monitoring Equipment [*Military*] .....DME
Distance Test .....DT
Distance Velocity Laboratory .....DVL
Distance at Which a Watch Is Heard with Left Ear [*Medicine*] .....HDLW
Distance at Which a Watch Is Heard with Right Ear [*Medicine*] .....HDRW
Distance Winner [*Horse racing*] .....D
Distanced [*Horse racing*] .....DIS
Distanced [*Horse racing*] .....DIST
Distant .....DSNT
Distant Central Office Transceivers .....DCOT
Distant-Control Boat .....DCB
Distant Drummer [*A publication*] .....Dist Drum
Distant Early Warning [*North American RADAR system*] [*Obsolete*] .....DEW
Distant Early Warning Identification Zone [*North American RADAR system*] [*Obsolete*] .....DEWIZ
Distant Early Warning Line [*North American RADAR system*] [*Obsolete*] .....DEW LINE
Distant Element .....DE
Distant Object Attitude Measuring System .....DOAMS
Distant Station Connected [*Data processing*] .....DSC
Distearoyl Phosphatidylcholine [*Biochemistry*] .....DSPC
Distearyl Thiodipropionate [*Organic chemistry*] .....DSTDP
Distemper Virus .....DV
Distill .....DSTL
Distillate .....DSTLT
Distillate Burner Manufacturers Association .....DBMA
Distillate plus Loss .....D & L
Distillation .....DISTN
Distillation Desalination System .....DDS
Distilled [*or Distillery*] .....DIST
Distilled .....DISTD
Distilled .....DSTLD
Distilled Fuel Oil .....DFO
Distilled Oil of Vitriol .....DOV
Distilled Spirits Council of the United States .....DISCUS
Distilled Spirits Institute [*Later, DISCUS*] .....DSI
Distilled Spirits Plant .....DSP
Distilled Water .....DW
Distiller and Rectifier .....D & R
Distillers Corporation-Seagrams Ltd. [*Later, VO*] [*NYSE symbol*] .....DCS
Distillers Dried Grain .....DDG
Distillers' Dried Grain with Solubles [*Feedstuff*] .....DDGS
Distillers Feed Research Council .....DFRC
Distillery, Rectifying, Wine, and Allied Workers International Union of America [*Later, DWAW*] .....DRWAW
Distillery, Wine, and Allied Workers International .....DWAW
Distillery, Wine, and Allied Workers' International Union .....DWW
Distilling Ship [*Navy symbol*] .....AW
Distinctive Insignia [*Military*] .....DI
Distinctive Ovarian Tumor with Sexual Precocity .....DOTSP
[*A*] Distinctly Empirical Prover of Theorems .....ADEPT
Distinguish .....DIST
Distinguish .....DISTING
Distinguished Conduct Medal [*British*] .....DCM
Distinguished Federal Civilian Service [*Award*] .....DFCS
Distinguished Flying Cross [*US and British*] .....DFC
Distinguished Flying Medal [*British*] .....DFM
Distinguished Graduate [*Military*] .....DG
Distinguished Guest [*Hotel term*] .....DG
Distinguished Marksmanship Badge .....DMB
Distinguished Military Graduate .....DMG
Distinguished Military Students .....DMS
Distinguished Naval Graduate .....DNG
Distinguished Pistol Badge .....DPB
Distinguished Pistol Shot Badge .....DPSBad
Distinguished Public Service Award .....DPSA
Distinguished Rifleman Badge .....DRflmnBad
Distinguished Service Cross [*US and British*] .....DSC
Distinguished Service Medal [*US and British*] .....DSM
Distinguished Service Order [*British*] .....DSO
Distinguished Unit Citation .....DUC
Distinguished Unit Citation Emblem .....DUCE
Distinguished Unit Emblem .....DUE
Distinguished University Professor .....DUP
Distinguished Visitor .....DV
Disto-Occlusal [*Dentistry*] .....DO
Distobuccal [*Dentistry*] .....DB
Distobucco-Occlusal [*Dentistry*] .....DBO
Distobuccopulpal [*Dentistry*] .....DBP

Distocervical [*Dentistry*] .....DC
Distogingival [*Dentistry*] .....DG
Distoincisal [*Dentistry*] .....DI
Distolabioincisal [*Dentistry*] .....DLAI
Distolabiopulpal [*Dentistry*] .....DLaP
Distolingual [*Dentistry*] .....DL
Distolinguo-Occlusal [*Dentistry*] .....DLO
Distolinguoincisal [*Dentistry*] .....DLI
Distolinguopulpal [*Dentistry*] .....DLP
Distolobial [*Dentistry*] .....DLA
Distopulpal [*Dentistry*] .....DP
Distopulpolabial [*Dentistry*] .....DPLa
Distopulpolingual [*Dentistry*] .....DPL
Distort .....DST
Distorted Wave-Borne Approximation .....DWBA
Distortion .....DISTN
Distortion-Eliminating Voltage Regulator .....DEVR
Distortion Transmission Impairment .....DTI
Distracted .....DISTR
Distress .....DTRS
Distress Alarm for Severely Handicapped [*British*] .....DASH
Distress Alerting and Locating System .....DALS
Distress Phase [*Aviation*] .....DETRESFA
Distressed British Seaman [*Granted a free passage home*] .....DBS
Distressed Vehicle .....DV
Distribuco, Inc. [*NASDAQ symbol*] .....DTIB
Distribuidora de Impresos, Sociedad Anonima [*Mexico*] .....DIMSA
Distribuion of Stockage Code .....DSC
Distributed Area Jamming System [*Air Force*] .....DAJS
Distributed Array RADAR .....DAR
Distributed Bragg Reflector [*LASER*] .....DBR
Distributed Budget at Complete .....DBAC
Distributed Budget Variance .....DBV
Distributed Communications Architecture .....DCA
Distributed Computer Systems .....DCS
Distributed Computer Systems [*NASDAQ symbol*] .....DCSI
Distributed Control Programing Language [*Data processing*] .....DCPL
Distributed Data Processing .....DDP
Distributed Emission Magnetron Amplifier .....DEMATRON
Distributed Energy Release [*Computer program*] .....DER
Distributed Feedback .....DFB
Distributed Graphics System .....DGS
Distributed Information System [*Data processing*] .....DIS
Distributed Interactive Secure Telecommunications Area Network .....DISTAN
Distributed Lab .....DL
Distributed Logic Corp. [*NASDAQ symbol*] .....DLOG
Distributed Microcomputer Network for Avionics .....DMNA
Distributed Office Support System [*IBM Corp.*] .....DISOSS
Distributed Operating System Kernel [*Data processing*] .....DOSK
Distributed Presentation Services [*IBM Corp.*] .....DPS
Distributed Processing Control Executive [*IBM Corp.*] .....DPCX
Distributed Processing Newsletter [*A publication*] .....Dist Proc
Distributed Processing Programing Executive Base [*IBM Corp.*] .....DPPX
Distributed Read Address Counter .....DRAC
Distributed State Response .....DSR
Distributed System Program [*Data processing*] .....DSP
Distributed Systems Environment .....DSE
Distributed Systems Executive [*IBM Corp.*] .....DSX
Distributed Time .....DIST
Distributed Time Division Multiple Access [*System*] [*DoD*] .....DTDMA
Distributed Write Address Counter .....DWAC
Distributing Post Office .....DPO
Distributing Terminal Assembly [*Electronics*] .....DTA
Distribution .....DISTN
Distribution [*A publication*] .....Distr
Distribution .....DISTRIB
Distribution .....DSTR
Distribution [*or Distributor*] .....DISTR
Distribution Age [*A publication*] .....Distrib Age
Distribution Amplifier .....DA
Distribution Assembly [*Ground Communications Facility, NASA*] .....DA
Distribution Assembly [*Ground Communications Facility, NASA*] .....DSTA
Distribution Authority [*Army*] .....DISTRA
Distribution Authority List .....DAL
Distribution Automation and Control .....DAC
Distribution Box [*Technical drawings*] .....DB
Distribution Chart File .....DCF
Distribution Construction Information System [*IBM Corp.*] .....DCIS
Distribution Contractors Association .....DCA
Distribution Control Analysis File .....DECAF
Distribution Control Assembly .....DCA
Distribution Control Center .....DCC
Distribution Control Unit .....DCU
Distribution Drop Point .....DDP
Distribution of Exact Classical Energy Transfer [*Physics*] .....DECENT
Distribution Frame .....DF
Distribution-Free Logic Design .....DFLD
Distribution Function [*Statistics*] .....DF
Distribution Fuse Board .....DFB
Distribution of Industry [*British*] .....DI

Distribution List ... DL
Distribution Manager [*A publication*] ... Distrib Mgr
Distribution Number Bank ... DNB
Distribution of Oceanographic Data at Isentropic Levels ... DODIS
Distribution Panel ... DPNL
Distribution Plot List ... DPL
Distribution Point ... DP
Distribution Point ... DSP
Distribution Register of Organic Pollutants [*In Water*] [*See also Water DROP*] [*Environmental Protection Agency*] ... DROP
Distribution Register of Organic Pollutants in Water [*See also DROP*] [*Environmental Protection Agency*] ... Water DROP
Distribution Tape Reel [*Data processing*] ... DTR
Distribution Unit ... DU
Distribution Worldwide [*A publication*] ... Distrib Worldwide
Distribution Worldwide [*A publication*] ... Distr Worldwide
Distributive Education ... DE
Distributive Education Clubs of America ... DECA
Distributive Education Clubs of America ... DECCA
Distributive Principle of Multiplication over Addition [*New math*] ... DPMA
Distributive, Processing, and Office Workers Union of America ... DPOWA
Distributive Trades [*Department of Employment*] [*British*] ... DT
Distributor ... DIST
Distributor Electronic Control ... DEC
Distributor-to-Group Display Generator ... DGDG
Distributor-Manufacturer-Representative ... DMR
Distributor-to-Printer Electronics ... DPE
District ... DIS
District ... DISC
District ... DISCT
District ... DIST
District ... DST
District Accounting Office [*or Officer*] [*Navy*] ... DAO
District Administrator ... DA
District Administrator ... DISTAD
District Agent [*Insurance*] ... DA
District Airport Engineer ... DAE
District Armament Supply Officer [*British*] ... DASO
District Attorney ... DA
District Authorities [*British*] ... DA
District Aviation Gas Office [*Navy*] ... DAGO
District Aviation Office [*or Officer*] [*Navy*] ... DAO
District Base Service Office ... DBSO
District Camouflage Office [*or Officer*] ... DCO
District Chaplain [*Navy*] ... DCH
District Chief Ranger [*Ancient Order of Foresters*] ... DCR
District Civil Readjustment Office [*or Officer*] ... DCRO
District Civilian Personnel Office [*or Officer*] ... DCPO
District Clothing Office [*or Officer*] ... DCO
District Coast Guard Officer ... DCGO
District of Columbia ... D of C
District of Columbia [*MARC country of publication code*] [*Library of Congress*] ... dcu
District of Columbia [*MARC geographic area code*] [*Library of Congress*] ... n-us-dc
District of Columbia [*Postal code*] ... DC
District of Columbia Health Sciences Information Network [*Library network*] ... DOCHSIN
District of Columbia Libraries [*A publication*] ... DC Lib
District of Columbia Manpower Administration ... DCMA
District of Columbia Military District ... DCMD
District of Columbia National Guard ... DCNG
District of Columbia Nursing Action [*A publication*] ... DC Nurs Action
District of Columbia Public Library, Washington, DC [*OCLC symbol*] ... DWP
District of Columbia Teachers College [*Later, University of the District of Columbia*] ... DCTC
District of Columbia Teachers College [*Later, University of the District of Columbia*]**, Washington, DC** [*Library symbol*] [*Obsolete*] ... DJOWT
District Commissioner [*British government*] ... DC
District Communication Officer ... DCO
District Communications Center [*Navy*] ... DCC
District Community Physician ... DCP
District Council ... DC
District Court ... DC
District Court Judge ... DCJ
District Court Law Library, Second Judicial District, Denver, CO [*Library symbol*] ... CoDDC
District Court-Martial ... DCM
District Degaussing Vessel [*Navy symbol*] ... YDG
District Dental Office [*or Officer*] [*Navy*] ... DDO
District Director ... DD
District Directors of Internal Revenue [*IRS*] ... DDIR
District Domestic Transportation Office [*or Officer*] ... DDTO
District Educational Services Officer [*Navy*] ... DESO
District Engineer [*Army*] ... DE
District Engineer [*Army*] ... DISTENGR
District Engineer Officer [*Army*] ... DEO
District Finance Officer ... DFO
District General Hospital ... DGH
District Headquarters ... DHQ
District Headquarters Induction and Recruiting Station [*Marine Corps*] ... DHIRS
District Heating [*A publication*] ... Dist Heat
District Historical Office [*or Officer*] [*Navy*] ... DHO
District Industrial Incentive Office [*or Officer*] [*Navy*] ... DIIO
District Industrial Manager [*Navy*] ... DIM
District Industrial Relations Officer [*Navy*] ... DIRO
District Inspector [*Navy*] ... DI
District Intelligence Officer ... DIO
District Intelligence Operations Centers [*Vietnam*] ... DIOC
District Judge ... DJ
District Labor Relations Office [*or Officer*] [*Navy*] ... DLRO
District Legal Office [*or Officer*] [*Navy*] ... DLO
District Management Office ... DMO
District Manager [*Insurance*] ... DM
District Marine Officer [*Navy*] ... DMO
District Material Officer [*Navy*] ... DMO
District Medical Officer [*Navy*] ... DMO
District Naval Material Office ... DNMO
District of North Vancouver Library, North Vancouver, BC, Canada [*Library symbol*] ... CaBNvD
District Nurse [*British*] ... DN
District Nursing Officer ... DNO
District Office [*or Officer*] ... DO
District Office/Area Office [*IRS*] ... DO/AO
District Office Direct Input [*Social Security computerized system*] ... DODI
District Office of Jurisdiction [*IRS*] ... DJ
District Office of Location [*IRS*] ... DL
District Officer Commanding ... DOC
District Officer for Reserve Communication Supplementary Activities ... DORCSA
District One Technical Institute, Eau Claire, Eau Claire, WI [*OCLC symbol*] ... WEC
District Operations Office [*or Officer*] [*Navy*] ... DOO
District Ordnance Office [*or Officer*] [*Navy*] ... DOO
District Personnel Office [*or Officer*] [*Navy*] ... DPO
District Port Director [*Navy*] ... DPD
District Postal Liaison Officer [*Navy*] ... DPLO
District Postal Office [*or Officer*] [*Navy*] ... DPO
District Power Equalizer [*Formula for school grants*] ... DPE
District Probate Registry ... DPR
District Property Transportation Office [*or Officer*] [*Navy*] ... DPTO
District Public Affairs Officer [*Military*] ... DPAO
District Public Information Office [*or Officer*] [*Navy*] ... DPIO
District Public Relations Office [*or Officer*] [*Navy*] ... DPRO
District Public Works Office ... DPWO
District Publications and Printing Office ... DPPO
District Railway [*London*] ... DR
District Records Management Office [*or Officer*] ... DRMO
District Recruiting Command [*Army*] ... DRC
District Registry ... DR
District Reserve Electronics Program Officer ... DREPO
District Reserve Equipment [*Army*] ... DRE
District Sales Office ... DSO
District Security Office [*or Officer*] [*Navy*] ... DSO
District Service Office [*or Officer*] [*Navy*] ... DSO
District Ships Service Office [*or Officer*] [*Navy*] ... DSSO
District Sub-Chief Ranger [*Ancient Order of Foresters*] ... DSCR
District Supply Office [*or Officer*] [*Navy*] ... DSO
District Traffic Superintendent [*British railroad term*] ... DTS
District Training Office [*or Officer*] [*Navy*] ... DTO
District Transportation Officer ... DTO
District War Bond Office [*or Officer*] [*Navy*] ... DWBO
District War Plans Officer ... DWPO
Distrito de Braga [*A publication*] ... DdB
Distrito Federal [*Federal District*] [*Mexico*] ... DF
Disturbance [*FBI standardized term*] ... DIST
Disturbance Accommodation Standard-Deviation Optimal Controller [*Space telescope*] [*NASA*] ... DASOC
Disturbance Analysis and Surveillance System [*NRC*] ... DASS
Disturbance Compensation System [*Navy satellite navigation*] ... DISCOS
Disturbed Gum [*Philately*] ... DG
Disyllable ... DISY
Ditch Mile [*Newmarket Racecourse*] [*Horseracing*] [*British*] ... DM
Ditchley Foundation ... DF
Dither ... DTER
Dithered Infrared Configuration ... DIRC
Dithiobis(nitrobenzoic acid) [*Analytical biochemistry*] ... DTNB
Dithioerythritol [*Organic chemistry*] ... DTE
Dithiothreitol [*Organic chemistry*] ... DTT
Ditridecyl Phthalate [*Organic chemistry*] ... DTDP
Dittenberger, Sylloge Inscriptionum Graecarum [*A publication*] ... SIG
Ditto ... DO
Diundecyl Phthalate [*Organic chemistry*] ... DUP
Divan [*A publication*] ... Div
Divanillylidenecyclohexanone [*or Divanillalcyclohexanone*] [*Pharmacology*] ... DVC
Divco-Wayne Corporation [*NYSE symbol*] [*Delisted*] ... DCO
Dive Auditory Location System ... DALS
Dive Bomb ... DB

Dive Bomber Aircraft ....DB
Dive Bomber Squadron [Navy symbol] ....VB
Diver..DVR
Diver Biographical Inventory [Navy] ....DBI
Diver Equipment Information Center [Battelle Memorial Institute] [Information service]....................................... DEIC
Diver Equivalent Manipulator System [General Electric] ......DEMS
Diver, Salvage [Navy rating]......................................DS
Diver, Second Class [Navy rating]..............................DT
Diverge ....DVRG
Divergence ....DIV
Divergence Source-Image Distortion [Crystal] ....DSID
Divergent Exhaust Nozzle Control...........................DENC
Divergent Lobed Suppressor [NASA]..........................DLS
Diverse ....DIV
Diversey Corp. [American Stock Exchange symbol] [Delisted]..................DIV
Diversified Economic and Planning Associates................DEPA
Diversified Energies [NYSE symbol]............................DEI
Diversified Industries, Inc. [NYSE symbol] ....DMC
Diversified Technology Management [NASDAQ symbol]......DTMI
Diversifoods, Incorporated [NASDAQ symbol]............. DFDI
Diversion..DVRSN
Diversion Investigative Unit [Drug Enforcement Administration]........... DIU
Diversion Order [Military].............................DIVERTORD
Diversity Combiner System ....DCS
Diversity Receiving Instrumentation for Telemetry ......DRIFT
Diversity Reception Receiver ....DRR
Diverted Force...DF
Diverter...DIV
Diverter Valve ....DV
Divested Operating Company ....DOC
Dividatur in Partes Aequales [Divide into Equal Parts] [Pharmacy]................................ DIV in PAR AEQ
Dividatur in Partes Aequales [Divide into Equal Parts] [Pharmacy]................................. DIV in PT AEQ
Dividatur in Partes Aequales [Divide into Equal Parts] [Pharmacy]....................................D in P AEQ
Divide...DIV
Divide..DV
Divide County Library, Crosby, ND [Library symbol].............NdCr
Divided Access Line Circuit ....DALC
Dividend ....D
Dividend ....DIV
Dividend ....DIVD
Dividend Investment Plan [Stock purchase]................DIP
Dividends from Space [An association]........................DFS
Divider Time Pulse Distributor................................DTPB
Divine [or Divinity]..DIV
Divine Light Mission [A cult]....................................DLM
Divine Saviour Seminary, Lanham, MD [Library symbol].............MdLaD
Divine Science Bachelor..DSB
Divine Science Doctor ....DSD
Divine Science Federation International....................DSFI
Divine Word College, Epworth, IA [Library symbol]............IaEpD
Divine Word Seminary, Bay St. Louis, MS [Library symbol]............MsBsS
Diving...DIV
Diving Duty [Military]..DVDY
Diving Equipment Manufacturers Association ....DEMA
Diving Information Center [Navy]...............................DIC
Diving Instrumentation Vehicle for Environmental and Acoustic Research..DIVAR
Diving Pay [Navy]..DIVPAY
Diving Saucer..DS
Diving Tender [Non-self-propelled] [Navy symbol] ....YDT
Divinitas [A publication] ....Div
Divinitatis Doctor [Doctor of Divinity] [Latin]...............DD
Divinylbenzene [Organic chemistry]...........................DVB
Divisao de Exploracao dos Transportes Aereos [Angolan airline]........ DETA
Divisao de Exploracao dos Transportes Aereos [Angolan airline]........... DTA
Divisao de Geologia e Mineralogia [Brazil] ....DGM
Divisi [Divide] [Music]..DIV
Division...D
Division...DIV
Division...DIVN
Division Administrative Assistant ....DAA
Division of Adult Education [Office of Education]..........DAE
Division of Adult Education Service [of NEA]..............DAES
Division of Adult and Vocational Research [Office of Education].......... DAVR
Division of Advanced Automotive Power Systems [Energy Research and Development Administration]......................DAAPS
Division Advisory Group ....DAG
Division Air Defense...DIVAD
Division Air Defense Artillery ....DIVADA
Division Air Defense Study ....DIVADS
Division Air Officer...DAO
Division of Air Pollution [Obsolete] [Public Health Service]................DAP
Division of Allied Health Manpower [Bureau of Health Professions Education and Manpower Training, HEW]...........DAHM
Division of Ambulatory Care [American Hospital Association]................DAC
Division Ammunition Office [Army] ....DAO
Division of Applied Technology [Coast Guard] ....DAT

Division through Army Group ....DIVTAG
Division Artillery [Army]...DA
Division Artillery [Army].....................................DIVART
Division Artillery Group [Military]...........................DAG
Division of Atmospheric Surveillance [Environmental Protection Agency]....................................... DAS
Division Aviation Officer......................................DAVNO
Division Base [Army]...DB
Division Base [Army]..DIVBASE
Division of Basic Grants [Office of Education] ....DBG
Division Beachhead [Army].......................................DBH
Division of Biological Effects [Bureau of Radiological Effects]........ DBE
Division of Biologics Standards [FDA]........................DBS
Division of Biomedical and Environmental Research [Later, Office of Health and Environmental Research] [Department of Energy]...............................DBER
Division for the Blind and Physically Handicapped [Later, NLS] [Library of Congress]...............DBPH
Division of Cancer Biology and Diagnosis [National Cancer Institute]...................... DCBD
Division of Career Education [Office of Education] .... DCE
Division of Cataloging and Classification [Later, CCS, RTSD] [ALA]......DCC
Division of Chemical Literature [ACS] ....DCL
Division for Children with Behavioral Disorders [of Council for Exceptional Children]........... DCBD
Division of Classification [Energy Research and Development Administration].................. DC
Division Classification Officer..................................DCO
Division of College and University Assistance [HEW] .... DCUA
Division Commander [Navy] ....DIVCOM
Division Communications-Electronics Officer [Military].............. DCEO
Division of Computer Research [Formerly, OCA] [National Science Foundation].............. DCR
Division of Computer Research and Technology [National Institutes of Health]....................DCRT
Division of Computer Research and Technology, Bethesda, MD [OCLC symbol]................... DCR
Division of Consumer Credit [FTC]............................DCC
Division Contract Termination Team........................DCTT
Division of Contracts .... DC
Division of Controlled Thermonuclear Research [Energy Research and Development Administration]....................DCTR
Division Crime Buffer...DCB
Division Data Center [Army]....................................DDC
Division of Defense Aid Reports [Abolished, 1941] [Military]...............DDAR
Division of Dental Health [Bureau of Health Professions Education and Manpower Training, HEW]........DDH
Division of Drug Advertising [FDA]............................DDA
Division of Drug Biology [Department of Health and Human Services]....DDB
Division of Drug Chemistry [Department of Health and Human Services].....................DDC
Division of Economic Research [Social Security Administration] ....DER
Division of Educational and Research Facilities [Bureau of Health Professions Education and Manpower Training, HEW]........DERF
Division of Electric Power Transmission and Distribution [Energy Research and Development Administration] ....DEPTD
Division of Electronic Products [Series] [A publication]...........DEP
Division of End Use Conservation [Energy Research and Development Administration]................DEUC
Division of Energy Storage [Energy Research and Development Administration]................DES
Division Engineer ....DIVE
Division Engineer [Army]..................................DIVENGR
Division of Engineering and Applied Physics [Harvard University].......DEAP
Division Engineering Planning Document ....DEPD
Division Entry .... DE
Division of Environmental Biology [National Science Foundation].........DEB
Division of Evaluation and Research [Department of Labor]..................DER
Division Final Fade..DFF
Division Flag [Navy] [British]......................................DV
Division Force Equivalents [Army]............................DFE
Division of Foreign Labor Conditions [Department of Labor]...............DFLC
Division Forms Control...DFC
Division Freight Agent..DFA
Division Funding Control Point ....DFCP
Division of General Medical Sciences [National Institutes of Health]......................DGMS
Division of Geothermal Research [Energy Research and Development Administration]...............DGR
Division for Girls' and Women's Sports [of American Association for Health, Physical Education, and Recreation; also used in a book title] [Later, NAGUS]...............DGWS
Division of Graduate Education in Science [National Science Foundation]....................DGES
Division of Handicapped Children and Youth [HEW]........DHCY
Division Headquarters [Military]...............................DHQ
Division Headquarters [Army]............................DIVHED
Division of Health Examination Statistics [HEW]..........DHES
Division of Improved Conversion Efficiency [Energy Research and Development Administration] .... DICE
Division of Industrial Cooperation [MIT]....................DIC

Division of Industrial Participation [*AEC*].................................DIP
Division of Information [*Marine Corps*] .... DIVINFO
Division of Information Science and Technology [*National Science Foundation*].................................DIST
Division of Institutional Development [*Office of Education*] .... DID
Division of Insured Loans [*Office of Education*].........................DIL
Division of International Education [*Office of Education*].................DIE
Division of International Finance [*of FRS*].........................DIF
Division of International Medical Education [*Association of American Medical Colleges*]....................................DIME
Division of International Security Affairs [*Energy Research and Development Administration*] .... DISA
Division of Isotopes Development [*AEC*]......................... DID
Division of Juvenile Delinquency Service [*of SSA*] ....DJDS
Division of Labor Relations [*Energy Research and Development Administration*] .... DLR
Division Liaison Officer....................................DLO
Division of Library Services and Educational Facilities [*Office of Education*].................................DLSEF
Division Logistical Operation Center................................DLOC
Division Logistics Control Center.................................DLCC
Division Logistics System.................................DLOGS
Division Logistics System Test [*Army*] ....DLST
Division Logistics System Test/Seventh Army Card Processor System.................................. DLST/SEACAPS
Division of Materials Research [*National Science Foundation*]...............DMR
Division Materiel Management Center [*Military*] ....DMMC
Division of Medical Radiation Exposure [*Bureau of Radiological Health*] .... DMRE
Division of Military Application [*Energy Research and Development Administration*] .... DMA
Division of Narcotic Addiction and Drug Abuse [*National Institute of Mental Health*] ....DNADA
Division of Naval Intelligence .... DNI
Division of Naval Reactors [*Energy Research and Development Administration*]...........................DNR
Division Notice ....DN
Division of Nuclear Education and Training [*AEC*] ....DNET
Division of Nuclear Materials Management [*AEC*] ....DNMM
Division of Nuclear Materials Safeguards [*AEC*]........................DNMS
Division Operating Instruction [*Air Force*] ....DOI
Division of Operational Safety [*Energy Research and Development Administration*].................................DOS
Division Ordnance Officer ....DIVOO
Division Ordnance Officer .... DOO
Division of Overseas Ministries [*National Council of Churches*]...............DOM
Division of Peaceful Nuclear Explosives [*AEC*]........................DPNE
Division of Physical Research [*Energy Research and Development Administration*].................................DPR
Division for Physically Handicapped [*Formerly, AEHHC, DOPHHH*] [*Council for Exceptional Children*] .... DPH
Division on Physically Handicapped, Homebound, and Hospitalized [*Later, DPH*] [*Council for Exceptional Children*] .... DOPHHH
Division Piece [*Rotary piston meter*]................................DV
Division of Policy Research and Analysis [*National Science Foundation*] .... PRA
Division Primary Standards.................................DPS
Division of Production and Materials Management [*Energy Research and Development Administration*]...........................DPMM
Division Property Book Officer [*Military*] .... DPBO
Division Quartermaster ....DQM
Division Rapid Reaction Force [*Army*] ....DRRF
Division of Reactor Development [*AEC*] .... DRD
Division of Reactor Development and Technology [*AEC*] ....DRDT
Division of Reactor Licensing [*AEC*] .... DRL
Division of Reactor Research and Development [*Energy Research and Development Administration*]...........................DRRD
Division Ready Force [*Army*] .... DRF
Division Reference Standards.................................DRS
Division of Rehabilitation Counseling [*of the APGA*] ....DRC
Division Reliability Policy Committee.................................DRPC
Division of Research [*Navy*]................................DR
Division of Research Facilities and Resources [*National Institutes of Health*].................................DRFR
Division of Research Grants [*National Institutes of Health*]........................DRG
Division of Research and Improvement, Vocational Education, and Rehabilitation [*Department of Education*].................................DRIVER
Division of Research Resources [*National Institutes of Health*]...............DRR
Division of Research Services [*National Institutes of Health*]...................DRS
Division of Resources, Centers, and Community Activities [*National Cancer Institute*].................................DRCCA
Division Restructuring Study Group [*TRADOC*] [*Army*]........................DRSG
Division of Retail Food Protection [*Food and Drug Administration*] ...... DRFP
Division of Retirement and Survivors Studies [*Social Security Administration*].................................DRSS
Division of Safeguards and Security [*Energy Research and Development Administration*].................................DSS
Division of Science Information [*National Science Foundation*]...................DSI
Division of Scientific Personnel and Education [*National Science Foundation*] .... DSPE

Division of Scientific and Technical Information [*International Atomic Energy Agency*] .... DSTI
Division Service Area [*Army*]................................DSA
Division Signal Officer [*Army*]................................DSO
Division of Solar Research [*Energy Research and Development Administration*].................................DSR
Division of Space Nuclear Systems [*Energy Research and Development Administration*]...........................DSNS
Division of Sponsored Research [*MIT*] .... DSR
Division Standard Practice.................................DSP
Division of State Systems Management [*Social and Rehabilitation Service, HEW*]................................ DSSM
Division of Student Support and Special Programs [*Office of Education*].................................DSSSP
Division of Supplemental Security Studies [*Department of Health and Human Services*] .... DSSS
Division Supply Control Point.................................DSCP
Division Supply Officer [*Army*]................................DSO
Division Supply Point.................................DIVSP
Division Support Area.................................DSA
Division Support Command [*Army*] .... DISCOM
Division Support Control Center [*Army*]........................DSCC
Division Tactical Area [*Army*] .... DTA
Division Tactical Operations Center.................................DTOC
Division Tactical Operations System .... DIVTOS
Division Tactical Zone [*Army*] .... DTZ
Division of Tax Research .... DTR
Division of Technical Information [*AEC*]................................DTI
Division of Technical Information Extension [*Later, Technical Information Center*] [*AEC*].................................DTIE
Division of Technology and Environmental Education [*Office of Education*].................................DTEE
Division of Training and Facilities [*Office of Education*].................DTF
Division Transportation Officer.................................DTO
Division of Tropical Agronomy. Technical Paper. Commonwealth Scientific and Industrial Research Organisation (Australia) [*A publication*].................................
     Div Trop Agron Tech Pap CSIRO (Aust)
Division of Tropical Crops and Pastures. Technical Paper. Commonwealth Scientific and Industrial Research Organisation (Australia) [*A publication*].................................
     Div Trop Crops Pastures Tech Pap CSIRO (Aust)
Division of Veterinary Medical Research [*Department of Health and Human Services*]........................ DVMR
Division for the Visually Handicapped [*Formerly, CEPS*] [*Council for Exceptional Children*] .... DVH
Division of Vocational Rehabilitation [*Later, DTVE*] [*Office of Education*].................................DVR
Division of Vocational and Technical Education [*Formerly, DVR*] [*Office of Education*].................................DVTE
Division of Waste Management and Transportation [*Energy Research and Development Administration*]........................DWMT
Division for Women in Medicine [*Defunct*].................................DWIM
Divisional Administrative Area [*Military*] [*British*] .... DAA
Divisional Administrative Contracting Officer [*Military*].................DACO
Divisional Agricultural Officer [*Ministry of Agriculture, Fisheries, and Food*] [*British*].................................DAO
Divisional Chief Superintendent [*British police*].................DCS
Divisional Detective Inspector [*British police*]................................DDI
Divisional Education Officer [*British*].................................DEO
Divisional Electronic Warfare Combat Model Test and Evaluation.................................DEWCOM T & E
Divisional Entertainments Officer [*British*]................................DEO
Divisional Executive Officer [*British*] .... DEO
Divisional-General [*British*].................................D-G
Divisional Interests Special Committee [*American Library Association*].................................DISC
Divisional Land Agent [*Ministry of Agriculture, Fisheries, and Food*] [*British*].................................DLA
Divisional Medical Officer [*British*].................................DMO
Divisional Officer [*Agricultural Development and Advisory Service*] [*British*].................................DO
Divisional Orders.................................DO
Divisional Pests Officer [*Ministry of Agriculture, Fisheries, and Food*] [*British*].................................DPO
Divisional Routine Order.................................DRO
Divisional Safety Inspector [*Ministry of Agriculture, Fisheries, and Food*] [*British*].................................DSI
Divisional Superintendent [*British police*] .... DS
Divisional Technical Conference. Society of Plastics Engineers. Technical Papers [*A publication*].................................
     Div Tech Conf Soc Plast Eng Tech Pap
Divisional Vendor Data Coordinator.................................DVDC
Divisional Veterinary Officer [*Ministry of Agriculture, Fisheries, and Food*] [*British*].................................DVO
Divisional Work Request.................................DWR
Divisions of Naval Staff Plans Division [*British*].................DNSPD
Divisionsverfuegung [*or Divisionsverordnung*] [*Divisional Order*] [*German military - World War II*].................................DV
Divorced ....D
Divorced ....DIV

Divorced	DV
Divorced Jewish Female [Classified advertising]	DJF
Divorced White Female [Classified advertising]	DWF
Divorced White Male [Classified advertising]	DWM
Divulgacion Pesquera Direccion General de Pesca (Bogota) [A publication]	Divulg Pesq Dir Gen Pesca (Bogota)
Divus [The Late] [Latin]	D
Divus Thomas [A publication]	DT
Divus Thomas [A publication]	DTh
Diwag [Germany] [Research code symbol]	WV
Dixhuitieme Siecle [A publication]	DHS
Dixico, Inc. [American Stock Exchange symbol]	DXC
Dixie [Australia] [Airport symbol] [Obsolete]	DXD
Dixie Airways [Nashville, TN] [FAA designator]	DEE
Dixie College, St. George, UT [Library symbol]	UStgD
Dixie Regional Library, Pontotoc, MS [Library symbol]	MsPon
Dixilyn Corp. [American Stock Exchange symbol] [Delisted]	DXL
Dixmont State Hospital, Sewickley, PA [OCLC symbol]	PHD
Dixmont State Hospital, Sewickley, PA [Library symbol]	PSewD
Dixon [USSR] [Geomagnetic observatory code]	DIK
Dixon, IL [Radio station call letters]	WIXN
Dixon, IL [Radio station call letters]	WIXN-FM
Dixon Ticonderoga Co. [NASDAQ symbol]	DIXY
Dixon, TN [Radio station call letters]	WTNQ
Dixon Unified School District Library, Dixon, CA [Library symbol]	CDi
Dixson, Inc. [NASDAQ symbol]	DIXS
Dixylylethane [Organic chemistry]	DXE
Diyarbakir [Turkey] [Airport symbol]	DIY
Dizionario Veterinario [A publication]	Dizion Vet
Dizygotic [Genetics]	DZ
Dizziness	DZ
Djakarta [Batavia] [Java] [Seismograph station code, US Geological Survey]	DJA
Djanet [Algeria] [Airport symbol]	DJG
Djerba [Tunisia] [Airport symbol]	DJE
Djibouti [Djibouti] [Airport symbol]	JIB
Djoemoe [Suriname] [Airport symbol]	DOE
DK Mitteilungen [A publication]	DK Mitt
DLSC [Defense Logistics Services Center] **Integrated Data System** [Military]	DIDS
DMG, Inc. [Formerly, Diversified Mortgage Investors] [NYSE symbol]	DMG
DMI Furniture [NASDAQ symbol]	DMIF
DNA Medical, Inc. [NASDAQ symbol]	DNAM
Do All Possible	DAP
Do It Now [Category of service call for maintenance or repair work] [Air Force]	DIN
Do It Now Foundation	DINF
Do-It-Yourself	DIY
Do-It-Yourself Research Institute	DIYRI
Do-List Item [Military]	DLI
Do Not Answer	DA
Do Not Duplicate	DND
Do Not Invite	DNI
Do Not Like	DNL
Do Not List	DNL
Do Not Load [Instruction re a freight car]	DNL
Do Not Publish	DNP
Do Not Resuscitate [Medicine]	DNR
Do Not Transmit by Radio	NOTWT
Do Not Use	DNU
Do the Right Thing [Also, DWIM] [In data processing context, translates as "Guess at the meaning of poorly worded instructions"]	DTRT
Do What I Mean [Also, DTRT] [In data processing context, translates as "Guess at the meaning of poorly worded instructions"]	DWIM
Doak Pharmacal Co. [NASDAQ symbol]	DOAK
Doane College, Crete, NE [Library symbol]	NbCrD
Doane College, Crete, NE [OCLC symbol]	NBD
Doany [Madagascar] [Airport symbol]	DOA
Dobbs Ferry Public Library, Dobbs Ferry, NY [Library symbol]	NDf
Doberman Pinscher Club of America	DPCA
Dobrovol'noe Obshchestvo Sodeistviia Armii, Aviatsii, i Flotu [Voluntary Society for Cooperation with the Army, Aviation, and the Fleet] [USSR]	DOSAAF
Dobson, NC [Radio station call letters]	WYZD
DOC Optics [NASDAQ symbol]	DOCO
Docent	Doc
Dock	DK
Dock of the Bay [A publication]	Dk of Bay
Dock and Harbour Authority [A publication]	Dock Harb Auth
Dock Mounted Loader	DML
Dock Receipt	DR
Dock Service	DS
Dock Warrant	DW
Docked Configuration Transfer	DCT
Docket	DOC
Docking	DCKG
Docking [NASA]	DCKNG
Docking	DKG
Docking Adapter [Aerospace]	DA

Docking Alignment Target [NASA]	DAT
Docking and Crew Transfer [Aerospace]	D & CT
Docking Initiate	DKI
Docking Lock Handle	DLH
Docking Mechanism	DM
Docking Mechanism Subsystem [NASA]	DMS
Docking Module [NASA]	DM
Docking Module Subsystem	DMS
Docking Survey	DS
Docking System	DS
Dockside Proofing Vehicle	DPV
Dockside Training Simulator	DSTS
Dockside Underway Replenishment Simulator [Navy]	DUS
Dockyard	DY
Dockyard	DYD
Dockyard Department [Navy] [British]	DD
Docosahexaenoic Acid	DHA
Docteur en Droit [Doctor of Law]	D en D
Doctor	D
Doctor	DOC
Doctor	DOC
Doctor of Accountancy [or Accounting]	D Acc
Doctor of Accounts	D Ac
Doctor of Administration	D Adm
Doctor of Administrative Engineering	D Adm Eng
Doctor in Administrative Sciences	DScAdm
Doctor of Aeronautical Engineering	D Ae E
Doctor of Aeronautical Engineering	D Ae Eng
Doctor of Aeronautical Engineering	D Aero E
Doctor of Aeronautical Science	D Ae S
Doctor of Aeronautical Science	D Ae Sc
Doctor of Aeronautical Science	Dr Ae S
Doctor of Aeronautical Science	Dr Ae Sc
Doctor of Aeronautics	D Ae
Doctor of Agricultural Engineering	D Agr E
Doctor of Agricultural Engineering	D Agr Eng
Doctor of Agricultural Science	D Agr S
Doctor of Agricultural Science	D Agr Sc
Doctor in Agricultural Sciences	DASc
Doctor of Agriculture	D Ag
Doctor of Agriculture	D Agr
Doctor of Agriculture	D Agric
Doctor of Agriculture	Dr Agr
Doctor of Air Conditioning Engineering	DACE
Doctor of Air Conditioning Engineering	DAC Eng
Doctor of Applied Arts	DAA
Doctor of Applied Chemistry	DA Chem
Doctor of Applied Science	DAS
Doctor of Applied Science	DA Sc
Doctor of Archaeology	DA
Doctor of Archaeology	D Ark
Doctor of Architectural Design	D Arch Des
Doctor of Architectural Engineering	D Arch E
Doctor of Architectural Engineering	D Arch Eng
Doctor of Architecture	D Arch
Doctor of Art Education	DAE
Doctor of Art of Oratory	DAO
Doctor of Arts	AD
Doctor of Arts	Art D
Doctor of Arts	Arts D
Doctor of Arts	DA
Doctor of Arts and Sciences	D Ar Sc
Doctor of Association Science	D As S
Doctor of Association Science	D As Sc
Doctor of Astronomy	D As
Doctor of Automobile Engineering	D Au E
Doctor of Automobile Engineering	D Au Eng
Doctor of Aviation	Dr Ae
Doctor of Ayurvedic Medicine	DAyM
Doctor of Beauty Culture	DBC
Doctor of Bible Philosophy	Ph BD
Doctor of Bio-Psychology	BPD
Doctor of Biochemistry	D Bi Ch
Doctor of Biochemistry	D Bi Chem
Doctor of Biological Chemistry	Dr Bi Ch
Doctor of Biological Engineering	D Bi E
Doctor of Biological Engineering	D Bi Eng
Doctor of Biological Physics	D Bi Phy
Doctor of Biological Sciences	D Bi S
Doctor of Biological Sciences	D Bi Sc
Doctor of Biophysics	Dr Bi Phy
Doctor of Business Administration	DBA
Doctor of Business Administration	DB Ad
Doctor of Business Administration	DB Adm
Doctor of Business Administration	DrBusAdmin
Doctor of Business Education	DB Ed
Doctor of Business Management	DBM
Doctor of Business Science	DBS
Doctor of Business Science	DB Sc
Doctor of Canon Law	D Can L
Doctor of Canon Law	DCL

Doctor of Canon Law	D Cn L
Doctor of Canon Law	Dr Can L
Doctor of Celtic Literature	DLC
Doctor of Cement Engineering	D Ce Eng
Doctor of Ceramic Engineering	D Cer E
Doctor of Ceramic Engineering	D Cer Eng
Doctor of Chemical Engineering	D Ch E
Doctor of Chemical Engineering	D Che E
Doctor of Chemical Engineering	D Chem E
Doctor of Chemical Engineering	D Ch Eng
Doctor of Chemistry	Ch D
Doctor of Chiropody	Cp D
Doctor of Chiropractic	DC
Doctor of Chiropractic and Physiological Therapeutics	DCPT
Doctor of Chiropraxis	DC
Doctor Chirurgiae Dentalis [Doctor of Dental Surgery] [British]	DChD
Doctor of Christian Archeology	DoctArch
Doctor of Christian Education	D Chr Ed
Doctor of Christian Science [Used only by those teachers who had received instruction directly from Mary Baker Eddy]	CSD
Doctor of Christian Science	DCS
Doctor of Christian Science	DSC
Doctor of Christian Service	DCS
Doctor of Christian Theology	DCT
Doctor of Christian Training	DCT
Doctor of Church History	DHE
Doctor of City Forestry	DCF
Doctor of City Planning	DCP
Doctor of Civil Engineering	DCE
Doctor of Civil Law	CLD
Doctor of Civil Law	DCL
Doctor of Classical Literature	DCL
Doctor of Commerce	D Com
Doctor of Commerce	DComm
Doctor of Commerce	Dr Com
Doctor of Commercial Administration	D Com Adm
Doctor of Commercial Arts	DCA
Doctor of Commercial Education	DC Ed
Doctor of Commercial Law	DCL
Doctor of Commercial Science	D Com Sc
Doctor of Commercial Science	DCS
Doctor of Commercial Science	DC Sc
Doctor of Commercial Science	DrComSc
Doctor of Commercial Science	Dr CS
Doctor of Commercial Science	DSC
Doctor of Commercial Science	SCD
Doctor of Commercial Service	DC Se
Doctor of Comparative Law	D Comp L
Doctor of Comparative Medicine	DCM
Doctor of Comparative Medicine	MCD
Doctor of Comparative Religion	DCR
Doctor of Cosmology	D Co
Doctor of Criminal Jurisprudence	CJD
Doctor of Criminal Jurisprudence	DCJ
Doctor of Criminal Jurisprudence	Dr Cr Jus
Doctor of Criminology	D Cr
Doctor of Cultural Science	Dr Cul S
Doctor of Cultural Science	Dr Cul Sc
Doctor of Dental Medicine	DDM
Doctor of Dental Medicine	DMD
Doctor of Dental Medicine	MDD
Doctor of Dental Science	DDS
Doctor of Dental Science	DD Sc
Doctor of Dental Surgery	DDS
Doctor of Dental Surgery	DD Sur
Doctor of Design	D Des
Doctor of Design	D Dn
Doctor of Didactics	D Did
Doctor of Diesel Engineering	D Di E
Doctor of Diesel Engineering	D Di Eng
Doctor of Diplomacy	D Dipl
Doctor of Divine Literature	DDL
Doctor of Divinity	DD
Doctor of Divinity	DDr
Doctor of Divinity	Dr D
Doctor of Divinity in Metaphysics	DD
Doctor of Dramatic Art	DDA
Doctor of Drugless Therapy	DDT
Dr. Dvorkovitz & Associates [Information service]	DDA
Doctor of Economic Science	D Econ Sc
Doctor of Economics	D Ec
Doctor of Economics	D Econ
Doctor of Economics	Dr Ec
Doctor of Education	D Ed
Doctor of Education	Ed D
Doctor of Electrical Engineering	DEE
Doctor of Electrical Engineering	DE Eng
Doctor of Electro-Chemical Engineering	DE Ch E
Doctor of Electro-Chemical Engineering	DE Ch Eng
Doctor of Elements	D El
Doctor of Elocution	D Elo

Doctor of Engineering	DE
Doctor of Engineering	D Eng
Doctor of Engineering	DEngg
Doctor of Engineering	Doc Eng
Doctor of Engineering	Dr of Eng
Doctor of Engineering	Dr Eng
Doctor of Engineering	Dr Ing
Doctor of Engineering	ED
Doctor of Engineering	Eng D
Doctor of Engineering	Engr D
Doctor of Engineering Physics	D Eng P
Doctor of Engineering Physics	DE Phy
Doctor of Engineering Science	D Eng Sc
Doctor of Engineering Science	DES
Doctor of Engineering Science	DE Sc
Doctor of Engineering Science	Eng Sc D
Doctor of English	D En
Doctor of English	Dr En
Doctor of English Divinity	DED
Doctor of English Literature	DEL
Doctor of Entomology	DE
Doctor of Entomology	D Ent
Doctor of Entomology	Dr Ent
Doctor of Expression	D Ex
Doctor of Family Life	DFL
Doctor of Finance	Dr Fi
Doctor of Financial Science	DFSc
Doctor of Financial Science	DScFin
Doctor of Fine Arts	AFD
Doctor of Fine Arts	DFA
Doctor of Foreign Science	DFS
Doctor of Foreign Service	DFS
Doctor of Forest Engineering	DFE
Doctor of Forest Engineering	DF Eng
Doctor of Forest Science	DFS
Doctor of Forestry	DF
Doctor of Forestry	Dr F
Doctor of Geography	Dr Geo
Doctor of Geological Engineering	D Ge E
Doctor of Geological Engineering	D Ge Eng
Doctor of Geology	Dr Ge
Doctor of Geopolitics	Dr GP
Doctor of Health Science	DHS
Doctor of Hebrew Letters	DHL
Doctor of Hebrew Letters [or Literature]	DH Litt
Doctor of Hebrew Literature	DHL
Doctor of Hebrew Literature	DH Lit
Doctor of Home Economics	DH Ec
Doctor of Honorary Humanities	DHH
Doctor of Honorary Humanities	HHD
Doctor of Horticulture	D Hor
Doctor of Horticulture	Dr Hor
Doctor of Hospital Administration	DHA
Doctor of Hospital Administration	DH Adm
Doctor of Household Economy	DH Ec
Doctor of Household Science	D Ho Sc
Doctor of Humane Letters	DHL
Doctor of Humane Letters	D Hu L
Doctor of Humane Letters	DHumLitt
Doctor of Humane Letters	HLD
Doctor of Humanics	DH
Doctor of Humanitarian Service	DHS
Doctor of Humanitarian Service	Dr HS
Doctor of Humanities	DH
Doctor of Humanities	D Hu
Doctor of Humanities	D Hum
Doctor of Humanities	HHD
Doctor of Humanities of Learning	Dr HL
Doctor of Hygiene	DHg
Doctor of Hygiene	D Hy
Doctor of Hygiene	D Hyg
Doctor of Hygiene	Dr Hy
Doctor of Industrial Arts	DIA
Doctor of Industrial Engineering	DIE
Doctor of Industrial Engineering	DI Eng
Doctor of Industrial Engineering	DInd
Doctor of Industrial Science	SID
Doctor of Industry	D Ind
Doctor of Industry	Dr Ind
Doctor Ingeniariae [Doctor of Engineering]	D Ing
Doctor of Interior Architectural Engineering	DI Arch E
Doctor of Interior Architectural Engineering	DI Arch Eng
Doctor of Interior Architecture	DI Arch
Doctor of International Law	DIL
Doctor of Irrigation Engineering	D Ir E
Doctor of Irrigation Engineering	D Ir Eng
Doctor of Jewish Pedagogy	DJP
Doctor of Jewish Theology	DJT
Doctor of Jewish Theology	DJ Th
Doctor of Judicial Science	DJS
Doctor of Judicial Science	DJ Sc

Doctor of Judicial Science ... Dr JS
Doctor of Judicial Science ... Dr J Sc
Doctor of Judicial [*or Juridical*] **Science** [*or Doctor of the Science of Law*] ... JSD
Doctor of Judicial Science [*or Doctor of Science of Jurisprudence*] ... Jur Sc D
Doctor of Juridical Science ... DJS
Doctor of Juridical Science ... D Jur Sc
Doctor of Juridical Science ... JDS
Doctor of Juridical Science ... J Sc D
Doctor of Juridical Science [*or Doctor of the Science of Jurisprudence or Doctor of the Science of Law*] ... SJD
Doctor Juris [*Doctor of Law*] ... DJ
Doctor Juris [*Doctor of Law*] ... DrJ
Doctor Juris Utriusque [*Doctor of Both Laws*] ... DrJU
Doctor of Jurisprudence ... D Jur
Dr. Karl Thomae GmbH [*Germany*] [*Research code symbol*] ... N
Dr. Karl Thomae GmbH [*Germany*] [*Research code symbol*] ... PB
Doctor of Landscape Architecture ... DL Arch
Doctor of Landscape Design ... DL Des
Doctor of Landscape Engineering ... DL Eng
Doctor of Landscape Management ... DLM
Doctor of Languages ... D Lang
Doctor of Late Laws ... DLL
Doctor of Latin Letters ... D La L
Doctor of Laws ... DL
Doctor of Laws ... Dr Iur
Doctor of Laws ... Dr Jur
Doctor of Laws ... Dr LL
Doctor of Laws ... LLD
Doctor of Laws and Political Science ... Dr Jur et Rer Pol
Doctor of Letters ... DL
Doctor of Letters ... D Let
Doctor of Letters ... D Lit
Doctor of Letters ... DLitt
Doctor of Letters ... Dr Litt
Doctor of Letters ... LD
Doctor of Letters ... Let D
Doctor of Letters in Economic Studies ... DLES
Doctor of Letters of Journalism ... LJD
Doctor of Liberal Arts ... DLA
Doctor of Library Economics ... DL Ec
Doctor of Library Science ... DLS
Doctor of Library Science ... DL Sc
Doctor of Library Science ... Dr LS
Doctor of Library Science ... LSD
Doctor of Life Science ... LSD
Doctor of Literary Interpretation ... DLI
Doctor of Literature ... DL
Doctor of Literature ... D Lit
Doctor of Literature ... DLitt
Doctor of Literature ... Dr Lit
Doctor of Lithuanian Philology ... Phil LD
Dr. Madaus & Co. [*Germany*] [*Research code symbol*] ... AS
Doctor of Management Sciences ... DManSc
Doctor of Marine Engineering ... D Ma E
Doctor of Marine Engineering ... D Ma Eng
Doctor Martin Luther College, New Ulm, MN [*OCLC symbol*] ... DML
Doctor Martin Luther College, New Ulm, MN [*Library symbol*] ... MnNeuL
Doctor of Mathematics ... DM
Doctor of Mathematics ... Math D
Doctor of Mathematics and Didactics ... DMD
Doctor of Mechanical Engineering ... DME
Doctor of Mechanical Engineering ... DM Eng
Doctor of Mechanical Science ... DMS
Doctor of Mechanics ... D Mech
Doctor of Mechanotherapy ... Dr MT
Doctor of Medical Dentistry ... DMD
Doctor of Medical Jurisprudence ... MJD
Doctor of Medical Science [*or Sciences*] ... DMS
Doctor of Medical Science ... DM Sc
Doctor of Medical Science [*or the Science of Medicine*] ... Med Sc D
Doctor of Medical Science ... M Sc D
Doctor of Medical Science ... MSD
Doctor of Medical Science ... Sc D (Med)
Doctor of Medical Technology ... DMT
Doctor of Medicine ... DM
Doctor of Medicine ... D Med
Doctor of Medicine ... Dr Med
Doctor of Metallurgical Engineering ... D Met E
Doctor of Metallurgical Engineering ... D Met Eng
Doctor of Metallurgy ... D Met
Doctor of Metaphysics ... D Me
Doctor of Metaphysics ... Ms D
Doctor of Microbiology ... D Mic
Doctor of Microbiology ... Mic D
Doctor of Military Science ... D Mil S
Doctor of Military Science ... DMS
Doctor of Mining Engineering ... D Mi E
Doctor of Mining Engineering ... D Mi Eng
Doctor of Missionary Science ... DMSc
Doctor in Missionology ... DMs
Doctor of Modern Languages ... DML
Doctor of Municipal Administration ... DMA
Doctor of Municipal Administration ... DM Adm
Doctor of Music ... DM
Doctor of Music ... D Mus
Doctor of Music ... Dr Mus
Doctor of Music Education ... Mus Ed D
Doctor of Musical Arts ... DMA
Doctor of Musical Arts ... D Mus A
Doctor of Musical Arts ... Mus AD
Doctor of Musical Education ... DM Ed
Doctor of Musical Education ... D Mus Ed
Doctor of Natural Philosophy ... Dr N Ph
Doctor of Natural Philosophy ... Dr Phil Nat
Doctor of Natural Philosophy ... NPhD
Doctor of Natural Science ... DrNatSc
Doctor of Natural Sciences ... Dr N Sc
Doctor of Natural Sciences ... Dr Sci Nat
Doctor of Natural Sciences ... RNDr
Doctor of Naturopathy ... D Nat
Doctor of Naturopathy ... ND
Doctor of Naval Architecture ... DN Arch
Doctor of Naval Engineering ... DNE
Doctor of Naval Engineering ... DN Eng
Doctor of Naval Science ... D Na S
Doctor of Naval Science ... D Na Sc
Doctor of Navigation ... D Na
Doctor of Nursing ... DN
Doctor of Nursing Education ... DN Ed
Doctor of Nursing Science ... DNS
Doctor of Nursing Science ... DN Sc
Doctor of Ocular Science ... D Oc S
Doctor of Ocular Science ... D Oc Sc
Doctor of Ocular Science ... DOS
Doctor Oeconomiae [*Doctor of Economics*] ... D Oec
Doctor of Ophthalmology ... DO
Doctor of Ophthalmology ... D Opth
Doctor of Ophthalmology ... Oph D
Doctor of Optical Science ... DOS
Doctor of Optometric Science ... DOS
Doctor of Optometric Science ... DO Sc
Doctor of Optometry ... DO
Doctor of Optometry ... OD
Doctor of Optometry ... Opt D
Doctor of Oral English ... DOE
Doctor of Oratory ... DO
Doctor of Oratory ... D Or
Doctor of Oriental Languages ... DOL
Doctor of Oriental Learning ... DOL
Doctor of Orthopaedic Medicine and Surgery ... DOMS
Doctor of Osteopathy ... DO
Doctor of Painting ... D Pa
Doctor of Painting ... Dr Pa
Doctor of Patent Law ... DPL
Doctor of Pedagogy ... DPaed
Doctor of Pedagogy ... D Pd
Doctor of Pedagogy ... D Ped
Doctor of Pedagogy ... PD
Doctor of Pedagogy ... Pd D
Doctor of Pedagogy ... Ped D
Dr. Pepper Bottlers Association ... DPBA
Dr. Pepper Co. [*NYSE symbol*] ... DOC
Doctor of Petroleum Engineering ... D Pe E
Doctor of Petroleum Engineering ... D Pe Eng
Doctor of Pharmaceutical Chemistry ... D Phar C
Doctor of Pharmaceutical Chemistry ... D Ph C
Doctor of Pharmacology ... D Phc
Doctor of Pharmacy ... DP
Doctor of Pharmacy ... D Phar
Doctor of Pharmacy ... PD
Doctor of Pharmacy ... Phar D
Doctor of Pharmacy ... Pharm D
Doctor of Pharmacy ... Ph D
Doctor of Philanthropy ... D Phil
Doctor of Philanthropy ... Dr Phi
Doctor of Philanthropy ... Phi D
Doctor of Philology ... Fil Dr
Doctor of Philosophy ... DP
Doctor of Philosophy ... D Ph
Doctor of Philosophy ... D Phil
Doctor of Philosophy ... DPhy
Doctor of Philosophy ... Dr Phil
Doctor of Philosophy ... Dr Philos
Doctor of Philosophy ... PD
Doctor of Philosophy [*Philosophae Doctor*] ... Ph D
Doctor of Philosophy ... PHDr
Doctor of Philosophy in Mechanics and Hydraulics ... PhDMH
Doctor of Philosophy in Metaphysics ... D Ph M
Doctor of Photography ... D Pho
Doctor of Photography ... Dr Pho

Doctor of Physical Biology	DPB
Doctor of Physical Education	DPE
Doctor of Physical Education	Dr of PE
Doctor of Physical Medicine	DPM
Doctor of Physical Science	D Ph S
Doctor of Physical Science	D Ph Sc
Doctor of Physical Science	Dr P Sc
Doctor of Physics	D Phy
Doctor of Physics	Dr Phy
Doctor of Podiatric Medicine	DPM
Doctor of Podiatry	Pod D
Doctor of Political Economy	DPEc
Doctor of Political Science	D Pol Sc
Doctor of Political Science	DPS
Doctor of Political Science	DP Sc
Doctor of Political Science	Dr Pol Sci
Doctor of Political Science	DScP
Doctor of Political Science	PSD
Doctor of Political Science	SPD
Doctor of Political Sciences	Dr Sc Pol
Doctor of Preventative Medicine	DPM
Doctor of Preventative Medicine	Dr Pr M
Doctor of Psychiatric Medicine	DPM
Doctor of Psycho-Therapy	D Ps Th
Doctor of Psychology	D Ps
Doctor of Psychology	Ps D
Doctor of Psychology	PsyD
Doctor of Psychology in Metaphysics	Ps D
Doctor of Public Administration	DPA
Doctor of Public Administration	DP Adm
Doctor of Public Administration	D Pub Adm
Doctor of Public Administration	Dr PA
Doctor of Public Health	DPH
Doctor of Public Health	Dr PH
Doctor of Public Health Education	DPH Ed
Doctor of Public Health Engineering	DPHE
Doctor of Public Health Engineering	DPH Eng
Doctor of Public Health and Hygiene	Dr PH Hy
Doctor of Public Health Nursing	DPHN
Doctor of Public Hygiene	DPH
Doctor of Public Hygiene	Dr PH
Doctor of Public School Art	DPSA
Doctor of Public School Music	DPSM
Doctor of Public Service	DPS
Doctor of Public Service	PSD
Doctor of Radio Engineering	D Ra E
Doctor of Radio Engineering	D Ra Eng
Doctor of Radio and Television Engineering	DRTE
Doctor of Radio and Television Engineering	DRT Eng
Doctor of Recreation	Dr of Rec
Doctor of Refrigeration Engineering	D Re E
Doctor of Refrigeration Engineering	D Re Eng
Doctor of Regional Planning	DRP
Doctor of Religion	D Re
Doctor of Religious Education	DRE
Doctor of Religious Education	DR Ed
Doctor of Religious Education	DRelEd
Doctor of Religious Education	Ed RD
Doctor Rerum Naturalium [Doctor of Natural Science]	Dr Rer Nat
Doctor Rerum Politicarum [Doctor of Political Science]	DocRerPol
Doctor Rerum Politicarum [Doctor of Political Science]	Dr Rer Pol
Doctor of the Royal College of Art	Dr RCA
Doctor of Rural Engineering	D Ru E
Doctor of Rural Engineering	D Ru Eng
Doctor Sacrae Scripturae [Doctor of Holy Scripture]	DSS
Doctor of Sacred Letters	DLittS
Doctor of Sacred Literature	DSL
Doctor of Sacred Literature	Sac Lit D
Doctor of Sacred Music	DSM
Doctor of Sacred Music	SMD
Doctor of Sacred Music	S Mus D
Doctor of Sacred Sciences	D Sa Sc
Doctor of Sacred Scripture	SSD
Doctor of Sacred Theology	DST
Doctor of Sanitary Engineering	DSE
Doctor of Sanitary Engineering	DS Eng
Doctor of Sanitary Science	DSS
Doctor of Sanitation	San D
Doctor of School Music	D Sch Mus
Dr. Schwarz Arzneimittelfabrik GmbH [Germany] [Research code symbol]	SM
Doctor of Science	Dr Sc
Doctor of Science	Dr Sci
Doctor of Science	DS
Doctor of Science	D Sc
Doctor of Science	D Sci
Doctor of Science	Sc D
Doctor of Science	Sci D
Doctor of Science	SD
Doctor of Science in Agriculture	DScA
Doctor of Science in Agriculture	D Sc Agr

Doctor of Science in Business Administration	DS in BA
Doctor of Science in Commerce	D Sc Com
Doctor of Science in Commerce	SD Comm
Doctor of Science in Economics	D Sc Econ
Doctor of Science in Economics	DSE
Doctor of Science in Education	Sc D in Ed
Doctor of Science in Education	Sc Ed D
Doctor of Science in Engineering	DScE
Doctor of Science (Engineering)	D Sc (Eng)
Doctor of Science and English Literature	DSEL
Doctor of the Science of Forestry	DSF
Doctor of Science in Geological Engineering	DS in Ge Engr
Doctor of Science in Geophysical Engineering	DS in Gp Engr
Doctor of Science in Government	Sc D Govt
Doctor of Science in Hygiene	D Sc Hyg
Doctor of Science and Hygiene	D Sci H
Doctor of Science in Hygiene	Sc D in Hyg
Doctor of Science in Industrial Medicine	DSIM
Doctor of the Science of Jurisprudence	Dr Sc Jur
Doctor of the Science of Jurisprudence	DSJ
Doctor of the Science of Law	D Sc L
Doctor of the Science of Law	L Sc D
Doctor of the Science of Medicine	M Sc D
Doctor of Science in Metallurgical Engineering	DS in Met Engr
Doctor of Science in Metallurgy	SD (Met)
Doctor of the Science of Oratory	D Or Sc
Doctor of the Science of Oratory	Dr O Sc
Doctor of the Science of Oratory	D Sc O
Doctor of the Science of Oratory	DSO
Doctor of the Science of Osteopathy	D Sc Os
Doctor of Science in Petroleum Engineering	DS in PE
Doctor of Science in Petroleum Refining Engineering	DS in PRE
Doctor of Science in Surgery	DSS
Doctor of the Science of Theology	STD
Doctor of Science in Veterinary Medicine	D Sc in VM
Doctor Scientiae [Doctor of Science] [Latin]	D Sc
Doctor of Scientific Didactics	DS Di
Doctor of Scientology	D Scn
Doctor of Secretarial Arts	D Se A
Doctor of Secretarial Science	D Se Sc
Doctor of Secretarial Science	DSS
Doctor of Secretarial Studies	D Se St
Doctor of Social Science	Dr So Sc
Doctor of Social Science	DScS
Doctor of Social Science	DScSoc
Doctor of Social Science	DSocS
Doctor of Social Science	D Soc Sc
Doctor of Social Science	DSocSci
Doctor of Social Science	D So Sc
Doctor of Social Science	DS Sc
Doctor of Social Science	ScSocD
Doctor of Social Sciences	RSDr
Doctor of Social Sciences	Sc SD
Doctor of Social Service	D So Se
Doctor of Social Service	DSS
Doctor of Social Welfare	DSW
Doctor of Social Work	DSW
Doctor of Sociology	Dr So
Doctor of Sociology	D So
Doctor of Speech	D Sp
Doctor of Statistics	D St
Doctor of Structural Engineering	D St E
Doctor of Structural Engineering	D St Eng
Doctor of Surgery	D Sur
Doctor of Surgical Chiropody	DSC
Doctor of Systematic Theology	D Sy Th
Doctor of Technical Chemistry	D Tech Chem
Doctor of Technical Science	Dr Rer Tech
Doctor of Technical Science	Dr Sc Techn
Doctor of Technical Science	D Sc Tech
Doctor of Technology	Dr Tech
Doctor of Technology	D Tech
Doctor of Textile Chemistry	DTC
Doctor of Textile Chemistry	DT Ch
Doctor of Textile Design	DT Des
Doctor of Textile Dyeing	DTD
Doctor of Textile Engineering	DTE
Doctor of Textile Engineering	DT Eng
Doctor of Textile Science	DTS
Doctor of Textile Technology	DTT
Doctor of Theology	Dr Theol
Doctor of Theology	DT
Doctor of Theology	D Th
Doctor of Theology	D Theol
Doctor of Theology	Th D
Doctor of Theology	THDr
Doctor of Thinkology [Honorary degree awarded the scarecrow by the wizard in 1939 film "The Wizard of Oz"]	ThD
Doctor of Tropical Medicine	Dr T Med
Doctor of Tropical Medicine	DTM
Doctor of the University	DU

Doctor of the University ... DUniv
Doctor of the University ... Univ D
Doctor of Veterinary Medicine ... D Vet Med
Doctor of Veterinary Medicine ... DVM
Doctor of Veterinary Medicine ... MDV
Doctor of Veterinary Medicine ... MVD
Doctor of Veterinary Medicine ... VMD
Doctor of Veterinary Medicine and Surgery ... DVMS
Doctor in Veterinary Radiology ... DVR
Doctor of Veterinary Science ... DVS
Doctor of Veterinary Science ... DV Sc
Doctor of Veterinary Science ... DV Sci
Doctor of Veterinary Surgery ... DVS
Doctor of Veterinary Surgery ... DVSC
Doctor of Vocational Education ... DV Ed
Dr. William M. Scholl College of Podiatric Medicine, Chicago, IL [*OCLC symbol*] ... JAV
Doctor of Zoology ... DZ
Doctoral Dissertations Accepted by American Universities [*A bibliographic publication*] ... DDAU
Doctors for Disaster Preparedness ... DDP
Doctors Emergency Service [*New York City*] ... DES
Doctors Hospital, Alexander Raxlen Memorial Library, Toronto, ON, Canada [*Library symbol*] ... CaOTDAR
Doctors Hospital, Freeport, NY [*Library symbol*] ... NFreeDH
Doctors Hospital, Milwaukee, WI [*Library symbol*] ... WMD
Doctors Officenters [*NASDAQ symbol*] ... DOCS
Doctor's Order Book ... DOB
Doctor's Orders ... DO
Doctors Ought to Care ... DOC
Doctrine and Command Systems [*Army*] ... DCS
Doctrine and Command Systems Directorate [*Army*] ... DCSD
Doctrine Improvement Program ... DIP
Doctrine of Incremental Reduction ... DIR
Doctrine and Systems Directorate [*Army*] ... DSD
Documation, Inc. [*NYSE symbol*] [*Delisted*] ... DCM
Document ... D
Document ... DCMT
Document [*or Documentation*] ... DOC
Document ... DOCT
Document ... DOCU
Document Abstract Retrieval Equipment ... DARE
Document Availability Code ... DAC
Document. Centre National de Recherches Forestieres [*A publication*] ... Docum Centre Nat Rech For
Document Change Notice ... DCN
Document Change Record ... DCR
Document Code [*Data processing*] ... DC
Document Composition Facility [*IBM Corp.*] ... DCF
Document Control ... DC
Document Control Book ... DCB
Document Control Center ... DCC
Document Control Chief [*NASA*] ... DCC
Document Control Number ... DCN
Document Control System [*Data processing*] ... DCS
Document Data Indexing Set ... DDIS
Document Disposal Indicator ... DDI
Document Distribution and Reproduction Branch [*NTIS*] ... DD & RB
Document Error Report ... DER
Document Generator ... DOCGEN
Document Handling and Information Services Facility [*General Accounting Office*] ... DHISF
Document Identification Number ... DIN
Document Identifier [*Military*] ... DI
Document Identifier Code [*Military*] ... DIC
Document Improvement Program [*DoD*] ... DIP
Document Indexing and Listing of Graphic Information Codes System [*Jet Propulsion Laboratory, NASA*] ... DIA-LOGICS
Document of Industrial Engineering ... DIE
Document Information Record ... DIR
Document Library Facility [*Data processing*] ... DLF
Document Locator Number [*Data processing*] ... DLN
Document Locator Number Counter File [*IRS*] ... DLNC
Document Log ... DL
Document Processing Branch [*NTIS*] ... DPB
Document Processing System [*Data processing*] ... DPS
Document Record Card ... DRC
Document Release Authorization ... DRA
Document Release Notice [*Jet Propulsion Laboratory, NASA*] ... DRN
Document Release Order ... DRO
Document Release Record ... DRR
Document Report ... DR
Document Requirement Description ... DRD
Document Requirement List ... DRL
Document Research Center, Bedford, MA [*Library symbol*] ... MBdD
Document Retention Unit [*IRS*] ... DRU
Document Retrieval System ... DRS
Document Revision Notice ... DRN
Document Service Center ... DSC
Document Signed ... DS
Document Status Report [*Military*] ... DSR
Document Storage Search and Retrieval [*Air Force*] ... DSS & R
Document Survey Data Sheet ... DSDS
Document Transmittal Record ... DTR
Document Validation Audit [*NASA*] ... DVA
Documenta Chemica Yugoslavica [*A publication*] ... Doc Chem Yugosl
Documenta Haematologica (Bucharest) [*A publication*] ... Doc Haematol (Bucharest)
Documenta de Medicina Geographica et Tropica [*A publication*] ... Doc Med Geogr Trop
Documenta et Monumenta Orientis Antiqui [*A publication*] ... DMOA
Documenta Neerlandica et Indonesica de Morbis Tropicis [*A publication*] ... Doc Neerl Indones Morb Trop
Documenta Ophthalmologica [*A publication*] ... Doc Ophthal
Documenta Ophthalmologica [*A publication*] ... Doc Ophthalmol
Documenta Ophthalmologica. Proceedings Series [*A publication*] ... Doc Ophthalmol Proc Ser
Documenta Veterinaria [*A publication*] ... Doc Vet
Documentacion Administrativa [*A publication*] ... Docum Adm
Documentacion Bibliotecologica [*A publication*] ... Doc Bibl
Documentacion Juridica [*A publication*] ... Docum Jur
Documentary Bill for Acceptance ... DA
Documentary Research Division [*Air Force*] ... DRD
Documentatio Geographica [*A publication*] ... Doc Geogr
Documentation Abstracts [*A publication*] ... DA
Documentation Abstracts [*A publication*] ... Doc Abstr
Documentation Associates Information Services, Inc. ... DA
Documentation Associates, Los Angeles, CA [*Library symbol*] ... CLDo
Documentation Automated Retrieval Equipment [*System*] [*Army*] ... DARE
Documentation and Automatization of Researches for Correlations [*For molecular structure*] [*Chemical physics*] ... DARC
Documentation et Bibliotheques [*A publication*] ... Doc et Bibl
Documentation et Bibliotheques [*A publication*] ... Docum et Biblio
Documentation Catholique [*A publication*] ... DC
Documentation Catholique [*A publication*] ... Doc Cath
Documentation Catholique [*A publication*] ... Docum Cath
Documentation Change Instruction ... DCI
Documentation Development Notification ... DDN
Documentation Distribution List ... DDL
Documentation Distribution System ... DDS
Documentation sur l'Europe Centrale [*A publication*] ... Docum Europe Centr
Documentation Europeenne [*A publication*] ... Docum Europ
Documentation Francaise Illustree [*A publication*] ... Docum Franc Illustr
Documentation Group [*Range Commanders Council*] [*NASA*] ... DG
Documentation Implementation Team [*Deep Space Network, NASA*] ... DIT
Documentation et Information Africaines [*African Documentation and Information*] [*Catholic News Agency*] ... DIA
Documentation et Information Pedagogiques [*A publication*] ... Docum Inform Pedag
Documentation Information Transmittal ... DIT
Documentation Management Officer [*Air Force*] ... DMO
Documentation Manager [*Air Force*] ... DM
Documentation of Molecular Spectroscopy ... DMS
Documentation Processing Center [*British*] ... DPC
Documentation of Programs in Core [*Data processing*] ... DOPIC
Documentation Research Project [*American Institute of Physics*] ... DRP
Documentation Research and Training Centre [*India*] ... DRTC
Documentation Staging Area [*Military*] ... DSA
Documentation Standards Committee [*British*] ... DSC
Documentation and Status ... D & S
Documentation Support Services ... DSS
Documentation Unit ... DU
Documentazione sui Paesi de l'Est [*A publication*] ... Docum Paesi Est
Documented Discount Notes [*Banking*] ... DDN
Documented Material Processed ... DMP
Documented Sample ... DS
Documentos Politicos [*A publication*] ... Doc Polit
Documents on Acceptance [*Banking*] ... DOA
Documents Against Acceptance [*Banking*] ... D/A
Documents Against Acceptance [*Banking*] ... DAA
Documents Against Discretion [*Banking*] ... DAD
Documents Against Payment [*Banking*] ... D/P
Documents Attached ... DA
Documents de Cartographie Ecologique [*A publication*] ... Doc Cartogr Ecol
Documents du Centre d'Etude des Revenus et des Couts [*A publication*] ... Doc Centre Et Revenus Couts
Documents CEPESS [*Centre d'Etudes Politiques, Economiques, et Sociales*] [*A publication*] ... Doc CEPESS
Documents d'Histoire [*A publication*] ... DH
Documents Information Accessing ... DIA
Documents d'Information et de Gestion [*A publication*] ... Doc Inform Gestion
Documents des Laboratoires de Geologie de la Faculte des Sciences de Lyon [*A publication*] ... Doc Lab Geol Fac Sci Lyon
Documents per Minute ... DPM
Documents on Payment [*Banking*] ... DOP
Documents to the People [*A publication*] ... DTTP
Documents et Rapports de la Societe Paleontologique et Archeologique de l'Arrondissement Judiciaire de Charleroi [*A publication*] ... DRSPAAJC
Documents Signed ... DSS

Documents Techniques Institut National de la Recherche Agronomique de Tunisie [*A publication*] ... Doc Tech Inst Natl Rech Agron Tunis
Docutel/Olivetti Corp. [*NASDAQ symbol*] ... DCTL
DoD [*Department of Defense*] **Automatic Addressing System** ... DAAS
DoD [*Department of Defense*] **Industrial Security Program** ... DISP
DoD [*Department of Defense*] **Information Security Advisory Board** ... DISAB
DoD [*Department of Defense*] **Logistics Data Element Standardization and Management Office** ... DESMO
DoD [*Department of Defense*] **Manager for Space Shuttle Support** ... DDMS
DoD [*Department of Defense*] **Officer Record Examination** ... DORE
DoD [*Department of Defense*] **Standard Data Repository System** ... DSDRS
DoD [*Department of Defense*] **Value Engineering Services Office** ... DVESO
DoD [*Department of Defense*] **Worldwide Energy Information System** ... DEIS
Dodaira [*Japan*] [*Seismograph station code, US Geological Survey*] ... DDR
Dodds Publishing Co., Hawthorne, NJ [*Library symbol*] ... NjHawD
Dodecadienyl Acetate [*Pheromone*] [*Organic chemistry*] ... DDDA
Dodecahedron [*Golf ball design*] ... DDH
Dodecandienol [*Pheromone*] [*Organic chemistry*] ... DDDOL
Dodecanoylsarcosyltaurine [*Crustacean detergent*] ... DST
Dodecenyl Acetate [*Pheromone*] [*Organic chemistry*] ... DDA
Dodecyl Benzenesulfonate [*Organic chemistry*] ... DBS
Dodecyl Sulfate [*Organic chemistry*] ... $DodSO_4$
(Dodecylbenzyl)trimethylammonium Chloride [*Organic chemistry*] ... DBT
Dodecyldimethylamine [*or Dimethyldodecylamine*] [*Organic chemistry*] ... DDA
Dodecyldimethylamine [*or Dimethyldodecylamine*] **N-Oxide** [*Organic chemistry*] ... DDNO
Dodecyloxyhydroxybenzophenone [*Organic chemistry*] ... DOBP
Dodecylpyridinium Chloride [*Also, LPC*] [*Organic chemistry*] ... DPC
Dodecylsuccinic Anhydride [*Organic chemistry*] ... DSA
Dodecyltrimethylammonium Chloride [*Organic chemistry*] ... DTAC
Dodekanesiakon Archeion [*A publication*] ... D Arch
Dodge City [*Kansas*] [*Airport symbol*] ... DDC
Dodge City College [*Kansas*] ... DCC
Dodge City, KS [*Radio station call letters*] ... KDCK-FM
Dodge City, KS [*Radio station call letters*] ... KEDD
Dodge City, KS [*Radio station call letters*] ... KGNO
Dodge City, KS [*Radio station call letters*] ... KINF
Dodge City, KS [*Radio station call letters*] ... KTTL
Dodge City Public Library, Dodge City, KS [*Library symbol*] ... KDc
Dodge County Mental Health Center, Juneau, WI [*Library symbol*] ... WJuMe
Dodge Wayfarer Sportabout Registry ... DWSR
Dodgeville, WI [*Radio station call letters*] ... WDMP
Dodgeville, WI [*Radio station call letters*] ... WDMP-FM
Dodoma [*Tanzania*] [*Airport symbol*] ... DOD
Dodoma [*Tanzania*] [*Seismograph station code, US Geological Survey*] [*Closed*] ... DOD
Dodrill, Charles T., Hurricane WV [*STAC*] ... DCT
Does Everything but Eat [*Superseded by DITTO*] [*Data processing*] ... DEBE
Does Not Answer [*Telephone operator's designation*] ... DNA
Does Not Apply ... DNA
Does Not Run ... DNR
Dog [*Phonetic alphabet*] [*World War II*] ... D
Dog Kidney Tissue Culture ... DKTC
Dog at Large [*Humorous notation put on letters that cannot be delivered*] [*British postmen's slang*] ... DAL
Dog Owners' Guild ... DOG
Dog Owners League of America [*Defunct*] ... DOLA
Dog Pound [*Multistory parking lot*] [*Slang*] [*British*] ... D-P
Dog Unit [*Veterinary medicine*] ... DU
Dog Vomit On Toast [*Creamed beef or tuna on toast*] [*Military slang*] ... DVOT
Dog Wags Tail [*Airspace effects*] ... DWT
Dog Writers' Association of America ... DWAA
Dogged ... DG
Dogmatic ... DOGM
Dogri [*MARC language code*] [*Library of Congress*] ... doi
Dogs for the Deaf ... DD
Dogs for Defense [*Organization which trained dogs for armed services*] [*World War II*] ... DFD
Dogs on Stamps Study Unit [*American Topical Association*] ... DOSSU
Dogwood [*Missouri*] [*Seismograph station code, US Geological Survey*] ... DWM
Dogwood Library System [*Library network*] ... DLS
Doha [*Qatar*] [*Airport symbol*] ... DOH
Doing Business As [*Followed by company name*] ... D/B/A
Doing Business As [*Followed by company name*] ... DBA
Doit [*Debit*] [*French*] ... DT
Doitsu Bungaku [*A publication*] ... DB
Doklady Academy of Sciences of the USSR. Earth Science Sections [*A publication*] ... Acad Sci USSR Dokl Earth Sci Sec
Doklady Academy of Sciences of the USSR. Earth Science Sections [*A publication*] ... Dokl Acad Sci USSR Earth Sci Sect
Doklady Akademii Nauk Armyanskoi SSR [*A publication*] ... Dokl Akad Nauk Arm SSR
Doklady Akademii Nauk Azerbaidzanskoj SSR [*A publication*] ... Dokl Akad Nauk Az SSR
Doklady Akademii Nauk Azerbajdzanskoj SSR [*A publication*] ... Dokl Akad Nauk Azerb SSR
Doklady Akademii Nauk Belorusskii SSR [*A publication*] ... Dokl Akad Nauk B SSR
Doklady Akademii Nauk Belorusskoi SSR [*A publication*] ... Dokl Akad Nauk Beloruss SSR
Doklady Akademii Nauk SSR [*A publication*] ... DANKA
Doklady Akademii Nauk SSSR [*A publication*] ... DAN
Doklady Akademii Nauk SSSR [*A publication*] ... DAN SSSR
Doklady Akademii Nauk SSSR [*A publication*] ... Dokl Akad Nauk SSSR
Doklady Akademii Nauk SSSR. Biochemistry Section (English Translation) [*A publication*] ... Dokl Akad Nauk SSR Biochem Sect (Engl Transl)
Doklady Akademii Nauk SSSR. Biological Science Section (English Translation) [*A publication*] ... Dokl Akad Nauk SSSR Biol Sci Sect (Engl Transl)
Doklady Akademii Nauk SSSR. Botanical Sciences Section (English Translation) [*A publication*] ... Dokl Akad Nauk SSR Bot Sci Sect (Engl Transl)
Doklady Akademii Nauk SSSR. Seriya Biologiya [*A publication*] ... Dokl Akad Nauk SSSR Ser Biol
Doklady Akademii Nauk Tadzhikskoi SSR [*A publication*] ... Dokl Akad Nauk Tadzh SSR
Doklady Akademii Nauk Uzbekskoi SSR [*A publication*] ... Dokl Akad Nauk Uzbek SSR
Doklady Akademii Nauk Uzbekskoi SSR [*A publication*] ... Dokl Akad Nauk Uzb SSR
Doklady Akademii Pedagogicheskikh Nauk RSFSR [*A publication*] ... DAPNA
Doklady Akademii Pedagogicheskikh Nauk RSFSR [*A publication*] ... Dokl Akad Pedagog Nauk RSFSR
Doklady Bolgarskoi Akademii Nauk [*A publication*] ... DAN Bolg
Doklady Bolgarskoi Akademii Nauk [*A publication*] ... Dokl Bolg Akad Nauk
Doklady Chemical Technology ... DCT
Doklady Chemical Technology. Academy of Sciences of the USSR. Chemical Technology Section [*A publication*] ... Dokl Chem Technol
Doklady Instituta Geografii Sibiri i Dal'nego Vostoka [*A publication*] ... Dokl Inst Geogr Sib Dal'n Vost
Doklady Moskovskoi Sel'skokhozyaistvennoi Akademii Imeni K. A. Timiryazeva [*A publication*] ... Dokl Mosk S-kh Akad Im K A Timiryazeva
Doklady na Naucnych Konferencijach [*A publication*] ... DNK
Doklady Otdelov i Komissii Geograficheskogo Obshchestva SSSR [*A publication*] ... Dokl Otd Kom Geogr O-va SSSR
Doklady Physical Chemistry ... DPC
Doklady Rossiiskoi Sel'skokhozyaistvennoi Akademii Imeni K. A. Timiryazeva [*A publication*] ... Dokl Ross S-kh Akad Im K A Timiryazeva
Doklady Soil Science (English Translation) [*A publication*] ... Dokl Soil Sci (Engl Transl)
Doklady i Soobscenija Filologoceskogo Fakul'teta Moskovskogo Universiteta [*A publication*] ... DoklMU
Doklady i Soobscenija Instituta Jazykozanija Akademiji Nauk SSSR [*A publication*] ... DSIJa
Doklady i Soobscenija Instituta Russkogo Jazyka [*A publication*] ... DoklIRuJa
Doklady i Soobscenija Uzgorodskogo Universiteta [*A publication*] ... DSUzU
Doklady Tbilisskogo Nauchnogo Obshchestva Anatomii, Gistologii, i Embriologii [*A publication*] ... Dokl Tbilis Nauchn O-va Anat Gistol Embriol
Doklady TSKHA [*Timiryazevskaya Sel'skokhozyaistvennaya Akademiya*] [*A publication*] ... Dokl TSKHA
Doklady Vsesoyuznoi Konferentsii "Fizika Khrupkogo Razrusheniya" [*A publication*] ... Dokl Vses Konf "Fiz Khrupkogo Razrusheniya"
Doklady Vsesoyuznoi Konferentsii po Teplofizicheskim Svoistvam Veshchestv [*A publication*] ... Dokl Vses Konf Teplofiz Svoistvam Veshchestv
Dokumantation Schweisstechnik [*Welding Documentation*] [*Germany*] [*Information service*] ... DS
Dokumentation Arbeitsmedizin [*A publication*] ... Dok Arbeitsmed
Dokumentation Fachbibliothek Werkbuecherei [*A publication*] ... Dok Fachbibl Werkbuech
Dokumentation/Information [*A publication*] ... Dok/Inf
Dokumentation zur Raumentwicklung [*A publication*] ... Dok Raum
Dokumentation Strasse [*A publication*] ... Dok Str
Dokumentation Zerstorungsfreie Prufung [*Nondestructive Testing Documentation*] [*West Germany*] [*Information service*] ... ZFP
Dokumentations- und Ausbildungszentrum fuer Theorie und Methode der Regionalforschung [*Documentation and Training Center for Theory and Methods of Regional Research*] [*Germany*] ... DATUM
Dokumentationsdienst Asien Mitteilugen [*A publication*] ... Dokum As Mitt
Dokumentationszentrale Feinwerktechnik [*Precision Technology Documentation Center*] [*West Germany*] [*Information service*] ... DZF
DOL Resources, Inc. [*NASDAQ symbol*] ... DOLS
Dolbeau, PQ [*Radio station call letters*] ... CHVD
Dolce [*Sweet*] [*Music*] ... DOL
Dolcissimo [*Very Sweetly*] [*Music*] ... DOLCIS
Dole [*France*] [*Airport symbol*] [*Obsolete*] ... DLE

Dolenti Parti [*To the Afflicted Part*] [*Pharmacy*] .... DOLENT PART
Dolichol [*Biochemistry*] .... DOL
Dolichos biflorus Agglutinin [*Immunology*] .... DBA
Doll Artisan Guild .... DAG
Doll Collectors of America .... DCA
Doll Supply Manufacturers Association .... DSMA
Dollar .... D
Dollar .... DO
Dollar .... DOL
Dollar [*Monetary unit in Malaya*] .... MS
Dollar General Corp. [*NASDAQ symbol*] .... DOLR
Dollar Tradeoff .... DTO
Dollars .... DLRS
Dollars .... DOLS
Dollars per Flight Hour .... DFH
Dollars and Sense [*A publication*] .... Dollars
Dollars and Sense [*A publication*] .... Doll & Sen
Dolly .... DLY
Dolly Back [*Films, television, etc.*] .... DB
Dolly In [*Films, television, etc.*] .... DI
Dolomite [*Lithology*] .... DOL
Dolore Urgente [*When the Pain Is Severe*] [*Pharmacy*] .... DOL URG
Dolores County Public Library, Dove Creek, CO [*Library symbol*] .... CoDc
Dolores County School District, Rico, CO [*Library symbol*] .... CoRicD
Dolores Public Library, Dolores, CO [*Library symbol*] .... CoDol
Dolpa [*Nepal*] [*Airport symbol*] .... DOP
Dolph-Tchebyscheff Pattern .... DTP
Dolphin .... Dol
Dolton Public Library District, Dolton, IL [*Library symbol*] .... IDol
Dom Perignon [*Champagne*] .... DP
Domain-Originated Functional Integrated Circuit .... DOFIC
Domain Tip Propagation Logic .... DTPL
Dombas [*Norway*] [*Geomagnetic observatory code*] .... DOB
Dome .... D
Dome Mines Ltd. [*NYSE symbol*] .... DM
Dome Petroleum Ltd. [*American Stock Exchange symbol*] .... DMP
Dome Petroleum Ltd., Calgary, AB, Canada [*Library symbol*] .... CaACDP
Dome Removal Tool .... DRT
Domesday Book [*Census-like record of the lands of England, 1085-86*] .... DB
Domesday Survey [*1085-86*] .... DS
Domestic .... DOM
Domestic Action Program [*Army*] .... DAP
Domestic Affairs Council [*Replaced Urban Affairs Council, Rural Affairs Council, and Cabinet Committee on Environment*] [*White House*] .... DAC
Domestic Android [*Quasar Industries*] .... DA
Domestic Annual Harvest .... DAH
Domestic Annual Processing .... DAP
Domestic Commerce [*A publication*] .... Dom Comm
Domestic Council [*Executive Office of the President*] [*Abolished 1978, functions transferred to the President*] .... DC
Domestic Council Committee on Veterans Services [*Veterans Administration*] .... DCCVS
Domestic Credit Expansion .... DCE
Domestic Door-to-Door [*Personal property*] .... DDD
Domestic Emergency Plan .... DEP
Domestic Engineering [*A publication*] .... Dom Eng
Domestic Escorted Tour [*Travel*] .... DET
Domestic and Foreign Missionary Society [*British*] .... DFMS
Domestic Hot Water .... DHW
Domestic Independent Tour [*or Travel*] .... DIT
Domestic Information Display System [*Data processing*] .... DIDS
Domestic and International Business Administration [*Terminated 1977, functions assumed by Industry and Trade Administration*] [*Department of Commerce*] .... DIBA
Domestic International Sales Corporation .... DISC
Domestic and International Scientific Planning and Cooperation .... DISPAC
Domestic Library Automation Functions [*Data processing*] .... DOMLIB
Domestic Policy Review .... DPR
Domestic Prelate .... DP
Domestic Presidential Directive [*Jimmy Carter Administration*] .... DPD
DOMESTIC Print Generator [*Data processing*] .... DOMPRINT
Domestic Route Order .... DRO
Domestic Satellite .... DOMSAT
Domestic Science [*Freight*] .... DOM SC
Domestic Service [*Equipment specification*] .... DS
Domestic Technology Institute .... DTI
Domestic Violence Project .... DVP
Domestic Water .... DW
Domestic Water Tank Manufacturers Council [*Defunct*] .... DWTMC
Domicile .... DOM
Domiciliary Visit [*Medicine*] .... DV
Dominance [*Psychology*] .... Do
Dominance [*Psychology*] .... DOM
Dominance and Submission .... D & S
Dominant [*Applied to a species*] .... D
Dominant .... DMNT
Dominant .... DOM
Dominant Feature Analysis .... DFA
Dominant Hand [*Psychometrics*] .... DH
Dominant Obstacle Allowance .... DOA
Dominant Wavelength .... DWL
Dominica [*Two-letter standard code*] .... DM
Dominica [*Three-letter standard code*] .... DMA
Dominica [*West Indies*] [*Airport symbol*] .... DOM
Dominica [*MARC country of publication code*] [*Library of Congress*] .... dq
Dominica [*MARC geographic area code*] [*Library of Congress*] .... nwdq---
Dominica [*West Indies*] [*Seismograph station code, US Geological Survey*] .... DOM
Dominica-Cane [*West Indies*] [*Airport symbol*] .... DCF
Dominical Letter .... DL
Dominican Campaign Medal .... DCM
Dominican College, Blauvelt, NY [*Library symbol*] .... NBlaD
Dominican College, Houston, TX [*Library symbol*] .... TxHDom
Dominican College of San Rafael [*California*] .... DCSR
Dominican College of San Rafael, San Rafael, CA [*Library symbol*] .... CSrD
Dominican Educational Association .... DEA
Dominican House of Studies, Immaculate Conception Convent Library, Washington, DC [*Library symbol*] [*OCLC symbol*] .... DDC
Dominican Junior College of Blauvelt [*Later, Dominican College*] [*New York*] .... DJCB
Dominican Oblates of Jesus [*Roman Catholic women's religious order*] .... DOJ
Dominican Republic [*Two-letter standard code*] .... DO
Dominican Republic [*Three-letter standard code*] .... DOM
Dominican Republic .... DOMREP
Dominican Republic [*MARC country of publication code*] [*Library of Congress*] .... dr
Dominican Republic [*Aircraft nationality and registration mark*] .... HI
Dominican Republic [*MARC geographic area code*] [*Library of Congress*] .... nwdr---
Dominican Republic Study Group [*Philately*] .... DRSG
Dominican Studies [*A publication*] .... DS
Dominick Fund, Inc. [*NYSE symbol*] [*Delisted*] .... DMK
Dominion .... DOM
Dominion Astrophysical Observatory, Victoria, BC, Canada [*Library symbol*] .... CaBViO
Dominion Atlantic Railway Co. [*Absorbed into CP Rail*] [*AAR code*] .... DA
Dominion Bankshares Corp. [*NASDAQ symbol*] .... DMBK
Dominion Bridge Co. Ltd., Montreal, PQ, Canada [*Library symbol*] .... CaQMDom
Dominion Bureau of Statistics [*Canada*] .... DBS
Dominion of Canada Rifle Association .... DCRA
Dominion Engineering Works Ltd., Montreal, PQ, Canada [*Library symbol*] .... CaQMDE
Dominion Foundries & Steel Ltd., Hamilton, ON, Canada [*Library symbol*] .... CaOHDF
Dominion Glass Co. Ltd., Mississauga, ON, Canada [*Library symbol*] .... CaOMDG
Dominion Holdings [*NASDAQ symbol*] .... DOMH
Dominion Land Surveyor [*Canada*] .... DLS
Dominion Mortgage & Realty [*NASDAQ symbol*] .... DMRTS
Dominion Museum Bulletin [*Wellington*] [*A publication*] .... Dom Mus Bull
Dominion Museum Records in Entomology (Wellington) [*A publication*] .... Dom Mus Rec Entomol (Wellington)
Dominion Museum Records in Zoology (Wellington) [*A publication*] .... Dom Mus Rec Zool (Wellington)
Dominion Naval Forces .... DNF
Dominion Observatory (Ottawa). Contributions [*A publication*] .... Dominion Observatory (Ottawa) Contr
Dominion Observatory. Seismological Series [*A publication*] .... Dominion Observatory Seismol Ser
Dominion Radio Astrophysical Observatory, Penticton, BC, Canada [*Library symbol*] .... CaBPO
Dominion Resources [*NASDAQ symbol*] .... DOMR
Dominion Resources, Inc. [*NYSE symbol*] .... D
Dominion Rubber Co. [*Canada*] [*Research code symbol*] .... D
Dominion Rubber Co. [*Canada*] [*Research code symbol*] .... F
Dominion Textile [*Montreal and Toronto Stock Exchanges symbol*] .... DTX
Dominion Textile, Montreal, PQ, Canada [*Library symbol*] .... CaQMDT
Dominions Office [*British*] .... DO
Dominis Nostris [*To Our Lords*] [*Latin*] .... DDNN
Domino Media, Incorporated [*NASDAQ symbol*] .... DOMI
Domino Nostro [*To Our Lord*] [*Latin*] .... DN
Dominquez Seminary, Compton, CA [*Library symbol*] .... CComD
Dominus [*The Lord*] [*Latin*] .... D
Dominus [*The Lord*] [*Latin*] .... DN
Dominus [*The Lord*] [*Latin*] .... DOM
Dominus [*The Lord*] [*Latin*] .... DS
Dominus Noster [*Our Lord*] [*Latin*] .... DN
Dominus Noster Jesus Christus [*Our Lord Jesus Christ*] [*Latin*] .... DNJC
Dominus Noster Papa Pontifex [*Our Lord the Pope*] [*Latin*] .... DNPP
Dominus Omnium Magister [*God the Master, or Lord, of All*] [*Latin*] [*Motto of the Benedictine Order*] .... DOM
Domodossola [*Italy*] [*Seismograph station code, US Geological Survey*] [*Closed*] .... DMD
Domtar Ltd. [*American Stock Exchange symbol*] .... DTC
Domtar Limited, Montreal, PQ, Canada [*Library symbol*] .... CaQMDL
Domtar Ltd., Research Centre, Senneville, PQ, Canada [*Library symbol*] .... CaQSeD
Domus Procerum [*The House of Lords*] [*Latin*] .... DP
Don [*Spanish*] .... D

Don Bosco College [*New Jersey*] ... DBC
Don Bosco College, Newton, NJ [*Library symbol*] ... NjNetDB
Don King Sports and Entertainment Network [*Cable TV programing service*] ... DKSEN
Donahue Library [*Catholic Library of San Francisco*], **San Francisco, CA** [*Library symbol*] ... CSfD
Donald W. Douglas Laboratory [*McDonnell Douglas Corp.*] ... DWDL
Donaldson Company, Incorporated [*NYSE symbol*] ... DCI
Donaldson, Lufkin, & Jenrette, Inc. [*NYSE symbol*] ... DLJ
Donaldsonville, GA [*Radio station call letters*] ... WGMK
Donaldsonville, LA [*Radio station call letters*] ... KSMI
Donalsonville, GA [*Radio station call letters*] ... WSEM
Donath-Landsteiner [*Hemolysin*] [*Hematology*] ... D-L
Donation on Discharge ... D/D
Donative ... DON
Doncaster Public Library, Doncaster, United Kingdom [*Library symbol*] ... UkDo
Donegal [*County in Ireland*] ... DON
Donegal Resources Ltd. [*NASDAQ symbol*] ... DONEF
Donelson, TN [*Radio station call letters*] ... WAMB
Donetsk [*USSR*] [*Airport symbol*] [*Obsolete*] ... DOK
Dongara [*Australia*] [*Airport symbol*] ... DOX
Dongguk Journal [*A publication*] ... Dongguk J
Dongola [*Sudan*] [*Airport symbol*] ... DOG
Dongola [*Missouri*] [*Seismograph station code, US Geological Survey*] ... DON
Doniphan, Kensett, & Searcy Railway [*AAR code*] ... DKS
Doniphan, MO [*Radio station call letters*] ... KDFN
Doniphan, MO [*Radio station call letters*] ... KOEA
Donizetti Society ... Donsoc
Donkey Red Cell [*s*] ... DRC
Donnees pour le Developpement [*Data for Development International Association - DFD*] ... DD
Donnees Statistiques du Limousin [*A publication*] ... Donnees Statist Limousin
Donnelley [*R. R.*] **& Sons Co.** [*NYSE symbol*] ... DNY
Donnellson Public Library, Donnellson, IA [*Library symbol*] ... IaDon
Donnely Dome [*Alaska*] [*Seismograph station code, US Geological Survey*] ... DDM
Donnkenny, Inc. [*American Stock Exchange symbol*] [*Delisted*] ... DON
Dono Dedit Dedicavit [*He Gave and Dedicated as a Gift*] [*Latin*] ... DDD
Donor ... D
Donor-Acceptor ... DA
Donor Energy Level ... DEL
Donora Southern R. R. [*AAR code*] ... DSO
Donor's Cells [*Medicine*] ... DC
Donor's Plasma [*Medicine*] ... DP
Donor's Serum [*Medicine*] ... DS
Donovan Cos. [*NASDAQ symbol*] ... DONOA
Donovan, Gerard J., Co., Inc., North Attleboro MA [*STAC*] ... DGJ
Donrey Media Group, Fort Smith, AR [*Library symbol*] ... ArFsD
Don't Answer ... DA
Don't-Care-a-Damn [*British naval slang term for torpedo-boat destroyer*] [*World War I*] ... DCD
Don't Ditch a Buddy [*Promise made by members of the Junior Woodchucks, organization to which comic strip character Donald Duck's nephews belonged*] ... DDB
Don't Give a Spit [*Slang*] [*Bowdlerized version*] ... DGS
Don't Knock It [*Slang*] ... DKI
Don't Know ... DK
Donum Dedit [*Gave, Dedicated*] [*Latin*] ... DD
Doolan Road [*California*] [*Seismograph station code, US Geological Survey*] ... DOO
Doomadgee Mission [*Australia*] [*Airport symbol*] ... DMD
Door ... DR
Door Closer ... DC
Door Closer ... DCL
Door County Library, Sturgeon Bay, WI [*Library symbol*] ... WSbD
Door in Flat [*Theater*] ... DF
Door Gunner [*Military*] ... DGR
Door and Hardware Institute [*Formerly, ASAHC, NBHA*] ... DHI
Door Insulating Systems Index ... DISI
Door Lock Rotary Actuator ... DLRA
Door Mounted Junction Panel ... DMJP
Door and Operator Dealers of America ... DODA
Door Operator and Remote Controls Manufacturers Association ... DORCMA
Door Stop ... DST
Door Switch ... DSW
Door or Window [*Freight*] ... DR WIND
Dopa Decarboxylase [*An enzyme*] ... DDC
Dopamine [*Biochemistry*] ... DA
Dopamine Beta-Hydroxylase [*An enzyme*] ... DBH
Doped Erbium Oxide ... DEO
Doped Glass LASER ... DGL
Dopo Cristo [*After Christ*] [*Italian*] ... DC
Dopovidi Akademii Nauk Ukrains'koi RSR [*A publication*] ... Dop Akad Nauk Ukr RSR
Dopovidi Akademii Nauk Ukrainskoi RSR [*A publication*] ... Dopov Akad Nauk Ukr RSR
Dopovidi Akademii Nauk Ukrainskoi RSR. Seriya A [*A publication*] ... Dop Ukr A
Dopovidi Akademii Nauk Ukrainskoi RSR. Seriya B [*A publication*] ... Dop Ukr B
Dopovidi ta Povidomlenniya L'vivs'koho Derzhavnoho Universytetu [*A publication*] ... Dopov Povidomlenniya L'viv Derzh Univ
Dopovidi ta Povidomlennja. Materialy Konferencij Drohobyc'koho Derzavnoho Pedahohicnoho Instytutu Imeni I. Ja. Franka. Serija Filolohicnych Nauk. Drohobyc [*A publication*] ... DPDroh
Doppel-Ring-Speicher [*Storage ring facility*] ... DORIS
Doppellafette [*Two-barreled mount*] [*German military - World War II*] ... DL
Doppelposten [*Double Sentry*] [*German military - World War II*] ... DP
Doppio Pedale [*Double Pedal*] [*Music*] ... DOPP PED
Doppler ... DOP
Doppler ... DOPP
Doppler ... DPLR
Doppler Acoustic Vortec Sensing System [*FAA*] ... DAVSS
Doppler Arrival Angle Spectral Measurement System [*Geophysics*] ... DAASM
Doppler Beam Sampling [*Air navigation*] ... DBS
Doppler Beam Sharpener ... DBS
Doppler Data Translator ... DDT
Doppler Detection Station [*Detection station on the Mid-Canada Line*] ... DDS
Doppler Detection System ... DDS
Doppler Direction-Finding Equipment ... DOPDF
Doppler Extractor ... DE
Doppler Filter Mixer-Oscillator [*Electronics*] ... DFMO
Doppler Inertial ... DI
Doppler Inertial LORAN ... DIL
Doppler Inertial LORAN System ... DILS
Doppler Inertial System ... DIS
Doppler LASER RADAR ... DLR
Doppler Location and Ranging System ... DOLARS
Doppler Martin RADAR [*Air Force*] ... DOMAR
Doppler Measurement System ... DMS
Doppler Microwave Landing System ... DMLS
Doppler Missile ... DM
Doppler Navigation System ... DNS
Doppler Optical Navigation ... DON
Doppler Optical Surveillance System ... DOSS
Doppler Phase Lock ... DOPLOC
Doppler Predict Voltage ... DPV
Doppler RADAR ... DRA
Doppler RADAR Equipment ... DRE
Doppler and Range Evaluation ... DARE
Doppler Range and Navigation [*Electronics*] ... DORAN
Doppler Ranging and Information System [*Navy*] ... DORIS
Doppler-Shifted Constant Frequency [*Biosonar research*] ... DSCF
Doppler SONAR Velocity Log ... DSVL
Doppler Spectrum Analyzer ... DSA
Doppler Spectrum Processor ... DSP
Doppler Techniques Proposal ... DTP
Doppler Tracking Station ... DTS
Doppler Translation Channel ... DTC
Doppler Unbeamed Search RADAR ... DOUSER
Doppler, Velocity and Position [*NASA*] ... DOVAP
Doppler Velocity Sensor ... DVS
Doppler VHF [*Very High Frequency*] **Omnirange** ... DVOR
Dora, AL [*Radio station call letters*] ... WPYK
Dorado [*Puerto Rico*] [*Airport symbol*] ... DDP
Dorado [*Constellation*] ... Dor
Dorado [*Constellation*] ... Dora
Dorado Wings [*Airline code*] ... KW
Doran Energy Corp. [*NASDAQ symbol*] ... DORE
Dorcas Welfare Society [*Later, Community Services*] ... DWS
Dorchester County Public Library, Cambridge, MD [*Library symbol*] ... MdCam
Dorchester Gas Corp. [*American Stock Exchange symbol*] ... DGS
Dorchester Hugoton DDR [*NASDAQ symbol*] ... DHULZ
Dordt College, Sioux Center, IA [*Library symbol*] ... IaSceD
Dordt College, Sioux Center, IA [*OCLC symbol*] ... IOT
Dori [*Upper Volta*] [*Airport symbol*] ... DOR
Doric ... DOR
Doric Corp. [*NYSE symbol*] [*Delisted*] ... DO
Doriden [*Glutethimide*] [*Sedative*] ... D
Doris Lessing Newsletter [*A publication*] ... DLN
Dormant Inertial Navigation System ... DINS
Dormit in Pace [*Sleeps in Peace*] [*Latin*] ... DIP
Dormitory ... DOR
Dormitory ... DORM
Dornier [*German airplane type*] ... DO
Dorobisoro [*Papua New Guinea*] [*Airport symbol*] ... DOO
Dorr-Oliver, Inc. [*NYSE symbol*] [*Delisted*] ... DOR
Dorr Township Library, Dorr, MI [*Library symbol*] ... MiDo
Dorsal ... D
Dorsal Column Stimulator [*Pain killer*] ... DCS
Dorsal Cutaneous Nerve ... DCN
Dorsal Fold ... DF
Dorsal Fold (Oesophagus) ... DFO

Dorsal (Kidney) ... DK
Dorsal Lateral Geniculate Nucleus [*Anatomy*] ... LGd
Dorsal Lip ... DL
Dorsal Motor Nucleus [*of the vagus*] ... DMN
Dorsal (Nephridial Gland) ... DNG
Dorsal Peristomial Collar Fold ... DPCF
Dorsal Pitt ... DP
Dorsal Raphe [*Brain anatomy*] ... DR
Dorsal Raphe Nucleus [*Brain anatomy*] ... DRN
Dorsal Respiratory Group [*Medicine*] ... DRG
Dorsal Root [*of spinal nerve*] [*Anatomy*] ... DR
Dorsal Root Ganglia [*Anatomy*] ... DRG
Dorsal Root Ganglion [*Neuroanatomy*] ... DRG
Dorsal Root Potential [*Anatomy*] ... DRP
Dorsal Velar Lobe ... DVL
Dorsch Memorial Public Library, Monroe, MI [*Library symbol*] ... MiMD
Dorsetshire [*County in England*] ... DORSET
Dorsey Corp. [*NYSE symbol*] ... DSY
Dorsey Laboratories [*Research code symbol*] ... HF
Dorsiflexion [*Medicine*] ... DF
Dorsolateral Funiculus [*Neuroanatomy*] ... DLF
Dorsomedial Nucleus [*Brain anatomy*] ... DMN
Dortmund [*West Germany*] [*Airport symbol*] ... DTM
Dortmund Data Bank [*West Germany*] [*Information service*] ... DDB
Dorunda Station [*Australia*] [*Airport symbol*] [*Obsolete*] ... DRD
Dos Bocas Dam [*Puerto Rico*] [*Seismograph station code, US Geological Survey*] ... DOS
Dosage [*Medicine*] ... DOS
Dose Commitment Factor [*Radioactivity calculations*] ... DCF
Dose Conversion Factor [*Radioactivity calculations*] ... DCF
Dose Detector System ... DDS
Dose Equivalent [*Radioactivity calculations*] ... DE
Dose Factor [*Radioactivity calculations*] ... DF
Dose Rate Instrumentation ... DRI
Dose Reduction Factor ... DRF
Dose Response Curve [*Medicine*] ... DRC
Doshida Joshidaigaku Gakujutsu Kenkyu Nenpo [*A publication*] ... DJGKN
Dosimetry Acquisition and Display System ... DADS
Dosimetry Applications Research Facility [*AEC*] ... DOSAR
Dosis [*Dose*] [*Pharmacy*] ... D
Doskocil Cos. [*NASDAQ symbol*] ... DOSK
Doslidzennja z Literaturoznavstava ta Movoznavstva [*A publication*] ... DLMov
Doslidzennja i Materijaly z Ukrjins'koji Movy [*A publication*] ... DMUkrM
Doslidzennja z Movoznavstva Zbirnyk Statej Aspirantiv i Dysertantiv [*A publication*] ... DMov
Dossier Mundo [*A publication*] ... Doss Mundo
Dossiers de l'Archeologie [*A publication*] ... Doss Archeol
Dossiers Bis Jeune Afrique et Economia [*A publication*] ... Doss Bis Jeune Afr Econ
Dossiers de l'Economie Lorraine [*A publication*] ... Doss Econ Lorraine
Dossiers de la Politique Agricole Commune [*A publication*] ... Doss Polit Agric Commune
Dothan [*Alabama*] [*Airport symbol*] ... DHN
Dothan, AL [*Radio station call letters*] ... WDBM
Dothan, AL [*Television station call letters*] ... WDHN-TV
Dothan, AL [*Radio station call letters*] ... WDIG
Dothan, AL [*Radio station call letters*] ... WOOF
Dothan, AL [*Radio station call letters*] ... WOOF-FM
Dothan, AL [*Radio station call letters*] ... WTVY
Dothan, AL [*Radio station call letters*] ... WWNT
Dothan, AL [*Television station call letters*] ... WTVY
Dotronix, Inc. [*NASDAQ symbol*] ... DOTX
Dottore Ingenieur [*Doctor of Engineering*] ... Dott Ing
Dottoressa [*Female Doctor*] ... Dssa
Douala [*Cameroon*] [*Airport symbol*] ... DLA
Douane [*Customs*] [*French*] ... D
Douay Version [*Bible*] ... DV
Double ... D
Double ... DBL
Double ... DUBL
Double Absorption Photofragment Spectroscopy ... DAPS
Double-Acting ... DA
Double-Acting Door [*Technical drawings*] ... DAD
Double-Acting Limit Switch ... DALS
Double-Acting Steam ... DASTM
Double-Action Cylinder ... DAC
Double Aged [*Metals*] ... DA
Double-Air Movement Valve ... DAMV
Double Aluminized Mylar ... DAM
Double Amplitude ... DA
Double-Amplitude Displacement ... DAD
Double-Amplitude Peak ... DAP
Double Anode Zener Diode ... DAZD
Double Arm Magnetic Spectrometer ... DASP
Double Balanced Mixer ... DBM
Double-Base Diode ... DBD
Double-Base Propellant ... DBP
Double-Base Solid Propellant ... DBSP
Double-Base Transistor ... DBT
Double Beam Spectrophotometer ... DBS
Double Beta Decay ... DBD
Double Biased ... DB
Double Bituminous Surface Treatment ... DBST
Double Black [*Pencil*] ... BB
Double Bottom ... DB
Double Bottoms [*Naval*] ... DB's
Double Bounce, Circularly Polarized ... DBCP
Double Braid ... DB
Double Break ... DB
Double Breasted [*Clothing industry*] ... DB
Double British Summer Time ... DBST
Double Cantilever Beam [*Stress condition of aluminum alloy*] ... DCB
Double Cap [*or Crown*] [*Paper size*] ... DC
Double Cash Ruled [*Stationery*] ... DX
Double Chain Branch-Oblong Master Link-Grab Hook ... DOG
Double Channel Duplex ... DCD
Double Channel Simplex ... DCS
Double-Check Valve ... DCV
Double-Coated Foam Tape ... DCFT
Double Column ... DC
Double Common Meter [*Music*] ... DCM
Double Compton Scattering ... DCS
Double Concave [*Medicine*] ... DCc
Double-Conductor, Heat and Flame-Resistant, Armor [*Cable*] ... DHFA
Double Contact [*Switch*] ... DC
Double Conversion Adapter ... DCA
Double Convex ... DCx
Double Cotton [*Wire insulation*] ... DC
Double Cotton Covered [*Wire insulation*] ... DCC
Double Cotton Double Silk [*Wire insulation*] ... DCDS
Double Cotton Single Silk [*Wire insulation*] ... DCS
Double Cotton Varnish [*Wire insulation*] ... DCV
Double Crochet ... DC
Double Current Generator ... DCG
Double Cylinder Deadlock ... DCDL
Double-Cylinder Tank [*Liquid gas carriers*] ... dc
Double Dacron Braid Lacquered ... DD
Double Dealer [*A publication*] ... Dble Dealer
Double Deck ... DD
Double Declining Balance [*Statistics*] ... DDB
Double Deflection Tube ... DDT
Double Defruit [*Aviation*] ... DDF
Double Density Modular Core Memory ... DMCM
Double Differential Cross Section ... DDCS
Double Diffused Mesa ... DDM
Double-Diffused Metal-Oxide Semiconductor ... DMOS
Double Diffusion [*Test*] ... DD
Double-Dipper [*Retired military-government employee*] ... DD
Double Dominance [*Ethology*] ... DD
Double-Doped Crystal ... DDC
Double Drift [*As used in a navigator's log*] ... DD
Double Eagle Petroleum & Mining Co. [*NASDAQ symbol*] ... DBLE
Double Edge Receiver ... DER
Double End [*Technical drawings*] ... DE
Double-Ended Pivot ... DEP
Double Entry [*Bookkeeping*] ... DE
Double Excellent ... XX
Double Extra Strong ... XXSTR
Double Face ... DBLF
Double Feeder [*Line*] [*Technical drawings*] ... DF
Double Frequency Shift Keying [*Radio*] ... DFSK
Double-Fronted ... D-F
Double-Gimbaled Momentum Wheel ... DGMW
Double Glass ... DG
Double Green Silk Covered [*Wire insulation*] ... DGS
Double Groove [*Insulators*] ... DG
Double Groove, Double Petticoat [*Insulators*] ... DGDP
Double-Gummed [*Envelopes*] ... DG
Double Gypsy Winch ... DGW
Double Heat-Sink Diode ... DHD
Double Heave Amplitude ... DHA
Double Helix [*Cytology, genetics*] ... DH
Double Heterostructure [*Physics*] ... DH
Double Hexagonal Close-Packed [*Metallography*] ... DHCP
Double-Hung [*Construction*] ... DH
Double-Hung Windows [*Technical drawings*] ... DHW
Double Indemnity ... DI
Double Injection ... DI
Double Injection Effect ... DIE
Double Injection Luminescence ... DIL
Double Isotope Derivative ... DID
Double Ledger [*Accounting*] ... DL
Double Leg Elbow Amplifier ... DLEA
Double Length Line ... DLL
Double Length Number ... DLN
Double Local Oscillator ... DLO
Double Long Meter [*Music*] ... DLM
Double Mark Blank Column ... DMBC
Double Mars Loiter ... DML
Double Master [*LORAN stations*] ... DM
Double Minute [*Cytology*] ... DM

Double Negation [Rule of replacement] [Logic]..............DN
Double Odd Pass Even [System in game of bridge] ....DOPE
Double Oil of Vitriol ....DOV
Double Outlet Right Ventricle [Cardiology] ....DORV
Double Overhead Camshaft [Automotive term]............DOHC
Double Paper [Wire insulation]...............................DP
Double Paper-Covered [Wire insulation]....................DPC
Double Paper, Double Cotton [Wire insulation] ....DPDC
Double Paper, Single Cotton [Wire insulation]...........DPSC
Double Petticoat [Insulators] ....DP
Double Play [Baseball]...DP
Double Pole [Switch]...DP
Double-Pole, Back Connected [Switch].....................DPBC
Double Pole, Both Connected [Switch] ....DPBC
Double-Pole, Double Throw [Switch].......................DPDT
Double-Pole, Double-Throw Switch ....DPDTSW
Double-Pole, Front Connected [Switch].....................DPFC
Double Pole, Single Throw [Switch] ....DPST
Double-Pole, Single-Throw Switch ....DPSTSW
Double-Pole Switch ....DPSW
Double Pole, Triple Throw [Switch] ....DPTT
Double-Precision Arithmetic...................................DPA
Double-Precision Automatic Interpretive System ....DAISY
Double-Precision Orbit Determination Program [NASA] ...DPODP
Double-Precision Quantity ....DPQ
Double-Precision Trajectory Program [NASA]...........DPTRAJ
Double [or Dual] Propellant Loading ....DPL
Double Pulse Duration Modulation ....DPDM
Double Pulse Operation ....DPO
Double Pulse Ranging ....DPR
Double Pumped Parametric Amplifier........................DPPA
Double-Purpose Gun ....DP
Double Reduced [Tinplate]....................................DR
Double Reduction-Locked Train ....DLT
Double Roll Out Arrays ....DORA
Double-Round Nose..DRN
Double-Screened [Coal] ....D/S
Double-Sealed Ball Valve....................................DSBV
Double Secondary Current Transformer.....................DSCT
Double Short Meter [Music]..................................DSM
Double Sideband...DSB
Double-Sideband Amplitude Modulation Reduced Carrier ....DSBAMRC
Double-Sideband Doppler Very-High-Frequency
   Omnidirectional Range [FAA]............................DSDVOR
Double-Sideband Suppressed Carrier.......................DSBSC
Double-Sideband Suppressed Carrier [Modulation] ....DSSC
Double-Sideband Transmitted Carrier......................DSBTC
Double-Sided, Double-Density Disk [Data processing]......DSDD
Double Silk [Wire insulation].................................DS
Double Silk Covered [Wire insulation]......................DSC
Double Silk Varnish [Wire insulation] ....DSV
Double Silver Plate...DSP
Double-Single-Dummy [in game of bridge] ....DSD
Double Single-Sideband......................................DSSB
Double Slave [LORAN stations]...............................DS
Double Spot System ....DSS
Double Spot Tuning ....DST
Double Stitch [Bookbinding]...................................DS
Double Strength [Medicine]....................................DS
Double Strokes per Minute...................................DSPM
Double Subdominance [Ethology]..............................DS
Double Summer Time [Daylight Saving Time two hours ahead of
   Standard Time] [British]......................................DST
Double Tape Armored [Heavy-duty telephone buried cable].........DTA
Double Test Position ....DTP
Double Throw [Switch]...DT
Double Throw Switch...DTS
Double Time ....DT
Double Tube ....DT
Double Uptake [Boilers] ....DU
Double Velocity Transit Time [Physics] ....DOVETT
Double Vessel Disease with an Abnormal Left Ventricle
   [Cardiology]..DVDALV
Double Vibrations [Cycles] ....DV
Double Vibrations [Cycles] ....VD
Double Vision..DV
Double Wall ....DBLW
Double Wall ....DW
Double-Wall Fiberboard ....DWLFBD
Double Weight ....DW
Double-Weight [Paper]..DWT
Double White Silk Covered [Wire insulation] ....DWS
Double Wipe Slide Switch...................................DWSS
Double-Wire Armor..DWA
Double Zigzag Rectifier ....DZR
Doublecross [i.e., to betray] [Criminal slang].................Y
Doubler...DBLR
Doublet...D
Doubly Buffered Ringer [Physiology]........................DBR
Doubtful..D
Doubtful...DBTF

Dough Rate of Reaction [Food science] ....DRR
Dougherty Brothers Company [American Stock Exchange symbol]........DBC
Dougherty County Court House, Albany, GA [Library symbol] ....GAID
Doughtie's Foods [NASDAQ symbol]........................DOBQ
Douglas [Arizona] [Airport symbol]..........................DUG
Douglas Advanced Research Laboratories [Obsolete] ....DARL
Douglas Aircraft Co. [of McDonnell Douglas Corp.] [NYSE
   symbol] [Delisted, see MD]....................................D
Douglas Aircraft Company [of McDonnell Douglas Corp.] .....DAC
Douglas Aircraft Co. of Canada [of McDonnell Douglas Corp.]..........DACAN
Douglas Aircraft Company Overseas [Obsolete] ....DACO
Douglas Aircraft Co., Santa Monica Division, Santa Monica, CA
   [Library symbol]...CStmoD
Douglas Aircraft Co., Technical Library, Long Beach, CA [Library
   symbol] ....CLobD
Douglas Airways Pty. Ltd. [ICAO designator]..................DB
Douglas, AZ [Radio station call letters]....................KAPR
Douglas, AZ [Radio station call letters]....................KDAP
Douglas, AZ [Radio station call letters]....................KKRK
Douglas College, New Westminster, BC, Canada [Library
   symbol]..CaBNWD
Douglas County Jarman Memorial Hospital, Tuscola, IL [Library
   symbol] ....ITuCoH
Douglas County Library, Minden, NV [Library symbol] ....NvMiD
Douglas County Library, Roseburg, OR [Library symbol].......OrRoD
Douglas County Museum, Roseburg, OR [Library symbol].......OrRoM
Douglas County Public Library, Castle Rock, CO [Library symbol]........CoCr
Douglas County Public Library, Castle Rock, CO [OCLC symbol]..........DAD
Douglas County Public Library, Parker Branch, Parker, CO
   [Library symbol]..CoParD
Douglas Elementary School, Princeton, IL [Library symbol]................IPriDS
Douglas Fir ....DF
Douglas Fir Export Company [Defunct] ....DFEC
Douglas Fir Plywood Association [Later, APA]..............DFPA
Douglas-Fir Tussock Moth ....DFTM
Douglas, GA [Location identifier] [FAA]......................DQH
Douglas, GA [Radio station call letters].....................WDMG
Douglas, GA [Radio station call letters].................WDMG-FM
Douglas, GA [Radio station call letters].....................WOKA
Douglas, GA [Radio station call letters].................WOKA-FM
Douglas Hospital, Montreal, PQ, Canada [Library symbol] ......CaQMDH
Douglas & Lomason [NASDAQ symbol] ....DOUG
Douglas [Arizona] Municipal [Airport symbol] ....DGL
Douglas Space Physics Laboratory ....DSPL
Douglas Space Vehicle ....DSV
Douglas United Nuclear, Inc....................................DUN
Douglas, WY [Radio station call letters]....................KWIV
Douglasville, GA [Radio station call letters]................WDGL
Dounreay Experimental Reactor Establishment [British]......DERE
Dounreay Fast Reactor [British].................................DFR
Dounreay Materials Testing Reactor [British]...............DMTR
Dourados [Brazil] [Airport symbol].............................DOU
Dourbes [Belgium] [Geomagnetic observatory code].............DOU
Dourbes [Belgium] [Seismograph station code, US Geological
   Survey]..DOU
Douro Litoral [A publication].....................................DL
Douro Litoral (Portugal) [A publication].......................DLP
Douzaine [Dozen] [French]....................................DZNE
DOVAP [Doppler Velocity and Position] Automatic Reduction
   Equipment ....DARE
Dove Creek, CO [Location identifier] [FAA]...................DVC
Dover Corp. [NYSE symbol]....................................DOV
Dover, DE [Radio station call letters].......................WDOV
Dover, DE [Radio station call letters].......................WDSD
Dover, DE [Radio station call letters].......................WKEN
Dover, ME [Radio station call letters]......................WDME
Dover, ME [Radio station call letters]..................WDME-FM
Dover, NH [Radio station call letters]......................WOKQ
Dover, NH [Radio station call letters]......................WTSN
Dover, NJ [Radio station call letters]......................WDHA
Dover, NJ [Radio station call letters]......................WRAN
Dover, OH [Radio station call letters].......................WJER
Dover, OH [Radio station call letters].................. WJER-FM
Dover Public Library, Dover, DE [OCLC symbol].............DOV
Dover Public Library, Dover, NH [Library symbol] ....NhDo
Dover Public Library, Dover, NJ [Library symbol]..............NjD
Dover Publications, New York, NY [Library symbol]..........NND
Dovetail...DVTL
Dow Chemical Co. [Research code symbol]....................A-E
Dow Chemical Company ....DCC
Dow Chemical Co. [Research code symbol] ....DH
Dow Chemical Co. [NYSE symbol]............................DOW
Dow Chemical Co., E and CS Information Center, Houston, TX
   [Library symbol]...TxHDC
Dow Chemical Co., Granville Research Center, Granville, OH
   [OCLC symbol] ....DOW
Dow Chemical Co., Library, Midland, MI [OCLC symbol].......MDC
Dow Chemical Co., Midland, MI [Library symbol]...........MiMidD
Dow Chemical Co., Rocky Flats Division, Golden, CO [Library
   symbol]..CoGD
Dow Chemical Co., Sarnia, ON, Canada [Library symbol]......CaOSD

Dow Chemical Co., Texas Division, Freeport, TX [*OCLC symbol*] .... DTF
Dow Chemical Co., Texas Division, Freeport, TX [*Library symbol*] .... TxFrD
Dow Corning Corp., Midland, MI [*Library symbol*] .... MiMidDC
Dow Education Systems [*Dow Chemical Corp.*] .... DES
Dow Epoxy Novolac .... DEN
Dow Jones Books, Princeton, NJ [*Library symbol*] .... DjB
Dow Jones Cable News [*Cable TV programing service*] .... DJCN
Dow Jones & Co., Inc. [*Also, the stock market averages compiled by this company*] .... D-J
Dow Jones & Co., Inc. [*NYSE symbol*] .... DJ
Dow Jones & Co., Inc., Chicopee, MA [*Library symbol*] .... MChiD
Dow Jones Index [*Stock market*] .... DJI
Dow Jones Index - Commodity [*Stock market*] .... CDJI
Dow Jones Index - Composite [*Stock market*] .... DJIC
Dow Jones Index - Industrials [*Stock market*] .... DJII
Dow Jones Index - Transport [*Stock market*] .... DJIT
Dow Jones Index - Utilities [*Stock market*] .... DJIU
Dow Jones Industrial Average [*Stock market*] .... DJIA
Dow-Lepetit [*Research code symbol*] .... DL
Dowager .... D
Dowager .... DOW
Dowagiac, MI [*Radio station call letters*] .... WDOW
Dowagiac, MI [*Radio station call letters*] .... WDOW-FM
Dowagiac Public Library, Dowagiac, MI [*Library symbol*] .... MiDow
Dowel .... DWL
Dowlais Central [*Cardiff*] [*Welsh depot code*] .... DLIS
Dowling College, Des Moines, IA [*Library symbol*] .... IaDmDC
Dowling College, Oakdale, NY [*Library symbol*] .... NOaD
Dowling College, Oakdale, NY [*OCLC symbol*] .... VXZ
Down .... DN
Down .... DWN
Down to Earth [*A publication*] .... Down Earth
Down Feeding Spindle .... DFS
Down-Island Communication System [*Taiwan*] .... DICS
Down Left [*The front left portion of a stage*] [*A stage direction*] .... DL
Down Link [*Data processing*] .... DL
Down-Link Communications [*Antisubmarine warfare*] .... DOLCO
Down-Link Television Terminal .... DLTT
Down (Quark) [*Atomic physics*] .... d
Down Right [*The front right portion of a stage*] [*A stage direction*] .... DR
Down Through [*Clairvoyance experiment*] .... DT
Down Through Sealed Packs [*Clairvoyance experiment*] .... DTSP
Downbeat [*A publication*] .... Dbt
Downdraft .... DNDFT
Downdrafts .... DWNDFTS
Downeast Airlines [*Rockland, ME*] [*FAA designator*] .... DEA
Downed Aircraft .... DAC
Downed Airman Power Source [*Navy*] .... DAPS
Downers Grove, IL [*Radio station call letters*] .... WDGC-FM
Downers Grove Public Library, Downers Grove, IL [*Library symbol*] .... IDow
Downey, CA [*Location identifier*] [*FAA*] .... JDY
Downey City Library, Downey, CA [*Library symbol*] .... CDo
Downey Savings & Loan Association [*American Stock Exchange symbol*] .... DSL
Downgrade .... DG
Downrange [*NASA*] .... DNR
Downrange .... D/R
Downrange Antimissile Measurement Program [*RADAR*] .... DAMP
Downrange Antimissile Program [*Army*] .... DAM
Downrange Computer Input System .... DCIS
Downrange Computer Output System .... DCOS
Downrange Data Report .... DDR
Downrange Distance During Launch [*NASA*] .... D
Downrange Error [*NASA*] .... DRE
Downrange Support Ship .... DRSS
Downrange Up Link [*Apollo*] [*NASA*] .... DRUL
Downriver Associated Narcotics Organization .... DRANO
Downriver Residents Against Bowling .... DRAB
Down's Syndrome [*Medicine*] .... DS
Down's Syndrome Congress .... DSC
Down's Syndrome International .... DSI
Downside Review [*A publication*] .... DoR
Downside Review [*A publication*] .... DownR
Downside Review [*A publication*] .... DR
Downslope .... DNSLP
Downspout .... DS
Downspout Rechargement Infusion Program [*Energy development program*] .... DRIP
Downstage [*Toward audience*] [*A stage direction*] .... DS
Downstage Center [*Toward audience*] [*A stage direction*] .... DSC
Downstage Left [*Toward audience*] [*A stage direction*] .... DSL
Downstage Right [*Toward audience*] [*A stage direction*] .... DSR
Downstate Medical Center, SUNY [*State University of New York*], **Brooklyn, NY** [*OCLC symbol*] .... VVD
Downstream .... DS
Downstream Heat Exchanger .... DSHE
Downtime .... DNT
Downtime .... DT
Downtown Area Short Hops [*Battery-powered bus service in Long Beach, California*] .... DASH
Downtown Development Foundation .... DDF
Downtown People Mover .... DPM
Downward Ejection Bomblet .... DEB
Downward-Looking Infrared [*Air Force*] .... DLIR
Downward-Looking Infrared System [*Air Force*] .... DLIS
Downward Vertical Velocity [*Meteorology*] .... DVV
Downwind .... DNWIND
Downwind Safety Limit .... DSL
Dows Community Library, Dows, IA [*Library symbol*] .... IaDo
Doxorubicin [*See also ADR, Adriamycin*] [*Antineoplastic drug*] .... D
Doyle Dane Bernbach, Inc. [*Advertising agency*] .... DDB
Doyle Dane Bernbach, Inc. [*NASDAQ symbol*] .... DOYL
Doylestown, PA [*Location identifier*] [*FAA*] .... DYL
Doylestown, PA [*Radio station call letters*] .... WBUX
Doyon, AK [*Location identifier*] [*FAA*] .... ADI
Dozen .... DOZ
Dozen .... DZ
Dozenal [*formerly, Duodecimal*] **Society of America** .... DSA
Dozier, AL [*Television station call letters*] .... WDIQ
DPF, Inc. [*Formerly, Data Processing Financial & General Corp.*] [*NYSE symbol*] [*Delisted*] .... DPF
Drachma [*Monetary unit in Greece*] .... D
Drachma [*Monetary unit in Greece*] .... DR
Drachma [*Monetary unit in Greece*] .... DRE
Drachma [*Monetary unit in Greece*] .... DRX
Drackett Co., Research and Development Library, Cincinnati, OH [*Library symbol*] .... OCDr
Draco [*Constellation*] .... Dra
Draco [*Constellation*] .... Drac
Draco [*Sweden*] [*Research code symbol*] .... KWD
Dracula Society .... DS
Draegerheft. Mitteilungen der Draegerwerk AG Luebeck [*A publication*] .... Draegerh
Draft .... DFT
Draft .... DR
Draft Action .... DA
Draft Change Notice .... DCN
Draft Collection Only [*Business and trade*] .... DCO
Draft Development Concept Paper .... DDCP
Draft Environmental Impact Statement .... DEIS
Draft Environmental Statement [*Bureau of Outdoor Recreation*] .... DES
Draft International Standard [*International Standards Organization*] .... DIS
Draft Presidential Memorandum [*DoD*] .... DPM
Draft Proposal .... DP
Draft Proposal Qualitative Materiel Requirement .... DPQMR
Draft Proposed Letter of Agreement .... DPLOA
Draft Proposed Training Device Requirement .... DPTDR
Draft Recommendation [*International Standards Organization*] .... DR
Draft Request for Proposal .... DRFP
Draft Stop [*Technical drawings*] .... DS
Draft Technical Manual .... DTM
Drafting .... DFTG
Drafting Machine .... DFMACH
Drafting Manual .... DM
Drafting, Pay and Records Office, Royal Marines [*British*] .... DPRORM
Drafting Practice Manual .... DPM
Drafting Program [*Association of Independent Colleges and Schools specialization code*] .... D
Drafting Request .... DR
Drafting [*or Drawing*] **Room Manual** .... DRM
Draftsman .... DFTMN
Draftsman .... DFTSMN
Drag .... D
Drag .... DRG
Drag Friction .... DF
Dragon Airways Ltd. .... DA
Dragonfly [*A publication*] .... Drag
Dragoon Guards [*Military unit*] [*British*] .... DG
Dragoons [*Military unit*] [*British*] .... D
Drain .... DR
Drain Cutoff Current .... DCOC
Drain Panel .... DP
Drain and Purge .... D & P
Drain Saturation Current .... DSC
Drain Tile [*Technical drawings*] .... DT
Drain, Waste, and Vent [*System*] .... DWV
Drainage and Water Supply Officer [*Ministry of Agriculture, Fisheries, and Food*] [*British*] .... DWSO
Drake Law Review [*A publication*] .... Drake Law R
Drake Law Review [*A publication*] .... Drake L Rev
Drake Public Library, Centerville, IA [*Library symbol*] .... IaCenv
Drake University, Des Moines, IA [*Library symbol*] .... IaDmD
Drake University, Des Moines, IA [*OCLC symbol*] .... IOD
Drake University, Law Library, Des Moines, IA [*OCLC symbol*] .... IWD
Drake University, Law School, Des Moines, IA [*Library symbol*] .... IaDmD-L
Dram .... DM
Dram .... DR
Dram, Apothecary .... DRAP
Dram, Avoirdupois .... DRAV
Drama .... D
Drama Book Specialists .... DBS
Drama Critique [*A publication*] .... DramC

Drama Desk [*An association*] ... DD
Drama: the Quarterly Theatre Review [*A publication*] ... DR
Drama Review [*A publication*] ... Drama R
Drama Review [*A publication*] ... DrR
Drama Review [*Formerly, Tulane Drama Review*] [*A publication*] ... TDR
Drama Survey [*A publication*] ... Drama Surv
Drama Survey [*A publication*] ... DramS
Drama Survey [*A publication*] ... DS
Drama and Theatre [*A publication*] ... D & T
Drama Tree [*An association*] ... DT
Dramatic ... DRAM
Dramatic Authors' Society [*British*] ... DAS
Dramatic Criticism Index [*A reference publication*] ... DCI
Dramatic Interpretation of the Ghetto through Improvisational Theater [*Washington, DC*] ... DIG-IT
Dramatic Order Knights of Khorassan ... DOKK
Dramatists Guild ... DG
Drammaturgia [*A publication*] ... D
Drammaturgia [*A publication*] ... Dram
Dranetz Technologies [*NASDAQ symbol*] ... DRAN
Draped [*Numismatics*] ... DR
Draper Fund Report [*A publication*] ... Draper Fund Rep
Draper Public Library, Draper, SD [*Library symbol*] ... SdDr
Drapery Hardware Manufacturers Association [*Defunct*] ... DHMA
Draught ... DT
Dravida Munnetra Kazhagam [*Political party in India seeking independent socialist state of Dravidanad*] ... DMK
Dravidian [*MARC language code*] [*Library of Congress*] ... dra
Dravo Corp. [*NYSE symbol*] ... DRV
Draw ... D
Draw-A-Person [*Psychology*] ... D-A-P
Draw-A-Person Quality Scale [*Psychology*] ... DPQS
Draw Die [*Tool*] ... DWDI
Draw Form [*Tool*] ... DWFM
Draw Out ... DO
Drawback [*Business and trade*] ... DBK
Drawbar Horsepower ... DBHP
Drawbar Pull ... DBP
Drawer ... DR
Drawer ... DWR
Drawing ... DRG
Drawing ... DRWG
Drawing ... DWG
Drawing for Army Training Aids ... DATA
Drawing Assembly List ... DAL
Drawing and Assembly Release Record ... DARR
Drawing Breakdown List ... DBL
Drawing Center [*An association*] ... DC
Drawing Change ... DC
Drawing Change List ... DCL
Drawing Change Notice ... DCN
Drawing Change Order ... DCO
Drawing Change Request ... DCR
Drawing Copy Request ... DCR
Drawing Data Required for Change ... DDRC
Drawing Departure Authorization ... DDA
Drawing Deviation ... DD
Drawing Error Report ... DER
Drawing List [*Engineering*] ... DL
Drawing Parts Release Ticket ... DPRT
Drawing Practice ... DRPR
Drawing Quality Audit ... DQA
Drawing Record Card ... DRC
Drawing Requirement Outline ... DRO
Drawing Society ... DS
Drawing and Specification Listing ... DSL
Drawing Stimulus Strategy Measure ... DSSM
Drawing Summary ... DS
Drawn ... DR
Drawn ... DWN
Drawn Cup Roller Bearing ... DCRB
Drawn over Mandrel [*Tubes*] ... DOM
Drayage Carriers Inc., Fort Wayne IN [*STAC*] ... DCR
Drayton Plains, MI [*Radio station call letters*] ... WTSD
Dream World [*A publication*] ... DWD
Dreco Energy Services Ltd. [*American Stock Exchange symbol*] [*Delisted*] ... DRE
Dredge [*Self-propelled*] [*Navy symbol*] ... YM
Dredged Material Research Program [*Waterways Experiment Station*] [*Army*] ... DMRP
Dredger ... DRGR
Dredging Operations Technical Support ... DOTS
Dredging Range [*Nautical charts*] ... DRDG RGE
Dreiser Newsletter [*A publication*] ... DreiN
Dresden [*East Germany*] [*Airport symbol*] ... DRS
Dresdner Bank AGADR [*NASDAQ symbol*] ... DRSDY
Dresdner Kunstblaetter. Monatsschrift der Staatlichen Kunstsammlungen Dresden [*A publication*] ... Dresdner Kunstbl
Dresher, Inc. [*NASDAQ symbol*] ... DRES
[*The*] **Dress Barn** [*NASDAQ symbol*] ... DBRN
Dress Rehearsal ... DR
Dressed [*Lumber*] ... DRS
Dressed and Headed [*Lumber*] ... D & H
Dressed and Matched [*Technical drawings*] ... D & M
Dressed or Tanned [*Freight*] ... DT
Dresser ... DR
Dresser ... DRSR
Dresser Industries, Inc. [*NYSE symbol*] ... DI
Dresser Industries, Inc., Dresser Clark Division, Olean, NY [*Library symbol*] ... NOID
Dresser Industries, Inc., Garland, TX [*Library symbol*] ... TxGarD
Dresser Industries, Inc., Harbison-Walker Refractories Co., West Mifflin, PA [*Library symbol*] ... PWesD
Dresser Industries, Inc., Lane-Wells Co., Houston, TX [*Library symbol*] ... TxHDE
Dressing [*Medicine*] ... DR
Dressing ... DREG
Dressing [*Medicine*] ... DRSG
Drevarsky Vyskum [*A publication*] ... Drev Vysk
Drevarsky Vyskum [*A publication*] ... Drev Vyskum
Drew Gateway [*A publication*] ... DrG
Drew, MS [*Radio station call letters*] ... WKZB
Drew National Corporation [*American Stock Exchange symbol*] [*Delisted*] ... DNC
Drew National Corp. [*NASDAQ symbol*] ... DRWN
Drew University, Madison, NJ [*OCLC symbol*] ... DRU
Drew University, Madison, NJ [*Library symbol*] ... NjMD
Drew University, Theological School, Madison, NJ [*Library symbol*] ... NjMD-T
Drewry Photocolor Corp. [*NASDAQ symbol*] ... DREW
Drewrys Ltd. USA, Inc. [*NYSE symbol*] [*Delisted*] ... DRE
Drexel Bond-Debenture Trading Fund [*NYSE symbol*] ... DBF
Drexel Institute of Technology [*Pennsylvania*] ... DIT
Drexel Library Quarterly [*A publication*] ... DLQ
Drexel Library Quarterly [*A publication*] ... Drexel Libr Q
Drexel Library Quarterly [*A publication*] ... Drex Lib Q
Drexel Technical Journal [*A publication*] ... Drexel Tech J
Drexel University, Philadelphia, PA [*OCLC symbol*] ... DXU
Drexel University, Philadelphia, PA [*Library symbol*] ... PPD
Drexel University, School of Library and Information Science, Philadelphia, PA [*OCLC symbol*] ... DRX
Drexel Utility Shares, Inc. [*American Stock Exchange symbol*] [*Delisted*] ... DUS
Drexler Technology [*NASDAQ symbol*] ... DRXR
Dreyer's Grand Ice Cream, Inc. [*NASDAQ symbol*] ... DRYR
Dreyfus Corp. [*NYSE symbol*] ... DRY
Dried Bakery Products [*An animal feed*] ... DBP
Dried Fruit Association of California [*Later, DFA of California*] ... DFA
Dried Fruit Association of California [*Later, DFA of California*] ... DFAC
Dried Skim Milk ... DSM
Driemaandelijkse Bladen [*A publication*] ... DmB
Drift ... DFT
Drift ... DRFT
Drift Angle [*Navigation*] ... DA
Drift Angle Indicator [*Navigation*] ... DAI
Drift Correction ... D/C
Drift Correction Angle ... DCA
Drift Cyclotron Loss Cone [*Plasma physics*] ... DCLC
Drift and Ground-Speed Measuring Airborne RADAR ... DAGMAR
Drift Rate ... DR
Drifting Automatic Radiometeorological Station ... DARMS
Drifting Low-Capability Buoys [*National Oceanic and Atmospheric Administration*] ... DLCB
Drifting Snow [*Meteorology*] ... DRSN
Drill ... DR
Drill Adapter ... DRAD
Drill Attendance Monitoring Procedure and Report [*National Guard*] ... DAMPRE
Drill Attendance Reporting Test [*National Guard*] ... DART
Drill Bushing ... DRBG
Drill Cluster Plate ... DCP
Drill Fixture ... DRFX
Drill Guidance System ... DGS
Drill Head ... DRHD
Drill Instructor [*Marine Corps*] ... DI
Drill Jig ... DJ
Drill Jig ... DRJG
Drill Jig ... DRJI
Drill Jig Bushing ... DJB
Drill Nonpay Status [*Naval Reserve*] ... DNP
Drill Pay ... DP
Drill Plate [*Tool*] ... DP
Drill Plate [*Tool*] ... DRPE
Drill Plate [*Tool*] ... DRPL
Drill Press Feed ... DPF
Drill Regulations ... DR
Drill Rod ... DR
Drill Sergeant [*Army*] ... DS
Drill Sergeant Identification Badge ... DSIdentBad
Drill Sergeant School [*Army*] ... DSS
Drill Shell ... DRSH
Drill Spacer Block ... DSB

Drill Template ... DRT
Drill Template ... DRTP
Drill Vise ... DRVS
Drillers, Inc. [*American Stock Exchange symbol*] ... DRL
[*A*] **Drink** ... AD
Drinker Library of Choral Music ... DLCM
Drinking Behavior Scale [*Test*] ... DBS
Drinking Fountain ... DF
Drinking Straw Institute [*Defunct*] ... DSI
Drinking Water ... DW
Drinking Water Quality Research Center [*Florida International University*] ... DWQRC
Drip Infusion Pyelography [*Radiography*] ... DIP
Drip Pan Pot [*of closed-loop ex-vessel machine*] [*Nuclear energy*] ... DPP
Drip-Proof ... DP
Dripproof Open ... DPO
Dripproof Protected ... DPP
Dripproof and Ratproof ... DPRP
Dripproof Semienclosed ... DPS
Dripproof Totally Enclosed ... DPT
Driptank ... DRTA
Driscoll Play Kit [*Psychological testing*] ... DPK
Dritte Welt Magazin [*A publication*] ... Dritte Welt Mag
Drive [*State*] [*Psychology*] ... D
Drive ... DR
Drive ... DRI
Drive Control Equipment ... DCE
Drive End ... DE
Drive Fit [*Technical drawings*] ... DF
Drive-Gearhead Package ... DGHP
Drive-Gearhead Package ... DGP
Drive Motor Assembly ... DMA
Drive Other Cars [*Insurance*] ... DOC
Drive System ... DS
Drive Tube ... DT
Drive Unit ... DRU
Driver [*Navy rating*] ... CD
Driver ... DRVR
Driver ... DVR
Driver Aid, Information, and Routing [*Data processing*] ... DAIR
Driver Augmented Readout [*Data processing*] ... DAR
Driver Badge, Amphibious Vehicles [*Military decoration*] ... DVRABAD
Driver Badge, Motorcycles [*Military decoration*] ... DVRMBAD
Driver Badge, Tracked Vehicles [*Military decoration*] ... DVRTBAD
Driver Badge, Wheeled Vehicles [*Military decoration*] ... DVRWBAD
Driver Control Area ... DCA
Driver Control Area Region Extension ... DCARE
Driver-Harris Co. [*American Stock Exchange symbol*] ... DRH
Driver Improvement Program [*American Automobile Association*] ... DIP
Driver, Master ... DM
Driver and Mechanic Badge, Amphibious Vehicles [*Military decoration*] ... DvrMechBadA
Driver and Mechanic Badge, Mechanic [*Military decoration*] ... DvrMechBadMech
Driver and Mechanic Badge, Motorcycles [*Military decoration*] ... DvrMechBadM
Driver and Mechanic Badge, Operator [*Military decoration*] ... DvrMechBadOp
Driver and Mechanic Badge, Tracked Vehicles [*Military decoration*] ... DvrMechBadT
Driver and Mechanic Badge, Wheeled Vehicles [*Military decoration*] ... DvrMechBadW
Driver Performance Measurement and Analysis System ... DPMAS
Driver Propulsion Unit ... DPU
Driver Screening Evaluator ... DSE
Driver Stage Silicon Transistor ... DSST
Driver and Traffic Safety Education Research Digest [*A publication*] ... DTSERD
Driver Units Speaker ... DUS
Driving ... D
Driving Away Auto without Owner's Permission [*FBI standardized term*] ... DAA w/o OP
Driving Car Intoxicated ... DCI
Driving Control Indicator ... DCI
Driving under the Influence of Liquor ... DUIL
Driving after License Revoked ... DLR
Driving after License Suspended ... DLS
Driving Point Admittance ... DPA
Driving Power ... DP
Driving School Association of America ... DSAA
Driving While Drunk [*Police term*] ... DWD
Driving While Intoxicated [*Police term*] ... DWI
Drizzle [*Meteorology*] ... DRZL
Drizzle [*Meteorology*] ... DZ
Drizzle [*Meteorology*] ... L
Drizzling [*Meteorology*] ... D
Drogue [*NASA*] ... DRG
Drogue Parachute Deployment ... DPR
Droit [*Right*] [*French*] ... D
Droit Maritime [*A publication*] ... Dr Marit
Droit Maritime Francais [*A publication*] ... Dr Marit Franc
Droit Ouvrier [*A publication*] ... Dr Ouvr
Droit et Pratique du Commerce International [*A publication*] ... Dr Pratique Com Int
Droit Sanitaire et Social [*A publication*] ... Dr Sanit Soc
Droit Social [*A publication*] ... Dr Soc
Drone [*Designation for all US military aircraft*] ... Q
Drone Aircraft Catapult Control Craft [*Navy symbol*] ... YV
Drone Antisubmarine Helicopter [*Air Force, Navy*] ... DASH
Drone Assisted Torpedo ... DAT
Drone Control and Data Retrieval System [*Later, CDRS*] [*Air Force*] ... DCDRS
Drone Control System ... DCS
Drone Deceptive Self-Screening Jammer ... DDSSJ
Drone Formation Control System ... DFCS
Drone Noise Jammers ... DNJ
Drone Plane [*Navy symbol*] ... D
Drone Recovery Platform ... DRP
Drone Target Control System ... DTCS
Drone Target Facility ... DTF
Drone Test Facility ... DTF
Drone Tracking and Control System ... DTCS
Drop ... D
Drop Altitude ... DALT
Drop Dead! ... DD
Drop Forge ... DF
Drop Forged Clamp ... DFC
Drop Forging Association [*Later, FIA*] ... DFA
Drop-Hammer Die ... DHD
Drop-Hammer Die ... DHDI
Drop-In-Maintenance ... DIM
Drop Landing Zone [*Air Force*] ... DLZ
Drop Manhole [*Technical drawings*] ... DMH
Drop Off ... D/O
Drop Out [*or Dropout*] ... DO
Drop Out ... DPO
Drop Out Generator ... DOG
Drop Point [*Air Force*] ... DP
Drop Siding ... DS
Drop Survival Time ... DST
Drop Tank ... DT
Drop Test Report ... DT
Drop-Weight Tear Test ... DWTT
Drop Wire ... DW
Drop Wood Siding [*Technical drawings*] ... DWS
Drop Zone [*For parachute troops and gliders*] [*Military*] ... DZ
Drop Zone Area [*Military*] ... DZA
Drop Zone Control Officer [*Military*] ... DZCO
Drop Zone Safety Officer [*Military*] ... DZSO
Droplet Countercurrent Chromatography ... DCCC
Droppable Fuel Tank [*Suffix to plane designation*] ... D
Dropped Own Request [*Navy*] ... DOR
Dropped from Rolls ... DFR
Dropping Mercury Electrode [*Electrochemistry*] ... DME
Dropsie University, Philadelphia, PA [*Library symbol*] ... PPDrop
Dror Young Zionist Organization [*Later, YKM*] ... DYZO
Drosophila Information Service [*Genetics*] ... DIS
Drowning Prevention and Beach Safety Program ... DPBSP
Drowsiness ... DRS
Druckzuender [*Pressure igniter*] [*German military - World War II*] ... DZ
Drug ... D
Drug Abuse Council [*Defunct*] ... DAC
Drug Abuse Council. Monograph Series [*A publication*] ... Drug Abu MS
Drug Abuse Council. Public Policy Series [*A publication*] ... Drug Abu PPS
Drug Abuse Current Awareness System [*A publication*] ... DACAS
Drug Abuse Epidemiology Data Center [*Texas Christian University*] ... DAEDAC
Drug Abuse Law Enforcement [*Department of Justice*] ... DALE
Drug Abuse Prevention Report [*A publication*] ... Drug Abuse Prev Rep
Drug Abuse Prevention Resource Unit [*Data bank*] [*National Institute on Drug Abuse*] ... DAPRU
Drug Abuse Warning Network [*Drug Enforcement Administration*] ... DAWN
Drug Addict ... DA
Drug Addiction Rehabilitation Enterprise ... DARE
Drug Addicts Yield to Persuasion [*of Daytop Village, Inc., a narcotics-addiction rehabilitation facility*] ... DAYTOP
Drug and Alcohol Abuse Program Advisor [*Navy*] ... DAPA
Drug and Alcohol Dependence [*A publication*] ... Drug Alcohol Depend
Drug and Alcohol Rehabilitation Testing System [*Navy*] ... DARTS
Drug and Allied Products Guild [*Later, NAPM*] ... DAPG
Drug, Chemical, and Allied Trades Association ... DCAT
Drug and Chemical Toxicology [*A publication*] ... Drug Chem Toxicol
Drug and Cosmetic Colors ... D & C
Drug and Cosmetic Industry [*A publication*] ... D & C Ind
Drug and Cosmetic Industry [*A publication*] ... Drug Cosmet
Drug and Cosmetic Industry [*A publication*] ... Drug Cosmet Ind
Drug Development Communications [*A publication*] ... Drug Dev C
Drug Development Communications [*A publication*] ... Drug Dev Commun
Drug Development and Industrial Pharmacy [*A publication*] ... Drug Dev Ind Pharm
Drug Digests [*A publication*] ... Drug Dig
Drug Discrimination [*Psychopharmacology*] ... DD

Drug Education Specialist [*Military*] .... DES
Drug Efficacy Study Implementation Notice [*Food and Drug Administration*] .... DESI
Drug Enforcement [*A publication*] .... Drug Enf
Drug Enforcement Administration [*Formerly, Bureau of Narcotics and Dangerous Drugs*] .... DEA
Drug Enforcement Administration - Special Operations Group .... DEA-SOG
Drug Evaluation .... DE
Drug Evaluation Center .... DEC
Drug Fair, Inc. [*American Stock Exchange symbol*] [*Delisted*] .... DF
Drug Identification Kit .... DIK
Drug Induced Diseases [*Elsevier Book Series*] [*A publication*] .... DID
Drug Information .... DI
Drug Information Association .... DIA
Drug Information Bulletin [*A publication*] .... Drug Inf Bull
Drug Information Journal [*A publication*] .... Drug Inf J
Drug Information Services [*University of Minnesota*] .... DIS
Drug Intelligence [*Later, Drug Intelligence and Clinical Pharmacy*] [*A publication*] .... Drug Intell
Drug Intelligence and Clinical Pharmacy [*Formerly, Drug Intelligence*] [*A publication*] .... Drug Intel
Drug Intelligence and Clinical Pharmacy [*Formerly, Drug Intelligence*] [*A publication*] .... Drug Intell Clin Pharm
Drug Interactions .... DI
Drug Mending Zone [*Drug abuse center*] .... DMZ
Drug Metabolism and Disposition [*A publication*] .... Drug Metab Dispos
Drug Metabolism and Disposition [*A publication*] .... Drug Metab Disposition
Drug Metabolism and Disposition [*A publication*] .... Drug Meta D
Drug Metabolism Reviews [*A publication*] .... Drug Metab
Drug Metabolism Reviews [*A publication*] .... Drug Metab Rev
Drug Product Information File [*American Society of Hospital Pharmacists*] [*Information service*] .... DPIF
Drug-Quaternary Carrier [*Biochemistry*] .... D-QC
Drug Research [*A publication*] .... Drug Res
Drug Supervisory Body .... DSB
Drug Supervisory Body of the United Nations .... DSB (UN)
Drug Systems, Inc. [*NASDAQ symbol*] .... DRGS
Drug and Therapeutic Information [*Later, Medical Letter*] .... DTI
Drug and Therapeutics Bulletin [*A publication*] .... Drug Ther Bull
Drug Therapy. Hospital Edition [*A publication*] .... Drug Ther Hosp Ed
Drug Therapy. Prescribing Practices and Problems [*A publication*] .... Drug Ther Prescr Pract Probl
Drug Therapy. Reviews [*A publication*] .... Drug Ther Rev
Drug Therapy. Reviews [*Elsevier Book Series*] [*A publication*] .... DTR
Drug Trade News [*A publication*] .... DTN
Drug Wholesalers Association .... DWA
Druggist's Guild of St. James [*Defunct*] .... DGSJ
Drugs Made in Germany [*A publication*] .... Drugs Made Ger
Drugs and the Pharmaceutical Sciences [*A publication*] .... Drugs Pharm Sci
Drugstore [*US maps*] .... DS
Druids [*Freemasonry*] .... D
Drum .... D
Drum .... DM
Drum .... DR
Drum [*Shipping*] .... DRM
Drum Control Unit .... DCU
Drum Demand .... DD
Drum Information Assembler and Dispatcher .... DIAD
Drum Information Display .... DID
Drum Interrogation, Alteration, and Loading System [*Honeywell, Inc.*] .... DIAL
Drum Major [*Marine Corps*] .... DRMAJ
Drum Memory Assembly [*Data processing*] .... DMA
Drum Memory System [*Data processing*] .... DMS
Drum Out of Service .... DOS
Drum Processor [*Data processing*] .... DP
Drum-Programed Automatic Tester .... D-PAT
Drum-Read Amplifier [*Data processing*] .... DRA
Drum-Read Driver [*Data processing*] .... DRD
Drum Seiners Association .... DSA
Drum Storage [*Data processing*] .... DS
Drum Storage System .... DSS
Drum Storage Unit .... DSU
Drum Switch .... DS
Drum Switch .... DSW
Drum Timing Pulse .... DTP
Drum Transfer .... DT
Drum Write [*Data processing*] .... DW
Drum Write Driver [*Data processing*] .... DWD
Drumheller, ON [*Radio station call letters*] .... CKDQ
Drummer [*Military*] [*British*] .... DMR
Drummond Island, MI [*Location identifier*] [*FAA*] .... DRM
Drummond Lighterage [*AAR code*] .... DLC
Drummond, MT [*Location identifier*] [*FAA*] .... DRU
Drummondville, PQ [*Radio station call letters*] CBF-FM-1
Drummondville, PQ [*Radio station call letters*] .... CHRD
Drummondville, PQ [*Radio station call letters*] .... CKRV
Drunk [*FBI standardized term*] .... DRK
Drunk in Charge .... DIC
Drunk and Dirty [*Military*] .... D & D
Drunk and Disorderly .... D & D
Drunk and Disorderly Conduct .... D & DC
Drunk and Proud .... D & P
Drury College. Bradley Geological Field Station. Bulletin [*A publication*] .... Drury Coll Bradley G Field Sta B
Drury College, Springfield, MO [*OCLC symbol*] .... MOD
Drury College, Springfield, MO [*Library symbol*] .... MoSpD
Drury Military Extension, Springfield, MO [*OCLC symbol*] .... MFT
Druzba Narodov [*A publication*] .... DN
Druzba Narodov [*A publication*] .... DrN
Drvna Industrija [*A publication*] .... Drvna Ind
Dry Adiabatic Lapse Rate [*Heat transfer*] .... DALR
Dry Basis .... DB
Dry Bath [*Instrumentation*] .... DB
Dry Bulb [*Thermometer, of a psychrometer*] [*Meteorology*] .... DB
Dry Bulb Temperature .... DBT
Dry Bulk Material .... DBM
Dry Cargo Loading Technical Committee [*NATO*] .... DCLTC
Dry Chemical .... DCHEM
Dry Color Manufacturers Association .... DCMA
Dry-Column Chromatography .... DCC
Dry Creek [*Idaho*] [*Seismograph station code, US Geological Survey*] .... DCI
Dry Discharge Pump .... DDP
Dry Diver Transport Vehicle [*Navy*] .... DDTV
Dry Dock Companion Craft [*Non-self-propelled*] [*Navy symbol*] .... YFND
Dry Dressing [*Medicine*] .... DD
Dry Electrolytic Capacitor .... DEC
Dry-Filled Capsules [*Pharmacy*] .... DFC
Dry Film Binder .... DFB
Dry Film Lubricant .... DFL
Dry Film Processor .... DFP
Dry Filter Processing .... DFP
Dry Gas Pump .... DGP
Dry Heat Sterilization .... DHS
Dry Honing Machine .... DHM
Dry Mass .... DM
Dry Matter Loss .... DML
Dry Photo Process .... DPP
Dry Pipe Valve .... DPV
Dry Point .... DP
Dry Process Ceramic and Steatite Manufacturers Association .... DPCSMA
Dry Reed Pushbutton Switch .... DRPS
Dry Reed Switch .... DRS
Dry Sterile Dressing [*Medicine*] .... DSD
Dry Tank Weight .... DTW
Dry Toned [*Copier*] [*Reprography*] .... DT
Dry Tortugas Island, FL [*Location identifier*] [*FAA*] .... DTF
Dry-Type Self-Cooled [*Transformer*] .... AA
Dry Vacuum Pump Discharge Filter .... DVPDF
Dry Vacuum Pump Filter .... DVPF
Dry Valley Drilling Project [*National Science Foundation*] .... DVDP
Dry Valley Drilling Project. Bulletin. Northern Illinois University. Department of Geology [*A publication*] .... Dry Valley Drill Proj Bull
Dry Weight .... DW
Dry Workshop [*NASA*] .... DWS
Dryden [*Canada*] [*Airport symbol*] .... YHD
Dryden Flight Research Center [*NASA*] .... DFRC
Dryden, ON [*Television station call letters*] .... CBWDT
Dryden, ON [*Radio station call letters*] .... CKDR
Dryden, ON [*Radio station call letters*] CKSB-FM-6
Dryden Public Library, Dryden, ON, Canada [*Library symbol*] .... CaODr
Dryden Township Library, Dryden, MI [*Library symbol*] .... MiDry
Drydock .... DD
Drydock Launch Facility .... DLF
Drying .... DYG
DSA [*Defense Supply Agency*] **Augmentation Element** .... DAE
DSA [*Defense Supply Agency*] **Central Regional Audit Office** .... DMRA
DSA [*Defense Supply Agency*] **Central Regional Telecommunications Office** .... DCRTO
DSA [*Defense Supply Agency*] **Civil Preparedness Office** .... DCPO
DSA [*Defense Supply Agency*] **Command Security Support Office** .... DCSO
DSA [*Defense Supply Agency*] **Disposal Operating Procedures** .... DDOP
DSA [*Defense Supply Agency*] **Eastern Regional Telecommunications Office** .... DERTO
DSA [*Defense Supply Agency*] **Objective Document** .... DPOD
DSA [*Defense Supply Agency*] **Performance Standards Support Office** .... DPSSO
DSA [*Defense Supply Agency*] **Planning Objective** .... DPO
DSH [*Deafness, Speech, and Hearing*] **Abstracts** [*A publication*] .... DSH
DSIF [*Deep Space Instrumentation Facility*] **Maintenance Facility** [*NASA*] .... DMF
DSIF [*Deep Space Instrumentation Facility*] **Monitor and Control Subsystem** [*NASA*] .... DMC
DSIF [*Deep Space Instrumentation Facility*] **Supply Depot** [*NASA*] .... DSD
DSIF [*Deep Space Instrumentation Facility*] **Telemetry and Command Subsystem** [*NASA*] .... DTC
DSIF [*Deep Space Instrumentation Facility*] **Tracking and Monitor-Control Subsystem** [*NASA*] .... DTS
DSS [*Deep Space Station*] **Communications Equipment Subsystem** .... DCES
DSS [*Deep Space Station*] **Communications Terminal Subsystem** .... DCT
DST Systems, Inc. [*NASDAQ symbol*] .... DSTS

DTW. Deutsche Tierarztliche Wochenschrift [*A publication*] .... DTW
Du Bois [*Pennsylvania*] [*Airport symbol*] .... DUJ
Du Bois Chemicals, Inc. [*NYSE symbol*] [*Delisted*] .... DU
Du Bois, PA [*Radio station call letters*] .... WCED
Du Bois, PA [*Radio station call letters*] .... WDBA
du Pont [*E. I.*] **de Nemours & Co., Inc.** [*NYSE symbol*] .... DD
du Pont [*E. I.*] **de Nemours & Co., Inc.** [*Research code symbol*] .... EXP
du Pont [*E. I.*] **de Nemours & Co., Inc.** [*Research code symbol*] .... GP
Du Quoin, IL [*Radio station call letters*] .... WDQN
Du Quoin, IL [*Radio station call letters*] .... WDQN-FM
Dual Aerospace Servo Amplifier .... DASA
Dual Air Density [*Explorer satellite*] [*NASA*] .... DAD
Dual Air Density Explorer [*Satellite*] [*NASA*] .... DADE
Dual Air Density Satellite [*NASA*] .... DADS
Dual Area Nozzle .... DAN
Dual Audio Cassette Interface .... DACI
Dual Axis Rate Transducer [*A gyroscope*] .... DART
Dual Beam Oscilloscope .... DBO
Dual Bowl Feeder .... DBF
Dual Bowl Vibratory Feeder .... DBVF
Dual Cam Clutch .... DCC
Dual Capable .... DC
Dual-Capable Aircraft .... DCA
Dual Capacity [*London Stock Exchange*] .... D
Dual Channel Dual Speed .... DCDS
Dual Channel Radiometer .... DCR
Dual Cycle Rifle .... DCR
Dual Displacement Engine .... DDE
Dual Diversity Comparator .... DDC
Dual Diversity Unit .... DDU
Dual Doctor Families .... DDF
Dual Emitter Transistor .... DUET
Dual Exciter System .... DES
Dual Fault Correction Actuator .... DFCA
Dual-Feed Coupler .... DFC
Dual Filament Ion Source .... DFIS
Dual Filter Hybrid .... DFH
Dual-Frequency Method .... DFM
Dual-Frequency Receiver .... DFR
Dual Fuel Quantity Indicating System .... DFQIS
Dual Function Jammer .... DFJ
Dual Gauge Expander .... DGE
Dual-Hardness Steel .... DHS
Dual Image System .... DIS
Dual In-Line .... DIL
Dual In-Line Package [*Data processing*] .... DILP
Dual In-Line Package [*Data processing*] .... DIP
Dual Independent Map Encoding [*Transportation*] .... DIME
Dual Input Describing Function [*Data processing*] .... DIDF
Dual Input Null Network .... DINN
Dual Input Transponder .... DIT
Dual Lite, Inc. [*NASDAQ symbol*] .... DUAL
Dual Loop Oscillator .... DLO
Dual Maneuvering Simulator .... DMS
Dual Maneuvering Unit [*A spacecraft*] .... DMU
Dual Miniature Inertial Navigation Systems .... DMINS
Dual Mode Display .... DMD
Dual Mode Hydrazine .... DMH
Dual Mode Imbedded Munitions .... DMIM
Dual Mode LASER .... DML
Dual Mode Lunar Roving Vehicle [*NASA*] .... DLRV
Dual Mode Recognizer .... DMR
Dual Mode Tracker .... DMT
Dual-Object Electronic Tracking System .... DOETS
Dual Path Protection Arrangement [*AT & T*] .... DUPPA
Dual Pen Recorder .... DPR
Dual Pilot .... DP
Dual Porosity Sinter .... DPS
Dual Pulse LASER Microwelder .... DPLM
Dual Pulse Ranging Fuse .... DPRF
Dual Purpose .... DP
Dual-Purpose Improved Conventional Munition .... DPICM
Dual Purpose Missile .... DPM
Dual Purpose Weapon System .... DPWS
Dual Radio Magnetic Indicator .... DRMI
Dual Readout Devices .... DRD
Dual Roll Idler .... DRI
Dual Roll Trough Idler .... DRTI
Dual Salvo Attack Tactic [*Navy*] .... DUALEXTAC
Dual Speed .... DSP
Dual-Speed Drive .... DSD
Dual-Speed Magnetic Transducer .... DSMT
Dual-Surface Attenuation Module .... DSAM
Dual Tandem Wheels [*Aviation*] .... DTW
Dual Thrust Rocket Motor .... DTRM
Dual Tires .... DT
Dual-Tone Multifrequency [*Telcommunications*] .... DTMF
Dual Trace Amplifier .... DTA
Dual Trace Display .... DTD
Dual Track Etcher .... DTE
Dual Track Geneva .... DTG
Dual Wheels [*Aviation*] .... DW
Duala [*MARC language code*] [*Library of Congress*] .... dua
Dualbowl Vibratory Feeder .... DVF
Duarte [*California*] [*Seismograph station code, US Geological Survey*] .... DUC
Dubai [*United Arab Emirates*] [*Airport symbol*] .... DXB
Dubai Riyal [*Monetary unit in Dubai*] .... QDR
Dubbo [*Australia*] [*Airport symbol*] .... DBO
Dubitans [*or Dubius*] [*Doubting or Dubious*] [*Latin*] .... DUB
Dublin [*City and county in Ireland*] .... DUB
Dublin [*City and county in Ireland*] .... DUBL
Dublin [*Ireland*] [*Airport symbol*] .... DUB
Dublin Castle .... DC
Dublin, GA [*Location identifier*] [*FAA*] .... DBN
Dublin, GA [*Radio station call letters*] .... WKKZ
Dublin, GA [*Radio station call letters*] .... WMLT
Dublin, GA [*Radio station call letters*] .... WXLI
Dublin Gazette [*A publication*] .... DG
Dublin Institute for Advanced Studies .... DIAS
Dublin Magazine [*A publication*] .... DM
Dublin Magazine [*A publication*] .... Dub Mag
Dublin Medical Press [*A publication*] .... Dublin Med Press
Dublin Pharmacopoeia .... PD
Dublin Quarterly Journal of Medical Science [*A publication*] .... Dublin Q J Med Sc
Dublin Quarterly Journal of Science [*A publication*] .... Dublin Q J Sc
Dublin Rathfarnham Castle [*Ireland*] [*Seismograph station code, US Geological Survey*] [*Closed*] .... DUB
Dublin Review [*A publication*] .... DR
Dublin Review [*A publication*] .... DubR
Dublin Review [*A publication*] .... Dub Rev
Dublin University Boat Club .... DUBC
Dublin University Law Review [*A publication*] .... DULR
Dublin University Magazine [*A publication*] .... Dub Univ
Dublin University Mission .... DUM
Dublin University Rowing Club .... DURC
Dubois, ID [*Location identifier*] [*FAA*] .... DBS
Dubois Oleic Albumin Complex [*Microbiology*] .... DOAC
Dubois Oleic Serum Complex [*Bacteriology*] .... DOSC
DuBois, PA [*Radio station call letters*] .... WOWQ
Dubrovnik [*Yugoslavia*] [*Seismograph station code, US Geological Survey*] [*Closed*] .... DBR
Dubrovnik [*Yugoslavia*] [*Airport symbol*] .... DBV
Dubuque [*Iowa*] [*Airport symbol*] .... DBQ
Dubuque [*Iowa*] [*Seismograph station code, US Geological Survey*] .... DBQ
Dubuque Area Library Consortium [*Library network*] .... DALC
Dubuque, IA [*Radio station call letters*] .... KDTH
Dubuque, IA [*Television station call letters*] .... KDUB-TV
Dubuque, IA [*Radio station call letters*] .... KFMD
Dubuque, IA [*Radio station call letters*] .... KLXL
Dubuque, IA [*Radio station call letters*] .... KLYV
Dubuque, IA [*Radio station call letters*] .... WDBQ
Ducati International Owners Club .... DIOC
Ducati Owners' Club of Canada .... DOCC
Duchenne Muscular Dystrophy .... DMD
Duchesne College, Omaha, NE [*Library symbol*] .... NbOD
Duchess .... D
Duchess .... DUC
Duchy .... D
Duchy .... DU
Duck .... DK
Duck Embryo Vaccine [*Immunology*] .... DEV
Duck Hepatic B Virus .... DHBV
Duck Hepatitis Virus .... DHV
Duck Virus Enteritis .... DVE
Ducks Unlimited .... DU
Ducktail [*Hair style*] [*Bowdlerized version*] .... DA
Duckwall-Alco Stores [*NASDAQ symbol*] .... DUCK
Ducommun, Inc. [*American Stock Exchange symbol*] .... DCO
Ducosyn Excitation Switch .... DES
Duct Burner Augmentation .... DBA
Duct Carcinoma [*Oncology*] .... DC
Duct Carcinoma In Situ [*Oncology*] .... DCIS
Duct Integrity and Nozzle Efficiency .... DIANE
Duct Transmission Loss [*Facility*] .... DTL
Duct Type .... DCTP
Ducted Propellers [*Aviation*] .... DP
Ductile to Brittle Transition Temperature .... DBTT
Ductile Iron Pipe Research Association .... DIPRA
Ductile Iron Society .... DIS
Ductus Deferens Tumor [*Type of cell line*] .... DDT
Dude Ranchers' Association .... DRA
Dudley Educational Journal [*A publication*] .... Dudley Ednl J
Dudley, Kenneth F., Ottumwa IA [*STAC*] .... DKF
Dudley, MA [*Radio station call letters*] .... WNRC
Dudley Observatory, Albany, NY [*Library symbol*] .... NAID
Due in Assets .... DIA
Due Date .... DD
Due Date .... DUDAT
Due In .... DI
Due-In from Maintenance [*Military*] .... DIFM
Due-In from Overhaul [*Military*] .... DIFO

Due-In Quantity ... DIQ
Due Out [*Army*] ... DO
Due-Out Cancellation [*Military*] ... DOC
Due-Out of Group [*Military*] ... DOG
Due-Out to Maintenance [*Military*] ... DOTM
Due West Motor Line [*AAR code*] ... DWML
Due West, SC [*Radio station call letters*] ... WARP
Duelmener Heimatblaetter [*A publication*] ... Duelmener Hb
Dues ... D
Duesseldorfer Jahrbuch [*A publication*] ... Duesseldorfer Jahrb
Duffryn Yard [*Welsh depot code*] ... PT
Duffy [*Blood group*] ... Fy
Dugway [*Utah*] [*Seismograph station code, US Geological Survey*] ... DUG
Dugway Proving Ground [*Utah*] [*Army*] ... DPG
Dugway Proving Ground [*Utah*] [*Army*] ... DPGR
Dugway/Tooele, UT [*Location identifier*] [*FAA*] ... DPG
Dugway/Tooele, UT [*Location identifier*] [*FAA*] ... MIJ
Duke ... D
Duke ... DU
Duke Bar Journal [*A publication*] ... Duke B J
Duke of Cambridge's Own [*Military unit*] [*British*] ... DCO
Duke of Connaught's Own [*Military unit*] [*British*] ... DCO
Duke of Cornwall's Light Infantry [*Military unit*] [*British*] ... DCLI
Duke Divinity School Review [*A publication*] ... Duke Div R
Duke of Edinburgh's Own [*Military unit*] [*British*] ... DEO
Duke of Edinburgh's Own Volunteer Rifles [*Military unit*] [*British*] ... DEOVR
Duke of Edinburgh's Royal Regiment [*Military unit*] [*British*] ... DERR
[*The*] **Duke Ellington Society** ... TDES
Duke of Lancaster's Own Yeomanry [*Military unit*] [*British*] ... DLOY
Duke Law Journal [*A publication*] ... Duke Law J
Duke Law Journal [*A publication*] ... Duke L J
Duke Mathematical Journal [*A publication*] ... Duke Math J
Duke, Nat, New York NY [*STAC*] ... DUK
Duke Power Co. [*NYSE symbol*] ... DUK
Duke University, Divinity School, Durham, NC [*Library symbol*] ... NcD-D
Duke University, Durham, NC [*Library symbol*] ... NcD
Duke University, Law Library, Durham, NC [*OCLC symbol*] ... NDL
Duke University Library, Durham, NC [*OCLC symbol*] ... NDD
Duke University Library Notes [*A publication*] ... DULN
Duke University Marine Station Bulletin [*A publication*] ... Duke Univ Mar Stn Bull
Duke University, Medical Center, Durham, NC [*Library symbol*] ... NcD-MC
Duke University, School of Law, Durham, NC [*Library symbol*] ... NcD-L
Duke University, Woman's College, Durham, NC [*Library symbol*] ... NcD-W
Duke of Wellington's Regiment [*Military unit*] [*British*] ... DWR
Duke of Wellington's West Riding Regiment [*Military unit*] [*British*] ... DW
Dukes County Historical Society, Edgartown, MA [*Library symbol*] ... MEdDHi
Dukovna Kultura [*A publication*] ... DK
Dulbecco-Vogt Modified Eagle's [*Medium for cell growth*] ... DVME
Dulbecco's Minimum Essential Medium ... DMEM
Dulbecco's Modified Eagle's Medium [*Also, DMEM, DMM*] [*Medium for cell growth*] ... DME
Dulbecco's Modified Eagle's Medium [*Also, DME, DMM*] [*Medium for cell growth*] ... DMEM
Dulbecco's Modified Eagle's Medium [*Also, DME, DMEM*] [*Medium for cell growth*] ... DMM
Dulce [*New Mexico*] [*Seismograph station code, US Geological Survey*] [*Closed*] ... DNM
Dulcis [*Dear One*] [*Latin*] ... D
Dulcis [*Sweet*] [*Pharmacy*] ... DULC
Dulcitol Lysine Lactose Iron [*Agar*] [*Microbiology*] ... DLLI
Dull ... D
Dull Black Finish Slate ... DBFS
Dull Men's Club ... DMC
Dulles International Airport [*FAA*] ... DIA
Duluth [*Minnesota*] [*Airport symbol*] ... DLH
Duluth [*Minnesota*] [*Seismograph station code, US Geological Survey*] [*Closed*] ... DUL
Duluth, Missabe & Iron Range Railway Co. ... DM & IR
Duluth, Missabe & Iron Range Railway Co. [*AAR code*] ... DMIR
Duluth, MN [*Location identifier*] [*FAA*] ... JUD
Duluth, MN [*Radio station call letters*] ... KDAL
Duluth, MN [*Television station call letters*] ... KDLH-TV
Duluth, MN [*Radio station call letters*] ... KDNW
Duluth, MN [*Radio station call letters*] ... KUMD-FM
Duluth, MN [*Radio station call letters*] ... WAKX-FM
Duluth, MN [*Radio station call letters*] ... WAVC
Duluth, MN [*Television station call letters*] ... WDIO-TV
Duluth, MN [*Television station call letters*] ... WDSE-TV
Duluth, MN [*Radio station call letters*] ... WEBC
Duluth, MN [*Radio station call letters*] ... WNCB
Duluth, MN [*Radio station call letters*] ... WNLT
Duluth, MN [*Radio station call letters*] ... WSCD-FM
Duluth, MN [*Radio station call letters*] ... WWJC
Duluth, MN-Superior, WI [*Television station call letters*] ... KBJR-TV
Duluth, MN-Superior, WI [*Radio station call letters*] ... KQDS-FM
Duluth & Northeastern Railroad Co. [*AAR code*] ... DNE
Duluth Public Library, Duluth, MN [*Library symbol*] ... MnDu
Duluth, South Shore, & Atlantic Railroad [*AAR code*] [*Obsolete*] ... DSA
Duluth, South Shore, & Atlantic Railroad [*Nickname: Damned Slow Service and Abuse*] [*Obsolete*] ... DSS & A
Duluth Weapons Calibration System ... DUWCAL
Duluth, Winnipeg & Pacific Railway ... DW & P
Duluth, Winnipeg & Pacific Railway [*AAR code*] ... DWP
Duly Authorized Officer ... DAO
Dumaguete [*Philippines*] [*Airport symbol*] ... DGT
Dumas, AR [*Radio station call letters*] ... KDDA
Dumas, AR [*Radio station call letters*] ... KDDA-FM
Dumas, TX [*Location identifier*] [*FAA*] ... DUX
Dumas, TX [*Radio station call letters*] ... KDDD
Dumas, TX [*Radio station call letters*] ... KMRE
Dumbarton Oaks Papers [*A publication*] ... DOP
Dumbarton Oaks Papers [*A publication*] ... DOPapers
Dumbarton Oaks Papers [*A publication*] ... Dumbarton OP
Dumbarton Oaks Research Library of Harvard University, Washington, DC [*Library symbol*] [*OCLC symbol*] ... DDO
Dumbwaiter ... DW
Dumbwaiter Door ... DWD
Dumfriesshire [*County in Scotland*] ... DUMF
Dummy [*in game of bridge*] ... D
Dummy ... DMY
Dummy ... DUM
Dummy Antenna ... DA
Dummy Director Set ... DDS
Dummy Firing Unit ... DFU
Dummy Guided Missile ... DGM
Dummy Load [*JETDS nomenclature*] [*Military*] ... DA
Dummy Load [*Military*] ... DL
Dummy Missile Firing ... DMF
Dummy Nose Plug ... DNP
Dummy Part ... DPT
Dummy Part Master ... DPMA
Dummy Stowage Receptacle ... DSR
Dummy Surface-to-Air Missile ... DUSAM
Dumont D'Urville [*Pointe Geologie, Adelie*] [*Antarctica*] [*Seismograph station code, US Geological Survey*] ... DRV
Dumont D'Urville [*France*] [*Geomagnetic observatory code*] ... DUM
DuMont Television Network [*1946-55*] ... DTN
Dump ... D
Dump Heat Exchanger [*Nuclear energy*] ... DHX
Dump Heat Exchanger Control System [*Nuclear energy*] ... DHXCS
Dump Revenues [*Solid waste management*] ... DR
Dump Telemetry ... DT
Dumping ... DMPG
Dumping ... DPG
Dumptruck ... DPTRK
Dun [*Thoroughbred racing*] ... D
Dun & Bradstreet, Inc. ... D & B
Dun & Bradstreet, Inc. [*NYSE symbol*] ... DNB
Dunbar [*Australia*] [*Airport symbol*] [*Obsolete*] ... DNB
Dunbarton College of Holy Cross [*Closed, 1973*] [*Washington, DC*] ... DCHC
Dunbartonshire [*County in Scotland*] ... DUNB
Duncan [*Oklahoma*] [*Airport symbol*] [*Obsolete*] ... DUC
Duncan Aviation, Inc. [*Lincoln, NE*] [*FAA designator*] ... PHD
Duncan, BC [*Radio station call letters*] ... CKAY
Duncan Memorial Library, Casey, IA [*Library symbol*] ... IaCa
Duncan, OK [*Radio station call letters*] ... KRHD
Duncan, OK [*Radio station call letters*] ... KRHD-FM
Duncan/Quamichan Lake [*Canada*] [*Airport symbol*] [*Obsolete*] ... DUQ
Dundas Public Library, Dundas, ON, Canada [*Library symbol*] ... CaOD
Dundee [*Scotland*] [*Airport symbol*] ... DND
Dundee [*Scotland*] [*Seismograph station code, US Geological Survey*] ... EDU
Dundee, IL [*Radio station call letters*] ... WCRM
Dundee, NY [*Radio station call letters*] ... WFLR
Dundee, NY [*Radio station call letters*] ... WFLR-FM
Dundo [*Angola*] [*Airport symbol*] ... DUE
Dundo [*Angola*] [*Seismograph station code, US Geological Survey*] ... DUN
Dunedin [*New Zealand*] [*Airport symbol*] ... DUD
Dunedin, FL [*Radio station call letters*] ... WWNN
Dunedin Public Library, Dunedin, FL [*Library symbol*] ... FDu
Duneland Post Card Club [*Defunct*] ... DPCC
Duneland School Corp., Chesterton, IN [*OCLC symbol*] ... ISC
Dunes Hotels & Casinos, Inc. [*American Stock Exchange symbol*] ... DHC
Dungeon Master [*In game Dungeons and Dragons*] ... DM
Dungeons and Dragons [*Game*] ... D & D
Dunhill International, Incorporated [*NYSE symbol*] [*Delisted*] ... DHI
Dunhuang [*China*] [*Airport symbol*] ... DNH
Dunk Island [*Australia*] [*Airport symbol*] ... DKI
Dunkin Donuts, Inc. [*NASDAQ symbol*] ... DUNK
Dunkirk, NY [*Radio station call letters*] ... WDOE
Dunlap & Associates, Inc. ... DA
Dunlap Public Library District, Dunlap, IL [*Library symbol*] ... IDun
Dunlap Public Library District, Dunlap, IL [*OCLC symbol*] ... IDV
Dunlap Society, Essex, NY [*Library symbol*] ... NEssDS
Dunlap, TN [*Radio station call letters*] ... WSVC
Dunlop Art Gallery, Regina, SK, Canada [*Library symbol*] ... CaSRDA
Dunlop Holdings Ltd. [*American Stock Exchange symbol*] ... DLP
Dunlop Research Centre, Sheridan Park, Mississauga, ON, Canada [*Library symbol*] ... CaOMDR

Dunn, NC [*Radio station call letters*] .... WCKB
Dunn, NC [*Radio station call letters*] .... WIDO
Dunnage .... DUN
Dunnage Board .... DB
Dunnellon, FL [*Radio station call letters*] .... WTRS
Dunnville Public Library, Dunnville, ON, Canada [*Library symbol*] .... CaODu
Dun's Business Month [*A publication*] .... DBM
DUNS [*Data Universal Numbering System*] **Industrial Affiliations Service** [*Dun & Bradstreet*] .... DIAS
Dun's International Review [*A publication*] .... Dun's Int R
Dun's Market Identifier [*Dun & Bradstreet*] .... DMI
Dun's Marketing Services [*Dun & Bradstreet Corp.*] [*Information service*] .... DMS
Dun's Review [*A publication*] .... DR
Dun's Review [*A publication*] .... Dun's
Dun's Review [*A publication*] .... Dun's R
Duns Scotus College [*Michigan*] .... DSC
Duns Scotus College, Detroit, MI [*Library symbol*] .... MiDDS
Dun's Statistical Review [*A publication*] .... Dun's Stat R
Dunsink Observatory [*Ireland*] [*Seismograph station code, US Geological Survey*] .... DDK
Duo-Mode Electric Transport System, Inc. .... DUETS
Duodecimo [*Book up to 20 centimeters in height*] .... D
Duodecimo [*Book up to 20 centimeters in height*] .... DUO
Duodenal Ulcer [*Medicine*] .... DU
Duodenum [*Anatomy*] .... D
Duodenum [*Anatomy*] .... DUOD
Duoplasmation Ion .... DPI
Duoplasmation Ion Source .... DPIS
Dupage Library System [*Library network*] .... DLS
Duplan Corp. [*NYSE symbol*] .... DUP
Duplex [*Radio*] .... DU
Duplex .... DUPLX
Duplex .... DX
Duplex-Drive [*Tank*] .... DD
Duplex-Drive Tank .... DDT
Duplex Line Control .... DLC
Duplex One-Tape System .... DOT
Duplex Products, Inc. [*American Stock Exchange symbol*] .... DPX
Duplexed Display Distributor .... DDD
Duplexer .... DPLXR
Duplexer .... DUPLXR
Duplicate .... DUP
Duplicate .... DUPE
Duplicate Aperture Card .... DAC
Duplicate Filing [*IRS*] .... DUP-FIL
Duplicate Title Transferred [*Library science*] .... DTT
Duplicates Exchange Union [*Library*] .... DEU
Duplicating Pattern Production .... DPP
Duplicating Requisition .... DR
Duplication Technician, Photolithography [*Navy rating*] .... DUT
Duplin County, Dorothy Wightman Library, Kenansville, NC [*Library symbol*] .... NcKeD
Dupo Junior-Senior High School, Dupo, IL [*Library symbol*] .... IDupHS
DuPont of Canada Ltd., Economist's Office Library, Montreal, PQ, Canada [*Library symbol*] .... CaQMDP
DuPont of Canada Ltd., Legal Library, Montreal, PQ, Canada [*Library symbol*] .... CaQMDPL
DuPont of Canada Ltd., Maitland, ON, Canada [*Library symbol*] .... CaOMD
DuPont of Canada Ltd., Research Centre Library, Kingston, ON, Canada [*Library symbol*] .... CaOKD
Dupree, SD [*Location identifier*] [*FAA*] .... DPR
Duquesne Hispanic Review [*A publication*] .... DHR
Duquesne Law Review [*Later, Duquesne University Law Review*] [*A publication*] .... Duquesne L Rev
Duquesne Light Co. [*NYSE symbol*] .... DQU
Duquesne Review [*A publication*] .... DR
Duquesne Science Counselor [*A publication*] .... Duquesne Sci Couns
Duquesne Studies in Language and Literature [*A publication*] .... DSLL
Duquesne Studies. Philological Series [*A publication*] .... DSPS
Duquesne University Law Review [*A publication*] .... Duquesne U L Rev
Duquesne University Library, Pittsburgh, PA [*OCLC symbol*] .... DUQ
Duquesne University, Pittsburgh, PA [*Library symbol*] .... PPiD
Duquesne University, School of Law, Pittsburgh, PA [*Library symbol*] .... PPiD-L
Durability .... DURA
Durability/Damage Tolerance Analysis [*Air Force*] .... D/DTA
Durable Medical Equipment .... DME
Durable Woods Institute .... DWI
Duralith Corp. [*NASDAQ symbol*] .... DRLH
Durand Free Library, Durand, WI [*Library symbol*] .... WDu
Durand, WI [*Radio station call letters*] .... WRDN
Durand, WI [*Radio station call letters*] .... WRDN-FM
Durango [*Colorado*] [*Seismograph station code, US Geological Survey*] [*Closed*] .... DGC
Durango [*Mexico*] [*Airport symbol*] .... DGO
Durango [*Colorado*] [*Airport symbol*] .... DRO
Durango, CO [*Radio station call letters*] .... KDGO
Durango, CO [*Radio station call letters*] .... KDUR
Durango, CO [*Radio station call letters*] .... KIUP
Durango, CO [*Television station call letters*] .... KREZ-TV
Durango, CO [*Radio station call letters*] .... KRSJ
Durango Public Library, Durango, CO [*Library symbol*] .... CoDu
Durant Family Registry .... DFR
Durant, OK [*Location identifier*] [*FAA*] .... DUA
Durant, OK [*Radio station call letters*] .... KEYD
Durant, OK [*Radio station call letters*] .... KHIB
Durant, OK [*Radio station call letters*] .... KLBC
Durant, OK [*Radio station call letters*] .... KLBC-FM
Durant, OK [*Radio station call letters*] .... KSEO-FM
Durante Dolore [*While Pain Lasts*] [*Pharmacy*] .... DUR DOL
Durante Dolore [*While Pain Lasts*] [*Pharmacy*] .... DUR DOLOR
Duration .... D
Duration .... DUR
Duration .... DURN
Duration Adjusting Type .... DAT
Duration of Disease Control .... DDC
Duration of the Present Emergency [*British*] [*World War II*] .... DPE
Duration of Tetany [*Medicine*] .... DT
Duration of Voluntary Apnea [*Physiology*] .... DVA
Duration of War .... DOW
Durban [*South Africa*] [*Airport symbol*] .... DUR
Durban City Council, Durban, South Africa [*Library symbol*] .... SaDDC
Durban Museum and Art Gallery. Annual Report [*A publication*] .... Durban Mus Art Gallery Annu Rep
Durban Museum Novitates [*A publication*] .... Durban Mus Novit
Durbin-Watson [*Procedure*] [*Statistics*] .... DW
Durchgangsvermittlung [*Long-distance telephone exchange*] [*German military - World War II*] .... DV
Durene Association of America .... DAA
Durex Abrasives Corporation [*Defunct*] .... DAC
Durham [*City and county in England*] .... DRHM
Durham [*City and county in England*] .... DUR
Durham [*City and county in England*] .... DURH
Durham [*England*] [*Seismograph station code, US Geological Survey*] .... DUR
Durham City-County Public Library, Durham, NC [*Library symbol*] .... NcDur
Durham College of Applied Arts and Technology, Oshawa, ON, Canada [*Library symbol*] .... CaOOshD
Durham Corporation [*NASDAQ symbol*] .... DUCO
Durham Downs [*Australia*] [*Airport symbol*] .... DHD
Durham Light Infantry [*Military unit*] [*British*] .... DLI
Durham, NC [*Radio station call letters*] .... WAFR
Durham, NC [*Radio station call letters*] .... WDBS
Durham, NC [*Radio station call letters*] .... WDCG
Durham, NC [*Radio station call letters*] .... WDNC
Durham, NC [*Radio station call letters*] .... WDUR
Durham, NC [*Television station call letters*] .... WPTF-TV
Durham, NC [*Radio station call letters*] .... WSRC
Durham, NC [*Radio station call letters*] .... WTIK
Durham, NC [*Television station call letters*] .... WTVD
Durham, NC [*Radio station call letters*] .... WXDU
Durham, NH [*Television station call letters*] .... WENH
Durham, NH [*Radio station call letters*] .... WUNH
Durham Public Library, Durham, ON, Canada [*Library symbol*] .... CaODur
Durham Research Review [*A publication*] .... Durham Res
Durham & Southern Railway Co. [*AAR code*] .... DS
Durham Technical Institute, Durham, NC [*Library symbol*] .... NcDurT
Durham University Biological Society Journal [*A publication*] .... Durham Univ Biol Soc J
Durham University Journal [*A publication*] .... DUJ
During .... DRG
During .... DUR
During .... DURG
During Climb [*Aviation*] .... DURGC
During Descent [*Aviation*] .... DURGD
During Reporting Period .... DRP
During the Temporary Absence Of [*Military*] .... DTAO
[*The*] **Duriron Co.** [*NASDAQ symbol*] .... DURI
Duro-Test Corp. [*American Stock Exchange symbol*] .... DUR
Durr-Fillauer Medical, Inc. [*NASDAQ symbol*] .... DUFM
Durrie [*Australia*] [*Airport symbol*] [*Obsolete*] .... DRR
Dursunbey [*Turkey*] [*Seismograph station code, US Geological Survey*] [*Closed*] .... DRB
Dursunbey [*Turkey*] [*Seismograph station code, US Geological Survey*] .... DST
Durum Growers Association of the United States .... DGA
Durum Wheat Institute .... DWI
Durus [*Hard*] [*Pharmacy*] .... DUR
Durzhavna Sigurnost [*Bulgarian secret service agency*] .... DS
Duscepoleznie Tchtenie [*A publication*] .... DT
Dushanbe [*Stalinabad*] [*USSR*] [*Seismograph station code, US Geological Survey*] .... DSH
Dushanbe [*USSR*] [*Airport symbol*] .... DYU
Dusheti [*USSR*] [*Seismograph station code, US Geological Survey*] .... DUS
Dusing [*New York*] [*Seismograph station code, US Geological Survey*] [*Closed*] .... DSN
Dusseldorf [*West Germany*] [*Airport symbol*] .... DUS
Dusseldorf-Main RR [*West Germany*] [*Airport symbol*] .... QDU
Dust [*Meteorology*] .... D
Dust Devils [*Aviation code*] .... PO
Dust-Free Chamber .... DFC
Dust-Free Room .... DFR

Dust Haze [*Aviation*]....HZ
Dust Infall Predominant....DIP
Dust Jacket [*Paper cover for a hardbound book*]....DJ
Dust and Moisture....DUMR
Dust, Thermal, and Radiation Engineering Measurements Package [*NASA*]....DTREM
Dust-Tight....DT
Dust Veil Index [*of atmosphere*]....DVI
Dust Wrapper [*Paper cover for a hardbound book*]....DW
Duster Class Yacht Racing Association....DCYRA
Dutch....D
Dutch....DU
Dutch....DUT
Dutch [*MARC language code*] [*Library of Congress*]....dut
Dutch-American Historical Commission....DAHC
Dutch Belted [*Rabbits*]....DB
Dutch Belted Cattle Association of America....DBCAA
Dutch Boy, Inc. [*NYSE symbol*] [*American Stock Exchange symbol*] [*Delisted*]....BOY
Dutch Door [*Technical drawings*]....DD
Dutch East Indies....DEI
Dutch Elm Disease....DED
Dutch Guilder [*Monetary unit*]....DG
Dutch Harbor [*Alaska*] [*Seismograph station code, US Geological Survey*] [*Closed*]....DHA
Dutch Harbor [*Alaska*] [*Airport symbol*]....DUT
Dutch, Middle [*MARC language code*] [*Library of Congress*]....dum
Dutch New Guinea [*Later, Irian Barat*]....DNG
Dutch Quarterly Review of Anglo-American Letters [*A publication*]....DQR
Dutch Reformed Church....DRC
Dutch State Mines....DSM
Dutch West Indies....DWI
Dutchess Community College, Poughkeepsie, NY [*Library symbol*]....NPDC
Dutchess County Mental Health Center, Poughkeepsie, NY [*Library symbol*]....NPDCM
Dutchess County Mental Health Center, Poughkeepsie, NY [*OCLC symbol*] [*Inactive*]....RVD
Duties Require Parachuting [*Army*]....DYRQRPRCHT
Duty [*Navy*]....D
Duty....DY
Duty Air Force Specialty....DAFS
Duty Air Force Specialty Code....DAFSC
Duty on Board that Vessel when Placed in Commission [*Navy*]....ONBOWCOM
Duty on Board that Vessel when Placed in Service [*Navy*]....ONBOWSERV
Duty Connection....DUCON
Duty Controller [*Tactical Air Command*]....DC
Duty Cycle Modulation Alternator....DCMA
Duty Cypher Officer [*Military*] [*British*]....DCO
Duty Directed Is Being Performed for Unit Issuing Order....DPUO
Duty Directed in Order Is Being Performed For....DOPF
Duty Driver [*Military*]....DD
Duty Flying Control Officer [*Navy*]....DFCO
Duty in a Flying Status Involving Operational or Training Flights [*Air Force*]....DIFOPS
Duty in a Flying Status Involving Operational or Training Flights as His Relief [*Air Force*]....DIFOTRELAS
Duty in a Flying Status Involving Operational or Training Flights under Instruction [*Air Force*]....DIFOTINS
Duty in a Flying Status Involving Operational or Training Flights Revoked [*Air Force*]....DIFOTRVK
Duty in a Flying Status Involving Operational or Training Flights as a Technical Observer [*Air Force*]....DIFOTECH
Duty in a Flying Status Involving Proficiency Flying [*Air Force*]....DIFPRO
Duty in a Flying Status Not Involving Flying [*Air Force*]....DIFDEN
Duty Free [*Business and trade*]....DF
Duty under Instruction....DUINS
Duty Intelligence Officer [*Air Force*]....DIO
Duty Involving Flying [*Military*]....DIF
Duty Involving Flying [*Military*]....DUFLY
Duty Involving Flying Crewman [*Military*]....DIFCREW
Duty Involving Flying as a Technical Observer [*Military*]....DUFLYTECH
Duty Involving Operational or Training Flights [*Air Force*]....DIFOT
Duty Involving Underway Operations in Submarines....DISUB
Duty Military Occupational Specialty....DMOS
Duty Officer [*Military*]....DO
Duty Officer [*Military*]....DTYO
Duty Operational Test Director....DOTP
[*For*] **Duty Outside the Continental Limits of the United States**....DUTOUT
Duty Paid....DP
Duty Pay....DP
Duty Salvage Ship [*Navy*]....SALV
Duty Section [*Air Force*]....DS
Duty Space Surveillance Officer [*Air Force*]....DSSO
Duty Station [*Navy*]....DUSTA
Duty Status [*Air Force*]....DS
Duxbury, MA [*Radio station call letters*]....WDBY
Duxbury Rural and Historical Society, Duxbury, MA [*Library symbol*]....MDuHi
Dvoracek Memorial Library, Wilber, NE [*Library symbol*]....NbWi
Dvorak Simplified Keyboard [*Typewriter keyboard developed by August Dvorak in the 1920's*]....DSK
Dwarf....D
Dwarf Fruit Trees Association [*Later, International Dwarf Fruit Trees Association*]....DFTA
Dwarf Iris Society....DIS
Dwell Time....DT
Dwelling....DWEL
Dwelling....DWLG
Dwelling Sculpture Institute....DSI
Dwelling Unit [*Household census*]....DU
DWG Corp. [*American Stock Exchange symbol*]....DWG
DWI Corporation [*NASDAQ symbol*]....DWIC
Dwight D. Eisenhower Library....DDEL
Dwight D. Eisenhower Library, Abilene, KS [*Library symbol*]....KAbE
Dwight D. Eisenhower Philatelic and Historical Society....DDEPHS
Dwight Health Care [*NASDAQ symbol*]....DWYT
Dwight, IL [*Location identifier*] [*FAA*]....DTG
Dwight T. Parker Public Library, Fennimore, WI [*Library symbol*]....WFe
Dwyer-Mercer County District Library, Celina, OH [*Library symbol*]....OCel
Dyadic Interaction Analysis....DIA
Dyatron Corp. [*NASDAQ symbol*]....DYTR
Dyco Petroleum Corporation [*NYSE symbol*]....DYC
Dye [*Classification key in textile printing*]....D
Dye-Binding Capacity....DBC
Dyer Hill [*Washington*] [*Seismograph station code, US Geological Survey*]....DHW
Dyer Library, Saco, ME [*Library symbol*]....MeSaco
Dyersburg [*Tennessee*] [*Seismograph station code, US Geological Survey*] [*Closed*]....DY1
Dyersburg, TN [*Location identifier*] [*FAA*]....DYR
Dyersburg, TN [*Radio station call letters*]....WASL
Dyersburg, TN [*Radio station call letters*]....WDSG
Dyersburg, TN [*Radio station call letters*]....WTRO
Dyes and Chemicals Technical Bulletin. Paper Industry Issue [*A publication*]....Dyes Chem Tech Bull
Dyess Air Force Base [*Texas*]....DAFB
Dyestuffs....DS
Dyestuffs Environmental and Toxicology Organization....DETO
Dyke College, Cleveland, OH [*Library symbol*]....OCID
Dymo Industries, Inc. [*NYSE symbol*] [*Delisted*]....DMO
Dynalectron Corp. [*American Stock Exchange symbol*]....DYN
Dynamic....DYN
Dynamic Accuracy Test Set [*or System*]....DATS
Dynamic Accuracy Tester [*GE*]....DYNAT
Dynamic Acoustic Response Trigger....DART
Dynamic Action Management Operations [*BSD*]....DYNAMO
Dynamic Active Index Matrix....DAIM
Dynamic Address Translation [*Data processing*]....DAT
Dynamic Air Blast Simulator....DABS
Dynamic Air War Game [*Military*]....DAWG
Dynamic Allocation Interface Routine [*Data processing*]....DAIR
Dynamic Analog Differential Equation Equalizer....DADEE
Dynamic Analysis Branch [*Redstone Arsenal*]....DA
Dynamic Analysis and Control Laboratory [*MIT*]....DACL
Dynamic Analysis and Design of Systems....DADS
Dynamic Analyzer....DYANA
Dynamic Analyzer....DYNA
Dynamic Antiresonant Vibration Isolator....DAVI
Dynamic Arm Programer [*Data processing*]....DYNARM
Dynamic Asynchronous Logic Circuit....DALC
Dynamic Automatic Monitoring....DYNAMO
Dynamic Balancing Equipment....DBE
Dynamic Braking....DB
Dynamic Braking....DYB
Dynamic Cardiogram....DCG
Dynamic Characteristic Load....DCL
Dynamic Checkout Unit [*Aerospace*]....DCU
Dynamic Cloud Free Line of Sight....DCFLOS
Dynamic Coercive Force....DCF
Dynamic Compression-Plate....DCP
Dynamic Computer Display....DCD
Dynamic Console for Operations Planners....DYCOP
Dynamic Control....DYCON
Dynamic Crew Procedures Simulator....DCPS
Dynamic Crossed-Field Electron Multiplication....DCFEM
Dynamic Crossed-Field Photomultiplier....DCFP
Dynamic Debugging Technique....DDT
Dynamic Demand Assignment [*Army*]....DDA
Dynamic Design Analysis Method [*Navy*]....DDAM
Dynamic Device Reconfiguration [*Data processing*]....DDR
Dynamic Diagnostic System....DDS
Dynamic Display Tester....DDT
Dynamic Docking Test Facility [*NASA*]....DDTF
Dynamic Docking Test System [*NASA*]....DDTS
Dynamic Dummy Director....DDD
Dynamic Economics [*Elsevier Book Series*] [*A publication*]....DE
Dynamic Electromagnetic Environment Simulator....DEES
Dynamic Electrospeaker....DES
Dynamic Energy Conversion....DEC
Dynamic Engineer....DE

Dynamic Environment Simulator [*Air Force*]............................ DES
Dynamic Environmental Laboratory Test..........................DELT
Dynamic Error-Free Transmission...............................DEFT
Dynamic Explorer [*NASA*]...DE
Dynamic Fault Diagnosis Technique .... DFDT
Dynamic Fermenter [*Microbiology*]................................. DF
Dynamic Flight Simulator ....DFS
Dynamic Flow Control Unit [*Chromatography*]...............DFCU
Dynamic Flow Parameter...DFP
Dynamic Forcing Function [*Information*] **Report** [*Nuclear energy*] .... DFFR
Dynamic Fuze Simulator [*RADAR*]...............................DYFUS
Dynamic Gas Disengagement [*Chemical engineering*]...............DGD
Dynamic Gravity Detector .... DGD
Dynamic Gravity Generator .... DGG
Dynamic Hardness Number .... DHN
Dynamic Homes [*NASDAQ symbol*]..............................DYHM
Dynamic Imagery Viewer...DIV
Dynamic Impedance Measurement .... DIM
Dynamic Instrumentation Data Automobile System
  [*Telemetering system for auto test tracks*]...............DIDAS
Dynamic Instrumentation Digital Analyzer ....DIDA
Dynamic Integrated Data Display ....DIDD
Dynamic Integrated Data Display System ....DIDDS
Dynamic Inventory Analysis System [*Data processing*]...............DIAS
Dynamic Line Regulation ....DLR
Dynamic Load Characteristic ....DL
Dynamic Load Characteristic ....DLC
Dynamic Load Regulation ....DLR
Dynamic Logic Chassis Analyzer.................................DLCA
Dynamic Map Display ....DMD
Dynamic Mapping System..DMS
Dynamic Mass Spectrometry [*A publication*] .... Dyn Mass Spectrom
Dynamic Mechanical Analysis .... DMA
Dynamic Mechanical Testing .... DMT
Dynamic Missile Simulator... DMS
Dynamic Model Continuous Time Simulation................DYNAMO
Dynamic Model Operations Section..............................DMOS
Dynamic Module Replacement ....DMR
Dynamic Motion Simulator .... DMS
Dynamic Noise Suppression [*Electronics*].........................DNS
Dynamic Nuclear Magnetic Resonance .... DNMR
Dynamic Nuclear Polarization .... DNP
Dynamic Octal Load.. DOL
Dynamic Operation Test .... DOT
Dynamic Operational Requirements and Cost Analysis
  [*Computer program*] [*NASA*]...............................DORCA
Dynamic Operator Response Apparatus.........................DORA
Dynamic Operator Response System.............................DORS
Dynamic Overload Controls ....DOC
Dynamic Personality Inventory [*Psychology*] ....DPI
Dynamic Phase Error .... DPE
Dynamic Philatelic Society ....DPS
Dynamic Preferential Runway System [*Aviation*]...............DPRS
Dynamic Pressure [*NASA*]...Q
Dynamic Pressure Feedback ....DPF
Dynamic Pressure Measurements .... DPM
Dynamic Processor Overload Control [*Telephone technology*] .... DPOC
Dynamic Programing [*Data processing*]..............................DP
Dynamic Quality Control ....DQC
Dynamic Random Access Mechanization ....DRAM
Dynamic Random Access Memory [*Data processing*]...............d-RAM
Dynamic Range ....DR
Dynamic Real-Time Information Processing Systems ....DRIPS
Dynamic Reflectance Spectroscopy...............................DRS
Dynamic Reliability Instantaneous Forecasting Technique .... DRIFT
Dynamic Research Console ....DRC
Dynamic Resolver Angle Digitizer ....DYRAD
Dynamic Response Index...DRI
Dynamic Scattering Mode ....DSM
Dynamic Science Fiction [*A publication*]...........................DSF
Dynamic Science Stories [*A publication*]...........................DSS
Dynamic Sequential Control ....DSC
Dynamic Shift Register ....DSR
Dynamic Sideband Regulator ....DSR
Dynamic Signal Analyzer ....DSA
Dynamic Simulation of Auto and Passenger Rail Transports ....DART
Dynamic Simulation System ....DSS
Dynamic Soaring [*Space flight*] ....DYNA-SOAR
Dynamic Spacial Reconstructor [*X-ray scanning machine*] ....DSR
Dynamic Spring Analysis ....DSA
Dynamic Standby Computer...DSC
Dynamic to Static..D/S
Dynamic Steady State ....DSS
Dynamic Storage Allocation Language [*in FORTRAN*] [*Data
  processing*]..DYSTAL
Dynamic Storage Analog Computer ....DYSAC
Dynamic Storage Analog Computer ....DYSTAC
Dynamic Stories [*A publication*]...................................DS
Dynamic Subscription Promotion.................................DSP
Dynamic Support Program [*Data processing*]......................DSP
Dynamic Support System...DSS

Dynamic System Electronics ....DSE
Dynamic Systems Analyzer [*General Electric Co.*]............DYNASAR
Dynamic Systems Test Rig [*Helicopters*] [*Army*]...............DSTR
Dynamic Test Fixture [*Military*]....................................DTF
Dynamic Test Model [*Spacecraft*]..................................DTM
Dynamic Test Panel ....DTP
Dynamic Test System ....DTS
Dynamic Test Vehicle ....DTV
Dynamic Tester ....DT
Dynamic Testing Program ....DTP
Dynamic Tongue and Palatometric Shapes [*System to help the
  deaf speak*]..DYTAPS
Dynamic Track Following [*Electronics*].............................DTF
Dynamic Universal Assembly Language [*Data processing*]...............DUAL
Dynamic Vacuum Seal ....DVS
Dynamic Visual Acuity ....DVA
Dynamic Weather Display ....DWD
Dynamical Tactical Simulator.................................DYNTACS
Dynamics Corp. of America [*NYSE symbol*]........................DYA
Dynamics Differential Analyzer.....................................DDA
Dynamics International Gardening Association ....DIGA
Dynamics Research Corporation ....DRC
Dynamics Research Corporation [*NASDAQ symbol*]...............DRCO
Dynamische Psychiatrie [*A publication*] ....Dynam Psych
Dynamische Psychiatrie [*A publication*] ....Dyn Psychiatr
Dynamite ....DYNMT
Dynamiting [*FBI standardized term*] ....DYN
Dynamo...DYN
Dynamo Alert System ....DAS
Dynamo Electric Amplifier ....DEA
Dynamo Management System .... DMS
Dynamogram ....DG
Dynamometer ....DYN
Dynamometer [*Engineering*] ....DYNMT
Dynamometer ....DYNO
Dynamotor ....DYNM
Dynamotors [*JETDS nomenclature*] [*Military*] ....DY
Dynascan Corp. [*NASDAQ symbol*].............................DYNA
Dynatech Corporation [*NASDAQ symbol*].......................DYTC
Dynatech Research/Development Co., Cambridge, MA [*Library
  symbol*]...MCD
Dynatrend, Incorporated [*NASDAQ symbol*].....................DYNI
Dynatronics LASER Corp. [*NASDAQ symbol*]...................DYNT
Dynayoke Deflection Yoke ....DDY
Dyne [*Unit of force*] [*Also, dyn*] [*Preferred unit is N, Newton*].....................D
Dyne [*Unit of force*] [*Also, D*] [*Preferred unit is N, Newton*] ....dyn
Dyneer Corp. [*American Stock Exchange symbol*]..................DYR
Dynell Electronics Corp. [*American Stock Exchange symbol*]
  [*Delisted*]...DNL
Dynes per Centimeter...DYN/CM
Dynes per Square Centimeter...............................DYN/CM²
D'Youville College, Buffalo, NY [*Library symbol*]..................NBuD
Dysan Corp. [*NASDAQ symbol*].................................DYSN
Dysart [*Australia*] [*Airport symbol*]................................DYA
Dysautonomia Foundation .... DF
Dysfunctional Uterine Bleeding [*Medicine*]........................DUB
Dysgerminoma [*Oncology*] ....DYS
Dyskaryosis, Index of [*Cytopathology*].............................DI
Dysmenorrhea [*Medicine*]...DYSM
Dyspnea on Exertion [*Medicine*]..................................DOE
Dysprosium [*Chemical element*] ....Dy
Dysrhythmic Aggressive Behavior ....DAB
Dystonia Medical Research Foundation ....DMRF
Dystrophic Epidermolysis Bullosa Research Association of
  America ....DEBRA
Dzaoudzi [*Comoro Islands*] [*Airport symbol*]......................DZA
Dzejas Diena [*A publication*] ....DzD
Dzhafr [*USSR*] [*Seismograph station code, US Geological Survey*]
  [*Closed*]...DZH
Dzhergetal [*USSR*] [*Seismograph station code, US Geological
  Survey*] [*Closed*]...DZT
Dziennik Literacki [*A publication*] ....Dz Lit
Dzis i Jutro [*A publication*] ....DiJ
Dzis i Jutro [*A publication*] ....DJ
Dzveli Kartuli Enis K'atedris Stomebi [*A publication*].....................DzKarSt

E

E. B. Eddy Co., Research and Technical Library, Hull, PQ, Canada [*Library symbol*].. CaQHE
E & B Marine, Incorporated. [*NASDAQ symbol*].........................EBMI
E. C. Brown Foundation ....ECBF
E. D'Appolonia Consulting Engineers, Pittsburgh, PA [*Library symbol*]...PPiE
E. F. Hutton & Co., Philadelphia, PA [*Library symbol*] [*Obsolete*].........PPEFH
E. F. Schumacher Society..EFSS
E-H International, Inc. [*NASDAQ symbol*]...............................EHIL
E. I. DuPont de Nemours & Co., Aiken, SC [*Library symbol*] .... ScAiD
E. I. DuPont de Nemours & Co., Benger Laboratory, Waynesboro, VA [*Library symbol*] .... ViWbD
E. I. DuPont de Nemours & Co., Carney's Point Development Laboratory, Carney's Point, NJ [*Library symbol*] .... NjCarpD
E. I. DuPont de Nemours & Co., Eastern Laboratory Library, Gibbstown, NJ [*Library symbol*]..NjGiD
E. I. DuPont de Nemours & Co., Electrochemical Department, Niagara Falls, NY [*Library symbol*]......................................NNiaD
E. I. DuPont de Nemours & Co., Haskell Laboratory, Newark, DE [*OCLC symbol*]...DLI
E. I. DuPont de Nemours & Co., Jackson Laboratory, Wilmington, DE [*Library symbol*] .... DeWDJ
E. I. DuPont de Nemours & Co., Jackson Laboratory, Wilmington, DE [*OCLC symbol*]..DUJ
E. I. DuPont de Nemours & Co., Lavoisier Library, Wilmington, DE [*Library symbol*].................................. DeWDL
E. I. DuPont de Nemours & Co., Lavoisier Library, Wilmington, DE [*OCLC symbol*]................................... DUP
E. I. DuPont de Nemours & Co., Marshall Laboratory, Philadelphia, PA [*Library symbol*] .... PPDM
E. I. DuPont de Nemours & Co., Martinsville, VA [*Library symbol*] .... ViMvD
E. I. DuPont de Nemours & Co., Sabine River Works, Orange, TX [*Library symbol*].. TXOrD
E. I. DuPont de Nemours & Co., Stine Laboratory, Newark, DE [*Library symbol*]...DeND
E. I. DuPont de Nemours & Co., Technical Library, Wilmington, DE [*Library symbol*]................................... DeWDT
E. I. DuPont de Nemours & Co., Yerkes Research Laboratory, Buffalo, NY [*Library symbol*]...NBuDY
E. & J. Gallo Winery, Modesto, CA [*Library symbol*].....................CMGW
E. J. Wilson High School Library, Spencerport, NY [*OCLC symbol*].....RWA
E. Jack Sharpe Public Library, White Cloud, MI [*Library symbol*] .... MiWhc
E Lacte [*With Milk*] [*Pharmacy*].. E LACT
E. Merck [*Laboratories*].. EM
E. Merck AG [*Germany*] [*Research code symbol*]............................AK
E. Merck AG [*Germany*] [*Research code symbol*].............................St
E. Merck AG, Darmstadt, Germany [*Library symbol*]............... GyDaM
E. O. Hulburt Center for Space Research ....HCSR
E Quolibet Vehiculo [*In Any Vehicle*] [*Pharmacy*].......... E QUOL VEH
E Quovis Liquido [*In Any Liquid*] [*Pharmacy*] .... E QUOV LIQ
E. R. Squibb & Sons [*Research code symbol*] C
E. R. Squibb & Sons [*Research code symbol*] ....SF
E. R. Squibb & Sons [*Research code symbol*] ....SQ
E. R. Squibb & Sons, Princeton, NJ [*Library symbol*]...................NjPERS
E. R. Squibb & Sons, Princeton, NJ [*OCLC symbol*] ....SQU
E-Systems, Inc. [*NYSE symbol*]..ESY
E-Tron Corp. Uts [*NASDAQ symbol*] ....ETONU
E Vino [*In Wine*] [*Pharmacy*] ....E VIN
E-Z-EM, Inc. [*NASDAQ symbol*]..EZEM
EAA [*Experimental Aircraft Association*] Aviation Foundation.............EAAAF
EAA [*Experimental Aircraft Association*] Ultralight Association .... EAAUA
EAAS [*European Association for American Studies*] Newsletter [*A publication*]...EAASN
EAC Industries, Inc. [*American Stock Exchange symbol*]....................EAC
Each ....EA
Each Community Helps Others [*Environmental Protection Agency*] .... ECHO
Each Face [*Technical drawings*]..EF
Each Layer [*Technical drawings*].. EL
Each Less Than ....ELT
Each More Than ....EMT

Each Thousand-Foot Level [*Aviation*] ....ETFL
Each Way ....EW
EADAS [*Engineering and Administrative Data Acquisition System*] Traffic Data Center [*Bell System*]...................................ETDC
Eadem [*The Same*] [*Pharmacy*].. EAD
Eagle [*Alaska*] [*Airport symbol*].. EAA
Eagle [*Colorado*] [*Seismograph station code, US Geological Survey*] [*Closed*].. EGC
Eagle Aviation [*Long Beach, CA*] [*FAA designator*] .... EGL
Eagle Aviation, Inc. [*Flint, MI*] [*FAA designator*]....................DAS
Eagle Butte [*South Dakota*] [*Seismograph station code, US Geological Survey*]... EBS
Eagle Butte, SD [*Television station call letters*]..............KPSD-TV
Eagle Clothes, Inc. [*American Stock Exchange symbol*] [*Delisted*] .... EGL
Eagle, CO [*Location identifier*] [*FAA*]....................................OWE
Eagle Commuter Airlines [*Brownwood, TX*] [*FAA designator*]..............ECA
Eagle Computer, Inc. [*NASDAQ symbol*]...............................EGLC
Eagle Corporation ADR [*NASDAQ symbol*]........................EGCLY
Eagle Elementary Consolidated School District 43, Streator, IL [*Library symbol*] .... IStrESD
Eagle Explorations Co. [*NASDAQ symbol*] ....EGLE
Eagle Forum ....EF
Eagle Grove Junior College [*Iowa*] ....EGJC
Eagle Grove Public Library, Eagle Grove, IA [*Library symbol*]................IaE
Eagle Pass [*Texas*] [*Airport symbol*] [*Obsolete*] ....EGP
Eagle Pass, TX [*Radio station call letters*]..............................KEPS
Eagle Pass, TX [*Radio station call letters*]................................KINL
Eagle-Picher Co. [*Later, EPI*] [*NYSE symbol*].............................EGP
Eagle-Picher Industries, Inc. [*NYSE symbol*]..............................EPI
Eagle Point, OR [*Radio station call letters*].............................KEPO
Eagle Public Library, Eagle, CO [*Library symbol*] ....CoEag
Eagle River, WI [*Radio station call letters*].............................WERL
Eagle River, WI [*Radio station call letters*]........................WERL-FM
Eagle Rock Public Library, Eagle Rock, CA [*Library symbol*] ....CEr
Eagle Telephonics, Inc. [*NASDAQ symbol*].............................EGLA
Eagle Valley Environmentalists...EVE
Eagleair Ltd. [*Arnarflug hf*] [*Iceland*] [*ICAO designator*]..................VL
Eagle's Basal Medium with Earle's Salts [*Culture medium*]................EBME
Eagle's Minimum Essential Medium [*Culture medium*]................EMEM
Eagle's Nest [*New York*] [*Seismograph station code, US Geological Survey*]... EGN
Ealing College of Higher Education [*England*] ....ECHE
Ealing Corp. [*NASDAQ symbol*]..EALG
EANHS [*East Africa Natural History Society*] Bulletin [*A publication*] .... EANHS Bull
Ear Falls Public Library, Ear Falls, ON, Canada [*Library symbol*] ....CaOEf
Ear Foundation ....EF
Ear and Hearing [*A publication*] ....Ear Hear
Ear, Nose, and Throat [*Medical Officer designation*] [*British*].......................E
Ear, Nose, and Throat Journal [*A publication*] .... Ear Nose Throat J
Ear, Nose, and Throat Journal [*A publication*] ....ENT J
Ear Research Institute [*Later, HEI*]..ERI
Earl ....E
Earl K. Long Hospital, Medical Library, Baton Rouge, LA [*Library symbol*].. LBrLH
Earl Marshal [*British*]..EM
Earl Township Public Library, Earlville, IL [*Library symbol*] ....IEar
Earl Warren Legal Training Program ....EWLTP
Earlham College, Richmond, IN [*OCLC symbol*].........................IEC
Earlham College, Richmond, IN [*Library symbol*].......................InRE
Earlham College. Science Bulletin [*A publication*].........Earlham Coll Sci Bull
[*The*] Earlham Review [*A publication*]...ER
Earliest Arrival Date .... EAD
Earliest Arrival Time ....EAT
Earliest Finish Date ....EFD
Earliest Possible Date ....EPD
Earliest Practicable Date .... EARLPRADATE
Earliest Scram Set Point [*Nuclear energy*]...............................ESSP
Earliest Start Date..ESD
Earliest Work Listed...EWL

Earlton [*Canada*] [*Airport symbol*] ... YXR
Earlville Community Unit, School District 9, Earlville, IL [*Library symbol*] ... IEarSD
Early ... ERY
Early Acquisition System [*Army*] ... EASY
Early American ... EA
Early American Coppers Club ... EAC
Early American Industries Association ... EAIA
Early American Life Insurance Association ... EAL
Early American Literature [*A publication*] ... EAL
Early American Literature [*A publication*] ... Early Am Lit
Early American Literature. Newsletter [*A publication*] ... EALN
Early American Society ... EAS
Early Antigen [*Immunochemistry*] ... EA
Early Apollo Scientific Experiments Package [*or Payload*] [*NASA*] ... EASEP
Early Birds of Aviation [*An association*] ... EBA
Early-Break-Make [*Data processing*] ... EBM
Early Burst [*Premature explosion of a warhead*] ... EB
Early California Industries [*NASDAQ symbol*] ... ERLY
Early Capability Orbital Manned Station ... ECOMS
Early Child Development and Care [*A publication*] ... Early Child Dev Care
Early Childhood Education ... ECE
Early Childhood Resource Center ... ECRC
Early Closing Association [*British*] ... ECA
Early-Closing Day [*British*] ... EC
Early-Closing Day [*British*] ... ECD
Early Decision Plan [*Medical school entrance program*] ... EDP
Early Departure Authorized ... EDA
Early Diastolic Murmur [*Medicine*] ... EDM
Early Dry Breakfast [*Medicine*] ... EDB
Early English [*Language, etc.*] ... EE
Early English Text Society ... EETS
Early Failure Detection ... EFD
Early Finish ... EF
Early Finish Time ... EFT
Early Four Cylinder Chevrolet Club, International ... EFCCCI
Early Fuel Evaporation [*Automotive technology*] ... EFE
Early Human Development [*A publication*] ... Early Hum Dev
Early Latent [*Medicine*] ... EL
Early Light Breakfast [*Medicine*] ... ELB
Early Lunar Flare ... ELF
Early Lunar Shelter [*NASA*] ... ELS
Early-Make-Break [*Data processing*] ... EMB
Early Manned Planetary-Interplanetary Round Trip Experiment ... EMPIRE
Early Missile Test ... EMT
Early Modern English [*Language, etc.*] ... EMNE
Early Morning Specimen [*Medicine*] ... EMS
Early Music [*A publication*] ... Early Mus
Early Music Gazette [*A publication*] ... Early Mus G
Early and Periodic Screening, Diagnosis, and Treatment ... EPSDT
Early Postsurgical Fitting [*Medicine*] ... EPSF
Early Pregnancy Test ... EPT
Early Programing Language [*Data processing*] ... EPL
Early Receptor Potential [*of the eye*] ... ERP
Early School Personality Questionnaire [*Psychology*] ... ESPQ
Early Scottish Text Society [*A publication*] ... ESTS
Early Settlers Association of the Western Reserve ... ESAWR
Early Site Review [*Nuclear energy*] ... ESR
Early Site Review Report [*Nuclear energy*] ... ESRR
Early Sites Research Society ... ESRS
Early Start Time ... EST
Early Thrust Termination ... ETT
Early Warning [*Air Force*] ... EW
Early Warning Air Defense ... EWAD
Early Warning Change Proposal ... EWCP
Early Warning and Control Aircraft System ... EWCAS
Early Warning/Control and Reporting Post ... EW/CRP
Early Warning Data Transmission ... EWDT
Early Warning Fighter ... EWF
Early Warning/Ground Control Intercept [*RADAR*] ... EW/GCI
Early Warning Observation Teams ... EWOTS
Early Warning RADAR [*Air Force*] ... EWR
Early Warning Squadron [*Symbol*] ... VW
Early Warning System ... EWS
Early Warning Threat Analysis Display ... EWTAD
Early Years [*A publication*] ... Early Yrs
Earned Income Credit ... EIC
Earned Income Tax Credit ... EITC
Earned Loss Ratio [*Insurance*] ... ELR
Earned Premium [*Insurance*] ... EP
Earned Premium to Incurred Loss Ratio [*Insurance*] ... E/I
Earned Run [*Baseball*] ... ER
Earned Run Average [*Baseball*] ... ERA
Earned Value Analysis ... EVA
Earnings [*Finance*] ... E
Earnings before Interest and Taxes ... EBIT
Earnings per Share [*Finance*] ... EPS
Earnings per Share Issued [*Finance*] ... EPSI
Earp, Joseph O., Seattle WA [*STAC*] ... EJO
Earphone Amplifier ... EA
Ears, Nose, and Throat ... EN & T
Ears, Nose, and Throat ... ENT
Earth [*Wind triangle problems and relative movement problems*] ... E
Earth [*Freight*] ... ERTH
Earth Aspect Sensor ... EAS
Earth Awareness Foundation ... EAF
Earth-Based Radio Guidance ... EBRG
Earth-Based Tug [*NASA*] ... EBT
Earth-Centered Inertial [*System*] ... ECI
Earth-Centered True ... ECT
Earth Coverage Horn [*Satellite communications*] ... ECH
Earth Crust Formation ... ECF
Earth Departure Window [*Aerospace*] ... EDW
Earth Dynamics Program [*Smithsonian Astrophysical Observatory*] ... EDP
Earth Entry Module [*NASA*] ... EEM
Earth Equatorial Plane ... EEP
Earth and Extraterrestrial Sciences. Conference Reports and Professional Activities [*A publication*] ... Earth Extraterr Sci
Earth Far Horizon [*NASA*] ... EFH
Earth First! ... EF!
Earth-Fixed Coordinate ... EFC
Earth-Fixed Coordinate System ... EFCS
Earth-Fixed System ... EFS
Earth or Geocentric Radius ... Re
Earth Geodetic Satellite [*Air Force*] ... ERGS
Earth Horizon Scanner ... EHS
Earth Inductor Compass ... EIC
Earth-Ionosphere Cavity ... EIC
Earth Landing Control Assembly [*NASA*] ... ELCA
Earth Landing Sequence Controller [*NASA*] ... ELSC
Earth Landing System [*or Subsystem*] [*NASA*] ... ELS
Earth Landmark [*NASA*] ... ELDMK
Earth Launch Date [*Aerospace*] ... ELD
Earth Launch Vehicle [*NASA*] ... ELV
Earth Launch Window [*Aerospace*] ... ELW
Earth Leakage Circuit Breaker ... ELCB
Earth Limb Measurement Satellite [*NASA/Air Force*] ... ELMS
Earth-Lunar Horizon Sensor ... EHS
Earth-Mars-Earth ... EME
Earth Mass ... EM
Earth Mean Orbital Speed ... EMOS
Earth and Mineral Sciences [*A publication*] ... Earth Miner Sci
Earth-Moon-Earth [*Extraterrestrial communications*] ... EME
Earth-Moon Space Exploration Study ... ESES
Earth Near Horizon [*NASA*] ... ENH
Earth Net Dial ... END
Earth Observations Aircraft Program [*NASA*] ... EOAP
Earth Observations Division [*Johnson Space Center*] [*NASA*] ... EOD
Earth Observations Programs [*NASA*] ... EOP
Earth Observatory Satellite [*NASA*] ... EOS
Earth-Observed Time [*NASA*] ... EOT
Earth and Ocean Physics [*NASA*] ... EOP
Earth and Ocean Physics Applications Program [*NASA*] ... EOPAP
Earth Orbit [*NASA*] ... EO
Earth Orbit Ejection [*Aerospace*] ... EOE
Earth Orbit Equipment [*Aerospace*] ... EOE
Earth Orbit Escape Device [*Aerospace*] ... EOED
Earth Orbit Insertion [*NASA*] ... EOI
Earth Orbit Launch [*NASA*] ... EOL
Earth Orbit Plane [*Aerospace*] ... EOP
Earth Orbit Rendezvous [*NASA*] ... EOR
Earth Orbital Flight [*Aerospace*] ... EOF
Earth Orbital Launch Configuration [*NASA*] ... EOLC
Earth Orbital Military Space Force ... EOMSF
Earth Orbital Mission [*NASA*] ... EOM
Earth Orbital Shuttle [*NASA*] ... EOS
Earth Orbital Space Station [*NASA*] ... EOSS
Earth Orbiting Recoverable Biological Satellite ... EORBS
Earth Orbiting Teleoperator System [*Spacecraft*] [*NASA*] ... EOTS
Earth-Orientated Applications Experiment ... EOAE
Earth Parking Orbit [*Apollo*] [*NASA*] ... EPO
Earth Path Indicator ... EPI
Earth-Penetrating Warhead ... EPW
Earth Physics and Physical Oceanography Program [*NASA*] ... EPPO
Earth Physics Program ... EPP
Earth-Physics Satellite Observation [*or Observing*] **Campaign** [*Smithsonian Astrophysical Observatory*] ... EPSOC
Earth and Planetary Science Letters [*A publication*] ... Earth Plan
Earth and Planetary Science Letters [*A publication*] ... Earth Planet Sci Lett
Earth-Pointing Instrument Carrier [*A satellite*] ... EPIC
Earth Prelaunch Calibration [*NASA*] ... EPC
Earth Probe near Limb of Venus [*Angle*] ... EPV
Earth-Probe-Mars [*Angle*] ... EPM
Earth-Probe-Sun [*Angle*] ... EPS
Earth Radiation Budget [*NASA*] ... ERB
Earth Radiation Budget Experiment [*NASA*] ... ERBE
Earth Radiation Budget Satellite System [*NASA*] ... ERBSS
Earth Radii ... ER
Earth Rate ... ER
Earth Rate Compensation ... ERC
Earth Rate Directional Reference ... ERDR
Earth Rate Unit [*NASA*] ... ERU

Earth Re-Entry Module ... ERM
Earth Received Time [*Astronomy*] ... ERT
Earth Recovery Subsystem [*NASA*] ... ERS
Earth-Reflecting Ionospheric Sounder [*Air Force*] ... ERIS
Earth Resistivity Meter ... ERM
Earth Resources ... ER
Earth Resources Aircraft Facility [*NASA*] ... ERAF
Earth Resources Aircraft Program [*NASA*] ... ERAP
Earth Resources Applications Mission [*NASA*] ... ERAM
Earth Resources Company [*American Stock Exchange symbol*] [*Delisted*] ... ERC
Earth Resources Data Center [*NASA*] ... ERDC
Earth Resources Experiment Package [*Skylab*] [*NASA*] ... EREP
Earth Resources Experiment Package Program [*Skylab*] [*NASA*] ... EREPP
Earth Resources Flight Data Processor [*NASA*] ... ERFDP
Earth Resources Image [*or Interactive*] **Processing System** ... ERIPS
Earth Resources Information Storage, Transformation, Analysis, and Retrieval ... ERISTAR
Earth Resources Laboratory [*Later, NSTL*] [*NASA*] ... ERL
Earth Resources Observation Systems [*Department of the Interior*] ... EROS
Earth Resources Project Office ... ERPO
Earth Resources Research Data Facility ... ERRDF
Earth Resources Satellite [*NASA*] ... ERS
Earth Resources Satellite System ... ERSS
Earth Resources Shuttle Imaging RADAR ... ERSIR
Earth Resources Survey [*NASA*] ... ERS
Earth Resources Survey Flights Program [*NASA*] ... ERSFP
Earth Resources Survey Program [*NASA*] ... ERSP
Earth Resources Technology Satellite [*Later, LANDSAT*] [*NASA*] ... ERTS
Earth Return Module [*NASA*] ... ERM
Earth Satellite Vehicle [*Air Force*] ... ESV
Earth Satellite Weapon Systems ... ESWS
Earth Science [*A publication*] ... Earth S
Earth Science [*A publication*] ... Earth Sci
Earth Science Bulletin [*A publication*] ... Earth Sci Bull
Earth Science Curriculum Project [*Education*] ... ESCP
Earth Science Digest [*A publication*] ... Earth Sci Digest
Earth Science Institute. Special Publication [*A publication*] ... Earth Sci Inst Special Pub
Earth Science Journal [*A publication*] ... Earth Sci Jour
Earth Science Reviews [*A publication*] ... Earth Sci R
Earth Science Reviews [*A publication*] ... Earth Sci Rev
Earth Sciences Assistance Office [*Department of the Interior*] ... ESAO
Earth Sciences Division [*Army Natick Laboratories*] ... ES
Earth Sciences, Incorporated [*NASDAQ symbol*] ... ESCI
Earth Sciences Laboratory ... ESL
Earth-Sighting Simulator [*NASA*] ... ESS
Earth Station ... ES
Earth Station - Arabia ... ESA
Earth Station - Brazil ... ESB
Earth Station - Chile ... ESCH
Earth Station - Colombia ... ESCO
Earth Station - Congo ... ESC
Earth Station - Ecuador ... ESEC
Earth Station - Egypt ... ESEG
Earth Station - Greece ... ESG
Earth Station - Hong Kong ... ESHK
Earth Station - Iran ... ESI
Earth Station - Israel ... ESIS
Earth Station - Ivory Coast ... ESIC
Earth Station - Jordan ... ESJ
Earth Station - Kenya ... ESK
Earth Station - Libya ... ESL
Earth Station - Mexico ... ESM
Earth Station - Morocco ... ESMO
Earth Station - Scandinavia ... ESSC
Earth Station - Senegal ... ESSE
Earth Station - South Africa ... ESSA
Earth Station - Sudan ... ESS
Earth Station - Syria ... ESSY
Earth Station - Turkey ... EST
Earth Station - Venezuela ... ESV
Earth Station - Yugoslavia ... ESY
Earth-Sun Coordinate System ... ESN
Earth Surface Processes [*A publication*] ... Earth Surf Process
Earth Surveillance and Rendezvous Simulator ... ESARS
Earth Terrain Camera [*NASA*] ... ETC
Earth Venus Transit [*Aerospace*] ... EVT
Earth Viewing Module ... EVM
Earth, Wind, and Fire [*Rock music group*] ... EWF
Earthenware [*Freight*] ... ERWRE
Earthquake Engineering Research Center [*National Science Foundation*] ... EERC
Earthquake Engineering Research Institute ... EERI
Earthquake Engineering and Structural Dynamics [*A publication*] ... Earthquake Eng Struct Dyn
Earthquake Information Bulletin [*A publication*] ... Earth Inf Bul
Earthquake Information Bulletin [*A publication*] ... Earthquake Inf Bull
Earthquake Information Bulletin [*A publication*] ... EIB
Earthquake Monitoring System ... EMS
Earthquake Notes [*A publication*] ... Earthqu Notes
Earthquake Prediction Research ... EPR
Earth's Physical Features Study Unit [*American Topical Association*] ... EPFSU
Earth's Polar Axis ... EPA
Earthwatch [*United Nations Environment Program*] ... EW
Earthwork/Center for Rural Studies ... ECRS
EASCO Corp. [*Formerly, Eastern Stainless Steel Corp.*] [*NYSE symbol*] ... ES
Eased Up [*Horse racing*] ... U
Easily ... E
Easley, SC [*Radio station call letters*] ... WELP
Easley, SC [*Radio station call letters*] ... WELP-FM
Eason Oil Co. [*American Stock Exchange symbol*] [*Delisted*] ... EAS
East [*or Eastern*] ... E
East Africa ... EA
East Africa Journal [*A publication*] ... EAJ
East Africa Protectorate [*Later, Kenya*] ... EAP
East African Agricultural and Forestry Journal [*A publication*] ... E Afr Agr Forest J
East African Agricultural and Forestry Journal [*A publication*] ... E Afric Agric & For J
East African Agricultural and Forestry Journal [*A publication*] ... East Afr Agric For J
East African Agricultural Journal [*A publication*] ... East Afr Agric J
East African Agriculture and Forestry Research Organization ... EAAFRO
East African Agriculture and Forestry Research Organization. Forestry Technical Note [*A publication*] ... East Afr Agric For Res Organ For Tech Note
East African Airways Corp. [*African airline*] ... EAA
East African Airways Corporation [*African airline*] ... EAAC
East African Common Services Organization [*Later, EAC*] ... EACSO
East African Community ... EAC
East African Development Bank ... EADB
East African Economic Community ... EAEC
East African Farmer and Planter [*A publication*] ... E Afr Farmer Plant
East African Freshwater Fisheries Research Organization ... EAFFRO
East African Freshwater Fisheries Research Organization. Annual Report [*A publication*] ... East Afr Freshw Fish Res Org Annu Rep
East African Geographical Review [*A publication*] ... East Afr Geogr R
East African Horn [*MARC geographic area code*] [*Library of Congress*] ... fh-----
East African Institute for Medical Research. Annual Report [*A publication*] ... East Afr Inst Med Res Annu Rep
East African Journal of Medical Research [*A publication*] ... East Afr J Med Res
East African Literature Bureau ... EALB
East African Marine Fisheries Research Organization ... EAMFRO
East African Medical Journal [*A publication*] ... E Afr Med J
East African Medical Journal [*A publication*] ... East Afr Med J
East African Natural Resources Research Council. Annual Report [*A publication*] ... East Afr Nat Resour Res Counc Annu Rep
East African Publishing House [*Kenya*] ... EAPH
East African Regional Committee for Conservation and Utilisation of Soil ... EARCCUS
East African Society of African Culture ... EASTASAC
East African Studies [*A publication*] ... E Afr Stud
East African Trypanosomiasis Research Organization. Annual Report [*A publication*] ... East Afr Trypanosomiasis Res Organ Annu Rep
East African Tuberculosis Investigation Centre. Annual Report [*A publication*] ... East Afr Tuberc Invest Cent Annu Rep
East African Veterinary Research Organization. Annual Report [*A publication*] ... East Afr Vet Res Organ Annu Rep
East African Virus Research Institute. Report [*A publication*] ... East Afr Virus Res Inst Rep
East African Wildlife Journal [*A publication*] ... E Afr Wildlife J
East African Wildlife Journal [*A publication*] ... East Afr Wildl J
East Albemarle Regional Library, Elizabeth City, NC [*Library symbol*] ... NcElc
East Alton Elementary 13, Alton, IL [*Library symbol*] ... IAIE
East Alton Public Library, East Alton, IL [*Library symbol*] ... IEa
East Alton-Wood River Community High School 14, Wood River, IL [*Library symbol*] ... IWorHS
East Asia Blocking Ridge [*Meteorology*] ... EABR
East Asia Christian Conference ... EACC
East Asia Journalism Program ... EAJP
East Asia Regional Organization for Planning and Housing ... EAROPH
East Asian Cultural Studies [*A publication*] ... East As Cult Stud
East Asian and Pacific [*Series*] [*A publication*] ... EA & P
East Asian Pastoral Review [*A publication*] ... EAPR
East Asian Review [*A publication*] ... East As R
East Australian Current [*Oceanography*] ... EAC
East Australian Standard Time ... EAST
East Baton Rouge Parish Public Library, Baton Rouge, LA [*Library symbol*] ... LBr
East Baton Rouge Parish Public Library, Baton Rouge, LA [*OCLC symbol*] ... LEB
East Bay Fan Guild ... EBFG
East Bay Information Service [*Library network*] ... EBIS
East Brunswick Public Library, East Brunswick, NJ [*Library symbol*] ... NjEb
East Camden & Highland Railroad Co. [*AAR code*] ... EACH
East Cape [*New Zealand*] [*Seismograph station code, US Geological Survey*] ... ECZ

East Carolina College [*Later, ECU*] [*North Carolina*] ... ECC
East Carolina Railway [*AAR code*] ... EC
East Carolina University [*Formerly, ECC*] [*North Carolina*] ... ECU
East Carolina University, Department of Library Science, Greenville, NC [*OCLC symbol*] ... NEL
East Carolina University, Greenville, NC [*OCLC symbol*] ... ERE
East Carolina University, Greenville, NC [*Library symbol*] ... NcGrE
East Carolina University, Health Sciences Library, Greenville, NC [*Library symbol*] ... NcGrE-H
East Carolina University, Health Sciences Library, Greenville, NC [*OCLC symbol*] ... NEH
East Carroll Parish Library, Lake Providence, LA [*Library symbol*] ... LLpEC
East Central [*Refers especially to London postal district*] ... EC
East Central Area Reliability Coordination Agreement [*Regional power council*] ... ECAR
East Central Junior College [*Mississippi*] ... ECJC
East Central Nuclear Group ... ECNG
East Central Oklahoma State University, Ada, OK [*OCLC symbol*] ... ECO
East Central Regional Library, Cambridge, MN [*Library symbol*] ... MnCaE
East Central Regional Library System [*Library network*] ... ECRL
East Central Reservoir Investigation [*Department of the Interior*] ... ECRI
East Central State College [*Later, East Central Oklahoma State University*] ... ECSC
East Central State College [*Later, East Central Oklahoma State University*]**, Ada, OK** [*Library symbol*] ... OkAdE
East Chicago Public Library, East Chicago, IN [*OCLC symbol*] ... INE
East Chicago Public Library, East Chicago, IN [*Library symbol*] ... InEc
East China Sea and Area [*MARC geographic area code*] [*Library of Congress*] ... an-----
East Cleveland Public Library, East Cleveland, OH [*OCLC symbol*] ... ECP
East Cleveland Public Library, East Cleveland, OH [*Library symbol*] ... OEac
East Coast ... EASTCO
East Coast ... EC
East Coast Base ... EASTCOBASE
East Coast Carriers Conference, New York NY [*STAC*] ... ECC
East Coast Coal Port [*Shipping*] [*British*] ... ECCP
East Coast Conference on Aerospace and Navigational Electronics ... ECCANE
East Coast Documents Distribution Center ... EDDC
East Coast of Great Britain [*Shipping*] ... ECGB
East Coast of Ireland [*Shipping*] ... ECI
East Coast Joint-Stock [*British railroad*] ... ECJS
East Coast Laboratory [*Environmental Science Services Administration*] ... ECL
East Coast Migrant Health Project ... ECMHP
East Coast Telecommunications Center [*Defense Communications System*] ... ECTC
East Coast of the United Kingdom [*Shipping*] ... ECUK
East Detroit Memorial Library, East Detroit, MI [*Library symbol*] ... MiEad
East Driefontein ADR [*NASDAQ symbol*] ... DRFNY
East End Environment [*A publication*] ... East End Environ
East Erie Commercial Railroad [*AAR code*] ... EEC
East Europe [*A publication*] ... EE
East Europe [*A publication*] ... E Eur
East Europe [*A publication*] ... Eu
East European Quarterly [*A publication*] ... East Europ Quart
East European Quarterly [*A publication*] ... E Europe Q
East European Quarterly [*A publication*] ... E Eur Q
East German Army ... EGA
East Grand Forks, MN [*Radio station call letters*] ... KRRK
East Grand Forks, MN [*Radio station call letters*] ... KRRK-FM
East Gwillimbury Public Libraries, Holland Landing, ON, Canada [*Library symbol*] ... CaOHIEG
East Hampton [*New York*] [*Airport symbol*] ... HTO
East Hampton Aire [*East Hampton, NY*] [*FAA designator*] ... EHA
East Hampton Free Library, East Hampton, NY [*Library symbol*] ... NEh
East Hanover Public Library, East Hanover, NJ [*Library symbol*] ... NjEh
East Hartford, CT [*Location identifier*] [*FAA*] ... RFX
East Hartford, CT [*Location identifier*] [*FAA*] ... UAZ
East Hartford Public Library, East Hartford, CT [*Library symbol*] ... CtEh
East India Company ... EIC
East India Company's Service ... EICS
East India Dock ... EID
East Indian Railway ... EIR
East Indies ... EI
East Integrated Test Stand ... EITS
East Islip Public Library, East Islip, NY [*Library symbol*] ... NEi
East Jersey Railroad & Terminal Co. [*AAR code*] ... EJR
East Jordan & Southern R. R. [*AAR code*] ... EJS
East Junior/Senior High School Library, Rochester, NY [*OCLC symbol*] ... RWC
East Kent Regiment ... EKR
East Kootenay Community College, Cranbrook, BC, Canada [*Library symbol*] ... CaBCrEK
East Kurupa, AK [*Location identifier*] [*FAA*] ... ACU
East Lansing, MI [*Radio station call letters*] ... WFMK
East Lansing, MI [*Radio station call letters*] ... WKAR
East Lansing, MI [*Radio station call letters*] ... WKAR-FM
East Lansing, MI [*Television station call letters*] ... WKAR-TV
East Lansing, MI [*Radio station call letters*] ... WVIC
East Lansing, MI [*Radio station call letters*] ... WVIC-FM
East Lansing Public Library, East Lansing, MI [*Library symbol*] ... MiE
East Liverpool Carnegie Public Library, East Liverpool, OH [*Library symbol*] ... OEal
East Liverpool, OH [*Location identifier*] [*FAA*] ... EVO
East Liverpool, OH [*Radio station call letters*] ... WELA
East Liverpool, OH [*Radio station call letters*] ... WOHI
East London [*South Africa*] [*Airport symbol*] ... ELS
East Longitude Date ... ELD
East Longmeadow, MA [*Radio station call letters*] ... WIXY
East Los Angeles College, Los Angeles, CA [*Library symbol*] ... CLELJ
East Machias [*Maine*] [*Seismograph station code, US Geological Survey*] ... EMM
East Main [*Canada*] [*Airport symbol*] ... ZEM
East Malaysia Geological Survey. Report [*A publication*] ... East Malays Geol Surv Rep
East Malling Research Station. Annual Report [*A publication*] ... East Malling Res Stn Annu Rep
East Meadow Public Library, East Meadow, NY [*Library symbol*] ... NEm
East Midland Geographer [*A publication*] ... East Midl Geogr
East Midlands [*England*] [*Airport symbol*] ... EMA
East Midlands [*England*] ... EMDL
East Midlands Airport [*England*] ... EMA
East Midlands Electricity Board [*British*] ... EMEB
East Mississippi Junior College ... EMJC
East Moline, IL [*Radio station call letters*] ... WDLM
East Moline, IL [*Radio station call letters*] ... WZZC
East Montpelier, VT [*Radio station call letters*] ... WVEP
East by North ... EbN
East-Northeast ... ENE
East-Northeastern [*Meteorology*] ... ENERN
East-Northeastward [*Meteorology*] ... ENEWD
East-Ocean Meeting Point ... EASTOMP
East Orange Free Public Library, East Orange, NJ [*Library symbol*] ... NjEo
East Orange, NJ [*Radio station call letters*] ... WFMU
East Pacific Rise [*Geology*] ... EPR
East Pennsylvania Psychiatric Institute, Philadelphia, PA [*OCLC symbol*] ... PIU
East Peoria Elementary Schools, East Peoria, IL [*OCLC symbol*] ... ILN
East Peoria, IL [*Television station call letters*] ... WEEK-TV
East Point, GA [*Radio station call letters*] ... WTJH
East Prairie, MO [*Radio station call letters*] ... KYMO
East Promontory [*Utah*] [*Seismograph station code, US Geological Survey*] ... EPU
East Providence, RI [*Radio station call letters*] ... WPRO
East Region Development Corporation ... ERDC
East Riding Yeomanry [*Military unit*] [*British*] ... ERY
East River [*New York*] ... ER
East Rockaway Public Library, East Rockaway, NY [*Library symbol*] ... NEr
East St. Louis, IL [*Radio station call letters*] ... WESL
East St. Louis, IL [*Radio station call letters*] ... WMRY
[*The*] **East St. Louis Junction R. R.** [*AAR code*] ... ESLJ
East St. Louis Public Library, East St. Louis, IL [*Library symbol*] ... IEs
East Saxon [*Dialect of Old English*] [*Language, etc.*] ... ESAX
East Siberian Region, RSFSR [*MARC geographic area code*] [*Library of Congress*] ... e-ure--
East by South ... EbS
East-Southeast ... ESE
East-Southeastern [*Meteorology*] ... ESERN
East-Southeastward [*Meteorology*] ... ESEWD
East Stroudsburg, PA [*Location identifier*] [*FAA*] ... ESP
East Stroudsburg, PA [*Radio station call letters*] ... WESS
East Stroudsburg State College, East Stroudsburg, PA [*OCLC symbol*] ... ETS
East Stroudsburg State College, East Stroudsburg, PA [*Library symbol*] ... PEsS
East Surrey Regiment [*Army*] [*British*] ... ESR
East Syracuse, NY [*Radio station call letters*] ... WSIV
East Tennessee Historical Society, Knoxville, TN [*Library symbol*] ... TKETHi
East Tennessee Historical Society. Publications [*A publication*] ... East Tenn Hist Soc Publ
East Tennessee State College [*Later, East Tennessee State University*] ... ETSC
East Tennessee State University [*Formerly, East Tennessee State College*] ... ETSU
East Tennessee State University, Johnson City, TN [*OCLC symbol*] ... TET
East Tennessee State University, Johnson City, TN [*Library symbol*] ... TJoS
East Tennessee State University, Medical Library, Johnson City, TN [*OCLC symbol*] ... MET
East Tennessee State University, Medical Library, Johnson City, TN [*Library symbol*] ... TJoS-M
East Tennessee & Western North Carolina Railroad Co. [*AAR code*] ... ETWN
East Texas Baptist College ... ETBC
East Texas, PA [*Location identifier*] [*FAA*] ... ETX
East Texas State College [*Later, East Texas State University*] ... ETSC
East Texas State University [*Formerly, East Texas State College*] ... ETSU
East Texas State University, Commerce, TX [*OCLC symbol*] ... IEA
East Texas State University, Commerce, TX [*Library symbol*] ... TxComS
East Texas State University, Metroplex Center, Commerce, TX [*OCLC symbol*] ... IEM

East Texas State University, Museum, Commerce, TX [*Library symbol*] ... TxComS-M
East Texas State University, Texarkana, Texarkana, TX [*OCLC symbol*] ... IET
East Timor Human Rights Committee ... ETHRC
East Timor News Agency ... ETNA
East Timor Project ... ETP
East Traverse Mountains [*Utah*] [*Seismograph station code, US Geological Survey*] ... ETU
East Troy Public Library, East Troy, WI [*Library symbol*] ... WEa
East Washington Railway Co. [*AAR code*] ... EW
East Wenatchee, WA [*Radio station call letters*] ... KTRW
East-West ... EW
East and West [*A publication*] ... EW
East and West [*A publication*] ... E & W
East-West Acceleration ... EWA
East-West Airlines Ltd. [*Australia*] [*ICAO designator*] ... EW
East-West Airlines Ltd. [*Australia*] ... EWA
East-West Center ... EWC
East West Center, Honolulu, HI [*OCLC symbol*] ... HWE
East-West Center, Population Institute, Honolulu, HI [*Library symbol*] ... HHE-P
East-West Center Review [*A publication*] ... EWCR
East-West Cultural Center ... EWCC
East-West Fine, Hundreds ... EWFH
East-West Fine, Tens ... EWFT
East-West Fine, Units ... EWFU
East West Journal [*A publication*] ... East West
East-West Population Institute ... EWPI
East-West Review [*A publication*] ... EWR
East-West Sign Language Association ... EWSLA
East-West Speed ... EWS
East-West Trade Council [*Defunct*] ... EWTC
East-West Trade Policy Committee ... EWTPC
East York Public Library, Toronto, ON, Canada [*Library symbol*] ... CaOTEY
East Yorkshire Regiment [*Military unit*] [*British*] ... EYR
Eastbound ... EB
Eastbound ... EBND
Eastchester Public Library, Eastchester, NY [*Library symbol*] ... NEa
Eastco Industrial Safety Corp. [*NASDAQ symbol*] ... ESTO
Easter ... E
Easter Island [*Seismograph station code, US Geological Survey*] ... EIC
Easter Island [*Airport symbol*] ... IPC
Easter Island [*MARC geographic area code*] [*Library of Congress*] ... poea---
Easter Island Committee ... EIC
Easter Offerings [*to a church*] ... EO
Easter Seal Research Foundation of the National Easter Seal Society ... ESRF
Easter Term ... ET
Easterly ... ELY
Eastern ... EASTN
Eastern ... ESTN
Eastern Academy of Sexual Therapy ... EAST
Eastern Africa Economic Review [*A publication*] ... EAER
Eastern Africa Economic Review [*A publication*] ... E Afr Econ
Eastern Africa Journal of Rural Development [*A publication*] ... East Afr J Rur Develop
Eastern Air Command [*CBI Theater*] [*World War II*] ... EAC
Eastern Air Defense Force ... EADF
Eastern Air Lines, Inc. [*ICAO designator*] ... EA
Eastern Air Lines, Inc. [*NYSE symbol*] [*Air carrier designation symbol*] ... EAL
Eastern Air Lines, Inc. Wts [*NASDAQ symbol*] ... ESALW
Eastern Air Procurement District ... EAPD
Eastern Air Transport ... EAT
Eastern Anthropologist [*A publication*] ... E Anthropol
Eastern Anthropologist [*A publication*] ... East Anthro
Eastern Anthropologist [*A publication*] ... East Anthropol
Eastern Anthropologist [*A publication*] ... Eastern Anthropol
Eastern Anthropologist. Lucknow University [*A publication*] ... EA
Eastern Apicultural Society of North America ... EAS
Eastern Area ... EA
Eastern Area Frequency Coordinator ... EAFC
Eastern Area Library Cooperative, Cedar Falls, IA [*Library symbol*] ... IaCfE
Eastern Area, Military Traffic Management and Terminal Service ... EAMTMTS
Eastern Arizona College [*Formerly, EAJC*] ... EAC
Eastern Arizona College, Thatcher, AZ [*Library symbol*] ... AzThE
Eastern Arizona Junior College [*Later, EAC*] ... EAJC
Eastern Association of Rowing Colleges ... EARC
Eastern Atlantic Area ... EASTLANT
Eastern Atlantic, Channel and North Sea Orders for Ships [*NATO*] ... ECNOS
Eastern Atlantic and Mediterranean [*Military*] ... ELM
Eastern Atlantic and Mediterranean Command [*Military*] ... EAMC
Eastern Atlantic and Mediterranean Command [*Military*] ... EASTLANTMEDCOM
Eastern Atlantic Planning Guidance [*NATO*] ... EAPG
Eastern Atlantic War Plan [*NATO*] ... EAWP
Eastern Baptist Theological Seminary, Philadelphia, PA [*OCLC symbol*] ... EBS
Eastern Baptist Theological Seminary, Philadelphia, PA [*Library symbol*] ... PPEB
Eastern Base Section [*Mediterranean and England*] [*Army*] [*World War II*] ... EBS
Eastern Basketball League ... EBL
Eastern Bird Banding Association ... EBBA
Eastern Buddhist [*A publication*] ... East Buddhist
Eastern Buddhist [*A publication*] ... EB
Eastern Carolina Aviation, Incorporated [*Richlands, NC*] [*FAA designator*] ... ECI
Eastern Catholic Life, Passaic, NJ [*Library symbol*] ... NjPasE
Eastern Central Motor Carriers Association ... ECMCA
Eastern Central Motor Carriers Association, Agent, Akron OH [*STAC*] ... ECA
Eastern Churches Review [*A publication*] ... East Ch R
Eastern Churches Review [*A publication*] ... ECR
Eastern Claims Conference ... ECC
Eastern Coast Breweriana Association ... ECBA
Eastern College Athletic Conference ... ECAC
Eastern College Basketball Association ... ECBA
Eastern College Hockey Association ... ECHA
Eastern College Personnel Officers ... ECPO
Eastern College, St. Davids, PA [*OCLC symbol*] ... EAS
Eastern College, St. Davids, PA [*Library symbol*] ... PstdE
Eastern College Soccer Association [*Formerly, ECSOB, ESOB*] ... ECSA
Eastern College Soccer Officials Bureau [*Later, ECSA*] ... ECSOB
Eastern Command [*World War II*] ... EASCOM
Eastern Command [*British*] ... EC
Eastern Communications Region [*Military*] ... EASTCOMMRGN
Eastern Commuter, Inc. [*Hasbrouck Heights, NJ*] [*FAA designator*] ... SVS
Eastern Co. [*American Stock Exchange symbol*] ... EML
Eastern Connecticut Clam Diggers Association [*Defunct*] ... ECCDA
Eastern Connecticut State College, J. Eugene Smith Library, Willimantic, CT [*OCLC symbol*] ... CTW
Eastern Connecticut State College, Willimantic, CT [*Library symbol*] ... CtWillN
Eastern Construction Company in Laos ... ECCOIL
Eastern Contract Management Region [*Air Force*] ... ECMR
Eastern Cosmetic Manufacturers Association ... ECMA
Eastern Counties Newspapers Ltd., Norwich, United Kingdom [*Library symbol*] ... UkNrE
Eastern Counties Regional Library, Mulgrave, NS, Canada [*Library symbol*] ... CaNSME
Eastern Dark-Fired Tobacco Growers Association ... EDFTGA
Eastern Daylight Saving Time ... EDST
Eastern Daylight Time ... EDT
Eastern Deciduous Forest Biome [*Ecological biogeographic study*] ... EDFB
Eastern Defense Command [*Army*] ... EDC
Eastern Development Division [*Air Force*] ... EDD
Eastern District [*ATSC*] ... ED
Eastern Dry Cleaning and Laundry Machinery Distributors Association [*Defunct*] ... EDCLMDA
Eastern Economic Association ... EEA
Eastern Economist [*A publication*] ... East Econ
Eastern Economist [*A publication*] ... EE
Eastern Educational Network [*Television*] ... EEN
Eastern Electricity Board [*British*] ... EEB
Eastern Environmental Radiation Facility [*Environmental Protection Agency*] ... EERF
Eastern Environmental Radiation Laboratory [*Environmental Protection Agency*] ... EERL
Eastern Equine Encephalomyelitis [*Virus*] ... EEE
Eastern Establishment [*Politics*] ... EE
Eastern European Economics [*A publication*] ... EEE
Eastern European Economics [*A publication*] ... E Eur Econ
Eastern European Mission ... EEM
Eastern Finance Association ... EFA
Eastern Football Conference ... EFC
Eastern Forest Products Laboratory (Canada). Report [*A publication*] ... East For Prod Lab (Can) Rep
Eastern Freight Inspection Bureau ... EFIB
Eastern Fruit Grower [*A publication*] ... East Fruit Grow
Eastern Gas & Fuel Associates [*NYSE symbol*] ... EFU
Eastern Gulf of Mexico ... EGMEX
Eastern Historical Commission, Prospect Park, NJ [*Library symbol*] ... NjPpE
Eastern Hockey League ... EHL
Eastern Horizon [*Hong Kong*] [*A publication*] ... EH
Eastern Illinois State College [*Later, EIU*] ... EISC
Eastern Illinois University [*Formerly, EISC*] ... EIU
Eastern Illinois University, Charleston, IL [*OCLC symbol*] ... IAD
Eastern Illinois University, Charleston, IL [*Library symbol*] ... ICharE
Eastern Independent Collegiate Basketball League ... EICBL
Eastern Intercollegiate Gymnastic League ... EIGL
Eastern Joint Computer Conference ... EJCC
Eastern Kentucky State College [*Later, EKU*] ... EKSC
Eastern Kentucky University [*Formerly, EKSC*] ... EKU
Eastern Kentucky University, Richmond, KY [*OCLC symbol*] ... KEU
Eastern Kentucky University, Richmond, KY [*Library symbol*] ... KyRE
Eastern League [*Baseball*] ... EL
Eastern Librarian [*A publication*] ... East Librn

Eastern Line of Communication [World War II]............ELOC
Eastern Long Island Hospital, Greenport, NY [Library symbol]........NGrpEH
Eastern Marathon Swimming Association...............EMSA
Eastern Mediterranean Area [NATO]...............MEDEAST
Eastern Mediterranean Special Service Intelligence Bureau [British] [World War I]............EMSIB
Eastern Megalopolis [Proposed name for possible "super-city" formed by growth and mergers of other cities]............EM
Eastern Mennonite College [Virginia]...............EMC
Eastern Mennonite College, Harrisonburg, VA [OCLC symbol]............VEM
Eastern Mennonite College, Harrisonburg, VA [Library symbol]............ViHarEM
Eastern Metals Review [A publication]............East Met Rev
Eastern Michigan University...............EMU
Eastern Michigan University, Ypsilanti, MI [OCLC symbol]............EYE
Eastern Michigan University, Ypsilanti, MI [Library symbol]............MiYEM
Eastern & Midlands Railway [British]............EMR
Eastern Montana College, Billings, MT [Library symbol]............MtBilE
Eastern Nazarene College, Wollaston, MA [OCLC symbol]............ENC
Eastern Nazarene College, Wollaston, MA [Library symbol]............MWollE
Eastern New Mexico University...............ENMU
Eastern New Mexico University, Portales, NM [OCLC symbol]............IPU
Eastern New Mexico University, Portales, NM [Library symbol]............NmPE
Eastern News Agency [Bangladesh]............ENA
Eastern Oklahoma District Library, Muskogee, OK [OCLC symbol]........OEA
Eastern Oklahoma District Library, Muskogee, OK [Library symbol]............OkMuE
Eastern Ontario Regional Library, Ottawa, ON, Canada [Library symbol]............CaOOEO
Eastern Oregon College...............EOC
Eastern Oregon College, La Grande, OR [Library symbol]............OrLgE
Eastern Pacific Area...............EASTPAC
Eastern Pacific Hurricane Center [San Francisco] [National Weather Service]............EPHC
Eastern Pacific Oceanic Conference...............EPOC
Eastern Peninsula Library System [Library network]............EPLS
Eastern Pennsylvania Psychiatric Institute...............EPPI
Eastern Pennsylvania Psychiatric Institute, Philadelphia, PA [Library symbol]............PPEP
Eastern Pilgrim College [Later, United Weslayan College] [Pennsylvania]............EPC
Eastern Plains Regional Library, Tucumcari, NM [Library symbol]....NmTuE
Eastern Primary Standards Laboratory...............EPSL
Eastern Procurement Division [Navy]...............EPD
Eastern Production District [Navy]...............EPD
Eastern Professional Hockey League...............EPHL
Eastern Professional River Outfitters Association...............EPRO
Eastern Professional Ski Instructors Association [Formerly, EPSTI]............EPSIA
Eastern Professional Ski Touring Instructors [Later, EPSIA]............EPSTI
Eastern Provincial Airways [Labrador]...............EPA
Eastern Provincial Airways [Labrador] [ICAO designator]............PV
Eastern Psychiatric Research Association...............EPRA
Eastern Psychological Association...............EPA
Eastern Railroad Association...............ERA
Eastern Railroad Presidents Conference [Later, ERA]............ERPC
Eastern Range Ships...............ERS
Eastern Recruiting Division...............ERD
Eastern Region [FAA]...............AEA
Eastern Region SEATO [Southeast Asia Treaty Organization] Field Forces............ERSFF
Eastern Regional Institute for Education...............ERIE
Eastern Regional Organization for Public Administration............EROPA
Eastern Regional Research Center [Department of Agriculture]............ERRC
Eastern Rugby Union of America...............ERU
Eastern Sea Frontier...............EASTSEAFRON
Eastern Sea Frontier...............ESF
Eastern Sea Frontier Control Local of Shipping in Gulf of Maine............EASTCON
Eastern Secondary Standards Laboratory...............ESSL
Eastern Shore Community College, Learning Resources Center, Melfa, VA [Library symbol]............ViMelE
Eastern Shore Public Library, Accomac, VA [Library symbol]............ViAc
Eastern Shore Regional Library Resource Center [Library network]....ESRL
Eastern Signal Corps Replacement Training Center............ESCRTC
Eastern Simulation Council...............ESC
Eastern Ski Area Operators Association...............ESAOA
Eastern Ski Association [Later, USSA]...............ESA
Eastern Soccer Officials Bureau [Later, ECSA]............ESOB
Eastern Space and Missile Center [Air Force]............ESMC
Eastern Special Passenger [Eastern Airlines]............ESP
Eastern Standard Time...............E
Eastern Standard Time...............EST
Eastern State Hospital, Medical Lake, WA [Library symbol]............WaMeH
Eastern State School and Hospital, Trevose, PA [OCLC symbol]............PHE
Eastern States Blast Furnace and Coke Oven Association............ESBFCOA
Eastern Surfing Association...............ESA
Eastern Tank Carrier Conference...............ETCC
Eastern Task Force...............ETF
Eastern Technical Net [Air Force]...............ETN
Eastern Tennis Patrons...............ETP
Eastern Test Range [Formerly, Atlantic Missile Range] [Air Force]............ETR

Eastern Test Range Operations Directive [Air Force]............ETROD
Eastern Time...............ET
Eastern Transport Air Force...............EASTAF
Eastern Tropical Pacific [Oceanographic expedition]............EASTROPAC
Eastern Underwriter [A publication]............East Underw
Eastern Underwriters Association [Later, ISO]............EUA
Eastern United States...............EUS
Eastern Utilities Associates [NYSE symbol]............EUA
Eastern Verbal Investigators League...............EVIL
Eastern Virginia Medical Authority, Norfolk, VA [OCLC symbol]............VNN
Eastern Virginia Medical School, Norfolk, VA [Library symbol]............ViNE
Eastern War Time [World War II]............EWT
Eastern Washington State College, Cheney, WA [Library symbol]............WaChenE
Eastern Washington State College, Cheney, WA [OCLC symbol]............WEA
Eastern Washington State Historical Society, Museum Library, Spokane, WA [Library symbol]............WaSpHiE
Eastern Women's Center [Women's health facility]............EWC
Eastern Women's Headwear Association [Later, AMMA]............EWHA
Eastern World [A publication]............EW
Eastern World [A publication]............E World
Eastern Wyoming College, Torrington, WY [Library symbol]............WyToE
Eastern Zone...............EZ
Eastfield College, Mesquite, TX [Library symbol]............TxMeE
EastGroup Properties SBI [American Stock Exchange symbol]............EGP
Eastland, TX [Location identifier] [FAA]............ETN
Eastland, TX [Radio station call letters]............KEAS
Eastland, TX [Radio station call letters]............KVMX
Eastman Dental Center, B. G. Bibby Library, Rochester, NY [OCLC symbol]............VQG
Eastman, GA [Radio station call letters]............WUFF
Eastman, GA [Radio station call letters]............WUFF-FM
Eastman Kodak Co. [NYSE symbol]............EK
Eastman Kodak Company...............EKC
Eastman Kodak Co., Apparatus Division, Rochester, NY [Library symbol]............NRE-A
Eastman Kodak Co., Business Library, Rochester, NY [OCLC symbol]...VQI
Eastman Kodak Co., Engineering Division, Library, Rochester, NY [OCLC symbol]............VQJ
Eastman Kodak Co., Engineering Division, Rochester, NY [Library symbol]............NRE-E
Eastman Kodak Co., Health and Safety Laboratory, Library, Rochester, NY [OCLC symbol]............VQK
Eastman Kodak Co., Health and Safety Laboratory, Rochester, NY [Library symbol]............NRE-M
Eastman Kodak Co., KAD Library, Rochester, NY [OCLC symbol]............VQH
Eastman Kodak Co., Photographic Technology Library, Rochester, NY [Library symbol]............NRE-P
Eastman Kodak Co., Photographic Technology Library, Rochester, NY [OCLC symbol]............VQL
Eastman Kodak Co., Research Laboratories, Library, Rochester, NY [OCLC symbol]............VQM
Eastman Kodak Co., Research Laboratories, Rochester, NY [Library symbol]............NRE-R
Eastman Kodak Co., Rochester, NY [Library symbol]............NRE
Eastman Kodak/Navy Ordnance District............EK/NOD
Eastman School of Music, Rochester, NY [OCLC symbol]............RES
Eastmet Corp. [NASDAQ symbol]............EMET
Easton Area Public Library, Easton, PA [OCLC symbol]............EAP
Easton Area Public Library, Easton, PA [Library symbol]............PE
Easton, MA [Radio station call letters]............WSHL-FM
Easton, MD [Location identifier] [FAA]............ESN
Easton, MD [Radio station call letters]............WCEI
Easton, MD [Radio station call letters]............WCEI-FM
Easton, PA [Radio station call letters]............WEEX
Easton, PA [Radio station call letters]............WEST
Easton, PA [Radio station call letters]............WJRH
Easton, PA [Radio station call letters]............WLEV
Easton, PA [Radio station call letters]............WQQQ
Easton, WA [Location identifier] [FAA]............ESW
Eastover Corp. SBI...............EASTS
Eastridge High School Library, Rochester, NY [OCLC symbol]............RWD
Eastsound [Washington] [Airport symbol]............ESD
Eastward Position...............EP
Easy [Phonetic alphabet] [World War II]............E
Easy [Slang]...............EZ
Easy Processing Channel...............EPC
Eat-In [Kitchen] [Classified advertising]............EI
Eat-In Kitchen [Classified advertising]............EIK
Eat Right and Slim Easily [Weight Watchers, Inc., competition]............ERASE
Eaton Corp. [Formerly, ENX] [NYSE symbol]............ETN
Eaton Financial Corp. [NASDAQ symbol]............EATO
Eaton Laboratories, Inc. [Research code symbol]............F
Eaton Laboratories, Inc. [Research code symbol]............NF
Eaton Laboratories, Inc. [Research code symbol]............U
Eaton Manufacturing Co. [Later, ETN] [NYSE symbol] [Delisted]............ENX
Eaton, OH [Radio station call letters]............WCTM
Eaton, OH [Radio station call letters]............WJAI
Eaton Public Library, Eaton, CO [Library symbol]............CoEa
Eaton Vance Corp. [NASDAQ symbol]............EAVN

Eatonton [Georgia] [Seismograph station code, US Geological Survey] .... ETG
Eatonton, GA [Radio station call letters] ....WXPQ
Eatontown, NJ [Radio station call letters] ....WHTG
Eatontown, NJ [Radio station call letters] .... WHTG-FM
Eatontown Public Library, Eatontown, NJ [Library symbol]................NjEa
Eau Claire [Wisconsin] [Airport symbol] .... EAU
Eau Claire County Hospital, Eau Claire, WI [Library symbol]................ WEC
Eau Claire Public Library, Eau Claire, WI [OCLC symbol]................GZF
Eau Claire Public Library, Eau Claire, WI [Library symbol] .... WE
Eau Claire, WI [Radio station call letters] ....WAXX-FM
Eau Claire, WI [Radio station call letters] ....WBIZ
Eau Claire, WI [Radio station call letters] ....WEAQ
Eau Claire, WI [Television station call letters] ....WEAU-TV
Eau Claire, WI [Radio station call letters] ....WIAL
Eau Claire, WI [Radio station call letters] ....WJJK
Eau Claire, WI [Radio station call letters] ....WOKL
Eau Claire, WI [Television station call letters] ....WQOW-TV
Eau Claire, WI [Radio station call letters] ....WUEC
Eau Gallie Public Library, Melbourne, FL [Library symbol]................FMeE
Eau et l'Industrie [A publication]................Eau Ind
Eau du Quebec [A publication] ....Eau Que
Eau-de-Vie [Taken from the French pronunciation and used to refer to brandy]................ODV
Eazor Express, Inc. [American Stock Exchange symbol] [Delisted] ....EAZ
Ebenburg, PA [Radio station call letters] ....WAJE
Ebenezer Society ....ES
Ebensburg, PA [Radio station call letters] ....WIYQ
Eboracum [York] [British]................EBOR
Ebro [Spain] [Geomagnetic observatory code] .... EBR
Ebro Roquetas [Tarragona] [Spain] [Seismograph station code, US Geological Survey]................ EBR
Ebstein's Anomaly [Cardiology]................EA
EBTA [Eastern Business Teachers Association] Journal [A publication]................EBTA J
EBTA [Eastern Business Teachers Association] Yearbook [A publication]................EBTA Y
EBU [European Broadcasting Union] Review. Technical [A publication] .... EBU Rev Tech
Eburnetoxin [Biochemistry]................ETX
EBV [Epstein-Barr Virus] Nuclear Antigen [Immunochemistry]................EBNA
ECC [Emergency Control Center] Bypass Test Facility [Nuclear energy]................EBTF
Eccentric ....ECC
Eccentric Geophysical Observatory [Also, EOGO] [NASA]................EGO
Eccentric Orbital Geophysical Observatory [Also, EGO] [NASA] ....EOGO
Eccentric Variable-Angle Thermionic Rheostat ....EVATRON
Eccentrically Stiffened Cylindrical Shell................ESCS
Eccentricity [of application of load] [Aerospace] ....e
Eccles-Jordan Circuit [Electronics]................EJC
Eccles-Jordan Trigger [Electronics] .... EJT
Eccles Public Library, Central Library, Eccles, United Kingdom [Library symbol]................UkEc
Ecclesiastes [Old Testament book]................Eccl
Ecclesiastes [Old Testament book]................Eccles
Ecclesiastical ....ECCL
Ecclesiastical ....ECCLES
Ecclesiastical and Admiralty Reports [Legal] [British]................E & A
Ecclesiastical Relations Branch [BUPERS]................ERB
Ecclesiastical Review [A publication] ....ER
Ecclesiasticos Pharos [A publication]................EPh
Ecclesiasticus [Old Testament book] [Apocrypha]................Ecclus
Echanges Internationaux et Developpement [A publication] .... Echanges Int Develop
Echangiste Universel. Revue Mensuelle des Collectionneurs de Timbres et des Numismates [A publication]................ Echang Univ
Echelon................ECH
Echelon Above Corps [Military]................EAC
Echelon Above Division [Military]................EAD
Echelons Above Division Study [Military]................EADS
Echery [France] [Seismograph station code, US Geological Survey]........ECH
Echlin, Inc. [NYSE symbol]................ECH
Echo [Phonetic alphabet]................E
Echo Bay Mines Ltd. [American Stock Exchange symbol]................ECO
Echo Depth Sounder................EDS
Echo Free Room ....EFR
Echo Glen Children's Center, Resident Library, Snoqualmie, WA [Library symbol]................WaSnqE-R
Echo Glen Children's Center, Staff Library, Snoqualmie, WA [Library symbol]................ WaSnqE
Echo Range Equipment ....ERE
Echo Ranging ....ER
Echo-Ranging Masked Acoustic Communications ....ERMAC
Echo des Recherches [A publication]................ Echo Rech
Echo Return Loss ....ERL
Echo Return Loss Enhancement................ERLE
Echo-Rhino-Coryza [Virus] [Usage obsolete]................ERC
Echo Sounding ....ES
Echo Sounding Device [Navigation]................ESD
Echo Teatrolne i Muzyczne [A publication]................ETiM
Echo Veterinaire [A publication]................Echo Vet

Echocardiogram [Cardiology]................ECHO
Echoencephalogram [Neurology]................ECHO
Echos d'Orient [A publication]................EchO
Echos d'Orient [A publication]................EO
Eckart [Berlin] [A publication]................Eck
Eckart Jahrbuch [Witten] [A publication]................Eckart J
Eckels Memorial Library, Oakland, IA [Library symbol]................IaOak
Eckerd College, St. Petersburg, FL [OCLC symbol]................FEC
Eckerd College, St. Petersburg, FL [Library symbol]................FSpE
Eckerd [Jack] Corp. [NYSE symbol]................ECK
Eckerd Drugs, Incorporated [NYSE symbol] [Delisted]................EDI
Eckley Public Library, Eckley, CO [Library symbol]................CoEck
Eclectic Engineering Magazine [Van Nostrand's] [A publication].... Ecl Engin
Eclectic Magazine [A publication] ....Ecl M
Eclectic Museum [A publication]................Ecl Mus
Eclectic Review [A publication]................Ecl R
Eclipse................EC
Eclogae Geologicae Helvetiae [A publication] ....Eclogae Geol Helv
Eco Cientifico [A publication]................Eco Cient
Eco-Energy System................EES
Ecodyne Corp. [American Stock Exchange symbol] [Delisted]................ECY
Ecole des Beaux-Arts, Montreal, PQ, Canada [Library symbol]...... CaQMBA
Ecole de Chimie, Geneva, Switzerland [Library symbol]................SzGE
Ecole Francaise d'Extreme-Orient................EFEO
Ecole des Hautes Etudes Commerciales [Paris]................HEC
Ecole des Hautes Etudes Commerciales, Montreal, PQ, Canada [Library symbol]................CaQMHE
Ecole Nationale d'Administration [National School of Administration] [France]................ENA
Ecole Nationale de l'Aviation Civile................ENAC
Ecole Nationale de Ski et d'Alpinisme................ENSA
Ecole Nationale de Theatre, Montreal, PQ, Canada [Library symbol]................CaQMENT
Ecole Normale Jacques Cartier ....ENJC
Ecole Normale M. L. Duplessis, Trois-Rivieres, PQ, Canada [Library symbol]................CaQTE
Ecole Normale Superieure [French teacher-training institution]................ ENS
Ecole Normale Superieure, Laboratoire de Chimie, Paris, France [Library symbol]................FrPE-C
Ecole Polytechnique Federale de Lausanne [Switzerland]................EPFL
Ecole Polytechnique, Montreal, PQ, Canada [Library symbol]................CaQMEP
Ecole Pratique des Hautes Etudes [A publication]................ EPHE
Ecole Pratique des Hautes Etudes. Institut de Montpellier. Memoires et Travaux [A publication] .... Ec Prat Hautes Etud Inst Montp Mem Trav
Ecole Pratique des Hautes Etudes IVe Section. Sciences Historiques et Philologiques. Annuaire [A publication] ...... EPHESHPhA
Ecole Pratique des Hautes Etudes Ve Section. Sciences Religieuses. Annuaire [A publication]................EPHESRA
Ecole Secondaire Saint-Francois, Sherbrooke, PQ, Canada [Library symbol]................ CaQSherSF
Ecole Secondaire Saint-Stanislas, Montreal, PQ, Canada [Library symbol]................CaQMES
Ecole Superieure d'Agriculture................ESA
Ecole Superieure d'Agriculture de la Suede. Annales [A publication]................Ec Super Agric Suede Ann
Ecole Superieure des Sciences Economiques et Commerciales [Paris]................ESSEC
Ecological Abstracts [A publication]................Ecol Abstr
Ecological Information and Analysis Center................EIAC
Ecological Modelling [A publication]................ Ecol Model
Ecological Monographs [A publication]................ Ecol Monogr
Ecological Research Committee. Bulletin [A publication]................ Ecol Res Comm Bull
Ecological Review [A publication]................ Ecol Rev
Ecological Sciences Division [Oak Ridge National Laboratory]................ ESD
Ecological Sciences Information Center [Oak Ridge National Laboratory]................ ESIC
Ecological Society of America [Later, Nature Conservancy]................ ESA
Ecological Society of Australia. Memoirs [A publication]................ Ecol Soc Aust Mem
Ecological Studies [A publication]................Ecol Stud
Ecological and Toxicological Association of the Dyestuffs Manufacturing Industry .... ETAD
Ecology ....ECOL
Ecology [A publication]................ECOL
Ecology Action/Common Ground [An association] .... EA/CG
Ecology Action East [An association]................EAE
Ecology Action Educational Institute ....EAEI
Ecology Action Newsletter [A publication] ....Ecol Action Newsl
Ecology and Analysis of Trace Contaminants [Program] [Oak Ridge National Laboratory]................ EATC
Ecology Center [An association]................EC
Ecology Center Communications Council [Defunct]................ECCC
Ecology Center of Louisiana ....EC
Ecology and Conservation [A publication]................ Ecol Conserv
Ecology of Food and Nutrition [A publication]................Ecol Food Nutr
Ecology Law Quarterly [A publication]................Ecol Law Q
Ecology Law Quarterly [A publication]................Ecology L Q
Ecology Review [A publication]................ Ecol Rev
Econo-Therm Energy Systems [NASDAQ symbol]................ ETHM

Econolite Automatic Sensing Equipment .... EASE
Econometric Society .... ES
Econometrica [*A publication*] .... EM
Econometrics and Operations Research [*A publication*] .... Econometrics Oper Res
Economia [*A publication*] .... Econ
Economia y Ciencias Sociales [*A publication*] .... Econ Cienc Soc
Economia Internazionale [*A publication*] .... EI
Economia Internazionale delle Fonti di Energia [*A publication*] .... Econ Int Fonti Energia
Economia Internazionale (Genova) [*A publication*] .... Econ Int (Genova)
Economia e Lavoro [*A publication*] .... Econ e Lav
Economia Salvadorena [*A publication*] .... Econ Salvad
Economia e Storia; Rivista Italiana di Storia Economica e Sociale [*A publication*] .... Ec Stor
Economic Abstracts [*A publication*] .... EconAb
Economic Activity Analysis .... EAA
Economic Activity in Western Australia [*A publication*] .... Econ Activity
Economic Adviser .... EA
Economic Advisers .... ECONADS
Economic Advisory Board [*Department of Commerce*] .... EAB
Economic Affairs [*A publication*] .... Econ Aff
[*African*] **Economic Affairs, Allied** [*World War II*] .... EFA
Economic Affairs Bureau .... EAB
Economic Analysis .... EA
Economic Analysis [*A publication*] .... Ec An
Economic Analysis Division [*Federal Emergency Management Agency*] [*Information service*] .... EAD
Economic Annalist [*A publication*] .... Econ Ann
Economic Batch Determination .... EBD
Economic Botany [*A publication*] .... Econ Bot
Economic Botany [*A publication*] .... Econ Botan
Economic Bulletin for Africa [*A publication*] .... Econ B Afr
Economic Bulletin for Asia and the Far East [*A publication*] .... EBAFE
Economic Bulletin for Asia and the Far East [*A publication*] .... Econ B Asia Far East
Economic Bulletin for Asia and the Pacific [*A publication*] .... Econ B Asia Pacific
Economic Bulletin. Commercial Bank of Greece (Athens) [*A publication*] .... Econ B (Athens)
Economic Bulletin for Europe [*A publication*] .... Econ B Europe
Economic Bulletin for Latin America [*A publication*] .... Econ B Latin Amer
Economic Bulletin. National Bank of Egypt (Cairo) [*A publication*] .... Econ B (Cairo)
Economic Bulletin (Oslo) [*A publication*] .... Econ B (Oslo)
Economic and Business Foundation .... EBF
Economic and Business Review [*A publication*] .... Econ Bus R
Economic Cabinet [*British*] .... ECOCAB
Economic Commission for Africa [*United Nations*] .... ECA
Economic Commission for Asia and the Far East [*Later, ESCAP*] [*United Nations*] .... ECAFE
Economic Commission for Europe [*United Nations*] .... ECE
Economic Commission for Latin America [*United Nations*] .... ECLA
Economic Commission for Western Asia [*United Nations*] .... ECWA
Economic Community for Livestock and Meat [*Africa*] .... ECLM
Economic Community of West African States [*Treaty signed May 28, 1975*] .... ECOWAS
Economic Community of West African States [*Treaty signed May 28, 1975*] .... ECWAS
Economic Computation and Economic Cybernetics Studies and Research [*A publication*] .... Econ Comput Econ Cybern Stud Res
Economic and Contingency Reserve Stock [*Military*] .... ECRS
Economic Control Agency [*Allied German Occupation Forces*] .... ECA
Economic Cooperation Act [*of 1948*] .... ECA
Economic Cooperation Administration [*Administered aid under Marshall Plan; abolished, 1951*] .... ECA
Economic Cooperation among Developing Countries [*United Nations*] .... ECDC
Economic Cooperation Organization .... ECO
Economic Council of Canada .... ECC
Economic Council of Canada, Ottawa, ON, Canada [*Library symbol*] .... CaOOEC
Economic Coverage Endorsement .... ECE
Economic Data Retrieval and Application System .... EDRAS
Economic Defense Board [*Later, Board of Economic Warfare*] [*World War II*] .... EDB
Economic Development [*A publication*] .... ED
Economic Development Administration [*Formerly, Office of Appalachian Assistance*] [*Terminated*] [*Department of Commerce*] .... EDA
Economic Development Committee [*Nickname: "Little Neddie"*] [*British*] .... EDC
Economic Development and Cultural Change [*A publication*] .... Econ Dev Cu
Economic Development and Cultural Change [*A publication*] .... Econ Dev Cult Change
Economic Development and Cultural Change [*A publication*] .... Econ Devel Cult Change
Economic Development and Cultural Change [*A publication*] .... Econ Develop Cult Change
Economic Development and Cultural Change [*A publication*] .... EDCC
Economic Development District [*EDA*] .... EDD
Economic Development of Equatorial and Southern Africa .... EDESA
Economic Development Financing Organization [*Greece*] .... EDFO
Economic Development Institute [*of the International Bank for Reconstruction and Development*] .... EDI
Economic Development Operations .... EDO
Economic Development Opportunity Committee [*Department of Labor*] .... EDOC
Economic Development Program .... EDP
Economic Dislocation Loans [*Small Business Administration*] .... EDL
Economic Education Foundation for Clergy [*Formerly, CEEF*] .... EEFC
Economic Engineering Branch .... EEB
Economic and Financial [*Plans*] [*British*] .... E & F
Economic and Financial Review. Central Bank of Nigeria [*A publication*] .... Econ Financ R Central Bank Nigeria
Economic and Financial Survey of Australia [*A publication*] .... Econ Finan Surv Aust
Economic General Staff [*British*] .... EGS
Economic Geography [*A publication*] .... Econ Geog
Economic Geography [*A publication*] .... Econ Geogr
Economic Geography [*A publication*] .... EG
Economic Geology [*A publication*] .... Econ Geol
Economic Geology and the Bulletin of the Society of Economic Geologists [*A publication*] .... Econ Geol Bull Soc Econ Geol
Economic Geology. Monograph [*A publication*] .... Econ Geology Mon
Economic History [*A publication*] .... Econ Hist
Economic History [*A publication*] .... EH
Economic History Association .... EHA
Economic History Review [*A publication*] .... Econ Hist R
Economic History Review [*A publication*] .... Econ Hist Rev
Economic History Review [*A publication*] .... EconHR
Economic History Review [*A publication*] .... EHR
Economic Impact Assessment .... EIA
Economic Impact Budget .... EIB
Economic Impact Forecast System [*Army*] .... EIFS
Economic Indicators [*A publication*] .... ECIN
Economic Indicators [*A publication*] .... Econ Indic
Economic Information System .... EIS
Economic Injury Disaster Loan [*Small Business Administration*] .... EIDL
Economic Inquiry [*A publication*] .... Econ Inq
Economic Inquiry [*A publication*] .... Econ Inquiry
Economic Inventory Policy .... EIP
Economic Inventory Procedures [*Army*] .... EIP
Economic Journal [*A publication*] .... Econ J
Economic Journal [*A publication*] .... EJ
Economic Load Dispatching .... ELD
Economic Manufacturing Quality .... EMQ
Economic Microbiology [*A publication*] .... Econ Microbiol
Economic and Monetary Union .... EMU
Economic News from Italy [*A publication*] .... Econ Italy
Economic Objectives Department [*Ministry of Economic Warfare*] [*British*] [*World War II*] .... EOD
Economic Opportunity Act [*1964*] [*Repealed, 1974*] .... EOA
Economic Opportunity Act Loan .... EOL
Economic Order Quantity .... EOQ
Economic Order and Stockage Procedure .... EOSP
Economic Order Van .... EOV
Economic Outlook [*A publication*] .... Econ Outlk
Economic Outlook USA [*A publication*] .... Econ Outlook
Economic Papers [*A publication*] .... Econ Pap
Economic Papers [*A publication*] .... EP
Economic Performance Indicator [*New York Stock Exchange*] .... EPI
Economic Planning .... EP
Economic Planning (Helsinki) [*A publication*] .... Econ Planning (Helsinki)
Economic Policy [*British*] .... EP
Economic Policy Board [*Department of the Treasury*] .... EPB
Economic Policy Committee [*OECD*] .... EPC
Economic Policy Council [*UNA-USA*] .... EPC
Economic Policy towards Eire [*British*] .... EPE
Economic Policy Group .... EPG
Economic and Political Weekly [*A publication*] .... Econ Polit Wkly
Economic and Political Weekly [*A publication*] .... Econ Pol W
Economic Power Dispatch Computer .... EPDC
Economic Power Transmission .... EPT
Economic Pressure on Germany Committee [*War Cabinet*] [*British*] [*World War II*] .... EPG
Economic Price Adjustment .... EPA
Economic Priorities Report [*A publication*] .... Econ Priorities Rep
Economic Proceedings. Royal Dublin Society [*A publication*] .... Econ Proc R Dublin Soc
Economic Procurement Item .... EPI
Economic Quotient .... EQ
Economic [*or Economical*] **Radioisotope Thermoelectric Generator** .... ERTG
Economic Record [*A publication*] .... Econ Rec
Economic Record [*A publication*] .... ER
Economic Recovery Tax Act [*1981*] .... ERTA
Economic Regulations [*Civil Aeronautics Board*] .... ER
Economic Regulatory Administration .... ERA
Economic Repair Quantity .... ERQ
Economic Report. Edinburgh School of Agriculture [*A publication*] .... Econ Rep Edinburgh Sch Agr

Economic Report. Geological Survey Department (Zambia) [A publication]......................Econ Rep Geol Surv Dep (Zambia)
Economic Research Journal [A publication]......................ERJ
Economic Research Round Table......................ERRT
Economic Research Service [Department of Agriculture]......................ERS
Economic Resources Corporation [OEO-Department of Labor project]......................ERC
Economic Retention Stock......................ERS
Economic Review [Helsinki] [A publication]......................Econ R
Economic Review. Bank of Israel [A publication]......................Econ R Bank Israel
Economic Review. Kansallis Osake-Pankki [A publication]......................Econ R Kansallis Osake-Pankki
Economic Road Maps [A publication]......................Road Maps
Economic and Sector Work......................ESW
Economic and Social Commission for Asia and the Pacific [Formerly, ECAFE] [United Nations]......................ESCAP
Economic and Social Council [United Nations]......................ECOSOC
Economic and Social Council [United Nations]......................ESC
Economic and Social Review [A publication]......................Econ Soc R
Economic Society of Australia and New Zealand, Melbourne University, Parkville, V, Australia [Library symbol]......................AuPaE
Economic Stabilization Act [Wage-price controls] [Expired April 30, 1974]......................ESA
Economic Stabilization Administration......................ESA
Economic Stabilization Agency [Terminated, 1953]......................ESA
Economic Stabilization Board [World War II]......................ESB
Economic Stabilization Program [Internal Revenue Service]......................ESP
Economic Studies [A publication]......................Econ Stud
Economic Studies [Bureau of the Census]......................ES
Economic Subregion [Bureau of the Census]......................ESR
Economic Support Fund......................ESF
Economic and Technical Review. Report EPS [Environmental Protection Service] (Canada) [A publication]......................Econ Tech Rev Rep EPS (Can)
Economic Warfare [British]......................EW
Economic Warfare Analysis Section......................EWAS
Economic Warfare Division [US] [London]......................EWD
Economic Week [A publication]......................EW
Economic Weekly [A publication]......................Ec W
Economic World [A publication]......................Econ W
Economica [A publication]......................EC
Economica (London) [A publication]......................Econ (London)
Economical Methods [A line of Varian spectrometers]......................EM
Economical Storage and Access System [Data processing]......................ECSTASY
Economics......................EC
Economics......................ECON
Economics of Distribution Foundation......................EDF
Economics Division [US Military Government, Germany]......................ED
Economics and Government [Office of Management and Budget]......................EG
Economics Laboratory, Inc. [NASDAQ symbol]......................ECON
Economics Laboratory, Inc.......................EL
Economics News Broadcasters Association......................ENBA
Economics of Planning [A publication]......................Econ Planning
Economics of Planning [A publication]......................EOP
Economics, Statistics, and Cooperatives Service [Later, ERS, SRS] [Department of Agriculture]......................ESCS
Economie Agricole (Paris) [A publication]......................Econ Agr (Paris)
Economie Appliquee [A publication]......................Econ Appl
Economie Appliquee [A publication]......................Econ Appliq
Economie-Geographie [A publication]......................Econ-Geogr
Economie et Humanisme [A publication]......................Econ et Human
Economie et Medecine Animales [A publication]......................Econ Med Anim
Economie et Politique [A publication]......................Econ et Polit
Economie Rurale [A publication]......................Econ Rur
Economie et Sante [A publication]......................Econ et Sante
Economie et Statistique [A publication]......................Econ et Statist
Economisch-Historisch Jaarboek [A publication]......................EHJ
Economisch en Sociaal Tijdschrift/Vie Economique et Sociale [A publication]......................Econ Soc Tijds
Economisch-Statistische Berichten [A publication]......................Econ-Sta Ber
Economisch-Statistische Berichten [A publication]......................Econ-Statist Ber
Economisch Technologisch Instituut in Limburg [Germany]......................ETIL
Economische Voorlichtingsdienst [Economic Information Service] [Netherlands] [Information service]......................EVD
Economist [A publication]......................Econ
Economist Intelligence Unit [British]......................EIU
Economist Newspapers, Chicago, IL [Library symbol]......................ICE
Economista Mexicano [A publication]......................Econ Mex
Economiste du Tiers-Monde [A publication]......................Econ Tiers-Monde
Economists' National Committee on Monetary Policy......................ENCMP
Economy......................ECON
Economy-Class Air Traveler......................Y
Economy and History [A publication]......................E & H
Economy and Society [A publication]......................Econ and Soc
Economy and Society [A publication]......................Econ Societ
Ecos de Valvanera [A publication]......................EV
Ecosystem of Machines Information System......................EMIS
Ecosystems of the World [Elsevier Book Series] [A publication]......................EW
Ecotoxicology and Environmental Safety [A publication]......................Ecotoxicol Environ Saf

Ecotoxicology and Environmental Safety [A publication]......................Ecotoxicol Environ Safety
Ecrits des Saints [A publication]......................EdS
Ectopic Focus [Cardiology]......................EF
Ectopic Pregnancy [Obstetrics]......................EP
Ector County Public Library, Odessa, TX [Library symbol]......................TxOE
Ecuador [MARC country of publication code] [Library of Congress]......................ec
Ecuador [Three-letter standard code]......................ECU
Ecuador......................ECUA
Ecuador [Aircraft nationality and registration mark]......................HC
Ecuador [MARC geographic area code] [Library of Congress]......................s-ec---
Ecuador [Two-letter standard code]......................EC
Ecuador. Direccion General de Geologia y Minas. Publication [A publication]......................Ecuador Dir Gen Geol Minas Publ
Ecuadorean American Association......................EAA
Ecumenical Celebrations......................EC
Ecumenical Church Loan Fund......................ECLOF
Ecumenical Clergy Association [Later, AGEI]......................ECA
Ecumenical Institute......................EI
Ecumenical Program for Inter-American Communication and Action......................EPICA
Ecumenical Review [A publication]......................Ec R
Ecumenical Review [A publication]......................Ec Rev
Ecumenical Review [A publication]......................Ecumenical R
Ecumenical Review [A publication]......................Ecumen Rev
Ecumenical Review [A publication]......................Ecum R
Ecumenical Review [A publication]......................ER
Ecumenical Satellite Commission......................ECUSAT
Ecumenical Voluntary Service [Defunct]......................EVS
Eczacilik Bulteni [A publication]......................Eczacilik Bul
Eczema [Medicine]......................EZ
Eczema, Asthma, Hay Fever......................EAHF
Eczematous Allergic Contact Dermatitis [Dermatology]......................EACD
Eday [Orkney Islands] [Airport symbol]......................EOI
Edda. Revue de Litterature [A publication]......................Ed
Eddy Current [Nuclear energy]......................EC
Eddy Current Brake......................ECB
Eddy Current Clutch......................ECC
Eddy Current Energy......................ECE
Eddy Current Flow Meter [Nuclear energy]......................ECFM
Eddy Current Loss......................ECL
Eddy Current Testing Instrument......................ECTI
Eddysville, KY [Radio station call letters]......................WEAK
Eddyville Public Library, Eddyville, IA [Library symbol]......................IaEdd
Ede-Aire Line [Detroit Lakes, MN] [FAA designator]......................EDE
Edema Factor [Medicine]......................EF
Eden, NC [Radio station call letters]......................WCBX
Eden, NC [Radio station call letters]......................WLOE
Eden, NC [Radio station call letters]......................WSRQ
Eden Theological Seminary, Webster Groves, MO [Library symbol]......................MoWgT
Edenton, NC [Radio station call letters]......................WBXB
Edenton, NC [Radio station call letters]......................WZBO
Edenton, NC [Radio station call letters]......................WZBO-FM
EDG, Inc. [American Stock Exchange symbol] [Delisted]......................EDG
Edgar Allan Poe Society of Baltimore......................EAPSB
Edgar Dale Media Center, Columbus, OH [OCLC symbol]......................EDM
Edgar Lee Masters Memorial Museum, Petersburg, IL [Library symbol]......................IPetM
Edgar Rice Burroughs [1875-1950] [Author of Tarzan books]......................ERB
Edgar Rice Burroughs Domain [as in organization, Friends of ERB-dom]......................ERB-dom
Edgar Rice Burroughs, Inc., Tarzana, CA [Library symbol]......................CTarB
Edge [Lumber]......................E
Edge and Center Bead on One Side [Technical drawings]......................E & CB1S
Edge and Center Bead on Two Sides [Technical drawings]......................E & CB2S
Edge and Center V on One Side [Technical drawings]......................E & CV1S
Edge and Center V on Two Sides [Technical drawings]......................E & CV2S
Edge Connector......................EC
Edge Crush Test [Packaging]......................ECT
Edge of Cutter......................EOC
Edge-Defined Film-Fed Growth [Photovoltaics]......................EFG
Edge Distance......................ED
Edge Gradient Analysis......................EGA
Edge Grain......................EG
Edge Guide System......................EGS
Edge-Lighted Display......................ELD
Edge-Lighted Status Board [Navy]......................ELSB
Edge-Mounted Threaded Inserts......................EMTI
Edge Oya [Norway] [Seismograph station code, US Geological Survey]......................EO1
Edge Reading Controller......................ERC
Edge Reading Meter......................ERM
Edge Thickness [Technical drawings]......................ET
Edge-Triggered......................ET
Edge Wear [Deltiology]......................ED/WR
Edgecliff College, Cincinnati, OH [Library symbol]......................OCE
Edgecombe County Memorial Library, Tarboro, NC [Library symbol]......................NcTA
Edgecombe County Technical Institute, Tarboro, NC [Library symbol]......................NcTaE

Edgefield County Library, Edgefield, SC [*Library symbol*] .... ScE
Edgemont High School, Edgemont, SD [*Library symbol*] .... SdEdH
Edgemont Public Library, Edgemont, SD [*Library symbol*] .... SdEd
Edgerton, Germeshausen, and Grier Report [*A publication*] .... Edgerton Germeshausen & Grier Rept
Edgewater Public Library, Edgewater, CO [*Library symbol*] .... CoEdg
Edgewise .... EDGW
Edgewise Meter .... EWM
Edgewood Arsenal [*Army*] .... EA
Edgewood Arsenal .... EWA
Edgewood Arsenal Nuclear Defense Center [*Army*] .... EANDC
Edgewood Arsenal Special Publication [*Army*] .... EASP
Edgewood Arsenal Technical Memorandum [*Army*] .... EATM
Edgewood Arsenal Technical Report [*Army*] .... EATR
Edgewood College of the Sacred Heart [*Wisconsin*] .... ECSH
Edgmoor & Manetta Railway [*AAR code*] .... EM
Edible Portion [*of a food*] .... EP
Edible Structure Material .... ESM
Ediciones Catedra [*A publication*] .... Ed Cat
Ediciones Espanolas SA [*A publication*] .... EDESA
Ediciones y Publicaciones Espanolas SA [*A publication*] .... EPESA
Edinaia Tovarnaia Nomenklatura Vneshney Torgovli [*Commodity nomenclature system used in international trade*] .... ETNVT
Edinboro, PA [*Radio station call letters*] .... WFSE
Edinboro State College, Edinboro, PA [*OCLC symbol*] .... EIB
Edinboro State College, Edinboro, PA [*Library symbol*] .... PEdiS
Edinburg, TX [*Radio station call letters*] .... KBFM
Edinburg, TX [*Radio station call letters*] .... KOIR
Edinburg, TX [*Radio station call letters*] .... KURV
Edinburg, TX [*Radio station call letters*] .... KVLY
Edinburgh [*City in Scotland*] .... ED
Edinburgh [*Scotland*] [*Airport symbol*] .... EDI
Edinburgh [*City in Scotland*] .... EDIN
Edinburgh [*Scotland*] [*Seismograph station code, US Geological Survey*] .... EDI
Edinburgh Bibliographical Society [*A publication*] .... EBS
Edinburgh Dental Hospital Gazette [*A publication*] .... Edinb Dent Hosp Gaz
Edinburgh Geological Society. Transactions [*A publication*] .... Edinb G Soc Tr
Edinburgh Geological Society. Transactions [*A publication*] .... Edinburgh Geol Soc Trans
Edinburgh Medical Journal [*A publication*] .... Edinb Med J
Edinburgh Medical and Surgical Journal [*A publication*] .... Edinb Med and S J
Edinburgh Monthly Review [*A publication*] .... Ed Mo
Edinburgh New Philosophical Journal [*Preceded by Edinburgh Philosophical Journal*] [*A publication*] .... Edinb N Ph J Edinb Ph J
Edinburgh New Philosophical Journal [*A publication*] .... Ed New Philos J
Edinburgh Paperback [*A publication*] .... EUP
Edinburgh Philosophical Journal [*A publication*] .... Ed Philos J
Edinburgh Public Library, Edinburgh, United Kingdom [*Library symbol*] .... UkE
Edinburgh Review [*A publication*] .... Edin Rev
Edinburgh Review [*A publication*] .... Ed R
Edinburgh Review [*A publication*] .... ER
Edinburgh School of Agriculture. Annual Report [*A publication*] .... Edinb Sch Agric Annu Rep
Edinburgh School of Agriculture. Experimental Work [*A publication*] .... Edinb Sch Agric Exp Work
Edincik [*Turkey*] [*Seismograph station code, US Geological Survey*] .... EDC
Edison Birthplace Association .... EBA
Edison Brothers Stores, Inc. [*NYSE symbol*] .... EBS
Edison Electric Institute .... EEI
Edison Electric Institute. Bulletin [*A publication*] .... EEI
Edison Electric Institute. Bulletin [*A publication*] .... EEI Bul
Edison Electric Institute. Electric Perspectives [*A publication*] .... EEI Elec P
Edison Institute [*Henry Ford Museum and Greenfield Village*] **Library, Dearborn, MI** [*Library symbol*] .... MiDbEI
Edison National Historic Site .... EDIS
Edison Responsive Environment [*Automated learning system*] .... ERE
Edison Sault Electric Co. [*NASDAQ symbol*] .... EDSE
Edison Screw .... ES
Edison State Community College, Piqua, OH [*Library symbol*] .... OPiE
Edison Technical and Occupational Educational Center Library, Rochester, NY [*OCLC symbol*] .... RWE
Edit Master and Activity Review List .... EMARL
Edit Program Generator .... EPG
EDITEC, Chicago, IL [*Library symbol*] .... ICEdit
Edited .... ED
Edited Collections Report File [*IRS*] .... ECRF
Editeurs Francais Reunis [*A publication*] .... EFR
Edith Stein Guild .... ESG
Editing Specifications .... EDITSPEC
Edition .... E
Edition .... ED
Edition .... EDIT
Edition .... EDN
Edition Bookbinders of New York .... EBNY
Edition Deluxe .... EDL
Editiones Arnamagnaeanae [*A publication*] .... Ed Arn
Editions du Boreal Express, Montreal, PQ, Canada [*Library symbol*] .... CaQTB
Editor .... ED
Editor and Compiler .... EDCOM
Editor and Publisher [*A publication*] .... Ed & Pub
Editor and Publisher [*A publication*] .... E & P
Editor and Publisher [*A publication*] .... EP
Editorial Cuadernos para el Dialogo [*A publication*] .... EDICUDA
Editorial Freelancers Association .... EFA
Editorial Layout Display System .... ELDS
Editorial Production Branch [*BUPERS*] .... EPB
Editorial Projects in Education .... EPE
Editorial Research Reports (Washington, DC) [*A publication*] .... Ed Res Rep (Wash DC)
Editorial Sudamericana, BA [*A publication*] .... SUDAM
Editorial Universitaria de Buenos Aires [*A publication*] .... EUDEBA
Editors Organizing Committee and Writers' and Publishers' Alliance for Disarmament .... EOC & WPA
Editor's Presentation Copy .... EPC
Edizioni Scientifiche Italiane [*A publication*] .... ESI
Edmond James Rothschild Memorial Group [*Foundation*] .... EJRMG
Edmond, OK [*Radio station call letters*] .... KCSC
Edmond, OK [*Radio station call letters*] .... KKLR
Edmond, OK [*Radio station call letters*] .... KOKF
Edmonds Community College, Edmonds, WA [*Library symbol*] .... WaEdE
Edmonds, WA [*Radio station call letters*] .... KBIQ
Edmonds, WA [*Radio station call letters*] .... KGDN
Edmonton [*Alberta*] [*Seismograph station code, US Geological Survey*] .... EDM
Edmonton [*Canada*] [*Airport symbol*] .... YEG
Edmonton, AB [*Radio station call letters*] .... CBX
Edmonton, AB [*Radio station call letters*] .... CBX-FM
Edmonton, AB [*Television station call letters*] .... CBXFT
Edmonton, AB [*Television station call letters*] .... CBXT
Edmonton, AB [*Radio station call letters*] .... CFRN
Edmonton, AB [*Television station call letters*] .... CFRN-TV
Edmonton, AB [*Radio station call letters*] .... CHED
Edmonton, AB [*Radio station call letters*] .... CHFA
Edmonton, AB [*Radio station call letters*] .... CHQT
Edmonton, AB [*Radio station call letters*] .... CIRK-FM
Edmonton, AB [*Television station call letters*] .... CITV-TV
Edmonton, AB [*Radio station call letters*] .... CJAX-FM
Edmonton, AB [*Radio station call letters*] .... CJCA
Edmonton, AB [*Radio station call letters*] .... CKER
Edmonton, AB [*Radio station call letters*] CKO-FM-6
Edmonton, AB [*Radio station call letters*] .... CKRA-FM
Edmonton, AB [*Radio station call letters*] .... CKST
Edmonton, AB [*Radio station call letters*] .... CKUA
Edmonton, AB [*Radio station call letters*] .... CKUA-FM
Edmonton, AB [*Radio station call letters*] .... CKXM-FM
Edmonton Catholic School District, Edmonton, AB, Canada [*Library symbol*] .... CaAECSD
Edmonton Catholic School District, Professional Library, Edmonton, AB, Canada [*Library symbol*] .... CaAEPL
Edmonton General Hospital, Edmonton, AB, Canada [*Library symbol*] .... CaAEGH
Edmonton Geological Society. Quarterly [*A publication*] .... Edmonton Geol Soc Quart
Edmonton [*Canada*] **Municipal Airport** [*Airport symbol*] .... YXD
Edmonton Power Co., Edmonton, AB, Canada [*Library symbol*] .... CaAEEP
Edmonton Public Library, Edmonton, AB, Canada [*Library symbol*] .... CaAE
Edmonton Public Library. News Notes [*A publication*] .... Edmonton P L News Notes
Edmore Public Library, Edmore, MI [*Library symbol*] .... MiEd
Edmos Corp. [*American Stock Exchange symbol*] [*Delisted*] .... EDM
Edmund Sixtus Muskie [*American politician*] .... ESM
Edmundston, NB [*Radio station call letters*] .... CJEM
Edna, TX [*Radio station call letters*] .... KQTI
Edna Zybell Memorial Library, Clarence, IA [*Library symbol*] .... IaClar
EDO Corp. [*American Stock Exchange symbol*] .... EDO
Edoth (Jerusalem) [*A publication*] .... EJ
EDP [*Electronic Data Processing*] **Audit, Control, and Security Newsletter** [*A publication*] .... EDP A C S
EDP [*Electronic Data Processing*] **Auditor** [*A publication*] .... EDP Aud
EDP [*Electronic Data Processing*] **Auditors Association** .... EDPAA
EDP [*Electronic Data Processing*] **In-Depth Reports** [*A publication*] .... EDP In-Depth Rep
EDP [*Electronic Data Processing*] **Industry Report** [*A publication*] .... EDP Indus Rep
EDP [*Electronic Data Processing*] **Performance Review** [*A publication*] .... EDP Perf Rev
Edsel Owner's Club .... EOC
Edson, AB [*Radio station call letters*] .... CJYR
Educable Mentally Handicapped .... EMH
Educable Mentally Retardate [*or Retarded*] .... EMR
Educable Neurologically Handicapped .... ENH
Educacion Dental (Ica, Peru) [*A publication*] .... Educ Dent (Ica)
Educacion Medica y Salud [*A publication*] .... Educ Med Salud
Educate People - Protect Innocent Children .... EPPIC
Educated .... E
Educated [*or Education*] .... EDUC

Education ... ED
Education ... EDN
Education [*A publication*] ... Educ
Education [*A publication*] ... Educa
Education ... EDUCN
Education [*A publication*] ... Ed
Education Abstracts [*A publication*] ... EdAb
Education Around the World [*A publication*] ... Ed World
Education Audit Institute [*Washington, DC*] ... EAI
Education through Aviation ... ETA
Education Canada [*A publication*] ... Ed Can
Education Canada [*A publication*] ... Educ Can
Education Center [*Army*] ... EDCEN
Education in Chemistry [*A publication*] ... Ed in Chem
Education in Chemistry [*A publication*] ... Educ Chem
Education Commission of the States ... ECS
Education Commission of the States, Denver, CO [*Library symbol*] ... CoDE
Education Consolidation and Improvement Act [*1981*] ... ECIA
Education Council of the Graphic Arts Industry [*Later, GATF*] ... ECGAI
Education Credit Union Council ... ECUC
Education and Culture [*A publication*] ... EC
Education et Culture [*A publication*] ... Educ et Cult
Education Department General Administrative Regulations ... EDGAR
Education and Development ... E & D
Education for Development [*A publication*] ... Ed for Dev
Education Development Associates [*Information service*] ... EDA
Education Development Center [*Formerly, ESI, IEI*] ... EDC
Education et Developpement [*A publication*] ... Educ et Develop
Education Digest [*A publication*] ... Ed Digest
Education Digest [*A publication*] ... Educ Dig
Education Digest [*A publication*] ... Educ Digest
Education Document Reproduction Service ... EDRS
Education Equivalency Test ... EET
Education and Experience in Engineering [*Illinois Institute of Technology program*] ... E³
Education Exploration Center ... EEC
Education Funding Research Council ... EFRC
Education of the Handicapped Act [*1968*] ... EHA
Education Index [*A publication*] ... EdI
Education Index [*A publication*] ... Educ Ind
Education and Industrial Television [*A publication*] ... E & ITV
Education Industries Association [*Later, NSSEA*] ... EIA
Education with Industry ... EWI
Education in Large Cities [*A publication*] ... Educ Lg Cit
Education Level ... EL
Education Liberation Front ... ELF
Education Libraries Bulletin [*A publication*] ... Ed Lib Bulletin
Education Libraries Bulletin [*A publication*] ... Educ Libr Bull
Education Manual [*Military*] ... EM
Education Media [*A publication*] ... EdM
Education and Medicine [*A publication*] ... Educ and Medicine
Education Music Magazine [*A publication*] ... Ed Mus Mag
Education Nationale [*A publication*] ... EN
Education and Neighborhood Action for Better Living Environment ... ENABLE
Education in the North [*A publication*] ... Ed in the North
Education Officer [*Military*] ... EO
Education Opportunity Center of the State University of New York, Syracuse, NY [*OCLC symbol*] ... ZUH
Education Permanente [*A publication*] ... Educ Perm
Education for Public Management [*Program*] [*Civil Service Commission*] ... EPM
Education Quarterly [*A publication*] ... Educ Q
Education Quarterly [*New Delhi*] [*A publication*] ... EQ
Education Quarterly. Katmandu Nepal College of Education [*A publication*] ... Educ Q Nepal
Education and Religious Affairs [*US Military Government, Germany*] ... ERA
Education Research [*A publication*] ... ERes
Education Review [*A publication*] ... Educ Rev
Education Service Group [*Bibliographic Retrieval Services*] [*Information service*] ... ESG
Education and Social Science [*A publication*] ... Ed & Social Science
Education Society [*Later, Psychology Society*] ... EMSO
Education Specialist ... Ed Sp
Education Specialist ... Ed Spec
Education for Teaching [*A publication*] ... Ed for Teaching
Education and Training [*A publication*] ... Ed & Training
Education and Training [*A publication*] ... Educ & Train
Education and Training [*Navy*] ... E & T
Education and Training Advisory Team ... ETAT
Education and Training of the Mentally Retarded [*A publication*] ... Ed & Train Men Retard
Education and Training of the Mentally Retarded [*A publication*] ... Educ & Train Men Retard
Education and Training of the Mentally Retarded [*A publication*] ... Educ & Train Mentally Retard
Education and Training in Quality Assurance Practices [*American Society for Quality Control*] ... ETQAP
Education and Urban Society [*A publication*] ... Educ Urban
Education and Urban Society [*A publication*] ... Educ & Urban Soc
Education and Urban Society [*A publication*] ... Educ Urb Soc
Education USA [*A publication*] ... Ed USA
Education for Victory [*A publication*] ... Educ Vict
Education of the Visually Handicapped [*A publication*] ... Educ Visual
Education of the Visually Handicapped [*A publication*] ... Ed Vis Hand
Education, Volunteerism, Employment Opportunities ... EVE
Education Voucher Institute ... EVI
Education and World Affairs [*Later, ICED*] [*An association*] ... EWA
Education Writers Association ... EWA
Educational ... EDUCL
Educational Administration Abstracts [*A publication*] ... EdAd
Educational Administration Abstracts [*A publication*] ... Educ Admin Abstr
Educational Administration Bulletin [*A publication*] ... Ednl Administration Bull
Educational Administration Quarterly [*A publication*] ... Ed Adm Q
Educational Administration Quarterly [*A publication*] ... Educ Admin
Educational Administration Quarterly [*A publication*] ... Educ Adm Q
Educational Administration and Supervision [*A publication*] ... Ed Adm & Sup
Educational Administration and Supervision [*A publication*] ... Educ Adm & Sup
Educational Advisor ... EA
Educational Advisory Committee [*AIAA*] ... EAC
Educational Age ... EA
Educational Alliance ... EA
Educational Analog Simulator ... EAS
Educational Awareness Project ... EAP
Educational Bi-Monthly [*A publication*] ... Ed Bi-Mo
Educational Broadcast Satellite ... EBS
Educational Broadcasting [*A publication*] ... EB
Educational Broadcasting [*A publication*] ... Educ Brdcstng
Educational Broadcasting Corporation ... EBC
Educational Broadcasting International [*A publication*] ... EBI
Educational Broadcasting International [*A publication*] ... Educ Broad Int
Educational Broadcasting Review [*A publication*] ... EBR
Educational Career Service [*Later, EHCS*] [*An association*] ... ECS
Educational Career Service/Health Career Service [*Later, EHCS*] [*An association*] ... ECS/HCS
Educational Center for Applied Ekistics ... ECAE
Educational Commission for Foreign Medical Graduates ... ECFMG
Educational Communication Association ... ECA
Educational Communication and Technology Journal [*A publication*] ... Educ Comm & Tech J
Educational Communications [*Inter-University Communications Council*] ... EDUCOM
Educational Communications on Exhibit [*Commercial firm*] ... ECOX
Educational Computer Corporation [*NASDAQ symbol*] ... EDCC
Educational and Cultural Development Program ... ECD
Educational Data Bank ... EDB
Educational Development [*A publication*] ... Ednl Dev
Educational Development Corporation [*An association*] ... EDCo
Educational Development Corporation [*NASDAQ symbol*] ... EDUC
Educational Development International [*A publication*] ... Ednl Dev International
Educational Development of Military Personnel ... EDOMP
Educational Developmental Laboratories [*of McGraw Hill, Inc.*] ... EDL
[*Center for*] **Educational Diffusion and Social Application of Satellite Telecommunications** [*University of Wisconsin*] ... EDSAT
Educational Digest [*A publication*] ... Edu D
Educational Directions for Dental Auxiliaries [*A publication*] ... Educ Dir Dent Aux
Educational Documentation and Information [*A publication*] ... EDI
Educational Documentation and Information [*A publication*] ... Educ Doc & Inf
Educational Documentation and Information Bulletin [*UNESCO*] [*A publication*] ... DI
Educational Employment Service ... EES
Educational Executive's Overview [*A publication*] ... Ed Exec Overview
Educational Expeditions International [*Later, Earthwatch*] ... EEI
Educational Facilities Laboratories ... EFL
Educational Film Library Association ... EFLA
Educational Forum [*A publication*] ... Ed F
Educational Forum [*A publication*] ... Ed Forum
Educational Forum [*A publication*] ... EducF
Educational Forum [*A publication*] ... Educ Forum
Educational Foundation for the Apparel Industry [*Later, EFFI*] ... EFAI
Educational Foundation for the Fashion Industries ... EFFI
Educational Foundation for Jewish Girls [*Later, Jewish Foundation for Education of Women*] ... EFJG
Educational Foundation for Nuclear Science ... EFNS
Educational Freedom Foundation ... EFF
Educational Fund for Individual Rights ... EFIR
Educational Futures, Incorporated ... EFI
Educational Gerontology [*A publication*] ... Educ Gerontol
Educational Guidance Associates School and College Advisory Center [*Formerly, SCAC*] ... EGASCAC
Educational Guidance Center for the Mentally Retarded [*Defunct*] ... EGC
Educational and Health Career Services ... EHCS
Educational Horizons [*A publication*] ... EdH
Educational Horizons [*A publication*] ... Ed Horiz
Educational Horizons [*A publication*] ... Educ Horiz

Educational Improvement Center - Northeast [*Information service*] .... EIC-NE
Educational Incentive Plan [*Red Cross*] .... EIP
Educational and Industrial Television [*A publication*] .... Educ Ind Telev
Educational and Industrial Television [*A publication*] .... Educ TV
Educational and Industrial Testing Service .... EDITS
Educational and Industrial Testing Service .... EITS
Educational Information Center [*Office of Education*] .... EIC
Educational Information Network [*Defunct*] .... EIN
Educational Institute of Scotland .... EIS
Educational/Instructional Broadcasting [*A publication*] .... EIB
Educational Jewelry Manufacturers Association [*Defunct*] .... EJMA
Educational Leadership [*A publication*] .... EdL
Educational Leadership [*A publication*] .... Ed Lead
Educational Leadership [*A publication*] .... Educ Lead
Educational Leadership [*A publication*] .... EL
Educational Leadership Institute .... ELI
Educational Management Information System .... EMIS
Educational Marketer [*A publication*] .... EM
Educational Materials Laboratory .... EML
Educational Media [*A publication*] .... Educ Media
Educational Media Council [*Defunct*] .... EMC
Educational Media Institutes Evaluation [*Project*] .... EMIE
Educational Media International [*A publication*] .... Educ Media Int
Educational Media Producers Council [*of the National Audio-Visual Association*] [*Later, NAVA Materials Council*] .... EMPC
Educational Media Research Information Center .... EMRIC
Educational Media Selection Center [*National Book Committee*] .... EMSC
Educational Media and Technology Center .... EMC
Educational Method [*A publication*] .... Ed Meth
Educational Modulation Center .... EMC
Educational Music Magazine [*A publication*] .... Educ Mus Mag
Educational Opportunity Bank .... EOB
Educational Opportunity Center [*Higher Education Act*] .... EOC
Educational Opportunity Center, Syracuse, NY [*Library symbol*] .... NSyEd
Educational Opportunity Grant .... EOG
Educational Outlook [*A publication*] .... Ed Outl
Educational Outlook [*A publication*] .... Educ Outl
Educational Paperback Association .... EPA
Educational Philosophy and Theory [*A publication*] .... Educ Phil Theor
Educational Planning Institute .... EPI
Educational Policies Commission [*Defunct*] .... EPC
Educational Premises [*Public-performance tariff class*] [*British*] .... N
Educational Press Association of America .... EDPRESS
Educational Press Association of America [*Later, EDPRESS*] .... EPAA
Educational Product Report [*A publication*] .... Ed Prod Rep
Educational Product Report [*A publication*] .... Educ Prod Rept
Educational Products Information Exchange .... EPIE
Educational Products Information Exchange Institute [*Later, EPIE Institute*] .... EPIEI
Educational Professional Development Assistance [*Office of Education*] .... EPDA
Educational Program in Systems Analysis .... EPSA
Educational and Psychological Measurement [*A publication*] .... Ed & Psychol M
Educational and Psychological Measurement [*A publication*] .... Educ & Psychol M
Educational and Psychological Measurement [*A publication*] .... Educ & Psychol Meas
Educational and Psychological Measurement [*A publication*] .... Educ Psyc M
Educational and Psychological Measurement [*A publication*] .... EPM
Educational and Psychological Measurement [*A publication*] .... EPMEA
Educational and Psychological Measurement [*A publication*] .... EPsM
Educational Psychologist [*A publication*] .... Educ Psychol
Educational Publication [*NASA*] .... EP
Educational Quotient [*Psychology*] .... EQ
Educational Radio Network .... ERN
Educational Ratio .... ER
Educational Record [*A publication*] .... EdR
Educational Record [*A publication*] .... Ed Rec
Educational Record [*A publication*] .... Educ Rec
Educational Record [*A publication*] .... Educ Recd
Educational Records Bureau .... ERB
Educational Records Bureau Bulletins [*Greenwich, Connecticut*] [*A publication*] .... Ed Rec Bur Bul
Educational Records Bureau Bulletins [*Greenwich, Connecticut*] [*A publication*] .... Educ Rec Bur Bull
Educational Reference Center [*National Institute of Education*] .... ERC
Educational Requirements Test .... ERT
Educational Research [*A publication*] .... Ednl Research
Educational Research [*Oxford*] [*A publication*] .... Ed Res
Educational Research [*Oxford*] [*A publication*] .... Educ Res
Educational Research Analysts .... EdReAn
Educational Research Bulletin [*A publication*] .... Ed Res B
Educational Research Bulletin [*A publication*] .... Educ Res Bul
Educational Research Bulletin [*A publication*] .... ERB
Educational Research Council of America .... ERCA
Educational Research Information .... ERI
Educational Research Quarterly [*A publication*] .... Educ Res Q
Educational Research Quarterly [*A publication*] .... Educ Res Quart
Educational Research Record [*A publication*] .... Ed Res Record
Educational Research Service .... ERS
Educational Researcher [*A publication*] .... Educ Researcher
Educational Resources Allocation Systems .... ERAS
Educational Resources [*formerly, Research*] **Information Center** [*Office of Education*] .... ERIC
Educational Review [*A publication*] .... Ednl R
Educational Review [*United Kingdom*] [*A publication*] .... Ed R
Educational Review [*A publication*] .... Educa R
Educational Review [*A publication*] .... Educ R
Educational Review [*A publication*] .... ER
Educational Review (China) [*A publication*] .... Ed R (China)
Educational Satellite .... EDUSAT
Educational Sciences [*A publication*] .... Ednl Sciences
Educational Screen [*A publication*] .... Ed Screen
Educational Screen [*A publication*] .... Educ Screen
Educational Screen and Audiovisual Guide [*Later, AV Guide: The Learning Media Magazine*] [*A publication*] .... AVG
Educational Screen and Audiovisual Guide [*Later, AV Guide: The Learning Media Magazine*] [*A publication*] .... Ed Screen AV G
Educational Series. Florida Department of Natural Resources. Marine Research Laboratory [*A publication*] .... Ed Ser Fla Dep Nat Resour Mar Res Lab
Educational Service Branch [*BUPERS*] .... ESB
Educational Services, Incorporated [*Later, EDC*] .... ESI
Educational Services, International .... ESI
Educational Services Office [*or Officer*] [*Navy*] .... ESO
Educational Services Section [*Navy*] .... ESS
Educational Specialist .... Ed S
Educational Specialist .... ES
Educational Statistics [*Search system*] .... EDSTAT
Educational Studies [*A publication*] .... Ed Studies
Educational Studies [*A publication*] .... Educ Stud
Educational Studies [*A publication*] .... ES
Educational Studies in Mathematics [*A publication*] ... Ednl Studies in Maths
Educational Studies in Mathematics [*A publication*] .... Educ Stud Math
Educational Subscription Service, Inc. .... ESS
Educational Survey [*A publication*] .... Ed Survey
Educational Systems Corporation [*Defunct*] .... ESC
Educational Talent Search .... ETS
Educational Technology [*A publication*] .... EdT
Educational Technology [*A publication*] .... Ed Tech
Educational Technology [*A publication*] .... Educ Tech
Educational Telecommunications Network .... ETN
Educational Television [*A publication*] .... ET
Educational Television .... ETV
Educational Television International [*A publication*] .... Ed TV Int
Educational Television for the Metropolitan Area .... ETMA
Educational Television and Radio Center [*Later, EBC*] .... ETRC
Educational Testing Service .... ETS
Educational Testing Service, Princeton, NJ [*Library symbol*] .... NjPE
Educational Testing Service Test Collection .... ETSTC
Educational Theatre Journal [*A publication*] .... Ed Theatre J
Educational Theatre Journal [*A publication*] .... Educ Theatre J
Educational Theatre Journal [*A publication*] .... ETJ
Educational Theory [*A publication*] .... Ed Theory
Educational Theory [*A publication*] .... Educ Theor
Educational Theory [*A publication*] .... Educ Theory
Educational Therapy .... ET
Educational Training .... ET
Educational and Training Establishment [*Military*] [*British*] .... ETE
Educational Travel, Incorporated .... ETI
Educational Video Corporation .... EVC
Educationally Handicapped .... EH
Educationally Impaired .... EI
Educationally Subnormal .... ESN
Educator [*A publication*] .... EDENA
Educators to Africa [*Later, ETAA*] .... EA
Educators to Africa .... ETAA
Educators Fund Management Corporation [*of NEA*] .... EFMC
Educator's Purchasing Master [*A publication*] .... EPM
Educators for Social Responsibility .... ESR
Educazione Musicale [*A publication*] .... Ed Mus
Educazione dei Sordomuti [*A publication*] .... Educ Sordomuti
EDUCOM [*Educational Communications*] **Bulletin** [*A publication*] .... EDUCOM
Educom Corp. [*NASDAQ symbol*] .... EDCM
Educreative Systems, Incorporated .... ESI
Eductor .... EDUC
Eduworld Society [*Later, CFB*] .... EWS
EDV [*Elektronische Datenverarbeitung*] **in Medizin und Biologie** [*A publication*] .... EDV Med Biol
Edvard Grieg Memorial Foundation .... EGMF
Edwald-Kornfeld Method .... EKM
Edward J. Meyer Memorial Hospital Medical Library, Buffalo, NY [*Library symbol*] .... NBuEMH
Edward Medal [*British*] .... EM
Edward Moore Kennedy [*American politician*] .... EMK
Edward River [*Australia*] [*Airport symbol*] .... EDR
Edward Walters College [*Florida*] .... EWC
Edwardian Drama and Literature Circle .... EDLC

Edwards [*California*] [*Airport symbol*] [*Obsolete*] ... EDW
Edwards Air Force Base [*California*] ... EAFB
Edwards Air Force Base Library, Edwards AFB, CA [*OCLC symbol*] ... CEB
Edwards Flight Research Center [*NASA*] ... EFRC
Edwards Flight Test Center [*NASA*] ... EFTC
Edwards Industries, Inc. [*NASDAQ symbol*] ... EDWR
Edwards Personal Preference Scale [*or Schedule*] [*Psychology*] ... EPPS
Edwards Personality Inventory [*Psychology*] ... EPI
Edwards Public Library, Henrietta, TX [*Library symbol*] ... TxHe
Edwards Rocket Base ... ERB
Edwards Rocket Test Site ... ERTS
Edwards [*A. G.*] **& Sons, Inc.** [*NYSE symbol*] ... AGE
Edwards Test Station [*NASA*] ... ETS
Edwardsville Community Unit, School District 7, Edwardsville, IL [*Library symbol*] ... IEdSD
Edwardsville Free Public Library, Edwardsville, IL [*Library symbol*] ... IEd
Edwardsville, IL [*Radio station call letters*] ... WSIE
Edwardus Rex [*King Edward*] [*Latin*] ... ER
Edwardus Rex et Imperator [*Edward King and Emperor*] [*Latin*] ... ER et I
Edwin A. Bemis Public Library, Littleton, CO [*Library symbol*] ... CoLi
EE/Systems Engineering Today [*A publication*] ... EE/Systems Eng
EECO, Inc. [*American Stock Exchange symbol*] ... EEC
EEG Aperiodic-Interval Spectrum Analysis [*Neurology*] ... EISA
Eek [*Alaska*] [*Airport symbol*] ... EEK
Eelam Tamils Association of America ... ETAA
Eenheidsvakcentrale [*United Dutch Trade Union Central*] ... EVC
EEO [*Equal Employment Opportunity*] **Spotlight** [*A publication*] ... EEO Spotl
Eesti NSV Teaduste Akadeemia Toimetised. Bioloogia [*A publication*] ... Eesti NSV Tead Akad Toim Biol
Eesti NSV Teaduste Akadeemia Toimetised. Uhiskonnateaduste Seeria [*A publication*] ... ETAT
Eestimaa Kommunistlik Partei ... EKP
Effect ... EFCT
Effect ... EFF
Effect ... EFT
Effect of Gravity on Methane-Air Combustion ... EGOMAC
Effect on Guarantees ... EOG
Effective Acoustic Center ... EAC
Effective Address [*Data processing*] ... EA
Effective Air Distance ... EAD
Effective Air Path ... EAP
Effective Angular Velocity ... EAV
Effective Atomic Charge ... EAC
Effective Atomic Number ... EAN
Effective Bandwidth ... EBW
Effective Buying Income [*Red Cross fund-raising*] ... EBI
Effective Citizens Organization [*Later, PAC*] ... ECO
Effective Complex Modulus ... ECM
Effective Concentration [*Instrumentation*] ... EC
Effective Concentration at which Light Emission Is Reduced by 50% [*Instrumentation*] ... EC_{50}
Effective Conductivity ... EC
Effective Control of Manpower ... ECONOMAN
Effective Creep Compliance ... ECC
Effective Cutoff Diameter [*Particulate measurement*] ... ECD
Effective Cutoff Frequency ... ECF
Effective Date ... E (Date)
Effective Date of Change ... EDC
Effective Date of Change ... EDOC
Effective Date of Change of Morning Report ... EDCMR
Effective Date of Change in Station Assignment [*Military*] ... EDSA
Effective Date of Change of Strength Accountability ... EDCSA
Effective Date of Federal Recognition ... EDFR
Effective Date of Release from Training ... EDRT
Effective Date of Supply ... EDOS
Effective Date of Training ... EDT
Effective Diameter of Objective [*Optics*] ... EDO
Effective Direct Radiation ... EDR
Effective Directives and Plans ... EDP
Effective Dose ... ED
Effective Dose, Median ... ED_{50}
Effective Elastic Modulus ... EEM
Effective Engineering Management ... EEM
Effective Equal Opportunity ... EEO
Effective Exposure Method ... EEM
Effective Filtration Pressure [*Physiology*] ... EFP
Effective Filtration Rate [*Physiology*] ... EFR
Effective Focal Length [*Optics*] ... EFL
Effective Full-Charge [*Weaponry*] ... EFC
Effective Full Power Day ... EFPD
Effective Full Power Month ... EFPM
Effective Halflife [*Nuclear science*] ... EHL
Effective Horsepower ... EHP
Effective Hydration Temperature [*Archeology, geology*] ... EHT
Effective Initial Value ... EIV
Effective Instantaneous Field of View ... EIFOV
Effective Kilogram ... EKG
Effective Management Responsibility ... EMR
Effective Mass Approximation ... EMA
Effective On or About ... EOA
Effective Perceived Noise [*Aviation*] ... EPN
Effective-Perceived-Noise Decibel Level [*Aviation*] ... EPNdB
Effective-Perceived-Noise Level [*Aviation*] ... EPNL
Effective Program Projections ... EPP
Effective Radiated Power [*Radio transmitting*] ... ERP
Effective Refractory Period ... ERP
Effective Relaxation Modulus ... ERM
Effective Renal Blood Flow [*Medicine*] ... ERBF
Effective Renal Plasma Flow [*Medicine*] ... ERPF
Effective Signal Radiated ... ESR
Effective SONAR Range [*Navy*] ... ESR
Effective Standard Deviation [*of chemical standardized solutions*] ... ESD
Effective Sunrise ... ESR
Effective Sunset ... ESS
Effective Temperature ... ET
Effective Thermal Expansion Coefficient ... ETEC
Effective Thyroxine Ratio [*Medicine*] ... ETR
Effective Transfer Date [*Military*] ... ETD
Effective True Airspeed ... ETAS
Effective United States Control Fleet ... EUSC
Effective Visual Transmission ... EVT
Effective Wavelength ... EWL
Effectiveness Evaluation System ... EES
Effectiveness and Maintainability ... E & M
Effectiveness of Navy Electronic Warfare Systems ... ENEWS
Effectiveness Report [*Military*] ... ER
Effectiveness Report - Performance Report [*Air Force*] ... ER-PR
Effectiveness Simulation Model ... ESM
Effectiveness Training Associates ... ETA
Effectiveness Training, Incorporated [*An association*] ... ETI
Effectiveness Training for Women [*A course of study*] ... ETW
Effectivity ... EFTV
Effects of Nuclear Weapons [*AEC-DoD book*] ... ENW
Effects of Subsurface Explosions [*Project*] [*Army and DNA*] ... ESSEX
Efferent [*Medicine*] ... EFF
Efferent Branchial Vein ... EBV
Efferent Renal Vein ... ERV
Efferent Vein from Nephridial Gland ... ENVG
Efferent Vessel ... EV
Effervescent Magnetic Peroxoborate ... EMPB
Efficiency [*or Efficient*] ... E
Efficiency ... EFF
Efficiency ... EFFCY
Efficiency Decoration [*Military*] [*British*] ... ED
Efficiency Medal ... EM
Efficiency Modulation ... EM
Efficiency of Plating [*Microbiology*] ... EOP
Efficient Assembly System ... EASY
Efficient Deck Hand ... EDH
Efficient Growth [*Computer program*] ... EFFGRO
Effigy Mounds National Monument ... EFMO
Effingham, IL [*Radio station call letters*] ... WBFG
Effingham, IL [*Radio station call letters*] ... WCRA
Effingham, IL [*Radio station call letters*] ... WCRC
Effluent ... EFL
Effluent [*or Evolved*] **Gas Analysis** ... EGA
Effluent Guidelines Division [*Environmental Protection Agency*] ... EGD
Effluent Inventory System [*Nuclear energy*] ... EIS
Effluent and Water Treatment Journal [*A publication*] ... Effluent Water Treat J
Effluent and Water Treatment Journal [*A publication*] ... Eff Wat Tre
Efik [*MARC language code*] [*Library of Congress*] ... efi
Efogi [*Papua New Guinea*] [*Airport symbol*] ... EFG
EFTA [*European Free Trade Association*] **Bulletin** [*A publication*] ... EFTA Bull
EG & G, Inc. [*NYSE symbol*] ... EGG
Egalitarian ... EGAL
Egan Machinery Co. [*American Stock Exchange symbol*] [*Delisted*] ... EGN
Ege Universitesi Fen Fakultesi Ilmi Raporlar Serisi [*A publication*] ... Ege Univ Fen Fak Ilmi Rap Ser
Egegik [*Alaska*] [*Airport symbol*] ... EGX
Eger's Yellow ... EY
Egg Harbor City, NJ [*Radio station call letters*] ... WRDR
Egg Harbor News, Egg Harbor City, NJ [*Library symbol*] ... NjEgN
Egg-Laying Hormone [*Endocrinology*] ... ELH
Egg-Laying Release Hormone [*Endocrinology*] ... ERH
Egg Length ... EL
Egg Lethal Dose ... ELD
Egg Producer [*A publication*] ... Egg Prod
Egg Stalk Length ... ESL
Egg Width ... EW
Egg Yolk ... EY
Eggs per Gram [*Parasitology*] ... EPG
Egilsstadir [*Iceland*] [*Seismograph station code, US Geological Survey*] ... EGI
Egilsstadir [*Iceland*] [*Airport symbol*] ... EGS
Eglin Air Force Base [*Florida*] ... EAFB
Eglin Air Force Base, Eglin, FL [*OCLC symbol*] ... FEA
Eglin Field [*Florida*] [*Air Force*] ... EF
Eglin Gulf Missile Test Range ... EGMTR
Eglin Gulf Test Range ... EGTR
Eglin RADAR Control Facility [*Air Force*] ... ERCF

Eglin Refugee Processing Center [*Air Force*] ERPC
Eglin Regional Hospital Library, Eglin AFB, FL [*OCLC symbol*] SCV
Eglin Test Facility [*NASA*] ETF
Eglise et l'Etat au Moyen Age [*A publication*] EEMA
Eglise et Theologie [*A publication*] Ee T
Eglise et Theologie [*A publication*] Eglise Th
Eglise et Theologie [*A publication*] E & Th
Ego Boost EGOBOO
Ego Control [*Psychology*] EC
Ego Overcontrol [*Psychology*] EO
Ego Resiliency [*Psychology*] ER
Ego Resources, Inc. [*NASDAQ symbol*] EGOR
Ego Strength [*Psychology*] Es
Ego Strength Q-Sort Test [*Psychology*] ESQST
Ego Support Value [*Psychology*] ESV
Egress EGRS
Egress Maintenance Vehicle EMV
Egyetemes Philologiai Koezloeny [*A publication*] EPhK
Egyetemes Philologiai Koezloeny [*A publication*] EPK
Egypt [*Two-letter standard code*] EG
Egypt [*Three-letter standard code*] EGY
Egypt ET
Egypt Air [*ICAO designator*] MS
Egypt Exploration Fund [*A publication*] EEF
Egypt Exploration Society EES
Egypt Exploration Society. Graeco-Roman Memoirs [*A publication*] EESGRM
Egypt Geological Survey. Annals [*A publication*] Egypt Geol Surv Ann
Egypt Geological Survey. Paper [*A publication*] Egypt Geol Surv Pap
Egypte Contemporaine [*A publication*] EC
Egypte Contemporaine [*A publication*] EgC
Egypte Contemporaine [*A publication*] Egypte Contemp
Egyptian E
Egyptian [*MARC language code*] [*Library of Congress*] egy
Egyptian Air Force EAF
Egyptian-American Chamber of Commerce EACC
Egyptian Army EA
Egyptian Confederation of Labor ECL
Egyptian Dental Journal [*A publication*] Egypt Dent J
Egyptian Expeditionary Force [*Military*] [*British*] EEF
Egyptian Federation of Labor - United Arab Republic [*Obsolete*] EFL-UAR
Egyptian General Petroleum Corporation EGPC
Egyptian Government Organization for Tourism and Hotels EGOTH
Egyptian Journal of Agronomy [*A publication*] Egypt J Agron
Egyptian Journal of Animal Production [*A publication*] Egypt J Anim Prod
Egyptian Journal of Bilharziasis [*A publication*] Egypt J Bilharz
Egyptian Journal of Bilharziasis [*A publication*] Egypt J Bilharziasis
Egyptian Journal of Botany [*A publication*] Egypt J Bot
Egyptian Journal of Chemistry [*A publication*] Egypt J Ch
Egyptian Journal of Chest Diseases and Tuberculosis [*A publication*] Egypt J Chest Dis Tuberc
Egyptian Journal of Food Science [*A publication*] Egypt J Food Sci
Egyptian Journal of Genetics and Cytology [*A publication*] Egypt J Genet Cytol
Egyptian Journal of Geology [*A publication*] Egypt J Geol
Egyptian Journal of Horticulture [*A publication*] Egypt J Hortic
Egyptian Journal of Microbiology [*A publication*] Egypt J Microbiol
Egyptian Journal of Pharmaceutical Sciences [*A publication*] Egypt J Pharm Sci
Egyptian Journal of Physics [*A publication*] Egypt J Phys
Egyptian Journal of Physiological Sciences [*A publication*] Egypt J Physiol Sci
Egyptian Journal of Phytopathology [*A publication*] Egypt J Phyopathol
Egyptian Journal of Psychiatry [*A publication*] Egypt J Psychiatry
Egyptian Journal of Soil Science [*A publication*] Egypt J Soil Sci
Egyptian Journal of Veterinary Science [*A publication*] Egypt J Vet Sci
Egyptian Order of Merit EOM
Egyptian Pharmaceutical Bulletin [*A publication*] Egypt Pharm Bull
Egyptian Pharmaceutical Journal [*A publication*] Egypt Pharm J
Egyptian Population and Family Planning Review [*A publication*] Egypt Popul Fam Plann Rev
Egyptian Religion [*A publication*] EgR
Egyptology EGY
Ehkonomika Neftyanoj Promyshlennosti [*A publication*] Ehkon Neft Prom-st
Ehksperimental'naya Khirurgiya i Anesteziologiya [*A publication*] Ehksp Khir Anesteziol
Ehkspress-Informatsiya. Laboratornye Tekhnologicheskie Issledovaniya i Obogashchenie Mineral'nogo Syr'ya [*A publication*] Ehkspress-Inf Lab Tekhnol Issled Obogashch Miner Syr'ya
Ehkspress-Informatsiya. Neftegazovaya Geologiya i Geofizika [*A publication*] Ehkspress-Inf Neftegazov Geol Geofiz
Ehkspress-Informatsiya. Seriya. Regional'naya. Razvedochnaya i Promyslovaya Geofizika [*A publication*] Ehkspress-Inf Ser Reg Razved Promysl Geofiz
Ehkspress-Informatsiya. Stroitel'stvo Teplovykh Ehlektrostantsij [*A publication*] Ehkspress-Inf Stroit Tepl Ehlektrostn
Ehkspress-Informatsiya. Svarochnye Raboty [*A publication*] Ehkspress-Inf Svar Rab
Ehlektricheskie Stantsii [*A publication*] Ehlektr Stn
Ehlektrofizicheskaya Apparatura [*A publication*] Ehlektrofiz Appar
Ehlektrokhimiya. Akademiya Nauk SSSR. Ezhemesyachnyj Zhurnal [*A publication*] Ehlektrokhim
Ehlektronnaya Obrabotka Materialov [*A publication*] Ehlektron Obrab Mater
Ehlektronnye i Ionnye Protessy v Tverdykh Telakh [*A publication*] Ehlektron Ionnye Protessy Tverd Telakh
Ehlektrosvyaz' i Radiotekhnika [*A publication*] Ehlektrosvyaz' Radiotekh
Ehlers-Danlos Syndrome [*Medicine*] EDS
Ehnergeticheskoe Stroitel'stvo [*A publication*] Ehnerg Stroit
Ehnergeticheskoe Stroitel'stvo za Rubezhom [*A publication*] Ehnerg Stroit Rubezhom
Ehnergetika i Ehlektrifikatsiya [*A publication*] Ehnerg Ehlektrif
Ehntomologicheskoe Obozrenie [*A publication*] Ehntomol Obozr
Ehrenfest Adiabatic Law [*Physics*] EAL
Ehrenreich Photo-Optical Industries, Inc. [*American Stock Exchange symbol*] [*Delisted*] EHR
Ehrenreich Photo-Optical Industries, Inc. EPI
Ehrenreich Photo-Optical Industries, Inc. EPOI
Ehrlich Ascites Carcinoma [*Cells*] EAC
Ehrlich Ascites Tumor [*Medicine*] EAT
Ehrlich Ascites Tumor Cell EATC
Ehrlich-Lettre Hyperdiploid [*Mouse ascites tumor*] ELD
Eibei Bungaku [*British and American Literature: The Rikkyo Review of Arts and Letters*] [*A publication*] EBB
Eibungaku Shicho [*Current Thoughts in English Literature*] [*A publication*] EBSC
Eicosapentaenoic Acid [*Biochemistry*] EPA
Eicosatetraynoic Acid [*Organic chemistry*] ETYA
Eidgenoessische Anstalt fuer das Forstliche Versuchswesen Mitteilungen [*A publication*] Eidg Anst Forstl Versuchswes Mitt
Eidgenoessische Technische Hochschule [*Swiss Federal Institute of Technology*] ETH
Eidgenoessische Technische Hochschule, Zurich, Switzerland [*Library symbol*] SzZE
Eidgenoessisches Institut fuer Reaktoforschung [*Switzerland*] EIR
EIFAC [*European Inland Fisheries Advisory Commission*] **Occasional Paper** [*A publication*] EIFAC Occas Pap
EIFAC [*European Inland Fisheries Advisory Commission*] **Technical Paper** [*A publication*] EIFAC Tech Pap
Eigen Schoon en de Brabander [*A publication*] ESB
Eigenvalue Change Analysis ECA
Eigenverstaendigung [*Intravehicular communication*] [*German military - World War II*] EIV
Eight Card Redrawing Test [*Psychology*] 8CRT
Eight Fathom Bight [*Alaska*] [*Airport symbol*] EFB
Eight-Parallel-Form Anxiety Battery [*Psychology*] 8PFAB
Eight Sheet Outdoor Advertising Association [*Formerly, JPOAA*] ESOAA
Eighteen-Nation Disarmament Committee [*or Conference*] [*Later, CCD*] [*Convened March 14, 1962; actually attended by 17 nations, with France absent*] ENDC
Eighteenth Century [*A publication*] E Cent
Eighteenth-Century Life [*A publication*] E-C Life
Eighteenth-Century Short-Title Catalogue [*A publication*] ESTC
Eighteenth-Century Studies [*A publication*] ECS
Eighteenth-Century Studies [*A publication*] Eighteenth-Cent Stud
Eighth Air Force Historical Society EAFHS
Eighth Lively Art [*Advertising award*] ELA
Eighth United States Army EUSA
Eighth United States Army USAEIGHT
Eighth United States Army in Korea EUSAK
Eighth United States Army Rear EUSAR
Eigo Seinen [*A publication*] Eigo S
Eigse [*A publication*] Eig
EIL Instruments [*NASDAQ symbol*] EILI
Eilat [*Israel*] [*Seismograph station code, US Geological Survey*] EIL
Eimac [*Division of Varian Associates*] **Technical Library, San Carlos, CA** [*Library symbol*] JScE
Ein Grosser Komponist [*A Great Composer*] **or Ein Genialer Komponist** [*A Great Genius of a Composer*] [*Suggested interpretations for the adopted surname of German composer Werner Egk. Egk maintained that he chose the name in honor of his wife, Elisabeth Karl*] EGK
EIN [*Employer Identification Number*] **Research and Assignment System** [*IRS*] ERAS
Ein Yahav [*Israel*] [*Airport symbol*] [*Obsolete*] EIY
Eindhoven [*Netherlands*] [*Airport symbol*] EIN
Eineiige Zwillinge [*Monozygotic Twins*] [*Psychology*] EZ
Einfache Lafette [*Single-barreled mount*] [*German military - World War II*] EL
Einfuehrungen zur Molekularbiologie [*A publication*] Einfuehr Molekularbiol
Einfuehrungen zur Molekularbiologie [*A publication*] Einfuehrung Molekularbiol
Eingang Vorbehalten [*Rights reserved, i.e., copyrighted*] [*German*] EV
Eingetragenes Warenzeichen [*Registered Trademark*] [*German*] EW
Einheitliche Systematik [*Library science*] ES
Einschluss-Korper [*Inclusion body*] [*Medicine*] EK
Einspritz [*Fuel-injection*] [*As in 280 E, the model number of a Mercedes-Benz automobile*] E

Einstein Equivalence Principle [*Gravity*] EEP
Einstein-Podolsky-Rosen [*Quantum mechanics*] EPR
Einstein Viscosity Equation EVE
Einsteinium [*Also see Es*] [*Chemical element*] E
Einsteinium [*Preferred form, but also see E*] [*Chemical element*] Es
Einzelsphaltrohrversuchsanlage [*Hydrogen generating reactor*] EVA
EIP Microwave, Inc. [*NASDAQ symbol*] EIPM
EIR- [*Eidgenoessisches Institut fuer Reaktorforschung*] **Bericht (Wuerenlingen)** [*A publication*] EIR-Ber (Wuerenlingen)
Eire Army Corps EAC
Eire Philatelic Association EPA
Eisai Co. Ltd. [*Japan*] [*Research code symbol*] PP
Eisenbahn-Ingenieur [*A publication*] Eisenbahn-Ing
Eisenbahn-Verkehrsordnung [*Germany*] EVO
Eisenbahnkesselwagen [*Railway tank car*] [*German military - World War II*] EKW
Eisenbahntechnische Rundschau [*A publication*] Eisenbahntech Rundsch
Eisenhower Consortium Bulletin [*A publication*] Eisenhower Consortium Bull
Eisenhower Exchange Fellowships EEF
Eisenhower Institute for Historical Research [*Smithsonian Institution*] EIHR
Eisenhower Public Library District, Harwood Heights, IL [*Library symbol*] IHh
Eiszeitalter und Gegenwart [*A publication*] Eiszeitalter Gegenw
Eject EJ
Eject EJCT
Eject Rocket Container ERC
Ejection EJN
Ejection Click [*Cardiology*] EC
Ejection Fraction [*Cardiology*] EF
Ejection Launch Test Vehicle ELTV
Ejection Sound [*Cardiology*] ES
Ejection Test Vehicle ETV
Ejector EJCTR
Ejector-Launcher, Guided Missile, Transporter EGLMT
Ejector Thrust Augmentation [*Air Force*] ETA
Ejector Unit EU
Ejercito Guerrillero de los Pobres [*Guerrilla Army of the Poor*] [*Guatemala*] EGP
Ejercito de Liberacion Nacional [*Bolivia*] ELN
Ejercito Popular de Liberacion [*Colombia*] EPL
Ejercito Revolucionario del Pueblo [*Argentina, El Salvador*] ERP
Ejus [*Of Him, or Of Her*] [*Latin*] EJ
Ejusdem [*Of the Same*] [*Pharmacy*] EJUSD
Ejusdem Generis [*Of the Same Kind*] [*Latin*] EG
Ekco Products Co. [*NYSE symbol*] [*Delisted*] EPO
Ekereku [*Guyana*] [*Airport symbol*] EKE
Ekistic Index [*A publication*] EKI
Ekistic Index [*A publication*] Ekist Ind
Ekistics [*A publication*] EKIS-A
Ekologia Polska [*A publication*] Ekol Pol
Ekologia Polska [*A publication*] Ekol Polska
Ekologia Polska. Seria A [*A publication*] Ekol Pol Ser A
Ekologia Polska. Seria B [*A publication*] Ekol Pol Ser B
Ekologicheskie i Fiziologicheskie Osobennosti Rastenii Yuzhnogo Urala i Ikh Resursy [*A publication*] Ekol Fiziol Osob Rast Yuzhn Urala Ikh Resur
Ekonomi. Forskningsstiftelsen Skogsarbeten [*A publication*] Ekon Forsknstift Skogsarb
Ekonomi dan Keuangan Indonesia [*A publication*] EKI
Ekonomi dan Keuangan Indonesia [*A publication*] Ekon Keuangan
Ekonomiceskie Nauki [*A publication*] Ekon Nauki
Ekonomiceskie Problemy Effektivnosti Proizvodstva [*A publication*] Ekon Probl Effekt
Ekonomicheskaya Gazeta [*A publication*] Ekon Gaz
Ekonomicko-Matematicky Obzor [*A publication*] Ekon-Mate O
Ekonomicky Casopis [*A publication*] Ekon Cas
Ekonomika i Matematiceskie Metody [*A publication*] Ekon Matem Metody
Ekonomika i Organizacija Promyslennogo Proizvodstva [*A publication*] Ekon Org Promysl Proizvodstva
Ekonomika Poljoprivrede [*A publication*] Ekon Poljopriv
Ekonomika Sel'skogo Hozjajstva [*A publication*] Ekon Sel'sk Hoz
Ekonomika Sel'skogo Khozyaistva [*A publication*] Ekon Sel'sk Khoz
Ekonomika Zemedelstvi [*A publication*] Ekon Zemed
Ekonomisk Revy (Stockholm) [*A publication*] Ekon R (Stockholm)
Ekonomisk Tidskrift [*A publication*] ET
Ekonomiska Samfundets Tidskrift [*A publication*] Ekon Samf T
Ekonomiska Samfundets Tidskrift [*A publication*] Ekon Samfund Ts
Ekonomska Revija (Ljubljana) [*A publication*] Ekon R (Ljubljana)
Ekranolytny Spassatyelny Kater Amphibiya [*Screen-Effect Amphibious Lifeboat*] [*USSR*] ESKA
Eksperimentalna Meditsina i Morfologiya [*A publication*] Eksp Med Morfol
Eksperimentalnaia Klinicheskaia Stomatologiia [*A publication*] Eksp Klin Stomatol
Eksperimental'naya Khirurgiya i Anesteziologiya [*A publication*] Eksp Khir Anesteziol
Ekuk [*Alaska*] [*Airport symbol*] KKU
Ekwok [*Alaska*] [*Airport symbol*] KEK
El Al Charter Services Ltd. [*Israel*] [*ICAO designator*] ER
El Al - Israel Airlines Ltd. [*ICAO designator*] LY
El Bagre [*Colombia*] [*Airport symbol*] EBG
El Banco [*Colombia*] [*Airport symbol*] ELB
El Bolson [*Argentina*] [*Airport symbol*] EHL
El Cajon [*California*] [*Airport symbol*] [*Obsolete*] CJN
El Cajon [*California*] [*Seismograph station code, US Geological Survey*] [*Closed*] ECA
El Cajon, CA [*Radio station call letters*] KECR
El Cajon, CA [*Radio station call letters*] KMJC
El Camino College [*California*] ECC
El Camino College, Torrance, CA [*Library symbol*] CEcaE
El Campo, TX [*Radio station call letters*] KULP
El Campo, TX [*Radio station call letters*] KXGC-FM
El Centro [*California*] [*Seismograph station code, US Geological Survey*] [*Closed*] ECC
El Centro [*Colombia*] [*Seismograph station code, US Geological Survey*] ETC
El Centro, CA [*Radio station call letters*] KAMP
El Centro, CA [*Television station call letters*] KECY-TV
El Centro, CA [*Radio station call letters*] KXO
El Centro, CA [*Radio station call letters*] KXO-FM
El Centro, CA [*Television station call letters*] XHBC-TV
El Centro College, Dallas, TX [*Library symbol*] TxDaE
El Centro Free Public Library, El Centro, CA [*Library symbol*] CEc
El Centro/Imperial [*California*] [*Airport symbol*] IPL
El Cerrito, CA [*Radio station call letters*] KECG
El Chico Corp. [*NASDAQ symbol*] ELCH
El Congreso Nacional de Asuntos Colegiales CONAC
El Debba [*Sudan*] [*Airport symbol*] [*Obsolete*] EDB
El Dorado [*Arkansas*] [*Airport symbol*] ELD
El Dorado, AR [*Radio station call letters*] KAYZ
El Dorado, AR [*Radio station call letters*] KDMS
El Dorado, AR [*Radio station call letters*] KELD
El Dorado, AR [*Radio station call letters*] KLBQ
El Dorado, AR [*Television station call letters*] KTVE
El Dorado County Free Library, Placerville, CA [*Library symbol*] CPla
El Dorado, KS [*Location identifier*] [*FAA*] EQA
El Dorado, KS [*Radio station call letters*] KOYY
El Dorado, KS [*Radio station call letters*] KSPG
El Dorado Springs, MO [*Radio station call letters*] KESM
El Dorado Springs, MO [*Radio station call letters*] KESM-FM
El Dorado & Wesson Railway Co. [*AAR code*] EDW
El Fasher [*Sudan*] [*Airport symbol*] ELF
El Geneina [*Sudan*] [*Airport symbol*] EGN
El Golfo De Santa Clara [*Mexico*] [*Seismograph station code, US Geological Survey*] EGM
El Hato [*Venezuela*] [*Seismograph station code, US Geological Survey*] EHV
El Maiten [*Argentina*] [*Airport symbol*] EMX
El Monte, CA [*Location identifier*] [*FAA*] EMT
El Monte Carmelo [*A publication*] EMC
El Morro National Monument ELMO
El Mundo Publishing Co., San Juan, PR [*Library symbol*] PrSE
El Museo Canario [*A publication*] EMC
El Nino - Southern Oscillation [*Coupled oceanic-atmospheric change*] ENSO
El Obeid [*Sudan*] [*Airport symbol*] EBD
El Oued [*Algeria*] [*Airport symbol*] ELU
El Palacio [*A publication*] El Pal
El Pangue [*Chile*] [*Seismograph station code, US Geological Survey*] ELP
El Paso [*Texas*] [*Airport symbol*] ELP
El Paso [*Texas*] [*Seismograph station code, US Geological Survey*] EPT
El Paso Community College, Colorado Springs, CO [*Library symbol*] CoCE
El Paso Community College, El Paso, TX [*OCLC symbol*] TXE
El Paso Community College, El Paso, TX [*Library symbol*] TxEC
El Paso Co. [*NYSE symbol*] [*Delisted*] ELG
El Paso Electric Co. [*NASDAQ symbol*] ELPA
El Paso Geological Society. Annual Field Trip (Guidebook) [*A publication*] El Paso Geol Soc Annu Field Trip (Guideb)
El Paso [*Texas*] **Intelligence Center** [*Drug Enforcement Administration; Border Patrol; US Customs Service; Bureau of Alcohol, Tobacco, and Firearms; FAA; US Coast Guard*] EPIC
El Paso Natural Gas Co. [*NYSE symbol*] ELPPrD
El Paso Natural Gas Co., Technical Information Center, El Paso, TX [*Library symbol*] TxENG
El Paso Products Co., Odessa, TX [*Library symbol*] TxOEP
El Paso Public Library, El Paso, TX [*Library symbol*] TxE
El Paso Public Library, El Paso, TX [*OCLC symbol*] TXP
El Paso Southern Railway Co. [*AAR code*] EPS
El Paso, TX [*Location identifier*] [*FAA*] BIF
El Paso, TX [*Radio station call letters*] KAMA
El Paso, TX [*Radio station call letters*] KAMZ
El Paso, TX [*Television station call letters*] KCIK-TV
EL Paso, TX [*Television station call letters*] KCOS
El Paso, TX [*Television station call letters*] KDBC-TV
El Paso, TX [*Radio station call letters*] KELP
El Paso, TX [*Radio station call letters*] KEZB
El Paso, TX [*Radio station call letters*] KFIM
El Paso, TX [*Radio station call letters*] KHEY
El Paso, TX [*Radio station call letters*] KHEY-FM

El Paso, TX [*Television station call letters*]....KINT-TV
El Paso, TX [*Radio station call letters*]....KISO
El Paso, TX [*Radio station call letters*]....KLAQ
El Paso, TX [*Radio station call letters*]....KLOZ
El Paso, TX [*Radio station call letters*]....KROD
El Paso, TX [*Radio station call letters*]....KSET
El Paso, TX [*Radio station call letters*]....KSET-FM
El Paso, TX [*Radio station call letters*]....KTEP
El Paso, TX [*Radio station call letters*]....KTSM
El Paso, TX [*Radio station call letters*]....KTSM-FM
El Paso, TX [*Television station call letters*]....KTSM-TV
El Paso, TX [*Television station call letters*]....KVIA-TV
El Paso, TX [*Radio station call letters*]....KYSP
El Paso, TX [*Radio station call letters*]....KYSR-FM
El Paso, TX [*Television station call letters*]....XEJ-TV
El Pinto [*Mexico*] [*Seismograph station code, US Geological Survey*]....IIP
El Quisco [*Chile*] [*Seismograph station code, US Geological Survey*] [*Closed*]....ELQ
El Real [*Panama*] [*Airport symbol*]....ELE
El Recreo [*Colombia*] [*Airport symbol*]....ELJ
El Reno College [*Oklahoma*]....ERC
El Reno, OK [*Radio station call letters*]....KCAN
El Salvador [*MARC country of publication code*] [*Library of Congress*]....es
El Salvador [*Chile*] [*Seismograph station code, US Geological Survey*] [*Closed*]....ESC
El Salvador [*Chile*] [*Airport symbol*]....ESR
El Salvador [*MARC geographic area code*] [*Library of Congress*]....nces---
El Salvador [*Three-letter standard code*]....SLV
El Salvador [*Two-letter standard code*]....SV
El Salvador [*Aircraft nationality and registration mark*]....YS
El Segundo Public Library, El Segundo, CA [*Library symbol*]....CEs
El Senoussi Multiphasic Marital Inventory [*Psychology*]....SMMI
El Tocuyo [*Venezuela*] [*Seismograph station code, US Geological Survey*]....TOV
El Torito Restaurant [*NYSE symbol*]....ET
El Toro International Yacht Racing Association....ETIYRA
El Urogallo (Madrid) [*A publication*]....ELM
El Yopal [*Colombia*] [*Airport symbol*]....EYP
El Yunque [*Puerto Rico*] [*Seismograph station code, US Geological Survey*] [*Closed*]....EYP
Ela Area Public Library District, Lake Zurich, IL [*OCLC symbol*]....IHY
Elabuzskii Gosudarstvennyi Pedagogiceskii Institut. Ucenye Zapiski [*A publication*]....Elabuz Gos Ped Inst Ucen Zap
Elamite [*MARC language code*] [*Library of Congress*]....elx
Elan Pharmaceutical [*NASDAQ symbol*]....ELAN
Elapsed Greenwich Mean Time....EGMT
Elapsed Ground Time....EGT
Elapsed Maintenance Time....EMT
Elapsed Method of Training....EMT
Elapsed Spacecraft Time....ESCT
Elapsed Time....ET
Elapsed Time....ETIM
Elapsed-Time Code Generator....ETCG
Elapsed-Time Indicator....ETI
Elapsed Time/Maintenance Action....ETMA
Elapsed-Time Meter....ETM
Elastase Inhibitory Capacity [*Physiology*]....EIC
Elastic....ELAS
Elastic Braid Manufacturers Association [*Later, EFMC or EFMCNTA*]....EBMA
Elastic Diaphragm Switch Technology....EDST
Elastic Fabric Manufacturers Council of the Northern Textile Association....EFMC
Elastic Fabric Manufacturers Council of the Northern Textile Association....EFMCNTA
Elastic Fabric Manufacturers Institute [*Later, EFMC or EFMCNTA*]....EFMI
Elastic Hysteresis Constant....EHC
Elastic Limit....EL
Elastic Loop Mobility System [*NASA*]....ELMS
Elastic Plastic Membrane....EPM
Elastic Space Vehicle....ESV
Elastic Stop Nut Corp. of America [*NYSE symbol*] [*Delisted*]....ESN
Elastic Stop Nut Corp. of America....ESNA
Elastic Suspensor....ES
Elastic Top and Bottom [*British naval slang for WREN's knickers*]....ETB's
Elasticities of Substitution [*Statistics*]....ES
[*Modulus of*] **Elasticity** [*Young's modulus*] [*Symbol*] [*IUPAC*] [*See also Y, YME*]....E
Elasticity, Viscosity, and Thixotropy....EVT
Elastohydrodynamic....EHD
Elastohydrodynamic Lubrication....EHL
Elastomeric Insulation Material....EIM
Elastomeric Reusable Surface Insulation....ERSI
Elastomeric Shield Material [*Ablative*]....ESM
Elastomerics [*A publication*]....Elast
Elastosis Perforans Serpiginosa [*Medicine*]....EPS
Elat [*Israel*] [*Airport symbol*]....ETH
Elazig [*Turkey*] [*Seismograph station code, US Geological Survey*] [*Closed*]....ELA
Elazig [*Turkey*] [*Seismograph station code, US Geological Survey*]....ELZ
Elazig [*Turkey*] [*Airport symbol*]....EZS
Elba, AL [*Radio station call letters*]....WELB
Elba Island [*Italy*] [*Airport symbol*] [*Obsolete*]....EBA
Elbert County Public Library, Kiowa, CO [*Library symbol*]....CoK
Elbert Hubbard Library Museum, East Aurora, NY [*Library symbol*]....NEAuH
Elbert Ivey Memorial Library, Hickory, NC [*Library symbol*]....NcHy
Elberta Public Library, Elberta, MI [*Library symbol*]....MiElb
Elberton, GA [*Radio station call letters*]....WSGC
Elberton, GA [*Radio station call letters*]....WWRK
Elbit Computers Ltd. [*NASDAQ symbol*]....ELBTF
Elbow....ELB
Elbow Jerk [*Medicine*]....EJ
Elbow Orthosis [*Medicine*]....EO
Elbow Pitch....EP
Elbow-Wrist-Hand-Orthosis [*Medicine*]....EWHO
Elcho Island [*Australia*] [*Airport symbol*]....ELC
Elco [*Illinois*] [*Seismograph station code, US Geological Survey*]....ELC
Elco Industries, Inc. [*NASDAQ symbol*]....ELCN
Elcor Corp. [*NYSE symbol*]....ELK
Elder....ER
Elder-Beerman Stores [*NASDAQ symbol*]....ELDR
Elder Cottage Housing Opportunity....ECHO
Elder Craftsmen [*An association*]....EC
Elderhostel, Incorporated [*An association*]....EI
Eldest....E
Eldest....ELD
Eldest Son....ES
Eldon Carnegie Library, Eldon, IA [*Library symbol*]....IaEld
Eldon Industrials, Inc. [*NASDAQ symbol*]....ELDN
Eldon, MO [*Radio station call letters*]....KLDN
Eldorado Bancorp [*NASDAQ symbol*]....ELDB
Eldorado Gold & Explorations, Inc. [*NASDAQ symbol*]....ELDG
Eldorado, IL [*Radio station call letters*]....WKSI
Eldorado Mining & Refining Co., Port Hope, ON, Canada [*Library symbol*]....CaOPhE
Eldorado Nuclear Ltd., Ottawa, ON, Canada [*Library symbol*]....CaOOEN
Eldoret [*Kenya*] [*Airport symbol*] [*Obsolete*]....EDL
Eldred Rock, AK [*Location identifier*] [*FAA*]....ERO
Eleanor Association....EA
Eleanor Roosevelt Institute....ERI
Eleanor Roosevelt Institute for Cancer Research....ERICR
Elected Public Official....EPO
Elected Spanish Speaking Officials....ESSO
Election....EL
Election....ELECT
Election District....ED
Election Laws....EL
Elective Cosmetic Surgery....ECS
Electra Data Management System....EDMS
Electric....EL
Electric....ELEC
Electric Accounting Machine [*or Methods*]....EAM
Electric Accounting Machine and Electronic Data Processing Machine....EAMEDPM
Electric Accounting Machine Unit....EAMU
Electric Arc Furnace [*Steelmaking*]....EAF
Electric Arc Metallizing Gun....EAMG
Electric Arc Shock Tunnel [*NASA*]....EAST
Electric Arc Weld....EAW
Electric Auto Association....EAA
Electric Beam Exposure System [*Integrated circuit*] [*Bell Laboratories*]....EBES
Electric Bilge Pump....EBP
Electric Bomb Fuze....EBF
Electric Bond & Share Co. [*NYSE symbol*] [*Delisted*]....EBS
Electric Brain Stimulator....EBS
Electric Car Racing Association....ECRA
Electric [*or Electronic*] **Cipher** [*or Coding*] **Machine**....ECM
Electric Cipher [*or Coding*] **Machine Repairman** [*Navy rating*]....EC
Electric Circuit Test Set....ECTS
Electric Clock Valve....ECV
Electric Comfort Conditioning Journal [*A publication*]....Electr Comf Cond J
Electric Comfort Conditioning News [*A publication*]....Elec Comft
Electric Comfort Conditioning News [*A publication*]....Electr Comf Cond News
Electric Companies' Advertising Program....ECAP
Electric Companies' Public Information Program....ECPIP
Electric Consumers Information Committee....ECIC
Electric Contact....ELCTC
Electric Contact Brush....ELCTCBR
Electric Contact Ring....ELCTRG
Electric Control Drive....ECD
Electric Current....EC
Electric Current [*Symbol*] [*IUPAC*]....I
Electric Current Density [*Symbol*] [*IUPAC*]....J
Electric Delay Line....EDL
Electric Depth Finder....EDF
Electric Diaphragm Switch Technique [*IBM Corp.*]....EDST
Electric-Discharge Convection LASER [*Navy*]....EDCL
Electric Displacement [*Symbol*]....D
Electric Displacement Density....EDD

Electric Double Layer ... EDL
Electric Drive Mechanism ... EDM
Electric Dynamic [*Motors*] ... ED
Electric Dynamometer [*Engineering*] ... EDYNMT
Electric Energy Association [*Later, EEI*] ... EEA
Electric Feedback ... EFB
Electric Field Gradient [*of crystals*] ... EFG
Electric Field-Induced Spectra ... EFS
Electric Field Meter ... EFM
Electric Field Strength [*Symbol*] ... E
Electric Field Strength ... EFS
Electric Field Vector ... EFV
Electric Flow Field ... EFF
Electric Flux Density ... EFD
Electric Forum [*A publication*] ... Electr Forum
Electric Furnace Conference Proceedings. Metallurgical Society of AIME. Iron and Steel Division [*A publication*] ... Elec Furnace Conf Proc AIME
Electric Furnace Conference Proceedings. Metallurgical Society of AIME. Iron and Steel Division [*A publication*] ... Electr Furn Proc Metall Soc AIME
Electric Fuse Manufacturers Guild [*Defunct*] ... EFMG
Electric Glue Gun ... EGG
Electric Ground Power System [*Aerospace*] ... EGPS
Electric Heart Vector [*Cardiology*] ... EHV
Electric Heater ... EH
Electric Heating Association ... EHA
Electric Heating Unit ... EHU
Electric Home and Farm Authority [*Terminated, 1947*] ... EHFA
Electric Horsepower ... EHP
Electric Hose & Rubber Co. [*American Stock Exchange symbol*] [*Delisted*] ... EH
Electric and Hybrid Vehicles ... EHV
Electric Induction Oven ... EIO
Electric Journal [*A publication*] ... Elect J
Electric Junction Equation ... EJE
Electric Light ... EL
Electric Light Orchestra [*Rock music group*] ... ELO
Electric Light and Power [*A publication*] ... Electr Light & Power
Electric Light and Power (Boston) [*A publication*] ... Electr Light Power (Boston)
Electric Light and Power Group ... ELPG
Electric Limit Switch ... ELS
Electric Machines and Electromechanics [*A publication*] ... Electr Mach Electromech
Electric Motor Driven ... EMD
Electric & Musical Industries [*later, EMI Ltd.*] **Analogue Computer** ... EMIAC
Electric Organ Discharge [*Electrophysiology*] ... EOD
Electric Overhead Crane Institute [*Later, Crane Manufacturers Association of America*] ... EOCI
Electric Overhead Travelling ... EOT
Electric Perspectives [*A publication*] ... Electr Perspect
Electric Plant Control Panel ... EPCP
Electric Polarization Vector ... EPV
Electric Potential [*Symbol*] [*IUPAC*] ... V
Electric [*or Electrical*] **Power** ... EP
Electric Power Database [*Research and Development Information System*] [*Electric Power Research Institute*] [*Information service*] ... EPD/RDIS
Electric Power Distribution ... EPD
Electric Power Generation System ... EPGS
Electric Power Research Institute ... EPRI
Electric Power Research Institute, Palo Alto, CA [*Library symbol*] ... CPaE
Electric Power Research Institute (Report) EPRI AF [*A publication*] ... Electr Power Res Inst (Rep) EPRI AF
Electric Power Research Institute (Report) EPRI EA [*A publication*] ... Electr Power Res Inst (Rep) EPRI EA
Electric Power Research Institute (Report) EPRI EL [*A publication*] ... Electr Power Res Inst (Rep) EPRI EL
Electric Power Research Institute (Report) EPRI EM [*A publication*] ... Electr Power Res Inst (Rep) EPRI EM
Electric Power Research Institute (Report) EPRI ER [*A publication*] ... Electr Power Res Inst (Rep) EPRI ER
Electric Power Research Institute (Report) EPRI FP [*A publication*] ... Electr Power Res Inst (Rep) EPRI FP
Electric Power Research Institute (Report) EPRI NP [*A publication*] ... Electr Power Res Inst (Rep) EPRI NP
Electric Power Source ... EPS
Electric Power Statistics [*A publication*] ... EPST
Electric Power Systems Research [*A publication*] ... Electr Power Syst Res
Electric Powered Vehicle ... EPV
Electric Pressure Wave ... EPW
Electric Primer ... EP
Electric Process Heating ... EPH
Electric Propulsion System ... EPS
Electric Propulsion Trajectory Analysis ... EPTA
Electric Quadrupole-Quadrupole ... EQQ
Electric Railroaders Association ... ERA
Electric Railway Journal [*A publication*] ... Elec Ry J
Electric Regulation Company ... ERC
Electric Reliability Council of Texas [*Regional power council*] ... ERCOT
Electric Space Heating and Air Conditioning ... ESHAC
Electric Storage Battery ... ESB
Electric Storage Battery Co., Yardley, PA [*Library symbol*] ... PYarE
Electric Surface Current ... ESC
Electric Technology (USSR) [*A publication*] ... Elec Technol (USSR)
Electric Technology (USSR) [*A publication*] ... Electr Technol (USSR)
Electric Telegraph ... ET
Electric Tension [*Symbol*] [*IUPAC*] ... U
Electric Test Installation ... ETI
Electric Test Vehicle [*Department of Energy*] ... ETV
Electric Tool Institute [*Later, Power Tool Institute*] ... ETI
Electric Utility Pump ... EUP
Electric Vacuum Gyro ... EVG
Electric Vehicle ... EV
Electric Vehicle Council ... EVC
Electric Vehicle News [*A publication*] ... Elec Veh
Electric Vehicles [*A publication*] ... Electr Veh
Electric Water Cooler ... EWC
Electric Water Systems Council ... EWSC
Electric Wave Section Filter ... EWSF
Electrical ... ELECT
Electrical ... ELECTL
Electrical ... ELECTRCL
Electrical [*in British naval officers' ranks*] ... L
Electrical Accounting for the Security Industry [*IBM Corp.*] ... EASI
Electrical Aerosol Analyzer [*Instrumentation*] ... EAA
Electrical Apparatus Service Association [*Formerly, NISA*] ... EASA
Electrical Artificer [*Navy*] [*British*] ... EA
Electrical Automatic Support Equipment ... EASE
Electrical Cable Test Set ... ECTS
Electrical Checkout Equipment ... ECE
Electrical [*or Electronic*] **Circuit Analysis Program** ... ECAP
Electrical Circuit Interrupter ... ECI
Electrical Communication [*A publication*] ... Elec Com
Electrical Communication [*A publication*] ... Elec Commun
Electrical Communication [*A publication*] ... Electr Commun
Electrical Communication Laboratories. Technical Journal [*A publication*] ... Electr Commun Lab Tech J
Electrical Conductivity ... EC
Electrical Connector Subassembly ... ECS
Electrical Construction and Maintenance [*A publication*] ... Elec Constr Maint
Electrical Contact Plate ... ECP
Electrical Control Activity ... ECA
Electrical Control Package ... ECP
Electrical Conversion Unit ... ECU
Electrical Coupling Display Unit ... ECDU
Electrical Deflection Indicator ... EDI
Electrical Department [*Navy*] [*British*] ... ED
Electrical Design Engineering ... EDE
Electrical Differential ... ED
Electrical Discharge LASER ... EDL
Electrical Discharge [*or Electrodischarge*] **Machine** [*or Machining*] ... EDM
Electrical Discharge Tube ... EDT
Electrical Distribution Unit ... EDU
Electrical and Electromagnetic Interference ... EEI
Electrical/Electronic ... E/E
Electrical and Electronic Abstracts [*United Kingdom*] [*A publication*] ... EEA
Electrical and Electronic Abstracts [*A publication*] ... Elec & Electron Abstr
Electrical, Electronic, and Electromechanical ... EEE
Electrical and Electronic Measurement and Test Instrumentation Conference ... EEMTIC
Electrical and Electronic Properties of Materials ... EEPM
Electrical and Electronics Commission ... EEC
Electrical/Electronics Insulation Conference [*Formerly, EIC*] ... EEIC
Electrical and Electronics Manufacturer [*A publication*] ... Elect Electron Mfr
Electrical-Electronics Materials Distributors Association ... EEMDA
Electrical Energy [*Symbol*] ... W
Electrical Engineer [*or Engineering*] ... EE
Electrical Engineer ... EENGR
Electrical Engineer [*A publication*] ... Electr Eng
Electrical Engineer (Johannesburg) [*A publication*] ... Electr Eng (Johannesburg)
Electrical Engineer (Melbourne) [*A publication*] ... Elec Eng (Melbourne)
Electrical Engineer (Melbourne) [*A publication*] ... Electr Eng (Melb)
Electrical Engineering [*A publication*] ... Elec Eng
Electrical Engineering Abstracts [*A publication*] ... EEA
Electrical Engineering Abstracts [*A publication*] ... Elec Eng Abstr
Electrical Engineering Exposition ... EEE
Electrical Engineering in Japan [*A publication*] ... Elec Eng Japan
Electrical Engineering in Japan [*A publication*] ... Elec En Jap
Electrical Engineering in Japan [*A publication*] ... Electr Eng Jap
Electrical Engineering Research Laboratory ... EERL
Electrical Engineering Review [*A publication*] ... Elec Eng Rev
Electrical Engineering Review [*A publication*] ... Electr Eng Rev
Electrical, Environmental, and Communications ... EECOM
Electrical, Environmental, Consumables, and Mechanical Systems ... EECOM
Electrical, Environmental Control, and Instrumentation Systems Specialist [*NASA*] ... EECIS
Electrical Equipment [*Fire classification*] ... C

Electrical Equipment [*A publication*]....Electr Equip
Electrical Equipment Representatives Association....EERA
Electrical Equipment Shelter....EES
Electrical Equipment Trailer....EET
Electrical Export Corporation [*Defunct*]....EEC
Electrical Field Current....EFC
Electrical Field-Flow Fractionation [*Electrochemical separation method*]....EFFF
Electrical Fitting Inventory Control Branch....EFICO
Electrical, General Instrumentation, and Lighting Engineer....EGIL
Electrical Generating Systems Marketing Association....EGSMA
Electrical Grapple Fixture....EGF
Electrical [*or Electronic*] **Ground-Support Equipment**....EGSE
Electrical Harness Assembly....EHA
Electrical Historical Foundation....EHF
Electrical Horology Society....EHS
Electrical Hull Penetration....EHP
Electrical India [*A publication*]....Electr India
Electrical Industry Study Board....EISB
Electrical Information Test....EIT
Electrical Installation Test....EIT
Electrical and Instrumentation Verification Tests [*NASA*]....EIVT
Electrical Insulation....EI
Electrical Insulation Conference [*Later, EEIC*]....EIC
Electrical Insulation Tape....EIT
Electrical Integration System....EIS
Electrical Interface Building [*NASA*]....EIB
Electrical Interface Verification Test [*NASA*]....EIVT
Electrical Intersystems Test....EIT
Electrical Journal [*A publication*]....Elec J
Electrical Kilowatts....EKW
Electrical Launch Support Equipment [*NASA*]....ELSE
Electrical Manufacturing [*A publication*]....Elec Manuf
Electrical Mate Test....EMT
Electrical Measurements and Standards Division [*National Bureau of Standards*]....EMSD
Electrical and Mechanical....E & M
Electrical and Mechanical Engineering [*or Engineers*]....EME
Electrical/Mechanical Power Generation Subsystem....EMPGS
Electrical Mechanical Tubing....EMT
Electrical Megawatt....EMW
Electrical Merchandising [*A publication*]....Elec Merch
Electrical Merchandising Week [*A publication*]....Elec Merch W
Electrical Metallic Tubing....EMT
Electrical Meter Kit....EMK
Electrical Multiplex....EMUX
Electrical News and Engineering [*A publication*]....Elec News Eng
Electrical News and Engineering [*A publication*]....Electr News Eng
Electrical Panel....EP
Electrical Potential Gradient Radiosonde [*Meteorology*]....EPGR
Electrical Power Conditioning, Distribution, and Control....EPCDC
Electrical Power and Distribution....EP & D
Electrical Power Distribution Box....EPDB
Electrical Power Distribution and Control....EPDC
Electrical Power Distribution and Control System....EPDCS
Electrical Power Distribution System....EPDS
Electrical Power Engineer [*A publication*]....Elect Pwr
Electrical Power Engineer [*A publication*]....Elect Pwr Engr
Electrical Power Generator....EPG
Electrical Power Level....EPL
Electrical Power Panel....EPP
Electrical Power Production Technician/Specialist....EPPT/S
Electrical Power/Pyro Sequential System....EPPS
Electrical Power Requirements Data....EPRD
Electrical Power Supply....EPS
Electrical Power System [*or Subsystem*]....EPS
Electrical Power System Test Facility [*NASA*]....EPSTF
Electrical Power Unit....EPU
Electrical Propulsion....EP
Electrical Prototype....EP
Electrical Quality Assurance Directorate [*British*]....EQD
Electrical [*or Electronic*] **Replaceable Assembly**....ERA
Electrical Reproduction Method of Accounting....ERMA
Electrical Research Association [*British*]....ERA
Electrical Research Association. ERA Report [*A publication*]....Elec Res Ass ERA Rep
Electrical Research Memorandum....ERM
Electrical Resistance....ER
Electrical Resistance Temperature....ERT
Electrical Resistance Temperature....TEMP
Electrical Resistance Weld....ERW
Electrical Response Activity....ERA
Electrical Review [*A publication*]....Elec R
Electrical Review [*A publication*]....Elec Rev
Electrical Review [*A publication*]....Elect Rev
Electrical Review [*A publication*]....Electr Rev
Electrical Review International [*A publication*]....Electr Rev Int
Electrical Rule Checker [*For integrated circuitry*]....ERC
Electrical Sign Manufacturers Association....ESMA
Electrical Simulation of the Brain....ESB
Electrical Spark Erosion....ELOX
Electrical Specification....ESPEC
Electrical Stimulating and Recording Unit....ESRU
Electrical Stimulation - Hot Boning [*Meat processing*]....ESHB
Electrical Stimulation of the Midbrain....ESM
Electrical Stimulus....ES
Electrical Stress Analysis....ESA
Electrical Supervisor [*A publication*]....Electr Superv
Electrical Supervisor [*A publication*]....Elect Supervis
Electrical Support Equipment....ESE
Electrical Survey-Net Adjuster....ESNA
Electrical System....ELS
Electrical System Design Report....ESDR
Electrical System Integration....ESI
Electrical Systems Branch [*NASA*]....ESB
Electrical Systems Panel [*Apollo Spacecraft Program Office*] [*NASA*]....ESP
Electrical Systems Repair Facilities....ESRF
Electrical Tactical Map....ETM
Electrical Technician/Electrician....ET/E
Electrical Techniques in Medicine and Biology....ETMB
Electrical Terminal Distributor....ETD
Electrical Terminal Nut....ETN
Electrical Test Setup [*NASA*]....ETS
Electrical Testing Laboratories, Inc.....ETL
Electrical Thermal Analysis....ETA
Electrical Thermal Generators....ETG
Electrical Time....ET
Electrical Time Base....ETB
Electrical Time Measurement....ETM
Electrical Time, Superquick....ETSQ
Electrical Times [*A publication*]....Electr Times
Electrical Times [*A publication*]....Elect Times
Electrical Tough Pitch [*Copper*]....ETP
Electrical Trades Union [*British*]....ETU
Electrical Transcription....ET
Electrical Welding Machine....EWM
Electrical West [*A publication*]....Elec West
Electrical and Wireless Operators [*Air Force*] [*British*]....EWO
Electrical Women's Round Table....EWRT
Electrical World [*A publication*]....Electr World
Electrical World [*A publication*]....Elec World
Electrical Zero....EZ
Electrically....ELECTLY
Electrically Activated Bank Release Device....EABRD
Electrically Alterable Device....EAD
Electrically Alterable Memory [*Data processing*]....EAM
Electrically Alterable Programable Read-Only Memory [*Data processing*]....EAPROM
Electrically Alterable Read-Only Memory [*Data processing*]....EAROM
Electrically Alterable Read-Only Store [*Data processing*]....EAROS
Electrically Calibrated Pyroelectric Radiometer....ECPR
Electrically Compensated Pyrometer....ECP
Electrically Conductive Film....ECF
Electrically Erasable, Programable, Read-Only Memory [*Data processing*]....EEPROM
Electrically Eraseable Read-Only Memory [*Data processing*]....EEROM
Electrically Initiated Explosive Device....EIED
Electrically Insulated Coating....EIC
Electrically Operated Depressurization Valve....ELDV
Electrically Operated Valve....ELV
Electrically Operated Valve....EOV
Electrically Polarized [*Relay*]....EP
Electrically Programable Read-Only Memory [*Data processing*]....EPROM
Electrically Scanned Microwave Radiometer [*NASA*]....ESMR
Electrically Steerable Antenna Feed Techniques....ESAFT
Electrically Supported [*or Suspended*] **Accelerometer**....ESA
Electrically Supported [*or Suspended*] **Gyro Accelerometer**....ESGA
Electrically [*or Electrostatically*] **Suspended Gyro**....ESG
Electrically Suspended Gyro Navigation....ESGN
Electrically Transmitted Message....ETM
Electrically Transmitted Unsatisfactory Report....EUR
Electrically Tuned Antenna Coupler....ETAC
Electrician....ELECN
Electrician's Mate [*Navy rating*]....EM
Electrician's Mate, Chief [*Navy rating*]....EMC
Electrician's Mate, Construction Battalion [*Navy rating*] [*Obsolete*]....EMCB
Electrician's Mate, Construction Battalion, Communications [*Navy rating*] [*Obsolete*]....EMCBC
Electrician's Mate, Construction Battalion, Draftsman [*Navy rating*] [*Obsolete*]....EMCBD
Electrician's Mate, Construction Battalion, General [*Navy rating*] [*Obsolete*]....EMCBG
Electrician's Mate, Construction Battalion, Line and Station [*Navy rating*] [*Obsolete*]....EMCBL
Electrician's Mate, Fireman [*Navy rating*]....EMFN
Electrician's Mate, Fireman Apprentice [*Navy rating*]....EMFA
Electrician's Mate, First Class [*Navy rating*]....EM1
Electrician's Mate, Master Chief [*Navy rating*]....EMCM
Electrician's Mate, Seaman [*Navy rating*]....EMSN
Electrician's Mate, Seaman Apprentice [*Navy rating*]....EMSA
Electrician's Mate, Second Class [*Navy rating*]....EM2
Electrician's Mate, Senior Chief [*Navy rating*]....EMCS

Electrician's Mate, Ship Repair [*Navy rating*] [*Obsolete*] .... EMSR
Electrician's Mate, Ship Repair, General Electrician [*Navy rating*] [*Obsolete*] ....EMSRG
Electrician's Mate, Ship Repair, I.C. Repairman [*Navy rating*] [*Obsolete*] .... EMSRT
Electrician's Mate, Ship Repair, Shop Electrician [*Navy rating*] [*Obsolete*] .... EMSRS
Electrician's Mate, Telephone [*Coast Guard rating*] [*Obsolete*].............. EMT
Electrician's Mate, Third Class [*Navy rating*]............... EM3
Electricien Industriel [*A publication*].................... Electr Ind
Electricite Automobile [*A publication*] .... Electr Automob
Electricite-Electronique Moderne [*A publication*]........... Electr-Electron Mod
Electricite de France [*National electric company*] ....EDF
Electricity ....ELECTY
Electricity Board [*British*] ....EB
Electricity Consumers Resource Council .... ELCON
Electricity Council [*British*] ....EC
Electricity Council Research Center [*British*].................ECRC
Electricity on the Farm Magazine [*A publication*].................. Elec Farm Mag
Electricity Supply Union [*British*] ....ESU
[*The*] Electrification Council ....EC
[*The*] Electrification Council ....TEC
Electro Audio Dynamics, Inc. [*American Stock Exchange symbol*]......... EAD
Electro-Biology, Incorporated [*NASDAQ symbol*]..................EBII
Electro-Catheter Corp. [*NASDAQ symbol*] ....ECTH
Electro-Flux Remelting [*Metal industry*] ....EFR
Electro-Machine Fixture ....EMF
Electro-Motive Division [*General Motors Corp.*]..................EMD
Electro-Motorische Kraft [*Electromotive Force*] [*German*] ....EMK
Electro-Nucleonics [*NASDAQ symbol*] ....ENUC
Electro-Optic Digital Deflector.............................EODD
Electro-Optic Direction Sensor..............................EODS
Electro-Optic Display ....EOD
Electro-Optic Display Test Chamber ....EODTC
Electro-Optic Force.......................................EOF
Electro-Optic Light Valve..................................EOLV
Electro-Optic Projector....................................EOP
Electro-Optic Test Chamber ....EOTC
Electro-Optical...EO
Electro-Optical Alignment Unit.............................EOAU
Electro-Optical Area Correlator [*Missile guidance system*] .... EAC
Electro-Optical Countermeasures..........................EOCM
Electro-Optical Glide Bomb ....EOGB
Electro-Optical Identification and Tracking System ....EOITS
Electro-Optical Light Modulator ....EOLM
Electro-Optical Modulator ....EOM
Electro-Optical Research ....EOR
Electro-Optical Sensor System [*Navy*]........................EOSS
Electro-Optical Sensors Atmospheric Effects Library .... E-O SAEL
Electro-Optical Simulation System [*for missiles*] [*Army*] ....EOSS
Electro-Optical Systems Design [*A publication*]...........Electro-Opt Syst Des
Electro-Optical Systems Design [*A publication*] ....Electro-Opt Systems
Electro-Optical Systems, Inc. [*Subsidiary of Xerox Corp.*]...................EOS
Electro-Optical Systems, Inc., Pasadena, CA [*Library symbol*]............ CPEI
Electro-Optical Technology Program Office [*Navy*]................EOPTO
Electro-Optical Tracking Device.............................EOTD
Electro-Optical Unit.......................................EOU
Electro-Optical Viewing System ....EOVS
Electro-Optical Viewing System ....EVS
Electro-Optical Visual Sensors [*Hughes Aircraft Co.*]................EVS
Electro-Optical Weapons System ....EOWS
Electro-Optics Series [*A publication*]..................Electro Opt Ser
Electro-Rent Corporation [*NASDAQ symbol*] .... ELRC
Electro-Revue [*A publication*]........................ Electro-Rev
Electro Science Laboratory [*Ohio State University*] ....ESL
Electro Scientific [*NASDAQ symbol*]..........................ESIO
Electro Sensor Panel [*Toyota*].............................ESP
Electro-Sensors [*NASDAQ symbol*] ....ELSE
Electro-Techniek [*A publication*]........................Electro-Tech
Electro-Technology [*A publication*].......................Electro-Tech
Electro-Technology (New York) [*A publication*].............. Electro-Technol (NY)
Electroacoustic Systems Laboratory .... EASL
Electroacoustic Torpedo Countermeasure ....ETC
Electroacupuncture ....EAP
Electroaerosol Therapy [*Medicine*] ....EAT
Electroanalytical Abstracts [*A publication*] .... Electroanal Abstr
Electroantennogram [*Entomology*] ....EAG
Electrocardiocorder [*Medicine*]...........................ECC
Electrocardiogram [*Also, EK, EKG*] [*Medicine*].................ECG
Electrocardiogram [*Also, ECG, EKG*] [*Medicine*]................EK
Electrocardiogram [*Also, ECG, EK*] [*Medicine*].................EKG
Electrocardiogram Simulator ....EKS
Electrocardiographic Amplifier ....EA
Electrocardiography and Basal Metabolism Technician [*Navy*] ....ELT
Electrocardioscanner ....ECS
Electrochemical [*or Electrochemistry*] ....EC
Electrochemical Cathodes ....ECC
Electrochemical Debarring ....ECD
Electrochemical Detector [*Instrumentation*]....................ED
Electrochemical Diffused-Collector Transistor ....ECDC
Electrochemical Fuel Cell ....EFC

Electrochemical Grinding ....ECG
Electrochemical Machining.................................ECM
Electrochemical Potential Gradient.........................ECPOG
Electrochemical Reaction ....ECR
Electrochemical Relaxation Methods ....ERM
Electrochemical Society...................................ECS
Electrochemical Society...................................ES
Electrochemical Society. Journal [*A publication*].............. Electrochem Soc J
Electrochemical Technology [*A publication*]................. Electrochem Tech
Electrochemical Technology [*A publication*].............. Electrochem Technol
Electrochemical Time Indicator [*Army*]......................ETI
Electrochemical Unit ....ECU
Electrochemically Modulated Infrared Reflectance Spectroscopy .... EMIRS
Electrochemiluminescence.................................ECL
Electrochemistry..ELECTROCHEM
Electrochemistry in Industrial Processing and Biology [*A publication*]....................Electrochem Ind Process & Biol
Electrochemistry in Industrial Processing and Biology (English Translation) [*A publication*] .... Electrochem Ind Process Biol (Engl Transl)
Electrochemistry of Molten and Solid Electrolytes [*A publication*]....................Electrochem Molten and Solid Electrolytes
Electrochimica Acta [*A publication*]....................Electr Act
Electrochimica Acta [*A publication*]....................Electrochim Acta
Electrochimica Metallorum [*A publication*] .... Electrochim Metal
Electrochromic Display [*For instruments*] ....ECD
Electrocoating...EC
Electrocomponent Science and Technology [*A publication*] .... Electrocomponent Sci Technol
Electrocomponent Science and Technology [*A publication*] .... Electrocompon Sci Technol
Electroconvulsive Shock ....ECS
Electroconvulsive Therapy [*or Treatment*] [*Medicine*]..............ECT
Electrocorticogram [*or Electrocorticographic*] ....ECOG
Electrode...ELCTD
Electrode Dark Current ....EDC
Electrode Electrostatic Precipitator ....EEP
Electrode Film Barrier ....EFB
Electrode Heater Kit ....EHK
Electrode Potential .... E
Electrode Track ....ET
Electrodeless Discharge Lamp ....EDL
Electrodeposition Memo ....EM
Electrodeposition and Surface Treatment [*A publication*] .... Electrodeposition & Surf Treat
Electrodermal Audiometry [*Otolaryngology*]...................EDA
Electrodermal Response ....EDR
Electrodesiccation [*Medicine*]............................EDN
Electrodiagnosis [*Medicine*].............................EDX
Electrodialysis...ED
Electrodialysis Reversing ....EDR
Electrodynamic ....ED
Electrodynamic Explorer [*NASA*] ....EE
Electroencephalogram [*or Electroencephalography*] [*Medicine*]............EEG
Electroencephalography and Clinical Neurophysiology [*A publication*]......................ECNEA
Electroencephalography and Clinical Neurophysiology [*A publication*] .... EEG Cl Neur
Electroencephalography and Clinical Neurophysiology [*A publication*]....................Electroencephalogr Clin Neurophysiol
Electroencephalography and Clinical Neurophysiology [*A publication*]....................Electroenceph Clin Neurophysiol
Electroencephalography and Clinical Neurophysiology. Supplement [*A publication*] .... Electroencephalogr Clin Neurophysiol Suppl
Electroencephalography Technician [*Navy*] ....ENC
Electroendosmosis [*Analytical biochemistry*] ....EEO
Electrofluid Converter ....EFC
Electrofluid Dynamic [*Process*]...........................EFD
Electrogasdynamic [*Generator*]...........................EGD
Electrograph...EOG
Electrographic Corp. [*American Stock Exchange symbol*] [*Delisted*] ...... EEG
Electrohydraulic...ELECTHYDR
Electrohydraulic...ELHYD
Electrohydraulic Actuator ....EHA
Electrohydraulic Forming..................................EHF
Electrohydraulic Motor....................................EHM
Electrohydraulic Pulse Motor...............................EHPM
Electrohydraulic Valve....................................EHV
Electrohydrodynamic Heat Pipe [*NASA*] ....EHDHP
Electrohydrodynamics....................................EHD
Electroimmunoassay [*Clinical medicine*] ....EIA
Electrokymogram...EKY
Electroless Nickel Plating..................................ENP
Electroluminescence......................................EL
Electroluminescent Diode..................................ELD
Electroluminescent Ferroelectric ....ELF
Electroluminescent Ferroelectric Cell ....ELFC
Electroluminescent-Photoconductive........................EL-PC
Electroluminescent-Photoelectric...........................ELPE
Electroluminescent Quantum Counter.......................ELQC

Electroluminescent Vertical Indication System ... ELVIS
Electrolysis Society of America ... ESA
Electrolyte ... ELCTLT
Electrolyte ... ELECT
Electrolyte Imbalance [*Physiology*] ... EI
Electrolyte and Steroid-Produced Cardiopathy [*Characterized by*] **Necrosis** [*Medicine*] ... ESCN
Electrolytic ... ELECTL
Electrolytic Biological Oxygen Demand ... E/BOD
Electrolytic Capacitor ... ELCO
Electrolytic Fused-Salt Process ... EFSP
Electrolytic Grinding ... ELG
Electrolytic Manganese Dioxide [*For use in batteries*] ... EMD
Electrolytic Plunge Grinder ... EPG
Electromagnetic ... ELECTMG
Electromagnetic ... EM
Electromagnetic Accelerometer [*Navigation*] ... EMA
Electromagnetic Amplifying Lens ... EAL
Electromagnetic Analysis ... EMA
Electromagnetic Compatibility ... EMC
Electromagnetic Compatibility Advisory Board ... EMCAB
Electromagnetic Compatibility Analysis Center [*FAA*] ... ECAC
Electromagnetic Compatibility Program [*Air Force*] ... ECP
Electromagnetic Compatibility Program [*Air Force*] ... EMCP
Electromagnetic Compatibility Standardization [*Program*] ... EMCS
Electromagnetic Compatibility Test Plan ... EMCTP
Electromagnetic Cyclotron ... EMC
Electromagnetic Effects Capability ... EMEC
Electromagnetic Effects Laboratory [*Army*] ... EEL
Electromagnetic Energy ... EME
Electromagnetic Energy Environment Criteria [*Army*] ... EEEC
Electromagnetic Environment Analysis ... EEA
Electromagnetic Environment Experiment [*NASA*] ... EEE
Electromagnetic Environment Generator ... EMEG
Electromagnetic Environment Recorder ... EMER
Electromagnetic Environment Simulator ... EES
Electromagnetic Environment Synthesizer ... ENSYN
Electromagnetic Environment Test Facility [*Army*] ... EMETF
Electromagnetic Flowmeter ... EMFM
Electromagnetic Form Factor ... EMFF
Electromagnetic Gyro ... EMG
Electromagnetic Induction Tweeter ... EMIT
Electromagnetic Intelligence ... ELMINT
Electromagnetic Intelligence ... EMINT
Electromagnetic Intelligence Collection System ... EICS
Electromagnetic Intelligence System ... EIS
Electromagnetic Intelligence System ... EMIS
Electromagnetic Interference ... EI
Electromagnetic Interference ... EMI
Electromagnetic Interference Control Engineer ... EMICE
Electromagnetic Interference Control Group ... EICG
Electromagnetic Interference Test System [*Navy*] ... EMITS
Electromagnetic Interference Testing ... EIT
Electromagnetic Interference Testing ... EMIT
Electromagnetic Intrusion Detector ... EMID
Electromagnetic Measurement ... EMM
Electromagnetic Performance of Air and Ship Systems ... EMPASS
Electromagnetic Propagation Working Group [*Army*] ... EPWG
Electromagnetic Pulse ... EMP
Electromagnetic Pulse Radiation Environment Simulator for Ships [*Navy*] ... EMPRESS
Electromagnetic Pulse Simulator ... EMPS
Electromagnetic Quiet ... EMQ
Electromagnetic Radiation ... EMR
Electromagnetic Radiation Advisory Council ... ERAC
Electromagnetic Radiation Generator ... EMRG
Electromagnetic Radiation Generator ... ERG
Electromagnetic Radiation Management Advisory Council [*US Government*] ... ERMAC
Electromagnetic Radiation Project Office [*Navy*] ... EMRPO
Electromagnetic Radiation Source Elimination ... ERASE
Electromagnetic Relief Valve [*Engineering instrumentation*] ... ERV
Electromagnetic Sciences [*NASDAQ symbol*] ... ELMG
Electromagnetic Simulation Unit ... EMSU
Electromagnetic Storage ... ES
Electromagnetic Submarine [*Navy*] ... EMS
Electromagnetic Surveillance [*Air Force*] ... EMS
Electromagnetic Susceptibility ... EMS
Electromagnetic Switching ... ES
Electromagnetic Systems Laboratories, Inc. ... ESL
Electromagnetic Technology ... EMTECH
Electromagnetic Test Environment ... EMTE
Electromagnetic Test Environment ... ETE
Electromagnetic Test Environment Data System ... EMTEDS
Electromagnetic Test Environment Data System ... ETEDS
Electromagnetic Thickness Tool [*Gas well*] ... ETT
Electromagnetic Unit ... EMU
Electromagnetic Velocity ... EMV
Electromagnetic Vibrating Feeder ... EVF
Electromagnetic Vulnerability ... EMV
Electromagnetic Warfare ... EMW
Electromagnetic Warfare and Communications Laboratory ... EWCL
Electromagnetic Wave ... EMW
Electromagnetic Wave Amplification by Stimulated Emission of Radiation ... EWASER
Electromagnetic Wave Energy Converter [*Solar energy conversion*] ... EWEC
Electromagnetic Wave Filter ... EWF
Electromagnetic Wave Form ... EMWF
Electromagnetic Window ... EMW
Electromechanical ... ELECTMECH
Electromechanical ... ELMCH
Electromechanical ... EM
Electromechanical Averaging Circuit ... EMAC
Electromechanical Design [*A publication*] ... Electromech Des
Electromechanical Laboratories ... EML
Electromechanical Linear Actuator ... EMLA
Electromechanical Mockup ... EMM
Electromechanical Optical ... EMO
Electromechanical Power ... EMP
Electromechanical Research ... EMR
Electromechanical Stop Clock ... EMSC
Electromechanical Stop Clock ... ESC
Electromechanical Technology ... EMT
Electromedica [*A publication*] ... Electromed
Electromedics, Inc. [*NASDAQ symbol*] ... ELMD
Electrometer ... ELT
Electromicroscopic ... EM
Electromolecular Instrument Space Simulator ... EMISS
Electromolecular Propulsion [*Electrochemistry*] ... EMP
Electromotive Difference of Potential ... EMDP
Electromotive Force [*Symbol*] [*See also EMF, V*] [*Electrochemistry*] ... E
Electromotive Force [*See also E, V*] [*Electrochemistry*] ... EMF
Electromotive Force [*Symbol*] [*See also E, EMF*] [*Electrochemistry*] ... V
Electromyogram [*or Electromyographic*] ... EMG
Electromyogram Sensors [*For control of artificial limbs*] ... EMGORS
Electromyography and Clinical Neurophysiology [*A publication*] ... Electromyogr Clin Neurophysiol
Electromyosignal [*Data processing*] ... EMS
Electron [*A nuclear particle*] ... e
Electron ... ELCTRN
Electron [*A nuclear particle*] ... ELTRN
Electron Affinity [*Chemistry*] ... EA
Electron Beam ... EB
Electron-Beam-Addressed Memory [*Air Force*] ... EBAM
Electron Beam Control ... EBC
Electron Beam Cutting [*Engraving*] ... EBC
Electron Beam Evaporation Equipment ... EBEE
Electron Beam Evaporation Module ... EBEM
Electron Beam Evaporator ... EBE
Electron Beam Fusion Accelerator ... EBFA
Electron Beam Generator ... EBG
Electron Beam Gun ... EBG
Electron Beam Membrane Light Modulator [*Army*] ... EBMLM
Electron Beam Method ... EBM
Electron Beam Microanalysis ... EBM
Electron Beam Mode Discharge ... EBMD
Electron Beam Parametric Amplifier ... EBPA
Electron Beam Pattern Generator ... EBPG
Electron Beam Readout ... EBR
Electron Beam Recorder [*or Recording*] ... EBR
Electron Beam Regulator ... EBR
Electron Beam Semiconductor ... EBS
Electron Beam System ... EBS
Electron Beam [*Fluorescence*] **Technique** ... EBT
Electron Beam Transmission ... EBT
Electron Beam Welding ... EBW
Electron Binding Energy ... EBE
Electron-Bombarded Semiconductor ... EBS
Electron-Bombardment-Induced Conductivity ... EBIC
Electron-Bombardment-Induced Conductivity ... EBICON
Electron-Bombardment Ion Thrustor ... EIT
Electron-Bombardment Silicon ... EBS
Electron-Bombardment Vehicle ... EBV
Electron Capture [*Radioactivity*] ... EC
Electron-Capture Detection [*Instrumentation*] ... ECD
Electron-Capture Gas Chromatography ... ECGC
Electron Capture Gas-Liquid Chromatography ... ECGLC
Electron Coupled ... EC
Electron-Coupled Oscillator ... ECO
Electron Cyclotron Heating [*Nuclear energy*] ... ECH
Electron Decay Profile ... EDP
Electron Decay Rate ... EDR
Electron Density Map [*Crystallography*] ... EDM
Electron Devices ... ED
Electron Devices Data Service [*National Bureau of Standards*] ... EDDS
Electron Devices Society ... EDS
Electron Diffraction Instrument ... EDI
Electron Dipole-Dipole Polarization ... EDDP
Electron Dipole-Dipole Reservoir ... EDDR
Electron Donor Acceptor Complex ... EDAC
Electron Electron Double Resonance [*Physics*] ... ELDOR

Electron Energy Loss Spectroscopy [Also, ELS]............................EELS
Electron Energy Loss Spectroscopy [Also, EELS] ....ELS
Electron Engineering Co. of California, Santa Ana, CA [Library
    symbol]............................CStaE
Electron-Hole Drop [Semiconductor physics]............................EHD
Electron-Hole Potential Method [Physics]............................EHP
Electron Impact [Mass spectrometry]............................EI
Electron Impact Desorption............................EID
Electron Injection LASER............................EIL
Electron-Ion Recombination............................EIR
Electron Ionization [Spectrometry]............................EI
Electron Ionization Cross Section............................EIC
Electron Ionization Mass Spectrometry............................EIMS
Electron Kilovolt............................eKv
Electron Linear Accelerator............................ELA
Electron Megavolt............................eMv
Electron Microprobe............................EM
Electron Microprobe............................EMP
Electron Microprobe X-Ray Analyzer............................EMX
Electron Microprobe X-Ray Analyzer............................EMXA
Electron Microprobe X-Ray Fluorescence............................EMXRF
Electron Microscope Tomography............................EMT
Electron Microscopy Congress............................EMCON
Electron Microscopy and Microanalysis............................EMMA
Electron Microscopy [formerly, Microscope] Society of America........EMSA
Electron Microscopy Society of America. Annual Meeting.
    Proceedings [A publication]............................
            Electron Microsc Soc Am Annu Meet Proc
Electron Microscopy Society of Southern Africa. Proceedings [A
    publication]............................Electron Micros Soc Southern Afr Proc
Electron Multiplex Switch............................EMS
Electron N-Type Semiconductor Material............................N
Electron-Nuclear Double Resonance............................ENDOR
Electron Optic Tracking System............................EOTS
Electron Optical Recording Facility............................EORF
Electron Paramagnetic............................EP
Electron Paramagnetic Resonance............................EPR
Electron Paramagnetic Resonance Spectroscopy............................EPRS
Electron Photon............................EP
Electron Photon Cascade............................EPC
Electron Photon Interaction............................EPI
Electron Polar Zone............................EPZ
Electron Probe Analysis Society of America [Later, MAS]............EPASA
Electron Probe Analyzer............................EPA
Electron Probe Microanalysis [Also, EPMA]............................EPM
Electron Probe Microanalysis [Also, EPM]............................EPMA
Electron Probe X-Ray Microanalyzer............................EPXMA
Electron/Proton............................E/P
Electron-Proton Spectrometer............................EPS
Electron-Ray Tuning Indicator............................ERTI
Electron Readout Measurement............................EROM
Electron Reflection Coefficient............................ERC
Electron Ring Accelerator............................ERA
Electron Scan Antenna [FAA]............................ESA
Electron Spectroscopic Imaging............................ESI
Electron Spectroscopy for Chemical Analysis............................ESCA
Electron Spectroscopy Theory, Techniques, and Applications
    [A publication]............................Electron Spectrosc Theory Tech Appl
Electron Spin Polarization............................ESP
Electron Spin Resonance............................ESR
Electron Steady-State Fermi Level............................ESSFL
Electron-Stimulated Desorption [Spectroscopy]............................ESD
Electron-Stimulated Desorption Ion Angular Distribution [For
    study of surfaces]............................ESDIAD
Electron Stream Potential............................ESP
Electron Synchrotron [Nuclear energy]............................ES
Electron Technology [A publication]............................Electron Technol
Electron Technology. Quarterly [A publication]............Electron Technol Q
Electron Transfer............................ET
Electron Transfer [or Transporting] Particle............................ETP
Electron-Transferring Flavoprotein [Biochemistry]............................ETF
Electron Transmission Spectroscopy............................ETS
Electron Transport System............................ETS
Electron [or Electronic] Tube............................ET
Electron Tube Klystron............................ETK
Electron Tube Panel............................ETP
Electron Tube Rectifier............................ETR
Electron Tube, Triode............................ETT
Electron Volt............................eV
Electron Yield............................EY
Electron Yield Measurement............................EYM
Electron Yield Measurement System............................EYMS
Electronegative Gas Detector............................EGAD
Electronic............................ELECT
Electronic............................ELEK
Electronic............................ELTRNC
Electronic Accounting Machine............................EAM
Electronic Aerospace Systems Convention............................EASTCON
Electronic Air Inlet Controller............................EAIC
Electronic Analog Simulating Equipment............................EASE
Electronic Applications [A publication]............................Electron Appl

Electronic Applications. Bulletin [A publication]................Electron Appl Bull
Electronic Area Support Base [Air Force]............................EASB
Electronic Article Surveillance............................EAS
Electronic Assembly............................EA
Electronic Asset Control Center............................EACC
Electronic Associates, Inc. [NYSE symbol]............................EA
Electronic Associates, Incorporated............................EAI
Electronic Attitude and Direction Indicator............................EADI
Electronic Audio Recognition............................EAR
Electronic Audit Gauger............................EAGER
Electronic Australia [A publication]............................Elec Austr
Electronic Automatic Exchange [Also known as ESS]
    [Telecommunications]............................EAX
Electronic Automatic Machinery............................EAM
Electronic Band Spectra............................EBS
Electronic Batch Control............................EBC
Electronic Bearing-Time Recorder............................EBTR
Electronic Business [A publication]............................Elec Busns
Electronic Business Communications System............................EBCS
Electronic Cabling Unit............................ECU
Electronic Calculating Punch............................ECP
Electronic Calculator............................EC
Electronic Calibration............................EC
Electronic Calibration Center [National Bureau of Standards]............ECC
Electronic Calibration and Normalization............................ECAN
Electronic Capability [Designation for all US military aircraft]............E
Electronic Cascade Impactor [For aerosol analysis]............................ECI
Electronic Cash Register............................ECR
Electronic Central Office............................ECO
Electronic Centralized Aircraft Monitoring System............................ECAM
Electronic and Chaff Jamming............................JAFF
Electronic Checkout............................ECO
Electronic Circuit-Making Equipment [Data processing]............................ECME
Electronic Circuit Plug-In Unit............................ECPIU
Electronic Circuit Protector............................ECP
Electronic Coding............................EC
Electronic Combat............................EC
Electronic Command Signal Programer............................ECSP
Electronic Communications Division [Air Force]............................ECD
Electronic Communications, Incorporated............................ECI
Electronic Comparator............................EC
Electronic Component Checkout Area............................ECCA
Electronic Component Group............................ECG
Electronic Component Industries Association............................ELCINA
Electronic Component Reliability Center [Battelle Memorial
    Institute]............................ECRC
Electronic Component Research and Development Grant
    [Canada]............................ECRDG
Electronic Components [A publication]............................Electron Compon
Electronic Components [A publication]............................Electron Components
Electronic Components Code............................ECC
Electronic Components Information Center [Battelle Memorial
    Institute]............................ECIC
Electronic Components Laboratory............................ECL
Electronic Composing System............................ECS
Electronic Computer-Originated Mail [Postal Service]............................E-COM
Electronic Computer Programming Institute [Ceased operation,
    1976]............................ECPI
Electronic Computers............................EC
Electronic Computing............................ELECOM
Electronic Computing Health-Oriented [An association]............................ECHO
Electronic Computing, Hospital-Oriented............................ECHO
Electronic Conductivity............................EC
Electronic Confusion Area............................ECA
Electronic Connector Study Group............................ECSG
Electronic Contact Operate............................ECO
Electronic Control............................ELECTC
Electronic Control Amplifier............................ECA
Electronic Control Assembly - Engine Thrust............................ECET
Electronic Control Assembly - Pitch and Yaw............................ECPY
Electronic Control Assembly - Roll............................ECAR
Electronic Control Instrumentation............................ECI
Electronic Control Module [Instrumentation]............................ECM
Electronic Control Products............................ECP
Electronic Control Relay............................ECR
Electronic Control Sensor............................ECS
Electronic Control Switch............................ECS
Electronic Control Systems, Inc. [NASDAQ symbol]............................ELCS
Electronic Control Unit............................ECU
Electronic Conversion Unit............................ECU
Electronic Coordinatograph and Readout System............................ECARS
Electronic Counter............................EC
Electronic Counter-Countermeasures [Military]............................ECCM
Electronic Counter-Countermeasures Operator [Military]............ECCMO
Electronic Countermeasures [Military]............................E
Electronic Countermeasures [Military]............................ECM
Electronic Countermeasures Environment [Military]............................ECME
Electronic Countermeasures Exercise [Military]............................ECMEX
Electronic Countermeasures Mission [Military]............................ECMSN
Electronic Countermeasures Observer [Military]............................ECMob
Electronic Countermeasures Officer [Navy]............................ECMO

Electronic Countermeasures Program [Military]	ECMP
Electronic Countermeasures System [Military]	ECS
Electronic Countermeasures Training [Military]	ECMTNG
Electronic Data Communications	EDC
Electronic Data Display	EDD
Electronic Data Gathering Equipment	EDGE
Electronic Data Information Technical Service	EDITS
Electronic Data Interchange	EDI
Electronic Data Local Communications Central	EDLCC
Electronic Data Processing	EDP
Electronic Data Processing Center	EDPC
Electronic Data Processing Equipment	EDPE
Electronic Data Processing Machine [Also translated by some users of such equipment as "Every Damn Problem Multiplied"]	EDPM
Electronic Data Processing Magnetic [Tape]	EDPM
Electronic Data Processing System	EDAPS
Electronic Data Processing System	EDPS
Electronic Data Processing Test	EDPT
Electronic Data Remote Communications Complex	EDRCC
Electronic Data System	EDS
Electronic Data Systems Corp. [NYSE symbol]	EDS
Electronic Data Traffic Control Center	EDTCC
Electronic Data Transmission	EDT
Electronic Data Transmission Communications Central	EDTCC
Electronic Data Transmission Working Party [Army]	ELDATRAWP
Electronic Decoy Rocket	EDR
Electronic Defense Evaluator	EDE
Electronic Dehydration Dryer	EDD
Electronic Depressurizing Valve	EDV
Electronic Design [A publication]	Elec Des
Electronic Design [A publication]	Electron Des
Electronic Desk Calculator	EDC
Electronic Development	ED
Electronic Development and Compatibility Test Unit	EDCTU
Electronic Devices Quality Assurance	EDQA
Electronic Dew Point Sensor	EDPS
Electronic Dial Tone Speed Register [Bell System]	EDTSR
Electronic Differential Analyzer	EDA
Electronic Digital Analyzer	EDA
Electronic Digital Computer	EDC
Electronic Digital Tracking and Ranging	EDITAR
Electronic Digital-Vernier Analog Plotter	EDVAP
Electronic Discrete Sequential Automatic Computer	EDSAC
Electronic Discrete Variable Automatic Computer	EDVAC
Electronic Display	ED
Electronic Display Assembly	EDA
Electronic Display Panel	EDP
Electronic Display Unit	EDU
Electronic Distance Measuring	EDM
Electronic Distance Measuring Equipment	EDME
Electronic Distributors' Research Institute	EDRI
Electronic Dive Angle Control	EDAC
Electronic Drafting Machine	EDM
Electronic Editing [Telecommunications]	EE
Electronic Egg Exchange [Computer program]	EEX
Electronic Electrical Termination Building [NASA]	EETB
Electronic, Electro-Optic, and Infrared Countermeasures [A publication]	Countrmsrs
Electronic, Electro-Optic, and Infrared Countermeasures [A publication]	Electron Electro-Opt Infrared Countermeas
Electronic Emission Control	EMCON
Electronic Emission Intelligence [Military]	EEI
Electronic Emission Security	EES
Electronic Emitter Location System	EELS
Electronic Engine Control	EEC
Electronic Engineer	ECENGR
Electronic Engineering	EE
Electronic Engineering [London] [A publication]	Electr Eng
Electronic Engineering Co. of California [American Stock Exchange symbol] [Delisted]	EEC
Electronic Engineering Division [Coast Guard]	EED
Electronic Engineering (London) [A publication]	Electron Eng (Lond)
Electronic Engineering (Philadelphia) [A publication]	Electron Eng (Phila)
Electronic Engineering Times [A publication]	Elec Eng T
Electronic Engineers Master	EEM
Electronic Environment Simulator	EES
Electronic Environmental Test Facility	EETF
Electronic Equipment Committee [NASA]	EEC
Electronic Equipment Engineering [A publication]	EEE
Electronic Equipment Environment Survey	EEES
Electronic Equipment Maintenance Kit	EEMK
Electronic Equipment Modification	EEM
Electronic Equipment Monitoring	EEM
Electronic Equipment News [A publication]	Electron Equip News
Electronic Equipment Technical Committee [NASA]	EETC
Electronic Explosive Device	EED
Electronic Exposure Timer	EET
Electronic Failure Report	EFR
Electronic Failure Report Only	EFRO
Electronic Family Security Program [of Sun Life Assurance Company of Canada]	EFSP
Electronic Fetal Monitoring [Medicine]	EFM
Electronic Fiber Fineness Indicator	EFFI
Electronic Final Zero	EFZ
Electronic Financial Control	EFICON
Electronic Financial Systems CI A [NASDAQ symbol]	EFSIA
Electronic Firing Switches [Military]	EFS
Electronic Flash Approach System	EFAS
Electronic Flash Illuminator	EFI
Electronic Flight Control System	EFCS
Electronic Flight Data Accumulation Service	EFDAS
Electronic Flight Data and Recording System	EFDARS
Electronic Flight Instrument System	EFIS
Electronic Forum for Industry [British]	EFFI
Electronic Frequency Control	EFC
Electronic Frequency Selection	EFS
Electronic Fuel Injection	EFI
Electronic Fund Transfers at Point-of-Sale	EFTPOS
Electronic Funds Transfer [Banking]	EFT
Electronic Funds Transfer Association	EFTA
Electronic Funds Transfer System [Banking] [National Science Foundation]	EFTS
Electronic Geographic Coordinate Navigation System	EGECON
Electronic-Glide Slope	EGS
Electronic Grading Operator	EGO
Electronic Ground Automatic Destruct [Air Force]	EGAD
Electronic Ground Automatic Destruct Sequencer [Air Force]	EGADS
Electronic Guidance	EG
Electronic Guides for Standardizing Items of Procurement and Supply	EGSIPS
Electronic Gyro Compass	EGC
Electronic Height Indicator	EHI
Electronic Horizontal Situation Indicator	EHSI
Electronic Image Generator	EIG
Electronic Industries Association	EIA
Electronic Industries Association of Canada	EIAC
Electronic Industries Association - Japan	EIA-J
Electronic Industries and Tele-Tech [A publication]	Electronic Ind & Tele-Tech
Electronic Industry Show Corporation [An association]	EISC
Electronic Information Bulletin [Navy]	EIB
Electronic Information Exchange System	EIES
Electronic Installation	EI
Electronic Installation Plan	EIP
Electronic Installation Technician	EIT
Electronic Installation Verification Test [NASA]	EIVT
Electronic Instruction	EI
Electronic Instrument Digest [A publication]	EID
Electronic Instrument Manufacturers Exhibit	EIME
Electronic Instruments Limited [as in EIL electrode, used in biochemistry] [British]	EIL
Electronic Intelligence [or Intercept] [Meaning of ELINT determined by reference to before (Intercept) and after (Intelligence) analysis of reconnaissance mission results]	ELINT
Electronic Intelligence Analysis Processing Subsystem	EAPSS
Electronic Interface	EI
Electronic Interface Unit	EIU
Electronic Interference	EI
Electronic Intrusion Detection	EID
Electronic Jamming	EJ
Electronic Journalism	EJ
Electronic Key Telephone System	EKTS
Electronic Keyboard	EKB
Electronic Keyboard System	EKBS
Electronic Keyboard System	EKS
Electronic Keyboarding, Incorporated [Information service]	EKI
Electronic Knowledge Bank	EKB
Electronic Laboratories and Services	EL & S
Electronic Launching Equipment	ELE
Electronic Letter Sorting and Indicator Equipment	ELSIE
Electronic Library Association	ELA
Electronic Lie Detector	ELD
Electronic Line Indicator [Tennis]	ELI
Electronic Location Finder	ELF
Electronic Mail	EM
Electronic Mail Association	EMA
Electronic Mail Corporation of America [NASDAQ symbol]	EMCA
Electronic Mail Facility [Postal Service]	EMF
Electronic Mail Handling	EMH
Electronic Mail System [Postal Service]	EMS
Electronic Maintenance Assembly	EMA
Electronic Maintenance Engineering Association	EMEA
Electronic Maintenance Engineering Center [Military]	EMEC
Electronic Maintenance Ground Equipment	EMGE
Electronic Maintenance Inspector	EMI
Electronic Maintenance Proficiency Test	EMPT
Electronic Maintenance Technician [FAA]	EMT
Electronic Management System	EMS
Electronic Map Display	EMD
Electronic Material Bulletin [Army]	EMB
Electronic Material Change	EMC
Electronic Material Data Service	EMDS

Electronic Material Sciences Laboratory ... EMSL
Electronic Material Shipment Request [*Navy*] ... EMSR
Electronic Materials Information Service [*Institution of Electrical Engineers*] ... EMIS
Electronic Measuring [*A publication*] ... Electron Meas
Electronic Mechanic Technician ... ELMT
Electronic-Media Literacy [*or Literate*] ... E-ML
Electronic Medical System ... EMS
Electronic Memories & Magnetics Corp. [*NYSE symbol*] ... EMM
Electronic Memory Systems Organization [*Burroughs Corp.*] ... EMSO
Electronic Mind Tester ... EMT
Electronic Missile Acquisition ... EMA
Electronic Modules Corp. [*NASDAQ symbol*] ... EMOD
Electronic Moisture Recorder ... EMR
Electronic Motion Control Association ... EMCA
Electronic MRO [*Maintenance Repair Operation*] **Distributors Association** ... EMRODA
Electronic Multiplying Punches ... EMP
Electronic Music Review [*A publication*] ... Elec Mus R
Electronic News [*A publication*] ... Elec News
Electronic News [*A publication*] ... Electronic N
Electronic News [*A publication*] ... EN
Electronic News Gathering [*Television news coverage*] ... ENG
Electronic Nuclear Instrumentation Group ... ENIG
Electronic Null Detector ... END
Electronic Numerical Integrator and Calculator [*Early computer*] ... ENIAC
Electronic Operations Center [*Military*] ... EOC
Electronic Order of Battle ... EOB
Electronic Original Equipment Market ... EOEM
Electronic Overload Protection ... EOP
Electronic Package ... EP
Electronic Package Housing ... EPH
Electronic Packaging and Production [*A publication*] ... Electron Packag Prod
Electronic Parts Distributors' Show ... EPDS
Electronic Parts and Equipment ... EPE
Electronic Parts Manual ... EPM
Electronic Parts Reliability ... EPR
Electronic Patrol, Experimental ... EPX
Electronic Pest Control Association ... EPCA
Electronic Photochromic Integrating Cathode-Ray [*Tube*] ... EPIC
Electronic Point-of-Sale [*Data processing*] ... EPOS
Electronic Position Indicator ... EPI
Electronic Preferred Parts List [*Jet Propulsion Laboratory, NASA*] ... EPPL
Electronic Private Automatic Branch Exchange [*Telecommunications*] ... EPABX
Electronic Private Branch Exchange [*Communications*] ... EPBX
Electronic Procurement Regulation [*Defense Supply Agency*] ... EPR
Electronic Production Methods and Equipment [*A publication*] ... Electron Prod Methods & Equip
Electronic Production Resources Agency [*Military*] ... EPRA
Electronic Products Magazine [*A publication*] ... Electron Prod
Electronic Products Magazine [*A publication*] ... Electr Prod
Electronic Program Control ... EPC
Electronic Program Guide [*Cable TV programing service*] ... EPG
Electronic Programed Procurement Information ... EPPI
Electronic Progress [*A publication*] ... Elec Prog
Electronic Progress [*A publication*] ... Electron Prog
Electronic Properties Information Center [*DoD*] ... EPIC
Electronic Proving Ground [*Army*] ... EPG
Electronic Publication Technology Group ... EPTG
Electronic Publishing and Bookselling [*A publication*] ... EPB
Electronic Quality Assurance Test Equipment [*System*] [*Army*] ... EQUATE
Electronic RADAR ... ELRA
Electronic and Radio Engineer [*A publication*] ... Electronic & Radio Eng
Electronic Random Action Control ... ERAC
Electronic Random Number and Indicating Equipment [*Used for selecting winning premium bond numbers*] [*British*] ... ERNIE
Electronic Range Scoring Device ... ERSD
Electronic Reading Automation [*Information retrieval*] ... ERA
Electronic Reconnaissance ... ER
Electronic Reconnaissance ... EREC
Electronic Reconnaissance Access Set ... ERAS
Electronic Reconnaissance Accessory System ... ELRAC
Electronic Reconnaissance Procurement Division ... ERPD
Electronic Reconnaissance Set ... ERS
Electronic Reconnaissance Unit ... ERU
Electronic Recording Beam ... ERB
Electronic Recording Machine Accounting ... ERMA
Electronic Remote and Independent Control ... ERIC
Electronic Remote Switching ... ERS
Electronic Remote Switching ... ERX
Electronic Repair Parts Allowance List [*Navy*] ... ERPAL
Electronic Representatives Association ... ERA
Electronic Requirement Plan [*Navy*] ... ERP
Electronic Research Associates, Inc. [*American Stock Exchange symbol*] [*Delisted*] ... ERA
Electronic Research Association [*British*] ... ERA
Electronic Research and Development Command [*Army*] ... ERDC
Electronic Research Directorate [*Air Force*] ... ERD
Electronic Research Supply Agency ... ERSA
Electronic Resources Development Agency ... ERDA
Electronic Retina Computing Reader ... ERCR
Electronic [*or Experimental*] **Route Guidance System** [*Road sign aid*] [*Bureau of Public Roads*] ... ERGS
Electronic Sales-Marketing Association [*Defunct*] ... ESMA
Electronic Satellite Image Analysis Console [*NASA*] ... ESIAC
Electronic Scan Converter ... ESC
Electronic Scanning RADAR ... ESR
Electronic Scanning RADAR System ... ESRS
Electronic Scanning Spectrometer ... ESS
Electronic Scanning and Stabilizing Antenna ... ESSA
Electronic Section [*National Weather Service*] ... ES
Electronic Security [*Air Force*] ... ELSEC
Electronic Security Alarm [*Automobile theft preventive*] ... ESA
Electronic Security Profile [*of Equitable Life Assurance Society*] ... ESP
Electronic Security Surveillance ... ESS
Electronic Security System ... ESS
Electronic Seismic Photography ... ESP
Electronic Selective Switching Unit ... ESSU
Electronic Sequence Switching ... ESS
Electronic Sequencer Timer ... EST
Electronic Sequencing Unit [*for helicopters*] [*Army*] ... ESU
Electronic Shop Computer ... ESC
Electronic Shop Major [*Coast Guard*] ... ES
Electronic Shop Major Telephone and Teletype [*Coast Guard*] ... EST
Electronic Shop Minor [*Coast Guard*] ... ESM
Electronic Shop Minor Telephone and Teletype [*Coast Guard*] ... ESMT
Electronic Signaling and Indicating Equipment ... ELSIE
Electronic Sky Screen Equipment [*Air Force*] ... ELSSE
Electronic Social Transformation ... EST
Electronic Solid-State Wide-Angle Camera System ... ESSWACS
Electronic Specialist ... ECSP
Electronic Specialty Co. [*NYSE symbol*] [*Delisted*] ... ELS
Electronic Specialty Products [*NASDAQ symbol*] ... ESPID
Electronic Stacked Beam RADAR ... ESBR
Electronic Standard ... ES
Electronic Standard Procedure ... ESP
Electronic Standards Office [*Navy*] ... ESO
Electronic Stock Evaluator Corp. ... ESE
Electronic Subsystems Analysis ... ESA
Electronic Supervisory Control ... ESC
Electronic Supervisory Panel ... ESP
Electronic Supply Segment of the Navy Supply System ... ESSNSS
Electronic Supply Support Base [*Air Force*] ... ESSB
Electronic Support Equipment ... ESE
Electronic Support Laboratory ... ESL
Electronic Supporting Systems Project Office [*Air Force*] ... ESSPO
Electronic Surge Arrester ... ESA
Electronic Surveillance Measures ... ESM
Electronic Surveillance System ... ESS
Electronic Sweep Generator ... ESG
Electronic Switch Module ... ESM
Electronic Switching ... ES
Electronic Switching Center ... ESC
Electronic Switching System [*Also known as EAX*] [*Telecommunications*] ... ESS
Electronic Switching System Flow Chart ... ESSFLO
Electronic Switching Unit ... ESU
Electronic System for Control of Receipt Transactions ... ESCORT
Electronic System Evaluator ... ESE
Electronic System Integration ... ESI
Electronic System Precision Orbit Determination [*Air Force*] ... ESPOD
Electronic System Test Unit ... ESTU
Electronic Systems Center [*Air Force*] ... ESC
Electronic Systems Command [*Also, NESC*] [*Navy*] ... ELECSYSCOM
Electronic Systems Command [*Also, NESC*] [*Navy*] ... ESC
Electronic Systems Compatibility Facility [*NASA*] ... ESCF
Electronic Systems Compatibility Laboratory [*NASA*] ... ESCL
Electronic Systems Division [*AFSC*] ... ESD
Electronic Systems Division, Technical Documentary Reports [*AFSC*] ... ESD TDR
Electronic Systems Laboratory ... ESL
Electronic Systems Mockup ... ESMU
Electronic Systems Planning ... ESP
Electronic Systems Test Laboratory [*NASA*] ... ESTL
Electronic Systems Test Program [*NASA*] ... ESTP
Electronic Systems Test Set ... ESTS
Electronic Tabulating Corporation [*NASDAQ symbol*] ... ETCO
Electronic Tactical Action Report ... ECTAR
Electronic Tactical Display [*Military*] ... ETD
Electronic Technical Institute ... ETI
Electronic Technical Suitability Test ... ETST
Electronic Technician ... ELT
Electronic Technology Laboratory [*Air Force*] ... ETL
Electronic Telecommunication Switching System ... ETSS
Electronic Telegraph System ... ETS
Electronic Teleprinter Cryptographic Regenerative Repeater Mixer ... ETCRRM
Electronic Temperature Control ... ETC
Electronic Temperature Offset ... ETO
Electronic Tensile Tester ... ETT

Electronic Terms for Space Age Language .... ETSAL
Electronic Test .... ET
Electronic Test Block .... ETB
Electronic Test Equipment .... ETE
Electronic Test Set .... ETS
Electronic Test Stand .... ETS
Electronic Test Station .... ETS
Electronic Time Delay .... ETD
Electronic Timing Set .... ETS
Electronic Toll Center [*AT & T*] .... ETC
Electronic Trajectory Measurements Working Group [*IRIG*] .... ETMWG
Electronic Transformers .... ET
Electronic Translator System [*Bell System*] .... ETS
Electronic Translator Unit [*Communications*] .... ETU
Electronic Trouble Report .... ETR
Electronic Tuning Fork .... ETF
Electronic Turbine Governor .... ETG
Electronic Typewriter .... ET
Electronic Unit .... EU
Electronic Unit Design Section .... EUDS
Electronic Valve Specification .... EVS
Electronic Velocity Analyzer .... EVA
Electronic Verification of Account Number [*Social Security*] .... EVAN
Electronic Vibration Cutoff [*Aerospace*] .... EVC-O
Electronic Video Recording [*CBS Laboratories' brand name for tape cartridges of TV programs*] .... EVR
Electronic-Visual-Auditory Training Aid .... EVATA
Electronic Voice Phenomena [*Parapsychology*] .... EVP
Electronic Voice Switching .... EVS
Electronic Voltmeter .... EVM
Electronic Voltohmmeter .... EVOM
Electronic Vote Analysis [*Election poll*] .... EVA
Electronic Warfare .... ELWAR
Electronic Warfare .... EW
Electronic Warfare .... EWF
Electronic Warfare Anechoic Chamber .... EWAC
Electronic Warfare Control Ship [*Navy*] .... EWCS
Electronic Warfare Coordination Center .... EWCC
Electronic Warfare Coordinator .... EWC
Electronic Warfare Element .... EWE
Electronic Warfare Evaluation Simulator .... EWES
Electronic Warfare Exercise .... EWEX
Electronic Warfare Exercise in Port .... EWEXIPT
Electronic Warfare Ground Environment Threat Simulator .... EWGETS
Electronic Warfare Integrated Reprograming Concept .... EWIRC
Electronic Warfare Interface Connection Box .... EWICB
Electronic Warfare Laboratory [*Army*] .... EWL
Electronic Warfare Management Information System [*Air Force*] .... EWMIS
Electronic Warfare Office [*or Officer*] .... EWO
Electronic Warfare Officer Training .... EWOT
Electronic Warfare Operational System [*Air Force*] .... EWOS
Electronic Warfare Operations .... EWOPS
Electronic Warfare Plans .... EWP
Electronic Warfare Quick Reaction Capability .... EWQRC
Electronic Warfare Support Measures [*Formerly, EWSM*] .... ESM
Electronic Warfare Support Measures [*Later, ESM*] .... EWSM
Electronic Warfare System .... EWS
Electronic Warfare Tactical Environment Simulation .... EWTES
Electronic Warfare Tactics Trainer .... EWTT
Electronic Warfare Trainer .... EWT
Electronic Warfare Warning System .... EWWS
Electronic Wind Direction Indicator .... EWDI
Electronic Wind Speed Indicator .... EWSI
Electronic Wiring Intercommunication .... EWI
Electronica y Fisica Aplicada [*A publication*] .... Electron Fis Apl
Electronically Agile RADAR .... EAR
Electronically Controlled Automatic-Switching System .... ECASS
Electronically Controlled Telephone Exchange .... ECX
Electronically Scanned Array RADAR .... ESAR
Electronically Scanned Stacked Beam RADAR [*Program*] .... ESSBR
Electronically Scanning Airborne Intercept RADAR Antenna .... ESAIRA
Electronically Steerable Array RADAR .... ESAR
Electronically Steerable Phased Array [*SPADATS*] .... ESPA
Electronically Steerable Phased Array RADAR [*SPADATS*] .... ESPAR
Electronically Stimulated Incarnation Recall .... ESIR
Electronically Tunable Filter .... ETF
Electronically Tunable Parametric Amplifier .... ETPA
Electronically Tuned Receiver .... ETR
Electronically Tuned Receiver Tuner .... ETRT
Electronically Tuned Tuner .... ETT
Electronics .... ELCT
Electronics .... ELEC
Electronics .... ELECTRO
Electronics [*A publication*] .... Electron
Electronics Abstracts Journal [*A publication*] .... Electron Abstr J
Electronics and Aerospace Systems Convention .... EASCON
Electronics Australia [*A publication*] .... Electron Aust
Electronics Chassis .... EC
Electronics Command [*Army*] .... ECOM
Electronics Command Meteorological Support Agency .... ECMSA
Electronics and Communications Abstracts Journal [*A publication*] .... Electron & Communic Abstr J
Electronics and Communications in Japan [*A publication*] .... Electr Co J
Electronics and Communications in Japan [*A publication*] .... Electron Commun Japan
Electronics and Communications in Japan [*A publication*] .... Electron Commun Jpn
Electronics Component Test Area .... ECTA
Electronics and Control .... EC
Electronics Control Assembly .... ECA
Electronics Control System .... ECS
Electronics Corporation of America [*American Stock Exchange symbol*] .... ECA
Electronics Corporation of Israel [*NASDAQ symbol*] .... ECILF
Electronics to Electronics .... EE
Electronics Engineering Division [*Coast Guard*] .... EE
Electronics Exercise [*Military*] .... ELEX
Electronics Information Branch [*Navy*] .... EIB
Electronics Information and Planning [*A publication*] .... Electron Inf Plann
Electronics Information Test .... ELIT
Electronics Installation Bulletin .... EIB
Electronics Installation and Maintenance Bulletin .... EIMB
Electronics and Instrumentation [*A publication*] .... Electron Instrum
Electronics Interface Integrated Validation .... EIIV
Electronics Laboratory .... EL
Electronics Letters [*A publication*] .... Electr Lett
Electronics Letters [*A publication*] .... Electron Lett
Electronics Manufacturer [*A publication*] .... Electron Mfr
Electronics Manufacturers Association [*Defunct*] .... EMA
Electronics Material Officer .... EMO
Electronics Materiel Agency [*Army*] .... EMA
Electronics Materiel Support Agency [*Army*] .... EMSA
Electronics for Medicine .... EFM
Electronics, Missiles & Communications [*NASDAQ symbol*] .... ECIN
Electronics Panel .... EP
Electronics and Power [*A publication*] .... Electron & Power
Electronics and Power [*A publication*] .... Electron Power
Electronics and Power [*A publication*] .... Electron Pwr
Electronics and Power [*A publication*] .... Electr Pow
Electronics Precedence List Agency .... EPLA
Electronics Program [*Association of Independent Colleges and Schools specialization code*] .... E
Electronics Research Center [*NASA*] .... ERC
Electronics Research and Development Activity [*Army*] .... ERDA
Electronics Research and Development Activity Analysis [*Army*] .... ERDAA
Electronics Research and Development Command [*Army*] .... ERADCOM
Electronics Research and Development Command Atmospheric Sciences Laboratory [*Army*] .... ERADCOM/ASL
Electronics Research and Development Laboratory .... ELRDL
Electronics Research Laboratory [*MIT*] .... ERL
Electronics Small Business Council .... ESBC
Electronics Supply Office [*or Officer*] .... ESO
Electronics Systems Source .... ESS
Electronics Technical Field Office [*FAA*] .... ETFO
Electronics Technician .... ELTEC
Electronics Technician [*Navy rating*] .... ET
Electronics Technician, Communications [*Navy rating*] .... ETN
Electronics Technician, Communications Seaman [*Navy rating*] .... ETNSN
Electronics Technician, Communications Seaman Apprentice [*Navy rating*] .... ETNSA
Electronics Technician, First Class [*Navy rating*] ET1
Electronics Technician, Master Chief [*Navy rating*] .... ETCM
Electronics Technician, (RADAR) [*Navy rating*] .... ETR
Electronics Technician, (RADAR) Seaman [*Navy rating*] .... ETRSN
Electronics Technician, (RADAR) Seaman Apprentice [*Navy rating*] .... ETRSA
Electronics Technician, Second Class [*Navy rating*] ET2
Electronics Technician, Senior Chief [*Navy rating*] .... ETCS
Electronics Technician, Third Class [*Navy rating*] ET3
Electronics Technicians Association, International .... ETA-I
Electronics Technician's Mate [*Navy rating*] .... ETM
Electronics Technician's Mate, Ship Repair [*Navy rating*] .... ETMSR
Electronics Technology and Devices Laboratory [*Army*] .... ETDL
Electronics Test Equipment Coordination Group [*Military*] .... ETECG
Electronics Today [*A publication*] .... Electron Today
Electronics Training Group .... ETG
Electronics Weekly [*A publication*] .... Electron Wkly
Electronics World [*A publication*] .... Electron World
Electronique Industrielle [*A publication*] .... Electron Ind
Electronique Medicale [*A publication*] .... Electron Med
Electronique et Microelectronique Industrielles [*A publication*] .... Electron Microelectron Ind
Electronique Nouvelle [*A publication*] .... Electron Nouv
Electronisch Meten [*A publication*] .... Electron Meten
Electronystagmography [*Medicine*] .... ENG
Electroocular Symbol Display .... ESD
Electrooculogram [*or Electrooculography*] [*Medicine*] .... EOG
Electroolfactogram .... EOG
Electrophoresis .... EP
Electrophoresis Experiment [*NASA*] .... EPE
Electrophoresis Operations in Space .... EOS

Electrophoretic Mobility [*Biochemical analysis*] ... EM
Electrophoretic Operations in Space [*Without gravity*] ... EOS
Electrophotography [*A publication*] ... Electrophotogr
Electrophrenic Respiration [*Medicine*] ... EPR
Electroplate ... EP
Electroplated Nickel Silver ... EPNS
Electroplating and Metal Finishing [*A publication*] ... Electroplat Met Finish
Electropneumatic ... ELPNEU
Electropneumatic ... EP
Electropneumatic Valve ... EPV
Electropneumogram [*Medicine*] ... EPG
Electroquimica e Corrasao [*A publication*] ... Electroquim Corrasao
Electroradioimmunoassay [*Clinical chemistry*] ... ERIA
Electroretinogram [*Medicine*] ... ERG
Electrosensitive Programing ... ESP
Electroshock [*Psychology*] ... ES
Electroshock Protection ... ESP
Electroshock Research Association [*Later, International Psychiatric Library Service*] ... ERA
Electroshock Therapy [*Psychology*] ... EST
Electroshock Therapy Apparatus [*Psychology*] ... ESTA
Electroslag Remelting [*Steel alloy*] ... ESR
Electrosonic Profiler ... ESP
ElectroSound Group [*American Stock Exchange symbol*] ... ESG
Electrospace Systems [*NASDAQ symbol*] ... ELEC
Electrostatic ... ES
Electrostatic Analyzer ... ESA
Electrostatic Collector ... ESC
Electrostatic Compatibility ... ESC
Electrostatic Discharge ... ESD
Electrostatic Discharge Effects ... ESDE
Electrostatic Electron Microscope ... EEM
Electrostatic Focusing [*Electronics*] ... ESF
Electrostatic Klystron ... ESK
Electrostatic Latent Image Photography ... ELIP
Electrostatic Loudspeaker ... ELS
Electrostatic Particle Size Analyzer ... EPSA
Electrostatic Plasma Oscillator ... EPO
Electrostatic Powder ... EP
Electrostatic Power Generator ... EPG
Electrostatic Precipitator [*Also, ESP*] ... EP
Electrostatic Precipitator [*Also, EP*] ... ESP
Electrostatic Printing Tube ... EPT
Electrostatic Probe Experiment ... EPE
Electrostatic Reversal Printing ... ERP
Electrostatic Spraying ... ES
Electrostatic Storage ... ES
Electrostatic Storage Deflection ... ESD
Electrostatic Storage Tube ... EST
Electrostatic Transistorized Voltmeter ... ETVM
Electrostatic Unit ... ESU
Electrostatic Vector Grid ... EVG
Electrostatic Voltmeter ... ESV
Electrostatically Enhanced Fabric Filtration ... EEFF
Electrostatically Focused Tube ... EFT
Electrostatically Supported Gyro Monitor [*Navy*] ... ESGM
Electrosurgical Unit [*Medicine*] ... ESU
Electrotechnical Journal of Japan [*A publication*] ... Electrotech J Jpn
Electrotechnical Laboratory ... ETL
Electrothermal Atomic Absorption [*Analytical technique*] ... ETAA
Electrothermal Engine ... ETE
Electrothermal Filter ... ETF
Electrothermal Hydrazine Thruster ... EHT
Electrothermie International. Edition B. Applications Industrielles de l'Electrothermie [*A publication*] ... Electrothermie Int Ed B
Electrovacuum Drive ... EVD
Electrovisual System ... ELVIS
Electrum [*Numismatics*] ... EL
Electuarium [*Electuary*] [*Pharmacology*] ... ELECT
Eleele, HI [*Radio station call letters*] ... KUAI
Elektricheskaya i Teplovoznaya Tyaga [*A publication*] ... Elektr & Teplovoznaya Tyaga
Elektrik Muhendisligi [*A publication*] ... Elektr Muhendisligi
Elektrische Ausruestung [*A publication*] ... Elektr Ausruestung
Elektrische Bahnen [*A publication*] ... Elek Bahnen
Elektrische Bahnen [*A publication*] ... Elektr Bahnen
Elektrische Energie-Technik [*A publication*] ... Elektr Energ-Tech
Elektrische Maschinen [*A publication*] ... Elektr Masch
Elektrisches Nachrichtenwesen [*A publication*] ... Elektr Nachrichtenwes
Elektrisitetsforsyningens Forskninginstitutt [*Research Institute of Electricity Supply*] [*Norway*] ... EFI
Elektro-Anzeiger [*A publication*] ... Elektro-Anz
Elektroenergetika i Avtomatika [*A publication*] ... Elektroenerget i Avtomat
Elektromeister und Deutsches Elektrohandwerk [*A publication*] ... Elektromeister & Dtsch Elektrohandwerk
Elektron International [*A publication*] ... Elektron Int
Elektronik-Anzeiger [*A publication*] ... Elektron Anz
Elektronik Industrie [*A publication*] ... Elektron Ind
Elektronik Informationen [*A publication*] ... Elektron Inf
Elektronik Journal [*A publication*] ... Elektron J
Elektronik (Muenchen) [*A publication*] ... Elektron (Muenchen)
Elektronik-Zeitung [*A publication*] ... Elektronik
Elektronik-Zeitung [*A publication*] ... Elektron-Ztg
Elektronika i Khimiya v Kardiologii [*A publication*] ... Elektron Khim Kardiol
Elektronikka Radio Television [*A publication*] ... ERT
Elektronische Datenverarbeitung [*Electronic Data Processing*] [*German*] ... EDV
Elektronische Datenverarbeitung [*Electronic Data Processing*] [*A publication*] ... Elektron Datenverarb
Elektronische Informationsverarbeitung und Kybernetik [*A publication*] ... EIK
Elektronische Informationsverarbeitung und Kybernetik [*A publication*] ... Elektron Informationsverarb Kybern
Elektronische Rechenanlagen [*A publication*] ... Elektron Rechenanlagen
Elektronische Rechenanlagen mit Computer Praxis [*A publication*] ... Elektron Rechenanlagen Comput Prax
Elektronisches Rechnen und Regeln [*A publication*] ... Elektron Rech Regeln
Elektronmikroskopievereniging van Suidelike Afrika. Verrigtings [*A publication*] ... Elektronmikroskopiever Suidelike Afr Verrig
Elektronnaya Obrabotka Materialov [*A publication*] ... Elektron Obrab Mater
Elektronno-Vychislitel'naya Mashina [*Electronic Calculating Machine*] [*Russian*] ... EVM
Elektrotechnicky Obzor [*A publication*] ... Elektrotech Obz
Elektrotechnik und Maschinenbau [*A publication*] ... Elektrotech Maschinenbau
Elektrotechniky Casopis [*A publication*] ... Elektrotech Cas
Elektrotechnische Zeitschrift [*A publication*] ... Elektrotech Zeit
Elektrotechnische Zeitschrift. A [*A publication*] ... Elektrotech Z A
Elektrotechnische Zeitschrift. Ausgabe A [*A publication*] ... Elektrotech Z Ausg A
Elektrotechnische Zeitschrift. Ausgabe B [*A publication*] ... Elektrotech Z Ausg B
Elektrotechnische Zeitschrift. Ausgabe B [*A publication*] ... Elektr Z B
Elektrotechnische Zeitschrift. B [*A publication*] ... Elektrotech Z B
Elektrotehnika u Industriji Pogonu [*A publication*] ... Elektroteh Ind Pogonu
Elektrotehniski Vestnik [*A publication*] ... Elektroteh Vestn
Elektroteknisk Tidsskrift [*A publication*] ... Elektrotek Tidsskr
Elektrowaerme International [*A publication*] ... Elektrowaerme Int
Elektrowaerme International. A [*A publication*] ... Elektrowaerme Int A
Elektrowaerme International. B [*A publication*] ... Elektrowaerme Int B
Elektrowaerme International. Edition A. Elektrowaerme im Technischen Ausbau [*A publication*] ... Elektrowaerme Int Ed A
Elektrowaerme International. Edition B. Industrielle Elektrowaerme [*A publication*] ... Elektrowaerme Int Ed B
Elektrowaerme im Technischen-Ausbau [*A publication*] ... Elektrowrm Tech-Ausbau
Elelmezesi Ipar [*A publication*] ... Elelmez Ipar
Elelmezesi Ipar [*A publication*] ... Elelm Ipar
Elelmiszervizgalati Kozlemenyek [*A publication*] ... Elelmiszervizgalati Kozl
Element ... EL
Element ... ELEM
Element ... ELM
Element ... ELT
Element ... L
Element Characteristics Equation ... ECE
Element Code ... ELECD
Element Contractor ... EC
Element of Expense ... EOE
Element of Expense/Investment Code ... EEIC
Element Interface Functional Analysis ... EIFA
Element Load Model ... ELM
Element Number [*Data processing*] ... EN
Element Project Office [*NASA*] ... EPO
Elemental Analysis Research Center [*Department of Health and Human Services*] ... EARC
Elemental Method of Training ... EMT
Elemental Standard Data System ... ESDS
Elemental X-Ray Analysis of Materials ... EXAM
Elementary ... EL
Elementary ... ELEM
Elementary Body ... EB
Elementary Charge [*of a proton*] [*Symbol*] [*IUPAC*] ... e
Elementary Circulation Mechanism ... ECM
Elementary Electrical and Radio Material [*Training School*] [*Navy*] ... EE & RM
Elementary English [*A publication*] ... EE
Elementary English [*A publication*] ... ElemE
Elementary English [*A publication*] ... El Engl
Elementary English Review [*A publication*] ... El Engl R
Elementary Flying Training College [*British*] ... EFTC
Elementary Flying Training School [*British*] ... EFTS
Elementary and High School [*Acronym refers to books published for this market*] ... ELHI
Elementary Perceiver and Memorizer [*Learning theory*] ... EPAM
Elementary Potential Digital Computing Component ... EPDCC
Elementary Processing Centers ... EPC
Elementary Renewal Theorem ... ERT
Elementary School Administrative Supervisory Certificate ... ESASC
Elementary School Behavior Rating Scale [*Devereaux*] [*Psychology*] ... ESBRS

Elementary School Guidance and Counseling [*A publication*]....................... El Sch Guid & Counsel
Elementary School Journal [*A publication*]....................................Elem Sch J
Elementary School Journal [*A publication*].......................................El Sch J
Elementary School Science Project ....ESSP
Elementary School Teacher [*A publication*] .... El School T
Elementary Science Study [*National Science Foundation*] ....ESS
Elementary and Secondary Education Act [*1965*] .... ESEA
Elementary Wiring Diagram .... EWD
Elemente der Mathematik [*A publication*] .... Elem Math
Elementos Electronics Mexicanos SA [*Mexico*]...................................ELMEX
Elements of Data... EOD
Elements of Expense [*Army*] .... EE
Elettronica e Telecomunicazioni [*A publication*]...........Elettron & Telecomun
Elettrotecnica [*A publication*] ....Elettrotecn
Eleutherian Mills Historical Library, Greenville, DE [*Library symbol*] ... DeGE
Elevated [*Railway*] [*Also, L*]... EL
Elevated [*Also, EL*] [*Railway*]... L
Elevated Glandular Epidermis .... EGE
Elevated Radiation Seeking Rocket.. ERASER
Elevated Radio System... ERS
Elevated Release Point [*Nuclear energy*] .... ERP
Elevated Stabilized Platform [*Aircraft*] ....ESP
Elevated Temperature.. ET
Elevated Temperature Strain Gauge.. ETSG
Elevated Training Platform...ETP
Elevation.. EL
Elevation...ELEV
Elevation Angle .... E
Elevation Angle Guidance Landing Equipment ....EAGLE
Elevation Console ....EC
Elevation Data Edit Terminals.. EDET
Elevation Finder [*Military*].. EF
Elevation Guidance for Approach and Landing [*Aviation*]..................... EGAL
Elevation Position Indicator [*Aviation*]...EPI
Elevation Versus Integrated Log.. EVIL
Elevator...ELEV
Elevon Load System [*Aviation*].. ELS
Elevtheros Kosmos [*A publication*] ....Elev Kosmos
Eley Game Advisory Service. Annual Report [*A publication*]......................... Eley Game Advis Serv Annu Rep
Eley Game Advisory Service. Booklet [*A publication*].. Eley Game Advis Serv Bookl
Eley Game Advisory Station. Annual Report [*A publication*]........................... Eley Game Advis Stn Annu Rep
Elfin Cove [*Alaska*] [*Airport symbol*]..ELV
Elgin Community College [*Illinois*] .... ECC
Elgin County Public Library, St. Thomas, ON, Canada [*Library symbol*] .... CaOStTE
Elgin, IL [*Radio station call letters*]...WEPS
Elgin, IL [*Radio station call letters*]..WJKL
Elgin, IL [*Radio station call letters*]... WJKL-FM
Elgin, IL [*Radio station call letters*]..WRMN
Elgin, Joliet, & Eastern Railway Co. [*AAR code*]....................................... EJE
Elgin National Industries, Inc. [*Formerly, Elgin National Watch Co.*] [*NYSE symbol*] .... ENW
Elgin, TX [*Radio station call letters*] .... KELG
Elginfield [*Ontario*] [*Seismograph station code, US Geological Survey*] ... ELF
Eli Lilly & Co. [*Research code symbol*].. A
Eli Lilly & Co. [*Research code symbol*].. EL
Eli Lilly & Co. [*Canada*] [*Research code symbol*].....................................VC-K
Eli Lilly & Co., Agricultural Library, Greenfield, IN [*OCLC symbol*] ....ILD
Eli Lilly & Co., Business Library, Indianapolis, IN [*OCLC symbol*] .... ILB
Eli Lilly & Co., Business Library, Indianapolis, IN [*Library symbol*] .... InILB
Eli Lilly & Co., Indianapolis, IN [*OCLC symbol*].. IES
Eli Lilly & Co., Library Agricultural Services, Greenfield, IN [*Library symbol*].. InGrefL
Eli Lilly & Co., Scientific Library, Indianapolis, IN [*Library symbol*].......... InIL
Eli Whitney Metrology Center .... EWMC
Eligibility Review and Reemployment Assistance Program [*Employment Service*] [*Department of Labor*] .... ERP
Eligible..ELIG
Eligible Individual [*Social Security Administration*] .... EI
Eligible for Overseas Service .... EOS
Eligible for Separation.. ES
Eligible Spouse [*Social Security Administration*] .... ES
Elim [*Alaska*] [*Airport symbol*] .... ELI
Eliminate...ELIM
Eliminate and Count [*Coding*] [*Data processing*]..................................ELCO
Elimination of Legal Files [*Lobbying effort of ARMA*]................................ELF
Elimination of Purchase Requirement [*Department of Agriculture*] .... EPR
Elimination of Range Zero System [*Aviation*]...EROS
Elin- Zeitschrift [*A publication*]...Elin-Z
Eline.. EI
ELINT [*Electronic Intelligence*] **Advisory Group** .... EAG
ELINT [*Electronic Intercept*] **Collection/Analysis Guide** [*Air Force*] ... ELCAG
ELINT [*Electronic Intelligence*] **- Ocean Reconnaissance Satellite** .... EORSAT
ELINT [*Electronic Intelligence*] **Receiver Test System** .... ERTS
Elisha D. Smith Public Library, Menasha, WI [*Library symbol*] .... WMe
Elisha Mitchell Scientific Society. Journal [*A publication*] .... Elisha Mitchell Sci Soc J
Elison Air Force Base [*Alaska*] .... EAFB
Elixir [*Pharmacology*] .... ELIX
Elixir Industries [*NYSE symbol*] [*Delisted*] ....EXR
[*An*] **Elizabeth Barrett Browning Concordance** [*A publication*]............BRCN
Elizabeth City, NC [*Location identifier*] [*FAA*].. IZE
Elizabeth City, NC [*Location identifier*] [*FAA*].. NOZ
Elizabeth City, NC [*Radio station call letters*]......................................WCNC
Elizabeth City, NC [*Radio station call letters*]...................................... WGAI
Elizabeth City, NC [*Radio station call letters*].................................... WMYK
Elizabeth City State University, Elizabeth City, NC [*Library symbol*] ....NcElcE
Elizabeth City State University, Elizabeth City, NC [*OCLC symbol*] .... NPE
Elizabeth Free Public Library, Elizabeth, NJ [*Library symbol*]................ NjEli
Elizabeth Jones [*Designer's mark, when appearing on US coins*]................ EJ
Elizabeth, NJ [*Radio station call letters*] ....WJDM
Elizabeth Public Library, Elizabeth, CO [*Library symbol*] .... CoEli
Elizabeth S. Priori-1 [*Virus named after one of the scientists who isolated it*] ESP-1
Elizabeth Seton College, Yonkers, NY [*Library symbol*] .... NYES
Elizabetha Regina [*Queen Elizabeth*] [*Latin*] ....ER
Elizabethan Club of Yale University..ECYU
Elizabethan Studies [*A publication*] .... ElizS
Elizabethton, TN [*Radio station call letters*] ....WBEJ
Elizabethton, TN [*Radio station call letters*] .... WIDD
Elizabethton, TN [*Radio station call letters*] ....WIDD-FM
Elizabethtown College, Elizabethtown, PA [*OCLC symbol*].....................ELZ
Elizabethtown College, Elizabethtown, PA [*Library symbol*]...................PEIC
Elizabethtown, KY [*Radio station call letters*] .... WIEL
Elizabethtown, KY [*Television station call letters*]................................. WKZT
Elizabethtown, KY [*Radio station call letters*] .... WQXE
Elizabethtown, NC [*Radio station call letters*] .... WBLA
Elizabethtown, PA [*Radio station call letters*]..WPDC
Elizabethtown, PA [*Radio station call letters*]....................................... WRKZ
Elizabethtown Water [*NASDAQ symbol*].. EWAT
Elizabethville [*Karavia*] [*Zaire*] [*Seismograph station code, US Geological Survey*] [*Closed*] .... ELI
Elizabethville [*Zaire*] [*Later, KVA*] [*Geomagnetic observatory code*] .... ELI
Elk Chute Ditch [*Missouri*] [*Seismograph station code, US Geological Survey*].. ECD
Elk City, OK [*Radio station call letters*] ....KADS
Elk City, OK [*Radio station call letters*] ....KECO
Elk Rapids District Library, Elk Rapids, MI [*Library symbol*]................ MiElk
Elk River Reactor.. ERR
Elk Township Library, Peck, MI [*Library symbol*].................................. MiPec
Elkader Historical Society, Elkader, IA [*Library symbol*]..................... IaElkHi
Elkader, IA [*Radio station call letters*]..KADR
Elkader Public Library, Elkader, IA [*Library symbol*].............................IaElk
Elkhart [*Indiana*] [*Airport symbol*]... EKI
Elkhart, IN [*Radio station call letters*]...WCMR
Elkhart, IN [*Radio station call letters*]... WFRN
Elkhart, IN [*Television station call letters*].......................................WSJV-TV
Elkhart, IN [*Radio station call letters*].. WTRC
Elkhart, IN [*Radio station call letters*].. WVPE
Elkhart, IN [*Radio station call letters*].. WYEZ
Elkhart Public Library, Elkhart, IN [*OCLC symbol*]..IEB
Elkhart Public Library, Elkhart, IN [*Library symbol*] .... InElk
Elkhorn City, KY [*Radio station call letters*].. WBPA
Elkhorn City, KY [*Radio station call letters*]... WECL
Elkhorn Ranch [*California*] [*Seismograph station code, US Geological Survey*].. EKH
Elkin, NC [*Radio station call letters*].. WIFM-FM
Elkin, NC [*Radio station call letters*].. WJOS
Elkins [*West Virginia*] [*Airport symbol*] .... EKN
Elkins, WV [*Location identifier*] [*FAA*]... OUW
Elkins, WV [*Radio station call letters*] ....WCDE
Elkins, WV [*Radio station call letters*] ....WDNE
Elkins, WV [*Radio station call letters*] ....WDNE-FM
Elkins, WV [*Radio station call letters*] .... WELK
Elko [*Nevada*] [*Airport symbol*]... EKO
Elko [*Nevada*] [*Seismograph station code, US Geological Survey*]............ELK
Elko [*Nevada*] [*Seismograph station code, US Geological Survey*] [*Closed*]... EKO
Elko County Library, Elko, NV [*Library symbol*].......................................NvE
Elko, NV [*Radio station call letters*].. KELK
Elko, NV [*Radio station call letters*]...KLKO
Elko, NV [*Radio station call letters*].. KRJC
Elkonix Corp. [*NASDAQ symbol*]... KONX
Elkton, KY [*Radio station call letters*]...WSRG
Elkton, MD [*Radio station call letters*]..WOEL-FM
Elkton, MD [*Radio station call letters*]... WSER
Elkton Public Library, Elkton, SD [*Library symbol*] ....SdEl
Ell .... E
Ellen Glasgow Newsletter [*A publication*]... EGN
Ellenikos Laikos Apeleutherotikos Stratos [*Hellenic Peoples Army of Liberation*] [*Military arm of EAM*] [*Greece*].......................... ELAS
Ellensburg Public Library, Ellensburg, WA [*Library symbol*] ....WaEl
Ellensburg, WA [*Radio station call letters*] .... KXLE
Ellensburg, WA [*Radio station call letters*] ....KXLE-FM
Ellenville, NY [*Radio station call letters*] .... WDRE

Ellenville, NY [*Radio station call letters*] ... WELV
Ellenville Public Library, Ellenville, NY [*Library symbol*] ... NElle
Ellery Queen's Mystery Magazine [*A publication*] ... EQMM
Ellesmere & Glyn Valley Railway [*Later, GVR*] [*Wales*] ... E & GVR
Ellijay, GA [*Radio station call letters*] ... WLEJ
Ellinghausen, McCullough, Johnson, Harris [*Medium*] [*Microbiology*] ... EMJH
Ellington Air Force Base [*Texas*] ... EAFB
Ellington Air Force Base, TX [*Location identifier*] [*FAA*] ... HKX
Elliot Lake [*Canada*] [*Airport symbol*] ... YEL
Elliot Lake, ON [*Television station call letters*] ... CBLFT-6
Elliot Lake, ON [*Television station call letters*] ... CKNC-TV-1
Elliot Lake Secondary School, Elliot Lake, ON, Canada [*Library symbol*] ... CaOELS
Elliott Lake, ON [*Television station call letters*] ... CICI-TV-1
Elliott Lake, ON [*Radio station call letters*] ... CKNR
Elliott Public Library, Elliott, IA [*Library symbol*] ... IaEll
Elliott Society of Natural History of Charleston. Proceedings [*A publication*] ... Elliott Soc N H Charleston Pr
Ellipsoid Collector Mirror ... ECM
Ellipsometry [*Surface analysis*] ... ELL
Ellipsometry, Low Field [*Microscopy*] ... ELF
Elliptic [*or Exact*] **Differential Equation** ... EDE
Elliptic Function First-Order Ripple Phase Approximation ... EFFORPA
Elliptic Function Second-Order Ripple Phase Approximation ... EFSORPA
Elliptical ... ELIP
Elliptical ... ELLIPT
Elliptical ... ELP
Elliptical Cavity Pump ... ECP
Elliptical Earth Orbit ... EEO
Elliptical Gear Planetary ... EGP
Elliptical Head ... ELPH
Elliptical Orbit [*Aerospace*] ... EO
Elliptically Polarized Light ... EPL
Elliptically Polarized Wave ... EPW
Ellis Air Lines ... ES
Ellis Banking Corp. [*NASDAQ symbol*] ... ELIS
Ellis College, Newtown, PA [*Library symbol*] [*Obsolete*] ... PNtE
Ellis Hospital, Schenectady, NY [*Library symbol*] ... NSchE
Ellison, R. A., Cincinnati OH [*STAC*] ... ERA
Ellisville, MS [*Radio station call letters*] ... WBSJ
Ellman's, Inc. [*NASDAQ symbol*] ... ELLM
Elloree-Santee, SC [*Radio station call letters*] ... WSOL
Ellsworth [*Connecticut*] [*Seismograph station code, US Geological Survey*] ... ECT
Ellsworth Air Force Base [*South Dakota*] ... ELAFB
Ellsworth Commumity College, Iowa Falls, IA [*Library symbol*] ... IaIfE
Ellsworth Community College [*Iowa*] [*Formerly, EJC*] ... ECC
Ellsworth Junior College [*Iowa*] [*Later, ECC*] ... EJC
Ellsworth, ME [*Radio station call letters*] ... WDEA
Ellsworth, ME [*Radio station call letters*] ... WWMJ
Ellsworth Public Library, Ellsworth, IA [*Library symbol*] ... IaEls
Ellwanger Jahrbuch: Ein Volksbuch fuer Heimatpflege in Virngau und Ries [*A publication*] ... Ellwanger Jb
Ellwood City Area Public Library, Ellwood City, PA [*Library symbol*] ... PEc
Ellwood City, PA [*Location identifier*] [*FAA*] ... EWC
Ellwood City, PA [*Radio station call letters*] ... WFEM
Elm [*Alabama*] [*Seismograph station code, US Geological Survey*] ... EMA
Elm Research Institute [*Supersedes EU*] ... ERI
Elma [*New York*] [*Seismograph station code, US Geological Survey*] [*Closed*] ... ELM
Elma Dill Russell Spencer Foundation Series [*A publication*] ... Elma Dill Russell Spencer Found Ser
Elmali [*Turkey*] [*Seismograph station code, US Geological Survey*] ... ELL
Elmbrook Memorial Hospital, Brookfield, WI [*Library symbol*] ... WBrE
Elmer Times, Elmer, NJ [*Library symbol*] ... NjElT
Elmhurst College, Elmhurst, IL [*OCLC symbol*] ... ICV
Elmhurst College, Elmhurst, IL [*Library symbol*] ... IElmC
Elmhurst, IL [*Radio station call letters*] ... WKDC
Elmhurst, IL [*Radio station call letters*] ... WRSE-FM
Elmhurst Public Library, Elmhurst, IL [*Library symbol*] ... IElm
Elmira [*New York*] [*Airport symbol*] ... ELM
Elmira College, Elmira, NY [*Library symbol*] ... NElmC
Elmira College, Elmira, NY [*OCLC symbol*] ... VXE
Elmira Heights-Horseheads, NY [*Radio station call letters*] ... WEHH
Elmira, NY [*Location identifier*] [*FAA*] ... UEK
Elmira, NY [*Radio station call letters*] ... WECW
Elmira, NY [*Radio station call letters*] ... WELM
Elmira, NY [*Radio station call letters*] ... WENY
Elmira, NY [*Television station call letters*] ... WENY-TV
Elmira, NY [*Television station call letters*] ... WETM-TV
Elmira, NY [*Radio station call letters*] ... WLEZ
Elmira, NY [*Radio station call letters*] ... WLVY
Elmira Psychiatric Center, Elmira, NY [*Library symbol*] ... NElmP
Elmo Bumpy Torus [*Nuclear energy*] ... EBT
Elmont Public Library, Elmont, NY [*Library symbol*] ... NElmo
Elms Unlimited [*Superseded by ERI*] ... EU
Elmwood Park, IL [*Radio station call letters*] ... WXFM
Elmwood Park Public Library, Elmwood Park, IL [*Library symbol*] ... IElwp
Elmwood Public Library, Providence, RI [*Library symbol*] ... RPE
Elmwood Township, MI [*Radio station call letters*] ... WLJN
Elocution ... E
Elohist Source [*Biblical scholarship*] ... E
Elon College, Elon College, NC [*Library symbol*] ... NcElon
Elon, NC [*Radio station call letters*] ... WSOE
Elongate ... ELNG
Elongated Die Bushing ... EDB
Elongated Punch ... EP
Elongated Single Domain ... ESD
Elongation ... ELONG
Elongation, Derotation, and Lateral Flexion [*Medicine*] ... EDF
Elongation Factor [*Biochemistry, genetics*] ... EF
Elongation in Two Inches ... EL2
Elorza [*Venezuela*] [*Airport symbol*] ... EOZ
Elron Electronics [*NASDAQ symbol*] ... ELRNF
Els Marges [*Barcelona*] [*A publication*] ... ELSM
Els Nostres Classics [*A publication*] ... ENC
Elsa Clubs of America ... ECA
Elsah, IL [*Radio station call letters*] ... WTPC
Elscint Ltd. [*NASDAQ symbol*] ... ELSTF
Else Good [*In good condition except for defects mentioned*] [*Antiquarian book trade*] ... EG
Elsevier Lexica [*Elsevier Book Series*] [*A publication*] ... EL
Elsevier Oceanography Series [*Elsevier Book Series*] [*A publication*] ... Elsevier Oceanogr Ser
Elsevier Oceanography Series [*Elsevier Book Series*] [*A publication*] ... EOS
Elsevier Oceanography Series (Amsterdam) [*Elsevier Book Series*] [*A publication*] ... Elsevier Oceanogr Ser (Amsterdam)
Elsevier Science Publishers ... ESP
Elsevier Series in Forensic and Police Science [*Elsevier Book Series*] [*A publication*] ... EFPS
Elsewhere ... ELSW
Elsie, MI [*Radio station call letters*] ... WOES
Elsinore [*A publication*] ... Els
Elsinore Corp. [*American Stock Exchange symbol*] ... ELS
Elsinore Free Public Library, Elsinore, CA [*Library symbol*] ... CEl
Elswick Quick-Firing Gun ... EQF
Elteknik Med Aktuell Elektronik [*A publication*] ... Eltek Aktuell Elektron
Elteknik Med Aktuell Elektronik [*A publication*] ... Elteknik Med Aktuel Elektron
Elting Memorial Library, New Paltz, NY [*Library symbol*] ... NNepa
Eltopia [*Washington*] [*Seismograph station code, US Geological Survey*] ... ETP
Eltra Corp. [*NYSE symbol*] [*Delisted*] ... ET
Eltsovka [*USSR*] [*Seismograph station code, US Geological Survey*] ... ELT
Elwood, IN [*Radio station call letters*] ... WBMP
Elwyn Institute, Elwyn, PA [*OCLC symbol*] ... PIE
Ely [*Nevada*] [*Airport symbol*] ... ELY
Ely [*Nevada*] [*Seismograph station code, US Geological Survey*] [*Closed*] ... ELY
Ely Junior College [*Minnesota*] [*Later, Vermilion Community College*] ... EJC
Ely, MN [*Radio station call letters*] ... WELY
Ely, NV [*Radio station call letters*] ... KELY
Elyria Library, Elyria, OH [*Library symbol*] ... OEly
Elyria, OH [*Radio station call letters*] ... WBEA
Elyria, OH [*Radio station call letters*] ... WEOL
EM and D [*Engineering Materials and Design*] **Journal of Engineering Materials, Components, and Design** [*A publication*] ... EM & D J Eng Mater Compon Des
EM and D [*Engineering Materials and Design*] **Product Data** [*A publication*] ... EM & D Prod Data
Emae [*Vanuata*] [*Airport symbol*] ... EAE
Emakeele Seltsi Aastaraamat [*A publication*] ... EmSA
Emakeele Seltsi Aastaraamat [*A publication*] ... ESA
Emanation Thermal Analysis ... ETA
Emanations Security ... EMSEC
Emanuel County Junior College, Swainsboro, GA [*Library symbol*] ... GSwE
Emanuel Einstein Free Public Library, Pompton Lakes, NJ [*Library symbol*] ... NjPl
Emanuel Hospital, Portland, OR [*Library symbol*] ... OrPEH
Emba Mink Breeders Association ... EMBA
Emballage Digest [*A publication*] ... Emballage Dig
Embalmer [*Navy rating*] ... EMT
Embalming Chemical Manufacturers Association [*Defunct*] ... ECMA
Embankment ... EMB
Embankment ... EMBKMT
Embark ... EMB
Embarkation Commandant [*Military*] [*British*] ... EC
Embarkation Medical Official [*Military*] [*British*] ... EMO
Embarkation Officer [*Marine Corps*] ... EMBO
Embarkation Order [*Marine Corps*] ... EMBO
Embarkation Staff Officer [*Military*] [*British*] ... ESO
Embarkation Supply and Stores Officer [*Military*] [*British*] ... ESSO
Embarked Mine Countermeasures Force ... EMCMF
Embarrassing Personal Question [*National Security Agency screening procedure*] ... EPQ
Embassy ... E
Embassy ... EMB
Embassy of Ghana, Washington, DC [*Library symbol*] ... DGhE
Embassy Officer ... EMBOFF
Embassy Social Secretaries Association ... ESSA
Embassy Telegram ... EMBTEL

Embassy of Zaire, Washington, DC [*Library symbol*] ... DZaE
Embden-Meyerhof [*Glycolytic pathway*] [*Biochemistry*] ... E-M
Embden-Meyerhof-Parnas [*Hexose metabolic pathway*] [*Biochemistry*] ... EMP
Embedded [*Meteorology*] ... EMBDD
Embedded-Alumina-Particle Aluminide [*Chemical coating*] ... EAPA
Embedded Computer Resources ... ECR
Embedded Figures [*Psychometrics*] ... EF
Embedded Figures Test [*Psychology*] ... EFT
Embedded in a Layer [*To indicate cumulonimbus embedded in layers of other clouds*] [*Aviation code*] ... EMBD
Embedded Sensor Technique ... EST
Embessa [*Papua New Guinea*] [*Airport symbol*] ... EMS
Embezzlement of Government Property ... EGP
Emboss ... EMB
Embossed [*Deltiology*] ... EMBS
Embossed Groove Recording ... EGR
Embossing Press Station ... EPS
Embroidered ... EMB
Embroiderers' Guild of America ... EGA
Embroidery ... EMBR
Embroidery Council of America ... ECA
Embroidery Manufacturers Promotion Board [*Later, SEMPB*] ... EMPB
Embry-Riddle Aeronautical University [*Formerly, ERSA*] [*Florida*] ... E-RAU
Embry-Riddle School of Aviation [*Later, E-RAU*] [*Florida*] ... ERSA
Embryo ... EMBR
Embryo Extract ... EE
Embryo Transfer ... ET
Embryology ... EMB
Embryology ... EMBRY
Embryonal Carcinoma [*Medicine*] ... EC
Embryonic Bovine Kidney ... EBK
Embryonic Chicken Kidney ... ECK
Embryonic Chicken Muscle ... ECM
Embryonic Growth and Development Factor [*Biochemistry*] ... EGDF
Embryonic Turkey Kidney ... ETK
EMC Energy, Inc. [*NASDAQ symbol*] ... EMCE
EMC Insurance Group [*NASDAQ symbol*] ... EMCI
Emden [*West Germany*] [*Airport symbol*] ... EME
Emder Jahrbuch [*A publication*] ... Emder Jb
Emendatio [*Emended*] ... EMEND
Emendation [*or Emended*] [*Change in spelling of name*] [*Taxonomy*] ... emend
Emerald [*Australia*] [*Airport symbol*] ... EMD
Emerald Airlines [*Austin, TX*] [*FAA designator*] ... EFF
Emergency [*Symbol placed in neighborhood windows to indicate that resident will aid passing schoolchildren in the event of an emergency*] ... E
Emergency ... EMER
Emergency ... EMERG
Emergency Action Console [*Navy*] ... EAC
Emergency Action Coordination Team [*Department of Energy*] ... EACT
Emergency Action File [*Air Force*] ... EAF
Emergency Action Message [*Navy*] ... EAM
Emergency Action Message Authentication System [*Military*] ... EAMAS
Emergency Action Notification [*Civil Defense*] ... EAN
Emergency Action Notification System [*White House Teletype network*] [*Civil Defense*] ... EANS
Emergency Action Procedure [*Military*] ... EAP
Emergency Action Reporting for Logistics Action Programing [*Military*] ... EARFLAP
Emergency Actions Noncommissioned Officer [*Army*] ... EANCO
Emergency Actions Officer [*Army*] ... EAO
Emergency Advisory Committee for Natural Gas [*Department of the Interior*] ... EACNG
Emergency Air Staff Actions ... EASA
Emergency Airborne Reaction System ... EARS
Emergency Alternate Command Center ... EACC
Emergency Area ... EA
Emergency Assistance [*or Assistant*] ... EMA
Emergency Bed Request System [*Data processing*] ... EMBERS
Emergency Bed Service [*Medicine*] ... EBS
Emergency Black Survival Fund ... EBSF
Emergency Bomb Release ... EBR
Emergency Box ... EB
Emergency Breathing Apparatus ... EBA
Emergency Breathing Subsystem ... EBS
Emergency Broadcast System [*Formerly, CONELRAD*] ... EBS
Emergency Call System [*AT & T*] ... ECS
Emergency Capability ... EC
Emergency Cardiac Care ... ECC
Emergency Care Research Institute ... ECRI
Emergency Category Designation ... ECD
Emergency Chaplain [*Army*] [*British*] ... EC
Emergency Civil Liberties Committee [*Later, NECLC*] ... ECLC
Emergency Coalition for Haitian Refugees ... ECHR
Emergency Combat Capability ... ECC
Emergency Combat Readiness ... ECR
Emergency Command Control Communications System ... ECCCS
Emergency Commission [*British*] ... EC
Emergency Committee for American Trade ... ECAT
Emergency Committee to Boycott Mother's Day ... ECBMD
Emergency Committee to Save America's Marine Resources ... ECSAMR
Emergency Communications Control [*Fictitious military unit in film "Seven Days in May"*] ... ECOMCON
Emergency Communications Key ... ECK
Emergency Communications Working Group [*DoD*] ... ECWG
Emergency Conditions [*Military*] ... EMERGCONS
Emergency Conservation Committee [*Defunct*] ... ECC
Emergency Conservation Measures ... ECM
Emergency Conservation Work [*Succeeded by CCC, 1937, now obsolete*] ... ECW
Emergency Control Center ... ECC
Emergency Coolant System ... ECS
Emergency Coordinator ... EC
Emergency Core Cooling [*Nuclear energy*] ... ECC
Emergency Core-Cooling System [*Nuclear energy*] ... ECCS
Emergency Council of Jewish Families ... ECJF
Emergency Decelerating [*Relay*] ... EDE
Emergency Decontamination Center [*Nuclear energy*] ... EDC
Emergency Decontamination Facility [*Energy Research and Development Administration*] ... EDF
Emergency Defense Plan [*Later, GDP*] ... EDP
Emergency Deorbit System [*NASA*] ... EDS
Emergency Department [*of a hospital*] ... ED
Emergency Department Nurses Association ... EDNA
Emergency Deployment Readiness Exercise [*Army*] ... EDRE
Emergency Detection and Decision System ... EDDS
Emergency Detection System ... EDS
Emergency Diesel Generator ... EDG
Emergency Digital Computer ... EDC
Emergency Dispersal Bases ... EDB
Emergency Drill in the Home [*Fire Department drill exercise*] ... EDITH
Emergency Earth Orbital Escape Device ... EEOED
Emergency Economic Committee for Europe [*A "Western Nation" organization*] [*Post-World War II*] ... EECE
Emergency Egress Air Pack [*NASA*] ... EEAP
Emergency Egress Working Group ... EEWG
Emergency Ejection Suits ... EES
Emergency Electrical Power System ... EEPS
Emergency Employment Act ... EEA
Emergency Energy Conservation Act [*1979*] ... EECA
Emergency Escape Device ... EED
Emergency Essential Personnel ... EEP
Emergency Establishment [*Military*] ... EE
Emergency Establishment Supplement Table of Personnel Distribution [*NATO*] ... EEST/PD
Emergency Establishment Supplements ... EES
Emergency Exposure Limits ... EEL
Emergency Facilities ... EF
Emergency Feeding Service [*Civil Defense*] ... EFS
Emergency Field Arresting Gear ... EFAG
Emergency Financial Control Board ... EFCB
Emergency Firing Panel ... EFP
Emergency Fix ... EF
Emergency Fleet Corporation [*Defunct, 1936*] ... EFC
Emergency Flight Termination ... EFT
Emergency Food and Medical Program ... EFMP
Emergency Food Supply Scheme [*World Food Program*] ... EFSS
Emergency Fund Request ... EFR
Emergency Gear ... EG
Emergency General Account of Advances ... EGAA
Emergency Global Rescue, Escape, and Survival System [*NASA*] ... EGRESS
Emergency Ground Egress ... EGE
Emergency Health Preparedness Advisory Committee [*Terminated, 1973*] ... EHPAC
Emergency Health Service [*HEW*] ... EHS
Emergency Highway Traffic Regulation [*Federal disaster planning*] ... EHTR
Emergency Highway Traffic Regulation Center [*Federal disaster planning*] ... EHTRC
Emergency Homes, Incorporated ... EHI
Emergency Hospital Scheme ... EHS
Emergency Housing Corporation ... EHC
Emergency Identification Light [*Aerospace*] ... EIDLT
Emergency Information Officer [*Civil Defense*] ... EIO
Emergency Information Readiness [*Civil Defense*] ... EIR
Emergency Jobs and Unemployment Assistance Act ... EJUAA
Emergency Land Fund ... ELF
Emergency Landing Ground ... ELG
Emergency Lead-Zinc Committee [*Later, Lead-Zinc Producers Committee*] ... ELZC
Emergency Legal Assistance Project ... ELAP
Emergency Legislation ... EL
Emergency Letter of Instructions ... ELOI
Emergency Librarian [*A publication*] ... Emergency Lib
Emergency Librarian [*A publication*] ... Emerg Lib
Emergency Librarian [*A publication*] ... Emer Libr
Emergency Life-Saving Instant Exit [*Aircraft*] [*Air Force*] ... ELSIE
Emergency Life Support System ... ELSS
Emergency Lighting Equipment ... ELE
Emergency Lighting Manufacturers Association [*Defunct*] ... ELMA

Emergency List *[Navy] [British]* .... EMY
Emergency Loading Procedure .... ELP
Emergency Loan Guarantee Board .... ELGB
Emergency Locator Transmitter .... ELT
Emergency Machine Tool Armament Corps *[British] [World War II]* .... EMTAC
Emergency Maintenance .... EM
Emergency Manning Level .... EML
Emergency Manual Release Handle .... EMRH
Emergency Maternity and Infant Care .... EMIC
Emergency Measures Organization *[Canada]* .... EMO
Emergency Medical Care and Rescue .... EMC & R
Emergency Medical Command and Communications System .... EMCCS
Emergency Medical Information .... EMI
Emergency Medical Information Devices .... EMID
Emergency Medical Kit .... EMK
Emergency Medical Service .... EMS
Emergency Medical Service System .... EMSS
Emergency Medical Services *[A publication]* .... Emerg Med Serv
Emergency Medical Tag .... EMT
Emergency Medical Technician .... EMT
Emergency Medical Technician Legal Bulletin *[A publication]* .... Emerg Med Tech Legal Bull
Emergency Medical Treatment *[Military]* .... EMT
Emergency Medicine *[A publication]* .... Emerg Med
Emergency Medicine Foundation .... EMF
Emergency Medicine Management Association .... EMMA
Emergency Medicine Residents' Association .... EMRA
Emergency Message .... EM
Emergency Message - Alert Message .... EM/AM
Emergency Message Authentication System *[USEUCOM]* .... EMAS
Emergency Message Automatic Transmission System *[Military]* .... EMATS
Emergency Message Automatic Transmission System - Air Force .... EMATS-AF
Emergency Message Automatic Transmission System - Joint Chiefs of Staff .... EMATS-JCS
Emergency Message Changes .... EMC
Emergency Message Initiation Terminal .... EMIT
Emergency Military Construction Program .... EMCP
Emergency Minerals Administration *[Department of the Interior]* .... EMA
Emergency Mission Control Center *[NASA]* .... EMCC
Emergency Mission Support *[Air Force]* .... EMS
Emergency Mission Support System *[Air Force]* .... EMSS
Emergency Mobilization Preparedness Board *[DoD]* .... EMPB
Emergency Movements Atomic *[Military]* .... EMA
Emergency Negative Thrust .... ENT
Emergency Nurse Legal Bulletin *[A publication]* .... Emerg Nurse Legal Bull
Emergency Nurse Legal Bulletin *[A publication]* .... ENLB
Emergency Officers' Retired List *[Army]* .... EORL
Emergency Operating Center *[Civil Defense]* .... EOC
Emergency Operating Facility *[Civil Defense]* .... EOF
Emergency Operation Headquarters *[Army]* .... EOH
Emergency Operational Capability .... EOC
Emergency Operations Center *[Military]* .... EOC
Emergency Operations Control Center *[Environmental Protection Agency]* .... EOCC
Emergency Operations Plan *[Civil Defense]* .... EOP
Emergency Operations Research Center .... EORC
Emergency Operations Simulation *[Civil Defense]* .... EOS
Emergency Operations Simulation Techniques *[Civil Defense]* .... EOST
Emergency Operations System .... EOS
Emergency Operations Systems Development *[Civil Defense]* .... EOSD
Emergency Oxygen Mask Assembly .... EOMA
Emergency Oxygen Pack *[NASA]* .... EOP
Emergency Oxygen Supply *[or System]* .... EOS
Emergency Parts Requisition .... EPR
Emergency Passenger Exit .... EPE
Emergency Petroleum Allocation Act .... EPAA
Emergency Petroleum and Gas Administration *[Department of the Interior]* .... EPGA
Emergency Petroleum Supply Committee *[Terminated, 1976]* .... EPSC
Emergency Planning .... EP
Emergency Planning Canada .... EPC
Emergency Planning Committee for Civil Transportation *[US and Canada]* .... EPCCT
Emergency Planning Digest *[A publication]* .... Emerg Plann Dig
Emergency Planning Officer *[Army]* .... EPO
Emergency Planning Zone *[Nuclear emergency planning]* .... EPZ
Emergency Plans and Readiness Division *[of OEP] [Terminated]* .... EPRD
Emergency Plant Facilities .... EPF
Emergency Position-Indicating Radio Beacon .... EPIRB
Emergency Positive Control Communications System .... EPCCS
Emergency Power .... EPWR
Emergency Power Cutoff *[NASA]* .... EPCO
Emergency Power Generator .... EPG
Emergency Power Level .... EPL
Emergency Power Off .... EPO
Emergency Power Package .... EPP
Emergency Power Ride-Through Capability System *[Nuclear energy]* .... EPRTCS
Emergency Power Supply .... EPS
Emergency Power Unit .... EPU
Emergency Powers Act *[British] [World War II]* .... EPA
Emergency Powers Defence Act *[British] [World War II]* .... EPDA
Emergency Preparedness .... EP
Emergency Pressurization System .... EPS
Emergency Pressurization Valve .... EPV
Emergency Priorities and Allocations Manual *[DoD]* .... EPAM
Emergency Procedure Trainer *[NASA]* .... EPT
Emergency Procedures .... EP
Emergency Procurement Service *[Later, Defense Materials Service]* .... EPS
Emergency Production Planning List *[Army]* .... EPPL
Emergency Production Planning Program *[Navy]* .... EPPP
Emergency Production Weapons Schedule *[Navy]* .... EPWS
Emergency Program Release Notice *[NASA]* .... EPRN
Emergency Project for Equal Rights .... EPER
Emergency Propaganda Committee *[London] [World War II]* .... EPC
Emergency Propellant Venting System .... EPVS
Emergency Proposal .... EMPRO
Emergency Propulsive Propellant Venting System .... EPPVS
Emergency Public Information *[Civil Defense]* .... EPI
Emergency Radiation Monitor .... ERM
Emergency Radio Beacon .... ERB
Emergency Recovery Display *[Bell System]* .... ERD
Emergency Recovery Force .... ERF
Emergency Recovery Group .... ERG
Emergency Recovery Section .... ERS
Emergency Recovery Unit .... ERU
Emergency Relief Administration .... ERA
Emergency Relocation Center .... ERC
Emergency Relocation Site *[Military]* .... ERS
Emergency Repair Overseer *[Navy]* .... ERO
Emergency Request .... ER
Emergency Rescue .... ER
Emergency Rescue Equipment .... ERE
Emergency Rescue Team Chief *[Air Force]* .... ERTC
Emergency Reserve .... ER
Emergency Reserve Decoration *[British]* .... ERD
Emergency Return Device *[Aerospace]* .... ERD
Emergency Road Service *[American Automobile Association]* .... ERS
Emergency Rocket Communications System .... ERCS
Emergency Room *[Medicine]* .... ER
Emergency Rubber Project *[National Research Council]* .... ERP
Emergency School Aid Act *[1972]* .... ESAA
Emergency School Assistance Program .... ESAP
Emergency Security Control of Air Traffic .... ESCAT
Emergency Security Operations .... ESO
Emergency Service .... ES
Emergency Ship Handling Unit *[Navy]* .... ESHU
Emergency Ship Salvage Material *[Navy]* .... ESSM
Emergency Ship Service *[Navy]* .... ESS
Emergency Short Stay *[in hospital] [British]* .... ESS
Emergency Shutoff Valve .... ESV
Emergency Signal .... EMS
Emergency Social Services *[Civil Defense]* .... ESS
Emergency Solid Fuels Administration .... ESFA
Emergency Standby Order - Federal Highway Administration *[Federal disaster planning]* .... ESO-FHWA
Emergency Standoff Range .... ESOR
Emergency Status Precedence Code *[DoD]* .... ESPC
Emergency Stop Indicator *[Aerospace]* .... ESI
Emergency Strike Effort *[Military]* .... ESE
Emergency Substitute in a Regular Position *[Education]* .... ESRP
Emergency Supply Operations Center *[Defense Supply Agency]* .... ESOC
Emergency Support Organization .... ESO
Emergency Survival System .... ESS
Emergency System of Control Allowing Pilot Escape and Recovery .... ESCAPER
Emergency Takeover .... ET
Emergency Task Force for Indochinese Refugees *[Defunct]* .... ETFIR
Emergency Technical Operations Center *[DoD]* .... ETOC
Emergency Test Operation .... ETO
Emergency Time Limit .... ETL
Emergency Traffic Coordinating Officer *[Army]* .... ETCO
Emergency Traffic Disposition Plan *[Military]* .... ETDP
Emergency Training Centre *[British]* .... ETC
Emergency Transceiver Equipment .... ETE
Emergency and Trauma Unit .... ETU
Emergency Treatment Unit .... ETU
Emergency Unemployment Compensation *[Account]* .... EUC
Emergency Unsatisfactory Material Report .... EUMR
Emergency Unsatisfactory Report *[Military]* .... EUR
Emergency Urgent Change Package *[Army]* .... EUCP
Emergency Use Only .... EUO
Emergency Venting System .... EVS
Emergency Veterinary Tag .... EVT
Emergency Virus Isolation Facility *[National Cancer Institute]* .... EVIF
Emergency War Operations .... EWO
Emergency War Order *[Air Force]* .... EWO
Emergency War Plan .... EWP
Emergency War Surgery Training Program *[Army]* .... EWSTP
Emergency Ward .... EW

Emergency Warnings Branch [*National Weather Service*] ... EWB
Emergency Water Supply ... EWS
Emergency Welfare Registration and Inquiry [*Civil Defense*] ... EWR & I
Emergency Welfare Service [*Civil Defense*] ... EWS
Emergency Window Escape [*NASA*] ... EWE
Emergent S Wave [*Earthquakes*] ... e(S)
Emerging Technology ... ET
Emerita [*A publication*] ... Em
Emerita [*A publication*] ... Emer
Emeritus ... EMER
Emerson College, Boston, MA [*OCLC symbol*] ... ECL
Emerson College, Boston, MA [*Library symbol*] ... MBE
Emerson Electric Company ... EEC
Emerson Electric Co. [*NYSE symbol*] ... EMR
Emerson, Lake, & Palmer [*Rock music group*] ... ELP
Emerson Radio Corp. [*Formerly, ERP*] [*NYSE symbol*] ... EME
Emerson Radio & Phonograph Corp. [*Later, EME*] [*NYSE symbol*] [*Delisted*] ... ERP
Emerson Radio & Phonograph Corporation [*Later, Emerson Radio Corporation*] ... ERPC
Emerson Society Quarterly [*A publication*] ... ESQ
Emery Air Freight Corp. [*NYSE symbol*] ... EAF
Emery County High School, Castle Dale, UT [*Library symbol*] ... UCdH
Emery County Library, Castle Dale, UT [*Library symbol*] ... UCdE
Emery Energy, Inc. [*NASDAQ symbol*] ... EMRY
Emery Industries, Inc. [*NYSE symbol*] [*Delisted*] ... EI
Emery Industries, Inc. [*Research code symbol*] ... Emfac
Emery Industries, Inc., Research Library, Cincinnati, OH [*Library symbol*] ... OCEmI
Emery Testing Machine [*Nineteenth-century hydraulic testing machine*] ... ETM
Emeryville Public Library, Emeryville, CA [*Library symbol*] ... CEv
Emetine [*Antiamebic compound*] ... EME
Emetine Bismuth Iodide [*Pharmacology*] ... EBI
Emett and Chandler Corporation [*NASDAQ symbol*] ... EMCC
EMF Corporation [*NASDAQ symbol*] ... EMFC
Emhart Corp. [*Formerly, EMM*] [*NYSE symbol*] ... EMH
Emhart Manufacturing Co. [*Later, EMH*] [*NYSE symbol*] ... EMM
Emhart Manufacturing Co. [*Later, Emhart Corp.*]**, Bloomfield, CT** [*Library symbol*] ... CtBlE
EMI [*formerly, Electric & Musical Industries Ltd.*] **Data Electronic Computer** [*Made by EMI Industries - Great Britain*] ... EMIDEC
EMI Ltd. [*Formerly, Electric & Musical Industries Ltd.*] [*NYSE symbol*] [*Delisted*] ... EMI
Emigrant Gap, CA [*Location identifier*] [*FAA*] ... BLU
Emigrant Institute [*Sweden*] ... EI
Emigrant's Assured Savings Estate [*Banking program*] ... EASE
Emily Dickinson Bulletin [*A publication*] ... EDB
Eminence ... EM
Eminence, KY [*Radio station call letters*] ... WSTL
Emirau [*Papua New Guinea*] [*Airport symbol*] ... EMI
Emission ... EM
Emission ... EMIS
Emission ... EMSN
Emission Characteristics Monitor ... ECM
Emission Computed Tomography ... ECT
Emission Control ... EMCON
Emission Control System ... ECS
Emission History Information System [*Environmental Information Agency*] ... EHIS
Emission Policy ... EP
Emission Release ... EMREL
Emission Security ... EMISEC
Emission Spectrograph ... EMS
Emissions Trading [*Environmental Protection Agency*] ... ET
Emissora Nacional de Radiodifusao [*Radio network*] [*Portugal*] ... ENR
Emitted Coherent Radiation ... ECR
Emitter ... E
Emitter ... EM
Emitter ... EMTR
Emitter-Controlled Negative Resistance Triode ... ECNRT
Emitter-Coupled Logic ... ECL
Emitter-Coupled Logic Operator ... ECLO
Emitter-Coupled Transistor Logic ... ECTL
Emitter Dip Effect ... EDE
Emitter-Emitter Coupled Logic ... EECL
Emitter Follower ... EF
Emitter Follower Logic ... EFL
Emitter Identification ... EID
Emitter Identification Guide ... EIG
Emitter Identification Program [*RADAR*] ... EIP
Emitter Isolated Difference Amplifier Paralleling [*Bell System*] ... EIDAP
Emitter Location Method ... ELME
Emitter Location System [*Air Force*] ... ELS
Emma Dorothy Eliza Nevitte Southworth [*American novelist, 1818-99*] [*Acronym used as pseudonym*] ... EDEN
Emmanuel College, Boston, MA [*OCLC symbol*] ... EMC
Emmanuel College, Boston, MA [*Library symbol*] ... MBEmm
Emmanuel College, Victoria University, Toronto, ON, Canada [*Library symbol*] ... CaOTE
Emmanuel School of Religion, Johnson City, TN [*OCLC symbol*] ... TEJ
Emmanuel School of Religion, Johnson City, TN [*Library symbol*] ... TJoE
Emmet [*California*] [*Seismograph station code, US Geological Survey*] ... EMT
Emmetropia [*Also, EM*] [*Ophthalmology*] ... E
Emmetropia [*Also, E*] [*Ophthalmology*] ... EM
Emmetsburg, IA [*Radio station call letters*] ... KEMB
Emmetsburg Public Library, Emmetsburg, IA [*Library symbol*] ... IaEm
Emmett, ID [*Radio station call letters*] ... KMFE
Emmitsburg, MD [*Radio station call letters*] ... WMTB-FM
Emmonak [*Alaska*] [*Airport symbol*] ... EMK
Emmonak, AK [*Location identifier*] [*FAA*] ... ENM
Emo [*Papua New Guinea*] [*Airport symbol*] ... EMO
EMO (Emergency Measures Organization) Digest (Canada) [*A publication*] ... EMO (Emerg Meas Organ) Dig
Emo Questionnaire [*Psychology*] ... EQ
Emons Industries, Inc. [*NASDAQ symbol*] ... EMON
Emory and Henry College [*Virginia*] ... EHC
Emory and Henry College, Emory, VA [*OCLC symbol*] ... VEH
Emory and Henry College, Emory, VA [*Library symbol*] ... ViEmoE
Emory Law Journal [*A publication*] ... Emory L J
Emory Sources and Reprints [*A publication*] ... ESR
Emory University, A. W. Calhoun Medical Library, Atlanta, GA [*OCLC symbol*] ... EMM
Emory University, A. W. Calhoun Medical Library, Atlanta, GA [*Library symbol*] ... GEU-M
Emory University, Atlanta, GA [*OCLC symbol*] ... EMU
Emory University, Atlanta, GA [*Library symbol*] ... GEU
Emory University, Candler School of Theology, Atlanta, GA [*Library symbol*] ... GEU-T
Emory University Division of Librarianship, Atlanta, GA [*OCLC symbol*] ... EML
Emory University, Division of Librarianship, Atlanta, GA [*Library symbol*] ... GEU-LS
Emory University, Division of Librarianship, Atlanta, GA [*OCLC symbol*] ... LEU
Emory University, Lamar School of Law, Atlanta, GA [*Library symbol*] ... GEU-L
Emory University, Pitts Theological Library, Atlanta, GA [*OCLC symbol*] ... EMT
Emory University Quarterly [*A publication*] ... Emory Univ Quart
Emory University Quarterly [*A publication*] ... EUQ
Emory University, School of Business Administration, Atlanta, GA [*Library symbol*] ... GEU-B
Emory University School of Dentistry, Atlanta, GA [*OCLC symbol*] ... EMD
Emory University, School of Dentistry, Atlanta, GA [*Library symbol*] ... GEU-D
Emory University, Yerkes Primate Research Center, Atlanta, GA [*Library symbol*] ... GEU-Y
Emosson [*Switzerland*] [*Seismograph station code, US Geological Survey*] ... EMO
Emotional ... EMOT
Emotional Disturbance ... ED
Emotional-Ethical Attitudes Test [*Psychometrics*] ... EEAT
Emotional Health Anonymous ... EHA
Emotionally Deprived ... ED
Emotionally Disturbed ... EM
Emotionally Disturbed/Learning Disabled ... ED/LD
Emotionally Handicapped [*Psychology*] ... EH
Emotionally Impaired ... EI
Emotionally Mentally Retarded [*Psychology*] ... EMR
Emotions Anonymous ... EA
Empathy Test [*Psychology*] ... ET
Empennage [*Aerospace engineering*] ... EMP
Empennage Support Beam ... ESB
Emperor [*or Empress*] ... EMP
Emperor's Clothes Syndrome ... ECS
Empfindichkeit [*Susceptibility to Stimulation*] [*Psychology*] ... E
Empfindlicher Aufschlagzuender [*Superquick impact fuze*] [*German military - World War II*] ... EAZ
Emphysema Anonymous, Incorporated ... EAI
Empi, Inc. [*NASDAQ symbol*] ... EMPI
Empire ... EMP
Empire Airlines [*NASDAQ symbol*] ... EAIR
Empire Airlines [*Oriskany, NY*] [*FAA designator*] ... EMP
Empire of Carolina [*American Stock Exchange symbol*] ... EMP
Empire Cotton Growing Corporation. Progress Reports from Experiment Stations [*A publication*] ... Emp Cotton Grow Corp Prog Rep Exp Stn
Empire Cotton Growing Review [*A publication*] ... Emp Cotton Grow Rev
Empire-Crown Auto [*NASDAQ symbol*] ... EMPC
Empire District Electric Co. [*NYSE symbol*] ... EDE
Empire Financial Corporation [*NYSE symbol*] [*Delisted*] ... EFC
Empire Forestry Journal [*A publication*] ... Emp For J
Empire Forestry Journal [*A publication*] ... Empire For J
Empire Forestry Review [*A publication*] ... Emp For Rev
Empire Gallantry Medal [*British*] ... EGM
Empire Gas Corporation [*NYSE symbol*] [*Delisted*] ... EGC
Empire Grade Road [*California*] [*Seismograph station code, US Geological Survey*] ... EGR
Empire Journal of Experimental Agriculture [*A publication*] ... Emp J Exp Ag

Empire Journal of Experimental Agriculture [*A publication*] ... Emp J Exp Agric
Empire Lines, Inc. ... EML
Empire Marketing Board [*For motion pictures in England*] ... EMB
Empire Producer [*A publication*] ... Empire Prod
Empire State Atomic Development Associates, Inc. ... ESADA
Empire State College, Saratoga Springs, NY [*Library symbol*] ... NSsE
Empire State College, Saratoga Springs, NY [*OCLC symbol*] [*Inactive*] ... YEM
Empire State Historical Publications [*Series*] ... ESHP
Empire Telecommunications [*British*] [*World War II*] ... ETS
Empire Test Pilots' School [*British*] ... ETPS
Empirical Distribution Function [*Statistics*] ... EDF
Empirical Kinetic Modeling Approach [*Air pollution research*] ... EKMA
Emplaced Instrument Complex [*Aerospace*] ... EIC
Emplaced Lunar Scientific Station [*Aerospace*] ... ELSS
Emplaced Scientific Station [*Aerospace*] ... ESS
Emplacement ... EMPL
Emplacement, Installation, and Test ... EI & T
Emplastrum [*Plaster*] [*Pharmacy*] ... EMP
Employ [*or Employee*] ... EMPL
Employ the Physically Handicapped ... EPH
Employability Development Services [*US Employment Service*] [*Department of Labor*] ... EDS
Employed Full Time [*Chiropody*] [*British*] ... EF
Employee ... EMPLEE
Employee Appraisal Record ... EAR
Employee Assistance Program ... EAP
Employee Attitude Research ... EAR
Employee Auxiliary Service Personnel ... EASP
Employee Benefit Plan Review [*A publication*] ... EBPR
Employee Benefit Plan Review [*A publication*] ... Em Benefit
Employee Benefit Plan Review [*A publication*] ... Employ Benefit Plan Rev
Employee Benefit Research Institute ... EBRI
Employee Benefits Journal [*A publication*] ... EBJ
Employee Benefits Journal [*A publication*] ... Employ Benefits J
Employee Daily Labor Distribution ... EDLD
Employee Data Record ... EDR
Employee Development Officer ... EDO
Employee Health Insurance ... EHI
Employee Health Maintenance Examination ... EHME
Employee Incident Report ... EIR
Employee Information System ... EIS
Employee-Management Cooperation ... EMC
Employee Number ... EMPNO
Employee Plan [*IRS*] ... EP
Employee Plan Administrators ... EPA
Employee Plans/Exempt Organization [*IRS*] ... EP/EO
Employee Profile Security File [*IRS*] ... EPSF
Employee Promotion Appraisal [*FAA*] ... EPA
Employee Record Change Notice ... ERCN
Employee Relations Index ... ERI
Employee Relations Law Journal [*A publication*] ... Employ Relat Law J
Employee Relocation Council [*Formerly, ERREAC*] ... E-R-C
Employee Relocation Real Estate Advisory Council [*Later, E-R-C*] ... ERREAC
Employee Retirement Income Security Act [*Also facetiously translated as Every Ridiculous Idea Since Adam*] ... ERISA
Employee Satisfaction ... ESAT
Employee Stock Ownership Plan [*Tax plan*] ... ESOP
Employee Stock Ownership Trust ... ESOT
Employee Suggestion ... ES
Employees' Compensation Appeals Board [*Department of Labor*] ... ECAB
Employees' Compensation Commission ... ECC
Employees' Compensation Fund ... ECF
Employees of Diplomatic Missions [*A publication*] ... EDMI
Employees' Plan Master File [*IRS*] ... EPMF
Employer ... EMPLR
Employer Identification Code ... EIC
Employer Identification Number [*IRS*] ... EIN
Employer Identification Number Assignment Control Card File [*IRS*] ... EACF
Employer Identification Number Key Index File [*IRS*] ... EKIF
Employer Identification Number Name and Address File [*IRS*] ... ENAF
Employer Identification Number Taxpayer Information File [*IRS*] ... ETIF
Employer Relations Representative ... ERR
Employers Casualty [*NASDAQ symbol*] ... ECRC
Employers Council on Flexible Compensation ... ECFC
Employer's Inventory of Critical Manpower ... EICM
Employers Labor Relations Information Committee ... ELRIC
Employer's Return File [*IRS*] ... ERF
Employers' Unemployment Compensation Council ... EUCC
Employing Photo-Engravers Association of America [*Defunct*] ... EPEAA
Employing Printers Association of America [*Defunct*] ... EPAA
Employment ... EMPLMNT
Employment Agencies Protective Association of the United States [*Later, National Employment Association*] ... EAPAUS
Employment Appeal Tribunal [*British*] ... EAT
Employment Code [*IRS*] ... EC
Employment and Earnings [*A publication*] ... EMEA
Employment Management Association ... EMA
Employment Medical Advisory Service [*Department of Employment*] [*British*] ... EMAS
Employment Policy Grievance Review Staff [*OSA*] ... EPGRS
Employment Protection [*Act*] [*British*] ... EP
Employment Relations Abstracts [*A publication*] ... EmAb
Employment Relations Abstracts [*A publication*] ... Employ Rel Abstr
Employment Relations Board [*Usually preceded by abbreviation of state name*] ... ERB
Employment Schedule ... EMPSKD
Employment Schedule ... EMPSKED
Employment Schedule ... EMSKED
Employment Security Administration Account ... ESAA
Employment Security Automation Project [*Department of Labor*] ... ESAP
Employment Security System [*Department of Labor*] ... ESS
Employment Security Systems Institute ... ESSI
Employment Service [*US*] ... ES
Employment Service Agency [*Department of Employment*] [*British*] ... ESA
Employment Service Automated [*or Automatic*] **Reporting System** [*Department of Labor*] ... ESARS
Employment Service Improvement Program [*Department of Labor*] ... ESIP
Employment Service On-Line Placement System [*Data processing*] ... ESOPS
Employment Service Potential [*Department of Labor*] ... ESP
Employment Service Representative ... ESR
Employment Service Review [*A publication*] ... EMSR
Employment Standards Administration [*Department of Labor*] ... ESA
Employment and Suitability Test [*Aerospace*] ... E & ST
Employment and Training ... E & T
Employment and Training Administration [*Formerly, Manpower Administration*] [*Department of Labor*] ... ETA
Employment and Training Administration Management System [*Department of Labor*] ... ETAMS
Employment and Training Administration Regional Office [*Department of Labor*] ... ETARO
Employment and Training Unit [*Work Incentive Program*] ... ETU
Employment Transfer Scheme [*British*] ... ETS
Employment at Will [*Worker protection from unjustified dismissal*] ... EAW
Emporia, KS [*Location identifier*] [*FAA*] ... EMP
Emporia, KS [*Radio station call letters*] ... KVOE
Emporia Public Library, Emporia, KS [*Library symbol*] ... KEm
Emporia State Research Studies [*A publication*] ... Emporia St Res Stud
Emporia State Research Studies [*A publication*] ... ESRS
Emporia State University, Emporia, KS [*Library symbol*] ... KEmU
Emporia State University, Emporia, KS [*OCLC symbol*] ... KKR
Emporia State University, School of Library Science, Emporia, KS [*OCLC symbol*] ... KEE
Emporia, VA [*Location identifier*] [*FAA*] ... EMV
Emporia, VA [*Radio station call letters*] ... WEVA
Emporium, PA [*Radio station call letters*] ... WLEM
Emporium, PA [*Radio station call letters*] ... WQKY
Empreendimentos Tecnicos de Estradas Limitada ... ETEL
Empresa Aero Uruguay SA [*ICAO designator*] ... UO
Empresa Aeroserivios Parrague [*Chile*] [*ICAO designator*] ... PE
Empresa Astilleros y Fabricas Navales del Estado SA ... AFNE
Empresa de Aviacion Aeronaves de Peru [*ICAO designator*] ... WP
Empresa Brasileira de Turismo [*Brazilian Tourist Authority*] ... EMBRATUR
Empresa Consolidada Cubana de Aviacion [*Cuba*] [*ICAO designator*] ... CU
Empresa Guatemalteca de Aviacion [*Guatemalan airline*] ... AVIATECA
Empresa Lineas Maritimas Argentinas ... ELMA
Empresa Nacional Mineral del Sahara [*Later, Fosfatos de Bucraa*] [*Corporation owned by the Spanish government*] ... ENMISA
Empresa de Transportes Aereao Catarinense [*Brazil*] ... TAC
Empresa de Transportes Aeros Norte [*Brazil*] ... AERONORTE
Empresade Transporte Aere de Peru [*ICAO designator*] ... PL
Empresas Nacionales de Energia [*Argentina*] ... ENDE
Empress Chinchilla Breeders Cooperative ... ECBC
Empty ... E
Empty ... EMT
Empty [*Slang*] ... MT
Empty ... MTY
Empty Net Goals [*Hockey*] ... ENG
Empty Sella Syndrome [*Medicine*] ... ESS
Empty Weight ... EW
EMT [*Emergency Medical Technician*] **Journal** [*A publication*] ... EMT J
Emulation Program ... EP
Emulex Corp. [*NASDAQ symbol*] ... EMLX
Emulsible Concentrate ... EC
Emulsified Liquid Propellant ... ELP
Emulsifying Capacity [*Food technology*] ... EC
Emulsifying Salts [*Food technology*] ... ES
Emulsion ... EMUL
Emulsion Butadiene Rubber ... EBR
Emulsion Polymers Institute ... EPI
Emunah Women of America ... EWA
En Cuenta [*On Account*] [*Business and trade*] [*Spanish*] ... EC
En Passant [*A publication*] ... En Pas
En Passant [*In Passing*] [*Chess*] ... EP
En Route ... ENR
En Route ... ENRT
En Route ... E/R
En Route Air Traffic Control [*A publication*] ... ENAT

En Route, Arrival at_____ [*Military*]	ENRAT
En Route Automated RADAR Tracking System [*Aviation*]	EARTS
En Route Chart [*Aviation*]	ERC
En Route Communications [*Aviation*]	ECOM
En Route Computer Identification	ECID
En Route Flight Advisory Services [*FAA*]	EFAS
En Route Guidance System	ERGS
En Route High Altitude	EHA
En Route Low Altitude	ELA
En Route Penetration [*Aviation*]	EP
En Route and Provide Service to Units Indicated [*Military*]	ENRSVC
En Route to/from Public Affairs Event [*Military*]	ENRPAE
En Route Radial [*Aviation*]	ERAD
En Route Secondary RADAR Beacon [*Aviation*]	ESEC
En Route Supplement	E-S
En Route Support Team [*Military*]	EST
En Route Surveillance RADAR	RSR
En Route This Station from Oversea Command	ENRFOSCOMD
En Route Weather Forecast [*Navy*]	WEAX
En Terre d'Islam [*A publication*]	ETI
Enable	ENBL
Enable Control System	ECS
Enamel	E
Enamel	ENAM
Enamel Bonded Double Cotton [*Wire insulation*]	EBDC
Enamel Bonded Double Paper [*Wire insulation*]	EBDP
Enamel Bonded Double Silk [*Wire insulation*]	EBDS
Enamel Bonded Single Cotton [*Wire insulation*]	EBC
Enamel Bonded Single Silk [*Wire insulation*]	EBS
Enamel Covered	EC
Enamel Double Cotton [*Wire insulation*]	EDC
Enamel Double Cotton Varnish [*Wire insulation*]	EDCV
Enamel Double Silk [*Wire insulation*]	EDS
Enamel Double Silk Varnish [*Wire insulation*]	EDSV
Enamel Insulated Wire	EIW
Enamel Insulating Compound	EIC
Enamel Single Cotton [*Wire insulation*]	EC
Enamel Single Cotton Varnish [*Wire insulation*]	ECV
Enamel Single Silk [*Wire insulation*]	ES
Enamel Single Silk Varnish [*Wire insulation*]	ESV
Enameled	ENMLD
Enameled Single-Covered [*Wire insulation*]	ESC
Enarotali [*Indonesia*] [*Airport symbol*]	EWI
Encampment for Citizenship [*An association*]	EFC
Encapsulated Harpoon Command and Launch System	EHCLS
Encapsulated Toroidal Inductor	ETI
Encapsulated Torpedo [*Antisubmarine*] [*Navy*]	CAPTOR
Encapsulated Variable Inductor	EVI
Encapsulation	ENCAP
Encased	ENCSD
Encased Elastic Cylinder	EEC
Encephale [*A publication*]	ENCEA
Encephalization Quotient	EQ
Encephalomyocarditis [*Virus*]	EMC
Encephalomyocarditis Virus	EMCV
Enchanted Village [*NASDAQ symbol*]	EVIA
Enciclopedia dell'Arte Antica, Classica, e Orientale [*A publication*]	EAA
Enciclopedia di Autori Classici [*A publication*]	EAC
Encino Energy & Development [*NASDAQ symbol*]	EEDC
Enciphered Facsimile Communications	CIFAX
Enclose	ENCL
Enclosed Cryocondenser for Air Recovery	ENCAR
Enclosed Track Conveyor	ETC
Enclosure	ENC
Enclosure	ENCLO
Encode	ENC
Encode	ENCD
Encoder	ENCDR
Encoder Address Translator	EAT
Encoder Coupler	E/C
Encoder Power Supply	EPS
Encontro com o Folclore [*A publication*]	EnF
Encore Industries, Inc. [*NASDAQ symbol*]	ENCRQ
Encounter [*Time*]	E
Encounter [*A publication*]	En
Encounter [*A publication*]	ENC
Encounter [*A publication*]	Encount
Encounter	ENCTR
Encounter (Christian Theological Seminary) [*A publication*]	Encounter (Chr Theol Sem)
Encounter in Health Education	ENHE
Encourage Coughing and Deep Breathing [*Medicine*]	EC & DB
Encouragement, Normalcy, Counselling, Opportunity, Reaching Out, Energies Renewed [*for mastectomy patients*]	ENCORE
Encrypt for Transmission Only [*Military*]	EFTO
Encrypted Traffic Report	ETR
Encryptic Secure Tracking RADAR Identification Friend or Foe	ESTRIFF
Encuentro Nacional de Desarrollo [*Colombia*]	ENDE
Encyclopaedia Biblica [*A publication*]	EB
Encyclopaedia Britannica [*A publication*]	EB
Encyclopaedia Judaica	EJ

Encyclopaedia of Veterinary Medicine, Surgery, and Obstetrics [*A publication*]	Encycl Vet Med Surg and Obst
Encyclopedia	ENC
Encyclopedia	ENCY
Encyclopedia	ENCYC
Encyclopedia of American Associations [*Later, EA*] [*A publication*]	EAA
Encyclopedia of Associations [*Formerly, EAA*] [*A publication*]	EA
Encyclopedia of Business Information Sources [*Formerly, EGIS*] [*A publication*]	EBIS
Encyclopedia Canadiana [*A publication*]	EC
Encyclopedia of Chemical Technology [*A publication*]	ECT
Encyclopedia of Chemical Technology [*A publication*]	Encycl Chem Technol
Encyclopedia of Governmental Advisory Organizations [*A publication*]	EGAO
Encyclopedia of Information Systems and Services [*A publication*]	EISS
Encyclopedia of Occultism and Parapsychology [*A publication*]	EOP
Encyclopedia of Polymer Science and Technology [*A publication*]	EPST
Encyclopedia of Religion and Ethics [*A publication*]	ERE
Encyclopedia of the Social Sciences [*A publication*]	ESS
Encyclopedia of Urology [*A publication*]	Encycl Urol
Encyclopedia of World Biography [*A publication*]	EWB
Encyclopedic Dictionary of Mathematics [*A publication*]	EDM
Encyclopedic Dictionary of Religion	EDR
Encyclopedie Biologique (Paris) [*A publication*]	Encycl Biol (Paris)
Encyclopedie Entomologique [*A publication*]	Encycl Entomol
Encyclopedie Medico-Chirurgicale [*A publication*]	Encycl Med-Chir
Encyclopedie Mycologique [*A publication*]	Encycl Mycol
Encyclopedie Ornithologique (Paris) [*A publication*]	Encycl Ornithol (Paris)
End [*Football*]	E
End of Address [*Data processing*]	EOA
End-Around Carry	EAC
End-Around Shift	EAS
End-Around Test	EAT
End of Block [*Data processing*]	EOB
End of Bombardment	EOB
End Breguet Cruise [*SST*]	EBC
End of Calendar Year	EOCY
End of Construction	EOC
End of Contract	EOC
End of Conversion	EOC
End of Course	EOC
End-of-Course Comprehensive Testing	EOCCT
End of Cycle	EOC
End of Data [*Data processing*]	EOD
End of Data Block [*Data processing*]	EDB
End of Day	EOD
End Delivery Date	EDD
End-Detonating Cartridge [*Explosive*]	EDC
End-Diastolic Count [*Cardiology*]	EDC
End-Diastolic Length [*Cardiology*]	EDL
End-Diastolic Pressure [*Cardiology*]	EDP
End-Diastolic Volume [*Cardiology*]	EDV
End-Diastolic Wall Thickness [*Medicine*]	EDWTH
End Effector	EE
End Effector Electronics Unit	EEEU
End to End	E-E
End to End [*Technical drawings*]	E to E
End of Equilibrium Cycle [*Nuclear energy*]	EEC
End of Equilibrium Cycle [*Nuclear energy*]	EOEC
End, Evening Civil Twilight [*Navigation*]	EECT
End, Evening Nautical Twilight [*Navigation*]	EENT
End Exercise Point	EEP
End of Extent [*Data processing*]	EOE
End of File [*Data processing*]	EOF
End of Fiscal Year	EFY
End of Fiscal Year	EOFY
End Forming Press	EFP
End Game Analysis	EGA
End Game Analysis Program	EGAP
End Half	EHF
End Injection	EI
End of Input	EOI
End-Inspiratory Pause [*Respiration*]	EIP
End Interruption Sequence	EIS
End Item	EI
End Item Allocation Document	EIAD
End Item Assembly Sequence Number	EIASN
End Item Contract	EIC
End Item Data Package	EIDP
End Item Delivery	EID
End Item Description	EID
End Item Designators	EID
End Item Documentation	EID
End Item Equipment	EIE
End Item Maintenance Form	EIMF
End Item Maintenance Sheets	EIMS
End Item Maintenance Transmittal Sheet	EIMTS
End Item Parameter	EIP
End Item Requirement	EIR

End Item Specification .....EIS
End Item Test Plan .....EITP
End of Job [Data processing] .....EOJ
End of Life .....EOL
End of Line [Communications] .....EOL
End of Line Block .....EOLB
End of Logical Tape [Data processing] .....EOLT
End of Magnetic Tape [Data processing] .....EMT
End Matched .....EM
End of Medium [Data processing] .....EM
End of Medium [Data processing] .....EOM
End of Message [Data processing] .....EOM
End-of-Message [Aviation code] .....NNNN
End of Message Sequence .....EOMS
End Mill .....ENML
End of Mission .....EOM
End of Month .....EOM
End of Month Payment .....EMP
End Output .....EOP
End of Overhaul .....EOH
End-Paper [Bibliography] .....E/P
End-Paper Rubbed, Else Good [Condition] [Antiquarian book
    trade] .....EPR/G
End of Paragraph .....EOP
End of Part .....EOP
End of Period .....EOP
End Piece of Equipment .....EPOE
End Plate Current .....EPC
End Plate Potential .....EPP
End Point [Distilling] .....EP
End Point Prediction .....EPP
End Poverty in California [Slogan used by Upton Sinclair during
    campaign as Democratic candidate for governor of California,
    1934] .....EPIC
End of Powered Flight .....EOPF
End Products Committee [of WPB] [World War II] .....EPC
End of Program [Data processing] .....EOP
End of Program .....EP
End of Programed Flight .....EPF
End of Push [Spectroscopy] .....EOP
End of Quarter .....EOQ
End of Record [Data processing] .....EOR
End of Recorded Information [Data processing] .....ERI
End of Reel .....EOR
End Reporting Period .....ERP
End Results Evaluation Program [Later, SEER] [National Cancer
    Institute] .....EREP
End of Screening Date [DoD] .....ESD
End Stage Renal Disease .....ESRD
End Strength .....ES
End-Systolic Length [Cardiology] .....ESL
End Systolic Pressure [Medicine] .....ESP
End-Systolic Volume [Cardiology] .....ESV
End of Tape [Data processing] .....EOT
End of Tape [Data processing] .....ET
End of Tape Test [Data processing] .....ETT
End of Tape Warning [Data processing] .....ETW
End of Task [Data processing] .....EOT
End of Test [Data processing] .....EOT
End of Text [Data processing] .....EOT
End of Text [Data processing] .....ETX
End of Tour [Air Force] .....EOT
End of Track .....EOT
End of Transmission [Data processing] .....EOT
End of Transmission Block [Data processing] .....ETB
End Use Check .....EUC
End Viewing Tube .....EVT
End Violence Against the Next Generation .....EVAN-G
End of Volume [Data processing] .....EOV
End Warning Area [Data processing] .....EWA
End of Word [Data processing] .....EOW
End of Work [Morse telephony] .....VA
End of Year .....EOY
Endangered Species Act Reauthorization Coordinating
    Committee .....ESARCC
Endangered Species Scientific Authority [US Fish and Wildlife
    Service] [Terminated 1979, functions transferred to
    Department of the Interior] .....ESSA
Endata, Inc. [NASDAQ symbol] .....DATA
Ende [Indonesia] [Airport symbol] .....ENE
Endeavour [A publication] .....ENDEA
Endemic Diseases Bulletin. Nagasaki University [A publication] .....
    Endem Dis Bull Nagasaki Univ
Endevco, Inc. [NASDAQ symbol] .....ENDV
Endicott Johnson Corp. [NYSE symbol] [Delisted] .....EJN
Endicott Junior College [Massachusetts] .....EJC
Endicott, NY [Radio station call letters] .....WENE
Endicott, NY [Radio station call letters] .....WMRV
Ending .....ENDG
Ending Period .....EP
Ending of Precipitation [Meteorology] .....E

Ending Tape Label [Data processing] .....ETL
Endings [of nerves] to Lip Muscle .....ELM
Endless Tangent Screw .....ETS
Endo-Atmospheric Decoy .....EAD
Endo Laboratories, Inc. [Research code symbol] .....EN
Endo Laboratories, Inc., Garden City, NY [Library symbol] .....NGcE
Endocardial Cushion Defect .....ECD
Endocardial Fibroelastosis [Medicine] .....EFE
Endocrine Bioassay Data. US Department of Health, Education,
    and Welfare [A publication] .....Endocr Bioassay Data
Endocrine Research Communications [A publication] .....Endocr Res
Endocrine Research Communications [A publication] .....
    Endocr Res Commun
Endocrine Reviews [A publication] .....Endocr Rev
Endocrine Society .....ES
Endocrinologia Experimentalis [A publication] .....Endocr Exp
Endocrinologia Experimentalis [A publication] .....Endocrinol Exp
Endocrinologia Japonica [A publication] .....Endocrinol Jpn
Endocrinologia Japonica [A publication] .....Endocr Jap
Endocrinologia e Scienza della Costituzione [A publication] .....
    Endocrinol Sci Cost
Endocrinology .....ENDOCRIN
Endocrinology [A publication] .....Endocrinol
Endocrinology Index [A publication] .....EDI
Endocrinology Index [A publication] .....Endocrinol Ind
Endocrinology and Metabolism [A publication] .....EM
Endogenous Inhibitor of Prostaglandin Synthase [Biochemistry] .....EIPS
Endogenous Limbic Potentials [Neurophysiology] .....ELP
Endogenous Morphine [or Endomorphin] [Also, ENM] [Brain
    peptide] .....ENDORPHIN
Endogenous Morphine [or Endomorphin] [Also, ENDORPHIN]
    [Brain peptide] .....ENM
Endogenous Pyrogen [Immunology] .....EP
Endokrinologie [A publication] .....Endokrinol
Endokrynologia Polska [A publication] .....Endokrynol Pol
Endolethelial Cell Growth Supplement [Cytochemistry] .....ECGS
Endomethylenetetrahydrophthalic Acid [Organic chemistry] .....EMTA
Endometriosis Association .....EA
Endoplasmic [Freeze etching in microscopy] .....E
Endoplasmic Fracture [Freeze etching in microscopy] .....EF
Endoplasmic Reticulum [Cytology] .....ER
Endoplasmic Surface [Freeze etching in microscopy] .....ES
Endorse .....END
Endorsement .....ENDT
Endorsement Irregular [Banking] .....E/I
Endorsers Conference for Veterans Administration Chaplaincy .....ECVAC
Endoscopic Retrograde Cholangiography [Medicine] .....ERC
Endoscopic Retrograde Cholangiopancreatographic [Exam]
    [Medicine] .....ERCP
Endoscopic Retrograde Pancreatography [Medicine] .....ERP
Endosperm Balance Number [Genetics] .....EBN
Endosteal Marrow [Hematology] .....EM
Endothelial Cell [Medicine] .....EC
Endothelial Cell Growth Factor [Cytochemistry] .....ECGF
Endothelial Proliferating Factor [Biochemistry] .....EPF
Endotracheal Tube [Medicine] .....ET
Endotronics, Inc. [NASDAQ symbol] .....ENDO
Endpaper Map [Publishing] .....ENDPRM
Endstone [Horology] .....ESTN
Endurance .....ENDCE
Endurance Horse Registry of America .....EHRA
Eneabba [Australia] [Airport symbol] .....ENB
Enema [Medicine] .....EN
Enema Saponis [Medicine] .....ES
Enemy .....EN
Enemy Aircraft .....EA
Enemy Civilian Internee Information Bureau [Military] .....ECIIB
Enemy Civilian Internee Information Bureau (Branch) [Military] .....ECIIB(Br)
Enemy Contact Report .....ECR
Enemy Countries Intelligence [Ministry of Economic Warfare]
    [British] [World War II] .....ECI
Enemy Dead .....ED
Enemy Equipment Identification Service [World War II] .....EEIS
Enemy Equipment Intelligence Branch [World War II] .....EEIB
Enemy Equipment Intelligence Service Team [World War II] .....EEIST
Enemy Exports Committee [British] [World War II] .....EEC
Enemy Forward Disposition [Military] .....EFD
Enemy/Friendly .....E/F
Enemy Fuels and Lubricants Technical Committee .....EF & LTC
Enemy Identification Friend or Foe .....EIFF
Enemy Initiated Incident [Vietnam] .....ENI
Enemy Initiated Incident Responded to by Friendly Forces
    [Vietnam] .....ENIRF
Enemy Intelligence .....EI
Enemy Objective Unit [of US] [in London] .....EOU
Enemy Occupied Europe [World War II] .....EOE
Enemy and Occupied Territories Department [Ministry of
    Economic Warfare] [British] [World War II] .....E & OT
Enemy-Occupied Territory .....EOT
Enemy Oil Committee [US] .....EOC

Enemy Oil Intelligence Group [*Ministry of Economic Warfare*] [*British*] [*World War II*] .... EOIG
Enemy Order of Battle .... EOB
Enemy Position .... EP
Enemy Prisoner of War [*Army*] .... EPW
Enemy Prisoner of War Information Bureau [*Army*] .... EPWIB
Enemy Prisoner of War Information Bureau (Branch) [*Army*] .... EPWIB(Br)
Enemy Situation Correlation Element [*DoD*] .... ENSCE
Enemy War Materials Branch [*Supreme Headquarters, Allied Expeditionary Force*] [*World War II*] .... EWMB
Ener-Mark Corp. [*NASDAQ symbol*] .... ENMK
Energas Co. [*NASDAQ symbol*] .... EGAS
Energetic Particles Detector [*Geophysics*] .... EPD
Energetic Particles Explorer [*Satellite*] [*NASA*] .... EPE
Energetic Particles Satellite [*NASA*] .... EPS
Energetic Storm Particle .... ESP
Energeticheskii Institut Imeni G. M. Krzhizhanovskogo. Sbornik Trudov [*A publication*] .... Energ Inst Im G M Krzhizhanovskogo Sb Tr
Energetics, Inc. [*NASDAQ symbol*] .... EJTX
Energetika i Transport [*A publication*] .... Energ Trans
Energex Minerals Ltd. [*NASDAQ symbol*] .... EGEXF
Energia es Atomtechnika [*A publication*] .... Energa Atom
Energia es Atomtechnika [*A publication*] .... Energ Atomtech
Energia Elettrica [*A publication*] .... Energ Elet
Energia Elettrica [*A publication*] .... Energ Elettr
Energia e Industria [*A publication*] .... Energ Ind
Energia e Industrias Aragonesas Sociedad Anonima [*Spain*] .... EIASA
Energia Nuclear e Agricultura [*A publication*] .... Energ Nucl Agric
Energia Nuclear. Boletim Informativo do Forum Atomico Portugues (Lisbon) [*A publication*] .... Energ Nucl (Lisbon)
Energia Nuclear (Madrid) [*A publication*] .... Energ Nucl (Madrid)
Energia Nucleare [*Milan*] [*A publication*] .... Energa Nu
Energia Nucleare [*Milan*] [*A publication*] .... Energa Nucl
Energia Nucleare (Milan) [*A publication*] .... Energ Nucl (Milan)
Energia Nucleare Sud Italia [*Italian nuclear power plant project*] .... ENSI
Energicamente [*With Energy*] [*Music*] .... ENERG
Energie-Brief [*A publication*] .... Energ-Brief
Energie Fluide [*A publication*] .... Energ Fluide
Energie Nucleaire (Paris) [*A publication*] .... Energ Nucl (Paris)
Energie und Technik [*A publication*] .... Energ Tech
Energie und Technik [*A publication*] .... Energ Technik
Energieonderzoek Centrum Nederland Report [*A publication*] .... Energieonder Cent Ned Rep
Energietechnik [*A publication*] .... Energietech
Energiewirtschaftliche Tagesfragen [*A publication*] .... Energiewirtsch Tagesfragen
Energize .... ENER
Energize .... ENRGZ
Energize Output M [*Symbol language*] .... EOM
Energy [*Symbol*] [*IUPAC*] .... E
Energy .... ENGY
Energy Absorbing Capacity .... EAC
Energy Absorption .... EA
Energy Absorption Characteristics .... EAC
Energy Abstracts for Policy Analysis [*National Science Foundation*] .... EAPA
Energy Action Educational Foundation [*Later, EAEP*] .... EAEF
Energy Action Educational Project [*Formerly, EAEF*] .... EAEP
Energy Analysis and Diagnostic Center [*Department of Energy*] .... EADC
Energy Assets International [*NASDAQ symbol*] .... EAIC
Energy Audit Report [*Navy*] .... EAR
Energy Bibliography and Index [*A publication*] .... EBI
Energy and Buildings [*A publication*] .... Energy Build
Energy Capital Development [*NASDAQ symbol*] .... ECDC
Energy Communications [*A publication*] .... Energy Commun
Energy Company [*Slogan and brand name used by Humble Oil & Refining Co.*] [*Later, Exxon*] .... ENCO
Energy Conservation Assessment of Systems, Technologies, and Requirements .... ECASTAR
Energy Conservation Caucus .... ECC
Energy Conservation Coalition .... ECC
Energy Conservation Council .... ECC
Energy Conservation Investment Program .... ECIP
Energy Conservation Opportunities [*Federal Energy Administration*] .... ECO
Energy Conservation and Production Act [*1976*] .... ECPA
Energy Conservation Program Guide for Industry and Commerce [*Department of Commerce*] .... EPIC
Energy Conservation Update [*A publication*] .... ECU
Energy Conservation Vehicle [*British Leyland*] .... ECV
Energy Consumers and Producers Association .... ECPA
Energy Consumption Rate .... ECR
Energy Control Report [*Navy*] .... ECR
Energy Conversion [*A publication*] .... Energy Conv
Energy Conversion [*A publication*] .... Energy Convers
Energy Conversion Alternatives Study [*NASA*] .... ECAS
Energy Conversion Devices [*Commercial firm*] .... ECD
Energy Conversion Devices [*NASDAQ symbol*] .... ENER
Energy Conversion Laboratory [*MIT*] .... ECL
Energy Conversion and Management [*A publication*] .... Energy Convers Manage
Energy Conversion and Utilization Technologies Program [*Department of Energy*] .... ECUT
Energy Coordinating Group [*Twelve-nation coalition*] .... ECG
Energy Crisis Assistance Program [*Federal government*] .... ECAP
Energy Daily [*A publication*] .... Energy Dly
Energy Data Reports. Coal, Bituminous and Lignite [*A publication*] .... EDR Coal B & L
Energy Data Reports. Distribution of Pennsylvania Anthracite [*A publication*] .... EDR Anthrc
Energy Data Reports. Liquefied Petroleum Sales [*A publication*] .... EDR LPS
Energy Data Reports. Sales of Fuel Oil and Kerosene [*A publication*] .... EDR Ker
Energy Data System [*Environmental Protection Agency*] .... EDS
Energy Depot Systems .... EDS
Energy and Development Journal [*A publication*] .... Energy Dev
Energy Development (New York). IEEE Power Engineering Society Papers [*A publication*] .... Energy Dev (New York)
Energy Developments [*A publication*] .... Energy Dev
Energy Developments in Japan [*A publication*] .... Energy Dev Jpn
Energy Digest [*A publication*] .... Energy Dig
Energy Digest (London) [*A publication*] .... Energy Dig (London)
Energy Dispersive Spectroscopy .... EDS
Energy Dispersive System [*Microscopy*] .... EDS
Energy-Dispersive X-Ray .... EDX
Energy Dispersive X-Ray Analysis [*or Analyzer*] [*Also, EDXRA*] .... EDXA
Energy Dispersive X-Ray Analysis [*or Analyzer*] [*Also, EDXA*] .... EDXRA
Energy Dispersive X-Ray Fluorescence [*Spectrometry*] .... EDXRF
Energy Dissipation Tests .... EDT
Energy Distribution Curve [*Electron*] .... EDC
Energy Economics [*A publication*] .... Energy Econ
Energy, Economics, and Environment Institute .... EEEI
Energy Efficiency [*Electrochemistry*] .... EE
Energy Efficiency Ratio [*Home appliance electric output*] .... EER
Energy Efficient Transport .... EET
Energy Engineering Program [*Navy*] .... EEP
Energy and the Environment [*A publication*] .... EAE
Energy and Environment [*South Africa*] [*A publication*] .... Energy Environ
Energy and the Environment. Proceedings of the National Conference [*A publication*] .... Energy Environ Proc Nat Conf
Energy Environmental [*NASDAQ symbol*] .... EECO
Energy Exchange Corp. Cl A [*NYSE symbol*] .... EEX
Energy Extension Service [*Department of Energy*] .... EES
Energy Factors, Inc. [*NASDAQ symbol*] .... EFAC
Energy Flux Density .... EFD
Energy Guideline Factors .... EGF
Energy Independence Authority .... EIA
Energy Index [*A publication*] .... Energy Ind
Energy Information Administration [*Department of Energy*] .... EIA
Energy Information Administration Clearinghouse .... EIAC
Energy Information Center [*Battelle Memorial Institute*] .... EIC
Energy International [*A publication*] .... Energy Int
Energy Law Institute .... ELI
Energy Level Diagram .... ELD
Energy Management .... EM
Energy Management Bumper System [*Automobile safety*] .... EMBS
Energy Management and Controls Society .... EMCS
Energy Management Corporation [*American Stock Exchange symbol*] .... EMC
Energy Management Display Indicator .... EMDI
Energy Management (India) [*A publication*] .... Energy Manage (India)
Energy Maneuverability .... EM
Energy and Man's Environment [*Utility-funded curriculum program*] .... EME
Energy Methods Corp. [*NASDAQ symbol*] .... EMTH
Energy Minerals [*American Stock Exchange symbol*] [*Delisted*] .... EM
Energy, Mines, and Resources [*Canadian government department*] .... EMR
Energy Mobilization Board .... EMB
Energy North, Incorporated [*NASDAQ symbol*] .... ENNI
Energy Oil [*NASDAQ symbol*] .... EOIL
Energy Optics, Inc. [*NASDAQ symbol*] .... EOPT
Energy Policy [*A publication*] .... Energ Polic
Energy Policy [*A publication*] .... Energy Pol
Energy Policy and Conservation Act [*1975*] .... EPCA
Energy Policy Information Center [*Defunct*] .... EPIC
Energy Policy Office [*Formerly, National Energy Office*] [*Executive Office of the President*] [*Abolished, 1974*] .... EPO
Energy Processing (Canada) [*A publication*] .... Energy Process (Can)
Energy Production Company [*NASDAQ symbol*] .... ENPC
Energy Progress [*A publication*] .... Energy Prog
Energy-Protein Malnutrition .... EPM
Energy Pulse Bonding [*Electronics*] .... EPB
Energy Quotient .... EQ
Energy Rate Input Controller .... ERIC
Energy-Related General [*National Science Foundation research office*] .... ERG
Energy-Related Graduate [*National Science Foundation trainee program*] .... ERG
Energy Reorganization Act [*1974*] .... ERA
Energy Research [*Elsevier Book Series*] [*A publication*] .... ER
Energy Research Abstracts .... ERA
Energy Research Advisory Board [*Department of Energy*] .... ERAB
Energy Research and Development .... ER & D
Energy Research and Development Administration [*Superseded by Department of Energy, 1977*] .... ERDA

Energy Research and Development Advisory Council ERDAC
Energy Research and Education Foundation EREF
Energy Research for the Governors ERG
Energy Research Institute ERI
Energy Research Management ERM
Energy Research Management Project [*Federal interagency group*] ... ERMP
Energy Research Reports [*A publication*] Energy Res Rep
Energy Reserve, Inc. [*NASDAQ symbol*] ERES
Energy Reserves Group [*NASDAQ symbol*] ERGS
Energy Resources Corp. [*American Stock Exchange symbol*] ENR
Energy Resources Council [*Terminated, 1977*] ERC
Energy Resources of North Dakota, Inc. [*NASDAQ symbol*] SAVE
Energy Resources and Technology [*A publication*] Energy Resourc Technol
Energy Review [*A publication*] ER
Energy Sciences Corporation [*NASDAQ symbol*] ESCG
Energy Security Act [*1980*] ESA
Energy Services Planning ESP
Energy Solutions, Inc. [*NASDAQ symbol*] ENSO
Energy Storage Modulator ESM
Energy Storage System ESS
Energy Supplies Allocation Board ESAB
Energy Supply and Environmental Coordination Act of 1974 ESECA
Energy Supply Planning Model [*National Science Foundation*] ESPM
Energy Systems Holding ADR [*NASDAQ symbol*] ESHLY
Energy Systems and Policy [*A publication*] Energy Systems Pol
Energy Systems and Policy [*A publication*] Energy Syst Policy
Energy Technology Center ETC
Energy Technology Conference. Proceedings [*A publication*] Energy Technol Conf Proc
Energy Technology Engineering Center [*Department of Energy*] ETEC
Energy Technology Review [*A publication*] Energy Technol Rev
Energy Technology Support Unit at Harwell [*British*] ETSU
Energy Telecommunications and Electrical Association [*Formerly, PIEA*] ENTELEC
Energy Transfer Control [*Aviation*] ETC
Energy Transfer Module [*Aviation*] ETM
Energy Transfer System ETS
Energy Transportation Systems, Incorporated ETSI
Energy User News [*A publication*] Energy
Energy-Variant Sequential Detection EVSD
Energy Ventures, Inc. [*NASDAQ symbol*] ENGY
Energy over Weight EOW
EnerServ Products [*American Stock Exchange symbol*] ESV
Enertech, Inc. [*NASDAQ symbol*] ENTK
Enex Resources Corp. [*NASDAQ symbol*] ENEX
Enfant en Milieu Tropical [*A publication*] Enfant Milieu Trop
Enfermedades del Torax [*A publication*] Enferm Torax
Enfield [*Borough of London*] ENFD
Enforced Dipole Moment EDM
Enforcement of Laws and Treaties [*Program*] [*Coast Guard*] ELT
Enforcement Management Subsystem [*Environmental Protection Agency*] EMS
Enforcement Notification EN
Engage ENGA
Engage Enemy Target EET
Engage High Yield EHY
Engage/Social Action [*A publication*] Engage/Soc Act
Engagement Control System [*Navy*] ECS
Engagement Controller [*Navy*] EC
Engagement Effectiveness [*Army*] EE
Engelhard Corporation [*Formerly, ENG*] [*NYSE symbol*] EC
Engelhard Industries. Technical Bulletin [*A publication*] Engelhard Ind Tech Bull
Engelhard Minerals & Chemicals Corp. [*Later, Engelhard Corp.*] EM & C
Engelhard Minerals & Chemicals Corp. [*Later, EC*] [*NYSE symbol*] ENG
Engelhard Minerals & Chemicals Corp. [*Later, Engelhard Corp.*], **Research Library, Edison, NJ** [*Library symbol*] NjEdE
Engenharia, Mineracao, Metalurgia [*A publication*] Eng Mineracao Met
Engert Aviation Services, Inc. [*Kansas City, MO*] [*FAA designator*] EAS
Engin Teleguide Anti-Char [*Antitank missile*] [*France*] ENTAC
Engine E
Engine ENG
Engine [*Shipping*] [*British*] E
Engine Air Intake Duct [*Hovercraft*] EAID
Engine Air Particle Separator EAPS
Engine Analytical Maintenance Program [*Navy*] EAMP
Engine Analyzer Systems [*Air Force*] EASY
Engine Assembly Vehicle EAV
Engine, Booster Maintenance Area EBMA
Engine Breather Separator EBS
Engine Bulletin EB
Engine Burn [*NASA*] EB
Engine Change EC
Engine Change Unit ECU
Engine Checkout System [*Aerospace*] ECO
Engine Combustion ECO
Engine Compartment Heater ECH
Engine Condition Monitoring ECM
Engine Control EC
Engine Control Development Area ECDA
Engine Control System ECS
Engine Cutoff EC
Engine Cutoff [*Aerospace*] ECO
Engine Cutoff Timer [*Aerospace*] ECT
Engine Deflector Nozzle EDN
Engine Detector EDET
Engine Drive ED
Engine Electronic Control EEC
Engine Failure Sensing and Shutdown System [*NASA*] EFSSS
Engine Firing Rate EFR
Engine-Generator E/G
Engine Hoods EH
Engine Identification Report [*Air Force*] ENGID
Engine In-Flight Condition Monitoring System EICMS
Engine Installation Vehicle EIV
Engine Interface Unit EIU
Engine Life Expectancy ELE
Engine Life Management Group [*Navy*] ELMG
Engine Lube Filter ELF
Engine Lube and Purge [*System*] ELP
Engine Maintenance EM
Engine Maintenance Area EMA
Engine Maintenance Center EMC
Engine Management Display EMD
Engine Management System [*Army*] EMS
Engine Manufacturers Association EMA
Engine Mixture Ratio EMR
Engine Model Derivative Program EMDP
Engine Monitor Display EMD
Engine-Mounted Gear Box EMGB
Engine Multiplexing Unit EMU
Engine Negative Torque Control ENTC
Engine Not Operationally Ready - Supply [*Air Force*] ENORS
Engine Oil EO
Engine Order EOR
Engine Order Capability EOC
Engine Out Capability EOC
Engine Out of Commission for Parts EOCP
Engine Parts Coordinating Office [*Navy*] EPCO
Engine Performance Indicator EPI
Engine Performance Monitoring System EPMS
Engine-Pressure Ratio EPR
Engine Program Information Center EPIC
Engine Project Office [*NASA*] EPO
Engine Propeller Order EPO
Engine Removal Report ERR
Engine Room [*Force*] ER
Engine Room ERM
Engine-Room Artificer [*Navy*] [*British*] ERA
Engine Rotor Tester ERT
Engine Sequence Panel ESP
Engine Service Association ESA
Engine Service Platform ESP
Engine Service Unit ESU
Engine-Sized [*Paper*] ES
Engine Start Command ESC
Engine Start Panel ESP
Engine Start Signal ESS
Engine Status Report [*Air Force*] ENGSTAT
Engine Status Word ESW
Engine Technical Commission ETC
Engine Test Chamber ETC
Engine Test Facility ETF
Engine Test Information ETI
Engine Test Panel [*Aerospace*] ETP
Engine Test Panel [*Aerospace*] ET-PNL
Engine Test Stand [*Nevada*] [*Seismograph station code, US Geological Survey*] [*Closed*] ETS
Engine Test Stands [*NERVA program*] ETS
Engine Transaction Report ETR
Engine V-Belt ENGV
Engine/Vehicle Test Stand E/VTS
Engine Vertical Scale EVS
Engine Vibration Monitor EVM
Engineer [*or Engineering*] E
Engineer [*or Engineering*] ENG
Engineer ENGNR
Engineer [*or Engineering*] ENGR
Engineer in Aeronautics and Astronautics EAA
Engineer Agency for Resources Inventories [*Army Corps of Engineers*] EARI
Engineer Amphibian Command [*Had logistical rather than engineering mission, namely, to load, carry, and unload a complete infantry division*] [*World War II*] EAC
Engineer Automation Support Activity [*Army Corps of Engineers*] EASA
Engineer Aviation Battalion [*Military*] EABN
Engineer Aviation Unit Training Center [*Military*] EAUTC
Engineer Battalion [*Military*] EB
Engineer Battalion [*Military*] ENGBAT
Engineer Battalion [*Military*] ENGRBN
Engineer Boat and Shore Regiment [*Army*] EB & SR

Engineer Boat and Shore Regiment [*Army*] ... EBSR
Engineer Captain [*Navy*] [*British*] ... EC
Engineer Change Order Request ... ECOR
Engineer-in-Charge [*Army*] ... E in C
Engineer-in-Charge ... EIC
Engineer-in-Chief ... E in C
Engineer Circular [*Army Corps of Engineers*] ... EC
Engineer Combat Battalions ... ECBS
Engineer Commissioner, District of Columbia [*Military*] ... ENGCOMDC
Engineer Construction Battalion ... ECB
Engineer Construction Command [*Army*] ... ENCOM
Engineer Control and Advisory Detachment [*Air Force*] ... ECAD
Engineer District, Far East ... EDFE
Engineer in Electrical Engineering ... E in EE
Engineer Element ... ENGRE
Engineer Functional Components System ... EPCS
Engineer, Furnish, and Install ... EF & I
Engineer Group, Construction [*Military*] ... EGC
Engineer Hill [*Alaska*] [*Seismograph station code, US Geological Survey*] ... ENG
Engineer Historical Division [*Army*] ... EHD
Engineer Information and Data Systems Office [*Army*] ... EIDSO
Engineer Intelligence Note ... EIN
Engineer Lieutenant [*Navy*] [*British*] ... EL
Engineer Lieutenant-Commander [*Navy*] [*British*] ... ELCR
Engineer-Maintenance Assembly-Disassembly [*NERVA program*] ... E-MAD
Engineer Maintenance Center ... EMC
Engineer Maintenance Control [*Army*] ... EMC
Engineer Manager ... EM
Engineer Manual [*Army Corps of Engineers*] ... EM
Engineer in Mechanical Engineering ... E in ME
Engineer of Metallurgy ... E Met
Engineer of Mines [*or Mining*] ... EM
Engineer-Officer [*Military*] [*British*] ... EO
Engineer Officers Reserve Corps ... ENGORC
Engineer Packaging Technical Office [*Merged with General Equipment Command*] ... EPTO
Engineer Pamphlet [*Army Corps of Engineers*] ... EP
Engineer Personnel [*Marine Corps*] ... EP
Engineer Photographic and Reproduction [*Marine Corps*] ... EPR
Engineer Procurement Office [*Army*] ... EPCO
Engineer and Railway Volunteer Staff Corps [*Army*] [*British*] ... ERVSC
Engineer Reactors Group [*Army*] ... ERG
Engineer Rear-Admiral [*Navy*] [*British*] ... EA
Engineer Rear-Admiral [*Navy*] [*British*] ... ERA
Engineer Repair Parts Packaging Office [*Merged with General Equipment Command*] ... ERPPO
Engineer Replacement Training Center ... ERTC
Engineer/Service [*Aerospace*] ... E/S
Engineer/Service Test Office [*Aerospace*] ... ESTO
Engineer Special Brigade [*Military*] ... ESB
Engineer Specialized Services ... ESS
Engineer Stores Assignment [*British*] ... ESA
Engineer Strategic Studies Group [*Army*] ... ESSG
Engineer Technical Letter [*Army Corps of Engineers*] ... ETL
Engineer Test/Service Test ... ET/ST
Engineer Topographic Laboratories [*Army*] ... ETL
Engineer-in-Training ... EIT
Engineer Training ... ET
Engineer/User [*Aerospace*] ... E/U
Engineer Vice-Admiral [*British*] ... EVA
Engineer Volunteer Corps [*British*] ... EVC
Engineered Fasteners Division [*Townsend Co.*] ... EFD
Engineered Military Circuit [*Leased long lines established in continental US*] [*Military*] ... EMC
Engineered Operating Cycle ... EOC
Engineered Restoration Procedure ... ERP
Engineered Safeguards Actuation System [*Nuclear energy*] ... ESAS
Engineered Safety Feature [*Nuclear energy*] ... ESF
Engineered Safety Features Actuation System [*Nuclear energy*] ... ESFAS
Engineered Time Standards ... ETS
Engineering ... ENGIN
Engineering ... ENGN
Engineering ... ENGNG
Engineering ... ENGRG
Engineering ... ENGRING
Engineering Abstract Report [*Defense Supply Agency*] ... EAR
Engineering Action Board ... EAB
Engineering and Administrative Data Acquisition System [*Bell System*] ... EADAS
Engineering Administrative Data Systems ... EADS
Engineering Advance Material Release ... EAMR
Engineering Aid [*Navy rating*] ... EA
Engineering Aid, Chief [*Navy rating*] ... EAC
Engineering Aid, Draftsman [*Navy rating*] [*Obsolete*] ... EAD
Engineering Aid, First Class [*Navy rating*] ... EA1
Engineering Aid, Master Chief [*Navy rating*] ... EACM
Engineering Aid, Second Class [*Navy rating*] ... EA2
Engineering Aid, Senior Chief [*Navy rating*] ... EACS
Engineering Aid, Surveyor [*Navy rating*] [*Obsolete*] ... EAS
Engineering Aid, Third Class [*Navy rating*] ... EA3
Engineering Analysis Report ... EAR
Engineering Analysis and Simulation Language [*Data processing*] ... EASL
Engineering Analysis Team [*NASA*] ... EAT
Engineering and Architects Association ... EAA
Engineering Aspects of Magnetohydrodynamics ... EAMHD
Engineering Assembly Parts List ... EAPL
Engineering Assistant ... EGA
Engineering Association of the South. Transactions [*A publication*] ... Eng As South Tr
Engineering Automated Systems ... EAS
Engineering Automatic System for Solving Equations ... EASE
Engineering and Boilerhouse Review [*A publication*] ... Eng Boilerhouse Rev
Engineering Capacity Exchange ... ECE
Engineering Casualty Control [*Military*] ... ECC
Engineering Casualty Control Training Team [*Navy*] ... ECCTT
Engineering Center ... ENGRCEN
Engineering Central Files ... ECF
Engineering Change ... EC
Engineering Change Analysis ... ECA
Engineering Change Announcement ... ECA
Engineering Change Authorization ... ECA
Engineering Change Committee ... ECC
Engineering Change Control ... ECC
Engineering Change Control Board ... ECCB
Engineering Change Incorporation ... ECI
Engineering Change Information ... ECI
Engineering Change Instruction ... ECI
Engineering Change List ... ECL
Engineering Change Management-Development ... ECM-D
Engineering Change Memo ... ECM
Engineering Change Notice ... ECN
Engineering Change Order ... ECO
Engineering Change Proposal ... ECP
Engineering Change Proposal Service Action Status ... EXPSAS
Engineering Change Proposal Work Statement ... ECPWS
Engineering Change Report ... ECR
Engineering Change [*or Correction*] **Request** [*or Requirement*] ... ECR
Engineering Change Request/Authorization ... ECR/A
Engineering Change Schedule ... ECS
Engineering Change Sheet ... ECS
Engineering Change Summary ... ECS
Engineering Cognizant Authority ... EC
Engineering College Administrative Council ... ECAC
Engineering College Magazines Associated ... ECMA
Engineering College Research Council ... ECRC
Engineering Command ... ENC
Engineering Command ... ENGCOM
Engineering Committee for the American Bicentennial ... ECAB
Engineering Committee on Oceanic Resources [*United Nations*] ... ECOR
Engineering Concept Review ... ECR
Engineering Concepts Curriculum Project ... ECCP
Engineering Configuration Data Control ... ECDC
Engineering Configuration List ... ECL
Engineering Construction ... EC
Engineering Construction and Related Industries Manpower [*British*] ... ECRIM
Engineering and Contract Record [*A publication*] ... Eng Contract Rec
Engineering Contractors Association ... ECA
Engineering Contracts Requirement Committee ... ECRC
Engineering Control Board ... ECB
Engineering Control Drawing ... ECD
Engineering Control System ... ECS
Engineering. Cornell Quarterly [*A publication*] ... Eng Cornell Q
Engineering Corps ... EC
Engineering Critical ... EC
Engineering Critical Component ... ECC
Engineering Cybernetics [*A publication*] ... Eng Cybern
Engineering Data ... ED
Engineering Data Bank [*GIDEP*] ... EDB
Engineering Data Control ... EDC
Engineering Data Depository ... EDD
Engineering Data File ... EDF
Engineering Data Information System ... EDIS
Engineering Data Management ... EDM
Engineering Data Management Information Control System [*DoD*] ... EDMICS
Engineering Data Management System [*Jet Propulsion Laboratory, NASA*] ... EDMS
Engineering Data Microreproduction System [*DoD*] ... EDMS
Engineering Data Plotting [*Data processing*] ... EDPLOT
Engineering Data Requirements ... EDR
Engineering Data Retrieval System [*Military*] ... EDRS
Engineering Data Service Center [*Air Force*] ... EDSC
Engineering Data Sheet ... EDS
Engineering Data Storage and Retrieval [*Military*] ... EDS & R
Engineering Data Support Center [*Air Force*] ... EDSC
Engineering Data Systems [*DoD*] ... EDS
Engineering Decision Integrator and Communicator ... EDIAC
Engineering Demonstrated Inspection ... EDI
Engineering Department [*Navy*] [*British*] ... ED
Engineering Department Interface Control Task [*or Technique*] ... EDICT

Engineering Department Notice ... EDN
Engineering Department [*or Division*] **Report** ... EDR
Engineering Depot ... ED
Engineering Design ... ED
Engineering Design Advisory Committee ... EDAC
Engineering Design and Analysis Laboratory Habitat ... EDALHAB
Engineering Design Change ... EDC
Engineering Design Change Proposal ... EDCP
Engineering Design Change Request ... EDCR
Engineering Design Change Schedule ... EDCS
Engineering Design Data ... EDD
Engineering Design Data Package ... EDDP
Engineering Design Documentation Procedures ... EDDP
Engineering Design Handbook Advisory Group ... EDHAG
Engineering, Design, and Inspection ... ED & I
Engineering Design Integration System [*NASA*] ... EDIN
Engineering Design Machine ... EDM
Engineering Design Memorandum ... EDM
Engineering Design Plan ... EDP
Engineering Design Proposal ... EDP
Engineering Design Review ... EDR
Engineering Design Review Board ... EDRB
Engineering Design Test ... EDT
Engineering Designer [*A publication*] ... Engng Des
Engineering Development ... ED
Engineering and Development Directorate [*NASA*] ... EDD
Engineering Development Integration Test ... EDIT
Engineering Development Laboratory ... EDL
Engineering Development Laboratory Program ... EDLP
Engineering Development Logic Network ... EDLN
Engineering Development Model ... EDM
Engineering Development Part Release ... EDPR
Engineering Development Phase ... EDP
Engineering and Development Services Department [*Naval Air Development Center*] ... EDSD
Engineering and Development Support Services ... EDSS
Engineering Development Systems Integration Laboratory ... EDSIL
Engineering Development Test ... EDT
Engineering Digest (Toronto) [*A publication*] ... Eng Dig (Toronto)
Engineering Directive ... ED
Engineering Division ... ED
Engineering Document ... ED
Engineering Document [*or Drawing*] **Information Collection Task** [*or Technique*] ... EDICT
Engineering Documentation Center [*NASA*] ... EDC
Engineering Drafting Machine ... EDM
Engineering Drafting Manual [*Air Force*] ... EDM
Engineering Draftsman ... ED
Engineering Drawing and Assembly Release Record ... EDARR
Engineering Drawing List ... EDL
Engineering Drawing Microfilm ... EDM
Engineering Drawing Release ... EDR
Engineering Drawing Release Authorization ... EDRA
Engineering Duty [*Navy*] ... ED
Engineering Duty Officer [*Military*] ... EDO
Engineering Duty Only [*Aerospace*] ... EDO
Engineering Economic Cost Analysis ... EECA
Engineering Economist [*A publication*] ... Eng Econ
Engineering Economist [*A publication*] ... Eng Economist
Engineering Education [*A publication*] ... Eng Educ
Engineering Electronics Laboratory ... EEL
Engineering Equipment Users Association ... EEUA
Engineering Evaluation Article ... EEA
Engineering Evaluation Model ... EEM
Engineering Evaluation Test ... EET
Engineering Evaluation Test Program ... EETP
Engineering Experiment Station ... EES
Engineering Experimental Memo ... EEM
Engineering Experimental Phase [*National Data Buoy Project*] ... EEP
Engineering Facilities Depot ... EFD
Engineering Facility ... ENGRFAC
Engineering Feasibility Model ... EFM
Engineering Field Divisions [*Military*] ... EFD
Engineering Flight Test ... EFT
Engineering Flight Test Inspector ... EFTI
Engineering Flight Test Instrumentation ... EFTI
Engineering Flight Test Report ... EFTR
Engineering Flow Diagram ... EFD
Engineering Foundation ... EF
Engineering Fracture Mechanics [*A publication*] ... Eng Fract Mech
Engineering Geologist ... EG
Engineering Geology [*A publication*] ... Eng Geol
Engineering Geology [*A publication*] ... Engng Geol
Engineering Geology and Soils Engineering Symposium. Proceedings [*A publication*] ... Eng Geol Soils Eng Symp Proc
Engineering Index [*A publication*] ... Ei
Engineering Index [*A publication*] ... Engl
Engineering Index [*A publication*] ... Eng Ind
Engineering Index of India [*A publication*] ... Eng Ind India
Engineering Index Thesaurus [*A publication*] ... EIT
Engineering Industries (Iraq) [*A publication*] ... Eng Ind (Iraq)
Engineering Industry Training Board [*British*] ... EITB
Engineering Information [*An association*] ... Ei
Engineering Information Center ... EIC
Engineering-Installation ... E-I
Engineering Installation Management System [*Air Force*] ... EIMS
Engineering Installation Plan ... EIP
Engineering Installation Workload Schedule ... EIWS
Engineering Institute of Canada ... EIC
Engineering Institute of Canada, Montreal, PQ, Canada [*Library symbol*] [*Obsolete*] ... CaQME
Engineering Institute of Canada. Transactions [*A publication*] ... Eng Inst Canada Trans
Engineering Instruction ... EI
Engineering Instruction Bulletin ... EIB
Engineering and Instrumentation [*A publication*] ... Eng & Instrumentation
Engineering Instrumentation Requirements Document ... EIRD
Engineering Interface Management Office ... EIMO
Engineering Investigation ... EI
Engineering Investigation Request ... EIR
Engineering Issues [*A publication*] ... Eng Issues
Engineering Item Description ... EID
Engineering Item Identification ... EII
Engineering Job Analysis ... EJA
Engineering Job Order ... EJO
Engineering Job Sheet ... EJS
Engineering Job Ticket ... EJT
Engineering Journal [*A publication*] ... Engng J
Engineering Journal. American Institute of Steel Construction [*A publication*] ... Eng J
Engineering Journal (Montreal) [*A publication*] ... Eng J (Montreal)
Engineering Laboratories [*Army*] ... EL
Engineering and Laboratory ... E & L
Engineering Laboratory Report ... ELR
Engineering Laboratory Technician ... ELT
Engineering Liaison Request ... ELR
Engineering Logic Diagram ... ELD
Engineering and Logistics Management Office [*MERDC*] [*Army*] ... ELMO
Engineering Lunar Model Surface ... ELMS
Engineering Magazine [*A publication*] ... Engin M
Engineering Magazine [*A publication*] ... Eng M
Engineering Malfunction Report ... EMR
Engineering Management ... EM
Engineering Management Information System [*Defense Supply Agency*] ... EMIS
Engineering Management Information Technique ... EMIT
Engineering Management Manual ... EMM
Engineering Management Network ... EMN
Engineering Manpower Bulletin [*Engineers' Joint Council*] [*A publication*] ... EMB
Engineering Manpower Commission ... EMC
Engineering Manual ... EM
Engineering Manual Preparation Instruction [*Army Materiel Command*] ... EMPI
Engineering and Manufacturing District Office [*FAA*] ... EMDO
Engineering Manufacturing Division Instruction ... EMDI
Engineering Manufacturing Liaison Release ... EMLR
Engineering Master Drawing ... EMD
Engineering Master Parts List ... EMPL
Engineering Master Schedule ... EMS
Engineering Materials and Design [*A publication*] ... Eng Mat Des
Engineering Materials and Design [*A publication*] ... Eng Mater & Des
Engineering Materials and Design [*A publication*] ... Eng Mater Des
Engineering Materials and Design [*A publication*] ... Engng Mater Des
Engineering Materials List [*Nuclear energy*] ... EML
Engineering Measurements [*NASDAQ symbol*] ... EMCX
Engineering Mechanics Laboratory [*National Bureau of Standards*] ... EML
Engineering in Medicine [*A publication*] ... Eng Med
Engineering in Medicine and Biology ... EMB
Engineering Memorandum ... EM
Engineering Methods Analysis ... EMA
Engineering and Mining Journal [*A publication*] ... EMJ
Engineering and Mining Journal [*A publication*] ... E & M Jour
Engineering and Mining Journal [*A publication*] ... Eng & Min J
Engineering and Mining Journal [*A publication*] ... Eng Min J
Engineering and Mining Journal [*A publication*] ... Engng Min J
Engineering Mock-Up ... EMU
Engineering Mock-Up Critical Experiment [*Nuclear energy*] ... EMC
Engineering Mock-Up and Manufacturing Aid ... EMMA
Engineering Model ... EM
Engineering Model Transport ... EMT
Engineering Modification Proposal ... EMP
Engineering Module ... EM
Engineering Narrative Report [*Defense Supply Agency*] ... ENR
Engineering News-Record [*A publication*] ... Engin N
Engineering News-Record [*A publication*] ... Eng N
Engineering News-Record [*A publication*] ... Eng New-Rc
Engineering News-Record [*A publication*] ... Eng News-Rec
Engineering Next Assembly ... ENA
Engineering Note [*or Notice*] ... EN
Engineering Officer of the Watch [*Navy*] ... EOOW
Engineering Officers Reserve Corps ... EORC

Engineering Operating Directives	EOD
Engineering Operating Procedure	EOP
Engineering Operational Casualty Control	EOCC
Engineering Operational Sequencing System	EOSS
Engineering and Operations Building [NASA]	EOB
Engineering Operations Control	EOC
Engineering/Operations - Information Management System	E/O-IMS
Engineering Operations Manual [NASA]	EOM
Engineering Opportunities [A publication]	E/O
Engineering Optimization [A publication]	Eng Optim
Engineering Optimization [A publication]	Eng Optimization
Engineering Order	EO
Engineering Order Delayed for Parts	EODP
Engineering Order Worksheet	EOW
Engineering Paper	EP
Engineering Part Card	EPC
Engineering Parts List	EPL
Engineering Parts List/Drawing Release List	EPL/DRL
Engineering Parts Release	EPR
Engineering Performance Measurement System	EPMS
Engineering Performance Standards	EPS
Engineering Personnel [Coast Guard]	EP
Engineering Planning Document	EPD
Engineering Power Reactor	EPR
Engineering Practice	EP
Engineering Practice Amendment	EPA
Engineering Print	EP
Engineering Print System [Xerox]	EPS
Engineering Procedure	EP
Engineering Procedures Manual	EPM
Engineering Procedures Services	EPS
Engineering Process Bulletin	EPB
Engineering and Process Economics [A publication]	Eng Process Econ
Engineering and Product Development Work Order	EPDWO
Engineering Production [A publication]	Engng Prod
Engineering Production [A publication]	Eng Prod
Engineering Program Definition Plan	EPDP
Engineering Progress. University of Florida. Bulletin [A publication]	Eng Progr Univ Fla Bull
Engineering Progress. University of Florida. Technical Progress Report [A publication]	Eng Progr Univ Fla Tech Progr Rep
Engineering Project	EP
Engineering Project Management System	EPMS
Engineering Proposal	EP
Engineering Purchase Specification	EPS
Engineering Qualification Test	EQT
Engineering Quality	EQ
Engineering Reference Branch [Department of the Interior]	ERB
Engineering Reference Number	ERN
Engineering Regulations [A publication]	ER
Engineering Release	ER
Engineering Release Authorization	ERA
Engineering Release Group	ERG
Engineering Release Notice	ERN
Engineering Release Operations	ERO
Engineering Release Order [Formerly, ROD]	ERO
Engineering Release Package	ERP
Engineering Release Record	ERR
Engineering Release System	ERS
Engineering Release Ticket	ERT
Engineering Release for Vendor Article Data [Later, PRVD]	ERVAD
Engineering Release Work Sheet	ERWS
Engineering Reliability and Quality Control	ERQC
Engineering Reliability Review	ER
Engineering and Repair [Department] [Navy]	E & R
Engineering Report	ER
Engineering Reprographic Management Association [Later, ERS]	ERMA
Engineering Reprographic Society [Formerly, ERMA]	ERS
Engineering Request Authorization	ERA
Engineering Requirements Plan [for Military Assistance Programs]	ERP
Engineering Research Associates	ERA
Engineering Research Council	ERC
Engineering Research and Development Laboratory [Army]	ERDL
Engineering Research Initiation Program [National Science Foundation]	ERIP
Engineering Research Institute	ERI
Engineering Research Report	ERR
Engineering Research Station [British]	ERS
Engineering Review Board [NASA]	ERB
Engineering Schedule Memo	ESM
Engineering Schedule Plan	ESP
Engineering Schoolship [Navy]	ENGSS
Engineering and Science [A publication]	Eng and Sci
Engineering, Science, and Management War Training	ESMWT
Engineering-Science News [A publication]	Eng-Sci News
Engineering Sciences Data Unit	ESDU
Engineering Sciences Data Unit. Data Items [A publication]	ESDU Data Items
Engineering and Scientific Career Continuation Pay [Air Force]	ESCCP
Engineering and Scientific Interpreter	ESI
Engineering Sequential Camera	ESC

Engineering Sequential Camera Coverage	ESCC
Engineering Service Circuit	ESC
Engineering Service [or Support] Group	ESG
Engineering Service Memo	ESM
Engineering Service Order	ESO
Engineering Service Project	ESP
Engineering Service Publications	ESP
Engineering Service Requests	ESR
Engineering/Service Test and Independent Evaluation Program [Army]	E/S TIEP
Engineering Services Laboratory [Air Force]	ESL
Engineering Services and Safety	ES & S
Engineering Shipping Notice	ESN
Engineering Signal Processor	ESP
Engineering Sketch	ESK
Engineering Societies Commission on Energy	ESCOE
Engineering Societies Library	ESL
Engineering Societies Library. ESL Bibliography [A publication]	Eng Soc Libr ESL Bibliogr
Engineering Societies Library, New York, NY [Library symbol]	NNE
Engineering and Society	ES
Engineering Society of Baltimore, Baltimore, MD [Library symbol]	MdBREC
Engineering Society of York. Proceedings [A publication]	Eng Soc York Pr
Engineering Special Test Equipment	ESTE
Engineering Specification [Air Force]	ENSP
Engineering Specification Control Document	ESCD
Engineering Specification Files	ESF
Engineering Standard	ES
Engineering Standard Specification	ESS
Engineering Standardization Directives	ESD
Engineering Statement of Work	ESOW
Engineering Statement of Work	ESW
Engineering Stop Order	ESO
Engineering Structures [A publication]	Eng Struct
Engineering Student Officer Program [Air Force]	ESOP
Engineering Study	ES
Engineering Study Authorization Division [NASA]	ESA
Engineering Sub Task	EST
Engineering Summary Report	ESR
Engineering Support Activity [Military]	ESA
Engineering Support Equipment	ESE
Engineering Support Field Office [Federal disaster planning]	ESFO
Engineering Support Request	ESR
Engineering Support Team	EST
Engineering Support Test Equipment [Deep Space Instrumentation Facility, NASA]	ETE
Engineering Surveillance Report	ENSURE
Engineering Tactical System	ETS
Engineering Task Assignment	ETA
Engineering and Technical Service	ETS
Engineering Technologist Certification Institute	ETCI
Engineering Technology	ET
Engineering Television Mode	ETV
Engineering Test	ET
Engineering Test Base Office	ETBO
Engineering Test Basis	ETB
Engineering Test Capsule	ETC
Engineering Test Directive	ETD
Engineering Test and Evaluation	ET & E
Engineering Test Evaluation	ETE
Engineering Test Facility [DoD]	ETF
Engineering Test Laboratory	ETL
Engineering Test Model	ETM
Engineering Test Program [NASA]	ETP
Engineering Test Reactor	ETR
Engineering Test Reactor Critical Facility	ETRC
Engineering Test Request [NASA]	ETR
Engineering Test Satellite	ETS
Engineering Test Unit	ETU
Engineering Test Vehicle	ETV
Engineering Test Vehicle Program	ETVP
Engineering Thermoplastic [Plastics technology]	ETP
Engineering Time Estimate	ETE
Engineering Time Standards [Navy]	ETS
Engineering Times (Calcutta) [A publication]	Eng Times (Calcutta)
Engineering Today [A publication]	Eng Today
Engineering and Training Center [NASA]	ETC
Engineering Unit	EU
Engineering Verification Test	EVT
[Qualified for] Engineering Watch [USNR officer classification]	WM
Engineering Waterways Experiment Station [Army]	EWES
Engineering Week [A publication]	Eng Week
Engineering Weekly Labor Distribution	EWLD
Engineering Work Assignment	EWA
Engineering Work Authorization	EWA
Engineering Work Order	EWO
Engineering Work Order - Drawing Summary	EWODS
Engineering Work Report [or Request]	EWR
Engineering Work Schedule	EWS

Engineering Work Statement ... EWS
Engineering Writer ... EGW
Engineering Writing and Speech ... EWS
Engineering Youth Day ... EYD
Engineers' Bulletin [*A publication*] ... Engineers' Bull
Engineers' Club of Dayton, Dayton, OH [*Library symbol*] ... ODaE
Engineers' Club, Philadelphia, PA [*Library symbol*] [*Obsolete*] ... PPEng
Engineers' Club of Philadelphia. Proceedings [*A publication*] ... Eng Club Phila Pr
Engineers Council for Professional Development [*Later, ABET*] ... ECPD
Engineers' Digest [*A publication*] ... Eng Dig
Engineers' Digest [*A publication*] ... Engrs Dig
Engineers' Digest (London) [*A publication*] ... Eng Dig (London)
Engineers Joint Council [*Superseded by AAES*] ... EJC
Engineers' Language for Automatic Test Equipment ... ELATE
Engineers Manual for Emergency Construction [*Army Corps of Engineers*] ... EMEC
Engineer's Order Wire ... EOW
Engineers Registration Board [*Council of Engineering Institutions*] [*British*] ... ERB
[*The*] **Engineers School** ... TES
Engineers and Scientists of America [*Defunct*] ... ESA
Engineers Society of Norway ... ESN
Engineers' Society of Western Pennsylvania. Proceedings [*A publication*] ... Eng Soc W Pa
Engineers Supply Control Office [*Army*] ... ESCO
Engineman [*Navy rating*] ... EN
Engineman, Chief [*Navy rating*] ... ENC
Engineman, First Class [*Navy rating*] ... EN1
Engineman, Master Chief [*Navy rating*] ... ENCM
Engineman, Second Class [*Navy rating*] ... EN2
Engineman, Senior Chief [*Navy rating*] ... ENCS
Engineman, Third Class [*Navy rating*] ... EN3
England [*or English*] ... ENG
England ... ENGL
England [*MARC country of publication code*] [*Library of Congress*] ... enk
England [*MARC geographic area code*] [*Library of Congress*] ... e-uk-en
England-Amerika-Institut [*A publication*] ... EAI
England, AR [*Radio station call letters*] ... KELC
England, France, Ireland, Scotland, Germany, and Aborigines [*See also TUPONA*] [*Suggested early name for Canada*] ... EFISGA
England and Wales ... E & W
Englehard, NC [*Location identifier*] [*FAA*] ... EQP
Englewood, CO [*Radio station call letters*] ... KWBZ
Englewood, FL [*Radio station call letters*] ... WENG
Englewood Library, Englewood, NJ [*Library symbol*] ... NjEn
Englewood Press, Englewood, NJ [*Library symbol*] ... NjEnP
Englewood Public Library, Englewood, CO [*Library symbol*] ... CoEn
Englewood, TN [*Radio station call letters*] ... WENR
Englische Studien [*A publication*] ... Engl Stud
Englische Studien [*A publication*] ... ES
Englische Studien [*A publication*] ... ESn
Englische Studien [*A publication*] ... EStn
Englisches Seminar [*A publication*] ... ES
English ... E
English [*A publication*] ... Eng
English [*A publication*] ... E
English [*MARC language code*] [*Library of Congress*] ... eng
English in Action ... EIA
English in Africa [*A publication*] ... E in A
English Association of American Bond and Share Holders [*Commercial firm*] ... EAABSH
English Association Pamphlets [*A publication*] ... EAP
English Bible ... EB
English Ceramic Circle ... ECC
English Chamber Choir ... ECC
English Chamber Orchestra ... ECO
English Church Union ... ECU
English Cocker Spaniel Club of America ... ECSCA
English Comprehension Level [*Army*] ... ECL
English Dance and Song [*A publication*] ... EDS
English Dance and Song [*A publication*] ... Eng Dance
English Dialect Dictionary [*A publication*] ... EDD
English Dialect Society ... EDS
English Education [*A publication*] ... Eng Educ
English in Education [*A publication*] ... English in Ed
English Electric Journal [*A publication*] ... Engl Elec J
English Fiction in Transition [*1880-1920*] [*Later, English Literature in Transition [1880-1920]*] [*A publication*] ... EFT
English Finish [*Paper*] ... EF
English Folk Dance and Song Society. Journal [*A publication*] ... Eng FD & S Soc Jl
English as a Foreign Language ... EFL
English for Foreigners ... EFF
English and Germanic Studies [*A publication*] ... EAGS
English and Germanic Studies [*A publication*] ... EG
English and Germanic Studies [*A publication*] ... E & Ger St
English and Germanic Studies [*A publication*] ... EGS
English and Germanic Studies [*A publication*] ... E and G Stud
English Historical Review [*A publication*] ... EHR
English Historical Review [*A publication*] ... Eng His R
English Historical Review [*A publication*] ... Eng Hist R
English Historical Review [*A publication*] ... Engl Hist R
English Historical Review [*A publication*] ... English His
English Hymnal [*Episcopalian*] ... EH
English Illustrated Magazine [*A publication*] ... Eng Illust
English Industrial Estates Corporation ... EIEC
English Institute ... EI
English Institute Essays [*A publication*] ... EIE
English Institute Materials Center ... EIMC
English Institute of the University of Uppsala. Essays and Studies on English Language and Literature [*A publication*] ... EIUES
English Journal [*A publication*] ... EJ
English Journal [*A publication*] ... Eng J
English Journal [*A publication*] ... Engl J
English Journal (College Edition) [*A publication*] ... Engl J (Col Ed)
English Journal (High School Edition) [*A publication*] ... Engl J (H S Ed)
English Language Books Abroad [*A publication*] ... ELBA
English Language Books by Title [*A publication*] ... ELBT
English Language Education Council. Bulletin [*A publication*] ... ELEC
English Language and Literature [*A publication*] ... ELL
English Language Notes [*A publication*] ... ELN
English Language Notes [*A publication*] ... Eng Lang Notes
English Language Notes [*A publication*] ... Engl Lang Notes
English Language Program ... ELP
English Language Teaching ... ELT
English Language Teaching [*Later, English Language Teaching Journal*] [*A publication*] ... Engl Lang Teach
English Language Teaching [*Later, English Language Teaching Journal*] [*A publication*] ... Eng L T
English Language Teaching [*Later, English Language Teaching Journal*] [*A publication*] ... ELT
English Language Teaching Journal [*A publication*] ... ELTJ
English Language Teaching Journal [*A publication*] ... Eng Lang Teach J
English Linguistics, 1500-1800: A Collection of Facsimile Reprints [*A publication*] ... ELCFR
English Literary Renaissance [*A publication*] ... ELR
English Literary Renaissance [*A publication*] ... Engl Lit Renaissance
English Literary Studies [*A publication*] ... ELS
English Literature and Language [*Tokyo, Japan*] [*A publication*] ... ELLS
English Literature in Transition [*1380-1920*] [*A publication*] ... ELiT
English Literature in Transition [*1880-1920*] [*A publication*] ... ELT
English Literature in Transition [*1880-1920*] [*A publication*] ... Eng Lit in Trans
English Literature in Transition [*1880-1920*] [*A publication*] ... Engl Lit Transition
English Market ... EM
English Market Selection [*Cigars*] ... EMS
English, Middle [*MARC language code*] [*Library of Congress*] ... enm
English Miscellany [*A publication*] ... EM
English Miscellany. St. Stephen's College (Delhi) [*A publication*] ... EMD
English Miscellany. St. Stephen's College (Delhi) [*A publication*] ... EMSCD
English National Opera ... ENO
English Newspaper Association ... ENA
English [*Communion*] **Office** [*Episcopalian*] ... EO
English Philological Studies [*A publication*] ... EPS
English Place-Name Society ... EPNS
English Prize Cases [*Legal*] ... EPC
English Record [*A publication*] ... Engl Rec
English Record [*A publication*] ... EngR
English Record [*A publication*] ... ERec
English Reports [*Legal*] ... ER
English Reprint Series [*A publication*] ... ERS
English Review [*A publication*] ... English R
English Review [*A publication*] ... Engl Rev
English Review [*A publication*] ... EngR
English Review [*A publication*] ... ER
English Review. Salem State College [*A publication*] ... Eng Rev
English Rugby Union ... ERU
English as a Second Language ... ESL
English as a Secondary Dialect ... ESD
English Setter Association of America ... ESAA
English to Speakers of Other Languages [*Program*] ... ESOL
English-Speaking Nations [*of NATO*] ... ESN
English-Speaking Union of the United States ... ESU
English Spelling Association [*Also known as Ingglish Spelling 3soesiaesh3n*] ... IS3
English Springer Spaniel Field Trial Association ... ESSFTA
English Standard Gauge ... ESG
English Studies [*A publication*] ... Engl Stud
English Studies [*Amsterdam*] [*A publication*] ... EngS
English Studies [*A publication*] ... Eng St
English Studies [*A publication*] ... Eng Stud
English Studies [*A publication*] ... ES
English Studies [*A publication*] ... ESs
English Studies [*A publication*] ... ESt
English Studies [*A publication*] ... EStud
English Studies [*A publication*] ... E Studies
English Studies in Africa [*A publication*] ... ESA
English Studies in Africa [*A publication*] ... ESAfr
English Studies in Canada [*A publication*] ... ESC
English Symposium Papers [*A publication*] ... ESP

English Teaching Abstracts [*A publication*] ETAb
English Text ET
English Tourist Board ETB
English Toy Spaniel Club of America ETSCA
English Translation ET
English Universities Press EUP
English Version EV
English Versions EVV
Englishwoman's Domestic Magazine [*A publication*] Eng Dom M
Engraph, Inc. [*NASDAQ symbol*] ENGH
Engrave ENG
Engrave ENGRV
Engraved ENGR
Engraved Stationery Manufacturers Association ESMA
Engraved Stationery Manufacturers Research Institute ESMRI
Engraving Master EM
Enhanced Cobra Armament Program [*Military*] ECAP
Enhanced Distant Early Warning EDEW
Enhanced Enlisted Master Tape Record EEMTR
Enhanced Oil Recovery [*Petroleum engineering*] EOR
Enhanced Private Switched Communications Service [*Pronounced "ep-sis"*] [*AT & T*] EPSCS
Enhanced-Radiation [*Weapon*] ER
Enhanced Radiation/Reduced Blast ER/RB
Enhanced-Radiation Weapon ERW
Enhanced Tactical Fighter ETF
Enhancement Metal-Oxide Semiconductor EMOS
Enhancement Ratio ER
Enid [*Oklahoma*] [*Airport symbol*] WDG
Enid Board of Trade EBT
Enid, OK [*Location identifier*] [*FAA*] END
Enid, OK [*Radio station call letters*] KCRC
Enid, OK [*Television station call letters*] KEQO
Enid, OK [*Radio station call letters*] KGWA
Enid, OK [*Radio station call letters*] KNID
Enid, OK [*Radio station call letters*] KUAL
Enid, OK [*Radio station call letters*] KXLS
Enid, OK [*Location identifier*] [*FAA*] LVC
Enid, OK [*Location identifier*] [*FAA*] WDG
Eniwetok [*Marshall Islands*] [*Airport symbol*] ENT
Eniwetok Proving Ground [*AEC*] EPG
Enkephalin [*Brain peptide, subclass of ENDORPHIN*] ENK
Enkephalin-Containing Polypeptide [*Physiological chemistry*] ECP
Enlarge ENLG
Enlarged ENL
Enlarged ENLGD
Enlarged Committee for Program and Coordination [*United Nations Development Program*] ECPC
Enlarged Heart [*Medicine*] EH
Enlightenment Essays [*A publication*] EE
Enlightenment Essays [*A publication*] Enl E
Enlisted [*Often in combination with numbers to denote serviceman's grade*] E
Enlisted Assignment System EAS
Enlisted Association of the National Guard of the United States EANGUS
Enlisted Classification Code ECC
Enlisted Correspondence Course ECC
Enlisted Dining Facility [*Military*] EDF
Enlisted Distribution and Verification Report EDAVR
Enlisted Distribution and Verification Report EDVR
Enlisted Efficiency Report [*Army*] EER
Enlisted Efficiency Report Weighted Average [*Army*] EERWA
Enlisted Evaluation Center [*Army*] EEC
Enlisted Evaluation Report EER
Enlisted Evaluation System [*Army*] EES
Enlisted Loss to Commissioned Status [*Military*] ELTC
Enlisted Loss to Warrant Status [*Military*] ELTW
Enlisted Man [*or Men*] EM
Enlisted Manning Report [*Air Force*] EMR
Enlisted Master File [*Army*] EMF
Enlisted Master Tape Record [*Army*] EMTR
Enlisted Member EM
Enlisted Men on Duty with the Counter Intelligence Corps [*Army*] DEML(CIC)
Enlisted Men on Duty with the National Guard [*Army*] DEML(NG)
Enlisted Men on Duty with the Organized Reserves [*Army*] DEML(OR)
Enlisted Men on Duty with the Reserve Officers' Training Corps [*Army*] DEML(ROTC)
Enlisted Personnel EP
Enlisted Personnel Assignment Document [*Navy*] EPAD
Enlisted Personnel Directorate [*Army*] EPD
Enlisted Personnel Distribution Office [*Navy*] EPDO
Enlisted Personnel Distribution Office, Atlantic Fleet [*Navy*] EPDOLANT
Enlisted Personnel Distribution Office, Continental United States [*Navy*] EPDOCONUS
Enlisted Personnel Distribution Office, Pacific Fleet [*Navy*] EPDOPAC
Enlisted Personnel Division [*Navy*] EPD
Enlisted Personnel Enlistment Eligibility Activity [*Army*] EPEEA
Enlisted Personnel Management Center [*Navy*] EPMAC
Enlisted Personnel Management Directorate EPMD
Enlisted Personnel Management System [*Army*] EPMS
Enlisted Programs Branch [*BUPERS*] EPB
Enlisted Record Brief [*Army*] ERB
Enlisted Records and Evaluation Center [*Army*] EREC
Enlisted Reserve Corps [*Later, Army Reserve*] ERC
Enlisted Signal Corps School ESCS
Enlisted Training Branch [*BUPERS*] ETB
Enlisted Transfer Manual [*Military*] TRANSMAN
Enlisted Woman [*or Women*] EW
Enlisted Women's Quarters [*Military*] EWQ
Enlistment ENL
Enlistment Allowance [*Military*] EA
Enlistment Bonus [*Military*] EB
Enlistment Canceled [*Military*] ENC
Enlistment Screening Test [*Military*] EST
Enlow Public Library, West Branch, IA [*Library symbol*] IaWb
Ennis Business Forms, Inc. [*NYSE symbol*] EBF
Eno Foundation for Transportation EFT
Enoch Pratt Free Library, Baltimore, MD [*OCLC symbol*] MDB
Enoch Pratt Free Library, Baltimore, MD [*Library symbol*] MdBE
Enoch Pratt Free Library, George Peabody Branch, Baltimore, MD [*Library symbol*] MdBP
Enolpyruvate [*Biochemistry*] ePrv
Enolpyruvylshikimic Acid Phosphate [*Organic chemistry*] EPSP
Enormously Entertaining Prodigy EEP
Enough ENO
Enough Is Enough Club EEC
Enquete Mensuelle de Conjoncture [*A publication*] Enquete Mens Conjonct
Enquetes du Musee de la Vie Wallonne [*A publication*] EMW
Enquiry ENQ
Enquiry Agency [*British*] EA
Enrico Fermi Atomic Power Plant [*Decommissioned*] EFAPP
Enrico Fermi Fast Breeder Power Reactor EFFBR
Enrico Fermi Institute [*University of Chicago*] EFI
Enrico Fermi International Summer School of Physics [*Elsevier Book Series*] [*A publication*] EFI
Enrolled Agent [*IRS*] EA
Enrolled Federal Tax Accountant [*Service mark designation of EFTA Institute*] EFTA
Enrolled Nurse EN
Enrollment ENRL
Enroute Air Traffic Regulation EATR
Ensayos y Estudios [*A publication*] Ensay Estud
Enschede [*Netherlands*] [*Airport symbol*] ENS
Enseignement Chretien [*A publication*] ECh
Enseignement Chretien [*A publication*] EChr
Enseignement Mathematique [*A publication*] Enseignement Math
Enseignement Public [*A publication*] EPubl
Enseignement Technique [*A publication*] Enseign Techn
Ensemble ENS
Ensenanza e Investigacion en Psicologia [*A publication*] Ensenanza Invest Psicol
Enserch Corp. [*Formerly, LSG*] [*NYSE symbol*] ENS
Enshi [*China*] [*Airport symbol*] ENH
Ensign ENS
Ensign, KS [*Television station call letters*] KTVC
Ensource, Inc. [*NYSE symbol*] EEE
Enstar Corp. [*NYSE symbol*] EST
Enstar Corp. Pfd [*NASDAQ symbol*] ESTRP
Enstar Indonesia [*American Stock Exchange symbol*] ESR
Enstatite [*CIPW classification*] [*Geology*] en
Ensun Corp. [*NASDAQ symbol*] ENSN
Entayant Institute EI
Ente Gestione Aziende Minerarie Metallurgiche [*Italy*] EGAM
Ente Italiano della Moda EIM
Ente Minerario Siciliano EMS
Ente Nazionale Assistenza Lavoratori [*Italy*] ENAL
Ente Nazionale Consulenza Assistenza Tecnica ENCAT
Ente Nazionale per l'Energia Elettrica [*National Electric Energy Agency*] [*Italy*] ENEL
Ente Nazionale Idrocarburi [*National Hydrocarbons Authority*] [*State-owned oil agency*] [*Italy*] ENI
Ente Nazionale Italiano per il Turismo [*Italy*] ENIT
Ente de Radiodiffusion y Television [*Radio and television network*] [*Argentina*] ERT
Ente per la Transformazione Fondiaria e Agraria in Sardegna [*Italy*] ETFAS
Entebbe [*Uganda*] [*Seismograph station code, US Geological Survey*] [*Closed*] ENT
Entebbe/Kampala [*Uganda*] [*Airport symbol*] EBB
Enter ENT
Enter Control Area [*Aviation*] ECA
Enter Exponent [*Data processing*] EE
Enteral Nutrition Council ENC
Entered ENTD
Entered without Inspection [*Usually applies to aliens who enter at other than a port of entry*] EWI
Entered in Service [*Military*] EIS
Enteric Coated [*Pharmacology*] EC
Enteric-Coated Microspheres of Pancrelipase ECMP
Enteric Coated Tablet [*Pharmacology*] ECT

Enteric Cytopathogenic Porcine Orphan [*Virus*]....................ECPO
Enteric Nervous System [*Neurobiology*]..................... ENS
Entering [*FBI standardized term*]............................. E
Entering [*FBI standardized term*]............................ENT
Entering Air Defense Identification Zone .... EADIZ
Entering Complaint [*Medicine*]...............................EC
Entering Office Date ....EOD
Enterochromaffin Cells [*Medicine*]...........................EC
Enterocytopathogenic Bovine [*Virus*]........................ECBO
Enterocytopathogenic Dog Orphan [*Virus*]...................ECDO
Enterocytopathogenic Human Orphan [*Virus*]................ECHO
Enterocytopathogenic Monkey Orphan [*Virus*]...............ECMO
Enterocytopathogenic Swine Orphan [*Virus*].................ECSO
Enterohepatic Circulation [*Medicine*]........................EHC
Enterohepatic Clearance [*Medicine*]..........................EHC
Enteropathogenic Escherichia coli [*Also, EPEC*] [*Food microbiology*] ... EEC
Enteropathogenic Escherichia coli [*Also, EEC*] [*Medicine*] ....EPEC
Enterostomal Therapist [*Gastroenterology*].....................ET
Enterotoxigenic Escherichia coli [*Water pollution indicator*]................ETEC
Enterprise, AL [*Location identifier*] [*FAA*]...................BVG
Enterprise, AL [*Radio station call letters*]....................WIRB
Enterprise, AL [*Radio station call letters*]...................WKMX
Enterprise, AL [*Radio station call letters*]................WLHQ-FM
Enterprise America...EA
Enterprise, OR [*Radio station call letters*]..................KWVR
Enterprise Statistics [*A publication*] ....ES
Enterprise Technology [*NASDAQ symbol*]......................ENTR
Enterprise Zone [*British*]....................................EZ
Enterra Corp. [*NYSE symbol*]................................EN
Entertainment ....ENT
[*The*] Entertainment Channel [*Pay-television network*] [*Obsolete*]..........TEC
Entertainment Publications [*NASDAQ symbol*]................EPUB
Entertainment Satellite [*Proposed*] ....ENT/SAT
Entertainment and Sports Programming Network [*Television*] ....ESPN
Entertainment Tonight [*Television program*] ....ET
Entertainments National Service Association [*For British military forces*]................................ENSA
Entertainments Officer [*Military*] [*British*]...................EO
Entex, Inc. [*Formerly, UG*] [*NYSE symbol*]...................ETX
Entgegen [*Opposed*] [*Chemistry*] ....(E)
Enthalpy [*Symbol*] [*IUPAC*].................................H
Enthronement of the Sacred Heart in the Home [*An association*].........ESHH
Entire ....ENTR
Entire Field Available [*Aviation*]..............................EFA
Entitle ....ENTL
Entitled to Severance Pay ....ETSP
Entity...ENT
Entity Module [*Data processing*].............................EM
Entner-Doudoroff [*Hexose metabolic pathway*] ....ED
Entologicke Listy [*A publication*] ....Entomol Listy
Entomologia Experimentalis et Applicata [*A publication*] .... Ent Exp App
Entomologia Experimentalis et Applicata [*A publication*] ....
              Entomol Exp Appl
Entomologia Experimentalis et Applicata [*A publication*] ....
              Entomologia Exp Appl
Entomologic..ENTOMOL
Entomologica Americana [*A publication*] ....Entomol Am
Entomologica Germanica [*A publication*] ....Entomol Ger
Entomologica Scandinavica [*A publication*] ....Entomol Scand
Entomologica Scandinavica. Supplementum [*A publication*] ....
              Entomol Scand Suppl
Entomological News [*A publication*]..................... Entom N
Entomological News [*A publication*].................... Entom News
Entomological News [*A publication*]................... Entomol News
Entomological Research Institute..............................ERI
Entomological Review [*A publication*] ....Entomol Rev
Entomological Review (English Translation of Entomologicheskoye Obozreniye) [*A publication*]................
        Entomol Rev (Engl Transl Entomol Obozr)
Entomological Society of America...........................ESA
Entomological Society of America. Annals [*A publication*].................
              Entom Soc Am Ann
Entomological Society of America. North Central State Branch. Proceedings [*A publication*]...... Entomol Soc Amer N Cent State Br Proc
Entomological Society of New Zealand. Bulletin [*A publication*].................
              Entomol Soc NZ Bull
Entomological Society of Nigeria. Occasional Publication [*A publication*]..................... Entomol Soc Nigeria Occas Publ
Entomological Society of Ontario. Annual Report [*A publication*]..................
              Entomol Soc Ont Annu Rep
Entomological Society of Ontario, Guelph, ON, Canada [*Library symbol*]... CaOGE
Entomologiceskoe Obozrenie [*A publication*] .... Ent Obozr
Entomologicheskoe Obozrenie [*A publication*] .... Entomol Obozr
Entomologicke Problemy [*A publication*]................ Entomol Probl
Entomologie et Phytopathologie Appliquees [*A publication*].................
              Entomol Phytopathol Appl
Entomologische Abhandlungen (Dresden) [*A publication*].................
              Entomol Abh (Dres)

Entomologische Arbeiten. Museum G. Frey (Tutzing-Bei Muenchen) [*A publication*]...................................
        Entomol Arb Mus G Frey (Tutzing-Bei Muench)
Entomologische Berichten (Amsterdam) [*A publication*]...................
              Entomol Ber (Amst)
Entomologische Berichten (Berlin) [*A publication*]...........Entomol Ber (Berl)
Entomologische Blaetter fuer Biologie und Systematik der Kaefer [*A publication*]...................... Entomol Bl Biol Syst Kaefer
Entomologische Mitteilungen. Zoologischen Museum Hamburg [*A publication*].................... Entomol Mitt Zool Mus Hamb
Entomologische Mitteilungen. Zoologischen Staatsinstitut und Zoologischen Museum (Hamburg) [*A publication*] ....
        Entomol Mitt Zool Staatsinst Zool Mus (Hamb)
Entomologische Nachrichten [*A publication*] .... Entomol Nachr
Entomologische Zeitschrift [*A publication*] ....Entomol Z
Entomologisk Tidskrift [*A publication*] ....Entomol Tidskr
Entomologisk Tidskrift [*A publication*] ....Ent Tidskr
Entomologiske Meddelelser [*A publication*].............Entomol Medd
Entomologist [*A publication*]...............................Entomol
Entomologist's Gazette [*A publication*].................Entomol Gaz
Entomologist's Monthly Magazine [*A publication*] ....Ent Mon Mag
Entomologist's Monthly Magazine [*A publication*]...........Entom Month Mag
Entomologist's Monthly Magazine [*A publication*] ....Entomol Mon Mag
Entomologist's Record and Journal of Variation [*A publication*]...................
              Entomol Rec J Var
Entomology ....ENT
Entomology ....ENTO
Entomology ....ENTOM
Entomology Abstracts [*A publication*] .... Entomol Abstr
Entomology Bulletin. British Museum (Natural History) [*A publication*]............. Entomol Bull Brit Mus (Natur Hist)
Entomophaga Memoire Hors Serie [*A publication*] ....
              Entomophaga Mem Hors Ser
Entorhinal Cortex [*Brain anatomy*]...........................EC
Entr'aide Universitaire Mondiale [*World University Service*]................EUM
Entrained-Flow Gasification Test Facility ....EFGTF
Entrance ....E
Entrance [*Maps and charts*]................................ENTR
Entrance National Agency Check [*Military*]................ENTAC
Entrance National Agency Check [*Military*]...............ENTNAC
Entre' Computer Centers [*NASDAQ symbol*] ....ETRE
Entreprise Miniere et Chimique [*France*].....................EMC
Entreprise de Recherches et d'Activites Petrolieres [*State-owned petroleum agency*] [*France*].....................ERAP
Entretiens de Bichat Chirurgie Specialites [*A publication*].................
              Entretiens Bichat Chir Spec
Entretiens de Bichat Medecine et Biologie [*A publication*].................
              Entretiens Bichat Med Biol
Entretiens de Bichat Therapeutique [*A publication*] ... Entretiens Bichat Ther
Entretiens de Chize Serie Physiologie [*A publication*].................
              Entretiens Chize Ser Physiol
Entropy [*Symbol*] [*IUPAC*] ....S
Entropy Unit ....EU
Entrucking Point [*Military*].................................EP
Entry [*Horse racing*]..E
Entry on Active Duty ....EAD
Entry Code [*Data processing*]...............................EC
Entry Computer...ECU
Entry Corridor Display ....ECD
Entry Data Subsystem ....EDS
Entry on Duty..EOD
Entry Elapsed Time ....EET
Entry Interface..EI
Entry Interface Time ....EIT
Entry Level Interactive Applications Systems [*Data processing*]........ ELIAS
Entry Level Training ....ELT
Entry Lock [*Diving apparatus*]...............................EL
Entry Military Occupational Specialty ....EMOS
Entry Monitor Display ....EMD
Entry Monitor System [*or Subsystem*] [*NASA*]................EMS
Entry Point...EP
Entry and Postlanding [*NASA*].............................E & PL
Entry Query Control Console ....EQCC
Entry and Recovery Simulation ....ERS
Entry Survival System ....ESS
Entry Time-Sharing System [*Data processing*]................ETSS
Entsprechend [*Corresponding*] [*German*]..................ENTSPR
Entwicklungsalter [*Developmental Age*] [*Psychology*] ....EA
Entwicklungsgeschichte und Systematik der Pflanzen [*A publication*].......................Entwicklungsgesch Syst Pflanz
Entwistle Co. [*NASDAQ symbol*] ....ENTW
Enugu [*Nigeria*] [*Airport symbol*].........................ENU
Enumclaw, WA [*Radio station call letters*]..................KENU
Enumeration ....ENUM
Enumeration Area [*Statistics*]...............................EA
Enumeration District [*Census*] ....ED
Envelope ....ENV
Envelope Delay Distortion ....EDD
Envelope Elimination and Restoration ....EER
Envelope Institute of America...............................EIA
Envelope Manufacturers Association ....EMA

Envirodyne Industries [*NASDAQ symbol*] ... ENVR
Environ [*About*] [*French*] ... ENV
Environic Foundation International ... EFI
Environment [*A publication*] ... Env
Environment ... ENVIR
Environment ... ENVMT
Environment Action Bulletin [*A publication*] ... Env Action
Environment and Behavior [*A publication*] ... EB
Environment and Behavior [*A publication*] ... EBEH
Environment and Behavior [*A publication*] ... Envir Behav
Environment and Behavior [*A publication*] ... Environ Behav
Environment and Behavior [*A publication*] ... Environ & Behavior
Environment Canada ... EC
Environment Canada. Annual Report [*A publication*] ... Environ Can Annu Rep
Environment and Change [*A publication*] ... Environ Change
Environment Coordination Board ... ECB
Environment Council of Alberta, Edmonton, AB, Canada [*Library symbol*] ... CaAEECA
Environment/Ecology [*A publication*] ... Env
Environment Generator ... EG
Environment and Heredity ... E & H
Environment Index [*A publication*] ... Envl
Environment Information Abstracts [*A publication*] ... EIA
Environment Information Access [*A publication*] ... Env
Environment Information Center [*Information service*] ... EIC
Environment International [*A publication*] ... Environ Int
Environment Law Review [*A publication*] ... Environ Law Rev
Environment Libraries Automated System [*Canada*] [*Information service*] ... ELIAS
Environment and Man [*A publication*] ... Environ Man
Environment Midwest [*A publication*] ... Environ Midwest
Environment and Planning [*A publication*] ... Environ and Planning
Environment and Planning [*A publication*] ... Envir Plann
Environment and Planning. A [*A publication*] ... ENVG
Environment and Pollution [*Republic of Korea*] [*A publication*] ... Environ Pollut
Environment Pollutions Agency [*British*] ... EPA
Environment Protection Engineering [*A publication*] ... Environ Prot Eng
Environment This Month [*A publication*] ... Environ This Mon
Environmental ... ENVR
Environmental ... ENVRNMTL
Environmental ... ENVT
Environmental Abstracts [*A publication*] ... Environ Abstr
Environmental Acceptance Test ... EAT
Environmental Action [*An association*] ... EA
Environmental Action [*A publication*] ... Environ Action
Environmental Action [*A publication*] ... Environmt
Environmental Action Coalition ... EAC
Environmental Action Foundation ... EAF
Environmental Action for Survival [*An association*] ... ENACT
Environmental Affairs [*A publication*] ... ENVA
Environmental Affairs [*A publication*] ... Environ Aff
Environmental Analog Recording System ... EARS
Environmental Analysis [*Program*] ... ENVANAL
Environmental Assessment ... EA
Environmental Assessment Data Systems [*Environmental Protection Agency*] [*Information service*] ... EADS
Environmental Awareness Reading List [*Department of the Interior*] ... EARL
Environmental Biology [*A publication*] ... Environ Biol
Environmental Biology of Fishes [*A publication*] ... Environ Biol Fishes
Environmental Biology and Medicine [*A publication*] ... Environ Biol Med
Environmental Chamber ... EC
Environmental Chemicals Data and Information Network [*Commission of the European Communities*] ... ECDIN
Environmental Chemicals. Human and Animal Health. Proceedings of Annual Conference [*A publication*] ... Environ Chem Hum Anim Health
Environmental Chemistry [*A publication*] ... Environ Chem
Environmental Clearinghouse, Incorporated [*An association*] ... ECI
Environmental Coalition on Nuclear Power ... ECNP
Environmental Communications Network [*Proposed environmental information exchange network*] ... ECN
Environmental Compatibility Assurance Program [*Navy*] ... ECAP
Environmental Complexity ... EC
Environmental Conditions Determination ... ECD
Environmental Conservation [*A publication*] ... Environ Conser
Environmental Conservation [*A publication*] ... Environ Conserv
Environmental Contaminant Evaluation [*Fish and Wildlife Service program*] ... ECE
Environmental Control ... EC
Environmental Control Administration [*Later, EPA*] ... ECA
Environmental Control Equipment ... ECE
Environmental Control and Life Support [*NASA*] ... ECLS
Environmental Control and Life Support Subsystem [*NASA*] ... ECLSS
Environmental Control Management [*A publication*] ... Environ Contr Manage
Environmental Control Organization [*Proposed in 1970 by Walter J. Hickel, Secretary of the Interior*] ... ECO
Environmental Control and Safety Management [*A publication*] ... Environ Contr Safety Manage
Environmental Control Shroud [*Nuclear energy*] ... ECS
Environmental Control Subsystem Group ... ECSG
Environmental Control System [*NASA*] ... ECS
Environmental Control Table ... ECT
Environmental Control Unit ... ECU
Environmental Crisis Operation [*University of British Columbia*] ... ECO
Environmental Criteria and Assessment Office [*Environmental Protection Agency*] ... ECAO
Environmental Data Book ... EDB
Environmental Data Collection and Processing Facility [*Army*] ... EDCPF
Environmental Data Index [*National Oceanic and Atmospheric Administration*] ... ENDEX
Environmental Data and Information Service [*Formerly, EDS*] [*National Oceanic and Atmospheric Administration*] ... EDIS
Environmental Data Service [*A publication*] ... EDS
Environmental Data Service [*A publication*] ... Env Data Serv
Environmental Data Service [*Later, EDIS*] [*National Oceanic and Atmospheric Administration*] ... EDS
Environmental Data Services Report [*A publication*] ... Environ Data Serv Rep
Environmental Defense Fund ... EDF
Environmental Design Alignment Process ... EDAP
Environmental Design Research Association ... EDRA
Environmental Disruption ... ED
Environmental-Ecological Education [*Office of Education program*] ... EEE
Environmental Education [*A publication*] ... Environ Educ
Environmental Education Group ... EEG
Environmental Effects Group [*Army*] ... EEG
Environmental Effects Laboratory [*Army*] ... EEL
Environmental and Energy Study Conference ... EESC
Environmental Engineering [*A publication*] ... Environ Eng
Environmental Engineering Intersociety Board ... EEIB
Environmental Engineering Section ... EES
Environmental Entomology [*A publication*] ... Env Entomol
Environmental Entomology [*A publication*] ... Environ Entomol
Environmental Equipment Institute [*Defunct*] ... EEI
Environmental and Experimental Botany [*A publication*] ... Envir & Exper Bot
Environmental and Experimental Botany [*A publication*] ... Environ Exp Bot
Environmental Experiments Program [*National Science Foundation*] ... EEP
Environmental Extremists ... ENVEX
Environmental Financing Authority [*Expired, 1975*] [*Environmental Protection Agency*] ... EFA
[*The*] **Environmental Fund** ... TEF
Environmental, General Instrumentation, Life Support [*NASA*] ... EGIL
Environmental Geology [*A publication*] ... Envir Geol
Environmental Geology [*A publication*] ... Environ Geol
Environmental Group, Pacific Command ... EGPACOM
Environmental Health [*London*] [*A publication*] ... Environ Health
Environmental Health Engineering Services [*Army*] ... EHES
Environmental Health Laboratory [*Air Force*] ... EHL
Environmental Health Laboratory, Kelly Air Force Base ... EHL(K)
Environmental Health Laboratory, McClellan Air Force Base ... EHL-M
Environmental Health (Nagpur) [*A publication*] ... Environ Health (Nagpur)
Environmental Health Perspectives [*A publication*] ... Env Health Persp
Environmental Health Perspectives [*A publication*] ... Environ Health Perspect
Environmental Health Service [*US Government*] ... EHS
Environmental Health Specialist ... EHS
Environmental Hygiene Agency [*Army*] ... EHA
Environmental Impact ... EI
Environmental Impact Analysis Program [*Department of the Interior*] ... EIAP
Environmental Impact Assessment ... EIA
Environmental Impact Review ... EIR
Environmental Impact Statement [*Environmental Protection Agency*] ... EIS
Environmental Impact Study ... EIS
Environmental Improvement Program ... EIP
Environmental Industry Council ... EIC
Environmental Information Analysis Center [*Battelle Memorial Institute*] ... EIAC
Environmental Information Division [*Air Force Air Training Command*] ... EID
Environmental Information Management System ... EIMS
Environmental Information Retrieval On-Line [*Environmental Protection Agency*] ... ENVIRON
Environmental Information System [*National Science Foundation*] ... EIS
Environmental Information System Office [*National Science Foundation*] ... EISO
Environmental Law [*A publication*] ... Environ Law
Environmental Law Institute ... ELI
Environmental Law Reporter [*Environmental Law Institute*] [*A publication*] ... ELR
Environmental Letters [*A publication*] ... Envir Lett
Environmental Letters [*A publication*] ... Environ Lett
Environmental Life Support Assembly [*NASA*] ... ELSA
Environmental Management ... EM
Environmental Management [*A publication*] ... Environ Manage
Environmental Management Association [*Formerly, ISE*] ... EMA
Environmental Measurements Experiment ... EME
Environmental Measurements Laboratory [*Department of Energy*] ... EML

Environmental Measurements Laboratory Impactor [*Sampling instrument*] ... EMLI
Environmental Medicine Branch [*NASA*] ... EMB
Environmental Medicine Officer [*Military*] ... EMO
Environmental Meteorological Support Unit [*National Weather Service*] ... EMSU
Environmental Modification ... ENMOD
Environmental Monitoring ... EM
Environmental Monitoring and Assessment [*A publication*] ... EMA
Environmental Monitoring Systems Laboratory [*Environmental Protection Agency*] ... EMSL
Environmental and Morale Leave [*Military*] ... E & ML
Environmental Mutagen Information Center [*Environmental Information System Office*] ... EMIC
Environmental Mutagen Society ... EMS
Environmental Mutagenesis [*A publication*] ... Environ Mutagen
Environmental Newsletter [*A publication*] ... Environ Newsl
Environmental Periodicals Bibliography [*A publication*] ... Environ Per Bibl
Environmental Periodicals Bibliography ... EPB
Environmental Physiology [*A publication*] ... Environ Physiol
Environmental Physiology and Biochemistry [*A publication*] ... Environ Physiol Biochem
Environmental Physiology and Biochemistry [*A publication*] ... Env Phys Bi
Environmental Policy Center ... EPC
Environmental Policy Institute ... EPI
Environmental Policy and Law [*A publication*] ... Environ Pol Law
Environmental Pollution [*A publication*] ... Environ Pollut
Environmental Pollution [*A publication*] ... Envir Pollu
Environmental Pollution Control [*A publication*] ... Envir Poll Control
Environmental Pollution Control ... EPC
Environmental Pollution Management [*A publication*] ... Environ Pollut Manage
Environmental Pollution. Series A. Ecological and Biological [*A publication*] ... Environ Pollut Ser A
Environmental Pollution. Series B. Chemical and Physical [*A publication*] ... Environ Pollut Ser B
Environmental, Population, and Organismic Biology ... EPO
Environmental Prediction Research Facility [*Navy*] ... ENVPREDRSCHF
Environmental Prediction Research Facility [*Navy*] ... EPRF
Environmental Progress [*A publication*] ... Environ Prog
Environmental Project Manager ... EPM
Environmental Protection Agency [*Government agency formed in 1970*] ... EPA
Environmental Protection Agency, Environmental Monitoring and Support Laboratory, Las Vegas, NV [*OCLC symbol*] ... ERB
Environmental Protection Agency, Environmental Research Laboratory, Narragansett, RI [*OCLC symbol*] ... EHB
Environmental Protection Agency, Environmental Research Laboratory, Gulf Breeze, FL [*OCLC symbol*] ... EKC
Environmental Protection Agency, Environmental Research Laboratory, Athens, GA [*OCLC symbol*] ... EKD
Environmental Protection Agency, ERC [*Environmental Research Center*] **Library, Corvallis, OR** [*OCLC symbol*] ... ESB
Environmental Protection Agency, ESRL [*Environmental Sciences Research Laboratory*], **Meteorology Laboratory, Research Triangle Park, NC** [*OCLC symbol*] ... EKF
Environmental Protection Agency Grants Administration Manual ... EPAGM
Environmental Protection Agency, Headquarters Library, Washington, DC [*OCLC symbol*] ... EJB
Environmental Protection Agency, Law Library, Washington, DC [*OCLC symbol*] ... EJC
Environmental Protection Agency, Library, Environmental Research Center, Cincinnati, OH [*OCLC symbol*] ... ELB
Environmental Protection Agency, Library, Environmental Research Laboratory, Duluth, MN [*OCLC symbol*] ... ELD
Environmental Protection Agency, Library, Research Triangle Park, NC [*OCLC symbol*] ... EKE
Environmental Protection Agency, Library Services, Research Triangle Park, NC [*OCLC symbol*] ... EKB
Environmental Protection Agency, Motor Vehicle Emission Laboratory, Ann Arbor, MI [*OCLC symbol*] ... ELC
Environmental Protection Agency, NEIC Library, Denver, CO [*OCLC symbol*] ... EOB
Environmental Protection Agency, OTS [*Office of Toxic Substances*] **Technical Information Center, Washington, DC** [*OCLC symbol*] ... EJE
Environmental Protection Agency - Pesticide Regional Division ... EPA-PRD
Environmental Protection Agency, R. S. Kerr Environmental Research Laboratory, Ada, OK [*OCLC symbol*] ... EMB
Environmental Protection Agency, Region I Library, Boston, MA [*OCLC symbol*] ... EHA
Environmental Protection Agency, Region II Field Office, Edison, NJ [*OCLC symbol*] ... EIC
Environmental Protection Agency, Region II Library, New York, NY [*OCLC symbol*] ... EIA
Environmental Protection Agency, Region III Field Office, Annapolis, MD [*OCLC symbol*] ... EJD
Environmental Protection Agency, Region III Library, Philadelphia, PA [*OCLC symbol*] ... EJA
Environmental Protection Agency, Region IV Library, Atlanta, GA [*OCLC symbol*] ... EKA
Environmental Protection Agency, Region IX Library, San Francisco, CA [*OCLC symbol*] ... ERA
Environmental Protection Agency, Region V Library, Chicago, IL [*OCLC symbol*] ... ELA
Environmental Protection Agency, Region VI Library, Dallas, TX [*OCLC symbol*] ... EMA
Environmental Protection Agency, Region VII Library, Kansas City, MO [*OCLC symbol*] ... ENA
Environmental Protection Agency, Region VIII Library, Denver, CO [*OCLC symbol*] ... EOA
Environmental Protection Agency, Region X Library, Seattle, WA [*OCLC symbol*] ... ESA
Environmental Protection Data Base [*Environmental Protection Agency*] ... EPDB
Environmental Protection Limit ... EPL
Environmental Protection Research Institute ... EPRI
Environmental Protection System ... EPS
Environmental Protection Technology Series. EPA [*Environmental Protection Agency*] [*A publication*] ... Environ Prot Technol Ser EPA
Environmental Psychology and Nonverbal Behavior [*A publication*] ... Environ Psychol Nonverbal Behav
Environmental Purification Systems, Inc. ... EPS
Environmental Qualification Test ... EQT
Environmental Quality ... EQ
Environmental Quality Abstracts [*A publication*] ... Environ Qual Abstr
Environmental Quality Abstracts [*A publication*] ... EQA
Environmental Quality Control ... EQC
Environmental Quality Council [*Terminated, 1970*] ... EQC
Environmental Quality Laboratory [*California Institute of Technology*] ... EQL
Environmental Quality Magazine [*A publication*] ... EQM
Environmental Quality and Safety [*A publication*] ... Environ Qual Saf
Environmental Quality and Safety. Supplement [*A publication*] ... Environ Qual Saf Suppl
Environmental Quarterly [*A publication*] ... Environ Q
Environmental Quarterly [*A publication*] ... Environ Quart
Environmental Radiation Ambient Monitoring System [*Environmental Protection Agency*] ... ERAMS
Environmental Recording, Editing, and Printing Program ... EREP
Environmental Report ... ER
Environmental Requirements/Capabilities Management Information System ... ERCMIS
Environmental Research [*A publication*] ... Environ Res
Environmental Research [*A publication*] ... Envir Res
Environmental Research [*A publication*] ... ENVRA
Environmental Research Assessment Committee [*National Research Council*] ... ERAC
Environmental Research Center [*Environmental Protection Agency*] ... ERC
Environmental Research Group ... ERG
Environmental Research Institute ... ERI
Environmental Research Institute of Michigan, Ann Arbor, MI [*Library symbol*] ... MiAaE
Environmental Research Institute of Michigan. Annual Report [*A publication*] ... Environ Res Inst Mich Annu Rep
Environmental Research Laboratory [*National Oceanic and Atmospheric Administration*] ... ERL
Environmental Research Papers ... ERP
Environmental Research Satellite [*NASA*] ... ERS
Environmental Research Ship [*Navy symbol*] ... AGER
Environmental Research and Technology ... ERT
Environmental Research and Technology, Information Center, Concord, MA [*OCLC symbol*] ... ERT
Environmental Resistance ... ER
Environmental Resistance Inherent in Equipment ... ERIE
Environmental Resource [*A publication*] ... Environ Resour
Environmental Resources Center ... ERC
Environmental Response Center [*Department of Energy*] ... ERC
Environmental Response and Referral Service [*Oak Ridge National Laboratory*] ... ERRS
Environmental Responsibility Program [*An association*] ... ERP
Environmental and Safety Business Opportunities [*Bureau of National Affairs*] ... ESBO
Environmental Science ... EVS
Environmental Science Information Center [*National Oceanic and Atmospheric Administration*] ... ESIC
Environmental Science Research [*A publication*] ... Environ Sci Res
Environmental Science Series [*Elsevier Book Series*] [*A publication*] ... ESS
Environmental Science Services Administration [*Later, National Oceanic and Atmospheric Administration*] ... ESSA
Environmental Science and Technology [*A publication*] ... Environ Sci & Tech
Environmental Science and Technology [*A publication*] ... Environ Sci Technol
Environmental Science and Technology [*A publication*] ... Envir Sci & Tech
Environmental Science and Technology [*A publication*] ... Env Sci Tec
Environmental Science and Technology [*A publication*] ... ES & T
Environmental Sciences Research Laboratory [*Environmental Protection Agency*] ... ESRL

Environmental Sciences Research Laboratory/Research Triangle Park [*Environmental Protection Agency*] ..... ESRL/RTP
Environmental Sensor Kit ..... ESK
Environmental Sex Determination [*Biology*] ..... ESD
Environmental Sketches in Perspective [*Computer program*] ..... ESP
Environmental and Societal Impacts Group [*National Center for Atmospheric Research*] ..... ESIG
Environmental Space Sciences [*A publication*] ..... Environ Space Sci
Environmental Standard Review Plan ..... ESRP
Environmental Stress Crack [*or Cracking*] [*Plastics*] ..... ESC
Environmental Stress-Crack Resistance [*Plastics*] ..... ESCR
Environmental Studies Board [*National Academy of Sciences*] ..... ESB
Environmental Study Area ..... ESA
Environmental Study Conference [*House of Representatives*] ..... ESC
Environmental Support System ..... ESS
Environmental Survey Satellite ..... ESSA
Environmental System and Effects Division [*NASA*] ..... ESED
Environmental System Resources [*National Science Foundation*] ..... ESR
Environmental Systems Applications Center [*NASA*] ..... ESAC
Environmental Systems Company [*NASDAQ symbol*] ..... ESCO
Environmental Systems Test Facility ..... ESTF
Environmental Technical Applications Center [*Air Force*] ..... ETAC
Environmental Technical Information System [*Army*] ..... ETIS
Environmental Technical Specifications ..... ETS
Environmental Technology and Economics [*A publication*] ..... ET & E
Environmental Technology Letters [*A publication*] ..... Environ Technol Lett
Environmental Technology Seminar ..... ETS
Environmental Tectonics [*NASDAQ symbol*] ..... ENVT
Environmental Teratology Information Center [*Department of Energy*] ..... ETIC
Environmental Test ..... ET
Environmental Test Chamber ..... ETC
Environmental Test Control Center ..... ETCC
Environmental Test Facility ..... ETF
Environmental Test Laboratory [*Jet Propulsion Laboratory, NASA*] ..... ETL
Environmental Test Program ..... ETP
Environmental Test Report ..... ETR
Environmental Testing Advisory Board [*Dow Chemical Co.*] ..... ETAB
Environmental Testing and Certification [*NASDAQ symbol*] ..... ETCC
Environmental Threat and Opportunity Profile ..... ETOP
Environmental Threshold of Measurement Accuracy ..... ETOMA
Environmental Toxicology and Chemistry [*A publication*] ..... ETC
Environmental Toxicology Research Laboratory [*National Environmental Research Center*] ..... ETRL
Environmental and Water Quality Operational Studies [*Army Corps of Engineers*] ..... EWQOS
Environmentalists for Full Employment ..... EFFE
Environments and Threats Directorate [*Army*] ..... ETD
Environnement Canada. Rapport Annuel [*A publication*] ..... Environ Can Rapp Annu
Envirosearch Corp. [*NASDAQ symbol*] ..... EVRO
Envirotech Corp. [*NYSE symbol*] ..... EVT
Envoy Extraordinary [*Department of State*] ..... EE
Envoy Extraordinary and Minister Plenipotentiary [*Department of State*] ..... EE & MP
Enzo Biochem, Inc. [*NASDAQ symbol*] ..... ENZO
Enzootic Bovine Leukemia ..... EBL
Enzymatic Deficiencies ..... ED
Enzyme Commission [*of the International Union of Biochemistry*] ..... EC
Enzyme-Digested Delta Endotoxin [*of Bacillus thuringiensis*] [*Biological control*] ..... EDD
Enzyme, Free [*Enzyme kinetics*] ..... E
Enzyme Immunoassay [*Clinical chemistry*] ..... EIA
Enzyme-Linked Immunoelectric Diffusion Assay [*Clinical chemistry*] ..... ELIEDA
Enzyme-Linked [*or -Labeled*] **Immunosorbent Assay** [*Immunochemistry*] ..... ELISA
Enzyme Membrane Immunoassay [*Biochemistry*] ..... EMIA
Enzyme-Modified Cheese ..... EMC
Enzyme Multiplied Immunoassay Technique [*Clinical chemistry*] [*Syva Company trademark*] ..... EMIT
Enzyme Presoak [*for laundry*] ..... EP
Enzyme-Product Complex [*Enzyme kinetics*] ..... EP
Enzyme Rate Analyzer ..... ERA
Enzyme-Substrate Complex [*Enzyme kinetics*] ..... ES
Enzyme Unit [*Analytical biochemistry*] ..... EU
Enzymes in Medicine [*A publication*] ..... Enzymes Med
Enzymic Radiochemical Assay [*Clinical chemistry*] ..... ERA
Enzymologia Acta Biocatalytica [*A publication*] ..... Enzymologia
Enzymologia Biologica et Clinica [*A publication*] ..... Enzymol Biol Clin
Eos. Commentarii Societatis Philologae Polonorum [*A publication*] ..... E
Eosin-Methylene Blue [*Dye combination*] ..... EMB
Eosinophil Chemotactic Factor [*Hematology*] ..... ECF
Eosinophil Chemotactic Factor of Anaphylaxis [*Immunochemistry*] ..... ECF-A
Eosinophilic Fasciitis [*Medicine*] ..... EF
Eosinophilic Granuloma [*Medicine*] ..... EG
Eosinophilic Lymphfolliculosis of the Skin [*Kimura disease*] [*Dermatology*] ..... ELS
Eosinophilic Nonallergic Rhinitis [*Medicine*] ..... ENR
Eosinophils [*Hematology*] ..... EOS
Eotros Number ..... Eo
EP/EO [*Employee Plans/Exempt Organization*] **Application Control System** [*IRS*] ..... EACS
EP Group of Companies, Microform Division, Wakefield, Yorkshire, United Kingdom [*Library symbol*] ..... EpG
EPA [*Environmental Protection Agency*] **Citizens' Bulletin** [*A publication*] ..... EPA Cit Bul
EPA [*Environmental Protection Agency*] **Journal** [*A publication*] ..... EPA J
Epatite "Degenerative-Proliferativa" [*A strain of mouse hepatitis virus*] ..... EDP
Epegrafika Vostika [*A publication*] ..... EV
Epeirotike Hestia [*A publication*] ..... EpH
Epena [*Congo*] [*Airport symbol*] ..... EPN
Epeteris tes Hetaireias Byzantinon Spoudon [*A publication*] ..... EHBS
Epeteris tes Hetaireias Byzantinon Spoudon [*A publication*] ..... Epet
Epeteris Hetaireias Kykladikon Meleton [*A publication*] ..... EHKM
Epeteris Hetaireias Stereoelladikon Meleton [*A publication*] ..... EHSM
Epeteris tou Kalabryton [*A publication*] ..... EtK
Epeteris tou Kentrou Epistemonikon Ereunon Kyprou [*A publication*] ..... EKEEK
Epeteris tou Kentrou Ereunes tes Hellenikes Laographias [*A publication*] ..... EKEHL
Epeteris tou Laographikov Arkheiov [*A publication*] ..... ETLA
Epeteris Mesaionikou Archeiou Akademias Athenon [*A publication*] ..... EMAAA
Ephemera Society of America ..... EPSOC
Ephemerides Carmeliticae [*A publication*] ..... ECarm
Ephemerides Carmeliticae [*A publication*] ..... EphC
Ephemerides Iuris Canonici [*A publication*] ..... EIC
Ephemerides Liturgicae [*A publication*] ..... EL
Ephemerides Liturgicae [*A publication*] ..... EphL
Ephemerides Theologicae Lovanienses [*A publication*] ..... Eph Th L
Ephemerides Theologicae Lovanienses [*A publication*] ..... EThL
Ephemerides Theologicae Lovanienses [*A publication*] ..... ETL
Ephemeris Dacoromana [*A publication*] ..... ED
Ephemeris Dacoromana [*A publication*] ..... Eph Dac
Ephemeris Epigraphica [*A publication*] ..... Eph Ep
Ephemeris - Orbit ..... EPHO
Ephemeris - Reentry ..... EPHR
Ephemeris Time [*Astronomy*] ..... ET
Ephemeris-Tuned Oscillator ..... ETO
Ephesians [*New Testament book*] ..... Eph
Ephphatha Services ..... ES
Ephraim, UT [*Radio station call letters*] ..... KEPH
Ephrata [*Washington*] [*Seismograph station code, US Geological Survey*] ..... EPW
Ephrata, PA [*Radio station call letters*] ..... WGSA
Ephrata, PA [*Radio station call letters*] ..... WIOV
Ephrata Public Library, Ephrata, WA [*Library symbol*] ..... WaEp
Ephrata, WA [*Location identifier*] [*FAA*] ..... EPH
Ephrata, WA [*Radio station call letters*] ..... KTBI
Ephrata, WA [*Radio station call letters*] ..... KTRM
Epiallopregnanolone [*Endocrinology*] ..... EAP
Epicardial Breakthrough [*Cardiology*] ..... EBT
Epichlorohydrin Ethylene Oxide [*Organic chemistry*] ..... ECO
Epichlorohydrin Triethanolamine [*Organic chemistry*] ..... ECTEOLA
Epidemic ..... EPID
Epidemic [*or Epizootic*] **Diarrhea of Infant Mice** ..... EDIM
Epidemic Hemorrhagic Fever [*Disease encountered by American troops during the Korean Conflict. The disease was suspected of being caused by the North Koreans in an early use of biological warfare.*] ..... EHF
Epidemic Hepatitis-Associated Antigen [*Immunochemistry*] ..... EHAA
Epidemic Intelligence Service [*of the Centers for Disease Control*] ..... EIS
Epidemic Keratoconjunctivitis [*Ophthalmology*] ..... EKC
Epidemic Observation Unit [*Medicine*] ..... EOU
Epidemiological ..... EPDML
Epidemiological Laboratory [*Air Force*] ..... EL
Epidemiological Report ..... EPIREPT
Epidemiological Review (English Translation of Przeglad Epidemiologiczny) [*A publication*] ..... Epidemiol Rev (Engl Transl Przegl Epidemiol)
Epidemiologija Mikrobiologija i Infekciozni Bolesti [*A publication*] ..... Epidem Mikrobiol
Epidemiologiya Mikrobiologiya i Infektsiozni Bolesti [*A publication*] ..... Epidemiol Mikrobiol Infekts Boles
Epidemiology ..... EPDMLGY
Epidemiology and Community Health [*A publication*] ..... Epidemiol Community Health
Epidemiology and Sanitation Technician [*Navy*] ..... EST
Epidermal Cell ..... EC
Epidermal Growth Factor [*Endocrinology*] ..... EGF
Epidermal Growth Factor - Urogastrone [*Endocrinology*] ..... EGF-URO
Epidermatophyton ..... TOE
Epidermis ..... E
Epidermolysis Bullosa [*Dermatology*] ..... EB
Epidermolysis Bullosa Dystrophia [*Dermatology*] ..... EBD
Epidermolysis Bullosa Dystrophic Dominant [*Dermatology*] ..... EBDD
Epidermolysis Bullosa Dystrophic Recessive [*Dermatology*] ..... EBDR
Epidermolysis Bullosa Simplex [*Dermatology*] ..... EBS
Epidural [*Brain anatomy*] ..... ED

Epigrafika Vostoka. Sbornik Statei [*A publication*] ..... Epigr Vostok
Epigraphia Indica [*A publication*] ..... EI
Epigraphia Indica [*A publication*] ..... Epig Indica
Epigraphical Museum [*Epigraphic notation*] ..... EM
Epikeraprosthesis [*Ophthalmology*] ..... EKP
Epilepsia [*A publication*] ..... EPILA
Epilepsy ..... EPIL
Epilepsy Association of America [*Later, EFA*] ..... EAA
Epilepsy Concern [*An association*] ..... EC
Epilepsy Foundation of America ..... EFA
Epilepsy International ..... EI
Epilepsy Partialis Continua [*Medicine*] ..... EPC
Epilogue ..... EPIL
Epinephrine [*Endocrinology*] ..... EPI
Epiphany ..... EPIPH
Epiphany Apostolic College [*New York*] ..... EAC
Epiphany Apostolic College, Newburgh, NY [*Library symbol*] ..... NNebgE
Epiphyllum Society of America ..... ESA
Epiphyllum Society of America ..... ESOA
Episcopal ..... EPIS
Episcopal ..... EPISC
Episcopal Actors' Guild of America ..... EAGA
Episcopal Church ..... EC
Episcopal Church Building Fund [*Formerly, ACBFC*] ..... ECBF
Episcopal Church Women ..... ECW
Episcopal Churchmen for South Africa ..... ECSA
Episcopal Communicators [*Formerly, NDP*] ..... EC
Episcopal Conference of the Deaf ..... ECD
Episcopal Council for Foreign Students and Other Visitors [*Defunct*] ..... ECFSOV
Episcopal Diocese of Massachusetts, Boston, MA [*Library symbol*] ..... MBD
Episcopal Diocese of Mississippi, Jackson, MS [*Library symbol*] ..... MsJPED
Episcopal Divinity School, Cambridge, MA [*OCLC symbol*] ..... BPS
Episcopal Divinity School, Cambridge, MA [*Library symbol*] ..... MCE
Episcopal Guild for the Blind ..... EGB
Episcopal Peace Fellowship ..... EPF
Episcopal Recorder [*A publication*] ..... ER
Episcopal Service for Youth ..... ESY
Episcopal Society for Cultural and Racial Unity [*Defunct*] ..... ESCRU
Episcopal Theological School ..... ETS
Episcopal Theological Seminary of the Southwest, Austin, TX [*Library symbol*] ..... TxAuE
Episcopal Women's Caucus ..... EWC
Episcopalian ..... EP
Episcopalians and Others for Responsible Social Action ..... EORSA
Episcopus [*Bishop*] ..... EP
Episcopus [*Bishop*] ..... EPUS
Episcopus et Martyr [*Bishop and Martyr*] ..... EM
Episiotomy [*Obstetrics*] ..... EPIS
Epistemonike Epeteris Kteniatrikes Scholes [*A publication*] ..... Epistemon Epeteris Kteniatr Sch
Epistemonike Epeteris tes Philosophikes Scholes tou Aristoteleiou Panepistemiou Thessalonikes [*A publication*] ..... EEPSAPT
Epistemonike Epeteris tes Philosophikes Scholes tou Panepistemiou Athenon [*A publication*] ..... EEPSPA
Epistle ..... E
Epistle ..... EP
Epistomium [*A Stopper*] [*Pharmacy*] ..... EPISTOM
Epitaph ..... EPIT
Epitaxial Mesa ..... EM
Epitaxial Passivated Integrated Circuits ..... EPIC
Epitaxial Planar [*Electronics*] ..... EP
Epitaxial Silicon Films on Insulators ..... ESFI
Epitaxial Tuning Varactor ..... ETV
Epithelial Focus-Forming Unit [*Oncology*] ..... EFFU
Epithelial Force (Assay) [*Oncology*] ..... EF
Epithelial Proliferation [*Histology*] ..... EP
Epithelial Stromal Junction [*Anatomy*] ..... ESJ
Epithelioma [*Medicine*] ..... EOA
Epithelium [*Medicine*] ..... EPITH
Epitheorese Logou Kai Technes [*A publication*] ..... ELkT
Epitheorese Technes [*A publication*] ..... ET
Epitheoresis Koinonikon Ereunon [*A publication*] ..... EPKE
Epithermal Critical Experiment Laboratory [*Nuclear energy*] ..... ECEL
Epitome ..... EPIT
Epizootic Hemorrhagic Disease [*Veterinary medicine*] ..... EHD
Eponyms Dictionaries Index [*A publication*] ..... EDI
Epoxide Hydrolase [*An enzyme*] ..... EH
Epoxidized Linseed Oil [*Organic chemistry*] ..... ELO
Epoxidized Soybean Oil [*Organic chemistry*] ..... ESO
Epoxy Bridge Rectifier ..... EBR
Epoxy Creosol Novolac [*Resin*] ..... ECN
Epoxy Curing Agent ..... ECA
Epoxy-Encapsulated Transistor ..... EET
Epoxy Experimental Kit ..... EEK
Epoxy Field Effect Transistor ..... EFET
Epoxy Spray Coater ..... ESC
Epoxy(nitrophenoxy)propane [*Organic chemistry*] ..... EPNP
EPPO [*European and Mediterranean Plant Protection Organization*] **Bulletin** [*A publication*] ..... EPPO Bull
EPPO [*European and Mediterranean Plant Protection Organization*] **Plant Health Newsletter Publications. Series B** [*A publication*] ..... EPPO Plant Health Newsl Publ Ser B
EPPO [*European and Mediterranean Plant Protection Organization*] **Publications. Series C** [*A publication*] ..... EPPO Publ Ser C
EPRI [*Electric Power Research Institute*] **Journal** [*A publication*] ..... EPRI J
Eprova Ltd. [*Switzerland*] [*Research code symbol*] ..... ES
Epsco, Inc. [*NASDAQ symbol*] ..... EPSC
Epsilon-Aminocaproic Acid [*Pharmacology*] ..... EACA
Epsilon Eta Phi [*Later, Phi Chi Theta*] ..... EEP
Epsilon Pi Tau ..... EPT
Epstein-Barr [*Virus*] ..... EB
Epstein-Barr Virus ..... EBV
EQL Memorandum. California Institute of Technology. Environmental Quality Laboratory [*A publication*] ..... EQL Memo Calif Inst Technol Environ Qual Lab
Equal ..... EQ
Equal ..... EQL
Equal Charge Displacement [*Fission*] ..... ECD
Equal Credit Opportunity Act [*1974, 1976*] ..... ECOA
Equal Educational Opportunities Program [*HEW*] ..... EEOP
Equal Employment Act ..... EEA
Equal Employment Advisory Council ..... EEAC
Equal Employment Officer ..... EEO
Equal Employment Opportunity ..... EEO
Equal Employment Opportunity Commission ..... EEOC
Equal Employment Opportunity Officer [*DoD*] ..... EEOO
Equal Interval [*Isophase navigation light*] ..... E Int
Equal Justice Foundation ..... EJF
Equal Life Group [*Depreciation class*] ..... ELG
Equal Listener Response [*Scale*] ..... ELR
Equal Mental Age [*Psychometrics*] ..... EMA
Equal Opportunities Commission [*British*] ..... EOC
Equal Opportunity ..... EO
Equal Opportunity Program Specialist [*Navy*] ..... EOPS
Equal Opportunity Programs ..... EOP
Equal Opportunity Quality Indicator [*Navy*] ..... EOQI
Equal Opportunity/Race Relations [*Navy*] ..... EO/RR
Equal Opportunity and Treatment [*Army program*] ..... EOT
Equal Payment Plan ..... EPP
Equal Rights Advocates ..... ERA
Equal Rights Amendment [*Proposed constitutional amendment which supports equal rights regardless of sex*] ..... ERA
Equal Rights Congress ..... ERC
Equal Section [*Technical drawings*] ..... ES
Equal-Time Commutation ..... ETC
Equal Time Point ..... ETP
Equal Time Spacing ..... ETS
Equal To or Greater Than ..... ETGT
Equal To or Less Than ..... ETLT
Equal Zero ..... E/Z
Equalization [*Electronics*] ..... EQ
Equalized Assessed Valuation ..... EAL
Equalized Sidelobe Antenna ..... ESA
Equalizer ..... EQ
Equate ..... EQU
Equation ..... EQ
Equation ..... EQN
Equation of State ..... EOS
Equation of Time [*Navigation*] ..... EQT
Equation of Time [*Navigation*] ..... ET
Equations of Motion ..... EOM
Equator Earth Terminal ..... EET
Equatorial [*Air mass*] ..... E
Equatorial ..... EQ
Equatorial Atlantic ..... EQUALANT
Equatorial Communications [*NASDAQ symbol*] ..... EQUA
Equatorial Countercurrent [*Oceanography*] ..... ECC
Equatorial Electrojet ..... EEJ
Equatorial Guinea [*Aircraft nationality and registration mark*] 3C
Equatorial Guinea [*MARC country of publication code*] [*Library of Congress*] ..... eg
Equatorial Guinea [*MARC geographic area code*] [*Library of Congress*] ..... f-eg---
Equatorial Guinea [*Three-letter standard code*] ..... GNQ
Equatorial Guinea [*Two-letter standard code*] ..... GQ
Equatorial Pacific ..... EQUAPAC
Equatorial Pacific Ocean Climate Studies [*National Oceanic and Atmospheric Administration*] ..... EPOCS
Equatorial Pitch Angle [*Geophysics*] ..... EPA
Equatorial Ring Current ..... ERC
Equatorial Scatter ..... EQS
Equerry ..... EQ
Equestrian Centers of America [*NASDAQ symbol*] ..... EQCA
Equifax, Inc. [*Formerly, Retail Credit Co.*] [*NYSE symbol*] ..... EFX
Equilibrium ..... EQUIL
Equilibrium Air Distillation ..... EAD
Equilibrium Air Total Radiation ..... EATR
Equilibrium Constant [*Symbol*] [*Chemistry*] ..... K
Equilibrium Dialysis [*Analytical chemistry*] ..... ED
Equilibrium-Line Altitude [*Glaciation*] ..... ELA

Equilibrium Moisture Content ... EMC
Equilibrium Problem Solver ... EPS
Equilibrium Problems of Linear Structures ... ELAS
Equilibrium Radiation Spectra ... ERS
Equilibrium Reflux Boiling Point [*Brake fluid*] ... ERBP
Equilibrium Surface Thermochemistry ... EST
Equilink Corporation [*NASDAQ symbol*] ... MACGC
Equimark Corp. [*NYSE symbol*] ... EQK
Equine Encephalitis ... EE
Equine Herpes Virus ... EHV
Equine Infectious Anemia ... EIA
Equine Lymphocyte Alloantigen [*Genetics, immunochemistry*] ... ELA
Equine Veterinary Journal [*A publication*] ... Equine Vet J
Equinetics, Inc. [*NASDAQ symbol*] ... EQNT
Equinox Solar, Inc. [*NASDAQ symbol*] ... EQIX
Equip and Install ... E & I
Equipage Category Number ... ECN
Equipement Industriel Achats et Entretien [*A publication*] ... Equip Ind Achats & Entretien
Equipement - Logement - Transports [*A publication*] ... Equipement
Equipes Medico-Sociales Itinerantes ... EMSI
Equipment ... EQ
Equipment ... EQP
Equipment ... EQPMT
Equipment ... EQPT
Equipment ... EQUIP
Equipment Acceptance Requirements and Inspections ... EARI
Equipment Accuracy Test Station ... EATS
Equipment Advisory Group ... EAG
Equipment Air Lock [*Nuclear energy*] ... EAL
Equipment Alignment ... EA
Equipment Allocation Document ... EAD
Equipment Allowance Revision Program ... EARP
Equipment Antiriot Projector [*British*] ... EARP
Equipment Applications List ... EAL
Equipment Approval Authority ... EAA
Equipment Authorization Inventory Data [*Air Force*] ... EAID
Equipment Authorization Inventory Data Listing [*Air Force*] ... EAIDL
Equipment Bay ... EB
Equipment Branch [*Air Force*] [*British*] ... EB
Equipment Building ... EB
Equipment Calibration [*Military*] ... ECAL
Equipment Calibration Maintenance Record ... ECMR
Equipment Category ... ECAT
Equipment Category Code [*Military*] ... ECC
Equipment Category Rollup Code [*Army*] ... ECRC
Equipment Certified ... EQCRT
Equipment Change Information ... ECI
Equipment Code Department Master ... EDM
Equipment Collecting Point [*Military*] [*British*] ... ECP
Equipment Company of America [*NASDAQ symbol*] ... ECOA
Equipment or Component ... E/C
Equipment Component List [*Army*] ... ECL
Equipment Concentration Sites [*Military*] ... ECS
Equipment Configuration Control ... ECC
Equipment Configuration Study ... ECS
Equipment Control Board ... ECB
Equipment Control Officer [*Air Force*] ... ECO
Equipment Control Record System [*Army*] ... ECRS
Equipment Controller ... EC
Equipment Deadlined for Maintenance [*Army*] ... EDM
Equipment Deadlined for Parts [*Army*] ... EDP
Equipment Density Data ... EQDD
Equipment Design Agent ... EDA
Equipment Design Information Memo ... EDIM
Equipment Development Division [*Britain's national phone-tapping center*] ... EDD
Equipment Development and Test Report [*Forest Service*] ... ED & T
Equipment Dictionary [*Navy*] ... EDIC
Equipment Disposition Authorization ... EDA
Equipment Distribution and Condition [*Statistical reporting system*] [*Military*] ... EDAC
Equipment Distribution Planning Studies [*Army*] ... EDPS
Equipment/Document Change Proposal ... E/DCP
Equipment Downtime ... EDT
Equipment, Environment, Velocity, Technique, Conditioning [*Sports medicine*] ... EEVeTec
Equipment Evaluation Report ... EER
Equipment Failure Rate ... EFR
Equipment Foreman ... EQPFOR
Equipment Functional Check ... EFC
Equipment Group Design Specifications ... EGDS
Equipment Guide List ... EGL
Equipment on Hand ... EOH
Equipment Identification Code ... EIC
Equipment Improvement Recommendations [*Military*] ... EIR
Equipment Improvement Report [*DoD*] ... EIR
Equipment Installation and Checkout ... EIC
Equipment Installation Notice ... EIN
Equipment Integration Design Section ... EIDS
Equipment Interchange Association ... EIA
Equipment Interstage Container ... EIC
Equipment Item ... EI
Equipment Item Material Requirements ... EIMR
Equipment Maintenance Agreement ... EMA
Equipment Maintenance Council ... EMC
Equipment Maintenance Facility [*Deep Space Instrumentation Facility, NASA*] ... EMF
Equipment Maintenance Log [*Army*] ... EML
Equipment Maintenance Record [*Army*] ... EMR
Equipment Maintenance Requirements List ... EMRL
Equipment Maintenance Squadron [*POMO*] ... EMS
Equipment Major Subdivision ... EMSD
Equipment Management Group ... EMG
Equipment Management System Training Requirements Program [*Navy*] ... EMSTRP
Equipment Manufacturers Design ... EMD
Equipment Manufacturers Workmanship ... EMW
Equipment Modification List ... EML
Equipment Mounting Plate ... EMP
Equipment Move Order ... EMO
Equipment Oil Analysis Program [*Air Force*] ... EOAP
Equipment Operating [*or Operational*] **Procedure** ... EOP
Equipment Operational Control ... EOC
Equipment Operationally Ready ... EOR
Equipment Operator [*Navy rating*] ... EO
Equipment Operator, Construction Equipment [*Navy rating*] ... EON
Equipment Operator, First Class [*Navy rating*] ... EO1
Equipment Operator, Hauling [*Navy rating*] ... EOH
Equipment Operator, Master Chief [*Navy rating*] ... EOCM
Equipment Operator, Second Class [*Navy rating*] ... EO2
Equipment Operator, Senior Chief [*Navy rating*] ... EOCS
Equipment Operator, Third Class [*Navy rating*] ... EO3
Equipment Performance Report ... EPR
Equipment Policy Statement [*Army*] ... EPS
Equipment Procurement Program ... EPP
Equipment Publication ... EP
Equipment Quality Analysis ... EQA
Equipment Readiness Date [*Army*] ... ERD
Equipment Readiness Drawing ... ERD
Equipment Recall Data System ... ERDS
Equipment Record Card ... ERC
Equipment Record System ... ERS
Equipment Reliability Status Report ... ERSR
Equipment Removal Tag ... ERT
Equipment Rental Agreement ... ERA
Equipment Repair Parts ... ERP
Equipment Repair Parts List ... ERPL
Equipment Repair Time ... ERT
Equipment Replacement and Enhancement Program [*Data processing*] ... EREP
Equipment Replacement Program [*Data processing*] ... ERP
Equipment Required on Site ... EROS
Equipment Requirement ... ER
Equipment Requirement List ... ERL
Equipment Requirement Program ... ERP
Equipment Requirement Specification ... ERS
Equipment Requirements Data [*Army*] ... ERD
Equipment Review and Authorization Activity [*Military*] ... ERAA
Equipment Review Board ... ERB
Equipment Section ... ES
Equipment Section Container ... ESC
Equipment Section Leakage Test ... ESLT
Equipment Section/Loaded Equipment Section ... ES/LES
Equipment Section Shell ... ESS
Equipment Service Association ... ESA
Equipment Serviceability Criteria [*Military*] ... ESC
Equipment Shipment Ready Date [*Army*] ... ESRD
Equipment Sliding Drawer Cabinet ... ESDC
Equipment Spare Package/Ground Communications and Electronic Equipment ... ESP/GC & EE
Equipment and Spare Parts ... E & SP
Equipment Specification ... ES
Equipment on Station Date [*Army*] ... EOSD
Equipment Statistical Data ... ESD
Equipment Statistical Data Card ... ESDC
Equipment Status Panel ... ESP
Equipment Status Report [*Air Force*] ... ESR
Equipment Storage Container ... ESC
Equipment Table Nomenclature ... ETN
Equipment Task Time ... ETT
Equipment Temporarily Removed ... ETR
Equipment Test ... ET
Equipment under Test ... EUT
Equipment Test Plan ... ETP
Equipment Time ... ET
Equipment and Tool Institute ... EATI
Equipment and Tool Institute ... ETI
Equipment Transfer Bag [*NASA*] ... ETB
Equipment Transfer or Change Order ... ETCO
Equipment Transfer or Loan Order ... ETLO
Equipment Trials Wing [*Military*] [*British*] ... ETW

Equipment Trust Certificate ... ETC
Equipment Unsatisfactory Report ... EUR
Equipment Visibility File ... EVF
Equipment Visibility System ... EVS
Equipment Working Group ... EWG
Equipo de Conferencias Sindicales de America Latina [*Committee for Latin American Trade Union Conferences*] ... ECOSAL
Equipotential Cathode ... EPC
Equipotential Kathode ... EPK
Equipotential Region ... EPR
Equipotential Surface ... EPS
Equipped with Search Light [*Suffix to plane designation*] [*Navy*] ... L
Equitable Bancorp [*NASDAQ symbol*] ... EBNC
Equitable Benefit-Based Financing ... EBBF
Equitable Gas Co. [*NYSE symbol*] ... EQT
Equitable Iowa Cl A [*NASDAQ symbol*] ... EQICA
Equitable Life Assurance Society of the United States, General Library, New York, NY [*OCLC symbol*] ... YEL
Equitable Life Assurance Society of the United States, Medical Library, New York, NY [*Library symbol*] ... NNEL
Equitable Life Assurance Society of the United States, Medical Library, New York, NY [*OCLC symbol*] ... ZEL
Equitable Life Interpreter [*Computer*] ... ELI
Equitable Life Mortgage & Realty Investors [*NYSE symbol*] [*Delisted*] ... EQ
Equitable Reserve Association ... ERA
Equitec Financial Group [*NASDAQ symbol*] ... EQTC
Equitex, Inc. [*NASDAQ symbol*] ... EQTX
Equitum Magister [*Master of the Horse*] [*British*] ... EM
Equity ... EQ
Equity Access Account [*Revolving mortgage-credit account*] [*Merrill Lynch & Co.*] ... EAA
Equity Capital for Industry [*British*] ... ECI
Equity Funding Corp. of America [*NYSE symbol*] [*Delisted*] ... EQF
Equity Oil Co. [*NASDAQ symbol*] ... EQTY
Equity Strategies Fund [*NASDAQ symbol*] ... EQSF
Equivalent ... EQ
Equivalent ... EQUIV
Equivalent Aerodynamic Median Diameter [*of atmospheric particulates*] ... EAMD
Equivalent Air Pressure ... EAP
Equivalent Air Speed ... EAS
Equivalent Atomic Number ... EAN
Equivalent Background Input ... EBI
Equivalent Binary Digit ... EBD
Equivalent Direct Radiation ... EDR
Equivalent Exposure Time ... EET
Equivalent Fatality Unit [*National Highway Traffic Safety Administration*] ... EFU
Equivalent Focal Length [*Optics*] ... EF
Equivalent Focal Length [*Optics*] ... EFL
Equivalent Full Charge ... EFC
Equivalent Full Power Hour [*FCC*] ... EFPH
Equivalent Gear Train ... EGT
Equivalent Input Offset Current ... EIOC
Equivalent Input Offset Voltage ... EIOV
Equivalent Instruction or Duty ... EIOD
Equivalent Isotropically Radiated Power [*Microwave transmission*] ... EIRP
Equivalent Loudness Level ... ELL
Equivalent Mean Time to Failure ... EMTTF
Equivalent Means Investment Period ... EMIP
Equivalent Megatonnage [*Military weapon index*] ... EMT
Equivalent Mission Cycle ... EMC
Equivalent Noise Input ... ENI
Equivalent Noise Level ... ENL
Equivalent Noise Resistance ... ENR
Equivalent Noise Sideband ... ENSB
Equivalent Noise Sideband Input ... ENSI
Equivalent Noise Temperature ... ENT
Equivalent Noise Voltage ... ENV
Equivalent Parallel Resistance ... EPR
Equivalent Passband ... EPB
Equivalent Pension Benefit [*British*] ... EPB
Equivalent Prior Sample [*Information*] [*Statistics*] ... EPS
Equivalent Quantum Efficiency ... EQE
Equivalent Residual Dose ... ERD
Equivalent Roentgen ... ER
Equivalent Round ... ER
Equivalent Series Resistance ... ESR
Equivalent Service Rounds [*A standard for indicating gun erosion*] ... ESR
Equivalent Shaft Horsepower [*Air Force*] ... ESHP
Equivalent Single Axle Load ... ESAL
Equivalent Single Wheel Load ... ESWL
Equivalent Snowline Altitude ... ESA
Equivalent Solar Hour [*NASA*] ... ESH
Equivalent Specific Fuel Consumption ... ESFC
Equivalent Spherical Diameter [*of a particle*] ... ESD
Equivalent Standard Hours ... ESH
Equivalent Station Location Error ... ESLE
Equivalent Threshold Sound Pressure Level ... ETSPL
Equivalent Top Product ... ETP
Equivalent Training ... EQT
Equivalent Training ... ET
Equivalent Ultraviolet Solar Hour [*NASA*] ... EUVSH
Equivalent Uranium ... eU
Equivalent Weight [*Chemistry*] ... equiv wt
Equivalent-Weight Factor ... EWF
Equuleus [*Constellation*] ... Equ
Equuleus [*Constellation*] ... Equi
ERA. Foerening foer Elektricitetens Rationella Anvaendning [*A publication*] ... ERA Foeren Elektr Ration Anvaendning
ERA Helicopter, Inc. [*Lake Charles, LA*] [*FAA designator*] ... ERH
ERA [*Equal Rights Amendment*] **Impact Project** ... EIP
Era Socialista [*A publication*] ... Era Social
Eranos [*A publication*] ... Er
Eranos-Jahrbuch [*A publication*] ... EranJb
Eranos-Jahrbuch [*A publication*] ... Eranos-Jb
Erasable Memory [*Data processing*] ... EM
Erasable Memory Octal Dump [*Data processing*] ... EMOD
Erasable Memory Program [*Data processing*] ... EMP
Erasable Programable Read-Only Memory [*Data processing*] ... EPROM
Erasable Read-Only Memory [*Data processing*] ... EROM
Erase [*British naval signaling*] ... EEEEE
Erase Digital [*Signal*] ... ED
Erase Gap [*Data processing*] ... ERG
Erased ... ERS
Erasmi Opera Omnia [*Elsevier Book Series*] [*A publication*] ... EOO
Erasmus [*A publication*] ... E
Erasmus in English [*A publication*] ... EE
Erasmus in English [*A publication*] ... Erasmus E
Erasmus Press, Lexington, KY [*Library symbol*] ... EP
Erasmus Review [*A publication*] ... ErasmusR
Erasmus Review [*A publication*] ... ErasR
Erave [*Papua New Guinea*] [*Airport symbol*] ... ERE
Erb Lumber Co. [*NASDAQ symbol*] ... ERBL
Erbamont, NV [*NYSE symbol*] ... ERB
Erbe und Auftrag [*A publication*] ... EA
Erbe der Vergangenheit [*A publication*] ... Erbe der V
Erbium [*Chemical element*] ... Er
Erbium Oxide Crystal ... EOC
Ercan [*Cyprus*] [*Airport symbol*] ... ECN
Erdbeernekrosevirus ... ENV
Erdek [*Turkey*] [*Seismograph station code, US Geological Survey*] ... ERD
Erdeszeti es Faipari Egyetem Kiadvanyai [*A publication*] ... Erdesz Faipari Egyetem Kiad
Erdeszeti es Faipari Egyetem Tudomanyos Kozlemenyei [*A publication*] ... Erdeszeti Faipari Egy Tud Kozl
Erdeszeti es Faipari Egyetem Tudomanyos Kozlemenyei [*A publication*] ... Erdesz Faipari Egyetem Tud Kozl
Erdeszeti Kutatasok [*A publication*] ... Erdeszeti Kut
Erdeszeti Kutatasok [*A publication*] ... Erdesz Kutatas
Erdeszettudomanyi Kozlemenyek [*A publication*] ... Erdeszettud Kozl
Erdoel-Erdgas Zeitschrift [*A publication*] ... Erdoel-Erdgas Z
Erdoel-Erdgas Zeitschrift. International Edition [*A publication*] ... Erdoel Erdgas Z Int Ed
Erdoel und Kohle, Erdgas, Petrochemie [*A publication*] ... Erdoel Kohle
Erdoel und Kohle, Erdgas, Petrochemie Vereinigt mit Brennstoff-Chemie [*A publication*] ... Erd Koh EPB
Erdoel und Kohle, Erdgas, Petrochemie Vereinigt mit Brennstoff-Chemie [*A publication*] ... Erdoel Kohle Erdgas Petrochem Brennst-Chem
Erdoel und Kohle, Erdgas, Petrochemie Vereinigt mit Brennstoff-Chemie [*A publication*] ... Erdoel Kohle Erdgas Petrochem Ver Brennst Chem
Erdoelverarbeitungswerk [*Crude Oil Processing Plant*] [*German*] ... EVW
Erect Posterior-Anterior ... EPA
Erecting ... ERCG
Erection ... ERECT
Erection Computer ... EC
Erection Counter Readout ... ECRO
Erection Digital Assembly ... EDA
Erection, Holddown, and Release [*Aerospace*] ... EHDR
Erection and Maintenance ... E & M
Erection Mechanism Motor Control Center ... EMMCC
Erection Subsystem ... ESS
Erection Timing Unit ... ETU
Erection Unit ... EU
Erector ... ERCR
Erector-Launcher, Guided Missile, Transportable ... ELGMT
Eregli Komurleri Isletmesi ... EKI
Eremitarum Camaldulensium [*Monk Hermits of Camaldoli*] [*Roman Catholic religious order*] ... ER CAM
Erevan [*USSR*] [*Seismograph station code, US Geological Survey*] ... ERE
Erevan [*USSR*] [*Airport symbol*] ... EVN
Erevanskii Gosudarstvennyi Universitet. Ucenye Zapiski. Estestvennye Nauki [*A publication*] ... Erevan Gos Univ Ucen Zap Estesv Nauki
Erevanskij Armjanskij Gosudarstvennyk Pedagogiceskij Institut Imeni Chacatur Abovjana. Sbornik Naucnych Trudov. Serija Russkogo Jazyka [*A publication*] ... EArmS
Erfahrung und Denken [*A publication*] ... Erfahr Denk
Erfahrungswissenschaftliche Blaetter [*A publication*] ... Erfahrungswiss Bl
Erfurt [*East Germany*] [*Airport symbol*] ... ERF

Erg .... E
Ergaenzungsbaende zur Zeitschrift fuer Veterinaerkunde [*A publication*] .... Ergnzngsbde Ztschr Veterinaerk
Ergebnisse der Allgemeinen Pathologie und Pathologischen Anatomie des Menschen und der Tiere [*A publication*] .... Ergebn Allg Path u Path Anat
Ergebnisse der Anatomie und Entwicklungsgeschichte [*A publication*] .... Ergeb Anat Entwicklungsgesch
Ergebnisse der Angiologie [*A publication*] .... Ergeb Angiol
Ergebnisse der Biologie [*A publication*] .... Ergeb Biol
Ergebnisse der Experimentellen Medizin [*A publication*] .... Ergeb Exp Med
Ergebnisse der Inneren Medizin und Kinderheilkunde [*A publication*] .... Ergeb Inn Med Kinderheilkd
Ergebnisse der Limnologie [*A publication*] .... Ergeb Limnol
Ergebnisse der Mathematik und Ihrer Grenzgebiete [*A publication*] .... Ergeb Math Grenzgeb
Ergebnisse der Mikrobiologie und Immunitaetsforschung [*A publication*] .... Ergeb Mikrobiol Immunitaetsforsch
Ergebnisse der Pathologie [*A publication*] .... Ergeb Pathol
Ergebnisse der Physiologie Biologischen Chemie und Experimentellen Pharmakologie [*A publication*] .... Ergeb Physiol Biol Chem Exp Pharmakol
Ergebnisse der Plasmaphysik und der Gaselektronik [*A publication*] .... Ergeb Plasmaphys Gaselektron
Ergocryptine [*Organic chemistry*] .... EC
Ergometer .... ERG
Ergonomics [*A publication*] .... ERGOA
Ergonomics Abstracts [*A publication*] .... Ergon Abstr
Ergs per Second .... ERG/S
Ergs per Square Centimeter Second .... ERG/(CM² S)
Erhard Seminars Training .... est
ERIC [*Educational Resources Information Center*] **Data Access System** [*Search system*] .... EDAS
ERIC [*Educational Resources Information Center*] **Document** .... ED
ERIC [*Educational Resources Information Center*] **Document Reproduction Service** .... EDRS
Erickson Educational Foundation [*Superseded by Janus Information Facility*] .... EEF
Erickson Gold Mines [*NASDAQ symbol*] .... ERGMF
Ericson Public Library, Boone, IA [*Library symbol*] .... IaBo
Ericsson Review [*A publication*] .... Ericsson Rev
Ericsson Technics [*A publication*] .... Ericsson Te
Ericsson Technics [*A publication*] .... Ericsson Tech
Ericsson [*L. M.*] **Telephone ADR** [*NASDAQ symbol*] .... ERICY
Eridamus [*Constellation*] .... Eri
Eridamus [*Constellation*] .... Erid
Erie [*Pennsylvania*] [*Airport symbol*] .... ERI
Erie Area Health Information Library Cooperative [*Library network*] .... EAHILC
Erie Army Depot .... ERAD
Erie Community College-North, Buffalo, NY [*Library symbol*] .... NBuEC
Erie Community College-North, Buffalo, NY [*OCLC symbol*] .... VVE
Erie Community College-North, City Campus, Buffalo, NY [*Library symbol*] .... NBuEC-C
Erie Community College-North, Urban Center, Buffalo, NY [*Library symbol*] .... NBuEC-U
Erie Community College-South, Orchard Park, NY [*Library symbol*] .... NOrcE
Erie County Historical Society, Erie, PA [*Library symbol*] .... PerHi
Erie County Library, Erie, PA [*OCLC symbol*] .... EPL
Erie County Technical Institute [*New York*] .... ECTI
Erie Lackawanna Inc. [*NASDAQ symbol*] .... ERIE
Erie-Lackawanna Railway Co. [*NYSE symbol*] [*Delisted*] .... E
Erie-Lackawanna Railway Co. [*AAR code*] [*Absorbed into Consolidated Rail Corp.*] .... EL
Erie, PA [*Location identifier*] [*FAA*] .... ERI
Erie, PA [*Radio station call letters*] .... WCCK
Erie, PA [*Radio station call letters*] .... WERG
Erie, PA [*Radio station call letters*] .... WEYZ
Erie, PA [*Television station call letters*] .... WICU-TV
Erie, PA [*Radio station call letters*] .... WJET
Erie, PA [*Television station call letters*] .... WJET-TV
Erie, PA [*Radio station call letters*] .... WLKK
Erie, PA [*Radio station call letters*] .... WLVU
Erie, PA [*Television station call letters*] .... WQLN
Erie, PA [*Radio station call letters*] .... WQLN-FM
Erie, PA [*Radio station call letters*] .... WRIE
Erie, PA [*Television station call letters*] .... WSEE-TV
Erie & Pittsburgh R. R. Co. [*NYSE symbol*] [*Delisted*] .... EPB
Erie Public Library, Erie, CO [*Library symbol*] .... CoEr
Erie Public Library, Erie, PA [*Library symbol*] .... PEr
Erie Western Railway Co. [*AAR code*] .... ERES
Erimo [*Japan*] [*Seismograph station code, US Geological Survey*] .... ERM
Eritrean Liberation Front [*Ethiopia*] .... ELF
Eritrean People's Liberation Front [*Ethiopia*] .... EPLF
Eritrean Relief Committee .... ERC
Eriu [*A publication*] .... Er
Erkennungssignal [*Recognition signal*] [*German military - World War II*] .... ES
Erlang [*Unit*] [*Statistics*] .... E
Erlanger Arbeiten zur Deutschen Literatur [*A publication*] .... EADL
Erlanger Beitrage zur Sprach- und Kunstwissenschaft [*A publication*] .... EBSK
Erlanger Geologische Abhandlungen [*A publication*] .... Erlanger Geol Abh
Erlanger, KY [*Radio station call letters*] .... WHKK
Erlanger Studien [*A publication*] .... ESt
Ermine [*Heraldry*] .... ERM
Ernaehrungs-Umschau [*A publication*] .... Ernaehr Umsch
Ernaehrungsforschung. Institut fuer Ernaehrung (Potsdam) [*A publication*] .... Ernaehrungsforsch Inst Ernaehr (Potsdam)
Ernaehrungslehre und- Praxis [*A publication*] .... Ernaehrungsl Prax
Ernaehrungswirtschaft. Lebensmitteltechnik (Hamburg) [*A publication*] .... Ernaehrungswirtsch Lebensmitteltech (Hamburg)
Ernest Bloch Society .... EBS
Ernest Hemingway Home, Key West, FL [*Library symbol*] .... FKwH
Ernest Orland Lawrence Livermore Laboratory [*University of California*] .... EOLLL
Ernestine [*Alaska*] [*Seismograph station code, US Geological Survey*] [*Closed*] .... ERN
Ernst [*E. C.*]**, Inc.** [*American Stock Exchange symbol*] [*Delisted*] .... ERN
Ernst Toller Memorial Society [*Later, ISSE*] .... ETMS
Ernst & Whinney, Cleveland, OH [*OCLC symbol*] .... OEE
Ero Industries, Inc. [*American Stock Exchange symbol*] .... ERO
Eroeterv Koezlemenyek [*A publication*] .... Eroeterv Koezl
Erotic Art Book Society [*Commercial firm*] .... EABS
Errata .... ER
Errata .... ERR
Erreur ou Omission Exceptee [*Error or Omission Excepted*] [*French*] .... EOOE
Errol, NH [*Location identifier*] [*FAA*] .... ERR
Erroneous .... ER
Erroneous .... ERRON
Error .... E
Error [*Aviation code*] .... EEE
Error .... ERR
Error Adaptive Control Computer .... EACC
Error Analysis Study .... EAS
Error Cause Identification [*Military*] .... ECI
Error Cause Removal [*Management*] .... ECR
Error of Closure .... EOC
Error Code [*Data processing*] .... EC
Error Control Receiver .... ECR
Error Control Translator .... ECT
Error Control Transmitter .... ECT
Error Correcting [*or Correction*] [*Data processing*] .... E/C
Error-Correcting Circuitry [*Data processing*] .... ECC
Error Correction .... ERRC
Error Correction Code .... ECC
Error Correction Information System [*NASA*] .... ECIS
Error Correction Servo [*or Signals*] .... ECS
Error Deletion by Iterative Transmission .... EDIT
Error Demodulator [*or Determination*] **Output** .... EDO
Error Detecting [*or Detection*] [*Data processing*] .... ED
Error Detecting Code .... EDC
Error Detection Code Generator .... EDCG
Error Detection and Correction .... EDAC
Error Detection and Correction .... EDC
Error Detection and Decision Feedback .... EDDF
Error Detection Encoder-Decoder [*Ground Communications Facility, NASA*] .... EDED
Error Detection System .... EDS
Error Detector Assembly .... EDA
Error and Dispersion Analysis .... EDA
Error, Freak, Oddity .... EFO
Error-Free Performance .... EFP
Error Function .... ERF
Error Function Complementary .... ERFC
Error Gap Probability Mass Function .... EGPMF
Error Logging Device .... ELD
Error Mean Square .... EMS
Error Monitor Register .... EMR
Error Multiplier .... EM
Error Protection Code .... EPC
Error Rate [*Statistics*] .... ER
Error Recorder .... ER
Error Recording Device .... ERD
Error Recovery .... ER
Error-Recovery Package [*Data processing*] .... ERP
Error-Recovery Procedure [*Data processing*] .... ERP
Error Relay .... ER
Error-Sensitive Test Case Analysis .... ESTCA
Error Sequence Number [*Data processing*] .... ESN
Error in Spelling [*Used in correcting manuscripts, etc.*] .... SP
Error Statistics by Tape Volume [*Data processing*] .... ESTV
Error Statistics by Volume .... ESV
Error Status Word [*Data processing*] .... ESW
Error Time Word .... ETW
Error in Use of Numbers [*Used in correcting manuscripts, etc.*] .... NUM
Error Variance Dependent on Level [*Statistical test*] .... ERRDEP
Error Vector Computer .... EVC
Error Volume Analysis [*Data processing*] .... EVA
Errors [*Baseball*] .... E

Errors Excepted [*Business and trade*] ... EE
Errors, Freaks, and Oddities Collector's Club ... EFOCC
Errors and Omissions [*Business and trade*] ... EO
Errors and Omissions Excepted [*Business and trade*] ... E and OE
Errors and Omissions Excepted [*Business and trade*] ... EOE
Erskine College, Due West, SC [*Library symbol*] ... ScDwE
Erskine College, Erskine Theological Seminary, Due West, SC [*Library symbol*] ... ScDwE-T
Erskine Register ... ER
ERT (Energy Resources and Technology) [*Formerly, Energy Resources Report*] [*A publication*] ... ERT (Energy Resour Technol)
Erume [*Papua New Guinea*] [*Airport symbol*] ... ERU
Erweiterte Oberschule [*Advanced Upper School*] [*German*] ... EOS
Erwin, TN [*Radio station call letters*] ... WEMB
Erwin, TN [*Radio station call letters*] ... WXIS
Erysipelas [*Medicine*] ... ERY
Erythema Chronicum Migrans [*Dermatology*] ... ECM
Erythema Dose [*Medicine*] ... ED
Erythema Nodosum [*Medicine*] ... EN
Erythema Nodosum Leproticum [*Medicine*] ... ENL
Erythematous-Edematous [*Reaction*] [*Medicine*] ... E-E
Erythroblastosis Fetalis [*Hematology*] ... EBF
Erythrocyte [*Hematology*] ... E
Erythrocyte [*Hematology*] ... ER
Erythrocyte Acid Phosphatase [*Hematology*] ... EAP
Erythrocyte-Antibody [*Complex*] [*Immunochemistry*] ... EA
Erythrocyte-Antibody Complement [*Immunochemistry*] ... EAC
Erythrocyte Creatine [*Clinical chemistry*] ... EC
Erythrocyte Glutatione Reductase [*An enzyme*] ... EGR
Erythrocyte Initiation Factor ... EIF
Erythrocyte Maturation Factor [*Hematology*] ... EMF
Erythrocyte Rosette [*Hematology*] ... ER
Erythrocyte Sedimentation Rate [*Hematology*] ... ESR
Erythrocyte-Sensitizing Substance [*Hematology*] ... ESS
Erythrocyte Superoxide Dismutase [*An enzyme*] ... ESOD
Erythro(hydroxynonyl)adenine [*Biochemistry*] ... EHNA
Erythroid Iron Turnover [*Hematology*] ... EIT
Erythromycin [*Also, ERYC*] [*Antibacterial compound*] ... ERY
Erythromycin [*Also, ERY*] [*Antibacterial compound*] ... ERYC
Erythromycin Ethylsuccinate [*Antimicrobial compound*] ... EES
Erythrophagocytosis [*Hematology*] ... EP
Erythropoietic Porphyria [*A genetic disorder*] ... EP
Erythropoietic Protoporphyria [*A genetic disorder*] ... EPP
Erythropoietic Stimulating [*or Erythropoietin Switching*] **Factor** [*Hematology*] ... ESF
Erythropoietin [*Endocrinology*] ... Ep
Erythropoietin-Responsive Cell [*Hematology*] ... ERC
Erythropoietin-Sensitive Stem Cells [*Hematology*] ... ESC
Erzurum [*Turkey*] [*Airport symbol*] ... ERZ
Erzurum [*Turkey*] [*Seismograph station code, US Geological Survey*] ... ERZ
Esa Ala [*D'Entrecasteaux Islands*] [*Seismograph station code, US Geological Survey*] ... ESA
Esa Ala [*D'Entrecasteaux Islands*] [*Seismograph station code, US Geological Survey*] ... ESB
ESA [*European Space Agency*] **Journal** [*A publication*] ... ESA J
Esa'Ala [*Papua New Guinea*] [*Airport symbol*] ... ESA
ESADA [*Empire State Atomic Development Associates, Inc.*] **Vallecitos Experimental Superheat Reactor** ... EVESR
Esalen Institute ... EI
ESB, Inc. [*Formerly, Electric Storage Battery Co.*] [*NYSE symbol*] [*Delisted*] ... ESB
Esbjerg [*Denmark*] [*Airport symbol*] ... EBJ
Escalade, Inc. [*NASDAQ symbol*] ... ESCA
Escanaba [*Michigan*] [*Airport symbol*] ... ESC
Escanaba & Lake Superior Railroad Co. [*AAR code*] ... ELS
Escanaba, MI [*Location identifier*] [*FAA*] ... ESC
Escanaba, MI [*Radio station call letters*] ... WBDN
Escanaba, MI [*Radio station call letters*] ... WDBC
Escanaba, MI [*Radio station call letters*] ... WFNN
Escanaba, MI [*Radio station call letters*] ... WGLQ
Escanaba, MI [*Television station call letters*] ... WJMN-TV
Escanaba, MI [*Radio station call letters*] ... WYKX
Escape ... ESC
Escape Character [*Data processing*] ... ESC
Escape and Evasion ... E & E
Escape Motor ... EM
Escape and Rescue ... EAR
Escape Road [*Hawaii*] [*Seismograph station code, US Geological Survey*] ... ESR
Escape Suit Ventilation System ... ESVS
Escape System ... ES
Escape System Test Article ... ESTA
Escape Tower [*NASA*] ... E/T
Escaped Federal Prisoner ... EFP
Escapees [*An association*] ... S-K-P's
Escherichia coli Polypeptides ... ECP
Escola de Agronomia da Amazonia. Boletim [*A publication*] ... Esc Agron Amazonia Bol
Escompte [*Discount*] [*French*] ... ESC
Escondido, CA [*Radio station call letters*] ... KOWN
Escondido, CA [*Radio station call letters*] ... KOWN-FM
Escondido Public Library, Escondido, CA [*Library symbol*] ... CEsc
Escorial [*A publication*] ... E
Escorial [*A publication*] ... Es
Escorial [*A publication*] ... Esc
Escort ... ESC
Escort Aircraft ... EA
Escort Aircraft Carrier [*Navy symbol*] ... CVE
Escort Carrier Force ... ESCARFOR
Escort Convoy ... EC
Escort Cost Model ... ESCOMO
Escort Destroyer [*Navy symbol*] ... DDE
Escort Division ... CORTDIV
Escort Division ... ESCORTDIV
Escort Fighter Squadron ... ESCORTFIGHTRON
Escort Fighter Squadron [*Navy symbol*] ... VGF
Escort Force Commander ... EFC
Escort Group ... EG
Escort Guard ... ESCRG
Escort Helicopter ... EH
Escort Helicopter Aircraft Carrier [*Navy symbol*] ... CVHE
Escort Mission ... ESM
Escort Oilers Supervising Officer [*Navy*] ... EOSO
Escort Research Ship [*Navy symbol*] ... AGDE
Escort-Scouting Squadron ... ESCORON
Escort-Scouting Squadron [*Navy symbol*] ... VGS
Escort Ship [*Destroyer Escort*] [*Navy symbol*] ... DE
Escort Ships ... ES
Escort Squadron ... CORTRON
Escort Towed Array Sensor [*Later, TACTAS*] [*Navy*] ... ETAS
Escort Trains ... ET
Escort Vessel Administration [*World War II*] ... EVA
Escort Vessels [*Enemy*] ... EV
Escuadron de la Morte [*Death Squad*] [*El Salvador*] ... EM
Escudo [*Monetary unit in Chile and Portugal*] ... E
Escudo [*Monetary unit in Chile and Portugal*] ... ESC
Escuela de Administracion de Negocios para Graduados [*A graduate school of business administration*] [*Lima, Peru*] ... ESAN
Escuela de Farmacia Guatemala [*A publication*] ... Esc Farm Guatem
Escuela Interamericana de Educacion Democratica ... EIDED
Escuela Nacional de Aeronautica [*Argentina*] ... ENA
Escuela Nacional de Agricultura (Chapingo). Monografias [*A publication*] ... Esc Nac Agric (Chapingo) Monogr
Escuela Nacional de Agricultura (Chapingo). Revista [*A publication*] ... Esc Nac Agric (Chapingo) Rev
Escuela Nacional de Agricultura (Chapingo). Serie de Apuntes [*A publication*] ... Esc Nac Agric (Chapingo) Ser Apuntes
Escuela Nacional de Agricultura (Chapingo). Serie de Investigaciones [*A publication*] ... Esc Nac Agric (Chapingo) Ser Invest
Escuela Nacional de Bellas Artes ... ENBA
Escuela Nacional de Biblioteconomia y Archivonomia ... ENBA
Escuela Superior de Administracion y Direccion de Empresas ... ESADE
Escuela Superior de Administracion Publica America Central [*Costa Rica*] ... ESAPAC
Escuela Tecnica y Superior de Arquitectura de Barcelona [*Spain*] ... ETSAB
Escuelas Radiofonicas de Bolivia ... ERBOL
Escutcheon ... ESC
Esen Bulak [*Mongolia*] [*Seismograph station code, US Geological Survey*] [*Closed*] ... EBM
Esic-Market, Estudios de Gestion Comercial y Empresa [*A publication*] ... Esic-Market Estud Gestion Com Empr
Eskdalemuir [*Scotland*] [*Geomagnetic observatory code*] ... ESK
Eskdalemuir [*Scotland*] [*Seismograph station code, US Geological Survey*] ... ESK
Eskdalemuir Array [*Scotland*] [*Seismograph station code, US Geological Survey*] ... EKA
Eskimo ... ESK
Eskimo [*MARC language code*] [*Library of Congress*] ... esk
Eskimo Dog Society of the Northwest Territories [*Defunct*] ... EDS-NWT
Eskimo Museum, Churchill, MB, Canada [*Library symbol*] ... CaMChE
Eskimo Point [*Canada*] [*Airport symbol*] ... YEK
ESL, Inc., Sunnyvale, CA [*Library symbol*] ... CSvE
Esmark, Inc. [*NYSE symbol*] ... ESM
Esmeraldas [*Ecuador*] [*Airport symbol*] ... ESM
Esophageal Gastric Tube Airway [*Medicine*] ... EGTA
Esophageal Motility Disorder [*Medicine*] ... EMD
Esophageal Valve ... ESV
Esophagogastroduodenoscopy [*Medicine*] ... EGD
Esophagus ... E
Esophagus ... ESOPH
Esophoria for Distance [*Ophthalmology*] ... E
Esotropia for Distance [*Ophthalmology*] ... ET
ESP [*Extrasensory Perception*] **Research Associates Foundation** ... ESPRAF
Espace Geographique [*A publication*] ... Espace Geogr
Espaces et Societes [*A publication*] ... Espaces et Soc
Espana [*Spain*] ... E
Espana Misionera [*A publication*] ... EM
Espanol Actual [*A publication*] ... EspA
Espanola, NM [*Radio station call letters*] ... KDCE
Espanola, NM [*Radio station call letters*] ... KEVR
Espanola, ON [*Radio station call letters*] ... CKNS
Espanola Public Library, Espanola, NM [*Library symbol*] ... NmE

Esparros [France] [Seismograph station code, US Geological Survey] .....EPF
Espe [Germany] [Research code symbol]......................... OMP
Especial [Designation on brandy labels]..................... E
Especialidades Farmaceuticas Espanolas Data Bank [Spanish
  Pharmaceutical Specialities Data Bank] [Information service]....... ESPES
Especially ....ESP
Especially ....ESPEC
Especially ....SPCLY
Esperance [Australia] [Airport symbol].................... EPR
Esperantic Studies Foundation............................ ESF
Esperantist Club of Veterans [See also VEK] .... ECV
Esperantist Movement for World Peace [See also MEM]....... EMWP
Esperantista Go-Ligo Internacia.......................... EGLI
Esperanto ....ESP
Esperanto [MARC language code] [Library of Congress]............esp
Esperanto Association of North America [Defunct] .... EANA
Esperanto en Komerco Kaj Industrio [Institute for Esperanto in
  Commerce and Industry]................................. EKI
Esperanto League for North America .... ELNA
Esperanto-Ligo Filatelista [Philatelic Esperanto League - PEL]....... ELF
Esperienza Poetica [A publication]...................... EPo
Espey Manufacturing & Electronics Corp. [American Stock
  Exchange symbol]...ESP
Espinosa [Brazil] [Airport symbol] .... ESI
Espionage [FBI standardized term]..........................ESP
Espionage ....ESPG
Espiritu Santo [Vanuata] [Airport symbol]................. SON
Espoir de la Jeunesse Camerounaise [Hope of the Cameroonese
  Youth].. EJC
Espressivo [With Expression] [Music]......................ESP
Espressivo [With Expression] [Music]...................ESPRESS
Esprit [A publication]...................................... E
Esprit Createur [A publication]........................... ECr
Esprit Createur [A publication]........................... EsC
Esprit Systems [American Stock Exchange symbol]........... ETI
Esquel [Argentina] [Airport symbol]...................... EQS
Esquimalt & Nanaimo Railway Co. [AAR code]............... EN
Esquire...ESQ
Esquire..ESQR
Esquire [A publication]................................... Esq
Esquire, Inc. [NYSE symbol]...............................ESQ
Esquire Radio & Electronics, Inc. [American Stock Exchange symbol] ...... EE
ESRO [European Space Research Organization] Advanced
  Imaging Detector [Satellite]............................ EAID
ESRO/ELDO [European Space Research Organization/European
  Launcher Development Organization] Bulletin [A publication] ....
                                                    ESRO/ELDO Bull
ESSA [Environmental Science Services Administration] Research
  Laboratories.. ERL
ESSA [Environmental Science Services Administration] Research
  Laboratories, Technical Memorandum [A publication]............... ERLTM
ESSA [Environmental Science Services Administration] Weather
  Wire Service.. EWWS
ESSA [Environmental Science Services Administration] World [A
  publication]..ESW
Essai Orgel [Orgel test reactor] [Italy].................. ESSOR
Essay and General Literature Index [A publication] .... EGLI
Essay-Proof Journal [A publication]....................... EPJ
Essay-Proof Society.......................................EPS
Essays in Arts and Sciences [A publication] .... EAS
Essays in Biochemistry [A publication]........... Essays Biochem
Essays on Canadian Writing [A publication]................ ECW
Essays on Canadian Writing [A publication]....... Essays Can Wri
Essays in Criticism [A publication]....................... EC
Essays in Criticism [A publication]....................... ECr
Essays in Criticism [A publication]....................... EIC
Essays in Criticism [A publication]................. Essays Crit
Essays in Criticism [A publication].................. Ess Crit
Essays by Divers Hands [A publication]................... EDH
Essays in French Literature [University of Western Australia] [A
  publication]..EFL
Essays in Fundamental Immunology [A publication] ....
                                          Essays Fundam Immunol
Essays in Literature. Western Illinois University [A publication] .... ELWIU
Essays in Neurochemistry and Neuropharmacology [A
  publication]............Essays Neurochem Neuropharmacol
Essays and Papers. Soong Jun University [Korea] [A publication]
                                                      Essays Pap
Essays in Physics [A publication].................Essays Phys
Essays and Studies [London] [A publication]............ E & S
Essays and Studies [London] [A publication]............... ES
Essays and Studies in English Language and Literature [A
  publication]..ESELL
Essays and Studies by the Faculty of Hiroshima Jogakuin
  College [A publication]...........Essays Stud Fac Hiroshima Jogakuin Coll
Essays in Toxicology [A publication]..............Essays Toxicol
Essence ....ESS
Essence [A publication]................................. Ess
Essences et Lubrifiants de France - Entreprise de Recherches
  et d'Activites Petrolieres [French oil company] ......ELF-ERAP
Essential ....ESN

Essential ....ESNTL
Essential ....ESS
Essential ....ESSEN
Essential Amino Acids [Nutrition] .... EAA
Essential Amino Acids plus Histidine [Nutrition] .... EAAH
Essential Elements of Analysis .... EEA
Essential Elements of Friendly Information [Army] .... EEFI
Essential Elements of Information [Military]............... EEI
Essential Fatty Acid Deficiency [Medicine] .... EFAD
Essential Fatty Acids [Biochemistry]...................... EFA
Essential Hypertension [Medicine]......................... EH
Essential Motor Control Center .... EMCC
Essential Oil Association of the United States .... EOA
Essential Performance Requirements .... EPR
Essential Repair Part Stockage List [Military]........... ERPSL
Essential Services Cooling Water Systems [Nuclear energy]...........ESCWS
Essential Switching Box .... ESB
Essential Technical Medical Data .... ETMD
Essential Thrombocythemia [Hematology] .... ET
Essential Work Order .... EWO
Essentiality Code .... EC
Essex [County in England]................................. ESS
Essex Archaeology and History [A publication]........ Essex Arch Hist
Essex Chemical Corp. [NYSE symbol].......................ESX
Essex Community College, Baltimore, MD [Library symbol] ....MdBEs
Essex Community College, James A. Newpher Library,
  Baltimore, MD [OCLC symbol].............................. ECC
Essex Corp. [NASDAQ symbol]............................. ESEX
Essex County College, Newark, NJ [OCLC symbol]...........ESX
Essex County College, Newark, NJ [Library symbol]........NjNE
Essex County Cooperating Libraries [Library network]..... ECCL
Essex County Gas Company [NASDAQ symbol].................ECGC
Essex County Natural History Society. Journal [A publication]...........
                                                  Essex Co N H Soc J
Essex County Newspapers Ltd., Colchester, United Kingdom
  [Library symbol]..UkCoE
Essex County Public Library, Essex, ON, Canada [Library
  symbol]...CaOEsE
Essex Institute. Bulletin [A publication] ....Essex Inst B
Essex Institute. Historical Collections [A publication] .... EIHC
Essex Institute. Historical Collections [A publication] ....Essex Inst Coll
Essex Institute. Historical Collections [A publication] ......Essex Inst Hist Coll
Essex Institute. Historical Collections [A publication] ....
                                              Essex Inst Hist Collect
Essex Institute. Proceedings [A publication] ....Essex Inst Pr
Essex Institute, Salem, MA [Library symbol]...............MSaE
Essex International, Inc. [NYSE symbol] [Delisted] .... EXC
Essex Naturalist (London) [A publication] ....Essex Nat (Lond)
Essex Review [A publication]............................ Ess R
Essex Scottish Regiment of Canada [Military unit] .... ESR
[The] Essex Terminal Railway Co. [AAR code]............... ETL
ESSO Agricola [A publication]........................ESSO Agr
ESSO Magazine [A publication]........................ESSO Mag
ESSO Oilways International [A publication]........ ESSO Oilways Int
Esso Resources Canada Ltd., Calgary, AB, Canada [Library
  symbol]...CaACERC
Esso Resources Canada Ltd., Production Research Division,
  Calgary, AB, Canada [Library symbol]...............CaACIPRD
Esso Turbo Oil [Standard Oil]............................ ETO
Essor Social des Bashi [Social Development of the Bashi]...............ESSOBA
Est Europeen [A publication].......................Est Europ
Est et Ouest. Bulletin de l'Association d'Etudes et
  d'Informations Politiques Internationales [A publication] .... Est-Ouest
Establish [or Establishment]............................ESTAB
Establish [or Establishment]............................ESTB
Established.. EST
Established...ESTBD
Established Church .... EC
Established Pattern of Psychodynamic Adaptation .... EPPA
Established Reliability .... ER
Establishment Date [IRS]................................. ED
Estacada High School, Estacada, OR [Library symbol]......OrEsHS
Estacada Public Library, Estacada, OR [Library symbol].........OrEs
Estacion Central de Ecologia. Boletin (Spain) [A publication]...............
                                              Estac Cent Ecol Bol (Spain)
Estacion Experimental Agricola de Tucuman. Boletin [A
  publication]............Estac Exp Agric Tucuman Bol
Estacion Experimental Agricola de Tucuman. Circular [A
  publication]............Estac Exp Agric Tucuman Circ
Estacion Experimental Agricola de Tucuman. Publicacion
  Miscelanea [A publication].............. Estac Exp Agric Tucuman Publ Misc
Estacion Experimental Agropecuaria Pergamino. Boletin de
  Divulgacion [A publication].... Estac Exp Agropecu Pergamino Bol Divulg
Estacion Experimental Agropecuaria Pergamino. Publicacion
  Tecnico [A publication]............ Estac Exp Agropecu Pergamino Publ Tec
Estacion Experimental de Aula dei Zaragoza. Boletin [A
  publication]............... Estac Exp Aula dei Zaragoza Bol
Estadistica Espanola [A publication].................Estadist Espanola
Estados Unidos Americanos [United States of America] [Spanish] .... EUA
Estados Unidos do Brasil [United States of Brazil] [Portuguese] .... EUB
Estafeta Literaria [A publication]........................ELit

Estafeta Literaria [*A publication*] ... EstLit
Estancia [*New Mexico*] [*Seismograph station code, US Geological Survey*] ... EST
Estate ... EST
Estate ... ESTE
Estate-Bottling [*Wine*] ... E-B
Estate Duties Investment Taxes [*British*] ... EDITH
Estate Duty Office [*British*] ... EDO
Estates, Powers, and Trusts Law [*A publication*] ... EPTL
Esteban's Mexican Foods [*NASDAQ symbol*] ... ESTB
Estel-Berichte aus Forschung und Entwicklung Unserer Werke [*A publication*] ... Estel-Ber Forsch Entwickl Unserer Werke
Estelline Public Library, Estelline, SD [*Library symbol*] ... SdEs
Esterase [*An enzyme*] ... EST
Esterline Corp. [*NYSE symbol*] ... ESL
Estes Park, CO [*Radio station call letters*] ... KSIR
Estes Park Public Library, Estes Park, CO [*Library symbol*] ... CoEp
Estevan, SK [*Radio station call letters*] ... CJSL
Esther [*Old Testament book*] ... Est
Esther [*Old Testament book*] ... Esth
Estherville, IA [*Location identifier*] [*FAA*] ... EST
Estherville, IA [*Radio station call letters*] ... KILR
Estherville, IA [*Radio station call letters*] ... KILR-FM
Estherville Junior College [*Iowa*] ... EJC
Estherville Public Library, Estherville, IA [*Library symbol*] ... IaEs
Esthetic ... ESTH
Estimate ... E
Estimate ... EST
Estimate of Adversary Sequence Interruption [*Nuclear energy*] ... EASI
Estimate Change Request ... ECR
Estimate at Completion ... EAC
Estimated ... ESTD
Estimated Acquisition Cost [*of drug products*] [*HEW*] ... EAC
Estimated Air Speed ... EAS
Estimated [*or Estimating*] **Approach Time** [*Aviation*] ... EAT
Estimated Arrival Carrier ... EAC
Estimated Arrival Date ... ESTAR
Estimated Availability Date [*Military*] ... EAD
Estimated [*or Expected*] **Average Life** ... EAL
Estimated on Berth ... EOB
Estimated Blood Loss [*Medicine*] ... EBL
Estimated Cloud Time [*Drinking slang*] ... ECT
Estimated Completion Date ... ECD
Estimated Completion Time ... ECT
Estimated Consumption [*of gasoline*] [*Computer model*] ... ESCON
Estimated Correction Cost ... ECC
Estimated Date ... ED
Estimated Date of Arrival ... EDA
Estimated Date of Availability ... EDA
Estimated Date of Completion ... EDC
Estimated [*or Expected*] **Date of Confinement** [*Obstetrics*] ... EDC
Estimated Date of Departure Far East Command [*Military*] ... EDDFEC
Estimated Date of Publication ... EDP
Estimated Date of Resumption ... EDR
Estimated Date of Separation ... EDS
Estimated Delivery Date ... EDD
Estimated Delivery Times ... EDT
Estimated Departure Clearance Time [*Aviation*] ... EDCT
Estimated Departure from Pacific ... EDPAC
Estimated Departure Time ... EDT
Estimated on Dock ... EOD
Estimated Effective Perceived Noise Level ... EEPNL
Estimated Elapsed Time [*Aviation*] ... EET
Estimated Expenditure of Ammunition ... EEA
Estimated Final Cost ... EFC
Estimated Gestational Age ... EGA
Estimated Ground Time ... EGT
Estimated Horsepower ... EHP
Estimated Information [*Aviation*] ... ETI
Estimated Latitude ... ELAT
Estimated Learning Potential ... ELP
Estimated Longitude ... ELONG
Estimated Mean Time to Failure ... EMTF
Estimated Month of Loss ... EML
Estimated Operational Date ... EOD
Estimated Position [*Navigation*] ... EP
Estimated Position Arc [*Navy*] ... EPA
Estimated Price Request ... EPR
Estimated Receival Date ... ERD
Estimated Release Date ... ERD
Estimated Release Schedule ... ERS
Estimated Shipping Date ... ESD
Estimated Surface Wheel Load ... ESWL
Estimated Takeoff ... ETO
Estimated Target Assurance ... ETA
Estimated Task Completion Date ... ETCD
Estimated Tax [*IRS*] ... ES
Estimated Tax Penalty [*IRS*] ... ESPEN
Estimated Time ... ET
Estimated Time of Acquisition ... ETA
Estimated [*or Expected*] **Time of Arrival** ... ETA
Estimated Time of Berthing [*Navigation*] ... ETB
Estimated Time in Commission [*Army*] ... ETIC
Estimated Time of Completion ... ETC
Estimated Time of Correction ... ETC
Estimated Time of Correction [*NASA*] ... ETOC
Estimated Time of Crew's Return ... ETCR
Estimated Time of Departure ... ETD
Estimated Time En Route ... ETE
Estimated Time of Flight ... ETF
Estimated Time of Interception ... ETI
Estimated Time Off ... ETO
Estimated Time of Operations [*NASA*] ... ETO
Estimated Time Out of Commission ... ETOC
Estimated Time Over [*Aviation*] ... ETO
Estimated Time Over [*Aviation*] ... ETOV
Estimated Time Over Target ... ETOT
Estimated Time of Ovulation [*Gynecology*] ... ETO
Estimated Time of Parachute Deployment ... ETPD
Estimated Time of Penetration [*Aviation*] ... ETP
Estimated Time and Point of DEWIZ [*Distant Early Warning Identification Zone*] **Penetration** ... ETDP
Estimated Time to Reach Altitude ... ETRA
Estimated Time of Repair ... ETR
Estimated Time of Return ... ETR
Estimated Time of Return to Operation [*Military*] ... ETRO
Estimated Time of Sailing [*Navigation*] ... ETS
Estimated Time of Separation [*Military*] [*Slang*] ... ETS
Estimated Time of Track ... ETT
Estimated Travel Time [*Army*] ... ETT
Estimated Turnaround Point ... ETP
Estimated Unit Price ... EUP
Estimated Warehouse Arrival ... EWA
Estimated Weight Report ... EWR
Estimated Yearly Cost of Operation [*of electrical appliance*] ... EYCO
Estimated Yearly Operating Cost [*of electrical appliance*] ... EYOC
Estimating Price Policy ... EPP
Estimation ... ESTN
Estivoautumnal [*Malaria*] ... EA
Estomatologia e Cultura [*A publication*] ... Estomatol Cult
Estonia ... EST
Estonian [*MARC language code*] [*Library of Congress*] ... est
Estonian Aid [*An association*] ... EA
Estonian American National Council ... EANC
Estonian Educational Society ... EHS
Estonian Learned Society of America ... ELSA
Estonian Relief Committee ... ERC
Estonian Soviet Socialist Republic [*MARC country of publication code*] [*Library of Congress*] ... err
Estonian Soviet Socialist Republic ... EstSSR
Estonian Soviet Socialist Republic [*MARC geographic area code*] [*Library of Congress*] ... e-ur-er
Estonian Student Association in the United States of America ... ESAUSA
Estradiol [*Endocrinology*] ... E-diol
Estradiol Benzoate [*Endocrinology*] ... EB
Estradiol-Binding Protein [*Biochemistry*] ... EBP
Estradiol Cyclopentanepropionate [*Endocrinology*] ... ECP
Estrogen Receptor [*Endocrinology*] ... ER
Estrogen Receptor Protein [*Endocrinology*] ... ERP
Estrogen Replacement Therapy [*Medicine*] ... ERT
Estrogen-Stimulated Neurophysin [*Endocrinology*] ... ESN
Estuarine Bulletin [*A publication*] ... Estuarine Bull
Estuarine and Coastal Marine Science [*A publication*] ... Est Coas M
Estuarine and Coastal Marine Science [*A publication*] ... Estuarine Coastal Mar Sci
Estuarine Research [*A publication*] ... Estuarine Res
Estuarine Research Federation ... ERF
Estuary [*Maps and charts*] ... EST
Estudio Agustiniano [*A publication*] ... Est Ag
Estudios [*A publication*] ... Est
Estudios Afrocubanos [*A publication*] ... EA
Estudios Americanos [*Sevilla*] [*A publication*] ... EAm
Estudios Andinos [*A publication*] ... Estud Andin
Estudios de Asia y Africa [*A publication*] ... Estud As Afr
Estudios Biblicos [*A publication*] ... EB
Estudios Biblicos [*A publication*] ... EBib
Estudios Clasicos [*A publication*] ... EClas
Estudios Clasicos [*A publication*] ... EsCl
Estudios Conjuntos sobre Integracion Economica Latinoamericana [*Program*] ... ECIEL
Estudios Cooperativos [*A publication*] ... Estud Coop
Estudios de Cultura Maya [*A publication*] ... ECM
Estudios de Cultura Maya [*A publication*] ... Est Cult Maya
Estudios de Cultura Nahuatl [*A publication*] ... ECN
Estudios de Cultura Nahuatl [*A publication*] ... Estud Cult Nahuatl
Estudios. Duquesne University [*A publication*] ... EstD
Estudios Ecclesiastico [*A publication*] ... EE
Estudios de Economia [*A publication*] ... Estud Econ
Estudios de Edad Media de la Corona de Aragon [*A publication*] ... EEMCA
Estudios Empresariales [*A publication*] ... Estud Empresar
Estudios Eruditos en Memoriam de Bonilla y San Martin [*A publication*] ... EE

Estudios Eruditos en Memoriam de Bonilla y San Martin [*A publication*] ... EEMB
Estudios Escenicos [*A publication*] ... EstE
Estudios Escenicos. Cuadernos del Instituto del Teatro [*A publication*] ... EECIT
Estudios Extremenos; Revista Historica, Literaria, y Artistica [*A publication*] ... Estud Extremenos
Estudios Filologicos [*A publication*] ... EFil
Estudios Filosoficos [*A publication*] ... Estud Filosof
Estudios Franciscanos [*A publication*] ... EstF
Estudios Geograficos [*A publication*] ... EG
Estudios Geograficos [*A publication*] ... Estud Geogr
Estudios Geologicos [*A publication*] ... Estudios Geol
Estudios Geologicos (Instituto de Investigaciones Geologicas "Lucas Mallada") [*A publication*] ... Estud Geol (Inst Invest Geol "Lucas Mallada")
Estudios Geologicos (Madrid) [*A publication*] ... Estud Geol (Madr)
Estudios de Hispanofila [*A publication*] ... EstdH
Estudios de Historia Moderna [*A publication*] ... EstHM
Estudios de Historia Social de Espana [*A publication*] ... EHSE
Estudios Internacionales [*A publication*] ... Estud Int
Estudios Josefinos [*A publication*] ... EJ
Estudios Lulianos [*A publication*] ... ELu
Estudios Lulianos [*A publication*] ... ELul
Estudios Orientales (Mexico City) [*A publication*] ... EOMC
Estudios Segovianos [*A publication*] ... ES
Estudios Sindicales [*A publication*] ... Estud Sindic
Estudios Sociales Centroamericanos [*A publication*] ... Estud Soc C
Estudios Sociales Centroamericanos [*A publication*] ... Estud Soc Centroamer
Estudios Sociales Revista de Ciencias Sociales [*A publication*] ... Estud Soc
Estudis Franciscans [*A publication*] ... EF
Estudis Romanics [*A publication*] ... ER
Estudis Universitaris Catalans [*A publication*] ... EUC
Estudos Agronomicos [*A publication*] ... Estudos Agron
Estudos Anglo-Americanos [*A publication*] ... EAA
Estudos Brasileiros [*A publication*] ... EBra
Estudos de Castelo Branco [*A publication*] ... ECB
Estudos sobre a Fauna Portuguesa [*A publication*] ... Estud Fauna Port
Estudos Ibero-Americanos [*A publication*] ... EIA
Estudos e Informacao. Servicos Florestais e Aquicolas (Portugal) [*A publication*] ... Estud Inform Serv Flor Aquic (Portugal)
Estudos Italianos em Portugal [*A publication*] ... EIP
Estudos Leopoldenses [*A publication*] ... Estud Leopold
Estudos Universitarios [*Recife*] [*A publication*] ... EU
Estudos Universitarios: Revista de Cultura da Universidade de Pernambuco [*A publication*] ... EURCUP
Esutoru [*Uglegorsk*] [*USSR*] [*Seismograph station code, US Geological Survey*] [*Closed*] ... ESU
Et Alia [*And Others*] [*Latin*] ... ET AL
Et Alibi [*And Elsewhere*] [*Latin*] ... ET AL
Et Cetera [*And So Forth*] [*Latin*] ... ETC
ET [*Enterostomal Therapy*] **Journal** [*A publication*] ... ET J
Et Sequens [*And The Following*] [*Latin*] ... ET SEQ
Et Uxor [*And Wife*] [*Latin*] ... ET UX
Eta Kappa Nu [*Fraternity*] ... EKN
Etaiyapuram [*India*] [*Geomagnetic observatory code*] ... ETT
Etat-Major [*Headquarters*] [*French military*] ... E-M
Etat-Major General [*General Headquarters*] [*French military*] ... E-MG
Etat Sanitaire des Animaux de la Belgique [*A publication*] ... Etat San Animaux Belgique
Etats Africains et Malgache Associes [*Associated African and Malagasy States*] ... EAMA
Etats-Unis [*United States*] [*French*] ... E-U
ETB - TUG (Equipement Technique du Batiment - Technische Uitrusting van het Gebouw) [*A publication*] ... ETB TUG
ETC: A Review of General Semantics [*A publication*] ... ERGS
ETC: A Review of General Semantics [*A publication*] ... ETC Rev Gen
Etch Template [*Tool*] ... ETTP
Etched Circuit Board ... ECB
Etched Circuit Society [*Defunct*] ... ECS
Etched Flexible Circuitry ... EFC
Etched Metal Circuit ... EMC
Etched Plate ... EP
Etched Sensitized Projected Image [*Circuit board manufacture*] ... ESPI
Etching by Transmitted Light ... ETL
Eterna International Foundation for Disabled Children ... EIFDC
Eternal Word Television Network ... EWTN
Eternelle Revue [*A publication*] ... ER
Eternity [*A publication*] ... Etr
Eternity [*A publication*] ... Ety
Eternity Magazine [*A publication*] ... Eter
Ethambutol [*An antituberculosis drug*] ... EMB
Ethanehydroxydiphosphonate [*or -diphosphonic Acid*] [*Also, HEDP*] [*Organic chemistry*] ... EHDP
Ethanolamine [*Biochemistry*] ... Etn
Ethanolamine [*Organic chemistry*] [*USAN*] ... OLAMINE
Ether-Chloroform [*Mixture*] ... E-C
Ethete, WY [*Radio station call letters*] ... KIEA
Ethical Record [*A publication*] ... Eth Rec
Ethical and Religious Classics of East and West [*A publication*] ... ERCEW
Ethical Society of Washington ... ESW
Ethicon, Inc., Somerville, NJ [*Library symbol*] ... NjSoE
Ethics [*A publication*] ... Et
Ethics ... ETH
Ethics Advisory Board [*HEW*] ... EAB
Ethics and Public Policy Center ... EPPC
Ethics Resource Center ... ERC
Ethics in Science and Medicine [*A publication*] ... Ethics Sci Med
Ethics and Values in Science and Technology [*National Science Foundation*] ... EVIST
Ethidium Bromide [*Trypanocide*] [*Also, ETB, Etd Br*] [*Biochemical analysis*] ... EB
Ethidium Bromide [*Trypanocide*] [*Also, EB, Etd Br*] [*Biochemical analysis*] ... ETB
Ethidium Bromide [*Trypanocide*] [*Also, EB, ETB*] [*Biochemical analysis*] ... Etd Br
Ethiopia [*Aircraft nationality and registration mark*] ... ET
Ethiopia [*Three-letter standard code*] ... ETH
Ethiopia [*MARC geographic area code*] [*Library of Congress*] ... f-et---
Ethiopia [*MARC country of publication code*] [*Library of Congress*] ... et
Ethiopia [*Two-letter standard code*] ... ET
Ethiopia Air Lines ... EAL
Ethiopia Geological Survey. Annual Report [*A publication*] ... Ethiop Geol Surv Annu Rep
Ethiopia Geological Survey. Bulletin [*A publication*] ... Ethiop Geol Surv Bull
Ethiopian Airlines Share Co. [*ICAO designator*] ... ET
Ethiopian Collectors Club ... ECC
Ethiopian Democratic Union ... EDU
Ethiopian Institute of Agricultural Research. Report [*A publication*] ... Ethiop Inst Agric Res Rep
Ethiopian Medical Journal [*A publication*] ... Ethiop Med J
Ethiopian News Agency ... ENA
Ethiopian People's Revolution Party ... EPRP
Ethiopian Standards Institution ... ESI
Ethiopian Students Union of North America ... ESUNA
Ethiopic [*MARC language code*] [*Library of Congress*] ... eth
Ethnic American Coalition (of Eastern Europeans) ... EAC
Ethnic Employees of the Library of Congress ... EELC
Ethnic Materials Information Exchange Task Force ... EMIETF
Ethnic Millions Political Action Committee ... EMPAC
Ethnic Minorities and Women in Science [*National Science Foundation*] ... EMWS
Ethnic Quotient ... EQ
Ethnic and Racial Studies [*A publication*] ... Ethnic & Racial Stud
Ethnic Studies [*A publication*] ... Ethnic Stud
Ethnike Organosis Kypriakou Agonos [*Greece*] ... EOKA
Ethnikon Apeleutherotikon Metopon [*National Liberation Front*] [*Greece*] ... EAM
Ethnikon Mouseion [*A publication*] ... EM
Ethnikos Demokratikos Ellenikos Stratos [*Hellenic National Democratic Army*] [*Greece*] ... EDES
Ethno-Psychologie [*A publication*] ... Ethno-Psych
Ethno-Psychologie [*A publication*] ... Ethno-Psychol
Ethnographic Museum. University of Oslo. Yearbook [*A publication*] ... Ethnogr Mus Univ Oslo Yb
Ethnographisch-Archaeologische Zeitschrift [*A publication*] ... EAZ
Ethnologia Americana [*A publication*] ... Ethnol Amer
Ethnologia Europaea [*A publication*] ... EthnoE
Ethnologia Europaea [*A publication*] ... Ethnol Europ
Ethnologia Fennica [*A publication*] ... Ethnol Fennica
Ethnologia Fennica/Finnish Studies in Ethnology [*A publication*] ... EthF
Ethnologia Scandinavica [*A publication*] ... Ethnol Scand
Ethnologia Scandinavica [*A publication*] ... Eth Sc
Ethnologia Slavia [*A publication*] ... Ethnol Slavia
Ethnologia Slavica [*A publication*] ... Eth S
Ethnologie Francaise [*A publication*] ... EthnoF
Ethnologie Francaise [*A publication*] ... Ethnol Franc
Ethnologische Zeitschrift [*A publication*] ... Ethnol Z
Ethnologischer Anzeiger [*A publication*] ... Ethnol Anz
Ethnology ... ETHNOL
Ethnomusicology [*A publication*] ... Em
Ethnomusicology [*A publication*] ... Ethmus
Ethnomusicology [*A publication*] ... Ethnomusic
Ethnomusicology [*A publication*] ... ETMSB
Ethoxy-meta-phenylenediamine [*Organic chemistry*] ... EMPD
(Ethoxybenylidene)butylaniline [*Organic chemistry*] ... EBBA
Ethoxybenzoic Acid [*Dental cement*] ... EBA
(Ethoxybenzylidene)cyanoaniline [*Also, PEBAB*] [*Organic chemistry*] ... EBCA
Ethoxycarbonylethoxydihydroquinone [*Pharmacology*] ... EEDQ
Ethoxyquin [*Antioxidant*] [*Organic chemistry*] ... EMQ
Ethoxy(trichloromethyl)thiadiazole [*Fungicide*] ... ETMT
Ethyl [*As substituent on nucleoside*] [*Biochemistry*] ... e
Ethyl [*Organic chemistry*] ... Et
Ethyl 2-(Diisopropylamino)ethylmethylphosphonite [*See EDMP*] [*Army symbol*] ... QL
Ethyl Acetamidocinnamate [*Organic chemistry*] ... EAC
Ethyl Acetimidate [*Biochemistry*] ... EAI
Ethyl Acetoacetate [*Organic chemistry*] ... EAA
Ethyl Acrylate [*Organic chemistry*] ... EA
Ethyl Alcohol ... ETOH

Ethyl Amyl Ketone [*Organic chemistry*] EAK
Ethyl Bromoacetate [*Organic chemistry*] EBA
Ethyl Corporation EC
Ethyl Corp. [*NYSE symbol*] EY
Ethyl Corp., Chemical Development Library, Baton Rouge, LA [*Library symbol*] LBrE
Ethyl Corp., Pasadena, TX [*Library symbol*] TxPE
Ethyl (Diisopropylamino)ethylmethyl-phosphonite [*Nerve gas intermediate*] [*Organic chemistry*] EDMP
Ethyl Dinitropentanoate [*An explosive*] EDNP
Ethyl Dipropylthiocarbamate [*Organic chemistry*] EPTC
Ethyl Methacrylate [*Organic chemistry*] EMA
Ethyl Methanesulfonate [*or Ethyl Methanesulfonic Acid*] [*Experimental mutagen*] EMS
Ethyl-nitronitrosoguanidine [*Organic chemistry*] ENNG
Ethyl para-Nitrophenyl Phenylphosphonothioate [*Insecticide*] EPN
Ethyl Phenylcarbamate [*Plant regulator*] [*Organic chemistry*] EPC
Ethyl-sec-butylamiline [*Organic chemistry*] ESBA
Ethyl Violet-Azide [*Broth*] [*Microbiology*] EVA
Ethylaluminum Dichloride [*Organic chemistry*] EADC
Ethylaluminum Sesquichloride [*Organic chemistry*] EASC
Ethylanthrahydroquinone [*Organic chemistry*] EAHQ
Ethylanthraquinone [*Organic chemistry*] EAQ
Ethylbenzene [*Organic chemistry*] EB
Ethylbenzene Hydroperoxide [*Organic chemistry*] EBHP
Ethyl(butyl)amine [*Organic chemistry*] EBA
Ethylcarboxylate Adenosine [*Biochemistry*] ECA
Ethyl(dimethylaminopropyl)carbodiimide [*Also, EDC*] [*Organic chemistry*] EDAC
Ethyl(dimethylaminopropyl)carbodiimide [*Organic chemistry*] EDC
Ethylene Bromide [*Same as DBE, EDB*] [*Organic chemistry*] EB
Ethylene Diacrylate [*Organic chemistry*] EDA
Ethylene Dibromide [*Same as DBE, EB*] [*Organic chemistry*] EDB
Ethylene Dichloride [*Organic chemistry*] EDC
Ethylene Dimethacrylate [*Organic chemistry*] EDMA
Ethylene-Ethyl Acetate [*Organic chemistry*] EEA
Ethylene-Ethyl Acrylate [*Copolymer*] [*Organic chemistry*] EEA
Ethylene Glycol [*Organic chemistry*] EG
Ethylene Glycol Bis(aminoethyl ether)tetraacetic Acid [*Also, EBONTA*] [*Organic chemistry*] EGTA
Ethylene Glycol Diacetate [*Organic chemistry*] EGDA
Ethylene Glycol Dimethacrylate [*Organic chemistry*] EDMA
Ethylene Glycol Dimethyl Ether [*Also, DME*] [*Organic chemistry*] GLYME
Ethylene Glycol Dinitrate [*Organic chemistry*] EGDN
Ethylene Glycol Monomethyl Ether [*A poison*] [*Organic chemistry*] EGME
Ethylene Glycol Succinate [*Organic chemistry*] EGS
Ethylene-Maleic Anhydride [*Copolymer*] [*Organic chemistry*] EMA
Ethylene Oxide [*Also, ETHO, ETO*] [*Organic chemistry*] EO
Ethylene Oxide [*Also, EO, ETO*] [*Organic chemistry*] ETHO
Ethylene Oxide [*Also, EO, ETHO*] [*Organic chemistry*] ETO
Ethylene Oxide Industry Council EOIC
Ethylene-Propylene-Diene Monomer [*Organic chemistry*] EPDM
Ethylene Propylene Rubber [*Organic chemistry*] EPR
Ethylene Propylene Terpolymer [*Organic chemistry*] EPT
Ethylene-Tetrafluoroethylene [*Organic chemistry*] ETFE
Ethylene Thiourea [*Organic chemistry*] ETU
Ethylene-Vinyl Acetate [*Copolymer*] [*Organic chemistry*] EVA
Ethylene-Vinyl Chloride [*Fire-retardant resin*] [*Organic chemistry*] EVCl
Ethyleneacrylic Acid [*Organic chemistry*] EAA
Ethylenebis(dithiocarbamate) [*Organic chemistry*] EBDC
Ethylenebis(hydroxyphenylglycine) [*Organic chemistry*] EHPG
(Ethylenebis(oxyethylenenitrilo))tetraacetic Acid [*Also, EGTA*] [*Organic chemistry*] EBONTA
Ethylenediamine [*Organic chemistry*] EDA
Ethylenediamine [*Organic chemistry*] en
Ethylenediamine Dihydriodide [*Organic chemistry*] EDDI
Ethylenediamine-Pyrocatechol-Water [*Mixture for etching silicon sensors*] EDPW
Ethylenediamine Tartrate [*Organic chemistry*] EDT
Ethylenediaminebis(hydroxyphenylacetic acid) [*Also, EDDHA, EDHPA*] [*Organic chemistry*] EDBHPA
Ethylenediaminedi-o-hydroxyphenylacetate [*or - hydroxyphenylacetic Acid*] [*Also, EDBHPA, EDHPA*] [*Organic chemistry*] EDDHA
Ethylenediaminedi-o-hydroxyphenylacetic Acid [*Also, EDBHPA, EDDHA*] [*Organic chemistry*] EDHPA
Ethylenediaminediacetic Acid [*Organic chemistry*] EDDA
Ethylenediaminedisuccinic [*Organic chemistry*] EDDS
Ethylenediaminetetraacetate [*Organic chemistry*] [*USAN*] EDETATE
Ethylenediaminetetraacetate [*or Ethylenediaminetetraacetic Acid*] [*Chelating agent*] [*Analytical biochemistry*] EDTA
Ethylenediaminetetraacetate [*Organic chemistry*] enta
Ethylenediaminetetraacetonitrile [*Organic chemistry*] EDTN
Ethylenediaminetetra(methylenephosphonic Acid) [*Organic chemistry*] EDTPO
(Ethylenedinitrilo)tetrakis(propanol) [*Organic chemistry*] ENTPROL
Ethyleneimine [*Organic chemistry*] EI
Ethylhexadecyldimethylammonium Bromide [*Blood count diluent*] EHDA
Ethylhexyl Diphenyl Phosphate [*Organic chemistry*] EHDPP
Ethyl(hydroxyethyl)cellulose [*Organic chemistry*] EHEC
Ethylisopropylaniline [*Organic chemistry*] EIPA
Ethylketocyclazocine [*Biochemistry*] EKC
Ethyl(methyl)-gamma-butyrolactone [*Biochemistry*] EMGBL
Ethylnitrolic Acid [*Organic chemistry*] ENA
Ethylnitrosourea [*Organic chemistry*] ENU
Ethylnorepinephrine [*Also, ENS*] [*Pharmacology*] ENE
Ethylnorsuprarenin [*Also, ENE*] [*Pharmacology*] ENS
Ethylpyridinium Bromide [*Organic chemistry*] EPB
Ethynodiol [*Pharmacology*] ED
Ethynyl Estradiol [*Endocrinology*] EE
Etimologiceskie Issledovanija po Russkomu Jazyku [*A publication*] EIRJa
Etiology ETIOL
Etna Free Library, Etna, CA [*Library symbol*] CEt
Etna & Montrose R. R. [*AAR code*] EM
Etnografia Polska [*A publication*] Etnogr Polska
Etnografia Polska [*A publication*] EtPol
Etnologia Antropologia Culturale [*A publication*] Etnol Antropol Cult
Etnologiska Studier [*A publication*] Etnol Stud
Etnoloski Pregled [*A publication*] EtP
Etobicoke Public Library, Etobicoke, ON, Canada [*Library symbol*] CaOTEtPL
Etoiles [*A publication*] Et
Eton College Chronicle [*A publication*] [*British*] ECC
Eton College, Windsor, Berks, United Kingdom [*Library symbol*] UkWE
Etowah, TN [*Radio station call letters*] WCPH
Etowah, TN [*Radio station call letters*] WMCC
Etruscan Foundation [*Formerly, AIEC*] EF
Etude. Centre National d'Etudes et d'Experimentation de Machinisme Agricole [*A publication*] Etude Cent Nat Etude Experim Machin Agr
Etude de la Langue Francaise [*A publication*] ELF
Etude Speciale Ministere des Richesses Naturelles du Quebec [*A publication*] Etude Spec Minist Richesses Nat Que
Etudes [*A publication*] Et
Etudes Anglaises [*A publication*] EA
Etudes Anglaises [*A publication*] EAn
Etudes Anglaises [*A publication*] EtA
Etudes Anglaises [*A publication*] Et Angl
Etudes Anglaises [*A publication*] Etud Ang
Etudes Anglaises [*A publication*] Etud Anglaises
Etudes Arabes [*A publication*] Et Ar
Etudes Archeologiques [*A publication*] EArch
Etudes Balkaniques [*A publication*] Et Balkan
Etudes Balkaniques Tchecoslovaques [*A publication*] EBT
Etudes Balkaniques Tchecoslovaques [*A publication*] E B Tch
Etudes Balzaciennes [*A publication*] EB
Etudes Byzantines [*A publication*] EByz
Etudes Byzantines [*A publication*] EtByz
Etudes Carmelitaines Historiques et Critiques [*A publication*] ECHC
Etudes Carmelitaines Mystiques et Missionnaires [*A publication*] ECMM
Etudes CEE [*Communaute Economique Europeenne*]**. Serie Agriculture** [*A publication*] Etude CEE Ser Agr
Etudes Celtiques [*A publication*] EC
Etudes Celtiques [*A publication*] ECelt
Etudes Celtiques [*A publication*] Et Celt
Etudes Cinematographiques [*A publication*] Etudes Cin
Etudes Classiques [*A publication*] E Cl
Etudes Classiques [*A publication*] ECLA
Etudes Classiques [*A publication*] EtCl
Etudes Classiques [*A publication*] Et Class
Etudes et Documents (Education Nationale) [*A publication*] Et et Doc (Educ Nat)
Etudes et Documents Tchadiens [*A publication*] E D Tch
Etudes Economiques (Mons) [*A publication*] Et Econ (Mons)
Etudes Franciscaines [*A publication*] EF
Etudes Franciscaines [*A publication*] EFran
Etudes Franciscaines [*A publication*] EtF
Etudes Gaulliennes [*A publication*] Et Gaul
Etudes Germaniques [*A publication*] EG
Etudes Germaniques [*A publication*] EGerm
Etudes Germaniques [*A publication*] Et Germ
Etudes Germaniques [*A publication*] Etud Germaniques
Etudes d'Histoire et de Philosophie Religieuses [*A publication*] EHPR
Etudes d'Histoire et de Philosophie Religieuses. Universite de Strausbourg [*A publication*] EHPRUS
Etudes Internationales [*A publication*] Et Int
Etudes Internationales [*A publication*] Etud Int
Etudes Irlandaises [*A publication*] EI
Etudes Italiennes [*A publication*] EI
Etudes Italiennes [*A publication*] Etud Ital
Etudes de Langue et de Litterature Francaises [*A publication*] ELLF
Etudes de Lettres [*A publication*] EL
Etudes de Lettres [*A publication*] EtL
Etudes de Lettres (Universite de Lausanne) [*A publication*] EdL
Etudes de Linguistique Appliquee [*A publication*] ELA
Etudes Linguistiques [*A publication*] ELing
Etudes Litteraires [*A publication*] ELit
Etudes de Litterature Etrangere et Comparee [*A publication*] ELEC
Etudes Maliennes [*A publication*] Et Mal
Etudes Mariales [*A publication*] Etud Mar
Etudes de Metaphysique et de Morale [*A publication*] EMM
Etudes Mongoles [*A publication*] E Mong

Etudes Normandes [*A publication*] ... Et Normandes
Etudes et Notes d'Information. Direction du Batiment et des Travaux Publics et de la Conjoncture [*A publication*] ... Et Notes Inform Batiment
Etudes Numismatiques [*A publication*] ... EN
Etudes de Papyrologie [*A publication*] ... EPap
Etudes Papyrologiques [*A publication*] ... EP
Etudes de Philosophie Medievale [*A publication*] ... EPM
Etudes Philosophiques [*A publication*] ... EP
Etudes Philosophiques [*A publication*] ... EPh
Etudes Philosophiques [*A publication*] ... Etud Phil
Etudes de Planning Familial [*A publication*] ... Et Planning Familial
Etudes Polemologiques [*A publication*] ... Et Polemol
Etudes Preliminaires aux Religions Orientales dans l'Empire Romain [*A publication*] ... EPROER
Etudes de Presse [*A publication*] ... EPr
Etudes Psychotherapiques [*A publication*] ... Etud Psychother
Etudes Rabelaisiennes [*A publication*] ... ER
Etudes Rabelaisiennes [*A publication*] ... ERab
Etudes et Recherches. Institut de Meteorologie. Part 2. Hydrologie [*A publication*] ... Etud Rech Inst Meteorol Part 2
Etudes de la Region Parisienne [*A publication*] ... Et Region Paris
Etudes Rhodaniennes [*A publication*] ... ER
Etudes Romanes de Brno [*A publication*] ... ERB
Etudes Romanes de Brno [*A publication*] ... ERBr
Etudes Romanes de Lund [*A publication*] ... ERL
Etudes Rurales [*A publication*] ... Et Rur
Etudes Rurales [*A publication*] ... Etud Rur
Etudes Slaves et Est-Europeennes [*A publication*] ... ESl
Etudes Slaves et Est-Europeennes [*A publication*] ... Etud Slav E
Etudes Slaves et Roumaines [*A publication*] ... ESLR
Etudes Slaves et Roumaines [*A publication*] ... ESR
Etudes Sociales (Paris) [*A publication*] ... Et Soc (Paris)
Etudes Sovietiques [*A publication*] ... ESov
Etudes et Statistiques. Banque des Etats de l'Afrique Centrale. Bulletin Mensuel [*A publication*] ... Et Statist Banque Etats Afr Centr
Etudes Statistiques. Institute National de la Statistique et des Etudes Economiques [*A publication*] ... Etude Stat Inst Nat Stat
Etudes Suisses d'Histoire Generale [*A publication*] ... ESHG
Etudes Techniques et Constructions Aerospatiales [*Belgium*] ... ETCA
Etudes Techniques et Economiques. Seria E. Hydrogeologie (Institut de Geologie et Geophysique) [*A publication*] ... Etud Tech Econ Ser E (Inst Geol Geophys)
Etudes Theologiques et Religieuses [*A publication*] ... EThR
Etudes Theologiques et Religieuses [*A publication*] ... ETR
Etudes Theologiques et Religieuses [*A publication*] ... E T Rel
Etudes Traditionnelles [*A publication*] ... ET
Etudes Tsiganes [*A publication*] ... ETs
Etudes d'Urbanisme de Developpement et d'Amenagement [*du Territoire*] ... EURDA
Etudes Zairoises [*A publication*] ... Et Zair
Etymology ... ETYM
ETZ [*Elektrotechnische Zeitschrift*]. **Archiv** [*A publication*] ... ETZ Arch
ETZ (Elektrotechnische Zeitschrift) [*A publication*] ... ETZ Elektrotech Z
Etz Lavud Ltd. [*American Stock Exchange symbol*] ... ETZ
Eua Tonga Island [*South Pacific*] [*Airport symbol*] ... EUA
Eucharistic Guard for Nocturnal Adoration ... EGNA
Euclid Public Library, Euclid, OH [*OCLC symbol*] ... ECU
Euclid Public Library, Euclid, OH [*Library symbol*] ... OEu
Euclid R. R. [*AAR code*] ... EUC
Euclidean [*Mathematics*] ... EUC
Eudora Welty Newsletter [*A publication*] ... Eu W N
Euer [*Your*] [*German*] ... EW
Euer Ehrwuerden [*Your Reverence*] [*German*] ... EE
Eufaula, AL [*Location identifier*] [*FAA*] ... EUF
Eufaula, AL [*Radio station call letters*] ... WKQK
Eufaula, AL [*Radio station call letters*] ... WULA
Eufaula, OK [*Radio station call letters*] ... KCES
Eufaula, OK [*Television station call letters*] ... KOET
Eugene [*Oregon*] [*Airport symbol*] ... EUG
Eugene Field House, St. Louis, MO [*Library symbol*] ... MoSFi
Eugene Isle, LA [*Location identifier*] [*FAA*] ... VUW
Eugene O'Neill Memorial Theater Center ... EOMTC
Eugene O'Neill Society ... EOS
Eugene, OR [*Location identifier*] [*FAA*] ... EUG
Eugene, OR [*Radio station call letters*] ... KASH
Eugene, OR [*Radio station call letters*] ... KBDF
Eugene, OR [*Radio station call letters*] ... KBMC
Eugene, OR [*Radio station call letters*] ... KEED
Eugene, OR [*Television station call letters*] ... KEZI-TV
Eugene, OR [*Radio station call letters*] ... KLCC
Eugene, OR [*Television station call letters*] ... KMTR-TV
Eugene, OR [*Radio station call letters*] ... KPNW
Eugene, OR [*Radio station call letters*] ... KPNW-FM
Eugene, OR [*Radio station call letters*] ... KQDQ
Eugene, OR [*Radio station call letters*] ... KRVM
Eugene, OR [*Radio station call letters*] ... KUGN
Eugene, OR [*Radio station call letters*] ... KUGN-FM
Eugene, OR [*Television station call letters*] ... KVAL
Eugene, OR [*Radio station call letters*] ... KWAX
Eugene, OR [*Radio station call letters*] ... KZEL-FM
Eugene Public Library, Eugene, OR [*OCLC symbol*] ... OEL
Eugene Public Library, Eugene, OR [*Library symbol*] ... OrE
Eugene-Springfield, MO [*Radio station call letters*] ... KSMU
Eugene V. Debs Foundation ... EVDF
Eugene V. Debs Foundation, Terre Haute, IN [*Library symbol*] ... InTD
Eugenics Laboratory. Memoirs [*A publication*] ... Eugen Lab Mem
Eugenics Quarterly [*A publication*] ... Eugen Q
Eugenics Review [*A publication*] ... Eugen Rev
Eugenics Review [*A publication*] ... Eug R
Eugenics Review [*A publication*] ... EUREA
Eugenics Society Symposia [*A publication*] ... Eugen Soc Symp
Eul Ji Medical Journal [*A publication*] ... Eul Ji Med J
Eulenspiegel-Jahrbuch [*A publication*] ... Eul J
EULEP [*European Late Effects Project Group*] **Newsletter** [*A publication*] ... EULEP Newsl
Euler Number ... E
Euler Number [*IUPAC*] ... Eu
Euler-Rodrigues Parameter [*Physics*] ... ERP
Eulerian Iterative Nonsteady [*Method*] [*Mathematics*] ... EIN
Eunice, LA [*Radio station call letters*] ... KEUN
Eunice, LA [*Radio station call letters*] ... KJJB
Eunice Public Library, Eunice, LA [*Library symbol*] ... LE
Euntes Docete [*A publication*] ... ED
Euphonium [*Musical instrument*] ... EUPH
Euphoria et Cacophoria (International Edition) [*A publication*] ... Euphoria Cacophoria (Int Ed)
Euphorion [*A publication*] ... Eu
Euphorion [*A publication*] ... Euph
Eupora, MS [*Radio station call letters*] ... WEPA
Eupora, MS [*Radio station call letters*] ... WEXA
Eurafrica et Tribune de Tiers-Monde [*A publication*] ... Eurafr Trib Tiers-Monde
Euralair [*France*] [*ICAO designator*] ... EL
Euralair International [*France*] [*ICAO designator*] ... EK
Eurasia [*MARC geographic area code*] [*Library of Congress*] ... me-----
Eurasia Septentrionalis Antiqua [*A publication*] ... ESA
EURATOM. Bulletin of the European Atomic Energy Community [*A publication*] ... EURATOM Bull Eur At Energy Community
EURATOM [*European Atomic Energy Community*] **Classified Information** ... ECI
Eureka [*Nevada*] [*Seismograph station code, US Geological Survey*] ... EUR
Eureka [*Washington*] [*Seismograph station code, US Geological Survey*] ... EUW
Eureka Aero Industries [*Eureka, CA*] [*FAA designator*] ... EKA
Eureka/Arcata [*California*] [*Airport symbol*] ... ACV
Eureka/Arcata [*California*] **Murray Field** [*Airport symbol*] [*Obsolete*] ... EKA
Eureka, CA [*Television station call letters*] ... KEET
Eureka, CA [*Radio station call letters*] ... KEKA
Eureka, CA [*Radio station call letters*] ... KFMI
Eureka, CA [*Television station call letters*] ... KIEM-TV
Eureka, CA [*Radio station call letters*] ... KINS
Eureka, CA [*Radio station call letters*] ... KPDJ
Eureka, CA [*Radio station call letters*] ... KRED
Eureka, CA [*Television station call letters*] ... KVIQ
Eureka Canyon [*California*] [*Seismograph station code, US Geological Survey*] ... EUC
Eureka City Library, Eureka, CA [*Library symbol*] ... CE
Eureka College, Eureka, IL [*OCLC symbol*] ... IBU
Eureka College, Eureka, IL [*Library symbol*] ... IEuC
Eureka Mesa [*New Mexico*] [*Seismograph station code, US Geological Survey*] ... EUM
Eureka, MT [*Location identifier*] [*FAA*] ... EUR
Eureka Pipe Line Co. [*American Stock Exchange symbol*] ... EKU
Eureka Public Library, Eureka, SD [*Library symbol*] ... SdEu
Eureka Ridge [*Idaho*] [*Seismograph station code, US Geological Survey*] [*Closed*] ... ERI
Euriam Bulteni [*A publication*] ... Euriam Bul
Euro American Cultural Exchange ... EACE
Euro-Latin American Bank Ltd. ... EULA
Euro-Spectra [*A publication*] ... Euro Spectr
Euroair Transport Ltd. [*Great Britain*] [*ICAO designator*] ... EZ
Eurobike Limited ... ELTD
Eurocard [*Credit card*] [*British*] ... E
Eurocheque [*Credit card*] [*British*] ... EC
Eurofund International, Inc. [*NYSE symbol*] [*Delisted*] ... EFD
Eurojet SA [*Spain*] [*ICAO designator*] ... JE
Euromicro Newsletters [*A publication*] ... Euromicro Newsl
Euromissiles Working Group ... EWG
Europa [*A publication*] ... E
Europa-Archiv [*A publication*] ... Eur Arch
Europa Chemie [*A publication*] ... Europ Chem
Europa Letteraria [*A publication*] ... EL
Europa Letteraria [*A publication*] ... ELet
Europa Nostra ... EN
Europa Study Unit [*American Topical Association*] ... ESU
Europaeische Chirurgische Forschung [*A publication*] ... Eur Chir Forsch
Europaeische Grundrechte [*A publication*] ... Eur Grundrechte
Europaeische Hochschulschriften [*A publication*] ... EH
Europaeische Hochschulschriften [*A publication*] ... EurH
Europaeische Konferenz ueber Mikrozirkulation [*A publication*] ... Eur Konf Mikrozirk

Europaeische Literatur [*A publication*] .... EL
Europaeische Organisation der Militaerverbaende .... EUROMIL
Europaeische Osten [*A publication*] .... EO
Europaeische Rundschau [*A publication*] .... Europ Rdsch
Europaeische Studentenvereinigung in Osterreich .... ESTO
Europaeische Wehrkunde [*A publication*] .... Europ Wehrkunde
Europaeische Wirtschaftsgemeinschaft [*European Economic Community*] .... EWG
Europaeische Zeitschrift fuer Forstpathologie [*A publication*] .... Eur Z Forstpathologie
Europaeische Zeitschrift fuer Kartoffelforschung [*A publication*] .... Eur Z Kartoffelforsch
Europaeischer Wissenschaftsdienst [*A publication*] .... EWD
Europaeisches Symposium fuer Pulvermetallurgie. Vorabdrucke [*A publication*] .... Eur Symp Pulvermetall Vorabdrucke
Europe [*MARC geographic area code*] [*Library of Congress*] .... e------
Europe .... EU
Europe .... EUR
Europe Aero Service [*France*] [*ICAO designator*] .... EY
Europe and Africa .... EURAFRICA
Europe-Africa-Middle East .... EAME
Europe, Asia, and Africa .... EURASAFRICA
Europe, Central [*MARC geographic area code*] [*Library of Congress*] .... ec-----
Europe, East Central [*MARC geographic area code*] [*Library of Congress*] .... et-----
Europe, Eastern [*MARC geographic area code*] [*Library of Congress*] .... ee-----
Europe Falcon Service [*France*] [*ICAO designator*] .... FK
Europe in the Middle Ages. Selected Studies [*Elsevier Book Series*] [*A publication*] .... EMA
Europe, Northern [*MARC geographic area code*] [*Library of Congress*] .... en-----
Europe Nouvelle [*A publication*] .... Eur Nouv
Europe and Oil [*A publication*] .... EO
Europe Orientale [*A publication*] .... EO
Europe-Outre-Mer [*A publication*] .... Europe-O-Mer
Europe, Southeastern [*MARC geographic area code*] [*Library of Congress*] .... ed-----
Europe, Southern [*MARC geographic area code*] [*Library of Congress*] .... es-----
Europe, Western [*MARC geographic area code*] [*Library of Congress*] .... ew-----
European Advisory Committee [*Allied German Occupation Forces*] .... EAC
European-African-Middle Eastern [*Communications area*] [*NASA*] .... E-A-ME
European-African-Middle Eastern Campaign Medal .... EAMECM
European Agricultural Aviation Centre [*Later, International Agricultural Aviation Centre*] .... EAAC
European Agricultural Guidance and Guarantee Fund [*Also known as FEOGA*] .... EAGGF
European Air Lines .... EURAL
European Air Transport Service .... EATS
European Airlines Research Bureau .... EARB
European Alliance of News Agencies .... EANA
European Allied Contacts Section [*Supreme Headquarters, Allied Expeditionary Force*] [*World War II*] .... EACS
European-American Committee on Reactor Physics .... EACRP
European-American Nuclear Data Committee [*OECD*] .... EANDC
European Application Satellite Systems .... EUROSAT
European Applied Research Reports. Nuclear Science and Technology Section [*A publication*] .... Eur Appl Res Rep-Nucl Sci Technol Sect
European Architectural Heritage Year [*1975*] .... EAHY
European Area Communications Plan [*Military*] .... EACP
European Area Headquarters [*Red Cross*] .... EUA
European Article Number [*Equivalent of Universal Product Code*] .... EAN
European Association of Advertising Agencies .... EAAA
European Association for American Studies .... EAAS
European Association for Animal Production .... EAAP
European Association for Animal Production. Publication [*A publication*] .... Eur Assoc Anim Prod Publ
European Association for Aquatic Mammals .... EAAM
European Association for Co-Operation .... EAC
European Association of Development Research and Training Institutes .... EADRI
European Association of Editors of Biological Periodicals .... EAEBP
European Association of Exploration Geophysicists .... EAEG
European Association of Management Training Centres .... EAMTC
European Association for Potato Research .... EAPR
European Association of Scientific Information Dissemination Centers .... EUSIDIC
European Association for Special Education .... EASE
European Athletic Association .... EAA
[*The*] **European-Atlantic Movement** .... TEAM
European Atomic Commission .... EAC
European Atomic Energy Community .... EAEC
European Atomic Energy Community .... EURATOM
European Atomic Energy Society .... EAES
European Bibliographical Center .... EBC
European Billiards Confederation .... EBC
European Boxing Union .... EBU
European Brazilian Bank .... EUROBRAZ
European Brewery Convention .... EBC
European Bridge League .... EBL
European Broadcasting Union .... EBU
European Bureau for the Allocation of International Long Lines .... EBAILL
European Bureau for Youth and Childhood .... EBYC
European Business [*A publication*] .... Europ Busin
European Calibration Line .... ECL
European Central Inland Movements of Transport .... ECIMOT
European Central Inland Transport Organization .... ECITO
European Central NOTAM [*Notice to Airmen*] **Facility** [*Military*] .... ECNF
European Centre for Population Studies .... ECPS
European Channel Tunnel Group [*Planning a proposed tunnel between England and France under the English Channel*] .... ECTG
[*The*] **European Chemical Industry Ecology and Toxicology Center** [*Brussels*] .... ECETOC
European Chemical Market Research Association .... ECMRA
European Chemical News [*A publication*] .... Eur Chem N
European Chemoreception Research Organization .... ECRO
European Christian Democratic Union .... ECDU
European Christian Mission .... ECM
European Civil Affairs .... ECA
European Civil Affairs Division [*US Military Government, Germany*] .... ECAD
European Civil Affairs Regiment .... ECAR
European Civil Aviation Conference .... ECAC
European Coal Organization .... ECO
European Coal and Steel Community [*France, West Germany, Italy, BENELUX*] .... ECSC
European Coil Coating Association .... ECCA
European Command [*Military*] .... EUCOM
European Command .... EURCOM
European Command and Control Console System [*DoD*] .... ECCCS
European Command Coordination Committee [*Military*] .... ECCC
European Commission on Agriculture [*FAO*] [*United Nations*] .... ECA
European Commission for the Control of Foot-and-Mouth Disease .... ECCFD
European Commission Host Organization [*Commission of the European Communities*] [*Information service*] .... ECHO
European Committee on Crime Problems .... ECCP
European Committee of Crop Protection .... ECP
European Committee on Future Accelerators [*Nuclear energy*] .... ECFA
European Committee on Milk-Butter-Fat Recording .... ECMBR
European Common Market .... ECM
European Common Market .... EUROMART
European Communication Satellite .... ECS
European Communication Security Agency .... ECSA
European Communications Area [*Military*] .... ECA
European Communications Security and Evaluation Agency of the Military Committee, London [*US Army*] .... EUSEC
European Communist Party Conference .... ECPC
European Community [*Formerly, EEC*] [*Common Market*] .... EC
European Community Information Service .... ECIS
European Community Research Council .... ECRC
European Computer Manufacturers Association .... ECMA
European Computer Manufacturers Association Algorithmic Language .... ECMALGOL
European Computing Congress .... EUROCOMP
European Confederation of Agriculture .... ECA
European Confederation of Free Trade Unions [*Later, ETUC*] .... ECFTU
European Conference on Animal Blood Groups and Biochemical Polymorphism [*A publication*] .... Eur Conf Anim Blood Groups Biochem Polymorphism
European Conference of Meteorological Experts for Aeronautics .... ECMEA
European Conference on Microcirculation [*A publication*] .... Eur Conf Microcirc
European Conference of Ministers of Transport .... ECMT
European Conference on Mixing and Centrifugal Separation .... ECMCS
European Conference on Molecular Biology .... ECMB
European Conference of Radiotelegraphy Experts for Aeronautics .... ECREA
European Conference on Satellite Communications .... ECSC
European Conference on Telecommunications by Satellite .... ECTS
European Congress of Biotechnology .... ECB
European Consortium for Political Research .... ECPR
European Cooperation Research Group [*European parliamentarians*] .... EUCORG
European Cooperation Space Environment Committee .... ECOSEC
European Coordinating Committee .... ECC
European Core Inventory of Existing Substances [*Chemicals which are exempt from new product regulations*] .... ECOIN
European Corn Borer [*Agronomy*] .... ECB
European Cultural Centre .... ECC
European Currency Unit [*European Monetary System*] .... ECU
European Defense Analysis Center .... EUDAC
European Defense Community [*NATO*] .... EDC
European Defense Force .... EDF
European Defense Improvement Program [*NATO*] .... EDIP
European Demographic Information Bulletin [*A publication*] .... Europ Demogr Inform B
European Development Fund .... EDF

European Disarmament Conference .... EDC
European Distribution and Accounting Agency of the Military Committee, London [*US Army*] .... EUDAC
European Distribution System [*DoD*] .... EDS
European Distribution System Aircraft [*DoD*] .... EDSA
European Division Naval Facilities Engineering Command .... DIREURDOCKS
European Division Naval Facilities Engineering Command .... EURNAVFACENGCOM
European Documentation and Information System for Education .... EUDISED
European Economic Community [*Later, EC*] [*Common Market*] .... EEC
European Economic and Political Survey [*A publication*] .... Europ Econ and Pol Survey
European Economic Review [*A publication*] .... Eur Econ R
European Economic Review [*A publication*] .... Europ Econ R
European Enterprises Development Co. [*Luxembourg*] .... EED
European Environmental Bureau .... EEB
European Exchange System .... EES
European Federalist Movement .... EFM
European Federation of Chemical Engineering .... EFCE
European Federation for the Protection of Waters .... EFPW
European Federation of Tile and Brick Manufacturers .... TBE
European Food Emulsifier Manufacturers' Association [*Common Market*] .... EFEMA
European Forestry Commission .... EFC
European Free Exchange Area .... EFEA
European Free Trade Area .... EFTA
European Free Trade Association [*Known as the "Outer Seven" as opposed to the "Inner Six" Common Market nations*] .... EFTA
European Furniture Federation .... EFF
European Geophysical Society. Meeting. Abstracts [*A publication*] .... Eur Geophys Soc Meet Abstr
European Glass Container Manufacturers' Committee .... EGM
European Heart Journal [*A publication*] .... Eur Heart J
European Host Operators Group [*EURONET*] .... EHOG
European Incoherent Scattering Scientific Association .... EISCAT
European Industrial Research Management Association .... EIRMA
European Industrial Space Study Group .... EUROSPACE
European Information Providers Association .... EURIPA
European Inland Fisheries Advisory Commission [*UN Food and Agriculture Organization*] .... EIFAC
European Inventory of Existing Commercial Chemical Substances [*Which will be exempt from new product regulations*] .... EINECS
European Investments Bank .... EIB
European Journal of Applied Microbiology [*A publication*] .... Eur J Appl Microbiol
European Journal of Applied Microbiology [*A publication*] .... Eur J App M
European Journal of Applied Microbiology and Biotechnology [*A publication*] .... Eur J Appl Microbiol Biotechnol
European Journal of Applied Physiology and Occupational Physiology [*A publication*] .... EJAPC
European Journal of Applied Physiology and Occupational Physiology [*A publication*] .... Eur J A Phy
European Journal of Applied Physiology and Occupational Physiology [*A publication*] .... Eur J Appl Physiol Occup Physiol
European Journal of Biochemistry [*A publication*] .... Eur J Bioch
European Journal of Biochemistry [*A publication*] .... Eur J Biochem
European Journal of Cancer [*A publication*] .... Eur J Canc
European Journal of Cancer [*A publication*] .... Eur J Cancer
European Journal of Cancer and Clinical Oncology [*A publication*] .... Eur J Cancer Clin Oncol
European Journal of Cardiology [*A publication*] .... Eur J Cardiol
European Journal of Cell Biology [*A publication*] .... Eur J Cell Biol
European Journal of Clinical Investigation [*A publication*] .... Eur J Cl In
European Journal of Clinical Investigation [*A publication*] .... Eur J Clin Invest
European Journal of Clinical Pharmacology [*A publication*] .... Eur J Clin Pharmacol
European Journal of Clinical Pharmacology [*A publication*] .... Eur J Cl Ph
European Journal of Drug Metabolism and Pharmacokinetics [*A publication*] .... Eur J Drug Metab Pharmacokinet
European Journal of Forest Pathology [*A publication*] .... Eur J For Pathol
European Journal of Immunology [*A publication*] .... Eur J Immun
European Journal of Immunology [*A publication*] .... Eur J Immunol
European Journal of Intensive Care Medicine [*A publication*] .... Eur J I Car
European Journal of Intensive Care Medicine [*A publication*] .... Eur J Intensive Care Med
European Journal of Marketing [*A publication*] .... Eur J Mktg
European Journal of Medicinal Chemistry [*A publication*] .... Eur J Med Chem
European Journal of Medicinal Chemistry. Chimica Therapeutica [*A publication*] .... Eur J Med Chem Chim Ther
European Journal of Nuclear Medicine [*A publication*] .... Eur J Nucl Med
European Journal of Obstetrics, Gynecology, and Reproductive Biology [*A publication*] .... Eur J Obstet Gynecol Reprod Biol
European Journal of Operational Research [*A publication*] .... Eur J Oper Res
European Journal of Operational Research [*A publication*] .... European J Oper Res
European Journal of Orthodontics [*A publication*] .... Eur J Orthod
European Journal of Pediatrics [*A publication*] .... Eur J Ped
European Journal of Pediatrics [*A publication*] .... Eur J Pediatr
European Journal of Pharmacology [*A publication*] .... Eur J Pharm
European Journal of Pharmacology [*A publication*] .... Eur J Pharmacol
European Journal of Political Research [*A publication*] .... Europ J Polit Res
European Journal of Respiratory Diseases [*A publication*] .... Eur J Respir Dis
European Journal of Respiratory Diseases. Supplement [*A publication*] .... Eur J Respir Dis Suppl
European Journal of Social Psychology [*A publication*] .... Eur J Soc P
European Journal of Social Psychology [*A publication*] .... Europ J Soc Psychol
European Journal of Sociology [*A publication*] .... Eur J Sociol
European Journal of Steroids [*A publication*] .... Eur J Steroids
European Journal of Toxicology [*A publication*] .... Eur J Toxicol
European Journal of Toxicology and Environmental Hygiene [*A publication*] .... Eur J Toxicol Environ Hyg
European Landworkers Federation .... ELF
European Large Orbiting Instrumentation for Solar Experiments .... ELOISE
European Launcher Development Organization [*Superseded by European Space Agency*] .... ELDO
European League for Economic Cooperation .... ELEC
European Letter Telegram .... ELT
European Liaison Group [*Army*] .... ELG
European Long Lines Agency [*NATO*] .... ELLA
European Malacological Union .... EMU
European Marine Biological Association .... EMBA
European Market Development .... EMD
European-Mediterranean [*Military*] .... EUM
European and Mediterranean Plant Protection Organization .... EPPO
European and Mediterranean Plant Protection Organization. Publications. Series A [*A publication*] .... Eur Mediterr Plant Prot Organ Publ Ser A
European and Mediterranean Plant Protection Organization. Publications. Series D [*A publication*] .... Eur Mediterr Plant Prot Organ Publ Ser D
European Mediterranean Troposphere .... EMT
European Military Communication .... EMC
European Military Communications Co-Ordinating Committee [*NATO*] .... EMCCC
European Mineworkers' Union [*Zambia*] .... EMU
European Missionary Fellowship .... EMF
European Mobility Service Office [*Army*] .... EMSO
European Molecular Biology Laboratory .... EMBL
European Molecular Biology Organization .... EMBO
European Monetary Agreement .... EMA
European Monetary Cooperation Fund .... EMCF
European Monetary Reserve Fund [*Common Market*] .... EMRF
European Monetary System .... EMS
European Monetary Union .... EMU
European Monetary Unit [*Proposed*] .... EMU
European Monetary Unit of Account .... EMUA
European Motel Federation .... EMF
European Motorcycle Association .... EMA
European Movement .... EM
European Municipal Credit Community .... EMCC
European Naval Communications Agency [*NATO*] .... ENCA
European Naval Communications Plan .... ENCP
European Neurology [*A publication*] .... Eur Neurol
European Nuclear Disarmament [*An association*] .... END
European Nuclear Documentation System [*Information service*] .... ENDS
European Nuclear Energy Agency [*Later, NEA*] .... ENEA
European Nuclear Society .... ENS
European Numismatics [*A publication*] .... EN
European Oceanographic Association .... EUROCEAN
European Office of Aerospace Research .... EOAR
European Office of Aerospace Research and Development .... EOARD
European On-Line Information Network [*Commission of the European Communities*] [*Information service*] .... EURONET
European Organization for Civil Aviation Electronics .... EUROCAE
European Organization for Quality Control .... EOQC
European Organization for Research on Treatment of Cancer .... EORTC
European Organization for Research on Treatment of Cancer. Monograph Series [*A publication*] .... Eur Organ Res Treat Cancer Monog Ser
European Organization for Research on Treatment of Cancer. Monograph Series [*A publication*] .... Eur Organ Treat Cancer Monogr Ser
European Organization for the Safety of Air Navigation .... EUROCONTROL
European Orthodontic Society .... EOS
European Parliament .... EP
European Participating Governments [*In the F-16 fighter program*] .... EPG
European Passenger Train Timetable Conference .... EPTTC
European Patent Convention .... EPC
European Patent Office [*Munich, West Germany*] .... EPO
European Payments Union .... EPU
European People's Party .... EPP
European Petrochemical Industry Computerized System [*Parpinelli Tecnon*] [*Italy*] [*Information service*] .... EPICS
European Physical Society .... EPS
European Plastics News [*A publication*] .... Eur Plast News
European Political Community .... EPC

European Polymer Journal [*A publication*] .... Eur Polym J
European Potato Journal [*A publication*] .... Eur Potato J
European Press Group .... EPG
European Primary Aluminum Association .... EPAA
European Productivity Agency .... EPA
European Programme Groupe [*NATO*] .... EPG
European Public Relations Advisory Committee .... EUPRAC
European Radio Frequency Agency [*Later, ARFA*] [*NATO*] .... ERFA
European Railway Passenger [*Ticket*] .... EURAILPASS
European Recovery Program .... ERP
European Red Mite [*Insect*] .... ERM
European Regional Organization of the ICFTU .... ERO
European Regional Test Center .... ERTC
European Requirements and Army Capabilities .... EURAC
European Requirements List [*Military*] .... ERL
European Research Associates .... ERA
European Research National Organization .... ERNO
European Research Office .... ERO
European Review of Agricultural Economics [*A publication*] .... Europ R Agric Econ
European Review of Endocrinology [*A publication*] .... Eur Rev Endocrinol
European Rubber Journal [*A publication*] .... Eur Rubb J
European Satellite Launching Organization .... ESLO
European Science Foundation .... ESF
European Scientific Information Referral [*EUSIDIC*] [*Information service*] .... EUSIREF
European Scientific Notes [*Navy*] .... ESN
European Security Conference [*Soviet-sponsored*] .... ESC
European Security Region [*Military*] .... ESR
European Shielding Information Service [*EURATOM*] .... ESIS
European Shipbuilding [*A publication*] .... Eur Shipbldg
European Social Fund .... ESF
European Society for Engineering Education .... ESEE
European Society for Opinion Surveys and Market Research .... ESOMAR
European Society for Rural Sociology .... ESRS
European Solid-State Circuits Conference .... ESSCIRC
European Solid State Device. Research Conference [*A publication*] .... Eur Solid State Device Res Conf
European Southern Observatory [*La Silla Mountain, Chile*] .... ESO
European Space Agency [*Superseded ESRO*] .... ESA
European Space Agency. Scientific and Technical Review [*A publication*] .... Eur Space Agency Sci Tech Rev
European Space Conference .... ESC
European Space Data Center .... ESDAC
European Space Laboratory .... ESLAB
European Space Launcher Organization .... ESLO
European Space Operations Center .... ESOC
European Space Range [*Sweden*] .... ESRANGE
European Space Research Institute .... ESRIN
European Space Research Organization [*Superseded by ESA*] .... ESRO
European Space Technology Centre [*Netherlands*] .... ESTC
European Space Technology Centre [*Netherlands*] .... ESTEC
European Space Tracking and Telemetry Network .... ESTRACK
European Space Vehicle Launcher Development Organization .... EUR/SV/LDO
European Standard Inventory List .... ESIL
European Standards on Nuclear Electronics .... ESONE
European Strategic Program for Research in Information Technology .... ESPRIT
European Studies in Law [*Elsevier Book Series*] [*A publication*] .... ESL
European Studies Newsletter [*A publication*] .... Europ Stud Newsl
European Studies Review [*A publication*] .... ESR
European Studies Review [*A publication*] .... Europ Stud R
European Studies Review [*A publication*] .... Eur Stud R
European Supply Agency .... ESA
European Surgical Research [*A publication*] .... Eur Surg Re
European Surgical Research [*A publication*] .... Eur Surg Res
European Symposium on Calcified Tissues. Proceedings [*A publication*] .... Eur Symp Calcif Tissues Proc
European Symposium on Chemical Reaction Engineering [*A publication*] .... Eur Symp Chem React Eng
European Symposium on Hormones and Cell Regulation [*A publication*] .... Eur Symp Horm Cell Regul
European Symposium on Lindane [*A publication*] .... Eur Symp Lindane
European Symposium for Powder Metallurgy. Preprints [*A publication*] .... Eur Symp Powder Metall Prepr
European Technical Operations Group .... ETOG
European Telephone System [*DoD*] .... ETS
European Television .... EUROVISION
European Theater .... ET
European Theater Air Command and Control Study [*DoD*] .... ETACCS
European Theater Bureau of Public Relations [*World War II*] .... ETBPR
European Theater of Operations [*World War II*] .... ETO
European Theater of Operations, United States Army [*World War II*] .... ETOUSA
European Trade Union Confederation [*Formerly, ECFTU*] .... ETUC
European Translation Centre [*Later, International Translation Centre*] .... ETC
European Translations Centre. Quarterly Index [*A publication*] .... ETC Quart Index
European Transport Organization [*ECE*] .... ETO
European Transuranium Institute [*West Germany*] .... ETI
European Travel Commission .... ETC
European Tropospheric - Army .... ETA
European Tyre and Rim Technical Organisation .... ETRTO
European Union of Federalists .... EUF
European Union Football Associations .... EUFA
European Union of Women .... EUW
European Units of Account [*Economics*] .... EUA
European Urology [*A publication*] .... Eur Urol
European Vegetable Protein Federation [*Common Market*] .... EUVEPRO
European Voluntary Worker .... EVW
European Weed Research Council [*Later, EWRS*] .... EWRC
European Weed Research Society [*Formerly, EWRC*] .... EWRS
European Wideband Communications System [*Army*] .... EWCS
European Wideband Transmission Media Improvement Program .... EWTMI
European Youth Campaign .... EYC
Europese Economische Gemeenschap [*European Economic Community*] .... EEG
Europhysics News [*A publication*] .... Europhys News
Europium [*Chemical element*] .... Eu
Europlastics Monthly [*A publication*] .... Europlast Mon
Eusko-Jakintza. Revista de Estudios Vascos [*A publication*] .... EJEV
Eustis, FL [*Radio station call letters*] .... WEUS
Eustis Memorial Library, Eustis, FL [*Library symbol*] .... FE
Euthanasia Society of America [*Later, SRD*] .... ESA
Euzkadi ta Azkatasuna [*Basque Fatherland and Freedom*] [*Spain*] .... ETA
Euzkadi ta Azkatasuna [*Basque Fatherland and Freedom*] **Military Front** [*Spain*] .... ETA-M
Euzkadi ta Azkatasuna [*Basque Fatherland and Freedom*] **Political-Military Front** [*Spain*] .... ETA-PM
Ev. Lutheran Good Samaritan Society .... ELGSS
Eva Brook Donly Museum, Simcoe, ON, Canada [*Library symbol*] .... CaOSiDM
EVA [*Extravehicular Activity*] **Life-Support System** [*NASA*] .... ELSS
Evacuation .... EVAC
Evacuation and Evasion .... E & E
Evacuation Hospital Ship [*Navy symbol*] .... AHP
Evacuation Mission [*Air Force*] .... EVM
Evacuation/Replacement [*Jar technique*] [*Microbiology*] .... E/R
Evacuation Ship [*Navy*] .... EVACSHIP
Evacuation Unit [*Army*] .... EU
Evadale, TX [*Location identifier*] [*FAA*] .... ETO
Evadale, TX [*Location identifier*] [*FAA*] .... EVA
Evaluate [*or Evaluation or Evaluator*] .... EVAL
Evaluated Maintenance Programing .... EMP
Evaluated Nuclear Data File [*AEC*] .... ENDF
Evaluating Fallout Protection in Homes [*Later, HFPS*] [*Civil Defense*] .... EFPH
Evaluation .... EVLTN
Evaluation of Air Defense Effectiveness .... EVADE
Evaluation and Analysis Group [*Navy*] .... EAG
Evaluation and Analysis Staff [*Navy*] .... EAS
Evaluation of the Army Study System .... ETASS
Evaluation Branch [*BUPERS*] .... EB
Evaluation Center .... EC
Evaluation Contractors Estimating System .... ECES
Evaluation Engineering [*A publication*] .... Eval Eng
Evaluation and Experiment. Some Critical Issues in Assessing Social Programs [*A publication*] .... Eval & Exper
Evaluation of Foreign Weapons Systems .... EFWS
Evaluation: A Forum for Human Services Decision-Makers [*A publication*] .... Evaluatn
Evaluation of Glide Reentry Structural Systems .... EGRESS
Evaluation and the Health Professions [*A publication*] .... Eval Health Prof
Evaluation Instrumentation .... EI
Evaluation Management Using Past History Analysis for Scientific Inventory Simulation .... EMPHASIS
Evaluation Modality Test [*Psychology*] .... EMT
Evaluation Model .... EM
Evaluation Monitoring Team .... EMT
Evaluation and Optimization .... EVOP
Evaluation and Program Planning [*A publication*] .... Eval Program Plann
Evaluation Project Report [*Air Force*] .... EPR
Evaluation Record [*LIMRA*] .... ER
Evaluation Report .... ER
Evaluation Research Corporation [*American Stock Exchange symbol*] .... ERC
Evaluation Research Corporation Uts [*NASDAQ symbol*] .... EVRCL
Evaluation Staff, War College [*Air Force*] .... ESAWC
Evaluation Studies. Review Annual [*A publication*] .... Evalu Stu
Evaluation Test Plan .... ETP
Evaluation Test Specification .... ETS
Evaluation Trainers .... ETS
Evaluation Vector Table .... EVT
Evaluation and Warning Team .... EWT
Evaluator Programer Integrated Circuit [*NASA*] .... EPIC
Evangel College, Springfield, MO [*OCLC symbol*] .... MOE
Evangel College, Springfield, MO [*Library symbol*] .... MoSpE
Evangelical [*or Evangelist*] .... EVAN
Evangelical [*or Evangelist*] .... EVANG
[*The*] **Evangelical Alliance Mission** .... TEAM

[*The*] **Evangelical Alliance Relief** [*of The TEAR Fund*] ... TEAR

Evangelical and Catholic Mission ... ECM

Evangelical Christian Publishers Association ... ECPA

Evangelical Church Library Association ... ECLA

Evangelical Congregational School of Theology, Myerstown, PA [*Library symbol*] ... PMyE

Evangelical Council for Financial Accountability ... ECFA

Evangelical Education Society of the Protestant Episcopal Church ... EES

Evangelical Foreign Missions Association ... EFMA

Evangelical Friends Alliance ... EFA

Evangelical Literature Overseas ... ELO

Evangelical Lutheran Synod ... ELS

Evangelical Lutheran Theological Seminary, Columbus, OH [*Library symbol*] ... OCoE

Evangelical Lutherans in Mission [*Group opposing the Missouri Synod of the Lutheran Church*] ... ELIM

Evangelical Missions Information Service ... EMIS

Evangelical Missions Quarterly [*A publication*] ... EMQ

Evangelical Press Association ... EPA

Evangelical Quarterly [*A publication*] ... EQ

Evangelical Quarterly [*A publication*] ... Evang Q

Evangelical and Reformed Historical Society ... ERHS

Evangelical and Reformed Historical Society, United Church of Christ ... ERHS-UCC

Evangelical Review [*A publication*] ... Evang R

Evangelical School of Nursing, Oak Lawn, IL [*Library symbol*] ... IOIE

Evangelical Seminary, Rio Piedras, PR [*Library symbol*] ... PrRe

Evangelical Teacher Training Association ... ETTA

Evangelical Theological Society ... ETS

Evangelical Union [*British*] ... EU

Evangelical United Brethren [*Church*] ... EUB

Evangelical Women's Caucus ... EWC

Evangelicals Concerned ... EC

Evangeline Parish Library, Ville Platte, LA [*Library symbol*] ... LVpE

Evangeline Railway Co. [*AAR code*] ... EVNG

Evangelische Kirche Deutschlands ... EKD

Evangelische Kirchenchor [*A publication*] ... Evan Kirchor

Evangelische Theologie [*A publication*] ... ET

Evangelische Theologie [*A publication*] ... Evang Th

Evangelism Center International ... ECI

Evangelist [*Church calendars*] ... E

Evangelist ... EV

Evangelist and Martyr [*Church calendars*] ... EM

"Evangelize China" Fellowship ... ECF

Evangelizing Today's Child [*A publication*] ... EvTC

Evans-Aristocrat Industries, Inc. [*American Stock Exchange symbol*] [*Delisted*] ... EVS

Evan's Blue [*Fluorescent dye*] ... EB

Evans Economics, Incorporated [*Information service*] ... EEI

Evans Electroselenium Limited [*as in EEL analyzer, used in biochemical analysis*] [*British*] ... EEL

Evans [*Bob*] **Farms** [*NASDAQ symbol*] ... BOBE

Evans, Inc. [*NASDAQ symbol*] ... EVAN

Evans Medical Ltd. [*Great Britain*] [*Research code symbol*] ... EM

Evans Memorial Library, Aberdeen, MS [*Library symbol*] ... MsAb

Evans Products Co. [*NYSE symbol*] ... EVY

Evans Public Library, Vandalia, IL [*Library symbol*] ... IV

Evans Signal Laboratory [*Army*] ... ESL

Evans & Sutherland Computer Corporation [*NASDAQ symbol*] ... ESCC

Evanston Early Identification Scale [*Psychology*] ... EEIS

Evanston, IL [*Radio station call letters*] ... WEAW

Evanston, IL [*Radio station call letters*] ... WNUR

Evanston, IL [*Radio station call letters*] ... WOJO

Evanston, IL [*Radio station call letters*] ... WONX

Evanston Public Library, Evanston, IL [*Library symbol*] ... IE

Evanston Public Library, Evanston, IL [*OCLC symbol*] ... IHE

Evanston Public Library, Extension (Bookmobile), Evanston, IL [*Library symbol*] ... IE-Ex

Evanston Public Library, North Branch, Evanston, IL [*Library symbol*] ... IE-N

Evanston Public Library, South Branch, Evanston, IL [*Library symbol*] ... IE-S

Evanston Public Library, West Branch, Evanston, IL [*Library symbol*] ... IE-W

Evanston, WY [*Location identifier*] [*FAA*] ... EVW

Evanston, WY [*Radio station call letters*] ... KEVA

Evanston, WY [*Radio station call letters*] ... KOTB

Evansville [*Indiana*] [*Airport symbol*] ... EVV

Evansville, IN [*Location identifier*] [*FAA*] ... DSO

Evansville, IN [*Location identifier*] [*FAA*] ... PXV

Evansville, IN [*Television station call letters*] ... WEHT-TV

Evansville, IN [*Television station call letters*] ... WEVV

Evansville, IN [*Television station call letters*] ... WFIE-TV

Evansville, IN [*Radio station call letters*] ... WGBF

Evansville, IN [*Radio station call letters*] ... WIKY-FM

Evansville, IN [*Radio station call letters*] ... WNIN

Evansville, IN [*Radio station call letters*] ... WPSR

Evansville, IN [*Radio station call letters*] ... WROZ

Evansville, IN [*Radio station call letters*] ... WSWI

Evansville, IN [*Television station call letters*] ... WTVW

Evansville, IN [*Radio station call letters*] ... WYNG

Evansville, IN [*Television station call letters*] ... WNIN

Evansville Public Library and Vanderburgh County Public Library, Evansville, IN [*OCLC symbol*] ... IEP

Evansville Public Library and Vanderburgh County Public Library, Evansville, IN [*Library symbol*] ... InE

Evansville, TN [*Radio station call letters*] ... WVHI

Evansville-Vanderburgh School Corp., Evansville, IN [*OCLC symbol*] ... IVA

Evaporate ... EVAP

Evaporated ... EVPD

Evaporated Milk Association ... EMA

Evaporation Control System [*Automobile antipollution device*] ... ECS

Evaporation [*or Evaporative*] **Emission Control** [*Automobile antipollution device*] ... EEC

Evaporative Cooling Garment [*Spacesuit*] [*NASA*] ... ECG

Evaporative Cooling Garment System [*NASA*] ... ECGS

Evaporative Cooling Processor ... ECP

Evaporative Cooling Techniques ... ECT

Evaporative Loss Control Device [*Automobile antipollution device*] ... ELCD

Evaporative Water Loss ... EWL

Evaporator [*Freight*] ... EVAPTR

Evart Public Library, Evart, MI [*Library symbol*] ... MiEv

Evasion and Escape [*Military*] ... E & E

Evasive Combat Maneuver ... ECM

Evasive Target Tank [*Army*] ... ETT

Eveleth Junior College [*Later, Mesabi Community College*] [*Minnesota*] ... EJC

Eveleth, MN [*Location identifier*] [*FAA*] ... EVM

Eveleth, MN [*Radio station call letters*] ... WEVE

Eveleth, MN [*Radio station call letters*] ... WEVE-FM

Evelyn Waugh Newsletter [*A publication*] ... EWN

Evelyn Waugh Society ... EWS

Even-Even Nucleus ... EEN

Even Positive Acknowledgment [*Data processing*] ... ACK0

Even Side Flat ... ESF

Evenes [*Norway*] [*Airport symbol*] ... EVE

Evening ... E

Evening ... EVE

Evening ... EVG

Evening ... EVNG

Evening Prayer ... EP

Evening Student Personnel Association [*Later, Evening Student Association*] ... ESPA

Evensong ... E

Event-Based Language [*Data processing*] ... EBL

Event Control Block [*Data processing*] ... ECB

Event Control Module [*Chromatography*] ... ECM

Event Elapsed Time ... EET

Event-by-Event Recording and Sorting [*Electronics*] ... EBERAS

Event Index Log [*NASA*] ... EIL

Event Processing System ... EPS

Event Queue Element ... EQE

Event Record Log ... ERL

Event-Related Potential [*Neurophysiology*] ... ERP

Event-Related Slow-Brain Potential [*Neurophysiology*] ... ERSP

Event Sequence Override ... ESO

Event Storage and Distribution Unit ... ESDU

Event Time Digitizer ... ETD

Event Timer ... ET

Events Control [*Subsystem*] [*NASA*] ... EVCON

Events Control Buffer [*NASA*] ... ECB

Events Controller ... EC

Events History Recorder ... EHR

Events Recorder Console ... ERC

Events Select Logic and Rates ... ESLR

Events per Time Unit ... EPTU

Events per Unit Time ... EPUT

Ever Heard of Him? [*Facetious criterion for determining insignificance of Supreme Court Justices*] [*Proposed by University of Chicago professor David P. Currie*] ... EHH

Ever-Lock ... EVRLK

Everest/Jennings International [*American Stock Exchange symbol*] ... EJ

Everett Community College [*Formerly, EJC*] [*Washington*] ... ECC

Everett Community College, Everett, WA [*Library symbol*] ... WaEE

Everett Junior College [*Later, ECC*] [*Washington*] ... EJC

Everett, PA [*Radio station call letters*] ... WSKE

Everett Public Library, Everett, WA [*Library symbol*] ... WaE

[*The*] **Everett Railroad Co.** [*AAR code*] ... EV

Everett, WA [*Radio station call letters*] ... KRKO

Everett, WA [*Television station call letters*] ... KUEV-TV

Everett, WA [*Radio station call letters*] ... KWYZ

Everett, WA [*Location identifier*] [*FAA*] ... SNJ

Everglades National Park ... EVER

Everglades Natural History [*A publication*] ... Everglades Nat History

Evergood Products Corp. [*NASDAQ symbol*] ... EVGD

Evergreen, AL [*Radio station call letters*] ... WEGN

Evergreen, AL [*Radio station call letters*] ... WEGN-FM

Evergreen International Airlines, Inc. [*ICAO designator*] ... EV

Evergreen Park Public Library, Evergreen Park, IL [*Library symbol*] ... IEvp

Evergreen Regional Library, Gimli, MB, Canada [*Library symbol*] ... CaMGE

Evergreen Resources [*NASDAQ symbol*] ... EVER

Evergreen Review [*A publication*] ... ER

Evergreen Review [*A publication*] ... EV
Evergreen Review [*A publication*] ... EvR
Evergreen State College, Olympia, WA [*Library symbol*] ... WaOE
Evergreen Valley College, San Jose, CA [*OCLC symbol*] ... CEV
Eversharp, Inc. [*NYSE symbol*] [*Delisted*] ... EVR
Everted [*or Eversion*] [*Medicine*] ... EV
Every ... EV
Every ... EVY
Every Day ... ED
Every-Day Life [*Psychological testing*] ... EDL
Every Good Boy Deserves Favour [*Title of play by Tom Stoppard*] ... EGBDF
Every Good Boy Does Fine [*or Deserves Favor*] [*Mnemonic guide to notes on the treble clef*] ... EGBDF
Every Hand an Adventure [*Bridge bidding method*] ... EHAA
Every Morning Fixum [*An old car*] [*Slang*] ... EMF
Every Other Day ... EOD
Every Other Week ... EOW
Every Saturday [*A publication*] ... Ev Sat
Everyman's Science [*A publication*] ... Everyman's Sci
Everything's Going to Be All Right ... EGBAR
Evidence [*Law*] ... E
Evidence ... EVCE
Evidence ... EVID
Evidence Photographers International Council ... EPIC
Evington, VA [*Location identifier*] [*FAA*] ... EVI
Evoked Action Potential [*Neurophysiology*] ... EAP
Evoked Potential [*Neurophysiology*] ... EP
Evoked Potential Index [*Neurophysiology*] ... EPI
Evoked Potential Technique [*Neurophysiology*] ... EPT
Evoked Response [*Neurophysiology*] ... ER
Evoked Response Audiometry [*Neurophysiology*] ... ERA
Evoked Response Detector [*Neurophysiology*] ... ERD
Evoked Synaptic Potential [*Neurophysiology*] ... ESP
Evoked Visual Potential [*Neurophysiology*] ... EVP
Evolution ... EV
Evolution [*A publication*] ... Evol
Evolution of Competing Hierarchical Organizations ... ECHO
Evolution Medicale [*A publication*] ... Evol Med
Evolution Psychiatrique [*A publication*] ... Evol Psychiatr
Evolution Psychiatrique [*A publication*] ... EVPSA
Evolutionary Biology [*A publication*] ... Evol Biol
Evolutionary Distance ... ED
Evolutionary Genetics Research Reports [*A publication*] ... Evol Genet Res Rep
Evolutionary Operation ... EVOP
[*An*] **Evolutionary System for On-Line Processing** [*Data processing*] ... AESOP
Evolutionary Theory [*A publication*] ... Evol Theory
Evolved ... EVOL
Evolved Gas Analysis Mass Spectrometry ... EGAMS
Evolvement by Understanding, Order, and Courage ... EUOC
Evreiskoe Kolonizatsionnoe Obshchestvo [*Jewish Colonization Association*] ... EKO
Evrytanian Association of America ... EAA
Ewa, HI [*Location identifier*] [*FAA*] ... NAX
Ewe [*MARC language code*] [*Library of Congress*] ... ewe
Ewo [*Congo*] [*Airport symbol*] ... EWO
Ex Affinis [*Of Affinity*] [*Latin*] ... EX AFF
Ex Air Ministry [*British*] ... ExAM
Ex Aqua [*In Water*] [*Pharmacy*] ... EX AQ
Ex-Cell-O Corp. [*NYSE symbol*] ... XLO
Ex Commissione [*Upon Order*] ... EC
Ex-Coupon [*Without the right to coupons, as of a bond*] [*Finance*] ... X-C
Ex-Coupon [*Without the right to coupons, as of a bond*] [*Finance*] ... XCP
Ex-Distribution [*NYSE symbol*] [*Delisted*] ... XDIS
Ex-Dividend [*Without the right to dividend*] [*Finance*] ... ED
Ex-Dividend [*Without the right to dividend*] [*Finance*] ... EX DIV
Ex-Dividend [*Without the right to dividend*] [*NYSE symbol*] ... X-D
Ex Grege [*Among the Rest*] [*Latin*] ... EG
Ex-Husband [*or Ex-Wife*] [*Slang*] ... X
Ex Idoneo Crasso Liquido [*In a Suitable Thick Liquid*] [*Pharmacy*] ... EX IDON CRASS LIQ
Ex Idoneo Liquido [*In a Suitable Liquid*] [*Pharmacy*] ... EX IDON LIQ
Ex-Interest [*Without the right to interest*] [*Finance*] ... X-I
Ex-Interest [*Without the right to interest*] [*Finance*] ... XIN
Ex-Interest [*Without the right to interest*] [*Finance*] ... XINT
Ex-Meridian [*Navigation*] ... EX-MER
Ex Modo Praescripto [*In the Manner Prescribed*] [*Pharmacy*] ... EMP
Ex-New [*Without the right to claim any new stocks or shares*] [*NYSE symbol*] ... XN
Ex Officio ... EO
Ex-Partners of Servicemen (Women) for Equality ... EXPOSE
Ex-Privileges [*Without the right to privileges*] [*Finance*] ... XPR
Ex Quay [*Seller's responsibility is to make goods available on the wharf at destination named*] [*"INCOTERM," International Chamber of Commerce official code*] ... EXQ
Ex-Rights [*Without rights*] [*Finance*] ... XR
Ex-Rights [*Without rights*] [*NYSE symbol*] ... XRT
Ex Senatus Consulto [*By Decree of the Senate*] [*Latin*] ... ESC
Ex Ship [*Seller's responsibility is to make goods available on board ship at destination named*] [*"INCOTERM," International Chamber of Commerce official code*] ... EXS
Ex-Tapol [*Political Prisoner*] [*Indonesia*] ... ET
Ex Testamento [*In Accordance with the Testament Of*] [*Latin*] ... EXTM
Ex-Vessel Flux Monitor [*Nuclear energy*] ... EVFM
Ex-Vessel Handling Machine [*Later, CLEM*] [*Nuclear energy*] ... EVHM
Ex-Vessel Transfer Machine [*Nuclear energy*] ... EVTM
Ex Voto [*In Fulfillment of a Vow*] [*Latin*] ... EV
Ex-Warrants [*Without warrants*] [*NYSE symbol*] ... XW
Ex Works [*Seller's only responsibility is to make goods available at his premises*] [*"INCOTERM," International Chamber of Commerce official code*] ... EXW
Ex-Young-Lady [*Wife*] [*Amateur radio slang*] ... XYL
Exa [*A prefix meaning multiplied by 10^{18}*] [*SI symbol*] ... E
Exact Cubic Search [*Mathematics*] ... ECS
Exact Quadratic Search [*Mathematics*] ... EQS
Exaggeration ... EXAG
Exaltation Newcastle Disease ... END
Examen de la Situacion Economica de Mexico [*A publication*] ... Exam Sit Econ Mexico
EXAMETNET [*Experimental Inter-American Meteorological Rocket Network*] **Executive Committee** [*NASA*] ... EEC
Examination ... EXAM
Examination ... EXAMN
Examination [*Slang*] ... X
Examination under Anesthesia [*Medicine*] ... EUA
Examination Division Planning Tape [*IRS*] ... EPT
Examination, Opinion, and Advice [*Medicine*] ... EOA
Examination Procedure Outline [*Weighing equipment*] ... EPO
Examination Status Verification Report ... ESVR
Examine and Repair as Necessary ... ERAN
Examine Your Zipper ... XYZ
Examined ... EX
Examined ... EXAMD
Examined ... EXD
Examiner [*Quezon City*] [*A publication*] ... Ex
Examiner ... EXAMR
Examining for Aphasia [*Psychology*] ... EA
Examining Circulars ... EC
Example ... EX
Examples ... EXX
Excalibur Technology Corp. [*NASDAQ symbol*] ... EXCA
Excavate ... EXC
Exceeding ... EX
Exceeding Speed Limit ... ESL
Exceedingly Rare [*Numismatics*] ... RRR
Excel Energy Corp. [*NASDAQ symbol*] ... EXLL
Excellence-in-Competition Badge (Pistol) [*Army*] ... ECB-P
Excellence-in-Competition Badge (Rifle) [*Army*] ... ECB-R
"Excellence in Production" [*Army-Navy "E" awarded manufacturers*] [*World War II*] ... E
Excellency ... E
Excellency ... EXC
Excellent ... E
Excellent [*Condition*] [*Deltiology*] ... EX
Excellent ... EXC
Excellent Skiing Conditions ... E
Excelsior Income Shares, Inc. [*NYSE symbol*] ... EIS
Excelsior Springs Genealogical Society, Excelsior Springs, MO [*Library symbol*] ... MoExGS
Excelsior Springs, MO [*Radio station call letters*] ... KEXS
Except ... EX
Except ... EXC
Except ... EXCP
Except ... XCP
Except ... XCPT
Except Change Departure to Read [*Aviation*] ... ECD
Except Change Route to Read [*Aviation*] ... ECR
Except as Otherwise Herein Provided ... EOHP
Except as Otherwise Noted ... EAON
Except Sixth Form [*For the wearing of schoolgirls' uniforms*] [*British*] ... Y
Exception ... EXCPT
Exception Monitor ... EM
Exception Noted ... EN
Exception Time Accounting ... ETA
Exceptional Child Education Abstracts [*A publication*] ... ECEA
Exceptional Child Education Abstracts [*A publication*] ... ExChAb
Exceptional Child Education Resources [*Data base*] [*Council for Exceptional Children*] ... ECER
Exceptional Children [*A publication*] ... EXCCA
Exceptional Children [*A publication*] ... Excep Child
Exceptional Children [*A publication*] ... Except Chil
Exceptional Children Abstracts [*A publication*] ... EC
Exceptional Civilian Service Award ... ECSA
Exceptional Parent [*A publication*] ... Except Parent
Exceptionally Well Qualified ... EWQ
Excerpta Botanica [*A publication*] ... Excerp Bot
Excerpta Criminologica [*A publication*] ... Excerp Criminol
Excerpta Medica [*Amsterdam*] [*A publication*] ... EM
Excerpta Medica (Amsterdam) [*A publication*] ... Excerpta Med (Amst)

Excerpta Medica Database [*Trademark*] ... EMBASE
Excerpta Medica Foundation ... EMF
Excerpta Medica. International Congress Series [*Amsterdam*] [*A publication*] ... Excerpta Med Int Congr Ser
Excerpta Medica Physicians Information Retrieval and Education Service [*Database*] ... EMPIRES
Excess ... EX
Excess ... XS
Excess and Casualty Reinsurance Association ... ECRA
Excess Current Liabilities [*Insurance*] ... XCL
Excess Lactate ... XL
Excess Leave [*Military*] ... EXLV
Excess Limit ... EL
Excess Noise Ratio ... ENR
Excess Personal Property ... EPP
Excess Profits ... EP
Excess Profits Duty ... EPD
Excess Profits Levy [*British*] ... EPL
Excess Profits Tax ... EPT
Excess Rent Allowance [*British*] ... ERA
Excess Reserves ... RX
Excess Speed of Advance Authorized [*Navy*] ... XSOA
Excess and Surplus Business [*Insurance*] ... E & S
Excess Transit Time ... XSTT
Excessive Daytime Sleepiness ... EDS
Exchange ... EX
Exchange ... EXC
Exchange ... EXCH
Exchange ... X
Exchange ... XCH
Exchange of Authenticated Electronic Component Performance Test Data [*European counterpart of GIDEP*] ... EXACT
Exchange Carrier Association ... ECA
Exchange Certificate [*Rate*] [*Value of the English pound*] ... EX/C
Exchange Chromatography ... EC
Exchange Control Logic ... ECL
Exchange Feeder Route Analysis Program [*Bell System*] ... EFRAP
Exchange Information Group ... EIG
Exchange of Information, Visits, and Reports ... EIVR
Exchange International Corp. [*NASDAQ symbol*] ... EXCG
Exchange Jump ... EJP
Exchange Key [*Word processing*] ... EXC
Exchange of Medical Information [*Program*] [*Veterans Administration*] ... EMI
Exchange Network Facilities for Interstate Access [*Communications*] ... ENFIA
Exchange of Ready for Issue in Lieu of Concurrent Overhaul ... ERILCO
Exchange and Repair ... E/R
Exchange Rolls ... ER
Exchange Sale Property ... ESP
Exchange of Technical Apollo Simulation Information [*NASA*] ... XTASI
Exchange Users Association ... EUA
Exchangeable General Linear Model [*Statistics*] ... EGLM
Exchangeable-Potassium-Percentage ... EPP
Exchangeable-Sodium-Percentage ... ESP
Exchanger ... XCNGR
Exchequer [*British*] ... EX
Exchequer [*British*] ... EXCH
Exchequer and Audit Department [*British government*] ... E and A
Exchequer and Audit Department [*British government*] ... E & AD
Excitability-Inducing Material [*Biochemistry*] ... EIM
Excitation ... EXC
Excitation ... XCIT
Excitation-Emission Matrix [*Fluorometry*] ... EEM
Excitation Power Supply ... EPS
Excitatory Junctional Potential [*Neurophysiology*] ... EJP
Excitatory Postsynaptic Potential [*Neurophysiology*] ... EPSP
Excitatory Receptive Field [*Physiology*] ... ERF
Excitement, Choreiform Movements, and Circling [*Characterizations of a medical syndrome*] ... ECC
Exciter [*Electricity*] ... EXCTR
[*The*] **Exciting Game Without Any Rules** [*Card game*] ... TEGWAR
Exclamation ... EXCL
Exclude ... EXCLD
Excluded from General Declassification Schedule ... XCL
Excluding ... EX
Excluding ... EXCL
Exclusion Area Boundary [*Nuclear energy*] ... EAB
Exclusive ... EXCL
Exclusive ... EXCLU
Exclusive ... EXCLV
Exclusive [*Concession in a circus or carnival*] ... X
Exclusive of Covering and Uncovering ... XC & UC
Exclusive Distribution [*Military security classification*] ... EXDIS
Exclusive Economic Zone [*Offshore sovereignty*] ... EEZ
Exclusive of Loading and Unloading ... XL & UL
Exclusive Or [*Gates*] [*Data processing*] ... EO
Exclusive Or [*Gates*] [*Data processing*] ... XOR
Exclusive of Sheeting ... ES
Excretory Cell ... EC
Excretory Urogram [*Medicine*] ... XU
Excudit [*He Engraved It*] [*Latin*] ... EXC
Excursion ... EX
Excursion ... EXCUR
Excursion Inlet [*Alaska*] [*Airport symbol*] ... EXI
Excursion Inlet, AK [*Location identifier*] [*FAA*] ... EXI
Excused from Duty ... ED
Excused from Duty ... EFD
Executair [*Nigeria*] [*ICAO designator*] ... EE
Execute ... EXCT
Execute ... EXEC
Execute ... XEQ
Execute Channel Program [*Data processing*] ... EXCP
Execute Command Request ... ECR
Execute Input/Output ... XI/O
Executed Out Of [*Business and trade*] ... EX
Executing Agency Identifier ... EXA
Executive ... EX
Executive ... EXEC
Executive ... EXTVE
Executive [*A publication*] ... Exec
Executive Agent ... EXAGT
Executive Air Charter [*Honolulu, HI*] [*FAA designator*] ... EAC
Executive Air Charter [*San Jose, CA*] [*FAA designator*] ... PAE
Executive Air Services, Inc. [*Jacksonville, FL*] [*FAA designator*] ... SRV
Executive Air Travel [*Denver, CO*] [*FAA designator*] ... RPA
Executive Assignment Service [*Civil Service Commission*] ... EAS
Executive Assistant ... EA
Executive Audial Rehabilitation Society ... EARS
Executive Board ... EB
Executive Bulletin ... EB
Executive Business Transport [*Aircraft*] ... EBT
Executive Chef Association [*Defunct*] ... ECA
Executive Chefs de Cuisine Association of America [*Later, Chefs de Cuisine Association of America*] ... ECCAA
Executive Committee ... EC
Executive Committee [*National Security Council*] ... EXCOM
Executive Committee on Commercial Policy [*Abolished, 1944*] ... ECCP
Executive Committee's Panel on Meteorological Aspects of Ocean Affairs [*WMO*] ... ECPMAOA
Executive Control Language [*Data processing*] ... ECL
Executive Control Program ... ECP
Executive Control Routines ... ECR
Executive Control System ... ECS
Executive Council ... EC
Executive Council on Foreign Diplomats ... ECFD
Executive Development [*Civil Service Commission*] ... XD
Executive Director ... ED
Executive Directorate Industrial Security ... EDIS
Executive Express [*ICAO designator*] ... EX
Executive Flight Detachment ... EFD
Executive Flight Service, Inc. [*Portland, OR*] [*FAA designator*] ... ORE
Executive Forum ... EF
Executive Generator ... EG
Executive Guide to Information Sources [*Later, EBIS*] [*A publication*] ... EGIS
Executive Housekeeper [*A publication*] ... Exec Housekeeper
Executive Independent Review Team ... EIRT
Executive Industries, Incorporated [*American Stock Exchange symbol*] [*Delisted*] ... EII
Executive Information Services [*Data processing system*] ... EIS
Executive Inventory File [*Civil Service Commission*] ... EIF
Executive Jet Aviation, Inc. [*Columbus, OH*] [*FAA designator*] ... EJA
Executive Jet Aviation, Inc. [*Great Britain*] [*ICAO designator*] ... EM
Executive-Legislative-Judicial ... ELJ
Executive Level Interactive Terminal ... ELITE
Executive Management Responsibility ... EMR
Executive Management Review ... EMR
Executive Manpower Management Technical Assistance Center [*Civil Service Commission*] ... EMMTAC
Executive Manpower Management Technical Assistance Plan [*Civil Service Commission*] ... EMMTAP
Executive Mansion and Grounds [*i.e., the White House and its grounds*] [*Executive Office of the President*] ... EMG
Executive Memorandum ... EM
Executive for National Military Representatives [*Supreme Headquarters Allied Powers Europe*] ... ENMR
Executive Office Building [*Washington, DC*] ... EOB
Executive Office of the President ... EOP
Executive Office of the President ... EXOP
Executive Office of the President, Washington, DC [*OCLC symbol*] ... EOP
Executive Office of the Secretary [*Navy*] ... EXOS
Executive Office of the Secretary [*Navy*] ... NAVEXOS
Executive Office for United States Attorneys [*Department of Justice*] ... EOUSA
Executive Officer ... EO
Executive Officer ... EXECO
Executive Officer ... EXO
Executive Officer [*Military*] ... XO
Executive Officers Council of the National Association of Real Estate Boards ... EOC

Executive Order [*Rule or regulation having the force of law, issued by the President with congressional authorization*]............EO
Executive Promotion Program [*FAA*]..........................EPP
Executive Protective Service [*Formerly, White House Police; later, USSS/UD*]..........................EPS
Executive Request [*Data processing*]..........................ER
Executive Reserve..........................ER
Executive Review of Overseas Programs [*Army*]..........EROP
Executive Schedule [*Job classification for certain Presidentially appointed executives*]..........................EX
Executive Sciences Institute [*A publication*].........Exec Sci Inst
Executive Secretary..........................ES
Executive Selection Inventory System..........................ESIS
Executive Seminar Center [*Civil Service Commission*]......ESC
Executive for Small Business..........................ESB
Executive Stewards' and Caterers' Association [*Later, IFSEA*]..........ESCA
Executive Subroutines for Afterheat Temperature Analysis [*Computer program*] [*NASA*]..........................ESATA
Executive System Problem-Oriented Language [*Data processing*]....ESPOL
Executive Systems Corporation [*An association*] [*Defunct*]..........ESC
Executive Vice President..........................EVP
Executive Vice President..........................XVP
Executive Volunteer Corps..........................EVC
Executive Women International [*Formerly, ESI*]..........EWI
Executive Working Group [*NATO*]..........................EWG
Executives Consultants, Incorporated [*An association*]..........ECI
Executives' Secretaries, Incorporated [*Later, EWI*]..........ESI
Executive's Shopping Service..........................ESS
Executone, Inc. [*American Stock Exchange symbol*] [*Delisted*]..........EXU
Executor..........................EXEC
Executor..........................EXOR
Executor..........................EXR
Executrix..........................EXECX
Executrix..........................EXOX
Executrix..........................EXRX
Executrix..........................EXTRIX
Executrix..........................EXX
Exemplary Rehabilitation Certificate [*Department of Labor*]..........ERC
Exempli Causa [*For the Sake of Example*] [*Latin*]..........EC
Exempli Gratia [*For Example*] [*Latin*]..........................EG
Exempli Gratia [*For Example*] [*Latin*]..........................EX GR
Exempt [*from traceability*] [*NASA*]..........................E
Exempt..........................EX
Exempt..........................EXM
Exempt..........................XMT
Exempt from General Declassification Schedule..........XGDS
Exempt Organization [*IRS*]..........................EO
Exempt Organization Master File [*IRS*]..........................EOMF
Exempted by Commanding Officer..........................ECO
Exercise..........................EX
Exercise..........................EXER
Exercise Code Word [*NATO*]..........................CODEX
Exercise Commander..........................EC
Exercise Control Center [*Military*]..........................EXCC
Exercise Control Group [*Military*]..........................EXCG
Exercise Director..........................EXDIR
Exercise Head..........................EH
Exercise Induced Asthma..........................EIA
Exercise-Induced Bronchiospasm [*Medicine*]..........................EIB
Exercise Intelligence Center [*Military*]..........................EIC
Exercise Limit [*Medicine*]..........................EL
Exercise Operating Area..........................EOA
Exercise Order [*Military*]..........................EXORD
Exercise Plan [*Military*]..........................EXPLAN
Exercise Planning Staff..........................EPS
Exercise and Plans..........................E & P
Exercise Readiness Condition [*Military*]..........EXREDCON
Exercise Simulation System for Flexible Nuclear Response..........ESSFNR
Exercise Specification..........................EXSPEC
Exercise and Sport Sciences Reviews [*A publication*]..........
    Exercise Sport Sci Rev
Exercise and Sport Sciences Reviews [*A publication*]....Exerc Sport Sci Rev
Exercise Tolerance Test [*Medicine*]..........................ETT
Exercise Torpedo..........................EXTORP
Exercise Weapon..........................EXWEP
Exerque [*Numismatics*]..........................EX
Exeter [*British depot code*]..........................EXE
Exeter [*England*] [*Airport symbol*]..........................EXT
[*The*] Exeter Abstract Reference System [*Exeter University*] [*Information service*]..........................TEARS
Exeter Hall Lectures [*A publication*]..........................Ex H Lec
Exeter, NH [*Radio station call letters*]..........................WERZ
Exeter, NH [*Radio station call letters*]..........................WPEA
Exeter, NJ [*Radio station call letters*]..........................WMYF
Exeter Oil Ltd. [*American Stock Exchange symbol*] [*Delisted*]..........ETR
Exeter, PA [*Radio station call letters*]..........................WASD
Exeter Public Library, Exeter, NE [*Library symbol*]..........NbE
Exeter Public Library, Exeter, ON, Canada [*Library symbol*]..........CaOE
Exhaust..........................EXH
Exhaust..........................EXHST
Exhaust..........................XHST

Exhaust Closes [*Valve position*]..........................EC
Exhaust Deflection Angle..........................EDA
Exhaust Fan..........................EF
Exhaust Gas Pressure..........................EGP
Exhaust Gas Recirculation [*Engines*]..........................EGR
Exhaust Gas Temperature..........................EGT
Exhaust Gas Temperature Indicator..........................EGTI
Exhaust Nozzle Control..........................ENC
Exhaust Nozzle Temperature..........................ENT
Exhaust Opens [*Valve position*]..........................EO
Exhaust Plume Interference Characterization [*NASA*]..........EPIC
Exhaust Pressure Ratio..........................EPR
Exhaust System Terminal..........................EST
Exhaust Systems Professional Association [*Defunct*]..........ESPA
Exhaust Trail Indicator [*Military*]..........................ETI
Exhaust Vent..........................EXHV
Exhibetur [*Let It Be Given*] [*Pharmacy*]..........................EXHIB
Exhibit..........................EXH
Exhibit Designers and Producers Association..........................EDPA
Exhibit Line Item Number..........................ELIN
Exhibited [*or Exhibition*]..........................EXHIB
Exhibition..........................EXHBN
Exhibition..........................EXHN
Exhibitions [*Trade fairs, etc.*] [*Public-performance tariff class*] [*British*]..........X
Exhibitors Advisory Council..........................EAC
Exhibits Round Table [*American Library Association*]..........ERT
Exidyne, Inc. [*NASDAQ symbol*]..........................EXID
Exigencies of the Service Having Been Such as to Preclude the Issuance of Competent Written Orders in Advance..........ESPWO
Existed Prior to Enlistment [*Especially, dependency*]..........EPTE
Existed Prior to Entry..........................EPTE
Existed Prior to Entry Service..........................EPTS
Existed Prior to Induction [*Especially, dependency or physical defect*]..........................EPTI
Existence Doubtful [*Navigation charts*]..........................ED
Existential Generalization [*Rule of quantification*] [*Logic*]..........EG
Existential Instantiation [*Rule of quantification*] [*Logic*]..........EI
Existential Psychiatry [*A publication*]..........Exist Psychiat
Existential Study [*Psychology*]..........................ES
Existing..........................EXIST
Existing..........................EXST
[*An*] Existing Generalized Information System [*Data processing*]..........AEGIS
Exit Guide Vane..........................EGV
Exit List [*Data processing*]..........................EXLST
Exmore, VA [*Radio station call letters*]..........................WEXM-FM
Exoatmospheric Interceptor Propulsion..........................EIP
Exoatmospheric Penetration Aid..........................EPA
Exodus [*Old Testament book*]..........................Ex
Exodus [*Old Testament book*]..........................Exod
Exomphalos, Macroglossia, and Giantism [*Syndrome*] [*Medicine*]..........EMG
Exonia [*Exeter*] [*British*]..........................EXON
Exophoria Distance [*Ophthalmology*]..........................X
Exophthalmos-Producing Factor [*Endocrinology*]..........EPF
Exophthalmos-Producing Substance [*Endocrinology*]..........EPS
Exoplasmic [*Freeze etching in microscopy*]..........................E
Exoplasmic Fracture [*Freeze etching in microscopy*]..........EF
Exoplasmic Surface [*Freeze etching in microscopy*]..........ES
Exospheric Composition Studies..........................ECS
Exospheric Satellite [*Japan*]..........................EXOS
Exothermic Bimetallic Ignition System..........................EBIS
Exotique Dancers League of America..........................EDLA
Exotropia Near [*Ophthalmology*]..........................XT
Exovir, Inc. [*NASDAQ symbol*]..........................XOVR
Expandable Computerized Automatic Test System..........ECATS
Expandable Polystyrene [*Plastics technology*]..........................EPS
Expandable Shelter Containers..........................ESC
Expandable Stored Program..........................ESP
Expandable Wing Tank..........................EWT
Expandable Wing Tank Structure..........................EWTS
Expanded Additional Skill Identifier [*Military*]..........EASI
Expanded Advanced Terminal Defense Study..........................EATDS
Expanded Alternative Minimum Tax..........................EAMT
Expanded Background Investigation..........................EBI
Expanded Bed Capacity..........................EXBEDCAP
Expanded Calculator Link Processing System [*Data processing*]....ECLIPS
Expanded Clay and Shale Association [*Later, LAPA*]..........ECSA
Expanded Communications - Electronics System [*DoD*]..........EXCELS
Expanded with Computers and Information Technology..........EXCITE
Expanded Direct Distance Dialing [*Telephone*]..........EDDD
Expanded Display..........................ED
Expanded Field [*Prism*] Telescopes [*Instrumentation*]..........EFT's
Expanded Flight Line Tester..........................XFLT
Expanded Food and Nutrition Education Program [*Department of Agriculture*]..........................EFNEP
Expanded Function Dental Auxiliary [*HEW program*]..........EFDA
Expanded Metal..........................EM
Expanded Metal [*Heavy gauge*]..........................XPM
Expanded Metal Manufacturers Association..........................EMMA
Expanded National Agency Check [*DoD*]..........................ENAC
Expanded Near-Term Prepositioning Ships..........................ENTPS
Expanded Plan Indicator..........................EPI

Expanded Position Indicator ... EPI
Expanded Program Evaluation and Review Technique ... EXPERT
Expanded Program of Technical Assistance [*United Nations*] ... EPTA
Expanded RADAR Service ... ERS
Expanded Reactance Series Resonator ... ERSER
Expanded Service Testing ... EST
Expanded Service Volume ... ESV
Expanded Shale Clay and Slate Institute ... ESCSI
Expanded Sweep Generator ... ESG
Expanded Technical Assistance Board [*United Nations*] ... ETAB
Expanded Technical Assistance Program [*United Nations*] ... ETAP
Expander Tube ... ET
Expanding and Specialty Paper Products Institute [*Defunct*] ... ESPPI
Expansion ... EXP
Expansion ... EXPSN
Expansion ... XPN
Expansion Anchor Manufacturers Institute ... EAMI
Expansion Deflection ... E-D
Expansion Joint Institute ... EJI
Expansion Joint Manufacturers Association ... EJMA
Expansion Rate Measuring Apparatus ... ERMA
Expansion Regionale [*A publication*] ... Expans Region
Expansion Regionale (Paris) [*A publication*] ... Expans Region (Paris)
Expansion Symbolic Compiling Assembly Program for Engineers ... ESCAPE
Expansionist Party of the United States ... XP
Expansive Classification ... EC
Expatriate Review [*A publication*] ... Exp R
Expect ... EXP
Expect ... EXPC
Expect ... EXPT
Expect ... XPC
Expect Approach Clearance Not Later Than [*Aviation*] ... EACNL
Expect to Arrive ... ETA
Expect Departure Clearance [*Aviation*] ... EDC
Expect Departure Release [*Aviation*] ... EDR
Expect Further Routing [*Aviation*] ... EFR
Expect Higher Altitude [*Aviation*] ... EHA
Expect Vector To [*Aviation*] ... EVT
Expectancy Age [*Education*] ... EA
Expectancy Phenomenon ... EP
Expectation ... E
Expected Amount of Sample Information [*Statistics*] ... EASI
Expected Approach Clearance [*Aviation*] ... EAC
Expected Approach Time [*Aviation*] ... EAT
Expected Confidence Interval Length [*Statistics*] ... ECIL
Expected Date of Delivery [*Obstetrics*] ... EDD
Expected Environmental Concentration [*Environmental science*] ... EEC
Expected Further Clearance [*Aviation*] ... EFC
Expected Grade Level [*Education*] ... EGL
Expected Loss ... EL
Expected Loss Ratio [*Insurance*] ... ELR
Expected Monetary Value ... EMV
Expected Occupancy Date ... EOD
Expected Operations Forecast [*Aviation*] ... EOF
Expected Output ... EO
Expected Pay-Off ... EP
Expected Present Multiattribute Utility ... EPMAU
Expected Provident Fund ... EPF
Expected Quality Level ... EQL
Expected Sample Size Ratio [*Statistics*] ... ESSR
Expected Turnaround [*Data processing*] ... ETA
Expected Upper Limit [*Clinical psychology*] ... EUL
Expected Value [*Statistics*] ... EV
Expected Value of Perfect Information [*Statistics*] ... EVPI
Expected Value of Sample Information [*Statistics*] ... EVSI
Expects to Enter on Duty ... EXEOD
Expedient Demise [*Used as title of novel by Len Deighton*] ... XPD
Expedite ... XPD
Expedite Delivery ... EXDLVY
Expedite Delivery by Telephone ... EXPHO
Expedite Engineering Order ... EEO
Expedite Mail Reply ... EXREP
Expedite Release Request Notice ... ERRN
Expedite Requirement ... ER
Expedite Shipment ... EXSHI
Expedite Shipping Request ... ESR
Expedite Travel Order ... EXPTO
Expedited Air Munitions ... EX-AM
Expedited Movement Report [*Army*] ... EXMOVREP
Expedited Non-Standard Urgent Requirements for Equipment [*Army*] ... ENSURE
Expediting ... EXPED
Expedition ... EXPDN
Expedition [*A publication*] ... Exped
Expeditionary ... EXPED
Expeditionary Airfield ... EAF
Expeditionary Equipment Report System ... EERS
Expeditionary Force ... EF
Expeditionary Force Canteens [*Official supply organization*] [*British*] [*World War I*] ... EFC
Expeditionary Force Institutions [*Military*] [*British*] ... EFI
Expeditionary Force Message [*Low-rate cable or radio message selected from a list of standard wordings*] ... EFM
Expeditionary Force Message [*Usually, EFM*] [*Low-rate cable or radio message selected from a list of standard wordings*] ... XFM
Expeditionary Logistics Facility ... ELF
Expeditionary Shelters [*Marine Corps*] ... EXSH
Expeditious Discharge Program [*Army*] ... EDP
Expeditious Monitor and Maintenance Analyst [*Computer*] [*NASA*] ... EMMA
Expeditious Sales, Catalog, and Property Evaluation [*Defense Logistics Services Center project*] [*DoD*] ... ESCAPE
Expend ... EXP
Expendability, Recoverability Cost Code ... ERCC
Expendability, Recoverability, Repairability Cost ... ERRC
Expendability, Recoverability, Repairability Cost Category ... ERRCC
Expendability Repair Classification ... ERC
Expendable ... EXPEN
Expendable Bathythermograph [*Naval Oceanographic Office*] ... XBT
Expendable Case ... XC
Expendable Cluster Aircraft Rocket Launcher ... ECARL
Expendable Communications Jammer [*Army*] ... EXJAM
Expendable Electronic Markers ... EEM
Expendable-Expendable-Reusable ... EER
Expendable Instrument System ... EIS
Expendable Launch Vehicle [*NASA*] ... ELV
Expendable Light Markers ... ELM
Expendable Reliable Acoustic Path Sensor [*or Sonobuoy*] ... ERAPS
Expendable Remote Operating Weather Station [*Air Force*] ... EROWS
Expendable Salinity/Temperature/Depth Probe ... XSTD
Expendable Second Stage [*Space shuttle*] [*NASA*] ... ESS
Expendable Sound Source ... ESS
Expendable Surface Current Probe [*Coast Guard*] ... ESCP
Expendable Turbine Engine ... ETE
Expended Core Facility [*Nuclear energy*] ... ECF
Expenditure ... EXPEND
Expenditure ... EXPND
Expenditure Account ... EXACCT
Expenditure Account Number ... EAN
Expenditure Order [*Military*] ... XO
Expense ... EXP
Expense Appropriation Management/Army Industrial Fund ... EAM/AIF
Expense Operating Budget ... EOB
Expense Report ... ER
Expense for Return of Absentee [*Military*] ... ERA
Expense for Return of Deserter [*Military*] ... ERD
Expenses ... EXS
Expenses ... XS
Experience ... E
Experience ... EXPC
Experience-Based Career Education ... EBCE
Experience Critique Orgel [*Nuclear reactor*] [*Italy*] ... ECO
Experience Demand Replacement Factor [*Navy*] ... EDRF
Experience Unit ... EU
Experience Usage Replacement Factor [*Navy*] ... EURF
Experienced ... EXP
Experienced ... EXPER
Experienced Export Manager [*Designation given by American Society of International Executives*] ... EEM
Experienced Playgoer [*Theatrical*] ... EP
Experienced Teacher Fellowship Program ... EXTFP
Experienced Worker Standard ... EWS
Experiences in Marketing Management ... EMM
Experientia [*A publication*] ... EXPEA
Experientia [*A publication*] ... Exper
Experientia Supplementum [*A publication*] ... Exper Suppl
Experientia Supplementum (Basel) [*A publication*] ... Exper Suppl (Basel)
Experiential World Inventory [*Psychodiagnostic questionnaire*] ... EWI
Experiment ... EXP
Experiment ... EXPER
Experiment ... EXPT
Experiment [*A publication*] ... Exp
Experiment Analysis Form ... EAF
Experiment Assembly ... EA
Experiment Assurance System [*Nuclear energy*] ... EAS
Experiment Canister ... EC
Experiment Checkout Equipment ... ECE
Experiment Compartment ... E
Experiment Computer ... EC
Experiment Computer Application Software ... ECAS
Experiment Computer Operating System ... ECOS
Experiment Data Facility [*NASA*] ... EDF
Experiment Data Record ... EDR
Experiment Data System ... EDS
Experiment and Development [*Flotilla*] [*Landing Craft*] ... X & D
Experiment Development Center [*NASA*] ... EDC
Experiment Flight Applications ... EFA
Experiment and Guidance Loop Evaluator ... EAGLE
Experiment Implementation Plan [*NASA*] ... EIP
Experiment, Inc., Richmond, VA [*Library symbol*] ... ViREx
Experiment Information System ... EIS

Experiment Integration Center .... EIC
Experiment Integration Requirements Document [*NASA*] .... EIRD
Experiment Interface Definition Document .... EIDD
Experiment in International Living .... EIL
Experiment Mock-Up Converters .... EMC
Experiment and Operations .... EXOP
Experiment Operations Handbook .... EOH
Experiment Operations Panel .... EOP
Experiment Performance Option .... EPO
Experiment Point Control [*NASA*] .... EPC
Experiment Point Control System [*or Subsystem*] [*NASA*] .... EPCS
Experiment Pointing Electronic Assembly [*NASA*] .... EPEA
Experiment Pointing System [*NASA*] .... EPS
Experiment Power Switching Panel .... EPSP
Experiment Procedures .... EXPRO
Experiment Requirements Document .... ERD
Experiment Segment and Pallet Simulator [*NASA*] .... ESPS
Experiment Sensing Platform .... ESP
Experiment Station Record [*A publication*] .... Exp Sta Record
Experiment Subsystem Simulator [*NASA*] .... ESS
Experiment Support Equipment .... ESE
Experiment Support System .... ESS
Experimental .... (E)
Experimental .... EXPTL
Experimental [*Military*] X
Experimental [*When preceding vessel classification*] [*Navy symbol*] .... E
Experimental Activity Proposal [*Nuclear energy*] .... EAP
Experimental Aerospace Multiprocessor .... EXAM
Experimental Aging Research [*A publication*] .... EAGRD
Experimental Aging Research [*A publication*] .... Exp Aging Res
Experimental Agriculture [*A publication*] .... Exp Ag
Experimental Agriculture [*A publication*] .... Exp Agric
Experimental Agriculture [*A publication*] .... Exper Agric
Experimental Agriculture [*A publication*] .... Expl Agric
Experimental Air-to-Air Missile [*Air Force, NASA*] .... XAAM
Experimental (Air Force) .... XA
Experimental Air Specification Weapons [*Navy*] .... XAS
Experimental Air-to-Surface Missile [*Air Force, NASA*] .... XASM
Experimental Aircraft Association .... EAA
Experimental Alcoholic Rhabdomyolysis [*Medicine*] .... EAR
Experimental Allergic Encephalomyelitis [*Medicine*] .... EAE
Experimental Allergic Neuritis [*Medicine*] .... EAN
Experimental Allergic Uveitis [*Ophthalmology*] .... EAU
Experimental Animals (Jikken Dobutsu) (Tokyo) [*A publication*] .... Exp Anim (Tokyo)
Experimental Army Satellite Tactical .... EAST
Experimental Army Satellite Tactical Terminals .... EASTT
Experimental Array RADAR [*Army*] .... EAR
Experimental Assembly and Sterilization Laboratory [*NASA*] .... EASL
Experimental Autoimmune Encephalitis [*Immunology*] .... EAE
Experimental Autoimmune Myasthenia Gravis [*Medicine*] .... EAMG
Experimental Autoimmune Thymitis [*Medicine*] .... EAT
Experimental Autonomous Vehicle [*Underwater robot*] .... EAVE
Experimental Ballistics Association .... EBA
Experimental Behavioral Analyzer .... EBA
Experimental Beryllium Oxide Reactor [*Later, BORE*] .... EBOR
Experimental Biology and Medicine [*A publication*] .... Exp Biol Med
Experimental Boiling Water Reactor .... EBWR
Experimental Bomber .... XB
Experimental Botany [*A publication*] .... Exp Bot
Experimental Botany: An International Series of Monographs [*A publication*] .... Exp Bot Int Ser Monogr
Experimental Brain Research [*A publication*] .... EXBRA
Experimental Brain Research [*A publication*] .... Exp Brain R
Experimental Brain Research [*A publication*] .... Exp Brain Res
Experimental Breeder Reactor .... EBR
Experimental Breeder Reactor .... XBR
Experimental Bridging Establishment [*British*] .... EBE
Experimental Buried Collector Gauge .... EBCG
Experimental Cargo Aircraft XC
Experimental Cargo Glider .... XCG
Experimental Cartographic Facility [*Air Force*] .... ECF
Experimental Cell Biology [*A publication*] .... Exp Cell Biol
Experimental Cell Research [*A publication*] .... Exp Cell Re
Experimental Cell Research [*A publication*] .... Exp Cell Res
Experimental Cell Research. Supplement [*A publication*] .... Exp Cell Res Suppl
Experimental Cities, Incorporated [*An association*] .... ECI
Experimental Communications Satellite [*NASA*] .... ECS
Experimental Computer Complex .... ECC
Experimental Consultative Conference of Industrialists .... ECCI
Experimental Contract Highlight Operation [*NASA*] .... ECHO
Experimental Cross Section Information Library [*University of California, Livermore*] .... ECSIL
Experimental Data Communications Network .... EDCN
Experimental Data Handling Equipment .... EDHE
Experimental Demolition Establishment [*British*] .... EDE
Experimental and Demonstration Projects .... E & D
Experimental Design .... ED
Experimental and Development .... XAD
Experimental and Development Operations .... E & DO
Experimental Development Requirements .... EDR
Experimental, Developmental, Test, and Research .... EDTR
Experimental Digital Television System .... EDITS
Experimental Display Concept [*Space shuttle*] [*NASA*] .... EDC
Experimental Display Generator .... EDGE
Experimental Diving Unit .... EDU
Experimental Diving Unit .... EXPDIVUNIT
Experimental Division .... EXDIV
Experimental Dynamic Processor .... EDP
Experimental Ecological Reserves [*Project*] [*National Science Foundation*] .... EER
Experimental Education Program .... EEP
Experimental Embryology and Teratology [*A publication*] .... Exp Embryol Teratol
Experimental Engine [*NASA*] .... XE
Experimental Engine - Cold Flow Configuration [*NERVA*] .... XECF
Experimental Establishment [*RAF*] [*British*] .... EE
Experimental Eye Research [*A publication*] .... Exp Eye Res
Experimental Fast Ceramic Reactor .... EFCR
Experimental Fighter .... XF
Experimental Firing Ship .... EFS
Experimental Flight .... EF
Experimental Flight Test .... EFT
Experimental Gas-Cooled Reactor .... EGCR
Experimental Geophysical Orbiting [*Vehicle*] .... EGO
Experimental Gerontology [*A publication*] .... Exp Geront
Experimental Gerontology [*A publication*] .... Exp Gerontol
Experimental Group .... EG
Experimental Guided Air Missiles .... XGAM
Experimental Health Services Delivery Systems [*HEW*] .... EHSDS
Experimental Helicopter .... XH
Experimental Hematology [*Lawrence, Kansas*] [*A publication*] .... Exp Hematol
Experimental Hematology (Copenhagen) [*A publication*] .... Exp Hematol (Copenh)
Experimental Horticulture [*A publication*] .... Exp Hort
Experimental Horticulture [*A publication*] .... Exp Hortic
Experimental Horticulture [*A publication*] .... Expl Hort
Experimental Horticulture Station [*British*] .... EHS
Experimental Husbandry [*A publication*] .... Exp Husb
Experimental Husbandry [*A publication*] .... Expl Husb
Experimental Husbandry Farm [*British*] .... EHF
Experimental Integrated Conformed Array .... EICA
Experimental Inter-American Meteorological Rocket Network [*NASA*] .... EXAMETNET
Experimental Intercom .... EIC
Experimental Library Management System .... ELMS
Experimental Light [*Navigation signal*] .... Exper
Experimental Liquid Rocket [*Air Force, NASA*] .... XLR
Experimental Low-Temperature Process Heat Reactor .... ELPHR
Experimental Lung Research [*A publication*] .... Exp Lung Res
Experimental Manned Space Station [*Air Force*] .... EMSS
Experimental Mechanics [*A publication*] .... Exper Mech
Experimental Mechanics [*A publication*] .... Exp Mech
Experimental Medical Care Review Organization [*Program of the National Center for Health Services Research and Development*] .... EMCRO
Experimental Medicine and Microbiology [*A publication*] .... Exp Med Microbiol
Experimental Medicine and Surgery [*A publication*] .... Exp Med Surg
Experimental Memo .... EM
Experimental Memory - Address Register .... EMAR
Experimental Meteorological Sounding Rocket Research Network .... EXMETNET
Experimental Meteorology Laboratory .... EML
Experimental Military Command Information System .... EMCIS
Experimental Miscellaneous Auxiliary [*Navy symbol*] .... EAG
Experimental Missile [*Air Force, NASA*] .... XM
Experimental Model .... XM
Experimental Model Basin [*Navy*] .... EMB
Experimental and Molecular Pathology [*A publication*] .... Exp Molecul Pathol
Experimental and Molecular Pathology [*A publication*] .... Exp Mol Pat
Experimental and Molecular Pathology [*A publication*] .... Exp Mol Pathol
Experimental and Molecular Pathology (Supplement) [*A publication*] .... Exp Mol Pathol (Suppl)
Experimental Monitoring Satellite .... EMS
Experimental Navigation Ship .... ENS
Experimental (Navy) .... XN
Experimental Negotiating Agreement [*Steelworkers contract*] .... ENA
Experimental Neurology [*A publication*] .... EN
Experimental Neurology [*A publication*] .... EXNEA
Experimental Neurology [*A publication*] .... Exp Neurol
Experimental Neurology. Supplement [*A publication*] .... Exp Neurol Suppl
Experimental Officer [*Also, ExO, XO*] [*Ministry of Agriculture, Fisheries, and Food*] [*British*] .... EO
Experimental Officer [*Also, EO, XO*] [*Ministry of Agriculture, Fisheries, and Food*] [*British*] .... ExO
Experimental Officer [*Also, EO, ExO*] [*Ministry of Agriculture, Fisheries, and Food*] [*British*] .... XO
Experimental On-Line Capabilities [*Data processing*] .... XOC

Experimental Operations Center .... EOC
Experimental Order .... EXPO
Experimental Organic Cooled Reactor .... EOCR
Experimental Packet Switching System .... EPSS
Experimental Parasitology [*A publication*] .... Exp Parasit
Experimental Parasitology [*A publication*] .... Exp Parasitol
Experimental Pathology (Jena) [*A publication*] .... Exp Pathol (Jena)
Experimental Patrol Craft, Escort and Rescue .... EPCER
Experimental Power Supply .... EPS
Experimental Procurement Service .... EPS
Experimental Project Apollo-Soyuz [*Acronym used as name of a cologne created to commemorate the first joint US/Russian manned space flight*] .... EPAS
Experimental Prototype Automatic Meteorological System .... EPAMS
Experimental Prototype Community of Tomorrow .... EPCOT
Experimental Prototype Gas-Cooled Reactor .... EPGCR
Experimental and Proving Establishment [*Canada*] .... EPE
Experimental Publications System [*Defunct*] .... EPS
Experimental RADAR Prediction Device .... ERPD
Experimental Record of the Department of Agriculture. South Australia [*A publication*] .... Exp Rec Dep Agric S Aust
Experimental Reflector Orbital Shot [*NASA project*] .... EROS
Experimental Remote Maneuvering Unit .... ERMU
Experimental Reports of Equine Health Laboratory [*A publication*] .... Exp Rep Equine Health Lab
Experimental Reproduction Film .... XRF
Experimental Research and Development Incentives Program [*National Science Foundation*] .... ERDIP
Experimental Research Kit .... ERK
Experimental Research Society [*Defunct*] .... ERS
Experimental Safety Vehicle [*Later, Research Safety Vehicle*] [*Department of Transportation*] .... ESV
Experimental SAGE [*Semi-Automatic Ground Environment*] **Sector** .... ESS
Experimental Solid Propellant Vehicle .... XSPV
Experimental Solid-State Exchange [*Communication system*] .... ESSEX
Experimental Sonic Azimuth Detector .... X-SONAD
Experimental Space Laboratory .... XSL
Experimental Space Station [*NASA*] .... XSS
Experimental Squadron [*Symbol*] VX
Experimental Station .... ES
Experimental Station [*ITU designation*] .... EX
Experimental Station .... EXSTA
Experimental Stations Committee on Organization and Policy [*National Association of State Universities and Land-Grant Colleges*] .... ESCOP
Experimental Strategic Missile .... XSM
Experimental Superconducting Accelerating Ring [*Atomic physics*] .... ESCAR
Experimental Superheat Reactor .... ESR
Experimental Surface Missile .... XSM
Experimental Tactic .... EXTAC
Experimental Target Designation Equipment .... ETDE
Experimental Target Drone [*Air Force, NASA*] .... XQ
Experimental Technology Incentives Program [*National Bureau of Standards*] .... ETIP
Experimental Test Model .... XTM
Experimental Time-Sharing System [*Data processing*] .... ETSS
Experimental Transmitting Antenna Modular Model .... ETAM
Experimental Tunneling Establishment [*British*] .... ETE
Experimental Underwater Pump Jet .... EUPJ
Experimental Unit .... EU
Experimental Use Computer, London Integrated Display .... EUCLID
Experimental Volunteer Army Training Program .... EVATP
Experimental Warhead .... XW
Experimental Weapon Specification .... XWS
Experimental Weapon System .... XWS
Experimental Yacht Society [*Defunct*] .... EYS
Experimentation Animale [*A publication*] .... Exp Anim
Experimentation Cerebrale [*A publication*] .... Exp Cereb
Experimentation Command [*Army*] .... EC
Experimentelle Hirnforschung [*A publication*] .... Exp Hirnforsch
Experimentelle Medizin, Pathologie, und Klinik [*A publication*] .... Exp Med Pathol Klin
Experimentelle Pathologie [*A publication*] .... Exp Path
Experimentelle Pathologie [*A publication*] .... Exp Pathol
Experimentelle Technik der Physik [*A publication*] .... Exp Tech Phys
Experiments in Art and Technology .... EAT
Experiments, Drill, and Maintenance .... EDAM
Experiments in Physiology and Biochemistry [*A publication*] .... Exp Physiol Biochem
Experiments in Progress. Grassland Research Institute (Hurley) [*A publication*] .... Exp Progr Grassland Res Inst (Hurley)
Experiments Systems Branch [*NASA*] .... ESB
Experiments Systems Monitor [*NASA*] .... ESM
Expert .... EX
Expert .... EXP
Expert Committee on Post Adjustments [*United Nations*] .... ECPA
Expert Field Medical Badge [*Military decoration*] .... EFMB
Expert Gunner [*Army*] .... EG
Expert Infantryman Badge [*Military decoration*] .... EIB
Expert Infantryman Badge [*Military decoration*] .... EIBAD
Expert Qualification Badge [*Military decoration*] .... ExpQualBad
Expert Rifleman .... ER
Expert Slope [*Skiing*] .... E
Expertutredningen Angaende Prisreglering av Foersvarsutgifterna [*Sweden*] .... EPAF
Expiration [*or Expiratory*] [*Medicine*] .... EXPIR
Expiration of Active Obligated Service [*Military*] .... EAOS
Expiration of Active Service [*Marine Corps*] .... EAS
Expiration of Enlistment .... E of E
Expiration of Enlistment .... EE
Expiration of Obligated Service [*Military*] .... EOS
Expiration of Service .... E of S
Expiration of Service Agreement [*Military*] .... ESA
Expiration of Term of Obligation [*Military*] .... ETO
Expiration of Term of Service [*Military*] .... ETS
Expiratory Center [*Physiology*] .... EC
Expiratory Reserve Volume [*Physiology*] .... ERV
Expire .... EXPR
Expired [*Gas*] [*Medicine*] .... E
Expired [*Medicine*] .... EXP
Explanation .... EX
Explanation .... EXPL
Explanation of Benefit Payments [*Blue Cross/Blue Shield*] .... EBP
Explanation Report [*NASA*] .... ER
Explicacion de Textos Literarios [*A publication*] .... ETL
Explicacion de Textos Literarios [*A publication*] .... ExTL
Explicator [*A publication*] .... Ex
Explicator [*A publication*] .... Exp
Explicator [*A publication*] .... Expl
Explicit 2-D Patterns Local Operations and Randomness [*Data processing*] .... EXPLOR
Explode .... EXPLD
Exploder .... EXPLR
Exploder Control Sensor .... ECS
Exploding Bridge-Wire .... EBW
Exploding Bridge-Wire .... XB
Exploding Bridge-Wire System .... EBWS
Exploding Wire Aerosol Generator [*Liquid suspension*] .... EWAG
Exploding Wire Phenomena .... EWP
Exploit .... XPLT
[*The*] **Exploration Corporation** [*NASDAQ symbol*] .... TXCO
Exploration and Economics of the Petroleum Industry [*A publication*] .... Explor Econ Petrol Ind
Exploration Geophysics [*A publication*] .... Explor Geophys
Exploration Map Data .... EMD
Exploration and Production [*In organization name Oil Industry International Exploration & Production Forum*] .... E & P
Exploration in Renaissance Culture [*A publication*] .... EIRC
Exploration Surveys [*American Stock Exchange symbol*] .... ESI
Explorations [*A publication*] .... Explor
Explorations in Economic History [*A publication*] .... EEH
Explorations in Economic History [*A publication*] .... Expl Ec His
Explorations in Economic History [*A publication*] .... Explo Econ Hist
Explorations in Economic History [*A publication*] .... Explor Econ Hist
Explorations in Economic Research [*A publication*] .... Explor Econ Res
Exploratory Committee on Assessing the Progress of Education [*Later, NAEP*] .... ECAPE
Exploratory Data Analysis [*Statistics*] .... EDA
Exploratory Development [*Military*] .... ED
Exploratory Development Goal [*Military*] .... EDG
Exploratory Development Model [*Military*] .... EDM
Exploratory Development Objective [*Military*] .... EDO
Exploratory Development Program Summary [*Military*] .... EDPS
Exploratory Development Request [*Military*] .... EDR
Exploratory Development Requirement [*Military*] .... EDR
Exploratory Development Summary Report [*Military*] .... EDSR
Exploratory Group .... EG
Exploratory Laparatomy [*Medicine*] .... Exp Lap
Exploratory Project for Economic Alternatives .... EPEA
Explorer .... EXPL
Explorer Gamma Ray Experiment Telescope [*NASA*] .... EGRET
Explorers Club .... EC
Explorers' Club, New York, NY [*Library symbol*] .... NNEC
Explorers Journal [*A publication*] .... Explor J
Exploring Human Nature [*National Science Foundation project*] .... EHN
Explosion .... EXPLN
Explosion Collapse, Underground Operations .... XCU
Explosion-Proof .... EP
Explosion-Proof Enclosure .... EPE
Explosion-Proof Housing .... EPH
Explosion-Proof Relay .... EPR
Explosion-Resistant Multi-Influence Sweep System .... ERMISS
Explosive .... EXP
Explosive .... EXPL
Explosive .... EXPLO
Explosive .... explos
Explosive .... XPL
Explosive .... XPLOS
Explosive-Actuated Light Filter .... ELF
Explosive-Actuated Valve .... EAV
Explosive Anchorage [*Buoy*] .... Explos Anch

Explosive Device ... ED
Explosive Device System ... EDS
Explosive Disposal Control ... EDC
Explosive Echo Ranging ... EER
Explosive Echo Ranging Charge ... EERC
Explosive-to-Electric Transducer ... EET
Explosive Excavation Research Agency [*Formerly, NCG*] [*Army*] ... EERA
Explosive Excavation Research Laboratory [*Army*] ... EERL
Explosive Excavation Research Office [*Army*] ... EERO
Explosive Fabricator [*NASDAQ symbol*] ... EXPL
Explosive Gas Indicator ... EGI
Explosive Investigative Laboratory [*Navy*] ... EIL
Explosive Lens Flashbinder ... ELF
Explosive Metal Forming ... EMF
Explosive Motor Behavior [*Neurochemistry*] ... EMB
Explosive Ordnance [*Military*] ... EO
Explosive Ordnance Components [*Military*] ... EOC
Explosive Ordnance Detachment [*Army*] ... EOD
Explosive Ordnance Device [*Military*] ... EOD
Explosive Ordnance Disposal [*Military*] ... EOD
Explosive Ordnance Disposal Bulletin [*Military*] ... EODB
Explosive Ordnance Disposal Control [*Military*] ... EODC
Explosive Ordnance Disposal Group [*Military*] ... EODG
Explosive Ordnance Disposal Group [*Military*] ... EODGRU
Explosive Ordnance Disposal Group, Atlantic [*Military*] ... EODGRULANT
Explosive Ordnance Disposal Group, Pacific [*Military*] ... EODGRUPAC
Explosive Ordnance Disposal, Nuclear ... EODN
Explosive Ordnance Disposal School [*Military*] ... EODS
Explosive Ordnance Disposal Specialist Badge [*Military decoration*] ... EODSBad
Explosive Ordnance Disposal Supervisor Badge [*Military decoration*] ... EODSupvBad
Explosive Ordnance Disposal Unit [*Military*] ... EODU
Explosive Ordnance Reconnaissance [*Military*] ... EOR
Explosive Ordnance Reconnaissance Agent [*Military*] ... EORA
Explosive Ordnance Safety Approval [*Military*] ... EOSA
Explosive Research and Development Establishment [*British*] ... ERDE
Explosive Safe Area [*NASA*] ... ESA
Explosive-Safe Facility ... ESF
Explosive Safety Approval ... ESA
Explosive Safety Survey ... ESS
Explosive Technology ... ET
Explosive Valve ... EV
Explosive Vapor Detector Systems ... EVDS
Explosives Corporation of America ... ECA
Explosives Corporation of America ... EXCOA
Explosives Engineer [*A publication*] ... Explosives Eng
Explosives Investigation Memorandum [*Navy*] ... EIM
Explosives Report ... ER
Explosives Research Center [*Bureau of Mines*] ... ERC
Explosives Research Memorandum ... ERM
Explosives Research Note ... ERN
Explosivstoffe [*A publication*] ... Explosivst
Expo Collectors and Historians Organization ... ECHO
Exponent ... E
Exponent ... EXPNT
Exponential ... EXP
Exponential Hazard Function ... EHF
Exponential Integral ... EI
Exponential Power Distribution [*Statistics*] ... EPD
Exponential Reliability Function ... ERF
Exponential-Slope Difference [*Statistics*] ... ESD
Exponentially Restored, Poisson-Released ... ERPR
Exponentially Retrograded Diode ... ERD
Export ... E
Export ... EX
Export ... EXP
Export ... XPT
Export Administration Regulation [*Department of Commerce*] ... EAR
Export Administration Review Board ... EARB
Export Business Relations Division [*Department of Commerce*] ... EBRD
Export of Commercial Samples ... ECS
Export Control Act ... ECA
Export Control Bulletin [*Department of Commerce*] ... ECB
Export Control Regulations [*Department of Commerce*] ... ECR
Export Control Review Board ... ECRB
Export Credits Guarantee Department [*British*] ... ECGD
Export Credits Insurance Corporation [*Canada*] ... ECIC
Export Development Corp., Ottawa, ON, Canada [*Library symbol*] ... CaOOEDC
Export Expansion Facility [*Export-Import Bank of the US*] ... EEF
Export Free Processing Zone ... EFPZ
Export Guarantees Act ... EGA
Export-Import Bank ... E-IB
Export-Import Bank ... EXIM
Export-Import Bank ... EXIMBANK
Export-Import Bank ... EXIMBK
Export-Import Bank of the United States [*Formerly, EIB(W)*] ... EIBUS
Export-Import Bank (of Washington) [*Later, EIBUS*] ... EIB(W)
Export Management Company ... EMC
Export Marketing Service [*Department of Agriculture*] ... EMS
Export Packers Association of New York [*Defunct*] ... EPANY
Export Pound Account [*Special type of currency*] [*United Arab Republic*] ... EPA
Export Processing Industry Coalition ... EPIC
Export Processing Zone Authority [*Philippines*] ... EPZA
Export Surpluses [*British*] ... ES
Export Task Force ... ETF
Export Trading Company [*Department of Commerce*] ... ETC
Export Traffic Release ... ETR
Export Transport Release ... ETR
Expose ... EXP
Exposed ... EXPD
Exposes Annuels de Biochimie Medicale [*A publication*] ... Expo Annu Biochim Med
Exposes Annuels de Biochimie Medicale [*A publication*] ... Expos Annu Biochim Med
Exposition ... EXPN
Exposition ... EXPO
Exposition of the Blessed Sacrament [*Roman Catholic*] ... EXP
Exposition and Conference Council ... ECC
Exposition Management Association ... EMA
Exposition Service Contractors Association ... ESCA
Expositor [*A publication*] ... Exp
Expositor [*A publication*] ... Expos
Expository Times [*A publication*] ... ET
Expository Times [*A publication*] ... Expos T
Expository Times [*A publication*] ... ExpT
Exposure ... E
Exposure ... EX
Exposure ... EXPSR
Exposure [*Symbol*] [*IUPAC*] ... H
Exposure Control Technique ... ECT
Exposure Draft [*Business and trade*] ... ED
Exposure Growth Curve ... EGC
Exposure Index [*Photography*] ... EI
Exposure Value [*System*] [*Photography*] ... EV
Express ... EX
Express ... EXP
Express ... EXPS
Express [*A publication*] ... Exp
Express Air Service (C.I.) Ltd. [*Great Britain*] [*ICAO designator*] ... LS
Express Delivery Service ... EDS
Express Group Newspapers [*British*] ... EGN
Express Paid ... XP
Express Paid Telegraph ... XPT
Express & Star Ltd., Wolverhampton, United Kingdom [*Library symbol*] ... UkWoE
Express Translation Service List [*A publication*] ... Express Transl Serv List
Express Transportation Order [*Army*] ... ETO
Expressed Breast Milk [*Medicine*] ... EBM
Expressible Moisture Index ... EMI
Expression ... EXPR
Expression of Anger [*Psychology*] ... AnE
Expression. Journal of the English Society [*A publication*] ... EESB
Expression-Linked Extra Copy [*Genetics*] ... ELC
Expression-Oriented Language [*Data processing*] ... EOL
Expressive-Regressive Index ... ERI
Expressway ... EXPY
Expressway ... X-WAY
Expulsion ... EXP
Extant ... EXT
Extend [*or Extension*] ... EXT
Extend [*or Extended*] ... EXTD
Extend [*or Extended*] ... XTND
Extendable Computer System Simulator ... ECSS
Extendable Debugging and Monitoring System [*Data processing*] ... EXDAMS
Extendable Nozzle Exit Cone ... ENEC
Extendable Stiff Arm Manipulator [*NASA*] ... ESAM
Extendable Tubular Member Device ... ETMD
Extende [*Spread*] [*Pharmacy*] ... EXT
Extended ... EXTND
Extended Abstracts and Program. Biennial Conference on Carbon [*A publication*] ... Extended Abstr Program Bienn Conf Carbon
Extended Active Duty ... EAD
Extended Air Surveillance Communications Intercept [*Air Force*] ... EASCOMINT
Extended Architecture [*Data processing*] ... XA
Extended Area Instrumentation RADAR ... EAIR
Extended Area Instrumentation System ... EAIS
Extended Area Service [*Telephone communications*] ... EAS
Extended Area Test System [*Navy*] ... EATS
Extended Arithmetic Element ... EAE
Extended Benefits [*Unemployment insurance*] ... EB
Extended Binary-Coded Decimal [*Data processing*] ... EBCD
Extended Binary-Coded Decimal ... EBCDC
Extended Binary-Coded Decimal Interchange Code [*Data processing*] ... EBCDIC
Extended Care Facility [*Medicine*] [*Obsolete*] ... ECF
Extended Cold/Wet Clothing Systems ... ECWC
Extended Communications Search [*Navy*] ... EXCOMMS

Extended Control [*Mode*] [*Data processing*]......EC
Extended Core Memory [*Data processing*]......ECM
Extended Core Memory Unit [*Data processing*]......ECMU
Extended Core Storage [*Data processing*]......ECS
Extended Coverage [*Insurance*]......EC
Extended Coverage Endorsement [*Insurance*]......ECE
Extended Data Management Facility......EDMF
Extended Defense Communication System......EDCS
Extended Disk Operating System......EDOS
Extended Electron Loss Fine Structure [*Spectrometry*]......EXELFS
Extended Family [*Unitarian Universalist program*]......XF
Extended Forecasts [*Symbol*] [*National Weather Service*]......FE
Extended Fund Facility [*International Monetary Fund*]......EFF
Extended General Purpose Simulator [*National Electronics Conference*]......EGPS
Extended Group Coded Recording [*Data processing*]......E/GCR
Extended Guide Projectile [*Navy*]......EGP
Extended Health Care [*Insurance*]......EHC
Extended Huckel Molecular Orbit......XHMO
Extended Hueckel [*Molecular orbit*] [*Atomic physics*]......EH
Extended Hueckel Molecular Orbit [*Atomic physics*]......EHMO
Extended Length Methods......ELM
Extended Life Attitude Control System [*NASA*]......ELACS
Extended Linear Expenditure System......ELES
Extended Lunar Mission [*NASA*]......ELM
Extended Lunar Orbital Rendezvous [*NASA*]......ELOR
Extended Lunar Orbital Rendezvous Mission [*NASA*]......ELORM
Extended Memory Unit......EMU
Extended Mercury Autocoder......EMA
Extended Mission Apollo [*NASA*]......EMA
Extended Mission Apollo Simulation [*NASA*]......XMAS
Extended Nylon Shaft......ENS
Extended Observation of Solar and Cosmic Radiation [*National Center for Atmospheric Research*]......EOSCOR
Extended Operating System [*DoD*]......EOS
Extended Operations......EO
Extended Overhaul Cycle......EOC
Extended Performance and Increased Capability......EPIC
Extended Planning Annex......EPA
Extended Play......EP
Extended Quasi-Static Approximation [*Materials research*]......EQSA
Extended Range......ER
Extended Range Anti-Armor Mine......ERAM
Extended Range Antitank Mine......ERAM
Extended-Range ASROC [*Antisubmarine Rocket*] [*Navy*]......ERA
Extended-Range Ballistic Missile......ERBM
Extended-Range Doppler......EXTRADOP
Extended-Range Doppler Velocity and Position......EXTRADOVAP
Extended-Range Floating Point Interpretive System......ERFPI
Extended-Range Juno [*Survey meter for radiation*]......ERJ
Extended-Range Lance [*Missile*]......ERL
Extended-Range Lance [*Missile*]......XRL
Extended Range Phase-Locked Demodulator......ERPLD
Extended-Range Poseidon [*Missile*] [*Navy*]......EXPO
Extended-Range and Space Communication......ERSC
Extended-Range Strike Aircraft [*for low-level missions*] [*Air Force*]......ERSA
Extended Reconnaissance Zone [*Army*]......ERZ
Extended Red Multialkali [*Cathode*]......ERMA
Extended Release [*Pharmacy*]......ER
Extended Research Telescope......ERT
Extended Salvage Depth Capability......ESDC
Extended School Year......ESY
Extended School Year Aid......ESYA
Extended Service Plan [*Ford Motor Co.*]......ESP
Extended Source Calibration Area [*Nuclear energy*]......ESCA
Extended Sterilization Qualification Test......ESQT
Extended Tape Operating System......ETOS
Extended Telecommunications Modules......EXTM
Extended Term Plan......ETP
Extended Time Tests......ETT
Extended Ultraviolet Transmission......EUVT
Extended Unemployment Compensation Account......EUCA
Extended Work Week......EWW
Extended X-Ray Absorption Fine Structure [*Spectrometry*]......EXAFS
Extender......EXTNR
Extendicare, Inc. [*NYSE symbol*] [*Delisted*]......XTC
Extensible Language Facility [*Data processing*]......ELF
Extensible Programing System [*Data processing*]......EPS
Extensible Structure Processing Language [*Data processing*]......ESPL
Extension [*A publication*]......Extensn
Extension......EXTN
Extension......EXTNS
Extension......EXTSN
Extension......X
Extension en las Americas [*A publication*]......Ext Amer
Extension of BASIC [*Data processing*]......XBASIC
Extension Bulletin. Delaware University. Agricultural Extension Service [*A publication*]......Ext Bull Del Univ Agr Ext Serv
Extension Bulletin. Iowa State University [*A publication*]......Ext Bull Iowa State Univ
Extension Bulletin. Maryland University. Cooperative Extension Service [*A publication*]......Ext Bull MD Univ Coop Ext Serv
Extension Bulletin. University of Minnesota. Agricultural Extension Service [*A publication*]......Ext Bull Univ Minn Agr Ext Serv
Extension Circular. Illinois University [*A publication*]......Ext Circ Ill Univ
Extension Circular. North Carolina State University. Agricultural Extension Service [*A publication*]......Ext Circ NC State Univ Agr Ext Serv
Extension Circular P. Auburn University. Agricultural Extension Service [*A publication*]......Ext Circ P Auburn Univ Agr Ext Serv
Extension Circular. Purdue University. Department of Agricultural Extension [*A publication*]......Ext Circ Purdue Univ Dept Agr Ext
Extension Circular. South Dakota State University. Cooperative Extension Service [*A publication*]......Ext Circ S Dak State Univ Coop Ext Serv
Extension Committee on Organization and Policy......ECOP
Extension and Conversion [*Public buildings*]......EC
Extension Course......EC
Extension Course Institute [*Air Force*]......ECI
Extension of Enlistment [*Military*]......EXTENL
Extension Folder. University of Minnesota. Agricultural Extension Service [*A publication*]......Ext Folder Univ Minn Agr Ext Serv
Extension Folder. University of New Hampshire. College of Agriculture. Extension Service [*A publication*]......Ext Folder Univ NH Coll Agr Ext Serv
Extension of the Gastric Shield......EGS
Extension Hose/Mouthpiece......EH/M
Extension Lay Volunteers......ELV
Extension Leaflet. Utah State University. Agricultural Extension Service [*A publication*]......Ext Leafl Utah State Univ Agr Ext Serv
Extension of Leave [*Military*]......EXTLV
Extension Management Information System [*Department of Agriculture*]......EMIS
Extension Publication. Illinois University. North Central Region [*A publication*]......Ext Publ Ill Univ N Cent Reg
Extension Publication. Louisiana State University. Agricultural Extension Service [*A publication*]......Ext Publ LA State Univ Agr Ext Serv
Extension Service [*Department of Agriculture*]......ES
Extension Service Review [*A publication*]......ESR
Extension Service Review [*A publication*]......Ext Serv R
Extension Service Review [*A publication*]......Ext Serv Rev
Extension Shaft Disconnect [*Nuclear energy*]......ESD
Extension Society Volunteers [*Defunct*]......ESV
Extension Training Materials [*Army*]......ETM
Extension Training Memorandum [*Civil Defense*]......ETM
Extension [*O Intercambio*] **Universitaria de la Plata** [*A publication*]......EUP
Extensions and Restrictions of Operators......EROP
Extensive......EXTSV
Extensive......EXTV
Extensive Air Shower [*Cosmic ray physics*]......EAS
Extensive Field Maintenance [*Military*]......EFM
Extensive Wound......EW
Extensor [*Anatomy*]......EXT
Extensor Carpi Radialis Brevis [*Muscle*]......ECRB
Extensor Digitorum Longus [*Anatomy*]......EDL
Extensor Pollicis Brevis [*Muscle*]......EPB
Extensor Pollicis Longus [*Muscle*]......EPL
Exterior......EXT
Exterior Insulation Manufacturers Association......EIMA
Exterior Surface......ES
External......EXT
External......EXTER
External......EXTNL
External Aerodynamic Diffusion......EAD
External Affairs [*A publication*]......Ext Affairs
External Affairs Department [*Canada*]......EA
External Auditory Canal [*Anatomy*]......EAC
External Auditory Meatus [*Anatomy*]......EAM
External Burning......EB
External Carotid - Middle Cerebral Artery [*Anatomy*]......EC-MCA
External Channels Ratio......ECR
External Combustion......EC
External Combustion Engine [*Steam bus*]......ECE
External Countdown Clock......ECDC
External Delay Factor [*Data processing*]......EDF
External Device [*Data processing*]......ED
External Device [*Data processing*]......EXD
External-Device Code [*Data processing*]......EDC
External-Device Control Word [*Data processing*]......EDCW
External Drug and Cosmetic [*Color*]......EXT D & C
External Economic Policy [*British*]......EEP
External Environment......EE
External Event Detection Module [*Data processing*]......EEDM
External Field Emission......EFE
External Finance Limit......EFL
External Finished Reports Information Subsystem [*Data processing*]......EFRIS
External Flaps......EF
External Function......EXF
External Function Translator......EFT
External Gauge......EXGA

External Hydrogen/Oxygen Tank ... EHOT
External Interlace ... EIN
External Limiting Membrane ... ELM
External Locus of Control [*Psychology*] ... ELC
External Memorandum ... EM
External-Mix Spray Nut ... EMSN
External Muon Identifier [*Atomic physics*] ... EMI
External Ocular Movement [*Medicine*] ... EOM
External Oxygen and Hydrogen Tanks ... EOHT
External Page Storage ... EPS
External Page Table [*Data processing*] ... XPT
External Pipe Thread [*Technical drawings*] ... EPT
External Pneumatic Compression [*Medicine*] ... EPC
External Pneumatic Intermittent Compression ... EPIC
External Polarization Modulation ... EPM
External Power Contractor ... EPC
External Power Relay ... EPR
External Pressure ... EP
External Pressure Circulatory Assist [*Cardiac treatment*] ... EPCA
External Pressure Vessel ... EPV
External Proton Beam ... EPB
External Publication ... EP
External Ramjet ... ERJ
External Ramjet Program ... ERP
External Reference ... EXTRN
External Regulation System ... ERS
External REM [*Radiology*] ... EXREM
External Report ... ER
External Representation of the Ukrainian Helsinki Group ... ERUHG
External Research Publication and Retrieval System [*Department of State*] ... XPARS
External Resistance [*Physics*] ... ER
External Standard Pulse [*Instrumentation*] ... ESP
External Standard Ratio ... ESR
External Symbol Dictionary [*A publication*] ... ESD
External Tank [*NASA*] ... ET
External Tank Door ... ETD
External Tank Lift-Off Weight [*NASA*] ... ETLOW
External Tank Separation Subsystem [*NASA*] ... ETSS
External Tank System ... ETS
External Technical Memorandum ... ETM
External Technical Report ... ETR
External Thermal Garment ... ETG
External Timing Register ... ETR
External Torpedo [*Formerly, DEXTOR*] ... EXTOR
External Transcribed Spacer [*Genetics*] ... ETS
External Transmit Clock ... XTC
External Urethral Sphincter [*Anatomy*] ... EUS
External Visual Display ... EVD
External Visual Display Equipment [*Used in Apollo mission*] [*NASA*] ... EVDE
External Visual Reference [*Motion sickness*] ... EVR
External Work ... EW
Externally Blown Flap [*Aviation*] ... EBF
Externally Caused Failure ... ECF
Externally Coupled Resonator Filter ... ECRF
Externally Quenched Counter ... EQC
Externally Specified Indexing ... ESI
Extinct ... EXT
Extinction [*Neurophysiology*] ... E
Extinguish ... EXT
Extinguish ... EXTG
Extinguish ... EXTGH
Extinguish ... EXTING
Extinguished Light [*Navigation signal*] ... Exting
Extinguisher ... EXTGR
Extortion [*FBI standardized term*] ... EXT
Extortionate Credit Transactions [*FBI standardized term*] ... ECT
Extra ... EX
Extra ... EXT
Extra [*As in XHVY, or extra-heavy*] ... X
Extra [*Designation on brandy labels*] ... X
Extra Best Best [*Steel wire*] ... EBB
Extra Coordination ... EC
Extra Deep Drawing [*Metal industry*] ... EDD
Extra Dense ... XD
Extra Duty [*Marine Corps*] ... ED
Extra-Extra Large [*Size*] ... XXL
Extra-Extra Strong ... XXS
Extra Fine [*Threads*] ... EF
Extra Fine ... XF
Extra Gentleman Usher to His Majesty [*British*] ... EGUHM
Extra Hard [*Pencil leads*] ... HH
Extra Hazardous ... EH
Extra Heavy ... XHVY
Extra-High Frequency ... XHF
Extra-High Potency ... EHP
Extra-High Reliability ... EHR
Extra-High Reliability ... XHR
Extra-High Tension ... EHT
Extra-High Voltage [*FPC*] ... EHV
Extra-Illustrated ... EI
Extra Large [*Size*] ... XL
Extra-Long Distance ... ELD
Extra-Long Staple [*Cotton*] ... ELS
Extra-Long Wheelbase ... XLWB
Extra-Low Carbon ... ELC
Extra-Low Dispersion [*Instrumentation*] ... ED
Extra-Low Impurity [*Metals*] ... ELI
Extra-Low Interstitial [*Alloy*] ... ELI
Extra-Low Interstitial [*Alloy*] ... XLI
Extra Milers ... EM
Extra Military Instruction ... EMI
Extra Old [*Designation on brandy labels*] ... XO
Extra Outsize [*Clothing*] ... XOS
Extra Parochial [*Geographical division*] [*British*] ... EXT P
Extra Point [*Football*] ... EP
Extra Police Duty [*Extra cleaning chores*] [*Military*] ... EPD
Extra-Regimentally Employed [*List*] [*Military*] [*British*] ... ERE
Extra Section ... EXSEC
Extra Series ... ES
Extra Soil Defense [*Fabric treatment*] ... ESD
Extra Strong ... XS
Extra Strong ... XSTR
Extra Time Allowance ... EXTAL
Extra Wide [*Women's shoe width*] [*More than one "E" indicates increasing wideness, up to EEE*] ... E
Extra Wide [*Size*] ... XW
Extra Years of Zest [*Gerontology*] ... XYZ
Extrabold [*Typography*] ... XBLD
Extracapillary Proliferative Glomerulonephritis [*Nephrology*] ... ExPGN
Extracellular [*Hematology*] ... EC
Extracellular Fluid [*Physiology*] ... ECF
Extracellular Material [*Physiology*] ... ECM
Extracellular Volume [*Hematology*] ... ECV
Extracorporeal Irradiation ... ECI
Extracorporeal Membrane Oxygenator [*Respirator*] ... ECMO
Extracorporeal Shockwave Lithotripsy [*Medicine*] ... ESWL
Extracranial-Intracranial [*Medicine*] ... ECIC
Extract [*or Extracted*] ... EXT
Extract ... EXTR
Extract of Requisition ... EXREQ
Extractable Fluorescence ... EF
Extractable Nuclear Antigen [*Immunology*] ... ENA
Extracted ... EXTD
Extracting ... EXTG
Extraction Dialysis [*For separation of mixtures*] ... ED
Extraction Tool Insert ... ETI
Extraction Zone [*Military*] ... EZ
Extraction Zone Control Officer [*Military*] ... EZCO
Extractive Fuels [*NASDAQ symbol*] ... FUEL
Extractive Metallurgy Institute ... EMI
Extractor Tool ... ETTO
Extractum [*Extract*] [*Latin*] ... EX
Extractum [*Extract*] [*Pharmacy*] ... EXT
Extradimensional Being ... EDB
Extradimensional Shift [*Psychometrics*] ... EDS
Extragalactic Light ... EGL
Extragalactic Radio Source ... EGRS
Extrahepatic Blood Flow [*Medicine*] ... EHBF
Extralymphatic [*Medicine*] ... E
Extraocular Movements [*Ophthalmology*] ... EOM
Extraocular Muscles [*Ophthalmology*] ... EOM
Extraoptic Photoreceptors ... EOP
Extraordinary Administrative Radio Conference [*ITU*] ... EARC
Extraordinary Electromagnetic Wave ... EEW
Extraordinary and Plenipotentiary ... E & P
Extraordinary Ray [*Direction of*] ... E
Extraordinary Wave ... XWAVE
Extrapolation [*A publication*] ... Ext
Extrapyramidal Symptoms [*Medicine*] ... EPS
Extraretinal Eye Position Information [*Ophthalmology*] ... EEPI
Extrasensory Perception ... ESP
Extraterrestrial [*Also used in film title "ET - The Extra-Terrestrial"*] ... ET
Extraterrestrial Civilization ... ETC
Extraterrestrial Hypothesis ... ETH
Extraterrestrial Intelligence ... ETI
Extraterrestrial Photographic Information Center [*NASA*] ... EPIC
Extraterrestrial Research Agency [*Army*] ... EXTERRA
Extrathyroidal Neck Radioactivity [*Radiology*] ... ENR
Extravascular [*Anatomy*] ... EV
Extravehicular ... EV
Extravehicular Activity [*Aerospace*] ... EVA
Extravehicular Aerospace Routing ... EAR
Extravehicular Communications [*Aerospace*] ... EVAC
Extravehicular Communications System [*NASA*] ... EVCS
Extravehicular Communications Umbilical ... EVCU
Extravehicular Communicator [*NASA*] ... EVC
Extravehicular Crew Transfer [*NASA*] ... EVCT
Extravehicular Crew Transfer Device [*NASA*] ... EVCTD
Extravehicular Engineering Activity [*Aerospace*] ... EVEA
Extravehicular Glove [*NASA*] ... EVG
Extravehicular Life Support System [*NASA*] ... EVLSS

Extravehicular Mobility Unit [NASA].............................EMU
Extravehicular Mobility Unit [NASA].............................EVMU
Extravehicular Operation [Aerospace]...........................EVO
Extravehicular Reference Information [NASA space program] ....ERI
Extravehicular Space Suit [Aerospace].........................EVSS
Extravehicular Suit..EVS
Extravehicular Suit Communications [Aerospace].................EVSC
Extravehicular Suit Telemetry Communications [Aerospace]...........EVSTC
Extravehicular Support Pack [or Package] [NASA] ....ESP
Extravehicular System [Aerospace]..............................EVS
Extravehicular Transfer [NASA].................................EVT
Extravehicular Visor Assembly [NASA]..........................EVVA
Extraversion-Introversion [Jungian psychology] ....E-I
Extreme ....EXT
Extreme ....EXTM
Extreme ....extr
Extreme ....EXTRM
Extreme ....XTRM
Extreme Close-Up [Television]..................................ECU
Extreme Fuel - Critical, Unspecified Area [NASA]...............EFCUA
Extreme High Vacuum ....XHV
Extreme High Water ....EHW
Extreme Low Water ....ELW
Extreme Pressure ....EP
Extreme Ultraviolet ....EUV
Extreme Ultraviolet ....XUV
Extreme Ultraviolet Photometer ....EUVP
Extreme Ultraviolet Telescope ....EUVT
Extreme Value Statistics......................................EVS
Extreme Width [of flight deck]................................EW
Extremely Fine [Condition] [Antiquarian book trade and numismatics] ......EF
Extremely High Frequency [Electronics, radio wave].............EHF
Extremely Low Frequency [Electronics, radio wave] ....ELF
Extremely Sensitive Information [Army]........................ESI
Extremely Severe [Rock climbing]..............................XS
Extremity [Medicine]..EXT
Extrinsic Allergic Alveolitis [Medicine]......................EAA
Extrinsic Factor [Vitamin B$_{12}$] [Also, APAF, LLD] ....EF
Extrinsic Hyperpolarizing Potential...........................EHP
Extrinsic Irradiated Silicon Vidicon..........................EISV
Extrinsic Plasminogen Activator [Hematology]..................EPA
Extroversion [Psychology].....................................Ex
Extrude ....EXTD
Extrude ....EXTR
Extruded Bar Solder ....EBS
Extruded Vinyl Bumper ....EVB
Extruded Vinyl Chamfer Strip ....EVCS
Extrusion Die...ED
Extrusion Trim and Drill Template.............................ETDT
Extrusion Trim Template.......................................ETT
Exudative Vitreoretinopathy [Ophthalmology]...................EV
Exxon Corp. [Formerly, Standard Oil of New Jersey] [NYSE
   symbol; formerly, J]......................................XON
Exxon Corp., Exploration Library, Denver, CO [Library symbol] ....CoDEx
Exxon Corp., Information Center, Technical Service
   Coordinator, New York, NY [OCLC symbol]...................ZXX
Exxon Donor Solvent Process [Coal liquefaction] ....EDS
Exxon Education Foundation ....EEF
Exxon Research and Development Laboratories [Formerly, Esso
   Research Laboratory]......................................ERDL
Exxon Research & Engineering Co., Company and Literature
   Information Center Library, Linden, NJ [Library symbol]............NjLinEx
Exxon Research & Engineering Co., Engineering Information
   Center, Florham Park, NJ [Library symbol]................NjFpEx
Exxon Research & Engineering Co., Medical Research Library,
   Linden, NJ [Library symbol] ....NjLinEx-M

Exzellenz [Excellency] [German] ....EXZ
Eye ....E
Eye Artifact Potential..EAP
Eye Ball Down...EBD
Eye Ball In...EBI
Eye Ball Left...EBL
Eye Ball Out..EBO
Eye Ball Right..EBR
Eye Ball Up...EBU
Eye Bank Association of America ....EBAA
Eye-Bank for Sight Restoration................................EBSR
Eye Care, Inc. [An association] ....EC
Eye and Ear...EE
Eye, Ear, Nose, and Throat Journal [A publication] ....EENTA
Eye, Ear, Nose, and Throat Monthly [A publication] ....Eye Ear Nos
Eye, Ear, Nose, and Throat Monthly [A publication] ....
                                                Eye Ear Nose Throat Mon
Eye Guard ....EGRD
Eye Infection [Classification system used by doctors on Ellis
   Island to detain, re-examine, and possibly deny entry to
   certain immigrants]......................................E
Eye Lens ....EL
Eye-Motion Camera ....EMC
Eye-Movement Device ....EMD
Eye-Movement Gauge ....EMG
Eye-Movement Measuring Apparatus ....EMMA
Eye Point of Regard [NASA]....................................EPR
Eye Protection Shutter..EPS
Eye Reference Point [NASA]....................................ERP
Eye Research [An association].................................ER
Eye Stalk...ES
Eye-Voice Span ....EVS
Eyelet..EYLT
Eyelet-Installing Machine.....................................EIM
Eyepiece ....EYPC
Eyepiece Box ....EB
[The] Eyes of the Army ....TEOTA
Eyes Closed [Ataxia]..EC
Eyes, Ears, Nose, and Throat [Medicine].......................EENT
Eyes Open [Ataxia]..EO
Eyes Right..ERI
Eyes in the Sky ....EIS
Eyewitness [A publication]....................................Eyewit
Eymard League ....EL
Eyrewell [New Zealand] [Geomagnetic observatory code].........EYR
Eysenck Personality Inventory [Psychology]....................EPI
Eysenck-Withers Personality Inventory [Psychology]............EWPI
Ezekiel [Old Testament book]..................................Ez
Ezekiel [Old Testament book]..................................Ezek
Ezhegodnik Gosudarstvennyi Istoricheskii Muzei [A publication]...............
                                                Ezhegodnik GIM
Ezhegodnik Imperatorskikh Teatrov [A publication].............EIT
Ezhegodnik Zoologicheskogo Muzeia Akademii Nauk Sofuza
   Sovetskikh Sotsialisticheskikh Respublik [A publication] ....
                                                Ezhegodnik Zool Muz Akad Nauk SSSR
Ezhegodnik Zoologicheskogo Muzeia Rossiiskoi Akademii
   Nauk [A publication]..................... Ezhegodnik Zool Muz Ross Akad Nauk
Ezik i Literatura [A publication] ....EiL
Ezik i Literatura [A publication] ....EL
Ezik i Stil na Balgarskite Pisateli [A publication]...........ESBP
Ezine [Turkey] [Seismograph station code, US Geological Survey] ....EZN
Ezra [Old Testament book].....................................Ez
Ezra [Old Testament book].....................................Ezr
Ezra Pound Society..EPS
Ezrat Nashim [An association].................................EN

F

Facility ... FCLTY
Facility for Accelerated Service Testing ... FAST
Facility Activation [*or Activity*] **Schedule** ... FAS
Facility Air Supply ... FAS
Facility for the Analysis of Chemical Thermodynamics [*McGill University*] [*Information service*] ... FACT
Facility for Analyzing Surface Texture [*National Bureau of Standards*] ... FAST
Facility for Automatic Sorting and Testing ... FAST
Facility Board [*Air Force*] ... FB
Facility Capability Report [*Military*] ... FCR
Facility Capability Review ... FCR
Facility Capital Funds ... FCF
Facility Change Authorization ... FCA
Facility Change Group ... FCG
Facility Change Initiation Request ... FCIR
Facility Change Order ... FCO
Facility Change Request ... FCR
Facility Checking Flight - Service Evaluation [*Air Force*] ... FCF SE
Facility Checkout ... FAC/CO
Facility Checkout Vehicle [*NASA*] ... FCOV
Facility Checkout Vehicle [*NASA*] ... FCV
Facility Chief [*Aviation*] ... FACF
Facility Clearance Board [*WPB*] ... FCB
Facility Contract End Item ... FCEI
Facility Coordination Offices [*FAA*] ... FCO
Facility Data Report [*Nuclear energy*] ... FDR
Facility Design Criteria ... FDC
Facility Design Criteria Document ... FDCD
Facility Drawing ... FD
Facility Emergency Organization [*Nuclear energy*] ... FEO
Facility Engineering Change Proposal ... FECP
Facility Engineering Command ... FACENGCOM
Facility and Environment ... F & E
Facility and Equipment Design Plan ... FEDP
Facility and Equipment Requirements Document ... FERD
Facility Forecast ... FF
Facility Gauge ... FCGA
Facility Group Control [*Military*] ... FGC
Facility Information Management System ... FIMS
Facility Installation Review ... FIR
Facility for Integrated Data Organization ... FIDO
Facility Interface Sheet ... FIS
Facility Interface Unit [*Telecommunications*] ... FIU
Facility Interference Review ... FIR
Facility Intrusion Detection System ... FIDS
Facility Need Date ... FND
Facility Operating License [*Nuclear energy*] ... FOL
Facility Planning and Design ... FP & D
Facility Portable Test Equipment ... FPTE
Facility Power Control ... FPC
Facility Power Monitor ... FPM
Facility Power Out Test ... FPOT
Facility Power Panel ... FPP
Facility Remote Control Panel ... FRCP
Facility Review Committee ... FRC
Facility Security Program [*World War II*] ... FSP
Facility Support Equipment ... FSE
Facility Terminal Cabinet ... FTC
Facility Training Equipment ... FTE
Facility Utilization Board ... FUB
Facility Utilization Plan ... FUP
Facility Working Group ... FWG
Facing ... FCG
Facing History and Ourselves National Foundation ... FHONF
Facing Identification Mark [*Postal Service*] ... FIM
Facing Tile Institute ... FTI
Faciundum Curavit [*He Caused To Be Made*] [*Latin*] ... FC
Facsimile ... FAC
Facsimile ... FACS
Facsimile ... FACSIM
Facsimile ... FAX
Facsimile ... FX
Facsimile Communications System ... FCS
Facsimile Reprints in Herpetology [*A publication*] ... Facsimile Repr Herpetol
Facsimile System [*Western Union trade name*] ... INTRAFAX
Facsimile Test Society ... FTS
Facsimile Transmission ... FAX
Facsimile Transmission ... TRANSFAX
Facsimile Transmission over AUTODIN ... FAXDIN
Facsimile Transmission System ... FACTS
Fact, Discussion, Recommendations ... FDR
Fact-Finding Bodies ... FFB
Fact Magazine [*A publication*] ... Fact Mag
Facteur Respiratoire Equilibre [*Ingredient in a cosmetic by Chanel*] ... FRE
Factor ... FAC
Factor ... FTR
Factor Analysis Chart Technique ... FACT
Factor [*Max*] **& Co.** [*NYSE symbol*] [*Delisted*] ... FAC
Factor of Safety ... FS
Factor/Test Procedure ... FTP
Factorial Moment Generating Function [*Statistics*] ... FMGF
Factory ... FAC
Factory ... Facty
Factory ... FCT
Factory ... FCTY
Factory Acceptance Checkout ... FACO
Factory Acceptance Test ... FAT
Factory Acceptance Test Procedure ... FATP
Factory Acceptance Test Specification ... FATS
Factory Aerospace Ground Equipment ... FAGE
Factory Assembly and Checkout ... FACO
Factory Automatic Checkout Equipment ... FACE
Factory Automation Systems Technology [*British*] ... FAST
Factory Damaged [*Slang*] ... FD'd
Factory Equipment Transfer Order ... FETO
Factory Ground Equipment ... FGE
Factory and Industrial Management [*A publication*] ... Factory and Ind Management
Factory-Installed Maintenance Automatic Test Equipment ... FIMATE
Factory Insurance Association [*Later, Industrial Risk Insurers*] ... FIA
Factory Management and Maintenance [*A publication*] ... Factory Mgt
Factory Manual ... FM
Factory Marriage Test ... FMT
Factory Materials Association ... FMA
Factory Mutual Engineering and Research ... FMER
Factory Mutual System [*Formerly, AFMFIC*] [*Group of four insurance companies and an engineering organization*] ... FM
Factory Mutual System [*Formerly, AFMFIC*] [*Group of four insurance companies and an engineering organization*] ... FMS
Factory Mutuals' Combined Fire-Boiler Policy [*Insurance*] ... FMB
Factory Order ... FO
Factory Pass ... FP
Factory and Plant [*A publication*] ... Fact Plant
Factory Serial Number ... FSN
Factory Space Allocation Plan ... FSAP
Factory Special Test Equipment ... FSTE
Factory Support Equipment ... FSE
Factory Test ... FT
Factory Test Equipment ... FTE
Factory Test Equipment Manufacturing ... FTEM
Factory Test Set ... FTS
Factory Training School ... FTS
Factory Training Unit ... FTU
Factory Work Group ... FWG
Facts of Bayonne Publishing Co., Bayonne, NJ [*Library symbol*] ... NjBaF
Facts on File [*A publication*] ... F on F
Facts on File [*Inc.*] ... FOF
Facts about Film Finland [*A publication*] ... Facts Finl
[*The*] **Facts of Life** [*NBC television program*] ... FOL
Factual Compiler ... FACT
Factum Similis [*Facsimile*] [*Latin*] ... FAC
Facture [*Invoice*] [*French*] ... FRE
Faculdade de Ciencias Agrarias do Para Boletim [*A publication*] ... Fac Cienc Agrar Para Bol
Faculdade de Filosofia e Letras [*Brazil*] ... FAFILE
Facultad de Agronomia, Balcarce [*Argentina*] ... FAB
Facultad de Ciencias Agrarias. Universidad Austral de Chile. Boletin [*A publication*] ... Fac Cienc Agrar Univ Austral Chile Bol
Facultad Latinoamericana de Ciencias Sociales [*Santiago, Chile*] ... FLACSO
Facultad de Odontologia [*A publication*] ... FO
Faculte de Medecine Veterinaire de l'Universite de Montreal, St.-Hyacinthe, PQ, Canada [*Library symbol*] ... CaQStHV
Faculty ... FAC
Faculty Exchange Center ... FEC
Faculty for Human Rights in El Salvador and Central America ... FACHRES-CA
Faculty of Law Review [*A publication*] ... Fac L Rev
Faculty Rating ... FR
Faculty Research Participation [*National Science Foundation program*] ... FRP
Faculty of Surgeons of England ... FSE
Fada Ngourma [*Upper Volta*] [*Airport symbol*] ... FNG
FADAC Automatic Test Analysis Language [*Data processing*] ... FATAL
Fade In [*Films, television, etc.*] ... FI
Fade In, Fade Out [*Films, television, etc.*] ... FIFO
Fade Out [*Films, television, etc.*] ... FO
Faded Prior to Interception [*RADAR*] ... FPI
Faellesforeningen for Danmarks Brugsforeninger [*Denmark*] ... FDB
Faellesraadet for Danske Tjenestemands-og Funktionaerorganisationer [*Federation of Civil Servants' and Salaried Employees' Organizations*] [*Denmark*] ... FTF
Faellesrepraesentationen for Danske Arbejdsleder-og Tekniske Funktinaerforeninger [*Council of Danish Supervisors' and Technical Employees' Associations*] ... FAF
Faenza [*Italy*] [*Seismograph station code, US Geological Survey*] [*Closed*] ... FAE
Faerie Queene [*A publication*] ... FQ
Faeroe Islands [*MARC country of publication code*] [*Library of Congress*] ... fa
Faeroe Islands [*MARC geographic area code*] [*Library of Congress*] ... infa---

Fafco, Inc. [*NASDAQ symbol*] ... FAFO
Fafnir Bearing Co. [*NYSE symbol*] [*Delisted*] ... FAF
Fagotto [*Bassoon*] ... FAG
Fahrdienstregelement [*Traffic Service Regulations*] [*German*] ... FDR
Fahrenheit ... F
Fahrenheit ... FAH
Fahrenheit ... FAHR
Fahrenheit Dry Bulb ... FDB
Fahrenheit Wet Bulb ... FWB
Fail As-Is [*Nuclear energy*] ... FAI
Fail Closed [*Nuclear energy*] ... FC
Fail Open [*Nuclear energy*] ... FO
Fail Operation [*NASA*] ... FO
Fail-Operational, Fail-Operational, Fail-Safe ... FO/FO/FS
Fail-Operational, Fail-Safe ... FO/FS
Fail-Passive Autoland System [*Aviation*] ... FPAS
Fail in Place [*Nuclear energy*] ... FI
Fail-Safe ... FS
Fail Sheer Ultimate ... FSU
Fail to Synchronize ... FS
Fail Tension Ultimate ... FTU
Failed Element Detection and Location [*In nuclear power reactors*] ... FEDAL
Failed Hardover ... FHO
Failed Item ... F/I
Fails to Break ... FTB
Fails to Drain ... FTD
Fails to Reproduce ... FTR
Failure ... F
Failure ... FAIL
Failure ... FLR
Failure Analysis ... FA
Failure Analysis Coordinator ... FAC
Failure Analysis Laboratory ... FAL
Failure Analysis Report ... FAR
Failure Analysis Report Summary [*Bell System*] ... FARS
Failure Analysis Section ... FAS
Failure Analysis by Statistical Techniques [*Data processing code*] ... FAST
Failure to Appear [*Court case*] ... FTA
Failure Cause Data Report ... FCDR
Failure and Consumption Data ... F & CD
Failure and Consumption Data Form ... FCDF
Failure and Consumption Data Inspection Report ... F & CD/IR
Failure and Consumption Inspector's Report ... F-CIR
Failure Consumption Sheets ... FCS
Failure Correction Panel ... FCP
Failure Count ... FC
Failure Definitions/Scoring Criteria ... FD/SC
Failure Density Function ... FDF
Failure Detection and Isolation ... FDI
Failure Diagnostic Team [*Aerospace*] ... FDT
Failure and Discrepancy Reporting ... F & DR
Failure Effect Analysis ... FEA
Failure Effects Summary List ... FESL
Failure Equation ... FE
Failure Equation ... FEQ
Failure Experience Data Bank [*GIDEP*] ... FEDB
Failure Factor ... FF
Failure Indicating Fuse ... FIF
Failure Indication Modules ... FIM
Failure Investigation Action Report [*NASA*] ... FIAR
Failure and Malfunction Report [*NASA*] ... FMR
Failure Mode Analysis ... FMA
Failure Mode and Effects ... FME
Failure Mode and Effects Analysis ... FMEA
Failure Mode, Effects, and Criticality Analyses ... FMECA
Failure Mode Indicator ... FMI
Failure Notification Sheet ... FNS
Failure Notification Telex ... FNT
Failure to Obtain Action ... FOA
Failure to Pay [*IRS*] ... FTP
Failure Probability Analysis ... FPA
Failure/Problem Report ... FPR
Failure Rate ... FR
Failure Rate Data ... FRD
Failure Rate Data Bank [*GIDEP*] ... FRDB
Failure Rate Data Program [*Navy*] ... FARADA
Failure and Rejection Report ... FARR
Failure and Rejection Report ... FRR
Failure Report ... FR
Failure Reporting Review ... FRR
Failure Review Board [*NASA*] ... FRB
Failure to Thrive [*Syndrome*] [*Medicine*] ... FTT
Failure or Unsatisfactory Report ... FUR
Failure or Unsatisfactory Report System ... FURS
Failure and Usage Data Report ... FUDR
Failure Warning and Analysis System ... FWAS
Faim-Developpement [*A publication*] ... Faim-Develop
Faint ... FT
Faipari Kutatasok [*A publication*] ... Faip Kutatas
Fair ... F
Fair Access to Insurance Requirements [*Government insurance program*] ... FAIR
Fair Average Quality ... FAQ
Fair Bluff, NC [*Radio station call letters*] ... WWKO
Fair Budget Action Campaign ... FBAC
Fair Campaign Practices Committee ... FCPC
Fair Copy ... FCO
Fair Credit Reporting Act ... FCRA
Fair Educational Practice Act [*New York, New Jersey, Massachusetts*] ... FEPA
Fair Employment Board [*of Civil Service Commission*] [*Abolished, 1955*] ... FEB
Fair Employment Practice ... FEP
Fair Employment Practices Act ... FEPA
Fair Employment Practices Code ... FEPC
Fair Employment Practices Committee [*or Commission*] ... FEPC
Fair, Fat, Fertile, and Forty [*Medical slang describing women most susceptible to gallbladder attacks*] ... 4F
Fair Housing Assistance Program [*HUD*] ... FHAP
Fair Housing, Incorporated ... FHI
Fair and Impartial Random Selection [*System*] [*Military draft*] ... FAIR
Fair International Trade Employment Committee ... FITE
Fair Isle [*Scotland*] [*Airport symbol*] ... FIE
Fair Labor Standards Act [*1938*] ... FLSA
Fair Lanes, Inc. [*NASDAQ symbol*] ... FAIR
Fair Lawn Free Public Library, Fair Lawn, NJ [*Library symbol*] ... NjF
Fair Market Value ... FMV
Fair Organ Preservation Society ... FOPS
Fair Packaging and Labeling Act ... FPLA
Fair Play [*Signature used on warning letters sent by George Metesky, the "Mad Bomber" of New York City in 1940's and 1950's*] ... FP
Fair and Simple Tax [*Type of flat tax proposed by Rep. Jack Kemp and Sen. Bob Kasten*] ... FAST
Fair Skiing Conditions ... F
Fair Wear and Tear ... FWT
Fair Weather Current ... FWC
Fairbanks [*Alaska*] [*Airport symbol*] ... FAI
Fairbanks [*Alaska*] [*Seismograph station code, US Geological Survey*] [*Closed*] ... FBK
Fairbanks Air Service [*Alaska*] ... FAS
Fairbanks Air Service [*Air carrier designation symbol*] ... FASX
Fairbanks, AK [*Location identifier*] [*FAA*] ... CNA
Fairbanks, AK [*Location identifier*] [*FAA*] ... CUN
Fairbanks, AK [*Location identifier*] [*FAA*] ... EAF
Fairbanks, AK [*Television station call letters*] ... KATN
Fairbanks, AK [*Radio station call letters*] ... KAYY
Fairbanks, AK [*Radio station call letters*] ... KCBF
Fairbanks, AK [*Radio station call letters*] ... KFAR
Fairbanks, AK [*Radio station call letters*] ... KGHX
Fairbanks, AK [*Radio station call letters*] ... KIAK
Fairbanks, AK [*Radio station call letters*] ... KQRZ
Fairbanks, AK [*Television station call letters*] ... KTTU-TV
Fairbanks, AK [*Television station call letters*] ... KTVF
Fairbanks, AK [*Radio station call letters*] ... KUAC
Fairbanks, AK [*Television station call letters*] ... KUAC-TV
Fairbanks, AK [*Location identifier*] [*FAA*] ... PII
Fairbanks [*Alaska*] **Metro Field** [*Airport symbol*] [*Obsolete*] ... MTX
Fairbanks, Morse, & Co. [*Later, COT*] [*NYSE symbol*] [*Delisted*] ... FKM
Fairbanks Museum of Natural Science, St. Johnsbury, VT [*Library symbol*] ... VtStjF
Fairbanks North Star Borough Library, Fairbanks, AK [*Library symbol*] ... AkF
Fairbanks Rhyme Test [*Hearing*] ... FRT
Fairbanks Whitney Corp. [*Delisted; later, Colt Industries, Inc.*] [*NYSE symbol*] [*Wall Street slang name: "Fuzzy Wuzzy"*] ... FW
Fairbourne Miniature Railway [*Wales*] ... FMR
Fairbury Junior College [*Nebraska*] ... FJC
Fairbury, NE [*Radio station call letters*] ... KCIE
Fairbury, NE [*Radio station call letters*] ... KGMT
Fairbury Public Library, Fairbury, NE [*Library symbol*] ... NbFb
Fairchild Air Force Base [*Washington*] ... FAFB
Fairchild Aircraft ... FA
Fairchild Automatic Intercept and Response System ... FAIRS
Fairchild Camera & Instrument Corp. [*NYSE symbol*] [*Delisted*] ... FCI
Fairchild Camera & Instrument Corporation ... FCIC
Fairchild Engine & Airplane Corporation ... FEAC
Fairchild-Hiller Corporation [*Later, Fairchild Industries, Inc.*] ... FHC
Fairchild-Hiller Corp. [*Later, Fairchild Industries, Inc.*], **Republic Aviation Division, Farmingdale, NY** [*Library symbol*] ... NFarF
Fairchild Industries, Inc. [*NYSE symbol*] ... FEN
Fairchild Semiconductor ... FCS
Fairchild Space and Defense System, Syosset, NY [*Library symbol*] ... NSyoF
Faire Suivre [*Please Forward*] [*French*] ... FS
Fairey Air Surveys Ltd. [*Great Britain*] [*ICAO designator*] ... FY
Fairfax County Public Library, Fairfax, VA [*Library symbol*] ... ViF
Fairfax Hall Junior College, Waynesboro, VA [*Library symbol*] ... ViWbF
Fairfax, VA [*Radio station call letters*] ... WEEL
Fairfax, VA [*Television station call letters*] ... WNVC
Fairfield, AL [*Radio station call letters*] ... WJLD

Fairfield Bay, AR [*Radio station call letters*] ... KFFB
Fairfield, CA [*Location identifier*] [*FAA*] ... SUU
Fairfield, CA [*Location identifier*] [*FAA*] ... TXV
Fairfield Communities, Incorporated [*American Stock Exchange symbol*] ... FCI
Fairfield County District Library, Lancaster, OH [*OCLC symbol*] ... OFA
Fairfield County District Library, Lancaster, OH [*Library symbol*] ... OLanF
Fairfield, CT [*Radio station call letters*] ... WSHU
Fairfield, CT [*Radio station call letters*] ... WVOF
Fairfield Free Public Library, Fairfield, NJ [*Library symbol*] ... NjFf
Fairfield, IA [*Radio station call letters*] ... KBCT
Fairfield, IA [*Radio station call letters*] ... KMCD
Fairfield, IL [*Radio station call letters*] ... WFIW
Fairfield, IL [*Radio station call letters*] ... WFIW-FM
Fairfield-Noble Corp. [*NASDAQ symbol*] ... FARF
Fairfield-Noble Corp. [*American Stock Exchange symbol*] [*Delisted*] ... FFN
Fairfield, OH [*Radio station call letters*] ... WCNW
Fairfield, OH [*Radio station call letters*] ... WLLT
Fairfield Public Library, Fairfield, CT [*Library symbol*] ... CtFa
Fairfield Public Library, Fairfield, IA [*Library symbol*] ... IaFair
Fairfield Public Library, Supervisor of Technical Services, Fairfield, CT [*OCLC symbol*] ... FRP
Fairfield, TX [*Radio station call letters*] ... KNES
Fairfield University, Fairfield, CT [*Library symbol*] ... CtFaU
Fairfield University, Fairfield, CT [*OCLC symbol*] ... FAU
Fairflight (Charters) Ltd. [*ICAO designator*] ... FC
Fairgrove Township Library, Fairgrove, MI [*Library symbol*] ... MiFg
Fairhope, AK [*Radio station call letters*] ... WZEW
Fairhope, AL [*Radio station call letters*] ... WABF
Fairing ... FAIR
Fairlane Club of America ... FCA
Fairleigh Dickinson University [*New Jersey*] ... FDU
Fairleigh Dickinson University, Madison, NJ [*Library symbol*] ... NjMF
Fairleigh Dickinson University, Rutherford, NJ [*OCLC symbol*] ... FDR
Fairleigh Dickinson University, Rutherford, NJ [*Library symbol*] ... NjRuF
Fairleigh Dickinson University, Teaneck, NJ [*OCLC symbol*] ... FDU
Fairleigh Dickinson University, Teaneck, NJ [*Library symbol*] ... NjTeaF
Fairleigh Dickinson University, Wayne, NJ [*Library symbol*] ... NjWF
Fairly Important Person ... FIP
Fairly Reliable Source of Intelligence Information ... C
Fairmont [*Minnesota*] [*Airport symbol*] ... FRM
Fairmont [*Washington*] [*Seismograph station code, US Geological Survey*] ... FTW
Fairmont Financial [*NASDAQ symbol*] ... FFIC
Fairmont Foods Co. [*NYSE symbol*] [*Delisted*] ... FMF
Fairmont, MN [*Location identifier*] [*FAA*] ... FRM
Fairmont, MN [*Radio station call letters*] ... KFMC
Fairmont, MN [*Radio station call letters*] ... KSUM
Fairmont, NC [*Radio station call letters*] ... WFMO
Fairmont State College [*West Virginia*] ... FSC
Fairmont State College, Fairmont, WV [*OCLC symbol*] ... WVF
Fairmont State College, Fairmont, WV [*Library symbol*] ... WvFS
Fairmont, WV [*Radio station call letters*] ... WFGM
Fairmont, WV [*Radio station call letters*] ... WMMN
Fairmont, WV [*Radio station call letters*] ... WTCS
Fairmount Chemical Co., Inc. [*American Stock Exchange symbol*] ... FMT
Fairmount, NC [*Radio station call letters*] ... WZYZ
Fairport High School Library, Fairport, NY [*OCLC symbol*] ... RWF
Fairport, Painesville, & Eastern Railway Co. [*AAR code*] ... FPE
Fairview College, Fairview, AB, Canada [*Library symbol*] ... CaAFAC
Fairview Hospital, Minneapolis, MN [*Library symbol*] ... MnMF
Fairview Park [*Nevada*] [*Seismograph station code, US Geological Survey*] [*Closed*] ... FPN
Fairview Park Regional Library, Fairview Park, OH [*Library symbol*] ... OFavp
Fairview State Hospital, Waymart, PA [*OCLC symbol*] ... PHF
Fairview, TN [*Radio station call letters*] ... WBLP
Fairwater Planes ... FWPLN
Fairway, KS [*Radio station call letters*] ... KCNW
Fairways Corp. [*Air carrier designation symbol*] ... FAIX
Fairways Corp. [*Washington, DC*] [*FAA designator*] ... FWY
Fairy Investigation Society ... FIS
Fairy Tale-Folklore Study Unit [*American Topical Association*] ... FTFSU
Faisalabad [*Pakistan*] [*Airport symbol*] ... LYP
Faith Baptist Bible College, Ankeny, IA [*Library symbol*] ... IaAnkFB
Faith for the Family [*A publication*] ... FFF
Faith and Form [*A publication*] ... FF
Faith-Man-Nature [*from F/M/N Papers, National Council of Churches*] ... F/M/N
Faith Theological Seminary ... FTS
Faithful Performance ... FP
Faithfully ... FFLY
Faithfully ... FFY
Fajardo [*Puerto Rico*] [*Airport symbol*] ... FAJ
Fajardo, PR [*Radio station call letters*] ... WDOY-FM
Fajardo, PR [*Radio station call letters*] ... WMDD
Fajardo, PR [*Television station call letters*] ... WMTJ
Fajardo, PR [*Television station call letters*] ... WSTE
Fak-Fak [*Indonesia*] [*Airport symbol*] ... FKQ
Fakarava [*French Polynesia*] [*Airport symbol*] ... FAV
Faker Track ... FK
Faktory Vneshnykh Sred Znachenie Zdorov'ya Naseleniya Respublikanskii Mezhvedomstvennyi Sbornik [*A publication*] ... Fakt Vneshn Sred Znach Zdor Nasel Resp Mezhved Sb
Falange Socialista Boliviana [*Bolivian Socialist Falange*] ... FSB
Falciparum Uganda - Palo Alto [*Plasmodium strain causing malaria*] ... FUP
Falcon Airways, Incorporated [*Addison, TX*] [*FAA designator*] ... FAI
Falcon Club of America ... FCA
Falcon Improvement Program ... FIP
Falcon Jet Centre Ltd. [*Great Britain*] [*ICAO designator*] ... FN
Falcon Launching Saber System ... FLSS
Falcon Oil & Gas Co. [*NASDAQ symbol*] ... FLOG
Falcon Products, Inc. [*NASDAQ symbol*] ... FLCP
Falcon Research & Development, Inc., Buffalo, NY [*Library symbol*] ... NBuF
Falcon/Sciences, Inc. [*NASDAQ symbol*] ... FSFS
Falcon Seaboard, Inc. [*NYSE symbol*] [*Delisted*] ... FSD
Falconbridge Nickel Mines Ltd. [*NASDAQ symbol*] ... FALCF
Falconbridge Nickel Mines Ltd., Information Centre, Toronto, ON, Canada [*Library symbol*] ... CaOTFN
Falconbridge Nickel Mines Ltd., Metallurgical Laboratory, Thornhill, ON, Canada [*Library symbol*] ... CaOThorF
Falconbridge Nickel Mines Ltd., Metallurgical Research Library, Falconbridge, ON, Canada [*Library symbol*] ... CaOFaF
Falfurrias, TX [*Location identifier*] [*FAA*] ... BKS
Falfurrias, TX [*Radio station call letters*] ... KPSO
Falfurrias, TX [*Radio station call letters*] ... KPSO-FM
Falkland Islands ... FI
Falkland Islands [*MARC country of publication code*] [*Library of Congress*] ... fk
Falkland Islands [*Three-letter standard code*] ... FLK
Falkland Islands [*MARC geographic area code*] [*Library of Congress*] ... lsfk---
Falkland Islands [*Two-letter standard code*] ... FK
Falkland Islands Dependencies Survey. Scientific Reports [*A publication*] ... Falkl Isl Depend Surv Sci Rep
Falkland Islands Philatelic Study Group [*of the American Philatelic Society*] ... FIPSG
Fall ... FL
Fall [*A publication*] ... FL
Fall Brook, CA [*Radio station call letters*] ... KAVO
Fall Exercise [*Military*] ... FALLEX
Fall Joint Computer Conference ... FJCC
Fall Reaction Spheres ... FRS
Fall River [*Massachusetts*] [*Seismograph station code, US Geological Survey*] ... FLR
Fall River, MA [*Location identifier*] [*FAA*] ... FLR
Fall River, MA [*Radio station call letters*] ... WALE
Fall River, MA [*Radio station call letters*] ... WSAR
Fall River Public Library, Fall River, MA [*Library symbol*] ... MF
Fall of Shot ... FOS
Fallen Building Clause ... FBC
Falling ... FLG
Falling Film Evaporation ... FFE
Falling Mass Hazard ... FMH
Falling to Pieces [*Slang*] ... FTP
Falling Sphere Trajectory Measurement ... FASTRAM
Fallon, NV [*Location identifier*] [*FAA*] ... FLX
Fallon, NV [*Radio station call letters*] ... KVLV
Fallon, NV [*Radio station call letters*] ... KVLV-FM
Fallout Forecast Data [*Civil Defense*] ... DF
Fallout Intensity Detector Oscillator ... FIDO
Fallout Monitoring Station [*Civil Defense*] ... FMS
Fallout Protection in Houses ... FPHS
Fallout Shelter Analysis [*or Analyst*] [*Civil Defense*] ... FSA
Fallout Studies Branch [*AEC*] ... FSB
Falls ... FLS
Falls Church, VA [*Radio station call letters*] ... WFAX
Falls City, NE [*Location identifier*] [*FAA*] ... FNB
Falls City, NE [*Radio station call letters*] ... KTNC
Falls City, NE [*Radio station call letters*] ... KTNC-FM
Falls City Press, Louisville, KY [*Library symbol*] ... FCP
Falls City Public Library, Falls City, OR [*Library symbol*] ... OrFc
Fallschirm [*Parachute*] [*German military*] ... FS
Fallschirmjaeger-Gewehr [*Parachutist's rifle*] [*German military - World War II*] ... FG
Fallschirmtruppen [*Parachute Troops*] [*German military*] ... FSTR
Falmouth, KY [*Radio station call letters*] ... WIOK
Falmouth, MA [*Location identifier*] [*FAA*] ... FMH
Falmouth, MA [*Radio station call letters*] ... WCIB
Falmouth Public Library, Falmouth, MA [*Library symbol*] ... MFal
Falsa Lectio [*False Reading, in a text*] [*Latin*] ... FL
False ... F
False [*FBI standardized term*] ... FLS
False Alarm Rate ... FAR
False Calves [*Padding worn under tights by actors, to improve shape of their legs*] ... FC's
False Cape [*NASA*] ... FC
False Entries in Records of Interstate Carriers [*FBI standardized term*] ... FERIC
False Negative [*Medicine*] ... FNEG
False Pass [*Alaska*] [*Airport symbol*] ... KFP
False Pretenses ... FP

False Target Can [*Navy*] FTC
Falsely Claiming [*US*] **Citizenship** FCC
Falsetto FALSET
Falstaff Brewing Corp. [*NASDAQ symbol*] FALB
Falwell Aviation, Inc. [*Lynchburg, VA*] [*FAA designator*] FAW
Familia Nova [*New Family*] [*Biology*] fam nov
Familial Dysautonomia [*Medicine*] FD
Familial Erythrophagocytic Lymphohistocytosis [*Medicine*] FEL
Familial Exudative Vitreoretinopathy [*Ophthalmology*] FEV
Familial Hypercholesteremia [*or Hypercholesterolemia*] [*Medicine*] FH
Familial Hypophosphatemic Rickets FHR
Familial Mediterranean Fever FMF
Familian Corporation [*NASDAQ symbol*] FAMC
Familiar FAM
Familiarization Exercise [*Military*] FAMEX
Familiarization Flight [*Aviation*] FFLT
Families in Action FIA
Families Adopting Children Everywhere FACE
Families Against Meat in New England [*Worcester, Massachusetts, group protesting high cost of food, 1973*] FAMINE
Families Anonymous FA
Families of Resisters for Amnesty FORA
Famille et Developpement [*A publication*] Fam Dev
Family F
Family FAM
Family FMLY
Family Adjustment Test [*Psychology*] FAT
Family Agency FA
Family Allowance [*Navy*] FA
Family Allowance, Class A [*Navy*] FAA
Family Allowance, Class A and B [*Navy*] FAAB
Family Allowance, Class B [*Navy*] FAB
Family America [*An association*] FA
Family of the Americas Foundation FAF
Family of Army Aircraft System FAAS
Family of Army Vehicles Study FAVS
Family Assessment Tool [*Kit*] [*Medicine*] FAT
Family Assistance Plan [*or Program*] [*Proposed during Nixon administration*] FAP
Family Auto Policy [*Insurance*] FAP
Family Camping Federation [*Later, FCFA*] FCF
Family Camping Federation of America [*Formerly, FCF*] [*Defunct*] FCFA
Family Circle [*A publication*] FC
Family Communion Crusade [*Defunct*] FCC
Family and Community Health [*A publication*] Fam Community Health
Family Coordinator [*A publication*] FADOA
Family Coordinator [*A publication*] Fam Coord
Family Crisis Intervention Unit [*New York Police Department*] FCIU
Family Dollar Stores, Inc. [*NYSE symbol*] FDO
Family Economics Research Group [*Department of Agriculture*] FERG
Family Economics Review [*A publication*] Fam Ec Rev
Family Education and Information Council of the United States FEICUS
Family Educational Rights and Privacy Act [*1974*] FERPA
Family Entertainment Centers [*NASDAQ symbol*] FMLY
Family Expenditure Survey [*Department of Employment*] [*British*] FES
Family of Faith Foundation FFF
Family Farm Movement FFM
Family Finance Corp. [*NYSE symbol*] [*Delisted*] FAM
Family Financial Statement FFS
Family Fitness Council FFC
Family Functioning Index FFI
Family Group Number FGN
Family Hands Off [*Indicates that a certain dish is not to be eaten by members of the family at a meal where guests are present*] FHO
Family Health [*A publication*] Fam Health
Family Health [*A publication*] Family Hlth
Family Health Bulletin [*A publication*] FHLBA
Family Health Insurance Plan FHIP
Family Health Systems [*NASDAQ symbol*] FHSY
Family History [*Medicine*] FH
Family Hold Back [*Indicates family should take small portions at a meal where guests are present*] FHB
Family Hold Off [*Indicates that a certain dish is not to be eaten by members of the family at a meal where guests are present*] FHO
Family Housing [*Army*] FHSG
Family Housing Division [*Army*] FHD
Family Housing Management Account [*Army*] FHMA
Family Income Security Plan FISP
Family Income Supplement [*British*] FIS
Family Involvement Process [*Used to encourage parent support in the education of their handicapped child*] FIP
Family Law Council FLC
Family Law Quarterly [*A publication*] Family LQ
Family Law Quarterly [*A publication*] Fam Law Q
Family Liaison Action Group [*An organization of the families of American hostages in Iran, 1980*] FLAG
Family Life Bureau [*Later, Family Life Division, United States Catholic Conference*] FLB
Family Life Income Patterns [*Economics simulation game*] FLIP
Family Life and Population Program/Church World Service FLPP/CWS
Family Location and Legal Service [*Formerly, FLS*] FLLS
Family Location Service [*Later, FLLS*] FLS
Family Manned Planetary Mission FMPM
Family Mediation Association FMA
Family Medical Treatment Centers of America [*NASDAQ symbol*] FAMM
Family of Military Engineer Construction Equipment FAMECE
Family of Military Engineer Construction Equipment/Universal Engineer Tractor FAMECE/UET
Family Motor Coach Association FMCA
Family Nurse Practitioner FNP
Family Physician [*A publication*] Fam Physician
Family Pitch In [*Indicates family may eat freely of a certain dish at a meal where guests are present*] FPI
Family Planning FP
Family Planning Association FPA
Family Planning Clinic [*British*] FPC
Family Planning Digest [*A publication*] Family Plann Digest
Family Planning Evaluation Branch [*Public Health Service*] FPEB
Family Planning Evaluation Division [*HEW*] FPED
Family Planning and Information Service FPIS
Family Planning International Assistance FPIA
Family Planning (London) [*A publication*] Fam Plann (Lond)
Family Planning Perspectives [*A publication*] Fam Plann Perspect
Family Planning Perspectives [*A publication*] Fam Plan Pe
Family Planning Resume [*A publication*] Fam Plann Resume
Family Planning Training Institute, Baltimore, MD [*Library symbol*] MdBFamP
Family Practice [*or Practioner*] FP
Family Practitioner Committee [*British*] FPC
Family Process [*A publication*] Fam Proc
Family Process [*A publication*] Fam Process
Family Protection League of USA [*Defunct*] FPL
Family Record Plan, Inc. [*American Stock Exchange symbol*] [*Delisted*] FRP
Family Relations [*A publication*] Fam Relat
Family Relations Indicator [*Psychology*] FRI
Family Relations Test [*Psychology*] FRT
Family Resource and Referral Center [*National Council on Family Relations*] [*Information service*] FR & RC
Family Resources Coalition FRC
Family Room [*Real estate*] FR
Family Rosary Crusade FRC
Family of Scatterable Mines [*Army*] FASCAM
Family Security Service FSS
Family Separation Allowance [*Military*] FSA
Family Service Association of America FSAA
Family Service Unit [*Medicine*] [*British*] FSU
Family Services and Assistance Officer FSAO
Family Services Center [*Military*] FSC
Family Services Program [*Military*] FSP
Family Showtime Theatre [*NASDAQ symbol*] EATS
Family of Special Weapons Atomic Contractors FOSWAC
Family Stop Eating [*A table signal at a meal where guests are present*] FSE
Family Strike Light [*Indicates family should take small portions at a meal where guests are present*] FSL
Family Suffering Index [*Economic measurement based on unemployment rate, plus costs of food, fuel, and housing*] FSI
Family of Systems Studies [*Military*] FOSS
Family Therapy Network FTN
Family Viewing Time [*Television*] FVT
Family of Weapons FOW
Famous Artists Schools [*Later, FAS International, Inc.*] FAS
Famous Fantastic Mysteries [*A publication*] FFM
Famous Personalities' Business Card Collectors of America FPBCCA
Famous Sayings [*Psychological testing*] FS
Famous Science Fiction [*A publication*] FMF
Fan Association of North America FANA
Fan Beam Scatterometer FBS
Fan Circle International FCI
Fan Club Associates [*Later, IFCA*] FCA
Fan Douche [*Medicine*] FD
Fan In FNI
Fan Inlet Variable Guide Vanes FIVGV
Fan Magazine [*Generic term for a publication of interest to science fiction fans*] FANZINE
Fan Marker [*Aviation*] FM
Fan Marker Approach [*Aviation*] FMAP
Fan Out FNO
Fan Out FO
Fan Pressure Ratio [*Aviation*] FPR
Fan Thrust Reverser FTR
Fan Turbine Inlet Temperature FTIT
Fan-Type Marker FTM
Fanciful Tales of Time and Space [*A publication*] FTT
Fanconi's Anemia [*Medicine*] FA
Fandom Is a Way of Life [*Science-fiction-fan slogan*] FIAWOL
Fane [*Papua New Guinea*] [*Airport symbol*] FNE
Fanfare [*A publication*] FF
Fanfulla della Domenica [*A publication*] FD
Fang [*MARC language code*] [*Library of Congress*] fan
Fangatau [*French Polynesia*] [*Airport symbol*] FGU

Fanned Beam Antenna ... FBA
Fannie Smith School, Bridgeport, CT [*Library symbol*] ... CtBFAST
Fanning Island [*Line Islands*] [*Seismograph station code, US Geological Survey*] [*Closed*] ... FAN
Fanny Farmer Candy Shops, Inc. [*American Stock Exchange symbol*] ... FFY
Fans Against the Strike ... FAST
Fanshawe College of Applied Arts and Technology, London, ON, Canada [*Library symbol*] ... CaOLFC
Fansteel, Inc. [*NYSE symbol*] [*Delisted*] ... FNL
Fansteel, Incorporated [*NASDAQ symbol*] ... FNLI
Fantastic Adventures [*A publication*] ... FA
Fantastic Adventures [*1939-1953*] [*A publication*] ... FAD
Fantastic Adventures Yearbook [*A publication*] ... FAY
Fantastic Novels [*A publication*] ... FN
Fantastic Novels Magazine [*A publication*] ... FNM
Fantastic Science Fiction [*A publication*] ... FASF
Fantastic Stories [*A publication*] ... FAS
Fantastic Story Magazine [*A publication*] ... FSM
Fantastic Story Quarterly [*A publication*] ... FSQ
Fantastic Universe Science Fiction [*A publication*] ... FAU
Fantasy [*A publication*] ... Fant
Fantasy Amateur Press Association ... FAPA
Fantasy Association ... FA
Fantasy Book [*A publication*] ... FB
Fantasy Book [*A publication*] ... FBK
Fantasy Fiction [*A publication*] ... FAN
Fantasy Fiction [*A publication*] ... FanF
Fantasy: The Magazine of Science Fiction [*A publication*] ... Fans
Fantasy and Science Fiction [*A publication*] ... Fant & Sci Fict
Fantasy and Science Fiction [*A publication*] ... F & SF
Fantasy Stories [*A publication*] ... FanS
Fantasy Stories [*A publication*] ... FFN
FAO [*Food and Agriculture Organization of the United Nations*] **Agricultural Development Papers** [*A publication*] ... FAO Agric Dev Pap
FAO [*Food and Agriculture Organization of the United Nations*] **Agricultural Studies** [*A publication*] ... FAO Agric Stud
FAO [*Food and Agriculture Organization of the United Nations*] **Association of Professional Staff** ... FAO/APS
FAO [*Food and Agriculture Organization of the United Nations*] **Development Program** [*A publication*] ... FAO Dev Program
FAO [*Food and Agriculture Organization of the United Nations*] **Documentation** [*A publication*] ... FAO Doc
FAO [*Food and Agriculture Organization of the United Nations*] **Fisheries Biology Synopsis** [*A publication*] ... FAO Fish Biol Synop
FAO [*Food and Agriculture Organization of the United Nations*] **Fisheries Biology Technical Paper** [*A publication*] ... FAO Fish Biol Tech Pap
FAO [*Food and Agriculture Organization of the United Nations*] **Fisheries Circular** [*A publication*] ... FAO Fish Circ
FAO [*Food and Agriculture Organization of the United Nations*] **Fisheries Reports** [*A publication*] ... FAO Fish Rep
FAO [*Food and Agriculture Organization of the United Nations*] **Fisheries Synopsis** [*A publication*] ... FAO Fish Synop
FAO [*Food and Agriculture Organization of the United Nations*] **Fisheries Technical Paper** [*A publication*] ... FAO Fish Tech Pap
FAO [*Food and Agriculture Organization of the United Nations*] **Food and Nutrition Paper** [*A publication*] ... FAO Food Nutr Pap
FAO [*Food and Agriculture Organization of the United Nations*] **Food and Nutrition Series** [*A publication*] ... FAO Food Nutr Ser
FAO [*Food and Agriculture Organization of the United Nations*] **Forestry Development Papers** [*A publication*] ... FAO For Developm Pap
FAO [*Food and Agriculture Organization of the United Nations*] **Forestry and Forest Products Studies** [*A publication*] ... FAO For & For Prod Stud
FAO [*Food and Agriculture Organization of the United Nations*] **General Fisheries Council for the Mediterranean. Studies and Reviews** [*A publication*] ... FAO Gen Fish Counc Mediterr Stud Rev
FAO [*Food and Agriculture Organization of the United Nations*] **Monthly Bulletin of Agricultural Economics and Statistics** [*A publication*] ... FAO Mo Bul Ag Econ & Stat
FAO [*Food and Agriculture Organization of the United Nations*] **Nutrition Meetings. Report Series** [*A publication*] ... FAO Nutr Meet Rep Ser
FAO [*Food and Agriculture Organization of the United Nations*] **Nutritional Studies** [*A publication*] ... FAO Nutr Stud
FAO [*Food and Agriculture Organization of the United Nations*] **Pasture and Fodder Crop Studies** [*A publication*] ... FAO Pasture Fodder Crop Stud
FAO [*Food and Agriculture Organization of the United Nations*] **Plant Protection Bulletin** [*A publication*] ... FAO Plant
FAO [*Food and Agriculture Organization of the United Nations*] **Plant Protection Bulletin** [*A publication*] ... FAO Plant Prot Bull
FAO [*Food and Agriculture Organization of the United Nations*] **Report** [*A publication*] ... FAO Rep
FAO [*Food and Agriculture Organization of the United Nations*] **Soils Bulletin** [*A publication*] ... FAO Soils Bull
Far East ... FE
Far East Air Force ... FEAF
Far East Air Logistical Force ... FEALOGFOR
Far East Air Materiel Command ... FEAMCOM
Far-East-America Council of Commerce and Industry ... FEACCI
Far East Area ... FEAREA
Far East Army and Air Force Exchange Service ... FEAAES
Far East Auto Owners Association ... FEAOA
Far East Broadcasting Association ... FEBA
Far East Broadcasting Company ... FEBC
Far East Combined Bureau [*Singapore, 1940*] [*Military*] ... FECB
Far East Command [*Military*] ... FEC
Far East Command [*Military*] ... FECOM
Far East Communications Region [*Air Force*] ... FECR
Far East Conference ... FEC
Far East Land Forces ... FARELF
Far East Liaison Group ... FELG
Far East Merchants Association [*Defunct*] ... FEMAS
Far East Network ... FEN
Far East Research Office ... FERO
Far East Science Center ... FESC
Far Eastern Advisory Council ... FEAC
Far Eastern Association of Tropical Medicine [*A publication*] ... Far East Ass Trop Med
Far Eastern Commission ... FEC
Far Eastern Economic Review [*A publication*] ... Far East Econ R
Far Eastern Economic Review [*A publication*] ... Far E Econ R
Far Eastern Economic Review [*A publication*] ... FEER
Far Eastern Freight Conference ... FEFC
Far-Eastern Prehistory Association [*Later, IPPA*] ... FEPA
Far Eastern Quarterly [*A publication*] ... Far East Q
Far Eastern Quarterly [*A publication*] ... FEQ
Far Eastern Region, RSFSR [*MARC geographic area code*] [*Library of Congress*] ... e-urf--
Far Eastern Review [*A publication*] ... Far East R
Far Eastern Shipping Company [*USSR*] ... FESCO
Far Eastern Survey [*A publication*] ... Far East S
Far Eastern Survey [*A publication*] ... FES
Far Eastern Technical Unit [*World War II*] ... FETU
Far Eastern University Faculty Journal [*A publication*] ... FEUFJ
Far-Encounter Planet Sensor ... FEPS
Far-End Crosstalk [*Bell System*] ... FEXT
Far-Field Pressure ... FFP
Far-Field Visibility [*Aviation*] ... FFV
Far Horizons Newsletter [*A publication*] ... FHNL
Far Infrared ... FIR
Far-Infrared Detector ... FID
Far-Infrared Detector ... FIRD
Far-Infrared MASER ... FIM
Far-Infrared Observation ... FIO
Far-Infrared Observation ... FIRO
Far-Infrared Pointer ... FIP
Far-Infrared Pointer ... FIRP
Far-Infrared Pointer Package ... FIPP
Far-Infrared Pointer Package ... FIRPP
Far-Infrared Radiometer ... FIR
Far-Infrared Search ... FIS
Far-Infrared Search and Track ... FIRST
Far-Infrared Spectrometer ... FIS
Far-Infrared Target Detector ... FITD
Far-Infrared Target Indicator ... FITI
Far-Infrared Technical Area [*Night Vision Laboratories*] [*Army*] ... FIRTA
Far-Infrared Track ... FIT
Far Point [*A publication*] ... FPt
Far Seas Fisheries Research Laboratory. S Series [*A publication*] ... Far Seas Fish Res Lab S Ser
Far Side ... FS
Far Ultraviolet Space Telescope ... FAUST
Far Ultraviolet Spectrometer [*NASA*] ... FUS
Far West Airlines [*Hillsboro, OR*] [*FAA designator*] ... FWA
Far West Financial Corp. [*NYSE symbol*] ... FWF
Far West Laboratory for Educational Research and Development [*Department of Education*] ... FWL
Far West Laboratory for Educational Research and Development ... FWLERD
Far Western Forum [*A publication*] ... FWF
Far and Wide Tape Club ... FWTC
Farad [*Symbol*] [*Unit of electric capacitance*] ... F
Faraday Constant [*Electrochemistry*] ... F
Faraday Dark Space ... FDS
Faraday Disc Machine ... FDM
Faraday Discussions of the Chemical Society [*A publication*] ... Faraday Dis
Faraday Discussions of the Chemical Society [*A publication*] ... Faraday Discuss
Faraday Discussions of the Chemical Society [*A publication*] ... Faraday Discuss Chem Soc
Faraday Laboratories [*NASDAQ symbol*] ... FDLB
Faraday Society Transactions [*A publication*] ... Faraday Soc Trans
Faraday Special Discussions of the Chemical Society [*A publication*] ... Faraday Spec Discuss Chem Soc
Faraday Symposia of the Chemical Society [*A publication*] ... Faraday Symp Chem Soc
Farads per Meter ... F/M
Faradyne Electronics [*NASDAQ symbol*] ... FARA
Farafangana [*Madagascar*] [*Airport symbol*] ... RVA
Farah Manufacturing Co., Inc. [*NYSE symbol*] ... FRA

Faratahi [*Tuamotu Archipelago*] [*Seismograph station code, US Geological Survey*] ... FRT
Farband Labor Zionist Order [*Later, Labor Zionist Alliance*] ... FLZO
Farbenfabriken Bayer [*Germany*] [*Research code symbol*] ... B
Farbenfabriken Bayer [*Germany*] [*Research code symbol*] ... BAY
Farbenfabriken Bayer [*Germany*] [*Research code symbol*] ... E
Farbenfabriken Bayer [*Germany*] [*Research code symbol*] ... FB
Farbenfabriken Bayer [*Germany*] [*Research code symbol*] ... FBA
Farbenfabriken Bayer [*Germany*] [*Research code symbol*] ... GEA
Farbenfabriken Bayer [*Germany*] [*Research code symbol*] ... P
Farbwerke Hoechst AG [*Germany*] [*Research code symbol*] ... HB
Farbwerke Hoechst AG [*Germany*] [*Research code symbol*] ... LB
Fare Automated Search Technique [*Airline travel service information system*] ... FAST
Fare Construction Unit [*Airlines*] ... FCU
Fare Quotation [*Airline*] ... FQ
Fared Robot Systems [*NASDAQ symbol*] ... FARE
Farewell [*Alaska*] [*Airport symbol*] ... FWL
Farfield Acoustic Measuring System ... FAMS
Fargo [*North Dakota*] [*Airport symbol*] ... FAR
Fargo, ND [*Location identifier*] [*FAA*] ... AAM
Fargo, ND [*Radio station call letters*] ... KDSU
Fargo, ND [*Radio station call letters*] ... KFGO
Fargo, ND [*Television station call letters*] ... KFME
Fargo, ND [*Radio station call letters*] ... KFNW
Fargo, ND [*Radio station call letters*] ... KFNW-FM
Fargo, ND [*Radio station call letters*] ... KQWB
Fargo, ND [*Television station call letters*] ... KVNJ-TV
Fargo, ND [*Radio station call letters*] ... WDAY
Fargo, ND [*Radio station call letters*] ... WDAY-FM
Fargo, ND [*Television station call letters*] ... WDAY-TV
Fargo Public Library, Fargo, ND [*Library symbol*] ... NdF
Farhang-E Iran-Zamin [*Revue Trimestrielle des Etudes Iranologiques*] [*A publication*] ... FIZ
Faribault, MN [*Radio station call letters*] ... KDHL
Faribault, MN [*Radio station call letters*] ... KDHL-FM
Farina-LaGrove Community Unit, School District 206, Farina, IL [*Library symbol*] ... IFaSD
Farm ... FM
Farm Advisory Committee [*MAFF*] [*British*] ... FAC
Farm Animal Reform Movement ... FARM
Farm Buildings Advisory Officer [*Ministry of Agriculture, Fisheries, and Food*] [*British*] ... FBAO
Farm Bulletin. Indian Council of Agricultural Research [*A publication*] ... Fm Bull Indian Coun Agric Res
Farm Bureau Services ... FBS
Farm Chemicals [*A publication*] ... Farm Chem
Farm Chemicals [*A publication*] ... Fm Chem
Farm Costs and Returns [*A publication*] ... FCR
Farm Credit Administration [*Independent government agency*] ... FCA
Farm Credit Corporation [*Canada*] ... FCC
Farm Credit Council ... FCC
Farm Credit System [*of FCA*] ... FCS
Farm Economics [*A publication*] ... Farm Econ
Farm Economics Research Division [*of ARS, Department of Agriculture*] ... FE
Farm Economist [*A publication*] ... Farm Econ
Farm Engineering [*A publication*] ... Farm Eng
Farm Equipment Dealer [*A publication*] ... Farm Equip Dealer
Farm Equipment Institute [*Later, FIEI*] ... FEI
Farm Equipment Manufacturers Association ... FEMA
Farm Equipment Wholesalers Association ... FEWA
Farm Film Foundation [*Later, Grange-Farm Film Foundation*] ... FFF
Farm and Food Research [*A publication*] ... Farm Food Res
Farm Forestry [*A publication*] ... Farm For
Farm Foundation ... FF
Farm Fresh, Inc. [*NASDAQ symbol*] ... FFSH
Farm and Garden Index [*A publication*] ... Farm & Garden Ind
Farm & Home Savings [*NASDAQ symbol*] ... FAHS
Farm and Home Science [*A publication*] ... Farm & Home Sci
Farm and Home Science [*A publication*] ... Farm Home Sci
Farm and Home Science [*A publication*] ... Fm Home Sci
Farm House Foods Corporation [*NASDAQ symbol*] ... FHFC
Farm Income Situation ... FIS
Farm Index [*A publication*] ... Farm In
Farm Index [*A publication*] ... FI
Farm and Industrial Equipment Institute ... FIEI
Farm Journal [*A publication*] ... Farm J
Farm Journal of British Guiana [*A publication*] ... Farm J Brit Guiana
Farm Journal (Eastern Edition) [*A publication*] ... Farm J (E Ed)
Farm Labor Contractor Registration Act [*1963*] [*US Employment Service*] [*Department of Labor*] ... FLCRA
Farm Labor Information [*US Employment Service*] [*Department of Labor*] ... FLI
Farm Labor Interstate Clearance System [*US Employment Service*] [*Department of Labor*] ... FLICS
Farm Labor Organizing Committee ... FLOC
Farm Labor Research Committee ... FLRC
Farm Labor Research Project ... FLRP
Farm Labor Service [*of USES*] ... FLS
Farm and Land Institute ... FLI
Farm Management and Finance [*British*] ... FMF
Farm Management Notes [*A publication*] ... Farm Manage Notes
Farm Mechanization [*A publication*] ... Farm Mech
Farm Policy Review Conference [*A publication*] ... Farm Policy Rev Conf
Farm and Power Equipment [*A publication*] ... Farm Power Equip
Farm Publications Reports ... FPR
Farm Quarterly [*A publication*] ... Farm Q
Farm Quarterly [*A publication*] ... Farm Quart
Farm Research [*A publication*] ... Farm Res
Farm Research News [*A publication*] ... Farm Res News
Farm Safety Review [*A publication*] ... Farm Safety Rev
Farm Security Administration [*Succeeded by Farmers Home Administration, 1946*] ... FSA
Farm Storage Facility Loan Program ... FSFLP
Farm Store Merchandising Association [*Commercial firm*] ... FSMA
Farm Technology [*A publication*] ... Farm Technol
Farm Underwriters Association [*Defunct*] ... FUA
Farm Workers Family Health Center ... FWFHC
Farmaceuticky Obzor [*A publication*] ... Farm Obz
Farmaceutski Glasnik [*A publication*] ... Farm Glas
Farmacevtisk Revy [*A publication*] ... Farm Revy
Farmacevtski Vestnik [*A publication*] ... Farm Vestn
Farmacia Nueva [*A publication*] ... Farm Nueva
Farmacja Polska [*A publication*] ... Farm Pol
Farmaco Edizione Pratica [*A publication*] ... Farmaco Pra
Farmaco Edizione Pratica [*A publication*] ... Farm Ed Prat
Farmaco Edizione Scientifica [*A publication*] ... Farmaco Sci
Farmaco Edizione Scientifica [*A publication*] ... Farm Ed Sci
Farmakeftikon Deltion. Edition Scientifique [*A publication*] ... Farm Delt Ed Sci
Farmakologiia i Toksikologiia [*A publication*] ... Farmakol Toksikol
Farmakologiya i Toksikologiya [*A publication*] ... Farmakol T
Farmakologiya i Toksikologiya (Moscow) [*A publication*] ... Farmakol Toksikol (Mosc)
Farmakologiya i Toksikologiya Respublikanskii Mezhvedomstvennyi Sbornick [*A publication*] ... Farmakol Toksikol Resp Mezhved Sb
Farmatsevtychnyi Zhurnal [*A publication*] ... Farm Z
Farmatsevtychnyi Zhurnal [*A publication*] ... Farm Zh
Farmatsevtychnyi Zhurnal (Kiev) [*A publication*] ... Farm Zh (Kiev)
Farmer Brothers Co. [*NASDAQ symbol*] ... FARM
Farmer City, FL [*Radio station call letters*] ... WZRO
Farmer Cooperative Service [*Later, ESCS*] [*Department of Agriculture*] ... FCS
Farmer Cooperatives [*A publication*] ... Farm Coop
Farmer and Forester [*A publication*] ... Fmr Forester
Farmer and Stockbreeder [*A publication*] ... Farmer Stockbr
Farmer's Advocate and Canadian Countryman [*A publication*] ... Farmer's Advocate Can Countryman
Farmers' Allied Meat Enterprises Cooperative ... FAME
Farmers' Bulletin [*A publication*] ... Farmers' B
Farmers' Bulletin [*A publication*] ... FB
Farmers' Bulletin. United States Department of Agriculture [*A publication*] ... Farmers Bull USDA
Farmers Chinchilla Cooperative of America [*Later, ECBC*] ... FCCA
Farmers' Educational and Cooperative Union of America ... FECUA
Farmers Federation Cooperative ... FFC
Farmers Group, Inc. [*NASDAQ symbol*] ... FGRP
Farmers Home Administration [*Later, FmHA*] [*Department of Agriculture*] ... FHA
Farmers Home Administration [*Formerly, FHA*] [*Department of Agriculture*] ... FmHA
Farmer's Insurance Group, Los Angeles, CA [*Library symbol*] ... CLF
Farmers and Manufacturers Beet Sugar Association ... FAMBSA
Farmers and Manufacturers Beet Sugar Association ... FMBSA
Farmers' and Scientists' Joint Conference [*A publication*] ... Farmers' Sci Joint Conf
Farmer's Weekly [*South Africa*] [*A publication*] ... Farmer's Wkly
Farmers and World Affairs [*An association*] [*Defunct*] ... FWA
Farmerville, LA [*Radio station call letters*] ... KTDL
Farmerville, LA [*Radio station call letters*] ... KWJM
Farming Progress [*A publication*] ... Farming Progr
Farming Review [*A publication*] ... Farming Rev
Farming Review [*A publication*] ... Fmg Rev
Farming in South Africa [*A publication*] ... Farming S Afr
Farming in South Africa [*A publication*] ... Fmg S Afr
Farmingdale, NY [*Location identifier*] [*FAA*] ... FRG
Farmingdale Public Library, Farmingdale, NY [*Library symbol*] ... NFar
Farmington [*New Mexico*] [*Seismograph station code, US Geological Survey*] ... FARG
Farmington [*New Mexico*] [*Airport symbol*] ... FMN
Farmington East High School, Farmington, IL [*OCLC symbol*] ... IQZ
Farmington Hills, MI [*Radio station call letters*] ... WORB
Farmington, ME [*Radio station call letters*] ... WKTJ
Farmington, ME [*Radio station call letters*] ... WKTJ-FM
Farmington, ME [*Radio station call letters*] ... WUMF-FM
Farmington, MO [*Radio station call letters*] ... KREI
Farmington, MO [*Radio station call letters*] ... KTJJ
Farmington, NM [*Location identifier*] [*FAA*] ... FMN
Farmington, NM [*Radio station call letters*] ... KENN
Farmington, NM [*Radio station call letters*] ... KNDN

Farmington, NM [*Radio station call letters*] .... KNMI
Farmington, NM [*Radio station call letters*] .... KRAZ
Farmington, NM [*Radio station call letters*] .... KRWN
Farmington, NM [*Radio station call letters*] .... KRZE
Farmington Public Library, Farmington, NM [*OCLC symbol*] .... FAR
Farmington Public Library, Farmington, NM [*Library symbol*] .... NmF
Farmington State Teachers College [*Merged with University of Maine*] .... FSTC
Farmington Village Library, Farmington, CT [*Library symbol*] .... CtF
Farmitalia [*Italy*] [*Research code symbol*] .... FI
Farmitalia [*Italy*] [*Research code symbol*] .... P
Farmland Industries [*An association*] .... FI
Farms .... FRMS
Farmstead Equipment Association [*Formerly, BCCFSUA, BEA*] .... FEA
Farmville, NC [*Radio station call letters*] .... WGHB
Farmville, NC [*Radio station call letters*] .... WRQR
Farmville, VA [*Location identifier*] [*FAA*] .... FVX
Farmville, VA [*Radio station call letters*] .... WFLO
Farmville, VA [*Radio station call letters*] .... WFLO-FM
Farmville, VA [*Radio station call letters*] .... WPAK
Farmville, VA [*Radio station call letters*] .... WUTA
Farnesyl Methyl Ether [*Juvenile hormone analog*] .... FME
Farnesynic Acid [*Juvenile hormone analog*] .... FA
Faro [*Portugal*] [*Airport symbol*] .... FAO
Faro [*Portugal*] [*Seismograph station code, US Geological Survey*] .... FAR
Faroe Islands [*Denmark*] [*Airport symbol*] .... FAE
Faroe Islands .... FI
Faroe Islands [*Two-letter standard code*] .... FO
Faroe Islands [*Three-letter standard code*] .... FRO
Faroese [*MARC language code*] [*Library of Congress*] .... far
Farr Company [*NASDAQ symbol*] .... FARC
Farrand Optical Company, Incorporated .... FOCI
Farrar, Straus & Giroux [*Publisher*] .... FS & G
Farrell, PA [*Radio station call letters*] .... WMGZ
Farris, Vaughan, Wills, & Murphy Law Firm, Vancouver, BC, Canada [*Library symbol*] .... CaBVaFV
Farsund [*Norway*] [*Airport symbol*] .... FAN
Farther .... FTHR
Farthest-On Circle .... FOC
Farthest on Point .... FOP
Farthing [*Monetary unit in Britain*] .... F
Farthing [*Monetary unit in Britain*] .... FAR
Farwell Public Library, Farwell, MI [*Library symbol*] .... MiFaw
Farwell, TX [*Radio station call letters*] .... KIJN-FM
Farwell, TX [*Radio station call letters*] .... KISN
FAS [*Fixed Airlock Shroud*] **Work Station** .... FWS
Fascia Dentata [*Brain anatomy*] .... FD
Fascicle .... FASC
Fasciculi Mathematici [*A publication*] .... Fasc Math
Fascioscapulohumeral [*Medicine*] .... FSH
FASEB [*Federation of American Societies for Experimental Biology*] **Monographs** [*A publication*] .... FASEB Monogr
Faserforschung und Textiltechnik [*A publication*] .... Faserforsch Textiltech
Fashion Coordination Institute [*Defunct*] .... FCI
Fashion Fabrics, Inc. [*American Stock Exchange symbol*] [*Delisted*] .... FAF
Fashion, Features, and Fluff [*Subject assignments to which female journalists were once limited*] .... 3F's
Fashion Glamour Set .... FGS
Fashion Group [*Later, TFG*] .... FG
[*The*] **Fashion Group** .... TFG
Fashion Institute of Technology [*New York*] .... FIT
Fashion Institute of Technology, New York, NY [*Library symbol*] .... NNFIT
Fashion Integrated Merchandising Planning and Control System .... FIMPACS
Fashion Merchandising, Fashion Design, and/or Interior Design Programs [*Association of Independent Colleges and Schools specialization code*] .... FM
Fashion Originators Guild of America [*Defunct*] .... FOGA
Fashion Reporters Award - New York .... FRANY
Fast .... F
Fast [*Horse racing*] .... FST
Fast [*Track condition*] [*Thoroughbred racing*] .... FT
Fast Access Information Retrieval .... FAIR
Fast Access Information Retrieval. Newsletter [*A publication*] .... FAIR Newsl
Fast Access to Systems Technical Information .... FASTI
Fast Accurate Refraction Correction [*NASA*] .... FARC
Fast Acquisition Search and Track .... FAST
Fast-Acting Fuse .... FAF
Fast Action on Comments of Technical Significance .... FACTS
Fast Action Procedures .... FAP
Fast Agricultural Communication Terminal System .... FACTS
Fast Announcement Service [*NTIS publication*] .... FAS
Fast Asymptotic Coherent Transmission .... FACT
Fast Atmospheric Pulsation .... FAP
Fast Atom Bombardment [*Mass spectrometry*] .... FAB
Fast Attack Class Submarine .... FACS
Fast Attack Submarine .... FASSN
Fast Attack Vehicle [*Army*] .... FAV
Fast Automatic Gain Control .... FAGC
Fast Automatic Shuttle Transfer [*System*] [*Navy*] .... FAST
Fast Automatic Transfer .... FAT
Fast Auxiliary Memory .... FAM
Fast Breeder Reactor .... FBR
Fast Burn Rate .... FBR
Fast Burst Reactor .... FBR
Fast Burst Reactor Facility .... FBRF
Fast as Can [*Business and trade*] .... FAC
Fast Capacitor Bank .... FCB
Fast Ceramic Reactor [*Program*] .... FCR
Fast Combat Support Ship [*Navy symbol*] .... AOE
Fast Component .... FC
Fast Critical Assembly [*Nuclear reactor*] [*Japan*] .... FCA
Fast Death Factor [*Medicine*] .... FDF
Fast Deployment Logistics Ship [*Navy symbol*] .... FDL
Fast Deployment Logistics Ship [*Navy*] .... FDLS
Fast Digital Processor [*Data processing*] .... FDP
Fast Diode Switch .... FDS
Fast Discrete Cosine Transform .... FDCT
Fast Economic Language [*Data processing*] .... FASTEL
Fast Eigensolution Extraction Routine [*Computer program*] .... FEER
Fast Erect System .... FES
Fast Extrusion Furnace .... FEF
Fast Fatigue [*Type of muscle contraction*] .... FF
Fast Field Program .... FFP
Fast Fission Factor .... FFF
Fast Flux Test Facility [*Nuclear energy*] .... FFTF
Fast Flying Vestibule [*Old railroad term for a deluxe coach*] .... FFV
Fast Food Operators [*NASDAQ symbol*] .... POPI
Fast Fourier Analyzer .... FFA
Fast Fourier Transform .... FFT
Fast Fractional Gaussian Noise [*Mathematics*] .... ffGn
Fast-Frequency Hopping .... FFH
Fast Frequency Shift Keying .... FFSK
Fast Frequency on Target .... FFOT
Fast Hydrofoil Escort .... FHE
Fast Information Retrieval for Surface Transportation [*IBM Corp.*] .... FIRST
Fast Interline Nonactivate Automatic Control [*AT & T*] .... FINAC
Fast Ion Bombardment .... FIB
Fast Luciferase Automated Assay of Specimens for Hospitals [*Bacteria analysis*] [*NASA*] .... FLASH
Fast Motor Launches .... MLF
Fast Moving Object .... FMO
Fast Neutron Breeder Reactor .... FNBR
Fast Neutron Cavity .... FNC
Fast Neutron Dose .... FND
Fast Operating [*Relay*] .... FO
Fast Order Radiation Effects Sampling Technique .... FOREST
Fast Patrol Boat [*Navy*] .... FPB
Fast Patrol Boat [*Ship symbol*] .... PBF
Fast-Payback Capital Investment Program [*Air Force*] .... FASCAP
Fast Prepotential [*Neurophysiology*] .... FPP
Fast Processor [*Instrumentation*] .... FP
Fast Protein, Peptide, and Polynucleotide Liquid Chromatography .... FPLC
Fast Pulse Electron Gun .... FPEG
Fast Reaction Fighting System .... FRFS
Fast Reaction Integrated Submarine Control .... FRISCO
Fast Reactivity Exclusion Device [*Nuclear energy*] .... FRED
Fast Reactor Core Test Facility [*Nuclear energy*] .... FRCTF
Fast Reactor Experiment Test [*Proposed but never built*] [*Nuclear energy*] .... FARET
Fast Reactor Thermal Engineering Facility [*Nuclear energy*] .... FRTEF
Fast Release [*Relay*] .... FR
Fast-Response Relief Valve .... FRRV
Fast-Response Solar Array Simulator .... FRSAS
Fast Retrieval Storage [*Data processing*] .... FRS
Fast Rise Balloon .... FRB
Fast Rise Pulse .... FRP
Fast Rise RADAR Reflective Balloon .... FRRRB
Fast Rise Reflective Balloon .... FRRB
Fast Screening .... FS
Fast at Sea Transfer [*Equipment*] .... FAST
Fast Sealift Ship .... TAKRX
Fast Settle Mode .... FSM
Fast Settle Operation .... FSO
Fast Slew .... FS
Fast Slew Rate .... FSR
Fast Supercritical Pressure Power Reactor .... FSPPR
Fast Supply [*Ships*] .... FS
Fast Test Reactor .... FTR
Fast Time Analysis .... FTA
Fast Time Analyzer System .... FTAS
Fast Time Constant [*RADAR*] .... FTC
Fast Track [*Insurance*] .... FT
Fast Transit Link [*Rapid-transit term*] .... FTL
Fast Wave Simple Harmonic Motion [*A microwave tube device*] .... FAWSHMOTRON
Fastener .... FSTNR
Fastener Installation Procedure [*Manual*] .... FIP
Fasteners Research Council [*Defunct*] .... FRC
Faster Than Light [*Science fiction*] .... FTL
Faster-Than-Light Drive .... FTLD
Fasti Archaeologici [*A publication*] .... FA

Fasting [Test] [Medicine]......F
Fasting Blood Sugar [Physiology]......FBS
Fat-Corrected Milk......FCM
Fat Free [Biochemistry]......FF
Fat-Free Body......FFB
Fat-Free Body Mass......FFBM
Fat-Free Dry Weight......FFDW
Fat-Free Solids......FFS
Fat-Free Supper [Medicine]......FFS
Fat-Free Wet Weight......FFWW
Fat Head Minnow......FHM
Fat-Induced Hyperglycemia [Medicine]......FIH
Fat-Mobilizing Hormone [Medicine]......FMH
Fat Mobilizing Substance......FMS
Fatal Accident Frequency Rate......FAFR
Fatal Accident Reduction Effort [or Enforcement] [Department of Transportation]......FARE
Fatal Accident Reporting System [National Highway Traffic Safety Administration]......FARS
Fatal Dose......FD
Fate of Atmospheric Pollutants Study [National Science Foundation]......FAPS
Father......F
Father......FR
Father of Chapel [Shop steward] [British]......FOC
Father of Sion [Roman Catholic]......FS
Fatherhood Project......FP
Fathers of the Church [A publication]......FC
Fathers Day Council......FDC
Fathom......F
Fathom......FAT
Fathom......FATH
Fathom......FM
Fathom......FTH
Fathometer Depth Sounder......FDS
Fathoms......fms
Fatigue Crack Growth Rate [Metals]......FCGR
Fatigue Cracking Test......FCT
Fatigue of Engineering Materials and Structures [A publication]......Fatigue Eng Mat Struct
Fatigue Life Expectancy [or Expended]......FLE
Fatigue Limit......FL
Fatigue Resistant......FR
Fatigue Scales Kit [Psychology]......FSK
Fatigue Test Article......FTA
FATIS [Food and Agriculture Technical Information Service] Review [A publication]......FATIS Rev
Fatphobia Awareness Training......FAT
Fats, Oils, and Grease [Food plant effluent]......FOG
Fats and Oils Situation......FOS
Fats and Proteins Research Foundation......FPRF
Fatstock Marketing Corporation [British]......FMC
Fatty Acid [Biochemistry]......FA
Fatty Acid Binding Protein [Biochemistry]......FABP
Fatty Acid-Free [Biochemistry]......FAF
Fatty Acid Methyl Ester [s] [Biochemistry]......FAME
Fatty Acid Producers' Council......FAPC
Fatty Oil......FO
Fault......FLT
Fault Detection......FD
Fault Detection and Annunciation......FDA
Fault Detection and Identification......FDI
Fault Detection and Isolation......FDI
Fault Detection, Isolation, Identification, and Recompensation......FDIIR
Fault Detection Tester......FDT
Fault Directory......FD
Fault Identification......FI
Fault Isolation Analysis......FIA
Fault Isolation Checkout System......FICS
Fault Isolation Code......FIC
Fault Isolation Detection......FID
Fault Isolation Maintainability Analysis......FIMA
Fault Isolation Meter......FIM
Fault Isolation Requirement Document......FIRD
Fault Isolation Routine......FIR
Fault Isolation by Semiautomatic Techniques [National Bureau of Standards]......FIST
Fault Isolation Test......FIT
Fault Isolation Test Adapter......FITA
Fault Localization......FLOC
Fault Location Facility [Aircraft]......FLF
Fault Location Indicating Console......FLIC
Fault Location Indicator......FLI
Fault Location through Interpretive Testing [Data processing]......FLIT
Fault Location and Monitoring......FLAM
Fault-Location Oscillator [Bell System]......FLO
Fault Location Panel [Aerospace]......FLP
Fault Location and Repair......FLAR
Fault Location Technology......FLT
Fault Location Unit [Aerospace]......FLU
Fault Location Word......FLW

Fault Locator Cable......FLC
Fault Locator System......FLS
Fault Logic Diagram......FLD
Fault of Management......FOM
Fault Message Line......FML
Fault Repair Service [Telecommunications] [British]......FRS
Fault Simulation Comparator......FSC
Fault Summary......FS
Fault Summary Page......FSP
Fault Tolerance System......FTS
Fault-Tolerant Computing......FTC
Fault Tree Analysis......FTA
Faulty Abbreviation [Used in correcting manuscripts, etc.]......AB
Faulty Agreement [Used in correcting manuscripts, etc.]......AGR
Faulty Capitalization [Used in correcting manuscripts, etc.]......CAP
Faulty Diction [Used in correcting manuscripts, etc.]......D
Faulty Punctuation [Used in correcting manuscripts, etc.]......P
Faulty Sentence Structure [Used in correcting manuscripts, etc.]......SS
Fauna Fennica [A publication]......Fauna Fenn
Fauna and Flora Preservation Society......FFPS
Fauna och Flora (Stockholm) [A publication]......Fauna Flora (Stockh)
Fauna and Flora (Transvaal) [A publication]......Fauna Flora (Transvaal)
Fauna Hungariae [A publication]......Fauna Hung
Fauna d'Italia [A publication]......Fauna Ital
Fauna Polski [A publication]......Fauna Pol
Fauna Preservation Society [Later, FFPS]......FPS
Faune de France [A publication]......Faune Fr
Faune du Quebec [A publication]......Faune Que
Faune du Quebec. Rapport Special [A publication]......Faune Que Rapp Spec
Faunistisch-Oekologische Mitteilungen [A publication]......Faun-Oekol Mitt
Faunistische Abhandlungen (Dresden) [A publication]......Faun Abh (Dres)
Faust Blaetter [A publication]......Faust B
Favorable......FAV
Fawick Corp. [NYSE symbol] [Delisted]......FAW
Fayalite [CIPW classification] [Geology]......fa
Fayette, AL [Radio station call letters]......WHKW
Fayette, AL [Radio station call letters]......WWWF
Fayette Community Library, Fayette, IA [Library symbol]......IaFay
Fayette County Court House, Fayette, AL [Library symbol]......AFC
Fayette County Free Library, Somerville, TN [Library symbol]......TSo
Fayette County Helpers Club and Historical Society, Fayette, IA [Library symbol]......IaFayHHi
Fayette County Public Library, Fayetteville, WV [Library symbol]......WvFa
Fayette Flying Service & Scheduled Skyways System [Fayetteville, AR] [FAA designator]......SKM
Fayette, MS [Radio station call letters]......WTYJ
Fayetteville [Arkansas] [Seismograph station code, US Geological Survey]......FAV
Fayetteville [Arkansas] [Seismograph station code, US Geological Survey] [Closed]......FAY
Fayetteville [Arkansas] [Airport symbol]......FYV
Fayetteville [North Carolina] [Airport symbol]......FAY
Fayetteville, AR [Location identifier] [FAA]......DAK
Fayetteville, AR [Television station call letters]......KAFT
Fayetteville, AR [Radio station call letters]......KFAY
Fayetteville, AR [Radio station call letters]......KHOG
Fayetteville, AR [Radio station call letters]......KKEG
Fayetteville, AR [Radio station call letters]......KKIX
Fayetteville, AR [Television station call letters]......KTVP
Fayetteville, AR [Radio station call letters]......KUAF
Fayetteville, AR [Location identifier] [FAA]......RZC
Fayetteville/Fort Bragg, NC [Location identifier] [FAA]......VRY
Fayetteville, NC [Location identifier] [FAA]......GRA
Fayetteville, NC [Location identifier] [FAA]......POB
Fayetteville, NC [Radio station call letters]......WFAI
Fayetteville, NC [Television station call letters]......WFCT
Fayetteville, NC [Radio station call letters]......WFLB
Fayetteville, NC [Radio station call letters]......WFNC
Fayetteville, NC [Radio station call letters]......WFSS
Fayetteville, NC [Radio station call letters]......WIDU
Fayetteville, NC [Television station call letters]......WKFT
Fayetteville, NC [Radio station call letters]......WQSM
Fayetteville State Teachers College [Later, Fayetteville State University] [North Carolina]......FSTC
Fayetteville State University, Fayetteville, NC [Library symbol]......NcFayS
Fayetteville State University, Fayetteville, NC [OCLC symbol]......NFS
Fayetteville Technical Institute, Fayetteville, NC [Library symbol]......NcFayT
Fayetteville, TN [Radio station call letters]......WEKR
Fayetteville, TN [Radio station call letters]......WIXC
Fayetteville, TN [Radio station call letters]......WYTM
Fay's Drug Co., Inc. [American Stock Exchange symbol]......FAY
FBA Pharmaceuticals Ltd. [Great Britain] [Research code symbol]......FBA
FBI [Federal Bureau of Investigation] Law Enforcement Bulletin [A publication]......FBI Law Enf Bul
FBM [Fleet Ballistic Missile] Support Ship......TAGS
FDA [Food and Drug Administration] Consumer [A publication]......FDA Consum
FDA [Food and Drug Administration] Drug Bulletin [A publication]......FDA Drug Bull
FDI, Inc. [American Stock Exchange symbol] [Delisted]......FDI
FDP Corporation [NASDAQ symbol]......FDPC

Fear [*A publication*] ... FER
Fear, Love, Anger, and Pain [*Cognitive system*] ... FLAP
Fear Survey Schedule [*Psychology*] ... FSS
Fear, Uncertainty, and Doubt [*Factors hindering sales of lesser-known computers*] ... FUD
Feasibility Demonstration Model ... FDM
Feasibility Demonstration Program ... FDP
Feasibility Study ... FS
Feasibility Study Change Proposal ... FSCP
Feasibility Validation Program ... FVP
Feasible ... FSBL
Feast ... F
Feather ... FTR
Feather and Down Association, Incorporated ... FDAI
Feather Falls [*California*] [*Seismograph station code, US Geological Survey*] [*Closed*] ... FEA
Feather River [*AAR code*] ... FR
Feather River Project ... FRP
Feathered ... FTHRD
Featherly Pass [*Alaska*] [*Seismograph station code, US Geological Survey*] ... FLP
Feature Analysis System [*Image analysis*] ... FAS
Feature Count [*Data processing*] ... FC
Feature Identification and Landmark Experiment [*NASA*] ... FILE
Feature Recognition Processor ... FRP
Febre Durante [*While the Fever Persists*] [*Pharmacy*] ... FEB DUR
Febris [*Fever*] [*Pharmacy*] ... FEB
February ... F
February ... FEB
FEBS [*Federation of European Biochemical Societies*] **Letters** [*A publication*] ... FEBS Lett
FEBS [*Federation of European Biochemical Societies*] **Proceedings of the Meeting** [*A publication*] ... FEBS Proc Meet
Fecal Coli [*Microbiology*] ... FC
Fecal Collection Device [*NASA*] ... FCD
Fecal Collection Receptacle Assembly [*NASA*] ... FCRA
Fecal Containment System [*NASA*] ... FCS
Fecal Emesis ... FE
Fecal Energy [*Nutrition*] ... FE
Fecal Management System [*NASA*] ... FMS
Fecal Pellet ... FP
Fecal Urobilinogen [*Clinical chemistry*] ... FU
Fecerunt [*They Did It*] [*Latin*] ... FF
Feces ... F
Fecit [*He Did It*] [*Latin*] ... F
Fecit [*He, or She, Did It*] [*Latin*] ... FEC
Fed-Mart Corp. [*American Stock Exchange symbol*] [*Delisted*] ... FMI
Fedders Corp. [*NYSE symbol*] ... FJQ
Feddes Repertorium [*A publication*] ... Feddes Repert
Feddes Repertorium. Specierum Novarum Regni Vegetabilis [*A publication*] ... Feddes Repert Specierum Nov Regni Veg
Federacion Anaquista Iberica [*Spain*] ... FAI
Federacion Cafetalera de America [*Central American Coffee Growers' Federation*] ... FEDECAME
Federacion Democratica Internacional de Mujeres [*Women's International Democratic Federation*] ... FDIM
Federacion de Estudiantes Universitaries de Ecuador ... FEUE
Federacion de Estudiantes de Venezuela ... FEV
Federacion Interamericana de la Industria de la Construccion [*Interamerican Federation of the Construction Industry*] ... FIIC
Federacion Interamericana de Periodistas y Escritores de Turismo [*Interamerican Federation of Journalists and Writers in the Tourist Trade*] ... FIPET
Federacion Interamericana de Touring y Automobil-Clubs [*Interamerican Federation of Automobile Clubs*] ... FITAC
Federacion Interamericana de Trabajadores del Espectaculo [*Interamerican Federation of Entertainment Workers*] ... FITE
Federacion Interamericana de Trabajadores de la Industria Textil, del Vestuario, y del Cuero [*Interamerican Textile, Garment, and Leather Workers Federation*] ... FITITV
Federacion Internacional de Asociaciones de Ferreteros y Almacenistas de Hierros [*International Federation of Ironmongers and Iron Merchants Associations*] ... FIDAF
Federacion Internacional de Medecina Fisica [*International Federation of Physical Medicine*] ... FIMF
Federacion Internacional de Periodistas [*International Federation of Journalists*] ... FIP
Federacion Internacional de Trabajadores de las Industrias Metalurgicas [*International Metalworkers' Federation*] ... FITIM
Federacion Internacional de Trabajadores Petroleros y Quimicos [*International Federation of Petroleum and Chemical Workers*] ... FITPQ
Federacion Internacional de Vivienda y Urbanismo [*International Federation for Housing and Planning*] ... FIVU
Federacion Latinoamericana de Bancos ... FELABAN
Federacion Latinoamericana de Parasitologos ... FLAP
Federacion Mundial Cristiana de Estudiantes [*World Student Christian Federation*] ... FMCE
Federacion Mundial de Instituciones Financieras de Desarrolla [*World Federation of Development Financing Institutions - WFDFI*] ... FEMIDE
Federacion Mundial de Sindicatos de Industrias [*World Federation of Industrial Workers' Unions*] ... FEMUSI
Federacion Nacional Velasquista [*Political party in Ecuador*] ... FNV
Federacion Obrera de la Industria Tabaquera de Filipinas [*Workers' Federation of the Tobacco Industry of the Philippines*] ... FOITAF
Federacion Obrera Revolucionaria [*Mexican political party*] ... FOR
Federacion Odontologica Centro America y Panama [*Odontological Federation of Central America and Panama*] ... FOCAP
Federacion Panamericana de Asociaciones de Arquitectos [*Panamerican Federation of Architects' Associations*] ... FPAA
Federacion Panamericana de Asociacions de Facultades de Medicina [*Pan American Federation of Associations of Medical Schools - PAFAMS*] ... FEPAFEM
Federacion de Sociedades Hispanas [*Defunct*] ... FSH
Federacion de Universidades Privadas de America Central ... FUPAC
Federacion Universitaria Democratica Espanola [*Spanish union of students*] ... FUDE
Federal ... FED
Federal Acquisition Regulation ... FAR
Federal Acquisitions Institute [*Formerly, FPI*] ... FAI
Federal Administrative Law Judges Conference ... FALJC
Federal ADP [*Automatic Data Processing*] **Users Group** ... FADPUG
Federal Advertising Committee on Ethics ... FACE
Federal Advisory Committee Act ... FACA
Federal Advisory Committee on False Identification [*Department of Justice*] ... FACFI
Federal Advisory Committee on Occupational Safety and Health ... FACOSH
Federal Advisory Council [*Department of Labor*] ... FAC
Federal Advisory Council on Employment Security ... FACES
Federal Advisory Council on Medical Training Aids ... FACMTA
Federal Advisory Council on Regional Economic Development ... FACRED
Federal Advisory Council on Scientific Information ... FACSI
Federal Advisory Council on Unemployment Insurance ... FACUI
Federal Agricultural Marketing Authority ... FAMA
Federal Aid to Airports Program [*FAA*] ... FAAP
Federal Aid Urban System [*Road improvement program*] [*Federal Highway Administration*] ... FAUS
Federal Air Regulations [*FAA*] ... FAR
Federal Airport Service ... FAS
Federal Alcohol Control Administration [*Established, 1933; abolished, 1935*] ... FACA
Federal Ambient Air Quality Studies ... FAAQS
Federal Archives and Records Center [*Regional depository of the National Archives and Records Service*] ... FARC
Federal Archives and Records Center, General Services Administration, Waltham, MA [*Library symbol*] ... MWalFAR
Federal Archives and Records Center, General Services Administration, Bayonne, NJ [*Library symbol*] ... NjBaFAR
Federal Archives and Records Center, General Services Administration, Philadelphia, PA [*Library symbol*] ... PPFAR
Federal Area Port Controller ... FAPC
Federal Art Project ... FAP
Federal Assistance Award Data System [*Department of Commerce*] [*Information service*] ... FAADS
Federal Assistance Information Reporting ... FAIR
Federal Assistance Program Retrieval System [*OMB*] ... FAPRS
Federal Assistance Review [*Program*] ... FAR
Federal Assistance for Staff Training [*Education*] ... FAST
Federal Assistance Streamlining Taskforce [*HEW*] ... FAST
Federal Association of Management Analysts [*Defunct*] ... FAMA
Federal Automated Career System ... FACS
Federal Aviation Act [*1958*] ... FAA
Federal Aviation Administration [*Formerly, Federal Aviation Agency*] [*Department of Transportation*] ... FAA
Federal Aviation Administration Aeronautical Center ... FAA-AC
Federal Aviation Administration Air Traffic Service ... FAA-AT
Federal Aviation Administration Aircraft Development Service ... FAA-ADS
Federal Aviation Administration Airports Service ... FAA-AS
Federal Aviation Administration Airway Facilities Service ... FAA-AAF
Federal Aviation Administration Airway Facilities Service ... FAA-AF
Federal Aviation Administration Canadian Air Services Committee ... FAA/CAS
Federal Aviation Administration Development Services ... FAA-DS
Federal Aviation Administration, Eastern Region Library, Jamaica, NY [*Library symbol*] ... NJFAA
Federal Aviation Administration Flight Standards Service ... FAA-AFS
Federal Aviation Administration Flight Standards Service ... FAA-FS
Federal Aviation Administration Flight Standards Service National Flight Inspection Division ... FAA-FS-NFID
Federal Aviation Administration National Airspace System Program Office ... FAA-NS
Federal Aviation Administration National Aviation Facilities Experimental Center ... FAA-NA
Federal Aviation Administration Office of Airports Programs ... FAA-AAP
Federal Aviation Administration Office of Airports Programs ... FAA-AP
Federal Aviation Administration Office of Aviation Medicine ... FAA-AM
Federal Aviation Administration Office of Aviation Policy ... FAA-AV
Federal Aviation Administration Office of Aviation Systems Plans ... FAA-ASP

Federal Aviation Administration Office of Environment and Energy ... FAA-AEE
Federal Aviation Administration Office of Environment and Energy ... FAA-EE
Federal Aviation Administration Office of Environmental Quality ... FAA-AEQ
Federal Aviation Administration Office of Environmental Quality ... FAA-EQ
Federal Aviation Administration Office of Management Systems ... FAA-MS
Federal Aviation Administration Office of Noise Abatement ... FAA-NO
Federal Aviation Administration Office of Supersonic Transport Development ... FAA-SST
Federal Aviation Administration Office of Systems Engineering Management ... FAA-AEM
Federal Aviation Administration Office of Systems Engineering Management ... FAA-EM
Federal Aviation Administration Quiet Short-Haul Air Transportation Systems Office ... FAA-QS
Federal Aviation Administration Requirements ... FAAR
Federal Aviation Administration, Southern Region, East Point, GA [*OCLC symbol*] ... GFA
Federal Aviation Administration Systems Research and Development Service ... FAA-ARD
Federal Aviation Administration Systems Research and Development Service ... FAA-RD
Federal Aviation Administration Technical Development Center ... FAATDC
Federal Aviation Commission [*Terminated, 1935*] ... FAC
Federal Aviation Procurement Regulations ... FAPR
Federal Aviation Service ... FAS
Federal Bar Association ... FBA
Federal Bar Journal [*A publication*] ... Fed B J
Federal Barge Lines, Inc. [*AAR code*] ... FBL
Federal Barge Lines, Inc., St. Louis MO [*STAC*] ... FBG
Federal Board of Hospitalization [*Coordinated hospitalization activities of Army, Navy, and various agencies; terminated, 1948*] ... FBH
Federal Bonding Program ... FBP
Federal Buildings Fund [*General Services Administration*] ... FBF
Federal Bureau of Advanced Paranoia [*Agency in film "Last Embrace"*] ... FBAP
Federal Bureau of Investigation ... FBI
Federal Bureau of Narcotics ... FBN
Federal Business Development Bank, Montreal, PQ, Canada [*Library symbol*] ... CaQMFBD
Federal Cabinet [*Australia*] ... FC
Federal Capital Press of Australia, Canberra, ACT, Australia [*Library symbol*] ... AuCF
Federal Capital Territory [*Later, ACT*] [*Australia*] ... FCT
Federal Carriers, Inc. [*White Lake, NY*] [*FAA designator*] ... SLV
Federal Catalog Number ... FCN
Federal Catalog System [*of GSA*] ... FCS
Federal Cataloging Handbook ... FCH
Federal Cataloging Program ... FCP
Federal City College [*Later, UDC*] [*Washington, DC*] ... FCC
Federal City College [*Later, UDC*], **Washington, DC** [*Library symbol*] [*Obsolete*] ... DFC
Federal Civil Defense Administration [*Transferred to Office of Defense and Civilian Mobilization, 1958; to Department of Defense and Office of Emergency Preparedness, 1961*] ... FCDA
Federal Civil Defense Guide ... FCDG
Federal Civil Service System ... FCSS
Federal Claims Settlement Commission of the United States ... FCSCUS
Federal Clean Car Incentive Program ... FCCI
Federal Clean Car Incentive Program [*Environmental Protection Agency*] ... FCCIP
Federal Coal Mine Safety Board of Review [*Independent government agency*] [*Inactive, 1970*] ... FCMSBR
Federal COBOL [*Common Business-Oriented Language*] **Compiler Testing Service** [*National Bureau of Standards*] ... FCCTS
Federal Columbia River Power System ... FCRPS
Federal Committee on Apprenticeship [*Department of Labor*] ... FCA
Federal Committee for Meteorological Services and Supporting Research ... FCMS & SR
Federal Committee on Pest Control ... FCPC
Federal Communications Act ... FCA
Federal Communications Bar Association ... FCBA
Federal Communications Bar. Law Journal [*A publication*] ... Fed Com B J
Federal Communications Commission [*Independent government agency*] ... FCC
Federal Communications Commission Network ... FCCN
Federal Communications Commission, Washington, DC [*OCLC symbol*] ... FCC
Federal Communications Systems ... FCS
Federal Co. [*NYSE symbol*] ... FFF
Federal Complaint Coordinating Center [*US Office of Consumer Affairs*] ... FCCC
Federal Constitutional Law ... FECL
Federal Construction Council ... FCC
Federal Consultative Council of South African Railways and Harbors Staff Association ... FCC
Federal Contract Research Center ... FCRC
Federal Coordinating Council for Science, Engineering, and Technology [*Office of Science and Technology Policy*] ... FCCSET
Federal Coordinating Council for Science and Technology ... FCCST
Federal Coordinating Officer [*Federal disaster planning*] ... FCO
Federal Coordination Committee on Instrumentation and Measurement ... FCCIM
Federal Council on the Aging [*Succeeded by President's Council on Aging, 1962*] ... FCA
Federal Council of Churches ... FCC
Federal Council for Science and Technology [*Later, FSPC, FCCSET*] [*Executive Office of President*] ... FCST
Federal Court of Canada ... FCT
Federal Court of Canada, Ottawa, ON, Canada [*Library symbol*] ... CaOOFC
Federal Court Clerks Association ... FCCA
Federal Credit Unions Bureau ... FCU
Federal Crop Insurance ... FCI
Federal Crop Insurance Corporation [*Department of Agriculture*] ... FCIC
Federal Cultural Policy Review Committee [*Canada*] ... FCPRC
Federal Data Processing Centers ... FDPC
Federal Deposit Insurance Corporation [*Independent government agency*] ... FDIC
Federal Deposit Insurance Corp., Washington, DC [*OCLC symbol*] ... FDI
Federal Design Council [*Formerly, SFAD*] ... FDC
Federal Directive ... FD
Federal Disaster Assistance Administration [*FEMA*] ... FDAA
Federal Document ... FD
Federal Document Retrievals, Inc. [*Information service*] ... FDR
Federal Economic Review [*A publication*] ... FER
Federal Editors Association [*Later, NAGC*] ... FEA
Federal Education Project ... FEP
Federal Elections Commission [*Formerly, OFE*] ... FEC
Federal Electric Company ... FEC
Federal Emergency Administration of Public Works [*Consolidated into Federal Works Agency and administered as PWA, 1939*] ... FEAPW
Federal Emergency Management Agency [*Independent government agency*] ... FEMA
Federal Emergency Relief Administration [*Liquidated, 1937*] ... FERA
Federal Emission Test Sequence and Selective Enforcement Audit [*General Motors Corp.*] ... FETS/SEA
Federal Employee Program ... FEP
Federal Employees' Appeal Authority [*Civil Service Commission*] ... FEAA
Federal Employees Association (Independent) ... FEA(I)
Federal Employees Compensation Act ... FECA
Federal Employees for a Democratic Society [*Defunct*] ... FEDS
Federal Employees' Group Life Insurance ... FEGLI
Federal Employees Health Benefits ... FEHB
Federal Employees Health Benefits Act ... FEHBA
Federal Employees Health Benefits Program ... FEHBP
Federal Employees Veterans Association [*Superseded by NAGE*] ... FEVA
Federal Employer Identification Number ... FEIN
Federal Employment Stabilization Office [*Functions transferred to National Resources Planning Board, 1939*] ... FESO
Federal Energy Administration [*Formerly, FEO*] [*Superseded by Department of Energy, 1977*] ... FEA
Federal Energy Bar Association ... FEBA
Federal Energy Emergency Administration ... FEEA
Federal Energy Information Locator Systems ... FEILS
Federal Energy Office [*Later, FEA*] ... FEO
Federal Energy Regulatory Commission [*Department of Energy*] ... FERC
Federal Environmental Pesticide Control Act [*1972*] ... FEPCA
Federal Equal Opportunity Recruitment Program ... FEORP
Federal Excise Tax ... FET
Federal Excise Tax Council [*Defunct*] ... FETC
Federal Executive Association ... FEA
Federal Executive Board ... FEB
Federal Executive Development Program [*Civil Service Commission*] ... FEDP
Federal Executive Drug Abuse Council ... FEDAC
Federal Executive Institute ... FEI
Federal Executive and Professional Association ... FEPA
Federal Executive Service ... FES
Federal Express Corp. [*Little Rock, AR*] [*FAA designator*] ... FDE
Federal Express Corp. [*NYSE symbol*] ... FDX
Federal Extension Service [*Department of Agriculture*] ... FES
Federal Facilities Corporation [*Dissolved, 1961*] ... FFC
Federal Farm Board [*Name changed to Farm Credit Administration, 1933*] ... FFB
Federal Farm Credit Board [*of FCA*] ... FFCB
Federal Farm Mortgage Corporation [*Established, 1934; assets transferred to Secretary of the Treasury, 1961*] ... FFMC
Federal Financial Participation ... FFP
Federal Financing Bank ... FFB
Federal Fire Council [*Defunct*] ... FFC
Federal Firearms Act ... FFA
Federal Fiscal Liability ... FFL
Federal Food Advisory Committee [*Cost of Living Council*] ... FFAC
Federal Food, Drug, and Cosmetic Act ... FFDCA
Federal German Navy ... FGN
Federal Government Accountants Association [*Later, AGA*] ... FGAA
Federal Grain Inspection Service [*Department of Agriculture*] ... FGIS

Federal Hall National Memorial .... FEHA
Federal Hazardous Substances Act .... FHSA
Federal Health Programs Service [*Health Services and Mental Health Administration, HEW*] .... FHPS
Federal Highway Administration [*Department of Transportation*] .... FHA
Federal Highway Administration [*Department of Transportation*] .... FHWA
Federal Highway Cost Allocation Study [*Also, HCAS*] .... FHCAS
Federal Home Loan Bank .... FHLB
Federal Home Loan Bank Board [*Independent government agency*] .... FHLBB
Federal Home Loan Bank Board, Accounts Payable, Washington, DC [*OCLC symbol*] .... HLB
Federal Home Loan Bank Board. Journal [*A publication*] .... Fed Home Loan Bk Bd J
Federal Home Loan Bank Board. Journal [*A publication*] .... FHLBB Jrl
Federal Home Loan Mortgage Corporation [*Federal Home Loan Bank Board*] [*Nickname: "Freddie Mac"*] .... FHLMC
Federal Housing Administration [*HUD*] .... FHA
Federal Housing Administration Matters [*FBI standardized term*] .... FHAM
Federal Housing Authority Insurance .... FHAI
Federal Housing Corporation .... FHC
Federal Housing Representative [*Australia*] .... FHR
Federal Income Tax .... FIT
Federal Income Tax Withholding .... FITW
Federal Information Center [*General Services Administration*] .... FIC
Federal Information Locator System .... FILS
Federal Information Processing Standards [*National Bureau of Standards*] .... FIPS
Federal Information Processing Standards Coordinating and Advisory Committee [*National Bureau of Standards*] .... FIPSCAC
Federal Information Processing Standards Publication [*National Bureau of Standards*] .... FIPS-PUB
Federal Information Processing Standards Register [*National Bureau of Standards*] .... FIPSR
Federal Information Requirements Management Council .... FIRMCO
Federal Insecticide, Fungicide, and Rodenticide Act [*1947*] [*Department of Agriculture*] .... FIFRA
Federal Institute for Snow and Avalanche Research .... FISAR
Federal Insurance Administration [*HUD*] .... FIA
Federal Insurance Administration, Office of Risk Assessment, Technical Operations Division, Production Control Branch of the Federal Emergency Management Agency .... FIA/ORA/TOD/PCB/FEMA
Federal Insurance Contributions Act [*Under which collections are made from employers and employees for OASDI benefits*] .... FICA
Federal Insured Student Loan Program .... FISLP
Federal Inter-Agency Sedimentation Conference [*Department of Agriculture*] .... FIASC
Federal Interagency Broadcast Committee .... FIBC
Federal Interagency Committee on Education .... FICE
Federal Interagency Media Committee .... FIMC
Federal Interagency Task Force on Inadvertent Modification of the Stratosphere .... FITFIMS
Federal Intermediate Credit Bank .... FICB
Federal Internal Security Board [*Formerly, Subversive Activities Control Board*] .... FISB
Federal Inventory Accounting .... FIA
Federal Item Identification .... FII
Federal Item Identification Guide System .... FIIGS
Federal Item Identification Guides .... FIIG
Federal Item Identification Guides for Supply Cataloging .... FIIGSC
Federal Item Identification Number .... FIIN
Federal Item Inventory Group .... FIIG
Federal Item Logistics Data .... FILD
Federal Item Logistics Data Record .... FILDR
Federal Item Name .... FIN
Federal Item Name Directory .... FIND
Federal Judicial Center .... FJC
Federal Labor Laws .... FELL
Federal Labor-Management Consultant [*A publication*] .... FLMC
Federal Labor Relations Authority [*Independent government agency*] .... FLRA
Federal Labor Relations Council [*Later, FLRA*] .... FLRC
Federal Lake Survey Center .... FLSC
Federal Land Bank .... FLB
Federal Land Bank Association .... FLBA
Federal Land Development Authority [*Malaysia*] .... FLDA
Federal Law Enforcement Officers Association .... FLEOA
Federal Law Enforcement Training Center [*Department of the Treasury*] .... FLETC
Federal Law Enforcement Training Center, Glynco, GA [*Library symbol*] .... GGIF
Federal Law Review [*A publication*] .... F L Rev
Federal League [*Major league in baseball, 1914-15*] .... FL
Federal Legal Information Through Electronics [*Air Force and Department of Justice*] .... FLITE
Federal Librarians Association [*Defunct*] .... FLA
Federal Librarians Round Table [*American Library Association*] .... FLIRT
Federal Librarians Round Table [*American Library Association*] .... FLRT
Federal Libraries' Experiment in Cooperative Cataloging [*Later, FEDLINK*] .... FLECC
Federal Library Committee [*Library of Congress*] .... FLC
Federal Library and Information Network [*Formerly, FLECC*] [*Library network*] .... FEDLINK
Federal Licensed Officers Association .... FLOA
Federal Licensing Examination [*for physicians*] .... FLEX
Federal Loan Administration .... FLA
Federal Loan Agency [*Abolished 1947, records transferred to Reconstruction Finance Corporation*] .... FLA
Federal Local Port Controller .... FLPC
Federal Management Circular .... FMC
Federal Managers Association .... FMA
Federal Manual for Supply Cataloging .... FMSC
Federal Manufacturers Code .... FMC
Federal Maritime Board [*1950-1961; functions transferred to FMC*] .... FMB
Federal Maritime Commission [*Independent government agency*] .... FMC
Federal Meat Inspection Act .... FMIA
Federal Mediation and Conciliation Service [*Independent government agency*] .... FMCS
Federal Merit Promotion Program .... FMPP
Federal Meteorological Handbook .... FMH
Federal-Mogul Corp. [*NYSE symbol*] .... FMO
Federal Motor Vehicle Safety Standard .... FMVSS
Federal Music Society .... FMS
Federal National Mortgage Association [*Wall Street slang name: "Fannie Mae"*] [*NYSE symbol*] .... FNM
Federal National Mortgage Association [*Wall Street slang name: "Fannie Mae"*] .... FNMA
Federal National Railroad Association [*Proposed railroad corporation*] [*Nickname: Fannie Rae*] .... FNRA
Federal Oceanographic Fleet Coordination Council .... FOFCC
Federal Office Building .... FOB
Federal Official .... FO
Federal Oil & Gas Corporation .... FOGCO
Federal Open Market Committee [*Also, OMC*] [*Federal Reserve System*] .... FOMC
Federal Pacific Electric Company [*NYSE symbol*] [*Delisted*] .... FPC
Federal Pacific Electric Company .... FPEC
Federal Paper Board Co., Inc. [*NYSE symbol*] .... FBO
Federal Parent Locator Service [*HEW*] .... FPLS
Federal Pattern Description .... FPD
Federal Pecan Growers .... FPG
Federal Personnel Council [*Abolished, 1954*] [*Civil Service Commission*] .... FPC
Federal Personnel Intern [*Program*] [*Civil Service Commission*] .... FPI
Federal Personnel Management Information System [*Civil Service Commission*] .... FPMIS
Federal Personnel Manual .... FPM
Federal Petroleum Board [*Department of the Interior*] .... FPB
Federal Photovoltaics Utilization Program [*Department of Energy*] .... FPUP
Federal Physicians Association .... FPA
Federal Plant Quarantine Inspectors National Association [*Later, NAAE*] .... FPQI
Federal Plant Quarantine Inspectors National Association [*Later, NAAE*] .... FPQINA
Federal Post Card Application [*For an absentee ballot*] .... FPCA
Federal Power Commission [*Superseded by Department of Energy, 1977*] .... FPC
Federal Power Commission Reports .... FPCR
Federal Preparedness Agency [*FEMA*] .... FPA
Federal Prison Industries, Inc. [*Department of Justice*] .... FPI
Federal Prison System .... FPS
Federal Probation [*A publication*] .... Fed Prob
Federal Probation [*A publication*] .... Fed Probat
Federal Probation Officers Association .... FPOA
Federal Procurement Eligibility .... FPE
Federal Procurement Institute [*Later, FAI*] .... FPI
Federal Procurement Regulations .... FPR
Federal Professional Association [*Later, FEPA*] .... FPA
Federal Property and Administrative Services Act [*1949*] .... FPASA
Federal Property Assistance [*Department of Health and Human Services*] .... FPA
Federal Property Council [*Terminated, 1977*] .... FPC
Federal Property Management Regulations .... FPMR
Federal Protective Officer [*General Services Administration*] .... FPO
Federal Protective Service [*General Services Administration*] .... FPS
Federal-Provincial Relations Office [*Canada*] .... FPRO
Federal Public Housing Authority [*Functions transferred to Public Housing Administration, 1947*] .... FPHA
Federal Publisher's Committee .... FPC
Federal Radiation Council [*Defunct*] .... FRC
Federal Radio Commission [*Functions transferred to FCC, 1934*] .... FRC
Federal Radio Education Committee .... FREC
Federal Railroad Administration .... FRA
Federal Ranch [*British Columbia*] [*Seismograph station code, US Geological Survey*] [*Closed*] .... FRC
Federal Real Estate Board [*Abolished, 1951*] .... FREB
Federal Realty Investment Trust SBI [*American Stock Exchange symbol*] .... FRT
Federal Records Center [*General Services Administration*] .... FRC
Federal Records Center, San Francisco, CA [*Library symbol*] .... CSfFRC
Federal Records Center, Seattle, WA [*Library symbol*] .... WaSFRC

Federal Records Council .... FRC
Federal Reference Method .... FRM
Federal Regional Center [*Office of Civil Defense*] .... FRC
Federal Regional Council [*for federal-state-local interchange*] [*Abolished, 1983*] .... FRC
Federal Regional Reconstitutional Area .... FRRA
Federal Register [*A publication*] .... Fed Regist
Federal Register .... FR
Federal Register Reprint .... FRR
Federal Regular Army [*Federation of South Arabia*] .... FRA
Federal Regulation of Lobbying Act .... FRLA
Federal Republic .... FR
Federal Republic of Germany [*Two-letter standard code*] .... DE
Federal Republic of Germany [*Three-letter standard code*] .... DEU
Federal Republic of Germany .... FRG
Federal Republic of Germany [*NATO*] .... GE
Federal Research on Biological and Health Effects of Ionizing Radiations .... FREIR
Federal Research Contract Center .... FRCC
Federal Reserve .... FR
Federal Reserve Act .... FRA
Federal Reserve Bank of Atlanta, Atlanta, GA [*OCLC symbol*] .... GFR
Federal Reserve Bank of Atlanta. Economic Review [*A publication*] .... Fed Atlant
Federal Reserve Bank of Atlanta, Research Library, Atlanta, GA [*Library symbol*] .... GAFR
Federal Reserve Bank of Boston, Boston, MA [*Library symbol*] .... MBFR
Federal Reserve Bank of Boston, Boston, MA [*OCLC symbol*] RF1
Federal Reserve Bank of Chicago Library, Chicago, IL [*OCLC symbol*] .... ITT
Federal Reserve Bank of Cleveland, Cleveland, OH [*Library symbol*] .... OCIFRB
Federal Reserve Bank of Dallas, Dallas, TX [*OCLC symbol*] .... FRD
Federal Reserve Bank of Dallas, Dallas, TX [*Library symbol*] .... TxDaFR
Federal Reserve Bank of Dallas. Farm and Ranch Bulletin [*A publication*] .... Fed Dallas
Federal Reserve Bank of Kansas City, Kansas City, MO [*OCLC symbol*] .... FRK
Federal Reserve Bank of Kansas City, Kansas City, MO [*Library symbol*] .... MoKFR
Federal Reserve Bank of Kansas City. Monthly Review [*A publication*] .... Fed KC
Federal Reserve Bank of New York. Quarterly Review [*A publication*] .... Fed Res Bank NY
Federal Reserve Bank of Philadelphia. Business Review [*A publication*] .... Fed Phila
Federal Reserve Bank of Philadelphia, Philadelphia, PA [*OCLC symbol*] .... FRC
Federal Reserve Bank of Philadelphia, Philadelphia, PA [*Library symbol*] .... PPFRB
Federal Reserve Bank of Richmond, Richmond, VA [*OCLC symbol*] .... FRR
Federal Reserve Bank of Richmond, Richmond, VA [*Library symbol*] .... ViRFR
Federal Reserve Bank of St. Louis. Monthly Review [*A publication*] .... Fed St L
Federal Reserve Bank of St. Louis, St. Louis, MO [*OCLC symbol*] .... FRS
Federal Reserve Bank of San Francisco, San Francisco, CA [*Library symbol*] .... CSfFB
Federal Reserve Banks [*of FRS*] .... FRB
Federal Reserve Board [*Later, BGFRS*] .... FRB
Federal Reserve Bulletin [*A publication*] .... Fed Res Bull
Federal Reserve Bulletin [*A publication*] .... Fed Reserve B
Federal Reserve District .... FRD
Federal Reserve Note .... FRN
Federal Reserve System [*Independent government agency*] .... FRS
Federal Reserve System Bank .... FRSB
Federal Reserve System, Board of Governors, Washington, DC [*OCLC symbol*] .... FRG
Federal Resources Corp. [*American Stock Exchange symbol*] .... FDR
Federal Rules Decisions [*A publication*] .... Fed R D
Federal Rules Decisions [*A publication*] .... FRD
Federal Safety Advisory Council [*Later, FACOSH*] .... FSAC
Federal Safety Council .... FSC
Federal Savings & Loan Insurance Corporation [*of FHLBB*] .... FSLIC
Federal Science Policy Council [*Later, FCCSET*] .... FSPC
Federal Screw Works [*NASDAQ symbol*] .... FSCR
Federal Secure Telephone System [*DoD*] .... FSTS
Federal Security Agency [*Functions and units transferred to HEW, 1953*] .... FSA
Federal Security Agency, Health, Education, and Welfare .... FSHEW
Federal Service Campaign for National Health Agencies [*Later, National Health Agencies for the Combined Federal Campaign*] .... FSCNHA
Federal Service Entrance Examination [*Later, PACE*] [*Civil Service*] .... FSEE
Federal Service Impasses Panel .... FSIP
Federal Sewage Research Association [*Later, Federal Water Quality Association*] .... FSRA
Federal Shelter Incentive Program .... FSIP
Federal Signal Corp. [*Formerly, Federal Sign & Signal Corp.*] [*NYSE symbol*] .... FSS
Federal Simulation Center .... FEDSIM
Federal Simulation Center .... FSC
Federal Software Exchange Center .... FSWEC
Federal Solar Energy Research Institute [*Energy Research and Development Administration*] .... FSERI
Federal Specification .... FEDSPEC
Federal Specification .... FS
Federal Specification Board .... FSB
Federal Specifications Executive Committee .... FSEC
Federal Standard .... FEDSTD
Federal Standard .... FS
Federal Standard Requisitioning and Issue Procedure .... FEDSTRIP
Federal Standard Stock Catalog .... FSSC
Federal Statistical Data Center .... FSDC
Federal Statistics Users' Conference .... FSUC
Federal Stock [*or Supply*] **Catalog** .... FSC
Federal Stock Classification .... FSC
Federal Stock Control .... FSC
Federal Stock Group .... FSG
Federal Stock Item .... FSI
Federal Stock Listings .... FSL
Federal Stock Number [*Later, NSN*] .... FSN
Federal Stock Number [*later, NSN*] **Master Data Record** .... FSNMDR
Federal Supplemental Benefits .... FSB
Federal Supply Classification .... FSC
Federal Supply Classification Code .... FSCC
Federal Supply Classification Group .... FSCG
Federal Supply Classification Listing .... FSCL
Federal Supply Classification/Material Management Aggregation .... FSC/MMAC
Federal Supply Code .... FSC
Federal Supply Code for Manufacturers .... FSCM
Federal Supply Code for Non-Manufacturers .... FSCNM
Federal Supply Group [*Air Force*] .... FSG
Federal Supply Group [*Air Force*] .... FSGp
Federal Supply Manufacturers' Code [*DoD*] .... FSMC
Federal Supply Schedule .... FSS
[*Office of*] **Federal Supply and Services** [*GSA*] .... FSS
Federal Supply Storage Depot .... FSSD
Federal Surplus Commodities Corporation .... FSCC
Federal Tax Deposit [*IRS*] .... FTD
Federal Tax Included .... FTI
Federal Telecommunications Laboratory [*Air Force*] .... FTL
Federal Telecommunications Records Center .... FTRC
Federal Telecommunications System [*of GSA*] .... FTS
Federal Telephone and Radio .... FTR
Federal Telephone System .... FTS
Federal Test Method Standards .... FTMS
Federal Test Procedure .... FTP
Federal Theater Project .... FTP
Federal Timber Purchasers Association .... FTPA
Federal Tobacco Inspectors Mutual Association .... FTIMA
Federal Tort Claims Act .... FTCA
Federal Trade Commission [*Independent government agency*] [*OCLC symbol*] .... FTC
Federal Trade Union Congress [*European*] .... FTUC
Federal Trade Zone .... FTZ
Federal Train Wreck Statute .... FTWS
Federal Travel Regulations .... FTR
Federal Trial Examiners Conference [*Later, FALJC*] .... FTEC
Federal Triangle [*Washington, DC*] .... FT
Federal Unemployment Account [*Unemployment insurance*] .... FUA
Federal Unemployment Benefit Account [*Unemployment insurance*] .... FUBA
Federal Unemployment Tax .... FUT
Federal Unemployment Tax Act .... FUTA
Federal Union of European Nationalities .... FUEN
Federal Wage Systems [*DoD*] .... FWS
Federal Warning Center .... FWC
Federal Water Pollution Control Act [*1965*] .... FWPCA
Federal Water Pollution Control Administration [*Later, OWP*] [*Department of the Interior*] .... FWPCA
Federal Water Quality Administration [*Later, OWP*] [*Environmental Protection Agency*] .... FWQA
Federal Water Quality Association .... FWQA
Federal Water Resources Council .... FWRC
Federal Way School District Central Library, Federal Way, WA [*Library symbol*] .... WaFwS
Federal Wholesale Druggists Association [*Later, DWA*] .... FWDA
Federal Wildlife Permit Office [*Department of the Interior*] .... FWPO
Federal Women's Program .... FWP
Federal Women's Program Committee/Coordinator .... FWOP
Federal Women's Program Committee/Coordinator .... FWPC
Federal Works Agency [*Abolished, 1949*] .... FWA
Federal Writers' Project [*Obsolete*] .... FWP
Federalist .... FED
Federally Assisted Code Enforcement [*Proposed HUD program*] .... FACE
Federally Employed Women [*An association*] .... FEW
Federally Funded Research and Development Center [*National Science Foundation*] .... FFRDC
Federally Insured Student Loan .... FISL
Federal's, Inc. [*NYSE symbol*] [*Delisted*] .... FDL
Federalsburg, MD [*Radio station call letters*] .... WCTD-FM

Federated Canadian Mining Institute. Journal [A publication]......................Fed Can M Inst J

Federated Clerks' Union of Australia.....................FCUA

Federated Council of Beth Jacob Schools [Formerly, NCBJS]............FCBJS

Federated Council of Israel Institutions ....FCII

Federated Department Stores, Inc. [NYSE symbol].....................FDS

Federated Development Co. [NYSE symbol] [Delisted].....................FDM

Federated Engineering Union ....FEU

Federated Funeral Directors of America ....FFD of A

[The] Federated Group [NASDAQ symbol].....................FEGP

Federated Guaranty Life [NASDAQ symbol].....................FEDG

Federated Institution of Mining Engineers. Transactions [A publication].....................Fed Inst M Eng Tr

Federated Ironworkers' Association of Australia ....FIA

Federated Malay States.....................FMS

Federated Natural Resources Cl B [NASDAQ symbol].....................FNRCB

Federated Pecan Growers' Associations of the United States ....FPGAUS

Federated Purchasers [NASDAQ symbol].....................FEDP

Federated Russian Orthodox Clubs.....................FROC

Federated States of Micronesia ....FSM

Federated Superannuation Scheme for Universities [British]..............FSSU

Federation ....FED

Federation ....FEDN

Federation Abolitionniste Internationale [International Abolitionist Federation].....................FAI

Federation for Accessible Nursing Education and Licensure............FANEL

Federation d'Action Nationale et Europeenne [Federation for National and European Action] [Neo-Nazi organization].................FANE

Federation Aeronautique Internationale [International Aeronautical Federation].....................FAI

Federation of All Okinawan Labor Unions.....................FAOLU

Federation of All Okinawan Military Employees' Labor Unions .... FAOMELU

Federation of Alpine and Schuhplattler Clubs in North America .... FASCNA

Federation of American Citizens of German Descent [Later, DANK].....................FACGD

Federation of American Controlled Shipping [Formerly, ACFN]...........FACS

Federation of American Hospitals ....FAH

Federation for American Immigration Reform ....FAIR

Federation of American Scientists ....FAS

Federation of American Societies for Experimental Biology ....FASEB

Federation of American Women's Clubs Overseas ....FAWCO

Federation of Americans Supporting Science and Technology ....FASST

Federation of Analytical Chemistry and Spectroscopy Societies ......FACSS

Federation of Apparel Manufacturers.....................FAM

Federation of Armenian Students Clubs of America.....................FASCA

Federation of Asian Pharmaceutical Associations ....FAPA

Federation of Asian Photographic Art ....FAPA

Federation of Asian Women's Associations ....FAWA

Federation des Associations de Chasseurs de la CEE [Federation of Hunting Associations of the European Economic Community] ....FACE

Federation of Associations of Health Regulatory Boards.................FAHRB

Federation des Associations Internationales Etablies en Belgique [Federation of International Associations Established in Belgium] ....FAIB

Federation d'Associations de Techniciens des Industries des Peintures, Vernis, Emaux, et Encres d'Imprimerie de l'Europe Continentale [Federation of Associations of Technicians in the Paint, Varnishes, Enamels, and Printing-Ink Industries of Continental Europe].....................FATIPEC

Federation des Associations Tribales des Originaires du Kasai [Federation of Associations of Kasai Tribes].....................FEDEKA

Federation of Astronomical and Geophysical Data Analysis Services ....FAGS

Federation of British Industries [Later, CBI].....................FBI

Federation Bulletin [A publication].....................Fed Bull

Federation of Cambodian Associations in North America ....FCANA

Federation of Canadian Artists ....FCA

Federation of Cash Grain Commission Merchants Associations [Defunct].....................FCGCMA

Federation of Catholic Physicians Guilds ....FCPG

Federation of Civil Service and Primary Aided School Teachers' Unions [Mauritius].....................FCSPASTU

Federation of Civil Service Unions of Mauritius.....................FCSUM

[The] Federation of Commodity Associations [Common Market] ....TFCA

Federation des Concours Internationaux de Musique [Federation of International Music Competitions].....................FCIM

Federation for Constitutional Government [Defunct] ....FCG

Federation Cynologique Internationale [International Federation of Kennel Clubs].....................FCI

Federation of Danish Trade Unions ....FDTU

Federation Democratique Internationale des Femmes [Women's International Democratic Federation] [See also WIDF].....................FDIF

Federation Dentaire Internationale [International Dental Federation].......FDI

Federation of Dental Diagnostic Sciences ....FDDS

Federation pour le Developpement de l'Artisanat Utilitaire [Federation for the Development of Utilitarian Crafts].....................FEDEAU

Federation of Digestive Disease Societies ....FDDS

Federation de l'Education Nationale [Federation of National Education].....................FEN

Federation of Egalitarian Communities.....................FEC

Federation des Employes Congolais des Banques [Federation of Congolese Bank Clerks].....................FECB

Federation Employment and Guidance Service ....FEGS

Federation des Enseignants d'Afrique Noire [Federation of Teachers of Black Africa].....................FEAN

Federation des Entreprises au Congo [Merger of AIIB and AICB]...........FEC

Federation Equestre Internationale [International Equestrian Federation].....................FEI

Federation des Etudiants d'Afrique Noire en France [Federation of Students of Black Africa in France].....................FEANF

Federation des Etudiants Revolutionaires [France].....................FER

Federation of European American Organizations ....FEAO

Federation of European Biochemical Societies ....FEBS

Federation of European Industrial Editors' Associations ....FEIEA

Federation of European Petroleum Equipment Manufacturers ....FEPEM

Federation of European Wholesale and International Trade Associations [Common Market].....................FEWITA

Federation Europeenne des Associations de Conseils en Organisation [European Federation of Management Consultants Associations].....................FEACO

Federation Europeenne des Associations d'Ingenieurs de Securite et de Chefs de Service de Securite [European Federation of Associations of Engineers and Heads of Industrial Safety Services].....................FEAICS

Federation Europeenne d'Associations Nationales d'Ingenieurs [European Federation of National Associations of Engineers].........FEANI

Federation Europeenne des Constructeurs d'Equipement Petrolier [European Federation of Petroleum Equipment Manufacturers].....................FECEP

Federation Europeenne des Fabricants d'Adjuvants pour la Nutrition Animale [European Federation of Manufacturers of Feed Additives] [Common Market].....................FEFANA

Federation Europeenne des Fabricants d'Aliments Composes pour Animaux [European Federation of Compound Animal Feeding Stuffs Manufacturers] [Common Market] ....FEFAC

Federation Europeenne des Fabricants de Carton Ondule [European Federation of Manufacturers of Corrugated Board]......FEFCO

Federation Europeenne des Fabricants de Ceramiques Sanitaires [European Federation of Sanitary Ceramic Manufacturers].....................FECS

Federation Europeenne des Fabricants de Produits Abrasifs ....FEPA

Federation Europeenne des Fabricants de Sacs en Papier a Grande Contenance [European Federation of Manufacturers of Multiwall Paper Sacks].....................EUROSAC

Federation Europeenne des Importateurs de Fruits Secs, Conserves, Epices et Miels [European Federation of Importers of Dried Fruits, Preserves, Spices, and Honey].....................FRUCOM

Federation Europeenne de l'Industrie des Aliments pour Animaux Familiers [European Pet Foods Industry Federation] [Common Market].....................FEDIAF

Federation Europeenne des Industries Techniques du Cinema..........FEITC

Federation Europeenne de la Manutention [European Mechanical Handling Federation] ....FEM

Federation Europeenne des Masseurskinesitherapeutes Praticiens en Physiotherapie ....FEMK

Federation Europeenne des Motels [European Motel Federation] ....FEM

Federation Europeenne pour la Protection des Eaux [European Federation for the Protection of Water] ....FEPE

Federation Europeenne de la Publicite Exterieure [European Federation of Outdoor Advertising].....................FEPE

Federation Europeenne des Syndicats de Fabricants de Parquets [European Federation of Parquet Manufacturers Unions].....................FESFP

Federation Europeenne des Transports Aeriens Prives [European Federation of Independent Air Transport].....................FETAP

Federation Europeenne des Unions Professionelles de Fleuristes [European Federation of Florists] [Common Market].... FEUPF

Federation Europeenne de Zootechnie [European Federation for Animal Production].....................FEZ

Federation of Family History Societies.....................FFHS

Federation Feminine Franco-Americaine [Federation of French American Women].....................FFFA

Federation of Fly Fishers ....FFF

Federation des Fondations pour le Sante Mondiale [Federation of World Health Foundations].....................FFSM

Federation of Former Jewish Fighters ....FFJF

Federation Francaise des Cooperatives Agricoles d'Approvisionnement.....................FFCAA

Federation Francaise des Cooperatives Agricoles de Cereales.........FFCAC

Federation of Franco-American Genealogical and Historical Societies.....................FFAGHS

Federation of Free African Trade Unions of South Africa ....FOFATUSA

Federation of Free Byelorussian Journalists ....FFBJ

Federation of Free Farmers [Philippines].....................FFF

Federation of Free Labor [Philippines].....................FFL

Federation of Free Workers [Philippines].....................FFW

Federation of French Alliances in the United States [Later, FIAF]......FFAUS

Federation of French War Veterans.....................FFWV

Federation of Genealogical Societies.....................FGS

Federation Generale du Congo [Congolese General Federation] ....FGC

Federation Generale du Travail de Belgique [*Belgian General Federation of Labor*] .... FGTB

Federation Generale du Travail du Kongo [*General Federation of Labor of the Congo*] [*Leopoldville*] .... FGTK

Federation Generale des Tribes du Haut Katanga [*General Federation of Tribes of North Katanga*] .... FETRIKAT

Federation of German Industries .... FGI

Federation Graphique Internationale [*International Graphical Federation*] [*See also IGF*] .... FGI

Federation des Gynecologues et Obstetriciens de Langue Francaise [*Federation of French-Language Gynaecologists and Obstetricians*] .... FGOLF

Federation Halterophile Internationale [*International Weightlifting Federation*] [*See also IWF*] .... FHI

Federation of Hellenic American Societies of Greater New York .... FHAS

Federation of Historical Bottle Clubs .... FOHBC

Federation of Homemakers .... FH

Federation of Independent Trade Unions [*Lebanon*] .... FITU

Federation Independente des Batetelas [*Independent Federation of Batetelas*] .... FIBAT

Federation de l'Industrie Dentaire en Europe [*Federation of the European Dental Industry*] .... FIDE

Federation de l'Industrie de l'Huile d'Olive de la CEE [*Federation of the European Economic Community Olive Oil Industry*] .... FEDOLIVE

Federation des Industries de Matieres Premieres et des Ameliorants pour la Boulangerie et la Patisserie dans la CEE [*European Federation of Manufacturers of Bakers' and Confectioners' Ingredients and Additives*] [*Common Market*] ...... FEDIMA

Federation of Information Users .... FIU

Federation des Ingenieurs des Telecommunications de la Communaute Europeenne [*Federation of Telecommunications Engineers in the European Community*] .... FITCE

Federation des Institutions Internationales Semi-Officielles et Privees Etablies a Geneve [*Federation of Semi-Official and Private International Institutions Established in Geneva*] .... FIIG

Federation of Insurance Counsel .... FIC

Federation of Insurance Counsel. Quarterly [*A publication*] ....
Federation Ins Couns Q

Federation of Insurance Counsel. Quarterly [*A publication*] .... FICQ

Federation Interalliee des Evades de Guerre et des Passeurs ..... FIDEGEP

Federation of International American Clubs .... FIAC

Federation of International Civil Servants' Associations .... FICSA

Federation of International Country Air Personalities .... FICAP

Federation of International Poetry Associations .... FIPA

Federation International de Trampoline [*International Trampoline Federation*] .... FIT

Federation of International Trampoline Technical Committee .... FITTC

Federation of International Youth Travel Organizations .... FIYTO

Federation Internationale des Acteurs [*International Federation of Actors*] .... FIA

Federation Internationale des Agences de Voyages [*International Federation of Travel Agencies*] .... FIAV

Federation Internationale Amateur de Cyclisme [*International Amateur Cycling Federation*] .... FIAC

Federation Internationale des Amies de la Jeune Fille .... FIAJF

Federation Internationale des Archives du Film [*International Federation of Film Archives*] .... FIAF

Federation Internationale des Archives de Television [*International Federation of Television Archives - IFTA*] .... FIAT

Federation Internationale de l'Art Photographique [*International Federation of Photographic Art*] .... FIAP

Federation Internationale de l'Artisanat [*International Federation of Master-Craftsmen*] .... FIA

Federation Internationale des Associations de Bibliothecaires [*International Federation of Library Associations*] .... FIAB

Federation Internationale des Associations de Chefs de Publicite d'Annonceurs [*International Federation of Advertising Managers Associations*] .... FIAPA

Federation Internationale des Associations des Chimistes du Textile et da la Couleur .... FIACTC

Federation Internationale des Associations des Distributeurs de Films [*International Federation of Associations of Film Distributors*] .... FIAD

Federation Internationale des Associations d'Etudes Classiques [*International Federation of Associations of Classical Studies*] .... FIEC

Federation Internationale des Associations d'Etudiants en Medecine [*International Federation of Medical Students Associations*] [*See also IFMSA*] .... FIAEM

Federation Internationale des Associations de Fabricants de Produits d'Entretien [*International Federation of Associations of Manufacturers of Household Products*] .... FIFE

Federation Internationale des Associations d'Instituteurs [*International Federation of Teachers' Associations*] .... FIAI

Federation Internationale des Associations des Medecins Catholiques [*International Federation of Catholic Doctors*] .... FIAMC

Federation Internationale des Associations Nationales d'Eleves Ingenieurs [*International Federation of National Associations of Engineering Students*] .... FIANEI

Federation Internationale des Associations de Pilotes de Ligne .... FIAPL

Federation Internationale des Associations de Producteurs de Films [*International Federation of Film Producers' Associations*] .... FIAPF

Federation Internationale des Associations de Quincailliers et Marchands de Fer [*International Federation of Ironmongers and Iron Merchants Associations*] [*See also IFIA*] .... FIDAQ

Federation Internationale des Associations de Thanatopraxie [*International Federation of Thanatopractic Associations*] .... FIAT

Federation Internationale des Associations Touristiques de Cheminots [*International Federation of Railwaymen's Travel Associations*] .... FIATC

Federation Internationale des Associations de Transitaires et Assimiles [*International Federation of Forwarding Agents Associations*] .... FIATA

Federation Internationale des Associations de Travailleurs Evangeliques .... FIATE

Federation Internationale des Associations de Vexillologie [*International Federation of Vexillological Associations*] .... FIAV

Federation Internationale d'Athletisme Amateur [*International Federation of Amateur Athletics*] [*See also IAAF*] .... FIAA

Federation Internationale des Auberges de la Jeunesse [*International Youth Hostel Federation*] [*See also IYHF*] .... FIAJ

Federation Internationale de l'Automobile [*International Automobile Federation*] .... FIA

Federation Internationale des Aveugles [*International Federation of the Blind*] .... FIA

Federation Internationale de Baseball [*International Baseball Federation*] .... FIB

Federation Internationale de Basketball Amateur [*International Amateur Basketball Federation*] .... FIBA

Federation Internationale du Batiment et des Travaux Publics .... FIBTP

Federation Internationale de Bobsleigh et de Tobogganing [*International Bobsledding and Tobogganing Federation*] .... FIBT

Federation Internationale de Boules [*International Bowling Federation*] .... FIB

Federation Internationale des Bourses de Valeurs [*International Federation of Stock Exchanges*] .... FIBV

Federation Internationale des Bureaux d'Extraits de Presse [*International Federation of Press-Cutting Agencies*] .... FIBEP

Federation Internationale des Cadres de la Chimie et des Industries Annexes .... FICCIA

Federation Internationale des Cadres des Mines .... FICM

Federation Internationale de Camping et de Caravanning [*International Federation of Camping and Caravanning*] .... FICC

Federation Internationale de Canoe [*International Canoe Federation*] [*See also ICF*] .... FIC

Federation Internationale Catholique d'Education Physique et Sportive [*International Catholic Federation for Physical and Sports Education*] .... FICEP

Federation Internationale des Centres Sociaux et Communautaires [*International Federation of Settlements and Neighborhood Centers*] .... FIS

Federation Internationale de Centres Touristiques [*International Federation of Tourist Centers*] .... FICT

Federation Internationale des Chasseurs de Son [*International Federation of Sound Hunters*] .... FICS

Federation Internationale des Cheminots Antialcooliques [*International Railway Temperance Union*] .... FICA

Federation Internationale de Chimie Clinique [*International Federation of Clinical Chemistry*] .... FICC

Federation Internationale des Choeurs d'Enfants [*International Federation of Children's Choirs*] .... FICE

Federation Internationale des Cine-Clubs [*International Federation of Film Societies*] .... FICC

Federation Internationale des Clubs de Publicite [*International Federation of Advertising Clubs*] .... FICP

Federation Internationale du Commerce et des Industries du Camping .... FICIC

Federation Internationale du Commerce des Semences [*International Federation of the Seed Trade*] .... FIS

Federation Internationale des Communautes Educatif [*International Federation of Educative Communities*] .... FICE

Federation Internationale des Communautes d'Enfants [*International Federation of Children's Communities*] .... FICE

Federation Internationale de Communautes de Jeunesse Catholique Paroissiales [*International Federation of Catholic Parochial Youth Communities*] .... FIMCAP

Federation Internationale des Conseils Juridiques et Fiscaux [*International Federation of Legal Fiscal Consultants*] .... FICJF

Federation Internationale des Conseils en Propriete Industrielle [*International Federation of Industrial Property Attorneys*] .... FICPI

Federation Internationale du Cyclisme Professionel [*International Federation of Professional Cycling*] .... FICP

Federation Internationale des Demenageurs Internationaux [*Federation of International Furniture Removers*] .... FIDI

Federation Internationale du Diabete [*International Diabetes Federation*] [*See also IDF*] .... FID

Federation Internationale des Directeurs de Journaux Catholiques .... FIDJC

Federation Internationale des Distributeurs de Presse [*International Federation of Wholesale Newspaper, Periodical, and Book Distributors*] .... DISTRIPRESS

Federation Internationale de Documentation [*International Federation for Documentation*] ....FID

Federation Internationale de Documentation. News Bulletin [*A publication*] .... FID News Bull

Federation Internationale de Documentation. Revue de la Documentation [*A publication*] .... FID R Doc

Federation Internationale pour le Droit Europeen [*International Federation for European Law*] ....FIDE

Federation Internationale des Droits de l'Homme [*International Federation for the Rights of Man*] .... FIDH

Federation Internationale des Echecs [*International Chess Federation*] ....FIDE

Federation Internationale des Echecs [*International Chess Federation*] .... FIE

Federation Internationale pour l'Economie Familiale [*International Federation for Home Economics*] [*See also IFHE*] .... FIEF

Federation Internationale des Editeurs de Journaux et Publications [*International Federation of Newspaper Publishers*] ..... FIEJ

Federation Internationale des Editeurs de Medailles [*International Federation of Medal Producers*] ....FIDEM

Federation Internationale pour l'Education Artistique...................FEA

Federation Internationale pour l'Education des Parents [*International Federation for Parent Education - IFPE*] ....FIEP

Federation Internationale d'Education Physique [*International Federation for Physical Education*] ....FIEP

Federation Internationale des Employes et des Techniciens ....FIET

Federation Internationale de l'Enseignement Menager ....FIEM

Federation Internationale d'Escrime [*International Fencing Federation*] .... FIE

Federation Internationale des Etudiants en Pharmacie ....FIEP

Federation Internationale des Etudiants en Sciences Politiques ....FIESP

Federation Internationale des Experts en Automobile [*International Federation of Automobile Experts*] ....FIEA

Federation Internationale des Fabricants de Papiers Gommes [*International Federation of Gummed Paper Manufacturers*] .... FIPAGO

Federation Internationale des Fabricants et Transformateurs d'Adhesifs et Thermocollants sur Papiers et Autres Supports [*International Federation of Manufacturers and Converters of Pressure-Sensitive and Heatseals on Paper and Other Base Materials*] .... FINAT

Federation Internationale des Femmes de Carrieres Liberales et Commerciales [*International Federation of Business and Professional Women*].. FIFCLC

Federation Internationale des Femmes Diplomees des Universites [*International Federation of University Women*]........... FIFDU

Federation Internationale du Film sur d'Art [*International Federation of Films on Art*] ....FIFA

Federation Internationale des Fonctionnaires Superieurs de Police [*International Federation of Senior Police Officers*]...............FIFSP

Federation Internationale de Football Association [*International Federation of Association Football*] ....FIFA

Federation Internationale des Geometres [*International Federation of Surveyors*] [*See also IFS*] ....FIG

Federation Internationale des Grandes Entreprises de Distribution [*International Federation of Distributors*] ....FIGED

Federation Internationale des Grossistes, Importateurs, et Exportateurs en Fournitures Automobiles [*International Federation of Wholesalers, Importers, and Exporters in Automobile Fittings*] .... FIGIEFA

Federation Internationale de Gymnastique [*International Gymnastic Federation*] [*See also IGF*] ....FIG

Federation Internationale de Gynecologie et d'Obstetrique [*International Federation of Gynecology and Obstetrics*] ....FIGO

Federation Internationale de l'Habitation et de l'Urbanisme .... FIHU

Federation Internationale pour l'Habitation, l'Urbanisme, et l'Amenagement des Territoires [*International Federation for Housing and Planning*]...FIHUAT

Federation Internationale Halterophile et Culturiste...........................FIHC

Federation Internationale de Handball [*International Handball Federation*] ....FIH

Federation Internationale de Hockey [*International Hockey Federation*] ....FIH

Federation Internationale des Hommes Catholiques [*International Council of Catholic Men - ICCM*]....................FIHC

Federation Internationale des Hopitaux [*International Hospital Federation*] ....FIH

Federation Internationale de l'Industrie du Medicament [*International Federation of Pharmaceutical Manufacturers Associations*] [*See also IFPMA*] .... FIIM

Federation Internationale de l'Industrie Phonographique ....FIIP

Federation Internationale des Industries et du Commerce en Gros des Vins, Spiritueux, Eaux-de-Vie et Liqueurs [*International Union of Wine, Spirits, Brandy, and Liqueur Industrialists and Wholesalers*] ....FIVS

Federation Internationale des Ingenieurs-Conseils [*International Federation of Consulting Engineers*] .... FIDIC

Federation Internationale des Ingenieurs-Conseils en Propriete Industrielle ....FIICPI

Federation Internationale des Ingenieurs Municipaux [*International Federation of Municipal Engineers*] .... FIIM

Federation Internationale des Instituts de Recherches Socio-Religieuses [*International Federation of Institutes for Socio-Religious Research*] .... FERES

Federation Internationale des Intellectuels Aveugles ....FIDIA

Federation Internationale de la Jeunesse Catholique ....FIJC

Federation Internationale des Jeunesses Musicales [*International Federation of Young Musicians*] .... FIJM

Federation Internationale des Journalistes [*International Federation of Journalists*] [*See also IFJ*]...................................FIJ

Federation Internationale des Journalistes et Ecrivains du Tourisme [*International Federation of Tourism Journalists and Writers*] .... FIJET

Federation Internationale des Journalistes Libres [*International Federation of Free Journalists*]...FIJL

Federation Internationale des Journalistes Professionnels de l'Aeronautique ....FIJPA

Federation Internationale de Judo [*International Judo Federation*]...........FIJ

Federation Internationale de Laiterie [*International Dairy Federation*] [*See also IDF*] .... FIL

Federation Internationale de Laiterie. Bulletin Annuel [*A publication*].. Fed Int Lait Bull Annu

Federation Internationale des Langues et Litteratures Modernes [*International Federation for Modern Languages and Literatures*] .... FILLM

Federation Internationale de Lawn Tennis [*International Lawn Tennis Federation*] .... FILT

Federation Internationale Libre des Deportes et Internes de la Resistance [*International Free Federation of Deportees and Resistance Internees*] .... FILDIR

Federation Internationale de Luge de Course [*International Luge Federation*] .... FIL

Federation Internationale de Lutte Amateur [*International Amateur Wrestling Federation*] ....FILA

Federation Internationale de Medecine Physique [*International Federation of Physical Medicine*] ....FIMP

Federation Internationale Medecine Sportive [*International Federation of Sportive Medicine*] ....FIMS

Federation Internationale des Mineurs [*Miners' International Federation - MIF*] .... FIM

Federation Internationale Motocycliste [*International Motorcycle Federation*] .... FIM

Federation Internationale des Mouvements d'Adultes Ruraux Catholiques [*International Federation of Adult Rural Catholic Movements*]..FIMARC

Federation Internationale des Mouvements d'Ecole Moderne ....FIMEM

Federation Internationale des Mouvements Ouvriers Chretiens [*International Federation of Christian Workers Movements*] .... FIMOC

Federation Internationale des Musiciens [*International Federation of Musicians*] .... FIM

Federation Internationale des Mutiles et Invalides du Travail et des Invalides Civils [*International Federation of Disabled Workmen and Civilian Cripples*] ....FIMITIC

Federation Internationale de Natation Amateur [*International Amateur Swimming Federation*] ....FINA

Federation Internationale d'Oleiculture [*International Olive Growers Federation*]...FIO

Federation Internationale des Organisateurs de Festivals [*International Federation of Festival Organizations*] .... FIDOF

Federation Internationale pour l'Organisation de Rencontres de Handicapes [*International Federation for the Organization of Meetings for the Handicapped*] ....FIORH

Federation Internationale des Organisations de Correspondances et d'Echanges Scolaires [*International Federation of Organizations for School Correspondence and Exchange*]...FIOCES

Federation Internationale des Organisations de Donneurs de Sang Benevoles [*International Federation of Blood Donors Organizations*] [*See also IFBDO*]..FIODS

Federation Internationale des Organisations d'Hoteliers, Restaurateurs, et Cafetiers [*International Union of Associations of Hotel, Restaurant, and Cafe Keepers*] .... HORECA

Federation Internationale des Organisations de Sciences Sociales [*International Federation of Social Science Organizations - IFSSO*] .... FIOSS

Federation Internationale des Organisations Syndicales du Personnel des Transporte [*International Federation of Trade Unions of Transport Workers - IFTUTW*] .... FIOST

Federation Internationale des Organisations de Travailleurs de la Metallurgie [*International Metalworkers Federation - IMF*].........FIOM

Federation Internationale des Ouvriers de la Chaussure et du Cuir [*International Shoe and Leather Worker's Federation*].........FIOCC

Federation Internationale des Ouvriers sur Metaux [*International Metalworkers' Federation*] ....FIOM

Federation Internationale des Petites et Moyennes Entreprises Commerciales [*International Federation of Small and Medium-Sized Commercial Enterprises*].................................. FIPMEC

Federation Internationale Pharmaceutique [*International Pharmaceutical Federation*] ....FIP

Federation Internationale des Pharmaciens Catholiques [*International Federation of Catholic Chemists*]......................FIPC

Federation Internationale de Philatelie [*International Philatelic Federation*]...FIP

Federation Internationale des Phonotheques [*International Federation of Record Libraries*]..................................FIP

Federation Internationale des Pietons [*International Federation of Pedestrians*]...FIP

Federation Internationale de Podologie [*International Federation of Podology*]...FIP

Federation Internationale de la Precontrainte [*International Federation of Prestressed Concrete*]...........................FIP

Federation Internationale de la Presse Agricole.....................................FIPRA

Federation Internationale de la Presse Cinematographique [*International Federation of the Cinematographic Press*]...........FIPRESCI

Federation Internationale de la Presse Gastronomique et Vinicole [*International Federation of Gastronomical and Vinicultural Press*]..FIPREGA

Federation Internationale de la Presse Periodique [*International Federation of the Periodical Press*].......................................FIPP

Federation Internationale de la Presse Technique et Periodique [*International Federation of the Technical and Periodical Press*]......FIPTP

Federation Internationale des Producteurs Agricoles [*International Federation of Agricultural Producers*].....................FIPA

Federation Internationale des Producteurs Auto-Consommateurs Industriels d'Electricite [*International Federation of Industrial Producers of Electricity for Own Consumption*]...FIPACE

Federation Internationale des Producteurs de Jus de Fruits [*International Federation of Fruit Juice Producers*].............................FIJU

Federation Internationale des Producteurs de Jus de Fruits [*International Federation of Fruit Juice Producers*].............................FIPJF

Federation Internationale des Professeurs de l'Enseignement Secondaire Officiel [*International Federation of Secondary Teachers*]..FIPESO

Federation Internationale des Professeurs de Francais [*International Federation of Teachers of French*]..............................FIPF

Federation Internationale des Professeurs de Langues Vivantes [*International Federation of Modern Language Teachers*].............FIPLV

Federation Internationale des Professions Immobilieres ....FIABCI

Federation Internationale pour la Protection des Populations ....FIPP

Federation Internationale de Psychotherapie Medicale [*International Federation for Medical Psychotherapy*]...............FIPM

Federation Internationale des Quilleurs [*International Bowlers' Federation*]...FIQ

Federation Internationale des Reconstructeurs de Moteurs [*International Federation of Engine Reconditioners - IFER*].............FIRM

Federation Internationale des Redacteurs en Chef ....FIREC

Federation Internationale des Resistants [*International Federation of Resistance Movements*]....................................FIR

Federation Internationale de Roller-Skating [*International Roller Skating Federation*]..FIRS

Federation Internationale de Rugby Amateur [*International Amateur Rugby Federation*]...FIRA

Federation Internationale de Sauvetage ....FIS

Federation Internationale des Semaines d'Art ....FISA

Federation Internationale de Ski [*International Ski Association*]...............FIS

Federation Internationale des Societes Aerophilateliques [*International Federation of Aero-Philatelic Societies*].....................FISA

Federation Internationale des Societes d'Amateurs d'Exlibris ....FISAE

Federation Internationale des Societes Artistiques et Intellectuelles de Cheminots [*International Federation of Railwaymen's Art and Intellectual Societies*]..................FISAIC

Federation Internationale des Societes d'Aviron [*International Rowing Federation*]...FISA

Federation Internationale des Societes d'Ecrivains-Medecins ....FISEM

Federation Internationale des Societes d'Ingenieurs des Techniques de l'Automobile [*International Federation of Automobile Engineers' and Technicians' Associations*]................FISITA

Federation Internationale des Societes et Instituts pour l'Etude de la Renaissance [*International Federation of Societies and Institutes for the Study of the Renaissance*].........................FISIER

Federation Internationale des Societes Magiques [*International Federation of Magical Societies*].......................................FISM

Federation Internationale des Societes de Philosophie [*International Federation of Philosophical Societies*] [*IFPS*].........FISP

Federation Internationale du Sport Medical pour l'Aide a la Recherche Cancerologique [*International Medical Sports Federation for Aid to Cancer Research*]...........................FISMARC

Federation Internationale du Sport Universitaire [*International University Sports Federation*]..FISU

Federation Internationale Sportive de l'Enseignement Catholique .... FISEC

Federation Internationale de Stenographie et de Dactylographie [*International Federation of Shorthand and Typewriting*]...................FISD

Federation Internationale de Stenographie et de Dactylographie [*International Federation of Shorthand and Typewriting*] .... INTERSTENO

Federation Internationale et Syndicale des Employes de Madagascar [*International Federation and Union of Malagasy Employees*] [*WFTU affiliate*]..FISEMA

Federation Internationale Syndicale de l'Enseignement [*International Federation of Teachers' Unions*]............................FISE

Federation Internationale des Syndicats Chretiens d'Employes, Techniciens, Cadres, et Voyageurs de Commerce [*International Federation of Christian Trade Unions of Salaried Employees, Technicians, Managers, and Commercial Travellers*]...FISCETCV

Federation Internationale des Syndicats Chretiens de la Metalurgie [*International Federation of Christian Metalworkers Unions*]..FISCM

Federation Internationale des Syndicats Chretiens d'Ouvriers Agricoles [*International Federation of Christian Agricultural Workers Unions*]..FISCOA

Federation Internationale des Syndicats Chretiens d'Ouvriers du Batiment et du Bois [*International Federation of Christian Trade Unions of Building and Wood Workers*].................FISCOBB

Federation Internationale des Syndicats Chretiens des Travailleurs du Textile et de l'Habillement [*International Federation of Christian Trade Unions of Textile and Clothing Workers*]..FISCTTH

Federation Internationale des Techniciens de la Bonneterie [*International Federation of Knitting Technologists - IFKT*]...........FITB

Federation Internationale de Tennis de Table [*International Table Tennis Federation*]...FITT

Federation Internationale du Thermalisme et du Climatisme [*International Federation of Thermalism and Climatism*].................FITEC

Federation Internationale de Tir a l'Arc [*International Archery Federation*]..FITA

Federation Internationale du Tourisme Social [*International Social Travel Federation*] [*See also ISTF*].............................FITS

Federation Internationale des Traducteurs [*International Federation of Translators*]..FIT

Federation Internationale des Transports Aeriens Prives [*International Federation of Private Air Transport*]......................FITAP

Federation Internationale des Travailleurs du Batiment et du Bois [*International Federation of Building and Woodworkers*].......FITBB

Federation Internationale des Travailleurs de l'Habillement ....FITH

Federation Internationale des Travailleurs des Industries du Textile de l'Habillement et du Cuir [*International Textile, Garment, and Leather Workers' Federation*]..........................FITITHC

Federation Internationale des Travailleurs des Industries du Textile, de l'Havillement, et du Cuir [*International Textile, Garment, and Leather Workers' Federation - ITGLWF*]...............FITTHC

Federation Internationale des Travailleurs du Petrole ....FITP

Federation Internationale des Travailleurs du Petrole et de la Chimie [*International Federation of Petroleum and Chemical Workers*]..FITPC

Federation Internationale des Travailleurs des Plantations ....FITP

Federation Internationale des Travailleurs des Plantations, de l'Agriculture, et des Secteurs Connexes [*International Federation of Plantation, Agricultural, and Allied Workers*].........FITPASC

Federation Internationale des Travailleurs de la Terre ....FITT

Federation Internationale des Universites Catholiques [*International Federation of Catholic Universities*].........................FIUC

Federation Internationale Veterinaire de Zootechnie...........................FIVZ

Federation Internationale de Volleyball [*International Volleyball Federation*]..FIVB

Federation of Interstate Truckers [*Acronym is title of film*]....................FIST

Federation of Islamic Associations in the US and Canada .... FIA

Federation des Jeunes Chefs d'Entreprises d'Europe [*European Federation of Young Managers*]..FJCEE

Federation of Jewish Charities, Philadelphia, PA [*Library symbol*] [*Obsolete*]...PPFJC

Federation of Jewish Philanthropies of New York ....FJP

Federation of Jewish Student Organizations [*Defunct*]....................FJSTO

Federation of Jewish Women's Organizations................................FJWO

Federation of Korean Trade Unions [*South Korea*]..........................FKTU

Federation of Labor Unions [*Lebanon*].....................................FLU

Federation of Labor Unions in Lebanon...................................FLUL

Federation Lainiere Internationale [*International Wool Textile Organization*] [*See also IWTO*]...................................... FLI

Federation of Libyan Labor Unions......................................FLLU

Federation Life Insurance of America ....FLIA

Federation of Lutheran Clubs ....FLC

Federation Lutherienne Mondiale [*Lutheran World Federation*] [*See also LWF*]...FLM

Federation of Masons of the World ....FMW

Federation of Materials Societies ....FMS

Federation des Medecins Omnipracticiens du Quebec, Montreal, PQ, Canada [*Library symbol*]...........................CaQMFMO

Federation des Medecins Specialistes du Quebec, Montreal, PQ, Canada [*Library symbol*]...................................CaQMFMS

Federation of Mental Health Centers [*Defunct*]..........................FMHC

Federation of Mobile Home Owners ....FMO

Federation of Modern Painters and Sculptors.............................FMPS

Federation Mondiale des Amis de Musees [*World Federation of Friends of Museums - WFFM*]...................................FMAM

Federation Mondiale des Anciens Combattants [*World Veterans Federation*] [*See also WVF*]......................................FMAC

Federation Mondiale des Associations pour les Nations Unies [*World Federation of United Nations Associations*]...................FMANU

Federation Mondiale des Communautes de Vie Chretienne [*World Federation of Christian Life Communities - WFCLC*].........FMCVC

Federation Mondiale de Jeunesse Catholique [*World Federation of Catholic Youth*] ....FMJC

Federation Mondiale de la Jeunesse Democratique [*World Federation of Democratic Youth*] [*See also WFDY*] ....FMJD

Federation Mondiale des Jeunesses Feminines Catholiques ....FMJFC

Federation Mondiale des Jeunesses Liberales et Radicales [*World Federation of Liberal and Radical Youth*] ....FMJLR

Federation Mondiale de Neurologie [*World Federation of Neurology*].....FMN

Federation Mondiale des Organisations d'Ingenieurs [*World Federation of Engineering Organizations*]......................................FMOI

Federation Mondiale pour la Protection des Animaux [*World Federation for the Protection of Animals*] [*Also known as WFPA and WTB*].. FMPA

Federation Mondiale pour la Sante Mentale [*World Federation for Mental Health*]...FMSM

Federation Mondiale des Sourds [*World Federation of the Deaf*] ....FMS

Federation Mondiale des Syndicats d'Industries [*World Federation of Industrial Workers' Unions*].............................FEMOSI

Federation Mondiale de Travailleurs Agricoles [*World Federation of Agricultural Workers - WFAW*]...............................FMTA

Federation Mondiale de Travailleurs des Industries Alimentaires, du Tabac, et de l'Hotellerie [*World Federation of Workers in Food, Tobacco, and Hotel Industries - WFFTH*]...........FMATH

Federation Mondiale des Travailleurs Non-Manuels [*World Federation of Trade Unions of Non-Manual Workers - WFNMW*] ....FMTNM

Federation Mondiale des Travailleurs Scientifiques [*World Federation of Scientific Workers*] [*See also WFSW*].........................FMTS

Federation Mondiale des Villes Jumelees [*United Towns Organization*]...FMDJ

Federation of Motion Picture Councils ....FMPC

Federation Museums Journal [*A publication*] ....FMJ

Federation of Mutual Fire Insurance Companies................................FMFIC

Federation of National Associations ....FNA

Federation of National Electrolysis Associations ....FNEA

Federation of National Professional Organizations for Recreation ... FNPOR

Federation Nationale d'Achats des Cadres [*Initials alone now used as name of discount-store chain in France*] [*Pronounced "f-nak"*]..FNAC

Federation Nationale des Centres d'Etudes Techniques Agricoles .... FNCETA

Federation Nationale des Cooperatives de Cereales ....FNCC

Federation Nationale des Cooperatives d'Utilisation de Materiel Agricole .... FNCUMA

Federation Nationale des Groupements Agricoles d'Approvisionnement .... FNGAA

Federation Nationale des Industries Electroniques Francaises [*National Federation of French Electronics Manufacturers*] ....FNIE

Federation Nationale des Organismes de Securite Sociale [*France*]..FNOSS

Federation Nationale des Patronages de Belgique..............................FNP

Federation Nationale des Syndicats du Commerce Ouest Africain [*National Federation of Commerce Unions - West Africa*] .... FENASYCOA

Federation Naturiste Internationale [*International Naturist Federation*].... FNI

Federation of NCR [*National Cash Register Corp.*] **User Groups** ....FNUG

Federation of NCR [*National Cash Register Corp.*] **User Groups** ....NUG

Federation of Nurses and Health Professionals ....FNHP

Federation of Organizations for Professional Women ....FOPW

Federation of Orthodontic Associations ....FOA

Federation of Outdoor Recreationists ....FOR

Federation of Paint and Varnish Production Clubs [*Later, FSCT*].......FPVPC

Federation of Pan-African Cinema [*of the Organization of African Unity*]...FEPACI

Federation of Parents and Friends of Lesbians and Gays .... P-FLAG

Federation des Personnels Africains de Police [*Federation of African Police*]...FAPAP

Federation of Postal Security Police..FPSP

Federation Proceedings [*A publication*]..Fed P

Federation Proceedings [*A publication*]......................................Fed Proc

Federation of Professional Writers of America ....FPWA

Federation for Progress...FFP

Federation of Progressive Trade Unions [*Zanzibar*]...........................FPTU

Federation Prohibitionniste Internationale [*International Prohibition Federation*]...FPI

Federation of Prosthodontic Organizations ....FPO

Federation of Protestant Welfare Agencies ....FPWA

Federation of Reconstructionist Congregations and Fellowships [*Later, FRCH*]..FRCF

Federation of Reconstructionist Congregations and Havurot ....FRCH

Federation of Regional Accrediting Commissions of Higher Education [*Later, COPA*] ....FRACHE

Federation of Rocky Mountain States..FRMS

Federation Royale des Associations Belges d'Ingenieurs [*Belgium*] ......FABI

Federation of Russian Charitable Organizations of the United States of America [*Defunct*] ....FRCOUSA

Federation des Salaries du Secteur Prive [*South Vietnam*]..................FSSP

Federation des Scouts du Congo...FEBOSCO

Federation Sephardite Mondiale [*World Sephardi Federation - WSF*] ....FSM

Federation of Sewage and Industrial Wastes Associations [*Later, Water Pollution Control Federation*] ....FSIWA

Federation des Societes Suisses d'Employes [*Federation of Swiss Employees' Societies*] .... FSSE

Federation of Societies for Coatings Technology [*Formerly, FPVPC, FSPT*] ....FSCT

Federation of Societies for Paint Technology [*Later, FSCT*] ....FSPT

Federation of Southern Cooperatives ....FSC

Federation Spirite Internationale [*International Spiritualist Federation*] ....FSI

Federation Sportive et Gymnique du Travail ....FSGT

Federation of State Associations of Independent Colleges and Universities [*Later, NAICU*]..FSAICU

Federation of State Medical Boards of the United States ....FSMB

Federation of State Medical Boards of the United States ....FSMBUS

Federation of Sterea Hellas ....FSH

Federation Suisse des Syndicats Chretiens-Nationaux [*Swiss Federation of National-Christian Trade Unions*] ....FSSCN

Federation of Swiss Employees' Societies...FSES

Federation Syndicale Mondiale [*World Federation of Trade Unions*] [*See also WFTU*]...FSM

Federation des Syndicats Libres des Travailleurs Luxembourgeois [*Free Luxembourg Workers' Federation*]...............FSL

Federation of Tax Administrators ....FTA

Federation of Telephone Workers ....FTW

Federation of Trainers and Training Programs in Psychodrama........ FTTPP

Federation of Turkish-American Societies [*Later, Turkish-American Associations*] .... FTAS

Federation of Turkish Revolutionary Youth...................................DEV GENC

Federation for Unified Science Education ....FUSE

Federation of Unions of Workers and Employees of North Lebanon.... FUNL

Federation Universelle des Associations d'Agences de Voyages [*Universal Federation of Travel Agents' Associations*] [*See also UFTAA*]...FUAAV

Federation Universelle des Associations Chretiennes d'Etudiants [*Universal Federation of Christian Students Associations*] ....FUACE

Federation of University Women...FUW

Federation des Veterinaires de la CEE [*Federation of Veterinarians of the European Economic Community*] .... FEVIR

Federation of West Indies ....FWI

Federation of Western Outdoor Clubs...FWOC

Federation of Westinghouse Independent Salaried Unions................FWISU

Federation of Westinghouse Independent Salaried Unions................WISU

Federation of Women Lawyers Judicial Screening Panel ....FWL

Federation of Women Shareholders in American Business...........FOWSAB

Federation of Women Shareholders in American Business.............FWSAB

Federation of Workers' Singing Societies of the USA ....FWSSUSA

Federation of World Health Foundations...FWHF

Federationa Narodna Republika Jugoslavija [*Yugoslavia*]...................FNRJ

Federazione Artisti e Professionisti Italiani [*Italian Federation of the Arts and Professions*]...FAPI

Federazione fra le Associazioni Nazionali Ufficiali e Sottufficiali in Congedo Provenienti dal Servizio Effettivo [*Federation of National Associations for Discharged Career Officers and Petty Officers*] [*Italy*]..FANUS

Federazione Autonoma Indossatrici [*Autonomous Federation of Models*] [*Italy*].. FAI

Federazione dei Chimici e Petrolieri [*Federation of Chemical and Petroleum Workers*] [*Italy*]..FCP

Federazione della Gente del Mare [*Federation of Seamen*] [*Italy*]... FEGEMARE

Federazione Giovanile Socialista [*Italy*].. FGS

Federazione Impiegati e Operai Metallurgici [*Federation of Metal Workers and Employees*] [*Italy*].......................................FIOM

Federazione Impiegati Operai Tessili [*Federation of Textile Workers*] [*Italy*]...FIOT

Federazione Internazionale della Stampa Gastronomica e Vinicola [*International Federation of Gastronomical and Vinicultural Press*]..FISGV

Federazione Italiana Addetti Industrie Zucchero e Alcole [*Italian Federation of Workers in the Sugar and Alcohol Industry*] .... FIAIZA

Federazione Italiana Agenti Rappresentanti Viaggiatorie e Paizzisti [*Italian Federation of Commercial Agents and Travelers*]...FIARVEP

Federazione Italiana Autoferrotramvieri e Internavigators [*National Federation of Busdrivers and Streetcar Conductors*] [*Italy*]...FIAI

Federazione Italiana Autonoma Lavoratori dello Spettacolo [*Italian Autonomous Federation of Entertainment Workers*]..........FIALS

Federazione Italiana Bancari [*Italian Federation of Bank Employees*] .... FIB

Federazione Italiana Dipendenti da Aziende di Credito [*Italian Federation of Credit Institution Employees*]..........................FIDAC

Federazione Italiana Dipendenti Aziende Elettriche [*Italian Federation of Electrical Workers*]...................................... FIDAE

Federazione Italiana Dipendenti Aziende Gas [*Italian Federation of Gas Workers*]..FIDAG

Federazione Italiana Dipendenti Aziende Telecomunicazioni [*Italian Federation of Communications Workers*]....................FIDAT

Federazione Italiana Dipendenti Enti Local [*Italian Federation of Local Government Employees*]..FIDEL

Federazione Italiana Dipendenti da Enti Parastatali e di Diritto Pubblico [*Italian Federation of Employees of Quasi-Governmental and State-Controlled Agencies*] .... FIDEP

Federazione Italiana della Gente dell'Aria [*Italian Federation of Airline Workers*] ....FIDGA

Federazione Italiana Lavoratori Abbigliamento [*Italian Federation of Garment Workers*] ....FILA

Federazione Italiana Lavoratori degli Acquedotti [*Italian Federation of Aqueduct Workers*] .... FILDA

Federazione Italiana Lavoratori Albergo Mensa e Termali [*National Union of Hotel and Restaurant Workers*] [*Italy*] ....FILAM

Federazione Italiana Lavoratori Ausiliari dell'Impiego [*Italian Federation of Auxiliary Services*] .... FILAI

Federazione Italiana Lavoratori Chimici [*Italian Federation of Chemical Workers*] ....FILC

Federazione Italiana Lavoratori Commercio e Aggregati [*Italian Federation of Commercial and Associated Workers*] ....FILCEA

Federazione Italiana Lavoratori Commercio Albergo Mensa e Servizi ....FILCAMS

Federazione Italiana Lavoratori Costruzioni e Affini [*Italian Federation of Construction and Related Workers*] ....FILCA

Federazione Italiana Lavoratori Industrie Alimentari [*Italian Federation of Food Processing Workers*] .... FILIA

Federazione Italiana Lavoratori Industrie Estrattive [*Italian Federation of Workers in Mining Industries*] .... FILIE

Federazione Italiana Lavoratori Legno-Boschivi - Artistiche e Varie [*National Federation of Carpenters, Lumbermen, and Cabinetmakers*] [*Italy*] ....FILLBAV

Federazione Italiana Lavoratori del Legno, dell'Edilizia e Industrie Affini [*Italian Federation of Construction and Allied Workers*] ....FILLEA

Federazione Italiana Lavoratori del Mare [*Italian Federation of Merchant Seamen*] .... FILM

Federazione Italiana Lavoratori Poligrafici e Cartai [*Italian Federation of Printers and Paperworkers*] ....FILPC

Federazione Italiana Lavoratori dei Porti [*Italian Federation of Longshoremen*] .... FILP

Federazione Italiana Lavoratori Sanatoriali [*Italian Federation of Public Health Workers - Hospital and Sanatorium Employees*] ....FILSA

Federazione Italiana Lavoratori Servizi Tributari e Assicuratori [*Italian Federation of Tax Workers*] .... FILSTA

Federazione Italiana Lavoratori dello Spettacolo [*Italian Federation of Entertainment Workers*] ....FILS

Federazione Italiana Lavoratori Statali [*Italian Federation of Government Employees*] ....FILS

Federazione Italiana del Lavoro [*Italian Federation of Labor*] ....FIL

Federazione Italiana Metal-Meccanici [*Italian Metal Mechanic Workers' Federation*] .... FIM

Federazione Italiana Pensionati [*Italian Federation of Pensioners*] ....FIP

Federazione Italiana Postelegrafonici [*Italian Federation of Postal, Telegraph, and Telephone Workers*] ....FIP

Federazione Italiana Salariati Braccianti Agricoli e Maestranze Specializzate Agricole e Forestali [*Italian Federation of Permanent Unskilled and Skilled Agricultural Workers*] .... FISBA

Federazione Italiana Salariati, Braccianti, e Tecnici Agricoli [*Italian Federation of Permanent, Daily, and Technical Agricultural Workers*] .... FISBTA

Federazione Italiana Servizi Pubblici [*Italian Federation of Public Services*] ....FISP

Federazione Italiana Sindacati Addetti Servizi Commerciali ed Affini [*Italian Federation of Commercial and Related Workers' Unions*] ....FISASCA

Federazione Italiana Sindacato Ospedalieri [*Italian Federation of Hospital Workers' Union*] ....FISO

Federazione Italiana Transportatori Artigiani ....FITA

Federazione Italiana Transporti ed Ausiliari del Traffico [*Italian Federation of Transportation and Auxiliary Services*] ....FILTAT

Federazione Italiana Venditori Ambulanti e Giornalai [*Italian Federation of Street Vendors and Newspaper Sellers*] ....FIVAG

Federazione Italiana Vigili del Fuoco [*Italian Federation of Firemen*] ...... FIVF

Federazione Lavoratori Aziende Elettriche Italiane [*Federation of Workers for Italian Electrical Firms*] ....FLAEI

Federazione Lavoratori Somali [*Somali Labor Federation*] ....FLS

Federazione Nazionale Dipendenti Enti Locali [*National Federation of Local Government*] [*Italy*] ....FNDEL

Federazione Nazionale Edili, Affini e del Legno [*National Federation of Building and Construction Workers*] [*Italy*] ....FENEAL

Federazione Nazionale dei Lavoratori Portuali [*National Federation of Port Workers*] [*Italy*] ....FENALPORTI

Federazione Nazionale delgi Statali [*Italian Federation of Government Employees*] ....FNDS

Federazione Nazionale Vetro e Ceramica [*National Federation of Glass and Pottery Workers*] [*Italy*] ....FNVCA

Federazione dei Sindacati Lavoratori Uniti della Somalia [*Somali Federation of United Trade Unions*] ....FSLUS

Federazione Svizzera dei Sindacati Cristiani [*Swiss Federation of National-Christian Trade Unions*] ....FSSC

Federazione Unitaria Italiana Lavoratori Abbigliamento [*Italian Amalgamated Federation of Garment Workers*] ....FUILA

Federazione Unitaria Lavoratori Chimici [*Italian union*] ....FULC

Federazione Unitaria Lavoratori Prodotti Industrie Alimentari e dello Zucchero e dell'Alcool [*Amalgamated Federation of Food Processing, Sugar and Liquor Industries' Workers*] [*Italy*] ....FULPIA

Federazione Unitaria Lavoratori dello Spettacolo [*Amalgamated Federation of Entertainment Workers*] [*Italy*] ....FULS

Fedetracao das Industrias do Estado do Espirito Santo ....FINDES

FEDLINK [*Federal Library and Information Network*], **Washington, DC** [*OCLC symbol*] ....FLC

FEDLINK [*Federal Library and Information Network*], **Washington, DC** [*OCLC symbol*] ....TPY

FEDLINK [*Federal Library and Information Network*], **Washington, DC** [*OCLC symbol*] ....TPZ

Fee Determination Official ....FDO

Fee Paid [*Classified advertising*] ....FP

Feed ....FD

Feed Assembly Modification ....FAM

Feed Efficiency Ratio ....FER

Feed Lines ....FL

Feed Management. Eastern Edition [*A publication*] ....Feed Manage E Ed

Feed Materials Production Center [*AEC*] ....FMPC

Feed Rate Number ....FRN

Feed Water ....FDW

Feed Water ....FW

Feed Water Heater Management ....FHM

Feed Water Heater Manufacturers Association ....FWHMA

Feed Water Pump ....FWP

Feedback ....F

Feedback ....FB

Feedback ....FDBK

Feedback Control Loop [*Data processing*] ....FCL

Feedback Control System ....FCS

Feedback Frequency Modulation ....FBFM

Feedback Inhibition Factor [*Immunochemistry*] ....FIF

Feedback Mechanism ....FM

Feedback, Multiple Loop ....FML

Feedback Network ....FBN

Feedback Node Set ....FNS

Feedback Positive ....FP

Feedback Potentiometer ....FP

Feedback Report ....FBR

Feedback Resistance ....FBR

Feedback Shift Register ....FSR

Feedback Signal ....FBS

Feedback, Stabilized ....FS

Feedback Summing Junction [*Data processing*] ....FSJ

Feedback System ....FBS

Feeder ....FDR

Feeder Distribution Interface [*Bell System*] ....FDI

Feeder Fault Sensing ....FFS

Feeder Lighter Aboard Ship ....FLASH

Feeding ....FDG

Feeding ....FDNG

Feedlot Waste ....FLW

Feedlot Waste Filtrate ....FLWF

Feeds Illustrated [*A publication*] ....Feed Illus

Feel Augmentation System [*Helicopters*] ....FAS

Feel, Inspect, Tighten, Clean, Adjust, Lubricate [*A keyword representing operations in preventive maintenance of communications equipment*] [*Military*] ....FITCAL

Feeler ....FELR

Feeley-Gorman [*Agar*] [*Microbiology*] ....F-G

Feeling Rough Inside [*Slang*] ....FRI

Feet [*or Foot*] ....F

Feet [*or Foot*] ....FT

Feet Board Measure ....FBM

Feet per Day ....FT/D

Feet per Hour ....FT/H

Feet per Minute ....FPM

Feet per Minute ....FT/MIN

Feet per Revolution ....FPR

Feet per Second ....FPS

Feet per Second ....FS

Feet per Second ....FT/S

Feet per Second ....FT/SEC

Feet per Second per Second ....FPSPS

Feet per Second per Second ....FPS/S

Feet per Year ....FT/A

Feingeraete Technik [*A publication*] ....Feingeraete Tech

Feingold Association of the United States ....FAUS

Feint [*of account book rulings*] ....FT

Feint and Cash [*of account book rulings*] ....FC

Feint and Cash [*of account book rulings*] ....FT & C

Feinwerktechnik und Messtechnik [*A publication*] ....Feinwerktech Messtech

Feinwerktechnik und Micronic [*A publication*] ....Feinwerktech & Micronic

Feldberg In Schwarzwald [*Federal Republic of Germany*] [*Seismograph station code, US Geological Survey*] ....FEL

Fel'dsher i Akusherka [*A publication*] ....Fel'dsher Akush

Feldspar Subgroup [*Orthoclase, albite, anorthite*] [*CIPW classification*] [*Geology*] .... F

[*The*] **Felician College** [*Illinois*]..TFC
Felician College, Chicago, IL [*OCLC symbol*]...............................IAE
Felician College, Chicago, IL [*Library symbol*] ....ICFC
Felician College, Lodi, NJ [*Library symbol*] ....NjLF
Feliciana Eastern Railroad Co. [*Later, FERR*] [*AAR code*]............FE
Feliciana Eastern Railroad Co. [*Formerly, FE*] [*AAR code*]......FERR
Felicidades Wildlife Foundation..FWF
Felicissimi Fratres [*Most Fortunate Brothers*] [*Latin*]..................FF
Feliciter [*Happily*]...F
Feline and Canine Friends..FCF
Feline Embryonic Fibroblast...FEF
Feline Fibrosarcoma Virus ....FSV
Feline Leukemia Virus [*Also, FeLV*]..FELV
Feline Orcornavirus-Associated Cell Membrane Antigen
   [*Immunology*]...FOCMA
Feline Practice [*A publication*]................................Feline Pract
Feline Sarcoma Virus [*Also, FeSV*]..FESV
Feline Urologic Syndrome..FUS
Feline Viral Rhinotracheitis [*Vaccine*]...................................FVR
Felix Ravenna [*A publication*]..Fel Rav
Felix Ravenna [*A publication*]..FR
Felix Schlag [*Designer's mark, when appearing on US coins*] .....FS
Fell [*Horse racing*]...F
Fellow...F
Fellow...FEL
Fellow..FELL
Fellow of the Academy of Arts and Sciences...........................FAAS
Fellow of the Academy of the Social Sciences in Australia ......FASSA
Fellow of the Accountants' and Executives' Corporation of Canada ......FAE
Fellow of the Actuarial Society...FAS
Fellow of Agricultural Institute of Canada..............................FAIC
Fellow of the American Academy of Allergy ....FAAA
Fellow of the American Academy of Arts and Sciences.........FAAAS
Fellow of the American Academy of Orthopedic Surgeons ....FAAOS
Fellow of the American Association for the Advancement of
   Science..FAA
Fellow of the American Association for the Advancement of
   Science...FAAAS
Fellow of the American Association of Criminology..................FAAC
Fellow of the American College of Allergists..........................FACAl
Fellow of the American College of Anesthesiologists ....FACAn
Fellow of the American College of Angiology..........................FACA
Fellow of the American College of Apothecaries......................FACA
Fellow of the American College of Cardiology.........................FACC
Fellow of the American College of Chest Physicians ....FACCP
Fellow of the American College of Chest Physicians ....FCCP
Fellow of the American College of Dentists.............................FACD
Fellow of the American College of Family Physicians.............FACFP
Fellow of the American College of Foot Surgeons....................FACFS
Fellow of the American College of Gastroenterology...............FACG
Fellow of the American College of Health Administrators ....FACHA
Fellow of the American College of Obstetricians and
   Gynecologists ....FACOG
Fellow of American College of Organists ....FACO
Fellow of the American College of Otolaryngology..................FACO
Fellow of the American College of Physicians..........................FACP
Fellow of the American College of Preventive Medicine ....FACPM
Fellow of the American College of Radiology...........................FACR
Fellow of the American College of Sports Medicine.................FACSM
Fellow of the American College of Surgeons ....FACS
Fellow of the American Geographical Society ....FAGS
Fellow of the American Institute of Actuaries ....FAIA
Fellow of the American Institute of Aeronautics and
   Astronautics [*Formerly, FIAes, FIAS*] ....FAIAA
Fellow of the American Institute of Architects.........................FAIA
Fellow of the American Institute of Criminology ....FAIC
Fellow of the American Institute of Electrical Engineers ....FAIEE
Fellow of the American Institute of Electrical Engineers ....F Am IEE
Fellow of the American Medical Association ....FAMA
Fellow of the American Neurological Association ....FANA
Fellow of the American Neurological Society ....FANS
Fellow of the American Ornithologists Union ....FAOU
Fellow of the American Physical Society ....FAPS
Fellow of the American Psychiatric Association ....FAPA
Fellow of the American Psychoanalytic Association ....FAPA
Fellow of the American Psychological Association ....FAPA
Fellow of the American Public Health Association ....FAPHA
Fellow of the American Society of Civil Engineers ....FAmSCE
Fellow of the American Society of Civil Engineers ....FASCE
Fellow of the American Sociological Association.......................FASA
Fellow of the Ancient Monuments Society [*British*] ....FAMS
Fellow of the Antiquarian Society [*British*] ....FAS
Fellow of the Antiquarian Society of Edinburgh ....FASE
Fellow Associate of the Institute of Chemistry ....FAIC
Fellow of the Association of Certified and Corporate
   Accountants [*British*]...FACCA
Fellow of the Association of International Accountants [*British*]............FAIA
Fellow of the Australian Academy of the Humanities................FAHA
Fellow of the Australian Academy of Science.............................FAA
Fellow of the Australian Chemical Institute [*Later, FRACI*].........FACI
Fellow of the Australian College of Education ....FACE

Fellow of the Australian Institute of Agricultural Science..................FAIAS
Fellow of the Australian Institute of Management ....FAIM
Fellow of the Australian Institute of Physics ....FAIP
Fellow of the Australian Insurance Institute [*British*]....................FAII
Fellow of the Australian and New Zealand College of
   Psychiatrists..FANZCP
Fellow of the Australian Planning Institute ....FAPI
Fellow of the Australian Psychological Society ....FAPsS
Fellow of the Australian Society of Accountants ....FASA
Fellow of the Birmingham School of Music [*British*] ....FBSM
Fellow of the Boot and Shoe Institution [*British*]......................FBSI
Fellow of the Botanical Society [*British*].....................................FBS
Fellow of the Botanical Society of Edinburgh ....FBSE
Fellow of the British Academy ....FBA
Fellow of the British Association of Accountants and Auditors...........FBAA
Fellow of the British Ballet Organisation ....FBBO
Fellow of the British Computer Society.....................................FBCS
Fellow of the British Horological Institute ....FBHI
Fellow of the British Institute of Management [*Formerly, FIIA*] ....FBIM
Fellow of the British Institution of Radio Engineers.................FBritIRE
Fellow of the British Interplanetary Society ....FBIS
Fellow of the British Optical Association ....FBOA
Fellow of the British Ornithologists Union.................................FBOU
Fellow of the British Psychological Society ....FBPsS
Fellow of the British Society of Commerce ....FBSC
Fellow of the British Society of Commerce ....FBSComm
Fellow of the Building Societies Institute [*British*].......................FBS
Fellow of the Cambridge Philological Society [*British*]..............FCPS
Fellow of the Canadian Aeronautics and Space Institute ....FCASI
Fellow of the Canadian Bankers' Association ....FCBA
Fellow of the Canadian College of Organists ....FCCO
Fellow of the Canadian College of Teachers ....FCCT
Fellow of the Canadian Credit Institute ....FCI
Fellow of the Canadian Institute of Actuaries ....FCIA
Fellow of the Canadian Institute of Realtors ....FRI
Fellow of the Canadian Psychological Association ....FCPA
Fellow of the Canadian Society of Radiological Technicians.............FCSRT
Fellow of the Casualty Actuarial Society ....FCAS
Fellow Chartered Accountant of New Zealand ....FCA(NZ)
Fellow of the Chartered Auctioneers' and Estate Agents'
   Institute [*British*]...FAI
Fellow of the Chartered Institute of Cost and Work Accountants
   [*British*] ....FCWA
Fellow of the Chartered Institute of Patent Agents [*British*]................FCIPA
Fellow of the Chartered Institute of Secretaries [*British*].........FCIS
Fellow of the Chartered Institute of Transport [*British*]..............FCIT
Fellow of the Chartered Insurance Institute [*British*]..................FCII
Fellow of the Chartered Land Agents' Society [*British*].............FLAS
Fellow of the Chartered Society of Physiotherapy [*British*].................FCSP
Fellow of the Chemical Institute of Canada ....FCIC
Fellow of the Chemical Society [*British*]..........................FChemSoc
Fellow of the Chemical Society [*British*]....................................FCS
Fellow of the City and Guilds of London Institute [*British*].........FCGI
Fellow of the College of American Pathologists ....FCAP
Fellow of the College of General Practitioners ....FCGP
Fellow of the College of Medicine and Surgery [*British*]............FCMS
Fellow of the College of Obstetricians and Gynecologists...........FCOG
Fellow of the College of Organists [*British*]...............................FCO
Fellow of the College of Osteopathy [*British*]............................FCO
Fellow of the College of Pathologists [*Later, Royal College of*
   Pathologists] [*British*]..FC Path
Fellow of the College of Physicians of South Africa ....FCP(SA)
Fellow of the College of Physicians of South Africa ....FCP(SoAf)
Fellow of the College of Physicians and Surgeons [*British*] ....FCPS
Fellow of the College of Physicians and Surgeons and
   Obstetricians of South Africa..................................FCPSO (SoAf)
Fellow of the College of Preceptors [*British*].............................FCP
Fellow of the College of Radiologists of Australia ....FCRA
Fellow of the College of Speech Therapists [*British*].................FCST
Fellow of the College of Surgeons of South Africa ....FCS(SA)
Fellow of the College of Surgeons of South Africa ....FCS(SoAf)
Fellow of the College of Teachers of the Blind...........................FCTB
Fellow of the Commonwealth Institute of Accountancy [*British*]...........FICA
Fellow of the Coopers Hill College [*British*] ....FCH
Fellow of the Corporation of Certified Secretaries [*British*].........FCCS
Fellow of the Corporation of Insurance Agents [*British*].............FCIA
Fellow of the Corporation of Insurance Brokers [*British*] ....FCIB
Fellow of Dental Surgery [*British*]..FDS
Fellow in Dental Surgery of the Royal College of Physicians and
   Surgeons of Glasgow...FDSRCPSGlas
Fellow in Dental Surgery of the Royal College of Physicians and
   Surgeons of Glasgow...FDSRCPS Glasg
Fellow in Dental Surgery of the Royal College of Surgeons of
   Edinburgh..FDSRCSE
Fellow in Dental Surgery of the Royal College of Surgeons of
   Edinburgh...FDSRCSEd
Fellow in Dental Surgery of the Royal College of Surgeons of
   Edinburgh...FDSRCS Edin
Fellow in Dental Surgery of the Royal College of Surgeons of
   England ....FDSRCS

Fellow in Dental Surgery of the Royal College of Surgeons of England ... FDSRCS Eng
Fellow of the Educational Institute of Scotland ... FEIS
Fellow [*or Fellowship*] **of Engineering** ... FEng
Fellow of the Engineering Institute of Canada ... FEIC
Fellow of the Engineering Institution of Zambia ... FEIZ
Fellow of the Entomological Society [*British*] ... FES
Fellow of the Ethnological Society [*British*] ... FES
Fellow of the Faculty of Actuaries [*British*] ... FFA
Fellow of the Faculty of Anaesthetists of the Royal Australian College of Surgeons ... FFARACS
Fellow of the Faculty of Anaesthetists of the Royal College of Surgeons of England ... FFARCS
Fellow of the Faculty of Anaesthetists of the Royal College of Surgeons of England ... FFARCS Eng
Fellow of the Faculty of Anaesthetists of the Royal College of Surgeons in Ireland ... FFARCSI
Fellow of the Faculty of Architects and Surveyors, London [*British*] ... FFAS
Fellow of the Faculty of Community Medicine [*British*] ... FFCM
Fellow in the Faculty of Dentistry [*British*] ... FFD
Fellow of the Faculty of Dentistry of the Royal College of Surgeons in Ireland ... FFDRCSI
Fellow of the Faculty of Dentistry of the Royal College of Surgeons in Ireland ... FFDRCS Irel
Fellow of the Faculty of Homoeopathy [*British*] ... FF Hom
Fellow of the Faculty of Physicians and Surgeons [*British*] ... FFPS
Fellow of the Faculty of Physiotherapists ... FFPh
Fellow of the Faculty of Radiologists [*British*] ... FFR
Fellow of the Franklin Society [*British*] ... FFS
Fellow of the Gemmological Association [*British*] ... FGA
Fellow of the Geographical Society ... FGS
Fellow of the Geographical Society of America ... FGSA
Fellow of the Geological Society [*British*] ... FGS
Fellow of the Geological Society of America ... FGSA
Fellow of the Guild of Organists [*British*] ... FGO
Fellow of Guildhall School of Music [*British*] ... FGSM
Fellow of Heriot-Watt College, Edinburgh ... FH-WC
Fellow of the Highland and Agricultural Society of Scotland ... FHAS
Fellow of the Horticultural Society [*British*] ... FHS
Fellow of the Illuminating Engineering Society [*Later, FIllumES*] [*British*] ... FIES
Fellow of the Illuminating Engineering Society [*Formerly, FIES*] [*British*] ... FIllumES
Fellow of the Imperial Institute [*British*] ... FIInst
Fellow of the Incorporated Association of Architects and Surveyors [*British*] ... FIAA & S
Fellow of the Incorporated Guild of Church Musicians [*British*] ... FIGCM
Fellow of the Incorporated Sales Managers' Association [*Later, F Inst MSM*] [*British*] ... FSMA
Fellow of the Incorporated Secretaries' Association [*British*] ... FISA
Fellow of the Incorporated Society of Auctioneers and Landed Property Agents [*British*] ... FALPA
Fellow of the Indian Academy of Medical Sciences ... FIAMS
Fellow of the Indian College of Dentists ... FICD
Fellow of the Indian National Science Academy [*Formerly, FNI*] ... FNA
Fellow of the Institute of Actuaries [*British*] ... FIA
Fellow of the Institute of Actuaries of New Zealand ... FIANZ
Fellow of the Institute of Aeronautical Sciences [*Later, FAIAA*] [*British*] ... FIAeS
Fellow of the Institute of Aeronautical Sciences [*Later, FAIAA*] [*British*] ... FIAS
Fellow of the Institute of Arbitrators ... FIArb
Fellow of the Institute of Auctioneers [*British*] ... FIA
Fellow of the Institute of Australian Agricultural Science ... FIAAS
Fellow of the Institute of Bankers [*British*] ... FIB
Fellow of the Institute of Banking Associations ... FIBA
Fellow of the Institute of Biology [*Formerly, FInstBiol*] [*British*] ... FI Biol
Fellow of the Institute of Biology [*Later, FI Biol*] [*British*] ... FInstBiol
Fellow of the Institute of British Decorators ... FIBD
Fellow of the Institute of British Photographers ... FIBP
Fellow of the Institute of Building [*British*] ... FIOB
Fellow of the Institute of Canadian Dentists ... FICD
Fellow of the Institute of Ceramics [*British*] ... FICeram
Fellow of the Institute of Certificated Grocers [*British*] ... FGI
Fellow of the Institute of Chartered Accountants [*British*] ... FCA
Fellow of the Institute of Chartered Accountants in Australia ... FCA(Aust)
Fellow of the Institute of Chartered Accountants in Canada ... FCA(Can)
Fellow of the Institute of Chartered Shipbrokers [*British*] ... FICS
Fellow of the Institute of Chemistry [*Later, FRIC*] [*British*] ... FIC
Fellow of the Institute of Chemistry of Ireland ... FICI
Fellow of the Institute of Chiropodists [*British*] ... FInstCh
Fellow of the Institute of Civil Defence [*British*] ... FICD
Fellow of the Institute of Commerce [*British*] ... FCI
Fellow of the Institute of Commerce ... FIC
Fellow of the Institute of Commerce [*British*] ... FInstC
Fellow of the Institute of Cost and Management Accountants [*British*] ... FCMA
Fellow of the Institute of Directors [*British*] ... FID
Fellow of the Institute of Directors [*British*] ... FInstD
Fellow of the Institute of Directors [*British*] ... F Inst Dir
Fellow of the Institute of Electrical and Electronic Engineers ... FIEEE
Fellow of the Institute of Electrical Engineers [*British*] ... FIEE
Fellow of the Institute of Engineers [*British*] ... FIE
Fellow of the Institute of Food Science and Technology [*British*] ... FIFST
Fellow of the Institute of Fuel [*British*] ... F Inst F
Fellow of the Institute of Health Education [*British*] ... FIHE
Fellow of the Institute of Health Service [*formerly, Hospital*] **Administrators** [*British*] ... FHA
Fellow of the Institute of Housing [*Later, FIHM*] [*British*] ... FIHsg
Fellow of the Institute of Housing Managers [*Formerly, FIHsg*] [*British*] ... FIHM
Fellow of the Institute of Hygiene [*British*] ... FIH
Fellow of the Institute of Industrial Administration [*Later, FBIM*] [*British*] ... FIIA
Fellow of the Institute of Industrial and Commercial Accountants [*British*] ... FIAI
Fellow of the Institute of Information Scientists [*British*] ... FIInfSc
Fellow of the Institute of Journalists [*British*] ... FIJ
Fellow of the Institute of Landscape Architects [*British*] ... FILA
Fellow of the Institute of Linguists [*British*] ... FIL
Fellow of the Institute of Management Consultants [*British*] ... FIMC
Fellow of the Institute of Marine Engineers [*British*] ... FIMarE
Fellow of the Institute of Marketing [*British*] ... FInstM
Fellow of the Institute of Marketing and Sales Management [*Formerly, FSMA*] [*British*] ... F Inst MSM
Fellow of the Institute of Mathematics and its Application [*British*] ... FIMA
Fellow of the Institute of Meat [*British*] ... FInstM
Fellow of the Institute of Metallurgists [*British*] ... FIM
Fellow of the Institute of Metals [*British*] ... FIM
Fellow of the Institute of Metals [*British*] ... FInstMet
Fellow of the Institute of the Motor Industry [*Formerly, FIMT*] [*British*] ... FIMI
Fellow of the Institute of Motor Trade [*Later, FIMI*] [*British*] ... FIMT
Fellow of the Institute of Municipal Treasurers and Accountants [*British*] ... FIMA
Fellow of the Institute of Municipal Treasurers and Accountants [*British*] ... FIMTA
Fellow of the Institute of Music Instrument Technology [*British*] ... FIMIT
Fellow of the Institute of Navigation [*British*] ... FIN
Fellow of the Institute of Operating Theatre Technicians [*British*] ... FIOT
Fellow of the Institute of Ophthalmic Opticians [*British*] ... FIO
Fellow of the Institute of Patentees and Inventors [*British*] ... F Inst PI
Fellow of the Institute of Personnel Management [*Later, CIPM*] [*British*] ... FIPM
Fellow of the Institute of Petroleum [*British*] ... F Inst Pet
Fellow of the Institute of Physics [*British*] ... FIP
Fellow of the Institute of Physics and the Physical Society [*British*] ... F Inst P
Fellow of the Institute of Practitioners in Advertising [*British*] ... FIPA
Fellow of the Institute of Professional Designers ... FIPD
Fellow of the Institute of Public Administration [*British*] ... FIPA
Fellow of the Institute of Public Relations [*British*] ... FIPR
Fellow of the Institute of Purchasing and Supply [*British*] ... FInstPS
Fellow of the Institute of Railway Auditors and Accountants (India) ... FIRA(Ind)
Fellow of the Institute of Road Transport Engineers [*British*] ... FIRTE
Fellow of the Institute of Science Technology [*British*] ... FIST
Fellow of the Institute of Statisticians [*British*] ... FIS
Fellow of the Institute of Water Engineers [*British*] ... FIWE
Fellow of the Institute of Welding [*British*] ... FInstW
Fellow of the Institute of Welfare Officers [*British*] ... FWI
Fellow of the Institute of Wood Science [*British*] ... FIWSc
Fellow of the Institution of Agricultural Engineers [*British*] ... FIAgrE
Fellow of the Institution of Chemical Engineers [*British*] ... FIChemE
Fellow of the Institution of Civil Engineers [*British*] ... FICE
Fellow of the Institution of Electronic and Radio Engineers [*British*] ... FIERE
Fellow of the Institution of Engineering Inspection [*British*] ... FIEI
Fellow of the Institution of Engineers of Australia ... FIEAust
Fellow of the Institution of Engineers, India ... FIE(India)
Fellow of the Institution of Gas Engineers [*British*] ... FIGasE
Fellow of the Institution of Heating and Ventilating Engineers [*British*] ... FIHVE
Fellow of the Institution of Mechanical Engineers [*British*] ... FI Mech E
Fellow of the Institution of Mining Engineers [*British*] ... FIMinE
Fellow of the Institution of Municipal Engineers [*British*] ... FIMunE
Fellow of the Institution of Nuclear Engineers [*British*] ... FI Nucl E
Fellow of the Institution of Production Engineers [*British*] ... FIProdE
Fellow of the Institution of Public Health Engineers [*British*] ... FIPHE
Fellow of the Institution of Radio and Electronics Engineers (Australia) [*Formerly, FIRE (Aust)*] ... FIREE (Aust)
Fellow of the Institution of Radio Engineers [*British*] ... FIRE
Fellow of the Institution of Radio Engineers (Australia) [*Later, FIREE (Aust)*] ... FIRE (Aust)
Fellow of the Institution of the Rubber Industry [*British*] ... FIRI
Fellow of the Institution of Sanitary Engineers [*British*] ... FISE
Fellow of the Institution of Structural Engineers [*British*] ... FIStructE
Fellow of the Institution of Works Managers [*British*] ... FIWM
Fellow of the Insurance Institute of Canada ... FIIC
Fellow of the International Academy of Management ... FIAM
Fellow of the International Academy of Wood Sciences ... FIAWS
Fellow of the International College of Dentists ... FICD

Fellow of the International College of Surgeons........................FICS
Fellow of the International Colonial Institute [British]...............FICI
Fellow of the International Criminal Justice Association.............FICJA
Fellow of the International Institute of Arts and Letters.............FIAL
Fellow of King's College [London].....................................FKC
Fellow of King's College, London......................................FKCL
Fellow of the King's and Queen's College of Physicians, Ireland......FKQCP
Fellow of the Library Association [British]...........................FLA
Fellow of the Library Association of Australia........................FLAA
Fellow, Life Management Institute [Designation conferred by Life
   Office Management Association]......................................FLMI
Fellow of the Linnaean Society [British]..............................FLS
Fellow of the Local Government Association [British]..................FLGA
Fellow of the London College of Music [British].......................FLCM
Fellow of the London and Counties Society of Physiologists
   [British]...FLCSP
Fellow of the London Historical Society [British].....................FLHS
Fellow of the Medical Council [British]...............................FMC
Fellow of the Medical Society [British]...............................FMS
Fellow of the Meteorological Society [British]........................FMS
Fellow of the Mineralogical Society of America........................FMSA
Fellow of the Museums Association [British]...........................FMA
Fellow of the National College of Rubber Technology [British].........FNCRT
Fellow of the National Institute of Arts and Letters [British]........FNIAL
Fellow of the National Institute of Medical Herbalists [British]......FNIMH
Fellow of the National Institute of Sciences in India [Later, FNA]....FNI
Fellow of the National Society of Art Education [British].............FSAE
Fellow of the National Society of Interior Designers..................FNSID
Fellow of the Nautical Institute [British]............................FNI
Fellow of the New Zealand Institute of Agricultural Science...........FNZIAS
Fellow of the New Zealand Institute of Architects.....................FNZIA
Fellow of the New Zealand Institute of Chemistry......................FNZIC
Fellow of the New Zealand Institution of Engineers....................FNZIE
Fellow of the New Zealand Library Association.........................FNZLA
Fellow of the Non-Destructive Testing Society of Great Britain........FNDTS
Fellow of the North East Coast Institution of Engineers and
   Shipbuilders [British]...FNECInst
Fellow of the Pakistan Academy of Sciences............................FPAS
Fellow of the Pathological Society of Great Britain...................FPS
Fellow of the Pharmaceutical Society [British]........................FPS
Fellow of the Philological Society [British]..........................FPS
Fellow of the Philosophical Society [British].........................F Ph S
Fellow of the Philosophical Society [British].........................FPS
Fellow of the Physical Society [British]..............................F Phys S
Fellow of the Physical Society [British]..............................FPS
Fellow of the Plastics Institute [British]............................FPI
Fellow, Public Accountant, New Zealand................................FPANZ
Fellow of the Real Estate Institute [Australia].......................FREI
Fellow, Registered Accountant, New Zealand............................FRANZ
Fellow of the Royal Academy of Dancing [British]......................FRAD
Fellow of the Royal Academy of Music [British]........................FRAM
Fellow of the Royal Academy of Physicians [British]...................FRAP
Fellow of the Royal Aeronautical Society [British]....................FRAeS
Fellow of the Royal Agricultural Societies [British]..................FRAgSs
Fellow of the Royal Agricultural Society of England...................FRASE
Fellow of the Royal Anthropological Institute [British]...............FRAI
Fellow of the Royal and Antiquarian Societies [British]...............FR and ASS
Fellow of the Royal Architectural Institute of Canada.................FRAIC
Fellow of the Royal Asiatic Society [British].........................FRAS
Fellow of the Royal Asiatic Society of Bengal.........................FRASB
Fellow of the Royal Astronomical Society [British]....................FRAS
Fellow of the Royal Australasian College of Physicians................FRACP
Fellow of the Royal Australasian College of Radiologists..............FRACR
Fellow of the Royal Australasian College of Surgeons..................FRACS
Fellow of the Royal Australian Chemical Institute [Formerly, FACI]....FRACI
Fellow of the Royal Australian College of Dental Surgeons.............FRACDS
Fellow of the Royal Australian Historical Society.....................FRAHS
Fellow of the Royal Australian Institute of Architects................FRAIA
Fellow of the Royal Botanic Society [British].........................FRBS
Fellow of the Royal College of Advanced Technology, Salford
   [British]...FRCATS
Fellow of the Royal College of Art [British]..........................FRCA
Fellow of the Royal College of Dentists [British].....................FRCD
Fellow of the Royal College of Dentists (Canada)......................FRCD(C)
Fellow of the Royal College of General Practitioners [British]........FRCGP
Fellow of the Royal College of Music [British]........................FRCM
Fellow of the Royal College of Obstetricians and Gynaecologists
   [British]..FRCOG
Fellow of the Royal College of Organists [British]....................FRCO
Fellow of the Royal College of Organists (Choir-Training
   Diploma) [British]..FRCO(CHM)
Fellow of the Royal College of Pathologists [British].................FRC Path
Fellow, Royal College of Pathologists, Australasia....................FRCPA
Fellow of the Royal College of Physicians [British]...................FRCP
Fellow of the Royal College of Physicians (Canada)....................FRCP(C)
Fellow of the Royal College of Physicians of Canada...................FRCPCan
Fellow of the Royal College of Physicians of Edinburgh................FRCPE
Fellow of the Royal College of Physicians of Edinburgh................FRCPEd
Fellow of the Royal College of Physicians of Edinburgh................FRCP Edin
Fellow of the Royal College of Physicians of Ireland..................FRCPI
Fellow of the Royal College of Physicians of Ireland..................FRCP Irel

Fellow of the Royal College of Physicians of London [British].........FRCP Lond
Fellow of the Royal College of Physicians and Surgeons of
   Glasgow..FRCPGlas
Fellow of the Royal College of Psychiatrists [British]................FRC Psych
Fellow of the Royal College of Radiologists [British].................FRCR
Fellow of the Royal College of Surgeons [British].....................FRCS
Fellow of the Royal College of Surgeons (Canada)......................FRCS(C)
Fellow of the Royal College of Surgeons of Canada.....................FRCSCan
Fellow of the Royal College of Surgeons of Edinburgh..................FRCSE
Fellow of the Royal College of Surgeons of Edinburgh..................FRCS Ed
Fellow of the Royal College of Surgeons of Edinburgh..................FRCS Edin
Fellow of the Royal College of Surgeons of England....................FRCS Eng
Fellow of the Royal College of Surgeons of Glasgow....................FRCSGlas
Fellow of the Royal College of Surgeons in Ireland....................FRCSI
Fellow of the Royal College of Surgeons in Ireland....................FRCS Irel
Fellow of the Royal College of Surgeons of London.....................FRCSL
Fellow of the Royal College of University Surgeons [Denmark]..........FRCUS
Fellow of the Royal College of Veterinary Surgeons [British]..........FRCVS
Fellow of the Royal Colonial Institute [British]......................FRCI
Fellow of the Royal Commonwealth Society [British]....................FRCSoc
Fellow of the Royal Economic Society [British]........................FR Econ S
Fellow of the Royal Economic Society [British]........................FR Ec(on) S(oc)
Fellow of the Royal Economic Society [British]........................FRES
Fellow of the Royal Empire Society [British]..........................FRES
Fellow of the Royal Entomological Society [British]...................FR Ent S
Fellow of the Royal Entomological Society [British]...................FRES
Fellow of the Royal Faculty of Physicians and Surgeons [British]......FRFPS
Fellow of the Royal Faculty of Physicians and Surgeons of
   Glasgow..FRFPS(G)
Fellow of the Royal Faculty of Physicians and Surgeons of
   Glasgow..FRFPSGlas
Fellow of the Royal Geographical Society [British]....................FRGS
Fellow of the Royal Geographical Society (Canada).....................FRGS(C)
Fellow of the Royal Historical Society [British]......................FRHistS
Fellow of the Royal Historical Society [British]......................FRHistSoc
Fellow of the Royal Historical Society [British]......................FRHS
Fellow of the Royal Horticultural Society [British]...................FRHortS
Fellow of the Royal Horticultural Society [British]...................FRHS
Fellow of the Royal Incorporation of Architects of Scotland...........FRIAS
Fellow of the Royal Institute of Architects of Ireland................FRIAI
Fellow of the Royal Institute of Architects of Scotland...............FRIAS
Fellow of the Royal Institute of British Architects...................FRIBA
Fellow of the Royal Institute of Chemistry [Formerly, FIC] [British]..FRIC
Fellow of the Royal Institute of Horticulture [New Zealand]...........FRIH
Fellow of the Royal Institute of Naval Architects [British]...........FRINA
Fellow of the Royal Institute of Public Health and Hygiene
   [British]..FRIPHH
Fellow of the Royal Institution [British].............................FRI
Fellow of the Royal Institution of Chartered Surveyors [Formerly,
   FSI] [British]...FRICS
Fellow of the Royal Manchester College of Music [British].............FRMCM
Fellow of the Royal Medical Society [British].........................FRMedSoc
Fellow of the Royal Meteorological Society [British]..................FR Met S
Fellow of the Royal Meteorological Society [British]..................FR Met Soc
Fellow of the Royal Meteorological Society [British]..................FRMS
Fellow of the Royal Microscopical Society [British]...................FRMS
Fellow of the Royal Numismatic Society [British]......................FRNS
Fellow of the Royal Philatelic Society, London........................FRPSL
Fellow of the Royal Photographic Society [British]....................FRPS
Fellow of the Royal Sanitary Institute [Later, FRSH] [British]........FRSanI
Fellow of the Royal School of Church Music [British]..................FRSCM
Fellow of the Royal School of Naval Architecture [British]............FRSNA
Fellow of the Royal Scottish Geographical Society.....................FRSGS
Fellow of the Royal Scottish Society of Arts..........................FRSSA
Fellow of the Royal Society [British].................................FRS
Fellow of the Royal Society of Antiquaries of Ireland.................FRSAI
Fellow of the Royal Society of Arts [British].........................FRSA
Fellow of the Royal Society of British Sculptors......................FRBS
Fellow of the Royal Society of Canada.................................FRSC
Fellow of the Royal Society of Canada.................................FRSCan
Fellow of the Royal Society of Edinburgh..............................FRSE
Fellow of the Royal Society of Edinburgh..............................FRS Edin
Fellow of the Royal Society of Health [Formerly, FRSanI] [British].....FRSH
Fellow of the Royal Society of Literature [British]...................FRSL
Fellow of the Royal Society, London [British].........................FRSL
Fellow of the Royal Society of Medicine [British].....................FRSM
Fellow of the Royal Society of Medicine [British].....................FRSocMed
Fellow of the Royal Society of New Zealand............................FRSNZ
Fellow of the Royal Society of Painter-Etchers and Engravers [British].RE
Fellow of the Royal Society of Radiographers..........................FSR
Fellow of the Royal Society of South Africa...........................FRSSAf
Fellow of the Royal Society of Teachers [British].....................FRST
Fellow of the Royal Society of Tropical Medicine and Hygiene
   [British]..FRSTM & H
Fellow of the Royal Statistical Society [British].....................FRSS
Fellow of the Royal Statistical Society [British].....................FSS
Fellow of the Royal Town Planning Institute [British].................FRTPI
Fellow of the Royal University of Ireland.............................FRUI
Fellow of the Royal Victorian Institute of Architects [British].......FRVIA
Fellow of the Royal Zoological Society of Scotland....................FRZSScot
Fellow of Sheffield Polytechnic [British].............................FSP

Fellow of the Society of Actuaries .... FSA
Fellow of the Society of Antiquaries [*British*] .... FSA
Fellow of the Society of Antiquaries, Edinburgh .... FSAE
Fellow of the Society of Antiquaries of Scotland .... FSAS
Fellow of the Society of Antiquaries of Scotland .... FSA Scot
Fellow of the Society of Architects [*British*] .... FSArc
Fellow of the Society of Art Masters [*British*] .... FSAM
Fellow of the Society of Arts [*British*] .... FSA
Fellow of the Society of Chiropodists [*British*] .... FChS
Fellow of the Society of Dyers and Colourists [*British*] .... FSDC
Fellow of the Society of Engineers [*British*] .... FSE
Fellow of the Society of Genealogists [*British*] .... FSG
Fellow of the Society of Glass Technology [*British*] .... FSGT
Fellow of the Society of Incorporated Accountants and Auditors [*British*] .... FSAA
Fellow of the Society of Industrial Artists [*British*] .... FSIA
Fellow of the Society of Industrial Artists and Designers [*British*] .... FSIAD
Fellow of the Society of Interior Designers .... FASID
Fellow of the Society of Licensed Aircraft Engineers and Technologists [*British*] .... FSLAET
Fellow of the Society of Metaphysicians [*British*] .... FSM
Fellow of the Society of Remedial Gymnasts [*British*] .... FSRG
Fellow of the Society of Science and Art [*British*] .... FSSA
Fellow of the South African Institute of Electrical Engineers .... F(SA)IEE
Fellow of the South African Institution of Civil Engineers .... F(SA)ICE
Fellow of the South African Institution of Mechanical Engineers .... F(SA)IME
Fellow of the South African Library Association .... FSALA
Fellow of the South Australian School of Mines .... FSASM
Fellow of the South Australian School of Mines (Metallurgy) .... FSASM (Met)
Fellow of the Surveyors' Institute [*Later, FRICS*] [*British*] .... FSI
Fellow of the Technical Publishing Society .... FTPS
Fellow of Technological Sciences .... FTS
Fellow of the Textile Institute [*British*] .... FTI
Fellow of the Theatrical Designers and Craftsmen's Association [*British*] .... FTDA
Fellow of Trinity College, Dublin .... FTCD
Fellow of Trinity College of Music, London .... FTCL
Fellow of the University of Manchester Institute of Science and Technology [*British*] .... FUMIST
Fellow of the Welding Institute [*British*] .... FIW
Fellow of the World Academy of Arts and Sciences .... FWA
Fellow of the Zoological Academy .... FZA
Fellow of the Zoological Society [*British*] .... FZS
Fellowes Athenaeum, Boston, MA [*Library symbol*] .... MBFA
Fellows of the American Bar Foundation .... FABF
Fellows in American Studies .... FAS
Fellows, CA [*Location identifier*] [*FAA*] .... FLW
Fellowship of the American Academy of Neurological and Orthopaedic Surgeons .... FAANaOS
Fellowship of Catholic Scholars .... FCS
Fellowship of Christian Athletes .... FCA
Fellowship of Christian Magicians .... FCM
Fellowship of Christian Musicians .... FCM
Fellowship of Christian Peace Officers .... FCPO
Fellowship of Christian Racers .... FCR
Fellowship of Concerned Churchmen .... FCC
Fellowship of Conservative Southern Baptists .... FCSB
Fellowship of First Fleeters .... FFF
Fellowship of Independent Evangelical Churches .... FIEC
Fellowship of Interdenominational Missionary Societies .... FIMS
Fellowship in Israel for Arab-Jewish Youth .... FIAJY
Fellowship of Missions .... FOM
Fellowship Party [*British*] .... FP
Fellowship in Prayer [*An association*] .... FIP
Fellowship in Prayer [*An association*] .... FP
Fellowship for Racial and Economic Equality [*Later, Southeast Institute*] .... FREE
Fellowship of Reconciliation .... FOR
Fellowship of Religious Humanists .... FRH
Fellowship of Religious Journalists .... FORJ
Fellowship of Southern Churchmen [*Later, Committee of Southern Churchmen*] .... FSC
Fellowship for Spiritual Understanding .... FSU
[*The*] **Fellowship of United Methodist Musicians** [*Later, Fellowship of United Methodists in Worship, Music, and Other Arts*] .... FUMM
Felmont Oil Corp. [*American Stock Exchange symbol*] .... FEL
Felon .... F
Felonious Assault .... FA
Felony [*FBI standardized term*] .... FEL
Fels Institute of Local and State Governments [*University of Pennsylvania*] .... FILSG
Fels Parent Behavior Rating Scales [*Psychology*] .... FPBRS
Fels Research Institute, Yellow Springs, OH [*Library symbol*] .... OYesF
Felsway Corp. [*American Stock Exchange symbol*] [*Delisted*] .... FLW
Felt Manufacturers Council .... FMC
Felt Reusable Surface Insulation .... FRSI
Feltman Research and Engineering Laboratory [*Army*] .... FREL
Feltman Research Laboratory [*Picatinny Arsenal*] [*Army*] .... FRL
Female .... F
Female [*or Feminine*] .... FEM
Female-Day-Equivalent [*Entomology*] .... FDE
Female Domination .... FD
Female Flared .... FFL
Female Groove .... FG
Female Liberal Arts Graduate .... FLAG
Female Pipe Thread .... FPT
Female Soldered .... FS
Female Voice Warning System .... FVWS
Females Opposed to Equality .... FOE
Feminine .... F
Feminine Deodorant Spray [*Initialism used as brand name*] .... FDS
Feminine Hygiene Spray .... FHS
Femininity Study [*Psychology*] .... FS
Feminist Alliance Against Rape .... FAAR
Feminist Center for Human Growth and Development .... FCHGD
Feminist Karate Union .... FKU
Feminist Press [*An association*] .... FP
Feminist Radio Network .... FRN
Feminist Resources on Energy and Ecology [*Defunct*] .... FREE
Feminist Review [*A publication*] .... Fem Rview
Feminist Studies [*A publication*] .... Feminist
Feminist Studies [*A publication*] .... Fem Stud
Feminist Studies [*A publication*] .... FS
Feminist Women's Health Center [*Later, FWHC/WCC*] .... FWHC
Feminist Women's Health Center/Women's Choice Clinic [*Defunct*] .... FWHC/WCC
Feminist Writers' Guild .... FWG
Feminists on Children's Media [*Defunct*] .... FOCM
Feminists for Life [*Later, FLA*] .... FFL
Feminists for Life of America [*Formerly, FFL*] .... FLA
Femmes [*or Feminin*] [*Initial used as title of a publication*] .... F
Femoral [*Anatomy*] .... FEM
Femoral Artery [*Anatomy*] .... FA
Femoral Ash per Centimeter .... FAC
Femoral Cortical Density .... FCD
Femoral Popliteal Bypass [*Medicine*] .... FPB
Femoral Popliteal Vein Bypass [*Medicine*] .... FPUB
Femoral Total Density .... FTD
Femoral Vein Ligation [*Medicine*] .... FVL
Femoribus Internus [*At the Inner Side of the Thigh*] [*Anatomy*] .... FEM INTERN
FEMS [*Federation of European Microbiological Societies*] **Microbiology Letters** [*A publication*] .... FEMS Microbiol Lett
Femto [*A prefix meaning divided by 10 to the 15th power*] [*SI symbol*] .... f
Femtometer [*Formerly, Fermi*] .... FM
Femtovolt .... FV
Fen [*Monetary unit in China*] .... F
Fenarete-Letture d'Italia [*A publication*] .... Fenarete
Fence Against Satellite Threats .... FAST
Fender [*s*] [*Freight*] .... FND
Fendi [*Italian couturier*] .... F
Fenestra, Inc. [*NYSE symbol*] [*Delisted*] .... FNT
Fengtien [*Hoten, Shenyang*] [*Republic of China*] [*Seismograph station code, US Geological Survey*] .... FEN
Fenian Brotherhood [*Irish*] .... FB
Fentanyl Isothiocyanate [*Biochemistry*] .... FIT
Fenton Art Glass Collectors of America .... FAGCA
Fenway Court [*A publication*] .... Fenway C
Fenway Library Consortium/Abbot Memorial Library [*Library network*] .... FLC
Feodosiya [*USSR*] [*Seismograph station code, US Geological Survey*] [*Closed*] .... FEO
Fera Island [*Solomon Islands*] [*Airport symbol*] .... FRE
Ferdinand Railroad Co. [*AAR code*] .... FRDN
Fergana [*USSR*] [*Seismograph station code, US Geological Survey*] .... FRG
Fergus Falls Community College, Fergus Falls, MN [*Library symbol*] .... MnFfC
Fergus Falls, MN [*Radio station call letters*] .... KBRF
Fergus Falls, MN [*Radio station call letters*] .... KBRF-FM
Fergus Falls, MN [*Radio station call letters*] .... KJJK
Fergus Falls Public Library, Fergus Falls, MN [*Library symbol*] .... MnFf
Ferguson Library, Stamford, CT [*OCLC symbol*] .... FEM
Ferguson, MO [*Radio station call letters*] .... KCFV
Fermanagh [*County in Northern Ireland*] .... FERMANH
Fermentation .... FRMNTN
Fermentnaya i Spirtovaya Promyshlennost' [*A publication*] .... Fermentn Spirt Prom-st'
Fermi [*Later, Femtometer*] [*Unit of length*] [*Nuclear physics*] .... F
Fermi-Dirac Gas .... FDG
Fermi-Dirac Statistics .... FDS
Fermi National Accelerator Laboratory [*Also, FNAL*] .... FERMILAB
Fermi National Accelerator Laboratory [*Also, FERMILAB*] .... FNAL
Fermi Selection Rules .... FSR
Fermium [*Chemical element*] .... Fm
Fermont, PQ [*Radio station call letters*] .... CBMR-FM
Fermont, PQ [*Radio station call letters*] .... CFMF-FM
Fern Gazette [*A publication*] .... Fern Gaz
Fern Ridge Community Library, Veneta, OR [*Library symbol*] .... OrV
Fernandina Beach, FL [*Radio station call letters*] .... WHOG

Fernbank Science Center, Atlanta, GA [*Library symbol*] .... GAFSC
Fernbank Science Center, Atlanta, GA [*OCLC symbol*] .... GFS
Ferndale [*Cardiff*] [*Welsh depot code*] .... FDL
Ferndale [*California*] [*Seismograph station code, US Geological Survey*] .... FER
Ferndale Public Library, Ferndale, CA [*Library symbol*] .... CFe
Fernie [*British Columbia*] [*Seismograph station code, US Geological Survey*] [*Closed*] .... FRN
Fernie, BC [*Radio station call letters*] .... CFEK
Fernmelde-Ingenieur [*A publication*] .... Fernmelde-Ing
Fernmelde-Praxis [*A publication*] .... Fernmelde-Prax
Fernschreiben [*Teletype message*] **or Fernschreiber** [*Teletype*] [*German military*] .... FS
Fernseh- und Kino- Technik [*A publication*] .... Fernseh- & Kino- Tech
Fernseh- und Kino- Technik [*A publication*] .... FKT
Fernwaerme International [*A publication*] .... Fernwaerme Int
Fernwood, Columbia, & Gulf R. R. [*AAR code*] .... FCG
Ferranti Ltd. [*Great Britain*] [*ICAO designator*] .... FB
Ferranti Sonobuoy Processing System .... FSPS
Ferrari Club of America .... FCA
Ferrari Owners Club .... FOC
Ferredoxin [*Biochemistry*] .... Fd
Ferret LASER Detector .... FLD
Ferri-Gas Duplexer .... FGD
Ferric Dimethyldithiocarbamate [*A fungicide*] .... FDDC
Ferric Ion Free .... FIF
Ferric-Leach Bacterial Regeneration [*Uranium extraction process*] .... FBR
Ferriday, LA [*Radio station call letters*] .... KFNV
Ferriday, LA [*Radio station call letters*] .... KFNV-FM
Ferris State College, Big Rapids, MI [*OCLC symbol*] .... EZF
Ferris State College, Big Rapids, MI [*Library symbol*] .... MiBrF
Ferrite Array Demonstration [*RADAR*] .... FAD
Ferrite Control Amplifier .... FCA
Ferrite Core .... FC
Ferrite Driver Amplifier .... FDA
Ferrite Manufacturers Association .... FMA
Ferrite Memory Core .... FMC
Ferrite Metal .... FM
Ferrite Phase Driver .... FPD
Ferrite Phase Shifter .... FPS
Ferrite Pot Core .... FPC
Ferrite Resonance Switch .... FRS
Ferro Corp. [*NYSE symbol*] .... FOE
Ferro Corp., Chemical Library, Bedford, OH [*Library symbol*] .... OBedF
Ferro Corp., Independence, OH [*Library symbol*] .... OInF
Ferroalloys Association .... FA
Ferrocarril de Chihuahua al Pacifico, SA de CV [*AAR code*] .... CHP
Ferrocarril Mexicano [*AAR code*] .... FCM
Ferrocarril Mexicano del Pacifico [*Mexican Pacific Railroad Co., Inc.*] [*AAR code*] .... MDP
Ferrocarril de Minatitlan al Carmen [*AAR code*] .... FDMA
Ferrocarril Nacional de Tehuantepec [*AAR code*] .... NDT
Ferrocarril de Nacozari [*AAR code*] .... FCDN
Ferrocarril Nor-Oeste de Mexico [*Mexico North Western Railroad*] [*AAR code*] .... NODM
Ferrocarril del Pacifico, SA de CV [*AAR code*] .... FCP
Ferrocarril Sonora Baja California SA de CV [*AAR code*] .... SBC
Ferrocarril del Sureste [*AAR code*] .... SCOP
Ferrocarriles Nacionales de Mexico [*National Railways of Mexico*] .... FNM
Ferrocarriles Nacionales de Mexico [*AAR code*] .... MGRS
Ferrocarriles Nacionales de Mexico [*AAR code*] .... NDM
Ferrocarriles Unidos del Sureste, SA de CV [*AAR code*] .... SE
Ferrocement .... FC
Ferrocene Polymer Cure Process .... FPCP
Ferrocenedicarboxylic Acid [*Organic chemistry*] .... FDA
Ferroelectric .... FE
Ferroelectric Ceramic .... FEC
Ferroelectric Ceramic Picture Device .... FERPIC
Ferroelectric-Electroluminescent .... FE-EL
Ferroelectric Variable Capacitor .... FEVAC
Ferroelectricity and Related Phenomena [*A publication*] .... Ferroelectr Relat Phenom
Ferroelectrics [*A publication*] .... Ferroelectr
Ferrofluidics Corp. [*NASDAQ symbol*] .... FERO
Ferromagnetic Contamination [*Medicine*] .... FC
Ferromagnetic Fluid Levitation Accelerometer .... FFLA
Ferromagnetic Material .... FMM
Ferromagnetic Object Recognition Matrix .... FORM
Ferromagnetic Resonance .... FMR
Ferrosan [*Sweden*] [*Research code symbol*] .... F
Ferrosan [*Sweden*] [*Research code symbol*] .... FG
Ferrosan [*Denmark*] [*Research code symbol*] .... NSD
Ferrosilite [*CIPW classification*] [*Geology*] .... fs
Ferrous Metal Detector .... FMD
Ferrous Metal Powder .... FMP
Ferrous Scrap Consumers Coalition .... FSCC
Ferrovanadium Corp. ADR [*NASDAQ symbol*] .... FERVY
Ferrovie dello Stato [*Italian State Railways*] .... FS
Ferroxcube Corp., Suagerties, NY [*Library symbol*] .... NSauF
Ferrum [*Iron*] [*Chemical element*] .... Fe
Ferrum [*Iron*] [*Pharmacy*] .... FER
Ferrum College, Ferrum, VA [*OCLC symbol*] .... VFC
Ferrum College, Ferrum, VA [*Library symbol*] .... ViFerF
Ferry .... FER
Ferry .... FRY
Ferry [*Nautical charts*] .... Fy
Ferry Command [*RAF*] [*British*] .... FC
Ferry Mission Equipment Store .... FMES
Ferry Movement Directive [*Navy*] .... FMD
Ferry-Porter Law [*Physics*] .... FPL
Ferry Range .... FR
Ferry Service Unit .... FSU
Ferry Squadron [*Navy symbol*] .... VRF
Ferry Training Unit [*British*] .... FTU
Ferryboat or Launch [*Self-propelled*] [*Navy symbol*] .... YFB
Fertile [*Medicine*] .... F
Fertilite Orthogenie [*A publication*] .... Fertil Orthogenie
Fertility and Contraception [*A publication*] .... Fert Contracept
Fertility Factor [*Genetics*] .... F
Fertility Research Foundation .... FRF
Fertility and Sterility [*A publication*] .... Fertil Steril
Fertility and Sterility [*A publication*] .... Fert Steril
Fertilized .... FERTD
Fertilizer .... FERT
Fertilizer Abstracts [*A publication*] .... Fert Abstr
Fertilizer Advisory Development Information Network for Asia and the Pacific .... FADINAP
Fertilizer and Feeding Stuffs Journal [*A publication*] .... Fert Feed Stuffs J
Fertilizer Grade Ammonium Nitrate .... FGAN
Fertilizer Green Book [*A publication*] .... Fert Green Bk
Fertilizer Industry Round Table .... FIRT
[*The*] **Fertilizer Institute** .... FI
[*The*] **Fertilizer Institute** .... TFI
Fertilizer News [*A publication*] .... Fert News
Fertilizer Review [*A publication*] .... Fert R
Fertilizer Solutions [*A publication*] .... Fert Solutions
Fertilizer Technology [*A publication*] .... Fert Technol
Ferulic Acid [*Biochemistry*] .... FA
Fervens [*Hot*] [*Pharmacy*] .... FERV
Festival .... FEST
Festkoerperprobleme [*A publication*] .... Festkoerperprobl
Festlegepunkt [*Reference point, a gunnery term*] [*German military - World War II*] .... FLP
Festpunkt [*Reference point, a surveying term*] [*German military - World War II*] .... FP
Festungsflak [*Fortress antiaircraft artillery*] [*German military - World War II*] .... FF
Festus, MO [*Radio station call letters*] .... KJCF
Fetal [*Medicine*] .... F
Fetal Activity Determination .... FAD
Fetal Alcohol Syndrome [*Medicine*] .... FAS
Fetal Bovine Serum .... FBS
Fetal Breathing Movements [*Gynecology*] .... FBM
Fetal Calf [*or Cow*] **Serum** .... FCS
Fetal Death in Utero [*Medicine*] .... FDIU
Fetal Electrocardiogram [*Medicine*] .... FEKG
Fetal Electrocardiography [*Medicine*] .... FECG
Fetal Erythroblastosis [*Medicine*] .... FE
Fetal Heart [*Medicine*] .... FH
Fetal Heart Heard [*Medicine*] .... FHH
Fetal Heart Not Heard [*Medicine*] .... FHNH
Fetal Heart Rate [*Medicine*] .... FHR
Fetal Heart Sounds [*Medicine*] .... FHS
Fetal Heart Tone [*Obstetrics*] .... FHT
Fetal Hydantoin Syndrome [*Medicine*] .... FHS
Fetal Maternal Hemorrhage [*Medicine*] .... FMH
Fetal Mouse Liver Cell [*Bioassay*] .... FMLC
Fetal Movement [*Gynecology*] .... FM
Fetal Movement Felt [*Medicine*] .... FMF
Fetal Occult Blood [*Medicine*] .... FOB
Fetal Sulfoglycoprotein Antigen [*Oncology*] .... FSA
Fetch/Load [*Data processing*] .... F/L
Fetlar [*Shetland Islands*] [*Airport symbol*] .... FEA
Fetoneonatal Estrogen-Binding Protein .... FEBP
Fette Seifen Anstrichmittel [*A publication*] .... Fette Seifen Anstrichm
Fette Seifen Anstrichmittel Verbunden mit der Zeitschrift die Ernahrungsindustrie [*A publication*] .... Fet Sei Ans
Feudal .... FEUD
Feuilles d'Histoire [*A publication*] .... FH
Feuillets du Praticien [*A publication*] .... Feuill Prat
Fever Therapy Technician [*Navy*] .... FTT
Fever of Undetermined Origin [*Medicine*] .... FUO
Fey Industries [*NASDAQ symbol*] .... FEYI
Fez [*Morocco*] [*Airport symbol*] .... FEZ
FFHC [*Freedom from Hunger Campaign*] **Basic Studies** [*A publication*] .... FFHC Basic Stud
FFI (Forsvarets Forskningsinstitutt) Mikroskopet (Norway) [*A publication*] .... FFI (Forsvarets Forskningsints) Mikrosk
FFTF [*Fast Flux Test Facility*] **Test Engineering** [*Nuclear energy*] .... FTE
FFTF [*Fast Flux Test Facility*] **Test Procedure** [*Nuclear energy*] .... FTP
FGI Investors [*Formerly, Fidelco Growth Investors*] [*American Stock Exchange symbol*] [*Delisted*] .... FGI

FhG [*Fraunhofer-Gesellschaft*] **Berichte** [*A publication*] ..... FhG Ber
Fianarantsoa [*Madagascar*] [*Airport symbol*] ..... WFI
Fiat [*Make*] [*Pharmacy*] ..... F
Fiat [*Make*] [*Pharmacy*] ..... FT
Fiat Cataplasma [*Let a Poultice Be Made*] [*Pharmacy*] ..... FT CAT
Fiat Ceratum [*Let a Cerate Be Made*] [*Pharmacy*] ..... FT CERAT
Fiat Chartula [*Let a Powder Be Made*] [*Pharmacy*] ..... FT CHART
Fiat Club of America ..... FCA
Fiat Collyrium [*Let an Eyewash Be Made*] [*Pharmacy*] ..... FT COLLYR
Fiat Emulsio [*Let an Emulsion Be Made*] [*Pharmacy*] ..... FT EMULS
Fiat Gargarisma [*Make a Gargle*] [*Pharmacy*] ..... FT GARG
Fiat Haustus [*Make a Drink*] [*Pharmacy*] ..... FH
Fiat Infusum [*Make an Infusion*] [*Pharmacy*] ..... FT INFUS
Fiat Lege Artis [*Do It by the Rules of the Art*] [*Pharmacy*] ..... FLA
Fiat Linimentum [*Let a Linament Be Made*] [*Pharmacy*] ..... FT LINIM
Fiat Massa [*Let a Mass Be Made*] [*Pharmacy*] ..... FT MAS
Fiat Massa et Divide in Pilulae [*Let a Mass Be Made and Divided into Pills*] [*Pharmacy*] ..... FT MAS DIV in PIL
Fiat Mistura [*Make a Mixture*] [*Pharmacy*] ..... FM
Fiat Mistura [*Make a Mixture*] [*Pharmacy*] ..... FT MIST
Fiat Pilula [*Make a Pill*] [*Pharmacy*] ..... FP
Fiat Pilula [*Make a Pill*] [*Pharmacy*] ..... F PIL
Fiat Pilulae [*Let Pills Be Made*] [*Pharmacy*] ..... FT PIL
Fiat Potio [*Let a Potion Be Made*] [*Pharmacy*] ..... FP
Fiat Pulvis [*Make a Powder*] [*Pharmacy*] ..... FT PULV
Fiat Pulvis Subtilis [*Make a Fine Powder*] [*Pharmacy*] ..... FT PULV SUBTIL
Fiat Secundum Artem [*Let It Be Done According to Art*] [*Pharmacy*] ..... FSA
Fiat Secundum Artem Reglas [*Let It Be Done According to the Rules of the Art*] [*Pharmacy*] ..... FSAR
Fiat Trochisci [*Make Lozenges*] [*Pharmacy*] ..... FT TROCH
Fiat Unguentum [*Make an Ointment*] [*Pharmacy*] ..... FT UNG
Fiat Venaesectio [*Let the Patient Be Bled*] [*Medicine*] ..... F VS
Fibber McGee and Molly [*Radio program*] ..... FM & M
Fiber ..... FBR
Fiber ..... FIB
Fiber Composite Material ..... FCM
Fiber-Embedding Approximation ..... FEA
Fiber and Integrated Optics [*A publication*] ..... Fiber Integr Opt
Fiber Optic Communications for Aerospace Systems ..... FOCAS
Fiber-Optic Rate Sensors [*Instrumentation*] ..... FORS
Fiber Optics Board ..... FOB
Fiber Optics Borescope ..... FOBS
Fiber Optics Guidance Demonstration ..... FOGD
Fiber Optics LASER ..... FOL
Fiber Optics LASER Gyros ..... FOLG
Fiber Optics Light ..... FOL
Fiber Optics Photo Pickup ..... FOPP
Fiber Optics Photo Transfer ..... FOPT
Fiber Optics Probe ..... FOP
Fiber Plan [*Used in title of book advocating a high-fiber diet*] ..... F (Plan)
Fiber Producer [*A publication*] ..... Fiber Prod
Fiber Producers Credit Association ..... FPCA
Fiber-Reinforced Composite ..... FRC
Fiber-Reinforced Composite Junction ..... FRCJ
Fiber-Reinforced Material ..... FRM
Fiber-Reinforced Polyethylene Terephthalate [*Glass*] ..... FR-PET
Fiber Society ..... FS
Fiber Volume Ratio ..... FVR
Fiberboard ..... FBRBD
Fiberboard, Corrugated ..... FBDC
Fiberboard, Double Wall ..... FDWL
Fiberboard, Solid ..... FBDS
Fiberglass Brush ..... FGB
Fiberglass Cone Brush ..... FGCB
Fiberglass Curtain ..... FGC
Fiberglass Fabrication Association ..... FFA
Fiberglass Hull ..... FGH
Fiberglass-Insulated Wire ..... FIW
Fiberglass-Reinforced Thermoplastic ..... FRTP
Fiberoptic Bronchoscopy [*Also, FOB*] [*Medicine*] ..... FB
Fiberoptic Bronchoscopy [*Also, FB*] [*Medicine*] ..... FOB
Fibonacci Quarterly [*A publication*] ..... Fibonacci Q
Fibre [*Classification key in textile printing*] ..... F
Fibre Box Association ..... FBA
Fibre Chemistry [*A publication*] ..... Fibre Chem
Fibre Containers and Paperboard Mills [*A publication*] ..... Fibre Containers
Fibre Drum Manufacturers Association [*Defunct*] ..... FDMA
Fibre Drum Technical Council ..... FDTC
Fibre Science and Technology [*A publication*] ..... Fibre Sci Technol
Fibreboard [*Freight*] ..... FIBRD
Fibreboard Corp. [*NYSE symbol*] [*Delisted*] ..... FBD
Fibreboard Paper Products Corp. [*NYSE symbol*] [*Delisted*] ..... FPP
Fibreboard and Wood [*Freight*] ..... FB WD
Fibrin [*or Fibrinogen*] **Degradation Products** [*Hematology*] ..... FDP
Fibrin-Stabilizing Factor [*Factor XIII*] [*Also, LLF*] [*Hematology*] ..... FSF
Fibrinogen [*Factor I*] [*Hematology*] ..... FBG
Fibrinogen [*Factor I*] [*Hematology*] ..... FIB
Fibrinogen-Split Products [*Hematology*] ..... FSP
Fibrinopeptide ..... FP
Fibrinopeptide A ..... FPA
Fibroblast [*Medicine*] ..... FB
Fibroblast Growth Factor [*Cytochemistry*] ..... FGF
Fibroblast Interferon [*Genetics*] ..... FIF
Fibroblast-Migration Inhibitory Factor [*Immunochemistry*] ..... FIF
Fibroelastic Connective Tissue [*Medicine*] ..... FECT
Fibronectin [*Biochemistry*] ..... FN
Fibronics International [*NASDAQ symbol*] ..... FBRX
Fibrositis [*Medicine*] ..... FIB
Fibrous ..... F
Fibrous ..... FBRS
Fibrous Material ..... FM
Fibrous Refractory Composite Insulation ..... FRCI
Fibrous Sausage Casing ..... FSC
Fibula [*Medicine*] ..... FIB
Fiches d'Identification du Zooplancton [*A publication*] ..... Fiches Identif Zooplancton
Fiches de Phytopathologie Tropicale [*A publication*] ..... Fiches Phytopathol Trop
Fiches Typologiques Africaines ..... FTA
Fichier Micropaleontologique General [*A publication*] ..... Fichier Micropaleontol Gen
Fick Diffusion Law ..... FDL
Fickle Hill [*California*] [*Seismograph station code, US Geological Survey*] ..... FHC
Fictilis [*Made of Pottery*] [*Latin*] ..... FICT
Fiction ..... F
Fiction ..... FICT
Fiction International [*A publication*] ..... Fic Int
Fiction Magazine [*Generic term for a publication covering science fiction*] ..... FICTIONZINE
Fidei Commissum [*Bequeathed in Trust*] [*Latin*] ..... FC
Fidei Defensor [*Defender of the Faith*] [*Latin*] ..... FD
Fidelcor, Inc. [*NASDAQ symbol*] ..... FICR
Fidelity Financial Corp. [*NYSE symbol*] ..... FDY
Fidelity [*to Living Condition*] **Index** [*Botany*] ..... FI
Fidelity Medical, Incorporated [*NASDAQ symbol*] ..... FMSI
Fidelity Mortgage Investors [*NYSE symbol*] [*Delisted*] ..... FID
Fidelity Mutual Life Insurance Co., Philadelphia, PA [*Library symbol*] ..... PPFML
Fidelity of Oklahoma [*NASDAQ symbol*] ..... FDOK
Fidelity Union Bancorporation [*NYSE symbol*] ..... FDU
Fidelity Union Life Insurance Company ..... FULICO
Fides et Historia [*A publication*] ..... FH
Fides et Historia [*A publication*] ..... FHist
Fiduciary Activity Simulation Training [*Investment banking simulation game*] ..... FAST
Fiduciary Identification Number [*IRS*] ..... FIN
Field ..... F
Field ..... FD
Field ..... FLD
Field Accelerator ..... FAC
Field Activities ..... F/A
Field Activity Missile Engineering ..... FAME
Field Activity Report ..... FAR
Field Activity War Emergency Program [*DoD*] ..... FAWEP
Field Activity War and Emergency Support Plan [*DoD*] ..... FAWESP
Field Advisory Element ..... FAE
Field Aircraft Services Ltd. [*Great Britain*] [*ICAO designator*] ..... FS
Field Alert Status [*Army*] ..... FAS
Field Alterable Control Element ..... FACE
Field Ambulance [*Military*] ..... FA
Field Analysis Report ..... FAR
Field Army ..... FA
Field Army Ballistic Missile Defense System [*Later, AADS*] [*Antimissile missile*] ..... FABMDS
Field Army Ballistic Missile Defense System [*Antimissile missile*] ..... FABMIDS
Field Army Calibration Team Support ..... FACTS
Field Army Communication System ..... FACS
Field Army Issuing Office ..... FAIO
Field Army Messenger Service ..... FAMS
Field Army Petroleum Office ..... FAPO
Field Army Replacement System ..... FARS
Field Army Service Area ..... FASA
Field Army Support Command ..... FASCOM
Field Army Tactical Operation Center ..... FATOC
Field Army Tactical Random Access Communications System ..... FATRACS
Field Artillery ..... FA
Field Artillery Acoustic Locating System ..... FAALS
Field Artillery Aerial Observer ..... FAAO
Field Artillery Airborne ..... FAA
Field Artillery Ammunition Support Vehicle ..... FAASV
Field Artillery Brigade ..... FAB
Field Artillery Computer Equipment ..... FACE
Field Artillery Digital Automatic Computer ..... FADAC
Field Artillery Fire Support Team [*Army*] ..... FIST
Field Artillery Group ..... FLDARTYGRU
Field Artillery Guided Missile [*Air Force*] ..... FAGMS
Field Artillery Intelligence Officer [*Military*] ..... FAIO
Field Artillery Logic Tester [*Army*] ..... FALT
Field Artillery Missile ..... FAM
Field Artillery Missile System ..... FAMS

Field Artillery Missile Systems Evaluation Group .... FAMSEG
Field Artillery Replacement Center .... FARC
Field Artillery School .... FAS
Field Artillery Tactical Data Systems [*Army*] .... FATDS
Field Artillery Target Acquisition Battalion [*Army*] .... FATAB
Field Artillery Target Acquisition Group [*Army*] .... FATAG
Field Artillery Tractor [*British*] .... FAT
Field Audit [*IRS*] .... FA
Field Audit and Completion Test [*Market research*] .... FACT
Field Audit Office .... FAO
Field Automated Intelligence File .... FAIF
Field Aviation Supply Office .... FASO
Field Bake Oven [*Military*] .... FBO
Field Base Visit .... FBV
Field Branch .... FLDBR
Field Cable Installation Platoon [*Army*] .... FCIP
Field Camera .... FC
Field Camera Control .... FCC
Field Carrier Landing Passes [*or Practice*] .... FCLP
Field Challenge Test Plan .... FCTP
Field Change .... FC
Field Change Analysis .... FCA
Field Change Kit .... FCK
Field Change Notification .... FCN
Field Change Order .... FCO
Field Change Proposal .... FCP
Field Checkout Equipment .... FCE
Field Columbian Museum. Publication. Geological Series. Zoological Series [*A publication*] .... Field Col Mus Pub G S Zool S
Field Command [*Military*] .... FC
Field Command, Defense Atomic Support Agency .... FC/DASA
Field Command, Defense Atomic Support Agency .... FLDCOMDASA
Field Command, Defense Nuclear Agency [*DoD*] .... FCDNA
Field Command, Defense Nuclear Agency [*DoD*] .... FLDCOMDNA
Field Command Post .... FCP
Field Communication Unit [*Military*] .... FCU
Field Configuration Control Board [*Army*] .... FCCB
Field Contract Administration Division [*of ONM*] .... FCAD
Field Control Center .... FCC
Field Cook [*Marine Corps*] .... FLDCK
Field Cook (Baker) [*Marine Corps*] .... FLDCK(B)
Field Cook (Commissary) [*Marine Corps*] .... FLDCK(C)
Field Coordination Group .... FCG
Field Crop Abstracts [*A publication*] .... Field Crop Abstr
Field Crop Abstracts [*A publication*] .... Fld Crop Abstr
Field Data Applications, Systems, and Techniques .... FAST
Field Data Computer .... FDC
Field Data Computer [*Army*] .... FIELDATA
Field Decelerator .... FDE
Field Depot Aviation Squadron [*Air Force*] .... FDAS
Field Designator Number [*Air Force*] .... FDN
Field Desorption .... FD
Field Desorption - Mass Spectrometry .... FD-MS
Field Developed Program [*Data processing*] .... FDP
Field Developed Programs [*Data processing*] .... FDPS
Field Development Program [*LIMRA*] .... FDP
Field Director .... FD
Field Director Overseas [*Red Cross*] .... FDO
Field Discharge .... FDI
Field Displacement Isolator .... FDI
Field of Drawing .... FD
Field Dressing Station [*Military*] .... FDS
Field Dynamic Braking .... FDB
Field Effect Amplifier .... FEA
Field Effect Device .... FED
Field Effect Transistor .... FET
Field Effect Transistors .... FETS
Field Electron Emission Microscope [*or Microscopy*] .... FEEM
Field Electron Microscope [*or Microscopy*] .... FEM
Field Electronic Maintenance Section [*National Weather Service*] .... FEMS
Field Emission Deposition [*Coating technique*] .... FED
Field Emission Microscope [*or Microscopy*] .... FEM
Field Emission Spectroscopy .... FES
Field Emitting Surface .... FES
Field Engineer [*or Engineering*] .... FE
Field Engineering Assistance Request .... FEAR
Field Engineering Bulletin .... FEB
Field Engineering Change .... FEC
Field Engineering and Equipment [*Military*] .... FEE
Field Engineering Maintenance .... FEM
Field Engineering Order .... FEO
Field Engineering Representative .... FER
Field Engineering Service .... FES
Field Engineering Theory of Operations .... FETO
Field-Enhanced Secondary Emission .... FESE
Field Enterprises Educational Corporation [*Later, World Book-Childcraft International, Inc.*] .... FEEC
Field Evaluation Agency [*Army*] .... FEA
Field Evaluation Model .... FEM
Field Exercise [*Military*] .... FEX
Field Exercise under Snow Conditions [*Military*] .... SNOWFLEX
Field Expedient .... FE
Field Exploitation of Elevation Data .... FEED
Field Extension Office [*DoD*] .... FEO
Field Failure .... FFL
Field of Fire [*Military*] .... F of F
Field Firing Exercise [*Military*] .... FFEX
Field-Flow Fractionation [*Chemical separation method*] .... FFF
Field Focusing Nuclear Magnetic Resonance .... FONAR
Field Force, Vietnam .... FFORCEV
Field Force, Vietnam .... FFV
Field Forces [*Military*] .... FF
Field Forcing (Decreasing) .... FFD
Field Forcing (Increasing) .... FFI
Field-Free Emission Current .... FFEC
Field Fresnel Lens Optical Platform .... FFLOP
Field Functional System Assembly and Checkout .... FFSA & C
Field General Court-Martial .... FGCM
Field Goal [*Football, basketball*] .... FG
Field Goals Attempted [*Football, basketball*] .... FA
Field Goals Attempted [*Football, basketball*] .... FGA
Field Goals Made [*Football, basketball*] .... FGM
Field Goals Missed [*Football, basketball*] .... M
Field Grade .... FG
Field Gun .... FG
Field Handling Design Objective .... FHDO
Field Handling Trainer [*Army*] .... FHT
Field Hockey Association of America .... FHAA
Field Illustrated [*A publication*] .... Field Il
Field-Induced Negative Ion Formation .... FINIF
Field Information Agency, Technical [*Under G-2, SHAEF*] .... FIAT
Field Information Release .... FIR
Field Information System .... FIS
Field Infrared Spectrometer .... FIS
Field Inspection Manual .... FIM
Field Inspection Procedure .... FIP
Field Installation Change Order .... FICO
Field Installation Simulator .... FIS
Field Installation and Test .... FIT
Field Installed Connector .... FIC
Field Instruction Memorandum .... FIM
Field Instruction System .... FIS
Field Integration Engineering Test .... FIET
Field Intelligence Department .... FID
Field Intelligence Simulation Test .... FIST
Field Intelligence Unit .... FIU
Field Intensity .... FI
Field Intensity Measuring System .... FIMS
Field Intensity Meter .... FIM
Field Intensity Receiver .... FIR
Field-of-Interest Register [*DoD*] .... FOIR
Field Interview .... FI
Field Ion Microscope [*or Microscopy*] .... FIM
Field Ionization .... FI
Field Ionization Kinetics .... FIK
Field Ionization Mass Spectrometry [*Air-pollutant detector*] .... FIMS
Field Judge [*Football*] .... FJ
Field and Laboratory [*A publication*] .... Field & Lab
Field Landing Practice .... FLP
Field Level Repair .... FLR
Field Level Training .... FLT
Field Library, Inc., Peekskill, NY [*Library symbol*] .... NPee
Field Loss Relay .... FLR
Field Main .... FM
Field Maintenance .... FM
Field Maintenance Equipment [*Military*] .... FME
Field Maintenance Party [*Aviation*] .... FMP
Field Maintenance Shop [*Army*] .... FLDMS
Field Maintenance Shop [*Army*] .... FMS
Field Maintenance Squadron [*Air Force*] .... FMS
Field Maintenance Squadron [*Air Force*] .... FMSq
Field Maintenance Technician .... FMT
Field Maintenance Test Station [*Army*] .... FMTS
Field Manual [*Military*] .... FM
Field Marching Pack .... FMP
Field Marshal .... FM
Field Medical Card [*Army*] .... FMC
Field Memorandum .... FM
Field Mirror Landing Practice .... FMLP
Field Missile System Test .... FMST
Field Modification .... FM
Field Modification Report .... FMR
Field Modification Request [*Military*] .... FMR
Field Modification Task .... FMT
Field Museum of Natural History, Chicago, IL [*OCLC symbol*] .... IBT
Field Museum of Natural History, Chicago, IL [*Library symbol*] .... ICF
Field Museum of Natural History, Edward E. Ayer Ornithological Library, Chicago, IL [*Library symbol*] .... ICF-A
Field Museum of Natural History Publications. Botanical Series [*A publication*] .... Field Mus Nat Hist Publ Bot Ser
Field Museum of Natural History Publications. Zoological Series [*A publication*] .... Field Mus Nat Hist Publ Zool Ser

Field Music [*Marine Corps*] ..... FM
Field Music Corporal [*Marine Corps*] ..... FMCORP
Field Music Corporal [*Marine Corps*] ..... FMCPL
Field Music School [*Marine Corps*] ..... FMS
Field Music Sergeant [*Marine Corps*] ..... FMSGT
Field Naturalist [*A publication*] ..... Field Nat
Field Network Evaluation Study [*Survey*] ..... FNES
Field Observing Facility [*of National Center for Atmospheric Research*] ..... FOF
Field Observing Support Facility [*National Center for Atmospheric Research*] ..... FOSF
Field Office [*or Officer*] ..... FO
Field Office Assistant [*Red Cross*] ..... FOA
Field Office Reporting-Management System [*HUD*] ..... FORMS
Field Office Sales and Service Costs Study [*LIMRA*] ..... FOSSCS
Field Officer ..... FLDO
Field Officer of the Day [*Army*] ..... FOD
Field Officers School [*Formerly, AOS*] [*LIMRA*] ..... FOS
Field On-Line Data Acquisition and Analysis System ..... FODAAS
Field Operating Cost Agency [*Army*] ..... FOCA
Field Operational [*Test*] ..... FO
Field Operations Department ..... FOD
Field Operations Group ..... FOG
Field Operations Intelligence ..... FOI
Field Operations Memorandum ..... FOM
Field Order ..... FO
Field Personnel Record ..... FPERR
Field Personnel Record ..... FPR
Field Post Office [*Military*] [*British*] ..... FDPO
Field Post Office [*Military*] [*British*] ..... FPO
Field Power Supply ..... FPS
Field Profit Analysis ..... FPA
Field-Programable Logic Array [*Data processing*] ..... FPLA
Field-Programable Read-Only Memory [*Data processing*] ..... F-PROM
Field Project Officer ..... FPO
Field Promotion Program [*FAA*] ..... FPP
Field Protective ..... FP
Field Punishment [*Military*] ..... FP
Field Record Group [*Air Force*] ..... FRGp
Field Repairable - Expendable Rotor Blade ..... FREB
Field Replaceable Unit [*IBM Corp.*] ..... FRU
Field Report ..... FR
Field Representative Europe ..... FRE
Field Representative Far East ..... FRFE
Field Requirements List ..... FRL
Field Research Projects. Man and Nature Series [*A publication*] ..... Field Res Proj Man Nat Ser
Field Research Projects. Natural Area Studies [*A publication*] ..... Field Res Proj Nat Area Stud
Field and Reservoir Reserve Estimate [*US Geological Survey*] ..... FRRE
Field Resistance ..... FR
Field Retrofit ..... FR
Field Reversing ..... FR
Field Security [*British Army detective police - a branch of Intelligence*] ..... FS
Field Security Officer [*Military*] ..... FSO
Field Security Personnel ..... FSP
Field Security Police ..... FSP
Field Selection Board [*Military*] ..... FSB
Field Service ..... FS
Field Service Addition ..... FSA
Field Service Bulletin ..... FSB
Field Service Engineer [*Military*] ..... FSE
Field Service Engineering ..... FSER
Field Service Modification Work Order ..... FSMWO
Field Service Operations ..... FSO
Field Service Regulations [*Army*] ..... FSR
Field Service Report ..... FSR
Field Service Representative ..... FSR
Field Service Section [*Military*] ..... FSS
Field Service Technical Report ..... FSTR
Field Service Technician ..... FST
Field Site Facility ..... FSF
Field Spectrometer System ..... FSS
Field Standard Weight and Force System ..... FSWFS
Field Station ..... FS
Field Station Materiel Requirements ..... FSMR
Field-Stimulated Exoelectron Emission [*Physics*] ..... FSEE
Field Storage Unit [*Military*] ..... FSU
Field and Stream [*A publication*] ..... Field & S
Field Strength Meter ..... FSM
Field Strength Radio ..... FSR
Field Studies [*A publication*] ..... Field Stud
Field Suitability Test ..... FST
Field Supply Group ..... FSG
Field Support Activity [*Military*] ..... FSA
Field Support Equipment [*Military*] ..... FSE
Field Support System ..... FSS
Field Survey Team ..... FST
Field Switch ..... FSW
Field Target Screen ..... FTS
Field Team Bulletin [*Military*] ..... FTB
Field Technical Authority ..... FTA
Field Technical Training Unit ..... FTTU
Field Test ..... FT
Field Test Administration ..... FTA
Field Test Exercise [*Military*] ..... FTX
Field Test Kit ..... FTK
Field Test Office ..... FTO
Field Test Operational Procedures [*Aerospace*] ..... FTP
Field Test Operations [*Aerospace*] ..... FTO
Field Test Operations Support [*Aerospace*] ..... FTOS
Field Test Support [*Aerospace*] ..... FTS
Field Testing and Development Center ..... FTDC
Field Torpedo Unit ..... FTU
Field Training [*AFROTC*] ..... FT
Field Training Command [*Military*] ..... FTC
Field Training Detachment [*Program*] [*Air Force*] ..... FTD
Field Training Equipment Concentration Site [*Army*] ..... FTECS
Field Training Services [*Army*] ..... FTS
Field Training Team [*Military*] ..... FTT
Field Trains ..... FLDTNS
Field Trip ..... FT
Field Turn-Around Time ..... FTAT
Field Verification Test Set ..... FVTS
Field of View [*or Vision*] ..... FOV
Field of Vision [*Medicine*] ..... F
Field Weakening ..... FW
Field Weakening ..... FWK
Field Wire Command Link [*Army*] ..... FWCL
Field Worship [*Army*] [*British*] ..... FW
Fieldcrest Mills, Inc. [*NYSE symbol*] ..... FLD
Fielder's Choice [*Baseball*] ..... FC
Fieldiana Botany [*A publication*] ..... Fieldiana Bot
Fieldiana Geology [*A publication*] ..... Fieldiana Geol
Fieldiana Geology. Memoirs [*A publication*] ..... Fieldiana Geol Mem
Fieldiana Geology. Memoirs [*A publication*] ..... Fieldiana Geology Mem
Fieldiana Zoology [*A publication*] ..... Fieldiana Zool
Fieldiana Zoology. Memoirs [*A publication*] ..... Fieldiana Zool Mem
Fieldiana Zoology. Memoirs [*A publication*] ..... Fieldiana Zoology Mem
Fielding Average [*Baseball*] ..... FA
Fields within Fields within Fields [*A publication*] ..... Field w Fie
Fields Plastics & Chemicals, Inc. [*American Stock Exchange symbol*] [*Delisted*] ..... FLP
Fields Point [*Washington*] [*Seismograph station code, US Geological Survey*] ..... FPW
Fiendishly Rapid Electronic Device ..... FRED
Fiera Letteraria [*A publication*] ..... FLe
Fiera Letteraria [*A publication*] ..... FLett
Fieri Curavit [*Caused to Be Made*] [*Latin*] ..... FC
Fieri-Facias [*Cause to Be Made*] [*Legal*] [*Latin*] ..... FI FA
Fieri Fecit [*Caused to Be Made*] [*Latin*] ..... FF
Fiesta-Air [*Air carrier designation symbol*] ..... FIAX
Fife Lake Public Library, Fife Lake, MI [*Library symbol*] ..... MiFil
Fifeshire [*County in Scotland*] ..... FIFES
Fifth Allied Tactical Air Force, Southern Europe ..... FIVEATAF
Fifth Amphibious Corps ..... VAC
Fifth Avenue Cards, Inc. [*NASDAQ symbol*] ..... FIVE
Fifth Avenue Coach Lines, Inc. [*NYSE symbol*] [*Delisted*] ..... FCL
Fifth Estate [*A publication*] ..... Fifth Est
Fifth-Order Theory ..... FOT
Fifth Third Bancorp [*NASDAQ symbol*] ..... FITB
Fifty [*Roman numeral*] L
Fifty-Plus Runners Association ..... FPRA
Fifty Upward Network ..... FUN
Figari [*Corsica*] [*Airport symbol*] ..... FSC
Figaro Litteraire [*A publication*] ..... FL
Figgie International Holdings [*NASDAQ symbol*] ..... FIGI
Figgie International, Inc. [*NYSE symbol*] [*Delisted*] ..... FIG
Fight to Advance the Nation's Sports [*Defunct*] ..... FANS
Fight to Advertise the Truth about Saturates [*Student legal action organization*] ..... FATS
Fight Against Dictating Designers [*Group opposing below-the-knee fashions introduced in 1970*] ..... FADD
Fight Inflation Together [*Group opposing high food prices in 1973*] ..... FIT
Fight for Sight [*An association*] ..... FS
Fighter [*Russian aircraft symbol*] ..... DI
Fighter [*Designation for all US military aircraft*] ..... F
Fighter ..... FH
Fighter ..... FIT
Fighter ..... FTR
Fighter [*Russian aircraft symbol*] I
Fighter [*Russian aircraft symbol*] ..... JP
Fighter [*Russian aircraft symbol*] ..... LA
Fighter [*Russian aircraft symbol*] ..... LAGG
Fighter Air Direction Center ..... FADC
Fighter Air Director [*Military*] ..... FAD
Fighter-Aircraft-Delivered Seismic Intrusion Detector ..... FADSID
Fighter Aircraft Structural Loads [*Program*] [*Air Force*] ..... FASTLODS
Fighter Alert ..... FA
Fighter Allocator ..... FA
Fighter Analysis Tactical Air Combat ..... FANTAC
Fighter, Attacker, Reconnaissance [*Requirements*] [*Air Force*] ..... FAR

Fighter Automatic Navigator .... FAN
Fighter Bomber .... FB
Fighter Bomber [*Advanced*] .... FBX
Fighter Bomber [*Obsolete*] .... FTB
Fighter Bomber Aircraft .... FBA
Fighter Bomber Attack .... FB/A
Fighter Bomber Program .... FBP
Fighter Bomber Strike .... FB/S
Fighter Bombing Plane [*Navy symbol*] .... VFB
Fighter Catapult [*Ship*] .... FC
Fighter Command [*Air Force*] .... FC
Fighter Command School [*Air Force*] .... FCS
Fighter Control Area [*Military*] .... FCA
Fighter Control Center .... FCC
Fighter Control Unit [*Military*] [*British*] .... FCU
Fighter Conveyor .... FICON
Fighter Development Program .... FDP
Fighter Direction .... FD
Fighter Direction Net [*Navy*] .... FDNET
Fighter Director Control Schools [*Navy*] .... FDCS
Fighter Director Officer [*Navy*] .... FDO
Fighter Director Post .... FDP
Fighter Director Ship [*Navy*] .... FDS
Fighter Director Tender [*Navy*] .... FDT
Fighter Dive-Bomber .... FDB
Fighter Duty Officer .... FDO
Fighter Engagement Zone [*Military*] .... FEZ
Fighter Escort .... FE
Fighter Experimental .... FX
Fighter Ground Attack .... FGA
Fighter Identification System .... FIS
Fighter Inertial Navigation System .... FINE
Fighter Interception Unit [*RAF*] [*British*] .... FIU
Fighter Interceptor .... FI
Fighter-Interceptor Squadron [*Air Force*] .... FIS
Fighter-Interceptor Squadron [*Air Force*] .... FISq
Fighter-Interceptor Wing .... FIW
Fighter Jet .... FJ
Fighter Missile System .... FMS
Fighter Multifunctional Inertial Reference Assembly .... FMIRA
Fighter Officer for Interceptors [*Member of the SAGE Command Post staff*] .... FOI
Fighter Officer for Missiles [*Member of the SAGE Command Post staff*] .... FOM
Fighter Operations .... FTRO
Fighter Plane [*Navy symbol*] .... VF
Fighter Plane (Two-Engine) [*Navy symbol*] .... VF(M)
Fighter Plans .... FTRP
Fighter Prop .... FP
Fighter Reconnaissance [*Air Force*] .... FR
Fighter Squadron [*Navy*] .... FITRON
Fighter Squadron [*Navy symbol*] .... VF
Fighter Squadron - All Weather [*Navy symbol*] .... VF AW
Fighter Squadron, Photo [*Navy symbol*] .... VFP
Fighter Tactical Wing .... FTW
Fighter Weapons .... FW
Fighter Weapons Training Command .... FWTC
Fighter Wing [*Navy*] .... FITWING
Fighting French .... FF
Fighting Landplane .... FLP
Fighting Squadron .... FIGHTRON
Fighting Vehicle Armament .... FVA
Fighting Vehicle Systems .... FVS
Fighting Vehicles Research and Development Establishment [*British*] .... FVRDE
Figural Bottle Association [*Defunct*] .... FBA
Figural Bottle Openers Collectors Club .... FBOC
Figurative .... FIG
Figure .... FIG
Figure Drawing Test [*Psychology*] .... FDT
Figure of Merit .... FM
Figure of Merit .... FOM
Figure of Merit [*Symbol*] .... Z
Figure Reading Electronic Device [*Information retrieval*] .... FRED
Figures or Images [*Freight*] .... FGIM
Figures Shift [*Teleprinters*] .... FIGS
Fiji [*MARC country of publication code*] [*Library of Congress*] .... fj
Fiji [*Three-letter standard code*] .... FJI
Fiji [*MARC geographic area code*] [*Library of Congress*] .... pofj---
Fiji [*Two-letter standard code*] .... FJ
Fiji Agricultural Journal [*A publication*] .... Fiji Agric J
Fiji Air Services Ltd. [*ICAO designator*] .... PC
Fiji Department of Agriculture. Bulletin [*A publication*] .... Fiji Dep Agric Bull
Fiji Federation of Labor .... FFL
Fiji Geological Survey Department. Bulletin [*A publication*] .... Fiji Geol Surv Dep Bull
Fiji Industrial Workers' Congress .... FIWC
Fiji Timbers and Their Uses [*A publication*] .... Fiji Timb
Fikambanan' Ny Mpanoratra Sy Mpamoron-Kira Ary Editora Malagasy [*Malagasy Republic*] .... FIMMEMA
Filament .... F
Filament .... FIL
Filament Center Tap .... FCT
Filament Composite Material .... FCM
Filament Ground .... FG
Filament Midtop .... FM
Filament-Reinforced Plastic .... FRP
Filament Wound .... FW
Filament-Wound Glass Fiber .... FGF
Filament-Wound Structure .... FWS
Filamentous Fungi [*A publication*] .... Filam Fungi
File Analysis and Selection Technique [*Data processing*] .... FAST
File Cabinet .... FC
File Code .... FC
File Control [*Microfilm*] .... FICO
File Control Block [*Data processing*] .... FCB
File Control Processor [*Data processing*] .... FCP
File Conversion [*Data processing*] .... FC
File Copy .... FC
File Definition [*Data processing*] .... FD
File Extended Control Block [*Data processing*] .... FECB
File Finish .... FF
File Gap [*Data processing*] .... FG
File of Industrial Data [*Data processing*] .... FIND
File Information Language Executive Routine [*Data processing*] .... FILER
File Information Table [*Data processing*] .... FIT
File Interrogation of Nineteen-Hundred Data [*Data processing*] .... FIND
File Interrogation and Reporting System [*Data processing*] .... FIRS
File de Istorie. Culegere de Studii, Articole si Comunicari [*A publication*] .... Fil Ist
File List Processor [*Data processing*] .... FLIST
File Location Code [*Data processing*] .... FLC
File Maintenance [*Data processing*] .... FM
File Maintenance System .... FMS
File Management Transaction Processor .... FMTP
File Manufacturers Association [*Defunct*] .... FMA
File Organization System .... FOS
File Organization Technique .... FORTE
File-Oriented Interpretive Language [*Data processing*] .... FOIL
File Processor [*Data processing*] .... FP
File Protect Memory [*Data processing*] .... FPM
File and Report Information Processing Generators [*Data processing*] .... FRINGE
File Separator [*Data processing*] .... FS
File Source [*Data processing*] .... FS
File Status Table [*Data processing*] .... FST
File System Control [*Data processing*] .... FSC
File System Control Block [*Data processing*] .... FSCB
File Utility Routines [*Data processing*] .... FUR
File Utility Routines, Program Utility Routines [*Data processing*] .... FURPUR
Filed Flight Plan Message [*Aviation code*] .... FPL
Filed IFR [*Instrument Flight Rules*] **Flight Plan** [*Aviation*] .... FIFP
Filed but Impracticable [*to transmit*] .... FIBI
Filene's [*Boston*] **Automatic Bargain Basement** .... FABB
Files Control Office .... FCO
Files Management Unit [*Data processing*] .... FMU
Filial Generation .... F
Filial Generation, First [*Biology*] .... F_1
Filial Generation, Second [*Biology*] .... F_2
Filii Divinae Providentiae [*Sons or Daughters of Divine Providence*] [*Roman Catholic religious order*] .... FDP
Filii Mariae Salutis Infirmorum [*Sons of Mary, Health of the Sick*] [*Roman Catholic religious order*] .... FMSI
Filing Requirement [*IRS*] .... FR
Filing Status [*IRS*] .... FS
Filing Status Code [*IRS*] .... FSC
Filing Time [*Time a message is presented for transmission*] .... FLT
Filing Time [*Time a message is presented for transmission*] .... FT
Filipinas Americas Science and Art Foundation .... FASAF
Filipino American Political Association .... FAPA
Filipino Employment Policy Instruction .... FEPI
Filipino Rehabilitation Commission [*Post-World War II*] .... FRC
Filipino Teacher [*A publication*] .... FT
Filius [*Son*] [*Latin*] .... F
Fill/Drain .... FD
Fill and Drain .... F & D
Fill Exit Entry [*Data processing*] .... FEE
Fill/Full [*or Full/Fill*] .... F/F
Fill Producers' Association .... FPA
Fill Start Entry [*Data processing*] .... FSE
Filled Quartz Helix .... FQH
Filled Thermal System [*Temperature sensor*] .... FTS
Filler .... FLR
Filler Sensor Nozzle .... FSN
Filler for Smoke Shells [*Weaponry*] .... FS
Filler Wire Addition .... FWA
Fillet .... FIL
Filling .... FILG
Filling .... FILL
Filling, Storage, and Remelt System [*Nuclear energy*] .... FS & R
Fillister .... FIL
Fillister Head [*Screws*] .... FILH

Fillmore City Library, Fillmore, UT [*Library symbol*] .... UFi
Filly .... F
Filly [*Thoroughbred racing*] .... F
Film .... FLM
Film Advisory Board .... FAB
Film, Air, and Package Carriers Conference .... FAPCC
Film Availability Services [*British Film Institute*] .... FAS
Film: British Documentary .... FBD
Film: British Feature .... FBF
Film: British Series .... FBS
Film Bulletin .... FB
Film Bulletin [*A publication*] .... F Bul
Film Capability Laboratories [*Bell System*] .... FCL
Film Carrousel Handle .... FCH
Film Coalition .... FILCO
Film Comment [*A publication*] .... FC
Film Comment [*A publication*] .... F Com
Film Comment [*A publication*] .... F Comment
Film Corp. of America [*American Stock Exchange symbol*] [*Delisted*] .... FIL
Film Council Film Circuit [*Library network*] .... FCFC
Film Culture [*A publication*] .... F CUL
Film Culture [*A publication*] .... F Culture
Film Culture Non-Profit Corporation .... FCNPC
Film Dope [*A publication*] .... F Dope
Film and Equipment Exchange [*Army*] .... F & EE
Film Fan Monthly [*A publication*] .... FFM
Film und Fernsehen [*A publication*] .... F & Fernsehen
Film: Foreign Documentary .... FFD
Film: Foreign Feature .... FFF
Film: Foreign Series .... FFS
Film Forum Review [*A publication*] .... FFR
Film Heritage [*A publication*] .... F Her
Film Input to Digital Automatic Computer .... FIDAC
Film Input to Digital Automatic Computer System .... FIDACSYS
Film Input/Output Unit .... FIOU
Film Inspection Apply Template .... FIAT
Film Integrated Circuit .... FIC
Film Journal [*A publication*] .... Film J
Film Journal [*A publication*] .... FJ
Film Journal [*A publication*] .... F Journal
Film Kultura [*A publication*] .... F Kultura
Film Liaison Officer [*Army*] .... FLO
Film Library Information Council .... FLIC
Film Library Instantaneous Presentation [*Data processing*] .... FLIP
Film Library Inter-College Cooperative of Pennsylvania [*Library network*] .... FLIC
Film Library Quarterly [*A publication*] .... Film Lib Q
Film Library Quarterly [*A publication*] .... F Lib Quarterly
Film Library Quarterly [*A publication*] .... FLQ
Film Literature Index [*A publication*] .... Film Lit Ind
Film Load .... F/L
Film-Lyd-Bilde [*A publication*] .... F-Lyd-Bild
Film Magazine Stowage Container .... FMSC
Film Magnetic Counter .... FMC
Film-Makers' Cooperative .... FMC
Film Making [*A publication*] .... F M
Film Music [*A publication*] .... Film Mus
Film Music Notebook [*A publication*] .... F Music Ntbk
Film Music Notes [*A publication*] .... Film Mus Notes
Film News [*A publication*] .... FN
Film News [*A publication*] .... F News
Film Optical Sensing Device for Input to Computers [*of the National Bureau of Standards*] .... FOSDIC
Film Pack [*Photography*] .... FP
Film Processing .... FLMPRS
Film Producers Association of New York [*Defunct*] .... FPANY
Film Quarterly [*A publication*] .... Film Q
Film Quarterly [*A publication*] .... FQ
Film Reader [*A publication*] .... F Reader
Film Reading Machine .... FRM
Film Recording .... FR
Film Report .... FR
Film and Sheet [*Plastics technology*] .... F/S
Film Society Review [*A publication*] .... F Soc Rev
Film Society Review [*A publication*] .... FSR
Film Sound .... FLMSD
Film Stowage Container .... FSC
Film Strip Sound Projector .... FSSP
Film en Televisie [*A publication*] .... F & TV
Film and Television Correlation Assessment Technique .... FATCAT
Film and Television Technician [*A publication*] .... F & TV Tech
Film Thickness Indicator .... FTI
Film Thickness Monitor .... FTM
Film und Ton [*A publication*] .... F & Ton
Film Tracing Reproduction .... FTR
Film Training Aid .... FTA
Film Transfer Boom [*NASA*] .... FTB
Film und TV Kameramann [*A publication*] .... F & TV Kam
Film Unit Secretary .... FUS
Film Weekly Award [*British*] .... FWA
Filmcritica [*A publication*] .... FCR
Filme Cultura [*A publication*] .... F Cultura
Filmfacts [*A publication*] .... FF
Filmfacts [*A publication*] .... Filmf
Filmkritik [*A publication*] .... Fkr
Filmkunst [*A publication*] .... F Kunst
Filmless Automatic Bond Inspection System .... FABIS
Filmmakers' Newsletter [*A publication*] .... FMN
Filmograph [*A publication*] .... FGR
Filmrutan [*A publication*] .... F Rutan
Films and Filming [*A publication*] .... FF
Films and Filming [*A publication*] .... Films & F
Films, Incorporated .... FI
Films in Review [*A publication*] .... Films in R
Films in Review [*A publication*] .... FIR
Filmstrip .... FS
Filmtec Corp. [*NASDAQ symbol*] .... FTEC
Filmways, Inc. [*NYSE symbol*] [*Delisted*] .... FWY
Filmwissenschaftliche Beitraege [*A publication*] .... F Wiss Beit
Filoil Free Workers [*Philippines*] .... FFW
Filoil Pipeline [*Manila*] [*A publication*] .... FP
Filologia [*A publication*] .... Fi
Filologia. Instituto de Filologia Romancia Facultad de Filosofia y Letras. Universidad de Buenos Aires [*A publication*] .... FUBA
Filologia e Letteratura [*A publication*] .... FeL
Filologia Moderna [*A publication*] .... FiM
Filologia Moderna [*A publication*] .... FMod
Filologia Romanza [*A publication*] .... FiR
Filologia Romanza [*A publication*] .... FRom
Filologiai Koezloeny [*A publication*] .... FK
Filologica [*A publication*] .... Filo
Filologiceskie Nauki [*A publication*] .... FN
Filologiceskie Vesti [*A publication*] .... Filol Vesti
Filologiceskij Sbornik [*Stat'i Aspirantov i Soiskatelej*]. **Alma-Ata** [*A publication*] .... FilSbAlm
Filologicke Studie [*A publication*] .... FILS
Filologija (Zagreb) [*A publication*] .... FilZ
Filologiskt Arkiv [*A publication*] .... FA
Filoloski Pregled [*Belgrade*] [*A publication*] .... FP
Filosofia [*A publication*] .... Fil
Filosofia y Letras [*A publication*] .... FyL
Filosofichnii Problemy Suchasnoho Przyrodoznavstva Mizhvidomchyi Naukovyi Zbirnyk [*A publication*] .... Filos Probl Suchasnoho Przyr Mizhvid Nauk Zb
Filosoficky Casopis CSAV [*Ceskoslovesnska Akademie Ved*] [*A publication*] .... Filosof Cas CSAV
Filosofija i Naucnyj Kommunizm [*A publication*] .... Filos Nauc Kommunizm
Filosofska Dumka [*A publication*] .... FD
Filosofska Misul [*A publication*] .... FM
Filosofski Problemy Suchasnoho Pryrodoznavstva [*A publication*] .... Filos Probl Suchasnoho Pryrodozn
Filosofskie Nauki [*A publication*] .... Filos Nauki
Filosofskie Problemy Obscestvennogo Soznanija [*A publication*] .... Filos Probl Obsc Soznanija
Filosofskie Voprosy Mediciny i Biologii [*A publication*] .... Filos Vopr Medicin Biol
Filson Club .... FC
Filson Club Historical Quarterly [*A publication*] .... FCHQ
Filson Club, Louisville, KY [*Library symbol*] .... KyLoF
Filson Club Quarterly [*A publication*] .... Filson C Q
Filter .... F
Filter .... FIL
Filter .... FL
Filter .... FLT
Filter .... FLTR
Filter Address Correction .... FAC
Filter-Band Eliminator .... FL-BE
Filter-Band Suppressor Assembly .... FBSA
Filter-Bandpass .... FL-BP
Filter Center .... FC
Filter Center .... FILCEN
Filter Change Kit .... FCK
Filter Gate .... FG
Filter-High Pass .... FL-HP
Filter-Low Pass .... FL-LP
Filter Output .... FO
Filter Paper .... FP
Filter Paper Activity .... FPA
Filter Paper Microscopic [*Test*] [*Medicine*] .... FPM
Filter Response Analysis for Continuously Accelerating Spacecraft [*NASA*] .... FRACAS
Filter Wedge Spectrometer .... FWS
Filter Wheels .... FW
Filterable Agent [*Virology*] .... FA
Filtertek, Inc. [*NASDAQ symbol*] .... FILTZ
Filtra [*Filter*] [*Pharmacy*] .... FILT
Filtration Fraction [*Physiology*] .... FF
Filtration and Separation [*A publication*] .... Filtr Sep
Filtration Society .... FS
Filtration et Techniques Separatives [*A publication*] .... Filtr Tech Separatives
Filtrol Corp. [*Wall Street slang name: "Flit"*] [*NYSE symbol*] [*Delisted*] .... FLT

Fin Creek, AK [*Location identifier*] [*FAA*] ... FNK
Fin Stabilized [*Rocketry*] ... FS
Fin Stabilized Rockets ... FSR
Finagle-Factor ... FF
Final Acceptance, Assembly Tests ... FAT
Final Acceptance Review [*NASA*] ... FAR
Final Address Register [*Data processing*] ... FA
Final Aerospace Trial ... FAT
Final Approach [*Aviation*] ... F
Final Approach [*Aviation*] ... FA
Final Approach [*Aviation*] ... FNA
Final Approach Display ... FAD
Final Approach Equipment [*Aviation*] ... FAE
Final Approach Fix [*Aviation*] ... FAF
Final Approach Path [*Aviation*] ... FAP
Final Approach Plane ... FAP
Final Assembly ... FA
Final Assembly Checkout [*NASA*] ... FACO
Final Assembly and Closeout System Installation ... FA/COSI
Final Assembly Test ... FAT
Final Asset Screen [*DoD*] ... FAS
Final Boiling Point ... FBP
Final Bomb Release Line ... FBRL
Final Braking ... FB
Final CAPE [*Capability and Proficiency Evaluation*] **Review Period** ... FCRP
Final Checkout ... FCO
Final Command and Sequencing [*Viking lander mission*] [*NASA*] ... FC & S
Final Common Pathway [*Neurology*] ... FCP
Final Configuration Review ... FCR
Final Contract Trials [*Navy*] ... FCT
Final Contractor's Trial ... FCTRL
Final Control Elements [*A publication*] ... Final Control Elem
Final Coordination Line [*Military*] ... FCL
Final Coordination Line [*Military*] ... FINALCL
Final Data Report ... FDR
Final Defense Guidance Memorandum [*Navy*] ... FDGM
Final Delivered Article ... FDA
Final Design Approval ... FDA
Final Design Criteria ... FDC
Final Design Review ... FDR
Final Development Test and Evaluation ... FDTE
Final Draft, Presidential Memorandum [*DoD*] ... FDPM
Final Engineering Acceptance Test [*Apollo*] [*NASA*] ... FEAT
Final Engineering Report ... FER
Final Environmental Impact Statement ... FEIS
Final Environmental Statement [*Bureau of Outdoor Recreation*] ... FES
Final Estimation of Data [*Data processing*] ... FED
Final Flight Certification [*Aerospace*] ... FFC
Final Hazards Summary Report [*Nuclear energy*] ... FHSR
Final Initial Operational Capability [*Aerospace*] ... FIOC
Final Issue ... FI
Final Limit, Down ... FLDO
Final Limit, Forward ... FLF
Final Limit, Hoist ... FLH
Final Limit, Lower ... FLL
Final Limit, Reverse ... FLR
Final Limit, Up ... FLU
Final Materials List [*NASA*] ... FML
Final Meteorological Radiation ... FMR
Final Meteorological Radiation Tape ... FMRT
Final Missile Deviation Report [*Aerospace*] ... FMDR
Final Multiple Score ... FMS
Final Operational Capability [*Military*] ... FOC
Final Opinion Inventory [*Psychometrics*] ... FOI
Final Parts List ... FPL
Final Power Amplifier ... FPA
Final Prediction Error [*Statistics*] ... FPE
Final Processing Center ... FPC
Final Procurement Action Approval ... FPAA
Final Program and Budget Guidance ... FPBG
Final Progress Report ... FPR
Final Project Design Description ... FPDD
Final Protective Fire [*Artillery term*] ... FPF
Final Protective Line [*Military*] ... FPL
Final Qualitative and Quantitative Personnel Requirements Information ... FQQPRI
Final Release ... FR
Final Report ... FINREP
Final Report ... FR
Final Safety Analysis Report [*NASA*] ... FSAR
Final Semester Temporary Duty [*Air Force*] ... FSTDY
Final Settlement ... FS
Final Site Acceptance ... FSA
Final Stage Vehicle ... FSV
Final Staging Base ... FSB
Final Statement [*Army*] ... F/S
Final Station [*Data processing*] ... FINST
Final System Release ... FSR
Final System Run ... FSR
Final Systems Check [*NASA*] ... FSC
Final Systems Installation [*NASA*] ... FSI
Final Target ... F
Final Technical Proposal ... FTP
Final Technical Report ... FTR
Final Test, Inc. [*NASDAQ symbol*] ... FNLT
Final Test Rack ... FTR
Final Work Statement ... FWS
Final Year Temporary Duty [*Military*] ... FYTDY
Finalco Group, Inc. [*NASDAQ symbol*] ... FLCO
Finance [*or Financial*] ... F
Finance [*or Financial*] ... FIN
Finance and Accounting ... FA
Finance and Accounting ... F & A
Finance and Accounting Group [*Air Force*] ... FAG
Finance and Accounting Group [*Air Force*] ... FAGp
Finance and Accounting Policy [*Army*] ... FAP
Finance and Accounts Office [*Army*] ... FAAO
Finance and Accounts Office [*or Officer*] [*Army*] ... FAO
Finance and Accounts Office [*or Officer*], **United States Army** ... FAOUSA
Finance Center, United States Army ... FCUSA
Finance Charge ... FC
Finance Committee [*UN Food and Agriculture Organization*] ... FC
Finance and Comptroller Information Systems Command [*Army*] ... FINCISCOM
Finance and Comptroller Information Systems Command, United States Army ... FACISCOM USA
Finance Corps ... FC
Finance Corps Board, United States Army ... FCBUSA
Finance Department ... FD
Finance and Development [*A publication*] ... Finance & Dev
Finance and Development [*A publication*] ... Fin Dev
Finance and Development [*A publication*] ... Fin & Devel
Finance and Development [*A publication*] ... FNDV-A
Finance Disbursing Section [*Army*] ... FDS
Finance Group Office ... FGO
Finance Image Processor [*Data processing*] ... FIP
Finance for Industry [*British*] ... FFI
Finance, Insurance, and Real Estate [*Insurance*] ... FIRE
Finance Officer [*Army*] ... FINO
Finance Officer [*Army*] ... FO
Finance Officer, United States Army ... FOUSA
Finance Replacement Training Center [*World War II*] ... FRTC
Finance School, United States Army ... FSUSA
Finance Service, Army ... FSA
Finance and Supply School [*Coast Guard*] ... FINSUPSCOL
Finance and Trade Review [*A publication*] ... Finance Trade R
Financial ... FINAN
Financial ... FINL
Financial [*Rate*] [*Value of the English pound*] ... FN
Financial Accounting and Control Techniques for Supply [*Army*] ... FACTS
Financial Accounting Data ... FAD
Financial Accounting Foundation ... FAF
Financial Accounting Standard ... FAS
Financial Accounting Standards Board [*Formerly, Accounting Principles Board*] [*American Institute of Certified Public Accountants*] ... FASB
Financial Accounts Receivable ... FAR
Financial Administrative Control ... FAC
Financial Advertising Committee on Ethics ... FACE
Financial Adviser ... FA
Financial Aid Form [*Of College Board*] ... FAF
Financial Aid Planning Service [*College Scholarship Service*] ... FAPS
Financial Analysis Language ... FINAL
Financial Analysis of Management Effectiveness [*Department of Agriculture*] ... FAME
Financial Analysis Program [*IBM Corp.*] ... FAP
Financial Analysts Federation ... FAF
Financial Analysts Journal [*A publication*] ... F Anal Jrl
Financial Analysts Journal [*A publication*] ... Fin Anal J
Financial Analysts Journal [*A publication*] ... Fin Analyst
Financial Analysts Journal [*A publication*] ... Fin Analysts J
Financial Analysts Journal [*A publication*] ... Financ Analysts J
Financial Assistance Program ... FAP
Financial Automation Systems Team for Writing Programs for Standardized Army-Wide Applications ... FAST RIPSAW
Financial Business Package ... FBP
Financial Controller ... FC
Financial Corp. of America [*NYSE symbol*] ... FIN
Financial Corp. of Santa Barbara [*NYSE symbol*] ... FSB
Financial Correlation Table ... FCT
Financial/Cost Management System ... F/CMS
Financial Data Records Folder ... FDRF
Financial and Economic Board ... FEB
Financial Evaluation Program [*IBM Corp.*] ... FEP
Financial Executive [*A publication*] ... Financial E
Financial Executive [*A publication*] ... Fin Exec
Financial Executives Institute ... FEI
Financial Executives Research Foundation ... FERF
Financial Federation, Inc. [*NYSE symbol*] [*Delisted*] ... FFI
Financial Funds Control ... FFC
Financial General Bankshares, Inc. [*American Stock Exchange symbol*] [*Delisted*] ... FGL

Financial General Ledger … FGL
Financial Industries Corp. [*NASDAQ symbol*] … FNIN
Financial Information Control System … FICS
Financial Information Reporting System … FIRST
Financial Information for Resources Management … FIRM
Financial Information Services Agency … FISA
Financial Institution Services [*NASDAQ symbol*] … FISI
Financial Institutions in the Nation's Economy [*Study initiated by House of Representatives*] … FINE
Financial Inter-Relations Ratio … FIR
Financial Inventory Accounting … FIA
Financial Inventory Control … FIC
Financial Inventory Control Report … FICR
Financial Inventory Report … FIR
Financial Inventory Subsidiary … FIS
Financial Mail [*A publication*] … Financ Mail
Financial Management [*A publication*] … Finan Manag
Financial Management … FM
Financial Management Association … FMA
Financial Management Information and Control System [*Navy*] … FMICS
Financial and Management Information System [*Naval Oceanographic Office*] … FAMIS
Financial Management Information System [*Army*] … FIMIS
Financial Management Manual [*NASA*] … FMM
Financial Management Office … FMO
Financial Management Plan … FMP
Financial Management Plan for Emergency Conditions [*Army*] … FMPEC
Financial Management Report … FMR
Financial Management System … FMS
Financial Management Systems [*A publication*] … FMSS
Financial Management Unit [*LIMRA*] … FMU
Financial Managers Society for Savings Institutions … FMS
Financial Marketing Association … FMA
Financial Network Manager … FNM
Financial News Network … FNN
Financial News Network [*NASDAQ symbol*] … FNNI
Financial Operating Plan … FOP
Financial Plan … FP
Financial Planning System [*IBM Corp.*] … FPS
Financial Post [*A publication*] … Fin Post
Financial Post Information Centre [*MacLean-Hunter Ltd.*] [*Information service*] … FPIC
Financial Programs Committee … FPC
Financial Public Relations Association [*Later, BMA*] … FPRA
Financial Relations Society [*Defunct*] … FRS
Financial Research Associates … FRA
Financial Responsibility … F/R
Financial Secretary … FS
Financial Secretary to the War Office [*British*] … FSWO
Financial Security Savings & Loan Association Cl A [*NASDAQ symbol*] … FSSLA
Financial Services Terminals Support [*IBM Corp.*] … FSTS
Financial Statement … F/S
Financial Suspense File [*Army*] … FSF
Financial Times [*A publication*] … Fin Times
Financial Times [*A publication*] … FT
Financial Times, Don Mills, Toronto, ON, Canada [*Library symbol*] … CaOTFT
Financial Times European Energy Report [*A publication*] … Financ Times Europ Energy Rep
Financial Weekly [*A publication*] … FW
Financial Women's Association of New York … FWA
Financial Working Arrangement … FWA
Financial World [*A publication*] … Fin World
Financially Limited Plan … FLIP
Financieel Dagblad [*A publication*] … Financ Dag
Financiera Industrial y Agropecuaria, SA [*Guatemala*] … FIASA
Financiera Nacional de la Vivienda [*El Salvador*] … FNV
Financing Adjustment Factor … FAF
Financing Agriculture [*A publication*] … Fin Agr
Financing Analysis Cost and Testing Service [*LIMRA*] … FACTS
Finanstidende [*A publication*] … Finanstid
Finanz-Archiv [*A publication*] … FA
Finch College, New York, NY [*Library symbol*] … NNFC
Finder … FDR
Finding of No Significant Impact … FNSI
Finding of No Significant Impact [*Office of Surface Mining*] … FONSI
Findings and Determination … F & D
Findlay College, Findlay, OH [*OCLC symbol*] … FIN
Findlay College, Findlay, OH [*Library symbol*] … OFiC
Findlay-Hancock County District Public Library, Findlay, OH [*OCLC symbol*] … FPL
Findlay-Hancock County District Public Library, Findlay, OH [*Library symbol*] … OFi
Findlay, OH [*Location identifier*] [*FAA*] … MAH
Findlay, OH [*Radio station call letters*] … WFIN
Findlay, OH [*Radio station call letters*] … WHMQ
Findlay, OH [*Radio station call letters*] … WLFC
Fine [*Condition*] [*Antiquarian book trade, numismatics, etc.*] … F
Fine [*Quality of the bottom*] [*Nautical charts*] … fne
Fine [*Designation on brandy labels*] … F
Fine [*End*] [*Music*] … F
Fine Alignment … FA
Fine Alignment Complete … FAC
Fine Alignment Equipment … FAE
Fine Alignment Subsystem … FASS
Fine Alignment Unit … FAU
Fine Art Aquisitions [*NASDAQ symbol*] … FAAA
Fine Arts … FA
Fine Arts Foundation … FAF
Fine Arts Gallery of San Diego, San Diego, CA [*Library symbol*] … CSdA
Fine Arts Journal [*A publication*] … Fine Arts J
Fine Arts Philatelists … FAP
Fine Arts Quarterly [*A publication*] … F Arts Q
Fine Attitude Control System [*Aerospace*] … FACS
Fine Bearing Servo … FBS
Fine Business [*i.e., excellent*] [*Amateur radio*] … FB
Fine Champagne … FC
Fine Cognac … FC
Fine Control … FC
Fine Control Damper [*Nuclear energy*] … FCD
Fine [*Condition*] **in Dust Wrapper** [*Antiquarian book trade*] … FDW
Fine Erection … FE
Fine Erection Complete … FEC
Fine Error Sensor … FES
Fine French Furniture … FFF
Fine Grain … FG
Fine Grain Data [*Equipment*] [*RADAR*] … FGD
Fine Hardwoods American Walnut Association [*Formerly, AWMA, FHA*] … FHAWA
Fine Hardwoods Association [*Later, FHAWA*] … FHA
Fine Measurement … FM
Fine Needle Aspiration [*Medicine*] … FNA
Fine-Needle Aspiration Biopsy [*Medicine*] … FNAB
Fine-Needle Cholangiography [*Gastroenterology*] … FNC
Fine Old … FO
Fine Old Blend [*Wines and spirits*] … FOB
Fine Old Extra Special … FOES
Fine Paper … FP
Fine Particulate Organic Matter … FPOM
Fine Point [*A publication*] … Fine Pt
Fine Pointing … FP
Fine Pointing Facility [*NASA*] … FPF
Fine and Specialty Wire Manufacturers Association [*Later, Specialty Wire Association*] … FSWMA
Fine Sun Sensor [*NASA*] … FSS
Fine Sun Sensor/Signal Conditioner [*NASA*] … FSS/S
Fine Track Sensor … FTS
Fineness Ratio … FR
Finest Foods of Virginia [*Brand name*] … FFV
FINFO Flight Inspection Aircraft [*Oklahoma City, OK*] [*FAA designator*] … FLC
Finger … F
Finger … FGR
Finger Breadth [*Medicine*] … FB
Finger Counting [*See also CF*] … FC
Finger Lake Library System, Ithaca, NY [*Library symbol*] … NIFL
Finger Lakes Library System [*Library network*] … FLLS
Finger Lakes Library System, Ithaca, NY [*OCLC symbol*] … VYG
Finger to Nose [*Medicine*] … F-N
Finger Sweat Print [*Psychometrics*] … FSP
Fingermatrix, Inc. [*NASDAQ symbol*] … FINX
Fingerprint Automatic Classification Technique [*Data processing*] … FACT
Fingerprint Reader … FIRE
Finis [*The End*] [*Latin*] … FIN
Finish … F
Finish … FIN
Finish … FNSH
Finish All Over [*Technical drawings*] … FAO
Finish Exercise [*Military*] … FINEX
Finish One Side [*Technical drawings*] … F1S
Finish Specification … FS
Finish Two Sides [*Technical drawings*] … F2S
Finished with Engines … FWE
Finished Goods Control … FGC
Finishing Industries [*A publication*] … Finish Ind
Finishing Industries [*A publication*] … Finshng Ind
Finite Area Solids Technology … FAST
Finite Automation … FA
Finite Automation Language … FAL
Finite Elastic Body … FEB
Finite Element Analysis [*Engineering*] … FEA
Finite Element Analysis Basic Library [*MIT*] … FEABL
Finite Element Data Generation [*Data processing*] … FEDGE
Finite Element Method … FEM
Finite Element Modeling Optimization … FEMO
Finite Element Structures Analysis Program [*Data processing*] … FESAP
Finite Energy Sum Rules [*Physics*] … FESR
Finite Flat Plate … FFP
Finite Fourier Transform … FFT
Finite Impulse Response … FIR
Finite Sampling Time … FST

Finite State Grammar ... FSG
Finite State Language ... FSL
Finkelstein Memorial Library, Spring Valley, NY [*Library symbol*] ... NSv
Finland [*MARC geographic area code*] [*Library of Congress*] ... e-fi---
Finland [*MARC country of publication code*] [*Library of Congress*] ... fi
Finland [*Three-letter standard code*] ... FIN
Finland [*Aircraft nationality and registration mark*] ... OH
Finland [*Two-letter standard code*] ... FI
Finland Geologinen Tutkimuslaitos. Opas [*A publication*] ... Finl Geol Tutkimuslaitos Opas
Finland Vesitutkimuslaitos. Julkaisuja [*A publication*] ... Finl Vesitutkimuslaitos Julk
Finlande Commission Geologique. Bulletin [*A publication*] ... Finlande Comm Geol Bull
Finlandia Foundation ... FF
Finlands Fiskerier [*A publication*] ... Fin Fisk
Finlay Fork [*British Columbia*] [*Seismograph station code, US Geological Survey*] [*Closed*] ... FNC
Finlay Revista Medico-Historica Cubana [*A publication*] ... Finlay Rev Med-Hist Cubana
Finnair [*Finland*] [*ICAO designator*] ... AY
Finnigan Corp. [*NASDAQ symbol*] ... FNNG
Finnisch-Ugrische Forschungen [*A publication*] ... FUF
Finnish [*MARC language code*] [*Library of Congress*] ... fin
Finnish ... FINN
Finnish Air Force ... FinAF
Finnish-American Historical Archives ... FAHA
Finnish American Historical Society of Michigan ... FAHSM
Finnish-American Historical Society of the West ... FAHSW
Finnish American League for Democracy ... FALD
Finnish-American Society [*Later, LFAS*] ... FAS
Finnish Chemical Letters [*A publication*] ... Finn Chem L
Finnish Chemical Letters [*A publication*] ... Finn Chem Lett
Finnish Fisheries Research [*A publication*] ... Finn Fish Res
Finnish Foundation for Alcohol Studies [*A publication*] ... Finn Found Alcohol Stud
Finnish Game Research [*A publication*] ... Finn Game Res
Finnish Journal of Dairy Science [*A publication*] ... Finn J Dairy Sci
Finnish Paper and Timber [*A publication*] ... Finnish Pap Timber
Finnish Paper and Timber [*A publication*] ... Finn Pap Timb
Finnish Plywood Development Association ... FPDA
Finnish Psychiatry [*A publication*] ... Finn Psychiatry
Finnish Radio Industries Association ... FRIA
Finnish Reactor ... FIR
Finnish Trade Review [*A publication*] ... Fin Trade
Finnish War Veterans in America ... FWVA
Finnish Workers' Educational Association [*Defunct*] ... FWEA
Finno-Ugrian [*MARC language code*] [*Library of Congress*] ... fiu
Finnsheep Breeders Association ... FSBA
Finommechanika-Mikrotechnika [*A publication*] ... Finommech-Mikrotech
Finommechanika-Mikrotechnika [*A publication*] ... FNMKA
Finschhafen [*Papua New Guinea*] [*Airport symbol*] ... FIN
Finsen Unit [*for ultraviolet light*] ... Fu
Finsk Tidskrift [*A publication*] ... FiTs
Finsk Tidskrift [*A publication*] ... FT
Finska Kemistsamfundets Meddelanden [*A publication*] ... Fin Kemistsamf Medd
Finska Lakaresallskapets Handlingar [*A publication*] ... Fin Lakaresallsk Handl
Finska Mosskulturforeningens Arsbok [*A publication*] ... Fin Mosskulturforen Arsb
Finskt Museum [*A publication*] ... Finskt Mus
Fir and Hemlock Door Association ... FHDA
FIRA [*Furniture Industry Research Association*] **Bulletin** [*A publication*] ... FIRA Bull Furn Ind Res Ass
FIRA [*Furniture Industry Research Association*] **Technical Report** [*A publication*] ... FIRA Tech Rep Furn Ind Res Ass
FIRA [*Furniture Industry Research Association*] **Transaction** [*A publication*] ... FIRA Trans Furn Ind Res Ass
Firaisan'ny Sendika eran'i Madagaskara [*Confederation of All Unions in Madagascar*] ... FISEMA
Firariana [*Madagascar*] [*Seismograph station code, US Geological Survey*] ... FRR
Fircrest School, Resident Library, Seattle, WA [*Library symbol*] ... WaSF-R
Fircrest School, Staff Library, Seattle, WA [*Library symbol*] ... WaSF
Fire ... F
Fire Alarm Bell ... FABL
Fire Alarm Box ... FABX
Fire Apparatus Manufacturers Association ... FAMA
Fire and Bilge ... F & B
Fire Brigade ... FB
Fire Brigade Hydrant ... FBH
Fire Brigade Union ... FBU
Fire and Casualty Insurance Library Edition ... FACILE
Fire Clay ... FC
Fire Command ... FCMD
Fire Control [*of guns*] ... FC
Fire Control Area [*Army*] ... FCA
Fire Control Check [*Military*] ... FCCK
Fire Control Code ... FCC
Fire Control Computer ... FCC
Fire Control Console ... FCC
Fire Control Control Console ... FCCC
Fire Control Control Subsystem ... FCCSS
Fire Control Data Converter ... FCDC
Fire Control Element ... FCE
Fire Control Equipment ... FCE
Fire Control Group ... FCG
Fire Control, Line-of-Sight ... FC/LOS
Fire Control Notes [*A publication*] ... FCN
Fire Control Operator [*Army*] ... FCO
Fire Control Optical Instrument ... FCOI
Fire Control Panel ... FCP
Fire Control Personnel [*Marine Corps*] ... FCP
Fire Control Platoon [*Army*] ... FCP
Fire Control RADAR ... FCR
Fire Control Reference Frame ... FCRF
Fire Control Sensor Group ... FCSG
Fire Control Simulation ... FICS
Fire Control Simulator ... FCS
Fire Control Simulator Unit ... FCSU
Fire Control and Small Caliber Weapon Systems Laboratory [*Army*] ... FC & SCWSL
Fire Control Switchboard ... FCSB
Fire Control Switchboard ... FCSWBD
Fire Control Switching Unit ... FCSU
Fire Control System ... FCS
Fire Control System Coordinator ... FCSC
Fire Control System Laboratory ... FCSL
Fire Control System Module ... FCSM
Fire Control Technician [*Navy rating*] [*Obsolete*] ... FCT
Fire Control Technician [*Navy rating*] ... FT
Fire Control Technician, Ballistic Missile [*Navy rating*] ... FTB
Fire Control Technician, Ballistic Missile Fire Control, Seaman Apprentice [*Navy rating*] ... FTBSA
Fire Control Technician, Ballistic Missile Fire Control, Seaman [*Navy rating*] ... FTBSN
Fire Control Technician, Chief [*Navy rating*] ... FTC
Fire Control Technician, First Class [*Navy rating*] ... FT1
Fire Control Technician, Gun [*Navy rating*] ... FTG
Fire Control Technician, Master Chief [*Navy rating*] ... FTCM
Fire Control Technician, Second Class [*Navy rating*] ... FT2
Fire Control Technician, Senior Chief [*Navy rating*] ... FTCS
Fire Control Technician, Surface Missile [*Navy rating*] ... FTM
Fire Control Technician, Third Class [*Navy rating*] ... FT3
Fire Control Test Equipment ... FCTE
Fire Control Test Package ... FCTP
Fire Control Test Set ... FCTS
Fire Control Trainer ... FCT
Fire Control Unit ... FCU
Fire Control Workshop ... FCW
Fire Controlman [*Navy rating*] [*Obsolete*] ... FC
Fire Controlman, Range-Finder Operator [*Navy rating*] [*Obsolete*] ... FCR
Fire Controlman, Submarine [*Navy rating*] [*Obsolete*] ... FCS
Fire Coordination Line [*Military*] ... FCL
Fire Department ... FD
Fire-Department Connection [*Technical drawings*] ... FDC
Fire Department Instructors Conference ... FDIC
Fire Detection Center ... FDC
Fire Detection System ... FDS
Fire Detector Control Unit ... FDCU
Fire Direction ... FD
Fire Direction Center [*Military*] ... FDC
Fire Direction Officer [*Army*] ... FDO
Fire Distribution System ... FDS
Fire Door ... FDR
Fire Drop ... FD
Fire Emergency Equipment Dispatch System ... FEEDS
Fire Engineering [*A publication*] ... Fire Eng
Fire Engineers Journal [*A publication*] ... Fire Eng J
Fire Equipment Manufacturers Association ... FEMA
Fire Extinguisher ... FE
Fire Extinguisher ... FEXT
Fire Extinguisher [*or Extinguishing System*] ... FIREX
Fire Fighting ... FF
Fire-Fighting Equipment ... FFE
Fire and Flushing ... F & F
Fire-and-Forget ... F & F
Fire Guardsman [*British*] [*World War II*] ... FG
Fire-in-the-Hole [*Burn*] [*NASA*] ... FITH
Fire Hose ... FH
Fire Hose Cabinet ... FHC
Fire Hose Rack ... FHR
Fire Hydrant ... FH
Fire Hydrant ... FHY
Fire Insurance Research and Actuarial Association [*Later, ISO*] ... FIRAA
Fire Island [*Alaska*] [*Seismograph station code, US Geological Survey*] [*Closed*] ... FIS
Fire Journal [*A publication*] ... Fire J
Fire Journal (Boston) [*A publication*] ... Fire J (Boston)
Fire Location RADAR ... FLORA
Fire Main ... FM

Fire Mark Circle of the Americas ... FMCA
Fire Marshal of Ontario, Toronto, ON, Canada [*Library symbol*] ... CaOTFM
Fire Marshals Association of North America ... FMANA
Fire and Materials [*A publication*] ... Fire Mater
Fire Operational Characteristics Using Simulation [*System for comparing organizations for wildland fire protection services in cost-effective terms*] [*Department of Agriculture, Forest Services*] ... FOCUS
Fire Philatelic Group ... FPG
Fire Plug ... FP
Fire Plug ... FPL
Fire Prevention Officer [*British*] ... FPO
Fire Prevention Science and Technology [*A publication*] ... Fire Prev Sci Technol
Fire Protection Yearbook [*A publication*] ... Fire Prot Yearb
Fire Rescue Air Pack [*NASA*] ... FRAP
Fire Research Abstracts and Reviews [*A publication*] ... Fire Res Abstr & Rev
Fire Research Information Services [*National Bureau of Standards*] ... FRIS
Fire Research (Lausanne) [*A publication*] ... Fire Res (Lausanne)
Fire Research Station ... FRS
Fire Resistant [*or Retardant*] ... FR
Fire Resistant ... FRES
Fire-Resistant Fuels ... FRF
Fire Resistive ... FR
Fire Resistive Protected [*Insurance classification*] ... XP
Fire Resistive Unprotected [*Insurance classification*] ... XU
Fire-Retardant and Smoke-Suppressant [*Chemicals*] ... FRSS
Fire Retardant Chemicals Association ... FRCA
Fire Risk on Freight [*Insurance*] ... FROF
Fire Room ... FRM
Fire Safety Evaluation System [*National Bureau of Standards*] ... FSES
Fire and Safety Test Detachment [*Coast Guard*] ... F & STD
Fire Sensor Control Panel ... FSCP
Fire Service ... FS
Fire Service Instructors ... FSI
Fire Service in Philately [*An association*] ... FSIP
Fire Station [*Maps and charts*] ... FS
Fire Support ... FS
Fire Support Aerial System ... FAS
Fire Support Area [*Military*] ... FSA
Fire Support Base [*Army*] ... FSB
Fire Support Combat Vehicle ... FSCV
Fire Support Coordination Center [*Military*] ... FSCC
Fire Support Coordination Element [*Military*] ... FSCE
Fire Support Coordination Line [*Military*] ... FSCL
Fire Support Coordination Section [*Military*] ... FSCS
Fire Support Coordinator [*Military*] ... FSC
Fire Support Coordinator [*Military*] ... FSCOORD
Fire Support Element [*Military*] ... FSE
Fire Support Officer [*Military*] ... FSO
Fire Support Ship ... FSS
Fire Support Station ... FSS
Fire Support Team ... FIST
Fire Support Team Vehicle [*Army*] ... FISTV
Fire Suppression ... FS
Fire Suppression System ... FSS
Fire Switch ... FS
Fire Team [*Marine Corps*] ... FT
Fire Technology [*A publication*] ... Fire Tech
Fire Technology [*A publication*] ... Fire Technol
Fire Technology Division [*National Bureau of Standards*] ... FTD
Fire and Theft ... F & T
Fire Thermostat ... FT
Fire-Tube [*Scotch-Type*] **Boiler** ... FT
Fire Unit Analyzer [*Military*] ... FUA
Fire Unit Integration Facility [*Military*] ... FUIF
Fire Until Touchdown [*Apollo*] [*NASA*] ... FUT
Fire Up Decoder ... FUD
Fire Wall [*Technical drawings*] ... FW
Fire Warning ... FWRNG
Fire, Water, Weather, Mildew Resistant ... FWWMR
Firearms and Individual Rights [*A California organization*] ... FAIR
Firearms Lobby of America [*Later, CCRKBA*] ... FLA
Firearms Research and Identification Association ... FRIA
Fireball Radius [*Military*] ... FBR
Firebrick ... FBCK
Fired ... FIR
Fired Vessel [*Insurance*] ... FV
Firefighter [*Army*] ... FFGT
Firefighter ... FFTR
Firefighter Breathing System [*NASA*] ... FBS
Firefighting [*Army*] ... FFTG
Fireman [*Navy rating*] ... F
Fireman [*Nonrated enlisted man*] [*Navy*] ... FN
Fireman Apprentice [*Navy rating*] ... FA
Fireman Apprentice, Boilermaker, Striker [*Navy rating*] ... BRFA
Fireman Apprentice, Boilerman, Striker [*Navy rating*] ... BTFA
Fireman Apprentice, Engineman, Striker [*Navy rating*] ... ENFA
Fireman Apprentice, Interior Communications Electrician, Striker [*Navy rating*] ... ICFA
Fireman Apprentice, Machinery Repairman, Striker [*Navy rating*] ... MRFA
Fireman Apprentice, Machinist's Mate, Striker [*Navy rating*] ... MMFA
Fireman Apprentice, Molder, Striker [*Navy rating*] ... MLFA
Fireman Apprentice, Patternmaker, Striker [*Navy rating*] ... PMFA
Fireman Apprentice, Shipfitter [*Navy rating*] ... SFFA
Fireman, Boilermaker, Striker [*Navy rating*] ... BRFN
Fireman, Boilerman, Striker [*Navy rating*] ... BTFN
Fireman, Engineman, Striker [*Navy rating*] ... ENFN
Fireman, Interior Communications Electrician, Striker [*Navy rating*] ... ICFN
Fireman, Machinery Repairman, Striker [*Navy rating*] ... MRFN
Fireman, Machinist's Mate, Striker [*Navy rating*] ... MMFN
Fireman, Molder, Striker [*Navy rating*] ... MLFN
Fireman, Patternmaker, Striker [*Navy rating*] ... PMFN
Fireman Recruit [*Navy rating*] ... FR
Fireman, Shipfitter, Striker [*Navy rating*] ... SFFN
Firenze Ximeniano [*Florence*] [*Italy*] [*Seismograph station code, US Geological Survey*] ... FIR
Fireplace ... FP
Fireplace [*Real estate*] ... FPL
Fireplace Association of America [*Later, WHA*] ... FAA
Firepower and Maneuver [*Army*] ... FIRMA
Firepower Potential ... FPP
Fireproof ... FPRF
Firestone Plastics Company ... FPC
Firestone Polyvinyl Chloride ... FPC
Firestone Tire & Rubber Co. [*NYSE symbol*] ... FIR
Firestone Tire & Rubber Co., Akron, OH [*Library symbol*] ... OAkF
FIREX [*Fire Extinguisher*] **and Launch Coolant Control Unit** [*Aerospace*] ... FLCCU
Firing ... FIRG
Firing ... FRNG
Firing Battery ... FB
Firing Circuit Test Set ... FCTS
Firing Error Indicator ... FEI
Firing Error Trajectory Recorder and Computer ... FIRETRAC
Firing Exercise ... FIREX
Firing in Extension [*Missiles*] ... FIX
Firing/Observation Port ... F/OP
Firing Order ... FO
Firing Out/Consolidate Operability Tests ... FO/COT
Firing Research Investigation, Navy ... FRIN
Firing Room [*NASA*] ... FR
Firing Set ... FS
Firing Set Maintenance Spares ... FSMS
Firing Site Command Post [*Army*] ... FSCP
Firing Station ... FS
Firing Tables [*Military*] ... FT
Firing Unit [*Military*] ... FU
Firing Unit Simulator ... FUS
Firing Unit Test Set ... FUTS
Firing Velocity ... FV
Firkin ... FIR
Firkin of Ale ... AF
Firland Correctional Center, Resident Library, Seattle, WA [*Library symbol*] ... WaSFC-R
Firland Correctional Center, Staff Library, Seattle, WA [*Library symbol*] ... WaSFC
Firm ... F
Firm [*Horse racing*] ... FM
Firm Contract Cost Proposal ... FCCP
Firm Cost Proposal ... FCP
Firm-Fixed Price [*Government contracting*] ... FFP
Firm-Fixed Price Contract ... FFPC
Firm-Fixed Price Letter [*Government contracting*] ... FFPLE
Firm Offer [*Business and trade*] ... FO
Firm Order [*Business and trade*] ... FO
First ... FST
First Advertising Agency Group ... FAAG
First Advertising Agency Network [*Later, First Network of Affiliated Advertising Agencies*] [*Defunct*] ... FAAN
First Aerodynamic Flight ... FAF
First Aid [*Medicine*] ... FA
First-Aid Box ... FAB
First-Aid Instructor [*Red Cross*] ... FAI
First-Aid Instructor Trainer [*Red Cross*] ... FAIT
First-Aid Nursing Yeomanry [*British women's organization formed to do medical transport work for the army; later did general transport work*] ... FANY
First-Aid Post ... FAP
First-Aid, Small Craft, and Water Safety [*Red Cross*] ... FASCWS
First-Aid and Water Safety [*Red Cross*] ... FAWS
First Alabama Bancshares [*NASDAQ symbol*] ... FABC
First Alarm Register ... FAR
First Allied Airborne Army [*World War II*] ... FAAA
First Amarillo Bancorp [*NASDAQ symbol*] ... FAMA
First Amendment Congress ... FAC
First Amendment Lawyers Association ... FALA
First of America Bank Corp. [*NASDAQ symbol*] ... FABK
First American Bank of Palm Beach County Cl A [*NASDAQ symbol*] ... FIAMA
First American Congress of Theater ... FACT
First American Corp. [*NASDAQ symbol*] ... FATN

First American Financial Corp. [*NASDAQ symbol*] ..... FAMR
First Approach and Landing [*Test*] [*NASA*] ..... FAL
First Arkansas Bankstock Corp. [*American Stock Exchange symbol*] ..... FAR
First Article Acceptance Test ..... FAAT
First Article Audit ..... FAA
First Article Capability Assessment Test ..... FACAT
First Article Configuration Inspection [*Gemini*] [*NASA*] ..... FACI
First Article Configuration Review [*Army*] ..... FACR
First Article Demonstration ..... FAD
First Article Factory Tests ..... FAFT
First Article Inspection [*NASA*] ..... FAI
First Article Master Scheduling Committee ..... FAMSCO
First Article Preproduction Sample [*DoD*] ..... FAPPS
First Article Production Inspection ..... FAPI
First Article Test ..... FAT
First Artillery Ammunition Resupply Vehicle [*Army*] ..... FASTV
First Atlanta Corporation [*NYSE symbol*] ..... FAC
First Atomic Power Industry Group [*Japan*] ..... FAPIG
First Atomic Ship Transport, Inc. ..... FAST
First Attack [*Men's lacrosse position*] ..... FA
First Available [*Military*] ..... FIRAV
First Available Air Transportation ..... FAIRTRANS
First Available Government Air Transportation [*Navy*] ..... FAGAIRTRANS
First Available Government Transportation ..... FAGT
First Available Government Transportation ..... FAGTRANS
First Available Transportation ..... FATRANS
First Bancgroup of Alabama [*NASDAQ symbol*] ..... FBGA
First Bancorp of Ohio [*NASDAQ symbol*] ..... FBOH
First Bancshares of Louisiana [*NASDAQ symbol*] ..... FBLA
First Bancshares of Texas [*NASDAQ symbol*] ..... FBTX
First Bank Systems [*NASDAQ symbol*] ..... FBKS
First Bankers Corp. of Florida [*American Stock Exchange symbol*] ..... FBF
First Bankshares Corp. of South Carolina [*NASDAQ symbol*] ..... FBSH
First Base [*or Baseman*] [*Baseball*] 1B
First Boston Corporation [*NYSE symbol*] ..... FBC
[*The*] **First Boston Corp., New York, NY** [*OCLC symbol*] ..... YFB
First Canadian Destroyer Flotilla ..... CANDESFLOT 1
First Capital Corp. [*NASDAQ symbol*] ..... FCAP
First Capital Holdings [*NASDAQ symbol*] ..... FCAH
First Captive Flight [*NASA*] ..... FCF
First Carolina Investors [*NASDAQ symbol*] ..... FCARS
First Catholic Slovak Ladies Association [*Formerly, FCSLU*] ..... FCSLA
First Catholic Slovak Ladies Union [*Later, FCSLA*] ..... FCSLU
First Catholic Slovak Union of the USA ..... FCSU
First Cavalry Division Association ..... FCDA
First Centennial Cl A [*NASDAQ symbol*] ..... FCLCA
First Cervical Vertebra [*Second cervical vertebra is C_2, etc., through C_7*] [*Medicine*] ..... C_1
First Chair of America ..... FCA
First Charter Financial Corp. [*NYSE symbol*] [*Delisted*] ..... FCF
First Chicago Corp. [*NYSE symbol*] ..... FNB
First Chicago Report [*A publication*] ..... First Chi
First Church of Christ, Scientist, Montreal, PQ, Canada [*Library symbol*] ..... CaQMFC
First City Bancorporation of Texas, Inc. [*NYSE symbol*] ..... FBT
First City Financial [*NASDAQ symbol*] ..... FCFN
First City Properties, Inc. [*NYSE symbol*] ..... FCP
First Class [*or First Quality*] A1
First-Class Air Traveler ..... F
First-Class Certificate ..... FCC
First Class Diver Badge [*Military decoration*] ..... FCDivBad
First Class Post Office ..... FCPO
First Class or Saloon Passengers [*Shipping*] [*British*] ..... FST
First Coinvestors [*NASDAQ symbol*] ..... COIN
First Columbia Financial [*NASDAQ symbol*] ..... FCLF
First Come, First Served ..... FCFS
First Commerce Corp. [*NASDAQ symbol*] ..... FCOM
First Commercial Bancorp [*NASDAQ symbol*] ..... FCOB
First Commercial Corp. [*NASDAQ symbol*] ..... FCLR
First Computer Interface Tester ..... FIT
First Connecticut Bancorp Inc. [*NASDAQ symbol*] ..... FCBC
First Connecticut Small Business Investment Co. [*American Stock Exchange symbol*] ..... FCO
First Customer Shipment [*Data processing*] [*IBM Corp.*] ..... FCS
First Czechoslovak Philatelic Club of North America ..... FCPCNA
First Data Management [*NASDAQ symbol*] ..... FDMC
First Data Resources [*NASDAQ symbol*] ..... FDRI
First Day [*Philately*] ..... FD
First-Day Cover [*Philately*] ..... FDC
First Day Cover Collectors Club ..... FDCCC
First Day of Issue [*Philately*] ..... FDI
First Day of Issue [*Philately*] ..... FDOI
First Defense [*Men's lacrosse position*] ..... FD
First Degree Relatives ..... FDR
First Destination Transportation [*Military*] ..... FDT
First Development Decade [*Ten-year plan designed to bring about self-sufficiency in developing countries*] [*United Nations*] DD1
First Division Association [*British*] ..... FDA
First Dorsal Vertebra [*Second dorsal vertebra is D_2, etc.*] [*Medicine*] ..... D_1
First Down [*Football*] ..... FD
First Dynamic Response and Kinematic Experiment in the Drake Passage [*Project of International Southern Ocean Studies*] ..... F-DRAKE
First Eastern Corporation [*NASDAQ symbol*] ..... FEBC
First Empire State Corp. [*NASDAQ symbol*] ..... FEMP
First-Ended First-Out [*Data processing*] ..... FEFO
First Engine to Test ..... FETT
First Executive Corporation [*NASDAQ symbol*] ..... FEXC
First Families [*i.e., the aristocracy*] [*Slang*] ..... FF
First Families [*i.e., the aristocracy*] [*Slang*] ..... FF's
First Families of Virginia [*Supposedly elite society*] [*Slang*] ..... FFV's
First Farwest Corp. [*NASDAQ symbol*] ..... FFWS
First Federal of Michigan [*NASDAQ symbol*] ..... FFOM
First Federal Savings Bank of California [*NASDAQ symbol*] ..... FFSB
First Federal Savings & Loan of Arizona [*NASDAQ symbol*] ..... FFAZ
First Federal Savings & Loan Association of Madison [*NASDAQ symbol*] ..... FFSA
First Federal Savings & Loan Association of Raleigh [*NASDAQ symbol*] ..... FFSR
First Federal Savings & Loan Association of Roanoke [*NASDAQ symbol*] ..... FFSL
First Federal Savings & Loan Association of Winter Haven [*NASDAQ symbol*] ..... FFWH
First Federal Savings & Loan of Austin [*NASDAQ symbol*] ..... FFAT
First Federal Savings & Loan of Charleston [*NASDAQ symbol*] ..... FFCH
First Federal Savings & Loan of Ft. Meyers [*NASDAQ symbol*] ..... FFMY
First Federal Savings & Loan of South Carolina [*NASDAQ symbol*] ..... FTSC
First Fidelity Savings & Loan [*NASDAQ symbol*] ..... APIO
First Financial Bancorp [*NASDAQ symbol*] ..... FFBC
First Financial Language [*Data processing*] ..... FFL
First Financial Management [*NASDAQ symbol*] ..... FFMC
First Financial Savings & Loan [*NASDAQ symbol*] ..... FFIN
First Fix Not Converted ..... FFNC
First Fleet [*Pacific*] [*Navy*] ..... FIRFLT
First Flight Cover [*Philately*] ..... FFC
First Flight Society ..... FFS
First Florida Banks [*NASDAQ symbol*] ..... FFBK
First Folio Edition [*1623*] [*Shakespearean work*] F1
First a Friend, Then a Host [*Safety slogan encouraging partygivers to prevent guests' overindulgence in alcohol*] ..... FAFTAH
First GARP [*Global Atmospheric Research Program*] **Global Experiment** [*National Academy of Sciences*] ..... FGGE
First General Resources [*NASDAQ symbol*] ..... FGNLS
First Grade Screening Test [*To detect learning disabilities*] ..... FGST
First Greatwest Corporation [*NASDAQ symbol*] ..... FGWC
First-Hand Distribution ..... FHD
First Hartford Corporation [*American Stock Exchange symbol*] [*Delisted*] ..... FHC
First Hawaiian, Inc. [*NASDAQ symbol*] ..... FHWN
First-in-the-Hole ..... FITH
First Horizontal Flight [*NASA*] ..... FHF
First Hungarian Literary Society ..... FHLS
First Illinois Corp. [*NASDAQ symbol*] ..... FTIL
First In, First Out [*Accounting*] ..... FIFO
First In, Last Out [*Accounting*] ..... FILO
First-In, Still-Here [*Facetious extension of FIFO definition*] [*Accounting*] ..... FISH
First-In, Still-There [*Facetious extension of FIFO definition*] [*Accounting*] ..... FIST
First Independent Political Success [*Political campaigning*] ..... FIPS
First Indiana Federal Savings [*NASDAQ symbol*] ..... FISB
First Indication of Trouble ..... FIT
First Installed Article, Tests [*NATO*] ..... FIAT
First Intermountain Holding [*NASDAQ symbol*] ..... FIHC
First International Bancshares, Inc. [*NYSE symbol*] [*Delisted*] ..... FIB
First International Conference of Economic History [*A publication*] ..... First Internat Econ Hist
First Interstate Bancorp. [*NYSE symbol*] I
First Interstate Bank of Arkansas [*NASDAQ symbol*] ..... FIBK
First Irish Families ..... FIF
First Jersey National Corporation [*NASDAQ symbol*] ..... FJNC
First Kentucky National Corp. [*NASDAQ symbol*] ..... FKYN
First Ladies' International Racing Team [*Group of women racing at Le Mans, France*] ..... FLIRT
First Level Adaptive Program ..... FLAP
First Lieutenant [*Army*] 1LT
First Lincoln Financial Corporation [*NASDAQ symbol*] ..... FLNC
First Lord of the Admiralty [*British*] ..... FLA
First Lot Procurement Status ..... FLPS
First Lumbar Vertebra [*Second lumbar vertebra is L_2, etc., through L_5*] [*Medicine*] ..... L_1
First Main Watch ..... FMW
First Manned Capture Flight ..... FMCF
First Manned Orbital Flight [*NASA*] ..... FMOF
First Manned Orbital Flight with EVA ..... FMOFEV
First Manned Orbital Flight with Payload ..... FMOFPL
First Marine Aircraft Wing ..... FMAW
First Maryland Bancorp [*NASDAQ symbol*] ..... FMDB
First Matagorda Corp. [*NASDAQ symbol*] ..... FMAT
First Menstrual Period [*Medicine*] ..... FMP
First Michigan Bank Corporation [*NASDAQ symbol*] ..... FMBC

First Midwest Bancorp [*NASDAQ symbol*] ... FMBI
First Midwest Corporation [*NASDAQ symbol*] ... FMWC
First Midwest Financial [*NASDAQ symbol*] ... FMFC
First Mississippi Corp. [*NYSE symbol*] ... FRM
First Mortgage Investors [*NYSE symbol*] [*Delisted*] ... FIM
First Motion ... F/M
First Mutual Savings Association of Florida [*NASDAQ symbol*] ... FMSA
First Name ... FN
First National Bancorp of Allentown [*NASDAQ symbol*] ... FNBA
First National Bancorp of Louisiana [*NASDAQ symbol*] ... FRNB
First National Bank Library, Phoenix, AZ [*Library symbol*] ... AzPhF
First National Boston Corp. [*NYSE symbol*] [*Delisted*] ... FB
First National of Cincinnati [*NASDAQ symbol*] ... FNAC
First National City Bank [*Later, Citibank*] [*New York City*] ... FNCB
First National City Bank [*Later, Citibank*] **of New York. Monthly Economic Letter** [*A publication*] ... First Nat City Bank
First National Corp. of California [*NASDAQ symbol*] ... FNBC
First National Corp. of Louisiana [*NASDAQ symbol*] ... FNCA
First National State Bancorporation [*NYSE symbol*] ... FNS
First National Stores, Inc. ... FINAST
First National Stores, Inc. [*NYSE symbol*] [*Delisted*] ... FST
First National Supermarkets [*NASDAQ symbol*] ... FOOD
First Nationwide Financial [*NASDAQ symbol*] ... FNFC
First New Hampshire Banks [*NASDAQ symbol*] ... FINH
First Northern Savings & Loan [*NASDAQ symbol*] ... FNGB
First of October Group of Anti-Fascist Resistance [*Spain*] ... GRAPO
First Officer [*Women's Royal Naval Service*] [*British*] ... 1/O
First Ohio Bancshares [*NASDAQ symbol*] ... FIRO
First Oklahoma Bancorp [*NASDAQ symbol*] ... FOKL
First Open Water [*Shipping*] ... FOW
First Operational Flight ... FOF
First Orbit Penetration System ... FOPS
First Orbital Flight [*NASA*] ... FOF
First Orbital Vehicle [*NASA*] ... FOV
First Order Gradient Technique ... FOGT
First-Order Polynomial Interpolator ... FOPI
First-Order Polynomial Predictor ... FOPP
First, Outer, Inner, Last [*Mathematical term used in factoring second degree trinomials*] ... FOIL
First Overtone Band ... FOB
First-Pass Radionuclide Angiogram [*Medicine*] ... FPRA
First Pennsylvania Corp. [*NYSE symbol*] ... FPA
First Pennsylvania Mortgage Trust [*NYSE symbol*] [*Delisted*] ... FPM
First Peoples Bank of New Jersey [*NASDAQ symbol*] ... FPNJ
First Periodic Inspection ... FPI
First Phone Corp. [*NASDAQ symbol*] ... FPHO
First Point of Aries [*Navigation*] ... FPA
First Port of Entry ... FPOE
First Printings of American Authors [*A publication*] ... FPAA
First Production Article ... FPA
First Production Unit ... FPU
First Quarter [*Moon phase*] ... FQ
First Railroad & Bank of Georgia [*NASDAQ symbol*] ... FRRG
First Reader ... FR
First Readiness State ... FRS
First Regional Library, Hernando, MS [*Library symbol*] ... MsHe
First Republic of Korea Army ... FROKA
First S & L Shares, Inc. [*American Stock Exchange symbol*] [*Delisted*] ... FSX
First Savings Association of Wisconsin [*NASDAQ symbol*] ... FSAW
First Savings Bank of Florida [*NASDAQ symbol*] ... FSBF
First Sea Level Test [*NASA*] ... FSLT
First Security Corporation [*NASDAQ symbol*] ... FSCO
First Security Corp. of Kentucky [*NASDAQ symbol*] ... FSKY
First Sergeant ... E8
First Sergeant [*Army*] ... 1SG
First Ship Configuration Review [*Navy*] ... FSCR
First Society of Whale Watchers [*Defunct*] ... FSWW
First Soprano, Second Soprano, and Alto [*in all-women choral groups*] ... SSA
First Source Corp. [*NASDAQ symbol*] ... SRCE
First Southern Federal Savings & Loan [*NASDAQ symbol*] ... FSFA
First Soviet Reactor ... FSR
First Special Service Force Association ... FSSFA
First Stage [*Aerospace*] ... FS
First-Stage Conduit [*Aerospace*] ... FSC
First-Stage Conduit Container [*Aerospace*] ... FSCC
First-Stage Engine Cutoff [*Aerospace*] ... FSECO
First-Stage Hydraulics [*Aerospace*] ... FSH
First-Stage Ignition System [*Aerospace*] ... FSIS
First-Stage Motor [*Aerospace*] ... FSM
First-Stage Motor Container [*Aerospace*] ... FSMC
First-Stage Rocket Motor [*Aerospace*] ... FSRM
First-Stage Separation [*Aerospace*] ... FSS
First-Stage Separation Device [*Aerospace*] ... FSSD
First Static Firing ... FSF
First Step ... FS
First Sunday [*An association*] ... FS
First Surface Mirror ... FSM
First Surrey Rifles [*Military unit*] [*British*] ... FSR
First Task Fleet ... FIRSTASKFLT
First Tennessee National Corp. [*NASDAQ symbol*] ... FTEN
First Tenor, Second Tenor, First Bass, and Second Bass [*in all-men choral groups*] ... TTBB
First-Time-Buy ... FTB
First Time Use ... FTU
First Training Unit ... FTU
First Trust Company Uts [*NASDAQ symbol*] ... FTCCU
First Tulsa Bancorp [*NASDAQ symbol*] ... FTBN
First Union Corporation [*NASDAQ symbol*] ... FUNC
First Union Real Estate Equity & Mortgage Investors SBI [*NYSE symbol*] ... FUR
First Unit Loading Cost ... FULC
First United, Incorporated [*NASDAQ symbol*] ... FIUN
First United States Army ... FUSA
First United States Army Group ... FUSAG
First Valley Corporation [*NASDAQ symbol*] ... FIVC
First Vermont Financial [*NASDAQ symbol*] ... FIVT
First Vertical Flight [*NASA*] ... FVF
First Virginia Bankshares Corp. [*NYSE symbol*] ... FVB
First Western Financial [*NASDAQ symbol*] ... FWES
First Wisconsin Corp. [*Formerly, First Wisconsin Bankshares*] [*NYSE symbol*] ... FWB
First Woman on the Supreme Court [*Sandra Day O'Connor*] ... FWOTSC
First Women's Bank [*New York City*] ... FWB
First Word Address ... FWA
First Wyoming Bancorporation [*American Stock Exchange symbol*] ... FWO
First-Year Algebra [*National Science Foundation project*] ... FYA
First York Corp. [*American Stock Exchange symbol*] ... FYK
First Zen Institute of America ... FZIA
Firstar Corp. [*NASDAQ symbol*] ... FSTW
Firstbancorp, Inc. [*NASDAQ symbol*] ... FBAN
Firstmark Corp. [*American Stock Exchange symbol*] [*Delisted*] ... FMK
Firsts and Seconds ... FAS
Firstsouth Federal Savings & Loan [*NASDAQ symbol*] ... FSTH
Fiscal ... FIS
Fiscal ... FISC
Fiscal Director of the Marine Corps ... FDMC
Fiscal Guidance ... FG
Fiscal Guidance Memo [*Navy*] ... FGM
Fiscal Pay Services of Armies [*World War II*] ... FPS
Fiscal Policy Council ... FPC
Fiscal Quarter ... FQ
Fiscal Station Number [*Military*] ... FSN
Fiscal Year ... FY
Fiscal Year Data Summary ... FYDS
Fiscal Year Design Objective ... FYDO
Fiscal Year Development Plan ... FYDP
Fiscal Year Ending ... FYE
Fiscal Year Month ... FYM
Fiscal Year Option ... FYO
Fiscal Year Transition Quarter ... FYTQ
Fiscalite Europeenne [*A publication*] ... Fisc Europ
Fischbach Corp. [*NYSE symbol*] ... FIS
Fischer [*Rat strain*] ... F
Fischer & Porter Co. [*American Stock Exchange symbol*] ... FP
Fischer Taschenbuecher [*A publication*] ... Fischer Taschenb
Fischer-Tropsch Type [*Class of chemical reaction*] ... FTT
Fischerei-Forschung [*A publication*] ... Fisch-Forsch
Fischerei-Geraete-Station ... FGS
Fish Disease Leaflet ... FDL
Fish Farming International [*A publication*] ... Fish Farming Int
Fish Oil Film ... FOF
Fish Protein Concentrate [*For use in antistarvation programs*] ... FPC
Fish Protein Hydrolysate ... FPH
Fish and Wildlife Service [*Department of the Interior*] ... F & WS
Fish and Wildlife Service [*Department of the Interior*] ... FWS
Fish and Wildlife Service/Office of Biological Services [*Department of the Interior*] ... FWS/OBS
Fisher Branch, MB [*Television station call letters*] ... CBWGT
Fisher Foods, Inc. [*NYSE symbol*] ... FHR
Fisher-Hirschfelder-Taylor [*Molecular model*] ... FHT
Fisher-Johns [*Melting point method*] ... FJ
Fisher Junior College [*Massachusetts*] ... FJC
Fisher-Price Toys, East Aurora, NY [*Library symbol*] ... NEAuF
Fisher Scientific Co. [*NYSE symbol*] [*Delisted*] ... FS
Fisher, WV [*Radio station call letters*] ... WELD
Fisheries Advisory Committee of the South Pacific Commission ... FAC/SPC
Fisheries Bulletin. South Africa [*A publication*] ... Fish Bull S Afr
Fisheries Conservation Zone ... FCS
Fisheries Loan Fund [*National Oceanic and Atmospheric Administration*] ... FLF
Fisheries Management [*A publication*] ... Fish Manage
Fisheries Newsletter [*A publication*] ... Fish Newsl
Fisheries Research Board of Canada. Annual Report [*A publication*] ... Fish Res Board Can Annu Rep
Fisheries Research Board of Canada. ARO [*Atlantic Regional Office*] **Circular** [*A publication*] ... Fish Res Board Can ARO Circ
Fisheries Research Board of Canada. Bulletin [*A publication*] ... Fish Res Board Can Bull
Fisheries Research Board of Canada. General Series Circular [*A publication*] ... Fish Res Board Can Gen Ser Circ

Fisheries Research Board of Canada. Miscellaneous Special Publication [*A publication*] ... Fish Res Board Can Misc Spec Publ
Fisheries Research Board of Canada. Review [*A publication*] ... Fish Res Board Can Rev
Fisheries Research Board of Canada. Technical Paper [*A publication*] ... Fish Res Board Can Tech Pap
Fisheries Research Division. Occasional Publication (New Zealand) [*A publication*] ... Fish Res Div Occas Publ (NZ)
Fisheries Research Institute ... FRI
Fisherman's Information Bureau ... FIB
Fishermen's Compensation Fund [*National Oceanic and Atmospheric Administration*] ... FCF
Fishermen's Guarantee Fund [*National Oceanic and Atmospheric Administration*] ... FGF
Fishers Island Library Association, Fishers Island, NY [*Library symbol*] ... NFisi
Fishers of Men ... FOM
Fishery Board ... FB
Fishery Board of Sweden. Institute of Marine Research. Report [*A publication*] ... Fish Board Swed Inst Mar Res Rep
Fishery Bulletin [*A publication*] ... Fish B
Fishery Bulletin [*A publication*] ... Fish Bull
Fishery Committee for the Eastern Central Atlantic ... FCECA
Fishery Conservation and Management Act [*1976*] [*Also, MFCMA*] ... FCMA
Fishery Conservation Zone ... FCZ
Fishery Council ... FC
Fishery Data Center [*FAO*] ... FDC
Fishery Flag [*Navy*] [*British*] ... FY
Fishery Industrial Research [*A publication*] ... Fishery Ind Res
Fishery Industrial Research [*A publication*] ... Fish Ind Res
Fishery Investigations. Ministry of Agriculture, Fisheries, and Food. (Great Britain) Series IV [*A publication*] ... Fish Invest Minist Agric Fish Food (GB) Ser IV
Fishery Management Plan ... FMP
Fishery Officer [*Ministry of Agriculture, Fisheries, and Food*] [*British*] ... FO
Fishery Protection Vessel ... FPV
Fishery Research Craft ... FRC
Fishery Technology [*A publication*] ... Fish Technol
Fishguard [*Goodwick*] [*British depot code*] ... FGD
Fishing News International [*A publication*] ... Fishg News Int
Fishing News International [*A publication*] ... Fish News Int
Fishing Research Vessel ... FRV
Fishing Stakes [*Nautical charts*] ... Fsh stks
Fishing Vessel and Gear Damage Compensation Fund [*National Oceanic and Atmospheric Administration*] ... FVGDCF
Fishman [*M. H.*] **Co., Inc.** [*American Stock Exchange symbol*] [*Delisted*] ... FSH
Fishpaper [*Insulation*] ... FPPR
Fisiologia e Medicina (Rome) [*A publication*] ... Fisiol Med (Rome)
Fisk University, Nashville, TN [*OCLC symbol*] ... FSK
Fisk University, Nashville, TN [*Library symbol*] ... TNF
Fiske Free Library, Claremont, NH [*Library symbol*] ... NhCla
Fiskeridirektoratet [*Directorate of Fisheries*], **Bergen-Nordens, Norway** [*Library symbol*] ... NoBeFi
Fiskeridirektoratets Skrifter. Serie Fiskeri [*A publication*] ... Fiskeridir Skr Ser Fisk
Fiskeridirektoratets Skrifter. Serie Havundersokelser [*A publication*] ... Fiskeridir Skr Ser Havunders
Fiskeridirektoratets Skrifter. Serie Teknologiske Undersokelser [*A publication*] ... Fiskeridir Skr Ser Teknol Unders
Fisons Pharmaceuticals Limited ... FPL
Fisons Pharmaceuticals plc Ltd. ADR [*NASDAQ symbol*] ... FISNY
Fissile Material ... FM
Fission ... FSSN
Fission-Fusion-Fission [*Bomb*] ... FFF
Fission-Fusion Ratio ... FFR
Fission Gas ... FG
Fission Gas Monitor ... FGM
Fission Product ... FP
Fission Product Control Screening Test Loop [*Nuclear energy*] ... FPCSTL
Fission Product Screening Loop [*Nuclear energy*] ... FPSL
Fission Products Conversion and Encapsulation [*Plant*] [*Nuclear energy*] ... FPCE
Fission Products Development Laboratory [*ORNL*] ... FPDL
Fission Yield Curve ... FYC
Fistula ... FIST
Fit to Be Detained [*Medicine*] ... FTBD
Fit Check [*NASA*] ... FC
Fit for Issue [*Navy*] ... FFI
Fitchburg Gas & Electric Light Co. [*American Stock Exchange symbol*] ... FGE
Fitchburg, MA [*Radio station call letters*] ... WEIM
Fitchburg, MA [*Radio station call letters*] ... WFGL
Fitchburg, MA [*Radio station call letters*] ... WFMP
Fitchburg Public Library and Regional Center for Central Massachusetts, Regional Library System, Fitchburg, MA [*Library symbol*] ... MFi
Fitchburg State College, Fitchburg, MA [*OCLC symbol*] ... FTB
Fitchburg State College, Fitchburg, MA [*Library symbol*] ... MFiT
Fitness for the Future [*Nursing Services Course*] [*Red Cross*] ... FFF
Fitness Motivation Institute of America Association ... FMIAA
Fitness Reports Branch [*BUPERS*] ... FRB
Fitopatologia [*A publication*] ... Fitopatol
Fitopatologia Brasileria [*A publication*] ... Fitopatol Bras
Fitopatologia Mexicana [*A publication*] ... Fitopatol Mex
Fitotecnia Latinoamericana [*A publication*] ... Fitotec Latinoam
Fitted ... FTD
Fitted as Flagship [*Suffix to plane designation*] ... F
Fitted for Oil Fuel [*Ships*] ... OF
Fitting ... FTG
Fitting Out [*Navy*] ... FO
Fitting Out Availability [*Navy*] ... FOA
Fitting Out Supply Assistance Team [*Navy*] ... FOSAT
Fitting Out Supply Assistance Team, Atlantic [*Navy*] ... FOSATLANT
Fitting Out Supply Assistance Team, Pacific [*Navy*] ... FOSATPAC
Fitzgerald, GA [*Radio station call letters*] ... WBHB
Fitzgerald-Hemingway Annual [*A publication*] ... FHA
Fitzgerald Newsletter [*A publication*] ... FitzN
Fitzgerald Newsletter [*A publication*] ... FNL
Fitzsimons Army Medical Center ... FAMC
Fitzsimons General Hospital, Medical Technical Library, Denver, CO [*Library symbol*] ... CoDFG-M
Fiume Study Group [*Philately*] ... FSG
Five [*Roman numeral*] ... V
Five Associated University Libraries [*State University of New York at Buffalo and Binghamton, Cornell University, Syracuse University, University of Rochester*] ... FAUL
Five Associated University Libraries, Rochester, NY [*OCLC symbol*] ... TPD
Five Associated University Libraries, Rochester, NY [*OCLC symbol*] ... TPE
Five Civilized Tribes Foundation ... FCTF
Five Dollars [*Slang*] ... V
Five Hundred [*Roman numeral*] ... D
Five International Associations Coordinating Committee ... FIACC
Five-Mile Camp, AK [*Location identifier*] [*FAA*] ... FVM
Five Task Test [*Psychology*] ... FTT
Five Towns College, Merrick, NY [*Library symbol*] ... NMerkF
Five-Year Defense Plan [*or Program*] [*Military*] ... FYDP
Five-Year Design Objectives ... FYDO
Five-Year Force Structure and Financial Program [*Military*] ... FYFS & FP
Five-Year Force Structure and Financial Program [*Military*] ... FYFSFP
Five-Year Materiel Program [*Military*] ... FYMP
Five-Year Plan [*Military*] ... FYP
Five-Year Planning Base [*Military*] ... FYPB
Five-Year Procurement Program [*Military*] ... FYPP
Five-Year Sentence [*Criminal slang*] ... V
Five-Year Test Program [*Military*] ... FYTP
Five-Year Training Development Plan [*Army*] ... FYTDP
Fivondronamben'ny Mpiasa Malagasy [*Confederation of Malagasy Workers*] ... FMM
Fix [*Navigation*] ... FX
Fix It Again Tony [*Reference to the alleged defects of Fiat automobiles*] ... FIAT
Fix-Radial-Distance ... FRD
Fix or Repair Daily [*Reference to the alleged defects of Ford automobiles*] ... FORD
Fix Up on Printer [*Have technician add or change an effect by means of optical printing*] [*Motion-picture production*] ... FUOP
Fixation Optokinetic Nystagmus [*Eye movement*] ... FOKN
Fixed ... FXD
Fixed Abrasive Slicing [*Semiconductor technology*] ... FAST
Fixed Acoustic Range ... FAR
Fixed Action Button ... FAB
Fixed Action Pattern ... FAP
Fixed Air Capacitor ... FAC
Fixed Airlock Shroud [*NASA*] ... FAS
Fixed Amount Reimbursement [*Agency for International Development*] ... FAR
Fixed-Angle Variable ... FAV
Fixed Area Scanning Alarm ... FASA
Fixed Array RADAR ... FAR
Fixed Asset Accounting Package [*Data processing*] ... FAAP
Fixed Asset Transfer ... FAT
Fixed Auto Transfer ... FATR
Fixed Autotransformer ... FATR
Fixed Base Aft Station ... FBAS
Fixed-Base Crew Station [*NASA*] ... FBCS
Fixed-Base Operator [*Provider of nonairline aviation services to users of airports*] ... FBO
Fixed Bathtub Capacitor ... FBC
Fixed Binary ... FXBIN
Fixed Camera ... FC
Fixed Center Drive ... FCD
Fixed Ceramic Capacitor ... FCC
Fixed Ceramic Disc Capacitor ... FCDC
Fixed Change Rate ... FCR
Fixed Coaxial Attenuator ... FCA
Fixed Code Processor ... FCP
Fixed Cost, Fixed Time ... FCFT
Fixed Cycle Operation ... FCO
Fixed Decade Capacitor ... FDC
Fixed Delay Line ... FDL
Fixed Distributed Subsystem [*Antisubmarine warfare*] ... FDS

Fixed Electrolytic Capacitor ... FEC
Fixed Federal Monitoring Network [*Aviation*] ... FFMN
Fixed Fee [*Business and trade*] ... FF
Fixed-Fee-Plus-Incentive [*Business and trade*] ... FFPI
Fixed Feed Through Capacitor ... FFTC
Fixed-Field Alternating Gradient [*Accelerator*] [*Nuclear energy*] ... FFAG
Fixed Film Capacitor ... FFC
Fixed and Flashing Light [*Navigation signal*] ... FFL
Fixed Flexion Deformity of the Knee [*Orthopedics*] ... FFDK
Fixed Focus [*Photography*] ... FF
Fixed Format Display ... FFD
Fixed Frequency Receiver ... FFR
Fixed Gain Control ... FGC
Fixed Gas-Filled Capacitor ... FGFC
Fixed Glass Capacitor ... FGC
Fixed Ground Radio Installations ... FGRI
Fixed and Group Flashing Light [*Navigation signal*] ... FGPFL
Fixed-Head Disk [*Data processing*] ... FHD
Fixed High-Temperature Capacitor ... FHTC
Fixed High-Volt Capacitor ... FHVC
Fixed Hub [*Rotary piston meter*] ... FH
Fixed Income Account ... FIA
Fixed Income Consumer Counseling [*ACTION*] ... FICC
Fixed Interim Baseline ... FIB
Fixed Interval ... FI
Fixed Interval Timer ... FIT
Fixed Laboratory Standard Capacitor ... FLSC
Fixed Length Cavity Resonance ... FLCR
Fixed-Length Field [*Data processing*] ... FLF
Fixed Light [*Navigation signal*] ... F
Fixed Line of Sight ... FLOS
Fixed Mica Capacitor ... FMC
Fixed Motor Run Capacitor ... FMRC
Fixed Motor Starting Capacitor ... FMSC
Fixed Mylar Capacitor ... FMC
Fixed Mylar Metallized Capacitor ... FMMC
Fixed Niobium Capacitor ... FNC
Fixed Nozzle Slow [*or Short*] **Landing** ... FNSL
Fixed Oil ... FO
Fixed Oil Capacitor ... FOC
Fixed Paper Capacitor ... FPC
Fixed Paper Metallized Capacitor ... FPMC
Fixed Path of Operation ... FPO
Fixed Photoflash Capacitor ... FPC
Fixed Photoflash Capacitor ... FPFC
Fixed Plasma Sheath ... FPS
Fixed Point ... FP
Fixed Point ... FXP
Fixed Point Calculation ... FPC
Fixed Point Operation ... FPO
Fixed Point Representation ... FPR
Fixed Point Station [*RADAR*] ... FPS
Fixed Point System ... FPS
Fixed Polycarbonate Capacitor ... FPC
Fixed Polycarbonate Capacitor ... FPCC
Fixed Porcelain Enamel Capacitor ... FPEC
Fixed Position Keyboard ... FPK
Fixed Precision Capacitor ... FPC
Fixed Price ... FP
Fixed Price Award Fee [*Contract*] ... FPAF
Fixed Price Basis ... FPB
Fixed Price Call ... FPC
Fixed Price Contracts ... FPC
Fixed Price with Escalation ... FPE
Fixed Price Firm ... FPF
Fixed Price Incentive ... FPI
Fixed Price Incentive Contract ... FPIC
Fixed Price Incentive Fee ... FPIF
Fixed Price Incentive Firm [*Award*] [*Government contracting*] ... FPIF
Fixed Price Incentive Force ... FPIF
Fixed Price Incentive Successive ... FPIS
Fixed Price Open ... FPO
Fixed Price with Price Revision ... FPPR
Fixed Price Redeterminable ... FPR
Fixed Price Redeterminable Article ... FPRA
Fixed-Price-Redeterminable-Prospective ... FPRP
Fixed-Price-Redeterminable-Retroactive ... FPRR
Fixed Price Redetermination Contract ... FPRC
Fixed Price Supply ... FPS
Fixed Printed Circuit Capacitor ... FPCC
Fixed Problem Report ... FPR
Fixed Program Computer ... FPC
Fixed Pulse RADAR Navigation Aid ... FPN
Fixed Pulse RADAR Search Equipment ... FPS
Fixed Radio Communication ... FRC
Fixed Radio Transmission Facility ... FRTF
Fixed Ratio ... FR
Fixed Safety Level ... FSL
Fixed Sample Rate ... FSR
Fixed Sample-Size Procedure ... FSP
Fixed Sequence Format ... FSF
Fixed Service Structure ... FSS
Fixed Service Tower ... FST
Fixed Silicon Capacitor ... FSC
Fixed Silver Mica Capacitor ... FSMC
Fixed Stand-Off Capacitor ... FSOC
Fixed Station [*ITU designation*] ... FX
Fixed Tantalum Capacitor ... FTC
Fixed Target Information [*Army*] ... FTI
Fixed Temperature Compensating Capacitor ... FTCC
Fixed Term Plan ... FTP
Fixed Throttle Point [*NASA*] ... FTP
Fixed Time of Arrival [*Aviation*] ... FTA
Fixed Tone ... FT
Fixed Transom ... FTR
Fixed Vacuum Capacitor ... FVC
Fixed Wavelength [*Electronics*] ... FW
Fixed Wing [*Aircraft*] ... FW
Fixed-Wing Aircraft [*Navy symbol*] ... V
Fixed-Wing Evaluation Exercise [*Aviation*] ... FIXWEX
Fixed-Wing Multiengine Qualification Course [*Aviation*] ... FWMQC
Fixed-Wing Special Instrument Flight Rules [*Aviation*] ... FW/SIFR
Fixed-Wing Special Visual Flight Rules [*Aviation*] ... FW/SVFR
Fixed-Wing Tactical Transport [*Aviation*] ... FWIT
Fixed Wing Tactical Transport ... FWTT
Fixed Word Length ... FWL
Fixing Fluid [*Histology*] ... FF
Fixity of Tenure, Fair Rents, and Free Sale [*Phrase used in Parliamentary discussions of Irish affairs, 1880-1882; opposition translated the initials as Fraud, Force, and Folly*] ... 3F's
Fixture ... FIX
Fixture ... FIXT
Fixture ... FXTR
Fixtures Manufacturers and Dealers ... FMD
Fizean Toothed Wheel ... FTW
Fizicheskaya Ehlektronika (Moskva) [*A publication*] ... Fiz Ehlektron (Moskva)
Fizichna Ehlektronika (L'vov) [*A publication*] ... Fiz Ehlektron (L'vov)
Fizika Aehrodispersnykh Sistem [*A publication*] ... Fiz Aehrodispers Sist
Fizika Ehlementarnykh Chastits i Atomnogo Yadra [*A publication*] ... Fiz Ehlem Chastits At Yad
Fizika i Fiziko-Khimiya Zhidkostei [*A publication*] ... Fiz Fiz-Khim Zhidk
Fizika Goreniya i Vzryva [*A publication*] ... Fiz Goreniya & Vzryva
Fizika i Khimiya Obrabotki Materialov [*A publication*] ... Fiz Khim Obrab Mater
Fizika i Khimiya Stekla [*A publication*] ... Fiz Khim Stekla
Fizika Kondensirovannogo Sostoyaniya [*A publication*] ... Fiz Kondens Sostoyaniya
Fizika Magnitnykh Plenok [*A publication*] ... Fiz Magn Plenok
Fizika Metallov i Metallovedenie [*A publication*] ... Fiz Metallov Metalloved
Fizika Metallov i Metallovedenie [*A publication*] ... Fiz Metal M
Fizika Metallov i Metallovedenie [*A publication*] ... Fiz Met & Metalloved
Fizika Molekul [*A publication*] ... Fiz Mol
Fizika Nizkikh Temperatur [*A publication*] ... Fiz Nizk Temp
Fizika Plazmy (Moskva) [*A publication*] ... Fiz Plazmy (Moskva)
Fizika Plazmy (Tbilisi) [*A publication*] ... Fiz Plazmy (Tbilisi)
Fizika i Tekhnika Poluprovodnikov [*A publication*] ... Fiz Tekh Poluprovo
Fizika Tverdogo Tela [*A publication*] ... Fiz Tverd T
Fizika (Zagreb) Supplement (Yugoslavia) [*A publication*] ... Fizika (Zagreb) Suppl
Fizika Zemli [*A publication*] ... Fiz Zemli
Fizika Zhidkogo Sostoyaniya [*A publication*] ... Fiz Zhidk Sostoyaniya
Fizikai Szemle [*A publication*] ... Fiz Sz
Fiziko-Khimicheskaya Mekhanika i Liofil'nost Dispersnykh Sistem [*A publication*] ... Fiz-Khim Mekh Liofil' Dispers Sist
Fiziko-Matematichesko Spisanie [*A publication*] ... Fiz-Mat Spis
Fiziko-Tekhnicheskie Problemy Razrabotki Polezynkh Iskopaemykh [*A publication*] ... Fiz-Tekh Probl Razrab Polez Iskop
Fiziologia Normala si Patologica [*A publication*] ... FZNPA
Fiziologicheskii Zhurnal SSSR Imeni I. M. Sechenova [*A publication*] ... Fiziol Zh SSSR
Fiziologicheskii Zhurnal SSSR Imeni I. M. Sechenova [*A publication*] ... Fiziol Zh SSSR Im I M Sechenova
Fiziologicheskii Zhurnal SSSR Imeni I. M. Sechenova [*A publication*] ... FZLZA
Fiziologichnij Zhurnal. Akademiya Nauk Ukrainskoj RSR [*A publication*] ... Fiziol Zh Akad Nauk Ukr RSR
Fiziologichnyi Zhurnal [*A publication*] ... Fiziol Zh
Fiziologija Rastenij [*A publication*] ... Fiziol Rast
Fiziologiya i Biokhimiya Kul'turnykh Rastenii [*A publication*] ... Fiziol Biokhim Kul't Rast
Fiziologiya Cheloveka [*A publication*] ... Fiziol Chel
Fiziologiya Normala si Patologica [*A publication*] ... Fiziol Norm Patol
Fiziologiya Rastenii (English Translation Plant Physiology) (Moscow) [*A publication*] ... Fiziol Rast (Engl Transl Plant Physiol)
Fiziologiya Rastenii (Moscow) [*A publication*] ... Fiziol Rast (Mosc)
Fiziologiya na Rasteniyata (Sofia) [*A publication*] ... Fiziol Rast (Sofia)
Fiziolohichnyi Zhurnal (Kiev) [*A publication*] ... Fiziol Zh (Kiev)
Fizyka Dielektrykow i Radiospektroskopia [*A publication*] ... Fiz Dielektr Radiospektrosk
Fjord [*Maps and charts*] ... Fd
Flaccid ... FLAC

Flag [*British naval signaling*] ... FL
Flag [*Data processing*] ... FLG
Flag Administrative Unit ... FAU
Flag Allowance ... FA
Flag Cancel Society ... FCS
Flag Communications Officer [*Navy*] ... FCO
Flag Engineering Officer [*British*] ... FEO
Flag Flange ... FLG
Flag Gunnery Officer ... FGO
Flag Hoist ... FH
Flag Lieutenant [*Navy*] ... FL
Flag-Lieutenant-Commander [*Navy*] [*British*] ... FLC
Flag Officer [*Navy*] ... FO
Flag Officer, Aircraft Carriers ... FOAC
Flag Officer, Atlantic Coast [*Canada*] ... CANFLAGLANT
Flag Officer, Atlantic Coast [*Canada*] ... FOAC
Flag Officer, British Assault Area ... FOBAA
Flag Officer, Central Europe ... FLAGCENT
Flag Officer-in-Charge [*British-controlled port*] ... FOIC
Flag Officer, Commander, Her Majesty's Australian Fleet ... FOCAF
Flag Officer Commanding West Africa [*British*] ... FOCWA
Flag Officer, Denmark ... FOD
Flag Officer, Germany ... FOG
Flag Officer, Gibraltar Mediterranean Area [*British*] ... FOGMA
Flag Officer, Naval Air Command [*British*] ... FONAC
Flag Officer, Naval Air, Pacific [*British*] ... FONAP
Flag Officer, Newfoundland [*British*] ... FONF
Flag Officer, Pacific Coast [*Canada*] ... CANFLAGPAC
Flag Officer, Pacific Coast [*Canada*] ... FOPC
Flag Officer, Soviet Middle East Forces ... FOSMEF
Flag Officer, Taranto and Adriatic and for Liaison ... FOTALI
Flag Officer, Western Area, British Pacific Fleet ... FOWABPF
Flag Plot ... FP
Flag Register Processing ... FRP
Flag Research Center ... FRC
Flag Tactical Data System ... FTDS
Flag Tower [*Maps and charts*] ... FTR
Flag Word ... FW
Flagg Industries, Inc. [*American Stock Exchange symbol*] [*Delisted*] ... FGG
Flagler College, St. Augustine, FL [*OCLC symbol*] ... FFC
Flagler Community Library, Flagler, CO [*Library symbol*] ... CoFla
Flagler Memorial Library, Miami, FL [*Library symbol*] ... FMF
Flagon and Trencher [*An association*] ... FT
Flagpole ... FP
Flagship [*Navy*] ... FLG
Flagstaff [*Arizona*] [*Airport symbol*] ... FLG
Flagstaff ... FLGSTF
Flagstaff ... FS
Flagstaff [*Arizona*] [*Seismograph station code, US Geological Survey*] [*Closed*] ... FLG
Flagstaff, AZ [*Radio station call letters*] ... KAFF
Flagstaff, AZ [*Radio station call letters*] ... KAXR
Flagstaff, AZ [*Radio station call letters*] ... KCLS
Flagstaff, AZ [*Radio station call letters*] ... KFLG
Flagstaff, AZ [*Radio station call letters*] ... KNAU
Flagstaff, AZ [*Television station call letters*] ... KNAZ-TV
Flagstaff, AZ [*Radio station call letters*] ... KSOJ
Flagstaff, AZ [*Radio station call letters*] ... KZKZ
Flagstaff City-Coconino County Public Library, Flagstaff, AZ [*Library symbol*] ... AzF
Flagstaff Corp. [*American Stock Exchange symbol*] [*Delisted*] ... FSF
Flagstaff National Park Service Group ... FLAG
Flagstone ... FLGSTN
Flah's Inc. [*NASDAQ symbol*] ... FLAH
Flair Resources Ltd. [*NASDAQ symbol*] ... RIALF
Flak RADAR Automatic Kanon ... FRAK
Flakey Jake's, Inc. [*NASDAQ symbol*] ... FJAK
Flakmessgerat [*Antiaircraft, gun-laying RADAR*] [*German*] ... FMG
Flame ... FL
Flame ... FLM
Flame Control System ... FCS
Flame Deflector ... FD
Flame Deflector Firex ... FDF
Flame Emission ... FE
Flame Emission Spectrometry ... FES
Flame/Furnace Autosampling Technique with Automatic Calibration [*Spectroscopy*] ... FASTAC
Flame Hardness Standard ... FHS
Flame Industries, Inc. [*NASDAQ symbol*] ... FLAMQ
Flame Ionization Analyzer and Detector ... FIAD
Flame Ionization Detector ... FID
Flame Launched Assault Shoulder or Hip-Fired Weapon [*Army*] ... FLASH
Flame Leak Proof ... FLP
Flame Photometric Detector ... FPD
Flame Retardancy of Polymeric Materials [*A publication*] ... Flame Retardancy Polym Mater
Flame Retardant ... FR
Flame Retardant Phosphonitratic Polymer ... FRPP
Flame Shielding ... FS
Flame Tight ... FLMTT
Flame Tight ... FT
Flame Tight ... MT
Flameless Alkali Sensitized Detector [*Instrumentation*] ... FASD
Flameless Atomic Absorption ... FAA
Flameless Gas Heater ... FGH
Flameless, Smokeless [*Gunpowder*] ... FS
Flameproof ... FLMPRF
Flameproof ... FP
Flamethrower ... FLMTHR
Flaming Gorge [*Utah*] [*Seismograph station code, US Geological Survey*] [*Closed*] ... FGU
Flamingo Airways Ltd. [*ICAO designator*] ... FE
Flammability Fabrics Act ... FFA
Flammable ... FL
Flammable ... FLMB
Flammable Fabric Accident Case and Testing System [*National Bureau of Standards*] ... FFACTS
Flammable Liquids [*Fire classification*] ... B
Flanagan Aptitude Classification Test [*Psychology*] ... FACT
Flange ... FLG
Flange Focal Distance ... FD
Flange Focal Distance ... FFD
Flanged Tongue Terminal ... FTT
Flanging Tube ... FT
Flanigan's Enterprises, Inc. [*Formerly, Big Daddy's Lounges, Inc.*] [*American Stock Exchange symbol*] ... BDL
Flanker [*Football*] ... FL
Flannery O'Connor Bulletin [*A publication*] ... FOB
Flapper ... FLPR
Flaps-Down Speed [*Aviation*] ... VF
Flare-Activated Radiobiological Observatory ... FARO
Flare Detection System ... FDS
Flare Die ... FLDI
Flare Dispenser Pod ... FDP
Flare Exercises [*Navy*] ... FLAREX
Flare, Inc. [*NASDAQ symbol*] ... FLAR
Flare/Shallow Glide Slope ... FSGS
Flared ... FLRD
Flared Slot Antenna ... FSA
Flared Tube Fitting ... FTF
Flared Tube Fitting Gasket Seal ... FTFGS
Flareout and Terminal Glide Beam Guidance [*Aerospace*] ... FTGBG
Flares ... FLR
Flarescan Instrument Landing System ... FILS
Flaring ... FLRG
Flash ... FLH
Flash Evaporator Plant ... FEP
Flash Evaporator System ... FES
Flash Financial Report [*for prospective overruns*] [*Navy*] ... FLASH FIRE
Flash Lights and Send Help [*Florida highway driving aid*] ... FLASH
Flash Mass Thermal Analysis ... FMTA
Flash-Nitrogen Supply ... FNS
Flash Photolysis System ... FPS
Flash Point ... FP
Flash Ranging ... FLRNG
Flash Ranging ... FR
Flash Ranging System ... FRS
Flash Triangulation Reduction ... FTR
Flash Vacuum Pyrolysis ... FVP
Flash-Vacuum Thermolysis ... FVT
Flash Welding [*Metallurgy*] ... FL/W
Flash X-Ray Device ... FXD
Flash X-Ray Facility ... FXF
Flashblindness Orientation Device ... FOD
Flashbulb [*Photography*] ... FB
Flashgun [*Photography*] ... FG
Flashing ... FLG
Flashing Light [*Navigation signal*] ... FL
Flashing Light System ... FLS
Flashless [*NASA*] ... FLHLS
Flashless ... FLHS
Flashless ... FLS
Flashless Nonhygroscopic [*Gunpowder*] ... FNH
Flashlight ... FLT
Flat ... F
Flat ... FL
Flat [*Alaska*] [*Airport symbol*] ... FLT
Flat [*Paper*] ... FT
Flat, AK [*Location identifier*] [*FAA*] ... FLT
Flat Back ... FBK
Flat Band Metallic Armor ... F
Flat Bar [*Technical drawings*] ... FB
Flat Cable Stripping Tool ... FCST
Flat Cars [*Freight*] ... FL CRS
Flat-Coated Retriever Society of America ... FCRSA
Flat Conductor Cable ... FCC
Flat Data Wing ... FDW
Flat Face [*Diamonds*] ... FF
Flat Fillister Head [*Screws*] ... FFILH
Flat or Folded Flat [*Freight*] ... FFF
Flat Glass Jobbers Association [*Later, FGMA*] ... FGJA
Flat Glass Marketing Association ... FGMA

Flat Grain [Lumber] ......FG
Flat Head [Screw] ......FH
Flat Head ......FLH
Flat Keel [Shipbuilding] ......FK
Flat Load Cell ......FLC
Flat Moving Target Screen [Weaponry] ......FMTS
Flat or Nested [Freight] ......FN
Flat Nose [Projectile] ......FN
Flat Oval [Technical drawings] ......FO
Flat Pack Diode ......FPD
Flat Pack Welder ......FPW
Flat Pack Welder System ......FPWS
Flat Pad ......FP
Flat Pattern ......F/P
Flat Plate [Medicine] ......FP
Flat-Plate Antenna [or Array] ......FPA
Flat-Plate Array Antenna ......FPAA
Flat-Plate Radiometer ......FPR
Flat-Plate Solar Array ......FSA
Flat Point [Technical drawings] ......FP
Flat Response Audio Pickup ......FRAP
Flat River [Missouri] [Seismograph station code, US Geological Survey] [Closed] ......FRM
Flat River, MO [Radio station call letters] ......KFMO
Flat Salary Payroll ......FSP
Flat Template ......FT
Flat-Tile Roof ......FTR
Flat-Topped [Frames] [Optometry] ......FT
Flat Trim Template ......FTT
Flat Veneer Products Association ......FVPA
Flat Washer ......FLW
Flat Work ......FLWK
Flateyri [Iceland] [Airport symbol] ......FLI
Flathead County Free Library, Kalispell, MT [Library symbol] ......MtK
Flathead Valley Community College, Kalispell, MT [Library symbol] ......MtKF
Flats [Utah] [Seismograph station code, US Geological Survey] [Closed] ......FLA
Flats ......FLT
Flatten ......FLN
Flatter, Squarer Tube [Television picture tube] ......FST
Flatware Importers Association [Defunct] ......FIA
Flavin-Adenine Dinucleotide [Biochemistry] ......FAD
Flavin-Adenine Dinucleotide [Reduced] [Biochemistry] ......$FADH_2$
Flavin Mononucleotide [Biochemistry] ......FMN
Flavin Mononucleotide [Reduced] [Biochemistry] ......FMNH
Flavin Phosphate [Biochemistry] ......FP
Flavoprotein [Biochemistry] ......FP
Flavor and Extract Manufacturers Association of the USA ......FEMA
Flavour Industry [A publication] ......Flavour Ind
Flavus [Yellow] [Pharmacy] ......FLAV
Flaw Detection Equipment ......FDE
Flax Institute of the United States [Defunct] ......FIUS
Flechette Area Neutralizing Gun ......FANG
Fleet ......F
Fleet ......FLT
Fleet Accountant Officer [British] ......FAO
Fleet Accounting and Disbursing Center [Navy] ......FAADC
Fleet Activities [Navy] ......CFA
Fleet Activities ......FLEACT
Fleet Activities ......FLTACT
Fleet Activities Command [Navy] ......FAC
Fleet Administration Office ......FAO
Fleet Admiral ......FADM
Fleet Air [Wing] ......FAIR
Fleet Air Arm [British] ......FAA
Fleet Air Arm Service Trials Unit [British] ......FAASTU
Fleet Air Base ......FAB
Fleet Air Base Unit ......FABU
Fleet Air Broadcast ......FAB
Fleet Air Control and Survey Facility ......FACSFAC
Fleet Air Defense ......FAD
Fleet Air Defense Exercise [Navy] ......FAIRDEX
Fleet Air Detachment ......FAD
Fleet Air Eastern Atlantic and Mediterranean ......FAIRELM
Fleet Air Gunnery Unit ......FAGU
Fleet Air Gunnery Unit, Pacific ......FAGUPAC
Fleet Air Intelligence Augmenting Unit ......FAIAU
Fleet Air Mediterranean Repair Area ......FAMRA
Fleet Air Photo Squadron ......FAPRON
Fleet Air Photographic Group ......FAPG
Fleet Air Reconnaissance Squadron ......FAIRECONRON
Fleet Air Reconnaissance Squadron [Navy symbol] ......VQ
Fleet Air [or Aircraft] Service Squadron [Obsolete] ......FASRON
Fleet Air Tactical Unit ......FATU
Fleet Air Western Pacific Repair Area ......FAWPRA
Fleet Air Wing ......FAIRWING
Fleet Air Wing ......FAW
Fleet Air Wing, Atlantic Fleet ......FAWAF
Fleet Air Wing, Western Pacific Area ......FAIRWESTPAC
Fleet Airborne Electronic Training Unit ......FAETU
Fleet Airborne Electronic Training Unit, Atlantic ......FAETUA

Fleet Airborne Electronic Training Unit, Atlantic ......FAETULANT
Fleet Airborne Electronic Training Unit Detachment ......FAETUDET
Fleet Airborne Electronic Training Unit, Pacific ......FAETUP
Fleet Airborne Electronic Training Unit, Pacific [Later, FASOTRAGRUPAC, FASOTRAGRUPACFLT] ......FAETUPAC
Fleet Aircraft Maintenance Unit ......FAMU
Fleet Aircraft Service Squadron ......FASTRON
Fleet Airship Wing ......FAIRSHIPWING
Fleet Airships ......FAIRSHIPS
Fleet Airships, Atlantic ......FASA
Fleet Airships, Pacific ......FASP
Fleet All Weather ......FAW
Fleet All-Weather Training Unit ......FAWTU
Fleet All-Weather Training Unit, Atlantic ......FAWTULANT
Fleet All-Weather Training Unit, Pacific ......FAWTUPAC
Fleet Ammunition Ship Training Unit, Atlantic ......FASTULANT
Fleet Ammunition Ship Training Unit, Pacific ......FASTUPAC
Fleet Antiair Warfare Training Center ......FAAWTC
Fleet Antiair Warfare Training Center ......FAAWTRACEN
Fleet Antisubmarine Data Analysis Program ......FADAP
Fleet Antisubmarine Warfare Command ......FASWC
Fleet Antisubmarine Warfare School ......FASWSCHOOL
Fleet Antisubmarine Warfare School ......FLEASWSCOL
Fleet Antisubmarine Warfare Tactical School ......FLEASWTACSCOL
Fleet Antiwarfare Training Center ......FAWTC
Fleet Application of Meteorological Observations from Satellites ......FAMOS
Fleet Assistance Group ......FAG
Fleet Assistance Group, Atlantic ......FAGLANT
Fleet Assistance Group, Pacific ......FAGPAC
Fleet ASW [Antisubmarine Warfare] Training Center [Navy] ......FLTASWTRACEN
Fleet Augmentation Component ......FAC
Fleet Auxiliary [British] ......FA
Fleet Aviation Accounting Office ......FAAO
Fleet Aviation Officer [British] ......FAVO
Fleet Aviation Specialized Operational Training Group, Pacific [Formerly, FAETUPAC] [Later, FASOTRAGRUPACFLT] [Navy] ......FASOTRAGRUPAC
Fleet Aviation Specialized Operational Training Group, Pacific Fleet [Formerly, FASOTRAGRUPAC, FAETUPAC] [Navy] ......FASOTRAGRUPACFLT
Fleet Aviation Support Unit ......FASU
Fleet Ballistic Missile ......FBM
Fleet Ballistic Missile Program ......FBMP
Fleet Ballistic Missile Submarine (Nuclear powered) [Navy symbol] ......SSBN
Fleet Ballistic Missile Submarine Tender Load List ......FBMSTLL
Fleet Ballistic Missile Submarine Training Center ......FLEBALMISUBTRACEN
Fleet Ballistic Missile System ......FBMS
Fleet Ballistic Missile Weapon System ......FBMWS
Fleet Ballistic Submarine [Navy symbol] ......SSB
Fleet Boat Pool ......FBP
Fleet Broadcast [Navy] ......FLTBCST
Fleet Broadcast [Navy] ......FLTBDCST
Fleet Civil Engineer ......FCE
Fleet Combat Direction Systems Support Activity [Navy] ......FCDSSA
Fleet Combat Direction Systems Support Activity, San Diego [California] [Navy] ......FCDSSA/SD
Fleet Combat Training Center [Navy] ......FCTC
Fleet Composite Squadron [Navy] ......FLECOMPRON
Fleet Computer Programing Center ......FCPC
Fleet Computer Programing Center, Atlantic [Navy] ......FCPCL
Fleet Computer Programing Center, Atlantic ......FCPCLANT
Fleet Computer Programing Center, Atlantic ......FLECOMPUTPROGCENLANT
Fleet Computer Programing Center, Pacific ......FCPCP
Fleet Computer Programing Center, Pacific [Navy] ......FCPCPAC
Fleet Computer Programing Center, Pacific ......FLECOMPUTPROGCENPAC
Fleet Computer Programming Center ......FLECOMPUTPROGCEN
Fleet Control ......FLTCON
Fleet Demonstration [Navy] ......FLTDEMO
Fleet Dental Officer ......FDO
Fleet Electromagnetic Radiation [Team] [Navy] ......FEMR
Fleet Electronic Warfare Support Group ......FEWSG
Fleet Electronics Calibration Laboratory ......FECL
Fleet Engineer Officer [British] ......FEO
Fleet Environmental Support System [Navy] ......FESS
Fleet Evaluation Trial [Navy] ......FET
Fleet Exercise [Navy] ......FEX
Fleet Exercise [Navy] ......FLEETEX
Fleet Exercise [Navy] ......FLTEX
Fleet Exercise Publication [Navy] ......FXP
Fleet Fighter [Air Force] ......FF
Fleet Fighter Reconnaissance [Air Force] ......FFR
Fleet Financial Group, Inc. [NYSE symbol] ......FLT
Fleet Flagship ......FF
Fleet Flash Net [Navy] ......FFN
Fleet Frequency Plans ......FFP
Fleet Gunnery Officer ......FGO
Fleet Gunnery School ......FLTGUNSCH

Fleet Gunnery School ... FLTGUNSCOL
Fleet Home Town News Center ... FHTNC
Fleet Hurricane Forecast Facility ... FHFF
Fleet Improved Readiness by Expediting Procurement, Logistics, and Negotiations [*Navy*] ... FIRE PLAN
Fleet Improvement Program [*Navy*] ... FIP
Fleet Indoctrination Program [*Navy*] ... FIP
Fleet Indoctrination Site [*Navy*] ... FIS
Fleet Induction Replacement Model [*Navy*] ... FIRM
Fleet Input and Reserve Support Training ... FIRST
Fleet Installation Budget [*Navy*] ... FIB
Fleet Intelligence Center [*Navy*] ... FIC
Fleet Intelligence Center, Europe [*Navy*] ... FICEUR
Fleet Intelligence Center, Pacific [*Navy*] ... FICPAC
Fleet Intelligence Center, Pacific Facility [*Navy*] ... FICPACFAC
Fleet Intelligence Officer ... FIO
Fleet Introduction Program ... FIP
Fleet Introduction Team [*Navy*] ... FIT
Fleet Issue Control [*Navy*] ... FIC
Fleet Issue Load List [*Navy*] ... FILL
Fleet Issue Requirements List [*Navy*] ... FIRL
Fleet Issue Requirements List/Shopping Guide [*Navy*] ... FIRL/SG
Fleet Issue Ship Shopping Guide [*Navy*] ... FISSG
Fleet Liaison Officer, Supreme Commander Allied Powers [*World War II*] ... FLTLOSCAP
Fleet Loading Center ... FLC
Fleet Location and Information Reporting [*Police term*] ... FLAIR
Fleet Logistic Air Wing ... FLAW
Fleet Logistic Support Improvement Program [*Navy*] ... FLSIP
Fleet Logistic Support Wing [*Navy*] ... FLSW
Fleet Logistics ... FLOG
Fleet Logistics Air Wing [*Navy*] ... FLOGAIR
Fleet Logistics Air Wing [*Obsolete*] [*Navy*] ... FLOGWING
Fleet Logistics Air Wing, Atlantic [*Navy*] ... FLOGWINGLANT
Fleet Logistics Air Wing, Pacific [*Navy*] ... FLOGWINGPAC
Fleet Logistics Support Department [*Naval Weapons Support Center*] ... FLS
Fleet Logistics Wing [*Navy*] ... FLW
Fleet Mail Office [*British*] ... FMO
Fleet Maintenance Assistance Group [*Navy*] ... FMAG
Fleet Maintenance Office [*or Officer*] ... FMO
Fleet Marine Air Wing ... FMAW
Fleet Marine Corps Reserve ... FMCR
Fleet Marine Force [*Military*] ... FMF
Fleet Marine Force, Atlantic [*Navy*] ... FMFLANT
Fleet Marine Force Manual [*Marine Corps*] ... FMFM
Fleet Marine Force, Pacific Fleet [*Navy*] ... FMFPAC
Fleet Marine Force, Western Pacific [*Navy*] ... FMFWESTPAC
Fleet Material Support [*Navy*] ... FMS
Fleet Material Support Office [*Navy*] ... FLEMATSUPPO
Fleet Material Support Office [*Navy*] ... FMSO
Fleet Material Support Office, Fleet Assistance Group, Atlantic [*Navy*] ... FLEMATSUPPOFAGLANT
Fleet Material Support Office, Fleet Assistance Group, Pacific [*Navy*] ... FLEMATSUPPOFAGPAC
Fleet Mechanical Calibration Laboratory ... FMCL
Fleet Medical Officer ... FMO
Fleet Minelayer [*Navy symbol*] ... MMF
Fleet Minesweeper (Steel-Hulled) [*Navy symbol*] ... MFS
Fleet Missile Systems Analysis and Evaluation Group [*Navy*] ... FMSAEG
Fleet Missile Systems Analysis and Evaluation Group Annex [*Navy*] ... FMSAEGA
Fleet Missile Systems Analysis and Evaluation Laboratory ... FMSAEL
Fleet Modernization Plan [*Navy*] ... FMP
Fleet Modernization Program ... FMP
Fleet Music School ... FMS
Fleet Naval Ordnance Inspecting Officer ... FNOIO
Fleet Numerical Weather Center [*Navy*] ... FNWC
Fleet Numerical Weather Facility ... FLENUMWEAFAC
Fleet Numerical Weather Facility ... FNWF
Fleet Observation of Oceanographic Data [*Navy*] ... FLOOD
Fleet Ocean Surveillance Information Facilities [*Navy*] ... FOSIF
Fleet Ocean Tug [*Navy symbol*] ... ATF
Fleet Operational Intelligence Training Center [*Navy*] ... FLEOPINTRACEN
Fleet Operational Intelligence Training Center [*Navy*] ... FOITC
Fleet Operational Investigation [*NOO*] ... FOI
Fleet Operational Readiness Accuracy Check Sites [*Navy*] ... FORACS
Fleet Operational Training Command, Atlantic [*Usually, COTCLANT*] ... OTCLANT
Fleet Operational Training Command, Pacific [*Usually, COTCPAC*] ... OTCPAC
Fleet Operations [*Navy*] ... FO
Fleet Operations Control Center ... FOCC
Fleet Operations Control Center, Europe ... FOCCEUR
Fleet Operations Control Center, Pacific Fleet ... FOCCPAC
Fleet Operations and Readiness ... FO & R
Fleet Oriented Consolidated Stock List [*Navy*] ... FOCSL
Fleet Post Office ... FPO
Fleet Probe Data System [*Navy*] ... FPDS
Fleet Program Support Material ... FPSM
Fleet Programing Center, Atlantic ... FPCLANT
Fleet Publication Supply Office ... FPSO
Fleet Radio Unit ... FRU
Fleet Radio Unit, Melbourne [*World War II*] ... FRUMEL
Fleet Radio Unit, Pacific ... FRUPAC
Fleet Readiness Analysis [*NORRS*] ... FRAN
Fleet Readiness Assistance Program ... FRAP
Fleet Readiness Enlisted Maintenance [*Trainees*] ... FREM
Fleet Readiness Improvement Plan ... FRIP
Fleet Readiness Representative ... FLTREADREP
Fleet Readiness Squadron [*Navy*] ... FRS
Fleet Records Office ... FRO
Fleet Recreation Officer [*British*] ... FRO
Fleet Rehabilitation and Modernization [*Navy*] ... FRAM
Fleet Repair Service ... FRS
Fleet Replacement Aviation Maintenance Program ... FRAMP
Fleet Replacement Pilot [*Navy*] ... FRP
Fleet Replacement Pilot Training [*Navy*] ... FRPTNG
Fleet Replacement RADAR Intercept Officer [*Navy*] ... FRRIO
Fleet Requirements Units [*Aircraft*] ... FRU
Fleet Reserve [*Navy*] ... FR
Fleet Reserve Association ... FRA
Fleet Reserve Association Auxiliary ... FRAA
Fleet Resources Office ... FRO
Fleet Return Evaluation Program ... FREP
Fleet Satellite Communications [*DoD*] ... FSC
Fleet Satellite Communications System [*Navy*] ... FLEETSATCOM
Fleet Satellite Communications System [*DoD*] ... FLTSATCOM
Fleet Secure Voice Communications [*Navy*] ... FLTSEVOCOM
Fleet Service Mine Test [*Navy*] ... FSMT
Fleet Service School ... FLTSERVSCOL
Fleet Service School ... FSS
Fleet Signals Officer [*Navy*] ... FSO
Fleet-Sizing Analysis and Sensitivity Technique [*Bell System*] ... FAST
Fleet SONAR School ... FLESONARSCOL
Fleet Sound School ... FLTSOUNDSCOL
Fleet Special Test and Checkout Equipment ... FSTACOE
Fleet Status [*Navy*] ... F/S
Fleet Street Letter [*A publication*] ... FSL
Fleet Submarine [*Navy symbol*] ... SF
Fleet Submarine Training Facility ... FLESUBTRAFAC
Fleet Supply Officer [*Navy*] ... FSO
Fleet Support ... FS
Fleet Support Material List ... FSML
Fleet Support Operations ... FSO
Fleet Supportability Evaluation ... FSE
Fleet Surgeon ... FS
Fleet Systems Capable ... FSC
Fleet Tactical Support [*Navy symbol*] ... VR
Fleet Tactical Support Squadron ... FLETACSUPPRON
Fleet Tactical Support Squadron Carrier [*Navy symbol*] ... VRC
Fleet Torpedo Bomber ... FTB
Fleet Torpedo Officer [*British*] ... FTO
Fleet Tracking Center ... FLTTRACKCEN
Fleet Training Base ... FLETRABASE
Fleet Training Center [*Navy*] ... FLETRACEN
Fleet Training Center [*Navy*] ... FLTTRACEN
Fleet Training Center [*Navy*] ... FTC
Fleet Training Command, Atlantic [*Navy*] ... TRALANT
Fleet Training Command, Pacific [*Navy*] ... TRAPAC
Fleet Training Exercise ... FTX
Fleet Training Group ... FLTTRAGRU
Fleet Training Group ... FTG
Fleet Training Group Services ... FTGSVC
Fleet Training Group and Underway Training Element ... FLETRAGRUWATE
Fleet Training Missile ... FTM
Fleet Training Publication ... FTP
Fleet Training Squadron [*Navy*] ... FTS
Fleet Training Unit ... FTU
Fleet Utility ... FUT
Fleet Weapon Armament Maintenance [*Navy*] ... FWAM
Fleet Weapons Center ... FLTWEPCEN
Fleet Weapons Center [*Navy*] ... FWC
Fleet Weather Center [*or Central*] ... FLEWEACEN
Fleet Weather Center [*Navy*] ... FWC
Fleet Weather Facility ... FLEWEAFAC
Fleet Weather Facility [*Navy*] ... FWF
Fleet Wireless Officer [*British*] ... FWO
Fleet Work Study [*Navy*] ... FWS
Fleet Work Study Group [*Navy*] ... FWSG
Fleet Work Study Group, Atlantic [*Navy*] ... FLEWORKSTUDYGRULANT
Fleetwood [*Alabama*] [*Seismograph station code, US Geological Survey*] ... FLT
Fleetwood Enterprises, Inc. [*NYSE symbol*] ... FLE
Fleischner Society ... FS
Fleming Community Library, Fleming, CO [*Library symbol*] ... CoFle
Fleming Companies [*NYSE symbol*] ... FLM
Fleming H. Revell Co., Old Tappan, NJ [*Library symbol*] ... NjOtR
Fleming International Airways, Inc. [*Air carrier designation symbol*] ... FLAX
Fleming International Airways, Inc. [*Lithonia, GA*] [*FAA designator*] ... FLM
Flemingsburg, KY [*Radio station call letters*] ... WFLE

Flemington, NJ [*Radio station call letters*] WCVH
Flemish FLEM
Flesh Public Library, Piqua, OH [*Library symbol*] OPi
Flesherton Public Library, Flesherton, ON, Canada [*Library symbol*] CaOFl
Fletcher [*Vermont*] [*Seismograph station code, US Geological Survey*] FLE
Fletcher Aviation Corporation FAC
Fletcher Free Library, Burlington, VT [*Library symbol*] VtB
Fletcher School of Law and Diplomacy, Tufts University, Medford, MA [*OCLC symbol*] TFF
Flettner Aircraft Corporation FAC
Fleur de Coin [*Mint state*] [*Numismatics*] FDC
Fleur-de-Lys [*Heraldry*] FDL
Flex Hose FH
Flex-Lead Torque FLT
Flex Multiplexer/Demultiplexer FMDM
Flexi-Filament FF
Flexi-Van Corp. [*NYSE symbol*] FLX
Flexible FLEX
Flexible Accelerator Path [*Economic theory*] FAP
Flexible Accounting Control System FACS
Flexible Adaptive RADAR FLEXAR
Flexible Aircraft Takeoff and Landing Analysis FATOLA
Flexible Algebraic Scientific Translator FAST
Flexible Automatic Circuit Tester FACT
Flexible Automatic Depot FAD
Flexible Computer Corp. [*NASDAQ symbol*] FLXXA
Flexible Critical Experiment FCE
Flexible Digital Receiving Terminal FDRT
Flexible Display System FDS
Flexible Drive Shaft FDS
Flexible Energy Management FLEXEM
Flexible Fiber Optic Borescope FFOB
Flexible Fiberoptic Bronchoscopy [*Medicine*] FFB
Flexible Guidance Software System FGSS
Flexible Gyro Header FGH
Flexible Gyro Header Assembly FGHA
Flexible Header Assembly FHA
Flexible Integrated Solar Cell Assembly FISCA
Flexible Linear Shaped Charge FLSC
Flexible Loan Insurance Program FLIP
Flexible Manufacturing System FMS
Flexible Mild Steel Wire Rope FMSWR
Flexible Monte Carlo [*Data processing*] FMC
Flexible Motor Coupling FMC
Flexible Nylon Coupling FNC
Flexible Packaging Association FPA
Flexible Pavements, Incorporated [*An association*] FPI
Flexible Payment Mortgage FPM
Flexible Polyurethane Foam FPF
Flexible Printed Circuit FPC
Flexible Real Estate Loan Plan FRELP
Flexible Reusable Surface Insulation FRSI
Flexible Rolled-Up Solar Array [*Air Force*] FRUSA
Flexible and Selective Targeting Options [*DoD*] FTO
Flexible Shielded Cable FSC
Flexible Sigmoidoscopy [*Proctoscopy*] FS
Flexible Solar Array FSA
Flexible Space Garment FSG
Flexible Steel Wire FSW
Flexible Steel Wire Rope FSWR
Flexible Test Station FTS
Flexible Test Station Test Procedure FTSTP
Flexible Theatre Missile FTM
Flexible Trunk [*Hovercraft*] FT
Flexible Waveguide FWG
Flexible Wing Recovery System [*Aerospace*] FWRS
Flexible Working Hours FWH
Flexicore Manufacturers Association FMA
Flexion [*Medicine*] FL
Flexion [*Medicine*] FLEX
Flexion-Extension Motion [*Orthopedics*] FEM
Flexographic Technical Association FTA
Flexor Digitorum Profundus [*Anatomy*] FDP
Flexor Digitorum Superficialis [*Anatomy*] FDS
Flexor Pollicis Brevis [*Anatomy*] FPB
Flexor Pollicis Longus [*Anatomy*] FPL
Flexowriter Equipment FLEX
Flexsteel Industries, Inc. [*NASDAQ symbol*] FLXS
Flexure [*Mechanics*] FLEX
Flexure Monitor Mounting Fixture FMMF
Flexwatt Corp. Units [*NASDAQ symbol*] FWATU
Flexweight Corp. [*NASDAQ symbol*] FLEX
Flicker Fusion Threshold FFT
Flickinger [*S. M.*] **Co., Inc.** [*NASDAQ symbol*] FLIC
Flickinger Foundation for American Studies FFAS
Flied Out [*Baseball*] F
Fliegerabwehrkanone [*German word for antiaircraft gun; acronym used in English for antiaircraft fire and as a slang term for dissension*] FLAK
Flight FLT
Flight Acceleration Safety Cutoff System FASCOS
Flight Acceptance FA
Flight Acceptance Composite Test [*NASA*] FACT
Flight Acceptance Profile FAP
Flight Acceptance Review FAR
Flight Acceptance Test FAT
Flight Accrual Payment Action [*Air Force*] FAPA
Flight Activities Officer [*NASA*] FAO
Flight Activities Scheduling System [*NASA*] FASS
Flight Advisory Service [*FAA*] FAS
Flight Advisory Service Test [*FAA*] FAST
Flight Advisory Weather Service FAWS
Flight Analysis Section FAS
Flight Anomalies Reporting FLARE
Flight Anomaly Investigation [*NASA*] FAI
Flight Application Software [*NASA*] FLAPS
Flight Aptitude Rating FAR
Flight Aptitude Selection Test [*Army*] FAST
Flight Article [*Army*] FLA
Flight Assistance Service FAS
Flight Attendant FA
Flight Attendant Volunteer Corps FAVC
Flight Attitude Table [*NASA*] FAT
Flight Augmentation Control System [*Aviation*] FACS
Flight Capsule FC
Flight Cargo Implementation Plan FCIP
Flight Certificate F/C
Flight Certificate FLTCERT
Flight Change Control Order FCCO
Flight Charts FC
Flight Check [*Aviation*] FLTCK
Flight Checkout Vehicle FCV
Flight Combustion Monitor FCM
Flight Combustion-Stability Monitor [*Apollo*] [*NASA*] FCSM
Flight Command School FCS
Flight Command Subsystem [*Spacecraft*] FCS
Flight Communications Center FCC
Flight Communications Operator FCO
Flight Communications Operator in Training FCO-T
Flight Composite Acceptance Test FCAT
Flight Computer [*NASA*] FC
Flight Computer Operating System [*NASA*] FCOS
Flight Condition Recognition [*Army aviation*] FCR
Flight Configuration Mode Test [*Gemini*] [*NASA*] FCMT
Flight Configuration Review FCR
Flight Control FC
Flight Control [*or Controller*] FLICON
Flight Control FLTCON
Flight Control FLYCON
Flight Control Applications Program [*NASA*] FCAP
Flight Control Assemblies FCA
Flight Control Center FCC
Flight Control Computer FCC
Flight Control Console FCC
Flight Control Container FCC
Flight Control Data Bus FCDB
Flight Control Electrical Package Container FCEPC
Flight Control Electronic Set FCES
Flight Control Electronics FCE
Flight Control Electronics Unit FCEU
Flight Control Equipment [*NASA*] FCE
Flight Control Group FCG
Flight Control Gyro Container FCGC
Flight Control Gyro Package Container FCGPC
Flight Control Hydraulics Laboratory [*NASA*] FCHL
Flight Control Indicator FCI
Flight Control Integration [*Apollo*] [*NASA*] FCI
Flight Control Interface Module FCIM
Flight Control Laboratory FCL
Flight Control Operating System [*NASA*] FCOS
Flight Control Operational Software FCOS
Flight Control Operations Branch [*NASA*] FCOB
Flight Control Panel FCP
Flight Control Programer FCP
Flight Control Ready Light [*System*] FCRL
Flight Control Ready Light System FCRLS
Flight Control Room FCT
Flight Control Sensor Group FCSG
Flight Control Set FCS
Flight Control System F/CS
Flight Control Systems Section FCSS
Flight Control Team FCT
Flight Control Test Stand [*Aviation*] FCTS
Flight Control Unit FCU
Flight Controller Confidence Test FCCT
Flight Controllers Handbook FCH
Flight Controllers Operations Handbook [*NASA*] FCOH
Flight Coordination Center FCC
Flight Coordination Control Central FCCC
Flight Correction Proposal FCP
Flight Crew FC

Flight Crew ... FLC
Flight Crew Compartment ... FCC
Flight Crew and Crew Equipment ... FC & CE
Flight Crew Equipment [*NASA*] ... FCE
Flight Crew Information File ... FCIF
Flight Crew Mission Simulator [*NASA*] ... FCMS
Flight Crew Operations [*NASA*] ... FCO
Flight Crew Operations Directorate [*NASA*] ... FCOD
Flight Crew Support Division [*NASA*] ... FCSD
Flight Crew System [*NASA*] ... FCS
Flight Crew Trainer [*NASA*] ... FCT
Flight Crew Trainer Simulator [*NASA*] ... FCTS
Flight Crew Training Building [*NASA*] ... FCTB
Flight Crew Workload [*Navy*] ... FCW
Flight Critical ... FC
Flight Critical Items ... FCI
Flight Data ... FDAT
Flight Data Acquisition Unit ... FDAU
Flight Data Center ... FDC
Flight Data Entry [*Device*] [*SAGE*] ... FLIDEN
Flight Data Entry and Printout [*Aviation*] ... FDEP
Flight Data File [*NASA*] ... FDF
Flight Data Management System [*Air Force*] ... FDMS
Flight Data Manager ... FDM
Flight Data Position ... FLIDAP
Flight Data Processing ... FDP
Flight Data Recorder ... FDR
Flight Data Recording System ... FDRS
Flight Data Storage Unit ... FDSU
Flight Data System [*NASA*] ... FDS
Flight Day ... FD
Flight Deck ... FD
Flight Deck ... FLDK
Flight Deck Assembly ... FDA
Flight Deck Hazardous Duty Billet ... FDHDB
Flight Deck Hazardous Duty Pay ... FDHDP
Flight Deck System Integration Simulator ... FDSIS
Flight Delay ... FD
Flight Demonstration Program ... FDP
Flight Demonstration Team ... FDT
Flight Design Operations Review ... FDOR
Flight Design and Scheduling ... FDS
Flight Determination Laboratory, Holloman Air Force Base ... FDLH
Flight Development Engineering Order ... FDEO
Flight Development Quality Assurance ... FDQA
Flight Direction and Altitude Indicator ... FDAI
Flight Direction Indicator ... FDI
Flight Director [*NASA*] ... FD
Flight Director Bombing Computer ... FDBC
Flight Director Computer ... FDC
Flight Director Group ... FDG
Flight Director Loop ... FDL
Flight Director Rate Indicator ... FDRI
Flight Director System ... FDS
Flight Display Cathode-Ray Tube ... FCRT
Flight Display Keyboard [*NASA*] ... FKB
Flight Display Research System ... FDRS
Flight Displays and Interface System ... FDIS
Flight Duty Officer [*Air Force*] ... FDO
Flight Dynamic Laboratory [*Air Force*] ... FDL
Flight Dynamics [*NASDAQ symbol*] ... FLYT
Flight Dynamics Branch [*NASA*] ... FDB
Flight Dynamics Group ... FDG
Flight Dynamics Officer [*NASA*] ... FDO
Flight Dynamics Officer [*NASA*] ... FIDO
Flight Dynamics Simulator ... FDS
Flight Dynamics Situation Complex ... FDSC
Flight Dynamics Software [*or System*] ... FDS
Flight Dynamics Staff Support Room [*Apollo*] [*NASA*] ... FDSSR
Flight Elapsed Time ... FET
Flight Element Set ... FES
Flight Engine Test Facility ... FETF
Flight Engineer [*or Engineering*] ... FE
Flight Engineer in Training ... FET
Flight Engineering Facility ... FEF
Flight Engineers' International Association ... FEIA
Flight Equipment Interface Device [*NASA*] ... FEID
Flight Evaluation Board ... FEB
Flight Evaluation Working Group ... FEWG
Flight Events Demonstration [*NASA*] ... FED
Flight Experiment Shielding Satellite ... FESS
Flight Express Cargo [*Philadelphia, PA*] [*FAA designator*] ... CFT
Flight Facilities Flight ... FFF
Flight Following Service [*FAA*] ... FFS
Flight Forecast ... FIFOR
Flight Forward ... FF
Flight Freedoms Foundation ... FFF
Flight Half Coupling ... FHC
Flight Hour ... FH
Flight Implementation Directive ... FID
Flight Incident Recorder/Crash Position Locator [*Navy*] ... FIR/CPL
Flight Information ... FLIFO
Flight Information Advisory Committee [*Terminated, 1977*] [*FAA*] ... FIAC
Flight Information Area ... FIA
Flight Information Bulletin ... FIB
Flight Information Center ... FIC
Flight Information and Control of Operations ... FICO
Flight Information Display ... FIND
Flight Information Manual ... FIM
Flight Information Plan ... FLIP
Flight Information Publication [*Air Force*] ... FIPUB
Flight Information Publication [*Air Force*] ... FLIP
Flight Information Region [*FAA*] ... FIR
Flight Information Region Boundary ... FIRB
Flight Information Report ... FIR
Flight Information Requirement ... FIR
Flight Information Service ... FIS
Flight Inspection ... F
Flight Inspection District Office [*FAA*] ... FIDO
Flight Inspection Field Office [*FAA*] ... FIFO
Flight Inspection Field Office, High Altitude [*FAA*] ... FIFO-H
Flight Inspection Group [*FAA*] ... FIG
Flight Inspection National Field Office [*FAA*] ... FINFO
Flight Inspection (Permanent) ... FI/P
Flight Inspection Positioning System ... FIPS
Flight Inspection Report ... FIR
Flight Inspection (Temporary) ... FI/T
Flight Inspector in Charge ... FIIC
Flight Instruction Program [*Air Force*] ... FIP
Flight Instrument Signal Converter ... FISC
Flight Instrument Trainer ... FIT
Flight Instrumentation Engineer ... FIE
Flight International [*A publication*] ... Flight Int
Flight International (London) [*A publication*] ... Flight Int (London)
Flight Investigation of Apollo Reentry Environment ... FIARE
Flight Investigation of the Reentry Environment ... FIRE
Flight and Laboratory Development ... F & LD
Flight Launched Infrared Probe ... FLIP
Flight Leader Identity [*RADAR*] ... FLI
Flight Level ... FL
Flight Level Pressure Altitude ... FLPA
Flight Level Sensing Subsystems ... FLSS
Flight Lieutenant ... FL
Flight Line ... FLTL
Flight Line Bunker ... FLB
Flight Line Detection and Isolation Techniques ... FLIDIT
Flight Line Maintenance ... FLM
Flight Line Printer ... FLP
Flight Line Reference ... FLR
Flight Line Taxi ... FLT
Flight Line Tester ... FLT
Flight Load Recorder ... FLR
Flight Loads Unit ... FLU
Flight Low-Level Image Receiver ... FLIR
Flight Management Office [*Air Force*] ... FMO
Flight Management Team [*Skylab*] [*NASA*] ... FMT
Flight Manifest and Hardware Tracking System ... FMAHTS
Flight Manual ... FM
Flight Manual Interim Changes ... FMIC
Flight Mechanic ... FM
Flight Mechanics, Dynamics, and Control ... FMD & C
Flight Medical Officer [*Air Force*] ... FMO
Flight Medicine Clinic ... FMC
Flight Mission Assignments Document ... FMAD
Flight Mission Rules Document [*NASA*] ... FMRD
Flight Model ... FM
Flight Motion Simulator ... FMS
Flight Nurse ... FN
Flight Officer [*Air Force*] ... FLTO
Flight Officer [*Air Force*] ... FO
Flight Operating Costs ... FOC
Flight Operations Building [*NASA*] ... FOB
Flight Operations Center ... FOC
Flight Operations Directorate [*or Division*] [*Apollo*] [*NASA*] ... FOD
Flight Operations Engineer ... FOE
Flight Operations Facility ... FOF
Flight Operations Group ... FOG
Flight Operations Integration Handbook ... FOIH
Flight Operations Management Room [*NASA*] ... FOMR
Flight Operations Plan ... FOP
Flight Operations Planner ... FLIOP
Flight Operations Planning Group [*NASA*] ... FOPG
Flight Operations and Planning Scheduling ... FOPS
Flight Operations Review ... FOR
Flight Operations Scheduling Office [*NASA*] ... FOSO
Flight Operations Support ... FOS
Flight Operations Support Personnel ... FOSP
Flight Operations Support Team ... FOST
Flight Operations Team ... FOT
Flight Order ... FO
Flight Orderly ... FO
Flight Orders [*Aviation*] ... FLTO

Flight Path Accelerometer	FPA
Flight Path Analysis	FPA
Flight Path Analysis Area [Space Flight Operations Facility, NASA]	FPAA
Flight Path Analysis and Command [Team] [NASA]	FPAC
Flight Path Angle	FPA
Flight Path Control	FPC
Flight Path Design Program	FPDP
Flight Path Deviation Indicator [Navigation]	DI
Flight Path Deviation Indicator [Navigation]	FPDI
Flight Path Marker	FPM
Flight Pay	FP
Flight Performance Reserve	FPR
Flight Plan [Aviation]	FP
Flight Plan [Aviation code]	PLN
Flight Plan Approval [Aviation]	FPA
Flight Plan Approved [Aviation]	FPAPVD
Flight Plan Filed in the Air [Aviation code]	AFIL
Flight Plan Gas Load [Air Force]	FPGL
Flight Plan Not Received [Aviation]	FPNO
Flight Plan Processing System [British]	FPPS
Flight Plan Support Specialist [NASA]	FLASP
Flight Planned Route [Aviation]	FPR
Flight Power Subsystem	FPS
Flight Preparation Sheet	FPS
Flight Programer	FLT/PG
Flight Programer	F/P
Flight Programer Computer	FPC
Flight Progress	FP
Flight Progress Board [Aviation]	FPB
Flight Progress Strip [Aviation]	FPS
Flight Proof Test Plan	FPTP
Flight/Propulsion Control Coupling [Air Force]	FPCC
Flight Propulsion Laboratory	FPL
Flight Qualification	FQ
Flight Qualification Instrumentation	FQI
Flight Qualification Recorder	FQR
Flight Qualification Reviews	FQR
Flight Qualification Tape Recorder [NASA]	FQTR
Flight Qualified System	FQS
Flight Qualities and Performance	FQ & P
Flight Quality Photomultiplier Assembly	FQPA
Flight in a Radiation Environment	FIRE
Flight Radio Officer [Aviation]	FRO
Flight Radio Subsystem	FRS
Flight Range and Endurance Data Indicator	FREDI
Flight Rated Bioinstrumentation	FRB
Flight Rating Test	FRT
Flight Readiness	FR
Flight Readiness Demonstration	FRD
Flight Readiness Firing Test [NASA]	FRF
Flight Readiness Firing Test	FRFT
Flight Readiness Review	FRR
Flight Readiness Review Item Disposition [NASA]	FRRID
Flight Readiness Test	FRT
Flight Readiness Vehicle	FRV
Flight Reference Stabilization Systems	FRSS
Flight Refueling	FR
Flight Refueling, Incorporated	FRI
Flight Related Element	FRE
Flight Reliability	FR
Flight Requirements Document	FRD
Flight Research Center [Later, DFRC] [NASA]	FRC
Flight Research and Development Instrumentation	FRDI
Flight Rule	FR
Flight Safety	FS
Flight Safety Foundation	FSF
Flight Safety Information Bulletin [NASA]	FSIB
Flight Safety Officer	FSO
Flight Safety Research	FSR
Flight Safety Review Board	FSRB
Flight Safety Training and Test Center	FSTTC
Flight Scheduling Precedence	FSP
Flight Sergeant [RAF] [British]	FS
Flight Service	FS
Flight Service Center	FSC
Flight Service Center	FSCEN
Flight Service Communications System	FSCS
Flight Service Station [FAA]	FSS
Flight Service Station Operations/Procedures Committee [FAA]	FSSCOM
Flight Services Handbook	FSH
Flight Simulated Training System [Military]	FSTS
Flight Simulation Engineer	FSE
Flight Simulation Report	FSR
Flight Simulation Test Data	FSTD
Flight Simulator	FS
Flight Simulator for Advanced Aircraft [NASA]	FSAA
Flight Software	FSW
Flight Software Readiness Review	FSRR
Flight Solar Reflectometer	FSR
Flight Space	FLSP
Flight Specific Requirements	FSR
Flight Standards District Office [FAA]	FSDO
Flight Standards National Field Office [FAA]	FSNFO
Flight Standards and Qualification [Army]	FS/Q
Flight Standards Service [FAA]	FS
Flight Standards Service [FAA]	FSS
Flight Steward	FLTST
Flight Strip Printer	FSP
Flight Suit with Integrated Flotation	FSIF
Flight Support Equipment	FSE
Flight Support Request	FSR
Flight Support Structure	FSS
Flight Support Tapes	FST
Flight Surgeon	FLS
Flight Surgeon	FLTSURG
Flight Surgeon	FS
Flight Surgeon Badge [Military decoration]	FltSurgBad
Flight System	FS
Flight System Interface Working Group	FSIWG
Flight System Mockup	FSM
Flight Systems Laboratory	FSL
Flight Systems Redundancy Test	FSRT
Flight Systems Simulator [NASA]	FSS
Flight Systems Software Requirement	FSSR
Flight Team	FT
Flight Team Operations Handbook	FTOH
Flight Telemetry Subsystem [Spacecraft]	FTS
Flight Television [NASA]	FTV
Flight Termination	FT
Flight Termination System	FTS
Flight Test	F/T
Flight Test Article	FTA
Flight [or Flying] Test Bed	FTB
Flight Test Center	FTC
Flight Test Change Proposal	FTCP
Flight Test Conductor	FTC
Flight Test Coordinating Committee [Air Force]	FTCC
Flight Test Data Recorder	FTDR
Flight Test Direction [or Directive]	FTD
Flight Test Division, Internal Project [Navy]	FTDIP
Flight Test Drawing	FTD
Flight Test Engineer	FTE
Flight Test Engineering Order	FTEO
Flight Test Equipment	FTE
Flight Test Evaluation	FTE
Flight Test Information Drawing	FTID
Flight Test Instrumentation System	FTIS
Flight Test Manual	FTM
Flight Test Missile [Air Force]	FTM
Flight Test Objective	FTO
Flight Test Operations	FTO
Flight Test Plan [or Procedure or Program]	FTP
Flight Test Planning and Evaluation	FTP & E
Flight Test Release Ticket	FTRT
Flight Test Report	FTR
Flight Test Report Guide	FTRG
Flight Test Reports Writer	FTRW
Flight Test Request Memorandum	FTRM
Flight Test Requirements [NASA]	FTR
Flight Test Requirements Document [NASA]	FTRD
Flight Test Review Board	FTRB
Flight Test Rocket Facilities Mechanical Engineering	FTRFME
Flight Test Sketch	FTS
Flight Test Station [ITU designation]	FAT
Flight Test Station	FTS
Flight Test Support	FTS
Flight Test Unit	FTU
Flight Test Vehicle [Air Force]	FTV
Flight Test Vehicle Safety Plan [Air Force]	FTVSP
Flight Test Work Order	FTWO
Flight Test Working Group	FTWG
Flight Time Constant	FTC
Flight Trace Contaminant Sensor System [NASA]	FTCSS
Flight Training Mission	FTM
Flight Unit	FU
Flight Vehicle	FV
Flight Vehicle Power Branch	FVPB
Flight Vehicles Systems	FVS
Flight Verification Vehicle	FVV
Flight Version	FV
Flight Watch Area	FWA
Flight Watch Control Station	FWCS
Flight Watch Outlet	FLTWO
Flight Watch Point	FWP
Flight Watch Specialist	FWS
Flight Watch Unit	FWU
Flight Weight	FW
Flight Worthiness Demonstration Test	FWDT
Flightsafety International, Inc. [Aerospace] [NYSE symbol]	FSI
Flin Flon [Manitoba] [Seismograph station code, US Geological Survey]	FFC

Flin Flon [*Manitoba*] [*Airport symbol*] ... YFO
Flin Flon, MB [*Television station call letters*] ... CBWBT
Flin Flon, MB [*Radio station call letters*] ... CFAR
Flin Flon Public Library, Flin Flon, MB, Canada [*Library symbol*] ... CaMFF
Flinders Island [*Australia*] [*Airport symbol*] ... FLS
Flinders University of South Australia, Bedford Park, SA, Australia [*Library symbol*] ... AuBpF
Flint ... F
Flint [*Michigan*] [*Airport symbol*] ... FNT
Flint Junior College [*Michigan*] ... FJC
Flint, MI [*Location identifier*] [*FAA*] ... BIQ
Flint, MI [*Location identifier*] [*FAA*] ... FNT
Flint, MI [*Location identifier*] [*FAA*] ... TUN
Flint, MI [*Radio station call letters*] ... WDZZ-FM
Flint, MI [*Radio station call letters*] ... WFBE
Flint, MI [*Radio station call letters*] ... WFDF
Flint, MI [*Radio station call letters*] ... WFLT
Flint, MI [*Television station call letters*] ... WFUM
Flint, MI [*Radio station call letters*] ... WGMZ
Flint, MI [*Television station call letters*] ... WJRT-TV
Flint, MI [*Radio station call letters*] ... WKMF
Flint, MI [*Radio station call letters*] ... WTAC
Flint, MI [*Radio station call letters*] ... WTRX
Flint, MI [*Radio station call letters*] ... WWCK
Flint, MI [*Radio station call letters*] ... WWMN
Flint Public Library, Flint, MI [*Library symbol*] ... MiFli
Flintkote Co. [*NYSE symbol*] ... FO
Flintshire [*County in Wales*] ... FLINTS
Flinty [*Quality of the bottom*] [*Nautical charts*] ... fly
Flip-Flop [*Data processing*] ... F-F
Flip-Flop [*Data processing*] ... FLF
Flip-Flop Complementary [*Data processing*] ... FFC
Flip-Flop Latch [*Data processing*] ... FFL
Flip-Flop - National Module [*Data processing*] ... FF-NM
Flip-Flop Position Indicator [*Data processing*] ... FFPI
Flip-Flop Relay Driver [*Data processing*] ... FFRD
Flippin, AR [*Location identifier*] [*FAA*] ... FLP
FLIR [*Forward-Looking Infrared RADAR*] **Augmented Cobra TOW** [*Tube-Launched, Optically-Tracked, Wire-Guided Weapon*] **Sight** ... FACTS
Float ... FLT
Float Bridge ... FLTBRG
Float On/Float Off ... FLO/FLO
Float Switch [*Aerospace*] ... FS
Floated Gyro [*Aerospace*] ... FG
Floated Inertial Measurement Ball ... FLIMBAL
Floated Integrating Gyro [*Aerospace*] ... FIG
Floated Lightweight Inertial Platform ... FLIP
Floated Rate Gyro [*Aerospace*] ... FRG
Floating ... FLTG
Floating Add ... FAD
Floating Aircraft Maintenance Facility [*Army*] ... FAMF
Floating Airfields [*British*] [*World War II*] ... FA
Floating Commutator ... FLOCOM
Floating Control Regulator ... FCR
Floating Crane [*Non-self-propelled*] [*Navy symbol*] ... YD
Floating Decimal Abstract Coding System ... FACS
Floating Digital Drive ... FDD
Floating Divide or Halt ... FDH
Floating Drift Tube Klystron ... FDTK
Floating Dry Dock [*Navy*] ... FDD
Floating Dry Dock Workshop (Hull) [*Non-self-propelled*] [*Navy symbol*] ... YRDH
Floating Dry Dock Workshop (Machine) [*Non-self-propelled*] [*Navy symbol*] ... YRDM
Floating Electronic Maintenance Facility ... FEMF
Floating Foundation of Photography ... FFP
Floating-Gate Avalanche-Injection Metal-Oxide Semiconductor ... FAMOS
Floating Hospital [*An association*] ... FH
Floating-In Rates ... FIR
Floating Indexed Point Arithmetic [*Data processing*] ... FLIP
Floating Input - Floating Output ... FIFO
Floating Input to Ground Output ... FITGO
Floating Instrument Platform [*Navy*] ... FLIP
Floating Interpretive Language [*Princeton University*] ... FLINT
Floating Laboratory Instrument Platform [*Movable oceanographic research station*] ... FLIP
Floating Machine Shop ... FMS
Floating Nuclear Plant [*or Powerplant*] [*ERDA*] ... FNP
Floating Ocean Research and Development [*Station*] ... FORD
Floating Ocean Research and Development Station ... FORDS
Floating Octal Point [*IBM Corp.*] ... FLOP
Floating Pile Driver [*Non-self-propelled*] [*Navy symbol*] ... YPD
Floating Platform No. 1 [*English bilingual film made in Germany with actor Conrad Veidt, 1933*] ... FP1
Floating Point [*Data processing*] ... FLP
Floating Point [*Data processing*] ... FP
Floating-Point Arithmetic ... FPA
Floating-Point Arithmetic Package ... FAP
Floating-Point Binary ... FLBIN
Floating-Point Calculation ... FPC
Floating-Point Decimal ... FLDEC
Floating-Point Interpretive Program [*Data processing*] ... FLIP
Floating-Point Means and Variance [*Biochemistry, genetics*] ... FMEVA
Floating-Point Processor [*Data processing*] ... FPP
Floating-Point Root Isolation [*Data processing*] ... FRTISO
Floating-Point Routine ... FPR
Floating-Point System ... FPS
Floating Point Systems, Inc. [*NYSE symbol*] ... FLP
Floating Point Systems, Inc., Beaverton, OR [*Library symbol*] ... OrBFP
Floating Point Unit ... FPU
Floating Policy [*Insurance*] ... FP
Floating Power Barge [*Non-self-propelled*] [*Navy symbol*] ... YFP
Floating Rate Certificate of Deposit ... FRCD
Floating Rate Note ... FRN
Floating Repair and Oil Storage Terminal ... FROST
Floating Round ... FRN
Floating Sign ... FS
Floating Spherical Gaussian Orbitals [*Atomic physics*] ... FSGO
Floating Units Division [*Coast Guard*] ... OFU
Floating Workshop [*Non-self-propelled*] [*Navy symbol*] ... YR
Floating Zone Melting ... FZM
Flocculation ... FLOCC
Flocculation Reaction [*Obsolete test for liver function*] ... FR
Flock Industries, Inc. [*American Stock Exchange symbol*] [*Delisted*] ... FLK
Flock Industries, Inc. [*NASDAQ symbol*] ... FLOK
Flomaton, AL [*Radio station call letters*] ... WPIK
Flood ... FL
Flood ... FLD
Flood Control ... FC
Flood Control District [*Florida*] ... FCD
Flood Insurance [*HUD*] ... FI
Flood Insurance Rate Map ... FIRM
Flood Plain Management Services [*Army*] ... FPMS
Flood Relief Punt [*Coast Guard*] ... FR
Flood Stage ... FLDST
Flood Stage ... FS
Flood Warnings Issued ... FLWIS
Flooding ... FLDNG
Floodlight ... FLDT
Floods ... F
Floor ... FL
Floor ... FLR
Floor Area Ratio [*in office buildings*] ... FAR
Floor Ataxia Test Battery ... FATB
Floor Covering Installation Contractors Association ... FCICA
Floor Drain [*Technical drawings*] ... FD
Floor Line ... FL
Floor Machine Manufacturers Association ... FMMA
Floor Manager ... FM
Floor Service Stations ... FSS
Floor and Vacuum Machinery Manufacturers' Association [*Defunct*] ... FVMMA
Floor Valve ... FV
Floor Valve Adapter ... FVA
Flooring ... FLG
Flooring ... FLRNG
Flooring Division, Rubber Manufacturers Association ... FDRMA
Floppy Disc Controller [*Data processing*] ... FDC
Floppy Disk [*Data processing*] ... FD
Floppy Disk Operating System [*Data processing*] ... FDOS
Flora oder Allgemeine Botanische Zeitung (Jena) [*A publication*] ... Flora Allg Bot Ztg (Jena)
Flora oder Allgemeine Botanische Zeitung (Jena) [*A publication*] ... Flora (Jena)
Flora Carnegie Library, Flora, IL [*Library symbol*] ... IFL
Flora Fennica [*A publication*] ... Flora Fenn
Flora, IL [*Location identifier*] [*FAA*] ... FOA
Flora, IL [*Radio station call letters*] ... WNOI
Flora Malesiana. Series I. Spermatophyta [*A publication*] ... Flora Malesiana Ser I Spermatophyta
Flora Malesiana. Series II. Pteridophyta [*A publication*] ... Flora Malesiana Ser II Pteridophyta
Flora van Nederland [*A publication*] ... Flora Ned
Flora Neerlandica [*A publication*] ... Flora Neerl
Flora North America Program [*Defunct*] ... FNA
Flora do Parana. Instituto Paranaense de Botanica Curitiba [*A publication*] ... Flora Parana Inst Parana Bot Curitiba
Flora Timarit um Islenzka Grasafraedi [*A publication*] ... Flora Timarit Isl Grasafraedi
Florafax International [*NASDAQ symbol*] ... FIIF
Floral Park Public Library, Floral Park, NY [*Library symbol*] ... NFlp
Florala, AL [*Radio station call letters*] ... WKWL
Flore Iconographique des Champignons du Congo [*A publication*] ... Flore Iconogr Champignons Congo
Flore Illustree des Champignons d'Afrique Centrale [*A publication*] ... Flore Illus Champignons Afr Cent
Florence [*South Carolina*] [*Airport symbol*] ... FLO
Florence [*Italy*] [*Airport symbol*] ... FLR
Florence Airlines [*Charlotte, NC*] [*FAA designator*] ... CLA
Florence, AL [*Radio station call letters*] ... WBCF
Florence, AL [*Television station call letters*] ... WFIQ

Florence, AL [*Television station call letters*] .... WOWL-TV
Florence, AL [*Radio station call letters*] .... WQLT
Florence, AL [*Television station call letters*] .... WTUK
Florence, AL [*Radio station call letters*] .... WXOR
Florence, AZ [*Radio station call letters*] .... KGUS
Florence County Library, Florence, SC [*OCLC symbol*] .... SCF
Florence County Library, Florence, SC [*Library symbol*] .... ScFl
Florence Crittenton Association of America .... FCAA
Florence-Darlington Technical College Library, Florence, SC [*Library symbol*] .... ScFIT
Florence-Darlington Technical College Library, Florence, SC [*OCLC symbol*] .... SFD
Florence Nightingale International Foundation .... FNIF
Florence Public Library, Florence, CO [*Library symbol*] .... CoFlo
Florence Public Library, Florence, OR [*Library symbol*] .... OrFl
Florence, SC [*Location identifier*] [*FAA*] .... GKF
Florence, SC [*Television station call letters*] .... WBTW
Florence, SC [*Radio station call letters*] .... WJMX
Florence, SC [*Television station call letters*] .... WJPM-TV
Florence, SC [*Radio station call letters*] .... WOLS
Florence, SC [*Television station call letters*] .... WPDE-TV
Florence, SC [*Television station call letters*] .... WSMF
Florence, SC [*Radio station call letters*] .... WSTN
Florence, SC [*Radio station call letters*] .... WYNN
Florence, SD [*Television station call letters*] .... KDLO-TV
Florence Williams Public Library, Christiansted, St. Croix, VI [*Library symbol*] .... VnSc
Florencia [*Colombia*] [*Airport symbol*] .... FLA
Florenville, LA [*Location identifier*] [*FAA*] .... FNA
Flores [*Flowers*] .... FL
Flores [*Guatemala*] [*Airport symbol*] .... FRS
Flores Assembly Program [*Data processing*] .... FLAP
Floresville, TX [*Radio station call letters*] .... KWCB
Florham Park Community News, Florham Park, NJ [*Library symbol*] .... NjFpN
Florham Park Public Library, Florham Park, NJ [*Library symbol*] .... NjFp
Florianopolis [*Brazil*] [*Airport symbol*] .... FLN
Florian's Own Statistically Oriented Language [*Data processing*] .... FOSOL
Florida [*Postal code*] .... FL
Florida .... FLA
Florida [*MARC country of publication code*] [*Library of Congress*] .... flu
Florida [*MARC geographic area code*] [*Library of Congress*] .... n-us-fl
Florida A & M University, Tallahassee, FL [*Library symbol*] .... FTaFA
Florida Academy of Sciences. Quarterly Journal [*A publication*] .... Fla Acad Sci Q J
Florida Agricultural Experiment Stations. Annual Report [*A publication*] .... Fla Agric Exp Stn Annu Rep
Florida Agricultural Experiment Stations. Bulletin [*A publication*] .... Fla Agric Exp Stn Bull
Florida Agricultural Experiment Stations. Circular [*A publication*] .... Fla Agric Exp Stn Circ
Florida Agricultural Experiment Stations. Monograph Series [*A publication*] .... Fla Agric Exp Stn Monogr Ser
Florida Agricultural Experiment Stations. Publications [*A publication*] .... Fla Ag Exp
Florida Agricultural Experiment Stations. Research Report [*A publication*] .... Fla Agric Exp Stn Res Rep
Florida Agricultural Extension Service. Bulletin [*A publication*] .... Fla Agric Ext Serv Bull
Florida Agricultural and Mechanical University .... FAMU
Florida Agricultural and Mechanical University, Tallahassee, FL [*OCLC symbol*] .... FCM
Florida Airlines, Inc. [*Tampa, FL*] [*FAA designator*] .... FDA
Florida Anthropologist [*A publication*] .... Florida Anthropol
Florida Anthropology [*A publication*] .... Fla Anthropol
Florida Aquanaut Research Expedition [*National Oceanic and Atmospheric Administration*] .... FLARE
Florida Area Cumulus Experiment [*National Science Foundation*] .... FACE
Florida Association of Marine Explorers .... FAME
Florida Atlantic University .... FAU
Florida Atlantic University, Boca Raton, FL [*Library symbol*] .... FBoU
Florida Atlantic University, Boca Raton, FL [*OCLC symbol*] .... FGM
Florida Automatic Computer [*Air Force*] .... FLAC
Florida Automotive Marketing [*NASDAQ symbol*] .... FLIM
Florida Bar Journal [*A publication*] .... Fla B J
Florida Board of Conservation. Marine Research Laboratory. Leaflet Series [*A publication*] .... Fla Board Conserv Mar Res Lab Leafl Ser
Florida Board of Conservation. Marine Research Laboratory. Professional Papers Series [*A publication*] .... Fla Board Conserv Mar Lab Prof Pap Ser
Florida Board of Conservation. Marine Research Laboratory. Special Scientific Report [*A publication*] .... Fla Board Conserv Mar Res Lab Spec Sci Rep
Florida Board of Conservation. Marine Research Laboratory. Technical Series [*A publication*] .... Fla Board Conserv Mar Res Lab Tech Ser
Florida Bureau of Geology. Information Circular [*A publication*] .... Fla Bur Geol Inf Circ
Florida Bureau of Geology. Report of Investigation [*A publication*] .... Fla Bur Geol Rep Invest
Florida Capital Corp. [*American Stock Exchange symbol*] .... FCC
Florida Christian College .... FCC
Florida Citrus Commission [*Later, Florida Department of Citrus*] .... FCC
Florida Citrus Mutual .... FCM
Florida Citrus Nurserymen's Association .... FCNA
Florida Citrus Packers .... FCP
Florida Coast Banks [*NASDAQ symbol*] .... FBNC
Florida College, Tampa, FL [*Library symbol*] .... FTFC
Florida Commercial Banks, Inc. [*NASDAQ symbol*] .... FLBK
Florida Commercial Fisheries Association .... FCFA
Florida Computer Catalog of Monographic Holdings [*Library network*] .... FLORIDA COMCAT
Florida Conservation News [*A publication*] .... Fla Conserv News
Florida Cypress Gardens [*NASDAQ symbol*] .... FCYP
Florida Dental Journal [*A publication*] .... Fla Dent J
Florida Department of Agriculture [*Tallahassee, FL*] [*FAA designator*] .... FFS
Florida Department of Agriculture and Consumer Services. Division of Plant Industry. Biennial Report [*A publication*] .... Fla Dep Agric Consum Serv Div Plant Ind Bienn Rep
Florida Department of Agriculture and Consumer Services. Division of Plant Industry. Bulletin [*A publication*] .... Fla Dep Agric Consum Serv Div Plant Ind Bull
Florida Department of Agriculture. Quarterly Bulletin [*A publication*] .... Fla Ag Dept Quar B
Florida Department of Citrus .... FDC
Florida Department of Natural Resources. Biennial Report [*A publication*] .... Fla Dep Nat Resour Bienn Rep
Florida Department of Natural Resources. Bureau of Geology. Bulletin [*A publication*] .... Fla Dep Nat Resour Bur Geol Bull
Florida Department of Natural Resources. Bureau of Geology. Geological Bulletin [*A publication*] .... Florida Bur Geology Geol Bull
Florida Department of Natural Resources. Bureau of Geology. Information Circular [*A publication*] .... Florida Bur Geology Inf Circ
Florida Department of Natural Resources. Bureau of Geology. Report of Investigations [*A publication*] .... Fla Dep Nat Resour Bur Geol Rep Invest
Florida Department of Natural Resources. Educational Series [*A publication*] .... Fla Dep Nat Resour Educ Ser
Florida Department of Natural Resources. Marine Research Laboratory. Leaflet Series [*A publication*] .... Fla Dep Nat Resour Mar Res Lab Leafl Ser
Florida Department of Natural Resources. Marine Research Laboratory. Professional Papers Series [*A publication*] .... Fla Dep Nat Resour Mar Res Lab Prof Pap Ser
Florida Department of Natural Resources. Marine Research Laboratory. Technical Series [*A publication*] .... Fla Dep Nat Resour Mar Res Lab Tech Ser
Florida Department of Natural Resources. Marine Research Laboratory. Special Scientific Report [*A publication*] .... Fla Dept Nat Resour Mar Res Lab Spec Sci Rep
Florida Designers Quarterly [*A publication*] .... FDQ
Florida East Coast Railway Co. [*AAR code*] .... FEC
Florida East Coast Railway Co. [*NYSE symbol*] .... FLA
Florida Employers Insurance [*NASDAQ symbol*] .... FLAEF
Florida Entomologist [*A publication*] .... Fla Entomol
Florida Facility [*NASA*] .... FF
Florida Federal Savings & Loan Association [*NASDAQ symbol*] .... FLFE
Florida Field Naturalist [*A publication*] .... Fla Field Nat
Florida Foliage Association .... FFA
Florida Foreign Language Reporter [*A publication*] .... FFLR
Florida Fresh Citrus Shippers Association [*Later, FCP*] .... FFCSA
Florida Fruit and Vegetable Association .... FFVA
Florida Gas Co. [*NYSE symbol*] [*Delisted*] .... FLG
Florida Geological Survey. Annual Report [*A publication*] .... Fla G S An Rp
Florida Geological Survey. Geological Bulletin [*A publication*] .... Fla Geol Surv Geol Bull
Florida Geological Survey. Information Circular [*A publication*] .... Fla Geol Surv Inf Circ
Florida Geological Survey. Information Circular [*A publication*] .... Fla Geol Surv Inform Circ
Florida Geological Survey. Report of Investigations [*A publication*] .... Fla Geol Surv Rep Invest
Florida Gift Fruit Shippers Association .... FGFSA
Florida Glass Industries [*NASDAQ symbol*] .... FGLS
Florida Group [*Navy*] .... FLAGRP
Florida Gulf Realty Trust [*NASDAQ symbol*] .... FGLFS
Florida Historical Quarterly [*A publication*] .... FHQ
Florida Historical Quarterly [*A publication*] .... Fla Hist Q
Florida Historical Quarterly [*A publication*] .... Fla Hist Quar
Florida Historical Society. Quarterly [*A publication*] .... Fla His S
Florida Historical Society, University of South Florida, Tampa, FL [*Library symbol*] .... FHi
Florida Industries Exposition .... FIE
Florida Institute of Oceanography .... FIO
Florida Institute of Technology .... FIT
Florida Institute of Technology, Melbourne, FL [*OCLC symbol*] .... FLT
Florida Institute of Technology, Melbourne, FL [*Library symbol*] .... FMeF
Florida Instructional League [*Baseball*] .... FIL
Florida International University .... FIU
Florida International University, Miami, FL [*Library symbol*] .... FMFIU
Florida International University, Miami, FL [*OCLC symbol*] .... FXG

Florida International University, North Campus, North Miami, FL [*OCLC symbol*] ... FXN
Florida Junior College at Jacksonville, DTC, Jacksonville, FL [*OCLC symbol*] ... FJD
Florida Junior College at Jacksonville, Jacksonville, FL [*Library symbol*] ... FJF
Florida Junior College at Jacksonville, Kent, Jacksonville, FL [*OCLC symbol*] ... FJK
Florida Junior College at Jacksonville, North, Jacksonville, FL [*OCLC symbol*] ... FJN
Florida Junior College at Jacksonville, South, Jacksonville, FL [*OCLC symbol*] ... FJS
Florida Libraries [*A publication*] ... Fla Lib
Florida Libraries [*A publication*] ... Fla Libr
Florida Library Information Network [*Library network*] ... FLIN
Florida Lime and Avocado Administrative Committee ... FLAAC
Florida Lychee Growers Association ... FLGA
Florida Mango Forum ... FMF
Florida Marine Aquarium Society ... FMAS
Florida Marine Research Publications [*A publication*] ... Fla Mar Res Publ
Florida Medical Entomology Laboratory, Vero Beach, FL [*Library symbol*] ... FVbF
Florida Memorial College, Miami, FL [*OCLC symbol*] ... FMC
Florida Memorial College, Miami, FL [*Library symbol*] ... FMFM
Florida Missile Test Range ... FMTR
Florida National Banks [*NASDAQ symbol*] ... FNBF
Florida Naturalist [*A publication*] ... Fla Nat
Florida Nurse [*A publication*] ... Fla Nurse
Florida Power & Light Co. [*NYSE symbol*] ... FPL
Florida Presbyterian College [*Later, Eckerd College*] ... FPC
Florida Progress [*Formerly, Florida Power Corporation*] [*NYSE symbol*] ... FPC
Florida Public Utilities [*NASDAQ symbol*] ... FPUT
Florida Quarterly [*A publication*] ... FloQ
Florida Quarterly [*A publication*] ... FlorQ
Florida Quarterly [*A publication*] ... FQ
Florida Rock Industries, Inc. [*American Stock Exchange symbol*] ... FRK
Florida Scientist [*A publication*] ... Fla Sci
Florida Solar Energy Center, Cape Canaveral, FL [*Library symbol*] ... FCaF
Florida Solar Energy Center, Cape Canaveral, FL [*OCLC symbol*] ... FSE
Florida Southern College ... FSC
Florida Southern College, Lakeland, FL [*Library symbol*] ... FLIS
Florida Southern College, Lakeland, FL [*OCLC symbol*] ... FSC
Florida Specialized Carriers Rate Conference, Inc., Jacksonville FL [*STAC*] ... FLS
Florida State Board of Conservation. Biennial Report [*A publication*] ... Fla State Board Conserv Bien Rep
Florida State Hospital, Chattahoochee, FL [*Library symbol*] ... FChH
Florida State League [*Baseball*] ... FSL
Florida State Library, Bureau of Book Processing, Tallahassee, FL [*Library symbol*] ... F-B
Florida State Library, Tallahassee, FL [*Library symbol*] ... F
Florida State Museum. Biological Sciences Bulletin [*A publication*] ... Fla State Mus Biol Sci Bull
Florida State Museum. Bulletin. Biological Sciences [*A publication*] ... Florida State Mus Bull Biol Sci
Florida State Plant Board. Publications [*A publication*] ... Fla State Plant Bd
Florida State University ... FSU
Florida State University, Law Library, Tallahassee, FL [*OCLC symbol*] ... FSL
Florida State University, Law Library, Tallahassee, FL [*Library symbol*] ... FTaSU-L
Florida State University Law Review [*A publication*] ... Fla St U L Rev
Florida State University, School of Library Science, Tallahassee, FL [*OCLC symbol*] ... FLS
Florida State University Slavic Papers [*A publication*] ... FSUSP
Florida State University. Studies [*A publication*] ... Fla State Univ Studies
Florida State University. Studies [*A publication*] ... FSUS
Florida State University, Tallahassee, FL [*OCLC symbol*] ... FDA
Florida State University, Tallahassee, FL [*Library symbol*] ... FTaSU
Florida Steel Corp. [*NYSE symbol*] ... FLS
Florida Supreme Court, Tallahassee, FL [*Library symbol*] ... F-SC
Florida Technological University ... FTU
Florida Technological University, Orlando, FL [*Library symbol*] ... FOFT
Florida Test Center [*NASA*] ... FTC
Florida Test Procedure [*Aerospace*] ... FTP
Florida Tomato Exchange ... FTE
Florida Trail Association ... FTA
Florida Tropical Fish Farms Association ... FTFFA
Florida Tropical Fish Industries ... FTFI
Florida Union List of Serials ... FULS
Florida Union List of Serials, Gainesville, FL [*Library symbol*] ... FGULS
Florida Union List of Serials, Gainesville, FL [*OCLC symbol*] [*Inactive*] ... FUL
Florida. University. Engineering and Industrial Experiment Station. Bulletin [*A publication*] ... Fla Univ Eng Exp Sta Bull
Florida West Coast Nuclear Group ... FWCNG
Florin [*Same as gulden, monetary unit in Netherlands*] ... F
Florin [*Same as gulden, monetary unit in Netherlands*] ... FL
Florissant [*Missouri*] [*Seismograph station code, US Geological Survey*] [*Closed*] ... FLO
Florissant, MO [*Radio station call letters*] ... KCFM
Florists' Exchange [*A publication*] ... Flor Exc
Florists' Review [*A publication*] ... Flor Rev
Florists' Transworld [*formerly, Telegraph*] **Delivery** [*Trademark*] ... FTD
Florists' Transworld [*formerly, Telegraph*] **Delivery Association** ... FTDA
Floro [*Norway*] [*Airport symbol*] ... FRO
Floruit [*He Flourished*] [*Latin*] ... FL
Floruit [*He Flourished*] [*Latin*] ... FLOR
Flossing, Brushing, and Irrigation [*Dentistry*] ... FBI
Flossmoor, IL [*Radio station call letters*] ... WHFH
Flossmoor Public Library, Flossmoor, IL [*Library symbol*] ... IFlo
Flota Aerea Mercane Argentina ... FAMA
Flotation ... FLOT
Flotilla ... FLOT
Flotilla Leader [*British*] ... FL
Flour Millers Export Association ... FMEA
Flourished ... FL
Flow [*of blood*] [*Medicine*] ... F
Flow ... FL
Flow Analysis Program [*Data processing*] ... FLAP
Flow Block ... FB
Flow Block Diagram ... FBD
Flow Coating ... FC
Flow Control Time of Arrival [*Aviation*] ... FCTA
Flow Control Valve ... FCV
Flow Cytometry [*Analytical biochemistry*] ... FCM
Flow-Diversion Valve ... FDV
Flow Gauge ... FG
Flow General, Inc. [*NYSE symbol*] ... FGN
Flow of Gold ... FOG
Flow Indicator ... FI
Flow Injection Analyzer [*Chemical analyses*] ... FIA
Flow Line [*Technical drawings*] ... FL
Flow Line ... FLL
Flow Measurement and Indication ... FMI
Flow Measuring System ... FMS
Flow Meter ... FL/MTR
Flow Meter ... FM
Flow Microfluorometer [*Instrumentation*] ... FMF
Flow Path Selector Valve ... FPSV
Flow Proportioning Value ... FPV
Flow Rate ... FLR
Flow Rate ... FL/RT
Flow Recorder ... FR
Flow Recorder Controller ... FRC
Flow Recording Transmitter ... FRT
Flow Switch ... FLS
Flow Switch ... FLSW
Flow Switch ... FS
Flow System, Inc. [*NASDAQ symbol*] ... FLOW
Flow and Temperature Removable Instrument Assembly [*Nuclear energy*] ... FTRIA
Flow-Through Tube Sampler [*Nuclear energy*] ... FTTS
Flow Totalizer ... FL/TOT
Flow Volume Loop [*Hemodialysis*] ... FVL
Flowcharting FORTRAN [*Data processing*] ... FLOTRAN
Flower ... F
Flower ... FLWR
Flower Essence Society ... FES
Flower Grower [*A publication*] ... Flower Grow
Flower Time, Inc. [*NASDAQ symbol*] ... FLWR
Flowering Plants of Africa [*A publication*] ... Flowering Plants Afr
Flowers Industries, Inc. [*American Stock Exchange symbol*] ... FLO
Flowers' Roguish Cultivator ... FRC
Flowing Gas Detonation Tube ... FDT
Flowing Gas Stream ... FGS
Flowmeter Calibration Stand ... FCS
Flowmeter Ordering and Indicating Unit ... FOIU
Flown ... FLN
Floyd Satellite Communications Terminal ... FSCT
Floydada, TX [*Radio station call letters*] ... KFBA
Fluctuate ... FLUC
Fluctuation ... FLCTN
Flue-Cured Tobacco Cooperative Stabilization Corporation ... FCTCSC
Flue-Cured Tobacco Growers Association ... FCTGA
Flue-Gas Desulfurization ... FGD
Flue-Gas Treatment ... FGT
Flugbetriebstoff-Kesselkraftwagen ... FBKKW
Flugfelag Islands H.F. [*Iceland Airways Ltd.*] ... FLUG
Flugzeug [*Airplane*] [*German military*] ... F
Fluid ... F
Fluid ... FL
Fluid ... FLD
Fluid Amplifier Control Engine Test ... FACET
Fluid Amplifier Control System ... FACS
Fluid Apparecchiature Idrauliche e Pneumatiche [*A publication*] ... Fluid Apparecch Idraul & Pneum
Fluid Catalytic Cracking [*Fuel technology*] ... FCC
Fluid Catalytic Cracking Unit [*Fuel technology*] ... FCCU
Fluid Checkout Unit ... FCU
Fluid Conductivity Indicator ... FCI

Fluid Controls Institute ... FCI
Fluid Controls Institute. FCI Standards [*A publication*] ... Fluid Contr Inst FCI Stand
Fluid Convection Cathode ... FCC
Fluid Corp. [*NASDAQ symbol*] ... FLUD
Fluid Digital Computer ... FDC
Fluid Distribution System ... FDS
Fluid Distribution Unit ... FDU
Fluid Dram ... FLDR
Fluid Dynamics [*A publication*] ... Fluid Dyn
Fluid Dynamics Research Group [*MIT*] ... FDRG
Fluid Dynamics Research Laboratory [*MIT*] ... FDRL
Fluid Dynamics. Transactions [*A publication*] ... Fluid Dyn Trans
Fluid to Electric Switch ... FES
Fluid Extract [*Pharmacy*] ... FE
Fluid Film Bearing ... FFB
Fluid Flow ... FDFL
Fluid Flow Indicator ... FFI
Fluid Inject Valve Actuator ... FIVA
Fluid Jet Amplifier ... FJA
Fluid Levitation Accelerometer ... FLA
Fluid Logic Industrial Control Relay ... FLICR
Fluid Mechanical ... FLMECH
Fluid Mechanics Laboratory [*MIT*] ... FML
Fluid Mechanics. Soviet Research [*A publication*] ... Fluid Mech Sov Res
Fluid Metering, Incorporated ... FMI
Fluid Modeling Facility [*Environmental Protection Agency*] ... FMF
Fluid Motion Panel [*of the British Aeronautical Research Council*] ... FMP
Fluid-Operated Digital Automatic Computer ... FLODAC
Fluid Ounce ... F
Fluid Ounce ... FLOZ
Fluid Phase Equilibria [*A publication*] ... Fluid Phase Equilib
Fluid Phase Equilibria [*Netherlands*] [*A publication*] ... Fluid Phase Equilibria
Fluid Power Distributors Association ... FPDA
Fluid Power International [*A publication*] ... Fluid Power Int
Fluid Power International [*A publication*] ... Fluid Pwr Int
Fluid Power Society ... FPS
Fluid Power Supply ... FPS
Fluid Power System ... FPS
Fluid Pressure Line ... FDPL
Fluid Properties Research, Inc. ... FPR
Fluid Purification System ... FPS
Fluid Rate Damper ... FRD
Fluid Resistant ... FR
Fluid Sealing Association ... FSA
Fluid Shaft Encoder ... FSE
Fluid Storage Container ... FSC
Fluid Supply System ... FSS
Fluid Switch ... FS
Fluid Thioglycolate [*Medium*] [*Microbiology*] ... FTG
Fluid Thioglycolate Medium [*Microbiology*] ... FTM
Fluid Transpiration Arc ... FTA
Fluid Vacancy Model ... FVM
Fluid Velocity Potential ... FVP
Fluid Volume Measurement System ... FVMS
Fluidextractum [*Fluidextract*] [*Pharmacy*] ... FLDEXT
Fluidextractum [*Fluidextract*] [*Pharmacy*] ... FLDXT
Fluidic Emergency Thruster [*Aviation*] ... FET
Fluidic Environmental Sensor ... FES
Fluidic Logic Module ... FLM
Fluidic Output Device ... FOD
Fluidic Proportional Thruster ... FPT
Fluidic Setting Device ... FSD
Fluidic Stability Augmentation System [*for helicopters*] ... FSAS
Fluidic Valve Operator ... FVO
Fluidics Inertial Bomb ... FIB
Fluidics Quarterly [*A publication*] ... Fluid Q
Fluidized Bed ... FB
Fluidized-Bed Combustion ... FBC
Fluidized-Bed Film Reactor [*For water purification*] ... FBFR
Fluidized-Bed Gasifier [*Coal gasification*] ... FBG
Fluidized-Bed Process ... FBP
Fluidized-Bed Reactor ... FBR
Fluidus [*Fluid*] [*Pharmacy*] ... FL
Fluidyne Engineering Corporation ... FDEC
Fluke [*John*] **Manufacturing Co., Inc.** [*American Stock Exchange symbol*] ... FKM
Fluked [*Naval architecture*] ... FLKD
Fluor Chrome Arsenate Phenol [*Wood preservative*] ... FCAP
Fluor Corp. Ltd. [*NYSE symbol*] ... FLR
Fluor Engineers & Constructors, Fluor Houston Library, Houston, TX [*Library symbol*] ... TxHFE
Fluor Ocean Services, Engineering Library, Houston, TX [*Library symbol*] ... TxHFO
Fluorenamine [*Also, AF*] [*Carcinogen*] ... FA
Fluorene [*Biochemistry*] ... Fln
Fluorenylacetamide [*Also, AAF, AcNHFln*] [*Organic chemistry*] ... FAA
Fluorenylmethyloxycarbonyl [*Organic chemistry*] ... FMOC
Fluorescamine [*Biochemical analysis*] [*Acronym is trademark of Roche Diagnostics*] ... FLURAM
Fluorescein Diacetate [*Organic chemistry*] ... FDA
Fluorescein Isothiocyanate [*Organic chemistry*] ... FITC
Fluorescein Isothiocyanate Conjugated Goat Antiserum to Rabbit Gamma Globulin [*Immunology*] ... FITC-gARGG
Fluorescein-Labeled Serum Protein [*Clinical chemistry*] ... FLSP
Fluorescein Mercury Acetate [*Analytical chemistry*] ... FMA
Fluorescein Thiourea [*Organic chemistry*] ... FTU
Fluorescence ... FL
Fluorescence-Activated Cell Sorter [*Becton, Dickinson Electronics Laboratory*] [*Instrumentation*] ... FACS
Fluorescence Correlation Spectroscopy ... FCS
Fluorescence Detection [*Spectrometry*] ... FD
Fluorescence plus Giemsa [*Cell-staining technique*] ... FPG
Fluorescence Microphotolysis ... FM
Fluorescence Photobleaching Recovery ... FPR
Fluorescence Recovery [*or Redistribution*] **After Photobleaching** ... FRAP
Fluorescent [*Freight*] ... FLORSENT
Fluorescent [*or Fluoresces or Fluorescence*] ... FLUOR
Fluorescent Antibody [*Clinical chemistry*] ... FA
Fluorescent Antibody Staining Technique [*Clinical chemistry*] ... FAST
Fluorescent Antibody Test [*Clinical medicine*] ... FAT
Fluorescent Antinuclear Antibody Test [*Serology*] ... FANA
Fluorescent Immunoassay [*Analytical biochemistry*] ... FIA
Fluorescent Lighting Association ... FLA
Fluorescent Mineral Society. Journal [*A publication*] ... Fluoresc Miner Soc J
Fluorescent Particle ... FP
Fluorescent Penetrant Inspection ... FPI
Fluorescent Rabies Antibody [*Immunology*] ... FRA
Fluorescent Runway Lighting ... FLORL
Fluorescent Target ... FT
Fluorescent Treponemal Antibody [*Clinical chemistry*] ... FTA
Fluorescent Treponemal Antibody - Absorption [*Test for syphilis*] ... FTA-ABS
Fluorescent Treponemal Antibody Test [*for syphilis*] ... FTAT
Fluorescent Whitening Agent [*Detergent*] ... FWA
Fluoride Quarterly Reports [*A publication*] ... Fluoride Q Rep
Fluorimetric Determination of Plasma Cortisol [*Clinical chemistry*] ... FDPC
Fluorinated Ethylene-Propylene [*Copolymer*] ... FEP
Fluorine [*Chemical element*] ... F
Fluorine-Liquid Oxygen ... FLOX
Fluorine One-Stage Orbital Space Truck ... FLOSOST
Fluorite [*CIPW classification*] [*Geology*] ... fr
Fluoro [*As substituent on nucleoside*] [*Biochemistry*] ... fl
Fluoroalanine [*Organic chemistry*] ... FA
Fluorocarbon Co. [*NASDAQ symbol*] ... FCBN
Fluorocarbons Technical Panel [*of Manufacturing Chemists Association*] ... FTP
Fluorochlorocarbon [*Organic chemistry*] ... FCC
Fluorocytosine [*Antifungal compound*] ... FC
Fluorocytosine Arabinoside [*Also, ara-FC*] [*Antitumor compound*] ... FCA
Fluorodeoxyglucose [*Organic chemistry*] ... FDG
Fluorodeoxyuridine [*Floxuridine*] [*Also, FUDR*] [*Antineoplastic drug*] ... FldUrd
Fluorodeoxyuridine [*Floxuridine*] [*Also, FldUrd*] [*Antineoplastic drug*] ... FUDR
Fluorodinitrobenzene [*Also, DFB, DNFB*] [*Organic chemistry*] ... FDNB
Fluorogenic Drug Reagent [*Clinical chemistry*] ... FDR
Fluoroiodoarabinosylcytosine ... FIAC
Fluoro(methyl)arabinosyluracil [*Biochemistry*] ... FMAU
Fluoroorotate [*Organic chemistry*] ... FO
Fluorophenylalanine [*Biochemistry*] ... FPA
Fluoropolymers [*Organic chemistry*] ... FP
Fluoroscopy ... FLUOR
Fluorouracil [*Also, FU*] [*Antineoplastic drug*] ... F
Fluorouracil [*Also, F*] [*Antineoplastic drug*] ... FU
Fluorouracil, Adriamycin, Cyclophosphamide [*Antineoplastic drug regimen*] ... FAC
Fluorouracil, Adriamycin (Doxorubicin), Mitomycin C, and Streptozotocin [*Antineoplastic drug regimen*] ... FAM-S
Fluorouracil, Adriamycin, Mitomycin [*Antineoplastic drug regimen*] ... FAM
Flurazepam [*Organic chemistry*] ... FZ
Flurry [*Meteorology*] ... FLRY
Flush ... FL
Flush Armor Balance Watertight Hatch ... FABWH
Flush Door Fastener ... FDF
Flush Joint [*Diamond drilling*] ... FJ
Flush Metal Threshold [*Technical drawings*] ... FMT
Flush Mount ... FLMT
Flush Oiltight Ventilation Hole ... FLOVTH
Flush Oiltight Ventilation Hole ... FOVH
Flush Threshold [*Technical drawings*] ... FT
Flush Type ... FLTP
Flush Valve [*Technical drawings*] ... FV
Flute Lead ... FL
Fluted ... FLTD
Fluted Socket ... FLUSOC
Fluted Socket Head ... FLUSOCH
Flutter ... FLUT
Flutter Exciter Control Unit ... FECU
Flutter and Matrix Algebra System [*Data processing*] ... FAMAS
Flutter Mode Control [*Aviation*] ... FMC
Flutter Speed Index [*Aerodynamics*] ... FSI

Flutter and Strength Optimization Program for Lifting Surface Structures ... FASTOP
Flutter Suppression System [*Aviation*] ... FSS
Flux [*Symbol*] [*IUPAC*] ... J
Flux Changes per Inch [*Data processing*] ... FCPI
Flux-Corrected Transport [*Algorithm*] ... FCT
Flux Current Loop ... FCL
Flux Logic Element Array ... FLEA
Flux Monitoring System [*Nuclear energy*] ... FMS
Flux Sensitive Resistor ... FSR
Flux Switch Alternator ... FSA
Flux Transfer Event [*Planetary physics*] ... FTE
Flux Valve ... FV
Fluxgate Magnetometer ... FGM
Fluxgate Magnetometer ... FMAG
Flxible Historic Association ... FHA
Fly-Along Infrared Program [*Army*] ... FAIR
Fly America's Supersonic Transport [*Student group*] ... FASST
Fly-Away Kit ... FAK
Fly Before You Buy [*Aerospace industry slogan*] ... FBYB
Fly without Fear [*An association*] ... FWF
Fly as Is ... FAI
Fly-to-Point ... FTP
Fly by Wire ... FBW
Flyable Engineering Model ... FEM
Flyable Orbital Vehicle ... FOV
Flyaway Factory ... FAF
Flyer Coil Winder ... FCW
Flygtekniska Forsoksanstalten [*Sweden*] ... FFA
Flygtekniska Forsoksanstalten, Meddelande [*A publication*] ... Flygtek Forsoksanst Medd
Flying ... FLG
Flying ... FLY
Flying [*A publication*] ... Fly
Flying Activity Category ... FAC
Flying Boat ... FB
Flying Boat [*Russian aircraft symbol*] ... GST
Flying Boat [*Russian aircraft symbol*] ... N
Flying Boat Alighting Area ... FBAA
Flying Chiropractors Association ... FCA
Flying Colonels [*Delta Air Lines' club for frequent flyers*] ... FC
Flying Control Officer [*Navy*] ... FCO
Flying-Deck Cruiser [*Navy symbol*] ... CF
Flying Dentists Association ... FDA
Flying Diamond Oil Corporation [*American Stock Exchange symbol*] [*Delisted*] ... FDC
Flying Division Air Training Command ... FDATC
Flying Evaluation Board ... FEB
Flying Fifteen International ... FFI
Flying Funeral Directors of America ... FFDA
Flying Hour ... FH
Flying Hour Program [*Army*] ... FHP
Flying Lunar Excursion Experimental Platform [*NASA*] ... FLEEP
Flying Officer [*British*] ... FO
Flying Optometrists Association of America ... FOAA
Flying Personnel Research Committee [*British*] ... FPRC
Flying Pharmacists of America ... FPA
Flying Physicians Association ... FPA
Flying Psychologists ... FP
Flying Relay Station ... FRS
Flying Runway Heading [*Aviation*] ... FRH
Flying Safety Officer [*Air Force*] ... FSO
Flying Saucers from Other Worlds [*A publication*] ... FSO
Flying Scot Sailing Association ... FSSA
Flying Senior Citizens of USA ... FSCUSA
Flying Spot Digitizer ... FSD
Flying Spot Scanner ... FSS
Flying Squadron ... FSq
Flying Status ... FS
Flying Status Code ... FSC
Flying Thread Loom ... FTL
Flying Tiger Corp. [*Later, TGR*] [*NYSE symbol*] ... FLY
Flying Tiger Line, Inc. [*ICAO designator*] ... FT
Flying Tiger Line, Inc. ... FTL
Flying Tiger Line, Inc. [*Air carrier designation symbol*] ... FTLX
Flying Training Air Force ... FLYTAF
Flying Training Air Force ... FTAF
Flying Training Command [*Air Force*] ... FTC
Flying Training School ... FTS
Flying Training Student Management System [*Air Force*] ... FTSMS
Flying Veterinarians Association ... FVA
Flying Wheel Casting [*Metallurgy*] ... FWC
Flyweight ... FLYWT
Flywheel ... FLYWHL
Flywheel Energy Storage System ... FESS
FM Broadcasting Station [*ITU designation*] ... BCF
FM Development Association [*Later, NRBA*] ... FMDA
FMC Corp. [*Formerly, Food Machinery Corporation*] [*NYSE symbol*] ... FMC
FMC Corp., Niagara Chemical Division, R and D Library, Middleport, NY [*Library symbol*] ... NMidpF
FMC Corp., Princeton, NJ [*OCLC symbol*] ... FMN
FMC Corp., Princeton, NJ [*Library symbol*] ... NjPF
FMC Corp., Santa Clara, CA [*Library symbol*] ... CStclF
FMG Telecomputer Ltd. [*NASDAQ symbol*] ... FMGTF
FMI Financial Corp. NQ ... FMIF
FOA [*Foersvarets Forskningsanstalt*] **Reports** [*A publication*] ... FOA Rep
Foam Laminators Association ... FLA
Foam Liquid ... FOLQ
Foam Stability Test ... FST
Foam in System ... FIS
Foam Tape ... FT
FOB Airport [*"INCOTERM," International Chamber of Commerce official code*] ... FOA
Focal ... FOC
Focal Diameter ... FD
Focal Distance ... FD
Focal Glomerulosclerosis [*Medicine*] ... FGS
Focal Length [*Photography*] ... F
Focal Length [*Photography*] ... FL
Focal Plane [*Photography*] ... FP
Focal-Plane Array ... FPA
Focal Proliferative Glomerulonephritis [*Medicine*] ... FPGN
Focal Region Investigation ... FRI
Focal Segmental Glomerulosclerosis [*Nephrology*] ... FSGS
Focke-Wulf [*A German fighter plane*] ... FW
Focolare Movement ... FM
Focsani [*Romania*] [*Seismograph station code, US Geological Survey*] ... FOC
Focus ... FOC
Focus on Arms Information and Reassurance ... FAIR
Focus on Exceptional Children [*A publication*] ... Foc Exc Chi
Focus on Exceptional Children [*A publication*] ... Focus Excep Child
Focus on Film [*A publication*] ... Foc F
Focus on Film [*A publication*] ... Focus on F
Focus-Forming Unit [*Medical/biochemical research*] ... FFU
Focus on Indiana Libraries [*A publication*] ... Focus
Focus on Indiana Libraries [*A publication*] ... Focus Indiana Libr
Focus-Inducing Cell [*Population*] [*Immunochemistry*] ... FIC
Focus on Mental Health [*Quezon City*] [*A publication*] ... FMH
Focus on Micronesia Coalition ... FMC
Focus/Midwest [*A publication*] ... Foc
Focus/Midwest [*A publication*] ... Focus
Focus Projection and Scanning ... FPS
Focused Ultrasonic Surgery ... FUS
Focusing ... FCSG
Focusing Array Study ... FAS
Focusing Mount [*Photography*] ... FM
Foederalistische Union Europaeischer Volksgruppen [*Federal Union of European Nationalities*] ... FUEV
Foeldrajzi Ertesito [*A publication*] ... Foeldrajzi Ertes
Foeldrajzi Ertesito [*A publication*] ... Foldrajzi Ertes
Foeldrajzi Koezlemenyek [*A publication*] ... Foeldrajzi Koezl
Foeldtani Koezlony [*A publication*] ... Foeldt Koezl
Foeldtani Kutatas [*A publication*] ... Foeldt Kut
Foersoeks- och Demonstrationsskolan [*Sweden*] ... FOD
Fog [*Meteorology*] ... F
Fog ... FG
Fog Bell [*Navigation charts*] ... FB
Fog Detector Light [*Nautical charts*] ... Fog Det Lt
Fog Diaphone [*Navigation charts*] ... FD
Fog Dispersal Operations [*Aviation code*] ... DENEB
Fog Factor ... FF
Fog Foam ... FOFM
Fog Gong [*Navigation charts*] ... FG
Fog Gun [*Navigation charts*] ... FG
Fog Horn [*Navigation charts*] ... FH
Fog, Intense, Dispersal Of [*NASA*] ... FIDO
Fog Investigation and Dispersal Operation [*System used on airfield landing strips*] [*World War II*] ... FIDO
Fog Nautophone [*Navigation charts*] ... FN
Fog Oil Smoke Generator ... FOSGEN
Fog Patches [*Aviation code*] ... BCFG
Fog Signal [*Station*] [*Maps and charts*] ... FS
Fog Signal Station [*Nautical charts*] ... FOGSIG
Fog Signal Station [*Coast Guard*] ... FSS
Fog Siren [*Navigation charts*] ... FS
Fog Trumpet [*Navigation charts*] ... FT
Fog Whistle [*Navigation charts*] ... FW
Fogarty International Center [*of National Institutes of Health*] ... FIC
Fogg Art Museum. Bulletin [*Harvard University*] [*A publication*] ... Fogg Mus Bul
Fogorvosi Szemle [*A publication*] ... Fogorv Sz
Foil [*Dentistry*] ... F
Foil Research Supercavitating Hydrofoil ... FRESH
Foil Wound Coil ... FWC
Foilborne Water Line ... FWL
Foilseachain Naisiunta Tta [*A publication*] ... FNT
Folclor Leterar [*A publication*] ... FolcL
Fold ... FD
Foldable Elastic Tube [*Satellite hinge*] ... FET
Foldback [*Genetics*] ... FB
Folded Dipole Antenna ... FDA

Folded File ... FF
Folded Flat [*Freight*] ... FF
Folded Flat or Nested [*Freight*] ... FFN
Folded Flow Reactor ... FFR
Folded and Gathered [*Printing*] ... F & G
Folded Other Than Flat [*Freight*] ... FOTF
Folded Sideband Modulation ... FSM
Folded, Trimmed, Packed [*Books*] ... FTP
Folder. Montana State College. Cooperative Extension Service [*A publication*] ... Folder Mont State Coll Coop Ext
Folder. University of Missouri. College of Agriculture. Extension Service [*A publication*] ... Folder Univ MO Coll Agr Ext Serv
Folding ... FG
Folding ... FLDG
Folding Chair Rental Association of America [*Later, RSA*] ... FCRAA
Folding-Fin Aerial Rocket ... FFAR
Folding-Fin Aircraft [*Rocket*] ... FFA
Folding Map [*Publishing*] ... FLDGM
Folding Paper Box Association of America [*Later, PPC*] ... FPBAA
Foldout ... FO
Foldtani Kozlony [*A publication*] ... Foldt Kozl
Foley, AL [*Radio station call letters*] ... WHEP
Foley Catheter [*Urology*] ... FC
Foley Catheter [*Medicine*] ... Fcath
Folger Documents of Tudor and Stuart Civilization [*A publication*] ... FDTSC
Folger Shakespeare Library, Washington, DC [*Library symbol*] ... DFo
Folha Medica [*A publication*] ... Folha Med
Folha Medica (Rio De Janeiro) [*A publication*] ... Folha Med (Rio De Janeiro)
Folhetas de Divulgacao. Servicos Florestais e Aquicolas (Portugal) [*A publication*] ... Folh Divulg Serv Flor Aquic (Portugal)
Folia [*Leaves*] ... FOL
Folia Allergologica [*A publication*] ... Folia Allergol
Folia Allergologica et Immunologica Clinica [*A publication*] ... Folia Allergol Immunol Clin
Folia Anatomica Japonica [*A publication*] ... Folia Anat Jpn
Folia Anatomica Universitatis Conimbrigensis (Coimbra) [*A publication*] ... Folia Anat Univ Conimbrigensis (Coimbra)
Folia Archaeologica [*Budapest*] [*A publication*] ... Folia Archaeol
Folia Archeologica [*Lodz*] [*A publication*] ... Folia Arch
Folia Biochimica et Biologica Graeca [*A publication*] ... Folia Biochim Biol Graeca
Folia Biologica [*A publication*] ... Fol Biol
Folia Biologica [*A publication*] ... Folia Biol
Folia Biologica (Cracow) [*A publication*] ... Folia Biol (Cracow)
Folia Biologica (Prague) [*A publication*] ... Folia Biol (Prague)
Folia Biologica (Praha) [*A publication*] ... Folia Biol (Praha)
Folia Cardiologica [*A publication*] ... Folia Cardiol
Folia Clinica et Biologica [*A publication*] ... Folia Clin Biol
Folia Clinica et Biologica. Nova Serie [*A publication*] ... Folia Clin Biol Nova Ser
Folia Clinica Internacional [*A publication*] ... FOCIA
Folia Clinica Internacional [*A publication*] ... Folia Clin Int
Folia Clinica Internacional (Barcelona) [*A publication*] ... Folia Clin Int (Barc)
Folia Endocrinologica [*A publication*] ... Folia Endocrinol
Folia Endocrinologica Japonica [*A publication*] ... Folia Endocrinol Jpn
Folia Endocrinologica (Pisa) [*A publication*] ... Folia Endocrinol (Pisa)
Folia Endocrinologica (Rome) [*A publication*] ... Folia Endocrinol (Rome)
Folia Entomologica Hungarica [*A publication*] ... Folia Entomol Hung
Folia Entomologica Mexicana [*A publication*] ... Folia Entomol Mex
Folia Facultatis Medicae [*A publication*] ... Folia Fac Med
Folia Facultatis Medicae. Universitatis Comenianae. Bratislaviensis [*A publication*] ... Folia Fac Med Univ Comenianae Bratisl
Folia Forestalia (Helsinki) [*A publication*] ... Folia For (Helsinki)
Folia Forestalia Instituti Forestalis Fenniae [*A publication*] ... Folia For Inst For Fenn
Folia Forestalia Polonica. Seria A (Lesnictwo) [*A publication*] ... Folia For Polon (Lesn)
Folia Forestalia Polonica. Seria A (Lesnictwo) [*A publication*] ... Folia For Pol Ser A (Lesn)
Folia Forestalia Polonica. Seria B (Drzewnictwo) [*A publication*] ... Folia For Polon (Drzewn)
Folia Forestalia Polonica. Seria B (Drzewnictwo) [*A publication*] ... Folia For Pol Ser B (Drzewnictwo)
Folia Geobotanica et Phytotaxonomica [*A publication*] ... Folia Geobot Phytotaxon
Folia Gynaecologica (Pavia) [*A publication*] ... Folia Gynaec (Pavia)
Folia Haematologica (Leipzig) [*A publication*] ... Folia Haematol (Leipz)
Folia Hereditaria et Pathologica [*A publication*] ... Folia Hered Pathol
Folia Histochemica et Cytochemica [*A publication*] ... Fol Hist Cy
Folia Histochemica et Cytochemica [*A publication*] ... Folia Histochem Cytochem
Folia Histochemica et Cytochemica (Krakow) [*A publication*] ... Folia Histochem Cytochem (Krakow)
Folia Humanistica [*A publication*] ... Fol Humanis
Folia Limnologica Scandinavica [*A publication*] ... Folia Limnol Scand
Folia Linguistica [*A publication*] ... FLin
Folia Linguistica [*A publication*] ... Fo Li
Folia Linguistica [*A publication*] ... Fol Ling
Folia Medica [*A publication*] ... FOMDA
Folia Medica Bialostocensia [*A publication*] ... Folia Med Bialostocensia
Folia Medica Cracoviensia [*A publication*] ... Folia Med Cracov
Folia Medica Facultatis. Medicinae Universitatis Saraeviensis [*A publication*] ... Folia Med Fac Med Univ Saraev
Folia Medica Lodziensia [*A publication*] ... Folia Med Lodz
Folia Medica (Naples) [*A publication*] ... Folia Med (Naples)
Folia Medica Neerlandica [*A publication*] ... Folia Med Neerl
Folia Medica (Plovdiv) [*A publication*] ... Folia Med (Plovdiv)
Folia Microbiologica [*A publication*] ... Folia Microbiol
Folia Microbiologica [*A publication*] ... Fol Microb
Folia Microbiologica (Prague) [*A publication*] ... Folia Microbiol (Prague)
Folia Morphologica (Prague) [*A publication*] ... Folia Morphol (Prague)
Folia Morphologica (Praha) [*A publication*] ... Folia Morphol (Praha)
Folia Morphologica (Warsaw) [*A publication*] ... Folia Morphol (Warsaw)
Folia Neuropsiquiatrica del Sur y Este de Espana [*A publication*] ... Folia Neuropsiquiatr Sur Este Esp
Folia Oeconomica Cracoviensia [*A publication*] ... Fol Oecon Cracov
Folia Ophthalmologica Japonica [*A publication*] ... Folia Ophthalmol Jpn
Folia Orientalia [*A publication*] ... FO
Folia Orientalia [*A publication*] ... Folia O
Folia Orientalia [*A publication*] ... Fol Or
Folia Parasitologica (Prague) [*A publication*] ... Folia Parasitol (Prague)
Folia Pharmaceutica (Istanbul) [*A publication*] ... Folia Pharm (Istanbul)
Folia Pharmacologica Japonica [*A publication*] ... Folia Pharmacol Jpn
Folia Pharmacologica Japonica [*A publication*] ... Fol Pharm J
Folia Phoniatrica [*A publication*] ... Folia Phoniatr
Folia Phoniatrica [*A publication*] ... Fol Phoniat
Folia Phoniatrica [*A publication*] ... FOPHA
Folia Phoniatrica [*A publication*] ... F Phon
Folia Phoniatrica (Basel) [*A publication*] ... Folia Phoniatr (Basel)
Folia Primatologica [*A publication*] ... Folia Primat
Folia Primatologica [*A publication*] ... Folia Primatol
Folia Primatologica [*A publication*] ... Fol Primat
Folia Psychiatrica et Neurologica Japonica [*A publication*] ... Folia Psychiatr Neurol Jpn
Folia Quaternaria [*A publication*] ... Folia Quat
Folia Societatis Scientiarum Lublinensis [*A publication*] ... Folia Soc Sci Lublinensis
Folia Universitaria Cochabamba [*A publication*] ... Folia Univ Cochabamba
Folia Veterinaria [*A publication*] ... Folia Vet
Folia Veterinaria Latina [*A publication*] ... Folia Vet Lat
Folia Veterinaria (Prague) [*A publication*] ... Folia Vet (Prague)
Folia Zoologica [*A publication*] ... Folia Zool
Foliage Penetration [*RADAR*] ... FOPEN
Foliage Penetration RADAR ... FPR
Foliage Penetration System [*Military*] ... FOLPES
Folic Acid [*Also, PGA, PteGlu*] [*Biochemistry*] ... FA
Folicular Basal Lamina [*Medicine*] ... FBL
Foligno [*Italy*] [*Seismograph station code, US Geological Survey*] [*Closed*] ... FOL
Folin-Ciocalteau [*Clinical chemistry*] ... FC
Folin-Denis [*Analytical chemistry*] ... FD
Folio [*A publication*] ... F
Folio ... FO
Folio ... FOL
Folio [*Book 30 centimeters and over in height*] ... F
Folio Recto [*Right-Hand Page*] [*Latin*] ... FR
Folio Verso [*On the back of the page*] ... FV
Folios [*Leaves*] ... FF
Folk Dance Guide [*A publication*] ... FDG
Folk Harp Journal [*A publication*] ... Folk Harp J
Folk Heritage Institute ... FHI
Folk og Kultur [*A publication*] ... F o K
Folk Life [*Cardiff*] [*A publication*] ... FoL
Folk-Liv [*A publication*] ... FLiv
Folk-Lore Journal [*A publication*] ... Folk-Lore J
Folk Music Journal [*A publication*] ... FMJ
Folk Music Journal [*A publication*] ... Folk Mus J
Folklore [*A publication*] ... FF
Folklore [*A publication*] ... FL
Folklore [*A publication*] ... Fo
Folklore [*A publication*] ... Folk
Folklore Americano [*A publication*] ... FA
Folklore Americano [*A publication*] ... FAm
Folklore Americano; Organo del Comite Interamericano de Folklore [*A publication*] ... FACI
Folklore Americas [*A publication*] ... FA
Folklore Americas [*A publication*] ... FAm
Folklore. Boletin del Departmento de Folklore del Instituto de Cooperacion Universitaria [*A publication*] ... FICU
Folklore Brabancon [*A publication*] ... FB
Folklore Brabancon [*A publication*] ... F Brab
Folklore (Calcutta) [*A publication*] ... FLC
Folklore (Calcutta) [*A publication*] ... Folklore C
Folklore Fellows Communications [*A publication*] ... FFC
Folklore and Folk Music Archivist [*A publication*] ... FFMA
Folklore and Folk Music Archivist [*A publication*] ... Folk Mus Arch
Folklore Forum [*A publication*] ... FF
Folklore Forum [*A publication*] ... FForum
Folklore Forum. Bibliographic and Special Series [*A publication*] ... FForumB
Folklore Institute. Journal [*A publication*] ... Folk Inst
Folklore Institute. Monograph Series [*A publication*] ... FIMS

Folklore Italiano [*A publication*]....FI
Folklore. Rivista di Tradizioni Popolari (Naples) [*A publication*]....FN
Folklore Studies [*A publication*]....Folkl Stud
Folklore Studies [*A publication*]....FolkS
Folklore Studies [*A publication*]....FS
Folklore Suisse [*A publication*]....Folkl Suisse
Folklore, Tribuna del Pensamiento Peruano [*A publication*]....FTPP
Folkmalsstudier [*A publication*]....FMSt
Folks Restaurants [*NASDAQ symbol*]....FOLK
Folktales of the World [*A publication*]....FW
Folkuniversitetet....FU
Folleto de Divulgacion. Instituto Forestal (Santiago De Chile) [*A publication*]....Foll Divulg Inst For (Chile)
Folletos Tecnicos Forestales. Administracion Nacional de Bosques (Argentina) [*A publication*]....Foll Tec For Adm Nac Bosques (Argent)
Follett, TX [*Location identifier*] [*FAA*]....FTE
Follicle-Stimulating Hormone [*Endocrinology*]....FSH
Follicle-Stimulating Hormone Releasing Factor [*Also, FSH-RF, FSH-RH*] [*Endocrinology*]....FRF
Follicle-Stimulating Hormone Releasing Factor [*Also, FRF, FSH-RH*] [*Endocrinology*]....FSH-RF
Follicle-Stimulating Hormone Releasing Hormone [*Also, FRF, FSH-RF*] [*Endocrinology*]....FSH-RH
Follow....FLW
Follow....FOL
Follow Copy [*Printing*]....FC
Follow-on-Development Test and Evaluation....FD & E
Follow-the-Leader Feedback [*Circuit theory*]....FLF
Follow-On Contract....FOC
Follow-On Evaluation....FOE
Follow-On Evaluation Test....FOET
Follow-On Interceptor [*Military*]....FOI
Follow-On Operational Test....FOOT
Follow-On Operational Test....FOT
Follow-On Parts Production....FOPP
Follow-On Production....FOP
Follow-On Spare Parts Selection List....FOSPSL
Follow-On Spares....FOS
Follow-On Test and Evaluation....FOT & E
Follow Through....F-T
Follow-Up....FLWP
Follow-Up....FOLUP
Follow-Up....FU
Follow-Up Alarm System....FAS
Follow-Up Amplifier....FUA
Follow-Up Error Alarm....FEA
Follow-Up Output....FUO
Follow-Up Report....FUR
Follow-Up Reporting System....FURS
Follow-Up on Supply Action Taken....FUPOSAT
Following [*Pages*] [*Also, FF*]....F
Following [*Pages*] [*Also, F*]....FF
Following....FLG
Following....FLWG
Following....FOLL
Following Amendment Authorized Effective [*Followed by date*]....FAMAE
Following Individual Reported This Station [*Army*]....FIRTS
Following Information Is Submitted [*Army*]....FOLIS
Following Items Not Available....FINA
Following Items Not Available....FOLNOAVAL
Following Landing Numbers [*Shipping*]....FLN
Following Named Airmen....FNA
Following Named Enlisted Men Are Relieved Assignment....FNERAS
Following Named Enlisted Men Organization Indicated....FNEORID
Following Named Enlisted Personnel....FNE
Following Named Individuals....FNI
Following Named Officers....FNO
Following Named Officers and Airmen....FNOA
Following Transmitted as Received....FTAR
Follows....FOLS
Folsom, PA [*Radio station call letters*]....WRSD
Fomento Industrial do Piani, SA....FOMINPI
Fon [*MARC language code*] [*Library of Congress*]....fon
Fonar Corp. [*NASDAQ symbol*]....FONR
Fond Du Lac Public Library, Fond Du Lac, WI [*Library symbol*]....WFon
Fond Du Lac, WI [*Radio station call letters*]....KFIZ
Fond Du Lac, WI [*Radio station call letters*]....WFON
Fonda, Johnstown, & Gloversville Railroad Co. [*AAR code*]....FJG
Fonda Public Library, Fonda, IA [*Library symbol*]....IaFon
Fondation pour l'Assistance Mutuelle en Afrique au Sud du Sahara [*Foundation for Mutual Assistance in Africa South of the Sahara*]....FAMA
Fondation Documentaire Dentaire....FDD
Fondation de l'Enseignement Superieur en Afrique Centrale....FESAC
Fondation Europeenne de la Culture....FEC
Fondation Europeenne pour l'Economie....FEE
Fondation Internationale pour un Autre Developpement [*International Foundation for Development Alternatives - IFDA*]....FIPAD
Fondation Internationale Penale et Penitentiaire [*International Penal and Penitentiary Foundation*] [*See also IPPF*]....FIPP
Fondation Internationale pour la Science [*International Foundation for Science - IFS*]....FIS
Fondation pour la Recherche en Endocrinologie Sexuelle et l'Etude de la Reproduction Humaine....FRESERH
Fondation Universitaire Luxembourgeoise. Serie Notes de Recherche [*A publication*]....Fond Univ Luxemb Ser Notes Rech
Fondazione Universale Hallesint [*Italy*]....FUH
Fonderia Italiana [*A publication*]....Fonderia Ital
Fondest Love and Kisses [*Correspondence*]....FLAK
Fondeur d'Aujourd'hui [*A publication*]....Fondeur
Fondo de Cultura Economica [*Mexico*] [*A publication*]....FCE
Fondren Science Series [*A publication*]....Fondren Sci Ser
Fonds Africain de Developpement [*African Development Fund*]....FAD
Fonds d'Aide et de Cooperation [*Aid and Cooperation Fund*] [*France*]....FAC
Fonds Europeen de Developpement pour les Pays et Territoires d'Outre-Mer [*European Development Fund for Overseas Countries and Territories*]....FEDOM
Fonds Europeen d'Orientation et de Garantie Agricole [*Also known as EAGGF*]....FEOGA
Fonds d'Investissement pour le Developpement Economique et Social [*United Nations*]....FIDES
Fonds Monetaire International [*International Monetary Fund*]....FMI
Fonds des Nations Unies pour l'Enfance [*United Nations Children's Fund*]....FISE
Fonds des Nations Unies pour les Refugies [*United Nations Funds for Refugees*]....FNUR
Fonds d'Orientation et de Regularisation des Marches Agricoles [*French government food agency*]....FORMA
Fonds de Recherches Forestieres de l'Universite Laval. Bulletin [*A publication*]....Fonds Rech For Univ Laval Bull
Fonds de Recherches Forestieres de l'Universite Laval. Contribution [*A publication*]....Fonds Rech For Univ Laval Contrib
Fonds Reine Elisabeth d'Assistance Medicale aux Indigenes [*Queen Elisabeth Funds for Medical Assistance to the Natives*]....FOREAMI
Fondulac District Library, East Peoria, IL [*Library symbol*]....IEp
Fondulac Public Library District, East Peoria, IL [*OCLC symbol*]....IDY
Fonetic English [*for spelling words the way they sound*]....FE
Fonetic English Spelling Association....FESA
Fonetica si Dialectologie [*A publication*]....F & D
Fonetica si Dialectologie [*A publication*]....FD
Fonetica si Dialectologie [*A publication*]....FsD
Font....F
Font Change....FC
Fontaine [*A publication*]....F
Fontaine [*A publication*]....Font
Fontana Aviation, Inc. [*Iron Mountain, MI*] [*FAA designator*]....FON
Fontana, CA [*Television station call letters*]....KTBN-TV
Fontana Public Library, Fontana, WI [*Library symbol*]....WFont
Fontana Regional Library, Bryson City, NC [*Library symbol*]....NcBcF
Fontane Blaetter [*A publication*]....FB
Fontanelle Observer, Fontanelle, IA Later,....IaFontO
Fontbonne College, St. Louis, MO [*OCLC symbol*]....MOF
Fontbonne College, St. Louis, MO [*Library symbol*]....MoSF
Fontes Artis Musicae [*A publication*]....FAM
Fontes Artis Musicae [*A publication*]....Fontes
Food....FD
Food Additive....FA
Food Additive Petition....FAP
Food Additives and Contaminants Committee [*British*]....FACC
Food and Agricultural Legislation [*A publication*]....Food Agric Leg
Food and Agricultural Organization of the United Nations, North American Regional Office, Washington, DC [*Library symbol*]....DFAO
Food and Agriculture....FA
Food and Agriculture Branch [*US Military Government, Germany*]....F & ABR
Food, Agriculture, and Nutrition Inventory [*Federal government*]....FANI
Food and Agriculture Organization [*United Nations*]....FAO
Food and Agriculture Planning Committee [*NATO*]....FAPC
Food Animal Concerns Trust....FACT
Food Awareness Training....FAT
Food and Beverage Trades Department [*of AFL-CIO*]....FBTD
Food from Britain....FFB
Food Business [*A publication*]....Food Bus
Food in Canada [*A publication*]....Food Canad
Food Chemicals Codex [*National Academy of Sciences*] [*A publication*]....FCC
Food Chemistry, Microbiology, Technology [*A publication*]....Food Chem Microbiol Technol
Food, Clothing, Maintenance [*Red Cross*]....FCM
Food Composition Table....FCT
Food and Container Institute....F & CI
Food Containment System....FCS
Food Control Diet....FCD
Food Controller [*British*] [*World War II*]....FC
Food and Cosmetics Toxicology [*A publication*]....Food Cosmet
Food and Cosmetics Toxicology [*A publication*]....Food Cosmet Toxicol
Food Defense Fund....FDF
Food Development [*A publication*]....Food Devel
Food Distribution Administration [*Terminated, 1945*]....FDA

Food Distribution Division [*of AMS, Department of Agriculture*] .... FD
Food Distribution Order .... FDO
Food Distribution Program [*Department of Agriculture*] .... FDP
Food Distribution Research Society .... FDRS
Food, Drink, Tobacco [*Department of Employment*] [*British*] .... FDT
Food and Drug Administration [*HEW*] .... FDA
Food and Drug Administration Medical Library, Rockville, MD [*OCLC symbol*] .... DDF
Food, Drug, and Consumer Product Agency [*Proposed successor to FDA*] [*HEW*] .... FDCPA
Food, Drug, and Cosmetic [*Act*] .... FDC
Food, Drug, Cosmetic Law Journal [*A publication*] .... Food Drug C
Food and Drug Law Institute .... FDLI
Food and Drug Packaging [*A publication*] .... F & D Pkg
Food Education and Service Training .... FEAST
Food and Energy Council .... FEC
Food Engineering [*A publication*] .... Food Eng
Food Engineering Laboratory [*Army*] .... FEL
Food Engineering (New York) [*A publication*] .... Food Eng (NY)
Food Engineering (Philadelphia) [*A publication*] .... Food Eng (Philadelphia)
Food Equipment Manufacturers Association .... FEMA
Food Facilities Consultants Society [*Later, FCSI*] .... FFCS
Food Facilities Engineering Society [*Later, FFCS*] .... FFES
Food Fair, Inc. [*Formerly, Food Fair Stores, Inc.*] [*NYSE symbol*] [*Delisted*] .... FFS
Food Farming and Agriculture. Journal for the Development of Food and Agriculture [*India*] [*A publication*] .... Food Farming Agric
Food Fish Market Review and Outlook [*A publication*] .... Food Fish Mark Rev & Outl
Food Giant Markets, Inc. [*NYSE symbol*] [*Delisted*] .... FGT
Food for the Hungry International .... FHI
Food Industries Journal [*A publication*] .... Food Ind J
Food Industries of South Africa [*A publication*] .... Food Ind S Afr
Food Industries Suppliers Association .... FISA
Food Industry Association Executives .... FIAE
Food Information and Early Warning System [*FAO*] [*United Nations*] .... FIEWS
Food Irradiation Information [*A publication*] .... Food Irradiat Inf
Food Irradiation (Japan) [*A publication*] .... Food Irradiat (Jpn)
Food Irradiation Reactor .... FIR
Food Laboratory [*Army*] .... FL
Food Law Institute [*Later, FDLI*] .... FLI
Food Lion, Inc. Cl A [*NASDAQ symbol*] .... FDLNA
Food Management [*A publication*] .... Food Manage
Food Management Area .... FMA
Food Management Compartment .... FMC
Food Management System [*or Subsystem*] .... FMS
Food Manufacture [*A publication*] .... Fd Mf
Food Manufacture [*A publication*] .... Food Manuf
Food Marketing Institute [*Formerly, NAFC, SMI*] .... FMI
Food Mart, Inc. [*NYSE symbol*] [*Delisted*] .... FMR
Food Merchandisers of America .... FMA
Food Monitor [*A publication*] .... Food Mon
Food and Nutrition [*A publication*] .... FN
Food and Nutrition [*A publication*] .... Food & Nutr
Food and Nutrition [*A publication*] .... Food Nutr
Food and Nutrition Board .... FNB
Food and Nutrition Information and Educational Materials Center [*Department of Agriculture*] .... FNIC
Food and Nutrition (Rome) [*A publication*] .... Food Nutr (Rome)
Food and Nutrition Service [*Department of Agriculture*] .... FNS
Food and Nutritional System [*Military*] .... FANS
Food Packaging Council .... FPC
Food for Peace [*Overseas food donation program*] .... FFP
Food Poisoning [*Medicine*] .... FP
Food for Poland .... FFP
Food Policy [*British*] .... FP
Food Preservation Quarterly [*A publication*] .... Food Preserv Q
Food Prices Review Board .... FPRB
Food Processing (Chicago) [*A publication*] .... Food Process (Chic)
Food Processing Development Irradiator .... FPDI
Food Processing Industry [*A publication*] .... Fd Process Ind
Food Processing Industry [*A publication*] .... Food Proc
Food Processing Machinery and Supplies Association .... FPM & SA
Food Processing and Marketing [*Chicago*] [*A publication*] .... Fd Process Market
Food Processing and Marketing [*Chicago*] [*A publication*] .... Food Processing Mktg
Food Processing and Marketing (Chicago) [*A publication*] .... Food Process Mark (Chic)
Food Processing and Packaging [*A publication*] .... Food Process Packag
Food Processors Institute .... FPI
Food Product Development [*A publication*] .... Food Prod
Food Product Development [*A publication*] .... Food Prod Devel
Food Production [*British*] .... FP
Food Production Administration [*World War II*] .... FPA
Food Protein Council [*Later, SPC*] .... FPC
Food Protein Research and Development Center [*Texas A & M University*] .... FPRDC
Food Ratio .... FR
Food Rationing Order [*British*] .... FRO
Food Research [*A publication*] .... Food Res
Food Research and Action Center .... FRAC
[*The*] **Food Research Institute** [*Agricultural Research Council*] [*British*] .... FRI
Food Research Institute. Studies [*A publication*] .... Food Res Inst Stud
Food Research Institute. Studies (Stanford) [*A publication*] .... Food Res Inst Stud (Stanford)
Food Reserves on Space Trips .... FROST
Food Safety Council [*Defunct*] .... FSC
Food Safety and Inspection Service [*Formerly, FSQS*] [*Department of Agriculture*] .... FSIS
Food Safety and Quality Service [*Later, FSIS*] [*Department of Agriculture*] .... FSQS
Food Sanitation Institute .... FSI
Food Science and Technology. Abstracts [*A publication*] .... Food Sci & Tech Abstr
Food Science and Technology. Abstracts [*A publication*] .... FSTA
Food Science + Technology (Zurich) [*A publication*] .... Food Sci + Technol (Zur)
Food Service Equipment Industry [*Later, FEDA*] .... FSEI
Food Service Executives' Association [*Later, IFSEA*] .... FSEA
Food Service/Lodging .... FS/L
Food Service Marketing [*A publication*] .... Food Serv Mkt
Food Service Marketing [*A publication*] .... Food S Mkt
Food Stamp Program .... FSP
Food Storage Cell .... FSC
Food Supply Board [*Ministry of Food*] [*British*] [*World War II*] .... FSB
Food Surplus Commodities Corporation .... FSCC
Food Technology [*A publication*] .... Food Tech
Food Technology [*A publication*] .... Food Technol
Food Technology in Australia [*A publication*] .... Food Technol Aust
Food Trade Review [*A publication*] .... Fd Trade Rev
Food Tray Association [*Defunct*] .... FTA
Food Tray and Board Association [*Later, SSI*] .... FTBA
Food, Water, and Waste [*NASA*] .... FWW
Food, Water, and Waste Management [*NASA*] .... FWWM
Food, Water, and Waste Management Subsystem [*NASA*] .... FWWMS
Foodarama Supermarkets, Inc. [*American Stock Exchange symbol*] .... FSM
Foodservice Consultants Society International [*Formerly, FFCS, ISFSC*] .... FCSI
Foodservice Equipment Distributors Association [*Formerly, FSEI*] .... FEDA
Foodservice and Lodging Institute .... FLI
Foodservice Organization of Distributors .... FOOD
Foodways National, Inc. [*American Stock Exchange symbol*] [*Delisted*] .... FYN
Fookien Times Yearbook [*Manila*] [*A publication*] .... FTY
Foolproof Auditing and Sale of Tickets [*in motion picture theaters*] .... FAST
Foolproof Identification [*System*] .... FID
Foolscap .... FCAP
Foolscap .... FCP
Foot [*or Feet*] .... FT
Foot-Candle [*Illumination*] .... FC
Foot-Candle [*Illumination*] .... FT-C
Foot-Controlled Maneuvering Unit [*Skylab*] [*NASA*] .... FCMU
Foot Groove .... FG
Foot Guards [*British*] .... FG
Foot-Lambert .... FL
Foot-Lambert .... FT-L
Foot-and-Mouth Disease [*Veterinary medicine*] .... FMD
Foot-and-Mouth Disease Virus [*Veterinary medicine*] .... FMDV
Foot Orthosis [*Medicine*] .... FO
Foot Patrol .... FP
Foot-Pound .... FP
Foot-Pound .... FT-LB
Foot-Pound Force .... FT LBF
Foot-Pound-Second [*System*] .... FPS
Foot-Poundal .... FT PDL
Foot-Pounds per Hour .... FT LB/H
Foot-Pounds per Minute .... FT LB/MIN
Foot-Pounds per Second .... FT LB/S
Foot Shock [*Biometrics*] .... FS
Foot Wide .... FW
Footage Dives [*Military*] .... FTGDV
Football [*Freight*] .... FT BAL
Football Association [*Controlling body of British soccer*] .... FA
Football Club [*British*] .... FC
Football Committee [*British*] .... FC
Football Grounds [*Public-performance tariff class*] [*British*] .... FG
Football Officials Association .... FOA
Football Writers Association of America .... FWAA
Foote, Cone & Belding Communications, Inc. [*Advertising agency*] .... FC & B
Foote, Cone & Belding Communications, Inc. [*Advertising agency*] [*NYSE symbol*] .... FCB
Foote Mineral Co. [*American Stock Exchange symbol*] .... FTE
Foothill Group Cl A [*NASDAQ symbol*] .... FTHLA
Foothills Pipe Lines (Yukon) Ltd., Calgary, AB, Canada [*Library symbol*] .... CaACF
Footing .... FTG
Footnote .... FN
Footwear and Accessories Council .... FAC
Footwear Caucus .... FC

Footwear Council	FC
Footwear Industries of America	FIA
Footwear Industry Traffic and Distribution Council	FITDC
Footwear News [*A publication*]	Ftwr News
For	F
For Action	FORAC
For Address, Write To	FAWT
For an Approach To [*Aviation*]	FAA
For the Benefit Of	FBO
For Better Living [*NASDAQ symbol*]	FBTR
For Carter Before Camp David [*Refers to Israeli-Egyptian agreements of 1978*]	FCBCD
For Duty	FORDU
For Duty or Such Other Duty as [*Command or Activity Indicated*] May Assign [*Military*]	DUSODA
For Early Domestic Dissemination	FEDD
For Engineering Information	FEI
For Further Assignment	FFA
For Further Assignment	FURAS
For Further Clearance [*Aviation*]	FFC
For Further Information	FFI
For Further Transfer [*to*] [*Military*]	FFT
For Illustrating Legal Methods [*Student legal action organization*]	FILM
For Improved Labeling to Terminate Hazards [*Student legal action organization*]	FILTH
For Information Only	FIO
For Instance	FI
For Internal Use Only	FIUO
For Life [*An association*]	FL
For Love of Children	FLOC
For NASA Personnel Only	FNPO
For Official Use Only [*Army*]	FOUO
For Official Use Only [*Army*]	OFLUSE
For Oily Hair Only [*Trademark of The Gillette Co.*]	FOHO
For Orders	FO
For Our Christian Understanding [*Program*]	FOCUS
For Possible Reclearance [*Aviation*]	FPRC
For Private Circulation	FPC
For the Purpose Of	FPUR
For Sale by Owner [*Real estate ads*] [*Pronounced "fizz-bo"*]	FSBO
For a Separate Peace Before Carter [*Refers to Israeli-Egyptian agreements of 1978*]	FSPBC
For Task Force [*Military*]	FORTSK
For Ultraviolet	FUV
For Your Attention	FYA
For Your Information	FYI
For Your Information and Guidance	FYIG
Forage Acre	FA
Foragers of America	FA
Foramen Ovale [*Anatomy*]	FO
Foraminifera [*Quality of the bottom*] [*Nautical charts*]	Fr
Foraminiferal [*Geology*]	FORAM
Forbes [*Australia*] [*Airport symbol*]	FRB
Forbes Air Force Base [*Kansas*]	FOAFB
Forbes Library, Northampton, MA [*Library symbol*]	MNF
Forbidden Combination Check	FCC
Forbush Decrease [*Geophysics*]	FD
Forca Aerea Brasileira [*Brazilian Air Force*]	FAB
Forca Expedicionaria Brasileira [*Brazilian Expeditionary Force, 1944-1955*]	FEB
Force [*Symbol*] [*IUPAC*]	F
Force	FOR
Force Accounting System [*Army*]	FAS
Force Accuracy Standards	FORACS
Force/Activity Designator [*Military*]	F/AD
Force/Activity Designators [*Military*]	F/ADS
Force Administration Data System [*Bell System*]	FADS
Force Aerienne Belge [*Belgium*] [*ICAO designator*]	EB
Force Air Intelligence Study [*Air Force*]	FAIS
Force Antiair Warfare Coordinator	FAAWC
Force Armee Nationale Khmer [*Cambodian army*]	FANK
Force Assessment in the Central Region [*NATO*]	FACR
Force Associated Control Communications [*Military*]	FACC
Force Automation and Communications [*Military*]	FACS
Force Beachhead Line [*Navy*]	FBHDL
Force Beachhead Line [*Navy*]	FBHL
Force Combat Air Patrol [*Military*]	FORCAP
Force of Concentrated Load	P
Force Control Unit	FCU
Force Development	FD
Force Development Management Information System [*Army*]	FDMIS
Force Development Testing and Experimentation [*Military*]	FDTE
Force Electronic Warfare Coordinator	FEWC
Force Electronic Warfare/Tactical SIGINT	FEWTS
Force Field	FF
Force Fighter Director Officer	FFDO
Force and Financial Program	F & FP
Force Flagship	FF
Force [*or Forced*] Fluid [*Medicine*]	FF
Force Generation Levels [*Military*]	FGLS
Force Headquarters [*Allied forces*] [*World War II*]	FH

Force Headquarters, Adjutant General [*World War II*]	FHAG
Force Headquarters, Adjutant General, Executive [*World War II*]	FHAGG
Force Headquarters, Adjutant General, Mail and Records [*World War II*]	FHAGR
Force Headquarters, Adjutant General, Miscellaneous [*World War II*]	FHAGM
Force Headquarters, Adjutant General, Personnel [*World War II*]	FHAGP
Force Headquarters, Air Commander-in-Chief, Mediterranean [*World War II*]	FHAIR
Force Headquarters, Antiaircraft [*World War II*]	FHAAO
Force Headquarters, Chemical Warfare [*World War II*]	FHCWS
Force Headquarters, Chief Administrative Officer [*World War II*]	FHCAO
Force Headquarters, Chief of Staff [*World War II*]	FHCOS
Force Headquarters, Civil Affairs [*World War II*]	FHCIV
Force Headquarters, Claims and Hirings [*World War II*]	FHCCH
Force Headquarters, Commander-in-Chief [*World War II*]	FHCIC
Force Headquarters, Commander-in-Chief, Mediterranean [*World War II*]	FHRNA
Force Headquarters, Deputy Allied Commander-in-Chief [*World War II*]	FHDCC
Force Headquarters, Deputy Chief of Staff [*World War II*]	FHDSC
Force Headquarters, Director of Harbor Craft [*World War II*]	FHDHC
Force Headquarters, Engineer [*World War II*]	FHENG
Force Headquarters, Expeditionary Forces Institute [*World War II*]	FHEFI
Force Headquarters, Field Artillery Section [*World War II*]	FHFLD
Force Headquarters, Headquarters Commandant [*World War II*]	FHHDC
Force Headquarters, Information and Censorship [*World War II*]	FHINC
Force Headquarters, Liaison [*World War II*]	FHLIA
Force Headquarters, Military Government Section [*World War II*]	FHMGS
Force Headquarters, Military Secretary Section [*World War II*]	FHDMS
Force Headquarters, Movements and Transportation [*World War II*]	FHGDM
Force Headquarters, North African Economic Board [*World War II*]	FHAEB
Force Headquarters, Ordnance [*World War II*]	FHORD
Force Headquarters, Petroleum [*World War II*]	FHPET
Force Headquarters, Psychological Warfare Office [*World War II*]	FHPWO
Force Headquarters, Public Relations [*World War II*]	FHPRO
Force Headquarters, "Q" Army Equipment Branch [*World War II*]	FHQAE
Force Headquarters, "Q" Maintenance [*World War II*]	FHGDQ
Force Headquarters, Quartermaster [*World War II*]	FHSUP
Force Headquarters, Secretary General Staff [*World War II*]	FHSGS
Force Headquarters, Signal [*World War II*]	FHSIG
Force Headquarters, Supply and Transport [*World War II*]	FHGDT
Force Headquarters, Surgeon [*World War II*]	FHMED
Force Headquarters, United States Naval Staff [*World War II*]	FHUSN
Force Headquarters, Works [*World War II*]	FHENW
Force Identification [*Military*]	FID
Force Information Service [*Military*]	FIS
Force de Liberation Nationale Kamerunaise [*National Cameroonian Liberation Force*]	FLNK
Force Logistics Command [*Marine Corps*]	FLC
Force Logistics Command [*Marine Corps*]	FORLOGMD
Force Logistics Support Group [*Marine Corps*]	FLSG
Force Logistics Support Unit [*Marine Corps*]	FLSU
Force Measurement Unit	FMU
Force Measuring System	FMS
Force Mobile (Canadian Forces)	FMC
Force Modernization Milestone Reporting System [*Army*]	FMMRS
Force Modernization Office [*Army*]	FMO
Force Modernization Program	FMP
Force Objective	F/O
Force Out [*Baseball*]	FO
Force Ouvriere [*French trade union*]	FO
Force Packaging Report [*Military*]	FOPREP
Force Planning Analysis [*Army*]	FPA
Force Planning Guide [*Army*]	FPG
Force Planning Package [*Military*]	FPP
Force Planning System	FORPA
Force Reaction Motor	FRM
Force Readiness Report [*DoD*]	FRR
Force Recon Association	FRA
Force Reconnaissance	FORECON
Force Reconnaissance Company [*Marine Corps*]	FORECONCO
Force Rendezvous Point [*Military*]	FRP
Force Requirement Number [*Army*]	FRN
Force Requirement Troop List Reporting System	FORTL
Force Requirements Generator	FRG
Force Requirements and Methodology [*Military*]	FOREM
Force and Rhythm [*of Pulse*] [*Medicine*]	F & R
Force Sensing Probe	FSP
Force Service Regiment [*Marine Corps*]	FSR
Force Service Support Group [*Military*]	FSSG
Force Spectral Density	FSD
Force Status and Identity Report	FORSTAR
Force Status Report [*Military*]	FORSTAT
Force Structure Committee	FSC
Force Structure Increase [*Military*]	FSI
Force Structure Planning Objective	FSPO
Force Structure Requirements Study [*Military*]	FSRS
Force Supply Officer	FSO

Force/Torque Module [*NASA*]....FTM
Force Track Coordinator [*Navy*]....FTC
Force Troops....FORTRPS
Force de l'Union National Cambodge [*Cambodia*]....FUNC
Force d'Urgence des Nations Unies....FUNU
Force and Weapon Analysis System....FOREWAS
Force Weapons Coordinator [*Navy*]....FORWEPCORD
Force Weapons Coordinator [*Navy*]....FWC
Forced-Air-Cooled [*Transformer*]....FA
Forced-Choice Preferential Looking....FPL
Forced Draft....FD
Forced-Draft Blower....FDB
Forced Equilibrating Expiration [*Physiology*]....FEE
Forced Expiratory Flow [*Physiology*]....FEF
Forced Expiratory Volume [*Physiology*]....FEV
Forced Fault Entry [*Data processing*]....FFE
Forced Inspiratory Oxygen [*Physiology*]....FIO_2
Forced Landing Incidents - Ground Accidents....FLIGA
Forced Oil Injection....FOI
Forced Out by a Reduction in Force....RIFFED
Forced Pair Copulation [*Sociobiology*]....FPC
Forced Removal....FR
Forced Test End....FTE
Forced Vital Capacity [*Physiology*]....FVC
Forced Whisper [*Medicine*]....FW
Forceps Delivery [*Obstetrics*]....FD
Forces Aeriennes Alliees Centre-Europe [*Allied Air Forces Central Europe*] [*NATO*]....FAACE
Forces Aeriennes Alliees Nord-Europe [*Allied Air Forces Northern Europe*] [*NATO*]....FAANE
Forces Aeriennes Alliees Sud-Europe [*Allied Air Forces Southern Europe*] [*NATO*]....FAASE
Forces Aeriennes Francaises [*ICAO designator*]....FA
Forces Armees Laotiannes [*Federated Army of Laos*]....FAL
Forces Armees Neutralist....FAN
Forces Armees Royal Khmere [*Cambodian Army*]....FARK
Forces Armees du Royaume [*Royal Armed Forces of Laos*]....FAR
Forces Command [*Formerly, CONARC*] [*Army*]....FORSCOM
Forces Courier Services [*Military*] [*British*]....FCS
Forces to Eliminate No-Deposit/No-Return....FENDRE
Forces Francaises en Allemagne [*French Forces in Germany*]....FFA
Forces Francaises de l'Interieur [*French Forces of the Interior*] [*World War II*]....FFI
Forces Francaises Libres [*Free French Forces*]....FFL
Forces Francaises de l'Ouest....FFO
Forces Intelligence Center....FORSIC
Forces des Nations Unies [*United Nations Forces*]....FNU
Forces Navales Francaises Libres [*Free French Naval Forces*] [*World War II*]....FNFL
Forces Post Office [*Military*] [*British*]....FPO
Forces and Weapons....FOREWON
Ford Aerosports Club....FAC
Ford-Aire [*Sidney, NY*] [*FAA designator*]....SQH
Ford, Bacon, & Davis, Inc., New York, NY [*Library symbol*]....NNFB
Ford of Europe, Inc. [*Great Britain*] [*ICAO designator*]....FD
Ford Foundation....FF
Ford Foundation, Ford Foundation Library, New York, NY [*Library symbol*]....NNFF-FL
Ford Foundation Library, New York, NY [*OCLC symbol*]....FOR
Ford Foundation, New York, NY [*Library symbol*]....NNFF
Ford Instrument Company....FICO
Ford Mercury Club of America....FMCA
Ford Motor Co. [*NYSE symbol*] [*Wall Street slang names: "Tin Lizzy" or "Flivver"*]....F
Ford Motor Company....FOMOCO
Ford Motor Co. [*Detroit, MI*] [*FAA designator*]....FRD
Ford Motor Co. of Canada Ltd. [*American Stock Exchange symbol*]....FC
Ford Motor Co., Dearborn, MI [*Library symbol*]....MiDbF
Ford Motor Co., Engineering and Research Library, Dearborn, MI [*OCLC symbol*]....EEF
Ford Nuclear Reactor....FNR
Ford [*Automobile*] **Operating Cost Analysis System**....FOCAS
Ford Satellite Plan [*Communications*]....FSP
Forde [*Norway*] [*Airport symbol*]....FDE
Fordham [*New York*] [*Seismograph station code, US Geological Survey*] [*Closed*]....FOR
Fordham Law Review [*A publication*]....Fordham L Rev
Fordham University, Bronx, NY [*OCLC symbol*]....VYF
Fordham University, Institute of Contemporary Russian Studies, New York, NY [*Library symbol*]....NNF-RS
Fordham University, Law Library, New York, NY [*Library symbol*]....NNF-L
Fordham University, Library at Lincoln Center, New York, NY [*Library symbol*]....NNF-LC
Fordham University, New York, NY [*Library symbol*]....NNF
Fordham Urban Law Journal [*A publication*]....Fordham Urban L J
Fordham Urban Solar Eco-System....FUSES
Ford's Theatre Society....FTS
Fordson Tractor Club....FTC
Fordyce, AR [*Radio station call letters*]....KBJT
Fordyce, AR [*Radio station call letters*]....KQEW
Fordyce & Princeton Railroad Co. [*AAR code*]....FP
Fore and Aft....F & A
Fore Edges Painted [*Paper*]....FEP
Fore Hatch [*Shipping*]....FH
Fore Perpendicular....FP
Fore River Railroad Corp. [*AAR code*]....FOR
Forearm Blood Flow [*Medicine*]....FBF
Forearm Pronated [*Medicine*]....fp
Forearm Supinated [*Medicine*]....FS
Forearm Vascular Resistance [*Medicine*]....FVR
Forecast....FCST
Forecast Office Facsimile [*National Weather Service*]....FOFAX
Forecast Sailing Report [*Navy*]....PRESAILEDREP
Forecast Support Date....FSD
Forecast/Surface....FS
Forecast Upper Air....FU
Forecast Wind Factor [*Meteorology*]....FRWF
Forecasting Control and Updating Schedule....FOCUS
Forecasting Information Retrieval of Management System....FIRMS
Forecasting International Ltd. [*Information service*]....FI
Forecasting and Inventory Control System....FICS
Forecasting and Modeling System....FAMS
Forecasting Passenger and Cargo....FORPAC
Forecasting and Scheduling Technique....FAST
Forecastle....F
Forecastle....FCSLE
Forecastle....FOCSL
Forecastle [*Navy*] [*British*]....FX
Forecastle....FXLE
Forecasts, Appraisals, and Management Evaluations....FAME
Foreground Initiated Batch [*Data processing*]....FIB
Foreign....FGN
Foreign....FOR
Foreign....FORGN
Foreign....FRGN
Foreign Adoption Center [*Later, FCVN*]....FAC
Foreign Affairs [*A publication*]....FA
Foreign Affairs [*A publication*]....For Aff
Foreign Affairs [*A publication*]....Foreign Aff
Foreign Affairs Bulletin [*Thailand*] [*A publication*]....FAB
Foreign Affairs Executive Seminar [*Department of State*]....FAES
Foreign Affairs Information Management Effort [*Computer*] [*Department of State*]....FAIME
Foreign Affairs Manual Circular [*A publication*] [*Department of State*]....FAMC
Foreign Affairs Programing System....FAPS
Foreign Affairs Recreation Association....FARA
Foreign Affairs Report [*A publication*]....For Aff Rep
Foreign Affairs Reports [*A publication*]....Foreign Aff Rep
Foreign Affairs Research Documentation Center [*Department of State*]....FAR
Foreign Affairs Specialist Corps [*Department of State*]....FASC
Foreign Agricultural Club....FAC
Foreign Agricultural Economic Reports....FAER
Foreign Agricultural Organization....FAO
Foreign Agricultural Relations Office....FAR
Foreign Agricultural Service [*Department of Agriculture*]....FAS
Foreign Agricultural Service Club [*Later, Foreign Agricultural Club*]....FASC
Foreign Agriculture [*A publication*]....For Agric
Foreign Agriculture [*A publication*]....Forgn Agr
Foreign Agriculture Including Foreign Crops and Markets [*A publication*]....FA
Foreign Agriculture Report [*Department of Agriculture*]....FAR
Foreign Agriculture Trade of the United States [*A publication*]....Foreign Agr Trade US
Foreign Aid Society [*British*]....FAS
Foreign Air Mail....FAM
Foreign Air Program....FAP
Foreign Area Consumer Dialing....FACD
Foreign Area Fellowship Program [*Later, SSRC*]....FAFP
Foreign Area and Language Study....FALS
Foreign Area Officer [*Army*]....FAO
Foreign Area Officer Management System [*Army*]....FAOMS
Foreign Area Research Coordination Group [*Department of State*]....FAR
Foreign Area Research Horizons [*A publication*]....FAR Horiz
Foreign Area Specialist [*Army*]....FAS
Foreign Area Specialist Training [*Army*]....FAST
Foreign Area Specialist Training Program [*Army*]....FASTP
Foreign Assignment Resources Employees [*FAA*]....FARE
Foreign Body [*Medicine*]....FB
Foreign Body Cornea Left Eye [*Medicine*]....FBCOS
Foreign Body Cornea Right Eye [*Medicine*]....FBCOD
Foreign Bondholders Protective Council....FBPC
Foreign-Born Irish....FBI
Foreign Broadcast Information Service....FBIS
Foreign Broadcast Intelligence Service [*FCC*] [*World War II*]....FBIS
Foreign Building Office [*Department of State*]....FBO
Foreign Car Haters Club of America....FCHCA
Foreign Claims Commission [*Canada*]....FGNCC
Foreign Claims Settlement Commission....FCSC
Foreign Clearance Base....FCB
Foreign Clearance Guide....FCG

Foreign Commerce Club of New York .... FCC
Foreign Commerce Weekly [*A publication*] .... For Comm
Foreign Commercial Service [*International Trade Administration*] .... FCS
Foreign and Commonwealth Office [*British*] .... FCO
Foreign Corporation Project [*IRS*] .... FCP
Foreign Correspondents' Club of Japan .... FCCJ
Foreign Corrupt Practices Act .... FCPA
Foreign Counterintelligence System [*Federal Bureau of Investigation*] .... FCIS
Foreign Credit Insurance Association [*Export-Import Bank*] .... FCIA
Foreign Credit Interchange Bureau .... FCIB
Foreign Criminal Jurisdiction .... FCJ
Foreign Currency .... FC
Foreign Currency Deposit Units .... FCDU
Foreign Disclosure Automated Data [*System*] .... FORDAD
Foreign Disclosure and Technical Information System .... FORDTIS
Foreign Document Division [*of CIA*] .... FDD
Foreign Duty Pay .... FDP
Foreign Economic Administration [*World War II*] .... FEA
[*Office of*] **Foreign Economic Coordination** .... FEC
Foreign Economic Development Service [*Department of Agriculture*] [*Abolished 1972, functions transferred to the Economic Research Service*] .... FEDS
Foreign Economic Trends and Their Implications for the United States [*A publication*] .... For Econ Trd
Foreign Escorted Tour [*Travel*] .... FET
Foreign Excess Personal Property .... FEPP
Foreign Exchange [*Business and trade*] .... FX
Foreign Exchange Brokers Association [*British*] .... FEBA
Foreign Exchange Brokers of New York City .... FEBNYC
Foreign Exchange Cost .... FEC
Foreign Exchange Operations Fund .... FEOF
Foreign Exchange Rate Service [*ContiCurrency*] [*Information service*] .... FX
Foreign Fishing Observer Fund [*National Oceanic and Atmospheric Administration*] .... FFOF
Foreign Flag .... FF
Foreign Force Reduction .... FFR
Foreign Freight Agent .... FFA
Foreign Funds Control .... FFC
Foreign General Agent .... FGA
Foreign General Average [*Insurance*] .... FGA
Foreign Independent Travel [*Air travel term*] .... FIT
Foreign Intelligence .... FI
Foreign Intelligence Advisory Board .... FIAB
Foreign Intelligence Office .... FIO
Foreign Intelligence Production Requirement [*Army*] .... FIPR
Foreign Intelligence Surveillance Act .... FISA
Foreign Investment Review Agency [*Canada*] .... FIRA
Foreign Language .... FL
Foreign Language Annals [*A publication*] .... FLA
Foreign Language Annals [*A publication*] .... Foreign Lan
Foreign Language Aptitude Test .... FLAT
Foreign Language Associates .... FLA
Foreign Language Bulletin .... FLB
Foreign Language Press of America .... FLPA
Foreign Language Program .... FLP
Foreign Language Training Program [*Air Force*] .... FLTP
Foreign Languages in Elementary Schools .... FLES
Foreign Languages (Nebraska) [*A publication*] .... FL (Neb)
Foreign Leave [*Military*] .... FLV
Foreign Legal Periodicals Index [*A publication*] .... Foreign Leg Per
Foreign Liaison Office [*Military*] .... FLO
Foreign Liquidation Commission .... FLC
Foreign Material Catalog .... FOMCAT
Foreign Materiel Branch [*Military*] .... FMB
Foreign Materiel Exploitation .... FME
Foreign Media Representatives Association .... FMRA
Foreign Medical Graduate [*doing residency in US hospital*] .... FMG
Foreign Military .... FM
Foreign Military Assistance Coordinating Committee .... FMACC
Foreign Military Assistance Steering Committee .... FMASC
Foreign Military Sales .... FMS
Foreign Military Sales Order [*Army*] .... FMSO
Foreign Military Sales Program [*Army*] .... FMSP
Foreign Military Service .... FMS
Foreign Military Training .... FMT
Foreign Minister [*or Ministry*] .... FM
Foreign Minister .... FOMIN
Foreign Mission .... FM
Foreign National Indirect .... FNI
Foreign National Weather Agency .... FNWA
Foreign Newspaper Microfilm Project, Association of Research Libraries, Center for Research Libraries, Chicago, IL [*Library symbol*] .... ICRL(ARL)
Foreign Numbering Plan Area [*AT & T*] .... FNPA
Foreign Object .... FO
Foreign Object Check .... FOC
Foreign Object Damage .... FOD
Foreign Object Inspection [*or Investigation*] .... FOI
Foreign Office .... FO
Foreign Office .... FONOFF
Foreign Office Research Department [*British*] .... FORD
Foreign Operating Committee [*World War II*] .... FOC
Foreign Operations Administration [*Later, ICA*] .... FOA
Foreign Organizations' Employees Union .... FOEU
Foreign Organizations Korean Employees' Union [*South Korea*] .... FOKEU
Foreign Ownership, Control, or Influence .... FOCI
Foreign Petroleum Supply Committee [*Terminated, 1976*] .... FPSC
Foreign Pharmacy Graduate Examination Commission .... FPGEC
Foreign Policy [*A publication*] .... Foreign Pol
Foreign Policy [*A publication*] .... For Pol
Foreign Policy .... FP
Foreign Policy Association .... FPA
Foreign Policy Briefs .... FPB
Foreign Policy Bulletin [*A publication*] .... For Policy Bul
Foreign Policy Clearing House [*Defunct*] .... FPCH
Foreign Policy Reports [*A publication*] .... For Policy Rep
Foreign Press Association .... FPA
Foreign Private Direct Investment .... FDI
Foreign Quarterly Review [*A publication*] .... For Q
Foreign Rations Not Available .... FRNA
Foreign Receiving Report .... FRR
Foreign Relations Committee [*US Senate*] .... FR
Foreign Requirements .... FR
Foreign Resources Associates .... FRA
Foreign Review [*A publication*] .... For R
Foreign Science Bulletin .... FSB
Foreign Science and Technology Center [*Army*] .... FSTC
Foreign Sea Duty .... FSD
Foreign Separate Rations .... FSR
Foreign Service [*Department of State*] .... FS
Foreign Service Allowances [*British*] .... FSA
Foreign Service Availability [*Military*] .... FSA
Foreign Service Credits [*Military*] .... FSC
Foreign Service Grievance Board [*Department of State*] .... FSGB
Foreign Service Information Officer [*Department of State*] .... FSIO
Foreign Service Inspection Corps [*Department of State*] .... FSIC
Foreign Service Institute [*Department of State*] .... FSI
Foreign Service Local .... FSL
Foreign Service Officer [*Department of State*] .... FSO
Foreign Service Officers' Training School .... FSOTS
Foreign Service Pay .... FSP
Foreign Service Research Institute .... FSRI
Foreign Service Reserve (Unlimited) [*Department of State*] .... FSRU
Foreign Service Reservists .... FSR
Foreign Service Sales Expense .... FSSE
Foreign Service Selection Date .... FSSD
Foreign Service Tour [*Military*] .... FST
Foreign Shore Service .... FSS
Foreign Staff College [*British*] .... FSC
Foreign State National .... FSN
Foreign Student Service Council .... FSSC
Foreign Tax Credit .... FTC
Foreign Technical Department [*Navy*] .... FTD
Foreign Technology Activity Office [*or Officer*] .... FTAO
Foreign Technology Division [*AFSC*] .... FTD
Foreign Technology Office [*Army Tank-Automotive Command*] .... FTO
Foreign Theater .... FT
Foreign Trade [*A publication*] .... Foreign Tr
Foreign Trade Association .... FTA
Foreign Trade Institute [*Mexico*] .... FTI
Foreign Trade Reports .... FTR
Foreign Trade Statistics [*Bureau of Census*] .... FTS
[*US*] **Foreign Trade Statistics, Classifications, and Cross-Classifications** [*A publication*] .... FTSC
Foreign Trade Statistics Regulations .... FTSR
Foreign Trade Zone Board .... FTZB
Foreign Traders Index [*Department of Commerce*] [*Information service*] .... FTI
Foreign Transaction .... FT
Foreign Weapon Development Program .... FWDP
Foreign Weapons Evaluation .... FWE
Foreland .... FRLD
Foreman .... FMAN
Foreman of Signals [*Military*] [*British*] .... F of S
Foreman's Association of America [*Defunct*] .... FAA
Foremanship Foundation [*Defunct*] .... FF
Foremost Corporation [*NASDAQ symbol*] .... FCOA
Foremost Dairies, Inc., San Francisco, CA [*Library symbol*] .... CSfFD
Foremost [*or Forward*] **Defended Localities** [*or Locations*] [*British*] .... FDL
Foremost-McKesson, Inc. [*NYSE symbol*] [*Delisted*] .... FOR
Foreningen Teknisk Information [*Swedish Society on Technical Communication*] .... FTI
Forenoon .... FORNN
[*The*] **Forensic Medicine Consultant-Advisor** [*Program*] .... FMCA
Forensic Pathology [*Medicine*] .... FOR
Forensic Science [*A publication*] .... Forensic Sci
Forensic Science International [*A publication*] .... Forensic Sci Int
Forensic Science Society Journal [*A publication*] .... Forensic Sci Soc J
Forensic Sciences Foundation .... FSF
Forepeak [*Naval architecture*] .... FP
Forer Structured Sentence Completion Test [*Psychology*] .... FSSCT

Forer Vocational Survey [*Psychology*] .... FVS
Foresight .... FS
Forest .... FRST
Forest City Enterprises, Inc. [*American Stock Exchange symbol*] .... FCE
Forest City, IA [*Radio station call letters*] .... KIOW
Forest City, NC [*Radio station call letters*] .... WAGY
Forest City, NC [*Radio station call letters*] .... WBBO
Forest City, NC [*Radio station call letters*] .... WBBO-FM
Forest Conservation Society of America .... FCSA
Forest Department Bulletin. Forest Department (Zambia) [*A publication*] .... For Dep Bull For Dep (Zambia)
Forest Division Technical Note. Forest Division. (Dar Es Salaam, Tanzania) [*A publication*] .... For Div Tech Note For Div (Tanz)
Forest Engineer .... FE
Forest Engineer .... F Eng
Forest Engineering Research Institute of Canada, Pointe-Claire, PQ, Canada [*Library symbol*] .... CaQMFER
Forest Environment Research [*Department of Agriculture*] .... FER
Forest Environmental Protection. US Forest Service. Northern Region [*A publication*] .... For Environ Prot US For Serv North Reg
Forest Farmers Association .... FFA
Forest Fire Control Abstracts [*A publication*] .... FFC Abstr
Forest Fire Control Abstracts [*A publication*] .... For Fire Control Abstr
Forest Fire Losses in Canada [*A publication*] .... Forest Fire Losses Can
Forest Genetics Research Foundation .... FGRF
Forest Hill Public Library, Toronto, ON, Canada [*Library symbol*] .... CaOTFH
Forest History [*A publication*] .... Forest Hist
Forest History Society .... FHS
Forest History Society, Santa Cruz, CA [*Library symbol*] .... CStcrF
Forest Hydrology Laboratory [*Forest Service*] .... FHL
Forest Industries [*A publication*] .... Forest Ind
Forest Industries Council .... FIC
Forest Industries Equipment Review [*A publication*] .... For Ind Rev
Forest Industries Radio Communications [*Later, FIT*] .... FIRC
Forest Industries Telecommunications [*Formerly, FIRC*] .... FIT
Forest Inventory and Regeneration System .... FIRS
Forest Laboratories, Inc. [*American Stock Exchange symbol*] .... FRX
Forest Lake, MN [*Radio station call letters*] .... WLKX-FM
Forest Lawn Museum, Glendale, CA [*Library symbol*] .... CGIF
Forest Management Note. British Columbia Forest Service [*A publication*] .... For Mgmt Note BC For Serv
Forest, MS [*Location identifier*] [*FAA*] .... FVS
Forest, MS [*Radio station call letters*] .... WJYV
Forest, MS [*Radio station call letters*] .... WQST
Forest Notes. New Hampshire's Conservation Magazine [*A publication*] .... For Notes
Forest Oil Corp. [*NASDAQ symbol*] .... FOIL
Forest and Outdoors [*A publication*] .... For & Outdoors
Forest Park Public Library, Forest Park, IL [*Library symbol*] .... IFop
Forest Patrol [*Activity of Civil Air Patrol*] .... FP
Forest Pest Leaflet. US Forest Service [*A publication*] .... For Pest Leafl US For Serv
Forest Pest Leaflets .... FPL
Forest Product Laboratory, Madison, WI [*OCLC symbol*] .... AGF
Forest Products Journal [*A publication*] .... Forest Prod J
Forest Products Journal [*A publication*] .... For Prod J
Forest Products Laboratory [*Department of Agriculture*] .... FPL
Forest Products Marketing Laboratory [*Forest Service*] .... FPML
Forest Products Radio Service .... FPRS
Forest Products Research and Industries Development Commission .... FORPRIDECOM
Forest Products Research Laboratory [*British*] .... FPRL
Forest Products Research Record. Division of Forest Products (Zambia) [*A publication*] .... For Prod Res Rec Div For Prod (Zambia)
Forest Products Research Reports. Department of Forest Research (Nigeria) [*A publication*] .... For Prod Res Rep Dep For Res (Nigeria)
Forest Products Research Society .... FPRS
Forest Products Safety Conference .... FPSC
Forest Quarterly [*A publication*] .... For Quar
Forest Range Environmental Production Analytical System .... FREPAS
Forest Record. Forestry Commission (London) [*A publication*] .... For Rec For Comm (Lond)
Forest Record (London) [*A publication*] .... For Rec (Lond)
Forest Research Bulletin. Forest Department (Zambia) [*A publication*] .... For Res Bull For Dep (Zambia)
Forest Research in India [*A publication*] .... For Res India
Forest Research Institute (Bogor) Communication [*A publication*] .... For Res Inst (Bogor) Commun
Forest Research News for the Midsouth [*A publication*] .... Forest Res News Midsouth
Forest Research Pamphlet. Division of Forest Research (Zambia) [*A publication*] .... For Res Pamphl Div For Res (Zambia)
Forest Resource Report. US Forest Service [*A publication*] .... For Resour Rep US For Serv
Forest Resources Newsletter [*A publication*] .... For Resour Newslett
Forest Science [*A publication*] .... Forest Sci
Forest Science [*A publication*] .... For Sci
Forest Science Monographs [*A publication*] .... Forest Sci Monogr
Forest Science Monographs [*A publication*] .... For Sci Monogr
Forest Service [*Later, Department of Natural Resources*] [*Department of Agriculture*] .... FS
Forest Service Research Notes .... FSRN
Forest Service Research Paper .... FSRP
Forest Survey Notes. British Columbia Forest Service [*A publication*] .... For Surv Note BC For Serv
Forest Tent Caterpillars .... FTC
Forest and Timber [*A publication*] .... For & Timb
Forest and Timber [*A publication*] .... For Timber
Forest Tree Improvement [*A publication*] .... For Tree Improv
Forester. Ministry of Agriculture of Northern Ireland [*A publication*] .... Forester N Ire
Foresters of America .... FOA
Forestry .... FOR
Forestry .... FORS
Forestry .... FORSTRY
Forestry Abstracts [*A publication*] .... For Abstr
Forestry Abstracts [*A publication*] .... Forest Abstr
Forestry Abstracts [*A publication*] .... Forestry Abstr
Forestry Chronicle [*A publication*] .... For Chron
Forestry Chronicle [*A publication*] .... Forest Chro
Forestry Chronicle [*A publication*] .... Forestry Chron
Forestry Commission [*British*] .... FC
Forestry, Conservation Communications Association .... FCCA
Forestry Digest (Philippines) [*A publication*] .... For Dig (Philippines)
Forestry Economics. New York State University. College of Forestry at Syracuse University [*A publication*] .... For Econ NY St Coll For
Forestry Equipment Notes. FAO [*Food and Agriculture Organization of the United Nations*] [*A publication*] .... For Equipm Note FAO
Forestry Incentive Program .... FIP
Forestry Note. University of Illinois. Agricultural Experiment Station [*A publication*] .... For Note Ill Agric Exp Sta
Forestry Occasional Paper. FAO [*Food and Agriculture Organization of the United Nations*] [*A publication*] .... For Occ Pap FAO
Forestry Quarterly [*A publication*] .... For Q
Forestry Remote Sensing Laboratory .... FRSL
Forestry Research Newsletter [*A publication*] .... Forestry Res Newsl
Forestry Research Notes. University of Wisconsin. College of Agriculture [*A publication*] .... For Res Note Wis Coll Agric
Forestry Research Report. Agricultural Experiment Station. University of Illinois [*A publication*] .... Forestry Res Rept Agr Expt Sta Univ Ill
Forestry in South Africa [*A publication*] .... For S Afr
Forestry Technical Notes. University of New Hampshire. Agricultural Experiment Station [*A publication*] .... For Tech Note NH Agric Exp Sta
Forestry Technical Papers. Forests Commission of Victoria [*A publication*] .... For Tech Pap For Comm Vict
Forests Commission Victoria. Bulletin [*A publication*] .... For Comm Victoria Bull
Forests Commission Victoria. Forestry Technical Papers [*A publication*] .... For Comm Victoria For Tech Pap
Forests Department of Western Australia Research Paper [*A publication*] .... For Dep West Aust Res Pap
Forestville [*Canada*] [*Airport symbol*] .... YFE
Forestville, PQ [*Radio station call letters*] .... CFRP
Foret-Conservation [*A publication*] .... Foret-Conserv
Foretop .... FT
Forever Yours .... FEY
Forex Association of North America .... FANA
Forfeiture .... FORF
Forfeiture of Pay .... FP
Forge .... FRG
Forged .... FGD
Forged Carbon Steel .... FCS
Forged Chrom-Moly .... FCM
Forged Steel .... FS
Forged Steel [*Technical drawings*] .... FST
Forget It, I've Got My Orders [*Bowdlerized version*] [*Military slang*] .... FIIGMO
Forging .... FORG
Forging Die [*Tool*] .... FGDI
Forging Industry Association .... FIA
Forging Industry Educational and Research Foundation .... FIERF
Forging Manufacturers Association [*Later, ODFI*] .... FMA
Forging Topics [*A publication*] .... Forg Top
Forgotten Americans Need Support .... FANS
Forgotten Boys of Iceland [*Nickname for US soldiers in Iceland*] [*World War II*] .... FBI's
Forgotten Fantasy [*A publication*] .... FF
Forgotten Generation .... FG
Forint [*Monetary unit in Hungary*] .... F
Forint [*Monetary unit in Hungary*] .... FT
Foristell, MO [*Location identifier*] [*FAA*] .... FTZ
Fork .... FK
Fork .... FRK
Forked .... FKD
Forklift .... FLFT
Forklift Truck .... FLT
Forks, WA [*Radio station call letters*] .... KLLM

Forks, WA [*Radio station call letters*] KVAC
Form [*Of*] F
Form FM
Form FRM
Form [*Rorschach*] [*Psychology*] F
Form Block FB
Form Block Check Template FBCT
Form Block Line FBL
Form Block Template FBT
Form Block Template Set FBTS
Form of Control Users System FOCUS
Form Cutter FMCU
Form Die FMDI
Form Die Forge FDF
Form Die Impact FDI
Form Die Press FDP
Form Feed FF
Form and Finish Grinding FFG
Form-Fit-Function [*Pronounced "f-cubed"*] F^3
Form und Geist [*A publication*] FG
Form Letter FL
Form Mandrel [*Tool*] FMMD
Form Molding Die FMD
Form Pads [*Tool*] FMPS
Form Retrieval and Manipulation Language FOREMAN
Form Roll FMRL
Form und Technik [*A publication*] Form Tech
Form Tool FMTO
Forma [*Also, f*] F
Forma et Function [*A publication*] Forma Functio
Forma Specialis [*Special Form*] [*Biology*] f sp
Formable Metallized Plastics [*Industrial technology*] FMP
Formage et Traitements des Metaux [*A publication*] Formage Trait Metaux
Formal Auto-Indexing of Scientific Texts FAST
Formal Change FCHG
Formal Design Review FDR
Formal Documents Issued [*Federal Power Commission*] FDI
Formal Evaluation Acceptance Test [*Apollo*] [*NASA*] FEAT
Formal Inspection FI
Formal Officer Career Utilization Structure [*Military*] FOCUS
Formal On-the-Job FOTJ
Formal On-the-Job Training FOJT
Formal Qualification FQ
Formal Qualification Reviews FQR
Formal Qualification Test FQT
Formal Semantic Language FSL
Formal Technical Documents FTD
Formal Technical Literature FTL
Formal Toxoid [*Medicine*] FT
Formal Training [*Military*] FT
Formal Training and Certification FT & C
Formal Training Data System FTDS
Formaldehyde-Glutaraldehyde-Dichromate [*Fixative*] FGD
Formaldehyde-Induced Fluorescence FIF
Formaldehyde Institute FI
Formaldehyde Task Force Fund FTFF
Formalin-Acetic Acid-Alcohol [*Fixative*] [*Botany*] FAA
Formalin Ammonium Bromide [*Fixative*] FAB
Formalin-Propionic Acid-Alcohol [*Fixative*] [*Botany*] FPA
Formalin-Treated Pyruvaldehyde-Stabilized Human Erythrocytes [*Immunology*] FPHE
Formality F
Formamidonitrofurylthiazole [*Organic chemistry*] FANFT
Forman Co., Monmouth, IL [*Library symbol*] FmC
Formaster Corp. [*NASDAQ symbol*] FMSR
Format FMT
Format FRMT
Format Code [*Data processing*] F/C
Format Control Buffer FCB
Format Control Word FCW
Format Effector [*Data processing*] FE
Format Identification [*Data processing*] FID
Format Request Element FRE
Formation [*Lithology*] FM
Formation FMN
Formation FORM
Formation FORMN
Formation FRMN
Formation pour l'Agriculture et le Developpement Rural [*A publication*] Formation Agric Develop Rur
Formation Continue [*A publication*] Format Continue
Formation Drone Control [*Navy*] FDC
Formation Flight Display FFD
Formation Flight Operation FFO
Formation Flight Trainer [*Air Force*] FFT
Formation Flying Simulator FFS
Formation Pennant [*Navy*] [*British*] FR
Formatted File System [*Data processing*] FFS
Formatted File System Commercial Users' Group [*Data processing*] FFSCUG
Formatted Teletypewriter FORTEL
Formazin Turbidity Unit [*Analytical chemistry*] FTU
Formazione Domani [*A publication*] Formazione Dom
Formed F
Formed FRMD
Formed Steel Institute FSI
Formed Steel Tube Institute [*Later, WSTI*] FSTI
Former FMR
Former FRMR
Former Live-In FLI
Former Members of Congress [*US*] [*Later, AFMC*] FMC
Former Priest FP
Former Pupil [*Alumnus*] [*British*] FP
Formerly FMLY
Formerly FMRLY
Formerly Fat Housewife [*Weight Watchers, International; advertising*] FFH
Formerly Married FM
Formerly Restricted Data [*Military*] FORESDAT
Formerly Restricted Data [*Military*] FRD
Formerly Utilized Sites Remedial Action Program [*Department of Energy*] FUSRAP
Formimino-L-glutamic Acid [*Organic chemistry*] FIGLU
Forming FRMG
Forming Up Place FUP
Formirovanie Celovska Kommunisticeskogo Obscestva [*A publication*] Formirov Celov Kom Obsc
Formosa [*MARC geographic area code*] [*Library of Congress*] a-ch---
Formosa [*Argentina*] [*Airport symbol*] FMA
Formosa Patrol Force, US Pacific Fleet FORMPATPAC
Formosan Agricultural Review [*A publication*] Formosan Agr Rev
Formosan Association for Human Rights FAHR
Formosan Science [*A publication*] Formosan Sci
Forms Control Buffer [*Data processing*] FCB
Forms Management FM
Forms Management Officer [*Army*] FMO
Forms Manufacturers Credit Interchange FMCI
Forms and Publications Supply Office [*Military*] FPSO
Formula F
Formula FORM
Formula Algebraic Processor [*Data processing*] FLAP
Formula Assembler Translator [*Data processing*] FAT
Formula Assembler Translator [*Data processing*] FORAST
Formula Calculator [*Data processing*] FOCAL
Formula Coder FORC
Formula Index [*Molecular formula indexing*] FORDEX
Formula Manipulation Compiler [*Data processing*] FORMAC
Formula Manipulation Language [*Data processing*] FORMAL
Formula One Spectators Association FOSA
Formula for Optimizing through Real-Time Utilization of Multiprograming FORUM
Formula and Statement Translator [*Data processing*] FAST
Formula Translation [*Data processing*] FORTRAN
Formula Weight [*Chemistry*] FW
Formulary FORMUL
Formyl [*As substituent on nucleoside*] [*Biochemistry*] f
Formylaminoacyl [*As substituent on nucleoside*] [*Biochemistry*] fa
Formyliminodiacetic Acid [*Organic chemistry*] FIDA
Formylmethionyl [*Biochemistry*] fMet
Formylmethionyl (sulfonyl) Methyl Phosphate [*Biochemistry*] FMMP
Formyl(methionyl)(leucyl)phenylalanine [*Biochemistry*] FMLP
Formyl(norleucyl)(leucyl)phenylalanine [*Biochemistry*] FNLLP
Formyltetrahydrofolate [*Biochemistry*] FTHF
Fornax [*Constellation*] For
Fornax [*Constellation*] Forn
Forney Army Airfield [*Fort Leonard Wood, MO*] FAAF
Fornication [*FBI standardized term*] FORN
Fornvannen [*A publication*] Fo
Foro Internacional [*A publication*] Foro Int
Forrest City, AR [*Radio station call letters*] KBFC
Forrest City, AR [*Radio station call letters*] KXJK
Forrest City, NC [*Television station call letters*] WSQY-TV
Forschner Group [*NASDAQ symbol*] FSNR
Forschung und Beratung. Forstwirtschaft [*A publication*] Forsch Berat Forstw
Forschung im Ingenieurwesen [*A publication*] Forsch Ingenieurw
Forschung im Ingenieurwesen [*A publication*] Forsch Ingenieurwes
Forschung in der Klinik und im Labor [*A publication*] Forsch Klin Lab
Forschungen und Berichte [*Graz*] [*A publication*] FB
Forschungen und Berichte [*A publication*] Fu B
Forschungen und Berichte Staatliche Museen zu Berlin [*A publication*] Forsch Ber Staatl Mus Berlin
Forschungen zur Brandenburgisch-Preussischen Geschichte [*A publication*] FBPG
Forschungen zur Deutschen Sprache und Dichtung [*A publication*] FDSD
Forschungen und Fortschritte [*A publication*] F & F
Forschungen und Fortschritte [*A publication*] FF
Forschungen und Fortschritte [*A publication*] Forsch u Fortschr
Forschungen und Fortschritte [*A publication*] Forsch Fortschr
Forschungen und Fortschritte [*A publication*] Fors u Fort
Forschungen und Fortschritte [*A publication*] FuF
Forschungen zur Geschichte Oberoesterreichs [*A publication*] FGO

Forschungen zur Kirchen- und Geistesgeschichte (Neue Folge) [*A publication*]....FKG(NF)
Forschungen zur Neueren Literaturgeschichte [*A publication*]....FNLG
Forschungen zur Osteuropaeischen Geschichte [*A publication*]....FOEG
Forschungen zur Osteuropaeischen Geschichte [*A publication*]....FOG
Forschungen zur Religion und Literatur des Alten und Neuen Testaments [*A publication*]....FRLANT
Forschungen zur Volks und Landeskunde [*A publication*]....Forsch Volks Land
Forschungen zur Volks und Landeskunde [*A publication*]....FVL
Forschungs-Gesellschaft Verfahrens-Technik [*West Germany*]....FGVT
Forschungs Kommission fuer Hochspannungsfragen [*Switzerland*]....FKH
Forschungs-Reaktor Berlin....FRB
Forschungsberichte zur Germanistik [*Osaka-Kobe*] [*A publication*]....FzG
Forschungsberichte des Landes Nordrhein-Westfalen [*A publication*]....Forschungsber Landes Nordrhein-Westfalen
Forschungshefte aus dem Gebiete des Stahlbaues [*A publication*]....Forschungsh Geb Stahlbaues
Forskning og Forsok i Landbruket [*A publication*]....Forsk Fors Landbruket
Forskningens Faellesudvalg [*Science Advisory Council*] [*Denmark*]....FFU
Forst- und Holzwirt [*A publication*]....Forst- u Holzw
Forsterite [*CIPW classification*] [*Geology*]....fo
Forstliche Bundesversuchsanstalt [*A publication*]....Forstl Bundesversuchsanst
Forstliche Bundesversuchsanstalt Wien. Jahresbericht [*A publication*]....Forstl Bundesversuchsanst Wien Jahresber
Forstlige Forsogsvaesen (Danmark) [*A publication*]....Forstl Forsogsv (Danm)
Forstlige Forsoksvaesen i Danmark [*A publication*]....Forst Forsokvaes Dan
Forsttechnische Informationen [*A publication*]....Forsttech Inform
Forstwirtschaftliches Centralblatt [*A publication*]....Forstw Centbl
Forstwissenschaftliche Forschungen [*A publication*]....Forstwiss Forsch
Forstwissenschaftliches Centralblatt [*A publication*]....Forstwiss Cbl
Forstwissenschaftliches Centralblatt (Hamburg) [*A publication*]....Forstwiss Centralbl (Hamb)
Forsvarets Forskningsrad [*Defense Board*] [*Denmark*]....FFR
Forsyth County Public Library System, Winston-Salem, NC [*Library symbol*]....NcWs
Forsyth Dental Center, Boston, MA [*Library symbol*]....MBFo
Forsyth, GA [*Radio station call letters*]....WFNE
Forsyth, MT [*Location identifier*] [*FAA*]....FOR
Forsyth, MT [*Radio station call letters*]....KIKC
Forsyth, MT [*Radio station call letters*]....KXXE
Forsyth Technical Institute, Winston-Salem, NC [*Library symbol*]....NcWsF
Forsythe Township Public Library, Gwinn, MI [*Library symbol*]....MiGw
Fort....FT
Fort Albany [*Canada*] [*Airport symbol*]....YFA
Fort Atkinson, WI [*Radio station call letters*]....WFAW
Fort Atkinson, WI [*Radio station call letters*]....WSJY
Fort Beausejour Museum, Sackville, NB, Canada [*Library symbol*]....CaNBSaB
Fort Belvoir, VA [*Location identifier*] [*FAA*]....DAA
Fort Benning Officers' Open Mess [*Pronounced "fuhboom"*]....FBOOM
Fort Bowie National Historic Site....FOBO
Fort Bragg, CA [*Radio station call letters*]....KDAC
Fort Bragg, CA [*Radio station call letters*]....KOZT
Fort Bragg Public Library, Fort Bragg, CA [*Library symbol*]....CFb
Fort Campbell, KY [*Radio station call letters*]....WABD
Fort Campbell, KY [*Radio station call letters*]....WABD-FM
Fort Campbell, KY [*Location identifier*] [*FAA*]....XRW
Fort Campbell Post Library, Fort Campbell, KY [*OCLC symbol*]....APK
Fort Caroline National Memorial....FOCA
Fort Carson Hospital, Medical Library, Colorado Springs, CO [*Library symbol*]....CoCFc-M
Fort Carson Library, Colorado Springs, CO [*Library symbol*]....CoCFc
Fort Chimo [*Canada*] [*Airport symbol*]....YVP
Fort Chipewyan [*Canada*] [*Airport symbol*]....YPY
Fort Churchill [*Manitoba*] [*Geomagnetic observatory code*]....FCC
Fort Churchill [*Manitoba*] [*Seismograph station code, US Geological Survey*]....FCC
Fort Clatsop National Memorial....FOCL
Fort Collins [*Colorado*] [*Airport symbol*]....FTC
Fort Collins, CO [*Radio station call letters*]....KCOL
Fort Collins, CO [*Radio station call letters*]....KCOL-FM
Fort Collins, CO [*Radio station call letters*]....KCSU-FM
Fort Collins, CO [*Radio station call letters*]....KIIX
Fort Collins, CO [*Radio station call letters*]....KTCL
Fort Collins/Loveland, CO [*Location identifier*] [*FAA*]....FNL
Fort Collins Public Library, Fort Collins, CO [*Library symbol*]....CoF
Fort Coulonge, PQ [*Radio station call letters*]....CHIP-FM
Fort Dauphin [*Madagascar*] [*Airport symbol*]....FTU
Fort Davis National Historic Site....FODA
Fort De France [*Martinique*] [*Airport symbol*]....FDF
Fort De France [*Morne Des Cadets*] [*Martinique*] [*Seismograph station code, US Geological Survey*]....FDF
Fort Dearborn Income Securities, Inc. [*NYSE symbol*]....FTD
Fort Detrick [*Maryland*] [*Army*]....FD
Fort Detrick Technical Library, Frederick, MD [*Library symbol*]....MdFreD
Fort Dodge [*Iowa*] [*Airport symbol*]....FOD
Fort Dodge Bio-Chemic Review [*A publication*]....Fort Dodge Bio-Chem Rev
Fort Dodge, Des Moines, & Southern Railway Co. [*AAR code*]....FDDM
Fort Dodge, IA [*Location identifier*] [*FAA*]....FOD
Fort Dodge, IA [*Radio station call letters*]....KICB
Fort Dodge, IA [*Radio station call letters*]....KKEZ
Fort Dodge, IA [*Radio station call letters*]....KSMX
Fort Dodge, IA [*Television station call letters*]....KTIN
Fort Dodge, IA [*Radio station call letters*]....KTPR
Fort Dodge, IA [*Radio station call letters*]....KVFD
Fort Dodge, IA [*Radio station call letters*]....KWMT
Fort Dodge Public Library, Fort Dodge, IA [*Library symbol*]....IaFd
Fort Donelson National Military Park....FODO
Fort Frances [*Canada*] [*Airport symbol*]....YAG
Fort Frances, ON [*Television station call letters*]....CBWCT
Fort Frances, ON [*Radio station call letters*]....CFOB
Fort Frances Public Library, Fort Frances, ON, Canada [*Library symbol*]....CaOFF
Fort Frederica National Monument....FOFR
Fort Gay, WV [*Radio station call letters*]....WFGH
Fort George [*Canada*] [*Airport symbol*]....YKU
Fort George G. Meade [*Maryland*]....FGGM
Fort Gordon, GA [*Location identifier*] [*FAA*]....FNJ
Fort Hamilton Post Library, Morale Support Activities, Brooklyn, NY [*OCLC symbol*]....TSK
Fort Hare Papers [*A publication*]....FHP
Fort Hare Papers [*A publication*]....Fort Hare Pap
Fort Hays State University, Hays, KS [*OCLC symbol*]....KFH
Fort Hays State University, Hays, KS [*Library symbol*]....KHayF
Fort Hays Studies. New Series. Science Series [*A publication*]....Fort Hays Stud New Ser Sci Ser
Fort Holabird Post Library, Baltimore, MD [*Library symbol*]....MdBFH
Fort Hood Post Library, Library Service Center, Fort Hood, TX [*OCLC symbol*]....APH
Fort Howard Paper Co. [*NYSE symbol*]....FHP
Fort Huachuca, AZ [*Location identifier*] [*FAA*]....DAO
Fort Huachuca/Sierra Vista [*Arizona*] [*Airport symbol*]....FHU
Fort Hunter-Liggett (Jolon), CA [*Location identifier*] [*FAA*]....HGT
Fort Indiantown Gap [*Army*]....FTIG
Fort Indiantown Gap (Annville), PA [*Location identifier*] [*FAA*]....MUI
Fort Jay, NY [*Location identifier*] [*FAA*]....GNY
Fort Jefferson National Monument....FOJE
Fort Kent, ME [*Radio station call letters*]....WLVC
Fort Kent, ME [*Radio station call letters*]....WUFK
Fort Knox, KY [*Location identifier*] [*FAA*]....FTK
Fort Knox, KY [*Location identifier*] [*FAA*]....GOI
Fort Knox, KY [*Radio station call letters*]....WSAC
Fort Knox, KY [*Radio station call letters*]....WWKK
Fort Laramie Historic Site, Fort Laramie, WY [*Library symbol*]....WyFIL
Fort Laramie National Historic Site....FOLA
Fort Larned National Historic Site....FOLS
Fort Lauderdale [*Florida*] [*Airport symbol*]....FLL
Fort Lauderdale, FL [*Location identifier*] [*FAA*]....LHI
Fort Lauderdale, FL [*Location identifier*] [*FAA*]....PJN
Fort Lauderdale, FL [*Radio station call letters*]....WAFG
Fort Lauderdale, FL [*Radio station call letters*]....WAXY
Fort Lauderdale, FL [*Radio station call letters*]....WFTL
Fort Lauderdale, FL [*Radio station call letters*]....WHYI
Fort Lauderdale, FL [*Radio station call letters*]....WSHE
Fort Lauderdale, FL [*Radio station call letters*]....WSRF
Fort Lauderdale, FL [*Radio station call letters*]....WWJF
Fort Lauderdale-Hollywood, FL [*Radio station call letters*]....WBSS
Fort Lauderdale Public Library, Fort Lauderdale, FL [*Library symbol*]....FFl
Fort Leonard Wood [*Missouri*] [*Airport symbol*]....TBN
Fort Leonard Wood Facilities Engineer Activity....FLWFEA
Fort Leonard Wood, MO [*Location identifier*] [*FAA*]....BHN
Fort Lewis College, Durango, CO [*Library symbol*]....CoDuF
Fort Liard [*Canada*] [*Airport symbol*]....YJF
Fort Logan Mental Health Center, Children's Library, Denver, CO [*Library symbol*]....CoDFC
Fort Logan Mental Health Center, Denver, CO [*Library symbol*]....CoDF
Fort Lupton Public Library, Fort Lupton, CO [*Library symbol*]....CoFlu
Fort Madison, IA [*Radio station call letters*]....KBKB
Fort Madison, IA [*Radio station call letters*]....KBKB-FM
Fort Malden National Historic Park, Amherstburg, ON, Canada [*Library symbol*]....CaOAmF
Fort Matanzas National Monument....FOMA
Fort McHenry National Monument....FOMC
Fort McMurray [*Canada*] [*Airport symbol*]....YMM
Fort McMurray, AB [*Television station call letters*]....CBXFT-6
Fort McMurray, AB [*Radio station call letters*]....CJOK
Fort McPherson [*Canada*] [*Airport symbol*]....ZFM
Fort McPherson Library System, Fort McPherson, GA [*OCLC symbol*]....APP
Fort Meade, MD [*Location identifier*] [*FAA*]....FME
Fort Meade, MD [*Location identifier*] [*FAA*]....ONN
Fort Meade, MD [*Location identifier*] [*FAA*]....TAU
Fort Mill, SC [*Location identifier*] [*FAA*]....FML
Fort Monmouth Procurement Division....FMPD
Fort Monmouth Procurement Office....FMPO
Fort Monmouth Signal Laboratory [*Army*]....FMSL
Fort Morgan Carnegie Public Library, Fort Morgan, CO [*Library symbol*]....CoFtm
Fort Morgan, CO [*Location identifier*] [*FAA*]....FMM

Fort Morgan, CO [*Radio station call letters*] ... KBRU
Fort Morgan, CO [*Radio station call letters*] ... KFTM
Fort Myer Library System and Fort McNair Post Library, Fort Myer, VA [*OCLC symbol*] ... MDW
Fort Myers [*Florida*] [*Airport symbol*] ... FMY
Fort Myers [*Florida*] [*Airport symbol*] ... RSW
Fort Myers Beach, FL [*Radio station call letters*] ... WQEZ
Fort Myers, FL [*Location identifier*] [*FAA*] ... FMY
Fort Myers, FL [*Television station call letters*] ... WBBH-TV
Fort Myers, FL [*Radio station call letters*] ... WCAI
Fort Myers, FL [*Radio station call letters*] ... WHEW
Fort Myers, FL [*Radio station call letters*] ... WINK
Fort Myers, FL [*Radio station call letters*] ... WINK-FM
Fort Myers, FL [*Television station call letters*] ... WINK-TV
Fort Myers, FL [*Radio station call letters*] ... WMYR
Fort Myers, FL [*Radio station call letters*] ... WSFP-FM
Fort Myers, FL [*Television station call letters*] ... WSFP-TV
Fort Myers, FL [*Radio station call letters*] ... WSOR
Fort Myers Southern Railroad Co. [*AAR code*] ... FMS
Fort Necessity National Battlefield ... FONE
Fort Necessity National Battlefield, Farmington, PA [*OCLC symbol*] ... FNB
Fort Nelson [*Hobart*] [*Tasmania*] [*Seismograph station code, US Geological Survey*] [*Closed*] ... FNT
Fort Nelson [*Canada*] [*Airport symbol*] ... YYE
Fort Nelson, BC [*Radio station call letters*] ... CFNL
Fort Payne, AL [*Radio station call letters*] ... WFPA
Fort Payne, AL [*Radio station call letters*] ... WZOB
Fort Pierce, FL [*Location identifier*] [*FAA*] ... FPR
Fort Pierce, FL [*Radio station call letters*] ... WFTP
Fort Pierce, FL [*Radio station call letters*] ... WIRA
Fort Pierce, FL [*Radio station call letters*] ... WIZD
Fort Pierce, FL [*Radio station call letters*] ... WOVV
Fort Pierce, FL [*Radio station call letters*] ... WQCS
Fort Pierce, FL [*Television station call letters*] ... WTVX
Fort Polk [*Louisiana*] [*Airport symbol*] ... POE
Fort Polk Army Airfield [*Fort Polk, LA*] ... FPAA
Fort Polk, LA [*Location identifier*] [*FAA*] ... POE
Fort Pulaski National Monument ... FOPU
Fort Raleigh National Historic Site ... FORA
Fort Richardson, AK [*Location identifier*] [*FAA*] ... FRN
Fort Riley, KS [*Location identifier*] [*FAA*] ... CVY
Fort Riley, KS [*Location identifier*] [*FAA*] ... FRI
Fort Riley, KS [*Location identifier*] [*FAA*] ... FTX
Fort St. James [*British Columbia*] [*Seismograph station code, US Geological Survey*] ... FSJ
Fort St. John [*Canada*] [*Airport symbol*] ... YXJ
Fort St. John, BC [*Radio station call letters*] ... CKNL
Fort St. Vrain [*Nuclear plant*] ... FSV
Fort Sam Houston Morale Support Library, Fort Sam Houston, TX [*OCLC symbol*] ... APX
Fort Scott Junior College [*Kansas*] ... FSJC
Fort Scott, KS [*Location identifier*] [*FAA*] ... FSK
Fort Scott, KS [*Radio station call letters*] ... KMDO
Fort Scott, KS [*Radio station call letters*] ... KOMB
Fort Severn [*Canada*] [*Airport symbol*] ... ZFV
Fort Sill, OK [*Location identifier*] [*FAA*] ... FSI
Fort Sill, OK [*Location identifier*] [*FAA*] ... XFS
Fort Simpson [*Canada*] [*Airport symbol*] ... YFS
Fort Simpson, NT [*Radio station call letters*] ... CFMR
Fort Smith [*Arkansas*] [*Airport symbol*] ... FSM
Fort Smith [*Canada*] [*Airport symbol*] ... YSM
Fort Smith, AR [*Location identifier*] [*FAA*] ... AFT
Fort Smith, AR [*Location identifier*] [*FAA*] ... FSM
Fort Smith, AR [*Radio station call letters*] ... KFPW
Fort Smith, AR [*Radio station call letters*] ... KFPW-FM
Fort Smith, AR [*Radio station call letters*] ... KFSA
Fort Smith, AR [*Television station call letters*] ... KFSM-TV
Fort Smith, AR [*Radio station call letters*] ... KISR
Fort Smith, AR [*Radio station call letters*] ... KMAG
Fort Smith, AR [*Television station call letters*] ... KPOM-TV
Fort Smith, AR [*Radio station call letters*] ... KTCS
Fort Smith, AR [*Radio station call letters*] ... KTCS-FM
Fort Smith, AR [*Radio station call letters*] ... KWHN
Fort Smith, AR [*Radio station call letters*] ... KXXI
Fort Smith Carnegie City Library, Fort Smith, AR [*Library symbol*] ... ArFs
Fort Smith Junior College [*Arkansas*] ... FSJC
Fort Smith National Historic Site ... FOSM
Fort Smith & Van Buren Railway Co. [*AAR code*] ... FSVB
Fort Steilacoom Community College, Tacoma, WA [*Library symbol*] ... WaTFS
Fort Stewart/Hunter AAF Library System, Fort Stewart, GA [*OCLC symbol*] ... APT
Fort Stockton, TX [*Location identifier*] [*FAA*] ... FST
Fort Stockton, TX [*Radio station call letters*] ... KFST
Fort Stockton, TX [*Radio station call letters*] ... KPJH
Fort Street Union Depot Co. [*AAR code*] ... FSUD
Fort Sumner, NM [*Location identifier*] [*FAA*] ... FSU
Fort Sumner Public Library, Fort Sumner, NM [*Library symbol*] ... NmFs
Fort Sumter National Monument ... FOSU
Fort Tejon [*California*] [*Seismograph station code, US Geological Survey*] [*Closed*] ... FTC
Fort Ticonderoga Association Museum and Library, Fort Ticonderoga, NY [*Library symbol*] ... NFtT
Fort Union National Monument ... FOUN
Fort Union Trading Post National Historic Site ... FOUS
Fort Valley, GA [*Radio station call letters*] ... WQBZ
Fort Valley, GA [*Radio station call letters*] ... WXKO
Fort Valley State College [*Georgia*] ... FVSC
Fort Valley State College, Fort Valley, GA [*Library symbol*] ... GFoF
Fort Valley State College, Fort Valley, GA [*OCLC symbol*] ... GFV
Fort Vancouver National Historic Site ... FOVA
Fort Vancouver Regional Library, Vancouver, WA [*Library symbol*] ... WaV
Fort Walton Beach [*Florida*] [*Airport symbol*] ... VPS
Fort Walton Beach, FL [*Radio station call letters*] ... WFTW
Fort Walton Beach, FL [*Radio station call letters*] ... WFTW-FM
Fort Walton Beach, FL [*Radio station call letters*] ... WNUE
Fort Walton Beach, FL [*Television station call letters*] ... WPAN
Fort Wayne [*Indiana*] [*Airport symbol*] ... FWA
Fort Wayne Bible College [*Indiana*] ... FWBC
Fort Wayne Bible College, Fort Wayne, IN [*OCLC symbol*] ... IFB
Fort Wayne Bible College, Fort Wayne, IN [*Library symbol*] ... InFwB
Fort Wayne, IN [*Location identifier*] [*FAA*] ... SMD
Fort Wayne, IN [*Radio station call letters*] ... WAFX
Fort Wayne, IN [*Television station call letters*] ... WANE-TV
Fort Wayne, IN [*Radio station call letters*] ... WBCL
Fort Wayne, IN [*Radio station call letters*] ... WBNI
Fort Wayne, IN [*Radio station call letters*] ... WEZV
Fort Wayne, IN [*Radio station call letters*] ... WFCV
Fort Wayne, IN [*Television station call letters*] ... WFFT-TV
Fort Wayne, IN [*Radio station call letters*] ... WFWQ
Fort Wayne, IN [*Radio station call letters*] ... WGL
Fort Wayne, IN [*Television station call letters*] ... WKJG-TV
Fort Wayne, IN [*Radio station call letters*] ... WLHI
Fort Wayne, IN [*Radio station call letters*] ... WMEE
Fort Wayne, IN [*Television station call letters*] ... WPTA
Fort Wayne, IN [*Radio station call letters*] ... WQHK
Fort Wayne, IN [*Radio station call letters*] ... WXKE
Fort Wayne, IN [*Location identifier*] [*FAA*] ... XBF
Fort Wayne Union [*AAR code*] ... FWU
Fort William [*Scotland*] [*Airport symbol*] ... FWM
Fort Wingate Army Depot [*New Mexico*] ... FTWIAD
Fort Wingate Army Depot [*New Mexico*] ... FWAD
Fort Worth Army Depot [*Texas*] ... FTWOAD
Fort Worth Art Museum, Fort Worth, TX [*Library symbol*] ... TxFF
Fort Worth Belt Railway Co. [*AAR code*] ... FWB
Fort Worth Christian College, Fort Worth, TX [*Library symbol*] ... TxFCC
Fort Worth & Denver Railway Co. [*AAR code*] ... FWD
Fort Worth Grain Exchange ... FWGE
Fort Worth Museum of Science and History, Fort Worth, TX [*Library symbol*] ... TxFM
Fort Worth Public Library, Fort Worth, TX [*OCLC symbol*] ... IFA
Fort Worth Public Library, Fort Worth, TX [*Library symbol*] ... TxF
Fort Worth Qualified Material List [*NASA*] ... FQML
Fort Worth, TX [*Location identifier*] [*FAA*] ... CNF
Fort Worth, TX [*Location identifier*] [*FAA*] ... FTW
Fort Worth, TX [*Radio station call letters*] ... KEGL
Fort Worth, TX [*Radio station call letters*] ... KESS
Fort Worth, TX [*Radio station call letters*] ... KJIM
Fort Worth, TX [*Radio station call letters*] ... KNOK-FM
Fort Worth, TX [*Radio station call letters*] ... KPLX
Fort Worth, TX [*Radio station call letters*] ... KSAX
Fort Worth, TX [*Radio station call letters*] ... KSCS
Fort Worth, TX [*Radio station call letters*] ... KTCU-FM
Fort Worth, TX [*Radio station call letters*] ... KTIA
Fort Worth, TX [*Television station call letters*] ... KTVT
Fort Worth, TX [*Television station call letters*] ... KTXA-TV
Fort Worth, TX [*Radio station call letters*] ... KTXQ
Fort Worth, TX [*Radio station call letters*] ... KUQQ
Fort Worth, TX [*Television station call letters*] ... KXAS
Fort Worth, TX [*Radio station call letters*] ... KXOL
Fort Worth, TX [*Location identifier*] [*FAA*] ... TCB
Fort Worth, TX [*Radio station call letters*] ... WBAP
Fort Wright College, Spokane, WA [*Library symbol*] ... WaSpN
Fort Yukon [*Alaska*] [*Seismograph station code, US Geological Survey*] ... FY1
Fort Yukon [*Alaska*] [*Seismograph station code, US Geological Survey*] ... FY2
Fort Yukon [*Alaska*] [*Seismograph station code, US Geological Survey*] ... FY3
Fort Yukon [*Alaska*] [*Seismograph station code, US Geological Survey*] ... FY4
Fort Yukon [*Alaska*] [*Seismograph station code, US Geological Survey*] ... FY5
Fort Yukon [*Alaska*] [*Airport symbol*] ... FYU
Fort Yukon [*Alaska*] [*Seismograph station code, US Geological Survey*] ... FYU
Fort Yukon, AK [*Location identifier*] [*FAA*] ... FTO
Fort Yukon Community/School Library, Fort Yukon, AK [*Library symbol*] ... AkFy
Fortaleza [*Brazil*] [*Airport symbol*] ... FOR
Fortasse [*Perhaps*] [*Latin*] ... F

Fortbildungskurse fuer Rheumatologie [*A publication*] ... Fortbildungskurse Rheumatol

Fortbildungskurse der Schweizerischen Gesellschaft fuer Psychiatrie [*A publication*] ... Fortbildungskurse Schweiz Ges Psychiatr

Forte [*Loud*] [*Music*] ... F

Forte [*Loud*] [*Music*] ... FOR

Forte Piano [*Loud, then Soft*] [*Music*] ... FFP

Forte Piano [*Loud, then Soft*] [*Music*] ... FP

FORTH Interest Group ... FIG

Fortid og Nutid [*A publication*] ... FN

Fortid og Nutid [*A publication*] ... FoN

Fortification ... FORT

Fortification ... FTN

Fortified ... FTD

Fortified Aqueous [*Pharmacology*] ... FA

Fortis [*Strong*] [*Pharmacy*] ... FORT

Fortissimo [*Very Loud*] [*Music*] ... FF

Fortissimo [*Very Loud*] [*Music*] ... FORTIS

Fortississimo [*As Loud as Possible*] [*Music*] ... FFF

Fortitudo Eius Rhodum Tenuit [*Motto of Lodovico family. Initials were used on gold coin struck by Duke Lodovico (1439-1465)*] ... FERT

Fortnight ... FRT

Fortnightly [*A publication*] ... F

Fortnightly [*A publication*] ... Fn

Fortnightly ... FORTN

Fortnightly Review [*A publication*] ... Fortn

Fortnightly Review [*A publication*] ... FortnR

Fortnightly Review [*A publication*] ... Fort Rev

Fortnightly Review [*A publication*] ... FR

Fortnightly Review of the Chicago Dental Society [*A publication*] ... Fortn Rev Chic Dent Soc

Fortpflanzung Besamung und Aufzucht der Haustiere [*A publication*] ... Fortpflanz Besamung Aufzucht Haustiere

FORTRAN-to-ALGOL Translator [*Data processing*] ... FALTRAN

FORTRAN [*Formula Translation*] **Analytical Cross Reference Tabulation System** [*Data processing*] ... FACTS

FORTRAN [*Formula Translation*] **Assembly Program** [*Data processing*] ... FAP

FORTRAN [*Formula Translation*] **Automatic Code Evaluation System** [*NASA*] [*Data processing*] ... FACES

FORTRAN [*Formula Translation*] **Automatic Timing System** [*Data processing*] ... FATS

FORTRAN Compiled Block-Oriented Simulation Language [*Data processing*] ... FORBLOC

FORTRAN [*Formula Translation*] **Graph Algorithmic Language** [*Data processing*] ... FGRAAL

FORTRAN Information Bulletin [*Data processing*] ... FIB

FORTRAN Input-Output Package [*Data processing*] ... FIOP

FORTRAN [*Formula Translation*] **Interactive Subroutine Library** [*Data processing*] ... FISLIB

FORTRAN and Internal Translator System [*Data processing*] ... FORTRANSIT

FORTRAN List Processing Language [*Data processing*] ... FLPL

FORTRAN Load and Go [*System*] [*Data processing*] ... FORGO

FORTRAN [*Formula Translation*] **Logical Information Retrieval Technique** [*Data processing*] ... FLIRT

FORTRAN Mathematical Programing System [*Data processing*] ... FMPS

FORTRAN [*Formula Translation*] **Matrix Abstraction Technique** [*Data processing*] ... FORMAT

FORTRAN [*Formula Translation*] **Matrix Abstraction Technique-FORTRAN** [*Data processing*] ... FORMAT-FORTRAN

FORTRAN [*Formula Translation*] **Matrix Analysis** [*Data processing*] ... FORMA

FORTRAN [*Formula Translation*] **Operating System** [*Data processing*] ... FOS

FORTRAN [*Formula Translation*] **Rules Used as a General Applications Language** [*Data processing*] ... FRUGAL

FORTRAN [*Formula Translation*] **Style Runcible** [*Data processing*] ... FORTRUNCIBLE

Fortress of Louisbourg, Canada Department of Indian Affairs and Northern Development, Fortress of Louisbourg, NS, Canada [*Library symbol*] ... CaNSLF

Fortschritte im Ackerund- Pflanzenbau [*A publication*] ... Fortschr Acker- Pflanzenbau

Fortschritte der Allergeilehre [*A publication*] ... Fortschr Allergeil

Fortschritte der Andrologie [*A publication*] ... Fortschr Androl

Fortschritte der Arzneimittelforschung [*A publication*] ... Fortschr Arzneimittelforsch

Fortschritte der Augenheilkunde [*A publication*] ... Fortschr Augenheilkd

Fortschritte Berichte. VDI Zeitschrift [*A publication*] ... Fortschr Ber VDI Z

Fortschritte der Botanik [*A publication*] ... Fortschr Bot

Fortschritte der Chemie Organischer Naturstoffe [*A publication*] ... Fortschr Chem Org Natr

Fortschritte der Chemie Organischer Naturstoffe [*A publication*] ... Fortschr Chem Org Naturst

Fortschritte der Chemischen Forschung [*A publication*] ... Fortschr Chem Forsch

Fortschritte der Evolutionsforschung [*A publication*] ... Fortschr Evolutionsforsch

Fortschritte der Experimentellen und Theoretischen Biophysik [*A publication*] ... Fortschr Exp Theor Biophys

Fortschritte der Experimentellen Tumorforschung [*A publication*] ... Fortschr Exp Tumorforsch

Fortschritte auf dem Gebiete der Roentgenstrahlen und der Nuklearmedizin [*A publication*] ... Fortschr Geb Roentgenstr Nuklearmed

Fortschritte auf dem Gebiete der Roentgenstrahlen und der Nuklearmedizin [*A publication*] ... F Roent Nuk

Fortschritte der Geburtshilfe und Gynaekologie [*A publication*] ... Fortschr Geburtshilfe Gynaekol

Fortschritte in der Geologie von Rheinland und Westfalen [*A publication*] ... Fortschr Geol Rheinl Westfalen

Fortschritte der Hals- Nasen Ohrenheilkunde [*A publication*] ... Fortschr Hals- Nasen Ohrenheilkd

Fortschritte der Hochpolymeren-Forschung [*A publication*] ... Fortschr Hochpolym-Forsch

Fortschritte der Kiefer und Gesichts Chirurgie [*A publication*] ... Fortschr Kiefer Gesichtschir

Fortschritte der Kieferorthopaedie [*A publication*] ... Fortschr Kieferorthop

Fortschritte der Krebsforschung [*A publication*] ... Fortschr Krebsforsch

Fortschritte der Medizin [*A publication*] ... Fortschr Med

Fortschritte der Medizinischen Virusforschung [*A publication*] ... Fortschr Med Virusforsch

Fortschritte der Mineralogie [*A publication*] ... Fortschr Mineral

Fortschritte der Neurologie, Psychiatrie, und Ihrer Grenzgebiete [*A publication*] ... F Neur Psyc

Fortschritte der Neurologie, Psychiatrie, und Ihrer Grenzgebiete [*A publication*] ... FNPGA

Fortschritte der Neurologie, Psychiatrie, und Ihrer Grenzgebiete [*A publication*] ... Fortschr Neurol Psychiatr Grenzgeb

Fortschritte der Neurologie, Psychiatrie, und Ihrer Grenzgebiete [*A publication*] ... Fortschr Neurol Psychiatr Ihrer Grenzgeb

Fortschritte der Pflanzenzuechtung [*A publication*] ... Fortschr Pflanzenzuecht

Fortschritte der Physik [*A publication*] ... Fortschr Ph

Fortschritte der Physik [*A publication*] ... Fortschr Phys

Fortschritte der Psychosomatischen Medizin [*A publication*] ... Fortschr Psychosom Med

Fortschritte in der Tierphysiologie und Tierernaehrung [*A publication*] ... Fortschr Tierphysiol Tierernaehr

Fortschritte der Tuberkuloseforschung [*A publication*] ... Fortschr Tuberkuloseforsch

Fortschritte der Verfahrenstechnik [*A publication*] ... Fortschr Verfahrenstech

Fortschritte der Verhaltensforschung [*A publication*] ... Fortschr Verhaltensforsch

Fortschritte der Veterinaermedizin [*A publication*] ... Fortschr Veterinaermed

Fortschritte der Zoologie [*A publication*] ... Fortschr Zool

Fortschrittsbericht fuer die Landwirtschaft [*A publication*] ... Fortschrber Landw

Fortsetzung Folgt [*To Be Continued*] [*German*] ... FF

Fortsetzung und Schluss Folgen [*To Be Continued and Concluded*] [*German*] ... FUSF

Fortuna, CA [*Location identifier*] [*FAA*] ... FOT

Fortuna, CA [*Radio station call letters*] ... KNCR

Fortune Federal Savings & Loan Association [*NASDAQ symbol*] ... FORF

Fortune National Corporation [*NASDAQ symbol*] ... FRNC

Fortune Society ... FS

Fortune Systems Corp. [*NASDAQ symbol*] ... FSYS

Forty Automatic Report Generating Operation ... FARGO

Forty-Eight Item Counseling Evaluation Test [*Psychology*] ... ICET

Forty-Mile Air [*Tok, AK*] [*FAA designator*] ... MLA

Forum for the Advancement of Toxicology in Colleges of Pharmacy ... FATCP

Forum Atomique Europeen [*European Atomic Forum*] ... FORATOM

Forum of Control Data Users [*Later, VIM, Inc.*] ... FOCUS

Forum for Death Education and Counseling ... FDEC

Forum, Denver, IA [*Library symbol*] ... IaDvF

Forum for the Discussion of New Trends in Education [*A publication*] ... Forum

Forum of Education [*A publication*] ... Forum Ed

Forum foer Ekonomi och Teknik [*A publication*] ... Forum Ekon Tek

Forum Group [*NASDAQ symbol*] ... FOUR

Forum (Houston) [*A publication*] ... ForumH

Forum Institute ... FI

Forum International: International Ecosystems University ... IEU

Forum International de Liaison des Forces de la Paix [*International Liaison Forum of Peace Forces - ILF*] ... FILFP

Forum Italiano dell'Energia Nucleare ... FIEN

Forum Italicum [*A publication*] ... FI

Forum Italicum [*A publication*] ... FoI

Forum der Letteren [*A publication*] ... FdL

Forum der Letteren [*A publication*] ... FL

Forum Linguisticum [*A publication*] ... For L

Forum Linguisticum [*A publication*] ... For Ling

Forum for Medical Affairs [*Formerly, CPOSMA*] ... FMA

Forum on Medicine [*A publication*] ... Forum Med

Forum for Modern Language Studies [*A publication*] ... FMLS

Forum on Public Affairs [*A publication*] ... Forum Pub Aff

Forum Romanum [*The Roman Forum*] ... FR

Forum Staedte-Hygiene [*A publication*] ... Forum Staedte-Hyg

Forum Theologiae Linguisticae [*A publication*] ..... FThL
Forum: A Ukrainian Review (Scranton, Pennsylvania) [*A publication*] ..... ForumS
Forum Umwelt Hygiene [*A publication*] ..... Forum Umwelt Hyg
Forum Umwelt Hygiene [*A publication*] ..... Forum Umw Hyg
Forum (Zagreb) [*A publication*] ..... ForumZ
Forward ..... F
Forward ..... FORD
Forward ..... FWD
Forward Acquisition RADAR ..... FAR
Forward Acquisition System ..... FAS
Forward/Aft ..... F/A
Forward Air Control [*or Controller*] [*Air Force*] ..... FAC
Forward Air Control Post ..... FACP
Forward Air Controller (Airborne) ..... FAC(A)
Forward Air Controller Terminal ..... FACTER
Forward Air Guide ..... FAG
Forward Air Strike Evaluation ..... FAST-VAL
Forward Air Strike Task ..... FAST
Forward Air Support Operations Center ..... FASOC
Forward Airborne Surveillance and Tracking ..... FAST
Forward Airfield Maintenance Organization ..... FAMO
Forward Airfield Supply Organization ..... FASO
Forward Airhead Maintenance Area [*Military*] [*British*] ..... FAMA
Forward America ..... FA
Forward Area Air Defense ..... FAAD
Forward Area Air Defense System ..... FAADS
Forward Area Air Defense Weapon ..... FAADW
Forward Area Alerting RADAR ..... FAAR
Forward Area Alerting System ..... FAAS
Forward Area Deployment, Spain ..... FADS
Forward Area LASER Systems - Tactical and Fiscal [*Military*] ..... FALSTAF
Forward Area LASER Weapon ..... FALW
Forward Area Rawinsonde Set [*Army*] ..... FARS
Forward Area Rearm and Refuel Point ..... FARRP
Forward Area Refueling Equipment [*Army*] ..... FARE
Forward Area Resupply Point ..... FARP
Forward Area SONAR Research ..... FASOR
Forward Area Support Coordination Officer [*Army*] ..... FASCO
Forward Area Support Helicopter ..... FASH
Forward Area Tactical Teletype ..... FATT
Forward Area Weapons [*Military*] ..... FAW
Forward Ballast Tank ..... FBT
Forward-Based Systems [*US aircraft based outside the US and capable of carrying nuclear weapons to the USSR*] ..... FBS
Forward Battle Zone [*British*] ..... FBZ
Forward Body ..... FB
Forward Bomb Line ..... FWDBL
Forward Brigade Administrative Area [*British*] ..... FWDBAA
Forward Calculation Request ..... FCR
Forward Collect ..... FWDC
Forward Combat Zone ..... FCZ
Forward Command Post ..... FCP
Forward Compartment ..... F
Forward Defended Locality [*Military*] [*British*] ..... FDL
Forward Defense Post ..... FDP
Forward Direction Center [*Air Force*] ..... FDC
Forward Director Post ..... FDP
Forward Distribution Point [*Military*] ..... FDP
Forward Echelon, Communications Zone [*Europe*] [*Army*] ..... FECOMZ
Forward Echelon, Communications Zone [*Europe*] [*Army*] ..... FECZ
Forward Edge of the Battle Area [*Army*] ..... FEBA
Forward End Cap ..... FEC
Forward Engine Room ..... FER
Forward Equipment Bay ..... FEB
Forward Error Correction [*Computer code*] ..... FEC
Forward Error Detection and Correction ..... FEDAC
Forward Events Controller ..... FEC
Forward of the FEBA [*Military*] ..... FOFEBA
Forward Fighting Aircraft Rocket ..... FFAR
Forward Fighting Operating Base [*Military*] ..... FFOB
Forward Firing Aircraft ..... FFAR
Forward Firing Ordnance ..... FFO
Forward Floating Depot [*Army*] ..... FFD
Forward Fuel Ballast Tank ..... FFBT
Forward Gate ..... FG
Forward Half-Line [*Feed*] ..... FHL
Forward Heat Shield [*NASA*] ..... FHS
Forward Heat Shield ..... FWDHTSHLD
Forward Heat-Shield Separation [*NASA*] ..... FHSS
Forward Industries, Inc. [*NASDAQ symbol*] ..... FORD
Forward Inspection Team [*Military*] ..... FIT
Forward Interpretation Unit [*Military*] ..... FIU
Forward Launched Aerodynamic Missiles ..... FLAM
Forward Line of Own Troops ..... FLOT
Forward Load Control ..... FLC
Forward Load Control Assembly ..... FLCA
Forward-Loading Infrared ..... FLIR
Forward-Looking Advanced Multimode RADAR ..... FLAMR
Forward-Looking Airborne Moving Target Indication ..... FLAMTI
Forward-Looking Airborne RADAR ..... FLAR
Forward-Looking Infrared [*Device*] ..... FLI
Forward-Looking Infrared ..... FLIR
Forward-Looking Infrared Attack Set ..... FLIRAS
Forward-Looking RADAR ..... FLR
Forward-Looking RADAR Set ..... FLRS
Forward Maintenance Area ..... FMA
Forward Master Events Controller [*NASA*] ..... FMEC
Forward Motion ..... FM
Forward Motion Compensation ..... FMC
Forward Observation Officer [*Military*] ..... FOO
Forward Observation Post [*Military*] ..... FOP
Forward Observer [*Military*] ..... FO
Forward Observer Bombardment ..... FOB
Forward Observer Colidar ..... FOC
Forward Observer LASER Range-Finder ..... FOLR
Forward Observer Target Survey Unit ..... FOBTSU
Forward Operating Base [*Air Force*] ..... FOB
Forward Operating Location [*Military*] ..... FOL
Forward Peak Tank [*On ships*] ..... FPT
Forward Perpendicular ..... FP
Forward Port Capabilities [*Navy*] ..... FORPORT
Forward Power Control Assembly ..... FPCA
Forward Power Controller ..... FPC
Forward Propagation by Ionospheric Scatter [*Radio communications technique*] ..... FPIS
Forward Propagation by Tropospheric Scatter [*Radio communications technique*] ..... FPTS
Forward Reaction Control Subsystem [*NASA*] ..... FRCS
Forward Reaction Jet Driver ..... FRJD
Forward Reconnaissance ..... FORECON
Forward Refueling Area ..... FRA
Forward Refueling Point ..... FRP
Forward Repair Team [*Military*] [*British*] ..... FRT
Forward Scatter ..... FS
Forward Scatter ..... FSC
Forward Scatter System ..... FSS
Forward-Scattering Spectrometer Probe [*Aerosol measurement device*] ..... FSSP
Forward Service Support Element ..... FSSE
Forward Skirt Adapter ..... FSA
Forward Supply Point [*Military*] ..... FSP
Forward Supply Support ..... FSS
Forward Support ..... FS
Forward Support Area [*Military*] ..... FSA
Forward Support Element ..... FSE
Forward Support Patrol Base ..... FSPB
Forward Swept Wing ..... FSW
Forward Transfer Admittance ..... FTA
Forward Traveling Wave ..... FTW
Forward Utility Bridge ..... FUB
Forward Visibility ..... FV
Forward Wave Amplifier ..... FWA
Forward Wave Tube ..... FWT
Forward Weapons Controller [*Military*] ..... FORWEPCON
Forward of Wing [*Aerospace*] ..... FW
Forwarded ..... FWDD
Forwarders Certificate of Receipt [*Shipping*] ..... FCR
Forzato [*Strongly Accented*] [*Music*] ..... FORZ
Forzato [*or Forzando*] [*Strongly Accented*] [*Music*] ..... FZ
Foss Launch & Tug [*AAR code*] ..... FLT
Fossil Energy Information Center [*ORNL*] ..... FEIC
Fossil Energy Update [*A publication*] ..... FEU
Fossil Fuel Resources Committee ..... FFRC
Fossil Oil & Gas Co. [*NASDAQ symbol*] ..... FOSL
Fosston, MN [*Location identifier*] [*FAA*] ..... FSE
Fosston, MN [*Radio station call letters*] ..... KEHG
Fosston, MN [*Radio station call letters*] ..... KEHG-FM
Foster Aviation [*Nome, AK*] [*FAA designator*] ..... FSA
Foster [*L. B.*] **Co. Cl A** [*NASDAQ symbol*] ..... FSTRA
Foster Father ..... FF
Foster Grandparent Program [*of ACTION*] ..... FGP
Foster Medical Corp. [*NASDAQ symbol*] ..... FMED
Foster Mother ..... FM
Foster Parents' Plan ..... FPP
Foster-Seeley Discriminator ..... FSD
Foster Wheeler-Bergbau Forschung [*Flue gas treatment*] ..... FW-BF
Foster Wheeler Corporation [*NYSE symbol*] ..... FWC
Fostering, or Fighting, Innovations and Experiment in Teaching [*Game*] ..... FIXIT
Foster's Monthly Reference Lists [*A publication*] ..... Foster Mo Ref
Fostoria Glass Society of America ..... FGSA
Fostoria, OH [*Radio station call letters*] ..... WFOB
Fostoria, OH [*Radio station call letters*] ..... WFOB-FM
Fotografia Industrial, Sociedad Anonima ..... FISA
Fotomat Corp. [*NYSE symbol*] ..... FOT
Foucault Rotating Mirror [*Physics*] ..... FRM
Fougamou [*Gabon*] [*Airport symbol*] ..... FOU
Fouilles de Delphes [*A publication*] ..... FdD
Fouilles de l'Institut Francais d'Archeologie Orientale [*A publication*] ..... FIFAO
Foul ..... F

Foul Bottom [*Navigation signal*] ... fb
Foul Fly [*Baseball*] ... FF
Fouled Up [*To describe a confused, mixed-up situation, person, or action*] [*Bowdlerized version*] ... FU
Fouled Up Beyond All Recognition [*Military slang*] [*Bowdlerized version*] ... FUBAR
Fouled Up Beyond Belief [*Military slang*] [*Bowdlerized version*] ... FUBB
Fouled Up More Than Usual [*See FU*] [*Bowdlerized version*] ... FUMTU
Foulwind [*New Zealand*] [*Seismograph station code, US Geological Survey*] [*Closed*] ... FLW
Found ... FND
Found Abandoned ... FA
Foundation ... FDN
Foundation ... FNDN
Foundation [*A publication*] ... FOU
Foundation ... FOUND
Foundation ... FOUNDN
Foundation for Accounting Education ... FAE
Foundation for Accredited Chiropractic Education [*Later, Foundation for Chiropractic Education and Research*] ... FACE
Foundation for Administrative Research ... FAR
Foundation for the Advancement of Artists ... FAA
Foundation for the Advancement of Chiropractic Tenets and Science ... FACTS
Foundation of America ... FA
Foundation for American Agriculture [*Later, FAAPFF*] ... FAA
Foundation for American Agriculture Program of the Farm Foundation [*Formerly, FAA*] ... FAAPFF
Foundation of American College of Nursing Home Administrators ... FACNHA
Foundation for American Communications ... FACS
Foundation of the American Economic Council ... FAEC
Foundation for America's Sexually Exploited Children ... FASEC
Foundation for the Arts of Peace ... FAP
Foundation Beefmasters Association ... FBA
Foundation for Better Living ... FBL
Foundation for Blood Irradiation ... FFBI
Foundation for Books to China ... FBC
Foundation Center ... FC
Foundation Center Library, New York, NY [*Library symbol*] ... NNFoC
Foundation for Character Education ... FCE
Foundation for Child Development ... FCD
Foundation for Child Mental Welfare ... FCMW
Foundation for Children with Learning Disabilities ... FCLD
Foundation for Chiropractic Education and Research ... FCER
Foundation for a Christian Civilization ... FCC
Foundation for Christian Living ... FCL
Foundation for Christian Theology ... FCT
Foundation Code [*IRS*] ... FC
Foundation for Commercial Banks ... FCB
Foundation for the Community of Artists ... FCA
Foundation for Community Creativity ... FCC
Foundation for Cooperative Housing [*Later, CHF*] ... FCH
Foundation for Cotton Research and Education [*Later, The Cotton Foundation*] ... FCRE
Foundation for Cure ... FFC
Foundation for Depression and Manic Depression ... FDMD
Foundation for Economic Education ... FEE
Foundation for Education and Research in Vision ... FERV
Foundation for the Establishment of an International Criminal Court ... FEICC
Foundation for Ethnic Dance ... FED
Foundation for Exceptional Children ... FEC
Foundation for Extension and Development of the American Professional Theatre ... FEDAPT
Foundation Facts [*A publication*] ... Found Facts
Foundation Faith of God ... FFG
Foundation of the Federal Bar Association ... FFBA
Foundation for Fire Safety ... FFS
Foundation of the Flexographic Technical Association ... FFTA
Foundation for Foreign Affairs ... FFA
Foundation for a Future ... FFF
Foundation for Gifted and Creative Children ... FGCC
Foundation for Giraffe Rescue ... FGR
Foundation for Hand Research ... FHR
Foundation for Health Services Research ... FHSR
Foundation of Human Understanding ... FHU
Foundation to Improve Television ... FIT
Foundation for Innovation in Medicine ... FIM
Foundation for Instrumentation Education and Research [*Defunct*] ... FIER
Foundation for Insurance Reform and Education ... FIRE
Foundation for Integrative Education ... FIE
Foundation for Interior Design Education Research ... FIDER
Foundation for International Cooperation ... FIC
Foundation for International Human Relations ... FIHR
Foundation for International Potash Research [*Later, PI*] ... FIPR
Foundation for International Trade Research ... FITR
Foundation for the Jewish National Fund ... FJNF
Foundation for Latin American Anthropological Research ... FLAAR
Foundation of Law and Society [*Defunct*] ... FLS
Foundation for Medical Technology ... FMT
Foundation Member ... FM
Foundation for Microbiology ... FFM
Foundation for Middle East Peace ... FMEP
Foundation of Motion Picture Pioneers ... FMPP
Foundation for National Progress ... FNP
Foundation News [*A publication*] ... Found News
Foundation for Non-Lethal Warfare ... FNLW
Foundation for Oceanographic Research and Education ... FORE
Foundation for the Peoples of the South Pacific ... FSP
Foundation for Preservation of the Archeological Heritage ... FPAH
Foundation for the Preservation and Protection of the Przewalski Horse ... FPPPH
Foundation for Public Affairs ... FPA
Foundation for Public Relations Research and Education ... FPRRE
Foundation for Rational Economics and Education ... FREE
Foundation for Reformation Research, St. Louis, MO [*Library symbol*] [*Obsolete*] ... MoSFRR
Foundation for Religious Action in the Social and Civil Order ... FRASCO
Foundation for Research in the Afro-American Creative Arts ... FRAACA
Foundation for Research on Human Behavior ... FRHB
Foundation for Research on the Nature of Man ... FRNM
Foundation Research Service ... FRS
Foundation for Science and the Handicapped ... FSH
Foundation for Scientific Relaxation ... FSR
Foundation for Student Communication ... FSC
Foundation for the Study of Cycles ... FSC
Foundation for the Study of Independent Social Ideas ... FSISI
Foundation for the Study of Presidential and Congressional Terms ... FSPCT
Foundation for the Study of Primitive Culture ... FSPC
Foundation for the Study of Wilson's Disease ... FSWD
Foundation for the Support of International Medical Training ... FSIMT
Foundation of Thanatology ... FT
Foundation of the Wall and Ceiling Industry ... FWCI
Foundation for World Literacy [*Defunct*] ... FWL
Foundation for Youth and Student Affairs [*Defunct*] ... FYSA
Foundations [*Baptist*] [*A publication*] ... Foun
Foundations of Control Engineering [*Poland*] [*A publication*] ... Found Control Eng
Foundations and Donors Interested in Catholic Activities ... FDICA
Foundations of Information Science [*American Society for Information Science*] ... FIS
Foundations of Language [*A publication*] ... F Lang
Foundations of Language [*A publication*] ... FoL
Foundations of Language [*A publication*] ... Found Lang
Foundations of Linguistics Series [*Elsevier Book Series*] [*A publication*] ... FLS
Foundations of Physics [*A publication*] ... Found Phys
Founded ... F
Founded ... FNDD
Founder ... FDR
Founder ... FNDR
Founders Financial Corp. [*NASDAQ symbol*] ... FOUN
Founding ... FNDG
Foundry ... FDRY
Foundry Educational Foundation ... FEF
Foundry Equipment Manufacturers Association ... FEMA
Foundry Facings Manufacturers Group [*Later, FSMG*] ... FFMG
Foundry Management and Technology [*A publication*] ... Foundry Manage Technol
Foundry Practice [*A publication*] ... Foundry Pract
Foundry Supply Manufacturers Group [*Formerly, FFMG*] ... FSMG
Foundry Trade Journal [*A publication*] ... Found Trade J
Fountain ... FTN
Fountain Inn, SC [*Radio station call letters*] ... WFIS
Fountainwell Drama Series [*A publication*] ... FDS
Fountainwell Drama Texts [*A publication*] ... FDT
Four-Address to SOAP [*Self-Optimizing Automatic Pilot*] **Translator** ... FAST
Four-Bar Cutter Device ... FCD
Four Bears, ND [*Radio station call letters*] ... KMHA
Four-Coil Differential Transformer ... FCDT
Four-Conductor [*Wire or cable*] ... 4/C
Four-Conductor Cables [*JETDS nomenclature*] [*Military*] ... WF
Four-Conductor, Heat-and-Flame-Resistant, Armor [*Cable*] ... FHFA
Four Corners Geological Society. Bulletin [*A publication*] ... Four Corners Geol Soc Bull
Four Corners Geological Society. Field Conference. Guidebook [*A publication*] ... Four Corners Geol Soc Field Conf Guideb
Four Corners Regional Commission [*Department of Commerce*] ... FCRC
Four County Library System, Binghamton, NY [*Library symbol*] ... NBiF
Four County Library System, Binghamton, NY [*OCLC symbol*] ... YXF
Four Cylinder Club of America ... FCCA
Four-Dimensional ... 4-D
Four-Horse Club [*British*] ... FHC
Four Island Air Ltd. [*Antigua*] [*ICAO designator*] ... FX
Four London Airport Group [*British*] ... FLAG
Four Mile Canyon [*Oregon*] [*Seismograph station code, US Geological Survey*] ... FMC
Four-Phase Systems, Inc. [*NYSE symbol*] [*Delisted*] ... FPS
Four Picture Test [*Psychology*] ... FPT
Four-Pole [*Switch*] ... 4P

Four-Pole, Double-Throw [*Switch*] 4PDT
Four-Pole, Single-Throw [*Switch*] 4PST
Four-Pole Switch 4PSW
Four Power Joint Military Commission .... FPJMC
Four-Quadrant Multiplier .... FQM
Four Quarters [*A publication*] .... Four Qt
Four Quarters [*A publication*] .... FQ
Four Rivers Area Library Services Authority [*Library network*] .... ALSA
Four Sigma Society .... FSS
Four Sons Flying Service [*Dodge City, KS*] [*FAA designator*] .... AKS
Four Star International, Inc. [*NASDAQ symbol*] .... FSTA
Four-Terminal Field-Effect Transistor .... FTFET
Four-Way RADAR Surveillance .... QUADRADAR
Four-Wheel Brake .... FWB
Four-Wheel Drive .... FWD
Four-Wheel Drive [*Vehicle*] 4WD
Four Winds Aviation Ltd. [*Colorado Springs, CO*] [*FAA designator*] .... WDS
Four-Wire 4W
Four-Wire, Shipboard, General Use, Armored [*Cable*] .... FSGA
Four-Year Plan .... FYP
Fourdrinier Kraft Board Group - American Paper Institute [*Formerly, FKBI*] .... FKBG-API
Fourdrinier Kraft Board Institute [*Later, FKBG-API*] .... FKBI
Fourdrinier Wire Council .... FWC
Fourier Coefficient Harmonic Analyzer .... FOCOHANA
Fourier Integral Estimate .... FIE
Fourier Ion Resonance Mass Spectrometer .... FIRMS
Fourier Number [*IUPAC*] .... Fo
Fourier Transform .... FT
Fourier Transform-Faradic Admittance Measurements [*Spectrometry*] .... FT-FAM
Fourier Transform Infrared [*Spectroscopy*] .... FT-IR
Fourier Transform-Ion Cyclotron Resonance [*Spectrometry*] .... FT-ICR
Fourier Transform/Mass Spectrometry .... FT/MS
Fourier Transform-Nuclear Magnetic Resonance [*Spectrometry*] .... FT-NMR
Fourier Transform Operator .... FTO
Fourier Transform Spectrometer [*or Spectroscopy*] .... FTS
Fourier Transform System .... FTS
Fourth Allied Tactical Air Force, Central Europe .... FOURATAF
Fourth Day [*NYSE symbol*] [*Delisted*] .... FD
Fourth Dimension [*Time*] .... FD
Fourth Financial Corp. [*NASDAQ symbol*] .... FRTH
Fourth of July Road .... F of JR
Fourth Section [*of Interstate Commerce Act*] .... FS
Fourth Stowage Adapter Container .... FSAC
Fowl Antimouse Lymphocyte Globulin [*Immunochemistry*] .... FALG
Fowl Plague Virus .... FPV
Fowler, A. R., Saint Paul MN [*STAC*] .... FAR
Fowler, CA [*Radio station call letters*] .... KLIP
Fowler, CA [*Radio station call letters*] .... KTED
Fowler Public Library, Fowler, CO [*Library symbol*] .... CoFow
Fowlerville Public Library, Fowlerville, MI [*Library symbol*] .... MiFow
Fox [*Phonetic alphabet*] [*World War II*] .... F
Fox, AK [*Location identifier*] [*FAA*] .... FOX
Fox Breeders Gazette [*A publication*] .... Fox Breeders Gaz
Fox-Stanley Photo Products, Inc. [*NYSE symbol*] .... FSP
Foxboro Co. [*NYSE symbol*] .... FOX
Foxmeyer Corp. [*NASDAQ symbol*] .... FOXM
Foxmoor International Films [*NASDAQ symbol*] .... FOXI
Foxtrot [*Phonetic alphabet*] .... F
Foya [*Liberia*] [*Airport symbol*] .... FOY
FPA Corp. [*American Stock Exchange symbol*] .... FPO
FR Liquidating Group SBI [*American Stock Exchange symbol*] [*Delisted*] .... FR
Fra Fysikkens Verden [*A publication*] .... Fra Fys Verden
Fra Ny-Carlsberg Glyptoteks Sammlingen [*A publication*] .... NCGS
Fra Randers Amt [*A publication*] .... FRA
Fra Sundhedsstyrelsen (Copenhagen) [*A publication*] .... Fra Sundhedsstyr (Copenhagen)
Fracana Oil & Gas Ltd. [*American Stock Exchange symbol*] [*Delisted*] .... FOG
Fracastoro [*A publication*] .... Fraca
Fracti Dosi [*In Divided Doses*] [*Pharmacy*] .... FRACT DOS
Fraction .... FRACT
Fraction Inspired Oxygen [*Physiology*] .... FIO
Fraction of Labeled Mitoses [*Measurement of cell labeling*] .... FLM
Fraction Optimizing .... FO
Fraction-Optimizing X-Y Collector [*Spectroscopy*] .... FOXY
Fraction Reliability Deviation .... FRD
Fraction Thereof .... FCT
Fractional .... FRAC
Fractional Brownian Motion [*Mathematics*] .... fBm
Fractional Doppler Gate .... FDG
Fractional Horsepower .... FHP
Fractional Orbital Bombardment .... FOB
Fractional Orbital Bombardment System .... FOBS
Fractional Shortening [*Cardiology*] .... FS
Fractional Test Meal [*Medicine*] .... FTM
Fractional and Unknown Nuclear [*Material in meteorites*] .... FUN
Fractional Urinalysis [*Medicine*] .... FU
Fractionator Reflux Analog Computer .... FRAC
Fractocumulus [*Meteorology*] .... FC
Fractocumulus [*Meteorology*] .... FRCU
Fractographic Examination .... FGE
Fractostratus [*Meteorology*] .... FS
Fracture .... F
Fracture [*Medicine*] .... FRAC
Fracture [*Medicine*] .... FRACT
Fracture [*Medicine*] .... FX
Fracture Appearance Transition Temperature .... FATT
Fracture, Simple [*Medicine*] .... FS
Fracture Toughness Parameter .... FTP
Fracture Zone [*Geophysics*] .... FZ
Fragile .... F
Fragile .... FRAG
Fragility Response Spectrum .... FRS
Fragment .... FR
Fragment [*Military*] .... FRAG
Fragment [*Used in correcting manuscripts, etc.*] .... FRAG
Fragment, Antigen-Binding [*Immunochemistry*] .... Fab
Fragment Connection Table [*Chemistry*] .... FCT
Fragment, Crystallizable [*of an antibody*] [*Immunochemistry*] .... Fc
Fragmenta Balcanica. Musei Macedonici Scientiarum Naturalium [*A publication*] .... Fragm Balc Mus Macedonici Sci Nat
Fragmenta Botanica [*A publication*] .... Fragm Bot
Fragmenta Entomologica [*A publication*] .... Fragm Entomol
Fragmenta Faunistica (Warsaw) [*A publication*] .... Fragm Faun (Warsaw)
Fragmenta Floristica et Geobotanica (Cracow) [*A publication*] .... Fragm Florist Geobot (Cracow)
Fragmenta Herbologica Jugoslavica [*A publication*] .... Fragm Herbol Jugosl
Fragmenta Mineralogica et Palaeontologica [*A publication*] .... Fragm Mineral Palaeontol
Fragmentary Order [*Military*] .... FRAGO
Fragmentation .... F
Fragmentation Bomb .... FRAGBOMB
Fragmentation Bomb, Parachute .... FRP
Fragmente der Griechischen Historiker [*A publication*] .... FGrHist
Fragmented Network .... FRAGNET
Fragmenting Offensive Aerial Mine .... FOAM
Fragmenting Warhead Rocket .... FRAGROC
Fragments .... FRAGM
Fragrance Foundation .... FF
Fragrance Materials Association of the US .... FMA
Fram Corporation [*NYSE symbol*] [*Delisted*] .... FRC
Frame .... FR
Frame .... FRM
Frame Check Sequence [*Data processing*] .... FCS
Frame Construction .... F
Frame Difference .... FD
Frame Difference Signal .... FDS
Frame Ground [*Data processing*] .... FG
Frame Protected [*Insurance classification*] .... FP
Frame Reference Line .... FRL
Frame Representation Language [*Data processing*] .... FRL
Frame Scan .... FS
Frame Storage System [*Television*] .... FSS
Frame Sync Indication .... FSI
Frame Synchronization Word .... FW
Frame Table Entry [*Data processing*] .... FTE
Frame Unprotected [*Insurance classification*] .... FU
Framed [*Construction*] .... FD
Framed .... FRMD
Frames to Come [*Optometry*] .... FTC
Frames per Inch [*Data processing*] .... FPI
Frames per Second [*Photography*] .... FPS
Framework .... FRWK
Framework Molecular Models .... FMM
Framing Camera Mopper .... FCM
Framingham, MA [*Radio station call letters*] .... WDJM-FM
Framingham, MA [*Radio station call letters*] .... WKOX
Framingham, MA [*Radio station call letters*] .... WVBF
Framingham Public Library, Framingham, MA [*OCLC symbol*] .... FRM
Framingham Relative Weight Index [*Cardiology*] .... FRWI
Framingham State College, Framingham, MA [*OCLC symbol*] .... FST
Framingham State College, Framingham, MA [*Library symbol*] .... MFmT
Framingham Town Library, Framingham, MA [*Library symbol*] .... MFm
Framycetin [*Neomycin B*] [*Antibacterial compound*] .... FRA
Framycetin [*Neomycin B*], **Colistin** [*Antineoplastic drug regimen*] .... FRACO
Framycetin [*Neomycin B*], **Colistin, Nystatin** [*Antineoplastic drug regimen*] .... FRACON
Fran Lee Foundation .... FLF
Franc [*Monetary unit in Belgium*] .... BF
Franc [*Monetary unit in Burundi*] .... BFU
Franc [*Monetary unit in France*] .... F
Franc [*Monetary unit in French Somaliland*] .... FD
Franc [*Monetary unit in Marie Galente*] .... FF
Franc [*Monetary unit in the Malagasy Republic*] .... FMG
Franc [*Monetary unit in France*] .... FR
Franc [*Monetary unit in Luxembourg*] .... L FR
Franc [*Monetary unit in Rwanda*] .... RF
Franc de Droits [*Free of charge*] [*French*] .... FDD
Franc Mali [*Monetary unit in Mali*] .... FM
Franca [*Brazil*] [*Airport symbol*] .... FRC

Francais [*French*] ... F
Francais Moderne [*A publication*] ... FM
Francais dans le Monde [*A publication*] ... FMonde
Francais au Nigeria [*A publication*] ... Fa N
France [*MARC geographic area code*] [*Library of Congress*] ... e-fr---
France ... F
France [*MARC country of publication code*] [*Library of Congress*] ... fr
France [*Three-letter standard code*] ... FRA
France [*Aircraft nationality and registration mark*] ... F
France [*Two-letter standard code*] ... FR
France-Amerique [*A publication*] ... FA
France-Asie [*A publication*] ... FrA
France, BENELUX ... FBX
France and Colonies Philatelic Society ... FCPS
France au Combat [*A publication*] ... FAC
France-Eurafrique [*A publication*] ... FE
France Franciscaine [*A publication*] ... FF
France Illustration [*A publication*] ... France Illus
France Illustration. Supplement [*A publication*] ... France Illus Sup
France, Italy, Netherlands, Belgium, and Luxembourg [*Economic agreement*] ... FINEBEL
France Latine [*A publication*] ... FrL
France Libre [*A publication*] ... FL
Franchise of Americans Needing Sports ... FANS
Franchise Industry Training [*High school dropout program*] [*Department of Labor*] ... FIT
Francis Bacon Foundation ... FBF
Francis Bacon Foundation, Inc., Claremont, CA [*Library symbol*] ... CCFB
Francis Bacon Society ... FBS
Francis Bitter National Magnet Laboratory [*MIT*] ... FBNML
Francis Grose Society [*Defunct*] ... FGS
Francis Marion College, Florence, SC [*Library symbol*] ... ScFIM
Francis Marion College, Florence, SC [*OCLC symbol*] ... SFM
Francis Marion National Forest [*South Carolina*] [*Seismograph station code, US Geological Survey*] [*Closed*] ... FMF
Francis Peak [*Utah*] [*Seismograph station code, US Geological Survey*] ... FPU
Franciscan ... FRANS
Franciscan Apostolate of the Way of the Cross ... FAWC
[*From the Latin for*] **Franciscan Brothers of the Holy Cross** [*Roman Catholic religious order*] ... FFSC
Franciscan Education Center, Lake Geneva, WI [*Library symbol*] ... WLagF
Franciscan Educational Conference [*Defunct*] ... FEC
Franciscan Handmaids of the Most Pure Heart of Mary [*Roman Catholic religious order*] ... FHM
Franciscan Hospitaller Sisters of the Immaculate Conception [*Roman Catholic religious order*] ... FHIC
Franciscan Missionaries of the Divine Motherhood [*Roman Catholic religious order*] ... FMDM
Franciscan Missionaries of Mary [*Roman Catholic women's religious order*] ... FMM
Franciscan Missionaries of St. Joseph [*Mill Hill Sisters*] [*Roman Catholic religious order*] ... FMSJ
Franciscan Missionary Sisters of Assisi [*Roman Catholic religious order*] ... SFMG
Franciscan Missionary Sisters of the Divine Child [*Roman Catholic religious order*] ... FMDC
Franciscan Missionary Sisters of the Sacred Heart [*Roman Catholic religious order*] ... FMSC
Franciscan Monastery, Washington, DC [*Library symbol*] ... DFM
Franciscan Preparatory Seminary ... FPS
Franciscan Sisters of Mary Immaculate of the Third Order of St. Francis of Assisi [*Roman Catholic religious order*] ... FMI
Franciscan Sisters of Our Lady of the Holy Angels [*Roman Catholic religious order*] ... BMVA
Franciscan Sisters of the Poor [*Roman Catholic religious order*] ... SFP
Franciscan Sisters of Ringwood [*Roman Catholic religious order*] ... FSR
Franciscan Sisters of St. Elizabeth [*Roman Catholic religious order*] ... FSSE
Franciscan Sisters of St. Joseph [*Roman Catholic religious order*] ... FSSJ
Franciscan Sisters of the Third Order of the Immaculate Conception [*Roman Catholic religious order*] ... FSIC
Franciscan Studies [*A publication*] ... FranS
Franciscan Studies [*A publication*] ... Fran Stds
Franciscan Studies [*A publication*] ... Fran Stud
Franciscan Studies [*A publication*] ... FS
Franciscan Studies [*A publication*] ... FSt
[*From the Latin for*] **Franciscan Tertiaries of the Holy Cross** ... TFSC
Franciscan Vocation Conference [*Formerly, AFSV*] [*Defunct*] ... FVC
Franciscana [*A publication*] ... Franc
Franciscansch Leven [*A publication*] ... FL
Francistown [*Botswana*] [*Airport symbol*] ... FRW
Francium [*Chemical element*] ... Fr
Franck Drawing Completion Test [*Psychology*] ... FDCT
Franco [*Free*] ... FCO
Franco American Committee for Educational Travel and Studies [*Later, FACETS Tour France*] ... FACETS
Franco Maria Ricci [*A publication*] ... FMR
Franconia Notch [*New Hampshire*] [*Seismograph station code, US Geological Survey*] [*Closed*] ... FNN
Frank Aviation, Inc. [*Dallas, TX*] [*FAA designator*] ... NHK
Frank Gasperro [*Designer's mark, when appearing on US coins*] ... FG
Frank J. Seiler Research Laboratory [*Air Force*] ... FJSRL
Frank L. Weyenberg Library, Mequon, WI [*Library symbol*] ... WMeq
Frank Lloyd Wright Association ... FLWA
Frank Lloyd Wright Foundation ... FLWF
Frank Nelson Doubleday [*American publisher*] ... FND
Frank Phillips College [*Texas*] ... FPC
Frank Phillips College, Borger, TX [*Library symbol*] ... TxBorF
Frank W. Horner Ltd. [*Canada*] [*Research code symbol*] ... FWH
Frank W. Horner Ltd., Montreal, PQ, Canada [*Library symbol*] ... CaQMFH
Frankford Arsenal [*Pennsylvania*] [*Army*] [*Closed*] ... FA
Frankford Arsenal ... FFA
Frankford Public Library, Frankford, PA [*Library symbol*] ... PF
Frankfort & Cincinnati Railroad Co. [*AAR code*] ... FCIN
Frankfort City Library, Frankfort, MI [*Library symbol*] ... MiFra
Frankfort Horizontal [*Eye-ear plane*] [*Anatomy*] ... FH
Frankfort, IN [*Radio station call letters*] ... WILO
Frankfort, IN [*Radio station call letters*] ... WSHW
Frankfort, KY [*Location identifier*] [*FAA*] ... JET
Frankfort, KY [*Radio station call letters*] ... WFKY
Frankfort, KY [*Radio station call letters*] ... WKED
Frankfort, KY [*Radio station call letters*] ... WKYW
Frankfort, MI [*Radio station call letters*] ... WBNZ
Frankfort Public Library District, Frankfort, IL [*Library symbol*] ... IFf
Frankfurt [*West Germany*] [*Airport symbol*] ... FRA
Frankfurter Allgemeine [*A publication*] ... FrankfAllg
Frankfurter Allgemeine Zeitung [*A publication*] ... FAZ
Frankfurter Arbeiten aus dem Gebiete der Anglistik und der Amerika-Studien [*A publication*] ... FAGAAS
Frankfurter Beitraege zur Anglistik und Amerikanistik [*A publication*] ... FBAA
Frankfurter Beitraege zur Germanistik [*A publication*] ... FBG
Frankfurter Hefte [*A publication*] ... FH
Frankfurter Hefte [*A publication*] ... Frankfurt H
Frankfurter Hefte. Zeitschrift fuer Kultur und Politik [*A publication*] ... Frankf Hefte
Frankfurter Historische Forschungen [*A publication*] ... Frankf Hist Forsch
Frankfurter Verein fuer Geographie und Statistik. Jahresbericht [*A publication*] ... Frankfurter Ver Geog Jber
Frankfurter Zeitschrift fuer Pathologie [*A publication*] ... Frankf Z Pathol
Frankische Forschungen [*A publication*] ... FF
Franklin [*Pennsylvania*] [*Airport symbol*] ... FKL
Franklin [*Also, sC, statC*] [*Unit of electric charge*] ... Fr
Franklin Bancorp of New Jersey [*NASDAQ symbol*] ... FRBC
Franklin College of Indiana ... FCI
Franklin College of Indiana, Franklin, IN [*OCLC symbol*] ... IFC
Franklin College of Indiana, Franklin, IN [*Library symbol*] ... InFrlC
Franklin Consolidated Mining [*NASDAQ symbol*] ... FKCM
Franklin Corp. [*NASDAQ symbol*] ... FKLN
Franklin D. Roosevelt Library ... FDRL
Franklin D. Roosevelt Library, Hyde Park, NY [*Library symbol*] [*Obsolete*] ... NHpR
Franklin D. Roosevelt Philatelic Society ... FDRPS
Franklin Delano Roosevelt ... FDR
Franklin Electric Co. [*NASDAQ symbol*] ... FELE
Franklin General Hospital, Valley Stream, NY [*Library symbol*] ... NVsFH
Franklin, IN [*Radio station call letters*] ... WFCI
Franklin, IN [*Radio station call letters*] ... WGAQ
Franklin Institute. Journal [*A publication*] ... Franklin Inst J
Franklin Institute Laboratories ... FIL
Franklin Institute Laboratories Universal Pulser ... FILUP
Franklin Institute, Philadelphia, PA [*Library symbol*] [*OCLC symbol*] ... PPF
Franklin Institute Research Laboratories ... FIRL
Franklin-Johnson County Public Library, Franklin, IN [*OCLC symbol*] ... IFJ
Franklin, KY [*Radio station call letters*] ... WFKN
Franklin, LA [*Radio station call letters*] ... KFRA
Franklin, LA [*Radio station call letters*] ... KFRA-FM
Franklin Lakes, NJ [*Radio station call letters*] ... WRRH
Franklin, MA [*Radio station call letters*] ... WGAO
Franklin and Marshall College [*Pennsylvania*] ... F and M
Franklin and Marshall College [*Pennsylvania*] ... FMC
Franklin and Marshall College, Lancaster, PA [*OCLC symbol*] ... LFM
Franklin and Marshall College, Lancaster, PA [*Library symbol*] ... PLF
Franklin McLean Memorial Research Institute ... FMMRI
Franklin Mint Corp. [*NYSE symbol*] ... FM
Franklin Mint Society ... FMS
Franklin, NC [*Radio station call letters*] ... WFSC
Franklin, NC [*Radio station call letters*] ... WLTM
Franklin, NC [*Radio station call letters*] ... WRFR
Franklin, NH [*Radio station call letters*] ... WFTN
Franklin, NJ [*Radio station call letters*] ... WSUS
Franklin, PA [*Radio station call letters*] ... WFRA
Franklin, PA [*Radio station call letters*] ... WVEN
Franklin Parish Library, Winnsboro, LA [*Library symbol*] ... LWinF
Franklin Pierce Adams [*1881-1960*] [*American newspaper columnist*] ... FPA
Franklin Public Library, Franklin, IN [*Library symbol*] ... InFrl
Franklin Public Library, Franklin, NH [*Library symbol*] ... NhFr
Franklin Public Library, Franklin, OH [*Library symbol*] ... OFr
Franklin Public Library, Franklin, PA [*Library symbol*] ... PFr
Franklin Realty & Mortgage Trust [*American Stock Exchange symbol*] [*Delisted*] ... FR
Franklin Resources [*NASDAQ symbol*] ... FRRI

Franklin Signal Corp. [*NASDAQ symbol*] .... FSIG
Franklin Simon & Co. [*NYSE symbol*] [*Delisted*] .... FKS
Franklin Simon & Co. [*Retail clothing stores*] .... FS
Franklin Square Public Library, Franklin Square, NY [*Library symbol*] .... NFs
Franklin Stores Corporation [*NYSE symbol*] [*Delisted*] .... FSC
Franklin, TN [*Radio station call letters*] .... WAKM
Franklin, TN [*Radio station call letters*] .... WIZO
Franklin, TN [*Radio station call letters*] .... WJKZ
Franklin Township Public Library, Malaga, NJ [*Library symbol*] .... NjMal
Franklin University, Columbus, OH [*Library symbol*] .... OCoF
Franklin University, Columbus, OH [*OCLC symbol*] .... OFU
Franklin, VA [*Radio station call letters*] .... WYSR
Franklinton, LA [*Radio station call letters*] .... WFCG
Frank's Nursery & Crafts, Inc. [*Formerly, Franks Nursery Sales, Inc.*] [*American Stock Exchange symbol*] [*Delisted*] .... FKS
Franse Boek [*A publication*] .... FB
Frantz Manufacturing Co. [*American Stock Exchange symbol*] .... FRZ
Franz Rosenzweig Society .... FRS
Franziskanische Studien [*A publication*] .... FrSt
Franziskanische Studien [*A publication*] .... FS
Franziskanische Studien. Muenster [*A publication*] .... FrSM
Franzoesisch Heute [*A publication*] .... FrH
Fraser [*James E.*] [*Designer's mark, when appearing on US coins*] .... F
Fraser-Hickson Institute, Montreal, PQ, Canada [*Library symbol*] .... CaQMF
Fraser Marketing Investments [*NASDAQ symbol*] .... FRASS
Fraser Public Library, Fraser, CO [*Library symbol*] .... CoFra
Fraser Public Library, Fraser, MI [*Library symbol*] .... MiFras
Fraser Valley College, Abbotsford, BC, Canada [*Library symbol*] .... CaBAbFV
Fraser Valley College, Clearbrook, BC, Canada [*Library symbol*] .... CaBClF
Fraser Valley Union Library, Abbotsford, BC, Canada [*Library symbol*] .... CaBAbF
Fraser's Magazine [*A publication*] .... Fraser
Frate Francesco [*A publication*] .... FF
Frater [*Brother*] [*Latin*] .... F
Frater [*Brother*] [*Latin*] .... FR
Fraternal Actuarial Association [*Defunct*] .... FAA
Fraternal Association of Steel Haulers .... FASH
Fraternal Field Managers' Association .... FFMA
Fraternal Insurance Counsellors Association [*Later, NAFIC*] .... FICA
Fraternal Insurance Counselor [*Designation given by Fraternal Field Managers' Association*] .... FIC
Fraternal and Military Club Managers Association [*Defunct*] .... FMCMA
Fraternal Order of Air Mail Pilots [*Defunct*] .... FOAMP
Fraternal Order of Eagles .... FOE
Fraternal Order of Orioles .... FOO
Fraternal Order of Police, Grand Lodge .... FOP
Fraternitatis Regiae Socius [*Fellow of the Royal Society*] [*Latin*] .... FRS
Fraternite Mondiale [*World Brotherhood*] .... FM
Fraternity .... FRAT
Fraternity Executives Association .... FEA
Fraternity of Recording Executives .... FORE
Fraternity Scholarship Association [*Later, College Fraternity Scholarship Officers Association*] .... FSA
Fraternity of the Wooden Leg .... FWL
Fratres [*Brothers*] [*Latin*] .... FF
Fratres Maristae a Scholis [*Marist Brothers*] [*Roman Catholic religious order*] .... FMS
Fratres Sancti Joseph [*Brothers of St. Joseph*] [*Roman Catholic religious order*] .... FSJ
Fratres Scholarum Christianarum [*Brothers of the Christian Schools*] [*Christian Brothers*] [*Roman Catholic religious order*] .... FSC
Fratrum Instructionis Christianae [*Brothers of Christian Instruction*] [*La Mennais Brothers*] [*Roman Catholic religious order*] .... FIC
Fraud [*FBI standardized term*] .... FRD
Fraud Against the Government .... FAG
Fraudulent Enlistment .... F/E
Fraulein [*Miss*] [*German*] .... FRL
Fraunhofer Line Discriminator [*Physics*] .... FLD
Fred B. Rothman & Co., South Hackensack, NJ [*Library symbol*] .... FbR
Fred. Olsen Flyselskap [*Norway*] [*ICAO designator*] .... FO
Frederic R. Harris, Inc., Lake Success, NY [*Library symbol*] .... NLsH
Frederick Air Taxi Service, Inc. [*Frederick, MD*] [*FAA designator*] .... FDC
Frederick Burk Foundation Research Center .... FBRC
Frederick Cancer Research Center .... FCRC
Frederick Cancer Research Center, Frederick, MD [*OCLC symbol*] .... FCR
Frederick Cancer Research Center, Frederick, MD [*Library symbol*] .... MdFreCR
Frederick Community College, Frederick, MD [*OCLC symbol*] .... FRE
Frederick Community College, Frederick, MD [*Library symbol*] .... MdFreFC
Frederick Douglass Memorial and Historical Association .... FDMHA
Frederick Eugene Lykes, Jr., Memorial County Library, Brooksville, FL [*Library symbol*] .... FBro
Frederick and Herrud [*NASDAQ symbol*] .... FKHD
Frederick Law Olmsted [*Nineteenth-century landscape architect*] .... FLO
Frederick Law Olmsted Association .... FLOA
Frederick, MD [*Radio station call letters*] .... WFMD
Frederick, MD [*Radio station call letters*] .... WFRE
Frederick, MD [*Radio station call letters*] .... WZYQ
Frederick, OK [*Radio station call letters*] .... KTAT
Frederick, OK [*Radio station call letters*] .... KYBE
Frederick Point, AK [*Location identifier*] [*FAA*] .... FPN
Frederick Research Center .... FRC
Frederick Ungar [*Publisher*] .... FU
Frederick's of Hollywood, Inc. [*American Stock Exchange symbol*] .... FHO
Fredericksburg [*Virginia*] [*Geomagnetic observatory code*] .... FRD
Fredericksburg and Spotsylvania County Battlefield Memorial National Military Park .... FRSP
Fredericksburg, TX [*Radio station call letters*] .... KFAN
Fredericksburg, TX [*Radio station call letters*] .... KNAF
Fredericksburg, VA [*Radio station call letters*] .... WFLS
Fredericksburg, VA [*Radio station call letters*] .... WFLS-FM
Fredericksburg, VA [*Radio station call letters*] .... WFVA
Fredericksburg, VA [*Radio station call letters*] .... WFVA-FM
Fredericksburg, VA [*Radio station call letters*] .... WJYJ
Fredericktown, MO [*Radio station call letters*] .... KFTW
Fredericton [*New Brunswick*] [*Seismograph station code, US Geological Survey*] .... UNB
Fredericton [*Canada*] [*Airport symbol*] .... YFC
Fredericton, NB [*Radio station call letters*] .... CBZ
Fredericton, NB [*Radio station call letters*] .... CBZF-FM
Fredericton, NB [*Radio station call letters*] .... CBZ-FM
Fredericton, NB [*Radio station call letters*] .... CFNB
Fredericton, NB [*Radio station call letters*] .... CIHI
Fredericton, NB [*Radio station call letters*] .... CKHJ-FM
Frederiksted, VI [*Radio station call letters*] .... WRRA
Frederiksted, VI [*Radio station call letters*] .... WVIS
Fredonia, NY [*Radio station call letters*] .... WBUZ
Fredonia, NY [*Radio station call letters*] .... WCVF-FM
Fredonia Veterans Association .... FVA
Free .... F
Free [*Rate*] [*Value of the English pound*] .... F
Free and Accepted Masons .... F & AM
Free and Accepted Masons .... FAM
Free and Accepted Masons of Pennsylvania, Grand Lodge Library, Philadelphia, PA [*Library symbol*] .... PPPFM
Free-Agent Market Simulator [*Computer programed to calculate the market value of free agents in the National Basketball Association*] .... FAMS
Free Air Delivered .... FAD
Free Air Facility Track [*Edwards Air Force Base*] .... FAFT
Free Air Suspension System .... FASS
Free Air Temperature .... FAT
Free Air Test Facility .... FATF
Free Albania Organization .... FAO
Free of All Average [*Insurance*] .... FA
Free of All Average [*Insurance*] .... FAA
Free All Toledoans - Committee to Help All Neglected Citizens Emigrate [*Group of Michigan citizens formed in 1973 to humorously protest results of the Toledo War of 1835*] [*Also see SCANDAL*] .... FAT CHANCE
Free Alongside .... FA
Free from Alongside .... FFA
Free Alongside Ship [*"INCOTERM," International Chamber of Commerce official code*] .... FAS
Free Aperture [*Technical drawings*] .... FA
Free Appropriate Public Education .... FAPE
Free the Army [*Bowdlerized version*] [*Barracks graffiti; also, title of antimilitary play*] .... FTA
Free Association [*A publication*] .... Free Assoc
Free-Association Strength [*Psychometrics*] .... FAS
Free Astray .... FA
Free Available Chlorine [*Analytical chemistry*] .... FAC
Free Available Chlorine Test with Syringaldazine [*Analytical chemistry*] .... FACTS
Free from Average [*Insurance*] .... FFA
Free Balloon [*Navy symbol*] .... ZF
Free Baptist .... FB
Free into Barge .... FIB
Free Beaches Information Center [*Later, The Naturists*] .... FBIC
Free-Binding Capacity [*Serology*] .... FBC
Free Board .... FBD
Free on Board [*"INCOTERM," International Chamber of Commerce official code*] .... FOB
Free Body Diagram .... FBD
Free into Bunker .... FIB
Free of Capture and Seizure [*Insurance*] .... FC & S
Free of Capture and Seizure [*Insurance*] .... FCS
Free of Capture, Seizure, Arrest, and Detainment [*Insurance*] .... FCSAD
Free of Capture, Seizure, Riots, and Civil Commotions [*Insurance*] .... FCSRCC
Free on Car .... FOC
Free Carrier [*Followed by a named point*] [*"INCOTERM," International Chamber of Commerce official code*] .... FRC
Free of Charge [*Business and trade*] .... FOC
Free China Assistance .... FCA
Free China Fund for Medical and Refugee Aid .... FCF
Free China Review [*A publication*] .... FCR
Free China Review [*A publication*] .... Free China R
Free from Chlorine .... FFC
Free Choice [*Psychology*] .... FC

Free Church ... FC
Free Church Federal Council ... FCFC
Free Congress Research and Education Foundation ... FCREF
Free into Container Depot [*Business and trade*] ... FID
Free Crystalline Silica ... FCS
Free Cuba Patriotic Movement ... FCPM
Free Cutting Brass ... FCB
Free of Damage [*Business and trade*] ... FOD
Free Delivery ... FD
Free Discharge ... FD
Free Dispatch ... FD
Free Dock [*Business and trade*] ... FD
Free Drop ... FD
Free Electron LASER ... FEL
Free Energy Change ... FEC
Free Energy Function ... FEF
Free Energy Minimization Procedure [*Data processing*] ... FEMP
Free Enterprise Awards Association ... FEAA
Free Enterprise Legal Defense Fund ... FELDF
Free Enterprise Personnel ... FEP
Free Erythrocyte Protoporphyrin [*Hematology*] ... FEP
Free Europe Committee [*Later, RFE/RL*] ... FEC
Free Europe Committee, New York, NY [*Library symbol*] ... NNFE
Free Europe, Incorporated [*Later, RFE/RL*] ... FEI
Free Expression of Appreciation or Revenge [*Customer opinion campaign operated by Bekins Van & Storage Co.*] ... FEAR
Free-Fall Grab [*Marine geology*] ... FFG
Free Fall Sensor ... FFS
Free Fatty Acid [*Biochemistry*] ... FFA
Free Field Analysis ... FFA
Free Field Room ... FFR
Free Fire Area ... FFA
Free Fire Zone [*Army*] ... FFZ
Free Flight ... FF
Free Flight Analysis Section ... FFAS
Free Flight Data ... FFD
Free Flight Facility ... FFF
Free Flight Rocket ... FFR
Free Flight Test Vehicle ... FFTV
Free Flood ... FF
Free-Flying [*Experiment*] **Module** [*NASA*] ... FFM
Free-Flying Teleoperator [*Program*] [*Electronics*] ... FFTO
Free Foil Switching Device ... FFSD
Free Foreign Agency [*or Agent*] [*Business and trade*] ... FFA
Free French [*World War II*] ... FF
Free French [*World War II*] ... FFR
Free French [*World War II*] ... FRF
Free French Forces [*World War II*] ... FFF
Free of General Average ... FGA
Free Harbor ... FH
Free in Harbor [*Navigation*] ... FIH
Free-Heave Amplitude ... FHA
Free-Heave Test ... FHT
Free Height ... FRHGT
Free In and Out [*Business and trade*] ... FIO
Free In and Out and Stowed [*Business and trade*] ... FIOS
Free In and Out and Trimmed [*Business and trade*] ... FIOT
Free In and Out of Trucks [*Business and trade*] ... FIOT
Free of Income Tax ... FIT
Free Induction Decay ... FID
Free from Infection ... FFI
Free Instrument Package ... FIP
Free Interprofessional Association of Workers [*Acronym represents Russian phrase*] ... SMOT
Free Interstitial Atom ... FIA
Free Jet Expansion ... FJE
Free Jet Test ... FJT
Free of Knots ... FOK
Free Lance ... F/L
Free Lance [*A publication*] ... Free L
Free Lance Exchange ... FLEX
Free Lance Finders Network ... FLFN
Free Learning Exchange [*An association*] [*Defunct*] ... FLEX
Free Library of Philadelphia, Carson Collection, Philadelphia, PA [*Library symbol*] ... PP-C
Free Library of Philadelphia, H. Josephine Widener Memorial Branch, Philadelphia, PA [*Library symbol*] [*Obsolete*] ... PP-W
Free Library of Philadelphia, Philadelphia, PA [*OCLC symbol*] ... PLF
Free Library of Philadelphia, Philadelphia, PA [*Library symbol*] ... PP
Free Library, Pittsfield, VT [*Library symbol*] ... VtPifi
Free-Machining Steel ... FMS
Free Man of Color [*Term of reference for blacks after the Civil War*] ... FMC
Free Men [*An association*] ... FM
Free Methodist Historical Center, Winona Lake, IN [*Library symbol*] ... InWinFM
Free Methodist World Fellowship ... FMWF
Free at Mill [*Business and trade*] ... FAM
Free Molecular Flow ... FMF
Free Motion Impedance ... FMI
Free Oceanographic Instrument Float ... FOIF
Free and Open Church Association [*British*] ... FOCA
Free Out [*Shipping*] ... FO
Free Overside ... FO
Free Pacific Association ... FPA
Free of Particular Average [*Insurance*] ... FPA
Free of Particular Average, American Conditions [*Insurance*] ... FPAAC
Free of Particular Average, English Conditions [*Insurance*] ... FPAEC
Free Polar Corticosteroids [*Endocrinology*] ... FPCS
Free Port ... FP
Free of Poundage Money Order ... FPMO
Free Press, Phillipsburg, NJ [*Library symbol*] ... NjPhP
Free Progressive Wave ... FPW
Free Propellers ... FP
Free from Prussic Acid ... FFPA
Free Public Library of the Borough of Madison, Madison, NJ [*Library symbol*] ... NjM
Free Public Library, Chariton, IA [*Library symbol*] ... IaCh
Free Public Library of the City of Orange, Orange, NJ [*Library symbol*] ... NjO
Free Public Library of Irvington, Irvington, NJ [*Library symbol*] ... NjI
Free Public Library of Livingston, Livingston, NJ [*Library symbol*] ... NjLi
Free Public Library, Mattapoisett, MA [*Library symbol*] ... MMat
Free Public Library, Metuchen, NJ [*Library symbol*] ... NjMe
Free Public Library of Newark, Newark, NJ [*OCLC symbol*] ... NPL
Free Public Library of the Township of Mahwah, Mahwah, NJ [*Library symbol*] ... NjMah
Free Public Library, West Liberty, IA [*Library symbol*] ... IaWl
Free Public Library of Woodbridge, Woodbridge, NJ [*Library symbol*] ... NjWoo
Free at Quay [*Business and trade*] ... FAQ
Free on Quay [*Business and trade*] ... FOQ
Free Radical Assay Technique [*Clinical chemistry*] ... FRAT
Free Radical Photography ... FRP
Free on Rail/Free on Truck [*"INCOTERM," International Chamber of Commerce official code*] ... FOR
Free on Rail/Free on Truck [*Business and trade*] ... FOR/FOT
Free Residual Chlorine ... FRC
Free of Riots and Civil Commotions [*Insurance*] ... FR & CC
Free of Riots and Civil Commotions [*Insurance*] ... FRCC
Free Rocket over Ground [*USSR missile*] ... FROG
Free Running Frequency ... FRF
Free Rural Delivery [*British*] ... FRD
Free Safety [*Football*] ... FS
Free Shear Layer ... FSL
Free Sons of Israel ... FSI
Free Southern Theater ... FST
Free Space Microwave Interferometer ... FSMWI
Free Space Transfer ... FST
Free Speech Movement [*University of California, Berkeley*] ... FSM
Free-Standing Ambulatory Surgical Center ... FASC
Free State Geduld Mines [*NASDAQ symbol*] ... FREEY
Free on Station ... FOS
Free on Steamer [*Business and trade*] ... FOS
Free in Store [*Business and trade*] ... FIS
Free Supersonic Jet ... FSJ
Free Support Area ... FSA
Free Surface Water Tunnel ... FSWT
Free of Tax ... FOT
Free Territory of Trieste ... FTT
Free Throw [*Basketball*] ... FT
Free Throws Attempted [*Basketball*] ... FTA
Free Throws Made [*Basketball*] ... FTM
Free Thyroxine [*Also, FT_4*] [*Endocrinology*] ... FT
Free Thyroxine Index [*Endocrinology*] ... FTI
Free-Time System [*GE/PAC*] ... FTS
Free Trade Area ... FTA
Free Trade Association [*European*] ... FTA
Free Trade Unions of Burma ... FTUB
Free Trade Unions of the Philippines ... FTUP
Free Trade Wharf ... FTW
Free in Truck [*Business and trade*] ... FIT
Free on Truck [*See also FOR*] [*Business and trade*] ... FOT
Free Turbine ... FT
Free Turn ... FT
Free University Network [*Later, LERN*] ... FUN
Free University of New York ... FUNY
Free Visayan Workers' Union [*Philippines*] ... FVWU
Free in Wagon [*Business and trade*] ... FIW
Free on Wagon [*Business and trade*] ... FOW
Free Wallenberg Committee ... FWC
Free-Wheel Bicycle ... FWB
Free-Wheel Rectifier ... FWR
Free-Will Baptist Bible College, Nashville, TN [*Library symbol*] ... TNFB
Free-Will Baptists ... FWB
Free Workers' Trade Union Congress [*Aden*] ... FWTUC
Free World Armed Forces ... FWAF
Free World Military Assistance ... FWMA
Free World Military Assistance Council ... FWMAC
Free World Military Assistance Forces [*Vietnam*] ... FWMAF
Free World Military Assistance Organization ... FWMAO
Freeboard ... FREEBD

Freeburg Community High School 77, Freeburg, IL [*Library symbol*] ... IFrHS
Freed-Hardeman College [*Tennessee*] ... FHC
Freedom Airlines, Inc. [*Binghamton, NY*] [*FAA designator*] ... FDM
Freedom Community Unit, School District 245, Earlville, IL [*Library symbol*] ... IEarFSD
Freedom Democratic Party [*in Mississippi*] ... FDP
Freedom of Faith: A Christian Committee for Religious Rights ... FFACCRR
Freedom House ... FH
Freedom from Hunger Campaign [*UN Food and Agriculture Organization*] ... FFHC
Freedom from Hunger Campaign - Action for Development [*UN Food and Agriculture Organization*] ... FFHC/AD
Freedom, Independence [*formerly, Integration*], **God, Honor, Today** [*Organization in Rochester, NY*] ... FIGHT
Freedom of Information [*Army*] ... FOI
Freedom of Information Act ... FIA
Freedom of Information Act ... FOIA
Freedom of Information Center [*University of Missouri*] [*An association*] ... FOI
Freedom of Information Clearinghouse [*An association*] ... FIC
Freedom of Information Clearinghouse [*An association*] ... FOIC
Freedom Information Service ... FIS
Freedom Leadership Foundation ... FLF
Freedom News [*A publication*] ... Free News
Freedom to Read Foundation ... FRF
Freedom to Read Foundation ... FTRF
Freedom from Religion Foundation ... FFRF
Freedom Savings & Loan Association [*NASDAQ symbol*] ... FRDM
Freedom Socialist [*A publication*] ... Free Soc
Freedom Socialist Party ... FSP
Freedoms Foundation at Valley Forge ... FFVF
Freehold ... FHLD
Freehold Public Library, Freehold, NJ [*Library symbol*] ... NjFr
Freeing the Spirit [*A publication*] ... Free Spir
Freelance Network ... FN
Freelance Research Service, Houston, TX [*OCLC symbol*] ... THF
Freeland League for Jewish Territorial Colonization [*Later, LY*] ... FLJTC
Freeland, PA [*Radio station call letters*] ... WQEQ
Freely Moving Human Subject ... FMHS
Freeman Anxiety Neurosis and Psychosomatic Test [*Psychology*] ... FANPT
Freeman Junior College [*South Dakota*] ... FJC
Freeman Public Library, Freeman, SD [*Library symbol*] ... SdFr
Freeman Time Unit [*Psychology*] ... FTU
Freeman [*Time*] **Unit** [*Psychology*] ... FU
Freemen Institute ... FI
Freeport [*Bahamas*] [*Airport symbol*] ... FPO
Freeport Hospital, Freeport, NY [*Library symbol*] ... NFreeH
Freeport, IL [*Radio station call letters*] ... WFPS
Freeport, IL [*Radio station call letters*] ... WFRL
Freeport, IL [*Television station call letters*] ... WIFR-TV
Freeport, IL [*Radio station call letters*] ... WXXQ
Freeport-McMoRan, Inc. [*NYSE symbol*] ... FMR
Freeport Memorial Library, Freeport, NY [*Library symbol*] ... NFree
Freeport Minerals Co. [*NYSE symbol*] [*Delisted*] ... FT
Freeport, NY [*Radio station call letters*] ... WGBB
Freeport, TX [*Radio station call letters*] ... KBRZ
Freer Gallery of Art, Washington, DC [*Library symbol*] ... DFG
Freestanding Ambulatory Surgical Association ... FASA
Freestate Aviation, Inc. [*Gaithersburg, MD*] [*FAA designator*] ... FST
Freetown [*Sierra Leone*] [*Airport symbol*] ... FNA
Freetown [*Sierra Leone*] **Hastings Airport** [*Airport symbol*] ... HGS
Freeway ... FRWY
Freeway ... FWY
Freeway Driver Information System ... FDIS
Freeze [*or Freezing*] ... FRZ
Freeze Desalination Plant ... FDP
Freeze-Dried ... FD
Freeze-Dried (Allogenic) Skin Graft [*Medicine*] ... FDSG
Freeze-Etch Technique ... FET
Freeze Thaw Lysate [*Cytology*] ... FTL
Freezer ... FRZR
Freezing ... FRZG
Freezing ... FZ
Freezing Drizzle [*Meteorology*] ... FZDZ
Freezing Drizzle [*Meteorology*] ... ZL
Freezing Fog [*Meteorology*] ... FZFG
Freezing Gas Jet ... FGJ
Freezing Level ... FRZLVL
Freezing Point ... FP
Freezing Point Calibration Standard ... FPCS
Freezing Point Osmometer ... FPO
Freezing Rain [*Meteorology*] ... FZRA
Freezing Rain [*Meteorology*] ... ZR
Fregate Island [*Seychelles Islands*] [*Airport symbol*] ... FRK
Freiberger Forschungshefte [*A publication*] ... Freiberger Forsch H
Freiberger Forschungshefte. Reihe A [*A publication*] ... Freiberg Forschungsh Reihe A
Freiberger Forschungshefte. Reihe C [*A publication*] ... Freiberg Forschungsh Reihe C
Freiburger Diozesanarchiv [*A publication*] ... FDA
Freiburger Forschungen zur Kunst und Literaturgeschichte [*A publication*] ... FFKL
Freiburger Zeitschrift fuer Philosophie und Theologie [*A publication*] ... Frei Z Phil Theol
Freiburger Zeitschrift fuer Philosophie und Theologie [*A publication*] ... FZPT
Freie Demokratische Partei [*Free Democratic Party*] [*West Germany*] ... FDP
Freie Deutsche Jugend [*Free German Youth*] ... FDJ
Freie-Koerper-Kultur [*Nudism, a pre-Nazi fad in Germany*] ... FKK
Freie Letzeburger Arbechterverband [*Free Luxembourg Workers' Federation*] ... FLA
Freie Universitat Berlin, Garystrasse, Berlin, Germany [*Library symbol*] ... GyBFU
Freier Christentum [*A publication*] ... FrChr
Freier Deutscher Gewerkschaftsbund [*Trade union confederation, East Germany*] ... FDGB
Freies Deutsches Hochstift: Reihe der Schriften [*A publication*] ... FDHRS
Freight ... FGT
Freight ... FRT
Freight Accounting Shipment Tracing System ... FAST
Freight Agent ... FA
Freight, All Kinds [*Railroad*] ... FAK
Freight Allowal ... FA
Freight Assurance Storage, United States ... FASUS
Freight Astray ... FA
Freight Automated System for Traffic Management ... FAST
Freight Bill ... FB
Freight on Board ... FOB
Freight or Carriage and Insurance Paid To_____ [*"INCOTERM," International Chamber of Commerce official code*] ... CIP
Freight or Carriage Paid To_____ [*"INCOTERM," International Chamber of Commerce official code*] ... DCP
Freight Claim Agent ... FCA
Freight Claim Association ... FCA
Freight Classification Guide System ... FCGS
Freight and Demurrage [*Shipping*] ... F & D
Freight Department ... FD
Freight and Equipment Reporting System for Transportation [*IBM Corp.*] ... FERST
Freight and Equipment Reporting System for Transportation/ Virtual Storage [*IBM Corp.*] ... FERST/VS
Freight Forwarder ... FF
Freight Forwarders Institute ... FFI
Freight Forwarders Tariff Bureau, Inc. ... FFTB
Freight Forwarders Tariff Bureau, Inc., New York NY [*STAC*] ... FFT
Freight, Insurance, Carriage ... FIC
Freight/Luggage Panniers [*Hovercraft*] ... F/LP
Freight Office ... FROF
Freight Pass-Through [*Publishing*] ... FPT
Freight and Passenger Vessels [*Army*] ... FP
Freight Receiving and Redistribution Unit ... FRRU
Freight Release ... FR
Freight Station Accounting Code [*Railroad term*] ... FSAC
Freight Supply Vessel ... FS
Freight Ton ... FT
Freight Traffic Committee - Trunk Line Territory Railroads ... FTC-TLTR
Freight Traffic Concurrence ... FX
Freight Traffic Department ... FTD
Freight Traffic Division [*Army*] ... FTD
Freight Traffic Manager ... FTM
Freight Transport ... FT
Freighter Travel Club of America ... FTC
Fremitus Vocalis [*Vocal Fremitus*] [*Medicine*] ... FREM
Fremont, CA [*Radio station call letters*] ... KDOS
Fremont, CA [*Radio station call letters*] ... KOHL
Fremont County Library, Lander, WY [*Library symbol*] ... WyLan
Fremont County Library, Riverton Branch, Riverton, WY [*Library symbol*] ... WyRi
Fremont General Corp. [*NASDAQ symbol*] ... FRMT
Fremont, MI [*Location identifier*] [*FAA*] ... FOJ
Fremont, MI [*Radio station call letters*] ... WSHN
Fremont, MI [*Radio station call letters*] ... WSHN-FM
Fremont, NE [*Radio station call letters*] ... KHUB
Fremont, NE [*Radio station call letters*] ... KHUB-FM
Fremont, OH [*Radio station call letters*] ... WFRO
Fremont, OH [*Radio station call letters*] ... WFRO-FM
Fremont Peak [*California*] [*Seismograph station code, US Geological Survey*] ... FRP
Fremont Public Library, Fremont, MI [*Library symbol*] ... MiFrem
Fremont Public Library, Fremont, NE [*Library symbol*] ... NbFr
French ... F
French ... FR
French ... FRE
French [*MARC language code*] [*Library of Congress*] ... fre
French Air Force ... FAF
French-American Foundation ... FAF
French-American Mid-Ocean Undersea Study [*Joint undersea program*] ... FAMOUS
French American Review [*A publication*] ... FAR
French American Review [*A publication*] ... French Am Rev

French-Anglo-United States Supersonic Transport ... FAUSST
French Army ... FA
French Australian and Antarctic Territories ... FAAT
French Bulldog Club of America ... FBDCA
French Chamber of Commerce of the United States [*Later, French-American Chamber of Commerce*] ... FCCUS
French Committee of National Liberation [*World War II*] ... FCNL
French Communist Party ... FCP
French Computing Association ... FCA
French Engineers in the United States ... FEUS
French Equatorial Africa ... FEA
French Expeditionary Corps ... FEC
French Expeditionary Force ... FEF
French Forum [*A publication*] ... Fr F
French Fourragere [*Military*] ... FF
French Franc [*Monetary unit*] ... FFr
French Fried ... FF
French Frigate Shoals, HI [*Location identifier*] [*FAA*] ... HFS
French Guiana [*MARC country of publication code*] [*Library of Congress*] ... fg
French Guiana [*Two-letter standard code*] ... GF
French Guiana [*Three-letter standard code*] ... GUF
French Guiana [*MARC geographic area code*] [*Library of Congress*] ... s-fg---
French Guiana Space Center ... GUY
French Historical Studies [*A publication*] ... FHS
French Historical Studies [*A publication*] ... Fr Hist Stud
French Institute/Alliance Francaise de New York/Federation of French Alliances in the United States ... FIAF
French Institute-Alliance Francaise, New York, NY [*Library symbol*] ... NNFI
French Institute in the United States [*Later, FIAF*] ... FIUS
French Library [*L'Alliance Francaise*], **San Francisco, CA** [*Library symbol*] ... CSfFL
French Lick, IN [*Location identifier*] [*FAA*] ... FRH
French Lick, IN [*Location identifier*] [*FAA*] ... JIF
French Lick, IN [*Radio station call letters*] ... WFLQ
French Literature on Microfiche [*A publication*] ... Fr LM
French Literature Series [*Columbia, South Carolina*] [*A publication*] ... FLS
French, Middle [*MARC language code*] [*Library of Congress*] ... frm
French Military Liaison Mission [*World War II*] ... FMLM
French Military Mission ... FMM
French Naval Liaison Officer ... FNLO
French Naval War College ... FRNWC
French Navy ... FN
French Navy ... FNY
French North Africa ... FNA
French, Old [*MARC language code*] [*Library of Congress*] ... fro
French Patent ... FP
French Polynesia [*MARC country of publication code*] [*Library of Congress*] ... fp
French Polynesia [*Two-letter standard code*] ... PF
French Polynesia [*MARC geographic area code*] [*Library of Congress*] ... pofp
French Polynesia [*Three-letter standard code*] ... PYF
French Pressure Cell ... FPC
French Quarterly [*A publication*] ... FQ
French Railway Techniques [*A publication*] ... Fr Railw Tech
French Research [*Satellite*] ... FR
French Review [*A publication*] ... FR
French Review [*A publication*] ... French R
French Sign Language ... FSL
French Socialist Party ... FSP
French Southern and Antarctic Lands [*Three-letter standard code*] ... ATF
French Southern and Antarctic Lands [*Two-letter standard code*] ... FQ
French Southern and Antarctic Lands [*MARC country of publication code*] [*Library of Congress*] ... fs
French Southern and Antarctic Lands [*MARC geographic area code*] [*Library of Congress*] ... i-fs---
French-Speaking Nations [*NATO*] ... FSN
French-Speaking Neuropsychological Society ... FSNS
French Studies [*A publication*] ... Fr St
French Studies [*A publication*] ... FS
French Studies in Southern Africa [*A publication*] ... FSSA
French Techniques [*A publication*] ... Fr Tech
French Territory of the Afars and Issas [*Three-letter standard code*] ... AFI
French Territory of the Afars and Issas [*Two-letter standard code*] ... AI
French Territory of the Afars and Issas [*Djibouti*] [*MARC geographic area code*] [*Library of Congress*] ... f-ft---
French Territory of the Afars and Issas [*Djibouti*] [*MARC country of publication code*] [*Library of Congress*] ... ft
French Togoland ... FRTO
French Training Mission [*Military*] ... FTM
French Union [*MARC geographic area code*] [*Library of Congress*] ... h------
French Village [*Missouri*] [*Seismograph station code, US Geological Survey*] ... FVM
French West Africa ... FWA
French West Indies ... FWI
Frenchville [*Maine*] [*Airport symbol*] ... WFK
Frenchville, ME [*Location identifier*] [*FAA*] ... FVE
Frente de Accion Popular [*Popular Action Front*] [*Chile*] ... FRAP
Frente Anti-Communista de Defensa Nacional [*Anti-Communist Front for National Defense*] [*Ecuador*] ... FADN
Frente de Izquierda Revolucionaria [*Peru*] ... FIR
Frente de Liberacion Nacional [*National Liberation Front*] [*Venezuela*] ... FLN
Frente de Libertacao de Mocambique [*Mozambique Liberation Front*] ... FRELIMO
Frente de Luta pela Independencia Nacional de Guinea [*Front for the Struggle for the National Independence of Guinea*] ... FLING
Frente Nacional de Libertacao da Angola [*Angolan National Liberation Front*] ... FNLA
Frente Patriotica de Libertacao Nacional [*Portugal*] ... FPLN
Frente Revolucionario Antifascista Patriotica [*Anti-Fascist and Patriotic Revolutionary Front*] [*Spain*] ... FRAP
Frente Sandinista de Liberacion Nacional [*Nicaragua*] ... FSLN
Frente Socialista Popular [*Portugal*] ... FSP
Frente Unita Angolana [*Angolan United Front*] ... FUA
Frente Urbana Zapatista [*Mexico*] ... FUZ
Freon Coolant Loop [*Space shuttle*] [*NASA*] ... FCL
Freon Coolant Servicing Unit ... FCSU
Freon Pump Package ... FPP
Freon Servicer ... FS
Freon Servicing Unit ... FSU
Freon Tank Container ... FTC
Frequency ... F
Frequency ... FRE
Frequency [*or Frequent*] ... FREQ
Frequency [*Spectroscopy*] ... V
Frequency [*Symbol*] [*IUPAC*] ... f
Frequency Adjusting Rheostat ... FAR
Frequency Agile Search and Track Seeker ... FAST
Frequency Agility ... FA
Frequency Agility RADAR Modifications to Existing RADAR Systems [*DoD*] ... FARMERS
Frequency Allocation Committee ... FAC
Frequency Allocation Coordinating Subcommittee [*Canada*] ... FACSC
Frequency Allocation List ... FAL
Frequency Allocation Panel ... FAP
Frequency Allocation Panel, United States ... FAPUS
Frequency Allocation Panel, United States Military Communications Electronics Board ... FAPUSMCEB
Frequency Allocation [*or Assignment*] **Subcommittee** ... FAS
Frequency Allocation and Uses ... FAU
Frequency Allocation and Wave Propagation Subcommittee ... FAWPSC
Frequency Analysis and Control ... FAC
Frequency Analysis of System Program [*NASA*] ... FASP
Frequency Angle Scanning, Tracking, and Ranging ... FASTAR
Frequency Application Index ... FAI
Frequency Assignment by Reference to Interference Charts ... FABRIC
Frequency-Azimuth Intensity [*RADAR*] ... FAI
Frequency Band of Emission ... FBOE
Frequency Coded Armaments System ... FCAS
Frequency Coded Firing System ... FCFS
Frequency Coded System ... FCS
Frequency Compression Demodulator ... FCD
Frequency Compressive Feedback ... FCF
Frequency Control [*NASDAQ symbol*] ... FCPI
Frequency Control and Analysis ... FCA
Frequency Control Analysis Facility ... FCAF
Frequency Control Analysis Subsystem ... FCAS
Frequency Control Officer ... FCO
Frequency Converter ... FC
Frequency Converter ... FREQCONV
Frequency Converter Excitation ... FCE
Frequency Converter Unit ... FCU
Frequency Coordination Working Group ... FCWG
Frequency Data Multiplexer ... FDM
Frequency Dependent Negative Conductance [*Physics*] ... FDNC
Frequency Dependent Negative Resistance [*Physics*] ... FDNR
Frequency Determining Unit ... FDU
Frequency Deviation Meter ... FDM
Frequency Discrimination [*Neurophysiology*] ... FD
Frequency Distortion Analyzer ... FDA
Frequency Distribution Analysis Sheet ... FDAS
Frequency Diversity ... FD
Frequency Diversity RADAR ... FDR
Frequency Divider ... FREQDIV
Frequency Division ... FD
Frequency-Division Data Link [*Radio*] ... FDDL
Frequency-Division Multiple Access ... FDMA
Frequency-Division Multiplex [*Communications*] ... FDM
Frequency-Division Multiplex Voice Communication ... FDMVC
Frequency-Division Multiplexing System [*Radio*] ... FDMS
Frequency Division Switching [*Radio and television broadcasting*] ... FDS
Frequency Domain Coding ... FDC
Frequency Domain Coding Technique ... FDCT
Frequency Domain Reflectometry ... FDR
Frequency Double LASER ... FDL
Frequency Doublers ... FD
Frequency Doubling LASER Device ... FDLD
Frequency Doubling Unit ... FDU
Frequency Drift ... FD

Frequency Electronics, Incorporated [*American Stock Exchange symbol*]	FEI
Frequency Engineering Laboratory	FEL
Frequency of Every Allowable Term	FEAT
Frequency of Fading [*Broadcasting*]	F
Frequency-Following Response [*Neurophysiology*]	FFR
Frequency Hopping [*Modulation*]	FH
Frequency Hopping Signal	FHS
Frequency Interference Control	FIC
Frequency Interference Control Center [*Air Force*]	FICC
Frequency Jumper Identification	FJI
Frequency Jumper Identification	FREJID
Frequency and Load Control Box	FLCB
Frequency and Load Controller	FLC
Frequency Management Advisory Council	FMAC
Frequency Management Branch [*White Sands Missile Range*]	FMB
Frequency Management Division [*White Sands Missile Range*]	FMD
Frequency Management Officer	FMO
Frequency Mass Spectrometer Tube	FMST
Frequency Measuring Devices [*JETDS nomenclature*] [*Military*]	FR
Frequency-Measuring Equipment	FME
Frequency Meter	FM
Frequency Meter	FREQM
Frequency Meter	FRM
Frequency of Minimum Delay	FMD
Frequency Mixer Stage	FMS
Frequency-Modulated Continuous-Wave [*RADAR*]	FMCW
Frequency-Modulated Cyclotron	FMC
Frequency-Modulated Quartz	FMQ
Frequency-Modulated RADAR	FMR
Frequency-Modulated Ranging	FMR
Frequency-Modulated Receiver	FMR
Frequency-Modulated Transmitter	FMT
Frequency-Modulated Transmitter	FMX
Frequency Modulation [*Radio*]	FM
Frequency Modulation Broadcasters	FMB
Frequency Modulation Deviation Meter	FMDM
Frequency Modulation Discriminator	FMD
Frequency Modulation with Feedback	FMFB
Frequency Modulation Feedback Discriminator	FMFD
Frequency Modulation - Frequency Modulation	FM-FM
Frequency Modulation Generator	FMG
Frequency Modulation Intercity Relay Broadcasting	FMI
Frequency Modulation and Narrowband Noise Analyzer	FMNBNA
Frequency Modulation - Phase Modulation [*RADAR*]	FM-PM
Frequency Modulation on the Pulse	FMOP
Frequency Modulation Signal Processor	FMSP
Frequency Monitoring and Interference Control [*Radio*]	FMIC
Frequency Multiplex	FM
Frequency-Multiplexed Subcarrier	FMS
Frequency Multiplier	FREQMULT
Frequency Multiplier	FRQMULT
Frequency Multiplier Storer	FMS
Frequency Network Analyzer	FNA
Frequency Offset Generator	FOG
Frequency of Optimum Operation	FOT
Frequency Optimum Traffic	FOT
Frequency Phase Lock	FPL
Frequency Programer	FQPR
Frequency Range	FR
Frequency Reference Protection	FRP
Frequency Response	FR
Frequency Response Function [*Statistics*]	FRF
Frequency Response Histogram [*Biometrics*]	FRH
Frequency Response Plotter	FRP
Frequency Response Survey	FRS
Frequency Response Test	FRT
Frequency Scan RADAR	FREQSCANRA
Frequency Scan RADAR	FSR
Frequency Scanning	FRESCAN
Frequency Scanning RADAR	FRESCANNAR
Frequency Select Control Unit	FSCU
Frequency Selective Receiver System	FSRS
Frequency Selective Relay	FSR
Frequency Selective Voltmeter	FSV
Frequency Selective Voltmeter	FSVM
Frequency Shift	FS
Frequency Shift Communications System	FSCS
Frequency Shift Converter	FSC
Frequency Shift Keying [*Radio*]	FSK
Frequency Shift Keying Low-Frequency [*Converter*]	FSKLF
Frequency Shift Modulation [*Radio*]	FSM
Frequency Shift Pulsing	FSP
Frequency Shift Receiver	FSR
Frequency Shift Reflector	FSR
Frequency Shift Transmission	FST
Frequency Space Characteristic Impedance	FSCI
Frequency Stability	FS
Frequency Stability Analyzer	FSA
Frequency Standard	FS
Frequency Standard, Primary	FSP

Frequency Sweep Oscillator	FSO
Frequency on Target	FOT
Frequency Threshold Curve	FTC
Frequency and Time	FT
Frequency Time Base	FTB
Frequency and Time Circuit Analysis Technique [*NASA*]	FATCAT
Frequency Time Control	FTC
Frequency and Time-Division Data Link	FATDL
Frequency Time Indicator [*RADAR*]	FTI
Frequency Time Intensity [*RADAR*]	FTI
Frequency and Time Measurement Counter	FTMC
Frequency Time Modulation	FTM
Frequency Time Schedule	FTS
Frequency Time Standard	FTS
Frequency and Timing Subsystem [*Deep Space Instrumentation Facility, NASA*]	FTS
Frequency Tolerance	FT
Frequency Tracker	FT
Frequency Transfer Unit	FTU
Frequency Translation Distortion	FTD
Frequency Translator	FRELATOR
Frequency Tuned Bandpass Filter	FTBF
Frequency to Voltage	F/V
Frequent [*In mention of occurrence of species*]	F
Frequent	FQT
Frequent	FR
Frequent	FRQ
Frequent Independent Traveler	FIT
Frequent Independent Travelers	FITS
Frequent Traveller [*on airlines*]	FT
Frequenting House of Ill Fame	FHIF
Frequently-Called-Numbers List [*Bell System*]	FCNL
Frequenz [*A publication*]	Freq
Freres [*Brothers*] [*French*]	FRES
Fresenius Zeitschrift fuer Analytische Chemie [*A publication*]	Fresenius Z Anal Chem
Fresenius Zeitschrift fuer Analytische Chemie [*A publication*]	Z Anal Chem
Fresh	FR
Fresh Frozen	FF
Fresh Frozen Plasma [*Medicine*]	FFP
Fresh Fruits and Vegetables	FF & V
Fresh Garlic Association	FGA
Fresh Off the Boat	FOB
Fresh Water [*Load line mark*]	F
Fresh Water [*Load line mark*]	FW
Fresh Water [*Technical drawings*]	FW
Fresh Water Bay [*Alaska*] [*Airport symbol*]	FRP
Fresh Water Damage	FWD
Fresh Water Drain Collecting Tank	FWDCT
Fresh Water Fish Wholesalers Association	FWFWA
Fresh Water Institute, Canada Fisheries Research Board, Winnipeg, MB, Canada [*Library symbol*]	CaMWFW
Fresh Water Pump	FWP
Freshwater Biological Association. Annual Report [*A publication*]	Freshw Biol Assoc Annu Rep
Freshwater Biological Association. Scientific Publication [*A publication*]	Freshw Biol Assoc Sci Publ
Freshwater Biology [*A publication*]	Freshw Biol
Freshwater Institute Report [*United Nations*]	FIR
Fresnel Lens Optical Landing System [*Navy*]	FLOLS
Fresnel Lens Optical Practice	FLOP
Fresnel Lens Optical Practice, Fleet	FLOPF
Fresnel Reflection Coefficient	FRC
Fresnillo Co. [*American Stock Exchange symbol*] [*Delisted*]	FRE
Fresno [*California*] [*Airport symbol*]	FAT
Fresno [*California*] [*Seismograph station code, US Geological Survey*] [*Closed*]	FRE
Fresno, AR [*Radio station call letters*]	KNAX
Fresno, CA [*Television station call letters*]	KAIL-TV
Fresno, CA [*Radio station call letters*]	KARM
Fresno, CA [*Radio station call letters*]	KBIF
Fresno, CA [*Radio station call letters*]	KEAP
Fresno, CA [*Radio station call letters*]	KFCF
Fresno, CA [*Radio station call letters*]	KFIG
Fresno, CA [*Radio station call letters*]	KFRE
Fresno, CA [*Radio station call letters*]	KFRY
Fresno, CA [*Television station call letters*]	KFSN-TV
Fresno, CA [*Radio station call letters*]	KFSR
Fresno, CA [*Radio station call letters*]	KFYE
Fresno, CA [*Radio station call letters*]	KGST
Fresno, CA [*Radio station call letters*]	KIRV
Fresno, CA [*Television station call letters*]	KJEO
Fresno, CA [*Radio station call letters*]	KKDJ
Fresno, CA [*Radio station call letters*]	KKNU
Fresno, CA [*Radio station call letters*]	KMAK
Fresno, CA [*Radio station call letters*]	KMJ
Fresno, CA [*Television station call letters*]	KMTF
Fresno, CA [*Television station call letters*]	KSEE
Fresno, CA [*Radio station call letters*]	KSJV
Fresno, CA [*Radio station call letters*]	KVPR-FM

Fresno, CA [*Radio station call letters*] .... KXEX
Fresno, CA [*Radio station call letters*] .... KYNO
Fresno, CA [*Radio station call letters*] .... KYNO-FM
Fresno City College, Fresno, CA [*Library symbol*] .... CFC
Fresno Community Hospital, Fresno, CA [*Library symbol*] .... CFH
Fresno County Department of Health, Fresno, CA [*Library symbol*] .... CFDH
Fresno County Department of Mental Health Services, Fresno, CA [*Library symbol*] .... CFDMH
Fresno County Free Library, Fresno, CA [*Library symbol*] .... CF
Fresno Service Center [*IRS*] .... FSC
Fresno State College [*Later, California State University, Fresno*] .... FSC
Fretted Instrument Guild of America .... FIGA
Freunde der Naturwissenschaften in Wien. Berichte ueber die Mittheilungen (W. Haidinger) [*A publication*] .... Freunde Naturw Ber (Haidinger)
Freund's Adjuvant [*Immunology*] .... FA
Freund's Complete Adjuvant [*Immunochemistry*] .... FCA
Frey Associates, Inc. [*NASDAQ symbol*] .... FRYA
Friant [*California*] [*Seismograph station code, US Geological Survey*] .... FRI
Friant, CA [*Location identifier*] [*FAA*] .... FRA
Friar .... F
Friar .... FR
Friars Club .... FC
Frick Art Reference Library, New York, NY [*Library symbol*] .... NNFr
Frick Chemical Laboratory .... FCL
[*Henry C.*] **Frick Educational Commission** .... FEC
Friction .... F
Friction .... FRICT
Friction Assessment Screening Test [*for brake linings*] .... FAST
Friction Cam Gear .... FCG
Friction Glaze .... FG
Friction Horsepower .... FHP
Friction Materials Standards Institute .... FMSI
Friction Materials Test Machine .... FMTM
Friction Measurement Test .... FMT
Friction Pressure Drop .... FPD
Friction Reducing Agent [*Chemicals*] .... FRA
Friction and Wear in Machinery [*A publication*] .... Frict Wear Mach
Friday .... F
Friday .... FR
Friday .... FRI
Friday Harbor [*Washington*] [*Airport symbol*] .... FRD
Fridays and Holidays Excepted [*Mohammedan*] .... F & HE
Fridays Only [*British railroad term*] .... FO
Friday's (TGI) [*NYSE symbol*] .... TGI
Friden, Inc. [*NYSE symbol*] [*Delisted*] .... FR
Fridericiana. Zeitschrift der Universitaet Karlsruhe [*A publication*] .... Fridericiana Z Univ Karlsruhe
Friedl Expert Committee .... FEC
Friedman Industries, Inc. [*American Stock Exchange symbol*] .... FRD
Friedman, John M., Hurricane WV [*STAC*] .... FJM
Friedman Library (Hugo Friedman Memorial), Tuscaloosa, AL [*Library symbol*] .... ATu
Friedman Test [*for pregnancy*] [*Obstetrics*] .... FRIED
Friedreich's Ataxia Group in America .... FAGA
Friedrich-Alexander-Universitat zu Erlangen-Nurnberg, Abteilung fur Wirtschafts- und Socialwissenschaften, Nurnberg, Germany [*Library symbol*] .... GyNU
Friedrich-Alexander-Universitat zu Erlangen-Nurnberg, Erlangen, Germany [*Library symbol*] .... GyEU
Friedrich-Ebert-Stiftung, Archiv der Sozialen Demokratie, Bonn, Germany [*Library symbol*] .... GyBoFE
Friedrich Miescher Institute [*Basle, Switzerland*] .... FMI
Friedrichshafen [*West Germany*] [*Airport symbol*] .... FDH
Friend .... FRD
Friend Disease Virus [*Also, FLV, FV*] .... FDV
Friend Leukemia Cells [*Cytology*] .... FLC
Friend Leukemia Virus [*Also, FDV, FV*] .... FLV
Friend Virus [*Also, FDV, FLV*] .... FV
Friendless, Isolated, Needy, Disabled [*Project of National Council on the Aging - acronym used as name of New York City coffeehouse*] .... FIND
Friendly Aircraft .... FA
Friendly Contacts Associates [*An association*] .... FCA
Friendly Foreign Government .... FFG
Friendly Forward Disposition .... FFD
Friendly Frost, Inc. [*American Stock Exchange symbol*] [*Delisted*] .... FF
Friendly Hand Foundation .... FHF
Friendly Initiated [*Incident*] [*Vietnam*] .... FRI
Friendly Laotian Forces .... FLF
Friendly Robot Educational Device [*Androbot, Inc.*] .... FRED
Friendly Society of Engravers and Sketchmakers [*Later, MPEA*] .... FSES
Friendly Strike or Support [*Military*] .... FSTK/SUP
Friends of Africa in America .... FAA
Friends of American Art in Religion .... FAAR
Friends of the American Museum in Britain .... FAMB
Friends of American Writers .... FAW
Friends of Animals .... FOA
Friends Association for Higher Education .... FAHE
Friends Bible College [*Kansas*] .... FBC
Friends of Books and Comics .... FBC
Friends of Buddhism .... FB
Friends of Cast Iron Architecture .... FCIA
Friends of Cathedral Music .... FCM
Friends of Children of Vietnam .... FCVN
Friends of Clara Barton .... FCB
Friends Committee on National Legislation .... FCNL
Friends of Community .... FC
Friends Coordinating Committee on Peace .... FCCP
Friends Council on Education .... FCE
Friends of the Earth .... FOE
Friends of the Earth Foundation .... FEF
Friends of the Everglades .... FE
Friends of Eye Research .... FER
Friends of Eye Research, Rehabilitation, and Treatment [*Later, FER*] .... FERRAT
Friends of Families .... FOF
Friends of Family Planning .... FFP
Friends of the FBI .... FOF
Friends of the Filipino People .... FFP
Friends of Free Asia [*Defunct*] .... FOFA
Friends of Free China .... FOFC
Friends' Free Library of Germantown, Philadelphia, PA [*Library symbol*] .... PPFr
Friends General Conference .... FGC
Friends of George Sand .... FGS
Friends of the Golden State .... FGS
Friends of Haiti .... FOH
Friends of Haitian Refugees .... FHR
Friends Historical Association .... FHA
Friends Historical Association. Bulletin [*A publication*] .... Friends Hist Assoc Bull
Friends Historical Library of Swarthmore College, Swarthmore, PA [*Library symbol*] .... PSC-Hi
Friends Historical Library of Swarthmore College, Swarthmore, PA [*OCLC symbol*] .... PSH
Friends of Historical Pharmacy .... FHP
Friends of India Society International .... FISI
Friends of Israel Gospel Ministry .... FIGM
Friends for Jamaica .... FFJ
Friends of the Land [*Later, IWLA*] .... FOL
Friends of Libraries USA .... FOL USA
Friends of the Library of Hawaii, Honolulu, HI [*Library symbol*] .... HHF
Friends of Little Gidding .... FLG
Friends Meeting House [*Quakers*] .... FMH
Friends Meeting, Stony Run, Baltimore, MD [*Library symbol*] .... MdBFr
Friends of the National Zoo .... FONZ
Friends of Nature .... FN
Friends of Old-Time Music [*Later, Society for Traditional Music*] .... FOTM
Friends Outside .... FO
Friends of Patrick Henry .... FPH
Friends Peace Committee .... FPC
Friends of the Peaceful Alternatives .... FPA
Friends of Photography .... FOP
Friends Program .... FP
[*The*] **Friends Program** .... TFP
Friends Reference Library, London, United Kingdom [*Library symbol*] .... UkLQ
Friends of the River .... FOTR
Friends of the Sea Lion .... FSL
Friends of the Sea Otter .... FSO
Friends Service Council [*Quakers*] .... FSC
Friends in Service Here .... FISH
Friends of Solidarity .... FS
Friends of the Superior Court .... FSC
Friends of the Third World .... FTW
Friends United Meeting .... FUM
Friends of the United States of Latin America .... FUSLA
Friends United Toward Understanding, Rights, and Equality .... FUTURE
Friends University, Wichita, KS [*OCLC symbol*] .... KFU
Friends University, Wichita, KS [*Library symbol*] .... KWiF
Friends of the Wilderness [*Defunct*] .... FOW
Friends World College .... FWC
Friends World Committee for Consultation .... FWCC
Friends of the World Council of Churches .... FWCC
Friendship Ambassadors .... FA
Friendship [*Airport*] **Annex** [*National Security Agency*] .... FANX
Friendship Facilities, Ottawa, IL [*Library symbol*] .... IOtF
Friendship House .... FH
Friendship Junior College [*South Carolina*] .... FJC
Friendship Loans to Latin American Endeavors, Inc. .... FLAME
Frigate [*Navy symbol*] .... DL
Frigate [*Navy symbol*] .... FF
Frigate .... FR
Frightened Little Man .... FLM
Frigidus [*Cold*] [*Pharmacy*] .... FRIG
Frigitemp Corp. [*American Stock Exchange symbol*] [*Delisted*] .... FTP
Frigitronics, Inc. [*NYSE symbol*] .... FRG
Frigorie [*Unit of rate of extraction of heat*] [*Thermodynamics*] .... fr
Frijoles Canyon [*New Mexico*] [*Seismograph station code, US Geological Survey*] [*Closed*] .... FCN
Fringe .... FRNG

Friona Industries, Inc. [*American Stock Exchange symbol*] .... FI
Frisch's Restaurants, Inc. [*American Stock Exchange symbol*] .... FRS
Frisian [*MARC language code*] [*Library of Congress*] .... fri
Frisian [*Language, etc.*] .... FRIS
Frisian .... FRS
Frisker-Monitor [*Radiation detection*] .... FM
Fritz Engineering Laboratory [*Lehigh University*] .... FEL
Fritzi of California [*NASDAQ symbol*] .... FRIT
Friuli Medico [*A publication*] .... Friuli Med
Frobisher [*Northwest Territories*] [*Seismograph station code, US Geological Survey*] .... FRB
Frobisher Bay [*Northwest Territories*] [*Seismograph station code, US Geological Survey*] [*Closed*] .... FBC
Frobisher Bay [*Canada*] [*Airport symbol*] .... YFB
Frobisher Bay, NT [*Radio station call letters*] .... CFFB
Froebel Journal [*A publication*] .... Froebel J
Frog [*Engineering*] .... FG
Frog Otolith Experiment Package [*NASA*] .... FOEP
Froid et la Climatisation [*A publication*] .... Froid Clim
From [*Use to precede the call sign of the calling station*] [*Aviation code*] .... DE
From .... F
From .... FM
From .... FR
From .... FRM
From Other Service Centers [*IRS*] .... FOSC
From Own Correspondent .... FOC
From Present Position [*Aviation*] .... FPP
From Unknown Worlds [*A publication*] .... FUN
Front .... F
Front .... FNT
Front .... FR
Front .... FRO
Front [*Deltiology*] .... FT
Front d'Action Politique .... FRAP
Front d'Alliberament Catala [*Spain*] .... FAC
Front of Board .... FOB
Front Communiste Revolutionnaire [*France*] .... FCR
Front-Connected .... FC
Front of Dash [*Technical drawings*] .... FD
Front End .... FRTN
Front End Analysis .... FEA
Front-End Network Processor .... FNP
Front-End Processor .... FEP
Front-End Screening [*DoD*] .... FES
Front Focal Length [*Optics*] .... FF
Front Focal Length [*Optics*] .... FFL
Front Jednosci Narodowej [*Polish Front of National Unity*] .... FJN
Front des Jeunes Nationalistes Africains [*National African Youth Front*] .... FJNA
Front de Liberation de la Bretagne - Armee Republicaine Bretonne [*France*] .... FLB-ARM
Front for the Liberation of the Cabinda Enclave .... FLEC
Front de Liberation de la Cote des Somalis [*Front for the Liberation of the Somali Coast*] [*Djibouti*] .... FLCS
Front de Liberation Nationale [*National Liberation Front*] [*Algeria*] .... FLN
Front de Liberation Nationale [*Chad*] .... FROLINAT
Front for the Liberation of Occupied South Yemen .... FLOSY
Front de Liberation Populaire [*Quebec separatist group*] .... FLP
Front de Liberation du Quebec [*Separatist group*] .... FLQ
Front for Liberation and Unity [*Western Sahara*] .... FLU
Front for the Liberation of Zimbabwe [*Zimbabwe is African term for Rhodesia*] .... FROLIZI
Front de Libertacao de Guinee [*Guinean Liberation Front*] [*Portuguese Guinea*] .... FLG
Front Line [*Revolutionary group*] [*Italy*] .... PL
Front de la Lutte pour l'Independence du Dahomey [*Battle Front for the Independence of Dahomey*] .... FLID
Front Mounting Light .... FML
Front for the National Liberation of the Congo .... FNLC
Front for National Salvation [*Uganda*] .... FRONASA
Front National Uni [*United National Front*] [*The Comoros*] .... FNU
Front Paisanu di Liberazione [*Corsica*] .... FPCL
Front Panel Control .... FPC
Front Populaire Soudanais [*Sudanese Popular Front*] .... FPS
Front for Popular Armed Struggle [*Iraq*] .... FPAS
Front du Quebec Francais .... FQF
Front Revolutionnaire Africain pour l'Independence Nationale des Colonies Portugaises [*African Revolutionary Front for the National Independence of Portuguese Colonies*] .... FRAIN
Front Royal, VA [*Location identifier*] [*FAA*] .... FRR
Front Royal, VA [*Radio station call letters*] .... WFFV
Front Royal, VA [*Radio station call letters*] .... WFTR
Front Royal, VA [*Radio station call letters*] .... WFTR-FM
Front Royal, VA [*Radio station call letters*] .... WIXV
Front Suspension Arm .... FSA
Front Uni Liberateur de la Guinee Portuguesa et des Isles du Cap Vert [*United Liberation Front of Portuguese Fuinea and Cape Verde*] .... FUL
Front Unifie de la Lutte de la Race Opprime [*United Front for the Struggle of Oppressed Races*] .... FULRO
Front d'Union Nationale de l'Angola [*National Union Front of Angola*] .... FUNA
Front de l'Unite Bangala [*Bangala United Front*] .... FUB
Front Upset Jaw .... FUJ
Front Vertex Back Focal Distance .... FVD
Front View .... FV
Front Wheel Drive .... FWD
Frontal Aviation [*Soviet tactical air force*] [*World War II*] .... FA
Frontal Groove of Pinnule .... FGP
Frontal Lobe [*Brain anatomy*] .... FL
Frontal National Democratic [*Rumania*] .... FND
Frontal Passage [*Meteorology*] .... FROPA
Frontal Surface [*Meteorology*] .... FROSFC
Frontenac County Public Library, Barriefield, ON, Canada [*Library symbol*] .... CaOBarF
Frontier .... FRON
Frontier [*A publication*] .... Front
Frontier Airlines, Inc. [*Air carrier designation symbol*] .... FAL
Frontier Airlines, Inc. [*ICAO designator*] .... FL
Frontier Armed and Mounted Police [*British government*] .... FAMP
Frontier Energy Corp. [*NASDAQ symbol*] .... FROG
Frontier Flying Service, Inc. [*Fairbanks, AK*] [*FAA designator*] .... FTA
Frontier Force .... FF
Frontier Holdings, Inc. [*American Stock Exchange symbol*] .... FA
Frontier Mining & Oil [*NASDAQ symbol*] .... FRMI
Frontier Nursing Service [*An association*] .... FNS
Frontier Nursing Service. Quarterly Bulletin [*A publication*] .... Front Nurs Serv Q Bull
Frontier Savings Association [*NASDAQ symbol*] .... FRNT
Frontiers of Biology [*Elsevier Book Series*] [*A publication*] .... FOB
Frontiers of Biology [*A publication*] .... Front Biol
Frontiers of Gastrointestinal Research [*A publication*] .... Front Gastrointest Res
Frontiers of Hormone Research [*A publication*] .... Front Horm Res
Frontiers International .... FI
Frontiers of Matrix Biology [*A publication*] .... Fron Matrix Biol
Frontiers of Oral Physiology [*A publication*] .... Front Oral Physiol
Frontiers in Physics [*A publication*] .... Front Phys
Frontiers of Plant Science [*A publication*] .... Frontiers Plant Sci
Frontiers of Plant Science [*A publication*] .... Front Plant Sci
Frontiers of Radiation Therapy and Oncology [*A publication*] .... Front Radiat Ther Oncol
Frontispiece [*Publishing*] .... FR
Frontispiece [*Publishing*] .... FRONT
Fronto-Dextra Anterior [*A fetal position*] [*Obstetrics*] .... FDA
Fronto-Dextra Posterior [*A fetal position*] [*Obstetrics*] .... FDP
Fronto-Dextra Transversa [*A fetal position*] [*Obstetrics*] .... FDT
Fronto-Occipital [*Anatomy*] .... FO
Frontogenesis [*Meteorology*] .... FNTGNS
Frontolysis [*Meteorology*] .... FNTLYS
Frost .... FRST
Frost X
Frost on Indicator [*Aviation*] .... FROIN
Frost & Sullivan, Inc. [*NASDAQ symbol*] .... FRSL
Frost & Sullivan, Inc. [*Information service*] .... F & S
Frost Warnings Issued .... FRWIS
Frost, WV [*Radio station call letters*] .... WVMR
Frostburg, MD [*Radio station call letters*] .... WFRB
Frostburg, MD [*Radio station call letters*] .... WFRB-FM
Frostburg State College, Frostburg, MD [*Library symbol*] .... MdFroS
Frostburg State College, Library, Frostburg, MD [*OCLC symbol*] .... MFS
Froude Number [*IUPAC*] .... F
Frozen .... FRZN
Frozen Cell .... FC
Frozen Concentrated Orange Juice .... FCOJ
Frozen Equilibrium Flow .... FEF
Frozen Fish Trades Association .... FFTA
Frozen Food Express [*NASDAQ symbol*] .... FEXP
Frozen Food Institute .... FFI
Frozen Foods [*A publication*] .... Frozen Fds
Frozen Granular Snow [*Skiing condition*] .... FRGR
Frozen Onion Ring Packers Council .... FORPC
Frozen Pea Council [*Defunct*] .... FPC
Frozen Plasma [*Medicine*] .... FP
Frozen Potato Products Institute .... FPPI
Frozen Red Cells [*Medicine*] .... FRC
Frozen Section [*Medicine*] .... FS
Frozen Storage .... FZSTO
Fructose [*A sugar*] .... Fru
Fructose Diphosphate [*Biochemistry*] .... FDP
Fructose Monophosphate [*Biochemistry*] .... FMP
Fruehauf Corp. [*NYSE symbol*] .... FTR
Fruehmittelalterliche Studien [*A publication*] .... FMAS
Fruit .... FRU
Fruit Pressure Tester .... FPT
Fruit Science Reports (Skierniewice) [*A publication*] .... Fruit Sci Rep (Skierniewice)
Fruit Varieties and Horticultural Digest [*A publication*] .... Fruit Var Hortic Dig
Fruit Varieties Journal [*A publication*] .... Fruit Var J
Fruit and Vegetable Division [*of Agricultural Research Service*] [*Department of Agriculture*] .... FV

Fruit World Annual and Orchardists' Guide [*A publication*] ... Fruit World Annu Orchardists' Guide
Fruit World and Market Grower [*A publication*] ... Fruit World Mark Grow
Fruita Public Library, Fruita, CO [*Library symbol*] ... CoFru
Fruitarian Network ... FN
Fruition Project ... FP
Fruits et Primeurs de l'Afrique du Nord [*A publication*] ... Fruits Prim Afr Nord
Fruits or Vegetables [*Freight*] ... FRU VEG
Frunze [*USSR*] [*Airport symbol*] ... FRU
Frunze [*USSR*] [*Seismograph station code, US Geological Survey*] ... FRU
Frustrated Multiple Internal Reflectance ... FMIR
Frustrated Total Reflection ... FTR
Frustration Tolerance Index [*Psychology*] ... FTI
Frustrillatum [*In Small Pieces*] [*Pharmacy*] ... FRUST
Frustula Entomologica [*A publication*] ... Frustula Entomol
Frustum Lifting Lug Kit ... FLLK
Fryeburg, ME [*Location identifier*] [*FAA*] ... FRY
Frysk Jierboek [*A publication*] ... FryskJb
Fryske Plaknammen [*A publication*] ... FPn
FSF Industries, Inc. [*Formerly, Flagstaff Corp.*] [*American Stock Exchange symbol*] [*Delisted*] ... FSF
FSS [*Flight Service Station*] **Assumes Control of Tower Frequencies and Lights** [*Aviation*] ... FATFL
FSS [*Flight Service Station*] **Returns Control of Tower Frequencies and Lights** [*Aviation*] ... FRTFL
FT Industries, Inc. [*NASDAQ symbol*] ... CLRS
Ftorafur [*Analog of 5-fluorourical deoxyribose*] [*Soviet anticancer drug*] ... FT
Fu Jen Studies [*A publication*] ... FJS
Fube [*Japan*] [*Seismograph station code, US Geological Survey*] ... FUB
Fuchu Air Force Weather Central ... FAFWC
Fucus [*Quality of the bottom*] [*Nautical charts*] ... Fu
Fuddruckers, Inc. [*NASDAQ symbol*] ... FUDD
Fuego [*Guatemala*] [*Seismograph station code, US Geological Survey*] ... FGO
Fuehrer der Luft [*Air liaison officer with Navy*] [*German military - World War II*] ... FDL
Fuel ... F
Fuel ... FL
Fuel Abstracts and Current Titles [*A publication*] ... FACT
Fuel Additive Blender Unit ... FABU
Fuel Additive Mixture Unit ... FAMU
Fuel Adjustment Clause ... FAC
Fuel Advisory Departure Procedures [*Aviation*] ... FAD
Fuel-Air [*Ratio*] ... F/A
Fuel Air Explosive ... FAE
Fuel Air Explosive ... FAX
Fuel Air Explosive System Helicopter Delivered ... FAESHED
Fuel Assembly ... F/A
Fuel Assembly Stability Test ... FAST
Fuel Bleed Valve ... FBV
Fuel on Board [*Aviation*] ... FOB
Fuel Booster Pump ... FBP
Fuel-Bound Nitrogen ... FBN
Fuel Building Filter System [*Nuclear energy*] ... FBFS
Fuel Capsule [*or Cell*] **Assembly** ... FCA
Fuel Cell ... FC
Fuel Cell ... FCL
Fuel Cell Battery ... FCB
Fuel Cell Catalyst ... FCC
Fuel Cell Module ... FCM
Fuel Cell Power Plant ... FCP
Fuel Cell Power Plant System ... FCPPS
Fuel Cell Power System [*or Subsystem*] ... FCPS
Fuel Cell Servicing System ... FCSS
Fuel Cell Test ... FCT
Fuel Cell Test Facility ... FCTF
Fuel Charge Kit ... FCK
Fuel Cladding Transient Tester [*Nuclear energy*] ... FCTT
Fuel Consuming Motor Vehicle ... FCMV
Fuel Consumption Unit ... FCU
Fuel Control Diaphragm Assembly ... FCDA
Fuel Coolant Interaction [*Nuclear energy*] ... FCI
Fuel Core Reserve [*Nuclear energy*] ... FCR
Fuel-Critical, Unspecified Area ... FCUA
Fuel Cycle ... FC
Fuel Cycle Facility [*Nuclear energy*] ... FCF
Fuel and Defueling ... F & DF
Fuel Desulphurization, Incorporated ... FDI
Fuel-Efficient Oil ... FEO
Fuel Element Failure Propagation [*Nuclear energy*] ... FEFP
Fuel Element Failure Propagation Loop [*Nuclear energy*] ... FEFPL
Fuel Element Rupture Detection [*Nuclear energy*] ... FERD
Fuel and Energy Abstracts [*A publication*] ... Fuel & Energy Abstr
Fuel Failure Detection ... FFD
Fuel Failure Mock-Up [*Nuclear energy*] ... FFM
Fuel Fill to Fuel Prefab ... FFP
Fuel Fill Line ... FFL
Fuel Fill to Missile [*Aerospace*] ... FFM
Fuel Flow ... FF
Fuel Flow Indicator ... FFI
Fuel Flow Totalizer [*Aerospace*] ... FFT
Fuel Flow Totalizer [*Aerospace*] ... FF/TOT
Fuel Gas ... FG
Fuel Handling and Radioactive Maintenance ... FH & RM
Fuel High Pressure ... FHP
Fuel Indicator Reading ... FIR
Fuel Injection Line ... FIL
Fuel Injection Pressure ... FIP
Fuel Injection Pump ... FIP
Fuel Insolation Valves ... FIV
Fuel Line ... FLN
Fuel Maintenance Panel ... FMP
Fuel Management Computer ... FMC
Fuel Oil ... FO
Fuel Oil Barge [*Self-propelled*] [*Navy symbol*] ... YO
Fuel Oil Barge [*Non-self-propelled*] [*Navy symbol*] ... YON
Fuel Oil Cooler ... FOC
Fuel Oil Equivalent Barrel ... FOEB
Fuel Oil Pump ... FOP
Fuel Oil Quick Closing Valve ... FOQCV
Fuel Oil Return ... FOR
Fuel Oil Route Delivery and Control System [*Computer-based system*] ... FORDACS
Fuel Oil Transfer ... FOT
Fuel Oil and Water Heater Manufacturers Association ... FOWHM
Fuel- Orr- Gegegyogyaszat [*Hungary*] [*A publication*] ... Fuel- Orr- Gegegyogy
Fuel to Oxidizer [*Ratio*] ... F/O
Fuel Packaging Facility [*Nuclear energy*] ... FPF
Fuel Preburner ... FPB
Fuel Preburner and Oxidizer Valve ... FPBOV
Fuel Preburner Oxidizer Valve ... FPOV
Fuel Pressure ... FP
Fuel Pressure Indicator ... FPI
Fuel Pressure Out ... FPO
Fuel Processing Technology [*Netherlands*] [*A publication*] ... Fuel Process Technol
Fuel Pump Control Unit ... FPCU
Fuel and Purchased Power Cost Adjustment ... FPPCA
Fuel Purification Unit [*Aerospace*] ... FPU
Fuel Quantity Indicator ... FQI
Fuel and Rearming Point [*Army*] ... FARP
Fuel Remaining [*Aviation*] ... FR
Fuel Reprocessing Plant [*Nuclear energy*] ... FRP
Fuel Rod Analysis Program [*Nuclear energy*] ... FRAP
Fuel Rod Analysis Program - Steady-State [*Nuclear energy*] ... FRAP-S
Fuel Rod Analysis Program - Transient [*Nuclear energy*] ... FRAP-T
Fuel Savings Advisory System ... FSAS
Fuel and Sensor, Tactical ... FAST
Fuel and Sensor Tactical Package ... FASTPACK
Fuel Service Nozzle ... FSN
Fuel Storage Area ... FSA
Fuel Storage Basin [*Nuclear energy*] ... FSB
Fuel Supply Depot [*Military*] ... FSD
Fuel Supply Exhausted [*Aviation*] ... FEXHA
Fuel Supply Module ... FSM
Fuel Supply Office [*Military*] ... FSO
Fuel Supply Unknown [*Aviation*] ... FENKIN
Fuel Supply Until [*Followed by time*] [*Aviation*] ... FENTL
Fuel System Supply Point ... FSSP
Fuel Systems Capability ... FSC
Fuel Tank ... FTK
Fuel Tank Helicopter ... FTH
Fuel Tanking [*Aerospace*] ... FT
Fuel Tanking Panel [*Aerospace*] ... FTP
Fuel Transfer Port ... FTP
Fuel Transfer Pump ... FTP
Fuel Transfer Tool ... FTT
Fuel Transfer Unit [*NASA*] ... FTU
Fuel and Transportation [*Navy*] ... FANDT
Fuel and Transportation [*Navy*] ... F & T
Fuel Treatment Apparatus ... FTA
Fuel Users Emergency Line [*Pennsylvania*] ... FUEL
Fuel Valve ... FV
Fuel Vapor Detector ... FVD
Fuel Wasting ... FW
Fueled Prototype Mock-Up System ... FPMS
Fueler [*Aircraft designation*] ... F
Fueling ... FLNG
Fueling Barge [*Navy symbol*] ... YCD
Fueling-at-Sea [*Navy*] ... FAS
Fueloil and Oil Heat and Solar Systems [*A publication*] ... Fueloil & Oil Heat
Fuels and Materials Examination Facility [*Department of Energy*] ... FMEF
Fuels Open Test Assembly [*Nuclear energy*] ... FOTA
Fuels Research Council [*Defunct*] ... FRC
Fuels Research Laboratory [*MIT*] ... FRL
Fuerstenfeldrruck [*Federal Republic of Germany*] [*Geomagnetic observatory code*] ... FUR
Fuerteventura [*Canary Islands*] [*Airport symbol*] ... FUE
Fuerza Democratica Nicaraguense [*Coalition of anti-Sandinista Nicaraguan exile groups*] ... FDN

Fuerzas Armadas de Liberacio [*Argentina*] ....FAL
Fuerzas Armadas de Liberacion Nacional [*National Liberation
    Armed Forces*] [*Venezuela*] ....FALN
Fuerzas Armadas de Liberacion Nacional Puertorriquena
    [*Armed Forces of Puerto Rican National Liberation*] ....FALN
Fuerzas Armadas Peronistas [*Argentina*] ....FAP
Fuerzas Armadas Rebeldes [*Rebel Armed Forces*] [*Guatemala*] ....FAR
Fuerzas Armadas Revolucionarias [*Argentina, Cuba, Mexico*] ....FAR
Fuerzas Armadas Revolucionarias Colombianas [*Colombia*] ....FARC
Fuerzas Revolucionarias Armadas del Pueblo [*Mexico*] ....FRAP
Fugacity [*Thermodynamics*] ....f
Fugitive Information Data Organizer [*Data base*] ....FIDO
Fugitive Intercept Net Deployment [*Philadelphia police program*] ....FIND
Fugitive Investigative Strike Team [*Operation conducted jointly
    by the US Marshals Service and local police*] ....FIST
Fugitive Other Authorities [*FBI standardized term*] ....FOA
Fuji Electric Journal [*A publication*] ....Fuji Electr J
Fuji Electric Review [*A publication*] ....Fuji Electr Rev
Fuji Photo Film ADR [*NASDAQ symbol*] ....FUJIY
Fujikura Technical Review [*A publication*] ....Fujikura Tech Rev
Fujisawa Pharmaceutical Co. [*Japan*] [*Research code symbol*] ....FK
Fujisawa Pharmaceutical Co. [*Japan*] [*Research code symbol*] ....NF
Fujisawa Pharmaceutical Co. [*Japan*] [*Research code symbol*] ....NTA
Fukien Province [*China, Mainland*] [*MARC geographic area code*]
    [*Library of Congress*] ....a-cc-fu
Fukue [*Japan*] [*Seismograph station code, US Geological Survey*] ....FKJ
Fukue [*Japan*] [*Airport symbol*] ....FUJ
Fukui [*Japan*] [*Seismograph station code, US Geological Survey*] ....FUK
Fukui Daigaku Gakugeigakubu Kiyo [*A publication*] ....FDGK
Fukui University, Fukui-shi, Japan [*Library symbol*] ....JFuU
Fukuoka [*Japan*] [*Seismograph station code, US Geological Survey*] ......FKK
Fukuoka [*Japan*] [*Airport symbol*] ....FUK
Fukuoka Acta Medica [*A publication*] ....Fukuoka Acta Med
Fukuoka Occupation Force ....FOF
Fukushima [*Japan*] [*Seismograph station code, US Geological
    Survey*] ....FKS
Fukushima Journal of Medical Science [*A publication*]
    ....Fukushima J Med Sci
Fukushima Medical Journal [*A publication*] ....Fukushima Med J
Fulbright Association of Alumni of International Educational
    and Cultural Exchange ....FAAIECE
Fulbright Newsletter [*A publication*] ....FulN
Fulcrum ....FUL
Fulcrum, Weight, Power ....FWP
Fulfillment Management Association [*Formerly, SFMA*] ....FMA
Full ....F
Full Action ....FA
Full Adder [*Data processing*] ....FA
Full Analog Video ....FAV
Full-Aperture Kicker [*Synchrotron*] ....FAK
Full Army Mobilization War Reserves ....FAM
Full Authority Electronic Control ....FAEC
Full Berth Terms [*Shipping*] ....FBT
Full of Brooklyns [*Coined by baseball broadcaster Red Barber,
    initialism refers to bases loaded with Brooklyn Dodgers*]
    [*Obsolete*] ....FOB
Full to Bursting [*Reply to question, "Have you had enough to eat?"*] ....FTB
Full Career Seaman Officer [*Navy*] [*British*] ....FCSO
Full Charge [*Bookkeeper*] ....FC
Full Circle Associates ....FCA
Full Cold Rolled [*Steel*] ....FCR
Full Container Load [*Shipping*] ....FCL
Full-Coverage Area [*Radio and TV*] ....FCA
Full-Coverage Film Cooling ....FCFC
Full Data Block ....FDB
Full Descriptive Method ....FDM
Full Dog Point ....FDP
Full Dress [*Colloquial reference to formal dress*] ....FD
Full Duplex ....FD
Full Duplex [*Data processing*] ....FDX
Full Duplex Teletype ....FDT
Full Duplex VOCODER ....FDV
Full Employment Action Council ....FEAC
Full Employment League ....FEL
Full Empty ....F/E
Full Face [*Photography*] ....FF
Full-Face Fire-Fighters' Mask ....FFFFM
Full Faith and Credit [*Finance*] ....FFC
Full-Fashioned ....FF
Full Field ....FF
Full Field Investigation ....FFI
Full Freight Allowed ....FFA
Full-Frequency Range Recording ....FFRR
Full-Frequency Stereophonic Sound ....FFSS
Full Fuzing Option [*Air Force*] ....FUFO
Full General-Emergency Striking Force Exercise [*Navy*] ....FLTSTRIKEX
Full Gospel Business Men's Fellowship International ....FGBMFI
Full Gospel Student Fellowship ....FGSF
Full Hard ....FH
Full Indicator Reading ....FIR
Full-Information Maximum Likelihood [*Econometrics*] ....FIML

Full Interest Admitted ....FIA
Full Joint Range of Movement [*Orthopedics*] ....FJRM
Full Length Emergency Cooling Heat Transfer [*Nuclear energy*] ......FLECHT
Full Lift ....FL
Full Liquid [*Medicine*] ....FL
Full Load [*Displacement*] ....F
Full Load ....F/L
Full Load ....FLLD
Full Load Frame Time [*Term used in SAGE operations*] ....FLFT
Full Marching Pack [*Military*] ....FMP
Full Maternal Behavior [*Physiology*] ....FMB
Full Mission Engineering Simulator ....FMES
Full Moon [*Moon phase*] ....FM
Full Mouth Extraction [*Dentistry*] ....FME
Full Mouth Radiograph [*Dentistry*] ....FMX
Full Mouth Series [*Dentistry*] ....FMS
Full Normal Plot [*Data processing*] ....FUNOP
Full Octave Filter ....FOF
Full Operational Capability Program [*Navy*] ....FOC
Full Operational Status ....FOS
Full Organ [*Music*] ....FO
Full Organ [*Music*] ....F ORG
Full Out [*Typesetting*] ....FO
Full Out Rye Terms [*Grain trade*] ....FORT
Full Outpatient Rate ....FOPR
Full Overlap Slotted Container [*Packaging*] ....FOSC
Full-Page Composition System [*Data processing*] ....FPCS
Full Paid [*NYSE symbol*] ....FPD
Full Period ....FP
Full Power ....FP
Full Power Days [*Nuclear energy*] ....FPD
Full Power Frequency ....FPF
Full Power Hours [*Nuclear energy*] ....FPH
Full Power Load ....FPL
Full Power Response ....FPR
Full Power Trial ....FPT
Full Pressure Suit [*Aerospace*] ....FPS
Full Pressure Suit Training Unit ....FPSTU
Full Propellant Requirement ....FPR
Full Range ....FR
Full Range Joint Movement [*Occupational therapy*] ....FRJM
Full Range of Motion [*or Movement*] [*Occupational therapy*] ....FROM
Full-Range Picture Vocabulary Test [*Education*] ....FRPVT
Full-Rate [*Telegrams and cables*] ....FR
Full Recovery Time [*Medicine*] ....FRT
Full Reimbursement Rate ....FRR
Full Remaining Radiation Service [*Unit*] [*Military*] ....FRRS
Full-Round Nose [*Diamond drilling*] ....FRN
Full Route Clearance Necessary [*Aviation*] ....FRC
Full Scale ....FS
Full Scale ....FSC
Full-Scale Deflection [*Instrumentation*] ....FSD
Full-Scale Development ....FSD
Full-Scale Engineering Development ....FSED
Full-Scale Output ....FSO
Full-Scale Production ....FSP
Full-Scale Record [*Instrumentation*] ....FSR
Full Scale Review ....FSR
Full-Scale Subsonic Wind Tunnel ....FSSWT
Full-Scale Test Vehicle [*NASA*] ....FSTV
Full-Scale Tunnel [*Aerospace*] ....FST
Full-Scale Unit ....FSU
Full Size ....FS
Full and Soft [*Dietetics*] ....FS
Full Stop Landing [*Aviation*] ....FSL
Full Straps Roosevelt Dime Club ....FSRDC
Full Term [*Pregnancy*] [*Medicine*] ....FT
Full Term Born Dead [*Medicine*] ....FTBD
Full Term License [*For nuclear power plant*] ....FTL
Full Term Normal Delivery [*Medicine*] ....FTND
Full Terms ....FT
Full Throttle Position ....FTP
Full Time [*Employment, education*] ....FT
Full-Time Equivalency Enrollment [*Education*] ....FTEE
Full-Time Equivalent [*Employment, education*] ....FTE
Full-Time Permanent [*Employment*] ....FTP
Full-Time Personnel [*Employment*] ....FTP
Full-Time Recruiting Force [*DoD*] ....FTRF
Full-Time Regular [*Civil Service employee category*] ....FTR
Full-Time Temporary [*Civil Service employee category*] ....FTT
Full-Time Temporary Personnel [*Employment*] ....FTTP
Full-Time Training Duty [*Army*] ....FTTD
Full-Time Unit Support [*Army Reserve*] ....FTUS
Full-Tracked Vehicle ....FTRAC
Full Transport Pack [*Military*] ....FTP
Full Truck Loads ....FTL
Full Up System Test ....FUST
Full Utilization of Rural Program Opportunities ....FURPO
Full Voltage ....FV
Full Wave ....FW
Full-Wave Alternating Current ....FWAC

Full-Wave Amplifier .... FWA
Full-Wave Balanced Amplifier .... FWBA
Full-Wave Bridge Rectifier .... FWBR
Full-Wave Direct Current .... FWDC
Full-Wave Rectified Unfiltered .... FWRU
Full-Wave Rectifier [*or Rectification*]......................... FWR
Full Weight Bearing [*Medicine*] .... FWB
Full Width at Half Maximum [*Spectroscopy*] .... FWHM
Full Width at Half Peak [*Spectroscopy*] .... FWHP
Full Width at Zero Intensity [*Spectroscopy*] .... FWZI
Full Year .... FY
Fullback [*Football*] .... FB
Fulleborn [*Papua New Guinea*] [*Airport symbol*] ..... FUB
Fuller [*H. B.*] Co. [*NASDAQ symbol*]........................ FULL
Fuller, R. H., Los Angeles CA [*STAC*] .... FRH
Fuller Theological Seminary, Pasadena, CA [*OCLC symbol*].................. CFT
Fuller Theological Seminary, Pasadena, CA [*Library symbol*]............... CPFT
Fullerton [*California*] [*Airport symbol*] .... FUL
Fullerton, CA [*Location identifier*] [*FAA*] .... FUL
Fullerton Junior College [*California*] .... FJC
Fullerton Junior College, Fullerton, CA [*Library symbol*] .... CFIJ
Fullerton Junior College Library, Fullerton, CA [*OCLC symbol*].......... CFU
Fullerton Public Library, Fullerton, CA [*Library symbol*]................. CFI
Fullrack System .... FS
Fully Automated Accounting Computer System .... FAACS
Fully Automated Computer Program .... FACP
Fully Automatic .... FA
Fully Automatic Cataloging Technique .... FACT
Fully Automatic Compiler [*or Computer*]-Translator .. FACT
Fully Automatic Compiling System .... FACS
Fully Automatic Compiling Technique .... FACT
Fully Automatic High Quality Machine Translation [*Data
 processing*] .... FAHQMT
Fully Automatic High Quality Translation [*Data processing*]..............FAHQT
Fully Buffered Channel .... FBC
Fully Good .... FG
Fully Good, Fair [*Business and trade*] .... FGF
Fully Heat Treated .... FHT
Fully Instrumented Submersible Housing [*An oceanographic
 instrument*] .... FISH
Fully Loaded Weight and Capacity [*Shipping*].......... FWC
Fully Mission Capable .... FMC
Fully Paid .... FP
Fully Proceduralized Job Performance Aid .... FPJPA
Fully Registered .... FR
Fully Separated Subsidiary .... FSS
Fully Tracked .... FT
Fulmer Research Institute .... FRI
Fulmer Research Institute. Newsletter [*A publication*] ....
                        Fulmer Res Inst Newsl
Fulminant Hepatic Failure [*Medicine*] .... FHF
Fulminant [*or Fulminating*] Viral Hepatitis [*Medicine*] ....FVH
Fulton County Court House, Atlanta, GA [*Library symbol*]................GAFC
Fulton County Law Library, Atlanta, GA [*Library symbol*]..............GAFL
Fulton County Medical Society, Atlanta, GA [*Library symbol*]...........GAFM
Fulton, KY [*Radio station call letters*].................... WFUL
Fulton, KY [*Radio station call letters*].................... WWKF
Fulton, MO [*Location identifier*] [*FAA*] .... FTT
Fulton, MO [*Radio station call letters*]................... KFAL
Fulton, MO [*Radio station call letters*]................... KKCA
Fulton-Montgomery Community College, Johnstown, NY
 [*Library symbol*] .... NJostF
Fulton-Montgomery Community College, Johnstown, NY [*OCLC
 symbol*] .... YJM
Fulton, MS [*Radio station call letters*].................... WFTA
Fulton, MS [*Radio station call letters*].................... WFTO
Fulton, NY [*Radio station call letters*].................... WKFM
Fulton, NY [*Radio station call letters*].................... WOSC
Fumaramido Oripavine [*Biochemistry*] .... FAO
Fumarate .... FUM
Fume-Tight [*Technical drawings*] .... FT
Fumigate .... FUM
Fumigation and Bath [*Military*] .... F & B
Fumigation and Bath [*Military*] .... FB
Fuming Nitric Acid .... FNA
Fun Fairs [*Public-performance tariff class*] [*British*] .... S
Fun, Travel, Adventure [*Sarcastic alternate to FTA - Free the Army*] ..... FTA
Funafuti Atol [*Tuvalu*] [*Airport symbol*].................. FUN
Funatsu [*Kawaguchuko*] [*Japan*] [*Seismograph station code, US
 Geological Survey*] .... FUN
Funbericht aus Schwaben [*A publication*] .... FS
Funchal [*Portugal*] [*Airport symbol*]....................... FNC
Funchal [*Madeira Island*] [*Seismograph station code, US
 Geological Survey*] .... FUL
Function .... F
Function .... FCT
Function .... FCTN
Function .... FNCTN
Function .... FUN
Function .... FUNC
Function .... FUNCT

Function of Astronaut Location [*NASA*] .... FAL
Function Button [*Data processing*]............................ FB
Function Circuit Diagram .... FCD
Function Control Block [*Data processing*] .... FCB
Function Control Package [*Data processing*] .... FCP
Function Designator .... FD
Function Designator Data Base .... FDDB
Function Generator .... FG
Function-on-Generator-Stop .... FOGS
Function Management Data .... FMD
Function-Oriented Organizational Structure .... FOOS
Function Safe-Release Panel [*Aerospace*]................ FS/RPNL
Function Set .... FS
Function Test Progress .... FTP
Function Timeline .... FCNTL
Functional Adhesive Bonding .... FAB
Functional Analysis .... FA
Functional Analysis and Its Applications [*A publication*] .... FAA
Functional Analysis and Its Applications [*A publication*].............
                        Functional Anal Appl
Functional Analysis System Technique .... FAST
Functional Area .... FA
Functional Area Breakdown .... FAB
Functional Area Code .... FAC
Functional Area Description .... FAD
Functional Area Documentation Manager [*Air Force*] .... FADM
Functional Arm Brace [*Medicine*] .... FAB
Functional Assembly .... FA
Functional Breadboard System [*Skylab*] [*NASA*] .... FBB
Functional Check Flight [*Air Force*] .... FCF
Functional Checkout .... FCO
Functional Code .... FC
Functional Configuration Audit .... FCA
Functional Configuration Identification .... FCI
Functional Data Coordinator .... FDC
Functional Demonstration and Acceptance .... FDA
Functional Demonstration Requirement .... FDR
Functional Description .... FD
Functional Design Activity [*Army*] .... FDA
Functional Design Criteria .... FDC
Functional Design Requirements .... FDR
Functional Design Review .... FDR
Functional Design Specifications .... FDS
Functional Differential Equation .... FDE
Functional Economic Area .... FEA
Functional Electronic Block .... FEB
Functional Electronic Blocks .... FEBS
Functional Element Test .... FET
Functional Engineering Interface Device [*NASA*] ... FEID
Functional Equipment Withholding Tab [*Obsolete*].............. FEWT
Functional Flow Block .... FFB
Functional Flow Block Diagram .... FFBD
Functional Flow Diagram .... FFD
Functional Individual Training System [*Navy*] .... FITS
Functional Input Report .... FIR
Functional Integration Test .... FIT
Functional Item Replacement [*Program*] [*Navy*] ... FIR
Functional Item Replacement Program [*Navy*] .... FIRP
Functional Job Analysis .... FJA
Functional Level Management .... FLM
Functional Line Diagram .... FLD
Functional Line Diagram .... FUNCTLINE
Functional Line Organization .... FLO
Functional Listing and Interconnection Wiring Record ....FLIWR
Functional Literacy [*Program to provide marginally literate
 soldiers with minimal literacy skills*] [*Army*] ..... FLIT
Functional Machine Representation Language [*Data processing*]........FMRL
Functional Maintenance Procedure .... FMP
Functional Manager .... FM
Functional Mathematical Programing System .... FM
Functional Mathematical Programing System [*Data processing*].........FMPS
Functional Mock-Up .... FMU
Functional Name Addresses .... FNA
Functional Neuromuscular Stimulation [*Physiotherapy*] ....FNS
Functional Nomenclature Signal .... FNS
Functional Objective .... FO
Functional Operational Sequence Diagram .... FOSD
Functional Path .... FP
Functional Performance Time .... FPT
Functional Photography [*A publication*].................... Funct Photgr
Functional Planning Matrices .... FPM
Functional Program Elements [*NASA*] .... FPE
Functional Proofing Vehicle .... FPV
Functional Query Language [*Data processing*] .... FQL
Functional Recovery Routine [*Data processing*] ...... FRR
Functional Reference Device .... FRD
Functional Requirement Specification .... FRS
Functional Requirements .... FR
Functional Reserve [*or Residual*] Capacity [*of the lungs*] [*Physiology*] .... FRC
Functional Schedules .... FS
Functional Schematic .... FS

Functional Selector...FS
Functional Sequence Diagram [*Data processing*]...........FSD
Functional Simulator...FSIM
Functional Simulator and Translator [*Data processing*]...........FST
Functional Specification Package [*Data processing*]...........FSP
Functional Stretch Reflex [*of muscles*].....................FSR
Functional Subsystem Software Requirements ....FSSR
Functional Supplementary Objective ....FSO
Functional Terminal Innervation Ratio [*Psychiatry*]....FTIR
Functional Test ....FT
Functional Test Change Request ....FTCR
Functional Test Data...FTD
Functional Test Equipment ....FTE
Functional Test Flight ....FTF
Functional Test Flight Checklist ....FTFC
Functional Test Objective ....FTO
Functional Test Procedure [*or Program*]....................FTP
Functional Test Report ....FTR
Functional Test Requirement ....FTR
Functional Test Specification ....FTS
Functional Training Branch [*BUPERS*]........................FTB
Functional User's Manual...FUM
Functional Uterine Bleeding [*Medicine*]....................FUB
Functional Validation Test [*Army*]...........................FVT
Functional Verification Unit [*Photography*].................FVU
Functional Vestibular Reserve [*Orientation*]...............FVR
Functionally Related Observable Difference [*between weapons*]........FROD
Functionally Significant Items ....FSI
Functiones et Approximatio Commentarii Mathematici [*A publication*]......Funct Approximatio Comment Math
Functions/Parameters/Characteristics ....FPC's
Functions and Responsibilities ....F & R
Fund for the Advancement of Camping ....FAC
Fund for the Advancement of Education [*Defunct*]........FAE
Fund for the Advancement of Music Education ....FAME
Fund for Artists' Colonies..FAC
Fund for Assuring an Independent Retirement ....FAIR
Fund Campaign [*Red Cross*].....................................FC
Fund Code ....FC
Fund for a Conservative Majority [*Formerly, YACC*].......FCM
Fund for Constitutional Government ....FCG
Fund for a Democratic Majority ....FDM
Fund for Education in World Order [*Later, FFP*]...........FEWO
Fund of Funds ....FOF
Fund for Human Dignity..FHD
Fund for Human Rights [*Later, WDL*]........................FHR
Fund for the Improvement of Postsecondary Education [*HEW*]...........FIPE
Fund for the Improvement of Postsecondary Education [*Department of Education*]...........FIPSE
Fund for Integrative Biomedical Research ....FIBER
Fund for Investigative Journalism ....FIJ
Fund Management Identification Code [*Military*].........FMIC
Fund for Modern Courts...FMC
Fund for Multinational Management Education ....FMME
Fund for New Priorities in America ....FFNPA
Fund for Objective News Reporting ....FONR
Fund for Open Information and Accountability ....FOIA
Fund for Peace [*Formerly, FEWO*].............................FFP
Fund for Peaceful Atomic Development [*Defunct*].......FPAD
Fund Raising [*Red Cross*].......................................FR
Fund Raising Management [*A publication*]...........Fund Raising Manage
Fund Raising Organization Graphics Service ....FROGS
Fund for the Relief of Russian Writers and Scientists in Exile ....LITFUND
Fund for the Replacement of Animals in Medical Experiments.........FRAME
Fund for the Republic [*Later, Robert Maynard Hutchins Center for the Study of Democratic Institutions*]...........FR
Fund to Restore an Educated Electorate.....................FREE
Fund for Special Operations [*Inter-American Development Bank*].........FSO
Fund for Theological Education ....FTE
Fund for UFO [*Unidentified Flying Object*] Research ....FUFOR
Fund for the United Nations for the Development of West Irian ......FUNDWI
Fundacao Brasileira para a Conservacao da Natureza Boletim Informativo [*A publication*]...........Fund Bras Conserv Nat Bol Inf
Fundacion Miguel Lillo Miscelanea [*A publication*].....Fund Miguel Lillo Misc
Fundamenta Informaticae [*A publication*]...........Fund Informat
Fundamenta Mathematicae [*A publication*]...........Fund Math
Fundamental ....FUND
Fundamental Aspects of Pollution Control and Environmental Science [*Elsevier Book Series*] [*A publication*]...........FAPCES
Fundamental Design Method......................................FDM
Fundamental Interpersonal Relations Orientation [*Psychology*]...........FIRO
Fundamental Material Controls ....FMC
Fundamental Order of Operation [*Mathematics game*]...........FOO
Fundamental Standard Data Link Working Group [*NATO*]...........FSDLWG
Fundamental Studies in Computer Science [*Elsevier Book Series*] [*A publication*]...........FSCS
Fundamental Studies in Engineering [*Elsevier Book Series*] [*A publication*]...........FSE
Fundamentally Analyzable Simplified English [*Data processing*].........FASE
Fundamentally Different Factors [*Environmental Protection Agency*]......FDF

Fundamentals of Aerospace Instrumentation [*A publication*]...........Fundam Aerosp Instrum
Fundamentals of Application and System Training [*Course*] [*Data processing*]...........FAST
Fundamentals of Cosmic Physics [*A publication*]...........Fundam Cosm Phys
Fundamentals Graduate..FG
Fundberichte aus Hessen [*A publication*]...........Fundber Hessen
Fundberichte aus Oesterreich [*A publication*]...........Fundber Oesterreich
Fundberichte aus Schwaben [*A publication*]...........Fundber Schwaben
Funded Delivery Period [*DoD*]..................................FDP
Funding..FDG
Funding...FNDG
Funding Authorization Document...............................FAD
Funding Exchange..FE
Funding Program Advice [*Military*]............................FPA
Funding Request..FR
Funding Sources Clearinghouse, Inc..........................FSC
Funds Flow Analysis...FFA
Funds Management Audit List [*Military*].....................FMAL
Funds Management Record [*Military*].........................FMR
Funds Net, Inc. [*NASDAQ symbol*].............................FNET
Funds Transfer System..FTS
Funds Will Not Be Entrusted to Others for Any Purpose [*Army*]...........FWNEOFAP
Funeral Telegraph Service ....FTS
Fungi Canadenses [*A publication*]...........Fungi Can
Fungus Proof...FP
Funk-Technik [*A publication*]...........Funk-Tech
Funksjonaerenes Sentralorganisasjoh [*Central Organization of Salaried Employees*] [*Norway*]...........FSO
Funksjonaersambandet i Norge [*Employees Federation of Norway*]........FSN
Funkstelle [*Radio Station*] [*German military - World War II*]...........FST
Funktionelle und Morphologische Organisation der Zelle [*A publication*]...........Funkt Morphol Organ Zelle
Funnel..FUNL
Funnel Cloud...FC
Funnel Length...FL
Funnel Length Index...FLI
Funny Looking Kid [*Medical slang*]............................FLK
Funter Bay [*Alaska*] [*Airport symbol*].......................FNR
Funter Bay, AK [*Location identifier*] [*FAA*].................FNR
Funtime, Inc. [*NASDAQ symbol*]................................FNTM
Fuqua Industries, Inc. [*NYSE symbol*].........................FQA
Fuquay Varina, NC [*Radio station call letters*].............WAKS
Fuquay Varina, NC [*Radio station call letters*].............WAKS-FM
Fuquene [*Colombia*] [*Geomagnetic observatory code*]...........FUQ
Fuquene [*Colombia*] [*Seismograph station code, US Geological Survey*]...........FUQ
Fur Brokers Association of America ....FBAA
Fur Buyers Association, Coat and Suit Industry ....FBACSI
Fur Dressers Guild ....FDG
Fur Garment Traveling Salesmen's Association............FGTSA
Fur Information and Fashion Council ....FIFC
Fur, Leather, and Machine [*Workers Joint Board*].........FLM
Fur Merchants Employers Council ....FMEC
Fur Takers of America ....FTA
Fur Trade Journal of Canada [*A publication*]...........Fur Trade J Can
Fur Wholesalers Association of America......................FWAA
Furanose [*One-letter symbol*] [*Biochemistry*]...........f
(Furfurylamino)purine [*Plant hormone*] [*Organic chemistry*]...........FAP
Furioso [*A publication*]...........Fur
Furlong..F
Furlong..FUR
Furlough Rations [*Army*]...FR
Furloughed Without Pay ....FWOP
Furman Studies [*A publication*]...........FS
Furman Studies [*A publication*]...........FurmS
Furman University Bulletin [*A publication*]...........FUB
Furman University, Greenville, SC [*Library symbol*]...........ScGF
Furman University, Greenville, SC [*OCLC symbol*]...........SFU
Furnace..FUR
Furnace..FURN
Furnace Atomic Nonthermal Excitation Spectrometry ....FANES
Furnace Explosion [*Insurance*].................................FE
Furnace Fuel Oil...FFO
Furness Railway [*Scotland*].....................................FR
Furnish..FURN
Furnish Assignment Instructions Without Delay ....FAWOD
Furnish Copies of Orders to Appropriate Commanders ....FCOAC
Furnished..FH
Furnished Hardware and Services List........................FH & SL
Furnished and Installed ....F & I
Furnished and Installed by Others.............................FIO
Furnished This Station [*Army*].................................FURTS
Furniture..FURN
Furniture and Bedding Spring Institute [*Defunct*]...........FBSI
Furniture Deliverers' Association ....FDA
Furniture and Fixtures [*Insurance*]...........................F & F
Furniture, Fixtures, and Equipment [*Insurance*]...........FF & E
Furniture History Society...FHS
Furniture Industry Consumer Advisory Panel ....FICAP

Furniture Industry Research Association..............................FIRA
Furniture Manufacturers Association of Grand Rapids..................FMAGR
Furniture Parts [*Freight*]...FURN PTS
Furniture Rental Association of America.............................FRAA
Furrier..FURR
Furriers Joint Council of New York...................................FJCNY
Furstenfeldbruck [*Federal Republic of Germany*] [*Seismograph
   station code, US Geological Survey*]...............................FUR
Further...FHR
Further...FTHR
Further...FUR
Further...FURR
Further Differentiated Fibroblast [*Cytology*].......................FDF
Further Education...FE
Further Finished Than Primed [*Freight*]................FHR FNSHD T PRMD
Further Finished Than Rough [*Freight*]................FHR FNSHD T RGH
Further Particulars When Available..................................FPWA
[*And*] Further Report To [*Army*]....................................FUREPT
Furtwaengler und Reichhold, Griechische Vasenmalerei [*A
   publication*]..FR
Furtwangen [*Schwarzwald*] [*Federal Republic of Germany*]
   [*Seismograph station code, US Geological Survey*]..................FWS
Fusable Read Only Memory [*Data processing*].......................FROM
Fuscaldo [*Italy*] [*Seismograph station code, US Geological Survey*]..........FSC
Fuse..F
Fuse...FS
Fuse...FU
Fuse Block...FB
Fuse Box..FUBX
Fuse Current Rating...FCR
Fuse Holder...FUHLR
Fuse on Jam..FOJ
Fuse Set Subsystem..FSSS
Fuse Voltage Rating...FVR
Fused Junction...FJ
Fused Quartz...FQ
Fused Quartz Incandescent Lamp......................................FQIL
Fused Quartz Tubing...FQT
Fuselage [*Aviation*]...FUS
Fuselage [*Aviation*]...FUSLG
Fuselage, Lower Forward..FUS/LF
Fuselage Reference Line [*Aviation*].................................FRL
Fuselage Reference Plane [*Aviation*]................................FRP
Fuselage Station [*Aviation*]..FS
Fuselage, Upper Forward...FUS/UF
Fusible..FSBL
Fusilier...FUS
Fusing Point...FP
Fusion Bonded Coaters Association....................................FBCA
Fusion Energy Foundation...FEF
Fusion Engineering Device [*Nuclear energy*].........................FED
Fusion-Fission Hybrid Reactor..FFHR
Fusion at the Inferred Threshold [*Test*] [*Medicine*]...............FIT
Fusion Materials Irradiation Test Facility [*Proposed*]..............FMIT
Fusion Point..FNP
Fusion Point..FNPT
Fusion Point..FUP
Fusobacteria Micro-Organisms [*Medicine*].............................FM
Fuss [*Feet of organ stops*]..F
Future..FUT
Future Abstracts [*A publication*]..............................Fut Abstr
Future American Magical Entertainers.................................FAME
Future Aviation Professionals of America.............................FAPA
Future Budget Year...FBY

Future Business Leaders of America - Phi Beta Lambda.............FBLA-PBL
Future Engineers of America...FEA
Future Farmers of America...FFA
Future Fiction [*A publication*].......................................Fut
Future Generations [*An association*]..................................FG
Future Homemakers of America...FHA
Future Horsemen of America...FHA
Future Impact Point...FIP
Future Issue Requirement..FIR
Future Journalists of America...FJA
Future Language Information Processing System.......................FLIPS
Future Lawyers Investigating Transportation Employment
   [*Student legal action organization*]..............................FLITE
Future Main Battle Tank..FMBT
Future Military Systems Authority....................................FMSA
Future Physicians Clubs...FPC
Future Production..FUPRO
Future Projects Office [*NASA*]..FPO
Future Science Fiction [*A publication*]..............................FUTF
Future Scientists of America [*Defunct*]..............................FSA
Future Scientists of America Foundation [*Defunct*]..................FSAF
Future Strategic Target List...FSTL
Future System [*Data processing*] [*IBM Corp.*].........................FS
Future Teachers of America [*Later, SAE*].............................FTA
Future Weapons Agency [*Army*]..FWA
Futures [*A publication*]..Fut
Futures [*A publication*]...FUTU
Futures for Children..FFC
Futures Commission Merchant..FCM
[*The*] Futures Group [*Commercial firm*]..............................TFG
Futures Industry Association..FIA
Futures Information Network...FIN
Futures Information Retrieval System [*Congressional Research
   Service*]..FIRST
Futures Network..FN
Futurist [*A publication*]..FTST
Futurist [*A publication*]...Fut
Futuristic Stories [*A publication*].................................FUTS
Fuyang [*China*] [*Airport symbol*]...................................FUG
Fuyun [*China*] [*Airport symbol*]....................................FYN
Fuze...FZ
Fuze Arming Test Experiment...FATE
Fuze Cavity Liner [*Projectile*].......................................FCL
Fuze Committee [*Military*]...FC
Fuze Control Device...FCD
Fuze Delay...FD
Fuze Firing Circuit...FFC
Fuze Maintenance Spares..FMS
Fuze Management Board [*Army*]..FMB
Fuze Management Organization [*Army*].................................FMO
Fuze Set Test Set..FSTS
Fuzed Alloy..FA
Fuzed Silica Tube...FST
Fuzhou [*China*] [*Airport symbol*]...................................FOC
Fuzing, Arming, and Firing..FAF
Fyizika Tverdogo Tyila [*A publication*]................Fyiz Tverd Tyila
Fyra Svenska Reformationskrifter Tryckta i Stockholm Ar 1562
   [*A publication*]..FSRTS
Fysiatricky a Reumatologicky Vestnik [*A publication*]....................
                                             Fysiatr Reumatol Vestn
Fysiatricky Vestnik [*A publication*]......................Fysiatr Vestn
Fysisk Tidsskrift [*A publication*]........................Fys Tidsskr
Fyzikalny Casopis [*A publication*]...........................Fyz Cas

G

G. & A. N. Scott Ltd., Rochdale, United Kingdom [*Library symbol*] ..... UkRoS
G-Cat Class Association ..... GCCA
G. D. Searle & Co., Inc., Skokie, IL [*Library symbol*] ..... ISkS
G. D. Searle & Co., Inc., Skokie, IL [*OCLC symbol*] ..... JAP
G & E Aviation [*Traverse City, MI*] [*FAA designator*] ..... LAK
G. G. Drayton Club ..... GGDC
G-I Manpower Management Information System ..... GIMMIS
G. K. Chesterton Society ..... GKCS
G. K. Hall Co. [*Publisher*] ..... GKH
G & K Services, Inc. [*NASDAQ symbol*] ..... GKSR
Gabbs [*Nevada*] [*Seismograph station code, US Geological Survey*] [*Closed*] ..... GAB
Gable ..... GAB
Gable Industries, Inc. [*Formerly, Central Foundry Co.*] [*NYSE symbol*] .... GBI
Gable Mountain [*Washington*] [*Seismograph station code, US Geological Survey*] ..... GBL
Gabon [*MARC geographic area code*] [*Library of Congress*] ..... f-go---
Gabon [*Two-letter standard code*] ..... GA
Gabon [*Three-letter standard code*] ..... GAB
Gabon [*MARC country of publication code*] [*Library of Congress*] ..... go
Gabon [*Aircraft nationality and registration mark*] ..... TR
Gaborone [*Botswana*] [*Airport symbol*] ..... GBE
Gabriel Garcia Moreno Memorial Association ..... GGMMA
Gabriel Gonzalez Videla [*Antarctica*] [*Seismograph station code, US Geological Survey*] [*Closed*] ..... GGV
Gabriel Industries, Inc. [*American Stock Exchange symbol*] [*Delisted*] ..... GAB
Gabriel Richard Institute ..... GRI
Gabungan Organisasi Buruh Serikat Islam Indonesia [*Federation of Indonesian Moslem Trade and Labor Unions*] ..... GOBSII
Gabungan SB2 Non-Vakcentral [*Federation of Non-Affiliated Trade Unions*] [*Indonesia*] ..... GASERBUN
Gabungan Serikat Buruh Indonesia [*Federation of Indonesian Trade Unions*] ..... GSBI
Gabungan Serikat Buruh Islam Indonesia [*Federation of Indonesian Islamic Trade Unions*] ..... GASBIINDO
GAC Corp. [*Formerly, General Acceptance Corporation*] [*NYSE symbol*] [*Delisted*] ..... GAC
GAC Liquidating UBI [*NASDAQ symbol*] ..... GACTZ
Gaceta Matematica (Madrid) [*A publication*] ..... Gac Mat (Madrid)
Gaceta Medica de Caracas [*A publication*] ..... Gac Med Caracas
Gaceta Medica Catalana [*A publication*] ..... Gac Med Catalana
Gaceta Medica (Guayaquil) Ecuador [*A publication*] ..... Gac Med (Guayaquil)
Gaceta Medica of Mexico [*A publication*] ..... Gac Med Mex
Gaceta Medica del Norte Bilbao [*A publication*] ..... Gac Med Norte Bilbao
Gaceta de Medicina Zoologica [*A publication*] ..... Gac Med Zool
Gaceta Numismatica [*A publication*] ..... Gac Num
Gaceta de Sanidad Militar [*A publication*] ..... Gac San Mil
Gaceta Veterinaria (Buenos Aires) [*A publication*] ..... Gac Vet (B Aires)
Gadolinium [*Chemical element*] ..... Gd
Gadolinium Gallium Garnet [*Substrate for magnetic film*] ..... GGG
Gadolinium Iron Garnet ..... GDLG
Gadolinium Molybdate ..... GMO
Gads Danske Magasin [*A publication*] ..... GDM
Gadsden [*Alabama*] [*Airport symbol*] ..... GAD
Gadsden, AL [*Location identifier*] [*FAA*] ..... DWY
Gadsden, AL [*Radio station call letters*] ..... WAAX
Gadsden, AL [*Radio station call letters*] ..... WEXP
Gadsden, AL [*Radio station call letters*] ..... WGAD
Gadsden, AL [*Radio station call letters*] ..... WQEN
Gadsden, AL [*Television station call letters*] ..... WTJP
Gadsden Purchase Refund Group [*Formerly, PRI*] [*Defunct*] ..... GPRG
Gadsden State Junior College, Gadsden, AL [*Library symbol*] ..... AGS
Gaede Diffusion Pump ..... GDP
Gaekwad's Oriental Series [*A publication*] ..... GOS
Gaelic ..... GAEL
Gaelic Athletic Association ..... GAA
Gaelic (Scots) [*MARC language code*] [*Library of Congress*] ..... gae
GAF Corp. [*Formerly, General Aniline & Film Corp.*] [*NYSE symbol*] ..... GAF
Gaffney, SC [*Radio station call letters*] ..... WAGI
Gaffney, SC [*Radio station call letters*] ..... WEAC
Gaffney, SC [*Radio station call letters*] ..... WFGN
Gaffney, SC [*Radio station call letters*] ..... WYFG
Gage Educational Publishing Ltd., Agincourt, ON, Canada [*Library symbol*] ..... CaOAgG
Gages Documentation Scheduling Committee ..... GADSCO
Gagnoa [*Ivory Coast*] [*Airport symbol*] ..... GGN
Gagnon [*Canada*] [*Airport symbol*] ..... YGA
Gahanna, OH [*Radio station call letters*] ..... WCVO
Gaigokugo Gaigoku Bungaku Kenkyu [*A publication*] ..... GGK
Gail Borden Public Library, Elgin, IL [*Library symbol*] ..... IElg
Gain ..... G
Gain Adjuster Adapter ..... GAA
Gain of Antenna ..... GA
Gain Band Merit ..... GBM
Gain Bandwidth ..... GB
Gain-Bandwidth Product ..... GBP
Gain Control ..... GC
Gain Control Amplifier ..... GCA
Gain Control Driver ..... GCD
Gain Control Range ..... GCR
Gain Factor [*Data processing*] ..... GF
[*Antenna*] **Gain-to-Noise Temperature Ratio** ..... G/T
Gain Time Control ..... GTC
Gained Output Ratio ..... GOR
Gainesville [*Florida*] [*Airport symbol*] ..... GNV
Gainesville, FL [*Television station call letters*] ..... WCJB
Gainesville, FL [*Radio station call letters*] ..... WDVH
Gainesville, FL [*Radio station call letters*] ..... WGGG
Gainesville, FL [*Radio station call letters*] ..... WKGR
Gainesville, FL [*Radio station call letters*] ..... WMFM
Gainesville, FL [*Radio station call letters*] ..... WMGI
Gainesville, FL [*Radio station call letters*] ..... WRUF
Gainesville, FL [*Radio station call letters*] ..... WRUF-FM
Gainesville, FL [*Television station call letters*] ..... WUFT
Gainesville, FL [*Radio station call letters*] ..... WUFT-FM
Gainesville, FL [*Radio station call letters*] ..... WYKS
Gainesville, GA [*Radio station call letters*] ..... WDUN
Gainesville, GA [*Radio station call letters*] ..... WFOX
Gainesville, GA [*Radio station call letters*] ..... WGGA
Gainesville, GA [*Radio station call letters*] ..... WLBA
Gainesville, GA [*Radio station call letters*] ..... WWLT
Gainesville Junior College [*Later, Cooke County Junior College*] [*Texas*] ..... GJC
Gainesville Midland Railroad Co. [*AAR code*] ..... GM
Gainesville Public Library, Gainesville, FL [*Library symbol*] ..... FG
Gainesville, TX [*Location identifier*] [*FAA*] ..... GLE
Gainesville, TX [*Radio station call letters*] ..... KDNG-FM
Gainesville, TX [*Radio station call letters*] ..... KGAF
Gaining Inventory Managers ..... GIM
Gaining Major Command [*Military*] ..... GMAJCOM
Gaining Motor Air Command ..... GMAC
Gaithersburg, MO [*Radio station call letters*] ..... WJOK
Gal/Guy Fridays [*Classified advertising*] ..... G/G/FRIS
Gala Law [*Scotland*] [*Seismograph station code, US Geological Survey*] ..... EGL
Galactic ..... GAL
Galactic Center ..... GC
Galactic Cosmic Radiation [*or Ray*] ..... GCR
Galactic Cosmic Ray Particle ..... GCRP
Galactic Jupiter Probe [*NASA*] ..... GJP
Galactic Probe ..... GP
Galactic Radiation Experiment Background Satellite [*Navy transit satellite*] ..... GREB
Galactic Radio Wave ..... GRW
Galactocerebroside [*Biochemistry*] ..... GC
Galactokinase [*Cell strain deficient in galactokinase*] ..... GALK
Galactose [*A sugar*] ..... Gal
Galactose-Binding Protein [*Biochemistry*] ..... GBP
Galactosemic Fibroblasts [*Medicine*] ..... GSF

Galactotransferase [*Cell strain deficient in galactose-1-phosphate uridyltransferase*] .... GALT
Galapagos Islands [*Ecuador*] [*Seismograph station code, US Geological Survey*] .... GIE
Galapagos Islands [*Ecuador*] [*Airport symbol*] .... GPS
Galapagos Islands [*MARC geographic area code*] [*Library of Congress*] .... pogg---
Galapagos Spreading Center [*Oceanography*] .... GSC
Galatians [*New Testament book*] .... Gal
Galax, VA [*Radio station call letters*] .... WBOB
Galax, VA [*Radio station call letters*] .... WBOB-FM
Galaxy [*A publication*] .... GAL
Galaxy Books [*Oxford University Press*] .... GB
Galaxy Carpet Mills, Inc. [*American Stock Exchange symbol*] .... GXY
Galaxy Oil [*American Stock Exchange symbol*] .... GOX
Galaxy Science Fiction [*A publication*] .... GSF
Galaxy Science Fiction Novels [*A publication*] .... GSFN
Galbraith Lake Camp, AK [*Location identifier*] [*FAA*] .... LCP
Gale [*Meteorology*] .... G
Gale Information Guide Library [*Publication series*] .... GIGL
Gale Research Company .... GRC
Galela [*Indonesia*] [*Airport symbol*] .... GLX
Galena [*Alaska*] [*Airport symbol*] .... GAL
Galena Air Service [*Galena, AK*] [*FAA designator*] .... GAS
Galena, AK [*Location identifier*] [*FAA*] .... BZP
Galerazamba [*Colombia*] [*Seismograph station code, US Geological Survey*] .... GAL
Galesburg [*Illinois*] [*Airport symbol*] .... GBG
Galesburg, IL [*Radio station call letters*] .... WAAG
Galesburg, IL [*Radio station call letters*] .... WAIK
Galesburg, IL [*Radio station call letters*] .... WGBQ
Galesburg, IL [*Radio station call letters*] .... WGIL
Galesburg, IL [*Radio station call letters*] .... WVKC
Galesburg Memorial Library, Galesburg, MI [*Library symbol*] .... MiGal
Galesburg Public Library, Galesburg, IL [*Library symbol*] .... IG
Galiceno Horse Breeders Association .... GHBA
Galileo [*Unit of acceleration*] .... gal
Galileo Electro-Optics [*NASDAQ symbol*] .... GAEO
Galileo Number .... Ga
Galion [*Ohio*] [*Airport symbol*] .... GQQ
Galion Crestline Service [*Galion, OH*] [*FAA designator*] .... GCS
Galion, OH [*Radio station call letters*] .... WGLX
Galion, OH [*Radio station call letters*] .... WQLX
Gall Bladder [*or a patient with an affliction of this organ*] [*Medicine*] .... GB
Gall Bladder Series [*Radiography*] .... GBS
Gall Bladder Visualization [*Medicine*] .... GBviz
Galla [*MARC language code*] [*Library of Congress*] .... gal
Gallard-Schlesinger [*Chemical manufacturing corporation*] .... G-S
Gallatin, TN [*Radio station call letters*] .... WAMG
Gallatin, TN [*Radio station call letters*] .... WHIN
Gallatin, TN [*Radio station call letters*] .... WVCP
Gallatin, TN [*Radio station call letters*] .... WWKX
Gallaudet College, Kendall Demonstration School, Washington, DC [*Library symbol*] .... DGC-K
Gallaudet College, Kendall Demonstration School, Washington, DC [*OCLC symbol*] .... GQK
Gallaudet College, Model Secondary School for the Deaf, Washington, DC [*Library symbol*] .... DGC-M
Gallaudet College, Montessori School, Washington, DC [*OCLC symbol*] .... GQM
Gallaudet College, Washington, DC [*Library symbol*] .... DGC
Gallaudet College, Washington, DC [*OCLC symbol*] .... GQG
Gallaudet Information Retrieval Service .... GIRS
Gallery .... GAL
Gallery .... GALL
Gallery of Living Catholic Authors [*Defunct*] .... GLCA
Galley .... GALY
Galley .... GY
Gallia County District Library, Gallipolis, OH [*Library symbol*] .... OGalG
Gallic .... GA
Gallic Acid Equivalent [*Wine analysis*] .... GAE
Gallipoli Society in the United States of America .... GSUSA
Gallipolis, OH [*Radio station call letters*] .... WJEH
Gallipolis, OH [*Radio station call letters*] .... WYPC
Gallium [*Chemical element*] .... Ga
Gallium Arsenide [*Semiconductor*] .... GaAs
Gallium Arsenide Diode .... GAD
Gallium Arsenide Illuminator System .... GAIS
Gallium Arsenide LASER .... GAL
Gallium Arsenide Microwave Diode .... GAMD
Gallium Arsenide Phosphide [*Semiconductor*] .... GaAsP
Gallium Substituted Yttrium Iron Garnet .... GAYIG
Gallivare [*Sweden*] [*Airport symbol*] .... GEV
Gallon .... GAL
Gallon .... GALL
Gallon .... GL
Gallons per Acre per Day [*Irrigation*] .... GPAD
Gallons per Capita .... GPC
Gallons per Capita per Day .... GPCD
Gallons per Day .... GPD
Gallons per Foot Day .... GAL/(FT D)
Gallons of Fuel [*"Energy equivalent" abbreviation - biomass agriculture and conversion*] [*Fuel chemistry*] .... GAL
Gallons per Horsepower-Hour .... GAL/(HP H)
Gallons per Hour .... GAL/H
Gallons per Hour .... GPH
Gallons per Mile .... GPM
Gallons per Minute .... GAL/MIN
Gallons per Minute .... G/M
Gallons per Minute .... GPM
Gallons per Second .... GAL/S
Gallons per Second .... GPS
Gallons per Second .... G/S
Gallons per Square-Foot per Day .... GAL/(FT² D)
Gallons per Square-Foot per Day .... GFD
Galloping Acronyms Save Paper .... GASP
Galloping Gourmet [*TV program*] .... GG
Galloway Cattle Society of America .... GCSA
Gallup [*New Mexico*] [*Airport symbol*] .... GUP
Gallup, NM [*Radio station call letters*] .... KGAK
Gallup, NM [*Radio station call letters*] .... KOVO
Gallup, NM [*Radio station call letters*] .... KQNM
Gallup, NM [*Radio station call letters*] .... KYVA
Gallup Poll .... GP
Gallup Public Library, Gallup, NM [*OCLC symbol*] .... GAL
Gallup Public Library, Gallup, NM [*Library symbol*] .... NmG
Gallup Report [*A publication*] .... Gallup Rpt
Gallus-adeno-like [*Avian virus*] .... GAL
Galpin Society .... GS
Galpin Society Journal [*A publication*] .... Galpin S J
Galpin Society Journal [*A publication*] .... GAVEA
Galpin Society Journal [*A publication*] .... GSJ
Galt Collegiate Institute, Cambridge, ON, Canada [*Library symbol*] .... CaOGalC
Galva Township Public Library, Galva, IL [*OCLC symbol*] .... ISK
Galvanic [*or Galvanized*] .... GALV
Galvanic Skin Potential [*Physiology*] .... GSP
Galvanic Skin Response [*Physiology*] .... GSR
Galvanic Stimulation Rate [*Physiology*] .... GSR
Galvanized [*Metallurgy*] .... GI
Galvanized Aircraft .... GAC
Galvanized Corrugated [*Metal industry*] .... GC
Galvanized Improved Plow [*Steel*] .... GIP
Galvanized Iron .... GALVI
Galvanized Iron .... GI
Galvanized Plain [*Metal industry*] .... GP
Galvanized Steel .... GALVS
Galvanized Steel .... GS
Galvanized Steel Fastenings .... GF
Galvanized Steel Wire Rope .... GSWR
Galvanized or Tinned [*Freight*] .... GALV TND
Galvanized Ware Manufacturers Council .... GWMC
Galvannealed .... GALVND
Galvano Tecnica [*A publication*] .... Galvano Tec
Galvanocutaneous Reaction .... GCR
Galvanometer .... GALV
Galvanometer .... GALVNM
Galvanometer-Mirror Lightbeam .... GML
Galvasay [*USSR*] [*Seismograph station code, US Geological Survey*] [*Closed*] .... GAY
Galveston [*Texas*] .... GALV
Galveston [*Texas*] [*Airport symbol*] .... GLS
Galveston Community College, Galveston, TX [*Library symbol*] .... TxGC
Galveston Cotton Exchange and Board of Trade .... GCEBT
Galveston Houston Co. [*NYSE symbol*] .... GHX
Galveston, Houston & Henderson Railroad Co. [*AAR code*] .... GHH
Galveston, TX [*Radio station call letters*] .... KGBC
Galveston, TX [*Radio station call letters*] .... KILE
Galveston, TX [*Radio station call letters*] .... KXKX
Galveston Wharves [*AAR code*] .... GWF
Galvo-Drive Amplifier .... GDA
Galway [*County in Ireland*] .... GALW
Gam-Anon International Service Office .... GAISO
Gamba [*Gabon*] [*Airport symbol*] .... GAX
Gambela [*Ethiopia*] [*Airport symbol*] .... GMB
Gambell [*Alaska*] [*Airport symbol*] .... GAM
Gambia [*MARC geographic area code*] [*Library of Congress*] .... f-gm---
Gambia [*MARC country of publication code*] [*Library of Congress*] .... gm
Gambia [*Three-letter standard code*] .... GMB
Gambia [*Two-letter standard code*] .... GM
Gambia Airways [*ICAO designator*] .... GW
Gambia Labour Union .... GLU
Gambia Workers' Union .... GWU
Gambier Island [*French Polynesia*] [*Airport symbol*] .... GMR
Gambier, OH [*Radio station call letters*] .... WKCO
Gambit [*A publication*] .... Gam
Gamble-Skogmo, Inc. [*NYSE symbol*] [*Delisted*] .... GSK
Gamblers Anonymous .... GA
Gambro, Inc. Cl B ADR [*NASDAQ symbol*] .... GAMBY
Game .... G
Game-A-Tron Corp. [*NASDAQ symbol*] .... GAME

Game Conservancy Annual Review [*A publication*] .... Game Conservancy Annu Rev
Game Conservation International .... GAMECOIN
Game Manufacturers Association .... GMA
Game Research Association. Annual Report [*A publication*] .... Game Res Assoc Annu Rep
Game Theory .... GT
Game-Tying Goals [*Hockey*] .... GTG
Game-Winning Goals [*Hockey*] .... GWG
Games Ahead [*Baseball*] .... GA
Games Behind [*Baseball*] .... GB
Games Behind Leader [*Baseball*] .... GBL
Games Finished [*Baseball*] .... GF
Games at Home [*Baseball*] .... GAH
Games Network, Inc. [*NASDAQ symbol*] .... GNET
Games of the New Emerging Forces [*A counter-attraction to the Olympic Games*] [*Indonesia*] .... GANEFO
Games Played [*Sports statistics*] .... G
Games Played [*Sports statistics*] .... GP
Games [*or Matches*] **Played** [*Sports statistics*] .... P
Games Started [*Baseball*] .... GS
Games Taken Out [*Baseball*] .... TO
Gamete Shedding Substance [*Endocrinology*] .... GSS
Gaming and Technology [*NASDAQ symbol*] .... GATI
Gamma .... G
Gamma .... GAM
Gamma [*Subgroup of IgG*] [*Immunology*] .... Gm
Gamma [*A publication*] .... GAM
Gamma Activation Materials Assay System [*Mobile laboratory*] .... GAMAS
Gamma-Amino-beta-hydroxybutyric Acid [*Pharmacology*] .... GABOB
Gamma-Aminobutyric Acid [*Biochemistry*] .... GABA
Gamma Atomic Radiation Detector .... GARD
Gamma Benzene Hexachloride [*Also, BHC, HCH*] [*Insecticide*] .... GBH
Gamma Biologicals [*NASDAQ symbol*] .... GAMA
Gamma-Butyrolactone [*Organic chemistry*] .... GBL
Gamma Cosmic Ray [*Geophysics*] .... GCR
Gamma Dose Detector System .... GDDS
Gamma Eta Gamma [*Fraternity*] .... GEG
Gamma Field Symposia [*A publication*] .... Gamma Field Symp
Gamma Globulin [*Medicine*] .... GG
Gamma-Glutamyl Transpeptidase [*Also, GGT, GT*] [*An enzyme*] .... GGTP
Gamma-Glutamyltransferase [*Also, GGTP, GT*] [*An enzyme*] .... GGT
Gamma-Glutamyltransferase [*Also, GGT, GGTP*] [*An enzyme*] .... GT
Gamma-Hydroxy-beta-aminobutyric Acid [*Pharmacology*] .... GOBAB
Gamma-Hydroxybutyric Acid [*Organic chemistry*] .... GHB
Gamma Inspection of Grain Integrity .... GIGI
Gamma LINAC Instrumentation .... GLI
Gamma-Linolenic Acid .... GLA
Gamma Radiation Source .... GRS
Gamma Radiation Spectrometer .... GRS
Gamma Ray [*or Roentgen*] .... GR
Gamma Ray Amplification .... GRA
Gamma Ray Amplification by Stimulated Emission of Radiation .... GRASER
Gamma Ray Attenuation Porosity Evaluator .... GRAPE
Gamma-Ray Burst .... GRB
Gamma Ray Experiment .... GRE
Gamma Ray Explorer .... GRE
Gamma Ray LASER .... GASER
Gamma Ray Logs .... GAMLOGS
Gamma Ray Observatory [*Terminated, 1979*] .... GRO
Gamma Ray Projector .... GRP
Gamma Ray Spectrometric Equipment .... GRSE
Gamma Ray Spectrum .... GRS
Gamma Ray Telescope .... GRT
Gamma Ray Tube .... GRT
Gamma Scintillation System .... GSS
Gamma Theta Upsilon .... GTU
Gamma-Vinyl-GABA [*Biochemistry*] .... GVG
Gammon Theological Seminary, Atlanta, GA [*Library symbol*] .... GAGTh
Gamow-Teller [*Transition*] [*Nuclear physics*] .... GT
Ganado High School Library, Ganado, AZ [*Library symbol*] .... AzGaH
Gandalf Technologies [*NASDAQ symbol*] .... GANDF
Gander [*Canada*] [*Airport symbol*] .... YQX
Gander Automated Air Traffic System .... GAATS
Gander, NF [*Radio station call letters*] .... CBG
Gander, NF [*Radio station call letters*] .... CJOS-FM
Gander, NF [*Radio station call letters*] .... CKGA
Gandhi Marg [*A publication*] .... GM
Gandhi Society for Human Rights .... GSHR
Gang Punch [*Data processing*] .... GP
Gangaw [*Burma*] [*Airport symbol*] .... GAW
Ganglion [*Medicine*] .... G
Ganglion [*Medicine*] .... GANG
Ganglion Cell [*Medicine*] .... GC
Gann Japanese Journal of Cancer Research [*A publication*] .... Gann
Gann Monograph [*A publication*] .... Gann Monogr
Gannett Company, Incorporated [*NYSE symbol*] .... GCI
Gannett News Service .... GNS
Gannett Newspaper Foundation .... GNF
Gannon University, Erie, PA [*Library symbol*] .... PErG
Gannon University, Nash Library, Erie, PA [*OCLC symbol*] .... PGU
Gantry Test Rack [*Aerospace*] .... GTR
Ganz [*White Blot*] [*Rorschach*] [*Psychology*] .... G
Ganzfeld [*Whole Field*] [*ESP test*] [*Germany*] .... GZ
Gao [*Mali*] [*Airport symbol*] .... GAQ
GAO [*General Accounting Office*] **Atlanta Regional Office, Atlanta, GA** [*OCLC symbol*] .... GAZ
GAO [*General Accounting Office*] **Boston Regional Office, Boston, MA** [*OCLC symbol*] .... GAF
GAO [*General Accounting Office*] **Denver Regional Office, Denver, CO** [*OCLC symbol*] .... GAE
GAO [*General Accounting Office*] **Norfolk Regional Office, Virginia Beach, VA** [*OCLC symbol*] .... GAN
GAO [*General Accounting Office*] **Philadelphia Regional Office, Philadelphia, PA** [*OCLC symbol*] .... GAG
GAO [*General Accounting Office*] **Review** [*A publication*] .... GAO Rev
GAO [*General Accounting Office*] **San Francisco Regional Office, San Francisco, CA** [*OCLC symbol*] .... GAR
GAO [*General Accounting Office*] **Seattle Regional Office, Seattle, WA** [*OCLC symbol*] .... GAX
Gap in Cell Cycle [*Cytology*] .... G
Gap Detector .... GD
Gap Filler [*RADAR*] .... GF
Gap-Filler Data [*RADAR*] .... GFD
Gap-Filler Input [*RADAR*] .... GFI
Gap-Filler Output [*RADAR*] .... GFO
Gap-Filler RADAR .... GFR
Gap Filler/Reporting Post [*RADAR*] .... GF/RP
Gap-Filler Satellite [*RADAR*] .... GAPSAT
Gap Junction [*Cytology*] .... GJ
GAP [*Group for the Advancement of Psychiatry*] **Report** [*A publication*] .... GAP
Gap Separation .... GS
[*The*] **Gap Stores, Inc.** [*NYSE symbol*] .... GPS
GAR Memorial Library, West Newbury, MA [*Library symbol*] .... MWn
Gar Wood Society .... GWS
Garachine [*Panama*] [*Airport symbol*] .... GHE
Garage .... G
Garage .... GAR
Garage Door Council .... GDC
Garage Door Opener .... GDO
Garage Forecourts [*Public-performance tariff class*] [*British*] .... GF
Garage Keeper's Legal Liability [*Insurance*] .... GKLL
Garaina [*Papua New Guinea*] [*Airport symbol*] .... GAR
Garan, Inc. [*American Stock Exchange symbol*] .... GAN
Garbage .... GBG
Garbage Collection [*Slang*] [*Data processing*] .... GC
Garbage In, Garbage Out [*Data processing*] .... GIGO
Garbage Lighter [*Self-propelled*] [*Navy symbol*] .... YG
Garbage Lighter [*Non-self-propelled*] [*Navy symbol*] .... YGN
Garbage Truck .... GT
Garbell Research Foundation .... GRF
Garberville, CA [*Radio station call letters*] .... KERG
Garble .... GRBL
Garboard [*Naval architecture*] .... GARBD
Garchy [*France*] [*Seismograph station code, US Geological Survey*] .... GRC
Garcia Corp. [*American Stock Exchange symbol*] [*Delisted*] .... GIA
Garcia Lorca Review [*A publication*] .... GLR
Garcia de Orta (Lisbon) [*A publication*] .... Garcia de Orta (Lisb)
Garcia de Orta. Serie de Botanica [*Lisbon*] [*A publication*] .... Garcia de Orta Ser Bot
Garcia de Orta. Serie de Estudos Agronomicos [*Lisbon*] [*A publication*] .... Garcia de Orta Ser Estud Agron
Garcia de Orta. Serie de Zoologia [*Lisbon*] [*A publication*] .... Garcia de Orta Ser Zool
Garcia's of Scottsdale [*NASDAQ symbol*] .... GMEX
Garden .... GDN
Garden Center of Greater Cleveland, Cleveland, OH [*Library symbol*] .... OClGC
Garden Centers of America .... GCA
Garden City [*Kansas*] [*Airport symbol*] .... GCK
Garden City [*New York*] [*Airport symbol*] .... JHC
Garden City, GA [*Radio station call letters*] .... WNMT
Garden City, KS [*Radio station call letters*] .... KANZ
Garden City, KS [*Radio station call letters*] .... KBUF
Garden City, KS [*Radio station call letters*] .... KBUF-FM
Garden City, KS [*Radio station call letters*] .... KIUL
Garden City, KS [*Television station call letters*] .... KSNG
Garden City, KS [*Television station call letters*] .... KUPK
Garden City, MI [*Radio station call letters*] .... WCAR
Garden City, NY [*Radio station call letters*] .... WBAU
Garden City, NY [*Radio station call letters*] .... WHPC
Garden City, NY [*Radio station call letters*] .... WLIR
Garden City, NY [*Television station call letters*] .... WLIW
Garden City Public Library, Garden City, MI [*Library symbol*] .... MiGc
Garden City Public Library, Garden City, NY [*Library symbol*] .... NGc
Garden City, SD [*Radio station call letters*] .... KEJA
[*The*] **Garden City Western Railway Co.** [*AAR code*] .... GCW
Garden Club of America .... GCA
Garden Digest [*A publication*] .... Gard Digest
Garden and Forest [*A publication*] .... Garden & F
Garden Grove, CA [*Radio station call letters*] .... KIKF

Garden and Home Builder [*A publication*]....Gard & Home B
Garden Journal [*A publication*]....Gard J
Garden Journal. New York Botanical Garden [*A publication*].... Gard J NY Bot Gard
Garden Journal. New York Botanical Garden [*A publication*].... Gdn J NY Bot Gdn
Garden Magazine [*A publication*]....Gard M
Garden Point [*Australia*] [*Airport symbol*]....GPN
Garden Seed Association....GSA
Garden State Airlines, Inc. [*Shrewsbury, NJ*] [*FAA designator*]....GSA
Garden Supply Dealers National....GSDN
Garden Writers Association of America....GWAA
Gardener's Abstracts [*A publication*]....Gard Abstr
Gardeners' Chronicle of America [*A publication*]....Gard Chron Am
Gardeners' Chronicle (London) [*A publication*]....Gard Chron (Lond)
Gardenia Society of America....GSA
Gardens....GDNS
Gardens for All [*Later, National Association for Gardening*]....GA
Gardens Bulletin [*A publication*]....Gdns Bull
Gardens Bulletin (Singapore) [*A publication*]....Gard Bull (Singapore)
Gardiner, ME [*Radio station call letters*]....WABK
Gardiner, ME [*Radio station call letters*]....WABK-FM
Gardiner Public Library, Gardiner, ME [*Library symbol*]....MeGar
Gardner-Denver Company [*NYSE symbol*] [*Delisted*]....GDC
Gardner, MA [*Radio station call letters*]....WGAW
Gardner, MA [*Radio station call letters*]....WMWC
Gardner Museum, Boston, MA [*Library symbol*]....MBG
Gardner-Webb College [*North Carolina*]....GWC
Gardner-Webb College, Boiling Springs, NC [*Library symbol*]....NcBsG
Gardner-Webb College, Boiling Springs, NC [*OCLC symbol*]....NGW
Gardner-Webb Junior College [*Later, Gardner-Webb College*] [*North Carolina*]....GWJC
Gardo [*Somalia*] [*Airport symbol*]....GSR
Garfield County Public Library, New Castle, CO [*Library symbol*]....CoNc
Garfield County System, New Castle, CO [*OCLC symbol*]....COG
Garfield Guardian, Garfield, NJ [*Library symbol*]....NjGaG
Garfield Memorial Public Library, Clare, MI [*Library symbol*]....MiCla
Garfinckel, Brooks Brothers, Miller & Rhoads, Inc. [*NYSE symbol*]....GBM
Gargarisma [*Gargle*] [*Pharmacy*]....GARG
Garin Arava [*Jewish youth organization*]....GA
Garissa [*Kenya*] [*Airport symbol*]....GAS
Garland Corp. [*American Stock Exchange symbol*] [*Delisted*]....GRK
Garland Reference Library of the Humanities [*A publication*]....GRLH
Garlock, Inc. [*NYSE symbol*] [*Delisted*]....GAK
Garm [*USSR*] [*Seismograph station code, US Geological Survey*]....GAR
Garment Dyers Guild of America....GDGA
Garment Salesmen's Guild of New York [*Later, Apparel Guild*]....GSG
Garmisch-Partenkirchen [*Federal Republic of Germany*] [*Seismograph station code, US Geological Survey*]....GAP
Garnavillo Historical Society, Garnavillo, IA [*Library symbol*]....IaGavoHi
Garnavillo, IA [*Radio station call letters*]....KCTN
Garner, NC [*Radio station call letters*]....WKBQ
Garner Public Library, Garner, IA [*Library symbol*]....IaGar
Garnes Mountain [*Idaho*] [*Seismograph station code, US Geological Survey*]....GMI
Garnish Molding....GMLDG
Garnisonsverwendungsfaehig Feld [*Fit for Garrison Duty in the Field*] [*German military - World War II*]....GVF
Garnisonsverwendungsfaehig Heimat [*Fit for Garrison Duty in Zone of Interior*] [*German military - World War II*]....GVH
Garoua [*Cameroon*] [*Airport symbol*]....GOU
GARP [*Global Atmospheric Research Program*] **Atlantic Tropical Experiment** [*National Academy of Sciences*]....GATE
GARP [*Global Atmospheric Research Program*] **International Sea Trial** [*National Science Foundation*]....GIST
GARP [*Global Atmospheric Research Program*] **Operational Control Center**....GOCC
Garrett Corp. [*NYSE symbol*] [*Delisted*]....GAR
Garrett-Evangelical Theological Seminary, Evanston, IL [*Library symbol*]....IEG
Garrett Memorial Library, Moulton, IA [*Library symbol*]....IaMou
Garrison....GAR
Garrison Adjutant [*Military*] [*British*]....GA
Garrison Hill [*Washington*] [*Seismograph station code, US Geological Survey*]....GHW
Garrison Military Police [*British*]....GMP
Garrison Sergeant-Major [*British*]....GSM
Garter....GTR
Garter King of Arms....GKA
Garuahi [*Papua New Guinea*] [*Airport symbol*]....GRH
Garuda Indonesian Airways Ltd. [*ICAO designator*]....GA
Garuda Indonesian Airways Ltd.....GIA
Garvie's Point Museum, Glen Cove, NY [*Library symbol*]....NGlcM
Gary Community School Corp., Gary, IN [*OCLC symbol*]....IGS
Gary, IN [*Radio station call letters*]....WGVE
Gary, IN [*Radio station call letters*]....WLTH
Gary, IN [*Radio station call letters*]....WWCA
Gary Public Library, Gary, IN [*OCLC symbol*]....IGP
Gary Public Library, Gary, IN [*Library symbol*]....InG
Gary School System, Gary, IN [*Library symbol*]....InGS
Garyville, LA [*Radio station call letters*]....WKQT
Gas [*Chemistry*]....(g)
Gas Abstracts [*A publication*]....Gas Abstr
Gas Acquisition System....GAS
Gas and Air [*Medicine*]....G and A
Gas or Air [*Transportation*]....GA
Gas Amplification....GA
Gas-Analysis Laboratory [*NASA*]....GAL
Gas-Analysis Sample Container [*Apollo*] [*NASA*]....GASC
Gas Annulus Sizing Program....GASP
Gas Appliance Engineers Society [*Later, ASGE*]....GAES
Gas Appliance Improvement Network....GAIN
Gas Appliance Manufacturers Association....GAMA
Gas Bearing Part....GBP
Gas Bearing System....GBS
Gas Bioassay System [*NASA*]....GBS
Gas Centrifuge Enrichment Plant [*Department of Energy*]....GCEP
Gas Chromatograph [*or Chromatography*]....GC
Gas Chromatograph Intoximeter [*Measure-of-intoxication test for drunk drivers*]....GCI
Gas Chromatography Abstracts [*A publication*]....Gas Chromat Abstr
Gas Chromatography in Biology and Medicine [*British*]....GCBM
Gas Chromatography with Electron Capture....GC-EC
Gas Chromatography/Infrared....GC/IR
Gas Chromatography. International Symposium [*A publication*].... Gas Chromatogr Int Sym
Gas Chromatography/Mass Spectrometry....GC/MS
Gas Component Test Stand....GCTS
Gas-Cooled Breeder Reactor....GCBR
Gas-Cooled Fast Breeder Reactor....GCFBR
Gas-Cooled Fast Reactor....GCFR
Gas-Cooled Fast Reactor Experiment....GCFRE
Gas-Cooled Loop [*Nuclear energy*]....GCL
Gas-Cooled Reactor....GCR
Gas-Cooled Reactor Experiment....GCRE
Gas Core Nuclear Rocket....GCNR
Gas Council [*British*]....GC
Gas Council (Great Britain) Research Communications [*A publication*]....Gas Counc (Gt Brit) Res Commun
Gas Cylinder System....GCS
Gas Discharge Counter....GDC
Gas Discharge Gauge....GDG
Gas Discharge Tube....GDT
Gas-Driven Gyro Inertial Platform [*Aerospace*]....GDGIP
Gas Dynamic Facility [*Air Force*]....GDF
Gas Dynamic LASER....GDL
Gas Dynamic Mixing LASER [*Navy*]....GDML
Gas Dynamic System....GDS
Gas Dynamics Laboratory....GDL
Gas Ejection [*Opening*] [*Technical drawings*]....GE
Gas, Electric, Telephones [*of GET, Inc., a consumer group*]....GET
Gas, Electricity, Water [*Department of Employment*] [*British*]....GEW
Gas Engineering and Management [*A publication*]....Gas Engine Manage
Gas Engineering and Management [*A publication*]....Gas Eng Manage
Gas Engineering and Management [*A publication*]....Gas Engng Mgmt
Gas Exchange....GEX
Gas Explosive Simulation Technique [*Air Force*]....GEST
Gas-Filled Counter....GFC
Gas-Filled Hydrophobic Region....GFHR
Gas-Filled Rectifier....GFR
Gas-Filled Rectifying Tube....GFRT
Gas Filter Correlation [*NASA*]....GFC
Gas Filter Correlation Radiometer [*NASA*]....GFCR
Gas-Fired Oven....GFO
Gas Fission Products Monitor....GFPM
Gas Flow Indicator [*NASA*]....GFI
Gas-Freeing System....GF
Gas-Gathering Pipeline....GGP
Gas Generator....GG
Gas Generator Valve....GGV
Gas-Guided Aircraft Rocket....GGAR
Gas High Pressure....GHP
Gas Hour Space Velocity [*Chemical engineering*]....GHSV
Gas Identification Officer....GIO
Gas-Insulated Flow Tube....GIFT
Gas Journal [*A publication*]....Gas J
Gas LASER....GL
Gas LASER Discharge Tube....GLDT
Gas LASER Tube....GLT
Gas Leak Detector....GLD
Gas-Liquid Chromatography [*Analytical chemistry*]....GLC
Gas Liquid Partition Chromatography....GLPC
Gas-Liquid Radiochromatography [*Analytical chemistry*]....GLRC
Gas [*or Grease*] **Lubricated Bearing**....GLB
Gas Measurement System....GMS
Gas Metal Arc....GMA
Gas Metal Arc Welding....GMAW
Gas Missile Tube....GMT
Gas, Nonpersistent....GNP
Gas Oil....G
Gas and Oil Power [*A publication*]....Gas Oil Pwr
Gas-Oil Ratio....GOR

Gas/Oil Tax Block Summary Record [*IRS*] ... G/OTBSR
Gas/Oil Tax Program Summary Record [*IRS*] ... G/OTPSR
Gas-Operated Core ... GOC
Gas and Oxygen [*Medicine*] ... G & O
Gas, Oxygen, Ether [*Anesthesiology*] ... GOE
Gas, Persistent ... GP
Gas Phase Titration ... GPT
Gas (Philadelphia) [*A publication*] ... Gas (Phila)
Gas Plasma Monitor ... GPM
Gas Power Exchange ... GPE
Gas Power Transfer ... GPT
Gas Power Unit ... GPU
Gas Pressure ... GP
Gas Pressure Activator ... GPA
Gas Pressure Bending System ... GPBS
Gas Processors Association ... GPA
Gas Processors Suppliers Association [*Formerly, NGPSA, NGSMA*] ... GPSA
Gas Proof ... GPF
Gas Properties [*NASA computer program*] ... GASP
Gas Quenching Process ... GQP
Gas Ratio ... GR
Gas Recycle Hydrogenation [*Petroleum engineering*] ... GRH
Gas Research Institute ... GRI
Gas Research Institute Digest [*Acronym is used as title of publication*] [*A publication*] ... GRID
Gas Scintillation Proportional Counter [*Instrumentation*] ... GSPC
Gas Service Co. [*NYSE symbol*] [*Delisted*] ... GSV
Gas Servicer ... GS
Gas Servicer Unit ... GSU
Gas-Solid Chromatography ... GSC
Gas Source Seismic Section Profiler ... GASSP
Gas Space Heater ... GSH
Gas Subject Pilot [*Aviation*] ... GASSP
Gas Sulfide [*Process for obtaining heavy water*] ... GS
Gas Tight ... GT
Gas Toggle Valve ... GTV
Gas Toxicity Analysis ... GTA
Gas Transport LASER ... GTL
Gas Tungsten Arc ... GTA
Gas Tungsten Arc Weld [*or Welding*] ... GTAW
Gas Turbine ... GT
Gas Turbine ... GTRB
Gas Turbine Compressor ... GTC
Gas Turbine Compressor and Power Unit ... GTCP
Gas Turbine Engine ... GTE
Gas-Turbine Engine-Driven [*Generator*] ... GTED
Gas Turbine and Engine Type Designation System ... GTETDS
Gas Turbine Generator ... GTG
Gas Turbine Generator Set ... GTGS
Gas-Turbine High-Temperature Gas-Cooled Reactor ... GT-HTGR
Gas Turbine International [*A publication*] ... Gas Turbine Int
Gas Turbine Laboratory [*MIT*] ... GTL
Gas Turbine Power System ... GTPS
Gas Turbine Power Unit ... GTP
Gas Turbine Power Unit ... GTPU
Gas Turbine Starter ... GTS
Gas Turbine Starting System ... GTSS
Gas Turbine Test Facility ... GTTF
Gas Under Pressure ... GUP
Gas, Undercarriage, Mixture, and Prop [*Checkout procedure*] ... GUMP
Gas Vent Institute ... GVI
Gas Waerme International [*A publication*] ... Gas Waerme Int
Gas Weld ... GAS/W
Gas World [*A publication*] ... Gas Wld
Gas World and Gas Journal [*A publication*] ... Gas World Gas J
Gascoyne Junction [*Australia*] [*Airport symbol*] [*Obsolete*] ... GSC
Gaseous Axisymmetric Jet ... GAJ
Gaseous Discharge Principle ... GDP
Gaseous Ejection ... GEJ
Gaseous Electronics Conference ... GEC
Gaseous Flow Measuring System ... GFMS
Gaseous Flowmeter Calibration Stand ... GFCS
Gaseous Helium ... GHE
Gaseous Hydrogen ... GH
Gaseous Hydrogen [*NASA*] ... GH_2
Gaseous Ion LASER ... GIL
Gaseous Mixture ... GM
Gaseous Nitrogen [*NASA*] ... GN_2
Gaseous Nitrogen Flow Measuring System ... GNFMS
Gaseous Nitrogen Measuring System ... GNMS
Gaseous Nuclear Rocket ... GNR
Gaseous Oxygen ... GOX
Gases, Fluids, and Propellants [*NASA*] ... GF & P
Gases in Research and Industry [*A publication*] ... Gases Res Ind
Gasket ... GSKT
Gasket Fabricators Association ... GFA
Gasmata [*Papua New Guinea*] [*Airport symbol*] ... GMI
Gasoffizier [*Gas Officer*] [*German military - World War II*] ... GO
Gasoline ... GAS
Gasoline ... GASO
Gasoline and Automotive Service Dealers Association ... GASDA
Gasoline Barge [*Self-propelled*] [*Navy symbol*] ... YOG
Gasoline Barge [*Non-self-propelled*] [*Navy symbol*] ... YOGN
Gasoline Engine ... GENG
Gasoline Engine, Close-Coupled ... GECC
Gasoline Engine Driven ... GED
Gasoline-Engine Heavy-Duty Vehicle ... GHDV
Gasoline/Ethanol [*Automotive fuel*] ... GASOHOL
Gasoline-Grade Tertiary-Butyl Alcohol [*Organic chemistry*] ... GTBA
Gasoline Pump Manufacturers Association ... GPMA
Gasoline Stowage and Fuel System Man [*Navy*] ... GA
Gasoline Supply ... GS
Gasoline Tanker [*Navy symbol*] ... AOG
Gasoline Tanker [*Military Sea Transportation Service*] ... TAOG
Gaspe [*Canada*] [*Airport symbol*] ... YGP
Gaspe-Nord, PQ [*Television station call letters*] ... CFER-TV-2
Gaspe, PQ [*Radio station call letters*] ... CJRG-FM
Gasschutzunteroffizier [*Gas Noncommissioned Officer*] [*German military - World War II*] ... GU
Gassim [*Saudi Arabia*] [*Airport symbol*] ... ELQ
Gaston College, Dallas, NC [*Library symbol*] ... NcDalG
Gaston, IN [*Radio station call letters*] ... WDHS
Gaston-Lincoln Regional Library, Gastonia, NC [*Library symbol*] ... NcGa
Gastonia, NC [*Location identifier*] [*FAA*] ... GHJ
Gastonia, NC [*Radio station call letters*] ... WGAS
Gastonia, NC [*Radio station call letters*] ... WGNC
Gastonia, NC [*Radio station call letters*] ... WLTC
Gastonia, NC [*Radio station call letters*] ... WZXI
Gastric Alcohol Dehydrogenase [*An enzyme*] ... GADH
Gastric Analysis ... GA
Gastric Emptying Time [*Medicine*] ... GET
Gastric [*or Gastrin*] **Inhibitory Principle** [*or Polypeptide*] [*Medicine*] ... GIP
Gastric Resection [*Medicine*] ... GR
Gastric Shield [*Medicine*] ... GS
Gastric Ulcer [*Medicine*] ... GU
Gastrocnemius [*Muscle*] [*Anatomy*] ... GASTROC
Gastroenterologia [*A publication*] ... Gastroenterol
Gastroenterologia Japonica [*A publication*] ... Gastroenterol Jpn
Gastroenterologie Clinique et Biologique [*A publication*] ... Gastroenterol Clin Biol
Gastroenterology [*Medicine*] ... GAS
Gastroenterology [*A publication*] ... Gastroenty
Gastroenterology [*Medicine*] ... GE
Gastroenterology. Abstracts and Citations [*A publication*] ... GAAC
Gastroenterology. Abstracts and Citations [*A publication*] ... Gastroenterol Abstr & Cit
Gastroenterology Japonica [*A publication*] ... Gastroenterol Jpn
Gastroenterology Research Group [*Defunct*] ... GRG
Gastroenteropancreatic System [*Medicine*] ... GEP
Gastrointestinal [*Medicine*] ... GI
Gastrointestinal Endoscopy [*A publication*] ... Gastroin En
Gastrointestinal Endoscopy [*A publication*] ... Gastrointest Endosc
Gastrointestinal Infection [*Medicine*] ... GII
Gastrointestinal and Liver Physiology [*A publication*] ... GLP
Gastrointestinal Radiology [*A publication*] ... Gastrointest Radiol
Gastrointestinal Series [*Radiology*] ... GIS
Gastrointestinal Tract [*Medicine*] ... GIT
Gate [*Electronics*] ... G
Gate ... GA
Gate Alarm Indicator [*RADAR*] ... GAI
Gate Assisted Turnoff Thyristor [*NASA*] ... GATT
Gate-Associated Transistor ... GAT
Gate Breakdown Voltage ... GBDV
Gate Breakdown Voltage ... GBV
Gate City, VA [*Radio station call letters*] ... WGAT
Gate-Controlled Switch ... GCS
Gate Craft [*Non-self-propelled*] [*Navy symbol*] ... YNG
Gate Driver ... GD
Gate Leads ... GL
Gate Leakage Current ... GLC
Gate-Modulated Bipolar Transistor ... GAMBIT
Gate Stealer Display ... GSD
Gate Turn Off [*Data processing*] ... GTO
Gate Valve ... GTV
Gated Attenuation [*Data processing*] ... GA
Gated Image Intensifier Viewer ... GIIV
Gated-Off Controlled Rectifier ... GOCR
Gated Video Tracker ... GVT
Gates-Chili Senior High School Library, Rochester, NY [*OCLC symbol*] ... RWG
Gates-LearJet Corp. [*American Stock Exchange symbol*] ... GLJ
Gates Memorial Library, Port Arthur, TX [*Library symbol*] ... TxPo
Gates Rubber Co., Technical Library, Denver, CO [*Library symbol*] ... CoDGR
Gatesville Public Library, Gatesville, TX [*Library symbol*] ... TxGat
Gatesville, TX [*Radio station call letters*] ... KPEP
Gateway ... GTWY
Gateway Army Ammunition Plant ... GAAP
Gateway Aviation Ltd. [*Edmonton, AB*] [*FAA designator*] ... GWY
Gateway Industries, Inc. [*NYSE symbol*] [*Delisted*] ... GAT

Gateway National Recreation Area [*New York*] [*Department of the Interior*] .... GNRA
Gateway Sporting Goods Co. [*American Stock Exchange symbol*] [*Delisted*] .... GAY
Gateway Technical Institute, Elkhorn Campus, Elkhorn, WI [*Library symbol*] .... WKenG-E
Gateway Technical Institute, Kenosha, WI [*Library symbol*] .... WKenG
Gateway Technical Institute, Racine Campus, Racine, WI [*Library symbol*] .... WKenG-R
GATF [*Graphic Arts Technical Foundation*] **Bulletin** [*A publication*] .... GATF Bull
GATF [*Graphic Arts Technical Foundation*] **Environmental Control Report** [*A publication*] .... GATF Envir Control Rept
GATF [*Graphic Arts Technical Foundation*] **Research Progress** [*A publication*] .... GATF Res Progr
GATF [*Graphic Arts Technical Foundation*] **Technical Service Information** [*A publication*] .... GATF Tech Serv Inform
Gathers Alarms, Reports, Displays, and Evaluates .... GARDAE
Gatineau/Hull [*Canada*] [*Airport symbol*] .... YND
Gating Half-Cycle [*Data processing*] .... GHC
Gating Waveform .... GWF
Gatlinburg, TN [*Radio station call letters*] .... WVTN
Gatling Gun .... GG
Gato, CA [*Location identifier*] [*FAA*] .... SAN
Gatooma Research Station. Annual Report [*A publication*] .... Gatooma Res Stn Annu Rep
GATX Corp. [*Formerly, General American Transportation Corp.*] .... GATX
GATX Corp. [*Formerly, General American Transportation Corp.*] [*NYSE symbol*] .... GMT
Gauche [*Chemical conformation*] .... g
Gauche [*Left*] [*French*] .... G
Gaucher's Disease Registry .... GDR
Gauge .... G
Gauge .... GA
Gauge .... GE
Gauge .... GGE
Gauge Board .... GABD
Gauge Code Number .... GCN
Gauge Control Analyzer .... GCA
Gauge Factor .... GF
Gauge-Invariant Atomic Orbital [*NASA*] .... GIAO
Gauge Length .... GL
Gauge Man [*Navy*] .... GA
Gauge Pressure Control .... GPC
Gauge Pressure Switch .... GPS
Gauhati [*India*] [*Airport symbol*] .... GAU
Gauribidanur Array [*India*] [*Seismograph station code, US Geological Survey*] .... GBA
Gauss [*Unit of magnetic flux density*] [*Preferred unit is T, Telsa*] .... G
Gauss [*Later, GTT*] [*Federal Republic of Germany*] [*Geomagnetic observatory code*] .... GAS
Gauss [*Unit of magnetic flux density*] [*Preferred unit is T, Telsa*] .... GS
Gauss Error Function [*Mathematics*] .... GEF
Gauss Hypergeometric Equation [*Mathematics*] .... GHE
Gauss Hypergeometric Function [*Mathematics*] .... GHF
Gauss-Jordan Elimination .... GJE
Gauss Quadrature Rule .... GQR
Gaussian Elimination .... GE
Gaussian Image Point [*Optics*] .... GIP
Gaussian Lens Formula [*Optics*] .... GLF
Gaussian Noise Generator [*Electronics*] .... GNG
Gaussian Orbitals [*Atomic physics*] .... GO
Gaussian Random Process [*Mathematics*] .... GRP
Gaussian-Type Orbitals [*Atomic physics*] .... GTO
Gaussian Wave Group [*Physics*] .... GWG
Gave Delivery .... GD
Gavel Clubs .... GC
Gavle [*Sweden*] [*Airport symbol*] .... GVX
Gavroche [*A publication*] .... Gav
Gay Academic Union .... GAU
Gay Activists' Alliance .... GAA
Gay Atheist League of America .... GALA
Gay Caucus of Members of the American Psychiatric Association .... GCMAPA
Gay Community News [*A publication*] .... Gay News
Gay Insurgent [*A publication*] .... Gay Insrg
Gay and Lesbian Association of Choruses .... GLAC
Gay Liberation [*A publication*] .... Gay
Gay Liberation Front .... GLF
Gay Literature [*A publication*] .... Gay L
Gay Male [*Classified advertising*] .... GM
Gay Media Task Force .... GMTF
Gay Men's Health Crisis .... GMHC
Gay Men's VD Clinic .... GMVDC
Gay Nurses' Alliance .... GNA
Gay Parents Legal and Research Group [*Defunct*] .... GPLRG
Gay People at Columbia .... GPC
Gay Press Association .... GPA
Gay Public Health Workers Caucus .... GPHW
Gay-Related Immunodeficiency [*Also, AID, AIDS*] [*Medicine*] .... GRID
Gay Rights National Lobby .... GRNL
Gay Sunshine [*A publication*] .... Gay Sun
Gay Theatre Alliance .... GTA
Gay Urban Professional [*Terminology used in "The Yuppie Handbook"*] .... Guppie
Gay White Male [*Classified advertising*] .... GWM
Gayana Botanica [*A publication*] .... Gayana Bot
Gayana Botanica Miscelanea [*A publication*] .... Gayana Bot Misc
Gayana Miscelanea [*A publication*] .... Gayana Misc
Gayana Zoologia [*A publication*] .... Gayana Zool
Gaylord Circulation Control System [*Gaylord Bros., Inc.*] [*Information service*] .... GLS
Gaylord, MI [*Location identifier*] [*FAA*] .... GLR
Gaylord, MI [*Radio station call letters*] .... WPOL
Gaylord, MI [*Radio station call letters*] .... WWRM
Gaylord, MI [*Radio station call letters*] .... WZXM
Gaylord-Otsego County Public Library, Gaylord, MI [*Library symbol*] .... MiGay
Gaylords National Corp. [*American Stock Exchange symbol*] .... GYL
Gayndah [*Australia*] [*Airport symbol*] .... GAH
Gaynor-Stafford Industries, Inc. [*American Stock Exchange symbol*] [*Delisted*] .... GNR
Gaz d'Aujourd'hui [*A publication*] .... Gaz Aujourd
Gaz Woda i Technika Sanitarna [*A publication*] .... Gaz Woda Tech Sanit
Gaza Strip [*MARC geographic area code*] [*Library of Congress*] .... awgz---
Gaza Strip [*MARC country of publication code*] [*Library of Congress*] .... gz
Gazdasag es Jogtudomany [*A publication*] .... Gazdasag es Jogtud
Gazeta do Agricultor (Angola) [*A publication*] .... Gaz Agr (Angola)
Gazeta Clinica (Sao Paulo) [*A publication*] .... Gaz Clin (S Paulo)
Gazeta Cukrownicza [*A publication*] .... Gaz Cukrow
Gazeta Cukrownicza [*A publication*] .... Gazeta Cukrown
Gazeta di Fisica [*A publication*] .... Gaz Fis
Gazeta Literara [*A publication*] .... GLit
Gazeta de Matematica [*A publication*] .... Gaz Mat
Gazeta Matematica Publicatie Lunara pentru Tineret [*A publication*] .... Gaz Mat Publ Lunara pentru Tineret
Gazeta Medica da Bahia [*A publication*] .... Gaz Med Bahia
Gazeta Musical [*A publication*] .... GM
Gazeta Musical e de Todas las Artes [*A publication*] .... Gaz Mus
Gazette [*or Gazetteer*] .... GAZ
Gazette Archeologique [*A publication*] .... Gaz Arch
Gazette des Beaux-Arts [*A publication*] .... Gaz Beaux-Arts
Gazette des Beaux-Arts [*A publication*] .... GBA
Gazette. Egyptian Paediatric Association [*A publication*] .... Gaz Egypt Paediatr Assoc
Gazette Hebdomadaire des Sciences Medicales de Bordeaux [*A publication*] .... Gaz Hebd Sc Med Bordeaux
Gazette. Institute of Medical Laboratory Science [*A publication*] .... Gaz Inst Med Lab Sci
Gazette de Lausanne [*A publication*] .... GLa
Gazette des Lettres [*A publication*] .... GL
Gazette Medicale de l'Algerie [*A publication*] .... Gaz Med Algerie
Gazette Medicale de France [*A publication*] .... Gaz Med Fr
Gazette Medicale de Nantes [*A publication*] .... Gaz Med Nantes
Gazette Medicale d'Orient [*A publication*] .... Gaz Med Orient
Gazette Medicale de Paris [*A publication*] .... Gaz Med Paris
Gazette Medicale de Picardie [*A publication*] .... Gaz Med Picardie
Gazette Numismatique Suisse [*A publication*] .... GNS
Gazette du Travail [*A publication*] .... Gaz Trav
Gaziantep [*Turkey*] [*Airport symbol*] .... GZT
Gazovaya Promyshlennost [*A publication*] .... Gazov Promst
Gazzetta Chimica Italiana [*A publication*] .... Gaz Chim It
Gazzetta Chimica Italiana [*A publication*] .... Gazz Chim Ital
Gazzetta Clinica dello Spedale Civico di Palermo [*A publication*] .... Gazz Clin Sped Civ Palermo
Gazzetta Commerciale [*A publication*] .... Gaz Com
Gazzetta Internazionale di Medicina [*A publication*] .... Gazz Internaz Med
Gazzetta Medica Italiana [*A publication*] .... Gazz Med Ital
Gazzetta Medica Italiana. Provincie Venete [*A publication*] .... Gazz Med Ital Prov Venete
Gazzetta del Mezzogiorno [*A publication*] .... GdM
Gazzetta degli Ospitali Milano [*A publication*] .... Gazz Osp Milano
Gazzetta Sanitaria (English Issue) [*A publication*] .... Gazz Sanit (Engl Issue)
Gazzetta Siciliana di Medicina e Chirurgia d'Igiene e d'Interessi Professionali [*A publication*] .... Gazz Sicil Med e Chir
Gazzetta Ufficiale della Repubblica Italiana [*A publication*] .... Gazz Uff Repub Ital
Gazzettino Numismatico [*A publication*] .... Gaz Num
Gbangbatok [*Sierra Leone*] [*Airport symbol*] .... GBK
GBC Closed Circuit TV [*NASDAQ symbol*] .... GBCC
GCA Corp. [*NYSE symbol*] .... GCA
GCN/Microfilm, Boston, MA [*Library symbol*] .... GcNM
Gdansk [*Poland*] [*Airport symbol*] .... GDN
Gdanskie Zeszyty Humanistyczne [*A publication*] .... GZH
Gduei Noar [*Youth Battalions*] [*Israel*] .... GADNA
GDV, Inc. [*Formerly, General Development Corp.*] [*NYSE symbol*] [*Delisted*] .... GDV
Gear .... G
Gear .... GR
Gear Assembly .... GA
Gear Down [*Aviation*] .... GD
Gear Rack .... GRK

Gear Test Data ... GTD
Gear Train Analyzer ... GTA
Gear Up [*Aviation*] ... GU
Gearbox ... GRBX
Gearcase ... GRC
Geared Radial [*Aircraft engine*] ... GR
Geared Roller Test Machine ... GRTM
Gearhart Industries, Inc. [*Formerly, Gearhart-Owen Industries, Inc.*] [*NYSE symbol*] ... GOI
Gearing ... GRG
Gearshaft ... GRSHFT
Geary 18 International Yacht Racing Association ... G18 IYRA
Geauga County Public Library, Chardon, OH [*OCLC symbol*] ... GEC
Geauga County Public Library, Chardon, OH [*Library symbol*] ... OChaG
Gebbies Pass [*New Zealand*] [*Seismograph station code, US Geological Survey*] ... GPZ
Geboren [*Born*] [*German*] ... GEB
Gebrauchlich [*Usual*] [*German*] ... GBR
Gebrauchsgraphik [*A publication*] ... Gebrauchs
Gebrauchsgraphik Novum [*A publication*] ... Gebrauchs Novum
Gebrueder [*Brothers*] [*German*] ... GEB
Gebunden [*Bound*] [*Bookbinding*] [*German*] ... GEB
Geburtshilfe und Frauenheilkunde [*A publication*] ... Geburtsh Fr
Geburtshilfe und Frauenheilkunde [*A publication*] ... Geburtshilfe Fraunheilkd
GEC [*General Electric Company*] **Journal of Science and Technology** [*A publication*] ... GEC J Sci & Technol
GEC [*General Electric Company*] **Telecommunications** [*A publication*] ... GEC Telecommun
Gedampft [*Muted*] [*Music*] ... GED
Gedeh [*Java*] [*Seismograph station code, US Geological Survey*] [*Closed*] ... GED
Gedrag-Tijdschrift voor Psychologie [*A publication*] ... Gedrag T P
Geehi [*Australia*] [*Seismograph station code, US Geological Survey*] [*Closed*] ... GEE
GEEIA [*Ground Electronics Engineering Installation Agency*] **Workload Schedule** ... GWS
Gegechkori [*USSR*] [*Seismograph station code, US Geological Survey*] [*Closed*] ... GEG
Gegenbaurs Morphologisches Jahrbuch [*A publication*] ... Gegenbaurs Morphol Jahrb
Gegenwart [*A publication*] ... Ge
Gegenwart der Dichtung [*A publication*] ... GdD
Gegenwartskunde Gesellschaft Staat Erziehung [*A publication*] ... Geg G S Erz
Geheime Staats Polizei [*Secret State Police*] [*Germany*] ... GESTAPO
GEICO Corporation [*NYSE symbol*] ... GEC
Geiger-Mueller [*Radiation counter*] ... G-M
Geiger-Mueller Tube ... GMT
Geigy Pharmaceuticals, Yonkers, NY [*Library symbol*] ... NYG
Geisinger Medical Center, Medical Library, Danville, PA [*OCLC symbol*] ... GEI
Geist und Leben [*A publication*] ... GL
Geist und Tat [*A publication*] ... GuT
Geist und Zeit [*A publication*] ... GuZ
Geistes- und Sozialwissenschaftliche Dissertationen [*A publication*] ... GSD
Geistige Arbeit [*A publication*] ... GA
Geistige Arbeit [*A publication*] ... GArb
Gel Chromatography ... GC
Gel Destainer [*Analytical chemistry*] ... GD
Gel Electrofocusing [*Analytical chemistry*] ... GEF
Gel Electrophoresis [*Analytical chemistry*] ... GE
Gel Filtration Chromatography ... GFC
Gel Frontal Analysis Chromatography ... GELFAC
Gel Permeation Chromatography ... GPC
Gel Tube [*Electrophoresis*] ... GT
Gelaendegaengig [*Having cross-country mobility*] [*German military - World War II*] ... G
Gelatin ... GEL
Gelatin Manufacturers Institute of America ... GMIA
Gelatin Matrix System ... GMS
Gelatin, Resorcinol, and Formaldehyde ... GRF
Gelatin Rigidized Panel ... GRP
Gelatina Quavis [*In Any Kind of Jelly*] [*Pharmacy*] ... GEL QUAV
Gelbe Hefte [*A publication*] ... GH
Gelbray Association ... GA
Gelco Corp. [*NYSE symbol*] ... GEL
Geldgeschichtliche Nachrichten [*A publication*] ... GN
Gelding ... G
Gelding [*Thoroughbred racing*] ... G
Gelled Liquid Propellant ... GLP
Gelling Temperature [*Analytical biochemistry*] ... GT
Gelman Sciences, Inc. [*American Stock Exchange symbol*] ... GSC
Gelre. Bijdragen en Mededeelingen [*A publication*] ... GBM
Gem State News Letter [*A publication*] ... Gem State News Lett
Gematologiya i Perelivanie Krovi Respublikanskoi Mezhvedomstvennyi Sbornik [*A publication*] ... Gematol Pereliv Krovi Resp Mezhved Sb
Gemco National [*American Stock Exchange symbol*] ... GNL
Gemeente Archief van Amsterdam, Amsterdam, Netherlands [*Library symbol*] ... NeAA
Gemeinsames Amtsblatt des Landes Baden-Wuerttemberg. Ausgabe A [*A publication*] ... Gemeinsames Amtsbl Landes Baden-Wuerttemb A
Gemeinsames Ministerialblatt A [*A publication*] ... Gemeinsames Ministerialbl A
Gemeinschaft Unabhangiger Beratender Ingenieurbueros [*Association of German Consulting Engineers*] ... GUBI
Gemeisamer Faktor [*General Factor*] [*Rorschach*] [*Psychology*] ... g
Gemena [*Zaire*] [*Airport symbol*] ... GMA
Geminate [*Chemistry*] ... gem
Gemini [*Constellation*] ... Gem
Gemini [*Constellation*] ... Gemi
Gemini Agena [*NASA*] ... GA
Gemini Agena Launch Vehicle Working Group [*NASA*] ... GALVWG
Gemini Agena Target [*NASA*] ... GAT
Gemini Agena Target Vehicle [*NASA*] ... GATV
Gemini Air Transport [*Ghana*] **Ltd.** [*ICAO designator*] ... GP
Gemini Atlas/Agena Target Vehicle [*NASA*] ... GAATV
Gemini Fund, Inc. [*NYSE symbol*] ... GEM
Gemini Hatch [*NASA*] ... GH
Gemini Inertial Guidance System [*NASA*] ... GIGS
Gemini Launch Data System [*NASA*] ... GLDS
Gemini Launch Vehicle [*NASA*] ... GLV
Gemini Management Panel [*NASA*] ... GMP
Gemini Mission Simulator [*NASA*] ... GMS
Gemini Pad Test [*NASA*] ... GPT
Gemini Problem Investigation Status [*NASA*] ... GPIS
Gemini Program Office [*NASA*] ... GPO
Gemini Program Planning Board [*NASA*] ... GPPB
Gemini Reentry Integration Program [*NASA*] ... GRIP
Gemini Slowscan Television [*NASA*] ... GEST
Gemini Spacecraft Project Office [*NASA*] ... GSPO
Gemini Stability Improvement Program [*NASA*] ... GEMSIP
Gemini-Titan [*NASA*] ... GT
Gemini-Titan-Agena [*NASA*] ... GTA
Gemmological Society of Japan. Journal [*A publication*] ... Gemmol Soc Jap J
Gemological Institute of America ... GIA
Gems and Gemology. Gemological Institute of America [*A publication*] ... Gems Gemol
Gems, Minerals, and Jewelry Study Unit [*American Topical Association*] ... GMJSU
Gemtec Corp. [*NASDAQ symbol*] ... GETC
Gen State Airlines [*Hayden Lake, ID*] [*FAA designator*] ... GMA
Genaire Ltd., Saint Catharines, ON, Canada [*Library symbol*] ... CaOStCGL
Genava [*A publication*] ... Gen
Gender ... G
Gender ... GEN
Gender Gap [*Refers to women's tendency to vote for Democratic over Republican candidates, a phenomenon noticed by pollsters beginning with the 1980 election*] ... GG
Gene Amplification and Analysis Series [*Elsevier Book Series*] [*A publication*] ... GAA
Gene Stratton-Porter Memorial, Rome City, IN [*Library symbol*] ... InRomS
Genealogical Enterprises, Morrow, GA [*Library symbol*] ... GMorGE
Genealogical Forum of Portland, Portland, OR [*Library symbol*] ... OrPGF
Genealogical and Heraldic Institute of America ... GHIA
Genealogical Information and Name Tabulating System ... GIANT
Genealogical Institute [*Publisher*] ... GI
Genealogical Periodical. Annual Index [*A publication*] ... Geneal Per Ind
Genealogical Society of Pennsylvania ... GSP
Genealogical Society of Pennsylvania, Philadelphia, PA [*Library symbol*] ... PPGen
Genealogische Recherche mit Magnetband-Speicherung [*Organic chemistry coding system*] ... GREMAS
Genealogy ... GEN
Genealogy ... GENEAL
Genealogy Club of America ... GCA
Geneeskunde en Sport [*A publication*] ... Geneeskd Sport
Geneeskundig Tijdschrift voor Nederlandsch-Indiee [*A publication*] ... Geneesk Tijdschr Nederl-Indiee
Geneeskundige Courant voor het Koningrijk der Nederlanden [*A publication*] ... Geneesk Courant
Geneeskundige Gids [*A publication*] ... GEGIA
Genentech, Inc. [*NASDAQ symbol*] ... GENE
General [*Military aircraft identification prefix*] [*Air Force*] ... A
General ... G
General ... GEN
General ... GENL
General Account of Advances ... GAA
General Accounting ... GA
General Accounting Instructions ... GAI
General Accounting Office [*of the US government*] ... GAO
General Accounting Office/Community and Economic Development Division ... GAO/CED
General Accounting Office/Federal Personnel and Compensation Division ... GAO/FPCD
General Accounting Office/Financial and General Management Studies Division ... GAO/FGMSD
General Accounting Office/Logistics and Communications Division ... GAO/LCD

General Accounting Office, Los Angeles Region, Los Angeles, CA [*OCLC symbol*] .... GAM
General Accounting Office/Procurement and Systems Acquisition Division .... GAO/PSAD
General Accounting Office Review .... GAOR
General Accounting Office, Technical Information Sources and Service, Washington, DC [*OCLC symbol*] .... GAO
General Accounting Office, Washington .... GAOW
General Activity Simulation Language [*Data processing*] ..... GASL
General Activity Simulation Program [*Data processing*] ...... GASP
General Adaptation Syndrome [*Medicine*] .... GAS
General Address Reading Devices [*Data processing*] .... GARD
General Adjustment Bureau [*Insurance*] .... GAB
General Administration Section [*of a joint military staff; also the officer in charge of this section*] J-5
General and Administrative .... G & A
General Administrative Expense [*A budget appropriation title*] ... GAE
General Administrative Order .... GAO
General Adverse Reaction [*Noise*] .... GAR
General Advisory Committee [*to the AEC, later, the Energy Research and Development Administration*] .... GAC
General Aerodynamic Lifting Surface .... GALS
General Aeronautical Material .... GAM
General Agency Agreement [*Navy*] .... GAA
General Agency Check [*Army*] .... GAC
General Agent [*Business and trade, especially insurance*] ...... GA
General Agents and Managers Conference of NALU .... GAMC
General Agreement on Tariffs and Trade [*Organization, and the concept it represents, concerned with adjustment of tariffs among 73 member nations*] .... GATT
General Agricultural Officer [*Ministry of Agriculture, Fisheries, and Food*] [*British*] .... GAO
General Agricultural Workers' Union [*Kenya*] .... GAWU
General Air Staff .... GAS
General Air Traffic [*Europe-Asia*] .... GAT
General Air Training .... GAT
General Alert .... GA
General Alert Order .... GAO
General All-Purpose Simulation Package [*McDonnell Douglas Automation Co.*] .... GASP
General Alpha-Numeric Direct Access Library Facility [*Search system*] .... GANDALF
General American English .... GAE
General American Investors Co., Inc. [*NYSE symbol*] .... GAM
General American Oil Co. of Texas [*NYSE symbol*] [*Delisted*] ... GAO
General American Transportation Corporation .... GATC
General Analine & Film Co., General Research Laboratory, Easton, PA [*Library symbol*] [*Obsolete*] .... PEG
General Analysis Technique .... GAT
General Analytical Evaluation .... GAE
General Analytical Model for Process Analysis .... GRAMPA
General Anesthesia [*Medicine*] .... GA
General Antenna Package [*COMSAT*] .... GAP
General Aptitude Test Battery .... GATB
General Aptitude Test Battery .... GATBY
General Arbitration Council of the Textile Industry .... GACTI
General of the Army .... GA
General Arrangement .... GA
General Arrangements to Borrow .... GAB
General Assembly .... GA
General Assembly of International Sports Federations [*Later, GAISF*] .... GAIF
General Assembly Library, Wellington, New Zealand, [*Library symbol*] .... NzWGAL
General Assembly Program .... GAP
General Assembly to Stop the Powerline .... GASP
General Assembly of the United Nations .... GA (UN)
General Assessment Tridimensional Analog Computer .... GATAC
General Assistance [*A form of public charity*] .... GA
General Association of International Sports Federations [*Formerly, GAIF*] .... GAISF
General Atomic Co., San Diego, CA [*Library symbol*] .... CSdGA
General Atomics [*Division of General Dynamics Corp.*] .... GA
General Attention [*Medicine*] .... GA
General Audiences [*All Ages Admitted*] [*Movie rating*] .... G
General Automation, Inc. .... GA
General Automation, Inc. [*NASDAQ symbol*] .... GENA
General Automation Users Group Exchange .... GAUGE
General Automotive Support .... GAS
General Average [*Insurance*] .... GA
General Aviation .... GA
General Aviation District Office [*FAA*] .... GADO
General Aviation Facilities Planning Group .... GAFPG
General Aviation, Inc. [*Greenville, TN*] [*FAA designator*] ...... GNL
General Aviation Inspection Aids Summary [*FAA*] .... GAIS
General Aviation Manufacturers Association .... GAMA
General Aviation Pilot Education [*Safety project*] .... GAPE
General Aviation Radio Magnetic Indicator .... GARMI
General Aviation Services Ltd. [*Great Britain*] [*ICAO designator*] ... DG
General Aviation Simulator [*Data processing*] [*NASA*] .... GAS
General Aviation Technical Training Conference .... GATTC

General Aviation Trainer .... GAT
General Aviation Transponder .... GAT
General Background .... GB
General Baking Co. [*NYSE symbol*] [*Delisted*] .... GBG
General Bancshares Corp. [*NYSE symbol*] .... GBS
General Bathymetric Chart of the Oceans [*International Hydrographic Bureau*] .... GEBCO
General Battery Corp. [*NYSE symbol*] [*Delisted*] .... GBY
General Bearing Line [*Navy*] .... GBL
General Bending Response Program [*Computer*] [*Navy*] .... GBRP
General Binding Corp. [*NASDAQ symbol*] .... GBND
General Board [*Military judicial or investigative body*] .... GB
General Board .... GBD
General Board of Christian Social Concerns of the Methodist Church .... GBCSCMC
General Bronze Corp. .... GB
General Bronze Corp. [*NYSE symbol*] [*Delisted*] .... GLZ
General Builders Corp. [*American Stock Exchange symbol*] [*Delisted*] .... GBD
General Builders Corporation [*NASDAQ symbol*] .... GBDC
General Care Corp. [*NYSE symbol*] [*Delisted*] .... GCE
General Certificate of Education [*British*] .... GCE
General Chairman-Member Pickwick Club [*From "The Pickwick Papers" by Charles Dickens*] .... GCMPC
General Cigar Co., Inc. [*Later, CUC*] [*NYSE symbol*] .... GCR
General Cinema Corp. [*NYSE symbol*] .... GCN
General Circular .... GC
General Circulation Model [*Data processing*] .... GCM
General Claim Agent .... GCA
General Classification Test [*Military*] .... GCT
General Combining Ability .... GCA
General Commission on Chaplains and Armed Forces Personnel [*Later, NCMAF*] .... GCC
General Commission on the Status and Role of Women [*United Methodist Church*] .... GCSRW-UMC
General Communication Subsystem [*Data processing*] .... GCS
General Communications Vessel [*Navy ship symbol*] [*World War II*] ... AGC
General and Comparative Endocrinology [*A publication*] ..... Gen C Endoc
General and Comparative Endocrinology [*A publication*] ..... Gen Comp Endocrinol
General and Complete Disarmament .... GCD
General Component Reference .... GCR
General Comprehensive Operating Supervisor .... GCOS
General Comprehensive Operating Supervisor .... GECOS
General Comprehensive Operating System .... GECOS
General Condition [*Medicine*] .... GC
General Conference Committee of the National Poultry Improvement Plan [*Department of Agriculture*] .... GCCNPIP
General Conference on Weights and Measures .... GCWM
General Constituency Section for Small or Rural Hospitals .... SSRH
General Contract Finance Corp. [*NYSE symbol*] [*Delisted*] ... GCF
General Control Unit .... GCU
General Council of British Shipping .... GCBS
General Counsel .... GC
General Counsel's Memorandum [*Internal Revenue Service*] ... GCM
General Court-Martial .... GCM
General Court-Martial Authority .... GCMA
General Court-Martial Order .... GCMO
General Court-Martial Prisoner .... GCMP
General Cueing .... GC
General Data Acquisition Unit .... GDAU
General Database Technology [*NASDAQ symbol*] .... GDTI
General DataComm Industries, Inc. [*NYSE symbol*] .... GDC
General Declassification Schedule .... GDS
General Defense Corp. [*American Stock Exchange symbol*] ..... GDF
General Defense Intelligence Program [*DoD*] .... GDIP
General Defense Plan [*Formerly, EDP*] .... GDP
General Delivery .... GD
General Dental Council [*British*] .... GDC
General Dentistry [*A publication*] .... Gen Dent
General Depot [*Military*] .... GENDEP
General Design .... GD
General Design Criteria .... GDC
General Detail [*Coast Guard*] .... GENDET
General Development .... GD
General Development Corporation .... GDC
General Development Map .... GDM
General Development Plan .... GDP
General Devices, Incorporated [*NASDAQ symbol*] .... GDIC
General Diagram .... GD
General [*Purpose*] Digital Computer .... GDC
General Discharge .... GD
General Dispensary [*Military*] .... GD
General Dispensary [*Military*] .... GENDISP
General Distribution [*Pentagon security classification code*] ... GENDIS
General Duties Medical Officer .... GDMO
General Duty .... GD
General Dynamics .... GENDYN
General Dynamics/Astronautics .... GD/A
General Dynamics/Convair .... GD/C

General Dynamics/Convair Aerospace Division, Fort Worth, TX [*Library symbol*] TxFG
General Dynamics/Convair Aerospace Division, San Diego, CA [*Library symbol*] CSdG
General Dynamics Corp. [*NYSE symbol*] GD
General Dynamics Corporation GDC
General Dynamics Corp., Pomona Division Library, Pomona, CA [*Library symbol*] CPomG
General Dynamics/Electric Boat Division GD/EB
General Dynamics/Fort Worth GD/FW
General Dynamics/General Atomic GD/GA
General Dynamics High-Speed Wind Tunnel GDHSWT
General Dynamics, Quincy Shipbuilding Division, Quincy, MA [*Library symbol*] MQG
General Dynamics/Telecommunications GD/T
General Education [*A publication*] General Ed
General Education Management System GEMS
General Education Provisions Act [*1970*] GEPA
General Educational Development [*Test*] GED
General Educational Development Program [*Army*] GEDP
General Educational Development Test GEDT
General Educational Services [*Corp.*] GES
General Election GE
General Electric Airborne Guidance GEAG
General Electric/Apollo Support Division GE/ASD
General Electric-ARSD, Sunnyvale, CA [*OCLC symbol*] GEA
General Electric Atomic Power GEAP
General Electric Chemical Engineering Calculation System GECECS
General Electric Co. [*NYSE symbol*] GE
General Electric Company GEC
General Electric Co., Electronics Park Library, Syracuse, NY [*OCLC symbol*] ZUI
General Electric Co., Information Resources Library, Utica, NY [*OCLC symbol*] ZUJ
General Electric Co., Knolls Atomic Laboratory, Technical Library, Schenectady, NY [*Library symbol*] NSchGEKA
General Electric Co., Light Research Laboratory, Cleveland, OH [*Library symbol*] OCIL
General Electric Co., Main Library, Schenectady, NY [*Library symbol*] NSchGEM
General Electric Co., Missile and Space Vehicle Department, Aerosciences Laboratory, Philadelphia, PA [*Library symbol*] PPGE-M
General Electric Co., Philadelphia, PA [*Library symbol*] PPGE
General Electric Co., Pittsfield, MA [*Library symbol*] MPG
General Electric Co., R and D Center, Branch Library, Schenectady, NY [*Library symbol*] NSchGERB
General Electric Co., Research Laboratory, Schenectady, NY [*Library symbol*] NSchGER
General Electric Co., Santa Barbara, CA [*Library symbol*] CStbGE
General Electric Co., Syracuse, NY [*Library symbol*] NSyGE
General Electric Co., Traveling Wave Tube Production Section, Palo Alto, CA [*Library symbol*] CPaGE
General Electric Co., Utica, NY [*Library symbol*] NUtGE
General Electric Computer Analysis Program GELAP
General Electric Detection and Automatic Correction GEDAC
General Electric Electronic Processor GEEP
General Electric Electronic System Evaluator GEESE
General Electric Flame Site GEFS
General Electric Gas [*Process*] GEGAS
General Electric Guidance System [*Aerospace*] GEGS
General Electric Laboratory GEL
General Electric Macro Assembly Language GMAL
General Electric Magnetically Anchored Gravity System GEMAGS
General Electric Manufacturing Simulator GEMS
General Electric Measurement and Control GE/MAC
General Electric Network [*Data processing*] GEN
General Electric Nose Cone [*Aerospace*] GENC
General Electric Parts Explosion System GEPEXS
General Electric Process Automation Computer GEPAC
General Electric Process Design System GEPDS
General Electric Range Safety Instrumentation System [*Aerospace*] GERSIS
General Electric Range Tracking System [*Aerospace*] GERTS
General Electric Reentry Vehicle [*Aerospace*] GERV
General Electric Remote Terminal System GERTS
General Electric Satellite Orbit Control [*Aerospace*] GESOC
General Electric Self-Adaptive Control System GESAC
General Electric Semiconductor GES
General Electric Six Hundred Users' Association [*Later, HLSUA*] [*Data processing*] GESHUA
General Electric Supply Corporation GESCO
General Electric Telemetering and Control GE/TAC
General Electric Test Engineering Language [*Data processing*] GETEL
General Electric Test Reactor GETR
General Electric Training Operational Logic GETOL
General Electric Variable Increment Computer GEVIC
General Electrical Review [*A publication*] Gen Elec R
General Electrodynamics Corporation GEC
General Emergency Operations Plan GEOP
General Employment Enterprises, Inc. [*American Stock Exchange symbol*] JOB
General Engine Bulletin GEB
General Engineering Research GER
General Environmental Statement for Mixed Oxide Fuel GESMO
General Epitaxial Monolith GEM
General Equipment Command [*Army*] GEC
General Equipment and Packaging Laboratory [*Army*] GEPL
General Equipment Test Activity [*Army*] GETA
General Equivalency Diploma [*For nongraduates*] GED
General Evaluation Equipment GEE
General Examination GE
General Expenses GE
General Exploration Co. [*American Stock Exchange symbol*] [*Delisted*] GEX
General Extrasensory Perception [*Psychical research*] GESP
General Failure Criteria GFC
General Federation of Labor Unions [*Syria*] GFLU
General Federation of Trade Unions [*Various countries*] GFTU
General Federation of Women's Clubs GFWC
General Finance Corp. of Delaware [*NYSE symbol*] [*Delisted*] GFN
General Fireproofing Co. [*Later, GFB*] [*NYSE symbol*] GLP
General Fisheries Council for the Mediterranean GFCM
General Fisheries Council for the Mediterranean. Session Report [*A publication*] Gen Fish Counc Mediterr Sess Rep
General Flight Work GFW
General Foods Corp. [*NYSE symbol*] GF
General Foods Corp., Hoboken, NJ [*Library symbol*] NjHoGF
General Foods Ltd., Cobourg, ON, Canada [*Library symbol*] CaOCoGF
General Foods Moisture Vapor Transmission GFMVT
General Foods Technical Center Library, Tarrytown, NY [*Library symbol*] NTaGF
General Foods Technical Center, White Plains, NY [*OCLC symbol*] YGF
General Forecasting Program GFP
General Foreign Policy [*A publication*] GFP
General Forestry Assistance GFA
General Freight Agent GFA
General Freight Department GFD
General Freight Office GFO
General Freight Traffic Committee - Eastern Railroads GFTC-ER
General Function System Requirement GFSR
General Functional Description [*Military*] GFD
General Functional Requirements GFR
General Genetics Corp. [*NASDAQ symbol*] GENG
General George A. Lincoln [*World War II*] GAL
General George C. Marshall [*World War II*] GCM
General Grant National Memorial GEGR
General Growth Properties SBI [*NYSE symbol*] GGP
General Headquarters [*Military*] GHQ
General Headquarters Air Force GHQAF
General Homes [*NASDAQ symbol*] GHOM
General Hospital [*Initialism also refers to a TV program*] GH
General Hospital Psychiatry [*A publication*] Gen Hosp Psychiatry
General Hospital, St. John's, NF, Canada [*Library symbol*] CaNfSGH
General Host Corp. [*NYSE symbol*] GH
General Hotel, Boarding House, and Apartments [*British*] HBA
General Household Survey [*Office of Population Census and Surveys*] [*British*] GHS
General Housekeeping Area [*NASA*] GHA
General Housewares Corp. [*American Stock Exchange symbol*] GHW
General Hydrocarbons of Minnesota [*NASDAQ symbol*] GHYD
General Improvement Contractors Association GIC
General Incentive for Research and Development [*Canada*] GIRD
General Index GI
General Indexing in Reciprocal Lattice Space GIRLS
General Industrial Equipment Reserve GIER
General Industry Advisory Committee GIAC
General Industry Applications GIA
General Information and Analysis Tool GIANT
General Information Booklet [*Navy*] GIB
General Information Retrieval System Simulation GIRSS
General Information Test GIT
General Inspection [*Military*] GI
General Inspectorate Section [*European Theater of Operations*] [*World War II*] GI Sec
General Installation Dolly GID
General Installation Subcontractor GIS
General Instruction Book GIB
General Instructions for Routing and Reporting Officers GIRO
General Instrument Corp. [*NYSE symbol*] GRL
General Insurance Fund [*Federal Housing Administration*] GIF
General Intelligence G
General Intelligence Unit [*US, London*] GIU
General Internal FORTRAN Translator [*Data processing*] GIFT
General Interpretative System for Matrix Operations [*Data processing system used in engineering*] [*Navy*] GISMO
General Issue GI
General Kinetics, Incorporated GKI
General Labor and Trades GLT
General Laboratory Associates GLA
General Land Office [*Became part of Bureau of Land Management, 1946*] GLO
General Layout Plan GLP

General Learning Ability..GLA
General Learning Corporation [of Time, Inc.]...............GLC
General Learning Disability..GLD
General Ledger..GENLED
General Ledger..GL
General Ledger Account...GLA
General Ledger Account Code..................................GLAC
General Ledger Identification Code...........................GLIC
General Ledger Subsidiary Account...........................GLSA
General Letter..GL
General Lew Wallace Studio, Crawfordsville, IN [Library symbol].......InCLW
General Liability [Insurance]..GL
General Lighting Service...GLS
General Line School...GLS
General Linear [Group theory, mathematics]................GL
General Linguistics [A publication]..............Gen Linguis
General Linguistics [A publication].............................GL
General List [Navy] [British]..G
General Machine Test...GMT
General Magnaplate Corporation [NASDAQ symbol].......GMCC
General Maintenance [Army]......................................GM
General Maintenance System......................................GMS
General Management Directive...................................GMD
General Management Plan [National Park Service].......GMP
General Manager...GM
General Maritime Stevedores' Union [Philippines].......GMSU
General Material Services...GMS
General Maximum Price Regulation [World War II].......GMPR
General Measurement Loop.......................................GML
General Mechanic..GMECH
General Medical Control [British]................................GMI
General Medical Corp. [NYSE symbol] [Delisted].......GMD
General Medical Council [British]................................GMC
General Medical Sciences and Atomic Energy Commission.....GeMSAEC
General Medical Services [British]...............................GMS
General Medicine...GM
General Medicine and Surgery..............................GM & S
General Meetings [Quakers]..GM
General Mental Ability..GMA
General Merchandise..GM
General Merchandise Distributors Council...............GMDC
General Microelectronics...GME
General Microfilm Co., Cambridge, MA [Library symbol].......GmC
General Microwave Corporation [NASDAQ symbol].......GMIC
General Military Course...GMC
General Military Science..GMS
General Military Subjects Test...................................GMST
General Military Training..GMT
General Military Training Office.................................GMTO
General Military Training Review Board....................GMTRB
General Milk Sales [An association] [Inactive].............GMS
General Mills, Inc. [NYSE symbol]................................GIS
General Mills, Incorporated, Minneapolis, MN [OCLC symbol].......GMI
General Mining Association of the Province of Quebec. Journal [A publication].......Gen M As Que J
General Mobilization Material Readiness [DoD].......GMMR
General Mobilization Reserve Acquisition Objective [DoD].......GMRAO
General Mobilization Reserve Materiel Objective [DoD].......GMRMO
General Mobilization Reserve Materiel Requirement [DoD].......GMRMR
General Mobilization Reserve Stock [DoD]................GMRS
General Mobilization Reserve Stockage Objective [DoD].......GMRSO
General Mobilization Reserves [DoD].........................GMR
General Model..GENMOD
General Monte Carlo Code [Data processing]..............GMC
General Mortgage [Bond]..GM
General Mortgage Bond...GMB
General Motors Acceptance Corporation..................GMAC
General Motors Allison Division................................GMAD
General Motors Assembly Division............................GMAD
General Motors Corp. [NYSE symbol]...........................GM
General Motors Corporation......................................GMC
General Motors Corp., Detroit Diesel Allison Division, Plant 8 Library, Indianapolis, IN [Library symbol].......InID
General Motors Corp., Engineering Staff Library, Warren, MI [Library symbol].......MiWarGMR-E
General Motors Corp., Inland Manufacturing Division, Engineering Library, Dayton, OH [Library symbol].......ODaGMI
General Motors Corp., Research Laboratories Division, Warren, MI [Library symbol].......MiWarGMR
General Motors Corporation. Research Laboratories. Research Publication [A publication].......Gen Mot Corp Res Lab Res Publ
General Motors Corp., Research Laboratory, Warren, MI [OCLC symbol].......EYG
General Motors Defense Research Laboratory.........GMDRL
General Motors Improvement Project [Investigating team sponsored by consumer-advocate Ralph Nader].......GMIP
General Motors Institute [Company-financed engineering school].......GMI
General Motors Research...GMR
General Motors Research Laboratories. Search [A publication].......GM Search
General and Municipal Workers' Union [British].......GMWU

General N. B. Baker Library, Sutherland, IA [Library symbol].......IaSu
General Nautical Chart [Navy]....................................GNC
General Naval Staff..GNS
General Neighborhood Renewal Plan........................GNRP
General Noise and Tonal System..............................GNATS
General Nonlinear Analysis of Two-Dimensional Structures [Computer program].......GNATS
General Notice..GENOT
General Nuclear Engineering Corporation..................GNEC
General Numerical Analysis of Transport [Computer program].......GNAT
General Nursing Care [Medicine]...............................GNC
General Nursing Council..GNC
General Nutrition [NYSE symbol]...............................GNC
General Obligation..GO
General Ocean Research [Navy ship symbol].............GOR
General Officer [Military]...GO
General Officer Command [US Army Reserve].........GOCOM
General Officer Commanding [Navy]...........................GOC
General Officer Commanding-in-Chief [British].......GOC-in-C
General Officer Commanding Royal Marines [British].......GOCRM
General Officer Money Allowance [Military]...............GOMA
General Officer Product Improvement Review Board.......GOPIRB
General Officers Branch [Air Force].............................GOB
General Officers' Protocol Roster................................GOPR
General Officers Review Group [Air Force].................GORG
General Operating Agency...GOA
General Operating Committee......................................GOC
General Operating Expenses..GOE
General Operating Language [Data processing]...........GOL
General Operating Room...GOR
General Operating Specification [Air Materiel Command].......GOS
General Operational Plot...GOP
General Operational Requirement................................GOR
General Operational Requirements [Army]...................GOR
General Operations and Logistics Simulation [Boeing].......GOALS
General Operator-Computer Interaction.....................GOCI
General Order...GO
General Order of Battle...GOB
General Ordination Examination.................................GOE
General Organization [Identification card used at Madison Square Garden].......GO
General Organizational Environment......................GEORGE
General Outdoor Advertising Co., Inc. [NYSE symbol] [Delisted].......GOU
General Outpost [Army]..GOP
General Outpost Line [Army].....................................GOPL
General Overhaul Specification...................................GOS
General Paralysis [or Paresis] [Medicine].......................GP
General Paralysis of the Insane [Literal translation, but also medical slang for eccentricity].......GPI
General Parent Ring System [Proposed chemical classification].......GPRS
General Passenger Agent...GPA
General Passenger Committee - Eastern Railroads [Defunct].......GPC-ERR
General Patents Index [A publication]..........................GPI
General Pause [Music]..GP
General Performance Number......................................GPN
General Petroleum Corp., Los Angeles, CA [Library symbol].......CLGP
General Petroleum & Mineral Organization [Saudi Arabia state-owned oil company].......PETROMIN
General Pharmacology [A publication]..................Gen Pharm
General Pharmacology [A publication]...............Gen Pharmacol
General Physical Condition [Medicine]..........................GPC
General Physics Corp. [NASDAQ symbol].....................GPHY
General Pico [Argentina] [Airport symbol]....................GPO
General Planning Group...GPG
General Plant Equipment Requirements.......................GPER
General Plant Projects...GPP
General Plywood Corp. [American Stock Exchange symbol].......GPY
General Political Warfare Department [Military].........GPWD
General Portland, Inc. [NYSE symbol] [Delisted]..........GPT
General Post Office [British] [Defunct]........................GPO
General Postal Union [Later, UPU]................................GPU
General and Practical Energy Information Data Base.......GAP
General Practice [A publication]....................................GP
General Practitioner [of medicine].................................GP
General Precision Equipment Corp. [NYSE symbol] [Delisted].......GPE
General Precision, Incorporated....................................GPI
General Precision, Inc., Librascope Division, Glendale, CA [Library symbol].......CGIL
General Precision Laboratory...................................GENPRL
General Precision Laboratory..GPL
General Preventive Medicine.......................................GPM
General Principles [FBI standardized term]....................GP
General Problem Solver [Data processing]...................GPS
General Procedures..G
General Process Simulation Studies...........................GPSS
General Processing Subsystem....................................GPS
General Product...GP
General Provision...GP
General Provisions..GP's
General Provisions Policy Statement..........................GPPS
General Public [Merchandising slang]............................GP

General Public Assistance [*A form of public charity*] GPA
General Public Service Corp. [*NYSE symbol*] [*Delisted*] GPV
General Public Utilities Corp. [*NYSE symbol*] GPU
General Public Visiting [*Navy*] GENVST
General Publication GP
General Pulaski Heritage Foundation GPHF
General Purchasing Agency [*Allied German Occupation Forces*] GPA
General Purchasing Board GPB
General Purpose GP
General-Purpose Airborne Simulator GPAS
General-Purpose Amplifier GPA
General-Purpose Analog Computer GPAC
General-Purpose Analysis GPA
General-Purpose Automatic Test [*Air Force*] GPAT
General-Purpose Automatic Test Equipment [*Army*] GATE
General-Purpose Automatic Test System [*Air Force*] GPATS
General-Purpose Barbed Tape Obstacle [*Army*] GPBTO
General-Purpose Buffer GPB
General-Purpose Buffer Interface Module [*Data processing*] GPBIM
General-Purpose Closed Loop [*Nuclear energy*] GPCL
General-Purpose Computer GPC
General-Purpose Digital Computer GPDC
General-Purpose Discipline [*IBM Corp.*] GPD
General-Purpose Display System GPDS
General-Purpose Electronic Test Equipment GPETE
General-Purpose Equipment GPE
General-Purpose Forces GPF
General-Purpose Function Code GPFC
General-Purpose Graphic Language [*Data processing*] GPGL
General-Purpose Heat Source [*Nuclear energy*] GPHS
General-Purpose Input/Output [*Data processing*] GPIO
General-Purpose Intercomputer [*Test*] GPIC
General-Purpose Interface GPI
General-Purpose Interface Bus [*Data processing*] GPIB
General-Purpose Inverter GPI
General-Purpose Keyboard and Display Control [*Data processing*] GPKD
General-Purpose Laboratory GPL
General-Purpose Language [*Data processing*] GPL
General-Purpose Linear Programing [*Data processing*] GPLP
General-Purpose Loop [*Nuclear energy*] GPL
General-Purpose Macrogenerator GPM
General-Purpose Maneuver GPM
General-Purpose Microprogram Simulator GPMS
General-Purpose Missile GPM
General-Purpose Mission Equipment GPME
General-Purpose Multiplex System [*Aviation*] GPMS
General-Purpose Oscilloscope GPO
General-Purpose Output [*Space Flight Operations Facility, NASA*] GPO
General-Purpose Programing [*Data processing*] GPP
General-Purpose Psychiatric Questionnaire GPPQ
General-Purpose Quarter-Ton Military Utility Vehicle JEEP
General-Purpose RADAR GPR
General-Purpose Radio Receiver GPRR
General-Purpose Radio Transmitter GPRT
General-Purpose Radiometer GPR
General-Purpose Receiver GPR
General-Purpose Register GPR
General-Purpose Relay GPR
General-Purpose Representative GPR
General-Purpose Satellite Communication System GPSCS
General-Purpose Scientific Document Image Code [*System*] [*National Bureau of Standards*] GPSDIC
General-Purpose Scientific Document Writer [*National Bureau of Standards*] GPSDW
General-Purpose Shelter GPS
General-Purpose Signal Processor GPSP
General-Purpose Simulation Environment [*Data processing*] GPSE
General-Purpose Simulation System [*formerly, Systems Simulator*] [*Data processing*] GPSS
General-Purpose Software Program [*Data processing*] GPSP
General-Purpose Surface-to-Surface Missile [*Army*] GPSSM
General-Purpose Terminal Interchanges [*Airline communication system*] [*Raytheon Co.*] GPTI
General-Purpose Test Equipment GPTE
General-Purpose Tool GPT
General-Purpose Vehicle GPV
General-Purpose Vehicle GPVEH
General-Purpose Video Buffer GPVB
General Quarters [*General Alert*] [*Navy*] GQ
General Radio GR
General Radio Service [*Canada*] GRS
General Railway Classification [*British*] GRC
General Railway Signal Co., Library, Rochester, NY [*OCLC symbol*] VQN
General Railway Signal Co., Rochester, NY [*Library symbol*] NRGR
General Railway Warrants [*US Military Government, Germany*] GRW
General Range Safety Plan [*NASA*] GRSP
General Re Corp. [*NYSE symbol*] GRN
General Reactor Technology GRT
General Real Estate SBI [*NASDAQ symbol*] GRELS
General Reconnaissance [*Marine Corps*] GR
General Records Schedules [*Military*] GRS
General Recreation, Inc. [*American Stock Exchange symbol*] [*Delisted*] GER
General Recursive Algebra and Differentiation GRAD
General Refractories Co. [*NYSE symbol*] GRX
General Register Office [*British*] GRO
General Register Set/Stack [*Data processing*] GRS
General Relativity [*Physics*] GR
General Relativity and Gravitation [*A publication*] Gen Relat G
General Relativity and Gravitation [*A publication*] Gen Relativ Gravitation
General Reports [*Military*] GENREP
General Repository [*A publication*] Gen Repos
General Requests for Ground-Based Electronics Equipment [*NASA*] GREE
General Research GR
General Reserve GR
General Resource Allocation and Selection Program [*NASA*] GRASP
General Retrieval and Information Processor for Humanities Oriented Studies GRIPHOS
General Retrieval of Information Program [*Data processing*] GRIP
General Retrieval Inquiry Negotiation Structure GRINS
General Revenue Sharing [*Office of Revenue Sharing*] GRS
General Roca [*Argentina*] [*Airport symbol*] GNR
General Rose Memorial Hospital, Medical Library, Denver, CO [*Library symbol*] CoDGRM-M
General Routine Order GRO
General [*Aviation*] **Safety District Office** GSDO
General Safety Inspector [*Aviation*] GSI
General Sales Manager GSM
General Santos [*Philippines*] [*Airport symbol*] GES
General Schedule [*Federal employee job classification GS-1 to GS-18*] GS
General Screening Test GST
General Secretary GS
General Semantic Problem GSP
General Semantics GS
General Semantics Bulletin [*A publication*] GSB
General Semantics Foundation GSF
General Series. Colorado State University. Agricultural Experiment Station [*A publication*] Gen Ser Colo State Agr Exp Sta
General Service [*Military*] GENSV
General Service [*Literal translation, but used in sense of "excessively keen," or "overly acute"*] [*Army*] [*British*] GS
General Service Corps [*Military unit*] [*British*] GSC
General Service Infantry [*Army*] GSI
General Service Medal [*British*] GSM
General Service Recruit [*Navy*] GSR
General Service School [*Army*] GSS
General Service Test GST
General Service Truck [*British*] GST
General Service Unit [*Marine Corps*] GSU
General Services Administration GSA
General Services Administration - Board of Contract Appeals GSA-BCA
General Services Administration - Civilian Personnel Office GSA-CPO
General Services Administration, National Archives and Record Service, Franklin D. Roosevelt Library, Hyde Park, NY [*Library symbol*] NHyF
General Services Administration - Office of Preparedness GSA-OP
General Services Administration - Public Building Service GSA-PBS
General Services Administration, Washington, DC [*OCLC symbol*] GSA
General Services Officer GSO
General Sessions GS
General Shale Products Corp. [*NASDAQ symbol*] GSHL
General Shoe Corporation [*Acronym now official name of firm*] GENESCO
General Signal Corp. [*NYSE symbol*] GSX
General Simulation Program [*Data processing*] GSP
General Situation [*Military*] GENSIT
General Situation Map [*Military*] GSM
General Society of Colonial Wars GSCW
General Society of Mayflower Descendants GSMD
General Society of Mechanics and Tradesmen GSMT
General Society of Mechanics and Tradesmen, New York, NY [*Library symbol*] NNMec
General Society, Sons of the Revolution SR
General Society of the War of 1812 GSW 1812
General Somatic Afferent [*Nerve*] [*Anatomy*] GSA
General Somatic Efferent [*Nerve*] [*Anatomy*] GSE
General Soviet [*Later, A Group*] [*Division of National Security Agency*] GENS
General Spin Orbitals [*Atomic physics*] GSO
General Staff [*Military*] GS
General Staff Branch [*Army*] [*British*] G
General Staff Committees on Army National Guard and Army Reserve Policy GSCARNGARP
General Staff Corps [*Military*] GSC
General Staff Council [*Military*] GSC
General Staff Identification Badge [*Military decoration*] GSIdentBad
General Staff Interpreter Officer [*Military*] [*British*] GSIO
General Staff Officer [*Military*] GSO
General Staff Operational Requirements [*Army*] GSOR
General Staff Requirement [*British*] GSR
General Staff Target GST
General Staff with Troops [*Army*] GST

General Staff with Troops [*Army*] ... GSWT
General Staff, United States Army ... GSUSA
General Statistics ... GS
General Steam Navigation Company [*British*] ... GSNC
General Steel Casting Corporation ... GSCC
General Steel Industries, Inc. [*NYSE symbol*] [*Delisted*] ... GSI
General Stock Ownership Plan ... GSOP
General Storekeeper [*Navy*] ... GSK
General Stores Issue Ship [*Navy symbol*] ... AKI
General Stores Issue Ship [*Navy symbol*] ... AKS
General Stores Material [*Navy*] ... GSM
General Stores Material List ... GSML
General Stores Supply Office ... GSSO
General Strike ... GS
General Strike for Peace ... GSP
General Strike Plan ... GSP
General Stud Book [*Horses*] ... GSB
General Superintendent ... GS
General Supply Depot ... GSD
General Supply Fund ... GSF
General Supply Office ... GSO
General Supply Schedule ... GSS
General Supply Stock Fund [*Air Force*] ... GSSF
General Support [*Army*] ... GENSUP
General Support [*Military*] ... GS
General Support Division [*Air Force*] ... GSD
General Support Equipment [*Military*] ... GSE
General Support Force [*Air Force*] ... GSF
General Support Group [*Army*] ... GSG
General Support Reinforcing [*Army*] ... GSR
General Support Rocket System ... GSRS
General Support Unit [*Army*] ... GSU
General Surgery ... GENSURG
General Surgery ... GS
General System Description [*Military*] ... GSD
General Systems [*A publication*] ... Gen Syst
General Systems Bulletin [*A publication*] ... Gen Syst
General Systems Division [*IBM Corp.*] ... GSD
General Systems Engineering and Technical Direction ... GSETD
General Systems Theory ... GST
General Tabulation System ... GTS
General Tariff Bureau Inc. Lansing MI [*STAC*] ... GTB
General Technical Advisory Committee [*for fossil energy*] [*Energy Research and Development Administration*] ... GTAC
General Technical Aptitude Area ... GT
General Technical Services, Inc. ... GTS
General Telephone of California [*NASDAQ symbol*] ... GTELN
General Telephone Call Processing ... GTCP
General Telephone Co. of Florida [*NYSE symbol*] ... GLF
General Telephone & Electronics Corp. ... GENTEL
General Telephone & Electronics Corp. ... GT & E
General Telephone & Electronics, GTE Sylvania, Inc., Towanda, PA [*Library symbol*] ... PToG
General Telephone & Electronics Laboratories, Inc., Waltham Research Center Library, Waltham, MA [*Library symbol*] ... MWalG
General Terms Agreement ... GTA
General Test Plan ... GTP
General Test Support ... GTS
General Theological Library, Boston, MA [*Library symbol*] ... MBGT
General Theological Seminary [*New York*] ... GTS
General Theological Seminary of the Protestant Episcopal Church, New York, NY [*Library symbol*] ... NNG
General Theological Seminary, St. Mark's Library, New York, NY [*OCLC symbol*] ... VXM
General Theory of Relativity ... GTR
General Time Corp. [*NYSE symbol*] [*Delisted*] ... GLI
General Time Sharing System [*Data processing*] ... GTSS
General Tire & Rubber Co. [*NYSE symbol*] ... GY
General Tire & Rubber Co. Wts [*NASDAQ symbol*] ... GENTW
General Tool ... GT
General Tool Experimental ... GTX
General Topology and Its Applications [*A publication*] ... General Topology and Appl
General Track Simulation [*NASA*] ... GETS
General Trade Books [*Publishing*] ... GTB
General Traffic Manager ... GTM
General Transistor Corporation ... GTC
General Transport Administrative Vehicle ... GTAV
General Transportation Importance ... GTI
General Troubleshooting ... GTS
General Unary Hypothesis Automation ... GUHA
General Union Democratic Students and Patriotic Afghans ... GUDSPA
General Unwanted Energy Rejection Analysis Program [*Air Force*] ... GUERAP
General Usage Inventory Director ... GUIDE
General-Use Consumable List [*Military*] ... GUCL
General Utility Library Program ... GULP
General Utility Mechanic ... GUM
General Visceral Afferent [*Neurology*] ... GVA
General Visceral Efferent [*Neurology*] ... GVE
General War Reserves [*Army*] ... GWR
General Warning ... GW
General Watch Officer [*Army*] ... GWO
General Water-Quality Engineering [*Survey*] [*Army*] ... GWQE
General Will [*Collectivist theory of government*] ... GW
General Work Area [*NASA*] ... GWA
General Workers Professional Unions [*Bulgaria*] ... GWPU
General Workers Union [*Malta*] ... GWU
General X-Ray Diagnosis [*Medicine*] ... GXD
General Yardmaster [*Railroading*] ... GYM
Generale Aeronautique Marcel Dassault [*Switzerland*] ... GAMD
Generale Congolaise des Minerais [*Congo*] ... GECOMIN
Generale Occidentale [*Commercial firm*] ... GO
Generality and Problem Solving ... GPS
Generalized Academic Simulation Program ... GASP
Generalized Activity Network ... GAN
Generalized Aerospace Program ... GASP
Generalized Algebraic Translator [*Data processing*] ... GAT
Generalized Algebraic Translator Extended [*Data processing*] ... GATE
Generalized Antisymmetric Potential ... GASP
Generalized Arteriosclerosis [*Medicine*] ... GAS
Generalized Assembly System ... GASS
Generalized Audit Software [*Data processing*] ... GAS
Generalized Circuit Analysis Program ... GCAP
Generalized Compiler [*Data processing*] ... GECOM
Generalized Computer Program ... GCP
Generalized Continuum Hypothesis [*Logic*] ... GCH
Generalized Data Base Management Systems [*Air Force*] ... GDBMS
Generalized Data Base System ... GDBS
Generalized Data Management System ... GDMS
Generalized Data Reduction, Manipulation, Evaluation ... GENDARME
Generalized Distributor Program [*Data processing*] ... GDP
Generalized Documentation Processor ... GDP
Generalized Engine [*Data processing*] ... GENENG
Generalized Environmental Impact Statement ... GEIS
Generalized Equipment Reliability Evaluation Procedure ... GEREP
Generalized Evaluation Model Simulator [*NASA*] ... GEMS
Generalized Fire-Control System Maintenance Trainer [*Spacecraft*] [*Navy*] ... GFCSMT
Generalized Glandular Enlargement [*Medicine*] ... GGE
Generalized Hyperbolic Class ... GHC
Generalized Immittance Converter ... GIC
Generalized Information Management System ... GIM
Generalized Information Processing System ... GIPSY
Generalized Information Retrieval and Listing System ... GIRLS
Generalized Information System [*IBM Corp.*] ... GIS
Generalized Input/Output Controller [*Data processing*] ... GIOC
Generalized Inquiry System [*Data processing*] ... GIS
Generalized Integrated Square Error [*Aeronautics*] ... GISE
Generalized Interrelated Flow Simulation ... GIFS
Generalized Lambda Family [*Statistics*] ... GLF
Generalized Least Squares [*Statistics*] ... GLS
Generalized Linear Model [*Statistics*] ... GLM
Generalized Mainline Framework [*Data processing*] ... GMF
Generalized Markup Language [*Data processing*] ... GML
Generalized Message Control System ... GEMCOS
Generalized Officer Assignment On-Line System [*Navy*] ... GOALS
Generalized One-Boson Exchange Potential ... GOBEP
Generalized Operations ... GO
Generalized Overhauser Orbitals [*Atomic physics*] ... GOO
Generalized Preference Scheme [*Tariff policy*] ... GPS
Generalized Process Control Programing [*Data processing*] ... GPCP
Generalized Production Function [*Industrial economics*] ... GPF
Generalized Programing [*Data processing*] ... GP
Generalized Programing Extended [*Data processing*] ... GPX
Generalized Programing Language [*Data processing*] ... GPL
Generalized Random Extract Device [*Data processing*] ... GRED
Generalized Reactor Analysis Subsystem ... GRASS
Generalized Reduced Gradient ... GRG
Generalized Reed-Muller [*Codes*] ... GRM
Generalized Reentry Application Simulation Program [*NASA*] ... GRASP
Generalized Remote Access Data Base ... GRAD
Generalized Remote Access Data Base ... GRADB
Generalized Remote Access Data Base System ... GRADS
Generalized Report Module Program [*Data processing*] ... GRM
Generalized Retrieval and Storage Program [*Data processing*] ... GRASP
Generalized Retrieval System [*Data processing*] ... GRS
Generalized Schartzman Reaction [*Medicine*] ... GSR
Generalized Simulation Language [*Data processing*] ... GSL
Generalized Sinusoidal Quantity ... GSQ
Generalized Sort/Merge [*Data processing*] ... GSM
Generalized Standard Addition Method [*Mathematics*] ... GSAM
Generalized Supervisor Calls [*Data processing*] ... GSVC
Generalized System of Preferences [*US Customs Service*] ... GSP
Generalized Trace Facility [*Data processing*] ... GTF
Generalized Transformation Function ... GTF
Generalized Upper Bounding [*Data processing*] ... GUB
Generalized Valence Bond [*Physics*] ... GVB
Generalized Weighted Least Squares Estimates [*Statistics*] ... GLSE
Generally ... GENY
Generally Accepted Accounting Principles [*or Procedures*] ... GAAP
Generally Labeled [*Radioactive compounds*] ... G

Generally Recognized [*or Regarded*] **as Safe** [*FDA term*] ..... GRAS
Generally Regarded as Effective [*Medicine*] ..... GRAE
Generaloberst [*Full general*] [*German military - World War II*] ..... GO
Generals of the Army and the Air Force and Admirals of the Navy [*A publication*] ..... Gen Arm
General's Branch, Quarter Master's Branch, and Adjutant's Branch [*Main divisions of Staff Duties*] [*Military*] [*British*] ..... GQ & A
Generals for Peace and Disarmament ..... GPD
Generate ..... GENR
Generated Data File [*Data processing*] ..... GEND
Generated Real-Time Output Operations on Voltage-Controlled Equipment [*Data processing*] ..... GROOVE
Generated Repeatable Exams [*Education*] ..... GRE
Generated Target Tracking ..... GTT
Generating and Analyzing Networks [*Data processing*] ..... GAN
Generating Power Unit ..... GPU
Generation ..... GEN
Generation Data Group [*Data processing*] ..... GDG
Generation Gather Group [*Data processing*] ..... GNG
Generation Management Station ..... GMS
Generation, Reduction, and Training Input System ..... GRATIS
Generation Strategy Language [*Data processing*] ..... GSL
Generation Time ..... GT
Generator ..... GEN
Generator ..... GNTR
Generator Control Breaker ..... GCB
Generator Control Switch ..... GCS
Generator Control Unit [*NASA*] ..... GCU
Generator Coordinate Method [*Physics*] ..... GCM
Generator Environmental Tester ..... GET
Generator Field ..... GF
Generator Field ..... GFLD
Generator Line Contractor ..... GLC
Generator Lorry [*British*] ..... GL
Generator Output Voltage ..... GOV
Generators, Power [*JETDS nomenclature*] [*Military*] ..... G
Generic ..... GEN
Generic Code ..... GC
Generic Failure ..... GF
Generic Pharmaceutical Industry Association ..... GPIA
Generics Corp. of America [*American Stock Exchange symbol*] [*Delisted*] ..... GNC
GENESCO, Inc. [*NYSE symbol*] ..... GCO
Genesee Brewing Cl B [*NASDAQ symbol*] ..... GENBB
Genesee Community College, Batavia, NY [*Library symbol*] ..... NBatC
Genesee County Landmark Society, East Bethany, NY [*Library symbol*] ..... NEabG
Genesee Hospital, Stabins Health Science Library, Rochester, NY [*OCLC symbol*] ..... VQO
Geneseo, IL [*Radio station call letters*] ..... WGEN
Geneseo, IL [*Radio station call letters*] ..... WGEN-FM
Geneseo Junior/Senior High School Library, Geneseo, NY [*OCLC symbol*] ..... RWH
Geneseo, NY [*Radio station call letters*] ..... WGSU
Genesis [*Old Testament book*] ..... Gen
Genesis [*Old Testament book*] ..... Gn
Genesis Project ..... GP
Genesis West [*A publication*] ..... GW
Genessee & Wyoming Railroad Co. [*AAR code*] ..... GNWR
Genetic Dynamics Corp. [*NASDAQ symbol*] ..... GEDY
Genetic Engineering [*NASDAQ symbol*] ..... GEEN
Genetic Laboratories, Inc. [*NASDAQ symbol*] ..... GENL
Genetic Prediabetes [*Endocrinology*] ..... GP
Genetic Psychology Monographs [*A publication*] ..... Genet Psych
Genetic Psychology Monographs [*A publication*] ..... Genet Psychol Monog
Genetic Psychology Monographs [*A publication*] ..... Genet Psychol Monogr
Genetic Psychology Monographs [*A publication*] ..... GPM
Genetic Systems [*NASDAQ symbol*] ..... GENS
Genetic Therapy ..... GT
Genetic Toxicology Association ..... GTA
Genetica Agraria [*A publication*] ..... Genet Agrar
Genetica Iberica [*A publication*] ..... Genet Iber
Genetica Polonica [*A publication*] ..... Genet Pol
Genetical Research [*A publication*] ..... Genet Res
Genetically Significant Concentration [*Mutagenesis*] ..... GSC
Genetically Significant Dosage [*X-Ray*] ..... GSD
Genetics ..... GEN
Genetics ..... GENET
Genetics [*A publication*] ..... Genet
Genetics Abstracts [*A publication*] ..... Genet Abstr
Genetics Lectures [*A publication*] ..... Genet Lect
Genetics and Physiology Notes [*A publication*] ..... Genet Physiol Notes
Genetics and Physiology Notes. Institute of Paper Chemistry [*A publication*] ..... Genet Physiol Note Inst Paper Chem
Genetics and Plant Breeding [*A publication*] ..... Genet Plant Breed
Genetics Society of America ..... GSA
Genetika i Selektsiya [*A publication*] ..... Genet Sel
Genetika i Selektsiya [*A publication*] ..... Genet Selektsiya
Genetika a Slechteni [*A publication*] ..... Genet Slechteni
Geneva [*City in Switzerland*] ..... GEN
Geneva [*Switzerland*] [*Airport symbol*] ..... GVA
Geneva, AL [*Radio station call letters*] ..... WGEA
Geneva, AL [*Radio station call letters*] ..... WGEA-FM
Geneva College, Beaver Falls, PA [*Library symbol*] ..... PBfG
Geneva College, Beaver Falls, PA [*OCLC symbol*] ..... PGC
Geneva Convention for the Amelioration of the Condition of the Wounded and Sick in Armed Forces in the Field, 12 August 1949 [*Army*] ..... GWS
Geneva Convention for the Amelioration of the Condition of the Wounded and Sick in Armed Forces in the Field, 27 July 1929 [*Army*] ..... GWS 1929
Geneva Convention for the Amelioration of the Condition of the Wounded, Sick, and Shipwrecked Members of the Armed Forces at Sea, 12 August 1949 [*Army*] ..... GWS Sea
Geneva Convention Relative to Protection of Civilian Persons in Time of War [*Army*] ..... GC
Geneva Convention Relative to Treatment of Prisoners of War, 12 August 1949 [*Army*] ..... GPW
Geneva Convention Relative to Treatment of Prisoners of War, 27 July 1929 [*Army*] ..... GPW 1929
Geneva Conventions [*Military*] ..... GENCONV
Geneva, IL [*Radio station call letters*] ..... WFXW
Geneva, NY [*Radio station call letters*] ..... WECQ
Geneva, NY [*Radio station call letters*] ..... WEOS-FM
Geneva, NY [*Radio station call letters*] ..... WGVA
Geneva Radio Regulations ..... GRR
Geneve-Afrique [*A publication*] ..... GAf
Geneve-Afrique [*A publication*] ..... Geneve-Afr
Geneve Capital Group [*NASDAQ symbol*] ..... GCGI
Genex Corp. [*NASDAQ symbol*] ..... GNEX
Genge, Inc. [*American Stock Exchange symbol*] [*Delisted*] ..... GII
Gengo Kenkyu [*A publication*] ..... GK
Gengo Seikatsu [*A publication*] ..... GS
Gengogaku Ronso [*A publication*] ..... GeR
Genie Biologique et Medical [*A publication*] ..... Genie Biol Med
Genie Civil [*A publication*] ..... Genie Civ
Genie Climatique International ..... GCI
Geniki Synomospondia Ergaton Hellados [*General Confederation of Greek Labor*] ..... GSEE
Genio Populi Romani [*To the Genius of the Roman People*] [*Latin*] ..... GPR
Genisco Technology Corp. [*American Stock Exchange symbol*] ..... GES
Genital ..... GEN
Genital Vein ..... GV
Genitalia [*Medicine*] ..... GENIT
Genitive [*Case*] [*Grammar*] ..... G
Genitive [*Case*] [*Grammar*] ..... GEN
Genitive [*Case*] [*Grammar*] ..... GENIT
Genitourinary [*Medicine*] ..... GU
Genoa [*Italy*] [*Seismograph station code, US Geological Survey*] [*Closed*] ..... GEN
Genoa [*Italy*] [*Airport symbol*] ..... GOA
Genoa City Public Library, Genoa City, WI [*Library symbol*] ..... WGc
Genova, Inc. [*NASDAQ symbol*] ..... GNVA
Genovese Drug Stores, Inc. [*American Stock Exchange symbol*] ..... GDX
GenRad, Inc. [*NYSE symbol*] ..... GEN
Genstar Corp. [*NYSE symbol*] ..... GST
Gentamicin [*Antibacterial compound*] [*Generic form*] ..... GE
Gentes Herbarum [*A publication*] ..... Gentes Herb
Gentex Corp. [*NASDAQ symbol*] ..... GNTX
Gentian Violet [*Also, MRC*] [*A dye*] ..... GV
Gentil Membre [*Guest of Club Mediterranee, a vacation cooperative*] ..... GM
Gentil Organisateur [*Employee of Club Mediterranee, a vacation cooperative*] ..... GO
Gentile Air Force Station [*Ohio*] ..... GAFS
Gentisic Acid [*Analgesic drug*] ..... GA
Gentleman ..... GENT
Gentleman Cadet [*British*] ..... GC
Gentleman Friend ..... GF
Gentleman Rider [*Horsemanship*] ..... GR
Gentleman's Magazine [*A publication*] ..... Gent M
Gentleman's Magazine [*A publication*] ..... GM
Gentleman's Magazine, New Series [*A publication*] ..... Gent M ns
Gentlemen's Quarterly [*A publication*] ..... GQ
Gentsche Bijdragen tot de Kunstgeschiedenis [*A publication*] ..... GBKG
Genuine Parts Company [*NYSE symbol*] ..... GPC
Genus ..... GEN
Genus Novum [*New Genus*] [*Biology*] ..... gen nov
GEO International [*NYSE symbol*] ..... GX
Geo Journal [*A publication*] ..... Geo J
Geoanomaly Interactive Data Analysis System ..... GIDAS
Geoballistic Input Unit ..... GBIU
Geoballistic Input Unit ..... GIU
Geobotanisches Institut Rubel Veroeffentlichungen [*A publication*] ..... Geobot Inst Rubel Veroeff
Geocentric Dust Cloud ..... GDC
Geocentric Pendulum Control ..... GPC
Geocentric Solar Ecliptic [*System*] [*NASA*] ..... GSE
Geocentric Solar Magnetospheric [*System*] [*NASA*] ..... GSM
Geochemical ..... GEOCHEM
Geochemical Journal [*A publication*] ..... Geochem J
Geochemical Journal (Geochemical Society of Japan) [*A publication*] ..... Geochem J (Geochem Soc Jap)

Geochemical Journal (Nagoya) [*A publication*] .... Geochem J (Nagoya)
Geochemical Journal (Tokyo) [*A publication*] .... Geochem J (Tokyo)
Geochemical News [*A publication*] .... Geochem News
Geochemical Ocean Sections Study [*Submarine ocean exploration by US for International Decade of Ocean Exploration*] .... GEOSECS
Geochemical Society .... GS
Geochemistry International [*A publication*] .... Geochem Int
Geochimica et Cosmochimica Acta [*A publication*] .... Geoch Cos A
Geochimica et Cosmochimica Acta [*A publication*] .... Geochim Cosmochim Acta
Geochimica et Cosmochimica Acta. Supplement [*A publication*] .... Geochim Cosmochim Acta Suppl
Geodaetisk Institut. Meddelelse [*A publication*] .... Geodaet Inst Medd
Geodaetisk Institut. Meddelelse [*A publication*] .... Geod Inst Medd
Geodaetisk Institut. Skrifter [*A publication*] .... Geod Inst Skr
Geodesic Isotensoid .... GI
Geodesy, Intelligence, and Mapping Research and Development Agency [*Army*] .... GIMRADA
Geodesy, Mapping, and Photogrammetry [*A publication*] .... Geodes Mapp Photogramm
Geodesy, Mapping, and Photogrammetry [*A publication*] .... Geod Mapp Photogramm
Geodetic .... GEOD
Geodetic Communications and Electronics Squadron [*Air Force*] .... GCESq
Geodetic Data Center [*Environmental Science Services Administration*] .... GDC
Geodetic Data Reduction .... GDR
Geodetic Data Site .... GDS
Geodetic Distance Measurement .... GDM
Geodetic Earth-Orbiting Satellite .... GEOS
Geodetic Engineer .... Geod E
Geodetic Inertial Survey and Horizontal Alignment .... GEISHA
Geodetic LASER Survey System .... GLASS
Geodetic Operations Control Center [*NASA*] .... GOCC
Geodetic Optical System .... GOS
Geodetic Receiver .... GEOCEIVER
Geodetic Satellite in Polar Geosynchronous Orbit [*NASA*] .... GEOPAUSE
Geodetic Satellite Program .... GSP
Geodetic Spacecraft .... GSC
Geodetic Survey Squadron [*Air Force*] .... GSSq
Geodeticky a Kartograficky Obzor [*A publication*] .... Geod Kartogr Obzor
Geodezia es Kartografia (Budapest) [*A publication*] .... Geod Kartogr (Budap)
Geodeziya i Kartografiya [*A publication*] .... Geod Kartogr
Geodome Resources [*NASDAQ symbol*] .... GOEDF
Geodyne Resources [*NASDAQ symbol*] .... GEOD
Geoexploration [*A publication*] .... Geoexplor
Geoexploration Monographs [*A publication*] .... Geoexplor Monogr
Geofisica International [*A publication*] .... Geofis Int
Geofisica e Meteorologia (Genoa) [*A publication*] .... Geofis Meteorol (Genoa)
Geofizicheskaya Apparatura [*A publication*] .... Geofiz Appar
Geofizikai Kozlemenyek [*A publication*] .... Geofiz Kozl
Geofysikalni Sbornik [*A publication*] .... Geofys Sb
Geofysiske Publikasjoner [*A publication*] .... Geofys Publ
Geograficheskii Sbornik Penzenskogo Otdeleniya Geograficheskogo Obshchestva SSSR [*A publication*] .... Geogr Sb Penz Otd Geogr O-va SSSR
Geografisk Tidsskrift [*A publication*] .... Geog Tidsskr
Geografisk Tidsskrift [*A publication*] .... GGTI-A
Geografisk Tidsskrift [*A publication*] .... GT
Geografiska Annaler [*A publication*] .... Geog Annaler
Geografiska Annaler [*A publication*] .... Geogr Annlr
Geografiska Annaler. Series B. Human Geography [*A publication*] .... Geogr Ann B
Geografiska Annaler. Series B. Human Geography [*A publication*] .... Geogr Ann Ser B Hum Geogr
Geografiske Casopis [*A publication*] .... Geogr Cas
Geographe Canadien [*A publication*] .... Geogr Can
Geographic .... GEO
Geographic Aerospace Search RADAR .... GASSER
Geographic Applications Program [*United States Geological Survey*] .... GAP
Geographic Area Code Index [*Bureau of Census*] .... GACI
Geographic Base File [*Civil Defense*] .... GBF
Geographic Data File [*List Processing Co.*] [*Information service*] .... GDF
Geographic Data Technology, Inc. [*Information service*] .... GDT
Geographic Digest [*A publication*] [*British*] .... GD
Geographic Distribution .... GD
Geographic Distribution of Federal Funds Information System [*Comptroller General of the United States*] .... GDFF
Geographic File [*DoD*] .... GEOFILE
Geographic Information System [*Data processing*] .... GEOIS
Geographic Information Systems [*United States Geological Survey*] .... GIS
Geographic Intelligence and Topographic System .... GIANT
Geographic Names Information Service [*US Geological Survey*] .... GNIS
Geographic Point .... GP
Geographic Position Locator [*Navigation*] .... GPL
Geographic Reference System [*Civil Defense*] .... GEOREF
Geographic Sciences Laboratory [*Army*] .... GSL
Geographic Society of Chicago. Bulletin [*A publication*] .... Geog Soc Chicago B
Geographic Systems, Incorporated [*Information service*] .... GSI
Geographica Helvetica [*A publication*] .... Geogr Helv
Geographica (Lisbon) [*A publication*] .... GeoL
Geographica Medica [*A publication*] .... Geogr Med
Geographical Abstracts [*A publication*] .... GeoAb
Geographical Abstracts [*A publication*] .... Geo Abstr
Geographical Abstracts [*A publication*] .... Geogrl Abstr
Geographical Analysis [*A publication*] .... Geogr Anal
Geographical Bulletin [*A publication*] .... Geog Bul
Geographical Journal [*A publication*] .... Geog J
Geographical Journal [*A publication*] .... Geog Jnl
Geographical Journal [*A publication*] .... Geogr J
Geographical Journal [*A publication*] .... Geogrl J
Geographical Journal [*A publication*] .... GGJO-A
Geographical Journal [*A publication*] .... GJ
Geographical Location [*Military*] .... GEOLOC
Geographical Magazine [*A publication*] .... GeM
Geographical Magazine [*A publication*] .... Geog M
Geographical Magazine [*A publication*] .... Geog Mag
Geographical Magazine [*A publication*] .... GGMA-A
Geographical Magazine [*A publication*] .... GM
Geographical Magazine (London) [*A publication*] .... Geogr Mag (Lond)
Geographical Pole .... GP
Geographical Position .... GP
Geographical Review [*A publication*] .... Geog R
Geographical Review [*A publication*] .... Geog Rev
Geographical Review [*A publication*] .... Geogr R
Geographical Review [*A publication*] .... Geogr Rev
Geographical Review [*A publication*] .... GeoR
Geographical Review [*A publication*] .... GR
Geographical Review of India [*A publication*] .... Geog R Ind
Geographical Review of India [*A publication*] .... GRI
Geographical Review of India [*A publication*] .... GRIN-A
Geographical Review of Japan [*A publication*] .... Geogr Rev Jap
Geographical Review (New York) [*A publication*] .... Geogr Rev (New York)
Geographical Section General Staff [*British*] .... GSGS
Geographical Society of Philadelphia. Bulletin [*A publication*] .... Geog Soc Phila
Geographical Society of Philadelphia. Bulletin [*A publication*] .... Geog Soc Phila B
Geographical Society of Philadelphia, Philadelphia, PA [*Library symbol*] [*Obsolete*] .... PPGeo
Geographical Specialist Team [*Army*] .... GST
Geographically Referenced Data Storage and Retrieval System [*Canada*] .... GRDSR
Geographically Separated Units [*Military*] .... GSU
Geographically Undesirable [*Slang*] .... GU
Geographie et Recherche [*A publication*] .... Georgr et Rech
Geographische Gesellschaft in Hamburg. Mitteilungen [*A publication*] .... Geog Gesell Hamburg Mitt
Geographische Gesellschaft in Hamburg. Mitteilungen [*A publication*] .... Geogr Ges Hamb Mitt
Geographische Gesellschaft in Muenchen. Jahresbericht [*A publication*] .... Geog Ges Muenchen Jber
Geographische Rundschau [*A publication*] .... Geogr Rundsch
Geographische Rundschau [*A publication*] .... Geog Rund
Geographische Zeitschrift [*A publication*] .... Geogr Z
Geographische Zeitschrift [*A publication*] .... Geog Z
Geographische Zeitschrift [*A publication*] .... GZ
Geographischer Anzeiger [*A publication*] .... GA
Geographisches Jahrbuch [*A publication*] .... GJb
Geography .... GEOG
Geography [*A publication*] .... GGHY-A
Geography and Map Division Bulletin [*Special Libraries Association*] [*A publication*] .... Geog Map Div Bull
Geography Remote Sensing Unit [*University of California, Santa Barbara*] .... GRSU
Geokhimiya [*A publication*] .... Geokhim
Geokhimiya. Akademiya Nauk SSSR [*A publication*] .... Geokhim Akad Nauk SSSR
Geokinetics, Inc. [*NASDAQ symbol*] .... GEOK
Geologia Applicata e Idrogeologia [*A publication*] .... Geol Appl Idrogeol
Geologia e Metalurgia. Boletim. Escola Politecnica. Universidade de Sao Paulo [*A publication*] .... Geol Met Bol
Geologia Sudetica (Warsaw) [*A publication*] .... Geol Sudetica (Warsaw)
Geologia Tecnica [*A publication*] .... Geol Tec
Geologic Names Committee [*US Geological Survey*] .... GNC
Geologica Balcanica [*A publication*] .... Geol Balc
Geologica Balcanica. Bulgarska Akademiya ne Naukite (Sofia) [*A publication*] .... Geol Balc (Sofia)
Geologica Bavarica [*A publication*] .... Geol Bavarica
Geologica Hungarica. Series Palaeontologica [*A publication*] .... Geol Hung Ser Palaeontol
Geologica et Palaeontologica [*A publication*] .... Geol Palaeontol
Geologica Romana [*A publication*] .... Geol Rom
Geologica Romana [*A publication*] .... Geol Roman
Geological Abstracts .... GA
Geological Association of Canada. Proceedings [*A publication*] .... Geol Assoc Canada Proc
Geological Association of Canada. Special Paper [*A publication*] .... Geol Assoc Can Spec Pap

Geological Bulletin of the Punjab University [A publication] ....
    Geol Bull Punjab Univ

Geological Center. Research Series [A publication] ....
    Geol Center Research Ser

Geological Data Center [Scripps Institution of Oceanography] ....GDC

Geological Engineer...Ge Engr

Geological Engineer...Geol E

Geological Journal [A publication]..Geol J

Geological Journal of Queen Mary College [A publication]....................
    Geol J Queen Mary Coll

Geological Long-Range Inclined ASDIC.....................................GLORIA

Geological Magazine [A publication]......................................Geol Mag

Geological Magazine [A publication]..G Mag

Geological, Mining, and Metallurgical Society of India. Quarterly
  Journal [A publication]............Geol Min Metall Soc India Q J

Geological and Mining Society of American Universities. Year
  Book and Directory [A publication] ....G M Soc Am Univ Y Bk

Geological Reference File [American Geological Institute]
  [Information service] ....GeoRef

Geological Report of the Hiroshima University [A publication] ....
    Geol Rep Hiroshima Univ

Geological Reports. Department of Natural Resources (Quebec)
  [A publication]............... Geol Rep Dep Nat Resour (Queb)

Geological and Scientific Bulletin [A publication]................................G Sc B

Geological Society of America...GSA

Geological Society of America. Abstracts with Programs [A
  publication]....................Geol Soc Am Abstr Programs

Geological Society of America. Abstracts with Programs [A
  publication]............Geol Soc America Abs with Programs

Geological Society of America. Annual Meeting. Field Trip
  Guidebook [A publication] ..... Geol Soc Am Annu Meet Field Trip Guideb

Geological Society of America. Bulletin [A publication]..............Geol S Am B

Geological Society of America. Bulletin [A publication]......Geol Soc Am Bull

Geological Society of America. Bulletin [A publication].........Geol Soc Bull

Geological Society of America. Bulletin [A publication]..............G Soc Am B

Geological Society of America. Cordilleran Section. Annual
  Meeting Guidebook [A publication]......................
    Geol Soc Am Cordilleran Sect Annu Meet Guideb

Geological Society of America. Engineering Geology Case
  Histories [A publication].....................Geol Soc Amer Eng Geol Case Hist

Geological Society of America. Map and Chart Series [A
  publication]....................Geol Soc Am Map Chart Ser

Geological Society of America. Memoir [A publication].... Geol Soc Am Mem

Geological Society of America. Microform Publication [A
  publication]......................................Geol Soc Am Microform Publ

Geological Society of America. Proceedings [A publication]......................
    Geol Soc Am Proc

Geological Society of America. Proceedings [A publication] ....
    Geol Soc Proc

Geological Society of America. Southeastern Section
  Guidebook [A publication] .... Geol Soc Am Southeast Sect Guideb

Geological Society of America. Special Paper [A publication] ....
    Geol Soc Am Spec Pap

Geological Society of America. Special Paper (Regional
  Studies) [A publication] ....Geol Soc Am Spec Pap (Reg Stud)

Geological Society of America. Special Papers [A publication] ....
    Geol Soc America Spec Paper

Geological Society of Australia. Journal [A publication]......................
    Geol Soc Australia J

Geological Society of Dublin. Journal [A publication]..............G Soc Dublin J

Geological Society of Egypt. Annual Meeting. Abstracts [A
  publication].........................Geol Soc Egypt Annu Meet Abstr

Geological Society of Finland. Bulletin [A publication] ....Geol Soc Finl Bull

Geological Society of Glasgow. Transactions [A publication]......................
    G Soc Glas Tr

Geological Society of Greece. Bulletin [A publication]......................
    Geol Soc Greece Bull

Geological Society of India. Bulletin [A publication] ....Geol Soc India Bull

Geological Society of India. Journal [A publication]..............Geol Soc India J

Geological Society of India. Journal [A publication].........Geol Soc India Jour

Geological Society of Iraq. Journal [A publication] ....Geol Soc Iraq J

Geological Society of Jamaica. Journal [A publication] .... Geol Soc Jam J

Geological Society of Japan. Journal [A publication] ....Geol Soc Jap J

Geological Society of Korea. Journal [A publication] ....Geol Soc Korea J

Geological Society of London. Journal [A publication] ....Geol Soc Lond J

Geological Society of London. Memoirs [A publication]......................
    Geol Soc London Mem

Geological Society of London. Quarterly Journal [A publication]...................
    Geol Soc Lond Q J

Geological Society of Malaysia. Bulletin [A publication]......................
    Geol Soc Malays Bull

Geological Society of Malaysia. Newsletter [A publication]......................
    Geol Soc Malays Newsl

Geological Society of New Jersey. Report [A publication]......................
    Geol Soc NJ Rept

Geological Society of Norfolk. Bulletin [A publication] ....
    Geol Soc Norfolk Bull

Geological Society of the Oregon Country. News Letter [A
  publication]....................Geol Soc Oregon Country News Letter

Geological Society of Pennsylvania. Transactions [A publication] ....
    G Soc PA Tr

Geological Society of the Philippines. Journal [A publication].......................
    Geol Soc Philipp J

Geological Society of South Africa. Congress Abstracts [A
  publication]....................Geol Soc S Afr Congr Abstr

Geological Society of South Africa. Quarterly News Bulletin [A
  publication].......................Geol Soc S Afr Q News Bull

Geological Society of South Africa. Transactions and
  Proceedings [A publication]...............Geol Soc So Africa Trans

Geological Society of Tokyo. Journal [A publication]..............G Soc Tokyo J

Geological Survey [Department of the Interior]...............................GS

Geological Survey of Canada. Bulletin [A publication]...... Geol Surv Can Bull

Geological Survey of Canada. Memoir [A publication].... Geol Surv Can Mem

Geological Survey of Canada, Ottawa, ON, Canada [Library
  symbol]..CaOOG

Geological Survey of Canada. Paper [A publication].........Geol Surv Can Pap

Geological Survey of Denmark. II Series [A publication]......................
    Geol Surv Den II Ser

Geological Survey of Denmark. III Series [A publication]......................
    Geol Surv Den III Ser

Geological Survey of Denmark. Report [A publication].....Geol Surv Den Rep

Geological Survey of Denmark. Yearbook [A publication]......................
    Geol Surv Den Yearb

Geological Survey of Finland. Bulletin [A publication] ....Geol Surv Finl Bull

Geological Survey of Guyana. Bulletin [A publication]......................
    Geol Surv Guyana Bull

Geological Survey of India. News [A publication].......... Geol Surv India News

Geological Survey of Israel. Bulletin [A publication] ....Geol Surv Isr Bull

Geological Survey of Japan. Hydrogeological Maps of Japan [A
  publication].....................Geol Surv Jap Hydrogeol Maps Jap

Geological Survey of Japan. Report [A publication] .... Geol Surv Jap Rep

Geological Survey of Japan. Report [A publication] .... Geol Surv Jpn Rep

Geological Survey of Malaysia. District Memoir [A publication]......................
    Geol Surv Malays Dist Mem

Geological Survey of New South Wales. Department of Mines.
  The Mineral Industry of New South Wales [A publication]......................
    Geol Surv of NSW Miner Ind NSW

Geological Survey of New South Wales. Geological Survey
  Report [A publication] .... Geol Surv NSW Geol Surv Rep

Geological Survey, Reston [Virginia] [Seismograph station code,
  US Geological Survey]..GSR

Geological Survey of Victoria. Memoir [A publication]......................
    Geol Surv Victoria Mem

Geological Survey - Water Resources Division ....GS-WRD

Geological Survey of Western Australia. Bulletin [A publication]...................
    Geol Surv W Aust Bull

Geological Survey of Wyoming. Bulletin [A publication]......................
    Geol Surv Wyo Bull

Geological Survey of Wyoming. Preliminary Report [A
  publication]....................Geol Surv Wyo Prelim Rep

Geologicheskaya Izuchennost SSR [A publication] ....Geol Izuch SSR

Geologicheskaya Literatura SSSR. Bibliograficheskiy
  Yezhegodnik [A publication]............ Geol Lit SSSR Bibliogr Yezhegodnik

Geologicheskii Sbornik [A publication]....................................Geol Sbornik

Geologicke Prace (Bratislava) [A publication]...................Geol Pr (Bratisl)

Geologicke Prace. Zpravy [A publication]...............................Geol Prace Zpr

Geologicky Pruzkum [A publication]....................................Geol Pruzkum

Geologicky Zbornik [A publication]....................................Geol Zb

Geologicky Zbornik - Geologica Carpathica [A publication] ....
    Geol Zb Geol Carpathica

Geologicky Zbornik - Geologica Carpathica. Slovenska
  Akademia Vied [A publication] .... Geol Zb Slov Akad Vied

Geologie Alpine [A publication]..Geol Alp

Geologie en Mijnbouw [A publication]...............................Geol Mijnbouw

Geologie en Mijnbouw [A publication]...............................Geologie Mijnb

Geologinen Tutkimuslaitos. Geoteknillisia Julkaisuja [A
  publication].....................Geol Tutkimuslaitos Geotek Julk

Geologische Blaetter fuer Nordost-Bayern und Angrenzende
  Gebiete [A publication]...........Geol Bl Nordost-Bayern

Geologische Blaetter fuer Nordost-Bayern und Angrenzende
  Gebiete [A publication]...........Geol Bl Nordost-Bayern Angrenzende Geb

Geologische und Paleontologische Abhandlungen [A
  publication]..G Pal Abh

Geologische Reichs-Museum in Leiden. Sammlungen [A
  publication].....................G Reichs-Mus Leiden Samm

Geologische Rundschau [A publication]...............................Geol Rundsch

Geologische Rundschau [A publication]...............................Geol Rundschau

Geologische Rundschau [A publication]...............................G Rundschau

Geologisches Jahrbuch [A publication] ....Geol Jahrb

Geologisches Jahrbuch [A publication]....................................Geol Jb

Geologisches Jahrbuch. Beihefte [A publication]..................Geol Jahrb Beih

Geologisches Jahrbuch. Reihe D. Mineralogie, Petrographie,
  Geochemie, Lagerstaettenkunde [A publication]...... Geol Jahrb Reihe D

Geologiska Foereningen i Stockholm. Foerhandlingar [A
  publication]....................Geol Foeren Stockh Foerh

Geologiska Foereningen i Stockholm. Foerhandlingar [A
  publication]....................Geol Foren Stockh Forh

Geologiska Foereningen i Stockholm. Foerhandlingar [A
  publication]..GFF

Geologiska Foereningen i Stockholm. Foerhandlingar [A
  publication]....................G Foeren Stockholm Foerh

Geologists' Association (London) Proceedings [*A publication*]..................... G As (London) Pr
Geologists' Association (London) Proceedings [*A publication*]..................... Geol Assoc (Lond) Proc
Geologists' Association of London. Proceedings [*A publication*]..................... Geologists' Assoc London Proc
Geologiya i Geofizika [*A publication*].............Geol Geofiz
Geologiya i Geokhimiya Goryuchikh Iskopayemykh. Akademiya Nauk Ukrainskoy SSR [*A publication*]...... Geol Geokhim Goryuch Iskop Akad Nauk Ukr SSR
Geologiya i Geokhimiya Goryuchikh Kopalin. Akademiya Nauk Ukrain'skoi RSR [*A publication*]...... Geol Geokhim Goryuch Kopalin Akad Nauk Ukr RSR
Geologiya Nefti i Gaza [*A publication*]..................... Geol Nefti Gaza
Geologiya Nefti i Gaza [*A publication*]..................... Geol Nefti Gaza
Geologiya i Razvedka Gazovykh i Gazokondensatnykh Mestorozhdenii [*A publication*]...... Geol Razved Gazov Gazokondens Mestorozhd
Geologiya Rudnykh Mestorozhdenij [*A publication*]...... Geol Rudn Mestorozhd
Geology..................GEOL
Geology Club of Puerto Rico. Bulletin [*A publication*]...... Geology Club Puerto Rico Bull
Geology. Exploration and Mining in British Columbia [*A publication*]............Geol Explor Min BC
Geology and Palaeontology of Southeast Asia [*A publication*]......Geol Palaeontol Southeast Asia
Geology of Pennsylvania [*A publication*]............ G PA
Geoloski Glasnik. Posebna Izdanja [*A publication*] ..... Geol Glas Posebna Izd
Geoloski Vjesnik (Zagreb) [*A publication*]............Geol Vjesn (Zagreb)
Geolshki Anali Balkanskoga Poluostrva [*A publication*]......Geol An Balk Poluostrva
Geomagnetic Airborne Survey System............GASS
Geomagnetic Bulletin. Institute of Geological Sciences [*A publication*]......Geogmagn Bull Inst Geol Sci
Geomagnetic Data Center [*National Oceanic and Atmospheric Administration*]......GDC
Geomagnetic Electrokinetograph [*Equipment for exploring ocean depths*]......GEEK
Geomagnetic Electrokinetograph [*Equipment for exploring ocean depths*]......GEK
Geomagnetic Reversal Time Scale......GRTS
Geomagnetism......GEOMAG
Geomagnetizm i Aeronomiya [*A publication*]......Geomag Aer
Geomagnetizm i Aeronomiya [*A publication*]......Geomagn Aeron
Geomarine Technology......GMT
Geometric Dilution of Precision......GDOP
Geometric Dimensioning and Tolerancing......GD & T
Geometric Mean......GM
Geometric Mean Distance......GMD
Geometric Mean Radii......GMR
Geometric Modulation Transfer Function......GMTF
Geometric and Positional Tolerance [*Drafting symbol*]......GPT
Geometric Progression......GP
Geometrical Acoustics......GA
Geometrical Theory of Diffraction......GTD
Geometrical and True Positioning Tolerance......GTPT
Geometrodynamics......GMD
Geometry......GEOM
Geometry......GMTRY
Geometry-Optimized [*Calculations*]......GO
Geometry Technology Module [*NASA*]......GTM
Geomorphological Abstracts [*A publication*]......Geomorph Abstr
Geon Process Butadiene......GPB
Geophysica Norvegica [*A publication*]......Geophys Norv
Geophysical......GEOPHYS
Geophysical Abstracts......GEAB
Geophysical Abstracts [*A publication*]......Geophys Abstr
Geophysical Associates International......GAI
Geophysical and Astrophysical Fluid Dynamics [*A publication*]......Geophys Astrophys Fluid Dyn
Geophysical Automatic Tracker Unit......GATU
Geophysical Case Histories [*A publication*]......Geophys Case Histories
Geophysical Data Center......GDC
Geophysical Engineer......Gp E
Geophysical Engineer......Gp Engr
Geophysical Exploration Manned Mobile Submersible......GEMMS
Geophysical Fluid Dynamics [*A publication*]......Geophys Fluid Dyn
Geophysical Fluid Dynamics Laboratory [*National Oceanic and Atmospheric Administration*]......GFD
Geophysical Fluid Dynamics Laboratory [*National Oceanic and Atmospheric Administration*]......GFDL
Geophysical Institute [*University of Alaska*]......GI
Geophysical Institute, University of Alaska [*Alaska*] [*Seismograph station code, US Geological Survey*] [*Closed*]......GIA
Geophysical Journal [*A publication*]......Geophys Jour
Geophysical Journal. Royal Astronomical Society [*A publication*]......Geophys J R
Geophysical Journal. Royal Astronomical Society [*A publication*]......Geophys J R Astron Soc
Geophysical Monitoring Satellite [*DoD, NOAA*]......GMS

Geophysical Monograph [*A publication*]......Geophys Monogr
Geophysical Note (Tokyo) [*A publication*]......Geophys Note (Tokyo)
Geophysical and Polar Research Center [*University of Wisconsin*]......GPRC
Geophysical Prospecting [*A publication*]......Geophys Prospect
Geophysical Research Bulletin [*A publication*]......Geophys R B
Geophysical Research Bulletin [*A publication*]......Geophys Res Bull
Geophysical Research Letters [*A publication*]......Geophys Res Lett
Geophysical Research Letters [*A publication*]......Geophys R L
Geophysical Sciences Laboratory [*New York University*]......GSL
Geophysical Service, Incorporated......GSI
Geophysical Society of Tulsa. Proceedings [*A publication*]......Geophys Soc Tulsa Proc
Geophysical Survey System [*Naval Oceanographic Office*]......GEOSS
Geophysical Surveys [*A publication*]......Geophys Surv
Geophysics [*A publication*]......Geophys
Geophysics and Astrophysics Monographs [*A publication*]......Geophys Astrophys Monogr
Geophysics Corporation of America......GCA
Geophysics Research Board......GRB
Geophysics Research Directorate [*US*]......GRD
Geophysics and Space Data Bulletin [*A publication*] [*Air Force*]......GSDB
Geophysik und Geologie [*A publication*]......Geophys Geol
Geophysikalische Arbeiten sowie Mitteilungen aus Meteorologie und Astrophysik [*A publication*]......Geophys Arb Mitt Meteorol Astrophys
Geopotential Meter......GPM
Geoppinger Akademische Beitraege [*A publication*]......GAB
Georesources, Incorporated [*NASDAQ symbol*]......GEOI
George [*Phonetic alphabet*] [*World War II*]......G
George [*South Africa*] [*Airport symbol*]......GRJ
George A. Zeller Zone Center, Professional Library, Peoria, IL [*Library symbol*]......IPZ
George Ade Hazeldon Home, Brook, IN [*Library symbol*]......InBroA
George Air Force Base [*California*]......GAFB
George Bernard Shaw [*Irish-born playwright, 1856-1950*]......GBS
George C. Marshall Research Foundation......GCMRF
George C. Marshall Space Flight Center [*Also known as MSFC*]......GCMSC
George C. Wallace Community College, Dothan, AL [*Library symbol*]......ADoW
George Cross [*British*]......GC
George Eastman House, Rochester, NY [*Library symbol*]......NRGE
George Eliot Fellowship Review [*A publication*]......GEFR
George Emerson's Old Grandmother Rode a Pig Home Yesterday [*Mnemonic guide for spelling "geography"*]......GEOGRAPHY
George Fox College [*Oregon*]......GFC
George Fox College, Newberg, OR [*Library symbol*]......OrNGF
George H. and Laura E. Brown Library, Washington, NC [*Library symbol*]......NcWa
George Hail Free Library, Warren, RI [*Library symbol*]......RWa
George Herbert Journal [*A publication*]......GHJ
George Junior Republic, Grove City, PA [*OCLC symbol*]......PIB
George Khoury Association of Baseball Leagues......GKABL
George MacDonald Society......GMS
George Marshall Space Flight Center [*Huntsville, AL*]......GMSFC
George Mason College [*Later, George Mason University*], Fairfax, VA [*Library symbol*]......ViFGM
George Mason University [*Virginia*]......GMU
George Mason University, Fairfax, VA [*OCLC symbol*]......VGM
George Medal [*British*]......GM
George Mercer, Jr., School of Theology, Garden City, NY [*Library symbol*]......NGcG
George Outram & Co. Ltd., Glasgow, United Kingdom [*Library symbol*]......UkGO
George Peabody College for Teachers [*Later, George Peabody College for Teachers of Vanderbilt University*] [*Tennessee*]......GPCT
George Pepperdine College, Los Angeles, CA [*Library symbol*]......CLGPC
George Risk Industries Cl A [*NASDAQ symbol*]......RISKA
George Rogers Clark National Historical Park......GERO
George S. Houston Memorial Library, Dothan, AL [*Library symbol*]......ADo
George Simon Kaufman [*American playwright, 1889-1961*]......GSK
George Town [*Bahamas*] [*Airport symbol*]......GGT
George Washington Birthplace National Monument......GEWA
George Washington Carver National Monument......GWCA
George Washington Corp. [*NASDAQ symbol*]......GWSH
George Washington Law Review [*A publication*]......George Wash
George Washington Law Review [*A publication*]......Geo Wash L Rev
George Washington Memorial Parkway [*National Park Service designation*]......GEWP
George Washington University [*Washington, DC*]......GW
George Washington University [*Washington, DC*]......GWU
George Washington University. Bulletin [*A publication*]......George Washington Univ Bull
George Washington University, Carnegie Endowment for International Peace Collection, Washington, DC [*Library symbol*]......DGW-C
George Washington University, Law Library, Washington, DC [*Library symbol*]......DGW-L
George Washington University, Law Library, Washington, DC [*OCLC symbol*]......GWL
George Washington University, Medical Center, Population Information Program, Washington, DC [*Library symbol*]......DGW-PIP

George Washington University, Medical Library, Washington, DC [*Library symbol*]...DGW-M
George Washington University, Medical Library, Washington, DC [*OCLC symbol*]..GWM
George Washington University, Washington, DC [*Library symbol*] [*OCLC symbol*].......................................DGW
George Williams College [*Illinois*]...................................GWC
George Williams College, Downers Grove, IL [*OCLC symbol*].................ICF
George Williams College, Downers Grove, IL [*Library symbol*]............IDowG
Georgetown [*District of Columbia*] [*Seismograph station code, US Geological Survey*]..GEO
Georgetown [*Delaware*] [*Seismograph station code, US Geological Survey*]...GTD
Georgetown [*Australia*] [*Airport symbol*]......................GTT
Georgetown [*Guyana*] [*Airport symbol*]......................GEO
Georgetown Automatic Translator [*Data processing*]...........GAT
Georgetown Clinical Research Institute [*FAA*]...........GCRI
Georgetown College, Georgetown, KY [*Library symbol*]..........KyGeC
Georgetown College Observatory.................................GCO
Georgetown County Memorial Library, Georgetown SC [*Library symbol*]...ScGeo
Georgetown, DE [*Radio station call letters*].................WJWL
Georgetown, DE [*Radio station call letters*].................WSEA
Georgetown Dental Journal [*A publication*].........Georgetown Dent J
Georgetown District High School, Georgetown, ON, Canada [*Library symbol*]...CaOGeG
Georgetown, KY [*Radio station call letters*]................WAXU-FM
Georgetown, KY [*Radio station call letters*].................WBBE
Georgetown, KY [*Radio station call letters*].................WRVG
Georgetown Law Journal [*A publication*].......................Geo LJ
Georgetown Law Journal [*A publication*].................Georget Law
Georgetown Medical Bulletin [*A publication*]...........Georgetown Med Bull
Georgetown, NY [*Location identifier*] [*FAA*]................GGT
Georgetown, OH [*Radio station call letters*]................WURD
Georgetown Railroad Co. [*AAR code*].........................GRR
Georgetown, SC [*Location identifier*] [*FAA*]................GGE
Georgetown, SC [*Radio station call letters*].................WAZX
Georgetown, SC [*Radio station call letters*]................WGMB
Georgetown, SC [*Radio station call letters*]................WGTN
Georgetown Township Library, Jenison, MI [*Library symbol*]..........MiJen
Georgetown, TX [*Radio station call letters*]................KGTN
Georgetown, TX [*Radio station call letters*].............KGTN-FM
Georgetown University [*Washington, DC*].......................GU
Georgetown University, Kennedy Institute, Center for Bioethics, Washington, DC [*Library symbol*]....................DGU-KIE
Georgetown University, Kennedy Institute, Center for Population Research, Washington, DC [*Library symbol*]..........DGU-Pop
Georgetown University, Law Library, Washington, DC [*Library symbol*]..DGU-L
Georgetown University, Law Library, Washington, DC [*OCLC symbol*]..GUL
Georgetown University, Medical Center Library, Washington, DC [*OCLC symbol*]..................................GTU
Georgetown University, Medical, Dental, and Nursing Library, Washington, DC [*Library symbol*]................DGU-M
Georgetown University, Medical Library Processing Center, Washington, DC [*OCLC symbol*]....................MPG
Georgetown University. Monograph Series on Languages and Linguistics [*A publication*]............................GMSLL
Georgetown University. Monograph Series on Languages and Linguistics [*A publication*]............................GUMSL
Georgetown University. Papers on Languages and Linguistics [*A publication*].................................GUP
Georgetown University. Round Table on Languages and Linguistics [*A publication*]............................GURT
Georgetown University, Science Library, Washington, DC [*Library symbol*]...DGU-S
Georgetown University, Washington, DC [*Library symbol*] [*OCLC symbol*]..DGU
Georgetown University, Woodstock Theological Center, Washington, DC [*Library symbol*]....................DGU-W
Georgetown Visitation Preparatory School, Washington, DC [*Library symbol*]....................................DGVC
Georgia [*Postal code*]..GA
Georgia [*MARC country of publication code*] [*Library of Congress*]..........gau
Georgia [*MARC geographic area code*] [*Library of Congress*]..........n-us-ga
Georgia Academy of Science. Bulletin [*A publication*].........GA Acad Sci Bull
Georgia Agricultural Experiment Station. Annual Report [*A publication*]..................GA Agric Exp Stn Annu Rep
Georgia Agricultural Experiment Station. Bulletin [*A publication*]..................GA Agric Exp Stn Bull
Georgia Agricultural Experiment Station. Circular [*A publication*]..................GA Agric Exp Stn Circ
Georgia Agricultural Experiment Station. Leaflet [*A publication*]..................GA Agric Exp Stn Leafl
Georgia Agricultural Experiment Station. Mimeograph Series [*A publication*]..................GA Agric Exp Stn Mimeogr Ser
Georgia Agricultural Experiment Station. Publications [*A publication*]..................GA Ag Exp
Georgia Agricultural Experiment Station. Research Bulletin [*A publication*]..................GA Agric Exp Stn Res Bull

Georgia Agricultural Experiment Station. Research Report [*A publication*]..................GA Agric Exp Stn Res Rep
Georgia Agricultural Experiment Station. Technical Bulletin [*A publication*]..................GA Agric Exp Stn Tech Bull
Georgia Agricultural Experiment Stations. Field Crops Variety Trials [*A publication*]...........GA Agric Exp Stn Field Crops Variety Trials
Georgia Agricultural Research [*A publication*]............GA Agric Res
Georgia Agricultural Research. University of Georgia [*A publication*]..................GA Agr Res
Georgia Air Freight [*Atlanta, GA*] [*FAA designator*]...........GEA
Georgia, Ashburn, Sylvester & Camilla R. R. [*AAR code*]................GASC
Georgia Baptist Hospital, Medical Library, Atlanta, GA [*Library symbol*]..GABH
Georgia Baptist Hospital, School of Nursing, Atlanta, GA [*Library symbol*]....................................GABH-N
Georgia Bar Journal [*A publication*]..........................GA B J
Georgia Bonded Fibers [*NASDAQ symbol*]...................GBFH
Georgia College, Milledgeville, GA [*OCLC symbol*]............GGC
Georgia College, Milledgeville, GA [*Library symbol*]........GMiW
Georgia Department of Education, Atlanta, GA [*OCLC symbol*]............GSL
Georgia Department of Human Resources, Atlanta, GA [*Library symbol*]..GAHR
Georgia Division, Lockheed Aircraft Corporation.............GELAC
Georgia & Florida R. R...G & F
Georgia & Florida R. R. [*AAR code*].............................GF
Georgia Forest Research Council. Annual Report [*A publication*]..................GA For Res Counc Annu Rep
Georgia Forest Research Council. Report [*A publication*]..................GA For Res Counc Rep
Georgia Forest Research. Paper [*A publication*]...........GA For Res Pap
Georgia Geological Survey. Bulletin [*A publication*]...........GA GSB
Georgia Historical Quarterly [*A publication*]...............GA His Q
Georgia Historical Quarterly [*A publication*].............GA Hist Quart
Georgia Historical Quarterly [*A publication*]................GAHQ
Georgia Historical Quarterly [*A publication*].................GHQ
Georgia Historical Society [*A publication*]................GA His S
Georgia Historical Society. Collections [*A publication*].........GA Hist Soc Coll
Georgia Historical Society, Savannah, GA [*Library symbol*]...................GHi
Georgia Institute of Technology................................GIT
Georgia Institute of Technology, Atlanta, GA [*Library symbol*] [*OCLC symbol*]..............................GAT
Georgia Institute of Technology. Engineering Experiment Station. Bulletin [*A publication*]............GA Inst Technol Eng Exp Sta Bull
Georgia Institute of Technology. Environmental Resources Center. ERC (Report) [*A publication*]..................GA Inst Technol Environ Resour Cent ERC (Rep)
Georgia Institute of Technology Research Reactor.............GTRR
Georgia Institute of Technology. Series in Nuclear Engineering [*A publication*]..................GA Inst Technol Ser Nucl Eng
Georgia Journal of International and Comparative Law [*A publication*]..................GA J Int & Comp L
Georgia Journal of Science [*A publication*]..................GA J Sci
Georgia Law Review [*A publication*].........................GA L Rev
Georgia Librarian [*A publication*]............................GA Libn
Georgia Librarian [*A publication*]............................GA Librn
Georgia Library Information Network [*Library network*]............GLIN
Georgia Mental Health Institute, Atlanta, GA [*Library symbol*]..............GAGM
Georgia Mental Health Institute, Atlanta, GA [*OCLC symbol*]..............GMH
Georgia Military College...GMC
Georgia Military College, Milledgeville, GA [*Library symbol*]..............GMiM
Georgia Mineral Newsletter [*A publication*]...........GA Mineral Newsletter
Georgia Motor Trucking Association [*STAC*]..................GAM
[*The*] Georgia Northern Railway Co. [*AAR code*]..................GANO
Georgia Nuclear Laboratory [*AEC*].............................GNL
Georgia Nursing [*A publication*]............................GA Nurse
Georgia-Pacific Corp. [*NYSE symbol*].............................GP
Georgia-Pacific Plywood Co. [*NYSE symbol*] [*Delisted*].............GXP
Georgia Peanut Commission...................................GPC
Georgia Power Co. [*NYSE symbol*]..............................GPE
Georgia Power Co., Atlanta, GA [*Library symbol*]............GAGP
Georgia Railroad Co. [*AAR code*]..................................GA
Georgia Regional Hospital at Atlanta, Atlanta, GA [*Library symbol*]....GARH
Georgia Retardation Center, Atlanta, GA [*Library symbol*]..........GAGR
Georgia Review [*A publication*]................................GA R
Georgia Review [*A publication*]................................Geo R
Georgia Review [*A publication*]..............................Georgia R
Georgia Review [*A publication*]..................................GR
Georgia Southern College, Statesboro, GA [*OCLC symbol*]..................GPM
Georgia Southern College, Statesboro, GA [*Library symbol*]..................GStG
Georgia Southern & Florida Railway Co.......................GS & F
Georgia Southern & Florida Railway Co. [*AAR code*]..............GSF
Georgia Southwestern College, Americus, GA [*Library symbol*].........GAmG
Georgia Southwestern College, Americus, GA [*OCLC symbol*]..........GHA
Georgia State Bar Journal [*A publication*]..................GA SBJ
Georgia State College of Agriculture. Publications [*A publication*]..................GA Ag Coll
Georgia State Department of Archives and History, Atlanta, GA [*Library symbol*]..................................G-Ar
Georgia State Department of Education, Division of Public Library, Library for the Blind and Physically Handicapped, Atlanta, GA [*Library symbol*]........................GAE-BPH

Georgia State Department of Education, Division of Public
  Library Services, Atlanta, GA [Library symbol]................GAE-P
Georgia State Library, Atlanta, GA [Library symbol]..................G
Georgia State University, Atlanta, GA [Library symbol]........GASU
Georgia State University, Atlanta, GA [OCLC symbol]............GSU
Georgia Tech Language [Data processing].............................GTL
Georgia Warm Springs Foundation................................GWSF
Georgian [MARC language code] [Library of Congress].........geo
Georgian Association in USA...GAUSA
Georgian Bay Regional Library, Barrie, ON, Canada [Library
  symbol]..CaOBaG
Georgian College of Applied Arts and Technology, Barrie, ON,
  Canada [Library symbol]...................................CaOBaGC
Georgian Court College [New Jersey]................................GCC
Georgian Court College, Lakewood, NJ [Library symbol].......NjLakG
Georgian Soviet Socialist Republic [MARC geographic area
  code] [Library of Congress]....................................e-ur-gs
Georgian Soviet Socialist Republic.............................GeoSSR
Georgian Soviet Socialist Republic [MARC country of publication
  code] [Library of Congress].......................................gsr
Georgians Unwilling to Surrender [Organization founded by
  former governor, Lester Maddox]................................GUTS
Georgikon Deltion [A publication]..................Georgikon Delt
Georgina Township Public Library, Keswick, ON, Canada
  [Library symbol]..CaOKes
Georgius Rex [King George]..GR
Georgius Rex et Imperator [George, King and Emperor].......GR et I
Geos Corp. [NASDAQ symbol].....................................GEOS
GEOS [Geodetic Earth-Orbiting Satellite] Data Adjustment
  Program..GDAP
Geoscience Abstracts [A publication]..............Geoscience Abs
Geoscience Canada [A publication]....................Geosci Can
Geoscience Documentation [A publication]............Geosci Doc
Geoscience Electronics..GE
Geoscience Electronics...GEO
Geoscience Information Society......................................GIS
Geoscience Information Society. Proceedings [A publication]........
  Geoscience Inf Soc Proc
Geoscience and Man [A publication]..................Geosci Man
Geoscience Research Institute.......................................GRI
GEOSECS [Geochemical Ocean Section Study] Operations Group.......GOG
Geosource, Inc. [NYSE symbol] [Delisted]..........................GSE
Geostationary Communications Satellite [WARC]..................GCS
Geostationary Earth Orbit...GEO
Geostationary European Meteorological Satellite................GEMS
Geostationary Meteorological Satellite [Japan]..................GMS
Geostationary Operational [or Orbit] Environmental Satellite
  [National Oceanic and Atmospheric Administration].........GOES
Geostationary Satellite..GSS
Geostationary Technology Satellite................................GTS
Geosynchronous Solar Electric Propulsion Stage [NASA].....GEOSEPS
Geosynchronous Very-High-Resolution Radiometer.........GVHRR
Geotechnical Abstracts [A publication]..............................GA
Geotechnical Abstracts [A publication]..............Geotech Abstr
Geotechnique [A publication].........................Geotechniq
Geotectonics [A publication]...........................Geotecton
Geoteknisk Institut. Bulletin [A publication].......Geoteknisk Inst Bull
Geotektonika [A publication]............................Geotekton
Geotektonika, Tektonofizika, i Geodinamika [A publication]........
  Geotektonika Tektonofiz Geodinamika
Geotektonische Forschungen [A publication].........Geotekton Forsch
Geotektonische Forschungen [A publication]......Geotektonische Forsch
Geotel, Inc. [NASDAQ symbol]...................................GETE
Geothermal Energy [A publication]..................Geotherm Energy
Geothermal Energy...GTE
Geothermal Energy Update [A publication]..........................GEU
Geothermal Loop Experimental Facility [Department of Energy]........GLEF
Geothermal Resources Council.....................................GRC
Geothermal Resources Council. Special Report [A publication]........
  Geotherm Resour Counc Spec Rep
Geothermal Resources International, Inc. [American Stock
  Exchange symbol]...GEO
Geothermal Resources International, Inc. Wts [NASDAQ symbol]........
  GEOWW
Geothermics [A publication]...........................Geotherm
Geraeteausgabestelle [Equipment distributing point] [German
  military - World War II]...GAST
Gerald R. Ford Library..GRFL
Geraldton [Australia] [Airport symbol]............................GET
Geraldton [Canada] [Airport symbol]..............................YGQ
Geraldton, ON [Television station call letters]................CBLAT
Gerard Parizeau Ltee., Montreal, PQ, Canada [Library symbol]......CaQMGP
Gerber Oscillogram Amplitude Translator........................GOAT
Gerber Products Co. [NYSE symbol]...............................GEB
Gerber Scientific Instrument Co. [NYSE symbol].................GRB
Gerber Systems Technology [NASDAQ symbol]....................GSTI
Gerbil Digest [A publication]..........................Gerbil Dig
Gercke und Norden, Einleitung in die Altertumswissenschaft [A
  publication]...............................Gercke Norden
Gerecht und Volkommen [Correct and Complete] [German].........GUV

Gereformeerd Theologisch Tijdschrift [A publication]............GTT
Geriatric Care...GC
Geriatric & Medical Centers [NASDAQ symbol]...................GEMC
Geriatric Nursing [A publication]...................Geriatr Nurs
Geriatric Order of Old Dolls Who Encourage the Generation Gap
  Singlemindedly [Tongue-in-cheek teachers' organization].........
  GOOD EGGS
Geriatric Research, Education, and Clinical Center [Veterans
  Administration]...GRECC
Geriatrics...GER
Geriatrics [A publication].......................................GERIA
Geriatrics...GERIAT
Gerichtsverfassungsgesetz [Judicial Organization Law] [Germany].......GVG
Gerkang Oktober [See also GESTAPU] [Plot against the
  government of Indonesia which began on September 30, 1965
  and continued into October]................................GESTOK
Gerkang, September, Tigapuluh [See also GESTOK] [Plot
  against the government of Indonesia beginning on September
  30, 1965]...GESTAPU
Gerlands Beitraege zur Geophysik [A publication]................
  Gerlands Beitr Geophys
Germ Warfare..GW
German [or Germanic]...G
German [MARC language code] [Library of Congress].............ger
German Air Defense Ground Environment.......................GEADGE
German Air Force [German Luftwaffe]...............................GAF
German Air Force Southern Command...........................GAFSC
German-American Football Association [Later, CSL]...............GAFA
German-American Studies [A publication]..........................GAS
German American Trade News [A publication]........German TN
German Army..GA
German Army..GAR
German Books in Print..GBiP
German Canadian Review [A publication]...........................GCR
German Cargo Services [ICAO designator]...........................GE
German Chemical Engineering [A publication].......Ger Chem Eng
German Colonies Collectors Group................................GCCG
German Convention Bureau...GCB
German Democratic Republic [East Germany] [Two-letter
  standard code]...DD
German Democratic Republic [East Germany]......................GDR
German Economic Review [A publication]..........................GER
German Economic Review [A publication]...............Ger Econ Re
German Economic Review [A publication]............German Econ R
German External Property Control Commission [Minden] [Allied
  German Occupation Forces].....................................GEPC
German Federal Republic [West Germany]...........................GFR
German Foreign Office [British] [World War II]....................GFO
German International [A publication].................German Int
German Life and Letters [A publication]................Ger L & L
German Life and Letters [A publication]..................GL & L
German Life and Letters [A publication].........................GLL
German Life and Letters. New Series [A publication]............GLLNS
German Medical Monthly [A publication]............Ger Med Mon
German Medical Monthly [A publication]........................GRMMA
German Medicine [A publication].......................Ger Med
German, Middle High [MARC language code] [Library of Congress].......gmh
German Military Documents Section [of AGO, Army] [World War
  II]..GMDS
German Mine Supplies Organization [Allied German Occupation
  Forces]...GMSO
German Minesweeping Administration [Allied German
  Occupation Forces]...GMSA
German Minimum Economy [Allied German Occupation Forces].......GME
German Ministry of Defense....................................GERMDF
German Naval Forces, North Sea Subarea..................GERNORSEA
German Navy...GNY
German, Old High [MARC language code] [Library of Congress].....goh
German Order of Harugari...GOH
German Quarterly [A publication].....................German Q
German Quarterly [A publication].........................Ger Q
German Quarterly [A publication]..................................GQ
German Reports..GR
German Research Satellite [NASA].................................GRS
German Rhine Coordination Directorate [Allied German
  Occupation Forces]...GRCD
German Shepherd Dog Club of America.........................GSDCA
German Shepherd Quarterly [A publication].........................GSQ
German Shorthaired Pointer Club of America.....................GSPCA
German Silver..GS
German Silver..GSIL
German Society of the City of New York.........................GSCNY
German Society of Pennsylvania....................................GSP
German Society of Pennsylvania, Philadelphia, PA [Library symbol].......PPG
German Student Travel Service...................................GSTS
German Studies in America [A publication].........................GSA
German Studies Review [A publication]..................Ger S R
German Telecommunications Statistics Agency...................GTSA
German Territorial Southern Command [NATO]....................GTSC
German Translation...GT
German Wirehaired Pointer Club of America.....................GWPCA

Germania [*A publication*] .... Ger
Germania Federal Savings & Loan [*NASDAQ symbol*]........................ GMFD
Germanic [*MARC language code*] [*Library of Congress*] .... gem
Germanic [*Language, etc.*] .... GMC
Germanic Notes [*A publication*] .... GN
Germanic Review [*A publication*] .... Germ R
Germanic Review [*A publication*] .... Ger Rev
Germanic Review [*A publication*] .... GR
Germanica Wratislaviensia [*A publication*] .... GeW
Germanica Wratislaviensia [*A publication*] .... GW
Germanisch-Romanische Monatsschrift [*A publication*] ....
　　　　　　　　　　　　　　　　　　　　　　　　　Germ-Rom Monat
Germanisch-Romanische Monatsschrift [*A publication*] .... GRM
Germanisch-Romanische Monatsschrift [*A publication*] .... G-R Mon
Germanisch-Romanische Monatsschrift [*A publication*] .... GRMS
Germanische Studien [*A publication*] .... GSt
Germanistic Society of America .... GSA
Germanistica Pragensia [*A publication*] .... GPrag
Germanistik [*A publication*] .... Ger
Germanistische Abhandlungen [*A publication*] .... GA
Germanistische Arbeitshefte [*A publication*] .... GA
Germanistische Linguistik [*A publication*] .... GermL
Germanistische Studien [*A publication*] .... GS
Germanistische Texte und Studien [*A publication*] .... GTS
Germanium [*Chemical element*] .... Ge
Germanium-Lithium Argon Scanning System ....GLASS
Germanium Rectifier.. GR
Germanium Stack Rectifier..................................... GSR
Germano Slavica [*A publication*] .... G Slav
Germanoslavica [*A publication*] .... G
Germanoslavica [*A publication*] .... Gsl
Germans-from-Russia Heritage Society.......................GFRHS
Germantown Laboratories, Inc., Philadelphia, PA [*Library symbol*].....PPF-G
Germantown Public Library, Germantown, OH [*Library symbol*] ....OGer
Germantown, TN [*Radio station call letters*]................... WLVS
Germany [*Aircraft nationality and registration mark*] .... D
Germany [*MARC geographic area code*] [*Library of Congress*] .... e-gx---
Germany ....GE
Germany ....GER
Germany Air Force Technical Order...........................GAFTO
Germany. Bundesanstalt fuer Bodenforschung und Geologische
　　Landesaemter. Geologisches Jahrbuch. Beiheft [*A
　　publication*].....................Ger Bundesanst Bodenforsch Geol Jahrb Beih
Germany, East [*MARC geographic area code*] [*Library of
　　Congress*] .... e-ge---
Germany, East [*MARC country of publication code*] [*Library of
　　Congress*] ....ge
Germany Philatelic Society ....GPS
Germany, West [*MARC geographic area code*] [*Library of
　　Congress*] ....e-gw---
Germany, West [*MARC country of publication code*] [*Library of
　　Congress*] ....gw
Germany. Zentrales Geologisches Institut. Abhandlungen [*A
　　publication*]...............................Ger Zent Geol Inst Abh
Germany. Zentrales Geologisches Institut. Jahrbuch fuer
　　Geologie [*A publication*] .... Ger Zent Geol Inst Jahrb Geol
Germfree [*Medicine*] .... GF
Germinal Vesicle Breakdown [*Cytology*] .... GVBD
Gerona [*Spain*] [*Airport symbol*] .... GRO
Gerontologia Clinica [*A publication*] .... Gerontol Clin
Gerontologia Clinica (Basel) [*A publication*] .... Gerontol Clin (Basel)
Gerontological Nurse Practitioner ....GNP
Gerontological Society [*Later, GSoA*] .... GS
Gerontological Society of America [*Formerly, GS*] .... GSoA
Gerontologist [*A publication*] .... Gerontol
Gerontologist [*A publication*] .... GRNTA
Gerontology ....GERONTOL
Gerontology Research Center [*Department of Health and Human
　　Services*] ....GRC
Gerontology Research Center, Baltimore, MD [*OCLC symbol*] .... GRL
Gerrish-Higgins School District Public Library, Roscommon, MI
　　[*Library symbol*] .... MiRosc
Gerrish House Society, Grand Harbour, Grand Manan Island,
　　NB, Canada [*Library symbol*] ....CaNBGG
Gerund ....GER
Gesammelte Aufsaetze zur Kulturgeschichte Spaniens [*A
　　publication*] .... GAKS
Gesamtdeutscher Block/Bund der Heimatvertriebenen und
　　Entrechteten [*All-German Bloc/Union of Expellees*]...........GB/BHE
Gesamtdeutsches Institut, Bonn, Germany [*Library symbol*] ....GyBoGI
Gesamthochschulbibliothek Duisburg, Duisburg, Germany
　　[*Library symbol*] ....GyDuiH
Gesamtverzeichnis Auslaendischer Zeitschriften [*Cumulative
　　List of Foreign Periodicals*] .... GAZ
Gesamtverzeichnis Auslaendischer Zeitschriften und Serien
　　[*Cumulative List of Foreign Periodicals and Serials*] ....GAZS
Geschichte [*History*] [*German*] ....GESCH
Geschichte und Gesellschaft [*A publication*].............Gesch Ges
Geschiedkundige Bladen [*A publication*]........................ GB
Gesell Developmental Schedules [*Education*] ....GDS
Gesellschaft [*Company*] [*German*] .... GES

Gesellschaft fuer Angewandte Mathematik und Mechanik
　　[*German Association for Applied Mathematics and Mechanics*] .... GAMM
Gesellschaft fuer Arsneipflanzenforschung [*Society for
　　Medicinal Plant Research*]................................... GA
Gesellschaft zur Befoerderung der Gesammten
　　Naturwissenschaften zu Marburg. Schriften [*A publication*].....................
　　　　　　　　　　　　　　　　　　　Ges Naturw Marburg Schrift
Gesellschaft mit Beschraenkter Haftung [*Company with limited
　　liability*] [*German*] ....GmbH
Gesellschaft fuer Deutsch-Sowjetische Freundschaft.........................GDSF
Gesellschaft Deutscher Chemiker............................GDCh
Gesellschaft Deutscher Metallhuetten- und Bergleute. Schriften
　　[*A publication*] .... Ges Dtsch Metallhuetten- und Bergleute Schr
Gesellschaft fuer Erdkunde zu Berlin. Verhandlungen.
　　Zeitschrift [*A publication*] ....Ges Erdk Berlin Verh Zs
Gesellschaft fuer Erdkunde zu Leipzig. Mitteilungen [*A
　　publication*] ....Gesell Erdk Leipz Mitt
Gesellschaft fuer Forstliche Arbeitswissenschaft ....GEFFA
Gesellschaft der Geologie- und Bergbaustudenten in Wien.
　　Mitteilungen [*A publication*] .... Ges Geol Bergbaustud Wien Mitt
Gesellschaft fuer die Geschichte und Bibliographie des
　　Brauwesens [*Berlin*] Jahrbuch [*A publication*]...................
　　　　　　　　　　　　　　Ges Gesch & Bibliog Brauwes Jahrb
Gesellschaft fuer Information und Dokumentation [*Society for
　　Information and Documentation*] [*West Germany*]
　　[*Information service*] .... GID
Gesellschaft fuer Kernenergieverwertung in Schiffbau und
　　Schiffahrt [*Atomic power*] [*Germany*]....................GKSS
Gesellschaft fuer Kernforschung [*West Germany*]...............KFK
Gesellschaft fuer Kernforschung mbH, Karlsruhe, Germany
　　[*Library symbol*] ....GyKG
Gesellschaft fuer Kieler Stadtgeschichte. Mitteilungen [*A
　　publication*]......................Gesell f Kieler Stadtgesch Mitt
Gesellschaft fuer Kieler Stadtgeschichte. Mitteilungen [*A
　　publication*] ....Gesell Kieler Stadtgesch Mitt
Gesellschaft fuer Mathematik und Datenverarbeitung [*Society
　　for Mathematics and Data Processing*] [*West Germany*]
　　[*Information service*] .... GMD
Gesellschaft fuer Musikalische Auffuhrung ....GEMA
Gesellschaft Naturforschender Freunde zu Berlin.
　　Sitzungsberichte [*A publication*] .... Ges Naturf Freund Berlin Szb
Gesellschaft fuer Naturkunde in Wuerttemberg. Jahreshefte [*A
　　publication*] ....Ges Naturkd Wuerttemb Jahresh
Gesellschaft fuer Nukleare Verfahrenstechnik [*Commercial firm*].........GNV
Gesellschaft Pro Vindonissa. Jahresbericht [*A publication*]................GPVJ
Gesellschaft fuer Programmierte Instruktion .... GPI
Gesellschaft fuer Schwerionenforschung [*Nuclear laboratory*] .... GSI
Gesellschaft fuer Weltraumforschung [*Society for Space
　　Research*] [*Germany*] ....GFW
Gesetz- und Verordnungsblatt fuer das Land Hessen. Teil 1 [*A
　　publication*] ....Gesetz- Verordnungsbl Land Hessen Teil 1
Gesetzblatt fuer Baden-Wuerttemberg [*A publication*] ....
　　　　　　　　　　　　　　　　　　　Gesetzbl Baden-Wuerttemb
Gesetzblatt der Deutschen Demokratischen Republik. Teil I
　　[*German Democratic Republic*] [*A publication*].......... Gesetzbl DDR Teil I
Gesneriad Hybridizers Association ....GHA
Gesneriad Saintpaulia News [*A publication*]....................GSN
Gesneriad Society International [*Formerly, AGS*] .... GSI
Gestalt und Gedanke: Ein Jahrbuch [*A publication*] .... GuG
Gestational [*Pediatrics*] ....GEST
Gestational Age [*Medicine*].................................. GA
Gestational Trophoblastic Neoplasia [*Medicine*] ....GTN
Gestioni e Partecipazioni Industriali [*Industrial Management and
　　Participation*] [*Italian government-sponsored agency to aid
　　ailing companies*] .... GEPI
Gestorben [*Died*] [*German*]..................................GEST
Gesunde Pflanzen [*A publication*] .... Gesunde Pflanz
Gesundheits-Ingenieur [*A publication*] .... Gesundheits-Ing
Gesundheits-Ingenieur [*A publication*]................Gesund-Ing
Gesundheits-Ingenieur. Haustechnik-Bauphysik-
　　Umwelttechnik [*A publication*] ....
　　　　　　　　　　Gesund-Ing Haustech-Bauphys-Umwelttech
Gesundheitswesen und Desinfektion [*A publication*] ....
　　　　　　　　　　　　　　　　　　　　Gesundheitswes Desinfekt
Get Away Special ....GAS
Get the Lead Out [*Of GLO week, sponsored by American Oil Co.*] ....GLO
Get Off Your After-End [*Slang*] [*Bowdlerized version*].........................GOYA
Get Oil Out [*Anti-oil-drilling group in Santa Barbara, CA*].....................GOO
Get Out of My Emergency Room [*Used as a noun in reference to
　　an elderly, chronically ill patient*] .... GOMER
Get Quick Answer [*Communications*] ....GQA
Get Set Day Care Program ....GSDC
Getheilt [*Divided*] [*Music*].................................GETH
Gethsemani [*Canada*] [*Airport symbol*] .... ZGS
Getreide Mehl und Brot [*A publication*]..............Getreide Mehl Brot
Getriebe Motoren Antriebselemente [*A publication*] ....
　　　　　　　　　　　　　　　　　　　Getriebe Mot Antriebselem
Getting Along [*Psychological testing*]......................... GA
Getting the Message [*A reading program*].....................GTM
Getty Oil Co. [*NYSE symbol*]................................. GET

Getty Oil Co., Exploration and Production Research Library, Houston, TX [Library symbol]............TxHTide(Res)
Getty Oil Co., Houston, TX [Library symbol]............TxHTide
Getty Oil Co., Los Angeles, CA [Library symbol]............CLGO
Gettysburg Battlefield Preservation Association [Defunct]............GBPA
Gettysburg College, Gettysburg, PA [OCLC symbol]............GDC
Gettysburg College, Gettysburg, PA [Library symbol]............PGC
Gettysburg National Military Park............GETT
Gettysburg, PA [Radio station call letters]............WGET
Gettysburg, PA [Radio station call letters]............WGET-FM
Gettysburg, PA [Radio station call letters]............WZBT
Gettysburg Railroad Co. [AAR code]............GETY
Geuzenpenning Munt- en Penningkundig Nieuws [A publication]............GP
GeV Electron Microtron [Atomic accelerator] [Proposed]............GEM
Gevic Arithmetic Simulation Program............GASP
Gevic Logic Operation Program............GLOP
Gewehrgranate [Rifle grenade] [German military - World War II]............GG
Gewerblicher Rechtsschutz und Urheberrecht [A publication]............
............Gewerbl Rechtsschutz Urheberrecht
Gewerkschaft Erdoel-Raffinerie Emsland [West Germany]............GERE
Gewerkschaftliche Monatshefte [A publication]............Gewerkschaftl Mh
Gewerkschaftliche Monatshefte [A publication]............Gewerksch Monatsh
Gewoya [Papua New Guinea] [Airport symbol]............GEW
Gey's Balanced Salt Solution [Medium] [Cell culture]............GBSS
Gezira Research Station and Substations. Annual Report [A publication]............Gezira Res Stn Substn Annu Rep
GF Corp. [Formerly, GF Business Equipment, Inc.] [NYSE symbol]............GFB
Ghadames [Libya] [Airport symbol]............LTD
Ghana [MARC geographic area code] [Library of Congress]............f-gh---
Ghana [Aircraft nationality and registration mark]............9G
Ghana [MARC country of publication code] [Library of Congress]............gh
Ghana [Three-letter standard code]............GHA
Ghana [Two-letter standard code]............GH
Ghana Airways Ltd. [ICAO designator]............GH
Ghana Animal Research Institute. Annual Report [A publication]............
............Ghana Anim Res Inst Annu Rep
Ghana Bulletin of Theology [A publication]............Ghana B Theol
Ghana Fishery Research Unit. Information Report [A publication]............
............Ghana Fish Res Unit Inf Rep
Ghana Fishery Research Unit. Marine Fishery Research Reports
[A publication]............Ghana Fish Res Unit Mar Fish Res Rep
Ghana Forestry Journal [A publication]............Ghana For J
Ghana Journal of Agricultural Science [A publication]............Ghana J Agric Sci
Ghana Journal of Science [A publication]............Ghana J Sci
Ghana Journal of Sociology [A publication]............Ghana J Sociol
Ghana Library Journal [A publication]............Ghana Libr J
Ghana Medical Journal [A publication]............Ghana Med J
Ghana News Agency............GNA
Ghana Publishing Company............GPC
Ghana Social Science Journal [A publication]............Ghana Soc S
Ghana Trades Union Congress............GTUC
Ghana Young Pioneers............GYP
Ghanaian Air Force............GhAF
Ghanian Cocoa Butter............GCB
Ghanian Nurse [A publication]............Ghana Nurse
Ghanzhou [China] [Airport symbol]............KOW
Ghardaia [Algeria] [Airport symbol]............GHA
Ghat [Libya] [Airport symbol]............GHT
Ghetto Arts Program [Later, Urban Arts Corps]............GAP
Ghetto Job Information [US Employment Service] [Department of Labor]............GJI
Ghost............G
Ghost Research Society............GRS
GI Civil Liberties Defense Committee............GICLDC
GI Export Corp. [American Stock Exchange symbol]............GON
Giannini Controls Corporation............GCC
Giannini Controls Corp., Duarte, CA [Library symbol]............CDuG
Giant Air Shower............GAS
Giant Attribute Survey............GAS
Giant Cell Arteritis [Medicine]............GCA
Giant Cell Reparative Granuloma [Oncology]............GCRG
Giant Cell Tumor [Oncology]............GCT
Giant Cerebral Neuron [Brain anatomy]............GCN
Giant Chinchilla Rabbit Association............GCRA
Giant Dipole Resonance............GDR
Giant Earth Mover [Machine]............GEM
Giant Food, Inc. [American Stock Exchange symbol]............GFS
Giant-to-Giant Interneuron Synaptic Potential [Neurochemistry]............GGSP
Giant Imperial Quart [of beer]............GIQ
Giant Motor Synapse [Anatomy]............GMS
Giant Piper Explorations [NASDAQ symbol]............GPPXF
Giant Portland & Masonry Cement Co. [NYSE symbol]............GPO
Giant Pulse............GP
Giant Pulse LASER............GPL
Giant Pulse LASER System............GPLS
Giant Reusable Air Blast Simulator [Air Force]............GRABS
Giant Schnauzer Club of America............GSCA
Giant Serotonin-Containing [Neuron]............GSC
Giant "Y" Boat [Navy symbol]............APY
Giant Yellowknife Mines Ltd. [American Stock Exchange symbol]............GYK
Gibb River [Australia] [Airport symbol] [Obsolete]............GBV

Gibberellic Acid [Also, GA$_3$] [Plant growth hormone]............GA
Gibberellin A$_3$ [Also, GA] [Plant growth hormone]............GA$_3$
Gibbon Ape Leukemia Virus............GALV
Gibbs Adsorption Equation [Physical chemistry]............GAE
Gibbs Adsorption Isotherm [Physical chemistry]............GAI
Gibbs-Duhem Equation [Physical chemistry]............GDE
Gibbs Energy [Symbol] [IUPAC]............G
Gibbs Free Energy [Physical chemistry]............GFE
Gibbs Function [Preferred term is Gibbs Energy]............G
Gibbs-Helmholtz Equation [Physical chemistry]............GHE
Gibilmanna [Sicily] [Seismograph station code, US Geological Survey]............GIB
Gibraltar [MARC geographic area code] [Library of Congress]............e-gi---
Gibraltar............GBZ
Gibraltar [MARC country of publication code] [Library of Congress]............gi
Gibraltar............GIB
Gibraltar [Gibraltar] [Airport symbol]............GIB
Gibraltar [Three-letter standard code]............GIB
Gibraltar [Two-letter standard code]............GI
Gibraltar Airways Ltd.............GIBAIR
Gibraltar Airways Ltd. [ICAO designator]............GT
Gibraltar Financial Corporation of California [NYSE symbol]............GFC
Gibraltar Mediterranean Command [NATO]............GIBMED
Gibraltar Savings Association [NASDAQ symbol]............GSTX
Gibson Community Hospital, Gibson City, IL [Library symbol]............IGibH
Gibson [C. R.] Co. [NASDAQ symbol]............GIBS
Gibson, Dunn & Crutcher, Los Angeles, CA [Library symbol]............CLGDC
Gibson Greeting Cards, Inc. [NYSE symbol] [Delisted]............GIB
Gibson Greeting Cards, Inc. [NASDAQ symbol]............GIBG
Gibson-Homans Co. [NASDAQ symbol]............GIBH
Gibson Spiral Maze [Psychology]............GSM
Giddings & Lewis, Inc. [NYSE symbol] [Delisted]............GID
Gideons International............GI
Gidroaeromehanika i Teorija Uprugosti [A publication]............
............Gidroaeromeh i Teor Uprogosti
Gidrobiologicheskii Zhurnal [A publication]............Gidrobiol Zh
Gidrobiologicheskij Zhurnal. Akademiya Nauk Ukrainskoj SSR [A publication]............Gidrobiol Zh Akad Nauk Ukr SSR
Gidrokhimicheskiye Materialy [A publication]............Gidrokhim Mater
Gidroliznaja i Lesokhimiceskaja Promyshlennost [A publication]............
............Gidrol Lesohim Prom
Gidroliznaya i Lesokhimicheskaya Promyshlennost [A publication]............Gidroliz Lesokhim Promysh
Gidrotekhnicheskoe Stroitel'stvo [A publication]............Gidrotekh Stroit
Gidrotekhnika i Melioratsiya [A publication]............Gidrotekh Melior
Gids [A publication]............G
Giemsa [Method] [Chromosome stain]............G
Gier-Dunkle Integrating Sphere............GDIS
Giessener Abhandlungen zur Agrar- und Wirtschaftsforschung des Europaischen Ostens [A publication]............
............Giessener Abh Agr WirtForsch Eur Ostens
Giessener Beitraege zur Deutschen Philologie [A publication]............GBDP
Giessener Beitraege zur Romanischen Philologie [A publication]............GBRP
Giessener Geologische Schriften [A publication]............Giessener Geol Schr
Giessener Schriftenreihe Tierzucht und Haustiergenetik [A publication]............Giessener Schriftenr Tierz Haustiergenet
Giesserei-Erfahrungsaustausch [A publication]............Giesserei-Erfah
Gifford-Hill & Co., Inc. [NYSE symbol]............GFH
Gift and Decorative Accessories Association of America............GDAA
Gift with Purchase............GWP
Gift Wrappings and Tyings Association............GWTA
Gifted Advocacy Information Network............GAIN
Gifted Child Quarterly [A publication]............GICQA
Gifted Child Quarterly [A publication]............Gift Child
Gifted Child Quarterly [A publication]............Gifted Child Q
Gifted Child Society............GCS
Gifted and Talented [Education]............GT
Giftware Manufacturers' Credit Interchange............GMCI
Giftware Manufacturers' Credit Interchange............GWCI
Gifu [Japan] [Seismograph station code, US Geological Survey]............GIF
Giga [A prefix meaning multiplied by 10^9] [SI symbol]............G
Giga Electron Volt............GeV
Giga-Tronics, Inc. [NASDAQ symbol]............GIGA
Gigacycle [Measurement]............Gc
Gigacycles per Second............GCPS
Gigacycles per Second [IEEE]............Gc/s
Gigacycles per Second [AIP]............Gc/sec
Gigagram............Gg
Gigahertz............GHz
Gigahertz [Preferred form is GHz]............GZ
Gigajoule............GJ
Gigameter............gm
Gigapascal [SI unit of pressure]............GPa
Gigaton............GTO
Gigavolt............GV
Gigawatt............GW
Gigawatt Electrical............GWe
Gigawatt-Hour............GWh
Gigawatt Thermal............GWt
Gigiena i Epidemiologiia [A publication]............Gig i Epidemiol

Gigiena Naselennykh Mest Respublikanskoi Mezhvedomstvennyi Sbornik [*A publication*] ... Gig Nasel Mest Resp Mezhved Sb
Gigiena i Sanitariya [*A publication*] ... Gig Sanit
Gigiena Truda i Professional'Nye Zabolevaniya [*A publication*] ... Gig Tr Prof Zabol
Gigiena Truda Respublikanskii Mezhvedomstvennyi Sbornik [*A publication*] ... Gig Tr Resp Mezhved Sb
Giglyena i Sanitariia [*A publication*] ... GISAA
Giglyena Truda i Professional'nyye Zabolevaniia [*A publication*] ... GTPZA
Gil Vicente [*A publication*] ... GV
Gila Cliff Dwellings National Monument ... GICL
Gilbert [*A unit of magnetomotive force*] ... G
Gilbert [*A unit of magnetomotive force*] ... Gb
Gilbert [*A unit of magnetomotive force*] ... Gi
Gilbert Associates, Incorporated ... GAI
Gilbert Associates, Inc. Cl A [*NASDAQ symbol*] ... GILBA
Gilbert Associates, Inc., Reading, PA [*Library symbol*] ... PRG
Gilbert and Ellice Islands [*Tuvalu*] [*gb (Gilbert Islands) or tu (Tuvalu) used in records cataloged after October 1978*] [*MARC country of publication code*] [*Library of Congress*] ... gn
Gilbert and Ellice Islands [*Tuvalu*] [*MARC geographic area code*] [*Library of Congress*] ... pogn---
Gilbert Flexi-Van Corp. [*NYSE symbol*] [*Delisted*] ... GIL
Gilbert Hill [*Idaho*] [*Seismograph station code, US Geological Survey*] [*Closed*] ... GHI
Gilbert Islands [*gn (Gilbert and Ellice Islands) used in records cataloged before October 1978*] [*MARC country of publication code*] [*Library of Congress*] ... gb
Gilbert Islands [*Two-letter standard code*] ... GE
Gilbert Islands [*Three-letter standard code*] ... GEL
Gilbert Keith Chesterton [*British journalist and author*] ... GKC
Gilbert M. Simmons Public Library, Kenosha, WI [*Library symbol*] ... WKen
Gilbert Public Library, Gilbert, AZ [*Library symbol*] ... AzGi
Gilbert and Sullivan ... G & S
Gilbert and Sullivan Journal [*A publication*] ... G & S J
Gilbert and Sullivan Society ... GSS
Gild of Ancient Suppliers of Gas Appliances, Skills, Gins, Accessories, and Substances ... GASGASGAS
Gildeboek [*A publication*] ... Gb
Gileppe [*Belgium*] [*Seismograph station code, US Geological Survey*] ... GIP
Giles [*Australia*] [*Seismograph station code, US Geological Survey*] ... GLS
Gilgit [*Pakistan*] [*Geomagnetic observatory code*] ... GIT
Gill ... GI
Gill [*Unit of weight*] ... GL
Gill Aviation Ltd. [*ICAO designator*] ... NG
Gill, CO [*Location identifier*] [*FAA*] ... GLL
Gill-Morell [*Valve oscillator*] ... GM
Gill-Morrell Oscillator ... GMO
Gill Withdrawal Reflex ... GWR
Gillam [*Canada*] [*Airport symbol*] ... YGX
Gillam-Grant Community Center Library, Bergen, NY [*Library symbol*] ... NBerG
Gillam, MB [*Radio station call letters*] ... CFIL-FM
Gillam Municipal Library, Gillam, MB, Canada [*Library symbol*] ... CaMGi
Gillespie Public Library, Gillespie, IL [*Library symbol*] ... IGill
Gillette [*Wyoming*] [*Airport symbol*] ... GCC
Gillette Co. [*NYSE symbol*] ... GS
Gillette Co., Boston R and D Laboratory, Boston, MA [*Library symbol*] ... MBGi
Gillette Company Research Institute ... GCRI
Gillette State Hospital for Crippled Children, St. Paul, MN [*Library symbol*] ... MnSG
Gillette, WY [*Radio station call letters*] ... KGWY
Gillette, WY [*Radio station call letters*] ... KIML
Gillette, WY [*Radio station call letters*] ... KOLL-FM
Gilley Airways Corp. [*Glen Falls, NY*] [*FAA designator*] ... GIL
Gilliam Center, Denver, CO [*Library symbol*] ... CoDGC
Gillies Bay [*Canada*] [*Airport symbol*] ... YGB
Gilmer, TX [*Radio station call letters*] ... KHYM
Gilmer, TX [*Radio station call letters*] ... KNIF
Gilmore [*Alaska*] [*Also, GLN*] [*Seismograph station code, US Geological Survey*] ... GLM
Gilmore [*Alaska*] [*Also, GLM*] [*Seismograph station code, US Geological Survey*] ... GLN
Gilmore, AR [*Location identifier*] [*FAA*] ... GQE
Gilmore City Public Library, Gilmore City, IA [*Library symbol*] ... IaGc
Gilmore Creek [*Alaska*] [*Seismograph station code, US Geological Survey*] ... GIL
Gilroy, CA [*Radio station call letters*] ... KAZA
Gilroy, CA [*Radio station call letters*] ... KFAT
Gilroy Free Public Library, Gilroy, CA [*Library symbol*] ... CGi
Gilroy Hot Springs [*California*] [*Seismograph station code, US Geological Survey*] ... GHS
Gilt [*Bookbinding*] ... G
Gilt ... GT
Gilt Beveled Edges [*Bookbinding*] ... GBE
Gilt Deckled Edge [*Bookbinding*] ... GDE
Gilt-Edged Securities [*Business and trade*] ... GES
Gilt Edges [*Bookbinding*] ... GE
Gilt Marbled Edges [*Bookbinding*] ... GME
Gilt Top [*Bookbinding*] ... GT
Gilt Top Edge [*Bookbinding*] ... GTE
Gimbal ... GIMB
Gimbal ... GMBL
Gimbal Angle ... GA
Gimbal Angle Change ... GAC
Gimbal Angle Controller ... GAC
Gimbal Angle Information Failure ... GAIF
Gimbal Angle Loss ... GAL
Gimbal Angle Matching Monitor ... GAMM
Gimbal Angle Rate ... GAR
Gimbal Angle Readout ... GAR
Gimbal Angle Runaway Detector ... GARD
Gimbal Angle Sequencing Transformation Assembly ... GASTA
Gimbal Assembly ... GA
Gimbal Assembly Storage System ... GASS
Gimbal Case ... GC
Gimbal Drive Actuator [*or Assembly*] ... GDA
Gimbal Electronics ... GE
Gimbal Limit Prearming Inhibiting Signal ... GL
Gimbal Mounted Electronics ... GME
Gimbal Package ... GP
Gimbal Pickoff Loop ... GPL
Gimbal Platform ... GP
Gimbal Point ... GP
Gimbal Position Display ... GPD
Gimbal Position Indicator ... GPI
Gimbal Positioning ... GIMP
Gimbal Trim System ... GTS
Gimbaled Electrostatic-Gyro Aircraft Navigation System [*Air Force*] ... GEANS
Gimbaled Integral Nozzle ... GIN
Gimbaled Night and Day Sight ... GNADS
Gimbaled Reaction Wheel Scanner ... GRWS
Gimballess Analytic Inertial Navigation System ... GAINS
Gimballess Inertial Measuring Unit ... GIMU
Gimballess Inertial Reference System ... GIRS
Gimbel Brothers, Inc. [*NYSE symbol*] [*Delisted*] ... GI
Gin and Tonic ... G & T
Ginecologia Brasileira [*A publication*] ... Ginecol Bras
Ginecologia y Obstetricia (Lima) [*A publication*] ... Ginecol Obstet (Lima)
Ginecologia y Obstetricia de Mexico [*A publication*] ... Ginecol Obstet Mex
Ginekologia Polska [*A publication*] ... Ginekol Pol
Ginekologia Polska. Suplement [*A publication*] ... Ginekol Pol Supl
Gingiva [*Dentistry*] ... GING
Gingival [*Dentistry*] ... G
Gingival-Periodontal Index [*Dentistry*] ... GPI
Gingivectomy [*Dentistry*] ... GVTY
Gingivoaxial [*Dentistry*] ... GA
Gingivobuccoaxial [*Dentistry*] ... GBA
Gingivolinguoaxial [*Dentistry*] ... GLA
Gingivoplasty [*Dentistry*] ... GPLY
Ginn & Co. [*NYSE symbol*] [*Delisted*] ... GNN
Ginn, Herbert E., South Portland ME [*STAC*] ... GHE
Gino's, Inc. [*NYSE symbol*] [*Delisted*] ... GNO
Ginseng Research Institute ... GRI
Ginzburg-Landau-Abrikosov-Gorkov [*Superconductivity theory*] ... GLAG
Giornale di Agricoltura [*A publication*] ... G Agr
Giornale di Agricoltura Domenica [*A publication*] ... G Agr Domen
Giornale della Arteriosclerosi [*A publication*] ... G Arterioscler
Giornale di Batteriologia e Immunologia [*A publication*] ... G Batteriol Immunol
Giornale di Batteriologia, Virologia, e Immunologia [*A publication*] ... G Batteriol Virol Immunol
Giornale di Batteriologia, Virologia, e Immunologia. Annali dell' Ospedale Maria Vittoria di Torino [*A publication*] ... G Batteriol Virol Immunol Ann Osp Maria Vittoria Torino
Giornale de Biochimica [*A publication*] ... G Biochim
Giornale di Bordo: Mensile di Storia, Letteratura, ed Arte [*A publication*] ... GdB
Giornale Botanico Italiano [*A publication*] ... G Bot Ital
Giornale de Clinica Medica [*A publication*] ... G Clin Med
Giornale de Clinica Medica [*A publication*] ... Gior Clin Med
Giornale di Clinica Medica (Bologna) [*A publication*] ... G Clin Med (Bologna)
Giornale Critico della Filosofia Italiana [*A publication*] ... GCFI
Giornale Critico della Filosofia Italiana [*A publication*] ... G Crit Filosof Ital
Giornale Critico della Filosofia Italiana [*A publication*] ... GFI
Giornale Dantesco [*A publication*] ... GD
Giornale degli Economisti e Annali di Economia [*A publication*] ... GE
Giornale degli Economisti e Annali di Economia [*A publication*] ... G Economisti
Giornale degli Economisti e Annali di Economia [*A publication*] ... Giorn Econom Ann Econom
Giornale di Fisica Sanitaria e Protezione Contro le Radiazioni [*A publication*] ... G Fis Sanit
Giornale di Fisica Sanitaria e Protezione Contro le Radiazioni [*A publication*] ... G Fis Sanit Protez Contro Radiaz
Giornale di Fisica Sanitaria e Protezione Contro le Radiazioni [*A publication*] ... G Fis Sanit Prot Radiaz
Giornale del Genio Civile [*A publication*] ... G Genio Civ

Giornale di Geologia (Bologna) [*A publication*] .... G Geol (Bologna)
Giornale di Gerontologia [*A publication*] .... G Gerontol
Giornale di Gerontologia [*A publication*] .... Gior Geront
Giornale di Gerontologia. Supplemento [*A publication*] ..... G Gerontol Suppl
Giornale di Igiene e Medicina Preventiva [*A publication*] .... G Ig Med Prev
Giornale Internazionale delle Scienze Mediche [*A publication*] .... Gior Internaz Sc Med
Giornale d'Italia [*A publication*] .... GdI
Giornale Italiano di Cardiologia [*A publication*] .... G Ital Cardiol
Giornale Italiano di Chemioterapia [*A publication*] .... G Ital Chemioter
Giornale Italiano di Dermatologia Minerva Dermatologica [*A publication*] .... G Ital Dermatol Minerva Dermatol
Giornale Italiano di Filologia [*A publication*] .... GIF
Giornale Italiano di Malattie Esotiche e Tropicali ed Iglene Coloniale [*A publication*] .... Gior Ital Mal Esot e Trop ed Ig Colon
Giornale Italiano delle Malattie del Torace [*A publication*] .... G Ital Mal Torace
Giornale Italiano delle Malattie del Torace. Supplemento [*A publication*] .... G Ital Mal Torace Suppl
Giornale Italiano delle Malattie Veneree e della Pelle [*A publication*] .... Gior Ital Mal Ven
Giornale Italiano di Psicologia [*A publication*] .... GIPSB
Giornale de Letterati d'Italia [*A publication*] .... Gior Lett Italia
Giornale di Malattie Infettive e Parassitarie [*A publication*] .... G Mal Infett Parassit
Giornale di Matematiche di Battaglini [*A publication*] ..... Giorn Mat Battaglini
Giornale di Medicina Practica [*A publication*] .... Gior Med Prat
Giornale di Medicina Veterinaria [*A publication*] .... Gior Med Vet
Giornale Medico del Regio Esercito e della Regia Marina [*A publication*] .... Gior Med R Esercito
Giornale di Metafisica [*A publication*] .... GdiM
Giornale di Metafisica [*A publication*] .... GM
Giornale di Metafisica [*A publication*] .... G Metaf
Giornale di Microbiologia [*A publication*] .... G Microbiol
Giornale dei Poeti [*A publication*] .... GP
Giornale dei Pollicoltori [*A publication*] .... G Pollicolt
Giornale di Psichiatria e di Neuropatologia [*A publication*] .... G Psichiatr Neuropatol
Giornale della Reale Accademia di Medicina di Torino [*A publication*] .... Gior R Accad Med Torino
Giornale della Reale Societa Italiana d'Igiene [*A publication*] .... Gior R Soc Ital Ig
Giornale di Scienze, Lettere, ed Arti per la Sicilia [*A publication*] .... Gior Sc Lett ed Arti Sicilia
Giornale della Societa Asiatica Italiana [*A publication*] .... GSAI
Giornale Storico e Letterario della Liguria [*A publication*] .... GSLL
Giornale Storico della Letteratura Italiana [*A publication*] .... Gior Storico
Giornale Storico della Letteratura Italiana [*A publication*] .... GSLI
Giornale Veneto di Scienze Mediche [*A publication*] .... G Veneto Sci Med
Girard College, Philadelphia, PA [*Library symbol*] [*Obsolete*] .... PPGi
Girard, PA [*Radio station call letters*] .... WGAE
Girard Township Library, Girard, IL [*Library symbol*] .... IGir
Girder [*Technical drawings*] .... G
Girdwood, AK [*Location identifier*] [*FAA*] .... AQY
Girl Friend [*Slang*] .... GF
Girl Friends [*An association*] .... GF
Girl Scouts of America .... GSA
Girl Scouts of the Philippines .... GSP
Girl Scouts of Racine County, Racine, WI [*Library symbol*] .... WRacGS
Girl Scouts of the USA .... GS
Girl Watchers Society - Ankle and Leg Division .... GWS-A & L
Girls Against More Skirt [*Group opposing below-the-knee fashions introduced in 1970*] .... GAMS
Girls Athletic Association [*Local school affiliates of National Girls Athletic Association*] [*Defunct*] .... GAA
Girls Clubs of America .... GCA
Girls' Friendly Society of the USA .... GFS
Girls' Friendly Society of the USA .... GFSUSA
Girls' Life Brigade [*British*] .... GLB
Girls Nation [*of the American Legion Auxiliary*] [*An association*] .... GN
Girls' Naval Training Corps [*British*] .... GNTC
Girls' Public Day School Trust [*British*] .... GPDST
Girls Rodeo Association [*Later, WPRA*] .... GRA
Girls' Service League [*Later, YCL*] .... GSL
Girls Together Outrageously [*or Organically*] [*Rock music group*] .... GTO's
Girozentrale Vienna [*Austrian bank*] .... GZ
Girth and Mirth [*An association*] .... G and M
Gisborne [*New Zealand*] [*Airport symbol*] .... GIS
Gisborne [*New Zealand*] [*Seismograph station code, US Geological Survey*] .... GNZ
Gish Biomedical, Inc. [*NASDAQ symbol*] .... GISH
Gissar [*USSR*] [*Seismograph station code, US Geological Survey*] [*Closed*] .... GIS
Gissing, Glen L., Evansville WI [*STAC*] .... GGL
Gissing Newsletter [*A publication*] .... Gissing N
GIT Industries, Inc. [*American Stock Exchange symbol*] [*Delisted*] .... GIM
Gitega [*Burundi*] [*Airport symbol*] .... GID
Gitut'yun ew Texnika [*A publication*] .... Gitut'yun Texnika
Give Better Address [*Communications*] .... GBA
Give Better Reference [*Communications*] .... GBR
Give Peace Holiday Project .... GPHP
Give Quick Answer [*Communications*] .... GQA
Given .... GIV
Givenchy [*Couturier*] .... G
Giving .... GVG
Gizan [*Saudi Arabia*] [*Airport symbol*] .... GIZ
Gizo [*Solomon Islands*] [*Seismograph station code, US Geological Survey*] .... GIZ
Gizo [*Solomon Islands*] [*Airport symbol*] .... GZO
Gjoa Haven [*Canada*] [*Airport symbol*] .... YHK
Gjogur [*Iceland*] [*Airport symbol*] .... GJR
Gjurmime Albanologjike [*A publication*] .... GAlb
Gjurmime Albanologjike [*Prishtina*] [*A publication*] .... GjA
GK Technologies, Inc. [*Formerly, General Cable Corp.*] [*NYSE symbol*] [*Delisted*] .... GK
Glacial .... GLAC
Glacial Debris Conjugate Region [*Oceanography*] .... GDCR
Glacier Bay National Monument .... GLBA
Glacier County Library, Cut Bank, MT [*Library symbol*] .... MtCG
Glacier National Park .... GLAC
Glacier Natural History Association. Special Bulletin [*A publication*] .... Glacier Nat History Assoc Special Bull
Glacier-Ocean-Atmosphere [*Global system used for modelling*] .... GOA
Gladding Corp. [*American Stock Exchange symbol*] [*Delisted*] .... GDD
Gladewater, TX [*Radio station call letters*] .... KEES
Gladstone [*Australia*] [*Airport symbol*] .... GLT
Gladstone-Dale Law .... GDL
Gladstone High School, Gladstone, OR [*Library symbol*] .... OrGlHS
Gladstone Public Library, Gladstone, OR [*Library symbol*] .... OrGl
Gladstone Stream [*New Zealand*] [*Seismograph station code, US Geological Survey*] .... GSP
Gladwin County Library, Gladwin, MI [*Library symbol*] .... MiGlad
Gladwin, MI [*Radio station call letters*] .... WGMM
Gladwin, MI [*Radio station call letters*] .... WJEB
Glamis [*California*] [*Seismograph station code, US Geological Survey*] ... GLA
Glamis Gold Ltd. [*NASDAQ symbol*] .... GLGVF
Glamorganshire [*County in Wales*] .... GLAM
Glamorganshire [*County in Wales*] .... GLAMS
Gland Anlage .... GA
Glare Shield .... GLRSHLD
Glas- und Instrumenten Technik Fachzeitschrift fuer das Laboratorium [*A publication*] .... GIT
Glas- und Instrumenten Technik Fachzeitschrift fuer das Laboratorium [*A publication*] .... GIT Fachz Lab
Glas Owners Club .... GOC
Glas Srpska Akademija Nauka [*A publication*] .... GlasSAN
Glas Srpska Akademija Nauka [*A publication*] .... GISAN
Glas Srpska Akademija Nauka i Umetnostii Odeljenje Medicinskih Nauka [*A publication*] .... Glas Srp Akad Nauk Umet Od Med Nauk
Glasers Annalen [*A publication*] .... Glasers Ann
Glasers Annalen ZEV [*Zeitschrift fuer Eisenbahnwesen und Verkehrstechnik*] [*A publication*] .... Glasers Ann ZEV
Glasgow [*Montana*] [*Airport symbol*] .... GGW
Glasgow [*Scotland*] [*Airport symbol*] .... GLA
Glasgow [*Scotland*] .... GLAS
Glasgow [*Scotland*] .... GLSGW
Glasgow Archaeological Journal [*A publication*] .... Glasgow Arch J
Glasgow Art Gallery and Museums Association. Review [*A publication*] .... Glasgow Art R
Glasgow Bibliographical Society [*A publication*] .... GBS
Glasgow City-County Library, Glasgow, MT [*Library symbol*] .... MtGl
Glasgow Coma Score [*Medicine*] .... GCS
Glasgow Dental Journal [*A publication*] .... Glasg Dent J
Glasgow, KY [*Location identifier*] [*FAA*] .... BVQ
Glasgow, KY [*Location identifier*] [*FAA*] .... GLW
Glasgow, KY [*Radio station call letters*] .... WCDS
Glasgow, KY [*Radio station call letters*] .... WGGC
Glasgow, KY [*Radio station call letters*] .... WKAY
Glasgow, KY [*Radio station call letters*] .... WOVO
Glasgow Mathematical Journal [*A publication*] .... Glas Math J
Glasgow, MT [*Radio station call letters*] .... KLAN
Glasgow, MT [*Radio station call letters*] .... KLTZ
Glasgow, MT [*Location identifier*] [*FAA*] .... MKR
Glasgow Naturalist [*A publication*] .... Glasg Nat
Glasgow [*Scotland*] **Prestwick Airport** [*Airport symbol*] .... PIK
Glasgow School of Art [*Scotland*] .... GSA
Glasgow & South-Western Railway [*Scotland*] .... G & SWR
Glashutten [*Austria*] [*Seismograph station code, US Geological Survey*] .... GHA
Glasnik [*A publication*] .... Gl
Glasnik [*A publication*] .... Glas
Glasnik Hemiskog Drustva (Beograd) [*A publication*] .... Glasn Hem Drust (Beogr)
Glasnik Khemijskog Drushiva (Beograd) [*A publication*] .... Glas Khem Drush (Beogr)
Glasnik Matematicki [*A publication*] .... Glas Mat
Glasnik Matematicki. Serija III. Drustvo Matematicara i Fizicara SR Hrvatske. [*A publication*] .... Glasnik Mat Ser III
Glasnik Pravoslavne Tzrkve u Kraljevini Srbiji [*A publication*] .... GPTKS
Glasnik za Sumske Pokuse [*A publication*] .... Glas Sumske Pokuse

Glasnik Tsentralnogo Khigiyenskog Zavoda (Beograd) [A publication] .... Glasnik Tsentral Khig Zavoda (Beograd)
Glasnik Zemaljskog Muzeja [Subseries] Etnologija [A publication] .... GZM
Glasrock Medical Services Corp. [American Stock Exchange symbol] [Delisted] .... GLA
Glass .... G
Glass .... GL
Glass Accumulation Rate [Oceanography] .... GAR
Glass Art Society .... GAS
Glass in Barrels [Freight] .... GLB
Glass Bead Rating .... GBR
Glass Bell Jar .... GBJ
Glass Block .... GLB
Glass-Bonded Mica .... GBM
Glass Bottle Blowers Association of the United States and Canada ... GBBA
Glass Bowl .... GB
Glass Capillary .... GC
Glass and Ceramics [A publication] .... Glass Ceram
Glass Cloth Tape .... GCT
Glass Container Industry Research Corporation [An association] ...... GCIRC
Glass Container Manufacturers Institute [Later, GPI] .... GCMI
Glass Crafts of America .... GCA
Glass Delay Line .... GDL
Glass Development LASER .... GDL
Glass Fabric Tape .... GFT
Glass Factor [Tissue culture] .... GF
Glass Fiber .... GF
Glass-Fiber Insulation Tubing .... GFIT
Glass-Fiber Material .... GFM
Glass-Fiber Reinforced .... GFR
Glass-Fiber-Reinforced Plastic [Also, GIFRP] .... GFRP
Glass-Fiber-Reinforced Plastic [Also, GFRP] .... GIFRP
Glass and Fiber Resin .... GFR
Glass Filter Covers .... GFC
Glass Hill [A publication] .... GIH
Glass Industry [A publication] .... Glass Ind
Glass-Insulated Wire .... GIW
Glass Insulation Material .... GIM
Glass LASER Rod .... GLR
Glass Manufacturers Federation .... GMF
Glass Oceanographic Buoy .... GOB
Glass Packaging Institute [Formerly, GCMI] .... GPI
Glass Plate Negative .... GPN
Glass, Pottery, Plastics, and Allied Workers International Union ..... GPPAW
Glass Precision Tubing .... GPT
Glass Probe Thermistor .... GPT
Glass-Reinforced Plastic .... GRP
Glass-Reinforced Plastic Joint .... GRPJ
Glass-Reinforced Structural Plastic .... GRSP
Glass Science and Technology [Elsevier Book Series] [A publication] .... GST
Glass-Silicone-Glass [Electronics] .... GSG
Glass Technology [A publication] .... Glass Tech
Glass Technology [A publication] .... Glass Technol
Glass Tempering Association .... GTA
Glass Tube .... GT
Glassboro, NJ [Radio station call letters] .... WGLS-FM
Glassboro Public Library, Glassboro, NJ [Library symbol] .... NjGb
Glassboro State College, Glassboro, NJ [OCLC symbol] .... NJG
Glassboro State College, Glassboro, NJ [Library symbol] .... NjGbS
Glasshouse Crops Research Institute. Annual Report [A publication] .... Glasshouse Crops Res Inst Annu Rep
Glassine and Greaseproof Manufacturers Association [Later, API] ... GGMA
Glassworks [A publication] .... Glass
Glassy Carbon Electrode .... GCE
Glastechnische Berichte [A publication] .... Glastech Ber
Glattfelter [P. H.] Co. [American Stock Exchange symbol] .... GLT
Glaucoma .... GLC
Glaucoma Society of the International Congress of Ophthalmology .... GSICO
Glavnaya Geofizicheskaya Observatory [Main Geophysical Observatory] [USSR] .... GGO
Glavnoe Razvedivatelnoe Upravlenie [Chief Administration for Intelligence] [Division of the General Staff of the Soviet Army] [USSR] .... GRU
Glavnoe Upravlenie Ispravitel'no-Trudovykh Lagerei [Main Administration of Corrective Labor Camps] [USSR] .... GULAG
Glavnoe Upravlenie Kontrrazvedkoi [Chief Administration for Counter-intelligence] [of the Ministry of War] [USSR] [World War II] .... GUKR
Glavny Universalny Magazin [Department store in USSR] .... GUM
Glaxo Holdings ADR [NASDAQ symbol] .... GLXOY
Glaxo Laboratories Ltd. [Great Britain] [Research code symbol] .... CG
Glaxo Laboratories Ltd. [Great Britain] [Research code symbol] .... GR
Glaxo Volume [A publication] .... Glaxo Vol
Glaze .... GL
Glaze .... GLZ
Glaze Icing [Aviation] .... GICG
Glazed .... GLZD
Glazed Facing Units [Technical drawings] .... GFU
Glazed Imitation Parchment .... GIP
Glazed Structural Facing Units [Technical drawings] .... GSFU

Glazed Structural Unit [Technical drawings] .... GSU
Glazed Structural Unit Base [Technical drawings] .... GSUB
Glazed Wall Tile [Technical drawings] .... GWT
Glazed Wall Tile Base [Technical drawings] .... GWTB
Glazed Wallboard [Technical drawings] .... GLWB
Gleaner Life Insurance Society .... GLIS
Gleanings in Bee Culture [A publication] .... Glean Bee Cult
Gleanings in Bee Culture [A publication] .... Gleanings
Gleanings in Bee Culture [A publication] .... Gleanings Bee Cult
Gleason Works [NYSE symbol] .... GLE
Gleb-Goldstein Color Sorting Test [Psychology] .... GGCST
Gledaliski List Akademije za Igralsko Umetnost [A publication] .... GLAIU
Gledaliski List Slovenskega Narodnega Gledalisca v Ljubljane [A publication] .... GLSNG-L
Gledaliski List Slovenskega Narodnega Gledalisca v Mariboru [A publication] .... GLSNG-M
Glen .... GLN
Glen Alden Corp. [NYSE symbol] [Delisted] .... GA
Glen Avon [California] [Seismograph station code, US Geological Survey] .... GAV
Glen Burnie, MD [Radio station call letters] .... WJRO
Glen Burnie, MD [Radio station call letters] .... WWIN-FM
Glen Canyon [Arizona] [Seismograph station code, US Geological Survey] .... GCA
Glen Canyon National Recreation Area .... GLCA
Glen Carbon Library, Glen Carbon, IL [Library symbol] .... IGlca
Glen County Library, Willows, CA [Library symbol] .... CWiWCL
Glen Cove [New York] [Seismograph station code, US Geological Survey] .... GCY
Glen Cove Public Library, Glen Cove, NY [Library symbol] .... NGlc
Glen Ellyn, IL [Radio station call letters] .... WDCB
Glen Ellyn, IL [Radio station call letters] .... WGHS
Glen Ellyn Public Library, Glen Ellyn, IL [Library symbol] .... IGle
Glen-Gery Corp. [American Stock Exchange symbol] [Delisted] .... GGB
Glen Innes [Australia] [Airport symbol] .... GLI
Glen Lake Community Library, Empire, MI [Library symbol] .... MiEm
Glen Oaks Community College, Centreville, MI [Library symbol] .... MiCeG
Glen Ridge Free Public Library, Glen Ridge, NJ [Library symbol] .... NjGlri
Glenbow Alberta Institute, Calgary, AB, Canada [Library symbol] ..... CaACG
Glencoe, MN [Radio station call letters] .... KQPM
Glencoe Public Library, Glencoe, IL [OCLC symbol] .... JAH
Glendale, AZ [Radio station call letters] .... KEZC
Glendale, AZ [Radio station call letters] .... KLFF
Glendale, AZ [Location identifier] [FAA] .... LUF
Glendale, CA [Radio station call letters] .... KIEV
Glendale, CA [Radio station call letters] .... KUTE
Glendale College, Glendale, CA [Library symbol] .... CGIC
Glendale College Library, Glendale, CA [OCLC symbol] .... CGN
Glendale Community College, Glendale, AZ [Library symbol] .... AzGC
Glendale Federal Savings & Loan [NASDAQ symbol] .... GLEN
Glendale Public Library, Glendale, CA [Library symbol] [OCLC symbol] .... CGI
Glendale Sanitarium and Hospital, Glendale, CA [Library symbol] .... CGIS
Glendive [Montana] [Airport symbol] .... GDV
Glendive, MT [Radio station call letters] .... KGLE
Glendive, MT [Radio station call letters] .... KIVE
Glendive, MT [Radio station call letters] .... KXGN
Glendive, MT [Television station call letters] .... KXGN-TV
Glendive Public Library, Glendive, MT [Library symbol] .... MtG
Glendora Public Library, Glendora, CA [Library symbol] .... CGle
Glengyle [Australia] [Airport symbol] .... GLG
Glenmary Research Center .... GRC
Glenmore Distilleries Co. [American Stock Exchange symbol] .... GDS
Glenmuick [New Zealand] [Seismograph station code, US Geological Survey] [Closed] .... GLE
Glenn A. Jones, MD, Memorial Library, Johnstown, CO [Library symbol] .... CoJo
Glenn Miller Birthplace Society .... GMBS
Glenn Mills School, Glenn Mills, PA [OCLC symbol] .... PIG
Glennallen, AK [Radio station call letters] .... KCAM
Glennville, GA [Radio station call letters] .... WKIG
Glennville, GA [Radio station call letters] .... WKIG-FM
Glens Falls, NY [Radio station call letters] .... WBZA
Glens Falls, NY [Radio station call letters] .... WGFR
Glens Falls, NY [Radio station call letters] .... WNIQ
Glens Falls, NY [Radio station call letters] .... WWSC
Glens Falls, NY [Radio station call letters] .... WYLR
Glenside Free Library, Glenside, PA [Library symbol] .... PGI
Glenview, IL [Location identifier] [FAA] .... NZE
Glenview, IL [Radio station call letters] .... WMWA
Glenville State College [West Virginia] .... GSC
Glenville State College, Glenville, WV [Library symbol] .... WvGIS
Glenwood, AR [Radio station call letters] .... KWXI
Glenwood, MN [Radio station call letters] .... KZZA
Glenwood Public Library District, Glenwood, IL [Library symbol] .... IGlw
Glenwood and Souris Regional Library, Souris, MB, Canada [Library symbol] .... CaMSoG
Glenwood Springs, CO [Radio station call letters] .... KCMK
Glenwood Springs, CO [Television station call letters] .... KCWS
Glenwood Springs, CO [Radio station call letters] .... KGLN
Glenwood Springs, CO [Radio station call letters] .... KMTS

Glenwood Springs Public Library, Glenwood Springs, CO [*Library symbol*] ... CoGs
Gli Archivi Italiani [*A publication*] ... GAI
Glia-Neuron Cell Adhesion Molecule [*Cytology*] ... GNCAM
Glial Fibrillary Acidic Protein [*Also, GFAP*] [*Biochemistry*] ... GFA
Glial Fibrillary Acidic Protein [*Also, GFA*] [*Biochemistry*] ... GFAP
Glidden Co. [*NYSE symbol*] [*Delisted*] ... GLN
Glidden Co. Research Library, Cleveland, OH [*Library symbol*] ... OCIG
Glide Angle [*Aviation*] ... GA
Glide Bomb [*Air Force*] ... GB
Glide Bomb [*Air Force*] ... GLOMB
Glide Bomb Unit [*Air Force*] ... GBU
Glide Path [*Aviation*] ... GP
Glide Path Indicator [*Aviation*] ... GPI
Glide Path Intercept Point [*Aviation*] ... GPIP
Glide Return to Launch Site ... GRTLS
Glide Slope [*Aviation*] ... GS
Glide Slope Antenna [*Aviation*] ... GSA
Glide Slope Indicator [*Aviation*] ... GSI
Glide Slope Receiver [*Aviation*] ... GSR
Glide Slope Reference Bar [*Aviation*] ... GSRB
Glidepath [*Slope*] **Station** [*ITU designation*] ... RLG
Glider ... G
Glider ... GLD
Glider ... GLDR
Glider ... GLI
Glider [*Special*] [*Navy symbol*] ... VLB
Glider Aircraft [*When first letter in Navy aircraft designation*] ... L
Glider Badge [*Military decoration*] ... GLIBAD
Glider Flight Control Electronics Subsystem ... GFCES
Glider Pilot Regiment [*Military unit*] [*British*] ... GPR
Gliding Horse and Pony Registry ... GHPR
Global Assessment [*Psychiatric evaluation test*] ... GA
Global Atmospheric and Aerosol Radiation Study ... GAARS
Global Atmospheric Measurements Experiment on Tropospheric Aerosols and Gases [*National Science Foundation*] ... GAMETAG
Global Atmospheric Measurements Program [*National Science Foundation*] ... GAMP
Global Atmospheric Research Program [*National Oceanic and Atmospheric Administration*] ... GARP
Global Atmospheric Sampling Program [*NASA*] ... GASP
Global Chart of the World [*Air Force*] ... GCW
Global Church Growth Bulletin [*A publication*] ... CGB
Global Circulation Model [*National Center for Atmospheric Research*] ... GCM
Global Citizens Association ... GCA
Global Communications Satellite System ... GCSS
Global Communications System [*Air Force*] ... GLOBECOM
Global Communications System [*Air Force*] ... GLOCOM
Global Community Health ... GCH
Global Data Area ... GDA
Global Data Link ... GDL
Global Data Processing System [*World Meteorological Organization*] ... GDPS
Global Digest [*A publication*] ... GD
Global Education Associates ... GEA
Global Energy Operations & Management Co. ... GEOMAN
Global Engineering Documents [*Information service*] ... GED
Global Environmental Monitoring System ... GEMS
Global Futures Network ... GFN
Global Horizontal Sounding Technique [*Meteorology*] ... GHOST
Global Impacts of Applied Microbiology [*International conferences*] ... GIAM
Global Intelligence ... GLINT
Global International Airways [*ICAO designator*] ... GX
Global Interrogation Recording and Location System ... GIRLS
Global Investigation of Pollution in the Marine Environment [*National Science Foundation*] ... GIPME
Global Land Use [*NASA*] ... GLU
Global Learning ... GL
Global Lightweight Airborne Navigation Computer Equipment ... GLANCE
Global Limb Photometric Scanning Experiment ... GLIMPSE
Global LORAN Navigation Chart [*Air Force*] ... GLC
Global Marine, Inc. [*NYSE symbol*] ... GLM
Global Meteorological Experiment [*Also known as GARP*] ... GLOMEX
Global Monitoring for Climatic Change ... GMCC
Global Natural Resources [*NASDAQ symbol*] ... GNRI
Global Navigation Chart [*Military*] ... GNC
Global Navigation and Planning Chart [*Military*] ... GNPC
Global Network for Environmental Monitoring [*Defunct*] ... GNEM
Global Observing Systems [*Weather*] ... GOS
Global Ocean Floor Analysis and Research [*Navy*] ... GOFAR
Global Ocean Surveillance System ... GLOSS
Global Perspectives in Education [*An association*] ... GPE
Global Plotting Chart [*Air Force*] ... GPC
Global Positioning Satellite ... GPS
Global Positioning System [*Formerly, NAVSTAR*] [*Air Force*] ... GPS
Global RADAR for Ocean Waves ... GLOW
Global Range Ballistic Missile [*Air Force*] ... GRBM
Global Range Missile [*Air Force*] ... GRM
Global Reference Code [*Developed by Smithsonian Institution*] ... GRC
Global Rescue Alarm Network [*Program*] [*Navy*] ... GRAN
Global Shared Resources [*Data processing*] ... GSR
Global Surveillance System [*Air Force*] ... GSS
Global Tape Recording Exchange ... GTRE
Global Telecommunication System [*World Meteorological Organization*] ... GTS
Global Tomorrow Coalition ... GTC
Global Tracking [*RADAR*] ... GLOTRAC
Global Weather Central ... GWC
Globe, AZ [*Radio station call letters*] ... KIKO-FM
Globe, AZ [*Radio station call letters*] ... KSML
Globe Ball Valve ... GBV
Globe Industries, Inc. [*American Stock Exchange symbol*] [*Delisted*] ... GLO
Globe and Mail, Toronto, ON, Canada [*Library symbol*] ... CaOTGM
Globe Microphone Evaluation ... GME
Globe Stop Valve ... GSV
Globe-Union, Inc. [*NYSE symbol*] [*Delisted*] ... GLB
Globe-Union, Inc., Milwaukee, WI [*Library symbol*] ... WMG
Globe Valve ... GLV
Globes [*Freight*] ... GLBS
Globetrotter Communications, Inc. [*NASDAQ symbol*] ... GCI
Globetrotter's Club ... GT's
Globigerina [*Quality of the bottom*] [*Nautical charts*] ... GI
Globin Insulin ... GI
Globular ... GLOB
Globular-Fibrous [*Biochemistry*] ... GF
Globulin ... G
Globulin ... GLOB
Globus Pallidus [*Brain anatomy*] ... GP
Globuscope, Incorporated [*NASDAQ symbol*] ... GPIX
Glomerular Basement Membrane [*Medicine*] ... GBM
Glomerular Basement Membrane-Reactive Antibodies [*Immunology*] ... GBM-rAb
Glomerular Filtrate [*Medicine*] ... GF
Glomerular Filtration Rate [*Nephrology*] ... GFR
Glomerular Nephritis [*Medicine*] ... GN
Glomerular Sclerosis [*Medicine*] ... GS
Glomerulo-Tubulo-Nephritis [*Medicine*] ... GITN
Glomerulo-Tubulo Nephritis [*Medicine*] ... GTN
Glomerulocystic Kidney [*Nephrology*] ... GCK
Gloom ... G
Gloria [*Glory*] [*Latin*] ... GL
Gloria Patri [*Glory to the Father*] [*Latin*] ... GP
Glos Anglii [*A publication*] ... GA
Glossa [*A publication*] ... GI
Glossaire des Patois de la Suisse Romande [*A publication*] ... GPSR
Glossari di Lingua Contemporanea [*A publication*] ... GLC
Glossaria Interpretum [*Elsevier Book Series*] [*A publication*] ... GI
Glossary ... GLOS
Glossary ... GLOSS
Glossary Function List ... GFL
Glosser Bros., Inc. [*American Stock Exchange symbol*] ... GEE
Glossopharyngeal Breathing ... GPB
GLOTRAC [*Global Tracking*] **Adjustment** ... GLAD
Glotta [*A publication*] ... GI
Gloucester [*British depot code*] ... GLO
Gloucester [*Massachusetts*] [*Seismograph station code, US Geological Survey*] ... GLO
Gloucester City Library, Gloucester City, NJ [*Library symbol*] ... NjGl
Gloucester City News, Gloucester City, NJ [*Library symbol*] ... NjGlN
Gloucester County College, Sewell, NJ [*Library symbol*] ... NjSewG
Gloucester County College, Voorhees, NJ [*OCLC symbol*] ... NGC
Gloucester County Historical Society, Woodbury, NJ [*Library symbol*] ... NjWdHi
Gloucester Engineering Company, Inc. [*American Stock Exchange symbol*] [*Delisted*] ... GEC
Gloucester Fisheries Association ... GFA
Gloucester Lyceum and Sawyer Free Public Library, Gloucester, MA [*Library symbol*] ... MGl
Gloucester, MA [*Radio station call letters*] ... WVCA
Gloucester Master Mariners Association ... GMMA
Gloucester Township [*Blackwood*] **Library, Blackwood, NJ** [*Library symbol*] ... NjBla
Gloucester, VA [*Radio station call letters*] ... WDDY
Gloucestershire [*County in England*] ... GLOS
Gloucestershire [*County in England*] ... GLOUCS
Gloucestershire Regiment [*Military unit*] [*British*] ... GR
Glover, Inc. [*American Stock Exchange symbol*] [*Delisted*] ... GLV
Gloversville, NY [*Radio station call letters*] ... WENT
Glow Discharge Lamp [*Spectrometry*] ... GDL
Glow International [*A publication*] ... Glow
Glow Plug ... GLPG
Glucagon-Like Immunoreactivity [*or Immunoreactant*] [*Endocrinology*] ... GLI
Glucinum [*Also, Gl*] [*Old name for chemical element beryllium*] ... G
Glucinum [*Also, G*] [*Old name for chemical element beryllium*] ... Gl
Gluckstadt, MS [*Radio station call letters*] ... WZXQ
Glucocorticoid [*Endocrinology*] ... GC
Glucoheptonate [*Organic chemistry*] [*USAN*] ... GLUCEPTATE
Gluconic Acid [*Biochemistry*] ... GlcA
Glucono-delta-Lactone [*Organic chemistry*] ... GDL

Glucophosphate Isomerase [An enzyme] .... GPI
(Glucopyranosyl)fluorothymine [Biochemistry] ..... GFT
Glucosamine [Biochemistry] .... GlcN
Glucose [Also, Glc, GLUC] [A sugar] ....G
Glucose [Also, G, GLUC] [A sugar] .... Glc
Glucose [Also, G, Glc] [A sugar] .... GLUC
Glucose-6-phosphate Dehydrogenase [Also, G6PD, G6PDH] [An
   enzyme] ....GPD
Glucose-6-phosphate Dehydrogenase [Also, GPD, G6PDH] [An
   enzyme] G6PD
Glucose-6-phosphate Dehydrogenase [Also, GPD, G6PD] [An
   enzyme] G6PDH
Glucose Electrolyte Solution [Medicine] .... GES
Glucose-Free Dialysate [Nephrology] .... GFD
Glucose-Free Hanks [Solution] [Cell incubation medium] ..... GFH
Glucose, Insulin, and Potassium [Solution] [Medicine] ..... GIK
Glucose Insulin Tolerance Test [Medicine] .... GITT
Glucose:Nitrogen [Ratio] .... G:N
Glucose Oxidase [Also, GOD] [An enzyme] .... GO
Glucose Oxidase [Also, GO] [An enzyme] .... GOD
Glucose Oxidase-Peroxidase [Also, PGO] [Enzyme mixture] ...... GOD-POD
Glucose Phosphate [Biochemistry] .... GP
Glucose-Ringer-Phosphate Solution .... GRPS
Glucose Tolerance [Medicine] .... GT
Glucose Tolerance Factor [Medicine] .... GTF
Glucose Tolerance Test [Medicine] .... GTT
Glucuronic Acid [Also, GlcUA] [Biochemistry] .... GA
Glucuronic Acid [Also, GA] [Biochemistry] .... GlcUA
Glucuronidase [An enzyme] .... GCR
Glue Line Heating .... GLH
Glue Weld Joint .... GWJ
Glutagen Sensitive Enteropathy [Medicine] .... GSE
Glutamate Acid Decarboxylase [An enzyme] .... GAD
[The] Glutamate Association - United States .... TGA
Glutamate Dehydrogenase [An enzyme] .... GDH
Glutamate Manufacturers Technical Committee .... GMTC
Glutamic Acid [One-letter symbol; see Glu] [An amino acid] ..... E
Glutamic Acid [See also Glu] [An amino acid] .... GA
Glutamic Acid [Also, E, GA] [An amino acid] .... Glu
Glutamic Acid [or Glutamine] [Also, Z] [An amino acid] ..... Glx
Glutamic Acid [or Glutamine] [Also, Glx] [Symbol] [An amino acid] .... Z
Glutamic Acid-Alanine-Tyrosine [Biopolymer] .... GAT$_{10}$
Glutamic-Oxaloacetic Transaminase [Also, AAT, AST] [An enzyme] ...... GOT
Glutamic-Pyruvic Transaminase [Also, ALT] [An enzyme] ..... GPT
Glutamine [or Glu(NH$_2$)] [Also, Q] [An amino acid] ..... Gln
Glutamine [or Gln] [Also, Q] [An amino acid] ..... Glu(NH$_2$)
Glutamine [One-letter symbol; see Gln] ....Q
Glutamine Synthetase [An enzyme] .... GS
Glutaraldehyde [Biochemistry] .... GA
Glutaraldehyde-Dichromate [Fixative] .... GD
Glutathione [Biochemistry] .... GSH
Glutathione [Oxidized] [Biochemistry] .... GSSG
Glutathione Reductase [An enzyme] .... GR
Glutathione S-Transferase [An enzyme] .... GST
Glutathione-SH [Reduced glutathione] [Biochemistry] ..... GSH
Gluten Intolerance Group .... GIG
Glyceraldehyde [Biochemistry] .... Gra
Glyceraldehyde Phosphate [Biochemistry] .... GAP
Glyceraldehyde-Phosphate Dehydrogenase [An enzyme] ..... GAPDH
Glyceric Acid [Biochemistry] .... Gri
Glycerin .... GLYC
Glycerine .... GLYCN
Glycerine Ball Memory .... GBM
Glycerine Producers Association .... GPA
Glycerine in Water [Medicine] .... GW
Glycerinisopropylidene Ether [Organic chemistry] ..... GIE
Glycerol [Biochemistry] .... Gro
Glycerol Monolaurate [Food-grade lipid] [Pharmacology] ..... GML
Glycerol Triacetate [Known as Triacetin] [Organic chemistry] ..... GTA
Glycerolphosphate Dehydrogenase [An enzyme] .... GPDH
Glycerone [Biochemistry] .... Grn
Glycerophosphate [Biochemistry] .... GP
Glyceryl Distearate [Organic chemistry] .... GD
Glyceryl Monooleate [Organic chemistry] .... GMO
Glyceryl Monostearate [Organic chemistry] .... GMS
Glyceryl Trinitrate [Also, NG, NTG] [Explosive, vasodilator] ..... GTN
Glyceryl Triricinoleate [Organic chemistry] .... GTRO
Glycerylphosphorylcholine [Biochemistry] .... GPC
Glycidyl Methacrylate [Organic chemistry] .... GMA
Glycinate [Organic chemistry] .... gly
Glycine [One-letter symbol; see Gly] ....G
Glycine [Also, G] [An amino acid] .... Gly
Glycine-Buffered Saline [Microbiology] .... GBS
Glycine-Rich Beta-Globulin [Immunology] .... GBG
Glycinecresol Red [An indicator] [Chemistry] .... GCR
Glycinenaphthol Violet [An indicator] [Chemistry] ..... GNV
Glycinethymol Blue [An indicator] [Chemistry] .... GTB
Glycinxylidide [Biochemistry] .... GX
Glycogen [Biochemistry] ....G
Glycogen Storage Disease [Medicine] .... GSD
Glycogen Synthase Kinase [An enzyme] .... GSK

Glycogenic Unit [Medicine] .... GU
Glycogenosis Type 1 [Medicine] GT1
Glycohemoglobin [Biochemistry, medicine] .... GHb
Glycol .... GLY
Glycol Dinitrate [Organic chemistry] .... GDN
Glycol Methacrylate [Organic chemistry] .... GMA
Glycol Trim Console .... GTC
Glycol Trim Unit .... GTU
Glycolic Aldehyde Dinitrophenylhydrazone [Organic chemistry] .... GADNPH
Glycolyl Phthalate [Organic chemistry] .... GP
Glycosaminoglycan [Biochemistry] .... GAG
Glycosaminoglycans, Glycoproteins, and Glycolipids Group
   [Informal name for organization that later became Society for
   Complex Carbohydrates] ....4G's
Glycosphingolipid [Biochemistry] .... GL
Glycotyrosine [Biochemistry] .... GT
Glycylglycine [Organic chemistry] .... GG
Glyn Valley Railway [Formerly, E & GVR] [Wales] ...... GVR
Glyoxal Bis(guanylhydrazone) [Organic chemistry] ..... GAG
Glyoxal Bis(o-hydroxyanil) [An indicator] [Chemistry] ..... GBHA
Glyoxalase [An enzyme] .... GLO
GMR Properties SBI [Formerly, Gulf Mortgage & Realty
   Investments] [NYSE symbol] [Delisted] .... GMR
GMT [Greenwich Mean Time] of Orbital Midnight .... TOM
GN & C [Guidance, Navigation, and Control] Flight Test Station ...... GNCFTS
GN & C [Guidance, Navigation, and Control] Test Station ..... GNCTS
Gnangara [Australia] [Geomagnetic observatory code] ..... GNA
GNC Energy Corporation [American Stock Exchange symbol] ..... GCE
Gnome Club .... GC
Gnome Engine [Hovercraft] .... GE
Gnomon [A publication] .... Gn
Gnomonic Tracking Chart [Air Force] .... GT
Go Ahead [or resume sending] [Communications] .... GA
Go Around .... GA
Go for Broke .... GFB
Go to Heaven [Name of missionary, "Professor Gotoh," for
   Worldwide Church of God] ....GOTOH
Go Like Hell [In model name Omni GLH, proposed for Dodge car
   designed by Carroll Shelby] .... GLH
Go Revista de Atualizacao em Ginecologia e Obstetricia [A
   publication] .... Go Rev Atualizacao Ginecol Obstet
Goa [Panjim] [India] [Seismograph station code, US Geological
   Survey] ....GOA
Goa [India] [Airport symbol] .... GOI
Goal [A position in lacrosse, soccer, hockey, etc.] .....G
GOAL [Ground Operations Aerospace Language] Automatic
   Procedure [NASA] .... GAP
Goal-Based Evaluation .... GBE
Goal-Directed Serial Alternation .... GDSA
GOAL [Ground Operations Aerospace Language] Language
   Processor .... GLP
Goal Post .... GP
GOAL [Ground Operations Aerospace Language] Processing
   Language .... GPL
GOAL [Ground Operations Aerospace Language] Program
   Control Block .... GPCB
Goal Programing .... GP
GOAL [Ground Operations Aerospace Language] Test Procedure
   Release Notice [NASA] .... GPRN
GOAL [Ground Operations Aerospace Language] Test Procedure
   Update Request .... GPUR
Goals Against [Hockey] ....A
Goals Against [Hockey] .... GA
Goals-Against Average [Hockey] .... AVG
Goals For [Hockey] ....F
Goals For [Hockey] .... GF
Goat [Veterinary medicine] ....G
Goat Anti-Rabbit [Also, GARb] [Immunology] .... GAR
Goat Anti-Rabbit [Also, GAR] [Immunology] .... GARb
Goat Antiserum to Rabbit Gamma-Globulin [Immunology] ..... GARGG
Goat Gamma-Globulin [Immunology] .... GGG
Gobel O'Malley Company [Entertainer George Gobel's firm;
   O'Malley is business manager] ....GOMALCO
Gobernador Gregores [Argentina] [Airport symbol] ..... GGS
God Bless You .... G-B-Y
God Damn .... GD
God Damned Independent [College slang for student not
   affiliated with a fraternity or sorority] .... GDI
God Only Knows [Facetious diagnosis for a puzzling medical case] ..... GOK
God Only Really Knows [Facetious diagnosis for a puzzling
   medical case] ....GORK
Goddard College, Plainfield, VT [Library symbol] ..... VtPlaG
Goddard Communications Center [NASA] .... GCC
Goddard Computing Center [NASA] .... GCC
Goddard Earth Model [NASA] .... GEM
Goddard Experiment Support System [NASA] .... GES
Goddard Experimental Package [NASA] .... GEP
Goddard Institute for Space Studies [NASA] .... GI for SS
Goddard Institute for Space Studies [NASA] .... GISS
Goddard Launch Operations [NASA] .... GLO
Goddard Management Instruction [NASA] .... GMI

Goddard Mission Control Facility [*NASA*] ... GMCF
Goddard Network Control [*NASA*] ... GNC
Goddard Network Operations Support [*NASA*] ... GNOS
Goddard Network Support Operations [*NASA*] ... GNSO
Goddard Optical Research Facility [*Goddard Space Flight Center*] [*NASA*] ... GORF
Goddard Range [*and Range Rate*] **Instrumentation Tracking System** [*NASA*] ... GRITS
Goddard Range and Range Data [*NASA*] ... GRARD
Goddard Range and Range Rate [*Tracking system*] [*NASA*] ... GRARR
Goddard Research and Engineering Management Exercise [*NASA*] ... GREMEX
Goddard Satellite Tracking [*NASA*] ... GOST
Goddard Space Flight Center [*NASA*] ... GSFC
Goddard Space Flight Center, Greenbelt, MD [*OCLC symbol*] ... NAG
Goddard Trajectory Determination System [*NASA*] ... GTDS
Gode [*Ethiopia*] [*Airport symbol*] ... GDE
Godecke AG [*Germany*] [*Research code symbol*] ... Go
Godey's Lady's Book [*A publication*] ... Godey
Godfrey Co. [*NASDAQ symbol*] ... GDFY
Godfrey, IL [*Radio station call letters*] ... WLCA
Godfrey Memorial Library, Middletown, CT [*Library symbol*] ... CtMG
Godhavn [*Greenland*] [*Geomagnetic observatory code*] ... GDH
Godhavn [*Greenland*] [*Seismograph station code, US Geological Survey*] ... GDH
Godisen Zbornik na Zemjodelsko-sumarskest. Fakultet na Univerzitetat Skopje [*A publication*] ... Godisen Zb Zemjod-sum Fak Univ Skopje
Godisen Zbornik ka Zemjodelsko-Sumarskoit. Fakultet na Univerzitetot Skoplje [*A publication*] ... God Zbor Zemjodel Sumar Fak Univ Skoplje
Godishen Zbornik Biologija Priridno-Matematichki. Fakultet na Univerzitetot Kiril i Metodij Skopje [*A publication*] ... God Zb Biol Prir-Mat Fak Univ Kiril Metodij Skopje
Godishen Zbornik na Meditsinskiot. Fakultet vo Skopje [*A publication*] ... God Zb Med Fak Skopje
Godishnik na Visshite Tekhnicheski Uchebni Zavedeniya. Prilozhna Mekhanika [*A publication*] ... God Vissh Tekh Uchebn Zaved Prilozh Mekh
Godishnik na Visshite Uchebni Zavedeniya. Prilozhna Matematika [*A publication*] ... God Vissh Uchebn Zaved Prilozh Mat
Godisnik na Ekonomski ot Fakultet (Skopje) [*A publication*] ... Godis Ekon Fak (Skopje)
Godisnik na Energoproekt [*A publication*] ... God Energoproekt
Godisnik na Sofiiskiya Universitet. Biologicheski Fakultet [*A publication*] ... God Sofii Univ Biol Fak
Godisnik na Sofijskiya Universitet. Fakultet po Slavjanski Filologii [*A publication*] ... GodSU
Godisnik na Sofijskiya Universitet. Fakultet po Zapadni Filologii [*A publication*] ... GSUFZF
Godisnik na Sofijskiya Universitet. Filologiceski Fakultet [*A publication*] ... GSU
Godisnik na Sofijskiya Universitet. Filologiceski Fakultet [*A publication*] ... GSUF
Godisnik na Sofijskiya Universitet. Istorikofilologiceski Fakultet [*A publication*] ... God
Godisnik Vissija Himikotehnologiceski Institut (Burgas) [*A publication*] ... Godisnik Viss Himikotehn Inst (Burgas)
Godisnik na Vissija Inzerno-Stroitelnija Institut [*A publication*] ... Godisnik Viss Inz-Stroitel Inst
Godisnik na Vissite Tehniceski Ucebni Zavedenija. Fizika [*A publication*] ... Godisnik Viss Tehn Ucebn Zaved Fiz
Godisnik na Vissite Tehniceski Ucebni Zavedenija. Matematika [*A publication*] ... Godisnik Viss Tehn Ucebn Zaved Mat
Godisnik na Vissite Ucebni Zavedenija. Prilozna Matematika [*A publication*] ... Godisnik Viss Ucebn Zaved Prilozna Mat
Godisnjak Bioloskog Instituta Univerziteta u Sarajevu [*A publication*] ... God Biol Inst Univ Sarajevu
Godisnjak Centra za Balkanoloska Ispitivanja [*A publication*] ... GCBI
Godisnjak Filozofskog Fakulteta u Novom Sadu [*A publication*] ... GFFNS
Godisnjak Filozofskog Fakulteta u Novom Sadu [*A publication*] ... GodFFNS
Godisnjak Naucnog Drustva Nr Bosne i Hercegovine [*A publication*] ... GNDBiH
Gods Narrows [*Canada*] [*Airport symbol*] ... YGO
God's Own Medicine [*Also, God's Medicine*] [*Morphine*] [*Slang*] ... GOM
Gods River [*Canada*] [*Airport symbol*] ... ZGI
Goebel Collectors' Club ... GCC
Goeppinger Arbeiten zur Germanistik [*A publication*] ... GAG
Goerz-Visier [*Bomb sight manufactured by Goerz Co.*] [*German military - World War II*] ... GV
Goes Over All Terrain [*Vehicle*] ... GOAT
Goeteborgs Handelstidning [*A publication*] ... GHT
Goeteborgs Hogskolas Arsskrift [*A publication*] ... GHA
Goeteborgs Kungliga Vetenskaps-och Vitterhets-Samhaelles Handlingar [*A publication*] ... GKVVH
Goeteborgs Kungliga Vetenskaps-och Vitterhets-Samhaelles Handlingar [*A publication*] ... Goeteborgs K Vetensk-o Vitterhets Samh Handl
Goeteborgs Universitets Arsskrift [*A publication*] ... GUA
Goethe-Almanach [*A publication*] ... Goethe-Al
Goethe House, German Cultural Institute, New York, NY [*Library symbol*] ... NNGoe
Goethe Institute, German Culture Institute, Atlanta, GA [*Library symbol*] ... GAGI
Goethe-Jahrbuch [*A publication*] ... Goethe-Jahrb
Goethe-Kalender [*A publication*] ... GK
Goethe Society of North America ... GSNA
Goethe, Vierteljahrsschrift der Goethe-Gesellschaft [*A publication*] ... Goe
Goettingen [*Federal Republic of Germany*] [*Geomagnetic observatory code*] ... GTT
Goettinger Arbeiten zur Geologie und Palaeontologie [*A publication*] ... Goett Arb Geol Palaeontol
Goettinger Floristische Rundbriefe [*A publication*] ... Goett Florist Rundbriefe
Goettingische Gelehrte Anzeiger [*A publication*] ... GGA
Goettingisches Journal der Naturwissenschaften [*A publication*] ... Goetting J Naturw
Gogebic Community College [*Michigan*] ... GCC
Goiania [*Brazil*] [*Airport symbol*] ... GYN
Going-Home Money ... GHM
Golay Pneumatic Cell ... GPC
Gold ... G
Gold ... GD
Gold ... GLD
Gold Beach, OR [*Location identifier*] [*FAA*] ... GOL
Gold Beach, OR [*Radio station call letters*] ... KGBR
Gold Bond [*Bond payable in gold coin*] ... GB
Gold Bondholders Protective Council ... GBPC
Gold Bulletin [*A publication*] ... Gold Bull
Gold C. Enterprises [*NASDAQ symbol*] ... GCEI
Gold Coast [*Australia*] [*Airport symbol*] ... OOL
Gold Coupling Dendrite ... GCD
Gold Field ... GF
Gold Fields of South Africa Ltd. [*NASDAQ symbol*] ... GLDFY
Gold-Filled Manufacturers Association ... GFMA
Gold Film Mercury Detector [*Spectrometry*] ... GFMD
Gold Hill [*Calfiornia*] [*Seismograph station code, US Geological Survey*] ... GHC
Gold Hill, OR [*Radio station call letters*] ... KRWQ
Gold Inlay [*Dentistry*] ... G
Gold Institute ... GI
Gold King River [*Alaska*] [*Seismograph station code, US Geological Survey*] ... GKC
Gold Life Saving Medal ... GLSM
Gold Medal ... GM
Gold Mining Association of America ... GMAA
Gold Mountain [*Washington*] [*Seismograph station code, US Geological Survey*] ... GMW
Gold Plated [*Freight*] ... GLD PLTD
Gold Prospectors Association of America ... GPAA
Gold Reserve ... GR
Gold Reserve Corp. [*NASDAQ symbol*] ... GLDR
Gold Standards ... GS
Gold Star Lapel Button [*Military decoration*] ... GSLB
Gold Star Mothers ... GSM
Gold Star Owners Club ... GSOC
Gold Star Parents for Amnesty [*Defunct*] ... GSPA
Gold Star Wives of America ... GSWA
Gold Surface Barrier ... GSB
Gold Thioglucose ... GTG
Gold Wing Road Riders Association ... GWRRA
Goldale Investments [*NASDAQ symbol*] ... GIAKF
Goldbarg-Rutenberg [*Enzyme unit*] ... G-R
Goldblatt Brothers, Inc. [*American Stock Exchange symbol*] [*Delisted*] ... GDB
Golden [*Colorado School of Mines*] [*Colorado*] [*Seismograph station code, US Geological Survey*] ... GLD
Golden [*New Mexico*] [*Seismograph station code, US Geological Survey*] ... GNM
Golden [*Bergen Park*] [*Colorado*] [*Seismograph station code, US Geological Survey*] ... GOL
Golden, BC [*Radio station call letters*] ... CKGR
Golden Book Magazine [*A publication*] ... GBM
Golden Book Magazine [*A publication*] ... Golden Bk
Golden Concord Mining [*NASDAQ symbol*] ... GCCVF
Golden Cycle Corp. [*American Stock Exchange symbol*] [*Delisted*] ... GCY
Golden Cycle Gold Corporation [*NASDAQ symbol*] ... GCGC
Golden Eagle Airlines [*Redding, CA*] [*FAA designator*] ... GEL
Golden Eagle Aviation [*Bedford, MA*] [*FAA designator*] ... SAJ
Golden Enterprises, Inc. [*NASDAQ symbol*] ... GLDC
Golden Fleece [*A publication*] ... GOF
Golden Gate Baptist Theological Seminary, Mill Valley, CA [*Library symbol*] ... CMIG
Golden Gate College [*California*] ... GGC
Golden Gate College, San Francisco, CA [*Library symbol*] ... CSfGG
Golden Gate Law Review [*A publication*] ... Golden Gate L Rev
Golden Gate National Recreation Area Advisory Commission [*Department of the Interior*] ... GGNRACAC
Golden Gate University, School of Law, San Francisco, CA [*Library symbol*] ... CSfGG-L

Golden Gate Youth Camp, Residents' Library, Golden, CO [*Library symbol*] CoGG
Golden Gloves Association of America GG
Golden Gloves Association of America GGAA
Golden Goose [*A publication*] GG
Golden Hour Tango GHT
Golden Meadow, LA [*Radio station call letters*] KLEB
Golden Meadow, LA [*Radio station call letters*] KZZQ
Golden Nugget, Inc. [*NYSE symbol*] GNG
Golden Number [*Number used to fix the date of Easter*] GN
Golden Oil Company [*NASDAQ symbol*] GOCO
Golden Retriever Club of America GRCA
Golden Ring Council of Senior Citizens Clubs GRCSCC
Golden Rule Foundation GRF
Golden Spike National Historic Site GOSP
Golden State Airlines, Inc. [*Burbank, CA*] [*FAA designator*] GSC
Golden State Mutual Life Insurance Co., Los Angeles, CA [*Library symbol*] CLGS
Golden Triangle Royalty & Oil [*NASDAQ symbol*] GTRO
Golden Valley Health Center, Golden Valley, MN [*Library symbol*] MnGvH
Golden Valley Lutheran College, Minneapolis, MN [*Library symbol*] MnMG
Golden Valley, MN [*Radio station call letters*] KGLD
Golden Valley, MN [*Radio station call letters*] KQRS-FM
Golden Valley, MN [*Radio station call letters*] KUXL
Golden West Airlines [*Los Angeles, CA*] [*FAA designator*] GWA
Golden West College Library, Huntington Beach, CA [*OCLC symbol*] CGW
Golden West Financial Corp. [*NYSE symbol*] GDW
Golden West Mobile Homes, Inc. [*American Stock Exchange symbol*] GWH
Golden West Subscription Television [*Cable TV programing service*] GWSTV
Goldendale, WA [*Radio station call letters*] KLCK
Goldene Keyt [*A publication*] Gold K
Golder, Brawner, & Associates Ltd., Vancouver, BC, Canada [*Library symbol*] CaBVaGB
Goldfield Corp. [*American Stock Exchange symbol*] GV
Goldfield Corp. Uts [*NASDAQ symbol*] GLDVU
Goldfish Society of America GFSA
Goldfish Society of America GSA
Goldflow GF
Goldman-Fristoe Test of Articulation [*Education*] GFTA
Goldman-Fristoe-Woodcock Test of Auditory Discrimination [*Education*] G-F-W
Goldome National Corp. Pfd [*American Stock Exchange symbol*] GDMR
Goldreich-Julian [*PULSAR theory*] GJ
Goldsboro, NC [*Radio station call letters*] WEQR
Goldsboro, NC [*Radio station call letters*] WFMC
Goldsboro, NC [*Radio station call letters*] WGBR
Goldsboro, NC [*Radio station call letters*] WOKN
Goldsboro, NC [*Radio station call letters*] WSSG
Goldschmidt Informiert [*A publication*] Goldschmidt Inf
Goldsil Mining & Milling [*NASDAQ symbol*] GSIL
Goldsmith Civic Garden Center, Memphis, TN [*Library symbol*] TMGG
Goldstein-Scheerer Cube Test [*Psychology*] GSCT
Goldstein-Scheerer Object Sorting Test [*Psychology*] GSOST
Goldstein-Scheerer Stick Test [*Psychology*] GSST
Goldstone [*California*] [*Seismograph station code, US Geological Survey*] GSC
Goldstone, California, Tracking Station [*NASA*] GDS
Goldstone Deep Space Communications Complex [*NASA*] GDSCC
Goldstone Duplicate Standard [*Deep Space Instrumentation Facility*] [*NASA*] GSDS
Goldstone Predict [*Orbit identification*] [*NASA*] GLPR
Goldstone-SFOF [*Space Flight Operations Facility*] **Microwave Assembly** [*NASA*] GSMA
Goldstone Tracking Station [*NASA*] GTS
Goldvein, VA [*Television station call letters*] WNVT
Goldwater, Barry [*Chemical symbols for gold and water; used to refer to the 1964 Republican presidential candidate*] AuH_2O
Goldwinn Resources Ltd. [*NASDAQ symbol*] GWNRF
Goleta, CA [*Radio station call letters*] KMGQ
Golf [*Phonetic alphabet*] G
Golf Ball Manufacturers Association GBMA
Golf Club GC
Golf Coaches Association of America GCAA
Golf Collectors' Society GCS
Golf Course Association GCA
Golf Course Builders of America GCBA
Golf Course Operations and Management Programs [*Association of Independent Colleges and Schools specialization code*] GM
Golf Course Reporter [*A publication*] Golf Course Rep
Golf Course Superintendents Association of America GCSAA
Golf Manufacturers and Distributors Association GMDA
Golf Products and Components Association GPCA
Golf Writers Association of America GWAA
Golfito [*Costa Rica*] [*Airport symbol*] GLF
Golgi-Associated Endoplasmic Reticulum Lysosomes GERL
Golgi Tendon Organ [*Anatomy*] GTO
Goliath Edison Screw GES
Golmud [*China*] [*Airport symbol*] GOQ
Golovin [*Alaska*] [*Airport symbol*] GLV
Golpazari [*Turkey*] [*Also, GPA*] [*Seismograph station code, US Geological Survey*] GLP
Golpazari [*Turkey*] [*Also, GLP*] [*Seismograph station code, US Geological Survey*] GPA
Goma [*Zaire*] [*Airport symbol*] GOM
Gonad-Stimulating Substance [*Endocrinology*] GSS
Gonadal Dysgenesis [*Endocrinology*] GD
Gonadal Steroid-Binding Globulin [*Medicine*] GSBG
Gonadotrophic Hormone [*Endocrinology*] GTH
Gonadotrophin [*Endocrinology*] Gn
Gonadotrophin Enhancing Factor [*Endocrinology*] GEF
Gonadotrophin-Releasing Factor [*Also, GnRH, LH-RF, LH-RH, LH-RH/FSH-RH, LRF, LRH*] [*Endocrinology*] GnRF
Gonadotrophin-Releasing Hormone [*Also, GnRF, LH-RF, LH-RH, LH-RH/FSH-RH, LRF, LRH*] [*Endocrinology*] GnRH
Gonalia [*Papua New Guinea*] [*Airport symbol*] GOE
Gondar [*Ethiopia*] [*Airport symbol*] GDQ
Gondi [*MARC language code*] [*Library of Congress*] gon
Gondola GOND
Gone for the Day GFD
Gone to Texas [*Sign on doors of New Englanders who had gone West, nineteenth century*] GTT
Gone with the Wind [*A novel by Margaret Mitchell; also, a motion picture*] GWTW
Gonidial [*With reference to colonies of bacteria*] G
Goniometer [*JETDS nomenclature*] [*Military*] GO
Gonococcal [*Clinical chemistry*] GC
Gonococcal Arthritis/Dermatitis Syndrome [*Medicine*] GADS
Gonococcal Base [*Broth*] [*Growth medium*] GCB
Gonococcal Ophthalmia Neonatorum [*Medicine*] GON
Gonococcal Urethritis [*Medicine*] GU
Gonorrhea Case [*Medical slang*] GC
Gonorrhea Complement Fixation Test [*Medicine*] GCFT
Gonzaga Law Review [*A publication*] Gonzaga L Rev
Gonzaga University, Law Library, Spokane, WA [*Library symbol*] WaSpG-L
Gonzaga University, Spokane, WA [*Library symbol*] WaSpG
Gonzales, CA [*Radio station call letters*] KKMC
Gonzales, LA [*Radio station call letters*] WSLG
Gonzales, TX [*Radio station call letters*] KCTI
Good [*Condition*] [*Antiquarian book trade, numismatics, etc.*] G
Good GD
Good [*Track condition*] [*Thoroughbred racing*] GD
Good American Helping Hands GAHH
Good Bears of the World GBW
Good-By [*Amateur radio*] GB
Good [*L. S.*] **& Co.** [*American Stock Exchange symbol*] [*Delisted*] GOO
Good Conduct [*Military decoration*] GC
Good Conduct Discharge GCD
Good Conduct Medal [*Military award*] GCM
Good Conduct Medal [*Military award*] GCMDL
Good Conduct Medal Clasp GCMC
Good Counsel College [*New York*] GCC
Good Delivery [*Business and trade*] GD
Good Evening [*Amateur radio*] GE
Good Fair Average [*Insurance*] GFA
Good Farming Quarterly [*A publication*] Good Farming Quart
[*The*] **Good Food Guide** [*A publication*] [*British*] GFG
Good Gay Poets GGP
[*The*] **Good Hotel Guide** [*A publication*] [*British*] GHG
Good Housekeeping [*A publication*] GH
Good Housekeeping [*A publication*] Good H
Good Housekeeping [*A publication*] Good House
Good Housekeeping Check Sheet GHCS
Good Industrial Relations Directors [*Meetings sponsored by Master Printers of America*] GIRD
Good Laboratory Practice [*FDA*] GLP
Good Manufacturing Practices [*FDA*] GMP
Good Marketable Quality [*Business and trade*] GMQ
Good Merchantable Brand [*Business and trade*] GMB
Good Morning [*Amateur radio*] GM
Good Morning America [*Television program*] GMA
Good Morning Britain [*Early morning television program*] [*ITV*] [*British*] GMB
Good Night [*Amateur radio*] GN
Good Old Friday [*Slang*] GOF
Good Ordinary Brand [*Business and trade*] GOB
Good Outdoor Manners Association GOMA
Good Packaging [*A publication*] Good Pkg
Good Sam Recreational Vehicle Club GSRVC
Good Samaritan Hospital, Corvallis, OR [*Library symbol*] OrCGSH
Good Samaritan Hospital, Dayton, OH [*Library symbol*] ODaGS
Good Samaritan Hospital and Medical Center, Portland, OR [*Library symbol*] OrPGH
Good Samaritan Hospital, Medical Library, Cincinnati, OH [*Library symbol*] OCGSH
Good Samaritan Hospital, West Islip, NY [*Library symbol*] NWiH
Good-Service Pension [*Navy*] [*British*] GSP

Good Skiing Conditions .... G
Good Sound Merchantable .... GSM
Good Taco Corp. [*NASDAQ symbol*] .... TACO
Good Templar .... GT
Good This Month .... GTM
Good This Week .... GTW
Good Till Canceled [*as in a brokerage order*] .... GTC
Good Times [*A publication*] .... Gd Times
Good Will In, Good Will Out [*Data processing*] .... GWIGWO
Goodall City Library, Ogallala, NE [*Library symbol*] .... NbOg
Goodenough-Harris Drawing Test [*Education*] .... G-H
Goodfellow Air Force Base [*Texas*] .... GAFB
Goodfellow Review of Crafts [*A publication*] .... Goodfellow
Goodheart-Wilcox Co. [*NASDAQ symbol*] .... GWOX
Gooding, ID [*Location identifier*] [*FAA*] .... GNG
Goodland [*Kansas*] [*Airport symbol*] .... GLD
Goodland, KS [*Radio station call letters*] .... KLOE
Goodland, KS [*Television station call letters*] .... KLOE-TV
Goodland, MN [*Radio station call letters*] .... KGKS-FM
Goodman, MS [*Radio station call letters*] .... WVTH
Goodnews Bay [*Alaska*] [*Airport symbol*] .... GNU
Goodrich [*B. F.*] **Co.** [*NYSE symbol*] .... GR
Goods .... GDS
Goods in Bad Order .... GBO
Goodwell, OK [*Radio station call letters*] .... KPSU
Goodwill Industries of America .... GIA
Goodwill Industries Volunteer Services .... GIVS
Goodwin Railroad, Inc. [*AAR code*] .... GWIN
Goodwood Data Systems Ltd., Carleton Place, ON, Canada [*Library symbol*] .... CaOCpG
Goodwyn Institute, Memphis, TN [*Library symbol*] .... TMG
Goody Products, Inc. [*NASDAQ symbol*] .... GOOD
Goodyear Aerospace Corporation .... GAC
Goodyear Associative Processor [*Data processing*] .... GAP
Goodyear Atomic Corp. .... GAT
Goodyear Atomic Corp., Portsmouth, OH [*Library symbol*] .... OPosmG
Goodyear Engineering Report .... GER
Goodyear-Reston-Winthrop [*Publishing group*] .... GRW
Goodyear Tire & Rubber Co. [*NYSE symbol*] .... GT
Goodyear Tire & Rubber Co., Akron, OH [*Library symbol*] .... OAkGy
Goofball [*Barbiturate pill*] .... GB
Goondiwindi [*Australia*] [*Airport symbol*] .... GOO
Goose Air Defense Sector .... GADS
Goose Bay [*Canada*] [*Airport symbol*] .... YYR
Goose Bay, NF [*Television station call letters*] .... CFLA-TV
Goose Bay, NF [*Radio station call letters*] .... CFLN
Goose Creek, SC [*Radio station call letters*] .... WBJX
Goose Red Blood Cell [*s*] .... GRBC
Gora [*Papua New Guinea*] [*Airport symbol*] .... GOC
Gorakhpur [*India*] [*Airport symbol*] .... GOP
Gordo Public Library, Gordo, AL [*Library symbol*] .... AGor
Gordon College, Wenham, MA [*Library symbol*] .... MWenhG
Gordon College, Wenham, MA [*OCLC symbol*] [*Inactive*] .... MWN
Gordon-Conwell Theological Seminary Library, South Hamilton, MA [*Library symbol*] .... MSohG
Gordon-Conwell Theological Seminary, South Hamilton, MA [*OCLC symbol*] .... BCT
Gordon Cooper Library, Carbondale, CO [*Library symbol*] .... CoCa
Gordon, E. S., Joplin MO [*STAC*] .... GES
Gordon, GA [*Radio station call letters*] .... WIZY
Gordon, GA [*Radio station call letters*] .... WIZY-FM
Gordon Jewelry Corp. [*NYSE symbol*] .... GOR
Gordon Military College [*Georgia*] .... GMC
Gordon, NE [*Radio station call letters*] .... KSDZ
Gordon Personal Inventory [*Psychology*] .... GPI
Gordon Personal Profile [*Psychology*] .... GPP
Gordon Review [*A publication*] .... Gor R
Gordon Setter Club of America .... GSCA
Gordonville, MO [*Radio station call letters*] .... KJAQ
Gore [*Ethiopia*] [*Airport symbol*] .... GOR
Gorge [*Board on Geographic Names*] .... GRGE
Gorham, ME [*Radio station call letters*] .... WASY
Gorham, ME [*Radio station call letters*] .... WMPG
Gorham State Teachers College [*Merged with University of Maine*] .... GSTC
Gori [*USSR*] [*Seismograph station code, US Geological Survey*] .... GOR
Gorilla Foundation .... GF
Gorin Stores, Inc. [*American Stock Exchange symbol*] [*Delisted*] .... GRN
Goris [*USSR*] [*Seismograph station code, US Geological Survey*] .... GRS
Gorje [*Yugoslavia*] [*Seismograph station code, US Geological Survey*] [*Closed*] .... GRJ
Gor'kovskii Gosudarstvennyi Universitet. Ucenye Zapiski [*A publication*] .... Gor'kov Gos Univ Ucen Zap
Gorman [*TACAN station*] .... GMN
Gorman, CA [*Location identifier*] [*FAA*] .... GMN
Gorman-Rupp Company [*American Stock Exchange symbol*] .... GRC
Gorna Orjachovica [*Bulgaria*] [*Airport symbol*] .... GOZ
Gorny [*USSR*] [*Seismograph station code, US Geological Survey*] [*Closed*] .... GOY
Gornyi Zhurnal [*A publication*] .... Gorn Zh
Gornyi Zhurnal (Moscow) [*A publication*] .... Gorn Zh (Mos)
Goroka [*Papua New Guinea*] [*Airport symbol*] .... GKA
Goroka [*Papua New Guinea*] [*Seismograph station code, US Geological Survey*] [*Closed*] .... GRK
Goroka [*Papua New Guinea*] [*Seismograph station code, US Geological Survey*] [*Closed*] .... GKA
Gorom-Gorom [*Upper Volta*] [*Airport symbol*] .... XGG
Gorontalo [*Indonesia*] [*Airport symbol*] .... GTO
Gorron [*France*] [*Seismograph station code, US Geological Survey*] .... GRR
Gorskostopanska Nauka [*A publication*] .... Gorskostop Nauka
Gorskostopanska Nauka Izvestiya na Akademiiata na Selskostopankite Nauke [*A publication*] .... Gorskostop Nauka Izv Akad Selskostop Nauke
Gosford [*Australia*] [*Airport symbol*] [*Obsolete*] .... GOS
Goshen College, Goshen, IN [*OCLC symbol*] .... IGC
Goshen College, Goshen, IN [*Library symbol*] .... InGo
Goshen, IN [*Radio station call letters*] .... WGCS
Goshen, IN [*Radio station call letters*] .... WKAM
Goshen, IN [*Radio station call letters*] .... WZOW
Goshen Library and Historical Society, Goshen, NY [*Library symbol*] .... NGos
Goshen Public Library, Goshen, IN [*Library symbol*] .... InGoP
Gospel Association for the Blind .... GAB
Gospel of the Hebrews [*Apocryphal work*] .... G Heb
Gospel Literature International; or Gospel Literature in National Tongues [*The organization's work*] [*Formerly, Gospel Light International*] .... GLINT
Gospel Music Association .... GMA
Gospel of Peter [*Apocryphal work*] .... G Pet
Gospel Recordings [*An association*] .... GR
Gospel Recordings, Incorporated .... GRI
Gospel of Thomas [*Apocryphal work*] .... G Thom
Gospel Truth Association .... GTA
Gospodarka Paliwami i Energia [*A publication*] .... Gospod Paliwami Energ
Gospodarka Planowa [*A publication*] .... Gosp Planowa
Gospodarka Wodna [*A publication*] .... Gospod Wodna
Gossudarstvenny Obstschessojusny Standart [*All-Union State Standard*] [*USSR*] .... GOST
Gosudarstvennaia Biblioteka SSR Imeni V. I. Lenina [*Lenin State Library of the USSR*], **Moscow, Soviet Union** [*Library symbol*] .... Ru
Gosudarstvennaia Publichnaia Biblioteka Imeni Saltykova-Shchedrina [*State Saltikov-Shchedrin Public Library*], **Leningrad, Soviet Union** [*Library symbol*] .... RuL
Gosudarstvennaia Publichnaia Nauchno-Tekhnicheskaia Biblioteka SSSR [*State Public Scientific and Technical Library*], **Moscow, Soviet Union** [*Library symbol*] .... RuMG
Gosudarstvennaja Planovaja Komissija [*Central Planning Commission*] [*USSR*] .... GOSPLAN
Gosudarstvennoe Knigoizdatelstvo [*State Publishing House*] [*USSR*] .... GEZ
Gosudarstvennoe Politicheskoe Upravlenie [*Government Political Administration*] [*Soviet secret service organization, also known as OGPU*] .... GPU
Gosudarstvennoe Strakhovanie [*State insurance*] [*USSR*] .... GOSSTRAKH
Gosudarstvennyi Institut Zhurnalistiki .... GIZH
Gosudarstvennyi Komitet Oborony [*State Defense Committee*] [*USSR*] [*World War II*] .... GKO
Gosudarstvennyi Universal'nyi Magazin [*Government Department Store*] [*Moscow*] .... GUM
Gosudartsvennaia Publichnaia Biblioteka Ukrainskoi SSR [*State Public Library of the Ukrainian SSR*], **Kiev, Soviet Union** [*Library symbol*] .... RuUk
Gosudorstvenuse Energeticheskoe Izdatel'stvo .... GEI
Got Ya Again [*Initialism used as name of second successful phony event staged by Washington, DC, law enforcement agents posing as fences*] [*See PFF Inc*] .... GYA
Gotaas-Larsen Shipping Corp. [*NASDAQ symbol*] .... GOTLF
Goteborg [*Sweden*] [*Seismograph station code, US Geological Survey*] [*Closed*] .... GOT
Goteborg Universitet. Naturgeografiska Institutionen. Rapport [*A publication*] .... Goteborg Univ Naturgeogr Inst Rapp
Goteborgs Naturhistoriska Museum Arstryck [*A publication*] .... Goteb Naturhist Mus Arstryck
Goteborgs Universititsbibliotek, Goteborg, Sweden [*Library symbol*] .... SwGU
Gotenba [*Japan*] [*Seismograph station code, US Geological Survey*] [*Closed*] .... GTN
Gothenburg [*Sweden*] [*Airport symbol*] .... GOT
Gothenburg Studies in English [*A publication*] .... Goth SE
Gothenburg Studies in English [*A publication*] .... GSE
Gothic [*MARC language code*] [*Library of Congress*] .... got
Gothic [*Language, etc.*] .... GOTH
Gothic Letter .... GL
Gott Corp. [*NASDAQ symbol*] .... GOTT
Gottesdienst und Kirchenmusik [*A publication*] .... Gottesd u Kir
Gottingen [*Federal Republic of Germany*] [*Seismograph station code, US Geological Survey*] .... GTT
Gottlieb Textiles .... GOTTEX
Gottwaldov [*Czechoslovakia*] [*Airport symbol*] .... GTW
Goucher College, Baltimore, MD [*Library symbol*] .... MdBG
Goudy Society .... GS
Goulburn Island [*Australia*] [*Airport symbol*] [*Obsolete*] .... GBL
Gould, Inc. [*NYSE symbol*] .... GLD

Gould, Incorporated, Gould Information Center, Cleveland, OH [*Library symbol*] .... OCIGI
Gould, Inc., Ocean Systems Information Center, Cleveland, OH [*OCLC symbol*] .... OGO
Gould Information Center, Cleveland, OH [*OCLC symbol*] .... OGI
Gould Investors Trust SBI [*American Stock Exchange symbol*] .... GTR
Gould Laboratory Materials Research, Cleveland, OH [*OCLC symbol*] .... CIE
Gould National Batteries, Inc. [*Later, GLD*] [*NYSE symbol*] .... GNB
Goulds, FL [*Radio station call letters*] .... WGLY
Goulds Pumps [*NASDAQ symbol*] .... GULD
Goundam [*Mali*] [*Airport symbol*] .... GUD
Gourd Society of America [*Superseded by AGS*] .... GSA
Gourde [*Monetary unit in Haiti*] .... G
Gourde [*Monetary unit in Haiti*] .... GDE
Gourmet Resources International [*NASDAQ symbol*] .... CHOK
Gouvernement Militaire de la Zone Francaise d'Occupation [*Military Government of the French Zone of Occupation*] [*of Germany*] .... GMZFO
Gouvernement Provisoire de la Republique Algerienne [*Provisional Government of the Algerian Republic*] .... GPRA
Gouvernement du Quebec, Ministere de l'Education, Service General des Moyens d'Enseignement, Montreal, PQ, Canada [*Library symbol*] .... CaQMSGME
Gouvernement de la Republique de l'Angola en Exile [*Government of the Republic of Angola in Exile*] .... GRAE
Gouverneur, NY [*Radio station call letters*] .... WIGS
Gouverneur, NY [*Radio station call letters*] .... WIGS-FM
Govalkot [*India*] [*Seismograph station code, US Geological Survey*] [*Closed*] .... GOV
Gove [*Australia*] [*Airport symbol*] .... GOV
Governador Valadares [*Brazil*] [*Airport symbol*] .... GVR
Governing .... GOVG
Governing Body .... GB
Governing Council for Environmental Programs [*United Nations*] .... GCEP
Government .... G
Government .... GOV
Government .... GOVT
Government Accountability Project .... GAP
Government Accountability Property System .... GAPS
Government Accounting Office .... GAO
Government Accounting Standards Board .... GASB
Government Accumulation Yard .... GAY
Government Actuary's Department .... GAD
Government Advisory Committee on International Book and Library Programs [*Terminated, 1977*] .... GAC
Government Affairs Branch [*European Theater of Operations*] [*World War II*] .... GAB
Government Affairs Foundation [*Defunct*] .... GAF
Government Agency .... GA
Government Agricultural Policy and Services for Farmers [*British*] .... GAPSF
Government Agricultural Research Centre. Ghent. Activity Report [*A publication*] .... Gov Agric Res Cent Ghent Act Rep
Government Aircraft Plant .... GAP
Government of American Samoa .... GAS
Government Astronomy Administration Round Table .... GAART
Government of Australia .... GOA
Government Authorized Representative .... GAR
Government Bill of Lading .... GBL
Government Bill of Lading .... GBLADING
Government Bill of Lading System .... GOBILS
Government Boat .... G/B
Government Bunkers .... GB
Government of Burma .... GOB
Government Clerical Services' Union [*Ceylon*] .... GCSU
Government Code and Cypher School [*Later, GCHQ*] [*British*] .... GCCS
Government Communications Headquarters [*British*] .... GCHQ
Government Competitive Testing .... GCT
Government Contract Committee [*Later, OFCCP*] [*Department of Labor*] .... GCC
Government Contract Management Association of America .... GCMA
Government Contractor .... GC
Government Contractors Subcontractors .... GCS
Government Contribution .... GC
Government Data Systems [*A publication*] .... Govt Data Sys
Government Document Publishing Service .... GDPS
Government Documents Round Table [*American Library Association*] .... GODORT
Government-Education-Medical .... GEM
Government Employee Relations Report [*A publication*] .... GERR
Government Employees Clinic Center [*British*] .... GECC
Government Employees Council [*Superseded by PED*] .... GEC
Government Employees Exchange .... GEX
Government Employees Insurance Company .... GEICO
Government Employees Training Act .... GETA
Government Employees United Against Discrimination [*An association*] .... GUARD
Government Evacuation Scheme [*British*] [*World War II*] .... GES
Government Excess Baggage Authorization .... GEBA
Government Facilities Brochure .... GFB
Government Facilities Request .... GFR
Government Fiscal Year .... GFY
Government Flight Representative .... GFR
Government Fluidic Coordinating Group .... GFCG
Government Form .... GF
Government Free Issue .... GFI
Government Full Period .... GFP
Government-Funded Procurement .... GFP
Government-Funded Program .... GFP
Government-Furnished Aeronautical Equipment .... GFAE
Government-Furnished Aeronautical Equipment List .... GFAEL
Government-Furnished Articles .... GFA
Government-Furnished Capital Equipment .... GFCE
Government-Furnished Data .... GFD
Government-Furnished Documentation .... GFD
Government-Furnished Equipment .... GFE
Government-Furnished Equipment List .... GFEL
Government-Furnished Equipment and Material .... GFE & M
Government-Furnished Equipment Records .... GFER
Government-Furnished Equipment Requirements Request .... GFERR
Government-Furnished Information .... GFI
Government-Furnished List .... GFL
Government-Furnished Material .... GFM
Government-Furnished Missile .... GFM
Government-Furnished Missile Equipment .... GFME
Government-Furnished Parts .... GFP
Government-Furnished Property .... GFP
Government-Furnished Property List .... GFPL
Government-Furnished Services .... GFS
Government-Furnished Software .... GFS
Government-Furnished Support Equipment .... GFSE
Government-Furnished Support Property .... GFSP
Government of the Gambia .... GOTG
Government Girl .... GG
Government Gold Mining Areas .... GGMA
Government Grade [*Followed by a number, 1-18; National Security Agency Employee Grade*] .... GG
Government House [*Canada*] .... GH
Government Idle Industrial Reserve .... GIIR
Government Imprinted Penalty Stationery Society .... GIPS
Government In-Service Library, Yellowknife, NT, Canada [*Library symbol*] .... CaNWYGI
Government of India .... GI
Government of Indonesia .... GOI
Government and Industrial .... GI
Government-Industry Cooperative Oyster Research Program .... GICORP
Government-Industry Coordinating Committee .... GICC
Government-Industry Data Exchange Program [*Later, IDEP*] .... GIDEP
Government and Industry Team .... GAIT
Government Information Organization [*Later, NAGC*] .... GIO
Government Information Services Committee [*Special Libraries Association*] .... GISC
Government Initiated .... GI
Government of Iran .... GOI
Government of Israel .... GOI
Government of Israel Furnished Equipment .... GOIFE
Government of Israel Trade Center .... GITC
Government Issue [*Army*] .... GI
Government Issue Technical Inspection .... GITI
Government of Japan .... GOJ
Government of Korea .... GOK
Government-Lent Property .... GLP
Government-Loaned Equipment .... GLE
Government-Loaned Material .... GLM
Government Maintenance Depot .... GMD
Government of Malaysia .... GOM
Government Management Information Sciences [*An association*] .... GMIS
Government Microcircuit Applications Conference .... GOMAC
Government Modification Authorization .... GMA
Government National Mortgage Association [*Nickname: Ginnie Mae*] .... GNMA
Government National Railway Association [*Proposed*] [*Nickname: Ginnie Rae*] .... GNRA
Government of New Zealand .... GNZ
Government of North Vietnam .... GNVN
Government Operations Committee [*US Senate*] .... GO
Government and Opposition [*A publication*] .... Govt & Oppos
Government and Opposition [*A publication*] .... Govt Oppos
Government and Opposition [*A publication*] .... Gvt and Opposition
Government Owned .... GO
Government-Owned Aircraft .... GOA
Government-Owned/Contractor-Operated [*Facility*] .... GO/CO
Government-Owned Depot .... GOD
Government-Owned Equipment .... GOE
Government-Owned Facility .... GOF
Government-Owned/Government-Operated [*Facility*] .... GO/GO
Government-Owned Installation .... GOI
Government-Owned Material .... GOM
Government-Owned Material Repair and Reimbursement .... GOMR & R
Government-Owned Plant Equipment .... GOPE
Government-Owned Property .... GOP
Government-Owned Terminal .... GOT

Government Paper Specification Standards ... GPS
Government Patents Board [*Functions transferred to Secretary of Commerce, 1961*] ... GPB
Government Pest Infestation Laboratory. Annual Report [*A publication*] ... Gov Pest Infest Lab Annu Rep
Government of the Philippines ... GOP
Government Printing Office ... GPO
Government Procurement Practices Board [*Proposed*] ... GPPB
Government Property ... GP
Government Property Administration ... GPA
Government Property Lost or Damaged [*or Destroyed*] ... GPLD
Government Property Yard ... GPY
Government Public Relations Association [*Defunct*] ... GPRA
Government Publications Review [*A publication*] ... Gov Pub R
Government Publications Review [*A publication*] ... Govt Pub R
Government Quality Assurance ... GQA
Government Rate Tender ... GRT
Government Regulation ... GR
Government Regulations ... GR's
Government Relations Note [*A publication*] ... Gov Relat Note
Government and Relief in Occupied Areas [*Post-World War II*] ... GARIOA
Government Report ... GR
Government Report Authorization and Record ... GRAR
Government Reports Announcements [*A publication*] ... Gov Rep Announce
Government Reports Announcements [*Formerly, USGRDR*] [*Department of Commerce*] ... GRA
Government Reports Index [*Formerly, USGRDR-I*] [*Department of Commerce*] ... GRI
Government Reports and Topical Announcements [*Later, WGA*] [*National Technical Information Service*] ... GRTA
Government of the Republic of China ... GRC
Government Research Centers Directory [*A publication*] ... GRC
Government Research Corporation [*Information service*] ... GRC
Government Research and Development Reports ... GRR
Government Research Institute of Formosa ... GRIF
Government Reservation Bureau ... GRB
Government Responsibility ... GR
Government Responsibility Authorized ... GRA
Government Rubber-Acrylonitrile [*Synthetic rubber*] ... GR-A
Government Rubber-Isobutylene [*Synthetic rubber*] ... GR-I
Government Rubber-Styrene [*Also, SBR*] [*Synthetic rubber*] ... GR-S
Government of the Ryukyu Islands ... GRI
Government Securities Trading [*Computer*] ... GST
Government Service ... GS
Government Service Insurance System Employees' Association [*Philippines*] ... GSISEA
Government of Singapore ... GOS
Government Source Inspection ... GSI
Government of Spain ... GOS
Government Spares Release ... GSR
Government Staffs [*British*] ... GS
Government Standard Parts ... GSP
Government Statistical Service [*British*] ... GSS
Government Steam Train [*British*] ... GST
Government on Taiwan ... GONT
Government Technical Report ... GTR
Government Telegraph Code [*British*] [*World War II*] ... GTC
Government Test Facility ... GTF
Government Training Centre [*British*] ... GTC
Government Transportation Request ... GTR
Government Union of Burma ... GUB
Government Vehicle ... GVH
Government Vehicle Service [*Postal Service*] ... GVS
Government of Vietnam ... GVN
Government White Paper ... GWP
Government-Wide Index [*Later, USGRDR*] ... GWI
Government-Wide Index to Research and Development ... GWIRD
Government Workers' Trade Union Federation [*Ceylon*] ... GWTUF
Government of the Yukon, Department of Territorial Affairs, Whitehorse, YT, Canada [*Library symbol*] ... CaYWTA
Government of the Yukon, Library Services Branch, Whitehorse, YT, Canada [*Library symbol*] ... CaYWLS
Governmental ... GOVTL
Governmental Affairs Institute ... GAI
Governmental Defence Council [*British*] ... GDC
Governmental Finance [*A publication*] ... GF
Governmental Finance [*A publication*] ... Govt Fin
Governmental Refuse Collection and Disposal Association ... GRCDA
Governmental Research Association ... GRA
Governor ... GOV
Governor General ... GG
Governor, Marshall Islands ... GOVMAR
Governors' Conference ... GC
Governor's Foot Guard ... GFG
Governors Harbour [*Bahamas*] [*Airport symbol*] ... GHB
Governor's Horse Guard ... GHG
Governors State University Energy Group ... GSUEG
Governors State University, Park Forest South, IL [*OCLC symbol*] ... IAF
Governors State University, Park Forest South, IL [*Library symbol*] ... IPfsG
Gowganda Resources [*NASDAQ symbol*] ... GOWGF
Goya [*Argentina*] [*Airport symbol*] ... OYA
Gozaisho [*Japan*] [*Seismograph station code, US Geological Survey*] [*Closed*] ... GZS
Gozdarski Vestnik [*A publication*] ... Gozd Vestn
GPETE End Item Replacement ... GEIR
GPz Owners of America ... GPZOA
Grab Rod ... GR
Grace A. Dow Memorial [*Public*] **Library, Midland, MI** [*Library symbol*] ... MiMid
Grace Balloch Memorial Library, Spearfish, SD [*Library symbol*] ... SdSpe
Grace Bible Institute [*Nebraska*] ... GBI
Grace College, Winona Lake, IN [*OCLC symbol*] ... IGR
Grace College, Winona Lake, IN [*Library symbol*] ... InWinG
Grace [*W. R.*] **& Co.** [*NYSE symbol*] ... GRA
Grace of God Movement for the Women of America [*Later, GGMWW*] ... GGMWA
Grace of God Movement for the Women of the World [*Formerly, GGMWA*] ... GGMWW
Grace Hospital, Winnipeg, MB, Canada [*Library symbol*] ... CaMWGH
Grace Theological Journal [*A publication*] ... GTJ
Graceland College, Lamoni, IA [*Library symbol*] ... IaLG
Graceland College, Lamoni, IA [*OCLC symbol*] ... IOF
Gracewood State School and Hospital, Gracewood, GA [*Library symbol*] ... GGraG
Graciosa Island [*Azores*] [*Airport symbol*] ... GRW
Graco, Inc. [*NASDAQ symbol*] ... GRAC
Gradatim [*Gradually*] [*Pharmacy*] ... GRAD
Gradco Systems, Inc. [*NASDAQ symbol*] ... GRCO
Grade ... GR
Grade Age [*Education*] ... GA
Grade Crossing Protection Device ... GCPD
Grade Level Equivalent [*Educational testing*] ... GLE
Grade Line ... GL
Grade-Point Average [*Education*] ... GPA
Grade of Service [*Military*] ... GOS
Grade System ... GS
Grade Teacher [*A publication*] ... Grade Teach
Graded Base Transistor ... GBT
Graded Exercise ... GRADEX
Graded Exercise ... Gx
Graded Exercise Testing ... GXT
Graded Program ... GP
Gradevinski Fakultet. Sarajevo. Radovi [*A publication*] ... Gradevinski Fak Sarajevo Rad
Gradient ... GRAD
Gradient Elution Fractionation ... GEF
Gradient Gel Electrophoresis ... GGE
Gradient Mixer [*Chromatography*] ... GM
Gradient Wind ... GDWND
Gradinarska i Lozarska Nauka [*A publication*] ... Gradinar Lozar Nauka
Grading ... GRD
Gradja za Povijest Knjizevnosti Hrvatske [*A publication*] ... Gradja
Gradual ... GRADU
Gradually ... GRDL
Graduate ... GR
Graduate ... GRAD
Graduate Aerospace Mechanical Engineering ... GAM
Graduate in Agriculture ... GA
Graduate in Architecture ... G Arch
Graduate in Arts ... BA
Graduate Assistant ... GA
Graduate Assistantship Directory [*A publication*] ... GAD
Graduate Business Admission Test ... GBAT
Graduate Certificate of Social Work ... GCSW
Graduate in Divinity ... GD
Graduate Employment and Training [*British*] ... GET
Graduate Engineering Education System ... GENESYS
Graduate English Papers [*A publication*] ... GEP
Graduate Fellowships for Black Americans ... GFBA
Graduate Grade-Point Average [*Higher education*] ... GGPA
Graduate of the Institution of Automobile Engineers [*British*] ... GradIAE
Graduate of the Institution of Electronic and Radio Engineers [*British*] ... Grad IERE
Graduate of the Institution of Mechanical Engineers [*British*] ... GI Mech E
Graduate of the Institution of Mechanical Engineers [*British*] ... Grad I Mech E
Graduate Jeweller ... GJ
Graduate in Law ... GL
Graduate in Letters ... BL
Graduate in Letters ... LB
Graduate in Liberal Arts ... BLA
Graduate Library School ... GLS
Graduate Management Admission Test ... GMAT
Graduate Medical Education [*Program*] [*Army*] ... GME
Graduate Medical Education National Advisory Committee [*Department of Health and Human Services*] ... GMENAC
Graduate Member of the Institute of British Engineers ... Grad Inst BE
Graduate Member of the Institute of Physics and the Physical Society [*British*] ... Grad Inst P
Graduate Member of the Institution of Mechanical Engineers [*British*] ... GMI Mech E

Graduate Member of the Non-Destructive Testing Society of Great Britain ... Grad MNDTS
Graduate Member of the Royal Institute of Chemistry [*British*] ... Grad RIC
Graduate Midwife ... Mid G
Graduate Nurse ... GN
Graduate Nurse ... Gr N
Graduate Nurse Transition Program ... GNTP
Graduate in Nursing ... G in N
Graduate Opportunities [*British*] ... GO
Graduate in Pharmacy ... G Ph
Graduate in Pharmacy ... Ph G
Graduate in Pharmacy ... Phm G
Graduate Practical Nurse ... GPN
Graduate Record Examination [*Higher education*] ... GRE
Graduate Reliability Engineering ... GRE
Graduate Research Assistant ... GRA
Graduate Research Center of the Southwest [*Formerly, Southwest Center for Advanced Studies; later, University of Texas at Dallas*] ... GRCSW
Graduate Research in Education and Related Disciplines [*A publication*] ... Grad Res Ed
Graduate Respiratory Therapist ... GRT
Graduate Resume Accumulation and Distribution [*Data processing*] ... GRAD
Graduate of the Royal Aeronautical Society [*British*] ... GR Aero S
Graduate of the Royal Air Force Staff College [*British*] ... FS
Graduate of the Royal College of Music [*British*] ... GRCM
Graduate of the Royal Naval Staff College, Greenwich [*British*] ... NS
Graduate of the Royal Schools of Music [*British*] ... GRSM
Graduate School Foreign Language Test ... GSFLT
Graduate in Science ... BS
Graduate in Science ... B Sc
Graduate Seminar Journal [*A publication*] ... Grad Sem J
Graduate Student of English [*A publication*] ... GSE
Graduate Teaching Assistant ... GTA
Graduate Texts in Mathematics [*A publication*] ... Grad Texts Math
Graduate Theological Union, Berkeley, CA [*Library symbol*] ... CBGTU
Graduate of Trinity College of Music, London ... GTCL
Graduated Equity Mortgage [*Also, Growing Equity Mortgage*] ... GEM
Graduated Length Method [*of learning to ski*] [*Later, Accelerated Length Method*] ... GLM
Graduated Payment Mortgage ... GPM
Graduated Reduction in Tensions [*Cold War term*] ... GRIT
Graduates of Italian Medical Schools [*An association*] ... GIMS
Graduation ... GRDTN
Graeber-Verwaltungsoffizier [*Graves Registration Officer*] [*German military - World War II*] ... GVO
Graecolatina et Orientalia [*A publication*] ... Ge O
Graecolatina et Orientalia [*A publication*] ... GLO
Graefenberg Array [*Erlangen*] [*Federal Republic of Germany*] [*Seismograph station code, US Geological Survey*] ... GRF
Graefenberg Spot [*Gynecology*] ... G (Spot)
Graefes Archiv fuer Klinische und Experimentelle Ophthalmologie [*A publication*] ... Graefes Arch Klin Exp Ophthalmol
Graettinger Public Library, Graettinger, IA [*Library symbol*] ... IaGra
Graetz Number [*Physics*] ... Gz
Grafische Technik Dokumentationsdienst [*A publication*] ... Grafische Tech
Grafiska Forskningslaboratoriets Meddelande [*A publication*] ... Grafiska Forskningslab Medd
Grafiske Hojskoles Smaskrifter [*A publication*] ... Grafiske Hojskoles Smaskr
Grafiskt Forum [*A publication*] ... GF
Graft (Polymer) [*Organic chemistry*] ... g
Graft Versus Host [*Immunology*] ... GVH
Graft-Versus-Host Disease [*Immunology*] ... GVHD
Graft-Versus-Host Reaction [*Immunology*] ... GVHR
Grafton [*Australia*] [*Airport symbol*] ... GFN
Grafton [*New York*] [*Seismograph station code, US Geological Survey*] [*Closed*] ... GFN
Grafton and Belington Railroad [*Initialism refers to a settlement of Indians who lived near this railroad*] ... G and B
Grafton, ND [*Radio station call letters*] ... KXPO
Grafton & Upton Railroad Co. [*AAR code*] ... GU
Grafton, WV [*Radio station call letters*] ... WKGA
Grafton, WV [*Radio station call letters*] ... WTBZ
Graham Brothers Truck and Bus Club ... GBTBC
Graham Center [*An association*] ... GC
Graham County Railroad Co. [*AAR code*] ... GC
Graham Evangelistic Association, Montreat, NC [*Library symbol*] ... NcMG
Graham Manufacturing Co., Inc. [*American Stock Exchange symbol*] ... GHM
Graham, NC [*Radio station call letters*] ... WSML
Graham Owners Club International ... GOCI
Graham Public Library, Union Grove, WI [*Library symbol*] ... WUg
Graham, TX [*Location identifier*] [*FAA*] ... GHX
Graham, TX [*Radio station call letters*] ... KSWA
Graham, TX [*Radio station call letters*] ... KWKQ
Grahamstown [*South Africa*] [*Seismograph station code, US Geological Survey*] [*Closed*] ... GRH
Grahamstown [*South Africa*] [*Geomagnetic observatory code*] ... GRM
Grahamstown [*South Africa*] [*Seismograph station code, US Geological Survey*] ... GRM
Grai si Suflet [*A publication*] ... G & S
Grai si Suflet [*A publication*] ... GS
Grail International Student Center [*Defunct*] ... GISC
Grain ... G
Grain ... GN
Grain ... GR
Grain Bin Manufacturers Council ... GBMC
Grain Boundary Dislocation ... GBD
Grain Boundary Relaxation ... GBR
Grain Count [*Measurement of cell labeling*] ... GC
Grain Elevator and Processing Society ... GEAPS
Grain and Feed Dealers National Association [*Later, National Grain and Feed Association*] ... GFDNA
Grain and Feed Journals Consolidated [*A publication*] ... Grain Feed J Consol
Grain and Feed Review [*A publication*] ... Grain Feed Rev
Grain Futures Administration [*Superseded by Commodity Exchange Administration, 1936*] ... GFA
Grain Income Stabilization Plan ... GISP
Grain Marketing Research Laboratory [*Department of Agriculture*] ... GMRL
Grain Neutral Spirits [*Alcohol*] ... GNS
Grain Processing Machinery Manufacturers Association ... GPMMA
Grain Producer News [*A publication*] ... Grain Prod News
Grain Products Irradiator [*Nuclear energy*] ... GPI
Grain Sorghum Producers Association ... GSPA
Grain Trade Buyers Guide and Management Reference [*A publication*] ... Grain Trade Buyers Guide Manage Ref
Grainger [W. W.] Co. [*NYSE symbol*] ... GWW
Grainger Journal [*A publication*] ... Grainger J
Grains per Foot ... GPF
Grains per Gallon [*Unit of measure for water hardness*] ... GPG
Gram ... g
Gram ... GM
Gram ... GR
Gram Atomic Weight [*Chemistry*] ... GAW
Gram Calorie ... GCAL
Gram Force per Square Centimeter ... GF/CM^2
Gram Meter ... GM-M
Gram Molecular Volume [*Chemistry*] ... GMV
Gram Molecular Weight [*Chemistry*] ... GMW
Gram-Negative [*Also, GRN*] [*Microbiology*] ... GN
Gram-Negative [*Also, GN*] [*Microbiology*] ... GRN
Gram-Negative Bacillary Meningitis [*Medicine*] ... GNBM
Gram-Negative Bacillus [*Microbiology*] ... GNB
Gram-Negative Intracellular Diplococci [*Microbiology*] ... GNID
Gram-Positive [*Also, GRP*] [*Microbiology*] ... GP
Gram-Positive [*Also, GP*] [*Microbiology*] ... GRP
Grambling, LA [*Radio station call letters*] ... KGRM
Grambling State University, Grambling, LA [*Library symbol*] ... LGra
Grambling State University, Grambling, LA [*OCLC symbol*] ... LGS
Gramicidin [*Antimicrobial compound*] ... GRD
Gramicidin A [*Antibiotic*] ... GA
Grammar ... GR
Grammar ... GRAM
Grammar School ... GS
Gramophone [*A publication*] ... GR
Gramophone Motor ... GM
Gramophone Records [*Music or sound effects*] ... GRAMS
Grams per Cubic Centimeter ... G/CM^3
Grams per Liter ... G/L
Grams per Square Centimeter ... G/CM^2
Grams per Square Meter ... GSM
Gran Quivira National Monument ... GRQU
Gran Turismo [*Grand Touring*] [*Automotive term*] ... GT
Gran Turismo Experimental [*Grand Touring, Experimental*] [*Automotive term*] ... GTX
Grana Palynologica [*A publication*] ... Grana Palynol
Granada [*Spain*] [*Airport symbol*] ... GRX
Granada Public Library, Granada, CO [*Library symbol*] ... CoGra
Granatbuechse [*Antitank grenade rifle*] [*German*] ... GRB
Granby, CO [*Location identifier*] [*FAA*] ... GNB
Granby Leader, Granby, PQ, Canada [*Library symbol*] ... CaQGL
Granby Mining Co. Ltd. [*NYSE symbol*] ... GB
Granby, PQ [*Radio station call letters*] ... CHEF
Grand [*Slang term for 1,000*] ... G
Grand ... GR
Grand ... GRND
Grand [*Title*] ... GR
Grand Accelerated Space Platform ... GASP
Grand American Handicap [*Shooting competition*] ... GAH
Grand Army of the Republic ... GAR
Grand Auto, Incorporated [*American Stock Exchange symbol*] ... GAI
Grand Bahama Island ... GBI
Grand Ballon [*France*] [*Seismograph station code, US Geological Survey*] [*Closed*] ... GBF
Grand Bank, NF [*Television station call letters*] ... CJOX-TV-1
Grand Bank, NF [*Radio station call letters*] ... CKYQ
Grand Banks [*FAA*] ... GRBNKS
Grand Bounce [*Suspension or dismissal*] [*Slang*] ... GB
Grand Cache, AB [*Radio station call letters*] ... CKYR-1
Grand Cadence de Tir [*Self-propelled howitzer*] ... GCT

Grand Canyon [*Arizona*] [*Airport symbol*] ... GCN
Grand Canyon [*Arizona*] [*Airport symbol*] ... JGC
Grand Canyon College [*Arizona*] ... GCC
Grand Canyon National Park ... GRCA
Grand Canyon Natural History Association. Bulletin [*A publication*] ... Grand Canyon Nat History Assoc Bull
Grand Cayman [*West Indies*] [*Airport symbol*] ... GCM
Grand Central, Inc. [*American Stock Exchange symbol*] ... GC
Grand Central Rocket Co. ... GCR
Grand Central Rocket Co., Redlands, CA [*Library symbol*] ... CRedlG
Grand Cess [*Liberia*] [*Airport symbol*] ... GRC
Grand Chancellor ... GC
Grand Chaplain ... GC
Grand Chapter ... GC
Grand Commander ... GC
Grand Commander of the Knights of Saint Patrick ... GCKP
Grand Conductor ... GC
Grand Coulee [*Washington*] [*Seismograph station code, US Geological Survey*] [*Closed*] ... GCW
Grand Coulee Public Library, Grand Coulee, WA [*Library symbol*] ... WaGc
Grand Coulee, WA [*Radio station call letters*] ... KEYF
Grand Coulee, WA [*Radio station call letters*] ... KEYG
Grand County Public Library, Granby Branch, Granby, CO [*Library symbol*] ... CoGranG
Grand County Public Library, Hot Sulphur Springs, CO [*Library symbol*] ... CoHsp
Grand Cross ... GC
Grand Cross of the French Legion of Honour ... GCFLH
Grand Cross, Order of the Niger [*British*] ... GCON
Grand-Dad's Day Council ... GDC
Grand Deacon [*Masonry*] ... GD
Grand Director of Ceremonies [*Masonry*] ... GDC
Grand Division ... GD
Grand Dixence [*Switzerland*] [*Seismograph station code, US Geological Survey*] ... DIX
Grand Duchess [*or Duke*] ... GD
Grand Duchy ... GD
Grand Encampment ... GE
Grand Falls Central Railway Co. Ltd. [*AAR code*] ... GFC
Grand Falls, NB [*Radio station call letters*] ... CKMV
Grand Falls, NF [*Television station call letters*] ... CBNAT
Grand Falls, NF [*Radio station call letters*] ... CBT
Grand Falls, NF [*Radio station call letters*] ... CIYQ
Grand Falls, NF [*Television station call letters*] ... CJCN-TV
Grand Falls, NF [*Radio station call letters*] ... CKCM
Grand Forks [*North Dakota*] [*Airport symbol*] ... GFK
Grand Forks [*Canada*] [*Airport symbol*] [*Obsolete*] ... ZGF
Grand Forks Airmotive, Inc. [*Grand Forks, ND*] [*FAA designator*] ... GFK
Grand Forks, BC [*Radio station call letters*] ... CKGF
Grand Forks Energy Research Center [*Energy Research and Development Administration*] ... GFERC
Grand Forks Energy Technology Center [*Department of Energy*] ... GFETC
Grand Forks, ND [*Radio station call letters*] ... KFJM
Grand Forks, ND [*Radio station call letters*] ... KFJM-FM
Grand Forks, ND [*Television station call letters*] ... KGFE
Grand Forks, ND [*Radio station call letters*] ... KKXL
Grand Forks, ND [*Radio station call letters*] ... KKXL-FM
Grand Forks, ND [*Radio station call letters*] ... KNOX
Grand Forks, ND [*Radio station call letters*] ... KYTN
Grand Forks, ND [*Location identifier*] [*FAA*] ... RDR
Grand Forks Public Library, Grand Forks, ND [*Library symbol*] ... NdG
Grand Forks United Hospital, Grand Forks, ND [*Library symbol*] ... NdGUH
Grand Haven, MI [*Radio station call letters*] ... WFMG
Grand Haven, MI [*Radio station call letters*] ... WGHN
Grand Haven, MI [*Radio station call letters*] ... WGHN-FM
Grand Island [*Nebraska*] [*Airport symbol*] ... GRI
Grand Island, NE [*Television station call letters*] ... KGIN-TV
Grand Island, NE [*Radio station call letters*] ... KMMJ
Grand Island, NE [*Radio station call letters*] ... KRGI
Grand Island, NE [*Radio station call letters*] ... KRGI-FM
Grand Island, NE [*Radio station call letters*] ... KROA
Grand Island, NE [*Radio station call letters*] ... KSYZ
Grand Island Public Library, Grand Island, NE [*Library symbol*] ... NbG
Grand Isle, LA [*Location identifier*] [*FAA*] ... GNI
Grand Isle, LA [*Location identifier*] [*FAA*] ... LEV
Grand Junction [*Colorado*] [*Airport symbol*] ... GJT
Grand Junction, CO [*Location identifier*] [*FAA*] ... FRU
Grand Junction, CO [*Radio station call letters*] ... KCIC
Grand Junction, CO [*Radio station call letters*] ... KEXO
Grand Junction, CO [*Television station call letters*] ... KJCT-TV
Grand Junction, CO [*Radio station call letters*] ... KJOL
Grand Junction, CO [*Radio station call letters*] ... KMSA
Grand Junction, CO [*Radio station call letters*] ... KQIL
Grand Junction, CO [*Radio station call letters*] ... KQIX
Grand Junction, CO [*Radio station call letters*] ... KREX
Grand Junction, CO [*Radio station call letters*] ... KREX-FM
Grand Junction, CO [*Television station call letters*] ... KREX-TV
Grand Junction, CO [*Radio station call letters*] ... KSTR
Grand Junction Office [*Energy Research and Development Administration*] ... GJO
Grand Junior Deacon [*Masonry*] ... GJD
Grand Junior Warden [*Masonry*] ... GJW
Grand Jury ... GJ
Grand Jury Project ... GJP
Grand Lake Public Library, Grand Lake, CO [*Library symbol*] ... CoGl
Grand Larceny ... GL
Grand Livre du Mois [*Best-selling book of the month*] [*French*] ... GLM
Grand Lodge [*Masonry*] ... GL
Grand Lodge of Ancient Free and Accepted Masons of Maryland, Masonic Library, Baltimore, MD [*Library symbol*] ... MdBFM
Grand Lodge of the Free and Accepted Masons of the State of Nevada, Reno, NV [*Library symbol*] ... NvRFM
Grand Lodge, Ladies Auxiliary, Fraternal Order of Police ... FOP
Grand Lodge of Mark Master Masons [*Masonry*] ... GLMMM
Grand Lodge of New York, F & AM Library and Museum, New York, NY [*Library symbol*] ... NNFM
Grand Lodge Order of the Sons of Hermann in Texas ... OSHT
Grand Lodge of Scotland [*Masonry*] ... GLS
Grand Lodge of Vermont, F & AM Library, Burlington, VT [*Library symbol*] ... VtBFB
Grand Lot ... GL
Grand Mal [*Epilepsy*] ... GM
Grand Marais, MN [*Location identifier*] [*FAA*] ... GRM
Grand Master [*Masonry*] ... GM
Grand Master of the Bath [*British*] ... GMB
Grand Master of the Knights of St. Patrick ... GMKP
Grand Master of the Order of the British Empire ... GMBE
Grand Master of the Order of the Indian Empire [*British*] ... GMIE
Grand Master of the Order of St. Michael and St. George [*British*] ... GMMG
Grand Master of the Order of St. Patrick ... GMP
Grand Master of the Order of the Star of India [*British*] ... GMSI
Grand Medal [*Ghana*] ... GM
Grand National [*Automobile racing*] ... GN
Grand National Curling Club of America ... GNCCA
Grand National Hunt [*British*] ... GNH
Grand Old Man [*A venerated man, especially in a specific field. Originally referred to William Gladstone, 1809-98, British statesman and prime minister, who was also sometimes known to his detractors as "Grand Old Muddler"*] [*See also HOM*] ... GOM
Grand Old Party [*The Republican Party*] ... GOP
Grand Old Woman [*England's Queen Victoria*] ... GOW
Grand Passion ... GP
Grand Past Master [*Masonry*] ... GPM
Grand Prairie, AB [*Radio station call letters*] ... CFGP
Grand Prairie Memorial Library, Grand Prairie, TX [*Library symbol*] ... TxGrp
Grand Prairie, TX [*Location identifier*] [*FAA*] ... GPM
Grand Prairie, TX [*Radio station call letters*] ... KKDA
Grand Prix ... GP
Grand Quartier-General [*French GHQ*] ... GQG
Grand Rapids [*Minnesota*] [*Airport symbol*] ... GPZ
Grand Rapids [*Michigan*] [*Airport symbol*] ... GRR
Grand Rapids Area Union List of Serials [*Library network*] ... GRAUL
Grand Rapids Baptist College, Grand Rapids, MI [*Library symbol*] ... MiGrB
Grand Rapids Baptist College and Seminary, Grand Rapids, MI [*OCLC symbol*] ... EXB
Grand Rapids Furniture Market Association ... GRFMA
Grand Rapids Junior College [*Michigan*] ... GRJC
Grand Rapids Junior College, Grand Rapids, MI [*Library symbol*] ... MiGrJC
Grand Rapids Law Library, Grand Rapids, MI [*Library symbol*] ... MiGrL
Grand Rapids, MI [*Location identifier*] [*FAA*] ... CYZ
Grand Rapids, MI [*Radio station call letters*] ... WCSG
Grand Rapids, MI [*Radio station call letters*] ... WCUZ
Grand Rapids, MI [*Radio station call letters*] ... WCUZ-FM
Grand Rapids, MI [*Radio station call letters*] ... WEHB
Grand Rapids, MI [*Radio station call letters*] ... WFUR
Grand Rapids, MI [*Radio station call letters*] ... WFUR-FM
Grand Rapids, MI [*Radio station call letters*] ... WGNR
Grand Rapids, MI [*Radio station call letters*] ... WGRD-FM
Grand Rapids, MI [*Television station call letters*] ... WGVC
Grand Rapids, MI [*Radio station call letters*] ... WJFM
Grand Rapids, MI [*Radio station call letters*] ... WLAV-FM
Grand Rapids, MI [*Radio station call letters*] ... WMAX
Grand Rapids, MI [*Radio station call letters*] ... WOOD
Grand Rapids, MI [*Radio station call letters*] ... WOOD-FM
Grand Rapids, MI [*Television station call letters*] ... WOTV
Grand Rapids, MI [*Radio station call letters*] ... WTWN
Grand Rapids, MI [*Radio station call letters*] ... WVGR
Grand Rapids, MI [*Television station call letters*] ... WXMI
Grand Rapids, MI [*Radio station call letters*] ... WXQT
Grand Rapids, MI [*Television station call letters*] ... WZZM-TV
Grand Rapids, MI [*Radio station call letters*] ... WZZR
Grand Rapids, MN [*Radio station call letters*] ... KAXE
Grand Rapids, MN [*Radio station call letters*] ... KNNS
Grand Rapids, MN [*Radio station call letters*] ... KOZY
Grand Rapids Public Library, Grand Rapids, MI [*OCLC symbol*] ... EXR
Grand Rapids Public Library, Grand Rapids, MI [*Library symbol*] ... MiGr
Grand Recorder ... GR
Grand Ridge Consolidated Community School District 95, Grand Ridge, IL [*Library symbol*] ... IGrSD
[*The*] **Grand River Railway Co.** [*AAR code*] ... GRNR
Grand Scale Integration ... GSI

Grand Scribe	GS
Grand Secretary	GS
Grand Seminaire, Montreal, PQ, Canada [Library symbol]	CaQMGS
Grand Seminaire des Saints-Apotres, Sherbrooke, PQ, Canada [Library symbol]	CaQSherG
Grand Senior Deacon [Masonry]	GSD
Grand Sentinel [Masonry]	GS
Grand Sentry [Masonry]	GS
Grand Slam Home Runs [Baseball]	GSHR
Grand Steward [Masonry]	GS
Grand Superintendent of Works [Masonry]	GS of W
Grand Sword-Bearer [Masonry]	GSB
Grand Teton National Park	GRTE
Grand Theft	GT
Grand Tiler [Masonry]	GT
Grand Treasurer [Masonry]	GT
Grand Trunk Railway	GTRY
Grand Trunk Western Railroad Co. [AAR code]	GTW
Grand Turk [British West Indies] [Airport symbol]	GDT
Grand Turk Island	GTI
Grand Ufficiale [Grand Officer]	GrUff
Grand Unified Monopoles [Cosmology]	GUM
Grand Unified Theories [Cosmology]	GUTs
Grand Unified Theory [Cosmology]	GUT
Grand Union Co. [NYSE symbol]	GUX
Grand United Order of Odd Fellows	GUOOF
Grand Valley State College, Allendale, MI [OCLC symbol]	EXG
Grand Valley State College, Allendale, MI [Library symbol]	MiAllG
Grand View College [Iowa]	GVC
Grand View College, Des Moines, IA [Library symbol]	IaDmG
Grand View College, Des Moines, IA [OCLC symbol]	IWG
Grandbury, TX [Radio station call letters]	KPAR
Granddaughter	GD
Granddaughter Of [Genealogy]	GR/D/O
Grande Centre, AB [Radio station call letters]	CILW
Grande Croix	GrCr
Grande Prairie [Canada] [Airport symbol]	YQU
Grande Prairie, AB [Television station call letters]	CBXAT
Grande Prairie, AB [Television station call letters]	CBXFT-8
Grande Prairie, AB [Television station call letters]	CFRN-TV-1
Grande Prairie, AB [Radio station call letters]	CJXX
Grande Prairie, AB [Radio station call letters]	CKUA-FM-4
Grande Prairie College, Grande Prairie, AB, Canada [Library symbol]	CaAGPC
Grande Puissance Filloux [World War II]	GPF
Grande Revue [A publication]	GR
Grande Vitesse [French high-speed train]	GV
Grandfather	GRF
Grandioso [Majestic] [Music]	GRANDO
Grandma Lee's, Incorporated [NASDAQ symbol]	GLICF
Grandmother	GRM
Grandmothers of America in War Service [World War II]	GAWS
Grandparents Anonymous	GPA
Grands Ballets Canadiens, Montreal, PQ, Canada [Library symbol]	CaQMGB
Grandson	GS
Grandson Of [Genealogy]	GR/S/O
Grandview Heights Library, Columbus, OH [Library symbol]	OCoG
Grandview Hospital, Dayton, OH [Library symbol]	ODaGH
Grandview, WV [Television station call letters]	WSWP-TV
Grange [or Manor, a religious residence]	GR
Granger Associates [American Stock Exchange symbol]	GRG
Granges-Gontardes [France] [Seismograph station code, US Geological Survey] [Closed]	GGF
Grangeville, ID [Radio station call letters]	KORT
Grangeville, ID [Radio station call letters]	KORT-FM
Granite	GRAN
Granite Butte [Montana] [Seismograph station code, US Geological Survey] [Closed]	GBM
Granite City Army Depot	GCAD
Granite City Community Unit 12, Granite City, IL [Library symbol]	IGracCU
Granite City, IL [Radio station call letters]	KWK-FM
Granite City, IL [Radio station call letters]	WGNU
Granite City, IL [Radio station call letters]	WWWK
Granite City Public Library, Granite City, IL [Library symbol]	IGrac
Granite City Steel Co. [NYSE symbol] [Delisted]	GRC
Granite Creek [California] [Seismograph station code, US Geological Survey]	GCC
Granite Cutters' International Association [Later, Tile, Marble, Terrazzo, Finishers, Shopworkers, and Granite Cutters International Union]	GCIA
Granite Falls, NC [Radio station call letters]	WKJK
Granite Grit Institute of America	GGIA
Granite Management Services, Inc. [American Stock Exchange symbol] [Delisted]	GMS
Granite Monthly [A publication]	Granite Mo
Granite Monthly [A publication]	Gran Mo
Granite Mountain [Alaska] [Seismograph station code, US Geological Survey]	GMA

Granite Mountain [Utah] [Seismograph station code, US Geological Survey]	GMU
Graniteville [South Carolina] [Seismograph station code, US Geological Survey] [Closed]	GVS
Graniteville Co. [NYSE symbol] [Wall Street slang name: "Grannie"]	GVL
Granodize	GRAN
Granolithic Base	GRB
Granolithic Finish Floor [Technical drawings]	GFF
Granos Semilla Selecta [A publication]	Granos Semilla Selec
Grant	GR
Grant Aid [Military]	GA
Grant Aid [Military]	GRA
Grant Air Program [DoD]	GAP
Grant [W. T.] Co. [NYSE symbol] [Delisted]	GTY
Grant-Illini School 110, Fairview Heights, IL [Library symbol]	IFhGS
Grant Industries [American Stock Exchange symbol]	GTX
Grant Information System [Oryx Press]	GIS
Grant Law Library, Davenport, IA [Library symbol]	IaDaGL
Grant MacEwan Community College, Edmonton, AB, Canada [Library symbol]	CaAEGM
Grant MacEwan Community College Library Technology Program, Edmonton, AB, Canada [OCLC symbol]	CGM
Grant, NE [Location identifier] [FAA]	GGF
Grant Parish Library, Colfax, LA [Library symbol]	LColfG
Grant Public Library, Grant, MI [Library symbol]	MiGran
Grantham High School, Saint Catharines, ON, Canada [Library symbol]	CaOStCG
Granting	GRTG
Grantree Corp. [NASDAQ symbol]	GTRE
Grants Administration Division [Environmental Protection Agency]	GAD
Grants Administration Manual [HEW]	GAM
Grants-in-Aid	GIA
Grants Magazine [A publication]	Grants Mag
Grants, NM [Location identifier] [FAA]	GNT
Grants, NM [Radio station call letters]	KMIN
Grants, NM [Radio station call letters]	KYKN
Grants Pass, OR [Location identifier] [FAA]	GNA
Grants Pass, OR [Radio station call letters]	KAGI
Grants Pass, OR [Radio station call letters]	KAJO
Grants Pass, OR [Radio station call letters]	KFMJ
Grants Pass, OR [Location identifier] [FAA]	OOO
Grantsmanship Center	GC
Granular Activated Carbon	GAC
Granular Snow [Skiing condition]	GR
Granulated	GNLTD
Granulated	GRANL
Granulation Time	G/T
Granulation Tissue	G/T
Granulatus [Granulated] [Pharmacy]	GRAN
Granulocyte Agglutination [Hematology]	GA
Granulocyte Cytotoxic [Hematology]	GC
Granulocyte/Macrophage [Ratio] [Hematology]	G/M
Granulocyte Turnover Rate [Hematology]	GTR
Granulocytosis-Promoting Factor [Hematology]	GPF
Granulomatous Angiitis [Medicine]	GA
Granulopoietin [Hypothetical substance] [Hematology]	GPO
Granulosis Virus	GV
Granum [Grain] [Latin]	GR
Granville, OH [Radio station call letters]	WDUB
Grape Berry Moth	GBM
Grapefruit Juice [Restaurant slang]	GJ
Graph Algorithmic Language [Data processing]	GRAAL
Graph Information Retrieval Language [Data processing]	GIRL
Graph Isomorphism Tester	GIT
Graphic	GRAPH
Graphic	GRPH
Graphic Addition to FORTRAN [Data processing]	GRAF
Graphic Aids for Investigating Networks [NASA]	GAIN
Graphic Ammeter	GA
Graphic Analysis of Three-Dimensional Data	GATD
Graphic Analyzer of Resistance Defects	GARD
Graphic Applications Subroutine Package [Data processing]	GASP
Graphic Artists Guild	GA
Graphic Arts Abstracts [A publication]	Graph Arts Abstr
Graphic Arts Advertisers Council [Later, GAAEC]	GAAC
Graphic Arts Advertisers and Exhibitors Council [Formerly, GAAC]	GAAEC
Graphic Arts Association Executives	GAAE
Graphic Arts Composing Equipment	GRACE
Graphic Arts Council of North America	GACNA
Graphic Arts Employers of America	GAE
Graphic Arts Equipment and Supply Dealers Association	GAESDA
Graphic Arts Guidance Kit	GAGK
Graphic Arts Industries Association	GAIA
Graphic Arts International Union [Merger of International Brotherhood of Bookbinders and Lithographers and Photoengravers International Union]	GAIU
Graphic Arts Literature Abstracts [A publication]	GALA
Graphic Arts Literature Abstracts [A publication]	Graphic Arts Lit Abstr
Graphic Arts Manufacturers' Representative Association	GAMRA

Graphic Arts Marketing Information Service [*Printing Industries of America*].................GAMIS
Graphic Arts Monthly [*A publication*].................GA
Graphic Arts Monthly [*A publication*].................Graphic Arts M
Graphic Arts Progress [*A publication*].................Graphic Arts Prog
Graphic Arts Research Center [*Later, T & E Center*] [*Rochester Institute of Technology*].................GARC
Graphic Arts Research Foundation.................GARF
Graphic Arts Spray Manufacturers [*Defunct*].................GASM
Graphic Arts Technical Foundation.................GATF
Graphic Arts Trade Association Executives [*Later, GAAE*].................GATAE
Graphic Arts Union Employers of America.................UEA
Graphic Communications Association [*of Printing Industries of America*] [*Formerly, GCCA*].................GCA
Graphic Communications Computer Association [*of Printing Industries of America*] [*Later, GCA*].................GCCA
Graphic Communications Weekly [*A publication*].................GC
Graphic Communications Weekly [*A publication*].................GCW
Graphic Communications Weekly [*A publication*].................Graphic Comm Wk
Graphic Controls Corp., Buffalo, NY [*Library symbol*].................NBuGC
Graphic Data System.................GDS
Graphic Demand Meter.................GD
Graphic Depth Recorder.................GDR
Graphic Display Processor.................GDP
Graphic Display Terminal.................GDT
Graphic Display Unit.................GDU
Graphic Export Center [*Netherlands*].................GEC
Graphic Expression Reading Improvement System.................GERIS
Graphic Firing Fan [*Weaponry*].................GFF
Graphic Firing Table [*Weaponry*].................GFT
Graphic Generator System.................GGS
Graphic Industries [*NASDAQ symbol*].................GRPH
Graphic Input System.................GIS
Graphic Interactive Display.................GRID
Graphic Interface for Finite Elements [*Graphics data processing*].................GIRAFFE
Graphic Job Processor.................GJP
Graphic Kilovolt-Ampere [*Meter*].................GVA
Graphic Layout and Engineering Aid Method.................GLEAM
Graphic Level Recorder.................GLR
Graphic Media, Inc. [*NASDAQ symbol*].................GMED
Graphic Microfilm Corp., Valley Stream, NY [*Library symbol*].................GmNY
Graphic Microfilm of New England, Waltham, MA [*Library symbol*].................GmNE
Graphic Numerical Control.................GNC
Graphic On-Line Language [*Data processing*].................GOLD
Graphic Output Circuit Analysis Program.................GOCAP
Graphic Programing Services [*Data processing*].................GPS
Graphic Reproduction by Integrated Design.................GRID
Graphic Retrieval and Information Display.................GRID
Graphic Scanning Corporation [*NASDAQ symbol*].................GSCC
Graphic Science [*A publication*].................Graphic Sci
Graphic Service Program.................GRASP
Graphic Service Routines.................GSR
Graphic Sketch Club, Philadelphia, PA [*Library symbol*] [*Obsolete*].................PPGraph
Graphic Stress Telethermometry [*Medicine*].................GST
Graphic Subroutine Package [*Data processing*].................GSP
Graphic Surface Kinetics [*Computer program*].................GASKET
Graphic Tablet Display.................GTD
Graphic Technology [*American Stock Exchange symbol*].................GRT
Graphic Training Aid.................GTA
Graphic Training Aids Officer [*Army*].................GTAO
Graphic Varmeter.................GRVA
Graphical Aid [*Data processing*].................GRAID
Graphical Analysis of Program Execution [*Data processing*].................GRAPE
Graphical Automatically Programed Tools [*Data processing*].................GAPT
Graphical Data Display Manager [*Data processing*].................GDDM
Graphical Data Entry [*Data processing*].................GRAPHDEN
Graphical Evaluation and Review Technique.................GERT
Graphical Input [*Language*] [*Data processing*].................GRIN
Graphical Input and Output in FORTRAN [*Data processing*].................GINO-F
Graphical Interaction [*Language*] [*Data processing*].................GRIN-2
Graphical Interactive NMR Analysis [*Data processing*].................GINA
Graphical Kernel System [*International Standards Organization*].................GKS
Graphical PERT [*Program Evaluation and Review Technique*] Analog [*Data processing*].................GPA
Graphically Oriented Design and Analysis System [*Data processing*].................GODAS
Graphics Access Method.................GAM
Graphics Action Request.................GAR
Graphics-Assisted Management Application.................GAMA
Graphics-Augmented Structural Post-Processing [*Module*].................GRASP
Graphics Flutter Analysis Methods [*Data processing*].................GFAM
Graphics Interaction with Proteins [*Computer graphics*].................GRIP
Graphics for the Multipicture System [*Computer graphics*].................GRAMPS
Graphics Nesting Program.................GNP
Graphics Philately Association.................GPA
Graphics Program for Aircraft Design.................GPAD
Graphics Terminal Scheduler.................GTS
Graphics Terminal Services.................GTS
Graphics Terminal System.................GTS

Graphics Vendor Control.................GVC
Graphite.................GPH
Graphite Fiber Composite.................GFC
Graphite-Fiber-Reinforced Plastic [*Also, GrFRP*].................GFRP
Graphite-Fiber-Reinforced Plastic [*Also, GFRP*].................GrFRP
Graphite-Furnace Atomic Absorption [*Spectroscopy*].................GFAA
Graphite Low-Energy Experimental Pile [*Nuclear reactor*] [*British*].................GLEEP
Graphite-Moderated Boiling and Superheating Reactor.................GBSR
Graphite Oxidation from Reactor Excursion [*Engineering computer code*].................GORX
Graphite-Reinforced Epoxy.................GRE
Graphitic Oxide.................GO
Graphitized Carbon Black.................GCB
Grapple Adapter [*Nuclear energy*].................GA
Grapple Adapter Handling Fixture [*Nuclear energy*].................GAHF
Grappling and Lock-On Validation.................GALOVAL
Grasas y Aceites [*A publication*].................Grasas Aceites
Grashof Number [*IUPAC*].................Gr
Grasonville, MD [*Radio station call letters*].................WBEY
Grass [*Maps and charts*].................GRS
Grass-Model Polygraph.................GMP
Grass Mountain [*Washington*] [*Seismograph station code, US Geological Survey*].................GSM
Grass Roots Association.................GRA
Grass Valley, CA [*Radio station call letters*].................KNCO
Grass Valley, CA [*Radio station call letters*].................KNCO-FM
Grass Valley Free Public Library, Grass Valley, CA [*Library symbol*].................CGr
Grasse River R. R. Corp. [*AAR code*].................GR
Grassi Block Substitution Test [*Psychology*].................GBST
Grassland.................GRSLND
Grassland Biome [*Ecological biogeographic study*].................GB
Grassland Heritage Foundation.................GHF
Grassland Husbandry Adviser [*Ministry of Agriculture, Fisheries, and Food*] [*British*].................GHA
Grassland Research Foundation.................GRF
Grassland Research Institute (Hurley). Annual Report [*A publication*].................Grassl Res Inst (Hurley) Annu Rep
Grassland Research Institute (Hurley). Experiments in Progress [*A publication*].................Grassl Res Inst (Hurley) Exp Prog
Grassland Research Institute (Hurley). Technical Report [*A publication*].................Grassl Res Inst (Hurley) Tech Rep
Grater.................GRTR
Grating.................GRTG
Gratio [*Tennessee*] [*Seismograph station code, US Geological Survey*].................GRT
Gratitude Patient [*A nonpaying patient*] [*Medical slang*].................GP
Gratuity.................GRAT
Gratz College. Annual of Jewish Studies [*A publication*].................GCAJS
Gratz College, Philadelphia, PA [*Library symbol*] [*Obsolete*].................PPGratz
Grave Record [*Genealogy*].................GR
Gravel [*Quality of the bottom*] [*Nautical charts*].................G
Gravel.................GRVL
Gravel.................GVL
Gravel-Surface Built-Up Roof [*Technical drawings*].................GSBR
Gravelbourg, SK [*Television station call letters*].................CBKFT-6
Gravelbourg, SK [*Radio station call letters*].................CFGR
Gravelbourg, SK [*Radio station call letters*].................CFRG
Graves Public Library, Mendota, IL [*Library symbol*].................IMen
Graves Registration [*Military*].................GR
Graves Registration [*Military*].................GRREG
Graves Registration and Effects Division [*Military*].................GRE & E Div
Graves Registration Officer [*Military*].................GRO
Graves Registration Service [*Military*].................GRS
Gravid [*Pregnant*] [*Medicine*].................GRAV
Gravida [*A publication*].................Gra
Gravimetric Density.................GD
Gravimetric Volume.................GV
Gravitational.................GRAV
Gravitational Mass.................GM
Gravitational Mass Sensor.................GMS
Gravitational Redshift Space Probe [*Also, GRAVR*].................GP
Gravitational Redshift Space Probe [*Also, GP*].................GRAVR
Gravitational Ulcer [*Medicine*].................GU
Gravito-Inertial Force.................GIF
Gravity [*or the force or acceleration produced by it*].................G
Gravity.................GR
Gravity-Assisted Space Probe [*NASA*].................GASP
Gravity Association for Universal Scientific Study.................GAUSS
Gravity-Controlled Gyro.................GCG
Gravity-Controlled Gyro System.................GCGS
Gravity Gradient.................GG
Gravity-Gradient Libration [*Damper*].................GGL
Gravity-Gradient Satellite.................GGS
Gravity-Gradient Sensor.................GGS
Gravity-Gradient Stabilization Experiment.................GGSE
Gravity-Gradient Test Satellite [*NASA*].................GGTS
Gravity-Gradient Torque.................GGT
Gravity Independent Photosynthetic Gas Exchanger.................GIPSE
Gravity Measuring System.................GMS
Gravity-Oriented Test Satellite [*NASA*].................GOTS
Gravity Reference Signal [*or System*].................GRS

Gravity Research Foundation ... GRF
Gravity per Second ... G/S
Gravity Sensors System [*Navigation*] ... GSS
Gravity Setting Culture ... GSC
Gravity Vacuum Tube System [*High-speed ground transportation*] ... GVT
Gravity-Velocity ... G-V
Gravure Engravers Association ... GEA
Gravure Research Institute ... GRI
Gravure Technical Association ... GTA
Gray ... GR
Gray ... GRA
Gray ... GY
Gray [*Symbol*] [*SI unit for absorbed dose acceleration*] ... Gy
Gray [*Thoroughbred racing*] ... GR
Gray Cast Iron ... GCI
Gray Communications Systems [*NASDAQ symbol*] ... GCOM
Gray Company, Inc. ... GRACO
Gray Court, SC [*Radio station call letters*] ... WSSL
Gray Drug Stores, Inc. [*NYSE symbol*] [*Delisted*] ... GRY
Gray and Ductile Iron Founders' Society [*Later, Iron Castings Society*] ... GDIFS
Gray Iron ... GI
Gray Iron Founders Society [*Later, GDIFS; then, Iron Castings Society*] ... GIFS
Gray Oral Reading Tests ... GORT
Gray Panther Network [*A publication*] ... Gray Pant
Gray Panthers [*Formerly, RPAG*] ... GP
Grayhill Exploration [*NASDAQ symbol*] ... GRAY
Grayling [*Alaska*] [*Airport symbol*] ... KGX
Grayling Creek [*Montana*] [*Seismograph station code, US Geological Survey*] ... GCR
Grayling, MI [*Radio station call letters*] ... WGRY
Grayling, MI [*Radio station call letters*] ... WQON
Grays Harbor College [*Washington*] ... GHC
Grays Harbor College, Aberdeen, WA [*Library symbol*] ... WaAG
Gray's Inn [*London*] [*One of the Inns of Court*] ... GI
Grayson County College, Denison, TX [*Library symbol*] ... TxDeniG
Grayson, KY [*Radio station call letters*] ... WGOH
Grayson, KY [*Radio station call letters*] ... WKCC
Grayson, KY [*Radio station call letters*] ... WUGO
Grayson Perceptualization Test [*Psychology*] ... GPT
Grayson Robinson Stores, Inc. [*NYSE symbol*] [*Delisted*] ... QGRB
Graysonia, Nashville, & Ashdown Railroad Co. [*AAR code*] ... GNA
Graz [*Steiermark*] [*Austria*] [*Seismograph station code, US Geological Survey*] [*Closed*] ... GRA
Graz [*Austria*] [*Airport symbol*] ... GRZ
Graz Landesmuseum Joanneum. Abteilung fuer Mineralogie. Mitteilungsblatt [*A publication*] ... Graz Landesmus Joanneum Abt Mineral Mitteilungsbl
Graz Landesmuseum Joanneum. Jahresbericht [*A publication*] ... Graz Landesmus Joanneum Jahresber
Graz Landesmuseum Joanneum. Museum fuer Bergbau, Geologie, und Technik. Mitteilungen [*A publication*] ... Graz Landesmus Joanneum Mus Bergbau Geol Tech Mitt
Grazer Beitraege [*A publication*] ... GB
Grazhdanskii Vozdushnyi Flot [*Civil Air Fleet*] [*USSR*] ... GVF
Graziano, R. M., Washington DC [*STAC*] ... GRM
Grazioso [*Gracefully*] [*Music*] ... GRAZ
Grazioso [*Gracefully*] [*Music*] ... GRAZO
Grease ... GRS
Grease Monkey Holding Uts [*NASDAQ symbol*] ... GMHCU
Grease Nozzle ... GNOZ
Grease Trap ... GT
Great ... G
Great ... GR
Great ... GT
Great American Airways [*Reno, NV*] [*FAA designator*] ... GRA
Great American Bancorp [*NASDAQ symbol*] ... GRTB
Great American Corp. [*NASDAQ symbol*] ... GTAM
Great American Dream ... GAD
Great American Federal Savings Bank [*NASDAQ symbol*] ... GRTA
Great American Industries, Inc. [*American Stock Exchange symbol*] ... GRI
Great American Management/Investment [*NASDAQ symbol*] ... GAMI
Great American Resources [*NASDAQ symbol*] ... GAMR
Great American Shoe Store [*Advertising slogan of Kinney Shoe Corp.*] ... GASS
Great American Wife and Mother [*Slang*] ... GAWAM
Great Analog Signal Saver ... GASS
Great Atlantic & Pacific Tea Co., Inc. ... A & P
Great Atlantic & Pacific Tea Co., Inc. [*NYSE symbol*] ... GAP
Great Atlantic Radio Conspiracy [*An association*] ... GARC
Great Barrier [*New Zealand*] [*Seismograph station code, US Geological Survey*] ... GBZ
Great Barrier Island [*Australia*] [*Airport symbol*] ... GBZ
Great Barrington, MA [*Radio station call letters*] ... WSBS
Great Basin Naturalist [*A publication*] ... Great Basin Nat
Great Basin Naturalist. Memoirs [*A publication*] ... Great Basin Nat Mem
Great Basins Petroleum Co. [*American Stock Exchange symbol*] [*Delisted*] ... GBR
Great Bend [*Kansas*] [*Airport symbol*] ... GBD
Great Bend, KS [*Location identifier*] [*FAA*] ... HIL
Great Bend, KS [*Television station call letters*] ... KSNC
Great Bend, KS [*Radio station call letters*] ... KVGB
Great Bend, KS [*Radio station call letters*] ... KVGB-FM
Great Big Star [*in the movies*] ... GBS
Great Books Foundation ... GBF
Great Britain [*United Kingdom*] [*Two-letter standard code*] ... GB
Great Britain Correspondence Club ... GBCC
Great Britain and the East [*A publication*] ... GBE
Great Britain and the East [*A publication*] ... Gt Brit & East
Great Britain Forestry Commission. Annual Report of the Forestry Commissioners [*A publication*] ... GB For Comm Annu Rep For Comm
Great Britain Forestry Commission. Booklet [*A publication*] ... GB For Comm Bookl
Great Britain Forestry Commission. Bulletin [*A publication*] ... GB For Comm Bull
Great Britain Forestry Commission. Forest Record [*A publication*] ... GB For Comm For Rec
Great Britain Forestry Commission. Leaflet [*A publication*] ... GB For Comm Leafl
Great Britain Forestry Commission. Report on Forest Research [*A publication*] ... GB For Comm Rep For Res
Great Britain Forestry Commission. Research and Development Paper [*A publication*] ... GB For Comm Res Dev Pap
Great Britain Institute of Geological Sciences. Annual Report [*A publication*] ... GB Inst Geol Sci Annu Rep
Great Britain Institute of Geological Sciences. Geomagnetic Bulletin [*A publication*] ... GB Inst Geol Sci Geomagn Bull
Great Britain Institute of Geological Sciences. Mineral Assessment Report [*A publication*] ... GB Inst Geol Sci Miner Assess Rep
Great Britain Institute of Geological Sciences. Report [*A publication*] ... GB Inst Geol Sci Rep
Great Britain and Ireland ... GB & I
Great Britain Land Resources Division. Land Resource Study [*A publication*] ... GB Land Resour Div Land Resour Study
Great Britain Ministry of Agriculture, Fisheries, and Food. Technical Bulletin [*A publication*] ... GB Minist Agric Fish Food Tech Bull
Great Britain Ministry of Aviation ... GBMA
Great Britain Ministry of Overseas Development. Land Resources Division. Progress Report [*A publication*] ... GB Minist Overseas Dev Land Resour Div Prog Rep
Great Britain Ministry of Technology. Forest Products Research. Bulletin [*A publication*] ... GB Minist Technol For Prod Res Bull
Great Britain Ministry of Technology. Forest Products Research. Special Report [*A publication*] ... GB Minist Technol For Prod Res Spec Rep
Great Britain Natural Environment Research Council. News Journal [*A publication*] ... GB Nat Environ Res Counc News J
Great Britain Natural Environment Research Council. Report [*A publication*] ... GB Nat Environ Res Counc Rep
Great Britain Soil Survey of England and Wales. Annual Report [*A publication*] ... GB Soil Surv Engl Wales Annu Rep
Great Britain Soil Survey. Special Survey [*A publication*] ... GB Soil Surv Spec Surv
Great Britain Water Resource Board. Publication [*A publication*] ... GB Water Resour Board Publ
Great British Public ... GBP
Great Bustard Trust [*An association*] ... GBT
Great Canadian Oil Sands Ltd. ... GCOS
Great Central Railway [*British*] ... GCR
Great Circle ... GC
Great Circle [*FAA*] ... GTCL
Great Circle Distance ... GCD
Great Circle Track ... GCT
Great Dane Club of America ... GDCA
Great Eastern Energy & Development [*NASDAQ symbol*] ... GREN
Great Eastern Mines ADR [*NASDAQ symbol*] ... GOLDY
Great Eastern Railway [*British*] ... GER
Great Exuma [*Bahama Islands*] ... GE
Great Falls [*Montana*] [*Airport symbol*] ... GTF
Great Falls, MT [*Radio station call letters*] ... KAAK
Great Falls, MT [*Radio station call letters*] ... KARR
Great Falls, MT [*Radio station call letters*] ... KEIN
Great Falls, MT [*Television station call letters*] ... KFBB
Great Falls, MT [*Radio station call letters*] ... KLFM
Great Falls, MT [*Radio station call letters*] ... KMON
Great Falls, MT [*Radio station call letters*] ... KNUW
Great Falls, MT [*Radio station call letters*] ... KOOZ
Great Falls, MT [*Radio station call letters*] ... KQDI
Great Falls, MT [*Television station call letters*] ... KRTV
Great Falls, MT [*Location identifier*] [*FAA*] ... SMR
Great Falls Public Library, Great Falls, MT [*Library symbol*] ... MtGr
Great Fire [*of London, 1666*] ... GF
Great Gatsby [*Describes clothing style modeled after the type worn by characters in F. Scott Fitzgerald's novel, "The Great Gatsby"*] ... GG
Great Granddaughter ... GGD
Great Grandson ... GGS
Great Gross [*144 dozen*] [*Also, GGR*] ... GG
Great Gross [*144 dozen*] [*Also, GG*] ... GGR

Great Harbour Cay [*Bahamas*] [*Airport symbol*] ... GHC
[*The*] **Great Ideas Today** [*A publication*] ... GIT
Great Indian Peninsular R. R. ... GIP
Great Indulgence ... GI
Great Irish Painter [*Reference to Jack B. Yeats, ca. 1905*] ... GIP
Great Keppel Island [*Australia*] [*Airport symbol*] ... GKL
Great Lakes [*Vessel load line mark*] ... GL
Great Lakes ... GLAKES
Great Lakes [*FAA*] ... GRTLKS
Great Lakes [*MARC geographic area code*] [*Library of Congress*] ... nl-----
Great Lakes Basin Commission ... GLBC
Great Lakes Bible College, Lansing, MI [*OCLC symbol*] ... EEG
Great Lakes Bible College, Lansing, MI [*Library symbol*] ... MiLG
Great Lakes Chemical Corp. [*American Stock Exchange symbol*] ... GLK
Great Lakes Colleges Association ... GLCA
Great Lakes Commission ... GLC
Great Lakes Entomologist [*A publication*] ... Great Lakes Entomol
Great Lakes Environmental Information Center ... GLEDIC
Great Lakes Environmental Information Sharing ... GLEIS
Great Lakes Environmental Research Laboratory [*National Oceanic and Atmospheric Administration*] ... GLERL
Great Lakes Federal Savings & Loan [*NASDAQ symbol*] ... GLFS
Great Lakes Fisheries Laboratory, Ann Arbor, MI [*OCLC symbol*] ... GLF
Great Lakes Fisheries Laboratory, Ann Arbor, MI [*Library symbol*] ... MiAaFL
Great Lakes Fishery Commission ... GLFC
Great Lakes Fishery Commission. Annual Report [*A publication*] ... Great Lakes Fish Comm Annu Rep
Great Lakes Fishery Commission. Technical Report [*A publication*] ... Great Lakes Fish Comm Tech Rep
Great Lakes Fishery Laboratory [*Department of the Interior*] ... GLFL
Great Lakes Freight Bureau Inc., Cleveland OH [*STAC*] ... GLB
Great Lakes Harbor Association ... GLHA
Great Lakes Historical Society ... GLHS
Great Lakes Intercollegiate Athletic Conference ... GLIAC
Great Lakes International, Inc. [*NYSE symbol*] ... GL
Great Lakes Licensed Officers' Organization ... GLLO
Great Lakes Maritime Institute ... GLMI
Great Lakes Megalopolis [*Proposed name for possible "super-city" formed by growth and mergers of other cities*] ... GLM
Great Lakes Mink Association ... GLMA
Great Lakes Naval Training Center ... GLNTC
Great Lakes Physical Information Analysis Center ... GLPIAC
Great Lakes Pilotage Administration [*Department of Transportation*] ... GLPA
Great Lakes Recreation Co. [*American Stock Exchange symbol*] [*Delisted*] ... GBW
Great Lakes Region [*FAA*] ... AGL
Great Lakes Review: a Journal of Midwest Culture [*A publication*] ... GrLR
Great Lakes - St. Lawrence Association ... GLASLA
Great Lakes Screw ... GLS
Great Lakes Seaplane Association ... GLSA
Great Lakes Ship Owners Association ... GLSOA
Great Lakes Study Group [*US, Canada*] ... GLSG
Great Lakes United ... GLU
Great Lakes Waterways Development Association ... GLWDA
Great Little Car [*Mazda Motors of America*] ... GLC
Great Neck Library, Great Neck, NY [*Library symbol*] ... NGrn
Great Nigeria People's Party ... GNPP
Great North of Scotland Railway ... GNSR
Great Northern Airlines, Inc. [*Anchorage, AK*] [*FAA designator*] ... GNA
Great Northern Iron Ore Properties [*NYSE symbol*] ... GNI
Great Northern Nekoosa Corp. [*NYSE symbol*] ... GNN
Great Northern Paper Co. [*Later, GNN*] [*NYSE symbol*] ... GPP
Great Northern Railway [*NYSE symbol*] [*Delisted*] ... GN
Great Northern Railway ... GNR
Great Northern Railway ... GNRY
Great Organ [*Music*] ... GO
Great Organ [*Music*] ... G ORG
Great Outdoor American Adventure, Inc. [*NASDAQ symbol*] ... GOAA
Great Plains [*AAR code*] ... GRIN
Great Plains [*MARC geographic area code*] [*Library of Congress*] ... np-----
Great Plains Agricultural Council ... GPAC
Great Plains Agricultural Council. Publication [*A publication*] ... Great Plains Agric Counc Publ
Great Plains Conservation Program ... GPCP
Great Plains Development Co. of Canada Ltd., Calgary, AB, Canada [*Library symbol*] ... CaACGP
Great Plains Historical Association [*Later, IGP*] ... GPHA
Great Plains Journal [*A publication*] ... GPJ
Great Plains Journal [*A publication*] ... Gt Plains Jour
Great Plains National Instructional Television Library ... GPNITL
Great Plains Wheat, Inc. ... GPW
Great Primer ... GP
Great Proletarian Cultural Revolution [*People's Republic of China*] ... GPCR
Great Pyrenees Club of America ... GPCA
Great Red Spot [*on planet Jupiter*] ... GRS
Great Revolutionary American Standard System [*Book title*] ... GRASS
Great River Library System [*Library network*] ... GRLS
Great River Library System, Quincy, IL [*Library symbol*] ... IQG
Great River Library System, Quincy, IL [*OCLC symbol*] ... ITA
Great River Regional Library, St. Cloud, MN [*Library symbol*] ... MnStclG
Great Roll [*of the Pipe*] [*British*] ... GR
Great Salt Lake [*Utah*] ... GSL
Great Sand Dunes National Monument ... GRSA
Great Science Fiction Stories [*A publication*] ... GSFS
Great Seal [*British*] ... GS
Great Sitkin [*Alaska*] [*Seismograph station code, US Geological Survey*] ... AD1
Great Smoky Mountains National Park ... GRSM
Great Somalia League ... GSL
Great Southwest Corporation ... GSC
Great Southwest Industries Corporation [*NASDAQ symbol*] ... GSIC
Great Southwest Railroad, Inc. [*AAR code*] ... GSW
Great Speckled Bird [*A publication*] ... Grt Bird
Great Universal Stores [*British*] ... GUSSIES
Great West Life Assurance Co., Winnipeg, MB, Canada [*Library symbol*] ... CaMWGW
Great Western Airlines, Inc. [*Tulsa, OK*] [*FAA designator*] ... GWS
Great Western Federal Savings Bank [*NASDAQ symbol*] ... GWSB
Great Western Financial Corp. [*NYSE symbol*] ... GWF
[*The*] **Great Western Railway Co.** [*Prior to nationalization*] [*AAR code*] ... GWR
Great Western Society ... GWS
Great Western Sugar Co., Technical Library, Denver, CO [*Library symbol*] ... CoDGW
Great Western Systems [*NASDAQ symbol*] ... GWSI
Great Western United Corp. [*NYSE symbol*] [*Delisted*] ... GWU
Great Whale [*Canada*] [*Airport symbol*] ... YGW
Great Whale River [*Quebec*] [*Geomagnetic observatory code*] ... GWC
Great Whale River [*Quebec*] [*Seismograph station code, US Geological Survey*] [*Closed*] ... GWC
Greate Bay Casino Cl A [*NASDAQ symbol*] ... GBAYA
Greater [*Freight*] ... GRTR
Greater ... GTR
Greater [*name of city*] **Alliance to Stop Pollution** ... GASP
Greater Antilles [*MARC geographic area code*] [*Library of Congress*] ... nwga---
Greater Blouse and Skirt Contractors Association [*Later, GBSUA*] ... GBSCA
Greater Blouse, Skirt, and Undergarment Association ... GBSUA
Greater Cincinnati Library Consortium [*Library network*] ... GCLC
Greater Cleveland Mathematics Program [*Education*] ... GCMP
Greater Clothing Contractors Association ... GCCA
Greater East Asia [*Used by Japanese in such terms as War of Greater East Asia and Greater East Asia Co-Prosperity Sphere*] [*World War II*] ... GEA
Greater than or Equal ... GE
Greater Greensboro [*North Carolina*] **Open** [*Golf tournament*] ... GGO
Greater Hartford [*Connecticut*] **Open** [*Golf tournament*] ... GHO
Greater Hartford Process [*An association*] ... GHP
Greater Heritage Corp. [*NASDAQ symbol*] ... GHER
Greater Independent Association of National Travel Services ... GIANTS
Greater Jacksonville [*Florida*] **Open** [*Golf tournament*] ... GJO
Greater London [*England*] ... GL
Greater London Council [*Formerly, LCC*] ... GLC
Greater-than-Lot Quantities ... GLQ
Greater Middle East ... GME
Greater Milwaukee Dental Bulletin [*A publication*] ... Greater Milw Dent Bull
Greater New England Society of Inhalation Therapists ... GNESIT
Greater New Orleans Microform Cooperative [*Library network*] ... GNOMAC
Greater New Orleans Microform Cooperative, Tulane University, New Orleans, LA [*Library symbol*] ... LNT-MC
Greater New York Council for Foreign Students [*Later, English in Action*] ... GNYCFS
Greater North American Aviculturist and Color Bred Judges Association [*Formerly, GNACBJA*] ... GNAACBJA
Greater North American Color-Bred Judge Association [*Later, GNAACBJA*] ... GNACBJA
Greater St. Louis Amateur Baseball Hall of Fame ... GSLABHF
Greater Super Six Club ... GSSC
Greater Than ... GT
Greater Toy Center ... GTC
Greater Trochanter [*Anatomy*] ... GT
Greater Underwater Propulsive Power [*Type of submarine*] ... GUPPY
Greater Vancouver Regional District, Planning Development Library, Vancouver, BC, Canada [*Library symbol*] ... CaBVaPD
Greater Victoria Public Library, Victoria, BC, Canada [*Library symbol*] ... CaBVi
Greater Washington Investments, Incorporated [*NASDAQ symbol*] ... GWII
Greater Washington Investors, Inc. [*NYSE symbol*] [*Delisted*] ... GRW
Greater World Christian Spiritualist Association ... GWCSA
Greatest Axial Linear Dimension ... GALD
Greatest Common Denominator ... GCD
Greatest Common Divisor ... GCD
Greatest Common Factor ... GCF
Greatest Common Measure ... GCM
Greatest Length ... GL
Greatest Response Amplitude Probability ... GRAP
Greatest Response Amplitude Probability Data ... GRAPD
Greatest Response Data ... GRD
Greatest Response Probability ... GRP

Greatest Upper Bound [*Data processing*] ..... GUB
Greatness Is Simplicity [*See also SIG*] ..... GIS
Greatwest Hospitals [*NYSE symbol*] ..... GHI
Greece [*MARC geographic area code*] [*Library of Congress*] ..... e-gr---
Greece [*MARC country of publication code*] [*Library of Congress*] ..... gr
Greece [*Three-letter standard code*] ..... GRC
Greece [*Aircraft nationality and registration mark*] ..... SX
Greece [*Two-letter standard code*] ..... GR
Greece-Arcadia Junior/Senior High School Library, Rochester, NY [*OCLC symbol*] ..... RWI
Greece-Athena Junior/Senior High School Library, Rochester, NY [*OCLC symbol*] ..... RWJ
Greece, NY [*Radio station call letters*] ..... WGMC
Greece-Olympia High School Library, Rochester, NY [*OCLC symbol*] ..... RWK
Greece and Rome [*A publication*] ..... G & R
Greece and Rome: New Surveys in the Classics [*A publication*] ..... Greece & Rome New Surv Class
Greek ..... G
Greek ..... GK
Greek ..... GR
Greek-American Progressive Association ..... GAPA
Greek, Ancient [*MARC language code*] [*Library of Congress*] ..... grc
Greek Atomic Energy Commission ..... GAEC
Greek and Byzantine Studies [*A publication*] ..... G & BS
Greek Catholic Union of the United States of America ..... GCUUSA
Greek, Modern [*MARC language code*] [*Library of Congress*] ..... gre
Greek Orthodox Ladies Philoptochos Society ..... GOLPS
Greek Orthodox Theological Review [*A publication*] ..... Gr Orth Th R
Greek Orthodox Theological Review [*A publication*] ..... GTR
Greek Orthodox Youth of America ..... GOYA
Greek Research Reactor ..... GRR
Greek, Roman, and Byzantine Monographs [*A publication*] ..... GRBM
Greek, Roman, and Byzantine Scholarly Aids [*A publication*] ..... GRBSA
Greek, Roman, and Byzantine Studies [*A publication*] ..... GR & BS
Greek, Roman, and Byzantine Studies [*A publication*] ..... GRBS
Greek, Roman, and Byzantine Studies [*A publication*] ..... Greek Rom & Byz Stud
Greeley, CO [*Radio station call letters*] ..... KFKA
Greeley, CO [*Radio station call letters*] ..... KGBS
Greeley, CO [*Radio station call letters*] ..... KGRE
Greeley, CO [*Radio station call letters*] ..... KUNC-FM
Greeley, CO [*Radio station call letters*] ..... KYOU
Greeley & Hansen, Chicago, IL [*OCLC symbol*] ..... IDR
Greeley & Hansen Engineering Library, Chicago, IL [*Library symbol*] ..... ICGH
Greeley Public Library, Greeley, CO [*Library symbol*] ..... CoGr
Green ..... G
Green [*Maps and charts*] ..... GN
Green ..... GR
Green ..... GRN
Green, Amber, Red, Blue [*Priority of the airways*] ..... GARB
Green Bank [*West Virginia*] [*Seismograph station code, US Geological Survey*] ..... GBV
Green Bay [*Wisconsin*] [*Airport symbol*] ..... GRB
Green Bay Aviation [*Green Bay, WI*] [*FAA designator*] ..... GBY
Green Bay & Western Railroad Co. ..... GB & W
Green Bay & Western Railroad Co. [*AAR code*] ..... GBW
Green Bay, WI [*Location identifier*] [*FAA*] ..... TUI
Green Bay, WI [*Television station call letters*] ..... WBAY-TV
Green Bay, WI [*Radio station call letters*] ..... WDUZ
Green Bay, WI [*Radio station call letters*] ..... WDUZ-FM
Green Bay, WI [*Television station call letters*] ..... WFRV-TV
Green Bay, WI [*Radio station call letters*] ..... WGBP-FM
Green Bay, WI [*Radio station call letters*] ..... WGBW
Green Bay, WI [*Radio station call letters*] ..... WGEE
Green Bay, WI [*Radio station call letters*] ..... WIXX
Green Bay, WI [*Television station call letters*] ..... WLRE-TV
Green Bay, WI [*Television station call letters*] ..... WLUK-TV
Green Bay, WI [*Radio station call letters*] ..... WNFL
Green Bay, WI [*Television station call letters*] ..... WPNE
Green Bay, WI [*Radio station call letters*] ..... WPNE-FM
Green Bulletin [*A publication*] ..... Green Bull
Green Circle Program [*Helps children develop self-worth and an awareness of human differences*] ..... GCP
Green Coffee Association [*of New York City*] ..... GCA
Green Coffee Association of New Orleans ..... GCA of NO
Green Cove Springs, FL [*Radio station call letters*] ..... WSVE
Green Giant Co. [*NYSE symbol*] [*Delisted*] ..... GG
Green Giant Corp., Le Sueur, MN [*Library symbol*] ..... MnLsG
Green Hill School, Staff Library, Chehalis, WA [*Library symbol*] ..... WaChehG
Green Hills Aviation Ltd. [*Kirksville, MO*] [*FAA designator*] ..... GHA
Green Hills Aviation Ltd. [*Kirksville, MO*] [*FAA designator*] ..... GRH
Green Hills Public Library District, Palos Hills, IL [*Library symbol*] ..... IPhi
Green Indicating Lamp ..... GIL
Green Island [*Plant pathology*] ..... GI
Green LASER System ..... GLS
Green Light ..... GL
Green, M. E., Jefferson City MO [*STAC*] ..... GME
Green Monkey Kidney Cell ..... GMK
Green Mountain Airlines [*Barre, VT*] [*FAA designator*] ..... GMT
Green Mountain College, Poultney, VT [*Library symbol*] ..... VtPouG
Green Mountain Junior College [*Vermont*] ..... GMJC
Green Mountain Power Corp. [*American Stock Exchange symbol*] ..... GMP
Green Mountain Railroad Corporation [*AAR code*] ..... GMRC
Green Mountain Textile Overseers Association ..... GMTOA
Green Olive Trade Association ..... GOTA
Green Phone [*NASA*] ..... G/P
Green Pulse Width [*Instrumentation*] ..... GPW
Green, Red, Orange, White, Blue, Yellow [*System devised by a military wife and used by the Army in commissaries of its European posts to indicate day on which packaged bread and rolls were baked. The twist ties on the packages are color-coded to represent the day, with Green indicating Monday, Red for Tuesday, etc., throughout the week.*] ..... GROWBY
Green Revolution [*A publication*] ..... Green Rev
Green River [*Papua New Guinea*] [*Airport symbol*] ..... GVI
Green River Community College, Auburn, WA [*Library symbol*] ..... WaAuG
Green River Review [*A publication*] ..... GRR
Green River Test Complex ..... GRTC
Green River, WY [*Radio station call letters*] ..... KUGR
Green Shoe Manufacturing Co. [*Later, Stride Rite Corp.*] [*NYSE symbol*] ..... GSR
Green Thumb [*An association*] ..... GT
Green Thumbs [*National Weather Service and Department of Agriculture Extension Service telecommunication system*] ..... GT
Green Tree Acceptance [*NASDAQ symbol*] ..... GTAC
Green Valley, AZ [*Radio station call letters*] ..... KEZG
Green Valley, AZ [*Radio station call letters*] ..... KGVY
Green Valley Road [*California*] [*Seismograph station code, US Geological Survey*] ..... GVR
Greenbrier [*West Virginia*] [*Airport symbol*] ..... LWB
Greenbrier College, Lewisburg, WV [*Library symbol*] ..... WvLeG
Greenbrier County Public Library, Lewisburg, WV [*Library symbol*] ..... WvLe
Greenburgh Public Library, Elmsford, NY [*Library symbol*] ..... NEI
Greencastle, IN [*Radio station call letters*] ..... WGRE
Greencastle, IN [*Radio station call letters*] ..... WJNZ
Greencastle, PA [*Radio station call letters*] ..... WKSL
Greene County District Library, Xenia, OH [*OCLC symbol*] ..... GRC
Greene County District Library, Xenia, OH [*Library symbol*] ..... OXe
Greene County Historical Society, Inc., Coxsakie, NY [*Library symbol*] ..... NCoxHi
Greene Public Library, Greene, IA [*Library symbol*] ..... IaGre
Greeneville, TN [*Location identifier*] [*FAA*] ..... DYQ
Greeneville, TN [*Radio station call letters*] ..... WGRV
Greeneville, TN [*Radio station call letters*] ..... WIKQ
Greenfield Community College [*Massachusetts*] ..... GCC
Greenfield Community College, Greenfield, MA [*Library symbol*] ..... MGrefC
Greenfield Community Unit, District 10, Greenfield, IL [*Library symbol*] ..... IGrefCU
Greenfield, IA [*Location identifier*] [*FAA*] ..... GFZ
Greenfield, IN [*Radio station call letters*] ..... WZPL
Greenfield, MA [*Radio station call letters*] ..... WHAI
Greenfield, MA [*Radio station call letters*] ..... WHAI-FM
Greenfield, MA [*Radio station call letters*] ..... WPOE
Greenfield, MA [*Radio station call letters*] ..... WRSI
Greenfield, MO [*Radio station call letters*] ..... KRFG
Greenfield Public Library, Greenfield, IL [*Library symbol*] ..... IGref
Greenfield Review [*A publication*] ..... Green R
Greenfield, WI [*Radio station call letters*] ..... WLZZ
Greenish Blue ..... GB
Greenish Yellow ..... GY
Greenland [*MARC country of publication code*] [*Library of Congress*] ..... gl
Greenland [*Three-letter standard code*] ..... GRL
Greenland [*MARC geographic area code*] [*Library of Congress*] ..... n-gl---
Greenland [*Two-letter standard code*] ..... GL
Greenland Base Command ..... GBC
Greenland Cruiser ..... GC
Greenland Ice Sheet Project [*National Science Foundation*] ..... GISP
Greenland-Iceland-United Kingdom [*NATO naval defense line*] ..... GIUK
Greenland Patrol [*Navy*] ..... GREPAT
Greenman Brothers, Inc. [*American Stock Exchange symbol*] ..... GMN
Greenpeace USA [*An association*] ..... GPUSA
Greenpond [*New Jersey*] [*Seismograph station code, US Geological Survey*] ..... GPD
Greensboro [*Georgia*] [*Seismograph station code, US Geological Survey*] ..... GBG
Greensboro College, Greensboro, NC [*Library symbol*] ..... NcGC
Greensboro, GA [*Radio station call letters*] ..... WGRG
Greensboro/High Point/West Salem [*North Carolina*] **Reynolds** [*Airport symbol*] ..... INT
Greensboro/High Point/Winston Salem [*North Carolina*] [*Airport symbol*] ..... GSO
Greensboro Justice Fund ..... GJF
Greensboro, NC [*Location identifier*] [*FAA*] ..... HIH
Greensboro, NC [*Location identifier*] [*FAA*] ..... LZY
Greensboro, NC [*Radio station call letters*] ..... WBIG
Greensboro, NC [*Radio station call letters*] ..... WCOG
Greensboro, NC [*Radio station call letters*] ..... WEAL
Greensboro, NC [*Television station call letters*] ..... WFMY-TV
Greensboro, NC [*Television station call letters*] ..... WGGT-TV
Greensboro, NC [*Radio station call letters*] ..... WKEW

Greensboro, NC [*Television station call letters*] ... WLXI-TV
Greensboro, NC [*Radio station call letters*] ... WNAA
Greensboro, NC [*Radio station call letters*] ... WPET
Greensboro, NC [*Radio station call letters*] ... WQFS
Greensboro, NC [*Radio station call letters*] ... WQMG
Greensboro, NC [*Radio station call letters*] ... WRQK
Greensboro, NC [*Radio station call letters*] ... WUAG
Greensboro Public Library, Greensboro, NC [*Library symbol*] ... NcG
Greensboro Public Library, Greensboro, NC [*OCLC symbol*] ... NGP
Greensburg, IN [*Radio station call letters*] ... WTRE
Greensburg, IN [*Radio station call letters*] ... WTRE-FM
Greensburg, KY [*Radio station call letters*] ... WGRK
Greensburg, KY [*Radio station call letters*] ... WGRK-FM
Greensburg, PA [*Radio station call letters*] ... WHJB
Greensburg, PA [*Radio station call letters*] ... WOKU
Greensburg, PA [*Television station call letters*] ... WPCB-TV
Greensward Foundation ... GF
Greenup, KY [*Radio station call letters*] ... WLGC
Greenville [*Mississippi*] [*Airport symbol*] ... GLH
Greenville [*Lake Wappapelo*] [*Missouri*] [*Seismograph station code, US Geological Survey*] [*Closed*] ... GRV
Greenville [*North Carolina*] [*Airport symbol*] ... PGV
Greenville, AL [*Radio station call letters*] ... WGYV
Greenville, AL [*Radio station call letters*] ... WKXN
Greenville Area Public Library, Greenville, PA [*Library symbol*] ... PGrev
Greenville College, Greenville, IL [*OCLC symbol*] ... IAG
Greenville College, Greenville, IL [*Library symbol*] ... IGreviC
Greenville County Library, Emporia, VA [*Library symbol*] ... ViEmP
Greenville County Library, Greenville, SC [*Library symbol*] ... ScG
Greenville County Library, Greenville, SC [*OCLC symbol*] ... SGR
Greenville, IL [*Location identifier*] [*FAA*] ... GRE
Greenville, IL [*Radio station call letters*] ... WGRN
Greenville, KY [*Location identifier*] [*FAA*] ... GMH
Greenville, KY [*Radio station call letters*] ... WGKY-FM
Greenville, ME [*Location identifier*] [*FAA*] ... XQA
Greenville, MI [*Radio station call letters*] ... WPLB
Greenville, MI [*Radio station call letters*] ... WPLB-FM
Greenville, MS [*Location identifier*] [*FAA*] ... MTQ
Greenville, MS [*Radio station call letters*] ... WBAQ
Greenville, MS [*Radio station call letters*] ... WDDT
Greenville, MS [*Radio station call letters*] ... WDMS
Greenville, MS [*Radio station call letters*] ... WGVM
Greenville, MS [*Radio station call letters*] ... WNIX
Greenville, MS [*Television station call letters*] ... WXVT
Greenville, NC [*Location identifier*] [*FAA*] ... AQE
Greenville, NC [*Radio station call letters*] ... WBZQ
Greenville, NC [*Radio station call letters*] ... WNCT
Greenville, NC [*Radio station call letters*] ... WNCT-FM
Greenville, NC [*Television station call letters*] ... WNCT-TV
Greenville, NC [*Radio station call letters*] ... WOOW
Greenville, NC [*Television station call letters*] ... WUNK-TV
Greenville, NC [*Radio station call letters*] ... WZMB
Greenville & Northern Railway Co. [*AAR code*] ... GRN
Greenville, OH [*Radio station call letters*] ... WDRK
Greenville, OH [*Radio station call letters*] ... WGVO
Greenville, OH [*Radio station call letters*] ... WLSN
Greenville, PA [*Radio station call letters*] ... WGRP
Greenville, PA [*Radio station call letters*] ... WGRP-FM
Greenville, PA [*Radio station call letters*] ... WTGP
Greenville Public Library, Greenville, IL [*Library symbol*] ... IGrevi
Greenville Public Library, Greenville, OH [*Library symbol*] ... OGr
Greenville, SC [*Location identifier*] [*FAA*] ... GMU
Greenville, SC [*Location identifier*] [*FAA*] ... GOX
Greenville, SC [*Radio station call letters*] ... WEPR
Greenville, SC [*Radio station call letters*] ... WESC
Greenville, SC [*Radio station call letters*] ... WESC-FM
Greenville, SC [*Radio station call letters*] ... WFBC
Greenville, SC [*Radio station call letters*] ... WFBC-FM
Greenville, SC [*Television station call letters*] ... WGGS-TV
Greenville, SC [*Radio station call letters*] ... WGVL
Greenville, SC [*Radio station call letters*] ... WHYZ
Greenville, SC [*Radio station call letters*] ... WLFJ
Greenville, SC [*Radio station call letters*] ... WMRB
Greenville, SC [*Radio station call letters*] ... WMUU
Greenville, SC [*Radio station call letters*] ... WMUU-FM
Greenville, SC [*Television station call letters*] ... WNTV
Greenville, SC [*Television station call letters*] ... WYFF-TV
Greenville/Spartanburg [*South Carolina*] [*Airport symbol*] ... GSP
Greenville/Spartanburg [*South Carolina*] **Downtown** [*Airport symbol*] ... SPA
Greenville, TN [*Television station call letters*] ... WOQP
Greenville, TN [*Radio station call letters*] ... WSMG
Greenville, TX [*Radio station call letters*] ... KGVL
Greenville, TX [*Location identifier*] [*FAA*] ... MJF
Greenville, VT [*Radio station call letters*] ... WPLS-FM
Greenwater Lake, SK [*Television station call letters*] ... CKBI-TV-3
Greenwich [*United Kingdom*] [*Later, HAD*] [*Geomagnetic observatory code*] ... GRW
Greenwich Apparent Time ... GAT
Greenwich Civil Noon ... GCN
Greenwich Civil Time ... GCT
Greenwich Conservatory Time ... GCT
Greenwich, CT [*Radio station call letters*] ... WGCH
Greenwich Hour Angle ... GHA
Greenwich & Johnsonville Railway Co. [*AAR code*] ... GJ
Greenwich Library, Greenwich, CT [*Library symbol*] ... CtGre
Greenwich Library, Greenwich, CT [*OCLC symbol*] ... GRN
Greenwich Mean Astronomical Time ... GMAT
Greenwich Mean Time ... GMT
Greenwich Mean Time ... Z
Greenwich Meridian [*Lower branch*] ... g
Greenwich Meridian ... GM
Greenwich Meridian [*Upper branch*] ... G
Greenwich Pharmaceutical [*NASDAQ symbol*] ... GRPI
Greenwich Sidereal [*or Standard*] **Time** ... GST
Greenwich Time ... G
Greenwich Time ... GT
Greenwich Time Signal ... GTS
Greenwich Zone Time ... GZT
Greenwood [*South Carolina*] [*Airport symbol*] ... GRD
Greenwood [*Mississippi*] [*Airport symbol*] ... GWO
Greenwood, AR [*Radio station call letters*] ... KACJ
Greenwood, AR [*Radio station call letters*] ... KAJJ
Greenwood Cotton Exchange ... GCE
Greenwood Lake Public Library, Greenwood, NY [*Library symbol*] ... NGrl
Greenwood-Leflore Public Library, Greenwood, MS [*Library symbol*] ... MsGwL
Greenwood, MS [*Radio station call letters*] ... WABG
Greenwood, MS [*Television station call letters*] ... WABG-TV
Greenwood, MS [*Radio station call letters*] ... WGRM
Greenwood, MS [*Television station call letters*] ... WMAO
Greenwood, MS [*Radio station call letters*] ... WMAO-FM
Greenwood, MS [*Radio station call letters*] ... WSWG
Greenwood, MS [*Radio station call letters*] ... WSWG-FM
Greenwood Publishing Corp., Westport, CT [*Library symbol*] ... GrP
Greenwood Resources [*NASDAQ symbol*] ... GRRL
Greenwood, SC [*Location identifier*] [*FAA*] ... GIW
Greenwood, SC [*Radio station call letters*] ... WCRS
Greenwood, SC [*Television station call letters*] ... WGCG-TV
Greenwood, SC [*Radio station call letters*] ... WGSW
Greenwood, SC [*Radio station call letters*] ... WMTY
Greenwood, SC [*Television station call letters*] ... WNEH
Greenwood, SC [*Radio station call letters*] ... WSCZ
Greer Hydraulics, Inc. [*American Stock Exchange symbol*] [*Delisted*] ... GRH
Greer, SC [*Radio station call letters*] ... WCKI
Greer, SC [*Radio station call letters*] ... WEAB
Greeting Card Association [*Later, National Association of Greeting Card Publishers*] ... GCA
Gregorian Institute of America ... GIA
Gregorianum [*A publication*] ... Greg
Gregorios ho Palamas [*A publication*] ... GP
Gregoriusblad [*A publication*] ... Gregor
Gregory Downs [*Australia*] [*Airport symbol*] [*Obsolete*] ... GGD
Gregory, SD [*Radio station call letters*] ... KKSD
GREIT Realty Trust [*American Stock Exchange symbol*] [*Delisted*] ... GRT
Grenada [*MARC country of publication code*] [*Library of Congress*] ... gd
Grenada [*Windward Islands*] [*Airport symbol*] ... GND
Grenada [*Three-letter standard code*] ... GRD
Grenada [*Seismograph station code, US Geological Survey*] ... GRE
Grenada [*MARC geographic area code*] [*Library of Congress*] ... nwgd
Grenada [*Two-letter standard code*] ... GD
Grenada Agricultural Department. Report [*A publication*] ... Grenada Agric Dep Rep
Grenada County Library, Grenada, MS [*Library symbol*] ... MsGren
Grenada, MS [*Location identifier*] [*FAA*] ... SBQ
Grenada, MS [*Radio station call letters*] ... WQXB
Grenada, MS [*Radio station call letters*] ... WYKC
Grenade ... GREN
Grenade Launcher ... GL
Grenade Safety Fuze ... GSF
Grenadier ... GRENDR
Grenadier Guards [*Military*] [*British*] ... GG
Grenadines [*MARC geographic area code*] [*Library of Congress*] ... nwgs---
Grenfell Association of America ... GAA
Grenoble [*France*] [*Airport symbol*] ... GNB
Grenoble [*France*] [*Seismograph station code, US Geological Survey*] ... GRN
Grenzpolizeihelfer [*Border Police Aide*] [*German*] ... GPH
Grenzschutzgruppe [*Border Protection Group*] [*German*] ... GSG
Grenzwache [*Frontier Guard*] [*German military - World War II*] ... GW
Gresham, OR [*Radio station call letters*] ... KMHD
Gresham, OR [*Radio station call letters*] ... KRDR
Gretna, LA [*Radio station call letters*] ... KGLA
Gretna, VA [*Radio station call letters*] ... WMNA
Gretna, VA [*Radio station call letters*] ... WMNA-FM
Grey Advertising [*NASDAQ symbol*] ... GREY
Grey Nuns of the Sacred Heart [*Roman Catholic religious order*] ... GNSH
Greybull, WY [*Radio station call letters*] ... KZMQ
Greyhound Club of America ... GCA
Greyhound Corp. [*NYSE symbol*] ... G
Greyhound Food Management ... GFM
Greyhound Package Express ... GPX

Greymouth [*New Zealand*] [*Seismograph station code, US Geological Survey*] [*Closed*] ... GRY
GRI Corp. [*American Stock Exchange symbol*] ... GRR
GRI [*Gravure Research Institute*] **Newsletter** [*A publication*] ... GRI Newsl
Gribair [*Switzerland*] [*ICAO designator*] ... GQ
Grid [*Electronics*] ... G
Grid Bearing [*Navigation*] ... GB
Grid Bias ... GB
Grid-Controlled Electron Gun ... GCEG
Grid-Controlled Klystron ... GCK
Grid Course [*Navigation*] ... GC
Grid-Dip Modulator ... GDM
Grid-Dip Oscillator ... GDO
Grid Driving Power ... GDP
Grid Heading [*Navigation*] ... GH
Grid Leak ... GDLK
Grid Leak ... GL
Grid Modulation ... GM
Grid Pool Tank ... GPT
Grid Reference Ship [*Navy*] ... GRS
Grid Resistor ... GR
Grid Return ... GR
Grid Space Relay ... GSR
Grid Sphere Drag [*DoD satellite*] ... GSD
Grid Spot Converter ... GSC
Grid Test of Schizophrenic Thought Disorder [*Psychology*] ... GTSTD
Grid Variation [*Navigation*] ... GV
Gridded Traveling-Wave Tube ... GTWT
Griddle ... GRDL
Gridiron Club of Washington, DC ... GCW
Gridley Public Library, Gridley, CA [*Library symbol*] ... CGrl
Grievance and Employment Policy Board [*Army*] ... GEPB
Grievous Body Harm ... GBH
Griffin, GA [*Radio station call letters*] ... WGRI
Griffin, GA [*Radio station call letters*] ... WHIE
Griffin, GA [*Radio station call letters*] ... WKEU
Griffin, GA [*Radio station call letters*] ... WKEU-FM
Griffin, GA [*Radio station call letters*] ... WKEZ-FM
Griffin Technology [*NASDAQ symbol*] ... GRIF
Griffiss Air Force Base [*New York*] ... GAFB
Griffith [*Australia*] [*Airport symbol*] ... GFF
Griffith Observatory [*California*] [*Seismograph station code, US Geological Survey*] ... GOC
Griffith University, Nathan, QLD, Australia [*Library symbol*] ... AuNaG
Grifora Umbellata Polysaccharide [*Antineoplastic drug*] ... GU-P
Grignard's Chemical Reaction ... GCR
Grigori Rasputin Society ... GRS
Grille ... GRL
Grilled American Cheese [*Sandwich*] [*Waitress's call to a short order cook*] ... GAC
Grillparzer Forum Forchtenstein [*A publication*] ... GFF
Grimsby Public Library and Art Gallery, Grimsby, ON, Canada [*Library symbol*] ... CaOGri
Grimsey [*Iceland*] [*Airport symbol*] ... GRY
Grind ... GRD
Grinder [*s*] [*Freight*] ... GRNDR
Grinding Arbor ... GRAR
Grinding Fixture ... GF
Grinding Fixture ... GRFX
Grinding Wheel Dresser ... GWD
Grinding Wheel Institute ... GWI
Grinnell College, Grinnell, IA [*Library symbol*] ... IaGG
Grinnell College, Grinnell, IA [*OCLC symbol*] ... IOG
Grinnell, IA [*Radio station call letters*] ... KDIC
Grinnell, IA [*Radio station call letters*] ... KGRN
Gritty [*Quality of the bottom*] [*Nautical charts*] ... gty
Grizzly Bear Club, San Francisco, CA [*Library symbol*] ... CSfGB
GRM Industries [*NASDAQ symbol*] ... GRMI
Grocery Manufacturers of America ... GMA
Grocery Prices Index [*British*] ... GPI
Grocery Update and Billing ... GRUB
Grocka [*Yugoslavia*] [*Geomagnetic observatory code*] ... GCK
Groenlands Geologiske Undersoegelse. Bulletin [*A publication*] ... Groenlands Geol Unders Bull
Groenlands Geologiske Undersoegelse. Bulletin [*A publication*] ... Groenlands Geol Undersoegelse Bull
Groenlands Geologiske Undersoegelse. Miscellaneous Papers [*A publication*] ... Groenlands Geol Unders Misc Pap
Groenlands Geologiske Undersoegelse. Rapport [*A publication*] ... Groenl Geol Unders Rap
Groff Industries [*NASDAQ symbol*] ... GROF
Grog [*i.e., entitled to draw a daily rum ration and doing so*] [*See also, T, UA*] [*Navy*] [*British*] ... G
Grolier Club ... GC
Grolier Club, New York, NY [*Library symbol*] ... NNGr
Grolier, Inc. [*NYSE symbol*] ... GLR
Groman Corp. [*NASDAQ symbol*] ... GROM
Gromer Aviation, Inc. [*Versailles, MO*] [*FAA designator*] ... GMR
Grommet ... GROM
Grondboor en Hamer [*Nederlandse Geologische Vereniging Tijdschrift*] [*A publication*] ... Grondboor Hamer
Groningen [*Netherlands*] [*Airport symbol*] ... GRQ
Groningsche Volksalmanach [*A publication*] ... GVA
Gronlandsfly Ltd. [*Denmark*] [*ICAO designator*] ... GL
Groom Lake Road [*Nevada*] [*Seismograph station code, US Geological Survey*] ... GLR
Groote Island [*Australia*] [*Airport symbol*] ... GTE
Grootfontein [*South-West Africa*] [*Airport symbol*] ... GFY
Groove ... GRV
Groove Gauge ... GG
Groove between Parallel Folds ... GPF
Grooved ... GRVD
Grooved for Iron Tongues ... GIT
Grooved Roofing [*Lumber*] ... GR
Groover ... GRVR
Grooving ... GRVG
Gros [*Large*] [*French*] ... G
Groschen [*Monetary unit in Austria*] ... G
Gross [*Leukemia antigen*] [*Immunochemistry*] ... G
Gross ... GR
Gross ... GRO
Gross Axle Weight Rating [*Auto safety*] ... GAWR
Gross Caloric Value ... GCV
Gross Capability Estimator [*Air Force*] ... GROCAP
Gross Cell-Surface Antigen [*Immunology*] ... GCSA
Gross Combination Weight [*for tractor and loaded trailer*] ... GCW
Gross Domestic Output [*Economics*] ... GDO
Gross Domestic Product [*Economics*] ... GDP
Gross Energy Product ... GEP
Gross Fixed Capital Formation ... GFCF
Gross Internal Product ... GIP
Gross Investment ... GI
Gross Lawyer Product [*Term for measurement of the income of attorneys*] ... GLP
Gross Leasable Area ... GLA
Gross Leukemia Virus ... GLV
Gross Lift-Off Mass [*NASA*] ... GLOM
Gross Lift-Off Weight [*NASA*] ... GLOW
Gross Logical Design ... GLD
Gross Maximum Shipping Weight ... GMSW
Gross National Effluent ... GNE
Gross National Expenditure [*Canada*] ... GNE
Gross National Income [*Economics*] ... GNI
Gross National Product [*Economics*] ... GNP
Gross National Recreation Experience [*Refers to cost of recreation in relation to gross national product*] ... GNRE
Gross Performance Measuring System [*Air Force*] ... GPMS
Gross Primary Productivity ... GPP
Gross Product Originating [*Department of Transportation*] ... GPO
Gross Rating Point [*Television*] ... GRP
Gross Regional Product ... GRP
Gross Registered Tons [*Navigation*] ... GRT
Gross Requirement ... GR
Gross Soluble Antigen ... GSA
Gross Takeoff Weight [*of an aircraft*] [*Also, GTW*] ... GTOW
Gross Takeoff Weight [*of an aircraft*] [*Also, GTOW*] ... GTW
Gross Telecasting, Inc. [*American Stock Exchange symbol*] ... GGG
Gross Ton [*or Tonnage*] ... GT
Gross Tons ... GRST
Gross Universal Cash Heist [*Techno-economic term coined by Buckminster Fuller*] ... GRUNCH
Gross Vehicle Weight ... GVW
Gross Vehicle Weight Rating ... GVWR
Gross Virus [*Leukemogenesis*] [*Immunochemistry*] ... GV
Gross Weight ... GRWT
Gross Weight ... GW
Gross Weight ... GWT
Gross World Product ... GWP
Grosses Zoologisches Praktikum [*A publication*] ... Grosses Zool Prakt
Grossesse Extra-Uterine [*Medicine*] ... GEU
Grosset & Dunlap [*Publisher*] ... G & D
Grosshandelsgesellschaft [*Wholesale Business Establishment*] [*German*] ... GHG
Grosshandelskontor [*Wholesale Business Office*] [*German*] ... GHK
Grosswetterlage [*Meteorology*] ... GWL
Grosvenor Reference Division, Buffalo and Erie County Public Library, Buffalo, NY [*Library symbol*] ... NBuG
Groszy [*Monetary unit in Poland*] ... G
Grotesque, Unbelievable, Bizarre, Unprecedented [*Term coined by an Irish politician to describe certain incidents in Irish politics*] ... GUBU
Groton, CT [*Radio station call letters*] ... WQBN-FM
Groton, CT [*Radio station call letters*] ... WSUB
Groton Public Library, Groton, CT [*Library symbol*] ... CtGr
Grouard Mission, AB [*Television station call letters*] ... CFRN-TV-8
Ground ... G
Ground ... GD
Ground ... GND
Ground ... GRD
Ground Acceptance [*or Article*] **Test Procedure** ... GATP
Ground Acquisition and Command Station ... GA & CS
Ground Adjutant General Section [*World War II*] ... GNAGS

Ground-Aided Acquisition ... GAA
Ground-to-Air [*Communications, weapons*] ... G-A
Ground-to-Air Communications ... G/A COMM
Ground Air Conditioning Unit ... GACU
Ground-to-Air Cycle ... GTAC
Ground-to-Air Data Link ... GADL
Ground-to-Air-to-Ground [*Aviation*] ... GAG
Ground-to-Air-to-Ground Data Terminal [*Air Force*] ... GAGDT
Ground-to-Air Missile ... GAM
Ground-to-Air Pilotless Aircraft [*Early US test missiles*] ... GAPA
Ground-to-Air Scanner Surveillance ... GRASS
Ground-to-Air Transmitter ... GAT
Ground-to-Air Transmitter Terminal ... GATT
Ground-to-Air Transmitting-Receiving [*Station*] ... GATR
Ground and Amphibious Military Operations [*Army*] ... GAMO
Ground Anchor Placement Equipment ... GAPE
Ground Area Attainable ... GAA
Ground Attack Night ... GAN
Ground Attack Tactics [*for air delivery of weapons against a ground target*] ... GAT
Ground Attacker Aircraft ... GA
Ground Attitude Control ... GAC
Ground Aviation Radio Exchange System ... GAREX
Ground Avoidance Simulation Program ... GASP
Ground Backup Instrument ... GBI
Ground-Based Computer ... GBC
Ground-Based Electro-Optical Deep Space Surveillance [*Satellite-tracking network*] ... GEODSS
Ground-Based Electronic Omnidirectional Satellite Communications Antenna ... GEOSCAN
Ground-Based Field ... GBF
Ground-Based Infrared Instrumentation ... GBII
Ground-Based Infrared Instrumentation System ... GBIIS
Ground-Based LASER ... GBL
Ground-Based Radiometer ... GBR
Ground-Based Scanner ... GBS
Ground-Based Software ... GBS
Ground-Based Telemetry ... GBT
Ground Beacon System ... GBS
Ground Check [*Aviation*] ... GNDCK
Ground Checkout [*NASA*] ... GCO
Ground Checkout [*NASA*] ... GND C/O
Ground Checkout Display and Control System ... GCDCS
Ground Checkout Equipment [*Aerospace*] ... GCE
Ground Checkout and Test [*Aerospace*] ... GCT
Ground Checkout Unit [*Aerospace*] ... GCU
Ground Clearance Intercept [*System similar to US commercial RADAR for ground control of aircraft*] [*North Vietnam*] ... GCI
Ground Command Facility ... GCF
Ground Command Guidance ... GCG
Ground Command System ... GCS
Ground Commanded [*or Controlled*] **Television Assembly** [*Apollo*] [*NASA*] ... GCTA
Ground Communications Controller ... GCC
Ground Communications Equipment ... GCE
Ground Communications Facility [*NASA*] ... GCF
Ground Communications Facility - Communications Switcher [*NASA*] ... GCF-CS
Ground Communications System ... GCS
Ground Communications Tracking Systems ... GCTS
Ground Composite Signal Mixer ... GCSM
Ground Computer Controller ... GCC
Ground Computer Operating System [*NASA*] ... GCOS
Ground Control ... GC
Ground Control ... GNDCON
Ground-Control Bombing System ... GCBS
Ground-Control Center ... GCC
Ground-Control Checkout ... GCCO
Ground-Control Computer Center ... GCCC
Ground-Control Equipment ... GCE
Ground-Control Intercept Squadron ... GCIS
Ground-Control Intercept Training ... GCITNG
Ground-Control Interface Logic ... GCIL
Ground-Control Interface Logic Controller ... GCILC
Ground-Control Interface Logic Unit ... GCILU
Ground-Control Landing ... GCL
Ground-Control Network [*NASA*] ... GCN
Ground-Control Unit ... GCU
Ground-Controlled Aircraft ... GCA
Ground-Controlled Apparatus [*RADAR*] ... GCA
Ground-Controlled Approach [*for lateral and vertical guidance of landing aircraft through use of ground RADAR and radio communications*] ... GCA
Ground-Controlled Interception [*RADAR*] ... GCI
Ground-Controlled RADAR ... GCR
Ground-Controlled Space System ... GCSS
Ground Coolant Loop ... GCL
Ground Cooling Heat Exchanger [*NASA*] ... GCHX
Ground Cooling Unit [*NASA*] ... GCU
Ground Cutout ... GCO
Ground Data Acquisition System ... GDAS
Ground Data Equipment [*Electronics*] ... GDE
Ground Data Handling ... GDH
Ground Data Handling Centre [*Canada*] ... GDHC
Ground Data Handling System ... GDHS
Ground Data Systems Manager ... GDSM
Ground Data Systems Officer ... GDSO
Ground Decommutation Facility ... GDF
Ground Defense Forces ... GDF
Ground Detector ... GD
Ground Detector ... GRD
Ground Detector Indicator ... GDI
Ground Display System ... GDS
Ground Diverted Force [*Military*] ... GDF
Ground Effect Machine ... GEM
Ground Effect Research Machine ... GERM
Ground Effect Takeoff and Landing ... GETOL
Ground Effect Vehicle ... GEV
Ground Effects Phenomenon ... GEP
Ground Elapsed Time [*Aerospace*] ... GET
Ground Elapsed Time of Ignition [*Aerospace*] ... GETI
Ground Electronic Maintenance Officer [*NASA*] ... GEMO
Ground Electronic System ... GES
Ground Electronics Engineering Installation Agency [*Air Force*] ... GEEIA
Ground Electronics Maintenance ... GEM
Ground Emitter Location and Identification System [*Army*] ... GELIS
Ground Emitter Location and Identification System - High [*Army*] ... GELIS-H
Ground Emplaced Mine Scattering System ... GEMMSS
Ground Emplaced Mine Scattering System ... GEMS
Ground-Emplaced Seismic Intrusion Detector ... GSID
Ground Engineering [*A publication*] ... Ground Eng
Ground Entry Point ... GEP
Ground Environment Complex ... GEC
Ground Environment Technical Installation System [*NATO*] ... GETIS
Ground and Environmental ... G & E
Ground Equipment ... GE
Ground Equipment Failure [*Air Force*] ... GEF
Ground Equipment System ... GES
Ground Equipment Test Set ... GETS
Ground Equipment Turn Off ... GETO
Ground Fault Circuit Breaker [*Electronics*] ... GFCB
Ground Fault Circuit Interrupter [*Electronics*] ... GFCI
Ground Fault Interrupter [*Electronics*] ... GFI
Ground-Fault Warning ... GFW
Ground Fire Locating System ... GFLS
Ground Fire Locator ... GFL
Ground Fog [*Meteorology*] ... GF
Ground Fog [*Meteorology*] ... GNDFG
Ground Fog Estimated_____ Feet Deep [*Meteorology*] ... GFDEP
Ground Forces Chief of Staff [*World War II*] ... GNGCS
Ground Forces Commanding General [*World War II*] ... GNDCG
Ground Forces Deputy Chief of Staff [*World War II*] ... GNGDC
Ground Forces Plans Section [*World War II*] ... GNGPS
Ground Forces Replacement Service [*World War II*] ... GFRS
Ground Forces Secretariat [*World War II*] ... GNGSE
Ground Fuel Start Tank ... GFST
Ground Fuel Ullage Tank ... GFUT
Ground Gained Forward [*Aerial photography*] ... GGF
Ground Gained Sideways [*Aerial photography*] ... GGS
Ground Glass ... GGL
Ground-to-Ground [*Communications, weapons, etc.*] ... G-G
Ground-to-Ground [*Communications, weapons, etc.*] ... GTG
Ground-to-Ground Missile ... GGM
Ground Guidance [*Aerospace*] ... GG
Ground Guidance Computer [*Aerospace*] ... GGC
Ground Guidance Equipment [*Aerospace*] ... GGE
Ground Guidance System [*Aerospace*] ... GGS
Ground Gunner [*Air Force*] [*British*] ... GG
Ground Gunnery Range ... GGR
Ground Half Coupling ... GHC
Ground Handling [*Aerospace*] ... GH
Ground Handling Equipment [*Aerospace*] ... GHE
Ground Handling System [*Aerospace*] ... GHS
Ground Handling and Transportation [*Aerospace*] ... GHAT
Ground Hazard Area ... GHA
Ground Heat Exchanger ... GHX
Ground Identification of Missions in Space ... GIMS
Ground Identification of Satellites ... GISAT
Ground Information Processing System ... GIPS
Ground Instrumentation Equipment ... GIE
Ground Integration Requirements Document ... GIRD
Ground Integration Test Program ... GITP
Ground LASER Attack Designator/Identification System ... GLADIS
Ground-LASER Designators ... GLD
Ground-LASER Tracking ... GLT
Ground-Launched Cruise Missile [*Pronounced "glick-em"*] ... GLCM
Ground Level ... GL
Ground-Level Attack, Reconnaissance, and Electronic Countermeasures ... GLARE
Ground-Level Event [*Geophysics*] ... GLE
Ground Liaison Officer [*Military*] ... GLO

Ground Liaison Section [Military] [British].................GLSECT
Ground Lift-Off Weight [NASA]...........................GLOW
Ground Line of Communications..........................GLOC
Ground Locator LASER Designator........................GLLD
Ground Logistics Operations [NASA].......................GLO
Ground Maintenance Support..............................GMS
Ground Malfunction..GM
Ground Mapping RADAR....................................GMR
Ground Mapping [or Marking] System......................GMS
Ground Measurements Command List......................GMCL
Ground Meat/Analyzer [USDA]............................GM/A
Ground Meteorological Detector [or Device]................GMD
Ground Mobil Forces Satellite Communications..........GMFSC
Ground Mobile Cenetheodolite.............................GMC
Ground Mobile Command Center..........................GMCC
Ground Mobile Forces [Military]...........................GMF
Ground Mobile RADAR....................................GMR
Ground Mode..GM
Ground Monitor Facility...................................GMF
Ground Moving Target Indicator..........................GMTI
Ground Munitions Analysis Study.........................GMAS
Ground Observation Reporting System.....................GORS
Ground Observer Aircraft Recognition [Army]..............GOAR
Ground Observer Corps....................................GOC
Ground Observer Organization.............................GOO
Ground Observer Post.....................................GOP
Ground Operation Order...................................GOO
Ground Operational Equipment [NASA].....................GOE
Ground Operational Equipment for the Orbiting Astronomical
   Observatory [NASA].............................GOE for OAO
Ground Operational Equipment/Real Property Installed
   Equipment [NASA]............................GOE/RPIE
Ground Operational [or Operations] Requirements Plan [NASA].......GORP
Ground Operational [or Operations] Support System [NASA]......GOSS
Ground Operations Aerospace Language [Data processing]
   [NASA]...GOAL
Ground Operations Control Area [NASA]....................GOCA
Ground Operations Coordinator [NASA].....................GOC
Ground Operations Management System [NASA].............GOMS
Ground Operations and Material Management System........GOMMS
Ground Operations Panel [NASA]...........................GOP
Ground Operations Planning Group [NASA].................GOPG
Ground Operations Review................................GOR
Ground Operations Working Group........................GOWG
Ground Optical Recorder for Intercept Determination........GORID
Ground Order of Battle...................................GOB
Ground Out [Baseball].....................................GO
Ground Passive Electronic Reconnaissance Facility.........GPERF
Ground Plane Antenna....................................GPA
Ground Plane Simulator..................................GPS
Ground Pneumatic...GP
Ground Point of Impact..................................GPI
Ground Point of Intercept................................GPI
Ground Position Indicator [Dead-reckoning computer].......GPI
Ground Potential Model [Physics].........................GPM
Ground Power Contactor.................................GPC
Ground Power Panel.....................................GPP
Ground Power Supply [NASA].............................GPS
Ground Power Supply Unit [NASA]........................GPSU
Ground Power Unit......................................GPU
Ground Processing Simulation...........................GPS
Ground Processing System [Aviation]....................GPS
Ground-Protective [Relay]................................GP
Ground Proximity Extraction System.....................GPES
Ground Proximity Warning System [FAA]..................GPWS
Ground RADAR Aerial Delivery System...................GRADS
Ground RADAR Emitter for Training Aviators [Army]........GRETA
Ground Range..GR
Ground-Received Times [Solar wind measurements]..........GRT
Ground Reconstruction Electronics [Used in photographing
   moon] [NASA].....................................GRE
Ground Reconstruction Equipment........................GRE
Ground Relay Panel [Aerospace]..........................GRP
Ground Resistance Tester................................GRT
Ground Resolved Distance [Satellite camera]..............GRD
Ground Return Area Suppression.........................GRAS
Ground Rods [JETDS nomenclature] [Military]...............GP
Ground Roll Guidance System............................GRGS
Ground Rule...GR
Ground Rule Double [Baseball]............................GRD
Ground Safety Approval.................................GSA
Ground Safety and Flight Safety Requirements.............GSFSR
Ground Safety Office [or Officer] [Air Force]..............GSO
Ground Safety Plan......................................GSP
Ground Saucer Watch [for UFOs] [An association]...........GSW
Ground Self-Defense Force [Japan].......................GSDF
Ground Self-Defense Force Japan........................GSDFJ
Ground Sensor Terminal..................................GST
Ground Service Equipment [Air Force].....................GSE
Ground Service Relay....................................GSR
Ground Shells [Quality of the bottom] [Nautical charts]......Grd

Ground Signal Mixer.....................................GSM
Ground to Slant...G/S
Ground Software Development Laboratory [NASA]............GSDL
Ground Sound Control, Incorporated......................GSCI
Ground Spacecraft Tracking and Data Network.............GSTDN
Ground Special Security Forces..........................GSSF
Ground Speed [Aviation]...................................GS
Ground Speed Continuing [Aviation]......................GSC
Ground-Speed Drift Angle [Aviation].....................GSDA
Ground-Speed Indicator [Aviation].......................GSI
Ground-Speed Oscillator [Aviation]......................GSO
Ground Speed Returning [Aviation].......................GSR
Ground Stabilized...GS
Ground Standard Interface Unit..........................GSIU
Ground Station [Aerospace]...............................GS
Ground Stub-Up Connection [Aerospace]...................GSUC
Ground Subsystem Evaluation Facility [Army]..............GSEF
Ground Support Cooling Unit.............................GSCU
Ground Support Engineering Change Proposal [Aerospace].....GSECP
Ground Support Equipment [Air Force, NASA]...............GSE
Ground Support Equipment Division [Naval Air Engineering
   Center]...GSED
Ground Support Equipment End Item [Military].............GSEEI
Ground Support Equipment Illustration [Military]..........GSEI
Ground Support Equipment Illustration Data [Military]......GSEID
Ground Support Equipment List [NASA]....................GSEL
Ground Support Equipment Recommendation Data [Military].......GSERD
Ground Support Facilities [Later, MGE] [Aerospace]........GSF
Ground Support Maintenance Equipment [Aerospace]........GSME
Ground Support Operations [Aerospace]....................GSO
Ground Support Simulation Computer [Aerospace]..........GSSC
Ground Support Software [NASA].........................GSS
Ground Support System [Aerospace].......................GSS
Ground Support System Integration.......................GSSI
Ground Support System Review [Aerospace]................GSSR
Ground Support System Specification [Aerospace]..........GSSS
Ground Support Verification Plan [NASA]..................GSVP
Ground-to-Surface Vessel [RADAR]........................GSV
Ground Surveillance Qualification Course [Army]...........GSQC
Ground Surveillance RADAR..............................GSR
Ground Surveillance and Target Acquisition...............GSTA
Ground Surveillance and Target Acquisition...............GS & TA
Ground Swell..G
Ground System..GS
Ground Systems Coordination Group......................GSCG
Ground Systems Group...................................GSG
Ground Systems Laboratory..............................GSL
Ground Systems Operations..............................GSO
Ground Takeoff and Landing.............................GTOL
Ground Target Detection................................GTD
Ground Target Marking System...........................GTMS
Ground Team...GT
Ground Team Manager...................................GTM
Ground Telemetry Subsystem.............................GTS
Ground Terminal System.................................GTS
Ground Test [NASA].....................................GNT
Ground Test [NASA]......................................GT
Ground Test and Acceptance [NASA]......................GT & A
Ground Test Access.....................................GTA
Ground Test Article [NASA]..............................GTA
Ground Test Conductor..................................GTC
Ground Test Equipment..................................GTE
Ground Test Instrumentation.............................GTI
Ground Test Missile....................................GTM
Ground Test Motor......................................GTM
Ground Test Plan.......................................GTP
Ground Test Plan Summary Sheets........................GTPSS
Ground Test Reactor [Air Force].........................GTR
Ground Test Station....................................GTS
Ground Test Unit.......................................GTU
Ground Test Vehicle....................................GTV
Ground Thermal Conditioning Unit [NASA].................GTCU
Ground Tilt Isolation Platform..........................GTIP
Ground Torquing Assembly...............................GTA
Ground Track..GT
Ground Track Plotter...................................GTP
Ground Tracking System.................................GTS
Ground Training Aid [Aerospace].........................GTA
Ground Transmit...GT
Ground Transport Equipment............................GTE
Ground Transport Express [Airport baggage computer].......GTX
Ground Transport Vehicle...............................GTV
Ground Umbilical Carrier Plate..........................GUCP
Ground Up-to-Space.....................................GUTS
Ground Vehicle Mine Dispensing System [Military].........GVMDS
Ground/Vehicular LASER Locator Designator..............G/VLLD
Ground Vibration Survey [Aerospace].....................GVS
Ground Vibration Test [Aerospace].......................GVT
Ground Vibration Test Article [Aerospace]................GVTA
Ground Visibility..GV
Ground Water Age [A publication]....................Ground Wat

Ground Water Council .... GWC
Ground Water Institute .... GWI
Ground Water Management District .... GWMD
Ground Water Resources Institute [*Later, Ground Water Council*] .... GWRI
Ground Wave Emergency Network .... GWEN
Ground Waves .... GW
Ground Winds Data Reduction System [*NASA*] .... GWDRS
Ground Winds Tower [*NASA*] .... GWT
Ground Zero [*Nevada*] [*Seismograph station code, US Geological Survey*] [*Closed*] .... GZN
Ground Zero [*Nevada*] [*Seismograph station code, US Geological Survey*] [*Closed*] .... ZOX
Ground Zero [*An association*] .... GZ
Ground Zero [*Atomic detonation*] .... GZ
Grounded [*Electronics*] .... GND
Grounded Base .... GB
Grounded Cathode Amplifier .... GCA
Grounded Collector .... GC
Grounded into Double Plays [*Baseball*] .... GDP
Grounded into Double Plays [*Baseball*] .... GIDP
Grounded Emitter .... GE
Grounded Grid [*Valve*] .... GG
Grounded Grid Amplifier .... GGA
Grounded Kathode Amplifier .... GKA
Grounded - Not Operationally Ready Maintenance .... G-NORM
Grounded - Not Operationally Ready Supply .... G-NORS
Grounded Plate Amplifier .... GPA
Groundwater Management Districts Association .... GMDA
Group .... G
Group .... GP
Group .... GR
Group .... GRP
Group .... GRU
Group Action Request Lists .... GARL
Group for the Advancement of Psychiatry .... GAP
Group Against Smokers' Pollution .... GASP
Group of Ancient Drama .... GOAD
Group Announcement Bulletin [*Defense Documentation Center*] .... GAB
Group Assembly Parts List .... GAPL
Group Attainment Program .... GAP
Group B Streptococci [*Medicine*] .... GBS
Group Capacity Assessment .... GCA
Group Captain .... GC
Group Change Control .... GCC
Group Coded Recording .... GCR
Group Cohesiveness [*Psychological testing*] .... GC
Group Commander .... GRUCOM
Group Control Center .... GCC
Group Dimensions Descriptions Questionnaire [*Psychology*] .... GDDQ
Group Display Generator .... GDG
Group Distributing Frames .... GDF
Group on Electronic Devices .... GED
Group Encounter Survey .... GES
Group Engineer .... GE
Group for Environmental Education .... GEE
Group to Establish Criteria for Certifying Munitions Systems to Electromagnetic Fields [*DoD*] .... GECCMSEF
Group of Experts .... GE
Group of Experts on Long-Term Scientific Policy and Planning [*UNESCO*] .... GELTSPAP
Group of Experts on Pollution of the Ocean Originating on Land [*IOC*] .... POOL
Group of Experts on the Scientific Aspects of Marine Pollution [*United Nations*] .... GESAMP
Group Finance Department .... GFD
Group Fire Distribution Center [*Army*] .... GFDC
Group Flashing [*Navigation signal lights*] .... GPFL
Group Fore Golf Foundation .... GFGF
Group Fore - Women's Pro Golf Tour .... WPGT
Group of Fourteen [*NATO countries minus France*] .... GF
Group Health Association of America .... GHAA
Group Health, Inc., St. Paul, MN [*Library symbol*] .... MnSGH
Group Inclusive Tour [*Airline fare*] .... GIT
Group Index .... GRIND
Group Insurance .... GI
Group Interaction Analysis .... GIA
Group Junction .... GJ
Group for Lunar Exploration and Planning .... GLEP
Group Mark [*Data processing*] .... GM
Group Medical Report .... GMR
Group Membership Scores [*Psychometrics*] .... GMS
Group Method of Determining Arguments [*Equation*] .... GMDA
Group Method of Data Handling [*Mathematical technique*] .... GMDH
Group Mobile .... GM
Group Number No Count [*Military communication*] .... GRNC
Group Occulting Lights [*Navigation signal*] .... GPOCC
Group Operational Access Tester System [*AT & T*] .... GOATS
Group, Operations Analysis [*Air Force*] .... GOA
Group Operations Center .... GOC
Group and Organization Studies [*A publication*] .... Group Org Stud
Group Pacific .... GROPAC

Group-Page-Line-Inserts .... GPLI
Group and Pension Marketing Conference [*LIMRA*] .... GPMC
Group Personality Projective Test [*Psychology*] .... GPPT
Group Practice [*A publication*] .... Group Pract
Group Practice Association [*Medicine*] .... GPA
Group Project for Holocaust Survivors and Their Children .... GPHSC
Group Psychotherapy [*Later, Group Psychotherapy, Psychodrama, and Sociometry*] [*A publication*] .... GRPSB
Group Psychotherapy and Psychodrama [*Later, Group Psychotherapy, Psychodrama, and Sociometry*] [*A publication*] .... Group Psych
Group Psychotherapy, Psychodrama, and Sociometry [*A publication*] .... Group Psychother Psychodrama Sociometry
Group Psychotherapy Suitability Evaluation Scale [*Psychology*] .... SES
Group Registration for Contributions to Periodicals [*US Copyright Office form*] .... GR/CP
Group Relations Ongoing Workshops .... GROW
Group Repetition Frequency .... GRF
Group Report .... GR
Group Routing and Charging Equipment [*British*] .... GRACE
Group Sail [*Navy*] .... GRUSL
Group Selective Register .... GSR
Group Separator [*Data processing*] .... GS
Group of Soviet Forces in Germany .... GSFG
Group Specific [*Antigen*] .... gs
Group Structured [*Counseling group*] .... GS
Group Study Course .... GSC
Group Talk Microphone .... GTM
Group Test Equipment Assembly .... GTEA
Group Therapy .... GpTh
Group Therapy .... GT
Group Training Command [*Air Force*] [*British*] .... GTC
Group-Transfer Polymerization [*Du Pont process*] [*1983*] .... GTP
Group Transformation .... GT
Group Translating Equipment .... GTE
Group Unit Simulator .... GUS
Group for the Use of Psychology in History .... GUPH
Group Value Engineering .... GVE
Group Velocity [*Symbol*] .... u
Groupe d'Action Nationale Comerounaise [*Cameroonian National Action Group*] .... GANC
Groupe de Chasse [*French aircraft fighter unit*] [*World War II*] .... GC
Groupe des Democrates Camerounais [*Cameroonian Democratic Group*] .... GDC
Groupe d'Etude des Problemes de l'Automatisme dans les Travaux Administratifs .... GEPATA
Groupe d'Etude et Recherches Sous-Marin .... GERS
Groupe d'Etudes Europeen des Recherches Spatiales .... GEERS
Groupe d'Etudes Mathematiques de Problemes Politiques et Strategiques [*France*] .... GEMPPS
Groupe des Independants et Ruraux Tchadiens [*Chadian Independent and Rural Group*] .... GIRT
Groupe Interdisciplinaire de Recherche Scientifique et Appliquee en Terminologie [*INFOTERM*] .... GIRSTERM
Groupe International Hachette [*France*] .... GIH
Groupe Linguistique d'Etudes Chamito-Semitiques. Comptes Rendus [*A publication*] .... GLECS
Groupe Revolutionnaire Socialiste [*France*] .... GRS
Groupe Romand pour l'Etude des Techniques d'Instruction [*Switzerland*] .... GRETI
Groupe d'Union Camerounaise [*Group for Cameroonian Union*] .... GUC
Groupement des Associations des Maisiers des Pays de la CEE [*Group of the Maize Processors Associations in the European Economic Community Countries*] .... EUROMAISIERS
Groupement Atomique Alsacienne Atlantique [*French*] .... GAA
Groupement pour l'Avancement de la Mecanique Industrielle [*A publication*] .... Group Avan Mec Ind
Groupement pour l'Avancement des Methods Physiques d'Analyse [*France*] .... GAMS
Groupement des Caisses d'Epargne de la CEE [*Savings Bank Group of the European Economic Community*] .... GCECEE
Groupement d'Etude du Synchrotron National [*France*] .... GESyN
Groupement Europeen des Associations Nationales des Fabricants de Pesticides [*European Group of National Pesticide Manufacturer' Associations*] [*Common Market*] .... GEFAP
Groupement Europeen des Maisons d'Alimentation et d'Approvisionnement a Succursales [*European Group of Food and Provision Chain Stores*] [*Common Market*] .... GEMAS
Groupement Francais des Producteurs de Bases et Banques de Donnees [*French Federation of Data Base Producers*] [*Information service*] .... GFPBBD
Groupement des Independants Africains [*Independent Africans Group*] .... GIA
Groupement de l'Industrie Chimique [*France*] .... GIC
Groupement International des Associations de Fabricants de Produits Agrochimiques [*International Group of National Associations of Agrochemical Manufacturers*] .... GIFAP
Groupement International de l'Industrie Pharmaceutique des Pays de la CEE [*International Pharmaceutical Industry Group for the EEC Countries*] .... GIIP

Groupement International pour la Recherche Scientifique en Stomatologie et Odontologie [*International Group for Scientific Research on Stomato-Odontology*].....GIRSO

Groupement Intersyndical de la Communication Audiovisuelle ....GICA

Groupement des Moyens Militaires de Transport Aerien [*France*].....GMMTA

Groupement des Opticiens du Marche Commun [*Common Market Opticians' Group*].....GOMAC

Groupement Professionnel de l'Industrie Nucleaire [*Also known as NIC*] [*Belgium*].....GPIN

Groups [*of code transmitted*] per Minute [*or Message*] [*Communications*].....GPM

Groups of Pulses per Second .....GPS

[*Sir George*] Grove [*When used in identifying Beethoven's compositions, refers to cataloging of his works by musicologist Grove*].....G

Grove .....GRO

Grove .....GRV

Grove City College [*Pennsylvania*] .....GCC

Grove City College, Grove City, PA [*Library symbol*] .....PGcC

Grove City, PA [*Radio station call letters*] .....WEDA

Grove City, PA [*Radio station call letters*] .....WSAJ

Grove City, PA [*Radio station call letters*] .....WSAJ-FM

Grove City Public Library, Grove City, OH [*Library symbol*] .....OGc

Grove City Public Library, Grove City, OH [*OCLC symbol*] .....OGC

Grove Explorations Ltd. [*NASDAQ symbol*] .....GRVXF

Grove, OK [*Radio station call letters*] .....KGVE

Grove Street College, Oakland, CA [*Library symbol*] .....COCiC

Grover City, CA [*Radio station call letters*] .....KLOI

Groves, TX [*Radio station call letters*] .....KTFA

Grow Group, Inc. [*NYSE symbol*] .....GRO

Grower Annual [*A publication*] .....Grower Annu

Growers' Directory. Illinois Crop Improvement Association [*A publication*] .....Growers' Dir Ill Crop Impr Ass

Growers' Handbook and Annual Proceedings. Ohio Vegetable and Potato Growers' Association [*A publication*] .....Growers' Handb Annu Proc

Growing Equity Mortgage [*Also, Graduated Equity Mortgage*] .....GEM

Growing, Improving, Maturing - Puppy of the Year [*Canine award*] ....GIMPY

Growing Point [*A publication*] .....GP

Grown Diffused .....GD

Grown Junction .....GJ

Growth [*Business and trade*] .....G

Growth of the American Family [*A study*] .....GAF

Growth Analysis and Review .....GAR

Growth-Associated Protein [*Cytochemistry*] .....GAP

Growth and Change [*A publication*] .....Growth Chan

Growth and Differentiation Hormone [*Endocrinology*] .....GDH

Growth, Economy, Management, and Customer Satisfaction [*Procedure for establishing management goals*] .....GEMS

Growth Fraction [*Endocrinology*] .....GF

Growth Fund of Florida [*NASDAQ symbol*] .....GFLA

Growth Hormone [*Somatotrophin*] [*Also, SH, STH*] [*Endocrinology*] .....GH

Growth-Hormone Release Inhibiting Factor [*Also, GH-RIH, GRIF, SRIF, SS*] [*Endocrinology*] .....GH-RIF

Growth-Hormone Release Inhibiting Factor [*Also, GH-RIF, GRIF, SRIF, SS*] [*Endocrinology*] .....GH-RIH

Growth-Hormone Release Inhibiting Factor [*Also, GH-RIF, GH-RIH, SRIF, SS*] [*Endocrinology*] .....GRIF

Growth-Hormone Releasing Factor [*Somatoliberin*] [*Also, GH-RH, GRF*] [*Endocrinology*] .....GH-RF

Growth-Hormone Releasing Factor [*Somatoliberin*] [*Also, GH-RF, GH-RH*] [*Endocrinology*] .....GRF

Growth-Hormone Releasing Hormone [*Somatoliberin*] [*Also, GH-RF, GRF*] [*Endocrinology*] .....GH-RH

Growth and Income [*Business and trade*] .....GI

Growth Inhibiting .....GI

Growth Rate [*Botany*] .....GRATE

Growth Realty Cos. [*NYSE symbol*] [*Delisted*] .....GRW

Growth Space Station .....GSS

Growth Test Vehicle .....GTV

Growth Vessel .....GV

Grozny [*USSR*] [*Seismograph station code, US Geological Survey*] .....GRO

GRS (Gesellschaft fuer Reaktorsicherheit). Kurz-Information. Reihe A [*A publication*] .....GRS (Ges Reaktorsicherheit) Kurz-Inf Reihe A

GRS (Gesellschaft fuer Reaktorsicherheit). Kurz-Information. Reihe B [*A publication*] .....GRS (Ges Reaktorsicherheit) Kurz-Inf Reihe B

GRS (Gesellschaft fuer Reaktorsicherheit). Kurz-Information. Reihe C [*A publication*] .....GRS (Ges Reaktorsicherheit) Kurz-Inf Reihe C

GRS (Gesellschaft fuer Reaktorsicherheit). Kurz-Information. Reihe D [*A publication*] .....GRS (Ges Reaktorsicherheit) Kurz-Inf Reihe D

GRS (Gesellschaft fuer Reaktorsicherheit). Kurz-Information. Reihe E [*A publication*] .....GRS (Ges Reaktorsicherheit) Kurz-Inf Reihe E

GRS (Gesellschaft fuer Reaktorsicherheit). Kurz-Information. Reihe F [*A publication*] .....GRS (Ges Reaktorsicherheit) Kurz-Inf Reihe F

GRS (Gesellschaft fuer Reaktorsicherheit). Kurz-Information. Reihe G [*A publication*] .....GRS (Ges Reaktorsicherheit) Kurz-Inf Reihe G

GRS (Gesellschaft fuer Reaktorsicherheit). Kurz-Information. Reihe H [*A publication*] .....GRS (Ges Reaktorsicherheit) Kurz-Inf Reihe H

Grubb & Ellis [*American Stock Exchange symbol*] .....GBE

Grudnaya Khirurgiya [*A publication*] .....Grudn Khir

Gruen Industries, Inc. [*American Stock Exchange symbol*] [*Delisted*] .....GRU

Grumman Aerospace Corporation [*of Grumman Corp.*] .....GAC

Grumman Aerospace Corp., Bethpage, NY [*Library symbol*] .....NBetG

Grumman Aircraft Engineering Corporation [*Later, Grumman Corp.*] .....GAEC

Grumman-Alderson Research Dummy [*Aircraft ejection seats*] .....GARD

Grumman Corp. [*NYSE symbol*] .....GQ

Grumman Submersible Vehicle .....GSV

Grunberg Hydrofoil System .....GHS

Grundarfjordur [*Iceland*] [*Airport symbol*] .....GUU

Grundlagen der Germanistik [*A publication*] .....GdG

Grundlagestudien aus Kybernetik und Geisteswissenschaft [*A publication*] .....Grund Kyber Geist

Grundlehren der Mathematischen Wissenschaften [*A publication*] .....Grundlehren Math Wiss

Grundrichtungslinie [*Base line, a gunnery term*] [*German military - World War II*] .....GRL

Grundrichtungspunkt [*Base point, a gunnery term*] [*German military - World War II*] .....GRP

Grundtvig Studier [*A publication*] .....GrSt

Grundy Center, IA [*Radio station call letters*] .....KGCI

Grundy Center Public Library, Grundy Center, IA [*Library symbol*] .....IaGrc

Grundy County-Jewett Norris Library, Trenton, MO [*Library symbol*] .....MoTr

Grundy, VA [*Radio station call letters*] .....WMJD

Grundy, VA [*Radio station call letters*] .....WNRG

Gruntal & Co. [*NYSE symbol*] .....GRU

Grupo de Convergencia Democratica en Uruguay [*Group of Democratic Convergence in Uruguay*] .....GCDU

Grupo Executivo de Trabalhos e Estudos de Projetos Espaciais [*Brazil*] .....GETEPE

Grupo Independente de Aviacao de Bombardeamento [*Portugal*] .....GIAB

Grupo de Oficiales Unidos [*Group of United Officers*] [*Argentina*] .....GOU

Grupos de Accion Revolucionaria Internacionalista [*Spain*] .....GARI

Gruppen-Hauptquartier [*Group Headquarters*] [*German military - World War II*] .....GRHQU

Gruppenfuehrer [*Squad Leader*] [*German military*] .....G

Gruppenpsychotherapie und Gruppendynamik [*A publication*] .....Gruppenpsyc

Grus [*Constellation*] .....Gru

GSA [*General Services Administration*] Procurement Regulations .....GSPR

GSA [*Geological Society of America*] Special Paper (Regional Studies) [*A publication*] .....GSA Spec Pap (Reg Stud)

GSA [*General Services Administration*] Stock Catalog .....GSC

GSE [*Ground Support Equipment*] Utilization List [*NASA*] .....GUL

GTA [*Grain Terminal Association*] Digest [*A publication*] .....GTA Dig

GTE [*General Telephone and Electronics Corp.*] Automatic Electric Technical Journal [*A publication*] .....GTE Autom Electr Tech J

GTE Corp. [*Formerly, General Telephone & Electronics Corp.*] [*NYSE symbol*] .....GTE

GTE-Sylvania, Electric Systems Group, Needham, MA [*Library symbol*] .....MNeeS

GTE Sylvania, Inc., Electronic Components Group, Seneca Falls, NY [*Library symbol*] .....NSnfG

GTECH Corp. [*NASDAQ symbol*] .....GTCH

GTI Corp. [*American Stock Exchange symbol*] .....GTI

GTI Corporation Uts [*NASDAQ symbol*] .....GTICU

GTO Association of America .....GAA

GTS Corporation [*NASDAQ symbol*] .....GTSC

Guacamayas [*Colombia*] [*Airport symbol*] .....GCA

Guadalajara [*Mexico*] [*Airport symbol*] .....GDL

Guadalajara [*Mexico*] [*Seismograph station code, US Geological Survey*] .....GUM

Guadeloupe [*Three-letter standard code*] .....GLP

Guadeloupe [*MARC country of publication code*] [*Library of Congress*] .....gp

Guadeloupe [*MARC geographic area code*] [*Library of Congress*] .....nwgp--

Guadeloupe [*Two-letter standard code*] .....GP

Guadeloupe Liberation Army .....GLA

Guaiacol-Linoleic Acid Hydroperoxide Oxidoreductase [*An enzyme*] .....GLO

Gualeguaychu [*Argentina*] [*Airport symbol*] .....GHU

Guam [*Three-letter standard code*] .....GUM

Guam [*Mariana Islands*] [*Seismograph station code, US Geological Survey*] .....GUMO

Guam [*MARC geographic area code*] [*Library of Congress*] .....pogu---

Guam [*MARC country of publication code*] [*Library of Congress*] .....gu

Guam [*Mariana Islands*] [*Geomagnetic observatory code*] .....GUA

Guam [*Santa Rosa*] [*Mariana Islands*] [*Seismograph station code, US Geological Survey*] .....GUA

Guam [*Two-letter standard code*] [*Postal code*] .....GU

Guam Agricultural Experiment Station. Publications [*A publication*] .....Guam Ag Exp

Guam Island [*Mariana Islands*] [*Airport symbol*] .....GUM

Guam Tracking Station [*NASA*] .....GTS

Guam Tracking Station [*NASA*] .....GWM

Guanambi [*Brazil*] [*Airport symbol*] .....GNM

Guanare [*Venezuela*] [*Airport symbol*] .....GUQ

Guangzhou [*China*] [*Airport symbol*] .....CAN

Guanidine [*Biochemistry*] .....Gdn

Guanidine Aluminum Sulfate Hexahydrate [*Insecticide*] .....GASH

Guanidine Aluminum Sulfate Hydrate [*Ferroelectrics*] .....GASH

Guanidine Hydrochloride [*Organic chemistry*] .....GHCl

Guanidinium Chloride [*Biochemistry*] ... GdmCl
Guanine [*Also, Gua*] [*Biochemistry*] ... G
Guanine [*Also, G*] [*Biochemistry*] ... Gua
Guanine, Cytosine [*Type*] [*Biochemistry*] ... GC
Guanine Phosphoribosyltransferase [*An enzyme*] ... GPRT
Guanosine [*One-letter symbol; see Guo*] ... G
Guanosine [*Also, G*] [*A nucleoside*] ... Guo
Guanosine Diphosphate [*Biochemistry*] ... GDP
Guanosine Diphosphomannose [*Biochemistry*] ... GDPMan
Guanosine Monophosphate [*Biochemistry*] ... GMP
Guanosine Triphosphate [*Biochemistry*] ... GTP
Guantanamo [*Cuba*] [*Airport symbol*] ... GAO
Guantanamo Bay [*Cuba*] [*Seismograph station code, US Geological Survey*] [*Closed*] ... GBC
Guantanamo Bay, Cuba ... GTMO
Guapi [*Colombia*] [*Airport symbol*] ... GPI
Guapiles [*Costa Rica*] [*Airport symbol*] ... GPL
Guarani [*Monetary unit in Paraguay*] ... G
Guarani [*MARC language code*] [*Library of Congress*] ... gua
Guarantee ... GU
Guarantee ... GUAR
Guarantee Bancorp. [*American Stock Exchange symbol*] [*Delisted*] ... GB
Guarantee Financial Corporation of California [*NASDAQ symbol*] ... GFCC
Guaranteed ... GTD
Guaranteed Annual Income ... GAI
Guaranteed Annual Income System ... GAINS
Guaranteed Annual Minimum ... GAM
Guaranteed Annual Wage ... GAW
Guaranteed Assignment Retention Detailing [*Navy*] ... GUARD
Guaranteed Hourly Minimum ... GHM
Guaranteed Hourly Wage ... GHW
Guaranteed Income Stream [*UAW program included in the union's 1982 contract with General Motors Corp.*] ... GIS
Guaranteed Income Supplement [*Program*] [*Canada*] ... GIS
Guaranteed Insurability Option ... GIO
Guaranteed Minimum Value ... GMV
Guaranteed One Coat [*Brand of house paint*] ... GOC
Guaranteed Purchase Option [*Insurance*] ... GPO
Guaranteed Retirement Income ... GRI
Guaranteed Student Loan ... GSL
Guaranteed Student Loan Program ... GSLP
Guaranteed Voltage Breakdown ... GVB
Guaranteed Weekly Minimum ... GWM
Guaranteed Weekly Wage ... GWW
Guaranty Commerce Corp. [*NASDAQ symbol*] ... GTCM
Guaranty National Corporation [*NASDAQ symbol*] ... GNIC
Guaratingueta [*Brazil*] [*Airport symbol*] ... GUJ
Guard [*Position in football, basketball, etc.*] ... G
Guard ... GD
Guard ... GRD
Guard-Cell Mother Cell [*Botany*] ... GMC
Guard Mail ... GM
Guard Rail ... GDR
Guard Ring Capacitor ... GRC
Guard, Tomb of the Unknown Soldier Identification Badge [*Military decoration*] ... GTUSIdentBad
Guard Vessel [*Nuclear energy*] ... GV
Guard Well Capacitor ... GWC
Guarded Relay Multiplexer ... GRM
Guardhouse ... GDHSE
Guardhouse ... GH
Guardhouse Lawyer [*Military slang*] ... GHL
Guardia Republicana [*Peru*] ... GRP
Guardian ... G
Guardian ... GDN
Guardian Angels ... GA
Guardian of Impressive Letters and Master of Excellent Replies ... GILMER
Guardian Industries Corp. [*NYSE symbol*] ... GRD
Guardian Mortgage Investors [*NYSE symbol*] [*Delisted*] ... GMI
Guardian Newspapers Ltd., Manchester, United Kingdom [*Library symbol*] ... UkMaG
Guardian Packaging [*NASDAQ symbol*] ... GPCK
Guardian Weekly [*A publication*] ... GW
Guards' Armoured Division [*Military unit*] [*British*] ... GAD
Guard's Expense in Returning Absentee [*Army*] ... GERA
Guardship ... GS
Guardsman [*Military*] ... GDSM
Guardsman Chemical, Inc. [*American Stock Exchange symbol*] ... GRV
Guari [*Papua New Guinea*] [*Airport symbol*] ... GUG
Guasdualito [*Venezuela*] [*Airport symbol*] ... GDO
Guatemala [*Three-letter standard code*] ... GTM
Guatemala ... GUAT
Guatemala [*MARC geographic area code*] [*Library of Congress*] ... ncgt---
Guatemala [*Aircraft nationality and registration mark*] ... TG
Guatemala [*MARC country of publication code*] [*Library of Congress*] ... gt
Guatemala [*Two-letter standard code*] ... GT
Guatemala City [*Guatemala*] [*Seismograph station code, US Geological Survey*] [*Closed*] ... GCG
Guatemala City [*Guatemala*] [*Airport symbol*] ... GUA
Guatemala News and Information Bureau ... GNIB
Guatemalan Human Rights Commission/USA ... GHR/USA
Guayama, PR [*Radio station call letters*] ... WBJA
Guayama, PR [*Radio station call letters*] ... WCRP
Guayama, PR [*Radio station call letters*] ... WXRF
Guayaquil [*Ecuador*] [*Airport symbol*] ... GYE
Guayaramerin [*Bolivia*] [*Airport symbol*] ... GYA
Guaymas [*Mexico*] [*Airport symbol*] ... GYM
Guaymas [*Mexico*] [*Seismograph station code, US Geological Survey*] ... GYM
Guaymas, Mexico [*Remote site*] [*NASA*] ... GYM
Gucci [*Designer*] ... G
Gudermannian Amplitude ... GD
Guelph, ON [*Radio station call letters*] ... CFRU-FM
Guelph, ON [*Radio station call letters*] ... CJOY
Guelph, ON [*Radio station call letters*] ... CKLA-FM
Guelph Public Library, Guelph, ON, Canada [*Library symbol*] ... CaOG
Guerilla ... GUER
Guerilla Urban Traffic System [*Refers to driving in Boston*] ... GUTS
Guernsey [*Channel Islands*] [*Airport symbol*] ... GCI
Guernsey Airlines Ltd. [*Great Britain*] [*ICAO designator*] ... HW
Guerrilla Art Action Group ... GAAG
Guerrilla Warfare ... GW
Guerrilla Warfare Operational Area [*Army*] ... GWOA
Guessed Average ... GA
Guest Aerovias Mexico, SA ... GAM
Guest Housing [*Army*] ... GHSG
Guest Option [*Hotel plan, Hilton hotels*] ... GO
Guest Supply, Inc. [*NASDAQ symbol*] ... GEST
Guevara-McInteer-Wageman ... GMW
Guggenheim Aeronautical Laboratory [*California Institute of Technology*] ... GAL
Guggenheim Aeronautical Laboratory, California Institute of Technology ... GALCIT
Guggenheim Institute of Flight Structures ... GIFS
Guidance ... GDNC
Guidance ... GDNCE
Guidance ... GUID
Guidance ... GUIDN
Guidance Acceptance Test Set ... GATS
Guidance Accuracy Study for SPRINT [*Missile*] [*Army*] ... GASS
Guidance Attitude Space Position Indicator ... GASPI
Guidance Capsule Handling ... GCH
Guidance Checkout Computer ... GCC
Guidance Checkout Junction Box ... GCJB
Guidance Command Test ... GCT
Guidance Computer ... GC
Guidance Computer Control Subsystem ... GUCCO
Guidance Computer Test ... GCT
Guidance Computer Test Equipment ... GCTE
Guidance Control ... GC
Guidance, Control, and Airframe ... GC & A
Guidance and Control Analysis Team [*Space Flight Operations, NASA*] ... GCAT
Guidance and Control Assembly ... GCA
Guidance and Control Computer ... GCC
Guidance and Control Coupler ... G & CC
Guidance and Control Equipment Performance ... G & CEP
Guidance and Control Flight Analysis Program [*Aerospace*] ... GCFAP
Guidance Control Group [*Military*] ... GCG
Guidance and Control Information [*DoD*] ... GACIA
Guidance, Control, and Information Systems Division [*NASA*] ... GCISD
Guidance Control Laboratory ... GCL
Guidance Control Officer ... GCO
Guidance Control Package ... GCP
Guidance Control and Sequencing Computer ... GCSC
Guidance and Control System ... G & CS
Guidance and Control Unit ... GCU
Guidance Correction Input Panel ... GCIP
Guidance Coupler Unit ... GCU
Guidance Cutoff Signal [*NASA*] ... GCS
Guidance Data Converter [*Aerospace*] ... GDC
Guidance Digital Evaluation Test ... GDEU
Guidance Engine Cutoff [*NASA*] ... GECO
Guidance Error Analysis Vehicles [*Air Force*] ... GEAV
Guidance Evaluation Missile ... GEM
Guidance Heater Control ... GHC
Guidance Inertial Data Analysis Program ... GIDAP
Guidance Information System [*Time Share Corp.*] ... GIS
Guidance Integration Unit ... GIU
Guidance Inventory [*Psychology*] ... GI
Guidance Monitor Set [*Aerospace*] ... GMS
Guidance and Navigation [*System*] [*Apollo*] [*NASA*] ... G & N
Guidance and Navigation Computer [*NASA*] ... GNC
Guidance, Navigation, and Control ... GN & C
Guidance, Navigation, and Control ... GNC
Guidance, Navigation, and Control Integration Simulator ... GNCIS
Guidance, Navigation, and Control System ... GNCS
Guidance and Navigation Electronics ... GNE
Guidance and Navigation Equipment ... GNE
Guidance and Navigation Officer [*NASA*] ... GUIDO
Guidance and Navigation System ... GNS
Guidance Officer ... GDO

Guidance Optical Alignment Shelter ... GOAS
Guidance Optics and Sighting ... GOST
Guidance and Orbit Determination for Solar Electric Propulsion [*NASA*] ... GODSEP
Guidance Package ... GP
Guidance Package Installation Dolly [*Polaris missile*] ... GPID
Guidance Platform Assembly [*Military*] ... GPA
Guidance Position Tracking [*Aerospace*] ... GPT
Guidance Positioning Assembly ... GPA
Guidance Power Supply ... GPS
Guidance Power Temperature Regulator ... GPTR
Guidance Rate Measurement ... GRM
Guidance Reference Release ... GRR
Guidance Regulator Unit ... GRU
Guidance and Reporting System [*Army*] ... G & RS
Guidance Shipping Container ... GSC
Guidance Signal Processor ... GSP
Guidance Signal Processor-Repeater ... GSP-R
Guidance Simulator ... GS
Guidance Spare Power Supply ... GSPS
Guidance Station [*Aerospace*] ... GS
Guidance Sustainer Cutoff [*Aerospace*] ... GSCO
Guidance System [*Aerospace*] ... GS
Guidance System Console [*Aerospace*] ... GSC
Guidance System Simulator ... GSS
Guidance System Test Equipment ... GSTE
Guidance System Test Set ... GSTS
Guidance System Test Unit ... GSTU
Guidance Systems Operation Plan [*NASA*] ... GSOP
Guidance Test Equipment ... GTE
Guidance Test Fixture ... GTF
Guidance Test Set ... GTS
Guidance Test Unit ... GTU
Guidance Test Vehicle ... GTV
Guidance Transfer Container ... GTC
Guidance Transmitter ... GT
Guidance Transmitter ... G/XMTR
Guidance Unit ... GU
Guidance Unit Assembly ... GUA
Guidance for Users of Integrated Data Processing Equipment ... GUIDE
Guidance Using Stable Tuning Oscillations ... GUSTO
Guide ... G
Guide to American Directories [*A publication*] ... GAD
Guide to Baseball Literature [*A publication*] ... GBL
Guide Dog Foundation for the Blind ... GDFB
Guide Dog Users ... GDU
Guide Dogs for the Blind ... GDB
Guide to Football Literature [*A publication*] ... GFL
Guide to Indian Periodical Literature [*A publication*] ... GInd
Guide to Indian Periodical Literature [*A publication*] ... G Indian Per Lit
Guide to International Scientific Publications and Associations [*A publication*] ... GISPA
Guide Light ... GLT
Guide Line Identification Program for Antimissile Research [*ARPA*] ... GLIPAR
Guide Line Paper [*of Washington Standardization Officers*] [*Military*] ... GLP
Guide to Microforms in Print [*A publication*] ... GMP
Guide to Performing Arts [*A publication*] ... GPerfArts
Guide to Religious Periodicals [*A publication*] ... G Rel Per
Guide Slope ... GS
Guidebook ... GB
Guided ... GDE
Guided Air Defense Rocket ... GADR
Guided Aircraft Missile [*Obsolete*] ... GAM
Guided Aircraft Rocket ... GAR
Guided Antiradiation Bomb ... GARB
Guided Antitank Projectile ... GAP
Guided Atomic Warhead ... GAW
Guided Bomb Unit ... GBU
Guided Flight Vehicle ... GFV
Guided Folding-Fin Aircraft Rocket ... GFFAR
Guided Missile ... GM
Guided Missile ... G/MSL
Guided Missile and Aerospace Intelligence Committee ... GMAIC
Guided Missile Ammunition ... GMA
Guided Missile Brigade [*Army*] ... GMB
Guided Missile Capital Ship [*Navy symbol*] ... BBG
Guided Missile Coastal Escort [*Ship symbol*] ... PCG
Guided Missile Control ... GMC
Guided Missile Control Facility ... GMCF
Guided Missile Control Officer ... GMCO
Guided Missile Countermeasures ... GMCM
Guided Missile Cruiser [*Navy symbol*] ... CG
Guided Missile Cruiser ... CGX
Guided Missile Cruiser (Nuclear Propulsion) [*Navy symbol*] ... CGN
Guided Missile Data Exchange Program [*Navy*] ... GMDEP
Guided Missile Destroyer [*Navy symbol*] ... DDG
Guided Missile Destroyer ... DDGX
Guided Missile Destroyer [*Navy symbol*] ... DXG
Guided Missile Destroyer, Nuclear-Propulsion [*Navy symbol*] ... DXGN
Guided Missile Development Division [*NASA*] ... GMDD
Guided Missile Escort Ship [*Navy symbol*] ... DEG
Guided Missile Evaluation Unit ... GMEVALU
Guided Missile Evaluator ... GME
Guided Missile Facilities ... GMF
Guided Missile Fast Patrol Boat [*Ship symbol*] ... PBFG
Guided Missile Fire Control ... GMFC
Guided Missile Fire Control System ... GMFCS
Guided Missile Firing Panel ... GMFP
Guided Missile Frigate [*Navy symbol*] ... DLG
Guided Missile Frigate [*Navy symbol*] ... FFG
Guided Missile Frigate (Nuclear Propulsion) [*Navy symbol*] ... DLGN
Guided Missile Group ... GMGRU
Guided Missile Heavy Cruiser [*Navy symbol*] ... CAG
Guided Missile Heavy Cruiser (Nuclear Propulsion) [*Navy symbol*] ... CAG(N)
Guided Missile Launcher ... GML
Guided Missile Launching System ... GMLS
Guided Missile Light Cruiser [*Navy symbol*] ... CLG
Guided Missile Light Cruiser (Nuclear Propulsion) [*Navy symbol*] ... CLGN
Guided Missile Officer ... GMO
Guided Missile Operation and Control Unit ... GMOCU
Guided Missile Operations Officer ... GMOO
Guided Missile Patrol Escort [*Ship symbol*] ... PFGM
Guided Missile Range Division [*NASA*] ... GMRD
Guided Missile Relay Working Group [*Navy*] ... GMRWG
Guided Missile School [*Dam Neck, VA*] ... GMS
Guided Missile Service Record ... GMSR
Guided Missile Service Report ... GMSER
Guided Missile Service Squadron ... GMSRON
Guided Missile Service Unit [*Air Force*] ... GMSU
Guided Missile Ship [*Navy symbol*] ... AVM
Guided Missile Squadron ... GMSQUAD
Guided Missile Strike Cruiser [*Navy symbol*] ... CSG
Guided Missile Submarine [*Navy symbol*] ... SSG
Guided Missile Submarine (Nuclear Propulsion) [*Navy symbol*] ... SSGN
Guided Missile System ... GMS
Guided Missile System Test Set ... GMSTS
Guided Missile Target ... GMT
Guided Missile Test Set ... GMTS
Guided Missile Trainer ... GMT
Guided Missile Training Unit [*Navy*] ... GMTU
Guided Missile Unit ... GMU
Guided Space Vehicle [*Air Force*] ... GSV
Guided Unified S-Band ... GUSB
Guided Weapon [*Air Force*] ... GW
Guidelines for Investigation, Planning, and Research ... GLIPAR
Guidelines Marketing Corporation ... GUIMARC
Guiding Eyes for the Blind ... GEB
Guidon Oil & Gas Co. [*NASDAQ symbol*] ... GUID
Guidotti & C. [*Italy*] [*Research code symbol*] ... LG
Guiglo [*Ivory Coast*] [*Airport symbol*] ... GGO
Guild ... GLD
Guild of Agricultural Journalists ... GAJ
Guild of Air Pilots and Air Navigators ... GAPAN
Guild of Air Traffic Control Officers [*British*] ... GATCO
Guild of All Souls [*British*] ... GAS
Guild of American Funeral Directors [*Defunct*] ... GAFD
Guild of American Luthiers ... GAL
Guild of Better Shoe Manufacturers ... GBSM
Guild of Book Workers ... GBW
Guild of Carillonneurs in North America ... GCNA
Guild of Carillonneurs in North America. Bulletin [*A publication*] ... GCNA
Guild of Catholic Lawyers ... GCL
Guild of Catholic Psychiatrists [*Later, National Guild of Catholic Psychiatrists*] ... GCP
Guild of Ethical Funeral Practice ... GEFP
Guild of the Infant Saviour ... GIS
Guild for Infant Survival [*Later, International Council for Infant Survival*] ... GIS
Guild of Natural Science Illustrators ... GNSI
Guild Notes [*A publication*] ... Guild Nts
Guild Practitioner [*A publication*] ... Guild Prac
Guild of Prescription Opticians of America [*Later, OAA*] ... GPOA
Guild for Religious Architecture [*Later, IFRAA*] ... GRA
Guild to Revive Exhausted Nurses ... GREEN
Guild of Saint Alban ... GSA
Guild of St. Ives ... GSI
Guild of Saint Matthew ... GSM
Guild of Television Cameramen [*British*] ... GTC
Guild of Temple Musicians ... GTM
Guild Vector Colorimeter ... GVC
Guild of Washington Incompetent Bureaucratic Ideal Throatcutters [*An organization rumored to have been active in World War II*] ... GWIBIT
Guilde Internationale des Cooperatrices ... GIC
Guilder [*Florin*] [*Monetary unit in the Netherlands*] ... FL
Guilder [*Modification of gulden*] [*Monetary unit in the Netherlands*] ... G
Guilder [*Florin*] [*Monetary unit in Netherlands Antilles*] ... NAF
Guildhall Library, Aldermanbury, London, United Kingdom [*Library symbol*] ... UkLG
Guildhall Museum [*London*] ... GMUS

Guildhall School of Music [*London*] GSM
Guilford College, Greensboro, NC [*Library symbol*] NcGG
Guilford Courthouse National Military Park GUCO
Guilford-Holley L Inventory [*Psychology*] GHLI
Guilford Industries, Inc. [*NASDAQ symbol*] GILD
Guilford-Martin Personnel Inventory [*Psychology*] GMPI
Guilford Mills, Inc. [*American Stock Exchange symbol*] GFD
Guilford Technical Institute, Jamestown, NC [*Library symbol*] NcJG
Guilford-Zimmerman Temperament Survey [*Psychology*] GZTS
Guilin [*China*] [*Airport symbol*] KWL
Guillain-Barre [*Syndrome*] [*Medicine*] GB
Guillain-Barre Syndrome [*Medicine*] GBS
Guillain-Barre Syndrome Support Group GBSSG
Guillotine GLTN
Guilty G
Guinea [*MARC geographic area code*] [*Library of Congress*] f-gv---
Guinea [*Monetary unit in Britain*] [*Obsolete*] G
Guinea [*Three-letter standard code*] GIN
Guinea [*Two-letter standard code*] GN
Guinea GU
Guinea [*MARC country of publication code*] [*Library of Congress*] gv
Guinea [*Aircraft nationality and registration mark*] 3X
Guinea Airways Limited GAL
Guinea-Bissau [*Three-letter standard code*] GNB
Guinea-Bissau [*Two-letter standard code*] GW
Guinea Pig GP
Guinea Pig Albumin GPA
Guinea Pig Complement [*Immunochemistry*] GPC
Guinea Pig Gamma Globulin [*Immunochemistry*] GPGG
Guinea Pig Myelin Basic Protein [*Immunochemistry*] GPBP
Guinea Pig Serum GPS
Guinea Pig Spinal Cord GPSC
Guinea Pig Spleen GPS
Guinea Pig Unit [*Endocrinology*] GPU
Guinean Trawling Survey [*United Nations*] GTS
Guineas [*Monetary unit in Britain*] [*Obsolete*] GNS
Guiria [*Venezuela*] [*Airport symbol*] GUI
Guirsh [*Monetary unit in Saudi Arabia*] G
Guitar G
Guitar and Accessory Manufacturers Association [*Formerly, NAMMM*] GAMA
Guitar Foundation of America GFA
Guitar Review [*A publication*] GTR
Guitar Review [*A publication*] Guitar R
Guitarra Magazine [*A publication*] Guitarra
Guiyang [*China*] [*Airport symbol*] KWE
Gujarat Statistical Review [*A publication*] Gujarat Statist Rev
Gujarati [*MARC language code*] [*Library of Congress*] guj
Gulden [*Monetary unit in the Netherlands*] G
Gulden Passer [*A publication*] GP
Gules [*Heraldry*] G
Gules [*Heraldry*] GU
Gulf [*Maps and charts*] G
Gulf GLF
Gulf of Alaska [*FAA*] GLFALSK
Gulf of Alaska Mesoscale Oceanographic Processes GAS-MOP
Gulf of Alaska SEASAT Experiment [*National Oceanic and Atmospheric Administration*] GOASEX
Gulf Applied Technology [*NASDAQ symbol*] GATS
Gulf Atomic Mobile Assay System GAMAS
Gulf Aviation Ltd. [*Great Britain*] [*ICAO designator*] GF
Gulf and Caribbean Fisheries Institute GCFI
Gulf Coast Association of Geological Societies. Transactions [*A publication*] Gulf Coast Assoc Geol Socs Trans
Gulf Coast Aviation, Inc. [*Gulfport, MS*] [*FAA designator*] GFC
Gulf Coast Base Service Unit GULFCOBASESERVUNIT
Gulf Coast Bible College, Houston, TX [*Library symbol*] TxHG
Gulf Coast Fisheries Center GCFC
Gulf Coast Hydroscience Center [*Department of the Interior*] GCHC
Gulf Coast Low Water Datum GCLWD
Gulf Coast Research Laboratory GCRL
Gulf Coast Waste Disposal Authority [*Governmental industrial waste disposal system*] GCWDA
Gulf, Colorado & Santa Fe Railway Co. GC & SF
Gulf, Colorado & Santa Fe Railway Co. [*AAR code*] GCSF
Gulf Control GULFCON
Gulf Cooperation Council [*Consists of Saudi Arabia, Bahrain, Kuwait, Oman, Qatar, and the United Arab Emirates*] GCC
Gulf Division Naval Facilities Engineering Command DIRGULFDOCKS
Gulf Division Naval Facilities Engineering Command GULFNAVFACENGCOM
Gulf Energy Corporation [*NASDAQ symbol*] GFEC
Gulf Energy & Minerals Co. GEM
Gulf Environmental Measurements Program GEP
Gulf-European Freight Association GEFA
Gulf General Atomic [*Commercial firm*] GGA
Gulf Intercoastal Conference GIC
Gulf International Bank [*Middle East*] GIB
Gulf Intracoastal Waterway GIW
Gulf Intracoastal Waterway GIWW
Gulf Islands Secondary School, Ganges, BC, Canada [*Library symbol*] CaBGS
Gulf It to FORTRAN [*Translator*] GIF
Gulf of Mexico [*FAA*] GLFMEX
Gulf of Mexico [*MARC geographic area code*] [*Library of Congress*] nm-----
Gulf, Mobile & Ohio Railroad [*NYSE symbol*] [*Delisted*] GFO
Gulf, Mobile & Ohio Railroad [*Later, Illinois Central Gulf Railroad*] GM & O
Gulf, Mobile & Ohio Railroad [*Later, Illinois Central Gulf Railroad*] [*AAR code*] GMO
Gulf Nuclear, Inc. [*NASDAQ symbol*] GNUC
Gulf Oil Canada Ltd. [*American Stock Exchange symbol*] GOC
Gulf Oil Canada Ltd., Calgary, AB, Canada [*Library symbol*] CaACGO
Gulf Oil Chemicals Co. GOCHEM
Gulf Oil Co.-US, Central Reference Library, Houston, TX [*Library symbol*] TxHGO
Gulf Oil Corp. [*NYSE symbol*] GO
Gulf Oil Real Estate Development Company GOREDCO
Gulf Oil Trading Company GOTCO
Gulf Organization for Development in Egypt GODE
Gulf Permanent Assistance Committee [*Persian Gulf*] GUPAC
Gulf Publishing Co., Houston, TX [*Library symbol*] TxHGP
Gulf Regional Planning Commission GRPC
Gulf Republic Financial Corp. [*American Stock Exchange symbol*] [*Delisted*] GRF
Gulf Research & Development Co., Pittsburgh, PA [*Library symbol*] PPiGulf
Gulf Research Reports [*A publication*] Gulf Res Rep
Gulf Resources & Chemical Corp. [*NYSE symbol*] GRE
Gulf of St. Lawrence [*FAA*] GLFSTLAWR
Gulf Science Year [*1970*] GSY
Gulf Sea Frontier GSF
Gulf Sea Frontier GULFSEAFRON
Gulf & Ship Island Railroad Co. G & SI
Gulf South Mortgage Investors [*American Stock Exchange symbol*] [*Delisted*] GSR
Gulf South Research Institute GSRI
Gulf South Research Institute, Baton Rouge, LA [*Library symbol*] LBrG
Gulf States Marine Fisheries Commission GSMFC
Gulf States Utilities Co. [*NYSE symbol*] GSU
Gulf States Utilities Co., Beaumont, TX [*OCLC symbol*] TGS
Gulf Transport [*AAR code*] GTC
Gulf Transportation Terminal Command GTTC
Gulf United Corp. [*Formerly, Gulf Life Holding Company*] [*NYSE symbol*] [*Delisted*] GHC
Gulf Universities Research Consortium GURC
Gulf & Western Industries, Inc. G & W
Gulf & Western Industries, Inc. G & WI
Gulf & Western Industries, Inc. [*NYSE symbol*] GW
Gulfcoast Pulpwood Association GPA
Gulfport/Biloxi [*Mississippi*] [*Airport symbol*] GPT
Gulfport-Carnegie-Harrison County Library, Gulfport, MS [*Library symbol*] MsGu
Gulfport, MS [*Radio station call letters*] WGCM
Gulfport, MS [*Radio station call letters*] WGUF
Gulfport, MS [*Radio station call letters*] WGUF-FM
Gulfport, MS [*Radio station call letters*] WROA
Gulfport, MS [*Radio station call letters*] WROA-FM
Gulfport, MS [*Radio station call letters*] WTAM
Gulfstream Aerospace Corp. [*NYSE symbol*] GA
Gulfstream Banks [*NYSE symbol*] [*Delisted*] GBK
Gulfstream Land & Development Corp. [*American Stock Exchange symbol*] GSD
Gulielmus Rex [*King William*] GR
Gulkana [*Alaska*] [*Airport symbol*] GKN
Gulkana, AK [*Location identifier*] [*FAA*] GKN
Gulkana, AK [*Location identifier*] [*FAA*] GLA
Gull Air [*South Yarmouth, MA*] [*FAA designator*] GUL
Gull, Inc. [*NASDAQ symbol*] GULL
Gullwing Group GWG
Gulmarg [*India*] [*Geomagnetic observatory code*] GUL
Gulton Industries, Inc. [*NYSE symbol*] GUL
Gulu [*Uganda*] [*Airport symbol*] ULU
Gum Skips [*Philately*] GS
Gummed All Over Flap [*Envelopes*] GAOF
Gummed Industries Association GIA
Gummed Only [*Envelopes*] GO
Gummi, Asbest, Kunststoffe [*A publication*] Gummi Asbest Kunstst
Gun G
Gun [*s*] [*Freight*] GN
Gun Accessory System GAS
Gun Aiming Sensor GAS
Gun Automatic GAU
Gun Board [*British*] GB
Gun, Bomb, and Rocket GBR
Gun-Bus [*Gun-carrying plane*] [*Air Force*] [*British*] GB
Gun Camera GC
Gun Captain GC
Gun Carriage GC
Gun Carriage GCRG
Gun Control GC

Gun Control Officer [*Navy*] GCO
Gun Cruiser [*Navy symbol*] CA
Gun Damage Assessment GDA
Gun-Defended Area GDA
Gun Direction Computer GDC
Gun Direction Officer GDO
Gun Director Pointer [*Naval gunnery*] GDP
Gun Director Pointer (Cross Leveler) [*Naval gunnery*] GDP(CL)
Gun Director Pointer (Leveler) [*Naval gunnery*] GDP(L)
Gun Director Pointer (Pointer) [*Naval gunnery*] GDP(P)
Gun Director Pointer (Sight Setter) [*Naval gunnery*] GDP(SS)
Gun Director Pointer (Trainer) [*Naval gunnery*] GDP(T)
Gun Electron-Induced Semiconductor Hybrid Amplifier GEISHA
Gun Lay [*or Laying*] GL
Gun-Laying Mark I [*RADAR*] GM
Gun-Laying (Turret) GL(T)
Gun Low-Altitude Air Defense System GLAADS
Gun Metal GMET
Gun Motor Carriage GMC
Gun Owners of America GOA
Gun Pointer [*Naval gunnery*] GP
Gun Position Officer GPO
Gun Range-Finder Operator GRFO
Gun Sight Aiming Point GSAP
Gun Sound Ranging [*An acoustic device*] GSR
Gun Target GT
Gun Target GTGT
Gun/Target Line [*Navy*] GTL
Gun Tractor [*British*] GT
Gun Turret GT
Gun Weapon System Replacement Program GWSRP
Gunboat [*Naval*] GB
Gunboat GBT
Gunboat [*Coast Guard*] WPB
Gundeck GD
Gunfire Area GFA
Gunfire Control System GFCS
Gunfire Detection Device GFDD
Gunfire Support GFS
Gunfire Support Ship GFSS
Gunite Contractors Association GCA
Gunma Journal of Liberal Arts and Science [*A publication*] Gunma J Libr Arts Sci
Gunma Journal of Medical Science [*A publication*] Gunma J Med Sci
Gunma Reports of Medical Sciences [*A publication*] Gunma Rep Med Sci
Gunma Symposium on Endocrinology [*A publication*] Gunma Symp Endocrinol
Gunmetal GM
Gunn-Diode X-Band Amplifier GXA
Gunn Effect Device GED
Gunn Effect Material GEM
Gunn, Hoffer & Associates, Winnipeg, MB, Canada [*Library symbol*] CaMWGHA
Gunn Oscillator GO
Gunnedah [*Australia*] [*Airport symbol*] GUH
Gunner GNR
Gunner GR
Gunner Instructor [*Navy*] [*British*] GI
Gunners Control Unit GCU
Gunner's Mate [*Navy rating*] GM
Gunner's Mate, Chief [*Navy rating*] GMC
Gunner's Mate, Construction Battalion [*Navy rating*] GMCB
Gunner's Mate, Construction Battalion, Armorer [*Navy rating*] GMCBA
Gunner's Mate, Construction Battalion, Powderman [*Navy rating*] GMCBP
Gunner's Mate, First Class [*Navy rating*] GM1
Gunner's Mate, Guns [*Navy rating*] GMG
Gunner's Mate, Master Chief [*Navy rating*] GMCM
Gunner's Mate, Missile [*Navy rating*] GMM
Gunner's Mate, Second Class [*Navy rating*] GM2
Gunner's Mate, Senior Chief [*Navy rating*] GMCS
Gunner's Mate, Ship Repair [*Navy rating*] [*Obsolete*] GMSR
Gunner's Mate, Ship Repair, Powderman [*Navy rating*] [*Obsolete*] GMSRP
Gunner's Mate, Technician [*Navy rating*] GMT
Gunner's Mate, Technician, Seaman [*Navy rating*] GMTSN
Gunner's Mate, Technician, Seaman Apprentice [*Navy rating*] GMTSA
Gunner's Mate, Third Class [*Navy rating*] GM3
Gunnerudssatern [*Sweden*] [*Seismograph station code, US Geological Survey*] GNN
Gunnery [*Navy*] [*British*] g
Gunnery GNRY
Gunnery GUN
Gunnery Exercise [*Navy*] GUNEX
Gunnery Flight GF
Gunnery Liaison Officer [*Navy*] GLO
Gunnery Officer's Console [*Army*] GOC
Gunnery Officers Ordnance School GOOS
Gunnery Range GR
Gunnery School [*Air Force*] GS
Gunnery Schoolship [*Navy*] GUNSS
Gunnery and Searchlight [*Control*] [*British*] [*World War II*] GS
Gunnery Sergeant GS
Gunnery Sergeant GUNSGT
Gunnery Sergeant GYSGT
Gunnery Support GS
Gunnery Weapon Control Switchboard GWCSWBD
Gunnison [*Colorado*] [*Airport symbol*] GUC
Gunnison, CO [*Radio station call letters*] KGUC
Gunnison, CO [*Radio station call letters*] KGUC-FM
Gunnison, CO [*Radio station call letters*] KVLE
Gunnison, CO [*Radio station call letters*] KWSB-FM
Gunnison County Public Library, Gunnison, CO [*Library symbol*] CoGu
Gunnison, UT [*Radio station call letters*] KGVH
Guns and Magnetic Material Alarm [*Weapon-detecting device to prevent skyjacking*] GAMMA
Gunshot Wound [*Medicine*] GSW
Gunshot Wound to the Abdomen GSWA
Guntersville, AL [*Radio station call letters*] WGSV
Guntersville, AL [*Radio station call letters*] WTWX
Gunton's Magazine [*A publication*] Gunton
Gurayat [*Saudi Arabia*] [*Airport symbol*] URY
Gure Herria [*A publication*] GH
Guri [*Venezuela*] [*Seismograph station code, US Geological Survey*] GUV
Gurkha Transport Regiment [*Military unit*] [*British*] GTR
Gusap [*Papua New Guinea*] [*Airport symbol*] [*Obsolete*] GAP
Gust Alleviation and Structural Dynamic Stability Augmentation [*Aviation*] GASDSAS
Gust Load Alleviation [*Aviation*] GLA
Gustav Freytag Blaetter [*A publication*] GFB
Gustavus [*Alaska*] [*Airport symbol*] GST
Gustavus Adolphus College [*Minnesota*] GAC
Gustavus Adolphus College, St. Peter, MN [*OCLC symbol*] MNG
Gustavus Adolphus College, St. Peter, MN [*Library symbol*] MnStpeG
Gustin-Bacon Manufacturing Co. [*NYSE symbol*] [*Delisted*] GBA
Gusts [*Meteorology*] G
Gusts [*Meteorology*] GSTS
Gusty [*Meteorology*] GSTY
Gut-Associated [*Medicine*] GA
Gut-Associated Lymphoid Tissue [*Medicine*] GALT
Gutenberg Gesellschaft GG
Gutenberg-Jahrbuch [*A publication*] GJ
Gutenkunst Public Library, State Center, IA [*Library symbol*] IaStc
Guthrie, C. B., Tariff Bureau Inc., Washington DC [*STAC*] GCB
Guthrie, OK [*Location identifier*] [*FAA*] GOK
Guthrie, OK [*Radio station call letters*] KOKC
Guthrie, OK [*Location identifier*] [*FAA*] LCY
Gutta [*Drop of Liquid*] [*Pharmacy*] GT
Guttae [*Drops of Liquid*] [*Pharmacy*] GTT
Guttae [*Drops of Liquid*] [*Pharmacy*] GUTT
Guttatim [*Drop by Drop*] [*Pharmacy*] GUTTAT
Guttenberg Public Library, Guttenberg, IA [*Library symbol*] IaGut
Gutter GUT
Gutter Pair [*Philately*] GP
Guttis Quibusdam [*With a Few Drops*] [*Pharmacy*] GUTT QUIBUSD
Gutturi [*To the Throat*] [*Pharmacy*] GUTT
Guy in the Back [*Copilot*] [*Air Force slang*] GIB
Guy in the Backseat [*Copilot*] [*Air Force slang*] GIBS
Guyana [*Three-letter standard code*] GUY
Guyana [*Aircraft nationality and registration mark*] 8R
Guyana [*MARC geographic area code*] [*Library of Congress*] s-gy---
Guyana [*MARC country of publication code*] [*Library of Congress*] gy
Guyana [*Two-letter standard code*] GY
Guyana Airways Corp. [*ICAO designator*] GY
Guyana Sugar Experiment Station's Bulletin [*A publication*] Guyana Sugar Exp Stn Bull
Guyanese Defense Force GDF
Guyman, OK [*Radio station call letters*] KKBS
Guymon City Library, Guymon, OK [*Library symbol*] OkGuy
Guymon, OK [*Radio station call letters*] KGYN
Guymon Public Library, Guymon, OK [*OCLC symbol*] GPL
Guy's Hospital Reports [*A publication*] GHREA
Guy's Hospital Reports [*A publication*] Guy's Hosp Rep
GVN [*Government of Vietnam*] **Liaison Officer** GLO
Gwadar [*Pakistan*] [*Airport symbol*] GWD
Gwalior [*India*] [*Airport symbol*] GWL
Gwelo [*Zimbabwe*] [*Airport symbol*] GWE
Gwinn, MI [*Location identifier*] [*FAA*] SAW
Gwynedd-Mercy College, Gwynedd, PA [*OCLC symbol*] GWY
Gwynedd-Mercy College, Gwynedd Valley, PA [*Library symbol*] PGwvG
Gymnasium GYM
Gymnasium [*A publication*] Gym
Gymnasium und Wissenschaft [*A publication*] GW
Gymnastic [*Freight*] GYMSTIC
Gynaecology GYNAE
Gynaecology GYNAECOL
Gynaekologische Rundschau [*A publication*] Gynaekol Rundsch
Gynecologic Investigation [*A publication*] Gynecol Inv
Gynecologic Investigation [*A publication*] Gynecol Invest
Gynecologic and Obstetric Investigation [*A publication*] Gynecol Obstet Invest
Gynecologic Oncology [*A publication*] Gynecol Oncol

Gynecologie et Obstetrique [*A publication*]........................... Gynecol Obstet
Gynecologie et Obstetrique de Langue Francaise [*A publication*].....GYOBA
Gynecologie Pratique [*A publication*]...............................Gynecol Prat
Gynecology..GYN
Gynecology..GYNCLGY
Gynoecium [*Botany*]..G
Gypsum..GYP
Gypsum Association..GA
Gypsum Community Library, Gypsum, CO [*Library symbol*]................. CoGy
Gypsum Drywall Contractors International [*Later, AWCI*]....................GDCI
Gypsum-Plaster Ceiling [*Technical drawings*].........................GPC
Gypsum-Plaster Wall [*Technical drawings*]............................GPW
Gypsum Roof Deck Foundation [*Later, National Roof Deck
     Contractors Association*]...GRDF
Gypsum Sheathing Board [*Technical drawings*].........................GSB
Gypsum Wallboard [*Technical drawings*]...............................GWB
Gypsy Lore Society, North American Section........................... GLS
Gypsy Moths [*An association*]...GM
Gypsy Scholar [*A publication*]..Gy S
Gyrate Atrophy [*Medicine*]..GA
Gyro Accelerometer Misalignment Erection Test ....GAMET
Gyro Assembly...GA
Gyro Compass..GC
Gyro Compass...GCMPS
Gyro-Compass Automatic Navigation [*System*]..........................GAN
Gyro-Compass, Desired Cluster Orientation.............................GCD
Gyro Control..GC
Gyro Control Assembly ....GCA
Gyro Control Gunsight...GCG
Gyro Coupling Unit ....GCU

Gyro Display Coupler..GDC
Gyro Drift Rate Compensation ....GDRC
Gyro Erected Optical Navigation ....GEON
Gyro Error...GE
Gyro Header Assembly ....GHA
Gyro International ....GI
Gyro Output Amplifier..GOA
Gyro Package..GP
Gyro Pitch Position ....GPP
Gyro Reference Assembly ....GRA
Gyro Reference System ....GRS
Gyro Storage Oven..GSO
Gyro Tilt Signal..GTS
Gyro Torque..GT
Gyro Transfer Table System ....GTTS
Gyro Yaw Position ....GYP
Gyrodyne Co. of America [*NASDAQ symbol*]..............................GYRO
Gyroless Control System..GCS
Gyromagnetic Kompass ....GMK
Gyromagnetic Ratio...G
Gyroscope...GY
Gyroscope...GYRO
Gyroscope Parameter Shift ....GPS
Gyroscope Pickoff Voltage ....GPV
Gyroscope Reference Unit ....GRU
Gyroscope Vibration Absorber ....GVA
Gyroscopes-Rate Bomb-Direction System ....GRBDS
Gyroscopic Low-Power Attitude Control ....GLOPAC
Gyrostabilizer...GS

H

H. A. Simons Ltd., Vancouver, BC, Canada [*Library symbol*].......... CaBVaHS
H. Allen Smith Jet Propulsion Laboratory [*Formerly, JPL, which
  laboratory is expected to continue using officially. Name had
  been changed in 1973 to honor retiring congressman*]................HASJPL
H. G. Wells Society .... HGWS
H. H. Franklin Club .... HHFC
H & H Oil Tool Co. [*NASDAQ symbol*] .... HHOT
H-Hour Coordinating Line [*Army*]..HHCL
H. J. Nugen Public Library, New London, IA [*Library symbol*].................. IaNI
H. Leslie Perry Memorial Library, Henderson, NC [*Library symbol*] ....NcHe
H. Lundbeck [*Denmark*] [*Research code symbol*] .... Lu
H. Lundbeck [*Denmark*] [*Research code symbol*] .... N
H. Mason [*Oregon*] [*Seismograph station code, US Geological
  Survey*]...HMO
H-Plane Tee Junction ....HTJ
H. Pordes, Publisher and Bookseller, London, United Kingdom
  [*Library symbol*]..UkLPo
H. W. Schroeder Junior/Senior High School Library, Webster,
  NY [*OCLC symbol*]..RWL
H. W. Wilson Co. [*Publisher*].. HWW
HAA [*Herpetological Association of Africa*] Journal [*A publication*]....... HAA J
Haadyai [*Thailand*] [*Airport symbol*]...HDY
Haarlemsch Bijdragen [*A publication*]..HBd
Habakkuk [*Old Testament book*] ....Hab
Habakkuk [*Old Testament book*] ....Hb
Habana Museo y Biblioteca de Malacologia Circulares [*A
  publication*].............................. Habana Mus y Biblioteca Malacologia Circ
Habana Museo y Biblioteca de Zoologia Circulares [*A
  publication*]................................Habana Mus y Biblioteca Zoologia Circ
Habeas Corpus [*You Have the Body*] [*Legal*] [*Latin*] .... HAB CORP
Habeat [*Let Him Have*] [*Pharmacy*]..HABT
Haber, Inc. [*NASDAQ symbol*]..HABE
Habitability/Crew Quarters .... H/CQ
Habitability Improvement .... HI
Habitability Improvement Plan [*Navy*]..HIP
Habitability Support System .... HSS
Habitability System [*NASA*] ....HS
Habitat [*A publication*]...HABT-A
Habitat Australia [*A publication*]... Habitat Aust
Habitat for Humanity .... HH
Habitat International Council ....HIC
Habitat et Vie Sociale [*A publication*]................................. Habitat Vie Soc
Habitation ....HAB
Habiter [*A publication*]..HBTF-A
Habitual [*FBI standardized term*] ....HAB
Habitual Abortion [*Medicine*]...HA
Habitual Criminal .... HC
Habituation Stimulus [*To light*]..HS
Haboro [*Japan*] [*Seismograph station code, US Geological
  Survey*] [*Closed*] ....HAB
Hac Nocte [*Tonight*] [*Pharmacy*]...HAC NOCT
Hacettepe Bulletin of Medicine-Surgery [*A publication*]...........................
  .... Hacettepe Bull Med-Surg
Hacettepe Bulletin of Social Sciences and Humanities [*A
  publication*]..Hacett B SS
Hach Co. [*NASDAQ symbol*] ....HACH
Hachijo Jima Island [*Japan*] [*Airport symbol*] ....HAC
Hachijojima [*Japan*] [*Seismograph station code, US Geological
  Survey*]...HJJ
Hachinohe [*Japan*] [*Seismograph station code, US Geological
  Survey*]..HAC
Hachtmann, J. I., Newark NJ [*STAC*] ....HJI
Hacienda Resorts, Incorporated [*NASDAQ symbol*] ....HRIC
Hack and Band Saw Manufacturers Association of America ....HBSMA
Hack and Band Saw Manufacturers Association of America ....HBSMAA
Hackensack, NJ [*Radio station call letters*] ....WWDJ
Hackensack Water Co. [*NYSE symbol*] [*Delisted*] ....HWA
Hackettstown, NJ [*Radio station call letters*] ....WNTI
Hackettstown, NJ [*Radio station call letters*] ....WRNJ
Hackley Public Library, Muskegon, MI [*Library symbol*] .... MiMu

Hackney [*Borough of London*] .... HACK
Hadashot Archaeologioth [*A publication*] .... Hadashot Arch
Hadassah Israel Education Services [*Jerusalem*] .... HIES
Hadassah Medical Relief Association ....HMRA
Hadassah, The Women's Zionist Organization of America .... HWZOA
Hadassah Zionist Youth Commission ....HZYC
Haddam [*Connecticut*] [*Seismograph station code, US Geological
  Survey*] ....HDM
Haddon Heights Public Library, Haddon Heights, NJ [*Library
  symbol*] ....NjHh
Haddon Township Free Library, Westmont, NJ [*Library symbol*] ....NjWem
Haddonfield Public Library, Haddonfield, NJ [*Library symbol*]................. NjH
Hadron, Inc. [*NASDAQ symbol*] .... HDRN
Hadson Petroleum Corp. [*NASDAQ symbol*] ....HADS
Haematocrit .... HAEMAT
Haematologica Latina [*A publication*] ....Haematol Lat
Haematologie und Bluttransfusion [*Haematology and Blood
  Transfusion*] [*A publication*] .... Haematol Bluttransfus
Haematology .... HAEMATOL
Haemolysis .... HAEM
Haemorrhage .... HAEMORRH
Haerterei-Technische Mitteilungen [*A publication*] ....Haerterei-Tech Mitt
Haerterei-Technische Mitteilungen [*A publication*] ....Haert-Tech Mitt
Haffkine Institute. Annual Report [*A publication*] .... Haffkine Inst Annu Rep
Hafnium [*Chemical element*] .... Hf
Hafuf [*Saudi Arabia*] [*Airport symbol*] .... HOF
Hagaman Memorial Library, East Haven, CT [*Library symbol*] ....CtEahav
Hageman Factor [*Factor XII*] [*Hematology*] .... HF
Hagerstown [*Maryland*] [*Airport symbol*]................................. HGR
Hagerstown Junior College [*Maryland*] .... HJC
Hagerstown, MD [*Radio station call letters*].............................. WARK
Hagerstown, MD [*Television station call letters*]...................... WHAG-TV
Hagerstown, MD [*Radio station call letters*].............................. WJEJ
Hagerstown, MD [*Radio station call letters*]............................ WWMD
Hagerstown, MD [*Television station call letters*]...................... WWPB
Hagerstown, MD [*Radio station call letters*]............................ WXCS
Hagfors [*Sweden*] [*Seismograph station code, US Geological Survey*]...HFS
Haggai [*Old Testament book*] ....Hag
Haggai [*Old Testament book*] .... Hg
Hague Conference on Private International Law .... CODIP
Hague Convention .... HC
Hague Resolutions .... HR
Hahn-Meitner-Institut fuer Kernforschung [*West Germany*] .... HMI
Hahnemann High School Behavior Rating Scale [*Psychology*] ....HHSB
Hahnemann Medical College and Hospital, Philadelphia, PA
  [*OCLC symbol*]...HHN
Hahnemann Medical College and Hospital, Philadelphia, PA
  [*Library symbol*]...PPHa
Hahnemann Symposium [*A publication*].............................Hahnemann Symp
Hahnium [*Proposed name for chemical element 105*] .... Ha
Haibara [*Japan*] [*Seismograph station code, US Geological Survey*]........HBR
Haida [*MARC language code*] [*Library of Congress*] ....hai
Haifa [*Israel*] [*Seismograph station code, US Geological Survey*]
  [*Closed*] .... HAF
Haifa [*Israel*] [*Airport symbol*]...HFA
Haikou [*China*] [*Airport symbol*]... HAK
Haiku Society of America ....HSA
Hail [*Meteorological symbol*] .... A
Hail [*Aviation code*]..GR
Hail [*Meteorology*]... H
Hail [*Saudi Arabia*] [*Airport symbol*]..HAS
Hail Insurance Adjustment and Research Association [*Later,
  NCIA*]...HIARA
Hailar [*China*] [*Airport symbol*]...HLD
Haile Selassie I University. Department of Geology. Annual
  Report [*A publication*] ....Haile Selassie I Univ Dep Geol Annu Rep
Hailey, ID [*Location identifier*] [*FAA*]..HLE
Hailey, ID [*Radio station call letters*]...KSKI
Hailey, ID [*Location identifier*] [*FAA*]..SUN

Haileybury Public Library, Haileybury, ON, Canada [*Library symbol*] .... CaOHai
Hailstones [*Meteorology*] .... HLSTO
Haines [*Alaska*] [*Airport symbol*] .... HNS
Haines, AK [*Radio station call letters*] .... KHNS
Haines Borough Public Library, Haines, AK [*Library symbol*] .... AkH
Haines City, FL [*Radio station call letters*] .... WFXI
Hair Space between Letters [*Proofreader's mark*] .... HR
Hair Tuning Bar .... HTB
Hairy Cell Leukemia [*Medicine*] .... HCL
Haiti [*Aircraft nationality and registration mark*] .... HH
Haiti [*MARC country of publication code*] [*Library of Congress*] .... ht
Haiti [*Three-letter standard code*] .... HTI
Haiti [*MARC geographic area code*] [*Library of Congress*] .... nwht---
Haiti [*Two-letter standard code*] .... HT
Haiti Air Transport [*ICAO designator*] .... HL
Haitian Air Corps .... HAC
Haitian-American Association [*Defunct*] .... HAA
Haitian-American Sugar Company .... HASCO
Haitian Campaign Medal .... HCM
Haitian Coalition on AIDS .... HCA
Haitian Medical Association Abroad .... HMAA
Haitian Philatelic Society .... HPS
Haitian Refugee Center .... HRC
Haitian Refugee Project .... HRP
Haitian Unity Council Incorporated [*Defunct*] .... HUCI
Haiwee [*California*] [*Seismograph station code, US Geological Survey*] [*Closed*] .... HAI
Hajji Baba Club .... HBC
Hajoca Corp. [*NYSE symbol*] [*Delisted*] .... HJA
Hakluyt Society .... HS
Hakodate [*Japan*] [*Seismograph station code, US Geological Survey*] .... HAK
Hakodate [*Japan*] [*Airport symbol*] .... HKD
Hal Roach Studios [*NASDAQ symbol*] .... HRSI
Halberd .... HLBRD
Halbfranzband [*Half-Calf*] [*Of books*] [*German*] .... HFRZ
Halbkettenfahrzeug [*Half-Track Vehicle*] [*German military - World War II*] .... HKF
Halbleinwand [*Half-Bound Cloth*] [*Of books*] [*German*] .... HLW
Halco Products Corp. [*American Stock Exchange symbol*] [*Delisted*] .... HCP
Halden Boiling Heavy-Water Reactor .... HBWR
Halden Reaktor Prosjekt [*Norway*] .... HPR
Haldimand County Museum Board, Cauga, ON, Canada [*Library symbol*] .... CaOCauHM
Hale Foundation .... HF
Hale Observatories [*Formerly, Mount Palomar and Mount Wilson Observatories*] .... HO
Hale Pohaku [*Hawaii*] [*Seismograph station code, US Geological Survey*] .... HPU
Hale Resources Ltd. [*NASDAQ symbol*] .... HALEF
Hale Systems, Inc. [*NASDAQ symbol*] .... HSYS
Haleakala [*Hawaii*] [*Seismograph station code, US Geological Survey*] .... HKL
Haleakala [*Hawaii*] [*Seismograph station code, US Geological Survey*] .... HLK
Haleakala National Park .... HALE
Haler [*Monetary unit in Czechoslovakia*] .... H
Haleyville, AL [*Radio station call letters*] .... WJBB
Haleyville, AL [*Radio station call letters*] .... WJBB-FM
Half .... H
Half .... HF
Half .... HLF
Half Add .... HA
Half-Amplitude Duration .... HAD
Half Bar Symbology .... HBS
Half Bound [*Bibliography*] .... HB
Half Breadth .... HB
Half Calf .... HC
Half Chest .... HC
Half Double Crochet .... HDC
Half Duplex .... HD
Half Duplex [*Transmission*] [*Data processing*] .... HDX
Half Duplex Teletype .... HDT
Half-Fare Order [*Aviation*] .... HFO
Half Hard [*Metallurgy*] .... HH
Half Hollow Hills Community Public Library, Huntington Station, NY [*Library symbol*] .... NHsH
Half-Life [*of radioactive elements*] .... HL
Half-Moon .... HLFM
Half Morocco .... HM
Half of 'O' Gauge [*Model railroading*] .... H-O
Half-Octave Bandwidth .... HOB
Half Page Printer .... HPP
Half Pay .... HP
Half Plate [*Photography*] .... HP
Half-Power Beamwidth .... HPBW
Half-Reversal [*Psychometrics*] .... HR
Half-Saddlebred Registry of America .... HSRA
Half-Sample plus Complement [*Statistics*] .... HS + C
Half-Shade Plate .... HSP
Half Strength .... HS
Half Subtractor .... HS
Half-Time [*Survey*] [*Shipping*] .... HT
Half-Time Survey [*Shipping*] .... HTS
Half-Title [*Publishing*] .... HT
Half-Track [*A type of military vehicle*] .... HTRAC
Half-Track .... HTRK
Half-Track [*A type of military vehicle*] .... HTRK
Half-Tracked [*Vehicle*] .... HT
Half-Truck [*British*] .... H-T
Half-Value Layer .... HVL
Half-Value Period .... HVP
Half-Value Thickness .... HVT
Half Wave .... HW
Half-Wave Bridge Rectifier .... HWBR
Half-Wave Plate .... HWP
Half-Wave Rectifier .... HWR
Half Word .... HW
Half-Word Designator [*Data processing*] .... H
Half-Yearly Review .... HR
Halfback [*Football*] .... HB
Halftone [*Photoengraving*] .... HT
Halfway, MD [*Radio station call letters*] .... WHAG
Halfway, MD [*Radio station call letters*] .... WQCM
Haliburton County Public Library, Hastings, ON, Canada [*Library symbol*] .... CaOHaH
Haliburton Public Library, Haliburton, ON, Canada [*Library symbol*] .... CaOHal
Halibut Association of North America .... HANA
Halifax [*Nova Scotia*] [*Seismograph station code, US Geological Survey*] .... HAL
Halifax [*Canada*] [*Airport symbol*] .... YHZ
Halifax City and Regional Library, Halifax, NS, Canada [*Library symbol*] .... CaNSH
Halifax Conservatory of Music .... HCM
Halifax County Library, Halifax, NC [*Library symbol*] .... NcHal
Halifax County Regional Library, Halifax, NS, Canada [*Library symbol*] .... CaNSHHC
Halifax County-South Boston Regional Library, Halifax, VA [*Library symbol*] .... ViHal
Halifax County Technical Institute, Weldon, NC [*Library symbol*] .... NcWelH
Halifax Engineering [*NASDAQ symbol*] .... HFAX
Halifax, NS [*Radio station call letters*] .... CBH
Halifax, NS [*Radio station call letters*] .... CBH-FM
Halifax, NS [*Television station call letters*] .... CBHFT
Halifax, NS [*Television station call letters*] .... CBHT
Halifax, NS [*Radio station call letters*] .... CHFX-FM
Halifax, NS [*Radio station call letters*] .... CHNS
Halifax, NS [*Radio station call letters*] .... CJCH
Halifax, NS [*Radio station call letters*] .... CJCH-FM
Halifax, NS [*Television station call letters*] .... CJCH-TV
Halifax Ocean Meeting Point .... HOMP
Halifax Regional Vocational School, Halifax, NS, Canada [*Library symbol*] .... CaNSHVH
Halite [*CIPW classification*] [*Geology*] .... hl
Hall .... H
Hall Beach [*Canada*] [*Airport symbol*] .... YUX
Hall & Co. [*Frank B.*] [*NYSE symbol*] .... FBH
Hall Effect Device .... HED
Hall Effect Function Generator .... HEFG
Hall Effect Generator .... HEG
Hall Effect Multiplier .... HEM
Hall Effect Probe .... HEP
Hall Electrolytic Conductivity Detector [*Analytical instrumentation*] .... HECD
Hall of Fame .... HOF
Hall of Fame for Great Americans .... HFGA
Hall [*W. F.*] **Printing Co.** [*NYSE symbol*] [*Delisted*] .... HPG
Hall of Records Commission, Annapolis, MD [*Library symbol*] .... MdAA
Hall Township High School District 502, Spring Valley, IL [*Library symbol*] .... ISprvHSD
Hallam Nuclear Power Facility [*AEC*] [*Decommissioned*] .... HNPF
Hallcraft Homes, Incorporated [*American Stock Exchange symbol*] [*Delisted*] .... HHI
Halle [*German Democratic Republic*] [*Seismograph station code, US Geological Survey*] .... HLE
Haller Muenzblaetter [*A publication*] .... Haller Mb
Hallett [*Antarctica*] [*Seismograph station code, US Geological Survey*] [*Closed*] .... HLL
Hallett [*Australia*] [*Seismograph station code, US Geological Survey*] .... HTT
Hallettsville, TX [*Radio station call letters*] .... KRJH
Halley Bay [*Antarctica*] [*Seismograph station code, US Geological Survey*] [*Closed*] .... HBA
Halley Bay [*United Kingdom*] [*Geomagnetic observatory code*] .... HLY
Halliburton Co. [*NYSE symbol*] .... HAL
Hallicrafters Co. [*NYSE symbol*] [*Delisted*] .... HLF
Hallicrafters Incremental Power Spectrum Analyzer .... HIPSA
Hallman, W. A., St. Paul MN [*STAC*] .... HWA
Hallmark .... HM
Halls Creek [*Australia*] [*Airport symbol*] [*Obsolete*] .... HCQ
Hall's Lagoon [*Australia*] [*Seismograph station code, US Geological Survey*] [*Closed*] .... HLA
Hall's Motor Transit Co. [*American Stock Exchange symbol*] [*Delisted*] .... HMT
Halls (Noncommercial) [*Public-performance tariff class*] [*British*] .... G

Hallucination ... HALLUC
Halmi [*Robert*]**, Inc.** [*NASDAQ symbol*] ... HLMI
Halmstad [*Sweden*] [*Airport symbol*] ... HAD
Halo Orbit Space Station [*NASA*] ... HOSS
Halogen Occulation Experiment ... HALOE
Halogen Quenched Tube ... HQT
Halogenated Cleaning Solvent Association ... HCSA
Halogenated Hydrocarbon ... HALON
Halogenated Solvent Industry Alliance ... HSIA
Halpern's AntiRADAR Point ... HARP
Halt ... H
Halt ... HLT
Halt Acknowledge [*Data processing*] ... HLTA
Halt and Jump [*Data processing*] ... HJ
HALT - An Organization of Americans for Legal Reform ... HALT-ALR
Halt and Transfer ... HT
Halt and Transfer ... HTR
Halverson Project [*World War II plan to bomb Japan from China*] ... HALPRO
Hamada [*Japan*] [*Seismograph station code, US Geological Survey*] ... HMD
Hamamatsu [*Japan*] [*Seismograph station code, US Geological Survey*] ... HMM
Hamann Newsletter [*A publication*] ... HN
Hamarein Air United [*Arab*] [*ICAO designator*] ... HM
[*Virus named for*] **Hamazaki, Sato, Takahashi, and Tani, principal investigators** [*Medicine*] ... HST
Hamburg [*West Germany*] [*Airport symbol*] ... HAM
Hamburg [*New York*] [*Seismograph station code, US Geological Survey*] [*Closed*] ... HMB
Hamburg [*West Germany*] [*Seismograph station code, US Geological Survey*] ... HAM
Hamburg-Amerika Linie [*Hamburg-America Steamship Co.*] ... HAL
Hamburg Geologischen Staatsinstitut. Mitteilungen [*A publication*] ... Hamburg Geol Staatsinstitut Mitt
Hamburg. Institut fuer Asienkunde. Mitteilungen [*A publication*] ... MIAH
Hamburg Public Library, Hamburg, IA [*Library symbol*] ... IaHamb
Hamburg Township Library, Hamburg, MI [*Library symbol*] ... MiHamb
Hamburg-Wechsler Intelligence Test [*Psychology*] ... HAWE
Hamburg-Wechsler-Intelligenztest fuer Kinder [*Intelligence test for children*] [*Psychology*] ... HAWIK
Hamburg in Zahlen [*A publication*] ... HMZA
Hamburger Akademische Rundschau [*A publication*] ... HAR
Hamburger Beitraege zur Numismatik [*A publication*] ... HBN
Hamburger Fremdenblatt [*A publication*] ... HF
Hamburger Geophysikalische Einzelschriften [*A publication*] ... Hamb Geophys Einzelschriften
Hamburger Hamlets [*NASDAQ symbol*] ... HAMB
Hamburger Ibero-Amerikanische Reihe [*A publication*] ... HIAR
Hamburger Jahrbuch fuer Wirtschafts- und Gesellschaftspolitik [*A publication*] ... Hamburg Jb Wirtsch- u Ges-Polit
Hamburger Philologische Studien [*A publication*] ... HPS
Hamburger Romanistische Dissertationen [*A publication*] ... HRD
Hamburger University [*McDonald's Corp.*] ... HU
Hamburger Verkehrsverbund [*Hamburg, West Germany, subway*] ... HVV
Hamburger Wirtschaft [*Mitteilungen der Handelskammer Hamburg*] [*A publication*] ... Hamb Wirtsch
Hamdard Medical Digest [*A publication*] ... Hamdard Med Dig
Hamden, CT [*Radio station call letters*] ... WKCI
Hamden, CT [*Radio station call letters*] ... WQAQ
Hamden, CT [*Radio station call letters*] ... WSCR
Hamden Testing Services, Inc. ... HTS
Hamer Butte [*Idaho*] [*Seismograph station code, US Geological Survey*] ... HID
Hamilton [*Bermuda*] [*Airport symbol*] ... BDA
Hamilton [*Australia*] [*Airport symbol*] ... HLT
Hamilton [*New Zealand*] [*Airport symbol*] ... HLZ
Hamilton [*Ontario*] [*Seismograph station code, US Geological Survey*] [*Closed*] ... HML
Hamilton [*New York*] [*Seismograph station code, US Geological Survey*] ... HNY
Hamilton [*Canada*] [*Airport symbol*] ... YHM
Hamilton Aeroservices [*Trenton, NJ*] [*FAA designator*] ... JNR
Hamilton, AL [*Radio station call letters*] ... WERH
Hamilton, AL [*Radio station call letters*] ... WERH-FM
Hamilton Association. Journal and Proceedings [*A publication*] ... Hamilton As J Pr
Hamilton Aviation, Inc. [*Hamilton, OH*] [*FAA designator*] ... HAM
Hamilton Brothers Petroleum [*NASDAQ symbol*] ... HAML
Hamilton College, Clinton, NY [*OCLC symbol*] ... YHM
Hamilton Digital Controls [*NASDAQ symbol*] ... HDIG
Hamilton Education Centre, Hamilton, ON, Canada [*Library symbol*] ... CaOHEC
Hamilton Grange National Memorial ... HAGR
Hamilton Island [*Australia*] [*Airport symbol*] ... HTI
Hamilton & Kirkland Colleges, Clinton, NY [*Library symbol*] ... NCH
Hamilton, MT [*Radio station call letters*] ... KLYQ
Hamilton, MT [*Radio station call letters*] ... KLYQ-FM
Hamilton Normal School ... HNS
Hamilton, NY [*Radio station call letters*] ... WRCU-FM
Hamilton, OH [*Radio station call letters*] ... WBLZ
Hamilton, OH [*Radio station call letters*] ... WHSS
Hamilton, OH [*Radio station call letters*] ... WMOH
Hamilton, OH [*Radio station call letters*] ... WSKS
Hamilton, ON [*Radio station call letters*] ... CFMU-FM
Hamilton, ON [*Radio station call letters*] ... CHAM
Hamilton, ON [*Television station call letters*] ... CHCH-TV
Hamilton, ON [*Radio station call letters*] ... CHML
Hamilton, ON [*Radio station call letters*] ... CKDS-FM
Hamilton, ON [*Radio station call letters*] ... CKOC
Hamilton Public Library, Hamilton, NY [*Library symbol*] ... NH
Hamilton Public Library, Hamilton, ON, Canada [*Library symbol*] ... CaOH
Hamilton Ranch [*California*] [*Seismograph station code, US Geological Survey*] ... HMR
Hamilton Scientific Association. Journal and Proceedings [*A publication*] ... Hamilton Sc As J Pr
Hamilton Spectator, Hamilton, ON, Canada [*Library symbol*] ... CaOHS
Hamilton, TX [*Radio station call letters*] ... KCLW
Hamilton Watch Co., Lancaster, PA [*Library symbol*] [*Obsolete*] ... PLH
Hamiltonian Function [*Mathematics*] ... H
Hamlet ... H
Hamlet [*Shakespearean work*] ... Ham
Hamlet ... HMLT
Hamlet Evaluation Survey [*South Vietnam*] ... HES
Hamlet, NC [*Radio station call letters*] ... WKDX
Hamlet Studies [*A publication*] ... H St
Hamline University, St. Paul, MN [*OCLC symbol*] ... MHA
Hamline University, St. Paul, MN [*Library symbol*] ... MnSH
Hamline University, School of Law, St. Paul, MN [*OCLC symbol*] ... MHL
Hamline University, School of Law, St. Paul, MN [*Library symbol*] ... MnSH-L
Hammer ... HMR
Hammer Form ... HF
Hammerfest [*Norway*] [*Airport symbol*] ... HFT
Hammermill Paper Co. [*NYSE symbol*] ... HML
Hammond Corp. [*NYSE symbol*] [*Delisted*] ... HMD
[*The*] **Hammond Corporation** [*NASDAQ symbol*] ... THCO
Hammond, IN [*Radio station call letters*] ... WJOB
Hammond, IN [*Radio station call letters*] ... WYCA
Hammond, LA [*Radio station call letters*] ... KSLU
Hammond, LA [*Location identifier*] [*FAA*] ... TAO
Hammond, LA [*Radio station call letters*] ... WFPR
Hammond, LA [*Radio station call letters*] ... WHMD
Hammond, LA [*Radio station call letters*] ... WTGI
Hammond Metallurgical Laboratory [*Yale*] ... HML
Hammond Public Library, Hammond, IN [*OCLC symbol*] ... IHP
Hammond Public Library, Hammond, IN [*Library symbol*] ... InHam
Hammondsport, NY [*Radio station call letters*] ... WVIN-FM
Hammonton, NJ [*Radio station call letters*] ... WTYO
Hammonton Public Library, Hammonton, NJ [*Library symbol*] ... NjHam
Hampden-Sydney College [*Virginia*] ... HSC
Hampden-Sydney College, Hampden-Sydney, VA [*OCLC symbol*] ... VHS
Hampden-Sydney College, Hampden-Sydney, VA [*Library symbol*] ... ViHdsC
Hampden-Sydney, VA [*Radio station call letters*] ... WWHS-FM
Hampshire [*County in England*] ... HAMPS
Hampshire [*County in England*] ... HANTS
Hampshire College, Amherst, MA [*OCLC symbol*] ... HAM
Hampshire College, Amherst, MA [*Library symbol*] ... MAH
Hampshire-Designers, Incorporated [*American Stock Exchange symbol*] [*Delisted*] ... HDI
Hampshire Hunt [*British*] ... HH
Hampshire Inter-Library Center [*Library network*] ... HILC
Hampshire Inter-Library Center, Inc., Amherst, MA [*Library symbol*] [*Obsolete*] ... MHILC
Hampshire Swine Registry ... HSR
Hampstead [*Region of London*] ... HAMP
Hampstead Public Libraries, Central Library, London, United Kingdom [*Library symbol*] ... UkLH
Hampton Bays, NY [*Radio station call letters*] ... WWHB
Hampton Bays Public Library, Hampton Bays, NY [*Library symbol*] [*Obsolete*] ... NHamB
Hampton Bays Public Library, Hampton Bays, NY [*Library symbol*] ... NHampB
Hampton & Branchville Railroad Co. [*AAR code*] ... HB
Hampton, IA [*Radio station call letters*] ... KWGG
Hampton Industries, Inc. [*American Stock Exchange symbol*] ... HAI
Hampton Institute, Hampton, VA [*Library symbol*] ... ViHal
Hampton Library, Bridgehampton, NY [*Library symbol*] ... NBrih
Hampton National Historic Site ... HAMP
Hampton-Norfolk, VA [*Television station call letters*] ... WHRO-TV
Hampton Roads Army Terminal ... HRART
Hampton Roads Army Terminal ... HRAT
Hampton, SC [*Radio station call letters*] ... WBHC
Hampton, SC [*Radio station call letters*] ... WJBW
Hampton, VA [*Location identifier*] [*FAA*] ... LFI
Hampton, VA [*Radio station call letters*] ... WHOV
Hampton, VA [*Radio station call letters*] ... WPEX
Hampton, VA [*Television station call letters*] ... WVEC-TV
Hampton, VA [*Radio station call letters*] ... WWDE-FM
Hampton's Magazine [*A publication*] ... Hampton
Hamster Leukemia Virus ... HaLV
Hamtramck Public Library, Hamtramck, MI [*Library symbol*] ... MiHam
Hana [*Hawaii*] [*Airport symbol*] ... HNM
Hanamaki [*Japan*] [*Airport symbol*] [*Obsolete*] ... HNA

Hancock [*Michigan*] [*Airport symbol*] ... CMX
Hancock Airbase Library, Hancock Field, NY [*OCLC symbol*] ... ZUR
Hancock, MI [*Location identifier*] [*FAA*] ... CMX
Hancock, MI [*Location identifier*] [*FAA*] ... CUT
Hancock, MI [*Radio station call letters*] ... WMPL
Hancock, MI [*Radio station call letters*] ... WZRK
Hand Book [*A publication*] ... Hand
Hand Carry ... H/C
Hand-Colored [*Photography*] ... HC
Hand or Computer Universal Simulation [*Simulation modeling method*] ... HOCUS
Hand Control [*Technical drawings*] ... HC
Hand County Library, Miller, SD [*Library symbol*] ... SdMi
Hand Crank ... HC
Hand Cut [*Envelopes*] ... HC
Hand-Deboned Meat ... HDM
Hand-Drawn ... HD
Hand-Emplaced Acoustic Intrusion Detector ... HAID
Hand-Emplaced Minefield Marking System ... HEMMS
Hand Form Block ... HFB
Hand Generator ... HG
Hand-Held Encryption and Authentication Device ... HEAD
Hand-Held Information Processor ... HHIP
Hand-Held LASER Range-Finder ... HHLR
Hand Hills-Drumheller, AB [*Television station call letters*] ... CFCN-TV-1
Hand Jewel Pusher ... HJP
Hand Lantern ... HL
Hand Movement(s) ... HM
Hand Orthosis [*Medicine*] ... HO
Hand Over ... HO
Hand Over Transmitter ... HOT
Hand-Printed Books ... HPB
Hand Rail ... HDR
Hand Rail ... HNDRL
Hand Receipt ... HR
Hand Reset ... HR
Hand and Shoe Monitor [*Radiation detection*] ... HSM
Hand-Starter ... HS
Hand Target Designator ... HTD
Hand Test [*Psychology*] ... HT
Hand Tool Carrier [*NASA*] ... HTC
Hand-Tool Dexterity [*Motor performance test*] ... HTD
Hand Tools Institute ... HTI
Hand Translation ... HT
Handbag Supply Salesmen's Association ... HSSA
Handbook ... HANDB
Handbook ... HB
Handbook ... HDBK
Handbook ... HNDBK
Handbook Art ... HBA
Handbook of Electronic Parts Reliability ... HELPR
Handbook on Emergency Measures ... HEM
Handbook of Environmental Isotope Geochemistry [*Elsevier Book Series*] [*A publication*] ... HEIG
Handbook of Exploration Geochemistry [*Elsevier Book Series*] [*A publication*] ... HEG
Handbook of Inflammation [*Elsevier Book Series*] [*A publication*] ... HOI
Handbook of Inspection Maintenance Requirements [*Navy*] ... HIMR
Handbook of Inspection Requirements [*Navy*] ... HIR
Handbook of Instructions for Aerospace Personnel Subsystem Designers ... HIAPSD
Handbook of Instructions for Aerospace Systems Design ... HIASD
Handbook of Instructions for Aerospace Vehicle Equipment Design ... HIAVED
Handbook of Instructions for Air Force Subsystem Designers ... HIAFSB
Handbook of Instructions for Aircraft Designers ... HIAD
Handbook of Instructions for Aircraft Ground Support Equipment Designers ... HIAGSED
Handbook of Instructions for Aircraft Ground Support Equipment Designers ... HIGSED
Handbook of Instructions for Ground Equipment Designers ... HIGED
Handbook of Instructions for Missile Designers ... HIMD
Handbook of Latin American Studies ... HLAS
Handbook of Maintenance Instructions ... HMI
Handbook of Occupational Groups and Series of Classes ... HOGC
Handbook of Occupational Keywords [*For use in employment services*] [*Department of Labor*] ... HOOK
Handbook of Operating Instructions [*Navy*] ... HOI
Handbook of Operating Instructions [*Navy*] ... HOPI
Handbook of Operating Procedures ... HOOP
Handbook of Overhaul Instructions [*Navy*] ... HOHI
Handbook of Overhaul Instructions [*Navy*] ... HOI
Handbook of Overhaul Instructions [*Navy*] ... HOVI
Handbook of Physiology [*A publication*] ... Handb Physiol
Handbook of Powder Technology [*Elsevier Book Series*] [*A publication*] ... HOPT
Handbook Production ... HBP
Handbook of Service Instructions ... HOSI
Handbook of Service Instructions ... HSI
Handbook of Soil Mechanics [*Elsevier Book Series*] [*A publication*] ... HSM
Handbook of Statistics [*Elsevier Book Series*] [*A publication*] ... HS
Handbook. United States National Bureau of Standards [*A publication*] ... Handb US Natn Bur Stand
Handbooks in Economics [*Elsevier Book Series*] [*A publication*] ... HE
Handbuch der Deutschen Literaturgeschichte [*A publication*] ... HDL
Handbuch der Literaturgeschichte in Einzeldarstellungen. Kroeners Taschenausgabe [*A publication*] ... HLEKT
Handbuch der Mineralogie [*A publication*] ... Handb Mineral
Handbuch der Orientalistik [*A publication*] ... HO
Handbuch der Pflanzenernahrung und Duengung [*A publication*] ... Handb Pflernahr Dueng
Handbuch der Physik [*A publication*] ... Handb Phys
Handbuch der Urologie [*A publication*] ... Handb Urol
Handcarried ... HCD
Handel and Haydn Society, Boston, MA [*Library symbol*] ... MBHH
Handel Jahrbuch [*A publication*] ... H Jb
Handel Wewnetrzny [*A publication*] ... Handel Wewn
Handel Zagraniczy [*A publication*] ... Handel Zagran
Handelinge van die Weidingsvereniging van Suidelikjke Agrika [*A publication*] ... Handel Weidingsver Suidelikjke Agr
Handelingen van het Genootschap voor Geschiedenis Gesticht Onder de Benaming Societe d'Emulation de Bruges [*A publication*] ... HGGSEB
Handelingen van de Koninklijke Commissie voor Toponymie en Dialectologie [*A publication*] ... HandKonCommTop-Dial
Handelingen van de Koninklijke Commissie voor Toponymie en Dialectologie [*A publication*] ... HKCTD
Handelingen der Koninklijke Zuidnederlandse Maatschappij voor Taal en Letterkunde en Geschiedenis [*A publication*] ... HKZM
Handelingen der Maatschappij voor Geschiedenis en Oudheidkunde te Gent [*A publication*] ... HMGOG
Handelingen en Mededeelingen van de Maatschappij der Nederlandsche Letterkunde te Leiden [*A publication*] ... HMMNL
Handelingen van het Nederlands Filologencongres [*A publication*] ... HandNFc
Handelingen van het Vlaamse Filologencongres [*A publication*] ... Hand Vl Fc
Handelingen der Zuidnederlandse Maatschappij voor Taal-En Letterkunde en Geschiedenis [*A publication*] ... HZM
Handelingen der Zuidnederlandse Maatschappij voor Taal-En Letterkunde en Geschiedenis [*A publication*] ... HZMTLG
Handelingen der Zuidnederlandse Maatschappij voor Taal-En Letterkunde en Geschiedenis [*A publication*] ... HZnMTL
Handels Kammer [*Chamber of Commerce*] [*German*] ... HK
Handelsblatt [*A publication*] ... Handelsblt
Handes Amsoriay [*A publication*] ... HA
Handgun Control, Incorporated [*Formerly, NCCH*] ... HCI
Handheld Computer ... HHC
Handheld Grenade-Launcher ... HAGL
Handheld LASER Range-Finder ... HLR
Handheld Maneuvering Unit [*NASA*] ... HHMU
Handheld RADAR ... HHR
Handheld Thermal Viewer ... HHTV
Handheld Viewer ... HHV
Handhole ... HH
Handicap ... HANDICP
Handicap ... HCP
Handicap ... HNDP
Handicap Problems Inventory [*Psychology*] ... HPI
Handicap Race [*Horse racing*] ... HCP
Handicapped [*Medicine*] ... HC
Handicapped ... HCAP
Handicapped Aid Program - USA ... HAP-USA
Handicapped Artists of America ... HAA
Handicapped Assistance Loan ... HAL
Handicapped Boaters Association ... HBA
Handicapped Children's Early Education Programs ... HCEEP
Handicapped Children's Home Service [*Later, Easter Seal Home Service*] ... HCHS
Handicapped Education Learner's Planning System [*Battelle Memorial Institute*] [*Information service*] ... HELPS
Handicapped Employe of the Year [*Award given to federal employees*] ... HEOY
Handicapped Introductions [*An association*] ... HI
Handicapped Person ... HP
Handily [*Horse racing*] ... H
Handkerchief ... HDKF
Handkerchief ... HKF
Handkerchief Industry Association [*Defunct*] ... HIA
Handle ... HDL
Handle Door Fastener ... HDF
Handleman Co. [*NYSE symbol*] ... HDL
Handler ... HDLR
Handley Library, Winchester, VA [*Library symbol*] ... ViWn
Handley-Page Ltd. ... H-P
Handling ... HDLG
Handling of Alarms with Logic [*Nuclear reactors*] ... HALO
Handling Capacity ... HC
Handling and Checkout Requirements ... H & CR
Handling Equipment ... HE
Handling Equipment Maintenance Facility [*Charleston Naval Shipyard*] ... HEMF

Handling Fee [*Coupon redemption*]....................H/F
Handling Fixture....................HF
Handling Ground Equipment....................HGE
Handling Instructions....................HI
Handling and Propulsion....................HP
Handling Quality Criteria....................HQC
Handling Room....................HR
Handling and Shipping [*Later, Handling and Shipping Management*] [*A publication*]....................Handl & Shipp
Handling and Shipping Management [*A publication*]........Handl & Shipp Mgt
Handling Time....................HT
Handling Tool....................HATO
Handling and Transportation....................H & T
Handmade....................HM
Handmade Paper....................HMP
Handmade Paper....................HP
Handmaids of Mary Immaculate [*Roman Catholic religious order*]....................AMI
Handmaids of the Precious Blood [*Roman Catholic religious order*]....................HPB
Handmaids of the Sacred Heart of Jesus [*Roman Catholic religious order*]....................ACJ
Handoff Point....................HOP
Handover Transfer and Receiver Accept Change [*SAGE*]....................HATRAC
Hands [*Units of measure, especially for the height of horses*]....................HH
Hands to Knee [*Medicine*]....................H-K
Hands Off - Automatic....................HOA
Hands-On Component....................HOC
Hands on Throttle and Stick....................HOTAS
Handschrift [*Manuscript*] [*German*]....................HS
Handset....................HNDST
Handset....................HS
Handweaver and Craftsman [*A publication*]....................Handweaver
Handweavers Guild of America....................HGA
Handwheel....................HNDWL
Handwoerterbuch [*Pocket Dictionary*] [*German*]....................HWB
Handwoerterbuch der Sozialwissenschaft [*Dictionary of the Social Sciences*] [*A publication*]....................HDSW
Handwriting Analysts, Incorporated....................HAI
Handwriting Foundation....................HF
Handy-Cap Horizons [*An association*]....................H-CH
Handy Dandy Orbital Computer....................HDOC
Handy & Harman [*NYSE symbol*]....................HNH
Hanes Corp. [*NYSE symbol*] [*Delisted*]....................HNS
Haney [*British Columbia*] [*Seismograph station code, US Geological Survey*]....................HYC
Hanford [*Washington*] [*Seismograph station code, US Geological Survey*]....................HAN
Hanford [*Washington*] **Atomic Metal Trades Council**....................HAMTC
Hanford Atomic Products Operations [*General Electric Co.*]....................HAPO
Hanford, CA [*Television station call letters*]....................KFTV
Hanford, CA [*Radio station call letters*]....................KKYS
Hanford, CA [*Radio station call letters*]....................KMGX
Hanford, CA [*Radio station call letters*]....................KNGS
Hanford Engineering Development Laboratory [*Department of Energy*]....................HEDL
Hanford Engineering Service [*Nuclear energy*]....................HES
Hanford Engineering Works [*Nuclear energy*]....................HEW
Hanford Environmental Health Foundation [*Nuclear energy*]....................HEHF
Hanford Gable Butte [*Washington*] [*Seismograph station code, US Geological Survey*]....................HGB
Hanford Isotopes Plant [*Nuclear energy*]....................HIP
Hanford Meteorology Surveys [*Nuclear energy*]....................HMS
Hanford Operations Office [*Nuclear energy*]....................HOO
Hanford Plant Standard [*Formerly, HWS*] [*Nuclear energy*]....................HPS
Hanford Public Library, Hanford, CA [*Library symbol*]....................CHan
Hanford Test Reactor....................HTR
Hanford Works Standard [*or Specification*] [*Later, HPS*] [*Nuclear energy*]....................HWS
Hang Alle Laffe Landverraders Op [*Hang All Cowardly Traitors to Their Country*] [*Greeting for Dutch Nazis allegedly coined by the Netherlands people during World War II*]....................HALLO
Hang Glider Association....................HGA
Hang Glider Manufacturers Association of America [*Defunct*]....................HGMAA
Hangar....................HGR
Hangar....................HNGR
Hangar Control Officer [*Navy*]....................HCO
Hangar Control Position [*Navy*]....................HCP
Hangar Engineering Item....................HEI
Hangar and Industrial Door Technical Council [*Defunct*]....................HIDTC
Hangar and Support Facility [*NASA*]....................HGR & SPTFAC
Hanger....................HGR
Hanging....................HNG
Hanging Loose [*A publication*]....................Hang L
Hanging Loose [*A publication*]....................HL
Hanging Mercury Drop Electrode [*Electrochemistry*]....................HMDE
Hangzhou [*China*] [*Airport symbol*]....................HGH
Hankins Air Service, Inc. [*Jackson, MS*] [*FAA designator*]....................HKN
Hanks Balanced Salt [*Solution*] [*Cell incubation medium*]....................HBS
Hanks Balanced Salt Solution [*Cell incubation medium*]....................HBSS
Hanksville, UT [*Location identifier*] [*FAA*]....................HVE
Hanna [*M. A.*] Co. [*NYSE symbol*] [*Delisted*]....................HNA
Hanna Mining Co. [*NYSE symbol*]....................HNM

Hannaford Bros., Inc. [*American Stock Exchange symbol*]....................HRD
Hannah Dairy Research Institute. Report [*A publication*]....................Hannah Dairy Res Inst Rep
Hannah Research Institute. Report [*A publication*]....................Hannah Res Inst Rep
Hannibal Connecting R. R. [*AAR code*]....................HC
Hannibal Free Public Library, Hannibal, MO [*Library symbol*]....................MoH
Hannibal-La Grange College [*Missouri*]....................HLGC
Hannibal, MO [*Radio station call letters*]....................KGRC
Hannibal, MO [*Radio station call letters*]....................KHMO
Hannibal, MO [*Television station call letters*]....................KHQA-TV
Hannoversche Geschichtsblaetter [*A publication*]....................HG
Hanoi [*North Vietnam*] [*Airport symbol*]....................HAN
Hanover [*West Germany*] [*Airport symbol*]....................HAJ
Hanover [*Former state in Germany*]....................HAN
Hanover [*New Hampshire*] [*Seismograph station code, US Geological Survey*]....................HNH
Hanover College, Hanover, IN [*OCLC symbol*]....................IHC
Hanover College, Hanover, IN [*Library symbol*]....................InHan
Hanover Insurance Co. [*NASDAQ symbol*]....................HINS
Hanover, NH [*Radio station call letters*]....................WDCR
Hanover, NH [*Radio station call letters*]....................WFRD
Hanover, NH [*Radio station call letters*]....................WTSL
Hanover, NJ [*Radio station call letters*]....................WHPH
Hanover, PA [*Radio station call letters*]....................WHVR
Hanover Planning Co., Inc. [*American Stock Exchange symbol*]....................HNV
Hanover Public Library, Hanover, ON, Canada [*Library symbol*]....................CaOHan
Hanover Shoe, Inc. [*American Stock Exchange symbol*] [*Delisted*]....................HAN
Hanover Square Realty Investors [*American Stock Exchange symbol*] [*Delisted*]....................HSQ
Hans Pfitzner-Gesellschaft. Mitteilungen [*A publication*]....................Pfitzner
Hansa Jet Corporation [*White Plains, NY*] [*FAA designator*]....................HJC
Hansard. House of Commons. Official Report [*Great Britain*] [*A publication*]....................Hansard House Commons Off Rep
Hanscom Air Force Base, Base Library, Hanscom AFB, MA [*OCLC symbol*]....................SCQ
Hansel Valley [*Utah*] [*Seismograph station code, US Geological Survey*]....................HVU
Hanseniase. Resumos e Noticias [*A publication*]....................Hanseniase Resumos Not
Hansenologia Internationalis [*A publication*]....................Hansenol Int
Hansen's Disease [*Leprosy*] [*Medicine*]....................HD
Hansische Geschichtsblaetter [*A publication*]....................HGB
Hansische Geschichtsblaetter [*A publication*]....................HGH
Hansoms of John Clayton [*An association*]....................HJC
Hanson-McCook County Regional Library, Spencer, SD [*Library symbol*]....................SdSpen
Hants Field Club and Archaeological Society [*A publication*]....................HFC
Hanzhong [*China*] [*Airport symbol*]....................HZG
Hao Island [*French Polynesia*] [*Airport symbol*]....................HOI
Hapag Lloyd Fluggesellschaft mbH [*ICAO designator*]....................HF
Haplequin Lake [*Alaska*] [*Seismograph station code, US Geological Survey*]....................HQN
Haploid Number [*Genetics*]....................N
Happiness of Womanhood [*Also known as LOH*] [*Antifeminist women's group*]....................HOW
Happy Bay [*Australia*] [*Airport symbol*]....................HAP
Happy Hours Brotherhood....................HHB
Happy Irish Celebration....................HIC
Happy New Year....................HNY
Happy Valley, AK [*Location identifier*] [*FAA*]....................HVY
Happy Valley, NF [*Radio station call letters*]....................CFGB
Haptoglobin [*Hematology*]....................Hp
Haptong Tongsin [*Press agency*] [*South Korea*]....................HAPTONG
Harare [*Zimbabwe*] [*Airport symbol*]....................HRE
Harassing Fire [*Military*]....................HF
Harassment and Interdiction....................H and I
Harbin [*Manchuria*] [*Airport symbol*]....................HRB
Harbison-Walker Refractories Co. [*NYSE symbol*] [*Delisted*]....................HKM
Harbor [*Maps and charts*]....................H
Harbor....................HAR
Harbor [*Maps and charts*]....................HBR
Harbor Advisory RADAR....................HAR
Harbor Airlines [*Oak Harbor, WA*] [*FAA designator*]....................HAR
Harbor Beach Public Library, Harbor Beach, MI [*Library symbol*]....................MiHb
Harbor Boat Service [*Military*]....................HBS
Harbor Carriers of the Port of New York....................HCPNY
Harbor Clearance Unit [*Navy*]....................HCU
Harbor Control Post....................HCP
Harbor Control Unit....................HCU
Harbor Craft....................HARCFT
Harbor Defense [*Military*]....................HD
Harbor Defense Command [*Army*]....................HDC
Harbor Defense Exercise [*Navy*]....................HARDEX
Harbor Defense Motor Launch....................HDML
Harbor Defense SONARman [*Navy*]....................ESH
Harbor Echo Ranging and Listening Devices....................HERALDS
Harbor Entrance Control Post [*Nautical charts*]....................HECP
Harbor Entrance Control Vessel....................HECVES
Harbor Master....................Hbr Mr
Harbor Master....................HM
Harbor Minesweepers [*Navy symbol*]....................AMH
Harbor Patrol Boat....................HPB

Harbor Patrol Fleet .... HPF
Harbor Survey Assistance Program [*Naval Oceanographic Office*] .... HARSAP
Harbor Tug [*Navy symbol*] .... YT
Harbor Utility Craft [*Self-propelled*] [*Navy symbol*] .... YFU
Harborfields Public Library, Greenlawn, NY [*Library symbol*] .... NGI
Harbour Grace, NF [*Radio station call letters*] .... CFIQ
Harcost Industries .... HI
Harcourt, Brace, Jovanovich, Inc. [*NYSE symbol*] .... HBJ
Harcourt, Brace & World, Inc. [*Later, HBJ*] [*NYSE symbol*] .... HBW
Harcum Junior College [*Pennsylvania*] .... HJC
Harcum, VA [*Location identifier*] [*FAA*] .... HCM
Hard [*or Hardness*] [*Pencil leads*] .... H
Hard .... HD
Hard [*Quality of the bottom*] [*Nautical charts*] .... hrd
Hard Black [*Pencil leads*] .... HB
Hard-Boiled [*Egg*] .... HB
Hard Chromium .... HDCR
Hard Copy .... HC
Hard Copy Printer .... HCP
Hard-Drawn [*Metallurgy*] .... HD
Hard Fibres Association .... HFA
Hard Filled [*Capsules*] .... HF
Hard Filled Capsules [*Pharmacy*] .... HFC
Hard Firm [*Pencil leads*] .... HF
Hard Freeze [*Meteorology*] .... HDFRZ
Hard of Hearing .... HH
Hard Labor .... HL
Hard Labor without Confinement .... HLW/OC
Hard Over .... H/O
Hard Point .... HP
Hard Point Decoys .... HAPDEC
Hard Point Defense .... HPD
Hard Point Defense Interceptor .... HPDI
Hard Point Defense System .... HPDS
Hard Point Demonstration Array RADAR .... HAPDAR
Hard Red Spring [*Wheat*] .... HRS
Hard Red Winter [*Wheat*] .... HRW
Hard Rock Silo Development .... HRSD
Hard Rolled .... HR
Hard and Soft Acids and Bases [*Chemistry*] .... HSAB
Hard Stability Augmentation System .... HSAS
Hard Stop .... HSTP
Hard Structure Munition .... HSM
Hard Structure Munition Weaponization Analysis .... HSM-WA
Hard Top [*Automobile ads*] .... HT
Hard Tube Modulator [*Electronics*] .... HTM
Hard Upper Torso .... HUT
Hard Valve .... HV
Hard X-Ray Imaging Spectrometer .... HXIS
Hard X-Ray Quanta .... HXQ
Hardee's Food Systems, Inc. [*NYSE symbol*] .... H
Hardeeville, SC [*Television station call letters*] .... WTGS
Harden .... HDN
Harden and Grind [*Technical drawings*] .... H & G
Hardened Amplifier for Radiation Transients .... HART
Hardened Compact Fiber .... HCF
Hardened and Dispersed .... H & D
Hardened Electronic Component .... HEC
Hardened Flexible Array .... HFA
Hardened Intersite Cable System .... HICS
Hardened Launch Control Facility .... HLCF
Hardened Memory System .... HMS
Hardened Operational Site Concept .... HOSC
Hardened Power System .... HPS
Hardened Reentry Kill [*Air Force*] .... HARK
Hardened Silo Missile .... HSM
Hardened Site .... HS
Hardened and Tempered [*Steel*] .... H & T
Hardened Voice Channel [*NASA*] .... HVC
Hardened Voice Circuit .... HVC
Hardening Technology Studies Program .... HARTS
Hardin County Historical Society, Eldora, IA [*Library symbol*] .... IaEldoHHi
Hardin, MT [*Radio station call letters*] .... KHDN
Hardin, MT [*Radio station call letters*] .... KHDN-FM
Hardin, MT [*Television station call letters*] .... KOUS-TV
Hardin Reading Center, Hardin, IL [*Library symbol*] .... IHardR
Hardin-Simmons University [*Texas*] .... HSU
Hardin-Simmons University, Abilene, TX [*Library symbol*] .... TxAbH
Hardin-Simmons University, Abilene, TX [*OCLC symbol*] .... TXS
Harding College, Searcy, AR [*OCLC symbol*] .... AHS
Harding College, Searcy, AR [*Library symbol*] .... ArSeH
Harding Graduate School of Religion, Memphis, TN [*Library symbol*] .... TMH
Harding Lake [*Alaska*] [*Seismograph station code, US Geological Survey*] .... HDA
Hardinsburg, KY [*Radio station call letters*] .... WHIC
Hardinsburg, KY [*Radio station call letters*] .... WHIC-FM
Hardline .... HL
Hardness [*Of precious stones*] .... H
Hardness .... HDNS
Hardness Assurance Test .... HAT
Hardness Assurance Verification Testing .... HAVT
Hardness Test Plan [*Army*] .... HTP
Hardover .... HDOV
Hards Memorial Library, Central City, NE [*Library symbol*] .... NbCen
Hardship .... HDSP
Hardsite Data Processor [*Army*] .... HSDP
Hardsite Defense [*Army*] .... HSD
Hardsite Missile Site RADAR [*Army*] .... HSMSR
Hardstand .... HS
Hardware .... H
Hardware .... HDW
Hardware .... HDWE
Hardware .... HW
Hardware Action Officer [*Military*] .... HAO
Hardware Affiliated Representatives .... HAR
Hardware Associative Memory [*Data processing*] .... HAM
Hardware Cloth .... HDWC
Hardware Description Sheet .... HDS
Hardware Design .... HD
Hardware Evaluator [*NASA*] .... HE
Hardware Executive .... HE
Hardware Indenture Code .... HIC
Hardware Interface Module [*NASA*] .... HIM
Hardware Logic Simulator .... HALSIM
Hardware in the Loop Simulation [*Data processing*] .... HITLS
Hardware Manufacturers Statistical Association [*Later, BHMA*] .... HMSA
[*A*] **Hardware Programing Language** [*Data processing*] .... AHPL
Hardware Reliability .... HR
Hardware Simulation Laboratory .... HSL
Hardware/Software Integration Review .... H/SIR
Hardware Status Register .... HSR
Hardware Usage Report .... HUR
Hardware Utilization List .... HUL
Hardware Virtualizer .... HV
Hardware Wholesalers, Incorporated .... HWI
Hardware Work Package .... HWP
Hardwell FORTRAN .... HARTRAN
Hardwood .... HDWD
Hardwood Dimension Manufacturers Association .... HDMA
Hardwood Plywood Institute [*Later, HPMA*] .... HPI
Hardwood Plywood Manufacturers Association [*Formerly, HPI*] .... HPMA
Hardwood Research Council .... HRC
Hardy, AK [*Radio station call letters*] .... KSRB
Hardy-Rand Rittler [*Test for color vision*] .... HRR
Harford Community College, Bel Air, MD [*OCLC symbol*] .... HAR
Harford Community College, Bel Air, MD [*Library symbol*] .... MdBaH
Harford County Library, Bel Air, MD [*Library symbol*] .... MdBaHC
Hargeisa [*Somalia*] [*Airport symbol*] .... HGA
Harken Oil & Gas [*NASDAQ symbol*] .... HOGI
Harker Geological Society. Journal [*A publication*] .... Harker Geol Soc J
Harlan, IA [*Radio station call letters*] .... KNOD
Harlan, KY [*Radio station call letters*] .... WFSR
Harlan, KY [*Radio station call letters*] .... WHLN
Harlan Public Library, Harlan, IA [*Library symbol*] .... IaHar
Harland Bartholomew & Associates, Memphis, TN [*Library symbol*] .... TMHB
Harland [*John H.*] **Co.** [*NYSE symbol*] .... JH
Harlech Television [*Wales*] .... HTV
Harlem Cultural Council .... HCC
Harlem Hospital Center, Health Sciences Library, New York, NY [*OCLC symbol*] .... VXA
Harlem Hospital Center, Medical Library, New York, NY [*Library symbol*] .... NNHH
Harlem Youth Opportunities Unlimited - Associated Community Teams [*A kind of Peace Corps for Harlem area of New York City*] .... HARYOU-ACT
Harlingen [*Texas*] [*Airport symbol*] .... HRL
Harlingen, TX [*Radio station call letters*] .... KELT
Harlingen, TX [*Radio station call letters*] .... KGBT
Harlingen, TX [*Television station call letters*] .... KGBT-TV
Harlingen, TX [*Radio station call letters*] .... KIWW
Harlingen, TX [*Television station call letters*] .... KLUJ
Harlingen, TX [*Television station call letters*] .... KZLN
Harlowton, MT [*Location identifier*] [*FAA*] .... HWQ
Harman International, Inc. [*American Stock Exchange symbol*] [*Delisted*] .... HAR
Harmonic .... HAR
Harmonic .... HMNC
Harmonic Distortion .... HD
Harmonic Distortion Meter .... HDM
Harmonic Frequency Generator .... HFG
Harmonic Generator .... HG
Harmonic Mean [*Music*] .... HM
Harmonic Multiplier Source .... HMS
Harmonic Oscillator .... HO
Harmonic Progression .... HP
Harmonic and Spurious Totalizer .... HST
Harmonically Varying Field .... HVF
Harmony .... HARM
Harmony-Emge-Ellis School District 175, Belleville, IL [*Library symbol*] .... IBelHSD

Harmony Heights [*Idaho*] [*Seismograph station code, US Geological Survey*] [*Closed*] ... HHI
Harness ... HARN
Harness ... HRN
Harness Assembly ... HA
Harness and Cable Assembly ... HCA
Harness Horsemen International ... HHI
Harness or Saddlery ... HS
Harness Tracks of America ... HTA
Harness Tracks Security [*An association*] ... HTS
Harnett County Public Library, Lillington, NC [*Library symbol*] ... NcLil
Harnischfeger Corp. [*NYSE symbol*] ... HPH
Harokeach Haivri. The Hebrew Pharmacist (Science Edition) [*A publication*] ... Harokeach Haivri Heb Pharm (Sci Ed)
Harold Institute ... HI
Harold L. Lyon Arboretum. Lecture [*A publication*] ... Harold L Lyon Arbor Lect
Harold's Air Service [*Galena, AK*] [*FAA designator*] ... HAS
Harp News [*A publication*] ... Harp N
Harp Renaissance Society ... HRS
[*The*] **Harper Group** [*NASDAQ symbol*] ... HARG
Harper Hospital, Department of Libraries, Detroit, MI [*Library symbol*] ... MiDHH
Harper & Row [*Publisher*] ... H & R
Harper & Row Publishers, Inc. [*NYSE symbol*] ... HPR
Harpers [*A publication*] ... Ha
Harper's Bazaar [*A publication*] ... Harp B
Harper's Bazaar [*A publication*] ... Harp Baz
Harpers Ferry Center [*National Park Service*] ... HFC
Harpers Ferry National Historical Park ... HAFE
Harper's Magazine [*A publication*] ... Harp
Harper's Magazine [*A publication*] ... Harper
Harper's Magazine [*A publication*] ... HM
Harper's Magazine Press ... HMP
Harper's New Monthly Magazine [*A publication*] ... Harper's Mag
Harper's Weekly [*A publication*] ... Harp W
Harpoon Aircraft Command and Launch Control Set [*Missiles*] ... HACLCS
Harpoon Aircraft Command and Launch Subsystem [*Missiles*] ... HACLS
Harpoon Check List [*Missiles*] ... HCL
Harpoon Data Processor [*Missiles*] ... HDP
Harpoon Data System Cabinet [*Missiles*] ... HDSC
Harpoon Fire Control System [*Missiles*] ... HFCS
Harpoon Firing Interlock Closed [*Missiles*] ... HFIC
Harpoon Indicator Panel [*Missiles*] ... HIP
Harpoon Logic Module [*Missiles*] ... HLM
Harpoon Missile Select Relay Rack [*Missiles*] ... HMSRR
Harpoon Shipboard Command and Launch Control Set [*Missiles*] ... HSCLCS
Harpoon Shipboard Command and Launch Subsystem [*Missiles*] ... HSCLS
Harpoon Trainer Module [*Missiles*] ... HTM
Harpoon Transfer Relay Rack [*Missiles*] ... HTRR
Harpoon Weapon Control Console [*Missiles*] ... HWCC
Harpoon Weapons System ... HWS
Harpsichord [*A publication*] ... HPD
Harrah's [*NYSE symbol*] ... HRR
Harrah's Automobile Collection and Pony Express Museum, Reno, NV [*Library symbol*] ... NvRH
Harriette Person Memorial Library, Port Gibson, MS [*Library symbol*] ... MsPog
Harriman College, Harriman, NY [*Library symbol*] ... NHarC
Harriman & Northeastern R. R. [*AAR code*] ... HNE
Harriman Public Library, Harriman, TN [*Library symbol*] ... TH
Harriman, TN [*Radio station call letters*] ... WHBT
Harriman, TN [*Radio station call letters*] ... WKCE
Harriman, TN [*Radio station call letters*] ... WKJS
Harriman and Vance [*Code name for 1968 Paris peace talks on Vietnam, derived from the surnames of US negotiators W. Averell Harriman and Cyrus R. Vance*] ... HARVAN
Harrington Harbour [*Canada*] [*Airport symbol*] ... YHR
Harrington Institute of Interior Design, Chicago, IL [*Library symbol*] ... ICHID
Harrington Institute of Interior Design, Design Library, Chicago, IL [*OCLC symbol*] ... IEX
Harrington Public Library, Harrington, DE [*OCLC symbol*] ... HRG
Harris Bankcorp, Inc. [*NYSE symbol*] ... HBC
Harris Corp. [*NYSE symbol*] ... HRS
Harris Institute, Woonsocket, RI [*Library symbol*] ... RWoH
Harris-Intertype Corp. [*Later, HRS*] [*NYSE symbol*] ... HI
Harris and Paulson [*NASDAQ symbol*] ... HAPI
Harris Ranch [*California*] [*Seismograph station code, US Geological Survey*] [*Closed*] ... HRC
Harris Teachers College [*Missouri*] ... HTC
Harris Teachers College, St. Louis, MO [*Library symbol*] ... MoSHT
Harris Transducer Corporation ... HTC
Harrisburg [*Pennsylvania*] [*Airport symbol*] ... MDT
Harrisburg Area Community College, Harrisburg, PA [*Library symbol*] ... PHarC
Harrisburg, IL [*Radio station call letters*] ... WEBQ
Harrisburg, IL [*Radio station call letters*] ... WEBQ-FM
Harrisburg, IL [*Television station call letters*] ... WSIL-TV
Harrisburg, PA [*Location identifier*] [*FAA*] ... CXY
Harrisburg, PA [*Radio station call letters*] ... WCMB
Harrisburg, PA [*Radio station call letters*] ... WFEC
Harrisburg, PA [*Radio station call letters*] ... WHP
Harrisburg, PA [*Radio station call letters*] ... WHP-FM
Harrisburg, PA [*Television station call letters*] ... WHP-TV
Harrisburg, PA [*Television station call letters*] ... WITF-TV
Harrisburg, PA [*Radio station call letters*] ... WKBO
Harrisburg, PA [*Radio station call letters*] ... WMSP
Harrisburg, PA [*Radio station call letters*] ... WSFM
Harrisburg, PA [*Radio station call letters*] ... WTPA
Harrisburg Polyclinic Hospital, Harrisburg, PA [*Library symbol*] ... PHarP
Harrison [*Arkansas*] [*Airport symbol*] ... HRO
Harrison, AR [*Radio station call letters*] ... KCWD
Harrison, AR [*Radio station call letters*] ... KHOZ
Harrison, AR [*Radio station call letters*] ... KHOZ-FM
Harrison Bay, AK [*Location identifier*] [*FAA*] ... HBA
Harrison County Historical Society, Logan, IA [*Library symbol*] ... IaLoHi
Harrison Fisher Society ... HFS
Harrison Memorial Library, Carmel, CA [*Library symbol*] ... CCarm
Harrison, MI [*Radio station call letters*] ... WKKM
Harrison Narcotic Act ... HNA
Harrison Public Library, Harrison, MI [*Library symbol*] ... MiHars
Harrison Public Library, Harrison, NY [*Library symbol*] ... NHarn
Harrison Township Historical Society, Mullica Hill, NJ [*Library symbol*] ... NjMuhHi
Harrisonburg [*Virginia*] [*Seismograph station code, US Geological Survey*] ... HBV
Harrisonburg, VA [*Radio station call letters*] ... WEMC
Harrisonburg, VA [*Radio station call letters*] ... WHBG
Harrisonburg, VA [*Television station call letters*] ... WHSV-TV
Harrisonburg, VA [*Radio station call letters*] ... WJSY
Harrisonburg, VA [*Radio station call letters*] ... WKCY
Harrisonburg, VA [*Radio station call letters*] ... WMRA
Harrisonburg, VA [*Radio station call letters*] ... WQPO
Harrisonburg, VA [*Radio station call letters*] ... WSVA
Harrisonville, MO [*Radio station call letters*] ... KIEE
Harrodsburg Historical Society, Harrodsburg, KY [*Library symbol*] ... KyHaHi
Harrodsburg, KY [*Radio station call letters*] ... WHBN
Harrodsburg, KY [*Radio station call letters*] ... WHBN-FM
Harrogate, TN [*Radio station call letters*] ... WSVQ
Harry Diamond Center [*Army*] ... HDC
Harry Diamond Laboratories [*Formerly, DOFL*] [*Washington, DC*] [*Military*] ... HDL
Harry S Truman ... HST
Harry S Truman College, Chicago, IL [*OCLC symbol*] ... IEG
Harry S Truman Library ... HSTL
Harry S Truman Library, Independence, MO [*Library symbol*] ... MoIT
Harry S Truman Memorial Veterans Hospital, Columbia, MO [*Library symbol*] ... MoCoV
Harry S Truman Scholarship Foundation ... HSTSF
Harsco Corporation [*NYSE symbol*] ... HSC
Harshaw Chemical Co. [*NYSE symbol*] [*Delisted*] ... HCM
Hart Crane Newsletter [*A publication*] ... HCN
Hart, MI [*Radio station call letters*] ... WCXT
Hart Public Library, Hart, MI [*Library symbol*] ... MiHa
Hart, Schaffner & Marx [*NYSE symbol*] [*Delisted*] ... HSM
Harte-Hanks Communications, Inc. [*NYSE symbol*] ... HHN
Hartebeesthoek [*South Africa*] [*Geomagnetic observatory code*] ... HBK
Hartford [*Connecticut*] [*Seismograph station code, US Geological Survey*] [*Closed*] ... HAR
Hartford Bar Library Association, Hartford, CT [*Library symbol*] ... CtHB
Hartford City, IN [*Radio station call letters*] ... WWHC
Hartford Conservatory, Hartford, CT [*Library symbol*] ... CtHHC
Hartford, CT [*Location identifier*] [*FAA*] ... AQD
Hartford, CT [*Location identifier*] [*FAA*] ... HFD
Hartford, CT [*Radio station call letters*] ... WCCC
Hartford, CT [*Radio station call letters*] ... WCCC-FM
Hartford, CT [*Radio station call letters*] ... WDRC
Hartford, CT [*Radio station call letters*] ... WDRC-FM
Hartford, CT [*Television station call letters*] ... WEDH
Hartford, CT [*Television station call letters*] ... WETG
Hartford, CT [*Television station call letters*] ... WFSB-TV
Hartford, CT [*Radio station call letters*] ... WHCN
Hartford, CT [*Television station call letters*] ... WHCT
Hartford, CT [*Radio station call letters*] ... WJMJ
Hartford, CT [*Radio station call letters*] ... WKSS
Hartford, CT [*Radio station call letters*] ... WLVH
Hartford, CT [*Radio station call letters*] ... WPOP
Hartford, CT [*Radio station call letters*] ... WQTQ
Hartford, CT [*Radio station call letters*] ... WRTC-FM
Hartford, CT [*Radio station call letters*] ... WTIC
Hartford, CT [*Radio station call letters*] ... WTIC-FM
Hartford Electric Light Company ... HELCO
Hartford, KY [*Radio station call letters*] ... WLLS
Hartford, KY [*Radio station call letters*] ... WLLS-FM
Hartford Medical Society, Hartford, CT [*Library symbol*] ... CtHM
Hartford Memorial Hospital, Hartford, WI [*Library symbol*] ... WHH
Hartford National Corp. [*NASDAQ symbol*] ... HNAT
Hartford Public Library, Hartford, CT [*Library symbol*] ... CtH
Hartford Public Library, Hartford, CT [*OCLC symbol*] ... HPL
Hartford Public Library, Hartford, IL [*Library symbol*] ... IHart

Hartford Public Library, Hartford, MI [*Library symbol*] .... MiHaf
Hartford Quarterly [*A publication*] .... Hart Q
Hartford Seminary Foundation .... HSF
Hartford Seminary Foundation, Hartford, CT [*Library symbol*] .... CtHC
Hartford Seminary Record [*A publication*] .... Hartf Sem Rec
Hartford & Slocomb Railroad Co. [*AAR code*] .... HS
Hartford [*Connecticut*]**/Springfield** [*Massachusetts*] [*Airport symbol*] [*Derived from name of airport: Bradley Field*] .... BDL
Hartford Steam Boiler [*NASDAQ symbol*] .... HBOL
Hartford Studies in Literature [*A publication*] .... HSL
Hartford, VT [*Television station call letters*] .... WNNE-TV
Hartford, WI [*Location identifier*] [*FAA*] .... HXF
Hartford, WI [*Radio station call letters*] .... WTKM
Hartford, WI [*Radio station call letters*] .... WTKM-FM
Hartford's Other Voice [*Superseded by Wild Raspberry*] [*A publication*] .... HO Voice
Hartland [*United Kingdom*] [*Geomagnetic observatory code*] .... HAD
Hartley Public Library, Hartley, IA [*Library symbol*] .... IaHart
Hartman Value Inventory [*Psychology*] .... HVI
Hartmann Dispersion Formula .... HDF
Hartmann Number [*IUPAC*] .... Ha
Hartman's Solution [*Dentistry*] .... HS
Hartmarx Corp. [*NYSE symbol*] .... HMX
Hartnell College, Salinas, CA [*Library symbol*] .... CSalH
Hartogen Energy Canada [*NASDAQ symbol*] .... HTENY
Hartree-Fock [*Orbitals*] [*Atomic structure*] .... HF
Harts Bluff [*South Carolina*] [*Seismograph station code, US Geological Survey*] .... HBF
Hartselle, AL [*Radio station call letters*] .... WHRT
Hartsville, SC [*Location identifier*] [*FAA*] .... HVS
Hartsville, SC [*Radio station call letters*] .... WHSC
Hartsville, SC [*Radio station call letters*] .... WSDC
Hartsville, TN [*Radio station call letters*] .... WJKM
Hartwell, GA [*Radio station call letters*] .... WKLY
Hartwell Railway Co. [*AAR code*] .... HRT
Hartwick College, Oneonta, NY [*Library symbol*] .... NOneoC
Hartwick College, Oneonta, NY [*OCLC symbol*] .... VZH
Hartwick Review [*A publication*] .... Hart R
Hartz Mountain Corp. [*American Stock Exchange symbol*] [*Delisted*] .... HTZ
Harvard Advocate [*A publication*] .... Harv Ad
Harvard Advocate [*A publication*] .... Harvard A
Harvard Air Cleaning Laboratory .... HACL
Harvard Black Rock Forest, Cornwall, NY [*Library symbol*] .... NCornB
Harvard Business Review [*A publication*] .... Har Bus R
Harvard Business Review [*A publication*] .... Harvard BR
Harvard Business Review [*A publication*] .... Harvard Bsns R
Harvard Business Review [*A publication*] .... Harvard Bus R
Harvard Business Review [*A publication*] .... Harv Bus Re
Harvard Business Review [*A publication*] .... Harv Bus Rev
Harvard Business Review [*A publication*] .... HBR
Harvard Business School .... HBS
Harvard Business School, Boston, MA [*OCLC symbol*] .... HBS
Harvard Civil Rights [*A publication*] .... Harv Civ Ri
Harvard Civil Rights - Civil Liberties Law Review [*A publication*] .... Harv Civil Rights L Rev
Harvard Civil Rights - Civil Liberties Law Review [*A publication*] .... Harv Civ Rights - Civ Liberties Law Rev
Harvard College. Museum of Comparative Zoology. Annual Report [*A publication*] .... Harvard Coll Mus CZ An Rp
Harvard College. Museum of Comparative Zoology. Bulletin [*A publication*] .... Harvard Coll Mus Comp Zoology Bull
Harvard College. Museum of Comparative Zoology. Bulletin [*A publication*] .... Harvard Coll Mus C Z B
Harvard College. Museum of Comparative Zoology. Memoirs [*A publication*] .... Harvard Coll Mus C Z Mem
Harvard College Observatory .... HCO
Harvard Divinity Bulletin [*A publication*] .... Harv Div B
Harvard Divinity School, Cambridge, MA [*OCLC symbol*] .... BHA
Harvard East Asian Series [*A publication*] .... HEAS
Harvard Educational Review [*A publication*] .... Harvard Ed R
Harvard Educational Review [*A publication*] .... Harvard Educ R
Harvard Educational Review [*A publication*] .... Harv Edu Re
Harvard Educational Review [*A publication*] .... HEdR
Harvard Educational Review [*A publication*] .... HER
Harvard Environmental Law Society .... ELS
Harvard Forest. Annual Report [*A publication*] .... Harv For Annu Rep
Harvard Forest. Bulletin [*A publication*] .... Harvard Forest Bull
Harvard Forest. Bulletin [*A publication*] .... Harv For Bull
Harvard Forest. Papers [*A publication*] .... Harv For Pap
Harvard Germanic Studies [*A publication*] .... HGS
Harvard Graduate School of Education .... HGSE
Harvard Graduates' Magazine [*A publication*] .... Harv Grad M
Harvard Group Scale of Hypnotic Susceptibility [*Psychology*] .... HGSHS
Harvard, IL [*Radio station call letters*] .... WMCW
Harvard Industries [*NASDAQ symbol*] .... HAVA
Harvard International Law Journal [*A publication*] .... Harv Int L J
Harvard Journal of Asiatic Studies [*A publication*] .... Harvard J Asiat Stud
Harvard Journal of Asiatic Studies [*A publication*] .... Harv J Asiatic Stud
Harvard Journal of Asiatic Studies [*A publication*] .... HJAS
Harvard Journal on Legislation [*A publication*] .... Harv J Leg
Harvard Journal on Legislation [*A publication*] .... Harv J Legis
Harvard Law Review [*A publication*] .... Harv Law R
Harvard Law Review [*A publication*] .... Harv Law Rev
Harvard Law Review [*A publication*] .... Harv L Rev
Harvard Law Review [*A publication*] .... HLR
Harvard Law School [*Massachusetts*] .... HLS
Harvard Law School. Bulletin [*A publication*] .... Harv LS Bull
Harvard Library. Bulletin [*A publication*] .... Harvard Lib Bul
Harvard Library. Bulletin [*A publication*] .... Harv Lib Bull
Harvard Library Bulletin [*A publication*] .... HL
Harvard Library Bulletin [*A publication*] .... HLB
Harvard Monographs in Applied Science [*A publication*] .... Harvard Mon Applied Sci
Harvard Monthly [*A publication*] .... Harv Mo
Harvard Musical Association, Boston, MA [*Library symbol*] .... MBHM
Harvard Negotiation Project .... HNP
Harvard - Oak Ridge [*Massachusetts*] [*Seismograph station code, US Geological Survey*] .... HRV
Harvard Project Physics .... HPP
Harvard Public Health Alumni. Bulletin [*A publication*] .... Harv Public Health Alumni Bull
Harvard Radio Meteor Project .... HRMP
Harvard Review [*A publication*] .... Harv R
Harvard Slavic Studies [*A publication*] .... HSLS
Harvard Slavic Studies [*A publication*] .... HSS
Harvard-Smithsonian Reference Atmosphere .... HSRA
Harvard Student Agencies [*Inc.*] .... HSA
Harvard Studies in Classical Philology [*A publication*] .... Harv Stud Class Philol
Harvard Studies in Classical Philology [*A publication*] .... HSCP
Harvard Studies in Classical Philology [*A publication*] .... HSPh
Harvard Studies in Comparative Literature [*A publication*] .... HSCL
Harvard Studies and Notes in Philology and Literature [*A publication*] .... HSNPL
Harvard Studies and Notes in Philology and Literature [*A publication*] .... HSPL
Harvard Studies in Romance Languages [*A publication*] .... HSRL
Harvard Theological Review [*A publication*] .... Harvard Theol R
Harvard Theological Review [*A publication*] .... Harv Theol R
Harvard Theological Review [*A publication*] .... Harv Th R
Harvard Theological Review [*A publication*] .... HThR
Harvard Theological Review [*A publication*] .... HTR
Harvard Ukrainian Research Institute .... HURI
Harvard Ukrainian Studies [*A publication*] .... HUS
Harvard University [*Massachusetts*] .... HARV
Harvard University [*Massachusetts*] .... HU
Harvard University [*Massachusetts*] .... HUX
Harvard University, Afro-American Studies, Lamont Undergraduate Library, Cambridge, MA [*Library symbol*] .... MH-AA
Harvard University, Andover-Harvard Theological Library, Cambridge, MA [*Library symbol*] .... MH-AH
Harvard University Archives, Cambridge, MA [*Library symbol*] .... MH-Ar
Harvard University, Arnold Arboretum, Cambridge, MA [*Library symbol*] .... MH-A
Harvard University, Arnold Arboretum, Horticultural Library, Jamaica Plain, MA [*Library symbol*] .... MH-HJ
Harvard University. Arnold Arboretum Journal [*A publication*] .... Arnold Arbor J
Harvard University, Biochemical Sciences Tutorial Library, Cambridge, MA [*Library symbol*] .... MH-BS
Harvard University, Biological Laboratories, Cambridge, MA [*Library symbol*] .... MH-BL
Harvard University, Blue Hill Meteorological Observatory, Cambridge, MA [*Library symbol*] .... MH-BH
Harvard University. Botanical Museum Leaflets [*A publication*] .... Harvard Univ Bot Mus Leaflets
Harvard University. Bulletin [*A publication*] .... Harvard Univ B
Harvard University, Busch-Reisinger Museum of Germanic Culture, Cambridge, MA [*Library symbol*] .... MH-BR
Harvard University, Cabot Science Library, Cambridge, MA [*OCLC symbol*] .... CLS
Harvard University, Cambridge, MA [*OCLC symbol*] .... HLS
Harvard University, Cambridge, MA [*OCLC symbol*] .... HUL
Harvard University, Cambridge, MA [*Library symbol*] .... MH
Harvard University, Career Reference Library, Cambridge, MA [*Library symbol*] .... MH-CL
Harvard University, Center for Analysis of Health Practices, Cambridge, MA [*Library symbol*] .... MH-HP
Harvard University, Center for European Studies, Cambridge, MA [*Library symbol*] .... MH-ES
Harvard University, Center for International Affairs, Semitic Museum, Cambridge, MA [*Library symbol*] .... MH-CI
Harvard University, Center for Middle Eastern Studies, Cambridge, MA [*Library symbol*] .... MH-ME
Harvard University, Center for Population Studies, Boston, MA [*Library symbol*] .... MH-CP
Harvard University Character Recognizer [*Data processing*] .... HUCR
Harvard University, Charles Warren Center for Studies in American History, Cambridge, MA [*Library symbol*] .... MH-WA
Harvard University, Chemistry Library, Cambridge, MA [*Library symbol*] .... MH-C

Harvard University, Child Memorial and English Tutorial Library, Cambridge, MA [*Library symbol*].................MH-CM

Harvard University, Commission on Extension Courses, Cambridge, MA [*Library symbol*].................MH-CE

Harvard University, Committee on Experimental Geology and Geophysics, Hoffman Laboratory, Cambridge, MA [*Library symbol*].................MH-GG

Harvard University. Department of Engineering. Publications [*A publication*].................... Harvard Univ Dep Eng Publ

Harvard University, East Asian Research Center, Cambridge, MA [*Library symbol*].................MH-EA

Harvard University, East Asian Studies Reading Room, Cambridge, MA [*Library symbol*].................MH-ER

Harvard University, Farlow Reference Library, Cambridge, MA [*Library symbol*].................MH-F

Harvard University, Fine Arts Library, Cambridge, MA [*Library symbol*].................MH-FA

Harvard University, Frances Loeb Library, Cambridge, MA [*OCLC symbol*].................FLL

Harvard University, Fred N. Robinson Celtic Seminar, Cambridge, MA [*Library symbol*].................MH-RC

Harvard University, Geological Sciences Library, Cambridge, MA [*Library symbol*].................MH-GS

Harvard University, George David Birkhoff Mathematics Library, Cambridge, MA [*Library symbol*].................MH-BM

Harvard University, George R. Agassiz Station, Cambridge, MA [*Library symbol*].................MH-AS

Harvard University, Godfrey Lowell Cabot Science Library, Cambridge, MA [*Library symbol*].................MH-CS

Harvard University, Gordon McKay Library, Cambridge, MA [*Library symbol*].................MH-GM

Harvard University, Graduate School of Business Administration, Boston, MA [*Library symbol*].................MH-BA

Harvard University, Graduate School of Design, Cambridge, MA [*Library symbol*].................MH-SD

Harvard University, Graduate School of Education, Cambridge, MA [*Library symbol*].................MH-Ed

Harvard University, Gray Herbarium, Cambridge, MA [*Library symbol*].................MH-G

Harvard University. Gray Herbarium. Contributions [*A publication*].................... Harvard Univ Gray Herbarium Contr

Harvard University, Gutman Library, Cambridge, MA [*OCLC symbol*].................HMG

Harvard University, Hamilton A. R. Gibb Islamic Seminar, Cambridge, MA [*Library symbol*].................MH-GI

Harvard University, Harvard College Observatory, Cambridge, MA [*Library symbol*].................MH-O

Harvard University, Harvard Forest Library, Petersham, MA [*Library symbol*].................MH-HF

Harvard University, Harvard Radio Astronomy Center, Fort Davis, TX [*Library symbol*].................MH-RA

Harvard University. Harvard Soil Mechanics Series [*A publication*].................... Harvard Univ Harvard Soil Mech Ser

Harvard University, Harvard-Yenching Institute [*Chinese-Japanese Library*], Cambridge, MA [*Library symbol*].................NH-HY

Harvard University, Harvard-Yenching Library, Cambridge, MA [*Library symbol*].................MH-HY

Harvard University, Herbert Weir Smyth Classical Library, Cambridge, MA [*Library symbol*].................MH-SC

Harvard University, Hilles Library of Radcliffe College, Cambridge, MA [*Library symbol*].................MH-Hi

Harvard University, History Department Library, Cambridge, MA [*Library symbol*].................MH-HD

Harvard University, History of Science Library, Cambridge, MA [*Library symbol*].................MH-HS

Harvard University, Houghton Library, Cambridge, MA [*Library symbol*].................MH-H

Harvard University, John Peabody Monks Library, Cambridge, MA [*Library symbol*].................MH-MH

Harvard University, Kennedy Inter-Faculty Program in Medical Ethics, Cambridge, MA [*Library symbol*].................MH-KM

Harvard University, Kennedy School for Government, Cambridge, MA [*OCLC symbol*].................KSG

Harvard University, Kennedy School of Government, Cambridge, MA [*Library symbol*].................MH-KG

Harvard University, Lamont Undergraduate Library, Cambridge, MA [*Library symbol*].................MH-Lm

Harvard University, Law School, Cambridge, MA [*Library symbol*].................MH-L

Harvard University, Linguistics Library, Cambridge, MA [*Library symbol*].................MH-Li

Harvard University, Littauer Library of the Kennedy School of Government, Cambridge, MA [*Library symbol*].................MH-PA

Harvard University, Lucien Howe Library of Ophthalmology, Boston, MA [*Library symbol*].................MH-HO

Harvard University Medical School, Countway Library of Medicine, Boston, MA [*OCLC symbol*].................HMS

Harvard University, Milman Parry Collection of Oral Literature, Cambridge, MA [*Library symbol*].................MH-PL

Harvard University, Monographic Cataloging Support Service, Cambridge, MA [*OCLC symbol*].................MCS

Harvard University. Museum of Comparative Zoology. Bulletin [*A publication*]....................Harvard Univ Mus Comp Zoology Bull

Harvard University. Museum of Comparative Zoology. Bulletin [*A publication*].................... Harv Univ Mus Comp Zool Bull

Harvard University. Museum of Comparative Zoology, Cambridge, MA [*Library symbol*].................MH-Z

Harvard University. Museum of Comparative Zoology. Memoirs [*A publication*].................... Museum Comp Zool Memoirs

Harvard University, Music Library, Cambridge, MA [*Library symbol*].................MH-Mu

Harvard University, Near Eastern Languages and Literatures Library, Cambridge, MA [*Library symbol*].................MH-NE

Harvard University, Nieman Collection of Contemporary Journalism, Cambridge, MA [*Library symbol*].................MH-NJ

Harvard University, Oakes Ames Library of Economic Botany, Cambridge, MA [*Library symbol*].................MH-EB

Harvard University, Oakes Ames Orchid Library, Cambridge, MA [*Library symbol*].................MH-AO

Harvard University, Palaeography Library, Cambridge, MA [*Library symbol*].................MH-PC

Harvard University. Papers of the Peabody Museum of Archaeology and Ethnology [*A publication*] ....HUPPAE

Harvard University, Peabody Museum, Cambridge, MA [*Library symbol*].................MH-P

Harvard University, Personnel Office Library, Cambridge, MA [*Library symbol*].................MH-PO

Harvard University, Physics Research Library, Cambridge, MA [*Library symbol*].................MH-PR

Harvard University, Program for Science and International Affairs Library, Cambridge, MA [*Library symbol*].................MH-SI

Harvard University, Psychology Research Library, Cambridge, MA [*Library symbol*].................MH-Ps

Harvard University, Public Policy Program, Cambridge, MA [*Library symbol*].................MH-PP

Harvard University, Robbins Library of Philosophy, Cambridge, MA [*Library symbol*].................MH-RP

Harvard University, Rubel Asiatic Research Bureau, Fogg Art Museum, Cambridge, MA [*Library symbol*] [*Obsolete*].................MH-RB

Harvard University, Russian Research Center, Cambridge, MA [*Library symbol*].................MH-R

Harvard University, Sanskrit Library, Cambridge, MA [*Library symbol*].................MH-SL

Harvard University, Schering Foundation Library, Boston, MA [*Library symbol*].................MH-SF

Harvard University. School of Public Health. Dean's Report [*A publication*].................... Harv Univ Sch Public Health Dean's Rep

Harvard University, Science and Public Police Program Library, Cambridge, MA [*Library symbol*].................MH-SP

Harvard University, Social Relations Library, Cambridge, MA [*Library symbol*].................MH-SR

Harvard University, Statistics Library, Cambridge, MA [*Library symbol*].................MH-S

Harvard University, Ticknor Library of Modern Languages, Cambridge, MA [*Library symbol*].................MH-ML

Harvard University, Tozzer Library, Cambridge, MA [*OCLC symbol*] ..... TOZ

Harvard University, Ukrainian Research Institute Reference Library, Cambridge, MA [*Library symbol*].................MH-UR

Harvard, Yale, and Princeton Universities.................HYP

Harvest Industries, Inc. [*NASDAQ symbol*].................HIND

Harvey Aluminum, Inc. [*NYSE symbol*] [*Delisted*].................HAR

Harvey Cushing Society [*Later, American Association of Neurological Surgeons*].................HCS

Harvey Group, Inc. [*American Stock Exchange symbol*].................HRA

Harvey, IL [*Radio station call letters*].................WBEE

Harvey Lectures [*A publication*].................Harvey Lect

Harvey Murine Sarcoma Virus.................HaMuSV

Harvey, ND [*Radio station call letters*].................KHND

Harvey Public Library, Harvey, IL [*Library symbol*].................IHa

Harvey Public Library, Harvey, ND [*Library symbol*].................NdHa

Harvey Society ....HS

Harwell Atomic Energy Establishment.................HAEE

Harwood Foundation, Taos, NM [*Library symbol*].................NmTHF

Harwyn Industries Corp. [*NASDAQ symbol*].................HAIC

Haryana Agricultural University. Journal of Research [*A publication*].................Haryana Agric Univ J Res

Has.................H

Has Been Drinking [*Medical notation*].................HBD

Has Been Reviewed.................HBR

Has Been Reviewed and Concurred With.................HBRACW

Has Not Voided [*Urology*].................HNV

Hasbro Industries, Inc. [*American Stock Exchange symbol*].................HAS

Hasbrouck Heights Free Public Library, Hasbrouck Heights, NJ [*Library symbol*].................NjHas

Hashomer Hatzair.................HH

Hashomer Hatzair Socialist Zionist Youth Movement.................HHSZYM

Hashomer Hatzair Zionist Youth Organization [*Later, HHSZYM*].................HZYO

Haskell, TX [*Radio station call letters*].................KVRP

Hasler Mitteilungen [*A publication*].................Hasler Mitt

Hasler Review [*A publication*].................Hasler Rev

Hassan Addakhil Dam [*Morocco*] [*Seismograph station code, US Geological Survey*].................HAD

Hasselblad Data Camera .... HDC
Hasselblad Electric Camera .... HEC
Hasselblad Electric Data Camera .... HEDC
Hasselblad Reflex Camera .... HRC
Hassi Messaoud [*Algeria*] [*Airport symbol*] .... HME
Hassle [*Sweden*] [*Research code symbol*] .... H
Hastings [*New Zealand*] [*Seismograph station code, US Geological Survey*] [*Closed*] .... HAS
Hastings [*Nebraska*] [*Airport symbol*] .... HSI
Hastings Center. Report [*A publication*] .... Hast Cent Rpt
Hastings Center. Report [*A publication*] .... Hastings Cent Rep
Hastings Center. Studies [*A publication*] .... Hast Cen St
Hastings Center. Studies [*A publication*] .... Hast Cent St
Hastings Center. Studies [*A publication*] .... Hastings Cent Stud
Hastings College, Hastings, NE [*OCLC symbol*] .... NBH
Hastings College, Hastings, NE [*Library symbol*] .... NbHC
Hastings Law Journal [*A publication*] .... Hastings L J
Hastings Law Journal [*A publication*] .... Hast Law J
Hastings Manufacturing Co. [*American Stock Exchange symbol*] .... HMF
Hastings, MI [*Radio station call letters*] .... WBCH
Hastings, MI [*Radio station call letters*] .... WBCH-FM
Hastings, MN [*Radio station call letters*] .... KDWA
Hastings, NE [*Radio station call letters*] .... KCNT
Hastings, NE [*Radio station call letters*] .... KEZH
Hastings, NE [*Radio station call letters*] .... KHAS
Hastings, NE [*Television station call letters*] .... KHAS-TV
Hastings, NE [*Television station call letters*] .... KHNE-TV
Hastings, NE [*Radio station call letters*] .... KICS
Hastings-On-Hudson Public Library, Hastings-On-Hudson, NY [*Library symbol*] .... NHas
Hastings Public Library, Hastings, MI [*Library symbol*] .... MiHas
Hastings Public Library, Hastings, NE [*Library symbol*] .... NbH
Hasvik [*Norway*] [*Airport symbol*] .... HAA
Hat Block and Die Makers Association .... HBDMA
Hat Corp. of America [*NYSE symbol*] [*Delisted*] .... HAT
Hat Institute .... HI
Hat Leather Association .... HLA
HAT [*Hypoxanthine-Aminopterin-Thymidine*] **with Ouabain** [*Growth medium*] [*Biochemistry*] .... HOT
Hatch [*Technical drawings*] .... H
Hatch Act [*1887*] .... HA
Hatch Public Library, Hatch, NM [*Library symbol*] .... NmHa
Hatchlike Experiment Module [*NASA*] .... HEM
Hateruma [*Japan*] [*Airport symbol*] .... HTR
Hathaway Corp. [*NASDAQ symbol*] .... HATH
Hatillo, PR [*Radio station call letters*] .... WMSW
Hatizyo [*Japan*] [*Geomagnetic observatory code*] .... HTY
Hato Corozal [*Colombia*] [*Airport symbol*] .... HTZ
Hatteras Income Securities, Inc. [*NYSE symbol*] .... HAT
Hatters' Fur Cutters Association of America [*Formerly, HFCAUS*] .... HFCAA
Hatters' Fur Cutters Association of the United States [*Later, HFCAA*] .... HFCAUS
Hatters Machinery and Equipment Association [*Defunct*] .... HMEA
Hattiesburg, MS [*Location identifier*] [*FAA*] .... HBG
Hattiesburg, MS [*Location identifier*] [*FAA*] .... HHB
Hattiesburg, MS [*Location identifier*] [*FAA*] .... LBY
Hattiesburg, MS [*Location identifier*] [*FAA*] .... SLJ
Hattiesburg, MS [*Radio station call letters*] .... WBKH
Hattiesburg, MS [*Radio station call letters*] .... WFOR
Hattiesburg, MS [*Radio station call letters*] .... WHER
Hattiesburg, MS [*Radio station call letters*] .... WHSY
Hattiesburg, MS [*Radio station call letters*] .... WHSY-FM
Hattiesburg, MS [*Radio station call letters*] .... WJMG
Hattiesburg, MS [*Television station call letters*] .... WLHT
Hattiesburg, MS [*Radio station call letters*] .... WMSU
Hattiesburg, MS [*Radio station call letters*] .... WORV
Hattiesburg, MS [*Radio station call letters*] .... WXXX
Hattiesburg Public Library, Hattiesburg, MS [*Library symbol*] .... MsHa
Haubitzgranate [*Howitzer Shell*] [*German military - World War II*] .... HGR
Hauch [*Antigen*] [*Immunology*] .... H
Haudompre [*France*] [*Seismograph station code, US Geological Survey*] .... HAU
Haugesund [*Norway*] [*Airport symbol*] .... HAU
Haul .... HL
Haunt of Horror [*A publication*] .... HOH
Haunt Hunters [*An association*] .... HH
Hauptbahnhof [*Main Railroad Station*] [*German*] .... HBF
Hauptpunkte [*Crystallography*] .... HP
Hauptverbandplatz [*Clearing Station*] [*German military - World War II*] .... HVB
Hauptverwaltung Aufklaerung [*Main Administration for Intelligence*] [*East Germany*] .... HVA
Hauptverwaltung Deutsche Grenzpolizei [*Central Administration of the Border Police*] [*Germany*] .... HVDGP
Hauptverwaltung fuer Schulung [*Central Administration for Education*] [*Germany*] .... HVS
Hauptverwaltung Seepolizei [*Central Administration of the Marine Police*] [*Germany*] .... HVS
Hauptwachtmeister [*First Sergeant*] [*German military - World War II*] .... HW
Hauptwerk [*Great Organ*] [*German*] .... HAUPTW
Hauptwerk [*Great Organ*] [*German*] .... HK
Hauptwerk [*Great Organ*] [*German*] .... HPTW
Hauptwerk [*Great Organ*] [*German*] .... HW
Hauptwiderstandslinie [*Main line of resistance in a delaying action*] [*German military - World War II*] .... HWL
Haus der Technik-Vortrags-Veroeffentlichungen [*A publication*] .... Haus Tech-Vortrag-Veroeff
Hausa [*MARC language code*] [*Library of Congress*] .... hau
Hauserman Inc. [*NASDAQ symbol*] .... HASR
Hausmitteilungen Jos Schneider [*A publication*] .... Hausmitt Jos Schneider
Hausmusik [*A publication*] .... Hausmus
Hausserman Aviation, Inc. [*Columbus, OH*] [*FAA designator*] .... HMS
Haustechnik, Bauphysik, Umwelttechnik [*A publication*] .... Haustech Bauphys Umwelttech
Haustus [*A Drink*] [*Pharmacy*] .... H
Haustus [*A Drink*] [*Pharmacy*] .... HAUST
Haustus [*A Drink*] [*Pharmacy*] .... HT
Haut-Commissaire des Nations Unies pour les Refugies .... HCR
Haut-Einheits-Dosis [*Unit Skin Dose*] .... HED
Haut Parleur [*Loudspeaker*] [*French*] .... HP
Hautboy [*Oboe*] .... HAUT
Haute-Contre [*Alto*] .... HC
Hauterive, PQ [*Radio station call letters*] .... CHLC
Havana [*Cuba*] [*Airport symbol*] .... HAV
Havana [*Cuba*] [*Geomagnetic observatory code*] .... HVN
Havana Biblioteca Nacional. Revista [*A publication*] .... Havana Bibl Nac R
Havana, FL [*Radio station call letters*] .... WHFL
Havana, IL [*Radio station call letters*] .... WDUK
Havana Rabbit Breeders Association .... HRBA
Havana Universidad. Ciencias. Serie 4. Ciencias Biologicas [*A publication*] .... Havana Univ Cienc Ser 4 Cienc Biol
Havana Universidad. Ciencias. Serie 7. Geografia [*A publication*] .... Havana Univ Cienc Ser 7 Geogr
Havana Universidad. Ciencias. Serie 8. Investigaciones Marinas [*A publication*] .... Havana Univ Cienc Ser 8 Invest Mar
Havana Universidad. Tecnologia. Serie 10. Ingenieria Hidraulica [*A publication*] .... Havana Univ Tecnol Ser 10 Ing Hidraul
Havasupai [*Arizona*] [*Airport symbol*] .... HAE
Have .... HV
Have Alimony, Will Keep .... HAWK
Have a Nice Day .... HAND
Have Not Yet Begun to Fight [*Simulated war game*] .... HOTBUN
Have You Stored Answers to Questions? [*Data processing*] .... HAYSTAQ
Haveg Industries, Inc. [*NYSE symbol*] [*Delisted*] .... HVG
Havelock, NC [*Radio station call letters*] .... WCPQ
Havelock, NC [*Radio station call letters*] .... WMSQ
Havelock North [*New Zealand*] [*Seismograph station code, US Geological Survey*] [*Closed*] .... HNZ
Haven [*Maps and charts*] .... Hn
Haven .... HVN
Haverford College, Haverford, PA [*OCLC symbol*] .... HVC
Haverford College, Haverford, PA [*OCLC symbol*] .... HVF
Haverford College, Haverford, PA [*Library symbol*] .... PHC
Haverford State Hospital, Haverford, PA [*OCLC symbol*] .... PHH
Haverford Township Free Library, Havertown, PA [*Library symbol*] .... PHav
Haverhill, MA [*Radio station call letters*] .... WHAV
Haverhill Public Library, Haverhill, MA [*Library symbol*] .... MHa
Haversine [*Mathematics*] .... HAV
Havertown, PA [*Radio station call letters*] .... WHHS
Haverty Furniture Co. [*NASDAQ symbol*] .... HAVT
Havilah [*California*] [*Seismograph station code, US Geological Survey*] [*Closed*] .... HAV
Having Been Assigned to This Organization [*or Headquarters*] .... HBAT
Havre [*Montana*] [*Airport symbol*] .... HVR
Havre, Antwerp, or Dunkirk [*Business and trade*] .... HA or D
Havre De Grace, MD [*Radio station call letters*] .... WASA
Havre De Grace, MD [*Radio station call letters*] .... WHDG
Havre to Hamburg [*Business and trade*] .... H/H
Havre, MT [*Radio station call letters*] .... KNOG
Havre, MT [*Radio station call letters*] .... KOJM
Havre, MT [*Radio station call letters*] .... KPQX
Havre, MT [*Radio station call letters*] .... KXEI
Havre, MT [*Location identifier*] [*FAA*] .... LDS
Havre Saint Pierre [*Canada*] [*Airport symbol*] .... YGV
Havsforskningsinstituets Skrift [*A publication*] .... Havforskningsinst Skr
Hawaii .... HAW
Hawaii .... HAWA
Hawaii [*Postal code*] .... HI
Hawaii [*MARC country of publication code*] [*Library of Congress*] .... hiu
Hawaii [*MARC geographic area code*] [*Library of Congress*] .... n-us-hi
Hawaii Aeronautics Commission .... HAC
Hawaii Agricultural Experiment Station. Biennial Report [*A publication*] .... Hawaii Agric Exp Stn Bienn Rep
Hawaii Agricultural Experiment Station. Bulletin [*A publication*] .... Hawaii Agric Exp Stn Bull
Hawaii Agricultural Experiment Station. Miscellaneous Publication [*A publication*] .... Hawaii Agric Exp Stn Misc Pub
Hawaii Agricultural Experiment Station. Progress Notes [*A publication*] .... Hawaii Agric Exp Stn Prog Notes
Hawaii Agricultural Experiment Station. Publications [*A publication*] .... Hawaii Ag Exp

Hawaii Agricultural Experiment Station. Research Bulletin [*A publication*] ...... Hawaii Agric Exp Stn Res Bull
Hawaii Agricultural Experiment Station. Research Report [*A publication*] ...... Hawaii Agric Exp Stn Res Rep
Hawaii Agricultural Experiment Station. Technical Bulletin [*A publication*] ...... Hawaii Agric Exp Stn Tech Bull
Hawaii Agricultural Experiment Station. Technical Progress Report [*A publication*] ...... Hawaii Agric Exp Stn Tech Prog Rep
Hawaii Air Defense ...... HAD
Hawaii Air Defense System ...... HADS
Hawaii Army National Guard ...... HARNG
Hawaii Bar Journal [*A publication*] ...... Hawaii B J
Hawaii Control Center [*Missiles*] ...... HCC
Hawaii County Library, Hilo, HI [*Library symbol*] ...... HHI
Hawaii Division of Water and Land Development. Report [*A publication*] ...... Hawaii Div Water Land Dev Rep
Hawaii Farm Science [*A publication*] ...... Hawaii Farm Sci
Hawaii Foundation for American Freedoms ...... HFAF
Hawaii Institute of Geophysics [*Hawaii*] [*Seismograph station code, US Geological Survey*] ...... HIG
Hawaii Institute of Geophysics. Publication [*A publication*] ...... Hawaii Inst Geophys Publ
Hawaii International Services Agency ...... HISA
Hawaii Landair [*Honolulu, HI*] [*FAA designator*] ...... LND
Hawaii Library Association. Journal [*A publication*] ...... Hawaii Lib Assn J
Hawaii Library Association Journal [*A publication*] ...... HLA J
Hawaii Medical Journal [*A publication*] ...... Hawaii Med J
Hawaii Medical Library, Inc., Honolulu, HI [*Library symbol*] ...... HHH
Hawaii Medical Library, Inc., Honolulu, HI [*OCLC symbol*] ...... HML
Hawaii Orchid Journal [*A publication*] ...... Hawaii Orchid J
Hawaii Regional Library for the Blind and Physically Handicapped, Honolulu, HI [*Library symbol*] ...... H-BPH
Hawaii State Library System, Honolulu, HI [*Library symbol*] ...... HH
Hawaii Surfing Association ...... HSA
Hawaii University. Cooperative Extension Service. Circular [*A publication*] ...... Hawaii Univ Coop Ext Serv Circ
Hawaii University. Institute of Geophysics. Contributions [*A publication*] ...... Hawaii Univ Inst Geophys Contrib
Hawaii University. Institute of Geophysics. Report [*A publication*] ...... Hawaii Univ Inst Geophys
Hawaii University. Sea Grant Program. Reports [*A publication*] ...... Hawaii Univ Sea Grant Prog Rep
Hawaii University. Water Resources Research Center. Annual Report [*A publication*] ...... Hawaii Univ Water Resour Res Cent Annu Rep
Hawaii University. Water Resources Research Center. Technical Report [*A publication*] ...... Hawaii Univ Water Resour Res Cent Tech Rep
Hawaii University. Water Resources Research Center. Technical Report [*A publication*] ...... Hawaii Uni Water Resour Cent Tech Rep
Hawaii Volcanoes National Park ...... HAVO
Hawaiian [*MARC language code*] [*Library of Congress*] ...... haw
Hawaiian Air Defense Division ...... HADD
Hawaiian Air Defense Identification Zone ...... HADIZ
Hawaiian Air National Guard ...... HANG
Hawaiian Air Tour Service [*Honolulu, HI*] [*FAA designator*] ...... RES
Hawaiian Airlines, Inc. [*ICAO designator*] [*American Stock Exchange symbol*] ...... HA
Hawaiian Airlines, Inc. ...... HAL
Hawaiian Archives for Tsunamis ...... HAT
Hawaiian Area Joint Committee [*Military*] ...... HAJC
Hawaiian Army and Air Force Exchange [*Military*] ...... HAAFE
Hawaiian Defense Area ...... HADA
Hawaiian Department [*Army*] [*World War II*] ...... HD
Hawaiian Development Irradiator [*AEC*] ...... HDI
Hawaiian Electric Co., Inc. [*NYSE symbol*] ...... HE
Hawaiian Environmental Analysis and Prediction System ...... HEAPS
Hawaiian Forester and Agriculturist [*A publication*] ...... Hawaiian For
Hawaiian Freight Tariff Bureau Inc., Maywood CA [*STAC*] ...... HIB
Hawaiian Historical Society, Honolulu, HI [*Library symbol*] ...... HHi
Hawaiian Integrated Air Defense System ...... HIADS
Hawaiian Islands ...... HI
Hawaiian Mission Children's Society, Honolulu, HI [*Library symbol*] ...... HHMC
Hawaiian Planters' Record [*A publication*] ...... Hawaii Plant Rec
Hawaiian Planters' Record [*A publication*] ...... Hawaii Plrs' Rec
Hawaiian Sea Frontier ...... HAWSEAFRON
Hawaiian Sea Frontier ...... HSF
Hawaiian Sky Tours [*Honolulu, HI*] [*FAA designator*] ...... VEN
Hawaiian Standard Time ...... HST
Hawaiian Sugar Planters' Association ...... HSPA
Hawaiian Sugar Planters' Association. Experiment Station. Annual Report [*A publication*] ...... Hawaii Sugar Plant Assoc Exp Stn Annu Rep
Hawaiian Sugar Planters' Association, Experiment Station, Honolulu, HI [*Library symbol*] ...... HHS
Hawaiian Telephone Co. [*NYSE symbol*] [*Delisted*] ...... HT
Hawaiian Territory [*Prior to statehood*] ...... HT
Hawaiian Theater [*Military*] ...... HT
Hawaiian Time ...... HT
Hawaiian Tracking Station ...... HTS
Hawaiian Volcano Observatory [*A publication*] ...... Hawaiian Vol Obs
Hawaiian Volcano Observatory [*Department of the Interior*] ...... HVO
Hawaiian Volcano Observatory [*Kilauea*] [*Hawaii*] [*Seismograph station code, US Geological Survey*] ...... HVO
Hawarden Public Library, Hawarden, IA [*Library symbol*] ...... IaHaw
Hawesville, KY [*Radio station call letters*] ...... WKCM
HAWK [*Homing All the Way Killer*] **Assembly and Missile Checkout** ...... HAMCO
HAWK [*Homing All the Way Killer*] **European Limited Improvement Program** [*NATO*] ...... HELIP
HAWK [*Homing All the Way Killer*] **Improvement Program** ...... HIP
Hawk Inlet, AK [*Location identifier*] [*FAA*] ...... HWI
HAWK [*Homing All the Way Killer*] **Intensified Management System Europe Program** [*Military*] ...... HIMSEUR
HAWK [*Homing All the Way Killer*] **Logistics Group** ...... HLG
Hawk Migration Association of North America ...... HMANA
Hawk Mountain Sanctuary Association ...... HMSA
Hawker [*Australia*] [*Airport symbol*] ...... HWK
Hawker-Siddeley Aviation Ltd. [*Great Britain*] [*ICAO designator*] ...... HQ
Hawker-Siddeley Dynamics ...... HSD
Hawker-Siddeley Electronics Ltd., Microform Division, Fairfield, V, Australia [*Library symbol*] ...... HsE
Hawker-Siddeley Nuclear Power Co. Ltd. [*British*] ...... HSNP
Hawker Siddeley Technical Review [*A publication*] ...... Hawker Siddeley Tech Rev
Hawkes Hospital of Mount Carmel, Mount Carmel Medical Center Library, Columbus, OH [*OCLC symbol*] ...... HHM
Hawkesbury Diploma in Agriculture [*Australia*] ...... HDA
Hawkesbury, ON [*Radio station call letters*] ...... CHPR
Hawkesbury Public Library, Hawkesbury, ON, Canada [*Library symbol*] ...... CaOHk
Hawkeye Bancorp [*NASDAQ symbol*] ...... HWKB
Hawkeye Institute of Technology, Area VII, Waterloo, IA [*Library symbol*] ...... IaWH
Hawkeye Public Library, Hawkeye, IA [*Library symbol*] ...... IaHweye
Hawkfarm One Design Association ...... HODA
Hawkins Chemical [*NASDAQ symbol*] ...... HWKN
Hawkinsville, GA [*Radio station call letters*] ...... WCEH
Hawkinsville, GA [*Radio station call letters*] ...... WCEH-FM
Hawser Laid ...... HL
Hawthorne [*Nevada*] [*Airport symbol*] [*Obsolete*] ...... HTH
Hawthorne Army Ammunition Plant ...... HWAAP
Hawthorne, CA [*Location identifier*] [*FAA*] ...... HHR
Hawthorne Financial Corp. [*NASDAQ symbol*] ...... HTHR
Hawthorne Press, Inc., Hawthorne, NJ [*Library symbol*] ...... NjHawP
Hawthorne Society Newsletter [*A publication*] ...... HSN
Haxtun Public Library, Haxtun, CO [*Library symbol*] ...... CoHa
Hay [*Australia*] [*Airport symbol*] ...... HXX
Hay Fever [*Medicine*] ...... HF
Hay Fever Prevention Society ...... HFPS
Hay River [*Canada*] [*Airport symbol*] ...... YHY
Hay River, NT [*Radio station call letters*] ...... CKHR-FM
Hayden Analysis and Reporting Tool [*Data processing*] ...... HART
Hayden, CO [*Location identifier*] [*FAA*] ...... HDN
Hayden, CO [*Radio station call letters*] ...... KRDZ
Hayden Public Library, Hayden, AZ [*Library symbol*] ...... AzHA
Hayden Public Library, Hayden, CO [*Library symbol*] ...... CoHay
Hayden's Viburnum Compound [*Medicine*] ...... HVC
Hayes-Albion Corp. [*NYSE symbol*] ...... HAY
Hayes Center, NE [*Location identifier*] [*FAA*] ...... HCT
Hayes Center, NE [*Television station call letters*] ...... KWNB-TV
Hayfield [*California*] [*Seismograph station code, US Geological Survey*] ...... HAY
Hayfields [*Papua New Guinea*] [*Airport symbol*] ...... HYF
Haygazean Hayagitagan Handes [*A publication*] ...... Haygaz Hayag Handes
Hayl Kashish [*Elderly Army*] [*Israel*] ...... HAKASH
Hayman Island [*Australia*] [*Airport symbol*] ...... HIS
Hayner Public Library, Alton, IL [*Library symbol*] ...... IAI
Haynes-Apperson Owners Club ...... HAOC
Haynesville, LA [*Radio station call letters*] ...... KLUV
Haynesville, LA [*Radio station call letters*] ...... KLUV-FM
Hays [*Kansas*] [*Airport symbol*] ...... HYS
Hays, KS [*Radio station call letters*] ...... KAYS
Hays, KS [*Television station call letters*] ...... KAYS-TV
Hays, KS [*Radio station call letters*] ...... KJLS
Hays, NE [*Television station call letters*] ...... KOOD
Haystack [*Washington*] [*Seismograph station code, US Geological Survey*] ...... HTW
Hayward [*Wisconsin*] [*Airport symbol*] ...... HYR
Hayward, CA [*Location identifier*] [*FAA*] ...... HWD
Hayward, CA [*Radio station call letters*] ...... KIQI
Hayward Map, CA [*Location identifier*] [*FAA*] ...... MBU
Hayward Public Library, Hayward, CA [*Library symbol*] ...... CH
Hayward, WI [*Location identifier*] [*FAA*] ...... SLY
Hayward, WI [*Radio station call letters*] ...... WHSM
Hayward, WI [*Radio station call letters*] ...... WHSM-FM
Hayward, WI [*Radio station call letters*] ...... WRLS
Haywood County Public Library, Canton Branch, Canton, NC [*Library symbol*] ...... NcWayH-C
Haywood County Public Library, Waynesville, NC [*Library symbol*] ...... NcWayH
Haywood Technical Institute, Clyde, NC [*Library symbol*] ...... NcClH
Hazard Analysis ...... HA

Hazard Analysis Critical Control Point [*Quality control*] ...... HACCP
Hazard Beacon .... HBN
Hazard Evaluation Division [*Environmental Protection Agency*] ...... HED
Hazard Function .... HF
Hazard, KY [*Television station call letters*] ...... WKHA
Hazard, KY [*Radio station call letters*] ...... WKIC
Hazard, KY [*Television station call letters*] ...... WKYH-TV
Hazard, KY [*Radio station call letters*] ...... WSGS
Hazard Reduction Precedence Sequence ...... HRPS
Hazard Warning Network ...... HWN
Hazardous [*Task classification*] [*NASA*] ...... (H)
Hazardous .... HAZ
Hazardous Air Traffic Report ...... HATR
Hazardous Area .... HA
Hazardous Cargo [*Shipping*] ...... H
Hazardous Cargo Bulletin [*A publication*] ...... Hazard Cargo Bull
Hazardous Chemical .... HAZCHEM
Hazardous Condition .... HAZCON
Hazardous Duty Incentive Pay [*Air Force*] ...... HDIP
Hazardous Exposure Reduction and Safety Criteria Plan [*NASA*] ...... HERSCP
Hazardous Gas Detection Systems .... HGDS
Hazardous Materials Advisory Council ...... HMAC
Hazardous Materials Information System ...... HMIS
Hazardous Materials Transportation Act [*1975*] ...... HMTA
Hazardous and Trace Emissions System [*Environmental Protection Agency*] ...... HATREMS
Hazardous Waste Disposal Management System [*Environmental Protection Agency*] ...... HWDMS
Hazardous Waste Management .... HWM
Hazardous Waste Services Association ...... HWSA
Hazardous Waste Treatment Council ...... HWTC
Hazards Analysis Board [*Air Force*] ...... HAB
Hazards of Electromagnetic Radiation to Ordnance ...... HERO
Hazards Monitoring System [*NASA*] ...... HMS
Haze [*Weather reports*] ...... H
Haze Filter [*Photography*] ...... HF
Haze Layer Aloft [*Aviation*] ...... HLYR
Haze Layer Estimated_____ Feet Deep [*Aviation*] ...... HDEP
Hazelden Foundation .... HF
Hazelhurst, GA [*Radio station call letters*] ...... WVOH-FM
Hazeltine Corp. [*NYSE symbol*] ...... HZ
Hazeltine Corp., Greenlawn, NY [*Library symbol*] ...... NGIH
Hazelton, PA [*Radio station call letters*] ...... WAZL
Hazelton, PA [*Television station call letters*] ...... WERF
Hazelton, PA [*Radio station call letters*] ...... WVCD
Hazelton Public Library, Hazelton, PA [*Library symbol*] ...... PHa
Hazen, NV [*Location identifier*] [*FAA*] ...... HZN
Hazlehurst, GA [*Radio station call letters*] ...... WVOH
Hazlehurst, MS [*Radio station call letters*] ...... WMDC
Hazlehurst, MS [*Radio station call letters*] ...... WMDC-FM
Hazlet, NJ [*Radio station call letters*] ...... WVRM
Hazleton [*Pennsylvania*] [*Airport symbol*] [*Obsolete*] ...... HZL
Hazleton Laboratories Corporation [*NYSE symbol*] ...... HLC
Hazleton, PA [*Location identifier*] [*FAA*] ...... HXM
HBO & Company [*NASDAQ symbol*] ...... HBOC
HCA Industries, Inc. [*NYSE symbol*] [*Delisted*] ...... HCA
HCC Industries [*NASDAQ symbol*] ...... HCCI
HCW Oil & Gas [*NASDAQ symbol*] ...... HCWO
Head [*Horse racing*] ...... H
Head .... HD
Head of Aircraft Department (Naval) [*British*] ...... HAD(N)
Head of Bed [*Medicine*] ...... HOB
Head Circumference [*Medicine*] ...... HC
Head to Come [*Publishing*] ...... HTC
Head Compartment Support Structure [*Nuclear energy*] ...... HCSS
Head of Contracting Activity [*Military*] ...... HCA
Head and Cover .... H & C
Head of Defence Sales [*British*] ...... HDS
Head of Department .... HOD
Head Diameter .... HD
Head-Down Display [*Aviation*] ...... HDD
Head, Ears, Eyes, Nose, Throat ...... HEENT
Head End Steering .... HES
Head End Treatment Plant [*Nuclear energy*] [*British*] ...... HETP
Head, Hand, and Chest Sets [*JETDS nomenclature*] [*Military*] ...... H
Head-to-Head [*Polymer structure*] ...... HH
Head, Heart, Hands, and Health [*as in 4H organizations*] 4H
Head, Heart, Hands, and Health [*As in 4H organizations*] ...... HHHH
Head of Household [*IRS*] ...... HOH
Head of Household Program [*IRS*] ...... HHP
Head to Kum [*Come*] [*Publishing*] ...... HTK
Head Linesman [*Football*] ...... HL
Head Motion [*Gravity*] ...... HM
Head, Neck, and Shaft [*of a bone*] [*Osteology*] ...... HNS
Head and Neck Surgery [*A publication*] ...... Head Nec Surg
Head Nigger in Charge [*Slang*] ...... HNIC
Head Nurse .... HN
Head, Nut, and Washer [*Construction*] ...... HNW
Head Office .... HO
Head Positioning Mechanism ...... HPM

Head Post Assembly .... HPA
Head Post Office .... HPO
Head of a Procuring Activity [*Army*] ...... HPA
Head Rotated Left [*Medicine*] ...... HRL
Head Rotated Right [*Medicine*] ...... HRR
Head Schoolmaster [*Navy*] [*British*] ...... HdSchm
Head and Shoulders [*Photography*] ...... H & S
Head Sling .... HS
Head Small Veins [*Anatomy*] ...... HSV
Head Suppression .... HS
Head Suppression Valve ...... HSV
Head-to-Tail [*Polymer structure*] ...... HT
Head Teachers' Review [*A publication*] ...... Head Teachers' R
Head per Track .... HPT
Head of Units Group [*American Library Association*] ...... HUG
Head-Up Display Unit ...... HUDU
Head Width .... HW
Head Width Index .... HWI
Head Wind [*Navigation*] ...... HW
Headache .... HA
Headache .... HDAC
Headache, Insomnia, Depression [*Syndrome*] ...... HID
Headcount .... HC
Headed Type .... HT
Header [*Data processing*] ...... HDR
Heading .... HDG
Heading Alignment Cylinder ...... HAC
Heading Axis Perturbation ...... HAP
Heading per Gyro Compass [*Navigation*] ...... HPGC
Heading Reference System ...... HRS
Heading per Standard Compass [*Navigation*] ...... HPSC
Heading per Steering Compass [*Navigation*] ...... HPSTGC
Headland [*Maps and charts*] ...... Hd
Headless .... HDLS
Headline Series [*A publication*] ...... Headline Ser
Headlining .... HLNG
Headmaster [*or Headmistress*] ...... HM
Headmaster Commander [*Navy*] [*British*] ...... HC
Headmaster-Lieutenant [*Navy*] [*British*] ...... HL
Headmaster Lieutenant-Commander [*Navy*] [*British*] ...... HLC
Headmasters Association ...... HA
Headquarters .... H
Headquarters [*Colorado*] [*Seismograph station code, US Geological Survey*] [*Closed*] ...... HDQ
Headquarters .... HDQR
Headquarters .... HDQRS
Headquarters .... HDQTRS
Headquarters .... HED
Headquarters .... HQ
Headquarters .... HQS
Headquarters .... HQTR
Headquarters Administration Division [*Coast Guard*] ...... HA
Headquarters Administration Office [*British police*] ...... HQ(A)
Headquarters, Air Force ...... HAF
Headquarters, Air Service Command [*Air Force*] ...... HASC
Headquarters, Air Support Command [*NATO*] ...... HQASC
Headquarters, Allied Air Force, Central Europe [*NATO*] ...... HAAFCE
Headquarters, Allied Forces ...... HAF
Headquarters, Allied Forces, Mediterranean ...... HAFMED
Headquarters, Allied Forces, Southern Europe ...... HAFSE
Headquarters, Allied Land Forces, Southeastern Europe ...... HALFSEE
Headquarters Area Command [*Military*] ...... HAC
Headquarters Area Command [*Military*] ...... HACOM
Headquarters, Australian Army Forces, Vietnam ...... HQAAFV
Headquarters Base Area ...... HQBA
Headquarters, Bomber Command [*Later, HQSTC*] [*British*] ...... HQBC
Headquarters British Element Trieste Forces ...... BETFOR
Headquarters Catalog Office ...... HCO
Headquarters, Civil Air Patrol ...... HQ-CAP
Headquarters, Coastal Command [*British*] ...... HQCC
Headquarters Command [*Military*] ...... HC
Headquarters Command [*Military*] ...... HEADCOM
Headquarters Command [*Military*] ...... HEDCOM
Headquarters Command [*Air Force*] ...... HQC
Headquarters Command [*Military*] ...... HQCMD
Headquarters Command [*Military*] ...... HQCOM
Headquarters Command [*Air Force*] ...... HQCOMD
Headquarters Command, United States Air Force ...... HQCOMDUSAF
Headquarters Commandant ...... HQCOMDT
Headquarters Data Manager ...... HQDM
Headquarters Defense Communications Agency, Washington, DC [*OCLC symbol*] ...... DFC
Headquarters, Defense Supply Agency ...... HQ DSA
Headquarters, Defense Traffic Management Service ...... HQDTMS
Headquarters, Department of the Army ...... HDA
Headquarters, Department of the Army ...... HQDA
Headquarters, Department of the Pacific [*Marine Corps*] ...... HQDP
Headquarters, Department of the Pacific [*Marine Corps*] ...... MARPAC
Headquarters, Equipment Authorization Review Center [*Army*] .... HQEARC
Headquarters Field Army ...... HFA
Headquarters, Fighter Command [*NATO*] ...... HQFC

Headquarters and Headquarters Battery [*Army*] ... HHB
Headquarters and Headquarters Company [*Army*] ... HHC
Headquarters and Headquarters Detachment [*Army*] ... HHD
Headquarters and Headquarters Squadron [*Marine Corps*] ... H & HS
Headquarters and Headquarters Troop [*Army*] ... HHT
Headquarters and Installation Support Activity [*Army*] ... HISA
Headquarters Library of the United Nations ... LIB (UN)
Headquarters and Maintenance Squad ... HAMS
Headquarters and Maintenance Squadron [*Marine Corps*] ... H & MS
Headquarters Management Directive [*NASA*] ... HQMD
Headquarters, Marine Corps ... HQMC
Headquarters, Naval Material Command ... HQNAVMATCOM
Headquarters Office Instruction ... HOI
Headquarters Operating Instructions [*Air Force*] ... HOI
Headquarters and Service [*Marine Corps*] ... HQ & SERV
Headquarters and Service [*Battery*] [*Army*] ... H & S
Headquarters and Service Squadron ... HS & SS
Headquarters and Service Troop [*Army*] ... H & STR
Headquarters Signal Officer ... HSO
Headquarters, Signals Command [*British*] ... HQSC
Headquarters Squadron [*Obsolete*] ... HEDRON
Headquarters Squadron ... HQSQ
Headquarters Squadron [*Marine Corps*] ... HQSQN
Headquarters Squadron Fleet Air Wing ... HEDRONFAIRWING
Headquarters Squadron Personnel Group ... HDNPRSGR
Headquarters Staff Instruction ... HSI
Headquarters Staff of the Royal Navy [*British*] ... HQSRN
Headquarters, Strike Command [*Formerly, HQBC*] [*British*] ... HQSTC
Headquarters Support Activity ... HEDSUPPACT
Headquarters Support Activity ... HSA
Headquarters Support Activity - Saigon [*Obsolete*] [*Military*] ... HSAS
Headquarters, Transport Command [*British*] ... HQTC
Headquarters, United States Air Force ... HQ USAF
Headquarters, United States Army Forces, Central Pacific Area ... HUSAFICPA
Headquarters, United States Army Forces, Middle Pacific [*World War II*] ... HUSAFMIDPAC
Heads of Services and Offices [*Red Cross*] ... HS & O
Heads-Up Display [*Aviation*] ... HUD
Heads-Up Display Unit [*Aviation*] ... HDU
Heads-Up Display Weapons Aiming System [*Air Force*] ... HUDWAS
Headseat Interface Unit ... HIU
Headset ... HDST
Headspace [*Above liquids*] ... HS
Headspace Sampler [*Instrumentation*] ... HS
Headwaiter ... HW
Headwear Institute of America ... HIA
Headwind [*Aviation*] ... HDWND
HEAF Emergency Service Tanks ... HEST
Healdsburg, CA [*Radio station call letters*] ... KREO
Healdsburg Carnegie Public Library, Healdsburg, CA [*Library symbol*] ... CHe
Health ... HLTH
Health and Accident [*Insurance*] ... H & A
Health Activation Network [*Later, WHAN*] ... HAN
Health Alliance Plan ... HAP
Health Aspects of Pesticides ... HAPS
Health Aspects of Pesticides Abstract Bulletin [*Environmental Protection Agency*] ... HAPAB
Health Associated Representatives ... HEAR
Health and Beauty Aid [*Retailing*] ... HBA
Health and Beauty Aids ... HABA
Health Board [*Ireland*] ... HB
Health Bulletin (Edinburgh) [*A publication*] ... Health Bull (Edinb)
Health Care in Canada [*A publication*] ... Health Care Can
Health Care Dimensions [*A publication*] ... Health Care Dimen
Health Care Education [*A publication*] ... Health Care Educ
Health Care Exhibitors Association ... HCEA
Health Care Financing Administration [*HEW*] ... HCFA
Health Care Financing Review [*A publication*] ... Health Care Financ Rev
Health Care Financing Study Group ... HCFSG
Health Care Fund SBI [*NASDAQ symbol*] ... HCFDS
Health Care Insurance Commission, Edmonton, AB, Canada [*Library symbol*] ... CaAEHCI
Health Care Literature Information Network [*West Germany*] [*Information service*] ... HECLINET
Health Care Management Review [*A publication*] ... HCMR
Health Care Management Review [*A publication*] ... Health Care Manage Rev
Health Care Material Management Society ... HCMMS
Health Care Newsletter [*A publication*] ... Health Care Newsl
Health Care Planning and Marketing [*A publication*] ... Health Care Plann Market
Health Care Research Division [*Brooke Army Medical Center*] ... HCRD
Health Care Research and Educational Foundation [*Later, AAMAREF*] ... HCREF
Health Care & Retirement [*NASDAQ symbol*] ... HCRX
Health Care Services Group [*NASDAQ symbol*] ... HCSG
Health Care Studies Division [*Academy of Health Sciences*] [*Army*] ... HCSD
Health Care Support [*System*] [*IBM Corp.*] ... HCS
Health Care Systems [*A publication*] ... Health Care Syst
Health Care Technology Study Section [*HEW*] ... HCTSS
Health Care Week [*A publication*] ... Health Care Wk
Health-Chem Corp. [*American Stock Exchange symbol*] ... HCH
Health Conference for Business and Industry [*Defunct*] ... HCBI
Health Education Assistance Loan ... HEAL
Health Education Bulletin [*A publication*] ... Health Educ Bull
Health Education Foundation ... HEF
Health Education Journal [*A publication*] ... Health Ed J
Health Education Journal [*A publication*] ... Health Educ
Health Education Journal [*A publication*] ... Health Educ J
Health Education Library Program [*Library network*] ... HELP
Health Education Media Association ... HEMA
Health Education Monographs [*A publication*] ... Heal Ed Mon
Health Education Monographs [*A publication*] ... Health Educ Monogr
Health-Education Telecommunications [*HEW*] ... HET
Health Effects of Environmental Pollutants [*A publication*] ... HEEP
Health Effects Research Laboratory [*Environmental Protection Agency*] ... HERL
Health Emergency & Dispensary, Inc. [*New Orleans clinic*] ... HEAD
Health and Energy Learning Project ... HELP
Health and Environment ... HEV
Health and Environmental Risk Analysis Program [*Department of Energy*] ... HERAP
Health and Environmental Studies Program [*Department of Energy*] ... HESP
Health Evaluation and Learning Program ... HELP
Health Evaluation and Referral Service ... HERS
Health Evaluation and Risk Tabulation ... HEART
Health Extension Services, Inc. [*American Stock Exchange symbol*] ... HLP
Health Facilities Planning and Construction Service ... HFPCS
Health Indication Test [*Engine system*] ... HIT
Health Industries Association [*Later, HIMA*] ... HIA
Health Industries Institute ... HII
Health Industry Manufacturers Association ... HIMA
Health Information Foundation ... HIF
Health Information Libraries of Westchester [*Library network*] ... HILOW
Health Information Library Network of Northeastern Pennsylvania [*Library network*] ... HILNNEP
Health Information Library Program [*Library network*] ... HILP
Health Information Series [*Federal government*] ... HIS
Health Information Systems [*NASDAQ symbol*] ... HISI
Health Insurance ... HI
Health Insurance Association of America ... HIAA
Health Insurance Benefits Advisory Council ... HIBAC
Health Insurance Council [*Later, Consumer and Professional Relations Division of HIAA*] ... HIC
Health Insurance Institute ... HII
Health Insurance Manual ... HIM
Health Insurance Persistency Award [*Later, HIQA*] [*LIMRA*] ... HIPA
Health Insurance Plan ... HIP
Health Insurance Quality Award [*Formerly, HIPA*] [*LIMRA*] ... HIQA
Health Interview Survey [*National Institutes of Health*] ... HIS
Health Laboratory Science [*A publication*] ... Health Lab
Health Laboratory Science [*A publication*] ... Health Lab Sci
Health Learning Systems ... HLS
Health Maintenance Organization ... HMO
Health Maintenance Organization Service [*Public Health Service*] ... HMOS
Health Manpower Advisory Council ... HMAC
Health Manpower Education Initiative Award ... HMEIA
Health Manpower Literature [*A publication*] ... Health Manpow Lit
Health Manpower Report [*Later, Health Planning and Manpower Report*] [*A publication*] ... Health Manpow Rep
Health Manpower Shortage Area ... HMSA
Health Media Education [*An association*] ... HME
Health and Medical Care Services Review [*A publication*] ... Health Med Care Serv Rev
Health Mobilization Series ... HMS
Health-Mor, Incorporated [*American Stock Exchange symbol*] ... HMI
Health of Munition Workers Committee [*British*] [*World War I*] ... HMWC
Health News Institute [*Defunct*] ... HNI
Health and Nutrition Examination Survey [*Public Health Service*] ... HANES
Health Occupations Students of America ... HOSA
Health Opportunity for People Everywhere [*Philanthropic project operating hospital ship*] ... HOPE
Health Organization to Preserve the Environment ... HOPE
Health-Oriented Libraries of San Antonio [*Library network*] ... HOLSA
Health-Oriented Physician Education ... HOPE
Health Perspectives [*Later, Consumer Health Perspectives*] [*A publication*] ... Health Perspect
Health Perspectives and Issues [*A publication*] ... Health Perspect Issues
Health, Physical Education, and Recreation ... HPER
Health Physics [*A publication*] ... Health Phys
Health Physics Research Reactor [*ORNL*] ... HPRR
Health Physics Society ... HPS
Health Physics (Tokyo) [*A publication*] ... Health Phys (Tokyo)
Health Planning and Manpower Report [*A publication*] ... Health Plann Manpow Rep
Health Policy Advisory Center ... HPAC
Health Policy Council ... HPC
Health Policy and Education [*A publication*] ... Health Policy Educ
Health Practitioner. Physician Assistant [*A publication*] ... Health Pract Physician Assist

Health Professions Scholarship Program [Army]................HPSP
Health Professions Student Loans.................................HPSL
Health Programs Systems Center..................................HPSC
Health Promotion and Disease Prevention Initiative [Pronounced "hippy dippy"] [Department of Health and Human Services]......HPDPI
Health Record..HELREC
Health Record..HREC
Health and Rehabilitative Library Services Division [Later, ASCLA] [American Library Association].........................HRLSD
Health Research Group..HRG
Health Resources Administration [Abolished, 1982, functions transferred to Health Resources and Services Administration] [HEW].......HRA
Health Resources and Services Administration [Department of Health and Human Services]..HRSA
Health and Safety Bulletin [A publication].........Health Saf Bull
Health and Safety Commission [Department of Employment] [British]..........HSC
Health and Safety Executive [Department of Employment] [British]........HSE
Health and Safety Laboratory [Nuclear energy]....................HASL
Health and Safety Research and Test Center [Bureau of Mines]....HSRTC
Health and Safety at Work [A publication]..........Health Saf Work
Health Science Centre, Children's Centre, Winnipeg, MB, Canada [Library symbol]...CaMWCCH
Health Science Libraries of Central Georgia [Library network]....HSLCG
Health Science Libraries Information Cooperative [Library network].........HSLIC
Health Sciences Advancement Award [National Institutes of Health].......HSAA
Health Sciences Centre, General Centre, Winnipeg, MB, Canada [Library symbol].......................................CaMWGCH
Health Sciences Communications Association......................HESCA
Health Sciences Computing Facility [UCLA]........................HSCF
Health Sciences Consortium..HSC
Health Sciences Library [Library network]......................MOHSLG
Health Security Action Council....................................HSAC
Health Service Action [Later, CNHS] [An association]..............HSA
Health Service Area [Military]....................................HSA
Health Service Laboratory [Army]..................................HSL
Health Service Region [Army]......................................HSR
Health Service Reports [A publication]...............Health Serv Rep
Health Services Administration [Abolished, 1982, functions transferred to Health Resources and Services Administration]....HSA
Health Services Administration. Publications [A publication].....HSA
Health Services Command [Army]....................................HSC
Health Services Manager [A publication]..........Health Serv Manager
Health Services Manpower Review [A publication]......Health Serv Manpow Rev
Health Services and Mental Health Administration [Later, ADAMHA] [Abolished, 1973] [HEW]........................HSM
Health Services and Mental Health Administration [Later, ADAMHA] [Abolished, 1973] [HEW]........................HSMHA
Health Services and Mental Health Administration. Publications [A publication].........HSM
Health Services Report [A publication]................Health Serv
Health Services Research [Chicago] [A publication].....Health Serv Res
Health Services Research and Development [Series] [A publication].........HSRD
Health and Social Service Journal [A publication]......Health Social Serv J
Health and Social Service Journal [A publication]......Health Soc Serv J
Health and Social Work [A publication]............Health Soc Work
Health and Social Work [A publication].............Hlth Soc Wrk
Health Standards and Quality Bureau [HEW]........................HSQB
Health Surveillance System [Shell Oil Co.]........................HSS
Health Systems Agency [New York City].............................HSA
Health Systems Agency of Western New York, Inc., Buffalo, NY [Library symbol]..NBuHSA
Health Systems Plan [HEW]...HSP
Health Systems Research Institute................................HSRI
Health-Tex, Inc. [NYSE symbol] [Delisted].........................HTX
Health Underserved Rural Areas...................................HURA
Health Visitor [A publication]...................Health Visit
Health Visitor's Certificate [British]...........................HVC
Health and Welfare Canada...HWC
HealthAmerica Corp. [NASDAQ symbol].............................HMOH
Healthdyne Inc. [NASDAQ symbol].................................HDYN
Healthgroup International [NASDAQ symbol].......................HGIS
Healthy America [An association]...................................HA
Healthy-Happy-Holy Organization...................................3HO
Hear..HR
Hear What I Mean [Speech recognition system]....................HWIM
Heard Island [Heard Island] [Seismograph station code, US Geological Survey] [Closed]...HII
Heard Island and McDonald Islands [MARC country of publication code] [Library of Congress].............................hm
Heard Island and McDonald Islands [Three-letter standard code]....HMD
Heard Island and McDonald Islands [Two-letter standard code].....HM
Heard and McDonald Islands [MARC geographic area code] [Library of Congress]...i-hm---
Hearing..HRNG
Hearing Aid Amplifier...HAA

Hearing Aid Battery...HAB
Hearing Aid with Compression......................................HAC
Hearing Aid Industry Conference [Later, HIA]......................HAIC
Hearing Aid Journal [A publication]...............Hear Aid J
Hearing Aid Microphone..HAM
Hearing Distance [Medicine].......................................HD
Hearing Dog Program...HDP
Hearing Education through Auditory Research Foundation [Later, HEAR Center]...HEAR
Hearing, Educational Aid and Research Foundation........HEAR-FOUND
Hearing Examiner [Also, ALJ]......................................HE
Hearing-Impaired Mentally Retarded...............................HIMR
Hearing Industries Association....................................HIA
Hearing Instruments [A publication]..................Hear Instrum
Hearing Rehabilitation Quarterly [A publication]....Hear Rehab Quart
Hearing Research [A publication]....................Hear Res
Hearing-for-Speech Test...HFST
Hearing Threshold Level...HTL
Hearing and Tinnitus Help Association............................HTHA
Hearst Free Library, Lead, SD [Library symbol]....................SdL
Hearst, ON [Television station call letters]...................CBLFT-5
Hearst, ON [Radio station call letters]..........................CFLH
Hearst's Magazine [A publication]................Hearst's M
Heart...HRT
Heart...HT
Heart Block [Medicine]..HB
Heart Bulletin [A publication]...................Heart Bull
Heart Cell Aggregate [Cytology]...................................HCA
Heart-Circulation-Training [Physical fitness].....................HCT
Heart Disease [Medicine]..HD
Heart Disease Research Foundation.................................HDRF
Heart Failure [Medicine]..HF
Heart Information Center..HIC
Heart Infusion Agar [Medicine]....................................HIA
Heart and Lung Foundation [Defunct]...............................HLF
Heart-Lung Resuscitation [Medicine]...............................HLR
Heart and Lungs [Medicine].......................................H & L
Heart Minute Output [Cardiology]..................................HMO
Heart Profile Recorder [Medicine].................................HPR
Heart Rate [Medicine]...HR
Heart Rate Acceleration...HRA
Heart Rate Audiometry...HRA
Heart Rate Range [Medicine].......................................HRR
Heart Sounds [Medicine]...HS
Heart of Texas Council of Governments...........................HOTCOG
Heart Tones [Medicine]..HT
Heart Transplantation...HT
Heart Trouble [Classification system used by doctors on Ellis Island to detain, re-examine, and possibly deny entry to certain immigrants]...H
Heart Valve Prostheses [Medicine].................................HVP
Hearth Electric Furnace...HEF
Heartless Old Man [Alternative sobriquet for William Gladstone, 1809-98, British statesman and prime minister, who was known to admirers as GOM, which see].......................HOM
Heat [or Heater]..H
Heat..HT
Heat [or q] [Symbol] [IUPAC]......................................Q
Heat-Actuated Device..HAD
Heat-Affected Zone..HAZ
Heat-Aggregated Gamma Globulin [Clinical chemistry]..............HAGG
Heat Capacity [Symbol] [IUPAC]....................................C
Heat Capacity Map Mission [NASA].................................HCMM
Heat Capacity Mapping Radiometer [NASA]..........................HCMR
Heat of Combustion..HOC
Heat Control Filter...HCF
Heat-Curing Epoxy Film..HEF
Heat Deflection Temperature [of plastics].........................HDT
Heat of Detonation..HOD
Heat Distortion Temperature.......................................HDT
Heat Engine...HE
Heat Engineering [A publication].................Heat Eng
Heat Escape Lessening Posture [First aid technique]..............HELP
Heat Exchange Institute...HEI
Heat Exchanger..HE
Heat Exchanger..HEX
Heat Exchanger..HTEXCH
Heat Exchanger...HTXGR
Heat Exchanger..HX
Heat Exchanger Method...HEM
Heat Flow [Physiology]..HF
Heat Flow and Convection..HFC
Heat-Flow Electronics...HFE
Heat-Flow Experiment..HFE
Heat-Flow Unit..HFU
Heat Flux Sensing Unit..HFSU
Heat Flux Sensor..HFS
Heat of Formation...HOF
Heat Generator Assembly...HGA
Heat-Inactivated Fetal Bovine Serum [Immunology].................HIFBS
Heat Index..HI

Heat Jacketed Proportioning Pump ... HJPP
Heat Jacketed Pump ... HJP
Heat-Labile Citrororum Factor [*Biochemistry*] ... HLCF
Heat-Labile Factor ... HLF
Heat Limiter Control Switch ... HLCS
Heat, Massage, Exercise [*Medicine*] ... HME
Heat, Massage, Exercise [*Medicine*] ... HMX
Heat Pipe Reactor ... HPR
Heat Protection System ... HPS
Heat Rate Variability ... HRV
Heat Recovery/Seed Recovery [*System*] ... HRSR
Heat Rejection Loop ... HRL
Heat Rejection Radiator ... HRR
Heat Rejection System ... HRS
Heat-Resistant Phenolic ... HRP
Heat Resisting [*Technical drawings*] ... HR
Heat-Resisting Plastic ... HRP
Heat Shield [*Aerospace*] ... HS
Heat Shield ... HTSHLD
Heat-Shield Boost [*Aerospace*] ... HSB
Heat-Shield Qualification [*NASA*] ... HSQ
Heat Shrinkable Tubing ... HST
Heat Sink Kit ... HSK
Heat of Solution ... HOS
Heat-Stable Fraction ... HSF
Heat Sterilizable Potting Compound ... HSPC
Heat Sterilization Compound ... HSC
Heat Sterilization Test Program ... HSTP
Heat Stress Index ... HSI
Heat Technology [*A publication*] ... Heat Technol
Heat Transfer ... HT
Heat Transfer Fluid ... HTF
Heat-Transfer and Fluid-Flow Service [*British*] ... HTFFS
Heat Transfer and Fluid Mechanics Institute ... HTFMI
Heat Transfer Instrument System ... HTIS
Heat Transfer. Japanese Research [*A publication*] ... Heat Transfer Jap Res
Heat Transfer. Japanese Research [*A publication*] ... Heat Transfer Jpn Res
Heat Transfer Laboratory [*MIT*] ... HTL
Heat Transfer Loop ... HTL
Heat Transfer Meter ... HTM
Heat Transfer Module [*Furnace*] ... HTM
Heat Transfer Reactor Experiment ... HTRE
Heat Transfer Research Institute ... HTRI
Heat Transfer Rotating Disc [*Engineering*] ... HTRD
Heat Transfer Section ... HTS
Heat Transfer. Soviet Research [*A publication*] ... Heat Transfer Sov Res
Heat Transfer System ... HTS
Heat Transfer Unit ... HTU
Heat Transport Section [*Apollo*] [*NASA*] ... HTS
Heat Transport System [*NASA*] ... HTS
Heat Treat ... HT
Heat Treat ... HTTR
Heat Treat Block ... HTB
Heat Treat Fixture ... HTF
Heat Treat Fixture ... HTFX
Heat-Treated Steel ... HTS
Heat Treating [*A publication*] ... Heat Treat
Heat Treatment of Metals [*A publication*] ... Heat Treat Met
Heat of Vaporization ... HOV
Heated ... HTD
Heated Experimental Carbon Thermal Oscillator Reactor [*British*] ... HECTOR
Heated Window Control Unit ... HWCU
Heater ... HTR
Heater Amplifier Assembly ... HAA
Heater Center Top ... HCT
Heater Cord ... HC
Heater Kit ... HK
Heath Educational Robot [*Heath Co.*] ... HERO
Heath, OH [*Radio station call letters*] ... WHTH
Heath Tecna Corporation [*NYSE symbol*] [*Delisted*] ... HTC
Heather Society ... HS
Heathlands [*Australia*] [*Airport symbol*] [*Obsolete*] ... HAT
Heating ... HTG
Heating and Air Conditioning Contractor [*A publication*] ... Heat Air Cond Contr
Heating and Air Conditioning Journal [*A publication*] ... Heat Air Condit J
Heating and Air Conditioning Journal [*A publication*] ... Heat Air Cond J
Heating Cabinet ... HC
Heating Coil ... HC
Heating, Piping, and Air Conditioning [*A publication*] ... Heating Piping
Heating, Piping, and Air Conditioning [*A publication*] ... Heat Piping Air Cond
Heating Plant ... HP
Heating Scow [*Navy symbol*] ... YHT
Heating Surface ... HS
Heating System ... HS
Heating and Ventilating [*A publication*] ... Heat & Vent
Heating, Ventilating, and Air Conditioning ... HVAC
Heating, Ventilating, and Cooling ... HV & C
Heating and Ventilating Engineer [*A publication*] ... Heat Vent Eng
Heating and Ventilating Engineer [*A publication*] ... Heat Vent Engr
Heating and Ventilating Engineer and Journal of Air Conditioning [*A publication*] ... Heat Vent Eng J Air Cond
Heating and Ventilating Research Association [*British*] ... HVRA
Heating and Ventilating Review [*A publication*] ... Heat Vent Rev
Heating and Ventilation ... HV
Heating and Ventilation ... H and V
Heating Ventilation Unit ... HVU
Heavier than Air [*Aircraft*] ... HTA
Heavier-than-Air Fighter/Attack/Experimental [*Aircraft*] ... VFAX
Heaviest Heavy Lift Helicopter ... HHLH
Heavily Armed Vessels ... HAV
Heaviside [*Ionosphere*] ... HS
Heaviside-Campbell Bridge [*Electronics*] ... HCB
Heavy ... H
Heavy ... HV
Heavy ... HVY
Heavy ... HY
Heavy [*Used to qualify interference or static reports*] [*Communications*] ... VIO
Heavy [*Used to qualify weather phenomena such as rain, e.g., heavy rain equals XXRA*] [*Aviation code*] ... XX
Heavy [*Chain*] [*Biochemistry, immunochemistry*] ... H
Heavy [*Track condition*] [*Thoroughbred racing*] ... HY
Heavy-Aggregate Concrete ... HAC
Heavy Air Training Unit ... HATU
Heavy Airborne Multipurpose System ... HAMPS
Heavy Aircraft Fuel ... HAF
Heavy Antiaircraft Artillery ... HAA
Heavy Antiarmor Weapon ... HAW
Heavy Antitank/Assault Weapon [*Army*] ... HAAW
Heavy Antitank Convoy ... HAC
Heavy Artillery ... HA
Heavy Assault Weapon ... HAW
Heavy Atom Method ... HAM
Heavy Atomic Demolition Munition [*Military*] ... HADM
Heavy Attack Aircraft Commander ... HAC
Heavy Attack Aircraft, Experimental ... VAX
Heavy Attack Squadron ... HATRON
Heavy Attack Squadron [*Symbol*] ... VAH
Heavy Attack Training Unit ... HATU
Heavy Attack Wing ... HATWING
Heavy Attack Wing, Atlantic Fleet ... HATWINGLANT
Heavy Attack Wing, Pacific Fleet ... HATWINGPAC
Heavy Automotive Maintenance ... HAM
Heavy Ballistic Missile ... HBM
Heavy Barrel [*In reference to a rifle*] ... HB
Heavy Bombardment [*or Bomber*] ... HB
Heavy Bomber Support ... HBS
Heavy Chain Disease [*Protein*] ... HCD
Heavy Construction Contractors Association ... HCCA
Heavy Cruiser, Guided Missile [*Navy symbol*] ... CAC
Heavy Drop [*Military*] ... HVDP
Heavy-Duty ... HD
Heavy-Duty ... HDY
Heavy-Duty Air Cylinder ... HDAC
Heavy-Duty Amplifier ... HDA
Heavy-Duty Automatic Press ... HDAP
Heavy Duty Business Forum ... HDBF
Heavy-Duty Contractor ... HDC
Heavy-Duty Detergent ... HDD
Heavy-Duty Diesel [*Vehicle*] ... HDD
Heavy-Duty Diesel Vehicle ... HDDV
Heavy-Duty Enzyme Detergent ... HDED
Heavy-Duty Gasoline [*Vehicle*] ... HDG
Heavy-Duty Industrial Filter ... HDIF
Heavy-Duty Industrial Relay ... HDIR
Heavy Duty Representatives Association ... HDRA
Heavy-Duty Truck Manufacturers Association ... HDTMA
Heavy Element and Radioactive Material Electromagnetic Separator [*British*] ... HERMES
Heavy Enamel ... HE
Heavy Enamel Bonded Cotton [*Wire insulation*] ... HEBC
Heavy Enamel Bonded Double Cotton [*Wire insulation*] ... HEBDC
Heavy Enamel Bonded Double Paper [*Wire insulation*] ... HEBDP
Heavy Enamel Bonded Double Silk [*Wire insulation*] ... HEBDS
Heavy Enamel Bonded Paper [*Wire insulation*] ... HEBP
Heavy Enamel Bonded Silk [*Wire insulation*] ... HEBS
Heavy Enamel Cotton Varnish [*Wire insulation*] ... HECV
Heavy Enamel Double Cotton [*Wire insulation*] ... HEDC
Heavy Enamel Double Cotton Varnish [*Wire insulation*] ... HEDCV
Heavy Enamel Double Silk [*Wire insulation*] ... HEDS
Heavy Enamel Double Silk Varnish [*Wire insulation*] ... HEDSV
Heavy Enamel Single Cellophane [*Wire insulation*] ... HEK
Heavy Enamel Single Cotton [*Wire insulation*] ... HEC
Heavy Enamel Single Glass [*Wire insulation*] ... HEG
Heavy Enamel Single Silk [*Wire insulation*] ... HES
Heavy Enamel Single Silk Varnish [*Wire insulation*] ... HESV
Heavy End Aviation Fuel ... HEAF
Heavy Equipment ... HE
Heavy Equipment Test Chamber ... HETC

Heavy Equipment Transporter ....HET
Heavy Expanded Mobility Tactical Truck [Army] .... HEMTT
Heavy Field Artillery ....HFA
Heavy Fire Team [Military] ....HFT
Heavy Flushing Spray ....HFS
Heavy Free Gas ....HFG
Heavy Fuel Oil ....HFO
Heavy Gauge Screwed Welded [Conduit] .... HGSW
Heavy Gauge Solid Drawn [Conduit] ....HGSD
Heavy Goods Vehicles ....HGV
Heavy Handy Deadweight [Scrap] [Shipping] ....HHDW
Heavy Hinged [Philately] ....HH
Heavy-Hull Repair Ship [Navy symbol] ....ARH
Heavy Hydrogen ....HH
Heavy Interdiction Missile ....HIM
Heavy Interdiction Missile System ....HIMS
Heavy-Ion Linear Accelerator [Nuclear energy] ....HILAC
Heavy-Ion Source ....HIS
Heavy Lift ....HL
Heavy Lift Airship ....HLA
Heavy-Lift Helicopter ....HLH
Heavy-Lift Helicopter Advanced Technology Component
  [Program] [Army] ....HLC-ATC
Heavy-Lift Helicopter System ....HLHS
Heavy-Lift Launch Vehicle ....HLLV
Heavy Lift Pontoon ....HLP
Heavy Lift System ....HLS
Heavy Logistics System ....HLS
Heavy Machine Gun ....HMG
Heavy Machinery Repair Ship [Navy symbol] ....ARM
Heavy Maintenance [Ordnance] ....HM
Heavy Meromyosin [Biochemistry] ....HMM
Heavy Military Electronic Equipment Division [General Electric
  Co.] ....HMEED
Heavy Mobile ....HM
Heavy Observation Aircraft ....HOA
Heavy Oil Cracking [Process] [Petroleum industry] ....HOC
Heavy Oil Engine Tractor [British] ....HOET
Heavy Operational Repair Squadron Engineer [Air Force] .... HORSE
Heavy Ordnance Gunship ....HOG
Heavy Photographic Squadron .... HEAVYPHOTORON
Heavy Positive Ion ....HPI
Heavy Primary Nuclei ....HPN
Heavy Replaceable [or Replacement] Assembly ....HRA
Heavy Sea [Navigation] ....H
Heavy SEAL [Sea-Air-Land] Support Craft ....HSSC
Heavy Section Steel Technology [Nuclear Regulatory Commission] ..... HSST
Heavy Specialized Carriers Conference [Later, SC & RA] ....HSCC
Heavy & Specialized Carriers Tariff Bureau .... H & SCTB
Heavy & Specialized Carriers Tariff Bureau, Washington DC [STAC] .... HSC
Heavy Tactical Transport ....HTT
Heavy Tank ....HT
Heavy Wall ....HW
Heavy Water ....HW
Heavy-Water Components Test Reactor .... HWCTR
Heavy-Water Moderated Gas-Cooled Reactor ....HWGCR
Heavy-Water Moderated Organic-Cooled Reactor ....HWOCR
Heavy-Water Plant [Nuclear energy] ....HWP
Heavy-Water Reactor ....HWR
Heavy Weather Patrol Boats ....HWPB
Hebbel-Jahrbuch [A publication] .... Hebbel-Jahrb
Hebbel-Jahrbuch [A publication] ....HJb
Hebdomada [A Week] [Pharmacy] .... HEBDOM
Heber City, UT [Radio station call letters] ....KLVR
Heber Springs, AR [Location identifier] [FAA] ....HBZ
Heber Springs, AR [Radio station call letters] ....KAWW
Heber Springs, AR [Radio station call letters] ....KAWW-FM
Hebrew ....HEB
Hebrew ....HEBR
Hebrew [MARC language code] [Library of Congress] ....heb
Hebrew Actors Union ....HAU
Hebrew Arts Foundation ....HAF
Hebrew Christian Alliance of America [Later, MJAA] ....HCAA
Hebrew Computational Linguistics [A publication] ....HCompL
Hebrew Culture Foundation ....HCF
Hebrew Free Burial Association ....HFBA
Hebrew Immigrant Aid Society ....HIAS
Hebrew Master Bakers Association ....HMBA
Hebrew Medical Journal [A publication] .... Heb Med J
Hebrew Order of David ....HOD
Hebrew Pharmacist [A publication] .... Heb Pharm
Hebrew Religious Protection Association of Greater New York ....HRPA
Hebrew Teachers College [Massachusetts] ....HTC
Hebrew Teachers College, Roxbury, MA [Library symbol] ....MRoxH
Hebrew Theological College, Skokie, IL [Library symbol] ....ISkH
Hebrew Union College [Later, HUC-JIR] ....HUC
Hebrew Union College Annual [A publication] ....HebrUCA
Hebrew Union College. Annual [A publication] ....HUCA
Hebrew Union College - Jewish Institute of Religion [Formerly,
  HUC] ....HUC-JIR

Hebrew Union College, Jewish Institute of Religion, Cincinnati,
  OH [OCLC symbol] ....HUC
Hebrew Union College - Jewish Institute of Religion, Cincinnati,
  OH [Library symbol] ....OCH
Hebrew Union College - Jewish Institute of Religion, Los
  Angeles, CA [Library symbol] ....CLHU
Hebrew Union College - Jewish Institute of Religion, New York,
  NY [Library symbol] ....NNHeb
Hebrew University (Jerusalem) [A publication] .... Hebrew Univ (Jerusalem)
Hebrew University. Studies in Literature [A publication] ....HUSL
Hebrew Veterans of the War with Spain ....HVWS
Hebrew Young Men's Association ....HYMA
Hebrews [New Testament book] ....Heb
Hebron, NE [Location identifier] [FAA] ....HJH
Hebronville, TX [Location identifier] [FAA] ....HBV
Hechalutz Organization of America [Defunct] ....HOA
Hechinger Co. Cl A [NASDAQ symbol] ....HECHA
Hechos y Dichos [A publication] ....HD
Heck's, Inc. [NYSE symbol] ....HEX
Heckscher-Ohlin-Samuelson [Theorem] ....HOS
Hecla Mining Co. [NYSE symbol] ....HL
Hectare ....HA
Hecto [A prefix meaning multiplied by 10²] [SI symbol] ....h
Hectocotylized Arm ....HA
Hectogram ....HECTOG
Hectogram ....HG
Hectograph ....HECTO
Hectoliter ....HECTOL
Hectoliter ....HL
Hectometer [100 meters] ....HECTOM
Hectometer [100 meters] ....HM
Hectometric Emissions [Radio astronomy] ....HOM
Hector, CA [Location identifier] [FAA] ....HEC
Hedeselskabets Tidsskrift [A publication] .... Hedeselsk Tidsskr
HEDL [Hanford Engineering Development Laboratory] Overpower
  [Nuclear energy] ....HOP
HEDL [Hanford Engineering Development Laboratory] Up
  Transient [Nuclear energy] ....HUT
Heel Breaster ....HLBR
Heel to Heel ....H to H
Heel Line ....HL
Heel Sanding ....HLSD
Heeres-Atmer [Service Oxygen Breathing Apparatus] [German
  military - World War II] ....HA
Heeres-Funkstelle [Army Radio Station] [German military - World
  War II] ....HFU
Heeres-Sauerstoffschutzgeraet [Service Oxygen Breathing
  Apparatus] [German military - World War II] ....HSS
Heeres-Sauerstoffschutzgeraet [Service Oxygen Breathing
  Apparatus] [German military - World War II] ....HSSG
Heeresbetriebsstofflager [Army Gasoline-Supply Depot] [German
  military - World War II] ....HBL
Heeresfahrzeug [Army Vehicle] [German military - World War II] ....HF
Heeresmunitionslager [Army Ammunition Depot] [German
  military - World War II] ....HML
Heeresnachrichtenwesen [Army Communications System]
  [German military - World War II] ....HNW
Heeresverpflegungslager [Army Ration Depot] [German military -
  World War II] ....HVL
Heeresverwaltungsamt [Army Administration Office] [German
  military - World War II] ....HVA
Heereswaffenamt [Army Ordnance Office] [German military -
  World War II] ....HWAA
Heerlen [Netherlands] [Seismograph station code, US Geological
  Survey] ....HEE
Hefei [China] [Airport symbol] ....HFE
Heflex Bioengineering Test [NASA] ....HBT
Heft [Part] [German] ....H
Hefte fuer Geschichte, Kunst, und Volkskunde [A publication] ....HGKV
Hefte fuer Literatur und Kritik [A publication] ....HLK
Hefte zur Unfallheilkunde [A publication] .... Hefte Unfallheilkd
Hegel-Jahrbuch [A publication] .... Hegel-Jrbh
Hegel Society of America ....HSA
Hegel-Studien [A publication] .... Hegel-Stud
Heho [Burma] [Airport symbol] ....HEH
HEI Corporation [NASDAQ symbol] ....HEIC
HEI, Incorporated [NASDAQ symbol] ....HEII
Heidelberg [Konigstuhl] [Federal Republic of Germany]
  [Seismograph station code, US Geological Survey] ....HEI
Heidelberg College, Tiffin, OH [OCLC symbol] ....HEI
Heidelberg College, Tiffin, OH [Library symbol] ....OTifH
Heidelberg Science Library [A publication] .... Heidelb Sci Libr
Heidelberger Abhandlungen [A publication] ....HA
Heidelberger Akademie der Wissenschaften. Sitzungsberichte
  [A publication] .... Heid Sitzb
Heidelberger Beitrage zur Mineralogie und Petrographie [A
  publication] .... Heidelberger Beitr Mineralogie u Petrographie
Heidelberger Forschungen [A publication] ....HF
Heidelberger Jahrbuecher [A publication] .... Heidelb Jahrb
Heidelberger Jahrbuecher [A publication] ....HeidJb
Heidelberger Taschenbuecher [A publication] .... Heidelb Taschenb

Heidelburg, MS [*Radio station call letters*] ... WEEZ
Heifer Project International, Inc. ... HPI
Height ... H
Height ... HGT
Height ... HT
Height [*Symbol*] [*IUPAC*] ... h
Height Adjustment Maneuver ... HAM
Height above Airport ... HAA
Height of Apogee ... HA
Height [*Depth*] **of Burst** ... HOB
Height Correction Factor ... HCF
Height Equivalent to a Theoretical Plate ... HETP
Height Equivalent to a Theoretical Stage ... HETS
Height of Eye [*Navigation*] ... HE
Height Finder [*or Finding*] [*RADAR*] ... HF
Height Finder Operator ... HFO
Height Finder RADAR ... HFR
Height of Fundus [*Obstetrics*] ... H of F
Height of Fundus [*Obstetrics*] ... HoF
Height Indicator ... HI
Height Integration Equipment ... HIE
Height above Landing [*Area*] ... HAL
Height-Length ... HL
Height Overlap Coverage [*RADAR*] ... HOC
Height of Perigee ... HP
Height-Position Indicator ... HPI
Height Range [*RADAR*] ... HR
Height-Range Indicator [*Electronics*] ... HRI
Height-Range Indicator Operator [*Electronics*] ... HRIO
Height Ranger Finder ... HRF
Height above Runway Touchdown Zone Elevation [*Aviation*] ... HAT
Height Sensing Device ... HSD
Height above Spherical Earth ... HS
Height Supervisor [*RADAR*] ... HTSUP
Height of Target ... HT
Height Technician [*Air Force*] ... HT
Height Telling [*RADAR*] ... HT
Height-Telling Surveillance ... HTS
Height-to-Time Converter ... HTC
Height Tracking Console ... HTC
Height of a Transfer Unit [*Distillation*] ... HTU
Height-Velocity ... H-V
Height-Velocity Diagram ... HVD
Height by Width by Length ... HXWXL
Heights ... HTS
Heights Finance Corp. [*NASDAQ symbol*] ... HFIN
Heileman [*G.*] **Brewing Co., Inc.** [*NYSE symbol*] ... GHB
Heilig [*Holy, Saint*] [*German*] ... HL
Heilig-Meyers Co. [*NYSE symbol*] ... HMY
Heilpaedagogische Forschung [*A publication*] ... Heilpaed For
Heilpaedagogische Werkblaetter [*A publication*] ... HPWBA
Heilungkiang Province [*China, Mainland*] [*MARC geographic area code*] [*Library of Congress*] ... a-cc-he
Heimatjahrbuch fuer den Kreis Hofgeismar [*A publication*] ... Hj Kreis Hofgeismar
Heimatstimmen aus dem Kreise Olpe [*A publication*] ... Hst Kreise Olpe
Heimlich-Armstrong-Rieveschl-Patrick [*Heart pump for aerospace use*] ... HARP
Hein-Werner Corp. [*American Stock Exchange symbol*] ... HNW
Heine-Jahrbuch [*A publication*] ... HeineJ
Heine-Jahrbuch [*A publication*] ... Heine-Jahrb
Heinemann, A. R., East Saint Louis IL [*STAC*] ... HAR
Heinicke Instruments Co. [*American Stock Exchange symbol*] ... HEI
Heinkel [*German aircraft type*] [*World War II*] ... HE
Heinkel-Messerschmitt-Isetta Club ... HMIC
Heinrich Hertz Institut Geophysical Data [*A publication*] ... HHI Geophys Data
Heinrich Hertz Institut Solar Data [*A publication*] ... HHI Sol Data
Heintz, M. H., Chicago IL [*STAC*] ... HMH
Heinz [*H. J.*] **Co.** [*NYSE symbol*] ... HNZ
Heir ... H
Heir Apparent ... HA
Heir-at-Law ... HL
Heir Presumptive ... HP
Heiseman Memorial Library, West Union, IA [*Library symbol*] ... IaWu
Heisey Collectors of America ... HCA
Heiss Island [*USSR*] [*Geomagnetic observatory code*] ... HIS
Heist [*C. H.*] **Corporation,** [*NASDAQ symbol*] ... CHHC
Heitler-London-Slater-Pauling [*Method*] [*Physics*] ... HLSP
Heitman Mortgage Investors [*American Stock Exchange symbol*] [*Delisted*] ... HTM
Heizer Corp. [*American Stock Exchange symbol*] ... HZR
Heizung, Lueftung, Klimatechnik, Haustechnik [*A publication*] ... H & L & H
Hel [*Poland*] [*Geomagnetic observatory code*] ... HLP
Held [*or Hold*] **in Abeyance** [*Military*] ... HIA
Held for Blueprint ... HBP
Held by Civil Authorities ... HCA
Held Covered ... HC
Held for Detail ... HFD
Held For ... H/F
Held by Manufacturer ... HBM
Held for Manufacturing ... HFM
Held for Material ... HFM
Held for Planning ... HFP
Held for Tooling ... HFT
Heldor Industries, Inc. [*American Stock Exchange symbol*] ... HDR
Heldor Industries, Inc. Wts [*NASDAQ symbol*] ... HLDRW
Helen Dwight Reid Educational Foundation ... HELDREF
Helen Kate Furness Free Library, Wallingford, PA [*Library symbol*] ... PWal
Helen Keller International ... HKI
Helen of Troy Corp. [*NASDAQ symbol*] ... HELE
Helen Thomas [*British author*] ... HT
Helena [*Montana*] [*Airport symbol*] ... HLN
Helena, AR [*Radio station call letters*] ... KFFA
Helena/Fort Harrison, MT [*Location identifier*] [*FAA*] ... ATN
Helena, MT [*Radio station call letters*] ... KBLL
Helena, MT [*Radio station call letters*] ... KBLL-FM
Helena, MT [*Radio station call letters*] ... KCAP
Helena, MT [*Radio station call letters*] ... KCAP-FM
Helena, MT [*Radio station call letters*] ... KHTC
Helena, MT [*Radio station call letters*] ... KMTX
Helena, MT [*Television station call letters*] ... KTVG
Helena Petrovna Blavatsky [*Famous 19th-century occultist*] ... HPB
Helena Public Library, Helena, MT [*Library symbol*] ... MtH
Helena Southwestern Railroad Co. [*AAR code*] ... HSW
Helena Township Public Library, Alden, MI [*Library symbol*] ... MiAld
Helena/West Helena, AR [*Location identifier*] [*FAA*] ... HEE
Helgoland [*West Germany*] [*Airport symbol*] ... HGL
Helgolander Wissenschaftliche Meeresuntersuchungen [*A publication*] ... Helgol Wiss Meeresunters
Helgolander Wissenschaftliche Meeresuntersuchungen [*A publication*] ... Helg W Meer
Heli-Home [*Recreational vehicle*] ... H-H
Heliax Coaxial Cable ... HCC
Heliborne Emitter Location/Countermeasures ... HEMLOC
Heliborne Illumination System ... HIS
Heliborne LASER Fire and Forget [*Missile system*] [*Army*] ... HELLFIRE
Helical ... HLCL
Helical Antenna System ... HAS
Helical Compression ... HLCPS
Helical Extension ... HLEXT
Helical Flight Path ... HFP
Helical Spring Lock Washer Institute ... HSLWI
Helical Washer Institute [*Defunct*] ... HWI
Helicon [*A publication*] ... Hel
Helicopter [*When the second letter or only letter*] [*Designation for all US military aircraft*] ... H
Helicopter ... H/C
Helicopter ... HCPTR
Helicopter ... HEL
Helicopter ... HELI
Helicopter ... HELO
Helicopter ... HLCPTR
Helicopter ... HP
Helicopter Action Group ... HAG
Helicopter Adverse-Weather Target Acquisition and Destruction System ... HAWTADS
Helicopter Aircraft Commander ... HAC
Helicopter Airline Association ... HAA
Helicopter Ambulance Medical Detachment ... HAMD
Helicopter Antisubmarine Squadron [*Navy*] ... HELANTISUBRON
Helicopter Antisubmarine Squadron [*Navy*] ... HELASRON
Helicopter Antisubmarine Squadron Light ... HSL
Helicopter Armored Experiment ... HAX
Helicopter Assault Force ... HAF
Helicopter Assault Wave ... HAW
Helicopter Association of America [*Later, HAI*] ... HAA
Helicopter Association International [*Formerly, HAA*] ... HAI
Helicopter Attack Squadron (Light) ... HA(L)
Helicopter Attack System ... HATS
Helicopter Attack Warning RADAR ... HAWR
Helicopter Attitude Indicator ... HAI
Helicopter Avionics System [*Air Force*] ... HAS
Helicopter Battle Damage Repair ... HBDR
Helicopter Blade Slap ... HBS
Helicopter Club of America ... HCA
Helicopter Collision Avoidance RADAR ... HELCAR
Helicopter Combat ... HC
Helicopter Combat Support Squadron [*Navy*] ... HELSUPPRON
Helicopter Command ... HC
Helicopter Command Instrumentation System ... HELCIS
Helicopter Control Center ... HCC
Helicopter Control Ship [*Navy*] ... HCS
Helicopter Control Unit ... HCU
Helicopter Coordinator (Airborne) ... HC(A)
Helicopter Council ... HC
Helicopter-Delivered Seismic Intrusion Detector ... HELOSID
Helicopter Direction Center ... HDC
Helicopter Electronic Landing Path [*Army*] ... HELP
Helicopter Employment and Assault Landing Table ... HEALT
Helicopter Expendable Bathythermograph [*Naval Oceanographic Office*] ... HXBT

Helicopter Experimental, Medium .... HXM
Helicopter Extended Area Platform .... HEAP
Helicopter Familiarization .... HFAM
Helicopter Gravity-Measuring System [*Naval Oceanographic Office*] .... HGMS
Helicopter In-Flight Monitoring System [*Army*] .... HIMS
Helicopter In-Flight Refueling .... HIFR
Helicopter Insecticide Dispersal Apparatus, Dry .... HIDAD
Helicopter Insecticide Dispersal Apparatus, Fog .... HIDAF
Helicopter Insecticide Dispersal Apparatus, Liquid .... HIDAL
Helicopter Instrument Rules .... HIR
Helicopter Integrated Direction Equipment .... HIDE
Helicopter Landing Exercise [*Amphibious*] [*Navy*] .... HELILEX
Helicopter Landing Zone .... HLZ
Helicopter Landing Zone Locator .... HLZL
Helicopter LASER Range-Finder .... HLR
Helicopter Logistic Support Center .... HLSC
Helicopter Long-Range Active SONAR .... HELRAPS
Helicopter Multifunction System .... HELMS
Helicopter Navigation System .... HELNAVS
Helicopter Night-Landing System .... HENILAS
Helicopter Operations .... HOP
Helicopter Optical Tracking and Control .... HOTAC
Helicopter Outlying Field .... HOLF
Helicopter Performance Computer .... HPC
Helicopter Pilot Control and Training .... HEPCAT
Helicopter Plane Commander .... HPC
Helicopter Position and Terrain Height .... HELIPATH
Helicopter Qualifications [*Navy*] .... HELOQUALS
Helicopter Request [*Military*] .... HR
Helicopter Safety Advisory Conference .... HSAC
Helicopter Sea Control Wing .... HSCW
Helicopter Sensor Development Program .... HESDEP
Helicopter SONAR Data Collection .... HESODAC
Helicopter Squadron, Antisubmarine .... HS
Helicopter Subcontrol Ship [*Navy*] .... HSCS
Helicopter Subcontrol Unit .... HSCU
Helicopter Support Team [*Navy*] .... HST
Helicopter System .... HS
Helicopter Team .... HELITEAM
Helicopter Training .... HELOTNG
Helicopter Training Squadron [*Navy*] .... HELTRARON
Helicopter Training Squadron [*Navy symbol*] .... HT
Helicopter Transportable Launcher .... HTL
Helicopter Utility (Piasecki) .... HUP
Helicopter Utility Squadron .... HUS
Helicopter Utility Squadron .... HUTRON
Helicopter Visual Rules .... HVR
Helicopter Weapons System .... HWS
Helicopter World [*A publication*] .... Helicop Wld
Heligoland [*Federal Republic of Germany*] [*Seismograph station code, US Geological Survey*] .... HLG
Helikopter Service A/S [*Norway*] [*ICAO designator*] .... HK
Heliocentric Orbit Rendezvous .... HOR
Heliogram .... HG
Helionetics, Inc. [*NASDAQ symbol*] .... HILX
Helipotentiometer .... HPOT
Helium [*Chemical symbol is He*] .... H
Helium [*Chemical element*] .... He
Helium Cadmium LASER .... HCL
Helium Charging Unit .... HCU
Helium Check Valve .... HECV
Helium Circulation [*System*] .... HC
Helium Emergency Supply .... HES
Helium Fill to Distribution Unit [*Aerospace*] .... HFD
Helium Fill Line .... HFL
Helium Flow Control Valve .... HFCV
Helium Fuel-Tank Pressurization .... HFP
Helium Gauge .... HEG
Helium Gauge Valve .... HEGV
Helium to Heat Exchanger .... HHE
Helium Latching Solenoid Valve .... HLSV
Helium Leak Detector .... HLD
Helium Level .... HL
Helium Liquid Program [*NASA*] .... HELP
Helium Manual Valve .... HEMV
Helium Neon Gas LASER .... HNGL
Helium Neon LASER .... HNL
Helium Oxidizer-Tank Pressure .... HOP
Helium Pressure Switch .... HPS
Helium Pressure Vessel .... HPV
Helium Rebottled [*System*] .... HR
Helium, Refrigerated .... HR
Helium Research Center .... HRC
Helium Service Unit .... HSU
Helium Underwater Speech Translating Equipment .... HUSTLE
Helium Vent Valve .... HVV
Helix Angle .... HLXA
Helix Countercurrent Chromatography .... HCCC
Helix Technology Corp. [*NASDAQ symbol*] .... HELX
Hellas-Jahrbuch [*A publication*] .... Hel
Hellas-Jahrbuch [*A publication*] .... HellasJB
Hellenic Affiliation Scale [*Psychology*] .... HAS
Hellenic Armed Forces .... HAF
Hellenic College of Arts and Sciences and Holy Cross Greek Orthodox Theological School, Brookline, MA [*Library symbol*] .... MBrHC
Hellenic Philatelic Society of America .... HPSA
Hellenic Veterinary Medicine [*A publication*] .... Hell Vet Med
Hellenika [*Salonika*] [*A publication*] .... Hellen
Hellenika (Salonika) [*A publication*] .... Hellenika (S)
Hellenika Stomatologika Chronika [*A publication*] .... Hell Stomatol Chron
Hellenike Kteniatrike [*A publication*] .... Hell Kteniatr
Hellenike Mikrobiologike kai Hygieinologike Hetaireia Deltion [*A publication*] .... Hell Mikrobiol Hygieinol Hetaireia Delt
Hellenike Trapeza Biomechanikes Anaptyxeos .... ETBA
Hellenis Adelphe [*A publication*] .... Hell Adelphe
Heller [*Walter E.*] **International Corp.** [*NYSE symbol*] [*Delisted*] .... HLR
HELLFIRE Fire and Forget Seeker [*Missile*] .... HFFS
HELLFIRE Modular Missile System .... HMMS
Hellmann-Feynmann Electrostatic Theorem [*Physics*] .... HFET
Helm Resources [*American Stock Exchange symbol*] .... H
Helme [*George W.*] **Co.** [*NYSE symbol*] [*Delisted*] .... GHH
Helme Products, Incorporated [*NYSE symbol*] [*Delisted*] .... HPI
Helmerich & Payne, Inc. [*NYSE symbol*] .... HP
Helmet Initiated Pointing System .... HIPS
Helmet-Mounted Display .... HMD
Helmet-Mounted Optical Projection System .... HOPS
Helmet-Mounted Sight [*Aviation*] .... HMS
Helmet-Position Sensing System .... HELPS
Helmet Shield .... HS
Helmet Sight Subsystem .... HSS
Helmet Stowage Bag [*NASA*] .... HSB
Helmholtz Energy [*Symbol*] [*IUPAC*] .... A
Helmholtz Free Energy .... HFE
Helmholtz Function [*Symbol*] .... F
Helmholtz Reciprocal Theorem [*Physics*] .... HRT
Helminthologia [*A publication*] .... Helminthol
Helminthological Abstracts [*A publication*] .... Helminth Abstr
Helms Athletic Foundation [*Later, Citizens Savings Athletic Foundation*] .... HAF
Helmut Attitude Tracking System .... HATS
Helmville [*Montana*] [*Seismograph station code, US Geological Survey*] [*Closed*] .... HLM
Help Abolish Legal Tyranny [*In organization name HALT-ALR*] .... HALT
Help Addicts Voluntarily End Narcotics .... HAVEN
Help the Aged .... HTA
Help Establish Lasting Peace .... HELP
Help Hospitalized Veterans .... HHV
Help through Industry Retraining and Employment [*Program*] [*Department of Labor*] .... HIRE
Help Obese People Everywhere .... HOPE
Help Our Wolves Live .... HOWL
Help Us Make a Nation .... HUMAN
Help Us Reach and Rehabilitate America's Handicapped [*State-Federal rehabilitation program*] .... HURRAH
Helper .... HLP
Helps for Bible Translators [*A publication*] .... HFBT
Helps International Ministries .... HIM
Helsingfors [*Helsinki*] [*Finland*] [*Seismograph station code, US Geological Survey*] .... HEL
Helsingin Sanomat [*A publication*] .... HSan
Helsingin Teknillinen Korkeakoulu Tieteellisia Julkaisuja [*A publication*] .... Helsingin Tek Korkeakoulu Tiet Julk
Helsingin Yliopisto [*University of Helsinki*], **Helsinki, Finland** [*Library symbol*] .... FiHU
Helsinki [*Finland*] [*Airport symbol*] .... HEL
Helsinki Guarantees for Ukraine Committee .... HGUC
Helsinki University of Technology Research Papers [*A publication*] .... Helsinki Univ Technol Res Pap
Helvetia Archaeologica [*A publication*] .... HA
Helvetia Archaeologica [*A publication*] .... Helvet Arch
Helvetia Association of North America [*Defunct*] .... HANA
Helvetica Chimica Acta [*A publication*] .... Helv Chim A
Helvetica Chimica Acta [*A publication*] .... Helv Chim Acta
Helvetica Chirurgica Acta [*A publication*] .... Helv Chir Acta
Helvetica Chirurgica Acta. Supplementum [*A publication*] .... Helv Chir Acta Suppl
Helvetica Medica Acta [*A publication*] .... Helv Med Acta
Helvetica Medica Acta. Supplementum [*A publication*] .... Helv Med Acta Suppl
Helvetica Odontologica Acta [*A publication*] .... Helv Odon A
Helvetica Odontologica Acta [*A publication*] .... Helv Odontol Acta
Helvetica Odontologica Acta. Supplementum [*A publication*] .... Helvetica Odontol Acta Suppl
Helvetica Paediatrica Acta [*A publication*] .... Helv Paed A
Helvetica Paediatrica Acta [*A publication*] .... Helv Paediatr Acta
Helvetica Paediatrica Acta. Supplementum [*A publication*] .... Helv Paediatr Acta Suppl
Helvetica Physica Acta [*A publication*] .... Helv Phys A
Helvetica Physica Acta [*A publication*] .... Helv Phys Acta

Helvetica Physiologica et Pharmacologica Acta [*A publication*] .... Helv Physiol Pharmacol Acta
Helvetica Physiologica et Pharmacologica Acta [*A publication*] .... HPPAA
Helvetische Muenzen-Zeitung [*A publication*] .... HMZ
Helwan [*Egypt*] [*Seismograph station code, US Geological Survey*] .... HLW
Hemadsorption [*Hematology*] .... HA
Hemadsorption [*Hematology*] .... HAD
Hemagglutinating [*Virology*] .... H
Hemagglutinating Unit [*Immunochemistry*] .... HU
Hemagglutinating Virus of Japan [*Medicine*] .... HVJ
Hemagglutination [*Hematology*] .... HA
Hemagglutination Inhibition [*Immunochemistry*] .... HAI
Hemagglutination Inhibition [*Immunochemistry*] .... HI
Hemagglutination Inhibition Test [*for pregnancy*] [*Medicine*] .... HIT
Hemagglutination Unit [*Hematology*] .... HAU
Hematite [*CIPW classification*] [*Geology*] .... hm
Hematocrit [*Medicine*] .... HCT
Hematology [*Medicine*] .... HEMAT
Hematoporphyrin Derivative [*Antineoplastic compound*] .... HPD
Hematoxylin and Eosin [*Biological stain*] .... H & E
Hematoxylin and Eosin [*Biological stain*] .... HE
Hemerdon Mining & Smelting [*NASDAQ symbol*] .... HMSLF
Hemet, CA [*Radio station call letters*] .... KHSJ
Hemet, CA [*Radio station call letters*] .... KHYE
Hemet Public Library, Hemet, CA [*Library symbol*] .... CHem
Hemic Subgroup [*Magnetite, chromite, hematite*] [*CIPW classification*] [*Geology*] .... H
Hemihydrate-Dihydrate [*Chemical technology*] .... HDH
Hemijska Industrija [*A publication*] .... Hem Ind
Hemin Controlled Repressor [*Biochemistry*] .... HCR
Hemingway Notes [*A publication*] .... HN
Hemingway, SC [*Location identifier*] [*FAA*] .... HEK
Hemingway, SC [*Radio station call letters*] .... WKYB
Hemingway, SC [*Radio station call letters*] .... WLGI
Hemingway Society .... HS
Hemiparalysis [*Medicine*] .... HEMI
Hemiplegia [*Medicine*] .... HEMI
Hemisphere .... HEM
Hemisphere .... HEMIS
Hemisphere Cylinder Body .... HCB
Hemisphere Development Corp. [*NASDAQ symbol*] .... HSDMF
Hemisphere Fund, Inc. [*NYSE symbol*] .... HEM
Hemispheres [*A publication*] .... Hs
Hemispheric Insurance Conference .... HIC
Hemispherical Reflective Antenna .... HRA
Hemispherical Search [*First frequency-scanning RADAR*] .... HEMISEARCH
Hemodialysis [*Nephrology*] .... HD
Hemodialysis Unit [*Medicine*] .... HDU
Hemoglobin [*Biochemistry, medicine*] .... Hb
Hemoglobin [*Biochemistry, medicine*] .... HG
Hemoglobin [*Biochemistry, medicine*] .... HGB
Hemoglobin, Adult [*Medicine*] .... HbA
Hemoglobin, Carboxy [*Biochemistry, medicine*] .... HbCO
Hemoglobin, Fetal [*Also, HgF*] [*Medicine*] .... HbF
Hemoglobin, Fetal [*Also, HbF*] [*Medicine*] .... HgF
Hemoglobin and Hematocrit [*Clinical chemistry*] .... H & H
Hemoglobin, Oxy [*Biochemistry, medicine*] .... HbO_2
Hemoglobin, Reduced [*Biochemistry, medicine*] .... HHb
Hemoglobin, Sickle [*Medicine*] .... HbS
Hemokinetics Cl A [*NASDAQ symbol*] .... HEMEA
Hemolysis [*Medicine*] .... HEM
Hemolysis, Elevated Liver Enzymes, and Low Platelet Count [*Clinical chemistry*] .... HELLP
Hemolytic Anemia [*Hematology*] .... HA
Hemolytic Anemia Antigen [*Immunochemistry*] .... HAA
Hemolytic Disease of Newborn [*Medicine*] .... HDN
Hemolytic Unit [*Hematology*] .... HU
Hemolytic-Uremic Syndrome [*Nephrology*] .... HUS
Hemolyzing Dose [*Medicine*] .... HD
Hemophilia Research [*An association*] [*Defunct*] .... HR
Hemorrhage [*Medicine*] .... HEMOR
Hemorrhage and Exudate [*Medicine*] .... H & E
Hemorrhagic Factor .... HF
Hemorrhagic Fever with Renal Syndrome [*Medicine*] .... HFRS
Hemorrhagic Retinopathy [*Ophthalmology*] .... HR
Hemotec Inc. [*NASDAQ symbol*] .... HEMO
Hemphill, TX [*Radio station call letters*] .... KAWS
Hempstead General Hospital, Medical Center, Hempstead, NY [*Library symbol*] .... NHemGH
Hempstead, NY [*Radio station call letters*] .... WHLI
Hempstead, NY [*Radio station call letters*] .... WRHU
Hempstead Public Library, Hempstead, NY [*Library symbol*] .... NHem
Hemstitched .... HS
Hen Egg-White Lysozyme [*An enzyme*] .... HEL
Hence .... H
Henceforth [*A publication*] .... He
Henderson County Junior College [*Texas*] .... HCJC
Henderson County Junior College, Athens, TX [*Library symbol*] .... TxAtH
Henderson County Public Library, Hendersonville, NC [*Library symbol*] .... NcHv
Henderson District Public Library, Henderson, NV [*Library symbol*] .... NvH
Henderson, KY [*Radio station call letters*] .... WHKC
Henderson, KY [*Radio station call letters*] .... WKDQ
Henderson, KY [*Radio station call letters*] .... WSON
Henderson, NC [*Radio station call letters*] .... WHNC
Henderson, NC [*Radio station call letters*] .... WIZS
Henderson, NC [*Radio station call letters*] .... WYFL
Henderson, NV [*Radio station call letters*] .... KILA
Henderson, NV [*Radio station call letters*] .... KMZQ-FM
Henderson, NV [*Radio station call letters*] .... KVEG
Henderson, NV [*Radio station call letters*] .... KVOV
Henderson, NV [*Television station call letters*] .... KVVU-TV
Henderson, NV [*Radio station call letters*] .... KXTZ
Henderson Petroleum Corp. [*NASDAQ symbol*] .... HEND
Henderson Regional Library, Winnipeg, MB, Canada [*Library symbol*] .... CaMWHR
Henderson State College [*Later, Henderson State University*] [*Arkansas*] .... HSC
Henderson State Teachers College [*Later, HSC*] [*Arkansas*] .... HSTC
Henderson State University [*Arkansas*] .... HSU
Henderson State University, Arkadelphia, AR [*OCLC symbol*] .... AKH
Henderson State University, Arkadelphia, AR [*Library symbol*] .... ArAT
Henderson, TN [*Radio station call letters*] .... WFHC-FM
Henderson, TN [*Radio station call letters*] .... WFKX
Henderson, TX [*Radio station call letters*] .... KGRI
Henderson, TX [*Radio station call letters*] .... KGRI-FM
Henderson, TX [*Radio station call letters*] .... KWRD
Hendersonville, NC [*Radio station call letters*] .... WHKP
Hendersonville, NC [*Radio station call letters*] .... WHVL
Hendersonville, NC [*Radio station call letters*] .... WKIT
Hendersonville, TN [*Radio station call letters*] .... WMAK-FM
Hendrick Hudson Free Library, Montrose, NY [*Library symbol*] .... NMontr
Hendrik Verwoerd Dam [*South Africa*] [*Seismograph station code, US Geological Survey*] .... HVD
Hendrix College, Conway, AR [*OCLC symbol*] .... AKE
Hendrix College, Conway, AR [*Library symbol*] .... ArCH
Hengchun [*Republic of China*] [*Seismograph station code, US Geological Survey*] .... HEN
Henkel Corporation, Minneapolis, MN [*OCLC symbol*] .... HKC
Hennepin Attendance Center, Hennepin, IL [*Library symbol*] .... IHennC
Hennepin County General Hospital, Minneapolis, MN [*Library symbol*] .... MnMHH
Hennepin County Library, Minneapolis, MN [*Library symbol*] .... MnMHCL
Hennepin County Medical Society, Minneapolis, MN [*Library symbol*] .... MnMH
Hennepin Lawyer [*A publication*] .... Hennepin Law
Hennessey Public Library, Hennessey, OK [*Library symbol*] .... OkHenn
Henniker, NH [*Radio station call letters*] .... WNEC-FM
Henoch-Schoenlein Syndrome [*Medicine*] .... HS
Henredon Furniture [*NASDAQ symbol*] .... HDON
Henrico County Public Library, Richmond, VA [*Library symbol*] .... ViRHC
Henrietta Lacks [*Pseudonym, Helen Lane*] [*Type of cell line*] .... HeLa
Henrietta, NY [*Radio station call letters*] .... WITR
Henrietta, NY [*Radio station call letters*] .... WRHR
Henry [*Symbol*] [*SI unit of inductance*] .... H
Henry .... HY
Henry Clay Memorial Foundation .... HCMF
Henry Draper Catalogue [*Astronomy*] .... HD
Henry E. Huntington Library, San Marino, CA [*Library symbol*] .... CSmH
Henry E. Sigerist Supplements. Bulletin of the History of Medicine [*A publication*] .... Henry E Sigerist Suppl Bull Hist Med
Henry, Edward, Mary, Philip, Elizabeth [*Bacon's prophecy*] .... HEMPE
Henry Energy Corp. [*NASDAQ symbol*] .... HNRY
Henry Ford Community College [*Michigan*] .... HFCC
Henry Ford Hospital, Detroit, MI [*Library symbol*] .... MiDHF
Henry Ford Hospital Medical Bulletin [*A publication*] .... Henry Ford Hosp Med Bull
Henry Ford Hospital Medical Journal [*A publication*] .... Henry Ford Hosp Med J
Henry Ford Hospital, Medical Library, Detroit, MI [*OCLC symbol*] .... EYF
Henry Francis DuPont Winterthur Museum, Joseph Downs Manuscript and Microfilm Collection, Winterthur, DE [*Library symbol*] .... DeWint-M
Henry Francis DuPont Winterthur Museum, Winterthur, DE [*Library symbol*] .... DeWint
Henry Francis DuPont Winterthur Museum, Winterthur, DE [*OCLC symbol*] .... DLH
Henry H. Warren Memorial Library, Massena, NY [*Library symbol*] .... NMas
Henry IV, Part I [*Shakespearean work*] 1H4
Henry IV, Part II [*Shakespearean work*] 2H4
Henry James Review [*A publication*] .... HJR
Henry Louis Mencken [*American author/critic*] .... HLM
Henry M. Seymour Library, Indianola, MS [*Library symbol*] .... MsIn
Henry per Meter .... H/m
Henry Phipps Institute, Philadelphia, PA [*Library symbol*] [*Obsolete*] .... PPHPI
Henry Public Library, Henry, IL [*OCLC symbol*] .... ISP
Henry Russell [*Astronomy*] .... HR
Henry Stephens Memorial Library, Almont, MI [*Library symbol*] .... MiAlmo
Henry V [*Shakespearean work*] H5
Henry VI, Part I [*Shakespearean work*] 1H6
Henry VI, Part II [*Shakespearean work*] 2H6

Henry VI, Part III [Shakespearean work] ... 3H6
Henry VIII [Shakespearean work] ... H8
Henry W. Grout Museum of History and Science, Waterlook, IA [Library symbol] ... IaWG
Henry Waldinger Memorial Library, Valley Stream, NY [Library symbol] ... NVs
Henryetta, OK [Location identifier] [FAA] ... HET
Henryetta, OK [Radio station call letters] ... KGCG-FM
Henryetta, OK [Radio station call letters] ... KHEN
Henryton State Hospital, Henryton, MD [Library symbol] ... MdHeH
Henson Aviation, Inc. [Hagerstown, MD] [FAA designator] ... HNA
HEP [Higher Education Publications] Higher Education Directory [A publication] ... HEP
Hepar Embryonis Bovis [Embryonic bovine liver cells used in tissue culture studies of viruses] [Medicine] ... HEB
Heparin Neutralizing Activity [Medicine] ... HNA
Heparin Sulfate [Biochemistry] ... HS
Hepatic Binding Protein [Biochemistry] ... HBP
Hepatic Blood Flow ... HBF
Hepatic Encephalography [Medicine] ... HE
Hepatic Encephalopathy [Medicine] ... HE
Hepatic Glucose Output [Physiology] ... HGO
Hepatic Stimulator Substance ... HSS
Hepatic Triglyceride Lipase [An enzyme] ... HTGL
Hepatitis A Virus ... HAV
Hepatitis A Virus Antigen [Immunochemistry] ... HAVAg
Hepatitis Associated [Virus] ... HA
Hepatitis Associated Antigen [Clinical chemistry] ... HAA
Hepatitis B [Medicine] ... HB
Hepatitis B Antibody [Immunology] ... HBAb
Hepatitis B Antigen [Immunology] ... HBAg
Hepatitis B Core Antigen [Immunology] ... HBCAg
Hepatitis B Immune Globulin [Immunology] ... HBIG
Hepatitis B Surface Antigen [Also, AA, Au, HBSAg] [Immunology] ... HB_S
Hepatitis B Surface Antigen [Also, AA, Au, HB_S] [Immunology] ... HBSAg
Hepatitis B Virus ... HBV
Hepatitis Contagiosa Canis [Virus] ... HCC
Hepatocellular Adenoma [Medicine] ... HCA
Hepatocellular Carcinoma [Oncology] ... HCC
Hepatojugular Reflex [Medicine] ... HJR
Hepatoma Tissue Culture [Medicine] ... HTC
Hepburn Library, Waddington, NY [Library symbol] ... NWadd
HEPES-Buffered EMEM ... HEM
HEPES-Saline-Albumin-Gelatin [Medium] [Microbiology] ... HSAG
Hepp [Alaska] [Seismograph station code, US Geological Survey] ... HPP
Heppner Public Library, Heppner, OR [Library symbol] ... OrHep
Heptadecapeptide Gastrin [Endocrinology] ... HG
Heptafluorobutyrate [or Heptafluorobutyric] [Organic chemistry] ... HFB
Heptafluorobutyric Acid [Organic chemistry] ... HFBA
Heptafluorobutyrylimidazole [Organic chemistry] ... HFBI
Heptagonal Games Association ... HGA
Heptamethylnonane [Fuel] ... HMN
Heptyl [Biochemistry] ... Hp
Heptylhydroxyquinoline N-Oxide [Analytical biochemistry] ... HOQNO
Her Netherlands Majesty's Ship ... HNMS
Heraklion [Greece] [Airport symbol] ... HER
Herald, Avalon, NJ [Library symbol] ... NjAvH
Herald of Holiness [A publication] ... H Hol
Herald of Library Science [A publication] ... Herald Lib Sci
Herald of Library Science [A publication] ... Her Libr Sci
Herald-Mitchellville Index, Altoona, IA [Library symbol] ... IaAltoH
Herald News, Passaic, NJ [Library symbol] ... NjPasH
Heraldic Quality Control System ... HQCS
Heraldry ... HER
Heraldry Society ... HS
Heralds' College [British] ... HC
Herat [Afghanistan] [Airport symbol] [Obsolete] ... HEA
Herb Research Foundation ... HRF
Herb Society of America ... HSA
Herb Trade Association ... HTA
Herba Hungarica [A publication] ... Herba Hung
Herba Polonica [A publication] ... Herba Pol
Herbage Abstracts [A publication] ... Herb Abstr
Herbarium Recentium [Of Fresh Herbs] [Pharmacy] ... HERB RECENT
Herbert H. Lehman College of the City University of New York, New York, NY [Library symbol] ... NNL
Herbert Hoover National Historic Site ... HEHO
Herbert Hoover Presidential Library Association ... HHPLA
Herbert Hoover Presidential Library, West Branch, IA [Library symbol] ... IaWbH
Herbert Wescoat Memorial Library, McArthur, OH [Library symbol] ... OMc
Herbicide Assessment Commission ... HAC
Hercules [Constellation] ... Her
Hercules [Constellation] ... Herc
Hercules, Inc. [Research code symbol] ... AC
Hercules, Inc. [Formerly, Hercules Powder Co.] [NYSE symbol] ... HPC
Hercules, Inc., Wilmington, DE [Library symbol] ... DeWHI
Hercules Powder Co. [Later, Hercules, Inc.], Cellulose Products Division, Hopewell, VA [Library symbol] ... ViHopHC
Hercules Powder Co. [Later, Hercules, Inc.], Experiment Station, Wilmington, DE [Library symbol] ... DeWH
Hercules Powder Co. [Later, Hercules, Inc.], Virginia Cellulose Division, Hopewell, VA [Library symbol] ... ViHopHV
Hercules on Water [Aircraft] ... HOW
Hercynia fuer die Fachgebiete Botanik-Geographie-Geologie Palaeontologie-Zoologie [A publication] ... Hercynia Fachgeb Bot-Geogr-Geol Palaeontol-Zool
Herd Test ... HT
Herder Korrespondez [A publication] ... Herder Korresp
Here [or Herewith] [Aviation code] ... ER
Here ... HR
Here and Now [A publication] ... H & N
Here and Now [A publication] ... HN
Hereafter ... HRAR
Hereby Detached from Duty Assigned [Military] ... HERDET
Hereditary Angioneurotic Edema [Medicine] ... HAE
Hereditary Angioneurotic Edema [Medicine] ... HANE
Hereditary Disease Foundation ... HDF
Hereditary Elliptocytosis [Medicine] ... HE
Hereditary Erythroblastic Multinuclearity Associated with a Positive Acidified-Serum Test [Hematology] ... HEMPAS
Hereditary Fructose Intolerance [Medicine] ... HFI
Hereditary Grand Almoner [Freemasonry] ... HGA
Hereditary Grand Master Mason [Freemasonry] ... HGMM
Hereditary Hemorrhagic Telangiectasia [Medicine] ... HHT
Hereditary Order of Armigerous Augustans ... OAA
Hereditary Osteo-Onychodysplasia [Medicine] ... HOOD
Hereditary Persistence of Fetal Hemoglobin [Hematology] ... HPFH
Hereditary Pyropoikilocytosis [Medicine] ... HPP
Hereditary Sensory Neuropathies [Neurology] ... HSN
Hereditary Spherocytosis [Medicine] ... HS
Hereditas [A publication] ... Hered
Heredity ... HERED
Heredity ... HRDTY
Heredity [A publication] ... Hered
Heredity and Environment ... H & E
Heredopathia Atactica Polyneuritiformis [Medicine] ... HAP
Hereford [British depot code] ... HFD
Hereford Otter Hounds ... HOH
Hereford, TX [Radio station call letters] ... KPAN
Hereford, TX [Radio station call letters] ... KPAN-FM
Herefordshire [County in England] ... HEREF
Herefordshire [County in England] ... HEREFORDS
Herefordshire [County in England] ... HEREFS
Hereinafter ... HRNAR
Herendeen Bay, AK [Location identifier] [FAA] ... HED
Herero [MARC language code] [Library of Congress] ... her
Heres [Heir] [Latin] ... H
Heres [Heir] [Legal] [Latin] ... HER
Heretofore ... HTOFORE
Herewith [Enclosures] ... HW
Herion Informationen [A publication] ... Herion Inf
Heritage Bancorp [NASDAQ symbol] ... HRTG
Heritage Bancorp of California [NASDAQ symbol] ... HRTB
Heritage Communications, Incorporated [NYSE symbol] ... HCI
Heritage Conservation Recreation Service [Abolished, 1981, functions transferred to National Park Service] [Department of the Interior] ... HCRS
Heritage Federal Savings & Loan Florida [NASDAQ symbol] ... HFLA
Heritage Financial Corporation [NASDAQ symbol] ... HFHC
Heritage Foundation ... HF
Heritage Hills Area Library Services Authority [Library network] ... HHALSA
Heritage of Indian Art Series [A publication] ... HIAS
Heritage of Kansas [A publication] ... HK
Heritage Papers, Danielsville, GA [Library symbol] ... GDanH
Heritage Roses Group ... HRG
Heritage Wisconsin [NASDAQ symbol] ... HWIS
Herkimer County Community College, Herkimer, NY [OCLC symbol] ... VXH
Herkimer County Community College, Ilion, NY [Library symbol] ... NIlH
Herkimer County Historical Society, Herkimer, NY [Library symbol] ... NHerkCHi
Herkimer, NY [Radio station call letters] ... WRMV
Herkimer, NY [Radio station call letters] ... WYUT
Herley Microwave Systems [NASDAQ symbol] ... HRLY
Herman Collegiate Institute, Windsor, ON, Canada [Library symbol] ... CaOWH
Herman Hospital, Houston, TX [Library symbol] ... TxHHH
Hermanas Catequistas Guadalupanas [Roman Catholic women's religious order] ... HCG
Hermanus [South Africa] [Geomagnetic observatory code] ... HER
Hermanus [South Africa] [Seismograph station code, US Geological Survey] ... HER
Hermathena [A publication] ... Ha
Hermes [A publication] ... Hm
Hermes Electronics Ltd., Dartmouth, NS, Canada [Library symbol] ... CaNSDH
Hermes. Messager Scientifique et Populaire de l'Antiquite Classique en Russie [A publication] ... HR
Hermes. Revista del Pais Vasco [A publication] ... HRPV
Hermes. Zeitschrift fuer Klassische Philologie [A publication] ... H
Hermes. Zeitschrift fuer Klassische Philologie [A publication] ... HZKP
Hermetic Pivoting Seal ... HPS

Hermetic-Sealed Container ..... HSC
Hermetically Sealed Bushing ..... HSB
Hermetically Sealed, Integrating Gyro ..... HIG
Hermetically Sealed Zener Diode ..... HSZD
Hermiston [*Oregon*] [*Seismograph station code, US Geological Survey*] ..... HRO
Hermiston, OR [*Radio station call letters*] ..... KOHU
Hermiston, OR [*Radio station call letters*] ..... KOHU-FM
Hermiston Public Library, Hermiston, OR [*Library symbol*] ..... OrHe
Hermit ..... H
Hermosillo [*Mexico*] [*Airport symbol*] ..... HMO
Hermsdorfer Technische Mitteilungen [*A publication*] ..... Hermsdorfer Tech Mitt
Hernandez Valley [*California*] [*Seismograph station code, US Geological Survey*] ..... HVC
Herndon, VA [*Radio station call letters*] ..... WVBK
Hernia [*or Herniated*] [*Medicine*] ..... HERN
Herniated Disc [*Medicine*] ..... HD
Herniated Nucleus Pulposus [*Medicine*] ..... HNP
Heroin [*Slang*] ..... H
Heroin Emergency Life Project ..... HELP
Heroin, Morphine, and Cocaine [*Mixture*] [*Slang*] ..... HMC
Heron (English Edition) [*A publication*] ..... Heron (Engl Ed)
Herpes Gestationis [*Medicine*] ..... HG
Herpes-Like Virus ..... HLV
Herpes Simplex ..... HS
Herpes Simplex Encephalitis [*Medicine*] ..... HSE
Herpes Simplex Genitalis ..... HSG
Herpes Simplex Labialis ..... HSL
Herpes Simplex Virus ..... HSV
Herpes Simplex Virus Encephalitis [*Medicine*] ..... HSVE
Herpes-Type Virus ..... HTV
Herpesvirus ..... HV
Herpesvirus Hominis ..... HVH
Herpesvirus of Saimiri ..... HVS
Herpetics Engaged in Living Productively [*Later, Herpes Research Center*] ..... HELP
Herpetological Information Search Systems ..... HISS
Herpetological Review [*A publication*] ..... Herpetol Rev
Herpetologists' League ..... HL
Herpetology ..... HERP
Herr [*Sir, Mr.*] [*German*] ..... HR
Herrick Public Library, Holland, MI [*Library symbol*] ..... MiHol
Herrin, IL [*Radio station call letters*] ..... WHPI
Herring Industries Board [*British*] ..... HIB
Herringbone [*Electronics, engineering*] ..... HGBN
Herringbone Strutting [*Construction*] ..... HBS
Herringbone Twill ..... HBT
Herringer-Hulster Effect ..... HHE
Herrold Hall Learning Resource Center, Zanesville, OH [*OCLC symbol*] ..... OHH
Herron School of Art, Indianapolis, IN [*Library symbol*] ..... InIJ
Herself ..... HERS
Hershey Foods Corp. [*NYSE symbol*] ..... HSY
Hershey Foods Corp., Hershey, PA [*OCLC symbol*] ..... HER
Hershey Medical Center, Hershey, PA [*Library symbol*] ..... PHeM
Hershey Oil [*American Stock Exchange symbol*] ..... HSO
Hershey, PA [*Radio station call letters*] ..... WITF-FM
Herstigte Nasionale Party [*Political party*] [*South Africa*] ..... HNP
Hertfordshire [*County in England*] ..... HERTS
Hertfordshire Archaeology [*A publication*] ..... Hertfordshire Arch
Hertz [*Symbol*] [*SI unit of frequency*] ..... Hz
Hertz Corp. [*NYSE symbol*] [*Delisted*] ..... HRZ
Hertzberg-New Method [*Standard periodical binding*] ..... HNM
Hertzler Research Foundation, Halstead, KS [*Library symbol*] ..... KHalH
Hertzsprung-Russell [*Diagram*] [*Astronomy*] ..... H-R
Hertzsprung-Russell Diagram [*Astronomy*] ..... HRD
Hervey Bay [*Australia*] [*Airport symbol*] ..... HVB
Herz Kreislauf [*A publication*] ..... Herz Kreisl
Heschl's Gyrus [*Brain anatomy*] ..... HG
Hesperia, CA [*Radio station call letters*] ..... KHSP
Hesperia Public Library, Hesperia, MI [*Library symbol*] ..... MiHe
Hesperian [*A publication*] ..... Hesp
Hesperian Foundation ..... HP
Hesperis-Tamuda [*A publication*] ..... H-T
Hess Oil & Chemical Corp. [*NYSE symbol*] [*Delisted*] ..... HES
Hesse Landesamt fuer Bodenforschung Notizblatt [*A publication*] ..... Hesse Landesamt Bodenforsch Notizblatt
Hessische Blaetter fuer Volkskunde [*A publication*] ..... HBV
Hessische Blaetter fuer Volkskunde [*A publication*] ..... HBVk
Hessische Chronik [*A publication*] ..... HC
Hessische Floristische Briefe [*A publication*] ..... Hess Florist Briefe
Hessische Landes- und Hochschulbibliothek, Darmstadt (Schloss), Germany [*Library symbol*] ..... GyDaH
Hessischer Rundfunk [*Radio network*] [*West Germany*] ..... HR
Hessisches Jahrbuch fuer Landesgeschichte [*A publication*] ..... Hess Jb Landesgesch
Hess's, Inc. [*American Stock Exchange symbol*] [*Delisted*] ..... HSS
Hesston Corp. [*NYSE symbol*] ..... HES
Het Boek [*A publication*] ..... Boek
Het Boek [*A publication*] ..... HB
Het Gildeboek. Tijdschrift voor Kerkelijke Kunst en Oudheidkunde [*A publication*] ..... HGB
Hetero-Atom-in-Context ..... HAIC
Heterodoxical Voice [*A publication*] ..... Het Voice
Heterodyne ..... HET
Heterodyne ..... HTN
Heterodyne Matrix Detector ..... HMD
Heterodyne Optical Optimization Communication System with Stops [*NASA*] ..... HOPS
Heterogeneous Element Processor [*Data processing*] ..... HEP
Heterogeneous Opposed Flow Diffusion ..... HOFD
Heterojunction Device ..... HJD
Heteropowered Earth-Launched Inter-Orbital Spacecraft ..... HELIOS
Heterosexual Attitudes toward Homosexuality [*Scale*] ..... HATH
Heterosexual Relations [*Scale*] ..... HR
Heterotrophic Intestinal Nitrification [*Metabolism*] ..... HIN
Heterozygosity [*Cytology*] ..... HET
Hetra Computer Commercial [*NASDAQ symbol*] ..... HETC
Hettinger, ND [*Location identifier*] [*FAA*] ..... HEI
Hettinger, ND [*Radio station call letters*] ..... KNDC
Heublein, Inc. [*NYSE symbol*] [*Delisted*] ..... HBL
Heuristic Concepts ..... HC
Heuristic Paper Trimming System ..... HUPATS
Heuristically-Programed Algorithmic [*Name of computer in film, "2001: A Space Odyssey." Acronym is also considered to have been formed by combining the letters preceding IBM in the alphabet*] ..... HAL
Heurtey Bulletin d'Informations. English Edition [*A publication*] ..... Heurtey Bull Inform
Heussler Air Service Corp. [*Buffalo, NY*] [*FAA designator*] ..... HUS
Hewitt-Robins, Inc. [*NYSE symbol*] [*Delisted*] ..... HEW
Hewlett-Packard Co. ..... HP
Hewlett-Packard Co. [*NYSE symbol*] ..... HWP
Hewlett-Packard Co., Corporate Library, Palo Alto, CA [*Library symbol*] ..... CPaHP
Hewlett-Packard Co., Fort Collins Division, Fort Collins, CO [*Library symbol*] ..... CoFHP
Hewlett-Packard Interface Bus [*Instrumentation*] ..... HP-IB
Hewlett Packard Journal [*A publication*] ..... Hewlett
Hewlett-Woodmere Public Library, Hewlett, NY [*Library symbol*] ..... NHew
Hex Aluminum Nut ..... HAN
Hex Head Electrical Squib ..... HHES
Hex Head Squib ..... HHS
Hexabromocyclododecane [*Flame retardant*] [*Organic chemistry*] ..... HBCD
Hexachloroacetone [*Organic chemistry*] ..... HCA
Hexachlorobenzene [*Organic chemistry*] ..... HCB
Hexachlorobutadiene [*Organic chemistry*] ..... HCBD
Hexachlorocyclohexane [*Also, BHC, GBH*] [*Insecticide*] ..... HCH
Hexachlorocyclopentadiene [*Also, HEX*] [*Organic chemistry*] ..... HCP
Hexachlorocyclopentadiene [*Also, HCP*] [*Organic chemistry*] ..... HEX
Hexachlorodibenzo-para-dioxin [*Organic chemistry*] ..... HxCDD
Hexachlorodibenzodioxin [*Organic chemistry*] ..... HCDD
Hexachloroepoxyoctahydro-exo-endo-dimethanonaphthalene [*Dieldrin*] [*Insecticide*] ..... HEOD
Hexachloroethane [*Organic chemistry*] ..... HC
Hexachlorophene [*Germicide*] ..... HCP
Hexadecadienyl Acetate [*Pheromone*] [*Organic chemistry*] ..... HDDA
Hexadecenal [*Pheromone*] [*Organic chemistry*] ..... HDAL
Hexadecenol [*Pheromone*] [*Organic chemistry*] ..... HDOL
Hexadecenyl Acetate [*Pheromone*] [*Organic chemistry*] ..... HDA
Hexadecimal ..... H
Hexadecimal [*System*] ..... HEX
Hexadecimal-to-Binary ..... H-B
Hexadecimal-to-Decimal ..... H-D
Hexadecyltrimethylammonium Chloride [*Organic chemistry*] ..... HTAC
Hexaethyl Tetraphosphate [*Organic chemistry*] ..... HETP
Hexafluorodiethyl Ether [*Convulsant*] ..... HFE
Hexafluoroisobutylene [*Organic chemistry*] ..... HFIB
Hexafluoroisopropanol [*or Hexafluoroisopropyl*] [*Organic chemistry*] ..... HFIP
Hexafluoropropylene [*Organic chemistry*] ..... HFP
Hexafluoropropylene Oxide [*Organic chemistry*] ..... HFPO
Hexagon ..... HEX
Hexagon Tungsten Honeycomb ..... HTH
Hexagonal Close-Packed [*Crystallography*] ..... HCP
Hexagonal Head ..... HEXHD
Hexahydrophthalic Anhydride [*Organic chemistry*] ..... HHPA
Hexamethylbenzene [*Organic chemistry*] ..... HMB
Hexamethyldisiloxane [*Organic chemistry*] ..... HMDS
Hexamethylene Bis(Acetamide) [*Organic chemistry*] ..... HMBA
Hexamethylene Diisocyanate [*Organic chemistry*] ..... HMDI
Hexamethylenediamine [*Organic chemistry*] ..... HMDA
Hexamethyleneimine [*Trademark*] [*Celanese Corp.*] ..... HMI
Hexamethylenetetramine [*Organic chemistry*] ..... HMT
Hexamethylenetetraselenafulvalenium [*Organic chemistry*] ..... HMTSF
Hexamethylmelamine [*Altretamine*] [*Also, HXM*] [*Antineoplastic drug*] ..... HMM
Hexamethylmelamine [*Altretamine*] [*Also, HMM*] [*Antineoplastic drug*] ..... HXM
Hexamethylphosphoramide [*or Hexamethylphosphoric Triamide*] [*Also, HEMPA, HMPA, HMPT, HPT*] [*Organic chemistry*] ..... HMP

Hexamethylphosphoramide [*or Hexamethylphosphoric Triamide*] [*Also, HEMPA, HMP, HMPT, HPT*] [*Organic chemistry*] ....HMPA
Hexamethylphosphoric Triamide [*Also, HMP, HMPA, HMPT, HPT*] [*Organic chemistry*] ....HEMPA
Hexamethylphosphoric Triamide [*Also, HEMPA, HMP, HMPA, HPT*] [*Organic chemistry*] ....HMPT
Hexamethylphosphoric Triamide [*Also, HEMPA, HMP, HMPA, HMPT*] [*Organic chemistry*] .... HPT
Hexamethyltrithiane [*Organic chemistry*]...................HMTT
Hexanediamine [*or Hexamethylenediamine*] [*Organic chemistry*] ....HDA
Hexanediol Diacrylate [*Also, HDODA*] [*Organic chemistry*]...................HDDA
Hexanediol Diacrylate [*Also, HDDA*] [*Organic chemistry*]...................HDODA
Hexanitroazobenzene [*Organic chemistry*] ....HNAB
Hexanitromannite [*Organic chemistry*]...................HNM
Hexanitrostilbene [*High explosive*] ....HNS
Hexasodium Metaphosphate [*Inorganic chemistry*] ....HMP
Hexcel ....HXCL
Hexcel Corp. [*NYSE symbol*]...................HXL
Hexcel Products, Technical Library, Berkeley, CA [*Library symbol*]......CBH
Hexobarbital Sleeping Time [*In experimental animals*] ....HST
Hexode...................Hx
Hexokinase [*An enzyme*] ....HK
Hexose Diphosphate [*Biochemistry*] ....HDP
Hexose Monophosphate [*Biochemistry*] ....HMP
Hexose Monophosphate Shunt [*Biochemistry*] ....HMPS
Hexyl [*Biochemistry*] ....Hx
Hexylene Glycol [*Organic chemistry*] ....HG
Heyden Antibiotic [*Pharmacology*] ....HA
Heyden Newport Chemical Corp. [*NYSE symbol*] [*Delisted*] ....HDN
Heythrop Journal [*A publication*]...................Heythrop
Heythrop Journal [*A publication*]...................Heythrop J
Heywood Public Library, Heywood, Lancashire, United Kingdom [*Library symbol*]...................UkHe
HF [*High Frequency*] Recovery Antenna...................HRA
HFIR Critical Experiment ....HFCE
HGIC Corp. [*NASDAQ symbol*] ....HGIC
Hi-Cor Resources Ltd. [*NASDAQ symbol*]...................HCORF
Hi Fi News and Record Review [*A publication*] ....HFN
Hi-G, Incorporated [*American Stock Exchange symbol*] ....HGI
Hi-Port Industries [*NASDAQ symbol*]...................HIPT
Hi-Pot Dwell Time ....HDT
Hi-Shear Industries, Inc. [*NYSE symbol*]...................HSI
Hi-Tech Robotics [*NASDAQ symbol*]...................HROB
Hiawatha, KS [*Radio station call letters*]...................KNZA
Hibbert Journal [*A publication*]...................HibbJ
Hibbert Journal [*A publication*]...................HibJ
Hibbert Journal [*A publication*]...................HJ
Hibbert Journal [*A publication*]...................HJI
Hibbing [*Minnesota*] [*Airport symbol*]...................HIB
Hibbing Community College, Hibbing, MN [*OCLC symbol*]...................HCC
Hibbing Community College, Hibbing, MN [*Library symbol*] ....MnHibC
Hibbing Junior College [*Later, Hibbing Community College*] [*Minnesota*] ....HJC
Hibbing, MN [*Television station call letters*]...................WIRT
Hibbing, MN [*Radio station call letters*]...................WKKQ
Hibbing, MN [*Radio station call letters*]...................WMFG
Hibbing, MN [*Radio station call letters*]...................WMFG-FM
Hibbing, MN [*Radio station call letters*]...................WTBX
Hibbing Public Library, Hibbing, MN [*Library symbol*]...................MnHib
Hibernation Induction Trigger [*Biochemistry*] ....HIT
Hibernation Information Exchange [*Later, IHS*] ....HIE
Hibernia Corporation CI A [*NASDAQ symbol*] ....HIBCA
Hibridni Kukuruz Jugoslavie [*A publication*].......... Hibridni Kukuruz Jugoslav
Hiburnium [*Supposed chemical element, discovered 1922*] ....Hi
Hic [*Here*] [*Latin*]...................H
Hic Conditus Est [*Here Lies Buried*] [*Latin*] ....HCE
Hic Est [*Here Is*] [*Latin*] ....HE
Hic Iacet [*Here Lies*] [*Latin*] ....HI
Hic Iacet Sepultus [*Here Lies Buried*] [*Latin*] ....HIS
Hic Jacet [*Here Lies*] [*Latin*] ....HJ
Hic Jacet Sepultus [*Here Lies Buried*] [*Latin*] ....HJS
Hic Requiescit in Pace [*Here Rests in Peace*] [*Latin*] ....HRIP
Hic Sepultus [*Here Is Buried*] [*Latin*] ....HS
Hic Sepultus Est [*Here Lies Buried*] [*Latin*] ....HSE
Hic Situs [*Laid Here*] [*Latin*] ....HS
Hic Verbis [*In These Words*] [*Latin*] ....HV
Hickenia (Boletin del Darwinion) [*A publication*]...... Hickenia (Bol Darwinion)
Hickory [*North Carolina*] [*Airport symbol*] ....HKY
Hickory Furniture [*NASDAQ symbol*] ....HFUR
Hickory Handle Association ....HHA
Hickory, NC [*Location identifier*] [*FAA*] ....BZM
Hickory, NC [*Radio station call letters*]...................WHKY
Hickory, NC [*Radio station call letters*] ....WHKY-FM
Hickory, NC [*Television station call letters*]...................WHKY-TV
Hickory, NC [*Radio station call letters*] ....WIRC
Hickory, NC [*Radio station call letters*] ....WSPF
Hickory, NC [*Radio station call letters*] ....WXRC
Hickory Task Force Report. Southeastern Forest Experiment Station [*A publication*]........Hickory Task Force Rep Stheast For Exp Sta
Hicks & Greist [*Advertising agency*] ....H & G
Hicksville Free Public Library, Hicksville, NY [*Library symbol*] ....NHick

Hid [*A publication*] ....Hi
Hidaka [*Japan*] [*Seismograph station code, US Geological Survey*]........HDK
Hidalgo County Library System, McAllen, TX [*OCLC symbol*]...................HDL
Hidden Bay [*Alaska*] [*Seismograph station code, US Geological Survey*]...................AD4
Hidden Lake [*Pennsylvania*] [*Seismograph station code, US Geological Survey*] [*Closed*] ....HKP
Hidden Variable Theory [*Physics*] ....HVT
Hidrologiai Koezloeny [*A publication*]...................Hidrol Koezl
Hienghene [*New Caledonia*] [*Airport symbol*] [*Obsolete*]...................HNG
Hierarchical Classification [*Indexing*] ....HICLASS
Hierarchical Direct Access Method [*Data processing*]...................HDAM
Hierarchical Distributed Control [*Data processing*] ....HDC
Hierarchical Indexed Direct Access Method [*Data processing*] ....HIDAM
Hierarchical Indexed Sequential Access Method [*Data processing*] ....HISAM
Hierarchical Intensive Search [*of the literature*] ....HIS
Hierarchical Memory Storage [*Data processing*] ....HMS
Hierarchical Sequential Access Method [*Data processing*]...................HSAM
Hierarchical Storage Manager ....HSM
Hierarchically Classified Index ....HCI
Hierarchy plus Input-Process-Output [*Data processing*] ....HIPO
Hierophant [*A publication*] ....Hiero
Higbee Co. [*NASDAQ symbol*]...................HIGB
Higginsville, MO [*Location identifier*] [*FAA*] ....HIG
Higginsville, MO [*Location identifier*] [*FAA*] LCX
High...................H
High...................HI
High [*Moody's bond rating*]...................Aa
High [*Standard & Poor's bond rating*] ....AA
High-Abrasion Furnace ....HAF
High-Absorption Integrated Defense Electromagnetic Warfare System...................HIDE
High-Acceleration Cockpit [*Air Force*] ....HAC
High-Acceleration Rocket-Missile ....HARM
High Accuracy [*RADAR*]...................HIAC
High-Accuracy Data [*System*]...................HAD
High-Accuracy Data Transmission System ....HADTS
High-Accuracy RADAR Data Transmission System ....HARDTS
High-Accuracy Targeting Subsystem...................HATS
High-Accuracy Voltmeter ....HAV
High-Affinity Choline Transport ....HAChT
High Air Pollution Potential ....HAPP
High Altitude ....HA
High Altitude ....HIALT
High-Altitude Abort [*NASA*] ....HAA
High-Altitude Air Pollution Program [*FAA*] ....HAAP
High-Altitude Air Traffic Control ....HAATC
High-Altitude Airborne Observation ....HAAO
High-Altitude Aircraft Detection ....HAAD
High-Altitude Application ....HAA
High-Altitude Balloon ....HIBAL
High-Altitude Bombing [*Military*]...................HAB
High-Altitude Bombsight...................HABS
High-Altitude Cerebral Edema [*Medicine*]...................HACE
High-Altitude Clear Air Turbulence [*Aviation*] ....HICAT
High-Altitude Delayed Opening Parachute Actuation Device.......HADOPAD
High-Altitude Density [*Sounding rocket*] ....HAD
High-Altitude Diagnostic [*Unit*] [*Rocket launcher*] ....HAD
High-Altitude Effects Simulation [*Defense Nuclear Agency*] ....HAES
High-Altitude Electromagnetic Pulse ....HEMP
High-Altitude Fluorescence ....HAF
High-Altitude Forecast Center ....HAFC
High-Altitude Fuze [*To activate weapons*]...................HAF
High-Altitude High-Speed Target [*Formerly, HAST*] ....HAHST
High-Altitude Infrared Detecting Set...................HAIRDS
High-Altitude Infrared Sensor System ....HAISS
High-Altitude Large Optics [*Air Force*] ....HALO
High-Altitude Long-Focus Convergent Mapping System ....HALCON
High-Altitude, Low-Opening [*Parachute*] ....HALO
High-Altitude Measurement Probe ....HAMP
High-Altitude Missile ....HAM
High-Altitude Navigation System ....HANS
High-Altitude Nuclear Detection Studies [*National Bureau of Standards*]...................HANDS
High-Altitude Nuclear Effects [*Study*]...................HANE
High-Altitude Nuclear Explosion ....HANE
High Altitude Observatory [*Boulder, CO*] [*National Center for Atmospheric Research*]...................HAO
High-Altitude Orbital Space Station ....HAOSS
High-Altitude Particle Program Experiment [*NASA*]...................HAPPE
High-Altitude Platform...................HAP
High-Altitude Pollution Project [*FAA*]...................HAPP
High-Altitude Powered Platforms ....HAPP
High-Altitude Probe ....HAP
High-Altitude Pulmonary Edema ....HAPE
High-Altitude RADAR Altimeter [*NASA*]...................HARA
High-Altitude RADAR Controller...................HARC
High-Altitude Radiological Instrumentation System ....HARIS
High-Altitude Ramjet Engine ....HARE
High-Altitude Recombination-Energy Propulsion ....HARE

High-Altitude Reconnaissance Platform ... HARP
High-Altitude Relay Point ... HARP
High-Altitude Research Program [*or Project*] [*Military*] ... HARP
High-Altitude Resonance Absorption Calculation ... HARAC
High-Altitude Rocket Probe [*Army*] ... HARP
High-Altitude Sampler ... HAS
High-Altitude Sampling Program [*Air Force*] ... HASP
High-Altitude Sounding Projectile ... HASP
High-Altitude Sounding Rocket ... HASR
High-Altitude Space Platform ... HASP
High-Altitude Space Velocity RADAR ... HASVR
High-Altitude Strike Indicator ... HASTI
High-Altitude Superpressure Powered Aerostat [*Navy*] ... HASPA
High-Altitude Supersonic Target [*Later, HAHST*] ... HAST
High-Altitude Surveillance Platform for Over-the-Horizon Targeting ... HISPOT
High-Altitude Target ... HAT
High-Altitude Target and Background [*Program*] ... HITAB
High-Altitude Terrain Contour Data Sensor ... HATS
High-Altitude Test and Evaluation of Infrared Sources ... HAIRS
High-Altitude Test Stand ... HATS
High-Altitude Test Vehicle ... HATV
High-Altitude Test Vehicle ... HTV
High-Altitude Testing [*Sounding rocket*] ... HAT
High-Altitude Transmitter ... HAT
High-Aluminous Concrete ... HAC
High Angle ... HA
High Angle of Attack [*Combat aircraft*] [*Navy*] ... HAOA
High-Angle Strafe ... HAS
High-Assault Risk Area [*DoD*] ... HARA
High Band ... HB
High-Band Jammer ... HBJ
High-Band Warning Antenna ... HBWA
High-Band Warning Receiver ... HBWR
High Bay ... HB
High BIT [*Binary Digit*] **Density Tape** [*Skylab*] [*NASA*] ... HBDT
High BIT [*Binary Digit*] **Rate** ... HBR
High Blood Pressure [*Medicine*] ... HBP
High Blood Pressure Information Center [*Public Health Service*] ... HBPIC
High Boilers ... HB
High Bridge Painting Co., High Bridge, NJ [*Library symbol*] ... NjHibP
High Calorific Value [*of a fuel*] ... HCV
High Capacity ... HC
High-Capacity Bomb ... HCB
High-Capacity Communication System ... HICAPCOM
High-Capacity Fog Foam [*Navy*] ... HCFF
High-Capacity Projectile ... HICAP
High Carbohydrate, High Fiber [*Nutrition*] ... HCF
High Carbohydrate, High Fiber [*Nutrition*] ... HCHF
High Carbohydrate, Low Fiber [*Nutrition*] ... HCLF
High Carbon [*Steel*] ... HC
High-Carbon Ferrochrome [*Metallurgy*] ... HCF
High Carbon, High Chrome ... HCHC
High-Carbon Steel ... HCS
High-Carbon Steel, Heat-Treated ... HCSHT
High Chief Ranger [*Ancient Order of Foresters*] ... HCR
High Church ... HC
High Clouds Visible [*Meteorology*] ... HCVIS
High [*Altitude*] **Combat Air Patrol** ... HICAP
High Command ... HICOM
High Command Secure Voice Network [*Navy*] ... HICOMSEVONET
High Commission [*or Commissioner*] ... HICOM
High Commission Territories Corps [*Military unit*] [*British*] ... HCT
High Commissioner ... HC
High Commissioner for Germany ... HICOG
High Commissioner of Ryukyu Islands ... HICOMRY
High Commissioner Trust Territory, Pacific Islands ... HICOMTERPACIS
High, Common, Low [*Relay*] ... HCL
High Compression ... HC
High Conditioners [*Psychology*] ... HC
High Conductivity [*Copper*] ... HC
High Control/Low Nurturance [*Psychology*] ... HC-LN
High Cost of Living ... HC
High Cost of Living ... HCL
High Court ... HC
High Court Junior Beadle [*Ancient Order of Foresters*] ... HCJB
High Court Junior Woodward [*Ancient Order of Foresters*] ... HCJW
High Court of Justice ... HCJ
High Court Secretary [*Ancient Order of Foresters*] ... HCS
High Court Senior Beadle [*Ancient Order of Foresters*] ... HCSB
High Court Senior Woodward [*Ancient Order of Foresters*] ... HCSW
High Court Treasurer [*Ancient Order of Foresters*] ... HCT
High Courts of Admiralty [*British*] ... HCA
High Cross Range ... HCR
High Cross-Range Orbiter ... HCRO
High Current ... HC
High-Current Density ... HCD
High-Current Diode ... HCD
High-Current Inductor ... HCI
High-Cycle Fatigue [*Rocket engine*] ... HCF
High Data Rate ... HDR
High-Data-Rate Assembly ... HDRA
High-Data-Rate LASER ... HDRL
High-Data-Rate Multiplexer ... HDRM
High-Data-Rate Storage System [*or Subsystem*] [*NASA*] ... HDRSS
High Data Register ... HDR
High Definition RADAR ... HDR
High-Definition Television [*Offers wider-screen pictures with high resolution that improves their depth, clarity, and detail*] ... HDTV
High Definition Video System ... HDVS
High Density ... HD
High-Density Acid ... HDA
High-Density Air Navigation ... HIDAN
High-Density Air Traffic Zone ... HDATZ
High-Density Data ... HDD
High-Density Data System ... HDDS
High-Density Digital Recording ... HDDR
High-Density Digital Tape ... HDDT
High-Density Electronic Packaging ... HDEP
High-Density Helicopter Landing [*Army*] ... HDHL
High-Density Lipoprotein [*Biochemistry*] ... HDL
High-Density Lipoprotein - Cell Surface Receptor [*Biochemistry*] ... HDL-c
High-Density Lipoprotein Cholesterol [*Physiology*] ... HDLC
High-Density/Low-Density Tariff ... HiD/LoD
High-Density Memory System ... HDMS
High-Density Moderated Reactor ... HDMR
High-Density Multitrack Recording ... HDMR
High-Density Polyethylene [*Plastics*] ... HDPE
High-Density Power Supply ... HDPS
High-Density Recorder [*Deep Space Instrumentation Facility, NASA*] ... HDR
High-Density Shock Tube ... HDST
High-Density Traffic Airport ... HDTA
High Detonation Pressure ... HDP
High Dirt Capacity [*A type of filter*] [*Pall Trinity Micro Corp.*] ... HDC
High-Dollar Value ... HDV
High Dose [*Medicine*] ... HD
High-Dose Immunological Paralysis [*Medicine*] ... HDIP
High Dose Methotrexate [*Antineoplastic drug regimen*] ... HDMTX
High Drag [*Navy*] ... HD
High Duty Alloys Ltd. ... HDA
High Efficiency ... HE
High-Efficiency Particle Accumulator ... HEPA
High-Efficiency Particulate Air [*Filter*] ... HEPA
High Egg Passage [*Rabies vaccine*] ... HEP
High Electroendosmosis [*Analytical biochemistry*] ... HEEO
High Electron Mobility Transistor [*Data processing*] ... HEMT
High Emission Cathode ... HEC
High-Endurance Coast Guard Cutter [*Later, WHEC*] ... WAPG
High-Endurance Coast Guard Cutter [*Formerly, WAPG*] ... WHEC
High Energy ... HE
High-Energy Accelerator and Reactor for Thermonuclear Fusion with Ion Beams of Relativistic Energies ... HEARTHFIRE
High-Energy Astronomy Observatory [*Pronounced "hee-oh"*] [*NASA*] ... HEAO
High-Energy Battery System ... HEBS
High-Energy Beam Transport [*For protons*] ... HEBT
High-Energy Benthic Boundary Layer Experiment [*Oceanography*] ... HEBBLE
High-Energy Chemistry ... HEC
High Energy Chemistry [*A publication*] ... High Energy Chem
High-Energy Cosmic Ray Experiment [*Balloon flight*] [*NASA*] ... HECRE
High-Energy Detector [*NASA*] ... HED
High-Energy Electrolyte Battery ... HEEB
High-Energy Electron Diffraction ... HEED
High-Energy Electronically Excited LASER ... HEEEL
High-Energy Firing Unit [*Army*] ... HEFU
High Energy Forming ... HEF
High-Energy Fuel [*Air Force*] ... HEF
High-Energy Gamma Ray ... HEGR
High-Energy Gas Fracturing [*For freeing natural gas from rock*] ... HEGF
High-Energy Ignition ... HEI
High-Energy LASER ... HEL
High-Energy LASER Beam ... HELB
High-Energy LASER Component Servicing ... HELCOS
High-Energy LASER Countermeasures ... HELCM
High-Energy LASER RADAR Acquisition and Tracking System ... HELRATS
High-Energy LASER Review Group [*Terminated, 1977*] [*DoD*] ... HELRG
High-Energy LASER System ... HELS
High-Energy LASER System Test Facility ... HELSTF
High-Energy LASER Tactical Air Defense System ... HELTADS
High-Energy LASER Technology Applications Study ... HELTAS
High-Energy Lightweight Propellant ... HELP
High-Energy Liquid Oxidizer ... HELO
High-Energy Neutron Reactions Experiment [*Nuclear energy*] ... HENRE
High Energy and Nuclear Physics Program [*Department of Energy*] ... HENP
High-Energy Orbit [*NASA*] ... HEO
High-Energy Organic Battery ... HEOB
High-Energy Organic Electrolyte Battery System ... HEOEBS
High-Energy Particle ... HEP
High-Energy Particle Spectrometer ... HEPS
High-Energy Phosphate [*Biochemistry*] ... HEP
High-Energy Physics ... HEP

High-Energy Physics Advisory Panel [*Department of Energy*]............HEPAP
High-Energy Physics Laboratory [*Stanford University*]............HEPL
High-Energy Proton Detection Experiment............HEPDEX
High-Energy Pulse............HEP
High-Energy Rate Forging [*Metalworking*]............HERF
High-Energy Rate Forming............HERF
High-Energy Ray............HER
High-Energy Rotor [*Helicopter*] [*Army*]............HER
High-Energy Solid Oxidizer............HESO
High-Energy Squib Simulator [*NASA*]............HESS
High-Energy Squib Simulators [*NASA*]............HESSES
High-Energy Telescope [*Geophysics*]............HET
High-Energy Telescope System [*Geophysics*]............HETS
High-Energy Transfer Stage............HETS
High-Energy Upper Stage [*NASA*]............HEUS
High Enthalpy Arc Tunnel [*NASA*]............HEAT
High Explosive............HE
High-Explosive, Antiaircraft [*Weaponry*]............HEAA
High-Explosive, Antipersonnel [*Weaponry*]............HEAP
High-Explosive, Antitank [*Weaponry*]............HEAT
High-Explosive Antitank-Tracer [*Weaponry*]............HEAT-T
High-Explosive Armor-Piercing [*Weaponry*]............HEAP
High-Explosive, Discarding Sabot [*Weaponry*]............HEDS
High-Explosive Dual-Purpose [*Cartridge*]............HEDP
High-Explosive, Incendiary [*Weaponry*]............HEI
High-Explosive, Incendiary Plug [*Weaponry*]............HEIP
High-Explosive, Incendiary Self-Destroying [*Weaponry*]............HEISD
High-Explosive, Incendiary [*Shell*] **Traced** [*i.e., fitted with tracer*] [*Weaponry*]............HEIT
High-Explosive, Incendiary Tracer, Dark Ignition, Self-Destroying [*Weaponry*]............HEITDISD
High-Explosive, Incendiary Tracer, Self-Destroying [*Weaponry*]............HEITSD
High-Explosive Plastic [*Weaponry*]............HEP
High-Explosive Plastic Antitank [*Weaponry*]............HEPAT
High-Explosive Plastic Tracer [*Weaponry*]............HEP-T
High-Explosive Plugged [*Weaponry*]............HEP
High-Explosive, Point Detonating Nose Plug [*Weaponry*]............HEPDNP
High-Explosive Ramjet [*Weaponry*]............HERJ
High-Explosive Rocket Assisted [*Weaponry*]............HERA
High-Explosive, Self-Destroying [*Weaponry*]............HESD
High-Explosive Spotting [*Weaponry*]............HES
High-Explosive, Squash Head [*Weaponry*]............HESH
High-Explosive [*Shell*] **Traced** [*i.e., fitted with tracer*] [*Weaponry*]............HET
High-Explosive, Tracer, Dark Ignition [*Weaponry*]............HETDI
High-Explosive Warhead [*Weaponry*]............HEWH
High-Explosives Research and Development............HERD
High Explosives Simulation Technique............HEST
High Fat [*Type of diet*]............HF
High Fidelity [*A publication*]............HF
High Fidelity [*A publication*]............Hi Fi
High-Fidelity [*Usually, in reference to home sound-reproducing equipment*]............HI-FI
High-Fidelity Amplitude Modulation............HIFAM
High Fidelity Institute............HFI
High-Fidelity Mock-Up [*NASA*]............HFMU
High Fidelity/Musical America [*A publication*]............Hi Fi
High Fidelity/Musical America [*A publication*]............Hi Fi/Mus Am
High Flight Foundation............HFF
High Flow Shutoff Valve............HFSV
High Flux Australian Reactor [*Sydney*]............HIFAR
High Flux Beam Reactor............HFBR
High Flux Experimental Facility [*Nuclear energy*]............HFEF
High Flux Isotope Reactor............HFIR
High Flux Reactor [*Netherlands*]............HFR
High Fragmentation............HIFRAG
High Frequency [*Electronics*]............HF
High-Frequency Accelerometer............HFA
High-Frequency Airborne Antenna............HFAA
High-Frequency Antenna System............HFAS
High-Frequency Choke............HFC
High-Frequency Correction............HFC
High-Frequency Current............HFC
High-Frequency Current............HFCUR
High-Frequency Direction Finding [*Electronics*]............HDF
High-Frequency Direction Finding [*Pronounced "huff duff"*] [*Electronics*]............HFDF
High-Frequency Direction Finding [*Electronics*]............HUFF-DUFF
High-Frequency Fixed Array RADAR............HIFAR
High-Frequency Furnace............HFF
High-Frequency Instruments and Measurements............HFIM
High-Frequency Jammer............HFJ
High-Frequency Jet Ventilation [*Pulmonary ventilation*]............HFJV
High-Frequency Oscillator............HFO
High-Frequency Positive Pressure Ventilation [*Medicine*]............HFPPV
High-Frequency Radio Transmitter............HFRT
High Frequency of Recombination [*Medicine*]............HFR
High-Frequency Recovery Antenna............HFA
High-Frequency Recovery Antenna............HFRA
High Frequency Relay............HEIFER
High-Frequency Repeater Distribution Frame............HFRDF
High-Frequency Resistor............HFR
High-Frequency Single Sideband [*Communications*]............HFSSB
High-Frequency Transceiver [*or Transducer*]............HFX
High-Frequency of Transduction [*Virology*]............HFT
High-Frequency Wave Analyzer............HFWA
High Frontier [*An association*]............HF
High-Fructose Corn Sweetener [*or Syrup*]............HFCS
High Gain Antenna............HGA
High Gain Antenna Controller............HGAC
High Gain Link............HGL
High Gelling Temperature [*Analytical biochemistry*]............HGT
High Geographic Aerospace Search RADAR............HIGH GASSER
High German [*Language, etc.*]............HG
High Go Low Test............HGL
High-Grade Plow Steel............HGPS
High-Gradient Magnetic Filtration............HGMF
High-Gradient Magnetic Separation............HGMS
High Group Receiving............HGR
High Group Transmitting............HGT
High Heat [*or Heating*] **Value**............HHV
High High-Altitude Clear Air Turbulence [*Aviation*]............HI-HICAT
High-Ignition-Temperature Propellants Self-Extinguishing at Atmospheric Pressure [*Cartridge*]............HITP-SEAP
High Impact............HI
High Impact............HIM
High Impact............HIMP
High-Impact Polystyrene [*Plastics technology*]............HIPS
High-Impact Pressure............HIP
High-Impedance Bridge............HIB
High-Impedance Follower............HIF
High-Impulse Booster Experiments [*DARPA/Army*]............HIBEX
High-Impulse Retrorocket System............HIRS
High Incidence Target [*Crime computer*]............HIT
High Index [*Aviation*]............HX
High Information Delta Modulation [*Data processing*]............HIDM
High Input Impedance............HII
High Input Shock Test............HIST
High-Integrating Gyroscope............HIG
High Intensity............HI
High Intensity............HIN
High Intensity............HINT
High-Intensity Approach Lighting System [*Airport runways*]............HIALS
High-Intensity Discharge [*Vapor lamp*]............HID
High-Intensity Food Irradiator............HIFI
High-Intensity Learning Systems............HILS
High-Intensity Light............HIL
High-Intensity Lighting System [*Aviation code*]............LSB
High-Intensity Microphone............HIM
High-Intensity Noise............HIN
High-Intensity Noise Generator............HING
High-Intensity Radiation Development Laboratory............HIRDL
High-Intensity Radiation Device............HIRD
High-Intensity Reciprocity Failure............HIRF
High-Intensity Runway Lights [*Aviation*]............HIRL
High-Intensity Sound Simulator............HISS
High-Intensity Sound System............HISS
High-Interest Books for Teens [*A publication*]............HIBT
High Interference Signaling Environment............HISE
High Internal Phase Ratio............HIPR
High Jump............HJ
High-Latitude Mode............HLM
High-Latitude Operation............HLO
High Level............HL
High Level [*Canada*] [*Airport symbol*]............YOJ
High Level Ad Hoc Working Group [*NATO*]............HLAHWG
High-Level Analog............HLA
High-Level Assembly Language............HLAL
High-Level Automatic Scheduling Program............HASP
High-Level Container Airdrop System [*Army*]............HLCADS
High-Level Data Link Control [*Data processing*]............HDLC
High-Level Flux Monitor............HLFM
High-Level Forecast [*Meteorology*]............HIFOR
High-Level Group [*NATO*]............HLG
High-Level Input Voltage............HLIV
High-Level Language............HLL
High-Level Liquid Wastes [*Nuclear energy*]............HLLW
High-Level Mixer............HLM
High-Level Output Voltage............HLOV
High-Level Radio Modulator............HLRM
High-Level, Single-Ended............HLSE
High-Level Test Language............HLTL
High-Level Transistor Logic............HLTL
High-Level Transistor Translator Logic............HLTTL
High-Level Waste [*Nuclear energy*]............HLW
High Loss Ferrite............HLF
High or Low............H/L
High Low............HL
High Mach Flow............HMF
High Magnetic Field............HMF
High Magnification Viewer............HMV
High Maneuvering Aircraft Technology............HIMAT
High-Meaningfulness [*Psychology*]............HM

High Medium [*Moody's bond rating*] .... A
High-to-Medium-Altitude Air Defense .... HIMAD
High Melting Point .... HMP
High-Mobility-Agility [*Test for combat vehicles*] .... HIMAG
High Mobility Group [*of nonhistone proteins*] [*Biochemistry*] .... HMG
High-Mobility Multipurpose Wheeled Vehicle [*Pronounced "humvee"*] [*Army*] .... HMMWV
High Modulus Glass Fiber .... HMGF
High Modulus Yarn .... HMY
High Molecular [*Weight*] [*Also, HMW*] [*Organic chemistry*] .... HM
High Molecular Weight [*Also, HM*] [*Organic chemistry*] .... HMW
High Molecular-Weight, High Density .... HMHD
High Museum of Art, Atlanta, GA [*Library symbol*] .... GAHM
High National Council .... HNC
High NATO Military Structure .... HNMS
High Needle Position [*on dial*] .... HNP
High Nickel Alloy .... HNA
High-Noise-Immunity Logic .... HINIL
High-Noise-Immunity Logic .... HNIL
High Noise-Level Margin .... HNLM
High Oblique [*Aerospace*] .... HO
High Occupancy Vehicle [*Commuter routes*] [*Acronym usually followed by a number indicating the minimum number of people per vehicle*] .... HOV
High Old Genius [*Slang*] [*British*] .... HOG
High-Orbital Bombardment System .... HOBS
High-Order Articulated Language .... HAL
High-Order Assembly Language [*Data processing*] .... HAL
High-Order Assembly Language for Shuttle Flight Computer .... HAL/S
High- [*or Higher-*] **Order Language** [*Data processing*] .... HOL
High- [*or Higher-*] **Order Language Working Group** [*Data processing*] .... HOLWG
High-Order Software [*Data processing*] .... HOS
High Output Current .... HOC
High Oxygen Pressure .... HOP
High Pass [*Electronics*] .... HP
High Pass Filter .... HPF
High Pass Network .... HPN
High-Passage Virus .... HPV
High-Passage Virus [*Grown in*] **Dog Kidney** [*Cells*] .... HPV-DK
High-Passage Virus [*Grown in*] **Duck Embryo** [*Cells*] .... HPV-DE
High Performance .... HP
High-Performance Adhesive System .... HPAS
High-Performance Advanced Attack Systems .... HIPAAS
High-Performance Aerial Attack System .... HPAAS
High-Performance Air-to-Ground .... HPAG
High-Performance Aircraft Cannon .... HIPAC
High-Performance Archiheater .... HIPERARC
High-Performance Control Center [*Aerospace*] .... HPCC
High-Performance Demonstration Facility .... HPDF
High-Performance Drone .... HPD
High-Performance Electrothermal Hydrazine Thruster .... HIPEHT
High-Performance External Gun .... HIPEG
High-Performance Fuel Cell .... HPFC
High-Performance Fuels Laboratory .... HPFL
High-Performance Insulation .... HPI
High-Performance Insulation System .... HPIS
High-Performance Intercept .... HI-PI
High-Performance Ion Exchange Chromatography .... HPIEC
High-Performance Liquid Affinity Chromatography .... HPLAC
High-Performance [*or High-Pressure*] **Liquid Chromatography** .... HPLC
High-Performance Low-Pressure Chromatography .... HPLPC
High-Performance Navigation System .... HIPERNAS
High-Performance Precision Approach Control RADAR .... HIPAR
High-Performance Preparative Liquid Chromatography .... HPPLC
High-Performance Reporting Post .... HPRP
High-Performance Reversed Phase Chromatography .... HPRPC
High-Performance Size Exclusion Chromatography .... HPSEC
High-Performance Space Feed .... HIPSF
High-Performance Thin-Layer Chromatography .... HPTLC
High-Performance Third Stage [*Rocket*] [*Army*] .... HPTS
High-Performance Throttleable Injector .... HIPERTHINO
High Permittivity .... HIK
High Plains Corporation [*NASDAQ symbol*] .... HIPC
High Plains Genetics Uts [*NASDAQ symbol*] .... XYXXU
High Point .... HPT
High Point College [*North Carolina*] .... HPC
High Point College, High Point, NC [*Library symbol*] .... NcHpC
High Point, NC [*Television station call letters*] .... WGHP-TV
High Point, NC [*Radio station call letters*] .... WGLD-FM
High Point, NC [*Radio station call letters*] .... WGOS
High Point, NC [*Radio station call letters*] .... WHPE-FM
High Point, NC [*Television station call letters*] .... WIUW
High Point, NC [*Radio station call letters*] .... WMFR
High Point, NC [*Radio station call letters*] .... WMFR-FM
High Point, NC [*Radio station call letters*] .... WOKX
High Point, NC [*Radio station call letters*] .... WWIH
High Point Public Library, High Point, NC [*Library symbol*] .... NcHp
High Point, Thomasville & Denton Railroad Co. [*AAR code*] .... HPTD
High Points [*A publication*] .... H Points
High Polar Latitude [*Geophysics*] .... HPL
High-Polymer Molecular [*Film*] .... HPM
High-Polymer Rheology .... HPR
High Polymers [*A publication*] .... High Polym
High Position .... H/P
High-Positive .... HP
High Potency .... HP
High Potential .... HIPOT
High-Potential Test .... HIPOTT
High-Potential Test [*or Tester*] .... HPT
High Power .... HP
High Power [*Water boiler atomic reactor*] [*Dismantled*] .... HYPO
High-Power Acquisition RADAR .... HIPAR
High-Power Amplifier .... HPA
High-Power Density .... HPD
High-Power Diffraction Limited Raman LASER .... HPDLRL
High-Power Effects [*Radio interference*] .... HPE
High-Power Field [*Microscopy*] .... HPF
High-Power Generator .... HPG
High-Power Group .... HPG
High-Power Illuminator .... HPI
High-Power Illuminator RADAR [*Army*] .... HIPIR
High-Power Illuminator RADAR [*Army*] .... HPIR
High-Power Illuminator Signal Source .... HPISS
High-Power Jammer .... HPJ
High-Power Klystron .... HPK
High-Power Klystron Amplifier .... HPKA
High-Power LASER .... HPL
High-Power/Low-Power .... HP/LP
High-Power Microelectronic Noise Jammer .... HPMNJ
High-Power Microwave Assembly .... HPMA
High-Power Noise Jammer .... HPNJ
High-Power Switching Device .... HPSD
High-Power Transistor-Transistor Logic .... HTTL
High-Power Veractor .... HPV
High-Powered Early Warning .... HPEW
High-Powered, Nondirectional Radio Homing Beacon [*Navigation*] .... HH
High-Powered RADAR .... HPR
High-Powered RADAR Post .... HPRP
High-Powered Radio Range (Adcock) .... RA
High-Powered Vehicle .... HPV
High Prairie, AB [*Television station call letters*] CBXAT-2
High-Precision SHORAN .... HIRAN
High Pressure .... HIPR
High Pressure .... HIPRES
High Pressure .... HP
High-Pressure Air .... HPA
High-Pressure Air Accumulator .... HPAA
High-Pressure Air Compressor .... HPAC
High-Pressure Chamber .... HPCBR
High-Pressure Coolant Injection [*Nuclear energy*] .... HPCI
High-Pressure Core Spray [*Nuclear energy*] .... HPCS
High-Pressure Cylinder [*Especially, a locomotive cylinder*] .... HP
High Pressure Data Center [*National Bureau of Standards*] [*Information service*] .... HPDC
High-Pressure Demineralized Water .... HDW
High-Pressure Fuel Pump .... HPFP
High-Pressure Fuel Turbopump .... HPFT
High-Pressure Fuel Turbopump .... HPFTP
High-Pressure Gas .... HPG
High-Pressure Gas System .... HPGS
High-Pressure High-Density .... HPHD
High-Pressure Hose .... HPH
High-Pressure Injection [*Nuclear energy*] .... HPI
High-Pressure Injection System [*Nuclear energy*] .... HPIS
High-Pressure Intensifier Pump .... HPIP
High-Pressure Jet .... HPJ
High-Pressure Liquid Jet .... HPLJ
High-Pressure Low-Flow .... HPLF
High-Pressure Mercury Vapor .... HPMV
High-Pressure Nervous Syndrome [*Deep-sea diving*] .... HPNS
High-Pressure Oil-Filled [*Cable*] .... HPOF
High-Pressure Oxidizer Pump .... HPOP
High-Pressure Oxidizer Turbopump .... HPOT
High-Pressure Oxidizer Turbopump .... HPOTP
High-Pressure Oxygen .... HPO
High-Pressure Oxygen .... HPOX
High-Pressure Relief Valve .... HPRV
High-Pressure Sodium .... HPS
High-Pressure Steam [*Technical drawings*] .... HPS
High-Pressure Tap .... HPT
High-Pressure Test .... HPT
High-Pressure Unit .... HPU
High-Pressure Valve .... HPV
High Priest .... HP
High Priority .... HIPRI
High Priority .... HP
High-Priority Key [*IRS*] .... HK
High-Priority Production Program [*NATO*] .... HPPP
High-Probability Behavior .... HPB
High Protein [*Nutrition*] .... HP
High-Protein Diet .... HPD

High-Protein Supplement [*Nutrition*] ... HPS
High Pulse Recurrence Frequency ... HPRF
High Purity ... H-P
High-Purity Dual Hardness Armor ... HP-DHA
High-Purity Germanium ... HPGe
High "Q" Circuit [*or Coil*] ... HQC
High "Q" Tuned Circuit ... HQTC
High Quality Bonus Point [*Advancement system*] [*Navy*] ... HQBP
High-Quality Epitaxial Silicon ... HQES
High-Quality Life ... HQL
High-Quality Silicon ... HQS
High Random Access ... HIRAC
High-Range [*RADAR*] ... HR
High-Range Juno [*Survey meter for radiation*] ... HRJ
High-Range Pressure Control ... HRPC
High-Rate Activated Sludge [*Waste treatment*] ... HRAS
High-Rate Data Assembly ... HRDA
High-Rate Demultiplexer ... HRDM
High-Rate Digital Recorder ... HRDR
High-Rate Discharge ... HRD
High-Rate Dosimeter ... HRD
High Rate of Fire ... HRF
High-Rate Heat ... HRH
High-Rate Multiplexer ... HRM
High-Rate Physical Vapor Deposition [*Metal*] ... HRPVD
High-Rate Station ... HRS
High-Rate Telemetry [*NASA*] ... HRT
High-Rate Telemetry System [*NASA*] ... HRTS
High Refraction Layer ... HRL
High-Reliability Relay ... HRR
High-Repetition Illuminator System ... HRIS
High-Repetition LASER ... HRL
High-Repetition LASER Illuminating System ... HRLIS
High-Repetition LASER Illuminator ... HRLI
High-Repetition LASER System ... HRLS
High Resistance ... HR
High Resolution [*Data processing*] ... HI-RES
High Resolution ... HR
High-Resolution Display ... HRD
High-Resolution Doppler Imager ... HRDI
High-Resolution Electrocardiography ... HRE
High-Resolution Electron Energy Loss Spectroscopy ... HREELS
High-Resolution Electron Microscopy ... HREM
High-Resolution Electronic System ... HRES
High-Resolution Facsimile ... HRF
High-Resolution Ground Map ... HRGM
High-Resolution Hemispherical Reflector Antenna Technique ... HIHAT
High-Resolution Image [*or Imager*] [*Astronomy*] ... HRI
High-Resolution Infrared Radiation Sounder ... HIRS
High-Resolution Infrared Radiation Sounder ... HRIRS
High-Resolution Infrared Radiometer ... HRIR
High-Resolution Mass Spectrometry ... HRMS
High-Resolution Pointable Imager ... HRPI
High-Resolution RADAR ... HRR
High-Resolution System ... HRS
High-Resolution Tracker ... HRT
High-Resolution Transmission Electron Microscope [*or Microscopy*] ... HRTEM
High Resolution Visible [*Imager*] ... HRV
High-Resolution Wind Measurement Program ... HIREWIMP
High Reynolds Number Transonic Wind Tunnel ... HRNTWT
High Reynolds Number Tunnel ... HIRT
High Risk ... HR
High-Risk Test Site [*Later, Research Test Site*] ... HRTS
High River, AB [*Radio station call letters*] ... CHRB
High Run ... HR
High-Rupturing Capacity ... HRC
High School ... HS
High School [*A publication*] ... H Sch
High School Diploma Graduate [*Military*] ... HSDG
High School Driver Education [*Department of Transportation*] ... HSDE
High School Education Program at University of Pennsylvania ... HEP-UP
High School Equivalency Program ... HEP
High School Evangelism Fellowship ... HSEF
High School Geography Project [*Defunct*] ... HSGP
High School Graduate [*Classified advertising*] ... HSG
High School for Health Professions ... HSHP
High School Journal [*A publication*] ... High Sch J
High School Journal [*A publication*] ... H Sch J
High School Journal [*A publication*] ... HSJ
High School Percentile Rank ... HSR
High School Personality Questionnaire [*Psychology*] ... HSPQ
High School Placement Test ... HSPT
High School Quarterly [*A publication*] ... H Sch Q
High School Red Cross ... HSRC
High School Student Information Center ... SIC
High School Teacher [*A publication*] ... H Sch Teach
High School Young Christian Students ... YCS
High-Scope Educational Research Foundation ... H/serf
High Seas Oil Recovery System ... HSORS
High-Similarity [*Psychology*] ... HS
High Solar Intensity ... HSI
High Specific Activity [*Radioisotope*] ... HSA
High Speed ... HS
High-Speed Analog Computer ... HSAC
High-Speed Antiradiation Missile ... HARM
High-Speed Automatic Monitor ... HAM
High-Speed Autoradiography ... HARG
High-Speed Bench Press ... HSBP
High-Speed Black and White [*Photography*] ... HBW
High-Speed Bombing RADAR ... HSBR
High-Speed Bus [*Data processing*] ... HSB
High-Speed Card Punch [*Data processing*] ... HSCP
High-Speed Card Reader [*Data processing*] ... HSCR
High-Speed Card Teletypewriter Terminal [*Data processing*] ... HSCTT
High-Speed Carry ... HSC
High-Speed Color Exterior ... HCEX
High-Speed Command Link ... HSCL
High-Speed Compound Terminal [*Data processing*] ... HSCT
High-Speed Data ... HSD
High-Speed Data Acquisition ... HSDA
High-Speed Data Acquisition and Reduction System ... HS-DARS
High-Speed Data Assembly [*Ground Communications Facility, NASA*] ... HSDA
High-Speed Data Line ... HSDL
High-Speed Data Regeneration Assembly [*Ground Communications Facility, NASA*] ... HSRA
High-Speed Die Mounter ... HSDM
High-Speed Digital Filter ... HSDF
High-Speed Displacement ... HSD
High-Speed Distributor Transmitter ... HSDT
High-Speed Electrostatic Printer ... HSEP
High-Speed Flight Station [*NASA*] ... HSFS
High-Speed Force Feed ... HSFF
High-Speed Fuel Air Explosive ... HSFAE
High-Speed Ground Test Center [*Pueblo, CO*] ... HSGTC
High-Speed Ground Transportation ... HSGT
High Speed Ground Transportation Journal [*A publication*] ... HSGTJ
High-Speed Integrated Test System ... HITS
High-Speed Interferometer [*Measures chemical components of smog*] ... HSI
High-Speed Launch [*Navy*] ... HSL
High-Speed Liquid Chromatography ... HSLC
High-Speed Liquid-Liquid Chromatography ... HSLLC
High-Speed Logic ... HSL
High-Speed Memory [*Data processing*] ... HSM
High-Speed Microwave Switch ... HSMS
High-Speed Minesweeper [*Navy symbol*] ... DMS
High-Speed Modular Interface Message Processor ... HSMIMP
High-Speed Nonimpact Printer [*Acronym pronounced "hisnip"*] [*Data processing*] ... HSNP
High-Speed Paper Tape Absolute Loader [*Data processing*] ... HSPTAL
High-Speed Paper Tape Punch [*Data processing*] ... HSPTP
High-Speed Paper Tape Reader [*Data processing*] ... HSPTR
High-Speed Parallel Adder ... HSPA
High-Speed Printer [*Data processing*] ... HSP
High-Speed Pulse ... HSP
High-Speed Rail ... HSR
High-Speed Reader [*Data processing*] ... HSR
High-Speed Relay ... HSR
High-Speed Repetitive Operation ... HSRO
High-Speed Rotary Prism ... HSRP
High-Speed Scintillation Autoradiography ... HSARG
High-Speed Steel ... HSS
High-Speed Storage ... HSS
High-Speed Symbol Generator ... HSSG
High-Speed System [*Ground Communications Facility, NASA*] ... HSS
High-Speed Telemetry ... HST
High-Speed Telemetry Link ... HSTL
High-Speed Test Track ... HSTT
High-Speed Train [*British*] ... HST
High-Speed Transistor-Transistor Logic ... HSTTL
High-Speed Transport [*Navy symbol*] ... APD
High-Speed Wire Guidance ... HSWG
High Spread Shears ... HSS
High Springs, FL [*Radio station call letters*] ... WKAE
High-Stability Temperature-Compensated Crystal Oscillator ... HSTCXO
High Strand Intensity ... HSI
High-Strength Adhesive ... HSA
High-Strength Low-Alloy [*or Light-Alloy*] [*Steel*] ... HSLA
High-Strength Quick Release ... HSQR
High-Strength Thermal-Resistant Alloy ... HSTRA
High-Stress Strain ... HSS
High Sub-Chief Ranger [*Ancient Order of Foresters*] ... HSCR
High Survivability Test Vehicle, Lightweight [*Military*] ... HSTVL
High Sustained G2 Acceleration [*NASA*] ... HSG
High-Swirl Combustion [*Engine*] ... HSC
High-Tar Content [*of cigarettes*] ... HTC
High Technology ... HTEC
High Technology Capital Corp. [*NASDAQ symbol*] ... HITK
High-Technology Escape System ... HTES
High-Technology Light Brigade [*Army*] ... HTLB
High Technology Light Division [*DoD*] ... HTLD

High Technology Professionals for Peace ....HTPFP
High Technology Recruitment Index [A publication]...............HTRI
High-Technology Test Bed [Army] ....HTTB
High Temperature [A publication] ....High Temp
High Temperature ....HT
High Temperature ....HTM
High-Temperature Adhesive ....HTA
High-Temperature Alloy ....HTA
High-Temperature Ashing ....HTA
High-Temperature Carbonization ....HTC
High-Temperature Catalyst ....HTC
High-Temperature Coil ....HTC
High-Temperature Detection Lens ....HTDL
High-Temperature Distillation ....HTD
High-Temperature Electrostatic Precipitator [Anti-smoke
   pollution device]...............HTESP
High-Temperature Fluid-Wall [Incineration process] ....HTFW
High-Temperature Fuel Cell ....HTFC
High-Temperature Gas-Cooled Reactor ....HTGCR
High-Temperature Gas-Cooled Reactor ....HTGR
High-Temperature Gas-Cooled-Reactor Critical Experiment ....HTGR-CX
High-Temperature Gas-Cooled Reactor Experiment ....HTGRE
High-Temperature Heater ....HTH
High-Temperature Isotropic ....HTI
High-Temperature Lacquer ....HTL
High-Temperature Lattice Test Reactor ....HTLTR
High-Temperature Mass Spectrometry ....HTMS
High-Temperature Materials ....HTM
High-Temperature Metallography ....HTM
High-Temperature Operating Test ....HTOT
High-Temperature Oxidation ....HTO
High-Temperature Reactor ....HTR
High-Temperature Reactor Development Associates ....HTRDA
High-Temperature Resistor ....HTR
High-Temperature Reusable Surface Insulation [Space shuttle]
   [NASA] ....HRSI
High Temperature Science [A publication]...............High Temp S
High Temperature Science [A publication]...............High Temp Sci
High-Temperature Short-Time [Pasteurization] [Food processing].......HTST
High-Temperature Sodium Facility [Nuclear energy]...............HTSF
High-Temperature Strain Gauge ....HTSR
High-Temperature Thermomechanical Processing [Alloy heat
   resistance] ....HTMP
High-Temperature Thermomechanical Treatment [Steel forging]...........HTT
High Temperature USSR [A publication]...............High Temp R
High-Temperature Water ....HTW
High-Temperature Wire ....HTW
High-Temperature X-Ray Diffraction ....HTXRD
High Temperatures - High Pressures [A publication]
   High Temp High Pressures
High Tensile [Mechanics]...............HTNSL
High-Tensile Cast Iron...............HTCI
High-Tensile Steel...............HTS
High Tensile Strength [Mechanics]...............HTS
High Tension ....HT
High-Tension Battery...............H-TB
High-Tension (Battery)...............HT(B)
High-Test Hydrogen-Peroxide ....HTP
High Test Level Language...............HTLL
High-Test Recorder and Simulator System ....HYTRESS
High Threshold Logic...............HTL
High Tide ....HT
High Times [A publication]...............HT
High-Titer, Low-Avidity [Hematology]...............HTLA
High Treason ....HT
High Turbulence Level...............HTL
High Twelve International...............HI-12
High-Usage [Telecommunications]...............Hi-U
High-Vacuum Environment ....HVE
High-Vacuum Evaporation System ....HVES
High-Vacuum Evaporator ....HVE
High-Vacuum Flame Sterilization [Food technology]...............HVFS
High-Vacuum Orbital Simulator...............HIVOS
High-Vacuum Pump ....HVP
High-Vacuum Rectifier ....HVR
High-Value Accounting Control ....HIVAC
High Value Asset Control ....HILAST
High-Value Asset Control ....HIVAC
High-Value Item ....HVI
High Value Target ....HVT
High-Value Unit [Torpedo defense system] ....HVU
High Velocity ....HV
High-Velocity Aircraft Rocket ....HVAR
High-Velocity Antitank [Projectile]...............HVAT
High-Velocity, Armor-Piercing [Projectile]...............HVAP
High-Velocity, Armor-Piercing, Discarding Sabot [Projectile].........HVAPDS
High-Velocity Detonation ....HVD
High-Velocity Hot-Air [Oven]...............HVHA
High-Velocity, Target-Practice [Projectile]...............HVTP
High-Velocity, Target-Practice, Discarding Sabot [Projectile].........HVTPDS
High- and Very-High-Frequency Direction Finding ....HVDF

High Video Pass ....HVP
High Viscosity Fuel ....H
High in Volatiles [Commercial grading] ....HV
High Voltage ....HV
High-Voltage Alternating Current ....HVAC
High-Voltage Bias ....HVB
High-Voltage Connector ....HVC
High-Voltage Control ....HVC
High-Voltage Direct Current ....HVDC
High-Voltage Electron Microscopy ....HVEM
High Voltage Engineering Corp. [NYSE symbol] ....HVE
High Voltage Engineering Corporation ....HVEC
High-Voltage Gradient ....HVG
High Voltage Laboratory [MIT] ....HVL
High-Voltage Mercury-Vapor Isolator ....HVMVI
High-Voltage Mode ....HVM
High-Voltage Paper Electrophoresis ....HVPE
High-Voltage Phase Retard ....HVPR
High-Voltage Photovoltaic Effect [Physics] ....HVPVE
High-Voltage Power Supply ....HVPS
High-Voltage Pump ....HVP
High-Voltage Rectifier ....HVR
High-Voltage Regulator ....HVR
High-Voltage Relay ....HVR
High Voltage Research Laboratory [MIT]...............HVRL
High-Voltage Resistor ....HVR
High-Voltage Selenium Cartridge Rectifier ....HVSCR
High-Voltage Solar Array ....HVSA
High-Voltage Solar Experiment ....HVSE
High-Voltage Solar Panel ....HVSP
High-Voltage Switch ....HVS
High-Voltage Switching Transistor ....HVST
High-Voltage Termination ....HVT
High-Voltage Tester ....HVT
High-Voltage Transformer ....HVT
High-Voltage Waveform ....HVW
High-Voltage Wire ....HVW
High Volume ....HV
High-Volume Printing System ....HVPS
High Water [Tides and currents] ....HW
High-Water-Content Fluid [Nonpetroleum lubricant] ....HWCF
High-Water Full and Change [Tides and currents]...............HWF & C
High-Water Interval ....HWI
High-Water Line [Technical drawings] ....HWL
High-Water Lunitidal Interval ....HWLI
High-Water Mark [Maps and charts] ....HWM
High-Water Neaps ....HWN
High-Water Ordinary Spring Tides [Maps and charts] ....HWOST
High-Water Quadrature ....HWQ
High Water of Spring Tide ....HWS
High-Yielding Varieties [Agriculture] ....HYV
High Z and E [Particles in outer space] ....HZE
High Z - High Energy ....HZE
Highamerica Balloon Club [Formerly, BPA] ....HBC
Higher Clerical Officer [Civil Service] [British] ....HCO
Higher Dental Diploma [British] ....HDD
Higher Diploma in Education [British]...............H Dip E
Higher Education [A publication]...............High Educ
Higher Education [A publication]...............Higher Ed
Higher Education Act [1965] ....HEA
Higher Education Administration Referral Service ....HEARS
Higher Education Coordinating Council of Metropolitan St.
   Louis [Library network] ....HECC
Higher Education Facilities Act ....HEFA
Higher Education Facilities Commission ....HEFC
Higher Education General Information Survey [Office of
   Education]...............HEGIS
Higher Education and the Handicapped [An association]...............HEATH
Higher Education Institution ....HEI
Higher Education Journal [A publication] ....Higher Ed J
Higher Education Learning Laboratory [of Youth Pride, Inc.] ....HELL
Higher Education Opportunities Committee ....HEOC
Higher Education Panel ....HEP
Higher Education Policy and Administration Library and
   Information Service ....HEPALIS
Higher Education Research Institute ....HERI
Higher Education Resource Services ....HERS
Higher Education Review [A publication]...............High Educ R
Higher Education Review [A publication]...............Higher Ed R
Higher Equal Opportunity Program [Education]...............HEOP
Higher Executive Officer [Civil service] [British] ....HEO
Higher Executive Order ....HEO
Higher Grade ....HG
Higher Harmonic Circulation Control [Rotor] [Navy] ....HHCC
Higher High Water [Tides and currents] ....HHW
Higher High-Water Interval ....HHWI
Higher Low Water ....HLW
Higher Low-Water Interval ....HLWI
Higher National Certificate [British] ....HNC
Higher National Diploma [British] ....HND
Higher Order Language Machine [Data processing] ....HOLM

Higher Order Laue Zone [Crystal diffraction lines]..............HOLZ
Higher Rate..............HR
Higher School Certificate [British]..............HSC
Higher Scientific Officer [British]..............HSO
Highest [Standard & Poor's bond rating]..............AAA
Highest Asymptomatic [Dose] [Medicine]..............HAS
Highest Common Factor [Mathematics]..............HCF
Highest Electroendosmosis [Analytical biochemistry]..............HE
Highest In, First Out [Accounting]..............HIFO
Highest Occupied Molecular Orbital [Atomic physics]..............HOMO
Highest Possible Frequency [Electronics]..............HPF
Highest Rank Aboard..............HRA
Highest Temperature..............HITMP
Highest Temperature Equaled for All Time [Meteorology]..............HIEAT
Highest Temperature Equaled for the Month [Meteorology]..............HIEFM
Highest Temperature Equaled So Early [Meteorology]..............HIESE
Highest Temperature Equaled So Late [Meteorology]..............HIESL
Highest Temperature Exceeded for All Time [Meteorology]..............HIXAT
Highest Temperature Exceeded for the Month [Meteorology]..............HIXFM
Highest Temperature Exceeded So Early [Meteorology]..............HIXSE
Highest Temperature Exceeded So Late [Meteorology]..............HIXSL
Highest Useful Compression Ratio [Aerospace]..............HUCR
Highhams Railway [Wales]..............HR
Highland Capital Corp. [American Stock Exchange symbol]..............HLD
Highland Community Unit, School District 5, Highland, IL
  [Library symbol]..............IHigSD
Highland County District Library, Hillsboro, OH [Library symbol]..............OHilH
Highland Free Library, Highland, NY [Library symbol]..............NHig
Highland Hospital, Williams Health Science Library, Rochester,
  NY [OCLC symbol]..............VQP
Highland, IL [Radio station call letters]..............WINU
Highland Junior College [Kansas]..............HJC
Highland Light Infantry [Military unit] [British]..............HLI
Highland Light Infantry of Canada [Military unit]..............HLIC
Highland Park, IL [Radio station call letters]..............WEEF
Highland Park, IL [Radio station call letters]..............WVVX-FM
Highland Park Junior College [Later, Highland Park College]
  [Michigan]..............HPJC
Highland Park, MI [Radio station call letters]..............WHPR
Highland Park, NJ [Radio station call letters]..............WVHP-FM
Highland Park Public Library, Highland Park, IL [Library symbol]..............IHigp
Highland Park Public Library, Highland Park, IL [OCLC symbol]..............IHV
Highland Park, TX [Radio station call letters]..............KVIL
Highland Park, TX [Radio station call letters]..............KVIL-FM
Highland Railway [Scotland]..............HR
Highland Ranch [Colorado] [Seismograph station code, US
  Geological Survey] [Closed]..............HLR
Highland Rim Regional Library Center, Murfreesboro, TN
  [Library symbol]..............TMurH
Highland Secondary School, Dundas, ON, Canada [Library
  symbol]..............CaODH
Highland Springs, VA [Radio station call letters]..............WHCE
Highland Springs, VA [Radio station call letters]..............WNWZ
Highland, WI [Radio station call letters]..............WHHI
Highlander Class International Association..............HCIA
Highlanders [British]..............HIGHRS
Highlands..............HGLDS
Highlands [Board on Geographic Names]..............HLND
Highlights of Agricultural Research. Alabama Agricultural
  Experiment Station [A publication]..............Highlights Agr Res
Highlights of Personal Experience in Agriculture Department..............HOPE
Highline..............HL
Highline Community College, Midway, WA [Library symbol]..............WaMiH
Highly Automated Logic [Data processing]..............HAL
Highly Desirable..............HD
Highly Eccentric Lunar Occultation Satellite..............HELOS
Highly Eccentric [or Elliptical] Orbit Satellite..............HEOS
Highly Enriched Reactor, Aldermaston [British]..............HERALD
Highly Enriched Uranium [Nuclear reactor technology]..............HEU
Highly Extendable Language Processor [Data processing]..............HELP
Highly Instrumented Orbiting Primate Experiment..............HOPE
Highly Ionized Plasma..............HIP
Highly Oriented Pyrolytic Graphite [Engineering]..............HOPG
Highly Protected Risk [Insurance]..............HPR
Highly Purified..............HP
Highly Qualified..............HQ
Highly Sensitive Refractive Index..............HSRI
Highly Unusual Geophysical Operation [A meteorological
  research vehicle]..............HUGO
Hightstown Gazette, Hightstown, NJ [Library symbol]..............NjHigG
Hightstown Memorial Library, Hightstown, NJ [Library symbol]..............NjHig
Highveld Steel & Vanadium Limited [NASDAQ symbol]..............HSVLY
Highway..............H/W
Highway..............HWY
Highway..............Hy
Highway Action Coalition..............HAC
Highway Advisory Radio [Federal program]..............HAR
Highway Communications..............HY-COM
Highway Cost Allocation Study [Also, FHCAS]..............HCAS
Highway Emergency Locating Paging Service [For motorist
  assistance]..............HELPS

Highway Emergency Locating Plan..............HELP
Highway Engineer [A publication]..............Highw Eng
Highway Engineering Exchange Program..............HEEP
Highway Fuel Economy Test [Environmental Protection Agency]..............HFET
Highway Geology Symposium Proceedings [A publication]..............
  Highway Geol Symp Proc
Highway and Heavy Construction [A publication]..............Highw Heavy Constr
Highway Loss Data Institute..............HLDI
Highway Post Office [Bus or truck equipped with mail distribution
  facilities]..............HIPO
Highway Post Office [Bus or truck equipped with mail distribution
  facilities]..............HPO
Highway Regulating Point..............HRP
Highway Research Abstracts [A publication]..............HwyResAb
Highway Research Board [Later, TRB]..............HRB
Highway Research Board Special Report [A publication]..............
  Highw Res Board Spec Rep
Highway Research Information Service [National Academy of
  Sciences]..............HRIS
Highway Research News [A publication]..............Highw Res News
Highway Research in Progress [British]..............HRIP
Highway Research Record [A publication]..............Highw Res Rec
Highway Safety Information Service [National Highway Safety
  Administration]..............HSIS
Highway Safety Literature..............HSL
Highway Safety Program Standard [Department of Transportation]..............HSPS
Highway Safety Research Institute [University of Michigan]..............HSRI
Highway Safety Statistical Indicator..............HSSI
Highway Tariff Bureau [Later, AMCTB]..............HTB
Highway Traffic Act..............HTA
Highway Traffic Control..............HTC
Highway Traffic Control..............HWTC
Highway Traffic Regulation..............HTR
Highway Traffic Safety Center [Michigan State University]..............HTSC
Highway Transportation Officer [Army]..............HTO
Highway Trust Fund..............HTF
Highway and Urban Mass Transportation [A publication]..............
  Hi Urb Mass Tran
Highway Users Federation for Safety and Mobility..............HUF
Highway Users Federation for Safety and Mobility..............HUFSM
Highways Design and Construction [A publication]..............Highw Des Constr
Highways and Public Works [A publication]..............Highw Publ Wks
Highways and Road Construction [A publication]..............Highw Rd Constr
Highways and Road Construction [A publication]..............Highw Road Const
Highways of Traffic Engineering [A publication]..............Highw Traff Engng
Highwood Resources [NASDAQ symbol]..............HIWDF
Hikone [Japan] [Seismograph station code, US Geological Survey]..............HIK
Hikone Ronso [A publication]..............HNR
Hilbert College, Hamburg, NY [Library symbol]..............NHamH
Hilda Doolittle [Initials used as pen name of American poet, 1886-1961]..............HD
Hilfspolizei [Auxiliary Police] [German]..............HIPO
Hilina Pali [Hawaii] [Seismograph station code, US Geological Survey]..............HLP
Hill..............HL
Hill [Board on Geographic Names]..............HLL
Hill-Burton [Federal grant and loan program for construction and
  modernization of medical facilities]..............HB
Hill City, KS [Location identifier] [FAA]..............HLC
Hill Corp. [NYSE symbol] [Delisted]..............HLL
Hill Engineering Test Facility [Air Force]..............HETF
Hill Interaction Matrix [Psychology]..............HIM
Hill Junior College, Hillsboro, TX [Library symbol]..............TxHiC
Hill & Knowlton, Inc. [Public relations firm]..............H & K
Hillenbrand Industries, Inc. [NYSE symbol]..............HB
Hiller Aviation [American Stock Exchange symbol] [Delisted]..............HIL
Hillhaven, Inc. [American Stock Exchange symbol] [Delisted]..............HIL
Hillman Public Library, Hillman, MI [Library symbol]..............MiHilm
Hills..............HLS
Hillsboro Community Unit, School District 3, Hillsboro, IL
  [Library symbol]..............IHilbSD
Hillsboro & North Eastern Railway Co. [AAR code]..............HLNE
Hillsboro, OH [Radio station call letters]..............WSRW
Hillsboro, OH [Radio station call letters]..............WSRW-FM
Hillsboro, OR [Location identifier] [FAA]..............HIO
Hillsboro, OR [Radio station call letters]..............KUIK
Hillsboro Public Library, Hillsboro, IL [Library symbol]..............IHilb
Hillsboro Public Library, Hillsboro, OR [Library symbol]..............OrHil
Hillsboro, TX [Radio station call letters]..............KHBR
Hillsboro, TX [Radio station call letters]..............KJNE-FM
Hillsboro, WI [Location identifier] [FAA]..............HBW
Hillsborough Public Library, Hillsborough, NJ [Library symbol]..............NjHb
Hillsdale College, Hillsdale, MI [Library symbol]..............MiHilC
Hillsdale College, Mossey Learning Center, Hillsdale, MI [OCLC
  symbol]..............EEI
Hillsdale County Railroad Company, Inc. [AAR code]..............HCRC
Hillsdale, MI [Radio station call letters]..............WCSR
Hillsdale, MI [Radio station call letters]..............WCSR-FM
Hillside Free Public Library, Hillside, NJ [Library symbol]..............NjHil
Hillside Hospital, Glen Oaks, NY [Library symbol]..............NGoH
Hillside Public Library, Hillside, IL [Library symbol]..............IHil
Hillside Public Library, New Hyde Park, NY [Library symbol]..............NNhpH
Hillside Times, Hillside, NJ [Library symbol]..............NjHilT

Hillsville, VA [Radio station call letters]	WHHV
Hilltop	HLTP
Hillyer College, Hartford, CT [Library symbol]	CtHHy
Hilo [Hawaii] [Seismograph station code, US Geological Survey]	HIL
Hilo [Hawaii] [Airport symbol]	ITO
Hilo, HI [Radio station call letters]	KFSH
Hilo, HI [Television station call letters]	KGMD-TV
Hilo, HI [Television station call letters]	KHAW-TV
Hilo, HI [Radio station call letters]	KHLO
Hilo, HI [Television station call letters]	KHVO
Hilo, HI [Radio station call letters]	KIPA
Hilo, HI [Radio station call letters]	KKBG
Hilo, HI [Television station call letters]	KOHA-TV
Hilo, HI [Radio station call letters]	KPUA
Hilton Davis Chemical Co., Cincinnati, OH [Library symbol]	OCHDC
Hilton Head Island [South Carolina] [Airport symbol]	HHH
Hilton Head Island, SC [Radio station call letters]	WHHQ
Hilton Head Island, SC [Radio station call letters]	WHHR
Hilton High School Library, Hilton, NY [OCLC symbol]	RWM
Hilton Hotels Corp. [NYSE symbol]	HLT
HIM [Hardware Interface Module] Equipment Rack [NASA]	HER
Himac Resources Ltd. [NASDAQ symbol]	HIMVF
Himachal Journal of Agricultural Research [A publication]	Himachal J Agric Res
Himachali [MARC language code] [Library of Congress]	him
Himalaya Mountain Region [MARC geographic area code] [Library of Congress]	ah-----
Himalayan Geology [A publication]	Himalayan Geol
Himeji [Japan] [Seismograph station code, US Geological Survey]	HIM
Himpunan Usahawan Muslimin Indonesia	HUSAMI
Himself	HIMS
Hincherton Hayfever Helmet [Clear plastic head-enclosing device that allegedly relieves hayfever symptoms]	HHH
Hinchinbrook, AK [Location identifier] [FAA]	HBK
Hinchinbrook Island [Alaska] [Seismograph station code, US Geological Survey]	HIN
Hind Mazdoor Sabha [India]	HMS
Hind Oil Kamger Sabha [India]	HOKS
Hindenberg Society	HS
Hindered Amine Light Stabilizers [for plastics]	HALS
Hinderliter Industries, Inc. [American Stock Exchange symbol]	HND
Hindi [MARC language code] [Library of Congress]	hin
Hindman, KY [Radio station call letters]	WKCB
Hindman, KY [Radio station call letters]	WKCB-FM
Hinds Junior College [Mississippi]	HJC
Hinds Junior College, Raymond, MS [OCLC symbol]	MRH
Hinds Junior College, Raymond, MS [Library symbol]	MsRH
Hindu Meal [Airline notation]	HNML
Hindustan Aeronautics Limited	HAL
Hindustan Antibiotics Bulletin [A publication]	Hind Antibiot Bull
Hindustan Bible Institute	HBI
Hindustani [Language, etc.]	HIND
Hines Administrative Center [Veterans Administration]	HAC
Hines [Edward] Lumber [NASDAQ symbol]	HINE
Hinesville, GA [Location identifier] [FAA]	LHW
Hinesville, GA [Radio station call letters]	WGML
Hinge	HNG
Hinge Jaw	HJ
Hinge Line [Technical drawings]	HL
Hinge Mount	HM
Hinge Pillar [Technical drawings]	HPLR
Hinge Side	HS
Hinged [Philately]	H
Hinged Plotting Board	HPB
Hinged Rotor Blade	HRB
Hinged Seat	HS
Hingham Marine Museum, Hingham, MA [Library symbol]	MHingM
Hinrichsen's Musical Year Book [A publication]	H M Y B
Hinsdale, IL [Radio station call letters]	WHSD
Hinsdale Public Library, Hinsdale, IL [Library symbol]	IH
Hinton [Test] [Medicine]	HINT
Hinton, AB [Radio station call letters]	CIYR
Hinton, WV [Radio station call letters]	WMTD
Hinton, WV [Radio station call letters]	WMTD-FM
Hip Disarticulation [Medicine]	HD
Hip-Knee-Ankle-Foot Orthosis [Medicine]	HKAFO
Hip-Knee-Ankle Orthosis [Medicine]	HKAO
Hip-Knee Orthosis [Medicine]	HKO
Hip Orthosis [Medicine]	HO
Hipotronics, Inc. [American Stock Exchange symbol]	HIP
Hippocampal	HC
Hippocampal Pyramidal Cell [Brain anatomy]	HPC
Hippocrates [Greek physician, 460?-377? BC]	HIPP
Hippokrates [A publication]	HIPPA
Hiradastechnikai Ipari Kutato Intezet Koezlemenyei [A publication]	Hiradastech Ipari Kut Intez Koezl
Hiram College, Hiram, OH [OCLC symbol]	HRM
Hiram College, Hiram, OH [Library symbol]	OHirC
Hiram Poetry Review [A publication]	Hiram Po R
Hiram Scott College, Scottsbluff, NE [Library symbol] [Obsolete]	NbSHS
Hire Purchase	HP
Hired Farm Working Force	HFWF
Hiring, Retention, and Tenure [of college professors]	HRT
Hiroo [Japan] [Seismograph station code, US Geological Survey]	HOO
Hirosaki Medical Journal [A publication]	Hirosaki Med J
Hiroshima [Japan] [Airport symbol]	HIJ
Hiroshima [Japan] [Seismograph station code, US Geological Survey]	HIR
Hiroshima Daigaku Bungakubu Kiyo [A publication]	HiroBK
Hiroshima Journal of Medical Sciences [A publication]	Hiroshima J Med Sci
Hiroshima Journal of Medical Sciences [A publication]	Hiros J Med
Hiroshima Mathematical Journal [A publication]	Hiroshima Math J
Hiroshima Peace Center Associates [Defunct]	HPCA
Hiroshima Studies in English Language and Literature [A publication]	HSELL
Hiroshima University Geological Report [A publication]	Hiroshima Univ Geol Rep
Hiroshima University Journal of Science. Series C. Geology and Mineralogy [A publication]	Hiroshima Univ J Sci Ser C
Hirsch Chemie Ltd. [NASDAQ symbol]	HCME
His Beatitude [or His Blessedness]	HB
His [or Her] Britannic Majesty	HBM
His [or Her] Britannic Majesty's Service	HBMS
His Bundle [Cardiology]	HB
His Bundle Electrogram [Cardiology]	HBE
His [or Her] Catholic Majesty	HCM
His Eminence	HE
His [or Her] Exalted Highness [Term applied only to personages of British India]	HEH
His [or Her] Excellency	HE
His [or Her] Grace	HG
His [or Her] Grand Ducal Highness	HGDH
His Hellenic Majesty's Ship	HHMS
His [or Her] Highness	HH
His Holiness	HH
His [or Her] Imperial Highness	HIH
His Imperial Japanese Majesty's Ship	HIJMS
His [or Her] Imperial Majesty	HIM
His [or Her] Imperial and Royal Highness	HI and RH
His [or Her] Majesty	HM
His [or Her] Majesty's Aircraft Carrier	HMAC
His [or Her] Majesty's Airship	HMA
His [or Her] Majesty's Armed Forces	HMAF
His [or Her] Majesty's Australian Ship	HMAS
His [or Her] Majesty's Boom Defence Vessel	HMBDV
His [or Her] Majesty's British Ship	HMBS
His [or Her] Majesty's Canadian Navy	HMCN
His [or Her] Majesty's Canadian Ship	HMCS
His [or Her] Majesty's Civil Service	HMCS
His [or Her] Majesty's Colonial Steamer [In use in 19th century]	HMCS
His [or Her] Majesty's Customs	HMC
His [or Her] Majesty's Drifter	HMD
His [or Her] Majesty's Factory Inspectorate [Department of Employment] [British]	HMFI
His [or Her] Majesty's Factory Inspectorate Headquarters [Department of Employment] [British]	HMFIHQ
His [or Her] Majesty's Forces	HMF
His [or Her] Majesty's Government	HMG
His [or Her] Majesty's Gunboat	HMGB
His [or Her] Majesty's Hospital Ship	HMHS
His [or Her] Majesty's Household	HMH
His [or Her] Majesty's Indian Military Forces	HMIMF
His [or Her] Majesty's Indian Navy	HMIN
His [or Her] Majesty's Inspector	HMI
His [or Her] Majesty's Land Registry	HMLR
His [or Her] Majesty's Lieutenant	HML
His [or Her] Majesty's Motor Launch	HMML
His [or Her] Majesty's Motor Mine Sweeper	HMMMS
His [or Her] Majesty's New Zealand Ship	HMNZS
His [or Her] Majesty's Overseas Civil Service	HMOCS
His [or Her] Majesty's Procurator General and Treasury Solicitor	HMPGTS
His [or Her] Majesty's Service	HMS
His [or Her] Majesty's Ship	HMS
His [or Her] Majesty's Stationery Office	HMSO
His [or Her] Majesty's Steamer	HMS
His [or Her] Majesty's Telegraph Ship	HMTS
His [or Her] Majesty's Transport	HMT
His [or Her] Majesty's Trawler	HMT
His Master's Voice [Phonograph records]	HMV
His [or Her] Royal Highness	HRH
His [or Her] Serene Highness [Used for certain Continental European princes or princesses]	HSH
His [or Her] Serene Majesty	HSM
Hispamerica. Revista de Literatura [A publication]	Hispam
Hispania [A publication]	H
Hispania [A publication]	Hi
Hispania [A publication]	His
Hispania [Madrid] [A publication]	Hisp
Hispania [Stanford, California] [A publication]	Hisp
Hispania Antiqua [A publication]	HAnt
Hispania (Baltimore) [A publication]	HBalt

Hispania (Madrid) [*A publication*]....HiM
Hispania (Madrid) [*A publication*]....HispM
Hispania (Madrid) [*A publication*]....HMad
Hispania Sacra [*A publication*]....HS
Hispania (Stanford, California) [*A publication*]....HCal
Hispania (Stanford, California) [*A publication*]....HispCal
Hispania (University of Kansas. Lawrence) [*A publication*]....HisK
Hispania (University of Kansas. Lawrence) [*A publication*]....HisL
Hispania (USA) [*A publication*]....HiUS
Hispanic American Historical Review [*A publication*]....HAHR
Hispanic American Historical Review [*A publication*]....Hisp Amer Hist Rev
Hispanic American Historical Review [*A publication*]....Hispan Am Hist R
Hispanic American Historical Review [*A publication*]....Hispanic Am His R
Hispanic American Report [*A publication*]....Hispan Am Rep
Hispanic Energy Forum....HEF
Hispanic Institute for the Performing Arts....HIFPA
Hispanic Institute in the United States....HIUS
Hispanic National Bar Association....HNBA
Hispanic Policy Development Project....HPDP
Hispanic Press Index [*A publication*]....Hisp Press Ind
Hispanic Public Affairs Association....HPAA
Hispanic Review [*A publication*]....HIR
Hispanic Review [*A publication*]....Hispan R
Hispanic Review [*A publication*]....Hisp Rev
Hispanic Review [*A publication*]....HR
Hispanic Society of America....HSA
Hispanic Society of America, New York, NY [*Library symbol*]....NNH
Hispaniola [*MARC geographic area code*] [*Library of Congress*]....nwhi---
Hispano-Suiza Society....HSS
Hispanofila [*Madrid*] [*A publication*]....Hispano
Hispanofila [*Madrid and Illinois*] [*A publication*]....Hispl
Hispunan Serikat Buruh Indonesia [*Federation of Indonesian Trade Unions*]....HISSBI
HISS [*Herpetological Information Search Systems*] **News-Journal** [*A publication*]....HISS News-J
Histadruth Ivrith of America....HI
Histadruth Ivrith of America....HIA
Histamine Club [*Later, HRSNA*]....HC
Histamine Research Society of North America [*Formerly, AC*]....HRSNA
Histidine [*One-letter symbol; see His*]....H
Histidine [*Also, H*] [*An amino acid*]....His
Histidine Decarboxylase [*An enzyme*]....HDC
Histidine-Rich Protein [*Biochemistry, immunochemistry*]....HRP
Histidinol Dehydrogenase [*An enzyme*]....HDH
Histochemical Journal [*A publication*]....Histochem J
Histochemical Society....HCS
Histochemistry [*A publication*]....Histochemis
Histocompatibility Locus [*Immunology*]....HL
Histocompatibility Locus Antigens [*System*] [*Immunology*]....HLA
Histocompatibility Y [*Immunology*]....H-Y
Histocytic Medullary Reticulosis [*Oncology*]....HMR
Histogram Average Ogive Calculator....HAVOC
Histoire de l'Academie Royale des Sciences [*A publication*]....Hist Acad Roy Sc
Histoire des Idees et Critique Litteraire [*A publication*]....HICL
Histoire Litteraire de la France [*A publication*]....HLF
Histoire Sociale/Social History [*A publication*]....Hist Soc
Histoire de la Spiritualite Chretienne [*A publication*]....HSC
Histology....HISTOL
Historia Agriculturae [*A publication*]....Hist Ag
Historia Judaica [*A publication*]....HJ
Historia Judaica [*A publication*]....HJud
Historia Mathematica [*A publication*]....Historia Math
Historia Medicinae Veterinariae [*A publication*]....Hist Med Vet
Historia Mexicana [*A publication*]....Hist Mex
Historia Mexicana [*A publication*]....H Mex
Historia i Teoria Literatury-Studia [*A publication*]....HTLStu
Historiae Societatis Socius [*Fellow of the Historical Society*]....HSS
Historian [*or History*]....HIS
Historian [*or History*]....HIST
Historian....HISTN
Historian's Microfilm Company, Cazenovia, NY [*Library symbol*]....HmC
Historic American Buildings [*Survey*] [*Library of Congress*]....HAB
Historic American Buildings Survey [*Library of Congress*]....HABS
Historic American Engineering Record [*Department of the Interior*]....HAER
Historic Buildings Bureau [*British*]....HBB
Historic Buildings Council [*British*]....HBC
Historic Commands of the American Revolution [*An association*]....HCAR
Historic Deerfield [*An association*]....HD
Historic Deerfield, Inc., Deerfield, MA [*Library symbol*]....MDeeH
Historic House Association of America....HHAA
Historic Mobile Preservation Society Headquarters, Mobile, AL [*Library symbol*]....AMobHi
Historic Naval Ships of the World [*An association*]....HINASW
Historic Preservation [*A publication*]....Hist Pres
Historic Preservation [*A publication*]....Hist Preservation
Historic Winslow House, Marshfield, MA [*Library symbol*]....MMarsW
Historica [*A publication*]....Hist
Historica Iberica [*A publication*]....HI
Historical....HISTL
Historical Abstracts [*A publication*]....HistAb
Historical Abstracts [*A publication*]....Hist Abstr
Historical Association of Southern Florida, Miami, FL [*Library symbol*]....FMHiS
Historical Branch [*Army*]....HB
Historical Bulletin [*A publication*]....HB
Historical Bulletin [*A publication*]....Hist Bull
Historical Commission....HC
Historical Commission, Southern Baptist Convention....HCSBC
Historical Committee of the Mennonite Church....MHC
Historical Data System [*Air Force*]....HDS
Historical Development....HD
Historical Division [*Air Force*]....HD
Historical English Dictionary [*A publication*]....HED
Historical Evaluation and Research Organization....HERO
Historical Foundation of the Presbyterian and Reformed Churches, Montreat, NC [*Library symbol*]....NcMHi
Historical Handbook....HH
Historical Journal [*A publication*]....Hist J
Historical Journal (Birmingham) [*A publication*]....Hist Ju (Birmingham)
Historical Magazine [*Dawson's*] [*A publication*]....Hist M
Historical Magazine of the Protestant Episcopal Church [*A publication*]....Hist Mag
Historical Magazine of the Protestant Episcopal Church [*A publication*]....HME
Historical Magazine of the Protestant Episcopal Church [*A publication*]....HMPEC
Historical Manuscripts Commission [*British*]....HMC
Historical Metallurgy [*A publication*]....Hist Metall
Historical Motion Picture Milestones Association....HMPMA
Historical New Hampshire [*A publication*]....Hist NH
Historical New Hampshire [*A publication*]....HNH
Historical Outlook [*A publication*]....His Outlook
Historical Outlook [*A publication*]....Hist Outl
Historical and Philosophical Society of Ohio Bulletin [*A publication*]....HPSO
Historical Preservation of America [*Publisher*]....HPA
Historical Record....HR
Historical Records and Studies [*A publication*]....HRS
Historical Report - Korea Military Advisory Group....HR-KMAG
Historical Review of Berks County [*A publication*]....HRBC
Historical and Scientific Society of Manitoba Transactions [*A publication*]....Hist Sc Soc Manit Tr
Historical Sea Surface Temperature Data Project [*WMO*]....HSSTD
Historical Society of Berks County, Reading, PA [*Library symbol*]....PRHi
Historical Society of Bloomfield, Bloomfield, NJ [*Library symbol*]....NjBlHi
Historical Society of Cheshire County, Keene, NH [*Library symbol*]....NhKeHi
Historical Society of Delaware, Wilmington, DE [*Library symbol*]....DeHi
Historical Society of Early American Decoration....HSEAD
Historical Society of the Episcopal Church [*Formerly, CHS*]....HSEC
Historical Society of the Evangelical and Reformed Church [*Later, ERHS-UCC*]....HSERC
Historical Society of the Evangelical United Brethren Church [*Later, General Commission on Archives and History of the United Methodist Church*]....HSEUBC
Historical Society of Frankford, Philadelphia, PA [*Library symbol*] [*Obsolete*]....PPFHi
Historical Society of Haddonfield, Haddonfield, NJ [*Library symbol*]....NjHHi
Historical Society of Montana Contributions [*A publication*]....Hist Soc Mont Contr
Historical Society of Montgomery County, Norristown, PA [*Library symbol*] [*Obsolete*]....PNortHi
Historical Society of New Mexico, Santa Fe, NM [*Library symbol*]....NmHi
Historical Society Nicholas Denis, Caraquet, NB, Canada [*Library symbol*]....CaNBCH
Historical Society of Ottawa Library and the Bytown Historical Museum, Ottawa, ON, Canada [*Library symbol*]....CaOOHI
Historical Society of Pennsylvania, Philadelphia, PA [*Library symbol*]....PHi
Historical Society of Princeton, Princeton, NJ [*Library symbol*]....NjPHi
Historical Society of Southern California, Los Angeles, CA [*Library symbol*]....CLHi
Historical Society of Southern California Quarterly [*A publication*]....HSSCQ
Historical Society of the Southern Convention, Congregation of Christian Churches, Elon College, NC [*Library symbol*]....NcElonCH
Historical Society of the Tarrytowns, Tarrytown, NY [*Library symbol*]....NTaHi
Historical Society of the Tonawandas, Tonawanda, NY [*Library symbol*]....NTonHi
Historical Society of Western Pennsylvania, Pittsburgh, PA [*Library symbol*]....PPiHi
Historical Society of York County, York, PA [*Library symbol*]....PYHi
Historical Studies [*A publication*]....Hist Stud
Historical Studies in the Physical Sciences [*A publication*]....HSPhS
Historical Survey....HS
Historical Wyoming [*A publication*]....HW
Historiche Avonden, Uitgegeven door het Historiche Genootschap te Groningen ter Gelegenheid van Zijn Twintigjarig Bestaan [*A publication*]....HAHGG
Historicky Casopis [*A publication*]....HC
Historiografia y Bibliografia Americanistas [*A publication*]....HBA

Historiographia Linguistica [*A publication*] ... HistL
Historiographia Linguistica [*A publication*] ... HL
Historisch-Politische Blaetter fuer das Katholische Deutschland [*A publication*] ... HPB
Historisch-Politische Blaetter fuer das Katholische Deutschland [*A publication*] ... HPBKD
Historisch-Politische Blaetter fuer das Katholische Deutschland [*A publication*] ... HPBL
Historische. Archiv fuer die Erzbistum Koeln [*A publication*] ... HAEK
Historische Vierteljahrschrift [*A publication*] ... HV
Historische Vierteljahrschrift [*A publication*] ... HVJ
Historische Vierteljahrschrift [*A publication*] ... HVJS
Historische Zeitschrift [*A publication*] ... Hist Z
Historische Zeitschrift [*A publication*] ... Hist Ztsch
Historische Zeitschrift [*A publication*] ... HZ
Historischer Verein fuer Mittelfranken. Jahresberichte [*A publication*] ... Hist Ver f Mittelfranken Jahresber
Historischer Verein fuer Nordingen und Umgebung [*A publication*] ... HVNU
Historisches Jahrbuch [*A publication*] ... HJ
Historisches Jahrbuch der Stadt Graz [*A publication*] ... Hist Jb Graz
Historisches Litteraturblatt [*A publication*] ... HLB
Historisk-Filosofiske Meddelelser Udgivet af det Kongelinge Danske Videnskabernes Selskab [*A publication*] ... HFM
Historisk-Filosofiske Meddelelser Udgivet af det Kongelinge Danske Videnskabernes Selskab [*A publication*] ... HFMKDVS
Historisk Tidskrift [*A publication*] ... Hist Tidskr
Historisk Tidskrift [*A publication*] ... HT
Historisk Tidskrift [*A publication*] ... HTK
Historisk Tidskrift foer Finland [*A publication*] ... HTF
Historisk Tidskrift foer Finland [*A publication*] ... HTsFi
Historisk Tidskrift (Oslo) [*A publication*] ... HTO
Historisk Tidskrift (Stockholm) [*A publication*] ... HTS
Historiska och Litteraturhistoriska Studier [*A publication*] ... HLS
History [*A publication*] ... H
History [*A publication*] ... Hist
History [*Medicine*] ... Hx
History [*Medicine*] ... Hy
[*The*] **History Book Club** ... HBC
History of Earth Sciences Society ... HESS
History of Economics Society ... HES
History of Education Journal [*A publication*] ... Hist Educ Jour
History of Education Quarterly [*A publication*] ... Hist Educ Q
History of Education Society ... HES
History of Education Society Bulletin [*A publication*] ... History of Ed Soc Bull
History of Ideas Newsletter [*A publication*] ... HINL
History of Medicine On-Line [*Data base*] [*National Library of Medicine*] ... HISTLINE
History of Medicine Series [*A publication*] ... His Med Ser
History Of [*Medicine*] ... H/O
History and Physical [*Examination*] [*Medicine*] ... H & P
History of Political Economy [*A publication*] ... Hist Pol Ec
History of Political Economy [*A publication*] ... Hist Pol Econ
History of Political Economy [*A publication*] ... Hist Polit
History of Present Illness ... HPI
History Quarterly [*A publication*] ... His Q
History Record Folder ... HRF
History of Religions [*A publication*] ... Hist Rel
History of Religions [*A publication*] ... Hist Relig
History of Religions [*A publication*] ... HR
History. Review of New Books [*A publication*] ... Hist R New Bk
History. Review of New Books [*A publication*] ... HRNB
History of Science [*A publication*] ... Hist of Sci
History of Science [*A publication*] ... Hist Sci
History of Science Cases ... HOSC
History of Science Society ... HSS
History Teacher [*A publication*] ... Hist Tchr
History Teacher [*A publication*] ... Hist Teach
History Teacher's Magazine [*A publication*] ... His Teach M
History Teacher's Magazine [*A publication*] ... HTM
History and Theory [*A publication*] ... Hist & T
History and Theory [*A publication*] ... Hist Theor
History and Theory [*A publication*] ... Hist and Theory
History and Theory [*A publication*] ... H & T
History Today [*A publication*] ... Hist Today
History Today [*A publication*] ... HT
History Workshop [*A publication*] ... History
Hit Batsman [*Baseball*] ... HB
Hit Indicator System ... HIS
Hit by Pitcher [*Baseball*] ... HBP
Hit by Pitcher [*Baseball*] ... HP
Hit Rate ... HR
Hit Scoring Device ... HSD
Hit Wicket ... HW
Hitachi Arithmetic Processor ... HARP
Hitachi Computer ... HITAC
Hitachi Ltd. ADR [*NYSE symbol*] ... HIT
Hitachi Ltd. Debs [*NASDAQ symbol*] ... HITAZ
Hitachi Parametron Automatic Computer ... HIPAC
Hitachi Review [*A publication*] ... Hitachi Rev
Hitachi Training Reactor [*Japan*] ... HTR
Hitachi Zosen Technical Review [*A publication*] ... Hitachi Zosen Tech Rev
Hitchhikers for America ... HFA
Hitotsubashi Academy. Annals [*A publication*] ... AHA
Hitotsubashi Journal of Arts and Sciences [*A publication*] ... Hitotsubashi J Arts Sc
Hitotsubashi Journal of Arts and Sciences [*A publication*] ... HJAS
Hitotsubashi Journal of Commerce and Management [*A publication*] ... Hitotsubashi J Com Manag
Hitotsubashi Journal of Commerce and Management [*A publication*] ... Hitotsubashi J Commer Manage
Hitotsubashi Journal of Commerce and Management [*A publication*] ... HJC
Hitotsubashi Journal of Economics [*A publication*] ... Hitots J Econ
Hitotsubashi Journal of Economics [*A publication*] ... Hitotsubashi J Econ
Hitotsubashi Journal of Economics [*A publication*] ... HJE
Hitotsubashi Journal of Social Studies [*A publication*] ... Hitotsubashi J Soc Stud
Hitotsubashi Journal of Social Studies [*A publication*] ... HJSS
Hitotsubashi University. Hitotsubashi Academy. Annals [*A publication*] ... HAA
Hits [*Baseball*] ... H
Hits per Gun per Minute ... HPGPM
Hittman Associates, Inc., Columbia, MD [*Library symbol*] ... MdCoH
Hizb Dastur Mustaghil Somalia [*Somali Independent Constitution Party*] ... HDMS
Hizbia Dighill e Mirifle [*Somali political party*] ... HDM
Hjalmar Bergman Samfundet Arsbok [*A publication*] ... HBSA
HLH Petroleum [*NASDAQ symbol*] ... HLHP
HMG Property Investors, Inc. [*Formerly, Hospital Mortgage Group*] [*American Stock Exchange symbol*] ... HMG
HMW Industries, Inc. [*Formerly, Hamilton Watch Co.*] [*NYSE symbol*] [*Delisted*] ... HMW
HNO (Hals-, Nasen-, Ohren-Heilkunde) [*A publication*] ... HNO
HNO: Wegweiser fuer die Fachaerztliche Praxis [*Later, HNO (Hals-, Nasen-, Ohren-Heilkunde)*] [*A publication*] ... HNO Weg Fac
Ho Chi Minh [*Vietnam*] [*Airport symbol*] ... SGN
Ho Eranistes [*A publication*] ... HoE
Ho Neos Koubaras [*A publication*] ... HNK
Hoan Products Ltd. [*NASDAQ symbol*] ... HOAN
Hoard Historical Museum, Fort Atkinson, WI [*Library symbol*] ... WFaH
Hoard's Dairyman [*A publication*] ... Hoard's D
Hobart [*Tasmania*] [*Airport symbol*] ... HBA
Hobart Bay [*Alaska*] [*Airport symbol*] ... HBH
Hobart Corp. [*NYSE symbol*] [*Delisted*] ... HOB
Hobart Mills [*California*] [*Seismograph station code, US Geological Survey*] ... HBM
Hobart Mills [*California*] [*Seismograph station code, US Geological Survey*] ... HBT
Hobart, OK [*Location identifier*] [*FAA*] ... HBR
Hobart, OK [*Radio station call letters*] ... KQTZ
Hobart, OK [*Radio station call letters*] ... KTJS
Hobart and William Smith Colleges, Geneva, NY [*Library symbol*] ... NGH
Hobart and William Smith Colleges, Geneva, NY [*OCLC symbol*] ... ZEM
Hobbies [*A publication*] ... Hob
Hobbs [*New Mexico*] [*Airport symbol*] ... HOB
Hobbs, NM [*Location identifier*] [*FAA*] ... HBB
Hobbs, NM [*Television station call letters*] ... KHFT
Hobbs, NM [*Radio station call letters*] ... KHOB
Hobbs, NM [*Radio station call letters*] ... KPER
Hobbs, NM [*Radio station call letters*] ... KUUX
Hobbs, NM [*Radio station call letters*] ... KZOR
Hobbs Public Library, Hobbs, NM [*OCLC symbol*] ... HOB
Hobbs Public Library, Hobbs, NM [*Library symbol*] ... NmHo
Hobby Clubs of America ... HCA
Hobby Greenhouse Owners Association of America ... HGA
Hobby Guild of America ... HGA
Hobby Horse Brigade of the Legion of Guardsmen ... HHBLG
Hobby Industry Association of America ... HIA
Hobby Industry Association of America ... HIAA
Hobie Class Association ... HCA
[*Anthony von*] **Hoboken** [*When used in identifying Haydn's compositions, refers to cataloging of his works by musicologist Hoboken*] ... H
Hoboken Free Public Library, Hoboken, NJ [*Library symbol*] ... NjHo
Hoboken Manufacturers [*AAR code*] ... HMR
Hoboken Shore Railroad [*AAR code*] ... HBS
Hoc Anno [*This Year*] [*Latin*] ... HA
Hoc Est [*That Is or This Is*] [*Latin*] ... HE
Hoc Loco [*In This Place*] [*Latin*] ... HL
Hoc Loco Situs [*Laid in This Place*] [*Latin*] ... HLS
Hoc Mense [*In This Month*] [*Latin*] ... HM
Hoc Monumentum Fieri Fecit [*Caused This Monument to Be Made*] [*Latin*] ... HMFF
Hoc Monumentum Posuit [*He, or She, Erected This Monument*] [*Latin*] ... HMP
Hoc Nocte [*Tonight*] [*Pharmacy*] ... HN
Hoc Quaere [*Look For This or See This*] [*Latin*] ... HQ
Hoc Sensu [*In This Sense*] [*Latin*] ... HS
Hoc Tempore [*At This Time*] [*Latin*] ... HT
Hoc Titulo [*In, or Under, This Title*] [*Latin*] ... HT
Hoc Verbum [*This Word*] [*Latin*] ... HV
Hoc Vespere [*Tonight*] [*Pharmacy*] ... HOC VESP

Hochland [*A publication*] .... HI
Hochland [*A publication*] .... Ho
Hochland [*A publication*] .... Hochl
Hochschulbuecher fuer Mathematik [*A publication*] .... Hochschulb Math
Hochschulbuecher fuer Physik [*A publication*] .... Hochschulb Phys
Hochschullehrbuecher fuer Biologie [*A publication*] .... Hochschullehrb Biol
Hochschulnachrichten [*A publication*] .... Hn
Hocker Federation International .... HFI
Hockessin, DE [*Radio station call letters*] .... WZZE
Hockey Club .... HC
Hockey Rules Board .... HRB
Hocking Technical College, Nelsonville, OH [*OCLC symbol*] .... HTN
Hockley [*Texas*] [*Seismograph station code, US Geological Survey*] .... HKT
Hodeidah [*Yemen Arab Republic*] [*Airport symbol*] .... HOD
Hodgenville, KY [*Radio station call letters*] .... WKMO
Hodges-Lehmann Estimator [*Statistics*] .... HL
Hodgkin's Disease [*Medicine*] .... HD
Hodgkin's Lymphoma [*Medicine*] .... HL
Hodgkins Public Library District, Hodgkins, IL [*Library symbol*] .... IHod
Hodowla Roslin Aklimatyzacja i Nasiennictwo [*A publication*] .... Hodowla Rosl Aklim Nasienn
Hoe [*R.*] **& Co., Inc.** [*American Stock Exchange symbol*] [*Delisted*] .... HOE
Hoe [*R.*] **& Company, Inc.** [*NASDAQ symbol*] .... HOEC
Hoechst-Roussel Pharmaceuticals, Inc. [*Research code symbol*] .... HOE
Hoechst-Roussel Pharmaceuticals, Inc. [*Research code symbol*] .... HR
Hoechst-Roussel Pharmaceuticals, Inc., Somerville, NJ [*Library symbol*] .... NjSoHR
Hoeheres Kommando [*Higher Command*] [*German military - World War II*] .... HK
Hoerner Waldorf Corporation [*NYSE symbol*] [*Delisted*] .... HWC
Hoesch, Arbeitskreis Forschung und Entwicklung, Berichte aus Forschung und Entwicklung Unserer Werke [*A publication*] .... Hoesch Ber Forsch Entwickl Werke
Hoessel und Winkler GmbH Luftverkehragesellschaft [*West Germany*] [*ICAO designator*] .... HD
Hof [*Federal Republic of Germany*] [*Seismograph station code, US Geological Survey*] .... HOF
Hof [*West Germany*] [*Airport symbol*] .... HOQ
Hofbibliothek, Aschaffenburg, Germany [*Library symbol*] .... GyAsH
Hoffer-Osmond Diagnostic Test [*Psychology*] .... HOD
Hoffman [*Reflex*] [*Medicine*] .... HOFF
Hoffman Core Driver .... HCD
Hoffman Electronics Corporation [*NYSE symbol*] [*Delisted*] .... HEC
Hoffman-La Roche Ltd., Vaudreuil, PQ, Canada [*Library symbol*] .... CaQVauH
Hoffman, NC [*Location identifier*] [*FAA*] .... HFF
Hoffmann-La Roche, Inc. [*Research code symbol*] .... LA
Hoffmann-La Roche, Inc. [*Research code symbol*] .... NIH
Hoffmann-La Roche, Inc. [*Research code symbol*] .... NSC
Hoffmann-La Roche, Inc. [*Switzerland, USA*] [*Research code symbol*] .... Ro
Hoffmann-La Roche, Inc., Scientific Library, Nutley, NJ [*Library symbol*] .... NjNuH
Hofmann Industries, Inc. [*American Stock Exchange symbol*] .... HOF
Hofmannsthal Blaetter [*A publication*] .... HBL
Hofn [*Iceland*] [*Airport symbol*] .... HFN
Hofstra Law Review [*A publication*] .... Hofstra L Rev
Hofstra University, Hempstead, NY [*Library symbol*] .... NHemH
Hofstra University, Hempstead, NY [*OCLC symbol*] .... ZIH
Hofstra University, Law School, Library, Hempstead, NY [*OCLC symbol*] .... ZHL
Hofstra University Yearbook of Business [*A publication*] .... Hofstra Univ Yrbk Bus
Hog Intrinsic Factor Concentrate .... HIFC
Hog Production [*A publication*] .... Hog Prod
Hogan Systems, Inc. [*NASDAQ symbol*] .... HOGN
Hogen Kenkyu Nenpo [*A publication*] .... HKN
Hogg's Instructor [*A publication*] .... Hogg
Hogshead .... HD
Hogshead .... HGD
Hogshead .... HHD
Hohenheim [*Federal Republic of Germany*] [*Seismograph station code, US Geological Survey*] [*Closed*] .... HOH
Hohenwald, TN [*Radio station call letters*] .... WMLR
Hohenzollern Society .... HS
Hohhot [*China*] [*Airport symbol*] .... HET
Hohkeppel [*Federal Republic of Germany*] [*Seismograph station code, US Geological Survey*] .... HOK
Hoisington, KS [*Radio station call letters*] .... KHOK
Hoist .... HO
Hoist .... HST
Hoist Manufacturers Association [*Later, HMI*] .... HMA
Hoist Manufacturers Institute [*Formerly, HMA*] .... HMI
Hoisting Tool .... HT
Hoja Tisiologica [*A publication*] .... Hoja Tisiol
Hokitika [*New Zealand*] [*Airport symbol*] .... HKK
Hokkai Gakuen University, Sapporo, Japan [*Library symbol*] .... JSHG
Hokkaido Daigaku Bungakubu Kiyo [*A publication*] .... HKDBK
Hokkaido Forest Products Research Institute Reports [*A publication*] .... Hokkaido Forest Prod Res Inst Rept
Hokkaido Geological Survey Report [*A publication*] .... Hokkaido Geol Surv Rep
Hokkaido Journal of Medical Science [*A publication*] .... Hokkaido J Med Sci
Hokkaido Mathematical Journal [*A publication*] .... Hokkaido Math J
Hokkaido National Agricultural Experiment Station Data [*A publication*] .... Hokkaido Natl Agric Exp Stn Data
Hokkaido National Agricultural Experiment Station Report [*A publication*] .... Hokkaido Natl Agric Exp Stn Rep
Hokkaido University [*Japan*] [*Seismograph station code, US Geological Survey*] .... HSS
Hokkaido University Faculty of Science Journal. Series 4. Geology and Minera logy [*A publication*] .... Hokkaido Univ Fac Sci J Ser 4
Hokkaido University Medical Library Series [*A publication*] .... Hokkaido Univ Med Libr Ser
Hokkaido University, Sapporo, Japan [*Library symbol*] .... JSU
Holborn Review [*A publication*] .... Holb Rev
Holbrook, AZ [*Radio station call letters*] .... KDJI
Holbrook High School Library, Holbrook, AZ [*Library symbol*] .... AzHH
Hold .... HLD
Hold Acknowledge [*Data processing*] .... HLDA
Hold for Arrival of Goods .... HAG
Hold Fire [*Military*] .... HF
Hold for Money [*Business and trade*] .... HFM
Hold Off Normal .... HON
Hold for Release .... HFR
Holddown .... H/D
Holddown .... HLDDN
Holddown .... HLDN
Holddown Alignment Support .... HAS
Holddown Arm .... HDA
Holddown Post .... HDP
Holddown and Release .... HDR
Holdenville, OK [*Location identifier*] [*FAA*] .... HDL
Holdenville, OK [*Radio station call letters*] .... KVYL
Holder .... HLDR
Holder .... HLR
Holder in Due Course [*Owner or holder of a negotiable instrument at some future time*] .... HDC
Holderlin-Jahrbuch [*A publication*] .... HoJb
Holderlin-Jahrbuch [*A publication*] .... Holderlin-Jahrb
Holding [*Electronics*] .... H
Holding .... HLDG
Holding Activity .... H/A
Holding Coil .... HC
Holding Fixture .... HF
Holding Instructions Issued [*Aviation*] .... H
Holding Out [*Cashier fraud*] .... HO
Holding Pattern [*Aviation*] .... HP
Holding as Previously Instructed [*Aviation*] .... HAPI
Holding under Promise of Payment .... HPP
Holding and Reconsignment [*Military*] .... H & R
Holding and Reconsignment Point [*Military*] .... H & RP
Holding and Reconsignment Point [*Military*] .... HRP
Holding and Reconsignment Point [*Military*] .... H & RPO
Holdover [*Theater*] .... HO
Holdrege, NE [*Location identifier*] [*FAA*] .... HDE
Holdrege, NE [*Radio station call letters*] .... KUVR
Holdrege, NE [*Radio station call letters*] .... KUVR-FM
Holdrege-Phelps County Library, Holdrege, NE [*Library symbol*] .... NbHo
Holdup [*FBI standardized term*] .... HDLP
Holdup Alert - Local Transmission [*Bank robbery alarm system*] .... HALT
Hole-Electron Pair .... HEP
Hole P-Type Semiconductor Material .... P
Holguin [*Cuba*] [*Airport symbol*] .... HOG
Holiday .... HOL
Holiday Airlines, Inc. [*Morristown, NJ*] [*FAA designator*] .... HOL
Holiday Airlines, Inc. [*Air carrier designation symbol*] .... HOLX
Holiday Camps [*Public-performance tariff class*] [*British*] .... HC
Holiday Caravan Parks [*Public-performance tariff class*] [*British*] .... HCP
Holiday, FL [*Radio station call letters*] .... WVTY
Holiday Inn University, Olive Branch, MS [*Library symbol*] .... TMHI-U
Holiday Inns of America, Memphis, TN [*Library symbol*] .... TMHI
Holiday Inns, Inc. [*NYSE symbol*] .... HIA
Holiday Institute of Yonkers .... HIY
Holiday and Leave [*Military*] .... HOL
Holiday Pay [*Army*] .... HP
Holiday, Upkeep [*Military*] .... HOLUPK
Holidays for Humanity [*An association*] .... HH
Holidays, Vacation, and Sick Leave .... HVSL
Holifield National Laboratory .... HNL
Holistic Dental Association .... HDA
Holistic Health Havens .... HHH
Holistic Health Organizing Committee .... HHOC
Holistic Life Foundation .... HLF
Holland .... HOLL
Holland America Cruises [*Formerly, Holland-America Line*] .... HAC
Holland-America Line [*Later, Holland America Cruises*] .... HAL
Holland Cheese Exporters Association .... HCEA
Holland College, Charlottetown, PE, Canada [*Library symbol*] .... CaPCHC
Holland Furnace Co. [*NYSE symbol*] [*Delisted*] .... HLN
Holland Info [*A publication*] .... Holld Info
Holland Lop Rabbit Specialty Club .... HLRSC

Holland, MI [*Location identifier*] [*FAA*] HLM
Holland, MI [*Radio station call letters*] WHTC
Holland, MI [*Radio station call letters*] WHTC-FM
Holland, MI [*Radio station call letters*] WJBL-FM
Holland, MI [*Radio station call letters*] WWJQ
Holland Mills [*Quebec*] [*Seismograph station code, US Geological Survey*] [*Closed*] HMC
Holland, OH [*Radio station call letters*] WPOS-FM
Holland Purchase Historical Society, Batavia, NY [*Library symbol*] NBatHHi
Holland Society of New York HSNY
Holland Society of New York, New York, NY [*Library symbol*] NNHol
Holland-Suco Color Co., Huntington, WV [*Library symbol*] WvHuH
Holland Vocational Preference Inventory [*Psychology*] HVPI
Hollands Maandblad [*A publication*] Hollands Maandbl
Hollerith Electronic Computer HEC
Hollidaysburg, PA [*Radio station call letters*] WHPA
Hollinger Mines Ltd. [*American Stock Exchange symbol*] [*Delisted*] HOL
Hollins College, Hollins College, VA [*OCLC symbol*] VHC
Hollins College, Hollins College, VA [*Library symbol*] ViHo
Hollins Critic [*A publication*] HC
Hollins Critic [*A publication*] Hol Crit
Hollis, AK [*Location identifier*] [*FAA*] HYL
Hollis & Eastern Railroad Co. [*AAR code*] HE
Hollister, CA [*Radio station call letters*] KHIP
Hollister, CA [*Radio station call letters*] KMPG
Hollister Public Library, Hollister, CA [*Library symbol*] CHo
Holliston, MA [*Radio station call letters*] WHHB
Holloman Air Development Center [*Air Force*] HADC
Holloman Air Force Base [*New Mexico*] HAFB
Holloman Air Force Test Base [*New Mexico*] HAFTB
Holloman Development Research Report [*Air Force*] HDRR
Holloman Symposium on Primate Immunology and Molecular Genetics [*A publication*] Holloman Symp Primate Immunol Mol Genet
Hollow HOL
Hollow HOLW
Hollow Cathode Discharge HCD
Hollow-Cathode Effect HCE
Hollow Cathode Lamp HCL
Hollow Cathode Tube HCT
Hollow Concrete Block HCB
Hollow Copper Conductor HCC
Hollow Electron Beam HEB
Hollow Fiber HF
Hollow Kathode Tube HKT
Hollow Metal [*Technical drawings*] HM
Hollow Metal Door and Buck Association HMDBA
Hollow Metal Door and Frame [*Technical drawings*] HMDF
Hollow Shaft Rotary Actuator HSRA
Hollow Tile [*Technical drawings*] HT
Holly Corporation [*American Stock Exchange symbol*] HOC
Holly Hill, SC [*Radio station call letters*] WKHJ
Holly Junior/Senior High School Library, Holly, NY [*OCLC symbol*] RWN
Holly Oil Co. [*NYSE symbol*] HLO
Holly Society of America HSA
Holly Springs, MS [*Location identifier*] [*FAA*] HLI
Holly Springs, MS [*Radio station call letters*] WKRA
Holly Springs, MS [*Radio station call letters*] WKRA-FM
Holly Sugar Corp. [*NYSE symbol*] HLY
Hollywood Comedy Club HCC
Hollywood, FL [*Location identifier*] [*FAA*] HWO
Hollywood, FL [*Radio station call letters*] WLQY
Hollywood Park Enterprises Paired Cert F [*NASDAQ symbol*] HTRFZ
Hollywood Quarterly [*A publication*] Hollywood Q
Hollywood Radio and Television Society HRTS
Hollywood Studio Collectors Club HSCC
Holman Island [*Canada*] [*Airport symbol*] YHI
Holmavik [*Iceland*] [*Airport symbol*] HVK
Holmes [*D. H.*] **Co.** [*NASDAQ symbol*] HLME
Holmes County Library, Durant, MS [*Library symbol*] MsD
Holmes County Public Library, Millersburg, OH [*Library symbol*] OMill
Holmes Junior College [*Mississippi*] HJC
Holmes Junior College, Goodman, MS [*Library symbol*] MsGoH
Holmes Library, Boonton, NJ [*Library symbol*] NjBoo
Holmes & Narver, Incorporated HNI
Holmium [*Chemical element*] Ho
Holmium LASER Illuminator HLI
Holocaust Information Network HIN
Holocaust Survivors of Auschwitz HSA
Holocaust Survivors Memorial Foundation HSMF
Holograph Assessment System HAS
Holograph Letter Signed HLS
Holograph Stress Strain Gauge HSSG
Holographic Horizontal Situation Display HHSD
Holographic Nondestructive Testing HNDT
Holographic Optical Element HOE
Holographic Visor Helmet-Mounted Display [*Air Force*] HVHMD
Holstein-Friesian Association of America HFAA
Holstein-Friesian World [*A publication*] Holstein World
Holston Army Ammunition Plant HAAP
Holston Army Ammunition Plant HSAAP
Holston Defense Corporation HDC
Holt [*Henry*] **& Co.** [*NYSE symbol*] [*Delisted*] HTY
Holt International Children's Services HICS
Holt, Rinehart & Winston, Inc. [*NYSE symbol*] [*Delisted*] HRW
Holton Inter-Urban Railway Co. [*AAR code*] HI
Holtzman Inkblot Test [*Psychology*] HIT
Holy H
Holy Childhood Association HCA
Holy Communion HC
Holy Cross HC
Holy Cross [*California*] [*Seismograph station code, US Geological Survey*] HCC
Holy Cross [*Alaska*] [*Airport symbol*] HCR
Holy Cross Foreign Mission Seminary, Washington, DC [*Library symbol*] DHCF
Holy Cross Foreign Mission Society HCFMS
Holy Cross Friary, Juniper Carol Library, New York, NY [*Library symbol*] NNHCF-C
Holy Cross Greek Orthodox School of Theology, Brookline, MA [*OCLC symbol*] BHC
Holy Day of Obligation HO
Holy Eucharist HE
Holy Family College [*California, Pennsylvania, Wisconsin*] HFC
Holy Family College, Philadelphia, PA [*OCLC symbol*] HFC
Holy Family College, Philadelphia, PA [*Library symbol*] PPHFC
Holy Family Convent, Benet Lake, WI [*Library symbol*] WBelH
Holy Family Hospital, Manitowoc, WI [*Library symbol*] WManiH
Holy Family Hospital, Spokane, WA [*Library symbol*] WaSpH
Holy Family School of Nursing, Manitowoc, WI [*Library symbol*] WManiHN
Holy Family Seminary [*Connecticut*] HFS
Holy Ghost HG
Holy Land Conservation Fund HLCF
Holy Name Society HNS
Holy Redeemer College, Washington, DC [*Library symbol*] DHR
Holy Redeemer College, Waterford, WI [*Library symbol*] WWatfH
Holy Roman Emperor [*or Empire*] HRE
[*The*] **Holy See** HS
Holy Shroud Guild HSG
Holy Spirit Association for the Unification of World Christianity HSA-UWC
Holy Trinity HT
Holy Trinity HTRIN
Holyoke, CO [*Location identifier*] [*FAA*] HEQ
Holyoke Community College [*Massachusetts*] HCC
Holyoke Community College, Holyoke, MA [*Library symbol*] MHolyC
Holyoke Junior College [*Later, Holyoke Community College*] [*Massachusetts*] HJC
Holyoke, MA [*Radio station call letters*] WCCH
Holyoke, MA [*Radio station call letters*] WREB
Holyoke Public Library, Holyoke, CO [*Library symbol*] CoHo
Holyoke Public Library, Holyoke, MA [*Library symbol*] MHoly
Holz als Roh- und Werkstoff [*A publication*] Holz Roh We
Holz als Roh- und Werkstoff [*A publication*] Holz Roh- Werkst
Holz als Roh- und Werkstoff [*A publication*] Holz Roh-Werkstoff
Holz-Zentralblatt [*A publication*] Holz Zbl
Holzblaser [*Players on Woodwind Instruments*] [*German*] HIZBL
Holzforschung [*A publication*] Holzforsch
Holzforschung und Holzverwertung [*A publication*] Holzf Holzv
Holzforschung und Holzverwertung [*A publication*] Holzforsch Holzverwert
Holzknecht [*Unit*] H
Holzmacher, McLendon & Murrell, Inc., Melville, NY [*Library symbol*] NMelH
Holztechnologie [*A publication*] Holztechnol
Holztechnologie [*German Democratic Republic*] [*A publication*] Holztechnologie
Homac, Inc. [*NASDAQ symbol*] HOMC
Homach Gap Lathe HGL
Homatropine Methylbromide [*Anticholinergic*] HMB
Hombre y Cultura [*A publication*] Hombre y Cult
Home H
Home Access Mortgage HAM
Home Accounting and Finance Office HAFO
Home Address HA
Home Amateur [*Radio*] HAM
Home and Auto Buyer Guide [*A publication*] Home Auto
Home Base [*Military*] HBA
Home Base Development Committee [*Navy*] HBDC
Home-Based Advanced Assignment Program [*Military*] HAAP
Home Beneficial Cl B [*NASDAQ symbol*] HBENB
Home Blood Glucose Monitoring [*Medicine*] HBGM
Home Box Office [*Cable-television system*] HBO
Home Care HC
Home Care Coordinator [*Medicine*] HCC
Home Center Institute HCI
Home Centers of America [*NASDAQ symbol*] HCOA
Home Civil Service [*British*] HCS
Home and Colonial School Society [*British*] HCSS
Home Counties Newspapers Ltd., Luton, United Kingdom [*Library symbol*] UkLuH
Home Defence [*British*] [*World War II*] HD

Home Defence Security Executive [*British*] [*World War II*] ..... HD(S)E
[*The*] **Home Depot, Inc.** [*NASDAQ symbol*] ..... HOMD
Home Dockyard Regulations [*Navy*] ..... HDR
Home Economics Education Association ..... HEEA
Home Economics News [*A publication*] ..... Home Econ News
Home Economics Reading Service [*Recipe clipping service*] ..... HERS
Home Economics Related Occupations ..... HERO
Home Economics Research Reports ..... HERR
Home Economists in Business ..... HEIB
Home Education Livelihood Program [*New Mexico*] ..... HELP
Home Education Resource Center [*Commercial firm*] ..... HERC
Home Emergency Ladies' Pal [*Book title*] ..... HELP
Home Entertainment Network [*Cable TV programing service*] ..... HEN
Home Fallout Protection Survey [*Formerly, EFPH*] [*Civil Defense*] ..... HFPS
Home Fashions Products Association [*Formerly, NCDAPA*] ..... HFPA
Home Federal Savings & Loan of Arizona [*NASDAQ symbol*] ..... HMAZ
Home Federal Savings & Loan Association of Meridian [*NASDAQ symbol*] ..... HMFD
Home Federal Savings & Loan Association of the Rockies [*NASDAQ symbol*] ..... HROK
Home Federal Savings & Loan of Atlanta [*NASDAQ symbol*] ..... HOMA
Home Federal Savings & Loan of California [*NASDAQ symbol*] ..... HFED
Home Fleet [*British*] ..... HF
Home Forces [*Military*] [*British*] ..... HF
Home and Foreign Review [*A publication*] ..... Ho & For R
Home of Franklin D. Roosevelt and Vanderbilt Mansion National Historic Sites ..... HOFR
Home Front ..... HF
Home Furnishings Industry Committee [*Defunct*] ..... HFIC
Home Garden [*A publication*] ..... Home Gard
Home and Garden Bulletins [*A publication*] ..... H & G
Home and Garden Show Executives International [*Formerly, NAPEM*] ..... HGSEI
Home Geographic Monthly [*A publication*] ..... Home Geog Mo
Home Group, Inc. Pfd [*NYSE symbol*] ..... HMEPr
Home Guard [*British*] ..... HG
Home Health Agency ..... HHA
Home Health Care of America [*NASDAQ symbol*] ..... HHCA
Home Health Care Services Quarterly [*A publication*] ..... Home Health Care Serv Q
Home Health Review [*A publication*] ..... Home Health Rev
Home Health Services Association [*Later, HHSSA*] ..... HHSA
Home Health Services and Staffing Association [*Formerly, HHSA*] ..... HHSSA
Home Help [*Medicine*] ..... HH
Home Improvement Dealers Association of America ..... HIDA
Home Improvement Products Association [*Defunct*] ..... HIPA
Home Instruction Program for Preschool Youngsters [*Israel*] ..... HIPPY
Home on Jamming ..... HOJ
Home Loan Bank Board ..... HLBB
Home Manufacturers Association [*Later, HMC*] ..... HMA
Home Manufacturers Council of NAHB [*Formerly, HMA*] ..... HMC
Home Mission ..... HM
Home Mission Association [*Episcopalian*] ..... HMA
Home Mortgage Disclosure Act ..... HMDA
Home News, New Brunswick, NJ [*Library symbol*] ..... NjNbH
Home Numbering Plan Area [*AT & T*] ..... HNPA
Home Nursing ..... HN
Home Nursing Supervisor [*Red Cross*] ..... HNS
Home Office [*British*] ..... HO
Home Office Life Underwriters Association ..... HOLUA
Home Oil Co. Ltd. [*American Stock Exchange symbol*] [*Delisted*] ..... HG
Home Oil Co. Ltd., Calgary, AB, Canada [*Library symbol*] ..... CaACH
Home Orchard Society ..... HOS
Home Oriented Maternity Experience ..... HOME
Home Owner Association ..... HOA
Home Owners Assistance Program [*Military*] ..... HAP
Home Owners' Loan Corporation [*Terminated, 1942*] ..... HOLC
Home Owners Warranty [*National Association of Home Builders*] ..... HOW
Home Ownership Assistance Program [*Farmers Home Administration*] ..... HOAP
Home Policy Committee of War Cabinet [*British*] [*World War II*] ..... HPC
Home Port [*Navy*] ..... HPO
Home Port [*Navy*] ..... HPT
Home Products Safety Council ..... HSC
Home Progress [*A publication*] ..... Home Prog
Home Radio Beacon ..... H
Home Radio Beacon - High Power ..... HH
Home of Record ..... HOR
Home Recording Rights Coalition ..... HRRC
Home Reunion Society [*British*] ..... HRS
Home Rule ..... HR
Home Run [*Baseball*] ..... HR
Home and School Institute ..... HSI
Home Secretary [*British*] ..... HS
Home of Selection and Completion of Travel within One Year Is Authorized [*Military*] ..... HOSTWOY
Home Sports Entertainment Network [*Cable TV programing service*] ..... HSEN
Home and Store News, Ramsey, NJ [*Library symbol*] ..... NjRamH
Home Surgeon [*Medicine*] [*British*] ..... HS
Home Theatre Network [*In network name "HTN Plus"*] [*Cable-television system*] ..... HTN
Home Total Parenteral Nutrition [*Medicine*] ..... HTPN
Home Town Honey [*Slang*] ..... HTH
Home Treatment [*Medicine*] ..... HT
Home User Groups [*Data processing*] ..... HUG's
Home Ventilating Institute ..... HVI
Home View Network [*Television programing subscription service*] ..... HVN
Homemakers Equal Rights Association ..... HERA
Homemakers & Mothers Cooperatives, Inc. ..... HOMOCO
Homenaje a Menendez Pidal [*A publication*] ..... HMP
Homeopathic Council for Research and Education ..... HCRE
Homeopathic Foundation ..... HF
Homeopathic Pharmacopoeia ..... HP
Homeopathy [*Medicine*] ..... HOMEOP
Homeostatic Regulators [*British*] ..... HR
Homeostatic Thymus Hormone [*Immunology*] ..... HTH
Homeowners' [*Insurance*] ..... HO
Homeowners Emergency Services, Inc. ..... HES
Homeowners Using Savings and Energy Information to Negotiate Fair Offers [*Student legal action organization*] ..... HOUSE-INFO
Homer [*Alaska*] [*Airport symbol*] ..... HOM
Homer [*Alaska*] [*Seismograph station code, US Geological Survey*] ..... HOM
Homer, AK [*Location identifier*] [*FAA*] ..... ACE
Homer, AK [*Radio station call letters*] ..... KBBI
Homer, AK [*Radio station call letters*] ..... KGTL
Homer, AK [*Radio station call letters*] ..... KGTL-FM
Homer City, PA [*Radio station call letters*] ..... WRID
Homer Hoyt Institute ..... HHI
Homer Public Library, Homer, AK [*Library symbol*] ..... AkHom
Homerville, GA [*Radio station call letters*] ..... WBTY
Homes of Private Enterprise [*As in HOPE, Inc.*] ..... HOPE
Homes Registration Office ..... HRO
Homes Using TV [*Television ratings*] ..... HUT
Homestake Mining Co. [*NYSE symbol*] ..... HM
Homestead [*Florida*] [*Airport symbol*] ..... HST
Homestead Financial Corp. [*NYSE symbol*] ..... HFL
Homestead Financial Corp. [*NASDAQ symbol*] ..... HOMF
Homestead, FL [*Radio station call letters*] ..... WQDI
Homestead National Monument ..... HOME
Homesteaders Association ..... HA
Hometown Public Library, Hometown, IL [*Library symbol*] ..... IHot
Homewood Public Library, Homewood, IL [*Library symbol*] ..... IHow
Homeworkers Organized for More Employment [*Crafts cooperative in Maine*] ..... HOME
Homiletic and Pastoral Review [*A publication*] ..... HPR
Homiletic Review [*A publication*] ..... Hom R
Homing ..... HOM
Homing All the Way Killer [*Small missile*] ..... HAWK
Homing Beacon [*Aviation*] ..... HB
Homing Bomb System [*Air Force*] ..... HOBOS
Homing Comparator Unit ..... HCU
Homing Fixture ..... HOF
Homing Guidance ..... HG
Homing Instrumentation Unit ..... HIU
Homing Level Gauge ..... HLG
Homing on Offset Beacon ..... HOB
Homing Optical Bomb ..... HOBO
Homing Optical Guidance ..... HOG
Homing Optical Guidance System ..... HOGS
Homing Optical System Study ..... HOSS
Homing Overlay Experiment [*Ballistic missile defense*] ..... HOE
Homing Position Indicator ..... HPI
Homing Terrier ..... HT
Homing Terrier/Improved Tartar [*Missile*] ..... HT/IT
Homing Terrier Retrofit [*Missile*] ..... HTR
Homing Test Vehicle ..... HTV
Homing Type ..... HT
Homing and Warning Computer ..... HAWC
Homing and Warning Programer ..... HAWP
Homing Weapons ..... HW
Homme et l'Oiseau [*A publication*] ..... Homme Oiseau
Homme et Societe [*A publication*] ..... Homme et Soc
Homme et Societe [*A publication*] ..... Homme Soc
Hommel AG [*Switzerland*] [*Research code symbol*] ..... HH
Hommes et Migrations [*A publication*] ..... Hommes et Migr
Hommes et Migrations. Documents [*A publication*] ..... Hommes et Migr Doc
Hommes et Mondes [*A publication*] ..... H & M
Hommes et Mondes [*A publication*] ..... HM
Hommes et Techniques [*A publication*] ..... Hommes Tech
Hommes et Techniques [*A publication*] ..... Hommes et Techn
Homoeopathic Digest [*A publication*] ..... Homoeopath
Homoeopathy [*Medicine*] ..... HOMOEO
Homogenate Survival Time ..... HST
Homogeneity of Variance [*Statistics*] ..... HOV
Homogeneous Assembly Zero Energy Level [*AERE*] ..... HAZEL
Homogeneous Boundary Condition ..... HBC
Homogeneous Catalysis in Organic and Inorganic Chemistry [*A publication*] ..... Homogeneous Catal Org Inorg Chem
Homogeneous Computer System ..... HCS

Homogeneous Differential Equation .... HDE
Homogeneous Reactor Equipment .... HRE
Homogeneous Reactor Experiments .... HRE
Homogeneous Reactor Test .... HRT
Homogeneous Thorium Reactor .... HTR
Homogeneously Staining Region [*Cytology*] .... HSR
Homogenization Medium .... HM
Homogenized Leaf Curing [*Tobacco industry*] .... HLC
Homogentisate [*Biochemistry*] .... HGA
Homolateral [*Medicine*] .... HOMOLAT
Homologous Canine Distemper [*Antiserum*] .... HCD
Homologous Leucocytic Antibodies .... HLA
Homologous Serum .... HS
Homonymous Hemianopsia [*Ophthalmology*] .... HH
Homophile Effort for Legal Protection [*An association*] [*Defunct*] .... HELP
Homopolar Disk Dynamo .... HDD
Homopolar Generator [*To power high-technology experiments*] .... HPG
Homoreactant [*Medicine*] .... HR
Homosassa Springs, FL [*Radio station call letters*] .... WXCV
Homosexual .... H
Homosexual .... HOMO
Homosexual Information Center .... HIC
Homosexual World Organization .... HWO
Homothetic-Constant Differences of Elasticities of Substitution [*Statistics*] .... HCDE
Homovanillic Acid [*Biochemistry*] .... HVA
Homozygous Diabetes Insipidus [*A genetic variety of rat*] .... HODI
Homozygous Typing Cells [*Immunochemistry*] .... HTC
Hon Industries, Inc. [*NASDAQ symbol*] .... HONI
Honan Province [*China, Mainland*] [*MARC geographic area code*] [*Library of Congress*] .... a-cc-ho
Honar va Mardom [*A publication*] .... HvM
Honda Civic Club [*Later, H-I*] .... HCC
Honda Motor Company Ltd. [*NYSE symbol*] .... HMC
Honda-Mrkos-Pajdusakova [*Comet*] .... HMP
Hondacar International [*Formerly, HCC*] .... H-I
Hondo, TX [*Location identifier*] [*FAA*] .... HDO
Hondo, TX [*Radio station call letters*] .... KRME
Honduran-American Association .... HAA
Honduras [*Two-letter standard code*] .... HN
Honduras [*Three-letter standard code*] .... HND
Honduras [*MARC country of publication code*] [*Library of Congress*] .... ho
Honduras [*Aircraft nationality and registration mark*] .... HR
Honduras [*MARC geographic area code*] [*Library of Congress*] .... ncho---
Hone-Finish Monolithic Floor [*Technical drawings*] .... HFMF
Honea Path, SC [*Radio station call letters*] .... WRIX
Honeoye Falls-Lima Senior High School Library, Honeoye Falls, NY [*OCLC symbol*] .... RWO
Honesdale, PA [*Radio station call letters*] .... WDNH
Honesdale, PA [*Radio station call letters*] .... WDNH-FM
Honest Ballot Association .... HBA
Honest John [*A type of short range, unguided Army rocket*] .... HJ
Honest John Launcher [*Army*] .... HJL
Honest John Rocket [*Army*] .... HJR
Honestly Significant Difference .... HSD
Honey Industry Council of America .... HICA
Honeycomb .... HNYCMB
Honeycomb Aluminum Panel .... HAP
Honeycomb Corrugated Construction .... HCC
Honeycomb Sandwich Aluminum Panel .... HSAP
Honeycomb-Supported Screen .... HSS
Honeycombed Sandwich Joint .... HSJ
Honeysuckle Creek Tracking Station [*NASA*] .... HSK
Honeywell Business Computer .... HBC
Honeywell Computer Journal [*A publication*] .... Honeywell Comput J
Honeywell Electro-Optics Center Library, Lexington, MA [*OCLC symbol*] .... HON
Honeywell Equipment Lease Plan .... HELP
Honeywell, Incorporated .... HI
Honeywell, Inc. [*Formerly, M-H*] [*NYSE symbol*] .... HON
Honeywell Information Systems .... HIS
Honeywell Information Systems, Phoenix, AZ [*Library symbol*] .... AzPhH
Honeywell Institute for Information Science .... HIIS
Honeywell Integrating Gyro .... HIG
Honeywell Large Systems Users Association .... HLSUA
Honeywell Time-Sharing System [*Data processing*] .... HTSS
Honeywell Users Group - Small and Medium Systems [*Later, NAHU*] .... HUG-SMS
Honeywell Verification Simulation Facility .... HVSF
Hong Kong [*MARC geographic area code*] [*Library of Congress*] .... a-hk---
Hong Kong [*MARC country of publication code*] [*Library of Congress*] .... hk
Hong Kong [*Hong Kong*] [*Geomagnetic observatory code*] .... HKC
Hong Kong [*Hong Kong*] [*Airport symbol*] .... HKG
Hong Kong [*Hong Kong*] [*Seismograph station code, US Geological Survey*] .... HKC
Hong Kong [*Three-letter standard code*] .... HKG
Hong Kong [*Two-letter standard code*] .... HK
Hong Kong Air International Ltd. [*ICAO designator*] .... HI
Hong Kong Airways Ltd. .... HKA
Hong Kong Economic Papers [*A publication*] .... HEP
Hong Kong Economic Papers [*A publication*] .... HK Econ Pap
Hong Kong Law Review [*A publication*] .... HK Law R
Hong Kong Nursing Journal [*A publication*] .... Hong Kong Nurs J
Hong Kong Seamen's Union .... HKSU
Hongik University Journal [*Republic of Korea*] [*A publication*] .... Hongik Univ J
Hongkong and Shanghai Banking Corporation .... HSBC
Hongo [*Japan*] [*Seismograph station code, US Geological Survey*] .... HGJ
Hongo [*Japan*] [*Seismograph station code, US Geological Survey*] [*Closed*] .... HNG
Honiara [*Guadalcanal*] [*Airport symbol*] .... HIR
Honiara [*Solomon Islands*] [*Seismograph station code, US Geological Survey*] .... HNR
Honningsvag [*Norway*] [*Airport symbol*] .... HVG
Honnold Library, Claremont, CA [*Library symbol*] CCC
Honolulu [*Hawaii*] [*Airport symbol*] .... HNL
Honolulu [*Hawaii*] [*Geomagnetic observatory code*] .... HON
Honolulu [*Hawaii*] .... HONO
Honolulu [*Hawaii*] [*Seismograph station code, US Geological Survey*] [*Closed*] .... HNL
Honolulu [*Hawaii*] [*Seismograph station code, US Geological Survey*] .... HON
Honolulu Community College, Honolulu, HI [*Library symbol*] .... HHC
Honolulu, HI [*Location identifier*] [*FAA*] .... EPC
Honolulu, HI [*Location identifier*] [*FAA*] .... HFO
Honolulu, HI [*Location identifier*] [*FAA*] .... HIK
Honolulu, HI [*Location identifier*] [*FAA*] .... HWN
Honolulu, HI [*Location identifier*] [*FAA*] .... IUM
Honolulu, HI [*Radio station call letters*] .... KAIM
Honolulu, HI [*Radio station call letters*] .... KAIM-FM
Honolulu, HI [*Radio station call letters*] .... KCCN
Honolulu, HI [*Radio station call letters*] .... KDUK
Honolulu, HI [*Television station call letters*] .... KGMB-TV
Honolulu, HI [*Radio station call letters*] .... KGU
Honolulu, HI [*Television station call letters*] .... KHAI-TV
Honolulu, HI [*Television station call letters*] .... KHET
Honolulu, HI [*Radio station call letters*] .... KHNL
Honolulu, HI [*Television station call letters*] .... KHON-TV
Honolulu, HI [*Radio station call letters*] .... KHPR
Honolulu, HI [*Radio station call letters*] .... KHVH
Honolulu, HI [*Radio station call letters*] .... KIKI
Honolulu, HI [*Television station call letters*] .... KIKU-TV
Honolulu, HI [*Radio station call letters*] .... KISA
Honolulu, HI [*Television station call letters*] .... KITV
Honolulu, HI [*Radio station call letters*] .... KKUA
Honolulu, HI [*Radio station call letters*] .... KMAI
Honolulu, HI [*Radio station call letters*] .... KNDI
Honolulu, HI [*Radio station call letters*] .... KOHO
Honolulu, HI [*Radio station call letters*] .... KORL
Honolulu, HI [*Radio station call letters*] .... KPOI
Honolulu, HI [*Radio station call letters*] .... KPOI-FM
Honolulu, HI [*Television station call letters*] .... KPRR-TV
Honolulu, HI [*Radio station call letters*] .... KQMQ
Honolulu, HI [*Television station call letters*] .... KSHO
Honolulu, HI [*Radio station call letters*] .... KSSK
Honolulu, HI [*Radio station call letters*] .... KTUH
Honolulu, HI [*Radio station call letters*] .... KUMU
Honolulu, HI [*Radio station call letters*] .... KUMU-FM
Honolulu, HI [*Radio station call letters*] .... KZHI
Honolulu, HI [*Radio station call letters*] .... KZOO
Honolulu, HI [*Location identifier*] [*FAA*] .... NPS
Honolulu Japanese Chamber of Commerce .... HJCC
Honolulu Magnetic Observatory .... HMO
Honolulu Magnetic and Seismological Observatory .... HMSO
Honolulu Star-Bulletin and Advertiser, Honolulu, HI [*Library symbol*] .... HHSA
Honor .... H
Honorable .... HON
Honorable .... HONBLE
Honorable Discharge [*Military*] .... HD
Honorable Discharge, under Age of Authorized Consent [*Military*] .... HDMU
Honorable Discharge, Convenience of Government [*Military*] .... HDCG
Honorable Discharge, Convenience of Man [*Military*] .... HDCM
Honorable Discharge, Dependency Arising Since Enlistment [*Military*] .... HDDS
Honorable Discharge, Dependency Existing Prior to Enlistment [*Military*] .... HDDP
Honorable Discharge, Expiration of Enlistment [*Military*] .... HDEE
Honorable Discharge, Medical Survey [*Military*] .... HDMS
Honorable Discharge, Minors Enlisted without Consent, under Eighteen at Discharge [*Military*] .... HDMW
Honorable Order of the Blue Goose, International .... HOBGI
Honorary [*Academic degree*] .... H
Honorary .... HON
Honorary Air Reserve [*Air Force*] .... HAR
Honorary Associate of the Royal Academy of Music [*British*] .... Hon ARAM
Honorary Associate of the Royal College of Veterinary Surgeons [*British*] .... HARCVS
Honorary Chaplain to the Forces [*British*] .... HCF
Honorary Fellow of the Educational Institute of Scotland .... Hon FEIS
Honorary Fellow of the Non-Destructive Testing Society of Great Britain .... Hon FNDTS
Honorary Fellow of the Royal Academy [*British*] .... HFRA

Honorary Fellow of the Royal Academy of Music [*British*] .... Hon FRAM
Honorary Fellow of the Royal College of Physicians and Surgeons [*Glasgow*] .... FRCPS(Hon)
Honorary Fellow of the Royal Photographic Society [*British*] .... Hon FRPS
Honorary Foreign Associate of Royal Academy [*British*] .... HFARA
Honorary Foreign Member of the Royal Academy .... HFMRA
Honorary Member of the Non-Destructive Testing Society of Great Britain .... Hon MNDTS
Honorary Member of the Royal Academy of Music [*British*] .... Hon RAM
Honorary Member of the Royal Hibernian Academy [*British*] .... HRHA
Honorary Member of the Royal Institute of Oil Painters [*British*] .... HROI
Honorary Member of the Royal Institute of Painters in Water Colours [*British*] .... HRI
Honorary Member of the Royal School of Church Music [*British*] .... Hon RSCM
Honorary Member of the Royal Scottish Academy .... HRSA
Honorary Member of the Royal Scottish Water Colour Society .... HRSW
Honorary Naval Aide-de-Camp [*British*] .... HNADC
Honorary Order of Trumpeters Living in Possible Sin .... HOTLIPS
Honorary Physician to the King [*British*] .... HPK
Honorary Physician to the King [*British*] .... KHP
Honorary Reserve Section .... HRS
Honorary Royal Academician [*British*] .... HRA
Honorary Royal Cambrian Academician [*British*] .... HRCA
Honorary Secretary .... HS
Honorary Surgeon of the King [*British*] .... HSK
Honorary Surgeon to the King [*British*] .... KHS
Honorary Surgeon to the Viceroy of India .... VHS
Honoris Causa [*For the Sake of Honor, Honorary*] [*Latin*] .... HC
Honors .... HONS
Honourable Artillery Company [*Military unit*] [*British*] .... HAC
Honourable East India Company [*British*] .... HEIC
Honourable East India Company's Service [*British*] .... HEICS
Honourable Society of Cymmrodorion. Transactions [*A publication*] .... Cym Trans
Hood College, Frederick, MD [*OCLC symbol*] .... HCF
Hood College, Frederick, MD [*Library symbol*] .... MdFreH
Hood River County Library, Hood River, OR [*Library symbol*] .... OrHr
Hood River, OR [*Radio station call letters*] .... KCGB-FM
Hood River, OR [*Radio station call letters*] .... KIHR
Hood's Texas Brigade Association .... HTBA
Hook .... HK
Hook Drugs, Inc. [*NASDAQ symbol*] .... HOOK
Hook Rail .... HR
Hook Tongue Terminal .... HTT
Hooker .... H
Hooker Air Services Ltd. [*Gimli, MB*] [*FAA designator*] .... HOS
Hooker Chemical Corp. [*NYSE symbol*] [*Delisted*] .... HKR
Hooker Chemical Corp. [*Later, Hooker Chemicals & Plastics Corp.*]**, Niagara Falls, NY** [*Library symbol*] .... NNiaH
Hooker Chemicals & Plastics Corp., Business Library, Niagara Falls, NY [*Library symbol*] .... NNiaHC
Hooker Chemicals & Plastics Corp., Corporate Technical and Services Center Research Library, Grand Island, NY [*Library symbol*] .... NGiHC
Hooker Chemicals & Plastics Corp., Durez Division Library, North Tonawanda, NY [*Library symbol*] .... NNotHC
Hooker Electro-Chemical Company .... HECC
Hooks, TX [*Radio station call letters*] .... KFFR
Hookup .... HKP
Hoonah [*Alaska*] [*Airport symbol*] .... HNH
Hoop-Iron Bond [*Construction*] .... HIB
Hoopa, CA [*Radio station call letters*] .... KIDE
Hooper Bay [*Alaska*] [*Airport symbol*] .... HPB
Hooper Visual Organization Test [*Psychology*] .... HVOT
Hoopes Conductivity Bridge [*Electronics*] .... HCB
Hoopeston, IL [*Radio station call letters*] .... WHPO
Hoopestown Community Memorial Hospital, Hoopestown, IL [*Library symbol*] .... IHoH
Hoopestown Public Library, Hoopestown, IL [*Library symbol*] .... IHo
Hoosac Tunnel & Wilmington R. R. [*AAR code*] .... HTW
Hoosier Folklore [*A publication*] .... HF
Hoosier Folklore Bulletin [*A publication*] .... HFB
Hoosier School Libraries [*A publication*] .... Hoosier Sch Lib
Hoover Ball & Bearing Co. [*NYSE symbol*] [*Delisted*] .... HBB
[*The*] **Hoover Co.** [*NASDAQ symbol*] .... HOOV
Hoover Co., Engineering Division, North Canton, OH [*Library symbol*] .... ONocHE
Hoover-Owens-Rentschler [*Engines*] .... HOR
Hoover Universal [*NYSE symbol*] .... HVU
Hop Growers of America .... HGA
Hope [*Jamaica*] [*Seismograph station code, US Geological Survey*] .... HOJ
Hope [*Jamaica*] [*Seismograph station code, US Geological Survey*] [*Closed*] .... HOP
Hope, AR [*Radio station call letters*] .... KHPA
Hope, AR [*Radio station call letters*] .... KXAR
Hope, BC [*Radio station call letters*] .... CKGO
Hope College, Holland, MI [*OCLC symbol*] .... EXH
Hope College, Holland, MI [*Library symbol*] .... MiHolH
Hopeh Province [*China, Mainland*] [*MARC geographic area code*] [*Library of Congress*] .... a-cc-hp
Hopewell Museum, Hopewell, NJ [*Library symbol*] .... NjHopM
Hopewell Public Library, Hopewell, NJ [*Library symbol*] .... NjHop
Hopewell, VA [*Radio station call letters*] .... WHAP
Hopewell Valley News, Hopewell, NJ [*Library symbol*] .... NjHopN
Hopewell Village National Historic Site .... HOVI
Hopital General Fleury, Montreal, PQ, Canada [*Library symbol*] .... CaQMHGF
Hopital Jean-Talon, Montreal, PQ, Canada [*Library symbol*] .... CaQMHJT
Hopital Louis-H.-LaFontaine, Montreal, PQ, Canada [*Library symbol*] .... CaQMHSJ
Hopital Maisonneuve-Rosemont, Montreal, PQ, Canada [*Library symbol*] .... CaQMHMR
Hopital Marie Enfant, Montreal, PQ, Canada [*Library symbol*] .... CaQMHME
Hopital Notre-Dame, Bibliotheque des Services Infirmiers, Montreal, PQ, Canada [*Library symbol*] .... CaQMHNDI
Hopital Notre-Dame de l'Esperance de Saint-Laurent, Montreal, PQ, Canada [*Library symbol*] .... CaQMNDE
Hopital Riviere des Prairies, Montreal, PQ, Canada [*Library symbol*] .... CaQMHRP
Hopital Sacre-Coeur, Montreal, PQ, Canada [*Library symbol*] .... CaQMHSC
Hopital Saint-Charles, Joliette, PQ, Canada [*Library symbol*] .... CaQJH
Hopital Saint-Joseph, Trois-Rivieres, PQ, Canada [*Library symbol*] .... CaQTHSJ
Hopital Saint-Luc, Montreal, PQ, Canada [*Library symbol*] .... CaQMHSL
Hopital du Saint-Sacrement, Quebec, PQ, Canada [*Library symbol*] .... CaQQHSS
Hopital Sainte-Justine, Centre d'Information sur l'Enfance et l'Adolescence Inadaptees, Montreal, PQ, Canada [*Library symbol*] [*Obsolete*] .... CaQMSTJC
Hopital Sainte-Justine, Centre d'Information sur la Sante de l'Enfant, Montreal, PQ, Canada [*Library symbol*] .... CaQMSTJ
Hopital Sainte-Marie, Trois-Rivieres, PQ, Canada [*Library symbol*] .... CaQTHSM
Hopital Santa Cabrini, Montreal, PQ, Canada [*Library symbol*] .... CaQMHSCA
Hopital Ste-Jeanne d'Arc, Montreal, PQ, Canada [*Library symbol*] .... CaQMHSJA
Hopkins Elementary School, Granville, IL [*Library symbol*] .... IGranHS
Hopkins Marine Station, Pacific Grove, CA [*Library symbol*] .... CPgH
Hopkins Research Bulletin [*A publication*] .... HRB
Hopkins Review [*A publication*] .... Hop R
Hopkins Ultraviolet Telescope .... HUT
Hopkinsville, KY [*Location identifier*] [*FAA*] .... HIX
Hopkinsville, KY [*Location identifier*] [*FAA*] .... HVC
Hopkinsville, KY [*Location identifier*] [*FAA*] .... HXW
Hopkinsville, KY [*Radio station call letters*] .... WHOP
Hopkinsville, KY [*Radio station call letters*] .... WHOP-FM
Hopkinsville, KY [*Radio station call letters*] .... WKOA
Hopkinsville, KY [*Radio station call letters*] .... WKOA-FM
Hopkinsville, KY [*Radio station call letters*] .... WNKJ
Hopkinsville, KY [*Television station call letters*] .... WNKJ-TV
Hoppe-Seyler's Zeitschrift fuer Physiologische Chemie [*A publication*] .... Hoppe-Seyler's Z Physiol Chem
Hoppe-Seyler's Zeitschrift fuer Physiologische Chemie [*A publication*] .... Hoppe-Seyler's Ztschr Physiol Chem
Hoppe-Seyler's Zeitschrift fuer Physiologische Chemie [*A publication*] .... H-S Z Physl
Hopper [*Freight*] .... HPR
Hops Marketing Board [*British*] .... HMB
Hoquiam, WA [*Radio station call letters*] .... KGHO
Hoquiam, WA [*Radio station call letters*] .... KGHO-FM
Hora [*Hour*] [*Latin*] .... h
Hora [*Hour*] [*Latin*] .... O
Hora Decubitus [*At Bedtime*] [*Pharmacy*] .... HD
Hora Decubitus [*At Bedtime*] [*Pharmacy*] .... HOR DECU
Hora Locoque Consuetis [*At the Usual Time and Place*] [*Latin*] .... HLQC
Hora Locoque Solitis [*At the Usual Time and Place*] [*Latin*] .... HLQS
Hora Somni [*At Bedtime*] [*Pharmacy*] .... HOR SOM
Hora Somni [*At Bedtime*] [*Pharmacy*] .... HS
Hora Somni [*At Bedtime*] [*Pharmacy*] .... H SOM
Horace Hardy Lestor Reactor .... HHLR
Horace Mann League of the USA .... HML
Horace Walpole Society [*A publication*] .... HWS
Horae Unius Spatio [*At the End of an Hour*] [*Pharmacy*] .... HOR UN SPAT
Horatio Alger Association of Distinguished Americans .... HAADA
Horatio Alger Society .... HAS
Horis Intermediis [*In the Intermediate Hours*] [*Pharmacy*] .... HOR INTERM
Horizon .... HOR
Horizon .... HRZN
Horizon [*A publication*] .... Hor
Horizon Air Service [*Honolulu, HI*] [*FAA designator*] .... KOK
Horizon Airways, Inc. [*Kirksville, MO*] [*FAA designator*] .... HZN
Horizon Bancorp. [*NYSE symbol*] .... HZB
Horizon Corp. [*NYSE symbol*] .... HZN
Horizon Crossing Ascending .... HCA
Horizon Crossing Descending .... HCD
Horizon Flight Director [*Aircraft*] .... HFD
Horizon Health Corporation [*NASDAQ symbol*] .... HORC
Horizon Industries [*NASDAQ symbol*] .... HRZN
Horizon Reference Indicator [*Aerospace*] .... HRI
Horizon Scanner .... HS

Horizon Sensor	HS
Horizon Sensor Assembly	HSA
Horizons Bancorp Pfd [*NASDAQ symbol*]	HZONP
Horizons in Biochemistry and Biophysics [*A publication*]	
	Horiz Biochem Biophys
Horizons Research [*NASDAQ symbol*]	HRES
Horizontal	H
Horizontal	HOR
Horizontal	HORIZ
Horizontal Access Kit	HAK
Horizontal Acoustic Range Depiction	HARD
Horizontal Alidade Tie	HAT
Horizontal Array of Dipoles	HAD
Horizontal Assembly Building [*NASA*]	HAB
Horizontal Axis Bearing	HAB
Horizontal Axis Electrical Hairspring	HAEH
Horizontal Axis Pivot	HAP
Horizontal Axis Wind Turbine	HAWT
Horizontal Baffle	HB
Horizontal Bands [*Navigation markers*]	HB
Horizontal Bomber	HB
Horizontal Boring Mill	HBM
Horizontal Candlepower	HCP
Horizontal Candlepower Seconds	HCPS
Horizontal Cargo Integration Test Equipment	HCITE
Horizontal Cask Lifting Fixture [*Nuclear energy*]	HCLF
Horizontal Cell [*Eye anatomy*]	HC
Horizontal Center Line	HCL
Horizontal Clearance [*Nautical charts*]	HOR CL
Horizontal Control Operator [*Military*]	HCO
Horizontal Correlation Distance	HCD
Horizontal Danger Angle [*Navigation*]	HDA
Horizontal Data Processing	HDP
Horizontal Deflection [*Symbol*]	X
Horizontal Display Indicator	HDI
Horizontal Distributing Frame	HDF
Horizontal Drive	HD
Horizontal Dynamic Balancing	HDB
Horizontal Dynamic Balancing Adjustment	HDBA
Horizontal Earth Rate	HER
Horizontal Electrical Dipole	HED
Horizontal Enlarger [*Photography*]	HOREN
Horizontal Equivalent	HE
Horizontal Flight	HF
Horizontal Flight Simulator	HFS
Horizontal Flight Test Facility [*NASA*]	HFTF
Horizontal Flight Test Simulator [*NASA*]	HFTS
Horizontal Flight Testing [*NASA*]	HFT
Horizontal Flight Vector	HFV
Horizontal Force of the Earth's Magnetism [*Amplitude of a tide*]	H
Horizontal Function Checkout	HOFCO
Horizontal Generator Mock-Up System [*NASA*]	HGMUS
Horizontal Ground Vibration Test [*NASA*]	HGVT
Horizontal Impulse	HIM
Horizontal Impulse	HZMP
Horizontal Impulse Reaction	HIR
Horizontal Injection Press	HIP
Horizontal Interval	HI
Horizontal Landing	HL
Horizontal Lights [*Navigation signal*]	Hor
Horizontal Line	HL
Horizontal Line Array	HLA
Horizontal Line Frequency	HLF
Horizontal Liquid Spring	HLS
Horizontal Location of Center of Gravity	HCG
Horizontal Lockout	HLO
Horizontal Mating Facility [*NASA*]	HMF
Horizontal Opposed [*Aircraft engine*]	O
Horizontal Output Transformer	HOT
Horizontal Output Tube	HOT
Horizontal Panel Mount	HPM
Horizontal Parallax [*Navigation*]	HP
Horizontal Plot Table	HPT
Horizontal Polarization	HP
Horizontal RADAR Display	HORAD
Horizontal Radiation Pattern [*Electronics*]	HRP
Horizontal Reaction	HZRN
Horizontal Recovery System	HRS
Horizontal Redundancy Check	HRC
Horizontal Reference Line [*Technical drawings*]	HRL
Horizontal Retort	HR
Horizontal Shear	HS
Horizontal Situation Display	HSD
Horizontal Situation Display System	HSDS
Horizontal Situation Indicator [*Aviation*]	HSI
Horizontal Sling Kit [*NASA*]	HSK
Horizontal Stabilizer Trim Setting	HSTS
Horizontal Static Balancing Adjustment	HSBA
Horizontal Stripes [*On buoys, beacons*]	HS
Horizontal Sweep Circuit Analyzer	HSCA
Horizontal Tabulation	HT

Horizontal Tactical Display	HTD
Horizontal Tactical Display Unit	HTDU
Horizontal Tactics Indicator	HTI
Horizontal Takeoff	HTO
Horizontal Takeoff, Horizontal Landing	HTOHL
Horizontal Trail Unit	HTU
Horizontal Volute Spring Suspension [*Projectile*]	HVSS
Horizontal Weather Depiction	HWD
Hormel [*Geo. A.*] & Co. [*American Stock Exchange symbol*]	HRL
Hormel Institute, University of Minnesota, Austin, MN [*Library symbol*]	MnAuH
Hormigueros, PR [*Radio station call letters*]	WGIT
Hormone [*Endocrinology*]	H
Hormone and Metabolic Research [*A publication*]	Horm Metab Res
Hormone and Metabolic Research [*A publication*]	Hormone Met
Hormone and Metabolic Research (Supplement) [*A publication*]	
	Horm Metab Res (Suppl)
Hormone Pregnancy Test	HPT
Hormone Receptor Site [*Endocrinology*]	HRS
Hormone Replacement Therapy [*Medicine*]	HRT
Hormone Research [*A publication*]	Hormone Res
Hormone Research (Basel) [*A publication*]	Horm Res (Basel)
Hormones and Behavior [*A publication*]	Horm Behav
Hormones and Behavior [*A publication*]	Hormone Beh
Horn	H
Horn of Africa [*A publication*]	Horn Afr
Horn Book [*A publication*]	HB
Horn Book [*A publication*]	Horn Bk
Horn Book Magazine [*A publication*]	Horn Bk
Horn Fiber	HNFBR
Horn Gap Switch	HGSW
Horn & Hardart Co. [*American Stock Exchange symbol*]	HOR
Horn-Hellersberg Test [*Psychology*]	HHT
Hornbeck Offshore Service [*NASDAQ symbol*]	HOSS
Hornell, NY [*Radio station call letters*]	WCKR
Hornell, NY [*Radio station call letters*]	WHHO
Hornell, NY [*Radio station call letters*]	WKPQ
Hornell, NY [*Radio station call letters*]	WLEA
Hornepayne [*Canada*] [*Airport symbol*]	YHN
Horner [*Horns*] [*Music*]	HR
Horner [*Horns*] [*Music*]	HRN
Horniman Museum [*London*]	HM
Horological Institute of America [*Later, AWI*]	HIA
Horological Journal [*A publication*]	Horol J
Horologium [*Constellation*]	Hor
Horologium [*Constellation*]	Horo
Horology	HOR
Horology	HOROL
Horology Program [*Association of Independent Colleges and Schools specialization code*]	HR
Horrific [*Film certificate*] [*British*]	H
Hors Concours [*Not Competing*] [*French*]	HC
Horse	H
Horse [*Thoroughbred racing*]	H
Horse of the Americas Registry	HAR
Horse Anti-Rhesus Lymphocyte Globulin [*Immunology*]	HoaRhLG
Horse Anti-Tetanus Toxoid Globulin [*Immunology*]	HoaTTG
Horse Antiserum to Rabbit Lymphocytes [*Immunology*]	HARLS
Horse Artillery	HA
Horse Canyon [*Utah*] [*Seismograph station code, US Geological Survey*]	HCU
Horse-Drawn	HD
Horse-Drawn Vehicle	HDV
Horse Guards [*British*]	HG
Horse Hemolyzate Supernatant	HHS
Horse Immunoglobulin [*Immunology*]	HoIg
Horse-Liver Alcohol Dehydrogenase [*An enzyme*]	HLALD
Horse Red Blood Cells [*Also, HRC*]	HRBC
Horse Red Blood Cells [*Also, HRBC*]	HRC
Horse Serum [*Immunology*]	HoS
Horse Serum [*Immunology*]	HS
Horse Serum Albumin [*Immunology*]	HSA
Horsed Transport [*Military*]	HT
Horseheads, NY [*Radio station call letters*]	WIQT
Horseheads, NY [*Radio station call letters*]	WQIX
Horseless Carriage Club of America	HCCA
Horseman's Abstracts [*A publication*]	HorsAb
Horsemanship Safety Association	HSA
Horsemen's Benevolent and Protective Association	HBPA
Horsepower	HP
Horsepower-Hour	HPH
Horsepower-Hour	HP-HR
Horsepower Nominal	HP
Horserace Betting Levy Board [*British*]	HBLB
Horserace Totalisator [*Set up in 1926 to provide alternative form of betting and to generate income from improvement of racing*] [*British*]	HT
Horseradish Peroxidase [*An enzyme*]	HRP
Horseshoe Bay [*British Columbia*] [*Seismograph station code, US Geological Survey*] [*Closed*]	HBC
Horseshoe Bend, AR [*Radio station call letters*]	KHAM

Horseshoe Bend National Military Park ... HOBE
Horsham [*Australia*] [*Airport symbol*] [*Obsolete*] ... HSM
Horta [*Azores*] [*Seismograph station code, US Geological Survey*] ... HOR
Horta [*Faial Island*] [*Azores*] [*Airport symbol*] ... HOR
Horticultural Abstracts ... HA
Horticultural Abstracts [*A publication*] ... Hort Abstr
Horticultural Advance (Sahranpur) [*A publication*] ... Hortic Adv (Sahranpur)
Horticultural Centre Loughgall Annual Report [*A publication*] ... Hortic Cent Loughgall Annu Rep
Horticultural Dealers Association ... HDA
Horticultural Marketing Inspectorate [*Ministry of Agriculture, Fisheries, and Food*] [*British*] ... HMI
Horticultural News [*A publication*] ... Hort N
Horticultural Research [*A publication*] ... Hortic Res
Horticultural Research [*A publication*] ... Hort Res
Horticultural Research (Edinburgh) [*A publication*] ... Hort Res (Edinb)
Horticultural Research Institute ... HRI
Horticultural Research Institute of Ontario Report [*A publication*] ... Hortic Res Inst Ont Rep
Horticultural Science (Calcutta) [*A publication*] ... Hortic Sci (Calcutta)
Horticultural Science (Stuttgart) [*A publication*] ... Hortic Sci (Stuttg)
Horticultural Society of New York, Inc., New York, NY [*Library symbol*] ... NNHor
Horticultural and Viticultural Sciences (Sofia) [*A publication*] ... Hortic Vitic Sci (Sofia)
Horticulture ... HORT
Horticulture [*Freight*] ... HORTI
Horticulture ... HORTIC
Horticulture [*A publication*] ... Hort
HortScience [*A publication*] ... HortSci
Hose Bib ... HB
Hose Clamp ... HC
Hose Connector ... HCONN
Hose Jacket ... HJ
Hose Rack ... HR
Hose Thread ... HSTH
Hosea [*Old Testament book*] ... Hos
Hoshina [*Japan*] [*Seismograph station code, US Geological Survey*] ... HSJ
Hosiery Wholesalers National Association ... HWNA
Hoskins [*Papua New Guinea*] [*Airport symbol*] ... HKN
Hoskins Manufacturing Co. [*American Stock Exchange symbol*] ... HOM
Hospital [*Traffic sign*] [*British*] ... H
Hospital ... HOSP
Hospital Abstract Service [*A publication*] ... Hosp Abstr Serv
Hospital Abstracts [*A publication*] ... HospAb
Hospital-Acquired Infection [*Medicine*] ... HAI
Hospital Activity Analysis [*British*] ... HAA
Hospital Adjustment Scale [*Psychology*] ... HAS
Hospital Administration [*or Administrator*] ... HAD
Hospital Administration in Canada [*A publication*] ... Hosp Adm Can
Hospital Administration (Chicago) [*A publication*] ... Hosp Adm (Chicago)
Hospital Administration Currents [*A publication*] ... Hosp Admin Curr
Hospital Administration (New Delhi) [*A publication*] ... Hosp Adm (New Delhi)
Hospital Administrative Services ... HAS
Hospital Affiliates International, Inc. [*NYSE symbol*] ... HAF
Hospital Apprentice [*Navy rating*] ... HA
Hospital Apprentice, High School ... HA(HS)
Hospital Audiences, Incorporated ... HAI
Hospital-Based Home Care ... HBHC
Hospital Benefits Payments ... HBP
Hospital Blood Bank ... HBB
Hospital Bureau, Incorporated [*Formerly, HBSS*] ... HBI
Hospital Bureau Research Institute [*Defunct*] ... HBRI
Hospital Bureau of Standards and Supplies [*Later, HBI*] ... HBSS
Hospital Car Service ... HCS
Hospital Care [*A publication*] ... Hosp Care
Hospital and Community Psychiatry ... H & CP
Hospital and Community Psychiatry [*A publication*] ... Hosp Commun
Hospital and Community Psychiatry [*A publication*] ... Hosp Community Psychiatry
Hospital and Community Psychiatry [*A publication*] ... HSCPA
Hospital Company [*Marine Corps*] ... HOSPCO
Hospital Computer Sharing System ... HCSS
Hospital Corporation of America [*NYSE symbol*] ... HCA
Hospital Corps [*or Corpsman*] [*Navy*] ... HC
Hospital Corpsman [*Navy rating*] ... HM
Hospital Corpsman, Chief [*Navy rating*] ... HMC
Hospital Corpsman, First Class [*Navy rating*] ... HM1
Hospital Corpsman, Master Chief [*Navy rating*] ... HMCM
Hospital Corpsman, Second Class [*Navy rating*] ... HM2
Hospital Corpsman, Senior Chief [*Navy rating*] ... HMCS
Hospital Corpsman, Third Class [*Navy rating*] ... HM3
Hospital Data Center [*American Hospital Association*] [*Information service*] ... HDC
Hospital Design/Hospital Equipment [*British*] ... HD/HE
Hospital Development [*A publication*] ... Hosp Dev
Hospital Development [*A publication*] ... Hosp Develop
Hospital Discharge Survey [*Public Health Service*] ... HDS
Hospital Educational and Research Fund, Inc., Albany, NY [*Library symbol*] ... NAIH
Hospital Educational Services Officer [*Navy*] ... HESO
Hospital Employees' Federation of Australia ... HEF
Hospital Engineering [*A publication*] ... Hosp Eng
Hospital Equipment Loan Project ... HELP
Hospital Equipment and Supplies [*A publication*] ... Hosp Equip Supplies
Hospital Field Director [*Red Cross*] ... HFD
Hospital Financial Management [*A publication*] ... Hosp Financ Manage
Hospital Financial Management [*A publication*] ... Hosp Fin Mgt
Hospital Financial Management Association ... HFMA
Hospital Food Directors Association ... HFDA
Hospital Formulary [*A publication*] ... Hosp Formul
Hospital Formulary Management [*A publication*] ... Hosp Formul Manage
Hospital Forum [*A publication*] ... Hosp Forum
Hospital General (Madrid) [*A publication*] ... Hosp Gen (Madr)
Hospital Health Care Newsletter [*A publication*] ... Hosp Health Care Newsl
Hospital and Health Services Administration [*A publication*] ... Hosp Health Serv Adm
Hospital and Health Services Administration [*A publication*] ... Hosp Health Serv Admin
Hospital and Health Services Review [*A publication*] ... Hosp Health Serv Rev
Hospital-Hygiene [*A publication*] ... Hosp-Hyg
Hospital Improvement ... HIP
Hospital In-Patient Enquiry [*British*] ... HIPE
Hospital In-Service Training ... HIST
Hospital Indicator for Physicians' Orders ... HIPO
Hospital Infection Control [*A publication*] ... Hosp Infect Control
Hospital Information System [*Data processing*] ... HIS
Hospital Information Systems Sharing Group ... HISSG
Hospital, Institution, and Educational Food Service Society ... HIEFSS
Hospital Insurance ... HI
Hospital Insurance Program ... HIP
Hospital International [*A publication*] ... Hosp Int
Hospital Libraries [*A publication*] ... Hosp Libr
Hospital Literature Index [*A publication*] ... Hosp Lit Ind
Hospital Management, Hospital Problems [*British*] ... HMHP
Hospital Management Systems Society ... HMSS
Hospital Materiel Management Quarterly [*A publication*] ... Hosp Mater Manage Q
Hospital Medical Staff [*A publication*] ... Hosp Med Staff
Hospital Medicine [*A publication*] ... Hosp Med
Hospital Music Newsletter [*A publication*] ... Hospital Mus News
Hospital Operating System - Structured Programing Language [*Data processing*] ... HOS-STPL
Hospital Participation [*Blood program*] [*Red Cross*] ... HP
Hospital Peer Review [*A publication*] ... Hosp Peer Rev
Hospital Pharmacy [*A publication*] ... Hosp Pharm
Hospital Physician [*A publication*] ... Hosp Physician
Hospital Plane [*When suffixed to Navy plane designation*] ... H
Hospital Practice [*A publication*] ... Hosp Pract
Hospital Progress [*A publication*] ... Hosp Progr
Hospital Purchasing Management [*A publication*] ... Hosp Purch Manage
Hospital Rations [*Navy*] ... HOSPRATS
Hospital Reading Society [*Defunct*] ... HRS
Hospital Recruit ... HR
Hospital Research and Educational Trust ... HRET
Hospital (Rio De Janeiro) [*A publication*] ... Hospital (Rio De J)
[*The*] **Hospital Satellite Network** [*Satellite television system*] ... HSN
Hospital Savings Association ... HSA
Hospital Service Plan [*British*] ... HSP
Hospital Services Commission, Edmonton, AB, Canada [*Library symbol*] ... CaAEHSC
Hospital Ship [*Navy symbol*] ... AH
Hospital Ship ... HS
Hospital Ship ... TAH
Hospital for Special Surgery, New York, NY [*Library symbol*] ... NNHS
Hospital and Specialist Services [*British*] ... HSS
Hospital Staffing Service [*NASDAQ symbol*] ... HSSI
Hospital Supervisors Bulletin [*A publication*] ... Hosp Superv Bull
Hospital Topics [*A publication*] ... Hosp Top
Hospital Topics [*A publication*] ... HOTOA
Hospital Train ... HT
Hospital Transfer Order ... HTO
Hospital Trustee [*A publication*] ... Hosp Trustee
Hospital Utilization Project [*Western Pennsylvania*] ... HUP
Hospital del Vina Del Mar [*A publication*] ... Hosp Vina Del Mar
Hospitality Committee for United Nations Delegations ... HCUND
[*The*] **Hospitality and Information Service** [*For diplomatic residents and families in Washington, DC*] ... THIS
Hospitality Lodging and Travel Research Foundation ... HLTRF
Hospitality Motor Inns, Inc. [*American Stock Exchange symbol*] [*Delisted*] ... HMN
Hospitalization Proneness Scale [*Psychometrics*] ... HPS
Hospitalization and Treatment ... H & T
Hospitalized Veterans Writing Project ... HVWP
Hospitaller Order of St. John of God [*Roman Catholic men's religious order*] ... OH
Hospitalman [*Nonrated enlisted man*] [*Navy*] ... HN
Hospitalman Recruit ... HR
Hospitals [*A publication*] ... HOSIA
Hospitals, Administration, and Organizations [*British*] ... HAO

Hospitals Staff ... HS
Host Country ... HC
Host Country Contributions [*Peace Corps*] ... HCC
Host International, Incorporated [*NYSE symbol*] [*Delisted*] ... HII
Host Nation ... HN
Host Nation Support [*Military*] ... HNS
Host to Network [*Data processing*] ... HN
Host-Plant Resistance [*Entomology, phytochemistry*] ... HPR
Host-Tenant Support Agreement [*Military*] ... HTSA
Host Ventures Ltd. [*NASDAQ symbol*] ... HOSTF
Host Versus Graft [*Medicine*] ... HVG
Hostage Bracelet Committee ... HBC
Hostage Rescue Team [*Pronounced "hurt"*] [*FBI standardized term*] ... HRT
Hostess ... HSTS
Hostesses Internationales [*French dating service*] ... HI
Hostile [*Military*] ... H
Hostile Artillery Positions ... HATLS
Hostile Electromagnetic Emission ... HEME
Hostile Fire Pay [*Special pay for hazardous duty*] [*Military*] ... HFP
Hostile, Unknown, Faker, and Pending [*Used in SAGE to designate certain tracks and raids*] ... HUKP
Hostile Weapons Locating System ... HWLS
Hostilities Only [*Applied to men who joined for duration of war only*] [*Navy*] [*British*] [*World War II*] ... HO
Hostility and Direction of Hostility Questionnaire [*Psychology*] ... HDHQ
Hostos Community College, New York, NY [*Library symbol*] ... NNHC
Hot ... H
Hot Air ... HA
Hot Air Balloon ... HAB
Hot Air Vulcanization ... HAV
Hot Blade Stripper ... HBS
Hot Boning [*Meat processing*] ... HB
Hot Bridgewire ... HBW
Hot-Carrier Diode ... HCD
Hot Carrier Quad ... HCQ
Hot Cathode Tube ... HCT
Hot and Cold ... HC
Hot and Cold Running Water ... HCRW
Hot Critical Experiments [*Nuclear energy*] ... HOTCE
Hot Dip Galvanization ... HDG
Hot Dry Rock [*Geothermal science*] ... HDR
Hot Electron Amplifier ... HEA
Hot Experimental Reaction of O Power ... HERO
Hot Firing ... HF
Hot Fuel Examination Facility [*Nuclear energy*] ... HFEF
Hot Gas Bonder ... HGB
Hot Gas Generator ... HGG
Hot Gas Manifold ... HGM
Hot Gas Radiating Facility ... HGRF
Hot Gas Soldering Equipment ... HGSE
Hot Gas System ... HGS
Hot Gas Thrust Vector Control ... HGTVC
Hot and Heavy [*In reference to a romance*] ... H^2
Hot Hydrogen Nozzle ... HHN
Hot Isostatic Compaction ... HIC
Hot Isostatic Pressing [*or Pressure*] [*Metals*] ... HIP
Hot Jet Exhaust ... HJE
Hot Jet Model ... HJM
Hot Kathode Tube ... HKT
Hot Leg [*Nuclear energy*] ... HLG
Hot Leg Check Valve [*Nuclear energy*] ... HLCV
Hot Leg Isolation Valve [*Nuclear energy*] ... HLIV
Hot Line [*Alert system*] ... HL
Hot Line Alert System ... HLAS
Hot Line Gunsight System ... HLGS
Hot Melt Applicator ... HMA
Hot Melt Equipment Manufacturers Association ... HEMA
Hot Pack [*or Pad*] [*Physical therapy*] ... HP
Hot Pilot [*An egotistic flying cadet*] [*Slang*] [*Air Force*] ... HP
Hot-Pressed [*Paper*] ... HP
Hot-Pressed Silicon Nitride ... HPSN
Hot Processing Plant [*Nuclear energy*] ... HPP
Hot Report ... HT
Hot Rolled ... HR
Hot Rolled, Pickled, and Oiled ... HRPO
Hot Rolled Steel ... HRS
Hot Shot Tunnel ... HST
Hot Side ... HSD
Hot Spot [*Washington*] [*Seismograph station code, US Geological Survey*] [*Closed*] ... HSW
Hot Spraying ... HS
Hot Springs [*Arkansas*] [*Airport symbol*] ... HOT
Hot Springs, AR [*Radio station call letters*] ... KACQ
Hot Springs, AR [*Radio station call letters*] ... KBHS
Hot Springs, AR [*Radio station call letters*] ... KSPA
Hot Springs, AR [*Radio station call letters*] ... KWBO
Hot Springs, AR [*Radio station call letters*] ... KXOW
Hot Springs, AR [*Radio station call letters*] ... KZNG
Hot Springs National Park ... HOSP
Hot Springs, SD [*Location identifier*] [*FAA*] ... FTA
Hot Springs, SD [*Radio station call letters*] ... KOBH
Hot Springs, SD [*Radio station call letters*] ... KOBH-FM
Hot Springs, VA [*Radio station call letters*] ... WWES
Hot Stamping Press ... HSP
Hot Stove Club ... HSC
Hot Stuff [*Slang*] [*Bowdlerized version*] ... HS
Hot Tin ... HT
Hot Tub Bath [*Medicine*] ... HTB
Hot Water ... HW
Hot Water Circulating [*Technical drawings*] ... HWC
Hot Water Heater ... HWH
Hot Water-Insoluble Nitrogen [*Analytical chemistry*] ... HWIN
Hot Water Line ... HWL
Hot Water Return ... HWR
Hot Water Soluble ... HWS
Hot Wire ... HW
Hot Wire Anemometer ... HWA
Hot Wire Emissive Probe ... HWEP
Hotan [*China*] [*Airport symbol*] ... HTN
Hotchkiss Public Library, Hotchkiss, CO [*Library symbol*] ... CoHotch
Hotel [*Phonetic alphabet*] ... H
Hotel Accountants Association of New York City ... HAA
Hotel Corporation of America [*NYSE symbol*] [*Delisted*] ... HCA
Hotel Credit Managers Association ... HCMA
Hotel-Dieu de Gaspe, Gaspe, PQ, Canada [*Library symbol*] ... CaQGaH
Hotel-Dieu Hospital, Montreal, PQ, Canada [*Library symbol*] ... CaQMHD
Hotel Dieu Medical-Nursing Educational Media Center, El Paso, TX [*Library symbol*] ... TxEHD
Hotel-Dieu de Quebec, Quebec, PQ, Canada [*Library symbol*] ... CaQQHD
Hotel-Dieu du Sacre Coeur, Quebec, PQ, Canada [*Library symbol*] ... CaQQHDS
Hotel Employees and Restaurant Employees International Union [*Formerly, HREBIU, HREU*] ... HERE
Hotel Greeters of America [*Later, HMGI*] ... HGA
Hotel Investors Trust SBI [*NYSE symbol*] ... HOT
Hotel-Motel Greeters International ... HMGI
Hotel and Motel Management [*A publication*] ... Hotel & Motel Mgt
Hotel and Restaurant Employees and Bartenders International Union [*Later, HERE*] ... HREBIU
Hotel and Restaurant Employees and Bartenders International Union [*Later, HERE*] ... HREU
Hotel Sales Management Association [*Later, HSMAI*] ... HSMA
Hotel Sundry Fund [*Air Force*] ... HSF
Hotels and Restaurants [*Public-performance tariff class*] [*British*] ... E
Hotot Rabbit Breeders International ... HRBI
Hotwell ... HWL
Houailou [*New Caledonia*] [*Airport symbol*] ... HLU
Houches. Ecole d'Ete de Physique Theoretique [*A publication*] ... Houches Ec Ete Phys Theor
Houdaille Industries, Inc. [*NYSE symbol*] [*Delisted*] ... HH
Hough Development Corporation [*Cleveland*] ... HDC
Hough-Powell Digitizer ... H-PD
Houghton College, Buffalo Campus, West Seneca, NY [*Library symbol*] ... NWsH
Houghton College, Buffalo Campus, West Seneca, NY [*OCLC symbol*] ... YXO
Houghton College, Houghton, NY [*OCLC symbol*] ... VXO
Houghton Lake, MI [*Location identifier*] [*FAA*] ... HTL
Houghton Lake, MI [*Radio station call letters*] ... WHGR
Houghton Lake, MI [*Radio station call letters*] ... WJGS
Houghton Lake Public Library, Houghton Lake, MI [*Library symbol*] ... MiHl
Houghton, MI [*Radio station call letters*] ... WCCY
Houghton, MI [*Radio station call letters*] ... WGGL-FM
Houghton, MI [*Radio station call letters*] ... WHUH
Houghton Mifflin Co. [*NYSE symbol*] ... HTN
Houghton Mifflin Co., Boston, MA [*OCLC symbol*] ... HMC
Houghton Mifflin Co., Boston, MA [*Library symbol*] ... MBHoM
Houghton, NY [*Radio station call letters*] ... WJSL
Houlton [*Maine*] [*Airport symbol*] ... HUL
Houlton, ME [*Location identifier*] [*FAA*] ... HUL
Houlton, ME [*Radio station call letters*] ... WHOU
Houlton, ME [*Radio station call letters*] ... WHOU-FM
Houlton, ME [*Radio station call letters*] ... WRNE-FM
Houma [*Louisiana*] [*Airport symbol*] ... HUM
Houma, LA [*Radio station call letters*] ... KCIL
Houma, LA [*Radio station call letters*] ... KHOM
Houma, LA [*Radio station call letters*] ... KJIN
Houn [*Libya*] [*Airport symbol*] ... HUQ
Hour [*Also, h*] ... H
Hour ... HR
Hour Angle [*Navigation*] ... HA
Hour Angle-Declination [*Type of antenna mounting*] ... HA-DEC
Hour Angle of the Mean Sun [*Navigation*] ... HAMS
Hour Angle of the True Sun [*Navigation*] ... HATS
Hour Circle ... HC
Hourglass Device [*Military decoration*] ... HGD
Hourly Difference [*Navigation*] ... HD
Hourly Noise Level ... HNL
Hourly Postflight ... HPO
Hourly Precipitation Data [*A publication*] ... HPD
Hours ... HRS
Hours, Minutes, Seconds ... HMS

Hours of Operation...HO
[*Service available during*] **Hours of Scheduled Operations** ......HS
Hours of Sleep [*Medicine*].......................................HS
Hours Waiting Parts ....HWP
House ....H
House ....HO
House ....HSE
House Appropriations Committee [*US Congress*].............HAC
House Armed Services Committee [*US Congress*] ....HASC
House Armed Services Investigation Subcommittee [*US
  Congress*]..HASIS
House Armed Services Permanent Investigations
  Subcommittee [*US Congress*]..........................HASPID
House Beautiful [*A publication*] ....House B
House Bill [*In state legislatures*].............................HB
House Boat [*Navy symbol*] ....YHB
House-Breaking Implements [*British police term*]............HBI
House Call [*Medicine*]..HC
House Call Tax Service ....HCTS
House Committee on Internal Security [*Formerly, HUAC*]
  [*Dissolved, 1975*] [*US Congress*]........................HCIS
House Committee on Space and Astronautics [*US Congress*]......HCSA
House Committee Substitute [*US Congress*] ....HCS
House of Commons [*British*]...........................H of C
House of Commons [*British*]..............................HC
House of Commons [*British*]..............................HOC
House of Commons Bill [*British*]..........................HCB
House Concurrent Resolution [*US Congress*]..............HCR
House of Correction ....HC
House Defense Appropriations Subcommittee [*US Congress*]......HDAS
House Democratic Research Organization ....HDRO
House Document ....HD
House Document ....HDOC
House Dress Institute ....HDI
House Dust Mite ....HDM
House Ear Institute...HEI
House of Fabrics, Inc. [*NYSE symbol*] ....HF
House and Garden [*A publication*].................House & G
House and Garden [*A publication*]............House & Gard
House Heating [*Freight*]......................................HHTG
House and Home [*A publication*]...................H & Home
House of Ill Fame...H of IF
House Information Systems [*Congress*] ....HIS
House Internal Security Committee ....HISC
House Joint Resolution ....HJR
House Joint Resolution ....HJ Res
House of Keys [*Isle of Man*] ....HK
House of Keys [*Isle of Man*] ....HOK
House of Lords [*British*]......................................HL
House of Lords [*British*]......................................HOL
House of Lords Cases [*Law*] [*British*] ....HLC
House of Lords Cases [*Law*] [*British*] ....HLCAS
House Magazine Institute [*Later, NY/IABC*]..............HMI
House Merchant Marine and Fisheries Committee ....HMMFC
House Nigger [*Derogatory nickname for an obsequious black person*] ......HN
House Officer...HO
House Physician...HP
House Report ....HR
House of Representatives...H
House of Representatives..HR
House of Representatives Bill ....HRB
House Resolution..HR
House Resolution, United States House of Representatives ......H Res
House of Ronnie, Inc. [*American Stock Exchange symbol*]......HRO
House of Ruth [*An association*] ....HR
House Science and Astronautics Committee [*US Congress*]......HSAC
House Space Committee [*US Congress*]..................HSC
House Spacecraft...HS/C
House Supervisor...HS
House Surgeon..HS
House Trailer...HT
[*A*] **House, a Tree, a Person** [*Psychological drawing test*] ......H-T-P
House Un-American Activities Committee [*Later, HCIS*] [*US
  Congress*]...HUAC
House of Vision, Inc. [*American Stock Exchange symbol*] [*Delisted*]......HOV
House Wednesday Group ....HWG
Houseboat Association of America...........................HAA
Housebreaking ....HB
Household...HH
Household..HHLD
Household..HSHLD
Household Cavalry [*British*]..................................HC
Household Earnings and Expenditure ....HEE
Household Economics Research Division [*of ARS, Department of
  Agriculture*]..HHE
Household Effects ....HHE
Household Employment Association for Reevaluation and
  Training [*Later, Personnel Resources*].................HEART
Household Finance Corporation [*NYSE symbol*] [*Delisted*] ......HFC
Household Finance Corporation, Chicago, IL [*Library symbol*]......ICHFC
Household Food Consumption................................HFC

Household Furniture [*Insurance*]............................HHF
Household Goods..HHG
Household Goods..HHGS
Household Goods/Baggage.....................................HB
Household Goods Carriers' Bureau ....HGCB
Household Goods Carriers' Bureau Agent, Arlington VA [*STAC*]......HGB
Household Goods Forwarders Association of America......HGFA
Household Goods Forwarders Association of America......HHGFAA
Household Goods Forwarders Tariff Bureau, Washington DC
  [*STAC*]..HGF
Household Goods Military and Government Rate Tariff......HGMGR
Household Goods Transportation Association, Washington DC
  [*STAC*]..HGT
Household International [*NYSE symbol*].....................HI
Household and Personal Products Industry [*A publication*]......HAPPI
Household Personal Products Industry [*A publication*] ......Household
[*Frank-Massy*] **Household Purchasing Characteristics
  Generating System** [*Marketing*]........................HPCGS
Household Words [*A publication*]....................House Words
Housekeeping ....HK
Housekeeping ....HSKPG
Housekeeping Data Acquisition..............................HDA
Houses of Parliament [*British*]...............................HP
Housewife...HW
Housewives Elect Lower Prices [*New York women's lobby group*]......HELP
Housing ....HOUS
Housing ....HOUSG
Housing ....HSG
Housing ....HSNG
Housing Allowance [*Military*]................................HA
Housing Assistance [*HUD*]..................................HA
Housing Assistance Administration [*HUD*]................HAA
Housing Assistance Council ....HAC
Housing Assistance Program ....HAP
Housing Authority ....HA
Housing Census ....HC
Housing Construction and Land Development..............HCLD
Housing Density ....HD
Housing and Development Administration [*New York City*]......HDA
Housing Development Corporation [*Washington, DC*]......HDC
Housing Guaranty ....HG
Housing and Home Finance Agency [*Terminated 1965, functions
  taken over by HUD*]..HHFA
Housing Improvement ....HI
Housing Improvement Program [*Federal government*]......HIP
Housing Industries of America [*NASDAQ symbol*].......HIAI
Housing Industry Association ....HIA
Housing Information Management System ....HIMS
Housing Intelligence Quotient..................................HIQ
Housing Investment Trust [*AFL-CIO*]......................HIT
Housing Management [*HUD*]................................HM
Housing Operation with Training Opportunity [*Office of
  Economic Opportunity*]..................................HOW-TO
Housing Opportunity Assistance Program [*Federal Home Loan
  Bank Board*] ....HOAP
Housing Our People Economically.............................HOPE
Housing and Planning References [*A publication*] ......HousP
Housing and Planning References [*A publication*].......HPR
Housing Production and Management Credit [*HUD*]......HPMC
Housing Referral Office [*Military*]............................HRO
Housing Referral Service [*Military*]..........................HRS
Housing Revenue Account [*British*]..........................HRA
Housing Scheme [*British*] ....HS
Housing Statistics...HS
Housing Study Tours [*British*]................................HST
Housing and Urban Development Association of Canada......HUDAC
Housing and Urban Development Department [*More commonly,
  HUD*] ....HUDD
Housing and Urban Development [*Department*] Procurement
  Regulations...HUDPR
Housman Society...HS
Housman Society Journal [*A publication*]..................HSJ
Houston [*Texas*] [*Airport symbol*] ....HOU
Houston [*Texas*] [*Seismograph station code, US Geological Survey*]......HOU
Houston Academy of Medicine, Houston, TX [*Library symbol*]......TxHMC
Houston Academy of Medicine for Texas Medical Center,
  Houston, TX [*OCLC symbol*].............................TMC
Houston Academy of Medicine for Texas Medical Center,
  Houston, TX [*Library symbol*]...........................TxHAM
Houston Aerospace Language [*NASA*].....................HAL
Houston [*Texas*] Allen Center [*Airport symbol*] ....JLC
Houston Area Library System [*Library network*].........HALS
Houston [*Texas*] Astrodome [*Airport symbol*]..........JMA
Houston Automatic Spooling Program [*Data processing*]......HASP
Houston Baptist University [*Texas*]..........................HBU
Houston Baptist University, Houston, TX [*OCLC symbol*]......TWH
Houston Baptist University, Houston, TX [*Library symbol*]......TxHBC
Houston Belt & Terminal Railway Co. ....HB & T
Houston Belt & Terminal Railway Co. [*AAR code*].........HBT
Houston Carnegie Public Library, Houston, MS [*Library symbol*]......MsHou
Houston Chronicle, Houston, TX [*Library symbol*]......TxHHC

Houston Community College System, Houston, TX [*Library symbol*]... TxHC
Houston Community College System, Learning Resource Center, Houston, TX [*OCLC symbol*]... THC
Houston Cotton Exchange and Board of Trade [*Defunct*]... HCEBT
Houston County Court House, Dothan, AL [*Library symbol*]... ADoC
Houston - ET [*Texas*] [*Seismograph station code, US Geological Survey*] [*Closed*]... HET
Houston-Galveston Area Council Library, Houston, TX [*Library symbol*]... TxHHG
Houston Geological Society. Bulletin [*A publication*]... Houston Geol Soc Bull
Houston [*Texas*] **Greenway** [*Airport symbol*]... JGP
Houston [*Texas*] **Guest Quarters** [*Airport symbol*]... JGQ
Houston Industries, Inc. [*NYSE symbol*]... HOU
Houston [*Texas*] **Intercontinental** [*Airport symbol*]... IAH
Houston Journal of Mathematics [*A publication*]... Houston J Math
Houston Law Review [*A publication*]... Houston Law
Houston Law Review [*A publication*]... Houston L Rev
Houston Lighting & Power Co., Houston, TX [*Library symbol*]... TxHHL
Houston Mission Control Center [*NASA*]... HMCC
Houston, MO [*Radio station call letters*]... KBTC
Houston, MO [*Radio station call letters*]... KSCM
Houston, MS [*Radio station call letters*]... WCPC
Houston, MS [*Radio station call letters*]... WCPC-FM
Houston Natural Gas Corp. [*NYSE symbol*]... HNG
Houston Network Controller [*NASA*]... HNET
Houston Oil Fields [*NASDAQ symbol*]... HOFC
Houston Oil & Minerals Corp. [*American Stock Exchange symbol*] [*Delisted*]... HOI
Houston Oil Royalty UBI [*NYSE symbol*]... RTH
Houston Oil Trust UBI [*American Stock Exchange symbol*]... HO
Houston [*Texas*] **Park-Ten** [*Airport symbol*]... JPT
Houston Post, Houston, TX [*Library symbol*]... TxHHP
Houston Public Library, Houston, TX [*Library symbol*]... TxH
Houston Public Library, Houston, TX [*OCLC symbol*]... TXN
Houston Research Institute, Houston, TX [*Library symbol*]... TxHRI
Houston Symphony. Program Notes [*A publication*]... Houston Sym
Houston Test for Language Development [*Education*]... HTLD
Houston [*Texas*] **Town/Country** [*Airport symbol*]... JTC
Houston, TX [*Location identifier*] [*FAA*]... AAP
Houston, TX [*Location identifier*] [*FAA*]... DWH
Houston, TX [*Location identifier*] [*FAA*]... HEW
Houston, TX [*Location identifier*] [*FAA*]... HUB
Houston, TX [*Radio station call letters*]... KBUK
Houston, TX [*Radio station call letters*]... KCOH
Houston, TX [*Radio station call letters*]... KEYH
Houston, TX [*Radio station call letters*]... KFMK
Houston, TX [*Radio station call letters*]... KHCB-FM
Houston, TX [*Television station call letters*]... KHOU-TV
Houston, TX [*Television station call letters*]... KHTV
Houston, TX [*Radio station call letters*]... KIKK-FM
Houston, TX [*Radio station call letters*]... KILT
Houston, TX [*Radio station call letters*]... KILT-FM
Houston, TX [*Radio station call letters*]... KKBQ
Houston, TX [*Radio station call letters*]... KLAT
Houston, TX [*Radio station call letters*]... KLEF
Houston, TX [*Radio station call letters*]... KLOL
Houston, TX [*Radio station call letters*]... KNUZ
Houston, TX [*Radio station call letters*]... KODA-FM
Houston, TX [*Radio station call letters*]... KPFT
Houston, TX [*Radio station call letters*]... KPRC
Houston, TX [*Television station call letters*]... KPRC-TV
Houston, TX [*Radio station call letters*]... KQUE
Houston, TX [*Radio station call letters*]... KRBE-FM
Houston, TX [*Television station call letters*]... KRIV-TV
Houston, TX [*Radio station call letters*]... KRLY
Houston, TX [*Radio station call letters*]... KSRR
Houston, TX [*Radio station call letters*]... KTRH
Houston, TX [*Television station call letters*]... KTRK-TV
Houston, TX [*Radio station call letters*]... KTRU
Houston, TX [*Radio station call letters*]... KTSU
Houston, TX [*Television station call letters*]... KTXH-TV
Houston, TX [*Radio station call letters*]... KUHF
Houston, TX [*Television station call letters*]... KUHT
Houston, TX [*Radio station call letters*]... KXYZ
Houston, TX [*Radio station call letters*]... KYOK
Houston, TX [*Location identifier*] [*FAA*]... LYD
Hoven & Company, Bakersfield, CA [*Library symbol*]... HoC
Hovenweep National Monument... HOVE
Hover... HVR
Hover Agility Rotor... HAR
Hover and Approach Coupler... HAC
Hover Augmentation System... HAS
Hover Out-of-Ground Effect... HOGE
Hover and Transition [*Simulator*]... HOTRAN
Hoverclub of America... HA
Hovercraft-Helicopter Carrier... HHC
Hovercraft World [*A publication*]... Hovercr Wld
Hovering... HVRNG
Hovering Craft and Hydrofoil [*A publication*]... Hov Craft Hydrof
Hovering Rocket System [*Army*]... HRS
Hovering Vehicle Versatile Automatic Control... HOVVAC
Hovnanian Enterprises, Inc. [*American Stock Exchange symbol*]... HOV
How [*Phonetic alphabet*] [*World War II*]... H
How Do We Stand?... HDWS
How to Evaluate Health Programs [*A publication*]... How Eval Health Programs
How-to-Fight [*Manuals*] [*Military*]... HTF
How Well Do You Know Yourself? [*Psychological testing*]... HWDYKY
How Will Arrival Report Be Filed Concerning____ [*Aviation*]... HIRIV
Howard BanCorporation [*NASDAQ symbol*]... HOBC
Howard Bank of New Jersey [*NASDAQ symbol*]... HWRD
Howard County Junior College [*Texas*]... HCJC
Howard County Junior College, Big Spring, TX [*Library symbol*]... TxBsH
Howard County Library, Big Spring, TX [*Library symbol*]... TxBs
Howard County Library, Simpsonville, MD [*Library symbol*]... MdSim
Howard Hughes Medical Institute... HHMI
Howard Ink Blot Test [*Psychology*]... HIBT
Howard Johnson [*Restaurant chain*] [*Slang*]... HOJO
Howard Johnson Co. [*NYSE symbol*] [*Delisted*]... HJ
Howard Law Journal [*A publication*]... Howard L J
Howard Payne College [*Texas*]... HPC
Howard Payne College, Brownwood, TX [*Library symbol*]... TxBrdH
Howard Public Library, Howard, SD [*Library symbol*]... SdHow
Howard Research Corporation... HRC
Howard Robard Hughes [*1905-1976*] [*American businessman*]... HRH
Howard Stores Corp. [*NYSE symbol*] [*Delisted*]... HOS
Howard Terminal [*Later, HT*] [*AAR code*]... HOWT
Howard Terminal [*AAR code*]... HT
Howard University, Washington, DC [*Library symbol*] [*OCLC symbol*]... DHU
Howard Young Medical Center, Woodruff, WI [*Library symbol*]... WWooH
Howe, IN [*Radio station call letters*]... WHWE
Howe Memorial Library, Breckenridge, MI [*Library symbol*]... MiBre
Howe Peak [*Idaho*] [*Seismograph station code, US Geological Survey*]... HPI
Howell Carnegie Library, Howell, MI [*Library symbol*]... MiHow
Howell Corp. [*NYSE symbol*]... HWL
Howell Industries, Inc. [*American Stock Exchange symbol*]... HOW
Howell-Jolly [*Bodies*] [*Hematology*]... HJ
Howell, MI [*Radio station call letters*]... WHMI
Howell, MI [*Radio station call letters*]... WHMI-FM
Howell Petroleum [*NYSE symbol*]... HPT
However... HOWR
However... HWVR
Howitt's Journal [*A publication*]... Howitt
Howitzer... HOW
Howitzer Motor Carriage... HMC
Howitzer Test Bed... HTB
Howler [*Communications; electronics*]... HW
Howmet Corp. [*NYSE symbol*] [*Delisted*]... HW
Howrah [*India*] [*Seismograph station code, US Geological Survey*]... HOW
Hoy Island [*Scotland*] [*Airport symbol*] [*Obsolete*]... HOY
Hoya Society International... HSI
Hoyt Peak [*Utah*] [*Seismograph station code, US Geological Survey*]... HTU
HPSC, Inc. [*NASDAQ symbol*]... HPSC
HRB-Singer, Inc., Science Park, State College, PA [*Library symbol*]... PStcH
Hristianskoe Ctenie [*A publication*]... HC
HRLSD [*Health and Rehabilitative Library Services Division*] **Journal** [*A publication*]... HRLSD J
Hroswitha Club... HC
HRS Industries Cl A [*NASDAQ symbol*]... HRIAF
HRT Industries [*Formerly, Hartfield-Zodys, Inc.*] [*NYSE symbol*]... HRT
Hruska Meat Animal Research Center [*Department of Agriculture*]... MARC
Hrvatski Dijalektoloski Zbornik [*A publication*]... HDZ
Hrvatski Dijalektoloski Zbornik [*A publication*]... HDZb
Hrvatsko Kolo [*A publication*]... HK
HSIA [*Halogenated Solvent Industry Alliance*] **Water Work Group**... WWG
Hsin-Li Hsueh-Pao [*Acta Psychologica Sinica*] [*A publication*]... APS
Hsin-Ya Shu-Yuan Hsueh-Shy Nien-K'an [*A publication*]... HYHN
Hsinchu [*Republic of China*] [*Seismograph station code, US Geological Survey*]... HSN
Hsinking [*Sirkyo, Chang Chun*] [*Republic of China*] [*Seismograph station code, US Geological Survey*]... HSK
Hsinkong [*Republic of China*] [*Also, SGK*] [*Seismograph station code, US Geological Survey*]... HSI
Hsinkong [*Republic of China*] [*Also, HSI*] [*Seismograph station code, US Geological Survey*]... SGK
Hsinying [*Republic of China*] [*Seismograph station code, US Geological Survey*]... TWK
HSMHA [*Health Services and Mental Health Administration*] **Report** [*United States*] [*A publication*]... HSMHA Health Report
Huahine [*French Polynesia*] [*Airport symbol*]... HUH
Hualalai [*Hawaii*] [*Seismograph station code, US Geological Survey*]... HUH
Hualien [*Taiwan*] [*Airport symbol*]... HUN
Hualien [*Republic of China*] [*Seismograph station code, US Geological Survey*]... TWD
Hualilan [*Argentina*] [*Seismograph station code, US Geological Survey*]... HLN
Huambo [*Angola*] [*Airport symbol*]... NOV
Huancayo [*Peru*] [*Geomagnetic observatory code*]... HUA
Huancayo [*Peru*] [*Seismograph station code, US Geological Survey*]... HUA
Huanuco [*Peru*] [*Airport symbol*]... HUU
Huaraz [*Peru*] [*Seismograph station code, US Geological Survey*]... HUZ

Hub Airlines, Inc. [*Fort Wayne, IN*] [*FAA designator*] .... HUB
Hubbard Brook Experimental Forest .... HBEF
Hubbard, OH [*Location identifier*] [*FAA*] .... HBD
Hubbard Public Library, Hubbard, OH [*Library symbol*] .... OHu
Hubbard Real Estate Investments [*NYSE symbol*] .... HRE
Hubbard Tank [*Medicine*] .... HT
Hubbell [*Harvey*], **Inc.** [*American Stock Exchange symbol*] .... HUB
Hubbell Trading Post National Historic Site .... HUTR
Hubbert Unit [*Petroleum technology*] .... HU
Hubcap Collector's Club .... HCC
HUBCO, Inc. [*NASDAQ symbol*] .... HUBC
Hubert Horatio Humphrey .... HHH
Huck Manufacturing Co. [*American Stock Exchange symbol*] [*Delisted*] .... HUX
HUD [*Housing and Urban Development*] **Challenge** [*A publication*] .... HUD Chal
HUD [*Housing and Urban Development*] **Clearinghouse Service** .... HCS
HUD [*Department of Housing and Urban Development*] **Mortgage Accounting Project** .... HUDMAP
HUD [*Housing and Urban Development*] **Newsletter** [*A publication*] .... HNL
HUD [*Department of Housing and Urban Development*] **Teleprocessing Network** .... HTN
Huddersfield Public Libraries, Huddersfield, United Kingdom [*Library symbol*] .... UkHu
Hudebni Revue [*A publication*] .... H R
Hudebni Rozhledy [*A publication*] .... H Ro
Hudebni Rozhledy [*A publication*] .... Hub Roz
Hudebni Rozhledy [*A publication*] .... Hud Roz
Hudebni Veda [*A publication*] .... Hud Veda
Hudebni Veda [*A publication*] .... HV
Hudeiba Research Station. Annual Report [*A publication*] .... Hudeiba Res Stn Annu Rep
Hudiksvall [*Sweden*] [*Airport symbol*] .... HUV
Hudson Bay [*AAR code*] .... HUBA
Hudson Bay [*MARC geographic area code*] [*Library of Congress*] .... n-cnh--
Hudson Bay Mining & Smelting Co. Ltd. [*NYSE symbol*] [*Delisted*] .... HD
Hudson-Essex-Terraplane Owners Club .... HETOC
Hudson Falls, NY [*Radio station call letters*] .... WENU
Hudson General Corporation [*American Stock Exchange symbol*] .... HGC
Hudson Institute .... HI
Hudson Institute, Croton-On-Hudson, NY [*Library symbol*] .... NCrohH
Hudson & Manhattan [*AAR code*] .... HDM
Hudson, NY [*Radio station call letters*] .... WHUC
Hudson, NY [*Radio station call letters*] .... WRVW
Hudson Public Library, Hudson, CO [*Library symbol*] .... CoHud
Hudson Public Library, Hudson, IA [*Library symbol*] .... IaHud
Hudson Public Library, Hudson, MI [*Library symbol*] .... MiHu
Hudson Public Library, Hudson, WI [*Library symbol*] .... WHud
Hudson Review [*A publication*] .... HR
Hudson Review [*A publication*] .... Hud R
Hudson Review [*A publication*] .... Hudson R
Hudson Review [*A publication*] .... HuR
Hudson River Day Line [*AAR code*] .... HRDL
Hudson River Sloop Clearwater [*An association*] .... HRSC
Hudson Star-Observer, Hudson, WI [*Library symbol*] .... WHudSO
Hudson Valley [*FAA*] .... HDSVLY
Hudson Valley Community College, Troy, NY [*Library symbol*] .... NTH
Hudson Valley Community College, Troy, NY [*OCLC symbol*] VXV
Hudson's Bay Company .... HBC
Hudson's Bay Oil & Gas Co. Ltd. [*American Stock Exchange symbol*] [*Delisted*] .... HBO
Hudson's Bay Oil & Gas Co. Ltd., Calgary, AB, Canada [*Library symbol*] .... CaACHB
Hudsonville Public Library, Hudsonville, MI [*Library symbol*] .... MiHudv
Hudspeth, TX [*Location identifier*] [*FAA*] .... HUP
Hueckel Molecular Orbital [*Atomic physics*] .... HMO
Huerfano County Public Library, Walsenburg, CO [*Library symbol*] .... CoWa
Huffy Corp. [*NYSE symbol*] .... HUF
Hug Club .... HC
Hug-a-Tree and Survive .... HTAS
Hughenden [*Australia*] [*Airport symbol*] .... HGD
Hughes [*Alaska*] [*Airport symbol*] .... HUS
Hughes Active RADAR Augmentation System .... HARAS
Hughes Air Corp. [*ICAO designator*] .... RW
Hughes Aircraft Company .... HAC
Hughes Aircraft Co., Communications Division Library, Airport Site, Inglewood, CA [*Library symbol*] .... CCuH-C
Hughes Aircraft Co., Culver City, CA [*Library symbol*] .... CCuH
Hughes Aircraft Co., Ground Systems Library, Fullerton, CA [*Library symbol*] .... CCuH-G
Hughes Aircraft Company, International Division .... HACI
Hughes Aircraft Co., Marketing Research Library, Airport Site, Inglewood, CA [*Library symbol*] .... CCuH-M
Hughes Aircraft Co., Research Laboratories Library, Malibu, CA [*Library symbol*] .... CCuH-R
Hughes Aircraft Co., Santa Barbara Research Center, Santa Barbara, CA [*Library symbol*] .... CCuH-RC
Hughes Aircraft Co., Semiconductor Division Library, Newport Beach, CA [*Library symbol*] .... CCuH-S
Hughes Automated Lunar Observer [*NASA*] .... HALO
Hughes Communications International [*Hughes Aircraft Co.*] .... HCI
Hughes Dynamic Imagery Viewer .... HDIV
Hughes Earth Station [*Aerospace*] .... HES
Hughes Emergency Locator Pack .... HELP
Hughes Hall Effect Function Generator .... HHEFG
Hughes Hall Effect Generator .... HHEG
Hughes & Hatcher, Inc. [*NYSE symbol*] [*Delisted*] .... HGH
Hughes Improved Terminal [*Aviation*] .... HIT
Hughes, Induced Turbulence .... HIT
Hughes Mining Barge [*Support vessel for Glomar Explorer*] .... HMB
Hughes NADGE [*NATO Air Defense Ground Environment*] **Consortium** .... HUCO
Hughes Photoelectric Reader .... HPR
Hughes Post Processor, Surveyor .... HPPS
Hughes Research Laboratories [*Hughes Aircraft Co.*] .... HRL
Hughes Research Library, Malibu, CA [*Library symbol*] .... CMalH
Hughes Satellite Communications Terminal .... HSCT
Hughes Satellite Earth Station .... HSES
Hughes Sports Network [*Formerly, SNI*] .... HSN
Hughes Supply, Inc. [*NASDAQ symbol*] .... HUGH
Hughes Television Network .... HTN
Hughes Tool Co. [*NYSE symbol*] .... HT
Hughes Tool Company .... HTC
Hughes Tool Co., Houston, TX [*Library symbol*] .... TxHHT
Hughes Transportable Link Terminal .... HTLT
Hughes Unit Malfunction Isolation Detector .... HUMID
Hugo, CO [*Location identifier*] [*FAA*] .... HGO
Hugo, OK [*Radio station call letters*] .... KIHN
Hugo, OK [*Radio station call letters*] .... KITX
Hugo Public Library, Hugo, CO [*Library symbol*] .... CoHu
Hugoniot Elastic Limit [*Thermodynamics*] .... HEL
Hugoton, KS [*Radio station call letters*] .... KHUQ
Huguenot Historical Society .... HHS
Huguenot, NY [*Location identifier*] [*FAA*] .... HUO
Huguenot Society of the Founders of Manakin in the Colony of Virginia .... HSFMCV
Huguenot-Thomas Paine Historical Association .... HTPHA
Huhner Test [*Gynecology*] .... HT
Huius Anni [*This Year's*] [*Latin*] .... HA
Huius Loci [*Of This Place*] [*Latin*] .... HL
Huius Mensis [*This Month's*] [*Latin*] .... HM
Hukbong Mapagpalaya ng Bayan [*People's Liberation Army, Philippines*] .... HUKS
Hulk [*Nautical charts*] .... Hk
Hull Check Valve .... HCV
Hull Collector Tank .... HCT
Hull Construction Certificate .... HCC
Hull Filter .... HF
Hull Gauge .... HG
Hull, Mechanical, Electrical [*Ship equipment*] [*Navy*] .... HME
Hull Moulding Release Note .... HMRN
Hull, PQ [*Television station call letters*] .... CHOT-TV
Hull, PQ [*Radio station call letters*] .... CIMF-FM
Hull, PQ [*Television station call letters*] .... CIVO-TV
Hull, PQ [*Radio station call letters*] .... CKCH
Hull Pressure Switch .... HPS
Hull Seal Section .... HSS
Hull Solenoid Valve .... HSV
Hull Test Vehicle [*for submarines*] .... HTV
Hull Urban Design Development Laboratory Enterprises, Inc. .... HUDDLE
Hultsfred [*Sweden*] [*Airport symbol*] .... HLF
Hum Modulation Factor .... HMF
Hum and Noise .... H & N
Humacao [*Puerto Rico*] [*Airport symbol*] .... HUC
Humacao-Palmas [*Puerto Rico*] [*Airport symbol*] .... PPD
Humacao, PR [*Radio station call letters*] .... WALO
Human .... H
Human .... HMN
Human Adaptability .... HA
Human Associative Memory .... HAM
Human Behavior [*A publication*] .... Hum Behav
Human Behavior [*A publication*] .... HB
Human Behavior [*National Science Foundation project*] .... HB
Human Being [*Rorschach*] [*Psychology*] .... H
Human Being [*Slang*] .... HB
Human Being Detail [*Rorschach*] [*Psychology*] .... B
Human Being Movement [*Rorschach*] [*Psychology*] .... M
Human Betterment Association for Voluntary Sterilization [*Later, AVS*] .... HBAVS
Human Biology [*A publication*] .... Human Biol
Human Biology [*A publication*] .... Hum Biol
Human Biology in Oceania [*A publication*] .... Hum Biol Oceania
Human Breast Tumor [*Type of cell line*] .... HBT
Human Calcitonin [*Endocrinology*] .... hCt
Human Cancer Immunology [*Elsevier Book Series*] [*A publication*] .... HCI
Human-Caused Error .... HCE
Human Chorionic Gonadotrophin [*Endocrinology*] .... HCG
Human Chorionic Somatomammotrophin [*Also, CGP, hcs, HPL*] [*Endocrinology*] .... HCS
Human Chorionic Thyrotrophin [*Endocrinology*] .... HCT
Human Communication Research [*A publication*] .... Human Comm Res
Human Communications [*A publication*] .... Hum Commun

Human Component Analysis ... HCA
Human Context [*A publication*] ... Human Cont
Human Context [*A publication*] ... Hum Context
Human Cord Serum ... HCS
Human Cultured Lymphoblastoid [*Cells*] ... HCL
Human Cytomegalovirus ... HCMV
Human Development ... HD
Human Development [*A publication*] ... HUDEA
Human Development [*A publication*] ... Human Dev
Human Development [*A publication*] ... Hum Dev
Human Development [*A publication*] ... HD
Human Development Institute ... HDI
Human Diploid Cell Strains [*Immunology*] ... HDCS
Human Diploid Cell Vaccine [*For rabies*] ... HDCV
Human Diploid Fibroblasts [*Cytology*] ... HDF
Human Disorientation Device ... HDD
Human/Dolphin Foundation ... H/DF
Human Ecology [*A publication*] ... Human Ecol
Human Ecology [*A publication*] ... Hum Ecol
Human Ecology Action League ... HEAL
Human Ecology Forum [*A publication*] ... Hum Ecol Forum
Human Ecology Fund ... HEF
Human Embryonic Kidney [*Type of cell line*] ... HEK
Human Embryonic Lung [*Type of cell line*] ... HEL
Human Embryonic Lung Fibroblasts [*Biochemistry*] ... HELF
Human Embryonic Palatal Mesenchymal [*Type of cell line*] ... HEPM
Human Engineering ... HE
Human Engineering Computer-Aided Design [*Air Force*] ... HECAD
Human Engineering Criteria for Maintenance and Repair [*GE, NASA*] ... HECMAR
Human Engineering Criteria for Maintenance and Repair [*GE, NASA*] ... HEMAR
Human Engineering Data ... HED
Human Engineering Information and Analysis Service [*Tufts University*] ... HEIAS
Human Engineering Institute ... HEI
Human Engineering Laboratories Battalion Artillery Test [*Army*] ... HELBAT
Human Engineering Laboratory [*Army*] ... HEL
Human Engineering Laboratory Armor Systems Test [*Army*] ... HELAST
Human Engineering Laboratory Helicopter Armament Test [*Army*] ... HELHAT
Human Engineering Laboratory Infantry System Test [*Army*] ... HELIST
Human Engineering Plan ... HEP
Human Engineering Systems Simulator [*Air Force*] ... HESS
Human Enteric [*Virology*] ... HE
Human Epithelial [*Cells*] ... HEp
Human Error Action Report [*NASA*] ... HEAR
Human Error Data Control Center [*NASA*] ... HEDCC
Human Error Rate ... HER
Human Error Research and Analysis Program ... HERAP
Human Erythrocyte Agglutination Test [*Hematology*] ... HEAT
Human Erythroleukemia [*Type of cell line*] ... HEL
Human Events [*A publication*] ... HE
Human Events [*A publication*] ... Hum Ev
Human Factor Division [*Air Research and Development Command*] [*Air Force*] ... HFD
Human Factor Evaluation Data for General Equipment ... HEDGE
Human Factors ... HF
Human Factors [*A publication*] ... Human Fact
Human Factors [*A publication*] ... Hum Factors
Human Factors Checklists [*Navy*] ... HFC
Human Factors in Electronics ... HFE
Human Factors Engineering ... HFE
Human Factors Group ... HFG
Human Factors Laboratory [*National Bureau of Standards*] ... HFL
Human Factors Measurement System ... HFMS
Human Factors Operation Research Laboratory [*Air Force*] ... HFORL
Human Factors and Operations Research [*Army*] ... HF & OR
Human Factors Research ... HFR
Human Factors Society ... HFS
Human Factors Study ... HFS
Human Factors Trade Studies [*Navy*] ... HFTS
Human Fetal Diploid Kidney [*Type of cell line*] ... HFDK
Human Fetal Diploid Lung [*Type of cell line*] ... HFDL
Human Fibroblast Interferon [*Cytology*] ... HFIF
Human Fibronectin [*Cytochemistry*] ... HFN
Human Gamma-Globulin [*Endocrinology*] ... HGG
Human Genetic Mutant Cell Repository ... HGMCR
Human Genetics [*A publication*] ... Hum Genet
Human Genetics. Supplement [*A publication*] ... Hum Genet Suppl
Human Gonadotrophin [*Endocrinology*] ... HG
Human Growth Foundation ... HGF
Human Growth Hormone [*Also, hGH*] [*Endocrinology*] ... HGH
Human Heredity [*A publication*] ... HUHEA
Human Heredity [*A publication*] ... Human Hered
Human Heredity [*A publication*] ... Hum Hered
Human Immunology [*A publication*] ... Hum Immunol
Human Individual Metamorphosis [*Flying saucer cult*] ... HIM
[*The*] **Human-Initiated Equipment Failures** ... THIEF
Human-Initiated Failure ... HIF
Human Intelligence ... HUMINT
Human Interest ... HI
Human Kidney ... HK
Human Lactation Center ... HLC
Human Leukocyte- [*or Lymphocyte-*] **Antigen** [*System for recognizing foreign tissue*] [*Immunology*] ... HL-A
Human Life Amendment ... HLA
Human Life Center ... HLC
Human Life Foundation of America [*Later, HLNFPF*] ... HLF
Human Life International ... HLI
Human Life and Natural Family Planning Foundation ... HLNFPF
Human Luteinizing Hormone [*Endocrinology*] ... HLH
Human Lymphocyte-Antigen Lymphocyte Defined [*Immunology*] ... HL-A LD
Human Lymphocyte-Antigen Serologically Defined [*Immunology*] ... HL-A SD
Human Lymphoid [*Immunology*] ... HL
Human Materials Resources Information System ... HUMARIS
Human Menopausal Gonadotrophin [*Endocrinology*] ... HMG
Human Metallothioneine [*Biochemistry*] ... HMT
Human Milk Lysozyme [*An enzyme*] ... HML
Human Milk Ribonuclease [*An enzyme*] ... HMR
Human Needs [*A publication*] ... Hum Needs
Human Neutrophil Elastase [*An enzyme*] ... HNE
Human Nutrition Information Service [*Department of Agriculture*] ... HNIS
Human Nutrition Research Division [*of ARS, Department of Agriculture*] ... HN
Human Old Tuberculin ... HOT
Human Organization [*A publication*] ... HO
Human Organization [*A publication*] ... Human Org
Human Organization [*A publication*] ... Human Organ
Human Organization [*A publication*] ... Hum Org
Human Osteosarcoma [*Medicine*] ... HOS
Human Outreach and Advancement Institute ... HOAI
Human Ovarian Antitumor Serum [*Antineoplastic compound*] ... HOATS
Human Ovarian Cancer [*Cytology*] ... HOC
Human Pancreas Growth Hormone-Releasing Factor [*Immunochemistry*] ... hpGRF
Human Pancreatic Polypeptide [*Endocrinology*] ... HPP
Human Papillomavirus ... HPV
Human Parotid Lysozyme [*An enzyme*] ... HPL
Human Pathology [*A publication*] ... Human Path
Human Pathology [*A publication*] ... Hum Pathol
Human Performance Reliability ... HPR
Human Peripheral Lymphocyte ... HPL
Human Physiology [*A publication*] ... Hum Physiol
Human Pituitary Gonadotrophin [*Endocrinology*] ... HPG
Human Placenta Thyrotrophin [*Endocrinology*] ... HPT
Human Placental Alkaline Phosphatase [*An enzyme*] ... HPLAP
Human Placental Lactogen [*Also, CGP, HCS*] [*Endocrinology*] ... HPL
Human Potential [*A publication*] ... Hum Potential
Human Potential Movement [*Psychotherapy*] ... HPM
Human Productivity Institute ... HPI
Human Prolactin [*Endocrinology*] ... HPR
Human Rabies Immune Globulin [*Immunology*] ... HRIG
Human Read/Machine Read [*Microfilm memory system*] ... HRMR
Human Relations [*A publication*] ... HR
Human Relations [*A publication*] ... Human Relat
Human Relations [*A publication*] ... Hum Relat
Human Relations Area Files [*Information service*] ... HRAF
Human Relations Area Files, New Haven, CT [*Library symbol*] ... CtNhH
Human Relations Education ... HRE
Human Relations Inventory [*Psychology*] ... HRI
Human Reliability ... HR
Human Reliability Program ... HRP
Human Reproductive Medicine [*Elsevier Book Series*] [*A publication*] ... HRM
Human Reproductive Medicine [*A publication*] ... Human Reprod Med
Human Research Need ... HRN
Human Resource Management [*A publication*] ... Hum Resource Mgt
Human Resource Management [*A publication*] ... Hum Resour Manage
Human Resource Planning Society ... HRPS
Human Resources Abstracts [*A publication*] ... Human Resour Abstr
Human Resources Administration [*New York City*] ... HRA
Human Resources Availability ... HRAV
Human Resources Center ... HRC
Human Resources Center, Albertson, NY [*Library symbol*] ... NAlbH
Human Resources Data ... HRD
Human Resources Development [*An affiliate of International Correspondence Schools*] ... HRD
Human Resources Development Institute [*AFL-CIO*] ... HRDI
Human Resources Laboratory [*Air Force*] ... HRL
Human Resources Management ... HRM
Human Resources Management Center [*Navy*] ... HRMC
Human Resources Management Specialist [*Navy*] ... HRMS
Human Resources Management Support System [*Navy*] ... HRMSS
Human Resources Network [*Information service*] ... HRN
Human Resources Research Center ... HRRC
Human Resources Research Institute ... HRRI
Human Resources Research Laboratory [*Air Force*] ... HRRL
Human Resources Research Office [*NASA*] ... HRRO
Human Resources Research Organization [*formerly, Office*] ... HumRRO

Human Resources, Veterans, and Labor [*Office of Management and Budget*] .... HRVL
Human Rights [*A publication*] .... Hum Rights
Human Rights Advocates .... HRA
Human Rights Advocates International .... HRAI
Human Rights Campaign Fund .... HRCF
Human Rights Commission .... HRC
Human Rights Group .... HRG
Human Rights International .... HRI
Human Rights International Documentation System .... HURIDOCS
Human Rights Internet .... HRI
Human Rights Journal [*A publication*] .... Hum Rights J
Human Rights Party [*Ann Arbor, MI*] .... HRP
Human Rights Political Action Committee .... HRPAC
Human Rights Resource Center .... HRRC
Human Rights for Women .... HRW
Human Rotaviruses .... HRV
Human Science [*Inkan Kwahak*] [*Republic of Korea*] [*A publication*] .... Hum Sci
Human Sciences Project [*National Science Foundation*] .... HSP
Human Serum Albumin .... HSA
Human Serum Prealbumin .... HSP
Human Service Personnel Association [*Defunct*] .... HSPA
Human Services Forum .... HSF
Human Settlements [*A publication*] .... Hum Settlements
Human Skeletal Growth Factor .... HSGF
Human Skin Collagen .... HSC
Human Standard Globulin [*Medicine*] .... HSG
Human Studies [*A publication*] .... Human S
Human T-Cell Leukemia/Lymphoma Virus .... HTLV
Human Therapeutic Dose .... HTD
Human Thrombin [*Cytochemistry*] .... HT
Human Thyroid Adenyl Cyclase Stimulator [*Endocrinology*] .... HTACS
Human Thyroid Stimulating Hormone [*Also, htsh*] [*Endocrinology*] .... HTSH
Human Thyroid Stimulator [*Endocrinology*] .... HTS
Human Toxicology [*A publication*] .... HT
Human Tumor Clonogenic Assay [*In-vitro testing system*] .... HTCA
Human Visual System .... HVS
Humana, Inc. [*NYSE symbol*] .... HUM
Humane Society of the United States .... HSUS
Humangenetik [*A publication*] .... Humangenet
Humanidades [*A publication*] .... Hum
Humanidades (Buenos Aires) [*A publication*] .... Hum(BA)
Humanidades. Serie 4. Logica Matematica [*A publication*] .... Humanidades Ser 4 Logica Mat
Humaniora Norvegica [*A publication*] .... HNorv
Humanisme et Entreprise [*A publication*] .... Human et Entr
Humanisme et Renaissance [*A publication*] .... H & R
Humanisme et Renaissance [*A publication*] .... HR
Humanisme et Renaissance [*A publication*] .... HRen
Humanisme et Renaissance [*A publication*] .... HuR
Humanist [*A publication*] .... Hum
Humanist Student Union of North America .... HSUNA
Humanistic Organization for Personal Expansion .... HOPE
Humanistica Lovaniensia [*A publication*] .... HL
Humanistica Lovaniensia [*A publication*] .... Hum Lov
Humanistisches Gymnasium [*A publication*] .... HG
Humanistiska Vetenskaps-Samfundet i Lund Arsberattelse [*A publication*] .... Hum Vetensk Samf i Lund Arsberatt
Humanitarian Deferment [*Military*] .... HD
Humanitarian Emergency Evacuation [*Military*] .... HUMEVAC
Humanitarian Reasons .... HUMS
Humanitarian Reassignment [*Military*] .... HR
Humanitas [*Pittsburgh*] [*A publication*] .... Hum
Humanitas (Brescia) [*A publication*] .... HumB
Humanitas International Human Rights Committee .... HIHRC
Humanitas: La Nouvelle Revue des Humanites [*A publication*] .... Hum(NRH)
Humanitas (Nuevo Leon) [*A publication*] .... HumNL
Humanitas. Revue Internationale de Philologie Classique et Humanites [*A publication*] .... Hum (RIPh)
Humanitas (Tucuman, Argentina) [*A publication*] .... HumT
Humanite Society .... HS
Humanites Chretiennes [*A publication*] .... Human Chr
Humanites. Revue d'Enseignement Secondaire et d'Education [*A publication*] .... Hum (RES)
Humanities .... HUM
Humanities Association. Bulletin [*A publication*] .... HAB
Humanities Center for Liberal Education .... HCLE
Humanities Index [*A publication*] .... Hum Ind
Humanities, Science, and Conservation [*Environment*] .... HUSICON
Humanities in Society [*A publication*] .... HIS
Humanities in the South [*A publication*] .... HS
Humanizacja Pracy [*A publication*] .... Human Pracy
Humber College of Applied Arts and Technology, Rexdale, Toronto, ON, Canada [*Library symbol*] .... CaOTHC
Humber Memorial Hospital, Weston, ON, Canada [*Library symbol*] .... CaOTHMH
Humberside [*England*] [*Airport symbol*] .... HUY
Humbert Humbert [*Character in Vladimir Nabokov's "Lolita"*] .... HH
Humble City, NM [*Radio station call letters*] .... KYKK
Humble Oil & Refining Co., Engineering Division Library, Baytown, TX [*Library symbol*] .... TxByH-E
Humble Oil & Refining Co., General Services Library, Houston, TX [*Library symbol*] .... TxHHO
Humble Oil & Refining Co., Marketing Research Library, Houston, TX [*Library symbol*] .... TxHHO-E
Humble Oil & Refining Co., Mineral Department Library, Denver, CO [*Library symbol*] .... CoDHO
Humble Oil & Refining Co., Technical Library, Baytown, TX [*Library symbol*] .... TxByH
Humble, TX [*Radio station call letters*] .... KSBJ
Humble, TX [*Radio station call letters*] .... KTUN
Humbligny [*France*] [*Seismograph station code, US Geological Survey*] .... HYF
Humboldt County Free Library, Eureka, CA [*Library symbol*] .... CEH
Humboldt, IA [*Radio station call letters*] .... KHBT
Humboldt, NE [*Location identifier*] [*FAA*] .... HBO
Humboldt State College [*Later, Humboldt State University*] [*California*] .... HSC
Humboldt State College, Arcata, CA [*Library symbol*] .... CArcHT
Humboldt State College, Arcata, CA [*OCLC symbol*] .... CHU
Humboldt State University [*California*] .... HSU
Humboldt, TN [*Location identifier*] [*FAA*] .... HDT
Humboldt, TN [*Radio station call letters*] .... WHMT
Humboldt, TN [*Radio station call letters*] .... WIRJ
Humboldt, TN [*Radio station call letters*] .... WZDQ
Humbolt County Historical Association, Humbolt, IA [*Library symbol*] .... IaHumHi
Humbolt Public Library, Humbolt, IA [*Library symbol*] .... IaHum
Hume Studies [*A publication*] .... Hume Stud
Humera [*Ethiopia*] [*Airport symbol*] .... HUE
Humeston Public Library, Humeston, IA [*Library symbol*] .... IaHume
Humic Acid [*Organic chemistry*] .... HA
Humid .... HMD
Humidity .... H
Humidity Control .... HC
Humidity-Electronic Indicator .... HEI
Humidity Index .... HI
Humidity Indicator Controller [*Aerospace*] .... HIC
Humidity Monitoring Panel .... HMP
Humidity, Relative .... HR
Humidity Test Procedure .... HTP
Humm-Wadsworth Temperament Scale [*Psychology*] .... HWTS
Hummel Collectors Club .... HCC
Humor Test of Personality [*Psychology*] .... HTP
Humphrey, Inc. [*NASDAQ symbol*] .... HUPH
Humphreys College, Stockton, CA [*Library symbol*] .... CStoH
Humphreys County Library, Belzoni, MS [*Library symbol*] .... MsBel
Hun-Stoffe [*Mustard gas*] [*Formerly, HS*] [*Also, HD, HT, M*] .... H
Hun-Stoffe [*US Chemical Corp. symbol for mustard gas*] [*Also, HD, HT, M*] [*Later, H*] .... HS
Huna Research, Inc. .... HUNA
Hunan Province [*China, Mainland*] [*MARC geographic area code*] [*Library of Congress*] .... a-cc-hu
Hundersingen [*Federal Republic of Germany*] [*Seismograph station code, US Geological Survey*] .... HUN
Hundred .... H
Hundred .... HD
Hundred .... HND
Hundred .... HUN
Hundred .... HUND
Hundred Club of Massachusetts .... HCM
Hundred Feet .... HF
Hundred Million Club .... HMC
Hundred Pounds .... HP
Hundred Woman Years [*of exposure*] [*Radiation*] .... HWY
Hundred Yards .... HY
Hundredweight .... CWT
Hungarian [*MARC language code*] [*Library of Congress*] .... hun
Hungarian .... HUNGN
Hungarian Agricultural Review [*A publication*] .... Hung Agric Rev
Hungarian Agricultural Review [*A publication*] .... Hung Agr Rev
Hungarian Airlines [*ICAO designator*] .... MA
Hungarian Baptist Union of America .... HBUA
Hungarian Boy Scout Association .... HBSA
Hungarian Catholic League of America .... HCLA
Hungarian Catholic Priests' Association in America .... HCPAA
Hungarian Central Committee for Books and Education .... HCCBE
Hungarian Committee of Socialist Labor Party [*Defunct*] .... HCSLP
Hungarian Cultural Foundation .... HCF
Hungarian Forest Scientifical Review [*A publication*] .... Hung For Sci Rev
Hungarian Freedom Fighters Federation .... HFFF
Hungarian Heavy Industries [*A publication*] .... Hung Heavy Ind
Hungarian Journal of Industrial Chemistry [*A publication*] .... Hung J Ind Chem
Hungarian Journal of Industrial Chemistry [*A publication*] .... Hung J Indus Chem
Hungarian Machinery [*A publication*] .... Hung Mach
Hungarian Medical Bibliography [*A publication*] .... Hung Med Biblio
Hungarian National Sports Federation .... HNSF
Hungarian Quarterly [*New York*] [*A publication*] .... HunQ

Hungarian Reformed Federation of America .... HRFA
Hungarian Review [*A publication*] .... Hung R
Hungarian Socialist Workers' Party .... HSWP
Hungarian Studies in English [*A publication*] .... HSE
Hungarian Survey [*A publication*] .... Hung S
Hungarologiai Intezet Tudomanyos Kozlemenyei [*A publication*] .... HITK
Hungary [*MARC geographic area code*] [*Library of Congress*] .... e-hu---
Hungary .... H
Hungary [*Aircraft nationality and registration mark*] .... HA
Hungary [*MARC country of publication code*] [*Library of Congress*] .... hu
Hungary [*Three-letter standard code*] .... HUN
Hungary .... HUNG
Hungary [*Two-letter standard code*] .... HU
Hungary. Magyar Allami Foeldtani Intezet. Evkoenyve [*A publication*] .... Hung Magy Allami Foeldt Intez Evk
Hunger Project .... HP
Hungry? Angry? Lonely? Tired? [*Slogan used by Alcoholics Anonymous members to determine whether their emotions are out of control to the point that they may be tempted to take a drink*] .... HALT
Hungry Horse [*Montana*] [*Seismograph station code, US Geological Survey*] .... HHM
Hungry Tiger, Inc. [*NASDAQ symbol*] .... HTIG
Hunt [*Philip A.*] **Chemical Corporation** [*NYSE symbol*] .... HCC
Hunt Foods & Industries, Inc. [*NYSE symbol*] [*Delisted*] .... HFI
Hunt, Harold, Jr., Bala-Cynwyd PA [*STAC*] .... HHJ
Hunt Manufacturing [*NYSE symbol*] .... HUN
Hunt [*J. B.*] **Transportation Services** [*NASDAQ symbol*] .... JBHT
Huntec Ltd., Toronto, ON, Canada [*Library symbol*] .... CaOTHu
Hunter Club of America .... HCA
Hunter College of the City University of New York, New York, NY [*Library symbol*] .... NNHuC
Hunter College of the City University of New York, New York, NY [*OCLC symbol*] .... ZHM
Hunter-Killer [*Missile*] .... H-K
Hunter-Killer [*Operations against submarines*] [*Navy*] .... HUK
Hunter-Killer Antisubmarine Warfare Exercise [*Navy*] .... HUKASWEX
Hunter-Killer Destroyer [*Navy ship symbol*] .... DDK
Hunter-Killer Forces [*Navy*] .... HUKFOR
Hunter-Killer Forces, Atlantic [*Navy*] .... HUKFORLANT
Hunter-Killer Forces, Pacific [*Navy*] .... HUKFORPAC
Hunter-Killer Ship [*Navy symbol*] .... CLK
Hunter-Killer Submarine [*Navy*] .... HUKS
Hunter-Leggitt Military Reservation .... HLMR
Hunter-Wheel .... HW
Hunterdon County Clerk, Flemington, NJ [*Library symbol*] .... NjFlCoC
Hunterdon County Democrat, Flemington, NJ [*Library symbol*] .... NjFlD
Hunterdon County Historical Society, Flemington, NJ [*Library symbol*] .... NjFlHi
Hunterdon County Library, Flemington, NJ [*Library symbol*] .... NjFlH
Hunterdon Medical Center, Flemington, NJ [*Library symbol*] .... NjFlM
Hunterdon Pharmaceuticals [*NASDAQ symbol*] .... HUNT
Hunterdon Review, Clinton, NJ [*Library symbol*] .... NjClinH
Hunterdon Review, Whitehouse Station, NJ [*Library symbol*] .... NjWhsH
Hunters Point Naval Shipyard .... HPNS
Hunting .... HNTG
Hunting-Clan Air Transport Ltd. .... HCA
Hunting Group Review [*A publication*] .... Hunting Group Rev
Hunting and Testing [*Apollo*] [*NASA*] .... HUNTEST
Huntingburg, IN [*Location identifier*] [*FAA*] .... FNZ
Huntingburg, IN [*Radio station call letters*] .... WBDC
Huntingdon College, Montgomery, AL [*Library symbol*] .... AMH
Huntingdon Gleaner, Sherbrooke, PQ, Canada [*Library symbol*] .... CaQSherH
Huntingdon, PA [*Radio station call letters*] .... WHUN
Huntingdon, PA [*Radio station call letters*] .... WKVR-FM
Huntingdon, PA [*Radio station call letters*] .... WRLR
Huntingdon Research Centre PLC ADR [*NASDAQ symbol*] .... HRCLY
Huntingdon, TN [*Radio station call letters*] .... WJPJ
Huntingdon, TN [*Radio station call letters*] .... WPBE
Huntingdonshire [*County in England*] .... HUNTS
Huntington [*West Virginia*] [*Airport symbol*] .... HTS
Huntington Bancshares [*NASDAQ symbol*] .... HBAN
Huntington Beach, CA [*Television station call letters*] .... KOCE-TV
Huntington Beach Public Library, Huntington Beach, CA [*Library symbol*] .... CHu
Huntington Beach Public Library, Huntington Beach, CA [*OCLC symbol*] .... HBL
Huntington College, Huntington, IN [*OCLC symbol*] .... IHH
Huntington College, Huntington, IN [*Library symbol*] .... InHuH
Huntington Galleries, Huntington, WV [*Library symbol*] .... WvHuG
Huntington Health Services, Inc. [*American Stock Exchange symbol*] [*Delisted*] .... HHS
Huntington Historical Society, Huntington, NY [*Library symbol*] .... NHuHi
Huntington Hospital, Huntington, NY [*Library symbol*] .... NHuH
Huntington, IN [*Radio station call letters*] .... WHLT
Huntington, IN [*Radio station call letters*] .... WHUZ
Huntington, IN [*Radio station call letters*] .... WVSH
Huntington Library Bulletin [*A publication*] .... HLB
Huntington Library Quarterly [*A publication*] .... HLQ
Huntington Library. Quarterly [*A publication*] .... Hunt Lib Q
Huntington Memorial Hospital, Pasadena, CA [*Library symbol*] .... CPH
Huntington, NY [*Radio station call letters*] .... WGSM
Huntington, PA [*Radio station call letters*] .... WQRO
Huntington Public Library, Huntington, IN [*Library symbol*] .... InHu
Huntington Public Library, Huntington, NY [*Library symbol*] .... NHu
Huntington, WV [*Location identifier*] [*FAA*] .... TUU
Huntington, WV [*Radio station call letters*] .... WEMM
Huntington, WV [*Radio station call letters*] .... WGNT
Huntington, WV [*Radio station call letters*] .... WHPW
Huntington, WV [*Radio station call letters*] .... WKEE
Huntington, WV [*Radio station call letters*] .... WKEE-FM
Huntington, WV [*Radio station call letters*] .... WMUL
Huntington, WV [*Television station call letters*] .... WOWK-TV
Huntington, WV [*Television station call letters*] .... WPBY-TV
Huntington, WV [*Television station call letters*] .... WSAZ-TV
Huntington, WV [*Radio station call letters*] .... WTCR
Huntington, WV [*Radio station call letters*] .... WWHY
Huntington's Disease [*Medicine*] .... HD
Hunt's Merchants' Magazine [*A publication*] .... Hunt
Huntsville [*Alabama*] [*Airport symbol*] .... HSV
Huntsville, AL [*Location identifier*] [*FAA*] .... BFZ
Huntsville, AL [*Location identifier*] [*FAA*] .... CWH
Huntsville, AL [*Location identifier*] [*FAA*] .... HUA
Huntsville, AL [*Radio station call letters*] .... WAAY
Huntsville, AL [*Television station call letters*] .... WAAY-TV
Huntsville, AL [*Radio station call letters*] .... WAED
Huntsville, AL [*Television station call letters*] .... WAFF-TV
Huntsville, AL [*Radio station call letters*] .... WAHR
Huntsville, AL [*Radio station call letters*] .... WBHP
Huntsville, AL [*Radio station call letters*] .... WEUP
Huntsville, AL [*Radio station call letters*] .... WFIX
Huntsville, AL [*Television station call letters*] .... WHIQ
Huntsville, AL [*Television station call letters*] .... WHNT-TV
Huntsville, AL [*Radio station call letters*] .... WLRH
Huntsville, AL [*Radio station call letters*] .... WNDA
Huntsville, AL [*Radio station call letters*] .... WOCG
Huntsville, AL [*Radio station call letters*] .... WTAK
Huntsville Association of Technical Societies [*Alabama*] .... HATS
Huntsville Nuclear Division [*Army Corps of Engineers*] .... HND
Huntsville, ON [*Radio station call letters*] .... CFBK
Huntsville Operations Support Center [*NASA*] .... HOSC
Huntsville Public Library, Huntsville, AL [*Library symbol*] .... AH
Huntsville Public Library, Huntsville, MO [*Library symbol*] .... MoHu
Huntsville, TX [*Radio station call letters*] .... KHUN
Huntsville, TX [*Radio station call letters*] .... KKNX
Huntsville, TX [*Radio station call letters*] .... KSAM
Huntsville, TX [*Radio station call letters*] .... KSHU
Hunza Research Society .... HRS
Hupa [*MARC language code*] [*Library of Congress*] .... hup
Hupeh Province [*China, Mainland*] [*MARC geographic area code*] [*Library of Congress*] .... a-cc-hh
Hupmobile Club .... HC
Hupp Corp. [*NYSE symbol*] [*Delisted*] .... H
Hurbanovo [*Czechoslovakia*] [*Geomagnetic observatory code*] .... HRB
Hurbanovo [*Ogyalla, Stara Dala*] [*Czechoslovakia*] [*Seismograph station code, US Geological Survey*] .... HRB
Hurco Manufacturing Co., Inc. [*NASDAQ symbol*] .... HURC
Hurdle .... HDLE
Hurghada [*Egypt*] [*Airport symbol*] .... HRG
Huron [*South Dakota*] [*Airport symbol*] .... HON
Huron College, Huron, SD [*Library symbol*] .... SdHuroC
Huron College, Huron, SD [*OCLC symbol*] .... SDU
Huron College, London, ON, Canada [*Library symbol*] .... CaOLH
Huron County Public Library, Goderich, ON, Canada [*Library symbol*] .... CaOGoH
Huron, Ontario, Michigan, Erie, Superior [*Great Lakes*] .... HOMES
Huron Public Library, Huron, OH [*Library symbol*] .... OHur
Huron Public Library, Huron, SD [*Library symbol*] .... SdHuro
Huron, SD [*Radio station call letters*] .... KIJV
Huron, SD [*Radio station call letters*] .... KOKK
Huron, SD [*Radio station call letters*] .... KURO
Huron Valley Library System [*Library network*] .... HVLS
Huron Valley Library System, Ann Arbor, MI [*OCLC symbol*] .... EYH
Huronia Historical Park, Midland, ON, Canada [*Library symbol*] .... CaOMiH
Hurricane [*Alaska*] [*Seismograph station code, US Geological Survey*] .... HUR
Hurricane .... HURCN
Hurricane Analog .... HURRAN
Hurricane Deck .... HD
Hurricane Evacuation .... HUREVAC
Hurricane Evacuation - General [*Military aircraft identification prefix*] .... H
Hurricane Hollow [*Tennessee*] [*Seismograph station code, US Geological Survey*] [*Closed*] .... HHT
Hurricane Microseismic Research Problem [*Aerology*] .... HMRP
Hurricane Operations Center .... HOC
Hurricane Report .... HUREP
Hurricane Supersonic Research Site .... HSRS
Hurricane Warning Office [*National Weather Service*] .... HWO
Hurricane, WV [*Radio station call letters*] .... WZTQ
Hurter and Driffield [*Chemists for whom H & D Curve and H & D Speed System are named*] .... H & D

Husavik [Iceland] [Airport symbol]............................HZK
Husband...H
Husband [Citizens band radio slang].........................XYM
Husbandman..HUSBN
Husbands of Airline Pilots...................................HALP
Husiki [Japan] [Seismograph station code, US Geological Survey]....HKI
Husky Oil Ltd. [American Stock Exchange symbol]..............HYO
Huslia [Alaska] [Airport symbol].............................HSL
Hussars [Military unit] [British]............................H
Hussars [Military unit] [British]............................HRS
Hussmann Refrigerator Co. [NYSE symbol] [Delisted]..........HRF
Husson College, Bangor, ME [OCLC symbol]....................HCL
Husson College, Bangor, ME [Library symbol].................MeBaH
Husson Review [Bangor, ME] [A publication]..................HussR
Huston-Tillotson College [Texas]............................HTC
Huston-Tillotson College, Austin, TX [OCLC symbol]..........HTC
Huston-Tillotson College, Austin, TX [Library symbol].......TxAuHT
Hutchinson [Kansas] [Airport symbol]........................HUT
Hutchinson Board of Trade Association.......................HBTA
Hutchinson Community Junior College, Hutchinson, KS [Library
    symbol]..KHuC
Hutchinson County Library, Borger, TX [Library symbol]......TxBor
Hutchinson Junior College [Kansas]..........................HJC
Hutchinson, KS [Radio station call letters].................KHCC
Hutchinson, KS [Radio station call letters].................KHUT
Hutchinson, KS [Television station call letters]............KPTS
Hutchinson, KS [Radio station call letters].................KSKU
Hutchinson, KS [Radio station call letters].................KWBW
Hutchinson, KS [Television station call letters]............KWCH-TV
Hutchinson, KS [Radio station call letters].................KWHK
Hutchinson, MN [Location identifier] [FAA]..................HCD
Hutchinson, MN [Radio station call letters].................KDUZ
Hutchinson, MN [Radio station call letters].................KDUZ-FM
[The] Hutchinson & Northern Railway Co. [AAR code]..........HN
Hutchinson Public Library, Hutchinson, KS [Library symbol]..KHu
Hutnicke Aktuality [Czechoslovakia] [A publication].........Hutn Aktual
Hutnicke Listy [A publication]..............................Hutn Listy
Hutnik (Katowice) [A publication]...........................Hutn (Katowice)
Hutsonville Community Unit, School District 1, Hutsonville, IL
    [Library symbol]...IHuSD
Hutt Adaptation of the Bender-Gestalt Test..................HABGT
Hutton [E. F.] Group, Inc. [NYSE symbol]....................EFH
Huyck Corp. [NYSE symbol] [Delisted]........................HYK
Huyck Felt Bulletin [A publication].........................Huyck Felt Bull
Hvalradets Skrifter [A publication].........................Hvalradets Skr
Hwalien [Karenko] [Republic of China] [Seismograph station
    code, US Geological Survey]..............................HWA
Hwange National Park [Zimbabwe] [Airport symbol]............WKM
Hyacinth Control Journal [A publication]....................Hyacinth Control J
Hyaline Membrane Disease [Later, RDS] [Medicine]............HMD
Hyaluronic Acid [Biochemistry]..............................HA
Hyannis [Massachusetts] [Airport symbol]....................HYA
Hyannis Aviation [Hyannis, MA] [FAA designator].............HAN
Hyannis, MA [Location identifier] [FAA].....................BZC
Hyannis, MA [Radio station call letters]....................WCOD
Hyannis Public Library, Hyannis, MA [Library symbol]........MHy
Hyborean Legion [An association]............................HL
Hybrid..HYB
Hybrid Analog Logic Language................................HYBALL
Hybrid Analog-Switching Attitude Control System for Space
    Vehicles...HYACS
Hybrid Combustion Process...................................HCP
Hybrid Computer...HC
Hybrid Computer Link..HYCOL
Hybrid Computer Translator..................................HYCOTRAN
Hybrid Digital-Analog Computing [System] [Satellite]........HYDAC
Hybrid Digital-Analog and Pulse Time........................HYDAPT
Hybrid Electromagnetic [Wave]...............................HEM
Hybrid Electromagnetic Antenna Coupler......................HEMAC
Hybrid Geotempered Envelope [Architecture]..................HGE
Hybrid Infrared Source......................................HIS
Hybrid Integrated Circuit...................................HIC
Hybrid Integrated Network [Bell System].....................HIN
Hybrid Language Assembler...................................HYLA
Hybrid Microcircuit...HMC
Hybrid Operating Program....................................HOP
Hybrid Orbital Rehybridization Method [Atomic physics]......HORM
Hybrid Programable Attitude Control Electronics [NASA].......HYPACE
Hybrid Programing Language [Data processing]................HPL
Hybrid Propulsion System....................................HPS
Hybrid Receiver Circuit.....................................HRC
Hybrid Simulation System....................................HSS
Hybrid Test Set...HTS
Hybridoma Sciences [NASDAQ symbol]..........................HYBD
Hybritech, Inc. [NASDAQ symbol].............................HYBR
Hycel, Inc. [American Stock Exchange symbol] [Delisted]......HCL
Hyconeechee Regional Library, Yanceyville, NC [Library symbol]....NcY
Hydaburg [Alaska] [Airport symbol]..........................HYG
Hydatidiform Mole [Gynecology]..............................HM
Hydco, Inc. [NYSE symbol] [Delisted]........................HYD
Hyde Athletic Industries [NASDAQ symbol]....................HYDE

Hyde County Library, Highmore, SD [Library symbol]..........SdHig
Hyde Park [Utah] [Seismograph station code, US Geological Survey]....HDU
Hyde Park, NY [Radio station call letters]..................WHVW
Hyde Park, NY [Radio station call letters]..................WJJB
Hyden, KY [Radio station call letters]......................WSLK
Hyderabad [Pakistan] [Airport symbol].......................HDD
Hyderabad [India] [Geomagnetic observatory code]............HYB
Hyderabad [India] [Airport symbol]..........................HYD
Hyderabad [India] [Seismograph station code, US Geological
    Survey] [Closed]...HYD
Hyderabad [National Geophysics Research Institute] [India]
    [Seismograph station code, US Geological Survey].........HYB
Hydralazine [Antihypertensive agent]........................HZ
Hydrant...H
Hydrargyrum [Mercury] [Chemical element]....................Hg
Hydrargyrum [Mercury] [Pharmacy]............................HYD
Hydrargyrum [Mercury] [Pharmacy]............................HYDRARG
Hydrated..HYD
Hydrated..HYDTD
Hydrated Textured Soy Flour.................................HTSF
Hydraulic...HYD
Hydraulic...HYDR
Hydraulic Actuator Assembly Container.......................HAAC
Hydraulic Actuator Test Fixture.............................HATF
Hydraulic Adjustable Speed..................................HAS
Hydraulic [or Hydrologic] Analysis..........................HYDRA
Hydraulic Bench Press.......................................HBP
Hydraulic Bore-Hole Mining [Coal]...........................HBM
Hydraulic Cement Concrete...................................HCC
Hydraulic Charging Unit.....................................HCU
Hydraulic Clean...HC
[The] Hydraulic Company [NYSE symbol].......................THC
Hydraulic Components Test...................................HCT
Hydraulic Control Unit [Nuclear energy].....................HCU
Hydraulic Control Valve.....................................HCV
Hydraulic Core Mock-Up [Nuclear energy].....................HCM
Hydraulic Cycling Unit......................................HCU
Hydraulic Cylinder..HC
Hydraulic Engineering Information Analysis Center [Army Corps
    of Engineers]..HEIAC
Hydraulic Engineering Laboratory [University of California at
    Berkeley]..HEL
Hydraulic Flight Control....................................HFC
Hydraulic Flight Control Test...............................HFCT
Hydraulic Fluid Filter......................................HFF
Hydraulic Fluid Replenishment Equipment.....................HFRE
Hydraulic Grade Elevations..................................HGE
Hydraulic Hand Pump...HHP
Hydraulic Institute...HI
Hydraulic Maintenance Panel.................................HMP
Hydraulic Mean Depth..HMD
Hydraulic Mock-Up...HMU
Hydraulic Package Container.................................HPC
Hydraulic Package Pressure Test Set.........................HPPTS
Hydraulic Package Servovalve Actuator.......................HPSA
Hydraulic Package Storage Container.........................HPSC
Hydraulic Performance Analysis Facility.....................HPAF
Hydraulic Piston Corer......................................HPC
Hydraulic Pneumatic Area....................................HPA
Hydraulic Pneumatic Mechanical Power [A publication]........
                                        Hydraul Pneum Mech Power
Hydraulic Pneumatic Panel...................................HPP
Hydraulic Pneumatic Power [Later, Hydraulic Pneumatic
    Mechanical Power] [A publication]............Hydraul Pneum Pwr
Hydraulic Power Control Relay Box...........................HPCRB
Hydraulic Power Section [Later, HPU]........................HPS
Hydraulic Power Supply......................................HPS
Hydraulic Power Supply Kit..................................HPSK
Hydraulic Power System......................................HPS
Hydraulic Power Transfer Panel..............................HPTP
Hydraulic-Power Transmission Fluid..........................HPTF
Hydraulic Power Unit..HPU
Hydraulic Pressure Indicator................................HPI
Hydraulic Pump Discharge....................................HPD
Hydraulic Pumping Unit......................................HPU
Hydraulic Punching Machine..................................HPM
Hydraulic Quick Coupler.....................................HQC
Hydraulic Rate Damper.......................................HRD
Hydraulic Relief Valve......................................HRV
Hydraulic Retention Time....................................HRT
Hydraulic Rotary Actuator...................................HRA
Hydraulic Selector Valve....................................HSV
Hydraulic Supply..HS
Hydraulic Supply and Checkout Unit..........................HSCU
Hydraulic Supply Unit.......................................HSU
Hydraulic System..HS
Hydraulic System Test and Repair Unit.......................HISTRU
Hydraulic System Test and Repair Unit [Army]................HSTRU
Hydraulic Tachometer..HYTAC
Hydraulic Temperature Control...............................HTC
Hydraulic Test Chamber......................................HTC

Hydraulic Test Equipment..HTE
Hydraulic Test Set [or Station]....................................HTS
Hydraulic Tool Manufacturers Association.....................HTMA
Hydraulic Valve Motor..HVM
Hydraulically Extendable Dipperstick [for tractors]..........HED
Hydraulically Operated Equipment..............................HOE
Hydraulics Engineer...HE
Hydraulics and Pneumatics [A publication]............Hydra Pneum
Hydraulics Research Laboratory [British]......................HRL
Hydraulics Research Station [British]...........................HRS
Hydrazine Auxiliary Rocket Engine............................HARE
Hydrazine Catalytic Plenum.....................................HCP
Hydrazine Electrolysis Plenum..................................HEP
Hydrazine Hand-Held Maneuvering Unit....................HHHMU
Hydrazine Monopropellant Thruster..........................HMT
Hydrazine Rocket Engine...HRE
Hydrazine Sulfate [Toxic substance] [Inorganic chemistry]...HS
HydrazinomethylDOPA [Biochemistry].........................HMD
Hydriodic Acid [Inorganic chemistry]...........................HI
Hydro-Air Library, Burbank, CA [Library symbol].............CBbH
Hydro-Electric Power Commission of Ontario, Toronto, ON,
     Canada [Library symbol]....................................CaOTH
Hydro Flame Corp. [NASDAQ symbol]........................HFLM
Hydro-Form Die...HFD
Hydro-Optics, Inc. [NASDAQ symbol].........................HOPC
Hydro-Quebec Bibliotheque, Montreal, PQ, Canada [Library
     symbol]...CaQMH
Hydrobiologia [A publication]..............................Hydrobiol
Hydrobiological Bulletin [A publication]..............Hydrobiol Bull
Hydrobiological Journal [A publication].................Hydrobiol J
Hydrobiological Journal (English Translation of
     Gidrobiologicheskii Zhurnal) [A publication]
                                    Hydrobiol J (Engl Transl Gidrobiol Zh)
Hydrobiological Studies [A publication]............Hydrobiol Stud
Hydrocarbon [Organic chemistry]...............................HC
Hydrocarbon Processing [A publication]......Hydrocarbon Process
Hydrocarbon Processing [A publication]............Hydroc Proc
Hydrocarbon Processing Industry...............................HPI
Hydrochemical Form Die [Tool].................................HCFD
Hydrochloric Acid [Inorganic chemistry]......................HCl
Hydrochlorothiazide [Drug] [Also, HCTZ, HCZ] [Organic chemistry]...HCT
Hydrochlorothiazide [Drug] [Also, HCT, HCZ] [Organic chemistry]......HCTZ
Hydrochlorothiazide [Drug] [Also, HCT, HCTZ] [Organic chemistry].....HCZ
Hydrocollator [Hot] Pack [Medicine]............................HY
Hydrocolloid Impression [Dentistry]...........................HcIMP
Hydrocortisone [Endocrinology]..................................HC
Hydrocyanic Acid [Inorganic chemistry]......................HCN
Hydrocylic Pressure Testing.....................................HPT
Hydrodenitrogenation [of chemical compounds]..............HDN
Hydrodesulfurization..HDS
Hydrodynamic Head...H
Hydrodynamic Interaction [Chemistry]..........................HI
Hydrodynamic Journal Bearing..................................HJB
Hydrodynamic Test System.......................................HTS
Hydrodynamic Welding..HDW
Hydrodynamically Modulated Voltammetry [Analytical chemistry]...HMV
Hydrodynamics...HYDRODYN
Hydrodynamics Laboratory [MIT]................................HL
Hydroelectric..HYDRELC
Hydroelectric..HYDROELEC
Hydroelectric Plant..HEP
Hydroelectric Power...HEP
Hydroelectric Unit...HEU
Hydrofluidic Stability Augmentation System...............HYSAS
Hydrofluoric Acid [Inorganic chemistry].........................HF
Hydrofoil Advanced Research Study Program.............HARPY
Hydrofoil Analysis and Design [Data processing]...........HANDE
Hydrofoil Motor Torpedo Boat [Ship symbol]..................PTH
Hydrofoil Ocean Combatant.......................................HOC
Hydrofoil-Operated Rocket Submarine.....................HORSE
Hydrofoil Research Ship [Navy symbol].......................AGEH
Hydrofoil Ship...HS
Hydrofoil Stabilization Device................................HYSTAD
Hydrofoil Tactical Data System................................HTDS
Hydrofoil Test Craft...HTC
Hydrogasification [Gas from coal fuel].......................HYAS
Hydrogen [Chemical element].....................................H
Hydrogen Bomb..H (Bomb)
Hydrogen Bond Donor [Solvent]................................HBD
Hydrogen Bubble Chamber.......................................HBC
Hydrogen Check Valve..HCV
Hydrogen Chloride..HC
Hydrogen Chloride [Inorganic chemistry].......................HCl
Hydrogen Convection Zone.......................................HCZ
Hydrogen Cyanide [Also, HCN] [Poison gas] [Army symbol].....AC
Hydrogen Cyanide [Also, AC] [Inorganic chemistry]..........HCN
Hydrogen Detection System......................................HDS
Hydrogen Drain..HD
Hydrogen Embrittlement..HE
Hydrogen Embrittlement Proof...................................HEP
Hydrogen Fill...HF

Hydrogen Fluid Distribution System...........................HFDS
Hydrogen Fluoride [Inorganic chemistry]........................HF
Hydrogen Fluoride/Deuterium Fluoride.....................HF/DF
Hydrogen-Fueled Aircraft...HFA
Hydrogen Gas Saver...HGS
Hydrogen Gas Valve...HGV
Hydrogen Gasification..HYGAS
Hydrogen Generator...HG
Hydrogen Iodide [Inorganic chemistry]..........................HI
Hydrogen, Ions, Helium, Oxygen in the Exosphere......HIHOE
Hydrogen Line..HL
Hydrogen Line Emission...HLE
Hydrogen Manual Valve...HMV
Hydrogen MASER..HM
Hydrogen Organization for Progress, Education, and
     Cooperation [Defunct]......................................HOPEC
Hydrogen-Oxygen [NASA]..HO
Hydrogen-Oxygen Fuel System [NASA].....................HOFS
Hydrogen-Oxygen Primary Extraterrestrial [Fuel cell] [NASA]...HOPE
Hydrogen-Oxygen Turbine: Super-High Operating
     Temperatures [Hydrogen utilization technology]....HOT-SHOT
Hydrogen Pressure Regulator.....................................HPR
Hydrogen Purge..HP
Hydrogen Relief..HR
Hydrogen Vent...HV
Hydrogenous Exponential Liquid Experiment [British].....HELEN
Hydrogenous Polyethylene..HPE
Hydrogeologicke Informace (Czechoslovakia. Ustav
     Geologickeho Inzenyrstvi) [A publication]......Hydrogeol Inf (Czech)
Hydrographer of the Navy [British].........................H of N
Hydrographer of the Navy [British].........................Hydrog
Hydrographic...HYD
Hydrographic...HYDROG
Hydrographic Center [Defense Mapping Agency].............HC
Hydrographic Data Acquisition System....................HDAS
Hydrographic Digital Positioning and Depth Recording [System]
     [NOO]..HYDRA
Hydrographic Information Committee [NATO]................HIC
Hydrographic Oceanographic Data Sheets..................HODS
Hydrographic Office [Terminated, 1963; later, NOO] [Navy]....HO
Hydrographic Office [Terminated, 1963; later, NOO] [Navy]..HYDRO
Hydrographic Office Publications [Obsolete] [Navy]..........HOP
Hydrographic Office Scale [Obsolete]..........................HOS
Hydrographic Personnel [Navy].............................HYPER
Hydrographic Precision Scanning Echo Sounder.........HYPSES
Hydrographic Survey [Navy] [British].............................H
Hydrographic Surveying and Charting [System] [NOO]..HYSURCH
Hydrography...HYDRO
Hydrologic...HYDROL
Hydrologic Engineering Center [Army]..........................HEC
Hydrologic Information Storage and Retrieval System...HISARS
Hydrologic Reports. State Bureau of Mines and Mineral
     Resources (New Mexico) [A publication]
                     Hydrol Rep St Bur Mines Miner Resour (New Mexico)
Hydrological and Meteorological Fixed Station [ITU designation]...FXH
Hydrological and Meteorological Mobile Station [ITU designation].....MOH
Hydrological Operational Multipurpose Subprogramme [World
     Meteorological Organization] [Information service]....HOMS
Hydrological Sciences. Bulletin des Sciences Hydrologiques [A
     publication]....................Hydrol Sci Bull Sci Hydrol
Hydrologist in Charge..HIC
Hydrology Symposium. Proceedings (Ottawa) [A publication]
                                            Hydrol Symp Proc (Ottawa)
Hydrology and Water Resources in Arizona and the Southwest
     [A publication].............Hydrol Water Resour Ariz Southwest
Hydrolysis...H
Hydrolyzed Animal Protein [Food technology].................HAP
Hydrolyzed Ethylene-Vinyl Acetate [Plastics technology]....HEVA
Hydrolyzed Vegetable Protein [Food additive].................HVP
Hydromechanical Control System...............................HCS
Hydromechanical Unit...HMU
Hydromer, Incorporated [NASDAQ symbol]...................HYDI
Hydrometer..HYDM
Hydrometer Erosion and Recession Test..................HEART
Hydronics Institute..HI
Hydroperoxyoctadecadienoic Acid [Organic chemistry]...HPOD
Hydroperoxyoctadecatrienoic Acid [Organic chemistry]....HPOT
Hydrophile/Lipophile [Followed by a number]...................H/L
Hydrophile-Lipophile Balance [Surface chemistry]............HLB
Hydrophobic Interaction Chromatography......................HIC
Hydrophone..HYPH
Hydrophone Effect [Navy]..HE
Hydropneumatic [Freight]................................HYDROPNEU
Hydropneumatic Suspension Device...........................HSD
Hydropneumatic Trailer..HPT
Hydroponic Society of America..................................HSA
Hydropress Accessory [Tool]..................................HPAC
Hydropress Form [Tool]..HPFM
Hydroquench Thrust Termination System [NASA].........HTTS
Hydroquinone [Organic chemistry]...............................HQ
Hydroquinone Monomethyl Ether [Organic chemistry]....HQMME

Hydroshift Gun ...HSG
Hydrospace Target Recognition, Evaluation, and Control ...HYTREC
Hydrostatic ...HYDRO
Hydrostatic ...HYDRST
Hydrostatic Impact Rocket ...HIR
Hydrostatic Indifference Point ...HIP
Hydrostatic Motor-Driven ...HMD
Hydrostatic Pressure ...HP
Hydrostatics ...HYD
Hydrotechnical Construction [A publication] ...Hydrotech Constr
Hydrotherapy [Medicine] ...HT
Hydrotherapy [Medicine] ...HYDRO
Hydrous ...HYD
Hydroxy [As substituent on nucleoside] [Also, oh] [Biochemistry] ... ho
Hydroxy [As substituent on nucleoside] [Also, HO] [Biochemistry] ...OH
Hydroxyalkylpropyl Sephadex [Analytical biochemistry] ...HAPS
Hydroxyaminoquinoline Oxide [Organic chemistry] ...HAQO
Hydroxyapatite [Also, HAP] [A mineral] ...HA
Hydroxyapatite [Also, HA] [A mineral] ...HAP
(Hydroxyazobenzene)benzoic Acid [Also, HBABA] [Organic chemistry] ...HABA
(Hydroxybenzeneazo)benzoic Acid [Also, HABA] [Organic chemistry] ...HBABA
Hydroxybenzoic Acid Hydrazide [Reagent] ...HBAH
Hydroxybenzotriazole [Organic chemistry] ...HBT
Hydroxybenzylbutanediol [Clinical chemistry] ...HBBD
Hydroxybenzylbutyrolactone [Clinical chemistry] ...HBBL
Hydroxybenzylpindolol [Neuropharmacology] ...HYP
Hydroxybutyrate Dehydrogenase [Also, HBDH] [An enzyme] ...HBD
Hydroxybutyrate Dehydrogenase [Also, HBD] [An enzyme] ...HBDH
Hydroxycholecalciferol [Biochemistry] ...HCC
Hydroxydaunomycin [See also ADR, Adriamycin] [Antineoplastic drug] ...H
Hydroxydaunomycin [Adriamycin], Oncovin [Vincristine], Prednisone [Antineoplastic drug regimen] ...HOP
Hydroxydimethylpyrimidine [Organic chemistry] ...HDP
Hydroxydopamine [Also, HDM, OHDA] [Biochemistry] ...HDA
Hydroxydopamine [Also, HDA, OHDA] [Biochemistry] ...HDM
Hydroxydopamine [Also, HDA, HDM] [Biochemistry] ...OHDA
Hydroxyecdysone [Endocrinology] ...HE
Hydroxyeicosatetraenoic Acid [Biochemistry] ...HETE
Hydroxyethyl Methacrylate [Organic chemistry] ...HEMA
Hydroxyethyl Starch [Plasma volume expander] ...HES
Hydroxyethyl Terephthalate [Organic chemistry] ...HET
(Hydroxyethyl)cellulose [Organic chemistry] ...HEC
Hydroxyethylenediaminetriacetic Acid [Organic chemistry] ...HEDTA
(Hydroxyethyl)ethylenediaminetetracetate [or -tetracetic] Acid [Organic chemistry] ...HEEDTA
Hydroxyethylflurazepam [Sedative] ...HEF
(Hydroxyethyl)hydrazine [Organic chemistry] ...HEH
(Hydroxyethylidene)diphosphonic Acid [Also, EHDP] [Organic chemistry] ...HEDP
(Hydroxyethyl)iminodiacetic Acid [Organic chemistry] ...HEIDA
Hydroxyethylmorpholine [Organic chemistry] ...HEM
(Hydroxyethyl)oxamic Acid [Organic chemistry] ...HOA
Hydroxyethylpiperazineethanesulfonic Acid [A buffer] ...HEPES
Hydroxyethylpiperazinepropanesulfonic Acid [A buffer] ...HEPPS
Hydroxyheptadecatrienoic Acid [Organic chemistry] ...HHT
Hydroxyindole O-Methyltransferase [An enzyme] ...HIOMT
Hydroxyindoleacetic Acid [Organic chemistry] ...HIAA
Hydroxyl-Terminated Polybutadiene [Organic chemistry] ...HTPB
Hydroxyl Value [Analytical chemistry] ...HV
Hydroxylamine-ortho-sulfonic Acid [Organic chemistry] ...HAOS
Hydroxylamine Perchlorate [Organic chemistry] ...HAP
Hydroxylamine Phosphate Oxime [Organic chemistry] ...HPO
Hydroxylysine [Also, Hylys] [An amino acid] ...Hyl
Hydroxylysine [or (OH)Lys] [Also, Hyl] [An amino acid] ...Hylys
Hydroxy(methoxy)benzaldehyde [Organic chemistry] ...HMB
Hydroxymethoxymandelic Acid [Also, VMA] [Biochemistry] ...HMMA
Hydroxymethyl [As substituent on nucleoside] [Biochemistry] ...hm
Hydroxymethyl Diacetone Acrylamide [Organic chemistry] ...HMDAA
(Hydroxymethyl)carboline [Biochemistry] ...HMC
Hydroxymethylcystosine [Organic chemistry] ...HMC
Hydroxymethylfuraldehyde [Organic chemistry] ...HMF
Hydroxymethylglutaryl [Biochemistry] ...HMG
Hydroxymethyl(methyl)benzanthracene [Organic chemistry] ...HMBA
Hydroxymethyluracil [Organic chemistry] ...HMU
Hydroxynitrobenzyl [Organic chemistry] ...HNB
Hydroxynonenal [Biochemistry] ...HNE
Hydroxyoxo-L-norvaline [Antibiotic] ...HON
Hydroxyperoxyeicosatetraenoic Acid [Biochemistry] ...HPETE
Hydroxyphenyl Pyruvate [Organic chemistry] ...HPP
Hydroxyphenylcinchoninic Acid [Pharmacology] ...HPC
Hydroxyphenylpyruvic Acid [Organic chemistry] ...HPPA
Hydroxyproline [Also, Hypro] [An amino acid] ...Hyp
Hydroxyproline [or (OH)Pro] [Also, Hyp] [An amino acid] ...Hypro
Hydroxypropyl Methacrylate [Organic chemistry] ...HPMA
Hydroxypropyl(methyl)cellulose [Synthetic food gum] [Organic chemistry] ...HMC
Hydroxypropyl(methyl)cellulose [Synthetic food gum] [Organic chemistry] ...HPMC
Hydroxypyrazolopyrimidine [Pharmacology] ...HPP

Hydroxypyrazolopyrimidine Ribonucleoside [Biochemistry] ...HPPR
Hydroxyquinoline Citrate [Antiseptic] ...HQC
Hydroxyquinolinesulfonic Acid [Organic chemistry] ...HQSA
Hydroxysteroid Dehydrogenase [An enzyme] ...HSD
Hydroxytryptamine [Biochemistry] ...HT
Hydroxytryptophan [Biochemistry] ...HTP
Hydroxyurea [Also, HYD] [Antineoplastic drug] ...HU
Hydroxyurea [Also, HU] [Antineoplastic drug] ...HYD
Hydrozene Monopropellant ...HMP
Hydrus [Constellation] ...Hya
Hydrus [Constellation] ...Hydi
Hygiene [Preventive and Industrial Medicine] [Medical Officer designation] [British] ...H
Hygiene ...HYG
Hygiene Institute, La Salle, IN [Library symbol] ...InLasH
Hygiene Institute, Medical Library, La Salle, IL [Library symbol] ...ILasH
Hygiene Mentale [A publication] ...Hyg Ment
Hygiene Mentale [A publication] ...HYMEA
Hygiene Mentale. Supplement de l'Encephale [A publication] ...Hyg Ment Suppl Encephale
Hygiene and Sanitation [A publication] ...Hyg Sanit
Hygienic Community Network ...HCN
Hygienic Laboratory [US] ...HL
Hygienische Rundschau [A publication] ...Hyg Rundschau
Hygienist ...HYGNST
Hygienist ...HYGST
Hygrade Food Products Corp. [American Stock Exchange symbol] [Delisted] ...HFO
Hygroscopic ...HYG
Hyland Laboratories, Los Angeles, CA [Library symbol] ...CLH
Hyman, TX [Location identifier] [FAA] ...HYM
Hymn [A publication] ...Hy
Hymn Society of America ...HSA
Hymn Society of Great Britain and Ireland [A publication] ...Hymn S
Hymnologiske Meddelelser. Vaerkstedsblad om Salmer [A publication] ...Hymn M
Hymns Ancient and Modern ...HA & M
Hymns Ancient and Modern ...HAM
Hyoscine [Organic chemistry] ...H
Hyoscine, Morphine, and Cactine [Tablets] [Medicine] ...HMC
Hyper-High-Frequency ...HHF
Hyperactive Child Syndrome ...HACS
Hyperbaric Oxygen [Medicine] ...HBO
Hyperbaric Oxygen Drenching ...HOD
Hyperbola [Mathematics] ...HYPERB
Hyperbolic Area Coverage [Navigation] ...HARCO
Hyperbolic Doppler ...HYPERDOP
Hyperbolic Grid System ...HGS
Hyperemia Unit ...HU
Hyperenvironmental RADAR ...HER
Hyperenvironmental Test Station [or System] [Air Force] ...HETS
Hypereosinophilic Syndrome [Medicine] ...HES
Hyperfine Structure ...HFS
Hyperglycemic-Glycogenolytic [Factor] [Endocrinology] ...HG
Hyperglycemic-Glycogenolytic Factor [Later, Glucagon] [Endocrinology] ...HGF
Hypergol Maintenance Facility [NASA] ...HMF
Hypergol Servicing Facility [NASA] ...HSF
Hypergolic ...HYGL
Hypergolic ...HYP
Hypergolic Clean ...HGC
Hypergolic Ignition ...HYPERIGN
Hypergolic Test Building ...HTB
Hyperimmune Antivariola Gamma Globulin ...HAGG
Hyperimmune Mice ...HM
Hyperintense Proximal Scanning ...HIPS
Hyperlipoproteinemia [Medicine] ...HLP
Hypermetropia [Ophthalmology] ...H
Hypermetropia [Medicine] ...Hy
Hypermetropia, Absolute [Ophthalmology] ...HA
Hypermetropia, Latent [Ophthalmology] ...HL
Hypermetropia, Total [Ophthalmology] ...Ht
Hyperparathyroidism [Endocrinology] ...HP
Hyperparathyroidism [or Hyperthyroidism] [Endocrinology] ...HPT
Hyperphoria ...HP
Hyperplastic Alveolar Nodules [Precancerous lesions in mice] ...HAN
Hyperplastic Liver Nodules [Medicine] ...HLN
Hyperpolarizing Afterpotential [Electrophysiology] ...HAP
Hyperpolarizing Bipolar Cell [In the retina] ...HPBC
Hyperpure Germanium ...HPG
Hyperquasicenter ...HQC
Hyperresonance ...HYP
Hyperresponse Electric Motor ...HYPREM
Hypersensitivity Lung Disease [Medicine] ...HLD
Hypersonic ...HS
Hypersonic Aerothermaldynamic Facility ...HAF
Hypersonic Air Data Entry System ...HADES
Hypersonic Air Data Sensor ...HADS
Hypersonic Arbitrary Body Program [NASA] ...HABP
Hypersonic Arc-Heated Tunnel [Langley Research Center] [NASA] ...HAHT
Hypersonic Boost-Glide Missile ...HBGM

Hypersonic Flight Environmental Simulator .... HYFES
Hypersonic Flow .... HSF
Hypersonic In-Flight Refueling System .... HIRES
Hypersonic Interference Technique .... HIT
Hypersonic Local Pressure .... HLP
Hypersonic Propulsion Research Facility .... HPRF
Hypersonic Rarefied Flow .... HRF
Hypersonic Research Airplane [*NASA*] .... HRA
Hypersonic Research Engine [*NASA*] .... HRE
Hypersonic Research Facilities [*NASA*] .... HYFAC
Hypersonic Research Vehicle .... HRV
Hypersonic Test Vehicle [*Air Force*] .... HTV
Hypersonic Transport [*Aircraft*] .... HST
Hypersonic Tunnel Facility [*NASA*] .... HTF
Hypersonic Vehicle Shield .... HVS
Hypersonic Wedge Nozzle .... HYWN
Hypersonic Wind Tunnel .... HWT
Hypersthene [*CIPW classification*] [*Geology*] .... hy
Hyperstriatum Vocalis [*Brain anatomy*] .... HVc
Hypertension [*Medicine*] .... HPN
Hypertension .... HYPN
Hypertension and Arteriosclerotic Heart Disease [*Medicine*] .... H & ASHD
Hypertension Detection and Follow-Up Program [*NHLBI*] .... HDFP
Hypertension and Proteinuria [*Medicine*] .... HP
Hypertension Secondary to Renal Disease [*Medicine*] .... HSRD
Hypertensive Arteriosclerotic [*Cardiology*] .... HAS
Hypertensive Cardiovascular Disease [*Medicine*] .... HCVD
Hypertensive Heart Disease [*Medicine*] .... HHD
Hypertensive Vascular Disease [*Medicine*] .... HVD
Hypertransfused Polycythemic [*Medicine*] .... HP
Hypertrichosis Lanuginosa [*Medicine*] .... HL
Hypertrophic Obstructive Cardiomyopathy [*Cardiology*] .... HOCM
Hypertrophic Subaortic Stenosis [*Medicine*] .... HSAS
Hypertrophic Subaortic Stenosis [*Cardiology*] .... HSS
Hypertrophy .... HYP
Hypertropia [*Medicine*] .... HT
Hypervariable [*Immunochemistry*] .... Hv
Hypervelocity .... HV
Hypervelocity .... HVEL
Hypervelocity Aircraft Rocket, Tactical .... HART
Hypervelocity Antiradiation Missile .... HARM
Hypervelocity Armor-Piercing [*Projectile*] .... HVAP
Hypervelocity Armor-Piercing - Tracer [*Projectile*] .... HVAP-T
Hypervelocity Countermeasures Program .... HCP
Hypervelocity Flow Field .... HFF
Hypervelocity Free Flight Facility .... HFFF
Hypervelocity Impulse Tunnel .... HIT
Hypervelocity Intercept Guidance .... HIG
Hypervelocity Intercept Guidance Simulator Study .... HIGSS
Hypervelocity Interceptor Armament .... HYVIA
Hypervelocity Interceptor Guidance Simulation .... HIGS
Hypervelocity Kill Mechanism [*Air Force*] .... HKM
Hypervelocity Missile .... HVM
Hypervelocity, Target-Practice [*Projectile*] .... HVTP
Hypervelocity Target-Practice - Tracer [*Projectile*] .... HVTP-T
Hyperventilation .... HV
Hyphenation and Justification [*Typography*] .... H & J

Hypnosis .... HYP
Hypnosis .... HYPNO
Hypnotism .... HYPNOT
Hypo-Osmotic Shock Treatment [*Analytical biochemistry*] .... HOST
Hypoascorbemia-Kwashiorkor [*Orthomolecular medicine*] .... H-K
Hypobranchial [*Gland*] .... HY
Hypobranchial Gland .... HG
Hypochondriasis [*Psychology*] .... Hs
Hypodermic .... H
Hypodermic .... HYPO
Hypodermic Tablet [*Medicine*] .... HT
Hypodermoclysis Infusion [*Medicine*] .... HINF
Hypofibrinogenic Plasma .... HFP
Hypogastric Nerve [*Anatomy*] .... HGN
Hypogonadotrophic Eunuchoidism [*Medicine*] .... HE
Hypoiodism [*Medicine*] .... HIO
Hyponex Corp. [*NASDAQ symbol*] .... HYPX
Hypoparathyroidism [*Endocrinology*] .... HOPT
Hypophysectomy [*Medicine*] .... HYPOX
Hypophysiotropic Area [*of hypothalamus*] [*Endocrinology*] .... HTA
Hypoplastic Left Heart [*Cardiology*] .... HLH
Hypoplastic Right Heart [*Cardiology*] .... HRH
Hypopressure Gas Chromatography .... HPGC
Hyporeninemic Hypoaldosteronism [*Endocrinology*] .... HH
Hypotenuse .... HYP
Hypothalamic-Pituitary-Adrenocortical [*Endocrinology*] .... HPA
Hypothalamic Secretory Factor [*Endocrinology*] .... HSF
Hypothalamo-Hypophyseal-Adrenal [*Endocrinology*] .... HHA
Hypothalamo-Neurohypophyseal Complex [*Endocrinology*] .... HNC
Hypothalamus [*Endocrinology*] .... HT
Hypothesis .... HYP
Hypothesis Testing Model .... HTM
Hypothetical .... HYPOTH
Hypothetical Core Disruptive Accident [*Nuclear energy*] .... HCDA
Hypothetical Future Samples [*Statistics*] .... HFS
Hypothetical Syllogism [*Rule of inference*] [*Logic*] .... HS
Hypothetico-Deductive .... H-D
Hypotonia-Hypomentia-Hypogonadism-Obesity [*Medicine*] .... HHHO
Hypotonic Lysis Buffer [*Analytical biochemistry*] .... HLB
Hypouricemia [*Medicine*] .... HUC
Hypoxanthine [*Biochemistry*] .... Hx
Hypoxanthine [*Biochemistry*] .... Hyp
Hypoxanthine-Aminopterin-Thymidine [*Medium*] [*Biochemistry*] .... HAT
Hypoxanthine-Guanine Phosphoribosyltransferase [*An enzyme*] .... HGPRT
Hypoxanthine Phosphoribosyltransferase [*An enzyme*] .... HPRT
Hypoxic Pulmonary Vasoconstriction [*Medicine*] .... HPV
Hypoxic Ventilatory Response [*Medicine*] .... HVR
Hyster Co. [*NASDAQ symbol*] .... HYST
Hysteresis Comparator .... HC
Hysteria .... HYS
Hysterical Personality .... HP
Hysteroid-Obsessoid Questionnaire [*Psychology*] .... HOQ
Hysterosalpingogram [*Gynecology*] .... HSG
Hysterotomy and Sterilization [*Medicine*] .... H & S
Hytek International Corp. [*NASDAQ symbol*] .... HYTK
Hytek Microsystems [*NASDAQ symbol*] .... HTEK
Hytone Film Lab, Inc., Des Moines, IA [*Library symbol*] .... HyF

I

I Am Chairman of Chrysler Corporation of America [*Acronym formed from name of Chrysler chairman Lee Iacocca*] .... IACOCCA
I-Beam [*Structural metal shape*] I
I Buy Money [*Humorous translation of the letters in IBM Corp., and referring to the appeal of investing in its stocks*] .... IBM
I Corps Tactical Zone [*Vietnamese designation for both a military zone and a political region*] .... ICTZ
I Got Mine [*Slang describing attitude of some nouveaux riches*] .... IGM
I Owe You [*Business and trade slang*] .... IOU
I. P. Sharp Associates Ltd., Carleton Place, ON, Canada [*Library symbol*] .... CaOCpS
I Quit [*Smoking*] .... IQ
I-T-E Imperial Corp. [*NYSE symbol*] [*Delisted*] .... ITE
I Wish Everyone Would Stop Using Letters of the Alphabet to Designate Their Organizations [*Originated by Bea von Boeselager in "Line o' Type," Chicago Tribune*] .... IWEWSULOTATDTO
Iacet Hic [*Here Lies*] [*Latin*] .... IH
IAG [*International Federation for Information Processing Administrative Data Processing Group*] Journal [*A publication*] .... IAG J
IAJRC [*International Association of Jazz Record Collectors*] Journal [*A publication*] .... IAJRC
IAL Boletim. Instituto Adolfo Lutz [*A publication*] ...... IAL Bol Inst Adolfo Lutz
Iamalele [*Papua New Guinea*] [*Airport symbol*] .... IMA
IAPA [*Industrial Accident Prevention Association*] Library, Toronto, ON, Canada [*Library symbol*] .... CaOTIAP
IARC [*International Agency for Research on Cancer*] Monographs [*A publication*] .... IARC Monogr
IARC [*International Agency for Research on Cancer*] Monographs. Evaluation of the Carcinogenic Risk of Chemicals to Humans [*A publication*]
.... IARC Monogr Eval Carcinog Risk Chem Hum
IARC [*International Agency for Research on Cancer*] Monographs. Evaluation of the Carcinogenic Risk of Chemicals to Humans. Supplement [*A publication*]...........................
.... IARC Monogr Eval Carcinog Risk Chem Hum Suppl
IARC [*International Agency for Research on Cancer*] Scientific Publications [*A publication*].............................. IARC Sci Publ
Iasi [*Romania*] [*Airport symbol*] .... IAS
Iasi [*Romania*] [*Seismograph station code, US Geological Survey*] .... IAS
Iasi Universitatea. Analele Stiintifice. Sectiunea 2-B. Geologie (Serie Noua) [*A publication*] .... Iasi Univ An Stiint Sect 2 B (Ser Noua)
IASLIC [*Indian Association of Special Libraries and Information Centres*] Bulletin [*A publication*] .... IASLIC Bull
Iasul Literar [*A publication*] .... I Lit
IATA [*International Air Transport Association*] Unit of Value [*International airline currency*] .... IUV
IAWA [*International Association of Wood Anatomists*] Bulletin [*A publication*] .... IAWA Bull
Iazyk i Literatura [*A publication*] .... I & L
IBA [*Independent Broadcasting Authority*] Technical Review [*A publication*] .... IBA Tech Rev
Ibadan [*Nigeria*] [*Airport symbol*] .... IBA
Ibadan [*Nigeria*] [*Geomagnetic observatory code*] .... IBD
Ibadan Review [*A publication*] .... Ibadan
Ibadan Studies in English [*A publication*] .... ISE
Ibadan University. Department of Forestry. Bulletin [*A publication*] .... Ibadan Univ Dep For Bull
Ibague [*Colombia*] [*Airport symbol*] .... IBE
Iberia Air Lines of Spain .... IBR
Iberia Parish Library, New Iberia, LA [*Library symbol*] .... LNiI
Iberian Atlantic Area .... IBERLANT
Iberian Atlantic Planning Guidance .... IAPG
Iberian Peninsula [*MARC geographic area code*] [*Library of Congress*] .... ei-----
Iberian Peninsula Operating Committee [*World War II*]................. IPOC
Iberica (New York) [*A publication*] .... IbNY
Iberiul-K'avk'asiuri Enatmecniereba [*A publication*] .... IKE
Ibero-American Association of Chambers of Commerce [*See also AICO*].. IAACC

Ibero-American Institute of Agrarian Law and Agrarian Reform [*See also IIDARA*].. IAIALAR
Ibero-Amerikanisches Archiv [*A publication*]......................... IAA
Ibero-Armorican Arc [*A geological area of western Europe*] .... IAA
Ibero-Romania [*A publication*] .... Ib
Ibero-Romania [*A publication*] .... Ibero
Iberville Parish Library, Plaquemine, LA [*Library symbol*] .... LPlaI
IBIA News, Ames, IA [*Library symbol*] .... IaAIBI
Ibidem [*In the Same Place*] [*Latin*] .... IB
Ibidem [*In the Same Place*] [*Latin*] .... IBID
Ibiza [*Spain*] [*Airport symbol*] .... IBZ
IBM Corp., Library Processing Center, White Plains, NY [*OCLC symbol*] .... XIB
IBM Corp., Office Products Division, Lexington, KY [*Library symbol*] .... KyLxI
IBM [*International Business Machines Corp.*] Journal of Research and Development [*A publication*] .... IBM J
IBM [*International Business Machines Corp.*] Journal of Research and Development [*A publication*].................................IBM J R D
IBM [*International Business Machines Corp.*] Journal of Research and Development [*A publication*] .... IBM J Res
IBM [*International Business Machines Corp.*] Journal of Research and Development [*A publication*] .... IBM J Res Dev
IBM [*International Business Machines Corp.*] Journal of Research and Development [*A publication*] .... IBM J Res Develop
IBM [*International Business Machines Corp.*] Nachrichten [*A publication*] .... IBM Nachr
IBM Recruitment Information System .... IRIS
IBM [*International Business Machines Corp.*] Systems Journal [*A publication*] ....IBM Systems J
IBM [*International Business Machines Corp.*] Systems Journal [*A publication*] .... IBM Syst J
IBM [*International Business Machines Corp.*] Technical Disclosure Bulletin [*A publication*] .... IBM Tech Disclosure Bull
IBM Technical Information Retrieval Center .... ITIRC
Ibsen-Aarboken [*A publication*] .... IA
Ibukiyama [*Ibukisan*] [*Japan*] [*Seismograph station code, US Geological Survey*] [*Closed*] .... IBU
IC Industries, Inc. [*Formerly, IL*] [*NYSE symbol*]..................... ICX
Ica [*Peru*] [*Seismograph station code, US Geological Survey*] ....ICA
ICA [*Instituto Colombiano Agropecuario*] Informa [*A publication*].........ICA Inf
Icabaru [*Venezuela*] [*Airport symbol*] .... ICA
Icard, NC [*Radio station call letters*].............................. WUIV
ICBM [*Intercontinental Ballistic Missile*] Blast Interference Test.............. IBIT
ICC [*Interstate Commerce Commission*] Practitioners' Journal [*A publication*] .... ICC Pract J
ICD [*International College of Dentists*] Scientific and Educational Journal [*A publication*] ....ICD Sci Educ J
Ice Age .... IA
Ice Breaker [*Freight*].. I BKR
Ice Chest... IC
Ice Cream [*Freight*].. I CRM
Ice Cream Review [*A publication*]................................ Ice Cream R
Ice Cream Review [*A publication*]............................... Ice Cream Rev
Ice Cream Trade Journal [*A publication*]...................... Ice Cream Trade J
Ice-Cream Van [*Slang*] [*British*] ICV
Ice Crystal Cloud... ICC
Ice Crystals.. IC
Ice-Cuber.. ICBR
Ice (Deposition) Nuclei [*Atmospheric science*].................... IN
Ice Fog... IF
Ice Pellets [*Meteorology*]....................................... IP
Ice Pellets [*Meteorology*]....................................... PE
Ice Point.. IP
Ice-Rafted Debris [*Oceanography*]................................ IRD
Ice Rinks [*Public-performance tariff class*] [*British*] .... IR
Ice on Runway [*Aviation*].. IR
Ice on Runway - Patchy [*Aviation*]............................... IRP
Ice Skating Institute of America.................................. ISIA
Ice and Snow on Runway [*Aviation*]............................... IASOR

Ice Water Content ..... IWC
Iceberg Athletic Club ..... IAC
Icebreaker [*Navy ship symbol*] ..... AGB
Icefield Ranges Research Project ..... IRRP
Iceland [*MARC geographic area code*] [*Library of Congress*] ..... e-ic---
Iceland [*MARC country of publication code*] [*Library of Congress*] ic
Iceland ..... ICE
Iceland IL
Iceland [*Two-letter standard code*] ..... IS
Iceland [*Three-letter standard code*] ..... ISL
Iceland [*Aircraft nationality and registration mark*] ..... TF
Iceland [*NATO*] IC
Iceland Base Command [*Army*] [*World War II*] ..... IBC
Iceland Defense Force ..... ICEDEFOR
Iceland Ocean Meeting Point [*Navy*] ..... ICOMP
Iceland Patrol [*Navy*] ..... ICEPAT
Iceland Veterans IV
Icelandair [*Iceland*] [*ICAO designator*] ..... FI
Icelandic [*MARC language code*] [*Library of Congress*] ..... ice
Icelandic ..... ICEL
Icelandic Air Defense Force ..... IADF
Icelandic Canadian [*A publication*] IC
Icelandic Federation of Labor ..... IFL
Icelandic Pony Trekkers ..... IPT
ICES [*Integrated Civil Engineering System*] **Users Group** ..... IUG
ICFTU [*International Confederation of Free Trade Unions*] **Economic and Social Bulletin** [*A publication*] ..... ICFTU Econ & Social Bul
ICH Corp. [*American Stock Exchange symbol*] ..... ICH
ICHCA [*International Cargo Handling Coordination Association*] **Journal** [*A publication*] ..... ICHCA J
ICHCA [*International Cargo Handling Coordination Association*] **Monthly Journal** [*A publication*] ..... ICHCA Mon J
Ichthyologica: The Aquarium Journal [*A publication*] ..... Ichthyol Aquarium J
Ichthyological Laboratory and Museum [*University of Miami*] ..... IL & M
Ichthyological Series. Department of Biology. College of Science. Tunghai University [*A publication*] ..... Ichthyol Ser Dep Biol Coll Sci Tunghai Univ
Ichthyology ..... ICH
Ichthyology ..... ICHTH
Ichud Habonim Labor Zionist Youth ..... IHLZY
ICI Americas, Inc., Wilmington, DE [*OCLC symbol*] ..... DLK
ICI Pharmaceuticals [*Great Britain*] [*Research code symbol*] ICI
ICIA [*International Center of Information on Antibiotics*] **Information Bulletin** [*A publication*] ..... ICIA Inf Bull
ICID [*International Commission on Irrigation and Drainage*] **Bulletin** [*A publication*] ..... ICID Bull
ICIDCA [*Instituto Cubano de Investigaciones de los Derivados de la Cana de Azucar*] **Boletin** [*A publication*] ..... ICIDCA Bol
Icing [*Meteorology*] ..... ICG
Icing in Clouds [*Meteorology*] ..... ICGIC
Icing in Clouds and in Precipitation [*Meteorology*] ..... ICGICIP
Icing in Precipitation [*Meteorology*] ..... ICGIP
ICM Realty [*American Stock Exchange symbol*] [*Delisted*] ..... ICM
ICN Pharmaceuticals, Inc. [*Formerly, International Chemical & Nuclear Corp.*] [*NYSE symbol; also, research code symbol*] ..... ICN
ICN-UCLA [*International Chemical and Nuclear Corp.-University of California at Los Angeles*] **Symposia on Molecular and Cellular Biology** [*A publication*] ..... ICN-UCLA Symp Mol Cell Biol
ICO, Inc. [*American Stock Exchange symbol*] ..... ICO
Icon [*Plate engraving*] IC
Iconclass [*Elsevier Book Series*] [*A publication*] IC
Iconic Store, Central [*Psychophysiology*] ..... ISc
Iconic Store, Peripheral [*Psychophysiology*] ..... ISp
Iconography ..... ICON
ICOT Corp. [*NASDAQ symbol*] ..... ICOT
ICRISAT [*International Crops Research Institute for the Semi-Arid Tropics*] **Annual Report** [*A publication*] ..... ICRISAT Annu Rep
ICRP [*International Commission on Radiological Protection*] **Publication** [*A publication*] ..... ICRP Publ
ICRS [*Institute of Contemporary Russian Studies*] **Medical Reports. Monographs in Soviet Medical Science** [*A publication*] ..... ICRS Med Rep Monogr Sov Med Sci
ICRU [*International Commission on Radiological Units*] **Report** [*A publication*] ..... ICRU Rep
Icterus [*Jaundice*] [*Medicine*] ..... ICT
Icterus Neonatorum [*Medicine*] ..... IN
Icterus Precox [*Medicine*] ..... IP
ICUIS [*Institute on the Church in Urban-Industrial Society*] **Abstract Service** [*A publication*] ..... ICUIS Abstr Service
Id [*That*] [*Latin*] I
Id, Ego, Superego [*Test*] [*Psychology*] ..... IES
Id Est [*That Is*] [*Latin*] ..... IE
Id Quod Erat Demonstrandum [*That Which Was to Be Proved*] [*Latin*] ..... IQED
Ida County Historical Society, Ida Grove, IA [*Library symbol*] ..... IaIdgIHi
Ida Grove, IA [*Location identifier*] [*FAA*] ..... IDG
Ida Grove, IA [*Radio station call letters*] ..... KIDA-FM
Ida Public Library, Belvidere, IL [*Library symbol*] ..... IBelv
Idabel, OK [*Location identifier*] [*FAA*] ..... IBO
Idabel, OK [*Radio station call letters*] ..... KBEL
Idabel, OK [*Radio station call letters*] ..... KWDG
Idaho I
Idaho [*Postal code*] ..... ID
Idaho ..... IDA
Idaho [*MARC country of publication code*] [*Library of Congress*] ..... idu
Idaho [*MARC geographic area code*] [*Library of Congress*] ..... n-us-id
Idaho Agricultural Experiment Station. Publications [*A publication*] ..... Idaho Ag Exp
Idaho Agricultural Experiment Station. Research Bulletin [*A publication*] ..... Idaho Agric Exp Stn Res Bull
Idaho Agricultural Research Progress Report. University of Idaho. College of Agriculture [*A publication*] ..... Idaho Agr Res Progr Rep
Idaho Agricultural Science. University of Idaho. College of Agriculture [*A publication*] ..... Idaho Agr Sci
Idaho Array [*Idaho*] [*Seismograph station code, US Geological Survey*] [*Closed*] ..... IDA
Idaho Bureau of Mines and Geology. Bulletin [*A publication*] ..... Idaho Bur Mines Geol Bull
Idaho Bureau of Mines and Geology. County Report [*A publication*] ..... Idaho Bur Mines Geol County Rep
Idaho Bureau of Mines and Geology. Earth Sciences Series [*A publication*] ..... Idaho Bur Mines and Geology Earth Sci Ser
Idaho Bureau of Mines and Geology. Information Circular [*A publication*] ..... Idaho Bur Mines Geol Inf Circ
Idaho Bureau of Mines and Geology. Pamphlet [*A publication*] ..... Idaho Bur Mines Geol Pam
Idaho Chemical Processing Plant [*AEC*] ..... ICPP
Idaho Department of Fish and Game Wildlife. Bulletin [*A publication*] ..... Idaho Dep Fish Game Wildl Bull
Idaho Department of Reclamation. Water Information Bulletin [*A publication*] ..... Idaho Dept Reclamation Water Inf Bull
Idaho Department of Water Administration. Water Information Bulletin [*A publication*] ..... Idaho Dep Water Adm Water Inf Bull
Idaho Department of Water Resources. Basic Data Release [*A publication*] ..... Idaho Dep Water Resour Basic Data Release
Idaho Department of Water Resources. Water Information Bulletin [*A publication*] ..... Idaho Dep Water Resour Water Inf Bull
Idaho Falls [*Idaho*] [*Airport symbol*] ..... IDA
Idaho Falls, ID [*Radio station call letters*] ..... KIBQ
Idaho Falls, ID [*Radio station call letters*] ..... KID
Idaho Falls, ID [*Radio station call letters*] ..... KID-FM
Idaho Falls, ID [*Television station call letters*] ..... KID-TV
Idaho Falls, ID [*Television station call letters*] ..... KIFI-TV
Idaho Falls, ID [*Radio station call letters*] ..... KQPI
Idaho Falls, ID [*Radio station call letters*] ..... KTEE
Idaho Falls, ID [*Radio station call letters*] ..... KUPI
Idaho Falls, ID [*Location identifier*] [*FAA*] ..... SWU
Idaho Falls Public Library, Idaho Falls, ID [*Library symbol*] ..... IdIf
Idaho Forest, Wildlife, and Range Experiment Station. Bulletin [*A publication*] ..... Idaho For Wildl Range Exp Stn Bull
Idaho Forest, Wildlife, and Range Experiment Station. Information Series [*A publication*] ..... Idaho For Wildl Range Exp Stn Inf Ser
Idaho Forest, Wildlife, and Range Experiment Station. Note [*A publication*] ..... Idaho For Wildl Range Exp Stn Note
Idaho Forest, Wildlife, and Range Experiment Station. Paper [*A publication*] ..... Idaho For Wildl Range Exp Stn Pap
Idaho Forest, Wildlife, and Range Experiment Station. Technical Report [*A publication*] ..... Idaho For Wildl Range Exp Stn Tech Rep
Idaho Genealogical Society, Boise, ID [*Library symbol*] ..... IdHi-G
Idaho Health Libraries Network [*Library network*] ..... IDA-HEAL-NET
Idaho Law Review [*A publication*] ..... Idaho L Rev
Idaho Librarian [*A publication*] ..... Idaho Libn
Idaho Librarian [*A publication*] ..... Idaho Librn
Idaho Mining Industry. Annual Report [*A publication*] ..... Idaho Min Industry Ann Rept
Idaho Motor Tariff Bureau, Boise ID [*STAC*] ..... IMT
Idaho Nuclear ..... IN
Idaho Nuclear Code Automation [*AEC*] ..... INCA
Idaho Nuclear Corporation ..... INC
Idaho Nuclear Engineering Laboratory ..... INEL
Idaho Operations Office [*Energy Research and Development Administration*] ..... ID
Idaho Operations Office [*Energy Research and Development Administration*] ..... IDO
Idaho Operations Office [*Energy Research and Development Administration*] ..... IOO
Idaho Potato Commission ..... IPC
Idaho Power Co. [*NYSE symbol*] ..... IDA
Idaho Power Company ..... IPCO
Idaho Power Company. Bulletin [*A publication*] ..... Idaho Power Co Bull
Idaho Springs Public Library, Idaho Springs, CO [*Library symbol*] ..... CoIs
Idaho State Historical Society, Boise, ID [*Library symbol*] ..... IdHi
Idaho State Library, Boise, ID [*Library symbol*] ..... Id
Idaho State University, Pocatello, ID [*Library symbol*] ..... IdPI
Idaho Supreme Court, Idaho State Law Library, Boise, ID [*Library symbol*] ..... Id-L
Idaho Test Station [*Nuclear energy*] ..... ITS
Idaho University. Agricultural Experiment Station. Current Information Series [*A publication*] ..... Idaho Univ Agric Exp Stn Curr Inf Ser

Idaho University. Engineering Experiment Station. Bulletin [*A publication*].................................Idaho Univ Eng Exp Sta Bull
Idaho University. Forest, Range, and Wildlife Experiment Station. Research Note [*A publication*]
　　　　　Idaho Univ For Range Wildl Exp Stn Res Note
Idaho Yesterdays [*A publication*]........................Idaho Yest
IDB Bankholding ADR [*NASDAQ symbol*]....................IDBBY
Idea [*Slang*]...ID
Ideal Basic Industries, Inc. [*NYSE symbol*]...............IDL
Ideal Body Weight [*Medicine*]..............................IBW
Ideal Cement Co. Research Library, Fort Collins, CO [*Library symbol*]...CoFI
Ideal Current Negative Immittance Converter...............INIC
Ideal Design of Effective and Logical Systems............IDEALS
Ideal Gas Law..IGL
Ideal Liquidus Structures...................................ILS
Ideal Low Pass Filter.....................................ILPF
Ideal Man Helicopter Engineering Project.................IMHEP
Ideal Solidus Structures...................................ISS
Ideal Toy Corp. [*NYSE symbol*] [*Delisted*]................ID
Idealistic Studies [*A publication*]..................Ideal Stud
Idealization to Frustration to Demoralization...............IFD
Ideas for Management [*A publication*]...........Ideas Manage
Ideas for Management [*A publication*]..........Ideas for Mgmt
Ideas, Resources, Exchange [*Computer*] [*British*]........IREX
Ideas y Valores [*A publication*]..........................I & V
Ideggyogyaszati Szemle [*A publication*].........Ideggyogy Sz
Idem [*The Same*] [*Latin*].................................ID
Idem Ac [*The Same As*] [*Latin*].......................ID AC
Idem Quod [*The Same As*] [*Latin*].......................IQ
Identical Location of Accelerometer and Force [*NASA*]....ILAF
Identification...I
Identification...ID
Identification...IDENT
Identification of Aircraft................................INDAIR
Identification Beacon.......................................IBN
Identification and Compliance Record.......................ICR
Identification Data..ID
Identification Dissector....................................ID
Identification, Distribution, and Exchange for Action [*Project*]............IDEA
Identification, Friend or Foe [*Military*].................IFF
Identification Friend or Foe or Neutral...................IFFN
Identification, Friend or Foe/Selective Identification Feature [*Military*]....................IFF/SIF
Identification, Friend or Foe, Switching Circuit [*Military*]...............IFS
Identification Light.......................................IDLT
Identification List..IL
Identification List...ILS
Identification Officer [*Military*].........................IDO
Identification Peculiarity..................................IP
Identification Point.......................................IP
Identification of Position..................................IP
Identification Record [*Data processing*]..................IDR
Identification Safety Range [*Military*]....................ISR
Identification Section.....................................IDS
Identification System for Questioned Documents [*Book title*]............ISQD
Identification Transponder..................................IT
Identified Flying Object [*Air Force*]......................IFO
Identified Friendly [*Military*]...........................IDFR
Identified Friendly Prior to Interception [*Military*]......IPI
Identified Parts List......................................IPL
Identifier [*Data processing*] [*Genetics*]................ID
Identity Preserved [*Wheat*] [*Department of Agriculture*]....IP
Ideological Survey [*Psychology*]...........................IS
Ideologies and Literature [*A publication*].................I & L
Ideology and Consciousness [*A publication*].............I and C
[*The*] **Ides**..ID
Idiopathic Congestive Cardiomyopathy [*Medicine*].........ICCM
Idiopathic Dilated Cardiomyopathy [*Cardiology*]...........IDC
Idiopathic Hypercalcemia [*Medicine*]......................IHC
Idiopathic Hyperplastic Aldosteronism [*Endocrinology*]....IHA
Idiopathic Hypertrophic Subaortic Stenosis [*Medicine*]...IHSS
Idiopathic Membranous Nephropathy [*Nephrology*]..........IMN
Idiopathic Orthostatic Hypotension [*Medicine*]............IOH
Idiopathic Pulmonary Fibrosis [*Medicine*].................IPF
Idiopathic Pulmonary Hemosiderosis [*Medicine*]...........IDPH
Idiopathic Respiratory Distress Syndrome [*Pediatrics*]...IRDS
Idiopathic Thrombocytopenic Purpura [*Medicine*]...........ITP
Idiopathic Ulcerative Colitis [*Medicine*].................IUC
Idle..IL
Idle Line Network...ILN
Idle Other Reasons [*Vessel status*] [*Navy*]............IDREA
Idle Used for Storage [*Shipping*].......................IDSTO
Idle Waiting Convoy Forward [*Vessel status*] [*Navy*]....IDFOR
Idle Waiting to Load [*Shipping*]........................IDLOD
Idle Wild Foods, Inc. [*NASDAQ symbol*]...................IDLE
Idler...IDL
IDMA [*Indian Drug Manufacturers' Association*] **Bulletin** [*A publication*]...........................IDMA Bull
IDOC [*International Documentation*] **Bulletin** [*A publication*]...........IDOC Bul
Idoneo-Vehiculo [*In a Suitable Vehicle*] [*Pharmacy*]....IDON VEHIC

Idoxuridine [*or Iododeoxyuridine*] [*Also, IDUR*] [*Pharmacology*]..............IDU
Idoxuridine [*or Iododeoxyuridine*] [*Also, IDU*] [*Pharmacology*]..............IDUR
IDRC [*International Development Research Centre*] **Reports** [*A publication*]...........................IDRC Rep
IDS [*Institute of Development Studies*] **Bulletin** [*A publication*].....IDS Bulletin
IDSA [*Institute for Defense Studies and Analyses*] **Journal** [*India*] [*A publication*]........................IDSA J
Iduronic Acid..IdUA
Idus [*The Ides*] [*Latin*]................................I
Idyllwild School of Music and the Arts [*California*]...ISOMATA
IE, Industrial Engineering [*A publication*]..........IE Ind Eng
IEC [*International Electrotechnical Commission*] **Bulletin** [*A publication*]...........................IEC Bull
IEE [*Institution of Electrical Engineers*] **Conference Publication (London)** [*A publication*]........IEE Conf Publ (Lond)
IEE [*Institution of Electrical Engineers*] **Electromagnetic Waves Series** [*A publication*]..........IEE Electromagn Waves Ser
IEE-IERE [*Institution of Electrical Engineers-Institution of Electronic and Radio Engineers*] **Proceedings (India)** [*A publication*]..................IEE-IERE Proc (India)
IEE [*Institution of Electrical Engineers*] **Journal on Computers and Digital Techniques** [*A publication*]....IEE J Comput Digital Tech
IEE [*Institution of Electrical Engineers*] **Journal on Electric Power Applications** [*A publication*]..........IEE J Electr Power Appl
IEE [*Institution of Electrical Engineers*] **Journal on Electronic Circuits and Systems** [*A publication*]....IEE J Electron Circuits Syst
IEE [*Institution of Electrical Engineers*] **Journal on Microwaves, Optics, and Acoustics** [*A publication*]....IEE J Microwaves Opt Acoust
IEE [*Institution of Electrical Engineers*] **Journal on Solid-State and Electron Devices** [*A publication*]
　　　　IEE J Solid-State Electron Devices
IEE [*Institution of Electrical Engineers*] **Monograph Series** [*A publication*]....................IEE Monogr Ser
IEE [*Institution of Electrical Engineers*] **Proceedings. A** [*A publication*]......................IEE Proc A
IEE [*Institution of Electrical Engineers*] **Proceedings. B. Electric Power Applications** [*A publication*]...IEE Proc B Electr Power Appl
IEE [*Institution of Electrical Engineers*] **Proceedings. C. Generation, Transmission, and Distribution** [*A publication*]....IEE Proc C Gener Transm Distrib
IEE [*Institution of Electrical Engineers*] **Proceedings. E. Computers and Digital Techniques** [*A publication*]
　　　　IEE Proc E Comput Digit Tech
IEE [*Institution of Electrical Engineers*] **Proceedings. I. Solid-State and Electron Devices** [*A publication*]
　　　　IEE Proc I Solid-State Electron Devices
IEE [*Institution of Electrical Engineers*] **Reviews** [*A publication*]..........IEE Rev
IEEE. Annual Textile Industry Technical Conference [*A publication*].............IEEE Annu Text Ind Tech Conf
IEEE. Cement Industry Technical Conference Paper [*A publication*]................IEEE Cem Ind Tech Conf Pap
IEEE. Communications Society Magazine [*A publication*]
　　　　IEEE Commun Soc Mag
IEEE. Computer Group News [*A publication*]........IEEE Comput Group News
IEEE. Conference Record. Annual Conference of Electrical Engineering Problems in the Rubber and Plastics Industries [*A publication*]
　　IEEE Conf Rec Annu Conf Electr Eng Probl Rubber Plast Ind
IEEE. Conference Record. Industrial and Commercial Power Systems. Technical Conference [*A publication*]
　　　　IEEE Conf Rec Ind Commer Power Syst Tech Conf
IEEE. Electromagnetic Compatibility Symposium. Record [*A publication*].................IEEE Electromagn Compat Symp
IEEE. Engineering Management Review [*A publication*]
　　　　IEEE Eng Manage Rev
IEEE. Intercon Technical Papers [*A publication*].......IEEE Intercon Tech Pap
IEEE. International Conference on Magnetics. Proceedings of the Intermag Conference [*A publication*]....IEEE Proc Intermag Conf
IEEE. International Convention. Record [*A publication*]....IEEE Int Conv Rec
IEEE. Journal of Oceanic Engineering [*A publication*]......IEEE J Ocean Eng
IEEE. Journal of Quantum Electronics [*A publication*]......IEEE J Q El
IEEE. Journal of Quantum Electronics [*A publication*]
　　　　IEEE J Quantum Electron
IEEE. Journal of Solid-State Circuits [*A publication*]......IEEE J Soli
IEEE. Journal of Solid-State Circuits [*A publication*]
　　　　IEEE J Solid-State Circuits
IEEE. Proceedings [*A publication*].....................IEEE Proc
IEEE. Proceedings. Annual Symposium on Reliability [*A publication*]........................IEEE Proc Annu Symp Rel
IEEE. Proceedings. Conference on Electrical Applications for the Textile Industry [*A publication*].....IEEE Proc Conf Elec Appl Text Ind
IEEE. Proceedings. Conference on Engineering in Medicine and Biology [*A publication*].......IEEE Proc Conf Eng Med Biol
IEEE. Proceedings. Electronic Components Conference [*A publication*].................IEEE Proc Electron Components Conf
IEEE. Proceedings. National Aerospace and Electronics Conference [*A publication*].....IEEE Proc Nat Aerosp Electron Conf
IEEE. Proceedings. National Aerospace and Electronics Conference [*A publication*]...........IEEE Proc Natl Aerosp Electron Conf
IEEE. Region Six (Western USA). Conference Record [*A publication*]...................IEEE Reg Six (West USA) Conf Rec

IEEE. Spectrum [*A publication*] .... IEEE S
IEEE. Spectrum [*A publication*] .... IEEE Spectr
IEEE. Standards Publications [*A publication*] .... IEEE Stand Publ
IEEE. Student Papers [*A publication*] .... IEEE Stud Pap
IEEE. Transactions on Acoustics, Speech, and Signal Processing [*A publication*] .... IEEE Acoust
IEEE. Transactions on Acoustics, Speech, and Signal Processing [*A publication*] .... IEEE Trans Acoust Speech Signal Process
IEEE. Transactions on Acoustics, Speech, and Signal Processing [*A publication*] .... IEEE Trans ASSP
IEEE. Transactions on Aerospace and Electronic Systems [*A publication*] .... IEEE Aer El
IEEE. Transactions on Aerospace and Electronic Systems [*A publication*] .... IEEE Trans Aerosp Electron Syst
IEEE. Transactions on Antennas and Propagation [*A publication*] .... IEEE Antenn
IEEE. Transactions on Antennas and Propagation [*A publication*] .... IEEE Trans Antennas Propag
IEEE. Transactions on Antennas and Propagation [*A publication*] .... IEEE Trans Antennas Propagat
IEEE. Transactions on Audio and Electroacoustics [*A publication*] .... IEEE Trans Audio Electroacoust
IEEE. Transactions on Automatic Control [*A publication*] .... IEEE Auto C
IEEE. Transactions on Automatic Control [*A publication*] .... IEEE Trans Automat Contr
IEEE. Transactions on Automatic Control [*A publication*] .... IEEE Trans Autom Control
IEEE. Transactions on Biomedical Engineering [*A publication*] .... IEBEA
IEEE. Transactions on Biomedical Engineering [*A publication*] .... IEEE Biomed
IEEE. Transactions on Biomedical Engineering [*A publication*] .... IEEE Trans Biomed Eng
IEEE. Transactions on Broadcast and Television Receivers [*A publication*] .... IEEE Trans Broadcast Telev Receivers
IEEE. Transactions on Broadcasting [*A publication*] .... IEEE Broadc
IEEE. Transactions on Broadcasting [*A publication*] .... IEEE Trans Broadcast
IEEE. Transactions on Cable Television [*A publication*] .... IEEE Trans Cable Telev
IEEE. Transactions on Cable Television [*A publication*] .... IEEE Trans CATV
IEEE. Transactions on Circuit Theory [*A publication*] .... IEEE Trans Circuit Theory
IEEE. Transactions on Circuits and Systems [*A publication*] .... IEEE Circ S
IEEE. Transactions on Circuits and Systems [*A publication*] .... IEEE Trans CAS
IEEE. Transactions on Circuits and Systems [*A publication*] .... IEEE Trans Circuits & Syst
IEEE. Transactions on Communication Technology [*A publication*] .... IEEE Trans Commun Technol
IEEE. Transactions on Communication Technology [*A publication*] .... IEEE Trans Com Tech
IEEE. Transactions on Communications [*A publication*] .... IEEE Commun
IEEE. Transactions on Communications [*A publication*] .... IEEE Trans Com
IEEE. Transactions on Components, Hybrids, and Manufacturing Technology [*A publication*] .... IEEE Trans Components Hybrids Manuf Technol
IEEE. Transactions on Computers [*A publication*] .... IEEE Comput
IEEE. Transactions on Computers [*A publication*] .... IEEE Trans
IEEE. Transactions on Computers [*A publication*] .... IEEE Trans Comput
IEEE. Transactions on Consumer Electronics [*A publication*] .... IEEE Cons E
IEEE. Transactions on Consumer Electronics [*A publication*] .... IEEE Trans CE
IEEE. Transactions on Consumer Electronics [*A publication*] .... IEEE Trans Consum Electron
IEEE. Transactions on Education [*A publication*] .... IEEE Educat
IEEE. Transactions on Education [*A publication*] .... IEEE Trans Educ
IEEE. Transactions on Electrical Insulation [*A publication*] .... IEEE El Ins
IEEE. Transactions on Electrical Insulation [*A publication*] .... IEEE Trans Elec Insul
IEEE. Transactions on Electrical Insulation [*A publication*] .... IEEE Trans Electr Insul
IEEE. Transactions on Electromagnetic Compatibility [*A publication*] .... IEEE Elmagn
IEEE. Transactions on Electromagnetic Compatibility [*A publication*] .... IEEE Trans Electromagn Compat
IEEE. Transactions on Electron Devices [*A publication*] .... IEEE Device
IEEE. Transactions on Electron Devices [*A publication*] .... IEEE T El Dev
IEEE. Transactions on Electron Devices [*A publication*] .... IEEE Trans Electron Devices
IEEE. Transactions on Engineering Management [*A publication*] .... IEEE Manage
IEEE. Transactions on Engineering Management [*A publication*] .... IEEE Trans Eng Manage
IEEE. Transactions on Engineering Writing and Speech [*A publication*] .... IEEE Trans Engng Wrtg Speech
IEEE. Transactions on Engineering Writing and Speech [*A publication*] .... IEEE Trans Eng Writing Speech
IEEE. Transactions on Geoscience Electronics [*A publication*] .... IEEE Geosci
IEEE. Transactions on Geoscience Electronics [*A publication*] .... IEEE Trans Geosci Electron
IEEE. Transactions on Industrial Electronics and Control Instrumentation [*A publication*] .... IEEE Ind El
IEEE. Transactions on Industrial Electronics and Control Instrumentation [*A publication*] .... IEEE Trans Ind Electron Control Instrum
IEEE. Transactions on Industry Applications [*A publication*] .... IEEE Ind Ap
IEEE. Transactions on Industry Applications [*A publication*] .... IEEE Trans Ind Appl
IEEE. Transactions on Industry and General Applications [*Later, IEEE. Transactions on Industry Applications*] [*A publication*] .... IEEE Trans Ind Gen Appl
IEEE. Transactions on Information Theory [*A publication*] .... IEEE Info T
IEEE. Transactions on Information Theory [*A publication*] .... IEEE Trans Inf Theory
IEEE. Transactions on Instrumentation and Measurement [*A publication*] .... IEEE Instr
IEEE. Transactions on Instrumentation and Measurement [*A publication*] .... IEEE Trans Instrum Meas
IEEE. Transactions on Magnetics [*A publication*] .... IEEE Magnet
IEEE. Transactions on Magnetics [*A publication*] .... IEEE Trans Magn
IEEE. Transactions on Man-Machine Systems [*A publication*] .... IEEE Trans Man-Mach Syst
IEEE. Transactions on Manufacturing Technology [*A publication*] .... IEEE Trans Manuf Technol
IEEE. Transactions on Microwave Theory and Techniques [*A publication*] .... IEEE Micr T
IEEE. Transactions on Microwave Theory and Techniques [*A publication*] .... IEEE Trans Microwave Theory Tech
IEEE. Transactions on Nuclear Science [*A publication*] .... IEEE Nucl S
IEEE. Transactions on Nuclear Science [*A publication*] .... IEEE T Nucl Sci
IEEE. Transactions on Nuclear Science [*A publication*] .... IEEE Trans Nucl Sci
IEEE. Transactions on Parts, Hybrids, and Packaging [*A publication*] .... IEEE Parts
IEEE. Transactions on Parts, Hybrids, and Packaging [*A publication*] .... IEEE Trans Parts Hybrids Packag
IEEE. Transactions on Parts, Materials, and Packaging [*A publication*] .... IEEE Trans Parts Mater Packag
IEEE. Transactions on Plasma Science [*A publication*] .... IEEE Plas S
IEEE. Transactions on Plasma Science [*A publication*] .... IEEE T Pl Sci
IEEE. Transactions on Plasma Science [*A publication*] .... IEEE Trans Plasma Sci
IEEE. Transactions on Plasma Science [*A publication*] .... IEEE Trans PS
IEEE. Transactions on Power Apparatus and Systems [*A publication*] .... IEEE Power
IEEE. Transactions on Power Apparatus and Systems [*A publication*] .... IEEE Trans Power App Syst
IEEE. Transactions on Professional Communications [*A publication*] .... IEEE Prof C
IEEE. Transactions on Professional Communications [*A publication*] .... IEEE Trans Prof Commun
IEEE. Transactions on Reliability [*A publication*] .... IEEE Reliab
IEEE. Transactions on Reliability [*A publication*] .... IEEE Trans Rel
IEEE. Transactions on Reliability [*A publication*] .... IEEE Trans Reliab
IEEE. Transactions on Software Engineering [*A publication*] .... IEEE Trans SE
IEEE. Transactions on Software Engineering [*A publication*] .... IEEE Trans Software Eng
IEEE. Transactions on Sonics and Ultrasonics [*A publication*] .... IEEE Son Ul
IEEE. Transactions on Sonics and Ultrasonics [*A publication*] .... IEEE Trans Sonics & Ultrason
IEEE. Transactions on Sonics and Ultrasonics [*A publication*] .... IEEE Trans Sonics Ultrason
IEEE. Transactions on Systems, Man, and Cybernetics [*A publication*] .... IEEE Syst M
IEEE. Transactions on Systems, Man, and Cybernetics [*A publication*] .... IEEE Trans Syst Man Cybern
IEEE. Transactions on Systems, Science, and Cybernetics [*A publication*] .... IEEE Trans Syst Sci Cybern
IEEE. Transactions on Ultrasonics Engineering [*A publication*] .... IEEE Trans Ultrasonics Eng
IEEE. Transactions on Vehicular Technology [*A publication*] .... IEEE Trans Veh Technol
IEEE. Transactions on Vehicular Technology [*A publication*] .... IEEE Veh T
IEEE. Wescon Convention Record [*A publication*] .... IEEE Wescon Conven Rec
IEEE. Wescon Technical Papers [*A publication*] .... IEEE Wescon Tech Pap
IEM SA ADR [*NASDAQ symbol*] .... IEMSY
IERE [*Institution of Electronic and Radio Engineers*] **Conference Proceedings (London)** [*A publication*] .... IERE Conf Proc (Lond)
IES [*Illuminating Engineering Society of Australia*] **Lighting Review** [*A publication*] .... IES Light Rev
Iesu Christo Duce [*With Jesus Christ as Leader*] [*Latin*] .... ICD
Iesu Christo Tutore [*With Jesus Christ as Protector*] [*Latin*] .... ICT
Iesus Christus [*Jesus Christ*] [*Latin*] IC
Iesus Christus [*Jesus Christ*] [*Latin*] IX
Iesus Nazarenus Rex Iudaeorum [*Jesus of Nazareth, King of the Jews*] [*Latin*] .... INRI
Iesus Salvator Mundi [*Jesus, Savior of the World*] [*Latin*] .... ISM
If Approach Missed Proceed [*Aviation*] .... IFAMP

If Authorized by Air Traffic Control, DME [*Distance Measuring Equipment*] **May Be Used** [*Aviation*] ....IAATCD
If Clause ....IFC
If Flight Visibility Becomes Less Than [*Aviation*] ....IFVLS
If Holding [*Aviation*] ....IFHOL
If I Tell You, Will You Buy Me a Drink? [*Tavern sign*] ....IITYWYBMAD
If Incorrect Advise [*Aviation*] ....IIA
If Incorrect Service Direct [*Aviation*] ....IISD
If Incorrect Service Originator [*Aviation*] ....IISO
If Instrument Conditions Encountered [*Aviation*] ....IFINS
If Not Already Processed, Orders Cancelled [*Military*]..............NOPROCAN
If Not Available Notify This Office at Once ....INOAVNOT
If Not Available Your Command, Obtain Accounting Data from Administrative Command [*Army*]..............NACOA
If Not Possible [*Aviation*] ....INP
If and Only If ....IFF
If Signal Source ....IFSS
If Unable [*Aviation*] ....IFUN
If Visibility Remains [*Aviation*] ....IFVR
Ife African Studies [*A publication*]..............Ife Afr Stud
IFF [*Institut fuer Festkoerperforschung*] **Bulletin** [*A publication*] ....IFF Bull
Iffley [*Australia*] [*Airport symbol*] [*Obsolete*] ....IFF
IFIP [*International Federation for Information Processing*] **Committee for International Liaison** ICIL
IFIP [*International Federation for Information Processing*] **Congress Series** [*Elsevier Book Series*] [*A publication*]..............IFIPC
IFIP [*International Federation for Information Processing*] **Medical Informatics Monograph Series** [*A publication*]..............IFIP Med Inf Monogr Ser
IFIP [*International Federation for Information Processing*] **World Conference Series on Medical Informatics** [*Elsevier Book Series*] [*A publication*] ....IFIPW
Ifni [*MARC geographic area code*] [*Library of Congress*] ....f-if---
IFR [*Instrument Flight Rules*] **Military Training Route** ....IR
Ifrane [*Morocco*] [*Seismograph station code, US Geological Survey*]..............IFR
IFS Industries, Inc. [*Formerly, International Funeral Services, Inc.*] [*American Stock Exchange symbol*] [*Delisted*] ....IFN
IGC, Incorporated [*NASDAQ symbol*] ....IIGC
Igiene Moderna [*A publication*] ....Ig Mod
Igiene e Sanita Pubblica [*A publication*] ....Ig Sanita Pubblica
Igiugig [*Alaska*] [*Airport symbol*] ....IGG
Iglesia Ni Cristo [*Religious organization*] ....INC
Igloo Environment Control Subsystem ....IECS
Igloo Thermal Control ....ITC
Igloolik [*Northwest Territories*] [*Seismograph station code, US Geological Survey*]..............IGL
Ignacio, CO [*Radio station call letters*]..............KSUT
Ignacio Public Library, Ignacio, CO [*Library symbol*] ....Colg
Igniter ....IGNR
Igniter ....IGNTR
Igniter Booster Assembly [*Aerospace*] ....IBA
Igniter-Fuel Assembly ....IFA
Igniter-Fuel Valve ....IFV
Igniter Initiator II
Igniter Initiator Cartridge [*or Container*]..............IIC
Igniter Initiator Test Set ....IITS
Igniter Nozzle Closure ....INC
Ignition ....IGN
Ignition Control Programer ....ICP
Ignition Detector ....IGNDET
Ignition Manufacturers Institute [*Later, TMI*] ....IMI
Ignition and Separation Assembly ....ISA
Ignition Shielding System ....ISS
Ignition Test Simulator ....ITS
Ignition Transmission Line ....ITL
Ignitron [*Electronics*] ....IGN
Ignorant ....IGN
Ignorant Bloody Aircrafthand [*British Royal Air Force slang*] ....IBA
Ignotus [*Unknown*] [*Latin*] ....IGN
Igor-Patrick Air Force Base ....IGPA
Iguassu Falls [*Brazil*] [*Airport symbol*] ....IGU
Iguazu [*Argentina*] [*Airport symbol*] ....IGR
Iguela [*Gabon*] [*Airport symbol*] [*Obsolete*] ....IGE
Iheringia. Serie Antropologia [*A publication*]..............Iheringia Ser Antropol
Iheringia. Serie Botanica [*A publication*]..............Iheringia Ser Bot
Iheringia. Serie Divulgacao [*A publication*] ....Iheringia Ser Divulg
Iheringia. Serie Geologia [*A publication*]..............Iheringia Ser Geol
Iheringia. Serie Zoologia [*A publication*]..............Iheringia Ser Zool
IHI [*Ishikawajima-Harima Heavy Industries*] **Engineering Review** [*A publication*]..............IHI Eng Rev
Ihr [*Your*] [*German*]..............I
Ihre Kingliche Hoheit [*His Royal Highness*] [*German*]..............IKH
Ihu [*Papua New Guinea*] [*Airport symbol*] ....IHU
IHVE [*Institution of Heating and Ventilating Engineers*] **Journal** [*A publication*]..............IHVE J
Iida [*Japan*] [*Seismograph station code, US Geological Survey*]..............IID
IIHR [*Iowa Institute of Hydraulic Research*] **Report** [*A publication*] ....IIHR Rep
Iinan [*Japan*] [*Seismograph station code, US Geological Survey*]..............INA
IIRB; Revue de l'Institut International de Recherches Betteravieres [*A publication*] ....IIRB Rev Inst Int Rech Better
IIT Chicago-Kent College of Law, Chicago, IL [*OCLC symbol*]..............ILK

Iizuka [*Japan*] [*Seismograph station code, US Geological Survey*] [*Closed*]..............IZK
IJS [*Institut "Jozef Stefan"*] **Report R** [*A publication*]..............IJS Rep R
Ijui [*Brazil*] [*Airport symbol*]..............IJU
Ikatan Buruh Kendaraan Bermotor [*Motor Transport Workers' Union*] [*Indonesia*]..............IBKB
Ikatan Buruh Kereta Api [*Railroad Workers' Union*] [*Indonesia*]..............IBKA
Ikatan Buruh Umum [*General Workers' Union*] [*Indonesia*]..............IBU
Ike Lovelady, Inc. [*NASDAQ symbol*]..............IKEL
Ike and Tina Turner [*Singers*]..............I & TT
Ikebana International..............II
Iki [*Japan*] [*Airport symbol*]..............IKI
Ikonomika i Mekhanizatsiya na Selskoto Stopanstvo [*A publication*]..............Ikon Mekh Selsk Stop
Ikusaka [*Japan*] [*Seismograph station code, US Geological Survey*]..............IKJ
Ikuska. Instituto Vasco de Investigaciones [*A publication*]..............IVI
Il Bollettino delle Cliniche [*A publication*]..............Boll Clin
Il Medico Veterinario (Torino) [*A publication*]..............Medico Vet (Torino)
Il Ponte [*A publication*]..............ILP
Il Tesaur [*A publication*]..............ILT
ILA [*Instruction Look Ahead*] **Associative Memory** [*Data processing*]..............IAM
ILA [*Instruction Look Ahead*] **Interrupt Address** [*Data processing*]..............IIA
Ilan [*Giran*] [*Republic of China*] [*Seismograph station code, US Geological Survey*]..............ILA
ILC Technology [*NASDAQ symbol*]..............ILCT
Ile Des Pins [*New Caledonia*] [*Airport symbol*]..............ILP
Ilerda [*A publication*]..............Ile
Iles De La Madeleine, PQ [*Radio station call letters*]..............CBIM-FM
Iles De La Madeleine, PQ, [*Television station call letters*]..............CBIMT
Iles De Madeleine [*Canada*] [*Airport symbol*]..............YGR
Ilheus [*Brazil*] [*Airport symbol*]..............IOS
Ili [*USSR*] [*Seismograph station code, US Geological Survey*] [*Closed*]..............ILI
Iliac Crest [*Anatomy*]..............ICR
Iliamna [*Alaska*] [*Airport symbol*]..............ILI
Iliamna [*Alaska*] [*Seismograph station code, US Geological Survey*]..............ILM
Iliamna Air Taxi, Inc. [*Iliamna, AK*] [*FAA designator*]..............IAR
Iliff Review [*A publication*]..............IR
Iliff School of Theology, Denver, CO [*Library symbol*]..............CoDI
Iliff School of Theology, Denver, CO [*OCLC symbol*]..............COI
Iligan [*Philippines*] [*Airport symbol*]..............IGN
Ilaga [*Indonesia*] [*Airport symbol*]..............ILA
Illegal Immigrant..............I-I
Illegal Possession of Government Property..............IPGP
Illegal Wearing of Uniform..............IWU
Illicit Diamond Buyer [*or Buying*]..............IDB
Illicit Gold Buyer [*or Buying*]..............IGB
Illicit Gold Dealer..............IGD
Illico Lagena Obturatur [*Stopper the Bottle at Once*] [*Pharmacy*]..............ILLIC LAG OBTURAT
Illinendus [*To Be Smeared*] [*Pharmacy*]..............ILLINEND
ILLINET [*Illinois Library Information Network*], **Springfield, IL** [*OCLC symbol*]..............TQA
ILLINET [*Illinois Library Information Network*], **Springfield, IL** [*OCLC symbol*]..............TQB
Illinois [*Postal code*]..............IL
Illinois..............ILL
Illinois [*MARC country of publication code*] [*Library of Congress*]..............ilu
Illinois [*MARC geographic area code*] [*Library of Congress*]..............n-us-il
Illinois Academy of Science. Transactions [*A publication*]..............Ill Ac Sc Tr
Illinois Agricultural Association & Affiliated Co., Bloomington, IL [*OCLC symbol*]..............JAE
Illinois Agricultural Economics [*A publication*]..............Ill Agr Econ
Illinois Agricultural Experiment Station. Bulletin [*A publication*]..............Ill Agric Exp Stn Bull
Illinois Agricultural Experiment Station. Department of Forestry. Forestry Research Report [*A publication*]..............Ill Agric Exp Stn Dep For For Res Rep
Illinois Agricultural Experiment Station. Publications [*A publication*]..............Ill Ag Exp
Illinois Baptist Historical Library, Springfield, IL [*Library symbol*]..............ISB
Illinois Bar Journal [*A publication*]..............Ill B J
Illinois Benedictine College, Lisle, IL [*OCLC symbol*]..............ICG
Illinois Benedictine College, Lisle, IL [*Library symbol*]..............ILS
Illinois Biological Monographs [*A publication*]..............Ill Biol Mon
Illinois Biological Monographs [*A publication*]..............Ill Biol Monogr
Illinois Catholic Historical Review [*A publication*]..............ICHR
Illinois Catholic Historical Review [*A publication*]..............Ill Cath His R
Illinois Central [*Illinois Central Gulf Railroad Co.*] [*AAR code*]..............IC
Illinois Central College, East Peoria, IL [*OCLC symbol*]..............IDB
Illinois Central College, East Peoria, IL [*Library symbol*]..............IEpl
Illinois Central Gulf Railroad Co. [*AAR code*]..............ICG
Illinois Central Industries, Inc. [*Later, ICX*] [*NYSE symbol*]..............IL
Illinois Central Railroad..............ICR
Illinois Classical Studies [*A publication*]..............ICS
Illinois Classical Studies [*A publication*]..............Ill Class Stud
Illinois Coal Mining Investigations. Cooperative Agreement. Bulletin [*A publication*]..............Ill Coal M Investigations B
Illinois College, Jacksonville, IL [*OCLC symbol*]..............ICH
Illinois College, Jacksonville, IL [*Library symbol*]..............IJI
Illinois College of Optometry..............ICO
Illinois College of Optometry, Chicago, IL [*Library symbol*]..............ICICO

Illinois College of Podiatric Medicine, Chicago, IL [*Library symbol*]......ICPM
Illinois Continuing Legal Education [*A publication*]............................... Ill CLE
Illinois Dental Journal [*A publication*]...Ill Dent J
Illinois Department of Conservation. Technical Bulletin [*A publication*]... Ill Dep Conserv Tech Bull
Illinois Division of Fisheries. Special Fisheries Report [*A publication*]... Ill Div Fish Spec Fish Rep
Illinois Division of Industrial Planning and Development. Atlas of Illinois Resources [*A publication*]... Ill Div Indus Plan and Devel Atlas Ill Res
Illinois Education [*A publication*]...Ill Educ
Illinois Farmer [*A publication*]... Illinois F
Illinois Geographical Society. Bulletin [*A publication*]..........Ill Geogr Soc Bull
Illinois Geological Survey. Oil and Gas Drilling in Illinois. Monthly Report [*A publication*]........ Ill Geol Surv Oil Gas Drill Ill Mon Rep
Illinois Health Libraries Consortium [*Library network*].............................IHL
Illinois Historical Survey, University of Illinois, Urbana, IL [*Library symbol*]...IU-HS
Illinois Institute for Advanced Computing .... ILLIAC
Illinois Institute for Environmental Quality, Chicago, IL [*Library symbol*]... ICIEQ
Illinois Institute of Technology.. IIT
Illinois Institute of Technology, Armour Research Foundation, Chicago, IL [*Library symbol*]... ICI-A
Illinois Institute of Technology, Chicago, IL [*OCLC symbol*] ....IAH
Illinois Institute of Technology, Chicago, IL [*Library symbol*]..................... ICI
Illinois Institute of Technology, Institute of Design, Chicago, IL [*Library symbol*].. ICI-D
Illinois Institute of Technology, Institute of Gas Technology, Chicago, IL [*Library symbol*]...ICI-G
Illinois Institute of Technology Research Institute .... IITRI
Illinois Integrator and Automatic Computer .... ILLIAC
Illinois Intrastate Motor Carrier Rate & Tariff Bureau, Springfield IL [*STAC*] .... IIB
Illinois Inventory of Parent Opinion .... IIPO
Illinois Journal of Mathematics [*A publication*].. ILJM
Illinois Journal of Mathematics [*A publication*]....................................Ill J Math
Illinois Law Review [*A publication*] .... Ill Law Rev
Illinois Libraries [*A publication*]..Ill Lib
Illinois Libraries [*A publication*]...Ill Libr
Illinois Library Association. Record [*A publication*] ....ILA Rec
Illinois Library and Information Network [*Library network*].............. ILLINET
Illinois Masonic Medical Center, Chicago, IL [*Library symbol*].............ICMM
Illinois Medical Journal [*A publication*] .... Illinois Med J
Illinois Medical Journal [*A publication*] .... Ill Med J
Illinois Medical Journal [*A publication*] ....IMJ
Illinois Monographs in Medical Sciences [*A publication*] .... Ill Monogr Med Sci
Illinois Monthly Magazine [*A publication*] ....Ill Mo
Illinois Motor Truck Operators Association, Chicago IL [*STAC*]..............ITA
Illinois Natural History Society. Transactions [*A publication*].... Ill N H Soc Tr
Illinois Natural History Survey. Biological Notes [*A publication*] .... Ill Nat Hist Surv Biol Notes
Illinois Natural History Survey. Bulletin [*A publication*] .... Ill Nat Hist Surv Bull
Illinois Natural History Survey. Circular [*A publication*]................................... Ill Nat Hist Surv Circ
Illinois Northern Railway [*AAR code*] .... IN
Illinois Power Company [*NYSE symbol*]..IPC
Illinois Prairie District Public Library, Metamora, IL [*OCLC symbol*] ....IEQ
Illinois Publications in Language and Literature [*A publication*]............ IPLL
Illinois Quarterly [*A publication*] .... Ill Q
Illinois Railway Museum .... IRM
Illinois Regional Library for the Blind and Physically Handicapped, Chicago Public Library, Chicago, IL [*Library symbol*] .... IC-BPH
Illinois Regional Library Council [*Library network*] .... IRLC
Illinois Research [*A publication*]...Ill Res
Illinois Research and Reference Center Libraries .... IRRN
Illinois Schools Journal [*A publication*]...Ill Sch J
Illinois Society of Engineers and Surveyors [*A publication*] ....Ill Soc Eng
Illinois State Academy of Science. Transactions [*A publication*]........... Illinois Acad Sci Trans
Illinois State Academy of Science. Transactions [*A publication*].................. Ill St Ac Sc Tr
Illinois State Academy of Science. Transactions [*A publication*]............... Ill State Acad Sci Trans
Illinois State Department of Conservation, Division of Parks and Memorials, Galena, IL [*Library symbol*]..IGaDC
Illinois State Geological Survey [*A publication*]...................................... Ill G S
Illinois State Geological Survey. Bulletin [*A publication*]...................Ill G S B
Illinois State Geological Survey. Bulletin [*A publication*]........................... Ill State Geol Surv Bull
Illinois State Geological Survey. Circular [*A publication*] .... Illinois Geol Survey Circ
Illinois State Geological Survey. Circular [*A publication*] .... Ill State Geol Surv Circ
Illinois State Geological Survey. Environmental Geology Notes [*A publication*]............................. Ill State Geol Surv Environ Geol Notes
Illinois State Geological Survey. Guide Leaflet [*A publication*] .... Ill Geol Surv Guide Leafl
Illinois State Geological Survey. Guidebook Series [*A publication*]... Ill State Geol Surv Guideb Ser
Illinois State Geological Survey. Illinois Petroleum [*A publication*]... Ill State Geol Surv Ill Petrol
Illinois State Geological Survey. Industrial Minerals Notes [*A publication*]...Ill State Geol Surv Ind Miner Notes
Illinois State Geological Survey. Report of Investigations [*A publication*]...Ill State Geol Surv Rep Invest
Illinois State Geological Survey. Review of Activities [*A publication*]...Ill Geol Surv Rev Act
Illinois State Geological Survey, Urbana, IL [*Library symbol*].................IUrG
Illinois State Historical Library. Collections [*A publication*] .... Ill His Col
Illinois State Historical Library. Collections [*A publication*] .... Ill Hist Coll
Illinois State Historical Library. Publications [*A publication*] .... Ill His L
Illinois State Historical Library, Springfield, IL [*Library symbol*]............... IHi
Illinois State Historical Society. Journal [*A publication*] .... Ill His J
Illinois State Historical Society. Journal [*A publication*] .... Ill State Hist Soc Jour
Illinois State Historical Society Journal [*A publication*]......................... ISHS
Illinois State Historical Society Journal [*A publication*]........................ ISHSJ
Illinois State Historical Society. Transactions [*A publication*]........................ Ill His S Trans
Illinois State Historical Society. Transactions [*A publication*]......Ill His Trans
Illinois State Horticultural Society. Newsletter [*A publication*] .... Ill State Hort Soc N L
Illinois State Laboratory of Natural History. Bulletin [*A publication*].. Ill St Lab N H B
Illinois State Library, Archives Division, Springfield, IL [*Library symbol*] .... I-Ar
Illinois State Library, Springfield, IL [*Library symbol*]..I
Illinois State Library, Springfield, IL [*OCLC symbol*]...................................SPI
Illinois State Museum of Natural History. Bulletin [*A publication*].................. Ill St Mus N H B
Illinois State Museum. Popular Science Series. Scientific Papers. Story of Illinois Series [*A publication*]... Ill State Mus Pop Sci Ser Sci Paper Story Ill Ser
Illinois State Museum. Reports of Investigations [*A publication*]................... Ill State Mus Rep Invest
Illinois State Normal University..ISNU
Illinois State Psychiatric Institute, Chicago, IL [*Library symbol*]........... ICSP
Illinois State University. Journal [*A publication*]................... Ill State Univ Jour
Illinois State University, Normal, IL [*OCLC symbol*]................................. IAI
Illinois State University, Normal, IL [*Library symbol*] ....INS
Illinois State Water Survey. Bulletin [*A publication*]..................................... Ill State Water Surv Bull
Illinois State Water Survey. Circular [*A publication*]...................................... Ill State Water Surv Circ
Illinois State Water Survey. Cooperative Ground-Water Report [*A publication*]..... Ill State Water Survey Cooperative Ground-Water Rept
Illinois State Water Survey. Division Bulletin. Circular. Reports of Investigations [*A publication*].. Ill State Water Survey Div Bull Circ Rept Inv
Illinois State Water Survey. Reports of Investigations [*A publication*].. Illinois Water Survey Rept Inv
Illinois State Water Survey. Reports of Investigations [*A publication*].. Ill State Water Surv Rep Invest
Illinois State Water Survey and State Geological Survey. Cooperative Resources Report [*A publication*] .... Ill State Water Surv State Geol Surv Coop Resour Rep
Illinois State Water Survey, Urbana, IL [*Library symbol*]........................ IUrW
Illinois Statewide Curriculum Study Center in the Preparation of Secondary School English Teachers..ISCPET
Illinois Studies in Anthropology [*A publication*] .... Ill Stud Anthropol
Illinois Studies in Anthropology [*A publication*] ....ISA
Illinois Studies in Language and Literature [*A publication*]...................... ISLL
Illinois Supreme Court, Springfield, IL [*Library symbol*]......................... I-SC
Illinois Teacher [*A publication*] .... Ill Teach
Illinois Terminal Railroad Co. .... ILLT
Illinois Terminal Railroad Company [*AAR code*] .... ITC
Illinois Test of Psycholinguistic Abilities..ITPA
Illinois Tool Works, Inc. [*NYSE symbol*] .... ITW
Illinois University .... ILU
Illinois University. Bulletin. University Studies [*A publication*]................... Ill Univ B Univ Studies
Illinois University (Chicago Circle). Department of Geological Sciences. Technical Report [*A publication*]............................. Ill Univ (Chicago Circle) Dep Geol Sci Tech Rep
Illinois University. Department of Electrical Engineering. Aeronomy Laboratory. Aeronomy Report [*A publication*]...................... Ill Univ Dep Electr Eng Aeron Lab Aeron Rep
Illinois University. Department of Theoretical and Applied Mechanics. TAM Report [*A publication*]...................... Ill Univ Dep Theor Appl Mech TAM Rep
Illinois University. Department of Theoretical and Applied Mechanics TAM Report [*A publication*]......................Ill Univ TAM Rep
Illinois University. Engineering Experiment Station. Bulletin [*A publication*]...Ill U Eng Exp Sta Bul
Illinois University. Engineering Experiment Station. Bulletin [*A publication*].. Ill Univ Eng Exp Sta Bull
Illinois University. Engineering Experiment Station Bulletin. Circulars [*A publication*] .... Ill Univ Eng Expt Sta Bull Circ

Illinois University. Engineering Experiment Station. Circular [*A publication*] ... Ill U Eng Exp Sta Circ
Illinois University. Proceedings of the Sanitary Engineering Conference [*A publication*] ... Ill Univ Proc Sanit Eng Conf
Illinois University. Water Resources Center. Research Report [*A publication*] ... Ill Univ Water Resour Cent Res Rep
Illinois Valley Community College, Oglesby, IL [*Library symbol*] ... IOgIV
Illinois Valley Community Hospital, Peru, IL [*Library symbol*] ... IPerIH
Illinois Valley Library System [*Library network*] ... IVLS
Illinois Valley Library System, Pekin, IL [*OCLC symbol*] ... IDM
Illinois Valley Library System, Peoria, IL [*Library symbol*] ... IPIV
Illinois Veterinarian [*A publication*] ... Ill Vet
Illinois Wesleyan University ... IWU
Illinois Wesleyan University, Bloomington, IL [*Library symbol*] ... IBloW
Illinois Wesleyan University, Bloomington, IL [*OCLC symbol*] ... ICO
Illinois Zinc Co. [*American Stock Exchange symbol*] ... ILZ
Illiterate ... ILLIT
Illiterati [*A publication*] ... Ill
Illness-Correctional Environments ... ICE
Illuminare [*A publication*] ... Im
Illuminate ... ILLUM
Illuminated Internal Graticule ... IIG
Illuminated Push Button ... IPB
Illuminating [*Ammunition*] ... ILL
Illuminating and Allied Glassware Manufacturers Association [*Defunct*] ... IAGMA
Illuminating Engineering [*Superseded by Illuminating Engineering Society. Journal*] [*A publication*] ... Illum Eng
Illuminating Engineering Research Institute ... IERI
Illuminating Engineering Society ... IES
Illuminating Engineering Society. Journal [*A publication*] ... Illum Eng Soc J
Illuminating Engineering Society of North America ... IESNA
Illuminating Engineering Society. Transactions [*A publication*] ... Illum Eng Soc Trans
Illumination Industries, Incorporated ... III
Illumination per Minute ... IPM
Illumination Unit ... LUU
Illuminator RADAR ... IR
Illusion ... ILL
Illustrate [*or Illustration*] ... ILLUS
Illustrated Archaeologist [*A publication*] ... Illus Archaeol
Illustrated London News [*A publication*] ... Illus Lond N
Illustrated London News [*A publication*] ... Illus London News
Illustrated London News [*A publication*] ... ILN
Illustrated Maintenance Parts List ... IMPL
Illustrated Parts Breakdown ... IPB
Illustrated Parts Catalog ... IPC
Illustrated Parts List ... IPL
Illustrated Provisioning Document ... IPD
Illustrated Shipboard Shopping Guide [*Navy*] ... ISSG
Illustrated Weekly of India [*A publication*] ... Illus W Ind
Illustrated Weekly of India (Annual) [*A publication*] ... Illus W Ind (A)
Illustrated World Encyclopedia [*A publication*] ... IWE
Illustration ... IL
Illustration ... ILL
Illustration ... ILLSTN
Illustration ... ILLUSTN
Illustration [*A publication*] ... ILL
Illustrator Draftsman [*Navy rating*] ... DM
Illustrator Draftsman, Seaman [*Navy rating*] ... DMSN
Illustrator Draftsman, Seaman Apprentice [*Navy rating*] ... DMSA
Illustrators Guild [*Later, GA*] ... IG
Illustrazione Biellese [*A publication*] ... IBi
Illustrazione Italiana [*A publication*] ... II
Illustrazione Vaticana [*A publication*] ... IV
Illustrazione Vaticana [*A publication*] ... IVat
Illustrissimo [*Most Illustrious*] [*Latin*] ... ILLMO
Illustrissimus [*Most Illustrious*] [*Latin*] ... ILL
Ilmenau, Technische Hochschule, Wissenschaftliche Zeitschrift [*A publication*] ... Ilmenau Tech Hochsch Wiss Z
Ilmenite [*CIPW classification*] [*Geology*] ... il
Ilmij Asarlari. V. I. Lenin Monidagi Toskent Davlat Universiteti [*A publication*] ... IIATos
Ilocano [*MARC language code*] [*Library of Congress*] ... ilo
Ilocos Review [*A publication*] ... Ilocos R
Iloilo [*Philippines*] [*Airport symbol*] ... ILO
Iloilo [*Philippines*] [*Seismograph station code, US Geological Survey*] [*Closed*] ... ILO
Ilorin [*Nigeria*] [*Airport symbol*] ... ILR
Ilyushin [*USSR aircraft type*] [*World War II*] ... IL
Im Auftrage [*By Order Of*] [*German*] ... IA
Im Jahre [*In the Year*] [*German*] ... IJ
Im Jahre der Welt [*In the Year of the World*] [*German*] ... IJDW
Im Mittel [*On an Average*] [*German*] ... IM
I'm Sorry, I'll Read That Again [*BBC radio comedy program*] ... ISIRTA
Image Analysing Computers, Inc. ... IMANCO
Image Converter Camera ... ICC
Image Converter Tube ... ICT
Image Data Processing System ... IDAPS
Image Data System Simulation [*NASA*] ... IDSS
Image Definition Device ... IDD
Image Digitizer [*Data processing*] ... ID
Image Discrimination, Enhancement, and Combination System [*Electronic optical system*] ... IDECS
Image Display and Manipulation System [*NASA*] ... IDAMS
Image Display System ... IDS
Image Dissector ... ID
Image Dissector Camera ... IDC
Image Dissector Camera System ... IDCS
Image Dissector Echelle Spectrograph [*Instrumentation*] ... IDES
Image Dissector Photomultiplier Tube ... IDPT
Image Dissector Tube ... IDT
Image Dynamics in Science and Medicine [*A publication*] ... Image Dyn Sci Med
Image Feature Extraction [*Air Force*] ... IFE
Image Feature Extraction System [*Air Force*] ... IFES
Image-to-Frame Ratio ... I/F
Image-to-Frame Ratio ... IFR
Image Input to Automatic Computers ... IMITAC
Image Intensified System ... IIS
Image Intensifier ... II
Image Intensifier Assembly ... IIA
Image Intensifier Device ... IID
Image Intensifier Night Sight ... IINS
Image Intensifier Orthicon ... IIO
Image Intensifier Plumbicon Camera ... IIPC
Image Intensifier Tube ... IIT
Image Intensifier Viewer ... IIV
Image Intensifier Viewing Device ... IIVD
Image Interpretation Cell ... IIC
Image Interpreter Response ... IIR
Image Motion Compensation [*or Compensator*] ... IMC
Image Motion Compensation and Calibration ... IMCC
Image Motion Configuration ... IMC
Image Motion Simulator ... IMS
Image Optical Scanner ... IOS
Image Orthicon ... IO
Image Orthicon Camera ... IOC
Image Orthicon Control ... IOC
Image Orthicon System ... IOS
Image Photon Counting System [*Instrumentation*] ... IPCS
Image Processing Laboratory ... IPL
Image Processing Program [*Computer program*] ... IMP
Image Processing System ... IPS
Image Products Company ... IPC
Image Quality Indicator ... IQI
Image Quality Merit Function [*Color image*] ... IQMF
Image Recording System, Low Light ... IRSLL
Image Rejection ... IR
Image Sensor System ... ISS
Image Storage Translation and Reproduction ... ISTAR
Image Technology [*A publication*] ... Image Technol
Image Technology Patent Information System [*Printing technology*] ... ITPAIS
Image Velocity Detector ... IVD
Image of Vocational Education [*ERIC*] ... IVE
Imagery Interpretation ... II
Imagery Interpretation Key ... IIK
Imagery Reconnaissance Objectives List ... IROL
Imaginamics, Inc. [*NASDAQ symbol*] ... IMGNF
Imaginary [*Mathematics*] ... Im
Imaginary ... IMAG
Imaginary Part [*of a complex number*] ... IP
Imagination [*A publication*] ... Im
Imagination Science Fiction [*A publication*] ... ISF
Imaging Infrared [*Air Force*] ... IIR
Imaging Infrared [*Pronounced "eye-squared ar"*] ... I^2R
Imaging Polarimeter [*or Photopolarimetry*] [*NASA*] ... IPP
Imaging Proportional Counter [*Astronomy*] ... IPC
Imaging Spectrometric Observatory ... ISO
Imago [*A publication*] ... Im
Imago Mundi [*A publication*] ... IM
Imark Industries, Inc. [*NASDAQ symbol*] ... IMAR
Imatron, Inc. [*NASDAQ symbol*] ... IMAT
Imbaimadai [*Guyana*] [*Airport symbol*] ... IMB
IMBLMS [*Integrated Medical Behavioral Measurement System*] **Digital Computer** ... IDC
Imbricated Program for Information Transfer [*Data processing*] ... IMPRINT
IMC Chemical Group, Inc., Technical Library, Terre Haute, IN [*Library symbol*] ... InTIMC
IMC Magnetics Corp. [*American Stock Exchange symbol*] ... IMG
Imex Medical Systems [*NASDAQ symbol*] ... IMEX
IMI of Philadelphia, Camp Hill, PA [*Library symbol*] ... ImI
Imidazole Glycerol Phosphate [*Biochemistry*] ... IGP
Imidazoleacetic Acid [*Biochemistry*] ... IAA
Imidazoleglycerol-phosphate Dehydratase [*An enzyme*] ... IGPD
Iminobispropylamine [*Organic chemistry*] ... IBPA
Iminodiacetic Acid [*Organic chemistry*] ... IDA
Iminodipropionitrile [*Biochemistry*] ... IDPN
Imipramine [*Antidepressant*] ... IMI
Imitation ... IMIT
Imitative Communication Deception [*Military*] ... ICD

IML Air Services Ltd. [*Great Britain*] [*ICAO designator*] .... JB
IMM Energy Service & Technology [*NASDAQ symbol*] .... IMME
Immaculata College, Immaculata, PA [*OCLC symbol*] .... IMM
Immaculata College, Immaculata, PA [*Library symbol*] .... PIm
Immaculate .... IMMAC
Immaculate Conception Junior College [*New Jersey*] .... ICJC
Immaculate Conception Seminary, College of Philosophy, Troy, NY [*Library symbol*] .... NTIC
Immaculate Conception Seminary, Huntington, NY [*Library symbol*] .... NHuI
Immaculate Conception Theological Seminary, Ramsey, NJ [*Library symbol*] .... NjRamI
Immaculate Heart College [*California*] .... IHC
Immaculate Heart College, Los Angeles, CA [*Library symbol*] CLI
Immaculate Heart College, Los Angeles, CA [*OCLC symbol*] [*Inactive*] CLI
Immanuel Lutheran College, Eau Claire, WI [*Library symbol*] .... WEI
Immaterial .... IMMAT
Immature .... IM
Immature .... IMMAT
Immature Brown-Fat [*Cells*] .... IBF
Immediate .... IMDT
Immediate .... IMM
Immediate .... IMMED
Immediate .... IMT
Immediate Access Storage .... IAS
Immediate Action Authority .... IAA
Immediate Action Directive .... IAD
Immediate Action Letter .... IAL
Immediate Commanding Officer .... ICO
Immediate Constituent IC
Immediate Constituent Analyzer [*Data processing*] .... ICA
Immediate Damage Assessment .... IDA
Immediate Delivery .... ID
Immediate Hypersensitivity [*Immunology*] .... IH
Immediate Identifiable Emergency Action [*Red Cross*] .... IIEA
Immediate Knowledge of Results .... IKOR
Immediate Operation Use .... IOU
Immediate Past Master [*Masonry*] .... IPM
Immediate Permanent Incapacitation [*Radiation casualty criterion*] [*Army*] .... IP
Immediate Photograph Intelligence Report [*Military*] .... IPIR
Immediate Postprandial Upper Abdominal Distress .... IPPUAD
Immediate Psychiatric Aid and Referral Center .... IMPAC
Immediate Reaction Force [*Military*] .... IRF
Immediate Ready Element [*Military*] .... IRE
Immediate Ready Reserve [*Army*] .... IRR
Immediate Replacement Support Requirement .... IRSR
Immediate Reserve [*Air Force*] [*British*] .... IR
Immediate Superior in Command [*Military*] .... ISIC
Immediate Superior in Command [*Military*] .... ISINC
Immediate Transient Incapacitation [*Radiation casualty criterion*] [*Army*] .... IT
Immediate Transient Incapacitation [*Radiation casualty criterion*] [*Army*] .... ITI
Immediate Transportation .... IT
Immediate Unit Commander [*Navy*] .... IUC
Immediately .... IMMY
Immediately Available .... IA
Immediately after Onset [*Medicine*] .... IAO
Immediately after Passing [*Aviation*] .... IMAP
Immediately Report .... IMREP
Immersion .... IMRS
Immigrant Inspector [*Immigration and Naturalization Service*] II
Immigrants in the Labour Force [*British*] .... ILF
Immigration .... IMG
Immigration .... IMMIG
Immigration Appeal Board [*Canada*] .... IAB
Immigration History Society .... IHS
Immigration and Naturalization [*Service*] [*Department of Justice*] .... I & N
Immigration and Naturalization Service [*Department of Justice*] .... INS
Immigration Patrol Inspector [*Immigration and Naturalization Service*] .... IPI
Immission Rate Measuring Apparatus [*Analytical chemistry*] .... IRMA
Immobile Suspension Feeders on Soft Substrata [*Oceanography*] .... ISOSS
Immobilize [*Medicine*] .... IMMOB
Immobilized .... IMO
Immobilized Knee [*Orthopedics*] .... IK
Immokalee, FL [*Radio station call letters*] .... WIKX
Immokalee, FL [*Radio station call letters*] .... WKEM
Immortalis Dei Auspicio [*With the Help of God*] [*Latin*] .... IDA
Immune [*or Immunization*] .... IMM
Immune Adherence [*Immunology*] .... IA
Immune Adherence Hemagglutination [*Immunochemistry*] .... IAHA
Immune Body .... IB
Immune Complex [*Immunology*] IC
Immune Complex Disease .... ICD
Immune Electron Microscopy .... IEM
Immune Interferon [*Cell biology*] .... IIF
Immune Precipitate [*Immunology*] .... IP
Immune Region Associated Antigen [*Immunology*] .... Ia
Immune Response [*Also, Ir*] [*Genetics*] .... IR
Immune Serum [*Also, IS*] .... ImS
Immune Serum [*Also, ImS*] .... IS
Immune Serum Globulin .... ISG
Immunekoerper [*Immune Bodies*] [*Medicine*] .... IK
Immunex Corp. [*NASDAQ symbol*] .... IMNX
Immunitaet und Infektion [*A publication*] .... Immun Infekt
Immunitaetseinheit [*Immunizing Unit*] [*Medicine*] .... IE
Immunity .... IMMUN
Immunity Test .... IT
Immunization Against Leprosy Program [*World Health Organization*] .... IMMLEP
Immunization Rate .... IR
Immunizing Unit [*Medicine*] .... IU
Immuno Nuclear Corp. [*NASDAQ symbol*] .... INUC
Immuno-Suppression Method [*For increasing fertility*] .... IM
Immunochemistry [*A publication*] .... Immunochem
Immunocytochemistry ICC
Immunodeficiency [*Immunology*] .... ID
Immunodiffusion [*Immunology*] .... ID
Immunodiffusion Procedure [*Immunochemistry*] .... IDP
Immunoelectroadsorption [*Analytical biochemistry*] .... IEA
Immunoelectroosmophoresis [*Analytical biochemistry*] .... IEOP
Immunoelectrophoresis [*Analytical biochemistry*] .... IE
Immunoelectrophoresis [*Analytical biochemistry*] .... IEP
Immunofixation [*Analytical biochemistry*] .... IMF
Immunofluorescence [*Immunochemistry*] .... IF
Immunofluorescence Assay [*Analytical biochemistry*] .... IFA
Immunofluorescent Antibody [*Immunochemistry*] .... IFA
Immunogenetics [*A publication*] .... Immunogenet
ImmunoGenetics, Inc. [*NASDAQ symbol*] .... IGEN
Immunoglobulin [*Immunology*] .... Ig
Immunoglobulin A [*Immunology*] .... IgA
Immunoglobulin A Immune Complex [*Immunochemistry*] .... IgAIC
Immunoglobulin A Nephropathy [*Nephrology*] .... IgAN
Immunoglobulin D [*Immunology*] .... IgD
Immunoglobulin E [*Immunology*] .... IgE
Immunoglobulin G [*Immunology*] .... IgG
Immunoglobulin G Immune Complex [*Immunochemistry*] .... IgGIC
Immunoglobulin M Immune Complex [*Immunochemistry*] .... IgMIC
Immunoglobulin Macro [*Also known as RF*] [*Immunology*] .... IgM
Immunoglobulin ND [*Immunology, provisional class*] .... IgND
Immunohematology .... IMMUNHMTLGY
Immunological Communications [*A publication*] .... Immunol Com
Immunological Communications [*A publication*] .... Immunol Commun
Immunological Distance [*in primate phylogeny*] .... ID
Immunological Distance Unit [*Genetics*] .... IDU
Immunological Reviews [*A publication*] .... Immunol Rev
Immunologically Mediated Disease [*Medicine*] .... IMD
Immunology .... IMMUNOL
Immunology Letters [*A publication*] .... Immunol Lett
Immunomedics, Inc. Uts [*NASDAQ symbol*] .... IMMUU
Immunoradiometric Assay [*Immunology*] .... IRMA
Immunoreactive .... IR
Immunoreactive Bovine Serum Albumin [*Immunochemistry*] .... IBSA
Immunoreactive Calcitonin [*Endocrinology*] .... ICT
Immunoreactive Glucagon [*Immunochemistry*] .... IRG
Immunoreactive Glucagon [*Immunochemistry*] .... IRGI
Immunoreactive Growth Hormone [*Immunology*] .... IRGH
Immunoreactive Insulin .... IRI
Immunoreactive Parathyroid Hormone [*Endocrinology*] .... IPTH
Immunoreactive Proinsulin [*Immunochemistry*] .... IRP
Immunoreactive Secretin [*Endocrinology*] .... IRS
Immunoregulatory alpha-Globulin [*Immunology*] .... IRA
Immunosuppressive [*Immunochemistry*] .... IS
Imonda [*Papua New Guinea*] [*Airport symbol*] .... IMD
Imono (Journal of the Japan Foundrymen's Society) [*A publication*] .... Imono (J Japan Foundrymen's Soc)
Impact .... IMP
Impact Agricultural Research in Texas. Annual Report [*A publication*] .... Impact Agric Res Tex Annu Rep
Impact Assessment Sheet .... IAS
Impact Energy Density .... IED
Impact Energy, Inc. [*NASDAQ symbol*] .... IMPT
Impact Excited Transmitter .... IET
Impact Force Measuring System .... IFMS
Impact Hand Tool .... IHT
Impact Ionization Avalanche Transit Time [*Solid state diodes*] [*Transistor technology*] .... IMPATT
Impact Ionization Diode .... IID
Impact Isolation Class [*Noise rating of insulation*] IIC
Impact Limit Lines ILL
Impact Mechanical Fuze .... IMF
Impact Noise Rating [*Of insulation*] .... INR
Impact Point .... IP
Impact Prediction Data .... IPD
Impact Prediction Point [*NASA*] .... IPP
Impact Predictor [*NASA*] .... IMP
Impact Predictor [*NASA*] .... IP
Impact Predictor Monitor Set [*NASA*] .... IPMS
Impact Predictor System [*NASA*] .... IPS
Impact Prognosticator [*Aerospace*] .... IP
Impact of Science on Society [*A publication*] .... Impact Sci
Impact of Science on Society [*A publication*] .... Impact Sci Soc

Impact of Science on Society [*A publication*] ... Imp Sci Soc
Impact Short Delay Fuze ... ISDF
Impact Warning System ... IWS
Impaction [*Dentistry*] ... IMPX
Impaired ... IMP
Impedance ... IMP
Impedance [*Electricity*] ... IMPD
Impedance [*Symbol*] [*IUPAC*] ... Z
Impedance Angle ... IA
Impedance Matching Attenuator ... IMA
Impedance Matching Unit ... IMU
Impedance Measuring Devices [*JETDS nomenclature*] [*Military*] ... ZM
Impedance Pneumograph [*Apollo*] [*NASA*] ... ZPN
Impedance Probe ... IP
Impedance Unit ... IU
Impeded Harmonic Operation ... IHO
Impedor ... IMPR
Impell Corp. [*NASDAQ symbol*] ... IMPL
Impeller ... IMP
Impeller [*Mechanical engineering*] ... IMPLR
Imperative ... IMP
Imperative ... IMPER
Imperator [*or Imperatrix*] [*Emperor or Empress*] [*Latin*] ... I
Imperator [*or Imperatrix*] [*Emperor or Empress*] [*Latin*] ... IMP
Imperator Napoleon Rex Italiae [*Emperor Napoleon, King of Italy*] [*Latin*] ... INRI
Imperatrix [*Empress*] [*Latin*] ... IMPX
Imperatriz [*Brazil*] [*Airport symbol*] ... IMP
Imperfect ... IMP
Imperfect ... IMPER
Imperfect ... IMPERF
Imperfect ... IMPF
Imperforate [*Philology*] ... IMPERF
Imperial ... I
Imperial ... IMP
Imperial ... IMPRL
Imperial Airlines [*Imperial, CA*] [*FAA designator*] ... IMP
Imperial Airways, Inc. [*St. Paul, MN*] [*FAA designator*] ... PNX
Imperial Airways Limited [*British*] ... IAL
Imperial Ballet of Canada, Ottawa, ON, Canada [*Library symbol*] ... CaOOIB
Imperial Bancorp [*NASDAQ symbol*] ... IBAN
Imperial Beach, CA [*Location identifier*] [*FAA*] ... NRS
Imperial, CA [*Radio station call letters*] ... KOZN
Imperial Cancer Research Fund [*British*] ... ICRF
Imperial Cancer Research Fund 159 [*Razoxane*] [*Antineoplastic drug*] ... ICRF 159
Imperial Chemical Industries [*American Stock Exchange symbol*] ... IMP
Imperial Chemical Industries [*Great Britain*] [*Research code symbol*] ... M
Imperial Chemical Industries [*British*] ... UCI
Imperial Chemical Industries of Australia and New Zealand Ltd. ... ICIANZ
Imperial Chemical Industries plc ADR [*NYSE symbol*] ... ICI
Imperial College of Science [*British*] ... ICS
Imperial Communications [*World War II*] ... ICC
Imperial Corporation of America [*NYSE symbol*] ... ICA
Imperial Council of the Ancient Arabic Order of the Nobles of the Mystic Shrine for North America ... AAONMS
Imperial County Free Library, El Centro, CA [*Library symbol*] ... CEcl
Imperial Court, Daughters of Isis ... ICDI
Imperial Defence College [*British*] ... IDC
Imperial Earthquake Investigation Committee. Bulletin [*A publication*] ... Imp Earthquake Investigation Com B
Imperial Ethiopian Air Force ... IEAF
Imperial Ethiopian Government ... IEG
Imperial Ethiopian Government Institute of Agricultural Research. Report [*A publication*] ... Imp Ethiop Gov Inst Agric Res Rep
Imperial and Foreign Money Orders ... IFMO
Imperial Gallon ... IG
Imperial Gallons per Minute ... IGPM
Imperial General Staff ... IGS
Imperial German Military Collector's Association ... IGMCA
Imperial Glass Collectors Society ... IGCS
Imperial Group Ltd. ... IMPG
Imperial Group Ltd. [*American Stock Exchange symbol*] ... IMT
Imperial Industries, Incorporated [*American Stock Exchange symbol*] ... III
Imperial Industries, Incorporated Pfd [*NASDAQ symbol*] ... IIIP
Imperial Institute of Entomology [*British*] ... IIE
Imperial Iranian Air Force ... IIAF
Imperial Iranian Ground Forces ... IIGF
Imperial Japanese Army [*World War II*] ... IJA
Imperial Japanese Navy [*World War II*] ... IJN
Imperial Measure ... IM
[*The*] **Imperial Merchant Service Guild** [*British*] ... MSG
Imperial Metal Industries Ltd. [*British*] ... IMI
Imperial Military Nursing Service [*British*] ... IMNS
Imperial Oil Enterprises Ltd., Engineering Division, Sarnia, ON, Canada [*Library symbol*] [*Obsolete*] ... CaOSIE
Imperial Oil Enterprises Ltd., Sarnia, ON, Canada [*Library symbol*] ... CaOSI
Imperial Oil Ltd. [*American Stock Exchange symbol*] ... IMO
Imperial Oil Ltd., Calgary, AB, Canada [*Library symbol*] ... CaACI
Imperial Oil Ltd., Toronto, ON, Canada [*Library symbol*] ... CaOTIOL
Imperial Oil Review [*A publication*] ... Imp Oil R
Imperial Order of the Crown of India ... CI
Imperial Order of Daughters of the Empire [*Canada*] ... IODE
Imperial Order of the Dragon ... IOD
Imperial Owners Club, International ... IOC
Imperial Pale Ale ... IPA
Imperial Public Library, Imperial, CA [*Library symbol*] ... CImp
Imperial Service College [*British*] ... ISC
Imperial Service Medal [*British*] ... ISM
Imperial Service Order [*British*] ... ISO
Imperial Smelting Furnace [*Zinc and lead*] ... ISF
Imperial Smelting Process ... ISP
Imperial Society of Teachers of Dancing ... ISTD
Imperial Standard Gallon ... ISG
Imperial Standard Wire Gauge ... ISWG
Imperial Tobacco Co. of Canada Ltd., Montreal, PQ, Canada [*Library symbol*] ... CaQMIT
Imperial Tobacco Co. of Canada Ltd., Research Library, Montreal, PQ, Canada [*Library symbol*] ... CaQMITR
Imperial Tobacco Company [*of Great Britain and Ireland*] **Ltd.** ... ITC
Imperial Valley College [*California*] ... IVC
Imperial Valley College, Imperial, CA [*OCLC symbol*] ... IVX
Imperial Valley Dune Buggy Association ... IVDBA
Imperial War Graves Commission [*British*] ... IWGC
Imperial War Museum [*England*] ... IWM
Imperial Yeomanry [*British*] ... IY
Imperium [*Empire*] [*Latin*] ... IMP
Impersonal ... IMP
Impersonal ... IMPERS
Impersonating [*FBI standardized term*] ... IMP
Impfondo [*Congo*] [*Airport symbol*] ... ION
Imphal [*India*] [*Airport symbol*] ... IMF
Impingement [*Engineering*] ... IGMT
Impingement Point ... IP
Implantable Artificial Heart ... IAH
Implantable Artificial Heart Energy System ... IAHES
Implantable Beacon Transmitter [*Oceanography*] ... IBT
Implantation Doping Technique ... IDT
Implanted Electrode Technique ... IET
Implanted Zener Diode ... IZD
Implement ... IMP
Implement ... IMPL
Implement and Tractor [*A publication*] ... Imp & Tractr
Implementation of Change ... IC
Implementation and Conversion ... IC
Implementation Instructions ... II
Implementation of Plan ... IP
Implementation Planning and Control Technique [*Data processing*] ... IMPACT
Implementation Support Package [*Army*] ... ISP
Implementing Agency ... IA
Implicit Continuous-Fluid Eulerian ... ICE
Implosive Therapy [*Type of behavior therapy*] ... IT
Import Cargo Electronic System ... ICES
Import Certificate Delivery Verification [*Military*] ... ICDV
Import Entitlement Agreement [*Special type of currency*] [*United Arab Republic*] ... IEA
Import Executive [*British*] ... IE
Import License ... I/L
Importance ... IMPCE
Importance Factor [*Statistics*] ... IF
Important ... IMP
Important ... IMPT
Important Risk Data Notice [*Insurance*] ... IRDN
Imported ... IMP
Imported Crude Oil Processing ... ICOP
Imported Food Regulations [*British*] ... IFR
Impose ... IMPS
Impossible Mission Force [*Fictitious group of undercover agents in TV series, "Mission: Impossible"*] ... IMF
Imposta sul Valore Aggiunto [*Value-Added Tax*] [*Italy*] ... IVA
Impotence Institute of America ... IIA
Impotent Grain Boundary Dislocation ... IGBD
Impotents Anonymous ... IA
Impoverished Conditions ... IC
Impracticable ... IMP
Impractical ... IMPR
Impregnate ... IMPG
Impregnate ... IMPRG
Impression ... IMP
Impression ... IMPRSN
Impressions per Hour [*Printing*] ... IPH
Imprest Fund ... IF
Imprimatur [*Let It Be Printed*] [*Latin*] ... IMP
Imprimerie et Industries Graphiques [*A publication*] ... Imprim Ind Graphiques
Imprint ... IMP
Improper Order ... IMO
Improper Use of Adjective [*Used in correcting manuscripts, etc.*] ... ADJ
Improper Use of Adverb [*Used in correcting manuscripts, etc.*] ... ADV
Improve ... IPV
Improved ... IMP

Improved ... IMPR
Improved Accuracy Program ... IAP
Improved Aerial Refueling System Program ... IARS
Improved Anode Catalyst ... IAC
Improved Antimateriel Warhead ... IAMW
Improved Antimateriel Warhead ... IAMWH
Improved Antimateriel Warhead ... IAW
Improved Antimateriel Warhead ... IAWH
Improved Benevolent Protective Order of Elks of the World ... IBPOEW
Improved Capability [*for aircraft*] ... ICAP
Improved Capability Missile [*Air Force*] ... ICM
Improved Capability Missile [*Air Force*] ... IMPCM
Improved Cobra Agility and Maneuverability [*Military*] ... ICAM
Improved Cobra Armament Program [*Military*] ... ICAP
Improved Combustion ... IMCO
Improved Continuous-Wave Acquisition RADAR [*Army*] ... ICWAR
Improved Conventional Munitions ... ICM
Improved Cost Estimate ... ICE
Improved-Cycle Boiling-Water Reactor [*Nuclear energy*] ... ICBWR
Improved Data Display System ... IDDS
Improved Data Effectiveness and Availability ... IDEA
Improved Data Interchange ... IDI
Improved Doppler Tracking System ... IDTS
Improved Effectiveness Nuclear Depth Bomb ... IMPEND
Improved Emergency Message Automatic Transmission System ... IEMATS
Improved Fiber Optics ... IFO
Improved Fiber Optics Bundle ... IFOB
Improved Fleet Ballistic Missile ... IFBM
Improved Flotation Chamber ... IFC
Improved Gray Scale ... IGS
Improved Guidance and Control ... IMPGAC
Improved HAWK [*Homing All the Way Killer*] **Simulator** [*Military*] ... IHS
Improved High-Speed Bombing RADAR ... IHSBR
Improved Holographic Image ... IHI
Improved Homing All the Way Killer [*Missile*] ... IHAWK
Improved Infrared Missile ... IIRM
Improved Infrared Source ... IIS
Improved Life Blower Bearing ... ILBB
Improved Light Antitank Weapon ... I-LAW
Improved Lighting System for Army Aircraft ... ILSAA
Improved Main Rotor Blade ... IMRB
Improved Maintenance Program [*Air Force*] ... IMP
Improved Management Procurement and Contracting Technique ... IMPACT
Improved Manned Interceptor [*Proposed plane*] [*Air Force*] ... IMI
Improved Manpower Production and Controller Technique [*Navy*] ... IMPACT
Improved Minimum Essential Medium [*Microbiology*] ... IMEM
Improved Mobile Telephone Service ... IMTS
Improved Mobility Package [*Wheelchair system*] ... IMP
Improved Navigational Satellite ... INS
Improved Night Sight ... INS
Improved Nike Hercules [*Missile*] ... INH
Improved Order of Red Men ... IORM
Improved Point Defense ... IPD
Improved Point Defense Surface Missile System ... IPDSMS
Improved Processing System ... IPS
Improved Programer Test Station ... IMPTS
Improved Programing Technologies ... IPT
Improved Pulse Acquisition RADAR ... IPAR
Improved Rearming Rate Program [*Military*] ... IRRP
Improved Rearming Rates [*Military*] ... IRR
Improved Reliability and Maintainability ... IRAM
Improved Replenishment-at-Sea Program ... IRP
Improved Risk Mutuals ... IRM
Improved Rotor Blade [*Rotorcraft*] ... IRB
Improved Saturn Launch Facility ... ISLF
Improved Sensing Munitions ... ISM
Improved Spartan Homing Sensor [*Missiles*] ... ISHS
Improved Stratospheric and Mesospheric Sounder ... ISAMS
Improved Symbolic Optimizing Assembly Routine ... ISOPAR
Improved Tartar ... IT
Improved Tartar Retrofit [*Missile*] ... ITR
Improved Third Stage [*of Minuteman rocket*] ... ITS
Improved TIROS [*Television Infrared Observation Satellite*] **Operational Satellite** [*National Oceanic and Atmospheric Administration*] ... ITOS
Improved TOW [*Tube-Launched, Optically-Tracked, Wire-Guided (Weapon)*] **Vehicle** ... ITV
Improved Transtage Injector Program ... ITIP
Improved Tube-Launched, Optically-Tracked, Wire-Guided (Weapon) ... ITOW
Improved Virtual Orbitals [*Atomic physics*] ... IVO
Improved Visible Marker ... IVM
Improved Water Analysis Kit ... IWAK
Improvement ... IMPROV
Improvement ... IMPRV
Improvement ... IMPRVMT
Improvement and Betterments ... I & B
Improvement Data Plan ... IDP
Improvement Data Plan Sheet ... IDPS
Improvement Data System ... IDS
Improvement Maintenance Program ... IMP
Improvement and Modernization ... I & M
Improvement Program ... IP
Improving College and University Teaching [*A publication*] ... ICUT
Improving College and University Teaching [*A publication*] ... Improv Coll & Univ Teach
Improving College and University Teaching [*A publication*] ... Improv Coll Univ Teach
Improving College and University Teaching [*A publication*] ... Improving Coll & Univ Teach
Improving the Definition of the Objective Force [*Military*] ... IDOFOR
Improving Human Performance [*A publication*] ... Impr Hum P
Improving Management Performance ... IMP
Improvised Explosive Device ... IED
Improvised Nuclear Device ... IND
Impulse ... IMP
Impulse ... IMPL
Impulse ... IMPLS
Impulse Balance System ... IBS
Impulse Bandwidth ... IBW
Impulse Base Flow Facility [*NASA*] ... IBFF
Impulse Conducting System [*Physiology*] ... ICS
Impulse Conductor ... IC
Impulse Duplexer Study ... IDS
Impulse Fast Reactor [*USSR*] ... IFR
Impulse Generator ... IMP
Impulse Modulation ... IM
Impulse P Wave [*Earthquakes*] [*Exclamation point signifies a very sharp earthquake*] ... iP!
Impulse Resistance Bridge ... IRB
Impulse Response Area Ratio ... IRAR
Impulse Sequencing Relay ... ISR
Impulse, Specific ... ISP
Impulse Transfer Function ... ITF
Impulse Transfer Orbit ... ITO
Impulses per Minute ... IPM
Impul'snaya Fotometriya [*A publication*] ... Impul'snaya Fotom
Impulstechniken [*A publication*] ... Impulstech
Impurity Study Experiment [*Oak Ridge National Laboratory*] ... ISX
IMR, Industrial Management Review [*A publication*] ... IMR Ind Manage Rev
Imre' Corp. Uts [*NASDAQ symbol*] ... IMREU
IMS [*Industrial Management Society*] **Clinical Proceedings** [*A publication*] ... IMS Clin Proc
IMS International [*NASDAQ symbol*] ... IMSI
In Absentia [*In Absence*] [*Latin*] ... IA
In Accordance With ... IAW
In Addition to Other Duties [*Military*] ... IAOD
In Addition to Other Duties [*Military*] ... IATOD
In Amenas [*Algeria*] [*Airport symbol*] ... IAM
In Amguel [*Issek Toufreg*] [*Algeria*] [*Seismograph station code, US Geological Survey*] [*Closed*] ... IAA
In Auri [*To the Ear*] [*Pharmacy*] ... IN AUR
In Bond [*Wines and Spirits*] ... IB
In Bono [*In Good Order*] ... INB
In the Business [*Refers to television and film industries*] ... ITB
In Case Of ... ICO
In Charge Of ... IC
In Christi Nomine [*In the Name of Christ*] [*Latin*] ... ICN
In Christo [*In Christ*] [*Latin*] ... IX
In-Circuit Emulator ... ICE
In Cloud [*Aviation*] ... INC
In-Commission ... IC
In Commission, In Reserve [*Vessel status*] [*Navy*] ... ICIR
In-Commission Rate ... ICR
In Compliance With ... ICW
In Connection With ... ICW
In-Core Shim Assembly [*Nuclear energy*] ... ICSA
In-Core Test Facility [*Nuclear energy*] ... INCOT
In-Core Thermionic Reactor ... ITR
In Dei Nomine [*In God's Name*] [*Latin*] ... IDN
In Dies [*Daily*] [*Pharmacy*] ... IN D
In the Ear [*Hearing aid*] ... ITE
In Excess ... IE
In Fine [*Finally*] [*Latin*] ... IN F
In Flagrante Delicto [*Caught in the Act*] [*Latin*] ... IFD
In-Flight ... IF
In-Flight Abort ... IFA
In-Flight Aeromedical Evacuation Team ... IAET
In-Flight Analysis ... IFA
In-Flight Calibration ... IFC
In-Flight Checkout System ... IFCS
In-Flight Coverall Garment [*Apollo*] [*NASA*] ... ICG
In-Flight Deployment ... IFD
In-Flight Diverted Force ... IDF
In-Flight Emergency ... IFE
In-Flight Experiments Panel ... IFEP
In-Flight Helium ... IFH
In-Flight Helmet Stowage Bag ... IHSB
In-Flight Insertion ... IFI

In-Flight Maintenance ... IFM
In-Flight Management System ... IFMS
In-Flight Management System ... IMS
In-Flight Medical Support System [*Skylab*] [*NASA*] ... IMSS
In-Flight Operable Bomb Rack Lock ... IFOBRL
In-Flight Operational Evaluation of a Space System ... INFOES
In-Flight Operations and Training ... IFOT
In-Flight Performance ... IFP
In-Flight Performance Monitor ... IFPM
In-Flight Refueling ... IFR
In-Flight Replaceable Unit ... IFRU
In-Flight Safety ... IFS
In-Flight Safety Inhibit Test ... IFSIT
In-Flight Test [*Air Force*] ... IFT
In-Flight Test and Maintenance ... IFTM
In-Flight Test System ... IFTS
In-Flight Thrust Augmentation ... IFTA
In-Flight Training Aid ... IFTA
In Folio Argenti Volvendae [*To Be Silvered*] [*Pharmacy*] ... IN FOL ARG VOLVEND
In Forma Pauperis [*As a Pauper*] [*Latin*] ... IFP
In Full ... IF
In-Ground Effect [*Aviation*] ... IGE
In Hands of Civil Authorities [*Military*] ... IHCA
In His Name ... IHN
In Hoc Signo [*By This Sign*] [*Latin*] ... IHS
In Home [*Men's lacrosse position*] ... IH
In-House ... IH
In-House Laboratories Independent Research Program [*Army*] ... ILIR
In-House Laboratory Independent Research ... ILIR
In Ladestreifen [*Loaded in Clips*] [*German military - World War II*] ... IL
In-Law ... I-L
In Liebe Vereint bis in dem Tod [*United in Love until Death*] [*German*] ... ILVBIDT
In Lieu Of ... ILO
In Lieu Of ... INLO
In Lieu Thereof [*Military*] ... ILT
In Lieu of Until Exhausted [*Military*] ... ILOUE
In Limine [*At the Outset*] [*Latin*] ... IN LIM
In-Line Instrument Package [*Nuclear energy*] ... ILIP
In-Line Integrated Circuit ... ILIC
In-Line Needle Valve ... INV
In-Line Printer ... ILP
In-Line Reciprocator ... ILR
In-Line Relief Valve ... ILRV
In Litteris [*In Correspondence*] [*Latin*] ... IN LITT
In-Lock ... IL
In-Lock Detector ... ILD
In Loco [*In the Place Of*] [*Latin*] ... IN LOC
In Maintenance ... IM
In Nomine Christi [*In the Name of Christ*] [*Latin*] ... INC
In Nomine Dei [*In the Name of God*] [*Latin*] ... IND
In Nomine Iesu [*In the Name of Jesus*] [*Latin*] ... INI
In Nomine Jesu [*In the Name of Jesus*] [*Latin*] ... INJ
In Nomine Sanctae Trinitatis [*In the Name of the Holy Trinity*] [*Latin*] ... INST
In-Orbit Plane ... IOP
In Order ... IO
In Other Words ... IOW
In Our Culture ... IOC
In Our Own Way [*An association*] ... IOOW
In and Out [*of clouds*] [*Aviation*] ... IAO
In-Out Converter ... IOC
In and Out Processing ... I & OP
In the Overcast [*Aviation*] ... IOVC
In Pace [*In Peace*] [*Latin*] ... INP
In Partibus Infidelium [*In the Countries, Lands, or Regions of Unbelievers*] [*Latin*] ... IPI
In Phase/Quadrature ... I/Q
In Place [*Dancing*] ... IP
In-Place Repair ... IPR
In-Place Repairable Assembly ... IPRA
In-Plant Powder Metallurgy Association ... IPPMA
In-Plant Printing Management Association ... IPMA
In-Plant Printing Management Association ... IPPMA
In-Plant Test ... IPT
In Port [*Navy*] ... INPT
In Port [*Navy*] ... IPT
In-Port Damage Control Training [*Navy*] ... DCLPT
In Practice [*A publication*] ... In Pract
In Praesentia Dominorum [*In the Presence of the Lords of Session*] [*Latin*] ... IPD
In Principio [*In the Beginning*] ... IN PR
In Process ... IP
In-Process Factor ... IPF
In-Process Quality Control ... IPQC
In-Process Review ... IPR
In-Process Self Test ... IPST
In Progress ... INPR
In Progress ... I/P
In Pulmento [*In Gruel*] [*Pharmacy*] ... IN PULM
In Reference To ... IN REF
In Reference To ... IRT
In Regard To ... IN RE
In Regard To ... IRT
In Reply To ... IRT
In Response To ... IRT
In Review. Canadian Books for Young People [*A publication*] ... In Rev
In Salah [*Algeria*] [*Airport symbol*] ... INZ
In-Service Engineering [*Navy*] ... ISE
In Service, In Reserve [*Vessel status*] [*Navy*] ... ISIR
In-Service Inspection ... ISI
In-Service Institute [*National Science Foundation*] ... ISI
In Situ [*In Place*] [*Latin*] ... IS
In Situ. Oil-Coal-Shale-Minerals [*A publication*] ... In Situ Oil Coal Shale Miner
In Status Quo ... ISQ
In-Store Promotions [*Marketing events for US goods held by retail establishments in foreign countries*] [*Department of Commerce*] ... ISP
In-Suit Drink Bag [*Aerospace*] ... IDB
In-Tank Solidification ... ITS
In Theory Only [*A publication*] ... INTGA
In These Times [*A publication*] ... ITT
In Touch Networks ... ITN
In-Track Contiguous ... ITC
In-Track Noncontiguous ... ITNC
In Transit ... INTNS
In-Transit Rendezvous ... ITR
In Transitu [*In Transit*] [*Latin*] ... IT
In Utero [*Gynecology*] ... IU
In Verbo [*Under the Word*] [*Latin*] ... IV
In-Vessel Handling Machine [*Nuclear energy*] ... IVHM
In-Vessel Handling Machine-Engineering Model [*Nuclear energy*] ... IVHM-EM
In-Vessel Storage [*Nuclear energy*] ... IVS
In-Vessel Storage Module [*Nuclear energy*] ... IVSM
In the Vicinity Of ... INVOF
In Visual Flight Rules Conditions ... IVFRC
In Vitro Fertilization [*Gynecology*] ... IVF
In Vitro Monograph [*A publication*] ... In Vitro Monogr
In Vitro Protein Digestibility [*Nutrition*] ... IVPD
In Vitro Rumen Digestibility [*Nutrition*] ... IVRD
INA Corp. [*NYSE symbol*] [*Delisted*] ... INA
INA Investment Securities, Inc. [*NYSE symbol*] ... IIS
Inactivated Fetal-Calf Serum [*Immunology*] ... IFS
Inactivated Horse Serum [*Immunology*] ... IHS
Inactivated Poliovirus Vaccine ... IPV
Inactivator Accelerator [*Immunology*] ... INA
Inactive [*Chemistry*] ... i
Inactive ... INACT
Inactive ... INACTV
Inactive Air Reserve ... IAR
Inactive Duty Training [*Military*] ... IDT
Inactive Duty Training [*Air Force*] ... INACDUTRA
Inactive Fleet, Atlantic Fleet ... INACTLANT
Inactive Fleet, Pacific Fleet ... INACTFLTPAC
Inactive Fleet, Pacific Fleet ... INACTPAC
Inactive - In Commission, In Reserve [*Vessel status*] [*Navy*] ... INA/IC
Inactive - In Service, In Reserve [*Vessel status*] [*Navy*] ... INA/IS
Inactive Materiel Request History and Status File [*Army*] ... IMRHS
Inactive National Guard ... ING
Inactive Nondisability Retirement Branch [*BUPERS*] ... INDRB
Inactive - Out of Commission, In Reserve [*Vessel status*] [*Navy*] ... INA/OC
Inactive - Out of Service, In Reserve [*Vessel status*] [*Navy*] ... INA/OS
Inactive Reserve Officer Status Branch [*BUPERS*] ... IROSB
Inactive Reserve Section [*Military*] ... IRS
Inactive Ship Maintenance Facility [*Navy*] ... INACTSHIPFAC
Inactive Ship Maintenance Facility ... ISMF
Inactive Ship Supply Overhaul Team ... ISSOT
Inactive Ships Navy Custody ... ISNAC
Inactive Status List ... ISL
Inactive Status List Reserve Section ... ISLRS
Inadequate ... INAD
Inadequate Core Cooling [*Requirements*] [*Nuclear energy*] ... ICC
Inadvertent ... INAD
Inadvertent Destruct [*Aerospace*] ... IDS
Inadvertent Ignition Panel ... IIP
Inadvertent Missile Ignition Detection ... IMID
Inadvertent Modification of the Stratosphere [*Interagency government task force*] ... IMOS
Inadvertent Separation and Destruct System [*Aerospace*] ... ISDS
Inagua [*Bahamas*] [*Airport symbol*] ... IGA
Inanities per Page [*Facetious criterion for determining insignificance of Supreme Court Justices*] [*Proposed by University of Chicago professor David P. Currie*] ... IPP
Inappropriate Gonadotrophin Secretion [*Endocrinology*] ... IGS
Inarco Corp. [*American Stock Exchange symbol*] [*Delisted*] ... IAC
Inboard ... INBD
Inboard Booster Engine Cutoff ... IBECO
Inboard Engine Cutoff ... IECO
Inboard Rotating Shield ... IRS
Inborn Error of Metabolism [*Medicine*] ... IEM

Inbound ... IB
Inbound ... IBND
Inbound ... INBD
Inbound/Outbound Traffic Analysis [*Military*] ... IOTA
Inbound Radial [*Aviation*] ... IRAD
Inbred Livestock Registry Association ... ILRA
Inca-Fiej Research Association ... IFRA
Inca Resources [*NASDAQ symbol*] ... INCRF
Incan Superior Ltd. [*AAR code*] ... NCAN
Incandescent ... INCAND
Incandescent ... INCD
Incandescent Lamp Manufacturers Association [*Defunct*] ... ILMA
Incapacitated Emergency Egress Practice [*NASA*] ... IEEP
Incarnate Word College [*Texas*] ... IWC
Incarnate Word College, San Antonio, TX [*Library symbol*] ... TxSaI
Incendiary [*Bomb*] ... I
Incendiary ... INC
Incendiary ... INCD
Incendiary ... INCND
Incendiary Bomb ... IB
Incendiary Bomb with Explosive Nose ... IBEN
Incendiary Fragmentation Bomb ... IFB
Incendiary Munitions Evaluation ... IME
Incentive Awards Program [*of the federal government, administered by CSC*] ... IAP
Incentive Compensation ... IC
Incentive Compensation Plan ... ICP
Incentive Cost Plus Fixed Fee [*Contracts*] ... ICPFF
Incentive Manufacturers Representatives Association [*Formerly, NPMR*] ... IMRA
Incentive Pay ... IP
Incentive PERT [*Program Evaluation and Review Technique*] **Events** ... IPE
Incentive Stock Option ... ISO
Inception-to-Date ... ITD
Incertae Sedis [*Uncertain Position*] [*Biology, taxonomy*] ... inc sed
Inch ... IN
Inch-Pound ... IN-LB
Inch Trim Moment [*Nautical*] ... ITM
Inches ... INS
Inches per Hour ... IN/H
Inches per Minute ... IPM
Inches per Revolution ... IPR
Inches per Second ... IN/S
Inches per Second ... IPS
Inches per Year ... IPY
Inchon [*Tyosen, Zinsen*] [*South Korea*] [*Seismograph station code, US Geological Survey*] [*Closed*] ... INC
Incide [*Cut*] [*Pharmacy*] ... INCID
Incident ... ICDT
Incident ... INCDT
Incident Report [*Military*] ... INCREP
Incident Report ... IR
Incident at Sea [*Navy*] ... INCSEA
Incident-Shock Equilibrium Expansion ... ISEE
Incident-Shock Frozen Expansion ... ISFE
Incidental Amplitude Modulation ... IAM
Incidental Phase [*or Pulse*] **Modulation** ... IPM
Incinerator ... INC
Incinerator ... INCIN
Incinerator Institute of America [*Later, NSWMA*] ... IIA
Incipient Fire Detection ... IFD
Incipient Heavies [*Slang for rising young bureaucrats in the foreign policy field*] ... IH
Incipient Lethal Concentration ... ILC
Incipient Nonequilibrium Index ... INI
Incisal Mandibular Plane Angle [*Dentistry*] ... IMPA
Incision and Drainage [*Medicine*] ... I & D
Incisolabial [*Dentistry*] ... ILa
Incisolingual [*Dentistry*] ... IL
Incisoproximal [*Dentistry*] ... IP
Incisopulpal [*Dentistry*] ... IP
Incisor (Deciduous) [*Dentistry*] ... i
Incisor (Permanent) [*Dentistry*] ... I
Incisors, Canines, Premolars, Molars [*Dentistry*] ... ICPMM
Inclinable Indexing Table ... IIT
Inclination ... I
Inclination [*Angular distance from equator in degrees*] ... INCL
Inclination of a Plane to the Plane of the Earth's Equator [*Aerospace*] ... IPEE
Incline Village, NV [*Radio station call letters*] ... KLKT
Inclined ... INCLN
Inclined Bottom Tank [*Fermenter*] ... IBT
Inclined Cleated Belt Conveyor ... ICBC
Inclined Ladder ... IL
Inclosure ... INC
Inclosure ... INCL
Inclosure ... INCLS
Include Accounting Data ... CLUDACTDAT
Include This Headquarters Information Addressee [*Army*] ... IHIA
Including ... INC
Including ... INCL
Including [*Freight*] ... INCLD
Including Air ... INCAIR
Including Loading ... IL
Including Particular Average [*Insurance*] ... IPA
Including Sheeting ... IS
Inclusion ... INCLN
Inclusion Body [*Cytology*] ... IB
Inclusion Body [*Cytology*] ... IncB
Inclusion Disease [*Medicine*] ... ID
Inclusive ... INC
Inclusive ... INCL
Inclusive ... INCLV
Inclusive ... INCV
Inclusive Tour [*Airline fare*] ... IT
Inclusive Tour Charter ... ITC
INCO Ltd. [*Formerly, International Nickel Co. of Canada Ltd.*] [*NYSE symbol*] ... N
INCO Limited Wts [*NASDAQ symbol*] ... INLWF
Inco Vitro v CSSR [*A publication*] ... Inco Vitro
Incognito ... INCOG
Incoherent ... INCOH
Incoherent Electronic Oscillator ... IEO
INCOLSA [*Indiana Cooperative Library Services Authority*] **Processing Center, Indianapolis, IN** [*OCLC symbol*] ... ICP
Income [*Business and trade*] ... I
Income Capital Certificate ... ICC
Income & Capital Shares, Inc. [*NYSE symbol*] [*Delisted*] ... ICS
Income Maintenance Unit [*Work Incentive Program*] [*Department of Labor*] ... IMU
Income Not Paying Interest [*Standard & Poor's bond rating*] ... C
Income Tax Unit ... ITU
Income Tax Unit Rulings [*US Internal Revenue Service*] ... IT
Incoming ... INC
Incoming ... INCM
Incoming ... INCMG
Incoming Capital Property Record ... ICPR
Incoming Correspondence Log ... ICL
Incoming Data ... INDAT
Incoming Letter ... IL
Incoming Line ... ICL
Incoming Orders ... IO
Incoming Procurement Authorization Document [*Air Force*] ... IPAD
Incoming Replacement [*Army*] ... INREPL
Incoming Teletype ... ITT
Incoming Transaction Listing ... ITL
Incoming Trunk ... ICT
Incompatibility Newsletter [*A publication*] ... Incompat Newsl
Incompatible [*Medicine*] ... INCOMPAT
Incomplete ... I
Incomplete ... INC
Incomplete ... INCOM
Incomplete ... INCOMP
Incomplete ... INCOMPL
Incomplete Freund's Adjuvant ... IFA
Incomplete Sequence ... IS
Incomplete Task Log ... ITL
Incompressible Turbulent Boundary Layer ... ITBL
Inconclusive ... INC
Inconclusive ... INCL
Incontinent [*Medicine*] ... I
Incontinent [*Medicine*] ... INC
Incontri Linguistici [*A publication*] ... ILing
Incontri Linguistici [*A publication*] ... InLi
Incontri Musicali [*A publication*] ... IM
Incorporated ... INC
Incorporated ... INCD
Incorporated ... INCOR
Incorporated ... INCORP
Incorporated Accountant ... IA
Incorporated Church Building Society [*British*] ... ICBS
Incorporated Law Society [*British*] ... ILS
Incorporated Linguist [*London*] [*A publication*] ... IncL
Incorporated Linguist [*A publication*] ... Inc Linguist
Incorporated Society of London Fashion Designers ... ISLFD
Incorporated Staff Sight-Singing College [*London*] ... ISC
Incorporating Your Business [*A publication*] ... Incorp Bus
Incorporeal Personal Agency [*Parapsychology*] ... IPA
Incorrect ... INCOR
Incorrect Negative Expectancy [*Psychometrics*] ... INE
Incoterm Corp. [*American Stock Exchange symbol*] [*Delisted*] ... IO
INCRA [*International Copper Research Association, Inc.*] **Research Report** [*A publication*] ... INCRA Res Rep
Increase ... INC
Increase ... INCR
Increase Feedback ... IncFB
Increase in Life-Span ... ILS
Increase Reliability of Operational Systems ... IROS
Increase and Replacement of Armor, Armament, and Ammunition [*Naval budget appropriation title*] ... IRAA & A
Increase and Replacement of Construction and Machinery [*Naval budget appropriation title*] ... IRC & M

Increase and Replacement of Emergency Construction [*Ships*] [*Naval budget appropriation title*] .... IREC
Increase and Replacement of Naval Vessels [*Naval budget appropriation title*] .... IRNV
Increased Capacity Drum Feed System .... ICDFS
Increased Combat Effectiveness .... ICE
Increased Hazard Rate .... IHR
Increased Maneuverability Kit .... IMK
Increased Readiness Information System .... IRIS
Increased Take-Home Pay .... ITHP
Increased Value IV
Increasing Failure Rate .... IFR
Increasing Failure Rate Average [*Statistics*] .... IFRA
Increasing Hazard Rate Average .... IHRA
Increment .... INC
Increment .... INCR
Increment-Decrement Life Table [*Statistics*] .... IDLT
Increment and Skip on Zero [*Data processing*] .... ISZ
Incremental Analysis [*Statistics*] .... IA
Incremental Cost IC
Incremental Cost Effectiveness Model .... ICEM
Incremental Critical Design Review .... ICDR
Incremental Differential Pressure System .... IDPS
Incremental Digital Recorder .... IDR
Incremental Financial Rate of Return .... IFR
Incremental Frequency Control .... IFC
Incremental Growth Vehicle .... IGV
Incremental Life Support Operations .... ILSO
Incremental Microwave Power Spectrum Analyzer [*Air Force*] .... IPSA
Incremental Proof Testing .... IPT
Incremental Range Summary .... IRS
Incremental Stretch Forming .... ISF
Incremental System Programing Language [*Data processing*] .... ISPL
Incremental Tape Recorder .... ITR
Incremental Velocity Indicator [*NASA*] IVI
Incubation Period [*Medicine*] .... IP
Incubator .... INCBR
Incumbent .... INCUMB
Incumbent Come Home [*Political humor*] [*Pronounced "itch"*] .... ICH
Incurable [*Medicine*] .... INCUR
Incurred but Not Reported [*Insurance*] .... IBNR
INDA, Association of the Nonwoven Fabrics Industry [*Formerly, International Nonwovens and Disposables Association*] .... INDA
Indagationes Mathematicae [*A publication*] .... Indag Math
Indagen [*Papua New Guinea*] [*Airport symbol*] .... IDN
Indecent [*FBI standardized term*] .... IND
Indecent Displays (Control) Act [*British*] .... ID(C)A
Indeclinable [*Grammar*] .... INDECL
Indefinite .... INDEF
Indefinite Ceiling [*Meteorology*] .... W
Indefinite Delivery .... ID
Indefinite Delivery Type Contract [*DoD*] .... IDTC
Indefinite Operations .... INDEFOPS
Indefinite Quantity .... IQ
Indefinite Substitute Temporary Mail Handler [*US Postal Service employee classification*] .... ISTMH
Indent .... INDT
Indent Load Deflection [*Measure of hardness*] .... ILD
Indenture .... INDRE
Indenture Part List .... IDP
Indentured Drawing List .... IDL
Indentured Parts List .... IPL
Indentured Parts Price List .... IPPL
Independants, et Paysans d'Action Sociale [*Right-wing political party of independents and peasants*] [*France*] .... IPAS
Independence [*Belize*] [*Airport symbol*] .... INB
Independence Bancorp [*NASDAQ symbol*] .... INBC
Independence Bank Group [*NASDAQ symbol*] .... IBGI
Independence, CA [*Radio station call letters*] .... KESR
Independence Community Junior College, Independence, KS [*Library symbol*] .... KIJ
Independence Holding [*NASDAQ symbol*] .... INHO
Independence, IA [*Radio station call letters*] .... KOUR
Independence, IA [*Radio station call letters*] .... KOUR-FM
Independence, KS [*Location identifier*] [*FAA*] .... IDP
Independence, KS [*Radio station call letters*] .... KIND
Independence, KS [*Radio station call letters*] .... KIND-FM
Independence Medical Center, Independence, MO [*Library symbol*] .... MoIMC
Independence, MO [*Radio station call letters*] .... KCCV
Independence National Historical Park .... INDE
Independence National Historical Park, Philadelphia, PA [*Library symbol*] .... PPIn
Independence Plan for Neighborhood Councils [*An association*] .... IPNC
Independence Public Library, Independence, OR [*Library symbol*] .... OrI
Independence Sanitarium and Hospital, Independence, MO [*Library symbol*] .... MoIS
Independence Square Income Securities [*NASDAQ symbol*] .... ISIS
Independent I
Independent .... IND
Independent .... INDEP
Independent [*A publication*] .... IND
Independent [*A publication*] .... INDEP
Independent Action [*An association*] .... IA
Independent Activities Questionnaire [*Psychology*] .... IAQ
Independent Aeronautical Dealers Association [*Defunct*] .... IADA
Independent Agent [*A publication*] .... IndA
Independent Air Carriers Association [*Defunct*] .... IACA
Independent Airlines Association .... IAA
Independent Aluminum Residential Fabricators Association .... IARFA
Independent American Whiskey Association .... IAWA
Independent Americans .... IA
Independent Armored Car Operators Association .... IACOA
Independent Association of Publishers' Employees .... IAPE
Independent Association of Questioned Document Examiners .... IAQDE
Independent Association of Stocking Manufacturers [*Defunct*] .... IASM
Independent Automotive Damage Appraisers Association .... IADA
Independent Automotive Service Association .... IASA
Independent Aviation Operators .... IAO
Independent Bakers Association .... IBA
Independent Bakery Employees Union .... BEU
Independent Bakery Employees Union .... IBEU
Independent Bankers Association of America .... IBAA
Independent Bankshares, Incorporated [*NASDAQ symbol*] .... IBSI
Independent Bar Association .... IBA
Independent Battery Manufacturers Association .... IBMA
Independent Board Authority [*Board granting franchises to new companies*] [*British*] .... IBA
Independent Broadcast Institute [*British*] .... IBI
Independent Broadcasting Authority [*Formerly, ITA*] [*British*] .... IBA
Independent Carbon-Dioxide Manufacturers Association .... ICDMA
Independent Cash Register Dealers Association .... ICRDA
Independent Cinema Artists and Producers .... ICAP
Independent Citizens Committee of the Arts, Sciences, and Professions [*Created to support Franklin D. Roosevelt's fourth-term Presidential candidacy*] [*Initialism often shortened to ASP*] .... ICCASP
Independent Citizens Research Foundation for the Study of Degenerative Diseases .... ICRFSDD
Independent Cluster Emission Model [*Atomic physics*] .... ICEM
Independent Cold Extruders Institute .... ICEI
Independent College Assistance Center .... ICAC
Independent College Funds of America .... ICFA
Independent Community Consultants ICC
Independent Component Release [*Data processing*] .... ICR
Independent Computer Consultants Association .... ICCA
Independent Corps Tactical Operations Center .... ICTOC
Independent Cosmetic Manufacturers and Distributors .... ICMAD
Independent Cost Assessment .... ICA
Independent Cost Estimate .... ICE
Independent Curators, Incorporated ICI
Independent Data Communications Manufacturers Association .... IDCMA
Independent Dealer Committee Dedicated to Action .... IDCDA
Independent Deployable Unit Detachment .... IDUD
Independent Distributor [*Bookselling*] .... ID
Independent Division Tactical Operations Center [*Army*] .... IDTOC
Independent Double Sideband .... IDSB
Independent Education [*A publication*] .... Indep Ed
Independent Educational Counselors Association .... IECA
Independent Educational Services [*An association*] .... IES
Independent Electrical Contractors [*Formerly, AIECA*] .... IEC
Independent Electrical Manufacturers Association .... IEMA
Independent Electron Pair Approximation [*Physics*] .... IEPA
Independent Electronic Music Center [*Defunct*] .... IEMC
Independent European Program Group [*NATO*] .... IEPG
Independent Evaluation .... IE
Independent Evaluation Plan .... IEP
Independent Evaluation Report .... IER
Independent Exploratory Development [*Navy*] .... IED
Independent Fabric Retailers Association [*Defunct*] .... IFRA
Independent Family Schools Resource Center .... IFSRC
Independent Federation of Flight Attendants .... IFFA
Independent Film Importers and Distributors of America [*Defunct*] .... IFIDA
Independent Film Journal [*A publication*] .... Indep F J
Independent Film Producers Export Corporation [*Defunct*] .... IFPEC
Independent Fire Control [*Area*] .... IFC
Independent Fission Yield .... IFY
Independent Fluorspar Producers Association .... IFPA
Independent Forward Bloc [*Mauritian political party*] .... IFB
Independent Foundation .... IF
Independent Free Papers of America .... IFPA
Independent Fuel Oil Marketers of America [*Defunct*] .... IFOMA
Independent Fuel Terminal Operators' Association .... IFTOA
Independent Garage Owners of America [*Later, Automotive Service Councils*] .... IGOA
Independent Gasoline Marketers Council .... IGMC
Independent Government Cost Estimate [*Army*] .... IGCE
Independent Grocers Alliance Distributing Co. .... IGA
Independent Health Plan [*NASDAQ symbol*] .... IHPI
Independent Hospital Workers Union .... IHWU
Independent Infantry Battalion .... IIB
Independent Innkeepers Association .... IIA

Independent Institute, NAD, Dublin, OH [*OCLC symbol*] .... OTH
Independent Insurance Agents of America [*Formerly, NAIA*] .... IIAA
Independent Insurance Conference IIC
Independent Insurance Group, Inc. [*NASDAQ symbol*] .... INDHK
Independent Investor Protective League .... IIPL
Independent Labor Congress [*Nigeria*] ILC
Independent Labour Party [*British*] .... ILP
Independent Landing Monitor [*RADAR-TV landing guidance*] [*NASA*] .... ILM
Independent Liquid Terminals Association .... ILTA
Independent Literary Agents Association .... ILAA
Independent Living Skills [*Needed by the handicapped*] .... ILS
Independent Local Radio [*British*] .... ILR
Independent Lubricant Manufacturers Association [*Formerly, IOCA*] .... ILMA
Independent Manned Manipulator [*NASA*] .... IMM
Independent Media Producers Association .... IMPA
Independent Medical Distributors Association .... IMDA
Independent Medical Examination [*British*] .... IME
Independent Military Air Transport Association [*Later, Independent Airlines Association*] .... IMATA
Independent Mixed Brigade [*Military*] .... IMB
Independent Motion Picture Co. .... IMP
Independent Motion Picture Distributors Association of America .... IMPDAA
Independent Motion Picture Producers Association .... IMPPA
Independent Network News [*Television*] .... INN
Independent Newsletter Association .... INA
Independent Oil Compounders Association [*Later, ILMA*] .... IOCA
Independent Order of B'nai B'rith [*Later, BBI*] .... IOBB
Independent Order of Foresters .... IOF
Independent Order Ladies of Vikings .... IOLV
Independent Order of Odd Fellows .... IOOF
Independent Order of Rechabites .... IOR
Independent Order of St. Luke .... IOSL
Independent Order of Sons of Malta .... IOSM
Independent Order of Svithiod .... IOS
Independent Order of Vikings .... IOV
Independent Parametric Cost Estimate .... IPCE
Independent Pet and Animal Transportation Association .... IPATA
Independent Petroleum Association of America .... IPAA
Independent Petroleum Association of America. Monthly [*A publication*] .... Independent Petroleum Assoc America Monthly
Independent Petroleum Association of Canada .... IPAC
Independent Political Entity [*Board on Geographic Names*] .... PCLI
Independent Postal System of America [*Alternative to US Postal Service*] .... IPSA
Independent Poster Exchanges of America .... IPEA
Independent Press, Bloomfield, NJ [*Library symbol*] .... NjBII
Independent Press, New Providence, NJ [*Library symbol*] .... NjNpI
Independent Professional Electronic Technicians .... IPET
Independent Professional Painting Contractors Association .... IPPCA
Independent Professional Typists Network .... IPTN
Independent Publishers' Association [*Canada*] .... IPA
Independent Publishers Group .... IPG
Independent Pump [*Liquid gas carriers*] i
Independent Rabbinate of America .... IROA
Independent Refiners Association of America .... IRAA
Independent Regulatory Agency [*US Government*] .... IRA
Independent Research .... IR
Independent Research and Development .... IRAD
Independent Research and Development .... IR & D
Independent Research/Independent Exploratory Development .... IR/IED
Independent Research Libraries Association [*Library network*] .... IRLA
Independent Research Service [*Defunct*] .... IRS
Independent Reservation System [*Hotels and motels*] .... INRES
Independent Retail Lumber Dealers Association .... IRLDA
Independent Retail Tobacconists Association of America [*Defunct*] .... IRTA
Independent Scheduled Exercises .... ISE
Independent Scholars of Asia .... ISA
Independent School Bulletin [*A publication*] .... Ind Sch Bull
Independent School Bulletin [*A publication*] .... ISB
Independent Schools Information Service [*British*] .... ISIS
Independent Schools Talent Search Program [*Later, A Better Chance*] .... ISTSP
Independent Search Consultants .... ISC
Independent Sector [*An association*] .... IS
Independent Sewing Machine Dealers of America [*Defunct*] .... ISMDA
Independent Shavian [*A publication*] .... I Sh
Independent Ship Exercise [*Navy*] .... ISE
Independent Shoemen of America [*Defunct*] .... IS
Independent Shoemen of America [*Defunct*] .... ISA
Independent Sideband .... ISB
Independent Signcrafters of America .... ISA
Independent Snowmobile Medical Research [*An association*] .... ISMR
Independent Spent Fuel Storage Facility [*Nuclear energy*] [*Department of Energy*] .... ISFSF
Independent Spent Fuel Storage Installation [*Nuclear energy*] .... ISFSI
Independent Studies Project [*Navy*] .... ISP
Independent Study Program [*IBM Corp.*] .... ISP
Independent Sweep System .... ISS
Independent Telephone Pioneer Association .... ITPA
Independent Television .... ITV
Independent Television Authority [*Later, IBA*] [*British*] .... ITA
Independent Television Companies Association [*British*] .... ITCA
Independent Television Corporation .... ITC
Independent Television News [*British*] .... ITN
Independent Television News Association [*News service*] .... ITNA
Independent Television Service Dealers' Association .... ITVSDA
Independent Television for Wales and the West of England .... TWW
Independent Terminal Operators Association .... ITOA
Independent Tour Excursion [*Airline fare*] .... ITX
Independent Trade Union Association [*Turkey*] .... ITUA
Independent Triggering System .... ITS
Independent Truckers Association .... ITA
Independent Union of Plant Protection Employees .... IUPPE
Independent Union of Plant Protection Employees in the Electrical and Machine Industry .... PPE
Independent United Labor Congress [*Nigeria*] .... IULC
Independent US Tanker Owners Committee .... IUSTOC
Independent Variable Depth SONAR .... IVDS
Independent Variable Hull [*Statistics*] .... IVH
Independent Vertical System .... IVS
Independent Visually Impaired Enterprisers .... IVIE
Independent Voters Association [*Political organization in North Dakota, 1918-1932*] .... IVA
Independent Watchmen's Association .... IWA
Independent Watchmen's Association .... WA
Independent Wire Drawers Association [*Later, AWPA*] .... IWDA
Independent Wire Producers Association [*Formerly, IWDA*] [*Later, AWPA*] .... IWPA
Independent Wire Rope Center [*or Core*] .... IWRC
Independent Wire Rope Manufacturers Association .... IWRMA
Independent Woman [*A publication*] .... Ind Woman
Independent Zinc Alloyers Association .... IZAA
Indeterminate .... INDET
Indeterminate Engineering Items .... IEI
Indeterminate Mass Particle .... IMP
Index I
Index .... IDX
Index .... IND
Index IX
Index to American Doctoral Dissertations [*A publication*] .... IADD
Index of American Periodical Verse [*A publication*] .... Ind Amer Per Verse
Index of Articles on Jewish Studies [*A publication*] .... IJewAr
Index of Body Build [*Anatomy*] .... IB
Index to Book Reviews in the Humanities [*A publication*] .... IBk
Index to Book Reviews in the Sciences [*A publication*] .... IBRS
Index Catalogue IC
Index on Censorship [*A publication*] .... Index Censor
Index Chemicus [*See also ICRS*] IC
Index Chemicus Registry System [*A publication of Institute for Scientific Information*] .... ICRS
Index of Codes for Research Drugs [*A publication*] .... ICRD
Index of Combat Effectiveness .... ICE
Index to Commonwealth Little Magazines [*A publication*] .... ICLM
Index of Community Noise .... ICN
Index to the Comtemporary Scene [*A publication*] .... ICS
Index Concordance [*International Serials Catalogue*] [*A publication*] .... I/C
Index Correction [*on a sextant*] [*Navigation*] IC
Index to Current Urban Documents [*A publication*] .... Ind Curr Urb Doc
Index to Dental Literature [*A publication*] .... IDL
Index for Design Engineering Applications [*Data retrieval service*] [*Product engineering*] .... IDEA
Index-Digest Quarterly System .... DQS
Index of Discrimination .... ID
Index of Dissimilarity .... ID
Index of Economic Articles [*A publication*] .... IEc
Index of Economic Journals [*A publication*] .... Ind Econ J
Index of Enrichment .... IE
Index Error [*Navigation*] .... IE
Index of Federal Specifications and Standards .... IFSS
Index India [*A publication*] .... IIn
Index India [*A publication*] .... Ind India
Index of Industrial Production .... IIP
Index Islamicus [*A publication*] .... Ind Islam
Index to Jewish Periodicals [*A publication*] .... IJewPer
Index to Jewish Periodicals [*A publication*] .... Ind Jew Per
Index to Latin American Periodicals [*A publication*] .... LatAm
Index to Legal Periodicals [*A publication*] .... ILP
Index to Legal Periodicals [*A publication*] .... LegPer
Index of Limited Distribution Reports [*A publication*] .... ILDR
Index Lists [*DoD*] IL
Index to Literature on the American Indian [*A publication*] .... Ind Lit Amer Indian
Index to Little Magazines [*A publication*] .... Ind Little Mag
Index to Little Magazines [*A publication*] .... LMags
Index to Maritime Publications [*A publication*] .... IMP
Index Medicus [*A publication*] .... IM
Index Medicus [*A publication*] .... IMed
Index Medicus [*A publication*] .... Ind Med
Index to New England Periodicals [*A publication*] .... INEP
Index to New Zealand Periodicals [*A publication*] .... Ind NZ Per

Index of Nutritional Quality ... INQ
Index of Performance ... IP
Index to Periodical Articles by and about Blacks [*A publication*] ... Ind Per Blacks
Index to Periodical Articles by and about Negroes [*Later, Index to Periodical Articles by and about Blacks*] [*A publication*] ... Ind Per Negroes
Index to Periodical Articles by and about Negroes [*Later, Index to Periodical Articles by and about Blacks*] [*A publication*] ... INeg
Index to Periodical Articles Related to Law [*A publication*] ... Ind Per Art Relat Law
Index of Production Industries [*Department of Employment*] [*British*] ... IPI
Index of Refraction ... IOR
Index to Religious Periodical Literature [*Data base*] ... IRPL
Index to Scientific Reviews [*A publication*] ... Ind Sci Rev
Index to Scientific Reviews [*A publication*] ... ISR
Index to Scientific and Technical Proceedings [*A publication*] ... IS & TP
Index to Selected Periodicals [*A publication*] ... Ind Sel Per
Index to South African Periodicals [*A publication*] ... Ind SA Per
Index of Specifications and Standards ... ISS
Index of Stability of Relative Magnitudes [*Statistics*] ... ISRM
Index of Status Characteristics ... ISC
Index Term [*Data processing*] ... IT
Index Translationum [*UNESCO*] ... IT
Index to US Government Periodicals [*A publication*] ... Ind US Gov Per
Index of Vertical Transmission [*Cultural evolution*] ... IVT
Index Veterinarius [*A publication*] ... Ind Vet
Indexed and Paged ... I & P
Indexed, Paged, and Titled ... IPT
Indexed References to Biomedical Engineering Literature [*A publication*] ... IRBEL
Indexed Sequential Access Method [*Pronounced "i-sam"*] [*Data processing*] ... ISAM
Indexed Sequential File Management System ... ISFMS
Indexes of Firepower Potential ... IFP
Indexing and Abstracting Services ... INAS
Indexing Slide Table ... IST
Indexing in Source ... IS
India [*MARC geographic area code*] [*Library of Congress*] ... a-ii---
India [*Phonetic alphabet*] ... I
India [*MARC country of publication code*] [*Library of Congress*] ... ii
India [*Two-letter standard code*] ... IN
India [*Three-letter standard code*] ... IND
India [*Aircraft nationality and registration mark*] ... VT
India-America Society ... IAS
India America Trade Council ... IATC
India-Burma [*World War II*] ... IB
India-Burma Theater [*World War II*] ... I-BT
India Chemists and Chemical Engineers Club ... ICCEC
India-China Wing [*World War II*] ... ICW
India Coffee Board. Annual Report [*A publication*] ... India Coffee Board Annu Rep
India Coffee Board. Research Department. Annual Detailed Technical Report [*A publication*] ... India Coffee Bd Res Dep Annu Detailed Tech Rep
India Coffee Board. Research Department. Annual Report [*A publication*] ... India Coffee Board Res Dep Annu Rep
India Coffee Board. Research Department. Bulletin [*A publication*] ... India Coffee Board Res Dep Bull
India Cultures Quarterly [*A publication*] ... Ind Cult Q
India Development Service ... IDS
India Directorate of Plant Protection. Quarantine and Storage. Plant Protection Bulletin [*A publication*] ... India Dir Plant Prot Quar Storage Plant Prot Bull
India Engineering Export Promotion Council ... EEPC
India Geological Survey. Bulletins. Series A. Economic Geology [*A publication*] ... India Geol Surv Bull Ser A
India Geological Survey. Bulletins. Series B. Engineering Geology and Ground-Water [*A publication*] ... India Geol Surv Bull Ser B
India Geological Survey. Memoirs [*A publication*] ... India Geol Surv Mem
India Geological Survey. Memoirs. Palaeontologia Indica. New Series [*A publication*] ... India Geol Surv Mem Palaeontol Indica New Ser
India Geological Survey. Miscellaneous Publication [*A publication*] ... India Geol Surv Misc Publ
India Geological Survey. News [*A publication*] ... India Geol Surv News
India International Philatelic Exhibition ... INDIPEX
India Office [*British*] ... IO
India Office Library and Records, Foreign and Commonwealth Office, London, United Kingdom [*Library symbol*] ... UkLIO
India Oil and Natural Gas Commission. Bulletin [*A publication*] ... India Oil Nat Gas Comm Bull
India Paper ... IP
India Paper Proofs ... IPP
India Press Agency ... IPA
India Quarterly [*A publication*] ... India Q
India Quarterly [*A publication*] ... India Quar
India Quarterly [*A publication*] ... Ind Q
India Quarterly [*A publication*] ... IQ
India-Rubber ... IR
Indian ... IND
Indian Academy of Geoscience. Journal [*A publication*] ... Indian Acad Geosci J
Indian Academy of Medical Sciences. Annual [*A publication*] ... Indian Acad Med Sci Ann
Indian Academy of Science. Proceedings [*A publication*] ... Indian Acad Sci Pro
Indian Administrative Service [*British*] ... IAS
Indian Affairs Record [*A publication*] ... IAR
Indian Agricultural Research Institute ... IARI
Indian Agricultural Research Institute (New Delhi). Annual Report [*A publication*] ... Indian Agric Res Inst (New Delhi) Annu Rep
Indian Agricultural Research Institute (New Delhi). Annual Scientific Report [*A publication*] ... Indian Agric Res Inst (New Delhi) Annu Sci Rep
Indian Agriculturist [*A publication*] ... Indian Agr
Indian Agriculturist [*A publication*] ... Indian Agric
Indian Air Force ... IAF
Indian Air Force ... InAF
Indian Airlines Corporation ... IAC
Indian Airlines Corporation [*India*] [*ICAO designator*] ... IC
Indian Anthropologist [*A publication*] ... Ind Anthro
Indian Army ... IA
Indian Army Medical Corps ... IAMC
Indian Army Ordnance Control [*British*] ... IAOC
Indian Army Reserve of Officers ... IARO
Indian Arts and Crafts Association ... IACA
Indian Arts and Crafts Board [*Department of the Interior*] ... IACB
Indian Association of America ... IAA
Indian Association of Special Libraries and Information Centres ... IASLIC
Indian Astronautical Society ... IAS
Indian Auxiliary Force [*British*] ... IAF
Indian Bee Journal [*A publication*] ... Indian Bee J
Indian Behavioural Science Abstracts [*A publication*] ... IBSA
Indian Biologist [*A publication*] ... Indian Biol
Indian Campaign Medal ... ICM
Indian Central Jute Committee. Annual Report of the Jute Agricultural Research Institute [*A publication*] ... Indian Cent Jute Comm Annu Rep Jute Agric Res Inst
Indian Ceramic Society. Transactions [*A publication*] ... Indian Ceramic Soc Trans
Indian Chemical Journal [*A publication*] ... Indian Chem J
Indian Chemical Manufacturer [*A publication*] ... Indian Chem Manuf
Indian Church History Review [*A publication*] ... Ind Ch HR
Indian Church History Review [*A publication*] ... Ind Chur Hist R
Indian Church History Review [*A publication*] ... Indian Church Hist R
Indian Civil Service [*British*] ... ICS
Indian Claims Commission [*Terminated, 1976*] ... ICC
Indian Claims Commission, Ottawa, ON, Canada [*Library symbol*] ... CaOOICC
Indian Coconut Journal [*A publication*] ... Indian Coconut J
Indian Communications Project ... ICP
Indian Community Action ... ICA
Indian Concrete Journal [*A publication*] ... Indian Concr J
Indian Cooperative Review [*A publication*] ... Ind Coop R
Indian Cotton Growing Review [*A publication*] ... Indian Cotton Grow Rev
Indian Cotton Journal [*A publication*] ... Indian Cott J
Indian Council of Agricultural Research. Animal Husbandry Series [*A publication*] ... Indian Counc Agric Res Anim Husb Ser
Indian Council of Agricultural Research. Annual Technical Report [*A publication*] ... Indian Counc Agric Res Annu Tech Rep
Indian Council of Agricultural Research. Cereal Crop Series [*A publication*] ... Indian Counc Agric Res Cereal Crop Ser
Indian Council of Agricultural Research. Entomological Monographs [*A publication*] ... Indian Counc Agric Res Entomol Monogr
Indian Council of Agricultural Research. Miscellaneous Bulletin [*A publication*] ... Indian Counc Agric Res Misc Bull
Indian Council of Agricultural Research. Monograph [*A publication*] ... Indian Counc Agric Res Monogr
Indian Council of Agricultural Research. Report Series [*A publication*] ... Indian Counc Agric Res Rep Ser
Indian Council of Agricultural Research. Research Series [*A publication*] ... Indian Counc Agric Res Res Ser
Indian Council of Agricultural Research. Review Series [*A publication*] ... Indian Counc Agric Res Rev Ser
Indian Council of Agricultural Research. Technical Bulletin [*A publication*] ... Indian Counc Agric Res Tech Bull
Indian Council of Historical Research ... ICHR
Indian Council of Medical Research. Annual Report [*A publication*] ... Indian Counc Med Res Annu Rep
Indian Council of Medical Research. Technical Report Series [*A publication*] ... Indian Counc Med Res Tech Rep Ser
Indian Council of Social Science Research ... ICSSR
Indian Cultural Center [*Defunct*] ... ICC
Indian Culture [*A publication*] ... IC
Indian Defense Rules ... IDR
Indian Distinguished Service Medal [*British*] ... IDSM
Indian and Eastern Engineer [*A publication*] ... Indian East Eng
Indian Ecologist [*A publication*] ... Indian Ecol
Indian Economic Journal [*A publication*] ... I Econ J
Indian Economic Journal [*A publication*] ... IEJ
Indian Economic Journal [*A publication*] ... Ind Econ J

Indian Economic Review [*A publication*] ... IER
Indian Economic Review [*A publication*] ... Ind Econ R
Indian Economic and Social History Review [*A publication*] ... IESH
Indian Economic and Social History Review [*A publication*] ... Ind Econ Soc Hist R
Indian Economic and Social History Review [*A publication*] ... India Econ Soc Hist R
Indian Economic and Social History Review [*A publication*] ... Indian Econ Soc Hist Rev
Indian Educational Service [*British*] ... IES
[*Order of the*] **Indian Empire** ... IE
Indian Engineer [*A publication*] ... Indian Eng
Indian-Eskimo Association of Canada [*Later, CASNP*] ... IEA
Indian Farm Mechanization [*A publication*] ... Indian Farm Mech
Indian Farmers Fertiliser Cooperative Ltd. [*Gujarat, India*] ... IFFCO
Indian Farming [*A publication*] ... Ind F
Indian Farming [*A publication*] ... Indian Fmg
Indian Federation of Working Journalists ... IFWJ
Indian Financial Questions [*British*] ... IF
Indian Foodgrain Requirements [*British*] ... IFR
Indian and Foreign Review [*A publication*] ... I & FR
Indian Foreign Review [*A publication*] ... Ind For R
Indian Forest Bulletin [*A publication*] ... Indian For Bull
Indian Forest Leaflet [*A publication*] ... Indian For Leafl
Indian Forest Records [*A publication*] ... Indian For Rec
Indian Forest Records. Botany [*A publication*] ... Indian For Rec Bot
Indian Forest Records. Entomology [*A publication*] ... Indian For Rec Entomol
Indian Forest Records. Forest Pathology [*A publication*] ... Indian For Rec For Pathol
Indian Forest Records. Mycology [*A publication*] ... Indian For Rec Mycol
Indian Forest Records. Silviculture [*A publication*] ... Indian For Rec Silvic
Indian Forest Records. Statistical [*A publication*] ... Indian For Rec Stat
Indian Forest Records. Timber Mechanics [*A publication*] ... Indian For Rec Timber Mech
Indian Forest Records. Wild Life and Recreation [*A publication*] ... Indian For Rec Wild Life Recreation
Indian Forest Records. Wood Anatomy [*A publication*] ... Indian For Rec Wood Anat
Indian Forest Service [*British*] ... IFS
Indian Forester [*A publication*] ... Indian For
Indian General Service Medal [*British*] ... IGSM
Indian Geographical Journal [*Madras*] [*A publication*] ... IGJ
Indian Geographical Journal [*A publication*] ... Ind Geog J
Indian Geohydrology [*A publication*] ... Indian Geohydrol
Indian Geological Index [*A publication*] ... Indian Geol Index
Indian Geologists Association. Bulletin [*A publication*] ... Indian Geol Assoc Bull
Indian Geotechnical Journal [*A publication*] ... Indian Geotech J
Indian Head Banks [*NASDAQ symbol*] ... IHBI
Indian Head, Inc. [*NYSE symbol*] [*Delisted*] ... IHD
Indian Head [*Maryland*] **- Quality Assurance Department** [*Naval ordnance station*] ... IH/QAS
Indian Health Service ... IHS
Indian Heart Journal [*A publication*] ... Indian Heart J
Indian Heart Journal. Teaching Series [*A publication*] ... Indian Heart J Teach Ser
Indian Highways [*A publication*] ... Indian Highw
Indian Historian [*A publication*] ... I Hist
Indian Historian [*A publication*] ... Indian Hist
Indian Historical Quarterly [*A publication*] ... IHQ
Indian Historical Quarterly [*A publication*] ... Indian Hist Q
Indian Horizons [*A publication*] ... Ind Hor
Indian Horizons [*A publication*] ... Ind Horizons
Indian Horticulture [*A publication*] ... Indian Hort
Indian Horticulture [*A publication*] ... Indian Hortic
Indian Industries [*A publication*] ... Indian Ind
Indian Journal of Agricultural Chemistry [*A publication*] ... Indian J Agric Chem
Indian Journal of Agricultural Economics [*A publication*] ... IJAE
Indian Journal of Agricultural Economics [*A publication*] ... Indian J Agr Econ
Indian Journal of Agricultural Economics [*A publication*] ... Ind J Agr Econ
Indian Journal of Agricultural Economics [*A publication*] ... Ind J Agric Econ
Indian Journal of Agricultural Research [*A publication*] ... Indian J Agric Res
Indian Journal of Agricultural Science [*A publication*] ... I J Agr Sci
Indian Journal of Agricultural Science [*A publication*] ... Indian J Agric Sci
Indian Journal of Agricultural Science [*A publication*] ... Indian J Agr Sci
Indian Journal of Agricultural Science [*A publication*] ... Ind J Ag Sci
Indian Journal of Agricultural and Veterinary Education [*A publication*] ... Indian J Agric Vet Educ
Indian Journal of Agronomy [*A publication*] ... Indian J Agron
Indian Journal of American Studies [*A publication*] ... IJAS
Indian Journal of Anaesthesia [*A publication*] ... Indian J Anaesth
Indian Journal of Animal Health [*A publication*] ... Indian J Animal Health
Indian Journal of Animal Research [*A publication*] ... Indian J Anim Res
Indian Journal of Animal Sciences [*A publication*] ... Indian J Anim Sci
Indian Journal of Applied Chemistry [*A publication*] ... Indian J Appl Chem
Indian Journal of Applied Psychology [*A publication*] ... Indian J Appl Psychol
Indian Journal of Biochemistry [*Later, Indian Journal of Biochemistry and Biophysics*] [*A publication*] ... Indian J Biochem
Indian Journal of Biochemistry and Biophysics [*A publication*] ... I J Bioch B
Indian Journal of Biochemistry and Biophysics [*A publication*] ... Indian J Biochem Biophys
Indian Journal of Cancer [*A publication*] ... Indian J Cancer
Indian Journal of Cancer Chemotherapy [*A publication*] ... Indian J Cancer Chemother
Indian Journal of Chemical Education [*A publication*] ... Indian J Chem Educ
Indian Journal of Chemistry [*A publication*] ... I J Chem
Indian Journal of Chemistry [*A publication*] ... Indian J Chem
Indian Journal of Chemistry. Section A. Inorganic, Physical, Theoretical, and Analytical Chemistry [*A publication*] ... Indian J Chem Sect A
Indian Journal of Chemistry. Section B [*A publication*] ... Indian J Chem Sect B
Indian Journal of Chemistry. Section B. Organic Chemistry, Including Medicinal Chemistry [*A publication*] ... Indian J Chem Sect B Org Chem incl Med Chem
Indian Journal of Chest Diseases [*Later, Indian Journal of Chest Diseases and Allied Sciences*] [*A publication*] ... Indian J Chest Dis
Indian Journal of Chest Diseases and Allied Sciences [*A publication*] ... Indian J Chest Dis Allied Sci
Indian Journal of Commerce [*Chandigarh*] [*A publication*] ... IJC
Indian Journal of Commerce [*A publication*] ... Ind J Commer
Indian Journal of Criminology [*A publication*] ... Indian J Criminol
Indian Journal of Cryogenics [*A publication*] ... Indian J Cryog
Indian Journal of Dairy Science [*A publication*] ... Indian J Dairy Sci
Indian Journal of Dermatology [*Later, Indian Journal of Dermatology, Venereology, and Leprology*] [*A publication*] ... Indian J Dermatol
Indian Journal of Dermatology and Venereology [*Later, Indian Journal of Dermatology, Venereology, and Leprology*] [*A publication*] ... Indian J Dermatol Venereol
Indian Journal of Dermatology, Venereology, and Leprology [*A publication*] ... Indian J Dermatol Venereol Leprol
Indian Journal of Earth Sciences [*A publication*] ... Indian J Earth Sci
Indian Journal of Ecology [*A publication*] ... Indian J Ecol
Indian Journal of Economics [*A publication*] ... IJE
Indian Journal of Economics [*A publication*] ... Ind J Econ
Indian Journal of Engineering Mathematics [*A publication*] ... Indian J Engrg Math
Indian Journal of English Studies [*Calcutta*] [*A publication*] ... IJES
Indian Journal of Entomology [*A publication*] ... Indian J Entomol
Indian Journal of Environmental Health [*A publication*] ... Indian J Environ Health
Indian Journal of Experimental Biology [*A publication*] ... I J Ex Biol
Indian Journal of Experimental Biology [*A publication*] ... Indian J Exp Biol
Indian Journal of Experimental Psychology [*A publication*] ... Indian J Exp Psychol
Indian Journal of Farm Sciences [*A publication*] ... Indian J Farm Sci
Indian Journal of Fisheries [*A publication*] ... Indian J Fish
Indian Journal of Genetics and Plant Breeding [*A publication*] ... I J Genet P
Indian Journal of Genetics and Plant Breeding [*A publication*] ... Indian J Genet Plant Breed
Indian Journal of Helminthology [*A publication*] ... Indian J Helminthol
Indian Journal of Heredity [*A publication*] ... Indian J Hered
Indian Journal of the History of Medicine [*A publication*] ... IJHM
Indian Journal of History of Science [*A publication*] ... Indian J Hist Sci
Indian Journal of Horticulture [*A publication*] ... Indian J Hortic
Indian Journal of Industrial Medicine [*A publication*] ... Indian J Ind Med
Indian Journal of Industrial Relations [*A publication*] ... I J Ind Rel
Indian Journal of Industrial Relations [*A publication*] ... Ind J Indus Rel
Indian Journal of Industrial Relations [*A publication*] ... Ind J Industr Relat
Indian Journal of International Law [*A publication*] ... IJIL
Indian Journal of Malariology [*A publication*] ... Indian J Malariol
Indian Journal of Marine Sciences [*A publication*] ... Indian J Mar Sci
Indian Journal of Mathematics [*A publication*] ... Indian J Math
Indian Journal of Mechanics and Mathematics [*A publication*] ... Indian J Mech Math
Indian Journal of Medical Research [*A publication*] ... I J Med Res
Indian Journal of Medical Research [*A publication*] ... Indian J Med Res
Indian Journal of Medical Research [*A publication*] ... Indian J Med Research
Indian Journal of Medical Sciences [*A publication*] ... Indian J Med Sci
Indian Journal of Medicine and Surgery [*A publication*] ... Indian J Med Surg
Indian Journal of Meteorology and Geophysics [*Later, Mausam*] [*A publication*] ... Indian J Meteorol Geophys
Indian Journal of Meteorology, Hydrology, and Geophysics [*Later, Mausam*] [*A publication*] ... Indian J Meteorol Hydrol Geophys
Indian Journal of Microbiology [*A publication*] ... Indian J Microbiol
Indian Journal of Mycological Research [*A publication*] ... Indian J Mycol Res
Indian Journal of Mycology and Plant Pathology [*A publication*] ... Indian J Mycol Plant Pathol
Indian Journal of Nematology [*A publication*] ... Indian J Nematol
Indian Journal of Nutrition and Dietetics [*A publication*] ... I J Nutr D
Indian Journal of Nutrition and Dietetics [*A publication*] ... Indian J Nutr Diet
Indian Journal of Occupational Health [*A publication*] ... Indian J Occup Health
Indian Journal of Ophthalmology [*A publication*] ... Indian J Ophthalmol
Indian Journal of Otolaryngology [*A publication*] ... Indian J Otolaryngol

Indian Journal of Pathology and Bacteriology [*Later, Indian Journal of Pathology and Microbiology*] [*A publication*] .... Indian J Pathol Bacteriol
Indian Journal of Pathology and Microbiology [*A publication*] .... Indian J Pathol Microbiol
Indian Journal of Pediatrics [*A publication*] .... Indian J Pediatr
Indian Journal of Pharmacy [*A publication*] .... Indian J Pharm
Indian Journal of Physical Anthropology and Human Genetics [*A publication*] .... Indian J Phys Anthropol Hum Genet
Indian Journal of Physics [*A publication*] .... I J Physics
Indian Journal of Physics [*A publication*] .... Indian J Phys
Indian Journal of Physics. Part A [*A publication*] .... Indian J Phys
Indian Journal of Physics. Part B [*A publication*] .... Indian J Phys Part B
Indian Journal of Physiology and Allied Sciences [*A publication*] .... Indian J Physiol Allied Sci
Indian Journal of Physiology and Pharmacology [*A publication*] .... Indian J Physiol Pharmacol
Indian Journal of Plant Physiology [*A publication*] .... Indian J Plant Physiol
Indian Journal of Political Science [*A publication*] .... IJPS
Indian Journal of Political Science [*A publication*] .... India J Pol Sci
Indian Journal of Political Science [*A publication*] .... Ind J Polit Sci
Indian Journal of Political Science [*A publication*] .... Ind J Pol Sci
Indian Journal of Politics [*A publication*] .... Ind J Polit
Indian Journal of Poultry Science [*A publication*] .... Indian J Poult Sci
Indian Journal of Power and River Valley Development [*A publication*] .... Indian J Power River Val Dev
Indian Journal of Power and River Valley Development [*A publication*] .... Indian J Power River Val Develop
Indian Journal of Psychology [*A publication*] .... I J Psychol
Indian Journal of Psychology [*A publication*] .... Indian J Psychol
Indian Journal of Psychology [*A publication*] .... INJPA
Indian Journal of Public Administration [*A publication*] .... IJPA
Indian Journal of Public Administration [*A publication*] .... Ind J Publ Adm
Indian Journal of Public Health [*A publication*] .... Indian J Publ Health
Indian Journal of Pure and Applied Mathematics [*A publication*] .... Indian J Pure Appl Math
Indian Journal of Pure and Applied Physics [*A publication*] .... I J PA Phys
Indian Journal of Pure and Applied Physics [*A publication*] .... Indian J Pure Appl Phys
Indian Journal of Radio and Space Physics [*A publication*] .... Indian J Radio Space Phys
Indian Journal of Radiology [*A publication*] .... Indian J Radiol
Indian Journal of Science and Industry. Section A. Agricultural and Animal Sciences [*A publication*] .... Indian J Sci Ind Sect A Agric Anim Sci
Indian Journal of Science and Industry. Section B. Animal Sciences [*A publication*] .... Indian J Sci Ind Sect B Anim Sci
Indian Journal of Sericulture [*A publication*] .... Indian J Seric
Indian Journal of Social Research [*A publication*] .... I J Soc Res
Indian Journal of Social Research [*A publication*] .... Ind J Soc Res
Indian Journal of Social Work [*A publication*] .... IJSW
Indian Journal of Social Work [*A publication*] .... Ind J Soc Wk
Indian Journal of Sugar Cane Research and Development [*A publication*] .... Indian J Sugar Cane Res Dev
Indian Journal of Surgery [*A publication*] .... Indian J Surg
Indian Journal of Technology [*A publication*] .... I J Techn
Indian Journal of Technology [*A publication*] .... Indian J Technol
Indian Journal of Textile Research [*A publication*] .... Indian J Text Res
Indian Journal of Theology [*A publication*] .... IJT
Indian Journal of Theology [*A publication*] .... Ind J Th
Indian Journal of Theoretical Physics [*A publication*] .... I J Theor P
Indian Journal of Theoretical Physics [*A publication*] .... Indian J Theor Phys
Indian Journal of Tuberculosis [*A publication*] .... Indian J Tuberculosis
Indian Journal of Veterinary Science [*A publication*] .... Ind J Vet Sci
Indian Journal of Veterinary Science and Animal Husbandry [*A publication*] .... Indian J Vet Sci Anim Husb
Indian Journal of Weed Science [*A publication*] .... Indian J Weed Sci
Indian Journal of Zoology [*A publication*] .... Indian J Zool
Indian Journal of Zootomy [*A publication*] .... Indian J Zootomy
Indian Labour Gazette [*A publication*] .... ILG
Indian Labour Journal [*A publication*] .... Ind Lab J
Indian Law Review [*A publication*] .... Indian L Rev
Indian Legal Information Development Service .... I-LIDS
Indian Librarian [*A publication*] .... I Lib
Indian Librarian [*A publication*] .... Indian Librn
Indian Librarian [*A publication*] .... Ind Lib
Indian Library Association. Bulletin [*A publication*] .... Indian Libr Ass Bull
Indian Library Association. Journal [*A publication*] .... Indian Lib Assn J
Indian Library Science Abstracts [*A publication*] .... Indian Lib Sci Abstr
Indian Linguistics [*A publication*] IL
Indian Linguistics [*A publication*] .... Ind Ling
Indian Linguistics [*A publication*] .... Ind Linguist
Indian Literature [*A publication*] .... I Lit
Indian Literature [*A publication*] .... Ind L
Indian Literature [*A publication*] .... IndLit
Indian Literature [*A publication*] .... InL
Indian Local Forces [*Military*] [*British*] .... ILF
Indian Medical Forum [*A publication*] .... Indian Med Forum
Indian Medical Gazette [*A publication*] .... Indian Med Gaz
Indian Medical Journal (Calcutta) [*A publication*] .... Indian Med J (Calcutta)
Indian Medical Service [*British*] .... IMS
Indian Mercantile Marine Training Ship [*British*] .... IMMTS
Indian Military Academy .... IMA
Indian Mineralogist [*A publication*] .... Indian Mineral
Indian Minerals [*A publication*] .... Indian Miner
Indian Minerals Yearbook [*A publication*] .... Indian Miner Yearb
Indian Mining and Engineering Journal [*A publication*] .... Indian Min Engng J
Indian Motorcycle Club of America .... IMCA
Indian Mountain [*Alaska*] [*Seismograph station code, US Geological Survey*] .... IMA
Indian Museum. Bulletin [*A publication*] .... Indian Mus Bull
Indian Museum. Records [*A publication*] .... Indian Mus Rec
Indian Music Quarterly [*A publication*] .... Indian Mus Q
Indian Musician [*A publication*] .... IPOGA
Indian Musicological Society. Journal [*A publication*] .... Indian M S
Indian Nation Restoration Committee .... INRC
Indian National Airways .... INA
Indian National Army [*World War II*] .... INA
Indian National Cement Workers' Federation .... INCWF
Indian National Electricity Workers' Federation .... INEWF
Indian National Iron and Steel Workers' Federation .... INISWF
Indian National Mine Workers' Federation .... INMWF
Indian National Oceanographic Data Centre [*Information service*] .... INODC
Indian National Satellite .... INSAT
Indian National Science Academy. Bulletin [*A publication*] .... Indian Nat Sci Acad Bull
Indian National Science Academy. Bulletin [*A publication*] .... INSA Bull
Indian National Science Academy. Proceedings. Part A. Physical Sciences [*A publication*] .... Indian Natl Sci Acad Proc Part A
Indian National Science Academy. Proceedings. Part B. Biological Sciences [*A publication*] .... Indian Natl Sci Acad Proc Part B
Indian National Scientific Documentation Centre [*New Delhi*] .... INSDC
Indian National Scientific Documentation Centre [*New Delhi*] .... INSDOC
Indian National Scientific Documentation Centre, New Delhi, India [*Library symbol*] .... IiNI
Indian National Textile Workers' Federation .... INTWF
Indian National Trades Union Congress .... INTUC
Indian Nations Council of Governments .... INCOG
Indian Navy .... IN
Indian and Northern Affairs Department [*Canada*] .... INA
Indian Numismatic Chronicle [*A publication*] .... INC
Indian Ocean [*MARC geographic area code*] [*Library of Congress*] .... i------
Indian Ocean .... IO
Indian Ocean Experiment .... INDEX
Indian Ocean Fisheries Commission .... IOFC
Indian Ocean/Persian Gulf .... IO/PG
Indian Ocean Region [*INTELSAT*] .... IOR
Indian Ocean Ship .... IOS
Indian Ocean Standard Net .... IOSN
Indian Ocean Station .... IOS
Indian Ocean Station Support .... IOSS
Indian Ocean Zone of Peace .... IOZP
Indian Order of Merit .... IOM
Indian Overseas Airways .... IOA
Indian Overseas Communication Project .... IOCP
Indian Pediatrics [*A publication*] .... Indian Pediatr
Indian PEN [*A publication*] .... InPEN
Indian PEN [*A publication*] .... IPEN
Indian People's Association in North America .... IPANA
Indian Philosophical Quarterly [*A publication*] .... Indian Phil Quart
Indian Philosophy and Culture [*A publication*] .... Indian Phil Cult
Indian Philosophy and Culture. Quarterly [*A publication*] .... IPC
Indian Phytopathology [*A publication*] .... Indian Phytopathol
Indian Police Service [*British*] .... IPS
Indian Political Science Review [*A publication*] .... India Pol Sci R
Indian Political Science Review [*A publication*] .... Ind Polit Sci R
Indian Political Science Review [*A publication*] .... Ind Pol Sci R
Indian Political Science Review [*A publication*] .... I Polit Sci
Indian Political Service [*British*] .... IPS
Indian Potash Journal [*A publication*] .... Indian Potash J
Indian Potato Journal [*A publication*] .... Indian Potato J
Indian Practitioner [*A publication*] .... Indian Pract
Indian Practitioner [*A publication*] .... IPRAA
Indian Preference [*Civil Service*] .... IP
Indian Psychological Abstracts [*A publication*] .... Indian Psychol Abstr
Indian Psychological Review [*A publication*] .... Indian Psychol R
Indian Psychological Review [*A publication*] .... Ind Psych R
Indian Psychological Review [*A publication*] .... I Psychol R
Indian Pulp and Paper [*A publication*] .... Indian Pulp Pap
Indian Pulp and Paper Technical Association. Journal [*A publication*] .... IPPTA
Indian Ridge Treatment Center, Resident Library, Arlington, WA [*Library symbol*] .... WArl-R
Indian Ridge Treatment Center, Staff Library, Arlington, WA [*Library symbol*] .... WaArl
Indian Rights Association .... IRA
Indian River Community College, Fort Pierce, FL [*Library symbol*] .... FFpI
Indian River Public Library, Indian River, MI [*Library symbol*] .... MiInr
Indian School of International Studies [*Delhi*] .... ISIS
Indian Science Abstracts [*A publication*] .... Indian Sci Abstr
Indian Science Congress Association. Proceedings [*A publication*] .... Indian Sci Cong Assoc Proc

Indian Science Congress Association. Proceedings [*A publication*] ... Indian Sci Congr Assoc Proc
Indian Science Index [*A publication*] ... Indian Sci Ind
Indian Scientific Satellite ... INDASAT
Indian Service of Engineers [*British*] ... ISE
Indian Society for Nuclear Techniques in Agriculture and Biology. Newsletter [*A publication*] ... Indian Soc Nuclear Tech Agric Biol Newsl
Indian Society of Soil Science. Bulletin [*A publication*] ... Indian Soc Soil Sci Bull
Indian Society of Soil Science. Journal [*A publication*] ... Indian Soc Soil Sci J
Indian Space Research Organization [*India*] ... ISRO
Indian Spring Low Water [*Tides and currents*] ... ISLW
Indian Staff Corps ... ISC
Indian Standard Time ... IST
Indian Standards Institution ... ISI
Indian Statistical Institute ... ISI
Indian Steel Training and Education Program [*India*] ... INSTEP
Indian Studies [*A publication*] ... Ind Stud
Indian Studies: Past and Present [*A publication*] ... Ind S
Indian Sugar [*A publication*] ... Indian Sug
Indian Supply Mission [*World War II*] ... ISM
Indian Territory [*in United States*] ... IT
Indian Textile Journal [*A publication*] ... Indian Text J
Indian Trails Public Library District, Wheeling, IL [*OCLC symbol*] ... JAG
Indian Transcontinental Airways ... ITCA
Indian University Association for Continuing Education ... IUACE
Indian Valley Colleges Library, Novato, CA [*OCLC symbol*] ... CIV
Indian Valley Public Library, Telford, PA [*Library symbol*] ... PTe
Indian Veterinary Journal [*A publication*] ... Indian Vet J
Indian Welding Journal [*A publication*] ... Indian Weld J
Indian Year Book of International Affairs [*A publication*] ... IYIA
Indian Youth of America ... IYA
Indian Zoological Memoirs [*A publication*] ... Indian Zool Mem
Indian Zoologist [*A publication*] ... Indian Zool
Indiana [*Postal code*] ... IN
Indiana ... IND
Indiana [*MARC country of publication code*] [*Library of Congress*] ... inu
Indiana [*MARC geographic area code*] [*Library of Congress*] ... n-us-in
Indiana Academy of Science, Indianapolis, IN [*Library symbol*] ... InIA
Indiana Academy of Science. Monograph [*A publication*] ... Indiana Acad Sci Monogr
Indiana Academy of Science. Proceedings [*A publication*] ... Ind Acad Sci Proc
Indiana Airways, Inc. [*Indiana, PA*] [*FAA designator*] ... INA
Indiana Army Ammunition Plant ... INAAP
Indiana Business Review [*A publication*] ... Indiana Busin R
Indiana Central University, Indianapolis, IN [*OCLC symbol*] ... III
Indiana Central University, Indianapolis, IN [*Library symbol*] ... InICC
Indiana Cooperative Library Service Authority (INCOLSA), Indianapolis, IN [*Library symbol*] ... InII
Indiana Cooperative Library Services Authority [*Library network*] ... INCOLSA
Indiana Cooperative Library Services Authority, Indianapolis, IN [*OCLC symbol*] ... INC
Indiana Cooperative Library Services Authority, Indianapolis, IN [*OCLC symbol*] ... TQC
Indiana Cooperative Library Services Authority, Indianapolis, IN [*OCLC symbol*] ... TQD
Indiana Division of Water. Bulletin [*A publication*] ... Indiana Div Water Bull
Indiana Division of Water Resources. Bulletin [*A publication*] ... Ind Div Water Res Bull
Indiana English Journal [*A publication*] ... IEJ
Indiana Financial Investors [*NASDAQ symbol*] ... IFII
Indiana Folklore [*A publication*] ... IndF
Indiana Gas Company, Inc. [*NYSE symbol*] ... IGC
Indiana Geological Survey. Mineral Economics Series [*A publication*] ... Indiana Geol Survey Mineral Economics Ser
Indiana Geological Survey. Mineral Economics Series [*A publication*] ... Indiana Geol Surv Miner Econ Ser
Indiana Geological Survey. Miscellaneous Map [*A publication*] ... Indiana Geol Surv Misc Map
Indiana Geological Survey. Occasional Paper [*A publication*] ... Indiana Geol Surv Occas Pap
Indiana Geological Survey. Special Report [*A publication*] ... Indiana Geol Surv Spec Rep
Indiana Harbor Belt Railroad Co. [*AAR code*] ... IHB
Indiana Historical Commission. Collections [*A publication*] ... Ind His Col
Indiana Historical Society, Indianapolis, IN [*Library symbol*] ... InHi
Indiana Historical Society, Indianapolis, IN [*OCLC symbol*] ... XHS
Indiana Historical Society. Publications [*A publication*] ... Ind His S
Indiana Historical Society. Publications [*A publication*] ... Ind Hist Soc Publ
Indiana History Bulletin [*A publication*] ... IHB
Indiana History Bulletin [*A publication*] ... Ind Hist Bull
Indiana, Illinois, Iowa [*Old baseball league*] ... 3-I
Indiana Information Retrieval System [*Library network*] ... INDIRS
Indiana Institute of Technology, Fort Wayne, IN [*Library symbol*] ... InFwI
Indiana Institute of Technology, McMillen Library, Fort Wayne, IN [*OCLC symbol*] ... IMX
Indiana Interstate Railroad Company, Inc. [*AAR code*] ... IIRC
Indiana Law Journal [*A publication*] ... Indiana Law
Indiana Law Journal [*A publication*] ... Ind Law Jour
Indiana Law Journal [*A publication*] ... Ind L J
Indiana Law Review [*A publication*] ... Ind L Rev
Indiana Legal Forum [*A publication*] ... Ind Legal F
Indiana Legislative Council, State House, Indianapolis, IN [*Library symbol*] ... In-LB
Indiana Limestone Institute of America ... ILI
Indiana Limestone Institute of America ... ILIA
Indiana Magazine of History [*A publication*] ... IMH
Indiana Magazine of History [*A publication*] ... Ind M
Indiana Magazine of History [*A publication*] ... Ind Mag Hist
Indiana & Michigan Electric Co. [*NYSE symbol*] ... IME
Indiana Motor Rate and Tariff Bureau Inc., Indianapolis IN [*STAC*] ... INB
Indiana Names [*Indiana State University*] [*A publication*] ... IN
Indiana National Corp. [*NASDAQ symbol*] ... INAT
Indiana, PA [*Location identifier*] [*FAA*] ... IDI
Indiana, PA [*Radio station call letters*] ... WDAD
Indiana, PA [*Radio station call letters*] ... WIUP-FM
Indiana, PA [*Radio station call letters*] ... WQMU
Indiana-Purdue University, Fort Wayne, IN [*Library symbol*] ... InFwIP
Indiana Slavic Studies [*A publication*] ... ISS
Indiana State Library, Indianapolis, IN [*Library symbol*] ... In
Indiana State Library, Indianapolis, IN [*OCLC symbol*] ... ISL
Indiana State Supreme Court, Law Library, Indianapolis, IN [*Library symbol*] ... In-SC
Indiana State University ... ISU
Indiana State University. Department of Geography and Geology. Professional Paper [*A publication*] ... Indiana State Univ Dep Geogr Geol Prof Pap
Indiana State University, Evansville Campus, Evansville, IN [*Library symbol*] ... InES
Indiana State University, Evansville, Evansville, IN [*OCLC symbol*] ... ISE
Indiana State University, Terre Haute, IN [*Library symbol*] ... InTI
Indiana State University, Terre Haute, IN [*OCLC symbol*] ... ISU
Indiana Theory Review [*A publication*] ... Indiana Theory R
Indiana Union List of Serials ... IULS
Indiana Union List of Serials, Indianapolis, IN [*OCLC symbol*] ... ILS
Indiana University ... IU
Indiana University, Anatomy-Physiology Laboratory, Bloomington, IN [*Library symbol*] ... InU-A
Indiana University, Biology Library, Bloomington, IN [*Library symbol*] ... InU-B
Indiana University, Bloomington, IN [*Library symbol*] ... InU
Indiana University, Bloomington, IN [*OCLC symbol*] ... IUL
Indiana University Bookman [*A publication*] ... IUB
Indiana University. Extension Division Bulletin [*A publication*] ... Ind Univ Extension Division Bull
Indiana University Folklore Series [*A publication*] ... IUFS
Indiana University, Fort Wayne Regional Campus, Fort Wayne, IN [*Library symbol*] ... InU-Fw
Indiana University Humanities Series [*A publication*] ... IUHS
Indiana University, Indianapolis Regional Campus, Indianapolis, IN [*Library symbol*] ... InU-I
Indiana University, Institute for Sex Research, Bloomington, IN [*Library symbol*] ... InU-ISR
Indiana University, Kokomo Regional Campus, Kokomo, IN [*Library symbol*] ... InU-K
Indiana University, Law Library, Indianapolis, IN [*Library symbol*] ... InU-L
Indiana University, Lilly Library, Bloomington, IN [*Library symbol*] ... InU-Li
Indiana University. Mathematics Journal [*A publication*] ... Indiana Univ Math J
Indiana University. Mathematics Journal [*A publication*] ... Indi Math J
Indiana University, Northwest Regional Campus, Gary, IN [*Library symbol*] ... InU-N
Indiana University, Optometry Library, Bloomington, IN [*Library symbol*] ... InU-O
Indiana University of Pennsylvania ... IUP
Indiana University of Pennsylvania, Indiana, PA [*Library symbol*] ... PInU
Indiana University of Pennsylvania, Indiana, PA [*OCLC symbol*] ... PZI
Indiana University Press ... IUP
Indiana University Publications. Anthropology and Linguistics [*A publication*] ... IUPAL
Indiana University Publications. Folklore Series [*A publication*] ... IUPFS
Indiana University Publications. Humanistic Series [*A publication*] ... IUPHS
Indiana University Publications. Language Science Monographs [*A publication*] ... IUPLSM
Indiana University Publications. Slavic and East European Series [*A publication*] ... IUPSEES
Indiana University Publications. Uralic and Altaic Series [*A publication*] ... IUPUAS
Indiana University - Purdue University at Indianapolis ... IUPUI
Indiana University - Purdue University at Indianapolis, Downtown Campus, Indianapolis, IN [*Library symbol*] ... InIU
Indiana University, Purdue University at Indianapolis, Indianapolis, IN [*OCLC symbol*] ... IUP
Indiana University - Purdue University at Indianapolis, School of Physical Education, Indianapolis, IN [*Library symbol*] ... InIPE
Indiana University. Research Center in Anthropology, Folklore, and Linguistics [*A publication*] ... IURCAFL

Indiana University, School of Business Administration, Bloomington, IN [*Library symbol*]..............InU-BA
Indiana University, School of Dentistry, Indianapolis, IN [*Library symbol*]..............InU-D
Indiana University, School of Dentistry, Indianapolis, IN [*OCLC symbol*]..............IUD
Indiana University. School of Education. Bulletin [*A publication*]..............Indiana Univ Ed Bul
Indiana University. School of Education. Bulletin [*A publication*]..............Ind Univ Sch Ed B
Indiana University, School of Law Library, Bloomington, IN [*OCLC symbol*]..............IUB
Indiana University, School of Law Library, Indianapolis, IN [*OCLC symbol*]..............ILI
Indiana University, School of Medicine, Health Library Cooperative, Indianapolis, IN [*OCLC symbol*]..............IUH
Indiana University, School of Medicine, Indianapolis, IN [*Library symbol*]..............InU-M
Indiana University, School of Medicine, Indianapolis, IN [*OCLC symbol*]..............IUM
Indiana University, School of Medicine, Medical Education Resources Program, Indianapolis, IN [*OCLC symbol*]..............XLC
Indiana University, South Bend Regional Campus, South Bend, IN [*Library symbol*]..............InU-Sb
Indiana University, Southeastern Regional Campus, Jeffersonville, IN [*Library symbol*]..............InU-Se
Indiana University Studies in the History and Theory of Linguistics [*A publication*]..............IUSHTL
Indiana Writing Today [*A publication*]..............IWT
Indianapolis [*Indiana*] [*Airport symbol*]..............IND
Indianapolis, IN [*Location identifier*] [*FAA*]..............BJP
Indianapolis, IN [*Location identifier*] [*FAA*]..............COA
Indianapolis, IN [*Location identifier*] [*FAA*]..............EYE
Indianapolis, IN [*Location identifier*] [*FAA*]..............TYQ
Indianapolis, IN [*Radio station call letters*]..............WAJC
Indianapolis, IN [*Radio station call letters*]..............WATI
Indianapolis, IN [*Radio station call letters*]..............WBDG
Indianapolis, IN [*Radio station call letters*]..............WBRI
Indianapolis, IN [*Radio station call letters*]..............WEDM
Indianapolis, IN [*Radio station call letters*]..............WFBQ
Indianapolis, IN [*Radio station call letters*]..............WFMS
Indianapolis, IN [*Television station call letters*]..............WFYI
Indianapolis, IN [*Television station call letters*]..............WHMB-TV
Indianapolis, IN [*Radio station call letters*]..............WIAN
Indianapolis, IN [*Radio station call letters*]..............WIBC
Indianapolis, IN [*Radio station call letters*]..............WICR
Indianapolis, IN [*Radio station call letters*]..............WIRE
Indianapolis, IN [*Television station call letters*]..............WISH-TV
Indianapolis, IN [*Radio station call letters*]..............WJEL
Indianapolis, IN [*Radio station call letters*]..............WMLF
Indianapolis, IN [*Radio station call letters*]..............WNAP
Indianapolis, IN [*Radio station call letters*]..............WNDE
Indianapolis, IN [*Radio station call letters*]..............WNTS
Indianapolis, IN [*Television station call letters*]..............WPDS-TV
Indianapolis, IN [*Radio station call letters*]..............WRFT
Indianapolis, IN [*Television station call letters*]..............WRTV
Indianapolis, IN [*Television station call letters*]..............WTHR
Indianapolis, IN [*Radio station call letters*]..............WTLC
Indianapolis, IN [*Radio station call letters*]..............WXLW
Indianapolis, IN [*Radio station call letters*]..............WXTZ
Indianapolis Law Catalog Consortium, Indiana University School of Law Library, Indianapolis, IN [*OCLC symbol*]..............IIL
Indianapolis Law School, Indianapolis, IN [*Library symbol*]..............InILS
Indianapolis-Marion County Public Library, Indianapolis, IN [*OCLC symbol*]..............IMD
Indianapolis-Marion County Public Library, Indianapolis, IN [*Library symbol*]..............InI
Indianapolis Museum of Art, Indianapolis, IN [*OCLC symbol*]..............IMO
Indianapolis Power & Light Co. [*NYSE symbol*] [*Delisted*]..............IPL
Indianapolis Public Schools, Indianapolis, IN [*OCLC symbol*]..............IPP
Indianapolis Union [*AAR code*]..............IU
Indianapolis Water [*NASDAQ symbol*]..............IWTR
Indianfields Public Library, Caro, MI [*Library symbol*]..............MiCa
Indianola, IA [*Radio station call letters*]..............KBAB
Indianola, MS [*Location identifier*] [*FAA*]..............IDL
Indianola, MS [*Radio station call letters*]..............WNLA
Indianola, MS [*Radio station call letters*]..............WNLA-FM
Indians into Communications Association..............IICA
Indians into Medicine [*Program*]..............INMED
Indiantown Gap, PA [*Location identifier*] [*FAA*]..............BZJ
Indic [*MARC language code*] [*Library of Congress*]..............inc
Indicate [*or Indicator*]..............IND
Indicate..............INDC
Indicate..............INDI
Indicate..............INDIC
Indicated [*or Indicative*]..............IND
Indicated Air Speed..............IAS
Indicated Air Temperature..............IAT
Indicated Altitude [*Navigation*]..............IA
Indicated Horsepower..............I
Indicated Horsepower..............IHP

Indicated Horsepower-Hour..............IHPH
Indicated Horsepower-Hour..............IHP-HR
Indicated Mach Number..............IMN
Indicated Main Engine..............I
Indicated Mean Effective Pressure [*Aerospace*]..............IMEP
Indicated Pressure Altitude..............IPA
Indicated True Air Speed [*Aviation*]..............ITAS
Indicateu Electronique de Pilotage [*Electronic Pilotage Indicator*] [*Aviation*]..............IEP
Indicateurs de l'Economie du Centre [*A publication*]..............Indicateurs Econ Centre
Indicating Device..............ID
Indicating Light..............IL
Indicating Light Relay..............ILR
Indication..............INDICN
Indications Review Committee [*Military*]..............IRC
Indicative [*Grammar*]..............INDIC
Indicative Planning Figure..............IPF
Indicative World Plan for Agricultural Development [*United Nations*]..............IWP
Indicator..............I
Indicator..............INDCTR
Indicator and Control..............IC
Indicator Control Unit..............ICU
Indicator Digest Average [*NYSE symbol*]..............IDA
Indicator Drive Screw..............IDS
Indicator Driver..............ID
Indicator Group..............IG
Indicator Group Speed..............IGS
Indicator Kit..............IK
Indicator Panel..............IP
Indicator Time Test [*Chemistry*]..............ITT
Indicator-Transmitter..............INDTR
Indicatore Cartotecnico [*A publication*]..............Indic Cartotec
Indicatore Grafico [*A publication*]..............Indic Grafico
Indice Agricole de America Latina y el Caribe [*A publication*]..............Ind Agri Am Lat Caribe
Indice de Arte y Letras [*A publication*]..............Ind
Indice Bibliografico de Lepra [*A publication*]..............Indice Bibliogr Lepra
Indice Historico Espanol [*A publication*]..............IHE
Indice de la Literatura Dental en Castellano [*A publication*]..............Ind Lit Dent
Indice Medico Espanol [*A publication*]..............Ind Med Esp
Indices of General Industrial Worth..............IGIW
Indices de Revista de Bibliotecologia [*A publication*]..............IREBI
Indies..............IND
Indigenous..............INDIG
Indigenous Peoples' Network..............IPN
Indio, CA [*Radio station call letters*]..............KRCQ
Indio Public Library, Indio, CA [*Library symbol*]..............CInd
Indirect..............IND
Indirect Addressing..............IA
Indirect Blood Pressure Measuring System..............IBPMS
Indirect Bomb-Damage Assessment..............IBDA
Indirect Centrifugal Flotation..............ICF
Indirect Component Improvement Program..............ICIP
Indirect Coombs' Test [*Immunochemistry*]..............ICT
Indirect Cost Management System..............ICMS
Indirect Coulometric Titration [*Analytical chemistry*]..............ICT
Indirect Damage [*Insurance*]..............ID
Indirect by Direct..............IDD
Indirect Fluorescent..............IF
Indirect Fluorescent Antibody Test [*Immunology*]..............IFAT
Indirect Hemagglutination [*Clinical chemistry*]..............IHA
Indirect Immunofluorescence [*Immunochemistry*]..............IIF
Indirect Immunofluorescence Technique [*Immunochemistry*]..............IIFT
Indirect Labor..............I/D
Indirect Maintenance Man-Hour..............IMMH
Indirect Manufacturing Expense..............IME
Indirect Material Purchasing Information Standards..............IMPIS
Indirect Measuring System..............IMS
Indirect Method..............IDM
Indirect Operating Costs..............IOC
Indirect Photometric Chromatography..............IPC
Indirect Plaque-Forming Cell [*Immunology*]..............iPFC
Indirect Proof [*Method in logic*]..............IP
Indirect Reading Pocket Chamber..............IRPC
Indirect Reference Word..............IRW
Indirect Target Damage Assessment..............ITDA
Indirect Waste..............IW
Indirect Work Breakdown Structure..............IWBS
Indirectly..............IDRTY
Indirectly Heated..............IH
Indirectly Heated Cathode..............IHC
Indium [*Chemical element*]..............In
Indium Antimode Varactor..............IAV
Indium Arsenide Filter..............IAF
Indium Arsenide Infrared Detector..............IAID
Indium Tin Oxide..............ITO
Individual [*Missile launch environment symbol*]..............F
Individual..............INDIV
Individual [*Freight*]..............INDIVL
Individual Acceptance Tests..............IAT

Individual Account Number File [*IRS*] ..... IANF
Individual Action Report ..... IAR
Individual Airplane Tracking Program ..... IATP
Individual Bias ..... IB
Individual Cleared for Access to Classified Material ..... ICFATCM
Individual Cleared for Access to Classified Material Up to and Including ..... ICFATCMUTAI
Individual/Collective Integration ICI
Individual/Collective Training Plan [*Army*] ..... ICTP
Individual Combat Actions [*Army*] ..... ICA
Individual Commitment to Excellence [*DoD*] ..... ICE
Individual Component Repair List [*DoD*] ..... ICRL
Individual Criterion-Referenced Test [*Education*] ..... ICRT
Individual Defense Counsel ..... IDC
Individual Development ..... ID
Individual Development Plan ..... IDP
Individual Development Program [*Civil Service Commission*] ..... IDP
Individual Documented Quality Assurance ..... IDQA
Individual Dose [*Radioactivity calculations*] ..... ID
Individual Drop Glider ..... IDG
Individual Education Record ..... IER
Individual Effective Dose ..... IED
Individual Evaluation Plan [*Army*] ..... IEP
Individual Evaluation Report ..... IER
Individual Field of View ..... IFOV
Individual Flight Activity Reporting System [*Navy*] ..... IFARS
Individual Flight Plans from This Point ..... IFPFP
Individual Housing Account ..... IHA
Individual Implementation Plan [*For the education of a handicapped person*] ..... IIP
Individual Inclusive Tour [*Air fare plan*] ..... IIT
Individual Instruction [*A publication*] ..... Indiv Inst
Individual Knowledge Evaluation Test ..... IKET
Individual Learning Disabilities Classroom Screening Instruments ..... ILDCSI
Individual and Marriage Counseling Inventory [*Psychology*] ..... IMCI
Individual Master File ..... IMF
Individual Material Readiness List [*DoD*] ..... IMRL
Individual Medical Record ..... IMR
Individual Medley [*Swimming*] ..... IM
Individual Merit Promotion ..... IMP
Individual Mobilization Augmentee [*DoD*] ..... IMA
Individual Motor Behavior Survey [*Test*] ..... IMBS
Individual Name and Address File [*IRS*] ..... INAF
Individual Name and Address Key Index File [*IRS*] ..... IKIF
Individual Nonrecurrence Action ..... INA
Individual Onsite Wastewater Systems [*A publication*] ..... Individ Onsite Wastewater Syst
Individual Operation Test ..... IOT
Individual Package Delivery ..... IPD
Individual Pay Record [*Military*] ..... IPR
Individual Personal Hygiene Equipment ..... IPHE
Individual Personal Hygiene Module ..... IPHM
Individual Practice Association [*A form of health maintenance organization*] ..... IPA
Individual Program Plan ..... IPP
Individual Psychologist [*A publication*] ..... Indiv Psych
Individual Psychologist [*A publication*] ..... IPSYA
Individual Psychology Association of New York ..... IPANY
Individual Ready Reserve [*Army*] ..... IRR
Individual Recorder [*Sports*] ..... IR
Individual Records Brief [*Military*] ..... IRB
Individual Reliability Test ..... IRT
Individual Repair Parts Ordering Data [*Program*] [*DoD*] ..... IRPOD
Individual Retirement Account ..... IRA
Individual Retirement Account File [*IRS*] ..... IRAF
Individual Retirement Account Register [*IRS*] ..... IRAR
Individual Retirement Arrangement ..... IRA
Individual Retirement Record [*Air Force*] ..... IRR
Individual Risk Premium Modification [*Insurance*] ..... IRPM
Individual Ship Exercises ..... ISE
Individual Soldier's Report ..... ISR
Individual Survival Vest for Aircrew [*Army*] ..... ISVESTA
Individual System Operation ..... ISO
Individual Task Authorization ..... ITA
Individual Taxpayer Information File [*IRS*] ..... ITIF
Individual Technical Training [*Military*] ..... ITT
Individual Tour Basing [*Fares*] ..... ITB
Individual Training [*Navy*] ..... INDTNG
Individual Training [*Army*] ..... IT
Individual Training and Performance Research Laboratory [*Army*] ..... ITPRL
Individual Training Plan [*Army*] ..... ITP
Individual Training Plan Proposal [*Army*] ..... ITPP
Individual Travel Order [*Military*] ..... ITO
Individual Treatment Plan [*For the medical care and the education of a handicapped person*] ..... ITP
Individual Viable Cells [*Metabolic studies*] IVC
Individual Weapons Captured ..... IWC
Individual Yield Coverage Program [*Department of Agriculture*] ..... IYC
Individualized Education Program [*For the education of a handicapped person*] ..... IEP
Individualized Instruction II
Individualized Mathematics System [*Education*] ..... IMS
Individualized Reading Program [*Education*] ..... IRP
Individualized Science Instructional System [*National Science Foundation project*] ..... ISIS
Individually ..... INDV
Individually Guided Education [*for upgrading students' skills*] ..... IGE
Individually Planned [*or Prescribed*] **Instruction** [*Education*] ..... IPI
Individually Planned Instruction/Management and Information System ..... IPI/MIS
Individually Quick-Frozen [*Food technology*] ..... IQF
Individuals for a Rational Society [*Defunct*] ..... IFRS
Indo-American Sports Association [*Later, FIA-USC*] ..... IASA
Indo-Asia [*A publication*] ..... Indo-As
Indo-Asian Culture [*A publication*] ..... IAC
Indo-European ..... IE
Indo-European [*MARC language code*] [*Library of Congress*] ..... ine
Indo-Germanic [*Language, etc.*] ..... IG
Indo-Iranian Journal [*A publication*] ..... IIJ
Indo-Pacific Council of the International Committee of Scientific Management ..... IPCCIOS
Indo-Pacific Fisheries Council ..... IPFC
Indo-Pacific Fisheries Council. Occasional Papers [*A publication*] ..... Indo-Pac Fish Counc Occas Pap
Indo-Pacific Fisheries Council. Proceedings [*A publication*] ..... Indo-Pac Fish Counc Proc
Indo-Pacific Fisheries Council. Regional Studies [*A publication*] ..... Indo-Pac Fish Counc Reg Stud
Indo-Pacific Fisheries Council. Special Publications [*A publication*] ..... Indo-Pac Fish Counc Spec Publ
Indo-Pacific International [*Tamuning, GU*] [*FAA designator*] ..... TMC
Indo-Pacific Mollusca [*A publication*] ..... Indo-Pac Mollusca
Indo-Pacific Prehistory Association [*Formerly, FEPA*] ..... IPPA
Indochina [*MARC geographic area code*] [*Library of Congress*] ..... ai-----
Indochina IC
Indochina Curriculum Group ..... ICG
Indochina Postwar Reconstruction ..... IPR
Indochina Refugee Action Center ..... IRAC
Indoctrinate ..... INDOC
Indocyanine Green [*Liver function test*] [*Medicine*] ..... ICG
Indogermanische Bibliothek [*A publication*] ..... IB
Indogermanische Forschungen [*A publication*] ..... Idg Forsch
Indogermanische Forschungen [*A publication*] ..... IF
Indogermanische Forschungen [*A publication*] ..... IGForsch
Indogermanische Jahrbuch [*A publication*] ..... IJ
Indogermanische Jahrbuch [*A publication*] ..... IJb
Indol Glycerophosphate [*Biochemistry*] ..... InGP
Indole, Methyl-Red, Voges-Proskauer, Citrate Test [*Bacteriology*] ..... IMViC
Indoleacetic Acid [*Plant growth promoter*] ..... IAA
Indolebutyric Acid [*Plant growth regulator*] ..... IBA
Indoleethanol [*Organic chemistry*] ..... IEA
Indoleglycerolphosphate Synthase [*Biochemistry*] ..... InGPS
Indomethacin-Treated Platelet Microsomes ..... IPM
Indonesia [*a-pt (Portuguese Timor) used in records cataloged before April 1980*] [*MARC geographic area code*] [*Library of Congress*] ..... a-io---
Indonesia [*Two-letter standard code*] ..... ID
Indonesia [*Three-letter standard code*] ..... IDN
Indonesia ..... INDO
Indonesia [*pt (Portuguese Timor) used in records cataloged before January 1978*] [*MARC country of publication code*] [*Library of Congress*] ..... io
Indonesia [*Aircraft nationality and registration mark*] ..... PK
Indonesia Direktorat Geologi. Publikasi Teknik. Seri Geofisika [*A publication*] ..... Indones Dir Geol Publ Tek Ser Geofis
Indonesia Direktorat Geologi. Publikasi Teknik. Seri Paleontologi [*A publication*] ..... Indones Dir Geol Publ Tek Ser Paleontol
Indonesian [*MARC language code*] [*Library of Congress*] ..... ind
Indonesian Air Force ..... IAF
Indonesian Institute of Marine Research. Oceanographical Cruise Report [*A publication*] ..... Indones Inst Mar Res Oceanogr Cruise Rep
Indonesian Journal of Geography [*A publication*] ..... Indo J Geog
Indonesian Journal of Geography [*A publication*] ..... Indonesian J G
Indonesian Petroleum Association. Annual Convention. Proceedings [*A publication*] ..... Indones Pet Assoc Annu Conv Proc
Indonesian Quarterly [*A publication*] ..... Indones Quart
Indonesian Quarterly [*A publication*] ..... Indo Q
Indonesian Students Association in the United States ..... ISAUS
Indoor Citrus and Rare Fruit Society ..... ICRFS
Indoor Light Gardening Society of America ..... ILGSA
Indoor Sports Club ..... ISC
Indoor Tennis Association [*Later, NTA*] ..... ITA
Indophenol Oxidase [*An enzyme*] ..... IPO
Indore [*India*] [*Airport symbol*] ..... IDR
Indore Mill Mazdoor Sangh [*Indore Textile Labour Association*] [*India*] ..... IMMS
Indorse ..... IND
Indorsement Irregular [*Banking*] ..... I/I
Induced Dipole Moment ..... IDM
Induced Directional FM ..... IDFM

Induced Draft .... ID
Induced Electrical Effect .... IEE
Induced Electromagnetic Pulse .... IEMP
Induced Electron Emission .... IEE
Induced Environmental Contamination Monitor .... IECM
Induced Fluid Flow .... IFF
Induced Muscular Tension [*Physiology*] .... IMT
Induced Nuclear Disintegration .... IND
Induced Polarization [*Geophysical prospecting*] .... IP
Induced Radiation Flux .... IRF
Induced Remanent Magnetization .... IRM
Induced Surface Effect .... ISE
Inductance .... IND
Inductance [*Symbol*] L
Inductance-Capacitance IC
Inductance/Capacitance .... L/C
Inductance-Capacitance-Resistance .... ICR
Inductance-Capacitance-Resistance .... LCR
Inductance Decade Box .... IDB
Inductance Regulator .... INDREG
Inductee Special Assignment .... ISA
Induction I
Induction .... IND
Induction .... INDN
Induction .... INDUC
Induction Communications System .... ICS
Induction Compass .... ICMPS
Induction-Conduction Heating .... ICH
Induction Ion LASER IIL
Induction Loop Communications System .... ILCS
Induction Output Tube .... IOT
Induction Period [*Medicine*] .... IP
Induction Plasma Gun .... IPG
Induction Plasma Torch .... IPT
Induction of Psychoneuroses by Conditioned Reflex under Stress [*In book and film "The Ipcress File"*] .... IPCRESS
Induction and Recruiting Station [*Marine Corps*] .... IRS
Induction System Deposit .... ISD
Induction Tube Modulation .... ITM
Inductive Coupling IC
Inductive Data Exploration and Analysis [*Data processing*] .... IDEA
Inductive Energy Storage .... IES
Inductive Energy Storage Modulator .... IESM
Inductive Loss Factor .... ILF
Inductive Null Voltage .... INV
Inductive Potentiometer .... IPOT
Inductive Storage Switch .... ISS
Inductively Coupled Argon Plasma [*Spectrometry*] .... ICAP
Inductively Coupled Plasma [*Spectrometry*] .... ICP
Inductively Coupled Plasma Emission Spectrometry .... ICPES
Inducto-Ratio Bridge .... IRB
Inductor .... IDCTR
Inductosyn .... ISYN
Inductosyn Angle Position Simulator .... IAPS
Inductosyn Linearity Checkout Kit .... ILCK
Indulin Agar [*Microbiology*] .... IA
Indus [*Constellation*] .... Ind
Indus [*Constellation*] .... Indi
Industri og Miljoe [*A publication*] .... Ind Miljoe
Industria Alimentaria [*A publication*] .... Ind Aliment
Industria Brasileira de Produtos Eletronicos e Electricos, SA .... IBRAPE
Industria della Carta [*A publication*] .... Ind Carta
Industria e Commercio de Mineros, SA .... ICOMI
Industria Conserve [*A publication*] .... Ind Conserve
Industria Conserve (Parma) [*A publication*] .... Ind Conserve (Parma)
Industria Electrica de Mexico, SA [*NYSE symbol*] [*Delisted*] .... IEX
Industria Farmaceutica y Bioquimica [*A publication*] .... Ind Farm Bioquim
Industria del Hierro [*Part of a large Mexican industrial complex*] .... I/H
Industria Italiana del Cemento [*A publication*] .... Ind Ital Cem
Industria Italiana Elettrotecnica ed Elettronica [*A publication*] .... Ind Ital Elettrotec & Elettron
Industria Lemnului [*A publication*] .... Ind Lemnului
Industria Libraria Tipografica Editrice .... ILTE
Industria Mineraria (Rome) [*A publication*] .... Ind Min (Rome)
Industria y Quimica (Buenos Aires) [*A publication*] .... Ind Quim (Buenos Aires)
Industrial I
Industrial .... INDL
Industrial .... INDUST
Industrial .... INDUSTL
Industrial Accident Board .... IAB
Industrial Accountable Property Officer [*Air Force*] .... IAPO
Industrial Acoustics [*NASDAQ symbol*] .... IACI
Industrial Advertising Research Institute [*Later, CMC*] .... IARI
Industrial Advisory Board [*World War II*] .... IAB
Industrial Aerodynamics Information Service [*British*] .... IAIS
Industrial Analysis and Control Council .... IACC
Industrial Appointment Full Time [*Chiropody*] [*British*] .... IF
Industrial Arbitration Board [*British*] .... IAB
Industrial Areas Foundation .... IAF
Industrial-Arts Magazine [*A publication*] .... Ind-Arts M
Industrial Arts and Vocational Education/Technical Education [*A publication*] .... Ind Arts & Voc Ed
Industrial Association of Juvenile Apparel Manufacturers .... IAJAM
Industrial Audio-Visual Association [*Later, AVMA*] .... IAVA
Industrial Bank of Japan .... IBJ
[*The*] **Industrial Bank of Kuwait** .... IBK
Industrial Base Engineering Activity .... IBEA
Industrial Bio-Test Laboratories, Inc. .... IBT
Industrial Biotechnology Association .... IBA
Industrial Business [*Insurance term*] [*British*] .... IB
Industrial Canada [*A publication*] .... Ind Can
Industrial Capacity Committee of the Production Council [*British*] [*World War II*] ICC
Industrial Chemist [*A publication*] .... Ind Chem
Industrial Civil Defense Management .... ICDM
[*The*] **Industrial College of the Armed Forces** [*Later, UND*] .... ICAF
[*The*] **Industrial College of the Armed Forces** [*Later, UND*] .... TICAF
Industrial and Commercial Company ICC
Industrial and Commercial Development Corporation [*Kenya*] .... ICDC
Industrial and Commercial Finance Corporation [*British*] .... ICFC
Industrial and Commercial Gas [*A publication*] .... Ind Comm Gas
Industrial and Commercial Photographer [*A publication*] .... Ind Commer Photogr
Industrial and Commercial Power Systems .... ICPS
Industrial Communication Association [*Later, International Communication Association*] .... ICA
Industrial Communication Council ICC
Industrial Compressor Distributors Association .... ICDA
Industrial and Construction Equipment Division [*Formerly, IEMC*] .... ICED
Industrial Control Products .... ICP
Industrial Control System .... ICS
Industrial Cooperation Division [*Navy*] .... ICD
Industrial Cooperative Association .... ICA
Industrial Cost Exclusion [*Amendment to Federal Clean Water Act which limits use of federal money*] .... ICE
Industrial Cost and Performance Report .... ICPR
Industrial Cost Recovery [*Environmental Protection Agency*] .... ICR
Industrial Coupling Program [*Refers to university-industry interaction*] .... ICP
Industrial Credit & Investment Corporation of India Ltd. ICICI
Industrial Damage Reports [*Formerly, ITR*] [*British*] [*World War II*] .... IDR
Industrial Data Bank Department [*Gulf Organization for Industrial Consulting*] [*Information service*] .... IDB
Industrial Data Processing .... IDP
Industrial Data Reduction .... IDR
Industrial Design [*A publication*] .... Ind Des
Industrial Design [*A publication*] .... Ind Design
Industrial Design Assistance Program [*National Design Council, Canada*] .... IDAP
Industrial Design Award .... IDA
Industrial Designers' Institute [*Later, IDSA*] .... IDI
Industrial Designers' Society of America .... IDSA
Industrial Development .... ID
Industrial Development [*A publication*] .... Ind Devel
Industrial Development Abstracts [*A publication*] .... Ind Develop Abstr
Industrial Development Advisory Board [*British*] .... IDAB
Industrial Development Authority [*Ireland*] .... IDA
Industrial Development Bank .... IDB
Industrial Development Center for Arab States .... IDCAS
Industrial Development Certificate [*Department of Industry*] [*British*] .... IDC
Industrial Development Corporation .... IDC
Industrial Development Division [*Vietnam*] .... IDD
Industrial Development Group .... IDG
Industrial Development Institute [*France*] .... IDI
Industrial Development and Manufacturers Record [*A publication*] .... Ind Dev
Industrial Development Organization [*United Nations*] .... IDO
Industrial Development Quotient .... IDQ
Industrial Development Research Council .... IDRC
Industrial-Development Revenue Bond [*Issued by a state or local government to finance construction by a private company, which then becomes responsible for repaying the debt*] .... IDRB
Industrial Development Unit .... IDU
Industrial Diamond Association of America .... IDA
Industrial Diamond Association of America .... IDAA
Industrial Diamond Review [*A publication*] .... Ind Diam Re
Industrial Diamond Review [*A publication*] .... Ind Diam Rev
Industrial Diamond Review [*A publication*] .... Indus Diamond Rev
Industrial Disputers Tribunal [*British*] .... IDT
Industrial Distribution [*A publication*] .... Ind Distr
Industrial Distribution [*A publication*] .... Ind Distrib
Industrial Documentation and Information Department [*Industrial Development Center for Arab States*] [*Information service*] .... IDID
Industrial Dynamics [*Management analysis*] .... ID
Industrial Editors Association .... IEA
Industrial Education Institute .... IEI
Industrial Education Magazine [*A publication*] .... Ind Ed M
Industrial Education Magazine [*A publication*] .... Ind Educ
Industrial Education Magazine [*A publication*] .... Ind Educ M
Industrial Electrification Council [*Later, TEC*] .... IEC

Industrial Electronic Hardware Corporation [*NASDAQ symbol*]............ IEHC
Industrial Electronic Security .... INDELSEC
Industrial Electronics.. IE
Industrial Electronics and Control Instrumentation............................... IECI
Industrial Engineer [*or Engineering*]... IE
Industrial Engineer .... Ind E
Industrial Engineering [*A publication*]..................................... Ind Eng
Industrial Engineering [*A publication*]..................................... Indus Eng
Industrial and Engineering Chemistry [*A publication*] .... I & EC
Industrial and Engineering Chemistry [*A publication*] ....Ind & Eng Chem
Industrial and Engineering Chemistry [*A publication*] ....Ind Eng Chem
Industrial and Engineering Chemistry [*A publication*] .... Indus and Eng Chemistry
Industrial and Engineering Chemistry. Fundamentals [*A publication*] ....Ind Eng Chem Fundam
Industrial and Engineering Chemistry. Fundamentals [*A publication*] ....Ind & Eng Chem Fundamentals
Industrial and Engineering Chemistry. Fundamentals [*A publication*] .... Ind Eng F
Industrial and Engineering Chemistry (International Edition) [*A publication*] ....Industr Engng Chem (Int Ed)
Industrial and Engineering Chemistry. Process Design and Development [*A publication*] .... Ind & Eng Chem Process Des Dev
Industrial and Engineering Chemistry. Process Design and Development [*A publication*] ....Ind & Eng Chem Process Design
Industrial and Engineering Chemistry. Process Design and Development [*A publication*] ....Ind Eng PDD
Industrial and Engineering Chemistry. Product Research and Development [*A publication*] ....Ind Eng Chem Prod Res Dev
Industrial and Engineering Chemistry. Product Research and Development [*A publication*] ....Ind Eng PRD
Industrial Engineering Institute .... IEI
Industrial Engineering Services... IES
Industrial Environmental Research Laboratory [*Environmental Protection Agency*]..IERL
Industrial Equipment Manufacturers Council [*Later, ICED*]..................IEMC
Industrial Equipment Materials and Services [*A publication*] .... Ind Equip Mater & Serv
Industrial Equipment News [*A publication*] ....IEN
Industrial Equipment Reserve...IER
Industrial Evaluation Board [*BDSA*]..IEB
Industrial Fabrics Association International ....IFAI
Industrial Facilities and Material Information System...................... IFMIS
Industrial Facilities Protection Program [*DoD*] ....IFPP
Industrial Fasteners Institute ....IFI
Industrial Finishing [*A publication*] ....Ind Finish
Industrial Finishing Equipment Manufacturers Association...............IFEMA
Industrial Finishing and Surface Coatings [*A publication*] .... Ind Finish Surf Coat
Industrial Finishing and Surface Coatings [*A publication*] .... Ind Finish & Surf Coatings
Industrial Fire Safety Library [*National Fire Protection Association*] .... IFSL
Industrial Fishery Products Market Review and Outlook [*A publication*]... Indus Fish Prod Mark Rev & Outl
Industrial Forestry Association... IFA
Industrial Frequency Changer .... IFC
Industrial Fund.. IF
Industrial Gas [*A publication*] .... Ind Gas
Industrial Gas Cleaning Institute .... IGCI
Industrial Gerontology [*A publication*] .... Ind Geront
Industrial Gerontology [*A publication*] .... Ind Gerontol
Industrial Gerontology [*A publication*] .... Industr Gerontol
Industrial Graphics International [*Later, IG*] [*An association*]..................IGI
Industrial Health [*A publication*] .... Ind Health
Industrial Health Advisory Council [*British*] .... IHAC
Industrial Health Foundation... IHF
Industrial Health (Kawasaki) [*A publication*] ....Ind Health (Kawasaki)
Industrial Health Research Board [*British*] .... IHRB
Industrial Heating [*A publication*]... Ind Heat
Industrial Heating Equipment Association.................................... IHEA
Industrial Heating (Pittsburg) [*A publication*].................. Ind Heat (Pittsburg)
Industrial Hygiene Digest [*A publication*].................................. Ind Hyg Dig
Industrial Hygienist [*Occupational Safety and Health Administration*]......... IH
Industrial Indemnity Co., San Francisco, CA [*Library symbol*] ....CSfII
Industrial India [*A publication*]...Ind India
Industrial Information and Advisory Services [*UNIDO*] .... INDIS
Industrial Information Service .... IIS
Industrial Information's Record Management System [*Data processing*]..IIRMS
Industrial Intelligence Centre [*British*] [*World War II*] IIC
Industrial Jacks Product Section of the Material Handling Institute .... IJPSMHI
Industrial and Labor Relations .... ILR
Industrial Labor Relations Office [*DoD*]...................................... ILRO
Industrial and Labor Relations Review [*A publication*]...........................ILRR
Industrial and Labor Relations Review [*A publication*].....Ind Labor Relat Rev
Industrial and Labor Relations Review [*A publication*]........ Ind & Labor Rel R
Industrial and Labor Relations Review [*A publication*].................. Ind Lab Rel
Industrial and Labor Relations Review [*A publication*]........Ind & Lab Rel Rev
Industrial and Labor Relations Review [*A publication*]...................... Industrial & Labor Rel Rev
Industrial and Labor Relations Review [*A publication*]..... Industr Lab Relat R
Industrial Laboratories [*Chicago*] [*A publication*] .... Ind Lab
Industrial Laboratory (United States) [*A publication*] ....Ind Lab (US)
Industrial Laboratory (USSR) [*A publication*] ....Ind Lab (USSR)
Industrial Law Review Quarterly [*A publication*]..................Industrial L Rev Q
Industrial Liaison Centre [*British*] ILC
Industrial Liaison Program [*Refers to university-industry interaction*]....... ILP
Industrial Lift and Loading Ramp Institute [*Defunct*] ....ILLRI
Industrial Lubrication [*A publication*]...................................... Ind Lubric
Industrial Lubrication and Tribology [*A publication*]....... Ind Lubric Tribology
Industrial Lubrication and Tribology [*A publication*]...............Ind Lubr Tribol
Industrial Management [*A publication*] .... Ind Manage
Industrial Management [*New York*] [*A publication*] .... Ind Management
Industrial Management [*New York*] [*A publication*] .... Ind Mgt
Industrial Management Assistance Survey [*Air Force*]......................IMAS
Industrial Management and Data Systems [*A publication*]............................ Ind Mgt & Data Syst
Industrial Management Improvement Program.................................. IMIP
Industrial Management (London) [*A publication*].............................. Ind Management (London)
Industrial Management Program ....IMP
Industrial Management Review [*A publication*] ....Ind Management R
Industrial Management Review [*A publication*] ....Ind Mgt R
Industrial Management Society .... IMS
Industrial Manager... IM
Industrial Manager.. INDMAN
Industrial Manager... INDMGR
Industrial Marketing [*A publication*]...................................... Ind Market
Industrial Marketing [*A publication*].. Ind Mktg
Industrial Marketing Associates ....IMA
Industrial Marketing Association...IMA
Industrial Marketing Management [*A publication*] .... Ind Mkt Man
Industrial Materials Handling Equipment......................................IMHE
Industrial Mathematics [*A publication*] .... Ind Math
Industrial Mathematics Society .... IMS
Industrial Medical Administrators' Association [*Later, OMAA*] .... IMAA
Industrial Medical Association [*Later, AOMA*] ....IMA
Industrial Medicine and Surgery [*A publication*] .... Ind Med
Industrial Medicine and Surgery [*A publication*] ....Ind Med Surg
Industrial Medicine and Surgery [*A publication*] .... Ind Med & Surg
Industrial Metal Containers Section of the Material Handling Institute ....IMC
Industrial Methylated Spirit.. IMS
Industrial Microfilm Company, Detroit, MI [*Library symbol*].....................ImC
Industrial Mineral Insulation Manufacturers Institute [*Later, TIMA*]..... IMIMI
Industrial Mineral Service [*Midland, ON*]..................................INDUSMIN
Industrial Minerals [*A publication*]... Ind Min
Industrial Minerals [*A publication*]...................................Indus Minerals
Industrial Minerals and Rocks [*A publication*] .... Ind Miner Rocks
Industrial Mobilization Planning .... IMP
Industrial Mobilization Production Planning [*DoD*] ....IMPP
Industrial Mobilization Training Program.......................................IMTP
Industrial National Corp. [*NYSE symbol*] [*Delisted*]..................................INB
Industrial Naval Air Stations...INAS
Industrial Obst- und Gemueseverwertung [*A publication*] .... Ind Obst- Gemueseverwert
Industrial Operations...IO
Industrial Participation [*Civil Defense*]... IP
Industrial Perforators Association ....IPA
Industrial Photographers Association of America [*Later, Industrial Photographers of New Jersey*] ....IPAA
Industrial Photographers of New Jersey ....IPNJ
Industrial Photography [*A publication*] .... Ind Phot
Industrial Photography [*A publication*] .... Ind Photogr
Industrial Planning... IP
Industrial Planning Committee [*NATO*]...IPC
Industrial Planning Specification... IPS
Industrial Plant [*or Production*] **Equipment** .... IPE
Industrial Plant Equipment Reutilization System [*DoD*]........................ IPERS
Industrial Plant Modernization Program [*Air Force*] ....IPMP
Industrial Police .... IP
Industrial Policy .... IP
Industrial Power Tube... IPT
Industrial Premises [*Public-performance tariff*] [*British*] I
Industrial Preparedness Measures ....IPM
Industrial Preparedness Planning [*DoD*] ....IPP
Industrial Preparedness Planning [*Military*] ....IPR
Industrial Process Control [*by computers*] ....IPC
Industrial Process Heat...IPH
Industrial and Process Heating [*A publication*] .... Ind Process Heat
Industrial Production... IP
Industrial and Production Engineering [*A publication*]............. Ind Prod Eng
Industrial Production Equipment Reserve ....IPER
Industrial Production Performance Reporting ....IPPR
Industrial Property Administration ....IPA
Industrial Property Committee [*US Military Government, Germany*].........IPC
Industrial Publicity Association ....IPA
Industrial Publishing Company...IPC
Industrial Quality Control [*A publication*].......................... Ind Quality Control
Industrial Quality Control ....IQC
Industrial Raw Materials Planning Committee [*NATO*] ....IRMPC

Industrial Rayon Corp., Covington, VA [*Library symbol*] ViCovl
Industrial Reactor Laboratories [*New Jersey*] IRL
Industrial Readiness and Mobilization Production Planning [*Military*] IRMP
Industrial Readiness Planning IRP
Industrial Readiness Planning Program IRPP
Industrial Readjustment Branch IRB
Industrial Reconstruction Corporation IRC
Industrial Rehabilitation Units [*British*] IRU
Industrial Relations [*A publication*] Ind Rel
Industrial Relations [*A publication*] Industr Relat
Industrial Relations IR
Industrial Relations [*A publication*] IR
Industrial Relations Advisory Committee IRAC
Industrial Relations Board IRB
Industrial Relations Bulletin IRB
Industrial Relations Council for the Plumbing and Pipe Fitting Industry IRC
Industrial Relations Council for the Plumbing and Pipe Fitting Industry IRCPPFI
Industrial Relations Counselors IRC
Industrial Relations Counselors, New York, NY [*Library symbol*] NNIR
Industrial Relations Office IRO
Industrial Relations and Personnel Development [*A publication*] IRPD
Industrial Relations Research Association IRRA
Industrial Relations Research Association. Proceedings [*A publication*] IRRA
Industrial Relations Review and Report [*A publication*] Ind Relat Rev Rep
Industrial Relations Review and Report [*A publication*] IRRR
Industrial Reorganization Corporation IRC
Industrial Reprocessing Group IRG
Industrial Research [*A publication*] Ind Res
Industrial Research Assistance Program [*Canada*] IRAP
Industrial Research and Development [*A publication*] Ind Res & Devel
Industrial Research and Development IR & D
Industrial Research Institute IRI
Industrial Research News [*Australia*] [*A publication*] Ind Res News
Industrial Research and Service Institute IRSI
Industrial Research Study. Timber Research and Development Association [*A publication*] Industr Res Study Timb Res Developm Ass
Industrial Resources [*NASDAQ symbol*] INDR
Industrial Retaining Ring Co. IRR
Industrial Revenue Bond [*Environmental Protection Agency*] IRB
Industrial Risk Insurers IRI
Industrial Robot [*A publication*] Ind Robot
Industrial Safety [*A publication*] Ind Saf
Industrial Safety Advisory Council [*British*] ISAC
Industrial Safety Chronicle [*A publication*] Ind Saf Chron
Industrial Safety Equipment Association ISEA
Industrial and Scientific Instruments [*A publication*] Ind Sci Instrum
Industrial, Scientific, and Medical ISM
Industrial Security Bulletin ISB
Industrial Security Clearance Review Office [*DoD*] ISCRO
Industrial Security Letter [*DoD*] ISL
Industrial Security Manual ISM
Industrial Security Plan [*Nuclear energy*] ISP
Industrial Security Program [*Air Force, Army*] ISP
Industrial Security Regulations [*DoD*] ISR
Industrial Security Section [*NATO*] ISS
Industrial Sentence Completion Form [*Psychology*] ISCF
Industrial Service [*Equipment specifications*] IS
Industrial Silencer Manufacturers Association ISMA
Industrial Situation in India [*A publication*] Indus Sit Ind
Industrial Specialist IS
Industrial Specialty Chemical Association ISCA
Industrial Standardization [*A publication*] Ind Stand
Industrial Stapling and Nailing Technical Association I-SANTA
Industrial Static Inverter ISI
Industrial Support Contractor ISC
Industrial Tachometer Generator ITG
Industrial Target Report [*Later, IDR*] [*British*] [*World War II*] ITR
Industrial Technical Information Service [*Singapore*] ITIS
Industrial Technological Associates, Inc. [*Information service*] ITA
Industrial and Technological Information Bank [*UNIDO*] INTIB
Industrial Television ITV
Industrial Television Society ITS
Industrial Test Laboratory [*Navy*] ITL
Industrial Training IT
Industrial Training Board [*British*] ITB
Industrial Training Council ITC
Industrial Transistor Value Automatic Computer ITVAC
Industrial Truck Association ITA
Industrial Union Department [*of AFL-CIO*] IUD
Industrial Union of Marine and Shipbuilding Workers of America IUMSWA
Industrial Union Party IUP
Industrial Unit of Tribology [*An association*] IUT
Industrial Utilisation of Sugar and Mill By-Products [*A publication*] Ind Util Sugar Mill By-Prod
Industrial Valley Bank [*NASDAQ symbol*] IBKT
Industrial Vegetation Management Association IVMA
Industrial Veterinarians' Association [*Later, AAIV*] IVA
Industrial View Camera IVC
Industrial Waste Conference Proceedings [*A publication*] Ind Waste Conf Proc
Industrial Wastes [*A publication*] Ind Wastes
Industrial Wastes (Chicago) [*A publication*] Ind Wastes (Chicago)
Industrial Water Engineering [*A publication*] Ind Water Eng
Industrial Water Supply IWS
Industrial Water System IWS
Industrial Water Wastes [*A publication*] Ind Water Wastes
Industrial Wire Cloth Institute [*Later, AWCI*] IWCI
Industrial Worker [*A publication*] Ind Wrkr
Industrial Workers of the World [*"Wobblies"*] IWW
Industrial X-Ray Film IXF
Industrialisation et Productivite [*A publication*] Industrial et Productiv
Industrialised Building [*A publication*] Ind Bldg
Industrialized Building Systems and Components IBSAC
Industrie-Anzeiger [*A publication*] Ind-Anz
Industrie Ceramique [*A publication*] Ind Ceram
Industrie Chimique Belge [*A publication*] Ind Chim Belge
Industrie Diamanten Rundschau [*A publication*] Ind Diamanten Rundsch
Industrie-Elektrik und Elektronik [*A publication*] Ind-Elektr Elektron
Industrie Francaise du Coton et des Fibres Alliees [*A publication*] Industr Franc Coton Fibres Alliees
Industrie Gewerkschaft Chemie, Papier, und Keramik [*West German union*] IGCPK
Industrie und Handel [*A publication*] Ind Handel
Industrie und Handelskammer IHK
Industrie-Lackier-Betrieb [*A publication*] Ind-Lackier-Betrb
Industrie Minerale [*A publication*] Ind Miner
Industrie Minerale. Mine [*A publication*] Ind Miner Mine
Industrie Minerale. Mineralurgie [*A publication*] Ind Miner Mineralurgie
Industrie Minerale (Paris) [*A publication*] Ind Miner (Paris)
Industriegewerkschaft [*Industrial Trade Union*] [*West Germany*] IG
Industries Alimentaires et Agricoles [*A publication*] Ind Aliment Agr
Industries Alimentaires et Agricoles (Paris) [*A publication*] Ind Aliment Agric (Paris)
Industries de l'Alimentation Animale [*A publication*] Ind Aliment Anim
Industries Atomiques [*A publication*] Ind At
Industries Atomiques et Spatiales [*A publication*] Ind At & Spat
Industries Atomiques et Spatiales [*A publication*] Ind At Spatiales
Industries Electriques et Electroniques [*A publication*] Ind Electr Electron
Industries Electroniques [*A publication*] Ind Electron
Industries et Techniques [*A publication*] Ind Tech
Industries Thermiques et Aerauliques [*A publication*] Ind Therm Aerauliques
Industries et Travaux d'Outre-Mer [*A publication*] Industr Trav O-Mer
Industrija Nafta [*State-owned company*] [*Yugoslavia*] INA
Industrija Secera [*A publication*] Ind Secera
Industry IND
Industry INDUS
Industry Advisory Committee [*World War II*] IAC
Industry Advisory Council [*Formerly, DIAC*] IAC
Industry Advisory Group for Air Logistics IAGAL
Industry Applications Programs [*Data processing*] IAP
Industry Center for Trade Negotiations [*Defunct*] ICTN
Industry Coalition for Fire Safety ICFS
Industry Cooperative Program [*United Nations*] ICP
Industry Crew Escape Systems Committee ICESC
Industry Data Exchange Program IDEP
Industry-Developed Equipment IDE
Industry of Free China [*Taipei*] [*A publication*] IFC
Industry of Free China [*A publication*] Indus Free China
Industry and General Applications IGA
Industry Manufacturers [*FCC*] IX
Industry Missile and Space Conference IMSC
Industry Motion Picture [*FCC*] IM
Industry Network for Social, Urban, and Rural Efforts INSURE
Industry-Organized Government-Approved IOGA
Industry Planning Representative [*DoD*] IPR
Industry Report. Chemicals [*A publication*] Ind Rept Chemicals
Industry Report. Containers and Packaging [*A publication*] Ind Rept Containers Pkg
Industry Report. Pulp, Paper, and Board [*A publication*] Ind Rept Pulp Pbd
Industry Sector Advisory Committee [*Established by Trade Reform Act for industry-to-government advice*] ISAC
Industry Service Bureaus ISB
Industry Service Package ISP
Industry Standard Item ISI
Industry Standard Specifications ISS
Industry Technology Group [*Air Force*] ITG
Industry Telephone Maintenance [*FCC*] IT
Industry and Trade Administration [*Later, International Trade Administration*] [*Department of Commerce*] ITA
Industry Trade and Commerce [*Canada*] IT & C
Industry, TX [*Location identifier*] [*FAA*] IDU
Industry/University Cooperation Research Center [*National Science Foundation*] IUCRC
Industry Week [*A publication*] Indus Week
Industry Week [*A publication*] Ind W
Industry Week [*A publication*] Ind Week

Ine [*Marshall Islands*] [*Airport symbol*] ... IMI
Inedible ... INED
Ineditus [*Not Made Known*] [*Latin*] ... INED
Inefficiency ... INEFFCY
Inefficiency ... INEFFY
Inelastic Electron Tunneling Spectroscopy ... IETS
Inelastic Mean Free [*or Face*] **Path** [*Surface analysis*] ... IMFP
INELEC Library Project, Menomonie, WI [*OCLC symbol*] [*Inactive*] ... WIN
Ineligible Reserve Section ... IRS
Inequality Constrained Least-Squares [*Statistics*] ... ICLS
Inequality in Education [*A publication*] ... Inequal Educ
Inert Building [*NASA*] ... IB
Inert Components Parts Building ... ICPB
Inert Filler ... INRTFLR
Inert Fluid Fill ... IFF
Inert Gas ... INRTG
Inert Gas Generator ... IGG
Inert Gas Receiving and Processing ... IGR & P
Inert Gas Storage ... IGS
Inert Nitrogen Protection ... INP
Inert Operational Missile ... IOM
Inert Ordnance Warehouse ... IOW
Inert Processing Building ... IPB
Inertia ... I
Inertia ... INRT
Inertia Compensated Balance ... ICB
Inertial ... IN
Inertial ... INER
Inertial ... INRTL
Inertial Attitude Control System [*Aerospace*] ... IACS
Inertial Component ... IC
Inertial Component Test Equipment ... ICTE
Inertial Components Temperature Controller ... ICTC
Inertial Confinement Fission [*Physics*] ... ICF
Inertial Coupling Data Unit ... ICDU
Inertial Coupling Display Unit ... ICDU
Inertial Dampened Servomotor ... IDSM
Inertial Data Box ... IDB
Inertial Data System ... IDS
Inertial Doppler System ... IDS
Inertial Flight Data System ... IFDS
Inertial Guidance ... IG
Inertial Guidance and Calibration Group [*Air Force*] ... IGCG
Inertial Guidance Mode ... IGM
Inertial Guidance Package ... IGP
Inertial Guidance Platform ... IGP
Inertial Guidance System [*NASA*] ... IGS
Inertial Guidance System Maintenance Area [*Aerospace*] ... IGSMA
Inertial Height Sensing Device ... IHSD
Inertial Instrument Assembly ... IIA
Inertial Laboratory [*NASA*] ... IL
Inertial Measurement Group ... IMG
Inertial Measurement Unit ... IMU
Inertial Measuring Set ... IMS
Inertial Navigation and Attack System ... INAS
Inertial Navigation Computer ... INC
Inertial Navigation Equipment ... INE
Inertial Navigation and Guidance [*Aerospace*] ... ING
Inertial Navigation Gyro ... ING
Inertial Navigation System ... INS
Inertial Navigation Unit ... INU
Inertial Navigation and Weapons Attack System ... INWAS
Inertial Platform ... IP
Inertial Processing ... IP
Inertial Quality Attitude ... IQA
Inertial Rate of Descent Sensor ... IRODS
Inertial Rate Gyro ... IRG
Inertial Rate Integrating Gyro ... IRIG
Inertial Reference ... INR
Inertial Reference and Control System [*Aerospace*] ... IRCS
Inertial Reference Package ... IRP
Inertial Reference Stabilization System ... IRSS
Inertial Reference System ... IRS
Inertial Reference Unit ... IRU
Inertial Sensing Unit ... ISU
Inertial Sensor System ... ISS
Inertial Start Command ... ISC
Inertial Subsystem ... ISS
Inertial Unit Assembly ... IUA
Inertial [*formerly, Interim*] **Upper Stage** [*Air Force*] ... IUS
Inertial Velocity ... INRTLVEL
Inertial Velocity ... VI
Inertial Velocity Measurement Unit ... IVMU
Inertialess Scanning, Tracking, and Ranging ... INSTAR
Inertialess Steerable Communications Antenna ... ISCAN
Inerting and Preheating [*Nuclear energy*] ... I & P
Inex Adria Aviopromet [*Yugoslavia*] [*ICAO designator*] ... JP
Inexco Oil Co. [*NYSE symbol*] ... INX
Inez, KY [*Radio station call letters*] ... WFJT
INF [*Inventario Nacional Forestal*] **Informacion Tecnica** [*A publication*] ... INF Inf Tec
Infamous [*FBI standardized term*] ... INF
Infant ... INF
Infant Behavior and Development [*A publication*] ... IBD
Infant of Diabetic Mother [*Medicine*] ... IDM
Infant Formula Action Coalition ... INFACT
Infant Formula Council ... IFC
Infant Hypercalcemia [*Medicine*] ... IHC
Infant Intensive Care Unit [*of a hospital*] ... IICU
Infant and Juvenile Manufacturers Association ... IJMA
Infant Soy Formula ... ISF
Infanterie-Ersatzbataillon [*Infantry Replacement Training Battalion*] [*German military - World War II*] ... IEB
Infanterie-Ersatzregiment [*Infantry Replacement Training Regiment*] [*German military - World War II*] ... IER
Infanterie-Lehrregiment [*Infantry Demonstration Regiment*] [*German military - World War II*] ... ILR
Infanteriegeschuetz - Kompanie [*Infantry Howitzer Company*] [*German military - World War II*] ... IGK
Infanteriegranate [*Infantry Howitzer Shell*] [*German military - World War II*] ... IGR
Infanteriekolonne [*Infantry Supply Column*] [*German military - World War II*] ... IK
Infantile Amaurotic Family Idiocy [*Medicine*] ... IAFI
Infantry ... I
Infantry [*Army*] ... IN
Infantry ... INF
Infantry Armored Fighting Vehicle ... IAFV
Infantry Battalion [*Army*] ... IB
Infantry Battalion [*Army*] ... INFBAT
Infantry Combat Developments Agency [*Pronounced "ick-da"*] [*Army*] ... ICDA
Infantry Drill Regulations ... IDR
Infantry Fighting Vehicle ... IFV
Infantry Liaison Team ... ILT
Infantry Manportable Antiarmor Weapon System ... IMAAWS
Infantry Mortar Platoon Course ... IMPC
Infantry Officer Advanced Course [*Army*] ... IOAC
Infantry Officer Basic Course [*Army*] ... IOBC
Infantry Officer Career Course [*Army*] ... IOCC
Infantry Officers Training Camp ... IOTC
Infantry Remote Targeting System [*Army*] ... IRETS
Infantry Replacement Training Center ... IRTC
Infantry Research and Development Liaison Office [*Army*] ... IRDLO
Infantry Rifle Unit Study [*Army*] ... IRUS
[*The*] **Infantry School** [*Army*] ... IS
[*The*] **Infantry School** [*Army*] ... TIS
Infantry Systems Program Review [*Army*] ... ISPR
Infantry Training Center [*Army*] ... ITC
Infantry Training Regiment [*Marine Corps*] ... ITR
Infantry Training Replacement ... ITR
Infants' and Children's Coat Association [*Later, ICGSCA*] ... ICCA
Infant's, Children's, and Girl's Sportswear and Coat Association [*Formerly, ICCA*] ... ICGSCA
Infants' and Children's Novelties Association ... ICNA
Infants', Children's, and Teens' Wear Buyers Association ... ICTBA
Infants' and Children's Wear Salesmen's Guild ... ICWSG
Infarct Size Index [*Cardiology*] ... ISI
Infaunal Trophic Index [*Marine pollution*] ... ITI
Infected Area ... IA
Infection [*Medicine*] ... INF
Infection Control [*A publication*] ... Infect Control
Infection-Control Practitioner [*Medicine*] ... ICP
Infection Control Rounds [*A publication*] ... Infect Control Rounds
Infection and Immunity [*A publication*] ... Infec Immun
Infection and Immunity [*A publication*] ... Infect Immun
Infection Prevention ... IP
Infectious Bovine Keratoconjunctivitis [*Veterinary medicine*] ... IBK
Infectious Bovine Rhinotracheitis [*Also, IBRV*] [*Virus*] ... IBR
Infectious Bovine Rhinotracheitis Virus [*Also, IBR*] ... IBRV
Infectious Bronchitis [*Veterinary medicine*] ... IB
Infectious Bronchitis Virus [*Avian*] ... IBV
Infectious Canine Hepatitis [*Veterinary medicine*] ... ICH
Infectious Disease [*Medicine*] ... ID
Infectious Disease Reviews [*A publication*] ... Infect Dis Rev
Infectious Diseases Society of America ... IDSA
Infectious Hepatitis [*Medicine*] ... IH
Infectious Mononucleosis [*Medicine*] ... IM
Infectious Pancreatic Necrosis [*Medicine*] ... IPN
Infectious Pancreatic Necrosis Virus ... IPNV
Infectious Pustular Vaginitis [*Medicine*] ... IPV
Infectious Pustular Vulvovaginitis [*Veterinary medicine*] ... IPV
Infective Dose ... ID
Infective Dose, Median ... ID_{50}
Infektionskrankheiten und Ihre Erreger [*A publication*] ... Infektionskr Ihre Erreger
Infektsionnye Gepatit Respublikanskoi Mezhvedomstvennyi Sbornik [*A publication*] ... Infekts Gepatit Resp Mezhved Sb
Infektsionnyi Gepatit [*A publication*] ... Infekts Gepatit
Inference ... INFRN
Inference Execution Language ... INFEREX
Inferential Value Testing ... IVT

Inferior ... INF
Inferior Angle [*Anatomy*] ... IA
Inferior Colliculus [*Brain anatomy*] ... IC
Inferior Mesenteric Artery [*Anatomy*] ... IMA
Inferior Mesenteric Ganglia [*Anatomy*] ... IMG
Inferior Mesenteric Vein [*Anatomy*] ... IMV
Inferior Oblique [*Muscle*] [*Anatomy*] ... IO
Inferior Rectus [*Muscle*] [*Anatomy*] ... IR
Inferior Thalamic Peduncle [*Anatomy*] ... ITP
Inferior Vena Cava [*Anatomy*] ... IVC
Infield ... I
Infielder [*Position in baseball*] ... IF
Infiltration Surveillance Center ... ISC
Infinite ... INF
Infinite Capitalism [*Book title*] ... IC
Infinite Periodic Minimal Surface ... IPMS
Infinite-Resolution Trimmer ... IRT
Infinite Time Span ... ITS
Infinitive ... INF
Infinitive [*Grammar*] ... INFIN
Infinity ... INF
Infinity Science Fiction [*A publication*] ... Inf
Infirmary ... INF
Infirmary ... INFIRM
Infirmary ... INFMRY
Infirmiere Canadienne [*A publication*] ... Infirm Can
Infirmiere Francaise [*A publication*] ... Infirm Fr
Inflammable ... INFL
Inflammable ... INFLAM
Inflammation of Connective Tissue [*Medicine*] ... ICT
Inflammatory Bowel Disease [*Medicine*] ... IBD
Inflatable ... IFL
Inflatable Boat Association ... IBA
Inflatable Boat, Small ... IBS
Inflatable Body and Head Restraint System [*Aviation*] ... IBAHRS
Inflatable Micrometeoroid Paraglide ... IMP
Inflatable Occupant Restraint System ... IORS
Inflating-Deflating ... IFL-DFL
Inflation Quotient ... IQ
Inflationary Impact Statement [*Economics*] ... IIS
Inflight Services, Inc. [*American Stock Exchange symbol*] ... INF
Influence ... INFL
Influx ... INFL
Info Designs [*NASDAQ symbol*] ... INFO
Infodata Systems, Inc. [*NASDAQ symbol*] ... INFD
Infodata Systems, Incorporated [*Information service*] ... ISI
Infor Journal [*Canadian Journal of Operational Research and Information Processing*] [*A publication*] ... Infor J
Informacao Cultural Portugues [*A publication*] ... ICP
Informacije Rade Koncar [*A publication*] ... Inf Rade Koncar
Informacio-Elektronika [*A publication*] ... Inf-Elektron
Informacio-Elektronika [*A publication*] ... Informac-Elektron
Informacion Comercial Espanola [*A publication*] ... ICE
Informacion Comercial Espanola [*A publication*] ... Inform Com Esp
Informacion de Quimica Analitica, Pura, y Aplicada a la Industria [*A publication*] ... Inf Quim Anal Pura Apl Ind
Informaciones Cientificas [*A publication*] ... Inf Cient
Informaciones sobre Grasas y Aceites [*A publication*] ... Inform Grasas Aceites
Informacni Bulletin pro Otazky Jazykovedne [*A publication*] ... IBOJ
Informacni Zpravodaj VLIS [*Vojenska Lekarska Informacni Sluzba*] [*A publication*] ... Inf Zp VLIS
Informal Communication ... IC
Informal Composite Negotiating Text [*United Nations Conference on the Law of the Sea*] ... ICNT
Informal Memo ... IM
Informal Memorandum Report ... IMR
Informal Policy Committee for Germany ... IPCOG
Informal Progress Report ... IPR
Informal Reading Inventory [*Education*] ... IRI
Informal Report ... IR
Informal Routing Slip ... IRS
Informal Spelling Inventory [*Education*] ... ISI
Informare si Documentare Selectiva. Tehnica Nucleara [*A publication*] ... Inf Doc Sel Teh Nucl
Informatech France-Quebec, Montreal, PQ, Canada [*Library symbol*] ... CaQMIFQ
Informatheque des Affaires Sociales du Quebec, Quebec, PQ, Canada [*Library symbol*] ... CaQQIAS
Informatics General Corp. [*NYSE symbol*] ... IG
Informatie en Communicatie Unie [*Information and Communication United*] [*Dutch publishing house*] ... ICU
Informatik-Fachberichte [*A publication*] ... Inf-Fachber
Informatik-Spektrum [*A publication*] ... Inf-Spektrum
Information ... IFN
Information ... INF
Information ... INFO
Information ... INFORMN
Information Access Corporation [*Information service*] ... IAC
Information Acquisition System ... IAS
Information and Action ... I & A
Information Activities Office [*or Officer*] ... IAO
Information Agency ... IA
Information Analysis Center [*DoD*] ... IAC
Information Assessment Team ... IAT
Information Associates of Ithaca [*Information service*] ... IAI
Information for Avionics Laboratory ... INFORMAL
Information Battelle Frankfurt [*A publication*] ... Inf Battelle Frankfurt
Information Bearing Radiation ... IBR
Information Bulletin ... IB
Information Bulletin: Appendices on Provisional Nomenclature, Symbols, Terminology, and Convention (International Union of Pure and Applied Chemistry) [*A publication*] ... Inf Bull: Append Provis Nomencl Symb Terminol Conv (IUPAC)
Information Bulletin. International Union of Pure and Applied Chemistry. Technical Reports [*A publication*] ... Inf Bull IUPAC Tech Rep
Information Bulletin. Library Automated Systems Information Exchange [*A publication*] ... Inf Bull Libr Autom Syst Inf Exch
Information Bulletin. Library Automated Systems Information Exchange [*A publication*] ... LASIE
Information Bulletin. Timber Research and Development Association [*A publication*] ... Inform Bull Timb Res Developm Ass
Information Canada, Publishing Division, Ottawa, ON, Canada [*Library symbol*] [*Obsolete*] ... CaOOQP
Information Card. Clemson Agricultural College. Extension Service [*A publication*] ... Inform Card Clemson Agr Coll Ext Serv
Information and Censorship [*Allied Forces*] [*World War II*] ... INC
Information Center ... IC
Information Center ... INFOCEN
Information Center on Children's Cultures ... ICCC
Information Center Complex [*ORNL*] ... ICC
Information Center on Crime and Delinquency [*National Council on Crime and Delinquency*] ... ICCD
Information Center for Individuals with Disabilities ... ICID
Information Center for Internal Exposure [*AEC*] ... ICIE
Information Center on Nuclear Standards [*American Nuclear Society*] [*Information service*] ... ICNS
Information Center on Nuclear Standards [*American Nuclear Society*] [*Information service*] ... ICONS
Information Center - Recreation for the Handicapped ... ICRH
Information Centers Service [*United States Information Agency*] ... ICS
Information Centre of the European Railways ... ICER
Information Chimie [*A publication*] ... Info Chimie
Information Circular ... IC
Information Circular. Economic Geology Research Unit. University of the Witwatersrand [*A publication*] ... Inf Circ Econ Geol Res Unit Univ Witwaters
Information Circular. Geology and Physiography Section. Nature Conservancy Council [*A publication*] ... Inf Circ Geol Physiogr Sect Nat Conserv Counc
Information Circular. United States Bureau of Mines [*A publication*] ... Inf Circ US Bur Mines
Information Clearing House, Inc. ... ICH
Information. Commission des Communautes Europeennes [*A publication*] ... Information Commun Europ
Information and Communication ... IAC
Information Concepts, Incorporated ... ICI
Information Consultants, Incorporated [*Information service*] ... ICI
Information Content ... IC
Information for the Contracting Officer ... ICO
Information and Control [*A publication*] ... Inf C
Information and Control [*A publication*] ... Inf Contr
Information and Control [*A publication*] ... Inf Control
Information and Control [*A publication*] ... Inform Contr
Information Council of the Americas ... INCA
Information des Cours Complementaires [*A publication*] ... ICC
Information and Data Exchange Experimental Activities ... IDEEA
Information Data Handling System ... IDHS
Information Data Processing ... IDP
Information Data Search, Inc. [*Information service*] ... IDS
Information, Decision, Action ... IDA
Information Definition Requirements Document ... IDRD
Information on Demand [*Information service*] ... IOD
Information Dentaire [*A publication*] ... Inf Dent
Information Design Change ... IDC
Information Design Change List ... IDCL
Information and Direction Center ... IDC
Information Display [*A publication*] ... Inf Disp
Information Display [*A publication*] ... Inf Display
Information Displays [*NASDAQ symbol*] ... IDPY
Information Displays Automatic Drafting System ... IDAS
Information Displays, Incorporated, Input-Output Machine ... IDIIOM
Information Dissemination and Retrieval [*System*] [*Reuters Ltd.*] ... IDR
Information Distributor ... ID
Information Document Matching Program [*IRS*] ... IDM
Information and Documentation [*British Film Institute*] ... IAD
Information et Documentation [*A publication*] ... Inf & Doc
Information/Documentation [*Information service*] ... INFO/DOC
Information Dynamics Corporation ... IDC
Information Dynamics Corp., Reading, MA [*Library symbol*] ... MRI
Information and Education [*Military*] ... I & E

Information and Education [*Army*] ... IE
Information Exchange Center ... IEC
Information Exchange Group [*National Institutes of Health*] ... IEG
Information Exchange List [*Military*] ... IEL
Information Exchange Program [*or Project*] [*Military*] ... IEP
Information Feedback ... IF
Information Film Producers of America [*Later, IFPA Film and Video Communicators*] ... IFPA
Information Flow Standards ... IFS
Information and Forwarding ... IAF
Information Gained per Unit Cost [*Data processing*] ... IGUC
Information Gatekeepers, Incorporated [*Information service*] ... IGI
Information General, Incorporated [*Information service*] ... IGI
Information Geographique [*A publication*] ... Inform Geogr
Information Grouping Logic [*Data processing*] ... IGL
Information Handling Project ... IHP
Information Handling Services ... IHS
Information Handling Services, Englewood, CO [*OCLC symbol*] ... CIH
Information d'Histoire de l'Art [*A publication*] ... IHA
Information and Historical [*Military*] ... I & H
Information Historique [*A publication*] ... IH
Information Historique [*A publication*] ... Inf Hist
Information Index [*LIMRA*] ... II
Information Industry Association [*Formerly, PRIM*] ... IIA
Information Intelligence, Incorporated [*Information service*] ... III
Information International, Incorporated ... III
Information International, Inc. [*NASDAQ symbol*] ... IINT
Information Item Only ... IIO
Information Lead Distance ... ILD
Information & Library Services [*Information service*] ... ILS
Information Litteraire [*A publication*] ... IL
Information Litteraire [*A publication*] ... Inf Litt
Information Logic Machine ... ILM
Information and Management [*A publication*] ... Inf Manage
Information and Management [*A publication*] ... Info & Mgmt
Information Management, Retrieval, and Dissemination System ... IMRADS
Information Management Simulation ... IMSIM
Information Management Specialists [*Information service*] ... IMS
Information Management Specialists, Denver, CO [*OCLC symbol*] ... DVI
Information Management System [*Data processing*] ... IMS
Information Management System/Virtual Storage ... IMS/VS
Information Manager ... IM
Information Manager [*A publication*] ... Info Mgr
Information Manager [*A publication*] ... IM
Information Memory ... IM
Information Network and File Organization ... INFO
Information Network for Freight Overhead Billing, Rating, and Message Switching ... INFORM
Information Network for Operations [*Data processing*] ... INFO
Information News and Sources [*A publication*] ... Inf News & Sources
Information Not Provided by Manufacturer ... INPBM
Information Numismatique [*A publication*] ... Inf Num
Information Officer ... IO
Information for Optimum Resource Management ... INFORM
Information Oriented Language [*Computer program*] ... INFOL
Information Overload Testing Aid [*or Apparatus*] ... IOTA
Information: Part 1: News/Sources/Profiles [*A publication*] ... Inf: Pt 1
Information: Part 2: Reports/Bibliographies [*A publication*] ... Inf: Pt 2
Information Parts Breakdown ... IPB
Information Process Analysis ... IPA
Information Processing ... IP
Information Processing Association [*Israel*] ... IPA
Information Processing Center ... IPC
Information Processing in the Central Nervous System ... INPRONS
Information Processing Code ... IPC
Information Processing in Command and Control [*Air Force*] ... IPCC
Information Processing in Command and Control Systems [*Air Force*] ... IPCCS
Information Processing and Control [*Systems Laboratory*] [*Northwestern University*] ... IPAC
Information Processing Equipment ... IPE
Information Processing Improvement Program ... IPIP
Information Processing Journal [*A publication*] ... InfP
Information Processing Language [*Data processing*] ... IPL
Information Processing Letters [*A publication*] ... Inf Process Lett
Information Processing and Management [*A publication*] ... Inf Pr Man
Information Processing and Management [*A publication*] ... Inf Processing & Mgt
Information Processing and Management [*A publication*] ... Inf Process Manage
Information Processing and Management [*A publication*] ... Inf Proc Man
Information Processing Society of Japan [*Information service*] ... IPSJ
Information Processing Standards for Computers ... IPSC
Information Processing System ... IPS
Information Processing Systems Standards Board [*Later, Board of Standards Review of ANSI*] [*American Standards Association*] ... IPSSB
Information Provider ... IP
Information Publication [*HUD*] ... IP
Information Publishing ... IP
Information and Records Management [*A publication*] ... Info Rec Mgmt
Information and Records Management ... IRM
Information and Records Management [*A publication*] ... IRM
Information Recovery Capsule ... IRC
Information Recovery [*or Retrieval*] **System** [*or Subsystem*] ... IRS
Information and Referral [*Services*] [*Used to assist the handicapped*] ... I & R
Information Referral Manual ... IRMA
Information Referral System for Technical Cooperation among Developing Countries [*United Nations*] [*Information service*] ... INRES/TCDC
Information Report ... INFOREP
Information Report ... IR
Information Report. Forest Fire Research Institute (Ottawa) [*A publication*] ... Inform Rep For Fire Res Inst (Ottawa)
Information Report. Forest Management Institute (Ottawa) [*A publication*] ... Inform Rep For Mgmt Inst (Ottawa)
Information Report. Forest Products Laboratory (Vancouver) [*A publication*] ... Inform Rep For Prod Lab (Vancouver)
Information Report. Forest Research Laboratory (Calgary) [*A publication*] ... Inform Rep For Res Lab (Calgary)
Information Report. Forest Research Laboratory (Quebec) [*A publication*] ... Inform Rep For Res Lab (Quebec)
Information Report. Forest Research Laboratory (Victoria, British Columbia) [*A publication*] ... Inform Rep For Res Lab (Victoria BC)
Information. Reports and Bibliographies [*A publication*] ... Inf Rept Bibliog
Information on Request ... INREQ
Information Request ... IR
Information Requested [*or Required*] ... INFOREQ
Information Requested ... INREQ
Information Requested in Above Referenced Message [*Army*] ... IRRM
Information Requests [*Army*] ... INREQS
Information Requirements Control Automated System [*Defense Supply Service/Pentagon*] ... IRCAS
Information Requirements Description [*or Document*] ... IRD
Information Requirements List ... IRL
Information Requirements of the Social Sciences [*British*] ... INFROSS
Information Research Center ... IRC
Information and Research Utilization Center in Physical Education and Recreation for the Handicapped [*American Association for Health, Physical Education, and Recreation*] ... IRUC
Information Researchers, Incorporated [*Information service*] ... IRI
Information Resource Management [*Data processing*] ... IRM
Information Resource Management Council [*DoD*] ... IRMC
Information Resources [*NASDAQ symbol*] ... IRIC
Information Resources Center [*of Mental Health Materials Center*] ... IRC
Information Resources Information System [*Library of Congress*] ... IRIS
Information Resources Management Office [*Army Corps of Engineers*] ... IRMO
Information Resources Press [*Washington, DC*] ... IRP
Information Retrieval ... IR
Information Retrieval Automatic Language [*Data processing*] ... INFRAL
Information Retrieval Center [*BBDO International*] [*Information service*] ... IRC
Information Retrieval Center on the Disadvantaged [*ERIC*] ... IRCD
Information Retrieval Data Bank ... IRDB
Information Retrieval and Display Language [*Data processing*] ... IRDL
Information Retrieval, Incorporated ... IRI
Information Retrieval Language [*Data processing*] ... IRL
Information Retrieval and Library Automation [*A publication*] ... IRLA
Information Retrieval and Library Automation Letter [*A publication*] ... Inf Retr Libr Automn
Information Retrieval Limited [*Information service*] [*British*] ... IRL
Information Retrieval Service [*European Space Agency*] ... IRS
Information Retrieval Technique ... IRT
Information Return Program [*IRS*] ... IRP
Information Returns Processing [*Data processing*] ... IRP
Information Revision and Manuscript Assembly ... IRMA
Information Science ... IS
Information Science Abstracts [*A publication*] ... Inform Sci
Information Science Abstracts [*A publication*] ... InfSciAb
Information Science Abstracts [*A publication*] ... ISA
Information Science and Automation Division [*Later, LITA*] [*American Library Association*] ... ISAD
Information Science, Inc. [*Information service*] ... InSci
Information Science and Technology ... IST
Information Sciences [*A publication*] ... Inform Sci
Information Sciences [*A publication*] ... InfoS
Information Sciences [*A publication*] ... Inf Sci
Information Sciences [*A publication*] ... Inf Sciences
Information Sciences [*NASDAQ symbol*] ... INSI
Information Scientist [*A publication*] ... Inf Scient
Information Scientist [*A publication*] ... Inf Scientist
Information Search Language ... ISL
Information Search and Recording System [*of UMREL*] ... ISRS
Information Security Oversight Office [*National Archives and Records Service*] ... ISOO
Information Separator [*Data processing*] ... IS
Information Series in Agricultural Economics. University of California. Agricultural Extension Service [*A publication*] ... Inform Ser Agr Econ Univ Calif Agr Ext Serv

Information Series. Department of Scientific and Industrial Research (New Zealand) [*A publication*] ... Inf Ser Dep Scient Ind Res (NZ)
Information Series. New Zealand Forest Service [*A publication*] ... Inform Ser NZ For Serv
Information Service ... IS
Information Service Computer System ... ISCS
Information Service of India ... ISI
Information Service in Mechanical Engineering [*Cambridge Scientific Abstracts*] ... ISMEC
Information Service for Physics, Electrotechnology, and Control [*IEE*] ... INSPEC
Information Service Representative [*Veterans Administration*] ... ISR
Information Service on Toxicity and Biodegradability [*British*] ... INSTAB
Information Services Control Branch [*Control Commission for Germany*] [*World War II*] ... ISC
Information Services to Education [*American Society for Information Science*] ... ISE
Information Services Officer ... ISO
Information Sheet. Mississippi Agricultural Experiment Station [*A publication*] ... Inform Sheet Miss Agr Exp Sta
Information Society of Canada ... ISC
Information Solutions [*NASDAQ symbol*] ... ISOL
Information Sort and Predict ... ISAP
Information Storage and Retrieval [*A publication*] ... Inform Stor Retrieval
Information Storage and Retrieval [*A publication*] ... Inf Storage
Information Storage and Retrieval [*A publication*] ... Inf Storage & Retr
Information Storage and Retrieval [*A publication*] ... Inf Storage Retr
Information Storage and Retrieval [*A publication*] ... Inf Stor Retr
Information Storage and Retrieval [*Data processing*] ... ISAR
Information Storage and Retrieval [*Data processing*] ... IS & R
Information Storage and Retrieval [*Data processing*] ... ISR
Information Storage and Retrieval System [*Data processing*] ... INSTARS
Information Storage, Selection, and Retrieval [*Data processing*] ... ISSR
Information Storage System ... ISS
Information (Swedish Pulp and Paper Association) [*A publication*] ... Inform (Swed)
Information System Access Lines [*Data processing*] ... ISAL
Information System for Adaptive, Assistive, and Rehabilitation Equipment [*For the handicapped*] ... ISAARE
Information System Language [*Data processing*] ... ISL
Information System Language Studies [*A publication*] ... ISLS
Information System Management Board [*NATO*] ... ISMB
Information System Manager ... ISM
Information System Plan ... ISP
Information System for Vocational Decisions Program ... ISVD
Information Systems [*A publication*] ... Information Syst
Information Systems [*Elmsford, NY*] [*A publication*] ... Info Systems
Information Systems [*A publication*] ... Inf Syst
Information Systems ... INS
Information Systems [*Subdivision*] ... ISS
Information Systems Consultants, Incorporated [*Information service*] ... ISCI
Information Systems Design Optimization System ... ISDOS
Information Systems Directorate [*Kennedy Space Center*] [*NASA*] ... IN
Information Systems Division [*NASA*] ... ISD
Information Systems for Management ... ISM
Information Systems Marketing, Inc. [*Information service*] ... ISM
Information Systems Office [*NASA*] ... IFO
Information Systems Office [*Library of Congress*] ... ISO
Information Systems Program [*National Science Foundation*] ... ISP
Information Systems Security Association ... ISSA
Information Systems and Services Division [*Department of Commerce*] ... ISSD
Information Technology ... IT
Information Technology Advisory Panel [*British*] ... ITAP
Information Technology Development [*Project*] [*DoD*] ... ITD
Information Technology Users Group [*Exxon Corp.*] ... ITUG
Information Technology Year [*1982*] ... ITY
Information Theory ... IT
Information Transfer Exchange [*Library science*] ... INTREX
Information Transfer Experiments ... INTREX
Information Transfer Satellite ... ITS
Information Transfer [*or Transmission*] **System** ... ITS
Information Transform [*Information service*] ... IT
Information Unlimited [*Information service*] ... IU
Information Unltd., Berkeley, CA [*Library symbol*] ... CBI
Information Viewing Device ... IVD
Information World [*A publication*] ... IW
Information Zukunfts- und Friedensforschung [*A publication*] ... Inf Zukunfts-Friedensforsch
Informational ... INFMTL
Informational Acquisition and Interpretation ... IAI
Informational Media Guaranty ... IMG
Informationen Bildung Wissenschaft [*A publication*] ... Inf Bild Wiss
Informationen fuer die Fischwirtschaft [*A publication*] ... Inf Fischwirtsch
Informationen Kerntechnische Normung [*A publication*] ... Inf Kerntech Normung
Informationen aus Orthodontie und Kieferorthopaedie mit Beitraegen aus der Internationalen Literatur [*A publication*] ... Inf Orthod Kieferorthop
Informationen zur Raumentwicklung [*A publication*] ... Inform Raumentwicklung
Informationen zur Raumentwicklung [*A publication*] ... Inf Raumentwickl
Informations Aerauliques et Thermiques [*A publication*] ... Inf Aerauliques Therm
Informations Catholiques Internationales [*A publication*] ... ICI
Informations Catholiques Internationales [*A publication*] ... Inform Cathol Int
Informations-Chimie [*A publication*] ... Inf-Chim
Informations Constitutionnelles et Parlementaires [*A publication*] ... Inform Constit Parl
Informations Cooperatives [*A publication*] ... Inform Coop
Informations et Documentation Agricoles [*A publication*] ... Inform Doc Agr
Informations et Documents [*A publication*] ... Inform et Doc
Informations sur l'Irradiation des Denrees [*A publication*] ... Inf Irradiat Denrees
Informations Sociales (Paris) [*A publication*] ... Inform Soc (Paris)
Informations Universitaires et Professionnelles Internationales [*A publication*] ... Inform Univ Profes Int
Informationszentrum Raum und Bau [*Information Center for Building and Space Planning*] [*West Germany*] [*Information service*] ... IRB
Informationszentrum fuer Schnittwertemachning [*Information Center for Machining*] [*Germany*] ... INFOS
Informatique et Gestion [*A publication*] ... Inf & Gestion
Informatique et Gestion [*A publication*] ... Informat et Gestion
Informativo do INT [*Instituto Nacional de Tecnologia*] [*Brazil*] [*A publication*] ... Inf INT
Informatologia Yugoslavica [*A publication*] ... Inform Yugoslav
Informatore Agrario [*A publication*] ... Inform Agr
Informatore Botanico Italiano [*A publication*] ... Inf Bot Ital
Informatore Fitopatologico [*A publication*] ... Inform Fitopatol
Informatore del Giovane Entomologo [*A publication*] ... Inf Giovane Entomol
Informatore Zootecnico [*A publication*] ... Inform Zootec
Informatsionnyi Byulleten'. Mikroelementy Sibirii [*A publication*] ... Inf Byull Mikroelem Sib
Informatsionnyi Byulleten'. Sovetskoi Antarkticheskoi Ekspeditsii [*A publication*] ... Inf Byull Sov Antarkt Eksped
Informe Anual de Labores. Costa Rica. Ministerio de Agricultura y Ganaderia [*A publication*] ... Informe Anu Labores Costa Rica Min Agr Ganad
Informe de Investigacion. Centro de Investigaciones Tecnologicas (Pando, Uruguay) [*A publication*] ... Inf Invest Cent Invest Tecnol (Pando Urug)
Informe Mensual. Estacion Experimental Agricola de "La Molina" (Lima) [*A publication*] ... Informe Mens Estac Exp Agr "La Molina" (Lima)
Informe Tecnico. Estacion Experimental Agropecuaria (Pergamino) [*A publication*] ... Informe Tec Estac Exp Agropecuar (Pergamino)
Informe Tecnico. Instituto Centroamericano de Investigacion y Tecnologia Industrial [*A publication*] ... Inf Tec ICAITI
Informe Tecnico. Instituto Centroamericano de Investigacion y Tecnologia Industrial [*A publication*] ... Inf Tec Inst Centroam Invest Tecnol Ind
Informe Tecnico. Instituto Forestal [*Chile*] [*A publication*] ... Informe Tec
Informed ... INF
Informed Birth and Parenting ... IBP
Informed Homebirth [*An association*] ... IH
Informes Cientificos y Tecnicos. Universidad Nacional de Cuyo [*A publication*] ... Infmes Cient Tec Univ Nac Cuyo
Informes. Provincia de Buenos Aires. Comision de Investigacions Cientificas [*A publication*] ... Inf Prov Buenos Aires Com Invest Cient
Inforonics Inc., Littleton, MA [*Library symbol*] ... MLitI
Infosystems [*Wheaton, IL*] [*A publication*] ... Infosys
Infotron Systems Corp. [*NASDAQ symbol*] ... INFN
Infra [*Beneath or Below*] [*Latin*] ... INF
Infra-Audible [*Sound*] ... IA
Infra Dignitatem [*Undignified*] [*Latin*] ... INFRA DIG
Infrablack Region ... IBR
Infrared ... IF
Infrared ... IFR
Infrared ... IR
Infrared Acquisition RADAR ... IRACQ
Infrared Active Homing ... IRAH
Infrared Advisory Center ... IRAC
Infrared Air Defense Detection System ... IRADDS
Infrared Alternate Head ... IRAH
Infrared Ambush Device ... IRAD
Infrared Amplification by Stimulated Emission of Radiation ... IRASER
Infrared Astronomical Satellite ... IRAS
Infrared Attack System ... IRAS
Infrared Auroral Emission ... IAE
Infrared Background Imaging Seeker ... IBIS
Infrared Calibration System ... ICS
Infrared Camera System ... ICS
Infrared Cell, Electronically Refrigerated ... ICER
Infrared Command Unit ... ICU
Infrared Communications System ... ICS
Infrared Communications System ... IRCS
Infrared Counter-Countermeasures [*Military electronics*] ... IRCCM

Infrared Countermeasures [Military electronics]	IRC
Infrared Countermeasures [Military electronics]	IRCM
Infrared Countermeasures System [Military electronics]	ICS
Infrared Decoy Evaluator	IDE
Infrared Detecting Set [or System]	IRDS
Infrared Detection Array	IDA
Infrared Detection Array	IRDA
Infrared Detection System	IDS
Infrared Detection Unit	IDU
Infrared Detection Unit	IRDU
Infrared Detector	IFD
Infrared Detector	IRD
Infrared Detector Cryostat	IDC
Infrared Display	IRD
Infrared Drying Oven	IDO
Infrared Drying Oven	IRDO
Infrared Early Warning System	IREWS
Infrared Electronic Warfare	IREW
Infrared Emission	IE
Infrared Emission	IRE
Infrared-Emitting Diode	IRED
Infrared Filter	IF
Infrared Filter Radiometer	IFR
Infrared Fire Control	IFC
Infrared Fire Control System	IFCS
Infrared Frequency Synthesis	IFS
Infrared Gas Analyzer	IRGA
Infrared Gas Radiation	IRGAR
Infrared Generator	IRG
Infrared Guided Projectile	IRGP
Infrared Gunfire Locator	IGL
Infrared Gunfire Locator	IRGL
Infrared Heater	IRH
Infrared Heterodyne Radiometer	IHR
Infrared Homing Bomb	IRBO
Infrared Homing System	IHS
Infrared Horizon Sensor	IHS
Infrared Image Converter	IRIC
Infrared Image Scanner	IRIS
Infrared Imagery	IRI
Infrared Imaging Seeker Head	IRISH
Infrared Imaging System	IIS
Infrared Industries, Inc. [NASDAQ symbol]	INFR
Infrared Information and Analysis	IRIA
Infrared Information and Analysis Center [University of Michigan]	IIAC
Infrared Information and Analysis Center [University of Michigan]	IRIAC
Infrared Information Exchange	IRIE
Infrared Information Symposia [Navy]	IRIS
Infrared Instrumentation	IRI
Infrared Instrumentation System	IIS
Infrared Interferometer Spectrometer	IRIS
Infrared Interferometer Spectrometer - Michelson	IRIS-M
Infrared Intruder System	IRIS
Infrared Intrusion Detection	IID
Infrared Jammer	IRJ
Infrared Jammer Equipment	IRJE
Infrared Kit	IRK
Infrared Lamp [or Light]	IRL
Infrared LASER	IRLAS
Infrared LASER Atmospheric Monitoring System	ILAMS
Infrared LASER Ranger	IRLR
Infrared LASER Spectrometer	IRLS
Infrared Lens	IRL
Infrared Line Scanner	IRLS
Infrared Mapper	IRM
Infrared Mapping System	IRMS
Infrared MASER	IRASER
Infrared Measurement	IRM
Infrared Measurement Instrument	IMI
Infrared Measurement Program	IRMP
Infrared Measuring System	IMS
Infrared Miniaturized Jammer	IMJ
Infrared Miniaturized Jammer	IRMJ
Infrared Miss-Distance Approximator	IRMA
Infrared Monochromatic Radiation	IMRA
Infrared Nondestructive Testing [Electrical technique]	INT
Infrared Nondestructive Testing [Electrical technique]	IRNDT
Infrared Optical Film	IOF
Infrared Oven	IRO
Infrared Physical Measurement	IRPM
Infrared Physics [A publication]	Infrared Phys
Infrared Physics [A publication]	Infrar Phys
Infrared Plume Target	IPT
Infrared Pointer Package	IPP
Infrared Pointer Package	IRPP
Infrared Preamplifier	IRP
Infrared Proximity Warning Indicator	IPWI
Infrared Quantum Counter	IRQC
Infrared RADAR Measurement Program	IRRMP
Infrared Radiation	IR
Infrared Radiation Profile	IRP

Infrared Radiometer	IR
Infrared Radiometer	IRR
Infrared Radiometer Clear Air Turbulence [Instrument]	IRCAT
Infrared Range and Detection	IRRAD
Infrared Receiver	IRR
Infrared Reconnaissance Set	IRS
Infrared Reconnaissance System	IRRS
Infrared Reflection Spectroscopy	IRRS
Infrared Reflective Spectra	IRS
Infrared Research Information Symposium	IRIS
Infrared Resolution Target System	IRRTS
Infrared Responsive Phosphor	IRP
Infrared Scanner	IRSCAN
Infrared Scanning Radiometer	ISR
Infrared Search Set	IRSS
Infrared Search Set Operator	IRSSO
Infrared Search and Track	IRST
Infrared Search and Track System	IRSTS
Infrared Sensitive Element Evaluation Program	ISEEP
Infrared Sensor System	IRSS
Infrared Sensor System	ISS
Infrared Sightline Control	ISC
Infrared Small Astronomical Spacecraft	ISAS
Infrared Solder Oven	IRSO
Infrared Source	IRS
Infrared Space Observatory	ISO
Infrared Spectrometer [or Spectroscopy]	IRS
Infrared Spectrometer [or Spectroscopy]	IRSP
Infrared Spectrometer [or Spectroscopy]	IRSPECT
Infrared Spectrophotometer	ISP
Infrared Structural Correlation Tables [A publication]	IRSCOT
Infrared Suppression Device	ISD
Infrared Surveillance Set	ISS
Infrared Surveillance Subsystem	IRSS
Infrared Systems Engineering	IRSE
Infrared Systems and Guidance Heads Laboratory	IRSGHL
Infrared Systems Manufacturing	IRSM
Infrared Systems Manufacturing	ISM
Infrared Tail Warning Set	IRTWS
Infrared on Target	IROT
Infrared Target Detector	IRTD
Infrared Target Detector	ITD
Infrared Target Seeker	IRTS
Infrared Telescope	IRT
Infrared Telescope Facility	IRTF
Infrared Temperature Profile Radiometer	ITPR
Infrared Thermal Mapper [NASA]	IRTM
Infrared Thermometer	IRT
Infrared Tracker	IRT
Infrared Tracking Display Unit	ITDU
Infrared Tracking System	ITS
Infrared Transmission	IRTRN
Infrared Transmitting	INTRAN
Infrared Transmitting	IRTRAN
Infrared Tube	IRT
Infrared Vidicon Tube	IRICON
Infrared Viewing Set	IVS
Infrared Warning Receiver [Aviation]	IRWR
Infrared Window	IRW
Infrasonic	IS
Infrasonic Frequency	ISF
Infrastructural, Logistics, Council Operations [NATO]	ILCO
Infrastructure Account Unit	IAU
Infrastructure Committee of the North Atlantic Council [NATO]	IC
Infrastructure Payments and Progress Committee [NATO]	IPPC
Infrastructure Special Committee [NATO]	ISC
Infricetur [Let It Be Rubbed In] [Pharmacy]	INFRIC
Infunde [Pour In] [Pharmacy]	INF
Infunde [Pour In] [Pharmacy]	INFUND
Infused Emitter Coupling	IEC
Infusion [Medicine]	INF
Infusionstherapie und Klinische Ernaehrung [A publication]	Infusionsther Klin Ernaehr
Infusionstherapie und Klinische Ernaehrung. Forschung und Praxis [A publication]	Infusionsther Klin Ernaer Forsch Prax
Infusionstherapie und Klinische Ernaehrung. Sonderheft [A publication]	Infusionsther Klin Ernaehr Sonderh
Infusoria Killing [Unit] [Medicine]	IK
Ingalls Memorial Hospital, Harvey, IL [Library symbol]	IHal
Inge Lehmann [Greenland] [Seismograph station code, US Geological Survey] [Closed]	ILG
Ingegneria Ferroviaria [A publication]	Ing Ferrov
Ingegneria Meccanica [A publication]	Ing Mecc
Ingegneria Nucleare [A publication]	Ing Nucl
Ingegneria Sanitaria [A publication]	Ing Sanit
Ingenieria Agronomica [A publication]	Ing Agron
Ingenieria Civil [A publication]	Ing Civil
Ingenieria Civil (Havana) [A publication]	Ing Civ (Havana)
Ingenieria Electrica y Mecanica [A publication]	Ing Electr & Mec
Ingenieria Forestal [A publication]	Ingen For
Ingenieria Hidraulica en Mexico [A publication]	Ingenieria Hidraul Mex

Ingenieria Hidraulica en Mexico [*A publication*] .... Ing Hidraul Mexico
Ingenieria Mecanica y Electrica [*A publication*] .... Ing Mec & Electr
Ingenieria Naval (Madrid) [*A publication*] .... Ing Nav (Madrid)
Ingenieur [*Engineer*] [*French*] .... ING
Ingenieur [*Engineer*] [*French*] .... Ir
Ingenieur-Archiv [*A publication*] .... Ing-Arch
Ingenieur Constructeur [*Academic degree*] IC
Ingenieur-Digest [*A publication*] .... Ing-Dig
Ingenieurs de l'Automobile [*A publication*] .... Ing Auto
Ingenieurs de l'Ecole Superieure de Physique et de Chimie Industrielles [*A publication*] .... Ing Ec Super Phys Chim Ind
Ingenieurs de l'Ecole Superieure de Physique et de Chimie Industrielles [*A publication*] .... Ing EPCI
Ingenieurs et Techniciens [*A publication*] .... Ing & Tech
Ingenieurs des Villes de France [*A publication*] .... Ingen Villes France
Ingenioerens Ugeblad [*A publication*] .... Ing Ugebl
Ingeniors Vetenskaps Akademien. Meddelande [*A publication*] .... Ing Vetenskaps Akad Medd
Ingenium Baccalaureus [*Bachelor of Engineering*] .... Ing B
Ingenium Doctor [*Doctor of Engineering*] .... Ing D
Ingenium Magister [*Master of Engineering*] .... Ing M
Ingenjoersveten Skapsakademien [*Sweden*] .... IVA
Ingersoll Public Library, Ingersoll, ON, Canada [*Library symbol*] .... CaOI
Ingersoll-Rand Co. [*NYSE symbol*] .... IR
Ingestion Exposure Pathway [*Nuclear emergency planning*] .... IEP
Ingglish Speling 3soesiaesh3n [*An organization to reform spelling*] .... IS
Ingham County Library, Mason, MI [*Library symbol*] .... MiMas
Inglewood, CA [*Radio station call letters*] .... KACE
Inglewood, CA [*Radio station call letters*] .... KTYM
Ingot .... IGT
Ingot Iron II
Ingram Ranch [*California*] [*Seismograph station code, US Geological Survey*] .... ING
Ingredient .... INGRD
Ingredient Technology Corporation [*NYSE symbol*] .... ITC
Ingress/Egress .... I/E
Inguinal [*Anatomy*] .... ING
Inhabitant .... INHAB
Inhabited Building Distance [*Army*] .... IBD
Inhalatio [*Inhalation*] [*Pharmacy*] .... INHAL
Inhalation .... INH
Inhalation Cycle Histogram [*Biometrics*] .... ICH
Inhalation Therapy [*Medicine*] .... IT
Inhalation Toxicology Research Institute .... ITRI
Inhaled Gas Analyzer .... IGA
Inhaled Particles [*A publication*] .... Inhaled Part
Inherent Corrective Maintenance Workload .... ICMW
Inherent Equipment Reliability .... IER
Inheritance of Acquired Characteristics .... IAC
Inherited Releasing Mechanism [*Psychiatry*] .... IRM
Inhibit .... IH
Inhibit .... INHB
Inhibit Halt Flip-Flop [*Data processing*] .... IHF
Inhibit Momentum Dump .... IMD
Inhibited .... INHBD
Inhibited Nitrogen Tetroxide .... INTO
Inhibited Red Fuming Nitric Acid [*Rocket fuel*] .... IRFNA
Inhibited Red Fuming Nitric Acid and Unsymmetrical Dimethylhydrazine [*Rocket fuel*] .... IRFN/UDMH
Inhibited Sexual Desire [*Sex therapy*] .... ISD
Inhibiting Factor .... IF
Inhibition .... INHIB
Inhibition Concentration [*Biochemistry*] IC
Inhibitor-Containing Minimal Medium [*Microbiology*] .... IMM
Inhibitor of DNA Synthesis [*Immunochemistry*] .... IDS
Inhibitory I
Inhibitory Dose [*Medicine*] .... ID
Inhibitory Junction Potential [*Neurophysiology*] .... IJP
Inhibitory Postsynaptic Current [*Neurophysiology*] .... IPSC
Inhibitory Postsynaptic Potential [*Neurophysiology*] .... IPSP
Initial I
Initial .... INIT
Initial Active Duty for Training [*Military*] .... IADT
Initial Aiming Point [*Gunnery*] .... IAP
Initial Appearance [*RADAR*] .... IA
Initial Approach [*Aviation*] I
Initial Approach [*Aviation*] .... IAP
Initial Approach [*Aviation*] .... INA
Initial Approach Course [*Aviation*] .... IAC
Initial Approach Fix [*Aviation*] .... IAF
Initial Approved Program .... IAP
Initial Attack Management System [*Weather system*] .... IAMS
Initial Authorization .... IA
Initial Beachhead [*Military*] .... IBH
Initial Beachhead [*Military*] .... IBHD
Initial Boiling Point .... IBP
Initial Boiling-Point Temperature .... IBT
Initial Bomb Release Line .... IBRL
Initial Capabilities Inspection [*Military*] ICI
Initial Cash Clothing Allowance [*Military*] .... ICCA
Initial Clothing Monetary Allowance [*Military*] .... ICMA
Initial Combat Employment [*of new munitions*] .... ICE
Initial Communications Connectivity [*DoD*] ICC
Initial Condition Evaluation [*Orbit identification*] .... ICEV
Initial Conditions IC
Initial Contact Control Time [*Aerospace*] .... ICCT
Initial Contingency Capability ICC
Initial Cooling Experiment [*Nuclear physics research*] .... ICE
Initial Course [*Navigation*] IC
Initial Defense Communications Satellite .... IDCS
Initial Defense Communications Satellite Program [*or Project*] .... IDCSP
Initial Defense Communications Satellite Program-Augmented .... IDCSP-A
Initial Defense Communications Satellite System .... IDCSS
Initial Defense Experiment .... IDEX
Initial Defense Satellite Communication .... IDSCM
Initial Defense Satellite Communication System .... IDSCS
Initial Delay Position [*Military*] .... IDP
Initial Denial Authority .... IDA
Initial Design Review .... IDR
Initial Distribution .... ID
Initial Dose [*Medicine*] .... IN
Initial Draft Presidential Memorandum .... IDPM
Initial Engine Development [*Air Force*] .... IED
Initial Engine Test .... IET
Initial Engine Test Facility .... IETF
Initial Entry Training .... IET
Initial Equipment [*Navy aircraft*] .... IE
Initial Fill Date [*Army*] .... IFD
Initial and Final Terminal Arrival Date [*Army*] .... IFTAD
Initial Graphics Exchange System [*National Standards Institute*] .... IGES
Initial Heading .... IH
Initial Ion Event .... IIE
Initial Issue II
Initial Launch Capability [*Aerospace*] ILC
Initial Launch Capability .... INLC
Initial Launch Capability Complex [*Aerospace*] ILCC
Initial Light Off Procedure .... ILOP
Initial Machine Load [*Data processing*] .... IML
Initial Marks [*Held*] **Constant** [*Psychology*] .... IMC
Initial Mass in Earth Orbit [*NASA*] .... IMEO
Initial Mass Function [*Galactic science*] .... IMF
Initial Materiel Support Office [*Army*] .... IMSO
Initial Measurement List .... IML
Initial Memory Protection .... IMP
Initial Microprogram Load [*Also, IMPL*] [*Data processing*] .... IML
Initial Microprogram Load [*Also, IML*] [*Data processing*] .... IMPL
Initial Military Assistance .... IMA
Initial Military Program .... IMP
Initial Missile Report .... IMR
Initial Navigation System .... INS
Initial Notification of an Aircraft Accident [*Aviation code*] .... ACCID
Initial Only .... IO
Initial Operating Production .... IOP
Initial Operating Test and Evaluation .... IOT & E
Initial Operation Capability Date [*Military*] .... IOCD
Initial Operational Capability [*Military*] .... IOC
Initial Operational Flight .... IOF
Initial Orbit Time [*Aerospace*] .... IOT
Initial Order Condition .... IOC
Initial Outfitting Allowance [*Navy*] .... IOA
Initial Outfitting List [*for advanced naval bases*] .... IOL
Initial Outfitting Technical Evaluation .... IOTE
Initial Phase .... IP
Initial Photographic Interpretation Report [*Air Force*] .... IPIR
Initial Point [*Military*] .... IP
Initial Point/H-Hour Control Line [*Aviation*] .... IP/HHCL
Initial Portable Equipment .... IPE
Initial Position .... IP
Initial Post [*Military*] .... IP
Initial Product Inspection .... IPI
Initial Production Facilities .... IPF
Initial Production Test [*Army*] .... IPT
Initial Program and Budget Estimate [*Army*] .... IP & BE
Initial Program Load [*Data processing*] .... INP
Initial Program Load [*Data processing*] .... IPL
Initial Project Design Description .... IPDD
Initial Protective Force .... IPF
Initial Provisioning .... IP
Initial Public Offering [*Business and trade*] .... IPO
Initial Quantity Order .... IQO
Initial Rate of Return .... IRR
Initial Receiving Point .... IRP
Initial Release .... IR
Initial Release Memorandum .... IRM
Initial Reserve .... IR
Initial Review Group [*National Institutes of Health*] .... IRG
Initial Satellite Communications Control Center .... ISACCC
Initial Satisfactory Performance Test .... ISPT
Initial Screening Training Effectiveness Analysis .... ISTEA
Initial Search Depth .... ISD
Initial Segment Membrane .... ISM
Initial Service Test .... IST

Initial Ship Design .... ISD
Initial Shipping Instructions .... ISI
Initial Shortage .... IS
Initial Software Configuration Map .... ISC
Initial Space Station .... ISS
Initial Spares and Repair Parts .... ISRP
Initial Spares Support List .... ISSL
Initial Specific Impulse .... ISP
Initial Stocks List .... ISL
Initial Subordinate Dominates Bystander [*Sociology*] .... ISDB
Initial Support Element .... ISE
Initial Support Increments [*Army*] .... ISI
Initial Support Team [*Military*] .... IST
Initial System Loading .... ISL
Initial Systems Checkout .... ISCO
Initial Systems Installation .... ISI
Initial Task Index .... ITI
Initial Teaching Alphabet [*A 44-symbol alphabet planned to simplify beginning reading by representing sounds more precisely*] .... i/t/a
Initial Track .... I/T
Initial Training Requirement .... ITR
Initial Trial Phase .... ITP
Initial Uniform Allowance [*Military*] .... INITUNIFALW
Initial Vapor Pressure .... IVP
Initial Velocity [*Ballistics*] IV
Initial Velocity .... Vo
Initial Ventricular Impulse IVI
Initial Voice Switched Network [*NATO Integrated Communications System*] .... IVSN
Initialization .... INIT
Initialization Load .... ILOAD
Initialize Reset Tape .... IRT
Initiating Reference Document .... IRD
Initiating Reference Letter .... IRL
Initiation .... INIT
Initiation Area Discriminator [*RADAR*] .... IAD
Initiation Factor [*Protein biosynthesis*] .... IF
Initiation a la Linguistique [*A publication*] .... I Ling
Initiation Supervisor .... IS
Initiative America Foundation .... IAF
Initiative Committee for National Economic Planning .... ICNEP
Initiative and Referendum .... I & R
Initiator Command Module .... ICM
Initiator Resistance Measuring Equipment .... IRME
Initio [*In the Beginning*] [*Latin*] .... INIT
Initio, Inc. [*NASDAQ symbol*] .... INTO
Iniziative [*A publication*] .... Iniz
Inject .... INJ
Injected Dose .... ID
Injected Electric Current Perturbation .... IECP
Injectio [*An Injection*] [*Pharmacy*] .... INJ
Injectio Hypodermica [*Hypodermic Injection*] [*Pharmacy*] .... INJ HYP
Injection [*Medicine*] .... INJ
Injection [*Medicine*] .... INJECT
Injection Electrode Catheter .... IEC
Injection LASER Illuminator ILI
Injection Luminescence Device .... ILD
Injection Microwave Plasma [*Oak Ridge National Laboratory*] .... IMP
Injection Mold .... IM
Injection Molding Kit .... IMK
Injector .... INJ
Injector Orifice .... IO
Injiciatur Enema [*Let an Enema Be Injected*] [*Pharmacy*] .... INJ ENEM
Injunction .... INJCT
Injure .... INJ
Injured on Duty .... IOD
Injured as Result of Hostile Action [*Military*] .... IRHA
Injury Control Research Laboratory [*HEW*] .... ICRL
Injury Control Research Laboratory Research Report [*HEW*] .... ICRL-RR
Injury Severity Index .... ISI
Ink Jet Printing .... IJP
Ink Receptivity .... IR
Inkopah [*California*] [*Seismograph station code, US Geological Survey*] .... IKP
Inkster, MI [*Radio station call letters*] .... WCHB
Inland .... INLD
Inland [*Aviation code*] .... LAN
Inland Airlines .... IAL
Inland and American Printer and Lithographer [*A publication*] .... Inland & Ptr & Lithog
Inland Bird Banding Association .... IBBA
Inland Bird-Banding News [*A publication*] .... Inl Bird-Banding News
Inland Clearance Depot [*Shipping*] .... ICD
Inland Commercial Fisheries Association .... ICFA
Inland Computer Service .... ICS
Inland Container Corp. [*NYSE symbol*] .... IN
Inland Daily Press Association .... IDPA
Inland Empire Airlines, Inc. [*La Verne, CA*] [*FAA designator*] .... IEA
Inland Forest Resource Council .... IFRC
Inland Library System [*Library network*] .... ILS
Inland Library System, Redlands, CA [*OCLC symbol*] .... LNI
Inland Marine Insurance Bureau [*Later, ISO*] .... IMIB
Inland Marine Underwriters Association [*Later, ISO*] .... IMUA
Inland Navigation Facility .... INF
Inland Printer [*A publication*] .... Inland Ptr
Inland Revenue [*British*] .... IR
Inland Revenue Commissioners [*British*] .... IRC
Inland Revenue Office [*or Officer*] [*British*] .... IRO
Inland Rivers, Ports, and Terminals [*An association*] .... IRPT
Inland Seas [*A publication*] .... InS
Inland Steel Co. [*NYSE symbol*] .... IAD
Inland Transport Committee [*United Nations*] .... ITC
Inland Transport War Council [*World War II*] .... ITWC
Inland Water Transport [*British*] .... IWT
Inland Waterway .... IWW
Inland Waterway Service .... IWS
Inland Waterways [*Organization that administered British canals during World War II. Since most of the barge crews were women, the initials were sometimes sardonically interpreted to mean "Idle Women"*] .... IW
Inland Waterways Common Carriers Association [*Defunct*] .... IWCCA
Inland Waterways Corporation [*Later, Federal Barge Lines, Inc.; liquidated, 1963*] .... IWC
Inlet [*Rotary piston meter*] I
Inlet [*Maps and charts*] .... IN
Inlet .... INL
Inlet [*Board on Geographic Names*] .... INLT
Inlet Absolute Pressure .... IAP
Inlet Contact IC
Inlet Gear Box .... IGB
Inlet Guide Valve .... IGV
Inlet Guide Vane .... IGV
Inlet Manhole [*Technical drawings*] .... IMH
Inlet and Outlet .... I & O
Inlet and Outlet .... IXO
Inlet and Outlet Head .... I & OH
Inlet and Outlet Head .... IXOH
Inlet Temperature Rise .... ITR
Inlet Valve .... I/V
Inlet Vane Actuator .... IVA
INLOGOV [*Institute of Local Government*] **Local Authority Game** .... ILAG
Inmersion y Ciencia [*A publication*] .... Inmersion Cienc
Inmont Corp. [*Formerly, Interchemical Corp.*] [*NYSE symbol*] [*Delisted*] .... IKN
Innate Release Mechanism [*Endocrinology*] .... IRM
Innateness Hypothesis [*Linguistics*] .... IH
Inner I
Inner .... INR
Inner Approach Channel .... IAC
Inner Artillery Zone .... IAZ
Inner Back End .... IBE
Inner [*Edge of*] **Basal Piece** .... IBP
Inner Bottom [*Technical drawings*] .... IB
Inner Cabin IC
Inner Cell Mass [*Embryology*] .... ICM
Inner Circle [*An association*] IC
Inner Circle [*Numismatics*] IC
Inner Circle of Advocates .... ICA
Inner Circle of American Revenuers .... ICAR
Inner City Business Improvement Forum .... ICBIF
Inner City Partnership [*EEC and British program to regenerate blighted areas*] .... ICP
Inner-City Simulation Laboratory [*Teacher training game*] .... ICSL
Inner Defense Zone .... IDZ
Inner Enamel Epithelium [*Dentistry*] .... IEE
Inner Front End .... IFE
Inner Gimbal .... IG
Inner Gimbal Angle .... IGA
Inner Gimbal Assembly .... IGA
Inner Gimbal Axis .... IGA
Inner Grid Injection .... IGI
Inner Guard [*Masonry*] .... IG
Inner Hair Cells [*of cochlea*] [*Anatomy*] .... IHC
Inner Integument [*Botany*] .... INI
Inner Keel .... IK
Inner London Education Authority [*British*] .... ILEA
Inner Marker [*Part of an instrument landing system*] [*Aviation*] .... IM
Inner Marker [*Part of an instrument landing system*] [*Aviation*] .... IMKR
Inner Mold Line .... IML
Inner Mongolia Autonomous Region [*China, Mainland*] [*MARC geographic area code*] [*Library of Congress*] .... a-cc-im
Inner Peace Movement .... IPM
Inner Pilot Valve .... IPV
Inner Plexiform Layer [*Retina*] .... IPL
Inner Quantum Number .... IQN
Inner Radiation Belt .... IRB
Inner Radiation Zone .... IRZ
Inner Seal Collar Tool [*Nuclear energy*] .... ISCT
Inner Temple .... IT
Inner Transport Area .... ITA
Innere Medizin [*A publication*] .... Innere Med

Innere Reich [*A publication*] ... IR
Innervation [*Medicine*] ... INNERV
Innings Pitched [*Baseball*] ... IP
Inniskilling Dragoons [*Military*] [*British*] ... ID
Innkeepers Society of America [*Defunct*] ... ISA
Innotron Diagnostics [*NASDAQ symbol*] ... INNO
Innovations in Land Use Management Symposium ... ILUMS
Innovative Design Fund ... IDF
Innovative Resources, Incorporated ... IRI
Innovative Software [*NASDAQ symbol*] ... INSO
Innovator of the Month ... IOM
Inns of Court and City Yeomanry [*Military unit*] [*British*] ... IC & CY
Innsbruck [*Austria*] [*Seismograph station code, US Geological Survey*] ... IBK
Innsbruck [*Austria*] [*Airport symbol*] ... INN
Innsbruck [*Austria*] [*Seismograph station code, US Geological Survey*] [*Closed*] ... INN
Innsbruecker Beitraege zur Kulturwissenschaft [*A publication*] ... IBK
Innsbruecker Beitraege zur Sprachwissenschaft [*A publication*] ... IBS
Inoculation ... INOC
Inolex Corp. [*American Stock Exchange symbol*] [*Delisted*] ... ILX
Inolex Pharmaceutical Co., Park Forest South, IL [*Library symbol*] ... IPfsI
Inongo [*Zaire*] [*Airport symbol*] ... INO
Inoperative ... INOP
Inorganic ... INORG
Inorganic Ablative Insulative Plastic ... IAIP
Inorganic Ablative Plastic ... IAP
Inorganic Carbon ... IC
Inorganic Chemistry [*A publication*] ... Inorg Chem
Inorganic Crystal Structure Database ... ICSD
Inorganic Halogen Oxidizer ... IHO
Inorganic Insulative Plastic ... IIP
Inorganic Macromolecules Reviews [*A publication*] ... Inorg Macromol Rev
Inorganic Materials [*A publication*] ... Inorg Mater
Inorganic and Nuclear Chemistry Letters [*A publication*] ... Inorg Nucl
Inorganic and Nuclear Chemistry Letters [*A publication*] ... Inorg Nucl Chem Lett
Inorganic Perspectives in Biology and Medicine [*A publication*] ... Inorg Perspect Biol Med
Inorganic Resin System [*Fire-resistant cement*] ... IRS
Inorganica Chimica Acta [*A publication*] ... Inorg Chim
Inorganica Chimica Acta [*A publication*] ... Inorg Chim Acta
Inosine [*One-letter symbol; see Ino*] ... I
Inosine [*Also, I*] [*A nucleoside*] ... Ino
Inosine Diphosphate [*Biochemistry*] ... IDP
Inosine Monophosphate [*Biochemistry*] ... IMP
Inosine Triphosphate [*Biochemistry*] ... ITP
Inositol [*Biochemistry*] ... Ins
Inositol Hexaphosphate [*Biochemistry*] ... IHP
Inostrannaya Literatura [*Moscow*] [*A publication*] ... InL
Inostrannye Jazyki v Skole [*A publication*] ... IJaS
Inostrannye Jazyki v Skole [*A publication*] ... IJS
Inostrannye Jazyki v Skole [*A publication*] ... InostrJazyki
Inostrannye Jazyki v Skole [*A publication*] ... IYaSh
Inozemna Filologiya [*L'vov*] [*A publication*] ... InF
Inozemna Filolohiji [*A publication*] ... InozF
Inpatient [*Medicine*] ... IP
Inpatient, Hospital ... IH
Inpatient Multidimensional Psychiatric Scale [*Psychology*] ... IMPS
Inpatient Unit [*Medicine*] ... IPU
Input ... I
Input ... IN
Input ... INP
Input ... I/P
Input Acknowledge ... IA
Input Axis ... IA
Input Bias Current ... IBC
Input Blocking Factor [*Data processing*] ... BI
Input-Checking Equipment ... ICE
Input Circuit ... IC
Input Collection Reports Data [*IRS*] ... ICRD
Input and Compare Register ... ICR
Input Contactor Switch ... ICS
Input Control Element ... ICE
Input Control System [*Military*] ... INC
Input Control Word [*Data processing*] ... ICW
Input Current ... IC
Input Current Offset [*Data processing*] ... ICO
Input Data Assembler ... IDA
Input Data Processor ... IDP
Input Data Request ... IDR
Input-Data Strobe ... IDS
Input Data Word ... IDWD
Input Display Console [*Data processing*] ... IDC
Input Expansion Unit ... IEU
Input Frequency Tolerance [*Data processing*] ... IFT
Input Impedance ... II
Input Interface Unit [*Data processing*] ... IIU
Input Logic Level ... ILL
Input Marginal Checking and Distribution ... IMCD
Input Memory Buffer [*Data processing*] ... IMB
Input Message Processor ... IMP
Input Offset Current ... IOC
Input Offset Voltage ... IOV
Input/Output [*Data processing*] ... I/O
Input/Output Access Unit [*Data processing*] ... IOAU
Input-Output Adapter [*Data processing*] ... IOA
Input-Output Address [*Data processing*] ... IOA
Input-Output Assembly [*Data processing*] ... IOA
Input-Output Box [*Data processing*] ... IOB
Input-Output Box and Peripheral Simulator [*Data processing*] ... IOBPS
Input-Output Buffer [*Data processing*] ... IOB
Input-Output Channels [*Data processing*] ... IOC
Input-Output Comparator [*Data processing*] ... IOC
Input-Output Control Center [*or Command*] [*Data processing*] ... IOCC
Input-Output Control System [*Data processing*] ... IOCS
Input-Output Control Unit [*Data processing*] ... IOCU
Input-Output Controller [*Data processing*] ... IOC
Input-Output Converter [*Data processing*] ... IOC
Input-Output Data Channel [*Data processing*] ... IODC
Input-Output Data Document [*Data processing*] ... IODD
Input-Output Delay Counter [*Data processing*] ... IODC
Input-Output Error Log Table [*Data processing*] ... IOE
Input-Output Gate [*Data processing*] ... IOG
Input-Output Module [*Data processing*] ... IOM
Input-Output Multiplexer [*Data processing*] ... I/OM
Input-Output Package [*Data processing*] ... IOP
Input-Output Port [*Data processing*] ... IOP
Input-Output Processor [*Data processing*] ... IOP
Input-Output Programing System [*Data processing*] ... IOPS
Input-Output Pulse [*Data processing*] ... IOP
Input-Output Queue [*Data processing*] ... IOQ
Input-Output Queue Element [*Data processing*] ... IOQE
Input-Output Register [*SAGE*] ... IOR
Input-Output Selector [*Data processing*] ... IOS
Input-Output Sense [*Data processing*] ... IOS
Input-Output Skip [*Data processing*] ... IOS
Input-Output Supervision [*Data processing*] ... IOS
Input-Output Switch [*Data processing*] ... IOS
Input/Output Systems Association ... IOSA
Input-Output Termination [*Data processing*] ... IOT
Input-Output Transfer [*Data processing*] ... IOT
Input-Output Unit [*Data processing*] ... IOU
Input-Output Utility [*Data processing*] ... IOU
Input Power ... IP
Input Processor ... IP
Input Processor Programs ... IPP
Input Read Submodule ... IRS
Input Revision Typewriter ... IRT
Input Secondary [*Electronics*] ... IS
Input Signal Voltage ... ISV
Input Simulator ... IS
Input Subsystem ... ISS
Input Test Equipment ... ITE
Input Translator [*Data processing*] ... INTRAN
Input Translator [*Data processing*] ... IT
Input Translator Program [*Data processing*] ... ITP
Input Voltage ... IV
Input Voltage Offset ... IVO
Input Voltage Supply ... IVS
Inquiry ... INQ
Inquiry [*A publication*] ... Inq
Inquiry Magazine [*A publication*] ... Inquiry Mag
Inquiry and Reporting System ... IRS
Inscribed ... INS
Inscribed [*or Inscription*] ... INSC
Inscription ... INSCR
Inscriptiones Creticae [*A publication*] ... ICr
Inscriptiones Graecae [*A publication*] ... IG
Inscriptiones Graecae [*Epigraphic notation*] ... IG
Inscriptiones Graecae ad Res Romanas Pertinentes [*A publication*] ... IGRR
Inscriptions Grecques et Latines de la Syrie [*A publication*] ... IGLSyr
Insect Balanced Salt Solution [*Cytology*] ... IBSS
Insect Biochemistry [*A publication*] ... Insect Bioc
Insect Biochemistry [*A publication*] ... Insect Biochem
Insect Carrier Toxicant ... ICT
Insect Disease Report. US Forest Service. Northern Region [*A publication*] ... Insect Dis Rep US For Serv North Reg
Insect Growth Regulator ... IGR
Insect Populations Management Research Unit [*Department of Agriculture*] ... IPM
Insect Screen ... IS
Insect Screening Weavers Association ... ISWA
Insect Visual System ... IVS
Insect Wire Screening Bureau [*Later, Insect Screening Weavers Association*] ... IWSB
Insecta Matsumurana. Supplement [*A publication*] ... Insecta Matsumurana Suppl
Insectes Sociaux [*A publication*] ... Insect Soc
Insecticide ... ICTCD
Insecticide(s) [*Freight*] ... INSECTI
Insects of Micronesia [*A publication*] ... Insects Micronesia
Insel-Almanach [*A publication*] ... IA

Insemnari Stiintifice [A publication].....................ISt
Insensitive High Explosive.............................IHE
Insensitive High Explosives and Propellants [DoD/DOE program].......IHEP
Insensitive Nuclei Enhanced by Polarization Transfer [Spectroscopy]............INEPT
Inseparable.............................INSEP
INSERM [Institut National de la Sante et de la Recherche Medicale] Colloque [A publication]............INSERM Colloq
INSERM [Institut National de la Sante et de la Recherche Medicale] Symposia [A publication]............INSERM Symp
INSERM [Institut National de la Sante et de la Recherche Medicale] Symposia [Elsevier Book Series] [A publication].............IS
Insert.............................INS
Insert.............................INSR
Insert Card Section.............................ICS
Insert Screw Thread.............................INST
Insert Storage Key.............................ISK
Insertable Nuclear Components.............................INC
Inserted Connection Losses [Telecommunications].............ICL
Insertion Loss.............................IL
Insertion Phase Delay.............................IPD
Insertion Sequence [Genetics].............................IS
Insertion Velocity Adjust Routine [NASA].............IVAR
Inshore Fire Support Ship [Later, LFR].............IFS
Inshore Fire Support Ship [Navy symbol].............LFR
Inshore Patrol.............................INSHOREPAT
Inshore Patrol.............................INSPAT
Inshore Undersea Warfare [Navy].............................IUW
Inshore Undersea Warfare Control Center [Navy].............IUWCC
Inshore Undersea Warfare Craft [Navy].............IUWC
Inshore Undersea Warfare Group [Navy].............INSHORUNSEAWARGRU
Inshore Undersea Warfare Group [Navy].............INSUWG
Inshore Undersea Warfare Group [Navy].............IUWG
Inside.............................I
Inside.............................INS
Inside Air Temperature.............................IAT
Inside Back Cover.............................IBC
Inside Continental United States [Military].............ICUS
Inside Diameter.............................ID
Inside Diameter of Outer Conductor.............IDOC
Inside Dimensions.............................ID
Inside Edge [Skating].............................I
Inside Edge.............................IE
Inside Frosted.............................IF
Inside Height.............................IH
Inside Home [Baseball].............................IH
Inside Layer [Technical drawings].............................IL
Inside Left [Soccer position].............................IL
Inside Length [Technical drawings].............................IL
Inside of Metal.............................I/M
Inside Mold Line [Technical drawings].............IML
Inside Nazi Germany [A publication].............................ING
Inside Radius [Technical drawings].............................IR
Inside Right [Soccer position].............................IR
Inside Sentinel [Masonry].............................IS
Inside Skin.............................ISS
Inside Surface.............................ISS
Inside Trim Template.............................ITT
Inside the United States.............................INUS
Inside Width.............................IW
Insiders' Chronicle [A publication].............Insiders' Chr
Insignia.............................ISGN
Insilco Corp. [Formerly, International Silver Co.] [NYSE symbol].............INR
Insituform East, Incorporated [NASDAQ symbol].............INEI
Insituform of North America CI A [NASDAQ symbol].............INSUA
Insoluble.............................I
Insoluble.............................INSOL
Insoluble Collagen [Biochemistry].............................ISC
Insoluble Metaphosphate [Inorganic chemistry].............IMP
Insoluble Residue.............................IR
Inspect [or Inspector].............................INSP
Inspect and Repair as Necessary [Aviation].............IRAN
Inspect and Repair Only as Necessary [Military].............IROAN
Inspect, Supervise, Generally Superintend Recruitment Methods.............INSUPGENCRUIT
Inspect, Test, and Correct as Necessary.............ITCAN
Inspected and Condemned [Military].............................I & C
Inspected and Condemned [Military].............................IC
Inspected Variety Purity [Agriculture].............................IVP
Inspecting Ordnance Officer.............................IOO
Inspecting Torpedo Officer [Navy].............................ITO
Inspection.............................INSPEC
Inspection Administration [Navy].............................IA
Inspection Analysis Review Board.............................IARB
Inspection Apply Template.............................IAT
Inspection by Attribute.............................IBA
Inspection Bulletin.............................IB
Inspection Card.............................IC
Inspection Check Fixture.............................ICF
Inspection Check Template.............................ICT
Inspection Committee.............................IC

Inspection Data Bulletin.............................IDB
Inspection Data Card.............................IDC
Inspection Departmental Instruction.............................IDI
Inspection Discrepancy Report.............................IDR
Inspection Discrepancy Tag.............................IDT
Inspection Division [Coast Guard].............................INS
Inspection and Enforcement.............................IE
Inspection Error.............................IE
Inspection Fixture.............................INFX
Inspection Gauge.............................IG
Inspection Gauge.............................INGA
Inspection Gauges Production.............................IGP
Inspection Instruction Sheet.............................IIS
Inspection Item Change Request.............................IICR
Inspection Item Sheet.............................IIS
Inspection Lot Size.............................ILS
Inspection and Maintenance.............................I & M
Inspection Manual.............................IM
Inspection Memorandum.............................IM
Inspection Operation Procedure.............................IOP
Inspection Operation Sheet.............................IOS
Inspection Operation System.............................IOS
Inspection Operation Tag.............................IOT
Inspection Order.............................IO
Inspection Outline.............................IO
Inspection, Palpation, Percussion, Auscultation [Medicine].............IPPA
Inspection Planning Order.............................IPO
Inspection Progress Notification.............................IPN
Inspection Quality Assurance.............................IQA
Inspection Record.............................IR
Inspection Record Card [Navy].............................IRC
Inspection Record Sheet.............................IRS
Inspection Rejection.............................IR
Inspection Rejection Report [NASA].............................IRR
Inspection Release.............................IR
Inspection, Repair, Overhaul, and Rebuild.............................IROR
Inspection [or Inspector's] Report.............................IR
Inspection Requirements Handbook [Navy].............................IRH
Inspection Requirements Manual.............................IRM
Inspection Review Board.............................IRB
Inspection and Security.............................I & S
Inspection Services, Inc. [An association].............................IS
Inspection Shell.............................INSH
[Board of] Inspection and Survey [Military].............................I & S
Inspection and Survey Board [Navy].............................PRESINSURV
Inspection and Survey Board Sub Board [Navy].............................SUBINSURV
Inspection Tag.............................IT
Inspection and Test.............................I & T
Inspection Test and Analysis Plan.............................IT & AP
Inspection and Test Instruction.............................ITI
Inspection and Test (Planning).............................I & T(P)
Inspection Test Procedure.............................ITP
Inspection Test Report.............................ITR
Inspection by Variables.............................IBV
Inspection Visual Aid.............................IVA
Inspection Zone.............................IZ
Inspections and Investigations Staff [Vietnam].............................IIS
Inspector.............................I
Inspector.............................INS
Inspector.............................INSPR
Inspector of Degaussing [Navy].............................IDG
Inspector of Dental Activities.............................INSDEN
Inspector General [Air Force, Army, Marine Corps].............................IG
Inspector General [Navy].............................INSGEN
[The] Inspector General [Army].............................TIG
Inspector General, Atlantic Fleet [Navy].............................INSGENLANTFLT
Inspector General Field Office [Military].............................IGFO
Inspector-General to the Forces for Training [British].............................IGT
Inspector General, Foreign Assistance [Department of State].............................IGFA
Inspector-General of Fortifications [British].............................IGF
Inspector General, Pacific Fleet and Pacific Ocean Areas [Navy].............................INSGENPAC
Inspector-General of the Royal Air Force [British].............................IGRAF
Inspector General, Supply Corps.............................IGSC
Inspector General's Department.............................IGD
Inspector General's Office [Air Force].............................IGO
Inspector-Instruction [Marine Corps].............................INSP-INSTR
Inspector-Instructor [Marine Corps].............................I-I
Inspector-Instructor, Naval Reserve.............................INSINSTR
Inspector/Killer.............................I/K
Inspector of Machinery.............................IM
Inspector of Naval Aircraft.............................INA
Inspector of Naval Aircraft.............................INSAIR
Inspector of Naval Engineering.............................INSENG
Inspector of Naval Machinery.............................INM
Inspector of Naval Machinery.............................INSMACH
Inspector of Naval Material.............................INM
Inspector of Naval Material.............................INSMAT
Inspector of Naval Material, Petroleum.............................INSMAT PET
Inspector of Naval Ordnance [British].............................INO
Inspector of Naval Ordnance.............................INSORD

Inspector of Navigational Material ... INSNAVMAT
Inspector of Navy Recruiting and Naval Officer Procurement ... INSCRUIT
Inspector of Ordnance ... INSORD
Inspector of Ordnance in Charge ... INSORDINC
Inspector of Petroleum Reserves ... INSPETRES
Inspector of Radio Material ... INSRADMAT
Inspector of the Royal Artillery [*British*] ... IRA
Inspector of Torpedoes and Mines [*Navy*] ... ITM
Inspector of Training Corps and Cadets [*Military*] [*British*] ... ITCA
Inspector of Works ... IW
Inspector's Report Addendum ... IRA
Inspekteur der Artillerie [*Inspector of Artillery*] [*German military - World War II*] ... IDA
Inspekteur der Ordnungspolizei [*Inspector of Uniformed Police*] [*German military - World War II*] ... IDO
Inspiration ... INSP
Inspiration Consolidated Copper Co. [*NYSE symbol*] [*Delisted*] ... IC
Inspiration Resources Corporation [*NYSE symbol*] ... IRC
Inspiratory Capacity [*Physiology*] ... IC
Inspiratory Center [*Physiology*] ... IC
Inspiratory Reserve Volume [*Physiology*] ... IRV
Inspired Partial Pressure [*Physiology*] ... IPP
Inspiretur [*Let It Be Inspired*] [*Pharmacy*] ... INSPIR
Instability ... INSTBY
Installation ... INSTAL
Installation ... INSTALLN
Installation ... INSTL
Installation ... INSTLN
Installation the Army Authorization Document System ... ITAADS
Installation, Assembly or Detail ... IAD
Installation Automated Budget System [*Army*] ... IABS
Installation Automated Manpower Utilization System [*Army*] ... IAMUS
Installation Calibration and Checkout ... IC & C
Installation Calibration and Checkout ... ICC
Installation and Checkout [*Military*] ... I & C
Installation and Checkout ... INSTL & C/O
Installation Completion Date ... ICD
Installation Confinement Facility [*Army*] ... ICF
Installation Console ... INCON
Installation and Construction [*Military*] ... I & C
Installation Damage Report [*Air Force*] ... INREP
Installation Data ... ID
Installation Data Record ... IDR
Installation Enhancement Release [*Data processing*] ... IER
Installation Equipment [*Army*] ... IE
Installation Fixtures ... IF
Installation Handbook ... IH
Installation Inspection Procedure Report ... IIPR
Installation Instruction ... II
Installation Lead Time ... ILT
Installation and Maintenance ... I & M
Installation and Maintenance Guide ... IMG
Installation and Maintenance Instruction ... IMI
Installation Maintenance Officer [*Military*] ... IMO
Installation Management Information System [*Army*] ... IMIS
Installation Master Planning [*Military*] ... IMP
Installation and Materiel District Office [*FAA*] ... IMDO
Installation Materiel Readiness Reporting System [*Army*] ... IMRRS
Installation, Modification, Maintenance, and Repair ... IMMR
Installation Notice Card ... INC
Installation Operating Program ... IOP
Installation Operation Budget ... IOB
Installation and Operational Checkout ... IOC
Installation Parts List ... IPL
Installation Performance Specification [*Data processing*] ... IPS
Installation Planning Order ... IPO
Installation Preflight Test ... IPT
Installation Procedure ... IP
Installation Production Order ... IPO
Installation Productivity Option [*IBM Corp.*] ... IPO
Installation Productivity Option/Extended [*IBM Corp.*] ... IPO/E
Installation Property Book [*Military*] ... IPB
Installation Readiness System [*Army*] ... IRS
Installation and Removal Record [*NASA*] ... IRR
Installation Report ... IR
Installation and Service Engineering ... I & SE
Installation Service Supply Support ... ISSS
Installation and Services ... I & S
Installation Shipping and Receiving Capability ... ISARC
Installation Specification Drawing ... ISD
Installation Start Date ... ISD
Installation Supply Accounting ... ISA
Installation Supply Division [*Military*] ... ISD
Installation Supply Officer [*Military*] ... ISO
Installation Support ... IS
Installation Support and Evaluation ... ISE
Installation Support School [*Army*] ... ISS
Installation Support Services ... ISS
Installation and Test [*Army*] ... I & T
Installation Test Program ... ITP
Installation Test Requirements Outline ... ITRO
Installation and Test Support Associate Contractor [*Air Force*] ... ITSA
Installation Transportation Office [*or Officer*] [*Air Force*] ... ITO
Installation Verification Procedure ... IVP
Installations Fragenkommission [*Later, International Commission on Rules for the Approval of Electrical Equipment*] [*CEE*] ... IFK
Installations and Logistics ... I & L
Installations Planning and Review Board [*DoD*] ... IPRB
Installations and Services Agency [*Army Materiel Command*] ... ISA
Installed ... INST
Installed User Program [*Data processing*] ... IUP
Installed User Programs [*Data processing*] ... IUPS
Installer ... INSTLR
Installment Agreement ... I/A
Instant ... INST
Instant Big Mouth [*Martini*] [*Slang*] ... IBM
Instant Control Point [*British police*] ... ICP
Instant Corn-Soya-Milk ... ICSM
Instant Data Access Control [*National Design Center, Inc.*] [*Information service*] ... IDAC
Instant Language [*Trademark*] [*Data processing*] ... INLAN
Instant Lead Vertical Speed Indicator ... ILVSI
Instant Lunar Ionosphere ... ILI
Instant Ocean Culture System ... IOCS
Instant Potato Products Association [*Defunct*] ... IPPA
Instant Private Network ... IPN
Instant Purchase Excursion Fares [*Aviation*] ... IPEX
Instant Research on Peace and Violence [*A publication*] ... Instant Res
Instant Research on Peace and Violence [*A publication*] ... Instant Res Peace Violence
Instant Response Information System ... IRIS
Instant Response Ordering System [*Brodart, Inc.*] [*Information service*] ... IROS
Instant Thin-Layer Chromatography ... ITLC
Instant Visual Index ... IVI
Instantaneous ... I
Instantaneous ... INST
Instantaneous Audience Measurement System ... IAMS
Instantaneous Automatic Frequency Control ... IAFC
Instantaneous Automatic Gain Control [*RADAR*] ... IAGC
Instantaneous Automatic Video Control ... IAVC
Instantaneous Automatic Volume Control [*Electronics*] ... IAVC
Instantaneous Center of Motion ... ICM
Instantaneous Center of Rotation ... ICR
Instantaneous Compressor Performance Analysis Computer ... ICPAC
Instantaneous Direction Finding ... IDF
Instantaneous Effective Photocathodes ... IEPC
Instantaneous Field of View ... IFOV
Instantaneous Frequency Correlation ... IFC
Instantaneous Frequency Correlation ... IFRC
Instantaneous Frequency Discriminator ... IFD
Instantaneous Frequency Measurement ... IFM
Instantaneous Frequency [*Indicating*] **Receivers** ... IFR
Instantaneous Geometric Field of View ... IGFOV
Instantaneous Impact Points ... IIP
Instantaneous Impact Predictor ... IIP
Instantaneous Launch Control Officer [*Aerospace*] ... ILCO
Instantaneous Overload ... IOL
Instantaneous Panoramic Display Unit ... IPDU
Instantaneous Power Output ... IPO
Instantaneous Readout Detector [*Satellite instrument*] ... IROD
Instantaneous Relay ... IR
Instantaneous Sound Pressure ... ISP
Instantaneous Spatial Transference ... IST
Instantaneous Unit Hydrograph ... IUH
Instantaneous Vertical Speed Indicator [*NASA*] ... IVSI
Instantaneous Vertical Velocity ... IVV
Instantaneous Vertical Velocity Indicator ... IVVI
Instantaneous Vertical Velocity Sensor ... IVVS
Instillandus [*To Be Dropped In*] [*Pharmacy*] ... INSTILL
Instituit voor de Toepassing van Atoomenergie in de Landboury [*Netherlands*] ... ITAL
Institut Agricole d'Oka, LaTrappe, PQ, Canada [*Library symbol*] [*Obsolete*] ... CaQTO
Institut za Alatne Masine i Alate. Monografije [*A publication*] ... Inst Alatne Masine Alate Monogr
Institut za Alatne Masine i Alate. Saopstenja [*A publication*] ... Inst Alatne Masine Alate Saopstenja
Institut Albert Prevost, Montreal, PQ, Canada [*Library symbol*] ... CaQMIAP
Institut Albert Tessier, Trois-Rivieres, PQ, Canada [*Library symbol*] ... CaQTI
Institut Archeologique Liegeois. Bulletin [*A publication*] ... IALBull
Institut des Arts Appliques, Montreal, PQ, Canada [*Library symbol*] ... CaQMIAA
Institut des Arts Graphiques, Montreal, PQ, Canada [*Library symbol*] ... CaQMIAG
Institut fuer Auslandsbeziehungen [*A publication*] ... IAB
Institut Belge pour l'Amelioration de la Betterave Publication Trimestrielle [*A publication*] ... Inst Belge Amelior Betterave Publ Trimest

Institut Belge d'Information et de Documentation [*Belgian Information Agency*] .... INBEL
Institut Belge de Normalisation [*Brussels, Belgium*] ....IBN
Institut Belles-Lettres Arabes. Revue [*Tunis*] [*A publication*] ....IBLA
Institut de Cardiologie de Montreal, Montreal, PQ, Canada [*Library symbol*] .... CaQMICM
Institut fuer Chemie der Treibstoffe [*West Germany*] ....ICT
Institut fuer Deutsche Sprache [*Institute for German Language*] [*Information service*] ....IDS
Institut fuer Dokumentation, Information, und Statistik [*Institute for Documentation, Information, and Statistics*] [*Information service on cancer research*] [*Germany*] ....IDIS
Institut de Droit International [*Institute of International Law*] .... IDI
Institut d'Egypte Bulletin [*A publication*] .... Inst d'Egypte Bull
Institut d'Elevage et de Medecine Veterinaire des Pays Tropicaux [*Institute of Stockraising and Veterinary Medicine in Tropical Countries*] [*France*] ....IEMVT
Institut Equatorial de Recherches et d'Etudes Geologiques et Minieres .... IEREGEM
Institut d'Estudis Catalans [*A publication*] ....IEC
Institut d'Etude du Developpement Economique et Social [*France*] ....IEDES
Institut pour l'Etude des Methodes de Direction de l'Enterprise [*A management development institute*] [*Lausanne, Switzerland*] .... IMEDE
Institut d'Etudes Congolaises [*Congolese Institute of Studies*] ....IEC
Institut des Etudes Medievales, Universite de Montreal, Montreal, PQ, Canada [*Library symbol*] .... CaQMUE
Institut Europeen des Industries de la Pectine [*European Institute of the Pectin Industries*] ....IEIP
Institut Europeen pour la Promotion des Entreprises ....IEP
Institut Federal de Recherches Forestieres. Memoires [*A publication*] .... Inst Fed Rech For Mem
Institut Fondamental d'Afrique Noire. Bulletin. Serie A. Sciences Naturelles [*Dakar*] [*A publication*] ....
Inst Fondam Afr Noire Bull Ser A
Institut Francais d'Afrique Noire [*French Institute of Black Africa*] .... IFAN
Institut Francais d'Archeologie Orientale. Bibliotheque d'Etude [*A publication*] ....IFAOBE
Institut Francais du Cafe et du Cacao. Bulletin [*A publication*] ....
Inst Fr Cafe Cacao Bull
Institut Francais d'Etudes Andines. Bulletin [*A publication*] ....
Inst Fr Etud Andines
Institut Francais d'Haiti. Memoires [*A publication*] ....
Inst Francais d'Haiti Mem
Institut Francais d'Opinion Publique [*French Institute of Public Opinion*] .... IFOP
Institut Francais du Petrole [*French Institute of Petroleum*] ....IFP
Institut Francais du Petrole. Revue et Annales des Combustible Liquides [*Later, Institut Francais du Petrole. Revue*] [*A publication*] .... Inst Francais Petrole Rev
Institut Francais du Petrole. Revue et Annales des Combustible Liquides [*Later, Institut Francais du Petrole. Revue*] [*A publication*] .... Inst Fr Pet Rev
Institut de France (Paris). Academie des Inscriptions et Belles-Lettres. Monuments et Memoires [*A publication*] ....
Acad Inscr (Paris) Mon et Mem
Institut Genealogique Drouin, Montreal, PQ, Canada [*Library symbol*] ....CaQMD
Institut de Geologie du Bassin d'Aquitaine. Bulletin [*A publication*] .... Inst Geol Bassin Aquitaine Bull
Institut des Hautes Etudes de l'Amerique Latine, Universite de Paris, Paris, France [*Library symbol*] .... FrPU-AL
Institut des Hautes Etudes Cinematographiques [*French institute for the study of the motion picture*] ....IDHEC
Institut des Hautes Etudes Scientifiques. Publications Mathematiques [*A publication*] .... Inst Hautes Etudes Sci Publ Math
Institut fuer Hydromechanik und Wasserwirtschaft. Eidgenoessische Technische Hochschule Zuerich [*A publication*] ....
Inst Hydromech Wasserwirtsch Eidg Tech Hochsch Zuerich
Institut Interafricain du Travail .... IIT
Institut International de Bibliographie .... IIB
Institut International des Brevets [*International Patent Institute*] ....IIB
Institut International des Caisses d'Epargne [*International Savings Banks Institute*] [*See also ISBI*] ....IICE
Institut International Catholique de Recherches Socio-Ecclesiales [*International Catholic Institute for Socio-Religious Research*] [*Later, FERES*] .... ICARES
Institut International des Civilisations Differentes [*International Institute of Differing Civilizations*] ....INCIDI
Institut International de Droit Humanitaire [*International Institute of Humanitarian Law - IIHL*] .... IIDH
Institut International de l'Epargne ....IIE
Institut International d'Etudes sur l'Education [*International Institute for Education Studies*] ....IIEE
Institut International d'Etudes Ligures [*International Institute for Ligurian Studies*] ....IIEL
Institut International du Froid [*International Institute of Refrigeration*] ....IIF
Institut International de Planification de l'Education [*International Institute for Educational Planning*] ....IIPE

Institut International de la Presse [*International Press Institute*] ....IIP
Institut International de Recherches Betteravieres [*International Institute for Sugar Beet Research*] ....IIRB
Institut International de Recherches Betteravieres. Revue [*A publication*] .... Inst Int Rech Better Rev
Institut International de Recherches Graphologiques ....IIRG
Institut International des Sciences Administratives [*International Institute for Administrative Sciences*] ....IISA
Institut International de la Soudure [*International Institute of Welding*] ..... IIS
Institut International de Statistique [*International Statistical Institute*] ......IIS
Institut International de Statistique. Revue [*A publication*] ....Inst Int Stat R
Institut International du Theatre [*International Theater Institute*] ....IIT
Institut International du Travail Temporaire - International Institute for Temporary Work ....IITT-IITW
Institut International pour l'Unification du Droit Prive [*International Institute for the Unification of Private Law*] ....UNIDROIT
[*Franco-German*] **Institut Laue-Langevin** ILL
Institut de Mecanique Statistique de la Turbulence [*France*] ....IMST
Institut Mehaniki Moskovskogo Gosudarstvennogo Universiteta. Naucnye Trudy [*A publication*] ....
Inst Meh Moskov Gos Univ Naucn Trudy
Institut de Microbiologie et d'Hygiene de Montreal, Montreal, PQ, Canada [*Library symbol*] ....CaQMIM
Institut Mondial du Phosphate [*World Phosphate Institute*] .... IMPHOS
Institut Napoleon. Revue [*A publication*] ....Inst Napoleon R
Institut National pour l'Amelioration des Conserves de Legumes. Bulletin Bimestriel (Belgium) [*A publication*] ....
Inst Natl Amelior Conserves Legumes Bull Bimest (Belg)
Institut National pour l'Amelioration des Conserves de Legumes. Bulletin Trimestriel (Belgium) [*A publication*] ....
Inst Nat Amelior Conserves Legumes Bull Trimest (Belg)
Institut National des Appellations d'Origine [*Semigovernmental organization that fixes the appellations on all French wines*] ....INAO
Institut National pour l'Etude Agronomique du Congo [*National Institute for the Study of Agronomy in the Congo*] ....INEAC
Institut National d'Etudes Demographiques .... INED
Institut National d'Etudes Demographiques, Paris, France [*Library symbol*] ....FrPED
Institut National Genevois. Bulletin [*A publication*] ..... Inst Natl Genevois Bull
Institut National Genevois. Bulletin. New Series [*A publication*] ....
Inst Natl Genevois Bull NS
Institut National de la Propriete Industrielle, Centre Regional, Marseilles, France [*Library symbol*] .... FrMC
Institut National de Radiodiffusion [*Belgium*] ....INR
Institut National de la Recherche Agronomique [*France*] .... INRA
Institut National de la Recherche Agronomique (Paris) [*A publication*] ....Inst Nat Rech Agron (Paris)
Institut National de la Recherche Agronomique au Service des Industries Agricoles et Alimentaires [*A publication*] ....
Inst Natl Rech Agron Serv Ind Agric Aliment
Institut National de la Recherche Agronomique de Tunisie [*A publication*] ....Inst Nat Rech Agron Tunisie
Institut National de la Recherche Agronomique de Tunisie. Documents Techiques [*A publication*] ....
Inst Natl Rech Agron Tunisie Doc Tech
Institut National de Recherche en Informatique et en Automatique [*National Institute for Research in Informatics and Automation*] [*France*] [*Information service*] ....INRIA
Institut National de la Sante et de la Recherche Medicale [*France*] ....INSERM
Institut National des Sciences Appliquees de Lyon .... INSA
Institut National des Sciences et Techniques Nucleaires [*France*] .....INSTN
Institut National de la Statistique et des Etudes Economiques [*National Institute of Statistics and Economic Research*] [*France*] .... INSEE
Institut National des Techniques de la Documentation [*National Institute for Documentation Techniques*] [*France*] [*Information service*] .... INTD
Institut Nauchnoi Informatsii po Obshchestvennym Naukam, Akademiia Nauk SSSR [*Institute of Scientific Information on Social Sciences, Academy of Sciences of the USSR*], **Moscow, Soviet Union** [*Library symbol*] .... RuMIN
Institut za Oceanografiju i Ribarstvo Split Biljeske [*A publication*] .... Inst Oceanogr Ribar Split Biljeske
Institut Oceanographique. Annales [*A publication*] .... Inst Oceanogr Ann
Institut Oecumenique pour le Developpement des Peuples [*Ecumenical Institute for the Development of Peoples*] .... INODEP
Institut fuer Oesterreichische Geschichtsforschung. Mitteilungen (Vienna) [*A publication*] ....Mitt Oesterr Ges (Vienna)
Institut fur Organische Chemie der Universitat Basel, Basel, Switzerland [*Library symbol*] ....SzBaU-IO
Institut Pasteur [*France*] [*Research code symbol*] C
Institut Pasteur Bangui. Rapport Annuel [*A publication*] ....
Inst Pasteur Bangui Rapp Annu
Institut Pasteur de la Republique Unie du Cameroun. Rapport sur le Fonctionnement Technique [*A publication*] ....
Inst Pasteur Repub Unie Cameroun Rapp Fonct Tech
Institut Philippe Pinel de Montreal, Montreal, PQ, Canada [*Library symbol*] .... CaQMIPP
Institut Politique Congolais [*Congolese Political Institute*] ....IPC

Institut de Recherche et Application des Methodes de Developpement ... IRAM
Institut de Recherche et de Coordination Acoustique/Musique [*Institute for Research and Coordination Acoustics/Music*] [*Paris*] ... IRCAM
Institut de Recherche et de Formation en Vue du Developpement Harmonise [*France*] ... IRFED
Institut de Recherche de l'Hydro-Quebec, Varennes, PQ, Canada [*Library symbol*] ... CaQVaH
Institut de Recherche d'Informatique et d'Automatique [*France*] ... IRIA
Institut de Recherche des Nations Unies pour le Developpement Social [*United Nations Research Institute for Social Development*] ... IRNU
Institut pour la Recherche Scientifique en Afrique Centrale [*Brussels*] ... IRSAC
Institut de Recherches Agronomiques Tropicales et des Cultures Vivrieres [*Food and agricultural research foundation supported by France and several African states*] ... IRAT
Institut de Recherches Cliniques, Montreal, PQ, Canada [*Library symbol*] ... CaQMIRC
Institut de Recherches pour les Huiles et Oleagineaux. Rapport Annual [*A publication*] ... Inst Rech Huiles Ol Rapp Annu
Institut de Recherches Scientifiques au Congo ... IRSC
Institut po Ribni Resursi (Varna). Izvestiya [*A publication*] ... Inst Ribni Resur (Varna) Izv
Institut Royal Colonial Belge. Bulletin des Seances [*A publication*] ... BICB
Institut Royal des Relations Internationales ... IRI
Institut Royal des Sciences Naturelles de Belgique. Bulletin [*A publication*] ... Inst Roy Sci Natur Belgique Bul
Institut Royal des Sciences Naturelles de Belgique. Documents de Travail [*A publication*] ... Inst R Sci Nat Belg Doc Trav
Institut Royal des Sciences Naturelles de Belgique. Memoires [*A publication*] ... Inst R Sci Nat Belg Mem
Institut Royal des Sciences Naturelles de Belgique. Memoires. Deuxieme Serie [*A publication*] ... Inst R Sci Nat Belg Mem Deuxieme Ser
Institut Russkogo Jazyka i Slovesnosti pri Akademii Nauk SSSR [*A publication*] ... IRJaSl
Institut de Science Economique Appliquee [*France*] ... ISEA
Institut fuer Steuerungstechnik der Werkzeugmaschinen ... ISW
Institut Suisse de Recherches Forestieres. Memoires [*A publication*] ... Inst Suisse Rech For Mem
Institut Superieur de Pedagogie du Hainaut [*Belgium*] ... ISPH
Institut Technique du Batiment et des Travaux Publics. Annales [*A publication*] ... Inst Tech Batim Trav Pub Ann
Institut de Technologie Agricole, La Pocatiere, PQ, Canada [*Library symbol*] ... CaQPES
Institut fuer Textil- und Faserforschung. Stuttgart. Berichte [*A publication*] ... Inst Text Faserforsch Stuttgart Ber
Institut du Transport Aerien [*Institute of Air Transport*] ... ITA
Institut po Tsvetna Metalurgiya. Plovdiv. Godishnik [*A publication*] ... Inst Tsvetna Metal Plovdiv God
Institut Unifie de Recherches Nucleaires ... IURN
Institut Universitaire de Technologie ... IUT
Institut fur Zeitgeschichte [*Institute of Modern History*], **Munchen, Federal Republic of Germany** [*Library symbol*] ... GyMIZ
Institut fur Zeitungsforschung, Dortmund, Germany [*Library symbol*] ... GyDIZ
Institute [*or Institution*] ... I
Institute [*or Institution*] ... INST
Institute for the Achievement of Human Potential ... IAHP
Institute of Actuaries [*British*] ... IA
Institute of Actuaries [*British*] ... InstAct
Institute for Advanced Concepts [*In 1980 film "Simon"*] ... IAC
Institute for Advanced Interdisciplinary Engineering Studies [*Purdue University*] ... IAIES
Institute of Advanced Marketing Studies - American Marketing Association ... IAMS
Institute for Advanced Materials, Mechanics, and Design [*Army Materiel Command*] ... IAMM & D
Institute for Advanced Pastoral Studies ... IAPS
Institute of Advanced Philosophic Research ... IAPR
Institute for Advanced Research in Asian Science and Medicine ... IARASM
Institute for Advanced Russian Studies [*Smithsonian Institution*] ... IARS
Institute for Advanced Studies [*Army*] ... IAS
Institute for Advanced Studies in the Theatre Arts ... IASTA
Institute of Advanced Studies of World Religions ... IASWR
Institute of Advanced Studies of World Religions, Stony Brook, NY [*Library symbol*] ... NSbIA
Institute for Advanced Study, Princeton, NJ [*Library symbol*] ... NjPI
Institute for Advanced Technology ... IAT
Institute for the Advancement of Engineering ... IAE
Institute for the Advancement of Human Behavior ... IAHB
Institute for Advancement of Medical Communication [*Defunct*] ... IAMC
Institute for the Advancement of Notary Public Education ... IANPE
Institute for the Advancement of Philosophy for Children ... IAPC
Institute for the Advancement of Sailing [*Commercial firm*] ... IAS
Institute of Aeronautical Engineers ... IAeE
Institute of Aerospace Safety and Management [*University of Southern California*] ... IASM
Institute of Aerospace [*formerly, Aeronautical*] **Sciences** [*Later, AIAA*] ... IAS
Institute of African Studies [*A publication*] ... Inst Afr Stud
Institute of African Studies. Occasional Publications [*A publication*] ... IASOP
Institute of Agricultural Research. Annual Report (Addis Ababa) [*A publication*] ... Inst Agric Res Annu Rep (Addis Ababa)
Institute of Agricultural Research. Progress Report (Addis Ababa) [*A publication*] ... Inst Agric Res Prog Rep (Addis Ababa)
Institute of Agricultural Research. Samaru. Annual Report [*A publication*] ... Inst Agric Res Samaru Annu Rep
Institute of Agriculture Remote Sensing Laboratory [*University of Minnesota*] ... IARSL
Institute of Air Weapons Research [*Air Force*] ... IAWR
Institute of Allegheny Life and Culture ... IALC
Institute for Alternative Futures ... IAF
Institute for American Democracy ... IAD
Institute on American Freedoms [*Defunct*] ... IAF
Institute of American Indian Arts ... IAIA
Institute of the American Musical ... IAM
Institute of American Poultry Industries [*Later, PEIA*] ... IAPI
Institute of American Relations ... IAR
Institute for American Strategy [*Later, ASCF*] ... IAS
Institute for American Universities ... IAU
Institute of the American West ... IAW
Institute of Andean Studies ... IAS
Institute of Animal Physiology [*British*] ... IAP
Institute of Animal Physiology. Report [*A publication*] ... Inst Anim Physiol Rep
Institute of Animal Technology [*London*] ... IAT
Institute of Appliance Manufacturers [*Later, GAMA*] ... IAM
Institute of Applied Clicheology ... IAC
Institute of Applied Natural Science ... IANS
Institute for Applied Research on Natural Resources. Technical Report (Bulletin) [*A publication*] ... Inst Appl Res Nat Resour Tech Rep (Bull)
Institute for Applied Technology [*Superseded by NEL*] [*National Bureau of Standards*] ... IAT
Institute of Arctic and Alpine Research [*University of Colorado*] ... INSTAAR
Institute of Arctic Mineral Resources [*University of Alaska*] ... IAMR
Institute for Art and Urban Resources ... IAUR
Institute of Association Management Companies [*Formerly, MAMI*] ... IAMC
Institute of Atmospheric Physics ... IAP
Institute for Atmospheric Sciences [*Environmental Science Services Administration*] ... IAS
Institute of Atomic Energy [*Academy of Sciences, USSR*] ... IAE
Institute for Atomic Sciences in Agriculture ... IASA
Institute of Automobile Engineers ... IAE
Institute of Aviation Medicine [*RAF*] [*British*] ... IAM
Institute for Basic Research [*National Bureau of Standards*] ... IBR
Institute for Basic Research on Mental Retardation ... IBRMR
Institute for Basic Standards [*Later, NSL*] [*National Bureau of Standards*] ... IBS
Institute in Basic Youth Conflicts ... IBYC
Institute for Behavioral Research ... IBR
Institute for Better Packaging [*Later, PPC*] ... IBP
Institute for Biblical Research ... IBR
Institute for Bioenergetic Analysis [*Later, IIBA*] ... IBA
Institute of Biology [*British*] ... IB
Institute of Biology [*London*]. **Journal** [*A publication*] ... Inst Biol J
Institute of Biology (London). Symposium [*A publication*] ... Inst Biol (Lond) Symp
Institute of Biology's Studies in Biology [*A publication*] ... Inst Biol Stud Biol
Institute of Black Studies ... IBS
Institute of the Black World ... IBW
Institute of the Blessed Virgin Mary [*Sisters of Loretto*] [*Roman Catholic religious order*] ... IBVM
Institute of Boiler and Radiator Manufacturers [*Later, Hydronics Institute*] ... IBR
Institute of Boiler and Radiator Manufacturers [*Later, Hydronics Institute*] ... IBRM
Institute of Brewing [*British*] ... IB
Institute for Briquetting and Agglomeration [*Formerly, International Briquetting Association*] ... IBA
Institute of British Architects ... IBA
Institute of British Engineers ... IBritishE
Institute of British Geographers. Liverpool. Transactions and Papers [*A publication*] ... Trans Papers L Brit G
Institute of British Geographers. Transactions [*A publication*] ... Inst Br Geogr Trans
Institute of British Industrial Art ... IBIA
Institute of Broadcasting Financial Management [*Later, BFM*] ... IBFM
Institute of Building [*British*] ... IB
Institute of Building [*British*] ... IOB
Institute of Business Appraisers ... IBA
Institute of Business Designers ... IBD
Institute for Business Planning ... IBP
Institute for Cancer Research ... ICR
Institute for Cancer Research, Philadelphia, PA [*Library symbol*] ... PPICR
Institute for Cancer Research (Philadelphia). Scientific Report [*A publication*] ... Inst Cancer Res (Phila) Sci Rep
Institute for Central European Research ... ICER
Institute for Certification of Computer Professionals ... ICCP

Institute for the Certification of Engineering Technicians [*Later, National Institute for Certification in Engineering Technologies*] ....ICET
Institute for Certification of Tax Professionals ....ICTP
Institute of Certified Financial Planners ....ICFP
Institute for Certified Park Operators ....ICPO
Institute of Certified Professional Business Consultants ....ICPBC
Institute of Certified Professional Managers ....ICPM
Institute of Certified Records Managers ....ICRM
Institute of Certified Travel Agents ....ICTA
Institute of Charity [*Rosminians*] [*Roman Catholic religious order*] IC
Institute of Chartered Accountants of Ontario, Toronto, ON, Canada [*Library symbol*] ....CaOTICA
Institute of Chartered Accountants of Quebec, Montreal, PQ, Canada [*Library symbol*] ....CaQMICA
Institute of Chartered Financial Analysts ....ICFA
Institute of Chartered Shipbrokers [*British*] ....ICS
Institute of Chemistry [*British*] IC
Institute for Child Behavior Research ....ICBR
Institute of Child Study Security Test [*Psychology*] ....ICSST
Institute for Childhood Resources ....INICR
Institute of Chinese Culture ICC
Institute on the Church in Urban-Industrial Society ....ICUIS
Institute of Cistercian Studies, Western Michigan University, Kalamazoo, MI [*Library symbol*] ....MiKCS
Institute of Civil War Studies ....ICWS
Institute of Clay Technology [*British*] ....ICT
Institute of Clinical Analysis ....ICA
Institute of Collective Bargaining and Group Relations ....ICB
Institute for College and University Administrators [*Later, CPAA*] ....ICUA
Institute of Combined Arms and Support [*Fort Leavenworth, KS*] [*Army*] ....ICAS
Institute of Commonwealth Studies, London, United Kingdom [*Library symbol*] ....UkLCS
Institute for Community Design Analysis ....ICDA
Institute for Community Economics ....ICE
Institute for the Community as Extended Family ....ICEF
Institute for the Comparative Study of Political Systems ....ICOPS
Institute of Complementary Sciences [*Defunct*] ....ICS
Institute for Composite Materials [*Defunct*] ....ICM
Institute for Comprehensive Planning ....ICP
Institute for Computer Applications in Science and Engineering [*NASA*] ....ICASE
Institute for Computer Research in the Humanities [*New York University*] ....ICRH
Institute [*formerly, Center*] **for Computer Sciences and Technology** [*National Bureau of Standards*] ....ICST
Institute of Computer Technology ....ICT
Institute for Computers in Jewish Life ....ICJL
Institute for Congress IC
Institute of Contemporary Arts [*British*] ....ICA
Institute of Contemporary Russian Studies [*Fordham University*] ....ICRS
Institute for Contemporary Studies ....ICS
Institute for Cooperative Research ....ICR
Institute of Corn and Agricultural Merchants. Journal [*A publication*] ....ICAM J
Institute of Cost Analysis ....ICA
Institute of Cost and Management Accountants [*British*] ....ICMA
Institute for Court Management ....ICM
Institute for Creation Research ....ICR
Institute of Cultural Affairs ....ICA
Institute for Cultural Exchange thru Photography ....ICEP
Institute of Current World Affairs ....ICWA
Institute of Data Processing [*British*] ....IDP
Institute for Defence Studies and Analyses. Journal [*A publication*] ....Inst Def Stud Anal J
Institute for Defense Analyses ....IDA
Institute for Defense Analyses. Paper [*A publication*] ....Inst Def Anal Pap
Institute for Defense Analysis-Communications Research Division ....IDA-CRD
Institute for Delphinid Research ....IDR
Institute for Democratic Education [*Absorbed by Anti-Defamation League of B'nai B'rith*] ....IDE
Institute for Democratic Socialism ....IDS
Institute of Dental Research. Biennial Report (Sydney) [*A publication*] ....Inst Dent Res Bienn Rep (Syd)
Institute for Development of Educational Activities [*of Charles F. Kettering Foundation*] ....I/D/E/A
Institute for the Development of Emotional and Life Skills ....IDEALS
Institute for the Development of Indian Law ....IN-DEV-IL
Institute of Directors [*British*] ....InstD
Institute of Distribution [*Defunct*] ....ID
Institute of Diving ....IOD
Institute of Early American History and Culture ....IEAHC
Institute of Early American History and Culture, Williamsburg, VA [*Library symbol*] ....ViWI
Institute for Earth Sciences [*Environmental Science Services Administration*] ....IES
Institute for Ecological Policies ....IEP
[*The*] **Institute of Ecology** ....TIE
Institute for Econometric Research ....IER
Institute for Economic Analysis ....IEA
Institute for the Editing of Historical Documents ....IEHD
Institute for Educational Development [*Defunct*] ....IED
Institute for Educational Innovation [*Later, Education Development Center*] ....IEI
Institute for Educational Leadership ....IEL
Institute of Educational Research ....IER
Institute of Educational Technology [*British*] ....IET
Institute of Electrical and Electronics Engineers ....IEEE
Institute of Electrical and Electronics Engineers, Piscataway, NJ [*Library symbol*] ....NjPwIE
Institute of Electrical and Electronics Engineers. Proceedings [*A publication*] ....Inst Elect & Electronics Eng Proc
Institute of Electrical and Electronics Engineers. Transactions on Industry Application [*A publication*] ....Inst Elect & Electronics Eng Trans IA
Institute of Electrical and Electronics Engineers. Transactions on Power Apparatus and Systems [*A publication*] ....Inst Elect & Electronics Eng Trans PAS
Institute of Electronic Communications Engineers of Japan ....IECEJ
Institute of Electronic Engineering ....IEE
Institute of Engineering Research [*University of California*] ....IER
Institute of Engineers of Chile ....IEC
Institute of Environmental Action ....IEA
Institute for Environmental Awareness ....IEA
Institute for Environmental Education ....IEE
Institute of Environmental Engineers [*Later, IES*] ....IEE
Institute of Environmental Medicine and Physiology ....IEMP
Institute for Environmental Research [*Environmental Science Services Administration*] ....IER
Institute for Environmental Research Technical Memorandum ....IERTM
Institute of Environmental Sciences [*Formerly, AACC, IEE*] ....IES
Institute of Environmental Sciences. Annual Technical Meeting. Proceedings [*A publication*] ....Inst Environ Sci Annu Tech Meet Proc
Institute for Epidemiologic Studies of Violence ....IESV
Institute for Esperanto in Commerce and Industry ....IECI
Institute on Estate Planning [*A publication*] ....Inst Estate Plan
Institute of Ethnomusicology. Selected Reports [*A publication*] ....Inst Ethmus Sel Repts
Institute of European Studies ....IES
Institute of Experimental Meteorology [*USSR*] ....IEM
Institute for Experimental Psychiatry ....IEP
Institute of Exploratory Research [*Army*] ....IER
Institute of Export [*British*] ....IE
Institute for Expressive Analysis ....IEA
Institute of Family History and Genealogy ....IFHG
Institute for Family Research and Education ....IFRE
Institute for Fermentation Research Communications (Osaka) [*A publication*] ....Inst Ferment Res Commun (Osaka)
Institute of Financial Education [*Formerly, ASLI*] ....IFE
Institute of Fire Engineers ....IFE
Institute of Fireplace Equipment Manufacturers ....IFEM
Institute of Fiscal and Political Education ....IFPE
Institute of Fisheries Research [*University of North Carolina*] ....IFR
Institute of Flight Structures [*Columbia University*] ....IFS
Institute of Fluid Power ....IFP
Institute for Fluitronics Education ....IFE
Institute for Food and Development Policy ....IFDP
Institute of Food Technologists ....IFT
Institute of Foreign Bankers ....IFB
Institute of Forest Zoology. Research Notes [*A publication*] ....Inst For Zool Res Notes
Institute of the Franciscan Sisters of the Eucharist [*Roman Catholic religious order*] ....FSE
Institute of Freight Forwarders [*British*] ....IFF
Institute of Freshwater Research. Drottningholm. Report [*A publication*] ....Inst Freshw Res Drottningholm Rep
Institute of Fuel [*British*] ....IF
Institute of Fuel [*British*] ....InstF
Institute of Fuel Symposium Series (London) [*A publication*] ....Inst Fuel Symp Ser (London)
Institute for the Future ....IFF
Institute for the Future ....IFTF
Institute of Gas Technology ....IGT
Institute of Gas Technology, Chicago, IL [*OCLC symbol*] ....IHF
Institute of General Semantics ....IGS
Institute of Geological Sciences [*British*] ....IGS
Institute of Geophysics [*Later, IGPP*] [*University of California*] ....IG
Institute of Geophysics and Planetary Physics [*University of California*] ....IGPP
Institute of Gerontology Series [*A publication*] ....Inst Gerontol Ser
Institute of Government Studies [*University of California at Berkeley*] ....IGS
Institute for Graphic Communication ....IGC
Institute for Gravitational Strain Pathology ....IGSP
Institute of the Great Plains [*Formerly, GPHA*] ....IGP
Institute of Groundsmanship ....IG
Institute of Heat Technology ....IHT
Institute of Heating and Air-Conditioning Industries ....IHAI
[*The*] **Institute of Heraldry** [*Military*] ....IOH
[*The*] **Institute of Heraldry** [*Military*] ....TIOH
Institute of High Energy Physics [*USSR*] ....IHEP
Institute of High Fidelity [*Formerly, IHFM*] [*Later, EIA*] ....IHF

Institute of High Fidelity Manufacturers [*Later, IHF*]....IHFM
Institute of Higher Education....IHE
Institute of Highway Engineers [*British*]....IHE
Institute of Historical Research. Bulletin [*A publication*]....IHRB
Institute for Historical Review....IHR
Institute of Home Economics [*of ARS, Department of Agriculture*]....IHE
Institute of Home Office Underwriters....IHOU
Institute on Hospital and Community Psychiatry....IHCP
Institute for Housing Management Innovations....IHMI
Institute of Human Origins....IHO
Institute for Human Progress [*Defunct*]....IHP
Institute of Human Rights Research....IHRR
Institute of Hydrology [*British*]....IH
Institute of Hypertension Studies - Institute of Hypertension School of Research [*Later, NIHS*]....IHS
Institute of Incorporated Photographers [*British*]....IIP
Institute for Independent Social Journalism....IISJ
Institute of Industrial Engineers [*Formerly, AIIE*]....IIE
Institute of Industrial Launderers....IIL
Institute of Industrial Race Relations....IIRR
Institute for Industrial Research and Standards [*American National Standards Institute*]....IIRS
Institute of Information Scientists [*British*]....IIS
Institute of Inter-American Affairs [*United Nations*]....IIAA
Institute for Interconnecting and Packaging Electronic Circuits [*Formerly, Institute of Printed Circuits*]....IPC
Institute for Intercultural Studies....IIS
Institute of Intermodal Repairers....IIR
Institute of Internal Affairs....IIA
Institute of Internal Auditors....IIA
Institute for Internal Combustion Engines....IICE
Institute of the International Conference on the Holocaust and Genocide....IICHG
Institute of International Container Lessors [*British*]....IICL
Institute of International Education....IIE
Institute of International Education, New York, NY [*Library symbol*]....NNIIE
Institute of International Education News Bulletin [*A publication*]....IIENB
Institute of International Education. News Bulletin [*A publication*]....Inst Int Educ N Bul
Institute of International Finance....IIF
Institute of International Labor Research....IILR
Institute of International Law....IIL
Institute of International Medical Education....IIME
Institute for International Order [*Later, IWO*]....IIO
Institute of International Relations. Proceedings [*A publication*]....Inst Int Rel Proc
Institute of International Studies....IIS
Institute of International Trade and Development....IITD
Institute for International Youth Affairs....IIYA
Institute of the Ironworking Industry....III
Institute of Jazz Studies....IJS
Institute of Jewish Affairs....IJA
Institute for Jewish-Christian Relations....IJCR
Institute for Jewish Life [*Later, Jewish Media Service*]....IJL
Institute for Jewish Policy Planning and Research....IJPPR
Institute of Judicial Administration....IJA
Institute for Juvenile Research, Chicago, IL [*Library symbol*]....ICIJ
Institute for Labor and Mental Health....ILMH
Institute for Labor Studies, Appalachian Center, Morgantown, WV [*Library symbol*]....WvMIL
Institute of Laboratory Animal Resources [*National Academy of Sciences*]....ILAR
Institute of Labour Management....ILM
Institute on Lake Superior Geology. Technical Sessions, Abstracts, and Field Guides [*A publication*]....Inst Lake Super Geol Tech Sess Abstr Field Guides
Institute of Land Combat [*Army*]....ILC
Institute of Landscape Architects [*British*]....ILA
Institute of Languages and Linguistics....ILL
Institute for Law and Social Research....INSLAW
Institute for Liberty and Community....ILC
Institute of Librarians [*India*]....IOL
Institute of Library Research....ILR
Institute of Life Insurance [*Later, ACLI*]....ILI
Institute of Lifetime Learning....ILL
Institute of Lithuanian Studies....ILS
Institute of Local Government Administration [*British*]....ILGA
Institute of Local Government Studies [*British*]....INLOGOV
Institute for Local Self-Reliance....ILSR
Institute of Logistics Research [*Army*]....ILR
Institute of Logopedics, Wichita, KS [*Library symbol*]....KWiIL
Institute of Makers of Explosives....IME
Institute of Man and Resources, Charlottetown, PE, Canada [*Library symbol*]....CaPCIMR
Institute on Man and Science [*Formerly, Council on World Tensions*]....IMS
Institute of Management Consultants....IMC
[*The*] **Institute of Management Sciences**....IMS
[*The*] **Institute of Management Sciences**....TIMS
Institute for Manpower Management....IMM
Institute of Manpower Studies [*Department of Employment*] [*British*]....IMS
Institute for Marine Biochemistry [*British*]....IMB
Institute of Marine Engineers [*British*]....IMarE
Institute of Marine Engineers [*British*]....IME
Institute of Marine Engineers. Annual Report [*A publication*]....Inst Mar Eng Annu Rep
Institute of Marine Engineers. Annual Volume [*A publication*]....Inst Mar Eng Annu Vol
Institute of Marine Engineers. Transactions [*A publication*]....Inst Mar Eng Trans
Institute of Marine Engineers. Transactions. Series C [*A publication*]....Inst Mar Eng Trans Ser C
Institute for Marine Environmental Research [*British*]....IMER
Institute for Marine Environmental Research. Report [*A publication*]....Inst Mar Environ Res Rep
Institute for Marine Information....IMI
Institute of Marine Research. Lysekil Series Biology Report [*A publication*]....Inst Mar Res Lysekil Ser Biol Rep
Institute of Marine Science....IMS
Institute of Marine Science. Publications [*A publication*]....Inst Marine Sci Pub
Institute of Marine Science. Report. University of Alaska [*A publication*]....Inst Mar Sci Rep Univ Alaska
Institute of Marine Science, University of Texas, Port Aransas, TX [*Library symbol*]....TxPaIMS
Institute of Marine Sciences and Technology....IMST
Institute of Masonry Research [*Defunct*]....IMR
Institute for Materials Research [*Later, NSL*] [*National Bureau of Standards*]....IMR
Institute of Materials Science....IMS
Institute of Mathematical Statistics....IMS
Institute of Mathematics and Its Applications [*British*]....IMIA
Institute of Mathematics and Its Applications. Bulletin [*A publication*]....Inst Math Its Appl Bull
Institute of Measurement and Control [*British*]....IMC
Institute of Measurement and Control....INSTMC
Institute for Mediation and Conflict Resolution....IMCR
Institute of Medical and Biological Illustration [*British*]....IMBI
Institute for Medical Research [*Camden, New Jersey*]....IMR
Institute of Medicine [*National Academy of Sciences*]....IM
Institute of Medicine [*National Academy of Sciences*]....IOM
Institute for Mediterranean Affairs....IMA
Institute for Mediterranean Art and Archaeology....IMAA
Institute of Metals [*British*]....InstMet
Institute of Metals [*British*]....IOM
Institute of Metals. Journal [*A publication*]....Inst Metals J
Institute Mexicano del Petroleo. Revista [*A publication*]....Inst Mex Petrol Rev
Institute of Microbiology....IMB
Institute for Microbiology [*USSR*]....INMI
Institute of Microbiology, Rutgers University [*New Jersey*]....IMRU
Institute of Microbiology. Rutgers University. Annual Report [*A publication*]....Inst Microbiol Rutgers Univ Annu Rep
Institute for Military Assistance [*Army*]....IMA
Institute on Mineral Law [*A publication*]....Inst Min L
Institute of Mining Engineers [*British*]....IME
Institute for Mining and Mineral Research. University of Kentucky. Technical Report [*A publication*]....Inst Min Miner Res Univ K Tech Rep
Institute for Minority Business Education [*Defunct*]....IMBE
Institute of Modern Languages....IML
Institute of Modern Procedures....IMP
Institute on Money and Inflation....IMI
Institute for Municipal Engineering....IME
Institute of Municipal Treasurers and Accountants [*Later, CIPFA*] [*British*]....IMTA
Institute for Muscle Disease [*Defunct*]....IMD
Institute for Muscle Disease, New York, NY [*Library symbol*] [*Obsolete*]....NNIMD
Institute of Museum Services [*National Foundation of the Arts and the Humanities*]....IMS
Institute of Natural Resources, Springfield, IL [*OCLC symbol*]....IFF
Institute of Nautical Archaeology [*Formerly, AINA*]....INA
Institute of Naval Medicine [*British*]....MedSch(N)
Institute for Naval Studies....INS
Institute of Navigation [*US and British*]....IN
Institute of Navigation [*US and British*]....ION
Institute for New Antibiotics [*USSR*]....INA
Institute for New Enterprise Development....INED
Institute of Newspaper Controllers and Finance Officers....INCFO
Institute of Noise Control Engineering....INCE
Institute of Non-Numerical Information Processing [*Switzerland*] [*Information service*]....INIP
Institute of Nuclear Materials Management....INMM
Institute of Nuclear Power Operations....INPO
Institute of Nuclear Research [*Poland*]....INR
Institute for Nuclear Study [*Japan*]....INS
Institute of Oceanographic Sciences [*British*]....IOS
Institute for Oceanography [*Environmental Science Services Administration*]....IO
Institute for the Officialization of Esperanto....IOE
Institute on Oil and Gas Law and Taxation [*A publication*]....Inst Oil & Gas L & Taxation

Institute of Operating Theatre Technicians [British]..............IOT
Institute of Ophthalmology, Presbyterian Hospital, New York,
  NY [Library symbol]............................ NNPH-O
Institute of Optimization and Systems Theory [Stockholm].....IOS
Institute of Outdoor Advertising ....IOA
Institute of Outdoor Drama................................IOD
Institute of Pacific Islands Forestry [Department of Agriculture]......IPIF
Institute of Pacific Relations............................IPR
Institute of Pacific Relations [A Publication]............IPR
Institute of Painters in Oil Colours [British]............IOP
Institute for Palestine Studies [Lebanon] ....IPS
Institute of Paper Chemistry..............................IPC
Institute of Paper Chemistry, Appleton, WI [Library symbol]......WAP
Institute of Paper Conservation..........................IOPC
Institute of Paralegal Training [Commercial firm]........IPT
Institute of Pastoral Care...............................IPC
Institute for Peace and Justice .... IPJ
Institute of the Pennsylvania Hospital, Philadelphia, PA [Library
  symbol]....................................... PPPH-I
Institute of Personal Image Consultants ....IPIC
Institute for Personality and Ability Testing [Champaign, IL].....IPAT
Institute of Personality Assessment and Research [University of
  California] .... IPAR
Institute of Petroleum [British] ....IP
Institute for Petroleum. Journal [A publication]..... Inst Pet J
Institute for Petroleum. Review [A publication].....Inst Petroleum Rev
Institute for Petroleum. Technical Paper. IP [A publication] ......
                                      Inst Pet Tech Pap IP
Institute of Petroleum Technologists ....IPT
Institute of Phonetics. Report [A publication]......Inst Phonet Rep
Institute of Physical Medicine and Rehabilitation, Peoria, IL
  [Library symbol] .... IPI
Institute of Physical Problems [USSR] ....IFP
Institute of Physics [USSR] ....IP
Institute for Physics of the Atmosphere ....IPA
Institute of Physics. Conference Digest [A publication].....Inst Phys Conf Dig
Institute of Physics. Conference Series [A publication].....Inst Phys Conf Ser
Institute for Physics and Nuclear Engineering Report (Romania)
  [A publication]........................Inst Phys Nucl Eng Rep (Rom)
Institute of Phytopathology Research. Annual Report [A
  publication]........................ Inst Phytopathol Res Annu Rep
Institute of Planetary and Space Science..................IPSS
Institute for Plasma Physics [West Germany]...............IPP
Institute on Pluralism and Group Identity ....IPGI
Institute for Polar Studies [Ohio State University].......IPS
Institute for Policy Studies ....IPS
Institute of Post Office Electrical Engineers [British]........IPOEE
Institute of Poultry Industries...........................IPI
Institute of Practitioners in Advertising ....IPA
Institute of Printed Circuits. Technical Report [A publication].....
                                      Inst Printed Circuits Tech Rep
Institute of Printing [British] ....IP
Institute of Printing Management [British].................IPM
Institute on Private Investments Abroad and Foreign Trade [A
  publication]........................Inst Private Investments
Institute of Production Engineers [British] ....IPE
Institute of Professional Designers ....IPD
Institute for Professional Development [Army].............IPD
Institute of Professional Librarians of Ontario. Newsletter [A
  publication]........................ Inst Prof Librn Ont Newsl
Institute of Property Taxation ....IPT
Institute for Psychiatry and Foreign Affairs ....IPFA
Institute for Psychoanalysis, Chicago, IL [Library symbol].....ICIP
Institute for Psychoanalytic Training and Research ....IPTAR
Institute for Psychohistory .... IP
Institute of Public Administration ....IPA
Institute of Public Administration of Canada ....IPAC
Institute of Public Administration of Canada, Toronto, ON,
  Canada [Library symbol].......................... CaOTPA
Institute of Public Administration, New York, NY [Library symbol]........NNIP
Institute of Public Affairs...............................IPA
Institute of Public Health Engineers [British]...........IPHE
Institute for Public Information ....IPI
Institute for Public Interest Representation [Later, CCCIPR]
  [Georgetown University]...........................INSPIRE
Institute for Public Interest Representation [Later, CCCIPR]
  [Georgetown University]...........................IPIR
Institute of Public Relations [British]...................IPR
Institute for Public Understanding.......................IPU
Institute of Public Utilities ....IPU
Institute of Purchasing and Supply [British]..............IPS
Institute of Pyramidology ....IOP
Institute of Quantity Surveyors [British].................IQS
Institute of Quarrying [British]..........................IOQ
Institute of Quarrying [British]...........................IQ
Institute of Radio Engineers [Later, IEEE]................IRE
Institute of Radio Engineers. Proceedings [A publication] ......
                                      Inst Radio Eng Proc
Institute for Radiological Technologists..................IRT
Institute for Rapid Transit [Later, APTA] ....IRT
Institute for Rational-Emotive Therapy ....IRET

Institute for Rational Living.............................IRL
Institute for Reactor Research [Switzerland]..............IRR
Institute of Real Estate Management ....IREM
Institute for Reality Therapy ....IRT
Institute of Refrigeration [British]......................IR
Institute of Registered Architects [British]..............IRA
Institute on Religion in an Age of Science ....IRAS
Institute on Religion and Democracy......................IRD
Institute of Religion, Texas Medical Center, Houston, TX [Library
  symbol]....................................... TxHIR
Institute for Religious Life..............................IRL
Institute for Religious and Social Studies ....IRSS
Institute of Reprographic Technology ....IRT
Institute for Research on Animal Diseases [British].......IRAD
Institute for Research on Educational Finance and Governance
  [Department of Education]..........................IFG
Institute for Research in History ....IRH
Institute for Research in Human Relations ....IRHR
Institute for Research in Hypnosis [Later, IRHP]..........IRH
Institute for Research in Hypnosis and Psychotherapy [Formerly,
  IRH]...IRHP
Institute for Research into Mental Retardation. Monograph
  (Oxford) [A publication] ....Inst Res Ment Retard Monogr (Oxford)
Institute for Research of Rheumatic Diseases ....IRRD
Institute for Resource Management ....IRM
Institute for Responsive Education ....IRE
Institute for Retired Professionals ....IRP
Institute of Risk Management Consultants ....IRMC
Institute of Road Safety Officers [British] ....IRSO
Institute of Road Transport Engineers [British]...........IRTE
Institute of Rubber Research..............................IRR
Institute for Rural Water ....IRW
Institute for Safety in Transportation ....IST
Institute of Salesian Studies ....ISS
Institute of Sanitation Management [Later, EMA]...........ISM
Institute of Science Magazine [A publication] ....Inst Sci Mag
Institute of Science and Technology ....IST
Institute for Scientific Analysis ....ISA
Institute for Scientific Humanism [Later, WISH]...........ISH
Institute for Scientific Information......................ISI
Institute of Scientific and Technical Information of China
  [INFOTERM].......................................ISTIC
Institute of Scrap Iron and Steel ....ISIS
Institute on Securities Regulation [A publication].........Inst Securities Reg
Institute of Sedimentary and Petroleum Geology, Calgary, AB,
  Canada [Library symbol]........................... CaACSP
Institute of Semiconductor Research [USSR]................ISR
Institute for Sex Research, Inc. [National Institute of Mental Health].........ISR
Institute of Shortening and Edible Oils...................ISEO
Institute of the Sisters of St. Dorothy [Roman Catholic religious
  order].. SSD
Institute for Social Dance Studies ....ISDS
Institute for Social Economic Change ....ISEC
Institute of Social, Economic, and Governmental Research
  [Later, ISER] [University of Alaska]...............ISEGR
Institute of Social and Economic Research [Formerly, ISEGR]
  [University of Alaska].............................ISER
Institute of Social Ethics................................ISE
Institute for Social Evaluation and Design ....ISED
Institute for Social Justice..............................ISJ
Institute of Social Order of the Society of Jesus [Later, JCSS].........ISOSJ
Institute for Social Research [University of Michigan]....ISR
Institute for Social Research and Development [University of
  New Mexico].......................................ISRAD
Institute of Social Services Alternatives ....ISSA
Institute of Society, Ethics, and Life Sciences...........ISELS
Institute of Society Ethnics and Life Sciences, Hastings Center,
  Hastings-On-Hudson, NY [Library symbol]...........NHasl
Institute for Socioeconomic Studies ....ISES
Institute for Socioeconomic Studies ....ISS
Institute for Software Engineering ....ISE
Institute for Solid Wastes ....ISW
Institute of Sound and Vibration [A publication] ....Inst Sound Vib
Institute of Sound and Vibration ....ISAV
Institute of Sound and Vibration Research [Southampton
  University, England].............................. ISVR
Institute of Southeast Asian Studies ....ISEAS
Institute for Southern Studies ....ISS
Institute for Soviet-American Relations ....ISAR
Institute of Space and Aeronautical Science [Japan].......ISAS
Institute of Space and Aeronautical Science. University of
  Tokyo. Report [A publication] ... Inst Space Aeronaut Sci Univ Tokyo Rep
Institute of Space Law....................................ISL
Institute for Space and Security Studies.................ISSS
Institute of Space Studies [NASA].........................ISS
Institute of Special Studies [Army].......................ISS
Institute of Statisticians [British]......................IS
Institute of Store Planners...............................ISP
Institute for Storm Research ....ISR
Institute of Strategic and Stability Operations [Army] ...ISSO
Institute for Strategic Studies [Later, IISS].............ISS

Institute for Studies in American Music ISAM
Institute for Studies in Psychological Testing ISPT
Institute for the Study of Animal Problems ISAP
Institute for the Study of Conflict [*British*] ISC
Institute for the Study of Conscious Evolution ISCE
Institute for the Study of Developing Nations ISDN
Institute for the Study of Drug Addiction [*Later, ISDM*] ISDA
Institute for the Study of Drug Dependence [*London*] ISDD
Institute for the Study of Drug Misuse [*Formerly, ISDA*] ISDM
Institute for the Study of Fatigue Fracture and Structural Reliability [*George Washington University*] ISFFSR
Institute for the Study of Genocide ISG
Institute for the Study of Human Issues ISHI
Institute for the Study of Human Knowledge ISHK
Institute for the Study of Inquiring Systems ISIS
Institute for the Study of Labor and Economic Crisis ISLEC
Institute for the Study of Man ISM
Institute for the Study of Matrimonial Laws ISML
Institute for the Study of Nonviolence [*Defunct*] ISNV
Institute for Study of Regulation ISR
Institute for the Study of Sexual Assault ISSA
Institute for the Study of Sport and Society ISSS
Institute for the Study of Universal History through Arts and Artifacts [*Defunct*] ISUH
Institute of Surgical Research [*Army*] ISR
Institute of Surplus Dealers ISD
Institute of Systems Analysis [*Army*] ISA
Institute for Systems Design and Optimization ISDO
Institute of Tax Consultants ITC
Institute Technical Group ITG
Institute of Technology [*Air Force*] IT
Institute for the Technology and Industrialization of Tropical Agricultural Products [*Ivory Coast*] ITIPAT
Institute of Technology, United States Air Force [*Wright-Patterson Air Force Base, Dayton, OH*] ITUSAF
Institute for Telecommunication Sciences [*Department of Commerce*] ITS
Institute for Telecommunication Sciences and Aeronomy [*Later, ITS*] [*National Oceanic and Atmospheric Administration*] ITSA
Institute for Telecommunications and Aeronomy [*ESSA*] ITA
Institute of Temporary Services [*Later, National Association of Temporary Services*] ITS
Institute of Terrestrial Ecology [*British*] ITE
Institute of Textile Technology ITT
Institute of Textile Technology, Charlottesville, VA [*Library symbol*] ViCT
Institute for Theological Encounter with Science and Technology ITEST
Institute for Theological and Philosophical Studies ITPS
Institute of Theoretical Astronomy [*University of Cambridge*] IOTA
Institute of Theoretical Astronomy [*Leningrad, USSR*] ITA
Institute of Thread Machiners [*Defunct*] ITM
Institute of Traditional Science, Cambridge, MA [*Library symbol*] MCIT
Institute of Traffic Administration [*British*] ITA
Institute of Traffic Engineers ITE
Institute for Training and Development INSTAD
Institute for Training in Municipal Administration ITMA
Institute of Transport Aviation ITA
Institute of Transport of Great Britain ITGB
Institute of Transportation and Regional Planning ITRP
Institute of Transportation Studies Library, University of California, Berkeley, CA [*OCLC symbol*] CBT
Institute of Transportation and Traffic Engineering [*UCLA*] ITTE
Institute of Transportation, Travel, and Tourism ITTT
Institute of Tropical Forestry [*Department of Agriculture*] ITF
Institute for Twenty-First Century Studies ITFCS
Institute on United States Taxation of Foreign Income [*Later, International Tax Institute*] IUSTFI
Institute for Urban Development IUD
Institute of Urban Life IUL
Institute of Vitreous Enamellers [*British*] IVE
Institute of Vitreous Enamellers. Bulletin [*A publication*] Inst Vitreous Enamellers Bull
Institute of Water Engineers [*British*] IWE
Institute of Water Pollution Control [*British*] IWPC
Institute for Water Resources [*Army*] IWR
Institute of Weights and Measures Administration [*Wales*] IWMA
Institute for Wholistic Education [*Later, SCIWE*] IWE
Institute of Women Today IWT
Institute of Work Study Practitioners IWSP
Institute for Workers' Control IWC
Institute of Works and Highways Superintendents [*British*] IWHS
Institute of World Affairs [*Later, UFSI-IWA*] IWA
Institute of World Affairs. Proceedings [*A publication*] Inst World Affairs Proc
Institute for World Order IWO
Institutes of Education of the Universities of Newcastle Upon Tyne and Durham. Journal [*A publication*] Newcastle Inst Ed J
Institutes of Religion and Health [*Formerly, ARMH, AFRP*] IRH
Institutes and Research Divisions [*National Institutes of Health*] I/RD
Institutet fuer Verkstadsteknisk Forskning [*Institute for Production Engineering Research*] [*Sweden*] IVF
Institutet fuer Verkstadsteknisk Forskning. IVF Resultat [*A publication*] Inst Verkstadstek Forsk IVF Resultat
Institution INSTN
Institution of Certificated Mechanical and Electrical Engineers. South Africa. Arthur Hallet Memorial Lectures [*A publication*] Inst Certif Mech Electr Eng S Afr Arthur Hallet Mem Lect
Institution of Chemical Engineers [*British*] I Ch E
Institution of Chemical Engineers [*British*] I Chem E
Institution of Chemical Engineers. Symposium Series [*A publication*] Inst Chem Eng Symp Ser
Institution of Chemical Engineers. Transactions [*A publication*] Inst Chem Eng Trans
Institution of Civil Engineers [*British*] ICE
Institution of Computer Sciences [*British*] ICS
Institution of Electrical and Electronics Technician Engineers IEETE
Institution of Electrical Engineers [*British*] IEE
Institution of Electrical Engineers. Conference Publication [*A publication*] Inst Elec Eng Conf Publ
Institution of Electrical Engineers. Journal [*A publication*] Inst E E J
Institution of Electrical Engineers. Journal [*A publication*] Inst Elec Eng J
Institution of Electrical Engineers. Proceedings [*A publication*] Inst E E Proc
Institution of Electrical Engineers. Student Quarterly Journal [*A publication*] Student Q J Instn Elec Engrs
Institution of Electronics and Telecommunication Engineers. Journal [*A publication*] Inst Electron Telecommun Eng J
Institution of Engineers of Australia IEAust
Institution of Engineers (Australia). Civil Engineering Transactions [*A publication*] Inst Eng (Aust) Civ Eng Trans
Institution of Engineers (Australia). Electrical Engineering Transactions [*A publication*] Inst Eng (Aust) Elec Eng Trans
Institution of Engineers (Australia). Electrical Engineering Transactions [*A publication*] Inst Eng (Aust) Electr Eng Trans
Institution of Engineers (Australia). General Engineering Transactions [*A publication*] Inst Eng (Aust) Gen Eng Trans
Institution of Engineers (Australia). Journal [*A publication*] Inst Eng (Aust) J
Institution of Engineers (Australia). Mechanical and Chemical Engineering Transactions [*A publication*] Inst Eng (Aust) Mech Chem Eng Trans
Institution of Engineers (Ceylon). Transactions [*A publication*] Inst Eng (Ceylon) Trans
Institution on Farm Training IOFT
Institution of Fire Engineers. Quarterly [*A publication*] Inst Fire Eng Q
Institution of Gas Engineers. Journal [*A publication*] Inst Gas Eng J
Institution of Heating and Ventilating Engineers [*British*] IHVE
Institution of Locomotive Engineers. Journal [*A publication*] Inst Locomotive Eng J
Institution of Mechanical Engineers [*British*] IME
Institution of Mechanical Engineers [*British*] I Mech E
Institution of Mechanical Engineers. Journal and Proceedings [*A publication*] Inst Mech Eng J & Proc
Institution of Mechanical Engineers (London). Proceedings [*A publication*] Inst Mech Eng (Lond) Proc
Institution of Mechanical Engineers. Proceedings [*A publication*] Inst Mech Eng Proc
Institution of Mechanical Engineers [*London*]**. Railway Division. Journal** [*A publication*] Inst Mech Eng Ry Div J
Institution of Mechanical Engineers. Railway Division. Journal [*A publication*] J Rly Div Instn Mech Engrs
Institution of Metallurgists. Autumn Review Course. Series 3 (London) [*A publication*] Inst Metall Autumn Rev Course Ser 3 (London)
Institution of Metallurgists. Course Volume. Series 3 (London) [*A publication*] Inst Metall Course Vol Ser 3 (London)
Institution of Metallurgists. Series 3 (London) [*A publication*] Inst Metall Ser 3 (London)
Institution of Metallurgists. Spring Residential Course. Series 3 (London) [*A publication*] Inst Metall Spring Resid Course Ser 3 (London)
Institution of Mining Engineers [*British*] IMIE
Institution of Mining Engineers [*British*] IMinE
Institution of Mining Engineers. Transactions [*A publication*] Inst M Eng Tr
Institution of Mining and Metallurgy IMM
Institution of Mining and Metallurgy. Transactions [*A publication*] Inst Min & Met Trans
Institution of Mining and Metallurgy. Transactions. Section A. Mining Industry [*A publication*] Inst Min Metall Trans Sect A
Institution of Mining and Metallurgy. Transactions. Section B. Applied Earth Science [*A publication*] Inst Min Metall Trans Sect B
Institution of Mining and Metallurgy. Transactions. Section C. Mineral Processing and Extractive Metallurgy [*A publication*] Inst Min Metall Trans Sect C
Institution of Municipal Engineers. South African District. Annual Journal [*A publication*] Inst Munic Eng S Afr Dist Annu J
Institution of Naval Architects [*British*] INA
Institution of Petroleum Technologists. Journal [*A publication*] Inst Petroleum Tech J
Institution of Post Office Electrical Engineers. Paper [*A publication*] Inst Post Office Elec Eng Paper

Institution of Professional Civil Servants [*British*] .... IPCS
Institution of Radio and Electronics Engineers (Australia). Proceedings [*A publication*] .... Inst Radio Electron Eng (Aust) Proc
Institution of the Rubber Industry [*British*] .... IRI
Institution of Structural Engineers [*British*] .... ISE
Institution of Structural Engineers [*British*] .... ISTRUCTE
Institution of Water Engineers. Journal [*Later, Institution of Water Engineers and Scientists. Journal*] [*A publication*] .... Inst Water Eng J
Institution of Water Engineers and Scientists. Journal [*Formerly, Institution of Water Engineers. Journal*] [*A publication*] .... Inst Water Eng Sci J
Institutional .... INSTNL
Institutional Biosafety Committee [*National Institutes of Health*] .... IBC
Institutional Brokers Estimate System [*Lynch, Jones & Ryan*] [*Information service*] .... IBES
Institutional Care [*British*] IC
Institutional Conduct of Fire Trainer [*Army*] .... I-COFT
Institutional Development and Economic Affairs Service .... IDEAS
Institutional Distribution [*A publication*] .... ID
Institutional Food Distributors of America [*Later, NAWGA*] .... IFDA
Institutional Investor [*A publication*] II
Institutional Investor [*A publication*] .... Inst Invest
Institutional Investor [*A publication*] .... Inst Invst
Institutional Investors Corp. [*NYSE symbol*] .... INV
Institutional Meat Purchase Specification [*Department of Agriculture*] .... IMPS
Institutional and Municipal Parking Congress .... IMPC
Institutional Networks [*NASDAQ symbol*] .... INET
Institutional Patent Agreements [*General Services Administration*] .... IPA
Institutional Research Council [*Defunct*] .... IRC
Institutional Review Board .... IRB
Institutional Revolutionary Party [*Political party*] [*Mexico*] .... IRP
Institutional and Service Textile Distributors Association .... ISTDA
Institutional Space Inventory Technique [*Data processing*] .... INSITE
Institutional Support Planning Group [*NASA*] .... ISPG
Institutionen foer Skoglig Matematisk Statistik Rapporter och Uppsatser [*A publication*] .... Inst Skoglig Mat Stat Rapp Uppsatser
Institutionen foer Skogsforyngring Rapporter och Uppsatser [*A publication*] .... Inst Skogsforyngring Rapp Uppsatser
Institutionen foer Skogszoologi Rapporter och Uppsatser [*A publication*] .... Inst Skogszool Rapp Uppsatser
Institutions [*A publication*] .... Inst
Institutions/Volume Feeding [*A publication*] .... Inst Vol Feed
Institutions/Volume Feeding Management [*Later, Institutions/ Volume Feeding*] [*A publication*] .... Inst/Vol Feeding Mgt
Instituto Antartico Argentino. Contribuciones [*A publication*] .... Inst Antart Argent Contrib
Instituto Antartico Chileno. Boletin [*A publication*] .... Inst Antart Chileno Bol
Instituto de Aposentadoria e Pensoes dos Comerciarios [*Brazil*] .... IAPC
Instituto de Asuntos Nucleares [*Colombia*] .... IAN
Instituto de Auxilios y Viviendas [*Institute for Help in Housing*] [*Dominican Republic*] .... IAV
Instituto de Biologia Aplicada. Publicaciones (Barcelona) [*A publication*] .... Inst Biol Apl Publ (Barcelona)
Instituto de Biologia Marina (Mar Del Plata). Memoria Anual [*A publication*] .... Inst Biol Mar (Mar Del Plata) Mem Anu
Instituto de Biologia Marina (Mar Del Plata). Serie Contribuciones [*A publication*] .... Inst Biol Mar (Mar Del Plata) Ser Contrib
Instituto Brasileiro de Bibliografia e Documentacao [*Brazilian Institute of Bibliography and Documentation*] .... IBBD
Instituto Brasileiro de Informacao em Ciencia e Tecnologia [*Brazilian Institute for Information in Science and Technology*] [*Information service*] .... IBICT
Instituto de Capacitacion e Investigacion en Reforma Agraria [*Agrarian Reform Training and Research Institute*] [*Chile*] .... ICIRA
Instituto Caro y Cuervo [*A publication*] ICC
Instituto Centroamericano de Administracion de Empresas [*Central American Institute of Business Administration*] [*Nicaragua*] .... INCAE
Instituto Centroamericano de Administracion Publica [*Central American Institute of Public Administration*] [*Costa Rica*] .... ICAP
Instituto Centroamericano de Investigacion y Tecnologia Industrial, Guatemala City, Guatemala [*Library symbol*] .... GuGIN
Instituto Centroamericano de Investigacion y Tecnologia Industrial [*Central American Research Institute for Industry*] [*Guatemala*] .... ICAITI
Instituto de Ciencia Animal [*Cuba*] .... ICA
Instituto Coimbra [*A publication*] IC
Instituto Colombiano Agropecuario. Boletin Tecnico [*A publication*] .... Inst Colomb Agropecu Bol Tec
Instituto Colombiano de Especializacion Tecnica en el Exterior .... ICETEX
Instituto Cubano de Investigaciones Tecnologicas .... ICIT
Instituto de Economia y Producciones Ganaderas del Ebro. Comunicaciones [*A publication*] .... Inst Econ Prod Ganad Ebro Comun
Instituto Ecuatoriano de Ciencias Naturales. Contribucion [*A publication*] .... Inst Ecuat Cienc Nat Contrib
Instituto de Energia Atomica [*Brazil*] .... IEA
Instituto de Energia Atomica Reactor [*Brazil*] .... IEAR
Instituto de Engenharia Nuclear [*Brazil*] .... IDEN
Instituto de Engenharia, Sao Paulo [*Brazil*] .... IESP
Instituto de Estudios Superiores de Administracion [*Institute of Higher Studies of Administration*] [*Venezuela*] .... IESA
Instituto de Estudos Brasileiros [*A publication*] .... Inst E B
Instituto Fisico-Geografico Nacional de Costa Rica. Anales [*A publication*] .... Inst Fisico-Geog Nac Costa Rica An
Instituto Florestal. Boletim Tecnico (Sao Paulo) [*A publication*] .... Inst Florest Bol Tec (Sao Paulo)
Instituto Florestal. Publicacao (Sao Paulo) [*A publication*] .... Inst Florest Publ (Sao Paulo)
Instituto de Fomento Algodonero (Bogota) [*A publication*] .... Inst Fom Algod (Bogota)
Instituto de Fomento Nacional [*Industrial promotion agency*] [*Nicaragua*] .... INFONAC
Instituto de Fomento Pesquero. Boletin Cientifico [*A publication*] .... Inst Fom Pesq Bol Cient
Instituto de Fomento Pesquero. Publicacion [*A publication*] .... Inst Fom Pesq Publ
Instituto Forestal de Investigaciones y Experiencias. Comunicacion [*A publication*] .... Inst For Invest Exp Comun
Instituto Forestal Nacional. Folleto Tecnico Forestal [*A publication*] .... Inst For Nac Foll Tec For
Instituto de Formacao Social e Corporativa [*Portugal*] .... IFSC
Instituto Gemologico Espanol. Boletin [*A publication*] .... Inst Gemol Esp Bol
Instituto Geofisico de los Andes Colombianos. Publicacion. Serie A. Sismologia [*A publication*] .... Inst Geofis Andes Colomb Publ Ser A
Instituto Geografico Nacional. Boletin Geologico (Guatemala) [*A publication*] .... Inst Geog Nac Bol Geol (Guatemala)
Instituto Iberoamericano de Derecho Agrario y Reforma Agraria [*Ibero-American Institute of Agrarian Law and Agrarian Reform - IAIALAR*] .... IIDARA
Instituto de Informacion y Documentacion en Ciencia y Tecnologia [*Institute for Information and Documentation in Science and Technology*] [*Spain*] [*Information service*] .... ICYT
Instituto para la Integracion de America Latina .... INTAL
Instituto Interamericano II
Instituto Interamericano de Ciencias Agricolas [*Inter-American Institute of Agricultural Sciences*] [*Costa Rica*] .... IICA
Instituto Interamericano del Nino [*Inter-American Children's Institute*] [*Uruguay*] .... IIN
Instituto Internacional de Ciencias Administrativas [*International Institute of Administrative Sciences*] .... IICA
Instituto Internacional de Literatura Iberoamericana [*International Institute of Iberoamerican Literature*] IILI
Instituto de Investigacao Agronomica (Angola). Serie Cientifica [*A publication*] .... Inst Invest Agron (Angola) Ser Cient
Instituto de Investigacao Agronomica (Angola). Serie Tecnica [*A publication*] .... Inst Invest Agron (Angola) Ser Tec
Instituto de Investigacao Agronomica (Mocambique). Serie Memorias [*A publication*] .... Inst Invest Agron (Mocambique) Ser Mem
Instituto de Investigacao Cientifica (Angola). Relatorios e Comunicacoes [*A publication*] .... Inst Invest Cient (Angola) Relat Comun
Instituto de Investigacion Aeronautica y Espacial [*Argentina*] .... IIAE
Instituto de Investigacion de los Recursos Marinos (Callao). Informe [*A publication*] .... Inst Invest Recur Mar (Callao) Inf
Instituto de Investigaciones Biomedicas. Universidad Nacional Autonoma de Mexico. Informe [*A publication*] .... Inst Invest Biomed Univ Nac Auton Mex Inf
Instituto Italiano di Cultura, Montreal, PQ, Canada [*Library symbol*] .... CaQMII
Instituto Latinoamericano de Planificacion Economica y Social [*Latin American Institute for Economic and Social Planning*] .... ILPES
Instituto Latinoamericano del Plastico .... ILAP
Instituto del Mar del Peru (Callao). Informe [*A publication*] .... Inst Mar Peru (Callao) Inf
Instituto de Materiales y Modelos Estructurales. Boletin Tecnico. Universidad Central de Venezuela [*A publication*] .... Inst Mater Modelos Estruct Bol Tec Univ Cent Venez
Instituto Mexicano de Minas y Metalurgia. Informes y Memorias [*A publication*] .... Inst Mex Minas Met Inf
Instituto Mexicano del Petroleo. Publicacion [*A publication*] .... Inst Mex Pet Publ
Instituto Mexicano de Planeacion y Operacion de Sistemas .... IMPOS
Instituto Mexicano de Recursos Naturales Renovables. Serie de Mesas Redondas [*A publication*] .... Inst Mex Recur Nat Renov Ser Mesas Redondas
Instituto Municipal de Ciencias Naturales Miscelanea. Zoologica [*A publication*] .... Inst Munic Cienc Nat Misc Zool
Instituto Nacional de Antropologia e Historia [*Mexico*] .... INAH
Instituto Nacional para la Conservacion de la Natureleza. Estacion Central de Ecologia. Boletin (Spain) [*A publication*] .... Inst Nac Conserv Nat Estac Cent Ecol Bol (Spain)
Instituto Nacional de Electricidad [*Guatemala*] .... INDE
Instituto Nacional de Industria [*National Institute for Industry*] [*Spain*] .... INI
Instituto Nacional de Investigaciones Agrarias. Comunicaciones. Serie: Proteccion Vegetal (Spain) [*A publication*] .... Inst Nac Invest Agrar Comun Ser Prot Veg (Spain)
Instituto Nacional de Investigaciones Agronomicas (Madrid). Conferencias [*A publication*] .... Inst Nac Invest Agron (Madr) Conf
Instituto Nacional del Libro Espanol .... INLE

Instituto Nacional do Livro [*A publication*].................... Inst N L
Instituto Nacional de Medicina Legal de Colombia. Revista [*A publication*]..................Inst Nac Med Leg Colomb Rev
Instituto Nacional de Nutricion. Caracas. Publicacion [*A publication*]..................Inst Nac Nutr Caracas Publ
Instituto Nacional de Pesca. Boletin Cientifico y Tecnico [*A publication*]..................Inst Nac Pesca Bol Cient Tec
Instituto Nacional de la Pesca. Cuba. Centro de Investigaciones Pesqueras. Contribucion [*A publication*]..................Inst Nac Pesca Cuba Cent Invest Pesq Contrib
Instituto Nacional de Pesca (Ecuador). Boletin Informativo [*A publication*]..................Inst Nac Pesca (Ecuador) Bol Inf
Instituto Nacional de Promocion [*National Institute of Industrial Promotion*] [*Peru*]..................INPI
Instituto Nacional de Proteccion a la Infancia [*Mexico*]..................INPI
Instituto Nacional de Reforma Agraria [*Cuba*]..................INRA
Instituto Nacional de Tecnica Aerospacial [*National Institute of Aerospace Technology*] [*Spain*]..................INTA
Instituto Nacional de Tecnologia Agropecuaria [*Argentina*]..................INTA
Instituto Nacional de Tecnologia Agropecuaria. Boletin Informativo [*A publication*]..................Inst Nac Tecnol Agropecu Bol Inf
Instituto Nacional de Tecnologia Agropecuaria. Suelos Publicacion [*A publication*]..................Inst Nac Tecnol Agropecu Suelos Publ
Instituto de Nutricion de Centro America y Panama [*Institute of Nutrition of Central America and Panama*] [*Guatemala*]..................INCAP
Instituto de Nutricion de Centro America y Panama, Guatemala City, Guatemala [*Library symbol*]..................GuGIC
Instituto per le Opere di Religione [*Institute for Religious Works*] [*The Vatican bank*]..................IOR
Instituto de Organizacion Racional [*Universidad de Chile*]..................INSORA
Instituto Panamericano de Geografia e Historia [*Pan American Institute of Geography and History*] [*Mexico*]..................IPGH
Instituto Pastoral Latinoamericano..................IPLA
Instituto Peruano-Norte Americano [*A publication*]..................IPNA
Instituto de Pesquisas Agronimicas (Recife). Boletim Tecnico [*A publication*]..................Inst Pesqui Agron (Recife) Bol Tec
Instituto de Pesquisas Agronomicas de Pernambuco. Boletim Tecnico [*A publication*]..................Inst Pesqui Agron Pernambuco Bol Tec
Instituto de Pesquisas Agropecuarias do Norte. Boletim Tecnico [*A publication*]..................Inst Pesqui Agropecu Norte Bol Tec
Instituto de Pesquisas Agropecuarias do Sul. Boletim Tecnico [*A publication*]..................Inst Pesqui Agropecu Sul Bol Tec
Instituto de Pesquisas Espaciais [*Formerly, CNAE*] [*Brazil*]..................INPE
Instituto de Pesquisas e Estudos Economicos [*Brazil*]..................IPEE
Instituto de Pesquisas e Experimentacao Agropecuarias do Norte (IPEAN). Serie Estudos e Ensaios [*A publication*]..................Inst Pesqui Exp Agropecu Norte (IPEAN) Ser Estud Ens
Instituto Politecnico Nacional [*National Polytechnic Institute*] [*Mexico*]..................IPN
Instituto Profesional para el Desarrollo [*Professional Development Institute*] [*Colombia*]..................INPRODE
Instituto Promotor de Inversiones en Bolivia..................INPIBOL
Instituto de Providencia e Assistencia dos Servidores do Estado [*Brazil*]..................IPASE
Instituto Provincial de Paleontologia de Sabadell. Boletin Informativo [*A publication*]..................Inst Prov Paleontol Sabadell Bol Inf
Instituto Salvadoreno de Fomento Industrial [*Industrial promotion agency*] [*El Salvador*]..................INSAFI
Instituto de Sistemas Audio-Visuales [*Institute of Audio-Visual Media*] [*Colombia*]..................ISAV
Instituto Sperimentale dei Metalli Leggeri..................ISML
Instituto Sudamericano del Petroleo [*South American Petroleum Institute*]..................ISAP
Instituto Superiore di Sanita [*Italy*]..................ISS
Instituto Tecnologica do Rio Grande Do Sul. Boletim [*A publication*]..................Inst Tecnol Rio Grande Sul Bol
Instituto Tecnologico Centroamericano [*El Salvador*]..................ITCA
Instituto Tecnologico y de Estudios Superiores de Monterrey. Departamento de Quimica. Boletin [*A publication*]..................Inst Tecnol Estud Super Monterrey Dep Quim Bol
Instituto Tecnologico y de Estudios Superiores de Monterrey, Monterrey, Mexico [*Library symbol*]..................MxMoT
Instituto Venezolano de Investigaciones Cientificas..................IVIC
Instituto Venezolano de la Petroquimica..................IVP
Instituto de Vivienda Urbana [*El Salvador*]..................IVU
Instituto Zimotecnico, Piracicaba, Brazil [*Library symbol*]..................BrPI
Instituto de Zootecnia Sao Paulo. Boletim Tecnico [*A publication*]..................Inst Zootec Sao Paulo Bol Tec
Institutt for Atomenergi [*Norway*]..................IFA
Institutul Agronomic Timisoara Lucrari Stiintifice. Seria Medicina Veterinara [*A publication*]..................Inst Agron Timisoara Lucr Stiint Ser Med Vet
Institutul de Fizica Atomica. Report (Romania) [*A publication*]..................Inst Fiz At Rep (Rom)
Institutul de Fizica si Inginerie Nucleara. Report (Romania) [*A publication*]..................Inst Fiz Ing Nucl Rep (Rom)
Institutul Geologic. Studii Tehnice si Economice. Seria E. Hidrogeologie [*A publication*]..................Inst Geol Stud Teh Econ Ser E
Institutul Geologic. Studii Tehnice si Economice. Seria I. Mineralogie-Petrografie [*A publication*]..................Inst Geol Stud Teh Econ Ser I

Institutul de Geologie si Geofizica. Studii Tehnice si Economice. Seria E. Hidrogeologie [*A publication*]..................Inst Geol Geofiz Stud Teh Econ Ser E
Institutul de Geologie si Geofizica. Studii Tehnice si Economice. Seria I. Mineralogie-Petrografie [*A publication*]..................Inst Geol Geofiz Stud Teh Econ Ser I
Institutul de Meteorologie si Hidrologie. Culegere de Lucrari de Meteorologie [*A publication*]..................Inst Meteorol Hidrol Culegere Lucr Meteorol
Institutul de Meteorologie si Hidrologie. Studii si Cercetari. Partea 1. Meteorologie [*A publication*]..................Inst Meteorol Hidrol Stud Cercet Partea 1
Institutul de Meteorologie si Hidrologie. Studii si Cercetari. Partea 2. Hidrologie [*A publication*]..................Inst Meteorol Hidrol Stud Cercet Partea 2
Institutul de Pathologie si Igiena Animala. Colectia Indrumari (Bucharest) [*A publication*]..................Inst Pathol Ig Anim Colect Indrumari (Buchar)
Institutul de Pathologie si Igiena Animala. Probleme de Epizootologie Veterinara (Bucharest) [*A publication*]..................Inst Pathol Ig Anim Probl Epizootol Vet (Buchar)
Institutul Politehnic din Iasi. Buletinul. Sectia 5. Constructii-Arhitectura [*A publication*]..................Inst Politeh Iasi Bul Sect 5
Institutul de Studii si Proiectari Energetice. Buletinul [*Romania*] [*A publication*]..................Inst Stud Proiect Energ Bul
Instituut voor Bodemvruchtbaarheid Haren-Groningen. Jaarverslag [*A publication*]..................Inst Bodemvruchtbaarheid Haren-Gr Jaarversl
Instituut voor Bodemvruchtbaarheid Haren-Groningen. Rapport [*A publication*]..................Inst Bodemvruchtbaarheid Haren-Gr Rapp
Instituut voor Toegepast Biologisch Onderzoek in de Natuur [*Institute for Biological Field Research*]. Mededeling [*A publication*]..................Inst Toegepast Biol Onderzoek Meded
Instron Corp. [*American Stock Exchange symbol*]..................ISN
Instruct [*or Instructor*]..................INSTR
Instruction [*or Instructor*]..................INST
Instruction..................INSTRN
Instruction..................INSTRUC
Instruction Address Register [*Data processing*]..................IAR
Instruction Bank [*Data processing*]..................IB
Instruction Bank [*Data processing*]..................I-BANK
Instruction Book..................IB
Instruction Card..................IC
Instruction Change Request..................ICR
Instruction Code..................IC
Instruction Control Unit..................ICU
Instruction Counter [*Data processing*]..................IC
Instruction/Data..................I/D
Instruction Folder..................IF
Instruction [*or Instructor*] Guide..................IG
Instruction Leaflet..................IL
Instruction Length Code [*Data processing*]..................ILC
Instruction Look-Ahead [*Unit*] [*Data processing*]..................ILA
Instruction Manual..................IM
Instruction in Motivation Achievement and General Education [*YMCA program*]..................IMAGE
Instruction Pamphlet..................IP
Instruction Plate..................IP
Instruction to Proceed..................ITP
Instruction Processing Unit..................IPU
Instruction Pulse..................IP
Instruction Register [*Data processing*]..................IR
Instruction Set Architecture [*Data processing*] [*Army*]..................ISA
Instruction Set Processor [*Data processing*]..................ISP
Instruction Set Processor Specification [*Data processing*]..................ISPS
Instruction Sheet..................IS
Instruction Staticizing Control..................ISC
Instruction Summary Sheet..................ISS
Instruction Tag..................IT
Instructional..................INSTRL
Instructional..................INSTRNL
Instructional-Based Appraisal System [*Education*]..................IBAS
Instructional Center Library..................ICL
Instructional Course Lectures [*A publication*]..................Instr Course Lect
Instructional Innovator [*A publication*]..................Instr Innov
Instructional Management System..................IMS
Instructional Material Adequacy Guide and Evaluation Standard..................IMAGES
Instructional Materials Center..................IMC
Instructional Materials Centers/Regional Media Centers..................IMC/RMC
Instructional Materials Reference Center..................IMRC
Instructional Media Laboratory..................IML
Instructional Procedures Preference Inventory..................IPPI
Instructional Program Development..................IPD
Instructional Resources Information System [*Environmental Protection Agency*]..................IRIS
Instructional Science [*A publication*]..................Instr Sci
Instructional Scientific Equipment Program [*National Science Foundation*]..................ISEP
Instructional System Package..................ISP
Instructional Systems Development..................ISD

Instructional Systems Language [*Data processing*] ... ISL
Instructional Technology ... IT
Instructional Telecommunications Consortium ... ITC
Instructional Television ... ITV
Instructional Television Fixed Service [*Educational TV*] ... ITFS
Instructions ... INSTNS
Instructions for Commodores of Convoys [*Navy*] [*Obsolete*] ... ICOC
Instructions for Mailers [*A publication*] ... IFOMA
Instructions per Second [*Data processing*] ... IPS
Instructions for Service ... IFS
Instructions to Ship ... IS
Instructor [*Navy*] [*British*] ... In
Instructor [*A publication*] ... Inst
Instructor [*A publication*] ... Instr
Instructor of Artillery [*British*] ... I of A
Instructor Control Panel ... ICP
Instructor Display Panel ... IDP
Instructor in Gunnery [*Military*] [*British*] ... IG
Instructor and Key Personnel ... IKP
Instructor and Key Personnel Training ... IKPT
Instructor-Lieutenant [*Navy*] [*British*] ... IL
Instructor Lieutenant-Commander [*Navy*] [*British*] ... ILC
Instructor of Musketry [*British*] ... I of M
Instructor Navigator ... IN
Instructor Operation Station [*Army*] ... IOS
Instructor-Patient [*Medicine*] ... IP
Instructor Pilot ... IP
Instructor Trainer [*Red Cross*] ... IT
Instructor Training Course ... ITC
Instructor Under Training [*Navy*] ... IUT
Instructors Basic Training Unit ... IBTU
Instructor's Journal [*Air Force*] ... IJ
Instrument ... INST
Instrument ... INSTR
Instrument ... INSTRMT
Instrument Abstracts ... IA
Instrument Abstracts [*A publication*] ... Instrum Abstr
Instrument Air Filter ... IAF
Instrument Air Receiver ... IAR
Instrument Approach Chart ... IAC
Instrument Approach and Landing Chart [*Aviation*] ... IAL
Instrument Approach and Landing Chart [*Aviation*] ... IALC
Instrument Approach Procedure [*Aviation*] ... IAP
Instrument Approach System ... IAS
Instrument Array Cable ... IAC
Instrument Bearing Jewel ... IBJ
Instrument Calibration Laboratory ... ICL
Instrument Calibration and Maintenance Record ... ICMR
Instrument Calibration Procedure ... ICP
Instrument Checkout Equipment [*NASA*] ... ICE
Instrument Compressed Air ... ICA
Instrument Control Center ... ICC
Instrument and Control Engineering [*A publication*] ... Instrum Control Engng
Instrument Correction ... I
Instrument Correction ... IC
Instrument Data Processing System ... IDPS
Instrument Data System ... IDS
Instrument Definition Team ... IDT
Instrument Development Laboratories ... IDL
Instrument Development Section ... IDS
Instrument and Electrical Technician ... IET
Instrument Engineering ... IE
Instrument for Evaluation of Photographs ... IEP
Instrument Field of View ... IFOV
Instrument Flag Motor ... IFM
Instrument Flight Center [*Air Force*] ... IFC
Instrument Flight Instructors School [*Navy*] ... IFIS
Instrument Flight Recovery [*NASA*] ... IFR
Instrument Flight Rules [*Aviation*] ... IFR
Instrument Flight Safety System ... IFSS
Instrument Flight Training ... INSTFLTNG
Instrument Formation Flight System for Helicopters ... IFFSH
Instrument und Forschung [*A publication*] ... Instrum Forsch
Instrument Ground ... IG
Instrument Ground Optical Recording ... IGOR
Instrument Ground Support Equipment ... IGSE
Instrument Head ... IH
Instrument Landing Aid ... ILA
Instrument Landing Approach ... ILA
Instrument Landing Approach System ... ILAS
Instrument Landing Guidance ... ILG
Instrument Landing System [*Aviation*] ... ILS
Instrument Landing System Approach [*Aviation*] ... ILSAP
Instrument Landing System - Partial [*Aviation*] ... ILSP
Instrument Landing System and TACAN ... ILSTAC
Instrument Low Approach [*Aircraft landing method*] ... ILA
Instrument Low-Approach System [*Aircraft landing method*] ... ILAS
Instrument Maintenance Management [*A publication*] ... Instrum Maint Manage
Instrument Marking Kit ... IMK
Instrument Material Bulletin ... IMB
Instrument [*Flight*] **Meteorological Conditions** [*Aviation*] ... IMC
Instrument Note ... IN
Instrument Operating Assembly ... IOA
Instrument Panel ... INSTPN
Instrument Panel Lighting ... IPL
Instrument Pilot Instructor School [*Air Force*] ... IPIS
Instrument Pointing System ... IPS
Instrument Practice [*A publication*] ... Instrum Pract
Instrument Reading ... IR
Instrument Servo System ... ISS
Instrument Society of America ... ISA
Instrument Society of America. Conference Preprint [*A publication*] ... Instrum Soc Amer Conf Preprint
Instrument Society of India. Journal [*A publication*] ... Instrum Soc India J
Instrument Standards Laboratory [*Space Flight Operations Facility, NASA*] ... ISL
Instrument Systems Corp. [*American Stock Exchange symbol*] ... ISY
Instrument Systems Corp. Uts [*NASDAQ symbol*] ... ISYNU
Instrument Takeoff ... ITO
Instrument Technician Service Organization ... ITSO
Instrument Test [*or Tree*] [*Nuclear energy*] ... IT
Instrument Test Repair Laboratory ... ITRL
Instrument Time (Actual) ... ITA
Instrument Time (Simulated) ... ITS
Instrument or on-Top-of-Clouds Authorized ... INSTOP
Instrument Transformer ... IT
Instrument Tree Flow and Temperature Removal Instrument Assembly [*Nuclear energy*] ... ITFTRIA
Instrument Tree Removable Instrument Assembly [*Nuclear energy*] ... ITRIA
Instrument Tree/Spool Piece [*Nuclear energy*] ... IT/SP
Instrument Unit [*NASA*] ... IU
Instrumental [*or Instrumentation*] ... I
Instrumental Activation Analysis ... IAA
Instrumental Engineering Division [*National Weather Service*] ... IED
Instrumental Magnitude [*Earthquakes*] ... M
Instrumental Neutron Activation Analysis ... INAA
Instrumental Photon Activation Analysis [*National Bureau of Standards*] ... IPAA
Instrumentalist [*A publication*] ... IN
Instrumentalist [*A publication*] ... Instrument
Instrumentalist [*A publication*] ... ISMTB
Instrumentarium Corp. ADR [*NASDAQ symbol*] ... INMRY
Instrumentation ... IM
Instrumentation ... INSTM
Instrumentation ... INSTMN
Instrumentation ... INSTN
Instrumentation ... INSTRU
Instrumentation in the Aerospace Industry [*A publication*] ... Instrum Aerosp Ind
Instrumentation Amplifier ... IA
Instrumentation and Automation [*A publication*] ... Instrum Autom
Instrumentation Calibration Incident Repair Service ... INSCAIRS
Instrumentation and Calibration Network ... ICN
Instrumentation Checkout Complex ... ICC
Instrumentation Checkout Station ... ICS
Instrumentation in the Chemical and Petroleum Industries [*A publication*] ... Instrum Chem Pet Ind
Instrumentation and Communication ... INST/COMM
Instrumentation Communication Equipment ... ICE
Instrumentation and Communication Subsystem [*NASA*] ... ICS
Instrumentation and Communication (System) ... I & C(S)
Instrumentation and Communications [*Cable system*] ... I & C
Instrumentation and Communications Monitor ... ICM
Instrumentation and Communications Officer [*NASA*] ... INCO
Instrumentation and Control [*Aerospace*] ... I & C
Instrumentation Control Center ... ICC
Instrumentation Control Document ... ICD
Instrumentation Control Officer ... ICO
Instrumentation Control Racks ... ICR
Instrumentation and Control Subsystem ... ICS
Instrumentation Controller ... IC
Instrumentation in the Cryogenic Industry [*A publication*] ... Instrum Cryog Ind
Instrumentation Data Distribution System ... IDDS
Instrumentation Data Items ... IDI
Instrumentation Data Test Station ... IDTS
Instrumentation Data Transmission System ... IDTS
Instrumentation Data Transmission System Controller ... IDTSC
Instrumentation Development Laboratory Report ... IDLR
Instrumentation Development Request ... IDR
Instrumentation Digital On-Line Transcriber [*Data processing*] ... IDIOT
Instrumentation/Displays and Controls [*Subsystem*] ... I/D & C
Instrumentation and Electronic Systems Division [*NASA*] ... IESD
Instrumentation Ground Equipment ... IGE
Instrumentation Ground System ... IGS
Instrumentation Habitability Power ... IHP
Instrumentation Inertial Reference Set [*Aviation*] ... IIRS
Instrumentation Laboratory ... IL
Instrumentation Manager [*NASA*] ... IM
Instrumentation and Measurement ... IM

Instrumentation in the Mining and Metallurgy Industries [*A publication*] ..... Instrum Min Metall Ind
Instrumentation Notice ..... IN
Instrumentation Operating Area ..... IOA
Instrumentation Operation Station ..... IOS
Instrumentation Operations Engineer ..... IOE
Instrumentation Package Container ..... IPC
Instrumentation Papers [*Air Force*] ..... IP
Instrumentation Plan ..... IP
Instrumentation Plan Number ..... IPN
Instrumentation Power ..... IP
Instrumentation in the Power Industry [*A publication*] ..... Instrum Power Ind
Instrumentation Power Supply ..... IPS
Instrumentation Power System [*or Subsystem*] [*NASA*] ..... IPS
Instrumentation Program and Component List ..... IPCL
Instrumentation Program and Components ..... IP & C
Instrumentation Program List ..... IPL
Instrumentation RADAR Set ..... IRS
Instrumentation and Range Safety [*NASA*] ..... I & RS
Instrumentation and Range Safety System [*NASA*] ..... IRSS
Instrumentation Report ..... IR
Instrumentation Requirements ..... IR
Instrumentation Ships Project [*Navy*] ..... IS
Instrumentation Ships Project Office [*Navy*] ..... ISPO
Instrumentation Specialties Company ..... ISCO
Instrumentation Status Report ..... ISR
Instrumentation Subsystem [*NASA*] ..... INSTRUM
Instrumentation Suitability Evaluation ..... ISE
Instrumentation Summary ..... IS
Instrumentation Support Instruction ..... ISI
Instrumentation Support Plan ..... ISP
Instrumentation Support Service ..... ISS
Instrumentation Support Team ..... IST
Instrumentation System ..... INSTSYS
Instrumentation System ..... IS
Instrumentation System Assessment Center ..... ISAC
Instrumentation System Corporation ..... ISC
Instrumentation Tape Recorder ..... ITR
Instrumentation Technology [*A publication*] ..... Instrn Technol
Instrumentation Technology [*A publication*] ..... Instr Tech
Instrumentation Technology [*A publication*] ..... Instrumentation Tech
Instrumentation Technology [*A publication*] ..... Instrum Tech
Instrumentation Technology [*A publication*] ..... Instrum Technol
Instrumentation Television ..... INTV
Instrumentation Test Equipment ..... ITE
Instrumentation Tracking Controller ..... ITC
Instrumentation Unit Updata Command System [*NASA*] ..... IUCS
Instrumented ..... INSTRM
Instrumented Bend Test ..... IBT
Instrumented Laboratory Training ..... IT
Instrumented Measuring System ..... IMS
Instrumented Monkey Pod ..... IMP
Instrumented Range Acquisition ..... IRACQ
Instrumented Vibration Measuring System ..... IVMS
Instrumentenbau Musik International [*A publication*] ..... INAUA
Instrumentenbau-Zeitschrift [*A publication*] ..... IZ
Instrumentman [*Navy rating*] ..... IM
Instrumentman, First Class [*Navy rating*] IM1
Instrumentman, Second Class [*Navy rating*] IM2
Instrumentman, Third Class [*Navy rating*] IM3
Instruments Authorized [*Aviation*] ..... INSTA
Instruments and Automation [*A publication*] ..... Instr & Autom
Instruments and Automation [*A publication*] ..... Instrum Automat
Instruments and Control Systems [*A publication*] ..... Instr Contr
Instruments and Control Systems [*A publication*] ..... Instrum Control Syst
Instruments and Control Systems [*A publication*] ..... Instrum Contr Syst
Instruments, Electronics, and Automation [*Exhibit*] ..... IEA
Instruments and Experimental Techniques [*A publication*] ..... Instr Exp Techn
Instruments and Experimental Techniques [*A publication*] ..... Instrum Exp Tech
Instruments India [*A publication*] ..... Instrum India
Instruments et Laboratoires [*A publication*] ..... Instrum Lab
Instytut Badan Literackick Polskiej Akademii Nauk [*A publication*] ..... IBL
Instytut Energetyki. Biuletyn [*A publication*] ..... Inst Energ Biul
Instytut Farb i Lakierow. Biuletyn Informacyjny [*A publication*] ..... Inst Farb Lakierow Biul Inf
Instytut Filozofii i Socjologii Pan [*A publication*] ..... IFiS
Instytut Informacji Naukowej, Technicznej, i Ekonomicznej [*Institute of Scientific, Technical, and Economic Information*] [*Poland*] [*Information service*] ..... IINTE
Instytut Informacji Naukowej Technicznej i Ekonomicznej, Warsaw, Poland [*Library symbol*] ..... PoWC
Instytut Metali Niezelaznych. Biuletyn [*A publication*] ..... Inst Met Niezelazn Biul
Instytut Metalurgii Zelaza. Prace [*A publication*] ..... Inst Metal Zelaza Pr
Instytut Przemyslu Organicznego. Prace [*A publication*] ..... Inst Przem Org Pr
Instytut Przemyslu Tworzyw i Farb. Biuletyn Informacyjny [*A publication*] ..... Inst Przem Tworzyw Farb Biul Inf
Instytut Przemyslu Wiazacych Materialow Budowlanych. Krakow. Biuletyn Informacyjny [*A publication*] ..... Inst Przem Wiazacych Mater Budow Krakow Biul Inf
Instytutow Hutniczych. Prace [*A publication*] ..... Inst Hutn Pr
Insufficient ..... INSUF
Insufflatio [*An Insufflation*] [*Pharmacy*] ..... INSUFF
Insula [*A publication*] ..... In
Insula [*A publication*] ..... Ins
Insulana [*A publication*] ..... Insul
Insular ..... INS
Insular Force ..... IF
Insulate ..... INS
Insulate ..... INSL
Insulated ..... INSUL
Insulated Binding Post ..... IBP
Insulated Cable Engineers Association [*Formerly, IPCEA*] ..... ICEA
Insulated Conductors IC
Insulated Core Reactor ..... ICR
Insulated [*or Insulating*] **Core Transformer** ..... ICT
Insulated Gate ..... IG
Insulated-Gate Field-Effect Transistor ..... IGFET
Insulated Power Cable Engineers Association [*Later, ICEA*] ..... IPCEA
Insulated Steel Door Systems Institute ..... ISDSI
Insulated Tank [*Liquid gas carriers*] I
Insulating Siding Association [*Defunct*] ..... ISA
Insulating Siding Core Board Association [*Defunct*] ..... ISCBA
Insulating Sleeve ..... IS
Insulating Transformer ..... IT
Insulation Board Institute [*Later, ABPA*] ..... IBI
Insulation Breakdown Tester ..... IBDT
Insulation Breakdown Tester ..... IBT
Insulation/Circuits [*A publication*] ..... Insul/Circuits
Insulation Contractors Association of America ..... ICAA
Insulation Distributor Contractors National Association [*Later, NICA*] ..... IDCNA
Insulation Fabricators Association [*Defunct*] ..... IFA
Insulation Resistance ..... IR
Insulation Specification ..... ISPEC
Insulation Test Specification ..... ITS
Insulator ..... INSULR
Insulators [*JETDS nomenclature*] [*Military*] IL
Insulin ..... In
Insulin Coma Therapy [*Medicine*] ..... ICT
Insulin-Dependent Diabetes ..... IDD
Insulin-Dependent Diabetes Mellitus ..... IDDM
Insulin Gene Family ..... IGF
Insulin-Like Activity ..... ILA
Insulin-Like Growth Factor ..... IGF
Insulin-Like Material ..... ILM
Insulin Shock Therapy [*Psychiatry*] ..... IST
Insulin Tolerance Test [*Physiology*] ..... ITT
Insulin Zinc Suspension ..... IZS
Insurance ..... INCE
Insurance ..... INS
Insurance ..... INSCE
Insurance [*A publication*] ..... INS
Insurance Accountants Association [*Later, SIA*] ..... IAA
Insurance Accounting Principles ..... IAP
Insurance Accounting and Statistical Association ..... IASA
Insurance Advertising Conference ..... IAC
Insurance Advocate [*A publication*] ..... IA
Insurance Agents International Union ..... IAIU
Insurance Asia [*Manila*] [*A publication*] ..... IA
Insurance Bureau of Canada ..... IBC
Insurance Company and Bank Purchasing Agents Association ..... ICBPA
Insurance Company Education Directors Society ..... ICEDS
Insurance Co. of North America ..... INA
Insurance Conference Planners ..... ICP
Insurance Counsel Journal [*A publication*] ..... ICJ
Insurance Counsel Journal [*A publication*] ..... Ins Counsel J
Insurance Counsel Journal [*A publication*] ..... Insur Couns J
Insurance Crime Prevention Institute ..... ICPI
Insurance Decisions [*A publication*] ..... Insurance D
Insurance Economics Society of America ..... IESA
Insurance Field (Fire and Casualty Edition) [*A publication*] ..... Ins Field (Fire Ed)
Insurance Field (Life Edition) [*A publication*] ..... Ins Field (Life Ed)
Insurance Forum [*A publication*] ..... IF
Insurance Information Institute III
Insurance Institute of America ..... IIA
Insurance Institute for Highway Safety ..... IIHS
Insurance Institute of the Province of Quebec, Montreal, PQ, Canada [*Library symbol*] ..... CaQMI
Insurance Institute of Winnipeg, Winnipeg, MB, Canada [*Library symbol*] ..... CaMWI
Insurance Law Journal [*A publication*] ..... ILJ
Insurance Law Journal [*A publication*] ..... Ins L J
Insurance Law Journal [*A publication*] ..... Insur Law J
Insurance Loss Control Association [*Formerly, AMFIE, AMIE*] ..... ILCA
Insurance Magazine [*A publication*] ..... IM
Insurance Management Decision Game ..... IMDEG

Insurance Market Risk Assessment ... IMRA
Insurance Patient [*Medicine*] ... IP
Insurance Premium Finance Association ... IPFA
Insurance Salesman [*A publication*] ... IS
Insurance Service Associates [*Later, Assurex International*] ... ISA
Insurance Service Association of America [*Later, Assurex International*] ... ISAA
Insurance Services Office [*A rating body*] ... ISO
Insurance Society of New York ... ISNY
Insurance Society of New York, New York, NY [*Library symbol*] ... NNInS
Insurance Society of Philadelphia, Philadelphia, PA [*Library symbol*] [*Obsolete*] ... PPPI
Insurance Underwriters Association of the Pacific, San Francisco, CA [*Library symbol*] ... CSfFU
Insurance Workers of America ... IWA
Insurance Workers International Union ... IWIU
Insure ... INS
Insured ... INSD
Insured Locksmiths and Safemen of America [*Defunct*] ... ILSA
Insurgency ... INSGCY
Insurgent Incident Data ... IID
Insurgent Sociologist [*A publication*] ... Insrg Soc
Insyte Energy Corp. [*NASDAQ symbol*] ... ISTE
INTA [*Instituto Nacional de Tecnologia Agropecuaria*] **Estacion Experimental Manfredi. Informacion Tecnica** [*A publication*] ... INTA Estac Exp Manfredi Inf Tec
INTA [*Instituto Nacional de Tecnologia Agropecuaria*] **Estacion Experimental Regional Agropecuaria (Parana). Serie Tecnica** [*A publication*] ... INTA Estac Exp Reg Agropecu (Parana) Ser Tec
INTA [*Instituto Nacional de Tecnologia Agropecuaria*] **Estacion Experimental Regional Agropecuaria (Pergamino). Informe Tecnico** [*A publication*] ... INTA Estac Exp Reg Agropecu Pergamino Inf Tec
INTA [*Instituto Nacional de Tecnologia Agropecuaria*] **Estacion Experimental Regional Agropecuaria (Pergamino). Publicacion Tecnica** [*A publication*] ... INTA Estac Exp Reg Agropecu Pergamino Publ Tec
INTA [*Instituto Nacional de Tecnica Aeronautica*] **Satellite** [*Spain*] ... INTASAT
Intact Educational Foundation ... IEF
Intact Ventricular System [*Cardiology*] ... IVS
Intake ... INT
Intake ... INTK
Intake Closes [*Valve position*] ... IC
Intake Opens [*Valve position*] ... IO
Intake and Output [*Medicine*] ... I & O
Intake (of a Unit of Food) Energy [*Nutrition*] ... IE
Intangible Drilling Costs [*Petroleum industry*] ... IDC
Intech, Inc. [*NASDAQ symbol*] ... INTE
InteCom, Inc. [*NASDAQ symbol*] ... INCM
Integon Corp. [*NYSE symbol*] [*Delisted*] ... ITG
Integral ... INT
Integral ... INTGL
Integral of Absolute Error ... IAE
Integral Boiling Reactor ... IBR
Integral Boiling and Superheat Reactor ... IBSHR
Integral Cesium Reservoir ... ICR
Integral Circuit Package ... ICP
Integral Error Squared ... IES
Integral Fire Control Equipment ... IFCE
Integral Frequency Scan Approach and Landing ... IFSAL
Integral [*or Integrated*] **Launch and Recovery** [*or Reentry*] **Vehicle** [*NASA*] ... ILRV
Integral [*or Integrated*] **Launch and Recovery** [*or Reentry*] **Vehicle System** [*NASA*] ... ILRVS
Integral Lift Fan [*Aviation*] ... ILF
Integral Pulse Frequency Modulation ... IPFM
Integral Radiative Heat Flux ... IRHF
Integral Rocket Ramjet [*Navy*] ... IRR
Integral Rocket Ramjet Surface-to-Air Missile ... IRRSAM
Integral Rocket Ramjet Surface-to-Surface Missile ... IRRSSM
Integral Rocket Ramjet Torpedo Tube Missile ... IRRTTM
Integral Spar Inspection System ... ISIS
Integral Squared Error ... ISE
Integral Superheat Reactor ... ISR
Integral Systems Experimental Requirements ... ISER
Integral Terminal Block ... ITB
Integral Trap Door [*Technical drawings*] ... ITD
Integral Weight and Balance System [*Aviation*] ... IWBS
Integrally Molded Insulation ... IMI
Integrally Stiffened ... IS
Integrate ... INTGR
Integrate-Transfer-Launch [*Complex*] [*NASA*] ... ITL
Integrated ... INT
Integrated ... INTGRD
Integrated Acoustic Communication System ... IACS
Integrated Advance Avionics for Aircraft ... IAAA
Integrated Air Defense System ... IADS
Integrated Airbase Defense ... IAD
Integrated Aircraft Armament System ... INTAAS
Integrated Aircraft Instrumentation ... IAI
Integrated Antiairborne Defense System ... IAADS
Integrated Armament Control System ... IACS
Integrated Automatic Documentation [*System*] ... IAD
Integrated Avionics Control System ... IACS
Integrated Avionics System ... IAS
Integrated Barter International [*NASDAQ symbol*] ... BRTRD
Integrated Basic Research [*of ASRA*] [*National Science Foundation*] ... IBP
Integrated Battlefield Control System [*Army*] ... IBCS
Integrated Bridge Rectifier ... IBR
Integrated Carrier Acoustic Prediction System [*Navy*] ... ICAPS
Integrated Catalog Algorithm ... INCA
Integrated Catapult Control Station ... ICCS
Integrated Checkout ... ICO
Integrated Checkout System ... ICOS
Integrated Checkout System ... ICS
Integrated Chip Circuit ... ICC
Integrated Chopper ... INCH
Integrated Circuit [*Electronics*] ... IC
Integrated Circuit Analysis [*Data processing*] ... ICAN
Integrated Circuit Array ... ICA
Integrated Circuit Mask ... ICM
Integrated Circuit and Message Switch ... ICMS
Integrated Circuit Test Set ... ICTS
Integrated Circuit Tester ... ICT
Integrated Circuits Engineering Corp. ... ICE
Integrated Circuits, Inc. [*NASDAQ symbol*] ... ICTM
Integrated Civil Engineering System [*Data processing*] ... ICES
Integrated Coal Gasification Combined Cycle [*Fuel technology*] ... IGCC
Integrated Combat Group [*Air Force*] ... ICG
Integrated Combat Ship ... ICS
Integrated Combat System ... ICS
Integrated Combat Systems Test Facility ... ICSTF
Integrated Combined System Test ... ICST
Integrated Command Accounting and Reporting ... ICAR
Integrated Command System ... ICS
Integrated Communication Control Panel ... ICCP
Integrated Communication, Navigation, Identification [*System*] ... ICNI
Integrated Communication/Navigation/Identification Control Panel ... ICNICP
Integrated Communication/Navigation/Identification Control Set ... ICNICS
Integrated Communications Access Method [*Data processing*] ... ICAM
Integrated Communications Adapter ... ICA
Integrated Communications Adapter Extended ... ICAE
Integrated Communications Agency [*Air Force*] ... INCA
Integrated Communications Control ... ICC
Integrated Communications System ... ICS
Integrated Communications System, Alaska [*Air Force, FAA*] ... ICSAL
Integrated Computer-Aided Manufacturing [*Program*] [*Air Force*] ... ICAM
Integrated Computer Telemetry ... ICT
Integrated Configuration List ... ICL
Integrated Configuration Summary ... ICS
Integrated Conformal Array ... ICA
Integrated Control ... ICON
Integrated Control and Display ... ICAD
Integrated Control Storage [*Data processing*] ... ICS
Integrated Control System [*Navy*] ... INCOS
Integrated Cooling for Electronics ... ICE
Integrated Cost Accounting ... ICA
Integrated Cost Accounting Application ... ICAA
Integrated Criminal Apprehension Program ... ICAP
Integrated Cryogenic Isotope Cooling Equipment ... ICICLE
Integrated Data Acquisition and Control [*Jet Propulsion Laboratory, NASA*] ... IDAC
Integrated Data Acquisition System ... IDAS
Integrated Data Base [*Data processing*] ... IDB
Integrated Data Coding System ... IDCS
Integrated Data Display System ... IDDS
Integrated Data File ... IDF
Integrated Data Generation Implementation Technique ... IDGIT
Integrated Data Handling System ... IDHS
Integrated Data Presentation ... IDP
Integrated Data Processing ... IDP
Integrated Data Processing Center ... IDPC
Integrated Data Processing System ... IDPS
Integrated Data Retrieval System [*Department of the Treasury*] ... IDRS
Integrated Data Store [*or System*] [*Data processing*] ... IDS
Integrated Data Transmittal Package ... IDTP
Integrated Database Management System ... IDMS
Integrated Defense System ... IDES
Integrated Design Analysis System [*Space shuttle*] [*NASA*] ... IDEAS
Integrated Design and Engineering Automated System ... IDEAS
Integrated Detection and Classification Station ... IDACS
Integrated Digital-Analog Converter ... IDAC
Integrated Digital Avionics ... IDA
Integrated Digital Avionics for Medium STOL Transport ... IDAMST
Integrated Digital Logic Circuit ... IDLC
Integrated Display Situation ... IDS
Integrated Displays and Controls ... IDC
Integrated Disposal Management System [*DoD*] ... IDMS
Integrated Drive Generator ... IDG

Integrated Drug Abuse Management Information Systems ... IDAMIS
Integrated Drug Abuse Reporting Process [*National Institutes of Health*] ... IDARP
Integrated Dynamic Tester ... IDT
Integrated Education [*A publication*] ... Integ Educ
Integrated Education [*A publication*] ... Integrated Educ
Integrated Education: Race and Schools [*A publication*] ... Integ Ed
Integrated Electronic Assembly [*NASA*] ... IEA
Integrated Electronic Components ... IEC
Integrated Electronic Control ... IEC
Integrated Electronic Signal Processor ... IESP
Integrated Electronic System ... IES
Integrated Electronic Vertical Display ... IEVD
Integrated Electronic Warfare System ... IEWS
Integrated Electronics ... INTEL
Integrated Energy, Incorporated [*American Stock Exchange symbol*] ... IEI
Integrated Engine Instrument System ... IEIS
Integrated Engineering Program ... IEP
Integrated Environmental Control ... IEC
Integrated Equipment Component ... IEC
Integrated Equipment Test [*Nuclear energy*] ... IET
Integrated Equipment Test Facility [*Department of Energy*] ... IETF
Integrated Facilities Management Information System ... IFMIS
Integrated Facilities System [*Army*] ... IFS
Integrated Feed Antenna ... IFA
Integrated File Adapter [*Data processing*] ... IFA
Integrated Financial Management System ... IFMS
Integrated Fire Control [*RADAR*] ... IFC
Integrated Flagship Data System [*Navy*] ... IFDS
Integrated Flight Control System ... IFCS
Integrated Flight Data Processing System [*Air Force*] ... IFDAPS
Integrated Flight Director [*Aviation*] ... IFD
Integrated Flight and Fire Control ... IFFC
Integrated Flight Instrument System ... IFIS
Integrated Flight System ... IFS
Integrated Force Administration System [*Bell System*] ... IFAMS
Integrated Fuel Cycle Facilities [*Nuclear energy*] ... IFCF
Integrated Genetics [*NASDAQ symbol*] ... INGN
Integrated Global Ocean Station System [*See also IGOSS*] [*UNESCO*] ... IGLOSS
Integrated Global Ocean Station System [*See also IGLOSS*] [*UNESCO*] ... IGOSS
Integrated Grant Administration ... IGA
Integrated Graphics System ... IGS
Integrated Ground/Airborne Avionics System ... IGAAS
Integrated Guidance and Control System [*Aerospace*] ... IGACS
Integrated Guidance and Control System [*Aerospace*] ... IGCS
Integrated Hazard Function ... IHF
Integrated Helicopter Avionics System [*Navy*] ... IHAS
Integrated Helmet and Display Sight System ... IHADSS
Integrated Helmet Display System ... IHDS
Integrated High-Frequency Antenna System ... IHFAS
Integrated Hit Indicator ... IHI
Integrated Hit Indicator System ... IHIS
Integrated Information Presentation and Control System [*Aviation*] ... IIPACS
Integrated Information Processing ... INTIP
Integrated Information Processing System ... INTIPS
Integrated Information System [*Marine Corps*] ... I2S
Integrated Information System (Financial) [*Marine Corps*] ... I2S(FIN)
Integrated Information System (Logistics) [*Marine Corps*] ... I2S(LOG)
Integrated Information System (Manpower) [*Marine Corps*] ... I2S(MPR)
Integrated Information System (Manpower and Functional Area Manpower Management System) [*Marine Corps*] ... I2S(MPR/MMS)
Integrated Information System (Operational) [*Marine Corps*] ... I2S(OPS)
Integrated Injection Logic [*Data processing*] ... IIL
Integrated Injection Logic [*Data processing*] ... I^2L
Integrated Installation Requirement Plan ... IIRP
Integrated Instrument Development ... IID
Integrated Instrument Development Program ... IIDP
Integrated Instrument Sheet ... IIS
Integrated Instrumentation RADAR ... IIR
Integrated Insulation System ... IIS
Integrated Joint Broadband System [*Army*] ... IJBS
Integrated Joint Communication System [*Military*] ... IJCS
Integrated Joint Communication System - Pacific [*Military*] ... IJCS-PAC
Integrated Key Set [*Data processing*] ... IKS
Integrated Laboratory Sequence [*A system of teaching chemistry devised by Mary L. Good at Louisiana State University in New Orleans*] ... ILS
Integrated Lake-Watershed Acidification Study ... ILWAS
Integrated LASER Optical Sight Set ... ILOSS
Integrated Launch Complex ... ILC
Integrated Launch Control and Checkout ... ILCC
Integrated Launch Control and Checkout System ... ILCCS
Integrated Library System [*National Library of Medicine*] [*Information service*] ... ILS
Integrated Life Support System [*NASA*] ... ILSS
Integrated Light Attack Aircraft [*or Attack Avionics*] **System** ... ILAAS
Integrated Light Attack Avionics System [*Navy*] ... ILASS
Integrated Logic Circuit ... ILC
Integrated Logistic Management Program ... ILMP
Integrated Logistic Support Management Plan ... ILSMP
Integrated Logistic Support Management Team ... ILSMT
Integrated Logistic Support Office [*DoD*] ... ILSO
Integrated Logistic Support Plan [*or Program*] ... ILSP
Integrated Logistics Data System ... ILDS
Integrated Logistics Management Team ... ILMT
Integrated Logistics Panel ... ILP
Integrated Logistics Support [*DoD*] ... ILS
Integrated Logistics Support Control Manual ... ILSCM
Integrated Logistics Support Coordination Meeting ... ILSCM
Integrated Logistics Support Data File ... ILSDF
Integrated Logistics System ... ILS
Integrated Low-Light-Level Television ... ILLLTV
Integrated Mail Preparation System ... IMPS
Integrated Maintenance Chart [*or Concept*] ... IMC
Integrated Maintenance Management ... IMM
Integrated Maintenance Management Information Retrieval System [*DoD*] ... IMMIRS
Integrated Maintenance Management Plan ... IMMP
Integrated Maintenance Management System [*Army*] ... IMMS
Integrated Maintenance Management Team ... IMMT
Integrated Maintenance Manual ... IMM
Integrated Maintenance Plan [*or Procedure*] ... IMP
Integrated Maintenance Program Operation ... IMPOP
Integrated Maintenance System ... IMS
Integrated Maintenance Test Plan ... IMTP
Integrated Maintenance Test Requirement Outline ... IMTRO
Integrated Management Information System [*Air Force*] ... IMIS
Integrated Management Planning and Control Technique [*British*] ... IMPACT
Integrated Management Planning Information Systems [*Data processing*] ... IMPIS
Integrated Managerial Programing Analysis Control Technique [*Air Force*] ... IMPACT
Integrated Maneuvering and Life Support System [*NASA*] ... IMLSS
Integrated Mapping System ... IMS
Integrated Master Programing and Scheduling ... IMPS
Integrated Materiel Management [*or Manager*] ... IMM
Integrated Medical and Behavioral Laboratory Measurement System ... IMBLMS
Integrated Medical Services ... IMS
Integrated Memory Processor ... IMP
Integrated Meteorological System [*Army*] ... IMS
Integrated Microelectronic Circuitry ... IMC
Integrated Microwave Amplifier Converter ... IMAC
Integrated Microwave Circuit ... IMC
Integrated Microwave Products ... IMP
Integrated Missile Control Center [*NASA*] ... IMCC
Integrated Missile Flight Safety System ... IMFSS
Integrated Missile Ground Control Network ... IMGCN
Integrated, Modification and Trial ... IMAT
Integrated Monitor and Control Panel ... IMCP
Integrated Monitoring Panel ... IMP
Integrated Monolithic Circuit ... IMC
Integrated Motorists' Information System [*Computerized guidance system to speed traffic and avoid tie-ups*] ... IMIS
Integrated Multifrequency RADAR ... IMFRAD
Integrated Multifunction Keyboard ... IMFK
Integrated Multisensor Airborne Display ... IMAD
Integrated Navigation and Communications, Automatic ... INCA
Integrated Navigation System ... INS
Integrated Network Fiber Optics ... INFO
Integrated Neutron Activation Prediction [*Code system*] ... INAP
Integrated Nuclear and Chemical Analysis ... INCA
Integrated Numerical Control Approach ... INCA
Integrated Observation Device ... IOD
Integrated Obstacle Plan [*Military*] ... IOP
Integrated Ocean Surveillance System [*Navy*] ... IOSS
Integrated On-Line Text Arrangement ... IOTA
Integrated Open Problem List ... IOPL
Integrated Operational Ground Equipment ... IOGE
Integrated Operational Intelligence Center ... IOIC
Integrated Operational Intelligence System ... IOIS
Integrated Operational Nuclear Detonation Detection System ... IONDS
Integrated Operator System [*Telecommunications*] ... IOS
Integrated Optical Circuit ... IOC
Integrated Optical Density [*Instrumentation*] ... IOD
Integrated Orbital Operations Simulation Facility ... IOOSF
Integrated Ordnance Package ... IOP
Integrated Passive Action Detection Acquisition Equipment ... IPADAE
Integrated Perceived Level [*Acoustics*] ... IPL
Integrated Perceived Noise Level [*Acoustics*] ... IPNL
Integrated Personnel Information Report ... IPIR
Integrated Personnel Planning and Budgeting System ... IPPBS
Integrated Personnel Requirement Report ... IPRR
Integrated Pest Control ... IPC
Integrated Pest Management [*Agronomy*] ... IPM
Integrated Photodetection Assemblies ... IPA
Integrated Pin Diode ... IPD
Integrated Planning Parts List ... IPPL

Integrated Plotting Package	IPP
Integrated Pneumatic Air System	IPAS
Integrated Position Indicator	IPI
Integrated Power and Attitude-Control System [*NASA*]	IPACS
Integrated Power and Environmental Control System	IPECS
Integrated Power System	IPS
Integrated Procedures Control	IPC
Integrated Process Demonstration [*Nuclear energy*]	IPD
Integrated Program, Budget, Manpower [*System*] [*Defense Supply Agency*]	IPBM
Integrated Program for Commodities [*UNCTAD*]	IPC
Integrated Program Management System [*Navy*]	IPMS
Integrated Programed Operational and Functional Appraisals	IPOFA
Integrated Programs for Aerospace-Vehicle Design	IPAD
Integrated Propulsion Control System [*Air Force*]	IPCS
Integrated Radio Control	IRC
Integrated Radio Room	IRR
Integrated RADOME [*RADAR Dome*] Antenna	IRA
Integrated RADOME [*RADAR Dome*] Antenna Structure	IRAS
Integrated Range Instrumentation	IRI
Integrated Range Missile	IRM
Integrated Range Mission [*Military*]	IRM
Integrated Rate System	IRS
Integrated Readiness Testing	IRT
Integrated Real-Time Contamination Monitor [*Module*]	IRTCM
Integrated Reconnaissance Intelligence System	IRIS
Integrated Record System	IRS
Integrated Regional Environmental Management Project	IREM
Integrated Reliability Data System	IRDS
Integrated Reliability Test Program	IRTP
Integrated Research Aircraft Control Technology	INTERACT
Integrated Resources, Inc. [*NYSE symbol*]	IRE
Integrated Safeguards Experiment	ISE
Integrated Satellite [*Military spacecraft*]	IS
Integrated Satellite System	ISS
Integrated Scientific Information System	ISIS
Integrated Sealift Study [*Army*]	ISS
Integrated Secure Voice System	ISVS
Integrated Sensor Interpretation Techniques	INSITE
Integrated Services Digital Network [*Telecommunications*]	ISDN
Integrated Services Satellite Digital Network	ISSDN
Integrated Shear Plate	ISP
Integrated Ship Design System	ISDS
Integrated Side-Lobe Ratio	ISLR
Integrated Sight Unit [*Weaponry*]	ISU
Integrated Site Facilities and Equipment	ISFE
Integrated Skills Method [*Education*]	ISM
Integrated Software Systems Corporation [*NASDAQ symbol*]	ISCX
Integrated Software Systems Corporation	ISSCO
Integrated Spacecraft Operations Plan [*NASA*]	ISOP
Integrated Start System	ISS
Integrated Status Reporting System	ISRS
Integrated Stock Listing	ISL
Integrated Storage Control	ISC
Integrated Stores Monitor and Management System [*Later, Armament Control Panel*]	ISMMS
Integrated Strike and Interceptor System	ISIS
Integrated Subject File	ISF
Integrated Submarine SONAR System Technician	ISSST
Integrated Subsystem Test Bed	ISTB
Integrated Support Area	ISA
Integrated Support Parts Requirement	ISPR
Integrated Support Plan	ISP
Integrated Support Requirements	ISR
Integrated Support Services Management Information System	ISSMIS
Integrated Surface Search and Attack Coordinate	ISSAC
Integrated Switching and Multiplexing [*IBM Corp.*]	ISAM
Integrated Symbolic Debugger [*Data processing*]	ISD
Integrative System for Automated Acquisition and Control	ISAAC
Integrated System Safety Engineering Plan	ISSEP
Integrated System Schematic	ISS
Integrated System Transformer	IST
Integrated Systems Demonstrator	ISD
Integrated Systems Test [*NASA*]	IST
Integrated Tactical Air Control System	ITACS
Integrated Tactical Amphibious Warfare Data System [*Navy*]	ITAWDS
Integrated Tactical Attack System	ITAS
Integrated Tactical Communications System [*Army*]	INTACS
Integrated Tactical Countermeasures [*Army*]	ITCM
Integrated Tactical Electronic Warfare System	ITEWS
Integrated Tactical Navigation System [*Navy*]	ITNS
Integrated Tactical Surveillance System	ITSS
Integrated Tank Insulation System	ITIS
Integrated Target System	ITS
Integrated Task Index	ITI
Integrated Technical Documentation and Training	ITDT
Integrated Telemetry Complex	ITC
Integrated Teleprocessing System	ITPS
Integrated Terminal Guidance	ITG
Integrated Test Area	ITA
Integrated Test Block	ITB

Integrated Test and Checkout Procedures	ITCP
Integrated Test Document	ITD
Integrated Test Equipment Facility	ITEF
Integrated Test/Evaluation Program	ITEP
Integrated Test Facility [*Data processing*]	ITF
Integrated Test Operate Panel	ITOP
Integrated Test Program	ITP
Integrated Test Program Board	ITPB
Integrated Test Requirements	ITR
Integrated Test Requirements Documents	ITRDS
Integrated Test Requirements Outline	ITRO
Integrated Testing	INT
Integrated Thermal Flux	ITF
Integrated Thermal Micrometeoroid Garment [*Spacesuit*]	ITMG
Integrated Thruster Assembly	ITA
Integrated Time and Absolute Error	ITAE
Integrated Torso Limb Suit Assembly [*NASA*]	ITLSA
Integrated Tracking System [*Obsolete*] [*ARTRAC*]	ITS
Integrated Training Brigade [*Navy*]	ITB
Integrated Trajectory Computations	ITC
Integrated Trajectory Error Display [*Aviation*]	ITED
Integrated Trajectory System	ITS
Integrated Transportation Management Information System [*Army*]	ITMIS
Integrated Tunnel Diode Amplifier	ITDA
Integrated Undersea Surveillance System	IUSS
Integrated Vacuum Circuit	IVC
Integrated Vehicle	IV
Integrated Vehicular Communication System	IVCS
Integrated Visual Approach and Landing Aid [*System*] [*RADAR*]	IVALA
Integrated Visual Testing Device	IVTD
Integrated Voltage Regulator	IVR
Integrated Warfare Requirements Methodology	IWRM
Integrated Weapon Secret Panel	IWSP
Integrated Weapon Support Management	IWSM
Integrated Weapon System Representative [*or Review*]	IWSR
Integrated Weapon System Training [*Air Force*]	IWST
Integrated Weapons Control System	IWCS
Integrated Weed Management System [*Agriculture*]	IWMS
Integrated Wideband Communications System [*Military*]	IWCS
Integrated Wideband Communications System/Southeast Asia	IWCS/SEA
Integrated Work Sequence/Inspection Traveler	IWS/IT
Integrated Work Statement	IWS
Integrated X-Ray Reflection	IXR
Integrating	INTEG
Integrating Assembly and Checkout Contractor	IACC
Integrating Assembly Contractor	IAC
Integrating Associate Contractor	IAC
Integrating Contractor	IC
Integrating Digital Voltmeter	IDV
Integrating Digital Voltmeter	IDVM
Integrating Fluctuation Meter	IFM
Integrating Gyro Accelerometer	IGA
Integrating Motor Pneumotachograph	IMP
Integrating Regulatory Transcription Units [*Genetics*]	IRTU
Integrating Support	IS
Integration Analog-to-Digital Converter	IADIC
Integration, Assembly, and Checkout	IAC
Integration Change Allowance	ICA
Integration and Checkout	I & C
Integration Control	IC
Integration with Controlled Error	ICE
Integration Hardware and Software Review	IH/SR
Integration Level Test Series [*Psychology*]	ILTS
Integration Support Service	ISS
Integration and Test	I & T
Integration Test Equipment	ITE
Integrative Control Functions of the Brain [*Elsevier Book Series*] [*A publication*]	ICFB
Integrator [*Aviation*]	INT
Integrator Cutoff	ICO
Integrity Entertainment Corporation [*NYSE symbol*] [*Delisted*]	IEC
Integrity Financial Group [*NASDAQ symbol*]	INTY
Integrity Loss Factor	ILF
Integro-Differential Analyzer	IDA
INTEK Diversified [*NASDAQ symbol*]	IDCC
Intel Corporation [*NASDAQ symbol*]	INTC
Intel Corp., Santa Clara, CA [*Library symbol*]	CStcll
Inteleplex Corp. [*NASDAQ symbol*]	ITPX
Intellectual Digest [*A publication*]	ID
Intellectual Freedom Committee [*American Library Association*]	IFC
Intellectual Freedom Round Table [*American Library Association*]	IFRT
Intellectual Observer [*A publication*]	Intel Obs
Intellectual Property	IP
Intellectual Property Owners [*Patent lobby*]	IPO
Intellectually Gifted Children	IGC
Intelligence	I
Intelligence	INT
Intelligence	INTEL
Intelligence Analysis	IA

Intelligence Automatic Data Processing Group	IADPG
Intelligence Bandwidth	IBW
Intelligence Branch	IB
Intelligence Bulletin	INTBUL
Intelligence Career Development Program	ICDP
Intelligence Case Control and Time Reporting System [*IRS*]	ICCTR
Intelligence Center	INTELCEN
Intelligence Center, Pacific Ocean Areas [*Obsolete*]	ICPOA
Intelligence Center, Pacific Ocean Areas [*Obsolete*]	INTELCENPAC
Intelligence Center and School [*Army*]	ICS
Intelligence Civilian Career Program [*Army*]	ICCP
Intelligence Collator [*British police term*]	IC
Intelligence Collection [*Military*]	INTCOL
Intelligence Collection Area [*Military*]	ICA
Intelligence Collection Plan [*Military*]	ICP
Intelligence Collection Requirement [*Army*]	ICR
Intelligence Committee [*NATO*]	IC
Intelligence Contingency Funds	ICF
Intelligence Coordination and Exploitation [*Joint CIA-MACV program*]	ICEX
Intelligence Corps [*Military unit*] [*British*]	IC
Intelligence Corps [*Army*]	IN
Intelligence Corps [*Army*]	INTC
Intelligence and Counterespionage [*Fictitious organization in the Matt Helm series of books and movies*]	ICE
Intelligence Cycle Time	ICT
Intelligence Data Handling System	IDHS
Intelligence Data Input Packages	IDIPS
Intelligence Data System	IDS
Intelligence Department [*Army*]	ID
Intelligence Digest [*A publication*]	Intell Dig
Intelligence Division [*NATO*]	ID
Intelligence Division Gaming Operations	INDIGO
Intelligence Duties	ID
Intelligence Duty Officer	IDO
Intelligence and Electronic Warfare [*System*] [*Military*]	IEW
Intelligence Evaluation Center [*Obsolete*] [*Saigon*]	IECS
Intelligence Evaluation Committee [*Department of Justice*]	IEC
Intelligence Evaluation Staff	IES
Intelligence Field Unit [*Navy*]	IFU
Intelligence Finished Reports Information Subsystem [*Data processing*]	IFRIS
Intelligence Generator	IG
Intelligence Information Report	IIR
Intelligence and Law Enforcement Division [*Coast Guard*]	INT
Intelligence Materiel Development and Support Office [*Army*]	IMDSO
Intelligence Memorandum	IM
Intelligence Office [*or Officer*]	IO
Intelligence Officer [*Army*]	INTO
Intelligence Oversight Board [*Federal government*]	IOB
Intelligence Priorities Committee [*British*] [*World War II*]	IPC
Intelligence Production Requests	IPR
Intelligence Publications	IP
Intelligence Publications Index [*Published January, 1953, through February, 1968, by the Defense Intelligence Agency*]	IPI
Intelligence Quotient [*Psychological and educational testing*]	IQ
Intelligence RADAR Reporting	IRR
Intelligence Ratio	IR
Intelligence and Reconnaissance	I & R
Intelligence Report	INTREP
Intelligence Report	INTREPT
Intelligence Report	IR
Intelligence Report Plan	IRP
Intelligence Reports Information Subsystem [*Data processing*]	IRIS
Intelligence Resources Advisory Committee [*To supervise US intelligence budget*]	IRAC
Intelligence Review	IR
Intelligence Review and Assessment Task Element [*Study of the effectiveness of the air war in Southeast Asia*]	IRATE
Intelligence School, United States Army Intelligence Center	ISUSAIC
Intelligence Section [*of an air staff; also, officer in charge of this section*] [*Air Force*]	A-2
Intelligence Section [*of a joint military staff; also, the officer in charge of this section*]	J-2
Intelligence Section [*in Army brigades or smaller units, and in Marine Corps units smaller than a brigade; also, the officer in charge of this section*]	S-2
Intelligence Section, Operations [*Control Commission for Germany*] [*World War II*]	IS(O)
Intelligence Section, Operations [*Joint Intelligence Subcommittee of Chiefs of Staff*] [*World War II*]	IS(Ops)
Intelligence and Security Board [*Army*]	INSB
Intelligence and Security Command [*Army*]	INSCOM
Intelligence in the Sky [*An extraterrestrial intelligence with whom Dr. Andrija Puharich and psychic Uri Geller claim to have communicated*]	IS
Intelligence for which the Source Reliability Cannot be Judged	F
Intelligence Subject Code	ISC
Intelligence Summary	INTSUM
Intelligence Summary	ISUM
Intelligence Support Activity [*Military*]	ISA

Intelligence Threat Analysis Detachment [*Army*]	ITAD
Intelligence Training [*Military*]	INTELTNG
Intelligence Watch Condition [*NATO*]	AIWC
Intelligence Working Group [*Military*]	IWG
Intelligenetics, Incorporated [*NASDAQ symbol*]	INAI
Intelligent Commercial Net [*NASDAQ symbol*]	ICNT
Intelligent Copier-Printer [*Electrophotography*]	IC-P
Intelligent Memory Manager [*Data processing*]	IMM
Intelligent Microimage Terminal [*Kodak*]	IMT
Intelligent Peripheral Controller [*Data processing*]	IPC
Intelligent Systems [*NASDAQ symbol*]	INTS
Intelligent Television [*Home video game*] [*Mattel, Inc.*]	INTELLIVISION
Intelligent Terminal [*Data processing*]	IT
Intelligent Time-Division Multiplexer	ITDM
Intelligenzalter [*Mental Age*] [*Psychology*]	IA
Intelligible Crosstalk Ratio	IXTR
INTELSAT Operations Center	IOC
Intemperate to Alcohol [*An alcoholic*] [*Slang*]	IA
Intendant-General	IG
Intended	INTDD
Intense	INTS
Intense Bunched Ion Source	IBIS
Intense Irregular Field	IIF
Intense Magnetic Field	IMF
Intense Neutron Generator	ING
Intense Product Inspection	IPI
Intense Pulsed Neutron Source	IPNS
Intense Relativistic Electron Beams [*Physics*]	IREB
Intense Thermal Radiation	ITR
Intensified Combat Training Program	ICTP
Intensified Confirmatory Troop Test	ICTT
Intensified Drug Inspection Program [*FDA*]	IDIP
Intensified Silicon Intensifier Target	ISIT
Intensifier Vidicon	IV
Intensify	INTSF
Intensify [*Meteorology*]	INTSFY
Intensity	I
Intensity	IN
Intensity	INT
Intensity	INTEN
Intensity	INTST
Intensity Duration (Curve)	I-D
Intensity of Magnetization [*Symbol*]	M
Intensity Measuring Devices [*JETDS nomenclature*] [*Military*]	IM
Intensity Modulation	IM
Intensity of Operational Employment [*Army*]	IOE
Intensity Unknown [*Meteorology*]	U
Intensive	INTENS
Intensive Agriculture [*A publication*]	Intensive Agr
Intensive Biometric Intertidal Survey [*Botany*]	IBIS
Intensive Care [*Medicine*]	IC
Intensive Care Facility [*Medicine*]	ICF
Intensive Care Medicine [*A publication*]	Intensive Care Med
Intensive Care Nursery	ICN
Intensive Care, Surgical [*Medicine*]	ICS
Intensive-Care Unit [*of a hospital*]	ICU
Intensive Employability Services [*Work Incentive Program*]	IES
Intensive Item Management System	IIMS
Intensive Student Jet Training Area	ISJTA
Intensivmedizin, Notfallmedizin, Anaesthesiologie [*A publication*]	Intensivmed Notfallmed Anaesthesiol
Intensivmedizinische Praxis [*A publication*]	Intensivmed Prax
Intent [*FBI standardized term*]	INT
Intent to Launch	ITL
Intention	INTN
Intentional Bases on Balls [*Baseball*]	IBB
Intentional Jitter Antijam [*Military*]	IJAJ
Intentional Jitter Jamming Unit [*Military*]	IJJU
Inter-African Advisory Committee on Epizootic Diseases	IACED
Inter-African Bureau for Animal Health and Protection	IBAHP
Inter-African Bureau of Animal Resources	IBAR
Inter-African Bureau for Epizootic Diseases	IBED
Inter-African Coffee Organization	IACO
Inter-African Labour Institute	ILI
Inter-African and Malagasy States Organization	IAMSO
Inter-African Phytosanitary Commission	IAPSC
Inter-African Phytosanitary Commission	IPC
Inter-Agency Air Cartographic Committee	IACC
Inter-Agency Consultative Board	IACB
Inter-Agency Data Processing Committee	IADPC
Inter Alia [*Among Other Things*] [*Latin*]	IA
Inter Alia [*Among Other Things*] [*Latin*]	INT AL
Inter-Allied Aeronautical Commission of Control	IAACC
Inter-Allied Committee on Post-War Requirements [*World War II*]	IACPWR
Inter-Allied Insurance Organization [*NATO*]	IIO
Inter-Allied Nuclear Force	IANF
Inter-Allied Personnel Board [*World War II*]	IAPB
Inter-Allied Postwar Requirements Bureau [*World War II*]	IPRB
Inter-Allied Reparations Agency [*Brussels*]	IARA
Inter-American [*A publication*]	Inter-Am

Inter-American Air Force Academy [*Operated by US Air Force to provide training for Latin American countries*]................IAAFA
Inter-American Association of Broadcasters ....IAAB
Inter-American Association for Democracy and Freedom.................IADF
Inter-American Association of Sanitary Engineering [*Later, Inter-American Association of Sanitary and Environmental Engineering*].....................IAASE
Inter-American Bank ....IAB
Inter-American Bar Association............................IABA
Inter-American Bar Foundation.............................IABF
Inter-American Bibliographical and Library Association.................IABLA
Inter-American Bibliographical and Library Association.................IBLA
Inter-American Center for Integral Development [*OAS*].............IACID
Inter-American Children's Institute [*OAS*].....................IACI
Inter-American Children's Institute [*OAS*].......................ICI
Inter-American College Association...........................IACA
Inter-American Commercial Arbitration Commission...............I-ACAC
Inter-American Commission on Human Rights [*OAS*].............IACHR
Inter-American Commission of Women [*OAS*]....................IACW
Inter-American Commission of Women [*OAS*].....................ICW
Inter-American Committee for the Alliance for Progress [*Superseded by Permanent Executive Committee of the Inter-American Economic and Social Council*]................IACAP
Inter-American Committee on Peaceful Settlement [*of the OAS*].......IACPS
Inter-American Congress of Radiology........................IACR
Inter-American Cooperative Institute...........................ICI
Inter-American Council of Commerce and Production..................IACCP
Inter-American Council of Jurists...........................IACJ
Inter-American Cultural Association.........................IACA
Inter-American Cultural Council [*Later, Inter-American Council for Education, Science, and Culture*].................IACC
Inter-American Defense Board.............................IADB
Inter-American Defense College [*Washington*]..................IADC
Inter-American Defense College, Fort McNair, Washington, DC [*Library symbol*]..........................DIAD
Inter-American Development Bank [*Also, IDB*]...................IADB
Inter-American Development Bank [*Also, IADB*]..................IDB
Inter-American Development Bank, Washington, DC [*OCLC symbol*]......BID
Inter-American Development Bank, Washington, DC [*Library symbol*].........................DIDB
Inter-American Development Commission......................IADC
Inter-American Economic Affairs [*A publication*]............ Inter-Amer Econ Aff
Inter-American Economic and Social Council [*United Nations*]...................IAECOSOC
Inter-American Economic and Social Council [*United Nations*]..........IAESC
Inter-American Education Association ....IAEA
Inter-American Emergency Advisory Committee for Political Defense.....................IAEACPD
Inter-American Federation for Adult Education ....IAFAE
Inter-American Federation of Entertainment Workers................IFEW
Inter-American Federation of Working Newspapermen's Organizations ....IAFWNO
Inter-American Foundation.................................IAF
Inter-American Foundation for the Arts [*Defunct*]...............IAFA
Inter-American Freight Conference..........................IAFC
Inter-American Geodetic Survey............................IAGS
Inter-American Hospital Association [*Defunct*].................IAHA
Inter-American Hotel Association...........................IAHA
Inter-American Human Rights Commission ....IAHRC
Inter-American Indian Institute [*OAS*].........................IAII
Inter-American Indian Institute [*OAS*]..........................III
Inter-American Institute of Agricultural Sciences [*Later, IICA*] [*OAS*]..........................IAIAS
Inter-American Institute of Ecology [*Ecological Society of America*].......IAIE
Inter-American Institute of Ecology [*Ecological Society of America*].........IIE
Inter-American Institute for Musical Research Yearbook [*A publication*]......................Intam Inst Mus Res
Inter-American Juridical Committee.........................IAJC
Inter-American Law Review [*A publication*].............. Inter-Am L Rev
Inter-American Legal Services Association.....................ILSA
Inter-American Literacy Foundation.........................IALF
Inter-American Municipal Organization.......................IMO
Inter-American Music Bulletin (English Edition) [*A publication*]...................Intam Mus B (Eng Ed)
Inter-American Music Review [*A publication*] .... Intam Mus R
Inter-American Musical Research. Yearbook [*A publication*]...................Intam Mus Res Yrbk
Inter-American Nuclear Energy Commission [*OAS*]...........IANEC
Inter-American Peace Committee [*Later, Inter-American Committee on Peaceful Settlement*] [*OAS*]....................IAPC
Inter-American Peacekeeping Force.........................IAPF
Inter-American Police Academy ....IAPA
Inter-American Press Association...........................IAPA
Inter-American Program for Social Progress [*AID*]...............IAPSP
Inter-American Quarterly [*A publication*]...............Inter-Am Q
Inter-American Review of Bibliography [*A publication*]...............IARB
Inter-American Safety Council ....IASC
Inter-American Social Development Institute [*Later, IAF*]............IASDI
Inter-American Statistical Institute [*OAS*]....................IASI
Inter-American Technical Council on Archives...................ITCA
Inter-American Translators Association ....AIT

Inter-American Travel Congress ....IATC
Inter-American Travel Congress ....ITC
Inter-American Travel Congresses..........................CIT
Inter-American Tropical Tuna Commission [*Scripps Institution of Oceanography*]..........................IATTC
Inter-American Tropical Tuna Commission [*Scripps Institution of Oceanography*]..........................ITTC
Inter-American Tropical Tuna Commission. Bulletin [*A publication*]...............Inter-Am Trop Tuna Comm Bull
Inter-American Tropical Tuna Commission. Special Report [*A publication*]...............Inter-Am Trop Tuna Comm Spec Rep
Inter-American University of Puerto Rico, San Juan Campus, San Juan, PR [*Library symbol*]...................PrIAU-SJ
Inter-Association Commission on Tsunami....................IACT
Inter-Association Committee on Health ....IACH
Inter-Association Group ....IAG
Inter Block Gap ....IBG
Inter-Bureau Citation of Funds [*Navy*]......................ICF
Inter-California Line in Mexico R. R. [*AAR code*]................ICLM
Inter-Channel Comparison Unit [*Nuclear energy*]................ICCU
Inter-Channel Time Displacement...........................ICTD
Inter Cibos [*Between Meals*] [*Pharmacy*].....................IC
Inter Cibos [*Between Meals*] [*Pharmacy*].................INT CIB
Inter-City Gas [*American Stock Exchange symbol*]................ICG
Inter-City Short Takeoff and Landing [*Aviation*].............INTERSTOL
Inter-Coastal Airways, Inc. [*Punta Gorda, FL*] [*FAA designator*].............ICA
Inter-Collegiate Yacht Racing Association [*of North America*] [*Later, ICYRA/NA*].........................ICYRA
Inter-Collegiate Yacht Racing Association of North America [*Formerly, ICYRA*].....................ICYRA/NA
Inter-Community Memorial Hospital, Newfane, NY [*Library symbol*]..........................NNefH
Inter-Company Correspondance ICC
Inter-Computer IC
Inter-Computer Compatibility Unit [*Data processing*].............ICCU
Inter-Continental Aerospacecraft-Range Unlimited System ....ICARUS
Inter-Department Data Exchange Program [*Air Force*].............IDEP
Inter Dependent [*A publication*].......................Inter Depend
Inter-Director Designation ....IDD
Inter Documentation Company, Ag, Zug, Switzerland [*Library symbol*]..........................IDC
Inter-Dynamic Balance ....IDB
Inter-Faith Compassionists...............................IFC
Inter-Faith Task Force ....IFTF
Inter-Fighter Director ....IFD
Inter-Gas System ....IG
Inter-Governmental Group for Indonesia ....IGGI
Inter-Governmental Marine Consultative Organization [*United Nations*].....................IMCO
Inter-Governmental Philatelic Corporation.....................IGPC
Inter-Granular ....IG
Inter-Industry Emission Control [*Program*]....................IIEC
Inter-Industry Highway Safety Committee.....................IIHSC
Inter-Institutional Committee on Nutrition.....................ICON
Inter-Island Air Services Ltd. [*Great Britain*] [*ICAO designator*]..............QW
Inter-Laboratory Committee on Editing and Publishing [*Navy*].........ILCEP
Inter-Laboratory Committee on Facilities [*Navy*]................ILCF
Inter-Lake Yachting Association...........................I-L YA
Inter-Mountain Airways [*Boulder, CO*] [*FAA designator*] ....IMA
Inter-NASA Data Exchange................................INDEX
Inter-Nation Simulation [*Simulation of international relations*]..........I-NS
Inter Noctem [*During the Night*] [*Pharmacy*] .... INTER NOCT
Inter Noctem [*During the Night*] [*Pharmacy*] ....INT NOCT
Inter-Nordic Standardization ....INSTA
Inter-Organization Board for Information Systems [*United Nations*].......IOB
Inter-Parliamentary Union [*British*].........................IPU
Inter-Professional Ad Hoc Group for Environmental Information Sharing.....................IPAHGEIS
Inter-Range Documentation Group [*White Sands Missile Range*].........IRDG
Inter-Range and Global Planning Group [*White Sands Missile Range*].....................IRGPG
Inter-Range Instrumentation Group [*White Sands Missile Range*].........IRIG
Inter-Range Instrumentation Group - Meteorological Working Group [*White Sands Missile Range*]...................IRIG-MWG
Inter-Range Missile Flight Safety Group [*White Sands Missile Range*].....................IRMFSG
Inter-Range Missile Ground Safety Group [*White Sands Missile Range*].....................IRMGSG
Inter-Range Operations Planning Group [*White Sands Missile Range*].....................IROPG
Inter-Range Vector [*NASA*]..............................IRV
Inter-Record Gap [*Data processing*]........................IRG
Inter-Regional Capital Account [*Inter-American Development Bank*].......IRC
Inter-Regional Financial Group, Inc. [*NYSE symbol*].............IFG
Inter-Regional Insurance Conference [*Later, ISO*]...............IRIC
Inter-Seamount Acoustic Range...........................ISAR
Inter-Secretariat Committee on Scientific Problems Relating to Oceanography [*United Nations*]...................ICSPRO
Inter-Service Communication [*British*] [*World War II*]..............ISC
Inter-Service Ionosphere Bureau [*Military*] ....ISIB
Inter-Service Metallurgical Research Council [*British*]............ISMET

Inter-Service Radio Measurements [*British*] [*World War II*] ... ISRM

Inter-Service Research Bureau [*British*] ... ISRB

Inter-Service Sports Council [*Military*] ... ISC

Inter-Service Topographical Department [*British*] ... ISTD

Inter-Service Working Group for Cooperation and Standardization of Foto Interpretation Procedures, Equipment, and Related Matters ... IWGCSFIPERM

Inter-Services Metallurgical Research Council [*British*] ... ISMRC

Inter-Society Color Council Newsletter [*A publication*] ... ISCC Newsl

Inter-Society Commission for Heart Disease Resources ... ICHD

Inter-Society Commission for Heart Disease Resources ... ISCHDR

Inter-State Manufacturers Association ... ISMA

Inter-Tel, Inc. [*NASDAQ symbol*] ... INTL

Inter-Theater Transfer [*Army*] ... ITT

Inter-Tribal Indian Ceremonial Association ... ITIC

Inter-Tropical Convergence Zone ... ITZ

Inter-Union Commission of Advice to Developing Countries ... IUCADC

Inter-Union Commission on Frequency Allocations for Radio Astronomy and Space Science ... IUCFA

Inter-Union Commission on Geodynamics. Scientific Report [*A publication*] ... Inter-Union Comm Geodyn Sci Rep

Inter-Union Commission on Solar-Terrestrial Physics ... IUCSTP

Inter-University Case Program ... ICP

Inter-University Committee for Debate on Foreign Policy [*Defunct*] ... IUC

Inter-University Committee on Israel [*Later, America-Israel Cultural Foundation*] ... IUCI

Inter-University Committee for Research on Consumer Behavior ... IUCRCB

Inter-University Committee on the Superior Student [*Defunct*] ... ICSS

Inter-University Committee on Travel Grants ... IUCTG

Inter-University Consortium for Political Research [*Later, ICPSR*] [*University of Michigan*] ... ICPR

Inter-University Consortium for Political and Social Research [*Formerly, ICPR*] [*University of Michigan*] ... ICPSR

Inter-University Council ... IUC

Inter-University Labor Education Committee ... IULEC

Inter-University Seminar on Armed Forces and Society ... IUS

Inter-User Reliability ... IUR

Inter-Varsity Christian Fellowship of the United States of America ... IVCF

Inter-Varsity Press [*British*] ... IVP

Inter-Vehicle Power Transfer ... IVPT

Interacting Boson Model [*Of nuclear structure*] ... IBM

Interacting Equipment Documents ... IED

Interaction Graphics Display ... IGD

Interaction Mean Free Path [*Astrophysics*] ... IMFP

Interaction Resources [*NASDAQ symbol*] ... INRLF

Interactive Algebraic Manipulation [*Data processing*] ... IAM

Interactive Alphanumeric Television ... IATV

Interactive Cable Television ... ICTV

Interactive Computer-Aided Design Evaluation ... ICADE

Interactive Computer Graphics ... ICG

Interactive Computer Presentation Panel [*To display computer-generated information for military use*] ... ICPP

Interactive Computer System [*Information science*] ... IACS

Interactive Computing [*A publication*] ... Int Comp

Interactive Computing and Control Facility [*IBM program product*] ... ICCF

Interactive Data Services, Incorporated [*Information service*] ... IDSI

Interactive Data System [*Data processing*] ... IDS

Interactive Dialogue Facility [*Data processing*] ... IDF

Interactive Differential Analyzer ... IDA

Interactive Digital Image Manipulation System [*Minicomputer*] ... IDIMS

Interactive Display Terminal ... IDT

Interactive Grafics Digitizer [*Data processing*] ... IGD

Interactive Graphics Finite Element System ... IGFES

Interactive Graphics Packaging Program [*Data processing*] ... IGPP

Interactive Graphics System [*Data processing*] ... IGS

Interactive Graphics Terminal [*Data processing*] ... IGT

Interactive Instructional System [*IBM Corp.*] ... IIS

Interactive International Banking System [*NCR Corp.*] ... IIBS

Interactive Keyboard and Terminal [*Data processing*] ... IKAT

Interactive Man/Computer Augmentation System ... IMCAS

Interactive Market Systems, Inc. [*Information service*] ... IMS

Interactive Microprogramable Control ... IMP

Interactive Planetary Image Processing System ... IPIPS

Interactive Problem-Control System [*IBM Corp.*] ... IPCS

Interactive Processing and Display System ... IPADS

Interactive Programing [*Data processing*] ... IAP

Interactive Query and Report Processor [*IBM Corp.*] ... IQRP

Interactive Radiation [*NASDAQ symbol*] ... INRD

Interactive Sciences Corporation [*Information service*] ... ISC

Interactive Simulation Language [*Data processing*] ... ISL

Interactive Structural Layout and Design [*Module*] ... ISLADE

Interactive Structural Sizing and Analysis System [*Data processing*] ... ISSAS

Interactive Synthesizer of Letterforms ... ITSYLF

Interactive System Productivity Facility [*Data processing*] ... ISPF

Interactive System Productivity Facility/Program Development Facility [*Data processing*] ... ISPF/PDF

Interactive Systems Corporation [*NASDAQ symbol*] ... ISCO

Interactive Terminal Facility ... ITF

Interactive Video Association ... IVA

Interagency ... INTAGCY

Interagency Advanced Power Group ... IAPG

Interagency Advisory Group [*Civil Service Commission*] ... IAG

Interagency Arctic Research Coordinating Committee [*National Science Foundation*] ... IARCC

Interagency Board of Examiners [*Civil Service Commission*] ... IAB

Interagency Chemical Rocket Propulsion Group ... ICRPG

Interagency Classification Review Committee [*Abolished, 1978*] [*DoD*] ... ICRC

Interagency Clean Car Advisory Committee [*HEW*] ... ICCAC

Interagency [*or Interdepartmental*] **Committee for Applied Meteorological Research** ... ICAMR

Interagency Committee on Automatic Data Processing [*Office of Management and Budget*] ... IAC/ADP

Interagency Committee on Back Contamination [*Aerospace*] ... ICBC

Interagency Committee on Climate Services and Research ... ICCSR

Interagency Committee on Excavation Technology [*Federal Council for Science and Technology*] ... ICET

Interagency Committee on Intelligence ... ICI

Interagency Committee on Intermodal Cargo ... ICIC

Interagency Committee for International Athletics [*Defunct*] ... IACIA

Interagency Committee on International Aviation Policy [*Department of State*] ... ICIAP

Interagency Committee on Marine Science and Engineering [*Federal Council for Science and Technology*] ... ICMSE

Interagency Committee on Marine Science, Research, Engineering, and Facilities ... ICMREF

Interagency Committee on Oceanography [*Later, ICMSE*] ... ICO

Interagency Committee for Outdoor Recreation [*Department of the Interior*] ... IAC

Interagency Committee on Product Information ... ICPI

Interagency Committee on Radiological Assistance ... ICRA

Interagency Committee on the Transportation of Radioactive Materials ... ICTRM

Interagency Committee on Transportation Security [*Department of Transportation*] ... ICOTS

Interagency Committee on Water Resources ... ICWR

Interagency Communications System [*Military*] ... ICS

Interagency Contingency Options Plan [*Military*] ... ICOP

Interagency Coordinating Committee for Astronomy [*Federal Council for Science and Technology*] ... ICCA

Interagency Coordinating Committee for Earth Resource Survey Programs [*National Aeronautics and Space Council*] ... ICCERSP

Interagency Coordinating Committee on US-Soviet Affairs [*Department of State*] ... ICCUSA

Interagency Council on Library Resources for Nursing ... ICLRN

Interagency Data Exchange Program [*Later, GIDEP*] ... IDEP

Interagency Dialing System ... IDS

Interagency Economic Growth Project [*Department of Transportation*] ... IEGP

Interagency Emergency Coordinating Group [*Federal disaster planning*] ... IECG

Interagency Emergency Planning Board [*Federal disaster planning*] ... IEPB

Interagency Emergency Planning Committee ... IEPC

Interagency Emergency Transportation Committee ... IETC

Interagency Geothermal Coordinating Council ... IGCC

Interagency Group [*Federal government*] ... IG

Interagency Group on International Aviation ... IGIA

Interagency Group on International Programs in Atmospheric Science ... IGIPAS

Interagency Life Sciences Supporting Space Research and Technology Exchange ... ILSE

Interagency Map and Publications Acquisitions Committee ... IMPAC

Interagency Materials Sciences Exchange ... IMSE

Interagency Mechanical Operations Group [*Lawrence Livermore Laboratory*] ... IMOG

Interagency Noise Abatement Program ... IANAP

Interagency Nuclear Safety Review Panel ... INSRP

Interagency Oil Policy Committee ... IOPC

Interagency Primate Steering Committee [*National Institutes of Health*] ... IPSC

Interagency Radiological Assistance Plan [*Nuclear energy*] ... IRAP

Interagency Radiological Assistance Program [*Nuclear energy*] ... IRAP

Interagency Rate ... IAR

Interagency Records Administration Conference [*Washington, DC*] ... IRAC

Interagency Regulatory Group ... IRG

Interagency Regulatory Liaison Group [*Comprising several federal agencies*] ... IRLG

Interagency Staff Committee on Public Law 480 [*Department of Agriculture*] ... ISC

Interagency Task Force [*for Indochina*] [*South Vietnam refugee relief*] ... IATF

Interagency Testing Committee [*Toxicology*] ... ITC

Interagency Textile Administrative Committee ... ITAC

Interagency Zero-Based Budgeting [*Federal government*] ... IZBB

Interallied Confederation of Reserve Officers [*See also CIOR*] ... ICRO

Interallied Force [*NATO*] ... IAF

Interallied Staff Communications Board [*World War II*] ... ISCB

Interallied Tactical Study Group [*NATO*] ... INTASGRO

Interamerican College of Physicians and Surgeons ... ICPS

Interamerican Confederation of Cattlemen ... IACC

Interamerican Federation of Public Relations Associations ... IFPRA
Interamerican Institute for Cooperation on Agriculture [*Formerly, IAIAS*] ... IICA
Interamerican Journal of Psychology [*A publication*] ... Interam J P
Interamerican Labour Institute ... ILI
Interamerican Naval Coordinating Authority ... IANCA
Interamerican Press Association ... IPA
Interamerican Program for Linguistics and Language Teaching ... IAPLLT
Interamerican Society of Cardiology ... ISC
Interamerican Society of Psychology ... ISP
Interamerican Travel Agents Society ... ITAS
Interamerican Underwater Festival ... IAUF
Interamerican Underwater Festival ... IUF
Interand Corp. [*NASDAQ symbol*] ... IRND
Interarray Communications ... IAC
Interarray Processor ... IAP
Interatrial Septal Defect [*Cardiology*] ... IASD
Interband Magneto-Optic [*Effect*] ... IMO
Interbank [*Credit cards*] ... I
Interbank Card Association ... ICA
Interbank National Authorization System ... INAS
Interboard Committee for Christian Work in Japan [*Later, JNAC*] ... IBC
Interboro Rapid Transit [*A New York City subway line*] ... IRT
Interbureau Insurance Advisory Group ... IIAG
Intercampus Committee for Handicapped Students ... ICCHS
Intercapital Income Securities, Inc. [*NYSE symbol*] ... ICB
Intercept ... INCPT
Intercept [*or Interceptor*] ... INT
Intercept ... INTCP
Intercept-Aerial [*Missile mission symbol*] ... I
Intercept Arm ... IA
Intercept Controller ... IC
Intercept Deployment Plan [*National Security Agency*] ... IDP
Intercept Director [*Military*] ... IND
Intercept During Boost [*Aerospace*] ... IDB
Intercept Ground Optical Recorder [*NASA*] ... IGOR
Intercept Ground Optical Recorder Tracking Telescope [*NASA*] ... IGORTT
Intercept Monitoring Display ... IMD
Intercept Officer ... IO
Intercept Point [*Air Force*] ... IP
Intercept Priorities Board [*Armed Forces Security Agency*] ... IPB
Intercept System Environment [*Army*] ... ISE
Intercept Target Optical Reader ... ITOR
Intercept Tracking and Control Group ... INTAC
Interception [*Football*] ... IN
Interception [*Football*] ... INTER
Interception Mission [*Air Force*] ... INM
Interception with Satellite Tracking ... INSATRAC
Interceptor [*Aircraft*] ... F
Interceptor ... I
Interceptor ... INCEP
Interceptor Aim Points ... IAP
Interceptor Command ... IC
Interceptor Day Fighter ... IDF
Interceptor Distance Computer ... IDC
Interceptor Identification Capability ... IIC
Interceptor Improvement Program ... IIP
Interceptor Missile ... IM
Interceptor Missile Direction Center ... IMDC
Interceptor Missile Interrogation RADAR ... IMIR
Interceptor Missile Squadron Operations Center [*Air Force*] ... IMSOC
Interceptor Missile Squadron and Supervisory Control Equipment ... IMSSCE
Interceptor Missile Squadron Supervisory Station ... IMSSS
Interceptor Night Fighter ... INF
Interceptor Pilot Simulator [*SSTM*] ... IPS
Interceptor Tactical Missile [*Air Force*] ... ITM
Interceptor Weapon Control System ... IWCS
Interceptor Weapons Instructor School [*Air Force*] ... IWIS
Intercessors for America ... IA
Interchange ... I/C
Interchange Center ... IC
Interchange File Separator [*Data processing*] ... IFS
Interchange Group Separator [*Data processing*] ... IGS
Interchange Record Separator [*Data processing*] ... IRS
Interchange Resource Center ... IRC
Interchange of Scientific and Technical Information in Machine Language ... ISTIM
Interchange State Bank [*NASDAQ symbol*] ... ISBJ
Interchange Unit Separator [*Data processing*] ... IUS
Interchangeability ... I
Interchangeability Document Change Notice ... IDCN
Interchangeability Document Change Request ... IDCR
Interchangeability and Replaceability [*or Replacement*] ... I & R
Interchangeability and Substitutability ... I & S
Interchangeability Survey Board ... ISB
Interchangeable ... INTCHG
Interchangeable at Attachment Point Only ... IAPO
Interchangeable Control Media ... ICM
Interchangeable Cycle Check ... ICC
Interchangeable Solid and Screen Panels [*Technical drawings*] ... IP
Interchangeable-Substitute Items ... INS
Interchangeable With ... I/W
Interchanger ... INTCHRG
Interchannel Communicator ... ICC
Interchannel Master Pulse ... ICMP
Interchannel Time Displacement [*Magnetic recording*] ... ITD
Interchannel Time Displacement Error [*Magnetic recording*] ... ITDE
Interchemical Printing Inks ... IPI
[*The*] **Interchurch Center** ... TIC
Interchurch Medical Assistance ... IMA
Interchurch News [*A publication*] ... Interchurch N
Interchurch Transportation Council [*Defunct*] ... ITC
Interciencia Association [*Latin America*] ... IA
Intercity Airlines ... ICA
INTERCO, Inc. [*Formerly, International Shoe Co.*] [*NYSE symbol*] ... ISS
Intercoastal Steamship Freight Association ... ISFA
Intercoastal Steamship Freight Association, New York NY [*STAC*] ... ISA
Intercoiffure America ... IA
Intercole, Inc. [*American Stock Exchange symbol*] ... IC
Intercollegiate Association of Amateur Athletes of America [*Also, IC4A, ICAAAA*] ... IAAAA
Intercollegiate Association of Amateur Athletes of America [*Also, IAAAA, ICAAAA*] ... IC4A
Intercollegiate Association of Amateur Athletes of America [*Also, IAAAA, IC4A*] ... ICAAAA
Intercollegiate Association for Study of the Alcohol Problem ... IASAP
Intercollegiate Association of Women Students ... IAWS
Intercollegiate Broadcasting System ... IBS
Intercollegiate Conference of Faculty Representatives ... ICFR
Intercollegiate Dramatic Association [*Defunct*] ... IDA
Intercollegiate Fencing Association ... IFA
Intercollegiate Horse Show Association ... IHSA
Intercollegiate Ice Hockey Association [*Later, ECHA*] ... IIHA
Intercollegiate Knights [*An association*] ... IK
Intercollegiate Musical Council ... IMC
Intercollegiate Opera Group [*Defunct*] ... IOG
Intercollegiate Outing Club Association ... IOCA
Intercollegiate Program of Graduate Studies ... IPGS
Intercollegiate Rowing Association ... IRA
Intercollegiate Soccer Association of America ... ISAA
Intercollegiate Soccer-Football Association of America [*Later, ISAA*] ... ISFAA
Intercollegiate Studies Institute ... ISI
Intercollegiate Tennis Coaches Association ... ITCA
Intercollegiate Women's Fencing Association [*Later, NIWFA*] ... IWFA
Intercolonial Medical Journal of Australasia [*A publication*] ... Intercolon Med J Australas
Intercom ... I/C
Intercomm User Group [*Later, SDAUG*] ... IUG
Intercommunication-Communication Control Group [*Navy*] ... ICCG
Intercommunication Control Station ... ICS
Intercommunication Devices ... ID
Intercommunication Flip-Flop [*Data processing*] ... ICF
Intercommunication System ... INTERCOM
Intercommunications ... IC
Intercommunications System ... ICS
Intercomponent Subcontractor ... ISC
Intercomputer Channel ... IC
Intercomputer Channel ... ICC
Intercomputer Communication ... ICC
Intercomputer Communication System ... ICCS
Interconexion Electrica, Sociedad Anonima ... ISA
Interconnected Business System ... ICBS
Interconnected Porosity Level ... IPL
Interconnected Systems Group ... ISG
Interconnecting Digital-Analog Converter ... IDAC
Interconnecting Station ... IS
Interconnection ... INTCON
Interconnection ... INTERCON
Interconnection Device ... ID
Interconnection Equipment ... IE
Interconnections Packaging Circuitry ... IPC
Intercontinental ... INTCNTL
InterContinental Airways, Inc. [*ICAO designator*] ... IL
Intercontinental Areas (Eastern Hemisphere) [*MARC geographic area code*] [*Library of Congress*] ... m------
Intercontinental Areas (Western Hemisphere) [*MARC geographic area code*] [*Library of Congress*] ... c------
Intercontinental Ballistic Missile ... IBM
Intercontinental Ballistic Missile ... ICBM
Intercontinental Ballistic Missile Operational Capability ... IBMOC
Intercontinental Ballistic Missile System ... ICBMS
Intercontinental Ballistic Transport ... ICBT
Intercontinental Diversified Corp. [*NYSE symbol*] [*Delisted*] ... ICD
Intercontinental Dynamics [*NASDAQ symbol*] ... ICDY
Intercontinental Energy Corporation [*NASDAQ symbol*] ... ICEC
Intercontinental Glide Bomber [*Unmanned*] ... IGB
Intercontinental Glide Missile ... ICGM
Intercontinental Jet Unmanned Bomber ... ICJUB
Intercontinental Life Corporation [*NASDAQ symbol*] ... ILCO
Intercontinental Medical Book Corp. ... IMB

Intercontinental Press [*A publication*]....Intercont
Intercontinental Press Publishing Association....IPPA
Intercontinental Services Corp. [*NASDAQ symbol*]....ICSR
Intercontinental Trailsea Corporation....ITC
Intercontract Material Transfer....ICMT
Intercooler....INCLR
Intercooler....INCOLR
Intercostal [*Between the ribs*] [*Medicine*]....IC
Intercostal Margin [*Anatomy*]....ICM
Intercostal Space [*Medicine*]....ICS
Intercostal Space [*Medicine*]....IS
Intercristo [*An association*]....ICO
Intercultural Action Learning Program....INTERALP
Intercultural Development Research Association....IDRA
Intercylinder....INTCYL
Interdenominational Church Ushers Association....ICUA
Interdenominational Foreign Mission Association of North America....IFMA
Interdenominational Theological Center, Atlanta, GA [*Library symbol*]....GAITh
Interdepartmental....INTDEPT
Interdepartmental....INTERDEPT
Interdepartmental Advisory Committee [*World War II*]....IAC
Interdepartmental Air Traffic Control Board....IATCB
Interdepartmental Committee....IDC
Interdepartmental Committee....INDEC
Interdepartmental Committee on Air Pollution Research [*British*]....ICAPR
Interdepartmental Committee for Atmospheric Sciences....ICAS
Interdepartmental Committee for Atmospheric Sciences. Report. United States [*A publication*]....Interdep Comm Atmos Sci Rep US
Interdepartmental Committee of External Relations [*Canada*]....ICER
Interdepartmental Committee on Internal Security....ICIS
Interdepartmental Committee on Labour Requirements [*British*] [*World War II*]....ICLR
Interdepartmental Committee on Manpower Requirements [*British*] [*World War II*]....MRC
Interdepartmental Committee for Meteorological Services [*National Weather Service*]....ICMS
Interdepartmental Committee on Nutrition for National Defense....ICNND
Interdepartmental Committee on the Status of Women [*Terminated, 1978*]....ICSW
Interdepartmental Committee on Weather Modification [*Military*]....ICWM
Interdepartmental Communication....IDC
Interdepartmental Dial System [*Telephones*]....IDS
Interdepartmental Memo....IM
Interdepartmental Planning Committee on Germany [*US*]....IPCOG
Interdepartmental Procurement Request....IPR
Interdepartmental Radio Advisory Committee [*Aviation*]....IRAC
Interdepartmental Regional Group [*Army*]....IRG
Interdepartmental Savings Bond Committee [*Military*]....ISBC
Interdepartmental Screw Thread Committee [*Departments of Commerce and Defense*]....ISTC
Interdepartmental Work Release Order....IWRO
Interdepartmental Workers' Compensation Task Force [*Department of Labor*]....IWCTF
Interdiction Mission [*Air Force*]....IDM
Interdiction Operations [*Navy*]....INTOPS
Interdigital Transducer [*Physics*]....IDT
Interdisciplinary....ID
Interdisciplinary....INTDISP
Interdisciplinary Committee on Institutes and Conferences....ICIC
Interdisciplinary Communications Program....ICP
Interdisciplinary Essays [*A publication*]....IE
Interdisciplinary Machine Processing for Research and Education in Social Sciences [*Data processing system*] [*Dartmouth College*]....IMPRESS
Interdisciplinary Materials Laboratory [*Various universities*]....IDL
Interdisciplinary Model Programs in the Arts for Children and Teachers....IMPACT
Interdisciplinary Programs in Health [*Harvard University*]....IPH
Interdisciplinary Research Equipment Program....IREP
Interdisciplinary Research Relevant to Problems of Our Society [*Later, RANN*] [*National Science Foundation*]....IRPOS
Interdisciplinary Research Relevant to Problems of Our Society [*Later, RANN*] [*National Science Foundation*]....IRRPOS
Interdisciplinary Science Reviews [*A publication*]....Interdiscip Sci Rev
Interdisciplinary Science Reviews [*A publication*]....ISR
Interdisciplinary Student-Originated Research Training [*National Science Foundation*]....ISORT
Interdisciplinary Team [*Education*]....IDT
Interdisciplinary Topics in Gerontology [*A publication*]....Interdiscip Top Gerontol
Interdisziplinaerer Sonderbereich Umweltschutz. Mitteilungen [*A publication*]....ISU Mitt
Interdivision Invoice....IDI
Interdivision Time [*Cytology*]....IDT
Interdivision Transfer....IDT
Interdivisional Information Unit [*Department of Justice intelligence unit*]....IDIU
Interdivisional Operations [*NASA*]....IDO
Interdivisional Sales Order [*NASA*]....IDSO
Interdivisional Technical Agreement [*NASA*]....IDTA
Interdivisional Work Authorization....IDWA
Interdyne Co. [*NASDAQ symbol*]....IDYN
Interessen Gemeinschaft....IG
Interessen Gemeinschaft der Farbenindustrie Aktiengesellschaft [*A dye trust*] [*Germany*]....IGFA
Interest....INT
Interest Assessment Scales....IAS
Interest-Bearing Eligible Liabilities....IBEL
Interest-Bearing Liability....IBL
Interest Checklist [*US Employment Service*] [*Department of Labor*]....ICL
Interest During Construction....IDC
Interest Equalization Tax....IET
Interest Inventory for Elementary Grades [*Psychology*]....IIEG
Interest by Member of Congress....CONGINT
Interested Future Attorneys Negotiating for Tot Safety [*Student legal action organization*]....INFANTS
Interexchange Mileage....IXC
Interface....I/F
Interface....INF
Interface....INTFC
Interface Agreement Document....IAD
Interface Amplifier....IA
Interface Analysis Document....IAD
Interface Assurance Contractor....IAC
Interface Change Notice....ICN
Interface Compatibility Record....ICR
Interface Control [*or Controller*]....IC
Interface Control Action Request....ICAR
Interface Control Board....ICB
Interface Control Chart....ICC
Interface Control Configuration List....ICCL
Interface Control Document [*Apollo*] [*NASA*]....ICD
Interface Control Documentation Log....ICDL
Interface Control Drawings....ICD
Interface Control Envelope Drawings....ICED
Interface Control Function....ICF
Interface Control Panel....ICP
Interface Control Specification....ICS
Interface Control Tooling....ICT
Interface Control Unit [*Army*]....ICU
Interface Control/Weapon Delivery....ICWD
Interface Control Working Group [*NASA*]....ICWG
Interface Control Working Group Action [*NASA*]....ICWGA
Interface Coordination and Control Procedure....ICCP
Interface Coordination Memo....ICM
Interface Coordinator....IC
Interface Data Sheet....IDS
Interface Definition Document....IDD
Interface Demonstration Unit....IDU
Interface Design Plan [*Air Force*]....IDP
Interface Designation Drawing....IDD
Interface Digital Processor....IDPS
Interface and Display Electronics Assembly....IDEA
Interface Document....ID
Interface Document Control....IDC
Interface Electronics Unit [*NASA*]....IEU
Interface Engineering Change Procedure....IECP
Interface Evaluation Report....IER
Interface Flooring Systems Cl A [*NASDAQ symbol*]....IFSIA
Interface Functional Analysis....IFA
Interface Keying Unit [*Data processing*]....IKU
Interface Management Agent....IMA
Interface Management Plan [*Air Force*]....IMP
Interface Message Processor [*Data processing*]....IMP
Interface Message Processors [*Data processing*]....IMPS
Interface Module....IM
Interface Noise Inverter....INI
Interface and Priority Unit....IPU
Interface Problem Status Log....IPSL
Interface Program Plan....IPP
Interface Requirement List....IRL
Interface Requirements Document....IRD
Interface Revision Notice [*NASA*]....IRN
Interface Signal Chart....ISC
Interface Specification....IFS
Interface Specification Control Document....ISCD
Interface Switching Assembly....ISA
Interface Switching Unit....ISU
Interface Systems [*NASDAQ symbol*]....INTF
Interface Technical Working Group....ITWG
Interface Test Adapters....ITA
Interface Timing Diagram....ITD
Interface Unit....I/FU
Interface Unit....IU
Interface Unit Adapter....IUA
Interface Unit Error Count Table....IUE
Interface Verification Equipment....IVE
Interface Volume....IV
Interface/Weapon Aiming Computer....I/WAC

Interfacial Surface Generation [*Instrumentation*]......................ISG
Interfacial Tension [*Physical chemistry*]......................IFT
Interfacial Test......................IFT
Interfacial Zone......................IZ
Interfacility Communication Network ....IFCN
Interfacility Data [*FAA*]......................IDAT
Interfaith Center on Corporate Responsibility [*Formerly, CIC, ICSRI*]......................ICCR
Interfaith Center to Reverse the Arms Race......................ICRAR
Interfaith Coalition on Energy......................ICE
Interfaith Committee on Social Responsibility in Investments [*Later, ICCR*]......................ICSRI
Interfaith Council for Human Rights......................ICHR
Interfaith Forum on Religion, Art, and Architecture ....IFRAA
Interfaith Hunger Appeal......................IHA
Interfaith Movement......................IM
Interference [*Broadcasting*]......................I
Interference......................INF
Interference......................INTEC
Interference......................INTFC
Interference......................INTFER
Interference......................INTFR
Interference......................INTRF
Interference Blanking Unit......................IBU
Interference Control Monitor......................ICM
Interference Detection and Interdiction Countermeasures Team [*Electromagnetic compatibility programs*]......................INTERDICT
Interference Frequency Rejection Unit [*Military*]......................IFRU
Interference Guard Bands......................IGB
Interference-to-Noise Ratio......................IN
Interference-to-Noise Ratio......................INR
Interference Prediction Model......................IPM
Interference Reporting Point......................IRP
Interference Suppressor......................IS
Interference Technology Engineer's Master......................ITEM
Interference Unit [*Military*]......................IU
Interferometer......................INTERF
Interferometer and Doppler......................ID
Interferometric LASER Source......................ILS
Interferon [*Also, IFN*] [*Biochemistry*]......................IF
Interferon [*Also, IF*] [*Biochemistry*]......................IFN
Interferon Foundation......................IF
Interferon Reference Unit......................IRU
Interferon Sciences [*NASDAQ symbol*]......................IFSC
Interfiber Distance......................IFD
InterFirst Corporation [*NYSE symbol*]......................IFC
Interflug, Gesellschaft fuer Internationalen Flugverkehr mbH [*Germany*] [*ICAO designator*]......................IF
Interfraternity Research and Advisory Council......................IRAC
Interfuture [*An association*]......................IF
Intergem, Inc. [*NASDAQ symbol*]......................IGEM
Intergovernmental......................INTERGOVT
Intergovernmental Affairs Fellowship Program......................IAFP
Intergovernmental Bureau for Informatics......................IBI
Intergovernmental Committee for European Migration [*Later, ICM*]......................ICEM
Intergovernmental Committee for Migration [*Formerly, ICEM*]......................ICM
Intergovernmental Committee on Refugees [*Post-World War II*]......................IGCR
Intergovernmental Conference on Oceanic Research......................ICOR
Intergovernmental Conference on Oceanographic Research ....INCOR
Intergovernmental Copyright Committee [*See also CIDA*]......................IGC
Intergovernmental Copyright Committee......................IGCC
Intergovernmental Council for ADP [*Automatic Data Processing*]......................ICA
Intergovernmental Council for the International Hydrological Programme......................IHP
Intergovernmental Health Policy Project......................IHPP
Intergovernmental Maritime Consultative Organization......................IMCO
Intergovernmental Oceanographic Commission [*See also COI*]......................IOC
Intergovernmental Oceanographic Commission - Bureau and Consultative Council [*UNESCO*]......................IOC/B & CC
Intergovernmental Oceanographic Commission. Technical Series [*A publication*]......................Intergov Oceanogr Comm Tech Ser
Intergovernmental Organization [*Generic term*]......................IGO
Intergovernmental Personnel Act [*1970*]......................IPA
Intergovernmental Perspective [*A publication*]......................Intergov Persp
Intergovernmental Refugee Committee [*London*] [*World War II*]......................IRC
Intergovernmental Science, Engineering, and Technology Advisory Panel [*National Science Foundation*]......................ISETAP
Intergovernmental Science Programs......................ISP
Intergovernmental Science and Public Technology [*of ASRA*] [*National Science Foundation*]......................ISPT
Intergovernmental Science and Research Utilization [*National Science Foundation*]......................ISRU
Intergovernmental Working Group [*United Nations*]......................IWG
Intergovernmental Working Group on Marine Pollution [*Inter-Governmental Maritime Consultative Organization*]......................IWGMP
Intergovernmental Working Group on Monitoring or Surveillance [*United Nations*]......................IWGM
Intergranular Attack [*Nuclear energy*]......................IGA
Intergranular Stress-Corrosion Cracking [*Plant engineering*]......................IGSCC
Intergraph Corp. [*NASDAQ symbol*]......................INGR
Intergroup Rhabdomyosarcoma Study [*Oncology*]......................IRS

Interim......................INT
Interim Acceptance Criteria......................IAC
Interim Access Authorization......................IAA
Interim Accessory Change......................IAYC
Interim Air Defense Weapon System [*Army*]......................IADWS
Interim Airframe Bulletin......................IAB
Interim Airframe Bulletin......................IAFB
Interim Airframe Change......................IAFC
Interim Amphibious Refresher Training [*Navy*]......................INTPHIBRFT
Interim Antenna Pointing Subsystem [*Deep Space Instrumentation Facility, NASA*]......................IAPS
Interim Antiradiation Missile......................IARM
Interim Armament Bulletin......................IAB
Interim Ballistic Instrumentation......................IBI
Interim Bomber Defense Missile......................IBDM
Interim Cargo Integration Operations ....ICIO
Interim Cargo Integrator......................ICI
Interim Catalog Module [*MEDLARS*]......................ICM
Interim Change......................IC
Interim Change Bulletin......................ICB
Interim Change Notice......................ICN
Interim Checkout Device......................ICD
Interim Circuit Order Control System [*Bell System*]......................ICOCS
Interim Co-ordinating Committee for International Commodity Arrangements......................ICCICA
Interim Command and Control System......................ICCS
Interim Command Switchboard [*Navy*]......................ICSB
Interim Commission......................IC
Interim Commission of the International Refugee Organization ....ICIRO
Interim Commission for the International Trade Organization......................ICITO
Interim Committee......................IC
Interim Communications Satellite Committee......................ICSC
Interim Contractor Support......................ICS
Interim Daily System Operational Test [*Navy*]......................IDSOT
Interim Data Communications Collection Center......................IDCCC
Interim Data Element [*Army*]......................IDE
Interim Decay Storage [*Nuclear energy*]......................IDS
Interim Decisions of the Department of Justice......................IDDJ
Interim Depot Repair......................IDR
Interim Development Report......................IDR
Interim Digital-Analog Converter......................IDAC
Interim Drydocking [*Navy*]......................IDD
Interim Engineering Order......................IEO
Interim Engineering Report......................IER
Interim Equipment Order Control System [*Bell System*]......................IEOCS
Interim Examination and Maintenance [*Nuclear energy*]......................IEM
Interim Examination and Maintenance Training Facility [*Nuclear energy*]......................IEMTF
Interim Expendable Emitter......................IEE
Interim Functional Alternate......................IFA
Interim Geophysical Data Record [*From spacecraft data*]......................IGDR
Interim Housing Allowance [*Military*]......................IHA
Interim Hypersonics Test Vehicle [*NASA*]......................IHTV
Interim Impact Predictor......................IIP
Interim Integrated Aircraft Instrumentation and Letdown System ....IIAILS
Interim International Information Service [*World War II*]......................IIIS
Interim Logistics Support Guide......................ILSG
Interim Low-Altitude Air Defense System......................ILAADS
Interim Maintenance Engineering Order......................IMEO
Interim Manpower Maintenance System......................IMMS
Interim Memorandum......................IM
Interim Meteorological Satellite......................IMS
Interim Military Microwave Landing System......................IMMLS
Interim Missile Guidance Test......................IMGT
Interim Monitoring Program......................IMP
Interim Narrow-Band Secure Voice......................INBSV
Interim National Space Surveillance Control Center ....INSSCC
Interim Operating Instructions......................IOI
Interim Operating Procedure ....IOP
Interim Operation Meteorological System......................IOMS
Interim Operational Capability......................IOC
Interim Operational System......................IOS
Interim Parts List [*Navy*]......................IPL
Interim Policy Statement......................IPS
Interim POMSEE [*Performance, Operating, and Maintenance Standards for Electronic Equipment*] Sheet ....IPS
Interim Problem Report......................IPR
Interim Progress Report......................IPR
Interim Range Operations ....IRO
Interim Rapid Action Change......................IRAC
Interim Refresher Training [*Navy*]......................INTRFT
Interim Refresher Training [*Navy*]......................IRFT
Interim Release Request......................IRR
Interim Reliability Evaluation Program [*Nuclear energy*]......................IREP
Interim Remote Area Terminal Equipment [*Air Force*]......................IRATE
Interim Repair Parts List......................IRPL
Interim Report......................IR
Interim Research Memo......................IRM
Interim Scientific and Management Group......................ISMG
Interim Scientific Report......................ISR
Interim Sea Control Ship......................ISCS

Interim Shipboard Availability	INSAV
Interim Shipyard Availability	INSAV
Interim Spare Parts List	ISPL
Interim Standard Airborne Digital Computer	ISADC
Interim Standard Microwave Landing System [Aviation]	ISMLS
Interim Standard Set	ISS
Interim Stowage Assembly	ISA
Interim Stowage Shelf	ISS
Interim Support Items List	ISIL
Interim Surface-to-Surface Missile System	ISSMS
Interim Tactical ELINT Processor	ITEP
Interim Tactical Information Processing and Interpretation	ITIPI
Interim Target Acquisition and Designation System	ITAADS
Interim Technical Memorandum	ITM
Interim Technical Note	ITN
Interim Technical Order	ITO
Interim Technical Order Field Change Notice [Air Force]	ITOFCN
Interim Technical Report	ITR
Interim Terminal Test Environment [FAA]	ITTE
Interim Test Procedure	ITP
Interim Test Report	ITR
Interim Towed Array Surveillance System [Military]	ITASS
Interim Training Program [Army]	ITP
Interim Use Item	IUI
Interim Use Material	IUM
Interim Use Material Authorization	IUMA
Interim Water Velocity Meter Test Set	IWVMTS
Interionic Attraction Theory	IAT
Interior	INT
Interior	INTR
Interior Ballistic Division [Ballistic Research Laboratory] [Army]	IBD
Interior Ballistics Laboratory [Aberdeen, MD] [Army]	IBL
Interior Committee on Research and Development	ICRD
Interior Communication	IC
Interior Communication and Fire Control Distribution	IC & FCD
Interior Communications Electrician [Navy rating]	IC
Interior Communications Electrician, Chief [Navy rating]	ICC
Interior Communications Electrician, First Class [Navy rating]	IC1
Interior Communications Electrician, Second Class [Navy rating]	IC2
Interior Communications Electrician, Third Class [Navy rating]	IC3
Interior Communications Switchboard	ICSWBD
Interior Control Board	ICB
Interior Department	ID
Interior Design [A publication]	Int Des
Interior Design [A publication]	Inter Des
Interior Design [A publication]	Interior Des
Interior Design Educators Council	IDEC
Interior Design Society	IDS
Interior Electromagnetic Pulse	IEMP
Interior and Insular Affairs	I & IA
Interior Landscape [An association]	IL
Interior Ministerial Real Estate Committee [Vietnam]	IMREC
Interior Plantscape Association	IPA
Interior Procurement Regulations [Department of the Interior]	IPR
Interior Surface	IS
Interior Upper Stage	IUS
Interior Voice Communications System	IVCS
Interiors [A publication]	Inter
Interiors Engineering and Industrial Design	IE & ID
Interjection	INT
Interjection	INTERJ
Interlaboratory Air-to-Air Missile Technology	ILAAT
Interlaced	INTRLCD
Interlake Development [NASDAQ symbol]	ILDCF
Interlake, Inc. [NYSE symbol]	IK
Interlake Sailing Class Association	ISCA
Interlake School, Staff Library, Medical Lake, WA [Library symbol]	WaMel
Interlaminar Adhesive Layer	IAL
Interleaver	INTLVR
Interleukin-2, Inc. [NASDAQ symbol]	ILTO
Interlibrary Delivery Service of Pennsylvania [Library network]	IDS
Interlibrary Loan	ILL
Interlibrary Network of Baltimore County [Library network]	INBC
Interlibrary Users Association [Library network]	IUA
Interline	IL
Interlingua [MARC language code] [Library of Congress]	int
Interlingua Institute	II
Interlingue Union	IU
Interlinked Computerized Storage and Processing System of Food and Agricultural Data [United Nations] [Information service]	ICS
Interlochen Center for the Arts	ICA
Interlochen, MI [Radio station call letters]	WIAA
Interlock	INTLK
Interlocked	INTRLKD
Interlocked Grain Index [Botany]	IGI
Interlocked Metallic Armor [Technical drawings]	I
Interlocking Paving Manufacturers Association	IPMA
Interlook Dormant Period	ILDP
Interloop Heat Exchanger [NASA]	IHX
Interlutheran Theological Seminary and Bible School, Minneapolis, MN [Library symbol]	MnMI

Intermagnetics General Corporation	IGC
Intermagnetics General Corp. [NASDAQ symbol]	INMA
Intermark, Incorporated [American Stock Exchange symbol]	IMI
Intermarket Association of Advertising Agencies	IAAA
Intermec Corp. [NASDAQ symbol]	INTR
Intermedco, Inc. [American Stock Exchange symbol] [Delisted]	ITM
Intermediaire des Chercheurs et des Curieux [A publication]	ICC
Intermediary Letter	IL
Intermediate [Car size]	I
Intermediate	INT
Intermediate	INTER
Intermediate	INTM
Intermediate	INTMD
Intermediate	INTMED
Intermediate [Vessel load line mark]	I
Intermediate Air Command [Air Force]	IAC
Intermediate Altitude Sounding Rocket	IASR
Intermediate BTU [British Thermal Unit] Gas	IBG
Intermediate Bulk Containers [Transportation]	IBC
Intermediate Cable Equalizers	ICE
Intermediate Capacity Automated Telecommunications System [Air Force]	ICATS
Intermediate Care Facility [Medicine]	ICF
Intermediate Care Facility for the Mentally Retarded	ICFMR
Intermediate Care Unit	ICU
Intermediate Configuration Control Board [Western Electric]	ICCB
Intermediate Coronary Care Unit [Medicine]	ICCU
Intermediate Current Stability Experiment	ICSE
Intermediate Density Lipoprotein [Biochemistry]	IDL
Intermediate Description	ID
Intermediate Design Review	IDR
Intermediate Distributing Frame	IDF
Intermediate Drum Storage	IDS
Intermediate Education Unit	IEU
Intermediate Erection	IE
Intermediate Examiner Training School [Federal Home Loan Bank Board]	IETS
Intermediate Fix	IF
Intermediate Flush and Fill	IF & F
Intermediate Focal Length Optical Tracker	IFLOT
Intermediate Focal Length Tracking Telescope	IFLTT
Intermediate Frame Memory [Data processing]	IFM
Intermediate Frequency [Electronics]	IF
Intermediate Frequency Amplifier [or Attenuator]	IFA
Intermediate Frequency Crystal Filter	IFCF
Intermediate Frequency/Medium Frequency	IF/MF
Intermediate Frequency Range	IFR
Intermediate Frequency Strip	IFS
Intermediate Frequency Time Averaged Clutter Coherent Airborne RADAR	IF TACCAR
Intermediate Frequency Transformer	IFT
Intermediate Frequency Video Microwave	IFVM
Intermediate Heat Exchanger [Nuclear energy]	IHE
Intermediate Heat Exchanger [Nuclear energy]	IHX
Intermediate Heat Exchanger Guard Vessel [Nuclear energy]	IHXGV
Intermediate Heat Transport System [Nuclear energy]	IHTS
Intermediate Infrared	IIR
Intermediate Intensive Care Unit [Medicine]	IICU
Intermediate Intercontinental Ballistic Missile	IICBM
Intermediate Language [Data processing]	IL
Intermediate Language Processor [Data processing]	ILP
Intermediare Level Avionics Support System	ILASS
Intermediate-Level Maintenance Training	ILMT
Intermediate Level Test Station	ILTS
Intermediate-Level Wastes	ILW
Intermediate Long-Range Interceptor System	ILRIS
Intermediate Loop	IL
Intermediate Lymphocytic Lymphoma [Medicine]	ILL
Intermediate Maintenance	IM
Intermediate Maintenance Activity	IMA
Intermediate Maintenance Availability	IMAV
Intermediate Maintenance Facility	IMF
Intermediate Maintenance Level	IML
Intermediate Maintenance Repair Level	IMRL
Intermediate Maintenance Requirements List	IMRL
Intermediate Maintenance Squadron	IMS
Intermediate Manned Interceptor	IMI
Intermediate Missile	IM
Intermediate Modulation	IM
Intermediate Moisture	IM
Intermediate Moisture Food	IMF
Intermediate Neglect of Differential Overlap [Quantum mechanics]	INDO
Intermediate Nuclear Force [Negotiations]	INF
Intermediate Objective Lens	IOL
Intermediate and Organizational Maintenance	I & OM
Intermediate Pallet	IP
Intermediate Payload Launch Vehicle	IPLV
Intermediate Postsurgical Fitting [Medicine]	IPSF
Intermediate Power Amplifier [Electronics]	IPA
Intermediate Pressure	IP
Intermediate Processing Centers	IPC

Intermediate Query Language [*Data processing*] ... IQL
Intermediate Range ... IR
Intermediate-Range Ballistic Missile ... IRBM
Intermediate-Range Intercontinental Ballistic Missile ... IRICBM
Intermediate-Range/Medium-Range Ballistic Missile ... IR/MRBM
Intermediate Range Monitor ... IRM
Intermediate-Range Nuclear Forces ... INF
Intermediate-Range Task Force ... IRTF
Intermediate Reference Structure ... IRS
Intermediate Related Power ... IRP
Intermediate Retention of Differential Overlap [*Physics*] ... IRDO
Intermediate Review ... IR
Intermediate Scale Facility [*Department of Energy*] ... ISF
Intermediate Scale Homogeneous Reactor ... ISHR
Intermediate Scale Warfare ... ISW
Intermediate School ... IS
Intermediate School District 101, Professional Materials Library, Spokane, WA [*Library symbol*] ... WaSpIn
Intermediate School District 113, Instructional Materials Center, Galvin, WA [*Library symbol*] ... WaGal
Intermediate Science Curriculum Study ... ISCS
Intermediate Section ... INTERSEC
Intermediate Service School [*Military*] ... ISS
(Intermediate) Shaft Horsepower ... (I)SHP
Intermediate Sideband ... ISB
Intermediate Slope [*Skiing*] ... I
Intermediate Sodium Disposal Facility [*Nuclear energy*] ... ISDF
Intermediate Specific Activity [*Radioisotope*] ... ISA
Intermediate Staging Base ... ISB
Intermediate Station ... INTERMSTA
Intermediate Super-Abrasion Furnace ... ISAF
Intermediate Support Base [*Military*] ... ISB
Intermediate Tape Store ... ITS
Intermediate Technology [*ITDG*] [*British*] ... IT
Intermediate Technology Development Group [*British*] ... ITDG
Intermediate Technology Development Group of North America ... ITDGNA
Intermediate Technology Industrial Services [*ITDG*] [*British*] ... IT-IS
Intermediate Test Facility ... ITF
Intermediate Thrust Arc ... ITA
Intermediate Training [*Naval Air*] ... INTERMTRA
Intermediate Transmission Block [*Data processing*] ... ITB
Intermediate Treatment [*Special provision of British law for juvenile offenders*] ... IT
Intermediate Upper Stage ... IUS
Intermediate Vector Boson [*Physics*] ... IVB
Intermediate Voltage ... IV
Intermediate Water Depth ... IWD
Intermediate Water Depth Mine ... IWDM
Intermediate Zone Yaw ... IZY
Intermedics, Inc. [*NYSE symbol*] ... ITM
Interment ... INTRMT
Interment Association of America [*Later, PIAA*] ... IAA
Interment Exchange of America ... IEA
Interment Is Authorized for the Remains Of [*Military*] ... IAR
Intermetrics [*NASDAQ symbol*] ... IMET
Intermittent ... INT
Intermittent ... INTER
Intermittent ... INTMT
Intermittent ... INTR
Intermittent Aortic Occlusion [*Cardiology*] ... IAO
Intermittent Bladder Irrigation [*Medicine*] ... IBI
Intermittent Commercial and Amateur Service [*Radio*] ... ICAS
Intermittent Demand Ventilation [*Medicine*] ... IDV
Intermittent Drive Unit ... IDU
Intermittent-Duty Rating ... IDR
Intermittent Instruments [*Aviation*] ... I/IFR
Intermittent Mandatory Ventilation [*Respiratory therapy*] [*Medicine*] ... IMV
Intermittent Motion Driver ... IMD
Intermittent Noise ... IN
Intermittent Operation during the Time Indicated [*Broadcasting*] ... I
Intermittent Peritoneal Dialysis [*Medicine*] ... IPD
Intermittent Positive Control [*Aviation*] ... IPC
Intermittent Positive Pressure Breathing [*Medicine*] ... IPPB
Intermittent Positive Pressure Breathing/Inspiratory ... IPPB/I
Intermittent Positive Pressure Respiration ... IPPR
Intermittent Positive Pressure Ventilation ... IPPV
Intermittent Reinforcement [*Psychology*] ... IRF
Intermodal Transportation Association ... ITA
Intermodulation ... IM
Intermodulation Distortion ... ID
Intermodulation Distortion ... IMD
Intermodulation Distortion Percentage ... IDP
Intermodulation Product ... IMP
Intermountain Aviation, Inc. [*Air carrier designation symbol*] ... ITAX
Intermountain Explorations [*NASDAQ symbol*] ... INTM
Intermountain Field Operations Center [*Bureau of Mines*] ... IFOC
Intermountain Gas [*NASDAQ symbol*] ... INMT
Intermountain Laboratories [*NASDAQ symbol*] ... IMLB
Intermountain Region [*Aviation*] ... INTRMTRGN
Intermountain Tariff Bureau, Inc. ... ITB
Intermountain Tariff Bureau, Inc., Salt Lake City UT [*STAC*] ... IMB
Intermountain Veterinary Medical Association ... IVMA
Intermuseum Conservation Association ... ICA
Internacia Asocio Monda Turismo [*International Association for World Tourism*] ... MT
Internacia Esperanto-Asocio de Bibliotekistoj [*International Association of Esperanto-Speaking Librarians*] [*Defunct*] ... IEAB
Internacia Esperanto-Asocio de Juristoj [*International Esperanto-Association of Jurists*] ... IEAJ
Internacia Esperanto Klubo Automobilista [*International Automobile Esperanto Club*] ... IEKA
Internacia Fervojista Esperanto Federacio [*International Federation of Esperantist Railwaymen*] ... IFEF
Internacia Katolica Unuigo Esperantista [*International Catholic Esperanto Union*] ... IKUE
Internacia Komitato por Etnaj Liberecoj [*International Committee for Ethnic Liberty - ICEL*] ... IKEL
Internacia Ligo de Esperantistaj Foto-Kino-Magnetofon-Amatoroj [*International League of Esperantist Amateur Photographers, Cinephotographers, and Tape-Recording*] ... ILEF
Internacia Ligo de Esperantistaj Instruistoj ... ILEI
Internacia Naturist Organizo Esperantista [*International Esperantist Organization of Naturalists - IEON*] ... INOE
Internacia Pedagogia Recuo [*A publication*] ... IPR
Internacia Scienca Asocio Esperantista [*International Association of Esperanto-Speaking Scientists*] ... ISAE
Internacia Socio de Juristoj-Esperantistoj [*International Association of Esperantist Lawyers*] ... IAJE
Internacia Unuigo de la Esperantistoj-Filologoj [*International Society of Esperantist-Philologists - ISEP*] ... IUEFI
Internacional de Aviacion [*Panama*] [*ICAO designator*] ... IX
Internal ... I
Internal ... INT
Internal ... INTER
Internal ... INTERN
Internal ... INTL
Internal ... INTR
Internal Absorbed Dose ... IAD
Internal Air Portability ... IAP
Internal Alignment Sensor ... IAS
Internal Audit ... IA
Internal Auditor [*A publication*] ... Auditor
Internal Auditor [*A publication*] ... Int Aud
Internal Auditor [*A publication*] ... Int Auditor
Internal Automation Operation ... IAO
Internal Bearing Stabilized Sighting Unit ... IBSSU
Internal Change Identifier ... ICI
Internal Combustion ... IC
Internal Combustion [*Freight*] ... INTL COMB
Internal Combustion Engine ... ICE
Internal Combustion Engine Institute [*Later, EMA*] ... ICEI
Internal Combustion Engine Repair Ship [*Navy symbol*] ... ARG
Internal Communication System [*Space Flight Operations Facility, NASA*] ... ICS
Internal Connection [*Electronics*] ... IC
Internal Conversion Coefficient [*Radiology*] ... ICC
Internal Coordination Control Drawing ... ICCD
Internal Correction Voltage ... ICV
Internal Countermeasures Set ... ICS
Internal Data Requirement Description ... IDRD
Internal Defense and Development [*Army*] ... IDAD
Internal Defense Plans ... IDP
Internal Delay Factor [*Data processing*] ... IDF
Internal Derangement of Knee Joint ... IDK
Internal Development and Assistance Program ... IDAP
Internal Development Report ... IDR
Internal Diameter ... ID
Internal Distribution Publication [*Navy*] ... IDP
Internal Distribution System [*Television*] ... IDS
Internal Document Control ... IDC
Internal Dose Information Center [*ORNL*] ... IDIC
Internal Economic Problems [*British*] ... IEP
Internal Economic Rate of Return ... IER
Internal Elastica [*Artery anatomy*] ... IE
Internal Electronic Countermeasure ... IECM
Internal Energy [*Symbol*] [*Thermodynamics*] ... U
Internal Environment ... IE
Internal Environment Monitoring ... IEM
Internal Environment Simulator ... IES
Internal Feed Rate Override ... IFRO
Internal Field Emission ... IFE
Internal Function Register ... IFR
Internal Gamma Flux Monitor ... IGFM
Internal Gravity Wave [*in the atmosphere*] ... IGW
Internal Guidance ... IG
Internal Locus of Control [*Psychology*] ... ILC
Internal Macedonian Revolutionary Organization [*World War II*] ... IMRO
Internal Magnetic Focus ... IMF
Internal Measuring Unit System ... IMUS
Internal Medicine ... IM
Internal Medicine ... INTMED
Internal Memorandum ... IM

Internal Message Distribution Center................................ IMDC
Internal Messenger Service [Hotels]............................... INTMS
Internal-Mix Nozzle.. IMN
Internal-Mix Spray Nozzle.. IMSN
Internal Navigation System... INS
Internal Noise Level.. INL
Internal Note... IN
Internal Operating Budget... IOB
Internal Operating Instruction.. IOI
Internal Operating Procedure.. IOP
Internal Pipe Thread... IPT
Internal Polarization Modulation................................... IPM
Internal Progress Report... IPR
Internal Quality.. IQ
Internal Rate of Return [Finance].................................. IRR
Internal Reference Number.. IRN
Internal Reflection Technique.. IRT
Internal Regenerative... INTEREGEN
Internal Reliability.. IR
Internal REM [Roentgen-Equivalent-Man] [Radiation dose] .... INREM
Internal Repeat [Genetics].. IR
Internal Report... IR
Internal Resistance.. IR
Internal Revenue.. IR
Internal Revenue Act... IRA
Internal Revenue Bulletin.. IRB
Internal Revenue Code.. IRC
Internal Revenue Department.. IRD
Internal Revenue Looseleaf Regulations System........... IRR
Internal Revenue Office [or Officer].............................. IRO
Internal Revenue Service [Department of the Treasury]...... IRS
Internal Revenue Service Centers............................... IRSC
Internal Revenue Service Library, Washington, DC [OCLC symbol]........ IRS
Internal Review [Army]... IR
Internal Review and Audit Compliance [Army] ....IR & AC
Internal Review and System Improvement [Army].......... IRASI
Internal Scientific Report... ISR
Internal Security.. INSEC
Internal Security [Military] [British].................................. IS
Internal Security Division [Abolished 1973; functions transferred
    to Criminal Division] [Department of Justice].............. ISD
Internal Security Plan... ISP
Internal Shape Components.. INSC
Internal Shield [Electronics].. IS
Internal Shutter Grid.. ISG
Internal Standard [Chemistry].. IS
Internal Standard Line.. ISL
Internal Surface... IS
Internal Switching System... ISS
Internal Technical Memorandum................................... ITM
Internal Technical Report.. ITR
Internal Test Directive.. ITD
Internal Thread... IT
Internal Translation Information Subsystem [Data processing]............. ITIS
Internal Translator.. IT
Internal Transmittance [Symbol] [IUPAC]........................ T
Internal Triangular Hinge Ligament [of scallops] .... ITHL
Internal Variable... IVAR
Internal Vibration Isolator... IVI
Internal Visual Reference [Motion sickness]................... IVR
Internal Working Paper... IWP
Internally Blown Flap [Aviation]..................................... IBF
Internally Linked Operation... ILO
Internally Specified Index.. ISI
Internally Stored Program... ISP
Internasjonal Politikk (Bergen) [A publication] ....Int Polit (Bergen)
Internasjonal Politikk (Oslo) [A publication].......... Int Polit (O)
Internationaal Tijdschrift voor Brouwertj en Mouterij [A
    publication]............................Int Tijdschr Brouw Mout
International I
International .... INT
International .... INTERN
International .... INTERNAT
International .... INTL
International Abolitionist Federation.............................. IAF
International Abstaining Motorists' Association............ IAMA
International Abstracting Board [Also, ICSU AB] [International
    Council of Scientific Unions].................................... IAB
International Abstracts of Biological Sciences [A publication] .... IABS
International Abstracts of Biological Sciences [A publication]
                                                        Int Abstr Biol Sci
International Abstracts in Operations Research [A publication]............ IAOR
International Abstracts in Operations Research [A publication]
                                                        Int Abstr Oper Res
International Academy of Astronautics............................ IAA
International Academy of Aviation and Space Medicine......IAASM
International Academy of Biological Medicine.............. IABM
International Academy of Ceramics [See also AIC]........ IAC
International Academy of Chest Physicians and Surgeons ...... IACPS
International Academy of Cosmetic Surgery................ IACS
International Academy of Cytology................................ IAC

International Academy of the History of Medicine............ IAHM
International Academy of History of Sciences.............. IAHS
International Academy of Management........................... IAM
International Academy of Metabology............................ IAM
International Academy of Myodontics............................ IAM
International Academy of Nutritional Consultants........ IANC
International Academy of Optimum Dentistry.............. IAOD
International Academy of Pathology.............................. IAP
International Academy of Pathology. Monograph [A publication]...........
                                            Int Acad Pathol Monogr
International Academy of Preventive Medicine............. IAPM
International Academy of Proctology.............................. IAP
International Academy for Quality.................................. IAQ
International Academy at Santa Barbara [Formerly, ISSI].....IASB
International Academy of Trial Lawyers......................... IATL
International Academy of Twirling Teachers................ IATT
International Accountants Society.................................. IAS
International Accounting Standards Committee.......... IASC
International Accounting Studies Institute................ INTASI
International Acetylene Association [Later, CGA].......... IAA
International Acronyms, Initialisms, and Abbreviations
    Dictionary [A publication]..................................... IAIAD
International Active Sun Years...................................... IASY
International Activities Committee [American Chemical Society]........... IAC
International Actuarial Association................................. IAA
International Administrative Aeronautical Radio Conference..........IAARC
International Advanced Life Information System........ INTERALIS
International Advanced Microlithography Society....... IAMS
International Advances in Nondestructive Testing [A
    publication]...........................Int Adv Nondestr Test
International Advances in Surgical Oncology [A publication]..................
                                                Int Adv Surg Oncol
International Advertiser [A publication]................Int Advertiser
International Advertising Association [Later, AAF]........... IAA
International Advisory Committee [ANSI]........................ IAC
International Advisory Committee on Documentation, Libraries,
    and Archives [UNESCO]....................................... IACDLA
International Advisory Committee on Marine Sciences..........IACOMS
International Aero Press... IAP
International Aerobatic Club... IAC
International Aeronautical Federation............................ IAF
International Aeronautical Telecommunications Switching
    Center.. IATSC
International Aerosol Association................................... IAA
International Aerospace Abstracts [A publication]........... IAA
International Aerospace Abstracts [A publication]......... IntAe
International Affairs [A publication] .... iA
International Affairs [A publication]................................. Int Aff
International Affairs (London) [A publication]....... Int Aff (London)
International Affairs (Moscow) [A publication].............. IAM
International Affairs. Studies [A publication].......... Int Aff Stud
International Affiliation of Independent Accounting Firms........IAIAF
International African Institute... IAI
International African Law Association.......................... IALA
International Afro-American Museum [Later, AAM]......... IAM
International Afroid Science Conference....................... IASC
International Agency for Research on Cancer............... IARC
International Agricultural Aviation Centre [Defunct]...... IAAC
International Agricultural Aviation Foundation............. IAAF
International Agricultural Development Service [Department of
    Agriculture]... IADS
International Agricultural Exchange Association........... IAEA
International Agricultural Research Center.................... IARC
International Agricultural Students Association of the Americas.......IASAA
International Aikido Federation....................................... IAF
International Air Bahama [ICAO designator] .... IW
International Air Cadet Exchange.................................. IACE
International Air Cargo Corporation [ICAO designator]........ CC
International Air Carrier Association............................. IACA
International Air Convention.. IAC
International Air Freight Forwarder.............................. IAFF
International Air Line Stewards and Stewardesses Association......IALSSA
International Air Safety Association............................. IASA
International Air Safety Seminar................................... IASS
International Air Service Co. [Napa, CA] [FAA designator]......... IAS
International Air Traffic Communications.................... IATC
International Air Traffic Communications Receiver Station........IATCR
International Air Traffic Communications Station........ IATCS
International Air Traffic Communications System...... IATCS
International Air Traffic Communications Transmitter Station.......IATCT
International Air Transport [formerly, Traffic] Association .... IATA
International Air Transport Association, Montreal, PQ, Canada
    [Library symbol].. CaQMIA
International Aircraft Leasing Company..................... IALCO
International Airforwarder and Agents Association...... IAAA
International Airline Navigators Council [Defunct]....... IANC
International Airline Passengers Association................ APA
International Airline Passengers Association............... IAPA
International Airport... IAP
International Airport Characteristics Data Bank [International
    Civil Aviation Organization] [Information service]....... ACDB

International Al Jolson Society .... IAJS
International Algebraic Compiler .... IAC
International Algebraic Language [*Replaced by ALGOL*] .... IAL
International Algorithmic Language [*Data processing*] .... IAL
International Alliance of Bill Posters, Billers, and Distributors of US and Canada [*Defunct*] .... BPBD
International Alliance of Bill Posters, Billers, and Distributors of US and Canada [*Defunct*] .... IABPBD
International Alliance of Film Producers [*Later, IAIP*] .... IAFP
International Alliance of Theatrical Stage Employees and Moving Picture Machine Operators of the United States and Canada [*Also, IATSE*] .... IA
International Alliance of Theatrical Stage Employees and Moving Picture Machine Operators of the United States and Canada [*Also, IA*] .... IATSE
International Alliance of Women [*See also AIF*] .... IAW
International Allied Printing Trades Association .... IAPTA
International Alphabet .... IA
International Aluminum Corp. [*NYSE symbol*] .... IAL
International Amateur Athletic Federation [*See also FIAA*] .... IAAF
International Amateur Boat Building Society [*Defunct*] .... IABBS
International Amateur Boxing Association .... IABA
International Amateur Cycling Federation .... IACF
International Amateur Karate Federation .... IAKF
International Amateur Radio Union .... IARU
International Amateur Surfing Federation .... IASF
International Amateur Swimming Federation .... IASF
International Amateur Theatre Association .... IATA
International American Saddlebred Pleasure Horse Association .... IASPHA
International Analysis Code [*Meteorology*] .... IAC
International Anatomical Nomenclature Committee .... IANC
International Anesthesia Research Society .... IARS
International Anesthesiology Clinics [*A publication*] .... Anesthesiol Clin
International Anesthesiology Clinics [*A publication*] .... Int Anesthesiol Clin
International Angstrom .... IA
International Animated Film Society .... IAFS
International Annealed Copper Standard .... IACS
International Antarctic Glaciological Project .... IAGP
International Anthropological and Linguistic Review [*A publication*] .... IALR
International Anti-Counterfeiting Coalition .... IAC
International Apple Association [*Later, IAI*] .... IAA
International Apple Institute .... IAI
International Arab Federation .... IAF
International Arabian Horse Association .... IAHA
International Archery Federation .... IAF
International Archives of Allergy and Applied Immunology [*A publication*] .... IAOHD
International Archives of Allergy and Applied Immunology [*A publication*] .... Int A Aller
International Archives of Allergy and Applied Immunology [*A publication*] .... Int Arch Allergy Appl Immunol
International Archives of the History of Ideas [*A publication*] .... IAHI
International Archives of Occupational and Environmental Health [*A publication*] .... Int A Occup
International Archives of Occupational and Environmental Health [*A publication*] .... Int Arch Occup Environ Health
International Archives of Occupational Health [*A publication*] .... Int Arch Occup Health
International Archives of Photogrammetry [*A publication*] .... Int Arch Photogramm
International Arms-Control Symposium .... IACS
International Aroid Society .... IAS
International Art Register .... IAR
International Arthur Schnitzler Research Association .... IASRA
International Artists' Cooperation .... IAC
International Arts Relations .... INTAR
International Arts and Sciences Press .... IASP
International Association of Accident and Health Underwriters [*Later, NAHU*] .... IAAHU
International Association for Accident and Traffic Medicine .... IAATM
International Association for Advancement of Appropriate Technology for Developing Countries .... IAAATDC
International Association for the Advancement of Earth and Environmental Sciences .... IAAEES
International Association for the Advancement of Educational Research .... IAAER
International Association Against Painful Experiments on Animals .... IAAPEA
International Association of Agricultural Economists .... IAAE
International Association of Agricultural Librarians and Documentalists .... IAALD
International Association of Agricultural Librarians and Documentalists. Quarterly Bulletin [*A publication*] .... IAALD Q Bull
International Association of Agricultural Medicine and Rural Health .... AAMRH
International Association of Agricultural Students [*See also AIEA*] .... IAAS
International Association of Aircraft Brokers and Agents .... IABA
International Association of Allergology [*Later, IAACI*] .... IAA
International Association of Allergology and Clinical Immunology .... IAACI
International Association of Amateur Boat Builders .... IAABB
International Association of Amusement Parks [*Later, IAAPA*] .... IAAP
International Association of Amusement Parks and Attractions .... IAAPA
International Association for Analytical Psychology .... IAAP
International Association of Applied Linguistics .... IAAL
International Association of Applied Psychology .... IAAP
International Association of Applied Social Scientists [*Later, CCI*] .... IAASS
International Association of Approved Basketball Officials .... IAABO
International Association for Aquatic Animal Medicine .... IAAAM
International Association of Arson Investigators .... IAAI
International Association of Art [*See also AIAP*] .... IAA
International Association of Art Critics .... IAAC
International Association of Assessing Officers .... IAAO
International Association of Assessing Officers, Chicago, IL [*OCLC symbol*] .... ILW
International Association of Astacology .... IAA
International Association of Auditorium Managers .... IAAM
International Association of Auto Theft Investigators .... IAATI
International Association of Automotive Modelers [*Defunct*] .... IAAM
International Association for Bear Research and Management .... IABRM
International Association for Better Basic Education .... IABBE
International Association of Biblicists and Orientalists .... IABO
International Association of Bibliophiles [*See also AIB*] .... IAB
International Association of Biological Oceanography [*of International Union of Biological Sciences*] .... IABO
International Association of Biological Standardization [*See also AISB*] .... IABS
International Association of Black and White Men Together .... IABWMT
International Association of Blue Print and Allied Industries [*Later, IRGBA, IRA*] .... IABPAI
International Association of Boards of Examiners in Optometry .... IAB
International Association of Bomb Technicians and Investigators .... IABTI
International Association of Botanic Gardens .... IABG
International Association for Bridge and Structural Engineering .... IABSE
International Association for Bridge and Structural Engineering. Publications [*A publication*] .... Int Ass Bridge Struct Eng Publ
International Association of Bridge, Structural, and Ornamental Iron Workers .... BSOIW
International Association of Bridge, Structural, and Ornamental Iron Workers .... IABSOIW
International Association of Broadcasting Manufacturers .... IABM
International Association of Buddhist Studies .... IABS
International Association of Building Companions [*See also IBO*] .... IABC
International Association of Business Communicators .... IABC
International Association of Businessmen and Professionals .... IABP
International Association of Buying Groups [*See also IVE*] .... IABG
International Association of Campus Law Enforcement Administrators .... IACLEA
International Association of Cancer Registries .... IACR
International Association of Cancer Victims and Friends .... IACVF
International Association of Chiefs of Police .... IACP
International Association for Child and Adolescent Psychiatry and Allied Professions .... IACAPAP
International Association for Child Psychiatry and Allied Professions [*Later, IACAPAP*] .... IACP
International Association for Child Psychiatry and Allied Professions [*Later, IACAPAP*] .... IACPAP
International Association of Circulation Managers .... IACM
International Association for Classical Archaeology [*See also AIAC*] .... IACA
International Association of Classified Societies .... IACS
International Association of Cleaning and Dye House Workers .... CDHW
International Association of Clerks, Recorders, Election Officials, and Treasurers .... IACREOT
International Association of Clothing Designers .... IACD
International Association to Combat Terrorism [*Defunct*] .... IACT
International Association for Comparative Research on Leukemia and Related Diseases .... IACRLRD
International Association of Computer Crime Investigators .... IACCI
International Association of Concert and Festival Managers [*Later, ISPAA*] .... IACFM
International Association of Concert Managers [*Later, ISPAA*] .... IACM
International Association of Conference Centers .... IACC
International Association of Convention Bureaus [*Later, IACVB*] .... IACB
International Association of Convention and Visitor Bureaus .... IACVB
International Association of Cooking Schools .... IACS
International Association of Coroners and Medical Examiners .... IACME
International Association of Counseling Services .... IACS
International Association of Crafts and Small and Medium-Sized Enterprises .... IACME
International Association of Credit Card Investigators .... IACCI
International Association for Cross-Cultural Psychology .... IACCP
International Association for Cultural Freedom [*Defunct*] .... IACF
International Association for Cybernetics [*See also AIC*] .... IAC
International Association of Democratic Lawyers .... IADL
International Association for Dental Research .... IADR
International Association of Dental Students .... IADS
International Association of Dentistry for Children. Journal [*A publication*] .... Int Assoc Dent Child J
International Association of Dentistry for the Handicapped .... IADH
International Association of Dento-Maxillo-Facial Radiology .... IADMFR
International Association of Department Stores .... IADS
International Association of Dollbaby Parents .... IADP

International Association of Dredging Companies ..... IADC
International Association of Drilling Contractors ..... IADC
International Association for Earthquake Engineering ..... IAEE
International Association for Ecology ..... IAE
International Association for Ecology ..... INTECOL
International Association for Educational Assessment ..... IAEA
International Association for Educational and Vocational Guidance [*See also AIOSP*] ..... IAEVG
International Association of Educators for World Peace ..... IAEWP
International Association of Electrical Contractors [*See also AIE*] ..... IAEC
International Association of Electrical Inspectors ..... IAEI
International Association of Electrical Leagues [*Later, ILEA*] ..... IAEL
International Association of Electrotypers and Stereotypers [*Later, Printing Platemakers Association*] ..... IAES
International Association of Energy Economists ..... IAEE
International Association of Engineering Geology ..... IAEG
International Association of Engineering Geology. Bulletin [*A publication*] ..... Int Assoc Eng Geol Bull
International Association for Enterostomal Therapy ..... IAET
International Association of Entertainment Lawyers ..... IAEL
International Association of Environmental Mutagen Societies ..... IAEMS
International Association for the Evaluation of Educational Achievement ..... IEA
International Association of Evening Student Councils [*Later, USAES*] ..... IAESC
International Association for the Exchange of Students for Technical Experience - United States [*Later, AIPT*] ..... IAESTE/US
International Association of Fairs and Expositions ..... IAFE
International Association of Family Sociology ..... IAFS
International Association of Filipino Patriots ..... IAFP
International Association of Financial Planners ..... IAFP
International Association of Fire Chiefs ..... IAFC
International Association of Fire Fighters ..... IAFF
International Association of Fish Meal Manufacturers ..... IAFMM
International Association of Fish and Wildlife Agencies ..... IAFWA
International Association on Food Distribution ..... IAFD
[*The*] **International Association of Forensic Toxicologists** ..... TIAFT
International Association of Game, Fish, and Conservation Commissioners [*Later, IAFWA*] ..... IAGFCC
International Association of Garment Manufacturers [*Absorbed by NOSA*] ..... IAGM
International Association on the Genesis of Ore Deposits ..... IAGOD
International Association of Geochemistry and Cosmochemistry ..... IAGC
International Association of Geodesy ..... IAG
International Association of Geomagnetism and Aeronomy ..... IAGA
International Association of Geophysical Contractors ..... IAGC
International Association of Germanic Languages and Literatures [*See also IVG*] ..... IAGLL
International Association of Gerontology ..... IAG
International Association of Golf Administrators ..... IAGA
International Association of Governmental Fair Agencies ..... IAGFA
International Association of Governmental Labor Officials [*Later, NAGLO*] ..... IAGLO
International Association of Great Lakes Ports ..... IAGLP
International Association for Great Lakes Research ..... IAGLR
International Association of Greeting Card Workers ..... IAGCW
International Association of Health Underwriters [*Later, NAHU*] ..... IAHU
International Association of Heart Patients [*Formerly, IAPP*] ..... IAHP
International Association of Heat and Frost Insulators and Asbestos Workers ..... HFIAW
International Association of Heat and Frost Insulators and Asbestos Workers ..... IAHFIAW
International Association of Hillel Directors ..... IAHD
International Association of Historians of Asia ..... IAHA
International Association for the History of Religions ..... IAHR
International Association for the History of Sport and Physical Education ..... HISPA
International Association of Holistic Health Practitioners [*Formerly, INA*] ..... IAHHP
International Association of Home Improvement Councils [*Defunct*] ..... IAHIC
International Association of Horticultural Producers ..... IAHP
International Association of Hospital Central Service Management ..... IAHCSM
International Association for Hospital Security ..... IAHS
International Association of Hospitality Accountants ..... IAHA
International Association for Housing Science ..... IAHS
International Association of Human Biologists ..... IAHB
International Association for Hydraulic Research ..... IAHR
International Association for Hydraulic Research. Congress. Proceedings [*A publication*] ..... Int Assoc Hydraul Res Congr Proc
International Association for Hydrogen Energy ..... IAHE
International Association of Hydrogeologists [*of International Union of Geological Sciences*] ..... IAH
International Association of Hydrogeologists. Memoirs [*A publication*] ..... Int Assoc Hydrogeol Mem
International Association of Hydrological Sciences ..... IAHS
International Association of Hydrological Sciences. Hydrological Sciences Bulletin [*A publication*] ..... Int Assoc Hydrol Sci Hydrol Sci Bull
International Association of Hydrological Sciences. Publication [*A publication*] ..... Int Assoc Hydrol Sci Publ
International Association of Hydrology ..... IAH
International Association of Ice Cream Manufacturers ..... IAICM
International Association for Identification ..... IAI
International Association for Impact Assessment ..... IAIA
International Association of Independent Colleges and Universities ..... IAICU
International Association of Independent Producers ..... IAIP
International Association of Independent Tanker Owners ..... INTERTANKO
International Association of Individual Psychology ..... IAIP
International Association of Industrial Accident Boards and Commissions ..... IAIABC
International Association of Institutes of Navigation ..... IAIN
International Association of Insurance Counsel ..... IAIC
International Association of Insurance and Reinsurance Intermediaries [*See also BIPAR*] ..... IAIRI
International Association for Integrative Education ..... IAIE
International Association of Intermodal Equipment Surveyors ..... IAIES
International Association for Iranian Art and Archaeology ..... IAIAA
International Association of Jazz Record Collectors ..... IAJRC
International Association of Jim Beam Bottle and Specialties Clubs ..... IAJBBSC
International Association of Judges ..... IAJ
International Association of Juvenile and Family Court Magistrates ..... IAJFCM
International Association of Labour History Institutions ..... IALHI
International Association of Laryngectomees ..... IAL
International Association of Law Enforcement Firearms Instructors ..... IALEFI
International Association of Law Enforcement Intelligence Analysts ..... IALEIA
International Association of Law Libraries ..... IALL
International Association of Legal Science ..... IALS
International Association of Liberal Religious Women ..... IALRW
International Association of Lighthouse Authorities ..... IALA
International Association of Lighting Designers ..... IALD
International Association of Linguistics ..... IAL
International Association of Lions Clubs ..... IALC
International Association of Logopedics and Phoniatrics ..... IALP
International Association of Lyceum Clubs ..... IALC
International Association of Machinists and Aerospace Workers ..... IAM
International Association of Marble, Slate and Stone Polishers, Rubbers and Sawyers, Tile and Marble Setters' Helpers, and Marble Mosaic and Terrazzo Workers' Helpers [*Later, Tile, Marble, Terazzo Finishers, Shopworkers, and Granite Cutters International Union*] ..... MSSP
International Association of Margaret Morris Method ..... IAMMM
International Association of Marine Science Libraries and Information Centers ..... IAMSLIC
International Association for Mass Communication Research ..... IAMCR
International Association of Master-Penmen and Teachers of Hand-Writing ..... IAMPTH
International Association for Mathematical Geology ..... IAMG
International Association for Mathematical Geology. Journal [*A publication*] ..... Int Assoc Math Geol J
International Association for Mathematics and Computers in Simulation [*Formerly, AICA*] ..... IMACS
International Association for Maxillo-Facial Surgery ..... IAMFS
International Association on Mechanization of Field Experiments ..... IAMFE
International Association for Medical Assistance to Travelers ..... IAMAT
International Association of Medical Esperantists ..... IAME
International Association of Medical Laboratory Technologists ..... IAMLT
International Association of Medical Museums [*Later, IAP*] ..... IAMM
International Association of Medical Museums. Bulletin and Journal of Technical Methods [*A publication*] ..... Internat Ass Med Mus Bull
International Association for Medical Research and Cultural Exchange ..... IAMR
International Association of Medicine and Biology of Environment [*See also AIMBE*] ..... IAMBE
International Association of Mercury Producers [*Spain, Italy, Turkey, Yugoslavia, Peru, Algeria*] ..... IAMP
International Association of Merger and Acquisition Consultants ..... INTERMAC
International Association of Meteorology and Atmosperic Physics ..... IAMAP
International Association of Metropolitan City Libraries ..... UNTAMEL
International Association for Metropolitan Research and Development ..... INTERMET
International Association of Microbiological Societies [*Later, IUMS*] ..... IAMS
International Association of Milk Control Agencies ..... IAMCA
International Association of Milk, Food, and Environmental Sanitarians ..... IAMFES
International Association for Mission Studies ..... IAMS
International Association of Mouth and Foot Painting Artists ..... IAMFPA
International Association of Municipal Statisticians [*Later, IARUS*] ..... IAMS
International Association of Museums of Arms and Military History ..... IAMAM

International Association of Music Libraries, Archives, and Documentation Centres [See also AIBM] ....IAML

International Association of Mutual Insurance Companies [See also AISAM] ....IAMIC

International Association for Near-Death Studies ....IANDS

International Association of Ocular Surgeons ....IAOS

International Association of Official Human Rights Agencies ....IAOHRA

International Association of Opera Directors..........................IAOD

International Association of Optometric Executives ....IAOE

International Association of Oral Surgeons ....IAOS

International Association of Organ Teachers USA ....IAOT

International Association of Orientalist Libraries ....IAOL

International Association of Orthodontics ....IAO

International Association of Pacemaker Patients [Later, IAHP].............IAPP

International Association of Paper Historians ....IPH

International Association of Parapsychologists ....IAP

International Association of Parents of the Deaf......................IAPD

International Association of Parents and Professionals for Safe Alternatives in Childbirth ....NAPSAC

International Association for Pattern Recognition......................IAPR

International Association of Personnel in Employment Security ....IAPES

International Association for Personnel Women ....IAPW

International Association of Pet Cemeteries [Formerly, NAPC]............IAPC

International Association for Philosophy and Literature....................IAPL

International Association of Photoplatemakers [Formerly, APA, PERI]....IAP

International Association of Physical Education and Sport for Girls and Women................IAPESGW

International Association of Physical Oceanography [Later, IAPSO] ....IAPO

International Association for the Physical Sciences of the Oceans [of International Union of Geodesy and Geophysics].........IAPSO

International Association of Pipe Smokers Clubs ....IAPSC

International Association of Planetology..................................IAP

International Association for Plant Physiology ....IAPP

International Association for Plant Taxonomy ....IAPT

International Association of Plumbing and Mechanical Officials ....IAPMO

International Association of Police Professors [Later, ACJS] ....IAPP

International Association of Political Consultants ....IAPC

International Association on the Political Use of Psychiatry ....IAPUP

International Association for Pollution Control [Defunct].....................IAPC

International Association of Ports and Harbors ....IAPH

International Association for the Prevention of Blindness ....IAPB

International Association of Printing House Craftsmen ....IAPHC

International Association of Professional Bureaucrats [Formerly, NATAPROBU]................INATAPROBU

International Association of Professional Congress Organizers ....IAPCO

International Association of Professional Numismatists [See also AINP] ....IAPN

International Association for the Promotion and Protection of Private Foreign Investments ....APPI

International Association for the Properties of Steam ....IAPS

International Association for the Protection of Industrial Property......IAPIP

International Association of Psycho-Social Rehabilitation Services................IAPSRS

International Association of Psychoanalytic Gerontology ....IAPG

International Association for Psychotronic Research ....IAPR

International Association of Public Cleansing ....INTAPUC

International Association of Public Pawnbroking Institutions..............IAPPI

International Association of Pupil Personnel Workers ....IAPPW

International Association for Quality Circles ....IAQC

International Association for Radiation Research ....IARR

International Association of Radiopharmacology......................IAR

International Association of Railway Employees ....IARE

International Association of Railway Employees ....IRE

International Association of Rattan Manufacturers and Importers [Defunct]................IARMI

International Association of Rebekah Assemblies [IOOF] ....IARA

International Association of Refrigerated Warehouses [Formerly, NARW]................IARW

International Association for Regional and Urban Statistics ....IARUS

International Association for Religion and Parapsychology ....IARP

International Association for Religious Freedom ....IARF

International Association of Religious Science Churches [Later, Religious Science International]................IARSC

International Association for Research in Income and Wealth ....IARIW

International Association of Research Institutes for the Graphic Arts Industry ....IARIGAI

International Association of Retired Persons [Superseded by IFA].......IARP

International Association of Rolling Stock Builders [See also AICMR] ....IARSB

International Association of Satellite Users ....IASU

International Association for Scandinavian Studies ....IASS

International Association of Scholarly Publishers....................IASP

International Association of School Librarianship ....IASL

International Association of School Security Directors [Later, NASSD]................IASSD

International Association of Schools in Advertising.....................IASA

International Association of Schools of Social Work ....IASSW

International Association of Science and Technology for Development ....IASTED

International Association of Scientific Hydrology [Later, International Association of Hydrological Sciences]................IASH

International Association of Scientific Hydrology. Bulletin [A publication]................Int Assoc Sci Hydrol Bull

International Association of Scientific Hydrology. Bulletin [A publication]................Internat Assoc Sci Hydrology Bull

International Association of Scientific Hydrology. Bulletin. Publication [A publication]........... Internat Assoc Sci Hydrology Bull Pub

International Association of Scientific Hydrology. Publications [A publication]................Internat Assoc Sci Hydrology Pub

International Association for the Scientific Study of Mental Deficiency................IASSMD

International Association of Security Service ....IASS

International Association of Sedimentologists.........................IAS

International Association of Seed Crushers ....IASC

International Association of Seismology and Physics of the Earth's Interior ....IASPEI

International Association for Semiotic Studies ....IASS

International Association of Service Companies........................IASCO

International Association for Shell and Spatial Structures ....IASS

International Association of Siderographers...........................IAS

International Association for Social Progress ....IASP

International Association for Social Science Information Service and Technology ....IASSIST

International Association of Soil Science.............................IASS

International Association of Sound Archives ....IASA

International Association of Space Philatelists ....IASP

International Association for Sports Information ....IASI

International Association for Statistical Computing ....IASC

International Association for Statistics in Physical Sciences.............IASPS

International Association of Strategic Planning Consultants ....IASPC

International Association for the Study of Anglo-Irish Literature......IASAIL

International Association for the Study of Cooperation in Education ....IASCE

International Association for the Study of the Italian Language and Literature [See also AISLLI]................IASILL

International Association for the Study of the Liver ....IASL

International Association for the Study of Pain ....IASP

International Association for Suicide Prevention ....IASP

International Association of Survey Statisticians ....IASS

International Association of Teachers of English as a Foreign Language................IATEFL

International Association of Technological University Libraries.........IATUL

International Association of Technological University Libraries Proceedings [A publication]................IATUL Proc

International Association of Telecomputer Networks ....IATN

International Association for Television Editors ....IATE

International Association for Temperance Education ....IATE

International Association of Terminology ....TERMIA

International Association for Testing Materials.......................IATM

International Association for Textile Care Labelling ....IATCL

International Association of Textile Dyers and Printers [See also AITIT]................IATDP

International Association of Theological Libraries ....IATL

International Association of Theoretical and Applied Limnology............IAL

International Association of Theoretical and Applied Limnology........IATAL

International Association of Theoretical and Applied Limnology Proceedings [A publication]................ Int Assoc Theor Appl Limnol Proc

International Association of Tool Craftsmen ....IATC

International Association of Torch Clubs ....IATC

International Association of Tour Managers ....IATM

International Association of Trade Exchanges ....IATE

International Association of Traffic and Safety Sciences.............IATSS

International Association for Training and Education in Distribution.....TED

International Association of Transport Museums [See also AIMT]........IATM

International Association of Trichologists ....IAT

International Association of Tungsten Producers ....IATP

International Association for a Union of Democracies ....IAUD

International Association of Universities.............................IAU

International Association of University Presidents....................IAUP

International Association of University Professors of English ....IAUPE

International Association of University Professors and Lecturers ......IAUPL

International Association for Vegetation Science [See also IVV]..........IAVS

International Association for Vehicle Systems Dynamics.............IAVSD

International Association of Veterinary Food Hygienists ....IAVFH

International Association of Visual Communications Management [Formerly, SRE]................IAVCM

International Association for Vocational Guidance....................IAVG

International Association of Voice Identification [Later, IAI]................IAVI

International Association of Volcanology [Later, IAVCEI]................IAV

International Association of Volcanology and Chemistry of the Earth's Interior ....IAVCEI

International Association of Volcanology and Chemistry of the Earth's Interior. Special Series [A publication]................ Int Assoc Volcanol Chem Earth's Inter Spe Ser

International Association for Volunteer Education.....................IAVE

International Association of Wall and Ceiling Contractors [Later, AWCI]................IAWCC

International Association of Wall and Ceiling Contractors - Gypsum Drywall Contractors International [Formerly, GDCI, IAWCC] [Later, AWCI]................IAWCC/GD

International Association for Water Law [See also AIDA]................IAWL

International Association on Water Pollution Research ....IAWPR

International Association of Wholesalers [Defunct]..................IAW
International Association of Wiping Cloth Manufacturers
[Formerly, NAWCM, SIA]....................IAWCM
International Association of Women and Home Page Journalists ....IAWHPJ
International Association of Women Ministers....................IAWM
International Association of Women Police....................IAWP
International Association of Wood Anatomists....................IAWA
International Association of Wood Anatomists. Bulletin [A
publication]....................Int Assoc Wood Anat Bull
International Association of Wool and Textile Laboratories
....................INTERWOOLABS
International Association of Word Processing Specialists
[Formerly, NAWPS]....................WPS
International Association of Workers for Maladjusted Children
[See also AIEJI]....................IAWMC
International Association of Youth Magistrates [Later, IAJFCM]..........IAYM
International Associations/Associations Internationales [A
publication]....................Int Assoc/Assoc Int
International Astrological Association....................IAA
International Astronautical Congress....................IAC
International Astronautical Congress. Proceedings [A
publication]....................Int Astronaut Congr Proc
International Astronautical Federation....................IAF
International Astronomical Union....................IAU
International Astronomical Union. Circular [A publication]..............IAU Circ
International Astronomical Union. Symposium [A publication]....................
Int Astron Union Symp
International Astrophysical Decade....................IAD
International Atlantic Salmon Foundation....................IASF
International Atlantic Salmon Foundation. Special Publication
Series [A publication]....................Int Atl Salmon Found Spec Publ Ser
International Atomic-Development Authority [Proposed by
Bernard M. Baruch, 1946, but never created]....................IADA
International Atomic Energy Agency....................IAEA
International Atomic Energy Agency. Bibliographical Series [A
publication]....................IAEA Bibliogr Ser
International Atomic Energy Agency. Bibliographical Series [A
publication]....................Int At Energy Ag Bibliogr Ser
International Atomic Energy Agency. Bulletin [A publication]........IAEA Bull
International Atomic Energy Agency. Bulletin [A publication]....................
Int At Energy Agency Bull
International Atomic Energy Agency. Proceedings Series [A
publication]....................IAEA Proc Ser
International Atomic Energy Agency. Proceedings Series [A
publication]....................Int At Energy Ag Proc Ser
International Atomic Energy Agency. Safety Series [A
publication]....................IAEA Saf Ser
International Atomic Energy Agency. Safety Series [A
publication]....................Int At Energy Agency Saf Ser
International Atomic Energy Agency. Technical Report Series
[A publication]....................IAEA Tech Rep Ser
International Atomic Energy Agency. Technical Report Series
[A publication]....................Int At Energy Agency Tech Rep Ser
International Atomic Energy Committee....................IAEC
International Atomic Time....................IAT
International Audio-Visual Technical Centre [Netherlands]..........IAVTC
International Audiovisual Society....................IAS
International Auto Show Producers Association....................IASPA
International Automotive Design....................IAD
International Auxiliary Language Association [Later, UMI]..........IALA
International Aviation Affairs [FAA]....................IAA
International Aviation Association....................INTAVA
International Aviation Corporation [Minneapolis, MN] [FAA
designator]....................IAC
International Aviation Service [FAA]....................IAS
International Aviation Services [Great Britain] [ICAO designator]..........FF
International Aviation Theft Bureau....................IATB
International B-24 Liberator Club....................IBLC
International Baby Food Action Network....................IBFAN
International Baccalaureate Office....................IBO
International Bach Society [Defunct]....................IBS
International Backpackers Association [Later, AHS]....................IBA
International Badminton Federation....................IBF
International Balance of Payments [Game]....................BALPAY
International Balance of Payments....................IBP
International Balance of Payments Reporting System....................IBOP
International Balint Federation....................IBF
International Ballet Competition....................IBC
International Balut Federation....................IBF
International Banana Association....................IBA
International Bandy Federation....................IBF
International Bank [NASDAQ symbol]....................IBKW
International Bank for Economic Cooperation....................IBEC
International Bank Note Society....................IBNS
International Bank Note Society. Quarterly Magazine [A
publication]....................IBNS
International Bank for Reconstruction and Development [Also
known as World Bank]....................IBRD
International Banker Association....................IBA
International Banking Facility....................IBF
International Banknote Co., Inc. [American Stock Exchange symbol].......IBK

International Bar Association....................IBA
International Bar Fly [Sign in Harry's New York Bar, Paris]....................IBF
International Barbed Wire Collectors Association....................IBWCA
International Barber Schools Association....................IBSA
International Barbie Doll Collectors Club....................IBDCC
International Basic Economy Corporation....................IBEC
International Basic Resources [NASDAQ symbol]....................IBRM
International Baton Twirling Association of America and Abroad..........IBTA
International Bauxite Association....................IBA
International Bee Research Association....................IBRA
International Beefalo Breeders' Registry....................IBBR
International Beer Tasting Society....................IBTS
International Behavioural Scientist [A publication]..........Int Behav Scientist
International Benchrest Shooters....................IBS
International Benjamin Franklin Society [Defunct]....................IBFS
International Benzoate Unit [Pharmacology]....................IBU
International Bible Reading Association....................IBRA
International Bible Students....................IBS
International Bibliographical Description....................IBID
International Bibliography of Historical Sciences [A publication]..........IBHS
International Bibliography, Information, and Documentation [A
publication]....................IBID
International Bibliography of the Social Sciences [A publication]....................
Int Bibl Soc Sci
International Bicycle Touring Society....................IBTS
International Bio-Environmental Foundation....................IBEF
International Biodeterioration Bulletin [A publication]....................Int Biod B
International Biodeterioration Bulletin [A publication].....Int Biodeterior Bull
International Biodeterioration Bulletin. Reference Index [A
publication]....................IBBRIS
International Biodeterioration Bulletin. Reference Index [A
publication]....................Intern Biodet Bull
International Biological Program [Concluded, 1974] [National
Academy of Sciences]....................IBP
International Biological Programme [A publication]........Int Biol Programme
International Biological Programme. Handbook [A publication]....................
Int Biol Programme Handb
International Biological Year....................IBY
International Biomass Institute....................IBI
International Biophysical Center....................IBC
International Biotoxicological Center....................IBC
International Bird Rescue Research Center....................IBRRC
International Black Peoples' Foundation....................IBPF
International Black Writers Conference....................IBWC
International Blind Sports Association [See also AISA]....................IBSA
International Blue Jay Class Association....................IBJCA
International Board of Auditors....................IBA
International Board on Books for Young People....................IBBY
International Board of Jewish Missions....................IBJM
International Board of Medicine and Psychology....................IBMP
International Board for Plant Genetic Resources [FAO]....................IBPGR
International Bobsled Federation....................IBF
International Bocce Association....................IBA
International Book Export Group....................IBEG
International Book Information Service....................IBIS
International Book Printers Association [Later, NABM]....................IBPA
International Book Service, Inc.....................IBS
International Book Year [1972] [UNESCO]....................IBY
International Booksellers Federation [Formerly, ICBA]....................IBF
International Border Fancy Canary Club....................IBFCC
International Botanical Congress. Recent Advances in Botany
[A publication]....................Int Bot Congr Recent Advan Bot
International Bottled Water Association....................IBWA
International Boundary and Water Commission....................IBWC
International Bowling Board....................IBB
International Boxing Guild....................IBG
International Boxing Writers Association....................IBWA
International Braille Chess Association....................IBCA
International Brain Research Organization....................IBRO
International Brain Research Organization. Monograph Series
[A publication]....................Int Brain Res Organ Monogr Ser
International Brancusi Society....................IBS
International Brangus Breeders Association....................IBBA
International Brecht Society....................IBS
International Brick Collectors' Association....................IBCA
International Bridge Academy....................IBA
International Bridge Press Association....................IBPA
[The] International Bridge & Terminal Co. [AAR code]....................IBT
International Bridge, Tunnel, and Turnpike Association....................IBTTA
International Brightness Coefficient....................IBC
International Broadcast Engineer [A publication]..............Int Broadcast Eng
International Broadcast Engineer [A publication]..............Int Broadc Engr
International Broadcast Institute [Later, IIC]....................IBI
International Broadcasting....................IB
International Broadcasting Corporation [NASDAQ symbol]..................IBCA
International Broadcasting Organization....................IBO
International Broadcasting Station [ITU designation]....................BCI
International Bronchoesophagological Society....................IBS
International Broom and Whisk Makers' Union of America
[Defunct]....................BWM

International Brotherhood of Boilermakers, Iron Shipbuilders, Blacksmiths, Forgers, and Helpers..................BBF
International Brotherhood of Bookbinders [Later, Graphic Arts International Union]..................IBB
International Brotherhood of Electrical Workers..................IBEW
International Brotherhood of Firemen and Oilers..................IBFO
International Brotherhood of Live Steamers..................IBLS
International Brotherhood of Longshoremen..................IBL
International Brotherhood of Magicians..................IBM
International Brotherhood of Motorcycle Campers..................IBMC
International Brotherhood of Old Bastards..................IBOB
International Brotherhood of Operative Potters [Later, IBPAW]..................IBOP
International Brotherhood of Painters and Allied Trades [Formerly, BPDP, B of PDPH of A]..................IBPAT
International Brotherhood of Painters and Allied Trades..................PAT
International Brotherhood of Papermakers [Later, United Paperworkers International Union]..................IBPM
International Brotherhood of Police Officers..................IBPO
International Brotherhood of Pottery and Allied Workers [Formerly, IBOP]..................IBPAW
International Brotherhood of Pulp, Sulphite, and Paper Mill Workers [Later, UPIU]..................PSPMW
International Brotherhood of Teamsters, Chauffeurs, Warehousemen, and Helpers of America..................IBT
International Bryozoology Association..................IBA
International Buckskin Horse Association..................IBHA
International Buddhist Meditation Center..................IBMC
International Builders Exchange Executives..................IBEE
International Building Classification Committee [Netherlands]..................IBCC
International Building Services Abstracts [A publication]..................Int Build Serv Abstr
International Bulletin of Bacteriological Nomenclature and Taxonomy [A publication]..................Int Bull Bacteriol Nomencl Taxon
International Bundle Branch Block Association..................IBBBA
International Bureau of Education..................IBE
International Bureau of Education. Bulletin [A publication]..................Int Bur Ed B
International Bureau for Epilepsy..................IBE
International Bureau of the Federations of Master Printers..................IBFMP
International Bureau of Fiscal Documentation..................IBFD
International Bureau of Legal Metrology..................IBLM
International Bureau for the Publication of Customs Tariffs..................IBPCT
International Bureau of Social Tourism [See also BITS]..................IBST
International Bureau of Weights and Measures..................IBWM
International Bus Collectors Club..................IBC
International Business Aviation Council..................IBAC
International Business Brokers Association..................IBBA
International Business Contact Club..................IBCC
International Business Contacts..................IBC
International Business Corporation..................IBC
International Business Council..................IBC
International Business Council Midamerica..................IBCM
International Business Forms Industries..................IBFI
International Business Machines Corp. [NYSE symbol]..................IBM
International Business Machines Corp., Components Division Library, Hopewell Junction, NY [Library symbol]..................NHjl
International Business Machines Corp., Corporation Library, Houston, TX [Library symbol]..................TxHI
International Business Machines Corp., Kingston, NY [Library symbol]..................NKil
International Business Machines Corp., Oswego, NY [Library symbol]..................NOsl
International Business Machines Corp., San Jose, CA [Library symbol]..................CSjIBM
International Business Machines Corp., Systems Development Library, Endicott, NY [Library symbol]..................NEnl
International Business Machines Corp., Systems Development Division, Poughkeepsie, NY [Library symbol]..................NPI
International Business Machines Corp., Systems Manufacturing Division, Boulder, CO [Library symbol]..................CoBIBM
International Business Machines Corp., Thomas J. Watson Research Center, Yorktown Heights, NY [Library symbol]..................NYhl
International Business Machines System..................IBSYS
International Business Unit [British] [Information service]..................IBU
International C Class Catamaran Association of America..................ICCCA
International Cable Protection Committee..................ICPC
International Call for Tenders..................ICT
International Camellia Society..................ICS
International Camp Counselor Program..................ICCP
International Cancer League..................ICL
International Cancer Patient Data Exchange System..................ICPDES
International Cancer Research Data Bank [National Cancer Institute]..................ICRDB
International Cancer Research Technology Transfer [Program]..................ICRETT
International Cancer Research Workshop..................ICREW
International Canoe Federation [See also FIC]..................ICF
International Capital Equipment [NASDAQ symbol]..................ICEYF
International Capital & Technology [NASDAQ symbol]..................ICTC
International Car Wash Institute..................ICWI
International Carbohydrate Organization..................ICO
International Cardiology Foundation..................ICF
International Cardiovascular Society..................ICS

International Cardiovascular Society..................ICVS
International Cargo Advisory Bureau..................ICAB
International Cargo Gear Bureau..................ICGB
International Cargo Handling Coordination Association..................ICHCA
International Caribbean Tourist, Inc. [Netherlands] [ICAO designator]..................IU
International Carnival Glass Association..................ICGA
International Carnivorous Plant Society..................ICPS
International Cartographic Association..................ICA
International Carwash Association [Formerly, AALA, ACWA]..................ICA
International Carwash Association/National Carwash Council..................ICA/NCC
International Cast Metals Journal [A publication]..................Int Cast Met J
International Casting Federation..................ICF
International Castles Institute..................ICI
International Castor Oil Association..................ICOA
[The] International Cat Association..................TICA
International Cataloguing [A publication]..................Int Cataloguing
International Catholic Auxiliaries..................ICA
International Catholic Child Bureau..................ICCB
International Catholic Confederation of Hospitals [Later, IHF]..................ICCH
International Catholic Deaf Association..................ICDA
International Catholic Girls' Society..................ICGS
International Catholic Migration Commission [See also CICM]..................ICMC
International Catholic Press Union [Later, UCIP]..................ICPU
International Catholic Rural Association..................ICRA
International Catholic Truth Society..................ICTS
International Catholic Union of the Press..................ICUP
International Catholic Youth Federation [Later, WFCY]..................ICYF
International CBX Owners Association..................ICOA
International Cell Research Organization..................ICRO
International Cello Centre..................ICC
International Cellulose Research Ltd., Hawkesbury, ON, Canada [Library symbol]..................CaOHkC
International Cemetery Supply Association [Formerly, CSA]..................ICSA
International Center for the Advancement of Management Education [Stanford University]..................ICAME
International Center for Agricultural Research in Dry Areas [Syria]..................ICARDA
International Center for Arid and Semi-Arid Land Studies [Texas Technological University]..................ICASALS
International Center for Arid and Semi-Arid Land Studies. Publication [A publication]..................Int Cent Arid Semi-Arid Land Stud Publ
International Center for Communication Arts and Sciences..................ICCAS
International Center for Comparative Criminology..................ICCC
International Center for the Disabled..................ICD
International Center for the Environment [Proposed]..................ICE
International Center of Free Trade Unionists in Exile..................ICFTUE
International Center of Genetic Epistemology [Geneva, Switzerland]..................ICGE
International Center for High Quality Scrap [Scrap salvage]..................INCH
International Center of Information on Antibiotics..................ICIA
International Center for Law in Development..................ICLD
International Center for Living Aquatic Resources Management [Philippines]..................ICLARM
International Center for Marine Resources Development [University of Rhode Island]..................ICMRD
International Center of Medical and Psychological Hypnosis..................ICMPH
International Center for Medicine and Law..................ICML
International Center of Medieval Art..................ICMA
International Center of the Neutral Esperanto Movement..................ICNEM
International Center in New York [Provides assistance to foreign visitors and diplomats]..................ICNY
International Center of Photography [Museum] [New York]..................ICP
International Center for Public Enterprises in Developing Countries..................ICPE
International Center for Research on Women..................ICRW
International Center for Science Information Services in Phytovirology..................ICSISP
International Center of Scientific and Technical Information..................ICSTI
International Center for Social Gerontology..................ICSG
International Center for the Solution of Environmental Problems..................ICSEP
International Center of Studies on Early Music..................ICSEM
International Center of Theatre Research..................ICTR
International Center for Theoretical Physics [Trieste]..................ICTP
International Center for the Typographic Arts..................ICTA
International Centre of Ancient and Modern Tapestry..................ICAMT
International Centre for Earth Tides..................ICET
International Centre for Economics [British]..................ICE
International Centre of Films for Children..................ICFC
International Centre for Industrial Studies [United Nations]..................ICIS
International Centre of Insect Physiology and Ecology [Kenya]..................ICIPE
International Centre for Mechanical Sciences. Courses and Lectures [A publication]..................Int Cent Mech Sci Courses Lect
International Centre of Research and Information on Collective Economy..................ICRICE
International Centre for Settlement of Investment Disputes..................ICSID
International Ceramic Association [Formerly, NCA]..................ICA
International Cerebral Palsy Society..................ICPS
International Chain of Industrial and Technical Advertising Agencies..................ICITA
International Chamber of Commerce [See also CCI]..................ICC
International Chamber of Commerce..................INCO

International Chamber of Shipping ... ICS
International Chaplain's Ministry ... ICM
International Cheerleading Foundation ... ICF
International Cheese and Deli Association ... ICDA
International Chefs' Association ... ICA
International Chemical Engineering [*A publication*] ... Int Chem En
International Chemical Engineering [*A publication*] ... Int Chem Eng
International Chemical Society [*Proposed*] ... ICS
International Chemical Workers Union ... ICW
International Chemical Workers Union ... ICWU
International Chessology Club ... ICC
International Childbirth Education Association ... ICEA
International Children's Centre ... ICC
International China Painting Teachers Organization [*Later, International Porcelain Artist Teachers*] ... ICPTO
International Chinese Snuff Bottle Society ... ICSBS
International Chiropractors Association ... ICA
International Christian Broadcasters [*Defunct*] ... ICB
International Christian Esperanto Association ... ICEA
International Christian Leadership ... ICL
International Christian Leprosy Mission ... ICLM
International Christian University [*Tokyo*] ... ICU
International Christian Youth ... ICY
International Christian Youth Exchange ... ICYE
International Churchill Society ... ICS
International Cigar Band Society [*Defunct*] ... ICBS
International Circulation Distributors, Inc. ... ICD
International Circulation Managers Association ... ICMA
International Citizens Committee of the Arts, Sciences, and Professions [*Also, ICCASP*] [*Created to support Franklin D. Roosevelt's fourth-term Presidential candidacy*] ... ASP
International City Management [*formerly, Managers*] **Association** ... ICMA
International Civil Airports Association ... ICAA
International Civil Aviation Organization ... ICAO
International Civil Aviation Organization, Montreal, PQ, Canada [*Library symbol*] ... CaQMIC
International Civil Defence Organization ... ICDO
International Civil Engineering Monthly [*A publication*] ... Int Civ Eng Mon
International Civil Service Advisory Board ... ICSAB
International Civil Service Commission ... ICSC
International Civil Service Training Organization ... ICSTO
International Claim Association ... ICA
International Claims Commission of the United States [*Abolished, 1954*] [*Department of State*] ... ICCUS
International Clarinet Society ... ICS
International Classification of Disease - Adopted Code for Hospitals ... H-ICDA
International Classification of Diseases [*A publication*] ... ICD
International Classification of Diseases Adapted ... ICDA
International Clearinghouse on Science and Mathematics Curricular. Developments Report [*A publication*] ... Int Clgh Sci Math Curricular Dev Rep
International Climate Zone ... ICZ
International Climatic Decades ... ICD
International Climatic Research Program ... ICRP
International Clinical Laboratories [*NASDAQ symbol*] ... ICLB
International Clinical Products Review [*A publication*] ... ICPR
International Clinics [*A publication*] ... Internat Clin
International Club for Collectors of Hatpins and Hatpin Holders ... ICCHHH
International Co-operative Alliance ... ICA
International Co-operative Bulletin [*A publication*] ... ICB
International Co-Operative Reinsurance Bureau ... ICRB
International Co-operative Women's Guild ... ICWG
International Coal Trade [*Bureau of Mines*] [*A publication*] ... ICT
International Cocoa Organization ... ICCO
International Cocoa Trades Federation ... ICTF
International Code of Medical Ethics ... ICME
International Code of Signals ... INTCO
International Coffee Agreement ... ICA
International Coffee Organization ... ICO
International Cogeneration Society ... ICS
International Coil Winding Association ... ICWA
International Cold Storage ... ICS
International College of Applied Nutrition ... ICAN
International College Art Program [*Red Cross Youth*] ... ICAP
International College in Copenhagen [*Denmark*] ... ICC
International College of Dentists ... ICD
International College of Officers [*Salvation Army*] ... ICO
International College of Real Estate Consulting Professionals ... RECP
International College of Surgeons ... ICS
International College of Surgeons, Chicago, IL [*Library symbol*] ... ICICS
International Collegiate Sports Foundation ... ICSF
International Colloquium of Plant Nutrition ... ICPN
International Color Computer Club ... ICCC
International Coma Recovery Institute ... ICRI
International Cometary Explorer [*Formerly, International Sun-Earth Explorer*] [*NASA*] ... ICE
International Commerce [*A publication*] ... Int Comm
International Commerce [*A publication*] ... Int Commer
International Commerce Term [*International Chamber of Commerce*] ... INCOTERM
International Commercial Bank of China [*Taiwan*] ... ICBC
International Commercial Exchange [*Defunct*] ... ICE
International Commission on Acoustics ... ICA
International Commission of Agricultural Engineering ... ICAE
International Commission for Agricultural Industries ... ICAI
International Commission for Air Navigation ... ICAN
International Commission for Bee Botany ... ICBB
International Commission on Civil Status [*See also CIEC*] ... ICCS
International Commission for Conformity of Certification of Electrical Equipment ... CEE
International Commission for the Conservation of Atlantic Tunas ... ICCAT
International Commission of Control and Supervision [*Composed of representatives of Canada, Hungary, Indonesia, and Poland, and charged with supervising the ceasefire in Vietnam, 1973*] ... ICCS
International Commission on Glass [*See also CIV*] ... ICG
International Commission on the History of the Geological Sciences ... INHIGEO
International Commission for the History of Representative and Parliamentary Institutions ... ICHRPI
International Commission for the History of Social Movements and Social Structures ... ICHSMSS
International Commission on Illumination [*Since 1951, has been known exclusively as CIE, which see*] ... ICI
International Commission on Illumination. Proceedings [*A publication*] ... Int Comm Illum Proc
International Commission on Irrigation and Drainage [*See also CIID*] ... ICID
International Commission of Jurists ... ICJ
International Commission of Jurists. Journal [*A publication*] ... JICJ
International Commission on Large Dams [*See also CIGB*] ... ICOLD
International Commission on Mathematical Instruction ... ICMI
International Commission on the Meteorology of the Upper Atmosphere ... ICMUA
International Commission on Microbiological Specifications for Foods ... ICMSF
International Commission on Mushroom Science [*Later, ISMS*] ... ICMS
International Commission on National Parks [*Later, CNPAA*] ... ICNP
International Commission for the Nomenclature of Cultivated Plants ... ICNCP
International Commission for the Northwest Atlantic Fisheries [*Superseded by NAFO*] ... ICNAF
International Commission for the Northwest Atlantic Fisheries. Annual Proceedings [*A publication*] ... Int Comm Northwest Atl Fish Annu Proc
International Commission for the Northwest Atlantic Fisheries. Annual Report [*A publication*] ... Int Comm Northwest Atl Fish Annu Rep
International Commission for the Northwest Atlantic Fisheries. Redbook. Part III [*A publication*] ... Int Comm Northwest Atl Fish Redb Part III
International Commission for the Northwest Atlantic Fisheries. Research Bulletin [*A publication*] ... Int Comm Northwest Atl Fish Res Bull
International Commission for the Northwest Atlantic Fisheries. Special Publication [*A publication*] ... Int Comm Northwest Atl Fish Spec Publ
International Commission for the Northwest Atlantic Fisheries. Statistical Bulletin [*A publication*] ... Int Comm Northwest Atl Fish Stat Bull
International Commission for Optics [*See also CIO*] ... ICO
International Commission for Orders of Chivalry ... ICOC
International Commission on Physics Education [*See also CIEP*] ... ICPE
International Commission for the Prevention of Alcoholism ... ICPA
International Commission for Protection Against Environmental Mutagens and Carcinogens ... ICPEMC
International Commission for the Protection of the Rhine Against Pollution [*See also IKSR*] ... ICPRAP
International Commission on Radiation Units and Measurements [*Formerly, ICRU*] ... ICRUM
International Commission on Radiological Protection ... ICRP
International Commission on Radiological Protection. Annals [*A publication*] ... Int Comm Radiol Prot Ann
International Commission on Radiological Protection. Publication [*A publication*] ... Int Comm Radiol Prot Publ
International Commission on Radiological Units [*Later, ICRUM*] ... ICRU
International Commission on Rules for the Approval of Electrical Equipment [*Later, CEE*] ... ICRAEE
International Commission on Signs and Symbols ... ICSS
International Commission for Small Scale Vegetation Maps ... ICSSVM
International Commission on Snow and Ice ... ICSI
International Commission for the Southeast Atlantic Fisheries [*See also CIPASE*] ... ICSAF
International Commission for the Southeast Atlantic Fisheries ... ICSEAF
International Commission for the Teaching of History ... ICTH
International Commission for Uniform Methods of Sugar Analysis ... ICUMSA
International Commission on Whaling Report [*A publication*] ... Int Comm Whaling Rep
International Commission on Yeasts and Yeast-Like Microorganisms ... ICYYLM
International Commission on Zoological Nomenclature ... ICZN
International Committee for Accounting Co-operation ... ICAC

International Committee on Aeronautical Fatigue .... ICAF
International Committee Against Apartheid, Racism, and
  Colonialism in Southern Africa .... ICSA
International Committee Against Mental Illness .... ICAMI
International Committee Against Racism ....INCAR
International Committee on Alcohol, Drugs, and Traffic Safety ......ICADTS
International Committee for the Anthropology of Food and Food
  Habits............ICAFFH
International Committee of Architectural Photogrammetry.............. ICAP
International Committee for Automobile Documentation............ ICAD
International Committee for Bird Preservation. Pan American
  Section. Research Report [A publication]............
  Int Comm Bird Preserv Pan Am Sect Res Rep
International Committee for Breaking the Language Barrier.............. ICBLB
International Committee of Catholic Nurses [See also CICIAMS].........ICCN
International Committee for the Centennial of Light ICCL
International Committee for the Check-List of the Fishes of the
  North-Eastern Atlantic and Mediterranean............CLOFNAM
International Committee on Chemical Warfare ....CCW
International Committee on Chemical Warfare, Crop
  Destruction............CCW(CD)
International Committee of Children's and Adolescents'
  Movements............ICCAM
International Committee for Coal Petrology. Proceedings [A
  publication]............Internat Comm Coal Petrology Proc
International Committee for Coal Research............ICCR
[The] International Committee for the Conservation of the
  Industrial Heritage............TICCIH
International Committee for the Conservation of Mosaics .... ICCM
International Committee for Contraceptive Research ....ICCR
International Committee for the Cooperation of Journalists ....ICCJ
International Committee for the Coordination of Clinical
  Application and Teaching of Autogenic Therapy .... ICAT
International Committee of Creole Studies ....ICCS
International Committee on Economic and Applied Microbiology..... ICEAM
International Committee of Electrochemical Thermodynamics
  and Kinetics............ICETK
International Committee on English in the Liturgy............ICEL
International Committee for Ethnic Liberty [See also IKEL]...............ICEL
International Committee on Food Microbiology and Hygiene .... ICFMH
International Committee on Future Accelerators [International
  Union of Pure and Applied Physics]............ ICFA
International Committee for Historical Sciences............ICHS
International Committee for the History of Technology ....ICOHTEC
International Committee for Horticultural Congresses............ICHC
International Committee for Human Rights in Taiwan ....ICHRT
International Committee for the Indians of the Americas ..... INCOMINDIOS
International Committee on Laboratory Animals .... ICLA
International Committee for Life Assurance Medicine .... ICLAM
International Committee on Microbial Ecology ....ICOME
International Committee of Military Medicine and Pharmacy............ ICMMP
International Committee on Nomenclature of Viruses ....ICNV
International Committee of Onomastic Sciences ....ICOS
International Committee for Outer Space Onomastics ....ICOSO
International Committee of Passenger Lines ....ICPL
International Committee for Recording the Productivity of Milk
  Animals [See also CICPLB]............ICRPMA
International Committee of the Red Cross............ICRC
International Committee on Refugees [World War II]............ICR
International Committee for the Release of Anatoly Scharansky ....ICRAS
International Committee for Research and Study on
  Environmental Factors............ICEF
International Committee on Sarcoidosis............ICS
International Committee for Social Science Information and
  Documentation [France] [Information service]............ICSSID
International Committee for the Sociology of Sport............ICSS
International Committee for Standardization in Haematology ....ICSH
International Committee for Standardization in Human Biology........ICSHB
International Committee on the Standardization of Physical
  Fitness Tests............ICSPFT
International Committee on Systematic Bacteriology ....ICSB
International Committee on Thrombosis and Hemostasis .... ICTH
International Committee on the University Emergency .... ICUE
International Committee on Veterinary Anatomical
  Nomenclature [See also CINAV]............ICVAN
International Committee on Weights and Measures ....ICWM
International Committee for World Day of Prayer ....ICWDP
International Commodities Clearing House ....ICCH
International Commodity Agreement ....ICA
International Common Law Exchange Society ....ICLES
International Communes Network ....ICN
International Communication Agency [Also known as USICA]
  [Formerly called BECA and USIA, it later became known again
  as USIA]............ICA
International Communication Association............ICA
International Communication of Orthodox Nations............ICON
International Communications Association............ICA
International Communications Satellite Consortium ....ICSC
International Communications Sciences............ICS
International Community of Booksellers' Associations [Later, IBF] ...... ICBA
International and Comparative Law Quarterly [A publication] .... I & CLQ

International and Comparative Law Quarterly [A publication] ....
  Int Comp Law Q
International and Comparative Law Quarterly [A publication] ....
  Int Comp Law Quart
International and Comparative Law Quarterly [A publication] ....
  Int & Comp L Q
International Comparative Literature Association .... ICLA
International Comparative Political Parties Project
  [Northwestern University]............ ICPP
International Competitive Bid ....ICB
International Computaprint Corporation ICC
International Computation Center [Sponsored by UNESCO]
  [Rome, Italy]............ ICC
International Computer Bibliography [A publication of National
  Computing Center]............ICB
International Computer Exhibition ....INCOMEX
International Computer Programs [Information service]............ICP
International Computer Symposium Proceedings [A publication]............
  Intl Comp Symp
International Computers Limited [Great Britain]............ICL
International Computing Center's Preparatory Committee...............ICCPC
International Concatenated Order of Hoo-Hoo [Later,
  International Order of Hoo-Hoo]............ICOHH
International Concentration Camp Committee ICCC
International Concept Study Team [for bridges] [US, Great
  Britain, Germany]............ICST
International Concerns Committee for Children ICCC
International Conciliation [A publication] .... Int Concil
International Confederation of Accordionists............ICA
International Confederation of Arab Labour Unions............ICALU
International Confederation of Arab Trade Unions............ICATU
International Confederation of Architectural Museums............ ICAM
International Confederation of Associations of Experts and
  Consultants............ICAEC
International Confederation of Book Actors ....ICOBA
International Confederation for Disarmament and Peace...............ICDP
International Confederation of Former Prisoners of War ....ICFPW
International Confederation of Free Trade Unions ....ICFTU
International Confederation of Genealogy and Heraldry [See
  also CIGH]............ICGH
International Confederation of Midwives ....ICM
International Confederation for Plastic and Reconstructive Surgery ... IPRS
International Confederation for Plastic Surgery ....IPS
International Confederation of Societies of Authors and
  Composers............ICSAC
International Confederation for Thermal Analysis............ICTA
International Conference............IC
International Conference on Acoustics, Speech, and Signal
  Processing............ ICASSP
International Conference of Administrators of Residential
  Centers for Youth [Formerly, NCSTSR]............ICA
International Conference of Agricultural Economists [Later, IAAE] ...... ICAE
International Conference on Automatic Control of Mines and
  Collieries............ICAMC
International Conference of Building Officials............ICBO
International Conference on Cataloging Principles ....ICCP
International Conference of Catholic Charities ICCC
International Conference. Center for High Energy Forming.
  Proceedings [A publication]............Int Conf Cent High Energy Form Proc
International Conference on Communications............ ICC
International Conference on Computer Applications [in
  developing countries] [1977]............ICCA
International Conference on Computers and the Humanities ....ICCH
International Conference of Coordination Chemistry ICCC
International Conference on Education in Chemistry ....ICEC
International Conference on Energy Use Management......................ICEUM
International Conference on Environmental Sensing and
  Assessment............ICESA
International Conference on Fire Safety. Proceedings [A
  publication]............Int Conf Fire Saf Proc
International Conference on Fluid Sealing. Proceedings [A
  publication]............Int Conf Fluid Sealing Proc
International Conference Group ....ICG
International Conference on High Energy Physics and Nuclear
  Structure............ICOHEPANS
International Conference on High Energy Rate Fabrication.
  Proceedings [A publication]............Int Conf High Energy Rate Fabr Proc
International Conference of Historians of the Labour Movement........ICHLM
International Conference Industry Association ....ICIA
International Conference on Information Processing [Paris, 1959].........ICIP
International Conference of Jewish Communal Service ....ICJCS
International Conference on Large Electrical Systems ....ICLES
International Conference on Machine Searching and Translation ..... ICMST
International Conference on Magnetics ....INTERMAG
International Conference on Medical Electronics ....ICME
International Conference on Organometallic Chemistry ....ICOMC
International Conference on the Peaceful Uses of Atomic
  Energy............ ICPUAE
International Conference on the Physics of Electronic and
  Atomic Collisions............ ICPEAC
International Conference of Police Associations [Defunct]...................ICPA

International Conference of Police Chaplains ... ICPC
International Conference for Promoting Technical Uniformity on Railways ... ICPTUR
International Conference on the Properties of Steam ... ICPS
International Conference on Scientific Information ... ICSI
International Conference of Social Work ... ICSW
International Conference of Sociology of Religion ... ICSR
International Conference on Soil Mechanics and Foundation Engineering. Proceedings [*A publication*] ... Int Conf Soil Mech Found Eng Proc
International Conference of Symphony and Opera Musicians ... ICSOM
International Conference on Thermal Analysis. Proceedings [*A publication*] ... Int Conf Therm Anal Proc
International Conference on Transfer of Water Resources Knowledge. Proceedings [*A publication*] ... Int Conf Transfer Water Resour Knowl Proc
International Conference on the Unity of the Sciences ... ICUS
International Conference on University Education for Public Relations ... ICUEPR
International Conference on Waste Oil Recovery and Reuse ... ICWORR
International Conference on Water Pollution Research [*A publication*] ... Int Conf Water Pollut Res
International Conference of Women Engineers and Scientists ... ICWES
International Congregational Council ... ICC
International Congress of Acarology ... ICA
International Congress of Africanists ... ICA
International Congress of Americanists ... ICA
International Congress on Animal Reproduction and Artificial Insemination [*A publication*] ... Int Congr Anim Reprod Artif Insemin
International Congress on Astronautics. Proceedings [*A publication*] ... Int Congr Astronaut Proc
International Congress of Biochemistry. Abstracts [*A publication*] ... Int Congr Biochem Abstr
International Congress on Catalysis. Preprints [*A publication*] ... Int Congr Catal Prepr
International Congress of Clinical Chemistry [*A publication*] ... Int Congr Clin Chem
International Congress on Combustion Engines ... ICCE
International Congress and Convention Association ... ICCA
International Congress of Dealers Associations ... ICDA
International Congress of Dealers Associations ... InCODA
International Congress of Electrical and Electronic Communications ... ICEEC
International Congress on Electron Microscopy. Proceedings [*A publication*] ... Int Congr Electron Micros Proc
International Congress of Entomology ... ICE
International Congress of Entomology. Proceedings [*A publication*] ... Int Congr Entomol Proc
International Congress on Fracture ... ICF
International Congress of Genetics ... ICG
International Congress of Hematology. Lectures [*A publication*] ... Int Congr Hematol Lect
International Congress on High-Speed Photography and Photonics ... ICHSPP
International Congress of Historical Sciences. Proceedings [*A publication*] ... Internatl Cong Hist Sci Proc
International Congress of Industrial Waste Water and Wastes ... ICIWWW
International Congress on Instrumentation in Aerospace Simulation Facilities ... ICIASF
International Congress on Large Dams [*A publication*] ... Int Congr Large Dams
International Congress of Maritime Museums ... ICMM
International Congress of Mathematicians ... ICM
International Congress for Measurement and Automation ... INTERMAMA
International Congress of Medical Laboratory Technologists ... ICMLT
International Congress for Microbiology Symposia [*A publication*] ... Int Congr Microbiol Symp
International Congress on Occupational Health ... ICOH
International Congress of Oral Implantologists ... ICOI
International Congress of Orientalists [*A publication*] ... ICO
International Congress of Orientalists. Proceedings [*A publication*] ... PICO
International Congress on Pteridines. Handbook [*A publication*] ... Int Congr Pteridines Handb
International Congress of Publishers ... ICP
International Congress of Radiology ... ICR
International Congress Series [*Elsevier Book Series*] [*A publication*] ... ICS
International Congress of Speleology. Abhandlungen [*A publication*] ... Int Congr Speleol Abh
International Congress of the Transplantation Society ... ICTS
International Congress of University Adult Education ... ICUAE
International Congress of Zoology. Proceedings [*A publication*] ... Int Cong Zool Pr
International Congresses on Tropical Medicine and Malaria ... ICTMM
International Conrad Society ... ICS
International Consommateurs Organization des Unions [*International Organization of Consumers Unions*] ... ICOU
International Construction [*A publication*] ... Int Constr
International Consultants Foundation ... ICF
International Consultative Council of Travel Agents ... ICCTA
International Consumer Credit Association ... ICCA
International Container Bureau ... ICB
International Contemporary Music Exchange ... ICME
International Control ... IC
International Control Commission [*Composed of representatives of Canada, India, and Poland, and charged with supervising the cease-fire in Laos established at Geneva Conference of 1962*] ... ICC
International Control Commission for Vietnam ... ICC
International Control Plan ... ICP
International Controls Corporation ... ICC
International Controls Corp. [*American Stock Exchange symbol*] ... INC
International Convention of Faith, Churches, and Ministers ... ICFCM
International Convention for Safe Containers ... CSC
International Convention on Transistors and Semiconductor Devices ... ICTASD
International Cooperation ... IC
International Cooperation Administration [*Later, Agency for International Development*] ... ICA
International Cooperation Council [*Later, UDC*] ... ICC
International Cooperation in Information Retrieval among Examining Patent Offices ... ICIREPAT
International Cooperation Year [*1965*] [*20th anniversary of UN*] ... ICY
International Cooperative Development Association [*Later, ACDI*] ... ICDA
International Cooperative Fracture Institute ... ICFI
International Cooperative Housing Development Association ... ICHDA
International Cooperative Insurance Federation ... ICIF
International Cooperative Investigations of the Tropical Atlantic [*Navy*] ... ICITA
International Cooperative Petroleum Association ... ICPA
International Cooperative Training Center ... ICTC
International Coordinating Committee for the Presentation of Science and the Development of Out-of-School Scientific Activities [*See also CIC*] ... ICC
International Coordinating Council of Aerospace Industries Associations ... ICCAIA
International Coordination Group [*IOC*] ... ICG
International Copper Research Association ... INCRA
International Copyrights Information Center [*UNESCO*] ... INCINC
International Cornish Bantam Breeders' Association ... ICBBA
International Corona Resources Ltd. [*NASDAQ symbol*] ... ICREF
International Corporation [*Generic term*] ... IC
International Correspondence Chess Federation ... ICCF
International Correspondence of Corkscrew Addicts ... ICCA
International Correspondence School ... ICS
International Correspondence Schools. Serial [*A publication*] ... Internat Correspondence Schools Serial
International Correspondence Society of Allergists ... ICSA
International Correspondence Society of Obstetricians and Gynecologists ... ICSOG
International Corrosion Council ... ICC
International Corrugated Case Association ... ICCA
International Cotton Advisory Committee ... ICAC
International Council for Adult Education ... ICAE
International Council for the Advancement of Surfing ... ICAS
International Council of the Aeronautical Sciences ... ICAS
International Council Against Bullfighting ... ICAB
International Council of Air Shows ... ICAS
International Council of Aircraft Owner and Pilot Associations ... IAOPA
International Council on Alcohol and Addictions ... ICAA
International Council of the Architects of Historical Monuments ... ICARMO
International Council on Archives [*UNESCO*] ... ICA
International Council of Ballroom Dancing ... ICBD
International Council for Bird Preservation ... ICBP
International Council for Building Research, Studies, and Documentation ... ICBRSD
International Council of Catholic Men [*See also FIHC*] ... ICCM
International Council for Children's Play ... ICCP
International Council of Christian Churches [*Later, National Council of Community Churches*] ... ICCC
International Council for Christian Leadership ... ICL
International Council of Christians and Jews ... ICCJ
International Council to Combat Lethal Yellowing ... ICCLY
International Council of Commerce Employers ... ICCE
International Council for Commercial Arbitration ... ICCA
International Council for Computer Communication ... ICCC
International Council for Computers in Education ... ICCE
International Council for Distance Education ... ICDE
International Council on Education for Teaching ... ICET
International Council for Education of the Visually Handicapped ... ICEVH
International Council for Educational Development ... ICED
International Council for Educational Films [*Later, ICEM*] ... ICEF
International Council for Educational Media [*Formerly, ICEF*] ... ICEM
International Council on Electrocardiology ... ICE
International Council of Environmental Law ... ICEL
International Council for Exceptional Children [*Later, CEC*] ... ICEC
International Council for the Exploration of the Sea ... ICES
International Council for the Exploration of the Sea. Cooperative Research Report [*A publication*] ... Int Counc Explor Sea Coop Res Rep
International Council for the Exploration of the Sea. Cooperative Research Report. Series A [*A publication*] ... Int Counc Explor Sea Coop Res Rep Ser A

International Council for the Exploration of the Sea. Cooperative Research Report. Series B [*A publication*] ... Int Counc Explor Sea Coop Res Rep Ser B
International Council of Fan Clubs [*Defunct*] ... ICFC
International Council of the French Language [*See also CILF*] ... ICFL
International Council on the Future of the University ... ICFU
International Council of Goodwill Industries ... ICGI
International Council of Graphic Design Associations ... ICOGRADA
International Council for Health, Physical Education, and Recreation ... ICHPER
International Council of Homehelp Services [*See also CISAF*] ... ICHS
International Council of Industrial Editors [*Later, IABC*] ... ICIE
International Council of Industrial Engineers ... ICIE
International Council of Infant Food Industries ... ICIFI
International Council for Infant Survival ... ICIS
International Council of Jewish Women ... ICJW
International Council of Jews from Czechoslovakia ... ICJC
International Council of Kinetography Laban ... ICKL
International Council of Marine Industries Associations ... ICOMIA
International Council of Monuments and Sites ... ICOMOS
International Council of Museums ... ICOM
International Council of the National Academy of Television Arts and Sciences ... IC/NATVAS
International Council of Nurses ... ICN
International Council for Philosophy and Humanistic Studies ... ICPHS
International Council for Physical Fitness Research ... ICPFR
International Council for Pressure Vessel Technology ... ICPVT
International Council of Psychologists ... ICP
International Council for Reprography ... ICR
International Council for Research in Agroforestry ... ICRAF
International Council for Research in the Sociology of Co-operation ... ICRSC
International Council of Scientific Unions ... ICSU
International Council of Scientific Unions Abstracting Board [*Also, IAB*] ... ICSU AB
International Council of Seamen's Agencies [*Formerly, NCSA*] ... ICOSA
International Council of Shopping Centers ... ICSC
International Council for Small Business [*Formerly, NCSBMD*] ... ICSB
International Council of Social Democratic Women [*Later, SIW*] ... ICSDW
International Council for the Social Studies ... ICSS
International Council on Social Welfare ... ICSW
International Council of Societies of Industrial Design ... ICSID
International Council of Societies of Pathology ... ICSP
International Council of Sport and Physical Education ... ICSPE
International Council of Tanners [*See also CIT*] ... ICT
International Council for Technical Communication ... INTECOM
International Council for Traditional Music [*Formerly, IFMC*] ... ICTM
International Council on United Fund Raising ... ICUFR
International Council of Voluntary Agencies ... ICVA
International Council of Women ... ICW
International Council of Women Psychologists [*Later, ICP*] ... ICWP
International Councils on Higher Education [*Formerly, CHEAR*] [*Defunct*] ... ICHE
International Country and Western Music Association ... ICWMA
International Couriers Corp. [*American Stock Exchange symbol*] [*Delisted*] ... ICR
International Court of Justice ... ICJ
International Courtly Literature Society ... ICLS
International Crane Foundation ... ICF
International Craniopathic Society ... ICS
International Creative Writers League ... ICWL
International Credit Insurance Association ... ICIA
International Cricket Conference ... ICC
International Criminal Justice Association ... ICJA
International Criminal Justice Clearinghouse [*Formerly, NCJRS*] [*Law Enforcement Assistance Administration*] ... ICJC
International Criminal Law Commission ... ICLC
International Criminal Police Commission [*Later, INTERPOL*] ... ICPC
International Criminal Police Organization ... ICPO
International Criminal Police Organization ... INTERPOL
International Critical Tables ... ICT
International Crocodilian Society [*Defunct*] ... ICS
International Crop Improvement Association [*Later, AOSCA*] ... ICIA
International Crops Research Institute for the Semi-Arid Tropics [*India*] ... ICRISAT
International Cross-Country Union ... ICCU
International Cruiser/Race Class [*Yachting*] ... IC/R
International Cryogenic Engineering Conferences [*A publication*] ... Int Cryog Eng Conf
International Cultural Centers for Youth ... ICCY
International Cultural Exchange ... ICE
International Cultural Exchange ... ICX
International Cultural Exchange Service ... ICES
International Currency Review [*A publication*] ... Int Currency R
International Current Meter Group. Report [*A publication*] ... Int Curr Meter Group Rep
International Customer Service Association ... ICSA
International Cycling Union ... ICU
International Cystic Fibrosis (Mucoviscidosis) Association ... ICF(M)A
International Dairy Committee ... IDC
International Dairy Development Scheme ... IDDS
International Dairy Federation [*See also FIL*] ... IDF
International Dairy Federation. Annual Bulletin [*A publication*] ... Int Dairy Fed Annu Bull
International Dairy Queen [*NASDAQ symbol*] ... INDQ
International Dance-Exercise Association ... IDEA
International Data and Analysis [*Bureau of Mines*] ... IDA
International Data Corporation [*Information service*] ... IDC
International Data Library and Reference Service ... IDL & RS
International Data Processing Institute ... IDPI
International Database Association ... IDA
International Date Line ... IDL
International Decade of Ocean Exploration [*1970's*] ... IDOE
International Decorative Accessories Center ... IDAC
International Deep Drawing Research Group ... IDDRG
International Defence and Aid Fund for Southern Africa ... IDAF
International Defenders of Animals ... IDA
International Defense and Aid Fund for Southern Africa, US Committee ... D & A
International Democratic Fellowship ... IDF
International Demographic Data Center [*Bureau of the Census*] [*Information service*] ... IDDC
International Demographic Data Directory [*Agency for International Development*] ... IDDD
International Dendrology Union ... IDU
International Dental Journal [*A publication*] ... Int Dent J
International Deployment of Accelerometers [*Project*] [*Seismography*] ... IDA
International Desalination and Environmental Association ... IDEA
International Desert Locust Information Service ... IDLIS
International Desert Racing Association [*Automobile racing*] ... IDRA
International Design Center, New York ... IDCNY
International Design Conference in Aspen ... IDCA
International Development Agency ... IDA
International Development and Assistance Program ... IDAP
International Development Association [*An agency of the International Bank for Reconstruction and Development*] ... IDA
International Development Conference ... IDC
[*US*] **International Development Cooperation Agency** [*Independent government agency*] ... IDCA
International Development Corporation [*Proposed corporation to combine Alliance for Progress and Agency for International Development*] ... IDC
International Development Data Center [*Georgia Institute of Technology*] ... IDDC
International Development - Economics Awareness System ... IDEAS
International Development Education Documentation Service [*University of Pittsburgh*] ... IDEDS
International Development Foundation ... IDF
International Development Institute [*Agency for International Development program*] ... IDI
International Development Research Centre [*Canada*] ... IDRC
International Development Research Centre, Ottawa, ON, Canada [*Library symbol*] ... CaOOID
International Development Review [*A publication*] ... Int Develop R
International Development Review [*A publication*] ... Int Dev Rev
International Development Services ... IDS
International Development Strategy [*United Nations*] ... IDS
International Diabetes Federation [*See also FID*] ... IDF
International Diagnostic Technology [*Medicine*] ... IDT
International Dialect Institute ... IDI
International Diamond Council ... IDC
International Die Sinkers' Conference ... DSC
International Die Sinkers' Conference ... IDSC
International Digest [*A publication*] ... Int Dig
International Digest of Health Legislation [*A publication*] ... Int Dig Health Legis
International Digital Data Service [*Western Union*] ... IDDS
International Direct Dialing [*Telecommunications*] ... IDD
International Direct Distance Dialing [*AT & T*] ... IDDD
International Directory of Research and Development Scientists [*A publication*] ... IDR & DS
International Disarmament Organization [*Proposed*] ... IDO
International Discotheque Association [*Defunct*] ... IDA
International Distress Frequency ... IDF
International District Heating Association ... IDHA
International District Heating Association. Official Proceedings [*A publication*] ... Int Dist Heat Assoc Off Proc
International District Office ... IDO
International Division [*Army Service Forces*] [*World War II*] ... ID
International DN [*Detroit News*] **Ice Yacht Racing Association** ... IDNIYRA
International Doctors in Alcoholics Anonymous ... IDAA
International Documentary Association ... IDA
International Documentation Center ... IDC
International Documentation in Chemistry ... IDC
International Documentation on the Contemporary Church ... IDOC
International Documentation and Information Centre ... INTERDOK
International Documents Service [*Defunct*] ... IDS
International Doll Association [*Defunct*] ... IDA
International Doll Makers Association [*Later, IDMA Internationals*] ... IDMA
International Dostoevsky Society ... IDS
International Dostoevsky Society Bulletin [*A publication*] ... IDSB

International Double Reed Society ... IDRS
International Downtown Executives Association ... IDEA
International Dragon Class Association ... IDCA
International Drapery Association ... IDA
International Dredging Abstracts [*A publication*] ... Int Dredg Abstr
International Dredging Association ... IDA
International Drivers' Behaviour Research Association ... IDBRA
International Driving Permit ... IDP
International Drug Regulatory Monitor [*A publication*] ... Int Drug Regul Monit
International Drycleaners Congress ... IDC
International Dwarf Fruit Trees Association ... IDFTA
International Ecology Society ... IES
International Economic Association ... IEA
International Economic Consultative Organization for Korea [*Ten-nation consortium*] ... IECOK
International Economic History Association ... IEHA
International Economic Indicators and Competitive Trends [*A publication*] ... Inter Econ Indic & Comp Tr
International Economic Policy ... IEP
International Economic Policy Association ... IEPA
International Economic Review [*A publication*] ... Int Econ R
International Economic Review [*A publication*] ... IntER
International Edsel Club ... IEC
International Education Act ... IEA
International Education Assembly [*World War II*] ... IEA
International Education Association ... IEA
International Education Exchange Service [*Department of State*] ... IEES
International Education Office [*World War II*] ... IEO
International Education Year [*UN designation*] ... IEY
International Educational and Cultural Exchange ... IEC
International Educational and Cultural Exchange [*Washington, DC*] [*A publication*] ... IECE
International Educational and Cultural Exchange [*A publication*] ... Int Ed & Cul Exch
International Educational and Cultural Exchange [*A publication*] ... Inter Ed & Cul Ex
International Egg Commission ... IEC
International Electronic Devices [*Conference*] ... IED
International Electronic Facsimile Users Association ... IEFUA
International Electronic Packaging Society ... IEPS
International Electronic Packaging Symposium ... IECPS
International Electronic Post [*Postal service*] ... INTELPOST
International Electronic Publishing Research Center ... IEPRC
International Electronic Research Corporation ... IERC
International Electronics Corporation ... IEC
International Electronics Engineering, Incorporated ... IEEI
International Electronics Manufacturing Company ... IEMC
International Electrotechnical Commission [*See also CEI*] ... IEC
International Electrotechnical Commission. Publications [*A publication*] ... Int Electrotech Comm Publ
International Electrotechnical Vocabulary ... IEV
International Embryo Transfer Society ... IETS
International Emergency Economic Powers Act [*1977*] ... IEEPA
International Emergency Food Council [*Post-World War II*] ... IEFC
International Encyclopedia of the Social Sciences [*A publication*] ... IESS
International Energy Agency ... IEA
International Energy Bank ... IEB
International Energy Program ... IEP
International English Shepherd Registry ... IESR
International Entrepreneurs Association [*Later, AEA*] ... IEA
International Environment Reporter [*A publication*] ... INER
International Environment and Safety [*A publication*] ... Int Environ Saf
International Environmental Bureau for the Non-Ferrous Metals Industry ... IEB
International Epidemiological Association ... IEA
International Ergonomics Association ... IEA
International Erosion Control Association ... IECA
International Esperantist Organization of Naturalists [*See also INOE*] ... IEON
International Esperanto Institute ... IEI
International Evaluations, Incorporated ... IEI
International Exchange Office ... IEO
International Exchange Service [*For publications*] [*Smithsonian Institution*] ... IES
International Exchangors Association ... INTEREX
International Executive Service Corps ... IESC
International Executives Association ... IEA
International Exhibition of Industrial Electronics ... INEI
International Exhibitions Bureau ... IEB
International Exhibitions Foundation ... IEF
International Explorers Society ... IES
International Eye Foundation ... IEF
International Fabricare Institute [*Formerly, AIL, NID*] ... IFI
International Facility Management Association ... IFMA
International Falcon Movement ... IFM
International Falcon Movement - Socialist Educational International ... IFM-SEI
International Fallout Warning Exercise ... INTEX
International Falls [*Minnesota*] [*Airport symbol*] ... INL
International Falls, MN [*Radio station call letters*] ... KGHS
International Falls, MN [*Radio station call letters*] ... KICC
International Falls, MN [*Television station call letters*] ... KITF
International Falls, MN [*Radio station call letters*] ... KSDM
International Falls Public Library, International Falls, MN [*Library symbol*] ... MnIf
International Family Planning Digest [*A publication*] ... Int Fam Plann Dig
International Family Planning Research Association [*Later, ISRM*] ... IFPRA
International Fan Club Association [*Formerly, FCA*] ... IFCA
International Fan Club Organization ... IFCO
International Fancy Guppy Association [*Supersedes AGA*] ... IFGA
International Farm Management Association ... IFMA
International Farmers Association for Education ... IFAE
International Federation of Accountants ... IFAC
International Federation of Actors ... IFA
International Federation of Advertising Agencies [*Formerly, NFAA*] ... IFAA
International Federation of Aestheticians ... INFA
International Federation on Ageing [*Formerly, IARP*] ... IFA
International Federation of Agricultural Producers ... IFAP
International Federation of Air Line Pilots Associations ... IFALPA
International Federation of Air Traffic Controllers' Associations ... IFATCA
International Federation of Air Traffic Safety Electronic Associations ... IFATSEA
International Federation of Airworthiness ... IFA
International Federation of Airworthiness Technology and Engineering ... IFATE
International Federation of American Homing Pigeon Fanciers ... IF
International Federation of American Homing Pigeon Fanciers ... IFAHPF
International Federation of Aquarium Societies ... IFAS
International Federation of Associations of Computer Users in Engineering Architecture and Related Fields ... FACE
International Federation of Associations of Textile Chemists and Colourists ... IFATCC
International Federation of Audit Bureaus of Circulations ... IFABC
International Federation on Automatic Control ... IFAC
International Federation of the Blind ... IFB
International Federation of Blood Donor Organizations [*See also FIODS*] ... IFBDO
International Federation of Boat Show Organisers ... IFBSO
International Federation of Bodybuilders ... IFBB
International Federation of Building and Wood Workers ... IFBWW
International Federation of Business and Professional Women ... IFBPW
International Federation of Camping and Caravanning ... IFCC
International Federation of Catholic Alumnae ... IFCA
International Federation of Catholic Journalists ... IFCJ
International Federation of Catholic Pharmacists ... IFCP
International Federation of Catholic Universities ... IFCU
International Federation of Cell Biology ... IFCB
International Federation of Chemical Workers' Unions ... IFCWU
International Federation of Children's Communities ... IFCC
International Federation of Christian Metalworkers Unions ... IFCM
International Federation of Christian Miners' Unions ... IFCMU
International Federation of Christian Trade Unions [*Often uses initialism CISC, based on name in French, to avoid confusion with ICFTU*] ... IFCTU
International Federation of Christian Trade Unions of Building and Wood Workers ... IFCTUBWW
International Federation of Christian Trade Unions of Graphical and Paper Industries ... IFCTUGP
International Federation of Christian Unions of Agricultural Workers ... IFCUAW
International Federation of Clinical Chemistry ... IFCC
International Federation of Commercial, Clerical, and Technical Employees ... IFCCTE
International Federation of Commercial Travelers Insurance Organizations [*Later, CTIF*] ... IFCTIO
International Federation of Community Centre Associations ... IFCCA
International Federation of Computer Sciences ... IFCS
International Federation of Cotton and Allied Textile Industries [*Later, ITMF*] ... IFCATI
International Federation of Data Organizations for the Social Sciences [*West Germany*] [*Information service*] ... IFDO
International Federation for Documentation ... IFD
International Federation of Electron Microscope Societies ... IFEMS
International Federation of Elvis Presley Fan Clubs ... IFEPFC
International Federation of Employees in Public Service ... INFEDOP
International Federation of Engine Reconditioners [*See also FIRM*] ... IFER
International Federation of Falerists ... IFF
International Federation for Family Health ... IFFH
International Federation for Family Life Promotion ... IFFLP
International Federation of Film Archives ... IFFA
International Federation of Film Producers' Associations ... IFFPA
International Federation of Film Societies ... IFFS
International Federation of Free Journalists of Central and Eastern Europe and Baltic and Balkan Countries ... IFFJ
International Federation of Free Teachers' Unions ... IFFTU
International Federation of Fruit Juice Producers ... IFFJP
International Federation of Fruit Juice Producers ... IFJU
International Federation of Gastronomical and Vinicultural Press ... IFGVP
International Federation of Grocers' Associations [*See also IVLD*] ... IFGA
International Federation of Gynecology and Obstetrics ... IFGO
International Federation of the Hard of Hearing ... IFHOH

International Federation of Health Professionals....IFHP
International Federation of Health Records Organizations....IFHRO
International Federation for Home Economics [*See also FIEF*]....IFHE
International Federation for Housing and Planning....IFHP
International Federation for Housing and Town Planning....IFHTP
International Federation of Hydraulic Platform Manufacturers....IFHPM
International Federation for Hygiene, Preventive Medicine, and Social Medicine....IFHPMSM
International Federation of Importers and Wholesale Grocers Associations....IFIWA
International Federation of Independent Air Transport....IFIAT
International Federation of Industrial Organizations and General Workers' Unions....IFIF
International Federation for Information Processing....IFIP
International Federation of Information Processing Societies [*Later, IFIP*]....IFIPS
International Federation of Institutes for Advanced Study....IFIAS
International Federation of Institutes for Socio-Religious Research....IFISRR
International Federation of Interior Architects Interior Designers....IFI
International Federation for Internal Freedom [*Later, Castalia Foundation*]....IFIF
International Federation of Inventors' Associations....IFIA
International Federation of Ironmongers and Iron Merchants Associations [*See also FIDAQ*]....IFIA
International Federation of Journalists [*See also FIJ*]....IFJ
International Federation of Kennel Clubs....IFKC
International Federation of Knitting Technologists [*See also FITB*]....IFKT
International Federation of Landscape Architects....IFLA
International Federation of Library Associations....IFLA
International Federation of Library Associations. News [*A publication*]....IFLA News
International Federation of Margarine Associations....IFMA
International Federation of Master-Craftsmen [*See also IFH*]....IFC
International Federation for Medical and Biological Engineering....IFMBE
International Federation for Medical Electronics....IFME
International Federation for Medical Psychotherapy [*See also IGAP*]....IFMP
International Federation of Medical Students Associations [*See also FIAEM*]....IFMSA
International Federation for Modern Languages and Literatures [*A publication*]....IFMLL
International Federation of Multiple Sclerosis Societies....IFMSS
International Federation of Municipal Engineers....IFME
International Federation for Narcotic Education....IFNE
International Federation of Netball Associations....IFNA
International Federation of Operational Research Societies....IFORS
International Federation of Ophthalmological Societies....IFOS
International Federation of Organic Agriculture Movements....IFOAM
International Federation of Oto-Rhino-Laryngological Societies....IFOS
International Federation for Parent Education [*See also FIEP*]....IFPE
International Federation of Park and Recreation Administration....IFPRA
International Federation of Pedestrians....IFP
International Federation of the Periodical Press....IFPP
International Federation of Petroleum and Chemical Workers....IFPCW
International Federation of Petroleum Workers....IFPW
International Federation of Pharmaceutical Manufacturers Associations [*See also FIIM*]....IFPMA
International Federation of Philosophical Societies [*See also FISP*]....IFPS
International Federation of Phonogram and Videogram Producers....IFPI
International Federation of Photographic Art....IFPA
International Federation of the Photographic Industry....IFPI
International Federation of Physical Medicine....IFPM
International Federation of Physical Medicine and Rehabilitation....IFPMR
International Federation of Plantation, Agricultural, and Allied Workers....IFPAAW
International Federation of Popular Travel Organisations....IFPTO
International Federation of Postcard Dealers....IFPD
International Federation of Press Cutting Agencies....IFPCA
International Federation of Professional and Technical Engineers....IFPTE
International Federation of Professional and Technical Engineers....PTE
International Federation of Protestant Workers' Associations....IFPWA
International Federation of Psychoanalytic Societies....IFPS
International Federation of Purchasing....IFP
International Federation of Purchasing and Materials Management....IFPMM
International Federation of Railway Advertising Companies....IFRAC
International Federation of Recreational Vehicle Users [*Later, FOR*]....IFORVU
International Federation of Resistance Movements....IFRM
International Federation of the Rights of Man....IFRM
International Federation of Roofing Contractors [*See also IFD*]....IFRC
International Federation of Sanitarians Organizations [*Defunct*]....IFSO
International Federation of Scientific Editors' Associations....IFSEA
International Federation of Senior Police Officers....IFSPO
International Federation of Settlements and Neighbourhood Centres [*Defunct*]....IFS
International Federation of Settlements and Neighbourhood Centres [*Defunct*]....IFSNC
International Federation of Shipmasters Associations....IFSMA
International Federation of Shorthand and Typewriting....IFST
International Federation of Social Science Organizations [*See also FIOSS*]....IFSSO
International Federation of Social Workers....IFSW
International Federation of the Socialist and Democratic Press....IFSDP
International Federation of the Societies of Classical Studies....IFSCS
International Federation of Societies of Cosmetic Chemists....IFSCC
International Federation of Societies for Electroencephalography and Clinical Neurophysiology....IFSECN
International Federation of Societies for Electron Microscopy....IFSEM
International Federation of Societies for Histochemistry and Cytochemistry....IFSHC
International Federation of Societies of Philosophy....IFSP
International Federation of Societies for Surgery of the Hand....IFSSH
International Federation of Sound Hunters....IFSH
International Federation of Sports Acrobatics....IFSA
International Federation of Sports Medicine....IFSM
International Federation of Stamp Dealers' Associations....IFSDA
International Federation of Students in Political Sciences....IFSPS
International Federation of Surgical Colleges....IFSC
International Federation of Surveyors [*See also FIG*]....IFS
International Federation of Teachers' Associations [*Later, WCOTP*]....IFTA
International Federation of Teachers' Unions....IFTU
International Federation of the Technical and Periodical Press....IFTPP
International Federation of Telephone Emergency Services....IFOTES
International Federation of Television Archives [*See also FIAT*]....IFTA
International Federation of the Temperance Blue Cross Societies....IFTBCS
International Federation of Textile Workers' Associations....IFTWA
International Federation of Thanatologists Associations....IFTA
International Federation for the Theory of Machines and Mechanisms....IFTOMM
International Federation of Thermalism and Climatism....IFTC
International Federation of Tobacco Workers....IFTW
International Federation of Trade Unions....IFTU
International Federation of Trade Unions of Transport Workers [*See also FIOST*]....IFTUTW
International Federation of Training and Development Organizations....IFTDO
International Federation of Translators....IFT
International Federation of Unions of Employees in Public and Civil Services....IFPCS
International Federation of University Women....IFUW
International Federation of Wargaming [*Defunct*]....IFW
International Federation for Weeks of Art....IFWA
International Federation of Women Lawyers....IFWL
International Federation of Women's Hockey Associations....IFWHA
International Federation of Women's Travel Organizations....IFWTO
International Federation of Workers' Educational Associations [*See also IVB*]....IFWEA
International Federation of Young Cooperators....IFYC
International Fellowship of Evangelical Students....IFES
International Fellowship of Former Scouts and Guides....IFOFSAG
International Fellowship of Reconciliation....IFOR
International Fence Industry Association....IFIA
International Fencing Federation....IFF
International Ferrocement Information Center....IFIC
International Fertility Association [*Defunct*]....IFA
International Fertility Research Program....IFRP
International Fertility Research Program, Durham, NC [*Library symbol*]....NcDurIF
International Fertilizer Development Center....IFDC
International Fertilizer Industry Association....IFA
International Fertilizer Supply Scheme [*FAO*] [*United Nations*]....IFSS
International Festivals Association....IFA
International Fiber Optics and Communications [*A publication*]....IFOC
International Fiction Review [*A publication*]....IFR
International Field Office [*FAA*]....IFO
International Field Year for the Great Lakes....IFYGL
International Field Year for the Great Lakes. Bulletin [*A publication*]....IFYGL Bull
International Field Year for the Great Lakes. Technical Manual Series [*A publication*]....Int Field Year Great Lakes Tech Man Ser
International Fighter Aircraft....IFA
International Fighter RADAR....IFR
International Fight'n Rooster Cutlery Club....IFRCC
International Figure Skating Writers Association [*Defunct*]....IFSWA
International Filariasis Association....IFA
International Film Foundation....IFF
International Film Guide [*A publication*]....Interntl F G
International Film Institute....IFI
International Film Seminars....IFS
International Film and Television Council....IFTC
International Finance Corporation [*Affiliate of International Bank for Reconstruction and Development*]....IFC
International Financial Institution....IFI
International Fire Administration Institute....IFAI
International Fire Buff Associates....IFBA
International Fire Photographers Association....IFPA
International Fire Service Training Association....IFSTA
International Fiscal Association....IFA
International Fisheries Commission [*Later, IPHC*] [*US and Canada*]....IFC

International Fisheries Commission, Seattle, WA [Library symbol].....WaSIF
International Fixed Public ....IFP
International Flame Research Foundation....................................IFRF
International Flat Earth Research Society....................................IFERS
International Flavors & Fragrances, Inc. [NYSE symbol] ....IFF
International Flavors & Fragrances, Inc., Union Beach, NJ
   [Library symbol] ....NjUbI
International Flight Attendants Association ....IFAA
International Flight Information Manual ....IFIM
International Flight Service Receiver Site...................................IFSR
International Flight Service Station [FAA]...................................IFSS
International Flight Service Transmitter Site...............................IFST
International Florists Association ....IFA
International Flying Dutchman Class Association of the US..........IFDCAUS
International Flying Dutchman Junior Class Organization ....FJUS
International Flying Dutchmen Class Organization.........................IFDCO
International Flying Farmers ....IFF
International Flying Nurses Association ....IFNA
International Foderation der Ausschusse Normenpraxis
   [International Federation for the Application of Standards]...............IFAN
International Folk Music Council [Later, ICTM]............................IFMC
International Folk Music Council. Journal [A publication] ....IFMCJ
International Folk Music Council. Journal [A publication]
                            Int Folk Mus Council Jl
International Folk Music Council. Yearbook [A publication].................IFMCY
International Food Additives Council ....IFAC
International Food Information Service ....IFIS
International Food Policy Research Institute.................................IFPRI
International Food Policy Research Institute, Washington, DC
   [Library symbol]..DIFP
International Food Service Executives Association ....IFSEA
International Foodservice Corp. [American Stock Exchange
   symbol] [Delisted]..IFS
International Foodservice Distributors Association ....IFDA
International Foodservice Editorial Council...................................IFEC
International Foodservice Manufacturers Association ....IFMA
International Footprint Association ....IFA
International Ford Retractable Club ....IFRC
International Fortean Organization..INFO
International Forum ....IF
International Forum Foundation ....IFF
International Forum on Information and Documentation [A
   publication]...Int Forum Inf Docum
[The] International Foundation..TIF
International Foundation for Art Research...................................IFAR
International Foundation for Cancer Research ....IFCR
International Foundation for the Conservation of Game ....IGF
International Foundation for Development Alternatives [See also
   FIPAD]..IFDA
International Foundation of Employee Benefit Plans ....IFEBP
International Foundation for Homeopathy ....IFH
International Foundation for Independence..................................IFI
International Foundation for Research in the Field of Advertising.........IFRA
International Foundation for Science [See also FIS]......................IFS
International Foundation for Telemetering ....IFT
International Foundation for Theatrical Research ....IFTR
International Fox-Tango Club ....IFTC
International Fragrance Association ....IFRA
International Franchise Association ....IFA
International Franchised Dealers Association [Later, SFDA].............IFDA
International Frankenstein Society ....IFS
International Free Trade Area ....IFTA
International Freight Airways SA [Belgium] [ICAO designator] ....FW
International Freighting Weekly [A publication] ....In Freight
International Frequency List ....IFL
International Frequency List Committee......................................IFLC
International Frequency Registration Board [of the ITU]...............IFRB
International Frequency Tables ....IFT
International Friends of Nature [See also NFI]..............................IFN
International Friendship League ....IFL
International Frisbee Association [Later, IFDA] ....IFA
International Frisbee Disc Association [Formerly, IFA]..................IFDA
International Frozen Food Association ....IFFA
International Fund for Agricultural Development...........................IFAD
International Fund for Animal Welfare...IFAW
International Fund for Concerned Photography [Later, ICP]..............IFCP
International Fund for Monuments ....IFM
International Fund-Raising Association ....IFRA
International Fund-Raising Institute [Later, IFRA] ....IFRI
International Fur and Leather Workers Union of United States
   and Canada..FLW
International Fur Trade Federation..IFTF
International Galdos Association...IGA
International Galvanizing Conference ....INTERGALVA
International Game Fish Association...IGFA
International Game Technology [NASDAQ symbol].............................IGAM
International Gamers Association...IGA
International Garden Club ....IGC
International Garment Workers' Federation ....IGWF
International Gas Union ....IGU
International Gay Information Center ....IGIC

International Gem Finders Society ....IGFS
International Genealogy Consumer Organization ....IGCO
International General [An association]..IG
International General Assembly of Spiritualists [Later, LDTF]..............IGAS
International General Aviation ....IGA
International General Industries, Inc. [American Stock Exchange
   symbol] [Delisted]..IGI
International Genetics Federation ....IGF
International Geneva Association ....IGA
International Geochemical Exploration Symposium.
   Proceedings [A publication]....................Int Geochem Explor Symp Proc
International Geodynamics Project ....IGP
International Geographical Association [Esperantist] ....IGA
International Geographical Congress. Papers - Congres
   International de Geographie. Communications [A publication]..............
              Int Geogr Congr Pap - Congr Int Geogr Commun
International Geographical Congress. Report. Verhandlungen [A
   publication]...Int Geog Cong Rp Verh
International Geographical Union..IGU
International Geological Congress ....IGC
International Geological Congress [A publication]......................Int G Cong
International Geological Correlation Program [See also PICG]
   [UNESCO/IUGS]..IGCP
International Geological/Geophysical Cruise Inventory ....IGGCI
International Geology Review [A publication]............... Internat Geology Rev
International Geology Review [A publication]..............................Int Geol Rev
International Geomagnetic Reference Field ....IGRF
International Geophysical Committee [Also, CIG].........................IGC
International Geophysical Cooperation [World Meteorological
   Organization]...IGC
International Geophysical Extension ....IGE
International Geophysical Union...IGU
International Geophysical Year ....IGY
International Geophysical Year, World Data Center.........................IGY-WDC
International Geophysical Year. World Data Center. A. General
   Report Series [A publication].......IGY World Data Center A Gen Rept Ser
International Geophysical Year. World Data Center. A.
   Glaciological Report Series [A publication]....................................
              IGY World Data Center A Glaciolog Rept Ser
International Geophysics Series: A Series of Monographs [A
   publication]...Int Geophys Ser
International Geranium Society ....IGS
International Glaciological Society..IGS
International Glaciospeleological Survey. Bulletin [A
   publication].................................Int Glaciospeleological Surv Bull
International Glaucoma Congress ....IGC
International Glove Workers' Union of America [Later, ACTWU]...........GWU
International Glove Workers' Union of America [Later, ACTWU]..........IGWU
International Golf Association ....IGA
International Golf Sponsors' Association [Later, AGS] ....IGSA
International Good Neighbor Council [See also CIBV]....................IGNC
International Good Templar Youth Federation ....IGTYF
International through Government Bill of Lading ....ITGBL
International Graduate Achievement [Defunct] ....IGA
International Graduate School, St. Louis, MO [OCLC symbol].................JNS
International Grail Movement ....IGM
International Grains Arrangement ....IGA
International Graphic Arts Education Association ....IGAEA
International Graphic Arts Society ....IGAS
International Graphical Federation [See also FGI].........................IGF
International Graphics [Formerly, IGI]..IG
International Graphoanalysis Society ....IGAS
International Grassland Congress ....IGC
International Great Lakes Datum ....IGLD
International-Great Northern [AAR code]......................................IGN
International Green Alliance ....IGA
International Green Party (Ecologism USA) ....IGP
International Grooving and Grinding Association ....IG & GA
International Grotius Foundation for the Propagation of
   International Law..IGFPIL
International Ground Environment Subcommittee [NATO]..........IGESUCO
International Group for Scientific Coordination ....IGSC
International Group of Scientific, Technical, and Medical
   Publishers...STM
International Group on Soil Sampling ....IGOSS
International Group for Studies in National Planning.................INTERPLAN
International Group of Users of Information Systems ....IGIS
International Guards Union of America...GUA
International Guards Union of America...IGUA
International Guide to Classical Studies [A publication] ....IGCS
International Guide to Classical Studies [A publication] ...... Int G Class Stud
International Guide to Classical Studies [A publication] ....IntGuC
International Guides' Club..IGC
International Guiding Eyes ....IGE
International Guild of Candle Artisans ....IGCA
International Guild of Craft Journalists, Authors, and
   Photographers...IGCJAP
International Guild of Dispensing Opticians ....IGDO
International Guild of Prestidigitators [Defunct] ....IGP
International Guild of Professional Electrologists ....IGPE
International Guild of Vatican Philatelists ....IGVP

International Gymnastic Federation [*See also FIG*] ....IGF
International Hahnemannian Association [*Defunct*] ....IHA
International Hajji Baba Society ....IHBS
International Halfway House Association ....IHHA
International Halley Watch [*Scientific liaison group to coordinate observations made during 1986 appearance of the comet*]...............IHW
International Handball Federation ....IHF
International Handgun Metallic Silhouette Association ......IHMSA
International Handicapped Net ....IHN
International Hardwood Products Association ....IHPA
International Harvester Co. [*NYSE symbol*] ....HR
International Harvester Co. ....IH
International Harvester Co., Memphis, TN [*Library symbol*]......TMI
International Health Centre of Socio-Economics Researches and Studies [*See also CIERSES*] ....IHCSERS
International Health Council ....IHC
International Health Evaluation Association ....IHEA
International Health Foundation ....IHF
International Health Industries Association ....IHIA
International Health Society ....IHS
International Hebrew Christian Alliance ....IHCA
International Heinrich Schutz Society ....IHSS
International Helicopter Foundation ....IHF
International Help for Children ....IHC
International Helsinki Federation for Human Rights ....IHFHR
International Henry Miller Letter [*A publication*] ....IHML
International Herald Tribune [*A publication*] ....IHT
International Heroines of Jericho [*Later, General Conference of Grand Courts Heroines of Jericho, Prince Hall Affiliation, USA*]..........IHJ
International Hibernation Society [*Formerly, HIE*] ....IHS
International Hide and Allied Trades Improvement Society ...IHATIS
International Hockey League ....IHL
International Hod Carriers', Building and Common Laborers' Union of America [*Later, Laborers' International Union of North America*] ....HCL
International Holdings Corp. [*NYSE symbol*] [*Delisted*] ....IH
International Home Furnishings Representatives Association ....IHFRA
International Homeopathic League ....IHL
International Hop Growers Convention ....IHGC
International Horn Society ....IHS
International Horticultural Advisory Board ....IHAB
International Hospital Federation ....IHF
International Hot Rod Association ....IHRA
International Hotel Association ....IHA
International Hotel and Motel Educational Exposition [*Later, IHM & RS*] ....IH & MEE
International Hotel/Motel and Restaurant Show ....IHM & RS
International House Association [*Defunct*] ....IHA
International House, Cunningham Library, New Orleans, LA [*Library symbol*] ....LNTC
International House of Pancakes [*Restaurant chain*] [*Pronounced "eye-hop"*]..IHOP
International House - World Trade Center ....IN
International Hug Center ....IHC
International Human Assistance Programs ....IHAP
International Human Powered Vehicle Association..............IHPVA
International Human Resources, Business, and Legal Research Association...IHRBLR
International Human Rights Law Group ....IHRLG
International Humanism Magazine [*Netherlands*] [*A publication*] .....IH
International Humanist and Ethical Union......................IHEU
International Hydrofoil Society ....IHS
International Hydrographic Bureau [*Later, IHO*] ....IHB
International Hydrographic Organization........................IHO
International Hydrographic Program.............................IHP
International Hydrographic Review [*A publication*].........Int Hyd Rev
International Hydrological Decade [*UNESCO*]....................IHD
International Hydrological Decade. Newsletter [*A publication*]........Int Hydrol Decade Newsl
International Hydron Corporation [*NASDAQ symbol*]............IHYC
International Hydronics Corp. [*American Stock Exchange symbol*] ....HYD
International Ice Hockey Federation.............................IIHF
International Ice Patrol [*Coast Guard*] IIC
International Ice Patrol ....IIP
International Illawarra Association ....IIA
International Imagery Association ....IIA
International Income Properties [*NASDAQ symbol*] ....IIPI
International Index [*A publication*] ....Int Ind
International Index to Film Periodicals [*A publication*]........Int Ind Film
International Indian Ocean Expedition [*Navy*]..................IIOE
International Indian Treaty Council ....IITC
International Industrial Marketing Club [*Formerly, MMEC*] [*Defunct*].....IIMC
International Industrial Relations Association ....IIRA
International Industrial Relations Institute ....IRI
International Industries [*NYSE symbol*] [*Delisted*]..............INT
International Information Administration [*Transferred to USIS, 1953*] [*Department of State*]...................................IIA
International Information Centre for Terminology [*UNESCO*].....INFOTERM
International Information on Peace-Keeping Operations ....IPKO
International Information Services for the Physics and Engineering Communities ....INSPEC

International Information System on Research in Documentation [*UNESCO*]....................................ISORID
International Information/Word Processing Association [*Formerly, IWPA*] [*Later, IWP*] ....IIWPA
International Information/Word Processing Association........................IWP
International Institute of Administrative Sciences ....IIAS
International Institute for Adult Literacy Methods.............IIALM
International Institute for Advanced Studies ....IIAS
International Institute of Agriculture ....IIA
International Institute of American Ideals ....IIAI
International Institute of Ammonia Refrigeration ....IIAR
[*The*] International Institute of Applied Linguistics ....TIIAL
International Institute for Applied Systems Analysis [*US/USSR*].........IIASA
International Institute for Applied Systems Analysis. Collaborative Publications [*A publication*] ....IIASA Collab Publ
International Institute for Applied Systems Analysis. Professional Paper [*A publication*] .... IIASA Prof Pap
International Institute for Applied Systems Analysis. Research Memorandum [*A publication*] .... IIASA Res Memo
International Institute for Applied Systems Analysis. Research Memorandum [*A publication*] .... Int Inst Appl Syst Anal Res Mem
International Institute for Applied Systems Analysis. Research Report [*A publication*] ....IIASA Res Rep
International Institute for Arab-American Relations ....IIAAR
International Institute of Arts and Letters ....IIAL
International Institute for Bioenergetic Analysis [*Formerly, IBA*] ....IIBA
International Institute of Biological Husbandry ....IIBH
International Institute for Children's Literature and Reading Research...IICLRR
International Institute of Children's Nature and Their Rights ....IICNTR
International Institute of Communications [*Formerly, IBI*] IIC
International Institute for Comparative Music Studies and Documentation ....IICMSD
International Institute for Conservation of Historic and Artistic Works IIC
International Institute for the Conservation of Historic and Artistic Works..IICHAW
International Institute for the Conservation of Museum Objects.................IIC
International Institute for Cotton IIC
International Institute for Economic Research ....IIER
International Institute for Educational Planning ....IIEP
International Institute of Embryology [*Later, ISDB*]............IIE
International Institute for Environment and Development [*Formerly, IIEA*]...IIED
International Institute for Environmental Affairs [*Later, IIED*]...............IIEA
International Institute for Ethnic Group Rights and Regionalism ....INTEREG
International Institute of Films on Art.........................IIFA
International Institute of Fisheries Economics and Trade ....IIFET
International Institute of Human Rights........................IIHR
International Institute of Humanitarian Law [*See also IIDH*] ....IIHL
International Institute of Intellectual Cooperation of the League of Nations [*Obsolete*]......................................IIIC (LN)
International Institute of Investment and Merchant Banking ....IIIMB
International Institute for Labor Studies ....IILS
International Institute for Land Reclamation and Improvement...........ILRI
International Institute for Land Reclamation and Improvement. Annual Report [*A publication*]...... Int Inst Land Reclam Improv Annu Rep
International Institute for Land Reclamation and Improvement. Publication [*A publication*]...............Int Inst Ld Reclam Improv
International Institute for Lath and Plaster ....IILP
International Institute for the Management of Technology [*Defunct*].....IIMT
International Institute of Maritime Culture....................IIMC
International Institute of Municipal Clerks....................IIMC
International Institute for Music, Dance, and Theatre in the Audio-Visual Media.......................................IMDT
International Institute of Nuclear Science and Engineering ....IINSE
International Institute for Peace ....IIP
International Institute of Philosophy...........................IIP
International Institute of Physical Oceanography...............IIPO
International Institute for Promotion and Prestige ....IIPP
International Institute of Public Finance ....IIPF
International Institute of Refrigeration ....IIR
International Institute of Rehabilitation ....IIR
International Institute for Resource Economics ....IIRE
International Institute for Robotics ....IIR
International Institute of Rural Reconstruction................IIRR
International Institute of Seismology and Earthquake Engineering [*Japan*] [*Seismograph station code, US Geological Survey*]... IIS
International Institute of Seismology and Earthquake Engineering. Bulletin [*A publication*]...................Int Inst Seismol Earthquake Eng Bull
International Institute of Seismology and Earthquake Engineering. Individual Studies by Participants [*A publication*]...............Int Inst Seismol Earthquake Eng Individ Stud
International Institute of Site Planning ....IISP
International Institute of Social Economics ....IISE
International Institute of Sociology............................IIS
International Institute of Space Law ....IISL
International Institute for Strategic Studies..................IISS
International Institute of Stress ....IIS

International Institute for Study and Research in the Field of Commercial Competition ... IICC
International Institute for Sugar Beet Research ... IISBR
International Institute for Sugar Beet Research. Journal [*A publication*] ... Int Inst Sugar Beet Res J
International Institute of Synthetic Rubber Producers ... IISRP
International Institute of Tropical Agriculture [*Ibadan, Nigeria*] ... IITA
International Institute of Valuers ... IIV
International Institute of Welding ... IIW
International Institutional Services [*An association*] ... IIS
International Insurance Intelligence ... III
International Insurance Monitor [*A publication*] ... IIM
International Insurance Seminars ... IIS
International Intelligence, Inc. ... INTERTEL
International Inter-Church Film Center ... INTERFILM
International Interdependent Research and Development ... IIRD
International Intersociety Committee on Pathology ... IICP
International Investment Bank ... IIB
International Investment Trust ... IIT
International Investments Association ... IIA
International Iron and Steel Institute ... IISI
International Irrigation Information Center ... IIIC
International Islamic Federation of Student Organizations ... IIFSO
International Jazz Federation ... IJF
International Jelly and Preserve Association ... IJPA
International Jet Air Ltd. [*ICAO designator*] ... JX
International Jet Ski Boating Association ... IJSBA
International Jewelry Workers Union [*Later, Service Employees International Union*] ... IJWU
International Jewelry Workers Union [*Later, Service Employees International Union*] ... JWU
International Jewish Committee on Interreligious Consultations ... IJCIC
International Jewish Labor Bund ... IJLB
International Joint Commission [*US/Canada*] ... IJC
International Joint Commission, Windsor, ON, Canada [*Library symbol*] ... CaOWIJC
International Joint Conference on Artificial Intelligence ... IJCAI
International Joint Rules Committee on Softball [*Later, ASA*] ... IJRCS
International Joseph Diseases Association ... IJDA
International Journal [*A publication*] ... IJ
International Journal [*A publication*] ... Internatl Jour
International Journal [*A publication*] ... Int J
International Journal of the Addictions [*A publication*] ... Int J Addic
International Journal of the Addictions [*A publication*] ... Int J Addict
International Journal of Adult and Youth Education [*A publication*] ... Int J Adult Youth Ed
International Journal of African Historical Studies [*A publication*] ... Int J Afr H
International Journal of African Historical Studies [*A publication*] ... Int J Afric Hist Stud
International Journal of African Historical Studies [*A publication*] ... Int J Afr Stud
International Journal of Aging and Human Development [*A publication*] ... Int J Aging
International Journal of Aging and Human Development [*A publication*] ... Int J Aging Hum Dev
International Journal of Agrarian Affairs [*A publication*] ... Int J A Aff
International Journal of Agrarian Affairs [*A publication*] ... Int J Ag Affairs
International Journal of Agrarian Affairs [*A publication*] ... Int J Agr Aff
International Journal of American Linguistics [*A publication*] ... IJAL
International Journal of American Linguistics [*A publication*] ... Int J Amer
International Journal of American Linguistics [*A publication*] ... Int J Am Ling
International Journal of Andrology [*A publication*] ... IJA
International Journal of Andrology [*A publication*] ... Int J Androl
International Journal of Applied Radiation and Isotopes [*A publication*] ... Int J Appl Radiat Isot
International Journal of Applied Radiation and Isotopes [*A publication*] ... Int J A Rad
International Journal of Artificial Organs [*A publication*] ... Int J Artif Organs
International Journal of Bio-Medical Computing [*A publication*] ... Int J Bio-M
International Journal of Bio-Medical Computing [*A publication*] ... Int J Bio-Med Comput
International Journal of Biochemistry [*A publication*] ... Int J Bioch
International Journal of Biochemistry [*A publication*] ... Int J Biochem
International Journal of Bioclimatology and Biometeorology [*A publication*] ... Int J Bioclim Biomet
International Journal of Biomedical Computing [*A publication*] ... IJBCB
International Journal of Biomedical Engineering [*A publication*] ... Int J Biomed Eng
International Journal of Biometeorology [*A publication*] ... Int J Biom
International Journal of Biometeorology [*A publication*] ... Int J Biometeorol
International Journal of Cancer [*A publication*] ... Int J Canc
International Journal of Cancer [*A publication*] ... Int J Cancer
International Journal of Chemical Kinetics [*A publication*] ... Int J Chem Kinet
International Journal of Chemical Kinetics [*A publication*] ... Int J Ch K
International Journal of Child Psychotherapy [*A publication*] ... Int J Child
International Journal of Chronobiology [*A publication*] ... IJCBA
International Journal of Chronobiology [*A publication*] ... Int J Chronobiol
International Journal of Circuit Theory and Applications [*A publication*] ... Int J Circuit Theory Appl
International Journal of Clinical and Experimental Hypnosis [*A publication*] ... IJEHA
International Journal of Clinical and Experimental Hypnosis [*A publication*] ... Int J C E Hy
International Journal of Clinical and Experimental Hypnosis [*A publication*] ... Int J Clin Exp Hypn
International Journal of Clinical and Experimental Hypnosis [*A publication*] ... Int J Clin & Exp Hypnosis
International Journal of Clinical Pharmacology and Biopharmacy [*A publication*] ... Int J Clin
International Journal of Clinical Pharmacology and Biopharmacy [*A publication*] ... Int J Clin Pharmacol Biopharm
International Journal of Clinical Pharmacology Therapy and Toxicology [*A publication*] ... Int J Clin Pharmacol Ther Toxicol
International Journal of Community Psychiatry and Experimental Psychotherapy [*A publication*] ... Int J Com P
International Journal of Comparative Sociology [*A publication*] ... Int J Comp
International Journal of Comparative Sociology [*A publication*] ... Int J Compar Sociol
International Journal of Comparative Sociology [*A publication*] ... Int J Comp Sociol
International Journal of Computer and Information Sciences [*A publication*] ... IJCIS
International Journal of Computer and Information Sciences [*A publication*] ... Int J C Inf
International Journal of Computer and Information Sciences [*A publication*] ... Int J Comput & Inf Sci
International Journal of Computer Mathematics [*A publication*] ... Int J Com M
International Journal of Computer Mathematics [*A publication*] ... Int J Comput Math
International Journal of Computer Mathematics. Section A. Programming Languages. Theory and Methods [*A publication*] ... Int J Comput Math Sect A
International Journal of Computer Mathematics. Section B. Computational Methods [*A publication*] ... Int J Comput Math Sect B
International Journal of Contemporary Sociology [*A publication*] ... Int J Con S
International Journal of Contemporary Sociology [*A publication*] ... Int J Contemp Sociol
International Journal of Control [*A publication*] ... Int J Contr
International Journal of Dermatology [*A publication*] ... Int J Dermatol
International Journal of Dravidian Linguistics [*A publication*] ... Int J Dravid Ling
International Journal of Earthquake Engineering and Structural Dynamics [*A publication*] ... Int J Earthquake Eng Struct Dyn
International Journal of Ecology and Environmental Sciences [*A publication*] ... Int J Ecol Environ Sci
International Journal of Electrical Engineering Education [*A publication*] ... Int J Elec Eng Educ
International Journal of Electrical Engineering Education [*A publication*] ... Int J Electr Eng Educ
International Journal of Electrical Engineering Education [*A publication*] ... Int J El En
International Journal of Electronics [*A publication*] ... Int J Elect
International Journal of Electronics [*A publication*] ... Int J Electron
International Journal of Energy Research [*A publication*] ... Int J Energy Res
International Journal of Engineering Science [*A publication*] ... Int J Eng S
International Journal of Engineering Science [*A publication*] ... Int J Eng Sci
International Journal of Environmental Analytical Chemistry [*A publication*] ... Int J Environ Anal Chem
International Journal of Environmental Studies [*A publication*] ... IJES
International Journal of Environmental Studies [*A publication*] ... Int J Environ Stud
International Journal of Environmental Studies [*A publication*] ... Int J Env S
International Journal of Epidemiology [*A publication*] ... Int J Epid
International Journal of Epidemiology [*A publication*] ... Int J Epidemiol
International Journal of Equilibrium Research [*A publication*] ... Int J Equilib Res
International Journal of Ethics [*A publication*] ... Int J Ethics
International Journal of Fatigue [*A publication*] ... Int J Fatigue
International Journal of Fertility [*A publication*] ... Int J Fert
International Journal of Fertility [*A publication*] ... Int J Fertil
International Journal of Forensic Dentistry [*A publication*] ... Int J Forensic Dent
International Journal of Fracture [*A publication*] ... Int J Fract
International Journal of Fracture Mechanics [*A publication*] ... Int J Fract Mech
International Journal of Fusion Energy [*A publication*] ... Int J Fusion Energy
International Journal of Game Theory [*A publication*] ... Internat J Game Theory
International Journal of General Systems [*A publication*] ... Int J Gen S
International Journal of General Systems [*A publication*] ... Int J Gen Syst
International Journal of Group Psychotherapy [*A publication*] ... IJGPA
International Journal of Group Psychotherapy [*A publication*] ... Int J Group Psychother
International Journal of Group Psychotherapy [*A publication*] ... Int J Grp P

International Journal of Group Tensions [*A publication*] ....
Int J Group Tensions
International Journal of Group Tensions [*A publication*] ....Int J Grp T
International Journal of Gynaecology and Obstetrics [*A publication*] ....Int J Gynaecol Obstet
International Journal of Health Education [*A publication*] .... Int J Healt
International Journal of Health Education [*A publication*] .... Int J Health Educ
International Journal of Health Services [*A publication*].......Int J Health Serv
International Journal of Health Services [*A publication*]............... Int J He Se
International Journal of Heat and Mass Transfer [*A publication*] .... Int J Heat
International Journal of Heat and Mass Transfer [*A publication*] .... Int J Heat & Mass Transfer
International Journal for Housing Science and Its Applications [*A publication*]...................................Int J Hous Sci Appl
International Journal of Hydrogen Energy [*A publication*] .... Int J Hydrogen Energy
International Journal of Immunopharmacology [*A publication*] .... Int J Immunopharmacol
International Journal of Insect Morphology and Embryology [*A publication*] .... Int J Insect Morphol Embryol
International Journal of Instructional Media [*A publication*]................................. Int J Instr Media
International Journal of Law Libraries [*A publication*] ....Int J Law Libr
International Journal of Law and Psychiatry [*A publication*] .... Int J Law Psychiatry
International Journal of Leprosy [*Later, International Journal of Leprosy and Other Mycobacterial Diseases*] [*A publication*]...... Int J Lepr
International Journal of Leprosy and Other Mycobacterial Diseases [*A publication*] .... Int J Lepr Other Mycobact Dis
International Journal of Machine Tool Design and Research [*A publication*]...............................Int J Mach
International Journal of Machine Tool Design and Research [*A publication*]...............................Int J Mach Tool Des Res
International Journal of Magnetism [*A publication*].......................Int J Magn
International Journal of Man-Machine Studies [*A publication*] .... Int J Man-M
International Journal of Man-Machine Studies [*A publication*] .... Int J Man-Mach Stud
International Journal of Mass Spectrometry and Ion Physics [*A publication*].................................... Int J Mass
International Journal of Mass Spectrometry and Ion Physics [*A publication*]...............................Int J Mass Spectrom Ion Phys
International Journal of Materials in Engineering Applications [*A publication*]...................................Int J Mater Eng Appl
International Journal of Materials Engineering Research [*A publication*]...............................Int J Mater Eng Res
International Journal of Mathematical Education in Science and Technology [*A publication*]...........................Internat J Math Ed Sci Tech
International Journal of Mathematical Education in Science and Technology [*A publication*]...........................Int J Math Educ Sci Technol
International Journal of Mechanical Sciences [*A publication*] ....Int J Mech
International Journal of Mechanical Sciences [*A publication*] .... Int J Mech Sci
International Journal of Mental Health [*A publication*].................. Int J Ment
International Journal of Mental Health [*A publication*]......... Int J Ment Health
International Journal of Middle East Studies [*A publication*] ....IJMES
International Journal of Middle East Studies [*A publication*] ....Int J M E St
International Journal of Middle East Studies [*A publication*] .... Int J Middle East Stud
International Journal of Middle East Studies [*A publication*] .... Int J Mid East Stud
International Journal of Middle East Studies [*A publication*] .... Int J Mid E Stud
International Journal of Mineral Processing [*A publication*]............................ Int J Miner Process
International Journal of Multiphase Flow [*A publication*]............................ Int J Multiphase Flow
International Journal of Multiphase Flow [*A publication*].... Int J Multiph Flow
International Journal of Nautical Archaeology and Underwater Exploration [*A publication*] ....IJNA
International Journal of Nautical Archaeology and Underwater Exploration [*A publication*] ....J Naut Arch
International Journal of Neurology [*A publication*].........................Int J Neuro
International Journal of Neurology [*A publication*].......................Int J Neurol
International Journal of Neuropharmacology [*A publication*]........................ Int J Neuropharmacol
International Journal of Neuropsychiatry [*A publication*] .... Int J Neuropsychiatr
International Journal of Neuropsychiatry. Supplement [*A publication*].................................Int J Neuropsychiatry Suppl
International Journal of Neuroscience [*A publication*] .... IJN
International Journal of Neuroscience [*A publication*] ....IJNUB
International Journal of Neuroscience [*A publication*] .... Int J Neurosci
International Journal of Neuroscience [*A publication*] .... Int J Neurs
International Journal of Non-Linear Mechanics [*A publication*] .... Int J Non-Linear Mech
International Journal of Nondestructive Testing [*A publication*]...................................Int J Nondestr Test
International Journal of Nondestructive Testing [*A publication*]....................................Int J Nondestruct Test

International Journal of Nuclear Medicine and Biology [*A publication*]...............................Int J Nucl Med & Biol
International Journal of Nuclear Medicine and Biology [*A publication*]...............................Int J Nucl Med Biol
International Journal of Nuclear Medicine and Biology [*A publication*]...............................Int J Nuc M
International Journal for Numerical and Analytical Methods in Geomechanics [*A publication*].........Int J Numer Anal Methods Geomech
International Journal for Numerical Methods in Engineering [*A publication*]...............................Int J Numer Methods Eng
International Journal of Nursing Studies [*A publication*]................. Int J Nurs
International Journal of Nursing Studies [*A publication*]........ Int J Nurs Stud
International Journal of Obesity [*A publication*] .... Int J Obes
International Journal of Occupational Health and Safety [*A publication*].................................Int J Occ H
International Journal of Occupational Health and Safety [*A publication*]................................ Int J Occup Health Saf
International Journal of Oceanology and Limnology [*A publication*]................................ Int J Oceanol Limnol
International Journal of Offender Therapy [*Later, International Journal of Offender Therapy and Comparative Criminology*] [*A publication*]...Int J Offen
International Journal of Offender Therapy and Comparative Criminology [*A publication*] ....Int J Offend Therapy
International Journal of Opinion and Attitude Research [*A publication*]...............................IJOAR
International Journal of Oral Myology [*A publication*].............. Int J Oral Myol
International Journal of Oral Surgery [*A publication*]............... Int J Oral Surg
International Journal of Oral Surgery [*A publication*].................... Int J Or Su
International Journal of Orthodontics [*A publication*]................... Int J Orthod
International Journal of Orthodontics [*A publication*]............Int J Orthodont
International Journal of Parapsychology [*A publication*] ....IJP
International Journal for Parasitology [*A publication*]................... Int J Paras
International Journal for Parasitology [*A publication*] .... Int J Parasitol
International Journal of Pediatric Otorhinolaryngology [*A publication*]...............................Int J Pediatr Otorhinolaryngol
International Journal of Peptide and Protein Research [*A publication*]................................ Int J Pept
International Journal of Peptide and Protein Research [*A publication*]................................ Int J Peptide Prot Res
International Journal of Peptide and Protein Research [*A publication*]................................ Int J Pept Protein Res
International Journal of Pharmaceutics [*A publication*]............... Int J Pharm
International Journal for Philosophy of Religion [*A publication*] .... Int J Phil Relig
International Journal of Physical Distribution. Journal Series [*A publication*]................................ Int J Phys Distrib J Ser
International Journal of Physical Distribution. Monograph Series [*A publication*] .... Int J Phys Distrib Monogr Ser
International Journal of Physical Education [*A publication*]................................ Int J Phys Educ
International Journal of Politics [*A publication*]................................ Int J Polit
International Journal of Polymeric Materials [*A publication*]................................ Int J Polym Mater
International Journal of Powder Metallurgy [*A publication*]............Int J Powd
International Journal of Powder Metallurgy [*A publication*]................................ Int J Powder Metall
International Journal of Powder Metallurgy and Powder Technology [*A publication*] .... Int J Powder Metall & Powder Tech
International Journal of Powder Metallurgy and Powder Technology [*A publication*] .... Int J Powder Metall Powder Technol
International Journal of Powder Metallurgy and Powder Technology [*A publication*]................Int J Powder Metall Technol
International Journal of Pressure Vessels and Piping [*A publication*].................................Int J Pressure Vessels Piping
International Journal of Production Research [*A publication*]................................ Int J Prod Res
International Journal of Protein Research [*A publication*] ....Int J Protein Res
International Journal of Psychiatry [*A publication*] .... Int J Psychiat
International Journal of Psychiatry [*A publication*] .... Int J Psychiatry
International Journal of Psychiatry [*A publication*] .... Int J Psyci
International Journal of Psychiatry in Medicine [*A publication*]...................... Int J Psychiatry Med
International Journal of Psychiatry in Medicine [*A publication*]....Int J Psy M
International Journal of Psychoanalysis [*A publication*] ....IJPsa
International Journal of Psychoanalysis [*A publication*] .... Int J Psych
International Journal of Psychoanalysis [*A publication*] .... Int J Psychoanal
International Journal of Psychoanalytic Psychotherapy [*A publication*]...............................Int J Ps Ps
International Journal of Psychoanalytic Psychotherapy [*A publication*].................................Int J Psychoanal Psychother
International Journal of Psychobiology [*A publication*] ....Int J Psychobiol
International Journal of Psychology [*A publication*]...................... Int J Psyco
International Journal of Quantum Chemistry [*A publication*].........Int J Quant
International Journal of Quantum Chemistry [*A publication*]...............................Int J Quant Chem
International Journal of Quantum Chemistry. Symposium [*A publication*]............... Int J Quant Chem Symp
International Journal of Quantum Chemistry. Symposium [*A publication*]............... Int J Quantum Chem Sym
International Journal of Radiation Biology [*A publication*].............Int J Rad B

International Journal of Radiation Biology and Related Studies in Physics, Chemistry, and Medicine [*A publication*]...... Int J Radiat Biol
International Journal of Radiation Biology and Related Studies in Physics, Chemistry, and Medicine [*A publication*]...... Int J Radiat Biol Relat Stud Phys Chem Med
International Journal of Radiation: Oncology-Biology-Physics [*A publication*]...... Int J Radiat Oncol-Biol-Phys
International Journal of Radiation: Oncology-Biology-Physics [*A publication*]......Int J Rad O
International Journal for Radiation Physics and Chemistry [*Later, Radiation Physics and Chemistry*] [*A publication*]...... Int J Radiat Phys Chem
International Journal for Radiation Physics and Chemistry [*Later, Radiation Physics and Chemistry*] [*A publication*]......Int J Rad P
International Journal of Rehabilitation Research [*A publication*]...... Int J Rehabil Res
International Journal of Religious Education [*A publication*]......IJRE
International Journal of Religious Education [*A publication*]..... Int J Relig Ed
International Journal of Religious Education [*A publication*].... Intl Jnl Rel Ed
[*The*] International Journal of Robotics Research [*A publication*]...........IJRR
International Journal of Rock Mechanics [*A publication*] .... Int J Rock
International Journal of Rock Mechanics and Mining Sciences [*Later, International Journal of Rock Mechanics and Mining Sciences and Geomechanics Abstracts*] [*A publication*]......Internat Jour Rock Mechanics and Mining Sci
International Journal of Rock Mechanics and Mining Sciences [*Later, International Journal of Rock Mechanics and Mining Sciences and Geomechanics Abstracts*] [*A publication*]......Int J Rock Mech Mining Sci
International Journal of Rock Mechanics and Mining Sciences [*Later, International Journal of Rock Mechanics and Mining Sciences and Geomechanics Abstracts*] [*A publication*]......Int J Rock Mech Min Sci
International Journal of Rock Mechanics and Mining Sciences and Geomechanics Abstracts [*A publication*]......Int J Rock Mech Min Sci Geomech Abstr
International Journal of Sexology [*A publication*]...... IJS
International Journal of Slavic Linguistics and Poetics [*A publication*]......IJSLP
International Journal of Social Economics [*A publication*]......IJSE
International Journal of Social Economics [*A publication*]...... Int J Soc Econ
International Journal of Social Psychiatry [*A publication*]......IJSPA
International Journal of Social Psychiatry [*A publication*]......Int J Social Psychiat
International Journal of Social Psychiatry [*A publication*]...........Int J Soc P
International Journal of Social Psychiatry [*A publication*]......Int J Soc Psych
International Journal of Social Psychiatry [*A publication*]......Int J Soc Psychiatry
International Journal of Sociology [*A publication*]......Int J Sociol
International Journal of Sociology of the Family [*A publication*]....Int J Soc F
International Journal of Sociology of the Family [*A publication*]......Int J Sociol Family
International Journal of the Sociology of Language [*A publication*]........IJSL
International Journal of the Sociology of Language [*A publication*]......Int J Sociol Lang
International Journal of the Sociology of Language [*A publication*]......Int J Soc L
International Journal of Solids and Structures [*A publication*]......Int J Solids Struct
International Journal of Speleology [*A publication*]......Int J Speleol
International Journal of Sport Psychology [*A publication*]...........Int J Sp Ps
International Journal of Symbology [*A publication*]......IJSym
International Journal of Symbology [*A publication*]......Int J Symb
International Journal of Systematic Bacteriology [*A publication*]......Intern J System Bacteriol
International Journal of Systematic Bacteriology [*A publication*]......Int J Sy B
International Journal of Systematic Bacteriology [*A publication*]......Int J Syst Bacteriol
International Journal of Systems Science [*A publication*]......Int J Syst
International Journal of Systems Science [*A publication*]..........Int J Syst Sci
International Journal of Theoretical Physics [*A publication*]......... Int J Theor
International Journal of Theoretical Physics [*A publication*]......Int J Theor Phys
International Journal on Tissue Reactions [*A publication*] ......Int J Tissue React
International Journal for Vitamin and Nutrition Research [*A publication*]...... Int J Vitam Nutr Res
International Journal for Vitamin and Nutrition Research [*A publication*]...... Int J Vit N
International Journal of Women's Studies [*A publication*]......IJWS
International Journal of Zoonoses [*A publication*]......Int J Zoonoses
International Judo Federation......IJF
International Jugglers Association......IJA
International Junior Brangus Breeders Association ......IJBBA
International Juridical Organization ......IJO
International Juvenile Officers' Association ......IJOA
International Juvenile Publications ......IJP
International Kart Federation......IKF
International Kennel Club of Chicago......IKC
International King's Table [*NASDAQ symbol*] ......IKNG

International Kirlian Research Association......IKRA
International Kitefliers Association ......IKA
International Knife and Fork Clubs ......IKFC
International Kolping Society [*See also IKW*]......IKS
International Kongress der Volkserzaehlungsforscher [*A publication*]....IKV
International Kraft Federation......IKF
International Labelling Centre [*Defunct*] ILC
International Labmate [*A publication*]...... Int Labmate
International Labor Conference [*A section of the International Labor Organization*] [*United Nations*] ILC
International Labor Defense [*An association*]......ILD
International Labor Office [*A section of the International Labor Organization*] [*United Nations*]......ILO
International Labor Organization......ILO
International Labor Organization. Occupational Safety and Health Series [*A publication*] .... Int Labor Organ Occup Saf Health Ser
International Labor Organization Staff Union ......ILOSU
International Labor Press Association ......ILPA
International Laboratory [*A publication*]...... Int Lab
International Laboratory of Genetics and Biophysics ......ILGB
International Laboratory for Research on Animal Diseases [*Kenya*]......ILRAD
International Labour Film Institute [*Defunct*] ...... ILFI
International Labour Office, Montreal, PQ, Canada [*Library symbol*]...... CaQMILO
International Labour Office. Occupational Safety and Health Series [*A publication*]...... Int Labour Off Occup Saf Health Ser
International Labour Review [*A publication*]......ILR
International Labour Review [*A publication*]......INLR-A
International Labour Review [*A publication*]...... Int Labour R
International Labour Review [*A publication*]......Int Lab R
International Labour Review [*A publication*]...... Int Lab Rev
International Labour Review. Statistical Supplement [*A publication*]......Int Labour R Stat Sup
International Ladies' Garment Workers' Union......ILGWU
International Land Development Consultants Ltd.......ILACO
International Landworkers' Federation [*Later, IFPAAW*]...... ILF
International Language for Aviation ......ILA
International Language Reporter [*A publication*] ......ILR
International Latex Corporation......ILC
International Latitude Service......ILS
International Laundry Association......ILA
International Law Association......ILA
International Law Commission [*United Nations*]......ILC
International Law Commission of the United Nations ......ILC (UN)
International Law Enforcement Stress Association ......ILESA
International Law Institute......ILI
International Law Quarterly [*A publication*]......ILQ
International Law Reports......ILR
International Lawn Hockey Federation......IHF
International Lawn Tennis Federation [*Later, ITF*]......ILTF
International Lawyer [*A publication*] ...... Int Law
International Lawyer [*A publication*]...... Int Lawyer
International Lead Zinc Research Organization ......ILZRO
International Lead and Zinc Study Group ......ILZSG
International League [*Baseball*]...... IL
International League Against Epilepsy ......ILAE
International League Against Rheumatism ......ILAR
International League of Agricultural Specialists-Esperantists...........ILASE
International League for Animal Rights ......ILAR
International League of Antiquarian Booksellers [*See also LILA*]...........ILAB
International League of Blind Esperantists [*See also LIBE*] ......ILBE
International League for Bolivarian Action ......ILBA
International League of Commercial Travelers and Agents...... ILCTA
International League of Dermatological Societies......ILDS
International League of Electrical Associations ......ILEA
International League of Esperantist Radio Amateurs......ILERA
International League for Human Rights [*Formerly, ILRM*]......ILHR
International League of New York......ILNY
International League of Professional Baseball Clubs ......ILPBC
International League of Religious Socialists ......ILRS
International League for the Rights and Liberation of Peoples......ILRLP
International League for the Rights of Man [*Later, ILHR*] ......ILRM
International League of Societies for Persons with Mental Handicap ......ILSPMH
International League of Women Composers [*Formerly, LWC*] ......ILWC
International Learning Systems......ILS
International Lease Finance [*NASDAQ symbol*]......ILFC
International Leather Goods, Plastic, and Novelty Workers' Union ......ILGPNWU
International Leather Goods, Plastic, and Novelty Workers' Union ......LGPN
International Legal Aid Association [*Defunct*]......ILAA
International Legal Center [*Formerly, SAILER*] [*Later, International Center for Law and Development*] ILC
International Legal Defense Counsel ......ILDC
International Legion of Intelligence [*Acronym is used as official name of association*]......INTERTEL
International Leisure Hosts [*NASDAQ symbol*]......ILHL
International Leprosy Association ......ILA
International Liaison Center of Schools of Cinema and Television..... ILOST
International Liaison Committee of Organizations for Peace ......ILCOP

International Liaison Committee for Research on Korea ... ILCORK
International Liaison Forum of Peace Forces [*See also FILFP*] ... ILF
International Library, Archives, and Museum of Optometry, St. Louis, MO [*Library symbol*] ... MoSIO
International Library Information Center ... ILIC
International Library Review [*A publication*] ... Int Lib R
International Library Review [*A publication*] ... Int Libr Re
International Library Review [*A publication*] ... Int Libr Rev
International Licensed Carrier [*Communications*] ... ILC
International Life Sciences Institute ... ILSI
International Lifeboat Conference ... ILC
International Lifesaving Museum and Water Safety Center ... ILMWSC
International Light Tackle Tournament Association ... ILTTA
International Lightning Class Association ... ILCA
International Lilac Society ... ILS
International Linen Promotion Commission ... ILPC
International Listening Association ... ILA
International Literary Annual [*London*] [*A publication*] ... ILA
International Literature [*USSR*] [*A publication*] ... IL
International Livestock Brand Conference ... ILBC
International Livestock Centre for Africa [*Ethiopia*] ... ILCA
International Log Rolling Association ... ILRA
International Logic Review [*A publication*] ... Int Log Rev
International Logistics ... IL
International Logistics Center [*Army*] ... ILC
International Logistics Control Office ... ILCO
International Logistics Field Office [*Army*] ... ILFO
International Logistics Negotiations [*Military export sales*] ... ILN
International Logistics Program ... ILP
International Logistics Supply Performance Improvement Program ... ILSPIP
International Logistics Training ... ILT
International Longshoremen's Association ... ILA
International Longshoremen's and Warehousemen's Union ... ILWU
International Longshoremen's and Warehousemen's Union, San Francisco, CA [*Library symbol*] ... CSfIL
International Low Water ... ILW
International Luge Federation ... ILF
International Luggage Registry [*Computer system for recovery of airline luggage*] ... ILR
International Lunar Society ... ILS
International Lutheran Deaf Association ... ILDA
International Lutheran Laymen's League ... ILLL
International Lutheran Women's Missionary League [*Formerly, LWML*] ... ILWML
International Machinery Insurers Association ... IMIA
International Magazine [*A publication*] ... Internat M
International Magic Dealers Association ... IMDA
International Magnesium Association [*Formerly, Magnesium Association*] ... IMA
International Magnetospheric Explorer [*NASA/ESRO*] ... IME
International Magnetospheric Study [*1976-78*] [*National Science Foundation*] ... IMS
International Mail [*A publication*] ... INTMA
International Mail Dealers Association ... IMDA
International Mailbag Club ... IMC
International Mailers Union [*Later, International Typographical Union*] ... IMU
International Maintenance Agency ... IMA
International Maintenance Control [*Communications*] ... IMC
International Maintenance Institute ... IMI
International Maledicta Society ... IMS
International Management [*A publication*] ... Int Manag
International Management [*A publication*] ... Int Mgt
International Management Association [*Later, AMA/I*] ... IMA
International Management Council ... IMC
International Management and Development Institute ... IMDI
International Management Institute [*Switzerland*] ... IMI
International Management Services, Inc. [*Information service*] ... IMS
International Management Systems Association [*Later, Internet-International Management Systems Association*] ... IMSA
International Manufacturers Representatives Association ... IMRA
International Map of the World ... IMW
International Maple Institute ... IMI
International Maple Syrup Institute ... IMSI
International Marine Expedition ... IMEX
International Marine Radio Aids to Navigation ... IMRAN
International Marine Science [*IOC*] [*A publication*] ... IMS
International Marine Transit Association ... IMTA
International Maritime Committee ... IMC
International Maritime Consultative Organization ... IMCO
International Maritime Dangerous Goods ... IMDG
International Maritime Industries Forum ... IMIF
International Maritime Organization [*See also OMI*] ... IMO
International Maritime Satellite System [*Department of Commerce*] ... INMARSAT
International Market Development Program [*Department of Energy*] ... IMD
International Marketing Audit Association ... IMAA
International Marketing Federation ... IMF
International Marketing Information Service ... IMIS
International Marketing Institute ... IMI
International Martial Arts Pen Pal Association ... IMAPPA
International Marxist Group ... IMG
International Masonry Institute ... IMI
International Masonry Institute Apprenticeship and Training ... IMIAT
International Mass Education Movement ... IMEM
International Master Printers Association ... IMPA
International Match Point [*Game of bridge*] ... IMP
International Material Management Society ... IMMS
International Materials Organization ... IMO
International Materiel Evaluation [*Program*] [*Military*] ... IME
International Materiel Evaluation Program [*Army*] ... IMEP
International Mathematical News [*A publication*] ... Internat Math News
International Mathematical Olympiad ... IMO
International Mathematical and Statistical Libraries, Inc. ... IMSL
International Mathematical Union ... IMU
International Meat Processors Association ... IMPA
International Mechanism for Appropriate Technology ... IMAT
International Media Buyers Association [*Defunct*] ... IMBA
International Medical Association for Radio and Television ... IMART
International Medical Exchange [*Defunct*] ... IME
International Medical Informatics Association ... IMIA
International Medical Information Center, Inc. [*Japan*] ... IMIC
International Medical Research ... IMR
International Medical and Research Foundation [*Later, AMRF*] ... IMRF
International Medical Systems [*NASDAQ symbol*] ... IMSX
International Medieval Bibliography [*A publication*] ... IMB
International Meditation Society ... IMS
International Meeting of Cataloging Experts ... IMCE
International Men's and Boys' Wear Exhibition ... IMBEX
International Messianic Outreach ... IMO
International Metal Union ... IMU
International Metallographic Society ... IMS
International Metallurgical Reviews [*A publication*] ... Int Metall Revs
International Metals Reviews [*A publication*] ... Int Met Rev
International Metalworkers' Federation [*See also FIOM*] ... IMF
International Meteorological Center [*India*] [*WMO*] ... IMC
International Meteorological Committee ... IMC
International Meteorological Organization [*Later, World Meteorological Organization*] ... IMO
International Meteorological Teletype Network Europe ... IMTNE
International Metered Communications ... IMCO
International Metric System ... IMS
International Micro-Print Preservation, Inc. ... IMP
International Micro-Print Preservation, Inc., New York, NY [*Library symbol*] ... IntMP
International Microelectronic Symposium. Proceedings [*A publication*] ... Int Microelectron Symp Proc
International Microfiche Parts Access Catalogue [*Auto parts*] [*A publication*] ... IMPAC
International Microfilm Journal of Legal Medicine, New York, NY [*Library symbol*] ... IntMJ
International Micrographic Congress ... IMC
International Microwave Power Institute ... IMPI
International Migration [*A publication*] ... INMI
International Migration Review [*A publication*] ... Int Migration R
International Migration Review [*A publication*] ... Int Migr Re
International Military Archives [*Formerly, AIMH*] [*An association*] ... IMA
International Military Assistance Office ... IMAO
International Military Club Executives Association ... IMCEA
International Military Education and Training Program [*DoD*] ... IMET
International Military Education and Training Program [*DoD*] ... IMETP
International Military Headquarters ... IMHQ
International Military Police [*NATO*] ... INTERMILPOL
International Military Recreation Association ... IMRA
International Military Services Ltd. [*Ministry of Defence*] [*British*] ... IMS
International Military Staff [*NATO*] ... IMS
International Military Staff Communication [*NATO*] ... IMSCOM
International Military Staff Memorandum [*NATO*] ... IMSM
International Military Staff Memorandum [*NATO*] ... MILSTAM
International Military Staff Summary [*NATO*] ... IMSUM
International Military Staff Working Memorandum [*NATO*] ... IMSWM
International Military Tribunal [*Post-World War II*] ... IMT
International Military Tribunal for Europe [*Post-World War II*] ... IMTE
International Military Tribunal for Japan [*Post-World War II*] ... IMTFJ
International Milling Association [*See also AIM*] ... IMA
International Mimes and Pantomimists [*Defunct*] ... IMP
International Mine Water Association ... IMWA
International Mineralogical Association ... IMA
International Minerals & Chemical Corp. [*NYSE symbol*] ... IGL
International Minerals & Chemical Corp. ... IMC
International Miniature Horse Registry ... IMHR
International Mining Congress [*A publication*] ... Int M Cong
International Mining Corp. [*NYSE symbol*] [*Delisted*] ... IM
International Mining Corporation [*Later, IM*] [*NYSE symbol*] [*Delisted*] ... IMC
International Mining Equipment [*A publication*] ... Int Min Equip
International Ministerial Federation [*Defunct*] ... IMF
International Mission Radio Association ... IMRA
International Missionary Council [*Later, CWME*] ... IMC
International Missions [*An association*] ... IM
International Mobile Air Conditioning Association [*Formerly, AACA*] ... IMACA

International Mobile Machines [*NASDAQ symbol*]....IMMC
International Model Power Boat Association....IMPBA
International Molders' and Allied Workers' Union [*AFL-CIO*]....IMAW
International Molders' and Allied Workers' Union [*AFL-CIO*]....IM & AWU
International Molders' and Foundry Workers' Union of North America [*Later, IM & AWU*]....IMFWUNA
International Monetary Fund....IMF
International Monetary Fund and International Bank for Reconstruction and Development....IMF/IBRD
International Monetary Fund. Staff Papers [*A publication*]....IMF
International Monetary Fund. Staff Papers [*A publication*]....IMF Staff Pa
International Monetary Fund. Staff Papers [*A publication*]....Int Monetar
International Monetary Fund. Staff Papers [*A publication*]....Int Monetary Fund Staff Pa
International Monetary Market [*Chicago Mercantile Exchange*]....IMM
International Monthly [*A publication*]....Internat Mo
International Moth Class Association - US....IMCA-US
International Motion Picture and Lecturers Association....IMPALA
International Motor Contest Association....IMCA
International Motor Press Association....IMPA
International Motor Sports Association....IMSA
International Motorcycle Federation....IMF
International Movement of Apostolate of Children....IMAC
International Movement for Atlantic Union....IMAU
International Movement of Catholic Agricultural and Rural Youth [*See also MIJARC*]....IMCAR
International Movement of Catholic Agricultural and Rural Youth [*See also MIJARC*]....IMCARY
International Movement of Esperantist Bicyclists [*See also BEMI*]....IMEB
International Movements Toward Educational Change....IMTEC
International Multifoods Corporation [*NYSE symbol*]....IMC
International Municipal Signal Association....IMSA
International Museum Photographers Association....IMPA
International Museum of Photography, Eastman House, Rochester, NY [*OCLC symbol*]....VZZ
International Music Association....IMA
International Music Council....IMC
International Music Educator [*A publication*]....Int Mus Ed
International Musician [*A publication*]....Int Mus
International Musician, Newark, NJ [*Library symbol*]....NjNIM
International Musicological Society....IMS
International Musicological Society. Report of the Congress [*A publication*]....IMS
International Mycological Association....IMA
International Mycophagist Association....IMA
International Myomassethics Federation....IMF
International Myopia Prevention Association....IMPA
International Narcotic Enforcement Officers Association....INEOA
International Narcotics Control Board....INCB
International Natural Sausage Casing Association....INSCA
International Naturist Federation....INF
International Naturopathic Association [*Later, IAHHP*]....INA
International Nautical Mile....INM
International Naval Research Organization [*Formerly, NRC*]....INRO
International Navigation System....INS
International Netsuke Collectors Society [*Commercial firm*]....INCS
International Network of Children of Jewish Holocaust Survivors....INCJHS
International Network of Feed Information Centers....INFIC
International Network for Social Network Analysis....INSNA
International Network for Terminology [*INFOTERM*]....TERMNET
International New Thought Alliance....INTA
International News Photo....INP
International News Service [*Merged with United Press to form UPI*]....INS
International Newsletter of Special Libraries [*A publication*]....INSPEL
International Newspaper Advertising Executives [*Later, INAME*]....INAE
International Newspaper Advertising and Marketing Executives [*Formerly, NAEA, INAE*]....INAME
International Newspaper Collectors' Club....INCC
International Newspaper and Colour Association....INCA
International Newspaper Promotion Association....INPA
International Newsreel and News Film Association....INA
International Nickel [*A publication*]....Int Nickel
International Nickel Company....INCO
International Nickel Co. of Canada, Mississauga, ON, Canada [*Library symbol*]....CaOMIN
International Nickel Co. of Canada, Toronto, ON, Canada [*Library symbol*]....CaOTIN
International Nickel Co., Technical Library, New York, NY [*Library symbol*]....NNIND
International Non-Governmental Organization....INGO
International Nonproprietary Names [*World Health Organization*]....INN
International Normal Atmosphere....INA
International North Pacific Fisheries Commission....INPFC
International North Pacific Fisheries Commission. Annual Report [*A publication*]....Int North Pac Fish Comm Annu Rep
International North Pacific Fisheries Commission. Bulletin [*A publication*]....Int North Pac Fish Comm Bull
International North Pacific Fisheries Commission, United States Section....INPFC-US
International North Pacific Fisheries, Vancouver, BC, Canada [*Library symbol*]....CaBVaI
International NOTAMS [*Notices to Airmen*] [*A publication*]....IN
International Nuclear Corp., Denver, CO [*Library symbol*]....CoDIN
International Nuclear Data Committee [*of International Atomic Energy Agency*]....INDC
International Nuclear and Energy Association....IN & EA
International Nuclear Forces....INF
International Nuclear Fuel Authority....INFA
International Nuclear Fuel Cycle Evaluation....INFCE
International Nuclear Information System....INIS
International Numismatic Commission....INC
International Numismatic Society Authentication Bureau....INSAB
International Nurse Education Program....INEP
International Nursing Index [*A publication*]....INI
International Nursing Index [*A publication*]....IntNurI
International Nursing Review [*A publication*]....Int Nurs Re
International Nursing Review [*A publication*]....Int Nurs Rev
International Nutrition Research Foundation....INRF
International Occultation Timing Association....IOTA
International Ocean Institute....IOI
International Oceanographic Data Exchange....IODE
International Oceanographic Foundation....IOF
International Oceanographic Foundation. Bulletin [*A publication*]....Internat Oceanog Found Bull
International Office for Audiophonology....IOA
International Office of Cocoa and Chocolate....IOCC
International Office of Epizootics....IOE
International Offshore Rule [*Yachting*]....IOR
International Oil Compensation Fund....IOCF
International Oil Pollution Compensation [*In association name IOPC Fund*]....IOPC
International Oil Scouts Association....IOSA
International Oil Scouts Association. Yearbook [*A publication*]....Int Oil Scouts Assoc Yearb
International Oil Tanker and Terminal Safety Guide....IOTTSG
International Old Lacers....IOL
International Olive Oil Council....IOOC
International Olympic Academy....IOA
International Olympic Committee....IOC
International Ombudsman Institute....IOI
International Omega Association....IOA
International Operations Simulation....INTOP
International Ophthalmology [*A publication*]....Int Ophthalmol
International Ophthalmology Clinics [*A publication*]....Int Ophthalmol Clin
International Ophthalmology Clinics [*A publication*]....IOPCA
International Optometric and Optical League....IOOL
International Order of Hoo-Hoo....IOHH
International Order of Job's Daughters....IOJD
International Order of Kabbalists....IOK
International Order of the King's Daughters and Sons....IOKDS
International Order of Runeberg....IOR
International Order of Saint Luke the Physician....OSL
International Organisation for the Elimination of All Forms of Racial Discrimination....EAFORD
International Organization [*A publication*]....Internatl Organ
International Organization [*A publication*]....Int Org
International Organization [*A publication*]....Int Organ
International Organization Against Trachoma....IOAT
International Organization for Biological Control of Noxious Animals and Plants [*See also OILB*]....IOBC
International Organization for Chemical Sciences in Development....IOCD
International Organization of Citrus Virologists....IOCV
International Organization of Consumers' Unions....IOCU
International Organization for Cultivating Human Spirit [*Later, OISCA*]....IOCHS
International Organization of Employers....IOE
International Organization of the Flavor Industry....IOFI
International Organization of Good Templars....IOGT
International Organization of Journalists [*See also OIJ*]....IOJ
International Organization for Legal Metrology....IOLM
International Organization for Masoretic Studies....IOMS
International Organization of Masters, Mates, and Pilots....IOMMP
International Organization of Masters, Mates, and Pilots....MMP
International Organization for Medical Cooperation....IOMC
International Organization for Medical Physics....IOMP
International Organization for Motor Trades and Repairs....IOMTR
International Organization for Mycoplasmology....IOM
International Organization of Old Testament Scholars....IOOTS
International Organization of Palaeobotany....IOP
International Organization of Plant Biosystematists....IOPB
International Organization for Pure and Applied Biophysics....IOPAB
International Organization for Rural Development....IORD
International Organization for Septuagint and Cognate Studies....IOSCS
International Organization of Space Communications....INTERSPUTNIK
International Organization for Standardization [*Official initialism is ISO*]....IOS
International Organization for Standardization....ISO
International Organization for the Study of Group Tensions....IOSGT
International Organization for the Study of Human Development....IOSHD
International Organization for the Study of the Old Testament....IOSOT
International Organization for Succulent Plant Study....IOS
International Organization of Supreme Audit Institutions....INTOSAI

International Organization for Vacuum Science and Technology .... IOVST
International Organization of Women Executives [*Defunct*] .... IOWE
International Organization of Women in Telecommunications .... IOWT
International Organization of Wooden Money Collectors .... IOWMC
International Orienteering Federation .... IOF
International Originating Toll Center [*Bell System*] .... IOTC
International Ornithological Congress .... IOC
International Orphans, Incorporated .... IOI
International Orthopaedics [*A publication*] .... Int Orthop
International Osteopathic Association .... IOA
International Oxygen Manufacturers Association .... IOMA
International Ozone Association .... IOA
International Ozone Institute [*Later, IOA*] .... IOI
International Pacific Halibut Commission .... IPHC
International Pacific Halibut Commission. Annual Report [*A publication*] .... Int Pac Halibut Comm Annu Rep
International Pacific Halibut Commission. Scientific Report [*A publication*] .... Int Pac Halibut Comm Sci Rep
International Pacific Halibut Commission. Technical Report [*A publication*] .... Int Pac Halibut Comm Tech Rep
International Pacific Salmon Fisheries Commission .... IPSFC
International Pacific Salmon Fisheries Commission. Annual Report [*A publication*] .... Int Pac Salmon Fish Comm Annu Rep
International Pacific Salmon Fisheries Commission. Bulletin [*A publication*] .... Int Pac Salmon Fish Comm Bull
International Pacific Salmon Fisheries Commission. Progress Report [*A publication*] .... Int Pac Salmon Fish Comm Prog Rep
International Packers Ltd. [*NYSE symbol*] [*Delisted*] .... IPK
International Pact Organization .... IPO
International Paddle Racket Association [*Later, AARA*] .... IPRA
International Paddleball Association [*Later, AARA*] .... IPA
International Palaeontological Association .... IPA
International Paleoclimatic Data Network .... IPDN
International Paleontological Union .... IPU
International Paper Board Industry [*European Edition*] [*A publication*] .... Intern Pbd Ind
International Paper Co. [*NYSE symbol*] .... IP
International Paper Co., Corporate Research and Development Division, Technical Information Center, Tuxedo Park, NY [*Library symbol*] .... NTuxpI
International Parents' Organization .... IPO
International Passenger Airline Reservations System .... IPARS
International Passenger Ship Association [*Merger of Atlantic Passenger Steamship Conference, Trans-Atlantic Passenger Steamship Conference, Caribbean Cruise Association*] .... IPSA
International Patent Classification .... IPC
International Patent Documentation Center [*Information service*] [*Austria*] .... INPADOC
International Patent Institute .... IPI
International Patent Research Office .... IPRO
International Patent and Trademark Association .... IPTA
International Payments Group .... IPG
International PBX [*Private Branch Exchange*] **Telecommunicators** .... IPC
International Peace Academy .... IPA
International Peace Bureau .... IPB
International Peace Campaign .... IPC
International Peace, Communication, and Coordination Center .... IPCCC
International Peace Research Association .... IPRA
International Peace Research Institution, Oslo [*Norway*] .... PRIO
International Peasant Union .... IPU
International Peat Society [*See also IMTG*] .... IPS
International Peat Society. Bulletin [*A publication*] .... Int Peat Soc Bull
International Pediatric Association [*See also AIP*] .... IPA
International Pediatric Nephrology Association .... IPNA
International PEN [*Official name; PEN, never spelled out in use, is said to stand for poets, playwrights, editors, essayists, novelists*] .... PEN
International Penal and Penitentiary Commission .... IPPC
International Penal and Penitentiary Foundation [*See also FIPP*] .... IPPF
International Penguin Class Dinghy Association .... IPCDA
International Pentecostal Press Association .... IPPA
International Percy Grainger Society .... IPGS
International Periodical Distributors Association .... IPDA
International Personnel Management Association .... IPMA
International Perspectives [*A publication*] .... Int Perspect
International Peruvian Paso Horse Association .... IPPHA
International Pest Control [*A publication*] .... Int Pest Contr
International Pest Control [*A publication*] .... Int Pest Control
International Pesticide Applicators Association .... IPAA
International Pesticide Institute .... IPI
International Petroleum Annual [*A publication*] .... Int Petrol Annu
International Petroleum Cartel .... IPC
International Petroleum Co. .... INTERPET
International Petroleum Industry Environmental Conservation Association .... IPIECA
International Petroleum Quarterly [*A publication*] .... IPQ
International Petroleum Times [*A publication*] .... Int Petr Tms
International Petroleum Times [*A publication*] .... Int Pet Times
International Pharmaceutical Abstracts [*A publication*] .... IPA
International Pharmaceutical Students' Federation .... IPSF
International Pharmacopoeia .... IP
International Pharmacopoeia .... PhI
International Pharmacopsychiatry [*A publication*] .... Int Pharmac
International Pharmacopsychiatry [*A publication*] .... Int Pharmacopsychiatry
International Phasor Telecom [*NASDAQ symbol*] .... IPTLF
International Phenomenological Society .... IPS
International Philatelic Press Club [*Formerly, PPC*] .... IPPC
International Philosophical Quarterly [*A publication*] .... Int Philo Q
International Philosophical Quarterly [*A publication*] .... Int Philos Q
International Philosophical Quarterly [*A publication*] .... Int Phil Quart
International Philosophical Quarterly [*A publication*] .... IPQ
International Phonetic Alphabet .... IPA
International Phonetic Association .... IPA
International Phonetic Association Journal [*A publication*] .... IPAJ
International Photo-Engravers Union [*Later, GAIU*] .... IPEU
International Photo Optical Show Association .... IPOSA
International Photosynthesis Committee .... IPC
International Phototherapy Association .... IPA
International Phototherapy Institute .... IPI
International Physical Fitness Association .... IPFA
International Physicians for the Prevention of Nuclear War .... IPPNW
International Physics Workshop Series [*A publication*] .... Int Phys Workshop Ser
International Piano Guild .... IPG
International Piano Teachers Association [*Defunct*] .... IPTA
International Pietenpol Association .... IPA
International Pig Veterinary Society .... IPVS
International Pilot Study of Schizophrenia [*WHO*] .... IPSS
International Pin Collectors Club .... IPCC
International Pinball Association .... IPA
International Pipe Association .... IPA
International Pipe Line Industry [*A publication*] .... Int Pipe Ln
International Pipe Line Industry [*A publication*] .... Pipeln Ind
International Pipe Standard .... IPS
International Pipe Thread .... IPT
International Planetarium Society .... IPS
International Planned Parenthood Federation .... IPPF
International Planned Parenthood Federation, Documentation and Publications Center, New York, NY [*Library symbol*] .... NNIPF
International Planned Parenthood Federation. Medical Bulletin [*A publication*] .... Int Plann Parent Fed Med Bull
International Planned Parenthood Federation, Western Hemisphere Region .... IPPF/WHR
International Planning Corporation .... IPC
International Planning Glossaries [*Elsevier Book Series*] [*A publication*] .... IPG
International Planning Group [*Belgium, Germany, Netherlands*] .... IPG
International Planning Team [*NATO*] .... IPT
International Plant Index [*A publication*] .... IPlx
International Plant Propagators' Society, Eastern Region .... IPPS
International Plasma Corporation .... IPC
International Plastic Modelers Society/US Branch .... IPMS/USA
International Plate Collectors Association .... IPCA
International Plate Printers, Die Stampers, and Engravers' Union of North America .... IPPDSEU
International Plate Printers, Die Stampers, and Engravers' Union of North America .... PPDSE
International Platform Association .... IPA
International Playing-Card Society .... IPCS
International Poetry Forum, Pittsburgh, PA [*Library symbol*] .... PPiI
International Polar Motion Service .... IPMS
International Polar Year .... IPY
International Police Academy [*Formerly, Inter-American Police Academy*] .... IPA
International Police Association .... IPA
International Police Dogs .... IPD
International Police Services .... INPOLSE
International Poliomyelitis Congress .... IPC
International Political Science Abstracts [*A publication*] .... IntPolSc
International Political Science Association .... IPSA
International Polka Association .... IPA
International Poplar Commission .... IPC
International Population Research Center [*University of California*] [*Defunct*] .... IPOR
International Porcelain Artist Teachers [*Formerly, NCPTO, ICPTO*] .... IPAT
International Portrait Gallery .... IPG
International Postage Stamp Exhibition .... INPEX
International Postal Collectors League [*Commercial firm*] .... IPCL
International Postcard Collectors Association .... IPCA
International Pot and Kettle Clubs [*Formerly, APKCA*] .... IPKC
International Potash Institute .... IPI
International Potash Institute. Bulletin [*A publication*] .... Int Potash Inst Bull
International Potash Institute. Colloquium. Proceedings [*A publication*] .... Int Potash Inst Colloq Proc
International Potash Institute. Research Topics [*A publication*] .... Int Potash Inst Res Top
International Power Machines [*American Stock Exchange symbol*] .... PWR
International Practical Scale of Temperature .... IPST
International Practical Temperature Scale [*National Bureau of Standards*] .... IPTS
International Prayer Fellowship .... IPF
International Precious Metals Institute .... IPMI
International Press Association [*Defunct*] .... IPA

International Press Institute ... IPI
International Press Telecommunications [*See also CIPT*] ... IPTC
International Primary Aluminium Institute ... IPAI
International Primate Protection League ... IPPL
International Primatological Society ... IPS
International Primitive Money Society ... IPMS
International Printers Supply Salesmen's Guild ... IPSSG
International Printing Exhibition ... IPEX
International Printing and Graphic Communications Union ... IPGCU
International Printing and Graphic Communications Union ... PGCU
International Printing Pressmen and Assistants' Union of North America [*Later, IPGCU*] ... IPPA
International Printing Pressmen and Assistants' Union of North America [*Later, IPGCU*] ... IPPAU
International Prisoners' Aid Association ... IPAA
International Probation Organization ... INTERPRO
International Problems (Belgrade) [*A publication*] ... Int Probl (Belgrade)
International Problems (Tel-Aviv) [*A publication*] ... Int Probl (Tel-Aviv)
International Processes Simulation [*Game*] ... IPS
International Production, Service, and Sales Union ... PSS
International Professional Ski Racers Association ... IPSRA
International Professional Surrogates Association ... IPSA
International Program for the Development of Communications [*United Nations*] ... IPDC
International Program in Environmental Management Education ... IPEME
International Program for Human Resource Development ... IPHRD
International Program of Laboratories for Population Statistics ... POPLAB
International Program of Ocean Drilling [*Formerly, DSDP*] [*National Science Foundation*] ... IPOD
International Program for Population Analysis ... IPPA
International Programs and Studies Office [*NASULGC*] ... IPSO
International Progress Organization ... IPO
International Progress in Urethanes [*A publication*] ... Int Prog Urethanes
International Project of the Association for Voluntary Sterilization ... IPAVS
International Project for Soft Energy Paths ... IPSEP
International Proteins Corp. [*American Stock Exchange symbol*] ... PRO
International Protocol ... PI
International Prototype Kilogram ... IPK
International Prototype Meter ... IPM
International Psychiatry Clinics [*A publication*] ... Int Psychiatry Clin
International Psycho-Analytical Association ... IPA
International Psychohistorical Association ... IPA
International Public Policy Institute ... IPPI
International Public Relations Association ... INPRA
International Public Relations Association ... IPRA
International Publishers Advertising Representatives Association ... IPARA
International Publishers Association [*See also UIE*] ... IPA
International Publishing Corporation [*England*] ... IPC
International "Q" Signal ... IQS
International Quail Foundation ... IQF
International Quality Award [*LIMRA*] ... IQA
International Quality Centre ... IQC
International Quarterly [*A publication*] ... Internat
International Quarterly [*A publication*] ... Int Q
International Quick Printing Foundation ... IQPF
International Quiet Sun Year [*1964-65*] [*Also, IYQS*] ... IQSY
International Quorum of Motion Picture Producers ... IQ
International Rabbinic Committee for the Safety of Israel ... IRCSI
International Race of Champions [*Auto racing*] ... IROC
International Racquet Sports Association ... IRSA
International Racquetball Association [*Later, AARA*] ... IRA
International Radiation Investigation Satellite [*NASA*] ... IRIS
International Radiation Protection Association ... IRPA
International Radio Air Safety Association ... IRASA
International Radio Call Sign ... IRCS
International Radio Club of America ... IRCA
International Radio Consultative Committee ... IRCC
International Radio Frequency Board ... IRFB
International Radio Scientific Union ... IRSU
International Radio Silence ... IRS
International Radio and Television Society ... IRTS
International Radium Unit ... IRU
International Raiffeisen Union ... IRU
International Railway Congress Association ... IRCA
International Railway Journal [*A publication*] ... Int Railw J
International Railway Temperance Union ... IRTU
International Railways of Central America [*NYSE symbol*] [*Delisted*] ... IRC
International Rainwear Council ... IRC
International Rating Class [*Yachting*] ... IRC
International Rayon and Synthetic Fibers Committee ... IRSFC
International Reading Association ... IRA
International Reading Association Conference. Papers [*A publication*] ... Int Read Assn Conf Pa
International Reading Association Convention. Papers [*A publication*] ... Int Read Assn Conv Pa
International Real Estate Federation ... IREF
International Reception Operators ... IRO
International Record Carrier ... IRC
International Record of Medicine [*A publication*] ... Int Rec Med
International Recreation Association [*Later, WLRA*] ... IRA
International Rectifier Corp. [*NYSE symbol*] ... IRF
International Red Cross ... IRC
International Red Cross Committee [*World War II*] ... IRCC
International Red Locust Control Service ... IRLCS
International Reference Center for Abortion Research ... IRCAR
International Reference Center for Water Supply [*Netherlands*] ... IRC
International Reference Collection of Soybean Arthropods [*INTSOY*] ... IRCSA
International Reference Organization in Forensic Medicine and Sciences ... INFORM
International Reference Preparation [*World Health Organization*] ... IRP
International Reference Zero [*Level for pure-tone audiometers*] ... IRZ
International Referral Center for Information Handling Equipment [*UNESCO*] ... IRCIHE
International Referral System [*United Nations Environment Programme*] ... IRS
International Reform Federation ... IRF
International Refugee Integration Resource Centre ... IRIRC
International Refugee Organization ... IRO
International Register of Manipulative Therapists ... IRMT
International Register of Potentially Toxic Chemicals [*United Nations Environment Program*] ... IRPTC
International Registry of Early Corvettes ... IREC
International Registry of Organization Development Professionals ... IRODP
International Registry for Religious Women Artists ... IRRWA
International Registry of World Citizens ... IRWC
International Regulations for Preventing Collisions at Sea [*1972*] ... COLREGS
International Rehabilitation Medicine [*A publication*] ... Int Rehabil Med
International Rehabilitation Medicine Association ... IRMA
International Rehabilitation Review [*A publication*] ... Int Rehab Rev
International Relations [*A publication*] ... Int Rel
International Relations [*A publication*] ... IR
International Relations Committee [*American Library Association*] ... IRC
International Relations and Foreign Policy [*Army*] [*British*] ... IRFP
International Relations Information System [*West Germany*] ... IRIS
International Relations (London) [*A publication*] ... Int Relat (London)
International Relations Office [*American Library Association*] ... IRO
International Relations (Prague) [*A publication*] ... Int Relat (Prague)
International Relations Round Table [*American Library Association*] ... IRRT
International Relations (Teheran) [*A publication*] ... Int Relat (Teheran)
International Relief Organization [*Post-World War II*] ... IRO
International Relief and Rescue Committee [*Post-World War II*] ... IRRC
International Relief Union ... IRU
International Religious Liberty Association ... IRLA
International Religious Studies Unit [*American Topical Association*] ... IRSU
International Remote Imaging Systems, Inc. [*NASDAQ symbol*] ... IRIS
International Remote Sensing Institute ... IRSI
International Rendezvous ... IR
International Rendezvous and Docking Mission [*Aerospace*] ... IRDM
International Reply Coupon ... IRC
International Reporting Information Systems ... IRIS
International Repro Graphic Blueprint Association [*Formerly, IABPAI; later, IRA*] ... IRGBA
International Reprographics Association ... IRA
International Rescue Committee [*Formerly, IRRC*] ... IRC
International Rescue and Emergency Care Association [*Formerly, IRFAA*] ... IRECA
International Rescue and First Aid Association [*Later, IRECA*] ... IRFAA
International Rescuer [*A publication*] ... Int Rescuer
International Research Career Development Program [*Public Health Service*] ... IRCDP
International Research Center for Energy and Economic Development ... ICEED
International Research Committee on the Biokinetics of Impacts ... IRCOBI
International Research Communications System ... IRCS
International Research on Communist Techniques ... IRCT
International Research Council [*Later, ICSU*] ... IRC
International Research Council of Neuromuscular Disorders ... IRCND
International Research and Development ... IRD
International Research & Development Corp. [*NASDAQ symbol*] ... IRDV
International Research, Development, and Standardization [*Division*] [*Army*] ... IRD & S
International Research and Education [*Information service*] ... IRE
International Research & Evaluation [*Information service*] ... IRE
International Research and Exchanges Board ... IREX
International Research Group on Colour Vision Deficiencies ... IRGCVD
International Research Group on Refuse Disposal ... IRGRD
International Research Group on Wood Preservation ... IRG
International Research Information Service [*American Foundation for the Blind*] ... IRIS
International Research Society for Children's Literature ... IRSCL
International Research and Technology, Inc. ... IRT
International Resistance Company ... IRC
International Resistor Center ... IRC
International Resource Development, Inc. [*Information service*] ... IRD
International Resources Bank ... IRB
International REST [*Restricted Environmental Stimulation Technique*] **Investigators Security** ... IRIS
International Review [*A publication*] ... Internat R
International Review [*A publication*] ... Int Rv

International Review of Administrative Sciences [*A publication*] .... Int R Admin Sci

International Review of Administrative Sciences [*A publication*] .... Int R Adm Sci

International Review of the Aesthetics and Sociology of Music [*A publication*] .... Int R Aesthetics & Soc

International Review of the Aesthetics and Sociology of Music [*A publication*] .... Int R Aesthetics & Soc Mus

International Review of the Aesthetics and Sociology of Music [*A publication*] .... IRAMD

International Review of the Aesthetics and Sociology of Music [*A publication*] .... IRASM

International Review of Agricultural Economics [*A publication*] .... Int R Ag Econ

International Review of Agriculture [*A publication*] .... Int R Ag

International Review of Applied Linguistics in Language Teaching [*A publication*] .... IRAL

International Review of the Army, Navy, and Air Force Medical Services [*A publication*] .... Int Rev Army Navy Air Force Med Serv

International Review of Biochemistry [*A publication*] .... Int Rev Biochem

International Review of Community Development [*A publication*] .... Int R Com Dev

International Review of Community Development [*A publication*] .... Int R Community Develop

International Review of Community Development [*A publication*] ..... IRCD-A

International Review of Connective Tissue Research [*A publication*] .... Int Rev Connect Tissue Res

International Review of Cytology [*A publication*] .... Int Rev Cyt

International Review of Cytology [*A publication*] .... Int Rev Cytol

International Review of Cytology. Supplement [*A publication*] .... Int Rev Cytol Suppl

International Review of Education [*A publication*] .... International R Ed

International Review of Education [*A publication*] .... Int R Ed

International Review of Education [*A publication*] .... Int R Educ

International Review of Education [*A publication*] .... Int Rev Edu

International Review of Educational Cinematography [*A publication*] .... Int R Ed Cinemat

International Review of Experimental Pathology [*A publication*] .... Int Rev Exp Pathol

International Review of Forestry Research [*A publication*] ..... Int Rev For Res

International Review of General and Experimental Zoology [*A publication*] .... Int Rev Gen Exp Zool

International Review of History and Political Science [*A publication*] .... Int Rev His

International Review of History and Political Science [*A publication*] .... Int R Hist Polit Sci

International Review of History and Political Science [*A publication*] .... Int R Hist Pol Sci

International Review of Industrial Property and Copyright Law [*A publication*] IIC

International Review of Missions [*A publication*] .... Int R Miss

International Review of Missions [*A publication*] .... Int R Missions

International Review of Missions [*A publication*] .... IRM

International Review of Modern Sociology [*A publication*] .... Int Rev Mod

International Review of Modern Sociology [*A publication*] .... Int R Mod Sociol

International Review of Music Aesthetics and Sociology [*Later, International Review of the Aesthetics and Sociology of Music*] [*A publication*] .... IRMAS

International Review of Neurobiology [*A publication*] .... Int Rev Neurobiol

International Review of Neurobiology. Supplement [*A publication*] .... Int Rev Neurobiol Suppl

International Review of Physiology [*A publication*] .... Int Rev Physiol

International Review of the Science and Practice of Agriculture [*A publication*] .... Int R Sci & Prac Ag

International Review of Slavic Linguistics [*A publication*] .... IRSL

International Review of Social History [*A publication*] .... Int Rev S H

International Review of Social History [*A publication*] .... Int R Soc Hist

International Review of Social History [*A publication*] .... IRSH

International Review of Sport Sociology [*A publication*] ..... Int R Sport Sociol

International Review of Trachoma [*A publication*] .... Int Rev Trach

International Review of Tropical Medicine [*A publication*] .... Int Rev Trop Med

International Rhinologic Society .... IRS

International Rice Commission .... IRC

International Rice Commission Newsletter [*A publication*] .... Int Rice Comm Newsl

International Rice Research Institute [*Philippines*] .... IRRI

International Rice Research Institute (Los Banos). Annual Report [*A publication*] .... Int Rice Res Inst (Los Banos) Annu Rep

International Rice Research Institute (Los Banos). Technical Bulletin [*A publication*] .... Int Rice Res Inst (Los Banos) Tech Bull

International Rice Research Institute. Research Paper Series [*A publication*] .... Int Rice Res Inst Res Pap Ser

International Right of Way Association .... IRWA

International Rights Information Service .... IRIS

International Risk Management Institute .... IRMI

International Road Documentation Center .... IRDC

International Road Federation .... IRF

International Road Research Documentation System [*OECD*] .... IRRD

International Road Transport Union .... IRU

International Robomation/Intelligence [*NASDAQ symbol*] .... ROBT

International Rock 'n' Roll Music Association .... IRMA

International Rocket Week .... IRW

International Rodeo Association .... IRA

International Rodeo Writers Association [*Later, RMA*] .... IRWA

International Roleo Association [*Later, International Log Rolling Association*] .... IRA

International Ropeway Review [*A publication*] .... Int Ropeway Rev

International Rorschach Society .... IRS

International Rose O'Neill Club .... IROC

International Rotary Engine Club [*Later, RX-7 Club of America*] .... IREC

International Round Table for the Advancement of Counseling .... IRTAC

International Rowing Federation .... IRF

International Royal Enterprises [*An association*] .... IRE

International Royalty & Oil [*NASDAQ symbol*] .... IROC

International Rubber Association .... IRA

International Rubber Development Committee .... IRDC

International Rubber Hardness Degree .... IRHD

International Rubber Regulation Committee [*World War II*] .... IRRC

International Rubber Research Board .... IRRB

International Rubber Research and Development Board .... IRRDB

International Rubber Study Group .... IRSG

International Rural Sociology Association .... IRSA

International Safety Academy .... ISA

International Safety Institute [*Defunct*] .... ISI

International Sailing Craft Association .... ISCA

International Salmonella Center .... ISC

International Salon of Cartoonists .... ISC

International Salt Co. [*NYSE symbol*] [*Delisted*] .... ILS

International Salzburg Conference [*A publication*] .... Int Salzburg Conf

International Sand Collectors Society .... ISCS

International Sanitary Convention for Air Navigation .... ISCAN

International Sanitary Regulations [*World Health Organization*] .... ISR

International Sanitary Supply Association .... ISSA

International Satellite Cloud Climatology Program .... ISCCP

International Satellite Geodesy Experiment .... ISAGEX

International Satellite for Ionospheric Studies [*NASA-Canada*] .... ISIS

International Satellite Verification Agency .... ISVA

International Save the Pun Foundation .... ISPF

International Savings Banks Institute [*See also IICE*] .... ISBI

International Savings & Loan Association Ltd. [*NASDAQ symbol*] .... ISLH

International Scheme for the Coordination of Dairy Development ...... ISCDD

International School Art Program [*Defunct*] .... ISAP

International Schools Association .... ISA

International Schools Service .... ISS

International Science and Engineering Fair .... ISEF

International Science Fiction [*A publication*] .... INT

International Science Foundation .... ISF

International Science Information Services [*Earth sciences data center in Dallas, TX*] .... ISIS

International Science Organization .... ISO

International Science and Technology [*A publication*] ...... Intern Sci Technol

International Science and Technology [*A publication*] .... Int Sci Technol

International Science Writers Association .... ISWA

International Scientific Council for Trypanosomiasis. Research Publication [*A publication*] .... Int Sci Counc Trypanosomiasis Res Publ

International Scientific Film Association .... ISFA

International Scientific Film Library .... ISFL

International Scientific Publications [*Tel Aviv, Israel*] .... ISC

International Scientific Radio Union [*Also, URSI*] .... ISRU

International Scientific Union .... ISU

International Scientific Vocabulary .... ISV

International Scleroderma Federation .... ISF

International Scotist Society [*See also SIS*] .... ISS

International Screen Advertising Producer's Association [*Defunct*] .... ISAPA

International Screen Publicity Association .... ISPA

International Seabed Area .... ISBA

International Seabed Authority .... ISA

International Seabed Research Authority .... ISRA

International Seal, Label, and Cigar Band Society .... ISLCBS

International Seaman's Union .... ISU

International Seaway Trading Corp. [*American Stock Exchange symbol*] .... INS

International Secretariat of Arts, Communications Media, and Entertainment Trade Unions .... ISACMETU

International Secretariat of Entertainment Trade Unions .... ISETU

International Secretariat for Research on the History of Agricultural Implements .... ISRHAI

International Secretariat for the University Study of Education .... ISUSE

International Secretariat for Volunteer Service [*Defunct*] .... ISVS

International Security [*A publication*] .... Int Sec

International Security [*A publication*] .... Int Secur

International Security Affairs [*DoD*] .... ISA

International Security Affairs Committee .... ISAC

International Security Agency .... ISA

International Security Review [*A publication*] .... Int Secur Rev

International Seed Testing Association .... ISTA

International Seismological Centre .... ISC

International Seismological Centre. Bulletin [*A publication*] .... Int Seismol Cent Bull

International Self-Service Organization ... ISO
International Self-Service Organization ... ISS
International Seminar on Reproductive Physiology and Sexual Endocrinology [*A publication*] ... Int Semin Reprod Physiol Sex Endocrinol
International Senior Citizens Association ... ISCA
International Sensitivity Index [*Hematology*] ... ISI
International Serials Catalogue [*A publication*] ... ISC
International Serials Data System [*UNESCO*] ... ISDS
International Sericultural Commission ... ISC
International Series on Materials Science and Technology [*A publication*] ... Int Ser Mater Sci Technol
International Series of Monographs in Analytical Chemistry [*A publication*] ... Int Ser Monogr Anal Chem
International Series of Monographs in Experimental Psychology [*A publication*] ... Int Ser Monogr Exp Psychol
International Series of Monographs in Natural Philosophy [*A publication*] ... Int Ser Monogr Nat Philos
International Series of Monographs in Nuclear Energy [*A publication*] ... Int Ser Monogr Nucl Energy
International Series of Monographs in Oral Biology [*A publication*] ... Int Ser Monogr Oral Biol
International Series of Monographs on Pure and Applied Biology. Division Biochemistry [*A publication*] ... Int Ser Monogr Pure Appl Biol Div Biochem
International Series of Monographs on Pure and Applied Biology. Division Botany [*A publication*] ... Int Ser Monogr Pure Appl Biol Div Bot
International Series of Monographs on Pure and Applied Biology. Zoology Division [*A publication*] ... Int Ser Pure Appl Biol Zool Div
International Series of Monographs in the Science of the Solid State [*A publication*] ... Int Ser Monogr Sci Solid State
International Series of Monographs in the Science of the Solid State [*A publication*] ... Int Ser Sci Solid State
International Series on Sport Sciences [*A publication*] ... Int Ser Sport Sci
International Service Agencies ... ISA
International Service Coordination Center [*Communications*] ... ISCC
International Services [*Red Cross*] ... IS
International Shade Tree Conference [*Later, ISA*] ... ISTC
International Shade Tree Conference. Proceedings [*A publication*] ... Int Shade Tree Conf Proc
International Ship Electric Service Association ... ISES
International Ship Painting and Corrosion Conference. Proceedings [*A publication*] ... Int Ship Painting Corros Conf Proc
International Ship Structure Congress ... ISSC
International Ship Suppliers Association ... ISSA
International Shipbuilding Progress [*A publication*] ... Int Shipbldg Progr
International Shipholding Corp. [*NASDAQ symbol*] ... INSH
International Shipmasters Association of the Great Lakes ... ISA
International Shipmasters Association of the Great Lakes ... ISAGL
International Shipmasters Association of the Great Lakes ... ISMA
International Shipowners' Association ... INSA
International Shipping Federation ... ISF
International Ships-in-Bottles Association ... ISBA
International Shoe and Leather Workers' Federation ... ISLWF
International Shooting Union ... ISU
International Shopfitting Organization ... ISO
International Show Car Association ... ISCA
International Shuffleboard Association ... ISA
International Siberian Husky Club ... ISHC
International Side-Saddle Organization ... ISSO
International Sight and Sound Exposition ... ISSE
International Sightseeing and Tours Association [*Defunct*] ... ISTA
International Sign Association [*Later, NESA*] [*Defunct*] ... ISA
International Silk Association ... ISA
International Silo Association ... ISA
International Silver Company [*Acronym now used as firm's name*] ... INSILCO
International Simulation and Gaming Association ... ISAGA
International Single Comb Black Minorca Club ... ISCBMC
International Six Days Trial [*Motorcycling*] ... ISDT
International Skateboard Association ... ISA
International Skating Union [*See also UIP*] ... ISU
International Skeeter Association ... ISA
International Skeletal Society ... ISS
International Ski Federation ... ISF
International Ski Racers Association [*Later, WPS-RA*] ... ISRA
International Ski Writers Association ... ISWA
International Sled Dog Racing Association ... ISDRA
International Slurry Seal Association ... ISSA
International Snowmobile Industry Association ... ISIA
International Soap Box Derby, Inc. ... ISBD
International Soccer League ... ISL
International Social Affiliation of Women Airline Pilots ... ISA + 21
International Social Development Institute ... ISDI
International Social Development Review [*A publication*] ... Int Soc Dev
International Social Science Council [*See also CISS*] ... ISSC
International Social Science Institute [*Later, International Academy at Santa Barbara*] ... ISSI
International Social Science Journal [*UNESCO*] [*A publication*] ... Int Social Sci J
International Social Science Journal [*UNESCO*] [*A publication*] ... Int Soc Sci
International Social Science Journal [*UNESCO*] [*A publication*] ... Int Soc Sci J
International Social Science Journal [*UNESCO*] [*A publication*] ... ISSJ
International Social Security Association ... ISSA
International Social Security Review [*A publication*] ... Int Soc Secur R
International Social Service [*See also SSI*] ... ISS
International Social Service, American Branch [*Formerly, TAISSA*] ... ISS/AB
International Social Travel Federation [*See also FITS*] ... ISTF
International Social Work [*A publication*] ... Int Soc Work
International Socialist [*A publication*] ... IS
International Socialist Organization ... ISO
International Socialist Review [*A publication*] ... Int Social R
International Socialist Review [*A publication*] ... I S Revw
International Socialists ... IS
International Society for the Abolition of Data Processing Machines ... ISADPM
International Society for the Advancement of Humanistic Studies in Gynecology ... ISFAHSIG
International Society for Aerosols in Medicine [*See also IGAeM*] ... ISAeM
International Society of Air Safety Investigators [*Formerly, SASI*] ... ISASI
International Society of Analytical Trilogy [*See also SITA*] ... ISAT
International Society for Animal Blood Group Research ... ISABR
International Society of Animal License Collectors ... ISALC
International Society of Antique Scale Collectors ... ISASC
International Society of Appraisers ... ISA
International Society of Arboriculture [*Formerly, ISTC, NSTC*] ... ISA
International Society of Art and Psychopathology ... ISAP
International Society for the Arts, Sciences, and Technology ... ISAST
International Society for Astrological Research ... ISAR
International Society for Autistic Children ... ISAC
International Society of Aviation Writers ... ISAW
International Society of Barristers ... ISOB
International Society of Bassists ... ISB
International Society of Bassists Newsletter [*A publication*] ... ISB
International Society of Bible Collectors ... ISBC
International Society for Biochemical Pharmacology ... ISBP
International Society of Bioclimatology and Biometeorology ... ISBB
International Society of Biometeorology ... ISB
International Society of Biorheology ... ISB
International Society of Blood Transfusion ... ISBT
International Society for Burn Injuries ... ISBI
International Society for Business Education ... ISBE
International Society of Cardiology ... ISC
International Society for Cell Biology ... ISCB
International Society of Certified Electronics Technicians ... ISCET
International Society of Certified Employee Benefit Specialists ... ISCEBS
International Society of Chemotherapy ... ISC
International Society of Christian Endeavor ... CE
International Society of Christian Endeavor ... ISCE
International Society for Chronobiology ... ISC
International Society of Citriculture ... ISC
International Society of City and Regional Planners [*See also AIU*] ... ISCRP
International Society of City and Regional Planners [*See also AIU*] ... ISoCaRP
International Society for Classical Bibliography ... ISCB
International Society for Clinical Electroretinography ... ISCERG
International Society for Clinical Enzymology ... ISCE
International Society for Clinical and Experimental Hypnosis ... ISCEH
International Society for Clinical Laboratory Technology ... ISCLT
International Society of Clinical Pathology [*Later, WASP*] ... ISCP
International Society for Community Development ... ISCD
International Society for the Comparative Study of Civilizations ... ISCSC
International Society for a Complete Earth ... ISCE
International Society for Contemporary Music ... ISCM
International Society of Continuing Education in Dentistry [*See also SIECD*] ... ISCED
International Society of Copier Artists ... ISCA
International Society of Cryosurgery ... ISC
International Society of Cryptozoology ... ISC
International Society of Cybernetic Medicine ... ISCM
International Society of Dermatologic Surgery ... ISDS
International Society of Development Biologists [*Formerly, IIE*] ... ISDB
International Society of Differentiation ... ISD
International Society for Diseases of the Esophagus ... ISDE
International Society for Education through Art ... INSEA
International Society for Educational Planners ... ISEP
International Society for Eighteenth Century Studies [*See also SIEDS*] ... ISECS
International Society of Electrochemistry ... ISE
International Society of Electromyographic Kinesiology ... ISEK
International Society for Electrostimulation ... ISE
International Society of Endocrinology ... ISE
International Society of Endoscopy ... ISE
International Society of Esperantist-Philologists [*See also IUEFI*] ... ISEP
International Society of Explosives Specialists ... ISES
International Society of Family Law ... ISFL

International Society for Fat Research .... ISF
International Society and Federation of Cardiology .... ISFC
International Society of Financiers .... ISF
International Society of Fine Arts Appraisers .... ISFAA
International Society of Fire Service Instructors .... FSI
International Society of Fire Service Instructors .... ISFSI
International Society for Fluoride Research .... ISFR
International Society of Flying Engineers .... ISFE
International Society for Folk-Narrative Research .... ISFNR
International Society of Food Service Consultants [*Later, FCSI*] .... ISFSC
International Society of Free Space Colonizers [*Superseded by Political Action Caucus*] .... ISFSC
International Society of Friendship and Good Will .... ISFGW
International Society of Gastroenterology .... ISGE
International Society for General Semantics .... ISGS
International Society of Geographic Ophthalmology .... ISGO
International Society for Geothermal Engineering .... ISGE
International Society of Guatemala Collectors .... ISGC
[*The*] **International Society Handling the Interchange of Remarkable T-Shirts** .... TSHIRTS
International Society for Heart Research .... ISHR
International Society for Heart Transplantation .... ISHT
International Society of Hematology .... ISH
International Society for the History of Ideas .... ISHI
International Society for Horticultural Science [*See also SISH*] .... ISHS
International Society of Hotel Association Executives .... ISHAE
International Society for Human and Animal Mycology .... ISHAM
International Society for Human Ethology .... ISHE
International Society for Human Rights [*See also IGM*] .... ISHR
International Society for Hybrid Microelectronics .... ISHM
International Society of Hypertension .... ISH
International Society of Industrial Fabric Manufacturers [*Formerly, ISIYM*] .... ISIFM
International Society of Industrial Yarn Manufacturers [*Later, ISIFM*] .... ISIYM
International Society of Interior Designers .... ISID
International Society of Internal Medicine .... ISIM
International Society for Japanese Philately .... ISJP
International Society of Jewish Librarians .... ISJL
International Society for Krishna Consciousness .... ISKCON
International Society for Labor Law and Social Legislation [*Later, International Society for Labor Law and Social Security United States National Branch*] .... ISLLSL
International Society of Literature .... ISL
International Society of Lymphology .... ISL
International Society of Mathematical Biology .... ISMB
International Society of Medical Hydrology [*Later, ISMHC*] .... ISMH
International Society of Medical Hydrology and Climatology [*Formerly, ISMH*] .... ISMHC
International Society on Metabolic Eye Disease .... ISMED
International Society for Metaphysics .... ISM
International Society of Mini- and Micro-Computers .... ISMM
International Society for Mushroom Science [*Formerly, ICMS*] .... ISMS
International Society for Musical Education .... ISME
International Society of Naturopathic Physicians .... ISNP
International Society for Neoplatonic Studies .... ISNS
International Society of Nephrology .... ISN
International Society for Neurochemistry .... ISN
International Society for Ophthalmic Ultrasound .... ISOU
International Society for Organ History and Preservation .... ISOHP
International Society of Organbuilders [*A publication*] .... ISO
International Society of Parametric Analysts .... ISPA
International Society for Pediatric Neurosurgery .... ISPN
International Society of Performing Arts Administrators [*Formerly, IACFM, IACM*] .... ISPAA
International Society of Pharmaceutical Engineers .... ISPE
International Society of Philology .... SP
International Society for Philosophical Enquiry .... ISPE
International Society of Phonetic Sciences .... ISPHS
International Society of Phonetic Sciences .... ISPS
International Society for Photogrammetry [*Later, ISPRS*] .... ISP
International Society for Photogrammetry and Remote Sensing [*Formerly, ISP*] .... ISPRS
International Society of Plant Morphologists .... ISPM
International Society for Plant Pathology .... ISPP
International Society of Plastic and Audio-Visual Art .... ISPAA
International Society for Portuguese Philately .... ISPP
International Society of Postmasters .... ISP
International Society of Preretirement Planners .... ISPP
International Society for Prevention of Child Abuse and Neglect .... ISPCAN
International Society for Preventive Oncology .... ISPO
International Society for Professional Hypnosis .... ISPH
International Society for Prosthetics and Orthotics .... ISPO
International Society for Prosthetics and Orthotics - US Committee .... ISPOUSC
International Society for the Protection of Animals [*Later, WSPA*] .... ISPA
International Society for the Protection of Mustangs and Burros .... ISPMB
International Society for the Psychology of Writing .... ISPW
International Society of Radiographers and Radiological Technicians .... ISRRT
International Society of Radiology .... ISR
International Society of Radiology Congress .... ISRC
International Society for Range Management .... ISRM
International Society for Rehabilitation of the Disabled [*Later, Rehabilitation International*] .... ISRD
International Society of Reply Coupon Collectors .... RCC
International Society of Reproductive Medicine .... ISRM
International Society for Research on Aggression .... ISRA
International Society for Respiratory Protection .... ISRP
International Society for Rock Mechanics .... ISRM
International Society for Rock Mechanics. Congress Proceedings [*A publication*] .... Int Soc Rock Mech Congr Proc
International Society for Sandwich Construction and Bonding .... ISSCB
International Society of Sculptors, Painters, and Gravers .... IS
International Society of Skilled Trades .... ISST
International Society for Socialist Studies .... ISSS
International Society for the Sociology of Knowledge .... ISSK
International Society for Soil Mechanics and Foundation Engineering .... ISSMFE
International Society of Soil Science [*See also AISS*] .... ISSS
International Society for Soilless Culture .... ISOSC
International Society of Sport Sponsors .... ISSS
International Society of Sports Psychology .... ISSP
International Society of Statistical Science in Economics .... ISSSE
International Society for Stereology .... ISS
International Society of Stress Analysts .... ISSA
International Society for the Study of Behavioural Development .... ISSBD
International Society for the Study of Church Monuments .... ISSCM
International Society for the Study of Expressionism [*Formerly, ETMS*] .... ISSE
International Society for the Study of the Human-Companion Animal Bond .... ISSHCAB
International Society for the Study of Symbols .... ISSS
International Society for the Study of Time .... ISST
International Society of Sugar Cane Technologists .... ISSCT
International Society of Surgery .... ISS
International Society for Terrain-Vehicle Systems .... ISTVS
International Society for Testing and Failure Analysis .... ISTFA
International Society for Testing Materials .... ISTM
International Society on Thrombosis and Hemostasis .... ISTH
International Society on Toxinology .... IST
International Society for Training and Culture .... ISTC
International Society of Transport Aircraft Traders .... ISTAT
International Society of Tropical Dermatology .... ISTD
International Society for Tropical Ecology .... ISTE
International Society of Tropical Foresters .... ISTF
International Society for Twin Studies .... ISTS
International Society of Urology [*See also SIU*] .... ISU
International Society of Videographers .... ISV
International Society of Violin and Bow Makers .... ISVBM
International Society of Wang Users .... ISWU
International Society of Weekly Newspaper Editors .... ISWNE
International Society for the Welfare of Cripples [*Later, Rehabilitation International*] .... ISWC
International Society of Wine Tasters .... ISWT
International Sociological Association .... ISA
International Softball Congress .... ISC
International Softball Federation .... ISF
International Software AG Users Group .... ISAGUG
International Soil Museum .... ISM
International Soil Tillage Research Organization .... ISTRO
International Solar Energy Society .... ISES
International Solar Polar [*Mission*] [*NASA*] .... ISP
International Solar Polar Mission [*NASA*] .... ISPM
International Solid State Circuits Conference .... ISSCC
International Solid Wastes and Public Cleansing Association .... ISWA
International Solidarity Committee with Algerian Youth .... ISCAY
International Soling Association .... ISA
International Sorghum and Millet Research .... INTSORMIL
International Sound Programming Center [*Communications*] .... ISPC
International Soundex Reunion Registry .... ISRR
International Sourcebook. Corrosion in Marine Environment [*A publication*] .... Int Sourceb Corros Mar Environ
International Sourdough Reunion .... ISR
International Southern Ocean Study [*National Science Foundation*] .... ISOS
International Soybean Program .... INTSOY
International Spa and Tub Institute .... ISTI
International Space Congress .... ISC
International Special Commission on Radio Interference .... ISPR
International Special Tooling Association .... ISTA
International Species Inventory System [*Data processing for animal mating*] .... ISIS
International Spectator [*A publication*] .... Int Spectator
International Spiritualist Federation .... ISF
International Sporting and Leisure Club .... ISLC
International Sporting Press Association .... ISPA
International Sports Exchange .... ISE
International Sports Organization for the Disabled .... ISOD
International Squash Rackets Federation .... ISRF
International Staff .... IS
International Staff Disaster Assistance Information Coordinator [*NATO*] .... ISDAIC

International Staff Duty Officer [*NATO*] ... ISDO
International Staff Planners Memo [*NATO*] ... ISPMEMO
International Staff Planners Message [*NATO*] ... ISPM
International Stained Glass Association ... ISGA
International Stamp Collectors Society ... ISCS
International Standard ... IS
International Standard Atmosphere ... ISA
International Standard Bibliographic Description [*Library of Congress*] ... ISBD
International Standard Bibliographic Description for Cartographic Materials [*Library of Congress*] ... ISBD(CM)
International Standard Bibliographic Description for Monographs [*Library of Congress*] ... ISBD(M)
International Standard Bibliographic Description for Serials [*Library of Congress*] ... ISBD(S)
International Standard Book Number [*Library of Congress*] ... ISBN
International Standard Classification of Education ... ISCED
International Standard Code for Information Interchange ... ISCII
International Standard Commodity Classification of All Goods and Services ... ISCC
International Standard Electric Corporation ... ISEC
International Standard Engineering, Incorporated ... ISEI
International Standard Industrial Classification ... ISIC
International Standard Orthopaedic Measurements [*Medicine*] ... ISOM
International Standard Paper Sizes ... ISPS
International Standard Resource [*NASDAQ symbol*] ... ISTRF
International Standard Serial Number ... ISSN
International Standard Statistical Classification of Aquatic Animals and Plants ... ISSCAAP
International Standard Thread ... INTSTDTHD
International Standard Thread ... IST
International Standards Association ... ISA
International Standing Committee on Distribution Problems [*International Water Supply Association*] ... ISCDP
International Standing Committee on Water Quality and Treatment [*International Water Supply Association*] ... ISCWQT
International Standing Conference on Philanthropy ... INTERPHIL
International Star Class Yacht Racing Association ... ISCYRA
International Star Registry ... ISR
International Statistical Classification ... ISC
International Statistical Education Centre [*India*] ... ISEC
International Statistical Institute ... ISI
International Statistical Institute. Review [*A publication*] ... RSIR
International Statistical Program Center [*Agency for International Development*] ... ISPC
International Statistical Programs Office [*Department of Commerce*] ... ISPO
International Statistical Review [*A publication*] ... Int Stat R
International Statistical Review [*A publication*] ... Int St Rvw
International Steel Guitar Convention ... ISGC
International Stereotypers and Electrotypers Union [*Later, IPGCU*] ... ISEU
International Stoke Mandeville Games Federation ... ISMGF
International Stop Continental Drift Society ... ISCDS
International Strabismological Association ... ISA
International Streptomyces Project ... ISP
International Stress and Tension Control Association [*Formerly, AAATC*] ... ISTC
International Stretch Products, Inc. [*American Stock Exchange symbol*] [*Delisted*] ... IST
International Stretch Products, Inc. [*NASDAQ symbol*] ... ISTP
International Student Conference ... ISC
International Student Exchange Program [*United States Information Agency*] ... ISEP
International Student Information Service ... ISIS
International Student Pugwash [*Formerly, USSPC*] ... ISP
International Student Relief [*Later, WUS*] ... ISR
International Student Service ... ISS
International Student Travel Conference ... ISTC
International Students, Incorporated ... ISI
International Students Peace Network ... ISPN
International Students Society [*Defunct*] ... ISS
International Studies [*New Delhi*] [*A publication*] ... Int Stud
International Studies [*A publication*] ... IS
International Studies Association ... ISA
International Studies. East Asian Series Research Publication [*A publication*] ... Int St E As
International Studies of Management and Organization [*A publication*] ... Int Stud Manage Org
International Studies (New Delhi) [*A publication*] ... Int Stud (New Delhi)
International Studies in Philosophy [*A publication*] ... Int Stud Phil
International Studies Quarterly [*A publication*] ... Int Stud Q
International Studies Quarterly [*A publication*] ... Int Stud Quart
International Studies on Sparrows [*A publication*] ... Int Stud Sparrows
International Studio [*A publication*] ... Int Studio
International Study Commission for Traffic Police ... ISCTP
International Study Group for Aerogrammes ... ISGA
International Study Group of Diabetes in Children and Adolescents ... ISGD
International Study Group for Steroid Hormones ... ISGSH
International Study Institution of the Middle Classes ... ISIMC
International Study of Kidney Disease in Children ... ISKDC
International Subcommittee on Lactobacilli and Closely Related Organisms ... ISL
International Subscriber Dialing [*Telephones*] ... ISD
International Sugar Agreement ... ISA
International Sugar Council ... ISC
International Sugar Journal [*A publication*] ... Int Sugar J
International Sugar Journal [*A publication*] ... Int Sug J
International Sugar Organization [*See also OIA*] ... ISO
International Sugar Research Foundation [*Defunct*] ... ISRF
International Sun-Earth Explorer [*NASA/ESRO satellite*] ... ISEE
International Sun-Earth Physics Satellite ... ISEPS
International Sunshine Society ... ISS
International Superphosphate Manufacturers' Association ... ISMA
International Supply Committee [*World War II*] ... ISC
International Supreme Council of World Masons ... ISC
International Surgery [*A publication*] ... Int Surg
International Survey Library Association ... ISLA
International Sweets Market [*Trade fair*] [*Cologne, West Germany*] [*1982*] ... ISM
International Swift Association ... ISA
International Swimming Hall of Fame ... ISHOF
International Switching Center [*Communications*] ... ISC
International Switching Maintenance Center [*Communications*] ... ISMC
International Switching and Testing Center [*Communications*] ... ISTC
International Symposium on Aerospace Nuclear Propulsion ... ISASNP
International Symposium on Antarctic Glaciological Exploration ... ISAGE
International Symposium on Biomembranes ... ISB
International Symposium on Chemical Reaction Engineering ... ISCRE
International Symposium on Chemiluminescence ... ISC
International Symposium on the Chemistry of the Organic Solid State ... ISCOSS
International Symposium on Chemotherapy [*A publication*] ... Int Symp Chemother
International Symposium on Circuits and Systems [*IEEE*] ... ISCAS
International Symposium on Combustion. Papers [*A publication*] ... Int Symp Combust Pap
International Symposium on Corals and Coral Reefs. Proceedings [*A publication*] ... Int Symp Corals Coral Reefs Proc
International Symposium on Crop Protection. Papers [*A publication*] ... Int Symp Crop Prot Pap
International Symposium on Flammability and Fire Retardants. Proceedings [*A publication*] ... Int Symp Flammability Fire Retard Proc
International Symposium on Homogeneous Catalysis ... ISHC
International Symposium on Humidity and Moisture [*A publication*] ... Int Symp Humidity and Moisture
International Symposium on Landslide Control. Proceedings [*A publication*] ... Int Symp Landslide Control Proc
International Symposium on Microtechniques ... ISM
International Symposium on Novel Aromatic Compounds ... ISNA
International Symposium on Olfaction and Taste ... ISOT
International Symposium on Purine Metabolism in Man ... ISPMM
International Symposium on Remote Sensing of Environment. Proceedings [*A publication*] ... Int Symp Remote Sensing Environ Proc
International Symposium on Rocket and Satellite Meteorology ... ISRSM
International Symposium on Space Electronics ... ISSET
International Symposium on Space Technology and Science ... ISTS
International Symposium on Ultrasonic Diagnostics in Ophthalmology [*Later, ISOU*] ... ISUDO
International Synthetic Rubber Co. [*United Kingdom*] ... ISR
International Synthetic Rubber Co. [*ICAO designator*] ... RQ
International System of Units ... ISU
International Systems & Controls Corp. [*American Stock Exchange symbol*] [*Delisted*] ... IS
International Systems Meeting [*Data processing*] ... ISM
International Table Calorie ... ITCAL
International Table Tennis Federation ... ITTF
International Table Tennis League ... ITTL
International Tanker Nominal Freight Scale Association ... ITNFSA
International Tanker Owners Pollution Federation ... ITOPF
International Tanning Manufacturers Association ... ITMA
International Tape/Disc Association ... ITA
International Tar Conference [*See also CIG*] ... ITC
International Tax Institute [*Formerly, IUSTFI*] ... ITI
International Taxicab Association ... ITA
International Tea Committee ... ITC
International Tea Promotion Association ... ITPA
International Technical Communications Conference [*Society for Technical Communication*] ... ITCC
International Technical Institute of Flight Engineers ... ITI
International Technical Tropical Timber Association ... ITTTA
International Technogeographical Society ... ITS
International Technology Corporation [*NASDAQ symbol*] ... ITCP
International Technology Resources, Inc. [*NASDAQ symbol*] ... ITRC
International Tele/Conferencing Association ... IT/CA
International Telecommunications Satellite [*Acronym is service mark and trade name of the International Telecommunications Satellite Organization and is used for communications services via satellite*] ... INTELSAT
International Telecommunications Satellite Consortium [*Superseded by International Telecommunications Satellite Organization*] ... ITSC

International Telecommunications Union [A specialized agency of the United Nations]....................ITU
International Telecommunications Users Group [Information service]....................INTUG
International Telegraph Alphabet....................ITA
International Telegraph and Telephonic Advisory Committee....................ITTAC
International Telephone Credit Union Association....................ITCUA
International Telephone and Telegraph Communication System.......ITTCS
International Telephone & Telegraph Corp. [NYSE symbol]....................IT and T
International Telephone & Telegraph Corp. [NYSE symbol] [Wall Street slang name: "It Girl," the sobriquet for early movie star Clara Bow]....................ITT
International Telephone & Telegraph Corp., Gilfillan Division, Engineering Library, Van Nuys, CA [Library symbol]....................CVnITT
International Telephone and Telegraph, Federal Laboratories....................ITTF
International Telephone and Telegraph Federal Laboratories....................ITTFL
International Telephone & Telegraph World Communications, Inc.....................ITTCOM
International Teletraffic Congress....................ITC
International Television Association....................ITVA
International Television Broadcasting....................ITVB
International Television Center [Communications]....................ITC
International Temperance Association....................ITA
International Temperance Union....................ITU
International Temperature Scale....................ITS
International Tennis Federation [Formerly, ILTF]....................ITF
International Test and Evaluation Association....................ITEA
International Textbook Co.....................INTEXT
International Textile, Garment, and Leather Workers' Federation [See also FITTHC]....................ITGLWF
International Textile and Garment Workers' Federation [Later, ITGLWF]....................ITGWF
International Textile Manufacturers Federation....................ITMF
International Theatre Institute....................ITI
International Theatre Institute of the United States....................ITI/US
International Thermographers Association....................ITA
International Thesaurus of Quotations [A publication]....................ITQ
International Thespian Society....................ITS
International Third World Legal Studies Association [Supersedes ALAA]....................INTWORLSA
International Thoroughbred [NASDAQ symbol]....................ITHB
International Thrift Institute....................ITI
International Thyroid Conference. Proceedings [A publication]....................Int Thyroid Conf Proc
International Time Bureau....................ITB
International Tin Agreement....................ITA
International Tin Council [See also CIE]....................ITC
International Tin Research Council....................ITRC
International Toastmistress Clubs....................ITC
International TOKAMAK Reactor [Thermonuclear-fusion system]....................INTOR
International Tolerance....................IT
International Totalizator Systems [NASDAQ symbol]....................ITSI
International Touring Alliance....................ITA
International Tourism Quarterly [A publication]....................INTQ
International Tourist Year....................ITY
International Towing Tank Conference....................ITTC
International Toy Buff's Association....................ITBA
International Tracing Service....................ITS
International Track Association [Defunct]....................ITA
International Track and Field Coaches Association....................ITFCA
International Trade Administration [Department of Commerce]....................ITA
International Trade Center....................ITC
International Trade Club of Chicago [Later, IBCM]....................ITC
International Trade Commission [Formerly, USTC]....................ITC
International Trade Commission, Washington, DC [Library symbol]....................DTC
International Trade Fairs Office [Department of Commerce]....................ITFO
International Trade Forum [A publication]....................Int Trade Forum
International Trade Information Service....................ITIS
International Trade Organization....................ITO
International Trade Reporter [A publication]....................ITR
International Trade Secretariat....................ITS
International Trade in Textiles [Textile trade agreement]....................ITT
International Trade Unions Committee of Social Tourism and Leisure [See also CSITSL]....................ITUCSTL
International Traders Association....................IT
International Traders Club....................ITC
International Traffic in Arms Regulation [US]....................ITAR
International Training Branch [Office of Education]....................ITB
International Training College [Salvation Army]....................ITC
International Training School....................ITS
International Transactional Analysis Association....................ITAA
International Transfer Printing Institute [Formerly, ATPI]....................ITPI
International Translations Centre [Formerly, ETC]....................ITC
International Transmission Maintenance Center [Communications].....ITMC
International Transport Workers' Federation....................ITF
International Transport Workers' Federation....................ITWF
International Travel Adventure Film Guild....................INTRAFILM
International Travel Market Research Council....................ITMRC
International Travel Orders....................ITO
International Travelers Health Institute [Formerly, THI]....................ITHI
International Travellers [YWCA]....................IT

International Tree Crops Institute USA....................ITCI
International Tree Disease Register System for Literature Retrieval in Forest Pathology [National Agricultural Library]...INTREDIS
International Tree-Ring Data Bank [University of Arizona]....................ITRDB
International Trombone Association....................ITA
International Trombone Association Journal [A publication]....................ITA J
International Trombone Association Newsletter [A publication]....................ITA N
International Tropical Fern Society....................ITFS
International Trotting and Pacing Association....................ITPA
International Truck Parts Association....................ITPA
International Truck Restorers Association....................ITRA
International Trumpet Guild....................ITG
International Trumpet Guild Journal [A publication]....................ITG J
International Trumpet Guild Newsletter [A publication]....................ITG N
International Tsunami Information Center [UNESCO]....................ITIC
International Tube Association....................ITA
International Tuberculosis Campaign....................ITC
International Tug Convention (Proceedings) [A publication]....................Int Tug Conv (Proc)
International Tunnelling Association....................ITA
International Turquoise Association....................ITA
International Turtle and Tortoise Society....................IT & TS
International Turtle and Tortoise Society. Journal [A publication]....................Int Turtle Tortoise Soc J
International Twins Association....................ITA
International Typeface Corporation....................ITC
International Typographic Association....................ITA
International Typographic Composition Association [Later, TIA]....................ITCA
International Typographical Union....................ITU
International Typographical Union Ruling Machine....................ITURM
International Ultraviolet Explorer [NASA]....................IUE
International Underwater Contractors, Inc.....................IUC
International Underwater Explorers Society....................UNEXSO
International Underwater Research Corporation....................IURC
International Underwater Spearfishing Association....................IUSA
International Union of Academies....................IUA
International Union of Advertisers Associations....................IUAA
International Union Against Cancer. Monograph Series [A publication]....................Int Union Cancer Monogr Ser
International Union Against Cancer. Technical Report Series [A publication]....................Int Union Cancer Tech Rep Ser
International Union Against Tuberculosis [See also UICT]....................IUAT
International Union Against the Venereal Diseases and the Treponematoses....................IUVDT
International Union of Agricultural Journalists....................IUAJ
International Union of Air Pollution Prevention Associations....................IUAPPA
International Union of Air Pollution Prevention Associations. International Clean Air Congress. Papers [A publication]....................Int Union Air Pollut Prev Assoc Int Clean Air Congr Pap
International Union, Allied Industrial Workers of America....................AIW
International Union of Allied Novelty and Production Workers....................IUANPW
International Union of Allied Novelty and Production Workers....................NPW
International Union of Alpine Associations....................IUAA
International Union of Anthropological and Ethnological Sciences [See also UISAE]....................IUAES
International Union for Applied Ornithology....................IUAO
International Union of Architects....................IUA
International Union of Associations of Doctor-Motorists....................IUADM
International Union of Aviation Insurers....................IUAI
International Union of Biochemistry....................IUB
International Union of Biological Sciences....................IUBS
International Union of Biological Sciences. Series B [A publication]....................Int Union Biol Sci Ser B
International Union of Biological Sciences. Series D. Newsletter [A publication]....................Int Union Biol Sci Ser D Newsl
International Union of Bricklayers and Allied Craftsmen [Formerly, BMP]....................BAC
International Union for Child Welfare....................IUCW
International Union for Conservation of Nature and Natural Resources....................IUCN
International Union for Conservation of Nature and Natural Resources. Annual Report [A publication]....................Int Union Conserv Nat Nat Resour Annu Rep
International Union of Crystallography....................IUC
International Union of Crystallography....................IU Cr
International Union of Directors of Zoological Gardens....................IUDZG
International Union of Doll and Toy Workers of the US and Canada [Later, IUANPW]....................IDTW
International Union of Electrical, Radio, and Machine Workers....................IUE
International Union of Electrical Workers....................IUEW
International Union for Electroheat [Also, IUE-H]....................IUE
International Union for Electroheat [Also, IUE]....................IUE-H
International Union of Elevator Constructors....................IUEC
International Union of Family Organizations....................IUFO
International Union of Food and Allied Workers' Associations [See also IUL]....................IUF
International Union of Food, Drink, and Tobacco Workers' Associations....................IUFDT
International Union of Food Science and Technology....................IUFOST
International Union of Forestry Research Organizations....................IUFRO
International Union of Game Biologists....................IUGB

International Union of Geodesy and Geophysics ... IUGG
International Union of Geological Sciences ... IUGS
International Union of Geological Sciences. International Subcommission on Stratigraphic Classification. Circular [*A publication*] ... Int Union Geol Sci Int Subcomm Stratigr Cl Circ
International Union of Gospel Missions ... IUGM
International Union for Health Education [*See also UIES*] ... IUHE
International Union of the History and Philosophy of Science ... IUHPS
International Union of Hotel, Restaurant, and Bar Workers ... IUHR
International Union of Immunological Societies ... IUIS
International Union of Journeymen Horseshoers of the United States and Canada ... IUJHUSC
International Union of Journeymen Horseshoers of the United States and Canada ... UJH
International Union for Land Value Taxation and Free Trade ... IULVTFT
International Union of Leather Chemists Societies ... IULCS
International Union of Liberal Christian Women ... IULCW
International Union of Life Insurance Agents ... IULIA
International Union of Life Insurance Agents ... LIA
International Union of Local Authorities ... IULA
International Union of Marine Insurance ... IUMI
International Union of Marine Sciences [*Proposed*] ... IUMS
International Union of Master Painters [*See also UNIEP*] ... IUMP
International Union of the Medical Press ... IUMP
International Union of Microbiological Societies ... IUMS
International Union of Mine, Mill, and Smelter Workers [*Later, USWA*] ... IUMMSW
International Union of Mine, Mill, and Smelter Workers [*Later, USWA*] ... MMSW
International Union for Moral and Social Action ... IUMS
International Union of Nutritional Sciences ... IUNS
International Union of Official Travel Organisations [*Later, WTO*] ... IUOTO
International Union of Operating Engineers ... IUOE
International Union of Petroleum and Industrial Workers ... IUPIW
International Union of Petroleum Workers [*Later, IUPIW*] ... IUPW
International Union of Pharmacology [*ICSU*] ... IUPHAR
International Union of Phlebology ... IUP
International Union of Physiological Sciences [*ICSU*] ... IUPS
International Union of Police Associations ... IUPA
International Union of Practitioners in Advertising ... IUPA
International Union of Prehistoric and Protohistoric Sciences ... IUPPS
International Union for Protecting Public Morality [*Later, International Union for Moral and Social Action*] ... IUPM
International Union for the Protection of Literary and Artistic Works ... IUPLAW
International Union of Psychological Science ... IUPS
International Union of Public Transportation ... IUPT
International Union of Pure and Applied Biophysics ... IUPAB
International Union of Pure and Applied Chemistry ... IUPAC
International Union of Pure and Applied Chemistry Information Bulletin [*A publication*] ... IUPAC Inf Bull
International Union of Pure and Applied Physics ... IUPAP
International Union for Quaternary Research ... INQUA
International Union of Railways ... IUR
International Union of Reticuloendothelial Societies ... IURES
International Union of School and University Health and Medicine [*See also UIHMSU*] ... IUSUHM
International Union for the Scientific Study of Population ... IUSSP
International Union of Security Officers ... IUSO
International Union of Social Democratic Teachers ... IUSDT
International Union of Socialist Youth ... IUSY
International Union of Societies of Foresters [*See also UISIF*] ... IUSF
International Union of Speleology ... IUS
International Union of Students [*See also UIE*] ... IUS
International Union for the Study of Social Insects ... IUSSI
International Union of Tenants ... IUT
International Union of Theoretical and Applied Mechanics ... IUTAM
International Union of Tool, Die, and Mold Makers ... IUTDMM
International Union of Tool, Die, and Mold Makers ... TDMM
International Union, United Automobile, Aerospace, and Agricultural Implement Workers of America ... UAW
International Union of United Brewery, Flour, Cereal, Soft Drink, and Distillery Workers of America [*Later, Brewery and Soft Drink Workers Conference - USA and Canada*] ... BFCSD
International Union, United Mine Workers of America ... UMWA
International Union, United Plant Guard Workers of America ... UPGWA
International Union, United Welders [*Later, IUOE*] ... IUUW
International Union for Vacuum Science, Technique, and Applications [*See also UISTAV*] ... IUVSTA
International Union of Young Christian Democrats ... IUYCD
International Unit ... IU
International Universities Bureau ... IUB
International Universities' Sports Board ... IUSB
International University of Communication [*Washington, DC*] ... IUC
International University Contact for Management Education ... IUC
International University Contact for Management Education ... IUCME
International University Foundation ... IUF
International Upper Mantle Program ... IUMP
International Urgency Signal ... XXX
International Urology and Nephrology [*A publication*] ... Int Urol Nephrol
International URSIgram and World Day Service ... IUWDS
International Vegetarian Union ... IVU
International Veterans Boxers Association ... IVBA
International Veterinary Acupuncture Society ... IVAS
International Veterinary Association for Animal Production [*See also AIVPA*] ... IVAAP
International Veterinary Federation of Zootechnics ... IVFZ
International Veterinary Students Association ... IVSA
International Veterinary Students Union ... IVSU
International Videotex Information Providers' Association [*British*] [*Information service*] ... IVIPA
International Vine and Wine Office ... IVWO
International Violin and Guitar Makers Association ... IVGMA
International Virology [*A publication*] ... Int Virol
International Visitors Information Service [*Name changed to International Visitors Service Council of Greater Washington Organizations, but initials retained for identification*] ... IVIS
International Visual Literacy Association ... IVLA
International Vitamin A Consultative Group ... IVACG
International Volleyball Association [*Defunct*] ... IVA
International Volleyball Association [*Defunct*] ... IVBA
International Volleyball Federation ... IVBF
International Voluntary Services [*Later, SCI-IVS*] ... IVS
International Walther League ... IWL
International War Crimes Tribunal ... IWCT
International War Veterans' Alliance ... IWVA
International Watch Fob Association, Incorporated ... IWFAI
International Water Pollution Research Conference. Papers [*A publication*] ... Int Water Pollut Res Conf Pap
International Water Power and Dam Construction [*A publication*] ... Int Water Power & Dam Constr
International Water Resources Association ... IWRA
International Water Supply Association ... IWSA
International Water Supply Association. Congress [*A publication*] ... Int Water Supply Assoc Congr
International Waterfowl Research Bureau ... IWRB
International Wattier [*Process*] [*A method of making transparencies for rotogravure plates*] ... IW
International Weddell Sea Oceanographic Expedition ... IWSOE
International Weed Science Society ... IWSS
International Weightlifting Federation [*See also FHI*] ... IWF
International Westward Development Corp. [*NASDAQ symbol*] ... IWWDF
International Whaling Commission ... IWC
International Whaling Commission Report [*A publication*] ... Int Whaling Comm Rep
International Wheat Agreement ... IWA
International Wheat Council [*See also CIB*] ... IWC
International Wheat Gluten Association ... IWGA
International Who's Who in Community Service [*A publication*] ... IWWCS
International Who's Who in Poetry [*A publication*] ... IWWP
International Wild Rice Association ... IWRA
International Wild Waterfowl Association ... IWWA
International Wildlife [*A publication*] ... Int Wildl
International Wildlife [*A publication*] ... Int Wildlife
International Windsurfer Class Association ... IWCA
International Wine Society ... IWS
International Wire and Cable Symposium. Proceedings [*A publication*] ... Int Wire Cable Symp Proc
International Wire and Machinery Association ... IWMA
International Wizard of Oz Club ... IWOC
International Women's Auxiliary to the Veterinary Profession ... IWA
International Women's Cricket Council ... IWCC
International Women's Film Project ... IWFP
International Women's Fishing Association ... IWFA
International Women's Health Coalition ... IWHC
International Women's Tribune Centre ... IWTC
International Women's Writing Guild ... IWWG
International Women's Year [*1975*] ... IWY
International Wood Collectors Society ... IWCS
International Woodworkers of America ... IWA
International Wool Secretariat [*Australia, New Zealand, South Africa*] ... IWS
International Wool Study Group ... IWSG
International Wool Study Group ... WSG
International Wool Textile Organization [*See also FLI*] ... IWTO
International Word Processing Association [*Later, IIWPA, IWP*] ... IWPA
International Work Group for Indigenous Affairs ... IWGIA
International Workers Sport Association ... IWSA
International Working Group [*NATO*] ... IWG
International Working-Group of Soilless Culture ... IWOSC
International Working Party ... IWP
International Working Team [*NATO*] ... IWT
International World Calendar Association ... IWCA
International World Day Service ... IWDS
International Writers Guild ... IWG
International Wrought Copper Council ... IWCC
International Yacht Racing Union ... IYRU
International Year of the Child [*1979*] [*United Nations*] ... IYC
International Year of the Disabled Person [*1981*] ... IYDP
International Year for the Preparation of Disarmament [*Pugwash Conference*] ... IYPD
International Year of the Quiet Sun [*1964-65*] [*Also, IQSY*] ... IYQS

International Yearbook of Agricultural Legislation [*A publication*] .... Int Yearbook Ag Leg
International Yearbook of Education [*A publication*] .... Int Yearbook of Ed
International Yearbook of Education [*A publication*] .... Int Yrbk Ed
International Youth Congress .... IYC
International Youth Federation for Environmental Studies and Conservation .... IYF
International Youth Hostel Federation [*See also FIAJ*] .... IYHF
International Youth Library .... IYL
International Youth and Student Movement for the United Nations .... ISMUN
International Zetcentrum [*International Typesetting Center, The Netherlands*] .... IZC
International Zoo Yearbook [*A publication*] .... Int Zoo Yearb
International Zoo Yearbook [*A publication*] .... IZY
International Zoological Congress [*A publication*] .... Int Zool Cong
Internationale Akademie fuer Bader-, Sport-, und Freizeitheitbau [*International Board for Aquatic, Sports, and Recreation Facilities*] .... IAB
Internationale des Amis de la Nature [*International Federation of Friends of Nature*] .... IAN
Internationale Arbeitsgemeinschaft Donauforschung [*International Working Association for Danube Research*] .... IAD
Internationale Arbeitsgemeinschaft von Sortimentsbuchhaendler Vereinigungen [*International Community of Booksellers' Associations*] .... IASV
Internationale Atomreactorbau [*Germany*] .... INTERATOM
Internationale Bibliographie der Zeitschriftenliteratur [*International Index to Periodicals*] [*A publication*] .... IBZ
Internationale Bouworde [*International Association of Building Companions - IABC*] .... IBO
Internationale Chretienne Professionelle pour les Industries Graphiques et Papetieres [*International Federation of Christian Trade Unions of Graphical and Paper Industries*] .... ICPIGP
Internationale Demokratische Frauenfoederation [*Women's International Democratic Federation*] .... IDFF
Internationale Dialog Zeitschrift [*A publication*] .... Int Dialog Z
Internationale Dokumentationsgesellschaft fuer Chemie [*West Germany*] .... IDC
Internationale Eisenbahn-Kongress-Vereinigung [*International Railway Congress Association*] .... IEKV
Internationale Elektronische Rundschau [*A publication*] .... Int Elektr
Internationale Elektronische Rundschau [*A publication*] .... Int Elektron Rundsch
Internationale Foderation des Handwerks [*International Federation of Master Craftsmen - IFC*] .... IFH
Internationale Foderation der Vereine der Textilchemiker und Coloristen [*International Federation of Associations of Textile Chemists and Colourists*] .... IFVTCC
Internationale Foederation fuer Kurzschrift und Maschinenschreiben [*International Federation of Shorthand and Typewriting*] .... IFKM
Internationale Frauenliga fuer Frieden und Freiheit [*Women's International League for Peace and Freedom*] .... IFFF
Internationale Gesellschaft fuer Aerosole in der Medizin [*International Society for Aerosols in Medicine - ISAeM*] .... IGAeM
Internationale Gesellschaft fuer Allgemeinmedizin [*International Society of General Medicine*] .... IGAM
Internationale Gesellschaft fuer Arztliche Psychotherapie [*International Federation for Medical Psychotherapy*] [*See also IFMP*] .... IGAP
Internationale Gesellschaft fuer Ingenieurpadogogik [*International Society for Engineering Education*] .... IGIP
Internationale Gesellschaft fuer Menschenrechte [*International Society for Human Rights - ISHR*] .... IGM
Internationale Gesellschaft fuer Moorforschung [*International Society for Research on Moors*] .... IGM
Internationale Gesellschaft der Schriftpsychologie [*International Society for the Psychology of Writing*] .... IGSP
Internationale Gesellschaft fuer Urheberrecht [*International Copyright Society*] .... INTERGU
Internationale Gewerbeunion [*International Association of Crafts and Small and Medium-Sized Enterprises*] .... IGU
Internationale Gustav Mahler Gesellschaft [*International Gustav Mahler Society*] .... IGMG
Internationale Hoptrenbaubuero [*International Hop Growers Convention*] .... IHB
Internationale Juristen-Kommission [*International Commission of Jurists*] .... IJK
Internationale Katholische Mittelstandsbewegung [*International Catholic Union of the Middle Class*] .... IKMB
Internationale Katholische Vereinigung fuer Soziale Arbeit [*Catholic International Union for Social Service*] .... IKVSA
Internationale Kirchliche Zeitschrift [*A publication*] .... IKZ
Internationale Kommission fuer Alpines Rettungswesen [*International Commission for Alpine Rescue*] .... IKAR
Internationale Kommission fuer Glas [*International Commission on Glass*] .... IKG
Internationale Kommission fuer Numismatik [*International Numismatic Commission*] .... IKN
Internationale Kommission zum Schutze des Rheins Gegen Verunreinigung [*International Commission for the Protection of the Rhine Against Pollution - ICPRAP*] .... IKSR
Internationale Kriminalpolizeiliche Organisation [*International Criminal Police Organization*] .... IKPO
Internationale Messtechnische Konfoderation [*International Measurement Confederation*] [*Hungary*] .... IMEKO
Internationale Monatsschrift [*A publication*] .... IMS
Internationale Moor und Torf-Gesellschaft [*See also IPS*] .... IMTG
Internationale Paracelsusgesellschaft zu Salzburg [*International Paracelsus Society*] .... IPS
Internationale du Personnel des Postes, Telegraphes, et Telephones [*Postal, Telegraph, and Telephone International*] [*See also PTTI*] .... IPTT
Internationale Rat fuer Vogelschutz [*International Council for Bird Preservation*] .... IRV
Internationale des Resistants a la Guerre [*War Resisters International*] .... IRG
Internationale Revue der Gesamten Hydrobiologie [*A publication*] .... Int Rev Gesamten Hydrobiol
Internationale Revue der Gesamten Hydrobiologie. Systematische Beihefte [*A publication*] .... Int Rev Gesamten Hydrobiol Syst Beih
Internationale Richard-Strauss-Gesellschaft Mitteilungen [*A publication*] .... Strauss
Internationale Seidenbau Kommission [*International Sericultural Commission*] .... ISK
Internationale des Services Publics [*Public Services International*] .... ISP
Internationale Spectator [*A publication*] .... Internat Spectator
Internationale Studiengemeinschaft fuer Pranatale Psychologie [*International Society for the Study of Prenatal Psychology*] .... ISPP
Internationale Tieraerztliche Vereinigung fuer Tierproduktion [*International Veterinary Association for Animal Production*] .... ITVTP
Internationale Union Junger Christlicher Demokraten [*International Union of Young Christian Democrats*] .... IUJCD
Internationale Union der Lebens- und Genussmittelarbeiter-Gewerkschaften [*International Union of Food and Allied Workers Associations*] [*See also IUF*] .... IUL
Internationale Vereinigung der Anschlussgeleise-Benuetzer [*International Association of Users of Private Sidings*] .... IVA
Internationale Vereinigung fuer Brueckenbau und Hochbau [*International Association for Bridge and Structural Engineering*] .... IVBH
Internationale Vereinigung von Einkaufsverbanden [*International Association of Buying Groups - IABG*] .... IVE
Internationale Vereinigung der Eisenwaren- und Eisenhaendlerverbaende [*International Federation of Ironmongers and Iron Merchants Association*] .... IVE
Internationale Vereinigung fuer Germanische Sprach - und Literaturwissenschaft [*International Association of Germanic Languages and Literatures - IAGLL*] .... IVG
Internationale Vereinigung fuer Gewerblichen Rechtsschultz [*International Association for the Protection of Industrial Property*] .... IVFGR
Internationale Vereinigung fuer Individualpsychologie [*International Association of Individual Psychology*] .... IVIP
Internationale Vereinigung fuer Jugendhilfe [*International Union for Child Welfare*] .... IVJH
Internationale Vereinigung der Klein- und Mittelbetriebe des Handels [*International Federation of Small and Medium-Sized Commercial Enterprises*] .... IVKMH
Internationale Vereinigung der Lehrerverbaende [*International Federation of Teachers' Associations*] IVL
Internationale Vereinigung der Musikbibliotheken [*International Association of Music Libraries*] .... IVMB
Internationale Vereinigung voor Nederlandistiek [*A publication*] .... IVN
Internationale Vereinigung der Organisationen von Lebensmittel-Detail-Listen [*International Federation of Grocers' Associations - IFGA*] .... IVLD
Internationale Vereinigung fur Rechts- und Sozialphilosophie [*International Association for Philosophy of Law and Social Philosophy*] .... IVR
Internationale Vereinigung fuer Soziale Sicherheit [*International Social Security Association*] .... IVSS
Internationale Vereinigung der Textileinkaufsverbande [*International Association of Textile Purchasing Societies*] .... IVT
Internationale Vereinigung fuer Theoretische und Angewandte Limnologie und Verhandlungen [*A publication*] .... Int Ver Theor Angew Limnol Verh
Internationale Vereinigung fuer Theoretische und Angewandte Limnologie [*International Association of Theoretical and Applied Limnology*] IVL
Internationale Vereinigung fuer Vegetationskunde [*International Association for Vegetation Science - IAVS*] IVV
Internationale Warenhaus-Vereinigung [*International Association of Department Stores*] .... IWV
Internationale Zeitschrift fuer Angewandte Physiologie [*A publication*] .... IZAPA
Internationale Zeitschrift fuer Angewandte Physiologie Einschliesslich Arbeitsphysiologie [*A publication*] .... Int Z Angew Phsyiol Einschl Arbeitsphysiol

Internationale Zeitschrift fuer Erziehungswissenschaft [*A publication*] ... Int Z Erzieh
Internationale Zeitschrift fuer Klinische Pharmakologie Therapie und Toxicologie [*A publication*] ... Int Z Klin Pharmakol Ther Toxicol
Internationale Zeitschrift der Landwirtschaft [*A publication*] ... Int Z Landwirtsch
Internationale Zeitschrift fuer Theoretische und Angewandte Genetik [*A publication*] ... Int Z Theor Angew Genet
Internationale Zeitschrift fuer Vitamin und Ernaehrungsforschung [*A publication*] ... Int Z Vitam-Ernaehrungsforsch
Internationale Zeitschrift fuer Vitaminforschung [*A publication*] ... Int Z Vitaminforsch
Internationale Zeitschrift fuer Vitaminforschung. Beiheft [*A publication*] ... Int Z Vitaminforsch Beih
Internationale Zeitschriften fuer Bibelwissenschaft und Grenzgebiete [*A publication*] ... Int Z Bibelwiss
Internationalen Foderation des Dachdeckerhandwerks [*International Federation of Roofing Contractors - IFRC*] ... IFD
Internationaler Arbeitskreis Sport- und Freizeiteninrichtungen [*International Working Group for the Construction of Sports and Leisure Facilities*] ... IAKS
Internationaler Bund der Bau-Haolzarbeiter [*International Federation of Building and Woodworkers*] ... IBBH
Internationaler Bund Freier Gewerkschaften [*International Confederation of Free Trade Unions*] ... IBFG
Internationaler Elektronik-Arbeitskreis [*International Electronics Association*] ... INEA
Internationaler Frauenrat [*International Council of Women*] ... IFR
Internationaler Genossenschaftsbund [*International Cooperative Alliance*] ... IGB
Internationaler Holzmarkt [*A publication*] ... Int Holzmarkt
Internationaler Jugendaustausch und Besucherdienst der Bundesrepublik Deutschland [*International Youth Exchange and Visitor Service of the Federal Republic of Germany*] ... IJAB
Internationaler Kongress ueber die Tierische Fortpflanzung und die Kuenstliche Besamung [*A publication*] ... Int Kongr Tier Fortpflanz Kuenstliche Besamung
Internationaler Kranckenhausverbaund [*International Hospital Federation*] ... IKV
Internationaler Metalarbeiterbund [*International Metalworkers' Federation*] ... IMB
Internationaler Metzgermeisterverband [*International Federation of Meat Traders' Associations*] ... IMV
Internationaler Milchwirtschaftverband [*International Dairy Federation*] ... IMV
Internationaler Rat der Hauspflegedienste [*International Council of Home-Help Services*] ... IRHD
Internationaler Ring fuer Landarbeit [*International Committee of Scientific Management in Agriculture*] ... IRL
Internationaler Staendiger Verband fuer Schiffahrt-Kongresse [*Permanent International Association of Navigation Congresses*] ... ISVSK
Internationaler Studentenbund [*International Union of Students*] ... ISB
Internationaler Turnerbund [*International Gymnastic Federation*] ... ITB
Internationaler Verband fuer Arbeiterbildung [*International Federation of Workers' Educational Associations - IFWEA*] ... IVB
Internationaler Verband der Gastronomie- und Weinbuau-Presse [*International Federation of Gastronomical and Vinicultural Press*] ... IVGWP
Internationaler Verband fuer Hauswirtschaft [*International Federation for Home Economics*] ... IVHW
Internationaler Verband der Petroleum- und Chemiearbeiter [*International Federation of Petroleum and Chemical Workers*] ... IVPC
Internationaler Verband der Stadt-, Sport-, und Mehrzweckhallen [*International Federation of City, Sport, and Multi-Purpose Halls*] ... VDSM
Internationaler Verband fuer Wohnungswesen, Staedtebau und Raumordnung [*International Federation for Housing and Planning*] ... IVWSR
Internationaler Zivildienst [*International Voluntary Service*] ... IZD
Internationales Afrika Forum [*A publication*] ... Int Afr Forum
Internationales Arbeiter-Hilfswerk [*International Workers Aid*] ... IAH
Internationales Archiv fuer Arbeits- und Umweltmedizin [*A publication*] ... Int Arch Arbeits-Umweltmed
Internationales Archiv fuer Arbeitsmedizin [*A publication*] ... Int Arch Arbeitsmed
Internationales Archiv fuer Ethnographie [*A publication*] ... IAE
Internationales Archiv fuer Ethnographie [*A publication*] ... Inst Arch Ethnog
Internationales Archiv fuer Ethnographie [*A publication*] ... Int Archiv Ethnog
Internationales Archiv fuer Ethnologie [*A publication*] ... Internat Archiv f Ethno
Internationales Archiv fuer Gewerbepathologie und Gewerbehygiene [*A publication*] ... Int Arch Gewerbepathol Gewerbehyg
Internationales Archiv fuer Sozialgeschichte der Deutschen Literatur [*A publication*] ... IASL
Internationales Asienforum [*A publication*] ... Int As For
Internationales Asienforum [*A publication*] ... Int Asienf
Internationales Asienforum [*A publication*] ... Int Asien Forum
Internationales Auschwitz-Komitee [*International Auschwitz Committee*] ... IAK
Internationales Burgen-Institut [*International Castles Institute*] ... IBI
Internationales Gewerkschafts Buro [*International Trades Union Office*] ... IGB
Internationales Institut der Sparkassen [*International Savings Banks Institute*] ... IIS
Internationales Institut fuer Verwaltungswissenschaften [*International Institute of Administrative Sciences*] ... IIVW
Internationales Jahrbuch fuer Religionssoziologie [*A publication*] ... Int Jb Relig Soziol
Internationales Journal fuer Prophylaktische Medizin und Sozialhygiene [*A publication*] ... Int J Prophyl Med Sozialhyg
Internationales Kolpingwerk [*International Kolping Society - IKS*] ... IKW
Internationales Komittee vom Roten Kreuz [*International Committee of the Red Cross*] ... IKRK
Internationales Kuratorium fuer das Jugendbuch [*International Board on Books for Young People*] ... IKJ
Internationales Musikzentrum [*International Music Center*] ... IMZ
Internationales Recht und Diplomatie [*A publication*] ... Int Recht u Diplom
Internationales Wissenschaftliches Kolloquium der Technischen Hochschule Ilmenau [*A publication*] ... Int Wiss Kolloq Tech Hochsch Ilmenau
Internationelle Studier (Stockholm) [*A publication*] ... Int Stud (Stockholm)
Interne [*Medicine*] ... INT
Interned ... INT
Internist [*Medicine*] ... I
Internist [*Medicine*] ... INT
Internistische Welt [*A publication*] ... Internist Welt
Internment Camp ... IC
Internment Serial Number ... ISN
Internordic Investment Bank [*Scandinavia*] ... IIB
InterNorth, Incorporated [*NYSE symbol*] ... INI
Interns for Peace ... IFP
Internuclear Company ... IC
Internuclear Double Resonance ... INDOR
Interocular Transfer [*Ophthalmology*] ... IOT
Interoffice Comment Sheet ... IOCS
Interoffice Correspondence ... IOC
Interoffice Memorandum ... IOM
Interorbital Space Vehicle ... ISV
Interorbital Vehicle Assembly Mode ... IVAM
Interorganizational Work Authorization ... IOWA
Interpace Corp. [*Formerly, International Pipe & Ceramics Corp.*] [*NYSE symbol*] [*Delisted*] ... INP
Interpenetrating Elastomeric Networks [*Organic chemistry*] ... IEN
Interpenetrating Polymer Network [*Organic chemistry*] ... IPN
Interpersonal Behavior Inventory [*Veterans Administration*] ... IBI
Interpersonal Check List [*Psychology*] ... ICL
Interpersonal Development [*A publication*] ... Interpers D
Interpersonal Diagnosis of Personality [*Psychology*] ... IDP
Interpersonal Perception Method [*Psychology*] ... IPM
Interpersonal Process Recall [*Psychology*] ... IPR
Interphalangeal [*Anatomy*] ... IP
Interphalangeal [*Anatomy*] [*Medicine*] ... IPH
Interpharm Laboratories Limited [*NASDAQ symbol*] ... IPLLF
Interphase Chromosome Volume ... ICV
Interphase Transformer [*Electronics*] ... INTPHTR
Interphase Unit ... IPU
Interphone ... IFO
Interphone ... INPH
Interphone ... INT
Interphone ... INTER
Interphone ... INTPH
Interphone Control Station ... ICS
Interphone Control System ... ICS
Interphoto Corp. [*American Stock Exchange symbol*] [*Delisted*] ... IPH
Interplanetary Ballistic Missile [*Air Force*] ... IPBM
Interplanetary Communications ... IPC
Interplanetary Craft for Advanced Research in Vicinity of Sun ... ICARVS
Interplanetary Dust Particle ... IDP
Interplanetary Magnetic Field ... IMF
Interplanetary Magnetometer Probe ... IMP
Interplanetary Measurement Probe ... IMP
Interplanetary Measurement Probes ... IMP's
Interplanetary Meteoroid Experiment [*NASA*] ... IME
Interplanetary Mission Support ... IMS
Interplanetary Mission Support Requirements ... IMSR
Interplanetary Monitoring Platform [*A spacecraft*] ... IMP
Interplanetary Monitoring Probe [*A spacecraft*] ... IMP
Interplanetary Scintillation ... IPS
Interplanetary Travel ... IPT
Interplant Material Requisition Order ... IMRO
Interplant Shipping Authority ... ISA
Interplant Shipping Notice ... ISN
Interplant Shipping Order ... ISO
Interplant Work Order ... IPWO
Interplatform Alignment System ... IPAS
Interpolated Data and Speech Transmission [*Data processing*] ... IDAST
Interpolated Learning [*Psychology*] ... IL
Interpolating Delta Modulator ... IDM

Interpolation .... INTRPL
Interpole [*Electromagnetics*] .... INTPO
Interpool Ltd. [*American Stock Exchange symbol*] [*Delisted*] .... ITP
Interpost Junction Panel .... IPJP
Interpret .... INTPR
Interpret Parity Error .... IPE
Interpret Sign Error .... ISE
Interpretation [*A publication*] .... In
Interpretation [*Richmond, Virginia*] [*A publication*] .... In
Interpretation [*A publication*] .... Interp
Interpretation .... INTPN
Interpretation: A Journal of Bible and Theology [*A publication*] .... Intpr
Interpretation Report .... IR
Interpreter I
Interpreter .... INT
Interpreter .... INTERP
Interpreter [*A publication*] .... Int
Interpreter Officer [*Military*] [*British*] .... IO
Interpreter's Bible .... IB
Interpreter's Dictionary of the Bible .... IDB
Interpretive Computer Simulator .... ICS
Interpretive Operation .... IO
Interpretive Programing System .... IPS
Interpretive Structural Modeling [*A computer-assisted learning process for structuring information*] .... ISM
Interprocessor Communication .... IPC
Interprocessor Communication and Control Routine ICC
Interprofessional Council on Environmental Design [*Formerly, Interprofessional Commission on Environmental Design*] .... ICED
Interprofessional Research Commission on Pupil Personnel Services [*Defunct*] .... IRCOPPS
Interproject Group .... IPG
Interprovincial Pipe Line Ltd. [*NASDAQ symbol*] .... IPIPF
Interpublic Group of Companies, Inc. [*NYSE symbol*] .... IPG
Interpulse Interval .... IPI
Interpupillary .... INTRPLRY
Interpupillary Distance .... PD
Interquartile Range .... IQR
Interracial Books for Children. Bulletin [*A publication*] .... Inter B C
Interracial Books for Children. Bulletin [*A publication*] .... Interracial Bks Child Bull
Interracial Council for Business Opportunity .... ICBO
Interracial Review [*A publication*] .... Interracial Rev
Interrange Communications Planning Committee .... ICPC
Interrange Instrumentation Group .... IRG
Interrange Telemetry Working Group .... IRTWG
Interrelated Flow Simulation .... IFS
Interrelated Logic Accumulating Scanner .... ILAS
Interreligious Committee of General Secretaries [*of the National Council of Churches of Christ, the Synagogue Council of America, and the US Catholic Conference*] .... ICGS
Interreligious Emergency Campaign for Economic Justice .... IECEJ
Interreligious Foundation for Community Organization .... IFCO
Interreligious Taskforce on US Food Policy .... ITUSFP
Interresponse Time [*Psychometrics*] .... IRT
Interrogate .... INT
Interrogate .... INTG
Interrogate .... INTRG
Interrogation [*British naval signaling*] .... INT
Interrogation .... INTERROG
Interrogation and Locating .... IRL
Interrogation Prisoner of War .... IPW
Interrogation, Recording, and Locating System [*Naval Oceanographic Office*] .... IRLS
Interrogation Repetition Frequency [*RADAR beacon*] .... IRF
Interrogation Report .... IR
Interrogation Side-Lobe Suppression .... ISLS
Interrogation Sign [*Question mark*] [*Aviation code*] .... IMF
Interrogation Sign [*Question mark*] [*Communications*] .... IMI
Interrogation-Translation Team [*Military*] .... ITT
Interrogative .... INTER
Interrogator [*Aviation*] .... INTERR
Interrogator-Responder .... IR
Interrogator-Responder-Transducer .... IRT
Interrogator-Transponder .... IT
Interrupt .... INTER
Interrupt [*Data processing*] .... INTR
Interrupt .... INTRP
Interrupt .... INTRPT
Interrupt .... RUPT
Interrupt Acknowledge [*Data processing*] .... INTA
Interrupt Control Block .... ICB
Interrupt Control Register [*Data processing*] .... ICR
Interrupt Control Register [*Data processing*] .... INCR
Interrupt Enable [*Data processing*] .... INTE
Interrupt Jet Sensor .... IJS
Interrupt Level Status Word .... ILSW
Interrupt Request [*Data processing*] .... IRQ
Interrupt Service Routine .... ISR
Interrupted Continuous Waves [*Electronics*] .... ICW
Interrupted Quick Flashing Light [*Navigation signal*] .... INTQKFL
Interrupted Quick Flashing Light [*Navigation signal*] .... I Qk Fl
Interrupted Quick [*Flashing*] **Light** [*Navigation signal*] .... Int Qk
Interrupted Quick [*Flashing*] **Light** [*Navigation signal*] .... IQ
Interrupted Quick [*Flashing*] **Light** [*Navigation signal*] .... I Qk
Interrupted Task Paradigm [*Psychometrics*] .... ITP
Interrupted Ultraquick [*Flashing*] **Light** [*Navigation signal*] .... IUQ
Interrupted Very Quick [*Flashing*] **Light** [*Navigation signal*] .... IVQ
Interrupter .... INT
Interruption of Air Traffic Service .... INATS
Interruptions per Minute .... IPM
Interruptions per Minute/Second .... IPM/S
Interruptions per Second .... IPS
Interscience Conference on Antimicrobial Agents and Chemotherapy. Proceedings [*A publication*] .... Intersci Conf Antimicrob Agents Chemother Proc
Interscience Monographs and Texts in Physics and Astronomy [*A publication*] .... Intersci Monogr Texts Phys Astron
Interscience Publishers .... IP
Intersect .... INTSCT
Intersect X
Intersecting Storage Accelerator [*In name of atomic reactor, Isabelle*] .... ISA
Intersecting Storage Ring [*High-energy physics*] .... ISR
Intersection .... INT
Intersection .... INTXN
Intersection of Air Routes [*Aviation*] .... IAR
Intersection of Range Legs .... IRL
Intersection of Runways [*Aviation*] .... IXR
Intersectional Transportation Service .... ITS
Interservice .... IS
Interservice Balkan Intelligence Committee [*World War II*] .... ISBIC
Interservice Committee on Technical Facilities [*Aerospace*] .... ISCTF
Interservice/Cross Service [*Support*] .... ISCS
Interservice Depot Maintenance Interrogation Systems .... ISMIS
Interservice Experiments Program .... ISEP
Interservice Group [*Military*] .... ISG
Interservice Group for Flight Vehicle Power [*Military*] .... IGFVP
Interservice Hovercraft Trials Unit [*Military*] .... IHTU
Interservice Hovercraft Unit [*Military*] .... IHU
Interservice Materiel Utilization Agency [*Military*] .... IMUA
Interservice Occupational Task Analysis Program [*Military*] .... ISOTAP
Interservice Procedures for Instructional Systems Development .... IPISD
Interservice Radiation Measurement Program .... IRMP
Interservice Radio Propagation Laboratory .... IRPL
Interservice Security Board [*World War II*] .... ISSB
Interservice Sports Council [*Later, ISC*] .... ISSC
Interservice Supply Support [*Military*] .... ISS
Interservice Supply Support Agreements [*Military*] .... ISSA
Interservice Supply Support Committee [*or Coordinator*] [*Military*] .... ISSC
Interservice Supply Support Program [*Military*] .... ISSP
Interservice Supply Support Records Office [*Military*] .... ISSRO
Interservice Supply Support Subcommittee [*Military*] .... ISSSC
Interservice Support Agreement [*Military*] .... ISA
Interservice Support Code [*Military*] .... ISC
Interservice Training Review Organization [*Military*] .... ITRO
Interservice Warehousing Support Services Agreement .... IWSSA
Intership .... INTSHP
Intersite Radio Communications System .... IRCS
Intersite Transmission Subsystem [*Ground Communications Facility, NASA*] .... ISTS
Intersociety Color Council .... ISCC
Intersociety Commission for Heart Disease Resources .... ICHDR
Intersociety Committee on Methods for Air Sampling and Analysis .... ICMASA
Intersociety Committee on Methods for Air Sampling and Analysis .... ISC
Intersociety Committee on Pathology Information .... ICPI
Intersociety Cytology Council .... ISCC
Intersociety Energy Conversion Engineering Conference .... IECEC
Intersociety Energy Conversion Engineering Conference. Proceedings [*A publication*] .... Intersoc Energy Convers Eng Conf Proc
[*An*] **Intersociety Liaison Committee on the Environment** .... AISLE
Interspecies Communication IC
Interstage .... INTRSTG
Interstage .... INTSTG
Interstage .... I/S
Interstage Section Container .... ISC
Interstage Section Shell .... ISS
Interstate [*Highways*] I
Interstate .... INSTA
Interstate .... IS
Interstate Airlines, Inc. [*Ypsilanti, MI*] [*FAA designator*] .... INT
Interstate Airmotive, Inc. [*St. Louis, MO*] [*FAA designator*] .... ITA
Interstate Airways Communications Station .... INSACS
Interstate Association of Commissions on the Status of Women .... IACSW
Interstate Bakeries Corporation [*Formerly, Interstate Brands Corporation*] [*NYSE symbol*] .... IBC
Interstate Clearing House on Mental Health [*Defunct*] .... ICHMH
Interstate Commerce .... ISC
Interstate Commerce Act .... ICA
Interstate Commerce Commission [*Independent government agency*] ... ICC
[*Designation used on tariffs filed with*] **Interstate Commerce Commission by Freight Forwarders** .... ICC-FF

Interstate Commerce Commission Transport Mobilization [*Federal emergency order*]...........................ICC-TM
Interstate Commission on the Delaware River Basin ....INCODEL
Interstate Commission on the Potomac River Basin ....ICPRB
Interstate Conference of Employment Security Agencies.................ICESA
Interstate Conference on Water Problems.....................ICWP
Interstate Congress for Equal Rights and Responsibilities.............ICERR
Interstate Council of State Boards of Cosmetology [*Later, NIC*].........ICSBC
Interstate Electronics Corporation ....IEC
Interstate Electronics Corp., Anaheim, CA [*Library symbol*].................CAnal
Interstate Financial Corporation [*NASDAQ symbol*].....................IFCO
Interstate Gambling Activities ....IGA
Interstate Helicopters, Inc. [*Roseland, NJ*] [*FAA designator*].................JYC
Interstate Job Bank ....IJB
Interstate Land Sales [*HUD*]..........................ILS
Interstate Loan Library [*Council of State Governments*] ILL
Interstate Mining Compact Commission ....IMCC
Interstate Motor Freight System [*NYSE symbol*] [*Delisted*] ....IMF
Interstate Motor Freight System [*NASDAQ symbol*].....................IMFS
Interstate Natural Gas Association of America ....INGAA
Interstate Oil Compact ....IOC
Interstate Oil Compact Commission ....IOCC
Interstate Oil Compact Commission. Committee Bulletin [*A publication*]...........................Interstate Oil Compact Comm Comm Bull
Interstate Oil Compact. Quarterly Bulletin [*A publication*]...........................Interstate Oil Compact Quart Bull
Interstate Organized Crime Index [*Computer data bank*].....................IOCI
Interstate Postgraduate Medical Association of North America .....IPMANA
Interstate Power Co. [*NYSE symbol*].....................IPW
Interstate Processing Center [*Department of Labor*] ....IPC
Interstate Producers Livestock Association ....IPLA
Interstate Railroad Co. [*AAR code*].....................INT
Interstate Revenue Research Center ....IRRC
Interstate Settlement Information System [*AT & T*].....................ISIS
Interstate Stores, Inc. [*NYSE symbol*] [*Delisted*].....................ISD
Interstate Tariff Bureau, Inc..........................ISTB
Interstate Tariff Bureau, Inc., Lakewood OH [*STAC*].....................ISB
Interstate Theft..........................IT
Interstate Towing Association ....ITA
Interstate Transmission of Wagering Information ....ITWI
Interstate Transportation in Aid of Racketeering ....ITAR
Interstate Transportation of Fireworks ....ITF
Interstate Transportation of Gambling Devices.....................ITGD
Interstate Transportation of Lottery Tickets ....ITLT
Interstate Transportation of Obscene Matter ....ITOM
Interstate Transportation of Prison-Made Goods ....ITPMG
Interstate Transportation of Prize Fight Films ....ITPFF
Interstate Transportation of Stolen Aircraft ....ITSA
Interstate Transportation of Stolen Cattle ....ITSC
Interstate Transportation of Stolen Motor Vehicle ....ITSMV
Interstate Transportation of Stolen Property ....ITSP
Interstate Transportation of Strikebreakers ....ITSB
Interstate Transportation of Unsafe Refrigerators ....ITUR
Interstate Transportation of Wagering Paraphernalia ....ITWP
Interstate United Corporation [*NYSE symbol*] [*Delisted*] ....IUC
Interstation Noise Suppression ....INS
Interstation Supersonic Track Conferences ....ISTRACON
Interstation Transmission ....IST
Interstellar Communications ....ISC
Interstellar Medium [*Planetary science*].....................ISM
Interstellar Travel..........................IST
Interstimulus Interval..........................ISI
Interstitial Cell Stimulating Hormone [*Also, LH, LSH*] [*Endocrinology*]..........................ICSH
Interstitial Cells [*Histology*]..........................IC
Interstitial Cells [*Histology*]..........................ISC
Interstitial Fluid [*Physiology*]..........................IF
Interstitial Fluid [*Physiology*]..........................ISF
Interstitial Lung Disease..........................ILD
Interstitial Transfer Facility [*Nuclear energy*] ....ITF
Interstrat Resources [*NASDAQ symbol*] ....ITERF
Interstudy, Minneapolis, MN [*Library symbol*] ....MnMln
Intersymbol Interference ....ISI
Intersymbol Interference Corrector..........................ISIC
Intersystem Crossing..........................ISC
Intertank..........................INTK
Intertank..........................I/T
Intertank Structural Tank Assembly..........................ISTA
Intertec Data Systems Corporation [*American Stock Exchange symbol*] ....IDC
Interthecal [*Anesthesiology*]..........................ITh
Intertherm, Inc. [*NASDAQ symbol*]..........................ITHM
Intertrial Interval [*Psychology*]..........................ITI
Intertropical Convergence [*Trade winds*] [*Meteorology*].....................ITC
Intertropical Convergence Zone [*Trade winds*] [*Meteorology*] ....ICZ
Intertropical Convergence Zone [*Trade winds*] [*Meteorology*] ....ITCZ
Intertropical Discontinuity [*Meteorology*].....................ITD
Intertuberous [*Diameter*] [*Medicine*]..........................IT
Intertype Corp. [*Later, HI*] [*NYSE symbol*].....................IRY
Intertype Fototronic Photographic System ....IFPTS
Intertype Training [*Navy*]..........................ITT

Interuniversity Library Council: Reference and Interlibrary Loan Service [*Library network*]...........................IULC-RAILS
Interuniversity Southeast Asia Committee [*of the Association for Asia*]...........................ISAC
Interval..........................INT
Interval..........................INTERV
Interval..........................INTVL
Interval Availability ....IA
Interval Embossed Tube ....IET
Interval International [*An association*] II
Interval Rate [*Army*]..........................IR
Interval Selection Circuit..........................ISC
Interval Service Value ....ISV
Interval Signal..........................IS
Interval Timer [*Data processing*]..........................IT
Interval Training [*Physical fitness program*].....................IT
Interval of Uncertainty [*Psychology*] ....IU
Intervalometer [*Military ordnance*].....................INTVLM
Intervalometer..........................IVL
Intervals between Aircraft in Stream Type Formation ....IBASF
Intervals of Pulsations of Diminishing Period ....IPDP
Intervalve Coupling..........................IC
Intervehicular Communication IVC
Intervehicular Transfer ....IVT
Intervening Sequence [*Genetics*].....................IVS
Interventricular [*Medicine*]..........................IV
Interventricular Septal Defect [*Cardiology*] ....IVSD
Interventricular Septum [*Cardiology*] ....IVS
Intervertebral [*Medicine*]..........................IV
Intervertebral Disc [*Medicine*]..........................IVD
Intervertebral Joint Complex [*Medicine*] ....IVJC
Interview..........................INT
Interview..........................INTERV
Interview..........................INTV
Interview..........................INTVW
Interview [*A publication*]..........................Interv
Interview-after-Combat ....IAC
Interview-Oriented Background Investigation ....IBI
Interviewer's Classification Guide..........................ICG
Intervirology [*A publication*]..........................Intervirolo
Interway Corp. [*American Stock Exchange symbol*] [*Delisted*].....................IWY
Interzonal Trade Office [*NATO*]..........................IZTO
Intestinal..........................INTEST
Intestinal Distress ....ID
Intestinal Groove ....IG
Intestinal Obstruction [*Medicine*]..........................IO
Intestine..........................I
Intext Educational Publishers ....IEP
Intimacy Potential Quotient..........................IPQ
Intimate Apparel Associates ....IAA
Intoxicated [*Airline notation*]..........................AL
Intoxication..........................INTOX
Intoxication and Intercourse ....I & I
Intra-Abdominal [*Artery*]..........................IAB
Intra-Alaska Facsimile [*National Weather Service*] ....IAF
Intra-Amniotic Saline [*Infusion*] [*Medicine*] ....IAS
Intra-Aortic Balloon [*Cardiology*] ....IAB
Intra-Aortic Balloon Counterpulsation [*Cardiology*] ....IABC
Intra-Aortic Balloon Pump [*Cardiology*] ....IABP
Intra-Arterial [*Cardiology*] ....IA
Intra-Arterial Chemotherapy [*Medicine*].....................IAC
Intra-Arterial Vasopressin [*Endocrinology*] ....IAV
Intra-Articular [*Medicine*] ....IA
Intra-Atrial [*Cardiology*] ....IA
Intra-Bureau Change Committee..........................IBCC
Intra-European Payments Agreement..........................IEPA
Intra-Government Procurement Advisory Council on Drugs.................IPAD
Intra-Governmental Professional Advisory Council on Drugs and Devices [*Inactive*] [*FDA*]..........................IPADD
Intra-Industry Management Program [*Small Business Administration*]....IMP
Intra-Science Chemistry Reports [*A publication*]............Intra-Sci Chem Rep
Intracardiac [*Medicine*]..........................IC
Intracavity [*Dentistry*]..........................ICAV
Intracellular..........................IC
Intracellular-Binding Proteins [*Medicine*]..........................ICBP
Intracellular Fluid [*Physiology*]..........................ICF
Intracerebral [*Medicine*]..........................IC
Intracerebroventricular [*Also, ICTV, ICV*] [*Brain anatomy*] ic
Intracerebroventricular [*Also, ic, ICV*] [*Brain anatomy*].....................ICTV
Intracerebroventricular [*Also, ic, ICTV*] [*Brain anatomy*].....................ICV
Intracoastal Waterway..........................IWW
Intracommunication System..........................ICS
Intracompany Correspondence ICC
Intracranial..........................IC
Intracranial Hemorrhage [*Medicine*] ....ICH
Intracranial Pressure [*Medicine*]..........................ICP
Intracranial Reinforcement..........................ICR
Intracranial Self-Administration [*Neurophysiology*].....................ICSA
Intracranial Self-Stimulation [*Also, ICSS*] [*Neurophysiology*].....................ICS
Intracranial Self-Stimulation [*Also, ICS*] [*Neurophysiology*] ....ICSS
Intracranial Stimulation [*Neurophysiology*] ....ICS

Intracutaneous [*Medicine*] ... IC
Intracytoplasmic Immunoglobulin ... ICIg
Intradermal [*Medicine*] ... ID
Intradermal Cancer Test [*Oncology*] ... ICT
Intraepithelial Carcinoma [*Medicine*] ... IEC
Intraepithelial Lymphocyte [*Hematology*] ... IEL
Intrafusal Muscle [*Anatomy*] ... IFM
Intramembranous Particle [*Cytology*] ... IMP
Intramural Law Review of American University [*A publication*] ... Intra L Rev (Am U)
Intramural Law Review of New York University [*A publication*] ... Intra L Rev (NYU)
Intramural Law Review of University of California at Los Angeles [*A publication*] ... Intra L Rev (UCLA)
Intramuscular [*Injection*] [*Medicine*] ... IM
Intranasal ... IN
Intransit Data Card ... IDC
Intransit Inventory ... II
Intransitive ... I
Intransitive ... INT
Intransitive ... INTR
Intranuclear Inclusion ... INI
Intraocular ... IO
Intraocular Foreign Body [*Medicine*] ... IOFB
Intraocular Lens [*Ophthalmology*] ... IOL
Intraocular Lens Manufacturers Association ... ILMA
Intraocular Pressure [*Ophthalmology*] ... IOP
Intraocular Tension Recorder ... ITR
Intrapair Interval ... IPI
Intraparenchymal Hemorrhage [*Medicine*] ... IPH
Intraperitoneal [*Medicine*] ... IP
Intraperitoneal Shock [*Psychology*] ... IPS
Intrapleural Pressure [*Biology*] ... IPP
Intrapulse Demodulation Analysis ... IPDA
Intrasite Cabling ... ISC
Intraspinal [*Injection*] ... IS
Intraspinal ... ISP
Intrasynovial [*Medicine*] ... ISY
Intrasystem Electromagnetic Compatibility Analysis Program [*Data processing*] [*Air Force*] ... IEMCAP
Intrathecal [*Within a sheath*] [*Medicine*] ... INTH
Intrathoracic [*Medicine*] ... IT
Intrathoracic [*Anatomy*] ... ITh
Intratracheal [*Medicine*] ... ITR
Intrauterine [*Medicine*] ... IU
Intrauterine Contraceptive Device [*Medicine*] ... ICD
Intrauterine Contraceptive Device [*Medicine*] ... IUCD
Intrauterine Death [*Medicine*] ... IUD
Intrauterine Device [*A contraceptive*] ... IUD
Intrauterine Foreign Body [*Gynecology*] ... IUFB
Intrauterine Growth Retardation [*Medicine*] ... IUGR
Intrauterine Pressure [*Gynecology*] ... IUP
Intrauterine Progesterone Contraceptive System [*Gynecology*] ... IPCS
Intrauterine Transfusion [*Gynecology*] ... IUT
Intravascular Bronchoalveolar Tumor [*Oncology*] ... IVBAT
Intravascular Coagulation and Fibrinolysis Syndrome [*Medicine*] ... ICF
Intravascular Erythrocyte Aggregation [*Hematology*] ... IEA
Intravascular Fluid [*Medicine*] ... IVF
Intravascular Papillary Endothelial Hyperplasia [*Medicine*] ... IPEH
Intravehicular ... IV
Intravehicular Activity ... IVA
Intravehicular Referenced Information [*NASA*] ... IRI
Intravehicular Umbilical [*NASA*] ... IVU
Intravenous [*Medicine*] ... INTRN
Intravenous [*Medicine*] ... IV
Intravenous Cholangiography [*Medicine*] ... IVC
Intravenous Glucose Tolerance Test [*Medicine*] ... IVGTT
Intravenous Hyperalimentation [*Medicine*] ... IVH
Intravenous Nutrition [*Medicine*] ... IVN
Intravenous Piggyback [*Medicine*] ... IVPB
Intravenous Push [*Medicine*] ... IVP
Intravenous Pyelogram [*Radiology*] ... IVP
Intravenous Transfusion [*Medicine*] ... IVT
Intravenous Vasopressin [*Endocrinology*] ... IVV
Intraventricular [*Cardiology*] ... IV
Intraventricular [*Cardiology*] ... IVT
Intraventricular Conduction Defect [*Pathology*] ... IVCD
Intraventricular Hemorrhage [*Cardiology*] ... IVH
IntraWest Financial [*NASDAQ symbol*] ... INTW
INTREC, Inc., Santa Monica, CA [*Library symbol*] ... CStmol
Intricate ... INTRC
Intrinsic Coercive Force ... ICF
Intrinsic Electric Strength ... IES
Intrinsic Energy [*Symbol*] [*Physics*] ... U
Intrinsic Factor [*Biochemistry*] ... IF
Intrinsic Heart Rate [*Cardiology*] ... IHR
Intrinsic Infrared Detector ... IID
Intrinsic Multiprocessing ... IMP
Intrinsic Payload Value ... IPV
Intrinsic Sympathomimetic Activity [*Biochemistry*] ... ISA
Intrinsic-Type, Semiconductor Material ... I
Introduction ... INTR
Introduction ... INTRO
Introduction ... INTROD
Introduction to the Federal Supply Catalog System ... IFSC
Introductory Physical Science [*Project*] [*Education*] ... IPS
Intromogenous Computer Network ... ICN
Intruder ... INTR
Intruder Monitoring and Guidance Equipment ... IMAGE
Intrusion Alarm System ... IAS
Intrusion Detection Alarm ... IDA
Intrusion Detection and Sensor Laboratory [*Army*] ... IDSL
Inuit Circumpolar Conference ... ICC
Inuvik [*Northwest Territories*] [*Seismograph station code, US Geological Survey*] ... INK
Inuvik [*Canada*] [*Airport symbol*] ... YEV
Inuvik, NT [*Radio station call letters*] ... CHAK
Inuvik, NT [*Television station call letters*] ... CHAK-TV
Inuyama [*Japan*] [*Seismograph station code, US Geological Survey*] ... INU
Invalid Children's Aid Association [*London*] ... ICAA
Invalided from Service [*Medicine*] [*Navy*] ... IS
Invariant ... INVAR
Invasion ... INV
Invasive Cancer of the Cervix [*Oncology*] ... ICC
Invasive Mole ... IM
Invective ... INV
Invenit [*He Designed It*] [*Latin*] ... INV
Invent ... INV
Inventaire Mineralogique de la France [*A publication*] ... Inventaire Mineral Fr
Inventario [*A publication*] ... Inv
Invention Design Engineering [*NASDAQ symbol*] ... IDEA
Invention Industry Association of America ... IIA
Invention Intelligence [*A publication*] ... Invention
Invention Marketing, Incorporated [*Information service*] ... IMI
Invention Report ... IR
Inventiones Mathematicae [*A publication*] ... Invent Math
Inventors Club of America ... ICA
Inventors' Workshop International ... IWI
Inventory ... I
Inventory ... INV
Inventory ... INVT
Inventory Adjustment ... INVADJ
Inventory Adjustment Document ... IAD
Inventory Adjustment Rate ... IAR
Inventory Adjustment Report [*Military*] ... IAR
Inventory Adjustment Voucher [*Military*] ... IAV
Inventory of Affective Tolerance [*Psychology*] ... IAT
Inventory Change Report ... ICR
Inventory Control Center [*of Field Army Support Command*] ... ICC
Inventory Control Manager ... ICM
Inventory Control Officer ... ICO
Inventory Control Point ... ICP
Inventory Control Point Europe ... ICPE
Inventory Control and Requirements Review Board [*CNO*] ... IC & RR
Inventory Control System [*Data processing*] ... ICS
Inventory Difference [*Formerly, MUF*] [*NRC/ERDA*] ... ID
Inventory Equipment Requirement ... IER
Inventory Equipment Requirement Specification ... IERS
Inventory Equipment Sheet ... IES
Inventory Forecasting and Replenishment Modules [*IBM Corp.*] ... INFOREM
Inventory Index ... IVI
Inventory and Inspection Report [*Army*] ... II
Inventory and Inspection Report [*Army*] ... IIR
Inventory of Job Attitudes [*LIMRA*] ... IJA
Inventory and Management Analysis ... I & MA
Inventory Management Program and Control Technique [*Data processing*] ... IMPACT
Inventory Management Record [*Military*] ... IMR
Inventory Management Responsibility Code ... IMRC
Inventory Management and Simulator ... IMS
Inventory Management System ... IMS
Inventory Manager [*Military*] ... IM
Inventory Manager Stock Control and Distribution [*Military*] ... IMSC & D
Inventory Manager Stock Control and Distribution System [*Military*] ... IMSC & DS
Inventory of Marriage and Family Literature [*University of Minnesota*] ... IMFL
Inventory Master File ... IMF
Inventory in Motion ... IIM
Inventory Objective ... IO
Inventory, Print, and Index [*System*] ... IPI
Inventory of Psychosocial Development ... IPD
Inventory Research Office [*Army*] ... IRO
Inventory Schedule ... IS
Inventory of Sources for History of Twentieth Century Physics [*University of California, Berkeley*] [*Information service*] ... ISHTCP
Inventory Status Report ... ISR
Inventory Stock Cataloging Program ... ISCP
Inventory Temporarily in Use [*Army*] ... ITIU
Inventory Transfer ... IT

Inventory Transfer Receipt ... IT/R
Inventory Trial Allowance List ... ITAL
Inventory Validation Listing [*Data processing*] ... IVL
Inventory Valuation Adjustments ... IVA
Inventory Verification Manual ... IVM
Inver Hills State Junior College, Inver Grove Heights, MN [*Library symbol*] ... MnIgS
Inveralochy [*Australia*] [*Seismograph station code, US Geological Survey*] ... INV
Invercargill [*New Zealand*] [*Airport symbol*] ... IVC
Inverell [*Australia*] [*Airport symbol*] ... IVR
Inverness [*Scotland*] [*Airport symbol*] ... INV
Inverness [*County in Scotland*] ... INVERN
Inverness, FL [*Radio station call letters*] ... WYSE
Inverness, NS [*Television station call letters*] ... CJCB-TV-1
Inverni & Della Beffa [*Italy*] [*Research code symbol*] ... IDB
Inverse [*or Invert*] ... INV
Inverse ... INVS
Inverse Check ... IC
Inverse Cosecant [*Mathematics*] ... ARCCSE
Inverse Cosine [*Mathematics*] ... ARCCOS
Inverse Cotangent [*Mathematics*] ... ARCCOT
Inverse Discrete Fourier Transform ... IDFT
Inverse Electrode Current ... IEC
Inverse Gain ... IG
Inverse Gaussian [*Statistics*] ... IG
Inverse Hyperbolic Function ... IHF
Inverse Joule Effect ... IJE
Inverse Kinetics Simulator ... IKS
Inverse Photoelectric Effect ... IPE
Inverse Polarity Protection ... IPP
Inverse Raman Scattering [*Spectroscopy*] ... IRS
Inverse Reflex Tetrode [*Physics*] ... IRT
Inverse Sampling Procedure ... ISP
Inverse Secant [*Mathematics*] ... ARCSEC
Inverse Sine [*Mathematics*] ... ARCSIN
Inverse Tangent [*Mathematics*] ... ARCTAN
Inverse Taper Lens ... ITL
Inverse Time Element ... ITE
Inverse Time Limit ... ITL
Inverse Time Relay ... ITR
Inverse Trigonometric Function ... ITF
Inversion ... INVRN
Invert ... INVT
Invert Sugar [*10%*] **in Saline** [*Medicine*] ... I-10/S
Invert Sugar [*5%*] **in Water** [*Medicine*] ... I5/W
Inverted Bowl Centrifuge ... IBC
Inverted Coaxial Magnetron ... ICEM
Inverted Energy Population ... IEP
Inverted Hand Position [*Neuropsychology*] ... IHP
Inverted Microscope [*Instrumentation*] ... IM
Inverted Vertical [*Aircraft engine*] ... IV
Inverted Y-Suspensor [*Medicine*] ... IYS
Inverter ... I
Inverter ... INV
Inverter ... INVTR
Inverter ... IV
Inverter Assembly ... IA
Inverter Distribution and Control Assembly ... ID & CA
Inverter Light Control Assembly ... ILCA
Inverter Power Supply ... IPS
Invest-in-America National Council ... IANC
Invest in Britain Bureau ... IBB
Investestate [*NASDAQ symbol*] ... INVT
Investex, Inc. [*NASDAQ symbol*] ... INVX
Investigacion Agricola (Santiago) [*A publication*] ... Invest Agric (Santiago)
Investigacion en la Clinica y en el Laboratorio [*A publication*] ... Invest Clin Lab
Investigacion Clinica (Maracaibo) [*A publication*] ... Invest Clin (Maracaibo)
Investigacion Economica [*A publication*] ... Invest Econ
Investigacion Pediatrica [*A publication*] ... Invest Pediatr
Investigacion Pesquera [*A publication*] ... Invest Pesq
Investigacion Pesquera [*A publication*] ... Inv Pesq
Investigacion y Progreso [*A publication*] ... IP
Investigacion y Progreso Agricola [*A publication*] ... Invest Prog Agric
Investigacion y Tecnica del Papel [*A publication*] ... Invest Tec Papel
Investigaciones Agropecuarias (Lima, Peru) [*A publication*] ... Invest Agropecu (Lima)
Investigaciones Agropecuarias (Lima, Peru) ... Invest Agropecu (Peru)
Investigaciones Marinas Universidad Catolica de Valparaiso [*A publication*] ... Invest Mar Univ Catol Valparaiso
Investigaciones Zoologicas Chilenas [*A publication*] ... Invest Zool Chil
Investigaciones Zoologicas Chilenas [*A publication*] ... Inv Zool Chilenas
Investigate [*or Investigation*] ... INVES
Investigate and Report ... INVSTAR
Investigating Officer ... IO
Investigation ... INV
Investigation ... INVESTIG
Investigation and Censure Review Branch [*BUPERS*] ... I & CRB
Investigation and Corrective Action Report ... ICAR
Investigation Record ... IR
Investigation Reports. CSIRO [*Commonwealth Scientific and Industrial Research Organisation*] **(Australia)** [*A publication*] ... Invest Rep CSIRO (Aust)
Investigation and Security Service Field Representative [*Veterans Administration*] ... I & SSFR
Investigation and Suspension ... I & S
Investigational New Drug [*Application*] [*FDA*] ... IND
Investigations of Indiana Lakes and Streams [*A publication*] ... Invest Indiana Lakes Streams
Investigations of Indiana Lakes and Streams [*A publication*] ... Inv Ind Lakes and Streams
Investigations in Ophthalmology and Visual Science [*A publication*] ... INOPA
Investigative and Cell Pathology [*A publication*] ... Invest Cell Pathol
Investigative and Corrective Action ... ICA
Investigative Ophthalmology [*Later, Investigative Ophthalmology and Visual Science*] [*A publication*] ... Invest Ophthalmol
Investigative Ophthalmology [*Later, Investigative Ophthalmology and Visual Science*] [*A publication*] ... Inv Ophth
Investigative Ophthalmology and Visual Science [*A publication*] ... Invest Ophthalmol Vis Sci
Investigative Ophthalmology and Visual Science [*A publication*] ... Invest Ophthalmol Visual Sci
Investigative Radiology [*A publication*] ... Invest Radiol
Investigative Radiology [*A publication*] ... Inv Radiol
Investigative Reporters and Editors ... IRE
Investigative Support Information System [*Federal Bureau of Investigation*] ... ISIS
Investigative Urology [*A publication*] ... Invest Urol
Investigative Urology [*A publication*] ... Inv Urol
Investigator ... IN
Investing Builders Association ... IBA
Investment ... INV
Investment ... INVEST
Investment Analysis Language [*Data processing*] ... IAL
Investment Bankers Association of America [*Later, Securities Industry Association*] ... IBA
Investment Bankers Association of America. Bulletin [*A publication*] ... IBA of A
Investment Banking [*A publication*] ... Inv Banking
Investment Casting Institute ... ICI
Investment Co-Operative Programme Office [*UNIDO*] ... ICPO
Investment Company ... IC
Investment Company Institute ... ICI
Investment Corporation of Florida [*American Stock Exchange symbol*] [*Delisted*] ... ICF
Investment Counsel Association of America ... ICAA
Investment Dealers Association of Canada ... IDA
Investment Education Institute ... IEI
Investment Equipment ... IVE
Investment Grant [*British*] ... IG
Investment Grant Office [*British*] ... IGO
Investment Guaranty Program [*AID*] ... IGP
Investment Promotion Zones ... IPZ
Investment Quality Trends [*A publication*] ... IQ
Investment Recovery Association ... IRA
Investment Strategy [*Game*] ... INSTRAT
Investment Tax Credit ... ITC
Investment Trust Units [*British*] ... ITU
Investor-Owned Hospital Review [*A publication*] ... Investor Owned Hosp Rev
Investor Responsibility Research Center, Inc. [*Pronounced "irk"*] [*Washington, DC*] ... IRRC
Investors Chronicle and Stock Exchange Gazette [*A publication*] ... Inv Chron
Investors Diversified Services, Inc. [*Mutual funds*] ... IDS
Investors GNMA Trust [*NASDAQ symbol*] ... INVG
Investors Heritage Life Insurance Co. [*NASDAQ symbol*] ... INLF
Investors Insurance Corp. [*NASDAQ symbol*] ... IINS
Investors Insurance Holding [*NASDAQ symbol*] ... IIHC
Investors Overseas Services Ltd. [*Firm which sells mutual funds in foreign countries*] ... IOS
Investors Planning Corporation ... IPC
Investors Savings & Loan Association [*NASDAQ symbol*] ... ISLA
Invicta International Airlines Ltd. [*Great Britain*] [*ICAO designator*] ... IM
Invisible Ministry [*An association*] ... IM
Invitation ... INV
Invitation ... INVIT
Invitation for Bid ... IFB
Invitation to Bid ... ITB
Invitation of Member Only ... IOMO
Invitation for Quote ... IFQ
Invitation to Quote ... ITQ
Invitation to Send [*Western Union*] ... ITS
Invitation to Transmit [*Communications*] ... K
Invitational Race [*Harness racing*] ... INV
Invitational Travel Order [*Army*] ... ITO
Invoice [*Business and trade*] ... INV
Invoice Book [*Business and trade*] ... IB
Invoice Book Inward [*Business and trade*] ... IBI
Invoice Book Outbound [*Business and trade*] ... IBO

Invoice Cost and Charges [Business and trade]	IC & C
Invoice Discrepancy Report [Business and trade]	IDR
Invoice Register Number [Business and trade]	IRN
Invoice Shipping Documentation [Business and trade]	ISD
Invoice Value [Business and trade]	IV
Involuntary	INV
Involuntary	INVOL
Involuntary Extension	INVOLEX
Involuntary Second SEA [Southeast Asia] Tour [Air Force]	ISST
Involuntary Servitude and Slavery	ISS
Involute	INVLT
Involve [Coat] [Pharmacy]	INVOLV
Involvement Limited to Bone [Oncology]	ILB
Inward	INWD
Inward Wide Area Telephone Service [Bell System]	INWATS
Inwestycje i Budownictwo [A publication]	Inwest i Budown
Inyo County Free Library, Bishop, CA [Library symbol]	CBisl
Inyo County Free Library, Independence, CA [Library symbol]	CInl
Inyokern [California] [Airport symbol]	IYK
Inyokern, CA [Location identifier] [FAA]	IYK
Inzenyrske Stavby [A publication]	Inz Stavby
Inzhenerno-Fizicheskii Zhurnal [A publication]	Inzh-Fiz Zh
Inzhenerno-Fizicheskii Zhurnal. Akademiya Nauk Beloruskoi SSR [A publication]	Inzh-Fiz Zh Akad Nauk Belorus SSR
Inzhenernyi Zhurnal, Mekhanika Tverdogo Tela [A publication]	Inzh Zh Mekh Tverd Tela
Inzynieria i Budownictwo [A publication]	Inz Budownictwo
Inzynieria Chemiczna [A publication]	Inz Chem
Ioannina [Greece] [Airport symbol]	IOA
Iodinated Human Serum Albumin	IHSA
Iodinated Serum Albumin [Medicine]	ISA
Iodine [Chemical element]	I
Iodine Azide Test [Medicine]	IAT
Iodine Binding Capacity [of starch]	IBC
Iodine Dextrin Color	IDC
Iodine Generating and Dispensing System	IGDS
Iodine Lotion [Medicine]	ILo
Iodine Value [Analytical biochemistry]	IV
Iodo [As substituent on nucleoside] [Biochemistry]	io
Iodoantipyrine [Biochemistry]	IAP
Iodocyanopindolol [Biochemistry]	ICYP
Iododacetic Acid [Organic chemistry]	IAA
Iododeoxyuridine [Biochemistry]	IdUrd
Iodohydroxybenzylpindolol [Organic chemistry]	IHYP
Iodonaphthyl Azide [Organic chemistry]	INA
Iodonitrotetrazolium Violet	INT
Iodosuccinyl CAMP Tyrosine Methyl Ester [Biochemistry]	ISCAMPME
Iokea [Papua New Guinea] [Airport symbol]	IOK
Iola, KS [Radio station call letters]	KIKS
Iola, KS [Radio station call letters]	KIOL
Ioma [Papua New Guinea] [Airport symbol]	IOP
IOMEC Users Association [Formerly, DUA] [Defunct]	IUA
Iomega Corp. [NASDAQ symbol]	IOMG
Ion Acoustic Plasma Pulse	IAPP
Ion Atom Interaction	IAI
Ion Beam Mass Spectrometer	IBMS
Ion Beam Projector	IBP
Ion Beam Scanning	IBS
Ion Beam Technology	IBT
Ion Beam Weapon	IBW
Ion Chamber [Nucleonics]	IC
Ion Chromatography	IC
Ion Chromatography Exclusion	ICE
Ion Chromatography Module	ICM
Ion Cluster Beam Deposition [Coating technique]	ICBD
Ion Conductance Modulator [Cytochemistry]	ICM
Ion Convection Electrodynamics	ICE
Ion Cyclotron Double Resonance	ICDR
Ion Cyclotron Radiation	ICR
Ion Cyclotron Resonance [Spectrometry]	ICR
Ion Cyclotron Resonance Frequency [Nuclear energy]	ICRF
Ion Cyclotron Resonance Heating	ICRH
Ion Density Electronics Package	IDEP
Ion Dipole Interaction	IDI
Ion Doping Technique	IDT
Ion Drift Semiconductor	IDS
Ion Energy Selector	IES
Ion Engine	IO
Ion Engine Simulator	IES
Ion Engine System	IES
Ion Engine System Section	IESS
Ion Exchange	INX
Ion Exchange Chromatography	IEC
Ion Exchange Desalination	IED
Ion Exchange Membrane	IEM
Ion Exchange and Membranes [A publication]	Ion Exch
Ion Exchange and Membranes [A publication]	Ion Exch Membr
Ion Exchange Resin	IER
Ion Exchange and Solvent Extraction [A publication]	Ion Exch Solvent Extr
Ion Exchange Unit	IEU

Ion Exchanger	IEX
Ion Focusing Technique	IFT
Ion-Getter-Pumping [Electron microscopy]	IGP
Ion Gun Assembly	IGA
Ion Gun Collector	IGC
Ion Implantation Doping	IID
Ion Implantation Doping Technique	IIDT
Ion Implantation Manufacturing System	IIMS
Ion Implantation Study	IIS
Ion-Implanted Base Transistor	IBT
Ion-Implanted Metal-Oxide Semiconductor	IMOS
Ion-Ion Collision	IIC
Ion Kinetic Energy Spectrometry	IKES
Ion Mass Spectrometer	IMS
Ion Microprobe Analyzer	IMA
Ion Microprobe Mass Analyzer	IMMA
Ion Microwelding Instrument	IMI
Ion Moderated Partition [Chromatography]	IMP
Ion-Neutralization Spectroscopy	INS
Ion Pair Yield	IPY
Ion Plating Supply	IPS
Ion Production Rate	IPR
Ion Pump Vacuum System	IPVS
Ion Recombination Chamber	IRC
Ion-Scattering Spectrometer [or Spectrometry]	ISS
Ion-Selective Electrode [Instrumentation]	ISE
Ion-Selective Field Effect Transistor	ISFET
Ion Source Injector	ISI
Ion Source Kit	ISK
Ion Thrust System	ITS
Ion Thruster Beam	ITB
Ion Time of Flight	ITOF
Ion Trap Detector [Spectroscopy]	ITD
Ion Vacuum Pump	IVP
Iona College, New Rochelle, NY [Library symbol]	NNerl
Iona College, New Rochelle, NY [OCLC symbol]	VXI
Iona Industries, Inc. [NASDAQ symbol]	IOAVF
Ionia, MI [Radio station call letters]	WION
Ionic	ION
Ionic Drive	IDRV
Ionic Heated Cathode	IHC
Ionic Heated Kathode	IHK
Ionic Strength	I
Ionic Thermoconductivity [or Thermocurrent]	ITC
Ionics, Inc. [American Stock Exchange symbol]	ION
Ionium [Th^{230}, radioactive isotope of thorium]	Io
Ionization Chamber	IC
Ionization Constant [Symbol] [Chemistry]	K
Ionization Energy [Chemistry]	IE
Ionization Gauge Tube	IGT
Ionization and Momentum Sensor	IMS
Ionization Potential	IP
Ionization Test Apparatus	ITA
Ionized Calcium Analyzer	ICA
Ionized Flow Field	IFF
Ionized Gas LASER	IGL
Ionized Yeast	IY
Ionizer, Slab Fabrication	ISF
Ionospharen-Institut Breisach [West Germany]	IIB
Ionosphere	IONO
Ionosphere and Aural Phenomena Advisory Committee [European Space Research Organization]	ION
Ionosphere Research Committee	IRC
Ionospheric Data [A publication]	ID
Ionospheric Dispersion Analysis [Air Force]	IDA
Ionospheric Electron Density	IED
Ionospheric Explorer [NASA/National Bureau of Standards]	IE
Ionospheric Ion Density	IID
Ionospheric Propagation Path	IPP
Ionospheric Radio Signal	IRS
Ionospheric Sounding Satellite [Japan]	ISS
Iosco-Arenac Regional Library, AuGres Branch Library, AuGres, MI [Library symbol]	MiTc-A
Iosco-Arenac Regional Library, East Tawas Branch Library, East Tawas, MI [Library symbol]	MiTc-E
Iosco-Arenac Regional Library, Oscoda Township Branch Library, Oscoda, MI [Library symbol]	MiTc-O
Iosco-Arenac Regional Library, Plainfield Township Branch Library, Hale, MI [Library symbol]	MiTc-P
Iosco-Arenac Regional Library, Standish Branch Library, Standish, MI [Library symbol]	MiTc-S
Iosco-Arenac Regional Library, Tawas City Branch Library, Tawas City, MI [Library symbol]	MiTc-T
Iosco-Arenac Regional Library, Tawas City, MI [Library symbol]	MiTc
Iosco-Arenac Regional Library, Whittemore Branch Library, Whittemore, MI [Library symbol]	MiTc-W
Iota-Cam Fiberscope [Also, ICFS]	ICF
Iota-Cam Fiberscope [Also, ICF]	ICFS
Iota-Cam Fiberscope Instrument	ICFI
Iowa [Postal code]	IA
Iowa [MARC country of publication code] [Library of Congress]	iau

Iowa...IO
Iowa [*MARC geographic area code*] [*Library of Congress*]...n-us-ia
Iowa Academy of Science. Proceedings [*A publication*]...Iowa Acad Sci Proc
Iowa Academy of Science. Proceedings [*A publication*]...Iowa Ac Sc Pr
Iowa Agricultural Experiment Station. Research Bulletin [*A publication*]...Iowa Agric Exp Stn Res Bull
Iowa Agriculture and Home Economics Experiment Station. Research Bulletin [*A publication*]...Iowa Agric Home Econ Exp Stn Res Bull
Iowa Agriculture and Home Economics Experiment Station. Special Report [*A publication*]...Iowa Agric Home Econ Exp Stn Spec Rep
Iowa Army Ammunition Plant...IAAP
Iowa Beef Processors, Inc. [*NYSE symbol*] [*Delisted*]...IBP
Iowa Central Community College, Fort Dodge, IA [*Library symbol*]...IaFdIC
Iowa City, IA [*Radio station call letters*]...KCJJ
Iowa City, IA [*Television station call letters*]...KIIN-TV
Iowa City, IA [*Radio station call letters*]...KKRQ
Iowa City, IA [*Radio station call letters*]...KRNA
Iowa City, IA [*Radio station call letters*]...KSUI
Iowa City, IA [*Radio station call letters*]...KXIC
Iowa City, IA [*Radio station call letters*]...WSUI
Iowa City Public Library, Iowa City, IA [*Library symbol*]...Iala
Iowa Conservationist [*A publication*]...Iowa Conserv
Iowa Dental Bulletin [*A publication*]...Iowa Dent Bull
Iowa Dental Journal [*A publication*]...Iowa Dent J
Iowa Electric Light & Power Co. [*NYSE symbol*]...IEL
Iowa English Bulletin. Yearbook [*A publication*]...IEBY
Iowa English Yearbook [*A publication*]...IEY
Iowa Falls, IA [*Radio station call letters*]...KIFG
Iowa Falls, IA [*Radio station call letters*]...KIFG-FM
Iowa Farm-to-Market Carriers Tariff Bureau, Ottumwa IA [*STAC*]...IFM
Iowa Farm Science [*A publication*]...Iowa Farm Sci
Iowa Foreign Language Bulletin [*A publication*]...IFLB
Iowa Geological Survey. Report of Investigations [*A publication*]...Iowa Geol Surv Rep Invest
Iowa Geological Survey. Water Atlas [*A publication*]...Iowa Geol Survey Water Atlas
Iowa Geological Survey. Water-Supply Bulletin [*A publication*]...Iowa Geol Survey Water-Supply Bull
Iowa Historical Record [*A publication*]...Iowa Hist Rec
Iowa-Illinois Gas & Electric Co. [*NYSE symbol*]...IWG
Iowa Institute of Hydraulic Research...IIHR
Iowa Journal of History [*A publication*]...IJH
Iowa Journal of History and Politics [*A publication*]...IA J
Iowa Journal of History and Politics [*A publication*]...IJHP
Iowa Journal of History and Politics [*A publication*]...Iowa Jour Hist and Pol
Iowa Law Review [*A publication*]...IA Law Rev
Iowa Law Review [*A publication*]...IA L Rev
Iowa Library Information Teletype Exchange [*Library network*]...I-LITE
Iowa Library Quarterly [*A publication*]...Iowa Lib Q
Iowa Masonic Library, Cedar Rapids, IA [*Library symbol*]...IaCrM
Iowa Medical Journal [*A publication*]...Iowa Med J
Iowa Mountaineers...IM
Iowa Naturalist [*A publication*]...Iowa Nat
Iowa Power & Light Co. [*NYSE symbol*] [*Delisted*]...IOP
Iowa Public Service Co. [*NYSE symbol*]...IPS
Iowa Quality [*Of pigs*]...IQ
Iowa Resources [*NYSE symbol*]...IOR
Iowa Review [*A publication*]...IowaR
Iowa Silent Reading Tests [*Education*]...ISRT
Iowa Southern Utilities [*Southern Industrial Railroad, Inc.*] [*AAR code*]...ISU
Iowa Southern Utilities [*NASDAQ symbol*]...IUTL
Iowa Starter, Iowa State University, Ames, IA [*Library symbol*]...IaAIS
Iowa State College of Agriculture and Mechanic Arts [*Later, Iowa State University*]...ISC
Iowa State College of Agriculture and Mechanic Arts. Agricultural Experiment Station. Publications [*A publication*]...IA Ag Exp
Iowa State College. Engineering Experiment Station. Engineering Report. Project [*A publication*]...Iowa State Coll Eng Expt Sta Eng Rept Proj
Iowa State Department of History and Archives, Des Moines, IA [*Library symbol*]...Ia-HA
Iowa State Education Association, Des Moines, IA [*Library symbol*]...IaDmE
Iowa State Genealogical Society, Genealogical Library, Des Moines, IA [*Library symbol*]...IaGen
Iowa State Historical Society, Iowa City, IA [*OCLC symbol*]...IOQ
Iowa State Institutions. Bulletin [*A publication*]...Iowa Institutions B
Iowa State Journal of Research [*A publication*]...Iowa State J Res
Iowa State Journal of Science [*A publication*]...Iowa State J Sci
Iowa State Journal of Science [*A publication*]...Iowa St J Sci
Iowa State Law Library, Des Moines, IA [*Library symbol*]...Ia-L
Iowa State Library Commission, Des Moines, IA [*Library symbol*]...Ia
Iowa State Medical Library, Des Moines, IA [*Library symbol*]...Ia-M
Iowa State University...ISU
Iowa State University. Department of Earth Sciences. Publication [*A publication*]...Iowa State Univ Dept Earth Sci Pub

Iowa State University. Laboratories of Natural History. Bulletin [*A publication*]...Iowa Univ Lab N H B
Iowa State University of Science and Technology, Ames, IA [*Library symbol*]...IaAS
Iowa State University of Science and Technology, Ames, IA [*OCLC symbol*]...IWA
Iowa State University of Science and Technology, Ames. Iowa Engineering Experiment Station. Bulletin [*A publication*]...Iowa State Univ Eng Exp Sta Bull
Iowa State University of Science and Technology. Doctoral Dissertations: Abstracts and References [*A publication*]...IDD
Iowa State University of Science and Technology, School of Veterinary Medicine, Ames, IA [*Library symbol*]...IaAS-V
Iowa State University. Statistical Laboratory. Annual Report [*A publication*]...Iowa State Univ Stat Lab Annu Rep
Iowa State Water Resources Research Institute. Annual Report [*A publication*]...Iowa State Water Resour Res Inst Annu Rep
Iowa Terminal Railroad Co. [*AAR code*]...IAT
Iowa Tests of Basic Skills...ITBS
Iowa Tests of Educational Development...ITED
Iowa Wesleyan College...IWC
Iowa Wesleyan College, Mount Pleasant, IA [*Library symbol*]...IaMpI
Iowa Wesleyan College, Mount Pleasant, IA [*OCLC symbol*]...IOI
Iowegian & Citizen, Centerville, IA [*Library symbol*]...IaCenvI
IPA [*International Pharmaceutical Abstracts*] Review [*A publication*]...IPA Rev
IPALCO Enterprises [*NYSE symbol*]...IPL
Ipargazdasagi Szemle [*A publication*]...Ipargazd Szle
Iparmueveszeti Muzeum Evkoenyvei [*A publication*]...IME
Iparmueveszeti Muzeum Evkoenyvei [*A publication*]...Iparmuveszeti Muz Ev
Ipatinga [*Brazil*] [*Airport symbol*]...IPN
IPC [*Institute of Philippine Culture*] Monographs [*A publication*]...IPC Mg
IPC Newspapers Ltd., London, United Kingdom [*Library symbol*]...UkLIP
IPC [*Institute of Philippine Culture*] Papers [*A publication*]...IPC Pap
Ipco Corp. [*Formerly, Ipco Hospital Supply Corp.*] [*NYSE symbol*]...IHS
IPE. Industrial and Production Engineering [*A publication*]...IPE Ind Prod Eng
Ipec Aviation Pty. Ltd. [*Australia*] [*ICAO designator*]...PD
IPEF [*Instituto de Pesquisas e Estudos Florestais*] Publicacao Semestral [*A publication*]...IPEF Publ Semest
IPI [*International Potash Institute*] Bulletin [*A publication*]...IPI Bull
IPI [*International Potash Institute*] Research Topics [*A publication*]...IPI Res Top
Ipiales [*Colombia*] [*Airport symbol*]...IPI
IPL Systems, Inc. Cl A [*NASDAQ symbol*]...IPLSA
IPLO [*Institute of Professional Librarians of Ontario*] Quarterly [*A publication*]...IPLO Q
IPM Technology [*American Stock Exchange symbol*]...IPM
Ipoh [*Malaysia*] [*Airport symbol*]...IPH
Ipota [*Vanuatu*] [*Airport symbol*]...IPA
IPP [*Max Planck Institut fuer Plasmaphysik*] Presseinformationen [*A publication*]...IPP Presseinf
IPPF [*International Planned Parenthood Federation*] Medical Bulletin [*A publication*]...IPPF Med Bull
Iproniazid Phosphate [*Organic chemistry*]...INPH
Ipse Fecit [*He Did It Himself*] [*Latin*]...IF
Ipsilateral Optic Tectum [*Medicine*]...IOT
Ipsilateral Routing of Signal...IROS
Ipso Facto [*By the Fact Itself*] [*Latin*]...IF
IPW [*Institut fuer Politik und Wirtschaft*] Berichte [*A publication*]...IPW Ber
IPW [*Institut fuer Politik und Wirtschaft*] Forschungshefte [*A publication*]...IPW Forsch-H
Iqbal Review [*A publication*]...Iqbal R
Iqbal Review [*A publication*]...IqR
Iquique [*Chile*] [*Airport symbol*]...IQQ
Iquique [*Chile*] [*Seismograph station code, US Geological Survey*]...IQQ
Iquitos [*Peru*] [*Airport symbol*]...IQT
Iran [*MARC geographic area code*] [*Library of Congress*]...a-ir---
Iran [*Aircraft nationality and registration mark*]...EP
Iran [*MARC country of publication code*] [*Library of Congress*]...ir
Iran [*Three-letter standard code*]...IRN
Iran [*Two-letter standard code*]...IR
Iran Aircraft Industries...IACI
Iran American Chamber of Commerce...IACC
Iran Electronics Industries...IEI
Iran Freedom Foundation...IFF
Iran Geological Survey. Report [*A publication*]...Iran Geol Surv Rep
Iran Long-Period Array [*Iran*] [*Seismograph station code, US Geological Survey*]...IR1
Iran Long-Period Array [*Iran*] [*Seismograph station code, US Geological Survey*]...IR2
Iran Long-Period Array [*Iran*] [*Seismograph station code, US Geological Survey*]...IR3
Iran Long-Period Array [*Iran*] [*Seismograph station code, US Geological Survey*]...IR4
Iran Long-Period Array [*Iran*] [*Seismograph station code, US Geological Survey*]...IR5
Iran Long-Period Array [*Iran*] [*Seismograph station code, US Geological Survey*]...IR6

Iran Long-Period Array [Iran] [Seismograph station code, US Geological Survey]..............................IR7
Iran National Airlines Corp. [ICAO designator]..............IR
Iran National Tourist Organization..............INTO
Iranian [MARC language code] [Library of Congress].......... ira
Iranian Aircraft Program [Military]..............IAP
Iranian Airways Co...............IRA
Iranian B'Nei Torah Movement..............IBTOM
Iranian Democratic Committee..............IDC
Iranian Documentation Centre..............IRANDOC
Iranian Documentation Centre, Tehran, Iran [Library symbol].............IrTD
Iranian Journal of Agricultural Research [A publication].......Iran J Agric Res
Iranian Journal of Plant Pathology [A publication].............Iran J Plant Pathol
Iranian Journal of Public Health [A publication].......Iran J Public Health
Iranian Journal of Science and Technology [A publication]..............
Iran J Sci Technol
Iranian Marine International Oil Company ....IMINICO
Iranian Oil Operating Companies..............IOOC
Iranian Oil Participants Ltd...............IOP
Iranian Peace Zebra Program [Military] ....IPZP
Iranian Research and Publication Group..............IRPG
Iranian Review of International Relations [A publication].......Iran R Int Relat
Iranian Students Association in the United States............ISAUS
Iranian Students Counseling Center ....ISCC
Iranian Studies [A publication]..............IranS
Iranian Studies [A publication]..............Iran Stud
Iranian Studies [A publication]..............Ira Stud
Iranica Antiqua [A publication]..............IA
Iranica Antiqua [A publication]..............Iran Antiq
Iranica Antiqua [A publication]..............Iranica Ant
Iraq [MARC geographic area code] [Library of Congress].....................a-iq---
Iraq [MARC country of publication code] [Library of Congress]..............iq
Iraq [Three-letter standard code]..............IRQ
Iraq [Aircraft nationality and registration mark]..............YI
Iraq [Two-letter standard code]..............IQ
Iraq Federation of Trade Unions ....IFTU
Iraq Natural History Museum. Publication [A publication]..............
Iraq Nat Hist Mus Publ
Iraq Natural History Museum. Report [A publication]..............
Iraq Nat Hist Mus Rep
Iraq-Saudi Arabia Neutral Zone [MARC geographic area code] [Library of Congress] ....awiy---
Iraq-Saudi Arabia Neutral Zone [MARC country of publication code] [Library of Congress]..............iy
Iraq-Saudi Arabia Neutral Zone [Two-letter standard code]..............NT
Iraq-Saudi Arabia Neutral Zone [Three-letter standard code] ....NTZ
Iraqi..............I
Iraqi Air Force..............IqAF
Iraqi Airways [ICAO designator] ....IA
Iraqi Chemical Society. Journal [A publication]..............Iraqi Chem Soc J
Iraqi Confederation of Trade Unions ....ICTU
Iraqi Dental Journal [A publication]..............Iraqi Dent J
Iraqi National Oil Company [Government company] ....INOC
Iraqi News Agency ....INA
Iraqi Petroleum Company..............IPC
IRCS [International Research Communications System] Medical Science-Library Compendium [A publication]..............
IRCS Med Sci-Libr Compend
IRE Financial [NASDAQ symbol]..............IREF
Iredell Public Library, Statesville, NC [Library symbol]..............NcSt
Ireland [Aircraft nationality and registration mark]..............EI
Ireland [MARC geographic area code] [Library of Congress]..............e-ie---
Ireland [Aircraft nationality and registration mark]..............EJ
Ireland..............I
Ireland [MARC country of publication code] [Library of Congress]..............ie
Ireland..............IRE
Ireland [Three-letter standard code]..............IRL
Ireland [Two-letter standard code]..............IE
Ireland Fund ....IF
Ireland: A Journal of Irish Studies [A publication] ....Eire
Ireland National Soil Survey. Soil Survey Bulletin [A publication]..............
Irel Natl Soil Surv Soil Surv Bull
Irenikon [A publication]..............Iren
Iridium [Chemical element]..............Ir
Iringa [Tanzania] [Airport symbol]..............IRI
Iris Diaphragm [Photography]..............ID
Irish..............IR
Irish [MARC language code] [Library of Congress]..............iri
Irish Agricultural and Creamery Review [A publication]..............
Irish Agr Creamery Rev
Irish American Cultural Association..............IACA
Irish American Cultural Institute..............IACI
Irish Astronomical Journal [A publication]..............Irish Astr
Irish Astronomical Journal [A publication]..............Irish Astron J
Irish Book [Bibliographical Society of Ireland] [A publication] ....IB
Irish Broadcasting Revenue ....IBR
Irish Church Missions..............ICM
Irish Congress of Trade Unions..............ICTU
Irish Council European Movement ....ICEM
Irish Digest [A publication]..............ID
Irish Ecclesiastical Record [A publication]..............IER

Irish Ecclesiastical Record [A publication] ....IrEccRec
Irish Economist [A publication]..............Irish Econ
Irish Emigrant Society ....IES
Irish Family History Society..............IFHS
Irish Family Names Society..............IFNS
Irish Features Agency [News agency]..............IFA
Irish Fisheries Investigations. Series A (Freshwater) [A publication] .... Ir Fish Invest Ser A (Freshwater)
Irish Fisheries Investigations. Series B (Marine) [A publication] ....
Ir Fish Invest Ser B (Mar)
Irish Forestry [A publication]..............Ir For
Irish Forestry [A publication]..............Irish For
Irish Free State [Later, Republic of Ireland]..............IFS
Irish Georgian Society ....IGS
Irish Guards [Military unit]..............IG
Irish Heritage Foundation ....IHF
Irish Historical Studies [A publication]..............IHS
Irish Historical Studies [A publication]..............Irish Hist Stud
Irish Institute II
Irish Journal of Agricultural Research [A publication] ....Irish J Agr
Irish Journal of Agricultural Research [A publication] ....Irish J Agr Res
Irish Journal of Agricultural Research [A publication] ....Ir J Agric Res
Irish Journal of Education [A publication]..............Irish J Ed
Irish Journal of Food Science and Technology [A publication] ....
Irish J Food Sci Technol
Irish Journal of Medical Science [A publication] ....Irish J Med
Irish Journal of Medical Science [A publication] ....Ir J Med Sci
Irish Journal of Psychology [A publication] ....Irish J Psy
Irish Journal of Psychology [A publication] ....Ir J Psychol
Irish Jurist [A publication]..............IJ
Irish Jurist [A publication]..............Irish Jur
Irish Jurist [A publication]..............Ir Jur
Irish Law Times [A publication]..............Ir L T
Irish Library Bulletin [A publication]..............Irish Lib Bul
Irish Linen Guild [Defunct]..............ILG
Irish Medical Association ....IMA
Irish Medical Journal [A publication]..............Irish Med J
Irish Medical Journal [A publication]..............Ir Med J
Irish Monthly [A publication]..............Irish Mo
Irish Monthly [A publication]..............IrM
Irish National Caucus..............INC
Irish National Liberation Army ....INLA
Irish National Teachers' Organisation ....INTO
Irish Naturalists' Journal [A publication]..............Ir Nat J
Irish Northern Aid..............INA
Irish Northern Aid Committee ....NORAID
Irish Numismatics [A publication] ....Irish Num
Irish Nursing News [A publication] ....Ir Nurs News
Irish Office..............IO
Irish Quarterly Review [A publication] ....Irish Q
Irish Railway Record Society..............IRRS
Irish Republican Army ....IRA
Irish Republican Brotherhood ....IRB
Irish Republican Socialist Party [Political party]..............IRSP
Irish Setter Club of America ....ISCA
Irish Society..............IS
Irish Statesman [A publication]..............IS
Irish Sword [A publication]..............Irish S
Irish Terrier Club of America..............ITCA
Irish Texts Society [A publication]..............ITS
Irish Theological Quarterly [A publication] ....I Th Q
Irish Theological Quarterly [A publication]..............ITQ
Irish Trade Union Congress..............ITUC
Irish University Press..............IUP
Irish University Review [A publication]..............IUR
Irish Water Spaniel Club of America ....IWSCA
Irish Wolfhound Club of America ....IWCA
Irisleabhar Mha Nuad [A publication]..............IMN
Irkutsk [USSR] [Airport symbol]..............IKT
Irkutsk [USSR] [Seismograph station code, US Geological Survey] ....IRK
Irkutskii Politehniceskii Institut. Trudy [A publication]..............
Irkutsk Politehn Inst Trudy
IRMA [Indian Refractory Makers Association] Journal [A publication]..............IRMA J
IRMMH [Institute for Research into Mental and Multiple Handicap] Monograph [A publication]..............IRMMH Monogr
Irodalmi Szemle [A publication]..............Irod Szle
Irodalmi Szemle [A publication]..............I Sz
Irodalomtorteneti Fuzetek [A publication]..............Irodal F
Irodalomtorteneti Kozlemenyek [A publication]..............IK
Iron [Chemical symbol is Fe]..............
Iron [CIPW classification] [Geology]..............ir
Iron Age..............IA
Iron Age Metalworking International [A publication]..............IAMI
Iron Age Metalworking International [A publication]..............Ir Age Int
Iron Age Metalworking International [A publication]..............
Iron Age Metalwork Int
Iron-Binding Capacity [Clinical chemistry]..............IBC
Iron-Binding Protein ....IBP
Iron Body Bronze-Mounted ....IBBM
Iron Bolts ....IB

Iron Canyon [*California*] [*Seismograph station code, US Geological Survey*] .... IRC
Iron Castings Society .... ICS
Iron City [*Pittsburgh, PA*] IC
Iron-Core Reactor .... ICR
Iron Hematoxylin [*A dye*] .... IH
Iron Information Center [*Battelle Memorial Institute*] [*Information service*] IIC
Iron Masters Board of Trade .... IMBT
Iron Mountain [*Michigan*] [*Airport symbol*] .... IMT
Iron Mountain, MI [*Television station call letters*] .... WIIM-TV
Iron Mountain, MI [*Radio station call letters*] .... WIMK-FM
Iron Mountain, MI [*Radio station call letters*] .... WJNR
Iron Mountain, MI [*Radio station call letters*] .... WMIQ
Iron Nickel Alloy .... INA
Iron Nickel System .... INS
Iron Ore Company of Canada [*Labrador*] .... IOC
Iron Overload Diseases Association .... IODA
Iron Phosphate Coating .... IPC
Iron Pipe .... IP
Iron Pipe Size .... IPS
Iron Pipe Thread .... IPT
Iron, Quinine, and Strychnine [*Elixir*] .... IQ & S
Iron Range Research Center, Chisholm, MN [*OCLC symbol*] .... IRR
Iron River, MI [*Radio station call letters*] .... WIKB
Iron River, MI [*Radio station call letters*] .... WIKB-FM
Iron Rotating Band .... IRB
Iron or Steel [*Freight*] .... IRN
Iron and Steel [*A publication*] .... Iron St
Iron and Steel [*A publication*] .... Iron Steel
Iron and Steel .... I & S
Iron and Steel Engineer [*A publication*] .... Iron Steel Eng
Iron, Steel and Heavy Transporters Association, Cleveland OH [*STAC*] .... IST
Iron and Steel Industry Profiles [*A publication*] .... ISIP
Iron and Steel Institute (London) Publication [*A publication*] .... Iron Steel Inst (London) Publ
Iron and Steel International [*A publication*] .... Iron Steel Int
Iron and Steel International [*A publication*] .... Iron St Int
Iron and Steel Society .... ISS
Iron and Steel Trades Confederation [*British*] .... ISTC
Iron and Steel Workers' Union [*India*] .... ISWU
Iron Trade Review [*A publication*] .... Iron Tr R
Iron Wire Gauge .... IWG
Iron or Wood [*Freight*] .... IWD
Ironbound Crier, Newark, NJ [*Library symbol*] .... NjNI
Ironclad .... IRC
Irondale, AL [*Radio station call letters*] .... WLPH
Ironing Board .... IB
Ironmaking Proceedings. Metallurgical Society of AIME. Iron and Steel Division [*A publication*] .... Ironmaking Proc AIME
Ironton, MO [*Radio station call letters*] .... KPIA
Ironton, OH [*Radio station call letters*] .... WIRO
Ironton, OH [*Radio station call letters*] .... WITO
[*The*] **Ironton Railroad Co.** [*Absorbed into Consolidated Rail Corp.*] [*AAR code*] .... IRN
Ironwood [*A publication*] .... Iron
Ironwood [*Michigan*] [*Airport symbol*] .... IWD
Ironwood, MI [*Location identifier*] [*FAA*] .... IWD
Ironwood, MI [*Radio station call letters*] .... WIMI
Ironwood, MI [*Radio station call letters*] .... WJMS
Ironwood, MI [*Radio station call letters*] .... WUPM
Iroquoian [*MARC language code*] [*Library of Congress*] .... iro
Iroquois Brands Limited [*American Stock Exchange symbol*] .... IBL
Iroquois Falls Public Library, Iroquois Falls, ON, Canada [*Library symbol*] .... CaOIf
Iroquois Memorial Hospital, Watseka, IL [*Library symbol*] .... IWatH
Iroquois Night Fighter and Night Tracker .... INFANT
Irradiance [*Symbol*] [*IUPAC*] .... E
Irradiance Measuring System .... IMS
Irradiated Fuel Processing Plant .... IFPP
Irradiated Fuels Storage Facility [*National Reactor Testing Station*] .... IFSF
Irradiated Fused Silica Open Tubular [*Column for chromatography*] .... IFSOT
Irradiated Materials Laboratory .... IML
Irradiated Silicon Vidicon .... ISV
Irradiation .... IRRADN
Irradiation des Aliments [*A publication*] .... Irradiat Aliments
Irradiation des Aliments (English Edition) [*A publication*] .... Irradiat Aliments (Engl Ed)
Irradiation Correction .... J
Irradiation Test Management Activity .... ITMA
Irrational Beliefs Test [*Psychology*] .... IBT
Irredundant Conjunctive Normal Formula .... ICNF
Irredundant Disjunctive Normal Formula .... IDNF
Irredundant Normal Formula .... INF
Irregular .... IREG
Irregular .... IRREG
Irregular Force [*Military*] .... IF
Irregular Light [*Navigation signal*] .... Irreg
Irregular Route Carrier .... IRC
Irregular Route Motor Carriers Bureau, Oklahoma City OK [*STAC*] .... IRB
Irregular Serials and Annuals [*A publication*] .... ISA
Irreversible Warmup Indicator [*To detect whether frozen foods have risen above an acceptable temperature level*] [*Pronounced "ee-wee"*] .... IWI
Irreversibly Sickled Cell [*Hematology*] .... ISC
Irrevocable Letter of Credit [*Business and trade*] ILC
IRRI [*International Rice Research Institute*] **Research Paper Series** [*A publication*] .... IRRI Res Pap Ser
Irrigate .... IRRIG
Irrigated Winter Wheat. Technical Publication [*A publication*] .... Irrig Winter Wheat Tech Publ
Irrigation .... IRRG
Irrigation Age [*A publication*] .... Irr Age
Irrigation Association [*Formerly, SIA*] .... IA
Irrigation Canal [*Board on Geographic Names*] .... CNLI
Irrigation Engineering and Maintenance [*A publication*] .... Irrig Eng Maint
Irrigation and Power [*A publication*] .... Irrig Power
Irritable Bowel Syndrome [*Medicine*] .... IBS
Irritant .... IRR
Irrotationally Bound Water [*Biophysics*] .... IBW
IRT Corporation [*NASDAQ symbol*] .... IRTC
IRT Property Co. [*Formerly, Investors Realty Trust*] [*American Stock Exchange symbol*] .... IRT
IRT Realty Services, Inc. [*NASDAQ symbol*] .... IRTR
Irvin Industries, Inc. [*American Stock Exchange symbol*] [*Delisted*] .... IRV
Irvine, CA [*Radio station call letters*] .... KUCI
Irvine, KY [*Radio station call letters*] .... WIRV
Irvine/Michigan/Brookhaven [*Experiment on proton decay*] .... IMB
Irvine Sensors Corp. [*NASDAQ symbol*] .... IRSN
Irving Bank Corp. [*NYSE symbol*] V
Irving Independent School District, Irving, TX [*OCLC symbol*] .... IJA
Irving Independent School District, Irving, TX [*Library symbol*] .... TxIrS
Irving Municipal Library, Irving, TX [*Library symbol*] .... TxIr
Irving Public Library System, Irving, TX [*OCLC symbol*] .... IJC
Irving Trust Company. Economic View from One Wall Street [*A publication*] .... Irving View
Irving, TX [*Television station call letters*] .... KLTJ
Irvington Public Library, Irvington, NY [*Library symbol*] .... NIr
Irwin Stone Foundation for Ascorbate Capability and Therapy .... IS-FACT
Irwin Toy Ltd. Non Vtg [*NASDAQ symbol*] .... IRWKF
Irwin Toy Ltd. Vtg [*NASDAQ symbol*] .... IRWJF
Is Amended to Add .... IATA
Is Amended to Delete .... IATD
Is Amended to Read .... IATR
Is Lietuviu Kulturos Istorijos [*A publication*] .... LKI
ISA [*Instrument Society of America*] **Conference Preprint** [*A publication*] .... ISA Prepr
ISA [*Instrument Society of America*] **Journal** [*A publication*] .... ISA J
ISA [*Instrument Society of America*] **Proceedings. International Power Instrumentation Symposium** [*A publication*] .... ISA Proc Int Power Instrum Symp
ISA [*Instrument Society of America*] **Transactions** [*A publication*] .... ISATA
ISA [*Instrument Society of America*] **Transactions** [*A publication*] .... ISA Trans
Isaac Newton Optical Telescope .... INT
Isabela, PR [*Radio station call letters*] .... WISA
Isabela, PR [*Radio station call letters*] .... WKSA-FM
Isabella [*California*] [*Seismograph station code, US Geological Survey*] .... ISA
Isafjordur [*Iceland*] [*Airport symbol*] .... IFJ
Isaiah [*Old Testament book*] .... Is
Isaiah [*Old Testament book*] .... Isa
Isaly Co. [*NASDAQ symbol*] .... ISLY
Isangel [*New Hebrides*] [*Seismograph station code, US Geological Survey*] .... INH
Isanmaallinen Kansanluke [*National Patriotic Movement*] [*Finland*] .... IKL
Isatin-beta-thiosemicarbazone [*Organic chemistry*] .... IBT
ISC Financial Corp. [*American Stock Exchange symbol*] [*Delisted*] .... ISC
ISC Systems Corp. [*NASDAQ symbol*] .... ISCS
Iscargo Ltd. [*Iceland*] [*ICAO designator*] .... KJ
Ischemic Heart Disease .... IHD
Ischial Tuberosity [*Medicine*] .... IT
Iscove's Modified Dulbecco's Medium [*For nematode culture*] .... IMDM
Ise [*Japan*] [*Seismograph station code, US Geological Survey*] .... ISE
Isethionyl Acetimidate [*Biochemistry*] .... IAI
Isfahan [*Iran*] [*Airport symbol*] .... IFN
Isfjord [*Norway*] [*Seismograph station code, US Geological Survey*] [*Closed*] .... ISF
Isham, Lincoln & Beale, Chicago, IL [*OCLC symbol*] .... ILZ
Ishigaki [*Japan*] [*Airport symbol*] .... ISG
Ishigakijima [*Ryukyu Islands*] [*Seismograph station code, US Geological Survey*] .... ISI
Ishihara [*Japan*] [*Seismograph station code, US Geological Survey*] [*Closed*] .... IHR
Ishikawajima-Harima Heavy Industries Co. Ltd. [*Japan*] .... IHI
Ishinomaki [*Japan*] [*Seismograph station code, US Geological Survey*] .... ISN
ISHM [*International Society for Hybrid Microelectronics*] **Journal** [*A publication*] .... ISHM J
ISHM [*International Society for Hybrid Microelectronics*] **Proceedings** [*A publication*] .... ISHM Proc
Ishpeming Carnegie Library, Ishpeming, MI [*Library symbol*] .... MIs

Ishpeming, MI [*Radio station call letters*] ... WJPD
Ishpeming, MI [*Radio station call letters*] ... WJPD-FM
Ishpeming, MI [*Radio station call letters*] ... WMQT
Ishpeming, MI [*Radio station call letters*] ... WMVN
Ishtion [*USSR*] [*Seismograph station code, US Geological Survey*] ... ISH
Ishurdi [*Bangladesh*] [*Airport symbol*] ... IRD
ISI [*Indian Standards Institution*] **Bulletin** [*A publication*] ... ISI Bull
Isiro [*Zaire*] [*Airport symbol*] ... IRP
Isis [*A publication*] ... I
Isis [*A publication*] ... Is
Isis-Chemie KG [*Germany*] [*Research code symbol*] ... S
Isisford [*Australia*] [*Airport symbol*] ... ISI
Iskusstvo Kino [*A publication*] ... Iskus K
Iskustvennyi Sputnik Zemil [*USSR*] ... ISZ
Isla De Pascua [*Easter Island*] [*Seismograph station code, US Geological Survey*] [*Closed*] ... PSC
Isla De Vieques, PR [*Location identifier*] [*FAA*] ... VQS
Isla Desecheo [*Puerto Rico*] [*Seismograph station code, US Geological Survey*] ... IDE
Isla Grande Flying School [*Hato Rey, PR*] [*FAA designator*] ... IGS
Isla Mona [*Puerto Rico*] [*Seismograph station code, US Geological Survey*] ... IMO
Isla Mona [*Puerto Rico*] [*Seismograph station code, US Geological Survey*] [*Closed*] ... IMR
Islam and the Modern Age [*A publication*] ... Islam Mod Age
Islamabad Journal of Sciences. Journal of Mathematics and Sciences [*A publication*] ... Islamabad J Sci
Islamabad/Rawalpindi [*Pakistan*] [*Airport symbol*] ... ISB
Islamic Center of New York ... ICNY
Islamic Congress ... IC
Islamic Council of Europe ... ICE
Islamic Culture [*A publication*] ... IC
Islamic Culture [*A publication*] ... Islam Cult
Islamic Development Bank ... IDB
Islamic Foundation for Science, Technology, and Development ... IFSTAD
Islamic Literature [*A publication*] ... Is Lit
Islamic Medical Association ... IMA
Islamic Mission of America ... IMA
Islamic Quarterly [*A publication*] ... IQ
Islamic Quarterly [*A publication*] ... IsQ
Islamic Republican Party ... IRP
Islamic Studies [*A publication*] ... Islam Stud
Islamic Studies [*A publication*] ... Isl St
Island [*Maps and charts*] ... I
Island [*Board on Geographic Names*] ... ISL
Island Air Transfer Ltd. [*Honolulu, HI*] [*FAA designator*] ... IAT
Island Airlines Hawaii [*Honolulu, HI*] [*FAA designator*] ... IAH
Island Base Section [*Navy*] ... IBS
Island Commander ... ISCOM
Island Commander Azores ... ISCOMAZORES
Island Commander Bermuda ... ISCOMBERMUDA
Island Commander Faroes ... ISCOMFAROES
Island Commander Greenland ... ISCOMGREENLAND
Island Commander Iceland ... ISCOMICELAND
Island Commander Madeira ... ISCOMADEIRA
Island Creek Coal Co. [*NYSE symbol*] [*Delisted*] ... ICR
Island Helicopter, Inc. [*Long Island, NY*] [*FAA designator*] ... MTP
Island Lagoon [*Australia*] [*Seismograph station code, US Geological Survey*] [*Closed*] ... ILN
Island Lake [*Canada*] [*Airport symbol*] ... YIV
Island Manager [*Aviation*] ... ISMGR
Island Pacific Air [*Maui, HI*] [*FAA designator*] ... PCR
Island Park Geothermal Area ... IPGA
Island Park Public Library, Island Park, NY [*Library symbol*] ... NIp
Island Resources Foundation ... IRF
Island Trees Public Library, Levittown, NY [*Library symbol*] ... NLevI
Island Tug & Barge [*AAR code*] ... ITB
Islands [*Maps and charts*] ... Is
Islands [*Board on Geographic Names*] ... ISLS
Islands Research Foundation [*Inactive*] ... IRF
Islay [*Scotland*] [*Airport symbol*] ... ILY
Isle ... I
Isle ... IS
Isle ... ISL
Isle Of Aran ... IA
Isle Of Man ... I of M
Isle Of Man ... IM
Isle Of Man [*England*] [*Airport symbol*] ... IOM
Isle Of Man ... IOM
Isle Of Man (Great Britain) ... GBM
Isle Of Skye [*Scotland*] [*Airport symbol*] ... SKL
Isle Of Wight ... IOW
Isle Of Wight ... I of W
Isle Of Wight ... IW
Isle Of Wight Railway [*British*] ... IWR
Isle Resources, Inc. [*NASDAQ symbol*] ... ISLE
Isle Royale National Park ... ISRO
Islenzk Tunga [*A publication*] ... IT
Islenzkar Landbunadarrannsoknir [*A publication*] ... Isl Landbunadarrannsoknir
Isles Of Scilly [*England*] [*Airport symbol*] ... ISC
Isles Of Scilly-Tresco [*Airport symbol*] ... TSO
Islet [*Maps and charts*] ... It
Islet Cell Antibodies [*Immunology*] ... ICA
Islet Cells [*of the pancreas*] [*Endocrinology*] ... IC
Islets of Langerhans [*Anatomy*] ... IS of LANG
Islip, NY [*Location identifier*] [*FAA*] ... RXN
Islip, NY [*Radio station call letters*] ... WLIX
Islip Public Library, Islip, NY [*Library symbol*] ... NIs
ISO Aero Service, Inc. [*Kingston, NC*] [*FAA designator*] ... ISR
Iso-Echo Contour ... IEC
ISO [*International Organization for Standardization*] **Information Network** [*Information service*] ... ISONET
ISO Status Accumulating Binaries [*Using*] **Extraordinary Logic** ... ISABEL
Isobaric Analog Resonance [*Nuclear structure*] ... IAR
Isobaric Multiplet Mass Equation ... IMME
Isobutene-Isoprene Rubber ... IIR
Isobutoxycarbonylation [*Organic chemistry*] ... IBOC
Isobutoxymethyl Acrylamide [*Organic chemistry*] ... IBMA
Isobutyl Vinyl Ether [*Organic chemistry*] ... IBVE
Isobutylamine [*Organic chemistry*] ... IBA
Isobutylidenediurea [*Organic chemistry*] ... IBDU
Isobutylmethylxanthine [*Also, MIX*] [*Biochemistry*] ... IBMX
Isocitrate Dehydrogenase [*Also, ICDH, IDH*] [*An enzyme*] ... ICD
Isocitrate Dehydrogenase [*Also, ICD, IDH*] [*An enzyme*] ... ICDH
Isocitrate Dehydrogenase [*Also, ICD, ICDH*] [*An enzyme*] ... IDH
Isodecyl Diphenyl Phosphate [*Organic chemistry*] ... IDDP
Isodensitracer ... IDT
Isoelectric Focusing [*Analytical chemistry*] ... IEF
Isoelectric Focusing in Polyacrylamide [*Gel*] [*Analytical chemistry*] ... IFPA
Isoelectric Point [*Also, IP*] [*Chemistry*] ... IEP
Isoelectric Point [*Also, IEP*] [*Chemistry*] ... IP
Isola [*France*] [*Seismograph station code, US Geological Survey*] ... ISO
Isolated ... ISOLD
Isolated Flow Responder [*Physiology*] ... IFR
Isolated-Gate Field-Effect Transistor [*Electronics*] ... IGFET
Isolated Safflower Protein [*Food technology*] ... ISP
Isolated Soy Protein [*Food technology*] ... ISP
Isolated Spontaneous Psychokinesis [*Parapsychology*] ... ISPK
Isolated Step ... IS
Isolated Volume Responders [*Physiology*] ... IVR
Isolation ... ISLN
Isolation ... ISO
Isolation ... ISOL
Isolation ... ISOLN
Isolation Amplifier ... IA
Isolation of Dimensions and Elimination of Alternatives ... IDEA
Isolation Pulse ... IP
Isolation Zone [*Nuclear energy*] ... IZ
Isolationer ... ISOLR
Isoleucine [*One-letter symbol; see Ile*] ... I
Isoleucine [*or iLeu, Ileu*] [*Also, I*] [*An amino acid*] ... Ile
Isoleucine [*or iLeu, Ile*] [*Also, I*] [*An amino acid*] ... Ileu
Isoleucyl-tRNA Synthetase [*An enzyme*] ... IRS
Isomedix, Inc. [*NASDAQ symbol*] ... ISMX
Isomeric Transition [*Radioactivity*] ... IT
Isomeric Transition Level [*Radioactivity*] ... ITL
Isomet Corp. [*NASDAQ symbol*] ... IOMT
Isometric ... ISO
Isometric ... ISOM
Isometric Piping Efficiency Program ... ISOPEP
Isomorphously Doped Ammonium Perchlorate ... IDAP
Isonicotinic Acid [*Organic chemistry*] ... INA
Isonicotinic Acid Hydrazide [*See also INH, ISONIAZID*] [*Antituberculous agent*] ... INAH
Isonicotinic Acid Hydrazide [*or Isonicotinylhydrazine*] [*See also INAH, ISONIAZID*] [*Antituberculous agent*] ... INH
Isonicotinic Acid Hydrazide [*See also INAH, INH*] [*Antituberculous agent*] ... ISONIAZID
Isooctyl Thioglycolate [*Organic chemistry*] ... IOTG
Isopentenyl [*As substituent on nucleoside*] [*Biochemistry*] ... i
Isopentenyl Pyrophosphate [*Organic chemistry*] ... IPP
Isopentenyladenosine [*Biochemistry*] ... IPA
Isophase ... Iso
Isophorone Diisocyanate [*Organic chemistry*] ... IPDI
Isophthalic Acid [*Organic chemistry*] ... IPA
Isophthalonitrile [*Organic chemistry*] ... IPN
Isoprene Rubber ... IR
Isopropyl Alcohol [*Organic chemistry*] ... IPA
Isopropyl Carbanilate [*Also, INPC, IPPC*] [*Herbicide*] ... IPC
Isopropyl Ether [*Organic chemistry*] ... IPE
Isopropyl Methyl Pyrimidinone [*Organic chemistry*] ... IMHP
Isopropyl Myristate [*Pharmacology*] ... IPM
Isopropyl N-phenylcarbamate [*Also, INPC, IPC*] [*Herbicide*] ... IPPC
Isopropyl Percarbonate [*or Diisopropyl Peroxydicarbonate*] [*Organic chemistry*] ... IPP
Isopropyl Phenylcarbamate [*Also, IPC, IPPC*] [*Herbicide*] ... INPC
Isopropyl(methyl)nitrobenzene [*Organic chemistry*] ... IMNB
Isopropylnoradrenaline ... IPNA
Isopropyl(phenyl)para-phenylene Diamine [*Organic chemistry*] ... IPPD
Isopropylthiogalactoside [*Also, IPTG*] [*Organic chemistry*] ... IPG
Isopropylthiogalactoside [*Also, IPG*] [*Organic chemistry*] ... IPTG

Isoproterenol [*Organic chemistry*] .... IPR
Isosceles [*Triangle*] .... ISOS
Isosorbide Dinitrate [*Coronary vasodilator*] .... ISDN
Isosorbide Dinitrite [*Coronary vasodilator*] .... ISD
Isotachophoresis [*Analytical biochemistry*] .... ITP
Isothermal .... ISOTH
Isothermal Community College, Spindale, NC [*Library symbol*] .... NcSpil
Isothermal Gas Chromatography .... IGC
Isothermal Pressure Profile .... IPP
Isothermal Remanence .... IRM
Isothermal Remanent Magnetization .... IRM
Isothermal Storage Test [*For hazardous chemicals*] .... IST
Isothermogravimetric Analysis .... ITGA
Isotope Development Limited .... IDL
Isotope Development Program [*AEC*] .... IDP
Isotope Dilution Mass Spectrometry .... IDMS
Isotope Exciter Light Source .... IELS
Isotope Heat Source .... IHS
Isotope-Heated Catalytic Oxidizer System .... IHCOS
Isotope in Industrie und Landwirtschaft [*A publication*] .... Isot Ind Landwirtsch
Isotope Power Generator .... IPG
Isotope Power Unit .... IPU
Isotope-Powered Device .... IPD
Isotope Radiography System .... IRS
Isotope Reactor [*USSR*] .... IR
Isotope Reentry Vehicle [*NASA*] .... IRV
Isotope Removal Service .... IRS
Isotope Separation Power .... ISP
Isotope-Shift, Zeeman-Effect Atomic Absorption .... IZAA
Isotope Thermoelectric Converter .... ISOTEC
Isotopenpraxis [*A publication*] .... Isotopenprax
Isotopes of Carbon, Oxygen, Nitrogen, and Sulfur [*AEC project*] .... ICONS
Isotopes Information Center [*ORNL*] IIC
Isotopes in Organic Chemistry [*Elsevier Book Series*] [*A publication*] .... IOC
Isotopes Process Development Laboratory [*AEC*] .... IPDL
Isotopes Radiation [*A publication*] .... Isotopes Radiat
Isotopes and Radiation Division [*American Nuclear Society*] .... IRD
Isotopes and Radiation Technology [*A publication*] .... Isotop Radiat Technol
Isotopes and Radiation Technology [*A publication*] .... Isot Radiat Technol
Isotopes and Radiation Technology [*A publication*] .... ISRT
Isotopic Atomic Weight .... IAW
Isotopic Dilution Analysis .... IDA
Isotopic Source Assay System .... ISAS
Isotopic Weight .... IW
Isotropic .... ISO
Isotropic Distribution Function .... IDF
Isotta Fraschini Owners' Association .... IFOA
Isozymes. Current Topics in Biological and Medical Research Isozymes [*A publication*] .... Isozymes Curr Top Biol Med Res Isozymes
Israel [*MARC geographic area code*] [*Library of Congress*] .... a-is---
Israel [*Two-letter standard code*] IL
Israel [*MARC country of publication code*] [*Library of Congress*] .... is
Israel [*Three-letter standard code*] .... ISR
Israel [*Aircraft nationality and registration mark*] 4X
Israel Agricultural Research Organization. Division of Forestry. Triennial Report of Research [*A publication*] .... Isr Agric Res Org Div For Trienn Rep Res
Israel Aircraft Industries Ltd. [*ICAO designator*] .... BK
Israel Aircraft Industries Ltd. .... IAI
Israel Aliya Center [*Formerly, COMOI*] .... IAC
Israel Annals of Psychiatry [*A publication*] .... Israel Ann Psychiat
Israel Annals of Psychiatry and Related Disciplines [*A publication*] .... Isr Ann Psy
Israel Annals of Psychiatry and Related Disciplines [*A publication*] .... Isr Ann Psychiatry Relat Discip
Israel Atomic Energy Commission, Soreq Nuclear Research Centre, Yavne, Israel [*Library symbol*] .... IsYAEC
Israel Book World [*A publication*] .... IBW
Israel Development Corporation [*American Stock Exchange symbol*] [*Delisted*] .... IDC
Israel Economic Conference .... IEC
Israel Education Fund .... IEF
Israel Exploration Journal [*A publication*] .... IEJ
Israel Exploration Journal [*A publication*] .... Isr Expl J
Israel Folk Dance Institute .... IFDI
Israel Geological Survey Bulletin [*A publication*] .... Isr Geol Surv Bull
Israel Geological Survey Geological Data Processing Unit Report [*A publication*] .... Isr Geol Surv Geol Data Process Unit Rep
Israel Geological Survey Report [*A publication*] .... Isr Geol Surv Rep
Israel Histadrut Foundation .... IHF
Israel Hydrological Service Report [*A publication*] .... Isr Hydrol Serv Rep
Israel Institute of Agricultural Engineering Scientific Activities [*A publication*] .... Isr Inst Agric Eng Sci Act
Israel Institute of Animal Science Scientific Activities [*A publication*] .... Isr Inst Anim Sci Sci Act
Israel Institute of Field and Garden Crops Scientific Activities [*A publication*] .... Isr Inst Field Gard Crops Sci Act
Israel Institute of Horticulture Scientific Activities [*A publication*] .... Isr Inst Hortic Sci Act
Israel Institute of Plant Protection Scientific Activities [*A publication*] .... Isr Inst Plant Prot Sci Act
Israel Institute of Soils and Water Scientific Activities [*A publication*] .... Isr Inst Soils Water Sci Act
Israel Institute of Technology .... IIT
Israel Investors Corporation [*NASDAQ symbol*] .... IICR
Israel-Jordan Demilitarized Zones [*MARC geographic area code*] [*Library of Congress*] .... awiw---
Israel-Jordan Demilitarized Zones [*is (Israel) used in records cataloged after January 1978*] [*MARC country of publication code*] [*Library of Congress*] .... iw
Israel Journal of Agricultural Research [*A publication*] .... Israel J Agric Res
Israel Journal of Agricultural Research [*A publication*] .... Israel J Agr Res
Israel Journal of Agricultural Research [*A publication*] .... Isr J Agric Res
Israel Journal of Botany [*A publication*] .... Israel J Bot
Israel Journal of Botany [*A publication*] .... Isr J Bot
Israel Journal of Chemistry [*A publication*] .... Isr J Chem
Israel Journal of Dental Medicine [*A publication*] .... Isr J Dent Med
Israel Journal of Earth-Sciences [*A publication*] .... Isr J Earth
Israel Journal of Earth-Sciences [*A publication*] .... Isr J Earth-Sci
Israel Journal of Entomology [*A publication*] .... Isr J Entomol
Israel Journal of Experimental Medicine [*A publication*] .... Isr J Exp Med
Israel Journal of Mathematics [*A publication*] .... Isr J Math
Israel Journal of Medical Sciences [*A publication*] .... IJMS
Israel Journal of Medical Sciences [*A publication*] .... Isr J Med S
Israel Journal of Medical Sciences [*A publication*] .... Isr J Med Sci
Israel Journal of Psychiatry and Related Sciences [*A publication*] .... Isr J Psychiatr Relat Sci
Israel Journal of Technology [*A publication*] .... Isr J Tech
Israel Journal of Technology [*A publication*] .... Isr J Technol
Israel Journal of Zoology [*A publication*] .... Isr J Zool
Israel Labor Party .... ILP
Israel Law Review [*A publication*] .... Israel Law R
Israel Law Review [*A publication*] .... Isr Law Rev
Israel Medical Journal [*A publication*] .... Isr Med J
Israel Music Foundation .... IMF
Israel National Committee on the Biosphere and Environment .... INCBE
Israel National Council for Research and Development Report [*A publication*] .... Isr Natl Counc Res Dev Rep
Israel News Agency .... INA
Israel Numismatic Journal [*A publication*] .... INJ
Israel Oceanographic and Limnological Research Annual Report [*A publication*] .... Isr Oceanogr Limnol Res Annu Rep
Israel-Palestine Philatelic Society of America [*Later, SIP*] .... IPPSA
Israel Pharmaceutical Journal [*A publication*] .... Isr Pharm J
Israel Plate Block Society .... IPBS
Israel Program for Scientific Translations [*An agency of the Government of Israel*] .... IPST
Israel Society of Special Libraries and Information Centers .... ISLIC
Israel Society of Special Libraries and Information Centers Bulletin [*A publication*] .... ISLIC Bull
Israel Society of Special Libraries and Information Centers Bulletin [*A publication*] .... Isr Soc Spec Libr Inf Cent Bull
Israel Student Tourist Association .... ISSTA
Israel Students Organization .... ISO
Israel-Syria Demilitarized Zones [*MARC geographic area code*] [*Library of Congress*] .... awiu---
Israel-Syria Demilitarized Zones [*is (Israel) used in records cataloged after January 1978*] [*MARC country of publication code*] [*Library of Congress*] .... iu
Israel Trade Commission .... ITC
Israel Universities Press .... IUP
Israeli I
Israeli Academy of Sciences and Humanities .... IASH
Israeli Air Force .... IsAF
Israeli Air Services .... IAS
Israeli Annals of Psychiatry [*A publication*] .... IPRDA
Israeli Defense Forces .... IDF
Israeli Journal of Mathematics [*A publication*] .... ISJM
Israeli Research Reactor .... IRR
Isramco, Inc. [*NASDAQ symbol*] .... ISRL
ISS-International Service System, Incorporated [*American Stock Exchange symbol*] .... ISI
ISSC Industries Solid State [*NASDAQ symbol*] .... ISSC
Issledovanie Kosmicheskogo Prostranstva [*A publication*] .... Issled Kosm Prostranstva
Issledovanija Nekotoryh Voprosov Matematiceskoi Kibernetiki [*A publication*] .... Issled Nekotoryh Voprosov Mat Kibernet
Issledovaniya Strukturnogo Sostoyaniya Neorganicheskikh Veshchestv [*A publication*] .... Issled Strukt Sostoyaniya Neorg Veshchestv
Issledovaniya po Uprugosti i Plastichnosti [*A publication*] .... Issled Uprug Plast
Issue .... ISS
Issue Date .... ID
Issue Definition Memorandum [*Jimmy Carter Administration*] .... IDM
Issue by Issue Tally .... IBIT
Issue Necessary Orders .... INO
Issue Paper .... IP
Issue Priority Designator .... IPD
Issue Priority Group [*Army*] .... IPG

Issue on Request [*or Requisition*] ... IOR
Issue While in Stock ... IWISTK
Issues in Comprehensive Pediatric Nursing [*A publication*] ... Issues Compr Pediatr Nurs
Issues in Criminology [*A publication*] ... Issues Crim
Issues in Health Care of Women [*A publication*] ... Issues Health Care Women
Issues Management Association ... IMA
Issues in Mental Health Nursing [*A publication*] ... Issues Ment Health Nurs
Issues in Radical Therapy [*A publication*] ... Rad Thera
Issues and Studies [*A publication*] ... Iss Stud
Issues and Studies [*A publication*] ... Issues and Stud
Issuing Agency ... IA
Issuing Office ... IO
Issuing Point ... IP
Issy-Les Moulineaux Airport [*France*] ... ISS
Istanbul [*Turkey*] [*Airport symbol*] ... IST
Istanbul [*Trabzon*] [*Turkey*] [*Seismograph station code, US Geological Survey*] ... TBZ
Istanbul [*Turkey*] [*Seismograph station code, US Geological Survey*] ... IST
Istanbul Arkeologi Muzeleri Yilligi [*A publication*] ... Istanbul Ark Muz Yilligi
Istanbul Asariatika Muzeleri Nesriyati [*A publication*] ... IAM
Istanbul-Kandilli [*Turkey*] [*Geomagnetic observatory code*] ... ISK
Istanbul-Kandilli [*Turkey*] [*Seismograph station code, US Geological Survey*] ... ISK
Istanbul Medical Faculty Medical Bulletin. Istanbul University [*A publication*] ... Istanbul Med Fac Med Bull Istanbul Univ
Istanbul Tip Fakultesi Mecmuasi [*A publication*] ... Istanbul Tip Fak Mecm
Istanbul Universitesi Dishekimligi Fakultesi Dergisi [*A publication*] ... Istanbul Univ Dishekim Fak Derg
Istanbul Universitesi Eczacilik Fakultesi Mecmuasi [*A publication*] ... Istanbul Univ Eczacilik Fak Mecm
Istanbul Universitesi Edegiyat Fakultesi Turk Dili ve Edebiyati Dergisi [*A publication*] ... TDED
Istanbul Universitesi Fen Fakultesi Mecmuasi. Seri A. Sirfi ve Tatbiki Matematik [*A publication*] ... Istanbul Univ Fen Fak Mecm Ser A
Istanbul Universitesi Fen Fakultesi Mecmuasi. Seri B. Tabii Ilimler [*A publication*] ... Istanbul Univ Fen Fak Mecm Ser B
Istanbul Universitesi Fen Fakultesi Mecmuasi. Seri B. Tabii Ilimler [*A publication*] ... Istanbul Univ Fen Fak Mecm Seri B Tabii Ilimler
Istanbul Universitesi Fen Fakultesi Mecmuasi. Seri C. Astronomi-Fizik-Kimya [*A publication*] ... Istanbul Univ Fen Fak Mecm Ser C
Istanbul Universitesi Orman Fakultesi Dergisi [*A publication*] ... Istanb Univ Orman Fak Derg
Istanbul Universitesi Veteriner Fakultesi Dergisi [*A publication*] ... Istanbul Univ Vet Fak Derg
Istanbul Universitesi Yaymlam (Orman Fakultesi) [*A publication*] ... Istanbul Univ Yay (Orm Fak)
Istanbul University Medical Bulletin [*A publication*] ... Istanbul Univ Med Bull
Istanbul University Medical Faculty Medical Bulletin [*A publication*] ... Istanbul Univ Med Fac Med Bull
Istanbul University. Review of the Geographical Institute. International Edition [*A publication*] ... Istanbul Univ Rev Geog Inst Internat Ed
Istanbuler Beitrage zur Klinischen Wissenschaft [*A publication*] ... Istanbuler Beitr Klin Wiss
Istanbuler Forschungen des Deutschen Archaeologischen Instituts [*A publication*] ... IFDAI
Istanbuler Mitteilungen [*A publication*] ... Ist Mit
Istanbuler Mitteilungen, Beiheft [*A publication*] ... Ist Mitt Bh
Isthmian Canal Zone ... ICZ
Isthmo-Optic Nucleus [*or Nuclei*] [*In midbrain of chick*] ... ION
Isthmus [*Board on Geographic Names*] ... ISTH
Istituto Affairi Internazionali [*Institute for International Affairs*] [*Italy*] ... IAI
Istituto de Angeli [*Italy*] [*Research code symbol*] ... DA
Istituto di Automatica dell'Universita di Roma Notiziario [*A publication*] ... Ist Autom Univ Roma Not
Istituto de Bologna. Reale Accademia delle Scienze. Classe di Scienze Fisiche. Memorie [*A publication*] ... Ist Bologna R Ac Sc Cl Sc Fis Mem
Istituto Centrale di Statistica [*Italy*] ... ISTAT
Istituto Chemioterapico Italiano [*Italy*] [*Research code symbol*] ... ICI
Istituto Elettrotecnico Nazionale [*Torino, Italy*] ... IEN
Istituto Federale di Ricerche Forestali Memorie [*A publication*] ... Ist Fed Ric For Mem
Istituto di Fisica dell'Atmosfera [*Institute of Atmospheric Physics*] [*Italy*] ... IFA
Istituto Internazionale di Studi Liguri [*International Institute for Ligurian Studies*] ... IISL
Istituto Lombardo. Accademia di Scienze e Lettere. Memorie della Classe di Lettere [*A publication*] ... ILML
Istituto Lombardo. Accademia di Scienze e Lettere. Rendiconti [*A publication*] ... Ist Lombardo Accad Sci e Lettere Rend
Istituto Lombardo. Accademia di Scienze e Lettere. Rendiconti della Classe de Lettere [*A publication*] ... ILRL
Istituto Lombardo. Accademia di Scienze e Lettere. Rendiconti. Scienze Biologiche e Mediche. B [*A publication*] ... Ist Lombardo Accad Sci Lett Rend Sci Biol Med B
Istituto Mobiliare Italiano [*Italy*] ... IMI
Istituto Nazional di Genetica per la Cerealicoltura Nazareno Strampelli [*A publication*] ... Ist Naz Genet Cerealicolt Nazareno Strampelli
Istituto Nazionale delle Assicurazioni ... INA
Istituto Nazionale di Assistenza Sociale ... INAS
Istituto Nazionale per il Commercio Estero [*Italy*] ... ICE
Istituto Nazionale Confederale di Assistenza ... INCA
Istituto Nazionale della Previdenza Sociale [*Italy*] ... INPS
Istituto di Patologia del Libro Bollettino [*A publication*] ... Ist Patologia Libro Boll
Istituto per le Pubbliche Relazioni [*Italian public relations institute*] ... IPR
Istituto per la Ricostruzione Industriale [*Institute for Industrial Reconstruction*] [*Government holding company*] [*Italy*] ... IRI
Istituto Storico della Resistenza in Toscana [*Italy*] ... ISRT
Istituto di Studi per lo Sviluppo Economico [*Institute for the Study of Economic Development*] [*Italy*] ... ISVE
Istituto Superiore di Sanita [*Italy*] [*Research code symbol*] ... IS
Istituto Svizzero di Ricerche Forestali Memorie [*A publication*] ... Ist Svizz Ric For Mem
Istituto Tecnico Agrario Statale (Macerata) [*A publication*] ... Ist Tec Agr Stat (Macerata)
Istituto Tecnico Statale Commerciale e per Geometri Roberto Valturio [*Rimini*] [*A publication*] ... IRV
Istituto Veneto di Scienze, Lettere, ed Arti. Venezia. Atti. Classe di Scienze Matematiche e Naturali [*A publication*] ... Ist Veneto Sci Lett Arti Atti Cl Sci Mat Natur
Istochniki Rudnogo Veshchestva Endogonnykh Mestorozhdenii [*A publication*] ... Istochniki Rudn Veshchestva Endog Mestorozhd
Istoriceskii Zapiski [*A publication*] ... IstZap
Istoriceskij Sbornik Instituta Istorii, Arheologii, i Etnografii [*A publication*] ... Ist Sb Inst Ist Arheol Etnogr
Istoriia, Arkheologiia, i Etnografiia Srednei Azii [*A publication*] ... Ist Ark Etnog Sred Azii
Istoriia Material-noj Kul'tury Uzbekistana [*A publication*] ... Ist Mat Kul't Uzbek
Istorija SSSR [*A publication*] ... Ist SSSR
Istoriko-Astronomiceskie Issledovanija [*A publication*] ... Istor-Astronom Issled
Istoriko-Filologiceskij Sbornik. Syktyvbar [*A publication*] ... IFSSykt
Istoriko-Filologiceskij Zurnal [*A publication*] ... IFZ
Istoriko-Filologiceskij Zurnal [*A publication*] ... Ist-Filol Z
Istoriko-Matematiceskie Issledovanija [*A publication*] ... Istor-Mat Issled
Istoriski Casopis [*A publication*] ... IC
Istoritcheskii Viestnik [*A publication*] ... IV
Istorycni Dzerela ta ich Vykorystannja [*A publication*] ... Ist Dzerela Vykorystannja
It Beaken [*A publication*] ... ItB
It Scale for Children [*Psychology*] ... ITSC
Ita Humanidades [*A publication*] ... IH
Itabuna [*Brazil*] [*Airport symbol*] ... ITN
Itaconic Acid [*Organic chemistry*] ... ITA
Italamerican [*A publication*] ... Italamer
Italfarmaco [*Italy*] [*Research code symbol*] ... ITF
Italia Agricola [*A publication*] ... Ital Agr
Italia Agricola [*A publication*] ... Ital Agric
Italia Antichissima [*A publication*] ... IA
Italia Che Scrive [*A publication*] ... ICS
Italia Che Scrive [*A publication*] ... It
Italia Dialettale [*A publication*] ... ID
Italia Forestale e Montana [*A publication*] ... Ital For Mont
Italia Francescana [*A publication*] ... IFr
Italia Intellettuale [*A publication*] ... II
Italia Medioevale e Umanistica [*A publication*] ... IMU
Italia Numismatica [*A publication*] ... IN
[*The*] **Italia Philatelic Society** ... TIPS
Italia Real Comitato Geologico Bollettino [*A publication*] ... Italia R Comitato G B
Italian ... IT
Italian [*MARC language code*] [*Library of Congress*] ... ita
Italian ... ITAL
Italian Actors Union ... IAU
Italian Air Force ... IAF
Italian-American Civil Rights League ... IACRL
Italian-American Cultural Society ... IACS
Italian American Forum ... IAF
Italian American Librarians Caucus ... IALC
Italian American Stamp Club ... IASC
Italian American War Veterans of the United States ... ITAMVETS
Italian Americana [*A publication*] ... Ital A
Italian Americana [*A publication*] ... Ital Am
Italian Army ... IA
Italian Baptist Association of America [*Later, Association of Evangelicals for Italian Missions*] ... IBAA
Italian Books and Periodicals [*A publication*] ... IBP
Italian Catholic Federation Central Council ... ICF
Italian Chamber of Commerce ... ICC
Italian Charities of America ... ICA
Italian Communist Party ... ICP
Italian Cultural Institute ... ICI
Italian Culture Council ... ICC
Italian Expeditionary Force ... IEF

Italian Expeditions to the Karakorum [K^2] **and Hindu Kush. Scientific Reports** [*A publication*]........ Ital Exped Karakorum Hindu Kush Sci Rep
Italian General Review of Dermatology [*A publication*]........ Ital Gen Rev Dermatol
Italian Greyhound Club of America........IGCA
Italian Historical Society of America........IHS
Italian Journal of Biochemistry [*A publication*]........Ital J Bioc
Italian Journal of Biochemistry [*A publication*]........Ital J Biochem
Italian Journal of Biochemistry (English Edition) [*A publication*]........ Ital J Biochem (Engl Ed)
Italian Journal of Orthopaedics and Traumatology [*A publication*]........Ital J Orthop Traumatol
Italian Journal of Orthopaedics and Traumatology. Supplementum [*A publication*]........Ital J Orthop Traumatol Suppl
Italian Journal of Zoology [*A publication*]........Ital J Zool
Italian Linguistics [*A publication*]........Ital L
Italian Lira [*Monetary unit*]........IL
Italian Navy........IN
Italian Quarterly [*A publication*]........IQ
Italian Quarterly [*A publication*]........Ital Q
Italian Quarterly [*A publication*]........ItQ
Italian Red Cross Society........IRCS
Italian Service Unit [*Italian prisoners of war who became volunteers in the Allied war effort*]........ISU
Italian Society of Physics........ISP
Italian Space Commission........ISC
Italian Studies [*A publication*]........IS
Italian Studies [*A publication*]........ISt
Italian Trade Commission........ITC
Italian Tribune, Newark, NJ [*Library symbol*]........NjNIT
Italian Welfare League........IWL
Italianistica: Revista di Letteratura Italiana [*A publication*]........IRLI
Italianistica: Revista di Letteratura Italiana [*A publication*]........Ital
Italians in Service of the US [*World War II*]........ITIS
Italic [*or Italics*]........ITAL
Italica [*A publication*]........I
Italica [*A publication*]........It
Italica [*A publication*]........Ital
Italics........ITAX
Italienische Studien [*A publication*]........IS
Italo-American National Union........IANU
Italy [*MARC geographic area code*] [*Library of Congress*]........e-it---
Italy........I
Italy [*MARC country of publication code*] [*Library of Congress*]........it
Italy [*Three-letter standard code*]........ITA
Italy [*Aircraft nationality and registration mark*]........I
Italy [*Two-letter standard code*]........IT
Italy. Servizio Geologico. Bollettino [*A publication*]........Italy Serv Geol Boll
Italy. Servizio Geologico. Memorie per Servire alla Descrizione della Carta Geologica d'Italia [*A publication*]........Italy Serv Geol Mem
Italyan Filolojisi [*A publication*]........ItF
Itasca Community College, Grand Rapids, MN [*OCLC symbol*]........MIC
Itasca Community College, Grand Rapids, MN [*Library symbol*]........MnGrI
Itasca Junior College [*Later, Itasca Community College*] [*Minnesota*]........IJC
Itawamba Junior College [*Mississippi*]........IJC
Itawamba Junior College, Tupelo Campus, Tupelo, MS [*Library symbol*]........MsTI
Itek Corp. [*NYSE symbol*] [*Delisted*]........ITK
Itel Corp. [*NYSE symbol*] [*Delisted*]........I
Itel Corp. [*NASDAQ symbol*]........ITEL
Item [*Phonetic alphabet*] [*World War II*]........I
Item........IT
Item Change Analysis........ICA
Item Characteristic Curve [*Statistics*]........ICC
Item Control Area........ICA
Item Control Point........ICP
Item Description........ID
Item Description Sheet........IDS
Item Design Change........IDC
Item Detail Card [*Military*]........IDC
Item Entry Control........IEC
Item [*or Items*] **on Hand**........IOH
Item Identification........II
Item Identification Code........IIC
Item Identification Number........IIN
Item Intelligence File [*DoD*]........IFF
Item Intelligence Maintenance [*DoD*]........IIM
Item Logistics Data Transmittal........ILDT
Item Logistics Data Transmittal Form........ILDTF
Item Logistics Management Data [*DoD*]........ILMD
Item Management........IM
Item Management Coding [*Military*]........IMC
Item Management Coding Program [*Military*]........IMCP
Item Management Control Code........IMCC
Item Management Data Element Standardization [*or System*] [*Military*]........IMDES
Item Management Statistical Series........IMSS
Item Mark........IM
Item Master Card [*Military*]........IMC
Item Name [*Military*]........IN
Item Name Code [*Military*]........INC
Item No Longer Required........INLR
Item Number........INO
Item Operation Trouble Report........IOTR
Item Processing........IP
Item Processing Card........IPC
Item Processing System........IPS
Item Responsibility Code........IRC
Item Selection List........ISL
Item Selection Working Group [*NATO*]........ISWG
Item Standardization Information System [*DoD*]........ISIS
Item Station and Indenture........ISI
Item Status Code........ISC
Item Study Listings........ISL
Item Transfer........IT
Item Urgently Required [*Army*]........IURGRQR
Items Not Available through Cannibalization, Fabrication, or Local Procurement or Replacement from Maintenance Float Stock........ICFLPRMFS
Iterated Ordinary Least Squares [*Statistics*]........IOLS
Iterated Proportional Fitting Procedure [*Statistics*]........IPFP
Iterative Differential Analyzer Control........IDACON
Iterative Differential Analyzer Pinboard........IDAP
Iterative Differential Analyzer Slave........IDAS
Iterative Guidance Mode [*NASA*]........IGM
Iterative Logic Array........ILA
Iterative Natural Orbital [*Atomic physics*]........INO
Iterative Operation........IO
Iterative Orbit Calculator........IOC
Iterative Scheme Using a Direct Solution........ISUDS
Iterative Self-Organizing Data Analysis Technique A [*Data processing*]........ISODATA
Iterative Time Optimal System........ITOS
Iterative Weighted Least Squares [*Statistics*]........IWLS
Ithaca [*New York*] [*Seismograph station code, US Geological Survey*]........INY
Ithaca [*New York*] [*Airport symbol*]........ITH
Ithaca [*New York*] [*Seismograph station code, US Geological Survey*] [*Closed*]........ITH
Ithaca College, Ithaca, NY [*Library symbol*]........NIIC
Ithaca College, Ithaca, NY [*OCLC symbol*]........XIM
Ithaca, NY [*Radio station call letters*]........WEIV
Ithaca, NY [*Radio station call letters*]........WHCU
Ithaca, NY [*Radio station call letters*]........WHCU-FM
Ithaca, NY [*Radio station call letters*]........WICB
Ithaca, NY [*Radio station call letters*]........WTKO
Ithaca, NY [*Radio station call letters*]........WVBR-FM
Ithaca Railroad Association [*Defunct*]........IRA
Ithomi [*Greece*] [*Seismograph station code, US Geological Survey*]........ITM
ITI Corp. [*American Stock Exchange symbol*] [*Delisted*]........IT
Itinerant........ITNRNT
Itinerant Recruiting Detail........IRD
Itinerari [*A publication*]........Itin
Itinerary........ITIN
Itinerary........ITRY
Ito [*Japan*] [*Seismograph station code, US Geological Survey*] [*Closed*]........ITO
Ito-Reenstierna [*Reaction*] [*Medicine*]........I-R
Ito System Color Television [*Japan*]........ISCT
Ito-Yokado Company Ltd. [*NASDAQ symbol*]........IYCOY
Itogi Nauki. Biologicheski Osnovy Rastenievodstva [*A publication*]........Itogi Nauki Biol Osn Rastenievod
Itogi Nauki. Embriologiya [*A publication*]........Itogi Nauki Embriol
Itogi Nauki. Geofizika [*A publication*]........Itogi Nauki Geofiz
Itogi Nauki. Khimicheskie Nauki [*A publication*]........Itogi Nauki Khim Nauki
Itogi Nauki. Obshchie Voprosy Patologii [*A publication*]........ Itogi Nauki Obshch Vopr Patol
Itogi Nauki i Tekhniki. Atomnaya Energetika [*A publication*]........ Itogi Nauki Tekh At Energ
Itogi Nauki i Tekhniki. Farmakologiya, Khimioterapevticheskie Sredstva [*A publication*]........ Itogi Nauki i Tekh Farmakol Khimioter Sredstva
Itogi Nauki i Tekhniki. Fiziologiya Rastenii [*A publication*]........ Itogi Nauki Tekh Fiziol Rast
Itogi Nauki i Tekhniki. Gidrogeologiya, Inzhenernaya Geologiya [*A publication*]........Itogi Nauki Tekh Gidrogeol Inzh Geol
Itogi Nauki i Tekhniki. Issledovanie Kosmicheskogo Prostranstva [*A publication*]........ Itogi Nauki Tekh Issled Kosm Prostranstva
Itogi Nauki i Tekhniki. Obshchaya Ekologiya, Biotsenologiya [*A publication*]........Itogi Nauki Tekh Obshch Ekol Biotsenol
Itogi Nauki i Tekhniki. Pozharnaya Okhrana [*A publication*]........ Itogi Nauki Tekh Pozharnaya Okhr
Itogi Nauki i Tekhniki. Seriya Issledovanie Kosmicheskogo Prostranstva [*A publication*]........ Itogi Nauk & Tekh Ser Issled Kosm Prostranstva
Itogi Nauki i Tekhniki. Toksikologiya [*A publication*]........ Itogi Nauki Tekh Toksikol
Itogi Nauki i Tekhniki. Zhivotnovodstvo i Veterinariya [*A publication*]........Itogi Nauki Tekh Zhivotnovod Vet
Itogi Nauki. Veterinariya [*A publication*]........Itogi Nauki Vet
Itogi Polevyh Rabot Instituta Etnografii [*A publication*]........ Itogi Polev Rabot Inst Etnogr

Itokama [Papua New Guinea] [Airport symbol]............................ITK
Itonut Yisrael Meugedet [ITIM News Agency of the Associated
   Israel Press Ltd.]..ITIM
It's Life, I Can't, I Must [Element of psychotherapist Joseph Bird's
   self-help theory]................................IL-IC-IM
It's That Man Again [Long-running English radio comedy, 1939-
   1949]...ITMA
ITT Consumer Services Corp. [NYSE symbol] [Delisted]............ITS
ITT Secure Ranging and Communications System...................ISRAC
IU International Corp. [NYSE symbol]..................................IU
IUCN [International Union for Conservation of Nature and Natural
   Resources] Bulletin [A publication]....................IUCN Bull
IUCN [International Union for Conservation of Nature and Natural
   Resources] Publications. New Series [A publication]...........
        IUCN Publ New Ser
IUCN [International Union for Conservation of Nature and Natural
   Resources] Yearbook [A publication]....................IUCN Yearb
Iugoslavica Physiologica Pharmacologica Acta [A publication]..........
        Iugosl Physiol Pharmacol Acta
Iuka, MS [Radio station call letters]............................WTIB
Iuka, MS [Radio station call letters]............................WVOM
Iuliu Maniu American Romanian Relief Foundation..................IMF
Iultin [USSR] [Seismograph station code, US Geological Survey]............ILT
IUMS [International Union of Microbiological Societies]
   Bacteriology Division.....................................IUMSBD
IUS [Interim Upper Stage] Processing Facility [NASA]..............IPF
IVA Tidskrift foer Teknisk-Vetenskaplig Forskning [A
   publication]...................... IVA Tidskr Tek-Vetenskaplig Forsk
Ivalo [Finland] [Airport symbol].................................IVL
Ivan [the Terrible], Borgia [the Poisoner], Attila [the Hun],
   Caligula [the Emperor] [Initials that form the name of the
   villain in "Captain Marvel" comic strip and also indicate the
   sources of his powers]...................................IBAC
Ivanovskii Gosudarstvennyi Universitet. Ucenye Zapiski [A
   publication]..................... Ivanov Gos Univ Ucen Zap
I've Never Seen One Like That [Antiques market].................INSOLT
Ives Laboratories [Research code symbol].........................IL
Ivigtut [Greenland] [Seismograph station code, US Geological
   Survey] [Closed]...IVI
Ivishak, AK [Location identifier] [FAA].........................IVH
IVL [Instituet foer Vatten och Luftvardsforskning] Bulletin [A
   publication]...IVL Bull
Ivory Coast [Two-letter standard code]...........................CI
Ivory Coast [Three-letter standard code].........................CIV
Ivory Coast [MARC geographic area code] [Library of Congress]...... f-iv---
Ivory Coast [MARC country of publication code] [Library of Congress]........iv
Ivory Coast [Aircraft nationality and registration mark]............TU
IVT [Instituut voor de Veredeling van Tuinbouwgewassen]
   Jaarverslag [A publication]............... IVT Jaarversl
IVT [Instituut voor de Veredeling van Tuinbouwgewassen]
   Mededeling [A publication]............... IVT Mededel
Ivugivik [Canada] [Airport symbol]...............................YIK
Iwate University. Faculty of Education. Annual Report [A
   publication]................... Annual Rep Fac Ed Iwate Univ
Iwate University Faculty of Engineering Technology Reports [A
   publication]...............................Iwate Univ Technol Rep
Ixtapalapa [Mexico] [Seismograph station code, US Geological
   Survey] [Closed]..IXT
Iz Istorii Kul'tury Narodov Uzbekistana [A publication]..............
        I Ist Kul't Narod Uzbek
Izaak Walton League of America..................................IWLA
Izaak Walton League of America Endowment...................... IWLAE
Izmenenie Pochvy pri Okyl'turivanii Ikh Klassifikatsiya i
   Diagnostika "Kolos" [A publication]...........................
        Izmen Pochv Okyl't Klassif Diagnostika "Kolos"
Izmeritel'naya Tekhnika [A publication]................Izmer Tekh
Izmir [Turkey] [Airport symbol]..................................IZM
Izmir [Turkey] [Seismograph station code, US Geological Survey]............IZM
Izmir [Turkey] Cigli Airport [Airport symbol].....................IGL
Izobreteniya Promyshlennye Obraztsy. Tovarnye Znaki [A
   publication]............... Izobret Prom Obraztsy Tovarnye Znaki
Izuhara [Japan] [Seismograph station code, US Geological Survey]..........IZU
Izumo [Japan] [Airport symbol]...................................IZO
Izvestiia na Balgarskite Muzei [A publication]............... Iz Balg Muz
Izvestiia na B'lgarskoto Istoricheskо Druzestvo [A publication]............IzBID
Izvestiia. Institut za Zhivotnovudstvo. Bulgarska Akademiia na
   Naukite [A publication]............... Izv Inst Zhivotn Bulg Akad Nauk
Izvestiia na Narodniia Muzei (Rousse) [A publication].................
        Iz Narod Muz (Rousse)
Izvestiia na Narodniia Muzei (Varna) [A publication].....Iz Narod Muz (Varna)
Izvestiia Rossiiskoi Akademii Nauk [A publication].....Izvest Ross Akad Nauk
Izvestija Abhazskogo Instituta Jazyka, Literatury, i Istorii [A
   publication]...............Izv Abhaz Inst Jaz Lit Ist
Izvestija. Akademii Nauk Estonskoj SSR. Obscestvennye Nauki
   [A publication]...............Izv Akad Nauk Eston SSR Obsc Nauki
Izvestija. Akademii Nauk Kazahskoi SSR. Serija Fiziko-
   Matematiceskaja [A publication]...............
        Izv Akad Nauk Kazah SSR Ser Fiz-Mat
Izvestija. Akademii Nauk SSSR. Serija Ekonomiceskaja [A
   publication]............... Izv Akad Nauk SSSR Ser Ekon

Izvestija. Akademii Nauk SSSR. Serija Geografii [A publication]............
        Izv Akad Nauk SSSR Ser Geogr
Izvestija. Akademii Nauk SSSR. Tekhniceskaja Kibernetika [A
   publication]............... Izv Akad Nauk SSSR Tehn Kibernet
Izvestija. Akademii Nauk UzSSR. Serija Fiziko-Matematiceskih
   Nauk [A publication]............... Izv Akad Nauk UzSSR Ser Fiz-Mat Nauk
Izvestija. Akademija Nauk Kirgizskoi SSR [A publication]..............
        Izv Akad Nauk Kirgiz SSR
Izvestija na Balgarskoto Istoricesko Druzestvo [A publication]...............IBID
Izvestija Kazanskogo Filiala Akademii Nauk SSSR. Serija
   Fiziko-Matematiceskih i Tehniceskih Nauk [A publication]............
        Izv Kazan Fil Akad Nauk SSSR Ser Fiz-Mat i Tehn Nauk
Izvestija Komi Filiala Geograficeskogo Obscestva SSSR [A
   publication]............... Izv Komi Fil Geogr Obsc SSSR
Izvestija Tomskogo Ordena Trudovogo Krasnogo Znameni
   Politehniceskogo Instituta Imeni S. M. Kirova [A publication]............
        Izv Tomsk Politehn Inst
Izvestija Voronezskogo Pedagogiceskogo Instituta [A
   publication]...............Izv Voronez Pedag Inst
Izvestija Vsesojuznogo Geograficeskogo Obscestva [A
   publication]............... Izv Vsesojuz Geogr Obsc
Izvestija Vyssih Ucebnyh Zavedenii. Aviacionnaja Tehnika [A
   publication]...............Izv Vyss Ucebn Zaved Aviacion Tehn
Izvestija Vyssih Ucebnyh Zavedenii. Fizika [A publication]..............
        Izv Vyss Ucebn Zaved Fizika
Izvestija Vyssih Ucebnyh Zavedenii. Matematika [A publication]............
        Izv Vyss Ucebn Zaved Matematika
Izvestiya [Moscow] [A publication]...............................Iz
Izvestiya. Academy of Sciences USSR. Atmospheric and
   Oceanic Physics [A publication]............................
        Izv Acad Sci USSR Atmos Oceanic Phys
Izvestiya. Academy of Sciences USSR. Physics of the Solid
   Earth [A publication]...............Izv Acad Sci USSR Phys Solid Earth
Izvestiya. Akademii Nauk Armjanskoj SSR. Obscestvennyh
   Nauk [A publication]...............IzvANArm
Izvestiya. Akademii Nauk Armyanskoi SSR. Biologicheskie
   Nauki [A publication]............... Izv Akad Nauk Arm SSR Biol Nauki
Izvestiya. Akademii Nauk Armyanskoi SSR. Biologicheskie i
   Sel'skokhozyaistvennye Nauki [A publication]...............
        Izv Akad Nauk Arm SSR Biol S-kh Nauki
Izvestiya. Akademii Nauk Azerbaidzhanskoi SSR [A publication]............
        Izv Akad Nauk Az SSR
Izvestiya. Akademii Nauk Azerbaidzhanskoi SSR. Seriya
   Biologicheskikh Nauk [A publication]...............
        Izv Akad Nauk Azerb SSR Ser Biol Nauk
Izvestiya. Akademii Nauk Azerbaidzhanskoi SSR. Seriya
   Biologicheskikh Nauk [A publication]...............
        Izv Akad Nauk Az SSR Ser Biol Nauk
Izvestiya. Akademii Nauk Azerbajdzhanskoj SSR. Seriya Nauk i
   Zemle [A publication]............. Izv Akad Nauk Azerb SSR Ser Nauk Zemle
Izvestiya. Akademii Nauk Azerbajdzhanskoj SSR. Seriya
   Obscestvennych Nauk [A publication]...............IzvANAzerb
Izvestiya. Akademii Nauk Belorusskoi SSR. Seriya
   Biologicheskikh Nauk [A publication]...............
        Izv Akad Nauk B SSR Ser Biol Nauk
Izvestiya. Akademii Nauk Belorusskoi SSR. Seriya
   Sel'skokhozyaistvennykh Nauk [A publication]...............
        Izv Akad Nauk B SSR Ser S Kh Nauk
Izvestiya. Akademii Nauk Ehstanskoj SSR. Khimiya i Geologiya
   [A publication]...............Izv Akad Nauk Ehst SSR Khim Geol
Izvestiya. Akademii Nauk Estonskoi SSR. Seriya
   Biologicheskaya [A publication]..........Izv Akad Nauk Eston SSR Ser Biol
Izvestiya. Akademii Nauk Estonskoi SSR. Seriya
   Biologicheskaya [A publication]...............Izv Akad Nauk Est SSR Ser Biol
Izvestiya. Akademii Nauk Gruzinskoi SSR. Seriya
   Khimicheskaya [A publication]...........Izv Akad Nauk Gruz SSR Ser Khim
Izvestiya. Akademii Nauk Kazakhskoi SSR. Seriya
   Biologicheskaya [A publication]...............Izv Akad Nauk Kaz SSR Ser Biol
Izvestiya. Akademii Nauk Kazakhskoi SSR. Seriya
   Biologicheskikh Nauk [A publication]...............
        Izv Akad Nauk Kaz SSR Ser Biol Nauk
Izvestiya. Akademii Nauk Kazakhskoi SSR. Seriya Botaniki i
   Pochvovedeniya [A publication]...............
        Izv Akad Nauk Kazakh SSR Ser Bot Pochvoved
Izvestiya. Akademii Nauk Kazakhskoi SSR. Seriya Botaniki i
   Pochvovedeniya [A publication]...............
        Izv Akad Nauk Kaz SSR Ser Bot Pochvoved
Izvestiya. Akademii Nauk Kazakhskoi SSR. Seriya Fiziko-
   Matematicheskaya [A publication]...............
        Izv Akad Nauk Kaz SSR Ser Fiz-Mat
Izvestiya. Akademii Nauk Kazakhskoi SSR. Seriya
   Geologicheskaya [A publication]......... Izv Akad Nauk Kaz SSR Ser Geol
Izvestiya. Akademii Nauk Kazakhskoi SSR. Seriya
   Khimicheskaya [A publication]...............Izv Akad Nauk Kaz SSR Ser Khim
Izvestiya. Akademii Nauk Kazakhskoi SSR. Seriya
   Meditsinskikh Nauk [A publication]...............
        Izv Akad Nauk Kaz SSR Ser Med Nauk
Izvestiya. Akademii Nauk Kazakhskoi SSR. Seriya Meditsiny i
   Fiziologii [A publication]...............Izv Akad Nauk Kaz SSR Ser Med Fiziol
Izvestiya. Akademii Nauk Kazakhskoj SSR. Seriya Filologii i
   Iskusstvovedeniya [A publication]...............IzvANKaz

Izvestiya. Akademii Nauk Kirgizskoi SSR [A publication]................
....Izv Akad Nauk Kirg SSR
Izvestiya. Akademii Nauk Kirgizskoi SSR. Seriya
Biologicheskikh Nauk [A publication].............................
...........................Izv Akad Nauk Kirgiz SSR Ser Biol Nauk
Izvestiya. Akademii Nauk Kirgizskoi SSR. Seriya
Biologicheskikh Nauk [A publication].............................
.............................Izv Akad Nauk Kirg SSR Ser Biol Nauk
Izvestiya. Akademii Nauk Latviiskoi SSR [A publication].........
....Izv Akad Nauk Latvii SSR
Izvestiya. Akademii Nauk Latviiskoi SSR [A publication].........
....Izv Akad Nauk Latv SSR
Izvestiya. Akademii Nauk Latviiskoi SSR. Seriya Fizicheskikh i
Tekhnicheskikh Nauk [A publication]............................
.........................Izv Akad Nauk Latv SSR Ser Fiz Tekh Nauk
Izvestiya. Akademii Nauk Latviiskoi SSR. Seriya Khimicheskaya
[A publication]......................Izv Akad Nauk Latv SSR Ser Khim
Izvestiya. Akademii Nauk Moldavskoi SSR [A publication].........
....Izv Akad Nauk Moldav SSR
Izvestiya. Akademii Nauk Moldavskoi SSR [A publication].........
....Izv Akad Nauk Mold SSR
Izvestiya. Akademii Nauk Moldavskoi SSR. Seriya
Biologicheskaya [A publication] ....Izv Akad Nauk Mold SSR Ser Biol
Izvestiya. Akademii Nauk Moldavskoi SSR. Seriya
Biologicheskikh i Khimicheskikh Nauk [A publication] ....
......................Izv Akad Nauk Mold SSR Ser Biol Khim Nauk
Izvestiya. Akademii Nauk Moldavskoi SSR. Seriya
Biologicheskikh i Sel'skokhozyaistvennykh Nauk [A
publication]........................ Izv Akad Nauk Mold SSR Ser Biol S-Kh Nauk
Izvestiya. Akademii Nauk Moldavskoi SSR. Seriya Fiziko-
Tekhnicheskikh i Matematicheskikh Nauk [A publication] ....
Izv Akad Nauk Mold SSR Ser Fiz-Tekh Mat Nauk
Izvestiya. Akademii Nauk SSSR [A publication] ....Izv Akad Nauk SSSR
Izvestiya. Akademii Nauk SSSR. Energetika i Transport [A
publication]........................ Izv Akad Nauk SSSR Energ Transp
Izvestiya. Akademii Nauk SSSR. Fizika Atmosfery i Okeana [A
publication]........................Izv Akad Nauk SSSR Fiz Atmos Okeana
Izvestiya. Akademii Nauk SSSR. Fizika Zemli [A publication]........
....Izv Akad Nauk SSSR Fiz Zemli
Izvestiya. Akademii Nauk SSSR. Mekhanika Tverdogo Tela [A
publication].....................Izv Akad Nauk SSSR Mekh Tverd Tela
Izvestiya. Akademii Nauk SSSR. Mekhanika Zhidkosti i Gaza [A
publication]....................Izv Akad Nauk SSSR Mekh Zhidk Gaza
Izvestiya. Akademii Nauk SSSR. Metally [A publication].............
....Izv Akad Nauk SSSR Met
Izvestiya. Akademii Nauk SSSR. Metally [A publication].............
....Izv Akad Nauk SSSR Metally
Izvestiya. Akademii Nauk SSSR. Neorganicheskie Materialy [A
publication]....................Izv Akad Nauk SSSR Neorg Mater
Izvestiya. Akademii Nauk SSSR. Otdelenie Literatury i Jazyka [A
publication]... IzvAN
Izvestiya. Akademii Nauk SSSR. Otdelenie Literatury i Jazyka [A
publication]....................Izvestiya Akad Nauk SSSR
Izvestiya. Akademii Nauk SSSR. Otdelenie Tekhnicheskikh
Nauk. Energetika i Transport [A publication].....................
Izv Akad Nauk SSSR Otd Tekh Nauk Energ Transp
Izvestiya. Akademii Nauk SSSR. Otdeleniya Gumanitarnykh
Nauk [A publication]......................................IAN-OGN
Izvestiya. Akademii Nauk SSSR. Otdeleniya Literatury i Jazyka
[A publication]....................................IAN-OLJa
Izvestiya. Akademii Nauk SSSR. Otdeleniya Obscestvennykh
Nauk [A publication]....................................IAN OON
Izvestiya. Akademii Nauk SSSR. Otdeleniya Russkogo Jazyka i
Slavesnosti Akademii Nauk [A publication]...................... IAN ORJaSL
Izvestiya. Akademii Nauk SSSR. Seriia Biologicheskaya [A
publication]....................Izv Akad Nauk SSSR Biol
Izvestiya. Akademii Nauk SSSR. Seriya Biologicheskaya [A
publication]...................................... IAN SSS Bio
Izvestiya. Akademii Nauk SSSR. Seriya Biologicheskaya [A
publication]....................Izv Akad Nauk SSSR Ser Biol
Izvestiya. Akademii Nauk SSSR. Seriya Fizicheskaya [A
publication]......................................IAN SSS Fiz
Izvestiya. Akademii Nauk SSSR. Seriya Fizicheskaya [A
publication]....................Izv Akad Nauk SSSR Ser Fiz
Izvestiya. Akademii Nauk SSSR. Seriya Fizika Atmosfery i
Okeana [A publication].....................IAN SSS FAO
Izvestiya. Akademii Nauk SSSR. Seriya Geograficheskaya [A
publication]....................Izv Akad Nauk SSSR Ser Geogr
Izvestiya. Akademii Nauk SSSR. Seriya Geograficheskaya i
Geofizicheskaya [A publication] ....
Izv Akad Nauk SSSR Ser Geogr Geofiz
Izvestiya. Akademii Nauk SSSR. Seriya Geologicheskaya [A
publication] ....Izv Akad Nauk SSSR Ser Geol
Izvestiya. Akademii Nauk SSSR. Seriya Geologicheskaya
(Translated Abstracts) [A publication]........................
Izv Akad Nauk SSSR Ser Geol (Transl Abstr)
Izvestiya. Akademii Nauk SSSR. Seriya Khimicheskaya [A
publication]....................Izv Akad Nauk SSSR Khim
Izvestiya. Akademii Nauk SSSR. Seriya Khimicheskaya [A
publication]....................Izv Akad Nauk SSSR Ser Khim

Izvestiya. Akademii Nauk SSSR. Seriya Literatury i Jazyka
[Moscow] [A publication]......................................IAN
Izvestiya. Akademii Nauk SSSR. Seriya Matematicheskaya [A
publication]....................Izv Akad Nauk SSSR Ser Mat
Izvestiya. Akademii Nauk SSSR. Tekhnicheskaya Kibernetika [A
publication]....................Izv Akad Nauk SSSR Tekh Kibern
Izvestiya. Akademii Nauk Tadzhickoi SSR. Otdelenie
Obscestvennych Nauk [A publication]....................IzvANTadz
Izvestiya. Akademii Nauk Tadzhikskoi SSR. Otdelenie
Biologicheskikh Nauk [A publication].....................
.........................Izv Akad Nauk Tadzhik SSR Otd Biol Nauk
Izvestiya. Akademii Nauk Tadzhikskoi SSR. Otdelenie
Biologicheskikh Nauk [A publication].....................
...........................Izv Akad Nauk Tadzh SSR Otd Biol Nauk
Izvestiya. Akademii Nauk Tadzhikskoi SSR. Otdelenie
Estestvennykh Nauk [A publication].....................
.........................Izv Akad Nauk Tadzh SSR Otd Estestv Nauk
Izvestiya. Akademii Nauk Tadzhikskoi SSR. Otdelenie
Fizichesko-Tekhnicheskikh Khimicheskikh Nauk [A
publication]........... Izv Akad Nauk Tadzhik SSR Otd Fiz-Tekh Khim Nauk
Izvestiya. Akademii Nauk Tadzhikskoi SSR. Otdelenie Fiziko-
Matematicheskikh i Geologo-Khimicheskikh Nauk [A
publication].......Izv Akad Nauk Tadzh SSR Otd Fiz-Mat Geol-Khim Nauk
Izvestiya. Akademii Nauk Tadzhikskoi SSR. Otdelenie
Sel'skokhozyaistvennykh i Biologicheskikh Nauk [A
publication].....................Izv Akad Nauk Tadzh SSR Otd S-Kh Biol Nauk
Izvestiya. Akademii Nauk Turkmenskoi SSR [A publication].........
....Izv Akad Nauk Turkm SSR
Izvestiya. Akademii Nauk Turkmenskoi SSR. Seriya
Biologicheskikh Nauk [A publication].....................
.........................Izv Akad Nauk Turkmen SSR Ser Biol Nauk
Izvestiya. Akademii Nauk Turkmenskoi SSR. Seriya
Biologicheskikh Nauk [A publication].....................
.........................Izv Akad Nauk Turkm SSR Ser Biol Nauk
Izvestiya. Akademii Nauk Turkmenskoi SSR. Seriya Fiziko-
Tekhnicheskikh. Khimicheskikh i Geologicheskikh Nauk [A
publication].......Izv Akad Nauk Turkm SSR Ser Fiz-Tekh Khim Geol Nauk
Izvestiya. Akademii Nauk Turkmenskoi SSR. Seriya
Obscestvennych Nauk [A publication]....................IAT
Izvestiya. Akademii Nauk Turkmenskoi SSSR. Seriya
Obscestvennych Nauk [A publication]....................IzvANTurkm
Izvestiya. Akademii Nauk Uzbekistanskoj SSSR [A publication] .... IANUz
Izvestiya. Akademii Nauk Uzbekskoi SSR [A publication]............
....Izv Akad Uzb SSR
Izvestiya. Akademii Nauk Uzbekskoi SSR. Seriya
Biologicheskaya [A publication] ....Izv Akad Nauk Uzb SSR Ser Biol
Izvestiya. Akademii Nauk Uzbekskoi SSR. Seriya Fiziko-
Matematicheskikh Nauk [A publication].....................
.........................Izv Akad Nauk Uzb SSR Ser Fiz-Mat Nauk
Izvestiya. Akademii Nauk Uzbekskoi SSR. Seriya
Tekhnicheskikh Nauk [A publication].....................
.........................Izv Akad Nauk Uzb SSR Ser Tekh Nauk
Izvestiya. Akademii Nauk UzSSR. Seriya Tekhnicheskikh Nauk
[A publication]....................Izv Akad Nauk UzSSR Ser Tekh Nauk
Izvestiya. Akademii Pedagogicheskikh Nauk RSFSR [A
publication]....................Izv Akad Pedagog Nauk RSFSR
Izvestiya. Akademiya Nauk Armyanskoi SSR. Biologicheskie
Nauk [A publication].................... Izv Akad Nauk Armyan SSR Biol Nauk
Izvestiya Altaiskogo Otdela Geograficheskogo Obshcestva
SSSR [A publication]....................Izv Altai Otd Geogr O-va SSSR
Izvestiya Armyanskogo Gosudarstvennogo Zaocnogo
Pedagogiceskogo Instituta [A publication]....................IzvArmZPI
Izvestiya na Balgarskiya Archeologiceski Institut [A publication]........ IzvBAI
Izvestiya Batumskogo Botanicheskogo Sada Akademii Nauk
Gruzinskoi SSR [A publication].....................
Izv Batum Bot Sada Akad Nauk Gruz SSR
Izvestiya na Botanicheskiya Instituta B'lgarska Akademiya na
Naukite [A publication]....................Izv Bot Inst B'lg Akad Nauk
Izvestiya Ceceno-Ingusskogo Naucno-Issledovatel-Skogo
Instituta Istorii, Jazyka, i Literatury [A publication]....................IzvCIngNII
Izvestiya na Druzestovoto na Filolozite-Slavisti v Bulgarija.
Sofija [A publication]......................................IDS
Izvestiya na Druzestovoto na Filolozite-Slavisti v Bulgarija.
Sofija [A publication]......................................IzvDS
Izvestiya Estestvenno-Nauchnogo Instituta pri Molotovskom
Gosudarstvennom Universiteta Imeni M. Gor'kogo [A
publication]....................Izv Estestv-Nauchn Inst Molotov Gos Univ Im M Gor'kogo
Izvestiya na Etnografskija Institut Muzej [A publication]....................IEIM
Izvestiya Fakul'teta Sel'skokhozyaistvennykh Nauk.
Moshonmad'yarovar. Vengriya [A publication]....................
Izv Fak S kh Nauk Moshonmad'yarovar Vengriya
Izvestiya na Fizicheskiya Instituta ANEB. Bylgarska Akademiya
na Naukite [A publication]....................Izv Fiz Inst ANEB Bylg Akad Nauk
Izvestiya na Geofizichniya Institut [A publication]....................Izv Geofiz Inst
Izvestiya na Geofizichniya Institut. Bylgarska Akademiya na
Naukite. Otdelenie a Matematicheski i Fizicheski Nauki [A
publication]....................Izv Geofiz Inst Bylg Akad Nauk
Izvestiya na Geologicheskiya Institut. Bulgarska Akademiya na
Naukite. Seria Geotektonika [A publication]....................
Izv Geol Inst Bulg Akad Nauk Ser Geotekton

Izvestiya na Geologicheskiya Institut. Seriya Paleontologiya
(Sofia) [*A publication*] ....Izv Geol Inst Ser Paleontol (Sofia)
Izvestiya na Geologicheskiya Institut. Seriya Prilozhna
Geofizika [*A publication*] .... Izv Geol Inst Ser Prilozh Geofiz
Izvestiya Glavnoj Astronomicheskoj Observatorii v Pulkove [*A
publication*]..Izv Gl Astron Obs Pulkove
Izvestiya Gorskogo Sel'skokhozyaistvennogo Instituta [*A
publication*] .... Izv Gorskogo S'kh Inst
Izvestiya Imperatorskoi Akademii Nauk St. Petersburg [*A
publication*]................................ Izvest Imp Akad Nauk S Petersburg
Izvestiya. Institut po Furazhite. Pleven [*A publication*]
Izv Inst Furazhite Pleven
Izvestiya. Institut po Pshenitsata i Slunchogleda (Tolbukhin) [*A
publication*]........................ Izv Inst Pshenitsata Slunchogleda (Tolbukhin)
Izvestiya. Institut Ribni Resursov. Varna [*A publication*]...................
Izv Inst Ribni Resur Varna
Izvestiya. Institut Rukopisej. Akademii Nauk Gruzinskoj SSR [*A
publication*]..IzvIRGruz
Izvestiya. Institut Rybnykh Resursov. Varna [*A publication*]...........
Izv Inst Rybn Resur
Izvestiya na Instituta za Belgarska Literatura [*A publication*]...................IIBL
Izvestiya na Instituta za Belgarski Ezik [*A publication*]....................IIBE
Izvestiya na Instituta za Belgarski Ezik [*A publication*]....................IzvIBE
Izvestiya na Instituta po Biokhimiya. Bylgarska Akademiya na
Naukite [*A publication*]............................Izv Inst Biokhim Bylg Akad Nauk
Izvestiya na Instituta po Biologiya "Metodii Popov" Bulgarskoi
Akademii Nauk [*A publication*]
Izv Inst Biol "Metod Popov" Bulg Akad Nauk
Izvestiya na Instituta po Elektronika [*A publication*]..............Izv Inst Elektron
Izvestiya na Instituta po Elektronika. Bylgarska Akademiya na
Naukite [*A publication*].......................... Izv Inst Elektron Bylg Akad Nauk
Izvestiya na Instituta po Fiziologiya. B'lgarska Akademiya na
Naukite [*A publication*] .... Izv Inst Fiziol B'lg Akad Nauk
Izvestiya na Instituta po Fiziologiya na Rasteniyata "Metodii
Popov." Bulgarska Akademiya na Naukite [*A publication*] ....
Izv Inst Fiziol Rast "Metodii Popov" Bulg Akad Nauk
Izvestiya na Instituta po Fiziologiya na Rasteniyata "Metodii
Popov". Bulgarskoi Akademii Nauk [*A publication*] ....
Izv Inst Fiziol Rast "Metod Popov" Bulg Akad Nauk
Izvestiya na Instituta po Khidrologiya i Meteorologiya.
Bylgarska Akademiya na Naukite [*A publication*].....................
Izv Inst Khidrol Meteor
Izvestiya na Instituta za Muzika [*A publication*]........................... IIM
Izvestiya na Instituta po Okeanografiya i Ribno Stopanstvo.
Bulgarska Akademiya na Naukite [*A publication*] ....
Izv Inst Okeanogr Ribno Stop Bulg Akad Nauk
Izvestiya na Instituta po Pamuka (Chirpan) [*A publication*]...................
Izv Inst Pamuka (Chirpan)
Izvestiya na Instituta po Rastenievudstvo. Bulgarska Akademiya
na Naukite [*A publication*].................... Izv Inst Rast Bulg Akad Nauk
Izvestiya na Instituta po Sravnitelna Patologiya na Zhivotnite [*A
publication*].....................................Izv Inst Sravn Patol Zhivotn
Izvestiya na Instituta po Tekhnicheska Kibernetika [*A
publication*]..Izv Inst Tekh Kibern
Izvestiya na Instituta po Tsarevitsata-Knezha [*A publication*]...............
Izv Inst Tsarevitsata-Knezha
Izvestiya na Instituta po Vodni Problemi Bylgarska Akademiya
na Naukite. Otdelenie za Tekhnicheskij Nauki [*A publication*]...............
Izv Inst Vodn Probl Bylg Akad Nauk
Izvestiya na Istoriseskoto Druzestvo [*A publication*].....................IID
Izvestiya Jugo-Osetinskogo Naucno-Issledovatel'skogo
Instituta [*A publication*]....................................IzvJOsNII
Izvestiya Jugo-Osetinskogo Naucno-Issledovatel'skogo
Instituta Akademii Nauk-Gruzinskoj SSR [*A publication*]...........IzvJuOsI
Izvestiya Kazanskogo Filiala Akademii Nauk SSR [*A publication*].................
Izv Kazan Fil Akad Nauk SSR
Izvestiya Komi Filiala Vsesoyuznogo Geograficheskogo
Obshchestva [*A publication*].................. Izv Komi Fil Vses Geogr Obshch
Izvestiya na Kompleksnja Selskostopanski
Nauchnoizsledvatelski Institut (Karnobat) [*A publication*].....................
Izv Kompleks Selskostop Nauchnoizsled Inst (Karnobat)
Izvestiya Krymskoi Astrofizicheskoi Observatorii [*A publication*] ....
Izv Krym Astrofiz Obs
Izvestiya Kuibyshevskogo Sel'skokhozyaistvennogo Instituta [*A
publication*]..................................... Izv Kuibyshev Sel'khoz Inst
Izvestiya Kuibyshevskogo Sel'skokhozyaistvennogo Instituta [*A
publication*]...................................... Izv Kuibyshev S-kh Inst
Izvestiya Leningradskogo Gosudarstvennogo Universiteta [*A
publication*].. ILGU
Izvestiya na Mikrobiologicheskiya Institut B'lgarska Akademiya
na Naukite [*A publication*].................... Izv Mikrobiol Inst B'lg Akad Nauk
Izvestiya na Nauchnoizsledovatelskiya Institut po
Okeanografiya i Ribno Stopanstvo. Varna [*A publication*]...................
Izv Nachnoizsled Inst Okeanogr Ribno Stop Varna
Izvestiya Omskogo Otdeleniya Geograficheskogo Obshchestva
SSR [*A publication*]...............................Izv Omsk Otd Geogr O-va SSR
Izvestiya na Otdelenieto za Khimicheski Nauki. Bulgarska
Akademiya na Naukite [*A publication*] ....
Izv Otd Khim Nauki Bulg Akad Nauk
Izvestiya. Physics of the Solid Earth [*A publication*] ....Izv Phys Solid Earth

Izvestiya na Sektsiyata po Astronomiya. Bylgarska Akademiya
na Naukite [*A publication*].....................Izv Sekts Astron Bylg Akad Nauk
Izvestiya Sel'skokhozyaistvennykh Nauk [*A publication*]......... Izv S-kh Nauk
Izvestiya Seminara po Slavjanske Filologija [*A publication*] ....IzvSLF
Izvestiya Severo-Osetinskogo Naucno-Issledovatel'skogo
Instituta [*A publication*].................................IzvSOsNII
Izvestiya Sibirskogo Otdeleniya Akademii Nauk SSSR [*A
publication*].................................Izv Sibir Otd Akad Nauk SSSR
Izvestiya Sibirskogo Otdeleniya Akademii Nauk SSSR [*A
publication*].................................Izv Sib Otd Akad Nauk SSSR
Izvestiya Sibirskogo Otdeleniya Akademii Nauk SSSR. Seriya
Biologo-Meditsinskikh Nauk [*A publication*] ....
Izv Sib Otd Akad Nauk SSSR Ser Biol-Med Nauk
Izvestiya Sibirskogo Otdeleniya Akademii Nauk SSSR. Seriya
Biologicheskikh Nauk [*A publication*] ....
Izv Sib Otd Akad Nauk SSSR Ser Biol Nauk
Izvestiya Sibirskogo Otdeleniya Akademii Nauk SSSR. Seriya
Khimicheskikh Nauk [*A publication*] ....
Izv Sibir Otd Akad Nauk SSSR Khim
Izvestiya Sibirskogo Otdeleniya Akademii Nauk SSSR. Seriya
Khimicheskikh Nauk [*A publication*] ....
Izv Sibir Otd Akad Nauk SSSR Ser Khim Nauk
Izvestiya Sibirskogo Otdeleniya Akademii Nauk SSSR. Seriya
Khimicheskikh Nauk [*A publication*] ....
Izv Sib Otd Akad Nauk SSSR Ser Khim Nauk
Izvestiya Sibirskogo Otdeleniya Akademii Nauk SSSR. Seriya
Tekhnicheskikh Nauk [*A publication*] ....
Izv Sibir Otd Akad Nauk SSSR Tekh
Izvestiya Sibirskogo Otdeleniya Akademii Nauk SSSR. Seriya
Tekhnicheskikh Nauk [*A publication*] ....
Izv Sib Otd Akad Nauk SSSR Ser Tekh Nauk
Izvestiya Tadzikskogo Filiala Akademii Nauk [*A publication*] .... IzvTadzikAN
Izvestiya Tikhookeanskog Nauchno-Issledovatel'Skogo
Instituta Rybnogo Khozyaistva i Okeanografii [*A publication*]...............
Izv Tikhookean Nauchno-Issled Ist Rybn Khoz Okeanogr
Izvestiya Timiryazevskoi Sel'skokhozyaistvennoi Akademii [*A
publication*]............................ Izv Timiryazev Sel'-khoz Akad
Izvestiya Timiryazevskoi Sel'skokhozyaistvennoi Akademii [*A
publication*].............................Izv Timiryazev S-kh Akad
Izvestiya Tomskogo Politekhnicheskogo Instituta Imeni S. M.
Kirova [*A publication*]............................. Izv Tomsk Politekh Inst
Izvestiya Tomskogo Politekhnicheskogo Instituta Mekhanika i
Mashinostroenia [*A publication*]...............................
Izv Tomsk Politekh Inst Mekh Mashinostr
Izvestiya na Tsentralnata Khelmintologichna Laboratoriya
B'lgarska Akademiya na Naukite [*A publication*].....................
Izv Tsentr Khelmintol Lab B'lg Akad Nauk
Izvestiya Vengerskikh Sel'skokhozyaistvennykh Nauchno-
Issledovatel'skikh Institutow. A. Rastenievodstvo [*A
publication*]............................. Izv Veng S'kh Nauchno-Issled Inst A
Izvestiya Vengerskikh Sel'skokhozyaistvennykh Nauchno-
Issledovatel'skikh Institutow. C. Sadovodstvo [*A publication*].................
Izv Veng S kh Nauchno-Issled Inst C
Izvestiya na Vmei "Lenin" [*A publication*] .... Izv Vmei "Lenin"
Izvestiya Voronezskogo Gosudarstvennogo Pedagogiceskogo
Instituta [*A publication*].................................. IVGPI
Izvestiya Voronezskogo Gosudarstvennogo Pedagogiceskogo
Instituta [*A publication*]................................... IzvVorPI
Izvestiya Vsesoyuznogo Geograficheskogo Obshchestva [*A
publication*]............................ Izv Vses Geogr Obshch
Izvestiya Vsesoyuznogo Geograficheskogo Obshchestva [*A
publication*]............................Izv Vses Geogr O-va
Izvestiya Vysshikh Uchebnykh Zavedenii. Aviatsionnaya
Tekhnika [*A publication*] .... Izv VUZ Aviats Tekh
Izvestiya Vysshikh Uchebnykh Zavedenii. Chernaya
Metallurgiya [*A publication*]................................Izv VUZ Chernaya Metall
Izvestiya Vysshikh Uchebnykh Zavedenii. Chernaya
Metallurgiya [*A publication*]............Izv Vyssh Uchebn Zaved Chern Metall
Izvestiya Vysshikh Uchebnykh Zavedenii. Chernaya
Metallurgiya [*A publication*]............Izv Vyssh Ucheb Zaved Chern Met
Izvestiya Vysshikh Uchebnykh Zavedenii. Ehlektromekhanika
[*A publication*].............. Izv Vyssh Uchebn Zaved Ehlektromekh
Izvestiya Vysshikh Uchebnykh Zavedenii. Ehnergetika [*A
publication*]................................Izv Vyssh Uchebn Zaved Ehnerg
Izvestiya Vysshikh Uchebnykh Zavedenii. Elektromekhanika [*A
publication*]................................Izv VUZ Elektromekh
Izvestiya Vysshikh Uchebnykh Zavedenii. Elektromekhanika [*A
publication*]............... Izv Vyssh Ucheb Zaved Elektromekh
Izvestiya Vysshikh Uchebnykh Zavedenii. Energetika [*A
publication*]................................Izv VUZ Energ
Izvestiya Vysshikh Uchebnykh Zavedenii. Energetika [*A
publication*]................................Izv Vyssh Ucheb Zaved Energ
Izvestiya Vysshikh Uchebnykh Zavedenii. Fizika [*A publication*]...... IVUZ Fiz
Izvestiya Vysshikh Uchebnykh Zavedenii. Fizika [*A publication*]...................
Izv VUZ Fiz
Izvestiya Vysshikh Uchebnykh Zavedenii. Geologiya i Razvedka
[*A publication*]............... Izv Vyssh Uchebn Zaved Geol Razved
Izvestiya Vysshikh Uchebnykh Zavedenii. Gornyi Zhurnal [*A
publication*]................................Izv VUZ Gornyi Zh
Izvestiya Vysshikh Uchebnykh Zavedenii. Gornyi Zhurnal [*A
publication*]............... Izv Vyssh Ucheb Zaved Gorn Zh

Izvestiya Vysshikh Uchebnykh Zavedenii. Khimiya i Khimicheskaya Tekhnologiya [*A publication*] ....
Izv VUZ Khim i Khim Tekhnol

Izvestiya Vysshikh Uchebnykh Zavedenii. Khimiya i Khimicheskaya Tekhnologiya [*A publication*] ....
Izv Vyssh Uchebn Zaved Khim Khim Tekhnol

Izvestiya Vysshikh Uchebnykh Zavedenii. Khimiya i Khimicheskaya [*A publication*] .... Izv Vyssh Ucheb Zaved Khim i Khim

Izvestiya Vysshikh Uchebnykh Zavedenii. Lesnoi Zhurnal [*A publication*] ....Izv VUZ Lesnoi Zh

Izvestiya Vysshikh Uchebnykh Zavedenii. Lesnoi Zhurnal [*A publication*] ....Izv Vyssh Uchebn Zaved Lesn Zh

Izvestiya Vysshikh Uchebnykh Zavedenii. Mashinostroenie [*A publication*] .... Izv VUZ Mashinostr

Izvestiya Vysshikh Uchebnykh Zavedenii. Mashinostroenie [*A publication*] .... Izv Vyssh Uchebn Zaved Mashinostr

Izvestiya Vysshikh Uchebnykh Zavedenii. Matematika [*A publication*] .... Izv VUZ Mat

Izvestiya Vysshikh Uchebnykh Zavedenii. Neft' i Gaz [*A publication*] ....Izv Vyssh Uchebn Zaved Neft' Gaz

Izvestiya Vysshikh Uchebnykh Zavedenii. Neft' i Gaz [*A publication*] ....Izv Vyssh Ucheb Zaved Neft i Gaz

Izvestiya Vysshikh Uchebnykh Zavedenii. Pishchevaya Tekhnologiya [*A publication*] ....Izv VUZ Pishch Tekhnol

Izvestiya Vysshikh Uchebnykh Zavedenii. Pishchevaya Tekhnologiya [*A publication*] .....Izv Vyssh Uchebn Zaved Pishch Tekhnol

Izvestiya Vysshikh Uchebnykh Zavedenii. Priborostroenie [*A publication*] ....Izv VUZ Priborostr

Izvestiya Vysshikh Uchebnykh Zavedenii. Priborostroenie [*A publication*] .... Izv Vyssh Uchebn Zaved Priborostr

Izvestiya Vysshikh Uchebnykh Zavedenii. Radioelektronika [*A publication*] ....Izv VUZ Radioelektron

Izvestiya Vysshikh Uchebnykh Zavedenii. Radiofizika [*A publication*] .... Izv VUZ Radiofiz

Izvestiya Vysshikh Uchebnykh Zavedenii. Radiotekhnika [*A publication*] ....Izv Vyssh Uchebn Zaved Radiotekh

Izvestiya Vysshikh Uchebnykh Zavedenii. Tekhnologiya Legkoi Promyshlennosti [*A publication*] ....Izv VUZ Tekhnol Legkoi Prom-st

Izvestiya Vysshikh Uchebnykh Zavedenii. Tekhnologiya Tekstil'noi Promyshlennosti [*A publication*]..........................
Izv VUZ Tekhnol Tekstil Prom

Izvestiya Vysshikh Uchebnykh Zavedenii. Tsvetnaya Metallurgiya [*A publication*]......................................Izv VUZ Tsvetn Metall

Izvestiya Vysshikh Uchebnykh Zavedenii. Tsvetnaya Metallurgiya [*A publication*]..........Izv Vyssh Uchebn Zaved Tsvetn Metall

Izvestiya Vysshikh Uchebnykh Zavedenii. Tsvetnaya Metallurgiya [*A publication*]..................Izv Vyssh Ucheb Zaved Tsvet Met

Izvestiya Vysshikh Uchebnykh Zavedenij. Fizika [*A publication*]....................
Izv Vyssh Uchebn Zaved Fiz

Izvestiya Vysshikh Uchebnykh Zavedenij. Gornyj Zhurnal [*A publication*].. Izv Vyssh Uchebn Zaved Gorn Zh

Izvestiya Vysshikh Uchebnykh Zavedenij. Radiofizika [*A publication*].. Izv Vyssh Uchebn Zaved Radiofiz

J

Jackson, MS [*Radio station call letters*]..............................WRBC
Jackson, MS [*Radio station call letters*]..............................WSLI
Jackson, MS [*Radio station call letters*]..............................WTYX
Jackson, MS [*Radio station call letters*]..............................WVLS
Jackson, MS [*Radio station call letters*]..............................WWCJ
Jackson, MS [*Radio station call letters*]..............................WYYN
Jackson Municipal Library, Jackson, MS [*Library symbol*].........MsJ
Jackson National Life [*NASDAQ symbol*]...........................JNAL
Jackson News, Jackson, NJ [*Library symbol*]......................NjJacN
Jackson, OH [*Radio station call letters*]..............................WCJO
Jackson, OH [*Radio station call letters*]..............................WLMJ
Jackson Parish Library, Jonesboro, LA [*Library symbol*].........LJo
Jackson Public Library, Jackson, MI [*Library symbol*]...........MiJa
Jackson Public Library, Jackson, OH [*Library symbol*]..........OJ
Jackson State College [*Later, Jackson State University*] [*Mississippi*] .....JSC
Jackson State College [*Later, Jackson State University*],
   Jackson, MS [*Library symbol*]....................................MsJS
Jackson State University, Jackson, MS [*OCLC symbol*].........MJU
Jackson, TN [*Location identifier*] [*FAA*].............................MKL
Jackson, TN [*Television station call letters*]....................WBBJ-TV
Jackson, TN [*Radio station call letters*]..............................WDXI
Jackson, TN [*Radio station call letters*]..............................WJAK
Jackson, TN [*Radio station call letters*]..............................WJHR
Jackson, TN [*Radio station call letters*]..............................WKIR
Jackson, TN [*Radio station call letters*]..............................WTJS
Jackson, TN [*Television station call letters*]......................WUAA
Jackson Township Publishing Co., Jackson, NJ [*Library symbol*].......NjJacP
Jackson Turbidity Unit [*Water pollution*].............................JTU
Jackson-Washabaugh County Library, Kadoka, SD [*Library
   symbol*]...SdKJ
Jackson, WI [*Radio station call letters*]..............................WYLO
Jackson, WY [*Location identifier*] [*FAA*]............................JAC
Jackson, WY [*Radio station call letters*]............................KMTN
Jackson, WY [*Radio station call letters*]............................KSGT
Jacksonville [*Florida*] [*Seismograph station code, US Geological
   Survey*] [*Closed*]...JAC
Jacksonville [*Florida*] [*Airport symbol*]...........................JAX
Jacksonville [*North Carolina*] [*Airport symbol*]..................OAJ
Jacksonville, AL [*Radio station call letters*].................WLJS-FM
Jacksonville, AR [*Radio station call letters*].......................KEZQ
Jacksonville, AR [*Radio station call letters*].......................KIEL
Jacksonville College, Jacksonville, TX [*Library symbol*]........TxJaC
Jacksonville, FL [*Location identifier*] [*FAA*]........................CZH
Jacksonville, FL [*Location identifier*] [*FAA*]........................HEG
Jacksonville, FL [*Location identifier*] [*FAA*]........................NZC
Jacksonville, FL [*Radio station call letters*].......................WAIV
Jacksonville, FL [*Radio station call letters*]...................WAIV-FM
Jacksonville, FL [*Radio station call letters*]......................WAPE
Jacksonville, FL [*Television station call letters*]............WAWS-TV
Jacksonville, FL [*Radio station call letters*]......................WBIX
Jacksonville, FL [*Radio station call letters*].....................WCGL
Jacksonville, FL [*Radio station call letters*]......................WCRJ
Jacksonville, FL [*Radio station call letters*]..................WCRJ-FM
Jacksonville, FL [*Radio station call letters*].....................WERD
Jacksonville, FL [*Radio station call letters*]......................WEXI
Jacksonville, FL [*Radio station call letters*].....................WFAM
Jacksonville, FL [*Radio station call letters*]..................WIVY-FM
Jacksonville, FL [*Radio station call letters*].....................WJAX
Jacksonville, FL [*Radio station call letters*].................WJAX-FM
Jacksonville, FL [*Television station call letters*]................WJCT
Jacksonville, FL [*Radio station call letters*]..................WJCT-FM
Jacksonville, FL [*Television station call letters*].............WJKS-TV
Jacksonville, FL [*Television station call letters*]................WJXT
Jacksonville, FL [*Radio station call letters*]......................WKTZ
Jacksonville, FL [*Radio station call letters*]..................WKTZ-FM
Jacksonville, FL [*Television station call letters*]................WNFT
Jacksonville, FL [*Radio station call letters*].....................WOKV
Jacksonville, FL [*Radio station call letters*].....................WOZN
Jacksonville, FL [*Radio station call letters*]....................WPDQ
Jacksonville, FL [*Radio station call letters*].....................WQIK
Jacksonville, FL [*Radio station call letters*]..................WQIK-FM
Jacksonville, FL [*Radio station call letters*].....................WROS
Jacksonville, FL [*Television station call letters*]...............WTLV
Jacksonville, FL [*Television station call letters*]............WUNM-TV
Jacksonville, IL [*Radio station call letters*]......................WEAI
Jacksonville, IL [*Radio station call letters*].......................WJIL
Jacksonville, IL [*Television station call letters*]................WJPT
Jacksonville, IL [*Radio station call letters*].....................WLDS
Jacksonville Museum, Jacksonville, OR [*Library symbol*]......OrJM
Jacksonville, NC [*Location identifier*] [*FAA*].......................NTL
Jacksonville, NC [*Location identifier*] [*FAA*]......................OAJ
Jacksonville, NC [*Radio station call letters*]......................WIIZ
Jacksonville, NC [*Radio station call letters*].....................WJNC
Jacksonville, NC [*Radio station call letters*].....................WLAS
Jacksonville, NC [*Radio station call letters*]....................WRCM
Jacksonville, NC [*Radio station call letters*]....................WXQR
Jacksonville Public Library System, Jacksonville, FL [*Library symbol*]......FJ
Jacksonville Public Library System, Jacksonville, FL [*OCLC symbol*] .... JPL
Jacksonville State University, Jacksonville, AL [*Library symbol*].....AJacT
Jacksonville State University, Jacksonville, AL [*OCLC symbol*] ....AJB
Jacksonville Terminal Company [*AAR code*].....................JTCO

Jacksonville, TX [*Location identifier*] [*FAA*].......................JSO
Jacksonville, TX [*Radio station call letters*].......................KEBE
Jacksonville, TX [*Radio station call letters*].......................KOOI
Jacksonville University, Jacksonville, FL [*Library symbol*] [*OCLC
   symbol*]..FJU
Jaclyn, Inc. [*American Stock Exchange symbol*]..................JLN
Jaco Electronics, Inc. [*NASDAQ symbol*]........................JACO
Jacob More Society...JMS
Jacob S. Mauney Memorial Library, Kings Mountain, NC [*Library
   symbol*]..NcKm
Jacob Simpson Payton Library, Alexandria, VA [*Library symbol*].........ViAIP
Jacobean Drama Studies [*A publication*]..........................JDS
Jacobi Elliptic Function [*Mathematics*]............................JEF
Jacobi Matrix Method [*Mathematics*]..............................JMM
Jacobi Polynomial [*Mathematics*]...................................JP
Jacobina [*Brazil*] [*Airport symbol*]................................JCM
Jacobs Engineering Group, Inc. [*American Stock Exchange symbol*] ......JEC
Jacobs Library, Clinton, SC [*Library symbol*] [*Obsolete*] ....ScCliJ
Jacobson Stores [*NASDAQ symbol*]...............................JCBS
Jacobus Rex [*King James*]..JR
Jacoby, Fragmente der Griechischen Historiker [*A publication*]........FGrHist
Jacor Communications [*NASDAQ symbol*].....................JCOR
Jacques-Yves Cousteau [*French marine explorer*] [*Initialism
   pronounced "Jheek" when used as nickname*].............JYC
Jacquinot Bay [*Papua New Guinea*] [*Airport symbol*]........... JAQ
Jadavpur Journal of Comparative Literature [*A publication*].....
                    Jadav J Comp Lit
Jadavpur Journal of Comparative Literature [*A publication*]....JJCL
Jaderna Energie [*A publication*] ....Jad Energ
Jadernaja Fizika [*A publication*] ....Jadernaja Fiz
Jaegdtiger [*Tank-destroyer*] [*German military - World War II*]...............JAEG
Jaeger Machine Co. [*NYSE symbol*]................................JAE
Jaeger Test Type One [*Ophthalmology*]..........................J-1
Jaffrey, NH [*Location identifier*] [*FAA*]............................AFN
JAG [*Judge Advocate General, US Air Force*] Bulletin [*A publication*] ..... JAG
JAG [*Judge Advocate General, US Navy*] Journal [*A publication*] ....JAG J
Jagdgeschwader [*Fighter wing*] [*German military - World War II*] ....JG
Jagdverband [*German aircraft fighter unit*] [*World War II*]................JV
Jaguar Clubs of North America.....................................JCNA
Jahr [*Year*] [*German*]...J
Jahrbuch [*Yearbook*] [*German*]..JB
Jahrbuch fuer Aesthetik und Allgemeine Kunstwissenschaft [*A
   publication*]...JAAK
Jahrbuch fuer Aesthetik und Allgemeine Kunstwissenschaft [*A
   publication*]..JAe
Jahrbuch fuer Aesthetik und Allgemeine Kunstwissenschaft [*A
   publication*]...JfAaK
Jahrbuch. Akademie der Wissenschaften in Goettingen [*A
   publication*]..JbAWG
Jahrbuch. Akademie der Wissenschaften und der Literatur
   [*Mainz*] [*A publication*]...JbAWL
Jahrbuch. Akademie der Wissenschaften und der Literatur
   (Mainz) [*A publication*].......................Jahrb Akad Wiss Lit (Mainz)
Jahrbuch. Albertus Universitaet zu Koenigsberg [*A publication*] ....JAUK
Jahrbuch fuer Amerikastudien [*A publication*]......................JA
Jahrbuch fuer Amerikastudien [*A publication*].................JahAs
Jahrbuch fuer Amerikastudien [*A publication*].......Jahrb Amerikastud
Jahrbuch fuer Amerikastudien [*A publication*]....................JAS
Jahrbuch fuer Amerikastudien [*A publication*].................Jb AS
Jahrbuch fuer Antike und Christentum [*A publication*]..........JAC
Jahrbuch fuer Antike und Christentum [*A publication*]..........JACh
Jahrbuch fuer Antike und Christentum [*A publication*]..........JbAC
Jahrbuch fuer Antike und Christentum [*A publication*].........JbAChr
Jahrbuch der Arbeitsgemeinschaft fuer Futterungsberatung [*A
   publication*]..................Jahrb Arbeitsgemein Futterungsberat
Jahrbuch der Arbeitsgemeinschaft der Rheinischen
   Geschichtsvereine [*A publication*]..............................JARGV
Jahrbuch der Barlach-Gesellschaft [*A publication*] ....JBG
Jahrbuch. Bayerischen Akademie der Wissenschaften [*A
   publication*]...................................Jahrb Bayer Akad Wiss
Jahrbuch. Bayerischen Akademie der Wissenschaften [*A
   publication*]...JBAW
Jahrbuch. Bayerischen Akademie der Wissenschaften [*A
   publication*]...JbBAW
Jahrbuch fuer Bergbau Energie Mineraloel und Chemie [*A
   publication*]....................Jahrb Bergbau Energ Mineraloel Chem
Jahrbuch. Berliner Museen [*A publication*].............Jahr Berliner Mus
Jahrbuch. Berliner Museen [*A publication*]..................J Berl M
Jahrbuch. Berliner Museen [*A publication*]......................JBM
Jahrbuch. Bernischen Historischen Museums [*A publication*].......................
                    JB Bern Hist Mus
Jahrbuch. Bernischen Historischen Museums [*A publication*]...............JBM
Jahrbuch fuer das Bistum (Mainz) [*A publication*]..............JBM
Jahrbuch fuer Brandenburgische Kirchengeschichte [*A
   publication*]..JBKG
Jahrbuch der Coburger Landesstiftung [*A publication*] ....
                  Jb Coburg Landesst
Jahrbuch der Dante Gesellschaft [*A publication*].................JbDG
Jahrbuch. Deutsche Akademie der
   Landwirtschaftwissenschaften zu Berlin [*A publication*]........
          Jahrb Deut Akad Landwirt Wiss Berlin

Jahrbuch. Deutschen Akademie fuer Sprache und Dichtung in Darmstadt [*A publication*].....................JDASD

Jahrbuch. Deutschen Akademie der Wissenschaften zu Berlin [*A publication*].....................JbDAW

Jahrbuch. Deutschen Archaeologischen Instituts [*A publication*]................. Jahr Deutsch Archaeol Inst

Jahrbuch. Deutschen Archaeologischen Instituts [*A publication*]..........JDAI

Jahrbuch. Deutschen Archaeologischen Instituts [*A publication*]..........JdI

Jahrbuch. Deutschen Archaeologischen Instituts. Ergaenzungsheft [*A publication*]..........JDI-EH

Jahrbuch. Deutschen Gesellschaft fuer Chronometrie [*A publication*].....................Jahrb Dtsch Ges Chronom

Jahrbuch der Deutschen Schiller-Gesellschaft [*A publication*] ....JDSG

Jahrbuch der Deutschen Shakespeare-Gesellschaft [*A publication*] ....JDSh

Jahrbuch der Deutschen Shakespeare-Gesellschaft Ost [*A publication*].....................SJO

Jahrbuch. Diplomatischen Akademie (Wien) [*A publication*] ....Jb Diplom Akad (Wien)

Jahrbuch der Droste-Gesellschaft [*A publication*].................... JDG

Jahrbuch des Evangelischen Vereins fuer Westfaelische Kirchengeschichte [*A publication*].....................JEVWK

Jahrbuch fuer Frankische Landesforschung [*A publication*].................JbFL

Jahrbuch fuer Frankische Landesforschung [*A publication*].................JFL

Jahrbuch fuer Frankische Landesforschung [*A publication*].................JFLF

Jahrbuch des Freien Deutschen Hochstifts [*A publication*].................JFDH

Jahrbuch fuer Friedens- und Konfliktforschung [*A publication*].....................Jb Friedens- u Konfliktforsch

Jahrbuch der Geologischen Bundesanstalt [*A publication*] ....Jahrb Geol Bundesanst

Jahrbuch der Geologischen Bundesanstalt. Sonderband [*A publication*].....................Jahrb Geol Bundesanst Sonderb

Jahrbuch fuer die Geschichte Mittel- und Ostdeutschlands [*A publication*] ....JGMOD

Jahrbuch der Gesellschaft fuer die Geschichte des Protestantismus in Oesterreich [*A publication*] ....JGGPO

Jahrbuch der Gesellschaft fuer die Geschichte des Protestantismus in Oesterreich [*A publication*] ....JGGPOes

Jahrbuch der Gesellschaft fuer Lothringische Geschichte und Altertumskunde [*A publication*].....................JGLGA

Jahrbuch der Gesellschaft fuer Lothringische Geschichte und Altertumskunde [*A publication*] ....JGLGAK

Jahrbuch der Gesellschaft fuer Niedersaechsische Kirchengeschichte [*A publication*].....................JGNSKG

Jahrbuch der Gesellschaft fuer Wiener Theater-Forschung [*A publication*] ....JGWT

Jahrbuch der Goethe-Gesellschaft [*A publication*] .... JGG

Jahrbuch der Grillparzer-Gesellschaft [*A publication*] ....JGG

Jahrbuch der Grillparzer-Gesellschaft [*A publication*] ....JGrG

Jahrbuch der Hamburger Kunstsammlungen [*A publication*].....................Jahrbuch Hamburger Kunstsam

Jahrbuch der Hamburger Kunstsammlungen [*A publication*].....................Jahr Hamburger Kunstsam

Jahrbuch der Heidelberger Akademie der Wissenschaften [*A publication*] ....JHAW

Jahrbuch des Historischen Verein Dillingen [*A publication*] .... JHVD

Jahrbuch des Historischen Vereins fuer das Fuerstbistum Bamberg [*A publication*].....................JHVFB

Jahrbuch fuer Internationale Germanistik [*A publication*].....................JIG

Jahrbuch fuer Internationales Recht [*A publication*].....................Jb Int Recht

Jahrbuch der Jean-Paul-Gesellschaft [*A publication*].....................JJPG

Jahrbuch der K. K. Heraldischen Gesellschaft, "Adler" [*A publication*].....................JHGA

Jahrbuch. Karl-May-Gesellschaft [*A publication*].....................JKMG

Jahrbuch fuer Kinderheilkunde und Physische Erziehung [*A publication*].....................Jahrb Kinderh

Jahrbuch fuer Kleinasiatische Forschung [*A publication*].....................JbKAF

Jahrbuch fuer Kleinasiatische Forschung [*A publication*].....................JKF

Jahrbuch fuer Kleinasiatische Forschung. Internationale Orientalistische Zeitschrift [*A publication*].....................JKAF

Jahrbuch der Kleist-Gesellschaft [*A publication*].....................JKG

Jahrbuch des Koelnischen Geschichtsvereins [*A publication*] ....JKGV

Jahrbuch der Kunsthistorischen Sammlungen [*A publication*]................JKS

Jahrbuch der Kunsthistorischen Sammlungen des Allerhochsten Kaiserhauses [*A publication*].....................Jahrb Kunsth Samml Kaiserh

Jahrbuch der Kunsthistorischen Sammlungen (Wien) [*A publication*].....................Jahr Kunsthist Sam Wien

Jahrbuch der Kunsthistorischen Sammlungen (Wien) [*A publication*].....................Jb Kunsthist Samml Wien

Jahrbuch der Kunsthistorischen Sammlungen (Wien) [*A publication*].....................JKSW

Jahrbuch fuer Kunstwissenschaft [*A publication*].....................JKW

Jahrbuch fuer Landeskunde von Niederdonau [*A publication*].....................Jahrbuch Niederdonau

Jahrbuch fuer Landeskunde von Niederoesterreich [*A publication*].....JbNo

Jahrbuch fuer Landeskunde von Niederoesterreich [*A publication*].....................JLKNO

Jahrbuch fuer Liturgiewissenschaft [*A publication*] ....JLW

Jahrbuch fuer Liturgik und Hymnologie [*A publication*] ....Jahrb Liturg & Hymnol

Jahrbuch fuer Liturgik und Hymnologie [*A publication*] ....JLH

Jahrbuch: Marburger Universitaetsbund [*A publication*].....................JbMu

Jahrbuch des Museums fuer Voilkerkunde zu Leipzig [*A publication*].....................JMVL

Jahrbuch fuer Musikalische Volks- und Voelkerkunde [*A publication*].....................Jb Musik Volks-u Voelkerk

Jahrbuch der Musikwelt [*A publication*].....................JDM

Jahrbuch fuer Niederdeutsche Sprachforschung [*A publication*].....................Jb f Niederdeut Spr

Jahrbuch fuer Niederdeutsche Sprachforschung [*A publication*].....................Jb f Niederdt Spr

Jahrbuch des Nordfriesischen Instituts [*A publication*].....................JNI

Jahrbuch fuer Numismatik und Geldgeschichte [*A publication*]............ JfNG

Jahrbuch fuer Numismatik und Geldgeschichte [*A publication*]............ JNG

Jahrbuch fuer Numismatik und Geldgeschichte [*A publication*]............ JNGG

Jahrbuch des Oberoesterreichischen Musealvereins [*A publication*].....................JOMV

Jahrbuch des Oeffentlichen Rechts der Gegenwart [*A publication*].....................Jb Oeff Rechts

Jahrbuch der Oesterreichischen Byzantinischen Gesellschaft [*A publication*].....................JOBG

Jahrbuch der Oesterreichischen Byzantinistik [*A publication*]..........JOEByz

Jahrbuch des Oesterreichischen Volksliedwerkes [*A publication*]..........JOV

Jahrbuch fuer das Oldenburger Muensterland [*A publication*].....................Jb Oldenburger Muensterland

Jahrbuch fuer Optik und Feinmechanik [*A publication*].....................Jahrb Opt Feinmech

Jahrbuch fuer Ostdeutsche Volkskunde [*A publication*].....................JOV

Jahrbuch fuer Ostrecht [*A publication*].....................Jb Ostrecht

Jahrbuch fuer Philologie [*A publication*].....................JP

Jahrbuch fuer Philosophie und Spekulative Theologie [*A publication*].....................JPST

Jahrbuch fuer Philosophie und Spekulative Theologie [*A publication*].....................JPT

Jahrbuch der Philosophischen Fakultaet der Universitaet zu Goettingen [*A publication*].....................JFG

Jahrbuch der Preussischen Kunstsammlungen [*A publication*].....................Jahrb Preuss Kunstsamml

Jahrbuch der Preussischen Kunstsammlungen [*A publication*] ....JPKS

Jahrbuch fuer Psychologie. Psychotherapie und Medizinische Anthropologie [*A publication*].....................JPPMB

Jahrbuch der Raabe-Gesellschaft [*A publication*].....................JRG

Jahrbuch der Rheinischen Denkmalpflege [*A publication*].....................JRD

Jahrbuch der Rheinischen Denkmalpflege [*A publication*] ....JRDP

Jahrbuch des Roemisch-Germanischen Zentralmuseums [*Mainz*] [*A publication*].....................JRGZ

Jahrbuch des Roemisch-Germanischen Zentralmuseums (Mainz) [*A publication*].....................JRGZMainz

Jahrbuch. Saechsische Akademie der Wissenschaften zu Leipzig [*A publication*].....................JbSAW

Jahrbuch der Sammlung Kippenberg Duesseldorf [*A publication*].........JSK

Jahrbuch der Schiffbautechnischen Gesselschaft [*A publication*].....................Jahrb Schiffbautech Ges

Jahrbuch der Schiller-Gesellschaft [*A publication*].....................JSG

Jahrbuch der Schlesischen Friedrich-Wilhelm Universitaet zu Breslau [*A publication*].....................JSFWUB

Jahrbuch der Schlesischen Friedrich-Wilhelm Universitaet zu Breslau [*A publication*].....................JSUB

Jahrbuch der Schweizerischen Gesellschaft fuer Ur- und Fruehgeschichte [*A publication*] ....Jb Schweiz Ges Ur Fruehgesch

Jahrbuch der Schweizerischen Gesellschaft fuer Urgeschichte [*A publication*].....................JSGU

Jahrbuch der Shakespeare Gesellschaft [*A publication*].....................JbShG

Jahrbuch fuer Sozialwissenschaft [*A publication*] ....Jahrb Sozia

Jahrbuch fuer Sozialwissenschaft [*A publication*] ....Jb Soz -Wiss

Jahrbuch der Staatlichen Kunstsammlungen Dresden [*A publication*].....................Jb St Kunstsamml Dresden

Jahrbuch. Technische Universitaet Muenchen [*A publication*].....................Jahrb Tech Univ Muenchen

Jahrbuch. Ungarischen Archaeologischen Gesellschaft [*A publication*].....................JUAG

Jahrbuch. Universitaet Duesseldorf [*A publication*].....................JUD

Jahrbuch des Vereins von Altertumsfreunden im Rheinlande [*A publication*].....................JVA

Jahrbuch des Vereins von Altertumsfreunden im Rheinlande [*A publication*].....................JVARh

Jahrbuch des Vereins fuer Landeskunde und Heimatpflege im Gau Oberdonau [*A publication*].....................JVLHOD

Jahrbuch des Vereins fuer Niederdeutsche Sprachforschung [*A publication*].....................JVNS

Jahrbuch des Vereins Schweizerischer Gymnasial-Lehrer [*A publication*].....................JVSch

Jahrbuch des Vereins fuer Westfaelische Kirchengeschichte [*A publication*].....................JVWK

Jahrbuch fuer Volkskunde der Heimatvertriebenen [*A publication*]......JbVH

Jahrbuch fuer Volkskunde der Heimatvertriebenen [*A publication*].......JVH

Jahrbuch fuer Volkskunde und Kulturgeschichte [*A publication*] ....Jb Volksk Kulturgesch

Jahrbuch fuer Volksliedforschung [*A publication*].....................JVF

Jahrbuch fuer Volksliedforschung [*A publication*].....................JY

Jahrbuch des Wiener Goethe-Vereins [*A publication*].....................JWGV

Jahrbuch der Wirtschaft Osteuropas [*A publication*] ... Jb Wirtsch Osteuropas
Jahrbuch fuer Wirtschaftsgeschichte [*A publication*] ... Jb Wirtsch -Gesch
Jahrbuch fuer Wirtschaftsgeschichte [*A publication*] ... JWG
Jahrbuch. Wissenschaftlichen Forschungsinstituts fuer Buntmetallurgie. Plovdiv [*A publication*] ... Jahrb Wiss Forschungsinst Buntmetall Plovdiv
Jahrbuch der Wittheit zu Bremen [*A publication*] ... JWB
Jahrbuecher fuer Geschichte Osteuropas [*A publication*] ... Jahrb Gesch Osteur
Jahrbuecher fuer Geschichte Osteuropas [*A publication*] ... Jahrb Gesch Osteurop
Jahrbuecher fuer Geschichte Osteuropas [*A publication*] ... JGO
Jahrbuecher fuer Geschichte Osteuropas [*A publication*] ... JGOE
Jahrbuecher fuer Kultur und Geschichte der Slaven [*A publication*] ... JKGS
Jahrbuecher fuer National-Oekonomie und Statistik [*A publication*] ... Jahrb N St
Jahrbuecher fuer National-Oekonomie und Statistik [*A publication*] ... Jb-r Nat-Oekon Statist
Jahresbericht des Bischoeflichen Gymnasiums und Dioezesanseminars am Kollegium Petrinum in Urfar [*A publication*] ... Jb Bischof Gymnas Kolleg Petrinum
Jahresbericht der Deutschen Mathematiker-Vereinigung [*A publication*] ... Jber Deutsch Math-Verein
Jahresbericht. Deutsches Hydrographisches Institut (Hamburg) [*A publication*] ... Jahresber Dtsch Hydrogr Inst (Hamburg)
Jahresbericht ueber die Fortschritte der Klassischen Altertumswissenschaft [*A publication*] ... JFA
Jahresbericht fuer Geschichtswissenschaft [*A publication*] ... JGW
Jahresbericht der Historisch-Antiquarischen Gesellschaft von Grabunden [*A publication*] ... Jahresbericht Grabunden
Jahresbericht des Historischen. Vereins fuer Mittelfranken [*A publication*] ... JBHVMF
Jahresbericht. Institut fuer Strahlen- und Kernphysik der Universitaet Bonn [*A publication*] ... Jahresber Inst Strahlenphys Kernphys Univ Bonn
Jahresbericht des Kurashiki-Zentralhospitals [*A publication*] ... Jahresber Kurashiki-Zentralhosp
Jahresbericht des Philologischen Vereins [*A publication*] ... JPhV
Jahresbericht. Schweizerische Gesellschaft fuer Vererbungsforschung [*A publication*] ... Jahresber Schweiz Ges Vererbungsforsch
Jahresbericht Veterinaer-Medizin [*A publication*] ... Jahresb Vet Med
Jahresberichte der Berliner Literatur Gesellschaft [*A publication*] ... JBLG
Jahresberichte des Deutschen Pflanzenschutzdienstes [*A publication*] ... Jahresber Dtsch Pflanzenschutzdienstes
Jahresberichte ueber die Erscheinungem auf dem Gebiete der Germanischen Literaturgeschichte [*A publication*] ... Jb u Ersch Ger Lit
Jahresberichte ueber die Fortschritte der Klassischen Altertumswissenschaft [*A publication*] ... JAW
Jahresberichte ueber die Fortschritte der Klassischen Altertumswissenschaft [*A publication*] ... JFKAW
Jahresberichte ueber das Hoehre Schulwesen [*A publication*] ... JHSch
Jahresberichte des Literarischen Zentralblattes [*A publication*] ... JLZ
Jahresberichte der Schlesischen Gesellschaft fuer Vaterlaendische Kultur [*A publication*] ... Jahresb Schles Gesellsch Vaterl Kult
Jahresheft des Vereins fuer Vaterlaendische Naturkunde in Wuerttemberg [*A publication*] ... J Ver Vaterl Naturk Wuertt
Jahreshefte der Gesellschaft fuer Naturkunde in Wuerttemberg [*A publication*] ... Jahresh Ges Naturkd Wuerttemb
Jahreshefte des Oesterreichischen Archaeologischen Instituts [*A publication*] ... OeJh
Jahreshefte des Oesterreichischen Archaeologischen Instituts. Beiblatt [*A publication*] ... Oe Jh Beibl
Jahreshefte des Oesterreichischen Archaeologischen Instituts in Wien [*A publication*] ... JhOAI
Jahreshefte des Oesterreichischen Archaeologischen Instituts in Wien [*A publication*] ... JOEAI
Jahresschrift fuer Mitteldeutsche Vorgeschichte [*A publication*] ... JMV
Jahresschrift fuer Mitteldeutsche Vorgeschichte [*A publication*] ... Jschr Mitteldtsch Vorgesch
Jahresverzeichnis der Deutschen Hochschulschriften [*A bibliographic publication*] [*Germany*] ... JVDHS
JAI Press [*Division of Johnson Associates, Inc.*] ... JAI
Jail Accounting Microcomputer System ... JAM
Jail Release Information ... JRI
Jaipur [*India*] [*Airport symbol*] ... JAI
Jaipur [*India*] [*Geomagnetic observatory code*] ... JAI
Jakarta [*Indonesia*] [*Airport symbol*] ... HLP
Jakarta [*Indonesia*] [*Airport symbol*] ... JKT
Jal Public Library, Jal, NM [*Library symbol*] ... NmJ
Jalkeen Puolenpaiuan [*Afternoon*] [*Finnish*] ... JPP
Jaluit [*Marshall Islands*] [*Airport symbol*] ... UIT
Jam Angle Tracking ... JAT
Jam Exceeds Threshold ... JET
Jam Frequency Hopper ... JFH
Jam, Jute, and Journalism [*3 major industries of Dundee, Scotland*] ... 3J's
Jam Resistant ... JR
Jam-Resistant Antenna ... JRA
Jam-Resistant Secure Communications ... JRSC
Jam-Resistant Secure Voice Communications ... JRSVC
Jam to Signal Ratio ... JSR
Jam Strobe ... JS
Jam Strobe Extractor ... JSE
Jam on Target ... JOT
Jamaica ... JA
Jamaica [*Three-letter standard code*] ... JAM
Jamaica [*MARC country of publication code*] [*Library of Congress*] ... jm
Jamaica [*MARC geographic area code*] [*Library of Congress*] ... nwjm
Jamaica [*Aircraft nationality and registration mark*] ... 6Y
Jamaica [*Two-letter standard code*] ... JM
Jamaica Agricultural Society. Journal [*A publication*] ... Jamaica Ag Soc J
Jamaica Association of Villas and Apartments [*Later, JRC*] ... JAVA
Jamaica Broadcasting Corporation ... JBC
Jamaica (BWI) Study Group ... JSG
Jamaica Geological Survey Department. Annual Report [*A publication*] ... Jamaica Geol Survey Dept Ann Rept
Jamaica Geological Survey Department. Bulletin [*A publication*] ... Jamaica Geol Survey Dept Bull
Jamaica Geological Survey Department. Occasional Paper [*A publication*] ... Jamaica Geol Survey Dept Occ Pap
Jamaica Geological Survey Department. Publication [*A publication*] ... Jamaica Geol Survey Pub
Jamaica Geological Survey Department. Short Paper [*A publication*] ... Jamaica Geol Survey Dept Short Pap
Jamaica Handbook [*A publication*] ... Jamaica Handb
Jamaica Labour Party ... JLP
Jamaica Library Service, Kingston, Jamaica [*Library symbol*] ... JamKLS
Jamaica Mines and Geology Division. Special Publication [*A publication*] ... Jam Mines Geol Div Spec Publ
Jamaica Ministry of Agriculture and Fisheries. Bulletin [*A publication*] ... Jam Minist Agric Fish Bull
Jamaica Ministry of Agriculture and Lands. Annual Report [*A publication*] ... Jam Minist Agric Lands Annu Rep
Jamaica Ministry of Agriculture and Lands. Bulletin [*A publication*] ... Jam Minist Agric Lands Bull
Jamaica Water Properties [*NASDAQ symbol*] ... JWAT
Jamair, Inc. [*Camden, AR*] [*FAA designator*] ... JMR
Jambi [*Indonesia*] [*Airport symbol*] ... DJB
James [*New Testament book*] ... Jas
James A. Ryder Transportation [*Acronym is trade name of truck-rental firm*] ... JARTRAN
James Arthur Lecture on the Evolution of the Human Brain [*A publication*] ... James Arthur Lect Evol Hum Brain
James B. Lansing Sound, Inc. ... JBL
James Branch Cabell Society ... JBCS
James Carson Breckinridge Library, Quantico, VA [*OCLC symbol*] ... QMC
James [*Fred S.*] **& Co., Inc.** [*NYSE symbol*] [*Delisted*] ... JMS
James Cook University of North Queensland, Townsville, QLD, Australia [*Library symbol*] ... AuTJC
James E. Wickson Memorial Library, Frankenmuth, MI [*Library symbol*] ... MiFram
James F. MacLaren Ltd., Willowdale, Toronto, ON, Canada [*Library symbol*] ... CaOTJFM
James Forrestal Research Center [*Princeton University*] ... JFRC
James Griffiths & Sons [*AAR code*] ... JGS
James J. Hill Reference Library, St. Paul, MN [*OCLC symbol*] ... MNR
James J. Hill Reference Library, St. Paul, MN [*Library symbol*] ... MnSJ
James Joyce Quarterly [*A publication*] ... James Joyce Q
James Joyce Quarterly [*A publication*] ... JJQ
James Joyce Review [*A publication*] ... JJR
James Joyce Society ... JJS
James Logan Morgan, Jr., Newport, AR [*Library symbol*] ... ArNeJM
James M. Peed [*Designer's mark when appearing on US coins*] ... JP
James Madison High School Library, Rochester, NY [*OCLC symbol*] ... RWP
James Madison Journal [*A publication*] ... James Madison J
James Madison University [*Virginia*] ... JMU
James Madison University, Harrisonburg, VA [*Library symbol*] ... ViHarT
James Madison University, Harrisonburg, VA [*OCLC symbol*] ... VMC
James McNeill Whistler [*Nineteenth-century American painter and etcher*] ... JMW
James Memorial Library, Williston, ND [*Library symbol*] ... NdWi
James Millikin University, Decatur, IL [*Library symbol*] ... IDecJ
James Monroe High School Library, Rochester, NY [*OCLC symbol*] ... RWQ
James Monroe Memorial Foundation ... JMMF
James Monroe Memorial Foundation, Fredericksburg, VA [*Library symbol*] ... ViFreJM
James Prendergast Free Library, Jamestown, NY [*Library symbol*] ... NJam
James River Corp. [*NYSE symbol*] ... JR
James Roosevelt Library, Hyde Park, NY [*Library symbol*] [*Obsolete*] ... NHpJR
James Sperry High School Library, Henrietta, NY [*OCLC symbol*] ... RWR
James Sprunt Historical Publications [*A publication*] ... James Sprunt Hist Publ
James Sprunt Technical Institute, Kenansville, NC [*Library symbol*] ... NcKeS
James Taylor [*Singer*] ... JT
James V. Brown Library of Williamsport and Lycoming County, Williamsport, PA [*OCLC symbol*] ... JVB
James V. Brown Library of Williamsport and Lycoming County, Williamsport, PA [*Library symbol*] ... PWmP

James Whitcomb Riley Home, Indianapolis, IN [*Library symbol*] .... InIR
James Willard Schultz Society .... JWSS
Jamesbury Corp. [*NASDAQ symbol*] .... JAME
Jamestown [*California*] [*Seismograph station code, US Geological Survey*] .... JAS
Jamestown [*New York*] [*Airport symbol*] .... JHW
Jamestown [*North Dakota*] [*Airport symbol*] .... JMS
Jamestown Area Furniture Haulers Association, Inc., Buffalo NY [*STAC*] .... JAF
Jamestown College, Jamestown, ND [*OCLC symbol*] .... NDJ
Jamestown College, Jamestown, ND [*Library symbol*] .... NdJC
Jamestown Community College [*New York*] .... JCC
Jamestown Community College, Jamestown, NY [*Library symbol*] .... NJamCC
Jamestown, KY [*Radio station call letters*] .... WJKY
Jamestown, KY [*Radio station call letters*] .... WJRS
Jamestown, ND [*Location identifier*] [*FAA*] .... JMS
Jamestown, ND [*Radio station call letters*] .... KQDJ
Jamestown, ND [*Radio station call letters*] .... KQDJ-FM
Jamestown, ND [*Radio station call letters*] .... KSJB
Jamestown, ND [*Radio station call letters*] .... KSJM
Jamestown, NY [*Location identifier*] [*FAA*] .... JHW
Jamestown, NY [*Radio station call letters*] .... WHUG
Jamestown, NY [*Radio station call letters*] .... WJTN
Jamestown, NY [*Radio station call letters*] .... WJWK
Jamestown, NY [*Radio station call letters*] .... WKSN
Jamestown, NY [*Radio station call letters*] .... WWSE
Jamestown Paint & Varnish Company .... JAPCO
Jamestown, TN [*Radio station call letters*] .... WCLC
Jamestown, TN [*Radio station call letters*] .... WDEB-FM
Jamestown Township Library, Jamestown, MI [*Library symbol*] .... MiJam
Jamestown-Williamsburg-Yorktown Celebration Committee .... JWYCC
Jamestowne Society .... JS
Jamesville, VA [*Radio station call letters*] .... WEXM
Jamesway Corp. [*NYSE symbol*] .... JMY
Jami'at Al Islan [*Defunct*] .... JAI
Jamin Effect [*Electronics*] .... JE
Jammer System Analysis .... JSA
Jammer System Analysis Simulator .... JSAS
Jammers Tracked by Azimuth Crossings [*RADAR*] .... JAMTRAC
Jamming [*Military*] .... JAM
Jamming .... JAMG
Jamming Amplitude Versus Azimuth .... JAVA
Jamming Avoidance Response .... JAR
Jamming Control Authority .... JCA
Jamming Equipment .... JE
Jamming Exercise [*Military*] .... JAMEX
Jamming Modulation Analysis .... JMA
Jamming Package [*Air Force*] .... JAMPAC
Jamming Package [*Air Force*] .... JAMPACK
Jamming RADAR Coverage Indicator .... JRCI
Jamming to Signal .... J/S
Jamming Tactics Evaluation .... JTE
Jamming and Warning System .... JAWS
Jammu [*India*] [*Airport symbol*] .... IXJ
Jammu and Kashmir University Review [*A publication*] .... JKUR
Jamnagar [*India*] [*Airport symbol*] .... JGA
Jamshedpur Mazdoor Union [*India*] .... JMU
Jan Mayen [*Jan Mayen Island*] [*Seismograph station code, US Geological Survey*] .... JMI
Jan Mayen [*MARC country of publication code*] [*Library of Congress*] .... jn
Jan Mayen [*MARC geographic area code*] [*Library of Congress*] .... lnjn---
Janak-Botkin-Wallis [*Data processing program regarding forest growth; named for three men involved in program*] .... JABOWA
Janakpur [*Nepal*] [*Airport symbol*] .... JKR
Janatha Vimukthi Peramuna [*People's Liberation Front*] [*Sri Lanka*] .... JVP
Jane Addams Peace Association .... JAPA
Jane Austen Society of North America .... JASNA
Janesbury Valve [*Aerospace*] .... JV
Janesville Public Library, Janesville, WI [*Library symbol*] .... WJa
Janesville, WI [*Radio station call letters*] .... WCLO
Janesville, WI [*Radio station call letters*] .... WJVL
Janina [*Greece*] [*Seismograph station code, US Geological Survey*] .... JAN
Janitor Closet .... JC
Janlen Enterprises, West Allis, WI [*Library symbol*] .... WWeaJ
Janney Cylinder Company .... JCC
Janssen [*Belgium*] [*Research code symbol*] .... R
Jantzen, Inc. [*NYSE symbol*] [*Delisted*] .... JAN
Janua Linguarum [*A publication*] .... JanL
January .... J
January .... JA
January .... JAN
January Assumption Budget [*Budget based on economic forecasts available as of January*] .... JAB
Janus. Archives Internationales pour l'Histoire de la Medecine [*A publication*] .... Jan
Janus Information Facility .... JIF
Janvier [*January*] [*French*] .... JANV
Japan [*MARC geographic area code*] [*Library of Congress*] .... a-ja---
Japan .... J
Japan .... JA
Japan .... JAP
Japan [*Two-letter standard code*] .... JP
Japan [*Three-letter standard code*] .... JPN
Japan [*Aircraft nationality and registration mark*] .... JA
Japan [*ry (Ryukyu Islands, Southern) used in records cataloged before January 1978*] [*MARC country of publication code*] [*Library of Congress*] .... ja
Japan Academy. Proceedings [*A publication*] .... Jap Acad Proc
Japan Air Defense Force .... JADF
Japan Air Lines .... JAL
Japan Air Lines [*ICAO designator*] .... JL
Japan Air Lines ADR [*NASDAQ symbol*] .... JAPNY
Japan-America Institute .... JAI
Japan-America Society of Southern California .... JASSC
Japan-America Society of Washington .... JASW
Japan-American Student Conference .... JASC
Japan Animal Welfare Society [*London, England*] .... JAWS
Japan Annual of Law and Politics [*A publication*] .... Ja Ann Law Pol
Japan Annual of Law and Politics [*A publication*] .... JALP
Japan Architect [*A publication*] .... JA
Japan Architect [*A publication*] .... Japan Arch
Japan Area .... JAPA
Japan Asia Airways Co. Ltd. [*ICAO designator*] .... EG
Japan Asia Sea Cable .... JASC
Japan Association for Radiation Research on Polymers .... JARRP
Japan Atomic Energy Commission .... JAEC
Japan Atomic Energy Insurance Pool .... JAEIP
Japan Atomic Energy Research Institute .... JAERI
Japan Atomic Energy Research Institute. Annual Report and Account [*A publication*] .... Jpn At Energy Res Inst Annu Rep Acc
Japan Atomic Fuel Corporation .... JAFC
Japan Atomic Industrial Forum .... JAIF
Japan Atomic Power Company .... JAPCO
Japan Auto Parts Industries Association .... JAPIA
Japan Automobile Tire Manufacturers Association .... JATMA
Japan Chemical Industry [*A publication*] .... Jpn Chem Ind
Japan Chemical Week [*A publication*] .... Japan Chem
Japan Chemical Week [*A publication*] .... JCW
Japan Christian Quarterly [*A publication*] .... Ja Christ Q
Japan Christian Quarterly [*A publication*] .... Jap Chr Q
Japan Christian Quarterly [*A publication*] .... JCQ
Japan Civil Aviation Bureau .... JCAB
Japan Documentation Center [*Columbia University*] .... JDC
Japan Echo [*A publication*] .... Ja Echo
Japan Economic Institute of America .... JEI
Japan Economic Journal [*A publication*] .... Jpn Econ J
Japan Electron Optics Laboratory Co. .... JEOL
Japan Electron Optics Laboratory Company .... JEOLCO
Japan Electronic Engineering [*A publication*] .... JEE
Japan Electronic Engineering [*A publication*] .... Jpn Electron Eng
Japan Electronic Parts Industry Association .... JEPIA
Japan Electronics Buyers' Guide .... JEBG
Japan Electronics Engineering .... JEE
Japan Electronics Industry .... JEI
Japan Electronics Industry [*A publication*] .... JEI
Japan Electronics Show .... JES
Japan Engineering Test Reactor .... JETR
Japan Environmental Systems .... JES
Japan External Trade Relations Organization .... JETRO
Japan Federation of Employers Association .... JFEA
Japan Foundation .... JF
Japan Foundation Newsletter [*A publication*] .... Ja Found Newsl
[*The*] **Japan Fund, Inc.** [*NYSE symbol*] .... JPN
Japan Geological Survey. Bulletin [*A publication*] .... Jap Geol Surv Bull
Japan Geological Survey. Report [*A publication*] .... Jap Geol Surv Rep
Japan Hour Association [*Later, JHB*] .... JHA
Japan Hour Broadcasting [*Formerly, JHA*] .... JHB
Japan Industrial Technology Association (Nyusu) [*A publication*] .... Jpn Ind Technol Assoc (Nyusu)
Japan Information Center of Science and Technology .... JICST
Japan Information Center of Science and Technology, Tokyo, Japan [*Library symbol*] .... JTJ
Japan Institute .... JI
Japan Institute for International Studies and Training .... JIIST
Japan International Christian University Foundation .... JICUF
Japan Interpreter [*A publication*] .... Japan Inter
Japan Interpreter [*A publication*] .... Jap Inter
Japan Interpreter [*A publication*] .... JI
Japan Journal of Nurses' Education [*A publication*] .... Jap J Nurses Educ
Japan Light Machinery Information Center .... JLMIC
Japan Medical World [*A publication*] .... Japan Med World
Japan Meteorological Agency .... JMA
Japan Meteorological Agency. Volcanological Bulletin [*A publication*] .... Jap Meteorol Agency Volcanol Bull
Japan Microfilm Service Center Co. Ltd., Tokyo, Japan [*Library symbol*] .... JmSC
Japan Microphotography Association .... JMA
Japan Missionary Bulletin [*A publication*] .... Ja Mission B
Japan Missionary Bulletin [*Tokyo*] [*A publication*] .... JMB
Japan National Railways .... JNR
Japan National Tourist Organization .... JNTO

Japan North American Commission on Cooperative Mission .... JNAC
Japan Nuclear Codes Group .... JNCG
Japan Oceanographic Data Center [*Information service*] .... JODC
Japan Paper .... JP
Japan Paper Proofs .... JPP
Japan Patient Information Center [*Information service*] .... JAPATIC
Japan Pesticide Information [*A publication*] .... Jpn Pestic Inf
Japan Petroleum Development Company .... JPDC
Japan Plastics Age [*A publication*] .... J Plas Age
Japan Power Demonstration Reactor .... JPDR
Japan Press Service .... JPS
Japan Procurement Agency .... JPA
Japan Public Works Research Institute. Report. Ministry of Construction [*A publication*] .... Jap Public Works Res Inst Rep (Minist Constr)
Japan Publications Guide Service [*Information service*] .... JPGS
Japan Quarterly [*A publication*] .... Japan Q
Japan Quarterly [*A publication*] .... Japan Quart
Japan Quarterly [*A publication*] .... Jap Q
Japan Quarterly [*A publication*] .... Jap Quart
Japan Quarterly [*A publication*] .... Ja Q
Japan Quarterly [*A publication*] .... JQ
Japan Scholarship Foundation .... JSF
Japan Science Review [*A publication*] .... JSR
Japan Science Review. Humanistic Studies [*A publication*] .... JSRHS
Japan Science Review. Literature, Philosophy, and History [*A publication*] .... JSR LPH
Japan Self-Defense Force .... JSDF
Japan Shipbuilding and Marine Engineering [*A publication*] .... Jap Shipbldg Mar Eng
Japan Silk Association .... JSA
Japan Socialist Party .... JSP
Japan Socialist Review [*A publication*] .... Ja Socialist R
Japan Socialist Review [*A publication*] .... JSR
Japan Society .... JS
Japan Society for Aeronautical and Space Sciences. Transactions [*A publication*] .... Jpn Soc Aeronaut Space Sci Trans
Japan Society Bulletin [*A publication*] .... Japan Soc B
Japan Society of London. Bulletin [*A publication*] .... Ja Soc Lond B
Japan Society of Mechanical Engineers .... JSME
Japan Society for the Promotion of Science .... JSPS
Japan Spectroscopic Company. Application Notes [*A publication*] .... JASCO Appl Notes
Japan Spectroscopic Company. Application Notes [*A publication*] .... Jpn Spectros Co Appl Notes
Japan Steel Bulletin [*A publication*] .... Jpn Steel Bull
Japan Synthetic Rubber Co. Ltd. .... JSR
Japan Techno-Economics Society .... JATES
Japan Telecommunications Review [*A publication*] .... Jap Telecom
Japan Telecommunications Review [*A publication*] .... Jpn Telecommun Rev
Japan Textile Federation .... JTF
Japan Welding Society. Transactions [*A publication*] .... Jap Weld Soc Trans
Japanese [*MARC language code*] [*Library of Congress*] .... jpn
Japanese Air Defense Environment .... JADE
Japanese Air Self-Defense Force .... JASDF
Japanese Airborne Early Warning .... JAEW
Japanese-American Citizens League .... JACL
Japanese American Curriculum Project .... JACP
Japanese American Philatelic Society [*Later, JASP*] .... JAPS
Japanese American Society for Legal Studies .... JASLS
Japanese American Society for Philately [*Formerly, JAPS*] .... JASP
Japanese Annals of Social Psychology [*A publication*] .... Japan A Soc Psychol
Japanese Annual of International Law [*A publication*] .... Ja Ann Int Law
Japanese Annual of International Law [*A publication*] .... Japan Annu Int Law
Japanese Antarctic Research Expedition .... JARE
Japanese, Arabic, Chinese, Korean, Persian, Hebrew, Yiddish [*Nonroman languages*] [*Library of Congress*] .... JACKPHY
Japanese Archives of Internal Medicine [*A publication*] .... Jpn Arch Intern Med
Japanese Army Air Force .... JAAF
Japanese Association for International Chemical Information .... JAICI
Japanese Association of Mineralogists, Petrologists, and Economic Geologists. Journal [*A publication*] .... Jap Assoc Mineral Petrol Econ Geol J
Japanese B Encephalitis [*Medicine*] .... JBE
Japanese Chin Club of America [*Formerly, JSCA*] .... JCCA
Japanese Circulation Journal [*A publication*] .... Jap Circ J
Japanese Circulation Journal [*A publication*] .... Jpn Circ J
Japanese Communist Party .... JCP
Japanese Defense Agency .... JDA
Japanese Economic Studies [*A publication*] .... Ja Econ Stud
Japanese Economic Studies [*A publication*] .... Japan Econ Stud
Japanese Economic Studies [*A publication*] .... Jap Econ St
Japanese Electronic Industries Association .... JEIA
Japanese Electronic Industries Development Association .... JEIDA
Japanese Electronic Information Processing Automatic Computer .... JEIPAC
Japanese Electrotechnical Committee .... JEC
Japanese Encephalitis [*Medicine*] .... JE
Japanese Encephalitis Virus [*Medicine*] .... JEV
Japanese Equine Encephalitis [*Medicine*] .... JEE
Japanese Expeditions to the Deep Sea .... JEDS
Japanese Fantasy Film Journal [*A publication*] .... JFFJ
Japanese Federation of Economic Organizations .... JFEO
Japanese Fermentation Institute .... JFI
Japanese Fiscal Year .... JFY
Japanese Ground Self-Defense Forces .... JGSDF
Japanese Heart Journal [*A publication*] .... Jap Heart J
Japanese Heart Journal [*A publication*] .... Jpn Heart J
Japanese Industrial Standard .... JIS
Japanese Industrial Standards Committee .... JISC
Japanese Industrial Technology Association .... JITA
Japanese Institute of Electrical Engineers .... JIEE
Japanese Journal of Allergology [*A publication*] .... Jpn J Allergol
Japanese Journal of Anesthesiology [*A publication*] .... Jpn J Anesthesiol
Japanese Journal of Antibiotics [*A publication*] .... Jpn J Antibiot
Japanese Journal of Applied Entomology and Zoology [*A publication*] .... Jap J Appl Entomol Zool
Japanese Journal of Applied Entomology and Zoology [*A publication*] .... Jpn J Appl Entomol Zool
Japanese Journal of Applied Physics [*A publication*] .... Jap J A Phy
Japanese Journal of Applied Physics [*A publication*] .... Jap J Appl Phys
Japanese Journal of Applied Physics [*A publication*] .... Jpn J Appl Phys
Japanese Journal of Applied Physics. Supplement [*A publication*] .... Jap J Appl Phys Suppl
Japanese Journal of Bacteriology [*A publication*] .... Jpn J Bacteriol
Japanese Journal of Botany [*A publication*] .... Jap J Bot
Japanese Journal of Botany [*A publication*] .... Jap J Botan
Japanese Journal of Botany [*A publication*] .... Jpn J Bot
Japanese Journal of Breeding [*A publication*] .... Jap J Breed
Japanese Journal of Breeding [*A publication*] .... Jpn J Breed
Japanese Journal of Cancer Research [*A publication*] .... Jpn J Cancer Res
Japanese Journal of Child Psychiatry [*A publication*] .... Jap J Child
Japanese Journal of Clinical and Experimental Medicine [*A publication*] .... Jpn J Clin Exp Med
Japanese Journal of Clinical Oncology [*A publication*] .... Jpn J Clin Oncol
Japanese Journal of Clinical Ophthalmology [*A publication*] .... Jpn J Clin Ophthalmol
Japanese Journal of Clinical Pathology. Supplement [*A publication*] .... Jpn J Clin Pathol Suppl
Japanese Journal of Clinical Pharmacology [*A publication*] .... Jpn J Clin Pharmacol
Japanese Journal of Constitutional Medicine [*A publication*] .... Jpn J Const Med
Japanese Journal of Dairy and Food Science [*A publication*] .... Jpn J Dairy Food Sci
Japanese Journal of Dairy Science [*A publication*] .... Jpn J Dairy Sci
Japanese Journal of Dermatology [*A publication*] .... Jpn J Dermatol
Japanese Journal of Dermatology. Series B (English Edition) [*A publication*] .... Jpn J Dermatol Ser B (Engl Ed)
Japanese Journal of Ecology [*A publication*] .... Jap J Ecol
Japanese Journal of Ecology [*A publication*] .... Jpn J Ecol
Japanese Journal of Educational Psychology [*A publication*] .... Jap J Edu P
Japanese Journal of Ethnology [*A publication*] .... JJE
Japanese Journal of Ethnology [*A publication*] .... Jpn J Ethnol
Japanese Journal of Experimental Medicine [*A publication*] .... Jap J Exp M
Japanese Journal of Experimental Medicine [*A publication*] .... Jpn J Exp Med
Japanese Journal of Fertility and Sterility [*A publication*] .... Jpn J Fertil Steril
Japanese Journal of Genetics [*A publication*] .... Jap J Genet
Japanese Journal of Genetics [*A publication*] .... Jpn J Genet
Japanese Journal of Geology and Geography [*A publication*] .... Japanese Jour Geology and Geography
Japanese Journal of Geology and Geography [*A publication*] .... Japan J Geol & Geog
Japanese Journal of Geology and Geography [*A publication*] .... Jap J Geol Geogr
Japanese Journal of Geology and Geography [*A publication*] .... Jpn J Geol Geogr
Japanese Journal of Geriatrics [*A publication*] .... Jpn J Geriatr
Japanese Journal of Herpetology [*A publication*] .... Jpn J Herpetol
Japanese Journal of Human Genetics [*A publication*] .... Jap J Hum G
Japanese Journal of Human Genetics [*A publication*] .... Jpn J Hum Genet
Japanese Journal of Hygiene [*A publication*] .... Jpn J Hyg
Japanese Journal of Ichthyology [*A publication*] .... Jpn J Ichthyol
Japanese Journal of Industrial Health [*A publication*] .... Jpn J Ind Health
Japanese Journal of Limnology [*A publication*] .... Jpn J Limnol
Japanese Journal of Mathematics [*A publication*] .... Japan J Math
Japanese Journal of Mathematics [*A publication*] .... Jpn J Math
Japanese Journal of Medical Electronics and Biological Engineering [*A publication*] .... Jap J Med Electron & Biol Eng
Japanese Journal of Medical Electronics and Biological Engineering [*A publication*] .... Jpn J Med Electron Biol Eng
Japanese Journal of Medical Mycology [*A publication*] .... Jpn J Med Mycol
Japanese Journal of Medical Science and Biology [*A publication*] .... Jap J Med S
Japanese Journal of Medical Science and Biology [*A publication*] .... Jpn J Med Sci Biol
Japanese Journal of Medical Sciences. Part IV. Pharmacology [*A publication*] .... Japan J Med Sc Pt IV Pharmacol

Japanese Journal of Medicine [*A publication*]....Jap J Med
Japanese Journal of Medicine [*A publication*]....Jpn J Med
Japanese Journal of Microbiology [*A publication*]....Jap J Micro
Japanese Journal of Microbiology [*A publication*]....Jpn J Microbiol
Japanese Journal for the Midwife [*A publication*]....Jap J Midwife
Japanese Journal for the Midwife [*A publication*]....Jpn J Midwife
Japanese Journal of Nuclear Medicine [*A publication*]....Jpn J Nucl Med
Japanese Journal of Nursing [*A publication*]....Jap J Nurs
Japanese Journal of Nursing [*A publication*]....Jpn J Nurs
Japanese Journal of Nursing Art [*A publication*]....Japan J Nurs Art
Japanese Journal of Nursing Research [*A publication*]....Jap J Nurs Res
Japanese Journal of Nursing Research [*A publication*]....Jpn J Nurs Res
Japanese Journal of Nutrition [*A publication*]....Jap J Nutr
Japanese Journal of Nutrition [*A publication*]....Jpn J Nutr
Japanese Journal of Ophthalmology [*A publication*]....Jpn J Ophthalmol
Japanese Journal of Oral Biology [*A publication*]....Jpn J Oral Biol
Japanese Journal of Palynology [*A publication*]....Jpn J Palynol
Japanese Journal of Parasitology [*A publication*]....Jpn J Parasitol
Japanese Journal of Pharmacognosy [*A publication*]....Jpn J Pharm
Japanese Journal of Pharmacology [*A publication*]....Jap J Pharm
Japanese Journal of Pharmacology [*A publication*]....JJPAA
Japanese Journal of Pharmacology [*A publication*]....Jpn J Pharmacol
Japanese Journal of Pharmacy and Chemistry [*A publication*]....Jpn J Pharm Chem
Japanese Journal of Physical Fitness and Sports Medicine [*A publication*]....Jpn J Phys Fitness Sports Med
Japanese Journal of Physiology [*A publication*]....Jap J Physi
Japanese Journal of Physiology [*A publication*]....JJPHA
Japanese Journal of Physiology [*A publication*]....Jpn J Physiol
Japanese Journal of Plastic and Reconstructive Surgery [*A publication*]....Jpn J Plast Reconstr Surg
Japanese Journal of Psychology [*A publication*]....Jap J Psych
Japanese Journal of Psychology [*A publication*]....Jpn J Psychol
Japanese Journal of Psychosomatic Medicine [*A publication*]....Jpn J Psychosom Med
Japanese Journal of Public Health [*A publication*]....Jpn J Public Health
Japanese Journal of Sanitary Zoology [*A publication*]....Jpn J Sanit Zool
Japanese Journal of Smooth Muscle Research [*A publication*]....Jpn J Smooth Muscle Res
Japanese Journal of Surgery [*A publication*]....Jpn J Surg
Japanese Journal of Thoracic Diseases [*A publication*]....Jpn J Thorac Dis
Japanese Journal of Tropical Agriculture [*A publication*]....Jap J Trop Agr
Japanese Journal of Tropical Agriculture [*A publication*]....Jpn J Trop Agric
Japanese Journal of Tropical Medicine and Hygiene [*A publication*]....Jpn J Trop Med Hyg
Japanese Journal of Tuberculosis [*A publication*]....Jpn J Tuberc
Japanese Journal of Tuberculosis and Chest Diseases [*A publication*]....Jpn J Tuberc Chest Dis
Japanese Journal of Veterinary Research [*A publication*]....Jap J Vet R
Japanese Journal of Veterinary Research [*A publication*]....Jpn J Vet Res
Japanese Journal of Veterinary Science [*A publication*]....Jap J Vet S
Japanese Journal of Veterinary Science [*A publication*]....Jpn J Vet Sci
Japanese Journal of Zoology [*A publication*]....Jap J Zool
Japanese Journal of Zoology [*A publication*]....Jpn J Zool
Japanese Journal of Zootechnical Science [*A publication*]....Jap J Zootech Sci
Japanese Keyword Indexing Simulator....JAKIS
Japanese Land-Based Test Site....JLBTS
Japanese Literature Today [*A publication*]....Ja Lit Today
Japanese Maritime Self-Defense Force....JMSDF
Japanese Military Administration....JMA
Japanese National Laboratory....JNL
Japanese National Railways. Railway Technical Research [*A publication*]....Jap Nat Ry Ry Tech Res
Japanese Periodicals Index [*A publication*]....Jap Per Ind
Japanese Poultry Science [*A publication*]....Jap Poultry Sci
Japanese Poultry Science [*A publication*]....Jpn Poult Sci
Japanese Progress in Climatology [*A publication*]....Jap Prog Climatol
Japanese Psychological Research [*A publication*]....Jap Psy Res
Japanese Psychological Research [*A publication*]....Jpn Psychol Res
Japanese Psychological Research [*A publication*]....JPREA
Japanese Railway Engineering [*A publication*]....Jpn Railw Eng
Japanese Religions [*A publication*]....Jap R
Japanese Religions [*A publication*]....Ja Rel
Japanese Research Reactor....JRR
Japanese Rocket Society....JRS
Japanese Self-Defense Agency....JSDA
Japanese Society for Tuberculosis. Annual Report [*A publication*]....Jpn Soc Tuberc Annu Rep
Japanese Sociological Review [*A publication*]....JSR
Japanese-Soviet Fisheries Commission for the Northwest Pacific....JSFC
Japanese Space Shuttle Utilization Program....JSSUP
Japanese Spaniel Club of America [*Later, JCCA*]....JSCA
Japanese Standard Time....JST
Japanese Studies [*A publication*]....Japan Stud
Japanese Studies in German Language and Literature [*A publication*]....JSGLL
Japanese Studies in the History of Science [*A publication*]....Ja Stud Hist Sci
Japanese Sword Society of the United States....JSS/US
Japanese Vellum....JV
Japanese Vellum Proofs....JVP
Japanese Victor Corporation....JVC
Japanese Yen [*Monetary unit*]....JY
Japanisch-Deutsche Medizinische Berichte [*A publication*]....Jpn Dtsch Med Ber
Jaque [*Panama*] [*Airport symbol*]....JQE
Jar....JR
Jardin Botanique de Montreal, Montreal, PQ, Canada [*Library symbol*]....CaQMJB
Jardin Zoologique de Quebec, Quebec, PQ, Canada [*Library symbol*]....CaQQZ
JARE [*Japanese Antarctic Research Expedition*] **Scientific Reports. Series E. Biology** [*A publication*]....JARE Sci Rep Ser E Biol
Jarmuevek, Mezoegazdasagi Gepek [*Hungary*] [*A publication*]....Jarmuevek Mezoegazd Gepek
Jaroslavskii Gosudarstvennyi Pedagogiceskii Institut. Doklady na Naucnyh Konferencijah [*A publication*]....Jaroslav Gos Ped Inst Dokl Naucn Konfer
Jaroslavskii Gosudarstvennyi Pedagogiceskii Institut Imeni K. D. Usinskogo. Ucenye Zapiski [*A publication*]....Jaroslav Gos Ped Inst Ucen Zap
Jaroslavskii Tehnologiceskii Institut. Fiziko-Matematiceskie Nauki. Sbornik Naucnyh Trudov [*A publication*]....Jaroslav Tehn Inst Fiz-Mat Nauk Sb Naucn Trudov
Jarrow Press, Inc.....JP
Jarvis Christian College [*Texas*]....JCC
Jarvis Christian College, Hawkins, TX [*OCLC symbol*]....JCC
Jarvis Christian College, Hawkins, TX [*Library symbol*]....TxHaJ
Jasper, AB [*Radio station call letters*]....CKYR
Jasper, AL [*Radio station call letters*]....WARF
Jasper, AL [*Radio station call letters*]....WWWB
Jasper, AL [*Radio station call letters*]....WWWB-FM
Jasper County Tribune, Colfax, IA [*Library symbol*]....IaColJ
Jasper, GA [*Radio station call letters*]....WYYZ
Jasper, IN [*Radio station call letters*]....WITZ
Jasper, IN [*Radio station call letters*]....WITZ-FM
Jasper Public Library, Jasper, IN [*OCLC symbol*]....XJP
Jasper, TN [*Location identifier*] [*FAA*]....APT
Jasper, TX [*Location identifier*] [*FAA*]....JAS
Jasper, TX [*Radio station call letters*]....KTXJ
Jasper, TX [*Radio station call letters*]....KWYX
Jasper, TX [*Location identifier*] [*FAA*]....PIN
Jaspers Society of North America....JSNA
Jaswant Singh and Bhattacharji [*Staining method for blood cells, named for its discoverers*] [*Medicine*]....JSB
Jauna Gaita [*A publication*]....J Ga
Jaundice [*Medicine*]....JAUND
JAVA Reservations Jamaica [*Formerly, JAVA*] [*An association*]....JRJ
Javan LASER....JL
Javanese....JAV
Javanese [*MARC language code*] [*Library of Congress*]....jav
Javelin Class Association....JCA
Javelin Rocket Vehicle....JRV
Jaw Jerk [*Medicine*]....JJ
Jawahrlal Institute of Postgraduate Medical Education and Research [*India*]....JIPMER
Jayapura [*Indonesia*] [*Airport symbol*]....DJJ
Jayapura [*West Irian*] [*Seismograph station code, US Geological Survey*]....JAY
Jayark Corp. [*NASDAQ symbol*]....JAYA
Jaycees International....JCI
Jayco Jafari International Travel Club....JJITC
Jaytex Oil & Gas [*NASDAQ symbol*]....JTEX
Jazyk i Literatura [*A publication*]....JaiL
Jazykovedny Aktuality [*A publication*]....JAk
Jazykovedny Aktuality. Zpravodaj Jazykovedneho Sdruzeni pri Ceskoslovenske Akademii Ved [*A publication*]....JazA
Jazykovedny Casopis [*A publication*]....JC
Jazykovedny Sbornik [*A publication*]....JazSB
Jazykovedny Sbornik [*A publication*]....JS
Jazykovedny Studie [*A publication*]....JazS
Jazykovedny Studie [*A publication*]....JS
Jazykovedny Zbornik [*A publication*]....JZ
Jazz Arts Society....JAS
Jazz Composers Orchestra Association....JCOA
Jazz di Ieri e di Oggi [*A publication*]....Jazz Ieri
Jazz Interactions [*An association*]....JI
Jazz International....JI
Jazz Journal [*Later, Jazz Journal International*] [*A publication*]....Jazz J
Jazz Journal [*Later, Jazz Journal International*] [*A publication*]....Jazz JI
Jazz Journal International [*A publication*]....Jazz J Int
Jazz-Lift [*Provides jazz records to persons in Iron Curtain countries*] [*Defunct*]....JL
Jazz Magazine [*A publication*]....Jazz Mag
Jazz Monthly [*A publication*]....Jazz Mo
Jazz at the Philharmonic....JATP
Jazz Report [*A publication*]....Jazz Rept
Jazz Research [*A publication*]....Jazz Res
Jazz Review [*A publication*]....Jazz R
Jazz Rytm i Piosenka [*A publication*]....Jazz Rytm
JBM. Jornal Brasileiro de Medicina [*A publication*]....JBM J Bras Med

JB's Restaurants [*NASDAQ symbol*] .... JBBB
Jealott's Hill Bulletin [*A publication*] .... Jealott's Hill Bull
Jean-Jacques Servan-Schreiber [*French publisher*] .... J-J S-S
Jean-Paul-Gesellschaft. Jahrbuch [*A publication*] .... Jean-Paul-Gesellsch Jahrb
Jean Piaget Society .... JPS
Jeanes Hospital, Philadelphia, PA [*Library symbol*] [*Obsolete*] .... PPJea
Jeannette Corp. [*American Stock Exchange symbol*] [*Delisted*] .... JGA
Jeannette, PA [*Radio station call letters*] .... WBCW
Jeans Viscosity Equation [*Physics*] .... JVE
JEC Lasers, Inc. [*NASDAQ symbol*] .... JECL
Jeddah [*Saudi Arabia*] [*Airport symbol*] .... JED
Jefferies Group, Inc. [*NASDAQ symbol*] .... JEFG
Jefferson Bancorp [*NASDAQ symbol*] .... JBNC
Jefferson Bankshares [*NASDAQ symbol*] .... JBNK
Jefferson City [*Missouri*] [*Airport symbol*] .... JEF
Jefferson City, IN [*Radio station call letters*] .... WKJQ
Jefferson City Junior College [*Discontinued operation, 1958*] [*Missouri*] .... JCJC
Jefferson City, MO [*Location identifier*] [*FAA*] .... JCQ
Jefferson City, MO [*Location identifier*] [*FAA*] .... JEF
Jefferson City, MO [*Television station call letters*] .... KBBM-TV
Jefferson City, MO [*Radio station call letters*] .... KJMO
Jefferson City, MO [*Radio station call letters*] .... KLIK
Jefferson City, MO [*Radio station call letters*] .... KLUM-FM
Jefferson City, MO [*Television station call letters*] .... KRCG-TV
Jefferson City, MO [*Radio station call letters*] .... KTXY
Jefferson City, MO [*Radio station call letters*] .... KWOS
Jefferson City, TN [*Radio station call letters*] .... WJFC
Jefferson College, Washington, MS [*Library symbol*] [*Obsolete*] .... MsWJ
Jefferson Community College, Library, Watertown, NY [*OCLC symbol*] .... VND
Jefferson Community College, Louisville, KY [*OCLC symbol*] .... KJC
Jefferson Community College, Louisville, KY [*Library symbol*] .... KyLoJ
Jefferson Community College, Watertown, NY [*Library symbol*] .... NWattJ
Jefferson County Court House, Birmingham, AL [*Library symbol*] .... ABC
Jefferson County Historical Society, Watertown, NY [*Library symbol*] .... NWattJHi
Jefferson County Law Library, Birmingham, AL [*Library symbol*] .... ABJ
Jefferson County Library, Fayette, MS [*Library symbol*] .... MsFa
Jefferson County Library, Golden, CO [*Library symbol*] .... CoGJ
Jefferson County Library, Madras, OR [*Library symbol*] .... OrMad
Jefferson County Youth Center, Golden, CO [*Library symbol*] .... CoGJY
Jefferson Davis Association .... JDA
Jefferson Davis County Library, Prentiss, MS [*Library symbol*] .... MsPr
Jefferson Davis Parish Library, Jennings, LA [*Library symbol*] .... LJJ
Jefferson Elementary School, LaSalle, IL [*Library symbol*] .... ILasJ
Jefferson Elementary School, Princeton, IL [*Library symbol*] .... IPriJS
Jefferson Lake Petrochemicals [*American Stock Exchange symbol*] .... JFL
Jefferson Lake Sulphur Co. [*See JFL*] [*NYSE symbol*] [*Delisted*] .... JEF
Jefferson Medical College of Philadelphia .... JMCP
Jefferson National Corp. [*NASDAQ symbol*] .... JEFF
Jefferson National Expansion Memorial National Historic Site .... JEFF
Jefferson National Life [*NASDAQ symbol*] .... JNAT
Jefferson, OH [*Location identifier*] [*FAA*] .... JFN
Jefferson, OH [*Radio station call letters*] .... WCVJ
Jefferson Parish Library, Metairie, LA [*Library symbol*] .... LMetJ
Jefferson Parish Public Library, Gretna, LA [*Library symbol*] .... LGrJ
Jefferson Parish Recreation Department, Metairie, LA [*Library symbol*] .... LMetR
Jefferson-Pilot Corp. [*NYSE symbol*] .... JP
Jefferson Proving Ground [*Indiana*] [*Military*] .... JPG
Jefferson Public Library, Jefferson, IA [*Library symbol*] .... IaJ
Jefferson Public Library, Jefferson, OR [*Library symbol*] .... OrJe
Jefferson School of Social Science, New York, NY [*Library symbol*] [*Obsolete*] .... NNJef
Jefferson Smurfit Corporation [*NASDAQ symbol*] .... JJSC
Jefferson State Junior College, Birmingham, AL [*Library symbol*] .... ABJS
Jefferson Township, OH [*Radio station call letters*] .... WLMB
Jefferson-Williams Energy Corporation [*NASDAQ symbol*] .... JWEC
Jeffersonville, IN [*Radio station call letters*] .... WQMF
Jeffersonville, IN [*Radio station call letters*] .... WXVW
Jeffersonville Township Public Library, Jeffersonville, IN [*OCLC symbol*] .... IJV
Jeffersonville Township Public Library, Jeffersonville, IN [*Library symbol*] .... InJe
Jeffrey Martin, Inc. [*NASDAQ symbol*] .... JFRY
Jegeroil Corp. [*NASDAQ symbol*] .... JEGR
Jehovistic and Elohistic [*Theology*] .... J & E
Jehuda [*On Hebrew coins of the fourth century*] .... JHD
Jejunum [*Medicine*] .... JEJ
Jellico, TN [*Radio station call letters*] .... WJJT
JEMF [*John Edwards Memorial Foundation*] **Quarterly** [*A publication*] .... JEMFA
JEMF [*John Edwards Memorial Foundation*] **Quarterly** [*A publication*] .... JEMFQ
JEMIC [*Japan Electric Meters Inspection Corporation*] **Technical Report** [*A publication*] .... JEMIC Tech Rep
Jemna Mechanika a Optika [*A publication*] .... Jemna Mech Opt
Jen-Sal Journal [*A publication*] .... Jen-Sal J
Jena [*German Democratic Republic*] [*Seismograph station code, US Geological Survey*] [*Closed*] .... JEN
Jena, LA [*Location identifier*] [*FAA*] .... JLY
Jena, LA [*Radio station call letters*] .... KCKW
Jena, LA [*Radio station call letters*] .... KJNA
Jena Nomina Anatomica [*Anatomy*] .... JNA
Jena Review [*A publication*] .... Jena Rev
Jenaer Germanistische Forschungen [*A publication*] .... JGF
Jenaer Rundschau [*A publication*] .... Jena Rundsch
Jenaische Zeitschrift fuer Medicin und Naturwissenschaft [*A publication*] .... Jenaische Ztschr Med u Naturw
Jenaische Zeitschrift fuer Naturwissenschaft [*A publication*] .... Jenaische Ztschr Naturw
Jenaische Zeitschrift fuer Naturwissenschaft [*A publication*] .... Jena Z Naturw
Jenkins, KY [*Radio station call letters*] .... WIFX
Jenkins, KY [*Radio station call letters*] .... WIFX-FM
Jenkinsville [*South Carolina*] [*Seismograph station code, US Geological Survey*] .... JSC
Jenkintown, PA [*Radio station call letters*] .... WIBF-FM
Jenks, OK [*Location identifier*] [*FAA*] .... JEX
Jenner & Block, Chicago, IL [*OCLC symbol*] .... IPB
Jenney Beechcraft, Inc. [*East Bedford, MA*] [*FAA designator*] .... JNY
Jennie Belle Stephens Smith Library, New Albany, MS [*Library symbol*] .... MsNa
Jennifer Jo [*In TV series "The Governor and JJ"*] .... JJ
Jennings County Public Library, North Vernon, IN [*Library symbol*] .... InNovJ
Jennings, LA [*Location identifier*] [*FAA*] .... JNZ
Jennings, LA [*Radio station call letters*] .... KJBQ
Jennings, LA [*Radio station call letters*] .... KJEF
Jennings, LA [*Radio station call letters*] .... KJEF-FM
Jennings Public Library, Jennings, LA [*Library symbol*] .... LJ
Jenny Hunter's Kindergarten and Primary Training School, New York, NY [*Library symbol*] [*Obsolete*] .... NNJHK
Jenolan [*Australia*] [*Seismograph station code, US Geological Survey*] .... JNL
Jenpeg, MB [*Radio station call letters*] .... CJEN-FM
Jensen Beach, FL [*Radio station call letters*] .... WHLG
Jensen Industries [*American Stock Exchange symbol*] .... JI
Jensen-Salsbery Laboratories, Kansas City, KS [*Library symbol*] .... KKcJS
Jentaculum [*Breakfast*] [*Pharmacy*] .... JENTAC
JEOL (Japan Electron Optics Laboratory Co.). News [*A publication*] .... JEOL News
Jequie [*Brazil*] [*Airport symbol*] .... JEQ
JerDon Air Service, Inc. [*Ardmore, OK*] [*FAA designator*] .... JNA
Jeremiah [*Old Testament book*] .... Jer
Jerez De La Frontera [*Spain*] [*Airport symbol*] .... XRY
Jericho Public Library, Jericho, NY [*Library symbol*] .... NJer
Jernal Antropoloji dan Sosioloji [*A publication*] .... J Antro Sos
Jernal Sejarah [*A publication*] .... J Sej
Jernel Sains Malaysia [*A publication*] .... Jernel Sains Malays
Jernkontorets Annaler [*A publication*] .... Jernkon Ann
Jernkontorets Annaler [*A publication*] .... Jernkontorets Ann
Jernkontorets Annaler. Edition A [*A publication*] .... Jernkontorets Ann Ed A
Jernkontorets Annaler. Edition B [*A publication*] .... Jernkontorets Ann Ed B
Jerome, ID [*Radio station call letters*] .... KART
Jerome, ID [*Radio station call letters*] .... KFMA
Jerrico, Inc. [*NASDAQ symbol*] .... JERR
Jersey [*Great Britain*] .... GBJ
Jersey [*Channel Islands*] [*Airport symbol*] .... JER
Jersey [*Channel Islands*] [*Seismograph station code, US Geological Survey*] [*Closed*] .... JRS
Jersey Bulletin [*A publication*] .... Jersey Bul
Jersey Bulletin and Dairy World [*A publication*] .... Jersey B
Jersey Central Power & Light Co. [*NYSE symbol*] .... JYP
Jersey City Free Public Library, Jersey City, NJ [*Library symbol*] .... NjJ
Jersey City State College, Jersey City, NJ [*OCLC symbol*] .... NJJ
Jersey City State College, Jersey City, NJ [*Library symbol*] .... NjJS
Jersey Community Hospital, Jerseyville, IL [*Library symbol*] .... IJeH
Jersey Community Unit, School District 100, Jerseyville, IL [*Library symbol*] .... IJeSD
Jersey European Airways [*Great Britain*] [*ICAO designator*] .... JY
Jersey Institute .... JI
Jersey Journal [*A publication*] .... Jersey J
Jersey Journal, Jersey City, NJ [*Library symbol*] .... NjJJJ
Jersey Microfilming, Clifton, NJ [*Library symbol*] .... JerM
Jersey Shore, PA [*Radio station call letters*] .... WJSA
Jersey Shore, PA [*Radio station call letters*] .... WSQV
Jerseyville & Eastern [*AAR code*] .... JE
Jerseyville Free Library, Jerseyville, IL [*Library symbol*] .... IJe
Jerseyville, IL [*Radio station call letters*] .... WJBM
Jerseyville, IL [*Radio station call letters*] .... WJBM-FM
Jerusalem .... JER
Jerusalem [*Airport symbol*] .... JRS
Jerusalem [*Israel*] [*Seismograph station code, US Geological Survey*] .... JER
Jerusalem Bible .... JB
Jerusalem and the East Mission .... JEM
Jerusalem Institutions for the Blind .... KEREN-OR
Jerusalem Journal of International Relations [*A publication*] .... Jerusalem J Int Relat

Jerusalem Journal of International Relations [*A publication*]............. Jerus J Int Rel

Jerusalem Symposia on Quantum Chemistry and Biochemistry [*A publication*]............ Jerus Symp Quantum Chem Biochem

Jervis Library Association, Rome, NY [*Library symbol*] .... NRom

Jervis Public Library, Rome, NY [*OCLC symbol*] ....ZVA

Jesness Inventory [*Psychology*]..................JI

Jesous Christos, Theou Uios Soter [*Jesus Christ, Son of God, Savior*]...............ICHTHYS

Jesse Stuart Foundation ....JSF

Jessore [*Bangladesh*] [*Airport symbol*]..................JSR

Jesuit Archives of the Province of Oregon, Spokane, WA [*Library symbol*]...............WaSpJ

Jesuit Association of Student Personnel Administrators [*Formerly, CJSPA*].................JASPA

Jesuit Center for Social Studies ....JCSS

Jesuit Educational Association [*Later split into AJCU and JSEA*] ....JEA

Jesuit-Krauss-McCormick Library, Chicago, IL [*Library symbol*].............ICJKM

Jesuit-Krauss-McCormick Library, Chicago, IL [*OCLC symbol*].............IDK

Jesuit Missions [*Formerly, AJMA*].............JM

Jesuit Office of Social Ministry [*Later, NOJSM*]........JOSM

Jesuit Philosophical Association of the United States and Canada ....JPA

Jesuit Scholastic Library, Spokane, WA [*Library symbol*] ....WaSpJS

Jesuit School of Theology in Chicago, Chicago, IL [*Library symbol*] ....ICJST

Jesuit Secondary Education Association ....JSEA

Jesuit Seismological Association ....JSA

Jesuit Seminary, Toronto, ON, Canada [*Library symbol*] ....CaOTJS

Jesuit Volunteer Corps: Northwest ....JVC

Jesuites Bibliotheque, St. Jerome, PQ, Canada [*Library symbol*] ....CaQStJeJ

Jesuits in Communication in North America ....JESCOM

Jesup, GA [*Location identifier*] [*FAA*].............JES

Jesup, GA [*Radio station call letters*]............WIFO

Jesup, GA [*Radio station call letters*]............WLOP

Jesup, GA [*Radio station call letters*]............WSOJ

Jesus [*First and third letters of His name in Greek*] IC

Jesus.............JES

Jesus Christ............JC

Jesus Christ Superstar [*Rock opera*] ....JCSS

Jesus to the Communist World [*An association*]............JTTCW

Jesus, Mary, and Joseph.............JMJ

Jet Age Conference ....JAC

Jet Aircraft Coating...............JAC

Jet Aircraft Noise..............JAN

Jet Aircraft Noise Survey ....JANS

Jet Aircraft Noise Survey Research Program ....JANSRP

Jet Aircraft Starting Unit ....JASU

Jet America, Inc. [*NASDAQ symbol*] ....JETA

Jet Approach and Landing Chart ....JAL

Jet Approach and Landing Chart ....JALC

Jet Assist Stop ....JASTOP

Jet-Assisted Takeoff..............JATO

Jet Attitude Control System ....JACS

Jet Augmented Wing Flap ....JAWF

Jet Barrier..............J-B

Jet Black [*Derogatory nickname for a black person*]..............JB

Jet Blast Deflector..............JBD

Jet Bomb...............JB

Jet Circulation Control ....JCC

Jet Courier Service, Inc. [*Cincinnati, OH*] [*FAA designator*]...........DWW

Jet Deflection Control..............JDC

Jet Driver..............JD

Jet Ejector System..............JES

Jet Engine..............JA

Jet Engine Base Maintenance ....JEBM

Jet Engine Control Bearing ....JECB

Jet Engine Duct..............JED

Jet Engine Exhaust..............JEE

Jet Engine Field Maintenance ....JEFM

Jet Engine Fuel..............JEF

Jet Engine Modulation ....JEM

Jet Engine Processor..............JEP

Jet Engine Smoke Abatement Program ....JESAP

Jet Exhaust...............JE

Jet Express Ticketing System...............JETS

Jet Flap..............JF

Jet Flap Model..............JFM

Jet Flap Rotor..............JFR

Jet Flight Information ....JFI

Jet Fuel..............J

Jet Fuel Starter...............JFS

Jet Fuel Thermal Oxidation Test [*or Tester*] [*Air Force*].............JFTOT

Jet Fuel Thermal Stability...............JFTS

Jet-Induced Circulation [*Combustor*]..............JIC

Jet-Induced Lift...............JIL

Jet Inlet System...............JIS

Jet Interaction ....JI

Jet Interaction Steering...............JIS

Jet Interaction Test Apparatus ....JITA

Jet Lift Aircraft...............JLA

Jet Lift Engine...............JLE

Jet Lift System ....JLS

Jet Mixing Flow ....JMF

Jet Navigation ....J-N

Jet Navigation Chart ....JN

Jet Navigation Chart ....JNC

Jet Noise Survey ....JNS

Jet Operations Requirements ....JOR

Jet Penetration ....JP

Jet Penetration Approach ....JPAP

Jet Petroleum ....JP

Jet-Piercing Machine ....JPM

Jet Pilot ....JP

Jet Pioneers Association of the United States of America..............JPA

Jet Pipe ....JP

Jet Pipe Temperature ....JPT

Jet Pipe Temperature Limiter ....JPTL

Jet Plume Simulation ....JPS

Jet Power ....JP

Jet Propellant [*or Propulsion*] ....JP

Jet-Propelled ....JETP

Jet-Propelled Takeoff ....JPTO

Jet Propulsion Laboratory [*Renamed H. Allen Smith Jet Propulsion Laboratory, 1973, after a retiring congressman. However, name is not expected to be used officially*] [*NASA*] ....JPL

Jet Propulsion Laboratory Field Station, Air Force Eastern Test Range ....JPL/ETR

Jet Propulsion Laboratory, Pasadena, CA [*Library symbol*]..............CPJP

Jet Propulsion Laboratory. Space Programs Summary [*A publication*]..............JPL Space Programs Summ

Jet Propulsion Laboratory. Technical Memorandum [*A publication*]..............Jet Propul Lab Tech Memo

Jet Reaction Control ....JRC

Jet Reaction Control System ....JRCS

Jet Refresher Training [*Navy*]..............JRFTNG

Jet Repair Service ....JRS

Jet Research Center, Inc., Arlington, TX [*Library symbol*] ....TxArJ

Jet Research Laboratory ....JRL

Jet Route [*Followed by identification*] ....J

Jet Runway Barrier..............J-BAR

Jet Select Logic ....JSL

Jet Show Assembly ....JSA

Jet Stabilization ....JS

Jet Steering System ....JSS

Jet STOL [*Short Takeoff and Landing*] Transport [*Aircraft*]..............JST

Jet Strategic Airlift Capability [*of Military Air Command*] ....JSAC

Jet Stream ....JS

Jet Stream ....JTST

Jet Stream ....JTSTR

Jet Study ....JS

Jet Tear Down Facility ....JTF

Jet Terminal Area [*Aviation symbol*]..............Z

Jet Test Vehicle ....JTV

Jet Training Unit ....JTU

Jet Transitional Training Unit [*Navy*]..............JTTU

Jet Transport Landing Approach Simulator ....JTLAS

Jet Utility Transport ....JUT

Jet Vane Actuators ....JVA

Jet Vane Control ....JVC

Jet Way, Inc. [*Ypsilanti, MI*] [*FAA designator*]..............DVR

Jet Way, Inc. [*Ypsilanti, MI*] [*FAA designator*]..............JWY

Jeta e Re ....J e R

Jetero Corp. [*American Stock Exchange symbol*] [*Delisted*]..............JTR

Jetevator ....JETR

Jetevator Assembly ....JA

Jetevator Null Position Indicator ....JNPI

Jetevator Sensor ....JS

JETP Letters [*English Translation of JETP Pis'ma v Redaktsiyu*] [*A publication*]..............JETP Lett

Jetronic Industries, Inc. [*American Stock Exchange symbol*]..............JET

Jettison ....JET

Jettison ....JETN

Jettison ....JETT

Jettison ....JTSN

Jettison Booster Package [*NASA*]..............JBP

Jettison Control Module ....JCM

Jettison Control Panel ....JCP

Jettison Motor ....J/M

Jettison Pushbutton Switch ....JPBS

Jettison Release Mechanism ....JRM

Jettison Signal ....JS

Jettison and Washing Overboard..............J & WO

Jeune Afrique [*A publication*] ....JA

Jeune Afrique [*A publication*] ....JeuneA

Jeune Cinema [*A publication*] ....Jeune C

Jeunes Travailleurs [*A publication*] ....Jeunes Trav

Jeunesse [*A publication*] ....J

Jeunesse Anarchiste Communiste [*French student group*] ....JAC

Jeunesse Chretienne Malgache [*Malagasy Christian Youth*] ....JCM

Jeunesse pour Christ [*Youth for Christ International - YFCI*]..............JPC

Jeunesse Communiste Revolutionnaire [*French student group*]..............JCR

Jeunesse Democratique Camerounaise [*Cameroonian Democratic Youth*]............JDC
Jeunesse Etudiante Catholique Internationale [*International Young Catholic Students*]............JECI
Jeunesse du Kwilu-Kwango-Bateke [*Kwilu-Kwango-Bateke Youth*]..... JKKB
Jeunesse du Mouvement National Congolaise - Lumumba [*Youth of the Lumumba Wing of the Congolese National Movement*]............ JMNCL
Jeunesse Nationale Katangaise [*Katangan National Youth*] .... JENAKAT
Jeunesse et Orgue [*A publication*]............Jeunesse
Jeunesse Ouvriere Chretienne [*Young Christian Workers*]............JOC
Jeunesse Ouvriere Marocaine [*Moroccan Working Youth*]............JOM
Jeunesse Ouvriere du Senegal [*Senegalese Working Youth*]............JOS
Jeunesse Populaire Senegalaise [*Senegalese People's Youth*]............JPS
Jeunesse Progressiste Casamancaise [*Casamance Progressive Youth*] [*Senegal*]............JPC
Jeunesse Progressiste Dahomeenne [*Dahomean Progressive Youth*].....JPD
Jeunesse du Rassemblement Democratique Africain [*Youth of the African Democratic Rally*]............ JRDA
Jeunesse du Rassemblement Democratique Africain de Cote d'Ivoire [*Youth of the African Democratic Rally of the Ivory Coast*]............JRDACI
Jeunesse Social Democrate [*Social Democratic Youth*] [*Malagasy*]........JSD
Jeunesse Socialiste Royale Khmer [*Cambodia*]............JSRK
Jeunesse du Sud-Kasai............JSK
Jeunesse Travailleuse Oubanguienne [*Ubangi Working Youth*]............JTO
Jeunesse d'Union Dahomeene [*Dahomean Youth Union*]............JUD
Jeunesse d'Union Nationale Congolaise [*Congolese National Youth Union*]............JUNC
Jeunesse de l'Unite Togolaise [*Togolese Unity Youth*]............JUT
Jeunesse Universelle............JU
Jeunesses Europeennes Federalistes .... JEF
Jeunesses Europeennes Liberales [*Liberal European Youth*]............ JEL
Jeunesses Federalistes Mondiales .... JFM
Jewel of Africa [*Zambia*] [*A publication*]............JoA
Jewel Bearing Assembly ....JBA
Jewel Cave National Monument ....JECA
Jewel Companies, Inc. [*NYSE symbol*]............JWL
Jewel Tea Co., Inc. [*Later, JWL*] [*NYSE symbol*] [*Delisted*]............JWT
Jewelcor, Inc. [*NYSE symbol*]............JC
Jeweled-Orifice Misting Nozzle ....JMN
Jeweled-Orifice Misting Nozzle .... JOMN
Jeweled-Orifice Nozzle............ JON
Jewelers of America .... JA
Jewelers Board of Trade ....JBT
Jewelers' Book Club ....JBC
Jewelers Memorandum Bureau ....JMB
Jewelers Security Alliance of the US............JSA
Jewelers Shipping Association ....JSA
Jewelers Vigilance Committee ....JVC
Jewelry Crafts Association [*Later, JMA*]............JCA
Jewelry Industry Council ....JIC
Jewelry Industry Tax Committee [*Defunct*]............JITC
Jewelry Manufacturers Association ....JMA
Jewish............J
Jewish Academy of Arts and Sciences .... JAAS
Jewish Agency for Israel [*Later, United Israel Appeal*]............ JAI
Jewish Agency for Palestine ....JAFP
Jewish Agency for Palestine ....JAP
Jewish Agricultural Society............JAS
Jewish-American Princess [*Slang*]............JAP
Jewish Association for Services for the Aged [*New York City*]............ JASA
Jewish Board of Guardians............ JBG
Jewish Book Council [*of the National Jewish Welfare Board*] [*Later, JWBJBC*]............JBC
Jewish Braille Institute of America ....JBIA
Jewish Chautauqua Society............JCS
Jewish Colonization Association ....JCA
Jewish Committee for Relief Abroad ....JCRA
Jewish Community Center............JCC
Jewish Community Center, Samuel and Rebecca Astor Judaica Library, San Diego, CA [*Library symbol*]............CSdJ
Jewish Community News, Union, NJ [*Library symbol*]............NjUJ
Jewish Conciliation Board of America ....JCBA
Jewish Convalescent Hospital, Chomedy, PQ, Canada [*Library symbol*]............ CaQChJC
Jewish Cultural Clubs and Societies ....JCCS
Jewish Currents [*A publication*] .... Jewish Cu
Jewish Defense League ....JDL
Jewish Education [*A publication*]............Jewish Ed
Jewish Education [*A publication*]............ Jewish Educ
Jewish Education Service of North America [*Formerly, AAJE*]............JESNA
Jewish Educators Assembly............JEA
Jewish Elite Person............JEP
Jewish Family Service ....JFS
Jewish Federation of Camden County, Cherry Hill, NJ [*Library symbol*]............NjChJ
Jewish Folk Schools of New York ....JFSNY
Jewish Foundation for Education of Women............JFEW
Jewish Free Loan Association............JFLA
Jewish Friends Society............JFS

Jewish Frontier [*A publication*]............J Fron
Jewish Funeral Directors of America............JFDA
Jewish General Hospital, Institute of Community and Family Psychiatry, Montreal, PQ, Canada [*Library symbol*]............CaQMJGI
Jewish General Hospital, Lady Davis Institute for Medical Research, Montreal, PQ, Canada [*Library symbol*]............ CaQMJGL
Jewish General Hospital, Montreal, PQ, Canada [*Library symbol*]............CaQMJG
Jewish Guild for the Blind............ JGB
Jewish Historical Society of England. Transactions [*A publication*]............Jew Hist Soc Engl Trans
Jewish Historical Society of England. Transactions [*A publication*]............Jewish Hist Soc of England Trans
Jewish Hospital, Louisville, KY [*OCLC symbol*]............KLJ
Jewish Hospital, Medical Library, Cincinnati, OH [*Library symbol*]............OCJH
Jewish Hospital, School of Nursing, Cincinnati, OH [*Library symbol*]............OCJH-N
Jewish Information Bureau............JIB
Jewish Information Society of America............JIS
Jewish Institute for National Security Affairs............JINSA
Jewish Institute of Religion............JIR
Jewish Journal of Sociology [*A publication*] .... Jew J Socio
Jewish Journal of Sociology [*A publication*]............JJS
Jewish Labor Bund............JLB
Jewish Labor Committee............JLC
Jewish Lawyers Guild............JLG
Jewish Ledger, Newark, NJ [*Library symbol*]............NjNJL
Jewish Librarians Association [*Later, AJL*]............JLA
Jewish Liturgical Music Society of America............JLMSA
Jewish Male [*Classified advertising*]............JM
Jewish Media Service [*Formerly, IJL*]............JMS
Jewish Ministers Cantors Association of America and Canada ....JMCA
Jewish Ministers Cantors Association of America and Canada ....JMCAAC
Jewish Music Alliance............JMA
Jewish Music Educators Association ....JMEA
Jewish Music Forum ....JMF
Jewish National Fund............JNF
Jewish National Home for Asthmatic Children ....JNHAC
Jewish National and University Library .... JNUL
Jewish National and University Library, Hebrew University, Jerusalem, Israel [*Library symbol*]............IsJJNL
Jewish Nazi Victims Organization of America ....JNVOA
Jewish News, Newark, NJ [*Library symbol*]............NjNJN
Jewish Occupational Council [*Later, NAJVS*] .... JOC
Jewish Peace Fellowship ....JPF
Jewish Pharmaceutical Society of America ....JPSA
Jewish Philanthropic Fund of 1933 ....JPF
Jewish Policy Planning and Research Institute [*Synagogue Council of America*]............JPPRI
Jewish Public Library, Montreal, PQ, Canada [*Library symbol*]............CaQMJ
Jewish Publication Society of America ....JPS
Jewish Quarterly Review [*A publication*]............JewQ
Jewish Quarterly Review [*A publication*]............Jew Q R
Jewish Quarterly Review [*A publication*]............Jew Quart R
Jewish Quarterly Review [*A publication*]............JQR
Jewish Reconstructionist Foundation ....JRF
Jewish Record, Atlantic City, NJ [*Library symbol*]............NjAcJ
Jewish Restitution Successor Organization ....JRSO
[*The*] Jewish Right............JR
Jewish Royalty Association ....JRA
Jewish Social Studies [*A publication*] ....Jewish Soc Stud
Jewish Social Studies [*A publication*]............Jew Soc Stu
Jewish Social Studies [*A publication*]............JSS
Jewish Socialist Verband of America ....JSVA
Jewish Socialist Youth Bund [*Later, MJSG*]............JSYB
Jewish Society of America............JSA
Jewish Society for the Blind ....JSB
Jewish Society for the Deaf [*Later, New York Society for the Deaf*]........JSD
Jewish Spectator [*A publication*]............J Spec
Jewish Standard, Jersey City, NJ [*Library symbol*] ....NjJJ
Jewish Statistical Bureau ....JSB
Jewish Student Press-Service ....JSPS
Jewish Teachers Association - Morim............JTA-M
Jewish Telegraphic Agency ....JTA
Jewish Television Network............JTN
Jewish Theological Seminary of America [*New York*]............JTSA
Jewish Theological Seminary of America, New York, NY [*Library symbol*]............NNJ
Jewish Theological Seminary of America, New York, NY [*OCLC symbol*]............ VXJ
Jewish Vacation Association [*Superseded by Association of Jewish Sponsored Camps*]............JVA
Jewish Vegetarian Society ....JVS
Jewish Visual Artists Association ....JVAA
Jewish Vocational Service Library, Chicago, IL [*Library symbol*]............ICJV
Jewish War Veterans of the USA............JWV
Jewish War Veterans of the USA - National Ladies Auxiliary............ JWVA
Jewish War Veterans USA National Memorial............JWVUSANM
Jewish Women's Resource Center ....JWRC
Jews' College, London, United Kingdom [*Library symbol*]............UkLJ
Jews for Jesus............JFJ

Jezebel [Sonobuoy] **Exercise** [Navy]..............JEZEX
Jezik [A publication]..............J
Jezik in Slovstvo [A publication]..............JiS
Jezyk Polski [A publication]..............JP
Jezyk Polski [A publication]..............JPol
Jezyk Rosyjski [A publication]..............JR
Jezyki Obce w Szkole [A publication]..............JOS
Jezykoznawca [A publication]..............Jz
JGC Corp. [Formerly, Japan Gasoline Company Ltd.]..............JGC
Jiffy Bag..............JB
Jiffy Foods Corp. [NASDAQ symbol]..............JIFFQ
Jiffy Industries [NASDAQ symbol]..............JIFY
Jiffy Junction Connector..............JJC
Jiffy Junction Single Wire Connector..............JJSWC
Jiffy Junction Wire Connector..............JJWC
Jig [Phonetic alphabet] [World War II]..............J
Jig Grinder Head..............JGH
Jig Grinding Machine..............JGM
Jig Template..............JT
Jig Transit Central Y-Plane..............JTCY-P
Jigging Information..............JI
Jihocesky Sbornik Historicky [A publication]..............JcSH
Jihocesky Sbornik Historicky [A publication]..............JSH
Jijel [Algeria] [Airport symbol]..............GJL
Jikeikai Medical Journal [A publication]..............Jikeikai Med J
Jim Creek [Washington] [Seismograph station code, US Geological Survey]..............JCW
Jim Smith Society..............JSS
Jim Walter Corporation [NYSE symbol]..............JWC
Jimma [Ethiopia] [Airport symbol]..............JIM
Jinan [China] [Airport symbol]..............TNA
Jinbun Gakuho [Journal of Social Science and Humanities] [A publication]..............JBGH
Jinbun Kenkyu [Studies in Humanities] [A publication]..............JBKK
Jinbungaku [Studies in Humanities] [A publication]..............JBG
Jindabyne [Australia] [Seismograph station code, US Geological Survey] [Closed]..............JIN
Jingdezhen [China] [Airport symbol]..............JDZ
Jinjiang [China] [Airport symbol]..............JJN
Jinotega [Nicaragua] [Seismograph station code, US Geological Survey]..............JIG
Jinruigaku Zasshi [Anthropological Journal] [A publication]..............JZ
Jiri [Nepal] [Airport symbol]..............JIR
Jishu Kanri [Voluntary Management] [Japanese method for increasing productivity of industrial workers by involving them in planning]..............JK
Jittered and Swept Active RADAR..............JASAR
Jiuquan [China] [Airport symbol]..............CHW
Jiwani [Pakistan] [Airport symbol]..............JIW
JLG Industries, Inc. [NASDAQ symbol]..............JLGI
JM Resources, Inc. [NASDAQ symbol]..............JMRE
JMB Realty Trust [NASDAQ symbol]..............JMBRS
JNKVV [Jawaharlal Nehru Krishi Vishwa Vidyalaya] **Research Journal** [A publication]..............JNKVV Res J
Joannou & Paraskevaides (Overseas) Ltd...............J & P
Joao Pessoa [Brazil] [Airport symbol]..............JPA
Job..............JB
Job [Old Testament book]..............Jb
Job Accounting System..............JAS
Job Activities Questionnaire..............JAQ
Job Aid..............JA
Job Analysis..............JA
Job Analysis and Interest Measurement..............JAIM
Job Analysis Memo Activity Chart..............JAMAC
Job Analysis Memorandum..............JAM
Job Analysis Schedule [Department of Labor]..............JAS
Job Analysis System [Computer program]..............JAS
Job Assignment Memo..............JAM
Job Bank Operations Review [Employment and Training Administration] [Department of Labor]..............JBOR
Job Banks Opening Summary [Department of Labor]..............JBOS
Job Book..............JB
Job Change Notice [Form]..............JCN
Job Control Block [Data processing]..............JCB
Job Control Card..............JCC
Job Control Language [Data processing]..............JCL
Job Control Number..............JCN
Job Corps [Department of Labor]..............JC
Job Corps Camp [Department of Labor]..............JCC
Job Corps Opportunity Specialist [Department of Labor]..............JCOS
Job Creation Scheme [Department of Employment] [British]..............JCS
Job Cylinder Map [Data processing]..............JCM
Job Data Sheet..............JDS
Job Delivery Orders..............JDO
Job Description [Department of Labor]..............JD
Job Description Card..............JDC
Job Description Language [Data processing]..............JDL
Job Development Program..............JDP
Job Drawing List..............JDL
Job Element Text..............JET
Job English Training..............JET

Job Entry Central Services..............JECS
Job Entry Peripheral Services..............JEPS
Job Entry System [or Subsystem] [Data processing]..............JES
Job Estimate..............JE
Job Express Transportation..............JET
Job File Control Block [Data processing]..............JFCB
Job and Function [Air Force]..............J & F
Job Function Manual..............JFM
Job Grading System for Trades and Labor Occupations..............JGTL
Job Improvement Plan..............JIP
Job Improvement Request..............JIR
Job Information Block [Data processing]..............JIB
Job Information Delivery System [US Employment Service] [Department of Labor]..............JIDS
Job Information Service [Department of Labor]..............JIS
Job Information Test [Military]..............JIT
Job Instruction..............JI
Job Instruction Manual..............JIM
Job Instruction Training..............JIT
Job Item Cost Code..............JICC
Job Knowledge Test [Military]..............JKT
Job Methods Training..............JMT
Job Operation Manual..............JOM
Job Operations Report..............JOR
Job Opportunities for Better Skills..............JOBS
Job Opportunities in the Business Sector [Program]..............JOBS
Job Opportunity for Youth [NASA employment program]..............JOY
Job Order..............JO
Job Order Cost Account System..............JOCAS
Job Order Number..............JON
Job Order/Program Control Number [Army]..............JO/PCN
Job Order Request..............JOR
Job Order Supplement..............JOS
Job Organization Language [Data processing]..............JOL
Job Orientation in the Neighborhoods..............JOIN
Job Oriented Basic Skills [Program] [Military]..............JOBS
Job-Oriented Manual..............JOM
Job-Oriented Organizational Structure..............JOOS
Job-Oriented Training Standards..............JOTS
Job Pack Area [Data processing]..............JPA
Job Parts List..............JPL
Job Performance Aid..............JPA
Job Performance [or Proficiency] **Guide**..............JPG
Job Performance Measure..............JPM
Job Planning Form..............JPF
Job Processing Word..............JPW
Job Progress Ticket..............JPT
Job Questionnaire..............JQ
Job Relations Training..............JRT
Job Release Analysis..............JRA
Job Safety and Health [A publication]..............Job Safe & H
Job Satisfaction Inventory [Guidance]..............JSI
Job Schedule Change Request..............JSCR
Job Schedule Items..............JSI
Job Search Information..............JSI
Job Sequence Number..............JSN
Job Service Improvement Program [Department of Labor]..............JSIP
Job Service Matching Systems [US Employment Service] [Department of Labor]..............JSMS
Job Shop Simulation Program Generator..............JSSPG
Job Shop Simulator..............JSS
Job-Site Component..............JSC
Job Specification [Department of Labor]..............JS
Job Step Control Block [Data processing]..............JSCB
Job Task Analysis..............JTA
Job Task Performance Test..............JTPT
Job Training Package..............JTP
Job Training Partnership Act [Formerly, CETA]..............JTPA
Job Training Standard..............JTS
Job Work Folder..............JWF
Job Work Order..............JWO
Jobbers [London Stock Exchange]..............J
Jobs-Education-Training [Organization in Buffalo, NY]..............JET
Jobs in Energy..............JIE
Jobs Evaluation and Training..............JET
Jobs with Peace National Network..............JWPNN
Jobs for Veterans National Committee [Defunct]..............JFV
Jobst Pump [Medicine]..............JP
Jockey Club..............JC
Jockey's Association [Defunct]..............JA
Jockeys' Guild..............JG
Jocose..............JOC
Jocular..............JOC
Jodhpur [India] [Airport symbol]..............JDH
Jodrell Bank Experimental Station [British]..............JBES
Joel [Old Testament book]..............JI
Joensuu [Finland] [Airport symbol]..............JOE
Joensuu [Finland] [Seismograph station code, US Geological Survey] [Closed]..............JOE
Joensuun Korkeakoulun Julkaisuja Sarja Bii [A publication]..............Joensuun Korkeakoulun Julk Sar Bii

Joggle [*Engineering*] .... JOG
Joggle Blocks .... JB
Joggle Die .... JD
JOGN [*Journal of Obstetric, Gynecologic, and Neonatal Nursing*] **Nursing** [*A publication*] .... JOGN Nurs
Jogtudomanyi Koezloeny [*A publication*] .... Jogtud Koezl
Johan Mangku Negara [*Malaysian Honour*] .... JMN
Johannesburg [*South Africa*] [*Airport symbol*] .... JNB
Johannesburg [*South Africa*] [*Seismograph station code, US Geological Survey*] [*Closed*] .... JOH
John [*New Testament book*] .... Jn
John [*New Testament book*] .... Jno
John A. Andrew Clinical Society .... JAACS
John Abbott College, Ste.-Anne-De-Bellevue, PQ, Canada [*Library symbol*] .... CaQSTAJ
John the Baptist .... JOBAPT
John Birch Society .... JBS
John Brown University [*Arkansas*] .... JBU
John Brown University, Siloam Springs, AR [*OCLC symbol*] .... AKK
John Brown University, Siloam Springs, AR [*Library symbol*] .... ArSsJ
John Bull [*The typical Englishman*] .... JB
John Burroughs Memorial Association .... JBMA
John C. Hart Memorial Library, Shrub Oak, NY [*Library symbol*] .... NShr
John Carroll University [*Ohio*] .... JCU
John Carroll University, Cleveland, OH [*Library symbol*] .... OClJC
John Carroll University, Grasselli Library, University Heights, OH [*OCLC symbol*] .... JCU
John Carter Brown Library, Providence, RI [*Library symbol*] .... RPJCB
John Crerar Library [*National Translation Center*] .... JCL
John Crerar Library, Chicago, IL [*OCLC symbol*] .... IAB
John Crerar Library, Chicago, IL [*Library symbol*] .... ICJ
John D. Rockefeller III [*American philanthropist, 1906-1978*] JDR3
John Day, OR [*Radio station call letters*] .... KJDY
John Dewey Society .... JDS
John Dewey Society. Yearbook [*A publication*] .... John Dewey Soc Yrbk
John the Divine .... JODIV
John E. Clegg Library, Central City, IA [*Library symbol*] .... IaCc
John E. Meyer Eye Foundation, Eye Foundation Hospital, Birmingham, AL [*Library symbol*] .... ABMF
John Ericsson Society .... JES
John the Evangelist .... JOEVANG
John F. Kennedy Library .... JFKL
John F. Kennedy Library, Waltham, MA [*Library symbol*] .... MWalK
John F. Kennedy Memorial Hospital, Stratford, NJ [*Library symbol*] .... NjStrK
John F. Kennedy Philatelic Society .... JFKPS
John Fitzgerald Kennedy .... JFK
John Fitzgerald Kennedy Center for the Performing Arts .... JFKC
John Fitzgerald Kennedy National Historical Site .... JOKI
John Fitzgerald Kennedy Spaceflight Center [*Also known as KSC*] .... JFKSC
John Flanagan [*Designer's mark, when appearing on US coins*] .... JF
John Fluke Manufacturing Co., Mountlake Terrace, WA [*Library symbol*] .... WaMtJF
John Fox, Jr. Memorial Library, Paris, KY [*Library symbol*] .... KyParF
John G. Shedd Aquarium, Chicago, IL [*Library symbol*] .... ICJSh
John G. Shedd Aquarium, Chicago, IL [*OCLC symbol*] .... IHW
John H. Burrows & Sons Ltd., Southend-On-Sea, United Kingdom [*Library symbol*] .... UkSsB
John Hancock Income Securities Corp. [*NYSE symbol*] .... JHS
John Hancock Investors, Inc. [*NYSE symbol*] .... JHI
John Henry Cardinal Newman Honorary Society [*Defunct*] .... JHCNHS
John Herron Art Institute. Bulletin [*Indianapolis*] [*A publication*] .... John Herron Art Inst Bul
John Howard Association .... JHA
John Innes Horticultural Institution. Annual Report [*A publication*] .... John Innes Hortic Inst Annu Rep
John Innes Institute. Annual Report [*A publication*] .... John Innes Inst Annu Rep
John J. Madden Mental Health Center, Training Staff Development Library, Hines, IL [*Library symbol*] .... IHineJ
John Jay College of Criminal Justice, New York, NY [*Library symbol*] .... NNJJ
John Jay College of Criminal Justice, New York, NY [*OCLC symbol*] .... VVJ
John Jermain Memorial Public Library, Sag Harbor, NY [*Library symbol*] .... NSh
John Judkyn Memorial .... JJM
John La Farge Institute .... JFI
John Lovell & Son, City Directories Ltd., Montreal, PQ, Canada [*Library symbol*] .... CaQMJL
John and Mable Ringling Museum of Art, Sarasota, FL [*Library symbol*] .... FSR
John Marshall High School Library, Rochester, NY [*OCLC symbol*] .... RWS
John Marshall Journal of Practice and Procedure [*A publication*] .... John Marshall J
John Marshall Law School, Chicago, IL [*OCLC symbol*] .... IUJ
John and Mary Kirby Hospital, Monticello, IL [*Library symbol*] .... IMoH
John McIntire Public Library, Zanesville, OH [*Library symbol*] .... OZav
John Mercanti [*Designer's mark, when appearing on US coins*] .... JM
John Milton Society for the Blind .... JMS
John Milton Society for the Blind .... JMSB
John Muir Institute for Environmental Studies .... JMI
John Muir National Historic Site .... JOMU
John Nurminen [*Finland*] [*ICAO designator*] .... JN
John O'Hara Journal [*A publication*] .... JOHJ
John Peter Smith Hospital, Fort Worth, TX [*Library symbol*] .... TxFJPS
John Phillip Tuba Corp. [*NASDAQ symbol*] .... TUBA
John R. Abney Collection, Edgefield County Library, Edgefield, SC [*Library symbol*] .... ScEA
John R. Kaufman, Jr., [*Sunbury*] **Public Library, Sunbury, PA** [*Library symbol*] .... PSu
John R. Sinnock [*Designer's mark, when appearing on US coins*] .... JRS
John R. Sinnock [*Designer's mark, when appearing on US coins*] .... JS
John R. Thompson Co. [*NYSE symbol*] [*Delisted*] .... THM
John Ronald Renel Tolkien [*British author, 1892-1973*] .... JRRT
John Ross Ewing, Jr. [*Character in TV series "Dallas"*] .... JR
John Rylands Library Bulletin [*A publication*] .... John Rylands Lib Bul
John Rylands Library Bulletin [*A publication*] .... JRLB
John Steinbeck House, Salinas, CA [*Library symbol*] .... CSalJS
John Steinbeck Society of America .... JSSA
John Swaney Attendance Center, McNabb, IL [*Library symbol*] .... IMcSC
John T. Mather Memorial Hospital, Port Jefferson, NY [*Library symbol*] .... NPjMH
John Tomay Memorial Public Library, Georgetown, CO [*Library symbol*] .... CoGeo
John Warner Hospital, Clinton, IL [*Library symbol*] .... IClH
John Wesley College Library, Owosso, MI [*OCLC symbol*] [*Inactive*] .... EYJ
John Wesley College, Owosso, MI [*Library symbol*] .... MiOwJW
John Wiley [*& Sons*] [*Publisher*] .... JW
John Wiley & Sons, New York, NY [*Library symbol*] .... JwS
JOHNNIAC [*John's Integrator and Automatic Computer*] **Open Shop System** [*Data processing*] .... JOSS
Johnny Come Lately [*Slang*] .... JCL
Johns and Call Girls United Against Repression .... JACGUAR
Johns Hopkins Magazine [*A publication*] .... JHMa
Johns Hopkins Medical Journal [*A publication*] .... Johns H Med
Johns Hopkins Medical Journal [*A publication*] .... Johns Hopkins Med J
Johns Hopkins Medical Journal. Supplement [*A publication*] .... Johns Hopkins Med J Suppl
Johns Hopkins Oceanographic Studies [*A publication*] .... Johns Hopkins Oceanogr Stud
Johns Hopkins Studies in Romance Language and Literature [*A publication*] .... JHSRLL
Johns Hopkins University [*Maryland*] .... JHU
Johns Hopkins University, Applied Physics Laboratory, Silver Spring, MD [*Library symbol*] .... MdBJ-A
Johns Hopkins University. Applied Physics Laboratory. Special Report [*A publication*] .... Johns Hopkins Univ Appl Phys Lab Spec Rep
Johns Hopkins University, Baltimore, MD [*OCLC symbol*] .... JHE
Johns Hopkins University, Baltimore, MD [*Library symbol*] .... MdBJ
Johns Hopkins University. Circular [*A publication*] .... Johns Hopkins Univ Cir
Johns Hopkins University, John Work Garrett Library, Baltimore, MD [*Library symbol*] .... MdBJ-G
Johns Hopkins University, School of Advanced International Studies, Washington, DC [*Library symbol*] .... MdBJ-AIS
Johns Hopkins University, School of Hygiene and Public Health, Maternal and Child Health-Population Dynamics Library, Baltimore, MD [*Library symbol*] .... MdBJ-H
Johns Hopkins University Studies in Historical and Political Science [*A publication*] .... J H U Studies
Johns Hopkins University Studies in Historical and Political Science [*A publication*] .... Johns Hopkins Univ Stud
Johns Hopkins University Studies in Historical and Political Science [*A publication*] .... Johns H U Stud
Johns Hopkins University, Welch Medical Library, Baltimore, MD [*OCLC symbol*] .... JHW
Johns Hopkins University, William H. Welch Medical Library, Baltimore, MD [*Library symbol*] .... MdBJ-W
John's [*Von Neumann*] **Integrator and Automatic Computer** .... JOHNNIAC
Johns-Manville Corp. [*Wall Street slang name: "Jump"*] [*NYSE symbol*] [*Delisted*] .... JM
Johns-Manville Corp., Corporate Information Center, Denver, CO [*OCLC symbol*] .... CJM
Johnson Associates, Incorporated, Greenwich, CT [*Library symbol*] .... Jai
Johnson Bible College [*Tennessee*] .... JBC
Johnson Bible College, Knoxville, TN [*Library symbol*] .... TKimJ
Johnson C. Smith University, Charlotte, NC [*Library symbol*] .... NcCJ
Johnson C. Smith University, James B. Duke Memorial Library, Charlotte, NC [*OCLC symbol*] .... NCJ
Johnson Canyon [*California*] [*Seismograph station code, US Geological Survey*] .... JHC
Johnson City, TN [*Radio station call letters*] .... WETB
Johnson City, TN [*Radio station call letters*] .... WETS
Johnson City, TN [*Radio station call letters*] .... WJCW
Johnson City, TN [*Television station call letters*] .... WJHL-TV
Johnson City, TN [*Radio station call letters*] .... WQUT
Johnson City, TX [*Location identifier*] [*FAA*] .... JCY
Johnson [*E. F.*] **Co.** [*NYSE symbol*] [*Delisted*] .... JEF
Johnson Controls, Incorporated [*NYSE symbol*] .... JCI
Johnson County Library, Buffalo, WY [*Library symbol*] .... WyBu
Johnson County Library, Kaycee Branch, Kaycee, WY [*Library symbol*] .... WyKc
Johnson County Library, Merriam, KS [*Library symbol*] .... KMrJ

Johnson County Mental Health Center, Mission, KS [*Library symbol*] ... KMiJ
Johnson Electronics [*NASDAQ symbol*] ... JHSN
Johnson Flying Service [*Air carrier designation symbol*] ... JOHX
Johnson Free Public Library, Hackensack, NJ [*Library symbol*] ... NjHack
Johnson & Johnson [*NYSE symbol*] ... JNJ
Johnson & Johnson Dental Products Co., Science Information Center, East Windsor, NJ [*OCLC symbol*] ... VJJ
Johnson & Johnson Ltd., Montreal, PQ, Canada [*Library symbol*] ... CaQMJJ
Johnson & Johnson, Research Center, New Brunswick, NJ [*Library symbol*] ... NjNbJJ
Johnson, KS [*Location identifier*] [*FAA*] ... JHN
Johnson Noise [*Thermal noise, that made by a resistor at a temperature above absolute zero*] ... JN
Johnson-O'Malley Act [*1934*] ... JOM
Johnson Products Company, Inc. [*American Stock Exchange symbol*] ... JPC
Johnson Reprint Corporation, New York, NY [*Library symbol*] ... JrC
Johnson Service Company [*Later, JCI*] [*NYSE symbol*] ... JSC
Johnson Society of London ... JSL
Johnson Space Center [*Formerly, Manned Spacecraft Center*] [*NASA*] ... JSC
Johnson State College, Johnson, VT [*OCLC symbol*] ... VTJ
Johnson State College, Johnson, VT [*Library symbol*] ... VtJoT
Johnson, VT [*Radio station call letters*] ... WJSC-FM
Johnsonian News Letter [*A publication*] ... JNL
Johnston Airways [*Chicago, IL*] [*FAA designator*] ... JMJ
Johnston Atoll [*MARC country of publication code*] [*Library of Congress*] ... ji
Johnston Atoll [*Two-letter standard code*] ... JT
Johnston Atoll [*Three-letter standard code*] ... JTN
Johnston Atoll [*MARC geographic area code*] [*Library of Congress*] ... poji---
Johnston City, IL [*Radio station call letters*] ... WDDW
Johnston County Technical Institute, Smithfield, NC [*Library symbol*] ... NcSmJ
Johnston Island [*Airport symbol*] ... JON
Johnston, SC [*Radio station call letters*] ... WJES
Johnstone Point, AK [*Location identifier*] [*FAA*] ... JOH
Johnstown [*Pennsylvania*] [*Airport symbol*] ... JST
Johnstown American Companies SBI [*NASDAQ symbol*] ... JOAMS
Johnstown Flood National Memorial ... JOFL
Johnstown, NY [*Radio station call letters*] ... WIZR-FM
Johnstown, NY [*Radio station call letters*] ... WMYL
Johnstown, OH [*Radio station call letters*] ... WWWJ
Johnstown, PA [*Location identifier*] [*FAA*] ... JST
Johnstown, PA [*Radio station call letters*] ... WCRO
Johnstown, PA [*Television station call letters*] ... WFAT-TV
Johnstown, PA [*Radio station call letters*] ... WGLU
Johnstown, PA [*Radio station call letters*] ... WJAC
Johnstown, PA [*Radio station call letters*] ... WJAC-FM
Johnstown, PA [*Television station call letters*] ... WJAC-TV
Johnstown, PA [*Radio station call letters*] ... WJNL
Johnstown, PA [*Radio station call letters*] ... WJNL-FM
Johnstown, PA [*Radio station call letters*] ... WKYE
Johnstown & Stony Creek Rail Road Co. [*AAR code*] ... JSC
Johore Bharu [*Malaysia*] [*Airport symbol*] ... JHB
Join ... J
Join ... JN
Join Airways ... JAWYS
Joined ... JD
Joined by Enlistment [*Military*] ... JDENL
Joined From [*Military*] ... JDFR
Joined by Induction [*Military*] ... JDIND
Joined by Reenlistment [*Military*] ... JDREENL
Joiner [*Machinery*] ... J
Joiner Pilaster Fumetight [*Technical drawings*] ... JPFT
Joiner Pilaster Nontight [*Technical drawings*] ... JPNT
Joining ... JNG
Joint ... J
Joint ... JNT
Joint ... JT
Joint Acceptance Plan ... JAP
Joint Account ... JA
Joint Action Armed Forces ... JAAF
Joint Action in Community Service ... JACS
Joint Action Company [*Marine Corps*] ... JAC
Joint Actions Control Office ... JACO
Joint Activity Briefing [*Military*] ... JAB
Joint Administration Services ... JAS
Joint Administrative Committee [*Military*] ... JADC
Joint Administrative Planning Section [*Joint Planning Staff*] [*World War II*] ... JAPS
Joint Advanced Study Group ... JASG
Joint Advanced Study Group ... JASGP
Joint Advanced Tactical Command, Control, and Communications Program [*Military*] ... JATCCCP
Joint Advanced Tactical Command, Control, and Communications System [*Military*] ... JATCCCS
Joint Advertising Directors of Recruiting [*Navy*] ... JADOR
Joint Advisory Survey Board [*British*] ... JASB
Joint Aeronautical Materials Activity [*Military*] ... JAMAC
Joint Agency for Municipal Securities Dealers ... JAMS
Joint Agent ... JA
Joint Air-to-Air Missile Requirement Study ... JAAMRS
Joint Air Attack Team Tactics ... JAATT
Joint Air Communications of the Pacific ... JACSPAC
Joint Air Control and Coordination Center [*Air Force*] ... JACCC
Joint Air Defense Board ... JADB
Joint Air Defense Force ... JADF
Joint Air Defense Interoperability Study ... JADIS
Joint Air Defense Operation Center ... JADOC
Joint Air Force-NASA ... JAFNA
Joint Air Force-Navy Committee ... JAFNC
Joint Air Force-Navy Experiment ... JANE
Joint Air-Ground Instruction Team ... JAGIT
Joint Air-Ground Operations System [*Military*] ... JAGOS
Joint Air Movements Board [*Military*] ... JAMB
Joint Air Operations Center ... JAOC
Joint Air Photo Center [*NATO*] ... JAPC
Joint Air Reconnaissance Center [*NATO*] ... JARC
Joint Air Reconnaissance Intelligence Centre [*British*] ... JARIC
Joint Air Sea Interaction [*National Science Foundation/United Kingdom*] ... JASIN
Joint Air-Surface Antisubmarine Action ... JASASA
Joint Air Traffic Control Center [*Military*] ... JATCC
Joint Air Training Plan ... JATP
Joint Air Transport Establishment [*Military*] [*British*] ... JATE
Joint Air Transportation Plan ... JATP
Joint Air Transportation Service ... JATS
Joint Airborne Advance Party [*Military*] ... JAAP
Joint Airborne Communications Center ... JACC
Joint Airborne Communications Center/Command Post ... JACC/CP
Joint Airborne Communications Center and Command Post ... JACKPOT
Joint Aircraft Committee [*World War II*] ... JAC
Joint Aircraft Hurricane Plan ... JAMHEP
Joint Airlift Allocations Board ... JAAB
Joint Airlift Allocations Committee ... JAAC
Joint Airlines Military Traffic Office ... JAMTO
Joint Airport Weather Studies [*National Center for Atmospheric Research*] ... JAWS
Joint Allied Communications Element ... JACE
Joint Allied Military Petroleum Office [*NATO*] ... JAMPO
Joint Allocation Committee Civil Intelligence [*of US and Great Britain*] [*World War II*] ... JACCI
Joint Alternate Command Center [*Military*] ... JACC
Joint Alternate Command Element ... JACE
Joint American-Chinese Foul Up [*World War II slang*] [*Bowdlerized version*] ... JACFU
Joint American Military Advisory Group ... JAMAG
Joint American Military Mission for Aid to Turkey ... JAMMAT
Joint Amphibious Board [*Military*] ... JAB
Joint Amphibious Task Force ... JATF
Joint Analog Numeric Understanding System ... JANUS
Joint Anglo-American Foul Up [*World War II slang*] [*Bowdlerized version*] ... JAAFU
Joint Antiaircraft Operation Center [*NATO*] ... JAAOC
Joint Antisatellite Study ... JASS
Joint Antisubmarine Action ... JASA
Joint Apprenticeship Committee ... JAC
Joint Apprenticeship Program [*Department of Labor*] ... JAP
Joint Apprenticeship and Training Committee [*Bureau of Apprenticeship and Training*] [*Department of Labor*] ... JATC
Joint Arctic Weather Stations [*Canada-US*] ... JAWS
Joint Area Petroleum Office ... JAPO
Joint Arms Control ... JAC
Joint Army-Air Force ... JAAF
Joint Army-Air Force Adjustment Regulations ... JAAFAR
Joint Army-Air Force Air-Ground Study ... JAGS
Joint Army-Air Force Commercial Traffic Bulletin ... JAAFCTB
Joint Army-Air Force Procurement Circular ... JAAFPC
Joint Army-Air Force Publication ... JAFPUB
Joint Army and Navy ... JAN
Joint Army-Navy-Air Force ... JANAF
Joint Army-Navy-Air Force Logistics Policy ... JANALP
Joint Army-Navy-Air Force Logistics Publication ... JANALP
Joint Army-Navy-Air Force, Pacific General Message [*Serially numbered*] ... JANAFPAC
Joint Army-Navy-Air Force Procedure [*NATO*] ... JANAP
Joint Army-Navy-Air Force Publication ... JANAP
Joint Army-Navy-Air Force Sea Transportation Message ... JANAST
Joint Army-Navy Aircraft Instrument Research ... JANAIR
Joint Army-Navy Assessment Committee [*World War II*] ... JANAC
Joint Army-Navy Ballistic Missile Committee ... JANBMC
Joint Army-Navy Board ... JB
Joint Army and Navy Committee on Welfare and Recreation ... JANCWR
Joint Army-Navy Communications ... JANCOM
Joint Army-Navy Experimental and Testing Board ... JANET
Joint Army-Navy Foul Up [*Military slang*] [*Bowdlerized version*] ... JANFU
Joint Army-Navy Grid ... JANGRID
Joint Army-Navy Information Center ... JANIC
Joint Army-Navy Intelligence Studies ... JANIS
Joint Army-Navy Machine Tools Committee ... JANMAT
Joint Army-Navy Material ... JANMAT
Joint Army and Navy Munitions Board [*Terminated, 1947*] ... JANMB

Joint-Army-Navy-NASA-Air Force Interagency Propulsion Committee ... JANNAF
Joint Army-Navy Ocean Terminal ... JANOT
Joint Army-Navy Petroleum Purchase Agency ... JANPPA
Joint Army-Navy Procedure ... JANP
Joint Army-Navy Publication ... JANP
Joint Army-Navy Specification ... JANSPEC
Joint Army-Navy Standard [*NATO*] ... JANSTD
Joint Army and Navy Technical Aeronautical Board ... JANTAB
Joint Army-Navy War Shipping Administration ... JANWSA
Joint Assault Signal Company [*Small unit in Pacific amphibious warfare*] [*World War II*] ... JASCO
Joint Association Survey [*American Petroleum Institute, Independent Petroleum Association of America, and Mid-Continent Oil and Gas Association*] ... JAS
Joint Atomic Energy Commission ... JAEC
Joint Atomic Energy Intelligence Center [*Military*] ... JAEIC
Joint Atomic Energy Intelligence Committee ... JAEIC
Joint Atomic Exercise [*NATO*] ... JAE
Joint Atomic Information Exchange Group [*DoD*] ... JAIEG
Joint Atomic Weapons Planning Manual ... JAWPM
Joint Atomic Weapons Publication System ... JAWPS
Joint Atomic Weapons Publications Board ... JAWPB
Joint Attack Weapon System [*Military*] ... JAWS
Joint Automated Planning Support System [*of JOPS*] [*Military*] ... JAPSS
Joint Automatic Control Conference ... JACC
Joint Automatic Language Processing Group ... JALPG
Joint Baltic American National Committee ... JBANC
Joint Bank-Fund Library, Washington, DC [*OCLC symbol*] ... DJB
Joint Bar ... JTB
Joint Blood Council [*Defunct*] ... JBC
Joint Board of Directors, Army-Air Force Exchange Service ... JBDAAFES
Joint Board on Future Storage of Atomic Weapons ... JBFSAW
Joint Bond ... JB
Joint Brazil-United States Defense Commission [*Terminated, 1977*] ... JBUSDC
Joint Brazil-United States Military Commission ... BMC
Joint Brazil-United States Military Commission ... JBUSMC
Joint Bus Military Traffic Office ... JBMTO
Joint Cadre Operation Control Group [*Military*] ... JCOCG
Joint Casualty Resolution Center ... JCRC
Joint Center for Political Studies ... JCPS
Joint Center for the Study of Law and Human Genetics ... JCSLHG
Joint Central Graves Registration Office [*Military*] ... JCGRO
Joint Chapters - Educational Council ... JCEC
Joint Chiefs of Staff [*United States*] [*Military*] ... JCS
Joint Chiefs of Staff [*Military decoration*] ... JCSIdentBad
Joint Chiefs of Staff Alerting Network [*Military*] ... JCSAN
Joint Chiefs of Staff Automatic Conference Arranger [*Military*] ... JCS-ACA
Joint Chiefs of Staff Interim Data Transmission Network [*Military*] ... JCSIDTN
Joint Chiefs of Staff Memorandum [*Military*] ... JCSM
Joint Chiefs of Staff Organization [*Military*] ... JCSO
Joint Chiefs of Staff Publications [*Military*] ... JCP
Joint Chiefs of Staff Publications [*Military*] ... JCSPUB
Joint Chiefs of Staff Representative, Europe [*NATO*] ... JCSRE
Joint Church Aid [*Biafra relief program in late 1960's*] [*Defunct*] ... JCA
Joint Church Aid - United States of America [*See also JCA*] [*Defunct*] ... JCA-USA
Joint Civil Affairs Committee ... JCAC
Joint Civil Defense Support Group ... JCDSG
Joint Civilian Employee Advisory Group [*Military*] ... JCEAG
Joint Civilian Orientation Conference [*DoD*] ... JCOC
Joint Combat Operations Center [*Navy*] ... JCOC
Joint Combat Systems Integrating ... JCSI
Joint Combined System Test ... JCST
Joint Command and Control Development Group [*DoD*] ... JCCDG
Joint Command and Control Requirements Group [*Joint Chiefs of Staff*] [*DoD*] ... JCCRG
Joint Command and Control Standards Committee ... JCCSC
Joint Command Operations Center [*NATO*] ... JCOC
Joint Command Post Exercise [*Military*] ... JCPX
Joint Commission on Accreditation of Hospitals ... JCAH
Joint Commission on Accreditation of Universities [*Military*] ... JCA
Joint Commission on Allied Health Personnel in Ophthalmology ... JCAHPO
Joint Commission on Applied Radioactivity ... JCAR
Joint Commission on Atomic Masses ... JCAM
Joint Commission for Black Sea Fisheries ... JCBSF
Joint Commission on Competitive Safeguards and the Medical Aspects of Sports ... JCCSMAS
Joint Commission on Dance and Theatre Accreditation ... JCDTA
Joint Commission on Hospital Accreditation ... JCHA
Joint Commission on Korea ... JCK
Joint Commission on Mental Health of Children ... JCMHC
Joint Commission on Mental Illness and Health [*Defunct*] ... JCMIH
Joint Commission on Political Prisoners and Refugees in French North Africa [*World War II*] ... JCPPRFNA
Joint Commission on Rural Reconstruction ... JCRR
Joint Committee on Agricultural Research and Development [*Agency for International Development*] ... JCARD
Joint Committee on Atomic Energy [*of the US Congress*] [*Terminated*] ... JCAE
Joint Committee of the Autonomous Federations and Unions [*Comite d'Entente des Federations et Syndicats Autonomes d'Algerie*] [*Algeria*] ... JCAFU
Joint Committee on Building Codes [*Later, Model Code Standardization Council*] ... JCBC
Joint Committee on College Teaching ... JCOT
Joint Committee on Contemporary China ... JCCC
Joint Committee on Continuing Legal Education [*Later, ALI-ABA Committee on Continuing Professional Education*] ... JCCLE
Joint Committee on Intersociety Coordination ... JCIC
Joint Committee [*of Congress*] **on the Library of Congress** ... JCLC
Joint Committee on Library Education ... JCLE
Joint Committee on New Weapons and Equipment ... JNW
Joint Committee on Powder Diffraction Standards ... JCPDS
Joint [*Congressional*] **Committee on Printing** ... JCP
Joint Committee of the States to Study Alcoholic Beverage Laws ... JCSSAB
Joint Committee on Television Transmission ... CMTT
Joint Committee on the Union List of Serials ... JCULS
Joint Communication Activity ... JCA
Joint Communications Agency [*Military*] ... JCA
Joint Communications Board ... JCB
Joint Communications Center ... JCC
Joint Communications-Electronics Committee [*Military*] ... JCEC
Joint Communications-Electronics Committee, Pacific [*Military*] ... JCECPAC
Joint Communications-Electronics Group [*Military*] ... JCEG
Joint Communications-Electronics Group [*Military*] ... JCEGP
Joint Communications-Electronics Nomenclature System ... JCENS
Joint Communications-Electronics Operating Instructions [*Military*] ... JCEOI
Joint Communications and Electronics Working Group [*NATO*] ... JCEWG
Joint Communications Instruction ... JCI
Joint Communications Support Element [*DoD*] ... JCSE
Joint Compound [*Plumbing*] ... JC
Joint Computer Conference ... JCC
Joint Concepts and Evaluation Group [*Military*] ... JCEG
Joint CONEX [*Container Express*] **Control Agency** ... JCCA
Joint Conference. Chemical Institute of Canada/American Chemical Society. Abstracts of Papers [*A publication*] ... J Conf Chem Inst Can Am Chem Soc Abstr Pap
Joint Conference. Chemical Institute of Canada/American Chemical Society. Abstracts of Papers [*A publication*] ... J Conf CIC/ACS Abstr Pap
Joint Congressional Atomic Energy Commission ... JCAEC
Joint Construction Agency ... JCA
Joint Consultative Board [*NATO*] ... JCB
Joint Consultative Committee [*of the National Joint Advisory Council*] [*British*] [*World War II*] ... JCC
Joint Continental Aerospace Defense Integration Staff [*Military*] ... JCADIS
Joint Continental Defense Systems Integration Planning Staff [*Air Force*] ... JCDSIPS
Joint Control Number ... JCN
Joint Conventional Ammunition Program [*Army*] ... JCAP
Joint Conventional Ammunition Program Coordinating Group [*Army*] ... JCAP-CG
Joint Coordinating Committee on Fundamental Properties of Matter [*US Department of Energy and USSR State Committee on Peaceful Uses of Atomic Energy*] ... JCC-FPM
Joint Coordination Center ... JCC
Joint Coordination Center Communications Network ... JCCOMNET
Joint Coordination Center, Far East [*Military*] ... JCCFE
Joint Council of Allergy and Immunology ... JCAI
Joint Council on Economic Education ... JCEE
Joint Council on Educational Broadcasting [*Later, JCET*] ... JCEB
Joint Council on Educational Telecommunications ... JCET
Joint Council to Improve Health Care of the Aged [*Defunct*] ... JCIHCA
Joint Council of Post Office Associations [*South Africa*] ... JCPOA
Joint Council for Repatriation ... JCR
Joint Council on Research in Pastoral Care and Counseling ... JCRPCC
Joint Council for Scientific and Technical Communication [*British*] ... JCSTC
Joint Countering Attack Helicopter Exercises ... J-CATCH
Joint Crisis Management Capability [*DoD*] ... JCMC
Joint Cruise Missile Project Office ... JCMPO
Joint Cultural Appeal [*Jewish fund-raising organization*] ... JCA
Joint Custody Association ... JCA
Joint Cutover Integrated Working Group [*Military*] ... JCIWG
Joint Defense Appeal [*Defunct*] ... JDA
Joint Defense Production Committee [*Later, Joint War Production Committee*] [*World War II*] ... JDPC
Joint Defense Staff [*NATO*] ... JDS
Joint Deployment System ... JDS
Joint Deputy Chiefs of Staff [*Military*] ... JDCS
Joint Design Team [*Military*] ... JDT
Joint Determination ... JD
Joint Development Agency [*DoD*] ... JDA
Joint Development Community [*DoD*] ... JDC

Joint Dictionary [*Dictionary of US Military Terms for Joint Usage*] [*A publication*] ... JD
Joint Diploma in Management Accounting Services [*British*] ... JDipMA
Joint Directory of Higher Education [*A publication*] ... JDHE
Joint Dissemination Review Panels ... JDRP
Joint Doppler Operational Project [*For tornado warning*] [*Meteorology*] ... JDOP
Joint Eastern Air Defense Force ... JEADF
Joint Economic Committee of Congress ... JEC
Joint Economic Committee of Congress ... JECC
Joint Economic Team ... JET
Joint Economy Board [*Abolished, 1947*] [*Army-Navy*] ... JEB
Joint Educational Development ... JED
Joint Effort Against Lefthanded Complications ... JELC
Joint Effort Evaluation Program [*Military*] ... JEEP
Joint Effort for Talent [*Navy*] ... JET
Joint Electron Device Engineering Council ... JEDEC
Joint Electron Tube Engineering Council [*Later, JEDEC*] ... JETEC
Joint Electronic Countermeasures Operation Section [*NATO*] ... JECMOS
Joint Electronics Board ... JEB
Joint Electronics Information Agency ... JEIA
Joint Electronics Type Designation System [*Military*] ... JETDS
Joint Electronics Type Designator [*Military*] ... JETD
Joint Electronics Type [*Designation*] **System** [*Military*] ... JETS
Joint Emergency Airlift Traffic Management Plan [*DoD*] ... JEAT
Joint Emergency Defense Plan Europe [*NATO*] ... JEDPE
Joint Emergency Evacuation Plan [*Military*] ... JEEP
Joint Emergency Personnel Augmentation Plan [*Military*] ... JEPAP
Joint Emergency Relocation Site ... JERS
Joint Endeavor for Welfare, Education, and Liberation [*In name of Grenadian political party, the New Jewel Movement, which governed from 1979 until ousted by a coup in 1983. Maurice Bishop, a founder of the party and prime minister under it, was killed during the overthrow*] ... JEWEL
Joint Engine Project Office ... JEPO
Joint Engineering Agency ... JEA
Joint Engineering Management Conference ... JEMC
Joint Enroute Terminal System [*Canada*] ... JETS
Joint Environmental Effects Program [*Military*] ... JEEP
Joint Environmental Research Unit ... JERU
Joint Equipment Identification Team [*Military*] ... JEIT
Joint Establishment Experimental Pile [*Nuclear reactor*] [*Norway*] ... JEEP
Joint Establishment for Nuclear Energy Research ... JENER
Joint European Operations Communications Network ... JEOCN
Joint European TOKAMAK [*or Torus*] [*Nuclear reactor*] ... JET
Joint Evaluation Committee [*NSF-UCAR*] ... JEC
Joint Executive Committee on Medicine and Biology ... JECMB
Joint Exercise ... JEX
Joint Exercise Control Group [*Military*] ... JXCG
Joint Exercise Planning Staff [*NATO*] ... JEPS
Joint Exploratory Group [*NATO*] ... JEG
Joint Export Agent ... JEA
Joint Export Association [*Department of Commerce*] ... JEA
Joint Export Establishment Promotion [*Trade exhibition*] [*Department of Commerce*] ... JEEP
Joint Export-Import Agency [*Munich*] [*Allied German Occupation Forces*] ... JEIA
Joint Facilities Utilization Board [*Military*] ... JFUB
Joint Feasibility Study Group [*Air Force*] ... JFSG
Joint Fiction Reserve ... JFR
Joint Field Training Exercise [*Military*] ... JFTX
Joint Field Trial ... JFT
Joint Financial Management Improvement Program ... JFMIP
Joint Flight Acceptance Composite Test [*Gemini*] [*NASA*] ... J-FACT
Joint Flight Test Control Group ... JFTCG
Joint Force [*Military*] ... JF
Joint Force Memo [*Military*] ... JFM
Joint Foreign Exchange Agency [*Berlin*] [*Post-World War II, Germany*] ... JFEA
Joint Foreign Intelligence Assistance Program ... JFIAP
Joint Formal Acceptance Inspection [*NATO*] ... JFAI
Joint Forward Air Controllers Training and Standards Unit [*British*] ... JFACTSU
Joint Foundation Support [*An association*] ... JFS
Joint Free Public Library of Morristown and Morris Township, Morristown, NJ [*Library symbol*] ... NjMo
Joint Frequency Allocation Panel ... JFAP
Joint Frequency List ... JFL
Joint Frequency Panel ... JFP
Joint Fuze Task Group [*Army*] ... JFTG
Joint General Staff [*Military*] ... JGS
Joint Government Liaison Committee [*Composed of Association of Brass and Bronze Ingot Manufacturers and Brass and Bronze Ingot Institute*] ... JGLC
Joint Group of Experts on the Scientific Aspects of Marine Pollution [*A publication*] ... J Group Experts Sci Aspects Mar Pollut
Joint Guidance and Control ... JG & C
Joint Health Library, New York, NY [*Library symbol*] [*Obsolete*] ... NNJH
Joint Household Goods Shipping Office [*Military*] ... JHHGSO
Joint Household Goods Shipping Office, Washington Area [*Military*] ... JHGSOWA
Joint Hurricane Warning Center ... JHWC
Joint Hypocenter Determination [*Earthquake study*] ... JHD
Joint In-Flight Data Transmission System [*Army*] ... JIFDATS
Joint In-Flight Transmission System [*Army*] ... JIFTS
Joint Industrial Conference on Hydraulic Standards ... JICHS
Joint Industrial Council [*Formerly, Joint Industry Conference*] ... JIC
Joint Industry Board of the Electrical Industry ... JIBEI
Joint Industry Committee for National Readership Surveys [*British*] ... JICNARS
Joint Industry-Government Tall Structures Committee ... JIGTSC
Joint Industry Research Committee for Standardization of Miniature Precision Coaxial Connectors ... JIRCSM
Joint Information Liaison Office [*Military*] ... JILO
Joint Information Office [*Military*] ... JIO
Joint Information and Retrieval System [*DoD*] ... JIRS
Joint Information Search Unit Retrieval System ... JISR
Joint Input Processing ... JIP
Joint Inspection Unit [*United Nations*] ... JIU
Joint Installation Plan ... JIP
Joint Institute for Acoustics and Flight Sciences ... JIAFS
Joint Institute for Laboratory Astrophysics [*Located at University of Colorado*] ... JILA
Joint Institute for Laboratory Astrophysics Information Center. Report [*A publication*] ... JILA Inf Cent Rep
Joint Institute for Laboratory Astrophysics. Report [*A publication*] ... JILA Rep
Joint Institute for Marine and Atmospheric Research [*National Oceanic and Atmospheric Administration*] ... JIMAR
Joint Institute of Nuclear Research [*USSR*] ... JINR
Joint Insurance Committee [*under the Trading with the Enemy Act*] [*World War II*] ... JIC
Joint Intelligence Bureau [*British*] ... JIB
Joint Intelligence Center ... JIC
Joint Intelligence Center, Africa ... JICA
Joint Intelligence Center, Pacific Ocean Areas ... JICPOA
Joint Intelligence Collecting Agency ... JICA
Joint Intelligence Collecting Agency, China, Burma, India [*World War II*] ... JICACBI
Joint Intelligence Collecting Agency, Middle East [*World War II*] ... JICAME
Joint Intelligence Collecting Agency, North Africa [*World War II*] ... JICANA
Joint Intelligence Collecting Agency, Reception Committee [*Navy*] ... JICARC
Joint Intelligence Committee ... JIC
Joint Intelligence Coordination Staff [*Central Intelligence Agency*] ... JICS
Joint Intelligence Estimate for Planning ... JIEP
Joint Intelligence Group [*Military*] ... JIG
Joint Intelligence Objectives Agency ... JIOA
Joint Intelligence Staff ... JIS
Joint Intelligence Studies Publishing Board ... JISPB
Joint Interest Test [*Navy*] ... JIT
Joint Interface Implementation Program [*Army*] ... JIIP
Joint Interface Test Facility [*Army*] ... JITF
Joint Interface Test Force [*Military*] ... JITF
Joint Interoperability of Tactical Command and Control Systems ... JINTACCS
Joint Interservice Task Force ... JITF
Joint Investigation of the Southeastern Tropical Atlantic [*Angola, US*] ... JISETA
Joint Labor Relations Board ... JLRB
Joint Landing Force ... JLF
Joint Landing Force Board ... JLFB
Joint Least Squares [*Statistics*] ... JLS
Joint Logistics Commanders [*Military*] ... JLC
Joint Logistics Committee [*Military*] ... JLC
Joint Logistics, Operations, Intelligence Center [*NATO*] ... JLOIC
Joint Logistics and Personnel Policy Guidance [*Military*] ... JLPPG
Joint Logistics Planning Board ... JLPB
Joint Logistics Plans Committee [*Military*] ... JLPC
Joint Logistics Plans Group [*Military*] ... JLPG
Joint Logistics Review Board [*Military*] ... JLRB
Joint Logistics over the Shore [*Military*] ... JLOTS
Joint Logistics Support Plan ... JLSP
Joint Long-Range Proving Ground ... JLRPG
Joint Long-Range Strategic Estimates [*Military*] ... JLRSE
Joint Long-Range Strategic Study [*Military*] ... JLRSS
Joint Management Team ... JMT
Joint Manpower Program [*Military*] ... JMP
Joint Manual Direction Center [*Air Force*] ... JMDC
Joint Maritime Commission ... JMC
Joint Materiel Priorities and Allocation Board [*Military*] ... JMPAB
Joint Maximum Effort ... JME
Joint Medical Regulating Office ... JMRO
Joint Merchant Vessels Board [*World War II*] ... JMVB
Joint Message Center ... JMC
Joint Meteorological Board ... JMB
Joint Meteorological Committee ... JMC
Joint Meteorological Group [*DoD*] ... JMG
Joint Meteorological Radio Propagation Committee [*British*] ... JMRP
Joint Meteorological Satellite Advisory Committee ... JMSAC
Joint Meteorological Satellite Program Office ... JMSPO
Joint Mexican-United States Defense Commission ... JMUSDC

Joint Military Aircraft Hurricane Evacuation Plan ... JMAHEP
Joint Military Assistance Affairs Division ... JMAAD
Joint Military Commission [*US, North Vietnam, South Vietnam, Viet Cong*] ... JMC
Joint Military Packaging Training Center ... JMPTC
Joint Military Procurements Control [*World War II*] ... JMPC
Joint Military Regulating Office ... JMRO
Joint Military Task Group ... JMTG
Joint Military Terminology Group ... JMTG
Joint Military Transportation Board ... JMTB
Joint Military Transportation Committee ... JMTC
Joint Mission Analysis ... JMA
Joint Mobile Communications Center [*NATO*] ... JMCC
Joint Monitor Display ... JMD
Joint Movements Branch [*NATO*] ... JMB
Joint Movements Coordinating Committee [*British*] ... JMCC
Joint Movements Staff [*British*] ... JMS
Joint Munitions Allocation Committee ... JMAC
Joint Munitions Effectiveness Manual [*Military*] ... JMEM
Joint Munitions Production Panel ... JMPP
Joint National Committee for Languages ... JNCL
Joint Navigation Satellite Committee ... JNSC
Joint North Sea Data Acquisition Program ... JONSDAP
Joint North Sea Wave Project ... JONSWAP
Joint Nuclear Accident Coordinating Center ... JNACC
Joint Nuclear Plot ... JNP
Joint Nuclear Research Center [*EURATOM*] ... JNRC
Joint Nuclear Research Institute [*USSR*] ... JNRI
Joint Nuclear Weapons Publication Systems ... JNWPS
Joint Numerical Weather Prediction Unit ... JNWPU
Joint Objective Area ... JOA
Joint Observing Program [*NASA*] ... JOP
Joint Occupancy Date ... JOD
Joint Occupancy Plan Memo ... JOPM
Joint Ocean [*or Overseas*] **Shipping Procedure** ... JOSPRO
Joint Ocean Surface Study ... JOSS
Joint Oceanographic Assembly ... JOA
Joint Oceanographic Institutions for Deep Earth Sampling ... JOIDES
Joint Oceanographic Research Group ... JORG
Joint Oil Analysis Program [*Military*] ... JOAP
Joint Oil Targets Committee [*World War II*] ... JOTC
Joint Operating Agreement ... JOA
Joint Operating Group [*SLA/ASIS*] ... JOG
Joint Operating Plan ... JOP
Joint Operation Procedure ... JOP
Joint Operation Procedure Memorandum ... JOPM
Joint Operation Procedure Report ... JOPR
Joint Operational Compatibility Tests ... J-OCT
Joint Operational Planning System [*Military*] ... JOPS
Joint Operational Report [*Military*] ... JOPREP
Joint Operational Report [*Military*] ... JOREP
Joint Operational Test and Evaluation ... JOT & E
Joint Operations Center ... JOC
Joint Operations Control Center ... JOCC
Joint Operations Evaluation Group ... JOEG
Joint Operations Evaluation Group, Vietnam [*Air Force*] ... JOEG-V
Joint Operations Graphics [*Military*] ... JOG
Joint Operations Group [*DoD*] ... JOG
Joint Operations Requirements [*Military*] ... JOR
Joint Operations Support Activity Frankfurt [*National Security Agency*] ... JOSAF
Joint Optical Information Network [*Army*] ... JOIN
Joint Optical Range Instrumentation Type Designation System ... JORITDS
Joint Organization ... JO
Joint Organization for Solar Observations ... JOSO
Joint Organization of Trade Unions [*Finland*] ... JOTU
Joint Organizing Committee [*Global Atmospheric Research Program*] ... JOC
Joint Overseas Shipping Control Office ... JOSCO
Joint Overseas Switching System [*Military*] ... JOSS
Joint Pacific [*Military*] ... JP
Joint Pacific Voice [*Military*] ... JPV
Joint Packaging Instruction ... JPI
Joint Parachute Test Facility [*DoD*] ... JPTF
Joint Passover Association of the City of New York ... JPA
Joint Personal Property Shipping Office, Washington, DC [*Military*] ... JPPSOWA
Joint Personnel Priority List ... JPPL
Joint Personnel Recovery Center [*Military*] ... JPRC
Joint Petroleum Coordination Center/Committee [*NATO*] ... JPCC
Joint Petroleum Office ... JPO
Joint Photographic Reconnaissance Organization [*World War II*] ... JPRO
Joint Photographic Type Designation System [*Military*] ... JPTDS
Joint Planning Activity [*DoD*] ... JPA
Joint Planning Board ... JPB
Joint Planning Committee ... JPC
Joint Planning Group [*NATO*] ... JPG
Joint Planning Process [*Military*] ... JPP
Joint Planning and Scheduling Group ... JPSG
Joint Planning Staff [*US and Great Britain*] [*World War II*] ... JPS
Joint Postwar Committee ... JPWC
Joint Power Generation Conference ... JPGC
Joint Procurement Board [*Military*] ... JPB
Joint Procurement Regulations [*of Army and Air Force*] ... JPR
Joint Production Board [*US and Great Britain*] ... JPB
Joint Production Survey Committee ... JPSC
Joint Program Assessment Memorandum ... JPAM
Joint Program Integration Committee [*NASA*] ... JPIC
Joint Program Plan ... JPP
Joint Program for the Study of Abortion ... JPSA
Joint Project Office [*or Officer*] ... JPO
Joint Projected Manpower Requirements [*Military*] ... JPMR
Joint Publications Research Service [*Department of Commerce*] ... JPRS
Joint Publications Research Service Translations - Government Use Only [*Department of Commerce*] ... JPRS-GUO
Joint Purchasing Board ... JPB
Joint RADAR Planning Group [*Military*] ... JRPG
Joint Radio Board ... JRB
Joint Rail Military Traffic Office ... JRMTO
Joint Railroad Conference ... JRC
Joint Reconnaissance Board [*Military*] ... JRB
Joint Reconnaissance Center [*Military*] ... JRC
Joint Reentry System Working Group ... JRSWG
Joint Regional Continuing Committee [*Later, RCEAC*] [*Civil defense*] ... JRCC
Joint Regional Reconnaissance Center [*NATO*] ... JRRC
Joint Registered Publications Memorandum ... JRPM
Joint Reporting Structure [*Military*] ... JRS
Joint Rescue Coordination Center [*Military*] ... JRCC
Joint Research and Development Board [*1946-1947*] ... JRDB
Joint Research and Development Objectives Document [*Military*] ... JRDOD
Joint Research and Test Activity ... JRATA
Joint Research and Test Agency [*Terminated, 1966*] [*Military*] ... JRATA
Joint Resolution [*Usually, of the US Senate and House of Representatives*] ... JR
Joint Resource Assessment Data Base Report [*Military*] ... JADREP
Joint Review Committee for Respiratory Therapy Education ... JRCRTE
Joint School District Number One, Lake Geneva, WI [*Library symbol*] ... WLagSD
Joint Schools Committee for Academic Excellence Now ... JSCAEN
Joint Sealer Manufacturers Association ... JSMA
Joint Sealift Movements Board [*Military*] ... JSMB
Joint Search and Rescue Center [*Military*] ... JSARC
Joint Security Control ... JSC
Joint Service Advisory Group ... JSAG
Joint Service Agreement Report [*Defense Supply Agency*] ... JSAR
Joint Service Civil Engineering Research and Development Coordination Group [*Military*] ... JSCERDCG
Joint Service Commendation Medal [*Military*] ... JSCM
Joint Service Committee [*Military*] ... JSC
Joint Service Fuze Plan [*Army*] ... JSFP
Joint Service Induction Area ... JSIA
Joint Service Intelligence Manual ... JSIM
Joint Service Interior Intrusion Detection Devices [*Military*] ... JSIID
Joint Service Interior Intrusion Detection System [*Military*] ... JSIIDS
Joint Service Office ... JSO
Joint Service Program Management Review Committee [*Military*] ... JSPMRC
Joint Service Small Arms Program ... JSSAP
Joint Services Actions Task Group ... JSATG
Joint Services Commendation Medal ... JSCOM
Joint Services Electronics Program [*Military*] ... JSEP
Joint Services Explosives Program ... JSEXP
Joint Services LASER Guided Weapons Countermeasures ... JSLGWCM
Joint Services Liaison Staff [*British*] ... JSLS
Joint Services Operational Requirement [*Military*] ... JSOR
Joint Services Reading Panel [*Military*] [*British*] ... JSRP
Joint Services Staff College [*or Course*] [*British*] ... JSSC
Joint Services Staff Manual [*Military*] [*British*] ... JSSM
Joint Setup Cost ... JSC
Joint Ship Operations Center ... JSOC
Joint Ship Operations Committee ... JSOC
Joint Ship Repair Committee ... JSRC
Joint Short-Range Technology ... JSRT
Joint Sobe Processing Center [*Okinawa*] [*Military*] ... JSPC
Joint Societies Employment Advisory Committee ... JSEAC
Joint Spacelab Working Group [*NASA*] ... JSLWG
Joint Special Operations Support Element [*DoD*] ... JSOSE
Joint Special Weapons Publications Board ... JSWPB
Joint Staff [*Military*] ... JS
Joint Staff Administrative Instruction [*Military*] ... JAI
Joint Staff Communications Office [*Military*] ... JSCO
Joint Staff Council [*Japanese*] [*Military*] ... JSC
Joint Staff Mission [*British*] [*World War II*] ... JSM
Joint Staff Pension Board [*United Nations*] ... JSPB
Joint Staff Pension Fund [*United Nations*] ... JSPF
Joint Staff Planners [*Joint Chiefs of Staff*] ... JSP
Joint Statement of Agreed Principles [*US-USSR*] ... JSAP
Joint-Stock Bank [*Banking*] ... JSB
Joint-Stock Company ... JSC
Joint Strategic Bomber Study ... JSBS
Joint Strategic Capabilities [*Military*] ... JSC

Joint Strategic Capabilities Plan [*Military*] ... JSCP
Joint Strategic Committee [*Military*] ... JSC
Joint Strategic Connectivity Committee [*Joint Chiefs of Staff*] ... JSCS
Joint Strategic Objectives Plans [*Military*] ... JSOP
Joint Strategic Planning Document ... JSPD
Joint Strategic Planning Document Supporting Analysis [*Military*] ... JSPDSA
Joint Strategic Planning System [*Military*] ... JSPS
Joint Strategic Plans Committee [*Military*] ... JSPC
Joint Strategic Plans Group [*Military*] ... JSPG
Joint Strategic Plans and Operations Group ... JSPOG
Joint Strategic Survey Committee [*or Council*] [*DoD*] ... JSSC
Joint Strategic Target Planning Agency ... JSTPA
Joint Strategic Target Planning Staff [*DoD*] ... JSTPS
Joint Strategy and Action Committee ... JSAC
Joint Study Group on Military Resources Allocation Methodology ... JSGOMRAM
Joint Subsidiary Plans Division [*Military*] ... JSPD
Joint Supply Council for Union of South Africa [*World War II*] ... JSCU
Joint Support [*Military*] ... JS
Joint Support Command [*Navy*] ... JSC
Joint Support List [*Military*] ... JSL
Joint [*Maritime Administration - Navy*] **Surface Effect Ship Program Office** ... JSESPO
Joint Surveillance System ... JSS
Joint Surveillance and Target Attack RADAR System ... JSTARS
Joint System Integration Planning Staff [*Air Force*] ... JSIPS
Joint Systematic Troop Review [*Military*] ... JSTR
Joint Systems Test ... JST
Joint Table of Allowance ... JTA
Joint Table of Distribution [*Military*] ... JTD
Joint Tactical Aids Detachment [*Military*] ... JTAD
Joint Tactical Air Control Center ... JTACC
Joint Tactical Air Support Board ... JTASB
Joint Tactical Command and Control and Communications System [*Military*] ... JTC³S
Joint Tactical Communications Program [*DoD*] ... TRITAC
Joint Tactical Fusion Program [*Military*] ... JTFP
Joint Tactical Information Distribution System [*DoD*] ... JTIDS
Joint Tactical Missile System ... JTACMS
Joint Tactical Operations Center ... JTOC
Joint Target Intelligence Group [*Military*] ... JTIG
Joint Targeting and Weapon Guidance ... JTAWG
Joint Task Force [*Military*] ... JTF
Joint Task Force Operating Area [*Military*] ... JTFOA
Joint Task Force Report [*Military*] ... JTFREP
Joint Task Groups [*Military*] ... JTG
Joint Technical Advisory Committee [*Electronics*] ... JTAC
Joint Technical Configuration Control Group [*Military*] ... JTCCG
Joint Technical Coordinating Group [*Military*] ... JTCG
Joint Technical Coordinating Group [*Military*] ... JTCGP
Joint Technical Coordinating Group for Air Launched Non-Nuclear Ordnance [*Military*] ... JTCG/ALNNO
Joint Technical Coordinating Group for Aircraft Survivability [*Military*] ... JTCG/AS
Joint Technical Coordinating Group for Munitions Development [*Military*] ... JTCG/MD
Joint Technical Coordinating Group for Munitions Effectiveness [*Military*] ... JTCG/ME
Joint Technical Coordinating Group for Munitions Effectiveness [*Military*] ... JTCGP/ME
Joint Technical Coordinating Group on Munitions Survivability [*Military*] ... JTCG/MS
Joint Technical Coordinating Group for Tactical Air Control System [*Military*] ... JTCGP-TACS
Joint Technical Development Plan ... JTDP
Joint Technical Evaluation ... JTE
Joint Technical Operations ... JTO
Joint Technical Support Activity ... JTSA
Joint Technology Demonstrator Engine [*Air Force*] ... JTDE
Joint Telecommunications Committee [*Military*] ... JTC
Joint Tenancy Agreement [*Military*] ... JTA
Joint Termination Regulation ... JTR
Joint Test and Evaluation Task Force [*Air Force*] ... JTETF
Joint Test and Evaluation [*DoD*] ... JT & E
Joint Theatre Reconnaissance Committee [*NATO*] ... JTRC
Joint Track Data Storage ... JTDS
Joint Trade Union Advisory Committee ... JTUAC
Joint Training Exercise [*Military*] ... JTX
Joint Training Standards [*Military*] ... JTS
Joint Transportation Board [*Military*] ... JTB
Joint Transportation Movements Board [*Military*] ... JTMB
Joint Travel Regulations ... JTR
Joint Travel Regulations ... JTRUS
Joint Travel Regulations, Department of Defense Civilian Personnel ... JTRCP
Joint Trials Subgroup [*NATO*] ... JTSG
Joint Tropical Trials Research Establishment [*Australia*] ... JTTRE
Joint Tsunami Research Effort ... JTRE
Joint Typhoon Warning Center ... JTWC
Joint UHF Modernization Project ... JUMP
Joint Unconventional Warfare Assessment Team [*Military*] ... JUWAT
Joint Unconventional Warfare Task Force ... JUWTF
Joint Unconventional Warfare Task Force, Atlantic ... JUWTFA
Joint Uniform Military Pay System ... JUMPS
Joint United States/Canada Civil Emergency Planning Committee ... JCEPC
Joint United States/Canada Industrial Mobilization Planning Committee [*NATO*] ... JUSCIMPC
Joint United States Military Advisory Group ... JUSMAG
Joint United States Military Advisory Group to the Republic of the Philippines [*World War II*] ... JUSMAGPHIL
Joint United States Military Advisory and Planning Group ... JUSMAP
Joint United States Military Aid Group, Greece ... JUSMAGG
Joint United States Military Assistance Advisory Group ... JUSMAAG
Joint United States Military Assistance Group, Thailand ... JUSMAGTHAI
Joint United States Military Group ... JUSMG
Joint United States Military Group ... JUSMGP
Joint United States Military Mission for Aid to Turkey ... JUSMMAT
Joint United States Public Affairs Office [*Vietnam*] ... JUSPAO
Joint United States Strategic Committee ... JUSSC
Joint University Libraries ... JUL
Joint University Libraries, George Peabody College for Teachers, Nashville, TN [*Library symbol*] ... TNJ-P
Joint University Libraries, Nashville, TN [*Library symbol*] ... TNJ
Joint University Libraries, Scarritt College for Christian Workers, Nashville, TN [*Library symbol*] ... TNJ-S
Joint University Libraries, Vanderbilt Medical Center, Nashville, TN [*Library symbol*] ... TNJ-M
Joint University Libraries, Vanderbilt School of Law, Nashville, TN [*Library symbol*] ... TNJ-L
Joint University Libraries, Vanderbilt School of Religion, Nashville, TN [*Library symbol*] ... TNJ-R
Joint Urban Manpower Program [*Course in architectural drafting for underprivileged youths*] ... JUMP
Joint Users Group [*Data processing*] ... JUG
Joint Users Requirements Group ... JURG
Joint Utility Notification for Excavators ... JUNE
Joint Utilization Coordination Group [*DoD*] ... JUCG
Joint Vertical Lift Aircraft [*Military*] ... JVX
Joint Vocational School ... JVS
Joint Vulnerability Board ... JVB
Joint War Games Agency [*JCS*] [*DoD*] ... JWGA
Joint War Games Control Group [*Military*] ... JWGCG
Joint War Plans Committee ... JWPC
Joint War Production Committee ... JWPC
Joint War Production Staff ... JWPS
Joint War Room [*Military*] ... JWR
Joint War Room Annex [*Military*] ... JWRA
Joint Warfare Establishment [*British*] ... JWE
Joint Warfare Staff [*British*] ... JWS
Joint Western Air Defense Force ... JWADF
Joint Whole Blood Center [*Military*] ... JWBC
Joint Wideband Circuit Allocation and Requirement Group, Thailand [*Military*] ... JOCARG
Joint Working Group ... JOWOG
Joint Working Group [*Military*] ... JWG
Joint Working Group Meeting [*NASA*] ... JWGM
Jointly ... JTLY
Jointly Endorsed Training [*Union-management*] ... JET
Jointly Sponsored Program for Foreign Libraries [*Defunct*] ... JSPFL
Joinville [*Brazil*] [*Airport symbol*] ... JOI
Joist [*Technical drawings*] ... J
Joists and Planks [*Technical drawings*] ... J & P
Jojoba Horizons, Inc. [*NASDAQ symbol*] ... JOJO
Joliet Army Ammunition Plant ... JAAP
Joliet, IL [*Location identifier*] [*FAA*] ... JOT
Joliet, IL [*Radio station call letters*] ... WAJP
Joliet, IL [*Television station call letters*] ... WFBN
Joliet, IL [*Radio station call letters*] ... WJOL
Joliet, IL [*Radio station call letters*] ... WJRC
Joliet, IL [*Radio station call letters*] ... WLLI
Joliet Junior College [*Illinois*] ... JJC
Joliet Public Library, Joliet, IL [*Library symbol*] ... IJol
Joliette, PQ [*Radio station call letters*] ... CJLM
Jolo [*Philippines*] [*Airport symbol*] ... JOL
Jolon [*California*] [*Seismograph station code, US Geological Survey*] ... JOL
Joly Black Screen ... JBS
Joly Steam Calorimeter ... JSC
Jolys Regional Library, St. Pierre, MB, Canada [*Library symbol*] ... CaMStPJ
Jomsom [*Nepal*] [*Airport symbol*] ... JMO
Jonah [*Old Testament book*] ... Jon
Jonathan Logan, Inc. [*NYSE symbol*] ... JOL
Jones County Junior College [*Mississippi*] ... JCJC
Jones/Hosplex Systems [*NASDAQ symbol*] ... JHPX
Jones Intercable [*NASDAQ symbol*] ... JOIN
Jones & Laughlin Steel Corp. ... J & L
Jones & Laughlin Steel Corp. [*NYSE symbol*] [*Delisted*] ... JL
Jones Library, Amherst, MA [*Library symbol*] ... MAJ
Jones Memorial Hospital, Wellsville, NY [*Library symbol*] ... NWelH
Jones Memorial Library, Lynchburg, VA [*Library symbol*] ... ViL
Jones Optical Co. [*NASDAQ symbol*] ... LENS

Jones, Paul H., Romulus MI [*STAC*] ... JPH
Jones & Vining, Inc. [*NASDAQ symbol*] ... JNSV
Jonesboro [*Arkansas*] [*Airport symbol*] ... JBR
Jonesboro, AR [*Location identifier*] [*FAA*] ... JBR
Jonesboro, AR [*Television station call letters*] ... KAIT-TV
Jonesboro, AR [*Radio station call letters*] ... KASU
Jonesboro, AR [*Radio station call letters*] ... KBTM
Jonesboro, AR [*Radio station call letters*] ... KFIN
Jonesboro, AR [*Radio station call letters*] ... KJBR
Jonesboro, AR [*Radio station call letters*] ... KNEA
Jonesboro, AR [*Television station call letters*] ... KTEJ
Jonesboro, GA [*Location identifier*] [*FAA*] ... JOO
Jonesboro, LA [*Location identifier*] [*FAA*] ... JBL
Jonesboro, LA [*Radio station call letters*] ... KTOC
Jonesboro, Lake City & Eastern Railroad ... JLC & E
Jonesboro, TN [*Radio station call letters*] ... WJSO
Joni Blair of California [*NASDAQ symbol*] ... JONB
Jonkheer [*Netherlands*] ... JR
Jonkoping [*Sweden*] [*Airport symbol*] ... JKG
Jonquiere, PQ [*Radio station call letters*] ... CHOC-FM
Jonquiere, PQ [*Radio station call letters*] ... CKRS
Jonquiere, PQ [*Television station call letters*] ... CKRS-TV
Joplin [*Missouri*] [*Airport symbol*] ... JLN
Joplin, MO [*Location identifier*] [*FAA*] ... JLN
Joplin, MO [*Radio station call letters*] ... KFSB
Joplin, MO [*Radio station call letters*] ... KKUZ
Joplin, MO [*Radio station call letters*] ... KOBC
Joplin, MO [*Radio station call letters*] ... KODE
Joplin, MO [*Television station call letters*] ... KODE-TV
Joplin, MO [*Radio station call letters*] ... KQYX
Joplin, MO [*Television station call letters*] ... KSNF-TV
Joplin, MO [*Radio station call letters*] ... KSYN
Joplin, MO [*Radio station call letters*] ... WMBH
Joplin Public Library, Joplin, MO [*Library symbol*] ... MoJo
Jordan [*MARC geographic area code*] [*Library of Congress*] ... a-jo---
Jordan [*MARC country of publication code*] [*Library of Congress*] ... jo
Jordan [*Three-letter standard code*] ... JOR
Jordan [*Aircraft nationality and registration mark*] ... JY
Jordan [*Two-letter standard code*] ... JO
Jordan Cosmological Theory ... JCT
Jordan Federation of Trade Unions ... JFTU
Jordan Information Bureau ... JIB
Jordan Medical Journal [*A publication*] ... Jordan Med J
Jordan, MT [*Location identifier*] [*FAA*] ... JDN
Jordan-Wentzel-Kramers-Brillouin [*Physics*] ... JWKB
Jordanian Air Force ... JAF
Jordanian News Agency ... JNA
Jordanian World Airways [*ICAO designator*] ... QJ
Jordbruksekonomiska Meddelanden [*A publication*] ... Jord-ekon Medd
Jordon Electronic Manufacturing Co. ... JEM
Jorgensen [*Earle M.*] **Co.** [*NYSE symbol*] ... JOR
Jorhat [*India*] [*Airport symbol*] ... JRH
Jornadas Agronomicas. Trabajos [*A publication*] ... Jornadas Agron Trab
Jornal Brasileiro de Ginecologia [*A publication*] ... J Bras Ginecol
Jornal Brasileiro de Neurologia [*A publication*] ... J Bras Neurol
Jornal Brasileiro de Psiquiatria [*A publication*] ... JBPSA
Jornal Brasileiro de Psiquiatria [*A publication*] ... J Bras Psiquiatr
Jornal Brasileiro de Urologia [*A publication*] ... J Bras Urol
Jornal do Commercio [*A publication*] ... J Commercio
Jornal de Filologia [*A publication*] ... JF
Jornal de Letras [*A publication*] ... JdL
Jornal de Letras [*A publication*] ... JL
Jornal de Letras e Artes [*A publication*] ... JLA
Jornal de Medicina de Pernambuco [*A publication*] ... J Med Pernambuco
Jornal do Medico (Porto) [*A publication*] ... J Med (Porto)
Jos [*Nigeria*] [*Airport symbol*] ... JOS
Josa Andras Muzeum Evkoenyve [*A publication*] ... Josa Andras Muz Ev
Jose De San Martin [*Argentina*] [*Airport symbol*] ... JSM
Joseph A. Yablonski Memorial Clinic, Fredericktown, PA [*Library symbol*] ... PFredY
Joseph Conrad Society of America ... JCSA
Joseph Mann Library, Two Rivers, WI [*Library symbol*] ... WTw
Joseph Pennell [*Specification-made paper*] ... JP
Joseph Quincy Adams Memorial Studies [*A publication*] ... AMS
Josephine County Library System, Grants Pass, OR [*OCLC symbol*] ... OJL
Josephine-Louise Public Library, Walden, NY [*Library symbol*] ... NWald
Josephson AttoWeber Switch [*Data processor circuitry*] ... JAWS
Josephson International, Inc. [*NASDAQ symbol*] ... JSON
Joshi Effect [*Physics*] ... JE
Joshua [*Old Testament book*] ... Jos
Joshua [*Old Testament book*] ... Josh
Joshua Tree [*Nevada*] [*Seismograph station code, US Geological Survey*] [*Closed*] ... NYJ
Joshua Tree National Monument ... JOTR
Joslin Diabetes Center [*Formerly, JDFI*] ... JDC
Joslin Diabetes Foundation, Incorporated [*Later, JDC*] ... JDFI
Joslyn Art Museum, Omaha, NE [*Library symbol*] ... NbOJ
Joslyn Manufacturing & Supply [*NASDAQ symbol*] ... JOSL
Jostens, Inc. [*NYSE symbol*] ... JOS
Josvafo [*Hungary*] [*Seismograph station code, US Geological Survey*] ... JOS
JOT. Journal fuer Oberflaechentechnik [*A publication*] ... JOT J Oberflaechentech
Jouf [*Saudi Arabia*] [*Airport symbol*] ... AJF
Joule [*Symbol*] [*SI unit of energy*] ... J
Joule-Clausius Velocity [*Physics*] ... JCV
Joule Cycle [*Physics*] ... JC
Joule Effect [*Physics*] ... JE
Joule Impulse Generator [*Physics*] ... JIG
Joule Impulse Generator System [*Physics*] ... JIGS
Joule per Kelvin [*Physics*] ... J/K
Joule per Kilogram [*Physics*] ... J/kg
Joule-Rowland Method [*Physics*] ... JRM
Joule-Thomson [*Physics*] ... J-T
Joule-Thomson Coefficient [*Physics*] ... JTC
Joule-Thomson Cooler [*Physics*] ... JTC
Joule-Thomson Effect [*Physics*] ... JTE
Joule-Thomson Flow [*Physics*] ... JTF
Joule-Thomson High Pressure [*Physics*] ... JTHP
Joules per Cubic Meter ... J/M^3
Joules per Kilogram Kelvin ... J/(KG K)
Joule's Law [*Physics*] ... JL
Joules per Mole ... J/MOL
Joules per Mole Kelvin ... J/(MOL K)
Joule's Own Version of the International Algorithmic Language [*Data processing*] ... JOVIAL
Joules per Square Meter ... J/M^2
Joullie [*France*] [*Research code symbol*] ... LJ
Jour [*Day*] [*French*] ... JR
Journal ... J
Journal [*Data processing*] ... JN
Journal ... JNL
Journal ... JOUR
Journal ... JOURN
Journal ... JRNL
Journal A. Presses Academiques Europeennes [*A publication*] ... J A
Journal of Abdominal Surgery [*A publication*] ... J Abdom Surg
Journal of Abnormal Child Psychology [*A publication*] ... J Abnorm Child Psychol
Journal of Abnormal Psychology [*A publication*] ... J Abnorm Psychol
Journal of Abnormal Psychology [*A publication*] ... J Abn Psych
Journal of Abnormal Psychology [*A publication*] ... JAbP
Journal of Abnormal Psychology [*A publication*] ... JAPCA
Journal of Abnormal Psychology. Monograph [*A publication*] ... J Abnorm Psychol Monogr
Journal of Abnormal and Social Psychology [*A publication*] ... J Abnorm Soc Psychol
Journal of Abnormal and Social Psychology [*A publication*] ... JASP
Journal of Academic Librarianship [*A publication*] ... J Acad Libnship
Journal of Academic Librarianship [*A publication*] ... J Acad Librarianship
Journal of Academic Librarianship [*A publication*] ... JAL
Journal. Academy of Natural Sciences of Philadelphia [*A publication*] ... J Acad Nat Sci Phila
Journal Access Service [*Center for Research Libraries*] ... JAS
Journal of Accountancy [*A publication*] ... J Account
Journal of Accountancy [*A publication*] ... J Accountancy
Journal of Accountancy [*A publication*] ... J Acctcy
Journal of Accountancy [*A publication*] ... J Accy
Journal of Accounting, Auditing, and Finance [*A publication*] ... Jrl Audit
Journal of Accounting Research [*A publication*] ... J Accountin
Journal of Accounting Research [*A publication*] ... J Accounting Res
Journal of Accounting Research [*A publication*] ... J Account Res
Journal. Acoustical Society of America [*A publication*] ... J Acoust So
Journal. Acoustical Society of America [*A publication*] ... J Acoust Soc Am
Journal. Acoustical Society of America [*A publication*] ... JAcS
Journal. Acoustical Society of America [*A publication*] ... JAS
Journal. Acoustical Society of America [*A publication*] ... JASA
Journal. Acoustical Society of America [*A publication*] ... JASMA
Journal. Acoustical Society of America [*A publication*] ... Jour Acoust Soc
Journal. Acoustical Society of America. Supplement [*A publication*] ... J Acoust Soc Am Suppl
Journal. Acoustical Society of Japan [*A publication*] ... J Acoust Soc Jap
Journal. Adelaide Botanic Gardens [*A publication*] ... J Adelaide Bot Gard
Journal of Adhesion [*A publication*] ... J Adhes
Journal of Adhesion [*A publication*] ... J Adhesion
Journal. Adhesion Society of Japan [*A publication*] ... J Adhes Soc Jpn
Journal of Administration Overseas [*A publication*] ... J Admin Overseas
Journal of Administration Overseas [*A publication*] ... J Adm Overs
Journal of Administration Overseas [*A publication*] ... J Adm Overseas
Journal of Administration Overseas [*A publication*] ... JADO
Journal of Adolescence [*A publication*] ... J Adolesc
Journal of Adolescence [*A publication*] ... J Adolescence
Journal of Adolescent Health Care [*A publication*] ... J Adolesc Health Care
Journal of Adult Education [*A publication*] ... J Adult Ed
Journal of Advanced Nursing [*A publication*] ... J Adv Nurs
Journal of Advertising [*A publication*] ... J Adv
Journal of Advertising Research [*A publication*] ... J Adv Res
Journal. Aero Medical Society of India [*A publication*] ... J Aero Med Soc India
Journal of the Aero/Space Sciences [*A publication*] ... J Aero/Space Sci
Journal of the Aeronautical Sciences [*A publication*] ... J Aero Sci
Journal of Aerosol Science [*A publication*] ... J Aerosol Sci

Journal of Aerospace Science [*A publication*] ... JAS
Journal. Aerospace Transport Division. American Society of Civil Engineers [*A publication*] ... J Aerosp Transp Div Am Soc Civ Eng
Journal of Aesthetic Education [*A publication*] ... JAE
Journal of Aesthetic Education [*A publication*] ... JAEDB
Journal of Aesthetic Education [*A publication*] ... J Aes Ed
Journal of Aesthetic Education [*A publication*] ... J Aes Educ
Journal of Aesthetic Education [*A publication*] ... J Aesth Educ
Journal of Aesthetic Education [*A publication*] ... J Aesthet E
Journal of Aesthetic Education [*A publication*] ... J Aesthetic Educ
Journal of Aesthetics and Art Criticism [*A publication*] ... JA
Journal of Aesthetics and Art Criticism [*A publication*] ... JAAC
Journal of Aesthetics and Art Criticism [*A publication*] ... J Aes Art Crit
Journal of Aesthetics and Art Criticism [*A publication*] ... J Aesth
Journal of Aesthetics and Art Criticism [*A publication*] ... J Aesth & Art C
Journal of Aesthetics and Art Criticism [*A publication*] ... J Aesthetics
Journal of Aesthetics and Art Criticism [*A publication*] ... JARCA
Journal of Aesthetics and Art Criticism [*A publication*] ... Jl Aesthetics
Journal of Aesthetics and Art Criticism [*A publication*] ... Jnl Aesthetics
Journal of Aesthetics and Art Criticism [*A publication*] ... Jnl Aesthetics & Art Crit
Journal of Aesthetics and Art Criticism [*A publication*] ... Jour Aesthetics and Art Crit
Journal of Affective Disorders [*A publication*] ... J Affective Disord
Journal of African Administration [*A publication*] ... JAA
Journal of African History [*A publication*] ... JAfrH
Journal of African History [*A publication*] ... J Afr Hist
Journal of African History [*A publication*] ... J Afric Hist
Journal of African Languages [*A publication*] ... JAfrL
Journal of African Languages [*A publication*] ... JAL
Journal of African Law [*A publication*] ... J Afr Law
Journal of African Studies [*A publication*] ... J Afr Stud
Journal. Agricultural Association of China [*A publication*] ... J Agr Ass China
Journal. Agricultural Association of China [*A publication*] ... J Agric Ass China
Journal. Agricultural Chemical Society of Japan [*A publication*] ... J Agr Che J
Journal. Agricultural Chemical Society of Japan [*A publication*] ... J Agr Chem Soc Jap
Journal. Agricultural Chemical Society of Japan [*A publication*] ... J Agric Chem Soc Japan
Journal. Agricultural Chemical Society of Japan [*A publication*] ... J Agric Chem Soc Jpn
Journal of Agricultural Economics [*A publication*] ... J Ag Econ
Journal of Agricultural Economics [*A publication*] ... J Agr Econ
Journal of Agricultural Economics [*A publication*] ... J Agric Econ
Journal of Agricultural Economics and Development [*A publication*] ... J Agr Econ Dev
Journal of Agricultural Engineering Research [*A publication*] ... J Agr Eng R
Journal of Agricultural Engineering Research [*A publication*] ... J Agr Eng Res
Journal of Agricultural Engineering Research [*A publication*] ... J Agric Engin Res
Journal of Agricultural Engineering Research [*A publication*] ... J Agric Engng Res
Journal of Agricultural Engineering Research [*A publication*] ... J Agric Eng Res
Journal. Agricultural Engineering Society of Japan [*A publication*] ... J Agr Eng Soc Jap
Journal. Agricultural Experiment Station of Chosen [*A publication*] ... J Agr Exp Sta Chosen
Journal of Agricultural and Food Chemistry [*A publication*] ... JA & FC
Journal of Agricultural and Food Chemistry [*A publication*] ... J Ag & Food Chem
Journal of Agricultural and Food Chemistry [*A publication*] ... J Agr Food
Journal of Agricultural and Food Chemistry [*A publication*] ... J Agr Food Chem
Journal of Agricultural and Food Chemistry [*A publication*] ... J Agric Fd Chem
Journal of Agricultural and Food Chemistry [*A publication*] ... J Agric Food Chem
Journal of Agricultural Laboratory [*A publication*] ... J Agr Lab
Journal of the Agricultural Laboratory (Chiba) [*A publication*] ... J Agric Lab (Chiba)
Journal of Agricultural Meteorology [*Tokyo*] [*A publication*] ... J Agric Meteorol
Journal of Agricultural Meteorology (Japan) [*A publication*] ... J Agr Meteorol (Japan)
Journal of Agricultural Meteorology (Tokyo) [*A publication*] ... J Agric Met (Tokyo)
Journal of Agricultural Research [*A publication*] ... J Ag Res
Journal of Agricultural Research [*A publication*] ... J Agr Res
Journal of Agricultural Research of China [*A publication*] ... J Agric Res China
Journal of Agricultural Research in Iceland [*A publication*] ... J Agric Res Icel
Journal of the Agricultural Research in the Tokai-Kinki Region [*A publication*] ... J Agr Res Tokai-Kinki Reg
Journal of Agricultural Science [*A publication*] ... J Agric Sci
Journal of Agricultural Science [*A publication*] ... J Agr Sci
Journal of Agricultural Science (Cambridge) [*A publication*] ... J Agric Sci (Camb)
Journal of Agricultural Science. Tokyo Nogyo Daigaku [*A publication*] ... J Agric Sci Tokyo Nogyo Daigaku
Journal of Agricultural Science. Tokyo Nogyo Daigaku [*A publication*] ... J Agr Sci Tokyo Nogyo Daigaku
Journal. Agricultural Society of Japan [*A publication*] ... J Agric Soc Jpn
Journal. Agricultural Society of Trinidad and Tobago [*A publication*] ... J Agric Soc Trinidad Tobago
Journal. Agricultural Society of Trinidad and Tobago [*A publication*] ... J Agric Soc Trin & Tobago
Journal. Agricultural Society of Trinidad and Tobago [*A publication*] ... J Agr Soc Trinidad Tobago
Journal. Agricultural Society. University College of Wales [*A publication*] ... J Agr Soc Wales
Journal of Agriculture and Horticulture [*A publication*] ... J Ag (Quebec)
Journal of Agriculture (Melbourne) [*A publication*] ... J Agr (Melbourne)
Journal d'Agriculture Pratique [*A publication*] ... J Ag Pratique
Journal d'Agriculture Pratique [*A publication*] ... J Agr Prat
Journal of Agriculture (South Australia) [*A publication*] ... J Agric (S Aust)
Journal of Agriculture (South Australia) [*A publication*] ... J Agr (S Aust)
Journal d'Agriculture Traditionnelle et de Botanique Appliquee [*A publication*] ... J Agr Trad Bot Appl
Journal d'Agriculture Tropicale et de Botanique Appliquee [*A publication*] ... J Agric Trop Botan Appl
Journal d'Agriculture Tropicale et de Botanique Appliquee [*A publication*] ... J Agric Trop Bot Appl
Journal d'Agriculture Tropicale et de Botanique Appliquee [*A publication*] ... J Agr Trop Bot Appl
Journal of Agriculture. University of Puerto Rico [*A publication*] ... J Agric Univ PR
Journal of Agriculture. University of Puerto Rico [*A publication*] ... J Agr Univ PR
Journal of Agriculture. University of Puerto Rico [*A publication*] ... J Ag Univ Puerto Rico
Journal of Agriculture (Victoria) [*A publication*] ... J Agric (Victoria)
Journal of Agriculture. Victoria Department of Agriculture [*A publication*] ... J Agric Vict Dep Agric
Journal of Agriculture (Western Australia) [*A publication*] ... J Agric (West Aust)
Journal of Agriculture (Western Australia) [*A publication*] ... J Agr (W Aust)
Journal of Agronomy and Crop Science [*A publication*] ... J Agron Crop Sci
Journal of Air Law and Commerce [*A publication*] ... J Air L
Journal. Air Pollution Control Association [*A publication*] ... J Air Pollu
Journal. Air Pollution Control Association [*A publication*] ... J Air Pollut Contr Ass
Journal. Air Pollution Control Association [*A publication*] ... J Air Pollut Control Assoc
Journal. Air Pollution Control Association [*A publication*] ... JAPCA
Journal of Air Traffic Control [*A publication*] ... JATC
Journal. Air Transport Division. American Society of Civil Engineers [*A publication*] ... J Air Transp Div Am Soc Civ Eng
Journal of Aircraft [*A publication*] ... J Aircraft
Journal. Alabama Academy of Science [*A publication*] ... J Ala Acad Sci
Journal. Alabama Dental Association [*A publication*] ... J Ala Dent Assoc
Journal. Albert Einstein Medical Center [*A publication*] ... J Albert Einstein Med Cent
Journal. Albert Einstein Medical Center (Philadelphia) [*A publication*] ... J Albert Einstein Med Cent (Phila)
Journal of Alcohol and Drug Education [*A publication*] ... J Alc Drug
Journal of Alcohol and Drug Education [*A publication*] ... J Alcohol & Drug Educ
Journal of Alcoholism [*A publication*] ... J Alc
Journal of Alcoholism [*A publication*] ... J Alcohol
Journal of Algebra [*A publication*] ... J Algebra
Journal of Allergy [*A publication*] ... J Allergy
Journal of Allergy and Clinical Immunology [*A publication*] ... J Allerg Cl
Journal of Allergy and Clinical Immunology [*A publication*] ... J Allergy Clin Immunol
Journal of Allied Health [*A publication*] ... J Allied Health
Journal of Altered States of Consciousness [*A publication*] ... J Altered States Conscious
Journal. Alumni Association. College of Physicians and Surgeons (Baltimore) [*A publication*] ... J Alumni Ass Coll Phys and Surg (Baltimore)
Journal of Ambulatory Care Management [*A publication*] ... J Ambulatory Care Manage
Journal. American Academy of Child Psychiatry [*A publication*] ... JACPA
Journal. American Academy of Child Psychiatry [*A publication*] ... J Am Acad Child Psych
Journal. American Academy of Child Psychiatry [*A publication*] ... J Am Acad Child Psychiatry
Journal. American Academy of Child Psychiatry [*A publication*] ... J Am A Chil
Journal. American Academy of Dermatology [*A publication*] ... J Am Acad Dermatol
Journal. American Academy of Psychoanalysis [*A publication*] ... J Am Acad P
Journal. American Academy of Psychoanalysis [*A publication*] ... J Am Acad Psychoanal
Journal. American Academy of Religion [*A publication*] ... JAAR

Journal. American Academy of Religion [*A publication*]..........J Am Acad Rel
Journal. American Academy of Religion [*A publication*]........J Am Acad Religion
Journal. American Academy of Religion [*A publication*]...............J Am A Rel
Journal. American Animal Hospital Association [*A publication*]........J Am Anim Hosp Assoc
Journal. American Association of Nephrology Nurses and Technicians [*A publication*]........J AANNT
Journal. American Association of Nephrology Nurses and Technicians [*A publication*]........J Am Assoc Nephrol Nurses Tech
Journal. American Audiology Society [*A publication*]........JAASD
Journal. American Audiology Society [*A publication*]........J Am Audiol Soc
Journal. American Ceramic Society [*A publication*]........J Am Ceram
Journal. American Ceramic Society [*A publication*]........J Amer Ceram Soc
Journal. American Chamber of Commerce. Philippines [*A publication*]........JAACP
Journal. American Chemical Society [*A publication*]........JACS
Journal. American Chemical Society [*A publication*]........J Am Chem S
Journal. American Chemical Society [*A publication*]........J Amer Chem Soc
Journal. American College of Dentists [*A publication*]........J Am Coll Dent
Journal. American College of Dentists [*A publication*]........J Amer Coll Dent
Journal. American College of Emergency Physicians and the University Association for Emergency Medical Services [*A publication*]........JACEP
Journal. American College Health Association [*A publication*]....J Am Coll H
Journal. American College Health Association [*A publication*]........J Am Coll Health Assn
Journal. American College Health Association [*A publication*]........J Am Coll Health Assoc
Journal. American College of Toxicology [*A publication*]........JACT
Journal. American Concrete Institute [*A publication*]........J Am Concr Inst
Journal. American Dental Association [*A publication*]........JADSA
Journal. American Dental Association [*A publication*]........J Am Dent A
Journal. American Dental Association [*A publication*]........J Am Dent Assoc
Journal. American Dental Hygienists' Association [*A publication*]........J Am Dent Hyg Assoc
Journal. American Dietetic Association [*A publication*]........J Am Diet A
Journal. American Dietetic Association [*A publication*]........J Am Diet Assoc
Journal. American Dietetic Association [*A publication*]........J Amer Diet Ass
Journal of American Folklore [*A publication*]........JAF
Journal of American Folklore [*A publication*]........JAFL
Journal of American Folklore [*A publication*]........J Am F-lore
Journal of American Folklore [*A publication*]........J Am Folk
Journal of American Folklore [*A publication*]........J Am Folklo
Journal of American Folklore [*A publication*]........Jnl Am Folklore
Journal of American Folklore [*A publication*]........Jour Am Folklore
Journal. American Geriatrics Society [*A publication*]........JAGSA
Journal. American Geriatrics Society [*A publication*]........J Am Geriatr Soc
Journal. American Geriatrics Society [*A publication*]........J Am Ger So
Journal. American Health Care Association [*A publication*]........J Am Health Care Assoc
Journal of American History [*A publication*]........JAH
Journal of American History [*A publication*]........J Am His
Journal of American History [*A publication*]........J Am Hist
Journal of American History [*A publication*]........Jnl Am Hist
Journal of American Humor [*A publication*]........JAHum
Journal of American Indian Education [*A publication*]........J Am Indian Ed
Journal. American Institute of Architecture [*A publication*]........Jour Am Inst Archit
Journal. American Institute of Homeopathy [*A publication*]........JAIHA
Journal. American Institute of Planners [*A publication*]........AIPJ-A
Journal. American Institute of Planners [*A publication*]........J Amer Inst Planners
Journal. American Institute of Planners [*A publication*]........J Am Inst P
Journal. American Institute of Planners [*A publication*]........J Am Inst Plann
Journal of American Insurance [*A publication*]........JAI
Journal of American Insurance [*A publication*]........J Am Ins
Journal of American Insurance [*A publication*]........J Am Insur
Journal. American Intraocular Implant Society [*A publication*]........J Am Intraocul Implant Soc
Journal. American Judicature Society [*A publication*]........J Am Jud Soc
Journal. American Killifish Association [*A publication*]........J Am Killifish Assoc
Journal. American Leather Chemists Association [*A publication*]........J Amer Leather Chem Ass
Journal. American Leather Chemists Association [*A publication*]........J Am Leath
Journal. American Leather Chemists Association [*A publication*]........J Am Leather Chem Assoc
Journal. American Leather Chemists Association. Supplement [*A publication*]........J Am Leather Chem Assoc Suppl
Journal. American Liszt Society [*A publication*]........J ALS
Journal. American Medical Association [*A publication*]........JAMA
Journal. American Medical Association [*A publication*]........JAMAA
Journal. American Medical Association [*A publication*]........J Am Med A
Journal. American Medical Association [*A publication*]........J Am Med Assoc
Journal. American Medical Record Association [*A publication*]........J Am Med Rec Assoc
Journal. American Medical Technologists [*A publication*]........J Am Med Technol
Journal. American Medical Women's Association [*A publication*]........J Am Med Wom Assoc
Journal. American Medical Women's Association [*A publication*]........J Am Med Women's Assoc
Journal. American Medical Women's Association [*A publication*]....JAMWA
Journal. American Musicological Society [*A publication*]........JAMS
Journal. American Musicological Society [*A publication*]........JMUSA
Journal of American Musicology [*A publication*]........JAM
Journal. American Oil Chemists' Society [*A publication*]........J Amer Oil
Journal. American Oil Chemists' Society [*A publication*]........J Amer Oil Chem Soc
Journal. American Oil Chemists' Society [*A publication*]........J Am Oil Ch
Journal. American Oil Chemists' Society [*A publication*]........J Am Oil Chem Soc
Journal. American Oil Chemists' Society [*A publication*]........JAOCS
Journal. American Optometric Association [*A publication*]........J Am Optom Assoc
Journal. American Oriental Society [*A publication*]........J Am Or Soc
Journal. American Oriental Society [*A publication*]........JAOS
Journal. American Osteopathic Association [*A publication*]........J Am Osteopath Assoc
Journal. American Osteopathic Association [*A publication*]........JAOA
Journal. American Peanut Research and Education Association [*A publication*]........J Am Peanut Res Educ Assoc
Journal. American Pharmaceutical Association [*A publication*]........J Am Pharm
Journal. American Pharmaceutical Association [*A publication*]........J Am Pharm Assoc
Journal. American Pharmaceutical Association. Scientific Edition [*A publication*]........J Amer Pharm Ass Sci Ed
Journal. American Pharmaceutical Association. Scientific Edition [*A publication*]........J Am Pharm Assoc Sci Ed
Journal. American Physical Therapy Association [*A publication*]....... JAPTB
Journal. American Planning Association [*A publication*]........J Am Plann Assoc
Journal. American Podiatry Association [*A publication*]........J Am Podiatry Assoc
Journal. American Psychoanalytic Association [*A publication*]........J Am Psycho
Journal. American Psychoanalytic Association [*A publication*]........J Am Psychonal Assoc
Journal. American Psychoanalytic Association [*A publication*]........JAPOA
Journal. American Research Center in Egypt [*A publication*]........JARCE
Journal. American Scientific Affiliation [*A publication*]........JASA
Journal. American Society of Agronomy [*A publication*]........J Amer Soc Agron
Journal. American Society of Chartered Life Underwriters [*A publication*]........J Am Soc CLU
Journal. American Society of Farm Managers and Rural Appraisers [*A publication*]....J Amer Soc Farm Manage Rural Appraisers
Journal. American Society for Horticultural Science [*A publication*]........J Amer Soc Hort Sci
Journal. American Society for Horticultural Science [*A publication*]........J Am S Hort
Journal. American Society for Horticultural Science [*A publication*]........J Am Soc Hortic Sci
Journal. American Society for Information Science [*A publication*]........J Amer Soc Inform Sci
Journal. American Society for Information Science [*A publication*]........J Am S Infor
Journal. American Society for Information Science [*A publication*]........J Am Soc Inf Sci
Journal. American Society for Information Science [*A publication*].....JASIS
Journal. American Society for Preventive Dentistry [*A publication*]........J Am Soc Prev Dent
Journal. American Society for Psychical Research [*A publication*]........J Am S Psyc
Journal. American Society of Psychosomatic Dentistry and Medicine [*A publication*]........J Am Soc Psychosom Dent
Journal. American Society of Psychosomatic Dentistry and Medicine [*A publication*]........J Am Soc Psychosom Dent Med
Journal. American Society of Safety Engineers [*A publication*]........J Amer Soc Safety Eng
Journal. American Society of Safety Engineers [*A publication*]........J Am Soc Saf Eng
Journal. American Society of Sugar Beet Technologists [*A publication*]........J Amer Soc Sugar Beet Tech
Journal. American Society of Sugar Beet Technologists [*A publication*]........J Am Soc Sugar Beet Technol
Journal. American Society of Sugar Beet Technologists [*A publication*]........J Am Soc Sug Beet Technol
Journal. American Statistical Association [*A publication*]........J Amer Statist Assoc
Journal. American Statistical Association [*A publication*]........J Am Stat A
Journal. American Statistical Association [*A publication*]....J Am Stat Assoc
Journal. American Statistical Association [*A publication*]........JASA
Journal of American Studies [*A publication*]........J Amer Stud
Journal of American Studies [*A publication*]........JAmS
Journal of American Studies [*A publication*]........J Am St
Journal of American Studies [*A publication*]........J Am Stud
Journal of American Studies [*A publication*]........JAS

Journal of American Studies [*A publication*] ... JAStud
Journal of American Studies [*A publication*] ... Jour Am Studies
Journal. American Studies Association of Texas [*A publication*] ... JASAT
Journal. American Venereal Disease Association [*A publication*] ... J Am Vener Dis Assoc
Journal. American Veterinary Medical Association [*A publication*] ... J Amer Vet Med Ass
Journal. American Veterinary Medical Association [*A publication*] ... J Am Vet Me
Journal. American Veterinary Medical Association [*A publication*] ... J Am Vet Med Assoc
Journal. American Veterinary Medical Association [*A publication*] ... JAVMA
Journal. American Veterinary Radiology Society [*A publication*] ... J Am Vet Ra
Journal. American Veterinary Radiclogy Society [*A publication*] ... J Am Vet Radiol Soc
Journal. American Water Works Association [*A publication*] ... J Am Water
Journal. American Water Works Association [*A publication*] ... J Am Water Works Assoc
Journal d'Analyse Mathematique [*A publication*] ... J Anal Math
Journal of Analytical Chemistry of the USSR [*A publication*] ... J Anal Chem
Journal of Analytical Psychology [*A publication*] ... J Anal Psych
Journal of Analytical Psychology [*A publication*] ... J Anal Psychol
Journal of Analytical Toxicology [*A publication*] ... J Anal Toxicol
Journal. Anatomical Society of India [*A publication*] ... J Anat Soc India
Journal of Anatomy [*A publication*] ... J Anat
Journal of Anatomy and Physiology [*A publication*] ... J Anat Phys
Journal of Ancient Indian History [*A publication*] ... J Anc Ind Hist
Journal. Ancient Near Eastern Society [*A publication*] ... JANES
Journal. Ancient Near Eastern Society of Columbia University [*A publication*] ... J Anc Near East Soc Columbia Univ
Journal. Andhra Historical Research Society [*A publication*] ... J Andhra Hist Res Soc
Journal of Andrology [*A publication*] ... JA
Journal. Anglo-Mongolian Society [*A publication*] ... J Anglo-Mongol Soc
Journal of Animal Breeding and Genetics [*A publication*] ... J Anim Breed Genet
Journal of Animal Ecology [*A publication*] ... J Animal Ecol
Journal of Animal Ecology [*A publication*] ... J Anim Ecol
Journal of Animal Morphology and Physiology [*A publication*] ... J Anim Morphol Physiol
Journal of Animal Physiology and Animal Nutrition [*A publication*] ... J Anim Physiol Anim Nutr
Journal of Animal Production. United Arab Republic [*A publication*] ... J Anim Prod Un Arab Repub
Journal of Animal Science [*A publication*] ... J Animal Sci
Journal of Animal Science [*A publication*] ... J Anim Sci
Journal of Animal Science [*A publication*] ... JANSA
Journal. Animal Technicians Association [*A publication*] ... J Anim Tech Ass
Journal. Animal Technicians Association [*A publication*] ... J Anim Tech Assoc
Journal. Annamalai University. Part B [*A publication*] ... J Annamalai Univ Part B
Journal of Anthropological Archaeology [*A publication*] ... JAA
Journal of Anthropological Research [*A publication*] ... J Anthropol Res
Journal of Anthropological Research [*A publication*] ... J Anthrop Res
Journal of Anthropological Research [*A publication*] ... J Anthro Res
Journal of Anthropological Research [*A publication*] ... J Anthr Res
Journal of Anthropological Research [*A publication*] ... JAR
Journal. Anthropological Society of Nippon [*A publication*] ... J Anthropol Soc Nippon
Journal. Anthropological Society of Nippon [*A publication*] ... J Anthr S N
Journal. Anthropological Society of Oxford [*A publication*] ... J Anthropol Soc Oxford
Journal of Antibiotics [*Tokyo*] [*A publication*] ... J Antibiot
Journal of Antibiotics. Series B (Japan) [*A publication*] ... J Antibiot Ser B (Japan)
Journal of Antibiotics (Tokyo) [*A publication*] ... J Antibiot (Tokyo)
Journal of Antibiotics (Tokyo). Series A [*A publication*] ... J Antibiot (Tokyo) Ser A
Journal of Antimicrobial Chemotherapy [*A publication*] ... J Antimicrob Chemother
Journal. Aoyama Gakuin Woman's Junior College [*A publication*] ... J Aoyama Gakuin Woman's Jr Coll
Journal of Apicultural Research [*A publication*] ... J Apic Res
Journal of Applied Bacteriology [*A publication*] ... J App Bact
Journal of Applied Bacteriology [*A publication*] ... J App Bacteriol
Journal of Applied Bacteriology [*A publication*] ... J Appl Bact
Journal of Applied Bacteriology [*A publication*] ... J Appl Bacteriol
Journal of Applied Behavior Analysis [*A publication*] ... J App Behav Anal
Journal of Applied Behavior Analysis [*A publication*] ... J App Behavior Anal
Journal of Applied Behavior Analysis [*A publication*] ... J Appl Be A
Journal of Applied Behavior Analysis [*A publication*] ... J Appl Behav Anal
Journal of Applied Behavioral Science [*A publication*] ... JABS
Journal of Applied Behavioral Science [*A publication*] ... J Ap Behav Sci
Journal of Applied Behavioral Science [*A publication*] ... J App Behavioral Sci
Journal of Applied Behavioral Science [*A publication*] ... J App Behav Sci
Journal of Applied Behavioral Science [*A publication*] ... J Appl Beh
Journal of Applied Behavioral Science [*A publication*] ... J Appl Behav Sci
Journal of Applied Biochemistry [*A publication*] ... JAB
Journal of Applied Biochemistry [*A publication*] ... J Appl Biochem
Journal of Applied Chemistry [*A publication*] ... JAC
Journal of Applied Chemistry [*A publication*] ... J Appl Chem
Journal of Applied Chemistry and Biotechnology [*A publication*] ... J Appl Ch B
Journal of Applied Chemistry and Biotechnology [*A publication*] ... J Appl Chem Biotechnol
Journal of Applied Chemistry (London) [*A publication*] ... J Appl Chem (London)
Journal of Applied Chemistry of the USSR [*A publication*] ... J Appl Chem
Journal of Applied Chemistry of the USSR [*A publication*] ... J Appl Chem USSR
Journal of Applied Crystallography [*A publication*] ... J Appl Crys
Journal of Applied Ecology [*A publication*] ... J Ap Ecol
Journal of Applied Ecology [*A publication*] ... J App Ecol
Journal of Applied Ecology [*A publication*] ... J Appl Ecol
Journal of Applied Educational Studies [*A publication*] ... J Applied Ednl Studies
Journal of Applied Electrochemistry [*A publication*] ... J Appl Elec
Journal of Applied Entomology [*A publication*] ... J Appl Entomol
Journal of Applied Mathematics and Mechanics [*A publication*] ... J Appl Math Mech
Journal of Applied Mechanics [*A publication*] ... J App Mech
Journal of Applied Mechanics and Technical Physics [*A publication*] ... J Appl Mech & Tech Phys
Journal of Applied Mechanics. Transactions. ASME [*A publication*] ... J Appl Mech
Journal of Applied Mechanics. Transactions. ASME [*A publication*] ... J Appl Mech Trans ASME
Journal of Applied Meteorology [*A publication*] ... J Ap Meterol
Journal of Applied Meteorology [*A publication*] ... J Appl Met
Journal of Applied Meteorology [*A publication*] ... J Appl Meteorol
Journal of Applied Meteorology [*A publication*] ... J App Meteor
Journal of Applied Microscopy (Rochester, New York) [*A publication*] ... J Applied Micr (Rochester NY)
Journal of Applied Nutrition [*A publication*] ... J Ap Nutrition
Journal of Applied Nutrition [*A publication*] ... J Appl Nutr
Journal of Applied Nutrition [*A publication*] ... J App Nutr
Journal of Applied Photographic Engineering [*A publication*] ... J Appl Photogr Eng
Journal of Applied Physics [*A publication*] ... JAP
Journal of Applied Physics [*A publication*] ... J Appl Phys
Journal of Applied Physiology [*Later, Journal of Applied Physiology: Respiratory, Environmental, and Exercise Physiology*] [*A publication*] ... J Appl Physiol
Journal of Applied Physiology [*Later, Journal of Applied Physiology: Respiratory, Environmental, and Exercise Physiology*] [*A publication*] ... J App Physiol
Journal of Applied Physiology [*Later, Journal of Applied Physiology: Respiratory, Environmental, and Exercise Physiology*] [*A publication*] ... JAPYA
Journal of Applied Physiology: Respiratory, Environmental, and Exercise Physiology [*A publication*] ... J Appl Physiol Respir Environ Exercise Physiol
Journal of Applied Polymer Science [*A publication*] ... J Appl Poly
Journal of Applied Polymer Science [*A publication*] ... J Appl Polym Sci
Journal of Applied Polymer Science. Applied Polymer Symposium [*A publication*] ... J Appl Polym Sci Appl Polym Symp
Journal of Applied Probability [*A publication*] ... J Appl Probab
Journal of Applied Probability [*A publication*] ... J App Prob
Journal of Applied Psychology [*A publication*] ... JAP
Journal of Applied Psychology [*A publication*] ... J Appl Psyc
Journal of Applied Psychology [*A publication*] ... J Appl Psychol
Journal of Applied Psychology [*A publication*] ... J App Psychol
Journal of Applied Psychology [*A publication*] ... J Ap Psychol
Journal of Applied Psychology [*A publication*] ... JAPs
Journal of Applied Psychology [*A publication*] ... JAPSA
Journal of Applied Science and Engineering. Section A. Electrical Power and Information Systems [*A publication*] ... J Appl Sci Eng A
Journal of Applied Social Psychology [*A publication*] ... J Appl So P
Journal of Applied Social Psychology [*A publication*] ... J App Soc Psychol
Journal of Applied Sociology [*A publication*] ... J Ap Sociol
Journal of Applied Spectroscopy [*A publication*] ... J Appl Spectrosc
Journal of Applied Toxicology [*A publication*] ... JAT
Journal of Approximation Theory [*A publication*] ... J Approx Th
Journal of Approximation Theory [*A publication*] ... JAPT
Journal of Aquatic Plant Management [*A publication*] ... J Aquat Plant Manage
Journal of Arabic Literature [*A publication*] ... JArabL
Journal of Arachnology [*A publication*] ... J Arachnol
Journal of Arboriculture [*A publication*] ... J Arboric
Journal. Archaeological Institute of America [*A publication*] ... JAIA
Journal of Archaeological Science [*A publication*] ... J Archaeol Sci
Journal of Archaeological Science [*A publication*] ... J Arch Sci
Journal of Architectural Research [*A publication*] ... JARR
Journal. Arizona Academy of Science [*A publication*] ... J Ariz Acad Sci
Journal of Arizona History [*A publication*] ... JArizH
Journal of Arizona History [*A publication*] ... J Ariz Hist
Journal. Arkansas Medical Society [*A publication*] ... J Arkansas Med Soc

Journal. Arnold Arboretum [*A publication*]....J Arn Arbor
Journal. Arnold Arboretum. Harvard University [*A publication*]....J Arnold Arbor Harv Univ
Journal of Asian Affairs [*A publication*]....J As Aff
Journal of Asian and African Studies [*A publication*]....JAAS
Journal of Asian and African Studies [*A publication*]....J Asian Afr
Journal of Asian and African Studies [*A publication*]....J Asian & Afric Stud
Journal of Asian and African Studies [*A publication*]....J Asian Afr Stud
Journal of Asian and African Studies (Tokyo) [*A publication*]....J As Afr Stud (T)
Journal of Asian Culture [*A publication*]....J As Cult
Journal of Asian History [*A publication*]....J As Hist
Journal of Asian History [*A publication*]....J Asian His
Journal of Asian-Pacific and World Perspectives [*A publication*]....J As Pac World
Journal of Asian Studies [*A publication*]....JAS
Journal of Asian Studies [*A publication*]....J Asian St
Journal of Asian Studies [*A publication*]....J Asian Stud
Journal of Asian Studies [*A publication*]....J Asia Stud
Journal of Asian Studies [*A publication*]....JASt
Journal of Asian Studies [*A publication*]....Jnl Asian Stu
Journal. Asiatic Society of Bangladesh [*A publication*]....J Asiat Soc Bangla
Journal. Asiatic Society of Bengal [*A publication*]....JASB
Journal. Asiatic Society of Bombay [*A publication*]....JAS B
Journal. Asiatic Society of Bombay [*A publication*]....J Asiat Soc Bombay
Journal. Asiatic Society (Calcutta) [*A publication*]....JASC
Journal. Asiatic Society (Calcutta) [*A publication*]....JAS (Calcutta)
Journal. Asiatic Society of Great Britain and Ireland [*A publication*]....JAS
Journal. Asiatic Society. Letters [*A publication*]....JASL
Journal. Asiatic Society of Pakistan [*A publication*]....JASP
Journal of Asiatic Studies [*A publication*]....J Asiat Stud
Journal Asiatique [*A publication*]....JA
Journal Asiatique [*A publication*]....J Asiat
Journal. Assam Research Society [*A publication*]....JARS
Journal. Assam Research Society [*A publication*]....J Assam Res Soc
Journal. Assam Science Society [*A publication*]....J Assam Sci Soc
Journal. Association for the Advancement of Medical Instrumentation [*A publication*]....J Ass Advan Med Instrum
Journal. Association for the Advancement of Medical Instrumentation [*A publication*]....J Assoc Adv Med Instrum
Journal. Association Canadienne des Radiologistes [*A publication*]....J Assoc Can Radiol
Journal. Association for the Care of Children in Hospitals [*A publication*]....J Assoc Care Child Hosp
Journal. Association for the Care of Children's Health [*A publication*]....J Assoc Care Child Health
Journal. Association for Computing Machinery [*A publication*]....JACM
Journal. Association for Computing Machinery [*A publication*]....J Ass Comput Mach
Journal. Association for Computing Machinery [*A publication*]....J Assoc Comput Mach
Journal. Association for Education by Radio-Television [*A publication*]....JAERT
Journal. Association of Engineers and Architects in Israel [*A publication*]....J Assoc Eng Archit Isr
Journal. Association of Engineers (India) [*A publication*]....J Assoc Eng (India)
Journal. Association for Hospital Medical Education [*A publication*]....J Assoc Hosp Med Educ
Journal. Association Medicale Canadienne [*A publication*]....J Assoc Med Can
Journal. Association of Official Agricultural Chemists [*A publication*]....J Assoc Off Agric Chem
Journal. Association of Official Agricultural Chemists [*A publication*]....J Ass Off Agric Chem
Journal. Association of Official Analytical Chemists [*A publication*]....J AOAC
Journal. Association of Official Analytical Chemists [*A publication*]....J Assoc Off Anal Chem
Journal. Association of Official Analytical Chemists [*A publication*]....J Assoc Offic Anal Chem
Journal. Association of Official Analytical Chemists [*A publication*]....J Ass Off Analyt Chem
Journal. Association of Official Analytical Chemists [*A publication*]....J Ass Offic Anal Chem
Journal. Association of Physicians of India [*A publication*]....J Assoc Physicians India
Journal. Association for the Study of Perception [*A publication*]....J Assoc Study Percept
Journal. Association for the Study of Perception [*A publication*]....J As Stud P
Journal. Association of Teachers of Italian [*A publication*]....JATI
Journal. Association of Teachers of Japanese [*A publication*]....J Asso Teach Ja
Journal of Asthma [*A publication*]....J Asthma
Journal of Asthma Research [*A publication*]....J Asthma Res
Journal of the Astronautical Sciences [*A publication*]....J Astronaut
Journal of the Astronautical Sciences [*A publication*]....J Astronaut Sci
Journal of Astrophysics and Astronomy [*A publication*]....JAA
Journal of Atherosclerosis Research [*A publication*]....J Atheroscler Res
Journal of the Atmospheric Sciences [*A publication*]....J Atmos Sci
Journal of Atmospheric and Terrestrial Physics [*A publication*]....J Atmos Terr Phys
Journal of Atmospheric and Terrestrial Physics [*A publication*]....J Atm Ter P
Journal. Atomic Energy Society of Japan [*A publication*]....J At Energy Soc Jap
Journal. Audio Engineering Society [*A publication*]....ADIOA
Journal. Audio Engineering Society [*A publication*]....JAES
Journal. Audio Engineering Society [*A publication*]....J Aud Eng S
Journal. Audio Engineering Society [*A publication*]....J Audio Eng Soc
Journal of Audiovisual Media in Medicine [*A publication*]....J Audiov Media Med
Journal of Auditory Research [*A publication*]....J Aud Res
Journal of Auditory Research [*A publication*]....JAURA
Journal of Auditory Research. Supplement [*A publication*]....J Aud Res Suppl
Journal. Australasian Institute of Metals [*A publication*]....J Australas Inst Met
Journal. Australasian Universities Modern Language Association [*A publication*]....JAUMLA
Journal. Australian Ceramic Society [*A publication*]....J Aust Ceram Soc
Journal. Australian Entomological Society [*A publication*]....J Aust Entomol Soc
Journal. Australian Institute of Agricultural Science [*A publication*]....J Aus I Agr
Journal. Australian Institute of Agricultural Science [*A publication*]....J Aust Inst Agric Sci
Journal. Australian Institute of Agricultural Science [*A publication*]....J Aust Inst Agr Sci
Journal. Australian Institute of Metals [*A publication*]....J Aus I Met
Journal. Australian Institute of Metals [*A publication*]....J Aust Inst Met
Journal. Australian Mathematical Society [*A publication*]....J Aust Math Soc
Journal. Australian Mathematical Society. Series A [*A publication*]....J Austral Math Soc Ser A
Journal. Australian Mathematical Society. Series B [*A publication*]....J Austral Math Soc Ser B
Journal of Austronesian Studies [*A publication*]....JAS
Journal of Autism and Childhood Schizophrenia [*A publication*]....JAUCB
Journal of Autism and Childhood Schizophrenia [*A publication*]....J Autism Ch
Journal of Autism and Childhood Schizophrenia [*A publication*]....J Autism & Child Schizo
Journal of Autism and Childhood Schizophrenia [*A publication*]....J Autism Child Schizophrenia
Journal of Autism and Developmental Disorders [*A publication*]....J Autism Dev Disord
Journal of Autism and Developmental Disorders [*A publication*]....J Autism & Devel Dis
Journal of Automotive Engineering [*A publication*]....J Automot Eng
Journal of the Autonomic Nervous System [*A publication*]....J Auton Nerv Syst
Journal of Bacteriology [*A publication*]....J Bact
Journal of Bacteriology [*A publication*]....J Bacteriol
Journal of Ballistics [*A publication*]....J Ballist
Journal of Baltic Studies [*A publication*]....JBalS
Journal of Baltic Studies [*A publication*]....J Bal Stud
Journal. Baltimore College of Dental Surgery [*A publication*]....J Baltimore Coll Dent Surg
Journal of Band Research [*A publication*]....J Band Res
Journal of Band Research [*A publication*]....JBASB
Journal. Bangladesh Academy of Sciences [*A publication*]....J Bangladesh Acad Sci
Journal of Bank Research [*A publication*]....J Bank Res
Journal. Bar Association of the District of Columbia [*A publication*]....J BADC
Journal. Bar Association of the State of Kansas [*A publication*]....J BA Kan
Journal of Basic Engineering [*A publication*]....J Basic Eng
Journal of Basic Engineering. Transactions. ASME [*American Society of Mechanical Engineers*] [*A publication*]....J Basic Eng Trans ASME
Journal of Basic Engineering. Transactions. ASME [*American Society of Mechanical Engineers*] **Series D** [*A publication*]....J Basic Eng Trans ASME Ser D
Journal of Behavior Therapy and Experimental Psychiatry [*A publication*]....J Behav Exp
Journal of Behavior Therapy and Experimental Psychiatry [*A publication*]....J Behav Ther Exp Psychiatry
Journal of Behavioral Medicine [*A publication*]....J Behav Med
Journal of Behavioural Science [*A publication*]....J Behav Sci
Journal Belge de Medecine Physique et de Rehabilitation [*A publication*]....J Belge Med Phys Rehabil
Journal Belge de Radiologie [*A publication*]....J Belge Radiol
Journal Belge de Radiologie [*A publication*]....J Belg Rad
Journal Belge de Rhumatologie et de Medecine Physique [*A publication*]....J Belge Rhumatol Med Phys
Journal. Bergen County Dental Society [*A publication*]....J Bergen Cty Dent Soc
Journal. Beverly Hills Bar Association [*A publication*]....J Beverly Hills Ba
Journal of Bible and Religion [*A publication*]....JBR
Journal of Biblical Literature [*A publication*]....J Bib Lit
Journal of Biblical Literature [*A publication*]....JBL

Journal. Bihar and Orissa Research Society [*Later, Journal. Bihar Research Society*] [*A publication*] ... JBORS
Journal. Bihar Research Society [*A publication*] ... JBIRS
Journal. Bihar Research Society [*A publication*] ... JBRS
Journal of Biochemical and Microbiological Technology and Engineering [*A publication*] ... J Biochem Microbiol Tech Eng
Journal of Biochemistry [*A publication*] ... J Biochem
Journal of Biochemistry (Tokyo) [*A publication*] ... J Biochem (Tokyo)
Journal of Biocommunication [*A publication*] ... J Biocommun
Journal of Bioenergetics [*A publication*] ... J Bioenerg
Journal of Bioenergetics and Biomembranes [*A publication*] ... J Bioenerg Biomembr
Journal of Bioengineering [*A publication*] ... J Bioeng
Journal of Biological Chemistry [*A publication*] ... J Biol Chem
Journal of Biological Education [*A publication*] ... J Biol Educ
Journal of Biological Education [*A publication*] ... J Biological Ed
Journal. Biological Photographic Association [*A publication*] ... J Biol Phot
Journal. Biological Photographic Association [*A publication*] ... J Biol Photogr Assoc
Journal of Biological Physics [*A publication*] ... J Biol Phys
Journal of Biological Psychology [*A publication*] ... J Biol Psychol
Journal of Biological Sciences [*A publication*] ... J Biol Sci
Journal of Biological Standardization [*A publication*] ... J Biol Stan
Journal of Biological Standardization [*A publication*] ... J Biol Stand
Journal de Biologie Buccale [*A publication*] ... J Biol Bucc
Journal of Biologie Buccale [*A publication*] ... J Biol Buccale
Journal of Biology (Bronx, NY) [*A publication*] ... J Biol (Bronx NY)
Journal of Biology. Osaka City University [*A publication*] ... J Biol Osaka City Univ
Journal of Biomechanics [*A publication*] ... J Biomech
Journal of Biomechanics [*A publication*] ... J Biomechan
Journal of Biomedical Materials Research [*A publication*] ... J Biomed Mater Res
Journal of Biomedical Materials Research [*A publication*] ... J Biomed MR
Journal of Biomedical Systems [*A publication*] ... J Biomed Syst
Journal of Biophysical and Biochemical Cytology [*A publication*] ... J Biophys Biochem Cytol
Journal of Biosocial Science [*A publication*] ... J Biosoc Sc
Journal. Birla Institute of Technology and Science [*A publication*] ... J Birla Inst Technol Sci
Journal of Black Poetry [*A publication*] ... J Black Poetry
Journal of Black Poetry [*A publication*] ... JnlOBP
Journal of Black Studies [*A publication*] ... J Black St
Journal of Black Studies [*A publication*] ... J Black Stud
Journal. Board of Agriculture [*Great Britain*] [*A publication*] ... J Bd Ag
Journal. Board of Agriculture (London) [*A publication*] ... J Bd Agric (London)
Journal. Board of Direction. American Society of Civil Engineers [*A publication*] ... J Board Dir Am Soc Civ Eng
Journal. Bombay Branch of the Royal Asiatic Society [*A publication*] ... JBRAS
Journal. Bombay Natural History Society [*A publication*] ... J Bombay Nat Hist Soc
Journal. Bombay University. Arts [*A publication*] ... JBUA
Journal of Bone and Joint Surgery [*A publication*] ... J Bone Joint Surg
Journal of Bone and Joint Surgery (American Volume) [*A publication*] ... J Bone-Am V
Journal of Bone and Joint Surgery (American Volume) [*A publication*] ... J Bone Joint Surg (Am)
Journal of Bone and Joint Surgery (American Volume) [*A publication*] ... J Bone Jt Surg (Am Vol)
Journal of Bone and Joint Surgery (British Volume) [*A publication*] ... J Bone-Br V
Journal of Bone and Joint Surgery (British Volume) [*A publication*] ... J Bone Joint Surg (Br)
Journal of Bone and Joint Surgery (British Volume) [*A publication*] ... J Bone Jt Surg (Br Vol)
Journal. Boston Society of Civil Engineers [*A publication*] ... J Boston Soc Civ Eng
Journal. Botanical Society of South Africa [*A publication*] ... J Bot Soc S Afr
Journal. British Archaeological Association [*A publication*] ... JAA
Journal. British Archaeological Association [*A publication*] ... JBAA
Journal. British Astronomical Association [*A publication*] ... J Br Astron Assoc
Journal. British Boot and Shoe Institution [*A publication*] ... J Br Boot Shoe Instn
Journal. British Ceramic Society [*A publication*] ... J Brit Ceram Soc
Journal. British Endodontic Society [*A publication*] ... J Br Endod Soc
Journal. British Grassland Society [*A publication*] ... J Br Grassl
Journal. British Grassland Society [*A publication*] ... J Br Grassl Soc
Journal. British Interplanetary Society [*A publication*] ... JBIS
Journal. British Interplanetary Society [*A publication*] ... J Brit Interplanet Soc
Journal. British Nuclear Energy Society [*A publication*] ... J Brit Nucl Energy Soc
Journal. British Nuclear Energy Society [*A publication*] ... J Br Nucl E
Journal. British Nuclear Energy Society [*A publication*] ... J Br Nucl Energy Soc
Journal. British Ship Research Association [*A publication*] ... J Brit Ship Res Ass
Journal. British Society for Phenomenology [*A publication*] ... J Brit Soc Phenomenol
Journal. British Society for Phenomenology [*A publication*] ... J Br Soc Ph
Journal of British Studies [*A publication*] ... J Brit Stud
Journal of British Studies [*A publication*] ... JBS
Journal of British Studies [*A publication*] ... Jour Brit Studies
Journal. British Thoracic and Tuberculosis Association [*A publication*] ... BTTA
Journal of Broadcasting [*A publication*] ... JB
Journal of Broadcasting [*A publication*] ... J Broadcast
Journal of Broadcasting [*A publication*] ... J Broadcasting
Journal of Bryology [*A publication*] ... J Bryol
Journal. Burma Research Society [*A publication*] ... JBRS
Journal. Busan Medical College [*A publication*] ... J Busan Med Coll
Journal of Business [*A publication*] ... JB
Journal of Business [*A publication*] ... J Bsns
Journal of Business [*A publication*] ... J Bus
Journal of Business [*A publication*] ... J Busin
Journal of Business Education [*A publication*] ... JBE
Journal of Business Education [*A publication*] ... J Bsns Ed
Journal of Business Education [*A publication*] ... J Bsns Educ
Journal of Business Education [*A publication*] ... J Bus Ed
Journal of Business Education [*A publication*] ... Jnl Business Ed
Journal of Business Law [*A publication*] [*British*] ... JBL
Journal of Business Law [*A publication*] [*British*] ... J Bus L
Journal of Business Research [*A publication*] ... J Bus Res
Journal of Byelorussian Studies [*A publication*] ... JBS
Journal of Byelorussian Studies [*A publication*] ... JByelS
Journal des Caisses d'Epargne [*A publication*] ... J Caisses Epargne
Journal. California Dental Association [*A publication*] ... J Calif Dent Assoc
Journal. California Horticultural Society [*A publication*] ... J Calif Hortic Soc
Journal. California State Dental Association [*A publication*] ... J Calif State Dent Assoc
Journal. Canadian Association for Music Therapy [*A publication*] ... JAMTD
Journal. Canadian Association of Radiologists [*A publication*] ... J Can Assoc Radiol
Journal. Canadian Bar Association [*A publication*] ... J Can Ba
Journal. Canadian Ceramic Society [*A publication*] ... J Can Ceram Soc
Journal. Canadian Ceramic Society [*A publication*] ... JCCS
Journal. Canadian Dental Association [*A publication*] ... J Can Dent Assoc
Journal. Canadian Dental Society [*A publication*] ... JCDA
Journal. Canadian Dietetic Association [*A publication*] ... J Can Diet Ass
Journal. Canadian Dietetic Association [*A publication*] ... J Can Diet Assoc
Journal of Canadian Fiction [*A publication*] ... JCF
Journal. Canadian Linguistic Association [*Edmonton*] [*A publication*] ... JCLA
Journal of Canadian Petroleum Technology [*A publication*] ... J Can Petrol Technol
Journal of Canadian Petroleum Technology [*A publication*] ... J Can Pet T
Journal of Canadian Petroleum Technology [*A publication*] ... J Can Pet Technol
Journal. Canadian Society of Forensic Science [*A publication*] ... J Can Soc Forensic Sci
Journal of Canadian Studies [*A publication*] ... J Can Stud
Journal Canadien de Biochimie [*A publication*] ... J Can Biochim
Journal Canadien de Botanique [*A publication*] ... J Can Bot
Journal Canadien de Chirurgie [*A publication*] ... J Can Chir
Journal Canadien de Genetique et de Cytologie [*A publication*] ... J Can Genet Cytol
Journal Canadien de Microbiologie [*A publication*] ... J Can Microbiol
Journal Canadien d'Ophtalmologie [*A publication*] ... J Can Ophtalmol
Journal Canadien d'Otolaryngologie [*A publication*] ... J Can Otolaryngol
Journal Canadien de Physiologie et Pharmacologie [*A publication*] ... J Can Physiol Pharmacol
Journal Canadien de la Recherche Forestiere [*A publication*] ... J Can Rech For
Journal Canadien des Sciences Appliquees au Sport [*A publication*] ... J Can Sci Appl Sport
Journal Canadien des Sciences Neurologiques [*A publication*] ... J Can Sci Neurol
Journal Canadien des Sciences de la Terre [*A publication*] ... J Can Sci Terre
Journal Canadien de Zoologie [*A publication*] ... J Can Zool
Journal of Cancer Research and Clinical Oncology [*A publication*] ... J Cancer Res Clin Oncol
Journal of Carbohydrates-Nucleosides-Nucleotides [*A publication*] ... J Carb-Nucl
Journal of Carbohydrates-Nucleosides-Nucleotides [*A publication*] ... J Carbohyd-Nucl-Nucl
Journal of Carbohydrates-Nucleosides-Nucleotides [*A publication*] ... J Carbohydr-Nucleosides-Nucleotides
Journal of Cardiography [*A publication*] ... J Cardiogr
Journal of Cardiovascular Pharmacology [*A publication*] ... J Cardiovasc Pharmacol
Journal of Cardiovascular Surgery [*A publication*] ... J Cardiovasc Surg
Journal of Cardiovascular Surgery [*A publication*] ... J Card Surg
Journal of Cardiovascular Surgery (Torino) [*A publication*] ... J Cardiovasc Surg (Torino)
Journal of Cataloging and Classification [*A publication*] ... J Cat & Class
Journal of Catalysis [*A publication*] ... J Catal
Journal of Catalysis [*A publication*] ... J Catalysis

Journal. Catch Society of America [*A publication*]....JCSA
Journal. Catholic Medical College [*A publication*]....J Cathol Med Coll
Journal of Cell Biology [*A publication*]....J Cell Biol
Journal of Cell Science [*A publication*]....J Cell Sci
Journal of Cellular and Comparative Physiology [*A publication*]....J Cell Comp Physiol
Journal of Cellular Physiology [*A publication*]....J Cell Phys
Journal of Cellular Physiology [*A publication*]....J Cell Physiol
Journal of Cellular Plastics [*A publication*]....J Cell Plast
Journal of Celtic Studies [*A publication*]....JCeltS
Journal of Celtic Studies [*A publication*]....JCS
Journal. Central Agricultural Experiment Station [*A publication*]....J Cent Agr Exp Sta
Journal. Central Agricultural Experiment Station [*A publication*]....J Cent Agric Exp Stn
Journal of Central European Affairs [*A publication*]....JCEA
Journal of Central European Affairs [*A publication*]....J Cent Eur Aff
Journal of Central European Affairs [*A publication*]....J Cent Eur Affairs
Journal. Central Mississippi Valley American Studies Association [*A publication*]....JCMVASA
Journal. Ceramic Society of Japan [*A publication*]....J Ceram Soc Jpn
Journal. Ceramic Society of Japan [*A publication*]....J Cer Soc Jap
Journal of Cerebral Blood Flow and Metabolism [*A publication*]....JCBF
Journal. Ceylon Branch. British Medical Association [*A publication*]....J Ceylon Br Brit Med Ass
Journal. Ceylon Branch. Royal Asiatic Society [*A publication*]....JCRAS
Journal. Chartered Institute of Transport [*A publication*]....J Chart Inst Transp
Journal of Chemical Documentation [*A publication*]....J Chem Doc
Journal of Chemical Documentation [*A publication*]....J Chem Docum
Journal of Chemical Ecology [*A publication*]....J Chem Ecol
Journal of Chemical Education [*A publication*]....J Chem Educ
Journal of Chemical and Engineering Data [*A publication*]....JC & ED
Journal of Chemical and Engineering Data [*A publication*]....J Chem En D
Journal of Chemical and Engineering Data [*A publication*]....J Chem Eng Data
Journal of Chemical Engineering of Japan [*A publication*]....J Chem Eng Jap
Journal of Chemical Engineering of Japan [*A publication*]....J Chem Eng Jpn
Journal of Chemical Information and Computer Sciences [*A publication*]....J Chem Inf
Journal of Chemical Information and Computer Sciences [*A publication*]....J Chem Inf Comput Sci
Journal of Chemical Information and Computer Sciences [*A publication*]....JCICS
Journal of Chemical Physics [*A publication*]....J Chem Phys
Journal of Chemical Physics [*A publication*]....JCPSA
Journal of Chemical Physics [*A publication*]....Jour Chem Physics
Journal of Chemical Research. Part M [*A publication*]....J Chem Res M
Journal of Chemical Research. Part S [*A publication*]....J Chem Res S
Journal of Chemical Research. Part S (Synopses) [*A publication*]....J Chem Res Part S
Journal. Chemical Society [*A publication*]....J Chem Soc
Journal. Chemical Society [*A publication*]....JCS
Journal. Chemical Society. Chemical Communications [*A publication*]....J Chem S Ch
Journal. Chemical Society. Chemical Communications [*A publication*]....J Chem Soc Chem Commun
Journal. Chemical Society. Chemical Communications [*A publication*]....JCS Chem Comm
Journal. Chemical Society. D. Chemical Communications [*A publication*]....J Chem Soc D Chem Commun
Journal. Chemical Society. Dalton Transactions [*A publication*]....J Chem S Da
Journal. Chemical Society. Dalton Transactions. Inorganic Chemistry [*A publication*]....JCS Dalton
Journal. Chemical Society. Faraday Transactions 1 [*A publication*]....J Chem S F1
Journal. Chemical Society. Faraday Transactions 2 [*A publication*]....J Chem S F2
Journal. Chemical Society. Faraday Transactions. I [*A publication*]....J Chem Soc Faraday Trans I
Journal. Chemical Society. Faraday Transactions. I. Physical Chemistry [*A publication*]....JCS Faraday I
Journal. Chemical Society. Faraday Transactions. II [*A publication*]....J Chem Soc Faraday Trans II
Journal. Chemical Society. Faraday Transactions. II. Chemical Physics [*A publication*]....JCS Faraday II
Journal. Chemical Society of Japan. Industrial Chemistry Section [*A publication*]....J Chem Soc Japan
Journal. Chemical Society of Japan. Industrial Chemistry Section [*A publication*]....J Chem Soc Jap Ind Chem Sect
Journal. Chemical Society (London) [*A publication*]....J Chem Soc (London)
Journal. Chemical Society. London. A. Inorganic, Physical, Theoretical [*A publication*]....J Chem Soc London A Inorg Phys Theor
Journal. Chemical Society. London. B. Physical, Organic [*A publication*]....J Chem Soc London B Phys Org
Journal. Chemical Society. London. C. Organic [*A publication*]....J Chem Soc London C Org
Journal. Chemical Society. London. Chemical Communications [*A publication*]....J Chem Soc London Chem Commun
Journal. Chemical Society. London. D. Chemical Communications [*A publication*]....J Chem Soc London D Chem Commun
Journal. Chemical Society. London. Dalton Transactions [*A publication*]....J Chem Soc London Dalton Trans
Journal. Chemical Society. London. Faraday Transactions. I [*A publication*]....J Chem Soc London Faraday Trans I
Journal. Chemical Society. London. Faraday Transactions. II [*A publication*]....J Chem Soc London Faraday Trans II
Journal. Chemical Society. London. Perkin Transactions. I [*A publication*]....J Chem Soc London Perkin Trans I
Journal. Chemical Society. London. Perkin Transactions. II [*A publication*]....J Chem Soc London Perkin Trans II
Journal. Chemical Society. Perkin Transactions 1 [*A publication*]....J Chem S P1
Journal. Chemical Society. Perkin Transactions 2 [*A publication*]....J Chem S P2
Journal. Chemical Society. Perkin Transactions I [*A publication*]....J Chem Soc Perkin Trans I
Journal. Chemical Society. Perkin Transactions. I. Organic and Bioorganic Chemistry [*A publication*]....JCS Perkin I
Journal. Chemical Society. Perkin Transactions. II [*A publication*]....J Chem Soc Perkin Trans II
Journal. Chemical Society. Perkin Transactions. II. Physical Organic Chemistry [*A publication*]....JCS Perkin II
Journal. Chemical Society. Section C. Organic Chemistry [*A publication*]....J Che Soc Sect C Org Chem
Journal of Chemical Technology and Biotechnology [*A publication*]....J Chem Technol Biotechnol
Journal of Chemical Thermodynamics [*A publication*]....J Chem Ther
Journal fuer Chemie und Physik [*A publication*]....J Chem Phys
Journal of Chemistry of the United Arab Republic [*A publication*]....J Chem UAR
Journal. Chester Archaeological Society [*A publication*]....J Chester Arch Soc
Journal. Chiba Medical Society [*A publication*]....J Chiba Med Soc
Journal of Child Development [*A publication*]....JCDVA
Journal of Child Language [*A publication*]....J Child Lang
Journal of Child Language [*A publication*]....J Child Language
Journal of Child Language [*A publication*]....J Ch L
Journal of Child Psychology and Psychiatry [*A publication*]....J Child Psy
Journal of Child Psychology and Psychiatry [*A publication*]....J Child Psychol
Journal of Child Psychology and Psychiatry [*A publication*]....J Child Psych & Psychiatry
Journal of Child Psychology and Psychiatry and Allied Disciplines [*Later, Journal of Child Psychology and Psychiatry*] [*A publication*]....J Child Psychol & Psych
Journal of Child Psychology and Psychiatry and Allied Disciplines [*Later, Journal of Child Psychology and Psychiatry*] [*A publication*]....J Child Psychol Psychiatry Allied Discipl
Journal of Child Psychology and Psychiatry and Allied Disciplines [*Later, Journal of Child Psychology and Psychiatry*] [*A publication*]....JPPDA
Journal of Child Psychology and Psychiatry. Book Supplement [*A publication*]....J Child Psychol Psychiatry Book Suppl
Journal of Child Psychotherapy [*A publication*]....J Child Psychotherapy
Journal of Children in Contemporary Society [*A publication*]....J Child Contemp Soc
Journal de Chimie Physique et de Physico-Chimie Biologique [*A publication*]....J Chim Phys
Journal de Chimie Physique et de Physico-Chimie Biologique [*A publication*]....J Chim Phys Phys-Chim Biol
Journal. Chinese Biochemical Society [*A publication*]....J Chin Biochem Soc
Journal. Chinese Chemical Society [*A publication*]....J Chin Chem
Journal. Chinese Chemical Society [*A publication*]....J Chin Chem Soc
Journal. Chinese Language Teachers Association [*A publication*]....J Chin Lang Teach Asso
Journal. Chinese Language Teachers Association [*A publication*]....JCLTA
Journal of Chinese Linguistics [*A publication*]....J Chinese Ling
Journal of Chinese Linguistics [*A publication*]....JChinL
Journal of Chinese Linguistics [*A publication*]....J Chin Ling
Journal of Chinese Philosophy [*A publication*]....JChinP
Journal of Chinese Philosophy [*A publication*]....J Chin Phil
Journal of Chinese Philosophy [*A publication*]....J Chin Philo
Journal. Chinese University of Hong Kong [*A publication*]....J Chin U HK
Journal de Chirurgie [*A publication*]....J Chir
Journal of Christian Education [*A publication*]....JCE
Journal. Christian Medical Association of India [*A publication*]....J Christ Med Assoc India
Journal of Christian Philosophy [*A publication*]....J Chr Philos
Journal of Christian Reconstruction [*A publication*]....JCR
Journal of Chromatographic Science [*A publication*]....J Chromatogr Sci
Journal of Chromatographic Science [*A publication*]....J Chromat Sci
Journal of Chromatographic Science [*A publication*]....J Chrom Sci
Journal of Chromatography [*A publication*]....J Chromat
Journal of Chromatography [*A publication*]....J Chromatogr
Journal of Chromatography. Biomedical Applications [*A publication*]....J Chromatogr Biomed Appl

Journal of Chromatography Library [*Elsevier Book Series*] [*A publication*]..JCL

Journal of Chromatography. Supplementary Volume [*A publication*]...........................J Chromatogr Suppl Vol

Journal of Chronic Diseases [*A publication*]..................................J Chron Dis

Journal of Chronic Diseases [*A publication*]..................................J Chronic Dis

Journal of Church Music [*A publication*]......................J Church Mus

Journal of Church and State [*A publication*]........................J Ch St

Journal of Church and State [*A publication*].........J Church & State

Journal of Church and State [*A publication*]...............................JCS

Journal of Church and State [*A publication*].........Jour Church and State

Journal Citation Reports [*A publication*].................................JCR

Journal. City Planning Division. American Society of Civil Engineers [*A publication*].................J City Plann Div Am Soc Civ Eng

Journal of Civil Engineering (Taipei) [*A publication*]...........J Civ Eng (Taipei)

Journal. Civil War Token Society [*A publication*]..............................JCWTS

Journal of Classical Studies [*Kyoto University*] [*A publication*]..................JCS

Journal of Clinical Chemistry and Clinical Biochemistry [*A publication*].....................J Clin Chem Clin Biochem

Journal of Clinical Child Psychology [*A publication*]........................ J Clin Chil

Journal of Clinical Electron Microscopy [*A publication*]......................J Clin Electron Microsc

Journal of Clinical Endocrinology [*A publication*] ....J Clin Endocr

Journal of Clinical Endocrinology and Metabolism [*A publication*] ......JCEM

Journal of Clinical Endocrinology and Metabolism [*A publication*]..........................J Clin Endocrinol Metab

Journal of Clinical Engineering [*A publication*] .... J Clin Eng

Journal of Clinical and Experimental Hypnosis [*A publication*]......................J Clin Exp Hypn

Journal of Clinical and Experimental Psychopathology and Quarterly Review of Psychiatry and Neurology [*A publication*] .... J Clin Exp Psychopathol Q Rev Psychiatry Neurol

Journal of Clinical Gastroenterology [*A publication*] ...... J Clin Gastroenterol

Journal of Clinical Hematology and Oncology [*A publication*]......................J Clin Hematol Oncol

Journal of Clinical and Hospital Pharmacy [*A publication*]......................J Clin Hosp Pharm

Journal of Clinical Investigation [*A publication*]................................J Clin Inv

Journal of Clinical Investigation [*A publication*]............................J Clin Invest

Journal of Clinical and Laboratory Immunology [*A publication*].......................J Clin Lab Immunol

Journal of Clinical Microbiology [*A publication*]....................... J Clin Micr

Journal of Clinical Microbiology [*A publication*].....................J Clin Microbiol

Journal of Clinical Neuropsychology [*A publication*] ...... J Clin Neuropsychol

Journal of Clinical Nutrition [*A publication*]....................................J Clin Nutr

Journal of Clinical Orthodontics [*A publication*]...................... J Clin Orthod

Journal of Clinical Pathology [*London*] [*A publication*] .... J Clin Path

Journal of Clinical Pathology (London) [*A publication*] ... J Clin Pathol (Lond)

Journal of Clinical Pathology (Supplement) [*A publication*]......................J Clin Pathol (Suppl)

Journal of Clinical Periodontology [*A publication*] ....J Clin Periodontol

Journal of Clinical Pharmacology [*A publication*].............................J Clin Phar

Journal of Clinical Pharmacology [*A publication*] ....J Clin Pharmacol

Journal of Clinical Pharmacology and New Drugs [*Later, Journal of Clinical Pharmacology*] [*A publication*] .....J Clin Pharmacol New Drugs

Journal of Clinical Psychiatry [*A publication*] ....J Clin Psychiatry

Journal of Clinical Psychology [*A publication*] ....J Clin Psyc

Journal of Clinical Psychology [*A publication*] ....J Clin Psychol

Journal of Clinical Psychology [*A publication*] ....JCP

Journal of Clinical Psychology [*A publication*] ....JCPs

Journal of Clinical Psychology [*A publication*] ....JCPYA

Journal of Clinical Psychopharmacology [*A publication*] ....J Clin Psychopharmacol

Journal of Clinical Ultrasound [*A publication*] ....JCLTB

Journal of Clinical Ultrasound [*A publication*] ....JCU

Journal of Coated Fabrics [*A publication*]...................J Coated Fabr

Journal of Coated Fibrous Materials [*A publication*]......................J Coated Fibrous Mater

Journal of Coatings Technology [*A publication*]......................J Coat Technol

Journal of Coffee Research [*A publication*]...............J Coffee Res

Journal of Collective Negotiations in the Public Sector [*A publication*]................J Collect Negotiations Public Sect

Journal. College of Agriculture. Tokyo Imperial University [*A publication*]......................J Coll Ag Tokyo

Journal. College of Arts and Sciences. Chiba University [*A publication*]......................J Coll Arts Sci Chiba Univ

Journal. College of Dairy Agriculture [*A publication*] .... J Coll Dairy Agr

Journal. College of Dairy Agriculture (Ebetsu, Japan) [*A publication*]......................J Coll Dairy Agri (Ebetsu Japan)

Journal. College of Dairy Agriculture (Nopporo) [*A publication*].......................J Coll Dairy Agric (Nopporo)

Journal. College of Dairying (Ebetsu, Japan) [*A publication*].......................J Coll Dairy (Ebetsu Japan)

Journal. College of Dairying (Nopporo) [*A publication*].......................J Coll Dairy (Nopporo)

Journal. College of Industrial Technology. Nihon University. Series A [*A publication*]...............J Coll Ind Technol Nihon Univ A

Journal. College of Industrial Technology. Nihon University. Series B [*A publication*]...............J Coll Ind Technol Nihon Univ B

Journal. College of Marine Science and Technology. Tokai University [*A publication*]......................J Coll Mar Sci Technol Tokai Univ

Journal of College Placement [*A publication*]......................J Coll Placement

Journal of College Placement [*A publication*]......................J Col Placement

Journal. College of Radiologists of Australasia [*A publication*]......................J Coll Radiol Australas

Journal of College Science Teaching [*A publication*]............J Coll Sci Teach

Journal of College Student Personnel [*A publication*]...................J Coll Stud

Journal of College Student Personnel [*A publication*] ....J Coll Student Personnel

Journal of College Student Personnel [*A publication*] ....J Coll Stud Personnel

Journal of College Student Personnel [*A publication*] ....J Col Stud Personnel

Journal. College of Surgeons of Australasia [*A publication*]......................J Coll Surgeons Australasia

Journal. College and University Personnel Association [*A publication*]...................... J Coll Univ

Journal. College and University Personnel Association [*A publication*]......................J Coll & Univ Personnel Assn

Journal of Colloid and Interface Science [*A publication*]..................J Coll I Sc

Journal of Colloid and Interface Science [*A publication*]......................J Colloid Interface Sci

Journal of Colloid Science [*A publication*].............................J Colloid Sci

Journal of Color and Appearance [*A publication*]...............................JCA

Journal of Color and Appearance [*A publication*].............................J Color

Journal of Color and Appearance [*A publication*]...........J Color Appearance

Journal. Colorado Dental Association [*A publication*].......J Colo Dent Assoc

Journal. Colorado-Wyoming Academy of Science [*A publication*]......................J Colo-Wyo Acad Sci

Journal of Combinatorial Theory [*A publication*].....................J Comb Theory

Journal of Combinatorial Theory. Series A [*A publication*].........J Comb Th A

Journal of Combinatorial Theory. Series B [*A publication*].........J Comb Th B

Journal of Combinatorics. Information and System Sciences [*A publication*]...................J Combinatorics Information Syst Sci

Journal of Combustion Toxicology [*A publication*] ...... J Combustion Toxicol

Journal of Combustion Toxicology [*A publication*] .... J Combust Toxicol

Journal of Commercial Bank Lending [*A publication*]......................J Comm Bank Lending

Journal of Common Market Studies [*A publication*] ....J Com Mkt S

Journal of Common Market Studies [*A publication*] ....J Common Market Stud

Journal of Common Market Studies [*A publication*] ...... J Common Mkt Stud

Journal of Commonwealth and Comparative Politics [*A publication*]...................J Commonw Comp Pol

Journal of Commonwealth and Comparative Politics [*A publication*]...................J Commonwealth Comp Polit

Journal of Commonwealth Literature [*A publication*] ....JCL

Journal of Commonwealth Literature [*A publication*] ....JComLit

Journal of Commonwealth Literature [*A publication*] .... J Commonwealth Lit

Journal of Communicable Diseases [*A publication*]..................J Commun Dis

Journal of Communication [*A publication*] ....JC

Journal of Communication [*A publication*] ....JCMNA

Journal of Communication [*A publication*] ....J Comm

Journal of Communication [*A publication*] ....J Communication

Journal of Communication Disorders [*A publication*]...........................JCDIA

Journal of Communication Disorders [*A publication*]........................J Comm Dis

Journal of Communication Disorders [*A publication*]........ J Commun Disord

Journal of Community Communications [*A publication*] .... Com Com

Journal of Community Health [*A publication*].................J Community Health

Journal of Community Psychology [*A publication*].........J Community Psychol

Journal of Comparative Administration [*A publication*]............. J Comp Adm

Journal of Comparative Economics [*A publication*].................. J Comp Econ

Journal. Comparative Education Society in Europe (British Section) [*A publication*] .... Compare

Journal of Comparative Ethology [*A publication*]....................J Comp Ethol

Journal of Comparative Family Studies [*A publication*]......................J Comp Family Stud

Journal of Comparative Family Studies [*A publication*]..... J Comp Fam Stud

Journal of Comparative Medicine and Veterinary Archives [*A publication*]...................J Comp Med and Vet Arch

Journal of Comparative Neurology [*A publication*]...........................JCNEA

Journal of Comparative Neurology [*A publication*]....................J Comp Neur

Journal of Comparative Neurology [*A publication*]................... J Comp Neurol

Journal of Comparative Pathology [*A publication*].................J Comp Path

Journal of Comparative Pathology [*A publication*]....................J Comp Pathol

Journal of Comparative Pathology and Therapeutics [*A publication*]......................J Comp Pathol Ther

Journal of Comparative Pathology and Therapeutics [*A publication*]......................J Comp Path and Therap

Journal of Comparative and Physiological Psychology [*A publication*]......................J Com Physl

Journal of Comparative and Physiological Psychology [*A publication*]......................J Comp & Physiol Psychol

Journal of Comparative and Physiological Psychology [*A publication*]......................J Comp Physiol Psychol

Journal of Comparative and Physiological Psychology [*A publication*]......................JCPP

Journal of Comparative and Physiological Psychology [*A publication*]......................JCPPA

Journal of Comparative Physiology [*A publication*] ....J Comp Phys

Journal of Comparative Physiology [*A publication*] ....J Comp Physiol

Journal of Comparative Physiology [*German Federal Republic*] [*A publication*]..J Comp Physiol
Journal of Comparative Physiology. A. Sensory, Neural, and Behavioral Physiology [*A publication*]............................
...........J Comp Physiol A Sens Neural Behav Physiol
Journal of Comparative Physiology. B. Metabolic and Transport Functions [*A publication*]...........J Comp Physiol B Metab Transp Funct
Journal of Comparative Psychology [*A publication*]...........J Comp Psychol
Journal of Composite Materials [*A publication*]......................J Compos Ma
Journal of Composite Materials [*A publication*]...................J Compos Mater
Journal of Computational and Applied Mathematics [*A publication*]...............................J Comput Appl Math
Journal of Computational Chemistry [*A publication*]...................................JCC
Journal of Computational Physics [*A publication*]....................J Comput Ph
Journal of Computational Physics [*A publication*]..................J Comput Phys
Journal of Computed Tomography [*A publication*].......................CT
Journal of Computer Assisted Tomography [*A publication*]......................
J Comput Assist Tomogr
Journal. Computer Society of India [*A publication*]..........J Comput Soc India
Journal of Computer and System Sciences [*A publication*].......J Comput Sy
Journal of Computer and System Sciences [*A publication*]...........................
J Comput Syst Sci
Journal of Computer and System Sciences [*A publication*]..................JCSS
Journal of Conchology [*A publication*]...........................J Conchol
Journal de Conchyliologie [*A publication*].......................J Conchyl
Journal de Conchyliologie [*A publication*]......................Jour Conchyliologie
Journal of Conflict Resolution [*A publication*]...............J Conflict Resol
Journal of Conflict Resolution [*A publication*]...............J Confl Res
Journal of Conflict Resolution [*A publication*]..........Jour Conflict Resolution
Journal des Connaissances Medico-Chirurgicales [*A publication*]......................J Conn Med Chir
Journal. Connecticut State Dental Association [*A publication*].....................
J Conn State Dent Assoc
Journal du Conseil [*A publication*]...............................J Conseil
Journal du Conseil [*A publication*]................................Jour Conseil
Journal du Conseil. Conseil International pour l'Exploration de la Mer [*A publication*].......................J Cons Cons Int Explor Mer
Journal du Conseil. Conseil International pour l'Exploration de la Mer [*A publication*]...........................J Cons Int Explor Mer
Journal of Constitutional and Parliamentary Studies [*A publication*].............................J Const Parl Stud
Journal of Constitutional and Parliamentary Studies [*India*] [*A publication*]................................ JCPS
Journal. Construction Division. American Society of Civil Engineers [*A publication*]......................J Cons ASCE
Journal. Construction Division. Proceedings. American Society of Civil Engineers [*A publication*]...............J Constr Div Am Soc Civ Eng
Journal of Consulting and Clinical Psychology [*A publication*]...........JCLPB
Journal of Consulting and Clinical Psychology [*A publication*]....J Cons Clin
Journal of Consulting and Clinical Psychology [*A publication*].......................
J Consult & Clin Psychol
Journal of Consulting and Clinical Psychology [*A publication*]......................
J Consult Clin Psychol
Journal of Consulting Psychology [*A publication*]...............J Consult Psychol
Journal of Consumer Affairs [*A publication*].......................J Con A
Journal of Consumer Affairs [*A publication*]...........................J Consum Af
Journal of Consumer Affairs [*A publication*]..........................J Consumer Aff
Journal of Consumer Affairs [*A publication*]..........................J Consumer Affairs
Journal of Consumer Product Flammability [*A publication*]..........................
J Consumer Prod Flammability
Journal of Consumer Product Flammability [*A publication*]..........................
J Consum Prod Flammability
Journal of Consumer Research [*A publication*]......................J Consumer Res
Journal of Contemporary Asia [*A publication*].......................J Contemp
Journal of Contemporary Asia [*A publication*].......................J Contemp Asia
Journal of Contemporary Business [*A publication*].......................J Cont Bus
Journal of Contemporary Business [*A publication*].......................J Contemp Bus
Journal of Contemporary Business [*A publication*].......................J Contemp Busin
Journal of Contemporary History [*A publication*]....................J Contemp Hist
Journal of Contemporary History [*A publication*]..................J Cont Hist
Journal of Contemporary History [*A publication*].............Jour Contemp Hist
Journal of Contemporary Law [*A publication*] ....J Contemp L
Journal of Contemporary Psychotherapy [*A publication*].............J Cont Psyt
Journal of Continuing Education in Nursing [*A publication*].......................
J Contin Educ Nurs
Journal of Cooperative Education [*A publication*].......................J Coop Educ
Journal of Coordination Chemistry [*A publication*]...........J Coord Ch
Journal. Cork Historical and Archaeological Society [*A publication*]..JCHAS
Journal. Cork Historical and Archaeological Society [*A publication*]........................Journal Cork Hist Soc
Journal of Corporate Taxation [*A publication*].............................J Corp Tax
Journal. Council for Scientific and Industrial Research (Australia) [*A publication*].......................J Counc Sci Ind Res (Australia)
Journal of Counseling Psychology [*A publication*]...........J Coun Psyc
Journal of Counseling Psychology [*A publication*]............J Counsel Psychol
Journal of Counseling Psychology [*A publication*]..................................JCP
Journal of Counseling Psychology [*A publication*]........................JLCPA
Journal of Counseling Psychology [*A publication*]............Jnl Counsel Psych
Journal of Country Music [*A publication*]........................JCM
Journal of Creative Behavior [*A publication*] ....JCB

Journal of Creative Behavior [*A publication*]..............................J Creat Beh
Journal of Creative Behavior [*A publication*] ....J Creative Behavior
Journal of Criminal Justice [*A publication*]..........................J Crim Jus
Journal of Criminal Law and Criminology [*A publication*]............J Crim Law
Journal of Criminal Law and Criminology [*A publication*].......................
J Crim Law & Criminol
Journal of Criminal Law, Criminology, and Police Science [*Later, Journal of Criminal Law and Criminology*] [*A publication*]..JCLCPS
Journal of Criminal Law, Criminology, and Police Science [*Later, Journal of Criminal Law and Criminology*] [*A publication*].................J Crim Law Criminol Police Sci
Journal of Criminal Law, Criminology, and Police Science [*Later, Journal of Criminal Law and Criminology*] [*A publication*]..Jour Crim Law
Journal of Criminal Law (English) [*A publication*]....................J Crim L (Eng)
Journal of Critical Analysis [*A publication*]........................J Crit Anal
Journal of Croatian Studies [*A publication*]........................JCS
Journal of Cross-Cultural Psychology [*A publication*].....................JCPGB
Journal of Cross-Cultural Psychology [*A publication*]...................J Cross-Cul
Journal of Cross-Cultural Psychology [*A publication*]......J Cross-Cult Psych
Journal of Cross-Cultural Psychology [*A publication*] ....
J Cross-Cult Psychol
Journal of Crystal Growth [*A publication*].............................J Cryst Gr
Journal of Crystal and Molecular Structure [*A publication*]..................JCMS
Journal of Crystal and Molecular Structure [*A publication*].........J Cryst Mol
Journal of Crystal and Molecular Structure [*A publication*].......................
J Cryst Mol Struct
Journal. Crystallographic Society of Japan [*A publication*]........................
J Crystallogr Soc Jap
Journal of Cuneiform Studies [*A publication*]........................JCS
Journal of Cuneiform Studies [*A publication*]................................J Cun S
Journal of Current Laser Abstracts [*A publication*]............J Curr Laser Abstr
Journal of Current Social Issues [*A publication*].................J Cur Soc Issues
Journal of Curriculum Studies [*A publication*].......................JCS
Journal of Curriculum Studies [*A publication*]............................J Curric St
Journal of Cutaneous Pathology [*A publication*] ....J Cutaneous Pathol
Journal of Cutaneous Pathology [*A publication*] ....J Cut Path
Journal of Cybernetics [*A publication*].......................J Cybern
Journal of Cybernetics and Information Science [*A publication*]..................
J Cybern Inf Sci
Journal of Cycle Research [*A publication*] ....J Cycle Res
Journal of Cyclic Nucleotide Research [*A publication*] ....
J Cyclic Nucleotide Res
Journal of Cyclic Nucleotide Research [*A publication*].................J Cycl Nucl
Journal of Dairy Research [*A publication*]...........................J Dairy Res
Journal of Dairy Science [*A publication*].....................................J Dairy Sci
Journal of Data Management [*A publication*].......................J Data Mgt
Journal of Data Management [*A publication*]...........................JDM
Journal des Debats [*A publication*] ....J Debats
Journal des Debats Politiques et Litteraires [*A publication*]..................JDPL
Journal of Defense Research [*A publication*]........................JDR
Journal Dentaire du Quebec [*A publication*]..................J Dent Que
Journal. Dental Association of South Africa [*A publication*]......................
J Dent Assoc S Afr
Journal. Dental Association of Thailand [*A publication*] .....J Dent Assoc Thai
Journal of Dental Education [*A publication*]........................J Dent Educ
Journal of Dental Engineering [*A publication*].....................................DE
Journal of Dental Engineering [*A publication*]...............................J Dent Eng
Journal. Dental Guidance Council on the Handicapped [*A publication*]........................J Dent Guid Counc Handicap
Journal of Dental Health (Tokyo) [*A publication*]...........J Dent Health (Tokyo)
Journal of Dental Medicine [*A publication*]........................J Dent Med
Journal of Dental Research [*A publication*].................................J Dent Res
Journal of Dental Technics [*A publication*]........................J Dent Tech
Journal of Dentistry [*A publication*]......................................J Dent
Journal of Dentistry for Children [*A publication*]...........................JDCHA
Journal of Dentistry for Children [*A publication*]...........................J Dent Chil
Journal of Dentistry for the Handicapped [*A publication*].....J Dent Handicap
Journal. Department of Agriculture and Fisheries (Dublin) [*A publication*]...........................J Dept Agr Fish (Dublin)
Journal. Department of Agriculture and Fisheries (Republic of Ireland) [*A publication*]......................J Dep Agric Fish (Irel)
Journal. Department of Agriculture (Puerto Rico) [*A publication*]......................
J Dept Ag (Puerto Rico)
Journal. Department of Agriculture (Republic of Ireland) [*A publication*]......................J Dep Agric (Repub Irel)
Journal. Department of Agriculture (South Africa) [*A publication*]......................J Dept Ag (S Africa)
Journal. Department of Agriculture (South Australia) [*A publication*]......................J Dep Agric (S Aust)
Journal. Department of Agriculture (South Australia) [*A publication*]......................J Dept Agr (S Aust)
Journal. Department of Agriculture (South Australia) [*A publication*]......................J Dept Ag (S Australia)
Journal. Department of Agriculture (Victoria) [*A publication*]......................
J Dept Agr (Victoria)
Journal. Department of Agriculture (Victoria) [*A publication*]......................
J Dept Ag (Victoria)
Journal. Department of Agriculture (Western Australia) [*A publication*]...................... J Dep Agric (W Aust)

Journal. Department of Agriculture (Western Australia) [*A publication*] ... J Dep Agric (West Aust)
Journal. Department of Agriculture (Western Australia) [*A publication*] ... J Dept Agr (W Aust)
Journal of Dermatologic Surgery and Oncology [*A publication*] ... J Dermatol Surg Oncol
Journal of Dermatology (Tokyo) [*A publication*] ... J Dermatol (Tokyo)
Journal of Design Automation and Fault-Tolerant Computing [*A publication*] ... J Des Autom Fault Tolerant Comput
Journal of Design Automation and Fault-Tolerant Computing [*A publication*] ... J Design Automat Fault-Tolerant Comput
Journal of Developing Areas [*A publication*] ... J Dev Areas
Journal of Developing Areas [*A publication*] ... J Devel Areas
Journal of Developing Areas [*A publication*] ... J Develop Areas
Journal of Development Economics [*A publication*] ... J Devel Econ
Journal of Development Planning [*A publication*] ... J Develop Plan
Journal of Development Studies [*A publication*] ... J Develop Stud
Journal of Development Studies [*A publication*] ... J Devel Stud
Journal of Development Studies [*A publication*] ... J Dev Stud
Journal of Development Studies [*A publication*] ... JDS
Journal of Developmental Areas [*A publication*] ... Jour Devel Areas
Journal of Developmental and Behavioral Pediatrics [*A publication*] ... JDBP
Journal of Developmental Physiology [*A publication*] ... J Dev Physiol
Journal of Developmental Reading [*A publication*] ... J Develop Read
Journal. Devon Trust for Nature Conservation [*A publication*] ... J Devon Trust Nat Conserv
Journal. Diabetic Association of India [*A publication*] ... J Diabetic Assoc India
Journal of Dialysis [*A publication*] ... J Dial
Journal. Dietetic Association (Victoria) [*A publication*] ... J Diet Assoc (Victoria)
Journal of Dietetics and Home Economics [*South Africa*] [*A publication*] ... J Diet Home Econ
Journal of Differential Equations [*A publication*] ... J Diff Equa
Journal of Differential Equations [*A publication*] ... J Differ Equations
Journal of Differential Geometry [*A publication*] ... J Differential Geometry
Journal of Dispersion Science and Technology [*A publication*] ... J Dispersion Sci Technol
Journal. District of Columbia Dental Society [*A publication*] ... J DC Dent Soc
[*The*] **Journal of Diverse Unsung Miracle Plants for Healthy Evolution among People** [*A publication*] ... DUMP HEAP
Journal of Documentation [*A publication*] ... JD
Journal of Documentation [*A publication*] ... J Doc
Journal of Documentation [*A publication*] ... J Docum
Journal du Droit International [*A publication*] ... J Dr Int
Journal of Drug Education [*A publication*] ... J Drug Educ
Journal of Drug Issues [*A publication*] ... J Drug Iss
Journal of Drug Issues [*A publication*] ... J Drug Issues
Journal of Drug Research (Cairo) [*A publication*] ... J Drug Res (Cairo)
Journal. Durham School of Agriculture [*A publication*] ... J Durham Sch Agr
Journal of Dynamic Systems, Measurement, and Control [*A publication*] ... J Dyn Syst Meas Control
Journal of Earth Sciences [*A publication*] ... J Earth Sci
Journal of Earth Sciences. Nagoya University [*A publication*] ... J Earth Sci Nagoya Univ
Journal of the Earth and Space Physics (Tehran) [*A publication*] ... J Earth Space Phys (Tehran)
Journal. East Africa Natural History Society and National Museum [*A publication*] ... J East Afr Nat Hist Soc Natl Mus
Journal. East African Swahili Committee [*A publication*] ... JEAfrSC
Journal of East Asiatic Studies [*A publication*] ... JEAS
Journal of East and West Studies [*A publication*] ... J East West Stud
Journal of Eastern African Research and Development [*A publication*] ... J East Afr Res Develop
Journal of Ecclesiastical History [*A publication*] ... J Eccl H
Journal of Ecclesiastical History [*A publication*] ... JEH
Journal of Ecclesiastical History [*A publication*] ... Jour Eccl Hist
Journal of Ecology [*A publication*] ... J Ecol
Journal of Ecology [*A publication*] ... Jour Ecology
Journal of Econometrics [*A publication*] ... J Econom
Journal of Econometrics [*A publication*] ... J Economet
Journal of Econometrics [*A publication*] ... J Econometrics
Journal of Economic Abstracts [*A publication*] ... J Econ Abstr
Journal of Economic Behavior [*A publication*] ... JEB
Journal of Economic and Business History [*A publication*] ... JEBH
Journal of Economic and Business History [*A publication*] ... Jour Econ and Bus Hist
Journal of Economic Education [*A publication*] ... J Econ Ed
Journal of Economic Entomology [*A publication*] ... J Econ Ent
Journal of Economic Entomology [*A publication*] ... J Econ Entom
Journal of Economic Entomology [*A publication*] ... J Econ Entomol
Journal of Economic History [*A publication*] ... J Econ H
Journal of Economic History [*A publication*] ... J Econ Hist
Journal of Economic History [*A publication*] ... JEH
Journal of Economic History [*A publication*] ... Jnl Econ Hist
Journal of Economic History [*A publication*] ... Jour Econ Hist
Journal of Economic History (Supplement) [*A publication*] ... JEH/S
Journal of Economic Issues [*A publication*] ... J Econ Iss
Journal of Economic Issues [*A publication*] ... JEI
Journal of Economic Literature [*A publication*] ... JEconLit
Journal of Economic Literature [*A publication*] ... J Econ Liter
Journal of Economic Literature [*A publication*] ... JEL
Journal of the Economic and Social History of the Orient [*A publication*] ... J Econ Soc Hist Or
Journal of the Economic and Social History of the Orient [*A publication*] ... J Econ Soc Hist Orient
Journal of the Economic and Social History of the Orient [*A publication*] ... JESHO
Journal of Economic Studies [*A publication*] ... JES
Journal of Economic Theory [*A publication*] ... J Econ Theo
Journal of Economics and Business [*A publication*] ... J Econ Bus
Journal of Economics Issues [*A publication*] ... J Econ Issues
Journal de Economistes [*A publication*] ... J Econ
Journal de Economistes [*A publication*] ... J Economistes
Journal of Ecumenical Studies [*A publication*] ... J Ec St
Journal of Ecumenical Studies [*A publication*] ... J Ecumen Stud
Journal of Ecumenical Studies [*A publication*] ... J Ecum Stud
Journal of Ecumenical Studies [*A publication*] ... JES
Journal of Education [*A publication*] ... JE
Journal of Education [*A publication*] ... J Ed
Journal of Education [*A publication*] ... J Educ
Journal of Education (Boston University School of Education) [*A publication*] ... JEB
Journal. Education Department. Niigata University [*A publication*] ... J Educ Dept Niigata Univ
Journal of Education Finance [*A publication*] ... J Educ Fin
Journal of Education for Librarianship [*A publication*] ... J Educ Libr
Journal of Education for Librarianship [*A publication*] ... J Educ Librarianship
Journal of Education (London) [*A publication*] ... J Ed (London)
Journal of Education (London) [*A publication*] ... J Educ (Lond)
Journal of Education and Psychology [*A publication*] ... J Educ Psych
Journal of Education for Social Work [*A publication*] ... J Educ Soc
Journal of Education for Social Work [*A publication*] ... J Educ Soc Work
Journal of Educational Administration [*A publication*] ... J Educ Adm
Journal of Educational Administration and History [*A publication*] ... J Ednl Admin and History
Journal of Educational Data Processing [*A publication*] ... J Ed Data Process
Journal of Educational Data Processing [*A publication*] ... J Educ Data Proc
Journal of Educational Data Processing [*A publication*] ... J Educ D P
Journal of Educational Measurement [*A publication*] ... J Ed M
Journal of Educational Measurement [*A publication*] ... J Educ M
Journal of Educational Method [*A publication*] ... J Educ Method
Journal of Educational Psychology [*A publication*] ... J Ed Psychol
Journal of Educational Psychology [*A publication*] ... J Educ Psyc
Journal of Educational Psychology [*A publication*] ... JEP
Journal of Educational Psychology [*A publication*] ... JEPs
Journal of Educational Research [*A publication*] ... J Ed Res
Journal of Educational Research [*A publication*] ... J Educ Res
Journal of Educational Research [*A publication*] ... JER
Journal of Educational Research [*A publication*] ... JOERA
Journal of Educational Sociology [*A publication*] ... J Ed Soc
Journal of Educational Sociology [*A publication*] ... J Educ Social
Journal of Educational Statisics [*A publication*] ... J Ed Stat
Journal of Educational Technology [*A publication*] ... J Ednl Technology
Journal of Educational Technology Systems [*A publication*] ... J Educ Technol Syst
Journal of Educational Technology Systems [*A publication*] ... J Educ Tech Syst
Journal of Educational Thought [*A publication*] ... J Educ Th
Journal of Egyptian Archaeology [*A publication*] ... JEA
Journal of Egyptian Archaeology [*A publication*] ... J Egypt Archaeol
Journal. Egyptian Medical Association [*A publication*] ... J Egypt Med Assoc
Journal of Egyptian Pharmacy [*A publication*] ... J Egypt Pharm
Journal. Egyptian Public Health Association [*A publication*] ... J Egypt Public Health Assoc
Journal. Egyptian Society of Parasitology [*A publication*] ... J Egypt Soc Parasitol
Journal. Eighteen Nineties Society [*A publication*] ... JENS
Journal of Elasticity [*A publication*] ... J Elast
Journal of Elastomers and Plastics [*A publication*] ... J Elastomers Plast
Journal of Elastoplastics [*Later, Journal of Elastomers and Plastics*] [*A publication*] ... J Elastoplast
Journal of Electrical and Electronics Engineering (Australia) [*A publication*] ... J Electr Electron Eng (Aust)
Journal of Electricity [*A publication*] ... J Elec
Journal of Electroanalytical Chemistry and Interfacial Electrochemistry [*A publication*] ... J Elec Chem
Journal of Electrocardiology [*A publication*] ... JECAB
Journal of Electrocardiology [*San Diego*] [*A publication*] ... J Elcardiol
Journal of Electrocardiology [*A publication*] ... J Electrocardiol
Journal of Electrocardiology (San Diego) [*A publication*] ... J Electrocardiol (San Diego)
Journal. Electrochemical Society [*A publication*] ... J Elchem So
Journal. Electrochemical Society [*A publication*] ... J Electrochem Soc
Journal. Electrochemical Society of India [*A publication*] ... J Electrochem Soc India
Journal. Electrochemical Society of Japan [*A publication*] ... J Electrochem Soc Japan
Journal of Electron Microscopy [*A publication*] ... J Elec Micr
Journal of Electron Microscopy [*A publication*] ... J Electron Microsc

Journal of Electron Microscopy [*A publication*]................... J Electron Micry
Journal of Electron Microscopy (Tokyo) [*A publication*]................
.... J Electron Microsc (Tokyo)
Journal of Electron Spectroscopy and Related Phenomena [*A publication*]..J Elec Spec
Journal of Electron Spectroscopy and Related Phenomena [*A publication*]........... J Electron Spectrosc Relat Phenom
Journal of Electron Spectroscopy and Related Phenomena [*A publication*]...................................J Electr Spectr
Journal of Electronic Engineering [*A publication*]............................J Elec E
Journal of Electronic Engineering [*A publication*]............ J Electron Eng
Journal of Electronic Materials [*A publication*].................J Elec Mat
Journal of Electronic Materials [*A publication*].................J Electron Mater
Journal of the Electronics Industry [*A publication*] .... Jrl Elec I
Journal of Electrostatics [*A publication*] .... J Electrostat
Journal. Elisha Mitchell Scientific Society [*A publication*] ....
.... J Elisha Mitchell Scient Soc
Journal. Elisha Mitchell Scientific Society [*A publication*] ....
.... J Elisha Mitchell Sci Soc
Journal of Embryology and Experimental Morphology [*A publication*].. J Emb Exp M
Journal of Embryology and Experimental Morphology [*A publication*]..........................J Embryol Exp Morphol
Journal of Emergency Nursing [*A publication*] .... J Emergency Nurs
Journal of Emergency Nursing [*A publication*] .... JEN
Journal of Emotional Education [*A publication*] .... JOEEA
Journal of Employment Counseling [*A publication*] .... J Empl Coun
Journal of Employment Counseling [*A publication*] ....J Employ Counsel
Journal of Endocrinological Investigation [*A publication*] ....
.... J Endocrinol Invest
Journal of Endocrinology [*A publication*]..............................J Endocr
Journal of Endocrinology [*A publication*]...................... J Endocrinol
Journal of Endocrinology [*A publication*]........................... JOENA
Journal of Endodontics [*A publication*] .... J Endod
Journal of Energy [*A publication*] .... J Energy
Journal of Energy and Development [*A publication*] .... J Energy Dev
Journal. Energy Division. ASCE [*American Society of Civil Engineers*] [*A publication*]..............J Energy Div ASCE
Journal of Energy Resources Technology [*A publication*] ....
.... J Energy Resources Technol
Journal of Engineering Education [*A publication*]...................................JEE
Journal of Engineering Education [*A publication*]........................ J Eng Ed
Journal of Engineering Education [*A publication*]...................... J Eng Educ
Journal of Engineering for Industry [*A publication*] .... J Eng Ind
Journal of Engineering for Industry. Transactions. ASME [*American Society of Mechanical Engineers*] [*A publication*]....................
.... J Eng Ind Tran ASME
Journal of Engineering Materials and Technology [*A publication*].................
.... J Eng Mater
Journal of Engineering Materials and Technology [*A publication*].................
.... J Eng Materials & Tech
Journal of Engineering Materials and Technology [*A publication*].................
.... J Eng Mater Technol
Journal of Engineering Materials and Technology [*A publication*].................
.... J Eng Mat & Tech
Journal of Engineering Mathematics [*A publication*] .... J Eng Math
Journal of Engineering Mathematics [*A publication*] .... JLEMA
Journal of Engineering Mechanics [*A publication*]........................J Eng Mech
Journal. Engineering Mechanics Division. Proceedings. American Society of Civil Engineers [*A publication*]....................
.... J Eng Mech Div Am Soc Civ Eng
Journal of Engineering Physics [*A publication*]..........................J Eng Phys
Journal of Engineering Physics [*A publication*] .... J Engrg Phys
Journal of Engineering for Power [*A publication*] .... J Eng Power
Journal of Engineering for Power. Transactions. ASME [*American Society of Mechanical Engineers*] [*A publication*]....................
.... J Eng Power Trans ASME
Journal of Engineering Psychology [*A publication*]...................J Eng Psychol
Journal of Engineering Sciences [*A publication*]...................J Eng Sci
Journal of Engineering Sciences (Saudi Arabia) [*A publication*] ....
.... J Eng Sci (Saudi Arabia)
Journal of English [*A publication*]..J En
Journal. English Folk Dance and Song Society [*A publication*] .... JEFDS
Journal. English Folk Dance and Song Society [*A publication*] .... JEFDSS
Journal. English Folk Dance and Song Society [*A publication*] .... JEFS
Journal of English and Germanic Philology [*A publication*]................... JEGP
Journal of English and Germanic Philology [*A publication*] .... JEG Ph
Journal of English and Germanic Philology [*A publication*]............JEG Phil
Journal of English and Germanic Philology [*A publication*]................
.... J Eng and Germ Philol
Journal of English and Germanic Philology [*A publication*]................
.... J Engl & Germ Philol
Journal of English and Germanic Philology [*A publication*]................
.... Jnl Engl Ger Philol
Journal of English Linguistics [*A publication*] .... JEL
Journal of English Linguistics [*A publication*] .... J Eng L
Journal of English Literary History [*A publication*] ....ELH
Journal of Enterostomal Therapy [*A publication*]...............J Enterostom Ther
Journal. Entomological Society of Australia (New South Wales) [*A publication*]..................J Entomol Soc Aust (NSW)

Journal. Entomological Society of British Columbia [*A publication*]..
.... J Entomol Soc BC
Journal. Entomological Society of British Columbia [*A publication*]..
.... J Ent Soc BC
Journal. Entomological Society of Southern Africa [*A publication*]..
.... J Entomol Soc S Afr
Journal. Entomological Society of Southern Africa [*A publication*]..
.... J Entomol Soc South Afr
Journal of Entomology. Series A. General Entomology [*A publication*]..
.... J Entomol A
Journal of Entomology. Series A. General Entomology [*A publication*]...................... J Entomol Ser A Gen Entomol
Journal of Entomology. Series A. Physiology and Behaviour [*A publication*]...................... J Entomol Ser A Physiol Behav
Journal of Entomology. Series B. Taxonomy [*A publication*].......J Entomol B
Journal of Entomology. Series B. Taxonomy and Systematics [*A publication*]...................J Entomol Ser B Taxon Syst
Journal of Environmental Economics and Management [*A publication*]...................... J Environ Econ Manage
Journal of Environmental Education [*A publication*].....................J Env Educ
Journal of Environmental Education [*A publication*].............. J Environ Educ
Journal. Environmental Engineering Division. American Society of Civil Engineers [*A publication*] .... J Envir Eng
Journal. Environmental Engineering Division. American Society of Civil Engineers [*A publication*] .... J Environ Eng Div Am Soc Civ Eng
Journal. Environmental Engineering Division. Proceedings. American Society of Civil Engineers [*A publication*]...................JEED
Journal of Environmental Health [*A publication*]...................J Environ Health
Journal of Environmental Management [*A publication*].............. J Envir Mgm
Journal of Environmental Management [*A publication*]..... J Environ Manage
Journal of Environmental Pathology and Toxicology [*A publication*]...................... J Environ Pathol Toxicol
Journal of Environmental Quality [*A publication*]......................J Environ Qual
Journal of Environmental Quality [*A publication*]...................... J Envir Q
Journal of Environmental Quality [*A publication*]...................... J Envir Quality
Journal of Environmental Science and Health. Part A. Environmental Science and Engineering [*A publication*] ....
.... J Environ Sci Health Part A
Journal of Environmental Science and Health. Part A. Environmental Science and Engineering [*A publication*] ....
.... J Environ Sci Health Part A Environ Sci Eng
Journal of Environmental Science and Health. Part B. Pesticides, Food Contaminants, and Agricultural Wastes [*A publication*]...................... J Environ Sci Health B
Journal of Environmental Science and Health. Part B. Pesticides, Food Contaminants, and Agricultural Wastes [*A publication*]........... J Environ Sci Health Part B
Journal of Environmental Science and Health. Part C. Environmental Health Sciences [*A publication*] ....
.... J Environ Sci Health (C)
Journal of Environmental Sciences [*A publication*] .... J Environ Sci
Journal of Environmental Sciences [*A publication*] ....J Envir Sci
Journal of Environmental Systems [*A publication*] .... J Environ Syst
Journal of Environmental Systems [*A publication*] ....J Environ Systems
Journal of Epidemiology and Community Health [*A publication*]....................
.... J Epidemiol Community Health
Journal of Equine Medicine and Surgery [*A publication*]....................
.... J Equine Med Surg
Journal of Ethiopian Studies [*A publication*] .... J Ethiop Stud
Journal of Ethiopian Studies [*A publication*] .... JEthS
Journal of Ethnic Studies [*A publication*]................................. JETCA
Journal of Ethnic Studies [*A publication*] .... J Ethnic Stud
Journal of Ethnic Studies [*A publication*] .... J Eth S
Journal of Ethnopharmacology [*A publication*] .... J Ethnopharmacol
Journal of European Studies [*A publication*] .... JES
Journal of European Studies [*A publication*] ....J Eur Stud
Journal of European Training [*A publication*] .... J Europ Training
Journal Europeen de Pathologie Forestiere [*A publication*] ....
.... J Eur Pathol For
Journal Europeen de Toxicologie [*A publication*].................J Eur Toxicol
Journal Europeen de Toxicologie. Supplement [*A publication*] ....
.... J Eur Toxicol Suppl
Journal. Evangelical Theological Society [*A publication*] ....ETS
Journal. Evangelical Theological Society [*A publication*] ....JETS
Journal. Evangelical Theological Society [*A publication*] ....J Evang Th S
Journal of Exceptional Children [*A publication*] ....J Excep Child
Journal of Existentialism [*A publication*]....................................JETXA
Journal of the Experimental Analysis of Behavior [*A publication*]...........JEAB
Journal of the Experimental Analysis of Behavior [*A publication*]....................
.... J Ex An Beh
Journal of the Experimental Analysis of Behavior [*A publication*]....................
.... J Exp Anal Behav
Journal of the Experimental Analysis of Behavior [*A publication*]....................
.... J Exper Anal Behav
Journal of Experimental Animal Science [*A publication*]........ J Exp Anim Sci
Journal of Experimental Biology [*A publication*] .... J Exp Biol
Journal of Experimental Biology [*A publication*] .... J Exper Biol
Journal of Experimental Botany [*A publication*] .... J Exp Bot
Journal of Experimental Botany [*A publication*]............................J Exper Bot
Journal of Experimental Child Psychology [*A publication*].................JECPA
Journal of Experimental Child Psychology [*A publication*].....J Exp Child Psy

Journal of Experimental Child Psychology [*A publication*]....J Exp Child Psychol
Journal of Experimental Child Psychology [*A publication*]....J Exp C Psy
Journal of Experimental Child Psychology [*A publication*]....J Exper Child Psychol
Journal of Experimental Education [*A publication*]....JEE
Journal of Experimental Education [*A publication*]....J Exp Ed
Journal of Experimental Education [*A publication*]....J Exper Educ
Journal of Experimental Marine Biology and Ecology [*A publication*]....J Exper Marine Biol & Ecol
Journal of Experimental Marine Biology and Ecology [*A publication*]....J Exp Mar B
Journal of Experimental Marine Biology and Ecology [*A publication*]....J Exp Mar Biol Ecol
Journal of Experimental Medical Sciences [*A publication*]....J Exp Med Sci
Journal of Experimental Medicine [*A publication*]....J Exper Med
Journal of Experimental Medicine [*A publication*]....J Exp Med
Journal of Experimental Psychology [*A publication*]....JEPSA
Journal of Experimental Psychology [*A publication*]....JExP
Journal of Experimental Psychology [*A publication*]....J Exp Psych
Journal of Experimental Psychology [*A publication*]....J Exp Psychol
Journal of Experimental Psychology: Animal Behavior Processes [*A publication*]....J Exp Psy A
Journal of Experimental Psychology: Animal Behavior Processes [*A publication*]....J Exp Psychol (Animal Behav Proc)
Journal of Experimental Psychology: Animal Behavior Processes [*A publication*]....JPAPD
Journal of Experimental Psychology: General [*A publication*]....J Exp Psychol Gen
Journal of Experimental Psychology: General [*A publication*]....J Exp Psy G
Journal of Experimental Psychology: Human Learning and Memory [*A publication*]....J Exper Psychol Human Learn Mem
Journal of Experimental Psychology: Human Learning and Memory [*A publication*]....J Ex P L
Journal of Experimental Psychology: Human Learning and Memory [*A publication*]....J Exp Psychol Hum Learn Mem
Journal of Experimental Psychology: Human Learning and Memory [*A publication*]....J Exp Psy H
Journal of Experimental Psychology: Human Perception and Performance [*A publication*]....J Exper Psychol Human Percept & Perf
Journal of Experimental Psychology: Human Perception and Performance [*A publication*]....J Ex P H P
Journal of Experimental Psychology: Human Perception and Performance [*A publication*]....J Exp Psychol Hum Percept Perform
Journal of Experimental Psychology: Human Perception and Performance [*A publication*]....J Exp Psychol Hum Perc Perf
Journal of Experimental Psychology: Human Perception and Performance [*A publication*]....J Exp Psy P
Journal of Experimental Psychology: Monograph [*A publication*]....J Exp Psychol Monogr
Journal of Experimental Research in Personality [*A publication*]....J Exp Res Pers
Journal of Experimental Social Psychology [*A publication*]....J Exper Social Psychol
Journal of Experimental Social Psychology [*A publication*]....J Exper Soc Psychol
Journal of Experimental Social Psychology [*A publication*]....J Exp Soc Psychol
Journal of Experimental Social Psychology [*A publication*]....J Exp S Psy
Journal of Experimental and Theoretical Physics [*A publication*]....JETP
Journal of Experimental Zoology [*A publication*]....J Exper Zool
Journal of Experimental Zoology [*A publication*]....J Exp Zool
Journal of Extension [*A publication*]....J Ext
Journal. Faculty of Agriculture. Hokkaido University [*A publication*]....J Fac Agric Hokkaido Univ
Journal. Faculty of Agriculture. Hokkaido University. Series Entomology [*A publication*]....J Fac Agric Hokkaido Univ Ser Entomol
Journal. Faculty of Agriculture. Iwate University [*A publication*]....J Fac Agric Iwate Univ
Journal. Faculty of Agriculture. Iwate University [*A publication*]....J Fac Agr Iwate Univ
Journal. Faculty of Agriculture. Kyushu University [*A publication*]....J Fac Agric Kyushu Univ
Journal. Faculty of Agriculture. Kyushu University [*A publication*]....J Fac Agr Kyushu Univ
Journal. Faculty of Agriculture. Shinshu University [*A publication*]....J Fac Agric Shinshu Univ
Journal. Faculty of Agriculture. Shinshu University [*A publication*]....J Fac Agr Shinshu Univ
Journal. Faculty of Agriculture. Tottori University [*A publication*]....J Fac Agric Tottori Univ
Journal. Faculty of Agriculture. Tottori University [*A publication*]....J Fac Agr Tottori Univ
Journal. Faculty of Arts. Royal University of Malta [*A publication*]....J Faculty Arts Roy Univ Malta
Journal. Faculty of Education. Tottori University. Natural Science [*A publication*]....J Fac Educ Tottori Univ Nat Sci
Journal. Faculty of Engineering. Chiba University [*A publication*]....J Fac Eng Chiba Univ
Journal. Faculty of Engineering. Shinshu University [*A publication*]....J Fac Eng Shinshu Univ
Journal. Faculty of Engineering. University of Tokyo [*A publication*]....J Fac Eng Univ Tokyo
Journal. Faculty of Engineering. University of Tokyo. Series A. Annual Report [*A publication*]....J Fac Eng Univ Tokyo Ser A
Journal. Faculty of Engineering. University of Tokyo. Series B [*A publication*]....J Fac Eng Univ Tokyo Ser B
Journal. Faculty of Fisheries and Animal Husbandry. Hiroshima University [*A publication*]....J Fac Fish Anim Husb Hiroshima Univ
Journal. Faculty of Fisheries. Prefectural University of Mie [*A publication*]....J Fac Fish Prefect Univ Mie
Journal. Faculty of Liberal Arts. Shinshu University. Part II. Natural Sciences [*A publication*]....J Fac Lib Arts Shinshu Univ Part II Nat Sci
Journal. Faculty of Marine Science and Technology. Tokai University [*A publication*]....J Fac Mar Sci Technol Tokai Univ
Journal. Faculty of Medicine (Baghdad) [*A publication*]....J Fac Med (Baghdad)
Journal. Faculty of Medicine. University of Ankara [*A publication*]....J Fac Med Univ Ankara
Journal. Faculty of Medicine. University of Ankara. Supplement [*A publication*]....J Fac Med Univ Ankara Suppl
Journal. Faculty of Oceanography. Tokai University [*A publication*]....J Fac Oceanogr Tokai Univ
Journal. Faculty of Pharmacy. Istanbul University [*A publication*]....J Fac Pharm Istanbul Univ
Journal. Faculty of Political Science and Economics. Tokai University [*A publication*]....J Fac Polit Sci Econ Tokai Univ
Journal. Faculty of Radiologists (London) [*A publication*]....J Fac Radiol (Lond)
Journal. Faculty of Science. Hokkaido University. Series 7. Geophysics [*A publication*]....J Fac Sci Hokkaido Univ Ser 7
Journal. Faculty of Science. Hokkaido University. Series IV. Geology and Mineralogy [*A publication*]....J Fac Sci Hokkaido Univ Ser IV Geol Mineral
Journal. Faculty of Science. Hokkaido University. Series V. Botany [*A publication*]....J Fac Sci Hokkaido Univ Ser V Bot
Journal. Faculty of Science. Hokkaido University. Series VI. Zoology [*A publication*]....J Fac Sci Hokkaido Univ Ser VI Zool
Journal. Faculty of Science. Imperial University of Tokyo. Section IV. Zoology [*A publication*]....J Fac Sci Imp Univ Tokyo Sect IV Zool
Journal. Faculty of Science. Niigata University. Series II. Biology, Geology, and Mineralogy [*A publication*]....J Fac Sci Niigata Univ Ser II Biol Geol Mineral
Journal. Faculty of Science. Shinshu University [*A publication*]....J Fac Sci Shinshu Univ
Journal. Faculty of Science. University of Tokyo. Section 1. Mathematics, Astronomy, Physics, Chemistry [*A publication*]....J Fac Tok 1
Journal. Faculty of Science. University of Tokyo. Section III. Botany [*A publication*]....J Fac Sci Univ Tokyo Sect III Bot
Journal. Faculty of Science. University of Tokyo. Section IV. Zoology [*A publication*]....J Fac Sci Univ Tokyo Sect IV Zool
Journal. Faculty of Science. University of Tokyo. Section V. Anthropology [*A publication*]....J Fac Sci Univ Tokyo Sect V Anthropol
Journal. Faculty of Textile Science and Technology. Shinshu University. Series A. Biology [*A publication*]....J Fac Text Sci Technol Shinshu Univ Ser A Biol
Journal. Faculty of Textile and Sericulture. Shinshu University. Series A. Biology [*A publication*]....J Fac Text Sericu Shinshu Univ Ser A Biol
Journal. Faculty of Veterinary Medicine. University of Ankara [*A publication*]....J Fac Vet Med Univ Ankara
Journal of Family Counseling [*A publication*]....J Fam Couns
Journal of Family Law [*A publication*]....J Family L
Journal of Family Law [*A publication*]....J Fam Law
Journal of Family Practice [*A publication*]....J Fam Pract
Journal of Family Welfare [*A publication*]....J Fam Wel
Journal of Family Welfare [*A publication*]....J Fam Welf
Journal of Farm Economics [*A publication*]....J Farm Econ
Journal of Farm Economics [*A publication*]....JFE
Journal of Farm History [*A publication*]....Jour Farm Hist
Journal. Farmers' Club [*A publication*]....J Farmers' Club
Journal. Federal Home Loan Bank Board [*A publication*]....JHLB
Journal of Fermentation Industries [*A publication*]....J Ferment Ind
Journal of Fermentation Technology [*A publication*]....J Ferment Technol
Journal of Fermentation Technology [*A publication*]....J Ferm Tech
Journal of Ferrocement [*A publication*]....J Ferrocem
Journal of Field Archaeology [*A publication*]....JFA
Journal of Field Archaeology [*A publication*]....J Field Arch
Journal of Finance [*A publication*]....JF
Journal of Finance [*A publication*]....J Fin
Journal of Finance [*A publication*]....J Finance
Journal of Financial and Quantitative Analysis [*A publication*]....J Financ Quant Anal
Journal of Financial and Quantitative Analysis [*A publication*]....J Fin Qu An
Journal of Financial and Quantitative Analysis [*A publication*]....JFQA
Journal of Fire and Flammability [*A publication*]....J Fire Flammability
Journal of Fire Retardant Chemistry [*A publication*]....J Fire Retardant Chem
Journal of Fish Biology [*A publication*]....J Fish Biol

Journal. Fisheries Research Board of Canada [*A publication*] ... J Fisheries Res Board Can
Journal. Fisheries Research Board of Canada [*A publication*] ... J Fish Res
Journal. Fisheries Research Board of Canada [*A publication*] ... J Fish Res Board Can
Journal. Florida Medical Association [*A publication*] ... J Fla Med Assoc
Journal. Florida Medical Association [*A publication*] ... JFMA
Journal of Flour and Animal Feed Milling [*A publication*] ... J Flour Anim Feed Milling
Journal of Fluency Disorders [*A publication*] ... J Fluency Dis
Journal of Fluid Mechanics [*A publication*] ... J Fluid Mec
Journal of Fluid Mechanics [*A publication*] ... J Fluid Mech
Journal of Fluids Engineering. Transactions. ASME [*American Society of Mechanical Engineers*] [*A publication*] ... J Fluid Eng Trans ASME
Journal of Fluids Engineering. Transactions. ASME [*American Society of Mechanical Engineers*] [*A publication*] ... J Fluids Eng
Journal of Fluorine Chemistry [*A publication*] ... J Fluorine
Journal of Fluorine Chemistry [*A publication*] ... J Fluorine Chem
Journal. Folk Song Society [*A publication*] ... JFSS
Journal. Folklore Institute [*A publication*] ... JFI
Journal. Folklore Institute [*A publication*] ... J Folkl Inst
Journal. Folklore Institute [*A publication*] ... Jour Folklore Inst
Journal. Folklore Society of Greater Washington [*A publication*] ... JFSGW
Journal of Food Biochemistry [*A publication*] ... J Food Biochem
Journal. Food Hygienic Society of Japan [*A publication*] ... J Food Hyg Soc Jap
Journal. Food Hygienic Society of Japan [*A publication*] ... J Food Hyg Soc Jpn
Journal of Food Process Engineering [*A publication*] ... J Food Process Eng
Journal of Food Processing and Preservation [*A publication*] ... J Food Process Preserv
Journal of Food Protection [*A publication*] ... J Food Prot
Journal of Food Protection [*A publication*] ... J Food Protect
Journal of Food Quality [*A publication*] ... J Food Qual
Journal of Food Resources Development [*A publication*] ... J Food Resour Dev
Journal of Food Science [*A publication*] ... J Food Sci
Journal of Food Science. Kyoto Women's University [*A publication*] ... J Food Sci Kyoto Women's Univ
Journal of Food Science and Technology [*A publication*] ... J Food Sci Technol
Journal of Food Science and Technology (Mysore) [*A publication*] ... J Food Sci Technol (Mysore)
Journal of Food Technology [*A publication*] ... J Food Technol
Journal of Foot Surgery [*A publication*] ... J Foot Surg
Journal of Foraminiferal Research [*A publication*] ... J Foraminiferal Res
Journal of Forensic Medicine [*A publication*] ... J Forensic Med
Journal of Forensic Medicine [*A publication*] ... J For Med
Journal. Forensic Science Society [*A publication*] ... J Forensic Sci Soc
Journal of Forensic Sciences [*A publication*] ... J Forensic Sci
Journal of Forensic Sciences [*A publication*] ... J For Sci
Journal Forestier Suisse [*A publication*] ... J For Suisse
Journal of Forestry [*A publication*] ... J For
Journal of Forestry [*A publication*] ... J Forest
Journal. Forestry Commission [*A publication*] ... J For Comm
Journal. Formosan Medical Association [*A publication*] ... J Formosan Med Assoc
Journal du Four Electrique [*A publication*] ... J Four Elec
Journal Francais de Biophysique et Medecine Nucleaire [*France*] [*A publication*] ... J Fr Biophys Med Nucl
Journal Francais de Medecine et Chirurgie Thoraciques [*A publication*] ... J Fr Med Chir Thorac
Journal Francais d'Ophtalmologie [*A publication*] ... J Fr Ophtalmol
Journal Francais d'Oto-Rhino-Laryngologie, Audiophonologie, et Chirurgie Maxillo-Faciale [*A publication*] ... JFOAB
Journal Francais d'Oto-Rhino-Laryngologie et Chirurgie [*A publication*] ... J Franc ORL
Journal Francais d'Oto-Rhino-Laryngologie et Chirurgie Maxillo-Faciale [*Later, Journal Francais d'Oto-Rhino-Laryngologie*] [*A publication*] ... J Fr Oto-Rhino-Laryngol
Journal Francais d'Otorhinolaryngologie [*A publication*] ... JFORL
Journal. Franklin Institute [*A publication*] ... JFI
Journal. Franklin Institute [*A publication*] ... J Frankl I
Journal. Franklin Institute [*A publication*] ... J Franklin Inst
Journal of Fuel and Heat Technology [*A publication*] ... J Fuel Heat Technol
Journal. Fuel Society of Japan [*Nenryo Kyokai-Shi*] [*A publication*] ... J Fuel Soc Jap
Journal of Functional Analysis [*A publication*] ... J Funct Ana
Journal of Fusion Energy [*A publication*] ... JFE
Journal of Fusion Energy [*A publication*] ... J Fusion Energy
Journal. Gakugei Tokushima University. Natural Science [*A publication*] ... J Gakugei Tokushima Univ Nat Sci
Journal. Ganganatha Jha Kendriya Sanskrit Vidyapeetha [*A publication*] ... J Gan Jha Kend Sans Vid
Journal. Ganganatha Jha Research Institute [*A publication*] ... JGJRI
Journal. Ganganatha Jha Research Institute [*A publication*] ... JGRI
Journal of Gas Chromatography [*A publication*] ... J Gas Chromatogr
Journal of Gemmology [*A publication*] ... J Gemmol
Journal of Gemmology and Proceedings. Gemmological Association of Great Britain [*A publication*] ... Jour Gemmology
Journal of General and Applied Microbiology [*A publication*] ... J Gen A Mic
Journal of General and Applied Microbiology [*A publication*] ... J Gen Appl Microbiol
Journal of General Chemistry [*A publication*] ... JGC
Journal of General Chemistry of the USSR [*A publication*] ... J Gen Chem USSR
Journal of General Education [*A publication*] ... JGE
Journal of General Education [*A publication*] ... J Gen Ed
Journal of General Education [*A publication*] ... J Gen Educ
Journal of General Education [*A publication*] ... Jnl Gen Ed
Journal of General Management [*A publication*] ... J Gen Manag
Journal General de Medecine, de Chirurgie, et de Pharmacie [*A publication*] ... J Gen Med Chir et Pharm
Journal of General Microbiology [*A publication*] ... J Gen Micro
Journal of General Physiology [*A publication*] ... J Gen Physiol
Journal of General Physiology [*A publication*] ... J Gen Physl
Journal of General Psychology [*A publication*] ... J Gen Psych
Journal of General Psychology [*A publication*] ... J Gen Psychol
Journal of General Psychology [*A publication*] ... JGP
Journal of General Psychology [*A publication*] ... JGPs
Journal of General Psychology [*A publication*] ... JGPSA
Journal of General Virology [*A publication*] ... J Gen Virol
Journal of Genetic Psychology [*A publication*] ... J Genet Psy
Journal of Genetic Psychology [*A publication*] ... J Genet Psychol
Journal of Genetic Psychology [*A publication*] ... J Gen Ps
Journal of Genetic Psychology [*A publication*] ... JGEPs
Journal of Genetic Psychology [*A publication*] ... JGPYA
Journal of Genetics [*A publication*] ... J Genet
Journal de Genetique Humaine [*A publication*] ... J Genet Hum
Journal de Geneve [*A publication*] ... JG
Journal of Geobotany [*A publication*] ... J Geobot
Journal of Geochemical Exploration [*A publication*] ... J Geochem E
Journal of Geochemical Exploration [*A publication*] ... J Geochem Explor
Journal Geographica [*A publication*] ... J Geog
Journal of Geography [*A publication*] ... JG
Journal of Geography [*A publication*] ... J Geog
Journal of Geological Education [*A publication*] ... J Geol Educ
Journal of Geological Education [*A publication*] ... Jour Geol Education
Journal. Geological Society of Australia [*A publication*] ... J Geol Soc Aust
Journal. Geological Society of India [*A publication*] ... J Geol S In
Journal. Geological Society of India [*A publication*] ... J Geol Soc India
Journal. Geological Society of Jamaica [*A publication*] ... J Geol Soc Jam
Journal. Geological Society of Japan [*A publication*] ... J Geol Soc Jpn
Journal. Geological Society (London) [*A publication*] ... J Geol Soc (Lond)
Journal of Geology [*A publication*] ... J Geo
Journal of Geology [*A publication*] ... J Geol
Journal of Geomagnetism and Geoelectricity [*A publication*] ... J Geomagn G
Journal of Geomagnetism and Geoelectricity [*A publication*] ... J Geomagn & Geoelectr
Journal of Geometry [*A publication*] ... J Geometry
Journal of Geophysical Research [*A publication*] ... J Geoph Res
Journal of Geophysical Research [*A publication*] ... J Geophys Res
Journal of Geophysical Research [*A publication*] ... JGR
Journal of Geophysical Research. Oceans and Atmosphere [*A publication*] ... J Geo R-O A
Journal of Geophysical Research. Space Physics [*A publication*] ... J Geo R-S P
Journal of Geophysics [*A publication*] ... J Geophys
Journal. Georgia Dental Association [*A publication*] ... J GA Dent Assoc
Journal. Georgia Entomological Society [*A publication*] ... J GA Entomol Soc
Journal of Geosciences. Osaka City University [*A publication*] ... J Geosci Osaka City Univ
Journal. Geotechnical Engineering Division. Proceedings. American Society of Civil Engineers [*A publication*] ... J Geotech Eng Div Am Soc Civ Eng
Journal of Geriatric Psychiatry [*A publication*] ... J Geriat Ps
Journal of Geriatric Psychiatry [*A publication*] ... J Geriatr Psychiatry
Journal of Gerontological Nursing [*A publication*] ... J Gerontol Nurs
Journal of Gerontology [*A publication*] ... J Geront
Journal of Gerontology [*A publication*] ... J Gerontol
Journal of Gerontology [*A publication*] ... JOGEA
Journal of Gesamte Oberflaechentechnik [*A publication*] ... J Gesamte Oberflaechentech
Journal of Glaciology [*A publication*] ... J Glaciol
Journal of Glaciology [*A publication*] ... Jour Glaciology
Journal of Glass Studies [*A publication*] ... J Glass Stud
Journal of Glass Studies [*A publication*] ... JGS
Journal. Graduate Music Students. Ohio State University [*A publication*] ... J GMS OSU
Journal. Graduate Research Center. Southern Methodist University [*A publication*] ... J Grad Res Cent South Methodist Univ
Journal of Graph Theory [*A publication*] ... J Graph Theory
Journal of Great Lakes Research [*A publication*] ... J Great Lakes Res
Journal. Greater India Society [*A publication*] ... Journal Greater India Soc
Journal of Growth [*A publication*] ... J Growth
Journal of Guidance and Control [*A publication*] ... J Guidance & Control
Journal. Gujarat Research Society [*India*] [*A publication*] ... JGRS
Journal. Gujarat Research Society [*India*] [*A publication*] ... J Gujarat Res Soc
Journal. Gujarat Research Society [*India*] [*A publication*] ... J Guj Res Soc

Journal. Gujarat Research Society [*India*] [*A publication*]....... Journal Gujarat Research Soc
Journal. Gyeongsang National University. Natural Sciences [*Republic of Korea*] [*A publication*] .... J Gyeongsang Natl Univ Nat Sci
Journal de Gynecologie, Obstetrique, et Biologie de la Reproduction [*Paris*] [*A publication*] .... JGOBA
Journal de Gynecologie, Obstetrique, et Biologie de la Reproduction [*Paris*] [*A publication*] ....J Gynecol Obstet Biol Reprod
Journal de Gynecologie, Obstetrique, et Biologie de la Reproduction (Paris) [*A publication*]....... J Gynecol Obstet Biol Reprod (Paris)
Journal. Gypsy Lore Society [*A publication*] .... JGLS
Journal. Gypsy Lore Society [*A publication*] ....JGyLS
Journal of Hand Surgery [*A publication*] .... J Hand Surg
Journal of Haryana Studies [*A publication*].......J Haryana Stud
Journal. Hattori Botanical Laboratory [*A publication*] ....J Hattori Bot Lab
Journal. Hawaii Dental Association [*A publication*].........J Hawaii Dent Assoc
Journal of Hazardous Materials [*A publication*].......J Hazard Mater
Journal of Hazardous Materials [*A publication*]....... J Hazard Materials
Journal of Health Care Marketing [*A publication*].......... J Health Care Market
Journal of Health and Human Behavior [*A publication*]....... J Health Hum Behav
Journal. Health and Human Resources Administration [*A publication*].......J Health Hum Resour Adm
Journal of Health, Physical Education, Recreation [*A publication*]....... J Health Phys Ed Rec
Journal of Health, Physical Education, Recreation [*A publication*]....... JOHPER
Journal of Health Physics and Radiation Protection [*A publication*]....... J Health Phys Radiat Prot
Journal of Health Politics, Policy, and Law [*A publication*] .... J Health Polit Policy Law
Journal of Health and Social Behavior [*A publication*] .... J Health So
Journal of Health and Social Behavior [*A publication*] .... J Health & Soc Behav
Journal of Health and Social Behavior [*A publication*]..... J Health Soc Behav
Journal of Health and Social Behavior [*A publication*] .... J Health & Social Behavior
Journal of Heat Transfer [*A publication*].......J Heat Transfer
Journal of Heat Transfer. Transactions. ASME [*American Society of Mechanical Engineers*] [*A publication*].......J Heat Tran
Journal of Heat Transfer. Transactions. ASME [*American Society of Mechanical Engineers*] [*A publication*]..... J Heat Transfer Trans ASME
Journal Hebdomadaire de Medecine [*A publication*] ....J Hebd Med
Journal of the Hellenic Diaspora [*A publication*].......JHD
Journal of Hellenic Studies [*A publication*].......JHEL
Journal of Hellenic Studies [*A publication*]....... J Hellenic Stud
Journal of Hellenic Studies [*A publication*]....... J Hellen Stud
Journal of Hellenic Studies [*A publication*]....... J Hell Stud
Journal of Hellenic Studies [*A publication*].......J Hel Stud
Journal of Hellenic Studies [*A publication*].......JHS
Journal of Hellenic Studies [*A publication*].......JoHS
Journal of Hellenic Studies. Archaeological Reports [*A publication*]....... JHS-AR
Journal of Helminthology [*A publication*]....... J Helminth
Journal of Helminthology [*A publication*]....... J Helminthol
Journal of Heredity [*A publication*] ....J Hered
Journal of Heredity [*A publication*] .... J Heredity
Journal of Heredity [*A publication*] ....JOHEA
Journal. Herpetological Association of Africa [*A publication*] .... J Herpetol Assoc Afr
Journal of Herpetology [*A publication*].......J Herpetol
Journal of Heterocyclic Chemistry [*A publication*]....... J Hetero Ch
Journal of Heterocyclic Chemistry [*A publication*]........... J Heterocycl Chem
Journal of Higher Education [*A publication*] .... J Hi E
Journal of Higher Education [*A publication*] .... J High Educ
Journal of Higher Education [*A publication*] ....J Higher Educ
Journal of Higher Education [*A publication*] ....Jnl Higher Ed
Journal. Highway Division. American Society of Civil Engineers [*A publication*]....... J Highw Div Am Soc Civ Eng
Journal fuer Hirnforschung [*A publication*].......J Hirnforsch
Journal. Hiroshima University. Dental Society [*A publication*] .... J Hiroshima Univ Dent Soc
Journal of Hispanic Philology [*A publication*] ....JHP
Journal of Histochemistry and Cytochemistry [*A publication*]...... J Hist Cyto
Journal of Histochemistry and Cytochemistry [*A publication*] .... J Histochem Cytochem
Journal of Historical Geography [*A publication*].......J Hist G
Journal of Historical Geography [*A publication*].......J Hist Geog
Journal of Historical Geography [*A publication*]....... J Hist Geogr
Journal of Historical Research [*A publication*] .... J Hist Res
Journal. Historical Society of the Church in Wales [*A publication*] .... JHSCW
Journal. Historical Society of Nigeria [*A publication*]..........J Hist Soc Nigeria
Journal of Historical Studies [*A publication*].......J Hist Stud
Journal of Historical Studies [*A publication*].......JHS
Journal of Historical Studies [*A publication*].......JHStud
Journal of History [*A publication*] .... JH
Journal for the History of Astronomy [*A publication*] ....J Hist Astron
Journal of the History of the Behavioral Sciences [*A publication*].......JHBSA
Journal of the History of the Behavioral Sciences [*A publication*]....... J Hist Beh
Journal of the History of the Behavioral Sciences [*A publication*]....... J Hist Beh Sci
Journal of the History of the Behavioral Sciences [*A publication*]....... Journ Hist Behavioral Sci
Journal of the History of Biology [*A publication*]....... J Hist Biol
Journal of the History of Ideas [*A publication*] .... JHI
Journal of the History of Ideas [*A publication*].......J Hist Ideas
Journal of the History of Ideas [*A publication*].......Jnl Hist Ideas
Journal of the History of Ideas [*A publication*]....... Jour Hist Ideas
Journal of the History of Medicine [*A publication*].......JHM
Journal of the History of Medicine [*A publication*].......Jour Hist Med
Journal of the History of Medicine and Allied Sciences [*A publication*] .... J Hist Med Allied Sci
Journal of the History of Philosophy [*A publication*] .... J Hist Phil
Journal of the History of Philosophy [*A publication*] ....J Hist Philos
Journal of the History of Philosophy [*A publication*] ....JHP
Journal of the History of Philosophy [*A publication*] ....JHPh
Journal of the History of Philosophy [*A publication*] .... Jour Hist Phil
Journal. Hokkaido Dental Association [*A publication*] .... J Hokkaido Dent Assoc
Journal. Hokkaido Forest Products Research Institute [*A publication*]....... J Hokkaido Forest Prod Res Inst
Journal. Hokkaido University of Education [*A publication*]....... J Hokkaido Univ Educ
Journal. Hokkaido University of Education. Section II-B [*A publication*] .... J Hokkaido Univ Educ Sect II-B
Journal of Home Economics [*A publication*] .... J Ho E
Journal of Home Economics [*A publication*] .... J Home Econ
Journal of Home Economics [*A publication*] .... Jnl Home Econ
Journal of Homosexuality [*A publication*] .... J Homosex
Journal of Homosexuality [*A publication*] ....J Homosexuality
Journal. Hong Kong Branch. Royal Asiatic Society [*A publication*]....... J HK Br Roy Asiat Soc
Journal. Hong Kong Branch. Royal Asiatic Society [*A publication*]....... J Hong Kong Branch Roy Asiatic Soc
Journal. Hongkong University. Geographical, Geological, and Archaeological Society [*A publication*]....... JGGAS
Journal of Horticultural Science [*A publication*].......J Hortic Sci
Journal of Horticultural Science [*A publication*].......J Hort Sci
Journal of Hospital Dental Practice [*A publication*]........... J Hosp Dent Pract
Journal of Housing [*A publication*]....... J Housing
Journal of Human Ergology [*A publication*].......J Hum Ergol
Journal of Human Ergology (Tokyo) [*A publication*] ....J Hum Ergol (Tokyo)
Journal of Human Evolution [*A publication*]....... J Hum Evol
Journal of Human Nutrition [*A publication*].......J Hum Nutr
Journal of Human Relations [*A publication*].......J of Human Rela
Journal of Human Relations [*A publication*].......J Hum Relat
Journal of Human Relations [*A publication*].......Jour Human Rel
Journal of Human Resources [*A publication*].......JHR
Journal of Human Resources [*A publication*]....... J Human Resources
Journal of Human Resources [*A publication*]....... J Hum Resources
Journal of Human Stress [*A publication*].......J Human Stress
Journal of Human Stress [*A publication*].......J Hum Stress
Journal of Humanistic Psychology [*A publication*]........ J Humanistic Psychol
Journal of Humanistic Psychology [*A publication*]....... J Hum Psy
Journal of Hydraulic Engineering (Peking) [*A publication*]....... J Hydraul Eng (Peking)
Journal of Hydraulic Research [*A publication*]....... J Hydraul Res
Journal. Hydraulics Division. American Society of Civil Engineers [*A publication*]....... J Hydr-ASCE
Journal. Hydraulics Division. American Society of Civil Engineers [*A publication*]....... J Hydraul Div Am Soc Civ Eng
Journal. Hydraulics Division. Proceedings. American Society of Civil Engineers [*A publication*] .... JYCE-A
Journal of Hydrological Sciences [*Poland*] [*A publication*].......... J Hydrol Sci
Journal of Hydrology [*New Zealand*] [*A publication*].......J Hydrol
Journal of Hydrology (New Zealand) [*A publication*]....... J Hydrol (NZ)
Journal of Hydronautics [*A publication*].......J Hydronaut
Journal of Hygiene [*A publication*]....... J Hyg
Journal of Hygiene (Cambridge) [*A publication*] ....J Hyg (Camb)
Journal d'Hygiene Clintologie (Paris) [*A publication*] .... J Hyg (Paris)
Journal of Hygiene, Epidemiology, Microbiology, and Immunology [*A publication*]....... J Hyg Ep Mi
Journal of Hygiene (London) [*A publication*] .... J Hyg (Lond)
Journal of Hygienic Chemistry [*A publication*] .... J Hyg Chem
Journal. IARI [*Indian Agricultural Research Institute*] **Post-Graduate School** [*A publication*].......J IARI Post-Grad Sch
Journal of Ichthyology (English Translation of Voprosy Ikhtiologii) [*A publication*]....... J Ichthyol (Engl Trans Vopr Ikhtiol)
Journal. Illinois State Historical Society [*A publication*] ....JIHS
Journal. Illinois State Historical Society [*A publication*].......J Ill Hist Soc
Journal. Illinois State Historical Society [*A publication*].......JILLHS
Journal. Illinois State Historical Society [*A publication*]....... JISHS
Journal. Illuminating Engineering Institute of Japan [*A publication*]....... J Illum Eng Inst Jap
Journal. Illuminating Engineering Society [*A publication*]......J Illum Eng Soc
Journal of Immunoassay [*A publication*] .... J Immunoassay
Journal of Immunogenetics [*A publication*] ....J Immunogen
Journal of Immunogenetics [*A publication*] .... J Immunogenet
Journal of Immunological Methods [*A publication*].......J Immunol M
Journal of Immunological Methods [*A publication*].........J Immunol Methods

Journal of Immunology [*A publication*] .... J Immunol
Journal of Immunopharmacology [*A publication*] .... J Immunopharmacol
Journal. Imperial Agricultural Experiment Station (Tokyo) [*A publication*] .... J Imp Agr Exp Sta (Tokyo)
Journal of Imperial and Commonwealth History [*A publication*] .... J Imp Commonw Hist
Journal Index .... JRNDEX
Journal. Indian Academy of Forensic Sciences [*A publication*] .... J Indian Acad Forensic Sci
Journal. Indian Academy of Philosophy [*A publication*] .... JIAP
Journal. Indian Academy of Philosophy [*A publication*] .... J Ind Acad Philo
Journal. Indian Academy of Philosophy [*A publication*] ......J Indian Acad Phil
Journal. Indian Academy of Sciences [*A publication*] ....J Indian Acad Sci
Journal. Indian Academy of Wood Science [*A publication*] .... J Indian Acad Wood Sci
Journal. Indian Anthropological Society [*A publication*] .... JIAS
Journal. Indian Anthropological Society [*A publication*] .... J Ind Anthropol Soc
Journal. Indian Anthropological Society [*A publication*] .... J Indian Anthropol Soc
Journal of Indian Art and Industry [*A publication*] .... Jour of Indian Art and Ind
Journal. Indian Botanical Society [*A publication*] .... J Ind Bot Soc
Journal. Indian Botanical Society [*A publication*] .... J Indian Bot Soc
Journal of Indian and Buddhist Studies [*A publication*] .... JIBS
Journal. Indian Chemical Society [*A publication*] .... J Ind Ch S
Journal. Indian Chemical Society [*A publication*] .... J Indian Chem Soc
Journal. Indian Dental Association [*A publication*] .... J Indian Dent Assoc
Journal. Indian Geophysical Union [*A publication*] .... J Indian Geophys Union
Journal of Indian History [*A publication*] .... JIH
Journal of Indian History [*A publication*] .... J Ind Hist
Journal of Indian History [*A publication*] .... J Indian Hist
Journal. Indian Institute of Bankers [*A publication*] .... JIIB
Journal. Indian Institute of Science [*A publication*] .... J Indian I
Journal. Indian Institute of Science [*A publication*] .... J Indian Inst Sci
Journal. Indian Law Institute [*A publication*] .... JILI
Journal. Indian Mathematical Society [*A publication*] .... JIMS
Journal. Indian Mathematical Society [*A publication*] .... J Indian Math Soc
Journal. Indian Medical Association [*A publication*] .... J Indian Med Ass
Journal. Indian Medical Association [*A publication*] .... J Indian Med Assoc
Journal. Indian Musicological Society [*A publication*] .... J Ind Musicol Soc
Journal of Indian Philosophy [*A publication*] .... J Indian Phil
Journal of Indian Philosophy [*A publication*] .... J Ind Philo
Journal of Indian Philosophy [*A publication*] .... JIP
Journal. Indian Potato Association [*A publication*] .... JIPA
Journal. Indian Refractory Makers Association [*A publication*] .... J Indian Refract Makers Assoc
Journal. Indian Roads Congress [*A publication*] ....J Indian Roads Congr
Journal. Indian Society of Agricultural Statistics [*A publication*] .... J Indian Soc Agric Stat
Journal. Indian Society of Agricultural Statistics [*A publication*] .... J Indian Soc Agr Statist
Journal. Indian Society of Soil Science [*A publication*] .... J Indian Soc Soil Sci
Journal. Indian Sociological Society [*A publication*] .... JISS
Journal. Indian Statistical Association [*A publication*] .... J Indian Statist Assoc
Journal. Indian Statistical Association [*A publication*] .... J Indn St A
Journal of Indian Textile History [*A publication*] .... JITH
Journal. Indiana Dental Association [*A publication*] ....J Indiana Dent Assoc
Journal. Indiana State Medical Association [*A publication*] .... J Indiana State Med Assoc
Journal. Indianapolis District Dental Society [*A publication*] .... J Indianap Dist Dent Soc
Journal of Individual Psychology [*A publication*] .... J Individ Psychol
Journal of Individual Psychology [*A publication*] .... J Indiv Psy
Journal of Indo-European Studies [*A publication*] .... JIES
Journal of Indo-European Studies [*A publication*] .... J Indo-European Stud
Journal of Industrial Aerodynamics [*A publication*] .... J Ind Aero
Journal of Industrial Aerodynamics [*A publication*] .... J Ind Aerodyn
Journal of Industrial Archaeology [*A publication*] .... JIA
Journal of Industrial Arts Education [*A publication*] .... J Ind Arts Ed
Journal of Industrial Economics [*A publication*] .... JIE
Journal of Industrial Economics [*A publication*] .... J Ind Econ
Journal of Industrial Economics [*A publication*] .... J Industr Econ
Journal of Industrial Engineering [*A publication*] .... J Ind Eng
Journal of Industrial Engineering [*A publication*] .... JLIEA
Journal. Industrial Explosives Society. Explosion and Explosives (Japan) [*A publication*] .... J Ind Explos Soc (Jap)
Journal of Industrial Hygiene [*A publication*] .... J Indust Hyg
Journal of Industrial Hygiene and Toxicology [*A publication*] .... J Ind Hyg
Journal of Industrial Hygiene and Toxicology [*A publication*] .... J Ind Hyg Toxicol
Journal of Industrial Relations [*A publication*] .... J Industr Relat
Journal of Industrial Relations [*A publication*] .... JIR
Journal of Industrial Teacher Education [*A publication*] ......J Ind Teach Educ
Journal of Industrial Teacher Education [*A publication*] .... J Industr Teacher Educ
Journal of Industrial Technology. Myong-Ji University [*Republic of Korea*] [*A publication*] ....J Ind Technol Myong-Ji Univ
Journal of Industry [*A publication*] ....J Ind

Journal of Industry and Trade [*A publication*] .... J Ind Trade
Journal of Infectious Diseases [*A publication*] ....J Infect Dis
Journal. Information Processing Society of Japan [*A publication*] .... J Inf Process Soc Jap
Journal des Ingenieurs [*A publication*] ....J Ing
Journal of Inherited Metabolic Disease [*A publication*] .... J Inherited Metab Dis
Journal. Inland Fisheries Society of India [*A publication*] .... J Inl Fish Soc India
Journal of Inorganic Biochemistry [*A publication*] .... J Inorg Biochem
Journal of Inorganic and Nuclear Chemistry [*A publication*] .... J Inorg Nuc
Journal of Inorganic and Nuclear Chemistry [*A publication*] .... J Inorg Nucl Chem
Journal of Inorganic and Nuclear Chemistry [*A publication*] .... Jour Inorganic and Nuclear Chemistry
Journal of Insect Pathology [*A publication*] .... J Insect Pathol
Journal of Insect Physiology [*A publication*] ....J Insect Ph
Journal of Insect Physiology [*A publication*] ....J Insect Physiol
Journal of Insect Physiology [*A publication*] .... JIPHA
Journal. Institut Canadien de Science et Technologie Alimentaire [*A publication*] .... J Inst Can Sci Technol Aliment
Journal. Institut Canadien de Technologie Alimentaire [*A publication*] .... J Inst Can Technol Aliment
Journal. Institute of Animal Technicians [*A publication*] ......J Inst Anim Tech
Journal. Institute of Brewing [*A publication*] ....J I Brewing
Journal. Institute of Brewing [*A publication*] ....J Inst Brew
Journal. Institute for Defence Studies and Analyses [*A publication*] .... J Inst Def Stud Anal
Journal. Institute of Draftsmen [*A publication*] .... J Inst Draftsmen
Journal. Institute of Electrical Communication Engineers of Japan [*Later, Journal. Institute of Electronics and Communication Engineers of Japan*] [*A publication*] .... J Inst Electr Commun Eng Jap
Journal. Institute of Electronics and Communication Engineers of Japan [*A publication*] ....J Inst Electron Commun Eng Jap
Journal. Institute of Energy [*United Kingdom*] [*A publication*] ....J Inst Energy
Journal. Institute of Fuel [*A publication*] ....J I Fuel
Journal. Institute of Fuel [*A publication*] ....J Inst Fuel
Journal. Institute of Highway Engineers [*A publication*] ....J Inst Highw Eng
Journal. Institute of Mathematics and Its Applications [*A publication*] .... J I Math Ap
Journal. Institute of Mathematics and Its Applications [*A publication*] .... J Inst Math Applic
Journal. Institute of Metals (London) [*A publication*] ....J Inst Met (Lond)
Journal. Institute of Mine Surveyors of South Africa [*A publication*] .... J Inst Mine Surv S Afr
Journal. Institute of Navigation [*A publication*] ....J Inst Navig
Journal. Institute of Petroleum [*A publication*] .... J Inst Pet
Journal. Institute of Transport [*A publication*] ....J Inst Transp
Journal. Institute of Wood Science [*A publication*] .... J Inst Wood Sci
Journal. Institute of Wood Science [*A publication*] .... J I Wood Sc
Journal. Institution of Computer Sciences [*A publication*] .... J Inst Comput Sci
Journal. Institution of Electronics and Telecommunication Engineers [*A publication*] .... J Inst Electron Telecommun Eng
Journal. Institution of Engineers (Australia) [*A publication*] .... J Inst Eng (Aust)
Journal. Institution of Engineers (India) [*A publication*] ....J Inst Eng (India)
Journal. Institution of Engineers (India). Chemical Engineering Division [*A publication*] .... J Inst Eng (India) Chem Eng Div
Journal. Institution of Engineers (India). Civil Engineering Division [*A publication*] ....J Inst Eng (India) Civ Eng Div
Journal. Institution of Engineers (India). Electrical Engineering Division [*A publication*] .... J Inst Eng (India) Elec Eng Div
Journal. Institution of Engineers (India). General Engineering Division [*A publication*] .... J Inst Eng (India) Gen Eng Div
Journal. Institution of Engineers (India). Mechanical Engineering Division [*A publication*] ....J Inst Eng (India) Mech Eng Div
Journal. Institution of Engineers (India). Mining and Metallurgy Division [*A publication*] .... J Inst Eng (India) Mining Met Div
Journal. Institution of Engineers (India). Mining and Metallurgy Division [*A publication*] .... J Inst Eng (India) Min Metall Div
Journal. Institution of Engineers (Malaysia) [*A publication*] .... J Inst Eng (Malaysia)
Journal. Institution of Gas Engineers [*A publication*] .... J Instn Gas Engrs
Journal. Institution of Heating and Ventilating Engineers [*A publication*] .... JIHVE
Journal. Institution of Heating and Ventilating Engineers [*A publication*] .... J Instn Heat Vent Engrs
Journal. Institution of Highway Engineers [*A publication*] .... J Instn Highw Engrs
Journal. Institution of Locomotive Engineers [*A publication*] .... J Instn Loco Engrs
Journal. Institution of Municipal Engineers [*A publication*] .... J Inst Munic Eng
Journal. Institution of Municipal Engineers [*A publication*] .... J Instn Munic Engrs
Journal. Institution of Nuclear Engineers [*A publication*] .... J Instn Nucl Engrs
Journal. Institution of Nuclear Engineers [*A publication*] ....J Inst Nucl Eng
Journal. Institution of Nuclear Engineers [*A publication*] ....J I Nucl En

Journal. Institution of the Rubber Industry [*A publication*]............................ J Instn Rubb Ind

Journal. Institution of the Rubber Industry [*A publication*]............................ J Inst Rubber Ind

Journal. Institution of Telecommunication Engineers [*A publication*]...................J Inst Telecommun Eng

Journal. Institution of Telecommunication Engineers [*A publication*].... JITE

Journal. Institution of Telecommunication Engineers (New Delhi) [*A publication*]...........................J Inst Telecommun Eng (New Delhi)

Journal. Institution of Water Engineers [*A publication*].......J Instn Wat Engrs

Journal. Institution of Water Engineers [*A publication*].........J Inst Water Eng

Journal of Instructional Psychology [*A publication*].................J Instr Psychol

Journal of Insurance [*A publication*]...JI

Journal of Interamerican Studies [*A publication*]..........................JIAS

Journal of Interamerican Studies and World Affairs [*A publication*]...J Intam St

Journal of Interamerican Studies and World Affairs [*A publication*]...J Interamer Stud

Journal of Interamerican Studies and World Affairs [*A publication*]...J Interam Stud

Journal of Interamerican Studies and World Affairs [*A publication*]...Jour Interam Studies

Journal. Interdenominational Theological Center [*A publication*]................... J Int Th C

Journal of Interdisciplinary Cycle Research [*A publication*]..........J Interd Cy

Journal of Interdisciplinary Cycle Research [*A publication*]...................... J Interdiscipl Cycle Res

Journal of Interdisciplinary History [*A publication*].............. J Interdiscip Hist

Journal of Interdisciplinary History [*A publication*]...................... J Interdis H

Journal of Interdisciplinary History [*A publication*]...................... J Interdis Hist

Journal of Intergroup Relations [*A publication*].....................J Intergroup Rel

Journal of International Affairs [*A publication*]................................ JIA

Journal of International Affairs [*A publication*].............................. J Int Aff

Journal of International Affairs [*A publication*].....................Jour of Int Affairs

Journal International d'Archeologie Numismatique [*A publication*].......JAN

Journal International d'Archeologie Numismatique [*A publication*].......JIAN

Journal. International Arthur Schnitzler Research Association [*A publication*]...JIASRA

Journal. International Association for Mathematical Geology [*A publication*]...J Int A Mat

Journal of International Business Studies [*A publication*]..................Jrl Int B

Journal International du Cancer [*A publication*]...........................J Int Cancer

Journal of International Economics [*A publication*] ....J Int Econ

Journal. International Folk Music Council [*A publication*]......................JIFC

Journal. International Folk Music Council [*A publication*]....................JIFM

Journal. International Folk Music Council [*A publication*]..................JIFMC

Journal. International Institute for Sugar Beet Research [*A publication*]..............................J Int Inst Sugar Beet Res

Journal of International Law and Economics [*A publication*] .... J Int Law E

Journal of International Law and Economics [*A publication*]...J Int Law & Econ

Journal of International Medical Research [*A publication*] .... J Int Med R

Journal of International Medical Research [*A publication*].........J Int Med Res

Journal of International Numismatics [*A publication*].....................J Int Num

Journal. International Phonetic Association [*A publication*]...................... J Int Phonetic Assoc

Journal. International Phonetic Association [*A publication*]...................JIPA

Journal International de Psychologie [*A publication*]..................J Int Psychol

Journal of International Relations [*A publication*] ....J Internat Rel

Journal of International Relations [*A publication*] ....J Intern Rel

Journal of International Relations [*A publication*] ....J Int Relations

Journal International de Vitaminologie et de Nutrition [*A publication*].............................. J Int Vitaminol Nutr

Journal of Invertebrate Pathology [*A publication*] .... J Inver Pat

Journal of Invertebrate Pathology [*A publication*]..............J Invertebr Pathol

Journal of Investigative Dermatology [*A publication*].........J Inves Der

Journal of Investigative Dermatology [*A publication*] .... J Invest Dermatol

Journal. Iowa Medical Society [*A publication*].......................J Iowa Med Soc

Journal. Iowa State Medical Society [*A publication*] .... J Iowa State Med Soc

Journal. Iraqi Chemical Society [*A publication*]....................J Iraqi Chem Soc

Journal. Iraqi Medical Professions [*A publication*] ....J Iraqi Med Prof

Journal. Irish Colleges of Physicians and Surgeons [*A publication*]...J Irish C P

Journal. Irish Dental Association [*A publication*].....................J Ir Dent Assoc

Journal. Irish Free State Department of Agriculture [*A publication*]...J Dept Ag Ireland

Journal of Irish Genealogy [*A publication*] ....JIG

Journal of Irish Literature [*A publication*] ....JIL

Journal. Irish Medical Association [*A publication*] ....JIMSA

Journal. Irish Medical Association [*A publication*] ....J Ir Med Assoc

Journal. Iron and Steel Institute [*A publication*] ....J Iron St Inst

Journal. Iron and Steel Institute (London) [*A publication*]...J Iron Steel Inst (London)

Journal. Irrigation and Drainage Division. Proceedings. American Society of Civil Engineers [*A publication*]...J Irrig Drain Div Am Soc Civ Eng

Journal. Irrigation and Drainage Division. Proceedings. American Society of Civil Engineers [*A publication*]........JRCE-A

Journal. Israel Medical Association [*A publication*] ....J Isr Med Assoc

Journal of Israel Numismatics [*A publication*] ....JIN

Journal. Iwate Medical Association [*A publication*]...........J Iwate Med Assoc

Journal. Japan Association for Philosophy of Science [*A publication*]...J Jap Assoc Philos Sci

Journal. Japan Broncho-Esophagological Society [*A publication*]...J Jpn Broncho-Esophagol Soc

Journal. Japan Contact Lens Society [*A publication*]...J Jpn Contact Lens Soc

Journal. Japan Diabetic Society [*A publication*] ....J Jpn Diabetic Soc

Journal. Japan Institute of Light Metals [*A publication*]...J Jap Inst Light Metals

Journal. Japan Institute of Light Metals [*A publication*]............J Jap Inst Met

Journal. Japan Institute of Light Metals [*A publication*]...J Jpn Inst Light Met

Journal. Japan Institute of Metals [*A publication*] ....J Jpn Inst Met

Journal. Japan Medical Association [*A publication*]............J Jpn Med Assoc

Journal. Japan Petroleum Institute [*A publication*].................J Jpn Pet Inst

Journal. Japan Research Association for Textile End-Uses [*A publication*]...J Jpn Res Assoc Text End-Uses

Journal. Japan Society of Air Pollution [*A publication*] ....J Jpn Soc Air Pollut

Journal. Japan Society of Blood Transfusion [*A publication*]...J Jpn Soc Blood Transfus

Journal. Japan Society for Cancer Therapy [*A publication*]...J Jpn Soc Cancer Ther

Journal. Japan Society of Civil Engineers [*A publication*]...J Jap Soc Civ Eng

Journal. Japan Society for Dental Apparatus and Materials [*A publication*]...J Jpn Soc Dent Appar Mater

Journal. Japan Society of Lubrication Engineers [*A publication*]...J Jap S Lub

Journal. Japan Society of Lubrication Engineers [*A publication*]...J Jpn Soc Lubr Eng

Journal. Japan Society of Mechanical Engineers [*A publication*]...J Jap Soc Mech Eng

Journal. Japan Society of Powder and Powder Metallurgy [*A publication*]...J Jap Soc Powder Met

Journal. Japan Society of Powder and Powder Metallurgy [*A publication*]...J Jpn Soc Powder Metall

Journal. Japan Society of Precision Engineering [*A publication*]...J Jap Soc Precis Eng

Journal. Japan Society of the Reticuloendothelial System [*A publication*]...J Jpn Soc Reticuloendothel Syst

Journal. Japan Society for Technology of Plasticity [*A publication*]...J Jap Soc Technol Plast

Journal. Japan Statistical Society [*A publication*]...........J Japan Statist Soc

Journal. Japan Turfgrass Research Association [*A publication*]...J Jpn Turfgrass Res Assoc

Journal. Japan Veterinary Medical Association [*A publication*]...J Jpn Vet Med Assoc

Journal. Japan Welding Society [*A publication*] ....J Jpn Weld Soc

Journal. Japan Wood Research Society [*A publication*]...J Japan Wood Res Soc

Journal. Japan Wood Research Society [*A publication*]...J Jap Wood Res Soc

Journal. Japan Wood Research Society [*A publication*]...J Jpn Wood Res Soc

Journal. Japanese Anodizing Association [*A publication*]...J Jpn Anodizing Assoc

Journal. Japanese Association for Infectious Diseases [*A publication*]...J Jap Assoc Infect Dis

Journal. Japanese Association for Infectious Diseases [*A publication*]...J Jpn Assoc Infect Dis

Journal. Japanese Association of Periodontology [*A publication*]...................J Jpn Assoc Periodontol

Journal. Japanese Association for Thoracic Surgery [*A publication*]...J Jpn Assoc Thorac Surg

Journal. Japanese Biochemical Society [*A publication*]...J Jap Biochem Soc

Journal. Japanese Biochemical Society [*A publication*]...J Jpn Biochem Soc

Journal of Japanese Botany [*A publication*].............................J Jpn Bot

Journal. Japanese Dental Anesthesia Society [*A publication*]...J Jpn Dent Anesth Soc

Journal. Japanese Forestry Society [*A publication*] .... J Jap For Soc

Journal. Japanese Forestry Society [*A publication*] .... J Jpn For Soc

Journal. Japanese Obstetrical and Gynecological Society [*A publication*]...JJOGA

Journal. Japanese Orthopaedic Association [*A publication*]...J Jpn Orthop Assoc

Journal. Japanese Psychosomatic Society [*A publication*]...J Jpn Psychosom Soc

Journal. Japanese Society of Food and Nutrition [*A publication*]...J Jap Soc Food Nutr

Journal. Japanese Society of Food and Nutrition [*A publication*]...J Jpn Soc Food Nutr

Journal. Japanese Society of Grassland Science [*A publication*]...J Jap Soc Grassland Sci

Journal. Japanese Society of Grassland Science [*A publication*]...J Jpn Soc Grassl Sci

Journal. Japanese Society of Herbage Crops and Grassland Farming [*A publication*].................J Jpn Soc Herb Crops Grassl Farming

Journal. Japanese Society for Horticultural Science [*A publication*]...J Jpn Soc Hortic Sci

Journal. Japanese Society for Strength and Fracture of Materials [*A publication*] .... J Jpn Soc Strength Fract Mater
Journal. Japanese Society of Veterinary Science [*A publication*] .... J Japan Soc Vet Sc
Journal of Japanese Studies [*A publication*] .... J Ja Stud
Journal of Japanese Studies [*A publication*] .... JJS
Journal. Japanese Surgical Society [*A publication*] .... J Jpn Surg Soc
Journal of Jazz Studies [*A publication*] .... J Jazz Studies
Journal of Jewish Communal Service [*A publication*] .... J Jew Commun Serv
Journal of Jewish Studies [*A publication*] .... JJewS
Journal of Jewish Studies [*A publication*] .... JJS
Journal of Jewish Studies [*A publication*] .... Jo Je S
Journal of Jinsen Medical Sciences [*A publication*] .... J Jinsen Med Sci
Journal. Jiwaji University [*A publication*] .... J Jiwaji Univ
Journal. Joint Panel on Nuclear Marine Propulsion [*A publication*] .... J Joint Panel Nucl Mar Propul
Journal of Juristic Papyrology [*A publication*] .... JJP
Journal of Juristic Papyrology [*A publication*] .... J Jur Pap
Journal of Juvenile Research [*A publication*] .... J Juvenile Res
Journal. Juzen Medical Society [*A publication*] .... J Juzen Med Soc
Journal. Kagawa Nutrition College [*A publication*] .... J Kagawa Nutr Coll
Journal. Kanagawa Prefectural Junior College of Nutrition [*A publication*] .... J Kanagawa Prefect J Coll Nutr
Journal. Kansai Medical University [*A publication*] .... J Kansai Med Univ
Journal. Kansas Bar Association [*A publication*] .... J Kan BA
Journal. Kansas Entomological Society [*A publication*] .... J Kans Entomol Soc
Journal. Kansas Medical Society [*A publication*] .... J Kans Med Soc
Journal. Kansas Medical Society [*A publication*] .... JKMSA
Journal. Kansas State Dental Association [*A publication*] .... J Kans State Dent Assoc
Journal. Kanto-Tosan Agricultural Experiment Station [*A publication*] .... J Kanto-Tosan Agr Exp Sta
Journal. Karnatak University [*Dharwar*] [*A publication*] .... JKU
Journal. Karnatak University. Humanities [*A publication*] .... J Karnatak U Hum
Journal. Karnatak University. Science [*A publication*] .... J Karnatak Univ Sci
Journal. Karnatak University. Social Sciences [*A publication*] .... J Karnatak U Soc Sci
Journal of Karyopathology. Especially Tumor and Tumorvirus [*A publication*] .... J Karyopathol Tumor Tumorvirus
Journal. Kentucky Medical Association [*A publication*] .... J KY Med Assoc
Journal. Kerala Academy of Biology [*A publication*] .... J Kerala Acad Biol
Journal. Kerry Archaeological and Historical Society [*A publication*] .... JKAHS
Journal. Kongju National Teachers College [*Republic of Korea*] [*A publication*] .... J Kongju Natl Teach Coll
Journal. Korea Electric Association [*Republic of Korea*] [*A publication*] .... J Korea Electr Assoc
Journal. Korea Merchant Marine College. Natural Sciences Series [*Republic of Korea*] [*A publication*] .... J Korea Merch Mar Coll Nat Sci Ser
Journal. Korea Military Academy [*Republic of Korea*] [*A publication*] .... J Korea Mil Acad
Journal. Korean Academy of Maxillofacial Radiology [*Republic of Korea*] [*A publication*] .... J Korean Acad Maxillofac Radiol
Journal. Korean Agricultural Chemical Society [*Republic of Korea*] [*A publication*] .... J Korean Agric Chem Soc
Journal. Korean Ceramic Society [*Republic of Korea*] [*A publication*] .... J Korean Ceram Soc
Journal. Korean Chemical Society [*A publication*] .... J Korean Chem Soc
Journal. Korean Dental Association [*Republic of Korea*] [*A publication*] .... J Korean Dent Assoc
Journal. Korean Forestry Society [*Republic of Korea*] [*A publication*] .... J Korean For Soc
Journal. Korean Institute of Chemical Engineers [*Republic of Korea*] [*A publication*] .... J Korean Inst Chem Eng
Journal. Korean Institute of Electrical Engineers [*Republic of Korea*] [*A publication*] .... J Korean Inst Electr Eng
Journal. Korean Institute of Electronics Engineers [*A publication*] .... J Korean Inst Electron Eng
Journal. Korean Institute of Metals [*Republic of Korea*] [*A publication*] .... J Korean Inst Met
Journal. Korean Institute of Mineral and Mining Engineers [*Republic of Korea*] [*A publication*] .... J Korean Inst Miner Mining Eng
Journal. Korean Institute of Mining [*Republic of Korea*] [*A publication*] .... J Korean Inst Min
Journal. Korean Mathematical Society [*A publication*] .... J Korean Math Soc
Journal. Korean Medical Association [*Republic of Korea*] [*A publication*] .... J Korean Med Assoc
Journal. Korean Nuclear Society [*Republic of Korea*] [*A publication*] .... J Korean Nucl Soc
Journal. Korean Ophthalmological Society [*A publication*] .... J Korean Ophthalmol Soc
Journal. Korean Physical Society [*A publication*] .... J Korean Phys Soc
Journal. Korean Radiological Society [*Republic of Korea*] [*A publication*] .... J Korean Radiol Soc
Journal. Korean Research Society of Radiological Technology [*Republic of Korea*] [*A publication*] .... J Korean Res Soc Radiol Technol
Journal. Korean Society of Civil Engineers [*Republic of Korea*] [*A publication*] .... J Korean Soc Civ Eng
Journal. Korean Society of Crop Science [*Republic of Korea*] [*A publication*] .... J Korean Soc Crop Sci
Journal. Korean Society of Mechanical Engineers [*Republic of Korea*] [*A publication*] .... J Korean Soc Mech Eng
Journal. Korean Society of Soil Science and Fertilizer [*A publication*] .... J Korean Soc Soil Sci Fert
Journal. Korean Society of Textile Engineers and Chemists [*Republic of Korea*] [*A publication*] .... J Korean Soc Text Eng Chem
Journal. Korean Surgical Society [*A publication*] .... J Korean Surg Soc
Journal. Koyasan University [*A publication*] .... J Koyasan Univ
Journal. Kumamoto Women's University [*A publication*] .... J Kumamoto Women's Univ
Journal. Kumasi University of Science and Technology [*A publication*] .... J Kumasi Univ Sci Technol
Journal. Kurume Medical Association [*A publication*] .... J Kurume Med Assoc
Journal. Kuwait Medical Association [*A publication*] .... J Kuwait Med Assoc
Journal. Kyorin Medical Society [*A publication*] .... J Kyorin Med Soc
Journal. Kyoto Prefectural University of Medicine [*A publication*] .... J Kyoto Prefect Univ Med
Journal. Kyungpook Engineering [*Republic of Korea*] [*A publication*] .... J Kyungpook Eng
Journal. Kyushu Hematological Society [*A publication*] .... J Kyushu Hematol Soc
Journal of Labelled Compounds [*Later, Journal of Labelled Compounds and Radiopharmaceuticals*] [*A publication*] .... J Label Com
Journal of Labelled Compounds [*Later, Journal of Labelled Compounds and Radiopharmaceuticals*] [*A publication*] .... J Labelled Compd
Journal of Labelled Compounds and Radiopharmaceuticals [*A publication*] .... J Label Compound Radiopharm
Journal of Labelled Compounds and Radiopharmaceuticals [*A publication*] .... J Labelled Compd Radiopharm
Journal of Laboratory and Clinical Medicine [*A publication*] .... J Lab Clin Med
Journal of Laboratory and Clinical Medicine [*A publication*] .... J La Cl Med
Journal of Labour Hygiene in Iron and Steel Industry [*A publication*] .... J Labour Hyg Iron Steel Ind
Journal. Lancashire Dialect Society [*A publication*] .... JLDS
Journal-Lancet [*A publication*] .... J-Lancet
Journal of Land and Public Utility Economics [*A publication*] .... J Land & Pub Util Econ
Journal of Land and Public Utility Economics [*A publication*] .... Jour Land Public Utility Econ
Journal. Language Association of Eastern Africa [*A publication*] .... JLAEA
Journal of Laryngology and Otology [*A publication*] .... J Laryngol Otol
Journal of Laryngology and Otology [*A publication*] .... J Laryng Ot
Journal of Laryngology and Otology [*A publication*] .... JLOTA
Journal of Laryngology and Otology. Supplement [*A publication*] .... J Laryngol Otol Suppl
Journal of Latin American Lore [*A publication*] .... JLAL
Journal of Latin American Studies [*A publication*] .... J Lat Am Stud
Journal of Latin American Studies [*A publication*] .... J Latin Amer Stud
Journal of Law and Economic Development [*A publication*] .... J L & Econ Develop
Journal of Law and Economic Development [*A publication*] .... Jour Law and Econ
Journal of Law and Economics [*A publication*] .... J Law & Econ
Journal of Law and Economics [*A publication*] .... J Law Econ
Journal of Law and Economics [*A publication*] .... JLE
Journal of Law and Economics [*A publication*] .... J L & Econ
Journal of Law and Education [*A publication*] .... J Law & Educ
Journal of Law and Education [*A publication*] .... J L & Educ
Journal of Learning Disabilities [*A publication*] .... JLD
Journal of Learning Disabilities [*A publication*] .... JLDIA
Journal of Learning Disabilities [*A publication*] .... J Lear Disabil
Journal of Learning Disabilities [*A publication*] .... J Learn Di
Journal of Learning Disabilities [*A publication*] .... J Learn Dis
Journal of Learning Disabilities [*A publication*] .... J Learn Disabil
Journal of Legal Education [*A publication*] .... J Legal Ed
Journal of Legal Education [*A publication*] .... J Leg Educ
Journal of Legal Education [*A publication*] .... Jour Legal Ed
Journal of Legal Medicine [*A publication*] .... J Leg Med
Journal of Legal Studies [*A publication*] .... J Leg Stud
Journal of Leisure Research [*A publication*] .... J Leis Res
Journal of Leisure Research [*A publication*] .... J Leisure
Journal of Leisure Research [*A publication*] .... JLER
Journal. Lepidopterists' Society [*A publication*] .... J Lepid Soc
Journal of the Less-Common Metals [*A publication*] .... J Less-C Met
Journal of the Less-Common Metals [*A publication*] .... J Less Common Met
Journal of Liberal Arts and Sciences. Kitasato University [*A publication*] .... J Lib Arts Sci Kitasato Univ
Journal of Librarianship [*A publication*] .... J Libnship
Journal of Librarianship [*A publication*] .... J Libr
Journal of Librarianship [*A publication*] .... J Librarianship
Journal of Library Automation [*A publication*] .... J Lib Automation
Journal of Library Automation [*A publication*] .... J Libr Aut
Journal of Library Automation [*A publication*] .... J Libr Auto
Journal of Library Automation [*A publication*] .... J Libr Automn
Journal of Library Automation [*A publication*] .... JOLA

Journal of Library History [*Later, Journal of Library History, Philosophy, and Comparative Librarianship*] [*A publication*] ... JLH
Journal of Library History [*Later, Journal of Library History, Philosophy, and Comparative Librarianship*] [*A publication*] ... J Lib Hist
Journal of Library History [*Later, Journal of Library History, Philosophy, and Comparative Librarianship*] [*A publication*] ... J Libr Hist
Journal of Library History [*Later, Journal of Library History, Philosophy, and Comparative Librarianship*] [*A publication*] ... Jnl Lib Hist
Journal of Library History [*Later, Journal of Library History, Philosophy, and Comparative Librarianship*] [*A publication*] ... Jour Lib Hist
Journal of Library History, Philosophy, and Comparative Librarianship [*A publication*] ... JLH
Journal of Library History, Philosophy, and Comparative Librarianship [*A publication*] ... J Libr Hist
Journal of Library and Information Science [*A publication*] ... J Libr Inf Sci
Journal. Library of Rutgers University [*A publication*] ... JLRU
Journal. Limnological Society of South Africa [*A publication*] ... J Limnol Soc South Afr
Journal of Linguistics [*A publication*] ... JL
Journal of Linguistics [*A publication*] ... J Ling
Journal of Linguistics [*A publication*] ... J Linguist
Journal of Linguistics [*A publication*] ... J Linguistics
Journal. Linnean Society of London. Botany [*A publication*] ... J Linn Soc Lond Bot
Journal. Linnean Society of London. Zoology [*A publication*] ... J Linn Soc Lond Zool
Journal of Lipid Research [*A publication*] ... J Lipid Res
Journal of Liquid Chromatography [*A publication*] ... J Liq Chromatogr
Journal of Liquid Chromatography [*A publication*] ... J Liquid Chromatogr
Journal of Literary Semantics [*A publication*] ... JLS
Journal. London Mathematical Society [*A publication*] ... JLMS
Journal. London Mathematical Society [*A publication*] ... J Lond Math
Journal. London School of Tropical Medicine [*A publication*] ... J London School Trop Med
Journal of Long Term Care Administration [*A publication*] ... J Long Term Care
Journal of Long Term Care Administration [*A publication*] ... J Long Term Care Admin
Journal. Louisiana State Medical Society [*A publication*] ... J LA State Med Soc
Journal. Louisiana State Medical Society [*A publication*] ... JLSMA
Journal of Low Temperature Physics [*A publication*] ... J Low Temp Phys
Journal of Low Temperature Physics [*A publication*] ... J L Temp Ph
Journal of Lubrication Technology [*A publication*] ... J Lubr Tech
Journal of Lubrication Technology [*A publication*] ... J Lubr Technol
Journal of Lubrication Technology. Transactions. ASME [*American Society of Mechanical Engineers*] [*A publication*] ... J Lubric Technol Trans ASME
Journal of Lubrication Technology. Transactions. ASME [*American Society of Mechanical Engineers*] [*A publication*] ... J Lub Tech
Journal of Luminescence [*A publication*] ... J Lumin
Journal of Luminescence [*A publication*] ... J Luminesc
Journal. Lute Society of America [*A publication*] ... J Lute
Journal. Macomb Dental Society [*A publication*] ... J Macomb Dent Soc
Journal of Macromolecular Science. Part A. Chemistry [*A publication*] ... J Macromol Sci Chem A
Journal of Macromolecular Science. Part A. Chemistry [*A publication*] ... J Macromol Sci Part A
Journal of Macromolecular Science. Part A. Chemistry [*A publication*] ... J Macr S Ch
Journal of Macromolecular Science. Part B. Physics [*A publication*] ... J Macromol Sci Part B
Journal of Macromolecular Science. Part B. Physics [*A publication*] ... J Macromol Sci Phys
Journal of Macromolecular Science. Part B. Physics [*A publication*] ... J Macr S Ph
Journal of Macromolecular Science. Part C. Reviews in Macromolecular Chemistry [*A publication*] ... J Macromol Sci Rev Macromol Chem
Journal of Macromolecular Science. Part C. Reviews in Macromolecular Chemistry [*A publication*] ... J Macr S Rm
Journal. MACT [*Maulana Azad College of Technology*] [*India*] [*A publication*] ... J MACT
Journal. Madras University [*A publication*] ... J Madras Univ
Journal. Madras University. Section B [*A publication*] ... J Madras Univ Sect B
Journal. Madras University. Section B. Contributions in Mathematics, Physical and Biological Science [*A publication*] ... J Madras Univ B
Journal of Magnetic Resonance [*A publication*] ... J Magn Res
Journal of Magnetism and Magnetic Materials [*A publication*] ... J Magn Magn Mater
Journal. Maharaja Sayajirao University of Baroda [*A publication*] ... J Maharaja Sayajirao Univ Baroda
Journal. Maharaja Sayajirao University of Baroda [*A publication*] ... JMSUB
Journal. Maharaja Sayayira University of Baroda [*A publication*] ... J Mahar Sayayira Univ Baroda
Journal. Maharashtra Agricultural Universities [*A publication*] ... J Maharashtra Agric Univ
Journal. Maine Medical Association [*A publication*] ... J Maine Med Assoc
Journal. Maine Medical Association [*A publication*] ... JMMAA
Journal. Malacological Society of Australia [*A publication*] ... J Malacol Soc Aust
Journal des Maladies Vasculaires [*A publication*] ... J Mal Vasc
Journal. Malayan Branch. Royal Asiatic Society [*A publication*] ... JMBRAS
Journal. Malayan Branch. Royal Asiatic Society [*A publication*] ... JMRAS
Journal. Malaysian Branch. Royal Asiatic Society [*A publication*] ... J Malay Branch Roy Asiatic Soc
Journal. Malaysian Branch. Royal Asiatic Society [*A publication*] ... J Malays Branch R Asiat Soc
Journal. Malaysian Branch. Royal Asiatic Society [*A publication*] ... J Mal Br Roy Asiat Soc
Journal of Maltese Studies [*A publication*] ... JMS
Journal. Mammalogical Society of Japan [*A publication*] ... J Mammal Soc Jpn
Journal of Mammalogy [*A publication*] ... J Mammal
Journal of Management Studies [*A publication*] ... J Manag Stu
Journal of Management Studies [*A publication*] ... JMS
Journal of Manipulative and Physiological Therapeutics [*A publication*] ... J Manipulative Physiol Ther
Journal. Manx Museum [*A publication*] ... JMM
Journal. Marine Biological Association [*United Kingdom*] [*A publication*] ... J Marine Bi
Journal. Marine Biological Association (India) [*A publication*] ... J Mar Biol Assoc (India)
Journal. Marine Biological Association (United Kingdom) [*A publication*] ... J Mar Biol Assoc (UK)
Journal. Marine Biological Association (United Kingdom) [*A publication*] ... J Marine Biol Ass (United Kingdom)
Journal of Marine Research [*A publication*] ... J Marine Re
Journal of Marine Research [*A publication*] ... J Marine Res
Journal of Marine Research [*A publication*] ... J Mar Res
Journal of Maritime Law and Commerce [*A publication*] ... J Maritime L
Journal. Market Research Society [*A publication*] ... J Market Res Soc
Journal. Market Research Society (London) [*A publication*] ... J Market (L)
Journal of Marketing [*A publication*] ... JM
Journal of Marketing [*A publication*] ... J Market
Journal of Marketing [*A publication*] ... J Marketing
Journal of Marketing [*A publication*] ... J Mkt
Journal of Marketing [*A publication*] ... J Mktg
Journal of Marketing [*A publication*] ... J Mkting
Journal of Marketing [*A publication*] ... Jnl Marketing
Journal of Marketing Research [*A publication*] ... J Marketing Res
Journal of Marketing Research [*A publication*] ... J Market R
Journal of Marketing Research [*A publication*] ... J Mktg Res
Journal of Marketing Research [*A publication*] ... J Mkting Res
Journal of Marketing Research [*A publication*] ... J Mkt Res
Journal of Marriage and the Family [*A publication*] ... J Mar Fam
Journal of Marriage and the Family [*A publication*] ... J Marr & Fam
Journal of Marriage and the Family [*A publication*] ... J Marriage
Journal of Marriage and the Family [*A publication*] ... J Marriage & Fam
Journal of Marriage and the Family [*A publication*] ... J Marriage Family
Journal of Marriage and the Family [*A publication*] ... JMF
Journal of Marriage and the Family [*A publication*] ... Jnl Marr & Fam
Journal. Maryland State Dental Association [*A publication*] ... J MD State Dent Assoc
Journal of Mass Spectrometry and Ion Physics [*A publication*] ... J Mass Spectrom Ion Phys
Journal of Mass Spectrometry and Ion Physics [*A publication*] ... J Mass Sp Ion P
Journal. Massachussetts Dental Society [*A publication*] ... J Mass Dent Soc
Journal of Materials [*A publication*] ... J Mater
Journal of Materials for Energy Systems [*A publication*] ... J Mater Energy Syst
Journal of Materials Science [*A publication*] ... J Materials Sci
Journal of Materials Science [*A publication*] ... J Mater Sci
Journal. Materials Science Society of Japan [*A publication*] ... J Mater Sci Soc Jpn
Journal of Mathematical Analysis and Applications [*A publication*] ... J Math Anal
Journal of Mathematical Analysis and Applications [*A publication*] ... J Math Anal Appl
Journal of Mathematical Biology [*A publication*] ... J Math Biol
Journal of Mathematical Economics [*A publication*] ... J Math Econom
Journal of Mathematical and Physical Sciences [*A publication*] ... J Mathematical and Physical Sci
Journal of Mathematical and Physical Sciences [*A publication*] ... J Math Phys Sci
Journal of Mathematical Psychology [*A publication*] ... J Math Psyc
Journal of Mathematical Psychology [*A publication*] ... J Math Psychol
Journal. Mathematical Society of Japan [*A publication*] ... J Math Jap
Journal. Mathematical Society of Japan [*A publication*] ... JMSJ
Journal of Mathematical Sociology [*A publication*] ... J Math Soci
Journal of Mathematical Sociology [*A publication*] ... J Math Sociol
Journal of Mathematics (Jabalpur) [*A publication*] ... J Math (Jabalpur)
Journal of Mathematics. Kyoto University [*A publication*] ... J Math Kyoto Univ
Journal of Mathematics. Kyoto University [*A publication*] ... JMKU

Journal of Mathematics and Mechanics [*A publication*] .... J Math Mech
Journal of Mathematics and Physics [*A publication*] .... J Math & Phys
Journal of Mathematics and Physics [*A publication*] .... J Math Phys
Journal of Mathematics and Sciences [*A publication*] .... J Math & Sci
Journal of Mathematics and Sciences [*A publication*] .... J Math Sci
Journal of Mathematics. Tokushima University [*A publication*] .... J Math Tokushima Univ
Journal de Mathematiques Pures et Appliquees [*A publication*] .... J Math P A
Journal de Mathematiques Pures et Appliques [*A publication*] .... J Math Pures Appl
Journal of Maxillofacial Surgery [*A publication*] .... J Maxillofac Surg
Journal de Mecanique [*A publication*] .... J Mec
Journal de Mecanique [*A publication*] .... J Mecanique
Journal de Mecanique Appliquee [*A publication*] .... J Mec Appl
Journal of Mechanical Design. Transactions. ASME [*American Society of Mechanical Engineers*] [*A publication*] .... J Mech Des Trans ASME
Journal. Mechanical Engineering Laboratory (Tokyo) [*A publication*] .... J Mech Eng Lab (Tokyo)
Journal of Mechanical Engineering Science [*A publication*] .... J Mech Eng
Journal of Mechanical Engineering Science [*A publication*] .... J Mech Eng Sci
Journal. Mechanical Laboratory of Japan [*A publication*] .... J Mech Lab Jap
Journal of Mechanical Working Technology [*A publication*] .... J Mech Work Technol
Journal of the Mechanics and Physics of Solids [*A publication*] .... J Mech Phys
Journal of the Mechanics and Physics of Solids [*A publication*] .... J Mech Phys Solids
Journal of Mechanisms [*A publication*] .... J Mech
Journal of Mechanochemistry and Cell Motility [*A publication*] .... J Mechanochem & Cell Motility
Journal of Mechanochemistry and Cell Motility [*A publication*] .... J Mechanochem Cell Motility
Journal de Medecine de Besancon [*A publication*] .... J Med Besancon
Journal de Medecine de Bordeaux [*A publication*] .... J Med Bordeaux
Journal de Medecine de Bordeaux et du Sud-Ouest [*A publication*] .... J Med Bord Sud-Ouest
Journal de Medecine de Caen [*A publication*] .... J Med Caen
Journal de Medecine, Chirurgie, Pharmacie (Paris) [*A publication*] .... J Med Chir Pharm (Paris)
Journal de Medecine et de Chirurgie Pratiques [*A publication*] .... J Med et Chir Prat
Journal de Medecine de Lyon [*A publication*] .... J Med Lyon
Journal de Medecine de Montpellier [*A publication*] .... J Med Montp
Journal de Medecine de Poitiers [*A publication*] .... J Med Poitiers
Journal de Medecine de Strasbourg [*A publication*] .... J Med Strasb
Journal de Medecine de Strasbourg [*France*] [*A publication*] .... J Med Strasbourg
Journal de Medecine Veterinaire et Comparee [*A publication*] .... J Med Vet et Comp
Journal de Medecine Veterinaire (Lyon) [*A publication*] .... J Med Vet (Lyon)
Journal de Medecine Veterinaire Militaire [*A publication*] .... J Med Vet Mil
Journal de Medecine Veterinaire et de Zootechnie (Lyon) [*A publication*] .... J Med Vet et Zootech (Lyon)
Journal for Medicaid Management [*A publication*] .... J Medicaid Manage
Journal. Medical Association of Georgia [*A publication*] .... J Med Assoc GA
Journal. Medical Association of Jamaica [*A publication*] .... J Med Assoc Jam
Journal. Medical Association of South Africa [*A publication*] .... J Med Ass South Africa
Journal. Medical Association of the State of Alabama [*A publication*] .... J Med Assoc State Ala
Journal. Medical Association of Thailand [*A publication*] .... J Med Assoc Thail
Journal of Medical Education [*A publication*] .... JMEDA
Journal of Medical Education [*A publication*] .... J Med Educ
Journal of Medical Electronics [*A publication*] .... J Med Electron
Journal of Medical Engineering and Technology [*A publication*] .... J Med Eng Technol
Journal of Medical Entomology [*A publication*] .... J Med Ent
Journal of Medical Entomology [*A publication*] .... J Med Entomol
Journal of Medical Entomology. Supplement [*A publication*] .... J Med Entomol Suppl
Journal of Medical Ethics [*A publication*] .... J Med Ethics
Journal Medical Francais [*A publication*] .... J Med Franc
Journal of Medical Genetics [*A publication*] .... J Med Genet
Journal of Medical Laboratory Technology [*A publication*] .... J Med Lab Technol
Journal Medical Libanais [*A publication*] .... J Med Liban
Journal of Medical Microbiology [*A publication*] .... J Med Micro
Journal of Medical Microbiology [*A publication*] .... J Med Microbiol
Journal of Medical Primatology [*A publication*] .... J Med Prim
Journal of Medical Primatology [*A publication*] .... J Med Primatol
Journal of Medical Sciences [*A publication*] .... J Med Sci
Journal of Medical Sciences. Banaras Hindu University [*A publication*] .... J Med Sci Banaras Hindu Univ
Journal. Medical Society of New Jersey [*A publication*] .... J Med Soc NJ
Journal. Medical Society of New Jersey [*A publication*] .... JMSNA
Journal. Medical Society of Toho University [*A publication*] .... J Med Soc Toho Univ
Journal of Medical Systems [*A publication*] .... J Med Syst
Journal of Medical Virology [*A publication*] .... J Med Virol
Journal of Medicinal Chemistry [*A publication*] .... JMC
Journal of Medicinal Chemistry [*A publication*] .... J Med Chem
Journal of Medicinal and Pharmaceutical Chemistry [*A publication*] .... J Med Pharm Chem
Journal of Medicine [*A publication*] .... J Med
Journal of Medicine. Experimental and Clinical (Basel) [*A publication*] .... J Med (Basel)
Journal of Medicine and Philosophy [*A publication*] .... J Med Philos
Journal of Medieval and Renaissance Studies [*A publication*] .... JMRS
Journal of Membrane Biology [*A publication*] .... J Membr Bio
Journal of Membrane Science [*A publication*] .... J Membr Sci
Journal of Mental Deficiency Research [*A publication*] .... J Mental Def Research
Journal of Mental Deficiency Research [*A publication*] .... J Ment Def
Journal of Mental Deficiency Research [*A publication*] .... J Ment Defic Res
Journal of Mental Health [*A publication*] .... J Ment Health
Journal. Mental Health Administration [*A publication*] .... J Ment Health Adm
Journal of Mental Science [*A publication*] .... J Ment Sci
Journal of Mental Science [*A publication*] .... JMSCA
Journal of Mental Subnormality [*A publication*] .... J Ment Subnorm
Journal of Mental Subnormality [*A publication*] .... JMSBA
Journal. Metal Finishing Society of Japan [*A publication*] .... J Met Finish Soc Jap
Journal. Metal Finishing Society of Japan [*A publication*] .... J Met Finish Soc Jpn
Journal. Metal Finishing Society of Korea [*A publication*] .... J Metal Finish Soc Korea
Journal of Metals [*A publication*] .... J Met
Journal of Metals [*A publication*] .... J Metals
Journal of Metals [*A publication*] .... JOM
Journal. Meteorological Society of Japan [*A publication*] .... J Meteorol Soc Jpn
Journal of Mexican American History [*A publication*] .... J Mex Am Hist
Journal. Michigan Dental Association [*A publication*] .... J Mich Dent Assoc
Journal. Michigan State Dental Association [*A publication*] .... J Mich State Dent Assoc
Journal. Michigan State Dental Society [*A publication*] .... J Mich State Dent Soc
Journal of Microbiology of the United Arab Republic [*A publication*] .... J Microbiol UAR
Journal of Micrographics [*A publication*] .... J Microgr
Journal of Micrographics [*A publication*] .... J Micrographics
Journal de Micrographie [*A publication*] .... J Microg
Journal de Microscopie [*France*] [*A publication*] .... J Microsc
Journal de Microscopie et de Biologie Cellulaire [*A publication*] .... J Microsc B
Journal de Microscopie et de Biologie Cellulaire [*A publication*] .... J Microsc Biol Cell
Journal de Microscopie (Paris) [*A publication*] .... J Microsc (Paris)
Journal de Microscopie et Spectroscopie Electronique (France) [*A publication*] .... J Microsc Spectrosc Electron (France)
Journal of Microscopy [*Oxford*] [*A publication*] .... J Micros
Journal of Microscopy [*A publication*] .... J Microsc
Journal of Microscopy and Natural Science [*A publication*] .... J Micr and Nat Sc
Journal of Microscopy (Oxford) [*A publication*] .... J Microsc (O)
Journal of Microscopy (Oxford) [*A publication*] .... J Microsc (Oxf)
Journal of Microsurgery [*A publication*] .... J Microsurg
Journal of Microwave Power [*A publication*] .... JLMPA
Journal of Microwave Power [*A publication*] .... J Microwave Power
Journal of Military Assistance [*A publication*] .... JOMA
Journal. Military Service Institution [*A publication*] .... J Mil Serv Inst
Journal of Milk and Food Technology [*Later, Journal of Food Protection*] [*A publication*] .... JMFT
Journal of Milk and Food Technology [*Later, Journal of Food Protection*] [*A publication*] .... J Milk Food
Journal of Milk and Food Technology [*Later, Journal of Food Protection*] [*A publication*] .... J Milk & Food Tech
Journal of Milk and Food Technology [*Later, Journal of Food Protection*] [*A publication*] .... J Milk Food Technol
Journal of Milk Technology [*A publication*] .... J Milk Tech
Journal. Mine Ventilation Society of South Africa [*A publication*] .... J Mine Vent Soc S Afr
Journal of Mines, Metals, and Fuels [*A publication*] .... J Mines Met Fuels
Journal. Mining and Metallurgical Institute of Japan [*A publication*] .... J Mining Met Inst Jap
Journal. Mining and Metallurgical Institute of Japan [*A publication*] .... J Min Metall Inst Jap
Journal. Ministere de l'Instruction Publique en Russie [*A publication*] .... JMIR
Journal. Minnesota Academy of Science [*A publication*] .... J Minn Acad Sci
Journal of Missile Defense Research [*A publication*] .... JMDR
Journal. Mississippi Academy of Sciences [*A publication*] .... J Miss Acad Sci
Journal of Mississippi History [*A publication*] .... JMH
Journal of Mississippi History [*A publication*] .... JMiH
Journal of Mississippi History [*A publication*] .... JMissH
Journal of Mississippi History [*A publication*] .... J Miss Hist
Journal of Mississippi History [*A publication*] .... Jour Miss Hist

Journal. Mississippi State Medical Association [*A publication*] ... J Mississippi Med Ass
Journal. Mississippi State Medical Association [*A publication*] ... J Miss State Med Assoc
Journal. Missouri Dental Association [*A publication*] ... J MO Dent Assoc
Journal of Modern African Studies [*A publication*] ... JMAS
Journal of Modern African Studies [*A publication*] ... J Mod Afric Stud
Journal of Modern African Studies [*A publication*] ... J Mod Afr S
Journal of Modern African Studies [*A publication*] ... J Mod Afr Stud
Journal of Modern History [*A publication*] ... JMH
Journal of Modern History [*A publication*] ... J Mod Hist
Journal of Modern History [*A publication*] ... Jnl Mod Hist
Journal of Modern History [*A publication*] ... Jour Mod Hist
Journal of Modern Literature [*A publication*] ... JML
Journal of Modern Literature [*A publication*] ... J Mod Lit
Journal of Molecular and Applied Genetics [*A publication*] ... JMAG
Journal of Molecular Biology [*A publication*] ... J Mol Biol
Journal of Molecular Catalysis [*A publication*] ... J Mol Catal
Journal of Molecular and Cellular Cardiology [*A publication*] ... J Mol Cel C
Journal of Molecular and Cellular Cardiology [*A publication*] ... J Mol Cell Cardiol
Journal of Molecular Evolution [*A publication*] ... J Mol Evol
Journal of Molecular Medicine [*A publication*] ... J Mol Med
Journal of Molecular Spectroscopy [*A publication*] ... J Mol Spect
Journal of Molecular Spectroscopy [*A publication*] ... J Mol Spectrosc
Journal of Molecular Structure [*A publication*] ... J Mol Struct
Journal of Molluscan Studies [*A publication*] ... J Molluscan Stud
Journal of Molluscan Studies. Supplement [*A publication*] ... J Molluscan Stud Suppl
Journal Mondial de Pharmacie [*A publication*] ... J Mond Pharm
Journal of Money, Credit, and Banking [*A publication*] ... J Money Cred Bank
Journal of Money, Credit, and Banking [*A publication*] ... J Money Credit & Banking
Journal of Moral Education [*A publication*] ... J Moral Ed
Journal of Moral Education [*A publication*] ... J Moral Educ
Journal of Morphology [*A publication*] ... J Morph
Journal of Morphology [*A publication*] ... J Morphol
Journal of Motor Behavior [*A publication*] ... J Mot Behav
Journal of Motor Behavior [*A publication*] ... J Motor Beh
Journal. Mount Sinai Hospital [*A publication*] ... J Mt Sinai Hosp
Journal of Multivariate Analysis [*A publication*] ... JMultiAn
Journal of Multivariate Analysis [*A publication*] ... J Multivar Anal
Journal of Muscle Research and Cell Motility [*A publication*] ... J Muscle Res Cell Motil
Journal. Music Academy (Madras) [*A publication*] ... JMAM
Journal of Music Theory [*A publication*] ... J Mus Theory
Journal of Music Theory [*A publication*] ... JMUTB
Journal of Music Therapy [*A publication*] ... JMT
Journal of Music Therapy [*A publication*] ... J Music Ther
Journal of Music Therapy [*A publication*] ... J Mus Therapy
Journal of Music Therapy [*A publication*] ... JMUTA
Journal Musical Francais [*A publication*] ... J Mus Francais
Journal of Musicology [*A publication*] ... Jl Musicology
Journal. Mysore Agricultural and Experimental Union [*A publication*] ... J Mysore Agr Exp Union
Journal. Mysore Medical Association [*A publication*] ... J Mysore Med Assoc
Journal. Mysore University. A. Arts [*A publication*] ... J Mysore U Arts
Journal. Nagari Pracarini Sabha [*A publication*] ... JNPS
Journal. Nagoya Medical Association [*A publication*] ... J Nagoya Med Assoc
Journal. Nara Medical Association [*A publication*] ... J Nara Med Assoc
Journal of Narrative Technique [*A publication*] ... JNT
Journal. National Academy of Administration [*India*] [*A publication*] ... JNAA
Journal. National Academy of Sciences [*Republic of Korea*] [*A publication*] ... J Natl Acad Sci
Journal of the National Academy of Sciences. Republic of Korea. Natural Sciences Series [*A publication*] ... J Natl Acad Sci Repub Korea Nat Sci Ser
Journal. National Agricultural Society of Ceylon [*A publication*] ... J Natl Agric Soc Ceylon
Journal. National Association of College Admissions Counselors [*A publication*] ... J Nat Assn Col Adm Counsel
Journal. National Association of College Admissions Counselors [*A publication*] ... J Natl Assn Coll Adm Counsel
Journal. National Association for Women Deans, Administrators, and Counselors [*A publication*] ... J Natl Assn Women Deans Adm & Counsel
Journal. National Association for Women Deans, Administrators, and Counselors [*A publication*] ... J NAWDAC
Journal. National Cancer Institute [*A publication*] ... J Nat Canc
Journal. National Cancer Institute [*A publication*] ... J Nat Cancer Inst
Journal. National Cancer Institute [*A publication*] ... J Natl Cancer Inst
Journal. National Cancer Institute [*A publication*] ... JNC
Journal. National Chiao Tung University [*A publication*] ... J Natl Chiao Tung Univ
Journal. National Institute of Agricultural Botany [*A publication*] ... J Natl Inst Agric Bot
Journal. National Institute of Hospital Administration [*A publication*] ... J Nat Inst Hospital Adm
Journal. National Institute for Personnel Research. South African Council for Scientific and Industrial Research [*A publication*] ... J Natl Inst Pers Res S Afr CSIR
Journal. National Institute of Social Sciences [*A publication*] ... J Nat Inst Soc Sci
Journal. National Intravenous Therapy Association [*A publication*] ... NITA
Journal. [*US*] **National Medical Association** [*A publication*] ... J Natl Med Assoc
Journal. National Research Council of Thailand [*A publication*] ... J Natl Res Counc Thail
Journal. National Research Council of Thailand [*A publication*] ... J Nat Res Coun Thai
Journal. National Science Council of Sri Lanka [*A publication*] ... J Natl Sci Counc Sri Lanka
Journal of Natural History [*A publication*] ... J Nat Hist
Journal of Natural History [*A publication*] ... J Natural Hist
Journal of Natural Products [*A publication*] ... J Nat Prod
Journal. Natural Science Research Institute. Yonsei University [*Republic of Korea*] [*A publication*] ... J Nat Sci Res Inst
Journal of Natural Sciences and Mathematics [*A publication*] ... J Natur Sci and Math
Journal of Natural Sciences and Mathematics (Lahore) [*A publication*] ... J Nat Sci Math (Lahore)
Journal of Navigation [*A publication*] ... J Navig
Journal of Near Eastern Studies [*A publication*] ... JNE
Journal of Near Eastern Studies [*A publication*] ... J Near Eastern Stud
Journal of Near Eastern Studies [*A publication*] ... J Near East Stud
Journal of Near Eastern Studies [*A publication*] ... J Near E St
Journal of Near Eastern Studies [*A publication*] ... JNES
Journal of Negro Education [*A publication*] ... JNE
Journal of Negro Education [*A publication*] ... JNEEA
Journal of Negro Education [*A publication*] ... J Negro Ed
Journal of Negro Education [*A publication*] ... J Negro Educ
Journal of Negro Education [*A publication*] ... Jnl Negro Ed
Journal of Negro History [*A publication*] ... J Negro Hist
Journal of Negro History [*A publication*] ... JNH
Journal of Negro History [*A publication*] ... Jnl Negro Hist
Journal of Nematology [*A publication*] ... J Nematol
Journal of Nervous and Mental Disease [*A publication*] ... J Nerv Ment
Journal of Nervous and Mental Disease [*A publication*] ... J Nerv Ment Dis
Journal of Nervous and Mental Disease [*A publication*] ... JNMD
Journal of Nervous and Mental Disease [*A publication*] ... JNMDA
Journal of Neural Transmission [*A publication*] ... J Neural Tr
Journal of Neural Transmission [*A publication*] ... J Neural Transm
Journal of Neural Transmission. Supplementum [*A publication*] ... J Neural Transm Suppl
Journal of Neuro-Visceral Relations [*A publication*] ... J Neuro-Visc Relat
Journal of Neurobiology [*A publication*] ... J Neurobiol
Journal of Neurochemistry [*A publication*] ... J Neurochem
Journal of Neurocytology [*A publication*] ... J Neurocyt
Journal of Neurocytology [*A publication*] ... J Neurocytol
Journal of the Neurological Sciences [*A publication*] ... J Neurol Sci
Journal of the Neurological Sciences [*A publication*] ... J Neur Sci
Journal of the Neurological Sciences [*A publication*] ... JNSCA
Journal of Neurology [*A publication*] ... J Neurol
Journal of Neurology (Berlin) [*A publication*] ... J Neurol (Berlin)
Journal of Neurology, Neurosurgery, and Psychiatry [*A publication*] ... J Ne Ne Psy
Journal of Neurology, Neurosurgery, and Psychiatry [*A publication*] ... J Neurol Neurosurg Psychiatry
Journal of Neurology, Neurosurgery, and Psychiatry [*A publication*] ... JNNPA
Journal of Neuropathology and Experimental Neurology [*A publication*] ... J Ne Exp Ne
Journal of Neuropathology and Experimental Neurology [*A publication*] ... J Neuropathol Exp Neurol
Journal of Neurophysiology [*A publication*] ... J Neurophysiol
Journal of Neurophysiology [*A publication*] ... J Neurphysl
Journal of Neurophysiology [*A publication*] ... JONEA
Journal of Neuropsychiatry [*A publication*] ... J Neuropsychiatry
Journal of Neuroradiology [*A publication*] ... J Neuroradiol
Journal of Neuroscience [*A publication*] ... JN
Journal of Neuroscience Methods [*A publication*] ... J Neurosci Methods
Journal of Neuroscience Research [*A publication*] ... J Neurosci Res
Journal of Neurosurgery [*A publication*] ... J Neurosurg
Journal of Neurosurgical Nursing [*A publication*] ... J Neurosurg Nurs
Journal of Neurosurgical Sciences [*A publication*] ... J Neurosurg Sci
Journal of the New African Literature and the Arts [*A publication*] ... JNALA
Journal of New Drugs [*A publication*] ... J New Drugs
Journal. New England Water Pollution Control Association [*A publication*] ... J NEngl Water Pollut Control Assoc
Journal. New England Water Works Association [*A publication*] ... J N Engl Water Works Assoc
Journal. New England Water Works Association [*A publication*] ... J New Engl Water Works Ass
Journal of New Jersey Poets [*A publication*] ... JnlONJP
Journal. New York Entomological Society [*A publication*] ... J NY Entomol Soc
Journal. New York Entomological Society [*A publication*] ... J NY Ent So
Journal. New Zealand Association of Bacteriologists [*A publication*] ... J NZ Assoc Bacteriol
Journal. New Zealand Institute of Medical Laboratory Technology [*A publication*] ... J NZ Inst Med Lab Technol

Journal-Newsletter. Association of Teachers of Japanese [*A publication*] ... JATJ
Journal. Nigerian Institute for Oil Palm Research [*A publication*] ... J Nigerian Inst Oil Palm Res
Journal. Nihon University School of Dentistry [*A publication*] ... J Nihon Univ Sch Dent
Journal of Non-Crystalline Solids [*A publication*] ... J Non-Cryst
Journal of Non-Crystalline Solids [*A publication*] ... J Non-Cryst Solids
Journal of Non-Destructive Inspection [*A publication*] ... J Non-Destr Insp
Journal of Non-Equilibrium Thermodynamics [*A publication*] ... J Non-Equilib Thermodyn
Journal of Non-Newtonian Fluid Mechanics [*A publication*] ... J Non-Newtonian Fluid Mech
Journal of Nonmetals [*A publication*] ... J Nonmet
Journal of Nonmetals and Semiconductors [*A publication*] ... J Nonmet Semicond
Journal. North China Branch. Royal Asiatic Society [*A publication*] ... J N Ch R A S
Journal of Northern Luzon [*A publication*] ... JNL
Journal of Northern Luzon [*A publication*] ... J No Luzon
Journal of Northwest Semitic Languages [*A publication*] ... J Nw SL
Journal of Nuclear Agriculture and Biology [*A publication*] ... J Nucl Agric Biol
Journal of Nuclear Biology and Medicine [*A publication*] ... J Nucl Biol
Journal of Nuclear Biology and Medicine [*A publication*] ... J Nucl Biol Med
Journal of Nuclear Energy [*A publication*] ... J Nucl Energy
Journal of Nuclear Materials [*A publication*] ... J Nucl Mat
Journal of Nuclear Materials [*A publication*] ... J Nucl Mater
Journal of Nuclear Medicine [*A publication*] ... J Nucl Med
Journal of Nuclear Medicine and Allied Sciences [*A publication*] ... J Nucl Med Allied Sci
Journal of Nuclear Medicine. Supplement [*A publication*] ... J Nucl Med Suppl
Journal of Nuclear Medicine Technology [*A publication*] ... J Nucl Med Technol
Journal of Nuclear Science and Technology [*A publication*] ... J Nucl Sci Technol
Journal of Nuclear Science and Technology [*A publication*] ... J Nuc Sci T
Journal of Nuclear Sciences (Seoul) [*A publication*] ... J Nucl Sci (Seoul)
Journal of Number Theory [*A publication*] ... J Number Th
Journal of Numismatic Fine Arts [*A publication*] ... JNFA
Journal. Numismatic Society of India [*A publication*] ... JNSI
Journal. Numismatic Society of Madhya Pradesh [*A publication*] ... JNSMP
Journal of Nurse Midwifery [*A publication*] ... J Nurse Midwife
Journal of Nursery Education [*A publication*] ... J Nurs Ed
Journal of Nursing Administration [*A publication*] ... J Nurs Adm
Journal of Nursing Care [*A publication*] ... J Nurs Care
Journal of Nursing Education [*A publication*] ... JNE
Journal of Nursing (Taipei) [*A publication*] ... J Nurs (Taipei)
Journal of Nutrition [*A publication*] ... J Nutr
Journal of Nutrition and Dietetics [*A publication*] ... J Nutr Diet
Journal of Nutrition Education [*A publication*] ... JNE
Journal of Nutrition Education [*A publication*] ... J Nutr Educ
Journal of Nutritional Science and Vitaminology [*A publication*] ... J Nutr Sci Vitaminol
Journal of Nutritional Science and Vitaminology [*A publication*] ... J Nutr Sc V
Journal of Nutritional Sciences [*A publication*] ... J Nutr Sci
Journal of Obstetrics and Gynaecology of the British Commonwealth [*A publication*] ... J Obstet Gynaec Brit Cmwlth
Journal of Obstetrics and Gynaecology of the British Commonwealth [*A publication*] ... J Obstet Gynaecol Br Commonw
Journal of Obstetrics and Gynaecology of the British Empire [*A publication*] ... J Obstet Gynaec Brit Emp
Journal of Obstetrics and Gynaecology of the British Empire [*A publication*] ... J Obstet Gynaecol Br Emp
Journal of Obstetrics and Gynaecology of India [*A publication*] ... J Obstet Gynaecol India
Journal of Occupational Accidents [*A publication*] ... J Occup Accid
Journal of Occupational Medicine [*A publication*] ... J Occupat Med
Journal of Occupational Medicine [*A publication*] ... J Occup Med
Journal of Occupational Medicine [*A publication*] ... JOCMA
Journal of Occupational Medicine [*A publication*] ... JOM
Journal of Occupational Psychology [*A publication*] ... J Occupa Psychol
Journal of Ocean Technology [*A publication*] ... J Ocean Technol
Journal. Oceanographical Society of Japan [*A publication*] ... J Oceanogr Soc Jpn
Journal. Oceanological Society of Korea [*A publication*] ... J Oceanol Soc Korea
Journal of Odor Control [*A publication*] ... J Odor Control
Journal. Office des Recherches sur les Pecheries du Canada [*A publication*] ... J Off Rech Pech Can
Journal Officiel de la Republique Francaise [*A publication*] ... J Off Repub Fr
Journal. Ohio Herpetological Society [*A publication*] ... J Ohio Herpetol Soc
Journal. Oil and Colour Chemists' Association [*A publication*] ... J Oil Col C
Journal. Oil and Colour Chemists' Association [*A publication*] ... J Oil Colour Chem Assoc
Journal. Operational Research Society [*A publication*] ... J Op Res Soc
Journal. Operations Research Society of Japan [*A publication*] ... J Oper Res Soc Jap
Journal. Operations Research Society of Japan [*A publication*] ... J Op Res So
Journal. Optical Society of America [*A publication*] ... J Opt Soc
Journal. Optical Society of America [*A publication*] ... J Opt Soc Am
Journal. Optical Society of America [*A publication*] ... JOSA
Journal. Optical Society of America [*A publication*] ... JOSAA
Journal of Optics [*A publication*] ... J Opt
Journal of Optimization Theory and Applications [*A publication*] ... J Optimization Theory Appl
Journal of Optimization Theory and Applications [*A publication*] ... J Optim Th
Journal of Optimization Theory and Applications [*A publication*] ... J Optim Theory Appl
Journal of Oral Implant and Transplant Surgery [*A publication*] ... J Oral Implant Transplant Surg
Journal of Oral Implantology [*A publication*] ... J Oral Implantol
Journal of Oral and Maxillofacial Surgery [*A publication*] ... JOMS
Journal of Oral Medicine [*A publication*] ... J Oral Med
Journal of Oral Pathology [*A publication*] ... J Oral Pathol
Journal of Oral Rehabilitation [*A publication*] ... J Oral Rehabil
Journal of Oral Surgery [*A publication*] ... J Oral Surg
Journal of Organic Chemistry [*A publication*] ... JOC
Journal of Organic Chemistry [*A publication*] ... J Org Chem
Journal of Organic Chemistry of the USSR [*A publication*] ... J Org Chem USSR
Journal of Organometallic Chemistry [*A publication*] ... J Organometal Chem
Journal of Organometallic Chemistry [*A publication*] ... J Organomet Chem
Journal of Organometallic Chemistry [*A publication*] ... J Orgmet Ch
Journal. Organometallic Chemistry Library [*A publication*] ... J Organomet Chem Libr
Journal. Oriental Institute (Baroda) [*A publication*] ... JOIB
Journal. Oriental Institute (Baroda) [*A publication*] ... J Orient Inst (Baroda)
Journal of Oriental Literature [*A publication*] ... JOL
Journal of Oriental Research [*A publication*] ... JOR
Journal. Oriental Society of Australia [*A publication*] ... J Or Soc Aust
Journal of Oriental Studies [*A publication*] ... J Or Stud
Journal of Oriental Studies [*A publication*] ... JOS
Journal fuer Ornithologie [*A publication*] ... J Ornithol
Journal of Orthomolecular Psychiatry [*A publication*] ... J Orthomol Psychiatry
Journal. Osaka City Medical Center [*A publication*] ... J Osaka City Med Cent
Journal. Osaka Dental University [*A publication*] ... J Osaka Dent Univ
Journal. Osaka Odontological Society [*A publication*] ... J Osaka Odontol Soc
Journal. Oslo City Hospital [*A publication*] ... J Oslo City Hosp
Journal. Oto-Laryngological Society of Australia [*A publication*] ... J Oto-Laryngol Soc Aust
Journal of Otolaryngology [*A publication*] ... J Otolaryngol
Journal of Otolaryngology of Japan [*A publication*] ... JOJAA
Journal of Otolaryngology. Supplement [*A publication*] ... J Otolaryngol Suppl
Journal. Otto Rank Association [*A publication*] ... J Otto Rank
Journal of Pacific History [*A publication*] ... Jour Pac Hist
Journal of Pacific History [*A publication*] ... J Pac Hist
Journal of Paint Technology [*A publication*] ... J Paint Tec
Journal de la Paix [*A publication*] ... J Paix
Journal. Pakistan Historical Society [*A publication*] ... J Pak Hist Soc
Journal. Pakistan Medical Association [*A publication*] ... J Pak Med Assoc
Journal of Paleontology [*A publication*] ... J Paleont
Journal of Paleontology [*A publication*] ... J Paleontol
Journal. Palestine Oriental Society [*A publication*] ... JPOS
Journal of Palestine Studies [*A publication*] ... J Pales Stu
Journal of Palestine Studies [*A publication*] ... J Palestine Stud
Journal of Palynology [*A publication*] ... Jour Palynology
Journal of Palynology [*A publication*] ... J Palynol
Journal of Parapsychology [*A publication*] ... J Parapsych
Journal of Parapsychology [*A publication*] ... J Parapsychol
Journal of Parasitology [*A publication*] ... J Parasitol
Journal of Parasitology [*A publication*] ... J Parasitology
Journal of Parenteral and Enteral Nutrition [*A publication*] ... JPEN
Journal of Parliamentary Information [*A publication*] ... J Parlia Info
Journal of Pastoral Care [*A publication*] ... J Past Care
Journal of Pastoral Care [*A publication*] ... J Pastoral Care
Journal of Pastoral Care [*A publication*] ... JPC
Journal of Pastoral Counseling [*A publication*] ... J Past Coun
Journal. Patent Office Society [*A publication*] ... J Pat Of So
Journal. Patent Office Society [*A publication*] ... J POS
Journal of Pathology [*A publication*] ... J Pathol
Journal of Pathology [*A publication*] ... J Pathology
Journal of Pathology and Bacteriology [*A publication*] ... J Path Bact
Journal of Pathology and Bacteriology [*A publication*] ... J Path and Bacteriol
Journal of Pathology and Bacteriology [*A publication*] ... J Pathol Bacteriol
Journal of Patient Account Management [*A publication*] ... J Patient Acc Manage
Journal of Peace Research [*A publication*] ... J Peace Res
Journal of Peace Science [*A publication*] ... J Peace Sci
Journal of Peasant Studies [*A publication*] ... J Peasant Stud
Journal of Peasant Studies [*A publication*] ... J Peas Stud

Journal of Pediatric Ophthalmology [A publication] ..... J Pediatr Ophthalmol
Journal of Pediatric Ophthalmology and Strabismus [A publication]..........................J Pediatr Ophthalmol Strabismus
Journal of Pediatric Psychology [A publication]....................J Pediat Psychol
Journal of Pediatric Surgery [A publication]............................J Pediatr Surg
Journal of Pediatric Surgery [A publication]..............................J Ped Surg
Journal of Pediatrics [A publication].....................................JOPDA
Journal of Pediatrics [A publication] .... J Pediat
Journal of Pediatrics [A publication] .... J Pediatr
Journal of Pedodontics [A publication] .... J Pedod
Journal of Perinatal Medicine [A publication] ....J Perinat Med
Journal of Periodontal Research [A publication] ....J Periodontal Res
Journal of Periodontal Research [A publication] ....J Period Re
Journal of Periodontal Research. Supplement [A publication]..........................J Periodontal Res Suppl
Journal of Periodontology [A publication].................................J Periodont
Journal of Periodontology [A publication]................................J Periodontol
Journal of Periodontology-Periodontics [A publication]..........................J Periodontol-Periodontics
Journal of Personality [A publication] ....JPer
Journal of Personality [A publication] .... JPers
Journal of Personality [A publication] .... J Personal
Journal of Personality Assessment [A publication] ....JNPAB
Journal of Personality Assessment [A publication]....................J Pers Asse
Journal of Personality and Social Psychology [A publication]....... J Pers Soc
Journal of Personality and Social Psychology [A publication].......................J Pers Soc Psychol
Journal of Personality and Social Psychology [A publication]...........JPSP
Journal of Personality and Social Psychology [A publication]............JPSPB
Journal of Personality and Social Systems [A publication]...............JPSS
Journal of Pesticide Science (Nihon Noyakugaku Kaishi) [A publication]..................J Pestic Sci (Nihon Noyakugaku Kaishi)
Journal of Petroleum Technology [A publication] .... J Petro Tec
Journal of Petroleum Technology [A publication] ....J Pet Tech
Journal of Petroleum Technology [A publication]....................J Pet Technol
Journal of Petroleum Technology [A publication] ....JPT
Journal of Petrology [A publication] ....J Petrol
Journal of Pharmaceutical Sciences [A publication]...................J Pharm Sci
Journal of Pharmaceutical Sciences [A publication].....................JPMSA
Journal of Pharmaceutical Sciences of the United Arab Republic [A publication]........................J Pharm Sci UAR
Journal. Pharmaceutical Society of Japan [A publication]..........................J Pharm Soc Jpn
Journal. Pharmaceutical Society of Korea [A publication]..........................J Pharm Soc Korea
Journal de Pharmacie de Belgique [A publication]...........J Pharm Belg
Journal de Pharmacie et des Sciences Accessoires (Paris) [A publication].......................J Pharm (Paris)
Journal of Pharmacokinetics and Biopharmaceutics [A publication]........................J Phar Biop
Journal of Pharmacokinetics and Biopharmaceutics [A publication]........................ J Pharmacokinet Biopharm
Journal de Pharmacologie [A publication] .... J Pharmacol
Journal de Pharmacologie Clinique [A publication] .... J Pharmacol Clin
Journal of Pharmacology and Experimental Therapeutics [A publication]........................J Pharmacol Exp Ther
Journal of Pharmacology and Experimental Therapeutics [A publication]........................J Pharm Exp
Journal of Pharmacy and Pharmacology [A publication] ....J Pharm Pha
Journal of Pharmacy and Pharmacology [A publication] ....J Pharm Pharmacol
Journal of Phenomenological Psychology [A publication]..........J Phenomen
Journal. Philippine Medical Association [A publication]........................J Philipp Med Assoc
Journal. Philippine Veterinary Medical Association [A publication] .... J Philipp Vet Med Assoc
Journal of Philology [A publication].. JP
Journal of Philosophical Logic [A publication] ....J Phil Log
Journal of Philosophical Logic [A publication] ....J Philos Lo
Journal of Philosophical Logic [A publication] ....JPL
Journal of Philosophy [A publication]..................................Jnl Philos
Journal of Philosophy [A publication]..................................Jour Philos
Journal of Philosophy [A publication]..JP
Journal of Philosophy [A publication].......................................JPh
Journal of Philosophy [A publication].......................................J Phil
Journal of Philosophy [A publication].......................................J Philos
Journal of the Philosophy of Sport [A publication].....................J Phil Sport
Journal of Phonetics [A publication]...JPh
Journal of Phonetics [A publication]..JPhon
Journal of Photochemistry [A publication]............................J Photochem
Journal of Photographic Science [A publication] .... J Photogr Sci
Journal of Photographic Science [A publication] .... J Phot Sci
Journal of Phycology [A publication]......................................J Phycol
Journal of Phycology [A publication]......................................J Phycology
Journal of Physical and Chemical Reference Data [A publication]......JPCRD
Journal of Physical and Chemical Reference Data [A publication].................J Ph Ch Ref Data
Journal of Physical and Chemical Reference Data [A publication].................J Phys & Chem Ref Data
Journal of Physical and Chemical Reference Data [A publication].................J Phys Chem Ref Data

Journal of Physical and Chemical Reference Data. Supplement [A publication].................... J Phys Chem Ref Data Suppl
Journal of Physical Chemistry [A publication]...................J Phys Chem
Journal of Physical Chemistry (Washington, DC) [A publication]........................J Phys Chem (Wash)
Journal of Physical and Colloid Chemistry [A publication]........................J Phys & Colloid Chem
Journal of Physical Education [A publication]..................J Phys Ed
Journal of Physical Education [A publication] ....J Phys Educ
Journal of Physical Education and Recreation [A publication]........................J Phys Educ & Rec
Journal of Physical Oceanography [A publication]..................J Phys Ocea
Journal. Physical Society of Japan [A publication]........................ J Phys Jap
Journal. Physical Society of Japan [A publication]................. J Phys Soc Jap
Journal of Physics. A: General Physics (London) [A publication]........................J Phys A (London)
Journal of Physics. A: Mathematical, Nuclear, and General [A publication]........................J Phys A Math Nucl Gen
Journal of Physics. A: Proceedings. Physical Society. General (London) [A publication] .... J Phys A (London) Proc Phys Soc Gen
Journal of Physics. B: Atomic and Molecular Physics [A publication]........................J Phys B
Journal of Physics. B: Atomic and Molecular Physics [A publication]........................ J of Phys B At Mol Phys
Journal of Physics. B: Atomic and Molecular Physics (London) [A publication]........................J Phys B (London)
Journal of Physics. C: Solid State Physics [A publication].................J Phys C
Journal of Physics. C: Solid State Physics (London) [A publication].......................... J Phys C (London)
Journal of Physics and Chemistry of Solids [A publication]........................J Phys Chem Sol
Journal of Physics and Chemistry of Solids [A publication]........................J Phys Chem Solids
Journal of Physics and Chemistry of Solids [A publication]........................J Phys Ch S
Journal of Physics. D: Applied Physics [A publication] .... J Phys D Appl Phys
Journal of Physics. D: Applied Physics (London) [A publication]........................J Phys D (London)
Journal of Physics. E: Scientific Instruments [A publication] ....J Phys E
Journal of Physics. E: Scientific Instruments [A publication]........................J Phys E Sci Instrum
Journal of Physics. E: Scientific Instruments [A publication] .... Sci Instrum
Journal of Physics. E: Scientific Instruments (London) [A publication]........................J Phys E (London) Sci Instrum
Journal of Physics of the Earth [A publication]..........................J Phys Earth
Journal of Physics. F: Metal Physics [A publication] ....J Phys F
Journal of Physics. G: Nuclear Physics [A publication]................J Phys G Nu
Journal. Physiological Society of Japan [A publication]...... J Physiol Soc Jpn
Journal de Physiologie [A publication].....................................JOPHA
Journal de Physiologie Experimentale et Pathologique [A publication]........................J Physiol Exper
Journal de Physiologie (Paris) [A publication].................... J Physiol (Paris)
Journal de Physiologie (Paris) [A publication]...........................J Physl (Par)
Journal de Physiologie et de Pathologie Generale [A publication]........................J Physiol et Path Gen
Journal of Physiology [A publication].....................................JPHYA
Journal of Physiology [A publication].................................... J Physiol
Journal of Physiology (London) [A publication].................J Physiol (Lond)
Journal of Physiology (London) [A publication]...........................J Physl (Lon)
Journal de Physique [A publication]......................................J Physique
Journal de Physique. Lettres [A publication] ....J Phys Lett
Journal de Physique. Lettres (Paris) [A publication]...........J Phys (Paris) Lett
Journal de Physique (Paris) [A publication].....................J Phys (Paris)
Journal de Physique (Paris). Colloque [A publication]........................J Phys (Paris) Colloq
Journal of Phytopathology (Berlin) [A publication]..........J Phytopathol (Berl)
Journal of Phytopathology (UAR) [A publication]..........J Phytopathol (UAR)
Journal. Pipeline Division. American Society of Civil Engineers [A publication]........................J Pipeline Div Am Soc Civ Eng
Journal of Pipelines [A publication] ....J Pipelines
Journal de la Planification du Developpement [A publication]........................J Planif Develop
Journal of Planning and Environment Law [A publication]........................J Plann Environ Law
Journal of Planning Law [A publication]....................................J P L
Journal of Plant Breeding [A publication] ....J Plant Breed
Journal of Plant Diseases and Protection [A publication].......J Plant Dis Prot
Journal of Plant Growth Regulation [A publication] ....JPGR
Journal of Plant Nutrition and Soil Science [A publication]........................J Plant Nutr Soil Sci
Journal of Plant Protection [A publication] ....J Plant Prot
Journal of Plantation Crops [A publication] ....J Platn Crops
Journal of Plasma Physics [A publication] ....J Plasma Ph
Journal of Plasma Physics [A publication] ....J Plasma Phys
Journal des Poetes (Brussels) [A publication]..............................JPB
Journal of Police Science and Administration [A publication]........................J Police Sci Adm
Journal of Police Science and Administration [A publication] ....J Polic Sci
Journal of Political Economy [A publication] ....Jnl Polit Econ
Journal of Political Economy [A publication] ....Jour Pol Econ
Journal of Political Economy [A publication] ....JPE
Journal of Political Economy [A publication] ....J Pol Econ

Journal of Political Economy [*A publication*] ... J Polit Ec

Journal of Political Economy [*A publication*] ... J Polit Econ

Journal of Political and Military Sociology [*A publication*] ... J Polit Mil

Journal of Political and Military Sociology [*A publication*] ... J Polit Milit Sociol

Journal of Political and Military Sociology [*A publication*] ... J Pol Mil Sociol

Journal of Political Studies [*A publication*] ... J Polit Stud

Journal of Political Studies [*A publication*] ... J Pol Stud

Journal of Politics [*A publication*] ... Jnl Politics

Journal of Politics [*A publication*] ... Jour Politics

Journal of Politics [*A publication*] ... JP

Journal of Politics [*A publication*] ... JPol

Journal of Politics [*A publication*] ... J Polit

Journal of Polymer Science [*A publication*] ... J Polym Sci

Journal of Polymer Science [*A publication*] ... JPS

Journal of Polymer Science. Macromolecular Reviews [*A publication*] ... J Polym Sci Macromol Rev

Journal of Polymer Science. Part A-1: Polymer Chemistry [*A publication*] ... J Polym Sci Part A-1: Polym Chem

Journal of Polymer Science. Part A-2: Polymer Physics [*A publication*] ... J Polym Sci Part A-2: Polym Phys

Journal of Polymer Science. Part B: Polymer Letters [*A publication*] ... J Polym Sci Part B: Polym Lett

Journal of Polymer Science. Part C: Polymer Symposia [*A publication*] ... J Pol Sci C

Journal of Polymer Science. Part C: Polymer Symposia [*A publication*] ... J Polym Sci Part C

Journal of Polymer Science. Part C: Polymer Symposia [*A publication*] ... J Polym Sci Part C: Polym Symp

Journal of Polymer Science. Part D: Macromolecular Reviews [*A publication*] ... J Polym Sci Part D

Journal of Polymer Science. Part D: Macromolecular Reviews [*A publication*] ... J Polym Sci Part D: Macromol Rev

Journal of Polymer Science. Polymer Chemistry Edition [*A publication*] ... J Pol Sc PC

Journal of Polymer Science. Polymer Chemistry Edition [*A publication*] ... J Polym Sci Polym Chem Ed

Journal of Polymer Science. Polymer Letters Edition [*A publication*] ... J Pol Sc PL

Journal of Polymer Science. Polymer Letters Edition [*A publication*] ... J Polym Sci Polym Lett Ed

Journal of Polymer Science. Polymer Physics Edition [*A publication*] ... J Pol Sc PP

Journal of Polymer Science. Polymer Physics Edition [*A publication*] ... J Polym Sci Polym Phys Ed

Journal of Polymer Science. Polymer Symposia [*A publication*] ... J Polym Sci Polym Symp

Journal. Polynesian Society [*A publication*] ... J Polynesia

Journal. Polynesian Society [*A publication*] ... J Polynes Soc

Journal. Polynesian Society [*A publication*] ... JPS

Journal of Pomology and Horticultural Science [*A publication*] ... J Pomology

Journal. Poona University [*A publication*] ... JPU

Journal of Popular Culture [*A publication*] ... JnlOPC

Journal of Popular Culture [*A publication*] ... JPC

Journal of Popular Culture [*A publication*] ... JPOCB

Journal of Popular Culture [*A publication*] ... J Pop Cul

Journal of Popular Culture [*A publication*] ... J Pop Cult

Journal of Popular Film [*Later, Journal of Popular Film and Television*] [*A publication*] ... JPF

Journal of Popular Film and Television [*A publication*] ... J Pop F & TV

Journal of Population Research [*A publication*] ... J Pop Res

Journal of Postgraduate Medicine (Bombay) [*A publication*] ... J Postgrad Med (Bombay)

Journal of Powder and Bulk Solids Technology [*A publication*] ... J Powder Bulk Solids Technol

Journal of Power Sources [*A publication*] ... J Power Sources

Journal of Practical Nursing [*A publication*] ... J Pract Nurs

Journal der Practischen Heilkunde [*A publication*] ... J Pract Heilk

Journal fuer Praktische Chemie [*A publication*] ... J Prak Chem

Journal fuer Praktische Chemie [*A publication*] ... J Prakt Chem

Journal of Pre-Medical Course. Sapporo Medical College [*A publication*] ... J Pre-Med Course Sapporo Med Coll

Journal. Presbyterian Historical Society [*A publication*] ... JPHS

Journal of Presbyterian History [*A publication*] ... Jour Presby Hist

Journal of Presbyterian History [*A publication*] ... JPH

Journal of Presbyterian History [*A publication*] ... J Pres H

Journal of Pressure Vessel Technology [*A publication*] ... J Pressure Vessel Technol

Journal of Pressure Vessel Technology. Transaction. ASME [*American Society of Mechanical Engineers*] [*A publication*] ... J Pressure Vessel Technol Trans ASME

Journal. Prestressed Concrete Institute [*A publication*] ... J Pre Concr

Journal. Prestressed Concrete Institute [*A publication*] ... J Prestressed Concr Inst

Journal of Preventive Dentistry [*A publication*] ... J Prev Dent

Journal. Printing Historical Society [*A publication*] ... J Print Hist Soc

Journal and Proceedings. Institute of Road Transport Engineers [*A publication*] ... J Proc Inst Rd Transp Engrs

Journal and Proceedings. Institute of Sewage Purification [*A publication*] ... J Proc Inst Sewage Purif

Journal and Proceedings. Royal Society of New South Wales [*A publication*] ... J Proc Roy Soc NSW

Journal and Proceedings. Royal Society of New South Wales [*A publication*] ... J Proc R Soc NSW

Journal of Products Liability [*A publication*] ... J Prod Liability

Journal of Projective Techniques [*A publication*] ... JPTEA

Journal of Projective Techniques and Personality Assessment [*A publication*] ... J Project Techniques

Journal of Property Management [*A publication*] ... J Prop Mgt

Journal of Prosthetic Dentistry [*A publication*] ... JPDEA

Journal of Prosthetic Dentistry [*A publication*] ... J Pros Dent

Journal of Prosthetic Dentistry [*A publication*] ... J Prosthet Dent

Journal of Protozoology [*A publication*] ... J Protozool

Journal of Psychedelic Drugs [*A publication*] ... J Psychedel Drugs

Journal of Psychedelic Drugs [*A publication*] ... J Psychedelic Drugs

Journal of Psychiatric Nursing and Mental Health Services [*A publication*] ... JPNNB

Journal of Psychiatric Nursing and Mental Health Services [*A publication*] ... J Psychiatr Nurs

Journal of Psychiatric Research [*A publication*] ... J Psychiatr Res

Journal of Psychiatric Research [*A publication*] ... J Psych Res

Journal of Psychiatry and Law [*A publication*] ... J Psych Law

Journal of Psychohistory [*A publication*] ... J Psychohist

Journal of Psycholinguistic Research [*A publication*] ... JPR

Journal of Psycholinguistic Research [*A publication*] ... JPRLB

Journal of Psycholinguistic Research [*A publication*] ... J Psycholin

Journal of Psycholinguistic Research [*A publication*] ... J Psycholing Res

Journal of Psycholinguistic Research [*A publication*] ... J Psycholinguist Res

Journal of Psycholinguistic Research [*A publication*] ... JPsyR

Journal of Psychological Researches [*A publication*] ... JPSRB

Journal of Psychological Researches [*A publication*] ... J Psychol Res

Journal fuer Psychologie und Neurologie [*A publication*] ... Jour f Psychol u Neurol

Journal fuer Psychologie und Neurologie [*A publication*] ... J Psychol u Neurol

Journal de Psychologie Normale et Pathologique [*A publication*] ... JP

Journal de Psychologie Normale et Pathologique [*A publication*] ... JPNP

Journal de Psychologie Normale et Pathologique [*A publication*] ... JPNPA

Journal de Psychologie Normale et Pathologique [*A publication*] ... JPsNP

Journal de Psychologie Normale et Pathologique [*A publication*] ... JPsych

Journal of Psychology [*A publication*] ... JOPSA

Journal of Psychology [*A publication*] ... JP

Journal of Psychology [*A publication*] ... JPs

Journal of Psychology [*A publication*] ... JPsy

Journal of Psychology [*A publication*] ... J Psychol

Journal of Psychology of the Blind [*A publication*] ... JPSBA

Journal of Psychology and Theology [*A publication*] ... J Psych Th

Journal of Psychology and Theology [*A publication*] ... JPT

Journal of Psychosocial Nursing and Mental Health Services [*A publication*] ... J Psychosoc Nurs

Journal of Psychosomatic Research [*A publication*] ... J Psychosom

Journal of Psychosomatic Research [*A publication*] ... J Psychosom Res

Journal of Public Economics [*A publication*] ... J Publ Econ

Journal of Public Health Dentistry [*A publication*] ... J Public Health Dent

Journal of Public Health and Medical Technology. Korea University [*A publication*] ... J Public Health Med Technol Korea Univ

Journal of Public Health Policy [*A publication*] ... J Public Health Policy

Journal of Public Law [*A publication*] ... Jour Pub Law

Journal of Public Law [*A publication*] ... J Pub L

Journal of Purchasing [*Later, Journal of Purchasing and Materials Management*] [*A publication*] ... J Purch

Journal of Purchasing and Materials Management [*A publication*] ... J Purchasing & Materials Mgt

Journal of Pure and Applied Algebra [*A publication*] ... J Pure Appl Algebra

Journal. Pusan Medical College [*A publication*] ... J Pusan Med Coll

Journal of Quality Technology [*A publication*] ... JQT

Journal of Quality Technology [*A publication*] ... J Quality Tech

Journal of Quality Technology [*A publication*] ... J Qual Tech

Journal of Quality Technology [*A publication*] ... J Qual Technol

Journal of Quantitative Spectroscopy and Radiative Transfer [*A publication*] ... J Quan Spec

Journal of Quantitative Spectroscopy and Radiative Transfer [*A publication*] ... J Quant Spectrosc Radiat Transfer

Journal of Quantum Electronics [*A publication*] ... JQE

Journal of Quantum Electronics [*A publication*] ... QE

Journal of Race Development [*A publication*] ... J Race Dev

Journal of Radiation Curing [*A publication*] ... J Radiat Curing

Journal of Radiation Research [*A publication*] ... J Radiat Res

Journal of Radiation Research (Tokyo) [*A publication*] ... J Radiat Res (Tokyo)

Journal. Radio Research Laboratories [*Japan*] [*A publication*] ... J Radio Res Lab

Journal. Radio Research Laboratories [*Japan*] [*A publication*] ... J Rad Res L

Journal of Radioanalytical Chemistry [*A publication*] ... J Rad Chem

Journal of Radioanalytical Chemistry [*A publication*] ... J Radioanal Chem

Journal de Radiologie [*A publication*] ... J Radiol

Journal de Radiologie et d'Electrologie [*A publication*] ... J Radiol Electrol

Journal de Radiologie, d'Electrologie, et de Medecine Nucleaire [*Later, Journal de Radiologie*] [*A publication*] ... J Radiol Electrol Med Nucl

Journal of Radiology and Physical Therapy. University of Kanazawa [*A publication*] J Radiol Phys Ther Univ Kanazawa
Journal. Rajasthan Institute of Historical Research [*A publication*] J Raj Inst Hist Res
Journal of Raman Spectroscopy [*A publication*] J Raman Sp
Journal of Range Management [*A publication*] J Range Man
Journal of Range Management [*A publication*] J Range Manage
Journal of Range Management [*A publication*] J Range Mgt
Journal of Reading [*A publication*] J Read
Journal of Reading Behavior [*A publication*] J Read Beh
Journal of Real Estate Taxation [*A publication*] Jrl RE Tax
Journal de Recherche Oceanographique [*A publication*] J Rech Oceanogr
Journal of Recreational Mathematics [*A publication*] J Recreational Math
Journal of Refrigeration [*A publication*] J Refrig
Journal. Regional Cultural Institute [*A publication*] JRCI
Journal of Regional Science [*A publication*] J Region Sci
Journal of Regional Science [*A publication*] J Reg Sci
Journal of Regional Science [*A publication*] JRS
Journal of Rehabilitation [*A publication*] JOREA
Journal of Rehabilitation [*A publication*] J Rehabil
Journal of Rehabilitation in Asia [*A publication*] J Rehabil Asia
Journal of Rehabilitation of the Deaf [*A publication*] J Rehabil D
Journal fuer die Reine und Angewandte Mathematik [*A publication*] J Reine Angew Math
Journal fuer die Reine und Angewandte Mathematik [*A publication*] J Rein Math
Journal of Religion [*A publication*] Jnl Relig
Journal of Religion [*A publication*] Jour of Relig
Journal of Religion [*A publication*] JR
Journal of Religion [*A publication*] J Rel
Journal of Religion [*A publication*] J Relig
Journal of Religion in Africa [*A publication*] J Rel Africa
Journal of Religion in Africa [*A publication*] J Relig Afr
Journal of Religion and Health [*A publication*] J Rel Health
Journal of Religious Ethics [*A publication*] J Rel Ethics
Journal of Religious Ethics [*A publication*] J Relig Ethics
Journal of Religious History [*A publication*] Jour Relig Hist
Journal of Religious History [*A publication*] J Rel H
Journal of Religious History [*A publication*] JRH
Journal of Religious Studies [*A publication*] J Re S
Journal of Religious Thought [*A publication*] J Rel Thot
Journal of Religious Thought [*A publication*] JRT
Journal of Religious Thought [*A publication*] J R Th
Journal of Remote Sensing [*A publication*] J Remote Sensing
Journal of the Remount and Veterinary Corps [*A publication*] J Remount Vet Corps
Journal of Renaissance and Baroque Music [*A publication*] JRBM
Journal of Renaissance and Baroque Music [*A publication*] J Ren & Bar Mus
Journal of Reproduction and Fertility [*A publication*] J Reprd & Fert
Journal of Reproduction and Fertility [*A publication*] J Repr Fert
Journal of Reproduction and Fertility [*A publication*] J Reprod Fertil
Journal of Reproduction and Fertility [*A publication*] JRPFA
Journal of Reproduction and Fertility. Supplement [*A publication*] J Reprod Fertil Suppl
Journal of Reproductive Medicine [*A publication*] J Reprod Med
Journal of Reproductive Medicine. Lying-In [*A publication*] J Reprod Med Lying-In
Journal of Research in Crime and Delinquency [*A publication*] J Res Crime
Journal of Research and Development in Education [*A publication*] J Res Dev E
Journal of Research and Development in Education [*A publication*] J Res & Devel Educ
Journal of Research and Development in Education [*A publication*] J Res Develop Educ
Journal of Research in Indian Medicine [*A publication*] J Res Indian Med
Journal. Research Institute for Catalysis. Hokkaido University [*A publication*] J Res Inst Catal Hokkaido Univ
Journal of Research on the Lepidoptera [*A publication*] J Res Lepid
Journal for Research in Mathematics Education [*A publication*] J Res Math Educ
Journal of Research in Music Education [*A publication*] Jl of Research
Journal of Research in Music Education [*A publication*] J Res Mus Ed
Journal of Research in Music Education [*A publication*] J Res Music
Journal of Research in Music Education [*A publication*] J Res Music Educ
Journal of Research in Music Education [*A publication*] JRME
Journal of Research in Music Education [*A publication*] JRMEA
Journal of Research. [*US*] **National Bureau of Standards** [*A publication*] J Res Nat Bur Stand
Journal of Research. [*US*] **National Bureau of Standards. A. Physics and Chemistry** [*A publication*] J Res Natl Bur Stand A
Journal of Research. [*US*] **National Bureau of Standards. A. Physics and Chemistry** [*A publication*] J Res NBS A
Journal of Research. [*US*] **National Bureau of Standards. B. Mathematical Sciences** [*A publication*] J Res NBS B
Journal of Research. [*US*] **National Bureau of Standards. B. Mathematics and Mathematical Physics** [*A publication*] J Res Natl Bur Stand B
Journal of Research. [*US*] **National Bureau of Standards. C. Engineering and Instrumentation** [*A publication*] J Res Natl Bur Stand C
Journal of Research. [*US*] **National Bureau of Standards (United States)** [*A publication*] J Res Natl Bur Stand (US)
Journal of Research in Personality [*A publication*] J Res Pers
Journal of Research. Punjab Agricultural University [*A publication*] J Res Punjab Agric Univ
Journal of Research. Punjab Agricultural University [*A publication*] J Res Punjab Agr Univ
Journal of Research. Science. Agra University [*A publication*] J Res Sci Agra Univ
Journal of Research in Science Teaching [*A publication*] J Res Sci Teach
Journal of Research. United States Geological Survey [*A publication*] J Res US Geol Surv
Journal of Research. United States Geological Survey [*A publication*] J Res US G S
Journal of Retailing [*A publication*] J Retail
Journal of Retailing [*A publication*] J Retailing
Journal. Reticuloendothelial Society [*A publication*] J Retic Soc
Journal. Reticuloendothelial Society [*A publication*] J Reticuloendothel Soc
Journal of Rheumatology [*A publication*] J Rheumatol
Journal. Rio Grande Valley Horticulture Society [*A publication*] J Rio Grande Val Hortic Soc
Journal of Risk and Insurance [*A publication*] JRI
Journal of Risk and Insurance [*A publication*] J Risk Ins
Journal of Risk and Insurance [*A publication*] J Risk & Insur
Journal of Roman Studies [*A publication*] J Roman Stud
Journal of Roman Studies [*A publication*] J Rom S
Journal of Roman Studies [*A publication*] J Rom Stud
Journal of Roman Studies [*A publication*] JRS
Journal of Root Crops [*A publication*] J Root Crops
Journal. Rossica Society of Russian Philately [*A publication*] J Rossica Soc
Journal. Royal Agricultural Society [*A publication*] J R Agric Soc
Journal. Royal Agricultural Society of England [*A publication*] Jl R Agric Soc
Journal. Royal Agricultural Society of England [*A publication*] J Roy Agr S
Journal. Royal Anthropological Institute of Great Britain and Ireland [*A publication*] JAI
Journal. Royal Anthropological Institute of Great Britain and Ireland [*A publication*] JAIB
Journal. Royal Anthropological Institute of Great Britain and Ireland [*A publication*] JAnthrI
Journal. Royal Anthropological Institute of Great Britain and Ireland [*A publication*] JRAI
Journal. Royal Anthropological Institute of Great Britain and Ireland [*A publication*] J R Anthropol Inst GB Irel
Journal. Royal Army Medical Corps [*A publication*] J R Army Med Corps
Journal. Royal Asiatic Society [*A publication*] J Roy Asiatic Soc
Journal. Royal Asiatic Society [*A publication*] J Roy Asiat Soc
Journal. Royal Asiatic Society of Bengal [*A publication*] JRASBengal
Journal. Royal Asiatic Society. Bombay Branch [*A publication*] JRASBB
Journal. Royal Asiatic Society. Ceylon Branch [*A publication*] JRASCB
Journal. Royal Asiatic Society of Great Britain and Ireland [*A publication*] JRAS
Journal. Royal Asiatic Society. Hong Kong Branch [*A publication*] JRASHKB
Journal. Royal Asiatic Society. Malayan Branch [*A publication*] JRASM
Journal. Royal Asiatic Society. Malayan Branch [*A publication*] JRASMB
Journal. Royal Astronomical Society of Canada [*A publication*] J Roy Astro
Journal. Royal Central Asian Society [*A publication*] JRCAS
Journal. Royal College of General Practitioners [*A publication*] J R Coll Gen Pract
Journal. Royal College of General Practitioners. Occasional Paper [*A publication*] J R Coll Gen Pract Occas Pap
Journal. Royal College of Physicians of London [*A publication*] J R Coll Physicians Lond
Journal. Royal College of Surgeons of Edinburgh [*A publication*] J R Coll Surg Edinb
Journal. Royal College of Surgeons in Ireland [*A publication*] J R Coll Surg Irel
Journal. Royal Horticultural Society [*A publication*] J R Hortic Soc
Journal. Royal Institute of British Architects [*A publication*] JRBA-A
Journal. Royal Institute of British Architects [*A publication*] J R Inst Br Archit
Journal. Royal Institute of Public Health and Hygiene [*A publication*] J R Inst Public Health Hyg
Journal. Royal Meteorological Society [*A publication*] JRMS
Journal. Royal Microscopical Society [*A publication*] J R Microsc Soc
Journal. Royal Microscopical Society [*A publication*] J Roy Micr Soc
Journal. Royal Naval Medical Service [*A publication*] J R Nav Med Serv
Journal. Royal Society of Antiquaries of Ireland [*A publication*] Journal Soc Antiq
Journal. Royal Society of Antiquaries of Ireland [*A publication*] JRSAI
Journal. Royal Society of Antiquaries of Ireland [*A publication*] JRSAntI
Journal. Royal Society of Arts [*A publication*] Jl R Soc Arts
Journal. Royal Society of Health [*A publication*] J R Soc Hlth
Journal. Royal Society of Medicine [*A publication*] J R Soc Med

Journal. Royal Society of New Zealand [*A publication*] .... J RSNZ
Journal. Royal Society of New Zealand [*A publication*] .... J R Soc NZ
Journal. Royal Society of Western Australia [*A publication*] .... J R Soc West Aust
Journal. Royal Statistical Society [*A publication*] .... J Roy Statis
Journal. Royal Statistical Society [*A publication*] .... JRSS
Journal. Royal Statistical Society. Series A. General [*A publication*] .... J Roy Sta A
Journal. Royal Statistical Society. Series B. Methodological [*A publication*] .... J Roy Sta B
Journal. Royal Statistical Society. Series C. Applied Statistics [*A publication*] .... J Roy Sta C
Journal. Royal Television Society [*A publication*] .... JR Telev Soc
Journal. Rubber Research Institute of Malaysia [*A publication*] .... J Rubber Res Inst Malays
Journal of Rural Cooperation [*A publication*] .... J Rur Coop
Journal of Rural Education [*A publication*] .... J Rural Educ
Journal of Russian Studies [*A publication*] .... JRS
Journal of Russian Studies [*A publication*] .... JRuS
Journal. Rutgers University Library [*A publication*] .... JRUL
Journal of Safety Research [*A publication*] .... J Safe Res
Journal of Safety Research [*A publication*] .... J Saf Res
Journal. Sanitary Engineering Division. Proceedings. American Society of Civil Engineers [*A publication*] .... J Sanit Eng Div Proc Am Soc Civ Eng
Journal des Savants [*A publication*] .... JdS
Journal des Savants [*A publication*] .... JS
Journal des Savants [*A publication*] .... JSav
Journal des Savants [*A publication*] .... J Savants
Journal of School Health [*A publication*] .... J Sch Healt
Journal of School Health [*A publication*] .... J Sch Health
Journal of School Health [*A publication*] .... JSHEA
Journal. School of Languages [*A publication*] .... JSL
Journal of School Psychology [*A publication*] .... J Sch Psych
Journal of School Psychology [*A publication*] .... J Sch Psychol
Journal of Science [*A publication*] .... J Sci
Journal of the Science Club [*A publication*] .... J Sci Club
Journal of Science. College of General Education. University of Tokushima [*A publication*] .... J Sci Coll Gen Educ Univ Tokushima
Journal of Science Education (Jeonju) [*A publication*] .... J Sci Educ (Jeonju)
Journal of Science Education. Science Education Research Institute Teacher's College. Kyungpook University [*A publication*] ...... J Sci Educ Sci Educ Res Inst Teach Coll Kyungpook Univ
Journal of the Science of Food and Agriculture [*A publication*] .... J Sci Fd Agric
Journal of the Science of Food and Agriculture [*A publication*] .... J Sci Food
Journal of the Science of Food and Agriculture [*A publication*] .... J Sci Food Agr
Journal of the Science of Food and Agriculture [*A publication*] .... J Sci Food Agric
Journal of the Science of Food and Agriculture [*A publication*] .... JSFA
Journal of the Science of Food and Agriculture. Abstracts [*A publication*] .... J Sci Food Agric Abstr
Journal of Science. Hiroshima University [*A publication*] .... J Sci Hiroshima Univ
Journal of Science. Hiroshima University. Series A-II [*A publication*] .... J Sci Hiroshima Univ Ser A-II
Journal of Science. Hiroshima University. Series A. Physics and Chemistry [*A publication*] .... J Sci Hiroshima Univ Ser A
Journal of Science. Hiroshima University. Series B. Division 1. Zoology [*A publication*] .... J Sc Hiroshima Univ S B Div 1 Zool
Journal of Science. Hiroshima University. Series B. Division 1. Zoology [*A publication*] .... J Sci Hiroshima Univ Ser B Div 1 Zool
Journal of Science. Hiroshima University. Series B. Division 2. Botany [*A publication*] .... J Sci Hiroshima Univ Ser B Div 2 Bot
Journal of Science (Karachi) [*A publication*] .... J Sci (Karachi)
Journal. Science Society of Thailand [*A publication*] .... J Sci Soc Thailand
Journal of the Science of Soil and Manure (Japan) [*A publication*] .... J Sci Soil Manure (Jap)
Journal of Science and Technology [*A publication*] .... J Sci Tech
Journal of Science and Technology [*A publication*] .... J Sci and Technol
Journal of Science and Technology (London) [*A publication*] .... J Sci Technol (London)
Journal des Sciences Medicales de Lille [*A publication*] .... J Sci Med Lille
Journal des Sciences de la Nutrition [*A publication*] .... J Sci Nutr
Journal for Scientific Agricultural Research [*A publication*] .... J Sci Agr Res
Journal. Scientific Agricultural Society of Finland [*A publication*] .... J Sci Agric Soc Finl
Journal of Scientific and Industrial Research [*A publication*] .... J Scient Ind Res
Journal of Scientific and Industrial Research [*A publication*] .... J Sci Ind R
Journal of Scientific and Industrial Research [*A publication*] .... J Sci Ind Res
Journal of Scientific and Industrial Research (India) [*A publication*] .... J Sci Ind Res (India)
Journal of Scientific and Industrial Research. Section B [*A publication*] .... J Sci Ind Res Sect B
Journal of Scientific Instruments [*A publication*] .... J Scient Instrum
Journal of Scientific Instruments [*A publication*] .... J Sci Instr
Journal of Scientific Instruments [*A publication*] .... J Sci Instrum
Journal. Scientific Laboratories. Denison University [*A publication*] .... J Sci Lab D
Journal. Scientific Laboratories. Denison University [*A publication*] .... J Sci Lab Denison Univ
Journal of Scientific Research. Banaras Hindu University [*A publication*] .... J Sci Res Banaras Hindu Univ
Journal of Scientific Research (Bhopal) [*A publication*] .... J Sci Res (Bhopal)
Journal of Scientific Research (Hardwar) [*A publication*] .... J Sci Res (Hardwar)
Journal of Scientific Research (Indonesia) [*A publication*] .... J Sci Res (Indones)
Journal for the Scientific Study of Religion [*A publication*] .... J Scient Stud Relig
Journal for the Scientific Study of Religion [*A publication*] .... J Sci St Re
Journal for the Scientific Study of Religion [*A publication*] .... J Sci Stud Rel
Journal for the Scientific Study of Religion [*A publication*] .... J Sci Stud Relig
Journal for the Scientific Study of Religion [*A publication*] .... JSSR
Journal for the Scientific Study of Religion [*A publication*] .... JSSRel
Journal of Secondary Education [*A publication*] .... J Sec Ed
Journal of Sedimentary Petrology [*A publication*] .... J Sediment Petrol
Journal of Sedimentary Petrology [*A publication*] .... J Sed Petrol
Journal of Seed Technology [*A publication*] .... J Seed Technol
Journal of Semitic Studies [*A publication*] .... J Sem St
Journal of Semitic Studies [*A publication*] .... JSS
Journal. Seoul Woman's College [*A publication*] .... J Seoul Woman's Coll
Journal of Sericultural Science of Japan [*A publication*] .... J Seric Sci Jpn
Journal of Sex and Marital Therapy [*A publication*] .... J Sex Marital Ther
Journal of Sex Research [*A publication*] .... J Sex Res
Journal. Sheffield University Metallurgical Society [*A publication*] .... J Sheffield Univ Met Soc
Journal. Shimonoseki College of Fisheries [*A publication*] .... J Shimonoseki Coll Fish
Journal. Shimonoseki University of Fisheries [*A publication*] .... J Shimonoseki Univ Fish
Journal of Ship Research [*A publication*] .... J Ship Res
Journal. Shivaji University [*A publication*] .... J Shivaji Univ
Journal. Siam Society [*A publication*] .... J Siam Soc
Journal. Siam Society [*Bangkok*] [*A publication*] .... JSS
Journal. Siam Society (Bangkok) [*A publication*] .... JSSB
Journal of Small Animal Practice [*A publication*] .... J Small Anim Pract
Journal of Small Animal Practice [*A publication*] .... J Sm Anim P
Journal of Small Business Management [*A publication*] .... J Small Bus Mgt
Journal. SMPTE [*Society of Motion Picture and Television Engineers*] [*A publication*] .... J SMPTE
Journal of Social Casework [*A publication*] .... J Social Casework
Journal of Social Forces [*A publication*] .... J Social Forces
Journal of Social History [*A publication*] .... Jour Soc Hist
Journal of Social History [*A publication*] .... J Soc Hist
Journal of Social Hygiene [*A publication*] .... J Soc Hygiene
Journal of Social Hygiene [*A publication*] .... J Social Hyg
Journal of Social Issues [*A publication*] .... Jour of Soc Issues
Journal of Social Issues [*A publication*] .... JSI
Journal of Social Issues [*A publication*] .... J Soc Iss
Journal of Social Issues [*A publication*] .... J Soc Issue
Journal of Social Philosophy [*A publication*] .... Jour Soc Philos
Journal of Social Philosophy [*A publication*] .... J Soc Phil
Journal of Social Policy [*A publication*] .... J Soc Pol
Journal of Social Policy [*A publication*] .... J Soc Polic
Journal of Social and Political Ideas in Japan [*A publication*] .... JSPIJ
Journal of Social Psychology [*A publication*] .... J Social Psychol
Journal of Social Psychology [*A publication*] .... J Soc Psych
Journal of Social Psychology [*A publication*] .... JSP
Journal of Social Psychology [*A publication*] .... JSPs
Journal of Social Psychology [*A publication*] .... JSPSA
Journal of Social Research [*A publication*] .... J Soc Res
Journal of Social Research [*A publication*] .... JSR
Journal of Social Sciences [*A publication*] .... Jour Soc Sci
Journal of Social Sciences [*A publication*] .... J Soc Sci
Journal of Social Sciences and Humanities [*A publication*] .... J Soc Sci Hum
Journal. Societe des Africanistes [*A publication*] .... JSAf
Journal. Societe des Africanistes [*A publication*] .... JSAfr
Journal. Societe des Africanistes [*A publication*] .... J Soc African
Journal. Societe des Americanistes [*A publication*] .... JSA
Journal. Societe des Americanistes [*A publication*] .... J Soc Amer
Journal. Societe des Americanistes de Paris [*A publication*] .... JSAm
Journal. Societe des Americanistes de Paris [*A publication*] .... JSAmP
Journal. Societe des Americanistes de Paris [*A publication*] .... JSAP
Journal. Societe Canadienne des Anesthesistes [*A publication*] .... J Soc Can Anesth
Journal. Societe Canadienne des Sciences Judiciaires [*A publication*] .... J Soc Can Sci Judiciaires
Journal. Societe Finno-Ougrienne [*A publication*] .... Journal Soc Finno-Ougr
Journal. Societe Finno-Ougrienne [*A publication*] .... JSFOu
Journal. Societe des Oceanistes [*A publication*] .... JSO
Journal. Societe des Oceanistes [*A publication*] .... JSOc
Journal. Societe des Oceanistes [*A publication*] .... J Soc Ocean
Journal. Societe Statistique de Paris [*A publication*] .... J Soc Statist Paris
Journal. Society of Archer-Antiquaries [*A publication*] .... J Soc Archer-Antiq
Journal. Society of Architectural Historians [*A publication*] .... Jour Society Archit Historians
Journal. Society of Architectural Historians [*A publication*] .... JSAH
Journal. Society of Arts [*A publication*] .... J Soc Arts

Journal. Society for the Bibliography of Natural History [*A publication*]...J Soc Bibliogr Nat Hist
Journal. Society of Brewing (Tokyo) [*A publication*].....J Soc Brew (Tokyo)
Journal. Society of Cosmetic Chemists [*A publication*]..............J S Cosm Ch
Journal. Society of Cosmetic Chemists [*A publication*]...J Soc Cosmet Chem
Journal. Society of Dairy Technology [*A publication*]...... J Soc Dairy Technol
Journal. Society of Dyers and Colourists [*A publication*]..............J S Dye Col
Journal. Society of Dyers and Colourists [*A publication*].......J Soc Dy Colour
Journal. Society of Engineers (London) [*A publication*] ...... J Soc Eng (Lond)
Journal. Society of Environmental Engineers [*A publication*] ....J Soc Env Engrs
Journal. Society of Environmental Engineers [*A publication*] ....J Soc Environ Eng
Journal. Society of Experimental Agriculturists [*A publication*] ....J Soc Exp Agric
Journal. Society of Industrial and Applied Mathematics [*A publication*]...JSIAM
Journal. Society for International Numismatics [*A publication*]..............JSIN
Journal. Society of Leather Technologists and Chemists [*A publication*]...........................J Soc Leath Technol Chem
Journal. Society of Leather Trades Chemists [*A publication*]..J Soc Leath Trades Chem
Journal. Society of Materials Science (Japan) [*A publication*]...J Soc Mater Sci (Jpn)
Journal. Society of Motion Picture and Television Engineers [*A publication*]........................ J Soc Motion Pict Telev Eng
Journal. Society of Occupational Medicine [*A publication*] ....J Soc Occup Med
Journal. Society of Oriental Research [*A publication*]............................JSOR
Journal. Society of Public Teachers of Law [*A publication*]...... J Soc Pub T L
Journal. Society of Public Teachers of Law. New Series [*A publication*].......................J Soc Pub Teach Law N S
Journal. Society for Radiological Protection [*A publication*] ....J Soc Radiol Prot
Journal. Society for the Study of State Governments [*Varanasi*] [*A publication*]...JSSSG
Journal. Soil Conservation Service (New South Wales) [*A publication*]..............................J Soil Conserv Serv (NSW)
Journal of Soil Science [*A publication*]..............................J Soil Sci
Journal of Soil Science of the United Arab Republic [*A publication*]........................... J Soil Sci UAR
Journal of Soil Science of the United Arab Republic [*A publication*]........................J Soil Sci Un Arab Repub
Journal of Soil and Water Conservation [*US*] [*A publication*] .... J Soil Wat
Journal of Soil and Water Conservation [*A publication*] ....J Soil & Water Conser
Journal of Soil and Water Conservation [*US*] [*A publication*] ....J Soil Water Conserv
Journal of Soil and Water Conservation in India [*A publication*] ....J Soil Water Conserv India
Journal. Solar Energy Society of Korea [*Republic of Korea*] [*A publication*]...................................J Sol Energy Soc Korea
Journal of Solid-Phase Biochemistry [*A publication*]..J Solid-Phase Biochem
Journal of Solid State Chemistry [*A publication*] ....J Solid State Chem
Journal of Solid State Chemistry [*A publication*] ....J Sol St Ch
Journal of Solid-State Circuits (IEEE) [*A publication*] .... JSSC
Journal of Solid Wastes [*A publication*].....................J Solid Wastes
Journal of Solution Chemistry [*A publication*]............................. J Sol Chem
Journal of Solution Chemistry [*A publication*] .... J Soln Chem
Journal of Solution Chemistry [*A publication*] .... J Solut Chem
Journal of Solution Chemistry [*A publication*] .... J Solution Chem
Journal of Sound and Vibration [*A publication*]..........................J Sound Vib
Journal of Sound and Vibration [*A publication*].........................JSVIA
Journal of South African Botany [*A publication*].................. J S Afr Bot
Journal of South African Botany. Supplementary Volume [*A publication*].....................................J S Afr Bot Suppl Vol
Journal. South African Chemical Institute [*A publication*]...........J SA Chem I
Journal. South African Forestry Association [*A publication*]..J SA For Assoc
Journal. South African Institute of Mining and Metallurgy [*A publication*]...................J S Afr Inst Mining Met
Journal. South African Institute of Mining and Metallurgy [*A publication*]......................... J SA I Min
Journal. South African Veterinary Association [*A publication*] ....J S Afr Vet Assoc
Journal. South African Veterinary Medical Association [*A publication*]........................ J S Afr Vet Med Assoc
Journal of South Asian Literature [*A publication*]........ J South Asian Lit
Journal of South Asian Literature [*A publication*]..................... J South As Lit
Journal. South Carolina Medical Association [*A publication*]..J SC Med Assoc
Journal of South-East Asia and the Far East [*A publication*]...........JSAFE
Journal of Southeast Asian History [*A publication*].............................. JSAH
Journal of Southeast Asian History [*A publication*]................ J SE Asian Hist
Journal of Southeast Asian Studies [*A publication*].............................. JSAS
Journal of Southeast Asian Studies [*A publication*]............J SE Asian Stud
Journal of Southeast Asian Studies [*A publication*] .... J SE Asia S
Journal of Southeast Asian Studies [*A publication*] ....J Se As Stud

Journal of Southeast Asian Studies [*A publication*]..J Southeast Asian Stud
Journal of Southern African Studies [*A publication*].............J South Afr Stud
Journal. Southern African Wildlife Management Association [*A publication*]....................J South Afr Wildl Manage Assoc
Journal of Southern History [*A publication*]..JSH
Journal of Southern History [*A publication*] .... J S Hist
Journal of Southern History [*A publication*] .... J So Hist
Journal of Southern History [*A publication*]...............................J Southern Hist
Journal of Southern History [*A publication*] .... J South His
Journal of Soviet Mathematics [*A publication*]......................... J Soviet Math
Journal of Space Law [*A publication*] ....J Space L
Journal of Space Law [*A publication*] .... J Space Law
Journal of Spacecraft and Rockets [*A publication*] .... J Spacecr Rockets
Journal of Spacecraft and Rockets [*A publication*] .... J Spac Rock
Journal of Spacecraft and Rockets [*A publication*] ....JSR
Journal of Spanish Studies. Twentieth Century [*A publication*]..............JSS
Journal of Spanish Studies. Twentieth Century [*A publication*].........JSSTC
Journal of Special Education [*A publication*] ....JSPEB
Journal of Special Education [*A publication*] .... J Spec Ed
Journal of Special Education [*A publication*] .... J Sp Educ
Journal for Special Educators [*A publication*] ....J Sp Educators
Journal for Special Educators of the Mentally Retarded [*Later, Journal for Special Educators*] [*A publication*]....... J Spec Ed Men Retard
Journal for Special Educators of the Mentally Retarded [*Later, Journal for Special Educators*] [*A publication*]....... J Sp Educ Men Retard
Journal of the Speculative Philosophy [*A publication*]...............J Spec Philos
Journal of Speech Disorders [*A publication*] ....Jour Speech Disorders
Journal of Speech and Hearing Disorders [*A publication*] .... JSHD
Journal of Speech and Hearing Disorders [*A publication*] ....JSHDA
Journal of Speech and Hearing Disorders [*A publication*] ....J Sp Disorders
Journal of Speech and Hearing Disorders [*A publication*] .... J Speech D
Journal of Speech and Hearing Disorders [*A publication*] ....J Speech & Hear Dis
Journal of Speech and Hearing Disorders [*A publication*] ....J Speech & Hear Disord
Journal of Speech and Hearing Disorders [*A publication*] ....J Speech Hear Disord
Journal of Speech and Hearing Research [*A publication*]..................... JSHR
Journal of Speech and Hearing Research [*A publication*]........... J Speech He
Journal of Speech and Hearing Research [*A publication*] ....J Speech & Hear Res
Journal of Speech and Hearing Research [*A publication*] ....J Speech Hear Res
Journal of Speech and Hearing Research [*A publication*]....................JSPHA
Journal of Sports Medicine and Physical Fitness [*A publication*] ....J Sports Med Phys Fitness
Journal of the Sports Turf Research Institute [*A publication*] ....J Sports Turf Res Inst
Journal of Starch Technology. Research Society of Japan [*A publication*]...................... J Starch Technol Res Soc Jpn
Journal of State Medicine [*A publication*] .... J St Med
Journal of Statistical Computation and Simulation [*A publication*]..............................J Stat Comput Simul
Journal of Statistical Physics [*A publication*] .... J Stat Phys
Journal of Statistical Planning Inference [*A publication*]..J Stat Plann Inference
Journal of Statistical Research [*A publication*]........................... J Statist Res
Journal of Statistical Research [*A publication*]........................J Stat Rsr
Journal. Statistical Society [*A publication*]................................. J Statis Soc
Journal of Steroid Biochemistry [*A publication*]................J Steroid B
Journal of Steroid Biochemistry [*A publication*]................J Steroid Biochem
Journal. Steward Anthropological Society [*A publication*] ....J Steward Anthropol Soc
Journal. Steward Anthropological Society [*A publication*] ....J Steward Anthro Soc
Journal of Stored Products Research [*A publication*] ....J Stored Pr
Journal of Stored Products Research [*A publication*] ....J Stored Prod Res
Journal of Strain Analysis [*A publication*] ....J Strain Anal
[*The*] Journal of Strain Analysis for Engineering Design [*A publication*]...JSAED
Journal of Strain Analysis for Engineering Design [*A publication*]..................J Strain Anal Eng Des
Journal of Structural Chemistry [*A publication*].....................................JSC
Journal of Structural Chemistry [*A publication*]...........................J Struct Ch
Journal of Structural Chemistry [*A publication*] .... J Struct Chem
Journal. Structural Division. ASCE [*American Society of Civil Engineers*] [*A publication*]...J Struct Di
Journal of Structural Learning [*A publication*]..............................J Struct Le
Journal of Structural Mechanics [*A publication*] .... J Struc Mec
Journal of Structural Mechanics [*A publication*] .... J Struct Mech
Journal of Studies on Alcohol [*A publication*] ....JSALO
Journal of Studies on Alcohol [*A publication*] .... J Stud Alc
Journal of Studies on Alcohol [*A publication*]............................. J Stud Alcohol
Journal of Studies on Alcohol (Supplement) [*A publication*] ....J Stud Alcohol (Suppl)
Journal for the Study of Judaism [*A publication*] .... J St Jud
Journal for the Study of the Old Testament [*A publication*].................. JSOT
Journal of Submicroscopic Cytology [*A publication*].................. J Submic Cy
Journal of Submicroscopic Cytology [*A publication*]........ J Submicrosc Cytol
Journal Suisse de Medecine [*A publication*]...........................J Suisse Med

Journal Supplement Abstract Service [*American Psychological Association*] .... JSAS
Journal of Supramolecular Structure [*A publication*] .... J Supramol Struct
Journal of Supramolecular Structure [*A publication*] .... J Supram St
Journal of Supramolecular Structure and Cellular Biochemistry [*A publication*] .... J Supramol Struct Cell Biochem
Journal of Supramolecular Structure (Supplement) [*A publication*] .... J Supramol Struct (Suppl)
Journal of Surgical Oncology [*A publication*] .... J Surg Oncol
Journal of Surgical Research [*A publication*] .... J Surg Res
Journal. Surveying and Mapping Division. ASCE [*American Society of Civil Engineers*] [*A publication*] .... J Surv Mapp
Journal of Symbolic Anthropology [*A publication*] .... J Symb Anthropol
Journal of Symbolic Logic [*A publication*] .... JSL
Journal of Symbolic Logic [*A publication*] .... J Symb Log
Journal of Symbolic Logic [*A publication*] .... J Symbolic Logic
Journal of Symbolic Logic [*A publication*] .... J Symbol Logic
Journal of Symbolic Logic [*A publication*] .... J Sym Log
Journal of Symbolic Logic. Quarterly [*A publication*] .... JSLQ
Journal of Synthetic Organic Chemistry (Japan) [*A publication*] .... J Syn Org J
Journal of Synthetic Organic Chemistry (Japan) [*A publication*] .... J Synth Org Chem (Jpn)
Journal of Systems Engineering [*A publication*] .... J Syst Eng
Journal of Systems Management [*A publication*] .... J Sys Mgmt
Journal of Systems Management [*A publication*] .... J Systems Mgt
Journal of Systems Management [*A publication*] .... J Syst Man
Journal of Taiwan Agricultural Research [*A publication*] .... J Taiwan Agric Res
Journal of Taiwan Agricultural Research [*A publication*] .... J Taiwan Agr Res
Journal. Takeda Research Laboratories [*A publication*] .... J Takeda Res Lab
Journal of Tamil Studies [*A publication*] .... J Tamil Stud
Journal of Tamil Studies [*A publication*] .... J Tam S
Journal of Taxation [*A publication*] .... J Taxation
Journal of Teacher Education [*A publication*] .... JTE
Journal of Teacher Education [*A publication*] .... J Teach Ed
Journal of Technical Writing and Communication [*A publication*] .... J Tech Writ Commun
Journal of Technology [*A publication*] .... J Technol
Journal of Technology. Bengal Engineering College [*A publication*] .... J Tech Bengal Engrg College
Journal of Technology and Engineering [*A publication*] .... J Technol Eng
Journal. Tennessee Academy of Science [*A publication*] .... J Tenn Acad Sci
Journal of Terramechanics [*A publication*] .... J Terramech
Journal of Testing and Evaluation [*A publication*] .... J Test Eval
Journal. Textile Institute [*A publication*] .... J Text Inst
Journal. Textile Machinery Society of Japan [*A publication*] .... J Text Mach Soc Jap
Journal of Texture Studies [*A publication*] .... J Texture Stud
Journal. Thailand Research Society [*A publication*] .... JTRS
Journal of Thanatology [*A publication*] .... J Thanatol
Journal of Theological Studies [*A publication*] .... JThS
Journal of Theological Studies [*A publication*] .... J Th St
Journal of Theological Studies [*A publication*] .... JTS
Journal of Theoretical Biology [*A publication*] .... J Theor Bio
Journal for the Theory of Social Behavior [*A publication*] .... J Theor Soc Behav
Journal for the Theory of Social Behavior [*A publication*] .... J T S Behav
Journal of Thermal Analysis [*A publication*] .... JTA
Journal of Thermal Analysis [*A publication*] .... J Therm Ana
Journal of Thermal Biology [*A publication*] .... J Therm Bio
Journal of Thoracic and Cardiovascular Surgery [*A publication*] .... J Thorac Cardiovasc Surg
Journal of Thoracic and Cardiovascular Surgery [*A publication*] .... J Thor Surg
Journal of Thoracic Surgery [*A publication*] .... J Thorac Surg
Journal of Thought [*A publication*] .... J Thought
Journal. Tokyo Dental College Society [*A publication*] .... J Tokyo Dent Coll Soc
Journal. Tokyo Medical College [*A publication*] .... J Tokyo Med Coll
Journal. Tokyo University of Fisheries [*A publication*] .... J Tokyo Univ Fish
Journal of Town Planning Institute [*A publication*] .... J Town Pl I
Journal of Toxicological Sciences [*A publication*] .... J Toxicol Sci
Journal of Toxicology and Environmental Health [*A publication*] .... J Tox Env H
Journal of Toxicology and Environmental Health [*A publication*] .... J Toxicol Environ Health
Journal of Transport Economics and Policy [*A publication*] .... J Transp Ec
Journal of Transport Economics and Policy [*A publication*] .... J Transport Econ Pol
Journal of Trauma [*A publication*] .... J Trauma
Journal of Tropical Geography [*A publication*] .... J Trop Geog
Journal of Tropical Medicine and Hygiene [*A publication*] .... J Trop Med
Journal of Tropical Medicine and Hygiene [*A publication*] .... J Trop Med Hyg
Journal of Tropical Medicine and Hygiene (London) [*A publication*] .... J Trop Med and Hyg (London)
Journal of Tropical Medicine (London) [*A publication*] .... J Trop Med (London)
Journal of Tropical Pediatrics [*A publication*] .... J Trop Pediatr
Journal of Tropical Pediatrics and African Child Health [*A publication*] .... J Trop Pediatr Afr Child Health
Journal of Tropical Pediatrics and Environmental Child Health [*A publication*] .... J Trop Pediatr
Journal of Tropical Pediatrics and Environmental Child Health [*A publication*] .... J Trop Pediatr Environ Child Health
Journal of Tropical Veterinary Science [*A publication*] .... J Trop Vet Sc
Journal of Turkish Phytopathology [*A publication*] .... J Turk Phytopathol
Journal of Typographic Research [*A publication*] .... JTR
Journal of Typographic Research [*A publication*] .... J Typogr Res
Journal of Ultrastructure Research [*A publication*] .... J Ultra Res
Journal of Ultrastructure Research [*A publication*] .... J Ultrastruct Res
Journal of Ultrastructure Research. Supplement [*A publication*] .... J Ultrastruct Res Suppl
Journal of Undergraduate Psychological Research [*A publication*] .... JUPOA
Journal. United Service Institution of India [*A publication*] .... JUSII
Journal. United States National Committee [*A publication*] .... JUSNC
Journal. University of Bombay [*A publication*] .... J Univ Bombay
Journal. University of Gauhati [*A publication*] .... J Univ Gauhati
Journal. University of Kuwait (Science) [*A publication*] .... J Univ Kuwait (Sci)
Journal. University of Poona. Science and Technology [*A publication*] .... J Univ Poona Sci Technol
Journal. University of Saugar [*A publication*] .... J Univ Saugar
Journal of University Studies [*A publication*] .... J Univ Stud
Journal of Urban Analysis [*A publication*] .... J Urban Anal
Journal of Urban Economics [*A publication*] .... J Urban Ec
Journal of Urban Economics [*A publication*] .... J Urban Econ
Journal of Urban Law [*A publication*] .... J Urban L
Journal. Urban Planning and Development Division. ASCE [*American Society of Civil Engineers*] [*A publication*] .... J Urban Pla
Journal d'Urologie et de Nephrologie [*A publication*] .... J Urol Neph
Journal d'Urologie et de Nephrologie [*A publication*] .... J Urol Nephrol
Journal of Urology [*A publication*] .... JUr
Journal of Urology [*A publication*] .... J Urol
Journal of Utilization of Agricultural Products [*A publication*] .... J Utiliz Agr Prod
Journal of Vacuum Science and Technology [*A publication*] .... J Vac Sci T
Journal of Vacuum Science and Technology [*A publication*] .... J Vac Sci Tech
Journal of Value Engineering [*A publication*] .... J Value Eng
Journal of Value Inquiry [*A publication*] .... J Value Inq
Journal of Verbal Learning and Verbal Behavior [*A publication*] .... J Verbal Learn
Journal of Verbal Learning and Verbal Behavior [*A publication*] .... J Verb Learn
Journal of Verbal Learning and Verbal Behavior [*A publication*] .... J Verb Learn Verb Behav
Journal of Verbal Learning and Verbal Behavior [*A publication*] .... JVLBA
Journal of Verbal Learning and Verbal Behavior [*A publication*] .... JVLVB
Journal of Vertebrate Paleontology [*A publication*] .... JVP
Journal des Veterinaires du Midi [*A publication*] .... J Vet Midi
Journal of Veterinary and Animal Husbandry Research (India) [*A publication*] .... J Vet Anim Husb Res (India)
Journal of Virological Methods [*A publication*] .... J Virol Methods
Journal of Virology [*A publication*] .... J Virol
Journal of Virology [*A publication*] .... J Virology
Journal of Vitaminology [*A publication*] .... J Vitaminol
Journal of Vitaminology (Kyoto) [*A publication*] .... J Vitaminol (Kyoto)
Journal of Vocational Behavior [*A publication*] .... J Vocat Beh
Journal of Vocational Behavior [*A publication*] .... J Voc Behav
Journal of Volcanology and Geothermal Research [*A publication*] .... J Volcanol Geotherm Res
Journal of Voluntary Action Research [*A publication*] .... J Volun Act
Journal Voucher [*Accounting*] .... JV
Journal. Wakayama Medical Society [*A publication*] .... J Wakayama Med Soc
Journal. Walters Art Gallery [*A publication*] .... JWAG
Journal. Walters Art Gallery [*A publication*] .... JWalt
Journal. Warburg and Courtauld Institute [*A publication*] .... JWarb
Journal. Warburg and Courtauld Institute [*A publication*] .... J Warburg and Courtauld Inst
Journal. Warburg and Courtauld Institute [*A publication*] .... J Warburg & Courtauld Inst
Journal. Warburg and Courtauld Institute [*A publication*] .... JWCI
Journal. Warburg and Courtauld Institute [*London*] [*A publication*] .... JWI
Journal. Washington Academy of Sciences [*A publication*] .... J Wash Acad Sci
Journal. Water Pollution Control Federation [*A publication*] .... J Water P C
Journal. Water Pollution Control Federation [*A publication*] .... J Water Pollut Control Fed
Journal. Water Pollution Control Federation [*A publication*] .... JWPCF
Journal. Water Pollution Control Federation [*A publication*] .... JWPF-A
Journal. Water Resources Planning and Management Division. American Society of Civil Engineers [*A publication*] .... J Water Resour Plann Manage Div ASCE
Journal. Water Resources Planning and Management Division. Proceedings. American Society of Civil Engineers [*A publication*] .... J Water Resour Plann Manage Div Am Soc Civ Eng
Journal. Waterways, Harbors, and Coastal Engineering Division. ASCE [*American Society of Civil Engineers*] [*A publication*] .... J Waterway
Journal. Welsh Bibliographic Society [*A publication*] .... JWBS
Journal of the West [*A publication*] .... Jour of West

Journal of the West [*A publication*]....J West
Journal. West African Institute for Oil Palm Research [*A publication*]....J West Afr Inst Oil Palm Res
Journal of West African Languages [*A publication*]....JWAfrL
Journal of West African Languages [*A publication*]....JWAL
Journal. West African Science Association [*A publication*]....J West Afr Sci Assoc
Journal. West China Border Research Society [*A publication*]....JWCBRS
Journal. West of Scotland Iron and Steel Institute [*A publication*]....J West Scot Iron Steel Inst
Journal. West Virginia Philosophical Society [*A publication*]....J W Vir Phil Soc
Journal of Western Speech [*A publication*]....JWS
Journal of Wildlife Diseases [*A publication*]....J Wildl Dis
Journal of Wildlife Management [*A publication*]....J Wildlife Mgt
Journal of Wildlife Management [*A publication*]....J Wildl Man
Journal of Wildlife Management [*A publication*]....J Wildl Manage
Journal. William Morris Society [*A publication*]....JWMS
Journal of Women's Studies in Literature [*A publication*]....JWSL
Journal of World History [*A publication*]....JWH
Journal of World History [*A publication*]....J World Hist
Journal of World Trade Law [*A publication*]....J Wld Trade Law
Journal of World Trade Law [*A publication*]....J World Tr
Journal of X-Ray Technology [*A publication*]....J X-Ray Technol
Journal. Yamagata Agriculture and Forestry Society [*A publication*]....J Yamagata Agric For Soc
Journal. Yonago Medical Association [*A publication*]....J Yonago Med Assoc
Journal of Youth and Adolescence [*A publication*]....J Youth Ado
Journal of Youth and Adolescence [*A publication*]....J Youth & Adolescence
Journal of Zoo Animal Medicine [*A publication*]....J Zoo Anim Med
Journal. Zoological Society of India [*A publication*]....J Zool Soc India
Journal of Zoology [*A publication*]....J Zool
Journalism....J
Journalism Association of Community Colleges [*Formerly, JAJC*]....JACC
Journalism Association of Junior Colleges [*Later, JACC*]....JAJC
Journalism Education Association....JEA
Journalism Educator [*A publication*]....Journalism Educ
Journalism Quarterly [*A publication*]....J-ism Quart
Journalism Quarterly [*A publication*]....Journalism Q
Journalism Quarterly [*A publication*]....Journ Q
Journalism Quarterly [*A publication*]....JQ
Journalist....JNLST
Journalist [*Navy rating*]....JO
Journalist....JRNIST
Journalist Biographies Master Index [*A publication*]....JBMI
Journalist, First Class [*Navy rating*]....JO1
Journalist, Second Class [*Navy rating*]....JO2
Journalist, Third Class [*Navy rating*]....JO3
Journalists, Authors, and Poets on Stamps Study Group [*American Topical Association*]....JAPOS
Journalistutbildningsutredningen [*Sweden*]....JUBU
Journals....JLS
Journals Access Service [*Center for Research Libraries*]....JAS
Journees Annuelles de Diabetologie Hotel-Dieu [*A publication*]....Journ Annu Diabetol Hotel-Dieu
Journees de Calorimetrie et d'Analyse Thermique. Preprints [*A publication*]....Journ Calorim Anal Therm Prepr
Journeyman....JOUR
Journeyman Training Program....JTP
Journeymen Barbers, Hairdressers, Cosmetologists and Proprietors' International Union of America....BHC
Journeymen Barbers, Hairdressers, Cosmetologists and Proprietors' International Union of America....JBHCPIUA
Journeymen Stone Cutters Association of North America [*Defunct*]....JSA
Journeymen Stone Cutters Association of North America [*Defunct*]....JSCA
JOVIAL [*Joule's Own Version of the International Algorithmic Language*] **Compiler** [*Data processing*]....JC
JOVIAL [*Joule's Own Version of the International Algorithmic Language*] **Compiler Implementation Tool** [*Data processing*]....JOCIT
JOVIAL [*Joule's Own Version of the International Algorithmic Language*] **Compiler Validation System** [*Data processing*]....JCVS
JOVIAL [*Joule's Own Version of the International Algorithmic Language*] **Control Program** [*Data processing*]....JCP
Jowett Car Club....JCC
Joy Manufacturing Co. [*NYSE symbol*]....JOY
Jozini [*South Africa*] [*Seismograph station code, US Geological Survey*]....JOZ
JP Industries, Incorporated [*NASDAQ symbol*]....JPII
JPL [*Jet Propulsion Laboratory*] **Astronautical Star Catalog**....JASC
JPL [*Jet Propulsion Laboratory*] **Quarterly Technical Review** [*A publication*]....JPL Q Tech Rev
JPL [*Jet Propulsion Laboratory*] **Technical Memorandum** [*A publication*]....JPL Tech Memo
JPL [*Jet Propulsion Laboratory*] **Technical Report** [*A publication*]....JPL Tech Rep
JPL [*Jet Propulsion Laboratory*] **Transient Radiation Analysis by Computer Program** [*NASA*]....JTRAC
JPT. Journal of Petroleum Technology [*A publication*]....JPT J Pet Technol
JSC [*Johnson Space Center*] **Payload Operations Center**....JPOC
Juana Diaz, PR [*Radio station call letters*]....WCGB
Juanjui [*Peru*] [*Airport symbol*]....JJI
Juba [*Sudan*] [*Airport symbol*]....JUB
Jucunde [*Pleasantly*] [*Latin*]....JUCUND
Judaeo-Arabic [*MARC language code*] [*Library of Congress*]....jrb
Judaeo-Persian [*MARC language code*] [*Library of Congress*]....jpr
Judah L. Magnes Memorial Museum, Rabbi Morris Goldstein Library, Berkeley, CA [*Library symbol*]....CBM
Judaica Historical Philatelic Society....JHPS
Judaism [*A publication*]....Ju
Judaism [*A publication*]....Jud
Judean Society....JS
Judean or Yahwistic [*Used in biblical criticism to designate Yahwistic material*]....J
Judex [*Judge*] [*Latin*]....J
Judge....JUDG
Judge Advocate....JA
Judge Advocate of the Fleet....JAF
Judge Advocate General [*Air Force, Army, Navy*]....JAG
[*The*] **Judge Advocate General** [*Army*]....TJAG
Judge Advocate General's Area Representatives....JAGAR
Judge Advocate General's Corps....JAGC
[*The*] **Judge Advocate General's Corps** [*Army*]....TJAGC
Judge Advocate General's Department [*Air Force, Army*]....JAGD
Judge Advocate General's Office....JAGO
Judge Advocate General's Office Publications [*Navy*]....NAVJAG
[*The*] **Judge Advocate General's School, Army**....TJAGSA
Judge Advocate Journal [*A publication*]....Ja J
Judge Advocate Library, Department of the Navy, Alexandria, VA [*OCLC symbol*]....JAL
Judge Advocates Association....JAA
Judged Utility Decision Generator....JUDGE
Judges [*Old Testament book*]....Jgs
Judges....JJ
Judges [*Old Testament book*]....Judg
Judges, Marshals, and Constables Association....JMCA
Judgment....JUD
Judgment....JUDGT
Judgment Analysis [*Psychology*]....JAN
Judicature....JUDRE
Judicial....JUD
Judicial....JUDIC
Judicial Appointments Project....JAP
Judicial Authority [*British*]....JA
Judicial Research Foundation [*Defunct*]....JRF
Judiciously Efficient Fixed Frame [*Data processing*]....JEFF
Judith [*Old Testament book*] [*Roman Catholic canon*]....Jdt
Judith [*Old Testament book*] [*Roman Catholic canon*]....Jud
Judo Black Belt Federation [*Later, USJE*]....JBBF
Judson College Library, Elgin, IL [*OCLC symbol*]....IFH
Judson College, Marion, AL [*Library symbol*]....AMaJ
Judy's, Inc. [*NASDAQ symbol*]....JUDY
Jugend Film Fernsehen [*A publication*]....JFF
Jugendarrestgeschaeftsordnung [*Germany*]....JAGO
Jugendgerichtgesetz [*Juvenile Court Law*] [*German*]....JGG
Jugenheim [*Federal Republic of Germany*] [*Seismograph station code, US Geological Survey*] [*Closed*]....JUG
Jugoslavenske Akademije Znanosti i Umjetnosti [*A publication*]....JAZU
Jugoslavia Study Group [*Philately*]....JSG
Jugoslovenska Ginekologija i Opstetricija [*A publication*]....Jugosl Ginekol Opstet
Jugoslovenska Pediajatrija [*A publication*]....Jugosl Pedijatr
Jugoslovenska Radio-Televizija [*Radio and television network*] [*Yugoslavia*]....JRT
Jugoslovenski Aerotransport [*Yugoslav Air Transport*]....JAT
Jugoslovenski Aerotransport [*Yugoslavia*] [*ICAO designator*]....JU
Jugoslovenski Pregled [*A publication*]....Jugosl Pregl
Jugoslovensko Pronalazastvo [*A publication*]....Jugosl Pronalazastvo
Jugular Vein [*Anatomy*]....JV
Jugular Vein [*or Venous*] **Pulse** [*Medicine*]....JVP
Jugulo [*To the Throat*] [*Pharmacy*]....JUG
Juice....J
Juilliard Review [*A publication*]....Juilliard R
Juilliard School of Music, New York, NY [*Library symbol*]....NNJu
Juist [*West Germany*] [*Airport symbol*] [*Obsolete*]....JUI
Juiz De Fora [*Brazil*] [*Airport symbol*]....JDF
Jujamcyn Theaters [*Established by William McKnight, and named for his three grandchildren, Judy, James, and Cynthia*]....JUJAMCYN
Jujuy [*Argentina*] [*Airport symbol*]....JUJ
Jujuy [*Argentina*] [*Seismograph station code, US Geological Survey*]....JUJ
Jukeboxes [*Public-performance tariff class*] [*British*]....JB
Jules Verne Circle....JVC
Julesburg Public Library, Julesburg, CO [*Library symbol*]....CoJu
Julia Creek [*Australia*] [*Airport symbol*]....JCK
Julia Morgan Association....JMA
Juliaca [*Peru*] [*Airport symbol*]....JUL
Julian [*Calendar*]....JUL
Julian, CA [*Location identifier*] [*FAA*]....JLI
Julian Date [*or Day*]....JD
Julian Day Number....JDN
Julian Ephemeris Data....JED
Julian & Kokenge Company [*NYSE symbol*]....JKC
Julianehab [*Denmark*] [*Later, NAQ*] [*Geomagnetic observatory code*]....JUL

Julich [Federal Republic of Germany] [Seismograph station code, US Geological Survey] .... JUE
Julie [Sonobuoy System] **Automatic Search and Attack Plotter** [Navy] .... JASAP
Julie [Sonobuoy System] **Automatic Sonic Data Analyzer** [Navy] .... JASDA
Julie [Sonobuoy System] **Exercise** [Navy] .... JULIEX
Julie/Jezebel [Sonobuoy Systems] **Airborne Maintenance Operator Trainee** [Navy] .... JAMOT
Juliet [Phonetic alphabet] .... J
Julius Caesar .... JC
Julius Caesar [Shakespearean work] .... JC
Julius Hartt Musical Foundation, Hartford, CT [Library symbol] .... CtHJH
Julius Kayser & Co. [NYSE symbol] .... JKS
July .... J
July .... JL
July .... JUL
July .... JY
Jumbo Jet Transport .... JJT
Jumbogroup Frequency Generator [Bell System] .... JFG
Jumbogroup Frequency Supply [Bell System] .... JFS
Jumbogroup Multiplex [Bell System] .... JMX
Jumla [Nepal] [Airport symbol] .... JUM
Jump Address .... JA
Jump on Condition [Data processing] .... JC
Jump on Condition [Data processing] .... JCN
Jump Indirectly [Data processing] .... JIN
Jump to Subroutine [Data processing] .... JSR
Jump to Subroutine Instruction [Data processing] .... JMS
Jump Unconditionally [Data processing] .... JUN
Jump Unit .... JU
Jumper .... JMPR
JUMPS [Joint Uniform Military Pay System] **Action Memorandum** .... JAM
JUMPS Automated Support System .... JASS
JUMPS Automated Support System - Reserve Corps .... JASS-RC
JUMPS [Joint Uniform Military Pay System] **Field Procedures Handbook** .... JFPH
JUMPS [Joint Uniform Military Pay System] **Monthly Compute Output Listing** .... JMCOL
Juncos, PR [Radio station call letters] .... WFAB
Junction .... JCT
Junction .... JCTN
Junction .... JN
Junction .... JUNC
Junction .... JUNCT
Junction [Texas] [Seismograph station code, US Geological Survey] .... JCT
Junction Box [Technical drawings] .... JB
Junction Box Assembly .... JBA
Junction City, KS [Radio station call letters] .... KJCK
Junction City, KS [Radio station call letters] .... KJCK-FM
Junction City, KY [Radio station call letters] .... WDFB
Junction City Public Library, Junction City, OR [Library symbol] .... OrJc
Junction Current Recovery [in silicon devices] .... JCR
Junction Devices [JETDS nomenclature] [Military] .... J
Junction Diode Circuit .... JDC
Junction Emitting Avalanche Light .... JEAL
Junction Field-Effect Device .... JFED
Junction Field-Effect Transistor .... JFET
Junction Gate Number .... JGN
Junction Growth Technique .... JGT
Junction and Insulated Gate Field Effect Transistor .... JIGFET
Junction Isolation [Electronics] .... JI
Junction Latching Circulator .... JLC
Junction Light Output .... JLO
Junction Module [Deep Space Instrumentation Facility, NASA] .... JM
Junction Panel [or Point] [Electronics] .... JP
Junction Rack .... JR
Junction Temperature, Operating .... JTO
Junction, TX [Location identifier] [FAA] .... JCT
Junction, TX [Radio station call letters] .... KMBL
Junction Wire Connector .... JWC
June .... J
June .... JE
June .... JU
June .... JUN
Juneau [Alaska] [Airport symbol] .... JNU
Juneau, AK [Location identifier] [FAA] .... JDL
Juneau, AK [Location identifier] [FAA] .... JNU
Juneau, AK [Radio station call letters] .... KINY
Juneau, AK [Radio station call letters] .... KJNO
Juneau, AK [Television station call letters] .... KJUD
Juneau, AK [Radio station call letters] .... KTOO
Juneau, AK [Television station call letters] .... KTOO-TV
Juneau Icefield Research Project .... JIRP
Juneau Memorial (Public) Library, Juneau, AK [Library symbol] .... AkJ
Juneau Public Library, Juneau, WI [Library symbol] .... WJu
Junge Pioniero .... JP
Jungle Aviation & Radio Service, Inc. [Mission plane service] .... JAARS
Jungle Canopy Penetration .... JCP
Jungle Environmental Survival Training [Military] .... JEST
Jungle and Guerrilla Warfare Training Center [Army] .... JGWTC
Jungle Message Encoder-Decoder .... JMED

Jungle Operations Training Center [Army] .... JOTC
Jungle Warfare Training Center [Army] .... JWTC
Jungsozialist [Young Socialist] [Germany] .... JUSO
Juniata College, Huntingdon, PA [Library symbol] .... PHuJ
Juniata College, Huntingdon, PA [OCLC symbol] .... PJU
Junior .... JNR
Junior .... JR
Junior .... JUN
Junior .... JUNR
Junior Achievement [A youth organization] .... JA
Junior Administrator Development Examination .... JADE
Junior Ambassadors .... JA
Junior American Coin Klub .... JACK
Junior Army-Navy Guild Organization [Organization of teenage daughters of military officers, who helped out in war work] [World War II] .... JANGO
Junior Beadle [Ancient Order of Foresters] .... JB
Junior Birdman [Slang] .... JB
Junior Bluejackets of America .... JBA
Junior Bookshelf [A publication] .... JB
Junior Bookshelf [A publication] .... Jr Bkshelf
Junior Catholic Daughters of the Americas .... JCDA
[United States] **Junior Chamber of Commerce** [Acronym is now used as official name of association] .... JAYCEES
Junior Chamber of Commerce .... JC of C
Junior Chamber of Commerce .... JCC
Junior Classical League .... JCL
Junior College .... JC
Junior College of Albany, Albany, NY [Library symbol] .... NAIJ
Junior College District .... JCD
Junior College District, Kansas City, MO [OCLC symbol] .... MJC
Junior College of Flat River [Missouri] .... JCFR
Junior College Journal [A publication] .... Jr Coll J
Junior College Journal [A publication] .... Jr Coll Jnl
Junior College Journal [A publication] .... Jun Col J
Junior College Journal [A publication] .... Junior Coll J
Junior College Libraries Section [Association of College and Research Libraries] .... JCLS
Junior Collegiate Players [Later, Associate Collegiate Players] .... JCP
Junior Common Room [in British colleges and public schools] .... JCR
Junior Deacon .... JD
Junior Dean .... JD
Junior Duty Officer .... JDO
Junior Engineering Technical Society .... JETS
Junior Engineers' and Scientists' Summer Institute .... JESSI
Junior Eysenck Personality Inventory [Psychology] .... JEPI
Junior Girls' Training Corps [British] [World War II] .... JGTC
Junior Grade .... JG
Junior Grand Warden [Masonry] .... JGW
Junior High Clearing House [A publication] .... J H Clearing House
Junior High School .... JHS
Junior Hospital Medical Officer .... JHMO
Junior Institute of Engineers .... JIE
Junior Institution of Engineers. London. Journal and Record of Transactions [A publication] .... Junior Inst Eng London J Rec Trans
Junior Libraries [A publication] .... Jr Lib
Junior Life Saving [Red Cross] .... Jr LS
Junior Lord of the Treasury .... JLT
Junior Management Assistant .... JMA
Junior Members Round Table [American Library Association] .... JMRT
Junior Military Aviator .... JMA
Junior National Association for the Deaf .... JrNAD
Junior Naval Reserve Officer Training Corps .... JNROTC
Junior Observers of Meteorology [Trainees for government service to replace Weather Bureau men who had gone to war] [World War II] .... JOOMS
Junior Officer .... JO
Junior Officer Council [Army] .... JOC
Junior Officer of the Day [or Deck] [Navy] .... JOOD
Junior Officer of the Watch [Navy] .... JOOW
Junior Officers and Professional Association .... JOPA
Junior Olympic Archery Development .... JOAD
Junior Optimist Clubs .... JOC
Junior Order United American Mechanics .... JOUAM
Junior Panel Outdoor Advertising Association [Later, ESOAA] .... JPOAA
Junior Participating Tactical Data System [Also known as "Jeep"] .... JPTDS
Junior Partner [i.e., a husband] [Slang] .... JP
Junior Philatelic Society of America [Later, JPA] .... JPSA
Junior Philatelists of America .... JPA
Junior Professional Officer [United Nations] .... JPO
Junior Red Cross .... JRC
Junior Reserve Officers' Training Corps .... JROTC
Junior Scholastic [A publication] .... JS
Junior Science and Humanities Symposium .... JSHS
Junior-Senior High School Clearing House [A publication] .... J-S H Sch Clearing House
Junior Slovak Catholic Sokol .... JSCS
Junior Staff Course [British] .... JSC
Junior Statesmen of America .... JSA
Junior Statesmen Foundation .... JSF

Junior Town Meeting League .... JTML
Junior Training Corps [British] .... JTC
Junior Varsity .... JV
Junior Vice Commander .... JVC
Junior Victory Army [World War II] .... JVA
Junior Warden [Masonry] .... JW
Junior Wolf [A young philanderer] [Slang] .... JW
Junior Woodward [Ancient Order of Foresters] .... JW
Junior Year Abroad [Collegiate term] .... JYA
Juniorat des Freres du Sacre-Coeur, Bromptonville, PQ, Canada
  [Library symbol] .... CaQBJ
Juniper Petroleum Corp. [American Stock Exchange symbol] .... JUN
Junk Acronyms When Speaking [Program] .... JAWS
Junker [German aircraft type] [World War II] .... JU
Junkers-Motor [Junkers aircraft engine] [German military - World
  War II] .... JUMO
Juno Lighting, Inc. [NASDAQ symbol] .... JUNO
Junta de Energia Nuclear [Spanish nuclear agency] .... JEN
Junta de Energia Nuclear. Report (Spain) [A publication] ....
  Junta Energ Nucl Rep (Spain)
Junta Internacional de Fiscalizacion de Estupefacientes
  [International Narcotics Control Board] .... JIFE
Junta Socialista Unida [United Socialist Party] [Spain] .... JSU
Jupiter .... J
Jupiter .... JUP
Jupiter Atmospheric Probe .... JAP
Jupiter Entry Probe .... JEP
Jupiter, FL [Radio station call letters] .... WCEZ
Jupiter, FL [Radio station call letters] .... WVSI
Jupiter, FL [Radio station call letters] .... WVSI-FM
Jupiter Flyby Mission [Aerospace] .... JFM
Jupiter Flyby Vehicle [Aerospace] .... JFV
Jupiter Industries, Inc. [American Stock Exchange symbol] .... JUP
Jupiter Inlet [NASA] .... JI
Jupiter Orbiter [NASA] .... JO
Jupiter Orbiter Probe [NASA] [Later, Project Galileo] .... JOp
Jupiter Orbiter Satellite Lander [NASA] .... JO/SL
Jupiter Orbiting Vehicle for Exploration .... JOVE
Jurassic [Period, era, or system] [Geology] .... JUR
Jurgensen's [NASDAQ symbol] .... JURG
Juridical Review [A publication] .... Jurid R
Juridical Review [A publication] .... Jurid Rev
Jurimetrics Journal [A publication] .... Jurimetrics
Jurin Law [Electronics] .... JL
Juris Baccalaureus [Bachelor of Laws] .... JB
Juris Canna Baccalaureus [Bachelor of Canon Law] .... J Can B
Juris Canna Baccalaureus [Bachelor of Canon Law] .... JCB
Juris Canna Doctor [Doctor of Canon Law] .... J Can D
Juris Canna Magister [Master of Canon Law] .... J Can M
Juris Canonici Doctor [Doctor of Canon Law] .... JCD
Juris Canonici Lector [Reader in Canon Law] .... JCL
Juris Canonici Licentiatus [Licentiate in Canon Law] .... JCL
Juris Civilis Baccalaureus [Bachelor of Civil Law] .... JCB
Juris Civilis Doctor [Doctor of Civil Law] .... JCD
Juris Civilis Licentiatus [Licentiate of Civil Law] .... JCL
Juris Civilis Magister [Master of Civil Law] .... JCM
Juris Doctor [A publication] .... JD
Juris Doctor [Doctor of Jurisprudence] .... JD
Juris Magister [Master of Laws] .... JM
Juris Utriusque Doctor [Doctor of Both Laws; i.e., Canon and Civil
  Law] .... DUJ
Juris Utriusque Doctor [Doctor of Both Laws; i.e., Canon and Civil
  Law] .... JUD
Juris Utriusque Doctor [Doctor of Both Laws; i.e., Canon and Civil
  Law] .... JUDr
Juris Utriusque Doctor [Doctor of Both Laws; i.e., Canon and Civil
  Law] .... Jur Utr Dr
Juris Utriusque Doctor [Doctor of Both Laws; i.e., Canon and Civil
  Law] .... JVD
Juris Utriusque Licentiatus [Licentiate in Both Laws; i.e., Canon
  and Civil Law] .... JUL
Jurisconsult .... JC
Jurisdiction .... JURIS
Jurisdiction .... JURISD
Jurisdictional Separation Process .... JSP
Jurisprudence .... JURISP
Juristisches Informationssystem [Judicial Information System]
  [West Germany] .... JURIS
Juror .... JR
Jurum Doctor [Doctor of Laws] .... JD
Jus [Law] [Latin] .... J
Jus Ecclesiasticum [A publication] .... Jus Eccl
Jus Liberorum Habens [Possessing the Right of Children] [Latin] .... ILH
Jussive .... JUSS
Just Another Break-Even Situation [Slang] .... JABES
Just Brand Names [Division of F. W. Woolworth Co.] .... J BRANNAM

Just a Drop in the Basket Helps Keep New York Clean [Antilitter
  campaign] .... JADITBHKNYC
Just Looking [A browser] [Retail slang] .... JL
Just Not Noticeable Difference .... JNND
Just Noticeable Difference [Psychology] .... JND
Just One Break [An association devoted to securing employment
  for physically handicapped workers] .... JOB
Just, Participatory, and Sustainable Society [World Council of
  Churches] .... JPSS
Just Prior Condition [Data processing] .... JPC
Just Publishable Unit .... JPU
Just Scale .... JS
Justerini and Brooks [Scotch] .... J & B
Justice [i.e., a judge; plural is JJ] .... J
Justice .... JUS
Justice Clerk .... JC
Justice Department .... JD
Justice Institute of British Columbia, Vancouver, BC, Canada
  [Library symbol] .... CaBVaJI
Justice Mortgage Investors SBI [NYSE symbol] .... JMI
Justice Party [Political party] [Turkey] .... JP
Justice of the Peace .... JP
Justice of the Peace [A publication] .... Just P
Justice Retrieval and Inquiry System [Department of Justice]
  [Information service] .... JURIS
Justice of the Supreme Court .... JSC
Justice System Improvement Act [1979] .... JSIA
Justice System Journal [A publication] .... Just Syst J
Justice System Training Association .... JSTA
Justices .... JJ
Justiciary Cases [Legal] [British] .... JC
Justification .... JUST
Justification for Authority to Negotiate [Military] .... JAN
Justin Industries, Inc. [NASDAQ symbol] .... JSTN
Justus Liebig Universitatsbibliothek Giessen, Giessen/Lahn,
  Federal Republic of Germany [Library symbol] .... GyGiU
Justus Liebigs Annalen der Chemie [A publication] ....
  Justus Liebigs Ann Chem
Jute-Asphalted [Nonmetallic armor] .... J
Jute Carpet Backing Council .... JCBC
Juvenile .... J
Juvenile .... JUV
Juvenile .... JUVE
Juvenile Amaurotic Idiocy [Medicine] .... JAI
Juvenile Court .... JC
Juvenile Court Judges Journal [A publication] .... Juv Ct Judges J
Juvenile Delinquency [or Delinquent] .... JD
Juvenile Delinquency Act .... JDA
Juvenile Delinquency Evaluation Project .... JDEP
Juvenile Delinquency and Youth Development Office [Federal
  government] .... JDYD
Juvenile Diabetes Foundation .... JDF
Juvenile Diabetes Mellitus [Medicine] .... JDM
Juvenile Hormone [Entomology] .... JH
Juvenile Hormone Analog [Entomology] .... JHA
Juvenile Hormone Mimic [Entomology] .... JHM
Juvenile Justice [A publication] .... Juven Just
Juvenile Justice and Delinquency Prevention .... JJDP
Juvenile Offenders .... JO
Juvenile Offenders Learn the Truth [Program] .... JOLT
Juvenile Onset Diabetes [Medicine] .... JOD
Juvenile Opportunities Endeavor .... JOE
Juvenile Products Manufacturers Association .... JPMA
Juvenile Rheumatoid Arthritis [Medicine] .... JRA
Juvenile Templar [Masonry] .... JT
Juveniles in Need of Supervision [Classification for delinquent
  children] .... JINS
Juvenis [Young] [Latin] .... JUV
Juventud Peronista [Peronist Youth] [Argentina] .... JP
Juventud Trabajadora Peronista [Working Peronist Youth]
  [Argentina] .... JTP
Juventud Universitaria Peronista [University Peronist Youth]
  [Argentina] .... JUP
Juvonen, K. W., Winnipeg, Manitoba CDA [STAC] .... JKW
Juxta [Near] [Pharmacy] .... JUXT
Juxtaglomerular [Histology] .... JG
Juxtaglomerular Apparatus [Histology] .... JGA
Juxtaglomerular Cells [Histology] .... JGC
Juznoslovenski Filolog [A publication] .... JF
Juznoslovenski Filolog [A publication] .... JslF
Jwalamukhi [India] [Seismograph station code, US Geological
  Survey] [Closed] .... JWA
JWB [Jewish Welfare Board] Jewish Book Council .... JWBJBC
JWT Group, Inc. [Formerly, J. Walter Thompson Co.] [NYSE symbol] .... JWT
Jydsk Teknologisk Institut [Technological Institute of Jutland]
  [Denmark] .... JTI
Jyvaskyla [Finland] [Airport symbol] .... JYV

K

K-Band Circulator .... KBC
K-Band Feed.. KBF
K-Band Waveguide Circulator .... KWC
K Capture [*A type of radioactive decay*] .... K
K, Li, and Na [*For the chemical elements potassium, lithium, and
    sodium*] [*Beckman flame system*] [*Trademark*] .... KLINA
K Mart Corp. [*NYSE symbol*].. KM
K-Tel International, Inc. [*American Stock Exchange symbol*]........... KTL
K-Tron International [*NASDAQ symbol*] .... KTII
K-V Pharmaceutical [*NASDAQ symbol*].................................. KVPH
Ka-Inertial Launch and Leave System .... KILLS
Kaanapali [*Hawaii*] [*Airport symbol*] .... HKP
Kaapuna [*Hawaii*] [*Seismograph station code, US Geological Survey*] ..... KUH
Kabaka Yekka [*The King Alone*] [*Ugandan political party*] [*Suspended*] ....KY
Kabala [*Sierra Leone*] [*Airport symbol*] .... KBA
Kabansk [*USSR*] [*Seismograph station code, US Geological Survey*] ...... KAB
Kabar Sebarang. Sulating Maphilindo [*A publication*] ....Kab Seb
Kabardino-Balkarskii Gosudarstvennyi Universitet. Ucenyi
    Zapiski [*A publication*] .... Kabardino-Balkarsk Gos Univ Ucen Zap
Kabataang Makabayan [*Nationalist Youth*] [*Philippines*] .... KM
Kabri Dar [*Ethiopia*] [*Airport symbol*] .... ABK
Kabul [*Afghanistan*] [*Seismograph station code, US Geological
    Survey*] .... KAAO
Kabul [*Afghanistan*] [*Airport symbol*]...................................... KBL
Kabul [*Afghanistan*] [*Seismograph station code, US Geological
    Survey*].. KBL
Kabul University. Faculty of Agriculture. Research Notes [*A
    publication*].. Kabul Univ Fac Agric Res Note
Kabul University. Faculty of Agriculture. Technical Bulletin [*A
    publication*].. Kabul Univ Fac Agric Tech Bull
Kabushiki Goshi Kaisha [*Partnership*] [*Japanese*].................... KGK
Kabushiki Kaishi [*Joint stock company*] [*Japanese*].................... KK
Kabwum [*Papua New Guinea*] [*Airport symbol*] .... KBM
Kachin [*MARC language code*] [*Library of Congress*] .... kac
Kadelpian Review [*A publication*].. Kadel R
Kadima of the United Synagogue of America .... KUSA
Kaduna [*Nigeria*] [*Airport symbol*] .... KAD
Kaedi [*Mauritania*] [*Airport symbol*] .... KED
Kaelte-Klima-Praktiker [*A publication*]........................... Kaelte-Klima-Prakt
Kaelte und Klimatechnik [*A publication*] .... Kaelte Klimatech
Kaeltetechnik-Klimatisierung [*A publication*] .... Kaeltetech-Klim
Kaena [*Hawaii*] [*Seismograph station code, US Geological Survey*] .... KAE
Kaena Point [*Hawaii*] [*Seismograph station code, US Geological
    Survey*] [*Closed*] .... KPH
Kafka Society of America .... KSA
Kagalaska [*Alaska*] [*Seismograph station code, US Geological
    Survey*]... AD3
Kagi [*Papua New Guinea*] [*Airport symbol*]............................. KGW
Kagoshima [*Japan*] [*Seismograph station code, US Geological
    Survey*] .... KAG
Kagoshima [*Japan*] [*Airport symbol*] .... KOJ
Kagoshima Daigaku Bunka Hokoku [*Cultural Science Reports.
    Kagoshima University*] [*A publication*] .... KagoBH
Kagoshima Space Center [*Japan*] .... KAG
Kahler Corp. [*NASDAQ symbol*] .... KHLR
Kahn Test of Symbol Arrangement [*Psychology*] .... KTSA
Kahuku [*Hawaii*] [*Seismograph station code, US Geological Survey*] .... KHU
Kahului [*Hawaii*] [*Airport symbol*] .... OGG
Kahului, HI [*Radio station call letters*] .... KNUI
Kahului, HI [*Location identifier*] [*FAA*] .... VYI
Kaibab Industries [*NASDAQ symbol*] .... KAIB
Kaieteur [*Guyana*] [*Airport symbol*] .... KAI
Kaikohe [*New Zealand*] [*Airport symbol*] [*Obsolete*] .... KKO
Kailua, HI [*Radio station call letters*] .... KLEI
Kailua, HI [*Radio station call letters*] .... KSHO-FM
Kailua Kona [*Hawaii*] [*Seismograph station code, US Geological
    Survey*] .... KKH
Kaimana [*Indonesia*] [*Airport symbol*] .... KNG
Kaimata [*New Zealand*] [*Seismograph station code, US
    Geological Survey*].. KAI

Kainokawa [*Japan*] [*Seismograph station code, US Geological
    Survey*] .... KKW
Kaintiba [*Papua New Guinea*] [*Airport symbol*] .... KZF
Kaisar-I-Hind [*Indian medal*] .... KIH
Kaiser Aluminum & Chemical Corporation .... KACC
Kaiser Aluminum & Chemical Corp. [*NYSE symbol*]................ KLU
Kaiser Aluminum & Chemical Corp., Permanente, CA [*Library
    symbol*].. CPermK
Kaiser Cement Corporation [*Formerly, KCG*] [*NYSE symbol*]....... KCC
Kaiser Cement & Gypsum Corp. [*Later, KCC*] [*NYSE symbol*]......... KCG
Kaiser Foundation Hospital, Doctor's Library, Los Angeles, CA
    [*Library symbol*].. CLK-D
Kaiser Foundation Hospital, Los Angeles, CA [*Library symbol*] ...... CLK
Kaiser Foundation Hospitals, Health Services Research Center,
    Portland, OR [*Library symbol*].. OrPKF
Kaiser-Frazer Owners Club International [*Formerly, KFOC*] .... KFOCI
Kaiser-Frazer Owners Clubs of America [*Later, Kaiser-Frazer
    Owners Club International*]... KFOC
Kaiser Industries Corp. [*American Stock Exchange symbol*] [*Delisted*] .... KI
Kaiser Koenigliche.. KK
Kaiser-Permanente .... K-P
Kaiser Permanente Medical Center, Health Science Library,
    Panorama City, CA [*Library symbol*] .... CPcK
Kaiser-Permanente Medical Center, Medical Library, Redwood
    City, CA [*Library symbol*] .... CRcK
Kaiser-Permanente Medical Center, San Francisco, CA [*Library
    symbol*] .... CSfK
Kaiser Steel Corporation [*NYSE symbol*] .... KSC
Kaiser Steel Corp., Fontana, CA [*Library symbol*] .... CFonK
Kaiser Steel Corp. Pfd [*NASDAQ symbol*] .... KASRP
Kaiserlich-Deutsches Archaologisches Institut. Jahrbuch [*A
    publication*]..................................... Kais-Deutsch Archaol Inst Jahrb
Kaiserlich-Koenigliche Geographische Gesellschaft in Wien.
    Mitteilungen [*A publication*]....................... K-K Geog Ges Wien Mitt
Kaiserlich-Koenigliche Naturhistorische Hofmuseum. Annalen
    [*A publication*].. K-K Naturh Hofmus An
Kaiserliche Akademie der Wissenschaften. Mathematische-
    Naturwissenschaftliche Classe. Sitzungsberichte [*A
    publication*]................................. K Ak Wiss Mat-Nat Cl Szb
Kaiserville [*Nevada*] [*Seismograph station code, US Geological
    Survey*] .... KVN
Kaitaia [*New Zealand*] [*Airport symbol*] .... KAT
Kajaani [*Finland*] [*Airport symbol*] .... KAJ
Kajaani [*Finland*] [*Seismograph station code, US Geological Survey*] .... KJF
Kajaani [*Finland*] [*Seismograph station code, US Geological
    Survey*] [*Closed*] .... KJN
Kajian Ekonomi Malaysia [*A publication*] .... Kaj Ekon Mal
Kajian Veterinaire [*A publication*]................................... Kajian Vet
Kakatiya Journal of English Studies [*A publication*] .... Kakatiya J Eng Stud
Kake [*Alaska*] [*Airport symbol*] .... KAE
Kaken Chemical Co. [*Japan*] [*Research code symbol*].................... K
Kakhk [*Iran*] [*Seismograph station code, US Geological Survey*]......... KHI
Kakhonak [*Alaska*] [*Airport symbol*] .... KNK
Kakioka [*Japan*] [*Geomagnetic observatory code*] .... KAK
Kakioka [*Japan*] [*Seismograph station code, US Geological Survey*] .... KAK
Kalabo [*Zambia*] [*Airport symbol*] .... KLB
Kalamata [*Greece*] [*Airport symbol*] .... KLX
Kalamazoo [*Michigan*] [*Airport symbol*]................................. AZO
Kalamazoo Area Library Consortium [*Library network*].............. KETAL
Kalamazoo College, Kalamazoo, MI [*OCLC symbol*]................. EXK
Kalamazoo College, Kalamazoo, MI [*Library symbol*] .... MiKC
Kalamazoo Library System, Kalamazoo, MI [*OCLC symbol*] .... EXZ
Kalamazoo, MI [*Radio station call letters*]............................. WIDR
Kalamazoo, MI [*Radio station call letters*].............................. WKDS
Kalamazoo, MI [*Radio station call letters*]............................. WKLZ
Kalamazoo, MI [*Radio station call letters*]............................ WKMI
Kalamazoo, MI [*Radio station call letters*]............................ WKPR
Kalamazoo, MI [*Radio station call letters*]............................ WKZO
Kalamazoo, MI [*Television station call letters*].................. WKZO-TV
Kalamazoo, MI [*Television station call letters*].................... WLLA

973

Kalamazoo, MI [*Radio station call letters*] ... WMUK
Kalamazoo, MI [*Radio station call letters*] ... WYYY
Kalamazoo Public Library, Kalamazoo, MI [*Library symbol*] ... MiK
Kalamazoo Public School District, Kalamazoo, MI [*Library symbol*] ... MiKPSc
Kalamazoo Stove & Furnace [*NYSE symbol*] ... KAL
Kalamazoo Valley Community College, Kalamazoo, MI [*Library symbol*] ... MiKV
Kalamein [*Trademark*] ... KAL
Kalamein [*Trademark*] **Door** ... KALD
Kalamein [*Trademark*] **Door and Frame** ... KDF
Kalaupapa [*Hawaii*] [*Airport symbol*] ... LUP
Kalbarri [*Australia*] [*Airport symbol*] ... KAX
Kaleidoscope Insert [*A publication*] ... Kal Inser
Kaleidoscope-Madison [*A publication*] ... Kal Mad
Kaleidoscope-Milwaukee [*A publication*] ... Kal Mil
Kalemi [*Zaire*] [*Airport symbol*] ... FMI
Kalemyo [*Burma*] [*Airport symbol*] ... KMV
Kalendae [*The Kalends*] [*First day of the ancient Roman month*] ... KAL
Kalendas [*Calends*] ... K
Kalevalaseuran Vuosikirja [*A publication*] ... KSVK
Kalevalaseuran Vuosikirja [*A publication*] ... KV
Kalgoorlie [*Australia*] [*Airport symbol*] ... KGI
Kalgoorlie [*Australia*] [*Seismograph station code, US Geological Survey*] ... KLG
Kalibo [*Philippines*] [*Airport symbol*] ... KLO
Kaliningrad [*USSR*] [*Geomagnetic observatory code*] ... KNG
Kaliningradskii Gosudarstvennyi Pedagogiceskii Institut. Ucenye Zapiski [*A publication*] ... Kaliningrad Gos Ped Inst Ucen Zap
Kaliningradskii Gosudarstvennyi Universitet. Trudy Kafedry Teoreticeskoi i Eksperimental'noi Fiziki [*A publication*] ... Kaliningrad Gos Univ Trudy Kaf Teoret i Eksper Fiz
Kaliningradskii Gosudarstvennyi Universitet. Ucenye Zapiski [*A publication*] ... Kaliningrad Gos Univ Ucen Zap
Kalininskii Gosudarstvennyi Pedagogiceskii Institut Imeni M. I. Kalinina. Ucenye Zapiski [*A publication*] ... Kalinin Gos Ped Inst Ucen Zap
Kaliophilite [*CIPW classification*] [*Geology*] ... kp
Kalispell [*Montana*] [*Airport symbol*] ... FCA
Kalispell, MT [*Radio station call letters*] ... KALS
Kalispell, MT [*Television station call letters*] ... KCFW-TV
Kalispell, MT [*Radio station call letters*] ... KGEZ
Kalispell, MT [*Radio station call letters*] ... KOFI
Kalispell, MT [*Location identifier*] [*FAA*] ... SAK
Kalispell Regional Hospital, Kalispell, MT [*Library symbol*] ... MtKH
Kalium [*Potassium*] [*Chemical element*] ... K
Kalium [*Potassium*] [*Pharmacy*] ... KAL
Kalkaska County Library, Kalkaska, MI [*Library symbol*] ... MiKa
Kalkaska, MI [*Radio station call letters*] ... WKLT
Kalkaska, MI [*Radio station call letters*] ... WTGE
Kalle Aktiengesellschaft, Litteraturabteilung, Wiesbaden-Biebrich, Germany [*Library symbol*] ... GyWK
Kallestad Laboratories, Inc. [*American Stock Exchange symbol*] [*Delisted*] ... KAL
Kallikrein Inactivator Unit [*Analytical biochemistry*] ... KIU
Kallikrein [*or Kininogenin*] **Inhibiting Unit** [*Hematology*] ... K
Kalltalsperre [*Federal Republic of Germany*] [*Seismograph station code, US Geological Survey*] ... KLL
Kalman Filter Theory ... KFT
Kalman Filtering System ... KFS
Kalmar [*Sweden*] [*Airport symbol*] ... KLR
Kalocsa [*Hungary*] [*Seismograph station code, US Geological Survey*] [*Closed*] ... KAL
Kalskag [*Alaska*] [*Airport symbol*] ... KLG
Kalt Wenig Loslich [*Not Very Soluble Cold*] [*German*] ... KWL
Kaltag [*Alaska*] [*Airport symbol*] ... KAL
Kalvar Corp. [*NASDAQ symbol*] ... KALV
Kamad Silver Co. Ltd. [*NASDAQ symbol*] ... KMADF
Kamakura [*Japan*] [*Seismograph station code, US Geological Survey*] [*Closed*] ... KMK
Kaman Aircraft Corporation ... KAC
Kaman Corp. Cl A [*NASDAQ symbol*] ... KAMNA
Kaman Sciences Corp., Nuclear Library, Colorado Springs, CO [*Library symbol*] ... CoCK
Kamarang [*Guyana*] [*Airport symbol*] ... KAR
Kamarata [*Venezuela*] [*Airport symbol*] ... KTV
Kamba [*MARC language code*] [*Library of Congress*] ... kam
Kambalda [*Australia*] [*Airport symbol*] ... KDB
Kamena [*A publication*] ... Kam
Kamerun National Congress ... KNC
Kamerun National Democratic Party [*Later, UNC*] ... KNDP
Kameshli [*Syria*] [*Airport symbol*] ... KAC
Kameyama [*Japan*] [*Seismograph station code, US Geological Survey*] ... KAM
Kamigamo [*Japan*] [*Seismograph station code, US Geological Survey*] [*Closed*] ... KMM
Kamikineusu Station [*Japan*] [*Seismograph station code, US Geological Survey*] ... KMU
Kamileroi [*Australia*] [*Airport symbol*] [*Obsolete*] ... KML
Kamimuroga [*Japan*] [*Seismograph station code, US Geological Survey*] ... KRJ
Kamina [*Papua New Guinea*] [*Airport symbol*] ... KMF
Kamina [*Zaire*] [*Airport symbol*] ... KMN
Kamiraba [*Papua New Guinea*] [*Airport symbol*] [*Obsolete*] ... KJU
Kamloops [*Canada*] [*Airport symbol*] ... YKA
Kamloops, BC [*Television station call letters*] ... CBUFT-2
Kamloops, BC [*Radio station call letters*] ... CFFM-FM
Kamloops, BC [*Radio station call letters*] ... CFJC
Kamloops, BC [*Television station call letters*] ... CFJC-TV
Kamloops, BC [*Television station call letters*] ... CHKM-TV
Kamloops, BC [*Radio station call letters*] ... CHNL
Kamloops Museum, Kamloops, BC, Canada [*Library symbol*] ... CaBKM
Kamloops Public Library, Kamloops, BC, Canada [*Library symbol*] ... CaBK
Kammer der Technik ... KDT
Kampfgeschwader [*Bombardment wing*] [*German military - World War II*] ... KG
Kampfwagen [*Tank*] [*German military - World War II*] ... KW
Kampfwagenkanone [*Tank Gun*] [*German military - World War II*] ... KWK
Kampground Owners Association ... KOA
Kampgrounds of America ... KOA
Kampsville Reading Center, Kampsville, IL [*Library symbol*] ... IKampR
Kampuchean National United Front for National Salvation [*Cambodia*] ... KNUFNS
Kamuela [*Hawaii*] [*Seismograph station code, US Geological Survey*] [*Closed*] ... KML
Kamuela [*Hawaii*] [*Airport symbol*] ... MUE
Kanab [*Utah*] [*Airport symbol*] ... KNB
Kanab [*Utah*] [*Seismograph station code, US Geological Survey*] ... KNB
Kanabea [*Papua New Guinea*] [*Airport symbol*] ... KEX
Kanaka Peak [*California*] [*Seismograph station code, US Geological Survey*] ... KPK
Kanamycin [*Antibacterial compound*] ... K
Kanamycin Acetyltransferase [*An enzyme*] ... KAT
Kanamycin-Vancomycin Blood Agar [*Microbiology*] ... KVBA
Kanamycin-Vancomycin Labeled Blood Agar [*Microbiology*] ... KVLBA
Kananga [*Zaire*] [*Airport symbol*] ... KGA
[*The*] **Kanawha Central Railway Co.** [*AAR code*] ... KC
Kanawha County Public Library, Charleston, WV [*Library symbol*] ... WvC
Kanawha County Public Library, Charleston, WV [*OCLC symbol*] ... WVK
Kanawha Public Library, Kanawha, IA [*Library symbol*] ... IaKan
Kanazawa [*Japan*] [*Seismograph station code, US Geological Survey*] ... KAN
Kanazawa Daigaku Hobungakubu Ronshu. Bungakuhen [*Studies and Essays. Faculty of Law and Literature. Kanazawa University. Literature*] [*A publication*] ... KanazHB
Kanazawa Daigaku Kyoyobu Ronshu. Jinbunkagakuhen [*Studies in Humanities. College of Liberal Arts. Kanazawa University*] [*A publication*] ... KanazJK
Kanazawa University Research Institute of Tuberculosis. Annual Report [*A publication*] ... Kanazawa Univ Res Inst Tuberc Annu Rep
Kanbum Gakkai Kaiho [*Journal. Sinological Society*] [*A publication*] ... KGH
Kandahar [*Afghanistan*] [*Airport symbol*] ... KDH
Kandavu [*Fiji*] [*Airport symbol*] ... KDV
Kandep [*Papua New Guinea*] [*Airport symbol*] [*Obsolete*] ... KDP
Kandrian [*Papua New Guinea*] [*Airport symbol*] ... KDR
[*The*] **Kandy-Kolored Tangerine-Flake Streamline Baby** [*Title of book by Tom Wolfe*] ... TKKTFSLB
Kane Miller Corp. [*NYSE symbol*] ... KML
Kane, PA [*Radio station call letters*] ... WKZA
Kane, PA [*Radio station call letters*] ... WRXZ
Kaneb Services, Inc. [*NYSE symbol*] ... KAB
Kangaku Kenkyu [*Sinological Studies*] [*A publication*] ... KGKK
Kangaroo Protection Foundation ... KPF
Kankakee, Beaverville & Southern Railroad Co. [*AAR code*] ... KBSR
Kankakee Community College, Kankakee, IL [*Library symbol*] ... IKC
Kankakee, IL [*Radio station call letters*] ... WBYG
Kankakee, IL [*Radio station call letters*] ... WKAN
Kankakee, IL [*Radio station call letters*] ... WKOC
Kannada [*MARC language code*] [*Library of Congress*] ... kan
Kannapolis, NC [*Radio station call letters*] ... WGTL
Kannapolis, NC [*Radio station call letters*] ... WJZR
Kannapolis, NC [*Radio station call letters*] ... WRKB
Kano [*Nigeria*] [*Airport symbol*] ... KAN
Kano, Nigeria [*Remote site*] [*NASA*] ... KNO
Kano Studies [*Nigeria*] [*A publication*] ... Kano S
Kanone [*Gun*] [*German military - World War II*] ... K
Kanonengranate [*Shell for a gun*] [*German military - World War II*] ... KGR
Kanoya [*Japan*] [*Geomagnetic observatory code*] ... KNY
Kanozan [*Japan*] [*Geomagnetic observatory code*] ... KNZ
Kanpur [*India*] [*Airport symbol*] ... KNU
Kansai Gaidai Kenkyu Ronshu [*Journal. Kansai University of Foreign Studies*] [*A publication*] ... KGKR
Kansai Research Reactor [*Japan*] ... KRR
Kansantaloudellinen Aikakauskirja [*A publication*] ... Kansantal Aikakausk
Kansas ... KAN
Kansas ... KANS
Kansas [*Postal code*] ... KS
Kansas [*MARC country of publication code*] [*Library of Congress*] ... ksu
Kansas [*MARC geographic area code*] [*Library of Congress*] ... n-us-ks
Kansas Academy of Science. Transactions [*A publication*] ... Kan Acad Sci Trans
Kansas Academy of Science. Transactions [*A publication*] ... Kans Acad Sci Trans

Kansas Academy of Science. Transactions [*A publication*]...Kans Ac Sc Tr

Kansas Academy of Science. Transactions [*A publication*]...Kansas Acad Sci Trans

Kansas Agricultural Experiment Station. Biennial Report of the Director [*A publication*]...Kans Agric Exp Stn Bienn Rep Dir

Kansas Agricultural Experiment Station. Bulletin [*A publication*]...Kans Agric Exp Stn Bull

Kansas Agricultural Experiment Station. Circular [*A publication*]...Kans Agric Exp Stn Circ

Kansas Agricultural Experiment Station. Research Publication [*A publication*]...Kans Agric Exp Stn Res Publ

Kansas Agricultural Experiment Station. Technical Bulletin [*A publication*]...Kans Agric Exp Stn Tech Bull

Kansas Agricultural Situation. Kansas State University of Agriculture and Applied Science. Extension Service [*A publication*]...Kans Agr Situation

Kansas Army Ammunition Plant...KAAP

Kansas Business Teacher [*A publication*]...Kansas Bus Tchr

Kansas City [*Missouri*] [*Slang*]...KAYSEE

Kansas City [*Missouri*] [*Slang*]...KC

Kansas City [*Missouri*] [*Airport symbol*]...MCI

Kansas City [*Missouri*] [*Airport symbol*]...MKC

Kansas City Area Hospital Association, Kansas City, MO [*Library symbol*]...MoKHA

Kansas City Area Office [*Energy Research and Development Administration*]...KCAO

Kansas City College of Osteopathic Medicine, Kansas City, MO [*Library symbol*]...MoKCO

Kansas City Connecting Railroad Co. [*AAR code*]...KCC

Kansas City General Hospital, Kansas City, MO [*Library symbol*]...MoKGH

Kansas City, Kaw Valley R. R., Inc. [*AAR code*]...KVW

Kansas City, KS [*Location identifier*] [*FAA*]...BGZ

Kansas City, KS [*Radio station call letters*]...KFKF

Kansas City, KS [*Radio station call letters*]...KFKF-FM

Kansas City, KS [*Radio station call letters*]...KUDL-FM

Kansas City Life Insurance [*NASDAQ symbol*]...KCLI

Kansas City Metropolitan Library Network Council [*Library network*]...KCMLN

Kansas City, Mexico, & Orient [*AAR code*]...KCMO

Kansas City, Missouri [*Airport symbol*]...MKC

Kansas City, MO [*Radio station call letters*]...KAYQ

Kansas City, MO [*Radio station call letters*]...KBEQ

Kansas City, MO [*Radio station call letters*]...KCMO

Kansas City, MO [*Radio station call letters*]...KCMO-FM

Kansas City, MO [*Television station call letters*]...KCPT

Kansas City, MO [*Radio station call letters*]...KCUR-FM

Kansas City, MO [*Television station call letters*]...KEKR-TV

Kansas City, MO [*Radio station call letters*]...KJLA

Kansas City, MO [*Radio station call letters*]...KLJC

Kansas City, MO [*Radio station call letters*]...KLSI

Kansas City, MO [*Television station call letters*]...KMBC-TV

Kansas City, MO [*Radio station call letters*]...KMBR

Kansas City, MO [*Radio station call letters*]...KMBZ

Kansas City, MO [*Radio station call letters*]...KPRS

Kansas City, MO [*Radio station call letters*]...KPRT

Kansas City, MO [*Television station call letters*]...KSHB-TV

Kansas City, MO [*Radio station call letters*]...KTSR

Kansas City, MO [*Radio station call letters*]...KXTR

Kansas City, MO [*Television station call letters*]...KYFC

Kansas City, MO [*Radio station call letters*]...KYYS

Kansas City, MO [*Location identifier*] [*FAA*]...MKM

Kansas City, MO [*Radio station call letters*]...WDAF

Kansas City, MO [*Television station call letters*]...WDAF-TV

Kansas City, MO [*Radio station call letters*]...WHB

Kansas City Philharmonic Program Notes [*A publication*]...KC Phil

Kansas City Power & Light Co. [*NYSE symbol*]...KLT

Kansas City Public Library, Kansas City, KS [*Library symbol*]...KKc

Kansas City Public Library, Kansas City, KS [*OCLC symbol*]...KKC

Kansas City Public Library, Kansas City, MO [*OCLC symbol*]...KCP

Kansas City Public Library, Kansas City, MO [*Library symbol*]...MoK

Kansas City Public Service R. R. [*AAR code*]...KCPS

Kansas City Records Center [*Military*]...KCRC

Kansas City Regional Council for Higher Education [*Library network*]...KCRCHE

Kansas City Review [*A publication*]...Kansas R

Kansas City Review of Science and Industry [*A publication*]...Kansas City Rv Sc

Kansas City Service Center [*IRS*]...KCSC

Kansas City Southern Industries, Inc. [*NYSE symbol*]...KSU

[*The*] **Kansas City Southern Railway Co.** [*AAR code*]...KCS

Kansas City Terminal Railway Co. [*AAR code*]...KCT

Kansas City Westport Belt [*AAR code*]...KCWB

Kansas Engineering Experiment Station. Bulletin [*A publication*]...Kans Eng Exp Stn Bull

Kansas Flight Research Laboratory...KFRL

Kansas Gas & Electric Co. [*NYSE symbol*]...KGE

Kansas Geological Survey. Bulletin [*A publication*]...Kans Geol Surv Bull

Kansas Geological Survey. Map [*A publication*]...Kansas Geol Survey Map

Kansas Geological Survey. Series on Spatial Analysis [*A publication*]...Kans Geol Surv Ser Spat Anal

Kansas Historical Quarterly [*A publication*]...Kan Hist Quar

Kansas Historical Quarterly [*A publication*]...Kans Hist Q

Kansas Historical Quarterly [*A publication*]...KHQ

Kansas Information Circuit [*Library network*]...KIC

Kansas Journal of Sociology [*A publication*]...Kansas J Sociol

Kansas Journal of Sociology...KJS

Kansas Judicial Council. Bulletin [*A publication*]...Kan Jud Council Bull

Kansas Law Review [*A publication*]...Kan Law Rev

Kansas Law Review [*A publication*]...Kan L Rev

Kansas Library Bulletin [*A publication*]...Kan Lib Bull

Kansas Library Bulletin [*A publication*]...Kan Libr Bull

Kansas Library Bulletin [*A publication*]...Kansas Lib Bul

Kansas Magazine [*A publication*]...KM

[*The*] **Kansas & Missouri Railway & Terminal Co.** [*Formerly, KMRT*] [*AAR code*]...KM

[*The*] **Kansas & Missouri Railway & Terminal Co.** [*Later, KM*] [*AAR code*]...KMRT

Kansas Motor Carriers Association, Topeka KS [*STAC*]...KSA

Kansas-Nebraska Natural Gas Co., Inc. [*NYSE symbol*] [*Delisted*]...KNB

Kansas Neurological Institute, Topeka, KS [*Library symbol*]...KTNI

Kansas Newman College [*Formerly, Sacred Heart College*]...KNC

Kansas Newman College, Wichita, KS [*OCLC symbol*]...KKN

Kansas Newman College, Wichita, KS [*Library symbol*]...KWiK

Kansas Nurse [*A publication*]...Kans Nurse

Kansas, Oklahoma & Gulf Railway Co....KO & G

Kansas, Oklahoma & Gulf Railway Co. [*AAR code*]...KOG

Kansas Power & Light Co. [*NYSE symbol*]...KAN

Kansas Quarterly [*A publication*]...KanQ

Kansas Quarterly [*A publication*]...KQ

Kansas River Basin...KRB

Kansas State Agricultural College. Agricultural Experiment Station. Publications [*A publication*]...Kan Ag Exp

Kansas State Board of Agriculture. Division of Entomology. Activities [*A publication*]...Kans State Board Agric Div Entomol Act

Kansas State Board of Agriculture. Transactions. Annual Report. Biennial Report [*A publication*]...Kans St Bd Agr Tr An Rp Bien Rp

Kansas State Geological Survey. Bulletin [*A publication*]...Kans State Geol Surv Bull

Kansas State Historical Society. Collections [*A publication*]...Kan State Hist Soc Coll

Kansas State Historical Society. Collections [*A publication*]...Kas His S

Kansas State Historical Society, Topeka, KS [*Library symbol*]...KHi

Kansas State Library, Law Department, Topeka, KS [*Library symbol*]...K-L

Kansas State Library, Topeka, KS [*Library symbol*]...K

Kansas State Teachers College...KSTC

Kansas State Teachers College, Emporia, KS [*Library symbol*] [*Obsolete*]...KEmT

Kansas State University...KSU

Kansas State University. Engineering Experiment Station. Bulletin [*A publication*]...Kans State Univ Eng Exp Stn Bull

Kansas State University, Farrell Library, Manhattan, KS [*OCLC symbol*]...KKS

Kansas State University, Manhattan, KS [*Library symbol*]...KMK

Kansas State University, Veterinary Medicine Library, Manhattan, KS [*Library symbol*]...KMK-V

Kansas State Water Resources Board. Bulletin [*A publication*]...Kansas Water Resources Board Bull

Kansas Stockman [*A publication*]...Kans Stockman

Kansas Teacher and Western School Journal [*A publication*]...Kans Teach

Kansas. University. Bulletin of Education [*A publication*]...Kans Univ B Ed

Kansas. University. Kansas Studies in Education [*A publication*]...Kan Univ Kan Studies Ed

Kansas. University. Museum of Natural History. Miscellaneous Publication [*A publication*]...Kansas Univ Mus Nat History Misc Pub

Kansas. University. Paleontological Contributions [*A publication*]...Kansas Univ Paleont Contr

Kansas University Quarterly [*A publication*]...Kans Univ Q

Kansas University. Science Bulletin [*A publication*]...Kans Univ Sc B

Kansas Water Resources Board. Bulletin [*A publication*]...Kans Water Res Board Bull

Kansas Wesleyan University...KWU

Kansas Wesleyan University, Salina, KS [*Library symbol*]...KSalW

Kansas Wheat Quality. Kansas State Board of Agriculture [*Kansas Wheat Commission*] [*A publication*]...Kans Wheat Qual Kans State Board Agr

Kansatieteellinen Arkisto [*A publication*]...K Ar

Kansu Province [*China, Mainland*] [*MARC geographic area code*] [*Library of Congress*]...a-cc-ka

Kant-Studien [*A publication*]...Kant-Stud

Kant-Studien [*A publication*]...KS

Kant-Studien [*A publication*]...KSt

Kanuri [*MARC language code*] [*Library of Congress*]...kau

Kaohsiung [*Takao*] [*Republic of China*] [*Seismograph station code, US Geological Survey*]...KAU

Kaohsiung [*Taiwan*] [*Airport symbol*]...KHH

Kaohsiung [*Republic of China*] [*Seismograph station code, US Geological Survey*] [*Closed*]...TWM

Kaohsiung [*Republic of China*] [*Seismograph station code, US Geological Survey*]...TWM1

Kaohsiung Export Processing Zone [*Reexport manufacturing complex*] [*Taiwan*]...KEPZ

Kap Tobin [*Greenland*] [*Seismograph station code, US Geological Survey*]....... KTG
Kapapala Ranch [*Hawaii*] [*Seismograph station code, US Geological Survey*]....... KLH
Kapiolani Community College, Honolulu, HI [*Library symbol*]....... HHK
Kapisanan ng mga Manggawa Sa MRR [*Manila Railroad Workers' Union*] [*Philippines*]....... KMSMRR
Kapit [*Malaysia*] [*Airport symbol*]....... KPI
Kapitalist Birokrat [*Capitalist Bureaucrat*] [*Term for foreigner*] [*Indonesia*]....... KABIR
Kapitalistate [*A publication*]....... Kapitalis
Kaplan Industries [*NASDAQ symbol*]....... KAPL
Kaplan, LA [*Radio station call letters*]....... KMDL
Kapok Corp. [*American Stock Exchange symbol*]....... KPK
Kapok Tree Inns Corp. [*American Stock Exchange symbol*]....... KTI
Kaposi's Sarcoma [*Medicine*]....... KS
Kappa Alpha Order....... KAO
Kappa Alpha Theta [*Sorority*]....... KAT
Kappa Beta Pi [*Society*]....... KBP
Kappa Beta Pi Quarterly [*A publication*]....... KBP Q
Kappa Delta Rho [*Fraternity*]....... KDR
Kappa Eta Kappa [*Fraternity*]....... KEK
Kappa Kappa Gamma [*Sorority*]....... KKG
Kappa Kappa Psi [*Society*]....... KKP
Kappa Mu Epsilon [*Society*]....... KME
Kappa Phi Kappa [*Fraternity*]....... KPK
Kappa Sigma Kappa [*Later, Theta Xi*] [*Fraternity*]....... KSK
Kapuskasing [*Canada*] [*Airport symbol*]....... YYU
Kapuskasing, ON [*Television station call letters*]....... CBLFT-4
Kapuskasing, ON [*Radio station call letters*]....... CFLK
Kapuskasing, ON [*Television station call letters*]....... CITO-TV-1
Kapuskasing, ON [*Radio station call letters*]....... CKAP
Kapuskasing Public Library, Kapuskasing, ON, Canada [*Library symbol*]....... CaOKap
Kar-Air [*Finland*] [*ICAO designator*]....... KR
Kar Kar [*Papua New Guinea*] [*Airport symbol*]....... KRX
Karabiner [*Carbine*] [*German military - World War II*]....... KAR
Karachi [*Pakistan*] [*Seismograph station code, US Geological Survey*]....... KAR
Karachi [*Pakistan*] [*Airport symbol*]....... KHI
Karad [*India*] [*Seismograph station code, US Geological Survey*]....... KAD
Karaganda [*USSR*] [*Geomagnetic observatory code*]....... KGD
Karakalpak [*MARC language code*] [*Library of Congress*]....... kaa
Karakoram Highway [*Asia*]....... KKH
Karakul Fur Sheep Registry [*Later, AKFSR*]....... KFSR
Karamay [*China*] [*Airport symbol*]....... KRY
Karapiro [*New Zealand*] [*Seismograph station code, US Geological Survey*]....... KRP
Karasabai [*Guyana*] [*Airport symbol*]....... KRG
Karasu [*USSR*] [*Seismograph station code, US Geological Survey*]....... KRU
Karat [*Variant of "carat," C, q.v.*]....... K
Karato [*Papua New Guinea*] [*Airport symbol*]....... KAF
Karavia [*Zaire*] [*Geomagnetic observatory code*]....... KVA
Kardiologia Polska [*A publication*]....... Kardiol Pol
Karen [*MARC language code*] [*Library of Congress*]....... kar
Karen Horney Clinic....... KHC
Karen National Defense Organization [*Burma*]....... KNDO
Karen National Unity Party [*Burma*]....... KNUP
Karen Silkwood Fund....... KSF
Kariba [*Rhodesia*] [*Seismograph station code, US Geological Survey*] [*Closed*]....... KRB
Kariba Dam [*Zimbabwe*] [*Airport symbol*]....... KAB
Kariba Studies [*A publication*]....... Kariba Stud
Karimui [*Papua New Guinea*] [*Airport symbol*]....... KMR
Karissimo Bene Merenti [*To the Most Dear and Well-Deserving*]....... KBM
Karkar Island [*Papua New Guinea*] [*Seismograph station code, US Geological Survey*]....... KKI
Karl-August-Forster-Lectures [*A publication*]....... Karl-August-Forster-Lect
Karlovy Vary [*Czechoslovakia*] [*Airport symbol*]....... KLV
Karlskoga [*Sweden*] [*Airport symbol*]....... KSK
Karlskrona [*Sweden*] [*Seismograph station code, US Geological Survey*] [*Closed*]....... KLS
Karlsruhe [*Federal Republic of Germany*] [*Seismograph station code, US Geological Survey*]....... KRL
Karlsruhe Isochronous Cyclotron....... KIC
Karlsruhe - West [*Federal Republic of Germany*] [*Seismograph station code, US Geological Survey*]....... KRW
Karlsruher Geographische Hefte [*A publication*]....... Karlsruher Geogr Hefte
Karlstad [*Sweden*] [*Airport symbol*]....... KSD
Karluk [*Alaska*] [*Airport symbol*]....... KYK
Karman Constant [*Physics*]....... KC
Karnatak University. Journal of Science [*A publication*]....... Karnatak Univ J Sci
Karnataka Medical Journal [*A publication*]....... Karnataka Med J
Karoi [*Rhodesia*] [*Seismograph station code, US Geological Survey*]....... KRR
Karolinska Institutets Bibliotek och Informationscentral [*Karolinska Institute Library and Information Center*] [*Sweden*] [*Information service*]....... KIBIC
Karolinska Symposia on Research Methods in Reproductive Endocrinology [*A publication*]....... Karolinska Symp Res Methods Reprod Endocrinol
Karonga [*Malawi*] [*Airport symbol*]....... KGJ
Karpathos [*Greece*] [*Airport symbol*]....... AOK
Karratha [*Australia*] [*Seismograph station code, US Geological Survey*] [*Closed*]....... KAA
Karratha [*Australia*] [*Airport symbol*]....... KTA
Karsanskaya [*USSR*] [*Later, TFS*] [*Geomagnetic observatory code*]....... KSI
Kartvelur Enata St'rukt'uris Sak'itxebi [*A publication*]....... KESS
Karuizawa [*Also, KRZ*] [*Japan*] [*Seismograph station code, US Geological Survey*]....... KAZ
Karuizawa [*Japan*] [*Also, KAZ*] [*Seismograph station code, US Geological Survey*]....... KRZ
Karumba [*Australia*] [*Airport symbol*]....... KRB
Karup [*Denmark*] [*Airport symbol*]....... KRP
Karyawan Pegawai Negeri [*Indonesia*]....... KARPEN
Karyopyknotic Index [*Cytology*]....... KPI
Kasaba Bay [*Zambia*] [*Airport symbol*]....... ZKB
Kasama [*Zambia*] [*Airport symbol*]....... KAA
Kaschechewan [*Canada*] [*Airport symbol*]....... ZKE
Kaschin-Beck Disease [*Medicine*]....... KBD
Kasernierte Volkspolizei....... KVP
Kasernierte Volkspolizei-Dienststelle....... KVPD
Kasese [*Uganda*] [*Airport symbol*]....... KSE
Kasetsart Journal [*A publication*]....... Kasetsart J
Kasetsart University. Fishery Research Bulletin [*A publication*]....... Kasetsart Univ Fish Res Bull
Kashi [*China*] [*Airport symbol*]....... KHG
Kashima [*Japan*] [*Seismograph station code, US Geological Survey*]....... KSJ
Kashiwara [*Japan*] [*Seismograph station code, US Geological Survey*]....... KAJ
Kashmir Science [*A publication*]....... Kashmir Sci
Kashmiri [*MARC language code*] [*Library of Congress*]....... kas
Kasigluk [*Alaska*] [*Airport symbol*]....... KUK
Kaskaskia Library System [*Library network*]....... KLS
Kaskaskia Library System, Smithton, IL [*OCLC symbol*]....... IFG
Kasler Corp. [*NASDAQ symbol*]....... KASL
Kaslo, BC [*Radio station call letters*]....... CKAL-FM-3
Kasos Island [*Greece*] [*Airport symbol*]....... KSJ
Kasperske Hory [*Czechoslovakia*] [*Seismograph station code, US Geological Survey*]....... KHC
Kasr El-Aini Journal of Surgery [*A publication*]....... Kasr El-Aini J Surg
Kassala [*Sudan*] [*Airport symbol*]....... KSL
Kassel [*West Germany*] [*Airport symbol*]....... KSF
Kassian Benevolent Society in America....... KBSA
Kastamonu [*Turkey*] [*Seismograph station code, US Geological Survey*]....... KAS
Kastoria [*Greece*] [*Airport symbol*]....... KSO
Kasturi and Sons [*India*] [*ICAO designator*] [*Obsolete*]....... KY
Katabatic Wind....... KW
Katadyn Pocket Filter....... KPF
Katal [*Unit of enzyme activity*]....... kat
Kataliticheskie Prevrascheniya Uglevodorodov [*A publication*]....... Katl Prevrashch Uglevodorodov
Katallagete [*A publication*]....... Katal
Katalog Fauny Polski [*A publication*]....... Kat Fauny Pol
Katalog Kandidatskikh i Doktorskikh Dissertatsii [*A bibliographic publication*]....... KKDD
Kate Greenaway Society....... KGS
Katherine [*Australia*] [*Airport symbol*]....... KTR
Kathodal Closing [*Medicine*]....... KC
Kathodal Closing Tetanus [*Medicine*]....... KCT
Kathodal Closure Contraction [*Medicine*]....... KCC
Kathodal Closure Tetanus [*Medicine*]....... KCTE
Kathodal Duration [*Medicine*]....... KD
Kathodal Duration Tetanus [*Medicine*]....... KDT
Kathodal Opening Contraction [*Medicine*]....... KOC
Kathode [*Cathode*]....... K
Kathode [*Cathode*]....... KA
Kathode Dark Space....... KDS
Kathode Flicker Effect....... KFE
Kathode Heating Time....... KHT
Kathode Pulse Modulation....... KPM
Kathode Ray Furnace....... KRF
Kathode Ray Lamp....... KRL
Kathode Ray Oscilloscope....... KRO
Kathode Ray Tube....... KRT
Kathode Ray Tube Oscillograph....... KRTO
Kathode Ray Tube Shield....... KRTS
Kathode Ray Tube Tester....... KRTT
Katholiek [*A publication*]....... Kat
Katholiek [*A publication*]....... Kath
Katholiek Cultureel Tijdschrift [*A publication*]....... KCT
Katholieke Arbeidersbewegung [*Netherlands*]....... KAB
Katholieke Film-Centrale [*Netherlands*]....... KFC
Katholieke Radio-Omroep [*Netherlands*]....... KRO
Katholische Gedanke [*A publication*]....... KG
Katholische Nachrichten-Agentur [*Press agency*] [*West Germany*]....... KNA
Katholischer Deutscher Akademikerinnen [*Bund*] [*Union of German Catholic University Women*] [*Germany*]....... KDA
Katholisk Nederlands Persbureau [*Press agency*] [*Netherlands*]....... KNP
Katilolehti. Tidskrift foer Barnmorskor [*A publication*]....... Katilolehti
Katipunang Manggagawang Pilipino [*Confederation of Trade Unions of the Philippines*]....... KMP

Katlanovo [Yugoslavia] [Seismograph station code, US Geological Survey] .... KAY
Katmai [Alaska] [Seismograph station code, US Geological Survey] .... KTM
Katmai National Monument .... KATM
Katmandu [Nepal] [Airport symbol] .... KTM
Kato [Guyana] [Airport symbol] .... KTO
Katonah Village Library, Katonah, NY [Library symbol] .... NKa
Katoptric System [Optics] .... KS
Katowice [Poland] [Airport symbol] .... KTW
Katubsanan sa Mamumio [Philippine United Labor Congress] .... KSM
Katuura [Japan] [Later, HTY] [Geomagnetic observatory code] .... KTR
Katuura [Japan] [Seismograph station code, US Geological Survey] [Closed] .... KTR
Katy Industries, Inc. [Formerly, Missouri-Kansas-Texas R. R. Co., with Wall Street slang name of "Kathy"] [NYSE symbol] .... KT
Katz Adjustment Scales [Psychology] .... KAS
Kauai Public Library Association, Linhue, HI [Library symbol] .... HLK
Kauai Test Facility [AEC] .... KTF
Kaufhaus des Westens [Department Store of the West] [Germany] .... KaDeWe
Kaufman Assessment Battery for Children .... KABC
Kaufman & Broad, Inc. [NYSE symbol] .... KB
Kaufman Ion Thrustor .... KIT
Kaukauna Public Library, Kaukauna, WI [Library symbol] .... WKa
Kaukauna, WI [Radio station call letters] .... WKAU
Kaukauna, WI [Radio station call letters] .... WKAU-FM
Kaukura [French Polynesia] [Airport symbol] .... KKR
Kaunakakai, HI [Location identifier] [FAA] .... MKK
Kauppakorkeakoulu [Helsinki School of Economics], Helsinki, Finland [Library symbol] .... FiHK
Kauri-Butanol Value [Measure of relative solvent power] .... KB
Kautschuk und Gummi Kunststoffe [A publication] .... Kaut Gum Ku
Kautschuk und Gummi Kunststoffe [A publication] .... Kautsch Gummi Kunstst
Kavak [Turkey] [Seismograph station code, US Geological Survey] .... KVT
Kavala [Greece] [Airport symbol] .... KVA
Kavieng [New Ireland] [Seismograph station code, US Geological Survey] [Closed] .... KAV
Kavieng [Papua New Guinea] [Airport symbol] .... KVG
Kavieng [Papua New Guinea] [Seismograph station code, US Geological Survey] .... KVG
Kawah Idjen [Java] [Seismograph station code, US Geological Survey] [Closed] .... KIJ
Kawasaki Disease [Also, MLNS] [Medicine] .... KD
Kawasaki Medical Journal [A publication] .... Kawasaki Med J
Kawasaki Steel. Technical Bulletin [A publication] .... Kawasaki Steel Tech Bull
Kaweah Delta District Hospital, Visalia, CA [Library symbol] .... CViKD
Kawecki Berylco Industries, Inc. [NYSE symbol] [Delisted] .... KBI
Kawneer Co. [NYSE symbol] .... KAW
Kawthaung [Burma] [Airport symbol] .... KAW
Kay Corp. [American Stock Exchange symbol] .... KAY
Kayak .... K
Kayak Island [Alaska] [Seismograph station code, US Geological Survey] .... KYK
Kayes [Mali] [Airport symbol] .... KYS
Kaypro Corp. [NASDAQ symbol] .... KAYP
Kayser .... K
Kayser-Roth Corp. [NYSE symbol] [Delisted] .... KYR
Kayseri [Turkey] [Airport symbol] .... ASR
Kazakhskii Gosudarstvennyi Pedagogiceskii Institut Imeni Abaja. Ucenye Zapiski [A publication] .... Kazah Gos Ped Inst Ucen Zap
Kazakh [MARC language code] [Library of Congress] .... kaz
Kazakh Soviet Socialist Republic [MARC geographic area code] [Library of Congress] .... e-ur-kz
Kazakh Soviet Socialist Republic .... KazSSR
Kazakh Soviet Socialist Republic [MARC country of publication code] [Library of Congress] .... kzr
Kazakhskii Nauchno-Issledovatel'skii Institut Lesnogo Khozyaistva. Trudy [A publication] .... Kaz Nauchno-Issled Inst Lesn Khoz Tr
Kazan [Formerly, Kazanskaya] [USSR] [Geomagnetic observatory code] .... KNS
Kazan [USSR] [Airport symbol] .... KZN
Kazan Aviation Institute .... KAI
Kazanskii Meditsinskii Zhurnal [A publication] .... Kazan Med Zh
Kazanskii Meditsinskii Zhurnal [A publication] .... Kazan Med Zhurnal
Kazanskii Ordena Trudovogo Krasnogo Znameni Gosudarstvennyi Universitet Imeni V. I. Ul'janova-Lenina. Ucenye Zapiski [A publication] .... Kazan Gos Univ Ucen Zap
Kazanskii Universitet. Issledovanija po Prikladnoi Matematike [A publication] .... Issled Prikl Mat
KC Piper Sales, Inc. [Olathe, KS] [FAA designator] .... KCE
KDD Technical Journal [A publication] .... KDD Tech J
KDI Corp. [NYSE symbol] .... KDI
KDT Industries, Inc. [NYSE symbol] [Delisted] .... KDT
Kealakekua [Hawaii] [Seismograph station code, US Geological Survey] [Closed] .... KLK
Kealakekua, HI [Radio station call letters] .... KOAS
Kealakekua-Kona, HI [Radio station call letters] .... KKON

Kealakomo [Hawaii] [Seismograph station code, US Geological Survey] [Closed] .... KEA
Kean College of New Jersey, Union, NJ [OCLC symbol] .... NJK
Kean College of New Jersey, Union, NJ [Library symbol] .... NjUN
Keanakolu [Hawaii] [Seismograph station code, US Geological Survey] .... KKU
Keane, Inc. [NASDAQ symbol] .... KEAN
Kearfott Acceleration Integrating Gyroscope .... KAIG
Kearney [Nebraska] [Airport symbol] .... EAR
Kearney-National [NASDAQ symbol] .... KERN
Kearney, NE [Radio station call letters] .... KGFW
Kearney, NE [Television station call letters] .... KHGI-TV
Kearney, NE [Radio station call letters] .... KQKY
Kearney, NE [Radio station call letters] .... KRNY
Kearney, NE [Radio station call letters] .... KRNY-FM
Kearney, NE [Radio station call letters] .... KSCV
Kearney Public Library, Kearney, NE [Library symbol] .... NbK
Kearney State College, Kearney, NE [OCLC symbol] .... KRS
Kearney State College, Kearney, NE [Library symbol] .... NbKS
Kearns, ON [Television station call letters] CFCL-TV-2
Kearns, ON [Television station call letters] CITO-TV-2
Kearny Observer, Kearny, NJ [Library symbol] .... NjKO
Kearny Public Library, Kearny, NJ [Library symbol] .... NjK
Keating, PA [Location identifier] [FAA] .... ETG
Keats-Shelley Association of America .... KSAA
Keats-Shelley Journal [A publication] .... Keats-Shelley J
Keats-Shelley Journal [A publication] .... KSJ
Keats-Shelley Journal. Annual Bibliography [A publication] .... Keats-Shelley J Ann Bibl
Keats-Shelley Memorial Bulletin [Rome] [A publication] .... KSMB
Keats-Shelley Memorial Bulletin (Rome) [A publication] .... KSMBR
Keban [Turkey] [Seismograph station code, US Geological Survey] .... KEB
Kebar [Indonesia] [Airport symbol] .... KEQ
Kechabta [Tunisia] [Seismograph station code, US Geological Survey] .... KCHT
Keck, Mahin, & Cate, Chicago, IL [OCLC symbol] .... ILT
Kecskemet [Hungary] [Seismograph station code, US Geological Survey] .... KEC
Kedougou [Senegal] [Seismograph station code, US Geological Survey] [Closed] .... KDG
Kedougou [Senegal] [Seismograph station code, US Geological Survey] .... KDS
Kedougou [Senegal] [Seismograph station code, US Geological Survey] [Closed] .... KED
Kedougou [Senegal] [Airport symbol] .... KGG
Kee Exploration, Inc. [NASDAQ symbol] .... KEEX
Keebler Co. [NYSE symbol] [Delisted] .... KBR
Keel .... K
Keel Depth Simulator .... KDS
Keel ja Kirjandus [A publication] .... KjK
Keel Shock Factor .... KSF
Keele ja Kirjanduse Instituudi Uurimused [A publication] .... KKIU
Keeley-Frontier Resources [NASDAQ symbol] .... KFRLF
Keen Mountain [Virginia] [Seismograph station code, US Geological Survey] [Closed] .... KMV
Keene [New Hampshire] [Airport symbol] .... EEN
Keene Corp. [NYSE symbol] [Delisted] .... KE
Keene, NH [Television station call letters] .... WEKW-TV
Keene, NH [Radio station call letters] .... WKBK
Keene, NH [Radio station call letters] .... WKNE
Keene, NH [Radio station call letters] .... WKNH
Keene, NH [Radio station call letters] .... WNBX-FM
Keene Public Library, Keene, NH [Library symbol] .... NhKe
Keene State College, Keene, NH [OCLC symbol] .... KNM
Keene State College, Keene, NH [Library symbol] .... NhKeK
Keene, TX [Radio station call letters] .... KSUC
Keeneland Association, Inc., Lexington, KY [Library symbol] .... KyLxK
Keene's Cement Plaster [Technical drawings] .... KCP
Keene's Cement Plaster Ceiling [Technical drawings] .... KCPC
Keep-Alive Anode .... KAA
Keep America Beautiful .... KAB
Keep America Independent .... KAI
Keep It Dark [Say Nothing About It] [Slang] .... KD
Keep It Short and Simple .... KISS
Keep It Short and Sweet [Radio messages] .... KISS
Keep It Simple, Make It Fun .... KISMIF
Keep It Simple, Sir [Data processing] .... KISS
Keep It Simple, Stupid [Bridge bidding term] .... KISS
Keep It Straight and Simple [Data processing] .... KISS
Keep Off [i.e., avoid assuming the risk on an application, pending further investigation] [Insurance] .... KO
Keep Off Pounds Sensibly [Club] .... KOPS
Keep Open .... KO
Keep This Office Advised .... KEPOA
Keep Type Standing [Printing] .... KS
Keep Up to Date .... KUTD
Keep Up the Good Work .... KUTGW
Keep Vein Open [Medicine] .... KVO
Keep in View .... KIV
Keeper of the Privy Purse [British] .... KPP
Keeping .... KPG

Keeping Abreast Journal of Human Nurturing [*A publication*] ...... Keep Abreast J
Keeping Abreast Journal of Human Nurturing [*A publication*] ...... Keep Abreast J Hum Nurt
Keeping House of Ill Fame ...... KHIF
Keeshond Club of America ...... KCA
Keesings Contemporary Archives [*British world-news digest service*] ...... KCA
Keesler Air Force Base [*Mississippi*] ...... KAFB
Keesler Technical Training Center ...... KTTC
Keesom Relationship ...... KR
Keetmanshoop [*South-West Africa*] [*Airport symbol*] ...... KMP
Keewatin [*FAA*] ...... KWTN
Keewatin Community College, The Pas, MB, Canada [*Library symbol*] ...... CaMTPK
Keg ...... K
Keg ...... KG
Kegaska [*Canada*] [*Airport symbol*] ...... ZKG
Kegoayah Kozga Public Library, Nome, AK [*Library symbol*] ...... AkN
Keighley Central Library, Keighley, United Kingdom [*Library symbol*] ...... UkK
Keio Business Review [*A publication*] ...... KBR
Keio Business Review [*Tokyo*] [*A publication*] ...... Keio Bus R
Keio Economic Studies [*A publication*] ...... Keio Econ S
Keio Economic Studies [*Tokyo*] [*A publication*] ...... Keio Econ Stud
Keio Economic Studies [*A publication*] ...... KES
Keio Engineering Reports [*A publication*] ...... Keio Eng Rep
Keio Engineering Reports [*A publication*] ...... Keio Engrg Rep
Keio Journal of Medicine [*A publication*] ...... Keio J Med
Keio Journal of Politics [*A publication*] ...... Keio J Polit
Keio Mathematical Seminar. Reports [*A publication*] ...... Keio Math Sem Rep
Keio University, Tokyo, Japan [*Library symbol*] ...... JTKU
Keiryo Kokugogaku [*Mathematical Linguistics*] [*A publication*] ...... Ke K
Keith Railway Equipment Co. [*AAR code*] ...... KTX
Keith Shipton Developments. Special Study [*A publication*] ...... Keith Shipton Dev Spec Study
KEK Annual Report (National Laboratory for High Energy Physics) [*A publication*] ...... KEK Annu Rep (Natl Lab High Energy Phys)
Kekaha, HI [*Location identifier*] [*FAA*] ...... BKH
Kelco Co. [*Research code symbol*] ...... B
Keleket X-Ray Corporation ...... KXC
Keles [*USSR*] [*Later, TKT*] [*Geomagnetic observatory code*] ...... KEL
Kell [*Blood group*] ...... K
Kelle [*Congo*] [*Airport symbol*] ...... KEE
Keller-Dorian, Berthon [*Method*] [*Photography*] ...... KDB
Keller Industries, Inc. [*NYSE symbol*] [*Delisted*] ...... KEL
Keller, N. L., Washington DC [*STAC*] ...... KNL
Keller's Language [*Data processing*] ...... KL
Kelley Island Time & Transport [*NYSE symbol*] ...... KIC
Kelley Memorial Library, Salem, NH [*Library symbol*] ...... NhS
Kellner Eye Piece ...... KEP
Kellogg [*Idaho*] [*Seismograph station code, US Geological Survey*] ...... KGI
Kellogg Community College, Battle Creek, MI [*OCLC symbol*] ...... EEK
Kellogg Community College, Battle Creek, MI [*Library symbol*] ...... MiBatK
Kellogg Co. [*NYSE symbol*] ...... K
Kellogg, ID [*Radio station call letters*] ...... KCJF
Kellogg, ID [*Radio station call letters*] ...... KGSF
Kellogg Switchboard and Supply ...... KSS
Kellwood Co. [*NYSE symbol*] ...... KWD
Kelly-Johnston Enterprises [*NASDAQ symbol*] ...... KEJO
Kelly Services, Inc. [*NASDAQ symbol*] ...... KELY
Kelly's Creek & Northwestern Railroad Co. [*AAR code*] ...... KCNW
Kelowna [*Canada*] [*Airport symbol*] ...... YLW
Kelowna, BC [*Television station call letters*] ...... CHBC-TV
Kelowna, BC [*Radio station call letters*] ...... CHIM-FM
Kelowna, BC [*Television station call letters*] ...... CHKL-TV
Kelowna, BC [*Radio station call letters*] ...... CKIQ
Kelowna, BC [*Radio station call letters*] ...... CKOV
Kelowna Centennial Museum and Archives, Kelowna, BC, Canada [*Library symbol*] ...... CaBKOM
Kelp [*Quality of the Bottom*] [*Nautical charts*] ...... K
Kelsey-Hayes Co. [*NYSE symbol*] [*Delisted*] ...... KW
Kelsey Institute of Applied Arts and Sciences, Saskatoon, SK, Canada [*Library symbol*] ...... CaSSSI
Kelseyville Free Library, Kelseyville, CA [*Library symbol*] ...... CKel
Kelso Public Library, Kelso, WA [*Library symbol*] ...... WaKel
Kelso, WA [*Radio station call letters*] ...... KLOG
Kelud [*Java*] [*Seismograph station code, US Geological Survey*] [*Closed*] ...... KEL
Kelvin [*Symbol*] [*SI unit of thermodynamic temperature*] ...... K
Kelvin Astatic Galvanometer [*Electronics*] ...... KAG
Kelvin Circulation Theorem [*Physics*] ...... KCT
Kelvin Double Bridge [*Physics*] ...... KDB
Kelvin-Helmholtz [*Waves*] [*Meteorology*] ...... KH
Kelvin Law [*Physics*] ...... KL
Kelvin Square Meters per Watt ...... K M^2/W
Kelvin Temperature Scale ...... KTS
Kelvin-Varley Slide [*Electronics*] ...... KVS
KEMA [*Keuring van Electrotechnische Materialien Arnhem*] **Publikaties** [*A publication*] ...... KEMA Publ
Kema Suspension Test Reactor [*Netherlands*] ...... KSTR
Kemerovskii Gosudarstvennyi Pedagogiceskii Institut. Ucenye Zapiski [*A publication*] ...... Kemerov Gos Ped Inst Ucen Zap
Kemi [*Finland*] [*Airport symbol*] ...... KEM
Kemia-Talajtani Tanszek [*A publication*] ...... Kem-Talajt
Kemiai Kozlemenyek [*A publication*] ...... Kem Kozl
Kemiai Kozlemenyek [*A publication*] ...... Kem Kozlem
Kemian Teollisuus [*Finland*] [*A publication*] ...... Kem Teollisuus
Kemija u Industrija (Zagreb) [*A publication*] ...... Kem Ind (Zagreb)
Kemisk Maandesblad og Nordisk Handelsblad foer Kemisk Industri [*A publication*] ...... Kem Maandesbl Nord Handelsbl Kem Ind
Kemisk Tidskrift [*A publication*] ...... Kem Tidskr
Kemmerer, WY [*Location identifier*] [*FAA*] ...... EMM
Kemmerer, WY [*Radio station call letters*] ...... KMER
Kemp Public Library, Wichita Falls, TX [*Library symbol*] ...... TxWic
Kemper Corporation [*NASDAQ symbol*] ...... KEMC
Kempsey [*Australia*] [*Airport symbol*] ...... KPS
Kenai [*Alaska*] [*Airport symbol*] ...... ENA
Kenai, AK [*Location identifier*] [*FAA*] ...... DRF
Kenai, AK [*Location identifier*] [*FAA*] ...... ENA
Kenai, AK [*Location identifier*] [*FAA*] ...... IWW
Kenai, AK [*Radio station call letters*] ...... KQOK
Kenai Community Library, Inc., Kenai, AK [*Library symbol*] ...... AkKe
Kenai Corp. [*NYSE symbol*] ...... KEN
Kenai Corp. Wts [*NASDAQ symbol*] ...... KENAW
Kenai Historical, Inc., Fort Kenai Museum, Kenai, AK [*Library symbol*] ...... AkKeHi
Kenai Peninsula Borough [*Alaska*] ...... KPB
Kenansville, NC [*Location identifier*] [*FAA*] ...... DPL
Kencope Energy Co. [*NASDAQ symbol*] ...... KCOP
Kendall Co. [*NYSE symbol*] ...... KEN
Kendall High School Library, Kendall, NY [*OCLC symbol*] ...... RWT
Kendall Whaling Museum, Sharon, MA [*Library symbol*] ...... MShaK
Kendall Young Library, Webster City, IA [*Library symbol*] ...... IaWec
Kendall's Compound E [*Cortisone*] ...... KE
Kendallville, IN [*Radio station call letters*] ...... WAWK
Kendallville, IN [*Radio station call letters*] ...... WAWK-FM
Kendari [*Indonesia*] [*Airport symbol*] ...... KDI
Kenedy-Karnes City, TX [*Radio station call letters*] ...... KAML
Kenedy, TX [*Radio station call letters*] ...... KTNR
Kenema [*Sierra Leone*] [*Airport symbol*] ...... KEN
Kengtung [*Burma*] [*Airport symbol*] ...... KET
Kenieba [*Mali*] [*Airport symbol*] ...... KNZ
Kenilworth Realty Trust SBI [*NYSE symbol*] [*Delisted*] ...... KRT
Kenilworth Systems Corp. [*NASDAQ symbol*] ...... KENSQ
Keningau [*Malaysia*] [*Airport symbol*] ...... KGU
Kenley Abstracts [*A publication*] ...... Kenley Abstr
Kenn Borek Air Ltd. [*Dawson Creek, BC*] [*FAA designator*] ...... KBA
Kennametal, Inc. [*NYSE symbol*] ...... KMT
Kennebunk, ME [*Location identifier*] [*FAA*] ...... ENE
Kennecott Co. Railroad [*AAR code*] ...... KENN
Kennecott Copper Corp. [*NYSE symbol*] [*Delisted*] ...... KN
Kennecott Copper Corp., Ledgemont Laboratory, Lexington, MA [*Library symbol*] ...... MLexK
Kennedy Air Service [*Valdez, AK*] [*FAA designator*] ...... KEN
Kennedy Approved Parts List [*NASA*] ...... KAPL
Kennedy Athletic Recreation and Social [*NASA*] ...... KARS
Kennedy-Heaviside Layer [*Electronics*] ...... KHL
Kennedy Institute of Ethics, Washington, DC [*OCLC symbol*] ...... KIE
Kennedy International Airport [*New York*] [*Airport symbol*] ...... JFK
Kennedy-King College of the City College of Chicago, Chicago, IL [*OCLC symbol*] ...... IAN
Kennedy-King College of the City College of Chicago, Chicago, IL [*Library symbol*] ...... ICKK
Kennedy Notice [*NASA*] ...... KN
Kennedy Operating Instructions [*NASA*] ...... KOI
Kennedy Program Directive [*NASA*] ...... KPD
Kennedy Program Requirements Document [*NASA*] ...... KPRD
Kennedy Resources [*NASDAQ symbol*] ...... KDDYF
Kennedy Space Center [*NASA*] ...... KSC
Kennedy Space Center/Unmanned Launch Operations [*NASA*] ...... KSC/ULO
Kennedy Space Center - Western Test Range Operations Division [*NASA*] ...... KSC-WTROD
Kennedy-Thorndike Experiment ...... KTE
Kennel Club ...... KC
Kennesaw College, Marietta, GA [*OCLC symbol*] ...... GKJ
Kennesaw College, Marietta, GA [*Library symbol*] ...... GMarK
Kennesaw Mountain National Battlefield Park ...... KEMO
Kenneth J. Lane [*Jewelry designer*] ...... KJL
Kennett, MO [*Radio station call letters*] ...... KBOA
Kennett, MO [*Radio station call letters*] ...... KBXM
Kennett, MO [*Radio station call letters*] ...... KTMO
Kennewick-Pasco-Richland, WA [*Radio station call letters*] ...... KONA
Kennewick-Pasco-Richland, WA [*Radio station call letters*] ...... KONA-FM
Kennewick, WA [*Radio station call letters*] ...... KOTY
Kennewick, WA [*Television station call letters*] ...... KVEW
Kennington Ltd. [*NASDAQ symbol*] ...... KENN
Kenny Rehabilitation Institute, Minneapolis, MN [*Library symbol*] ...... MnMK
Keno Hill, YT [*Television station call letters*] ...... CBKHT
Kenora [*Canada*] [*Airport symbol*] ...... YQK
Kenora, ON [*Radio station call letters*] ...... CBQX-FM

Kenora, ON [Television station call letters] ....CBWAT
Kenora, ON [Radio station call letters] ....CJRL
Kenora Public Library, Kenora, ON, Canada [Library symbol] ....CaOKe
Kenosha County Historical Association, Kenosha, WI [Library symbol] ....WKenHi
Kenosha Memorial Hospital, Kenosha, WI [Library symbol] ....WKenM
Kenosha Public Library, Kenosha, WI [OCLC symbol] ....WIK
Kenosha, WI [Location identifier] [FAA] ....ENW
Kenosha, WI [Location identifier] [FAA] ....PKW
Kenosha, WI [Radio station call letters] ....WGTD
Kenosha, WI [Radio station call letters] ....WJZQ
Kenosha, WI [Radio station call letters] ....WJZQ-FM
Kenosha, WI [Radio station call letters] ....WLIP
Kenova, WV [Radio station call letters] ....WHEZ
Kensett Public Library, Kensett, IA [Library symbol] ....IaKen
Kent County Library and Kent County Library System, Grand Rapids, MI [OCLC symbol] ....EXE
Kent and County of London Yeomanry [Military unit] [British] ....KCLY
Kent County Public Library, Chatham, ON, Canada [Library symbol] ....CaOChaKC
Kent, OH [Radio station call letters] ....WKNT
Kent, OH [Radio station call letters] ....WKSU-FM
Kent, OH [Radio station call letters] ....WNIR
Kent-Rosanoff Free Association Test [Psychology] ....K-R
Kent State University [Ohio] ....KSU
Kent State University, Ashtabula Regional Campus, Ashtabula, OH [Library symbol] ....OAshtK
Kent State University, Columbiana Regional Campus, Salem, OH [Library symbol] ....OSalK
Kent State University, East Liverpool Regional Campus, East Liverpool, OH [Library symbol] ....OEalK
Kent State University, Kent, OH [OCLC symbol] ....KSU
Kent State University, Kent, OH [Library symbol] ....OKentU
Kent State University, School of Library Science, Kent, OH [OCLC symbol] ....KSS
Kent State University, Stark County Regional Campus, Canton, OH [Library symbol] ....OCanK
Kent State University, Stark County Regional Campus, Canton, OH [OCLC symbol] ....OCK
Kent State University, Trumbull Regional Campus, Warren, OH [Library symbol] [OCLC symbol] ....OWK
Kent State University, Tuscarawas County Regional Campus, New Philadelphia, OH [Library symbol] ....ONpK
Kent Technical Review [A publication] ....Kent Tech Rev
Kent Yeomanry [Military unit] [British] ....KY
Kentfield [California] [Seismograph station code, US Geological Survey] ....KFC
Kentish ....K
Kenton County Public Library, Covington, KY [Library symbol] ....KyCov
Kenton, DE [Location identifier] [FAA] ....ENO
Kenton, OH [Radio station call letters] ....WKTN
Kentron International, Inc. [American Stock Exchange symbol] ....KTN
Kentron Programmatismou kai Oikonomikon Ereunon [Indonesia] ....KEPE
Kentucky ....KEN
Kentucky [Postal code] ....KY
Kentucky [MARC country of publication code] [Library of Congress] ....kyu
Kentucky [MARC geographic area code] [Library of Congress] ....n-us-ky
Kentucky Academy of Science. Transactions [A publication] ....Kentucky Acad Sci Trans
Kentucky Agricultural Experiment Station Annual Report [A publication] ....KY Agric Exp Stn Annu Rep
Kentucky Agricultural Experiment Station Bulletin [A publication] ....KY Agric Exp Stn Bull
Kentucky Agricultural Experiment Station Miscellaneous Publications [A publication] ....KY Agric Exp Stn Misc Pubs
Kentucky Agricultural Experiment Station Progress Report [A publication] ....KY Agric Exp Stn Prog Rep
Kentucky Agricultural Experiment Station Publications [A publication] ....KY Ag Exp
Kentucky Agricultural Experiment Station Regulatory Bulletin [A publication] ....KY Agric Exp Stn Regul Bull
Kentucky Agricultural Experiment Station Results of Research [A publication] ....KY Agric Exp Stn Results Res
Kentucky Bar Journal [A publication] ....KY B J
Kentucky Central Life [NASDAQ symbol] ....KENCA
Kentucky Cooperative Library and Information Project [Library network] ....KENCLIP
Kentucky Department of Fish and Wildlife Resources Fisheries Bulletin [A publication] ....KY Dep Fish Wildl Resour Fish Bull
Kentucky Department of Libraries, Frankfort, KY [Library symbol] ....Ky
Kentucky Department of Libraries, Library Extension Division, Frankfort, KY [OCLC symbol] ....KSL
Kentucky Department of Libraries, Processing Center, Frankfort, KY [OCLC symbol] ....KSP
Kentucky Economic Information System [Information service] ....KEIS
Kentucky Farm and Home Science [A publication] ....KY Farm Home Sci
Kentucky Folklore Record [A publication] ....KFR
Kentucky Folklore Record [A publication] ....KY Folk Rec
Kentucky Folklore Series [A publication] ....KFS
Kentucky Foreign Language Quarterly [A publication] ....KFLQ

Kentucky Geological Survey. Bulletin [A publication] ....Kentucky Geol Survey Bull
Kentucky Geological Survey. County Report [A publication] ....Kentucky Geol Survey County Rept
Kentucky Geological Survey. Information Circular [A publication] ....Kentucky Geol Survey Inf Circ
Kentucky Geological Survey. Report of Investigations [A publication] ....Kentucky Geol Survey Rept Inv
Kentucky Geological Survey Report of Investigations [A publication] ....KY Geol Surv Rep Invest
Kentucky Geological Survey Report of Progress. Bulletin [A publication] ....KY G S Rp Prog B
Kentucky Geological Survey. Special Publication [A publication] ....Kentucky Geol Survey Spec Pub
Kentucky Geological Survey Thesis Series [A publication] ....KY Geol Surv Thesis Ser
Kentucky Historical Society, Frankfort, KY [Library symbol] ....KyHi
Kentucky Historical Society. Register [A publication] ....KHS
Kentucky Historical Society. Register [A publication] ....KHSR
Kentucky Historical Society Register [A publication] ....KY Hist Soc Reg
Kentucky Historical Society Register [A publication] ....KYHS
Kentucky Horse Center [NASDAQ symbol] ....HORS
Kentucky & Indiana Terminal Railroad Co. [AAR code] ....KIT
Kentucky Investors [NASDAQ symbol] ....KINV
Kentucky Law Journal [A publication] ....KY Law J
Kentucky Law Journal [A publication] ....KY L J
Kentucky Library Association Bulletin [A publication] ....KY Lib Assn Bull
Kentucky Library Association Bulletin [A publication] ....KY Libr Ass Bull
Kentucky Library for the Blind and Physically Handicapped, Frankfort, KY [Library symbol] ....Ky-BPH
Kentucky Medical Journal [A publication] ....Kentucky Med J
Kentucky Nurses' Association Newsletter [A publication] ....KY Nurses Assoc Newsl
Kentucky, Ohio, Michigan [Medical library network] ....KOM
Kentucky-Ohio-Michigan Regional Medical Library [Library network] ....KOMRMLN
Kentucky Philological Association. Bulletin [A publication] ....KPAB
Kentucky Review [A publication] ....KYR
Kentucky Romance Quarterly [A publication] ....KRQ
Kentucky School Journal [A publication] ....KY Sch J
Kentucky State Historical Society Register [A publication] ....KSHSR
Kentucky State Historical Society Register [A publication] ....KY Reg
Kentucky State University, Frankfort, KY [Library symbol] ....KyFSC
Kentucky State University, Frankfort, KY [OCLC symbol] ....KYS
Kentucky & Tennessee Railway [AAR code] ....KT
Kentucky Union List of Serials [Library network] ....KULS
Kentucky. University. Office of Research and Engineering Services. Bulletin [A publication] ....KY Univ Off Res Eng Serv Bull
Kentucky Utilities Co. [NYSE symbol] ....KU
Kentucky Warbler [A publication] ....KY Warbler
Kentucky Wesleyan College ....KWC
Kentucky Wesleyan College, Owensboro, KY [Library symbol] ....KyOwK
Kentville, NS [Radio station call letters] ....CKEN
Kentville, NS [Radio station call letters] ....CKWM-FM
Kentwood, MI [Radio station call letters] ....WKWM
Kenwin Shops, Inc. [American Stock Exchange symbol] ....KWN
Kenya [MARC geographic area code] [Library of Congress] ....f-ke---
Kenya [MARC country of publication code] [Library of Congress] ....ke
Kenya [Three-letter standard code] ....KEN
Kenya [Aircraft nationality and registration mark] 5Y
Kenya [Two-letter standard code] ....KE
Kenya African Democratic Union [A political party] [Absorbed by KANU] ....KADU
Kenya African Movement ....KAM
Kenya African National Union [A political party] ....KANU
Kenya Air Force ....KAF
Kenya Airways Ltd. [ICAO designator] ....KQ
Kenya Department of Agriculture. Annual Report [A publication] ....Kenya Dep Agric Annu Rep
Kenya and East African Medical Journal [A publication] ....Kenya and East African Med J
Kenya Federation of Labour ....KFL
Kenya Information Services Bulletin [A publication] ....Kenya Inform Serv Bull
Kenya Medical Journal [A publication] ....Kenya Med J
Kenya National Museum ....KNM
Kenya News Agency ....KNA
Kenya Nursing Journal [A publication] ....Kenya Nurs J
Kenya People's Union ....KPU
Kenya Petroleum and Oil Workers' Union ....KPOWU
Kenya Rangeland Ecological Monitoring Unit ....KREMU
Kenya Trades Union Congress ....KTUC
Kenyon College, Gambier, OH [OCLC symbol] ....KEN
Kenyon College, Gambier, OH [Library symbol] ....OGK
Kenyon Review [A publication] ....Kenyon R
Kenyon Review [A publication] ....KR
Keokuk Community College [Iowa] ....KCC
Keokuk, IA [Location identifier] [FAA] ....EOK
Keokuk, IA [Radio station call letters] ....KIMI
Keokuk, IA [Radio station call letters] ....KOKX
Keokuk Public Library, Keokuk, IA [Library symbol] ....IaK

Keosippi Library Cooperative, Keokuk, IA [*Library symbol*] .... IaKK
Kepi [*Indonesia*] [*Airport symbol*] .... KEI
Kerala Journal of Veterinary Science [*A publication*] .... Kerala J Vet Sci
Keramische Zeitschrift [*A publication*] .... Keram Z
Keratin, Myosin, Epidermin, Fibrin [*Biochemistry*] .... KMEF
Keratinizing Desquamative Squamous Metaplasia [*Medicine*] .... KDSM
Keratitis Precipitate [*s*] [*Ophthalmology*] .... KP
Keratitis Punctata [*Ophthalmology*] .... KP
Kerato-Refractive Society .... KRS
Keravat [*New Britain*] [*Seismograph station code, US Geological Survey*] [*Closed*] .... KET
Keravat [*New Britain*] [*Seismograph station code, US Geological Survey*] [*Closed*] .... KRT
Kerema [*Papua New Guinea*] [*Airport symbol*] .... KMA
Kerema [*Papua New Guinea*] [*Seismograph station code, US Geological Survey*] [*Closed*] .... KRG
Kerikeri [*New Zealand*] [*Airport symbol*] .... KKE
Kerkyraika Chronika [*A publication*] .... KerC
Kermadec Islands [*MARC geographic area code*] [*Library of Congress*] .... poki---
Kerman [*Iran*] [*Airport symbol*] .... KER
Kermanshah [*Iran*] [*Seismograph station code, US Geological Survey*] .... KER
Kermit [*Texas*] [*Seismograph station code, US Geological Survey*] .... KIT
Kermit [*Texas*] [*Seismograph station code, US Geological Survey*] KM2
Kermit [*Texas*] [*Seismograph station code, US Geological Survey*] KM5
Kermit [*Texas*] [*Seismograph station code, US Geological Survey*] KM6
Kermit [*Texas*] [*Seismograph station code, US Geological Survey*] KM9
Kermit [*Texas*] [*Seismograph station code, US Geological Survey*] [*Closed*] .... KME
Kermit [*Texas*] [*Seismograph station code, US Geological Survey*] KT1
Kermit [*Texas*] [*Seismograph station code, US Geological Survey*] [*Closed*] KT2
Kermit [*Texas*] [*Seismograph station code, US Geological Survey*] KT4
Kermit [*Texas*] [*Seismograph station code, US Geological Survey*] [*Closed*] KT5
Kermit [*Texas*] [*Seismograph station code, US Geological Survey*] KT7
Kermit [*Texas*] [*Seismograph station code, US Geological Survey*] KT8
Kermit [*Texas*] [*Seismograph station code, US Geological Survey*] [*Closed*] KT9
Kermit [*Texas*] [*Seismograph station code, US Geological Survey*] .... KTE
Kermit [*Texas*] [*Seismograph station code, US Geological Survey*] [*Closed*] .... KTT
Kermit [*Texas*] [*Seismograph station code, US Geological Survey*] .... KTX
Kermit, TX [*Radio station call letters*] .... KERB
Kern County Department of Health, Bakersfield, CA [*Library symbol*] .... CBaKH
Kern County Land Co. [*NYSE symbol*] [*Wall Street slang name: "Casey"*] [*Defunct*] [*Delisted*] .... KCL
Kern County Library, Bakersfield, CA [*Library symbol*] .... CBaK
Kern County Library System [*Library network*] .... KCLS
Kern County Library System, Bakersfield, CA [*OCLC symbol*] .... KLC
Kern County Museum, Reference Library, Bakersfield, CA [*Library symbol*] .... CBaKM
Kern Medical Center, Bakersfield, CA [*Library symbol*] .... CBaH
Kern Wave [*Earthquakes*] .... K
Kernel Multiple Processing System [*Data processing*] .... KMPS
Kernenergie [*A publication*] .... Kernenerg
Kernforschungsanlage [*Julich, Germany*] .... KFA
Kernforschungsanlage Julich, Julich, Germany [*Library symbol*] .... GyJuK
Kernforschungszentrum Karlsruhe [*West Germany*] .... KFK
Kernkraftwerk Baden-Wuerttemberg Planungsgesellschaft .... KBWP
Kerntechnik, Isotopentechnik, und Chemie [*A publication*] .... Kerntechnik Isotpentech Chem
Kerosene .... K
Kerosene .... KRSN
Kerr Cell [*Optics*] .... KC
Kerr Constant [*Optics*] .... K
Kerr Effect [*Optics*] .... KE
Kerr Electro-Optical Effect [*Optics*] .... KEE
Kerr Glass Manufacturing Corp. [*NYSE symbol*] .... KGM
Kerr Industrial Applications Center [*Southeastern Oklahoma State University*] [*Information service*] .... KIAC
Kerr Magneto-Optical Effect [*Optics*] .... KME
Kerr-McGee Corp. [*NYSE symbol*] .... KMG
Kerr-McGee Corp., Oklahoma City, OK [*Library symbol*] .... OkOkK
Kerr Vector [*Optics*] .... KV
Kerrville, TX [*Location identifier*] [*FAA*] .... ERV
Kerrville, TX [*Radio station call letters*] .... KERV
Kerrville, TX [*Radio station call letters*] .... KERV-FM
Kershaw, SC [*Radio station call letters*] .... WKSC
Kerteszeti es Szoleszeti Foiskola Evkoryve [*A publication*] .... Kertesz Szolesz Foisk
Kerteszeti es Szoleszeti Foiskola Kozlemenyei [*A publication*] .... Kertesz Szolesz Foisk Kozl
Kerukunan Nasional [*Campaign for National Harmony*] [*Indonesia*] .... KERUK-NASI
Kerygma und Dogma [*A publication*] .... K D
Kerygma und Dogma [*A publication*] .... KerDo
Kesatuan Aksi Guru Indonesia [*Action Front of Indonesian Teachers*] .... KAGI
Kesatuan Aksi Mahasiswa Indonesia [*Action Front of Indonesian University Students*] .... KAMI
Kesatuan Aksi Pemuda Peladjar Indonesia .... KAPPI
Kesatuan Aksi Sardjana Indonesia [*Action Front of Indonesian Scholars*] .... KASI
Kesatuan Buruh Kerakjatan Indonesia [*Indonesian Democratic Workers' Federation*] .... KBKI
Kesatuan Persekutuan Guru Melayu, Persekutuan Tanah Melayu [*Federation of Malay Teachers' Unions, Federation of Malaya*] .... KPGMPTM
Keshequa Junior/Senior High School Library, Nunda, NY [*OCLC symbol*] .... RWU
Keshod [*India*] [*Airport symbol*] .... IXK
Kessel, WV [*Location identifier*] [*FAA*] .... ESL
Ketapang [*Indonesia*] [*Airport symbol*] .... KTG
Ketch .... KCH
Ketchikan [*Alaska*] [*Airport symbol*] .... KTN
Ketchikan, AK [*Location identifier*] [*FAA*] .... CMJ
Ketchikan, AK [*Radio station call letters*] .... KETH
Ketchikan, AK [*Radio station call letters*] .... KRBD
Ketchikan, AK [*Radio station call letters*] .... KTKN
Ketchikan Public Library, Ketchikan, AK [*Library symbol*] .... AkK
Ketchum & Co., Inc. [*American Stock Exchange symbol*] .... KCH
Ketchum, McLeod, & Grove, Inc., Pittsburgh, PA [*Library symbol*] .... PPiK
Ketoacidosis [*Medicine*] .... KA
Ketobutyraldehyde Dimethyl Acetal [*Biochemistry*] .... KBA
Ketodeoxyoctonate [*Biochemistry*] .... KDO
Ketogenic to Anti-Ketogenic [*Ratio*] [*In diets*] .... K/A
Ketogenic Steroid [*Endocrinology*] .... KGS
Ketoglutaric [*Biochemistry*] .... KG
Ketoisocaproate [*Biochemistry*] .... KIC
Ketoisovalerate [*Biochemistry*] .... KIV
Ketone Bodies [*Clinical chemistry*] .... KB
Ketosteroid [*Endocrinology*] .... KS
Ketothiomethylbutyric Acid [*Organic chemistry*] .... KTBA
Kettering Industries [*NASDAQ symbol*] .... KETT
Kettering Memorial Hospital, Kettering, OH [*Library symbol*] .... OKetH
Kettering, OH [*Radio station call letters*] .... WCXL
Kettering, OH [*Radio station call letters*] .... WKET
Kettering, OH [*Television station call letters*] .... WPTD
Kettering, OH [*Radio station call letters*] .... WVUD-FM
Kettledrum .... KD
Kettleson Memorial Library, Sitka, AK [*Library symbol*] .... AkS
Keuka College, Keuka Park, NY [*Library symbol*] .... NKpK
Keuka College, Lightner Library, Keuka Park, NY [*OCLC symbol*] .... ZKC
Keuringsinstituut voor Waterleidingartikelen .... KIWA
Kevex Corp. [*NASDAQ symbol*] .... KEVX
Kevlin Microwave Corp. [*NASDAQ symbol*] .... KVLM
Kevo [*Finland*] [*Seismograph station code, US Geological Survey*] .... KEV
Kew [*England*] [*Seismograph station code, US Geological Survey*] [*Closed*] .... KEW
Kew Bulletin [*A publication*] .... Kew Bull
Kew Bulletin. Additional Series [*A publication*] .... Kew Bull Addit Ser
Kewanee, IL [*Location identifier*] [*FAA*] .... EZI
Kewanee, IL [*Radio station call letters*] .... WJRE
Kewanee, IL [*Radio station call letters*] .... WKEI
Kewanee Industries, Inc. [*American Stock Exchange symbol*] [*Delisted*] .... KOC
Kewanee, MS [*Location identifier*] [*FAA*] .... EWA
Kewanee Public Library, Kewanee, IL [*OCLC symbol*] .... IEV
Kewanee Public Library, Kewanee, IL [*Library symbol*] .... IKe
Kewaunee, Green Bay & Western R. R. [*AAR code*] .... KGB
Kewaunee Science Equipment [*NASDAQ symbol*] .... KEQU
Kewaunee, WI [*Radio station call letters*] .... WAUN
Keweenaw Research Center [*Michigan Technological University*] .... KRC
Keweenaw Rocket Launch Site [*University of Michigan*] .... KRLS
Kex National Association .... KNA
Key .... K
Key .... KY
Key Airlines [*Salt Lake City, UT*] [*FAA designator*] .... KEY
Key-Auto-Key [*Data processing*] .... KAK
Key Banks, Inc. [*NYSE symbol*] .... KEY
Key to Christian Education [*A publication*] .... Key
Key-Click Filter .... KCF
Key Club International .... KCI
Key Collectors International .... KCI
Key Company [*American Stock Exchange symbol*] .... KC
Key Configuration Studies .... KCS
Key Display System [*Data processing*] .... KDS
Key District Office [*IRS*] .... KDO
Key Element Search .... KES
Key Energy Enterprises [*NASDAQ symbol*] .... KEEI
Key Essential Item List [*Defense Supply Agency*] .... KEIL
Key Facilities List [*AEC*] .... KFL
Key Image Systems Cl A [*NASDAQ symbol*] .... KIMGA
Key Integrative Social Systems .... KISS
Key Intelligence Position .... KIP
Key Intelligence Question [*CIA*] .... KIQ
Key Length [*Data processing*] .... KL
Key Lock Switch .... KLS
Key Locker .... KL

Key Officers of Foreign Service Posts [*A publication*] ... KOFS
Key Operated Valve ... KOV
Key Personnel ... KP
Key Personnel Course ... KPC
Key Personnel Upgrade Program [*National Guard*] ... KPUP
Key Pharmaceuticals, Inc. [*American Stock Exchange symbol*] ... KPH
Key Prep on Campus [*Slang*] ... KPOC
Key Pulsing ... KP
Key Resource People [*US Chamber of Commerce*] ... KRP
Key Result Area ... KRA
Key Seated [*Freight*] ... KS
Key Station Terminal [*Data processing*] ... KST
Key Symbol Out of Context [*Data processing*] ... KSOC
Key System Control Unit [*Telecommunications*] ... KSU
Key Telephone System Modules ... KTS
Key Telephone Unit ... KTU
Key Tronic Corporation [*NASDAQ symbol*] ... KTCC
Key Verifier [*Data processing*] ... KV
Key Way ... KWY
Key West [*Florida*] [*Airport symbol*] ... EYW
Key West [*Florida*] ... KW
Key West Art and Historical Society, Key West, FL [*Library symbol*] ... FKwHi
Key West, FL [*Location identifier*] [*FAA*] ... EYW
Key West, FL [*Location identifier*] [*FAA*] ... NQX
Key West, FL [*Radio station call letters*] ... WFYN
Key West, FL [*Radio station call letters*] ... WIIS
Key West, FL [*Radio station call letters*] ... WKWF
Key West, FL [*Television station call letters*] ... WQHJ
Key West, FL [*Television station call letters*] ... WTKW
Key West, FL [*Radio station call letters*] ... WVFK
Keyboard [*Data processing*] ... KB
Keyboard [*A publication*] ... KEYRA
Keyboard ... KYBD
Keyboard Button [*Data processing*] ... KB
Keyboard Cathode Ray Tube ... KCRT
Keyboard Change Button [*Data processing*] ... KCB
Keyboard Common Contact [*Data processing*] ... KCC
Keyboard Data Recorder [*Data processing*] ... KDR
Keyboard and Display [*Data processing*] ... KAD
Keyboard Encoder [*Data processing*] ... KBE
Keyboard Entry [*Data processing*] ... KBE
Keyboard Immortals [*Recording label*] ... KBI
Keyboard Input Matrix [*Data processing*] ... KIM
Keyboard Input Printout [*Data processing*] ... KIPO
Keyboard Input Simulation [*Data processing*] ... KIS
Keyboard Interface Module ... KBIM
Keyboard Monitor [*Data processing*] ... KBM
Keyboard/Printer Control [*Data processing*] ... KPC
Keyboard Process [*Data processing*] ... KBP
Keyboard Send and Receive [*Data processing*] ... KSR
Keyboard Simulated Lateral Telling [*Data processing*] ... KSL
Keyboard Typing Reperforator [*Data processing*] ... KTR
Keyboard Unit [*Data processing*] ... KBU
Keychart Educational Equipment [*for use with an electronic typewriter*] ... KEE
Keyed Display Console ... KDC
Keyed Sequential Access Mode [*Data processing*] ... KSAM
Keyed Video Generator ... KVG
Keyhole Limpet Hemocyanin [*Immunology*] ... KLH
Keying Devices [*JETDS nomenclature*] [*Military*] ... KY
Keying Material [*Data processing*] ... KEYMAT
Keying Relay ... KR
Keying Switching Station ... KSS
Keyletter-in-Context [*Data processing*] ... KLIC
Keyona College, Fort McMurray, AB, Canada [*Library symbol*] ... CaAFmK
Keyport Free Public Library, Keyport, NJ [*Library symbol*] ... NjKey
Keypunch [*Data processing*] ... KP
Keypunch Cabinet [*Data processing*] ... KPC
Keypunch Operator [*Data processing*] ... KPO
Keyseat ... KST
Keyser-Mineral County Public and Potomac Valley Regional Library, Keyser, WV [*Library symbol*] ... WvK
Keyser, WV [*Radio station call letters*] ... WKLP
Keyser, WV [*Radio station call letters*] ... WQZK-FM
Keyset [*Navy*] ... KS
Keyset Central Multiplexer ... KCMX
Keyset Panel ... KSP
Keysort Multiple Selector ... KMS
Keystation Adapter Unit [*Data processing*] ... KAU
Keystation On-Line Business-Oriented Language [*Data processing*] ... KOBOL
Keystone Aviation, Inc. [*New Cumberland, PA*] [*FAA designator*] ... KAC
Keystone Aviation, Inc. [*New Cumberland, PA*] [*FAA designator*] ... KAI
Keystone Bituminous Coal Association ... KBCA
Keystone Consolidated Industries, Inc. [*NYSE symbol*] ... KES
Keystone Folklore Quarterly [*A publication*] ... KFQ
Keystone Foods Corporation [*NYSE symbol*] [*Delisted*] ... KFC
Keystone Industries, Inc. [*American Stock Exchange symbol*] [*Delisted*] ... KEY
Keystone International, Incorporated [*NYSE symbol*] ... KII
Keystone Junior College [*Pennsylvania*] ... KJC
Keystone Junior College, La Plume, PA [*Library symbol*] ... PLapK
Keystone Medical Corporation [*NASDAQ symbol*] ... KMEC
Keystone Portland Cement [*NASDAQ symbol*] ... KCMT
Keystone Public Library, Keystone, IA [*Library symbol*] ... IaKey
Keystone Visual Survey Test [*Ophthalmology*] ... KVST
Keyword and Context [*Indexing*] ... KWAC
Keyword in Context [*Indexing*] ... KWIC
Keyword Out of Context [*Indexing*] ... KWOC
Keyword in Title [*Indexing*] ... KWIT
Keyword out of Title [*Indexing*] ... KWOT
Keywords Permuted ... KEYPER
KFC Corp. [*Formerly, Kentucky Fried Chicken Corp.*] ... KFC
KFK [*Kernforschungszentrum Karlsruhe*] **Nachrichten** [*A publication*] ... KFK Nachr
KFKI [*Kozponti Fizikai Kutato Intezet*] **Kozlemenyek** [*A publication*] ... KFKI Kozl
Khabarovsk [*USSR*] [*Geomagnetic observatory code*] ... KHB
Khabarovsk [*USSR*] [*Airport symbol*] ... KHV
Khadi Gramodyong [*India*] [*A publication*] ... Khadi Gram
Khajuraho [*India*] [*Airport symbol*] ... HJR
Khamtis [*Burma*] [*Airport symbol*] ... KHM
Khancoban [*Australia*] [*Seismograph station code, US Geological Survey*] ... KHA
Khapcheranga [*USSR*] [*Seismograph station code, US Geological Survey*] ... KPC
Kharchova Promyslovist [*A publication*] ... Kharchova Promst
Khark [*Iran*] [*Airport symbol*] [*Obsolete*] ... KHK
Kharkov [*USSR*] [*Airport symbol*] ... HRK
Khar'kovskii Meditsinskii Institut. Trudy [*A publication*] ... Khar'k Med Inst Tr
Khartoum [*Sudan*] [*Airport symbol*] ... KRT
Khasi [*MARC language code*] [*Library of Congress*] ... kha
Kheis [*USSR*] [*Seismograph station code, US Geological Survey*] ... KHE
Khidrologiya i Meteorologiya [*A publication*] ... Khidrol Met
Khidrologiya i Meteorologiya [*A publication*] ... Khidrol Meteorol
Khigiena i Zdraveopazvane [*A publication*] ... Khig Zdraveopaz
Khigiena i Zdraveopazvane [*A publication*] ... Khig Zdraveopazvane
Khimicheskaya Nauka i Promyshlennost [*A publication*] ... Khim Nauka Prom-st
Khimicheskaya Promyshlennost [*A publication*] ... Khim Prom
Khimicheskaya Promyshlennost' Ukrainy [*A publication*] ... Khim Prom-st' Ukr
Khimicheskaya Svyaz' v Kristallakh i Ikh Fizicheskie Svojstva [*A publication*] ... Khim Svyaz' Krist Fiz Svoj
Khimicheskie Produkty Koksovaniya Uglei Vostoka SSSR [*A publication*] ... Khim Prod Koksovaniya Uglei Vostoka SSSR
Khimicheskie Volokna [*A publication*] ... Khim Volokna
Khimicheskii Poglotitel Izvestkovyi [*Chemical absorbent*] [*USSR*] ... KHPI
Khimicheskoe Mashinostroenie. Moskovskii Institut Khimicheskogo Mashinostroeniya [*A publication*] ... Khim Mashinostr Mosk Inst Khim Mashinostr
Khimicheskoe i Neftyanoe Mashinostroenie [*A publication*] ... Khim Neft Mashinostr
Khimicheskoe i Neftyanoe Mashinostroenie [*A publication*] ... Khim i Neft Mashinostr
Khimiko-Farmatsevticheskii Zhurnal [*A publication*] ... Khim-Farm Zh
Khimiko-Farmatsevticheskii Zhurnal [*A publication*] ... Khim-Far Zh
Khimiya Drevesiny [*A publication*] ... Khim Drev
Khimiya Elementoorganicheskikh Soedinenii [*A publication*] ... Khim Elementoorg Soedin
Khimiya Geterotsiklicheskikh Soedinenii [*A publication*] ... Khim Geterotsiklich Soedin
Khimiya Geterotsiklicheskikh Soedineniya [*A publication*] ... Khim Getero
Khimiya i Industriya [*A publication*] ... Khim Ind
Khimiya i Khimicheskaya Tekhnologiya (Alma-Ata) [*A publication*] ... Khim Khim Tekhnol (Alma-Ata)
Khimiya Plazmy. Sbornik Statej [*A publication*] ... Khim Plazmy
Khimiya Prirodnykh Soedinenii [*A publication*] ... Khim Prirod Soed
Khimiya Prirodnykh Soedinenii [*A publication*] ... Khim Prir S
Khimiya Prirodnykh Soedinenii (Tashkent) [*A publication*] ... Khim Prir Soedin (Tashk)
Khimiya v Sel'skom Khozyaistve [*A publication*] ... Khim Sel'Khoz
Khimiya v Sel'skom Khozyaistve [*A publication*] ... Khim Sel'sk Khoz
Khimiya i Tekhnologiya Neorganicheskikh Proizvodstv [*A publication*] ... Khim Tekhnol Neorg Proizvod
Khimiya i Tekhnologiya Topliv i Masel [*A publication*] ... Khim i Tekhnol Topliv i Masel
Khimiya i Tekhnologiya Topliv i Masel [*A publication*] ... Khim Tekhnol Topl Masel
Khimiya Tverdogo Topliva (Leningrad) [*A publication*] ... Khim Tverd Topl (Leningrad)
Khimiya Tverdogo Topliva (Moscow) [*A publication*] ... Khim Tverd Topl (Moscow)
Khimiya Vysokikh Ehnergij [*A publication*] ... Khim Vys Ehnerg
Khirurgicheskaia Lietopis [*A publication*] ... Khir Lietop
Khlebopekarnaya i Konditerskaya Promyshlennost' [*A publication*] ... Khlebopekar Konditer Prom
Khlopkovodstvo [*A publication*] ... Khlopkovod
Khmer Insurgents [*Cambodian rebel force*] ... KI
Khmer Kampuchea Krom [*Cambodian group*] ... KKK

Khodzhikent [*USSR*] [*Seismograph station code, US Geological Survey*] [*Closed*] ... KDK
Khon Kaen [*Thailand*] [*Airport symbol*] ... KKC
Khorog [*USSR*] [*Seismograph station code, US Geological Survey*] ... KHO
Khorongon [*USSR*] [*Seismograph station code, US Geological Survey*] [*Closed*] ... KHR
Khost [*Afghanistan*] [*Airport symbol*] [*Obsolete*] ... KHT
Khotanese [*MARC language code*] [*Library of Congress*] ... kho
Khranitelna Promishlenost [*A publication*] ... Khranit Prom
Khranitelna Promishlenost [*A publication*] ... Khranit Prom-st
Khristianskoe Tchtenie [*A publication*] ... KT
Khronika VOZ [*Vsemirnoj Organisatsij Zdravookhraneniya*] [*A publication*] ... Khron VOZ
Kiana [*Alaska*] [*Airport symbol*] ... IAN
Kiangsi Province [*China, Mainland*] [*MARC geographic area code*] [*Library of Congress*] ... a-cc-ki
Kiangsu Province [*China, Mainland*] [*MARC geographic area code*] [*Library of Congress*] ... a-cc-ku
Kibernetika i Avtomatika [*A publication*] ... Kibern Avtom
Kibernetika i Vycislitel'naja Tehnika [*A publication*] ... Kibernet i Vycisl Tehn
Kibris Turk Ischi Birlikleri Federasyonu [*Cyprus Turkish Trade Unions Federation*] ... KTIBF
Kick in the Afterdeck [*Bowdlerized version*] ... KITA
Kick Plate ... KP
Kick Plate [*Building construction*] ... KPL
Kick Plate and Drip ... KP & D
Kick Stage [*NASA*] ... K/S
Kickback Racket Act ... KRA
Kicker [*Football*] ... K
Kickoff ... KO
Kickoff Point [*Diamond drilling*] ... KOP
Kickpipe [*Building construction*] ... KP
Kidde, Inc. [*NYSE symbol*] ... KDE
Kidderminster [*British depot code*] ... KDR
Kiddie Products, Inc. [*NASDAQ symbol*] ... KIDD
Kidnaping [*FBI standardized term*] ... KID
Kidnaping and Ransom [*Insurance policy*] ... K and R
Kidney Disease Control Program [*Public Health Service*] ... KDCP
Kidney International [*A publication*] ... Kidney Int
Kidney International. Supplement [*A publication*] ... Kidney Int Suppl
Kidney, Liver, Spleen [*Medicine*] ... KLS
Kidney Lobe ... KL
Kidney Plasminogen Activator [*Anticlotting agent*] ... KPA
Kidney Pore ... KP
Kidney Sac ... KS
Kidney and Upper Bladder ... KUB
Kidney, Ureter, Bladder ... KUB
Kidney Valve ... KV
Kids of Preachers ... KP
Kidsgrove ALGOL [*Algorithmic Language*] **Digital Analogue Simulation** [*Data processing*] [*British*] ... KALDAS
Kiel Public Library, Kiel, WI [*Library symbol*] ... WKi
Kieler Beitraege zur Anglistik und Amerikanistik [*A publication*] ... KBAA
Kieler Meeresforschungen [*A publication*] ... Kiel Meeresforsch
Kieler Milchwirtschaftliche Forschungsberichte [*A publication*] ... Kiel Milchwirtsch Forschungsber
Kieler Notizen zur Pflanzenkunde in Schleswig Holstein [*A publication*] ... Kiel Not Pflanzenkd Schleswig Holstein
Kieler Studien zur Deutschen Literaturgeschichte [*A publication*] ... KSDL
Kierkegaardiana [*A publication*] ... Kie
Kierunki [*A publication*] ... Ki
Kieta [*Papua New Guinea*] [*Airport symbol*] ... KIE
Kiev [*USSR*] [*Airport symbol*] ... IEV
Kiev [*USSR*] [*Geomagnetic observatory code*] ... KIV
Kiev [*USSR*] **Borispol Airport** [*Airport symbol*] ... KBP
Kiev Universitet. Visnik. Seriya Geografi [*A publication*] ... Kiev Univ Visn Ser Geogr
Kiffa [*Mauritania*] [*Airport symbol*] ... KFA
Kigali [*Rwanda*] [*Airport symbol*] ... KGL
Kigoma [*Tanzania*] [*Airport symbol*] ... TKQ
Kihei, HI [*Radio station call letters*] ... KHEI
Kikaiga Shima [*Japan*] [*Airport symbol*] ... KKX
Kikori [*Papua New Guinea*] [*Airport symbol*] ... KRI
Kikuyu [*MARC language code*] [*Library of Congress*] ... kik
Kikwit [*Zaire*] [*Airport symbol*] ... KKW
Kilbourn Public Library, Wisconsin Dells, WI [*Library symbol*] ... WWd
Kilderkin [*Unit of measurement*] [*British*] ... KILD
Kilenge Mission [*New Britain*] [*Seismograph station code, US Geological Survey*] ... KCM
Kilgore College, Kilgore, TX [*Library symbol*] ... TxKilC
Kilgore, TX [*Radio station call letters*] ... KKTX-FM
Kilgore, TX [*Radio station call letters*] ... KOCA
Kili [*Marshall Islands*] [*Airport symbol*] ... KIO
Kilimanjaro [*Tanzania*] [*Airport symbol*] ... JRO
Kilkenny [*County in Ireland*] ... KILK
Kill Probability ... KP
Killearn Properties, Incorporated [*American Stock Exchange symbol*] ... KPI
Killed ... K
Killed ... KD
Killed in Action [*Military*] ... KIA
Killed by Air [*Military*] ... KBA
Killed by Helicopter [*In reference to the enemy*] [*Vietnam*] ... KBH
Killed by Hostile Action [*Military*] ... KHA
Killed; Not Enemy Action [*Military*] ... KNA
Killeen [*Texas*] [*Airport symbol*] ... ILE
Killeen, TX [*Location identifier*] [*FAA*] ... GRK
Killeen, TX [*Radio station call letters*] ... KIIZ
Killeen, TX [*Radio station call letters*] ... KIXS-FM
Killeen, TX [*Radio station call letters*] ... KNCT-FM
Killer as an Organized Sport [*Campus game*] ... KAOS
Killing Federal Officer ... KFO
Killing Frost [*Meteorology*] ... KFRST
Killing Zone [*Military*] [*British*] ... KZ
Kilmarnock Public Library, Central Library, Dick Institute, Kilmarnock, United Kingdom [*Library symbol*] ... UkKi
Kilmarnock, VA [*Radio station call letters*] ... WKWI
Kiln-Dried [*Lumber*] ... KD
Kilo [*A prefix meaning multiplied by* 10^3] [*SI symbol*] ... k
Kilo [*Phonetic alphabet*] ... K
Kilo Accounting Units ... KAU
Kilo-Instructions per Second ... KIPS
Kilo Yard ... KYD
Kiloampere ... kA
Kilobar ... kb
Kilobase ... kb
Kilobase Pairs [*Genetics*] ... kbp
Kilobit ... kb
Kilobits per Second ... kbps
Kilobits per Second ... kbs
Kilobyte [*Data processing*] ... K
Kilocalorie ... kc
Kilocalorie ... kcal
Kilocharacter ... KC
Kilocurie ... kCi
Kilocycle [*Radio*] ... kc
Kilocycles per Second [*Aviation code*] ... K
Kilocycles per Second [*Aviation code*] ... KC
Kilocycles per Second ... kcps
Kilocycles per Second ... kcs
Kiloelectron Volt ... keV
Kiloelectron Watt ... keW
Kilogauss ... kG
Kilogram [*Also, kg*] [*Symbol*] [*SI unit for mass*] ... k
Kilogram [*Also, k*] [*Symbol*] [*SI unit for mass*] ... kg
Kilogram ... KIL
Kilogram ... KILO
Kilogram-Calorie ... kgcal
Kilogram-Foot ... kg-f
Kilogram-Force [*Unit of force*] ... kgf
Kilogram Force per Meter ... KGF/M
Kilogram Force per Square Centimeter ... KGF/CM^2
Kilogram Force per Square Meter ... KGF/M^2
Kilogram-Meter ... kg-m
Kilograms per Cubic Meter ... kg/cum
Kilograms per Cubic Meter ... KG/M^3
Kilograms per Joule ... KG/J
Kilograms per Pascal Second Square Meter ... KG/(PA S M^2)
Kilograms per Second ... kgps
Kilograms per Second ... kg/s
Kilograms per Square Meter ... KG/M^2
Kilohertz [*Electronics*] ... kHz
Kilohertz [*Preferred form is kHz*] [*Electronics*] ... KZ
Kilohm ... k
Kilohm ... KOHM
Kilojoule ... kJ
Kilokayser ... kK
Kilolambert ... kL
Kiloliter ... KILOL
Kiloliter ... kL
Kilomega ... kM
Kilomega Hertz ... kMHZ
Kilomegacycle ... kMc
Kilomegacycles per Second ... kMcs
Kilometer ... KIL
Kilometer ... KILOM
Kilometer ... KLM
Kilometer ... km
Kilometer Post ... KP
Kilometer-Wave Orbiting Telescope [*NASA*] ... KWOT
Kilometers per Hour ... kmh
Kilometers per Hour ... kmph
Kilometers per Hour ... kph
Kilometers per Second ... kmps
Kilometers per Second ... km/s
Kilometers per Second ... KPS
Kilometric Wavelength [*Radio astronomy*] ... KOM
Kilonewton ... kN
Kilooersted ... kOe
Kilopascal ... kPa
Kilopond ... KP
Kilopondmeter ... Kpm
Kilopound ... KLB

Kilopulse ... kp
Kilopulses per Second ... kpps
Kilorayleigh ... kR
Kiloroentgen ... kR
Kiloton [*Nuclear equivalent of 1000 tons of high explosives*] ... KLT
Kiloton [*Nuclear equivalent of 1000 tons of high explosives*] ... kt
Kilovar ... kvar
Kilovar-Hour ... kvarh
Kilovolt ... kV
Kilovolt Ampere ... kVA
Kilovolt-Ampere Hour ... kVAH
Kilovolt-Ampere Hour Meter ... kVAhm
Kilovolt-Ampere Meter ... kVAM
Kilovolt-Ampere Reactive ... kVAr
Kilovolt Constant Potential ... kVCP
Kilovolt Direct Current ... kVdc
Kilovolt Meter ... kVM
Kilovolts, Direct Current ... kDVC
Kilovolts Peak ... kVP
Kilowatt ... kW
Kilowatt-Hour ... kWh
Kilowatt-Hour ... kWhr
Kilowatt-Hour Electric ... kWhe
Kilowatt-Hour Meter ... KWHM
Kilowatt Meter ... kWm
Kilowatt, Thermal ... kWt
Kilowatt, Thermal ... kW(th)
Kilowatts of Electric Energy ... kWe
Kilowatts Reactive ... kWr
Kilowatts per Square Meter ... KW/M²
Kiloword ... KW
Kilwa [*Tanzania*] [*Airport symbol*] ... KIY
Kimam [*Indonesia*] [*Airport symbol*] ... KMM
Kimball International [*NASDAQ symbol*] ... KBALB
Kimball, NE [*Location identifier*] [*FAA*] ... IBM
Kimball, NE [*Radio station call letters*] ... KIMB
Kimball Public Library, Kimball, NE [*Library symbol*] ... NbKi
Kimball's Dairy Farmer [*A publication*] ... Kimball's D F
Kimbark Oil & Gas [*NASDAQ symbol*] ... KIMB
Kimbe [*New Britain*] [*Seismograph station code, US Geological Survey*] [*Closed*] ... KMB
Kimbell Art Museum, Fort Worth, TX [*Library symbol*] ... TxFK
Kimberley [*South Africa*] [*Airport symbol*] ... KIM
Kimberley [*South Africa*] [*Seismograph station code, US Geological Survey*] ... KIM
Kimberly-Clark Corp. [*NYSE symbol*] ... KMB
Kimberly-Clark Corp., Memphis, TN [*Library symbol*] ... TMK
Kimberly-Clark Corp., Research and Engineering Library, Neenah, WI [*Library symbol*] ... WNKC
Kimberly, WI [*Radio station call letters*] ... WYNE
Kimble Method for Controlled Devacuation ... KIMCODE
Kin Seeking Missing Military Personnel [*Organization of parents with sons missing in action with purpose of supplementing US government search for missing personnel*] [*Post-World War II*] ... KSMMP
Kinark Corp. [*American Stock Exchange symbol*] ... KIN
Kincaid Furniture Co. [*NASDAQ symbol*] ... KNCD
Kindamba [*Congo*] [*Airport symbol*] ... KNJ
Kinder-Care Learning [*NASDAQ symbol*] ... KNDR
Kinderaerztliche Praxis [*German Democratic Republic*] [*A publication*] ... Kinderaerztl Prax
Kinderaerztliche Praxis [*A publication*] ... Kinderaerztl Prax
Kindergarten ... K
Kindergarten ... KG
Kindergarten Evaluation for Learning Potential [*McGraw Hill*] ... KELP
Kindergarten and First Grade [*A publication*] ... Kind and First Grade
Kindergarten Primary Magazine [*A publication*] ... Kind M
Kindly Old Gentleman [*Slang*] ... KOG
Kindness in Nature's Defense [*Elementary school course*] ... KIND
Kindu [*Zaire*] [*Airport symbol*] ... KND
Kinematic Analysis Method ... KAM
Kinematic Bombing System ... KBS
Kinematic Viscosity ... KV
Kinematical Analysis Program ... KAP
Kinematograph Renter's Society ... KRS
Kinescope ... KIN
Kinescope ... KINE
Kinescope Image Test and Evaluation System ... KITES
Kinesitherapie Scientifique [*A publication*] ... Kinesither Sci
Kinesthetic ... K
Kinesthetic Figural Aftereffects [*Also, KFAE*] [*Psychometrics*] ... KFA
Kinesthetic Figural Aftereffects [*Also, KFA*] [*Psychometrics*] ... KFAE
Kinetic Analysis Using Over-Relaxation [*FORTRAN computer program*] [*Physical chemistry*] ... KORE
Kinetic Energy [*Symbol*] [*IUPAC*] ... K
Kinetic Energy ... KE
Kinetic Energy [*Symbol*] [*IUPAC*] ... T
Kinetic Energy Released per Unit Mass ... KERMA
Kinetic Experiment on Water Boiler [*Nuclear reactor*] ... KEWB
Kinetic Family Drawing [*Psychology*] ... KFD
Kinetic Intense Neutron Generator ... KING
Kinetic Isotope Effect [*Physical chemistry*] ... KIE
Kinetic Minerals, Inc. [*NASDAQ symbol*] ... KMNL
Kinetic Momentum ... KM
Kinetic Potential ... KP
Kinetic Potential [*Symbol*] ... L
Kinetic Process Control ... KPC
Kinetic Reaction ... KR
Kinetic Ring Energy Storage System ... KRESS
Kinetic Theory ... KT
Kinetically Designed Nozzle ... KDN
Kinetics and Catalysis ... KAC
Kinetics and Catalysis [*A publication*] ... Kinet Catal
Kinetika i Kataliz [*A publication*] ... Kinet Katal
Kinetin [*Plant growth regulator*] ... KT
King ... K
King [*Chess, card games*] ... K
King ... KG
King [*Phonetic alphabet*] [*World War II*] ... K
King of Arms ... KA
King-Armstrong Unit [*Clinical chemistry*] ... KA
King-Armstrong Unit [*Clinical chemistry*] ... KAU
King City, CA [*Radio station call letters*] ... KLFA
King City, CA [*Radio station call letters*] ... KRKC
King City Public Library, King City, CA [*Library symbol*] ... CK
King College, Bristol, TN [*Library symbol*] ... TBriK
King County Library System, Seattle, WA [*Library symbol*] ... WaSKC
King County Medical Society, Seattle, WA [*Library symbol*] ... WaSK
King Cove [*Alaska*] [*Airport symbol*] ... KVC
King Edward Point [*South Georgia Island*] [*Seismograph station code, US Geological Survey*] ... KEP
King Edward's Horse Regiment [*Military unit*] [*British*] ... KEH
King George's Fund for Sailors [*British*] ... KGFS
King International Corp. [*NASDAQ symbol*] ... KITL
King Island [*Tasmania*] [*Airport symbol*] ... KNS
King James Version [*or Authorized Version of the Bible, 1611*] ... KJV
King John [*Shakespearean work*] ... Jn
King Kullen Grocery [*NASDAQ symbol*] ... KKUL
King Lear [*Shakespearean work*] ... Lr
King and Martyr [*Church calendars*] ... KM
King, NC [*Radio station call letters*] ... WKTE
King Optical Corp. [*American Stock Exchange symbol*] [*Delisted*] ... KNG
King Post ... KP
King, Queen, Jack Meld [*Canasta*] ... KQJM
King Radio Corporation [*American Stock Exchange symbol*] ... KRC
King Ranch [*California*] [*Seismograph station code, US Geological Survey*] [*Closed*] ... KRC
King Research, Incorporated [*Information service*] ... KRI
King Salmon [*Alaska*] [*Airport symbol*] ... AKN
King-Seeley Thermos Co. [*NYSE symbol*] [*Delisted*] ... KST
King Township Public Library, King City, ON, Canada [*Library symbol*] ... CaOKcKT
King of Video [*NASDAQ symbol*] ... KOVI
Kingaroy [*Australia*] [*Airport symbol*] ... KGY
Kingcome Navigation [*AAR code*] ... KNC
Kingdom ... KINGD
Kingdom ... KM
Kingman [*Arizona*] [*Airport symbol*] ... IGM
Kingman, AZ [*Radio station call letters*] ... KAAA
Kingman, AZ [*Radio station call letters*] ... KZZZ
Kingman City-Mohave County Library, Kingman, AZ [*Library symbol*] ... AzKiM
Kings [*Old Testament book*] ... Kgs
Kings [*Old Testament book*] ... Ki
Kings ... KK
King's African Rifles [*Military unit*] [*British*] ... KAR
Kings Bay Army Terminal ... KBART
King's Bench [*of law courts*] [*British*] ... KB
King's Bench Court [*British*] ... KBC
King's Bench Divisional Court [*British*] ... KBDC
King's Bishop [*Chess*] ... KB
King's College, Briarcliff Manor, NY [*Library symbol*] ... NBmK
King's College, Briarcliff Manor, NY [*OCLC symbol*] ... VZK
King's College Hospital ... KCH
King's College, London ... KCL
King's College, London, ON, Canada [*Library symbol*] ... CaOLK
King's College School [*British*] ... KCS
King's College, Wilkes-Barre, PA [*OCLC symbol*] ... KOL
King's College, Wilkes-Barre, PA [*Library symbol*] ... PWbK
King's Counsel [*British*] ... KC
Kings County Free Library, Hanford, CA [*Library symbol*] ... CHanK
Kings County Free Library, Hanford, CA [*OCLC symbol*] ... CKC
King's Daughters Public Library, Del Norte, CO [*Library symbol*] ... CoDn
King's Dragoon Guards [*Later, QDG*] [*Military unit*] [*British*] ... KDG
King's Harbour Master [*British*] ... KHM
King's Hard Bargain [*British military slang for undesirable sailor or soldier*] ... KHB
King's Honorary Chaplain [*British*] ... KHC
King's Honorary Dental Surgeon [*British*] ... KHDS
King's Honorary Nursing Sister [*British*] ... KHNS
King's Hussars [*Military unit*] [*British*] ... KH
King's Knight [*Chess*] ... KKT

King's Light Infantry [*Military unit*] [*British*] .... KLI
Kings Mountain National Military Park .... KIMO
Kings Mountain, NC [*Radio station call letters*] .... WKMT
King's National Roll .... KNR
King's Own [*Military unit*] [*British*] .... KO
King's Own Light Infantry [*Military unit*] [*British*] .... KOLI
King's Own Royal [*Military unit*] [*British*] .... KOR
King's Own Royal Regiment [*Military unit*] [*British*] .... KORR
King's Own Scottish Borderers [*Military unit*] [*British*] .... KOSB
King's Own Yorkshire Light Infantry [*Military unit*] [*British*] .... KOYLI
Kings Park State Hospital, Kings Park, NY [*Library symbol*] .... NKpaH
King's Pleasure [*British*] .... KP
King's Police Medal .... KPM
King's Proctor [*British*] .... KP
King's and Queen's College of Physicians [*Ireland*] .... KQCP
King's Regiment [*Military unit*] [*British*] .... KR
King's Regulations and Admiralty Instructions [*Navy*] [*British*] .... KR & AI
King's Regulations for the Army and the Army Reserves [*British*] .... KR
King's Regulations and Orders for the Royal Canadian Air Force .... KR Air
King's Regulations and Orders for the Royal Canadian Army .... KR & O (Can)
King's Regulations and Orders for the Royal Canadian Navy .... KRCN
King's Remembrancer [*British*] .... KR
King's Rook [*Chess*] .... KR
King's Royal Irish [*Military unit*] [*British*] .... KRI
King's Royal Rifle Corps [*Military unit*] [*British*] .... KRRC
King's Royal Rifles [*Military unit*] [*British*] .... KRR
King's Scholar [*British*] .... KS
King's Shropshire Light Infantry [*Military unit*] [*British*] .... KSLI
King's Speech [*British*] .... KS
Kings View Hospital, Reedley, CA [*Library symbol*] .... CReeK
Kingsbay [*Spitsbergen*] [*Seismograph station code, US Geological Survey*] .... KBS
Kingsborough Community College of the City University of New York, Brooklyn, NY [*Library symbol*] .... NBK
Kingsborough Community College of the City University of New York, Brooklyn, NY [*OCLC symbol*] .... YKC
Kingsbrook Jewish Medical Center, Brooklyn, NY [*Library symbol*] .... NBJ
Kingscote [*Australia*] [*Airport symbol*] .... KGC
Kingsley, Kinsella, and Keeney [*Prominent citizens of Brooklyn; all three died within a year of each other, 1884-1885*] .... 3K's
Kingsley Public Library, Kingsley, MI [*Library symbol*] .... MiKins
Kingsport Public Library, Kingsport, TN [*Library symbol*] .... TKi
Kingsport, TN [*Radio station call letters*] .... WCSK
Kingsport, TN [*Radio station call letters*] .... WGOC
Kingsport, TN [*Radio station call letters*] .... WKIN
Kingsport, TN [*Radio station call letters*] .... WKPT
Kingsport, TN [*Television station call letters*] .... WKPT-TV
Kingsport, TN [*Radio station call letters*] .... WTFM
Kingsport, TN [*Radio station call letters*] .... WZXY
Kingstip, Inc. [*American Stock Exchange symbol*] .... KTP
Kingston [*Jamaica*] [*Airport symbol*] .... KIN
Kingston [*Canada*] [*Airport symbol*] .... YGK
Kingston [*Jamaica*] [*Seismograph station code, US Geological Survey*] .... KIN
Kingston Community Public Library, Kingston, MI [*Library symbol*] .... MiKin
Kingston Hospital Libraries, Kingston, NY [*Library symbol*] .... NKiHL
Kingston, NY [*Radio station call letters*] .... WBPM
Kingston, NY [*Radio station call letters*] .... WFGB
Kingston, NY [*Radio station call letters*] .... WGHQ
Kingston, NY [*Radio station call letters*] .... WKNY
Kingston, ON [*Radio station call letters*] .... CBBK-FM
Kingston, ON [*Radio station call letters*] .... CFLY-FM
Kingston, ON [*Radio station call letters*] .... CFMK-FM
Kingston, ON [*Radio station call letters*] .... CFRC
Kingston, ON [*Radio station call letters*] .... CFRC-FM
Kingston, ON [*Radio station call letters*] .... CKLC
Kingston, ON [*Radio station call letters*] .... CKWS
Kingston, ON [*Television station call letters*] .... CKWS-TV
Kingston Public Library, Kingston, ON, Canada [*Library symbol*] .... CaOK
Kingston, RI [*Radio station call letters*] .... WRIU
Kingston-Tinson [*Jamaica*] [*Airport symbol*] .... KTP
Kingston, TN [*Radio station call letters*] .... WTNR
Kingstree, SC [*Location identifier*] [*FAA*] .... CKI
Kingstree, SC [*Radio station call letters*] .... WDKD
Kingstree, SC [*Radio station call letters*] .... WKSP
Kingstree, SC [*Radio station call letters*] .... WWKT
Kingsville, TX [*Radio station call letters*] .... KINE
Kingsville, TX [*Radio station call letters*] .... KINE-FM
Kingsville, TX [*Radio station call letters*] .... KODK
Kingsville, TX [*Radio station call letters*] .... KTAI
Kingsville, TX [*Location identifier*] [*FAA*] .... NQI
Kingwood, WV [*Radio station call letters*] .... WFSP
Kinnard Investments [*NASDAQ symbol*] .... KINN
Kinnear Public Library, McGill, NV [*Library symbol*] .... NvMcK
Kinney Co., Inc. [*NYSE symbol*] .... KNX
Kinney Services, Inc. [*Later, WCI*] [*NYSE symbol*] .... KNS
Kinney System, Inc. [*NASDAQ symbol*] .... KINY
Kinomoto [*Japan*] [*Seismograph station code, US Geological Survey*] [*Closed*] .... KMT
Kinsel Drug Co. [*NYSE symbol*] .... KSL
Kinshasa [*Zaire*] [*Airport symbol*] .... FIH
[*Georg*] **Kinsky** [*When used in identifying Beethoven's compositions, refers to cataloging of his works by musicologist Kinsky*] .... K
Kinston [*North Carolina*] [*Airport symbol*] .... ISO
Kinston-Lenoir County Public Library, Kinston, NC [*Library symbol*] .... NcK
Kinston, NC [*Radio station call letters*] .... WELS
Kinston, NC [*Radio station call letters*] .... WFTC
Kinston, NC [*Radio station call letters*] .... WISP
Kinston, NC [*Radio station call letters*] .... WKNS
Kinston, NC [*Radio station call letters*] .... WQDW
Kinston, NC [*Radio station call letters*] .... WRNS
Kinyarwanda [*MARC language code*] [*Library of Congress*] .... kin
Kiowa County Public Library, Eads, CO [*Library symbol*] .... CoE
Kip [*1000 lbs.*] .... K
Kip [*Monetary unit in Laos*] .... K
Kipapa [*Hawaii*] [*Seismograph station code, US Geological Survey*] .... KIP
Kipling Journal [*A publication*] .... KJ
Kipling Society .... KS
Kipnuk [*Alaska*] [*Airport symbol*] .... KPN
Kipp Relay .... KR
Kips [*Thousands of Pounds*] **per Square Foot** .... ksf
Kips [*Thousands of Pounds*] **per Square Inch** .... kpi
Kips [*Thousands of Pounds*] **per Square Inch** .... KPSI
Kips [*Thousands of Pounds*] **per Square Inch** .... KSI
Kipuka Nene [*Hawaii*] [*Seismograph station code, US Geological Survey*] .... KNH
Kira [*Papua New Guinea*] [*Airport symbol*] .... KIQ
Kira Kira [*Solomon Islands*] [*Airport symbol*] .... IRA
Kirbati Philatelic Society .... KPS
Kirby Exploration Co. [*American Stock Exchange symbol*] .... KEX
Kirby Industries, Inc. [*American Stock Exchange symbol*] [*Delisted*] .... KVS
Kirbyville, TX [*Location identifier*] [*FAA*] .... BKB
Kirchenchor [*A publication*] .... Kirchor
Kirchenmusikalische Jahrbuch [*A publication*] .... K Jb
Kirchenmusikalische Jahrbuch [*A publication*] .... Km J
Kirchenmusiker [*A publication*] .... Kirmus
Kirchhoff Radiation Law [*Physics*] .... KRL
Kirchliche Zeitschrift [*A publication*] .... KZ
Kirchner-French Memorial Library, Peterson, IA [*Library symbol*] .... IaPet
Kirchner, Prosopographia Attica [*A publication*] .... Kirch PA
Kirchoff, H. H., St. Paul MN [*STAC*] .... KHH
Kirghiz [*MARC language code*] [*Library of Congress*] .... kir
Kirghiz Soviet Socialist Republic [*MARC geographic area code*] [*Library of Congress*] .... e-ur-kg
Kirghiz Soviet Socialist Republic [*MARC country of publication code*] [*Library of Congress*] .... kgr
Kirghiz Soviet Socialist Republic .... KirSSR
Kiri [*Zaire*] [*Airport symbol*] .... KRZ
Kirin Brewery Co. ADR [*NASDAQ symbol*] .... KNBWY
Kirin Province [*China, Mainland*] [*MARC geographic area code*] [*Library of Congress*] .... a-cc-kr
Kirjallisuudentutkijain Seuran Vuosikirja [*A publication*] .... KSV
Kirkcaldy [*Seaport in Scotland*] .... KIRK
Kirkcudbrightshire [*County in Scotland*] .... KIRKCUDB
Kirke og Kultur [*A publication*] .... KK
Kirke og Kultur [*A publication*] .... KoK
Kirkendall Public Library, Ankeny, IA [*Library symbol*] .... IaAnk
Kirkenes [*Norway*] [*Airport symbol*] .... KKN
Kirkenes [*Norway*] [*Seismograph station code, US Geological Survey*] [*Closed*] .... KRK
Kirkens Verden [*A publication*] .... KV
Kirkland & Ellis, Chicago, IL [*OCLC symbol*] .... IBM
Kirkland & Ellis, Chicago, IL [*Library symbol*] .... ICKE
Kirkland Lake [*Ontario*] [*Seismograph station code, US Geological Survey*] [*Closed*] .... KLC
Kirkland Lake [*Canada*] [*Airport symbol*] .... YKX
Kirkland Lake, ON [*Radio station call letters*] .... CJKL
Kirkland, WA [*Radio station call letters*] .... KGAA
[*Ralph*] **Kirkpatrick** [*When used in identifying D. Scarlatti's compositions, refers to cataloging of his works by musicologist Kirkpatrick*] .... K
Kirksville [*Missouri*] [*Airport symbol*] .... IRK
Kirksville College of Osteopathy and Surgery, Kirksville, MO [*Library symbol*] .... MoKiCO
Kirksville, MO [*Radio station call letters*] .... KIRX
Kirksville, MO [*Radio station call letters*] .... KRXL
Kirksville, MO [*Radio station call letters*] .... KTUF
Kirksville, MO [*Television station call letters*] .... KTVO
Kirkus Reviews [*A publication*] .... Kirkus R
Kirkus Reviews [*A publication*] .... KR
Kirkwall [*Orkney Islands*] [*Airport symbol*] .... KOI
Kirkwood Community College, Cedar Rapids, IA [*Library symbol*] .... IaCrK
Kirovabad [*USSR*] [*Seismograph station code, US Geological Survey*] .... KRV
Kirsch Co. [*NYSE symbol*] [*Delisted*] .... KIR
Kirsten Murine Sarcoma Virus .... KiMSV
Kirtland Air Force Base [*New Mexico*] .... KAFB
Kirtland Community College, Roscommon, MI [*Library symbol*] .... MiRoscK
Kiruna [*Sweden*] [*Geomagnetic observatory code*] .... KIR
Kiruna [*Sweden*] [*Airport symbol*] .... KRN
Kiruna [*Sweden*] [*Seismograph station code, US Geological Survey*] .... KIR
Kisan Mazdoor Praja Party [*India*] .... KMPP

Kisangani [Zaire] [Airport symbol].. FKI
Kiserletes Orvostudomany [A publication] .... Kiserl Orvostud
Kiserletugyi Koezlemenyek [A publication] ....Kiserletugyi Koezlem
Kiserletugyi Koezlemenyek [A publication] .... Kiserl Kozl
Kiserletugyi Koezlemenyek. A Kotet. Novenytermesztes [A publication]... Kiserletugyi Kozl A
Kiserletugyi Koezlemenyek. C Kotet. Kerteszet [A publication] ....
　　Kiserletugyi Kozl C
Kish Island [Iran] [Airport symbol]................................KIH
Kishinev [USSR] [Seismograph station code, US Geological Survey] ....KIS
Kishinev [USSR] [Airport symbol]..............................KIV
Kisinevskii Gosudarstvennyi Universitet. Ucenye Zapiski [A publication]....................... Kisinev Gos Univ Ucen Zap
Kismayu [Somalia] [Airport symbol]...........................KMU
Kissel Kar Klub..KKK
Kissimmee, FL [Radio station call letters] ....WFIV
Kissimmee, FL [Radio station call letters] ....WMJK
Kisumu [Kenya] [Airport symbol]...............................KIS
Kit...KT
Kit Carson Memorial Foundation, Inc., Taos, NM [Library symbol] ....NmTKC
Kit Configuration Notice..KCN
Kit Control Number [Navy]......................................KCN
Kit Design Approach..KDA
Kit Engineering Change Proposal..............................KECP
Kit Karson Corp. [NASDAQ symbol]..........................KITK
Kit Manufacturing Co. [American Stock Exchange symbol] ....KIT
Kit Munition Unit [Air Force]...................................KMU
Kit Quotation Request ....KQR
Kit Shortage Notice...KSN
Kita-Daito [Japan] [Airport symbol]..........................KTD
Kita Kyushu [Japan] [Airport symbol] [Obsolete].........KKJ
Kitakanto Medical Journal [A publication].............. Kitakanto Med J
Kitano Hospital Journal of Medicine [A publication] ....Kitano Hosp J Med
Kitasato Archives of Experimental Medicine [A publication] ....
　　Kitasato Arch Exp Med
Kitasato Medicine [A publication].........................Kitasato Med
Kitchen...K
Kitchen...KI
Kitchen and Bathroom..KB
Kitchen Biddy [Female kitchen worker] [Restaurant slang]..........KB
Kitchen Guild of America.......................................KGA
Kitchen Klutzs of America [Inactive]........................KKA
Kitchen Mechanic [Restaurant slang] ....KM
Kitchen Police [Kitchen helpers] [Military] ....KP
Kitchener, ON [Radio station call letters]................CFCA-FM
Kitchener, ON [Radio station call letters].................CHYM
Kitchener, ON [Television station call letters]..........CKCO-TV
Kitchener, ON [Radio station call letters].................CKGL-FM
Kitchener, ON [Radio station call letters].................CKKW
Kitchener, ON [Radio station call letters].................CKWR-FM
Kitchener-Paris, ON [Television station call letters].....................CICO-TV-28
Kitchener Public Library, Kitchener, ON, Canada [Library symbol] ....CaOKit
Kitchener-Waterloo Academy of Medicine, Waterloo, ON, Canada [Library symbol].................. CaOWtA
Kitchener-Waterloo General Hospital, Waterloo, ON, Canada [Library symbol]............................. CaOWtG
Kitchener-Waterloo Record, Kitchener, ON, Canada [Library symbol].................................. CaOKitW
Kitchigami Regional Library, Pine River, MN [Library symbol]..............MnPr
Kite Balloon [Air Force]..KB
Kite Balloon [Air Force]..KYTOON
Kite and Balloon Officer [Navy] ....KBO
Kite Balloon Pilot...KBP
Kite-Supported Antenna ....KSA
Kithira [Greece] [Airport symbol]..............................KIT
Kitimat, BC [Radio station call letters].....................CKTK
Kitoi [Alaska] [Airport symbol].................................KKB
Kitsap Regional Library, Bremerton, WA [Library symbol] ...... WaBr
Kitt Peak National Observatory [Arizona] ....KPNO
Kitt Peak National Observatory [Arizona] ....KPNOB
Kitt Peak National Observatory, Tucson, AZ [OCLC symbol] ....KPO
Kittanning, PA [Radio station call letters]..................WACB
Kittila [Finland] [Airport symbol]..............................KTT
Kitting Instruction Sheet [NASA].............................KIS
Kitto's Journal of Sacred Literature [A publication] ....Kitto
Kittrell College, Kittrell, NC [Library symbol] ....NcKiK
Kittrell Junior College, Kittrell, NC [OCLC symbol] [Inactive]..........KIT
Kitty Hawk Airways, Inc. [Dallas, TX] [FAA designator] ....KHA
Kitwe [Zambia] [Airport symbol]...............................KIW
Kiunga [Papua New Guinea] [Airport symbol] ....UNG
Kivalina [Alaska] [Airport symbol]............................KVL
Kives-Television [In company name K-Tel International. Derived from name of company president and fact that it markets its products on television] .... K-TEL
Kiwai Island [Papua New Guinea] [Airport symbol].........KWX
Kiwanis International ....KI
Kiwi Growers of California....................................KGC
Kiyosumi [Japan] [Seismograph station code, US Geological Survey] [Closed] ....KIY
Kiyosumi - Telemeter [Japan] [Seismograph station code, US Geological Survey]......................KYS

Kizyl-Arvat [USSR] [Seismograph station code, US Geological Survey]....................... KAT
Kjeller Research Establishment [Norway]...................KR
KLA Instruments [NASDAQ symbol].........................KLAC
Klagenfurt [Austria] [Airport symbol].......................KLU
Klamath County Library, Klamath Falls, OR [OCLC symbol]..............KCL
Klamath County Library, Klamath Falls, OR [Library symbol] ....OrK
Klamath Falls [Oregon] [Seismograph station code, US Geological Survey]................................. KFO
Klamath Falls [Oregon] [Airport symbol]....................LMT
Klamath Falls, OR [Radio station call letters] ....KAGO
Klamath Falls, OR [Radio station call letters]............KAGO-FM
Klamath Falls, OR [Radio station call letters] ....KFLS
Klamath Falls, OR [Radio station call letters] ....KJSN
Klamath Falls, OR [Radio station call letters] ....KKRB
Klamath Falls, OR [Radio station call letters] ....KLAD
Klamath Falls, OR [Television station call letters].......KOTI-TV
Klamath Falls, OR [Radio station call letters] ....KTEC
Klamath Falls, OR [Location identifier] [FAA]............LFA
Klamath Northern Railway Co. [Later, KNOR] [AAR code]...........KN
Klamath Northern Railway Co. [AAR code]................KNOR
Klank en Weerklank [A publication]..........................Klank
Klasicni Naucn. Spisi. Matematicki Institut (Beograd) [A publication]............... Klasicni Naucn Spisi Mat Inst (Beograd)
Klasse [Class] [German]..KL
Klassizismus und Kulturverfall [A publication].............KuKv
Klaus-Groth-Gesellschaft Jahresgabe [A publication]......KGGJ
Klawock [Alaska] [Airport symbol]............................KLW
KLD Associates, Inc., Huntington Station, NY [Library symbol] ....NHusk
Klebs-Loeffler [Bacteriology] ....KL
Kleer-Vu Industries, Inc. [American Stock Exchange symbol] ....KVU
Klein-Gordon Equation [Physics] ....KGE
Klein-Nishina Formula [Physics]..............................KNF
Klein Paradox [Physics]...KP
Klein-Rydberg Method [Physics]..............................KRM
Kleinasiatische Forschungen [A publication]................KAF
Kleinasiatische Forschungen [A publication]................KF
Kleine Beitrage zur Droste-Forschung [Munster] [A publication]...........KBDF
Kleine Deutsche Prosadenkmaeler des Mittelalters [A publication]....KDPM
Kleine Flote [Piccolo] [German]...............................KF
Kleine Schriften der Gesellschaft fuer Theatergeschichte [A publication]..KSGT
Kleine Texte fuer Vorlesungen und Uebungen [A publication].............KTVU
Kleinert's, Inc. [NYSE symbol] [Delisted].....................KLR
Kleinert's, Inc. [NASDAQ symbol]............................KLRT
Kleinkaliber [Small caliber] [German military] ....KK
Kleinmann-Low [Astronomy].................................KL
Kleinzee [South Africa] [Airport symbol] ....KLZ
Klepzig Fachberichte fuer die Fuehrungskraefte aus Maschinenbau und Huettenwesen [A publication]......... Klepzig Fachber
Kliatt Paperback Book Guide [A publication] ....Kliatt
Kliatt Paperback Book Guide [A publication] ....KPG
Kligler Iron Agar [Medium]......................................KIA
Klima, Kaelte, Heizung [German Federal Republic] [A publication] ....
　　Klima Kaelte Heiz
Klima und Kaelte Ingenieur [A publication] .... Klim Kaelte Ing
Klima-Kaelte-Technik [A publication]................Klima-Kaelte-Tech
Klima und Kaelteingenieur [A publication] .... Klima Kaelteing
Klima-Technik [A publication]........................Klima-Tech
Klinge [Germany] [Research code symbol]...................K
Klinge [Germany] [Research code symbol]...................KD
Klinicheskaya Khirurgiya [Kiev] [A publication]...........Klin Khir
Klinicheskaya Khirurgiya (Kiev) [A publication].......Klin Khir (Kiev)
Klinicheskaya Meditsina (Moscow) [A publication] ....Klin Med (Mosc)
Klinicheskoi Rentgenologii Respublikanskoi Mezhvedomstvennyi Sbornik [A publication]...................
　　Klin Rentgenol Resp Mezhved Sb
Klinika i Lechenie Zlokachestvennykh Novoobrazovanii [A publication]............... Klin Lech Zlokach Novoobraz
Klinika Oczna [A publication]........................... Klin Oczna
Klinika Oczna. Acta Ophtalmologica Polonica [A publication]...........KOAOA
Klinisch-Therapeutische Wochenschrift [A publication].....................
　　Klin Therap Wchnschr
Klinische Anaesthesiologie und Intensivtherapie [A publication]...................
　　Klin Anaesthesiol Intensivther
Klinische Medizin (Vienna) [A publication].........Klin Med (Vienna)
Klinische Monatsblaetter fuer Augenheilkunde [A publication]...................
　　Klin Monats
Klinische Monatsblaetter fuer Augenheilkunde [A publication]...................
　　Klin Monatsbl Augenheilkd
Klinische Monatsblaetter fuer Augenheilkunde [A publication]...........KMAUA
Klinische Paediatrie [A publication]................Klin Paediat
Klinische Paediatrie [A publication]................Klin Paediatr
Klinische Wochenschrift [A publication]............Klin Wchnschr
Klinische Wochenschrift [A publication]............ Klin Woch
Klinische Wochenschrift [A publication]............ Klin Wochenschr
Klinisches Jahrbuch [A publication] ....Klin Jahrb
Klio. Beitrage zur Alten Geschichte [A publication]..........K
Klio. Beitrage zur Alten Geschichte [A publication]..........KI
KLM [Koninklijke Luchtvaart Maatschappij] **Royal Dutch Airlines** [ICAO designator]................................KL

KLM [*Koninklijke Luchtvaart Maatschappij*] **Royal Dutch Airlines** [*NYSE symbol*] ..... KLM
Klondike Air, Inc. [*Anchorage, AK*] [*FAA designator*] ..... KNK
Kloof Gold Mining Co. Ltd. ADR [*NASDAQ symbol*] ..... KLOFY
Kloss, Low, and Hofmann [*Initialism is name of electronics company and brand name of its products*] ..... KLH
Kloss Video Corp. [*NASDAQ symbol*] ..... KLOS
Kluang [*Malaysia*] [*Seismograph station code, US Geological Survey*] ..... KGM
Klung Kidney-Heart-Lung [*Machine*] ..... KKHL
Klutina [*Alaska*] [*Seismograph station code, US Geological Survey*] ..... KLU
Klystron ..... K
Klystron Amplifier ..... KLA
Klystron Frequency Multiplier ..... KFM
Klystron Life Test ..... KLT
Klystron Mount ..... KM
Klystron Oscillator ..... KLO
Klystron Oscillator ..... KO
Klystron Phase Control ..... KPC
Klystron Power Amplifier ..... KPA
Klystron Power Supply ..... KPS
Klystron Power Supply Modulator ..... KPSM
Klyuchi [*USSR*] [*Seismograph station code, US Geological Survey*] ..... KLY
KMED Centers, Inc. [*NASDAQ symbol*] ..... KMED
KMS Fusion, Inc., Ann Arbor, MI [*Library symbol*] ..... MiAaK
KMS Industries [*NASDAQ symbol*] ..... KMSI
KMW Systems Corp. [*NASDAQ symbol*] ..... KMWS
KN Energy, Inc. [*NYSE symbol*] ..... KNE
Knape & Vogt Manufacturing [*NASDAQ symbol*] ..... KNAP
Knapp, Drewett, & Sons Ltd., Kingston-Upon-Thames, United Kingdom [*Library symbol*] ..... UkKuK
Knapp Time Metaphor Scale ..... KTMS
Knee-Ankle-Foot Orthosis [*Medicine*] ..... KAFO
Knee Brace [*Technical drawings*] ..... KB
Knee Disarticulation [*Medicine*] ..... KD
Knee Jerk [*Medicine*] ..... KJ
Knee Kick [*Neurology*] ..... KK
Knee Orthosis [*Medicine*] ..... KO
Knickerbocker Magazine [*A publication*] ..... Knick
Knickerbocker Toy Company, Inc. [*American Stock Exchange symbol*] [*Delisted*] ..... KTC
Knife Blade ..... KNBL
Knife Collectors Club ..... KCC
Knife Edge ..... KNED
Knife and Fork Club International ..... KFCI
Knife Switch ..... KNSW
Knifemakers Guild ..... KG
Kniga i Proletarskaya Revolyutsiya [*A publication*] ..... KPR
Kniga i Revoljucija [*A publication*] ..... KiR
Knight [*Chess, card games*] ..... K
Knight [*British title*] ..... KNT
Knight [*British title*] ..... KT
Knight [*Chess*] ..... N
Knight [*Chess*] ..... KT
Knight Bachelor ..... Kt Bach
Knight Bachelor [*or Knight Companion*] **of the Order of the Bath** [*British*] ..... KB
Knight of the Black Eagle [*Obsolete*] [*Russia*] ..... KBE
Knight of the Blessed Sacrament ..... KBS
Knight of [*the Order of*] **Charles III of Spain** ..... KCS
Knight Commander ..... KC
Knight Commander of the [*Order of the*] **Bath** [*British*] ..... KCB
Knight Commander of the [*Order of the*] **British Empire** ..... KBE
Knight Commander of Court of Honor [*British*] ..... KCCH
Knight Commander of the [*Order of the*] **Crown** [*Belgium*] ..... KCC
Knight Commander of the Guelphic Order of Hanover [*British*] ..... KCH
Knight Commander of the Holy Sepulchre ..... KCHS
Knight Commander of the [*Order of the*] **Indian Empire** [*British*] ..... KCIE
Knight Commander of the Lion and the Sun ..... KCLS
Knight Commander of [*the Order of*] **Pius IX** ..... KCP
Knight Commander of the Royal Victorian Order [*British*] ..... KCVO
Knight Commander of [*the Order of*] **St. Gregory** [*British*] ..... KCSG
Knight Commander of [*the Order of*] **St. John of Jerusalem** [*British*] ..... KStJ
Knight Commander of St. Michael and St. George [*Facetiously translated, "Kindly Call Me God"*] [*British*] ..... KCMG
Knight Commander of [*the Order of*] **St. Sylvester** ..... KCSS
Knight Commander of the [*Order of the*] **Star of India** [*British*] ..... KCSI
Knight of the Crescent [*Turkey*] ..... KC
Knight of the Eagle ..... KE
Knight of the Elephant [*Denmark*] ..... KE
Knight of Ferdinand [*Spain*] ..... KF
Knight of [*the Order of*] **the Garter** [*British*] ..... KG
Knight of the Golden Circle ..... KGC
Knight of the Golden Fleece [*Spain and Austria*] ..... KGF
Knight of Grace, Order of St. John of Jerusalem ..... KGStJ
Knight Grand Commander ..... KGC
Knight Grand Commander of the [*Order of the*] **Indian Empire** [*British*] ..... GCIE
Knight Grand Commander of the [*Order of the*] **Star of India** [*British*] ..... GCSI
Knight of the Grand Cross ..... KGC
Knight Grand Cross of the [*Order of the*] **Bath** [*British*] ..... GCB
Knight Grand Cross of the [*Order of the*] **Bath** [*British*] ..... KGCB
Knight Grand Cross of the [*Order of the*] **British Empire** ..... GBE
Knight Grand Cross of the Guelphic Order of Hanover [*British*] ..... GCH
Knight Grand Cross of the Legion of Honour [*British*] ..... GCLH
Knight Grand Cross of the Royal Victorian Order [*British*] ..... GCVO
Knight Grand Cross of St. Gregory the Great [*British*] ..... GCSG
Knight Grand Cross of [*the Order of*] **St. John of Jerusalem** [*British*] ..... GCStJ
Knight Grand Cross of St. Michael and St. George [*Facetiously translated "God Calls Me God"*] [*British*] ..... GCMG
Knight Grand Cross of St. Sylvester [*British*] ..... GCSS
Knight of the Guelphic Order of Hanover [*British*] ..... KGH
Knight of the Guelphic Order of Hanover [*British*] ..... KH
Knight of Gustavus Vasa [*Sweden*] ..... KCV
Knight of Gustavus Vasa [*Sweden*] ..... KGV
Knight of Hanover ..... K of H
Knight of the Holy Sepulchre ..... KHS
Knight Industries Two Thousand [*Acronym is name of computerized car in TV series "Knight Rider"*] ..... KITT
Knight of Justice, Order of St. John of Jerusalem ..... KJStJ
Knight-Knott Hotels Corp. [*NYSE symbol*] ..... KNT
Knight of the Legion of Honor [*France*] ..... KLH
Knight of [*the Order of*] **Leopold** [*Belgium*] ..... KLB
Knight of [*the Order of*] **Leopold of Austria** ..... KL
Knight of [*the Order of*] **Leopold of Austria** ..... KLA
Knight of Malta ..... KM
Knight of Maria Theresa [*Austria*] ..... KMT
Knight of Maximilian Joseph [*Bavaria*] ..... KMJ
Knight of Merit of Holstein ..... KMH
Knight of the Netherlands Lion ..... KNL
Knight of the [*Order of the*] **Oak Crown** ..... KOC
Knight of Pius IX ..... KP
Knight of Polonia Restituta [*British*] ..... KPR
Knight of the Red Cross ..... KRC
Knight of the Red Eagle [*Prussia*] ..... KRE
Knight of the [*Order of the*] **Redeemer** [*Greece*] ..... KR
Knight-Ridder Newspapers, Inc. [*Later, KRN*] [*NYSE symbol*] ..... KNI
Knight-Ridder Newspapers, Inc. [*Formerly, KNI*] [*NYSE symbol*] ..... KRN
Knight of [*the Order of*] **the Royal Northern Star** [*Sweden*] ..... KNS
Knight Royalty Corporation [*NASDAQ symbol*] ..... KROC
Knight of St. Alexander Nevsky [*Obsolete*] [*Russia*] ..... KAN
Knight of St. Andrew [*Obsolete*] [*Russia*] ..... KA
Knight of St. Anne [*Obsolete*] [*Russia*] ..... KSA
Knight of St. Benedict of Avis ..... KBA
Knight of St. Columba ..... KSC
Knight of Saint-Esprit [*France*] ..... KSE
Knight of St. Ferdinand and Merit [*Italy*] ..... KFM
Knight of St. Ferdinand and Merit [*Italy*] ..... KSFM
Knight of St. George [*Russia*] [*Obsolete*] ..... KSG
Knight of St. Gregory ..... KSG
Knight of St. Hubert [*Bavaria*] ..... KSH
Knight of St. Januarius [*Naples*] ..... KSJ
Knight of St. Joachim ..... KJ
Knight of [*the Order of*] **St. Lazarus of Jerusalem** [*British*] ..... KLJ
Knight of [*the Order of*] **St. Lazarus of Jerusalem** [*British*] ..... KSLJ
Knight of Saint Michael and Saint George [*Ionian Islands*] ..... KSM & SG
Knight of St. Patrick [*British*] ..... KP
Knight of St. Stanislaus of Poland ..... KSP
Knight of St. Sylvester ..... KSS
Knight of St. Vladimir [*Obsolete*] [*Russia*] ..... KSV
Knight of St. Wladimir [*Obsolete*] [*Russia*] ..... KSW
Knight of San Fernando [*Spain*] ..... KSF
Knight of the Southern Star [*Brazil*] ..... KSS
Knight of [*the Order of*] **the Star of India** [*British*] ..... KSI
Knight of the Sun and Lion [*Persia*] ..... KSL
Knight of the Sword [*of Sweden*] ..... KS
Knight of the Sword of Sweden ..... KSS
Knight of the Thistle [*British*] ..... KT
Knight of the Tower and Sword [*Portugal*] ..... KTS
Knight of the White Eagle [*Poland*] ..... KWE
Knight of William [*Netherlands*] ..... KW
Knights of the Altar ..... K/A
Knights of Columbus ..... K of C
Knights of Columbus ..... KC
Knights of Equity and Friendly Sons of St. Patrick ..... KE
Knights of the Golden Eagle ..... KGE
Knights of Jurisprudence ..... KJ
Knights of King Arthur ..... KKA
Knights of Labor ..... K of L
Knights of Lithuania ..... K of L
Knights of Lithuania ..... KL
Knights of Lithuania ..... KOL
Knights of Peter Claver ..... KPC
Knights of Pythias ..... K of P
Knights of Pythias ..... KP
Knights of St. John ..... KSJ
Knights of St. John Supreme Commandery ..... KSJSC
Knights in the Service of Satan [*Rock music group*] ..... KISS
Knights of the Square Table ..... NOST
Knights Templar ..... KT
Knights of Vartan ..... KV

Knights York Cross of Honour KYCH
Knik Glacier [*Alaska*] [*Seismograph station code, US Geological Survey*] KNK
Knit K
Knitgoods Dyers and Processors Association KDPA
Knitted Outerwear Foundation KOF
Knitted Textile Association KTA
Knitting International [*A publication*] Knitting Int
Knitting Machine Manufacturers Association [*Defunct*] KMMA
Knitting Times [*A publication*] Knit Times
Knitwear Employers Association KEA
Knitwear Mill Representatives Association [*Defunct*] KMRA
Knitwise [*Knitting*] KW
Kniznice Odbornych a Vedeckych Spisu Vysokeho Uceni Technickeho v Brne [*A publication*] Kniznice Odborn Ved Spisu Vysoke Uceni Tech v Brne
Kniznice a Vedecke Informacie [*A publication*] Kniznice & Ved Inf
Knjizevna Istorija [*A publication*] KnjIst
Knjizevne Novine [*A publication*] KnjiNov
Knjizevne Novine [*A publication*] KnN
Knjizevnost [*A publication*] K
Knjizevnost [*A publication*] Knji
Knjizevnost i Jezik [*A publication*] KiJ
Knjizevnost i Jezik [*A publication*] KJ
Knjizevnost i Jezik u Skoli [*A publication*] KJS
Knob Door Fastener KDF
Knob Noster, MO [*Radio station call letters*] KLUK
Knob Noster, MO [*Location identifier*] [*FAA*] SZL
Knobby Lake Mines [*NASDAQ symbol*] KNOBF
Knock [*Cardiology*] K
Knocked-on-Atom KOA
Knocked Down [*i.e., disassembled*] KD
Knocked Down, in Carloads KDCL
Knocked Down Flat KDF
Knocked Down, in Less than Carloads KDLCL
Knockout [*Boxing*] KO
Knockout [*Partly cut out or loosened area which can be easily removed, as in a junction box*] [*Technical drawings*] KO
Knockout Drops [*A drug producing unconsciousness*] [*Slang*] KO's
Knocks Eczema [*Acronym, brand name for skin cream, said to be taken from this phrase*] NOXZEMA
Knogo Corp. [*American Stock Exchange symbol*] KNO
Knoll AG [*Germany*] [*Research code symbol*] D
Knoll International Cl A [*American Stock Exchange symbol*] KNL
Knolls KNLS
Knolls Atomic Power Laboratory [*AEC*] KAPL
Knoop Hardness Number HK
Knoop Hardness Number KHN
Knot KN
Knots [*Also, KT*] [*Nautical speed unit*] K
Knots [*Also, K*] [*Nautical speed unit*] KT
Knots Calibrated Airspeed KCAS
Knots End Airspeed KEAS
Knots Equivalent Airspeed KEAS
Knots Indicated Airspeed KIAS
Knots per Revolution KPR
Knots True Airspeed [*Navy*] KTAS
Knotted List Structure KLS
Knotty Pine KP
Know Problems of Hydrocephalus KPH
Know Your Endorsers - Require Identification [*Advice to businessmen and others who cash checks for the public*] KYERI
Knowledge [*A publication*] Knowl
Knowledge, Attitude, Skills, Habits [*Formula*] [*LIMRA*] KASH
Knowledge, Attitudes, and Practice [*Sociology*] KAP
Knowledge Availability Systems Center [*University of Pittsburgh*] KASC
Knowledge Industry Publications, Inc. KIP
Knowledge Industry Publications, Incorporated KIPI
Knowledge Industry Systems Concept [*Publishing and education*] [*Pronounced "kiss"*] KISC
Knowledge Information Processing Systems KIPS
Knowledge of Results [*Visual monitoring*] KOR
Knowledge of Results KR
Knowledge of Results Feedback KRF
Knowles Electronics Manikin for Acoustic Research KEMAR
Known KN
Known Datum Point KDP
Known-Distance [*Range*] [*Weaponry*] KD
Known Enemy Dead [*Military*] KED
Known Enemy Location [*Military*] KEL
Known Gambler [*Police slang*] KG
Known Geothermal Resource Area [*Department of the Interior*] KGRA
Knox College, Galesburg, IL [*OCLC symbol*] IBK
Knox College, Galesburg, IL [*Library symbol*] IGK
Knox College, University of Toronto, Toronto, ON, Canada [*Library symbol*] CaOTK
Knox County Public Library, Vincennes, IN [*OCLC symbol*] IMW
Knox, IN [*Location identifier*] [*FAA*] OXI
Knox, IN [*Radio station call letters*] WKVI-FM
Knox Ranch [*California*] [*Seismograph station code, US Geological Survey*] [*Closed*] KNO
Knoxville [*Tennessee*] [*Airport symbol*] TYS
Knoxville Academy of Medicine, Knoxville, TN [*Library symbol*] TKAM
Knoxville Area Health Science Consortium [*Library network*] KAHSLC
Knoxville City School, Knoxville, TN [*OCLC symbol*] TKS
Knoxville, IA [*Radio station call letters*] KNIA
Knoxville, IA [*Radio station call letters*] KRLS
Knoxville, IA [*Radio station call letters*] KTAV
Knoxville, IA [*Location identifier*] [*FAA*] OXV
Knoxville International Energy Exposition [*1982*] KIEE
Knoxville-Knox County Public Library, Knoxville, TN [*OCLC symbol*] TKL
Knoxville Public Library, Knoxville, IA [*Library symbol*] IaKn
Knoxville, TN [*Location identifier*] [*FAA*] BUI
Knoxville, TN [*Television station call letters*] WATE
Knoxville, TN [*Radio station call letters*] WBMK
Knoxville, TN [*Radio station call letters*] WEZK
Knoxville, TN [*Radio station call letters*] WIMZ
Knoxville, TN [*Radio station call letters*] WIMZ-FM
Knoxville, TN [*Radio station call letters*] WITA
Knoxville, TN [*Radio station call letters*] WIVK
Knoxville, TN [*Radio station call letters*] WIVK-FM
Knoxville, TN [*Television station call letters*] WKCH-TV
Knoxville, TN [*Radio station call letters*] WKCS
Knoxville, TN [*Radio station call letters*] WKGN
Knoxville, TN [*Radio station call letters*] WKXV
Knoxville, TN [*Radio station call letters*] WNOX
Knoxville, TN [*Radio station call letters*] WRJZ
Knoxville, TN [*Radio station call letters*] WSKT
Knoxville, TN [*Television station call letters*] WTVK
Knoxville, TN [*Radio station call letters*] WUOT
Knoxville, TN [*Radio station call letters*] WUTK
Knudsen Absolute Manometer [*Physics*] KAM
Knudsen Cosine Law [*Physics*] KCL
Knudsen Flow [*Physics*] KF
Knudsen Leaf Gauge [*Physics*] KLG
Knudsen Number [*IUPAC*] Kn
Knurl [*Engineering*] KNRL
Knurling Tool KLTO
Kobacher Stores, Inc. [*NYSE symbol*] KOB
Kobe [*Japan*] [*Seismograph station code, US Geological Survey*] KOB
Kobe Economic and Business Review [*A publication*] KEBR
Kobe Gaidai Ronso [*Kobe City University Journal*] [*A publication*] KGR
Kobe Journal of Medical Science [*A publication*] Kobe J Med Sci
Kobe Research Development [*A publication*] Kobe Res Dev
Kobe University Economic Review [*A publication*] Kobe Univ Econ R
Kobe University Economic Review [*A publication*] KUER
Kobe University Medical Mission to Indonesia KUMMI
Kobenhavns Universitetsbibliotekets [*University of Copenhagen*], **Afdeling, Fiolstraede, Kobenhavn, Denmark** [*Library symbol*] DnKU-S
Kobenhavns Universitetsbibliotekets [*University of Copenhagen*], **Afdeling, Norre Alle, Kobenhavn, Denmark** [*Library symbol*] DnKU
Koblenz Procurement Center [*Military*] [*Federal Republic of Germany*] KPC
Kobuan [*Solomon Islands*] [*Seismograph station code, US Geological Survey*] [*Closed*] KOA
Kobuk [*Alaska*] [*Airport symbol*] OBU
Kobunshi Ronbunshu [*A publication*] Kobunsh Ron
Kochi [*Japan*] [*Airport symbol*] KCZ
Kochi [*Japan*] [*Seismograph station code, US Geological Survey*] KOC
Kodai Mathematical Journal [*A publication*] Kodai Math J
Kodaikanal [*India*] [*Geomagnetic observatory code*] KOD
Kodaikanal [*India*] [*Seismograph station code, US Geological Survey*] KOD
Kodaikanal Observatory Bulletin. Series A [*A publication*] Kodaikanal Obs Bull A
Kodaikanal Observatory Bulletin. Series B [*A publication*] Kodaikanal Obs Bull B
Kodak Industrial Film KIF
Kodak Industrial X-Ray Film KIXF
Kodak Infrared Phosphor KIRP
Kodak Infrared Scope KIRS
Kodak Infrared Scope KIS
Kodak International Newspaper Snapshot Awards KINSA
Kodak Job Sheet KJS
Kodak Ltd., Recordak Division, London, United Kingdom [*Library symbol*] NRE-L
Kodak Metal Etch Resist KMER
Kodak (Near East) Ltd., Beirut, Lebanon [*Library symbol*] NRE-B
Kodak Ortho Resist KOR
Kodak Photo Resist KPR
Kodak Photofabrication Center KPC
Kodak Reflex Camera KRC
Kodak Relief Plate KRP
Kodak Special Plate KSP
Kodak Standard [*Photography*] KS
Kodak Thin-Film Resist [*Cathode coating*] KTFR
Kodak Timing Negative Film KTNF
Kodak Unitized Engineering Data KUED
Kodak Vacuum Probe KVP
Kodak Versamat Processor KVP
Kodak Wratten Light Filter KWLF

Kodak X-Ray Film..KXF
Kodiak [Alaska] [Airport symbol]..ADQ
Kodiak [Alaska] [Seismograph station code, US Geological Survey].......KDC
Kodiak Airways, Inc. [Kodiak, AK] [FAA designator] ....KDK
Kodiak, AK [Radio station call letters] ....KMXT
Kodiak, AK [Radio station call letters] ....KVOK
Kodiak, AK [Location identifier] [FAA]................................NOJ
Kodiak, AK [Location identifier] [FAA]..............................RWO
Kodiak Historical Society, Kodiak, AK [Library symbol] ....AkKoHi
Kodiak [Alaska] Municipal Airport [Airport symbol] [Obsolete]......KDK
Kodiak Public Library (A. Holmes Johnson Memorial Library),
   Kodiak, AK [Library symbol] ....AkKo
Kodiak Tracking Station [NASA]..KTS
Kodiak-Western Alaska Airlines, Inc. [CAB official abbreviation].......KO
Kodiak-Western Alaska Airlines, Inc. [Air carrier designation
   symbol] ....KWA
[Ludwig Ritter von] Koechel [When used in identifying Mozart's
   compositions, refers to cataloging of his works by
   musicologist Koechel]...K
Koedoe Monograph [A publication]..................... Koedoe Monogr
Koehler Air Taxi Co., Inc. [Columbus, OH] [FAA designator] ......KAT
Koehring Co. [NYSE symbol] [Delisted]................................KOE
Koeln. Vierteljahrschrift fuer Freunde der Stadt [A publication]..........Koeln
Koelner Geographische Arbeiten [A publication]............. Koeln Geogr Arb
Koelner Germanistische Studien [A publication].....................KGS
Koelner Jahrbuch fuer Vor- und Fruehgeschichte [A publication]......
   Koln Jb Vor Fruh Gesch
Koelner Romanistische Arbeiten [A publication] ....KRA
Koelner Zeitschrift fuer Soziologie und Sozial-Psychologie [A
   publication]..Koelner Z Soz
Koelner Zeitschrift fuer Soziologie und Sozial-Psychologie [A
   publication]............................ Koelner Z Soziol u Soz-Psychol
Koelner Zeitschrift fuer Soziologie und Sozial Psychologie [A
   publication]..KZSS
Koenig, Inc. [NASDAQ symbol] ....KOEN
Koeniglich [Royal] [German]..KGL
Koeniglich-Bayerische Akademie der Wissenschaften zu
   Muenchen. Mathematisch-Physikalische Klasse.
   Sitzungsberichte. Abhandlungen [A publication] ....
   K-Bayer Ak Wiss Muenchen Mat-Phys Kl Szb Abh
Koeniglich-Boehmische Gesellschaft der Wissenschaften in
   Prag. Mathematisch-Naturwissenschaftliche Classe.
   Sitzungsberichte [A publication].......K-Boehm Ges Wiss Mat-Nat Cl Szb
Koeniglich-Preussische Akademie der Wissenschaften (Berlin).
   Abhandlungen [A publication]...................................AWBAbh
Koeniglich-Preussische Akademie der Wissenschaften (Berlin).
   Sitzungsberichte [A publication].................................AWBSb
Koeniglich-Saechsische Gesellschaft der Wissenschaften zu
   Leipzig. Mathematisch-Physische Classe. Berichte ueber
   die Verhandlungen [A publication].............................
   K-Saechs Ges Wiss Leipzig Mat-Phys Cl Ber
Koenigliche Akademie der Wissenschaften (Wien).
   Denkschriften [A publication] ....AWWDs
Koenigliche Gesellschaft der Wissenschaften zu Goettingen.
   Abhandlungen [A publication] ....K Ges Wiss Goettingen Abh
Koenigsberg Universitaet. Jahrbuch [A publication] ....
   Konigsberg Univ Jahrb
Koenigsberger Deutsche Forschungen [A publication] ....KDF
Koezgazdasagi Szemle [A publication]...................Koezgazd Szle
Kofu [Japan] [Seismograph station code, US Geological Survey]...........KOF
Koger Co. [American Stock Exchange symbol] ....KGR
Koger Properties [NYSE symbol]....................................KOG
Kohala [Hawaii] [Seismograph station code, US Geological Survey] ....KOH
Kohles, F. S., Montebello CA [STAC]................................KFS
Koinambe [Papua New Guinea] [Airport symbol] ....KMB
Koingnaas [South Africa] [Airport symbol].........................KIG
Koinonia Foundation...KF
Kokka Gakkai Zassi [Journal. Association of Political and Social
   Science] [A publication].................................Kok Gak Zas
Kokkola [Finland] [Airport symbol] ....KOK
Koko Head, HI [Location identifier] [FAA].........................CKH
Kokoda [Papua New Guinea] [Airport symbol] ....KKD
Kokomo [Indiana] [Airport symbol] ....OKK
Kokomo, IN [Radio station call letters].........................WHSK
Kokomo, IN [Radio station call letters].........................WIOU
Kokomo, IN [Radio station call letters]........................WWKI
Kokomo, IN [Radio station call letters].......................WZWZ
Kokomo Public Library, Kokomo, IN [OCLC symbol] ....IKP
Kokomo Public Library, Kokomo, IN [Library symbol] ....InKo
Kokoro [Papua New Guinea] [Airport symbol] ....KOR
Kokugo Kokubun no Kenkyu [Studies in Japanese Language and
   Literature] [A publication].....................................KKK
Kokugo to Kokubungaky [Japanese Language and Literature] [A
   publication]..KtoK
Kokuritsu Kokkai Toshokan [National Diet Library], Tokyo,
   Japan [Library symbol]..JTNDL
Kokusai Denshin Denwa [Telegraph & Telephone Corp.] [Japan]..........KDD
Kol [Papua New Guinea] [Airport symbol]..........................KQL
Kolel Shomre Hachomos [An association]...........................KSH
Koleopterologische Rundschau [A publication] .... Koleopterol Rundsch
Kolff Medical, Inc. [NASDAQ symbol]..............................KOLF

Kolhospnyk Ukrainy [A publication].....................Kolhospnyk Ukr
Koliganek [Alaska] [Airport symbol].................................KGK
Kolkhozno-Sovkhoznoe Proizvodstvo [A publication]..................
   Kolkhoz-Sovkhoz Proizvod
Kolkhozno-Sovkhoznoe Proizvodstvo Kirgizii [A publication]..........
   Kolkhoz-Sovkhoz Proizvod Kirgizii
Kolkhozno-Sovkhoznoe Proizvodstvo Moldavil [A publication]..........
   Kolkhoz-Sovkhoz Proizvod Mold
Kolkhozno-Sovkhoznoe Proizvodstvo RSFSR [A publication]..........
   Kolkhoz-Sovkhoz Proizvod RSFSR
Kolkhoznoe Proizvodstvo [A publication] .... Kolkhoz Proizvod
Kollektsioner Azerbaidzhana [A publication] ....Koll Azerb
Kollmorgen Corp. [NYSE symbol] ....KOL
Kolloid-Zeitschrift und Zeitschrift fuer Polymere [A publication] ....Kolloid-Z
Kolloid-Zeitschrift und Zeitschrift fuer Polymere [A publication]..........
   Kolloid-Z & Z Polym
Kolloidnyi Zhurnal [A publication] ....Kolloidnyi Zh
Kolloidnyi Zhurnal [A publication] ....Kolloid Zh
Kollsman [When followed by altimeter setting] [See also KOL] [Aviation].....K
Kollsman [See also K] [Aviation]....................................KOL
Kollsman Integrated Flight Instrumentation System [Aviation].......KIFIS
Kolmer [Test with] Reiter Protein [Serology]......................KRP
Kolmogorov-Arnol'd-Moser [Statistical mechanics]..................KAM
Kolmogorov - Smirnov Test [Statistics].............................KS
Kolomenskii Pedagogiceskii Institut. Ucenye Zapiski [A
   publication]........................Kolomen Ped Inst Ucen Zap
Kolorisztikai Ertesitoe [A publication]....................Kolor Ert
Kolson Quick Modality Test [Education].............................KQM
Komaba [Japan] [Seismograph station code, US Geological
   Survey] [Closed] ....KOM
Komando Operasi Projek-Projek Sandang [Indonesia] ....KOPROSAN
Komando Pertahanan Maritim Nasional [Indonesia]..........KOHANMARNAS
Komarom Megyei Muzeumok Koezlemenei [A publication]..........
   Komarom Meg Muz Koz
Komatsu [Japan] [Airport symbol]..................................KMQ
Kombinatornyi Analiz [A publication]................. Kombinatornyi Anal
Komisja Krystalografii PAN [Polska Akademia Nauk]. Biuletyn
   Informacyjny [A publication]..............Kom Krystalogr PAN Biul Inf
Komite Olahraga Nasional Indonesia ....KONI
Komitet Gossudarstvennoi Bezopasnosti [Committee of State
   Security] [Russian Secret Police] [Also satirically interpreted
   as Kontora Grubykh Banditov, or "Office of Crude Bandits"]...........KGB
Kommunalekonomiska Utredningen [Sweden]........................KEU
Kommunismus und Klassenkampf [A publication] ....
   Kommun u Klassenkampf
Kommunist Azerbajdzana [A publication] ....Kommunist Azerbajd
Kommunist Sovetskoj Latvii [A publication]..........Kommunist Sov Latvii
Kommunista Ifjusagi Szovetseg [Communist Youth Organization]
   [Hungary] ....KISZ
Kommunisticheskaia Partiia Sovetskogo Soiuza [Communist
   Party of the Soviet Union].....................................KPSS
Kommunisticheskaia Partiia Ukrainy [Communist Party of the
   Ukraine]...KPU
Kommunisticheskaia Partiia Uzbekistana [Communist Party of
   Uzbekistan]...KPUZ
Kommunistikon Komma Ellada [Communist Party of Greece] ....KKE
Kommunistische Jugend Oesterreich [Austrian Communist Youth] ......KJO
Kommunistische Partei [Communist Party] [German]...................KP
Kommunistische Partei Deutschlands [Communist Party of
   Germany]..KPD
Kommunistische Partei Oesterreichs [Communist Party of Austria].......KPO
Kommunistische Partei der Sowjetunion [Communist Party of
   the Soviet Union] ....KPDSU
Kommunistische Jugendverband Deutschlands [Communist
   Youth Club of Germany] ....KJVD
Komo-Manda [Papua New Guinea] [Airport symbol] [Obsolete].........KOM
Komondor Club of America...KCA
Kompartimen Perindustrian Rakjat [Indonesia] ....KOMPERINDRA
Kompleksnoe Ispol'zovanie Mineral'nogo Syr'ya [A publication]..........
   Kompleksn Ispol'z Miner Syr'ya
Komunikaty Mazursko-Warminskie [A publication]........ Kom Mazur-Warmin
Komunist (Belgrade) [A publication].................................KB
Komunisticka Partija Jugoslavije...................................KPJ
Komunisticka Strana Ceskoslovenska.................................KSC
Komunisticke Partija Hrvatske......................................KPH
Komunistycha Spilka Molodi Ukrainy...............................KSMU
Komunistyczna Partia Polski [Communist Party of Poland]............KPP
Kona [Hawaii] [Airport symbol] ....KOA
Konan Women's College. Researches [A publication] ....
   Konan Women's Coll Res
Konawaena [Hawaii] [Seismograph station code, US Geological
   Survey] [Closed] ....KNW
Konawaruk [Guyana] [Airport symbol] [Obsolete] ....KKG
Kone [New Caledonia] [Airport symbol] [Obsolete]...............KNQ
Konedobu [Papua New Guinea] [Seismograph station code, US
   Geological Survey]..KDB
Konfederasi Serikat Serikat Buruh Islam [Confederation of
   Islamic Trade Unions of Indonesia]............................KSSBI
Konge [Papua New Guinea] [Airport symbol] ....KGB
Kongelige Bibliotek [Royal Library], Kobenhavn, Denmark
   [Library symbol]...Dn

Kongelige Danske Videnskabernes Selskab. Biologiske Skrifter
[A publication].................................. K Dan Vidensk Selsk Biol Skr

Kongelige Danske Videnskabernes Selskab. Historisk-
Filosofiske Meddelelser [Copenhagen] [A publication]..................KDVS

Kongelige Danske Videnskabernes Selskab. Oversigt
Selskabets Virksomhed [A publication]..............................
Kgl Danske Vidensk Selsk Oversigt

Kongelige Norske Videnskabers Selskabs Foerhandlinger [A
publication]............................ K Nor Vidensk Selsk Foerhandl

Kongelige Norske Videnskabers Selskabs Foerhandlinger [A
publication]............................... K Nor Vidensk Selsk Forh

Kongelige Norske Videnskabers Selskabs Foerhandlinger
(Trondheim) [A publication] .... Norske Vid Selsk Forh (Trondheim)

Kongelige Norske Videnskabers Selskabs Museet Miscellanea
[A publication]........................ K Nor Vidensk Selsk Mus Misc

Kongelige Norske Videnskabers Selskabs Skrifter [A
publication]................................... K Nor Vidensk Selsk Skr

Kongelige Norske Videnskabers Selskabs Skrifter (Trondheim)
[A publication]........................ Norske Vid Selsk Skr (Trondheim)

Kongelige Norske Videnskapers Selskap [A publication].....................KNVS

Kongelige Veterinaer-og Landbohojskole Arsskrift [A
publication]...............................K Vet-Landbohojsk Arsskr

Kongiganak [Alaska] [Airport symbol]............................... KKH

Konglomerati Florida Foundation for Literature and the Book
Arts ....KFFLBA

Kongo [MARC language code] [Library of Congress]................ kon

Kongo-Overzee. Tijdschrift voor en Over Belgisch-Kongo en
Andere Overzeese Gewesten [A publication].................. KO

Kongolo [Zaire] [Airport symbol]................................KOO

Kongres Buruh Islam Merdeka [Free Islamic Trade Union
Congress] [Indonesia]..KBIM

Kongres Buruh Karata Api [Congress of Railway Workers]
[Indonesia]..KBKA

Kongres Buruh Seluruh Indonesia [All Indonesia Congress of
Workers]..KBSI

Kongres Wanita Indonesia..KOWANI

Kongresszentralblatt fuer die Gesamte Innere Medizin und Ihre
Grenzgebiete [A publication] .... Kong Zentralbl Ges Innere Med

Kongsberg [Norway] [Seismograph station code, US Geological
Survey]...KON

Kongsberg Vaapenfabrikk [Norway].................................KV

Konigsberg [Kaliningrad] [USSR] [Seismograph station code, US
Geological Survey] [Closed]..................................KNG

Koninklijk Academie van Belgie Jaarboek [A publication] ....
K Acad Belg Jaarb

Koninklijk Belgisch Instituut voor Natuurwetenschappen
Studiedocumenten [A publication]........ K Belg Inst Natuurwet Studiedoc

Koninklijk Belgisch Instituut voor Natuurwetenschappen
Verhandelingen [A publication]..........K Belg Inst Natuurwet Verh

Koninklijk Instituut voor Taal-, Land-, en Volkenkunde, Leiden,
Netherlands [Library symbol]................................NeLV

Koninklijk Instituut voor de Tropen, Amsterdam, Netherlands
[Library symbol]... NeAT

Koninklijk Instituut voor de Tropen Mededeling. Afdeling
Tropische Producten [A publication] ....
K Inst Tropen Meded Afd Tropische Producten

Koninklijk Museum voor Midden-Afrika Tervuren Belgie
Annalen Reeks in Octavo Geologische Wetenschappen [A
publication]...
K Mus Midden-Afr Tervuren Belg Ann Reeks Octavo Geol Wet

Koninklijk Nederlands Verbond van Drukkerijen [Royal
Netherlands Printing Association]...........................KNVD

Koninklijke Belgische Commissie voor Volkskunde, Vlaamse
Afdeling Jaarboek [A publication]...........................KBCJ

Koninklijke Bibliotheek [Royal Library], The Hague, Netherlands
[Library symbol]...NeHKB

Koninklijke Java-China-Paketvaart Lijnen.........................KJCPL

Koninklijke Luchtvaart Maatschappij [Royal Dutch Airlines]..................KLM

Koninklijke Nederlandse Akademie van Wetenschappen [A
publication]..KNAW

Koninklijke Nederlandse Akademie van Wetenschappen.
Indagationes Mathematicae ex Actis Quibus Titulus [A
publication]..............................Nederl Akad Wetensch Indag Math

Koninklijke Nederlandse Akademie van Wetenschappen.
Proceedings. Series C. Biological and Medical Sciences [A
publication]...KNWCA

Koninklijke Nederlandse Akademie van Wetenschappen.
Proceedings [A publication]...................................
Koninkl Nederlandse Akad Wetensch Proc

Koninklijke Nederlandse Akademie van Wetenschappen.
Proceedings. Series A. Mathematical Sciences [A publication]..............
Nederl Akad Wetensch Proc Ser A

Koninklijke Nederlandse Akademie van Wetenschappen.
Proceedings. Series B. Physical Sciences [A publication]....................
Nederl Akad Wetensch Proc Ser B

Koninklijke Nederlandse Akademie van Wetenschappen.
Verslag van de Gewone Vergadering van de Afdeling
Natuurkunde [A publication].................................
Nederl Akad Wetensch Verslag Afd Natuurk

Koninklijke Nederlandse Natuurhistorische Vereniging Uitgave
[A publication]........................... K Ned Natuurhist Ver Uitg

Koninklijke Vlaamse Academie voor Taal- en Letterkunde [A
publication]..KVATL

Koninklijke Zout-Organon, NV [Later, AKZO] [Netherlands].................KZO

Koninklijke Zuidnederlandse Maatschappij voor Taal- en
Letterkunde en Geschiedenis [A publication] ....KZMTLG

Konkani [MARC language code] [Library of Congress]....................kok

Konservnaya i Ovoshchesushil'naya Promyshlennost' [A
publication].......................Konservn Ovoshchesush Prom-st

Konservnaya i Ovoshchesushil'naya Promyshlennost' [A
publication]..............................Konserv Ovoshchesush Prom

Konsthistorisk Tidskrift [A publication].................... Konsthist Tid

Konsthistorisk Tidskrift [A publication]................Konsthist Tidskrift

Konstitutsiya i Svojstva Mineralov [A publication]...............Konst Svoj Miner

Konstruktion, Elemente, Methoden [A publication] ... Konstr Elem Methoden

Konstruktion im Maschinen-, Apparate-, und Geraetebau [A
publication]........................ Konstr Masch-Appar- Geraetebau

Konstruktion im Maschinen-, Apparate-, und Geraetebau [A
publication]........................ Konstr Masch App Geraetebau

Konstruktiver Ingenieurbau Berichte [A publication] ....
Konstr Ingenieurbau Ber

Konstruktsionnye Materialy na Osnove Grafita [A publication].................
Konstr Mater Osn Grafita

Konstruktsionnye Materialy na Osnove Ugleroda [A publication].................
Konstr Mater Osn Ugleroda

Konstruktsionnye Uglegrafitovye Materialy. Sbornik Trudov [A
publication]...................... Konstr Uglegrafitovye Mater Sb Tr

Konyvtari Figyelo [A publication]........................ Konyvtari Figy

Konyvtartudomanyi es Modszertani Kozpont [Center for Library
Science and Methodology] [Hungary] [Information service]............. KMK

Konzentrationslager [Concentration Camp] [Initials also used in
medicine to indicate a psychiatric syndrome found in
surviving victims of the World War II camps]....................KZ

Konzerv- es Paprikaipar [A publication] .... Konzerv-Paprikaip

Koolatah [Australia] [Airport symbol] [Obsolete].....................KOH

Kooperativno Zemedelie [A publication] .... Kooper Zemed

Koordinatsionnaya Khimiya [A publication]........................ Koord Khim

Kopasker [Iceland] [Airport symbol]...............................OPA

Kopeck [Monetary unit in Russia]................................. K

Kopeck [Monetary unit in Russia]................................KOP

Kopenhagener Beitrage zur Germanistischen Linguistik [A
publication]..KGBL

Kopenhagener Germanistische Studien [A publication]..................KopGS

Kopiago [Papua New Guinea] [Airport symbol].......................KPA

Koppel [Federal Republic of Germany] [Seismograph station
code, US Geological Survey]..................................KOE

Koppers Co., Inc. [NYSE symbol]................................KOP

Koppers Co., Inc., Research Department, Monroeville, PA
[Library symbol]...PMvK

Koppers Hydrate Process..KHP

Koracorp Industries, Inc. [NYSE symbol] [Delisted]...................KOR

Korea [MARC geographic area code] [Library of Congress] ....a-kr---

[Republic of] Korea [Aircraft nationality and registration mark]..................HL

Korea Advanced Institute of Science ....KIAS

Korea Air Defense System..KADS

Korea-American Commerce and Industry Association [Later,
USKEC]...KACIA

Korea, Australia, New Zealand, and the United States ....KANZUS

Korea Development Bank..KDB

Korea Development Finance Corporation.............................KDFC

Korea Institute of Forest Genetics. Research Reports [A
publication]........................... Korea Inst Forest Genet Res Rept

Korea Journal [A publication] .... KoJ

Korea Journal [A publication] .... Korea J

Korea Journal [Republic of Korea] [A publication] ....Kor J

Korea Journal of Comparative Law [Republic of Korea] [A
publication]..Kor J Comp Law

Korea Journal of International Studies [Republic of Korea] [A
publication].. Kor J Int Stud

Korea Limited Identification Zone ....KLIZ

Korea Microforms, Seoul, Korea [Library symbol]....................KoM

Korea Military Academy .... KMA

Korea Military Advisory Group [United States].....................KMAG

Korea, North [MARC geographic area code] [Library of Congress] ...... a-kn---

Korea, North [MARC country of publication code] [Library of Congress] .....kn

Korea Observer [Republic of Korea] [A publication] .... Kor Obs

Korea Oil Corporation..KOCO

Korea Oil Storage Company...KOSCO

Korea Procurement Agency...KPA

Korea Scientific and Technological Information Center ....KORSTIC

Korea, South [MARC geographic area code] [Library of Congress]...... a-ko---

Korea, South [MARC country of publication code] [Library of Congress].... ko

Korea Stamp Society..KSS

Korea Trade Promotion Center ....KOTRA

Korea University Medical Journal [A publication] .... Korea Univ Med J

Korean [MARC language code] [Library of Congress].....................kor

Korean Affairs [A publication].....................................KA

Korean Affairs Institute...KAI

Korean Air Lines, Inc...KAL

Korean Air Lines, Inc. [ICAO designator]...........................KE

Korean-American Chamber of Commerce [Later, AAACC]..............KACC

Korean-American Cultural Foundation ....KACF

Korean-American Technical Cooperation Association .... KATCA
Korean Army Training Center .... KATC
Korean Augmentation to the United States Army .... KATUSA
Korean Biochemical Journal [*A publication*] .... Korean Biochem J
Korean Broadcasting System .... KBS
Korean Central Intelligence Agency .... KCIA
Korean Central Journal of Medicine [*A publication*] .... Korean Cent J Med
Korean Central News Agency [*North Korea*] .... KCNA
Korean Civic Action Group .... KCAG
Korean Civil Action Corps .... KCAC
Korean Communications Zone [*Military*] .... KCOMZ
Korean Conflict Research Foundation [*Defunct*] .... KCRF
Korean Council of Organization [*South Korea*] .... KCLU
Korean Cultural and Freedom Foundation .... KCFF
Korean Direct Hire .... KDH
Korean Federation of Education Associations .... KFEA
Korean Federation of Trade Unions [*North Korea*] .... KFTU
Korean Hemorrhagic Fever [*Medicine*] .... KHF
Korean Institute for Human Rights .... KIHR
Korean Institute of International Studies .... KIIS
Korean Institute of Mineral and Mining Engineers. Journal [*Republic of Korea*] [*A publication*] .... Korean Inst Miner Min Eng J
Korean Institute for Research in the Behavioral Sciences .... KIRBS
Korean Institute for Science and Technology .... KIST
Korean Journal of Animal Sciences [*A publication*] .... Korean J Anim Sci
Korean Journal of Applied Microbiology and Bioengineering [*Republic of Korea*] [*A publication*] .... Korean J Appl Microbiol Bioeng
Korean Journal of Biochemistry [*A publication*] .... Korean J Biochem
Korean Journal of Botany [*A publication*] .... Korean J Bot
Korean Journal of Breeding [*Republic of Korea*] [*A publication*] .... Korean J Breed
Korean Journal of Dermatology [*A publication*] .... Korean J Dermatol
Korean Journal of Entomology [*A publication*] .... Korean J Entomol
Korean Journal of Environmental Health Society [*Republic of Korea*] [*A publication*] .... Korean J Environ Health Soc
Korean Journal of Food Science and Technology [*A publication*] .... Korean J Food Sci Technol
Korean Journal of Horticultural Science [*A publication*] .... Korean J Hortic Sci
Korean Journal of Internal Medicine [*A publication*] .... Korean J Intern Med
Korean Journal of Microbiology [*A publication*] .... Korean J Microbiol
Korean Journal of Nuclear Medicine [*A publication*] .... Korean J Nucl Med
Korean Journal of Obstetrics and Gynecology [*A publication*] .... Korean J Obstet Gynecol
Korean Journal of Parasitology [*A publication*] .... Korean J Parasitol
Korean Journal of Pharmacognosy [*A publication*] .... Korean J Pharmacogn
Korean Journal of Pharmacology [*A publication*] .... Korean J Pharmacol
Korean Journal of Public Health [*A publication*] .... Korean J Public Health
Korean Journal of Urology [*Republic of Korea*] [*A publication*] .... Korean J Urol
Korean Journal of Veterinary Research [*Republic of Korea*] [*A publication*] .... Korean J Vet Res
Korean Journal of Zoology [*A publication*] .... Korean J Zool
Korean Labor Party [*Communist*] .... KLP
Korean Logistic Service Corps .... KLSC
Korean Marine Corps [*North Korea*] .... KMC
Korean Medical Abstracts [*A publication*] .... KOMAB
Korean National Airlines .... KNA
Korean National Association .... KNA
Korean Patriotic Women's Association in America .... KPWA
Korean Presidential Unit Citation [*Military award*] .... KPUC
Korean Scientific Abstracts [*A publication*] .... KOSAB
Korean Scientists and Engineers Association in America .... KSEA
Korean Service Corps .... KSC
Korean Service Medal .... KSM
Korean Student Federation of the United States .... KSFUS
Korean Studies Forum [*Republic of Korea*] [*A publication*] .... Korean Stud For
Korean Survey [*A publication*] .... KS
Korean War .... KW
Korean Wideband Network [*Communications*] [*Military*] .... KWN
Koreana Quarterly [*A publication*] .... Koreana Quart
Koreana Quarterly [*A publication*] .... KQ
Korhaz- es Orvostechnika [*Hungary*] [*A publication*] .... Korh Orvostech
Korhogo [*Ivory Coast*] [*Airport symbol*] .... HGO
Korintji-Kaba-Dempo [*Sumatra*] [*Seismograph station code, US Geological Survey*] [*Closed*] .... KKD
Korla [*China*] [*Airport symbol*] .... KRL
Korma i Kormlenie Sel'skokhozyaitvennykh Zhivotnykh [*A publication*] .... Korma Korml Skh Zhivotn
Kormi ta Godivlya Sil's'kogospodars'kikh Tvarin [*A publication*] .... Kormi Godivlya Sil's'kogospod Tvarin
Korn Magasinet [*A publication*] .... Korn Mag
Koro [*Fiji*] [*Airport symbol*] .... KXF
Koroba [*Papua New Guinea*] [*Airport symbol*] [*Obsolete*] .... KDE
Koror [*Palau Islands*] [*Seismograph station code, US Geological Survey*] [*Closed*] .... KOR
Koror [*Palau Islands*] [*Airport symbol*] .... ROR
Koroze a Ochrana Materialu [*A publication*] .... Koroze Ochr Mater
Korps Karyawan Pemerintahan Dalam Negeri [*Indonesia*] .... KOKARMINDAGRI
Korrespondenzblatt des Gesamtvereins der Deutschen Geschichte und Altertumsvereine [*A publication*] .... KBDA
Korrespondenzblatt fuer die Hoeheren Schulen Wuerttembergs [*A publication*] .... KBW
Korrespondenzblatt des Vereins fuer Niederdeutsche Sprachforschung [*A publication*] .... Kbl
Korrespondenzblatt des Vereins fuer Niederdeutsche Sprachforschung [*A publication*] .... KVNS
Korrosionsinstitutet. Rapport [*A publication*] .... KI Rapp
Korrosionsinstitutet. Rapport [*A publication*] .... Korrosionsinst Rapp
Korrozios Figyelo [*A publication*] .... Korroz Figyelo
Korroziya i Zashchita v Neftegazovoi Promyshlennosti Nauchno-Tekhnicheskii Sbornik [*A publication*] .... Korroz Zashch
Korsakoff's Disease [*Medicine*] .... KD
Korte Mededeling Stichting Bosbouwproefstation "De Dorschkamp" [*A publication*] .... Korte Meded Bosbouwproefsta
Korteweg-deVries [*Equation*] [*Mathematics*] .... KdV
Koruna [*Monetary unit in Czechoslovakia*] .... K
Koruna Ceskoslovensky [*Monetary unit in Czechoslovakia*] .... KC
Kos [*Greece*] [*Airport symbol*] .... KGS
Kosan Boka [*Ivory Coast*] [*Seismograph station code, US Geological Survey*] .... KIC
Kosciusko, MS [*Location identifier*] [*FAA*] .... OSX
Kosciusko, MS [*Radio station call letters*] .... WKOZ
Kosciusko, MS [*Radio station call letters*] .... WKOZ-FM
Kosciuszko Foundation .... KF
Kosher .... K
Kosher Meal [*Airline notation*] .... KSML
Kosher Wine Institute .... KWI
Kosice [*Czechoslovakia*] [*Airport symbol*] .... KSC
Kosmetik Journal [*A publication*] .... Kosmet J
Kosmicheskaya Biologiya i Aviakosmicheskaya Meditsina [*A publication*] .... KBAMA
Kosmicheskaya Biologiya i Aviakosmicheskaya Meditsina [*A publication*] .... Kosm B Av M
Kosmicheskaya Biologiya i Aviakosmicheskaya Meditsina [*A publication*] .... Kosm Biol Aviakosm Med
Kosmicheskaya Biologiya i Meditsina [*A publication*] .... Kosm Biol Med
Kosmicheskie Issledovaniya [*A publication*] .... Kosm Issled
Kosmicheskie Issledovaniya Zemnykh Resursov. Metody i Sredstva Izmerenii i Obrabotki Informatsii [*A publication*] .... Kosm Issled Zemnykh Resur
Kosmodemyansk [*USSR*] [*Seismograph station code, US Geological Survey*] [*Closed*] .... KOS
Kosmos Bibliothek [*A publication*] .... Kosmos Bibl
Kosmos. Seria A. Biologia (Warsaw) [*A publication*] .... Kosmos Ser A Biol (Warsaw)
Kosmos. Seria A. Biologia (Warsaw) [*A publication*] .... Kosmos Ser A (Warsaw)
Koss Corp. [*NASDAQ symbol*] .... KOSS
Kossuth County Advance, Algona, IA [*Library symbol*] .... IaAlgKA
Kossuth Foundation .... KF
Koster [*South Africa*] [*Seismograph station code, US Geological Survey*] .... KSR
Kostromskoi Gosudarstvennyi Pedagogiceskii Institut Imeni N. A. Nekrasova. Ucenye Zapiski [*A publication*] .... Kostrom Gos Ped Inst Ucen Zap
Koszalin [*Poland*] [*Airport symbol*] .... OSZ
Kota [*India*] [*Airport symbol*] .... KTU
Kota Bharu [*Malaysia*] [*Airport symbol*] .... KBR
Kota Kinabalu [*Malaysia*] [*Airport symbol*] .... BKI
Kota Kinabalu [*Malaysia*] [*Seismograph station code, US Geological Survey*] .... KKM
Kotlik [*Alaska*] [*Airport symbol*] .... KOT
Kotzebue [*Alaska*] [*Seismograph station code, US Geological Survey*] .... KTA
Kotzebue [*Alaska*] [*Airport symbol*] .... OTZ
Kotzebue, AK [*Location identifier*] [*FAA*] .... HHM
Kotzebue, AK [*Radio station call letters*] .... KOTZ
Koula Moutou [*Gabon*] [*Airport symbol*] .... KOU
Koumac [*New Caledonia*] [*Airport symbol*] .... KOC
Koumac [*New Caledonia*] [*Seismograph station code, US Geological Survey*] .... KOU
Kourday [*USSR*] [*Seismograph station code, US Geological Survey*] [*Closed*] .... KRD
Kousour [*Djibouti*] [*Seismograph station code, US Geological Survey*] .... KSU
Koussevitzky Music Foundation .... KMF
Koutaba [*Cameroon*] [*Airport symbol*] .... KOB
Kovats [*Retention*] **Index** .... KI
Kovcezic [*A publication*] .... Ko
Kovcezic [*A publication*] .... Kov
Kovove Materialy [*A publication*] .... Kovove Mater
Kowanyama [*Australia*] [*Airport symbol*] .... KWM
Koyala Mazdoor Panchayat [*India*] .... KMP
Koyama [*Japan*] [*Seismograph station code, US Geological Survey*] [*Closed*] .... KOY
Koyna Nagar [*India*] [*Seismograph station code, US Geological Survey*] [*Closed*] .... KNI
Koyuk [*Alaska*] [*Airport symbol*] .... KKA
Koyukuk [*Alaska*] [*Airport symbol*] .... KYU
Kozani [*Greece*] [*Airport symbol*] .... KZI
Kozani [*Greece*] [*Seismograph station code, US Geological Survey*] .... KZN

Kozawa, Iwatsuru, and Kawaguchi [*Factor involving injection of cancerous gastric juices into rabbits, named for its discoverers*] [*Medicine*] ... KIK
Kozyrevsk [*USSR*] [*Seismograph station code, US Geological Survey*] ... KOZ
Kpelle [*MARC language code*] [*Library of Congress*] ... kpe
Kradschuetzen-Bataillon [*Motorcycle Battalion*] [*German military - World War II*] ... KSB
Kraemer System ... KS
Kraevye Zadachi dlya Differentsial'nykh Uravnenij [*A publication*] ... Kraev Zadachi Differ Uravn
Kraft durch Freude [*Strength through Joy Movement*] [*Pre-World War II, Germany*] ... KDF
Kraft, Inc. [*NYSE symbol*] [*Delisted*] ... KRA
Kraft Mill Effluent [*Pulp and paper processing*] ... KME
Kraft Paper Association [*Later, API*] ... KPA
Kraftco Corp., Research and Development Library, Glenview, IL [*Library symbol*] ... IGlvK
Kraftfahrwesen [*Motor transport*] [*German military - World War II*] ... K
Kraftrad [*Motorcycle*] [*German military - World War II*] ... K
Kraftwagen [*Motor Vehicle*] [*German military - World War II*] ... KW
Kraftwerksunion [*West Germany*] ... KWU
Krag-Jorgensen Rifle ... KRAG-JORG
Krakow [*Poland*] [*Seismograph station code, US Geological Survey*] ... KRA
Krakow [*Poland*] [*Airport symbol*] ... KRK
Kramfors [*Sweden*] [*Airport symbol*] ... KRF
Krasnaja Nov' [*A publication*] ... KN
Krasnaya Polyana [*USSR*] [*Seismograph station code, US Geological Survey*] [*Closed*] ... KPR
Krasnodar [*USSR*] [*Airport symbol*] ... KRR
Krasnogorka [*USSR*] [*Seismograph station code, US Geological Survey*] [*Closed*] ... KRS
Kratkie Soobscenija Instituta Arheologii [*A publication*] ... Kr Soobsc Inst Arheol
Kratkie Soobshcheniia Instituta Arkheologii. Akademii Nauk SSSR [*A publication*] ... Krat Soob Inst Ark A N SSSR
Kratkie Soobshcheniia o Polevykh Arkheologicheskikh Issledovaniiakh Odesskogo Gosudarstvennogo Arkheologicheskogo Muzeia [*A publication*] ... Krat Soob OGAM
Kratkie Soobshcheniya po Fizike [*A publication*] ... Kratk Soobshch Fiz
Kratkije Soobscenija Breves Communications de l'Institute d'Archeologie (Kiev) [*A publication*] ... KrSoob(Kiev)
Kratkije Soobscenija Instituta Narodov Azii [*A publication*] ... KSINA
Kratkije Soobscenija Instituta Slajanovednija. Akademija Nauk SSSR [*A publication*] ... KSISL
Kratkije Soobscenija Instituta Vostokovedenija. Akademija Nauk SSSR [*A publication*] ... KSIV
Kratkir Soobscenija Burjatskogo Kompleksnogo Naucnoissledovatel'skogo Instituta. Serija Storiko-Filologiceskaja [*A publication*] ... KSBurNII
Kratos, Inc. [*NASDAQ symbol*] ... KTOS
Kraus-Thomson Organization [*Publishing*] ... KTO
Krazy Kat [*Cartoon character by George Herriman*] ... K
Krebs-Henseleit Bicarbonate [*A buffer*] [*Analytical biochemistry*] ... KHB
Krebs-Ringer-Bicarbonate [*Buffer solution*] ... KRB
Krebs-Ringer-Bicarbonate Glucose-Albumin [*Buffer solution*] ... KRB-GA
Krebs-Ringer-Glucose [*Buffer solution and growth medium*] ... KRG
Krebs-Ringer-Phosphate [*Buffer solution*] ... KRP
Krebs-Ringer-Phosphate Buffer [*Solution*] ... KRPB
Krebsforschung [*A publication*] ... Krebsforsch
Kreeger, George W., Atlanta GA [*STAC*] ... KGW
Kreisinger Development Laboratory ... KDL
Kreisler Manufacturing Co. ... KRSL
Kremmling Public Library, Kremmling, CO [*Library symbol*] ... CoKr
Kremsmuenster [*Austria*] [*Seismograph station code, US Geological Survey*] ... KMR
Kresge Art Center Bulletin [*A publication*] ... Kresge Art Bull
Kresge [*S. S.*] **Co.** [*NYSE symbol*] [*Delisted*] ... KG
Kresge Eye Institute ... KEI
Kresge Hearing Research Institute [*University of Michigan*] ... KHRI
Kress [*S. H.*] **& Company** [*NYSE symbol*] [*Delisted*] ... KSC
Kreutzer [*Monetary unit in Germany*] ... KR
Kribi [*Cameroon*] [*Airport symbol*] ... KBI
Kriegs Dekoration [*War Decoration*] [*German*] ... KD
Kriegsausruestungsnachweisung [*Table of basic allowances*] [*German military - World War II*] ... KAN
Kriegsgefangener [*Prisoner of War*] [*German*] ... KGF
Kriegsgericht [*War Tribunal*] [*German*] ... KrG
Kriegsoffizier-Bewerber [*Applicant for wartime commission*] [*German military - World War II*] ... KOB
Kriegsstaerke-Nachweisung [*Table of organization*] [*German military - World War II*] ... KSTN
Kriegstagebuch [*War Diary*] [*German military - World War II*] ... KTB
Kriegsverdienstkreuz [*War Service Cross*] [*German military decoration - World War II*] ... KVK
Kriegsverwendungsfaehig [*Fit for Active Service*] [*German military - World War II*] ... KV
Kriminalistik und Forensische Wissenschaften [*A publication*] ... Krim Forensische Wiss
Kriminalpolizei [*Ordinary Criminal Police*] [*Germany*] ... KRIPO
Krishnamurti Foundation of America ... KFA
Kristall und Technik [*A publication*] ... Krist Tech
Kristallografiya [*A publication*] ... Kristallogr
Kristallographie. Grundlagen und Anwendung [*A publication*] ... Kristallogr Grundl Anwend
Kristelig Forening for Unge Kvinder [*Young Women's Christian Associations*] [*Denmark*] ... KFUK
Kristelig Forening for Unge Maend [*Young Men's Christian Associations*] [*Denmark*] ... KFUM
Kristiansand [*Norway*] [*Airport symbol*] ... KRS
Kristianstad [*Sweden*] [*Airport symbol*] ... KID
Kristiansund [*Norway*] [*Airport symbol*] ... KSU
Kriterion [*A publication*] ... Krit
Kritik (Copenhagen) [*A publication*] ... KritC
Kritika Chronika [*A publication*] ... KC
Kritika Chronika [*A publication*] ... Kr Chron
Kritika Phylla [*A publication*] ... KP
Kritikas Gadagramata [*A publication*] ... K Gad
Kritische Berichte zur Kunstgeschichtlichen Literatur [*A publication*] ... KBKL
Kritische Blaetter zur Literatur der Gegenwart [*A publication*] ... KBLG
Kritische Justiz [*A publication*] ... Krit Justiz
Kritische Vierteljahresschrift [*A publication*] ... KVJS
Kritische Vierteljahresschrift fuer Gesetzgebung [*A publication*] ... KVG
KRM Petroleum Corporation [*NASDAQ symbol*] ... KRMC
Kroc Foundation Series [*A publication*] ... Kroc Found Ser
Kroc Foundation Symposia [*A publication*] ... Kroc Found Symp
Kroeber Anthropological Society ... KAS
Kroeber Anthropological Society Papers [*A publication*] ... Kroeber Anthro Soc Pap
Kroehler Manufacturing Co. [*NYSE symbol*] [*Delisted*] ... KFM
Kroenig's Isthmus [*Of resonance*] [*Medicine*] ... KI
Kroger Co. [*NYSE symbol*] ... KR
Krolikovodstvo i Zverovodstvo [*A publication*] ... Krolikovod Zverovod
Krona [*Monetary unit in the Faroe Islands*] ... F KR
Krona [*Monetary unit in Iceland, Sweden*] ... K
Krona [*Monetary unit in Iceland, Sweden*] ... KR
Krona [*Monetary unit in Sweden*] ... S KR
Krone [*Monetary unit in Denmark, Norway*] ... K
Krone [*Monetary unit in Denmark, Norway*] ... KR
Krone [*Monetary unit in Norway*] ... N KR
Kroniek van Kunst en Kultur [*A publication*] ... KVKEK
Kronig-Penny Model ... KPM
Kronika [*A publication*] ... Kron
Kroon [*Monetary unit in Estonia*] ... K
Kroy, Inc. [*NASDAQ symbol*] ... KROY
Krs Jugoslavije Carsus Iugoslaviae [*A publication*] ... Krs Jugosl Carsus Iugosl
Kru [*MARC language code*] [*Library of Congress*] ... kro
Krueger Brewing Co. [*NYSE symbol*] ... KRU
Krueger [*W. A.*] **Co.** [*NASDAQ symbol*] ... KRUE
Krupp Gun ... K
Krupp Quick-Firing Gun ... KQF
Krypton [*Chemical element*] ... Kr
Krypton Exposure Technique ... KET
Krypton Ion LASER ... KIL
Krypton LASER System ... KLS
Ksar Es Souk [*Seismograph station code, US Geological Survey*] [*Closed*] ... KES
Ksara [*Lebanon*] [*Geomagnetic observatory code*] ... KSA
Ksara [*Lebanon*] [*Seismograph station code, US Geological Survey*] ... KSA
KSC [*Kennedy Space Center*] **Handbook** [*NASA*] ... KHB
KSC [*Kennedy Space Center*] **Management Instruction** [*NASA*] ... KMI
KSC [*Kennedy Space Center*] **Shuttle Management** [*Document*] [*NASA*] ... K-SM
KSC [*Kennedy Space Center*] **Space Transportation System Management** [*Document*] [*NASA*] ... K-STSM
KSC [*Kennedy Space Center*] **Station Set Specification** [*NASA*] ... KSSS
Ksiaz [*Poland*] [*Seismograph station code, US Geological Survey*] ... KSP
Ksiazka i Wiedza [*A publication*] ... KiW
Ktavim Records of the Agricultural Research Station [*A publication*] ... Ktavim Rec Agric Res Stn
KTO Microform, Millwood, NY [*Library symbol*] ... KtO
Ku-Band Antenna Feed Horn ... KAFH
Ku-Band Feed Horn ... KFH
Ku-Band Signal Processor ... KUSP
Ku Klux Klan ... KKK
Kuala Lumpur [*Malaysia*] ... KL
Kuala Lumpur [*Malaysia*] [*Seismograph station code, US Geological Survey*] ... KLM
Kuala Lumpur [*Malaysia*] [*Airport symbol*] ... KUL
Kuala Trengganu [*Malaysia*] [*Airport symbol*] ... TGG
Kuantan [*Malaysia*] [*Airport symbol*] ... KUA
Kubota Ltd. [*NYSE symbol*] ... KUB
Kuching [*Malaysia*] [*Airport symbol*] ... KCH
Kuching Employees and Labourers' Union [*Sarawak*] ... KELU
Kucino [*USSR*] [*Seismograph station code, US Geological Survey*] [*Closed*] ... KUC
Kudat [*Malaysia*] [*Airport symbol*] ... KUD
Kuder Preference Record - Personal [*Psychology*] ... KPR-P
Kuehn-Archiv [*A publication*] ... Kuehn-Arch
Kufrah [*Libya*] [*Airport symbol*] ... AKF
Kugellager-Zeitschrift [*A publication*] ... Kugellager-Z

Kuh Shi [*Republic of China*] [*Seismograph station code, US Geological Survey*].....................KSH
Kuhlman Corporations [*NYSE symbol*].....................KUH
Kuhlmann-Anderson Intelligence Tests [*Education*].....................K-A
Kuhner, J. J., Cleveland OH [*STAC*].....................KJJ
Kuhn's Big K Stores Corp. [*American Stock Exchange symbol*] [*Delisted*].....................KBK
Kuiper Airborne Observatory [*NASA*].....................KAO
Kulanka Afka Somalyed.....................KAS
Kulicke & Soffa Industries [*NASDAQ symbol*].....................KLIC
Kullback-Leibler [*Mathematics*].....................KL
Kullback-Leibler Nearest Neighbor [*Mathematics*].....................KL-NN
Kultur [*A publication*].....................K
Kultur og Folkeminder [*A publication*].....................KOF
Kultur og Klasse [*A publication*].....................Ku KI
Kultur in Literatur [*A publication*].....................KL
Kultura [*A publication*].....................KA
Kultura Slova [*A publication*].....................KS
Kultura Slova [*A publication*].....................KSI
Kultura i Spoleczenstwo [*A publication*].....................KiS
Kultura i Spoleczenstwo [*A publication*].....................Kult i Spolecz
Kultura (Warsaw) [*A publication*].....................KulturaW
Kulturas Biroja Biletins [*Bulletin. Cultural Bureau of the American Latvian Association in the US*] [*A publication*].....................KBB
Kulturbund.....................KB
Kulturni Politika [*A publication*].....................KP
Kulturny Zivot [*Bratislava*] [*A publication*].....................KZ
Kulturos Barai [*A publication*].....................KB
Kulturpflanze Beiheft [*A publication*].....................Kulturpflanze Beih
Kultuurpatronen. Bulletin Etnografisch Museum (Delft) [*A publication*].....................KBEMD
Kulyab [*USSR*] [*Seismograph station code, US Geological Survey*].....................KUL
Kumagaya [*Japan*] [*Seismograph station code, US Geological Survey*].....................KMG
Kumamoto [*Japan*] [*Airport symbol*].....................KMJ
Kumamoto [*Japan*] [*Seismograph station code, US Geological Survey*].....................KUM
Kumamoto Journal of Science [*A publication*].....................Kumamoto J Sci
Kumamoto Journal of Science. Biology [*A publication*].....................Kumamoto J Sci Biol
Kumamoto Journal of Science. Geology [*A publication*].....................Kumamoto J Sci Geol
Kumamoto Journal of Science. Series A. Mathematics, Physics, and Chemistry [*A publication*].....................Kumamoto J Sci Ser A
Kumamoto Journal of Science. Series B. Section 2. Biology [*A publication*].....................Kumamoto J Sci Ser B Sect 2 Biol
Kumamoto Medical Journal [*A publication*].....................Kumamoto Med J
Kumano [*Japan*] [*Seismograph station code, US Geological Survey*].....................KMN
Kumasi [*Ghana*] [*Airport symbol*].....................KMS
Kume Jima [*Ryukyu Islands*] [*Seismograph station code, US Geological Survey*].....................KMJ
Kume Jima [*Japan*] [*Airport symbol*].....................UEO
Kummer, Kneser, and Kodaira [*Surfaces*] [*Mathematics*].....................K-3
Kundiawa [*Papua New Guinea*] [*Airport symbol*].....................CMU
Kundu's Neurotic Personality Inventory [*Psychology*].....................KNPI
Kunduz [*Afghanistan*] [*Airport symbol*] [*Obsolete*].....................UND
K'ung Meng Msueh-Pao [*Journal. Confucius Mencius Society*] [*A publication*].....................KMHP
Kungliga Automobil Klubben.....................KAK
Kungliga Biblioteket, Bibliotheca Regia Holmiensis, Stockholm, Sweden [*Library symbol*].....................SwSKB
Kungliga Fysiografiska Sallskapets i Lund. Arsbok [*A publication*].....................K Fysiogr Sallsk Lund Arsb
Kungliga Fysiografiska Sallskapets i Lund. Foerhandlingar [*A publication*].....................K Fysiogr Sallsk Lund Forh
Kungliga Gustav Adolfs Akademiens. Minnesbok [*A publication*].....................KGAAM
Kungliga Humanistiska Vetenskapssamfundet i Lund. Arsberattelse [*A publication*].....................AHVsLund
Kungliga Humanistiska Vetenskapssamfundet i Uppsala [*A publication*].....................KHVSU
Kungliga Humanistiska Vetenskapssamfundet i Uppsala. Arsbok [*A publication*].....................AHVsUppsala
Kungliga Karolinska Mediko-Kirurgiska Institutes, Stockholm, Sweden [*Library symbol*].....................SwSKM
Kungliga Lantbruksakademiens Tidskrift [*A publication*].....................K Lantbruksakad Tidskr
Kungliga Lantbrukshogskolans Annaler [*A publication*].....................K Lantbrhogsk Annlr
Kungliga Lantbrukshogskolans Annaler [*A publication*].....................K Lantbrukshogsk Ann
Kungliga Skogs- och Lantbruksakademiens Tidskrift [*A publication*].....................K Skogs o Lantbr Akad Tidskr
Kungliga Svenska Vetenskaps-Akademiens. Handlingar. Oefversigt til Handlingar [*A publication*].....................K Svenska Vet-Ak Hdl Oefv
Kungliga Svenska Vetenskapsakademiens. Handlingar [*A publication*].....................K Sven Vetenskapsakad Handl
Kungliga Tekniska Hoegskolan [*Royal Institute of Technology*] [*Stockholm*].....................KTH
Kungliga Tekniska Hoegskolan [*Royal Institute of Technology*], **Stockholm, Sweden** [*Library symbol*].....................SwSK

Kungliga Vetenskaps-Academiens. Handlingar [*A publication*].....................K Vetensk Acad Handl
Kungliga Vetenskaps-Academiens. Nya Handlingar (Stockholm) [*A publication*].....................K Vetensk N Handl (Stockholm)
Kungliga Vetenskaps-Societetens. Arsbok [*A publication*].....................K Vetensk-Soc Arsb
Kungliga Vetenskapssamhaellets i Uppsala. Arsbok [*A publication*].....................K Vetenskapssamh Uppsala Arsb
Kungliga Vitterhets Historie och Antikvitets Akademiens. Handlingar [*A publication*].....................KVHAAH
Kunia Operations Control Center Coordination Group.....................KOCCCG
Kunlun Mountain Region [*China, Mainland*] [*MARC geographic area code*] [*Library of Congress*].....................a-cck--
Kunming [*Republic of China*] [*Airport symbol*].....................KMG
Kunming [*Republic of China*] [*Seismograph station code, US Geological Survey*].....................KUN
Kunst en Cultuur [*A publication*].....................K & C
Kunst und Kultur der Hethiter [*A publication*].....................KKH
Kunst und Kunstler [*A publication*].....................K & K
Kunst und Literatur [*A publication*].....................KuL
Kunst und Literatur [*A publication*].....................Kunst u Lit
Kunst der Nederlanden [*A publication*].....................KN
Kunst und Sprache [*A publication*].....................K & S
Kunstchronik [*A publication*].....................KC
Kunstgeschichtliche Anzeigen [*A publication*].....................KAnz
Kunstgeschichtliche Anzeigen [*A publication*].....................KGA
Kunstliteratur [*A publication*].....................KI
Kunstmuseets Arsskrift [*A publication*].....................KA
Kunststoff-Berater [*A publication*].....................Kunstst-Berat
Kunststoff-Berater Vereinigt mit Kunststoff-Rundschau und Kunststoff-Technik [*A publication*].....................Kunstst-Berat Rundsch Tech
Kunststoff Journal [*A publication*].....................Kunstst J
Kunststoff-Rundschau [*A publication*].....................Kunstst-Rundsch
Kunststoffberater, Rundschau, und Technik [*A publication*].....................Kunststoffberat Rundsch Tech
Kunststoffe [*A publication*].....................Kunstst
Kunststoffe im Bau [*A publication*].....................Kunstst Bau
Kunststoffe - German Plastics [*A publication*].....................Kunstst Ger Plast
Kunststoffe-Plastics [*A publication*].....................Kunstst-Plast
Kunstwissenschaftliches Jahrbuch der Gorresgesellschaft [*A publication*].....................KJG
Kununurra [*Australia*] [*Seismograph station code, US Geological Survey*].....................KNA
Kununurra [*Australia*] [*Airport symbol*].....................KNX
Kuo Ming Tang [*or Kuomintang*] [*Nationalist Party of China*].....................KMT
Kuopio [*Finland*] [*Airport symbol*].....................KUO
Kupang [*Indonesia*] [*Airport symbol*].....................KOE
Kupang [*Timor*] [*Seismograph station code, US Geological Survey*].....................KUG
Kupang [*Timor*] [*Seismograph station code, US Geological Survey*] [*Closed*].....................KUP
Kuparuk, AK [*Location identifier*] [*FAA*].....................PYC
Kuparuk, AK [*Location identifier*] [*FAA*].....................UBW
Kupiano [*Papua New Guinea*] [*Seismograph station code, US Geological Survey*].....................KPN
Kupiano [*Papua New Guinea*] [*Airport symbol*].....................KUP
Kuranda [*Australia*] [*Seismograph station code, US Geological Survey*] [*Closed*].....................KDA
Kuratorium fuer Technik in der Landwirtschaft.....................KTL
Kuratorium fuer Technik in der Landwirtschaft. Berichte ueber Landtechnik [*A publication*].....................KTL Ber Landtech
Kuratorium fuer Technik in der Landwirtschaft. Flugschrift [*A publication*].....................Kurator Tech Landwirt Flugschr
Kurchatovium [*See also Rf*] [*Proposed name for chemical element 104*].....................Ku
Kurdish [*MARC language code*] [*Library of Congress*].....................kur
Kurdish Democratic Party [*Iran*].....................KDP
Kurdish Democratic Party of Syria.....................KDPS
Kurdzhali [*Bulgaria*] [*Seismograph station code, US Geological Survey*].....................KDZ
Kure [*Japan*] [*Seismograph station code, US Geological Survey*] [*Closed*].....................KRE
Kuria [*Kiribati*] [*Airport symbol*].....................KUC
Kurie Plot [*Physics*].....................KP
Kurilsk [*USSR*] [*Seismograph station code, US Geological Survey*].....................KUR
Kurme Medical Journal [*A publication*].....................Kurme Med J
Kurmenty [*USSR*] [*Seismograph station code, US Geological Survey*].....................KRM
Kurortologiya i Fizioterapiya [*Bulgaria*] [*A publication*].....................Kurortol Fizioter
Kurskii Gosudarstvennyi Pedagogiceskii Institut. Ucenye Zapiski [*A publication*].....................Kursk Gos Ped Inst Ucen Zap
Kurt Weill Foundation for Music.....................KWFM
Kurth Memorial Library, Lufkin, TX [*Library symbol*].....................TxLufK
Kurtis-Kraft Register.....................KKR
Kurtosis [*The relative degree of flatness in the region about the mode of a frequency curve*].....................Ku
Kurukh [*MARC language code*] [*Library of Congress*].....................kru
Kurukshetra [*India*] [*Seismograph station code, US Geological Survey*].....................KKR
Kurupung [*Guyana*] [*Airport symbol*].....................KPG
Kurus [*Monetary unit in Turkey*].....................K
Kurze Sicht [*Short Sight*] [*German*].....................KS
Kurzweil Data Entry Machine.....................KDEM
Kurzweil Reading Machine.....................KRM

Kushiro [Japan] [Airport symbol]..KUH
Kushiro [Japan] [Seismograph station code, US Geological Survey].......KUS
Kuskokwin Consortium Library, Bethel, AK [Library symbol] ....AkB
Kustom Electronics [NASDAQ symbol] ....KUST
Kustom Kemps of America ....KKOA
Kutchino [USSR] [Later, MOS] [Geomagnetic observatory code] ....KTC
Kutenai [MARC language code] [Library of Congress].............................kut
Kutsu-Ga-Hara [Japan] [Seismograph station code, US
   Geological Survey]..KUT
Kutta-Joukowski Force...KJF
Kutztown [Pennsylvania] [Seismograph station code, US
   Geological Survey]..KTZ
Kutztown State College, Kutztown, PA [OCLC symbol]....................KZS
Kutztown State College, Kutztown, PA [Library symbol] ....PKuS
Kuusamo [Finland] [Airport symbol]...KAO
Kuwait [MARC geographic area code] [Library of Congress]............a-ku---
Kuwait [Aircraft nationality and registration mark].................................9K
Kuwait [MARC country of publication code] [Library of Congress]............ku
Kuwait [Two-letter standard code]..KW
Kuwait [Kuwait] [Airport symbol]...KWI
Kuwait [Three-letter standard code]...KWT
Kuwait Airways Corp..KA
Kuwait Airways Corporation...KAC
Kuwait Airways Corp. [ICAO designator]...KU
Kuwait Fund for Arab Economic Development ....KFAED
Kuwait International Investment Company.......................................KIIC
Kuwait National Petroleum Company...KNPC
Kuwait Oil Company...KOC
Kuyper [Indonesia] [Later, TNG] [Geomagnetic observatory code] ....KUY
Kuznechno-Shtampovochnoe Proizvodstvo [A publication]...................
                                   Kuznechno-Shtampov
Kuznica [A publication] ....Kuz
Kvantovaya Ehlektronika [A publication]......................Kvantovaya Ehlektron
Kvantovaya Elektronika (Kiev) [A publication].....Kvantovaya Elektron (Kiev)
Kvantovaya Elektronika (Moskva) [A publication]..............................
                          Kvantovaya Elektron (Moskva)
Kvantovia Elektronika [A publication]...................................Kvan Elektr
KVP Sutherland Paper Co. [NYSE symbol] [Delisted]......................KSP
Kwacha [Monetary unit in Malawi and Zambia]......................................K
Kwajalein [Marshall Islands] [Airport symbol] ....KWA
Kwajalein Atoll..KWAJ
Kwajalein Missile Range..KMR
Kwajalein Standard Atmosphere..KSA
Kwajalein Test Site..KTS
Kwangsi Chuang Autonomous Region [China, Mainland] [MARC
   geographic area code] [Library of Congress] ....a-cc-kc
Kwangtung Province [China, Mainland] [MARC geographic area
   code] [Library of Congress]...a-cc-kn
Kwansei Gakuin Sociology Department Studies [A publication] ....
                    Kwansei Gakuin Sociol Dept Stud
Kwansei Gakuin University. Annual Studies [A publication] ....KGUAS
Kwansei Gakuin University Annual Studies [A publication] ....
                        Kwansei Gakuin U Ann Stud
Kwartalnik Geologiczny [A publication]...............................Kwart Geol
Kwartalnik Geologiczny (Poland. Instytut Geologiczny) [A
   publication]......................................Kwart Geol (Pol Inst Geol)
Kwartalnik Historii Kultury [A publication] ....Kwart Hist Kult
Kwartalnik Historii Kultury Materialnej [A publication]...........................
                          Kwart Hist Kult Mater
Kwartalnik Historii Nauki i Techniki [A publication]............................
                        Kwart Hist Nauki i Tech
Kwartalnik Historyczny [A publication]..KH
Kwartalnik Instytutu Polsko-Radzieckiego [A publication] ....KIPR
Kwartalnik Klasyczny [A publication]...KK
Kwartalnik Muzyczny [A publication]...KM
Kwartalnik Naucyzciela Opolskiego [A publication]............................KNO
Kwartalnik Neofilologiczny [A publication]..KN
Kwartalnik Neofilologiczny [A publication].......................................KNf

Kwartalnik Opolski [A publication]....................................Kwart Opolski
Kwartalnik Opolski [A publication]...KwO
Kwartalnik Prasoznawczy [A publication]..KP
Kweichow Province [China, Mainland] [MARC geographic area
   code] [Library of Congress]..a-cc-kw
Kweiyang [Republic of China] [Seismograph station code, US
   Geological Survey]..KWA
Kwethluk [Alaska] [Airport symbol] ....KWT
Kwigillingok [Alaska] [Airport symbol] ....KWK
Kwigillingok, AK [Location identifier] [FAA]....................................GGV
KWU [Kraftwerk Union AG, Muehlheim] Report [A publication]........KWU Rep
KXE6S Verein Chess Society ....KVCS
Kyakhta [USSR] [Seismograph station code, US Geological
   Survey] [Closed] ....KYA
Kyasanur Forest Disease ....KFD
Kyat [Monetary unit in Burma]...K
Kyaukpyu [Burma] [Airport symbol] ....KYP
Kyauktaw [Burma] [Airport symbol] ....KYT
Kybernetika [A publication]..Kyb
Kybernetika [A publication]...KYBNA
Kyburz Flat [California] [Seismograph station code, US
   Geological Survey]...KBF
Kyklos [A publication] ....Kyk
Kyle Classification [Library science]..KC
Kyle Technology Corp. [NASDAQ symbol] ....KYLE
Kyocera Corp. ADR [NYSE symbol]...KYO
Kyorin Journal of Medicine and Medical Technology [A
   publication]...Kyorin J Med Med Technol
Kyosato Education Experiment Project [Self-help program for
   Japanese farmers established by Americans in 1948] ....KEEP
Kyoto [Japan] [Seismograph station code, US Geological Survey]...........KYO
Kyoto Ceramic Co. Ltd. [NYSE symbol] [Delisted]...........................KYO
Kyoto University Economic Review [A publication].............................Kyo
Kyoto University Economic Review [A publication]........... Kyoto Univ Econ R
Kyoto University Faculty of Science Memoirs. Series of Geology
   and Mineralogy [A publication]..
                    Kyoto Univ Fac Sci Mem Ser Geol Mineral
Kyoto University Geophysical Research Station Reports [A
   publication]....................................Kyoto Univ Geophys Res Stn Rep
Kyoto University. Jimbun Kagaku Kenkyu-sho. Silver Jubilee
   Volume [A publication]...SJV
Kyoto University, Kyoto, Japan [Library symbol]...............................JKU
Kyoto University Reactor ....KUR
Kypriaka Chronika [A publication] ....KyC
Kypriakai Spoudai [A publication]...KyS
Kypriakos Logos [A publication] ....KL
Kyrkohistorisk Arsskrift [A publication]..KA
Kyrkohistorisk Arsskrift [A publication]............................Kyrkohist Arsskr
Kysor Industrial Corp. [NYSE symbol] ....KZ
Kyungpook Mathematical Journal [A publication] .... Kyungpook Math J
Kyungpook University Medical Journal [A publication]........................
                          Kyungpook Univ Med J
Kyushu Agricultural Research [A publication].....................Kyushu Agr Res
Kyushu American Literature [Fukuoka, Japan] [A publication]..............KAL
Kyushu Chugokugakkaiho [Journal of the Sinological Society of
   Kyushu] [A publication]..KSCGH
Kyushu Journal of Medical Science [A publication]............Kyushu J Med Sci
Kyushu University. College of General Education. Reports on
   Earth Science [A publication]...
                    Kyushu Univ Coll Gen Educ Rep Earth Sci
Kyushu University. Department of Geology. Science Reports [A
   publication]...................................Kyushu Univ Dep Geol Sci Rep
Kyushu University. Faculty of Agriculture. Science Bulletin [A
   publication].....................................Kyushu Univ Fac Agr Sci Bull
Kyushu University Faculty of Science Memoirs [A publication].................
                        Kyushu Univ Faculty Sci Mem
Kyushu University. Faculty of Science. Memoirs. Series D.
   Geology [A publication]...........................Kyushu Univ Fac Sci Mem Ser D
KZ Owners' Association ....KZOA